THE NEW BIBLE DICTIONARY

The New BIBLE Dictionary

Organizing Editor

J. D. DOUGLAS, M.A., B.D., S.T.M., Ph.D.

Formerly Librarian, Tyndale House, Cambridge

Consulting Editors

F. F. BRUCE, M.A., D.D.

Rylands Professor of Biblical Criticism and Exegesis, University of Manchester

R. V. G. TASKER, M.A., D.D.

Emeritus Professor of New Testament Exegesis, University of London

J. I. PACKER, M.A., D.Phil.

Librarian, Latimer House, Oxford

D. J. WISEMAN, O.B.E., M.A.

Professor of Assyriology, University of London

WM. B. EERDMANS PUBLISHING CO.

GRAND RAPIDS, MICHIGAN

First Edition, May 1962
Reprinted, July 1963
Reprinted, January 1964

Photolithoprinted by Grand Rapids Book Manufacturers
Grand Rapids, Michigan, United States of America

PREFACE

The New Bible Dictionary is the latest, and thus far the major, product of the Tyndale Fellowship for Biblical Research, which was founded in 1945 in close association with the Inter-Varsity Fellowship to stimulate evangelical biblical scholarship in Great Britain and elsewhere. The project of a Bible Dictionary was mooted even before the Tyndale Fellowship was founded, but several years had to elapse before adequate manpower was available for its production. Even so, the contributors to this Dictionary have not been drawn exclusively from the ranks of the Tyndale Fellowship; we are deeply indebted to the generous co-operation of colleagues in America, Europe, the Commonwealth, and other lands.

The word 'New' in the title of the Dictionary is used in no conventional way. This is not in any sense a revision of any older work. Each of its 2,300 articles has been specially written for this volume. The intention has been to take full advantage of the considerable advances made in biblical studies in recent years, particularly in the realm of archaeology. Here we have been fortunate in having the help of a number of younger scholars who are actively concerned with Near Eastern archaeology, and who have been able to present the later findings in a way that makes this work, among other things, an up-to-date handbook on this subject.

The aim of Editors and contributors alike has been to produce a volume, written in a spirit of loyalty to Holy Scripture, which would contribute substantially to the understanding of God's Word to men. No attempt has been made, however, to impose a rigid uniformity upon the whole work, or to exclude the occasional expression of different viewpoints.

Our special thanks are due to the Organizing Editor, Dr. J. D. Douglas, formerly Librarian of Tyndale House, Cambridge. For more than three years he has devoted the greater part of his time to the preparation of this volume, planning the form which the contents should take and generally co-ordinating the work of the many contributors.

Mention must also be made of Mr. Andrew F. Walls, who shared with the Organizing Editor the preliminary work of planning, and of Mr. Ronald Inchley, Publications Secretary of the Inter-Varsity Fellowship, whose assistance at every stage of the production has gone far beyond the normal limits of a publisher's responsibility and interest and has contributed materially to the finished work.

An illustrated volume of this kind cannot be produced without a considerable amount of careful research. Our thanks are due to Mr. Alan Millard and Mr. Terence Mitchell, both of the British Museum staff, who helped to prepare the lists of illustrations, and especially to Mrs. Gillian Potter, the artist responsible for the majority of the drawings. And among the considerable number of editorial helpers and proof-readers who have assisted in the work, special mention must be made of Miss P. J. Holmes, to whom we are greatly indebted for her careful preparation of copy for our efficient printers and her accuracy in checking proofs and the multitudinous points of detail associated with a volume of this nature.

F. F. B.
J. I. P.
R. V. G. T.
D. J. W.

CONTENTS

Sixteen pages of photographs and sixteen pages of coloured maps will be found at the end of the volume.

EXPLANATIONS

TRANSLITERATION

The following systems of transliteration have been adopted throughout the volume. In fairness to our contributors it should be said that some have disagreed on philological grounds with our transliteration of Hebrew words generally and of the divine name *Yahweh* in particular (see p. 478), but they have graciously subordinated their own convictions to editorial policy.

Hebrew

א	=	’	ד	=	ḏ	י	=	y	ס	=	s	ר	=	r
בּ	=	b	ה	=	h	כּ	=	k	ע	=	‘	שׂ	=	ś
ב	=	ḇ	ו	=	w	כ	=	ḵ	פּ	=	p	שׁ	=	š
גּ	=	g	ז	=	z	ל	=	l	פ	=	p̄	תּ	=	t
ג	=	ğ	ח	=	ḥ	מ	=	m	צ	=	ṣ	ת	=	t
דּ	=	d	ט	=	ṭ	נ	=	n	ק	=	q			

Long Vowels						Short Vowels			Very Short Vowels		
ָ(ה)	=	â	ָ	=	ā	ַ	=	a	ֲ	=	^{a}
ֵי	=	ê	ֵ	=	ē	ֶ	=	e	ֱ	=	^{e}
ִי	=	î				ִ	=	i	ְ	=	^{e} (if vocal)
וֹ	=	ô	ֹ	=	ō	ָ	=	o	ֳ	=	^{o}
וּ	=	û				ֻ	=	u			

Greek

α	=	a	ι	=	i	ρ	=	r	ῥ	=	rh
β	=	b	κ	=	k	σ, ς	=	s	‘	=	h
γ	=	g	λ	=	l	τ	=	t	γξ	=	nx
δ	=	d	μ	=	m	υ	=	y	γγ	=	ng
ε	=	e	ν	=	n	φ	=	ph	αυ	=	au
ζ	=	z	ξ	=	x	χ	=	ch	ευ	=	eu
η	=	ē	ο	=	o	ψ	=	ps	ου	=	ou
θ	=	th	π	=	p	ω	=	ō	υι	=	yi

Arabic

ا	=	’	خ	=	ḫ	ش	=	š	غ	=	ġ	ن	=	n
ب	=	b	د	=	d	ص	=	ṣ	ف	=	f	ه	=	h
ت	=	t	ذ	=	ḏ	ض	=	ḍ	ق	=	ḳ	و	=	w
ث	=	t	ر	=	r	ط	=	ṭ	ك	=	k	ى	=	y
ج	=	ğ	ز	=	z	ظ	=	ẓ	ل	=	l	ة	=	t
ح	=	h	س	=	s	ع	=	‘	م	=	m			

AUTHORSHIP OF ARTICLES

The key to the initials appended to articles is printed on pp. x–xiii. Very short articles without initials are generally the work of the Organizing Editor.

BIBLIOGRAPHIES

To assist those wishing to study particular subjects in greater detail bibliographies have been appended to most of the longer articles. These usually provide references to the recent general works on the subject but may include detailed studies or books which take up a position differing from that of the contributor.

ABBREVIATIONS

A full list of abbreviations used in the Dictionary will be found on pp. xiv–xvi. To this has been added a list of some of the ancient writers and their works to which contributors have referred in their articles. This will be found on pp. 1362 ff.

LIST OF CONTRIBUTORS

Entries are made in alphabetical order of authors' initials

A.A.J. A. A. Jones, M.A., B.D., Ph.D., Vicar of St. Silas', Nunhead, London.

A.C. R. A. Cole, B.A., M.Th., Ph.D., Lecturer, Moore Theological College, Sydney.

A.E.W. A. E. Willingale, B.A., B.D., M.Th., Romford, Essex.

A.F. A. Flavelle, B.A., Minister of Mourne Presbyterian Church, Kilkeel, Co. Down.

A.F.W. A. F. Walls, M.A., B.Litt., Lecturer in Theology, Fourah Bay College, The University College of Sierra Leone, Freetown.

A.G. A. Gelston, M.A., Curate of St. Mary's Church, Chipping Norton, Oxfordshire.

A.K.C. A. K. Cragg, M.A., D.Phil., Warden of St. Augustine's College, Canterbury.

A.P.W. A. P. Waterson, M.D., M.R.C.P., Lecturer in Pathology, University of Cambridge.

A.R. A. Ross, M.A., B.D., D.D., formerly Professor of New Testament, Free Church College, Edinburgh.

A.R.M. A. R. Millard, B.A., Temporary Assistant Keeper, Department of Western Asiatic Antiquities, The British Museum.

A.S. A. Saarisalo, Teol. Dr., Professor of Oriental Literature, University of Helsinki.

A.St. A. Stuart, M.Sc., F.G.S., Emeritus Professor of Geology, University of Exeter.

A.S.W. A. S. Wood, B.A., Ph.D., F.R.Hist.S., Minister of Southlands Methodist Church, York.

A. van S. A. van Selms, D.D., Professor of Semitic Languages, University of Pretoria.

B.F.C.A. B. F. C. Atkinson, M.A., Ph.D., formerly Under-Librarian in the University of Cambridge.

B.F.H. B. F. Harris, M.A., B.D., Senior Lecturer in Classics, University of Auckland.

B.L.S. B. L. Smith, B.D., Th.Schol., Lecturer, Moore Theological College, Sydney.

B.O.B. B. O. Banwell, B.A., Methodist Minister in Fish Hoek, Cape Town.

C.D.W. C. de Wit, Docteur en Philologie et Histoire Orientales, Bruxelles. Attaché aux Musées Royaux d'Art et d'Histoire de Belgique; Chef de la section de l'Égypte Pharaonique à la Fondation Égyptologique Reine Elisabeth, Bruxelles.

C.F.P. C. F. Pfeiffer, B.A., B.D., Ph.D., Associate Professor of Old Testament, Gordon Divinity School, Beverly Farms, Massachusetts.

C.H.D. C. H. Duncan, M.A., B.D., Ph.D., Registrar of the Australian College of Theology; Senior Lecturer of Ridley College, Melbourne.

C.L.F. C. L. Feinberg, Th.D., Ph.D., Professor of Semitics and Old Testament; and Dean of Talbot Theological Seminary, Los Angeles.

D.A.H. D. A. Hubbard, Th.M., Ph.D., Chairman, Division of Biblical Studies and Philosophy, Westmont College, Santa Barbara, California.

D.B.K. D. B. Knox, B.A., B.D., M.Th., D.Phil., Principal of Moore Theological College, Sydney; Canon of St. Andrew's Cathedral, Sydney.

D.C. D. Calcott, B.Sc., N.D.A., Tutor in charge of Commonwealth Bursars' Course, University of Reading, Institute of Education.

D.F. D. Freeman, Ph.D., Orthodox Presbyterian Minister in Philadelphia.

D.F.P. D. F. Payne, M.A., Assistant Lecturer in Biblical History and Literature, University of Sheffield.

D.G. D. Guthrie, B.D., M.Th., Ph.D., Lecturer in New Testament Language and Literature, London Bible College.

D.G.S. D. G. Stradling, M.A., Magdalen College, Oxford.

D.H.T. D. H. Tongue, M.A., Vicar of Locking, Somerset, and Lecturer in New Testament at Tyndale Hall, Bristol.

D.H.W. D. H. Wheaton, M.A., B.D., Tutor at Oak Hill College, London.

D.J.V.L. D. J. V. Lane, B.D., Ll.B., Missionary with the China Inland Mission (O.M.F.) in Malaya.

D.J.W. D. J. Wiseman, O.B.E., M.A., A.K.C., F.S.A., Professor of Assyriology, University of London.

D.K.I. D. K. Innes, M.A., B.D., Curate of St. John's, Ealing Dean, London.

D.O.S. D. O. Swann, B.A., B.D., Minister of Pontnewydd Congregational Church, Cwmbran, Monmouthshire.

D.R.H. D. R. Hall, M.A., Methodist Minister in South Ferriby, Lincolnshire.

D.W.B.R. D. W. B. Robinson, M.A., Vice-Principal of Moore Theological College, Sydney.

D.W.G. D. W. Gooding, M.A., Ph.D., Lecturer in Classics, The Queen's University, Belfast.

E.A.J. E. A. Judge, M.A., Senior Lecturer in History, University of Sydney.

E.E.E. E. E. Ellis, Ph.D., Visiting Professor of New Testament Interpretation, Bethel Seminary, St. Paul, Minnesota.

E.M.B. E. M. Blaiklock, M.A., Litt.D., Professor of Classics, University of Auckland.

E.M.B.G. E. M. B. Green, M.A., Lecturer, The London College of Divinity, Middlesex.

E.S.P.H. E. S. P. Heavenor, M.A., B.D., Minister of the Abbey Church, North Berwick, East Lothian.

E.J.Y. E. J. Young, B.A., Th.M., Ph.D., Professor of Old Testament, Westminster Theological Seminary, Philadelphia.

F.C.F. F. C. Fensham, M.A., Ph.D., D.D., University of Stellenbosch, South Africa.

F.F. F. Foulkes, M.A., B.D., M.Sc., Principal, Vining Christian Leadership Centre, Akure, Nigeria.

F.F.B. F. F. Bruce, M.A., D.D., Rylands Professor of Biblical Criticism and Exegesis, University of Manchester.

F.H.P. F. H. Palmer, M.A., Chaplain of Fitzwilliam House, Cambridge.

F.N.H. F. N. Hepper, B.Sc., F.L.S., The Herbarium, Royal Botanic Gardens, Kew, London.

F.R.S. F. R. Steele, Ph.D., Home Secretary of the American Branch, North Africa Mission; formerly Associate Curator, University Museum, Philadelphia.

F.S.F. F. S. Fitzsimmonds, B.A., B.D., M.Th., Tutor in Biblical Languages and Exegesis, Spurgeon's College, London.

G.C. G. S. Cansdale, B.A., B.Sc., F.L.S., formerly Superintendent, Zoological Society of London.

G.C.D.H. G. C. D. Howley, Editor of *The Witness*.

G.E.L. G. E. Ladd, Th.B., B.D., Ph.D., Professor at Fuller Theological Seminary, Pasadena, California.

G.I.E. Mrs. Grace I. Emmerson, M.A., Dip.Heb., Fazakerley, Liverpool.

G.O. G. Ogg, M.A., B.Sc., D.D., D.Litt., Minister at Anstruther Easter, Fife.

G.S.M.W. G. S. M. Walker, M.A., B.D., Ph.D., Lecturer in Church History, University of Leeds.

G.T.M. The late G. T. Manley, M.A., sometime Fellow of Christ's College, Cambridge.

G.W. G. Walters, B.A., B.D., Ph.D., Professor of Pastoral Theology, Gordon Divinity School, Beverly Farms, Massachusetts.

G.W.G. G. W. Grogan, B.D., M.Th., Lecturer, Bible Training Institute, Glasgow.

H.A.G.B. H. A. G. Belben, M.A., B.D., Tutor at Cliff College, Calver, Derbyshire.

H.D.McD. H. D. McDonald, B.A., B.D., Ph.D., Vice-Principal of London Bible College.

H.L.E. H. L. Ellison, B.D., B.A., Lecturer and Writer on Old Testament.

H.M.C. H. M. Carson, B.A., B.D., Vicar of St. Paul's, Cambridge.

H.R. H. Ridderbos, Dr. Theol., Professor of New Testament, Kampen Theological Seminary, The Netherlands.

I.H.M. I. H. Marshall, M.A., B.D., Assistant Tutor at Didsbury College, Bristol.

J.A.B. J. A. Balchin, M.A., B.D., Lecturer in Old Testament and Hebrew, Bible Training Institute, Glasgow.

J.A.M. J. A. Motyer, M.A., B.D., Vice-Principal of Clifton Theological College, Bristol.

J.A.T. J. A. Thompson, M.A., B.Ed., M.Sc., B.D., Lecturer in the Baptist Theological College of New South Wales.

J.B.J. J. B. Job, M.A., Wesley College, Headingley, Leeds.

LIST OF CONTRIBUTORS

J.B.P. J. B. Payne, M.A., Th.D., Associate Professor of Old Testament, Wheaton College, Illinois.

J.B.T. J. B. Torrance, M.A., B.D., Lecturer in Divinity and Dogmatics, New College, University of Edinburgh.

J.B.TT. J. B. Taylor, M.A., Vicar of Henham and Elsenham, Essex.

J.C.C. J. C. Connell, M.A., Lecturer in Biblical Exegesis, London Bible College.

J.C.J.W. J. C. J. Waite, B.D., Principal, South Wales Bible College.

J.C.W. J. C. Whitcomb, Jr., Th.D., Professor of Old Testament, Grace Theological Seminary, Winona Lake, Indiana.

J.D.D. J. D. Douglas, M.A., B.D., S.T.M., British Editorial Associate, *Christianity Today.*

J.G.G.N. J. G. G. Norman, B.D., M.Th., Minister of George Road Baptist Church, Birmingham.

J.G.S.S.T. J. G. S. S. Thomson, M.A., B.D., B.A., Ph.D., Minister of St. David's, Knightswood, Glasgow.

J.H. J. W. L. Hoad, M.A., Methodist Chaplain to the University College of the West Indies.

J.H.H. J. H. Harrop, M.A., Lecturer in Classics, Fourah Bay College, The University College of Sierra Leone.

J.H.P. J. H. Paterson, M.A., Lecturer in Geography, University of St. Andrews.

J.H.S. J. H. Skilton, Th.B., A.M., Ph.D., Associate Professor of New Testament, Westminster Theological Seminary, Philadelphia.

J.H.SR. J. H. Stringer, M.A., B.D., Methodist Minister in Ventnor, Isle of Wight.

J.I.P. J. I. Packer, M.A., D.Phil., Librarian, Latimer House, Oxford.

J.L.K. J. L. Kelso, Th.D., Ll.D., Professor of Old Testament History and Biblical Archaeology, Pittsburgh Theological Seminary, Pittsburgh, Pennsylvania.

J.M. J. Murray, M.A., Th.M., Professor of Systematic Theology, Westminster Theological Seminary, Philadelphia.

J.M.H. J. M. Houston, M.A., B.Sc., D.Phil., Lecturer in Geography, University of Oxford.

J.N.B. J. N. Birdsall, M.A., Ph.D., Lecturer in Theology, University of Birmingham.

J.N.G. J. N. Geldenhuys, B.A., B.D., Th.M., Manager of Publications of the Dutch Reformed Church, South Africa.

J.P. J. Philip, M.A., Minister of Holyrood Abbey Church, Edinburgh.

J.P.U.L. J. P. U. Lilley, M.A., A.C.A., Magdalen College, Oxford.

J.R. J. Rea, Th.D., Moody Bible Institute, Chicago, Illinois.

J.S.W. J. S. Wright, M.A., Principal of Tyndale Hall, Bristol.

J.T. J. A. Thompson, B.A., Th.M., Ph.D., Professor of Old Testament Language in the Evangelical Theological Seminary, Cairo, Egypt.

J.W.C. J. W. Charley, M.A., Assistant Curate of All Souls', Langham Place, London.

J.W.M. J. W. Meiklejohn, M.A., Secretary of the Scripture Union Inter-School Fellowship in Scotland.

K.A.K. K. A. Kitchen, B.A., Lecturer in Egyptian and Coptic, University of Liverpool.

K.L.MCK. K. L. McKay, M.A., Senior Lecturer in Classics, School of General Studies, Australian National University, Canberra, Australia.

L.C.A. L. C. Allen, M.A., Tutor in Hebrew, London Bible College.

L.M. L. L. Morris, B.Sc., M.Th., Ph.D., Warden of Tyndale House, Cambridge.

M.A.M. M. A. MacLeod, M.A., Minister of Tarbert Free Church of Scotland, Argyll.

M.G. Miss M. Gray, B.A., B.D., Senior Lecturer in Divinity, Cheshire County Training College, Alsager.

M.G.K. M. G. Kline, Ph.D., Associate Professor of Old Testament, Westminster Theological Seminary, Philadelphia.

M.H.C. M. H. Cressey, M.A., Minister of St. Columba's Presbyterian Church of England, Coventry.

M.J.S.R. M. J. S. Rudwick, M.A., Ph.D., Fellow of Trinity College, Cambridge.

M.R.G. M. R. Gordon, B.D., Principal of the Bible Institute of South Africa, Kalk Bay, South Africa.

M.R.W.F. M. R. W. Farrer, M.A., Tutor in Clifton Theological College, Bristol.

M.T.F. M. T. Fermer, B.A., B.Sc., A.R.C.S., Vicar of Tamerton Foliot, Plymouth.

N.H.R. N. H. Ridderbos, D.D., Professor of Old Testament, Free University, Amsterdam.

P.A.B. P. A. Blair, M.A., Chaplain and Assistant Master, Oundle School.

P.E. P. Ellingworth, M.A., Tutor at École Pastorale Évangélique, Porto-Novo, Dahomey, West Africa.

P.E.H. P. E. Hughes, M.A., B.D., D.Litt., Editor of *The Churchman*.

P.W. P. Woolley, Th.M., Professor of Church History, Westminster Theological Seminary, Philadelphia.

R.A.F. R. A. Finlayson, M.A., Professor of Systematic Theology, Free Church College, Edinburgh.

R.A.H.G. R. A. H. Gunner, M.Th., B.A., Assistant Lecturer in Brooklands Technical College, Weybridge, Surrey.

R.A.S. R. A. Stewart, M.A., B.D., M.Litt., Minister of Victoria Tollcross, Glasgow.

R.E.N. R. E. Nixon, M.A., Tutor in Cranmer Hall, Durham.

R.F.H. R. F. Hosking, B.A., Assistant Keeper, Department of Oriental Printed Books and Manuscripts, The British Museum.

R.H.M. R. H. Mounce, B.A., B.D., Th.M., Ph.D., Associate Professor of Biblical Literature and Chairman of the Department of Christianity, Bethel College and Seminary, St. Paul, Minnesota.

R.J.A.S. R. J. A. Sheriffs, B.A., B.D., Ph.D., formerly Lecturer in Old Testament, Rhodes University, Grahamstown, Cape Province.

R.J.C. R. J. Coates, M.A., formerly Warden of Latimer House, Oxford.

R.J.McK. R. J. McKelvey, B.A., M.Th., D.Phil., Lecturer at Adams United Theological School, Modderpoort, Orange Free State.

R.J.T. R. J. Thompson, B.A., B.D., Dr.Theol., Th.M., New Zealand Baptist Theological College, Auckland.

R.J.W. R. J. Way, M.A., Westminster College, Cambridge.

R.K.H. R. K. Harrison, M.Th., Ph.D., Professor of Old Testament, Wycliffe College, University of Toronto.

R.N.C. R. N. Caswell, M.A., Ph.D., Principal of Belfast Bible College.

R.P.M. R. P. Martin, M.A., Lecturer in Theology, London Bible College.

R.S.W. R. S. Wallace, M.A., B.Sc., Ph.D., Minister of Lothian Road Church, Edinburgh.

R.T.B. R. T. Beckwith, M.A., Tutor in Tyndale Hall, Bristol.

R.V.G.T. R. V. G. Tasker, M.A., D.D., Emeritus Professor of New Testament Exegesis, University of London.

S.S.S. S. S. Smalley, M.A., B.D., Chaplain of Peterhouse, Cambridge.

T.C.M. T. C. Mitchell, M.A., Research Assistant, Department of Western Asiatic Antiquities, The British Museum.

T.H.J. T. H. Jones, B.A., B.D., Scripture Specialist, King Edward VII Grammar School, Coalville, Leicestershire.

W.G. W. H. Gispen, D.Theol., Doctorandus Semitic Languages. Professor of Old Testament Exegesis, The Free University, Amsterdam.

W.G.P. W. G. Putman, B.A., B.D., Methodist Minister in Dudley, Worcestershire.

W.J.C. W. J. Cameron, M.A., B.D., Professor of New Testament Language, Literature and Theology, Free Church College, Edinburgh.

W.J.M. W. J. Martin, M.A., Ph.D., Senior Rankin Lecturer in Hebrew and Ancient Semitic Languages, University of Liverpool.

W.W.W. W. W. Wessel, Ph.D., Professor of Biblical Literature, North American Baptist Seminary, Sioux Falls, South Dakota.

ABBREVIATIONS

I. REFERENCE BOOKS AND JOURNALS

AASOR	*Annual of the American Schools of Oriental Research*
A.f.O.	*Archiv für Orientforschung*
A. J. Arch.	*American Journal of Archaeology*
AJSL	*American Journal of Semitic Languages and Literatures*
ANEP	*The Ancient Near East in Pictures* (J. B. Pritchard), 1954
ANET	*Ancient Near Eastern Texts* (J. B. Pritchard), 1950
ANT	*The Apocryphal New Testament* (M. R. James), 1924
ARAB	*Ancient Records of Assyria and Babylonia* (D. D. Luckenbill), 1926
ARE	*Ancient Records of Egypt* (J. H. Breasted), 5 vols., 1906–7
Arndt	Arndt–Gingrich, *Greek-English Lexicon of the New Testament*, 1957
AS	*Anatolian Studies*
BA	*Biblical Archaeologist*
BASOR	*Bulletin of the American Schools of Oriental Research*
BC	*The Beginnings of Christianity* (ed. Foakes-Jackson and Lake), 5 vols., 1920–33
BDB	Brown, Driver and Briggs, *Hebrew–English Lexicon of the Old Testament*, 1907
Bib	*Biblica*
BIES	*Bulletin of the Israel Exploration Society*
BJRL	*Bulletin of the John Rylands Library*
BO	*Bibliotheca Orientalis*
BS	*Bibliotheca Sacra*
BTh	*Biblical Theology*
BZAW	*Beiheft, Zeitschrift für die alttestamentliche Wissenschaft*
CAH	*Cambridge Ancient History*, 12 vols., 1923–39
CBP	*Cities and Bishoprics of Phrygia* (W. M. Ramsay), 1895–7
CBQ	*Catholic Biblical Quarterly*
CBSC	*Cambridge Bible for Schools and Colleges*
CDC	*Cairo Geniza Documents of the Damascus Covenanters*
CE	*Chronique d'Égypte*
CGT	*Cambridge Greek Testament*
CIG	*Corpus Inscriptionum Graecarum*
CIL	*Corpus Inscriptionum Latinarum*
CQ	*Crozer Quarterly*
CRE	*The Church in the Roman Empire before A.D. 170* (W. M. Ramsay), 1903
DAC	*Dictionary of the Apostolic Church* (J. Hastings), 2 vols., 1915–18
DCG	*Dictionary of Christ and the Gospels* (J. Hastings), 2 vols., 1906–8
BS	*Bible Studies*[2] (A. Deissmann), 1909
DOTT	*Documents from Old Testament Times* (ed. D. W. Thomas), 1958
EB	*Expositor's Bible*
EBi	*Encyclopaedia Biblica*, 4 vols., 1899–1903
EBr	*Encyclopaedia Britannica*
EEP	*The Earlier Epistles of St. Paul* (K. Lake), 1911
EGT	*Expositor's Greek Testament*
EH	*Historia Ecclesiastica* (Eusebius)
EIs	*Encyclopaedia of Islam*, 1954–
EQ	*Evangelical Quarterly*
ERE	*Encyclopaedia of Religion and Ethics* (J. Hastings), 13 vols., 1908–26
ExpT	*Expository Times*
GB	*Ginsburg's Bible* (*New Massoretico-Critical Text of the Hebrew Bible*), 1896
GTT	*Geographical and Topographical Texts of the Old Testament* (J. Simons), 1959
HDB	Hastings' *Dictionary of the Bible*, 5 vols., 1898–1904
HES	*Harvard Expedition to Samaria*, 1924
HHT	*Horae Hebraicae et Talmudicae* (J. Lightfoot), 1658–64
HJ	*Hibbert Journal*
HJP	*History of the Jewish People in the Time of Jesus Christ* (E. Schürer), E.T., 1892–1901
HNT	*Handbuch zum Neuen Testament* (H. Lietzmann), 1911
HTR	*Harvard Theological Review*
HUCA	*Hebrew Union College Annual*
IB	*Interpreter's Bible*, vols. I–XII, 1952–
IBA	*Illustrations from Biblical Archaeology* (D. J. Wiseman), 1958
ICC	*International Critical Commentary*
IEJ	*Israel Exploration Journal*
IG	*Inscriptiones Graecae*
ISBE	*International Standard Bible Encyclopaedia*[2], 5 vols., 1930
JAOS	*Journal of the American Oriental Society*
JBL	*Journal of Biblical Literature*
JCS	*Journal of Cuneiform Studies*
JEA	*Journal of Egyptian Archaeology*
JEH	*Journal of Ecclesiastical History*

JewE *Jewish Encyclopaedia*, 12 vols., 1901–6
JHS *Journal of Hellenic Studies*
JNES *Journal of Near Eastern Studies*
Jos., *Ant.* Josephus, *Antiquities of the Jews*
Jos., *BJ* Josephus, *Jewish Wars*
JPOS *Journal of the Palestine Oriental Society*
JQR *Jewish Quarterly Review*
JRAS *Journal of the Royal Asiatic Society*
JRS *Journal of Roman Studies*
JSS *Journal of Semitic Studies*
JTS *Journal of Theological Studies*
JTVI *Journal of the Transactions of the Victoria Institute*
KB Köhler-Baumgartner, *Lexicon in Veteris Testamenti Libros*, 1953
KEK *Kritisch-exegetischer Kommentar über das Neue Testament* (H. A. W. Meyer), 1951
LAE *Light from the Ancient East*[4] (A. Deissmann), 1929
LOT *Introduction to the Literature of the Old Testament*[9] (S. R. Driver), 1913
LSJ Liddell, Scott and Jones, *Greek-English Lexicon*, 1940
MM Moulton and Milligan, *The Vocabulary of the Greek Testament*, 1930
MNT *Moffatt New Testament Commentary*
NBC *New Bible Commentary* (ed. F. Davidson), 1953
Nestle *Nestle's Novum Testamentum Graece*[22], 1956
NH *Historia Naturalis* (Pliny)
NIC *New International Commentary*
NLC *New London Commentary*
NovT *Novum Testamentum*
NTS *New Testament Studies*
OCD *The Oxford Classical Dictionary* (ed. M. Cary, *etc.*), 1949
ODCC *The Oxford Dictionary of the Christian Church* (ed. F. L. Cross), 1957
OTMS *The Old Testament and Modern Study* (ed. H. H. Rowley), 1951
OTS *Oudtestamentische Studiën*
PEQ *Palestine Exploration Quarterly*
PG *Patrologia Graeca* (Migne)
PJB *Palästina-Jahrbuch*
PRU *Palais Royale d'Ugarit*
PTR *Princeton Theological Review*
RA *Revue d'Assyriologie*
RAr *Revue d'Archéologie*
RAC *Reallexicon für die Antike und Christentum*
RB *Revue Biblique*
RE *Realencyclopaedie der klassischen Altertumswissenschaft* (Pauly-Wissowa-Kroll)
RHR *Revue de l'Histoire des Religions*
SB (or Strack–Billerbeck) H. L. Strack and P. Billerbeck, *Kommentar zum Neuen Testament aus Talmud und Midrasch*, 5 vols., 1922–56
SHERK *The New Schaff–Herzog Encyclopaedia of Religious Knowledge*[2], 1949–52
SJT *Scottish Journal of Theology*
SPEM *St. Paul's Ephesian Ministry* (G. S. Duncan), 1929
SPT *St. Paul the Traveller and Roman Citizen* (W. M. Ramsay), 1920
ST *Studia Theologica*
TB *Babylonian Talmud*
TCERK *The Twentieth Century Encyclopaedia of Religious Knowledge*, 1955
Th.L. *Theologische Literaturzeitung*
TJ *Jerusalem Talmud*
TNTC *Tyndale New Testament Commentary*
TS *Texts and Studies*
TU *Texte und Untersuchungen zur Geschichte der altchristlichen Literatur*
TWNT *Theologisches Wörterbuch zum Neuen Testament* (G. Kittel and G. Friedrich), 1932–
VC *Vigiliae Christianae*
VT *Vetus Testamentum*
WC *Westminster Commentaries*
WDB *Westminster Dictionary of the Bible*, 1944
Wett J. J. Wettstein's *Novum Testamentum Graecum*, 1751–2
WH Westcott and Hort, *The New Testament in Greek*, 1881
WTJ *Westminster Theological Journal*
ZA *Zeitschrift für Assyriologie*
ZAW *Zeitschrift für die alttestamentliche Wissenschaft*
ZDM *Zeitschrift der deutschen morgenländischen Gesellschaft*
ZDPV *Zeitschrift des deutschen Palästina-Vereins*
ZNW *Zeitschrift für die neutestamentliche Wissenschaft*
ZTK *Zeitschrift für Theologie und Kirche*

Editions have been indicated by small superior figures thus: *LOT*[9]

II. GENERAL ABBREVIATIONS

ad loc. at the place
Akkad. Akkadian
Apocr. Apocrypha(l)
Aq. Aquila's Greek Translation of the Old Testament
Arab. Arabic
Aram. Aramaic
ARV American Revised Version
Assyr. Assyrian
ASV American Standard Version
AV Authorized Version
Bab. Babylonian

ABBREVIATIONS

BM	British Museum
c.	about (of time)
cf.	compare
Com.	Commentary
D	Deuteronomist
DSS	Dead Sea Scrolls
E	Elohist
Egyp.	Egyptian
E.T.	English Translation
Eth.	Ethiopic
EVV	English Versions
Gk.	Greek
H	Law of Holiness
Heb.	Hebrew
Lat.	Latin
L.L.	Late Latin
LXX	Septuagint
mg	margin
MS, MSS	manuscript(s)
MT	Massoretic Text
NEB	New English Bible
NS	New Series
op. cit.	in the work cited above
P	Priestly Narrative
par.	parallel
Pesh.	Peshitta
Phoen.	Phoenician
q.v.	which see
Rom.	Roman
RSV	Revised Standard Version
RV	Revised Version
Sem.	Semitic
s.v.	under the word
Symm.	Symmachus' Greek Translation of the Old Testament
Syr.	Syriac
Targ.	Targum
Theod.	Theodotion's Greek Translation of the Old Testament
tr.	translated or translation
TR	Textus Receptus
VSS	Versions
Vulg.	Vulgate

III. BIBLICAL BOOKS

Books of the Old Testament

Gn., Ex., Lv., Nu., Dt., Jos., Jdg., Ru., 1, 2 Sa., 1, 2 Ki., 1, 2 Ch., Ezr., Ne., Est., Jb., Ps. (Pss.), Pr., Ec., Ct., Is., Je., La., Ezk., Dn., Ho., Joel, Am., Ob., Jon., Mi., Na., Hab., Zp., Hg., Zc., Mal.

Books of the New Testament

Mt., Mk., Lk., Jn., Acts, Rom., 1, 2 Cor., Gal., Eph., Phil., Col., 1, 2 Thes., 1, 2 Tim., Tit., Phm., Heb., Jas., 1, 2 Pet., 1, 2, 3 Jn., Jude, Rev.

THE NEW BIBLE DICTIONARY

AARON. Probably the eldest son of Amram and Jochebed and three years older than his brother, Moses (Ex. vi. 20, vii. 7). Miriam was probably the older sister of both (Nu. xxvi. 59; 1 Ch. vi. 3), for she cared for the infant Moses (Ex. ii. 4 ff.). According to Ex. vi. 16–20 and 1 Ch. vi. 1–3, Aaron was the third in descent from Levi (Levi–Kohath–Amram–Aaron), but the genealogy is probably not intended to be complete (*cf.* Ru. iv. 18–20; 1 Ch. ii).

We first meet Aaron in connection with God's commission to Moses to go to Egypt. Moses complains that he is not eloquent (Ex. iv. 10), and Aaron is introduced as one who can speak well (Ex. iv. 14). Aaron is to serve as the 'prophet' or mouthpiece through whom Moses will speak to Pharaoh (Ex. vii. 1 ff.).

Aaron is commanded to meet Moses in the wilderness (Ex. iv. 27) and without hesitation or objection obeys. Moses instructs Aaron as to the work which they are to perform, and together they approach the people, gathering the elders about them, and informing them of what God will do. The people believe their words (Ex. iv. 27–31).

The first blush of belief, however, passed away. By reason of hard oppression the Israelites came to hearken not —'for anguish of spirit, and for cruel bondage' (Ex. vi. 9b). The Lord therefore gave a charge to Moses and Aaron, and the two of them went before the Egyptian king. It was Aaron who was to perform the miracles. Thus, he appears as an accredited spokesman, and acts in concert with Moses before Pharaoh.

We next hear of Aaron when the Amalekites attacked Israel. Together with Hur, Aaron held up the hands of Moses so that Israel prevailed against the enemy (Ex. xvii. 8 ff.). To Aaron, as also to Moses, to Aaron's two sons, Nadab and Abihu, and to the seventy elders, it was granted to behold the Lord's glory. Moses alone could approach the glory of the Lord, whereas the others were to worship from afar. Yet they beheld the Lord's glory (Ex. xxiv. 1, 9, 10).

Aaron, however, was not as strong a character as Moses. When Moses remained in the mount, Aaron yielded, albeit probably reluctantly, to the entreaties of the people to construct a god for them. Aaron may have thought that under the newly-fashioned gods he was worshipping the Lord (Ex. xxxii. 5), but he partook of idolatry nevertheless. When Moses called for those who were on the Lord's side, Aaron's people, the sons of Levi, quickly volunteered. The episode reveals Aaron not as a leader, but as a weak, pliable character.

Yet God uses servants who are sinful, and it was His purpose that Aaron should serve as high priest. Befitting the sacredness of the office, elaborate vestments were prepared for the high priest, as described in Ex. xxxix. The induction into office was a solemn occasion, and was conducted at the hands of Moses. Aaron in particular was anointed that he might be set apart for the sacred office (Lv. viii).

Aaron therefore was the spiritual leader of the nation. It comes as somewhat of a shock to learn that he associated with his sister Miriam in making a jealous complaint against Moses. As a pretext Miriam and Aaron murmured because Moses had married a Cushite woman (probably a woman who had joined the Israelites). Really, however, they were jealous of Moses' position in the divine economy. The Lord makes clear to Miriam and Aaron the nature of Moses' exalted office, and because of her part in the complaint Miriam is punished with leprosy. Aaron pleaded with Moses on his sister's behalf, and Moses prayed to God, with the result that Miriam was shut out from the camp for seven days (Nu. xii).

In Nu. xvi we read that both Moses and Aaron were the objects of a revolt on the part of Korah, Dathan and Abiram, but the Lord showed by a plague that Moses and Aaron were in positions of rightful authority. Aaron took a censer and ran into the midst of the congregation, thus making atonement for the people, and the plague was stayed. It must now be made clear to the people that Aaron is the legitimate high priest. This is done by the fact that, from among the rods of the different sons of Israel, Aaron's alone budded (Nu. xvii. 8). This rod was to be kept by the ark as a testimony against future rebels.

Together with Moses, Aaron, because of his unbelief, is precluded from entering the promised land (Nu. xx. 12). He died at the age of one hundred and twenty-three. There are three statements concerning his death. Moses announces his death and he is taken unto Mt. Hor, where his garments are taken from him and put upon his son and successor Eleazar. There on the top of the mountain Aaron died (Nu. xx. 28). The exact location of Mt. Hor is not known, although tradition puts it near Petra. The statement of his death is repeated in Nu. xxxiii. 38, 39 and again in Dt. x. 6.

Aaron appears as a somewhat secondary figure, living in the shadow of the greater figure, Moses. He seems to have exhibited true devotion to his priestly duties. The episode of the golden calf, however, would indicate that he was not a leader of the same calibre as his brother. E.J.Y.

AARON'S ROD. The rebellion of Korah, Dathan and Abiram made it clear that the supremacy of Aaron's priesthood must be emphasized. Moses is commanded (Nu. xvii. 1 ff., in Heb. verses 16 ff.) to take a rod (*maṭṭeh*) for each tribe of Israel and to write each prince's name upon it. Upon a thirteenth rod he is to write Aaron's name, and all are to be placed in the tabernacle. On the morrow Aaron's rod had budded, blossomed, and borne almonds. It was to be kept therefore before the testimony as a token against rebels. In Solomon's day this command was still observed, and only the two tables of the law were in the ark (1 Ki. viii. 9). Later, however, the rod also was kept in the ark (Heb. ix. 4). E.J.Y.

AB. See CALENDAR.

ABADDON. The satanic angel of the bottomless pit (Rev. ix. 11) whose Greek name is given as Apollyon, 'destroyer'. In Hebrew *'ᵃḇaddôn* means '(place of) destruction', and is usually translated thus in the AV Old Testament to signify the region of the dead—a familiar concept in later Jewish literature. See HELL. J.D.D.

ABANA, ABANAH. One of two Syrian rivers mentioned by the leprous Naaman in 2 Ki. v. 12. Named Chrysorrhoas ('Golden River') by the Greeks, it is probably identical with the modern Barada, which rises in the Anti-Lebanon mountains 18 miles north-west of Damascus, and then, after flowing through the city, enters a marshy lake, *Bahret el-Kibliyeh*, some 18 miles to the east. The fertile gardens and orchards which it waters may explain Naaman's boast. J.D.D.

ABARIM (*'ᵃḇārîm*). The plural form of a word meaning 'across' or 'beyond'; hence in Je. xxii. 20 the RV rightly renders it 'passages'. It can signify also 'the parts beyond' or 'distant places', and be used as a proper noun. In the itinerary of Nu. xxxiii. 44 ff., the Israelites camped at Iye-Abarim (*q.v.*), a station on the eastern border of Moab, then on 'the mountains of Abarim'—that is, on the central plateau. Thereafter they descended to the plains or grazing-grounds, facing Jericho. The plural form suggests a range, and this word is too general to be limited to a single spot. See also NEBO. G.T.M.

ABBA. An Aramaic word, in the emphatic state, meaning 'father', and used as a vocative in each of its three New Testament occurrences. The Aramaic word passed into Hebrew, and is used in TB, by a child to his father, and also, frequently, as an honorific style of address to Rabbis. In the New Testament it is always used to address God, and is followed immediately by the Greek translation. This double expression was common in the early Church, including the Greek-speaking section. Regarding the double expression in Mk. xiv. 36, some question if this was what the Lord actually said, or if the Evangelist added the Greek translation to aid his readers. D.F.P.

ABDON. 1. One of the Judges (Jdg. xii. 13). **2.** One of the heads of fathers' houses of Benjamin (1 Ch. viii. 23). **3.** A Benjamite ancestor of Saul (1 Ch. viii. 30, *cf.* ix. 35–39). **4.** A member of Josiah's court (2 Ch. xxxiv. 20). R.F.H.

ABDON. A levitical city in the portion of Asher (Jos. xxi. 30), identified with Khirbet 'Abdeh nearly 4 miles inland from Achzib on the coast of Phoenicia. R.F.H.

ABED-NEGO. The name given Azariah, companion of Daniel in exile (Dn. i. 7). Made an official of a Babylonian province until deposed on refusing to bow to an image (Dn. iii. 13), but restored after escaping the furnace (iii. 30). Most consider the name, unknown in Neo-Babylonian texts, to be a dissimulation from common Abed-Nebo (= Arad-Nabu), 'servant of the god Nabu', to avoid giving a heathen name to a Jew. He is mentioned in 1 Macc. ii. 59 and, by implication, in Heb. xi. 33, 34. D.J.W.

ABEL. The second son of Adam and Eve, and the brother (perhaps the twin, Gn. iv. 1, 2) of Cain. The name is sometimes connected with Akkadian *aplu*, 'son', or Sumerian *ibila*, but as there can be no knowledge of what language was spoken at the time this remains a conjecture. Abel was a righteous (*dikaios*, Mt. xxiii. 35) man and when he, as a shepherd (Gn. iv. 2), brought an offering of the firstlings of his flock, God accepted it (Gn. iv. 4; Heb. xi. 4). He was subsequently murdered by Cain, leaving, so far as we know, no offspring. It is clear that to Christ he was a historical person (Mt. xxiii. 35; Lk. xi. 51). See CAIN.

BIBLIOGRAPHY. L. Köhler and W. Baumgartner, *Lexicon in Veteris Testamenti Libros*, 1953, p. 224; and *cf.* S. Landersdorfer, *Sumerisches Sprachgut im Alten Testament*, 1916, pp. 67, 68.
T.C.M.

ABEL (*'āḇēl*, 'meadow'). Used as a prefix in several place-names, *e.g.* Abel-shittim, 'meadow of acacias', Nu. xxxiii. 49. See also 1 Sa. vi. 18; where the Heb. mentions 'the great meadow' and the Gk. 'the great stone', AV renders 'the great stone of Abel'. J.D.D.

ABEL-BETH-MAACHAH (*'āḇēl bêṯ ma'ᵃḵâ*, 'meadow of the house of oppression'). The place in N Palestine to which Joab pursued Sheba, son of Bichri (2 Sa. xx. 14); taken by the Syrians under Ben-hadad (1 Ki. xv. 20; 2 Ch. xvi. 4, where it is called Abel-maim); later by the Assyrians under Tiglath-pileser (2 Ki. xv. 29). Generally identified with the modern Tell Abil near Lake Huleh. J.D.D.

ABEL-MEHOLAH. Usually identified with Tel Abu Sifri, west of Jordan, about half-way between the Sea of Galilee and the Dead Sea. It is mentioned in the flight of the Midianites before Gideon (Jdg. vii. 22), was on the boundary of Solomon's fifth district (1 Ki. iv. 12), and was the birth-place of Elisha (1 Ki. xix. 16). A new identification, Tell el-Maqlūb on the Wadi el-Jābis, has been proposed by N. Glueck in *AASOR*, xxv–xxviii, 1951, p. 216, and for a discussion of the problem see *GTT*, pp. 293, 294. R.F.H.

ABEL-SHITTIM. See SHITTIM.

ABIATHAR (*'eḇyāṯār*, 'father of excellence'). Son of Ahimelech and with him priest at Nob. He alone escaped from the massacre of his family by Saul and joined David at Keilah, bringing with him an ephod (1 Sa. xxii. 20–22, xxiii. 6, 9). He helped to take the ark to Jerusalem, where he was one of David's counsellors (1 Ch. xv. 11, xxvii. 34). He was sent back to Jerusalem with his son Jonathan, when David fled, to act in the king's interests against Absalom (2 Sa. xv. 35 ff., xvii. 15). At the close of David's reign he conspired to make Adonijah king, and was expelled from office by Solomon (1 Ki. i, ii). Abiathar may have been high priest during David's reign; he seems to have been senior to Zadok (1 Ki. ii. 35; *cf.* Mk. ii. 26). It is uncertain whether he had a son Ahimelech or whether the two names have been transposed in 2 Sa. viii. 17; 1 Ch. xxiv. 6. A.R.M.

ABIB. See CALENDAR.

ABIEL (*'aḇî'ēl*, 'God is my father'). **1.** Saul's grandfather, mentioned in 1 Sa. ix. 1 and xiv. 51. **2.** A member of David's body-guard in 1 Ch. xi. 32, called Abi-albon in 2 Sa. xxiii. 31, where some codices of LXX have Abiel. R.A.H.G.

ABIEZER (*'aḇî'ezer*, 'father is help'). **1.** A clan of Manasseh (Jos. xvii. 2; 1 Ch. vii. 18). It was Gideon's clan (Jdg. vi. 11). He said it was the poorest in Manasseh (Jdg. vi. 15), though this may simply be typical of Gideon's humility, as with Saul in 1 Sa. ix. 21 (*cf.* Moore, *ICC*). In Gideon's time the seat of the clan was at Ophrah, west of Jordan (Jdg. vi. 11, 24). Jeezer (*'î'ezer*) in Nu. xxvi. 30 is a contraction. Abiezrite is the gentilic name.

2. The Anethothite (2 Sa. xxiii. 27) or Antothite (1 Ch. xi. 28). One of the 'Thirty' of David's mighty men, from Anathoth of Benjamin (*cf.* Je. i. 1), 2 miles north of Jerusalem. He commanded David's army in the ninth month (1 Ch. xxvii. 12). J.G.G.N.

ABIGAIL (*'aḇîgayil*, 'my father is joy'(?)).

1. The wife of Nabal the Carmelite or Calebite, a wealthy boor who lived in Maon, and a contrast to her husband. She realized that his veiled insult in his refusal to give gifts to David's men, at the time of sheepshearing, endangered the whole household, and so, on her own responsibility, she took gifts of loaves, wine, sheep, corn, raisins, and figs, and waylaid David as he was planning his attack, thus preventing bloodshed. Her wisdom, beauty, and dignity impressed him and he blessed God. When she told Nabal of her action he appreciated the narrowness of their escape, and from fright fell into an apoplectic fit and died—at the hand of God. David then married her and thus secured a new social position and a rich estate. With Ahinoam, the Jezreelite, she shared David's life at Gath. They were captured by the Amalekites near Ziklag and rescued (1 Sa. xxx. 18). She was the mother of Chileab (2 Sa. iii. 3), or Daniel (1 Ch. iii. 1), David's second son.

2. The wife of Ithra (2 Sa. xvii. 25) or Jether (1 Ch. ii. 17; 1 Ki. ii. 5) the Ishmaelite—terms easily confused in Hebrew—and mother of Amasa. She was a daughter of Nahash (2 Sa. xvii. 25) or Jesse (1 Ch. ii. 13–16). Modern critics dismiss Nahash (*q.v.*) as a scribal error. M.G.

ABIHAIL (*'aḇîḥayil*, 'my father is might'). **1.** A Levite (Nu. iii. 35). **2.** The wife of Abishur (1 Ch. ii. 29). **3.** A Gadite living in Bashan (1 Ch. v. 14). **4.** The mother of Rehoboam's wife Mahalath and daughter of Eliab, the son of Jesse (2 Ch. xi. 18). **5.** Esther's father (Est. ii. 15, ix. 29). R.A.H.G.

ABIHU (*'aḇîhû'*, 'my father is he' [*sc.* Yahweh]). Son of Aaron, a priest. He saw God in His glory (Ex. xxiv. 1, 9) yet acted independently of the requirements of the ritual law and was killed by holy fire (Lv. x. 1–8). A.R.M.

ABIJAH (*'aḇîyâ*, 'my father is Yahweh', or 'Yahweh is father'). A name borne by several men and women in the Old Testament. Chief among them are the second son of Samuel (1 Sa. viii. 2; 1 Ch. vi. 28), a descendant of Eleazar who gave his name to the eighth of the twenty-four courses of priests (1 Ch. xxiv. 10; *cf.* Lk. i. 5), the son of Jeroboam I (1 Ki. xiv. 1–18), and the son and successor of Rehoboam king of Judah (1 Ch. iii. 10; 2 Ch. xi. 20, xiii. 1). The name of the latter appears as Abijam (*'aḇîyām*, 'father of sea', or 'father of west') in 1 Ki. xiv. 31, xv. 1, 7, 8. Several Heb. MSS, however, read Abijah here and this reading is supported by the LXX *Abiou*.

Abijah reigned three years over Judah (1 Ki. xv. 2; 2 Ch. xiii. 2). The accounts of his reign in Kings and Chronicles stand in marked yet reconcilable contrast to each other. In the former he is censured for his adherence to the corrupt religious policy of his father (1 Ki. xv. 3). The account in Chronicles (2 Ch. xiii) is almost wholly concerned with a decisive victory with Yahweh's help over the numerically stronger army of

Jeroboam I. Abijah's oration before the battle condemns the apostasy of the northern kingdom and affirms the divine sanction attaching to the Davidic dynasty and the worship offered at the Temple at Jerusalem. J.C.J.W.

ABILENE. A region of Anti-Lebanon, attached to the city of Abila (*cf.* Heb. *'āḇēl*, 'meadow'), on the bank of the Abana (mod. Barada), some 18 miles north-west of Damascus (its ruins still stand round the village of Es-Suk). Abilene belonged to the Ituraean kingdom of Ptolemy Mennaeus (*c.* 85–40 BC) and his son Lysanias I (40–36 BC); it was later detached to form the tetrarchy of a younger Lysanias, mentioned in Luke iii. 1 (see LYSANIAS). In AD 37 it was given by the Emperor Gaius to Herod Agrippa I as part of his kingdom, and in 53 by Claudius to Herod Agrippa II. *Cf.* Jos., *BJ* ii. 11. 5, ii. 12. 8; *Ant.* xviii. 6. 10, xix. 5. 1, xx. 7. 1. F.F.B.

ABIMELECH (*'aḇîmeleḵ*, 'the (divine) king is my father'). **1.** A common cognomen of Philistine kings (*cf.* Pharaoh in Egypt and Agag among the Amalekites); it is used in the Old Testament in this sense for three different persons: (*a*) King of Gerar in the time of Abraham (*q.v.*), at whose court the latter tried to pass off Sarah as his sister (Gn. xx. 1–18). Both later made a covenant (Gn. xxi. 22–24). (*b*) Another Philistine king at Gerar with whom Isaac (*q.v.*) attempted a similar stratagem. Again the king and the Patriarch entered into a covenant (Gn. xxvi. 1–33). While there are many similarities between the two incidents, there are also significant differences. See, *e.g.*, A. H. Finn, *The Unity of the Pentateuch*, p. 28. (*c*) The name given to Achish in the title of Ps. xxxiv.

2. A son of Gideon by a Shechemite concubine. He secured the aid of his mother's family in murdering all his seventy brothers, except Jotham the youngest, who escaped. He assumed the title of king, but how far his hegemony extended is doubtful. After three years, dissension arose in Shechem, resulting in a revolt led by Gaal. This was cruelly suppressed, but in another engagement at Thebez, Abimelech was mortally wounded by a millstone thrown by a woman, and to save his honour commanded his armour-bearer to end his life (Jdg. ix).

3. A priest, the son of Abiathar (1 Ch. xviii. 16) according to *MT*, but perhaps a scribal error for A*h*imelech (*cf.* 2 Sa. viii. 17). M.A.M.

ABIRAM (*'aḇîrām*, 'the exalted one is (my) father'). **1.** A son of Eliab, a Reubenite. With his brother Dathan (*q.v.*) and the Levite Korah (*q.v.*), he took part in a rebellion against Moses, Nu. xvi. **2.** Firstborn son of Hiel the Bethelite, the rebuilder of Jericho *c.* 870 BC. The foundations of the city were laid at the cost of Abiram's life, 1 Ki. xvi. 34.

ABISHAG (*'aḇîšaḡ*; possibly, 'father has wandered'). A beautiful Shunammite girl brought by David's servants to minister to the aged king (1 Ki. i. 1–4). After Solomon's accession, Adonijah, David's eldest son, sought her for his wife. Solomon interpreted this as an attempt on the throne, and had him executed (1 Ki. ii. 12–24), for by ancient custom a man's concubines became the inheritance of his heir (*cf.* 2 Sa. xvi. 20 ff.). J.G.G.N.

ABISHAI (*'aḇîšay*, 'father of gift' or 'my father is Jesse'). Son of Zeruiah and brother of Joab and Asahel (2 Sa. ii. 18). 2 Sa. xxiii. 18; 1 Ch. xi. 20, 21, show him to be chief of 'the three', which must mean (as the Vulgate translates) 'the second group of three', next in order to 'the three' of 2 Sa. xxiii. 8–12. However, two Hebrew MSS and the Syriac of 2 Sa. xxiii. 18, 19 and the Syriac of 1 Ch. xi. 20 make him the chief of 'the thirty'. He had an eventful career as a high officer in David's army. G.W.G.

ABISHALOM. Found in 1 Ki. xv. 2, 10 as an alternative name for Absalom (*q.v.*).

ABNER (*'aḇnēr*, but *'aḇînēr* in 1 Sa. xiv. 50). The cousin of Saul. Their paternal grandfather was Abiel (1 Sa. ix. 1, 2, xiv. 51), a descendant of Ner the son of Jeiel, and this Ner is referred to in 1 Ch. viii. 33, ix. 39. The intermediate generations are not mentioned. Abner was given the post of 'captain of the host' under Saul, and on the death of the king he obtained for Ishbosheth the allegiance of all the tribes except Judah (2 Sa. ii. 8–10). During the war which followed he conducted the campaign for Ishbosheth, but was alienated from him by the insinuation that he himself was aiming at the crown by taking Saul's concubine (2 Sa. iii. 7; *cf.* 1 Ki. ii. 13–25). He then offered to win all Israel over to David, but was treacherously slain by Joab. His reluctance to kill Asahel (2 Sa. ii. 18–23) and his generosity in votive offerings for the future temple (1 Ch. xxvi. 28) reveal the finer aspects of his character. M.A.M.

ABOMINATION. Four Hebrew words are translated thus. 1. *piggûl* is used of sacrificial flesh which has been left too long (Lv. vii. 18, *etc.*). 2. *šiqqûṣ* refers to idols ('Milcom the abomination of the Ammonites', 1 Ki. xi. 5), and to customs derived from idolatry (Je. xvi. 18). 3. The related word *šeqeṣ* is used in much the same way, a notable extension of meaning being its application to food prohibited for Israelites as being 'unclean' (Lv. xi. 10 f.). 4. *tô'ēḇâ* is the most important word of the group. This may denote that which offends anyone's religious susceptibilities: 'every shepherd is an abomination unto the Egyptians' (Gn. xlvi. 34; so with eating with foreigners, Gn. xliii. 32). Or it may be used of idols (in 2 Ki. xxiii. 13 *šiqqûṣ* is used of Ashtoreth and Chemosh and *tô'ēḇâ* of Milcom). It denotes practices derived from idolatry, as when Ahaz 'made his son to pass through the fire, according to the abominations of the heathen' (2 Ki. xvi. 3), and all magic and divination (Dt. xviii. 9–14). But the word is not confined to heathen customs. Sacrifice offered to Yahweh in the wrong spirit is 'abomination' (Pr. xv. 8; Is. i. 13). So is sexual sin (Lv. xviii. 22). And the word attains a strongly ethical connotation when such things as 'lying lips' and 'divers weights' are said to be an abomination to the Lord (Pr. xii. 22, xx. 23, *cf.* also vi. 16 ff., *etc.*). L.M.

ABOMINATION OF DESOLATION. A description of some act of profanity which Jesus tells His disciples will be the sign that they must leave Jerusalem and escape to the hills. The key to its meaning, the reader of Mk. xiii. 14 and Mt. xxiv. 15 is told, is to be found in Daniel in the Hebrew expression *šiqqûṣ šōmēm*, which probably means 'the abomination that causes horror'. The LXX rendering, *to bdelygma tēs erēmōseōs*, 'the abomination that causes desolation', is followed in the Gospels. No certain conclusions have been reached regarding the meaning of the term *bdelygma* in this context. It has been identified with antichrist (*cf.* 2 Thes. ii. 1–4); and the fact that the original text of Mk. xiii. 14 could be translated 'standing where he ought not', gives plausibility to this view. It has also been regarded as a profanation of the Temple by the erection of an idol, similar to that perpetrated by Antiochus Epiphanes; and the expression 'stand (neuter) in the holy place' in Mt. xxiv. 15 is in keeping with this. Others regard the expression as prophetic of the desecration wrought by the Roman army previous to the destruction of Jerusalem. Some scholars, accepting as genuine the Syriac text of Mt. xxiv. 15, which omits 'standing in the holy place' and reads 'the sign of abomination', interpret 'the sign' as the Roman ensign to which the image of the emperor was attached—an abomination indeed to a Jew.

BIBLIOGRAPHY. For a recent and very full discussion see G. R. Beasley-Murray, *A Commentary on Mark Thirteen*, 1957, pp. 54–72.

R.V.G.T.

ABRAHAM. A descendant of Shem and son of Terah, who became the ancestor of the Hebrew and other nations (Gn. xvii. 5). He lived a life of outstanding faith and was known as the 'Friend of God' (2 Ch. xx. 7). His life history is recorded in Gn. xi. 26–xxv. 10 and summarized in Acts vii. 2–8. A list of his immediate descendants through his sons Isaac and Ishmael is given in Gn. xxv. 11–19.

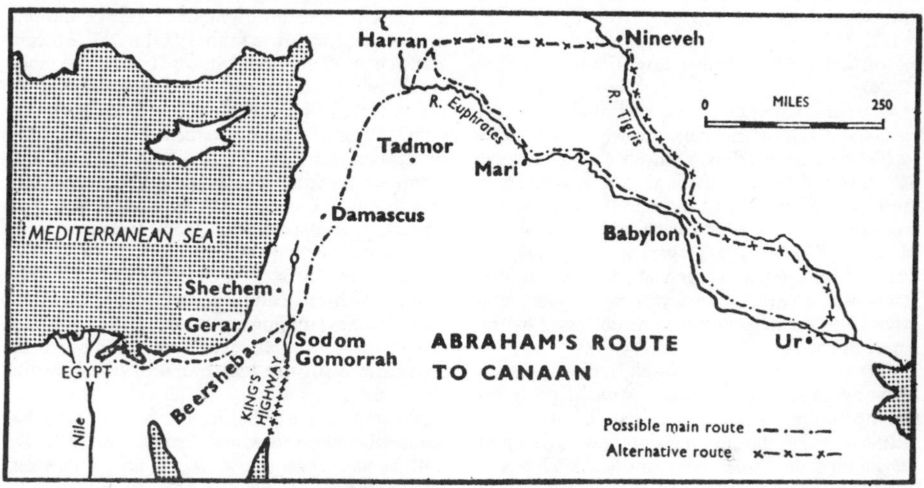

Fig. 1. The journeys of Abraham.

I. NAME

The etymology of the name Abram (Heb. *'aḇrām*, Gn. xi. 27–xvii. 5) is uncertain, but probably means 'the father is exalted' and is a variant of the W Semitic names Abiram, Ab(a)ram(a), found also in cuneiform texts of the 19th–18th centuries. With the promise of the divine covenant and future progeny his name was changed to Abraham (*'aḇrāhām*), which is explained as 'father of multitudes' (Gn. xvii. 5). This has been considered a variant or dialectical form of Abram (the *h* denoting a long vowel as in S Arabic) or as a popular etymology, since no *rhm*, 'multitude', is known. It is, however, likely that the root (*cf.* Arab. *ruhām*, 'multitude') exists but is unattested in biblical Hebrew. Halévy's derivation, *'aḇîr hām*, 'chief of a multitude' (*cf.* Gn. xlix. 24; Is. xli. 24), is doubtful.

II. CAREER

Abraham was born in Ur of the Chaldees (see UR), where he lived with his father Terah and brothers Nahor and Haran and married Sarai. On Haran's death he moved with his wife, father, and nephew Lot to Harran, where Terah died

(Gn. xi. 26–32). At God's call Abraham, aged 75, left Harran with Lot and moved by stages *via* Shechem and Bethel into Canaan (xii. 1–9). Famine drove him through the Negeb into Egypt, where he and Sarai escaped from the pharaoh only through the intervention of plagues (verses 10–20). After his return to Bethel there was a dispute between Abraham's camp and Lot, which was resolved by allowing the latter to choose the fertile Jordan valley for pasturage (xiii. 1–14).

Yahweh promised Abraham the possession of the whole land from the Euphrates southwestwards, and Abraham returned to Mamre near Hebron (xiii. 15–18). Following the oppression, and sack, of Sodom and Gomorrah by a coalition of four kings under Chedorlaomer, Abraham, with his servants and Amorite friends from Mamre, pursued and defeated the raiders near Damascus and recovered the booty (xiv. 1–16). On his return Abraham received the blessing of Melchizedek, priest-king of Salem (verses 17–24).

Abraham, being childless, had made a home-born slave, Eliezer, his heir, but was now given a special assurance from Yahweh that he would have a son of his own through whom would rise the future nation. This and the promise of the land was confirmed by a covenant (xv). Meanwhile Sarai gave him Hagar, a concubine, by whom Abraham, now aged 86, had a son Ishmael. Hagar, mocking Sarai's barrenness, was driven into the desert only to be delivered by the Angel of the Lord (xvi).

Thirteen years later Yahweh again appeared to Abraham to reaffirm His covenant promises for the future of his family, nation, and land, setting as a sign the circumcision of all males and the change of names to Abraham and Sarah (xvii). The promise of a son is again confirmed by another theophany at Mamre, despite Sarah's disbelief (xviii. 1–19). When the imminent judgment on Sodom and Gomorrah was revealed to him, Abraham interceded for Lot, who now lived there (verses 20–33). From Mamre he witnessed the overthrow of the cities from which Lot escaped (xix. 27–29).

Abraham journeyed through the Negeb, halting near Kadesh and Gerar, where a dispute over Sarah, similar to that in his earlier visit to Egypt, almost resulted in the defilement of Sarah (xx). Isaac was borne by Sarah to Abraham now aged 100. To guard the succession he dismissed Hagar and Ishmael, an action contrary to the prevailing custom (see HAMMURABI), which required a direct injunction by God to Abraham, who reluctantly took this seemingly hard action (xxi). At this time also Abraham made a treaty with the Philistine Abimelech to secure rights in Beersheba (xxi. 22–34).

The great test of Abraham's faith came when Yahweh ordered him to sacrifice Isaac at Moriah. He obeyed, his hand being stayed at the moment of slaughter when a ram was provided as a substitute (xxii. 1–14). Thereupon the covenant between Yahweh and Abraham was reaffirmed (verses 15–20). Sarah died, aged 127, and was buried in a cave at Machpelah, the freehold of which Abraham purchased from Ephron (xxiii). As his death approached Abraham made Eliezer swear to obtain a wife for Isaac from his kinsfolk near Harran. Thus Abraham's great-niece Rebekah became the bride of Isaac (xxiv).

Abraham himself in his advanced age married Keturah, whose sons became the ancestors of the tribes of Dedan and Midian. After giving 'all he had' to Isaac and gifts to his other sons Abraham died, aged 175, and was buried at Machpelah (xxv. 1–10).

III. CHARACTER

Abraham declared his faith in God as almighty (Gn. xvii. 1), eternal (xxi. 33), the most high (xiv. 22), possessor (Lord) of heaven and earth (xiv. 22, xxiv. 3), and the righteous judge of nations (xv. 14) and of all mankind (xviii. 25). To him Yahweh was just (xviii. 25), wise (xx. 6), righteous (xviii. 19), good (xix. 19), and merciful (xx. 6). He accepted the judgment of God upon sin (xviii. 19, xx. 11) yet interceded with Him for erring Ishmael (xvii. 20) and Lot (xviii. 27–33). Abraham communed with God in close fellowship (xviii. 33, xxiv. 40, xlviii. 15), and was granted special revelation from Him in visions (xv. 1) and visits in human (xviii. 1) or angelic ('messenger') form (xxii. 11, 15). Abraham worshipped Yahweh, calling upon Him by that name (xiii. 4) and building an altar for this purpose (xii. 8, xiii. 4, 18). His clear monotheism is to be contrasted with the polytheism of his ancestors (Jos. xxiv. 2).

Abraham's faith is perhaps best seen in his ready obedience whenever called by God. By faith he left Ur (xi. 31, xv. 7), an act emphasized by Stephen (Acts vii. 2–4, see MESOPOTAMIA). Similarly he was guided to leave Harran (Gn. xii. 1, 4). By faith also he accepted the semi-nomadic or 'pilgrim' life even when the land of Canaan had been promised him (xiii. 15, xv. 18); a promise of which he lived to see only a partial fulfilment in the occupation of a small plot of land at Machpelah and rights near Beersheba. The supreme trial of his faith came when he was asked to sacrifice Isaac his only son, who was, humanly speaking, the only means whereby the divine promises could be fulfilled. His faith rested in a belief in God's ability, if need be, to raise his son from the dead (Gn. xxii. 12, 18; Heb. xi. 19).

Towards his own family Abraham showed deep affection. He was acknowledged as one able 'to command his children and his household after him, that they might keep the way of the Lord in doing justice and judgement' (Gn. xviii. 19). His servant Eliezer, and his allies at Mamre, respected his commands. Abraham was hospitable and respectful to strangers (xviii. 2–8, xxi. 8), and generous without seeking personal gain (xiii. 9, xiv. 23). He was rich in servants (xiv. 14) and possessions (xiii. 2), and able and brave enough to wage war against superior numbers (xiv. 15).

Incidents which have been considered grave weaknesses in Abraham's character are the apparent deception of pharaoh in Egypt and of Abimelech of Gerar, by passing Sarah off as his sister and thus saving his own life (Gn. xii. 11–13, xx. 2–11). While this may well be an example of the way the Scriptures portray the failures of even the great heroes (see DAVID), the exact nature of these incidents may as yet be imperfectly understood. Sarah might have been Abraham's step-sister, and such marriages were contemporary practice in Egypt and Assyria (Nuzi). Abraham's statement to Isaac in Gn. xxii. 7, 8 may be attributed to faith (verse 5 reads 'we will come again') rather than to any deception of Isaac in face of the task ahead. The whole chapter, and Isaac's submission (verse 3), is an early condemnation of child-sacrifice.

IV. SIGNIFICANCE

Israel was considered 'the seed of Abraham', and Yahweh's action in raising much people from one man was held to be a particularly significant fulfilment of His word (Is. li. 2; Ezk. xxxiii. 24). 'The God of Abraham' designated Yahweh throughout Scripture and was the name whereby He revealed Himself to Moses (Ex. iii. 15). Abraham's monotheism amid idolatry (Jos. xxiv. 3), the way God appeared to him (Ex. vi. 3), chose (Ne. ix. 7), redeemed (Is. xxix. 22), and blessed him (Mi. vii. 20), and Abraham's faith were a constant theme of exhortation and discussion (1 Macc. ii. 52).

In New Testament times also Abraham was revered as the ancestor of Israel (Acts xiii. 26), of the levitical priesthood (Heb. vii. 5), and of the Messiah Himself (Mt. i. 1). Though the popular Jewish superstition that racial descent from Abraham brought divine blessing with it is refuted by the Baptist (Mt. iii. 9) and Paul (Rom. ix. 7), the unity of the Hebrews as his descendants was a picture of the unity of believers in Christ (Gal. iii. 16, 29). The oath (Lk. i. 73), covenant (Acts iii. 13), promise (Rom. iv. 13), and blessing (Gal. iii. 14) granted Abraham by God's free choice are inherited by his children by faith. Abraham's faith was a type of that which leads to justification (Rom. iv. 3–11), a pre-Christ proclamation of the universal gospel (Gal. iii. 8). His obedience by faith to his call from Ur to the nomadic life of a 'stranger and pilgrim' and his offering of Isaac are listed as an outstanding example of faith in action (Heb. xi. 8–19; Jas. ii. 21).

As a great prophet and recipient of the divine covenant Abraham plays a unique rôle in both Jewish (Ecclus. xliv. 19–21; *Bereshith Rabba*; *Pirqe Aboth* v. 4; Jos., *Ant*. i. 7, 8) and Muslim traditions (188 refs. in Qur'an).

V. CHRONOLOGY

As a result of archaeological discoveries the life and times of Abraham as recorded in Genesis can be shown to accord well with the recent knowledge of the second millennium BC. Albright and de Vaux place Abraham between 1900 and 1700 BC; Rowley 1800–1600 BC, and Gordon as late as the Amarna age (late 14th century). However, the known occupation of sites in the plain of Jordan (Gn. xiv), in the Middle Bronze Age but not later, seems to favour the 20th–19th centuries BC. Many of the customs observed by Abraham, his action over Hagar, choice of Eliezer as heir, and purchase of Machpelah have been compared with evidence of these same customs at Nuzi (see ARCHAEOLOGY). See also PATRIARCHAL AGE.

The evidence of archaeology and increasing knowledge of the period means that most modern scholars accept the substantial historicity of the narratives; this has led to a weakening of the position of those who hold the theory that Abraham personifies a tribe, or an early tribal deity (the mythical theory of Nöldeke), or is the product of a cycle of sagas. It is to be observed that the majority of Abraham's deeds are recorded as those of an individual (*e.g.* Gn. xv. 1–18, xviii. 1–19, xx. 1–17, xxii. 1–14).

BIBLIOGRAPHY. D. J. Wiseman, *The Word of God for Abraham and To-day*, 1959. D.J.W.

ABRAHAM'S BOSOM. A figure of speech used by Jesus in the parable of Lazarus and Dives (Lk. xvi. 22, 23), illustrating the 'great gulf fixed' between the bliss of paradise and the misery of Hades (*cf.* Mt. viii. 11). The dead Lazarus is portrayed as reclining next to Abraham at the feast of the blessed, after the Jewish manner, which brought the head of one person almost into the bosom of the one who sat above him, and placed the most favoured guest in such a relation to his host (*e.g.* Jn. xiii. 23). To sit in Abraham's bosom, in Talmudic language, was to enter paradise (*cf.* 4 Macc. xiii. 17). Such Oriental imagery should not be regarded as evidence of Jewish belief in an interim state. See LAZARUS AND DIVES. J.D.D.

ABRECH. An obscure term proclaimed before Joseph as Pharaoh's chief minister (Gn. xli. 43). W. Spiegelberg interpreted it as Egyp. *ỉb-r.k*, 'attention!', 'look out!' Perhaps better, as J. Vergote suggests, *ỉ.brk*, 'pay homage!', 'kneel!', an Egyptian imperative of a Semitic loanword. For fuller details see J. Vergote, *Joseph en Égypte*, 1959, pp. 135–141. K.A.K.

ABSALOM (*'aḇšālôm*, 'father is/of peace'). **1.** Third son of David, with a foreign mother, Maacah, daughter of Talmai, king of Geshur (2 Sa. iii. 3). His personal comeliness was shared by Tamar, his sister, and was the cause of her being assaulted by Amnon, David's firstborn son by another mother (2 Sa. xiii. 1–18). When Absalom learned of this incident, he brought about the death of Amnon, thus incurring the displeasure of his father, before which he fled to Geshur (2 Sa. xiii. 19–39). The first part of

Nathan's prophecy had come true (2 Sa. xii. 10). After three years of exile, and a further two years of banishment from the court, David received his son back into favour, and was repaid by a plot against his throne (2 Sa. xv. 1–15). The 'forty years' of verse 7 does not seem to square with xviii. 5, and the reading 'four' has been suggested. The second part of Nathan's prophecy now came true (2 Sa. xii. 11a). The third part (verse 11b) was also soon fulfilled (2 Sa. xvi. 20–23) and there was now no turning back. There is pathos and spiritual profit in the words of David when the Levites sought to take the Ark into flight with the deposed king (2 Sa. xv. 25–26). The end of Absalom is well known. With the help of Hushai (2 Sa. xv. 32–37 and xvii. 1–16) and Joab (2 Sa. xviii. 1–21; see also xix. 1–7) David was able to defeat him in battle. 2 Sa. xviii. 9–17 describes his ignominious death. The third Psalm purports to come from the period of Absalom's rebellion.

2. Rehoboam's father-in-law. 1 Ki. xv. 2, 10; 2 Ch. xi. 20, 21.

3. In the Apocrypha, an ambassador of Judas Maccabaeus, the father of Mattathias and Jonathan. 1 Macc. xi. 70, xiii. 11; 2 Macc. xi. 17.

T.H.J.

ABYSS (Gk. *abyssos*, 'bottomless (pit)', 'deep'). Appearing nine times in the New Testament, the Greek word is rendered in AV twice as 'deep', seven times as 'bottomless pit'; by RV always as 'abyss'. It is used to describe the abode of demons (Lk. viii. 31), the place of the dead (Rom. x. 7), and in the Apocalypse as the place of torment (ix. 1, *etc.*). LXX renders Heb. *tᵉhôm*, 'deep place', as 'abyss' (Gn. i. 2, *etc.*), with reference to the primitive idea of a vast mass of water on which the world floated, or to the underworld (Ps. lxxi. 20). See HELL.

J.D.D.

ACCAD, AKKAD. One of the major cities, with Babylon and Erech, founded by Nimrod (Gn. x. 10). It bore the Semitic name of *Akkadu*, Sumerian *Agade*. Its precise location near Sippar or Babylon is uncertain, though some identify it with the ruins of Tell Dēr, Tell Šešubār or even Babylon itself.

Inscriptions show that an early Semitic Dynasty founded by Sargon I (*c.* 2350 BC) flourished here. At this time Akkad controlled all Sumer (S Babylonia), and its armies reached Elam, Syria, and S Anatolia. With the great trade and prosperity which followed the rule of Sargon and his successor Naram-Sin the Dynasty became symbolic of a 'golden age'. When Babylon later became the capital the term 'Akkad' continued to be used to describe the whole of N Babylonia until the late Persian period. See ASSYRIA; BABYLONIA.

Akkadian (Accadian) is now used as a convenient term for the Semitic Assyrian and Babylonian languages, the dialect of the famous Dynasty of Agade being designated 'Old Akkadian'.

D.J.W.

Fig. 2. Bronze head of an Akkadian ruler, probably Sargon, king of Agade *c.* 2350 BC.

ACCEPTANCE. The English words 'accept', 'accepted', 'acceptable', and 'acceptance' translate a variety of Hebrew and Greek words of cognate meaning. God is normally the subject; and the object may be the worshipper's sacrifices (Ps. cxix. 108), his prayers (Gn. xix. 21), the whole tenor of his life, and particularly his person. In contrary distinction to the pagan viewpoint, the biblical doctrine is that the prayers and sacrifices are acceptable to God because a man's person is acceptable. Thus 'the Lord had respect unto Abel and to his offering: but unto Cain and to his offering he had not respect' (Gn. iv. 4, 5). The acceptance of Abel's offering was a witness that Abel's person had already been accepted. Through his offerings 'he had witness borne to him that he was righteous, God bearing witness in respect of his gifts' (Heb. xi. 4), and Cain was admonished that his offering would be accepted if his life were acceptable (Gn. iv. 7).

The Old Testament prophets inveighed against the notion, so congenial to the natural man, that God can be persuaded to accept a man's person through accepting a correctly-offered ritual worship. They constantly affirmed that the divine order was the reverse. The offerings were acceptable only when the persons were acceptable (Ho. viii. 13; Mal. i. 10, 13). Throughout the Bible the teaching is underlined that God does not accept a man's person because of his social status or importance. He does not respect persons (Gal. ii. 6). This is a virtue which all are to imitate. However, it was not till the Cornelius incident that the early Church apprehended the truth that God does not require Jewish nationality, nor circumcision, as a prerequisite for acceptance with Him (Acts x. 35).

The well-doing that God requires for acceptance must not in any point fall short of His perfections. Only those who by patience persist in well-doing may claim the reward of eternal life for their works (Rom. ii. 6, 7). None achieve this. All fall short of the glory of God through sin (Rom. iii. 9–23). Our Lord alone is accepted. He alone has merited God's verdict: 'In thee I am well pleased'.

Ezekiel foretold that it would be the work of God to make sinners acceptable to Him (Ezk. xx. 40, 41, xxxvi. 23–29). It is through incorporation into Christ, and the gift of His righteousness (Rom. v. 17), that believers are accepted with God. This is the work of God, who through His grace makes us 'accepted in the beloved' (Eph. i. 6). D.B.K.

ACCESS. An intermediary in the Oriental court introduced suppliants and guaranteed their genuineness (*cf.* Barnabas, Acts ix. 27, 28). The Old Testament portrait of God as King (Ps. xlvii. 7) posed to New Testament writers the problem of the sinner's *prosagōgē* or access into His presence. He has no independent right of personal approach, and obtains introduction only through Christ (Rom. v. 2; Eph. ii. 18, iii. 12; 1 Pet. iii. 18), whose death removes the barriers of hostility (Eph. ii. 16), and enables believers to draw near with confidence to the throne of grace (Heb. iv. 16). D.H.T.

ACCHO, ACCO. See PTOLEMAIS.

ACELDAMA. See AKELDAMA.

ACHAIA. A small region of Greece, on the south coast of the gulf of Corinth, which twice gave its name to the whole country. In Homer the Greeks are frequently called Achaeans. Again, in the age of the Hellenistic kings, the Achaean confederacy championed the freedom of the republics, and after its defeat by the Romans (146 BC) the name was used by them for Greece in general. The area was administered with Macedonia at first, and even after organization as a separate province (27 BC) is linked in common usage with Macedonia (Acts xix. 21; Rom. xv. 26; 1 Thes. i. 8). The province was in the regular senatorial allotment, and was hence governed by a proconsul (*anthypatos*, Acts xviii. 12), with two exceptions: from AD 15 to 44 it was under the Caesarian legate of Moesia; and from AD 67 Roman supervision was entirely suspended for several years by Nero's benevolence, and the forty or so republics in the area enjoyed their liberty without even the appearance of permission.

The old confederacy was maintained under the Romans, with its capital at Argos, the seat of the imperial cult, but the much larger province was governed from Corinth. It is always in connection with Corinth that the name occurs in the New Testament, and it is uncertain whether anything more is meant (see 2 Cor. i. 1, ix. 2, xi. 10). We know, however, that there was a church at Cenchreae (Rom. xvi. 1), and apparently there were Christians at Athens (Acts xvii. 34). We may assume, therefore, that in referring to Stephanas as the 'firstfruits of Achaia' (1 Cor. xvi. 15), Paul is applying the term to Corinth as having a primacy due to its position as the Roman capital. He is not thinking of the rest of the province.

BIBLIOGRAPHY. Pausanias, vii. 16. 10–17. 4; Strabo, viii; J. Keil, *CAH*, xi, pp. 556–558. E.A.J.

ACHAICUS. A Corinthian Christian (1 Cor. xvi. 17): on his position see FORTUNATUS. The name suggests a slave or ex-slave of Achaia, or possibly in the service of the Mummii: it was the title of L. Mummius, creator of Roman Achaia (and destroyer of Corinth, *q.v.*), and was retained in his family in Paul's lifetime (*cf.* Suetonius, *Galba*, 3). A.F.W.

ACHAN (*'āḵān*). A Judahite of clan Zerah, who was in the assault on Jericho and violated the sacrificial ban, stealing gold, silver, and fine clothing. This was discovered when inquiry was made by lot after the failure to take Ai. Achan with his family and possessions was stoned and cremated in the valley south of Gilgal (Jos. vii). Joshua, in pronouncing sentence, used the similarity of his name to the verb *'āḵar*, 'to distress', and the valley was called Achor thereafter. The event is recalled in Jos. xxii. 20 and by the Chronicler (1 Ch. ii. 7), who writes the man's name *'āḵār*. J.P.U.L.

ACHISH. King of Gath, son of Maoch (1 Sa. xxvii. 2), or Maachah (1 Ki. ii. 39); also called Abimelech in the title of Ps. xxxiv. He lived during the reigns of David and Solomon. David dwelt *incognito* with him when fleeing from Saul's anger, and subsequently escaped by feigning madness upon being discovered as the slayer of Goliath (1 Sa. xxi. 10–15). On the occasion of David's second flight from Saul's anger, Achish gave him Ziklag on the Philistine–Israelite border (1 Sa. xxvii). After the death of Saul (1 Sa. xxxi) David left Ziklag for Hebron, where he received the sovereignty over Judah (2 Sa. ii. 1–4). R.J.W.

ACHMETHA. Called Ecbatana by the Greeks and Romans, this was from 700 BC the capital of Media. The modern Hamadan, 180 miles west-south-west of Tehran. Herodotus (i. 98) described it as a magnificent city with seven concentric walls. Depository of the royal archives, here was discovered the Decree of Cyrus, authorizing the rebuilding of the Temple in Ezra's day (Ezr. vi. 2). J.D.D.

ACHOR. The Vale of Achor in NE Judah, where Achan was executed, mentioned in Jos. xv. 7, is probably not Wadi Qilt (as G. A. Smith thought), but El Buqei'a; some 4 miles from north to south, centred on the Wadi Qumran

10 miles south of Jericho, with outlets to the north and east. The strongholds Middin, Secacah, and Nibshan were built there, with irrigation-works and forts; the area was and is called *'arab* (wilderness). See *GTT*, pp. 137 ff., 271; Noth, *ZDPV*, LXXI, p. 49. Achor is the first place-name mentioned on the copper scroll from Qumran. J.P.U.L.

ACHSAH. 1. The daughter of Caleb son of Jephunneh (Jos. xv. 16; Jdg. i. 12–15). **2.** The daughter of Caleb son of Hezron (1 Ch. ii. 49; *cf.* ii. 18 [unless, indeed, the same Caleb is in view throughout]). R.F.H.

ACHSHAPH (*'akšāp̄*, 'place of magic'). A city assigned to Asher (Jos. xix. 25); its king joined the coalition under Jabin and Sisera against Israel, and was slain (Jos. xi. 1, xii. 20). Possibly the modern Tell Keisān, near Acre (*cf.* Amarna Letters; *Papyrus Anastasi*, I). J.D.D.

ACHZIB. 1. A city of Asher (Jos. xix. 29) which the tribe never occupied (Jdg. i. 31), on the coast road about 10 miles north of Acco (Acre); taken by Sennacherib in 702 BC; the modern ez-Zib. **2.** A city of Judah (Jos. xv. 44; *cf.* Mi. i. 14) in the Shephelah near Mareshah; probably the Chezib of Gn. xxxviii. 5 and the modern Tell el-Beida. J.D.D.

ACRE. See WEIGHTS AND MEASURES.

ACTS, BOOK OF THE. 'The Acts of the Apostles' (Gk. *praxeis apostolōn*) is the title given, since the latter years of the second century AD, to the second volume of a history of Christian beginnings whose first volume we know as 'The Gospel according to St. Luke'.

I. OUTLINE OF CONTENTS

The book takes up the story where the Gospel (the 'former treatise' of Acts i. 1) ends, with the resurrection appearances of Jesus, and goes on to record His ascension, the coming of the Holy Spirit, and the rise and early progress of the church of Jerusalem (i–v). Then it describes the dispersal of the Hellenistic members of that church which followed the execution of their leader Stephen, their evangelization of more distant regions as far north as Antioch, and the beginning of the Gentile mission in that city. In the course of this narrative we have also the account of Paul's conversion and Peter's evangelization of the plain of Sharon, culminating in the conversion of the first Gentile household in Caesarea. This section of Acts ends with Paul's arrival in Antioch to take part in the Gentile mission there, and Peter's departure from Jerusalem after his escape from death at the hands of Herod Agrippa I (vi–xii). From then on Paul's apostolic ministry is the main subject of Acts: with Barnabas he evangelizes Cyprus and South Galatia (xiii–xiv), takes part in the Council of Jerusalem (xv), with Silas crosses to Europe and evangelizes Philippi, Thessalonica, and Corinth (xvi–xviii), with other colleagues evangelizes provincial Asia from his headquarters in Ephesus (xix), pays a visit to Palestine, where he is rescued from mob-violence and kept in custody for two years (xx–xxvi), is sent to Rome to have his case heard by the Emperor at his own request, and spends two years there under house arrest, with complete liberty to make the gospel known to all who visit him (xxvii, xxviii). While the gospel was no doubt carried along all the roads which branched out from its Palestinian homeland, Acts concentrates on the road from Jerusalem to Antioch and thence to Rome.

II. ORIGIN AND PURPOSE

The preface to the 'former treatise' (Lk. i. 1–4) applies equally to both parts of the work: the whole work was undertaken in order that one Theophilus (*q.v.*) might have a consecutive and reliable account of the rise and progress of Christianity—a subject on which he already possessed a certain amount of information.

The date is not indicated precisely; Acts cannot have been written earlier than the latest event it records, Paul's spending two years in custody in Rome (Acts xxviii. 30), covering probably the years 60 and 61, but how much later it was written is uncertain. If its dependence on the *Antiquities* of Josephus were established, then its date could not be earlier than AD 93, but such a dependence is most improbable. We might think of a time when something had happened to stimulate special interest in Christianity among responsible members of Roman society, of whom Theophilus may be regarded as a representative. One such time was the latter part of Domitian's principate (AD 81–96), when Christianity had penetrated the imperial family. It has even been suggested that Theophilus might be a pseudonym for Domitian's cousin, Flavius Clemens. An earlier occasion may be found in the later sixties, when the moment seemed opportune to dissociate Christianity from the Jewish revolt in Palestine, or (better still) nearer the beginning of the sixties, when the leading propagator of Christianity came to Rome as a Roman citizen to have his appeal heard by the imperial tribunal. The optimistic note on which Acts ends, with Paul proclaiming the kingdom of God in Rome without let or hindrance, suggests a date before the outbreak of persecution in AD 64. The internal evidence for the dating of Luke is relevant here, but if it be felt that Luke, as we have it now, must be dated after AD 70, it might be considered whether the 'former treatise' of Acts i. 1 could not be 'Proto-Luke' (so C. S. C. Williams and others). The remitting of Paul's case to Rome would certainly make it needful for certain imperial officials to look more seriously into the nature of Christianity than had previously been necessary; the author of Acts may well have thought it wise to provide such people with an account of the matter.

The author, from the second century onwards,

has been identified (rightly, in all probability) with Luke, Paul's physician and fellow-traveller (Col. iv. 14; Phm. 24; 2 Tim. iv. 11). Luke was a Greek of Antioch, according to the late second-century anti-Marcionite prologue to his Gospel (his Antiochene origin is also implied by the 'Western' reading of Acts xi. 28). His presence at some of the events which he records is indicated unobtrusively by the transition from the third person to the first person plural in his narrative; the three 'we-sections' of Acts are xvi. 10–17, xx. 5–xxi. 18, xxvii. 1–xxviii. 16. Apart from the periods covered by these sections, he had ample opportunity of tracing the course of events from the first, as he had access to first-hand information from people he met from time to time, not only in Antioch but also in Asia Minor and Macedonia, in Jerusalem and Caesarea, and finally in Rome. Among these informants an important place should doubtless be given to his hosts in various cities, such as Philip and his daughters in Caesarea (xxi. 8 f.) and Mnason, a foundation-member of the church in Jerusalem (xxi. 16). He does not appear to have used Paul's Epistles as a source.

III. HISTORICAL CHARACTER

The historical trustworthiness of Luke's account has been amply confirmed by archaeological discovery. While he has apologetic and theological interests, these do not detract from his detailed accuracy, although they control his selection and presentation of the facts. He sets his narrative in the framework of contemporary history; his pages are full of references to city magistrates, provincial governors, client kings, and the like, and these references time after time prove to be just right for the place and time in question. With a minimum of words he conveys the true local colour of the widely differing cities mentioned in his story. And his description of Paul's voyage to Rome (xxvii) remains to this day one of our most important documents on ancient seamanship.

IV. APOLOGETIC EMPHASIS

Luke is obviously concerned, in both parts of his work, to demonstrate that Christianity is not a menace to imperial law and order. He does this particularly by citing the judgments of governors, magistrates, and other authorities in various parts of the Empire. In the Gospel Pilate thrice pronounces Jesus not guilty of sedition (Lk. xxiii. 4, 14, 22), and when similar charges are brought against His followers in Acts they cannot be sustained. The praetors of Philippi imprison Paul and Silas for interference with the rights of private property, but have to release them with an apology for their illegal action (xvi. 19 ff., 35 ff.). The politarchs of Thessalonica, before whom Paul and his companions are accused of sedition against the Emperor, are content to find citizens of that place who will guarantee the missionaries' good behaviour (xvii. 6–9). A more significant decision is taken by Gallio, proconsul of Achaia, who dismisses the charge of propagating an illicit religion brought against Paul by the Jewish leaders of Corinth; the practical implication of his decision is that Christianity shares the protection assured by Roman law to Judaism (xviii. 12 ff.). At Ephesus, Paul enjoys the friendship of the Asiarchs (*q.v.*) and is exonerated by the town clerk from the charge of insulting the cult of Ephesian Artemis (xix. 31, 35 ff.). In Judaea the governor Festus and the client king Agrippa II agree that Paul has committed no offence deserving either death or imprisonment, and that in fact he might have been liberated forthwith had he not taken the jurisdiction out of their hands by appealing to Caesar (xxvi. 32).

It might well be asked, however, why the progress of Christianity had so frequently been marked by public riots if Christians were so law-abiding as Luke maintained. His reply is that, apart from the incident at Philippi and the demonstration stirred up by the silversmiths' guild at Ephesus, the tumults which attended the proclamation of the gospel were invariably instigated by its Jewish opponents. Just as the Gospel represents the Sadducean chief priests of Jerusalem as compelling Pilate to sentence Jesus to death against his better judgment, so in Acts it is Jews who are Paul's bitterest enemies in one place after another. While Acts records the steady advance of the gospel in the great Gentile centres of imperial civilization, it records at the same time its progressive rejection by the majority of the Jewish communities throughout the Empire.

V. THEOLOGICAL INTEREST

On the theological side, the dominating theme of Acts is the activity of the Holy Spirit. The promise of the outpouring of the Spirit, made by the risen Christ in i. 4 ff., is fulfilled for Jewish disciples in chapter ii and for Gentile believers in chapter x. The apostles discharge their commission in the power of the Spirit, which is manifested by supernatural signs; their converts' acceptance of the gospel is likewise attended by visible manifestations of the Spirit's power. The book might indeed be called 'The Acts of the Holy Spirit', for it is the Spirit who controls the advance of the gospel throughout; He guides the movements of the preachers, *e.g.* of Philip (viii. 29, 39), Peter (x. 19 f.), Paul and his companions (xvi. 6 ff.); He directs the church of Antioch to set Barnabas and Saul apart for the more extended service to which He Himself has called them (xiii. 2); He receives pride of place in the letter conveying the decision of the Jerusalem Council (*q.v.*) to the Gentile churches (xv. 28); He speaks through prophets (xi. 28, xx. 23, xxi. 4, 11) as He did in Old Testament days (i. 16, xxviii. 25); He it is in the first instance who appoints the elders of a church to take spiritual charge of it (xx. 28); He is the principal witness to the truth of the gospel (v. 32).

The supernatural manifestations which accompany the spread of the gospel signify not only the Spirit's activity but also the inauguration of the new age in which Jesus reigns as Lord and Messiah. The miraculous element, as we should expect, is more prominent in the earlier than in the later part of the book: 'we have a steady reduction of the emphasis on the miraculous aspect of the working of the Spirit which corresponds to the development in the Pauline Epistles' (W. L. Knox, *The Acts of the Apostles*, 1948, p. 91).

VI. ACTS IN THE EARLY CHURCH

Unlike most of the New Testament books, the two parts of Luke's history do not appear to have been primarily associated with Christian churches, whether as addressed to them or as circulating within them. Martin Dibelius may be right in thinking that the work circulated through the contemporary book trade for the benefit of the Gentile reading public for which it was intended. There may thus have been some lapse of time between the first publication of the twofold work and its more general circulation in the churches as an authoritative Christian document.

Early in the second century, when the four Gospel writings were collected and circulated as a fourfold group, the two parts of Luke's history were separated from each other, to pursue their several paths. While the future of Luke was assured by reason of its incorporation with the other three Gospels, Acts proved increasingly to be such an important document that it can justly be called, in Harnack's words, the pivot-book of the New Testament.

The wider circulation of Acts in the churches may have had much to do, towards the end of the first century, with the move to collect the Pauline Epistles to form a *corpus*. If Paul tended to be forgotten in the generation following his death, Acts would certainly bring him back to Christian memory and also emphasize what an interesting and extraordinarily important man he was. But, while emphasizing the importance of Paul's rôle, Acts bore witness to the work of other apostles too, especially Peter.

For this last reason Marcion (*c*. AD 140) could not include Acts in his Canon, although he did include his edition of Luke as a preface to the Pauline *corpus*. Acts, while it bore eloquent witness to the apostleship of Paul, at the same time cut right across Marcion's insistence that the original apostles of Jesus had proved unfaithful to their Master's teaching. Marcion and his followers are probably the main target of Tertullian's charge of inconsistency against those heretics who confidently appeal to the exclusive apostolic authority of Paul while rejecting the one book above all others which provides independent testimony of his apostleship (*Prescription*, 22 f.).

To the champions of the catholic faith, on the other hand, the value of Acts now appeared greater than ever. For not only did it present irrefragable evidence of Paul's status and achievement as an apostle, but it also safeguarded the position of the other apostles and justified the inclusion of non-Pauline apostolic writings alongside the Pauline collection in the volume of Holy Writ. It was from this time that it came to be known as 'The Acts of the Apostles', or even, as the Muratorian list calls it with anti-Marcionite exaggeration, 'The Acts of *all* the Apostles'.

VII. ITS ABIDING VALUE

The title of Acts to occupy its traditional place between the Gospels and the Epistles is clear. On the one hand, it is the general sequel to the fourfold Gospel (as it is the proper sequel to one of the four); on the other hand, it supplies the historical background to the earlier Epistles, and attests the apostolic character of most of the writers whose names they bear.

Moreover, it remains a document of incalculable value for the beginnings of Christianity. When we consider how scanty is our knowledge of the progress of the gospel in other directions in the decades following AD 30, we may appreciate our indebtedness to Acts for the relatively detailed account which it gives of the progress of the gospel along the road from Jerusalem to Rome. The rise and progress of Christianity is a study beset with problems, but some of these problems would be even more intractable than they are if we had not the information of Acts to help us. For example, how did it come about that a movement which began in the heart of Judaism was recognized after a few decades as a distinctively Gentile religion? And how has it come about that a faith which originated in Asia has been for centuries predominantly associated, for better or worse, with European civilization? The answer is largely, though not entirely, bound up with the missionary career of Paul, apostle to the Gentiles and citizen of Rome; and of that career Luke, in Acts, is the historian. His narrative is, in fact, a source-book of the highest value for a significant phase of the history of world civilization.

BIBLIOGRAPHY. Foakes-Jackson and Kirsopp Lake, *The Beginnings of Christianity*, 5 vols. 1920–33; F. F. Bruce, *The Acts of the Apostles*, 1951, and *Commentary on the Book of the Acts*, 1954; E. M. Blaiklock, *Commentary on the Acts of the Apostles*, 1959; C. S. C. Williams, *Commentary on the Acts of the Apostles*, 1957; H. J. Cadbury, *The Book of Acts in History*, 1955; M. Dibelius, *Studies in the Acts of the Apostles*, 1956.

F.F.B.

ACTS, APOCRYPHAL. See NEW TESTAMENT APOCRYPHA.

ADAH. 1. One of the wives of Lamech and mother of Jabal and Jubal (Gn. iv. 19 ff.). **2.** One of the wives of Esau, daughter of Elon a Hittite and mother of Eliphaz (Gn. xxxvi. 2 ff.).

T.C.M.

ADAM.

I. IN THE OLD TESTAMENT

The first man, created (*bārā'*, Gn. i. 27) by God in His own image (*ṣelem*), on the sixth day (see CREATION), by means of forming him (as a potter forms, *yāṣar*, Gn. ii. 7) of dust from the ground (*'ᵃḏāmâ*), and breathing into his nostrils the breath of life (*nišmaṯ ḥayyîm*). The result of this was that 'the man' became a living being (*nep̄eš ḥayyâ*). Sumerian and Babylonian myths of the creation of man are known, but compared with the creation story in the Bible all are crude and polytheistic.

a. Etymology

The name Adam (*'āḏām*), in addition to being a proper name, also has the connotation 'mankind', a sense in which it occurs in the Old Testament some 500 times, so that when the noun occurs with the definite article (*hā'āḏām*) it is to be translated as the proper noun rather than as the name. The word *'adm* occurs also in Ugaritic in the sense 'mankind'. In the accounts of the creation in Gn. i and ii the article is used with *'āḏām* in all but three cases: i. 26, where 'man' in general is evidently intended; ii. 5, where 'a man' (or 'no man') is clearly the most natural sense; and ii. 20, the first permissible use of the proper name according to the text. The AV has projected this use back into the preceding verse (ii. 19) in spite of the article there, whereas the RV, observing that in this occurrence, and indeed in all those (iii. 17, 21) without the article up to Gn. iv. 25 the name is prefixed by the preposition *lᵉ-*, which might be read (*lā-*<*lᵉhā-*) to include the article without alteration to the consonantal text, prefers to assume that the Massoretes have wrongly pointed the text and that the proper name does not occur until Gn. iv. 25. Though attempts have been made to determine the etymology of the name, there is no agreement, and the fact that the original language of mankind was not Hebrew renders such theories academic. It is clear, however, that the use of the word *'ᵃḏāmâ*, 'ground', in juxtaposition to the name *'āḏām* in Gn. ii. 7 is intentional, a conclusion reinforced by Gn. iii. 19.

b. Adam's early condition

Adam was distinguished from the animals, but this not because the epithets *nep̄eš* and *rûaḥ* were applied to him, for these terms are also used on occasion of the animals, but because he was made in God's image, given dominion over all the animals, and perhaps also because God individually breathed the breath (*nᵉšāmâ*) of life into his nostrils. God made a garden for Adam in Eden (*q.v.*; Gn. ii. 8–14) and put him in it to work it and watch over it. The word 'to work it' (*'āḇaḏ*) is that commonly used for labour (*e.g.* Ex. xx. 9), so Adam was not to be idle. His food was apparently to be fruit from the trees (Gn. ii. 9, 16), berries and nuts from the shrubs (*śîaḥ*, EVV 'plant') and cereals from the herbs (*'ēśeḇ*, Gn. ii. 5). God then brought all the animals and birds to Adam for him to give them names, and presumably in the process to familiarize himself with their characteristics and potentialities (Gn. ii. 19, 20). It is possible that some dim reflection of this is to be found in a Sumerian literary text which describes how the god Enki set the world in order, and among other things put the animals under the control of two minor deities.

c. The fall

God said 'It is not good that the man should be alone' (Gn. ii. 18), so He made a woman (ii. 22), to be a help to him (see EVE). At the inducement of the serpent the woman persuaded Adam to eat from the fruit of the tree which he had been commanded by God not to touch (Gn. iii. 1–7) (see FALL), and as a result he and the woman were banished from the garden (Gn. iii. 23, 24). It is evident that until this time Adam had had direct communion with God. When Adam and the woman recognized their nakedness they took fig leaves and sewed them together to make loin cloths (*ḥᵃgôrâ*, Gn. iii. 7), evidence perhaps for the practice of such simple skills as sewing. Adam was punished by expulsion from the garden and subjection to the future lot of obtaining his livelihood in painful toil and in the sweat of his face, since the ground (*'ᵃḏāmâ*), to which he would now return at his death, was cursed and would bring forth thorn bushes and thistles. He was still to be a farmer, therefore, though his labours would be now more arduous than they had been (Gn. iii. 17–19, 23). Parallels have been drawn between these episodes and the Akkadian myth of Adapa, who mistakenly refused the bread and water of life, thus losing immortality for mankind; but the connections are remote. God provided the two with leather tunics (Gn. iii. 21), implying that they would now need protection from uncontrolled vegetation or cold weather.

Adam had two sons, Cain and Abel (*qq.v.*), but as Cain killed Abel he had another son, Seth (*q.v.*), to take Abel's place (Gn. iv. 25) and to carry on the faithful line of descent. Adam was 130 (LXX 230) years old when Seth was born and he lived 800 (LXX 700) years after this event, making 930 years in all (Gn. v. 2–5 agreeing with LXX and Samaritan Pentateuch, the latter agreeing with *MT* in all three figures; see GENEALOGY). In comparison, it is to be noted that the first pre-flood king, Alulim, in the Sumerian king list is given a reign of 28,800 years (a variant text gives 67,200), and his counterpart, Alōros, in Berossos' *Babylōniaka*, is credited with 36,000 years. It is to be presumed that Adam had other children than the three specifically mentioned in Genesis. The date of Adam's existence and the exact area in which he lived are at present disputed.

BIBLIOGRAPHY. C. H. Gordon, *Ugaritic Manual*, 1955, III, p. 233; *cf.* J. Gray, *The Legacy of Canaan*, 1957, p. 118; S. Landersdorfer, *Sumerisches Sprachgut im Alten Testament*, 1916, pp. 59, 60, for early theories; for the creation of man, see A. Heidel, *The Babylonian Genesis*[2], 1951, pp. 46, 47, 66–72, 118–126; S. N. Kramer, 'Sumerian Literature and the Bible', *Analecta Biblica*, XII, 1959, pp. 191, 192; for Enki and the world order, see *History Begins at Sumer*, 1958, pp. 145–147; for Adapa, see Heidel, *Genesis*, pp. 147–153; E. A. Speiser in *ANET*, pp. 101–103; for king list, see T. Jacobsen, *The Sumerian King List*, 1939, pp. 70, 71, A. L. Oppenheim in *ANET*, p. 265. T.C.M.

II. IN THE NEW TESTAMENT

The name Adam occurs nine times, eight times with reference to the first man (Lk. iii. 38; Rom. v. 14 (2); 1 Cor. xv. 22, 45; 1 Tim. ii. 13, 14; Jude 14) and once with reference to Christ (1 Cor. xv. 45). On several occasions, however, there are allusions to Adam, the first man, though the name does not occur (Mt. xix. 4–8; Mk. x. 6–8; Rom. v. 12, 15, 16, 17 (2), 19). Certain conclusions are to be drawn from these references.

a. Adam is represented as the first man (1 Cor. xv. 45, 47) and his unique origin as being without father or mother is intimated by drawing attention to the fact that, while others in human genealogy are said to be the son of the forebear in each case, Adam is said to be the son of God (Lk. iii. 38). Adam did not come by human generation.

b. Adam sustained a unique relation to the human race, comparable to the relation which Christ as the last Adam sustains to the redeemed. On these two unique relationships the history of the human race turns (1 Cor. xv. 45–49; Rom. v. 12–19). There is none before Adam, for he is the first man. There is none between Adam and Christ, because Christ is the second Man. There is none after Christ, for He is the last Adam. Adam was, therefore, the type of the One to come, namely, Christ.

c. By Adam sin and death entered into the world. The explicit mention of 'the transgression of Adam' in Rom. v. 14 makes clear that the 'one man' mentioned in Rom. v. 12 is Adam and the sin his first sin.

d. In Adam all men sin and die. Through the disobedience of the one man Adam they were made sinners (Rom. v. 19), through his one trespass the judgment of condemnation passed upon them (Rom. v. 16, 18) and death reigned over them (Rom. v. 15, 17; 1 Cor. xv. 22).

e. Union with Adam in his sin, condemnation, and death is the pattern in terms of which by union with Christ believers come into possession of righteousness, justification, and life (Rom. v. 15–19; 1 Cor. xv. 22, 45, 49). In the constitution which God has established, solidarity with Adam lays the basis for that by which the superabundance of grace reigns through righteousness unto eternal life (Rom. v. 21).

f. The New Testament confirms the historicity of the account given in the early chapters of Genesis pertaining to Adam. In 1 Cor. xv. 45, 47 we have allusion to Gn. ii. 7, in Jude 14 to Gn. v. 3–18 (*cf.* 1 Ch. i. 1–3), in 1 Tim. ii. 13 to Gn. ii. 20–23, in 1 Tim. ii. 14 to Gn. iii. 1–6, 13, in Mt. xix. 4, Mk. x. 6 to Gn. i. 27, in Mt. xix. 5, 6, Mk. x. 7, 8 (*cf.* Eph. v. 31) to Gn. ii. 24, in Rom. v. 12–19, 1 Cor. xv. 22 to Gn. ii. 17, iii. 19. This pervasive allusion, sometimes explicit and sometimes implicit, demonstrates that the New Testament assumes the historicity of Adam and of the events pertaining to him as well as the authenticity of the record which the early chapters of Genesis provide. It is not feasible to maintain the doctrine which our Lord and the apostles elicit from these assumed facts and propound in connection with them if we deny the historicity of the events themselves. We cannot so dissociate the lessons for faith and practice from the historicity of the events to which these lessons are attached, that we may retain the doctrinal and practical significance while rejecting the historical character of the alleged events. Herein rests the importance of the New Testament witness respecting Adam. J.M.

ADAM. A city in the Jordan valley about 18 miles from Jericho, where the waters were miraculously held back (Jos. iii. 16, in which the RV more accurately refers to it as 'the city that is beside Zarethan'). Usually identified with the modern Kh. Tell ed-Dâmiyeh. J.D.D.

ADAMAH. A fortified city of Naphtali listed in Jos. xix. 36.

ADAMANT. See under 'Diamond' in JEWELS AND PRECIOUS STONES.

ADAMI-NEKEB. A place mentioned in Jos. xix. 33, on the border of Naphtali. It was apparently a pass and has been identified with the modern Kh. ed-Dâmiyeh. R.A.H.G.

ADAR. See CALENDAR.

ADDER. See SERPENT.

ADMAH. One of the Cities of the Plain (*q.v.*) (Gn. xiv. 2, 8; Dt. xxix. 23), linked specially with Zeboim (*q.v.*) (Ho. xi. 8). The association with Gaza (Gn. x. 19) suggests the correctness of the modern locating of the pentapolis as submerged beneath the southern waters of the Dead Sea. J.A.M.

ADONI-BEZEK ('*ᵃḏōnî-ḇezeq*, 'my lord is Bezek'). After the death of Joshua the tribes of Judah and Simeon slew ten thousand Canaanites in the town of Bezek in southern Palestine (Jdg. i. 4–7). The king fled, but was captured, and his thumbs and great toes cut off. Adoni-bezek acknowledged that this was a just requital for his own action of cutting off the thumbs and great toes of seventy kings who had gathered crumbs (?) under his table. He was brought to Jerusalem and died there. This is the only instance of such cruelty having been practised by the Israelites. E.J.Y.

ADONIJAH (*'ᵃḏōniyyâ*, 'my lord is Yahweh'). **1.** The fourth son of David, by his wife Haggith. After the death of the three eldest he regarded himself as the heir-presumptive. (Amnon had been murdered by his brother Absalom, who himself died in the rebellion against his father. As no mention is made of Chileab, the son of Abigail, it is assumed that he died before any question of the succession arose.) It would appear, however, that David had promised Bathsheba (1 Ki. i. 17) that her son Solomon should succeed him. It may have been knowledge of this that provoked Adonijah to make his futile attempt at gaining the crown while his father was alive. His supporters included two of his father's right-hand men, Joab the commander-in-chief of the army, and Abiathar the priest, and no doubt Adonijah hoped that they would draw the power of the army and the sanction of the priesthood. But before that hope materialized those faithful to the king, Nathan his prophet-counsellor, Zadok the priest, and Benaiah the commander of the royal bodyguard, took action. While Adonijah was making a feast for his supporters, Bathsheba was instructed to approach David and remind him of his oath, and while she was yet speaking Nathan came in and reproached the king for his not having told him of his (supposed) plans for Adonijah. David confirmed his oath to Bathsheba and secured the accession of Solomon. The noise and the news of the acclamation reached Adonijah and his guests in En-rogel, and threw them into a panic. The would-be aspirant for the throne fled for sanctuary to the altar, and Solomon promised to spare his life on condition of future loyalty (1 Ki. i). No sooner was his father dead than his former ambitions again made themselves apparent. Thus at least did Solomon interpret his request for Abishag, his father's young concubine who had nursed him in his old age. This charge of a renewed attempt on the throne was probably not without foundation in the light of oriental custom (*cf.* 2 Sa. iii. 7, xvi. 21). The sentence of death on the ambitious and tactless Adonijah was speedily carried out (1 Ki. ii. 13–25).

2. One of the Levites whom Jehoshaphat sent to teach in the cities of Judah (2 Ch. xvii. 8).

3. One of those who sealed the covenant (Ne. x. 16). This is the same as Adonikam (Ezr. ii. 13, *etc.*). M.A.M.

ADONIRAM (*'ᵃḏōnîrām*, 'my lord is exalted'). Official in charge of forced labour under Solomon (1 Ki. iv. 6, v. 14), and identified with Adoram, who held a similar position under David (2 Sa. xx. 24) and Rehoboam (1 Ki. xii. 18, 'Hadoram' in 2 Ch. x. 18). The rebellious people stoned him to death, precipitating Jeroboam's revolt about 922 BC. J.D.D.

ADONI-ZEDEK (*'ᵃḏōnî-ṣeḏeq*, 'my lord is righteous'). An Amorite king of Jerusalem who led four other Canaanite kings against the Israelites and their allies of Gibeon. The five kings were defeated by divine intervention and hid themselves in a cave at Makkedah (*q.v.*). They were humbled and then executed by Joshua, who had them buried in the cave (Jos. x). The meaning of the name may be compared with Melchizedek ('my king is righteous'), king of Salem (*q.v.*; Gn. xiv. 18). There is not sufficient evidence for the existence of a god Zedek ('righteousness') to give a meaning 'my king is Zedek'. A.R.M.

ADOPTION. This word (used only by Paul) does not occur in the Bible as a legal technical term in quite the modern sense, for in Semitic society actual blood-relationship was unnecessary for the possession of family privileges. The covenant with Abraham and his seed (Gn. xvii. 9) was valid not only for those born of Abraham but also for purchased slaves of alien stock (Gn. xvii. 12 f.). The Hebrew word for father (*'āḇ*) 'does not imply physical fatherhood so much as protector and nurturer. In fact the words "Thou art the father of the fatherless" exactly explain what fatherhood meant' (A. Guillaume, *Prophecy and Divination*, 1938, p. 75).

The discovery of the Nuzi archives has, however, thrown some light on a Semitic form of adoption, which had not previously been thought to exist. At Nuzi it was the custom for a childless couple to adopt a son, who should serve them while they lived and bury them when they died, and receive in return the inheritance, though any son born to the couple after the adoption became the chief heir (W. H. Rossell, *JBL*, LXXI, 1952, pp. 233 f.). Some procedure such as this must be envisaged in the relationship of Abraham and Eliezer (Gn. xv. 2 ff.), while something closely akin to legal adoption occurs at Gn. xlviii. 5 (Ephraim and Manasseh), Ex. ii. 10 (Moses), 1 Ki. xi. 20 (Genubath), and Est. ii. 7 (Esther).

The germ of the use of the term in a religious sense is clearly present in the Old Testament description of Israel as a son of God (Ex. iv. 22; Is. i. 2 f.; Je. iii. 19; Ho. xi. 1) and the focus of this relationship in the king, representative of his people (2 Sa. vii. 14; 1 Ch. xxviii. 6; Ps. ii. 6 f.), so that Paul can speak of his kinsmen the Israelites, 'to whom pertaineth the adoption' (Rom. ix. 4).

For Paul, adoption as a son of God is a relationship of grace, unlike the Sonship of Christ, who was Son by nature (*cf.* Jn. i. 14). It involves a change of status, planned from eternity and mediated by Jesus Christ (Eph. i. 5), from slavery to sonship; though potentially men were sons before Christ's coming (Gal. iv. 1), actually they were only slaves (Gal. iv. 3). The cry 'Abba, Father' (Rom. viii. 15 and Gal. iv. 6 in the context of adoption) may perhaps be the traditional cry of the adopted slave. Once adopted, the son of God possesses all family rights, including access to the Father (Rom. viii. 15) and sharing with Christ in the divine inheritance (Rom. viii. 17). The presence of the Spirit of God is both the instrument (Rom. viii. 14) and the consequence (Gal. iv. 6) of this possession of sonship. However complete in status this adoption may be, it has yet to be finally realized and promulgated in fact in the deliverance of the creation itself from bondage (Rom. viii. 21 ff.).

Though adoption as a theological formula occurs only in Paul, it is implicit as a relationship of grace in John's teaching about 'becoming a son' (Jn. i. 12; 1 Jn. iii. 1 f.), in the prodigal's acceptance into full family rights (Lk. xv. 19 ff.), and in Jesus' oft-repeated title of God as Father (Mt. v. 16, vi. 9; Lk. xii. 32). F.H.P.

ADORAIM. City of SW Judah fortified by Rehoboam (2 Ch. xi. 9). Robinson identifies it with the village of Dura, about 7 miles west of Hebron. J.D.D.

ADORAM. See ADONIRAM.

ADRAMMELECH. 1. A god brought from Sepharvaim (*q.v.*) to Samaria, where the colonists sacrificed children to him (2 Ki. xvii. 31). Possibly corresponds to a divine name Atar (Atr) found in personal names from Harran and Syria (Alalaḫ and Ugarit). Atarmilki would mean 'Atar is King' (*RA*, XXX, p. 72). Eissfeldt compares the name with the palm-god Demarus (*Mélanges Isidore Lévy*, 1953, pp. 153–159).

2. One of the sons of Sennacherib, brother of Sharezer, who murdered their father in 681 BC (2 Ki. xix. 37; Is. xxxvii. 38). This event is also recorded in the Babylonian Chronicle without naming the son (*DOTT*, pp. 70–73). A West Semitic name for one of the sons is likely, as Sennacherib's wife Naqi'a-Zakutu was of West Semitic origin. D.J.W.

ADRAMYTTIUM. Seaport in Mysia, in Roman Asia, facing Lesbos: the site is Karatash, but the modern inland town, Edremid, preserves the name. Rendel Harris suggested a S Arabian origin for the original settlement (*Contemporary Review*, CXXVIII, 1925, pp. 194 ff.). Its commercial importance, once high, was declining by New Testament times.

An Adramyttian ship conveyed Julius and Paul from Caesarea (Acts xxvii. 2). It was doubtless homeward bound, engaging in coastwise traffic with 'the ports along the coast of Asia' (*cf.* RSV), where a connection for Rome might be obtained—an expectation soon justified (verses 5 f.).

BIBLIOGRAPHY. Strabo, xiii. 1. 51, 65, 66; Pliny, *Nat. Hist.* xiii. 1. 2 (for a local export); W. Leaf, *Strabo on the Troad*, 1923, pp. 318 ff. A.F.W.

ADRIA. This name, probably derived from that of the town of Adria on the river Po, first denoted the gulf at the head of the Adriatic Sea. Later it was extended to cover the whole of that sea, and by the first century AD it appeared to include also the central Mediterranean below the gulf of Otranto. It is used in this sense in Acts xxvii. 27 and also by Josephus (*Vita* iii. 15). It was the scene of the dramatic shipwreck in which Paul and his companions were involved, their ship being tossed about for fourteen days in the waters between Crete and Malta. B.F.C.A.

ADULLAM. A Canaanite city (Gn. xxxviii. 1, 2) in the territory of Judah (Jos. xii. 15); fortified by Rehoboam (2 Ch. xi. 7); mentioned by Micah (Mi. i. 15) and inhabited after the Exile (Ne. xi. 30). Identified with Tell esh-Sheikh Madhkur, midway between Jerusalem and Lachish, the place is usually associated with the cave in which David hid when pursued by Saul (1 Sa. xxii. 1). J.W.M.

ADULTERY. See MARRIAGE.

ADUMMIM. A steep pass on the boundary between Judah and Benjamin (Jos. xv. 7, xxviii. 17) on the road from Jericho to Jerusalem. Traditionally the scene of the Good Samaritan story (Lk. x. 34), it is known today as Tal'at ed-Damm ('ascent of blood'), probably from the colour of the soil, though Jerome attributed the name to the murders and robberies said to have taken place there. J.D.D.

ADVOCATE. The word *paraklētos* in the Johannine writings, derived from the verb *parakaleō*, literally 'to call beside', has been interpreted both actively and passively; actively as meaning one who stands by and exhorts or encourages, whence the AV 'comforter' in Jn. xiv. 16, 26, xv. 26, xvi. 7; passively as meaning one called to stand by someone, particularly in a law-court (though as a friend of the accused rather than a professional pleader), whence the AV 'advocate' in 1 Jn. ii. 1. Many versions simply transliterate the Greek; hence the name 'Paraclete' for the Holy Spirit.

Parakaleō is frequently used in the New Testament to mean 'exhort', 'encourage', and Acts ix. 31 speaks expressly of the *paraklēsis* of the Holy Spirit, which probably means the 'exhortation' or 'encouragement' of the Spirit (though it may mean the invocation of the Spirit's aid).

There is little evidence for an active use of *paraklētos* outside the New Testament or the patristic commentators on the Gospel passages, who seem to derive the sense 'consoler' or 'encourager' simply from the general context, which speaks of the disciples' sense of desolation at Jesus' departure and of their need to be taught more about Him. This derivation from the context is quite reasonable, though it should be noted that it finds no true support in AV 'comfortless' at Jn. xiv. 18 for *orphanous*, better translated 'orphans'.

On the other hand, the help of the Spirit promised in Mt. x. 19, 20; Mk. xiii. 11; Lk. xii. 11, 12 is precisely that of an advocate before the Jewish and secular authorities. Even Jn. xvi. 8–11 has a forensic tone, though admittedly rather of prosecution than defence. The translation 'advocate' is more appropriate in 1 Jn. ii. 1, where the sinner is thought of as arraigned before God's justice. Even here, however, the more general sense is not impossible.

The evidence is nicely balanced, and since so many words in the fourth Gospel seem intended to suggest more than one meaning an ambiguous rendering such as RSV 'Counsellor' is probably to be preferred.

Critics have argued that the application of the word *paraklētos* in the Gospel to the Spirit and in the Epistle to Jesus Christ indicates the different authorship of the two works. But: (i) the Spirit's *paraklēsis* is amid earthly dangers and difficulties: Jesus appears for us in heaven; (ii) these different but parallel offices are reflected also in Rom. viii. 26, 34: the Spirit makes intercession in us and the risen Christ for us in heaven; (iii) the words *allos paraklētos* used in Jn. xiv. 16, though Greek usage permits the translation 'another, a Paraclete', may mean simply 'another Paraclete', implying that Jesus Himself is a Paraclete. See also HOLY SPIRIT.

BIBLIOGRAPHY. A good survey of the evidence is in C. K. Barrett, 'The Holy Spirit in the Fourth Gospel', *JTS*, N.S., I, 1950, pp. 7–15.

M.H.C.

AENON (*ainōn*, 'springs'). The place on the west side of Jordan where John was baptizing because water was plentiful (Jn. iii. 23). The site is uncertain, but see under SALIM. J.D.D.

AFRICA.

I. EARLY KNOWLEDGE AND NOMENCLATURE

The Greeks designated the continent 'Libya', but of its extent and its relation to Asia there was doubt. Herodotus (5th century BC) is already convinced of its being almost surrounded by sea, and cites (*Hist.* iv. 42) an alleged circumnavigation by a Phoenician crew in the service of Pharaoh Necho (*q.v.*). A translation of a Punic document, the Periplus of the Erythraean Sea, recounts a Carthaginian voyage, evidently as far as Sierra Leone, before 480 BC. The Romans applied 'Africa' to the whole continent (Pomponius Mela, i. 4), but far more regularly to Proconsular Africa, comprising the area (roughly modern Tunisia) annexed from Carthage in 146 BC, plus the Numidian and Mauretanian domains later added. But, though the Carthaginians may have known more about the Trans-Sahara than we realize, the knowledge of Africa possessed by the ancient peoples who have left most literary remains was largely confined to the areas participating in, or accessible to, the Mediterranean civilizations, rarely penetrating the colossal barriers of the Atlas Mountains, the Sahara, and the perils of the Upper Nile.

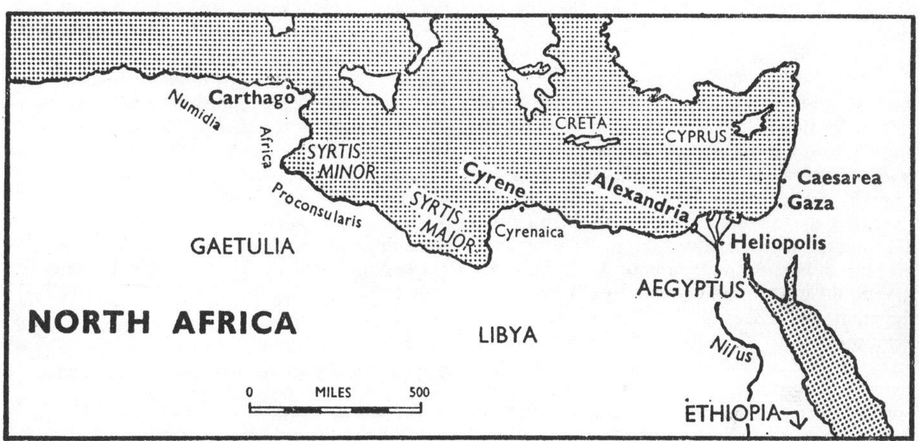

Fig. 3. The north coast of Africa in Roman times.

II. AFRICA IN THE OLD TESTAMENT

Similarly, Israel's main concerns in Africa were naturally with her powerful neighbour, Egypt. Whether as the granary of the Patriarchs, the oppressor of the bondage, or the broken reed of the period of Assyrian advance, the changing rôles of Egypt could not be ignored. Despite the cruel past, a tender feeling towards Egypt remained (Dt. xxiii. 7), which prepares us for the prophecies of Egypt's eventually sharing with Israel, in the knowledge and worship of the Lord (Is. xix—note the changing tone as the chapter proceeds). Other African peoples are mentioned from time to time (see, *e.g.*, LUBIM, PUT), but the most frequent allusions are to Cush (see ETHIOPIA), the general designation for the lands beyond Egypt. The characteristic skin and physique of the inhabitants was remarked (Je. xiii. 23; Is. xlv. 14, and probably Is. xviii. 2, 7).

At some periods historical circumstances linked Egypt and Ethiopia in Hebrew eyes, and they stand together, sometimes with other African peoples, as representative nations on which God's righteous judgments will be executed (Is. xliii. 3; Ezk. xxx. 4 ff.; Na. iii. 9), as those who will one day recognize the true status of God's people (Is. xlv. 14), and as those who will ultimately receive Israel's God (Ps. lxxxvii. 4, see RV; and especially Ps. lxviii. 31). The picture of Ethiopia, symbol of the great African unknown beyond the Egyptian river, stretching out hands to God, was like a trumpet call in the missionary revival of the 18th and 19th centuries. Even within the biblical period it had a measure of fulfilment; not only were there Jewish settlements in Africa (*cf.* Zp. iii. 10) but an Ethiopian in Jewish service did more for God's prophet than true-born Israelites (Je. xxxviii), and the high-ranking Ethiopian of Acts viii was evidently a devout proselyte.

Despite a long tradition of perverted exegesis in some quarters, there is nothing to connect the curse of Ham (Gn. ix. 25) with a permanent divinely instituted malediction on the negroid peoples.

III. AFRICA IN THE NEW TESTAMENT

Jesus Himself received hospitality on African soil (Mt. ii. 13 ff.). The Jewish settlements in Egypt and Cyrene, prefigured, perhaps, in Is. xix. 18 f. *et alia*, were evidently a fruitful field for the early Church. Simon who bore the cross was a Cyrenian, and that his relationship with Christ did not stop there may be inferred from the fact that his children were apparently well known in the primitive Christian community (Mk. xv. 21). Egyptian and Cyrenian Jews were present at Pentecost (Acts ii. 10); the mighty Apollos (*q.v.*) was an Alexandrian Jew (Acts xviii. 24); Cyrenian converts, probably including the prophet Lucius (*q.v.*), shared in the epoch-making step of preaching to pure pagans at Antioch (Acts xi. 20 f.). But we know nothing certain about the foundation of the Egyptian and North African churches, some of the most prominent in the world by the late 2nd century. The tradition, which cannot be traced very early, that Mark was the pioneer evangelist of Alexandria (Eus., *EH* ii. 16) is itself, when applied to 1 Pet. v. 13, the only support for the theory of Peter's residence there (but *cf.* G. T. Manley, *EQ*, XVI, 1944, pp. 138 ff.). Luke's vivid picture in Acts of the march of the gospel through the northern lands of the Mediterranean may obscure for us the fact that the march through the southern lands must have been quite as effective and probably almost as early. There were Christians in Africa about as soon as there were in Europe.

But Luke does not forget Africa. He shows how, by means the apostolic Church never anticipated, and before the real Gentile mission began, the gospel went to the kingdom of Meroë (Acts viii. 26 ff.), as if in earnest of the fulfilment of the purpose of God for Africa declared in the Old Testament.

BIBLIOGRAPHY. M. Cary and E. H. Warmington, *The Ancient Explorers*, 1929; C. K. Meek, *Journal of African History*, I, 1960, pp. 1 ff.; C. P. Groves, *The Planting of Christianity in Africa*, I, 1948, pp. 31 ff. A.F.W.

AGABUS. Derivation uncertain; possibly equals Old Testament Hagab, Hagabah. A Jerusalem prophet whose prediction of 'great dearth' was fulfilled in the reign of Claudius (Acts xi. 27, 28). Suetonius, Dio Cassius, Tacitus, and Eusebius mention famines at that time. At Caesarea he acted a prediction of Paul's fate at Jerusalem (Acts xxi. 10, 11). In late traditions, one of the 'Seventy' (Lk. x. 1) and a martyr. G.W.G.

AGAG. From Balaam's use of the name (Nu. xxiv. 7, *etc.*) it would appear to be the common title of the kings of Amalek as 'Pharaoh' was in Egypt. In particular, the name is used of the king of the Amalekites taken by Saul and, contrary to God's command, spared along with the spoil. He was slain by Samuel. Saul's disobedience was the occasion of his rejection by God (1 Sa. xv). M.A.M.

AGAGITE. An adjective applied to Haman in Est. iii. 1, 10, viii. 3, 5, ix. 24. Josephus (*Ant.* xi. 6. 5) makes him an Amalekite, presumably descended from Agag, whom Saul spared (1 Sa. xv). Mordecai, who brought about Haman's fall, was, like Saul, descended from Kish (Est. ii. 5; 1 Sa. ix. 1). The LXX has *Bougaios* (meaning obscure) in iii. 1, and *Makedōn* (Macedonian) in ix. 24; elsewhere it omits the adjective. J.S.W.

AGAPE. See LOVE FEAST.

AGATE. See JEWELS AND PRECIOUS STONES.

AGE, OLD AGE. The Jews, and Orientals generally, held old age in honour, and respect was required for the aged (*cf.* Lv. xix. 32; Herodotus, ii. 80). 'Who is sure of heaven?' asks the Talmud. 'He that honours the aged.' The cruelty of the Chaldeans is expressed by their having no compassion on 'him who stooped for age' (2 Ch. xxxvi. 17). Old age was greatly desired, and its attainment regarded as a reward for piety and a token of the divine favour (Gn. xv. 15; Ex. xx. 12); communities are represented as greatly blessed in which old people abound (Is. lxv. 20; Zc. viii. 4).

The disabilities of age are not overlooked (*cf.* Ps. lxxi. 9), and are graphically described in Ec. xii. 2–7, but divine assurance is given of God's concern for the aged (Is. xlvi. 4); hence age was looked forward to in faith and hope (Ps. lxxi. 18).

Superior wisdom was believed to belong to the old (Jb. xii. 20, xv. 10, xxxii. 7; 1 Ki. xii. 6, 8); thus positions of guidance and authority were given to them, as indicated by the terms 'elders' and 'presbyters'. Age formed under Moses the main qualification of those who acted as representatives of the people in all matters of difficulty and deliberation.

The Jews, however, never lost sight of the fact that length of days alone did not entitle a man to consideration. It was always understood that God may give a man wisdom independently of his years; Job was held in such high esteem for his goodness that even old men stood up as he passed by (xxix. 8). That there was no indiscriminate veneration of the old is seen in another way. While the young were taught to regard grey hairs as the 'beauty of old men' (Pr. xx. 29), and constantly reminded that it is an evil time when youth bears itself insolently towards age (Is. iii. 5; La. v. 12), there always followed some such condition, as in 'the hoary head is a crown of glory, if it be found in the way of righteousness' (Pr. xvi. 31; *cf.* Ec. iv. 13). J.D.D.

AGES. See TIME.

AGRAPHA. See NEW TESTAMENT APOCRYPHA.

AGRICULTURE. The excavations of Old Testament Jericho have demonstrated that Palestine was one of the earliest agricultural centres yet discovered. Good farming can be dated here around 7500 BC. Jericho represents irrigation culture which was common in the prehistoric period in the Jordan valley, not along the river itself but beside the streams that flowed into it. About the same time the hill country also was showing signs of agriculture, for the Natufian culture shows flint sickle-blades and hoes. Irrigation as an ancient science reached its peak and held it in Egypt and Babylonia. By Abraham's time, however, in Palestine irrigation farming was declining in importance, and even dry farming, as in the Negeb, was coming in.

Most of Palestine's farmers depended on rain. The drought of a six months' summer ended with the 'early rains', and as soon as the sun-baked earth could be farmed (late November or December) the seed was broadcast and ploughed under. Sometimes the land was also ploughed before seeding. The heavy winter rains gave the crops their major moisture, but the 'latter rains' of March and April were needed to bring the grain to head.

The principal grain crops were wheat and barley, the former the more valuable, but the latter had the advantage of a shorter growing season and the ability to grow on poorer soil. Various legumes, such as lentils, peas, and beans, formed a secondary crop. Vegetables added variety to the meal, with onions and garlic playing a prominent part. Herbs, seeds, and other condiments gave variety to a menu that was basically bread. Newly-sprouting wild flowers and spring plants served as salads.

After the invention of the sickle, where flint teeth were set into a bone or wooden haft, the next improvement was the plough. The best tree from which to fashion a wooden plough was the holm oak. The poorest farmer never had a metal ploughshare. By the time of David, however, iron was sufficiently plentiful, and a good-sized iron one could be used. The result was much better crops and a heavier population on the same land area.

The single-handled wooden plough had a virtue in its lightness, as the fields were often stony and the plough could be easily lifted over boulders. On level land, as in Bashan, excess rocks were gathered into piles in the fields. But on the hillsides they were built into terraces to keep the good soil from washing away. Large stones served as boundary marks of a grain field, and no fencing was used. The single-handled plough left the farmer's other hand free to use the ox-goad.

Fig. 4. A Babylonian seed plough of the 7th century BC from an obelisk of Esarhaddon.

Grain crops matured first in the deep hot Jordan valley, and then the harvest season followed up the rising elevation of the land, first the coastal and Esdraelon areas, then the low hills, and finally the higher mountains. The barley harvest of April and May preceded the wheat by several weeks or even a month. By that time a summer crop of millet had often been sown on other land which had been left fallow through the winter.

To harvest the crop, the grain was grasped in one hand and then cut with the sickle held in the other hand. These bundles were tied into sheaves, which in turn were loaded on to donkeys or camels to be carried to the threshing-floor. Amos mentions the use of wagons. Gleaners followed the reapers, and then animals were let into the stubble in the following order: sheep, goats, and camels.

Threshing-floors were located near the village at a point where the winds would be helpful for winnowing. The floor itself was either a rock outcropping or a soil area coated with marly clay. The sheaves were scattered about a foot deep over the floor and protected at the edges by a ring of stones. The animals, which were sometimes shod for this purpose, were driven round and round until the grain was loosened and the stocks chopped into small pieces. A faster method was to use a wooden sled with stones or iron fragments fastened into the under side. The grain was winnowed by tossing it into the wind with wooden pitchforks. The grain might be sifted then before being bagged for human use.

The straw was saved as fodder for the animals. Fire in a ripening field or a threshing-floor was a major crime, as that year's food supply was lost. Samson's fox-fire episode (Jdg. xv. 4, 5) was a catastrophe to the Philistines. Threshing might last to the end of August or even later with bumper harvests. See also CALENDAR.

The best grain lands were the benches of the Jordan valley that could be irrigated by the tributaries of the Jordan, the Philistine plain, Esdraelon (although part of it was then marshy), Bashan, and Moab. But since bread was the principal food of the country, even poor bench land was often cultivated to produce grain. Narrow stair-like terraces were erected on the mountainside, and in Lebanon today they still creep up the mountains to the very snow-line. The lower hills, such as the Shephelah, gave a wider distribution to crops, adding the vine and the olive to the grains. The better sections of the higher land were farmed, but much was left for grazing or forestry. See figs. 158, 159.

The heavy summer dews in many parts of the country supplemented the sub-soil moisture from the winter rains and made possible the cultivation of grapes, cucumbers, and melons. These were far more valuable crops than many Bible readers realize, for Palestine has no summer rain, and most of the streams dry up. These fruits and vegetables then become an extra water ration to both man and beast. Many varieties of grapes were grown, and they were not only a valuable food item in summer but, when dried as raisins, they were also winter food. The wine made from the grape was an item of export. Grapes were usually a hillside crop, with beans and lentils often grown between the vines. Is. v. 1–6 provides a good picture of the vineyard. See also figs. 156, 157.

Fruits and nuts were other means of adding variety to the menu. The olive tree and the sesame plant were principal sources of cooking oil; animal fat was very expensive. Nuts, although rich in oil, were primarily used as condiments. The beans of the carob tree were an excellent food for animals. Flax was the only plant grown for cloth.

The farmer's major enemy was drought. The failure of any one of the three rain seasons was serious, and prolonged droughts were not uncommon, especially in certain sections of the land. The farmer was also plagued by locust invasions, plant diseases, such as the mildew, and the hot sirocco winds. War, too, was a common enemy of the farmer, for war was usually conducted at the harvest season so that the invading army could live off the land. Palestine's chief exports were wheat, olive oil, and wine. These were not only shipped to other countries, but large quantities of these items were consumed by the caravans traversing the land of Palestine itself.

BIBLIOGRAPHY. Denis Baly, *The Geography of the Bible*, 1957. J.L.K.

AGRIPPA. See HEROD.

AHAB (*'aḥ'āḇ*; Assyr. *Aḫābu*, 'the (divine) brother is father').

1. The son and successor of Omri, founder of the dynasty, who reigned as seventh king of Israel for twenty-two years, *c.* 874–852 BC (1 Ki. xvi. 28 ff.). He married Jezebel, daughter of Ethbaal, king of Sidon and priest of Astarte.

I. POLITICAL HISTORY

Ahab fortified Israelite cities (1 Ki. xvi. 34, xxii. 39) and undertook extensive work at his own capital, as is shown also by excavation (1 Ki. xvi. 32; see SAMARIA). His own palace was adorned with ivory (1 Ki. xxi. 1, xxii. 39; *cf.* Am. iii. 15). Throughout his reign there were frequent wars with Syria (*cf.* 1 Ki. xxii. 1) especially against Ben-hadad who, with his allies, besieged Samaria but was driven off (1 Ki. xx. 21). Later, in battle near Aphek, Ahab heavily defeated Ben-hadad but spared his life (1 Ki. xx. 26–30), perhaps in return for commercial concessions in Damascus similar to those allowed to the Syrian merchants in Samaria. Economic ties were maintained with the Phoenician ports through his marriage.

The Assyrian annals show that in 854 BC, at the battle of Qarqar on the Orontes, Ahab supported Ben-hadad with 2,000 chariots and 10,000 men in the successful, though temporary, effort to stay the Assyrian advance south-westwards (see SHALMANESER; *cf. ANET*, pp. 278–281). This intervention was to be one of the first causes of the later Assyrian advances against Israel. The preoccupation with Syrian affairs enabled Moab, once Ahab's vassal, to revolt (see MOABITE STONE). Later in his reign, however, Ahab, with Jehoshaphat of Judah, once more warred against Syria (1 Ki. xxii. 3). Though warned by Micaiah's prophecy of the fatal outcome, Ahab entered the final battle, but in disguise. He was mortally wounded by a random arrow, and his body taken to Samaria for burial. His son Ahaziah succeeded to the throne (1 Ki. xxii. 28–40).

II. RELIGIOUS AFFAIRS

Throughout his reign Ahab had Elijah as the divine prophet. He was influenced by his wife Jezebel whom he allowed to build a temple dedicated to Baal (of Tyre) in Samaria with its pagan altar, *asherah* and attendants (1 Ki. xvi. 32). She encouraged a large group of false prophets together with the devotees of Baal (1 Ki. xviii. 19, 20), and later instigated open opposition to Yahweh. The true prophets were slain, altars of the Lord were torn down and Elijah forced to flee for his life. One hundred prophets were, however, hidden by Obadiah, Ahab's godly minister (1 Ki. xviii. 3, 4).

Ahab's failure to stand for the law and true justice was exemplified in the fake trial and subsequent death of Naboth whose vineyard was annexed to the adjacent palace grounds at Jezreel (1 Ki. xxi. 1–16). This brought Elijah once again into open opposition; his stand was vindicated by Yahweh at the test at Carmel which routed the claims of the false prophets. Elijah prophesied the fate of Ahab, his wife and the dynasty (1 Ki. xxi. 20–24). The reign, marked by idolatry and the evil influence of Jezebel (1 Ki. xxi. 25–26), affected succeeding generations for evil, and was also condemned by Hosea (i. 4) and Micah (vi. 16).

2. Ahab, son of Kolaiah, was one of the two false prophets denounced by Jeremiah for using the name of Yahweh. His death, by fire, at the hand of the king of Babylon was foretold by the prophet (Je. xxix. 21). D.J.W.

AHASUERUS (*'ªḥašwērôš*, the Hebrew equivalent of the Persian *khshayarsha*). In the Elephantine Aramaic papyri the consonants appear as *kšy'rš*. The resemblance of the latter to the Greek Xerxes is reasonably close, and the Babylonian version of Xerxes' name on the Behistun inscription is close to the Hebrew as above. Xerxes I was king of Persia (485–465 BC). The name occurs in three different contexts:

1. Ezra iv. 6. It is probable that in Ezr. iv. 6–23 the author has deliberately introduced two later examples of opposition in the reigns of Xerxes I and his successor, Artaxerxes I. The context speaks of opposition to the building of the city walls, and not of the temple, as in iv. 1–5, 24 (see J. Stafford Wright, *The Date of Ezra's Coming to Jerusalem*, 1958, pp. 17 f.). An alternative but improbable theory is that the king here is Cambyses, the successor of Cyrus (529–522 BC).

2. The book of Esther. The LXX reads throughout 'Artaxerxes', and some identify Ahasuerus here with Artaxerxes II (404–359 BC). Traditionally, however, it is again Xerxes to whom the writer refers. See ESTHER.

3. Daniel ix. 1. The father of Darius the Mede. See DARIUS. J.S.W.

AHAVA. A river or alluvial region in Mesopotamia where the returning exiles were mustered by Ezra and a census taken (Ezr. viii. 15–31). This census disclosed a lack of Levites, the deficiency being made good from those yet in Babylon, and a time of fasting and supplication was held. The site is probably the modern Hit on the Euphrates (Herodotus i. 80). R.J.W.

AHAZ (*'āḥaz*, 'he has grasped'). He became king of Judah on the death of his father Jotham *c.* 735 BC. His name is an abbreviated form of Jehoahaz. This is confirmed by an inscription of Tiglath-pileser III (see *ANET*, p. 282). His age at the time of his accession and the length of his reign (2 Ki. xvi. 2; 2 Ch. xxviii. 1) both give rise to chronological problems (see CHRONOLOGY OF THE OLD TESTAMENT).

Early in his reign, Pekah, king of Israel, and Rezin, king of Syria, tried to force him to join their anti-Assyrian alliance. Failing in this, the allies invaded Judah (2 Ki. xvi. 5). The Judaeans suffered heavy casualties and many were taken prisoner. The intervention of the prophet Oded secured the repatriation of the prisoners (2 Ch. xxviii. 5–15). Isaiah sought vainly to encourage Ahaz at the height of the crisis to put his trust in Yahweh (Is. vii. 1–12), but the faithless king preferred to appeal to Assyria for help. The price of Assyrian aid, besides being a heavy drain on the exchequer, was a century of vassalage for Judah. The Philistines and the Edomites took advantage of Judah's weakened condition to make hostile incursions (2 Ch. xxviii. 17, 18).

These calamities are represented as divine judgment on Ahaz for his flagrant apostasy. He 'made his son to pass through the fire', encouraged corrupt worship of the high places, placed an Assyrian-type altar in the temple court, used the displaced Solomonic bronze altar for divination, and closed the temple sanctuary (2 Ki. xvi. 3, 4, 10–16; 2 Ch. xxviii. 2–4, 23–25). J.C.J.W.

AHAZIAH (*'ªḥazyâ* or *'ªḥazyāhû*, 'Yahweh has grasped'). **1.** The son and successor of Ahab, king of Israel (1 Ki. xxii. 51–2 Ki. i. 18). His name belies his character. The influence of his mother Jezebel is seen in his sending messengers to consult Baalzebub, the god of Ekron, about the chances of his recovery after his fall through the lattice of his upper apartment in Samaria (see ELIJAH). His brief reign of barely two years is notable for the revolt of Moab (2 Ki. i. 1) and for the ill-fated maritime alliance with Jehoshaphat of Judah (2 Ch. xx. 35, 36).

2. The youngest son of Jehoram, king of Judah. He was placed on the throne by the inhabitants of Jerusalem as the sole surviving heir (2 Ch. xxii. 1). His religious policy during his short reign of one year plainly indicates his complete domination by his mother Athaliah and is epitomized in Chronicles as walking 'in the ways of the house of Ahab' (2 Ch. xxii. 3). He met his death at the hands of Jehu while visiting his uncle Jehoram, who was convalescing in Jezreel. The accounts of his death (2 Ki. ix. 16–28; 2 Ch. xxii. 6–9) are complementary and not contradictory. J.C.J.W.

AHIJAH, AHIAH. 1. A prophet from Shiloh who protested against the idolatry of Solomon. Ahijah symbolically divided his robe into twelve parts, ten of which he gave to Jeroboam, a minor official in Solomon's government (1 Ki. xi. 28 ff.). Ahijah stated that the kingdom of Solomon would be divided and that ten of the tribes would become subject to Jeroboam (1 Ki. xi. 30–40). To escape the wrath of Solomon, Jeroboam fled to Egypt, where he was granted asylum by Pharaoh Shishak. After Solomon's death, Ahijah's prophecy was fulfilled when the ten northern tribes revolted from Rehoboam, Solomon's son, and Jeroboam became king of Israel (922–901 BC). Jeroboam, however, led Israel into idolatry and was also denounced by Ahijah. The prophet foretold the death of Jeroboam's son, the extinction of his house, and the future captivity of Israel (1 Ki. xiv. 6–16).

2. In 1 Sa. xiv. 3, 18 Ahiah appears as the name of the great-grandson of Eli, who is elsewhere called Ahimelech, priest of Nob and father of Abiathar (1 Sa. xxi. 1 ff., xxii. 9 ff.).

3. Other men bearing the name are mentioned briefly: one of Solomon's secretaries (1 Ki. iv. 3); the father of Baasha (1 Ki. xv. 27, 33); the son of Jerahmeel (1 Ch. ii. 25, where the rendering is uncertain); the son of Ehud (1 Ch. viii. 4, 7, AV respectively 'Ahoah' and 'Ahiah'); one of David's heroes (1 Ch. xi. 36); a guardian of the temple treasure (1 Ch. xxvi. 20, where again the text is dubious); and one of Nehemiah's fellow-signatories to the covenant (Ne. x. 26, RV 'Ahiah').

C.F.P.

AHIKAM (*'ᵃḥîqām*, 'my brother has arisen'). Son of Shaphan and member of Josiah's deputation to Huldah the prophetess (2 Ki. xxii. 12, 14; 2 Ch. xxxiv. 20). Later, Jeremiah's protector (Je. xxvi. 24). Father of Gedaliah, the governor appointed by Nebuchadrezzar (2 Ki. xxv. 22; Je. xxxix. 14). Some scholars, *e.g.* J. Skinner (*Prophecy and Religion*, 1948, p. 236), N. J. D. White (art. 'Gedaliah', *HDB*), infer that he was the son of the scribe Shaphan (2 Ki. xxii. 3, 8–11), but J. A. Montgomery (*Kings*, *ICC*, p. 524) says that the relationship cannot be determined.

J.G.G.N.

AHIMAAZ (*'ᵃḥîma'aṣ*, 'my brother is wrath'). **1.** Father of Saul's wife, Ahinoam (1 Sa. xiv. 50).

2. Son of Zadok. Famed for his swift running (2 Sa. xviii. 27). With Jonathan, Abiathar's son, he acted as messenger from David's secret allies in Jerusalem during Absalom's rebellion (2 Sa. xv. 27, 36), and escaped capture at En-rogel only by hiding in a well (2 Sa. xvii. 17–21). He was one of the two messengers who brought news of Absalom's defeat, though he did not report his death, either through ignorance of the fact or a natural reluctance to tell David (2 Sa. xviii. 19–32).

3. Solomon's commissariat officer for Naphtali, who married his daughter, Basemath (1 Ki. iv. 15). Some identify with Zadok's son.

J.G.G.N.

AHIMELECH (*ᵃḥîmeleḵ*, 'brother of a king', 'my brother is king'). The name is also found on the ostraca from Samaria. **1.** Son of Ahitub, father of Abiathar. The priest at Nob who gave David the shewbread and Goliath's sword, for which he was killed by Saul (1 Sa. xxi, xxii); see AHIJAH. **2.** Son of Abiathar, a priest under David, perhaps grandson of (1) (2 Sa. viii. 17); see ABIATHAR. **3.** A Hittite in David's service before he became king (1 Sa. xxvi. 6).

A.R.M.

AHIRAM. A son of Benjamin (Nu. xxvi. 38), possibly corrupted to Ehi in Gn. xlvi. 21 and to Aharah in 1 Ch. viii. 1.

J.D.D.

AHITHOPHEL (*ᵃḥîṯōp̄el*, possibly 'brother of foolish talk'). A native of Giloh and David's respected counsellor (2 Sa. xvi. 23). When he conspired with Absalom, David prayed that his advice might be rendered useless, perhaps playing on the name (2 Sa. xv. 12, 31 ff.). Ahithophel suggested that Absalom should assert his authority by taking possession of his father's harem. His plan for attacking David before he could muster his forces was thwarted by the king's friend Hushai. Ahithophel, perceiving that Absalom had taken a disastrous course, went home and hanged himself lest he fall into the hands of his former lord (2 Sa. xvi, xvii). Jehoiada and Abiathar took his place as David's counsellors (1 Ch. xxvii. 33, 34). His son, Eliam, evidently remained faithful to David, as he was one of the thirty heroes (2 Sa. xxiii. 34).

A.R.M.

AHITUB. (*'ᵃḥîṭûḇ*, 'brother of good', 'my brother is good'. LXX *Achitōb* and Assyr. *Aḫu-ṭāb* suggest a reading Ahitob.) **1.** Son of Phinehas, grandson of Eli, father of Ahijah (1 Sa. xiv. 3); see AHIJAH. **2.** Father of Ahimelech, perhaps the same person as (1) (1 Sa. xxii. 9). **3.** A Levite, son of Amariah (1 Ch. vi. 7, 8), father of Meraioth and 'chief officer of the house of God'. Zadok was evidently his grandson (2 Sa. viii. 17; 1 Ch. xviii. 16; Ezr. vii. 2; *cf.* 1 Ch. ix. 11; Ne. xi. 11).

A.R.M.

AHLAB. Situated in the territory of Asher (Jdg. i. 31), it is probably to be identified with Khirbet el-Mahalib, 5 miles north-east of Tyre, the Mahalib captured by Tiglath-pileser III in 734 BC and later by Sennacherib (*Iraq*, XVIII, 1956, p. 129).

D.J.W.

AHOLAH. See OHOLAH.

AI. The name is always written with the definite article in Hebrew, *hā'ay*, the heap, ruin. The city lay east of Bethel and the altar which Abram built (Gn. xii. 8) adjacent to Bethaven (Jos. vii. 2) and north of Michmash (Is. x. 28). The Israelite attack upon it, immediately following the sack of Jericho, was at first repulsed, but after Achan's sin had been punished a successful stratagem was employed. The people of Ai were killed, their king executed, and their city burned and made into 'an heap' (Heb. *tēl*; Jos. vii. 1–viii. 29). It became an Ephraimite town (1 Ch. vii. 28, 'Ayyah', RSV), but was inhabited by the Benjamites after the Exile (Ne. xi. 31). Isaiah pictured the Assyrian armies advancing on Jerusalem by way of Ai (Is. x. 28, 'Aiath').

Modern Et-Tell (Arab. *tall*, heap, mound) about 2 miles south-east of Bethel (Tell Beitīn) is usually identified with Ai on topographical grounds and on the correspondence in the meanings of the ancient and modern names. Excavations in 1933–35 by Mme J. Marquet-Krause revealed a city which prospered in the third millennium BC. There was a triple city-wall and a temple containing stone bowls and ivories imported from Egypt. It was destroyed *c.* 2200 BC, perhaps by Amorite invaders. No traces of later occupation were found except for a small settlement which made use of the earlier ruins about 1100 BC. Those who believe in this identification have made various attempts to explain the discrepancy between the biblical account of Joshua's conquest and the archaeological evidence. It has been suggested that the story originally referred to Bethel but was later adapted to suit Ai or even invented to explain the impressive ruin as the result of an attack by the hero Joshua. There is no evidence to support these hypotheses; indeed, it would be strange to credit a hero with failure at first. More plausible is the explanation that Ai was used as a temporary stronghold by the surrounding population; but the account points rather to an inhabited town with its own king. While it is possible that Late Bronze Age strata have been removed by erosion or that Ai is to be located elsewhere, no completely satisfactory solution has yet been proposed. The later town (Ezr. ii. 28; Ne. vii. 32) may be identified with Khirbet Ḥayyān 1 mile south-east of Et-Tell. Occupation of this site was confined to the Iron Age. For a summary of the excavation results and proposed solutions of the problem they raise, see W. F. Albright, *BASOR*, 74, 1939, pp. 11–23.

Ai is also the name of a city in Moab (Je. xlix. 3) of unknown location. A.R.M.

AIJALON, AJALON. 1. A town on a hill commanding from the south the entrance to the Vale of Aijalon; called in the Amarna letters Aialuna, its modern name is Yalo. Tell el-Qoq'a, near the village, has traces of the earliest remains (*c.* 2000 BC). In successive phases of Israel's history it was inhabited by Danites (who could not expel the Amorites), Ephraimites, and Benjamites (Jos. xix. 42; Jdg. i. 35; 1 Ch. vi. 69, viii. 13). Fortified by Rehoboam to guard the NW approaches to Jerusalem, it was occupied by the Philistines in the reign of Ahaz (2 Ch. xi. 10, xxviii. 18).

BIBLIOGRAPHY. Abel, *Géographie*, II, p. 241; *GTT*, p. 205.

2. Aijalon in Zebulun (Jdg. xii. 12), spelt Ailom by LXX, where the judge Elon (same Heb. letters) was buried. Possibly Kh. el-Lōn.

BIBLIOGRAPHY. Abel, *Géographie*, II, p. 241; *JPOS*, IX, 1929, pp. 38 ff. J.P.U.L.

AKELDAMA. Acts i. 19 gives the meaning of the word (in AV Aceldama) as 'field of blood'—the Aramaic phrase being *ḥaqēl dᵉmâ*. The ground was previously known as the Potter's Field, and this has been equated with the Potter's House (Je. xviii. 2) in the Hinnom Valley. Jerome placed it on the south side of this valley; and the site accepted today is there. Eusebius, however, said this ground was north of Jerusalem. The traditional site certainly can provide potter's clay; and it has long been used for burials. D.F.P.

AKHENATEN. See EGYPT (IV, *d*).

AKRABBIM (*'aqrabbîm*, 'scorpions'), 'Acrabbim' in Jos. xv. 3. An ascent on the southern end of the Dead Sea between the Arabah and the hill-country of Judah, identified with the modern Naqb eṣ-ṣâfâ. J.D.D.

ALABASTER. See JEWELS AND PRECIOUS STONES.

ALEXANDER. A common Hellenistic name. Its widespread adoption among Jews displeased some strict Rabbis and gave rise to an amusing aetiological story that a demand by Alexander the Great for a golden statue in the Temple was countered with the proposal that all boys born that year should be called Alexander (see E. Nestle, *ExpT*, X, 1898–9, p. 527). The frequency is reflected in the New Testament.

1. The son of Simon of Cyrene (see RUFUS). **2.** A member of the high priestly family, unknown apart from Acts iv. 6. **3.** The would-be spokesman of the Jewish interest in the Ephesian riot (Acts xix. 33 f.). His function was presumably to dissociate the regular Jewish community from the Christian trouble-makers: the anti-Semitism of the mob, however, allowed him no voice. **4.** A pernicious teacher of subverted morals (1 Tim. i. 20), whom Paul 'delivers to Satan' (on this see HYMENAEUS).

5. A bitter enemy of Paul and the gospel (2 Tim. iv. 14 f.), evidently (since Timothy is put on guard against him) operating in the Ephesus–Troas area. Had he been responsible for an arrest in Ephesus? He was a coppersmith (the word was then used to designate all kinds of metal-worker), though some have read the title as a proper name, 'Alexander Chalceus'. When Paul adds 'God will render him due judgment', the tense marks this as a prediction (RV), not a curse (AV).

Those identifying (3) and (5) (*e.g.* P. N. Harrison, *Problem of the Pastoral Epistles*, 1921, pp. 118 f.) can point to the Ephesian location, the origin of the riot with the craft-guilds, and the introduction of Alexander in Acts xix. 33 as if well known; but nothing there indicates the sort of opposition betokened in 2 Tim. iv. 14. Little can be said for or against identifying (4) and (5); but (3) and (4) cannot be identical, for the latter would claim to be a Christian.

A.F.W.

ALEXANDER THE GREAT. The youthful king of Macedon whose pan-hellenic expedition of 336 BC to liberate the Greeks of Asia Minor unexpectedly demolished the Persian Empire. Only the mutiny of his troops stopped him at the Ganges, and he died in 323 while planning the conquest of the west. His generals established the concert of Hellenistic kingdoms to which the Herods performed the epilogue. Probably from necessity rather than idealism, Alexander abandoned the isolationism of the Greeks in favour of racial co-operation. Hellenism became an international norm of civilization. Hence the agonies of the Jews in the Maccabean age, and the tensions that surrounded the crucifixion. Hence also the inspiration of the cosmopolitan philosophies that chimed in with Christian ideals.

Presumably it is Alexander to whom reference is made in Dn. viii. 21, xi. 3.

Bibliography. Arrian, *Anabasis*; Plutarch, *Life of Alexander*; W. W. Tarn, *Alexander the Great*, 2 vols., 1948; E. Barker, *From Alexander to Constantine*, 1956; H. E. Stier, *RAC*, I, pp. 261–270.

E.A.J.

ALEXANDRIA.

I. THE CITY

a. Location

A great seaport on the north-west coast of the Egyptian Delta, on the narrow isthmus between the sea and Lake Mareotis. It was founded in 332 BC by Alexander (the Great) of Macedon and named after himself. A small Egyptian settlement, Rakotis, was its only predecessor on the site and was absorbed into the west side of the new city; in native Egyptian parlance (exemplified by Coptic, centuries later), the name Rakotis was extended to Alexandria. The city was apparently laid out on a 'grid' plan of cross-streets and *insulae*; but as the remains of the ancient city are inextricably buried underneath its modern successor, any reconstruction of its lay-out and location of its great buildings must draw heavily on the none-too-precise literary references virtually by themselves, and hence cannot be exact. Not until the time of Ptolemy II (*c.* 285–245 BC) did Alexandria first attain to the architectural splendours so famed in later writers' accounts. Between the shore and the Pharos

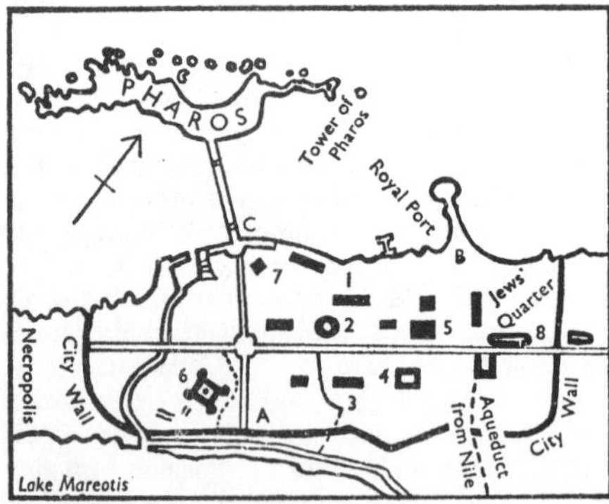

Fig. 5. Ancient Alexandria. *Key:* (1) Exchange; (2) Amphitheatre; (3) Gymnasium; (4) Hall of Justice; (5) Library and Museum; (6) Serapeum; (7) City dockyards and quays; (8) Stadium. (A) Gate of the Sun; (B) Royal Docks; (C) Gate of the Moon.

island stretched a connecting causeway, the 'Heptastadion' ('seven stadia', 1,300 metres long); this divided the anchorage into a West harbour and an East or Great harbour, whose entrance was dominated by the Pharos lighthouse-tower. It contained also the Royal harbour, and was flanked on the east by the royal palace. South of the shore-line, extending all along behind it and as far as Lake Mareotis, stretched the city. See fig. 5.

b. Population

Right from the start, Alexandria was a thoroughly cosmopolitan city. Besides its Greek citizens and numerous poor Greek immigrants, there was a considerable Jewish community (*cf.* later, Acts vi. 9, xviii. 24) under their own ethnarch and having their own quarter (though not restricted to it until AD 38), and quite a large native Egyptian populace, especially in the Rakotis district in the west. In Rakotis was localized the Serapeum, temple of the Egypto-Hellenistic deity Sarapis, whose cult was specifically promoted by Ptolemy I, just possibly to serve as a common bond for both Greeks and Egyptians (Sir H. I. Bell).

c. The city's rôle

Politically, Alexandria became capital of Egypt under the Ptolemies, Graeco-Macedonian kings of Egypt, *c.* 323–30 BC (see Ptolemy). Under the first and energetic kings of this line it became the greatest Hellenistic city of the day. Alexandria continued as Egypt's administrative capital into the Roman imperial and Byzantine epochs. Alexandria was the banking-centre of all Egypt, an active manufacturing city (cloths, glass, papyrus, *etc.*), and a thriving port. Thence were transhipped the exotic products of Arabia, India, and the East, and thence in Roman times sailed the great grain-ships of Alexandria (*cf.* Acts xxvii. 6, xxviii. 11) to bring cheap corn for the Roman plebeians. Finally, Alexandria quickly became and long remained a brilliant seat of learning. To the reign of either Ptolemy I (323/04–285 BC) or Ptolemy II (285–245 BC) belongs the founding of the 'Museum', where scholars researched and taught in arts and sciences, and of the Library which eventually contained thousands of works upon many tens of thousands of papyrus rolls.

II. JUDAISM AND CHRISTIANITY

Alexandria had, as stated above, a very large Jewish community, concentrated in the eastern sector, but with places of worship all over the city (Philo, *Legatio ad Gaium* 20). One famous synagogue, magnificently fitted, was so vast that flags had to be used to signal the Amen (*BC*, I, pp. 152 f.). But beyond this, Alexandria was the intellectual and literary centre of the Dispersion. It was there that the Greek Old Testament, the Septuagint (see under Text and Versions), was produced, and from there came such works as the Book of Wisdom (see Apocrypha) with its Platonic modifications of Old Testament categories and its Greek interest in cosmology and immortality. It was the home of the voluminous Philo (*q.v.*), perhaps the first considerable scholar to use the biblical material as philosophic data—though 'his object is not to investigate but to harmonize' (Bigg, p. 7)—and the first major exponent of the allegorical exegesis of Scripture. Whatever the demerits of the attempted synthesis of Athens and Jerusalem by Alexandrian Jews (and some of them amount to enormities), the literary remains testify to intellectual energy, missionary concern, and, despite audacious departures from traditional formulation, a profound seriousness about the Scriptures.

These features had considerable indirect influence on early Greek Christianity. It is significant that the eloquent travelling Rabbi Apollos (*q.v.*), who became an important figure in the apostolic church, was an Alexandrian Jew, and 'mighty in the Scriptures' (Acts xviii. 24). The Epistle to the Hebrews, because of its use of terminology beloved at Alexandria, and its characteristic use of the Old Testament, has been associated, if not necessarily with him, at least with an Alexandrian background; and so, with less reason, have other New Testament books (*cf.* J. N. Sanders, *The Fourth Gospel in the Early Church*, 1943; S. G. F. Brandon, *The Fall of Jerusalem and the Christian Church*, 1951). Apart, however, from unreliable traditions about the agency of the evangelist Mark, the origin and early history of the Alexandrian church is completely hidden (see AFRICA).

It has been suggested that Alexandrian Judaism had so philosophized away the messianic hope that the earliest Christian preaching made slow headway there. There is not sufficient evidence to test this hypothesis. It is unmistakable, however, that when Alexandrian Christianity comes into full view it is patently the heir of Alexandrian Judaism. The missionary zeal, the philosophic apologetic, the allegorical exegesis, the application to biblical commentary, and the passion for intellectual synthesis which sometimes leads doctrine to disaster, are common to both. Some thoroughfare, at present unlit, links Philo and Clement of Alexandria; but it is hardly too bold a conjecture that the road lies through the conversion to Christ of a substantial number of Jews or their adherents in Alexandria during the apostolic or sub-apostolic period.

BIBLIOGRAPHY. For a standard historical and cultural background for Alexandria, Ptolemaic and Byzantine, see respectively *CAH*, VII, 1928, chapter IV, sect. vii, pp. 142–148, and chapters VIII–IX, pp. 249–311, and *ibid.*, XII, 1939, chapter XIV, sect. i, pp. 476–492. Useful and compact, with reference to actual remains is E. Breccia, *Alexandrea ad Aegyptum, A Guide . . .*, 1922. A popular, readable account of the history and manner of life in ancient Alexandria is H. T. Davis, *Alexandria, the Golden City*, 2 vols., 1957. An excellent study of paganism, Judaism, and the advent and triumph of Christianity in Egypt generally, and Alexandria also, is provided by Sir Harold Idris Bell, *Cults and Creeds in Graeco-Roman Egypt*, 1953. On Alexandria and Christianity, see also J. M. Creed in S. R. K. Glanville (ed.), *The Legacy of Egypt*, 1942, chapter XII. 1, pp. 300–316; C. Bigg, *The Christian Platonists of Alexandria*, 1886; J. E. L. Oulton and H. Chadwick, *Alexandrian Christianity*, 1954. K.A.K.

A.F.W.

ALGUM. See TREES.

ALLELUIA. See HALLELUJAH.

ALLIANCE. The word alliance is not used in the AV, though *b^erîṯ*, *qešer*, *nûaḥ*, *ḥāṯan* are variously translated 'covenant', 'affinity', 'confederacy' (see Gn. xiv. 13; 1 Ki. iii. 1; 2 Ch. xviii. 1; Ezr. ix. 14; Is. viii. 12). Alliances with other nations were made as early as the time of the Patriarchs. In Abraham's covenant with Abimelech (Gn. xxi. 22–24; *cf.* Isaac's alliance with the same king, Gn. xxvi. 26–34) is seen one of the early forms of covenant-making, involving the giving and receiving of 'sevens' in which objects of any kind could be given. See COVENANT for ceremonies connected with alliances. Though the Mosaic law forbade alliances with foreign powers because of the consequent faithlessness and idolatry (Ex. xxiii. 32, xxxiv. 12, 15; Dt. vii. 2), many were contracted in Israel's subsequent history with just those results. Sometimes the very existence of Israel as a distinct people was in jeopardy (see WAR).

Some alliances were entered into freely and loosely, as that of David with Achish of Gath (1 Sa. xxvii. 2–12). Trade was greatly advanced through such alliances, especially that between Solomon and Hiram (1 Ki. v. 12–18). Marriages cemented these treaties (1 Ki. ix. 16), sometimes with disastrous results, as in the marriage between Ahab and Jezebel, the Phoenician queen, who brought with her the worship of the Tyrian Baal. Other alliances included those between Asa and Ben-hadad (1 Ki. xv. 18–20); Ahab and Ben-hadad (1 Ki. xx. 31–34); and the Syro-Ephraimitic alliance against Judah (Is. vii. 1 ff.). The prophets and Ezra preached much against this constant tendency of alliance and fraternization with their attendant evils (Is. vii. 3 ff., xxx. 15; Je. xiii. 18–36; Ho. viii. 9; Ezr. x). This prefigures the stern prohibition of allying with evil on the basis of the impossibility of mixture between righteousness and unrighteousness, light and darkness, Christ and Belial (2 Cor. vi. 14–16). J.A.B.

ALLON. AV in Jos. xix. 33; see ELON (4).

ALMIGHTY. A name of God used forty-eight times in the Old Testament (*e.g.* Gn. xlix. 25; Jb. v. 17) to translate Heb. *šaddai*, of which the root meaning is uncertain. It is sometimes used in conjunction with *'el*, 'God', and rendered as 'God Almighty' (Gn. xxviii. 3) or 'Almighty God' (Ezk. x. 5). In the New Testament the word is found eight times in the Apocalypse and also in 2 Cor. vi. 18 to render Gk. *pantokratōr*, 'all-powerful'. See N. Walker, 'A New Interpretation of the Divine Name "Shaddai" ', *ZATW*, 1960, pp. 64–66. J.D.D.

ALMOND, ALMOND TREE. Of the same genus as the peach, the almond (*Amygdalus communis*) blooms in the Holy Land as early as January. Its Hebrew name, *šāqēḏ*, 'waker', suggests the first of the fruit trees to awake in the winter. Blossoms are pink and sometimes white, demonstrating an analogy with the hoary-headed Patriarch (Ec. xii. 5). The almond's beauty was often copied in ornamental work (Ex. xxv. 33, 34). As well as being oil-producing, the kernel was a favourite food in Palestine, and an acceptable gift when sent by Jacob to Egypt (Gn. xliii. 11), where it may have been unknown. It is probably denoted in Gn. xxx. 37, where AV renders 'hazel', and is mentioned in Je. i. 11, 12, where a play on words (*šāqēḏ* and *šōqēḏ*) illustrates God's prompt fulfilment of His promises. J.D.D.

ALMS, ALMSGIVING. From Gk. *eleēmosynē* via eccl. Lat. *eleemosyna* and Old English *ælmysse*. The Greek word signifies pity, prompting relief given in money or kind to the poor.

Though not explicitly mentioned in the English Old Testament, almsgiving is implied as an expression of compassion in the presence of God. It had a twofold development: (*a*) The Mosaic legislation looked on compassion as a feeling to be cherished in ideal conduct (*cf.* Dt. xv. 11); (*b*) The prophets considered almsgiving as a right which the needy might justly claim.

From the fusion of these two concepts there arose in the intertestamental age the idea of righteousness secured through almsgiving as efficacious in annulling the guilt of sin, and as ensuring divine favour in time of trouble (*cf.* Ps. cxii. 9; Dn. iv. 27). Righteousness and almsgiving were at times regarded as synonymous terms, as in the LXX (and in our modern use of 'charity' to denote almsgiving), but this is scarcely justifiable from either the Hebrew Old Testament or from the true text of the New Testament.

After the cessation of sacrifice, almsgiving seems to have ranked among the Jews as the first of religious duties. In every city there were collectors who distributed alms of two kinds, *i.e.* money collected in the synagogue chest every sabbath for the poor of the city, and food and money received in a dish. 'Therefore no disciple should live in a city where there is no alms-box' (*Sanh.* 17b). It is significant that in the Old Testament scarcely a trace of beggars and begging in the street can be found (but see 1 Sa. ii. 36; Ps. cix. 10). Ps. xli. 1 can be taken as not merely an exhortation to almsgiving, but also as an adjuration to take a personal interest in the poor.

In the New Testament Jesus does not reject almsgiving as futile in the search for right standing with God, but stresses the necessity for right motive, 'in my name'. He rebuked the ostentatious charity of His day (Mt. vi. 1–4; note RV 'righteousness' for AV 'alms'), and emphasized the blessedness of giving (*cf.* Acts xx. 35), and its opportunities.

In the early Christian community the first election of officers was made to ensure a fair distribution of alms; the needs of the poor were met (Acts iv. 32, 34); and every Christian was exhorted to lay by on the first day of each week some portion of his profits to be applied to the wants of the needy (Acts xi. 30; Rom. xv. 25–27; 1 Cor. xvi. 1–4).

'Alms' are equated with 'righteousness', not because they justify a man (Rom. iii–v), but because they constitute an action which is right and for which our neighbour has a rightful claim on us in the eyes of God who gives us means for this very end (Eph. iv. 28).

See also POVERTY; COMMUNITY OF GOODS; COMPASSION. J.D.D.

ALMUG. See TREES.

ALOES (*'ahālîm* in Pr. vii. 17; Nu. xxiv. 6, 'lign aloes'; *'ahālôṯ* in Ps. xlv. 8; Ct. iv. 14; *aloē* in Jn. xix. 39). Probably the modern eagle-wood (*Aquilaria agallochum*) found today in E Bengal, Malaya, and part of China. From it was derived a precious spice used in biblical times for perfuming garments and beds. The perplexing question of the reference in Nu. xxiv. 6 may suggest that the tree (or one similar) grew in the Jordan valley, but Balaam need not have actually seen the tree of which he spoke. J.D.D.

ALPHA AND OMEGA. A central theological term, meaning 'first and last', which is causal as well as chronological in its significance (*cf.* Rom. xi. 36; Eph. i. 10). It is used in this way in the Apocalypse (Rev. i. 8, xxi. 6, xxii. 13; it does not appear in the best MSS at Rev. i. 11). In the first of these passages the phrase refers to the Father, in the others to the Son. The term derives from the first and last letters of the Gk. alphabet, corresponding to the Heb. *'alep̄* and *tāw* (*cf.* a Rabbinic comment in the *Yalkut*, which tells us that Adam transgressed the whole law from *aleph* to *tāw*). The Hebrews, the Greeks, and the Romans all used their alphabetic letters as numerals, which accounts for the ease with which 'alpha and omega' also represented 'first and last'. Biblically, the term denotes the eternal, creative existence of God (*cf.* Is. xliv. 6), as well as, eschatologically, the redemptive activity of Christ (*cf.* Rev. ii. 8). S.S.S.

ALPHABET. See WRITING.

ALPHAEUS. 1. The father of Levi, the tax collector (Mk. ii. 14), who is generally identified with the apostle Matthew. Nothing else is known about him.

2. The father of the apostle James, who is called 'the son of Alphaeus', to distinguish him from James the son of Zebedee (Mt. x. 3; Mk. iii. 18; Lk. vi. 15; Acts i. 13). There is no valid reason for identifying him with the father of Levi (1). Attempts have also been made to identify him with Cleopas (Lk. xxiv. 18) and

Clopas (Jn. xix. 25). However, it is improbable that Cleopas and Clopas are the same person and that Alphaeus is the same as either of them. The Aramaic of Alphaeus is *Ḥalphai*, which could be transliterated as *Klōpas*, but even if the same individual is signified, we cannot assume from Jn. xix. 25 that this James was in any way related to our Lord and certainly not that he was James the Lord's brother. R.E.N.

ALTAR.

I. IN THE OLD TESTAMENT

In all but four of the Old Testament occurrences of the word 'altar', the Hebrew is *mizbēaḥ*, which means 'place of sacrifice' (from *zāḇaḥ*, 'to slaughter for sacrifice'), and one of the remaining occurrences (Ezr. vii. 17) is simply its Aramaic cognate *maḏbaḥ*. While etymologically the term involves slaughter, in usage it was not always so restricted, being applied also to the altar for burning incense (Ex. xxx. 1). For the other three occurrences of 'altar' in the EVV, see *g* below.

a. The Patriarchs

The Patriarchs built their own altars and offered their own sacrifices on them without having any recourse to a priesthood. Noah built one after the flood and made burnt offerings on it (Gn. viii. 20). Abraham built altars to Yahweh at Shechem, between Bethel and Ai, at Hebron, and at Moriah, where he offered a ram instead of Isaac (Gn. xii. 6–8, xiii. 18, xxii. 9). Isaac did likewise at Beersheba (Gn. xxvi. 25), Jacob erected altars at Shechem and Bethel (Gn. xxxiii. 20, xxxv. 1–7), and Moses erected one at Rephidim after the victory of the Israelites over Amalek (Ex. xvii. 15). The altars were evidently erected mainly to commemorate some event in which the principal had had dealings with God. No information is given as to their construction, but it is reasonable to suppose that they were of the same type as those later allowed in the Mosaic law (see *d* below).

b. Pre-Israelite altars in Palestine

In the early days of Palestine exploration it was customary to see altars in many things which today are understood as domestic, agricultural, or industrial installations. True altars have, however, been uncovered at several sites from different periods. At Ai, Mme J. Marquet-Krause discovered a small temple of the Early Bronze Age in which was an altar of plastered stones, against the wall, on which animal and food-offerings had been made. In Middle Bronze Age Megiddo (*q.v.*; level xv) two temples were found containing rectangular altars, one of mud bricks and the other of lime-plastered stones. Temples of the Late Bronze Age containing altars of similar type have been found at Lachish, Beth-shan, and Hazor. In the levels of this period at Hazor a great hewn block of stone was discovered, with two hollowed basins on one face, perhaps for catching the blood of sacrificed animals. At Megiddo and Nahariyeh great platforms of stones which were probably used as places of sacrifice were uncovered, but these were more 'high places' (*q.v.*) than altars.

A number of hewn limestone altars with four horns at the upper corners, dating from about the period of the conquest, were found at Megiddo (see fig. 6). These, however, to judge from their relatively small size (largest *c.* 2 feet 3 inches high), were probably incense altars. Numerous clay stands which may have been for burning

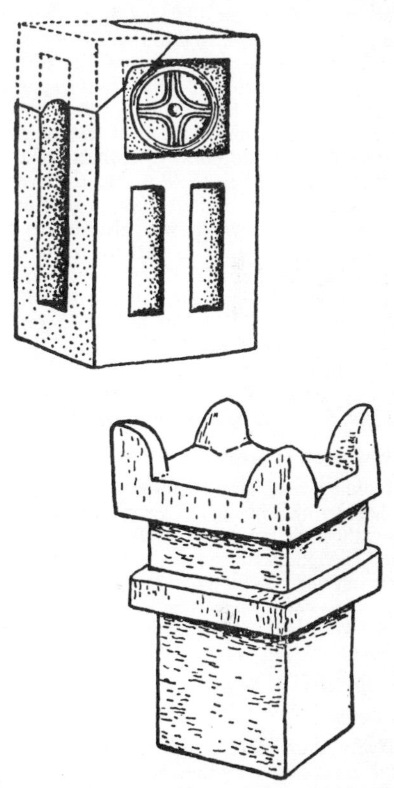

Fig. 6. *Above:* Incense altar of basalt with emblem of the sun-god carved in relief, from Canaanite Hazor of the 14th–13th centuries BC. Height *c.* 4 feet 7 inches. *Below:* A Canaanite incense altar of limestone from Megiddo of the 10th–9th centuries BC. Height *c.* 21 inches.

incense have been uncovered at such sites as Megiddo, Beth-shan, and Lachish, from Bronze and Iron Age Levels.

Thus altars were in use among the Canaanites in the promised land, a fact that gives point to the careful regulations on this matter in the Sinai revelation. That altars were not limited to Palestine is shown by the discoveries at such sites as Eridu, Ur, Khafajah, and Assur in Mesopotamia, and the episode in which Balaam erected, and offered bullocks on, seven altars at Kiriath-huzoth (Nu. xxiii) may perhaps be understood in this light.

c. The altars of the Tabernacle

At Sinai God revealed to Moses the specifications for two altars which were to be used in the Tabernacle: the altar of burnt offering and the altar of incense. For accounts of these, see TABERNACLE.

d. Built altars

In Ex. xx. 24–26, God instructed Moses to tell the people to make an altar of earth (*mizbaḥ 'ᵃdāmâ*) or (unhewn) stones (*mizbaḥ 'ᵃbānîm*), upon which to sacrifice their offerings. In neither case were there to be steps, so that the 'nakedness' of the offerer might not be uncovered. The form of this passage, in which God tells Moses to pass on this instruction to the people, suggests that it, like the Ten Commandments at the beginning of the chapter, was addressed to each Israelite individually, rather than to Moses as their representative as in Ex. xxvii. It may be that under this provision the layman was permitted to perform this himself, and it is perhaps in the light of this that the altars built by Joshua on Mt. Ebal (Jos. viii. 30, 31; *cf.* Dt. xxvii. 5), by Gideon in Ophrah (Jdg. vi. 24–26), by David on the threshing-floor of Araunah (2 Sa. xxiv. 18–25), and by Elijah on Mt. Carmel (1 Ki. xviii), as well as the episodes described in Jos. xxii. 10–34 and 1 Sa. xx. 6, 29, are to be viewed (*cf.* Ex. xxiv. 4).

e. The Temple of Solomon

In building his Temple, Solomon, though influenced by his Phoenician associates, sought to follow the basic lay-out of the Tabernacle and its court. Though David had already built an altar of burnt offerings (2 Sa. xxiv. 25), Solomon probably built a new one, as is indicated by 1 Ki. viii. 22, 54, 64 and ix. 25 (not mentioned in the main description 1 Ki. vi–vii). For a description of this, see TEMPLE.

f. False altars

Unlawful altars were in use in both Israel and Judah, as is shown by the condemnations of the prophets (Am. iii. 14; Ho. viii. 11) and the account of Jeroboam's sins in 1 Ki. xii. 28–33.

g. Ezekiel's vision

During the Exile, Ezekiel had a vision of Israel restored and the Temple rebuilt (Ezk. xl–xliv; see fig. 81), and while no incense altar is mentioned, the altar of burnt offering in this visionary temple is described in detail (xliii. 13–17). It consisted of three stages reaching to a height of eleven cubits on a base eighteen cubits square. It was thus in form reminiscent of a Babylonian ziggurat, and this impression is furthered by the names of some of its parts. The base, *ḥêq hā'āreṣ* (Ezk. xliii. 14, AV 'bottom upon the ground', literally 'bosom of the earth') recalls the Akkadian *irat irṣiti* with the same meaning, and the terms *har'ēl* and *'ᵃri'êl* translated 'altar' in verses 15, 16 may be Hebraized forms of Akkadian *arallu*, one of the names for the underworld, which had the secondary meaning 'mountain of the gods'. Such borrowings from the Babylonian vocabulary, which would be independent of their etymological meaning, would have been normal after an exile of many years in Babylonia. The altar was ascended by a flight of steps, and the four upper corners bore horns.

h. The second Temple

When the Temple was rebuilt after the Return it was presumably provided with altars. These are referred to in Josephus (*Contra Apionem* i. 198) and in the Letter of Aristeas, but on this period neither of these authors can be followed uncritically. In 169 BC Antiochus Epiphanes carried off the 'golden altar' (1 Macc. i. 21), and two years later he surmounted the altar of burnt offering with an 'abomination of desolation' (1 Macc. i. 54), probably an image of Zeus. The Maccabees built a new altar and restored the incense altar (1 Macc. iv. 44–49), and these must have continued in use when Herod enlarged the Temple in the latter part of the 1st century BC. In his time the altar of burnt offering was a great pile of unhewn stones, approached by a ramp. See TEMPLE.

II. IN THE NEW TESTAMENT

In the New Testament two words for altar are used, that most frequently found being *thysiastērion*, which is used often in the LXX for *mizbēaḥ*. This word is used of the altar on which Abraham prepared to offer Isaac (Jas. ii. 21), of the altar of burnt offering in the Temple (Mt. v. 23, 24, xxiii. 18–20, 35; Lk. xi. 51; 1 Cor. ix. 13, x. 18; Heb. vii. 13; Rev. xi. 1), and of the altar of incense not only in the earthly Temple (Lk. i. 11) but also in the heavenly (Rev. vi. 9, viii. 5, ix. 13, xiv. 18, xvi. 7; *cf.* also Rom. xi. 3; Heb. xiii. 10). The other word, *bōmos*, is used once (Acts xvii. 23). It was employed in the LXX for both *mizbēaḥ* and *bāmâ* (see HIGH PLACE), and had primarily the meaning of a raised place.

BIBLIOGRAPHY. R. de Vaux, *Les Institutions de l'Ancien Testament*, II, 1960, pp. 279–290, 451; B. F. Westcott, *The Epistle to the Hebrews*, 1889, pp. 453 ff.; A. Edersheim, *The Temple, Its Ministry and Services as they were at the Time of Jesus Christ*, 1874, pp. 32, 33. T.C.M.

AMALEK, -ITES. Amalek (*'ᵃmālēq*) was the son of Eliphaz and the grandson of Esau (Gn. xxxvi. 12, 16). The name is used as a collective noun for his descendants, Amalekites (Ex. xvii. 8; Nu. xxiv. 20; Dt. xxv. 17; Jdg. iii. 13, *etc.*).

Some writers distinguish the nomadic Amalekites normally found in the Negeb and Sinai area, from the descendants of Esau, because Gn. xiv. 7, which pre-dates Esau, refers to 'the country of the Amalekites' (*'ᵃmālēqî*). The distinction is unnecessary if we regard the phrase as a later editorial description.

Israel first met the Amalekites at Rephidim in the wilderness of Sinai (Ex. xvii. 8–13; Dt. xxv. 17, 18). Because of this attack, the Amalekites came under a permanent ban and were to be destroyed (Dt. xxv. 19; 1 Sa. xv. 2, 3). On that occasion Aaron and Hur held up Moses' hands and Israel prevailed. A year later, after the report of the spies, Israel ignored Moses' command and sought to enter southern Palestine. The Amalekites defeated them at Hormah (Nu. xiv. 43, 45).

From the days of the Judges two encounters are recorded. The Amalekites assisted Eglon, king of Moab, to attack Israelite territory (Jdg. iii. 13), and later combined forces with the Midianites and the children of the East to raid Israelite crops and flocks. Gideon drove them out (Jdg. vi. 3–5, 33, vii. 12, x. 12).

From the Exodus onwards, Amalekites were to be found in the Negeb, but for a time they gained a foothold in Ephraim (Jdg. xii. 15). Balaam, the foreign prophet, looked away to their lands from his vantage-point in Moab, and described them as 'the first of the nations' (Nu. xxiv. 20), which may mean in regard either to origin or to status.

Samuel commanded Saul to destroy the Amalekites in the area south of Telaim (see TELAIM). Booty was forbidden. Saul pursued them from Havilah to Shur but captured their king alive. Later, Samuel slew Agag and rebuked Saul (1 Sa. xv).

David fought the Amalekites in the area of Ziklag which Achish, king of Gath, had given him (1 Sa. xxvii. 6, xxx. 1–20). The Amalekites declined later, and in Hezekiah's day the sons of Simeon attacked 'the remnant of the Amalekites that escaped', taking their stronghold in Mount Seir (1 Ch. iv. 43).

BIBLIOGRAPHY. F. M. Abel, *Géographie de la Palestine*, 1933, II, pp. 270–273. J.A.T.

AMARNA. See ARCHAEOLOGY.

AMASA. 1. Son of Jether (or Ithra) an Ishmaelite, and of David's sister Abigail, Amasa commanded Absalom's rebel army (2 Sa. xvii. 25), was defeated by Joab (2 Sa. xviii. 6–8), pardoned by David, and replaced Joab as commander of the army (2 Sa. xix. 13). Taken off his guard, he was slain by the double-dealing Joab at 'the great stone of Gibeon' (2 Sa. xx. 9–12). Amasa may possibly be the Amasai of 1 Ch. xii. 18, but the evidence is inconclusive.

2. An Ephraimite who, among others, obeyed the prophet Oded and opposed the entry into Samaria of the Jewish prisoners taken by Pekah, king of Israel, in his campaign against Ahaz (2 Ch. xxviii. 9–15). J.D.D.

AMAZIAH. 1. King of Judah (2 Ki. xiv. 1–20; 2 Ch. xxv). His name (*'ᵃmaṣyâ* or *'ᵃmaṣyāhû*) means 'Yahweh is mighty'. He succeeded his father Joash when the latter was assassinated. He mobilized and organized the Judaean militia for the re-conquest of Edom. Mercenaries from Israel, hired in addition, were dismissed in deference to a prophetic warning (2 Ch. xxv. 7–10). The expedition resulted in a complete victory over Edom. The Edomite idols which Amaziah appropriated as a mark of his supremacy proved his undoing. His war with Israel was probably precipitated by the depredation of the dismissed Israelite mercenaries (2 Ch. xxv. 13). His overwhelming defeat, the dismantling of part of Jerusalem's defences, and the plundering of the palace and the Temple earned him extreme unpopularity and led to the conspiracy which ended in his assassination at Lachish.

2. The priest of Jeroboam II who sought to silence the prophet Amos at Bethel (Am. vii. 10–17). J.C.J.W.

AMBASSADOR (*mal'āḵ*, 'messenger'; *lûṣ*, 'interpreter'; *ṣîr*, 'to go'). A term used to describe envoys sent to other nations on special occasions, *e.g.* to congratulate (1 Ki. v. 1; 2 Sa. viii. 10), solicit favours (Nu. xx. 14), make alliances (Jos. ix. 4), or protest against wrongs (Jdg. xi. 12). Usually men of high rank, ambassadors became more common after Israel had developed relations with Syria, Babylon, *etc.* They did not represent the person of their sovereign, nor, as a general rule, were they empowered to negotiate (but see 2 Ki. xviii. 17–xix. 8). They were nevertheless treated with respect, and the only biblical infringement of this brought severe retribution (2 Sa. x. 2–5). The word (*presbeuō*, 'to be a senior') occurs metaphorically in the New Testament (2 Cor. v. 20; Eph. vi. 20), applied to the representative of Christ. The collective term 'ambassage' is found in Lk. xiv. 32. J.D.D.

AMBER. Heb. *ḥašmal*, occurring only in Ezk. i. 4, 27, viii. 2. The context requires *ḥašmal* to be something shining, but the exact denotation of the word has puzzled scholars from the rabbinic to present times. LXX renders *ēlektron*, meaning 'amber' or 'an alloy of gold and silver' (*LSJ*). The Talmud (*Ḥagigah* 13b) supposes it to be a composite word meaning 'beasts which send forth fire', but this is merely a flight of fancy. Delitzsch suggests the Assyrian *ešmaru* as a cognate, which is phonologically possible, and which denotes a shining metallic alloy. G. R. Driver suggests 'brass', comparing Akkadian *elmešu* (*VT*, I, 1951, pp. 60–62). R.J.W.

AMEN. Heb. *'āmēn*, 'surely', from a root meaning 'to be firm, steady, trustworthy'; *cf.* *'ᵉmûnâ*, 'faithfulness', *'ᵉmeṯ*, 'truth'. Rendered also in AV 'truth' (Is. lxv. 16 twice, lit. 'God of Amen') and 'so be it' (Je. xi. 5). The Gk. word is a transliteration of the Heb. and is rendered 'verily' in the frequent formula, 'Verily, verily, I say unto you'.

It is used: (*a*) as a responsive formula with which a listener acknowledges the validity of an oath or curse and declares himself willing to accept its consequences (Nu. v. 22; Dt. xxvii. 15, *etc.*; Ne. v. 13; Je. xi. 5); (*b*) to welcome an announcement or a prophecy of good (1 Ki. i. 36; Je. xxviii. 6); (*c*) as an expression of agreement with a doxology or benediction, and often duplicated for emphasis (1 Ch. xvi. 36; Ps. xli. 13, *etc.*). In this last usage it became an accepted part of synagogue worship and thence passed into the life of the early Church (*cf.* 1 Cor. xiv. 16).

In the New Testament the ascriptional use is frequent, although several instances are additions by a later hand. In Rev. i. 7, xxii. 20 it expresses confirmation of the writer's hope in the parousia. Christ's use of it is unique and seems to imply that He is endowing His words with His own (messianic) authority, a thing no scribe or Rabbi would ever have done. That is why in Him the promises of God are authoritative and will undoubtedly be fulfilled (2 Cor. i. 20); He can therefore be called 'the Amen' (Rev. iii. 14), and if the *MT* is correct the same meaning must underlie the description of God in Is. lxv. 16.

J.B.Tr.

AMETHYST. See Jewels and Precious Stones.

AMMINADIB. A charioteer in Ct. vi. 12 according to AV, RVmg, LXX, Vulg. RV and RSV do not read as proper name, but translate it: 'my princely people' (*'ammî nādîḇ*) and 'beside my prince' (*'im n^e^dîḇî*, a slight alteration of the text).

D.A.H.

AMMON, AMMONITES. Ammon (*'ammôn*) was the name of the descendants of Ben-ammi, Lot's younger son by his daughter, born in a cave near Zoar (Gn. xix. 38). They were regarded as relatives of the Israelites, who were commanded to treat them kindly (Dt. ii. 19).

At an early date the Ammonites occupied the territory of the Zamzummim between the Arnon and Jabbok rivers (Dt. ii. 20, 21, 37, iii. 11). Later, part of this territory was taken from them by the Amorites, and they were confined to an area to the east of the river Jabbok (Nu. xxi. 24; Dt. ii. 37; Jos. xii. 2, xiii. 10, 25; Jdg. xi. 13, 22). Modern archaeology shows that the Ammonites, like others, surrounded their territories by small fortresses (Nu. xxi. 24).

At the time of the Exodus, Israel did not conquer Ammon (Dt. ii. 19, 37; Jdg. xi. 15). However, the Ammonites were condemned for joining the Moabites in hiring Balaam, and were forbidden to enter the congregation of Israel to the tenth generation (Dt. xxiii. 3–6).

Their chief town was Rabbath Ammon, mod. *'Ammān* (see Rabbah), where, in the days of the judges, the ironstone sarcophagus ('bedstead of iron') of Og, the king of Bashan, rested (Dt. iii. 11).

In the days of the Judges, the Ammonites assisted Eglon of Moab to subdue Israelite territory (Jdg. iii. 13). Again, at the time of Jephthah they encroached on Israelite lands east of Jordan (Jdg. xi) and were driven out. Their religion influenced some of the Israelites (Jdg. x. 6), and this caused the Ammonite oppression in Gilead which led to Jephthah's campaign (Jdg. x). Later Nahash, king of the Ammonites, besieged Jabesh Gilead just before Saul became king. Saul rallied Israel and drove off Nahash (1 Sa. xi. 1–11, xii. 12, xiv. 47). A few years later Nahash was a friend of David (2 Sa. x. 1, 2), but his son Hanun rejected a kindly visit of David's ambassadors and insulted them. He hired Syrian mercenaries and went to war, but David's generals Joab and Abishai defeated them (2 Sa. x; 1 Ch. xix). A year later the Israelites captured Rabbah, the Ammonite capital (2 Sa. xii. 26–31; 1 Ch. xx. 1–3) and put the people to work. Some Ammonites befriended David, however, *e.g.* Shobi son of Nahash, who cared for him when he fled from Absalom (2 Sa. xvii. 27, 29), and Zelek, who was one of his thirty mighty men (2 Sa. xxiii. 37; 1 Ch. xi. 39).

Solomon included Ammonite women in his harem, and worshipped Milcom (Molech) and Chemosh (1 Ki. xi. 1, 5, 7, 33). An Ammonitess, Naamah, was the mother of Rehoboam (1 Ki. xiv. 21, 31; 2 Ch. xii. 13).

In the days of Jehoshaphat, the Ammonites joined Moabites and Edomites in a raid on Judah (2 Ch. xx. 1–30). About 800 BC, Zabad and Jehozabad, both sons of an Ammonitess, conspired to slay Joash king of Judah (2 Ch. xxiv. 26). Later in the century, both Uzziah and Jotham of Judah received tribute from the Ammonites (2 Ch. xxvi. 8, xxvii. 5). Josiah defiled the high place that Solomon erected (2 Ki. xxiii. 13). Ammonites joined others in troubling Jehoiakim (2 Ki. xxiv. 2), and after the fall of Jerusalem in 586 BC, Baalis their king provoked further trouble (2 Ki. xxv. 25; Je. xl. 11–14). They were bitterly attacked by the prophets as inveterate enemies of Israel (Je. xlix. 1–6; Ezk. xxi. 20, xxv. 1–7; Am. i. 13–15; Zp. ii. 8–11).

After the return from exile Tobiah, the governor of Ammon, hindered the building of the walls by Nehemiah (Ne. ii. 10, 19, iv. 3, 7). Intermarriage between the Jews and the Ammonites was censured by both Ezra and Nehemiah (Ezr. ix. 1, 2; Ne. xiii. 1, 23–31).

The Ammonites survived into the second century BC. Important graves, seals, and inscribed statues from the seventh and sixth centuries BC suggest vitality and political significance. The Tobiad family persisted till the second century BC, as important archaeological evidence from Transjordan and Egypt shows (see fig. 14), and Judas Maccabaeus fought the Ammonites in his day (1 Macc. v. 6).

Bibliography. F. M. Abel, *Géographie de la Palestine*, 1933, I, pp. 277, 278; D. Baly, *The Geography of the Bible*, 1958, chapter xix; Nelson Glueck, *The Other Side of Jordan*, 1940; *id.*, *AASOR*, XVIII, XIX, XXV–XXVIII; W. F. Albright, Article on Ammon in the *Miscellanea Biblica*, 1953.

J.A.T.

AMON. The son of Manasseh, Amon reigned for two years over Judah (2 Ki. xxi. 19–26; 2 Ch. xxxiii. 21–25). Before his reign was cut short by assassination, he gave the clearest evidence of his complete acceptance of the gross idolatry of his father's earlier years. It is not certainly known what motive inspired his assassins, but the fact that they were in turn put to death by 'the people of the land' suggests that Amon was the victim of court intrigue rather than of a popular revolution. J.C.J.W.

AMON (Egyp. *Amūn*, 'the hidden'). An Egyptian god whose essential nature is as unclear as his name indicates. Often associated with the wind, and in certain forms embodying the power of generation, he was first prominent as a local god of Thebes (see No), whence came the powerful XIIth Dynasty pharaohs (1991–1786 BC). Through union with the cosmic and royal sun-god Rē' as Amen-Rē', Amūn became chief god. Later, when the XVIIIth Dynasty Theban pharaohs established the Egyptian Empire (1570 BC ff.), Amūn became state god, 'king of the gods', gathering up many of their powers and attributes, while his priesthood accumulated vast wealth and lands. Hence, the fall of Thebes (No) and the wealth of its priesthoods to the Assyrians in 663 BC was fittingly selected by Nahum (iii. 8, RV) in prophesying the crash of equally mighty Nineveh. After this, Amūn and Thebes, still his holy city, regained some measure of prosperity, but even this was doomed by prophecy of Jeremiah (xlvi. 25, RV). See also EGYPT. K.A.K.

AMORITES. A people of Canaan (Gn. x. 16) often listed with the Hittites, Perizzites, *etc.*, as opponents of Israel (Ex. xxxiii. 2). They were scattered throughout the hill country on either side of the Jordan. Abraham had an alliance with the Amorites of Hebron and, with their aid, routed the four kings who had attacked the Dead Sea plain, including the Amorite town of Hazazon-Tamar (Gn. xiv. 5–7). The name was also used as a general term for the inhabitants of Canaan (Gn. xlviii. 22; Jos. xxiv. 15). Ezekiel well indicates the mixed population of Palestine (caused largely by the continuous infiltrations of desert dwellers), describing Jerusalem as the offspring of Amorite and Hittite (Ezk. xvi. 3, 45).

During the latter half of the third millennium BC, Sumerian and Akkadian inscriptions refer to the Amorites (Sum. *mar-tu*, Akkad. *amurru*) as a desert people unacquainted with civilized life, grain, houses, cities, government. Their headquarters were in the mountain of Basar, probably Jebel Bishri north of Palmyra. About 2000 BC these people, who had been infiltrating for centuries, moved into Babylonia in force. They were partly responsible for the collapse of the powerful IIIrd Dynasty of Ur and took over the rule of several towns (*e.g.* Larsa). An 'Amorite' dynasty was established at Babylon (*q.v.*), and its most powerful king, Hammurabi, conquered the two other important 'Amorite' states of Assur and Mari (*c.* 1750 BC). Amorites are traceable by linguistic, mainly onomastic, evidence. Such is not always reliable or conclusive and, while these dynasties were clearly of western origin, their right to the name 'Amorite' is disputed. The 20,000 texts found at Mari (see ARCHAEOLOGY) are mostly written in Akkadian with many west-Semitic features. The Hebrew Patriarchs may well have spoken this language, and their names include distinctive 'Amorite' forms (*e.g.* termination in *-el*, 'god'). The Mari texts give information about nomadic tribes in Syria, notably the *Mare-Yamina* (or possibly *Bene-Yamina*) connected with the area of Mount Basar. Another group had settled in the Lebanon and engaged in the trading of horses. This kingdom survived into the period of the Amarna letters and the XIXth Dynasty of Egypt when tribute is recorded from the state of Amor. The capital of this seems to have been the port of Ṣumur (modern Tell Simiriyân) south of Arvad. This is the country mentioned in Jos. xiii. 4.

The general unrest of the years *c.* 2100–1800 BC both in Mesopotamia and in Palestine was closely connected with increased Amorite movement. The break in occupation of several Palestinian cities between the Early and Middle Bronze Age was caused by an influx of nomadic folk who left only graves behind them. The pottery of these people has clear affinities with pottery from Syria, which may indicate that they were related 'Amorites' (see K. M. Kenyon, *Jericho I*, British School of Archaeology in Jerusalem, 1960, pp. 150 ff.). The journeys of Abraham may be associated with the latter part of this period.

At the time of the Israelite invasion of Palestine, Amorite kings (Sihon of Heshbon and Og of Bashan) ruled most of Transjordan (Jos. xii. 1–6; Jdg. i. 36). The conquest of these two kings was the first stage of the possession of the Promised Land and was looked upon as a most important event in Israelite history (Am. ii. 9; Pss. cxxxv. 11, cxxxvi. 19). Gad, Reuben, and half of Manasseh occupied this territory (Nu. xxxii. 33), and it later formed one of the twelve regions supporting Solomon's court (1 Ki. iv. 19). The men of Ai are called Amorites (Jos. vii. 7) and Jerusalem, Hebron, Jarmuth, Lachish, and Eglon were Amorite principalities which Israel overcame (Jos. x. 1–27). Northern Amorites aided the king of Hazor (Jos. xi. 1–14; see HAZOR). After the land was settled, the Amorites became menials and were gradually absorbed (1 Ki. ix. 20). Their evil memory remained, providing comparison for the idolatry of Ahab and Manasseh (1 Ki. xxi. 26; 2 Ki. xxi. 11; *cf.* Gn. xv. 16).

Invasions of other peoples, the Kassites, Hurrians, and Indo-Europeans in Mesopotamia, the Israelites in Palestine, and the Aramaeans in Syria weakened the Amorites as a power by 1000 BC. The name survived in Akkadian as a designation for Syria–Palestine until superseded by *Ḫatti* (Hittite), and was also a word for 'west'.

BIBLIOGRAPHY. S. Moscati, *The Semites in Ancient History*, 1959; J. R. Kupper, *Les Nomades en Mésopotamie au temps des Rois de Mari*, 1957; and the review by A. Goetze in *JSS*, IV, 1959, pp. 142–147. A.R.M.

AMOS, BOOK OF.

I. OUTLINE OF CONTENTS

On the whole the Hebrew text of Amos' prophecies has been well preserved. In addition, the progressive orderliness of his writings makes it possible to divide the book up into sections which are not artificial. It falls into four parts.

a. i. 1–ii. 16. After a simple introduction (i. 1 f.) in which Amos tells who he is, when he prophesied, and wherein resided his authority to preach, he announces judgment upon the surrounding peoples (i. 3–ii. 3), upon his native Judah, and upon Samaria (ii. 4–16), to whom Yahweh had sent him to preach. The sins upon which divine judgment will fall are ethical in character and offend against the moral laws which are the cement of society.

b. iii. 1–vi. 14. The series of addresses in this section are each introduced by a clearly defined formula (iii. 1, iv. 1, v. 1, vi. 1). Here the emphasis is upon Samaria's privileges, but the nation's sinfulness has turned privilege into a ground upon which Amos bases his doctrine of judgment. Privilege involves God's people in penalty, hence Amos' proclamation of the 'Day of the Lord' when Assyria will be the rod with which Yahweh will smite Israel.

c. vii. 1–ix. 10. This section contains a series of five visions of judgment, in each of which the judgment is set forth under a symbol. These five symbols are locusts (vii. 1–3), fire (vii. 4–6), a plumbline (vii. 7–9), summer fruit (viii. 1–14), and a smitten sanctuary (ix. 1–10). In vii. 10–17 Amos adds a long autobiographical note.

d. ix. 11–15. This division consists of an epilogue which describes the restoration of the Davidic kingdom.

II. AUTHORSHIP AND DATE

Nothing is known of the prophet Amos outside of his writings. He was a native of Tekoa (i. 1), situated about 10 miles south of Jerusalem. Its elevated position made it a natural 'city for defence' (2 Ch. xi. 6). The surrounding countryside yielded pasture for the flocks, to tend which was part of Amos' calling (i. 1). In addition, he was 'a dresser of sycomore trees'. The significance of this information is that Amos was not brought up in the class from which prophets usually came, nor was he trained for the prophethood in the prophetic schools or guilds (vii. 14 f.). We know from i. 1 that he lived during the reigns of Uzziah, king of Judah (779–740 BC) and Jeroboam II, king of Samaria (783–743 BC). Uzziah and Jeroboam II reigned concurrently for thirty-six years (779–743). Since Uzziah's leprosy necessitated a co-regency in the latter years of his reign (2 Ki. xv. 1–7), perhaps Amos' ministry should be placed about midway between the concurrent reigns of Uzziah and Jeroboam II. We have no means of determining how long he had been preaching in Samaria when he was peremptorily ordered to return to his native Judah (vii. 10–13). Doubtless this brought to a close his ministry as a prophet of Yahweh.

III. CIRCUMSTANCES

Since a Hebrew prophet's ministry and message were intimately bound up with the conditions in which the people to whom he preached lived, his writings mirror faithfully the circumstances of his own day. In this Amos' book is no exception.

a. Political and social conditions. It is generally conjectured that Amos began to preach in Samaria about 760 BC. Over forty years earlier Assyria had crushed Syria, Samaria's northern neighbour. This permitted Jeroboam II to extend his frontiers (2 Ki. xiv. 25), and to build up a lucrative trade which created a powerful merchant class in Samaria. Unfortunately the wealth that came to Samaria was not evenly distributed among the people. It remained in the hands of the merchant princes, who spent the new-found riches on improving their own living standards (iii. 10, 12, 15, vi. 4), and neglected completely the peasant class which had hitherto been the backbone of Samaria's economy. The unmistakable symptoms of a morally sick society began to declare themselves in Samaria. In Amos' day oppression of the poor by the rich was common (ii. 6 f.), and heartless indifference among the wealthy towards the affliction of the hungry (vi. 3–6). Justice went to the highest bidder (ii. 6, viii. 6). In drought (iv. 7–9) the poor had recourse only to the moneylender (v. 11 f., viii. 4–6), to whom he was often compelled to mortgage his land and his person.

b. The state of religion. Naturally the social conditions in Samaria affected religious habits. Religion was being not neglected but perverted. At the national religious shrines (v. 5) ritual was being maintained (iv. 4 f.), but it went hand in hand with godlessness and immorality; therefore it must be abolished, not reformed (iii. 14, vii. 9, ix. 1–4). In fact, this was not Yahweh-worship at all, it was transgression (iv. 4). God was not to be found at the national shrines (v. 4 f.) because He could not accept the worship there (v. 21–23); it was being offered to another deity (viii. 14). In addition, this rich ceremonial and the costly sacrifices were being offered at the expense of the poor (ii. 8, v. 11).

IV. AMOS AND THE PENTATEUCH

It is instructive to notice the number of references in Amos' prophecies to facts which are contained in the first five books of the Old Testament.

a. References to earlier history. In the course of his message he notices the destruction of Sodom and Gomorrah (iv. 11). He also has references to the Exodus (iii. 1), to the wilderness wanderings (v. 25), and to the eventual conquest of Canaan (ii. 9 f.). These, together with the mention of

Isaac, Jacob, and Joseph (vii. 16, iii. 13, v. 6), and an oblique reference to the enmity between Jacob and Esau (i. 11), bespeak familiarity with important events in Hebrew history, and a fairly widespread knowledge of that history among the Hebrews of Amos' day.

b. References to the law. His allusions to ritual (v. 21), to the statutory sacrifices and tithes (iv. 4 f., v. 22), to the new moons and sabbaths (viii. 5), point to a familiarity with those parts of the Pentateuch where these religious institutions are regulated. His references to the moral conditions of his own day also may well be echoes of the ethics of the Pentateuch. *Cf.* ii. 8 with Ex. xxii. 26; viii. 5 with Lv. xix. 35 f.; ii. 4 with Dt. xvii. 19; *etc.*

V. THE PROPHET'S MESSAGE

a. Amos' concept of God is fundamental to an understanding of his message to Samaria. The Lord is the Creator of the world (iv. 13), but He is still actively present as its Sustainer. He it is who brings day and night to pass, and controls the waves of the sea (v. 8, ix. 6). He determines whether famine (iv. 6–11) or plenty (ix. 13) shall prevail. The Lord also controls the destinies of the nations. He restrains this nation (i. 5), raises up that (vi. 14), and puts down another (ii. 9). He also controls their distribution (ix. 7). He is therefore their Judge (i. 3–ii. 3) when they offend against His moral laws.

b. Naturally Amos' message betrays a particular interest in Israel. In a quite special sense Yahweh is the God of Israel. It was His will to elect her to covenant relation with Himself (iii. 2). Through His servants He has made known His will to her (ii. 11, iii. 7). But these high privileges involve Israel in heavy responsibility; and failure to accept this brings upon His people a far more severe judgment than that which was to fall upon pagan nations. When Israel broke Yahweh's laws (ii. 4) there could be only a fearful looking forward to judgment (iv. 12).

c. Amos was also concerned to proclaim that a law broken through unrighteousness could not be mended by means of ritual, festival, or offering alone. Indeed, Yahweh was already standing at the altar waiting to smite it (ix. 1–4). The most elaborate ritual was an abomination to Him so long as it was offered by a people who had no intention of measuring up to the ethical standards laid down in His holy laws. Such a religion of ceremonial and ritual was divorced from morality, and this Yahweh could only hate (v. 21 f.).

d. The foregoing means that Amos' main concern was to demand righteousness in the name of the Lord from the people of the Lord (v. 24). Righteousness was for Amos the most important moral attribute of the divine nature. Every outrage of the moral law, whether perpetrated by pagan nations (i. 3–ii. 3) or by Israel (ii. 4–16), was an outrage upon the nature of God and was, therefore, a provocation of divine justice. If Yahweh is righteous, then injustice, dishonesty, immorality, cannot be tolerated by Him, and must receive stern retribution from Him.

e. But judgment was not Amos' final word to Samaria (v. 4). Indeed, he closes with a promise of a brighter day for her (ix. 11–15). However, his actual ministry ended in apparent failure. While no-one contradicted his message, and while, doubtless, the national conscience witnessed to the truth and the justice of his preaching, at the end Amaziah the priest insisted that Amos should leave Samaria in peace and return to Judah to proclaim his message there (vii. 10 ff.).

BIBLIOGRAPHY. W. R. Harper, *Amos and Hosea*, in the *ICC*; S. R. Driver, *Joel and Amos*, in *CBSC*; G. Adam Smith, *The Book of the Twelve Prophets*, in *EB*; Adam C. Welch, *Kings and Prophets of Israel*, pp. 107–129; R. S. Cripps, *Critical and Exegetical Commentary on Amos*[2], 1955; J. D. W. Watts, *Vision and Prophecy in Amos*, 1958. J.G.S.S.T.

AMPHIPOLIS. An important strategic and commercial centre at the north of the Aegean, situated on the river Strymon (Struma) about 3 miles inland from the seaport Eion. Prized by the Athenians and Macedonians as the key both to the gold, silver, and timber of Mt. Pangaeus and also to the control of the Dardanelles, it became under the Romans a free town and the capital of the first district of Macedonia. Amphipolis is about 30 miles west-south-west of Philippi on the Via Egnatia, a great Roman highway, and Paul passed through it on his way to Thessalonica (Acts xvii. 1). K.L.McK.

AMPLIAS, AMPLIATUS. Paul's friend, affectionately greeted (Rom. xvi. 8). The best MSS show 'Ampliatus', a Latin slave name: 'Amplias' is a Greek pet-form. Lightfoot (*Philippians*, p. 174) finds the name in inscriptions of 'Caesar's household' (*cf.* Phil. iv. 22); but it was common. Those addressing Rom. xvi to Ephesus can find one there (*CIL*, iii, 436). A tomb-inscription 'Ampliati', perhaps late first century, in the catacomb of Domitilla, is ornate for a slave, perhaps reflecting his honour in the Church (*cf.* Sanday and Headlam, *Romans*, p. 424). A connection with Paul's Ampliatus or his family is not impossible (*cf.* R. Lanciani, *Pagan and Christian Rome*, 1895, pp. 342 ff.). Amplias, Stachys, and Urbanus (*cf.* verse 9) were commemorated together as martyrs (*Acta Sanctorum*, Oct. xiii, p. 687). A.F.W.

AMRAM (*'amrām*, 'people exalted'). **1.** The husband of Jochebed, and father of Moses, Aaron, and Miriam (Ex. vi. 20; Nu. xxvi. 59; 1 Ch. vi. 3, xxiii. 13). He was a son (*i.e.* probably to be understood in the sense of descendant, *cf.* 1 Ch. vii. 20–27) of Kohath (Ex. vi. 18; Nu. iii. 19), and so of Levi. **2.** An Amram is mentioned in Ezr. x. 34 as having taken a foreign wife.

In 1 Ch. i. 41 the word Amram should be Hamran. E.J.Y.

AMRAPHEL. In Gn. xiv. 1 ff. a king of Shinar (? Singar in Upper Mesopotamia) who, along with Chedorlaomer (*q.v.*) and other eastern kings, attacked Sodom and her neighbour cities, but was routed by Abram. See HAMMURABI.

AMULETS. The practice of wearing amulets was common throughout the Ancient Near East, and the Hebrews were unique in condemning their use, which was thought to protect the owner or wearer from evil. The amulets, generally worn on the head or neck, were usually small ornaments or gems, stones, seals, beads, plaques, or emblems which might be inscribed with a prayer or incantation. The Heb. *laḥaš*, commonly denoting the whispering sound used to charm snakes (Ps. lviii. 5; Ec. x. 11), is once applied to amulets (AV 'earrings') worn by women and condemned by Isaiah (iii. 20).

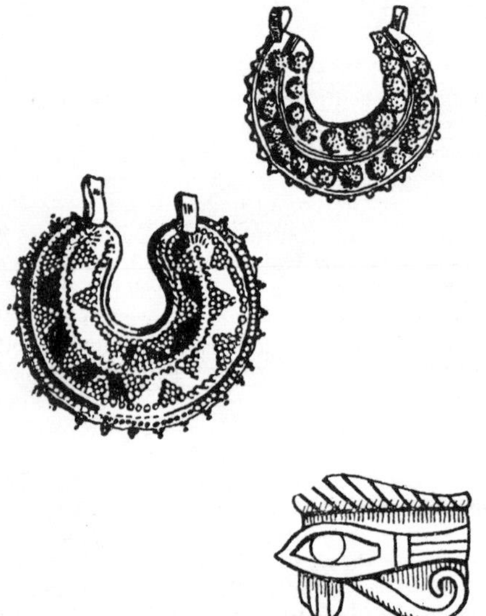

Fig. 7. *Above:* Pendants or earrings, some worn as inverted moon crescents, were used as amulets in Palestine in the 14th–13th centuries BC (Tell el-'Ajjul). *Below:* A blue glaze *ujat* or eye amulet from Lachish.

Amulets may be inferred in 'stones conferring favour' (Pr. xvii. 8; AVmg, 'stone of grace'), for most stones were thought to have magical properties. Thus all seal-stones and rings were considered as amulets (*cf.* Je. xxii. 24; Hg. ii. 23), as were most personal ornaments like those used to make the golden calf (Ex. xxxii. 2) or buried by Jacob (Gn. xxxv. 4). In common with the condemnation of those who employed charms (see Is. iii. 3, RSV), the bronze serpent made by Moses was destroyed as soon as it became an object of superstitious reverence in itself (2 Ki. xviii. 4).

A common amulet was an inverted crescent-shaped ornament, symbol of the goddess Astarte-Ishtar, worn by women or hung on animals to increase their fertility (Jdg. viii. 21, 26). The fringe phylacteries (*t^epillîn*) introduced by Moses (Nu. xv. 38, 39) were designed to act as a reminder of the Law and as a deterrent to superstition and idolatry, which it condemned (Ex. xiii. 9; Dt. vi. 8 ff.; Pr. iii. 3). The Heb. *m^ezûzâ* is used of the 'doorpost' itself, but not of the amulet put upon it by later Jews. See PHYLACTERIES. D.J.W.

ANAH. 1. Mentioned in Gn. xxxvi. 2, 14, 18, 25 (AV) as a daughter of Zibeon and mother of Oholibamah, one of Esau's wives. The Samaritan Septuagint and Syriac Peshitta read 'son' for 'daughter' of the Heb. text. This would identify this Anah with **(2)**, a son of Zibeon, Gn. xxxvi. 24; 1 Ch. i. 40, who found hot springs in the wilderness, as he fed the asses of Zibeon his father (Gn. xxxvi. 24, RV). If we identify Oholibamah of Gn. xxxvi. 2 with Judith, Gn. xxvi. 34, Beeri the Hittite mentioned in this latter verse will be another name for Anah, and commemorates the discovery of the hot springs (Heb. *b^e'ēr* means 'well'). **3.** A Horite duke, the son of Seir, and brother of Zibeon, Gn. xxxvi. 20, 29; 1 Ch. i. 38. R.A.H.G.

ANAK, ANAKIM. The Anakim (*'^anāqîm*), descendants of an eponymous ancestor Anak, were among the pre-Israelite inhabitants of Palestine. The name Anak occurs without the article only in Nu. xiii. 33 and Dt. ix. 2, but elsewhere it appears in the form 'the Anak' (*hā'^anāq*), where it is presumably to be taken as the collective, equivalent to Anakim. The phrase 'the city of Arba (*qiryaṯ 'arba'*, see KIRIATH-ARBA), father of Anak' in Jos. xv. 13 apparently indicates that an individual named Arba was the ultimate ancestor of the Anakim, unless the noun 'father' is taken to qualify the city, in which case this city, later known as Hebron (*q.v.*), was considered the ancestral home of the Anakim.

The stature and formidable nature of the Anakim was almost proverbial, for they were taken as a standard for comparison to stress the size of such other peoples as the Emim (Dt. ii. 10) and the Rephaim (Dt. ii. 21), and there was a saying, 'Who can stand before the sons of Anak?' (see Dt. ix. 2). In the account of the promised land brought back by the ten faint-hearted spies, emphasis was laid on the fact that the Anakim were there (Dt. i. 28; the LXX here renders *'^anāqîm* by *gigantes*, see GIANT). It was even stated that they were descended from the Nephilim (*q.v.*), who were also claimed as sons of Anak, and the spies said that they felt like grasshoppers beside them (Nu. xiii. 33). They were settled in the hill-country, particularly at Hebron (Nu. xiii. 22), where Ahiman, Sheshai, and Talmai, 'offspring of the Anak', were found. Joshua cut the Anakim off from the hill-country (from Hebron, Debir, and Anab), but some were left in Gaza, Gath, and Ashdod (Jos. xi. 21 f.), and it fell to Caleb finally to drive them out from Hebron, which had been allotted to him. Nothing is known of these people outside the Bible, unless they are, as some scholars hold, among the peoples mentioned in the Egyptian 18th-century execration texts.

BIBLIOGRAPHY. *KB*, p. 722; *ANET*, p. 328.

T.C.M.

ANAMMELECH. A deity worshipped, with Adrammelech, by Sepharvaim colonists placed in Samaria by the Assyrians (2 Ki. xvii. 31). If Sepharvaim (*q.v.*) is interpreted as the Babylonian Sippar the name is 'Anu is king'. Since this view is unsupported, a connection with the Syrian-Arabian goddess Anat is possible, especially as a consort for Adrammelech (*q.v.*) is likely in the context. D.J.W.

ANANIAS, Gk. form of Hananiah ('Yahweh has dealt graciously'). **1.** In Acts v. 1 ff. a member of the primitive church of Jerusalem whose contribution to the common fund was less than he pretended; he fell dead when his dishonesty was exposed. **2.** In Acts ix. 10 ff. a follower of Jesus in Damascus, 'a devout man according to the law', who befriended Saul of Tarsus immediately after his conversion and conveyed Christ's commission to him. **3.** In Acts xxiii. 2, xxiv. 1, Ananias the son of Nedebaeus, high priest AD 47–58, president of the Sanhedrin when Paul was brought before it, notorious for his greed; killed by Zealots in 66 for his pro-Roman sympathies. F.F.B.

ANATHEMA. 1. *Anathēma* originally meant 'something set up (in a temple)', hence a votive offering, a form and sense preserved in Lk. xxi. 5 (AV 'gifts').

2. *Anathema* (short *e*) is later; the forms are distinguished by lexicographers such as Hesychius, but are related in meaning and often confused in practice.

The LXX often uses *anathema* to represent *ḥērem* (see CURSE), 'the devoted thing', the thing to be put to the ban, involving total destruction (*e.g.* Lv. xxvii. 28 f.; Nu. xxi. 3, of Hormah; Dt. vii. 26, and *cf.* the striking Judith xvi. 19). Pagan imprecatory texts show that the word was used as a cursing formula outside Judaism (see Deissmann, *LAE*, pp. 95 ff.; and *MM*).

So it was that Christians might hear, Hellenistic syncretism being what it was, the horrid blasphemy 'Anathema Jesus' from the lips of apparently 'inspired' preachers (1 Cor. xii. 3): whether as an abjuration of allegiance (Pliny, *Ep.* x. 96 and other sources show persecuted Christians were called on to 'curse Christ'), or a Judaistic taunt at the crucified, or in sheer hatred. Whatever the condition of the speaker, no message degrading Christ came from the Holy Spirit. Again, Paul could wish himself for the sake of his unconverted brethren 'under the ban', involving separation from Christ (Rom. ix. 3), and could call the ban, involving the abolition of Christian recognition, on preachers of 'any other gospel' (Gal. i. 8, 9). In all these cases RV transliterates *anathema*, while AV renders it 'accursed'.

In one place, 1 Cor. xvi. 22, AV has transliterated *anathema* putting haters of Christ under the ban, attaching the following *maranatha* (*q.v.*) to it. This would perhaps give the general sense 'and may our Lord swiftly execute His judgments' (*cf.* C. F. D. Moule, *NTS*, VI, 1960, pp. 307 ff.). But *maranatha* may be a separate sentence (*cf.* RV). In view of the contents of 1 Corinthians, these words amid the affectionate closing greetings are quite appropriate, without any special connection of the anathema with the dismissal before the Eucharist, which some find (*cf.* G. Bornkamm, *Th.L.*, LXXV, 1950, pp. 227 ff.; J. A. T. Robinson, *JTS*, NS, IV, 1953, pp. 38 ff.).

The conspirators in Acts xxiii. 14 put themselves under an *anathema* (EVV 'curse'): *i.e.* they called the curse upon themselves if they failed (*cf.* the Old Testament phrase 'So do the Lord to me and more if I do not . . .').

The ecclesiastical sense of excommunication is an extension, not an example, of biblical usage, though it is not impossible that synagogue practice (*cf.* *SB*, IV, pp. 293 ff.) gave some early colouring to it.

The cognate verb appears in Mk. xiv. 71; Acts xxiii. 12, 14, 21. A.F.W.

ANATHOTH. Town in the territory of Benjamin assigned to Levites (Jos. xxi. 18). The home of Abiathar (1 Ki. ii. 26) and Jeremiah (Je. i. 1, xi. 21), Abiezer (2 Sa. xxiii. 27), Jehu (1 Ch. xii. 3), and some of David's warriors (1 Ch. xi. 28, xxvii. 12, RV). Repopulated after the Exile (Ne. xi. 32). The modern site, Ras el-Ḥarrūbeh, *c.* 3 miles north of Jerusalem, lies near the village of 'Anāta (Photo. Grollenberg, *Atlas*, pl. 250).

D.J.W.

ANCESTOR WORSHIP. Most primitive pagan peoples believe in the existence of spirits, good and evil, and many consider that among these are the spirits of the dead. The desire to provide for the comfort of the benevolent, and to placate the ill-will of the malevolent, among these, often leads to a 'cult of the dead', where such services as fitting burial and provision of food and drink are performed to achieve these ends. The overt worship of the dead in the sense of adoration or even deification is, however, comparatively rare; the best-known example is that of Confucian China. It is more appropriate therefore to speak of a 'cult of the dead' than of 'ancestor worship', since there is no question of the latter's being found in the Bible.

In the latter part of the 19th and early years of the 20th century the reports of travellers and missionaries of the beliefs of modern primitive peoples gave material for anthropologists to speculate on the 'development' of religion. In the light of the resultant theories the Bible was re-examined, and the supposed traces of early stages in the development of Israelite religion detected.

Among these traces were indications of ancestor worship. Thus it has been claimed that evidence of this is to be found in the translation of Enoch (*q.v.*) to be with God (Gn. v. 24), which is taken as an indication that he was deified, but this is entirely gratuitous. It has been suggested likewise that the teraphim (*q.v.*) were originally worshipped as ancestor images, but there is again no foundation for such a view.

With the rediscovery of the civilizations of the Ancient Near East, which formed the *milieu* of the Old Testament, the customs of modern primitive peoples were seen to be largely irrelevant, but many of the theories of the development of religion remained, though now the religion of the Old Testament was viewed as something of an amalgam of the beliefs and practices of the surrounding peoples.

In the Ancient Near East belief in the after-life led to widespread cult practices connected with the dead. The provisions by the Egyptians for the comfort of the deceased, in what was believed to be a basically enjoyable future existence, were elaborate. In Mesopotamia less is known of the funeral rites of individuals, but a gloomy view was taken of the life to come, and it was in consequence important to ensure, by the provision of necessities as well as by ritual and liturgy, that the dead did not return as dissatisfied spirits to molest the living. The case of kings was different, and there was a tendency, in form at least, to their deification. The names, for example, of such early rulers as Lugalbanda and Gilgamesh were written with the divine determinative, an honour also accorded particularly to the kings of the IIIrd Dynasty of Ur, and prayers were on occasion offered to them. In Syria also a cult of the dead is well attested, as, for instance, in the discoveries at Ras Shamra, where tombs were found provided with pipes and gutters to make it possible for libations to be poured from the surface into the tomb vaults.

Few cemeteries or tombs of the Israelite period have been excavated in Palestine, but those which have show, perhaps, a decline in furniture from the Canaanite Bronze Age or, in other words, a decline in the cult of the dead. That the Israelites, however, were continually falling away from the right path and adopting the religious practices of their neighbours is clearly stated by the Bible. It is to be expected that among these practices should have been some associated with the cult of the dead. Thus, the declarations in Dt. xxvi. 14 suggest that it was necessary to prohibit offerings to the dead; it appears that it was expected that incense would be burned for (*l*[e]) Asa at his burial (2 Ch. xvi. 14), and at Zedekiah's funeral (Je. xxxiv. 5); and Ezekiel xliii. 7–9 implies that there was worship of the dead bodies of kings. The practice of necromancy (see DIVINATION) is also attested (1 Sa. xxviii. 7), though clearly condemned (Is. viii. 19, lxv. 4).

Other biblical passages are sometimes cited as evidence that such practices were acquiesced in, or accepted as legitimate. Thus, in Gn. xxxv. 8 it is described how the oak under which Rebekah's nurse was buried was called Allon-bacuth, 'Oak of weeping', and again in Gn. xxxv. 20 Jacob set up a *maṣṣēḇâ* (see PILLAR) over Rachel's grave. These actions have been taken to indicate a belief in the sanctity of graves, and, as a consequence, cult practices associated with the dead. But weeping over the dead may just as well be genuine as ritual, and there is no evidence to suggest that the raising of a memorial pillar necessarily implies a cult practice. The custom of levirate marriage (Dt. xxv. 5–10; see MARRIAGE, IV) has been interpreted as partly aimed at providing someone to carry out the cult of the dead for the deceased. This interpretation, however, is again one which exceeds the simple testimony of the text. Despite various theories, the participation in family sacrifices (*e.g.* 1 Sa. xx. 29) provides no evidence of a cult of the dead. It has been further suggested that some of the mourning customs (see BURIAL AND MOURNING) show signs of a cult of, or even worship of, the dead. But such of these practices as were legitimate (*cf.* Lv. xix. 27, 28; Dt. xiv. 1) may just as well be explained as manifestations of sorrow over the loss of a dear one.

It is thus clear that neither ancestor worship nor a cult of the dead played any part in the true religion of Israel.

BIBLIOGRAPHY. R. H. Lowie, *An Introduction to Cultural Anthropology*, 1940, pp. 308–309 (modern primitives); J. N. D. Anderson (ed.), *The World's Religions*, 1950, pp. 12, 13 (modern primitives), 144, 145 (Shinto), 169–172 (Confucian); A. H. Gardiner, *The Attitude of the Ancient Egyptians to Death and the Dead*, 1935; H. R. Hall in *ERE*, I, pp. 440–443 (Egypt); A. Heidel, *The Gilgamesh Epic and Old Testament Parallels*², 1949, pp. 137–223; H. W. F. Saggs, 'Some Ancient Semitic Conceptions of the After-life', *Faith and Thought*, XC, 1958, pp. 157–182; C. F. A. Schaeffer, *The Cuneiform Texts of Ras Shamra*, 1939, pp. 49–54; G. Margoliouth in *ERE*, I, pp. 444–450; M. Burrows, *What Mean These Stones?*, 1941, pp. 238–242; R. de Vaux, *Les Institutions de l'Ancien Testament*, I, 1958, p. 100.

T.C.M.

ANCIENT OF DAYS. See GOD, NAMES OF.

ANDREW. One of the twelve apostles. The name is Greek (meaning 'manly'), but it may have been a 'Christian name' like 'Peter'. He was the son of Jonas or John and came from Bethsaida in Galilee (Jn. i. 44), but afterwards went to live with his brother Simon Peter at Capernaum (Mk. i. 29), where they were in partnership as fishermen (Mt. iv. 18). As a disciple of John the Baptist (Jn. i. 35–40) he was pointed by him to Jesus as the Lamb of God. He then found Simon and brought him to Jesus (Jn. i. 42). Later he was called to full-time discipleship (Mt. iv. 18–20; Mk. i. 16–18) and became one of the twelve apostles (Mt. x. 2; Mk. iii. 18; Lk. vi. 14). His practical faith is shown in Jn. vi. 8, 9, xii. 21, 22. He was one of those who asked about the judgment coming on Jerusalem (Mk. xiii. 3, 4). He is mentioned finally as being with the other apostles after the ascension (Acts i. 13).

It is probable that he was crucified in Achaia. The Synoptic Gospels say little about him, but in John he is shown as the first home missionary (i. 42) and the first foreign missionary (xii. 21, 22). Of the former, William Temple wrote, 'Perhaps it is as great a service to the Church as ever any man did' (*Readings in St. John's Gospel*, p. 29).

R.E.N.

ANDRONICUS AND JUNIA, JUNIAS. (AV 'Junia' is feminine—perhaps Andronicus' wife? RV 'Junias' would be masculine, contracted from Junianus.) Affectionately greeted by Paul (Rom. xvi. 7) as (1) 'kinsmen', *i.e.* probably fellow-Jews, as in Rom. ix. 3 (but see *MM*, *syngenēs*, for this word as a title of honour); Ramsay (*Cities of St. Paul*, pp. 176 ff.) infers membership of the same Tarsian civic tribe; (2) 'fellow-prisoners of war', probably to be understood of literal imprisonment (see Abbott, *ICC*, in Col. iv. 10), but at what time this occurred is unknown; (3) 'distinguished among the apostles' ('well-known *to* the apostles' is improbable): on this see APOSTLE; and (4) Christians before him, as one might expect of apostles. For hypotheses connecting them with the foundation of the Ephesian or Roman churches, see B. W. Bacon, *ExpT.* XLII, 1931, pp. 300 ff., and G. A. Barton, *ibid.*, XLIII, 1932, pp. 359 ff. A.F.W.

ANGEL. A biblical angel (Heb. *mal'āḵ*, Gk. *angelos*) is, etymologically and conceptually, a messenger of God, familiar with Him face to face, therefore of an order of being higher than that of man. Certainly he is a creature, but also holy and uncorrupted spirit in original essence, yet endowed with free will, and therefore not necessarily impervious to temptation and sin. There are many indications of an angelic fall, under the leadership of Satan (Jb. iv. 18; Mt. xxv. 41; 2 Pet. ii. 4; Rev. xii. 9), but its effects belong strictly to the realm of demonology (see DEVIL). The word is used also, in both Testaments, for mortal messengers.

I. IN THE OLD TESTAMENT

There are two broad phases of the doctrine of angels in the Old Testament, roughly divided by the Babylonian Exile. An exact differentiation of their features would involve much discussion of chronology. The notes which follow do not claim to do more than distinguish approximately.

a. In the pre-exilic period

The Angel of God (*mal'aḵ Yahweh*) is the direct agent of His will, but remains nameless and almost without revealed personality. In many passages God and His emissary are practically interchangeable concepts—*cf.* notably the appearances to Hagar in the wilderness (Gn. xvi. 7–13, xxi. 17–20); to Abraham on Mt. Moriah (Gn. xxii. 11–18); to Moses at the burning bush (Ex. iii. 2 ff.); and to Gideon at Ophrah (Jdg. vi. 11 ff.). Some would argue that the angel in such contexts is a device to soften the seeming anthropomorphism of the sacred record. More commonly, Scripture conceives of a spiritual being separate from God, but of unquestioned integrity, goodwill, and obedience to Him (*cf.* 1 Sa. xxix. 9; 2 Sa. xiv. 17, 20, xix. 27). Angels may appear to men as bearers of God's specific commands and tidings (Jdg. vi. 11–23, xiii. 3–5, *etc.*, see II below). They may bring specific succour to needy mortal servants of God (1 Ki. xix. 5–7, see II below). They may undertake commissions of military assistance (2 Ki. xix. 35, *etc.*) or, more rarely, active hostility (2 Sa. xxiv. 16 f.) towards Israel. The men of Sodom (Gn. xix *passim*) or any other evil-doers may be smitten by them. Their warlike potential, implied in Gn. xxxii. 1 f.; 1 Ki. xxii. 19, is more specific in Jos. v. 13–15; 2 Ki. vi. 17—hence the familiar title of deity, Lord God of hosts.

Man's early reflective judgment associated angels with stars. This prompted one of the poetic thoughts of Job, where the angels are also witnesses of creation (Jb. xxxviii. 7, see below; *cf.* Jdg. v. 20; Rev. ix. 1). Balaam's ass may be more immediately perceptive of the angelically numinous than her master, who stands in need of divine rebuke (Nu. xxii. 21–35). Very familiar are the angels in converse with Abraham (Gn. xviii. 1–16) or on Jacob's ladder (Gn. xxviii. 12). Individual guardian angels (*cf.* Ps. xci. 11) and the angel of death (*cf.* Jb. xxxiii. 22; Pr. xvi. 14) remain rudimentary concepts in the Old Testament, but become firm, rounded doctrines in the rabbinic literature. The term 'sons of God' means simply angels—the descent implied is mental or spiritual, not physical. The beings thus denoted may be clearly good angels (Jb. xxxviii. 7, see above), possibly good angels (Jb. i. 6, ii. 1) or clearly fallen angels (Gn. vi. 2, 4). Another special term is *qᵉḏôšîm*, 'holy ones'—AV 'saints' (Jb. v. 1; Ps. lxxxix. 5, 7; Dn. viii. 13, *etc.*). The technicality of the designation is suggested by the fact that it may be used when the implication is not exactly saintly (Jb. xv. 15).

The ideas so far examined are probably pre-exilic, at least in origin, though some later examples are included. The angels still remain for the most part echoes of a higher will, and have not yet advanced in man's interpretation to the personality of a later envisaging.

b. In the exilic and later books

In this later period the angel unquestionably gains in firmness and contour. The 'man' who acts as Ezekiel's divinely appointed guide to the ideal temple is a midway concept (chapters xl ff.) which becomes a distinctive interpreting angel in Zc. i–vi. The intercessory function on behalf of Israel in Zc. i. 12 calls for special mention. If it be remembered that 'saints' means 'angels' in that context, the last words of Zc. xiv. 5 make interesting reading in the light of the Synoptic predictions of the second coming.

Old Testament angelology reaches its fullest development in Daniel, which is the earliest flowering of Jewish apocalyptic. Here angels are first endowed with proper names, and attain to something like personality. Gabriel explains many things to Daniel, much in the spirit of Zechariah's divine visitant (Dn. viii. 16 ff., ix. 21 ff.). In both books the angel is the fluent mouthpiece of God, and may be questioned—but the Danielic Gabriel is more rounded and convincing. Michael has a special function as guardian angel of Israel (Dn. x. 13, 21, xii. 1), and other nations are similarly equipped (Dn. x. 20). This became rabbinic commonplace. There is a visionary glimpse into the heavenly places, where there are countless myriads of throne angels (Dn. vii. 10; *cf.* Dt. xxxiii. 2; Ne. ix. 6; Ps. lxviii. 17 for slighter echoes).

II. IN THE NEW TESTAMENT

The New Testament largely endorses and underlines the Old—though the intervening centuries must not be forgotten. Heb. i. 14 defines the angel both as messenger of God and as minister to man, while the totality of passages suggests a deepening bond of sympathy and service (*cf.* Rev. xix. 10; Lk. xv. 10). The concept of the personal guardian angel has sharpened, as in the rabbinic literature (Mt. xviii. 10; *cf.* Strack-Billerbeck *ad loc.*; and on Acts xii. 15). Special missions of communication to individuals are not lacking—the visitation of Gabriel to Daniel may be compared with that to Zacharias (Lk. i. 11–20) and Mary (Lk. i. 26–38; *cf.* also Mt. i, ii, *passim*; Acts viii. 26, x. 3 ff., xxvii. 23, *etc.*). The rôle of more active succour to humanity is perceived in Acts v. 19 f., xii. 7–10, which recalls Elijah under the juniper tree. God's throne is surrounded by countless myriads of angels, as Daniel had already declared (Heb. xii. 22; Rev. v. 11, *etc.*).

The Old Testament implies that angels were the joyful witnesses of, though not necessarily active participants in, God's act of creation (Jb. xxxviii. 7). In the New Testament they are closely associated with the giving of the law (Acts vii. 53; Gal. iii. 19; Heb. ii. 2), and it is not inconsistent that they should be frequently coupled with final judgment (Mt. xvi. 27; Mk. viii. 38, xiii. 27; Lk. xii. 8 f.; 2 Thes. i. 7 f.; and numerous parallels). It may be their special task also to carry the righteous dead into Abraham's bosom (Lk. xvi. 22 f.). Little is attempted by way of direct description of the angelic form. The references to lustre of countenance or apparel suggest rather than postulate an awesome beauty which is not of this world (Mt. xxviii. 2 f. and parallels; Lk. ii. 9; Acts i. 10). The Old Testament shows a comparable restraint in dealing with the cherubim (Ezk. x) and seraphim (Is. vi) (*qq.v.*; the words are already plural, and the 's' in the AV is superfluous). The splendour on the face of the condemned Stephen reflects the angelic loveliness (Acts vi. 15).

The incarnate Christ received the angelic ministry on several occasions (Mt. iv. 11; Lk. xxii. 43) and He could have commanded thousands of angels, had He been prepared, at Gethsemane or anywhere else, to deviate from the appointed sacrificial path (Mt. xxvi. 53).

There is a strange undertone of hostility or suspicion towards angels in certain passages. This has interesting though unconnected parallels in the rabbinic literature. Rom. viii. 38 refers to fallen angels, and this explains also the puzzling passage 1 Cor. xi. 10, which should be read in the light of Gn. vi. 1 ff. It is still necessary to account for Gal. i. 8 and 1 Cor. xiii. 1, and the stern warning of Col. ii. 18. It was doubtless through doctrinal errors on the part of his readers that the writer to the Hebrews urged so forcefully the superiority of the Son to any angel (Heb. i).

The essential meaning of Jude 9 (partial parallel 2 Pet. ii. 10 f.) would seem to be that fallen angels retain from their first condition a status and dignity such that even their unfallen former companions may not speak against them in unrestrained terms, but must leave the final condemnation to God. The incident referred to by Jude is said to have been recorded in the *Assumption of Moses*, a fragment of apocalyptic midrash. There Satan claims the body of Moses for his kingdom of darkness, because Moses killed the Egyptian (Ex. ii. 12) and was therefore a murderer, whatever his subsequent virtues may have been. The final honours do not go to Satan, but even Michael the archangel must bridle his tongue before the foe of mankind.

BIBLIOGRAPHY. Hodge, *Systematic Theology*, I, 1883, pp. 637 ff.; Strack und Billerbeck, *Kommentar zum N.T. aus Talmud und Midrasch*, 1926, gives Rabbinic parallels to New Testament passages; art. '*Angelos*' in *TWNT*, I, pp. 72–87; R. A. Stewart, *Rabbinic Theology*, 1961; Heppe, *Reformed Dogmatics*, 1950, pp. 201–219. R.A.S.

ANGEL OF THE LORD. The angel of the Lord, sometimes 'the angel of God' or 'my (or 'his') angel', is represented as a heavenly being sent by God to deal with men as His personal agent and spokesman. In many passages he is virtually identified with God as an extension of the divine personality, and speaks not merely in the name of God but as God in the first person singular (*e.g.* with Hagar, Gn. xvi. 7 ff., xxi. 17 f.; at the sacrifice of Isaac, Gn. xxii. 11 ff.; to Jacob, Gn. xxxi. 13, 'I am the God of Beth-el'; at the burning bush, Ex. iii. 2; with Gideon, Jdg. vi. 11 ff.). Sometimes, however, he is distinguished from God, as in 2 Sa. xxiv. 16; Zc. i. 12, 13. Zechariah, however, does not distinguish them in iii. 1, 2 (*cf.* also xii. 8).

In the New Testament there is no suggestion of identity, the angel of the Lord being personalized as Gabriel (*q.v.*) in Lk. i. 19. But from Acts viii. 26, 29 identification with the Holy Spirit could be inferred.

In function, the angel of the Lord is the agent of destruction and judgment (2 Sa. xxiv. 16; 2 Ki. xix. 35; Ps. xxxv. 5, 6; Acts xii. 23); of protection and deliverance (Ex. xiv. 19; Ps. xxxiv. 7; Is. lxiii. 9, 'the angel of his presence'; Dn. iii. 28, vi. 22; Acts v. 19, xii. 7, 11); he offers guidance and gives instructions (Gn. xxiv. 7, 40; Ex. xxiii. 23; 1 Ki. xix. 7; 2 Ki. i. 3, 15; Mt. ii. 13, 19; Acts viii. 26); he gives prior information about the birth of Samson (Jdg. xiii. 3 ff.) John Baptist (Lk. i. 11) and Jesus (Mt. i. 20, 24; Lk. ii. 9). He is not recognized at once in Jdg. xiii. 3 ff. and is not even visible to Balaam (Nu. xxii. 22 ff.); but mostly when appearing to men he is recognized as a divine being and addressed as God (Gn. xvi. 13, *etc.*). J.B.Tr.

ANGER. See WRATH.

ANISE. See PLANTS.

ANNA (Gk. form of Heb. *ḥannâ*, 'grace'). An aged widow, daughter of Phanuel, of the tribe of Asher (Lk. ii. 36–38). Like Simeon, who also belonged to the remnant which 'waited for the consolation of Israel', she had prophetic insight, and was a regular attender at the morning and evening services in the Temple. On hearing Simeon's words at the presentation of Jesus, she commended the child as the long-awaited Messiah, and praised God for the fulfilment of His promises. J.D.D.

ANNAS. Annas or Ananos, son of Seth, was appointed high priest in AD 6 and deposed in AD 15. In the New Testament he is still referred to as high priest after AD 15. This may be for one of three reasons. First, though the Romans deposed high priests and appointed new ones, the Jews thought of the high priesthood as a life office. The Mishnah (*Horayoth* iii. 4) says: 'A high priest in office differs from the priest that is passed from his high priesthood only in the bullock that is offered on the Day of Atonement and the tenth of the ephah.' Secondly, the title 'high priest' is given in Acts and Josephus to members of the few priestly families from which most high priests were drawn, as well as to those exercising the high-priestly office. Thirdly, Annas had great personal influence with succeeding high priests. Five of his sons and Caiaphas his son-in-law became high priest. At the trial of Jesus we find Annas conducting a preliminary investigation before the official trial by Caiaphas (Jn. xviii. 13–24). When Lk. iii. 2 says that the high priest was Annas and Caiaphas, the singular is probably deliberate, indicating that, though Caiaphas was the high priest officially appointed by Rome, his father-in-law shared his high-priestly power, both *de facto* by his personal influence and, according to strict Jewish thought, also *de jure* (*cf.* Acts iv. 6). D.R.H.

ANNUNCIATION. The vision of Mary (Lk. i. 26–38) 'announces' the conception of a Messiah-Son and describes with poetic imagery Messiah's human (Lk. i. 32) and divine (Lk. i. 34 f.) character and the eternal nature of His kingdom (Lk. i. 33). Machen and Daube give the most helpful treatment of the literary questions. For reference to Virgin Birth, see INCARNATION.

BIBLIOGRAPHY. D. Daube, *The New Testament and Rabbinic Judaism*, 1956; M. Dibelius, *Botschaft und Geschichte*, 1953, pp. 1–78; J. G. Machen, *The Virgin Birth*, 1931; *DCG*; *ODCC*. E.E.E.

ANOINTING, ANOINTED. Persons and things were anointed, in the Old Testament, to signify holiness, or separation unto God: pillars (*cf.* Gn. xxviii. 18); the tabernacle and its furniture (Ex. xxx. 22 ff.); shields (2 Sa. i. 21; Is. xxi. 5: probably to consecrate them for the 'holy war', see Dt. xxiii. 9 ff.); kings (Jdg. ix. 8; 2 Sa. ii. 4; 1 Ki. i. 34); priests (Ex. xxviii. 41); prophets (1 Ki. xix. 16). The importance and solemnity of the anointing is shown, first, by the fact that it was a criminal offence to compound the holy oil for a common purpose (Ex. xxx. 32, 33); secondly, by the authority which the anointing carried, such that, for example, while Jehu's fellow-commanders scorned the prophet as a 'madman', they did not dare resist the implications of his action, but accepted without question that he who was anointed as king must indeed be king (2 Ki. ix. 11–13); thirdly, by the effect produced in the anointed, the person or thing becoming holy (Ex. xxx. 22–33) and sacrosanct (1 Sa. xxiv. 7, *etc.*). Fundamentally the anointing was an act of God (1 Sa. x. 1)—which explains the awe in which it was held—and the word 'anointed' was even used metaphorically to mean the bestowal of divine favour (Pss. xxiii. 5, xcii. 10) or appointment to a special place or function in the purpose of God (Ps. cv. 15; Is. xlv. 1). Further, the anointing symbolized equipment for service, and is associated with the outpouring of the Spirit of God (1 Sa. x. 1, 9, xvi. 13; Is. lxi. 1; Zc. iv. 1–14). This usage is carried over into the New Testament (Acts x. 38; 1 Jn. ii. 20, 27). The use of oil in anointing the sick (Jas. v. 14) is best understood in the same way, as pointing to the Holy Spirit, the Lifegiver. J.A.M.

ANT (Heb. *n*ᵉ*mālâ*). Mentioned only in Pr. vi. 6 and xxx. 25. The term is properly applied to a group of insects belonging to the order *Hymenoptera.* They vary greatly in size and habits, but all are social, living in colonies ranging from a dozen or so to hundreds of thousands. Many types of ants are found in Palestine, but the reference is clearly to the Harvester Ant, sometimes called the Agricultural Ant, which collects seeds of many kinds during summer and stores them in underground galleries, often after removing and discarding the husks. Such colonies are common in the coastal regions of Israel. G.C.

ANTICHRIST. The expression *antichristos* is found in the Bible only in the Johannine Epistles

(1 Jn. ii. 18, 22, iv. 3; 2 Jn. 7), but the idea behind it is widespread. We should probably understand the force of *anti* as indicating opposition, rather than a false claim, *i.e.* the antichrist is one who opposes Christ rather than one who claims to be the Christ. If this is so, then we should include under the heading 'antichrist' such Old Testament passages as Dn. vii. 7 f., 21 f., and those in 2 Thes. ii and Revelation which deal with the strong opposition that the forces of evil are to offer Christ in the last days.

The concept is introduced in John as already well known ('ye have heard that antichrist shall come', 1 Jn. ii. 18). But though he does not dispute the fact that at the end of this age there will appear an evil being, called 'antichrist', John insists that there is a temper, an attitude, characteristic of antichrist, and that already exists. Indeed, he can speak of 'many antichrists' as already in the world (1 Jn. ii. 18). He gives something in the nature of a definition of antichrist when he says, 'He is antichrist, that denieth the Father and the Son' (1 Jn. ii. 22). This becomes a little more explicit when the criterion is made the denial that 'Jesus Christ is come in the flesh' (1 Jn. iv. 3; 2 Jn. 7). For John it is basic that in Jesus Christ we see God acting for man's salvation (1 Jn. iv. 9 f.). When a man denies this he is not simply guilty of doctrinal error. He is undercutting the very foundation of the Christian faith. He is doing the work of Satan in opposing the things of God. At the end of the age this will characterize the work of the supreme embodiment of evil. And those who in a smaller way do the same thing now demonstrate by that very fact that they are his henchmen.

Paul does not use the term 'antichrist', but the 'man of sin' of whom he writes in 2 Thes. ii. 3 ff. clearly refers to the same being. The characteristic of this individual is that he 'opposeth and exalteth himself above all that is called God, or that is worshipped' (verse 4). He claims to be God (*ibid.*). He is not Satan, but his coming 'is after the working of Satan' (verse 9). It cannot be said that all the difficulties of this passage have been cleared up, and, in particular, the identification of the man of sin is still hotly debated. But for our present purpose the main points are clear enough. Paul thinks of the supreme effort of Satan as not in the past, but in the future. He does not think of the world as gradually evolving into a perfect state, but of evil as continuing right up till the last time. Then evil will make its greatest challenge to good, and this challenge will be led by the mysterious figure who owes his power to Satan, and who is the instrument of Satan's culminating challenge to the things of God. Paul is sure of the outcome. Christ will consume the man of sin 'with the spirit of his mouth' (verse 8). The last, supreme challenge of Satan will be defeated.

That is surely the meaning of some, at least, of the imagery of the book of Revelation. Biblical students are far from unanimous about the right way to interpret this book, but nearly all are agreed that some of the visions refer to the final struggle of the forces of evil with Christ. Sometimes the symbolism refers plainly to Satan. Thus the 'great red dragon' of Rev. xii. 3 is expressly identified with Satan (verse 9). But the 'beast' of Rev. xi. 7 is not. He is closely related to Satan, as his works show. Other similar figures appear (Rev. xiii. 11, *etc.*). It is not our purpose here to identify any particular one with the antichrist, but simply to point to the fact that this book too knows of one empowered by Satan who will oppose Christ in the last days. This may fairly be said to be characteristic of the Christian view of the last days.

BIBLIOGRAPHY. W. Bousset, *The Antichrist Legend*; art. 'Antichrist' in *EBi*; M. R. James, art. 'Man of Sin and Antichrist' in *HDB*; G. Vos, *The Pauline Eschatology*, chapter V. L.M.

ANTIOCH (PISIDIAN). Strabo described this Asia Minor city as being in Phrygia towards Pisidia. It was one of several Antiochs founded by a Macedonian cavalry leader, Seleucus I Nicator (312–280 BC), in honour of his father. Situated on an important trading route between Ephesus and Cilicia, it was a prominent centre of Hellenism. The Seleucids had encouraged Jewish colonists to settle throughout Phrygia for political and commercial reasons. The more tolerant descendants of these received Paul kindly on his first missionary journey (Acts xiii. 14). Under the Roman Empire Pisidian Antioch was included in the Province of Galatia (in the region Phrygia Galatica). The Emperor Augustus gave it the status of a Roman colony.

In Phrygia, women enjoyed considerable prestige and sometimes occupied civic offices. The opponents of Paul enlisted some of these influential persons (Acts xiii. 50) to secure his expulsion from the city. The ruined site is near Yalovach in modern Turkey. R.K.H.

ANTIOCH (SYRIAN). Antioch on the Orontes, as this celebrated city was often known, was founded *c.* 300 BC by Seleucus I Nicator after his victory over Antigonus at Issus (310 BC). It was the most famous of sixteen Antiochs established by Seleucus in honour of his father. Built at the foot of mount Sylphus, it overlooked the navigable river Orontes and boasted a fine seaport, Seleucia Pieria. While the populace of Antioch was always mixed, Josephus records that the Seleucids encouraged Jews to emigrate there in large numbers, and gave them full citizenship rights. Other Jews probably fled to Antioch during the Maccabean wars.

Antioch fell to Pompey in 64 BC, and he made it a free city. Subsequently it became the capital of the Roman province of Syria, and was the third largest city of the Empire. The Seleucids and Romans erected magnificent temples and other buildings, enhancing the already imposing appearance of the city.

Even under the Seleucids the inhabitants had gained a reputation for energy, insolence, and instability, which manifested itself in a series of revolts against Roman rule. Nevertheless, Antioch was renowned for its culture, being commended in this respect by no less a person than Cicero. Close by the city were the renowned groves of Daphne, and a sanctuary dedicated to Apollo, where orgiastic rites were celebrated in the name of religion. Despite the bad moral tone, life in Antioch at the beginning of the Christian era was rich and varied.

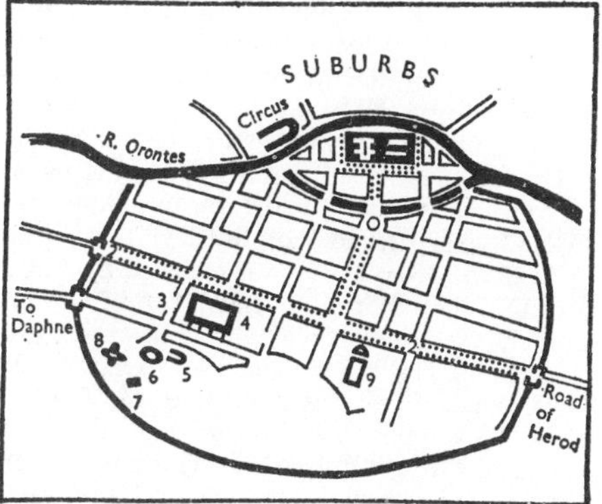

Fig. 8. Plan of Syrian Antioch in New Testament Times. *Key:* (1) Palace; (2) Street of Colonnades; (3) Forum; (4) Museum; (5) Theatre; (6) Amphitheatre; (7) Baths of Caesar; (8) Baths of Caligula; (9) Basilica of Caesar.

Apart from Jerusalem itself, no other city was so intimately connected with the beginnings of Christianity. Acts vi. 5 records that a certain Nicolas had abandoned Greek paganism and become a member of the Jewish synagogue at Antioch. During the persecution which followed the death of Stephen, some of the disciples went as far north as Antioch (Acts xi. 19), about 300 miles from Jerusalem, and preached to the Jews. Later arrivals also took Christianity to the Greek populace, and when numerous conversions occurred the Jerusalem church sent Barnabas to Antioch. When he had assessed the situation he went to Tarsus and brought Saul back with him, where both of them taught for over a year.

The energetic nature of the Christians in Antioch was displayed in the way in which alms were sent to the mother church in Jerusalem when famine struck (Acts xi. 27–30). It was fitting that the city in which the first Gentile church was founded, and where the Christians were given, perhaps sarcastically, their characteristic name, should be the birthplace of Christian foreign missions (Acts xiii. 1). Paul and Barnabas set out from the seaport of Antioch and sailed for Cyprus. This first journey into Asia Minor concluded when Paul and Barnabas returned to Antioch and presented a report of their doings to the assembled church.

While Antioch acknowledged the spiritual primacy of Jerusalem, it did not subscribe in every detail to the evangelistic views current there. From the beginning the church at Antioch had favoured a ministry to Jews and Gentiles alike, and matters came to a head when some Jews visited Antioch and proclaimed the necessity of circumcision for Gentiles as a prerequisite to becoming Christians. Resisting this principle, the church at Antioch sent a deputation headed by Paul and Barnabas to Jerusalem to debate the matter.

With James presiding, the question of whether or not circumcision was to be obligatory for Gentile Christians was discussed thoroughly. Peter had already encountered the difficulties involved in the relationships between Jews and Gentiles at other than commercial levels (Acts x. 28). Although appearing favourable to such contacts, he had been censured by the Jerusalem church for eating in uncircumcised company (Acts xi. 3; *cf.* Gal. ii. 12). While uncertain about the Gentiles having equality with Jewish Christians, he nevertheless acknowledged that God had not differentiated between them in the days after Pentecost.

Probably this recognition ultimately decided the issue. After Paul had related the blessings which the Gentiles had received, James ruled that abstinence from blood, things strangled, idolatry, and immorality would alone be required of Gentile converts. Paul returned to Antioch as the recognized apostle to the uncircumcision (Acts xv. 22–26).

Paul began and ended his second missionary journey at Antioch. This notable city saw also the start of his third missionary visitation. Its evangelistic zeal afforded Antioch great status in the subsequent history of the church. Archaeological excavations at the site (Antakya) have unearthed over twenty ruined churches dating from the fourth century AD. R.K.H.

ANTIOCHUS was the name of thirteen kings of the Seleucid Dynasty which in the forty years following the death of Alexander the Great in 323 BC had become master of Asia Minor, Syria, and the more westerly of Alexander's eastern dominions. Being a Hellenistic Dynasty, they sought to maintain hold of this vast empire by founding or resettling a chain of Graeco-Macedonian cities throughout its length and breadth. Antioch on the Orontes was their capital, with Seleucia on the Tigris a second capital administering the eastern provinces.

Antiochus I was the son of Seleucus I, founder of the dynasty, and Apama I. Joint-king with his father from 292, he succeeded him early in 280 and ruled until his death on 1 or 2 June, 261. About 275 he was honoured with the title *Sōtēr* ('saviour') for delivering several cities of Asia Minor from the Gauls: he founded many Hellenistic cities. During his reign there was much conflict with the Ptolemaic Dynasty of Egypt.

Antiochus II, the younger son of Antiochus I and Stratonice, succeeded his father in 261. He liberated Ephesus, Ionia, Cilicia, and Pamphylia from Egyptian domination, and in return for their autonomy the cities of Asia Minor gave him the title *Theos* ('god'). He banished his first wife, his cousin Laodice, and her two sons and two daughters, and in 252 married Berenice, daughter of Ptolemy II Philadelphus of Egypt. He died in 246.

Antiochus III, the younger son of Seleucus II and grandson of Antiochus II and Laodice, succeeded his older brother Alexander Seleucus III Soter on the latter's assassination in 223. While reducing southern Syria and Palestine in 217 he was defeated at Raphia by Ptolemy IV Philopator of Egypt, but a victory at Panion (the New Testament Caesarea Philippi) in 198 BC gave him secure control of those regions, formerly part of the empire of the Ptolemies. After putting down two domestic revolts, he led a victorious army east as far as Bactria to regain the old Seleucid Empire: for this he was called by the Greeks 'the Great' as he had assumed the Achaemenid title of the 'Great King'. Campaigns in Asia Minor and Greece resulted in successive defeats by Rome, culminating in the battle of Magnesia (189) and the subsequent Treaty of Apamea, by which he ceded to Rome all Asia Minor north and west of the Taurus Mountains. In 187 he died and was succeeded by his son Seleucus IV Philopator.

Antiochus IV, the youngest son of Antiochus III and Laodice III, succeeded his brother Seleucus IV in 175. Until 170/169 he reigned with his nephew Antiochus, Seleucus' baby son, who was murdered in Antiochus' absence by Andronicus, who arranged also the assassination of Onias III, the illegally deposed high priest, and was himself rewarded with execution (2 Macc. iv. 32–38). During his reign there was much intrigue for the high-priesthood on the part of Jason and Menelaus, and because of their misbehaviour Antiochus visited Jerusalem in 169 and insisted on entering the holy of holies, and carried off some of the gold and silver vessels. Pressure from Egypt convinced him of the necessity to hellenize Palestine, and measures against the old religion resulted in the cessation of the sacrifices in the Temple and the erection of a Greek altar on the site of the old one on 25 December 167. The revolt led by Mattathiah of the house of Hashmon and his five sons led to the reconsecration of the Temple just three years later. Antiochus, who on coins of the later years of his reign called himself (*Theos*) *Epiphanēs*, '(god) manifest', died on campaign in Media in 164.

Fig. 9. Coin of Antiochus IV Epiphanes, showing him beardless and wearing a diadem.

Antiochus V Eupator, son of Epiphanes and Laodice, was put to death by the army in 162 on the arrival in Syria of his cousin Demetrius I Soter, the younger son of Seleucus IV and Epiphanes' rightful successor.

Antiochus VI Epiphanes Dionysus, the infant son of the pretender Alexander Balas (ruled 150–145), was put forward as king by Diodotus (Tryphon) in 143, dethroned by him in 142 and murdered by him in 138.

Antiochus VII Sidetes, son of Demetrius I Soter, deposed Tryphon in 138 and ruled until 130/129. After his decree to the Jews (1 Macc. xv. 1–9), permitting them to coin their own money for the first time, he invaded and subdued Judaea in 134, granting the people religious freedom.

The rest of the history of the dynasty is a story of constant rivalry for the throne. Antiochus VIII Grypus (nephew of Sidetes) ruled from 123/122 to 113, when he was expelled by Antiochus IX Philopator (Cyzicenus), son of Grypus' mother, Cleopatra Thea, and Sidetes. Grypus returned in 111 and regained all except Coele-Syria, which Cyzicenus ruled until his death in 95. In 96 Grypus died, and among subsequent contestants for the throne bearing this name were two sons of Grypus (Antiochus XI Epiphanes Philadelphus and Antiochus XII Dionysus), and a son and grandson of Cyzicenus (Antiochus X Eusebes Philopator and Antiochus XIII Asiaticus). The last-named ruled from 69 to 65 and was the last of the Seleucid monarchs: in his settlement of the East in 63 Pompey annexed Syria to Rome.

BIBLIOGRAPHY. *Cambridge Ancient History*, VI–IX *passim*; J. Bright, *History of Israel*, chapters iii, iv; D. J. Wiseman in *Iraq*, XVI, 1954, pp. 202–211. D.H.W.

ANTIPAS. An abbreviation of Antipater. **1.** Herod Antipas, who ordered the execution of

Fig. 10. Coin of Herod Antipas. *Obverse* shows a palm-branch, surrounded by the legend *Herodou Tetrarchou* ('Of Herod the Tetrarch'), and in the field, to left and right, the abbreviation for 'Year 33' (*i.e.* AD 30). *Reverse* shows a wreath surrounding the legend *Tiberias* (the city of Tiberias, on the Lake of Galilee, founded by Antipas in AD 22).

John the Baptist. See HEROD. **2.** A martyr of the church of Pergamum (Rev. ii. 13), who tradition states was roasted in a brazen bowl during Domitian's reign. J.D.D.

ANTIPATRIS. Formerly Kaphar-Saba, the modern Ras el-'Ain, this city, about 26 miles south of Caesarea on the road to Lydda, was rebuilt by Herod the Great in memory of his father Antipater (Josephus, *Ant.* xvi. 5. 2; *BJ* i. 21. 9). Paul was taken there on his way from Jerusalem to Caesarea (Acts xxiii. 31). Vespasian occupied it in AD 68 (*BJ* iv. 8. 1). Codex Sinaiticus reads *Antipatris* instead of *patris* (home-country) in Mt. xiii. 54, with *anti-* subsequently crossed out. See also APHEK.

D.H.W.

ANTONIA, TOWER OF. See JERUSALEM.

APE. Listed among the valuable cargo brought home by Solomon's trading vessels (1 Ki. x. 22; 2 Ch. ix. 21). Heb. *qôp̄* is a loan-word from Egyp. *g(i)f, gwf,* 'monkey'. We know also that these animals featured among cargoes brought back to Egypt by her Red Sea fleets from 'Punt', a land possibly located in Somaliland or SW Arabia, or both.

K.A.K.

APELLES. Greeted by Paul as a tried Christian (Rom. xvi. 10). Lightfoot (*Philippians*, p. 174) found the name—which was often adopted by Jews (*cf.* Horace, *Sat.* i. s. 100)—in Imperial household circles: Lagrange *in loc.* notes the sculptured contemporary Apelles in *CIL*, VI, 9183, just possibly Christian. Some MSS have 'Apelles' for 'Apollos' at Acts xviii. 24, xix. 1, perhaps through Origen's guess that they might be identical.

A.F.W.

APHEK, APHEKAH (*'ᵃp̄ēq[â]*, 'fortress, enclosure'). Aphek occurs as a place-name in Egyptian Texts (execration texts, inscriptions of Amen-hotep II, Rameses II and III), and in an Aramaic letter of *c.* 600 BC. An inscription of Esarhaddon mentions '*Apku* in the territory of Samaria' (see *ANET*, 242, 246, 292, 329). The biblical references are as follows:

1. Jos. xiii. 4. Defining the land remaining to be occupied to the north. Probably Afqa north-east of Beirut at the source of Nahr Ibrahim (*BDB*; Abel, *Géographie de la Palestine*, p. 247). By a different interpretation of the text it is located at Ras el-'Ain (*cf. GTT*, p. 110).

2. Jos. xii. 18; 1 Sa. iv. 1, xxix. 1. Later Antipatris (*q.v.*), modern Ras el-'Ain at the source of the Nahr el-'Auǵā (Jarkon of Jos. xix. 46) on the trunk road to Egypt.

3. Jos. xix. 30; Jdg. i. 31 (Aphik). In Asher, modern Tell Kurdaneh at the source of Nahr Na'amein which flows into the Bay of Haifa.

4. 1 Ki. xx. 26, 30; 2 Ki. xiii. 17. Fīq or Afīq at the head of Wadi Fīq, east of the sea of Galilee.

5. Jos. xv. 53 (Aphekah). South-west of Hebron, either Khirbet eḍ-ḍarrame (A. Alt, *Palästinajahrbuch*, 28, pp. 16 f.) or Khirbet Kana'an (Abel, *op. cit.*, p. 247).

A.R.M.

APOCALYPSE. See REVELATION, BOOK OF.

APOCALYPTIC. The word designates both a distinct type of Jewish and Christian literature and the kind of religion usually expressed in this literature.

Jewish apocalyptic is a product of a distinct historical situation. After the post-exilic prophets, no further prophets appeared in Israel. Prophetic inspiration had ceased; God no longer spoke through a living voice. Furthermore, the times were evil. The promised messianic salvation did not appear. Instead of God's kingdom, a succession of pagan kings ruled over God's people; and in the days of Antiochus Epiphanes (168 BC), the Jewish faith was proscribed and faithful Jews suffered fearful persecution. To fill this vacuum, apocalyptic writings appeared between 200 BC and AD 100, which purported to bring revelations from God explaining the reason for the prevalence of evil, disclosing heavenly secrets, and promising the imminent coming of His kingdom and the salvation of the afflicted.

The most outstanding of the Jewish apocalypses are *First or Ethiopic Enoch*, a composite work written during the last two centuries BC, but probably compiled in the first century AD, *Jubilees*, second century BC, *Assumption of Moses*, late first century BC, *4 Ezra* or *2 Esdras* and the *Apocalypse of Baruch*, both written in the late first century AD, and *2 or Slavonic Enoch*, date uncertain. *The Testaments of the Twelve Patriarchs*, second century BC, includes forecasts of the future destiny of each tribe. Other apocalypses have been found in the Qumran literature but have not yet been published. The *Psalms of Solomon*, mid-first century BC, and *Sibylline Oracles* are often included in this genre of literature, but they are not really apocalypses, although they include elements of apocalyptic eschatology. Certain characteristics mark this literature.

1. It is professedly *revelatory*. In the absence of a living prophetic voice, these writings relate alleged revelations attained through dreams, visions, and heavenly journeys.

2. It is *imitative*. Modern scholarship recognizes that with the possible exception of *4 Ezra*, this literature does not record real visionary experiences. The revelations are an imitative literary device to convey a message to the author's contemporaries. The visions of the prophets, especially of Daniel, provided an archetype which these authors imitated.

3. It is *pseudonymous*. Since the Spirit of inspiration no longer spoke through living prophets, the apocalyptists placed their revelations in the mouth of an Old Testament saint. This technique was employed to validate the message to its own generation.

4. It habitually employs *symbolism*. The prophets had made frequent use of symbolism, and the visions of Daniel had employed symbolism in a new way to outline the course of history and its great redemptive crises. The apocalyptists drew heavily upon this type of symbolism, often going to bizarre extremes in the employment of a veritable menagerie picturing Israel's history and prophesying the coming of God's kingdom.

5. It is *pseudo-predictive*. Because the revelations were placed in the mouths of Old Testa-

ment saints, they embodied alleged disclosures of the future from the pseudo-author's time to the days of the actual author when the kingdom of God was expected immediately to appear. The apocalyptists rewrote history under the guise of prophecy to interpret to their contemporaries their evil plight and to assure them that God was about to bring His kingdom.

'Apocalyptic' is used also to describe the religious outlook of this literature. 'Eschatology' refers to the last things; 'apocalyptic' is a particular kind of eschatology embodying a number of distinctive characteristics which are developments of elements found in prophetic religion.

1. *Dualism.* The prophets placed the final redemption in this world. The new order to be established by the coming of God's kingdom, however, while continuous with the present historical order, would nevertheless be different in that suffering, violence, and evil would be no more (Is. xi. 6–9). This new era would be introduced by a visitation of God, not by forces working immanently in history (Is. xxvi. 21, xxiv. 1–3). The apocalyptists further developed this contrast between the present and the future until there emerged the concept of two ages: this age and the age to come. This so-called dualism is temporal and historical, not metaphysical or cosmic, and apart from the New Testament attains fully developed form in *4 Ezra* and the *Apocalypse of Baruch*. This age is evil; the age to come will be the age of God's kingdom.

2. *Determinism.* The coming of the new age rests entirely in God's hands and cannot be hastened or delayed by men. The evil age must run its course and the kingdom must await the end of this age. This idea often led to speculations about the times and to the dividing of time into a series of predetermined periods by which the time of the end could be calculated.

3. *Pessimism.* The apocalyptists looked for the ultimate triumph of God's kingdom in the age to come but were pessimistic about this age. God had withdrawn His help from the righteous and the problem of evil was a complete enigma apart from the coming of the new age.

4. *Ethical passivity.* The apocalyptic writings did not announce God's judgments on His people as did the prophets. The problem of the apocalyptists consisted in the fact that Israel was righteous but still suffered undeservedly. Most apocalyptic writings lack a strong note of moral and ethical urgency; the *Testaments of the Twelve Patriarchs* is a notable exception.

A distinction must be drawn between biblical and non-biblical apocalyptic, although this is not always recognized. The characteristics listed above describe Jewish apocalyptic but do not apply at all points to biblical apocalyptic. New Testament religion is apocalyptic in that it shares the dualistic structure of the two ages; but it is not deterministic or pessimistic or ethically passive. Although God's kingdom comes from without and is not the product of history, it is now working in history and will finally transform it.

The Apocalypse of John, while sharing certain of the apocalyptic traits, stands apart at other points. It is not pseudonymous but bears the name of the author, who writes as a prophet. It employs apocalyptic symbolism, but John takes his stand in his own day and looks into the future rather than rewrites history as pseudo-prophecy. John does not share the pessimism of the apocalyptists who despaired of history and saw hope only in the age to come. God was working redemptively both in history and at the end of history. This is portrayed by the lion who is the slain lamb (Rev. v. 5, 6). History is the scene of redemption. Only the Crucified One can solve the riddle of history. Finally, John possesses the moral urgency of the prophets, rebuking a faithless Church and demanding repentance to avoid the divine judgment (ii. 5, 16, 21, 22, iii. 3, 19). See also ESCHATOLOGY; PSEUDEPIGRAPHA.

BIBLIOGRAPHY. H. H. Rowley, *The Relevance of Apocalyptic*, 1947; R. H. Charles, *The Apocrypha and Pseudepigrapha of the Old Testament*, 1913; G. E. Ladd, 'Why Not Prophetic-Apocalyptic?', *JBL*, LXXVI, 1957, pp. 192–200; *id.*, 'The Revelation and Jewish Apocalyptic', *EQ*, XXIX, 1957, pp. 94–100; S. B. Frost, *Old Testament Apocalyptic*, 1952.

G.E.L.

APOCRYPHA.

I. DEFINITION

The term 'apocrypha' (neuter plural of the Gk. adjective *apokryphos*, 'hidden') is a technical term concerning the relation of certain books to the Old Testament Canon, signifying that, while they are not approved for public lection, they are nevertheless valued for private study and edification. The term covers a number of additions to canonical books in their LXX form (*viz.* Esther, Daniel, Jeremiah, Chronicles), and other books, legendary, historical, or theological, many originally written in Hebrew or Aramaic but preserved or known until recently only in Greek; these figure in the loosely defined LXX Canon, but were rejected from the Hebrew Canon at Jamnia (see CANON). Christian usage and opinion about their status were somewhat ambiguous until the 16th century, when twelve works were included in the Canon of the Roman Church by the Council of Trent; but Protestant thought (*e.g.* Luther, and the English Church in the Thirty-Nine Articles) admitted them only for private edification. Works other than the twelve here under discussion are nowadays usually termed 'pseudepigrapha' (*q.v.*). These, too, were freely drawn upon before the 16th century in the outlying Eastern churches in whose languages alone they have been preserved (*e.g.* Ethiopic, Armenian, Slavonic).

II. CONTENTS

We may proceed to summarize the contents and chief critical problems of the twelve books which go to make up what we know today as the Apocrypha.

1 Esdras in EVV is called 2 Esdras in the Lucianic recension of the LXX, and 3 Esdras in Jerome's Vulg. This gives a parallel account of events recorded in Chronicles–Ezra–Nehemiah, with one large addition (*viz.* the 'Debate of the Three Youths' in iii. 1–v. 6). i. 1–20, 23–25 = 2 Ch. xxxv. 1–xxxvi. 21; ii. 1–11 = Ezr. i. 1–11; ii. 12–26 = Ezr. iv. 7–24; v. 7–71 = Ezr. ii. 1–iv. 5; vi. 1–ix. 36 = Ezr. v. 1–x. 44; ix. 37–55 = Ne. vii. 72–viii. 13. The 'Debate of the Three Youths' is an adaptation of a Persian tale, and in its details evidence of this may still be discerned: it is adapted as the means whereby Zerubbabel, guardsman of Darius, by winning a debate on the strongest power (wine, women, or Truth?), gains opportunity to remind the Persian monarch of his obligation to allow the Temple to be rebuilt. Detailed comparison of it with the LXX Ezra shows that the two are independent translations from the *MT*: 1 Esdras is probably the earlier of the two. They present contrasts not only of text but also in chronological order of events and of the Persian kings. In a number of these cases scholarship is still undecided as to which work to follow. Certainly in some cases 1 Esdras provides good textual evidence. It is a free and idiomatic translation, and was known to Josephus.

2 Esdras in EVV is 4 Esdras in the Vulg.; it is also called the Apocalypse of Ezra. This version, as it now stands in the Old Latin, is an expansion by Christian writers of an original Jewish apocalyptic work found in chapters iv–xiv. The other chapters, *i.e.* the Christian additions, are lacking in some Oriental versions. The original body of the book consists of seven visions. In the first (iii. 1–v. 19) the seer demands an explanation of the suffering of Zion, whose sin is not greater than that of her oppressor. The angel Uriel answers that this cannot be understood, but that the era shortly to dawn will bring salvation. The second (v. 20–vi. 34) deals with a similar problem —why Israel, God's chosen, has been delivered up to other nations; this, too, is declared to be incomprehensible to men. The age to come will follow this age without interval, preceded by signs of the end and a time of conversion and salvation. This should give comfort to the seer. The third vision (vi. 35–ix. 25) asks why the Jews do not possess the earth; the answer is given that they will inherit it in the age to come. Various other matters about the after-life and the age to come are dealt with, including the fewness of the elect. The fourth vision (ix. 26–x. 59) is of a mourning woman who recounts her woes, and is thereupon transformed into a glorious city. This is a symbol of Jerusalem. The fifth vision (x. 60–xii. 51) is of a twelve-winged and three-headed eagle—the symbol of Rome, which is explicitly declared by the interpreting angel to be the fourth kingdom of Daniel vii. The Messiah is to supplant it. By the most probable interpretation, this vision is to be dated in the reign of Domitian. The sixth vision (xiii. 1–58) is of a man arising from the sea, and annihilating an antagonistic multitude. This is an adaptation of the Son of Man vision of Daniel vii. The final vision (xiv) deals with the distinct topic of Ezra's restoration of the sacred books of the Hebrews, by means of a vision and with the help of supernaturally aided scribes. There are ninety-four such books, *viz.* the twenty-four of the Hebrew Canon and seventy esoteric or apocalyptic works.

Tobit is a pious short story of a righteous Hebrew of the northern captivity, Tobit, and his son Tobias. Tobit suffers persecution and privations because of his succour of fellow Israelites under the tyranny of Esarhaddon. At length he is blinded accidentally; and to his shame, his wife is obliged to support him. He prays that he may die. At the same time, prayer is offered by Sarah, a young Hebrew woman in Ecbatana, who is haunted by the demon Asmodaeus, who has slain seven suitors on their wedding night with her. The angel Raphael is sent 'to heal them both'. Tobias is sent by his father to collect ten silver talents left in Media. Raphael takes on the form of Azariah, who is hired as a travelling companion. In the Tigris a fish is caught, and its heart, liver, and gall are preserved by Tobias on Azariah's advice. Tobias arrives in Ecbatana and becomes betrothed to Sarah, who is found to be his cousin. On the bridal night he burns the heart and liver of the fish, the stench of which drives the demon away to Egypt. On his return home (preceded by his dog), where he had been given up as lost, Tobias anoints his father's eyes with the fish-gall and restores his sight. The story apparently originated in the Babylonian or Persian Exile, and its original language is likely to have been Aramaic. Three Greek recensions are known, and fragments in Hebrew and Aramaic have been found by the Dead Sea.

Judith tells the story of a courageous young Jewess, a widow, and the overthrow of Nebuchadrezzar's host by her guile. A native of Bethulia, besieged by Holofernes, she visits him in his camp, under the ruse of giving military secrets away: she then begins to entice him by her charms, until at length, banqueting with him alone at night, she is able to behead him. She then returns with his head to the city, greeted by rejoicing. The Assyrian(!) host retreats on the discovery of its general's assassination. Judith and the women of Bethulia rejoice in a psalm before God. The story is frank fiction—otherwise its inexactitudes would be incredible—and dates from the 2nd century BC. Its original was Hebrew, and a Greek translation in four recensions has preserved the tale for us.

Additions to Daniel are found in the LXX and Theodotion's translation. To chapter iii is added the **Prayer of Azariah** uttered in the furnace and the **Song of the Three Holy Children** (*i.e. paidōn*, 'servants') sung to God's praise as the three walk about in the fire. This is the Benedicite of Christian worship. These two additions evidently existed in a Hebrew original. Prefaced to Daniel in Theodotion but following in LXX, is the story of **Susanna.** She is the beautiful and virtuous wife of a wealthy Jew in Babylon. Two elders of the people who lust after her come upon her bathing and offer her the alternatives of yielding to their desire or facing false accusation as an adulteress. She chooses the latter: her detractors are believed, and she is condemned protesting her innocence. Daniel, though but a mere youth, cries out against the injustice of this, and in a second trial before him the lie is uncovered and the woman justified. The stories of **Bel and the Dragon** are plainly written to ridicule idolatry. Daniel shows that the priests of Bel, and not the image of the god, devour the nightly offering of food; the king thereupon destroys the image. A mighty dragon worshipped in Babylon is destroyed by Daniel. He is thrown into the lions' den and is preserved alive for six days; on the sixth the prophet Habakkuk is miraculously transported from Judaea to give him food; on the seventh he is released by the king. These two stories are probably translated from a Semitic original, but the matter is not finally decided. These additions are examples of pious legendary embroidery of the Daniel story and date from about 100 BC.

Additions to Esther considerably increase the size of the Greek version of the book. There are six additional passages. The first deals with Mordecai's dream and his prevention of a conspiracy against the king; it precedes chapter i. The second is the king's edict for the destruction of all Jews in his realm. This follows iii. 13 of the Hebrew. The third comprises prayers of Esther and Mordecai to follow chapter iv. The fourth describes Esther's audience with the king, to supplement v. 12. The fifth is the king's edict permitting Jewish self-defence, to follow viii. 12. The sixth includes the interpretation of Mordecai's dream; and an historical note giving the date of the bringing of the Greek version into Egypt. The majority of scholars consider that all this is in fact addition to the shorter work of the Hebrew Canon, and that some, if not all, was composed in Greek. Scholars of the Roman obedience and a minority of others (including C. C. Torrey) argue, however, that the Hebrew is an abbreviation of a larger work, in Hebrew or Aramaic, of which the Greek is a translation. The colophon claims that the work was translated in Palestine some time before 114 BC, by one Lysimachus, son of Ptolemy, a Jerusalemite.

The Prayer of Manasses claims to give the prayer of which record is made in 2 Ch. xxxiii. 11–19. In the opinion of most scholars it is a Jewish composition and probably was written originally in Hebrew. However this may be, it is first attested in the Syriac Didascalia (3rd century AD), and found also among the Odes (*i.e.* hymns from the Old and New Testaments used in Christian worship) appended to the Psalms in some LXX MSS, such as the Codex Alexandrinus.

The Epistle of Jeremiah is a typical Hellenistic–Jewish attack on idolatry in the guise of a letter from Jeremiah to the exiles in Babylon, similar to that mentioned in Je. xxix. Idols are ridiculed; the evils and follies connected with them are exposed, and the captive Jews are told neither to worship nor to fear them. It is written in good Greek, but it may have had an Aramaic original.

The Book of Baruch is allegedly the work of the friend and scribe of Jeremiah. The work is brief, but, in the opinion of most scholars, it is a composite work, variously attributed to two, three, or four authors. It falls into the following sections. (*a*) i. 1–iii. 8. In the setting of the Babylonian Exile of 597, Baruch is depicted as addressing the exiles, setting out a confession of sins, a prayer for forgiveness, and a prayer for salvation. (*b*) iii. 9–iv. 4. This section sets out the praises of Wisdom which may be found in the law of Moses, and without which the heathen have come to naught, but with which Israel will be saved. (*c*) iv. 5–v. 9. A lament of Jerusalem over the exiles, followed by an exhortation to Jerusalem to be comforted, since her children will be brought back to their home. The first part was patently written in Hebrew, and, although the Greek of the two later sections is more idiomatic, a plausible case for a Hebrew original can be made.

Ecclesiasticus is the name given in its Greek dress to the Wisdom of Joshua ben-Sira. He was a Palestinian living in Jerusalem, and parts of his work survive in the original Hebrew in MSS of the Cairo Geniza. The work figures in Greek among the apocrypha in the translation made by his grandson, who furnishes chronological details in a preface. The most likely date for Ben-Sira himself is *c.* 180 BC, since his grandson apparently migrated to Egypt in the reign of Ptolemy VII Euergetes (170–117 BC). The author composed his work in two parts, chapters i–xxiii and xxiv–l, with a short appendix, chapter li. Like the Wisdom books, it is advice for a successful life conceived in the widest sense; fear of the Lord and the observance of His law are allied in the author's experience and teaching with practical 'wisdom' drawn from observation and his own life. Personal piety will express itself in the observance of the law, in which Wisdom is revealed; and in daily living moderation will be the key-note of all aspects of life. The second book concludes with the praise of famous men, a list of the worthies of Israel, ending with Simon II the high priest (*c.* 200 BC), who is known also from the Mishnah (*Aboth* i. 2) and Josephus (*Ant.* xii. 3. 4). The book represents the beginnings of the ideal of the scribe, such as Ben-Sira himself, which became the type of orthodox Jewry—devoted to God, obedient to the law, sober in living, and setting the highest value on learning in the law. It became a favourite Christian book, as its title ('the Church-book') shows; and though never canonical among the Jews, it was held in high honour by them, being occasionally cited by the Rabbis as if it were Scripture. The Syriac version is of Jewish origin and is based directly upon the Hebrew text.

The Wisdom of Solomon is perhaps the highlight of Jewish Wisdom writing. Its roots are in the stream of Wisdom literature which is to be found in the Old Testament and Apocrypha, but here under the influence of Greek thought the book achieves a greater formality and precision than other examples of this literary type. The book is an exhortation to seek Wisdom. Chapters i–v declare the blessings which accrue upon the Jews who are the seekers after Wisdom; chapters vi–ix speak the praises of the divine Wisdom, hypostatized as a feminine celestial being, foremost of the creatures and servants of God; chapters x–xix review Old Testament history in illustration of the theme that throughout it Wisdom has helped her friends the Jews, and has brought punishment and damnation upon her adversaries. The work may thus be interpreted as an encouragement to Jews not to forsake their ancestral faith, but the missionary motive so evident in Hellenistic Judaism is not lacking. The author drew on sources in Hebrew, but it appears clear that the work as it stands was composed in Greek, since its prosody is Greek, and it makes use of Greek terms of philosophy and depends on the Greek version of the Old Testament. The description of Wisdom, in which Stoic and Platonic terminology is utilized, and the author's convictions about the immortality of the soul, are the points at which his dependence on Greek thought is most clearly in evidence. In the opinion of most scholars there are no conclusive arguments for subdividing the authorship of the book, but various sources may be discerned. The author of the book is unknown, but an Alexandrian origin is most likely.

Several works are entitled **Maccabees**: of these, two figure in the Apocrypha as printed in the English versions. These are the historical works **1 and 2 Maccabees. 1 Maccabees** covers events between 175 and 134 BC, *i.e.* the struggle with Antiochus Epiphanes, the wars of the Hasmonaeans, and the rule of John Hyrcanus. The book ends with a panegyric on John and was evidently written just after his death in 103 BC. Originally written in Hebrew, it is translated in the literal style of parts of the LXX. The aim of the work is to glorify the family of the Maccabees seen as the champions of Judaism. **2 Maccabees** is a work of different origin: its subject-matter covers much of the same history as its namesake, but does not continue the history beyond the campaigns and defeat of Nicanor. Its unknown author is sometimes called the 'epitomist', since much of his book is excerpted from the otherwise unknown work of Jason of Cyrene. There are a number of discrepancies in chronological and numerical matters between the two works, and it is customary to place more reliance on 1 Maccabees. There is debate also over the historical value of the letters and edicts which figure in the two works. Nevertheless, neither work is to be discredited as an historical source. **3 and 4 Maccabees** are found in a number of MSS of the LXX. The former is an account of pogroms and counter-pogroms under Ptolemy IV (221–204 BC) not unlike the book of Esther in tone and ethos. 4 Maccabees is not a narrative but a diatribe or tract on the rule of reason over the passions, illustrated from biblical stories and the martyr stories of 2 Maccabees vi and vii. The writer seeks to enhance the law, though he is greatly influenced by Stoicism. (See also NEW TESTAMENT APOCRYPHA.)

BIBLIOGRAPHY. R. H. Charles (ed.), *The Apocrypha and Pseudepigrapha of the Old Testament*, 1913; *id.*, *Religious Development between the Old and New Testaments*, 1914; C. C. Torrey, *The Apocryphal Literature*, 1945; R. H. Pfeiffer, *History of New Testament Times with an Introduction to the Apocrypha*, 1949; B. M. Metzger, *An Introduction to the Apocrypha*, 1957.

J.N.B.

APOLLONIA. A town on the Via Egnatia some 27 miles west-south-west of Amphipolis. It lay between the rivers Strymon and Axius (Vardar), but its site is not known for certain. Paul and Silas passed through it on their way from Philippi to Thessalonica (Acts xvii. 1). There were several other towns named Apollonia in the Mediterranean area. K.L.McK.

APOLLOS. An Alexandrian Jew (Acts xviii. 24). The name is abbreviated from Apollonius. He came to Ephesus in AD 52 during Paul's hasty visit to Palestine (Acts xviii. 22). He had accurate knowledge of the story of Jesus, which may have come to him (possibly at Alexandria) either from Galilaean disciples of our Lord or from some early written Gospel. He combined natural gifts of eloquence (or learning) with a profound understanding of the Old Testament, and he was enthusiastic in proclaiming such truth as he knew (Acts xviii. 24, 25). The conspicuous gap in his knowledge concerned the outpouring of the Holy Ghost and the consequent rite of Christian baptism. This was made good by the patient instruction of Priscilla and Aquila (Acts xviii. 26). From Ephesus Apollos went on to Corinth, where he showed himself to be an expert at Christian apologetics in dealing with the Jews (Acts xviii. 27, 28). At Corinth there sprang up factions in the names of Paul, Apollos, Cephas, and Christ Himself (1 Cor. i. 12). Paul seeks to show that this was not due to himself or Apollos, who were both working together under the hand of God (1 Cor. iii. 4–6). All belonged to the Corinthians, including himself and Apollos (1 Cor. iii. 21–23), and there could be no cause for party spirit (1 Cor. iv. 6). The factions were probably due to the preference of some for the polished eloquence of Apollos. His desire to lessen the controversy may be the reason for his not returning to Corinth despite Paul's request (1 Cor. xvi. 12). He is mentioned finally as making some sort of journey in Tit. iii. 13.

Since the time of Luther, Apollos has often been suggested as the author of the Epistle to the Hebrews. This is possible, if he used the allegorical exegesis of his native Alexandria, but it is by no means proved. R.E.N.

APOLLYON. See ABADDON.

APOSTASY. The English word does not appear in AV. In classical Gk. *apostasia* is a technical term for political revolt or defection. In LXX it always relates to rebellion against God (Jos. xxii. 22; 2 Ch. xxix. 19), originally instigated by Satan, the apostate dragon of Jb. xxvi. 13.

There are two New Testament instances. Acts xxi. 21 records that Paul was maliciously accused of teaching the Jews to forsake Moses by abandoning circumcision and other traditional observances. 2 Thes. ii. 3 describes the great apostasy of prophecy, prior to the revelation of the man of lawlessness (*cf.* Mt. xxiv. 10–12). The allusion is neither to the political nor to the religious infidelity of the Jews, but is entirely eschatological in character and refers to 'the final catastrophic revolt against the authority of God which in apocalyptic writings is a sign of the end of the world' (E. J. Bicknell, *The First and Second Epistles to the Thessalonians*, 1932, p. 74). It may be regarded as the earthly counterpart of the heavenly rebellion in Rev. xii. 7–9.

Apostasy is a continual danger to the Church, and the New Testament contains repeated warnings against it (*cf.* 1 Tim. iv. 1–3; 2 Thes. ii. 3; 2 Pet. iii. 17). Its nature is made clear: falling 'from the faith' (1 Tim. iv. 1) and 'from the living God' (Heb. iii. 12). It increases in times of special trial (Mt. xxiv. 9, 10; Lk. viii. 13) and is encouraged by false teachers (Mt. xxiv. 11; Gal. ii. 4), who seduce believers from the purity of the Word with 'another gospel' (Gal. i. 6–8; 2 Tim. iv. 3, 4; 2 Pet. ii. 1, 2; Jude 3, 4). The impossibility of restoration after apostasy is solemnly urged (Heb. vi. 4–6, x. 26). A.S.W.

APOSTLE. There are over eighty occurrences of the Greek word *apostolos* in the New Testament, seven-eighths of them in Luke and Paul. It derives from the very common verb *apostellō*, to send, but in non-Christian Greek, after Herodotus in the 5th century BC, there are few recorded cases where it means 'a person sent', and it generally means 'fleet', or perhaps occasionally 'admiral'. The sense of 'sent one, messenger' may have survived in popular speech: at least, isolated occurrences in the LXX and Josephus suggest that this meaning was recognized in Jewish circles. Only with Christian literature, however, does it come into its own. In the New Testament it is applied to Jesus as the Sent One of God (Heb. iii. 1), to those sent by God to preach to Israel (Lk. xi. 49), and to those sent by churches (2 Cor. viii. 23; Phil. ii. 25); but above all it is applied absolutely to the group of men who held the supreme dignity in the primitive Church. Since *apostellō* seems frequently to mean 'to send with a particular purpose', as distinct from the neutral *pempō* (save in the Johannine writings, where the two are synonyms), the force of *apostolos* is probably 'one commissioned'—it is implied, by Christ.

It is disputed whether *apostolos* represents in the New Testament a Jewish term of similar technical force. Rengstorf, in particular, has elaborated the theory that it reflects the Jewish *šālîaḥ*, an accredited representative of religious authority, entrusted with messages and money and empowered to act on behalf of the authority (for the idea, *cf.* Acts ix. 2); and Dom Gregory Dix and others have applied ideas and expressions belonging to the *šālîaḥ* concept (*e.g.* 'a man's *šālîaḥ* is as himself') to the apostolate and eventually to the modern episcopate. Such a process is full of perils, and not least because there is no clear evidence that *šālîaḥ* was used in this sense until post-Christian times. *Apostolos*, in fact, may well be the earlier as a technical term, and it is safest to seek its significance in the meaning of *apostellō* and from the contexts of the New Testament occurrences.

a. The origin of the Apostolate

Essential to the understanding of all the Gospels as they stand is the choice by Jesus, out of the wider company of His followers, of a group of twelve men whose purpose was to be with Him, to preach, and to have authority to heal and to exorcize (Mk. iii. 14 f.). The only occasion on which Mark uses the word 'apostle' is on the successful return of the Twelve from a mission of preaching and healing (Mk. vi. 30; *cf.* Mt. x. 2 ff.). This is usually taken as a non-technical use (*i.e.* 'those sent on this particular assignment'), but it is unlikely that Mark would use it without evoking other associations. This preparatory mission is a miniature of their future task in the wider world. From this preliminary training they return 'apostles' indeed. There is then nothing incongruous in Luke (who speaks of the 'apostles' in ix. 10, xvii. 5, xxii. 14, xxiv. 10) declaring that Jesus conferred the title (already in Greek?) Himself (vi. 13).

b. The functions of the Apostolate

Mark's first specification on the choice of the Twelve is 'that they might be with him' (Mk. iii. 14). It is no accident that the watershed of Mark's Gospel is the apostolic confession of the Messiahship of Jesus (Mk. viii. 29), or that Matthew follows this with the 'Rock' saying about the apostolic confession (Mt. xvi. 18 f.; see PETER). The primary function of the apostles was witness to Christ, and the witness was rooted in years of intimate knowledge, dearly bought experience, and intensive training.

This is complementary to their widely recognized function of witness to the resurrection (*cf.*, *e.g.*, Acts i. 22, ii. 32, iii. 15, xiii. 31); for the special significance of the resurrection lies, not in the event itself, but in its demonstration, in fulfilment of prophecy, of the identity of the slain Jesus (*cf.* Acts ii. 24 ff., 36, iii. 26; Rom. i. 4). Their witness *of* the resurrection of Christ made them effective witnesses *to* His Person, and He

Himself commissions them to world-wide witness (Acts i. 8).

The same commission introduces a factor of profound importance for the apostolate: the coming of the Spirit. Curiously enough, this is most fully treated in John xiv–xvii, which does not use the word 'apostle' at all. This is the great commissioning discourse of the Twelve (*apostellō* and *pempō* are used without discrimination): their commission from Jesus is as real as His from God (*cf.* Jn. xx. 21); they are to bear witness from their long acquaintance with Jesus, yet the Spirit bears witness of Him (Jn. xv. 26, 27). He will remind them of the words of Jesus (Jn. xiv. 26), and guide them into all the truth (a promise often perverted by extending its primary reference beyond the apostles) and show them the age to come (of the Church) and Christ's glory (Jn. xvi. 13–15). Instances are given in the Fourth Gospel of this process, where the significance of words or actions was recalled only after Christ's 'glorification' (Jn. ii. 22, xii. 16, *cf.* vii. 39). That is, the witness of the apostles to Christ is not left to their impressions and recollections, but to the guidance of the Holy Spirit, whose witness it is also—a fact of consequence in assessing the recorded apostolic witness in the Gospels.

For this reason the apostles are the norm of doctrine and fellowship in the New Testament Church (Acts ii. 42; *cf.* 1 Jn. ii. 19). In their own day they were regarded as 'pillars' (Gal. ii. 9—*cf.* C. K. Barrett, in *Studia Paulina*, 1953, pp. 1 ff.)—perhaps translate 'marking posts'. The Church is built on the foundation of the apostles and prophets (Eph. ii. 20; probably the witness of the Old Testament is intended, but the point remains if Christian prophets are in mind). The apostles are the assessors at the messianic judgment (Mt. xix. 28), and their names are engraved on the foundation stones of the holy city (Rev. xxi. 14).

Apostolic doctrine, however, originating as it does with the Holy Spirit, is the *common* witness of the apostles, not the perquisite of any individual. (For the common preaching, *cf.* C. H. Dodd, *The Apostolic Preaching and its Developments*; for the common use of the Old Testament, C. H. Dodd, *According to the Scriptures.*) The chief apostle could by implication betray a fundamental principle he had accepted, and be withstood by a colleague (Gal. ii. 11 ff.).

The Synoptists, as already noted, view the incident of Mk. vi. 7 ff. and parallels as a miniature of the apostolic mission, and healing and exorcism, as well as preaching, were included. Healing, and other spectacular gifts, such as prophecy and tongues, are abundantly attested in the apostolic Church, related, like the apostolic witness, to the special dispensation of the Holy Spirit; but they are strangely missing in the 2nd-century Church, the writers of those days speaking of them as a thing in the past—in the apostolic age, in fact (*cf.* J. S. McEwan, *SJT*, VII, 1954, pp. 133 ff.; B. B. Warfield, *Miracles Yesterday and Today*). Even in the New Testament, we see no signs of these gifts except where apostles have been at work. Even where there has previously been genuine faith, it is only in the presence of apostles that these gifts of the Spirit are showered down (Acts viii. 14 ff., xix. 6—the contexts show that visual and audible phenomena are in question).

By contrast, the New Testament has less to say than might be expected of the apostles as ruling the Church. They are the touchstones of doctrine, the purveyors of the authentic tradition (*q.v.*) about Christ: apostolic delegates visit congregations which reflect new departures for the Church (Acts viii. 14 ff., xi. 22 ff.). But the Twelve did not appoint the Seven; the crucial Jerusalem Council consisted of a large number of elders as well as the apostles (Acts xv. 6, *cf.* 12, 22): and two apostles served among the 'prophets and teachers' of the church at Antioch (Acts xiii. 1). Government was a distinct gift (1 Cor. xii. 28), normally exercised by local elders: apostles were, by virtue of their commission, mobile. Nor are they even prominent in the administration of the sacraments (*cf.* 1 Cor. i. 14). The identity of function which some see between apostle and 2nd-century bishop (*cf.* K. E. Kirk in *The Apostolic Ministry*, p. 10) is by no means obvious.

c. Qualifications

It is obvious that the essential qualification of an apostle is the divine call, the commissioning by Christ. In the case of the Twelve, this was given during His earthly ministry. But with Matthias, the sense of the divine commissioning is not less evident: God has already chosen the apostle (Acts i. 24), even though His choice is not yet known. No laying on of hands is mentioned. The apostle, it is assumed, will be someone who has been a disciple of Jesus from the time of John's baptism ('the beginning of the gospel') to the ascension. He will be someone acquainted with the whole course of the ministry and work of Jesus (Acts i. 21, 22). And, of course, he must be specifically a witness of the resurrection.

Paul equally insists on his direct commission from Christ (Rom. i. 1; 1 Cor. i. 1; Gal. i. 1, 15 ff.). He in no sense derived his authority from the other apostles; like Matthias, he was accepted, not appointed by them. He did not fulfil the qualifications of Acts i. 21 f., but the Damascus road experience was a resurrection appearance (*cf.* 1 Cor. xv. 8), and he could claim to have 'seen the Lord' (1 Cor. ix. 1); he was thus a witness of the resurrection. He remained conscious that his background—an enemy and persecutor, rather than a disciple—was different from that of the other apostles, but he counts himself with their number and associates them with his own gospel (1 Cor. xv. 8–11).

d. The number of the apostles

'The Twelve' is a regular designation of the apostles in the Gospels, and Paul uses it in 1 Cor. xv. 5. Its symbolic appropriateness is obvious, and recurs in such places as Rev. xxi. 14. The whole Matthias incident is concerned with making up the number of the Twelve. Yet Paul's consciousness of apostleship is equally clear. Further, there are instances in the New Testament where, *prima facie*, others outside the Twelve seem to be given the title. James the Lord's brother appears as such in Gal. i. 19, ii. 9, and, though he was not a disciple (*cf.* Jn. vii. 5), received a resurrection appearance personal to himself (1 Cor. xv. 7). Barnabas is called an apostle in Acts xiv. 4, 14, and is introduced by Paul into an argument which denies any qualitative difference between his own apostleship and that of the Twelve (1 Cor. ix. 1–6). The unknown Andronicus (*q.v.*) and Junias are probably called apostles in Rom. xvi. 7, and Paul, always careful with his personal pronouns, may so style Silas in 1 Thes. ii. 6. Paul's enemies in Corinth evidently claim to be 'apostles of Christ' (2 Cor. xi. 13).

On the other hand, some have argued strongly for the limitation of the title to Paul and the Twelve (*cf., e.g.*, Geldenhuys, pp. 71 ff.). This involves giving a subordinate sense ('accredited messengers of the Church') to 'apostles' in Acts xiv. 14 and Rom. xvi. 7, and explaining otherwise Paul's language about James and Barnabas. Some have introduced more desperate expedients, suggesting that James replaced James bar-Zebedee as Matthias replaced Judas, or that Matthias was mistakenly hurried into the place which God intended for Paul. Of such ideas there is not the remotest hint in the New Testament. However it may be explained, it seems safest to allow that there *were*, at an early date, apostles outside the Twelve. Paul's own apostleship makes such a breach in any more restrictive theory that there is room for others of God's appointment to pass with him. A hint of this may be given in the distinction between 'the Twelve' and 'all the apostles' in 1 Cor. xv. 5, 7. But everything suggests that an apostle was a witness of the resurrection, and the resurrection appearance to Paul was clearly exceptional. Whether, as old writers suggested, some who are later called 'apostles' belonged to the Seventy sent out by the Lord (Lk. x. 1 ff.), is another matter. The special significance of the Twelve for the first establishment of the Church is beyond question.

e. Canonicity and continuity

Implied in apostleship is the commission to witness by word and sign to the risen Christ and His completed work. This witness, being grounded in a unique experience of the incarnate Christ, and directed by a special dispensation of the Holy Spirit, provides the authentic interpretation of Christ, and has ever since been determinative for the universal Church. In the nature of things, the office could not be repeated or transmitted: any more than the underlying historic experiences could be transmitted to those who had never known the incarnate Lord, or received a resurrection appearance. The origins of the Christian ministry and the succession in the Jerusalem Church are beyond the scope of this article; but, while the New Testament shows the apostles taking care that a local ministry is provided, there is no hint of the transmission of the peculiar apostolic functions to any part of that ministry.

Nor was such transmission necessary. The apostolic witness was maintained in the abiding work of the apostles and, what became normative for later ages, its written form in the New Testament (see Geldenhuys, pp. 100 ff.; O. Cullmann, 'The Tradition', in *The Early Church*, 1956). No renewal of the office or of its special gifts has been called for. It was a foundational office: and Church history ever since has been its superstructure.

See further, BISHOP, TRADITION.

BIBLIOGRAPHY. K. H. Rengstorf, *TWNT* (*Apostleship*, E.T. by J. R. Coates, 1952); J. B. Lightfoot, *Galatians*, pp. 92 ff.; K. Lake in *BC*, V, pp. 37 ff.; K. E. Kirk (ed.), *The Apostolic Ministry*², 1957, especially essays I and III; A. Ehrhardt, *The Apostolic Succession*, 1953 (see chapter I for a trenchant criticism of Kirk); J. N. Geldenhuys, *Supreme Authority*, 1953. A.F.W.

APOSTOLIC FATHERS. See PATRISTIC LITERATURE.

APOTHECARY. See COSMETICS AND PERFUMERY.

APPHIA. Addressed in Phm. 2 in a manner suggesting that she was Philemon's wife, and hostess to the Colossian church (but see under PHILEMON, EPISTLE TO). RV's text 'our sister' is probably to be preferred to AV's 'our beloved'. The name was common in W Asia and is probably native Phrygian. (See examples in Lightfoot, *Colossians*, p. 304, *MM*, and the Colossian inscription, *CIG*, III, 4380K, 3.) A.F.W.

APPII FORUM. A market town and staging-post in Latium, a foundation of Appius Claudius Caecus, the builder of the Via Appia, on which the town stands. It is 27 miles from Rome, a place 'packed with bargees and extortionate innkeepers', if the poet Horace is to be believed. The town was the northern terminus of the canal through the Pontine Marshes. It was here that the Roman Christians met Paul (Acts xxviii. 15).

E.M.B.

APPLE (*tappûaḥ*). Referred to in Canticles chiefly, this fruit's identity has long been discussed in view of the objection that Palestine is too hot and dry to allow satisfactory cultivation of the true apple (*Pyrus malus*). The Hebrew and Arabic words, however, favour this reading; the tree affords good shade, the fruit is sweet (Ct. ii. 3), and the perfume is much appreciated in the East (Ct. vii. 8), where the apple was well known and extensively cultivated in ancient times. Though most of these conditions apply also to the apricot, about which the image in Pr. xxv. 11 concerning 'apples of gold' would be more apposite, it is questionable whether the apricot was established in Palestine at this time. This objection is even more serious in the case of the citron, a third possibility. An indigenous fruit, the quince, has been suggested also, but its taste is somewhat bitter, and the Mishnah renders it by a different Hebrew word. Finally, some argue that *tappûaḥ* is used for 'gall-apple' grown in the hill-country, but this seems even less likely than the interpretations cited above. J.D.D.

AQABAH, GULF OF. See RED SEA.

AQUILA AND PRISCA, PRISCILLA. A Jewish leatherworker (AV 'tent-maker', Acts xviii. 3) and his wife, staunch friends of Paul. Aquila came from Pontus, but the couple were in Rome when Claudius's edict of *c.* AD 49 expelled all Jews from the city. Obscure words of Suetonius (*Claudius* xxv. 4) suggest that the purge followed disturbances in the Roman Jewish community over Christianity, and there is every likelihood that Aquila and Prisca were already Christians on meeting Paul in Corinth. He stayed with them and shared in their craft (Acts xviii. 1–3; an inferior reading in verse 7 adds that Paul left them after the split in the synagogue). It was doubtless in this period that they endangered their lives for his sake (Rom. xvi. 3); perhaps, too, they turned the apostle's mind to the needs and opportunities of Rome.

When Paul left, they accompanied him as far as Ephesus, where they received and assisted to a fuller faith the very influential Apollos (*q.v.*) (Acts xviii. 18–28). They were still at Ephesus, and a church was meeting in their house, when 1 Corinthians was written, and they had not forgotten their Corinthian friends (1 Cor. xvi. 19 —a gloss claims that Paul was again their guest). Not long afterwards, perhaps taking advantage of relaxations towards Jews after Claudius's death, they seem to be back in Rome (Rom. xvi. 3). Since 2 Tim. iv. 19 evidently indicates a renewal of the Ephesian residence, the references to the couple have been a primary argument for regarding Rom. xvi as a separate letter to Ephesus (*cf.* especially K. Lake, *EEP*, pp. 327 ff.); but the force of it is much reduced by the obvious propensity of Aquila and Prisca for travel.

Aquila's name is attested in Pontus (*cf. MM*)—his namesake, the translator, also came from there. The best MSS indicate that Paul uses the proper form, Prisca, for the lady, Luke, characteristically, the diminutive, Priscilla.

Rom. xvi. 3 shows how widely this peripatetic and ever-hospitable Jewish couple were known and loved in the Gentile churches, and the temptation to fill in the blanks in our knowledge about them has proved irresistible. The curious fact that Prisca is usually named first has been interpreted as indicating that she was a Roman lady of higher rank than her husband (*cf.* Ramsay, *CBP*, I, p. 637, for a contemporary analogy), or that she was more prominent in the Church. The true reason is undiscoverable. Attempts have been made to trace their final return to Rome (*cf.* Sanday and Headlam, *Romans*, pp. 418 ff., for archaeological data), or even Pontus, or to show that Aquila was a member or freedman of the *gens Pontia* or the *gens Acilia.* While some are attractive, none are conclusive; and still less is Harnack's attribution to the couple, with the lady in the lead, of the Epistle to the Hebrews.

BIBLIOGRAPHY. A. Harnack, *ZNW*, I, 1900, pp. 16 ff.; Ramsay, *SPT*, pp. 241, 253 ff. A.F.W.

AQUILA'S VERSION. See TEXT AND VERSIONS.

AR. The chief city of Moab, whose exact site is unknown. Something of the early history of the city was known to the Hebrews from records in the Book of the Wars of the Lord (Nu. xxi. 15), and popular proverbs (Nu. xxi. 28). Isaiah appears to have had access to similar sources (Is. xv. 1). In the later stages of the wilderness wanderings the Hebrews were forbidden to dispossess the Moabite inhabitants of the city and settle there themselves, for this was not the land which the Lord their God had given them. (Dt. ii. 9, 18, 29.) R.J.W.

ARABAH. In the AV the word is used only once in its original form (Jos. xviii. 18), although it is of frequent occurrence in the Hebrew text.

1. The root *'rb*, meaning 'dry', 'burnt up' and therefore 'waste land', is used to describe the desert steppe (Jb. xxiv. 5, xxxix. 6; Is. xxxiii. 9, xxxv. 1, 6; Je. li. 43).

2. Used with the article (*hā-'ᵃrāḇâ*), the name is applied generally to the rift valley which runs from the Sea of Tiberias to the Gulf of Aqabah. Although the topographical significance of this word was ignored by the earlier commentators, it has a precise connotation in many Old Testament references. Its location is connected with the lake of Tiberias (Dt. iii. 17; Jos. xi. 2, xii. 3) and as far south as the Red Sea and Elath (Dt. i. 1, ii. 8). The Dead Sea is called the Sea of Arabah (Jos. iii. 16, xii. 3; Dt. iv. 49; 2 Ki. xiv. 25). Today, the valley of the Jordan downstream to the Dead Sea is called the Ghôr, the 'depression', and the Arabah more properly begins south of the Scorpion cliffs and terminates in the Gulf of Aqabah. For its physical features see JORDAN. See also ARCHAEOLOGY.

3. The plural of the same word, 'Araboth, without the article, is used in its primary meaning to describe certain waste areas within the Arabah, especially around Jericho (Jos. v. 10; 2 Ki. xxv. 5; Je. xxxix. 5), and the wilderness of Moab. The Araboth Moab is plainly distinguished from the pastoral and cultivated lands of the plateaux above the Rift Valley, the Sede-Moab (see Nu. xxii. 1, xxvi. 3, 63, xxxi. 12, xxxiii. 48–50; Dt. xxxiv. 1, 8; Jos. iv. 13, v. 10, *etc.*).

4. Beth-arabah (the house of Arabah) refers to a settlement situated near Ain el-Gharba (Jos. xv. 6, 61, xviii. 22). J.M.H.

ARABIA.

I. IN THE OLD TESTAMENT

a. Geography

In structure the Arabian peninsula consists of a mass of old crystalline rock which forms a range of mountains on the west, rising above 10,000 feet in places, with a series of strata of younger formation uptilted against its eastern side. In the western mountains, and particularly in the south-western corner of the peninsula, where the annual rainfall exceeds 20 inches in parts, settled life based on irrigation is possible, and it was in this area, modern Yemen and the W Aden protectorate, that the ancient kingdoms of S Arabia chiefly flourished. The capitals of three of these, Qarnāw (of Ma'īn), Mārib (of Saba'), and Timna' (of Qatabān), were situated on the eastern slopes of the mountain range, on water-courses running off to the east, and Shabwa the capital of Ḥaḍramaut lay farther to the south-east on a water-course running north-westwards off the Ḥaḍramaut table-land. An area of rainfall of between 5 and 10 inches extends northwards along the western mountains and eastwards along the coast, and here settled life is also possible. In

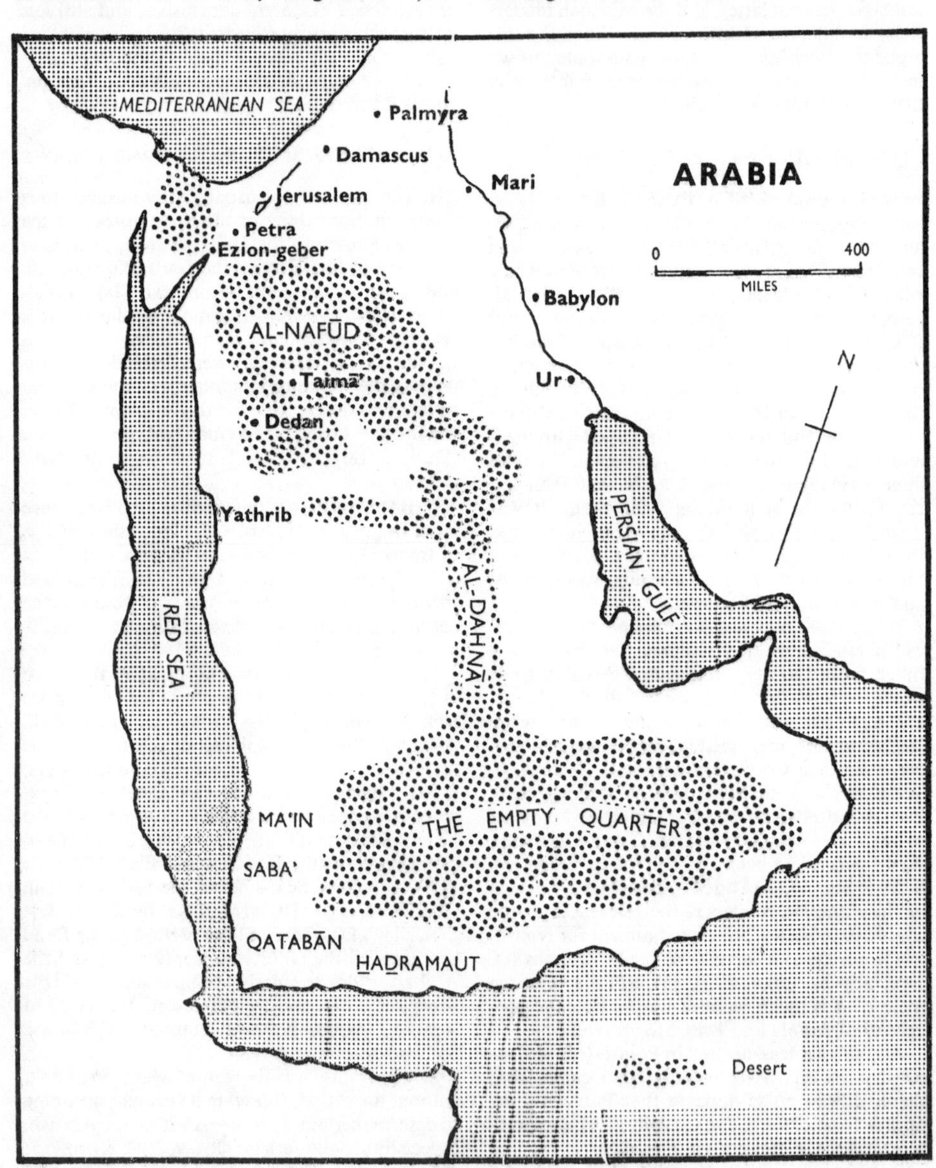

Fig. 11.

the whole of the rest of the peninsula the annual rainfall is negligible and life depends upon oases and wells.

Between the escarpments formed by the uptilted strata and the east coast the scarp slope of the uppermost provides level areas ranging from steppe to sandy desert. The zones of desert which exist in this area and between the central escarpments widen out in the south into the barren sand desert of al-Rab' al-Ḥāli ('the empty quarter'), and in the north to the smaller desert of al-Nufud. At various points along the foot of the escarpments springs provide oases, and consequent trade routes. Apart from the areas of sandy and rocky desert, the terrain of the peninsula is largely steppe, yielding grass under the sporadic annual rains, and supporting a poor nomadic population (see NOMADS), particularly in the northern area between Syria and Mesopotamia. It was where this zone graded into the settled areas of Syria that such metropolises as Petra, Palmyra, and Damascus flourished.

b. Exploration

The first notable exploration in the Arabian peninsula was carried out by the 18th-century Danish orientalist, Carsten Niebuhr, who visited the Yemen in the sixties, but it was not until the 19th century that this work was continued. In the north J. L. Burckhardt rediscovered Petra in 1812, but interest was focused on the south when Lt. J. R. Wellsted published in 1837 the first S Arabian inscriptions to be seen in Europe, an event which led to their decipherment in 1841 by W. Gesenius and E. Rödiger. These inscriptions were known as 'Ḥimyaritic', from the name of the kingdom which came to dominate the whole of the south-west of the peninsula in the last centuries BC, and was therefore considered by later historians to be the source of the inscriptions, though in fact they stemmed from the earlier kingdoms. Some thousands of these inscriptions are now known, chiefly as a result of the explorations of J. Halévy and E. Glaser in the second half of the last century, but also from numerous individual explorers, and recently from the investigations of the American Foundation for the Study of Man in Aden and the Yemen. Excavations in S Arabia have been few. In 1928 C. Rathjens and H. v. Wissmann excavated at Ḥugga near San'â in the Yemen, and in 1937–8 Miss G. Caton Thompson uncovered a temple of the moon god *(syn)* at Ḥureyḍa in the Ḥaḍramaut, but the most spectacular have been those of the American Foundation for the Study of Man at Timna' and surrounding sites (1950–1), at Mārib, where the temple of the Sabaean moon god *'lmqh* was uncovered (1952), and in subsequent expeditions in Oman.

Many explorations have been made in other parts of Arabia, notable among which are those of the Czech orientalist A. Musil, who travelled extensively in central and N Arabia (1909–14), those of N. Glueck, who since 1932 has made an exhaustive archaeological survey of Transjordan, and those of G. Ryckmans and H. St. J. Philby, who collected some thousands of Arabic inscriptions from Sa'udi Arabia in 1951–2, not to mention the travels on a lesser scale of such men as Burton, Hurgronje, Doughty, Rutter, and Thomas. Important among inscriptions from the north is the Taima' Stone, which bears an Aramaic inscription of about the 5th century BC, obtained by Huber in 1883 (see TEMA).

c. History and civilization

Apart from the nomads of the steppe lands of Arabia, whose life has continued with little change for millennia (see NOMADS), the main areas of historical civilization were in the south-west corner of the peninsula, and in the zone to the north where the steppe merges into the settled regions of Syria.

In the second millennium BC various Semitic-speaking tribes arrived from the north in the area of modern Yemen and western Aden, and formed the settlements which were later to emerge as the kingdoms of Saba' (see SABAEANS and SHEBA), Ma'īn (see MINAEANS), Qatabān, and Ḥaḍramaut (Hazarmaveth, Gn. x. 26). The main cause of their prosperity was their intermediate position on the trade routes from the frankincense lands of the south coast and Ethiopia (see FRANKINCENSE and MYRRH), to the civilizations in the north. The first of these kingdoms to emerge was Saba', as revealed by the appearance in the 8th century of native inscriptions which indicate a well-organized polity under a ruler *(mkrb)* who evidently combined certain priestly functions in his office. The extent of Sabaean trading commitments at this date is indicated by the mention of the name, perhaps referring to a northern trading colony, as a tributary in the annals of Tiglath-pileser III. Its continuing prosperity is indicated by the fact that it paid tribute also to Sargon and Sennacherib. In the 5th century the *mkrb* gave place to a king *(mlk)*, but *c.* 400 BC the neighbouring kingdom of Ma'īn came into prominence and infringed on much of Sabaean authority. In the 4th century the monarchy was founded at Qatabān, and in the last quarter of the first millennium the dominion of Saba', Ma'īn, Qatabān, and Ḥaḍramaut fluctuated with turn of fortune, until the area came under the control of the Ḥimyarites. At their height, the S Arabian kingdoms had colonies as far afield as Oman and N Arabia, and inscriptions in their characters have been found in Mesopotamia (Ur) and Palestine (Bethel). The alphabets of the Thamūdian, Liḥyānite, and Ṣafāitic inscriptions also show their influence in the north, and the Ethiopic language and script offer similar evidence from Africa.

In the north the history is one of the contacts made by nomads with the settled civilizations of Mesopotamia and Syria. In Transjordan the process of infiltration and settlement is evident, though there were periods when this was very sparse. In the early part of the Middle Bronze

Age the whole of Transjordan was dotted with settlements (see ABRAHAM), but this was followed by a barren period, *c.* 1900–1300 BC, until settlement increased again in the 13th century (see EXODUS). The 'Arabs' first appear in the contemporary inscriptions in the annals of Shalmaneser III, when one Gindibu (*(m)gin-in-di-bu-' (māt)ar-ba-a-a*; Kurkh Stele ii. 94) fought against him at Qarqar (853 BC), and thereafter they frequently appear in the Assyrian inscriptions as camel-borne raiding nomads, and they are so depicted in the bas-reliefs of Ashurbanipal at Nineveh (see CAMEL and fig. 50). One of the unusual episodes in Mesopotamian history was the sojourn at Taima' (see TEMA) in the northern Nejd of Nabonidus king of Babylon (556–539 BC), who stayed there for ten years while his son Bêl-šar-uṣur (see BELSHAZZAR) ruled for him in Babylon.

In the latter part of the 4th century BC the Aramaic-speaking Arab kingdom of the Nabataeans (*q.v.*), with its capital at Petra, began to emerge, and throve as a trading state from the 2nd century until well into the Roman period. Farther south in the same period was the Liḥyānite kingdom of Dedan (*q.v.*), which was formed by Arabs settling on top of an ancient Minaean colony. In the 1st century BC another Arab state, which adopted Aramaic as its official language, began to come to prominence at Palmyra (see TADMOR), and in the Christian era it largely replaced Petra as the trading state, and became a serious rival to Rome.

d. Biblical references

Arabia is not often referred to by this name in the Bible, since its inhabitants were generally known by the political or tribal names of the smaller groups to which they belonged. The first biblical passage to refer to the inhabitants of Arabia is the Table of the Nations (*q.v.*) in Gn. x, which lists a number of S Arabian peoples as the descendants of Joktan (*q.v.*) and of Cush (*q.v.*). Later on, a number of mainly N Arabian tribes are listed as being descended from Abraham through Keturah and Hagar (*qq.v.*; Gn. xxv). Again among the descendants of Esau (*q.v.*; Gn. xxxvi) a number of Arabian peoples are mentioned. In the time of Jacob two groups of Abraham's descendants, the Ishmaelites (see ISHMAEL) and the Midianites (*q.v.*), are found as caravan merchants (Gn. xxxvii. 25–36; see NOMADS). It is, however, in the time of Solomon that contacts with Arabia become prominent in the Old Testament narrative, mainly as a result of his extensive trade relations, particularly from his port of Ezion-geber (*q.v.*) on the Red Sea. This is emphasized by the famous visit of the Queen of Sheba (*q.v.*; 1 Ki. ix. 26–28, x), and nearer home by the tribute he received from the *malᵉḵê ʿarab* (2 Ch. ix. 14) which the EVV render 'kings of Arabia'. The name *ʿᵃrāḇ*, *ʿᵃrāḇî* seems to have originally meant 'desert' or 'steppe' and by extension 'steppe dweller', and therefore in the biblical context it referred chiefly to those people who occupied the semi-desert areas to the east and south of Palestine (see also EAST, CHILDREN OF). It is not possible, however, to say whether the word is always to be taken as a proper name 'Arab', or as a collective noun 'steppe dweller'. The matter is further complicated by the fact that there is an etymologically distinct root *'rb*, 'to intermix', one of whose forms is vocalized *'ēreḇ*, which is taken in some contexts to mean 'mixed multitude'. Indeed, this is the form that occurs in 1 Ki. x. 15, the parallel passage to 2 Ch. ix. 14, the distinction depending entirely upon the Massoretic vocalization. Each occurrence of the word has therefore to be judged from its context rather than its form, and in this case there is no reason why it should not be taken as 'Arabia', or perhaps better 'Arabs'.

In the 9th century, Jehoshaphat of Judah received tribute from the *ʿᵃrāḇî* (2 Ch. xvii. 11), but his successor Jehoram suffered a raid in which the *ʿᵃrāḇî* carried off his wives and sons (2 Ch. xxi. 16, 17), and only Ahaziah, the youngest, was left (2 Ch. xxii. 1). In the 8th century Uzziah reversed the situation and restored Elath (see EZION-GEBER) to his dominion (2 Ki. xiv. 22).

Though the S Arabian kingdoms were known (*e.g.* Joel iii. 8), most of the contacts of Israel with Arabia were with the nomadic tribes of the north. In the time of Hezekiah these people were very familiar (Is. xiii. 20, xxi. 13), and some even served as mercenaries in the defence of Jerusalem against Sennacherib (*(amêl)ur-bi*; Taylor Prism iii. 31). In the time of Josiah (Je. iii. 2), and in the closing days of the kingdom of Judah, the Arabians were coming to prominence as traders (Je. xxv. 23, 24; Ezk. xxvii; see also KEDAR).

The growing tendency of the Arabs to settle and build trading centres is illustrated by Geshem (*q.v.*), the Arab who tried to hinder Nehemiah rebuilding Jerusalem (Ne. ii. 19, vi. 1), presumably because he feared trade rivals. The kingdom of the Nabataeans was to follow, and in the Apocrypha the term 'Arab' usually refers to these people (1 Macc. v. 39; 2 Macc. v. 8), and indeed the 'Arabian' desert to which Paul retired (Gal. i. 17) was probably part of the Nabataean dominion.

See also JOB. For maps, see figs. 11, 149 and the coloured plates which follow the text.

BIBLIOGRAPHY. (*a*) General: W. B. Fisher, *The Middle East. A . . . Geography*, 3rd edn., 1956, pp. 431–453; H. Field, *Ancient and Modern Man in Southwestern Asia*, 1956, pp. 97–124, and folding pocket map; P. K. Hitti, *History of the Arabs*, 6th edn., 1956, pp. 1–86; J. A. Montgomery, *Arabia and the Bible*, 1934; 'The Present State of Arabian Studies' in E. Grant (ed.), *The Haverford Symposium on Archaeology and the Bible*, 1938, pp. 188–201; D. S. Margoliouth, *The Relations between Arabs and Israelites Prior to the Rise of Islam*, 1924; S. Moscati, *Ancient Semitic Civilizations*, 1957, pp. 181–207, 243; *The Semites in Ancient History*, 1959, pp. 104–132. (*b*) S Arabia: M. Höfner, *Altsüdarabische Grammatik*,

1943; G. Ryckmans, *Les Noms propres sud-sémitiques*, 1934–5; J. Bright, *A History of Israel*, 1960, pp. 194–195; the American excavations in S Arabia are being published by the Johns Hopkins Press under the general editorship of W. F. Albright; the first volume to appear is R. le B. Bowen and F. P. Albright, *Archaeological Discoveries in South Arabia*, 1958; other preliminary matter and discussion by Albright and others appears in *BASOR*, 119, 1950, pp. 5–15; 120, 1950, pp. 26–27; 128, 1952, pp. 25–45; 129, 1953, pp. 20–24; 143, 1956, pp. 6–10; 145, 1957, pp. 25–30; 151, 1958, pp. 9–16; 153, 1959, pp. 11–19; 155, 1959, pp. 29–33; *BA*, XV, 1952, pp. 2–18; XXIII, 1960, pp. 70–95; and a popular account is given in W. Phillips, *Qataban and Sheba*, 1955. (*c*) N Arabia: W. Wright, *A Grammar of the Arabic Language* (3rd edn.), rev. by W. R. Smith and M. J. de Goeje, 1896; A. Guillaume, in G. Ryckmans (ed.), *L'Ancien Testament et l'Orient. Études presentées aux VIes Journées Bibliques de Louvain . . .* 1954, 1957; A. Musil, *Oriental Explorations and Studies*, 1–6, 1926–8; N. Glueck, *Explorations in Eastern Palestine*, I–IV (*AASOR*, XIV, XV, XVIII–XIX, XXV–XXVIII), 1934–51; and more popular accounts—*The Other Side of the Jordan*, 1940; *The River Jordan*, 1946; and *Rivers in the Desert*, 1959; see also *BA*, XXII, 1959, pp. 98–108; on Tema, see R. P. Dougherty, *Nabonidus and Belshazzar*, 1929, pp. 105–166; C. J. Gadd, in *Anatolian Studies*, VIII, 1958, pp. 79–89.

T.C.M.

II. IN THE NEW TESTAMENT

Arabia did not, as it does today, denote the whole of the great peninsula between the Red Sea and the Persian Gulf, but only the area to the immediate east and south of Palestine. This territory was occupied by an Arab tribe or tribes called the Nabataeans (*q.v.*), who had settled in the area during the 3rd century BC. By the first century they had established their control over an area which stretched from Damascus on the north to Gaza to the south and far into the desert to the east. Their capital was the red-rock city of Petra.

Arabia is mentioned only twice in the New Testament. Paul relates how, after his conversion, he went away into Arabia (Gal. i. 17). No other account of this incident occurs in the New Testament. The exact location of this event is very uncertain. Since Arabia to the Graeco-Roman mind meant the Nabataean kingdom, it is likely that he went there, possibly to Petra, the capital city. Why he went is not revealed. Perhaps his purpose was to be alone to commune with God. K. Lake suggests that Paul conducted a preaching mission there, because in the Epistle to the Galatians, where he mentions this incident, the antithesis is not between conferring with the Christians at Jerusalem and conferring with God in the desert, but between obeying immediately his commission to preach to the Gentiles and going to Jerusalem to obtain the authority to do this (*The Earlier Epistles of St. Paul*, 1914, pp. 320 f.).

In the only other occurrence of the word Arabia in the New Testament (Gal. iv. 25) it is used in the narrower sense to denote the Sinai Peninsula, or the territory immediately to the east of it, across the Gulf of Aqabah.

BIBLIOGRAPHY. G. A. Smith, *The Historical Geography of the Holy Land*, 1931, pp. 547 f., 649; *HDAC*; J. A. Montgomery, *Arabia and the Bible*, 1934.

W.W.W.

ARABS. See ARABIA.

ARAD. 1. A South Canaanite settlement whose king suffered defeat at the hand of the invading Hebrews (Nu. xxi. 1–3 RV, RSV, xxxiii. 40 RV, RSV; Jos. xii. 14; Jdg. i. 16). The battle took place at Hormah, also known as Zephath (Jdg. i. 17), perhaps modern Tell esh-Sheri'ah, 15 miles south-east of Gaza. **2.** A descendant of Benjamin through Beriah (1 Ch. viii. 15, 16). R.J.W.

ARAM, ARAMAEANS.

I. ANCESTRAL AND PERSONAL

a. The son of Shem, so named with Elam, Assyria, and others in Gn. x. 22, 23 and 1 Ch. i. 17, having four others grouped under him. On this association of Aram with the eastern and north-eastern parts of the Ancient East, see section II*a* (i) below.

b. A personal name borne by individuals and heads of later clans in the patriarchal age and after, thus: Aram, grandson of Nahor, Abraham's brother (Gn. xxii. 21); an 'Aramitess' was mother of Machir by Manasseh (1 Ch. vii. 14); another Aram is mentioned as a descendant of Asher (1 Ch. vii. 34). In the genealogies of Mt. i. 3, 4 and Lk. iii. 33 (AV) Aram is simply the misleading Gk. form of Ram, an entirely different name.

II. PEOPLE, LANDS, AND LANGUAGE

a. Origins

Aram and Aramaeans are usually called 'Syria(ns)' in the English Old Testament—a misleading appellation when applied to the period before *c.* 1000 BC. During the third—as later in the second and first—millennium BC, Western Semitic-speaking semi-nomadic peoples are known from cuneiform sources to have been constantly infiltrating into Syria and Mesopotamia from almost the whole of the Arabian desert-fringe. In Mesopotamia under the kings of Akkad and of the IIIrd Dynasty of Ur (*c.* 2400–2000 BC) these 'Westerners' (*MAR.TU* in Sumerian, *Amurru* in Babylonian) eventually penetrated right across the Tigris to the steppe-lands farther east, reaching the Iranian mountains. Evidence shows that they became well established there; so much so that Landsberger (followed by Bauer) have rather surprisingly suggested it as their place of origin. (For a good discussion of this see J.-R. Kupper, *Les Nomades en*

Mésopotamie au Temps des Rois de Mari, 1957, pp. 147, 148, 166, 177, 178, 196.) But these north-eastern regions were no empty land. In the steppes and hills beyond, the Hurrians were at home, and the two populations doubtless mingled. These facts provide an illuminating background for the origins of the Aramaeans of biblical and external sources.

Under the Akkad and IIIrd Ur Dynasties (*c.* 2400–2000 BC) mention is made of a settlement called Aram(e/i) in the eastern Tigris region north of Elam and east-north-east of Assyria. If this fact is linked with the presence of Western Semitic-speaking settlers there, these may justifiably be considered as proto-Aramaeans. Kupper rejects this interpretation, but has apparently overlooked the importance of some Old Testament passages here. This association of the earliest 'Aramaeans' with the east and north-east is evident in Gn. x. 22, 23, where Aram, Elam, and Assyria occur together—a mark of very early date. Am. ix. 7 carries on this tradition in later times; God brought Israel from Egypt (south), the Philistines from Caphtor (west), and the Aramaeans from Qir (north-east). Qir occurs only once more (Is. xxii. 6)—standing for Assyria—along with Elam, so Amos is in line with Gn. x and with the ascertainable north-eastern occurrences of proto-Aramaeans. On the cuneiform evidence (but not using the biblical passages adduced here), these earliest Aramaeans are accepted by A. Dupont-Sommer, *VT*, Supplement Volume I, 1953, pp. 40–49; by S. Moscati, *The Semites in Ancient History*, 1959, pp. 66, 67, and in earlier works; and by M. McNamara, *Verbum Domini*, XXXV, 1957, pp. 129–142.

Aramu is attested as a personal name in the IIIrd Dynasty of Ur (*c.* 2000 BC) and at Mari (18th century BC); at Alalaḫ in N Syria about this time occurs the form Arammu—for the doubled 'm' *cf.* the Heb. *'arammî*, 'Aramaean'. This corresponds with Aram as an Old Testament personal name about that time. The name Aram may even be Hurrian; at Alalaḫ and at Nuzi appear a series of Hurrian-type names compounded with initial Aram- or Arim- (Kupper, *Nomades*, p. 113). 'Aram' may have been the name of a tribal group that first crossed the Tigris into the Hurrian regions, and its name have been applied by the Hurrians to all such W Semitic-speaking infiltrators and settlers (*cf.* Sumerian and Babylonian use of terms *MAR.TU* and *Amurru*, above)—hence its occurrence in place-names, or it might even have been a Hurrian epithet, which would better explain its occurrence in personal names. As the Hurrians spread right across upper Mesopotamia and into Syria by the beginning of the second millennium, they would then perhaps use this term of the many W Semitic settlers in these regions—known from non-Hurrian cuneiform sources (*e.g.* Mari), Haneans, Suteans, and others; but this must remain wholly uncertain as yet.

b. Early history, 19th–12th centuries BC

The Hebrew Patriarchs, after leaving Ur, first settled in this upper Mesopotamian area, at Harran (Gn. xi. 28–32), in 'Aram-naharaim' (see below on this). One part of the family stayed on here (Nahor, Bethuel, Laban) as 'Aramaeans', while the other (Abraham) went on to Canaan. But the wives of both Isaac and Jacob came from the Aramaean branch of the family (Gn. xxiv, xxviii ff.), thoroughly justifying the later Israelite confession of descent from 'a wandering Aramaean' (= Jacob) in Dt. xxvi. 5 (RSV). The speech of Jacob's and Laban's families already showed dialectal differences ('Canaanite' and 'Aramaic'), see Gn. xxxi. 47; note the early form of this Aramaic phrase, using direct (construct) genitive and not circumlocution with *dî*.

Aram-naharaim ('Aram of the two rivers') or Paddan-aram was basically the area within the great bend of the river Euphrates past Carchemish bounding it on the west, with the river Habur as limit in the east (see fig. 27). In this area arose the Hurrian kingdom of Mitanni (16th–14th centuries BC). In the Amarna Letters (*c.* 1360 BC) it is called *Naḫrima* with Canaanitic dual in 'm' (like Heb.), while in Egyptian texts of *c.* 1520–1170 BC appears the form *Nhrn*, clearly exhibiting an Aramaic-type dual in 'n', not assimilated to Canaanite as in the Amarna Letters. The form in Egyptian is clear evidence—deriving directly from Egyptian military contact with Aram-naharaim—for Aramaic dialect-forms there from the 16th century BC. The forms *Naḫrima/Nhrn* are mentioned briefly in Gelb, *Hurrians and Subarians*, 1944, p. 74 and n. 208. Further hints of (proto-)Aramaic forms in the early second millennium in this area are found in Albright, *Archiv für Orientforschung*, VI, 1930–1, p. 218, note 4.

From Ugarit (14th–13th centuries BC) come personal names Armeya and B(e)n-Arm(e)y(a), and a plot of land called 'fields of Aramaeans' (Kupper, *Nomades*, p. 114), which continue the story. But the place-name 'the Aram' or 'Pa-Aram' in the Egyptian Papyrus Anastasi III (13th century BC) is probably only a graphic error for Amurru/Amor. It was in the 13th century BC that Balaam was hired from Pethor (*q.v.*) (in 'Amaw?) by the Euphrates in Aram (-naharaim) and the 'mountains of the east', in order to curse Israel (Nu. xxii. 5, RSV, xxiii. 7; Dt. xxiii. 4).

In the chaos that befell the western part of the Ancient East just after *c.* 1200 BC when the sea peoples destroyed the Hittite Empire and disrupted Syria-Palestine (see CANAAN, EGYPT: History), one of Israel's oppressors was the opportunist Cushan-Rishathaim, king of Aram-naharaim, whose far-flung but fragile dominion lasted only eight years (Jdg. iii. 7–11) (see CUSHAN-RISHATHAIM). Still later in the judges' period, the gods of Syria proper could already be called 'the gods of Aram' (*c.* 1100 BC?) in Jdg. x. 6 (Heb.); this ties up with the accelerating inflow of Aramaeans and settling in the later 12th and 11th centuries BC in Syria and Mesopotamia, culminating in the founding of Aramaean states. Just at this time, Tiglath-pileser I of Assyria (1100 BC) was trying unavailingly to stem the advance of 'Akhlamu, Aramaeans' across the length of the middle Euphrates (*ANET*, p. 275). The Akhlamu occur in the 13th, 14th, and (as personal name) 18th centuries BC as Aramaean-type people, thus further witnessing to an Aramaean continuity from earlier to later times. On this section see also Kupper, *Nomades*; R. T. O'Callaghan, *Aram Naharaim*, 1948; in modern Hebrew, A. Malamat, *The Aramaeans in Aram Naharaim and the Rise of Their States*, 1952; M. F. Unger, *Israel and the Aramaeans of Damascus*, 1957; *ANET*, p. 259 and note 11.

c. Israel and the Aramaean States, c. 1000–700 BC

(i) *Saul* (*c. 1050–1010 BC*). During his reign, Saul had to fight many foes for Israel: Moab, Ammon, and Edom in the east, the Philistines in the south-west, and the 'kings of Zobah' in the north (1 Sa. xiv. 47; or 'king', if LXX be followed). This was probably at the height of his power (*c.* 1025 BC?), before the final disasters of his reign.

(ii) *David* (*c. 1010–970 BC*). David's first known Aramaean contact is with Talmai son of Ammihur, king of Geshur, whose daughter he married (Absalom being her son by him) within his first seven years' reign at Hebron (1010–1003 BC), 2 Sa. iii. 3, 5. Talmai still ruled Geshur late in David's reign when Absalom fled there for three years (2 Sa. xiii. 37–39). In the second half of his reign, David clashed with Hadadezer son of Rehob, king of Aram-Zobah (north of Damascus). This king had already extended his rule as far as the Euphrates (subduing the hostile Toi, king of Hamath, 2 Sa. viii. 10), but his northern subjects must have revolted, for when David attacked him Hadadezer was then going to 'restore' his conquests there (2 Sa. viii. 3). Perhaps David and Toi found Hadadezer too dangerous; at any rate, David annexed Damascus and Toi of Hamath became his (subject-)ally, 2 Sa. viii. 5–12. The revolt against Hadadezer probably followed the two heavy defeats that David inflicted on him as ally of Ammon (2 Sa. x; 1 Ch. xix) with other Aramaean states (see Unger, pp. 42–46). No direct time-relation between 2 Sa. viii. 3–12 and ix–xii is stated. For evidence that the Ammonite war preceded that of 2 Sa. viii, see Kitchen, *Hittite Hieroglyphs, Aramaeans and Hebrew Traditions*, Table IV, commentary. Henceforth, David was doubtless overlord of Hadadezer and all Syria. The earlier wide but ephemeral power of Hadadezer may be reflected in later Assyrian texts which report how, under Ashur-rabi II (*c.* 1012–972 BC), 'the king of Aram' gained control of Pethor (Pitru) and Mutkinu on either side of the Euphrates; this may mark the foundation there of the Aramaean kingdom of Bit-Adini—perhaps the source of Hadadezer's troops from beyond the Euphrates. For further discussion, see Landsberger, *Sam'al I*, 1948, p. 35, note 74; and Malamat, *BA*, XXI, 1958, pp. 101, 102.

(iii) *Solomon* (*c. 970–930 BC*). Probably it was in the first half of his reign that Solomon overcame 'Hamath-Zobah', *i.e.* presumably crushed a revolt in the southern part of the country of Hamath that adjoined Zobah—perhaps a rising against Hamath's subject-ally status? At any rate Solomon's overlordship was effective enough for him to have store-cities built there (2 Ch. viii. 3, 4). But in the last part of David's reign, after the discomfiture of Hadadezer of Zobah, a mere youth, Rezon, went off and gathered a marauding band around himself. For some time, into Solomon's earlier years, he was probably little more than a petty, roving insurgent. But for the latter half of Solomon's reign he gained control of Damascus and became king there, briefly surviving Solomon, whom he had always opposed (1 Ki. xi. 23–25); Rezon, it seems, played bandit till *c.* 955 BC, reigning in Damascus perhaps *c.* 955–925 BC, till at last—full of years —he passed away, and a new 'strong man', Hezion, seized the Damascus throne.

(iv) *The Dynasty of Hezion.* The new opportunist founded a dynasty that lasted a century. Hezion (*c.* 925–915?), his son Tabrimmon (*c.* 915–900?), and grandson Ben-hadad I (*c.* 900–860?) are attested in this order and relationship, both from 1 Ki. xv. 18 and from Ben-hadad's 'Melqart Stele' of *c.* 860 BC, for which see Albright and della Vida, *BASOR*, 87, 1942, pp. 23–29; 90, 1943, pp. 30–34; Black in Thomas (ed.), *DOTT*, pp. 239–241 and plate 15, also Parrot, *Samaria*, 1958, p. 25, fig. III. These kings speedily made of Damascus the paramount kingdom in Syria proper, rivalled only by Hamath. When attacked by Baasha of Israel, Asa of Judah sought aid from Ben-hadad I (1 Ki. xv. 18 ff.).

The Ben-hadad who clashed with Ahab (1 Ki. xx) and was murdered by Hazael in Joram's time, *c.* 843 BC (2 Ki. vi. 24 ff., viii. 7–15) is probably a different king, a Ben-hadad II (*c.* ?860–843), but it is possible to argue, as does Albright, that this is still Ben-hadad I (then, *c.* 900–843 BC—a long reign but not unparalleled); see BEN-HADAD. This Ben-hadad II/I is almost certainly the Adad-idri ('Hadad-ezer') of Damascus whom Shalmaneser III attacked in 853, 849, 848, and 845 BC, and whose murder and replacement by Hazael are also alluded to by the Assyrian (see HAZAEL). Double names are common among Ancient Near Eastern rulers; Ben-hadad/Adad-idri is but one more example. It was Ben-hadad of Damascus and Urhilen̆i of Hamath who led the opposition to Assyria and contributed the largest armed contingents, though their efforts were handsomely matched in this respect by Ahab of Israel in 853 BC at Qarqar (*ANET*, pp. 278–281; Wiseman in *DOTT*, p. 47).

(v) *Hazael to Rezin.* The usurper Hazael (*c.* 843–796 BC) almost immediately clashed with Joram of Israel (842/1 BC), *cf.* 2 Ki. viii. 28, 29, ix. 15. Jehu gained the Israelite throne at this time, but he and others paid tribute to Assyria

(*ANET*, p. 280; *DOTT*, p. 48; *IBA*, p. 57, fig. 51), leaving Hazael of Damascus to oppose Assyria alone in 841 and 837 BC (Unger, *op. cit.*, pp. 76–78). Thereafter, Hazael savagely attacked Israel under Jehu, seizing Transjordan (2 Ki. x. 32, 33), and throughout the reign of Jehoahaz, *c.* 814/3–798 BC (2 Ki. xiii. 22). But temporary relief did occur; the 'deliverer' sent by God then (2 Ki. xiii. 5) may have been Adad-nirari III of Assyria who intervened against Hazael (called 'Mari'; see HAZAEL) about 805–802 BC.

In the Israelite Joash's early years the pressure was at first maintained by Hazael's son Ben-hadad III (2 Ki. xiii. 3). But as promised by God through Elisha, Joash (*c.* 798–782/1 BC) was able to recover from Ben-hadad the lands previously lost to Hazael (2 Ki. xiii. 14–19, 22–25). Ben-hadad acceded *c.* 796 BC (see HAZAEL), and reigned till roughly 770 BC on evidence of Zakir's stele. Ben-hadad headed a powerful coalition against Zakir of Hamath, a usurper from Lu'ash who had seized control of the whole kingdom Hamath-Lu'ash. But Zakir and his allies defeated Ben-hadad's coalition and so spelt the end of the dominance in Syria of the Aramaean kingdom of Damascus. For Zakir's stele, see Unger, *op. cit.*, pp. 85–89, and Black in *DOTT*, pp. 242–250.

Shortly after this, discredited Damascus came under the overlordship of Jeroboam II of Israel (2 Ki. xiv. 28). Still later, perhaps after Jeroboam II's death in 753 BC, a King Rezin (Assyrian *Raḫianu*) appeared in Damascus and menaced Judah as Israel's ally, even (like Hazael) conquering Transjordan again; but Ahaz of Judah appealed to Tiglath-pileser III of Assyria, who then in 732 BC defeated and slew Rezin (2 Ki. xvi. 5–9; *ANET*, p. 283), deporting the unhappy Aramaeans to Qir, ironically their ancient homeland, as prophesied by Amos (i. 4, 5).

(vi) *Other Aramaean kingdoms.* These included Arpad (Bit-Agusi) between north of Aleppo and Carchemish, Bit-Adini in the bend of the Euphrates, and Guzanu (Gozan) somewhat east of Harran. But these barely appear in Scripture. Sennacherib in 701 BC mocked Hezekiah over the impotence of the kings and gods of Arpad, Hamath, Gozan, Harran, Rezeph (Assyr. *Raṣappa*), and the 'children of Eden in Telassar' (2 Ki. xviii. 34, xix. 12, 13). The last-named, the *Bᵉnē-'Eden* dwelling in Telassar, are the people of the Aramaean province (former kingdom) of Bit-Adini, the 'House of Eden' or Beth-Eden of Am. i. 5. The 'sceptre-holder of Beth-Eden' whose doom Amos (*c.* 790–740 BC, roughly) prophesied was apparently the almost-independent Assyrian governor of Bit-Adini called Shamshi-ilu (*c.* 780–743 BC), doubtless suppressed by Tiglath-pileser III; *cf.* A. Malamat, *BASOR*, 129, 1953, pp. 25, 26.

BIBLIOGRAPHY. M. F. Unger, R. T. O'Callaghan, A. Malamat (works cited at end of IIb); A. Dupont-Sommer, *Les Araméens*, 1949. Specific studies include: R. de Vaux, *RB*, XLIII, 1934, pp. 512–518, and A. Jepsen, *Archiv für Orientforschung*, XIV, 1941–4, pp. 153–172, and *ib.*, XVI, 1952–3, pp. 315–317, for Aram-Damascus and Israel; E. O. Forrer, in Ebeling and Meissner, *Reallexikon der Assyriologie*, I, 1932, pp. 131–139 (*Aramu*), and B. Landsberger, *Sam'al I*, 1948, on cuneiform references; W. F. Albright in *AS*, VI, 1956, pp. 75–85, on Assyrian penetration of Aramaean politics and art; Kitchen, *Hittite Hieroglyphs, Aramaeans and Hebrew Traditions*, forthcoming, on Neo-Hittite and Aramaean states as Old Testament background and allied matters.

d. Language

See LANGUAGE OF THE OLD TESTAMENT, for a fuller account; the following observations are historically and archaeologically complementary to that entry.

(i) *Aramaisms in the Old Testament.* The occurrence of these often indicates an early, not a late, date. Note the second-millennium traces of Aramaic forms (IIb, above). Aramaean states in Syria which existed from at least Saul's reign, and marriages in the time of David (Talmai), imply Aramaic linguistic influence in Palestine then. Finally, some 'Aramaisms' are actually Hebraisms (or Canaanisms) in Aramaic.

(ii) *Extended Use of Aramaic.* In the 9th and following centuries BC, Aramaic and its script (taken from alphabetic Hebrew/Phoenician) rapidly became the international medium of commerce and diplomacy. Already in the 9th century BC, Israel and Damascus had merchants in each other's capitals (1 Ki. xx. 34), and in 701 BC Hezekiah's officers sought to be addressed in Aramaic—understood by rulers or merchants, but not by (Hebrew) 'men in the street' (2 Ki. xviii. 26). In Assyria itself from *c.* 730 BC under Tiglath-pileser III, Aramaic steadily came into official use: Aramaic dockets on cuneiform tablets, Aramaic annotations by high Assyrian officials, and Assyrian sculptures showing the recording of tribute by scribes who write (Aramaic) with pen on parchment as well as in cuneiform on clay tablets. (For full references, see R. A. Bowman, *JNES*, VII, 1948, pp. 73–76, to which add the new ostracon listing Hebrew exiles in Assyria found at Calah, J. B. Segal, *Iraq*, XIX, 1957, pp. 139–145, and Albright, *BASOR*, 149, 1958, pp. 33–36.) Note here, too, the Aramaic letter of Adon of Ascalon to the pharaoh of Egypt in 604(?) BC (W. D. McHardy in *DOTT*, pp. 251–255 with bibliography). Unless it is a note to readers that Aramaic directly follows, the note in Dn. ii. 4 'in Aramaic' when the Chaldeans address Nebuchadrezzar would fit in perfectly with Assyro-Babylonian court use of Aramaic. Besides examples above, Aramaic epigraphs occur on the very bricks used in constructing the great buildings of Nebuchadrezzar's Babylon and testify to the common use of that language there then (see R. Koldewey, *The Excavations at Babylon*, 1914, pp. 80, 81, figs. 52, 53). Aramaic ('Reichsaramäisch') became the official medium of communication throughout the polyglot

Persian Empire—Ezra is the classic biblical example. This is vividly illustrated by Aramaic papyri from Egypt (5th century BC); for these see A. Cowley, *Aramaic Papyri of the Fifth Century BC*, 1923; H. L. Ginsberg in *ANET*, pp. 222, 223, 427–430, 491, 492; E. G. Kraeling, *The Brooklyn Museum Aramaic Papyri*, 1953; G. R. Driver and others, *Aramaic Documents of the Fifth Century BC*, 1954, and abridged and revised, 1957.

(iii) *Old Testament Aramaic.* This has often been a subject of dispute. Recent evidence on one matter must suffice here. In early Aramaic there was a sound *ḏ* (*dh*) which by Persian times had become identical with ordinary 'd' in pronunciation. In the West (Syria) this consonant was written as 'z' (even in a non-Aramaic name, as Miliz for Milid(h), 'Melitene' in Zakir's stele), and this persisted as a 'historical' spelling in the Aramaic papyri of the Persian Empire. But in the East, 'dh' was already represented by the Assyrians as 'd' from the 9th century BC (Adad-idri for (H)adad-ezer). The real pronunciation 'd' in Persian times is betrayed by various hints: a remarkable Aramaic text in Egyptian demotic script, 5th century BC, writes 't'/'d' (Bowman, *JNES*, III, 1944, pp. 224, 225 and note 17), while in some of the normal Aramaic papyri there are cases of false archaism in writing 'z' for original 'd' (not 'dh'), *cf.* Kutscher, *JAOS*, LXXIV, 1954, p. 235 (*zyn wzbb*).

Old Testament Aramaic writes a phonetically true 'd', not a Western historic 'z'; this is no indicator of late date, but signifies one of two things. Either Daniel, Ezra, *etc.*, simply put Aramaic as spoken in 6th/5th-century Babylonia into a directly phonetic spelling, or else they used the historic spelling largely eliminated by a subsequent spelling-revision of rather later date. On spelling-revision as attested in Ancient Near Eastern usage, see EGYPT: Literature. For Aramaic, see H. H. Schaeder, *Iranische Beiträge*, I, 1930; full evaluation of pre-war literature in F. Rosenthal, *Die Aramaistische Forschung*, 1939; more recent still are R. A. Bowman, *JNES*, VII, 1948, pp. 65–90, on 'Aramaic, Arameans and the Bible' and E. G. Kraeling's survey, *Brooklyn Museum Aramaic Papyri*, 1953, pp. 3–119, including historical matter on the Jews in Egypt.

e. Aramaean culture

The Aramaeans' one major contribution to ancient Oriental culture was their language: at first, in commerce and diplomacy, then for communication over wide areas (see above), but also as a literary medium. The story and proverbs of Ahiqar are set in the Assyria of Sennacherib and certainly go back in origin to almost that time; from the 5th century BC come the religious texts in demotic (Egyptian) script (Bowman, *JNES*, III, 1944, pp. 219–231) and the Papyri Blacassiani (G. A. Cooke, *A Textbook of North-Semitic Inscriptions*, 1903, pp. 206–210, No. 76). Still later come magical texts, including one in cuneiform script of the Seleucid era (C. H. Gordon, *Archiv für Orientforschung*, XII, 1937–9, pp. 105–117). Syriac in the Christian epoch was a great province of Christian literature. The chief gods of the Aramaeans were Baal-shamain and other forms of Baal, Hadad the storm-god, Canaanite deities such as Ashtaroth, and Mesopotamian ones, including Marduk, Nebo, Shamash, *etc.* (Dupont-Sommer, *Les Inscriptions Araméennes de Sfiré*, 1958, p. 19, *etc.*). See Dupont-Sommer, *Les Araméens*, pp. 106–119; Dhorme and Dussaud, *Religions, Babylonie, etc.*, 1949, pp. 389 ff.

K.A.K.

ARAMAIC. See LANGUAGE OF OLD TESTAMENT.

ARARAT.

I. BIBLICAL EVIDENCE

The name Ararat occurs four times in the Bible. It was the mountainous or hilly area (*hārê ʾᵃrārāṭ*, 'mountains of Ararat') where Noah's ark came to rest (Gn. viii. 4; see FLOOD); the land (*'ereṣ*) to which Adrammelech and Sharezer, the parricides of Sennacherib, fled for asylum (2 Ki. xix. 37 = Is. xxxvii. 38); and a kingdom (*mamlāḵâ*) grouped by Jeremiah with Minni and Ashkenaz in a prophetic summons to destroy Babylon (Je. li. 27). The AV reads 'Armenia' in both Kings and Isaiah in deference to *Armenian* in the LXX of Isaiah.

II. EXTRA-BIBLICAL EVIDENCE

There is little doubt that biblical *ʾᵃrārāṭ* was the *Urarṭu* of the Assyrian inscriptions, a kingdom which flourished in the time of the Assyrian Empire in the neighbourhood of Lake Van in Armenia. While it is frequently mentioned by the Assyrian kings as a troublesome northern neighbour, it was much influenced by Mesopotamian civilization, and in the 9th century the cuneiform script was adopted and modified for writing Urarṭian (also called 'Vannic' or 'Chaldian', not to be confused with 'Chaldean'), a language unrelated to Akkadian. Nearly 200 Urarṭian inscriptions are known, and in these the land is referred to as *Biai-nae* and the people as 'children of Ḫaldi', the national god. Little excavation has been done in Urarṭian territory, but examples of art and architecture have been uncovered at Toprak Kale, which represents part of the ancient capital, Ṭušpa, near the shore of Lake Van, and at Karmir Blur, a town site near Erivan in the U.S.S.R.

III. URARṬU

In the 13th century, when Urarṭu is first mentioned in the inscriptions of Shalmaneser I, it appears as a small principality between the lakes of Van and Urmia, but it seems to have grown in power in the following centuries when Assyria was suffering a period of decline. In the 9th century reports of Assyrian campaigns against Urarṭu, whose territory now extended well to the north and west, become more frequent, and about 830 BC a new dynasty was founded by Sardur I, who established his capital at Ṭušpa. His immediate successors held the frontiers, but the kingdom was badly shaken at the end of the 8th century by the Cimmerian (see GOMER) invasions, and was only briefly revived in the mid-7th century by Rusa II, who may have been the king who gave asylum to Sennacherib's assassins. The end of Urarṭu is obscure, but though its inhabitants are probably to be seen in the *Alarodioi* of Herodotus (iii. 94), the Old Persian cuneiform inscriptions of the 6th century name the area Armenia, indicating that by then the Indo-European Armenians had become dominant. Urarṭu probably disappeared as a state in the early 6th century, at about the time of Jeremiah's prophetic summons.

BIBLIOGRAPHY. A. Goetze, *Kleinasien*[2], 1957, pp. 187–200, 215–216; F. W. König, *Handbuch der chaldischen Inschriften* (AfO, Beiheft 8), I, 1955, II, 1957. T.C.M.

ARAUNAH (*'ᵃrawnâ*, also *hā'ᵃwarnâ*, *'ᵃranyâ*). In 2 Sa. xxiv. 16 ff. a Jebusite whose threshing-floor was bought by David when he saw the destroying angel hold his hand there, so that he might build an altar on the spot and offer a sacrifice to check the pestilence which broke out after his numbering of the people. In 1 Ch. xxi. 18 ff. (where Araunah is called Ornan) David buys the area surrounding the threshing-floor too, to be the site of the future Temple which, in due course, Solomon built there (1 Ch. xxii. 1; 2 Ch. iii. 1).

Araunah's name has been derived from Hittite *arawanis*, 'freeman', 'noble'. In 2 Sa. xxiv. 16 it is preceded by the definite article, and in verse 23 it is glossed by *hammeleḵ* ('the king'), whence it has been conjectured that he was the last king of Jebusite Jerusalem. See HITTITES. F.F.B.

ARCHAEOLOGY.

I. GENERAL

Within the rapidly developing science of archaeology the special study of 'Biblical Archaeology' selects those material remains of Palestine and its neighbouring countries which relate to the biblical period and narrative. These include the remains of buildings, art, inscriptions, and every artefact which helps the understanding of the history, life, and customs of the Hebrews and those peoples who, like the Egyptians, Phoenicians, Syrians, Assyrians, and Babylonians, came into contact with and influenced them. Interest in places and times mentioned in the Bible provided the initial incentive to many of the earlier excavations, and the broad picture of the historical, religious, and ethical background to the Bible now available from archaeological discoveries has done much to explain, illustrate, and sometimes to corroborate biblical statements and counteract theories insufficiently based on facts.

The limitations of archaeology are due to the vast span of time and area to be covered. No biblical site has ever been, or probably can be, completely excavated. Only in recent years have accurate methods of stratification and recording enabled detailed comparisons to be made between sites. Moreover, the dearth of inscriptions from Palestine itself means that direct extra-biblical insight into the thoughts and life of the early peoples is rare. As archaeology, a branch of history, deals primarily with materials, it can never test such great biblical truths as the existence and redeeming activity of God and Christ, the incarnate Word.

In Palestine (taking this term to include the modern states of Israel and Jordan), a special archaeological technique has been worked out. Flinders Petrie in 1890 evolved a system of sequence dating at Tell el-Hesi by which different levels of occupation can be distinguished by the characteristic pottery and other dateable criteria (architecture, seals, *etc.*) found in each level (see fig. 12). This scheme of stratigraphy and typology has been subsequently improved by later excavations, especially those at Gibeah, Beit Mirsim, Samaria, Lachish, Jericho, and Hazor, and by comparisons with other Near Eastern sites. The resultant ceramic index and chronology of finds is remarkably closely knit from the fourth millennium BC, and between the 12th and 7th centuries pottery can be dated within narrow limits. Dates before that, including those provided by the Carbon-14 method, are still only comparative. The following table gives the currently-accepted designations for these archaeological periods:

II. CLASSIFICATION OF ARCHAEOLOGICAL PERIODS (ISRAEL)

	c. BC
I Stone Age	
Palaeolithic = Old Stone Age	250000
Mesolithic = Middle Stone Age = Natufian	10000
Neolithic = New Stone Age (Tahunian and Jerichoan):	
a. Prepottery	7000
b. Pottery	5000
II Chalcolithic (in part, Ghassulian)	4000–3200
III Bronze Age or Canaanite Period	
Early Bronze (EB) = Early Canaanite (EC)—I	3200–2900
Early Bronze (EB) = Early Canaanite (EC)—II	2900–2600
Early Bronze (EB) = Early Canaanite (EC)—III–IV	2600–2200
Intermediate Bronze (Canaanite); EB–MB / EC–MC	2200–1950

	c. BC
Middle Bronze (MB) = Middle Canaanite (MC)—I	1950–1750
Middle Bronze (MB) = Middle Canaanite (MC)—II	1750–1550
Late Bronze (LB) = Late Canaanite (LC)—I	1550–1400
Late Bronze (LB) = Late Canaanite (LC)—IIa	1400–1300
Late Bronze (LB) = Late Canaanite (LC)—IIb	1300–1200
IV Iron Age or Israelite Period	
Iron Age (IA) I {Early Israelite (EI) I = Israelite I	1200–1050
Iron Age (IA) I {Early Israelite (EI) II = Israelite II	1050–970
Iron Age (IA) II {Middle Israelite (MI) I = Israelite II	970–840
Iron Age (IA) II {Middle Israelite (MI) II = Israelite III	840–580
Iron Age (IA) III = Late Israelite (LI) = Israelite IV	580–330
V Hellenistic Period	
Hellenistic I	330–165
Hellenistic II = Maccabean Period	165–63
VI Hellenistic–Roman Period	63–AD 70
VII Roman Period	AD 70–330

III. PREHISTORY

Palaeolithic implements have been found at a number of sites and caves (Carmel, 'Evron, 'Oren) in Palestine, but little is known of cultural advances until the 'Natufians', Mesolithic hunters, are found building houses with stone substructures (Eynan). Having no metal, these people used flint tools and lived primarily by hunting, later adopting agriculture and animal domestication. They made unusually moulded figurines of mud, bone, or stone. Neolithic sites are found near the Jordan in Galilee (Yarmuk and Sha'ar Haggolan), and are roughly parallel with the early sites in the Nile and Tigris (Jarmo) valleys. An impressive stone tower and defences (at Jericho) at a time before pottery was known, and the remarkable plaster moulded skulls and figurines from Jericho show how skilful were these early peoples (*c.* 5000 BC).

Metal first appears in the Chalcolithic (Aenolithic) age, which has been traced in most parts of the country. At the village site of Teleilat Ghassul (Jordan) painted pottery, realistic polychrome wall paintings, a wealth of flints, and a few simple copper axeheads were discovered. Similar pottery has been found in the Jordan valley (near Jericho), Esdraelon, and in the N Negeb and Wadi Ghazzeh near Gaza. By this time agriculture and the metal industry were relatively advanced and painted model house ossuaries, some with curving vaulted roofs, show the early architectural forms adopted (Ḥedēra, 'Azor). At some sites near Beersheba underground dwellings and stores (Abu Matar, Zafad, Horvat Beter) or rock-cut cisterns (Gezer) are also found for the first time.

The transition to the Bronze Age is traceable at a number of settlements which later grew into city states (Megiddo, Jericho, Beth-shan, Beth-yeraḥ, and Tell el-Far'a near Shechem) or were later abandoned for a time (Samaria and Tell en-Nasbeh). Invaders, probably former nomads from the north or east, brought a new type of pottery and buried their dead in mass graves cut in the rocks. These tombs sometimes included pottery types known from the previous Late Chalcolithic period, Esdraelon burnished wares and painted pottery later found in abundance (EB I). The term Proto-Urban, corresponding to the Protoliterate (Jemdet Nasr) period in Iraq *c.* 3200 BC has been used to describe this phase.

IV. THE CANAANITE (BRONZE) AGE

Towns with mud-brick walls begin to appear in the Early Bronze Age I. At the same time the pottery in the North (Beth-yeraḥ, level II; Beth-shan, level XI) differs from that in the South, found at Ophel (Jerusalem), Gezer, Ai, Jericho (VI–VII) and Tell en-Nasbeh. The towns in the North continued to flourish in EB II *c.* 2900 BC (Megiddo, XVI–XVII; Beth-yeraḥ, III; Beth-shan, XII) although in the South a strong Egyptian influence can be seen (Jericho, IV). There were striking developments, notably in a fine new 'Khirbet Kerak' ware which shows the gradual improvement in pottery technique in Palestine and Syria, and in the layout of the Canaanite temple found at Ai (EB III).

About 2200 BC the arrival of the Amorites in Palestine is marked by burials which include a distinct type of pottery and weapons (Tell Ajjul, Jericho, Megiddo). These were the invading nomadic groups whose presence in the Palestinian hills was later noted by the incoming Israelites (Nu. xiii. 29; Jos. v. 1, x. 6) and by the Egyptians in their execration texts (see EGYPT). Another group of people, mainly from Syria and Phoenicia, brought with them their own types of pottery, weapons, and burial customs, but these concentrated in the towns which formed the Canaanite city-states first mentioned in the Old Testament and letters from Mari. It was a time of wealth (see ARCHITECTURE, Old Testament) though of frequent inter-city warfare. The newcomers included the Asiatic 'foreign rulers' (Hyksos), who by *c.* 1730 BC had overrun Egypt. The characteristic Hyksos defences unearthed at

Hazor, Jericho, Lachish, and Megiddo have a steep outer ramp or glacis, probably designed to prevent the use by attackers of battering-rams and chariots.

This Middle Bronze Age was a time when semi-nomadic groups, including Habiru, among whom may well have been the Patriarchs, infiltrated the valleys between the defended towns (see also PATRIARCHAL AGE). The tombs of such people have been found at Jericho. The towns and their houses (*e.g.* Beit Mirsim, Megiddo, and Jericho) remained small but with little change until they were violently destroyed (LB) probably by the Egyptians (Tuthmosis III) repulsing the Hyksos, *c.* 1450 BC. Despite trade contacts with the E Mediterranean (Mycenaean pottery), the hill towns of Palestine were now poorer than the neighbouring Phoenician cities.

Once again the major cities were reoccupied, but only to be sacked again later in the 14th century. The heavy destruction at this time at Hazor, Bethel, Beit Mirsim (Debir?), and Lachish fits well with the record of the assaults of the incoming Israelites under Joshua. At Jericho the town has been found to have been abandoned *c.* 1325 BC, but the fallen walls once thought to belong to this LB period (Garstang) are now known to have been destroyed in EB (Kenyon).

The Canaanites in this Late Bronze Age could have employed five different systems of writing: (1) Mesopotamian (Akkadian)—cuneiform-inscribed tablets found at Megiddo, Jericho, Shechem, Taanach, Tell el-Hesi, Gezer, and Hazor (pot), see also Amarna letters, VIII *b*, below; (2) Egyptian hieroglyphs—Beth-shan, Chinnereth; (3) 'Proto-Hebrew'—Lachish, Hazor; (4) the Ugaritic cuneiform alphabet—found on a tablet from Beth-shemesh (see Ras Shamra, VIII *e*, below); (5) the Byblos script—but so far no example of its use inland has been found (see GEBAL).

The religious practices of the Canaanites can be seen in the many 'Astarte' plaques found during excavations, in the temples at Lachish, Megiddo, and Shechem and in the representations of Baal, including that on a cylinder seal from Bethel, *c.* 1300 BC.

V. THE ISRAELITE (IRON) AGE

By *c.* 1200 BC a locally made and highly decorated pottery, similar in style to that found in Cyprus and Rhodes, was found above ash at Ashkelon and other coastal sites between the Wadi Ghazzeh and Jaffa, showing that invaders had destroyed and then occupied Canaanite cities. This is convincing evidence for the arrival of the Philistines among the 'Sea Peoples' who earlier had settled in E Cyprus and probably at points on the Palestinian shores. Their pottery, other than small amounts attributable to trade, is not found at first in the central hills (Gibeah, Jerusalem, Beth-zur, Tell en-Nasbeh), but by 1050 BC traces of their inroads to Shiloh and Beth-shan have been discovered. These Philistines were the first people to use iron in Palestine (an iron dagger and knife in a Tell el-Far'a tomb) and the Israelites were slow to break this monopoly and their consequent economic superiority (1 Sa. xiii. 18–22). Wealthy and well-constructed Canaanite strongholds held out for at least another century (Beth-shan). The Israelites in the time of the Judges either built poor houses (Bethel), lived on the ground floor of captured Canaanite buildings (Beit Mirsim), or squatted in roughly constructed villages of their own (Gat, Raqqat). Their pottery also was rough and poor compared with that of the Canaanites.

Saul's citadel at Gibeah (Tell el-Fûl) shows how the Israelites adopted a northern system of casemate walls for their defences (see ARCHITECTURE, Old Testament, and fig. 95). Life here was simple, though marked by the importation of a few iron weapons. Similar casemate walls at Shechem may have been built by Abimelech (Jdg. ix), while those at Beit Mirsim and Beth-shemesh may indicate David's work of fortifying Judah against the Philistines. Otherwise, except for the defences at Ophel, no building which can certainly be attributed to David's reign has so far been identified.

The age of Solomon shows an increase in the use of iron and improved building techniques. The same plan was used for the casemate walls and city gateways he built at Hazor, Gezer, and Megiddo (1 Ki. ix. 15; see fig. 102). Residences for district-governors were constructed at Megiddo and Hazor, with massive granaries for storing the taxes, paid in grain, at Lachish and Beth-shemesh. Large stables, for 500 or more horses, were found at Megiddo (1 Ki. ix. 15, 19); these, though generally attributed to Solomon, may well date to the reign of Ahab. There is also evidence of an extensive programme for the building of regional administrative offices. The material prosperity of Solomon's reign must have been largely due to the construction of many copper- and iron-smelting plants in the Wadi leading to Ezion-geber at Aqabah. The busy port there was used for importing many commodities (see SHIPS). A pot found at Tell Qasileh inscribed 'gold from Ophir' attests this trade.

The defeat of the Philistines opened the way for an undisputed expansion of Phoenician trade, and this is reflected in the building of Solomon's Temple. The plan followed a Syro-Phoenician style already adopted at Hazor and Tell Tainat (see fig. 13). The entrance, flanked by twin free-standing pillars (see JACHIN AND BOAZ) led by a direct axis through a vestibule into the large sanctuary (*hêḵāl*) into the small, inner sanctuary (*d*ᵉ*ḇîr*). A peculiar Solomonic development was the provision of considerable storage space for the treasuries along the sides of this building. The decoration of the Temple, with its cherubim, palms, open-work patterns or furnishings, can be paralleled from contemporary ivories found at Samaria, Ras Shamra, Arslan Tash (Syria) or Nimrud (Iraq). See ART, Old Testament. Other items, altars, stands, tongs, and utensils, have been found during excavations.

The invasion of Shishak I of Egypt, *c.* 926 BC, resulted in destruction as far north as Tell Abu Hawan and at Beit Mirsim (B) and Beth-shemesh (IIA). The period of the divided Monarchy has been illuminated by a number of excavations. At Tirzah (Tell el-Far'a) de Vaux has shown that after the 10th century the town was abandoned, as would be expected when Omri transferred his capital to Samaria (1 Ki. xvi. 23, 24) which gave him better communications with the Phoenician sea-ports. At Samaria the summit was laid out as a royal quarter surrounded by a wall of fine masonry. The Omri-Ahab palace and gateway incorporated 'proto-Ionic' pilasters. Many ivories found here may have come from the decorations or furnishings of Ahab's 'ivory house' (1 Ki. xxii. 39; Am. vi. 4), and some are inscribed with Phoenician marks which assist in dating them to this reign (see IVORY). The script is identical with that of the inscription of Mesha, found at Dibhan, which describes relations between that king and Israel *c.* 825 BC (see MOAB). In the palace courtyard at Samaria was an open cistern or 'pool', perhaps that in which Ahab's chariot was washed down (1 Ki. xxii. 38). Official buildings similar to those at Samaria (I) have been found at Beth-shan (V) and Megiddo (V). At Hazor (VIII) Ahab appears to have extended the town by building new fortifications round the whole of the high ground around the citadel. There, as at Samaria (II = Jehu), the solid defence walls now built were to stand until the Hellenistic reconstructions, *c.* 150 BC. About 800 BC Tell el-Far'a was reoccupied as a local residence for a governor with excellent private houses near by. The pottery found there is similar to that at Samaria (IV), where Jeroboam II was in residence. Sixty-three inscribed ostraca, accounts of the import of wine and oil, show that the city was still a vigorous trading centre.

Tell en-Nasbeh (Mizpah) and Gibeah were strongly refortified as frontier towns during the divided Monarchy. Both sites were reconstructed on an identical plan and with similar material which may show that this was the work of Asa after he had destroyed the nearby fort of Baasha at Ramah (1 Ki. xv). The invasion of Tiglath-pileser III of Assyria, *c.* 734 BC, resulted in the heavy destruction of Hazor (V) and Megiddo (IV). In the debris of the former a sherd inscribed *lpqḥ* ('belonging to Pekah'; see fig. 163) is reminiscent of the fact that, according to 2 Ki. xv. 29, xvi. 5–8 and the Assyrian Annals, Pekah ruled there at this time. The same Assyrian king mentioned (Jeho)ahaz whose tribute is recorded in 2 Ki. xvi. 8.

In 722 BC Sargon II concluded the siege of Samaria and, as he claims, removed 27,290 prisoners 'and their gods' from the city and district, importing foreigners to take their place (2 Ki. xvii. 24). Archaeologically, this can be seen by the poorer and partial habitation of the site, which included imported Assyrian and foreign pottery types. Henceforth Israel was under Assyrian domination and influence. When Judah threatened the Assyrian advance into Egypt, Sennacherib led his army south, sacking Megiddo (IV), Samaria, and Gibeah *en route* for Judah in 701 BC. The fall of Lachish, an event shown on the Assyrian palace reliefs (see fig. 127), has been confirmed by the armour, weapons, and helmets of fallen attackers near the ramp leading to the main city gate. A communal grave for 1,500 victims may be dated to this time. Hezekiah, whom Sennacherib claims to have 'shut up in his capital Jerusalem like a bird in a cage', was helped to withstand the Assyrian siege of his capital by the tunnel he had had the foresight to have cut to bring water 1,700 feet into the city from the Virgin's Spring (2 Ki. xx. 20; 2 Ch. xxxii. 30). The inscription found here in 1880 is one of the longest monumental Hebrew texts extant (*DOTT*, 209–211; see SILOAM). For other contemporary Hebrew inscriptions, see SHEBNA, WRITING.

The ardour of Josiah's opposition to Egypt is seen in the destruction of Megiddo (II) by Necho in 609 BC while on his way to Carchemish, a city which excavation shows to have been destroyed by fire soon afterwards (C. L. Woolley; 1931–2). This was during the battle in 605 BC when Nebuchadrezzar II captured the city and overran Syria and Palestine, which became subject to the Babylonians (so the Babylonian Chronicle). When Judah rebelled, stern punishment was inevitable. The Babylonian Chronicle describes the capture of Jerusalem on 16 March 597 BC. Many towns and fortresses in Judah, but not in the North, show the ravages of the Babylonian attacks at this time and, following Zedekiah's revolt, during the war of 589–587, some were destroyed and never again reoccupied (Beth-shemesh, Tell Beit Mirsim). In the debris at Lachish (III) twenty-one inscribed potsherds bear witness to the anxiety of the defenders at this time (*DOTT*, pp. 211–217; see LACHISH and fig. 161).

Archaeological surveys show that the country was greatly impoverished during the Exile, although the royal estates in Judah continued to be administered on behalf of Jehoiachin, who is named in texts from his prison in Babylon. Stamp sealings of 'Eliakim, steward of Yaukin'; seals of Jaazaniah from Tell en-Nasbeh and of Gedaliah from Lachish (2 Ki. xxv. 22–25; see figs. 76, 115) are witnesses to the activities of these leaders (see SEAL).

The resettlement of Judah was slow, and excavations show that it was not until the 3rd century that Judah was repopulated to the same density as in former times. Samaria, Bethel, Tell en-Nasbeh, Beth-zur, and Gezer were, however, occupied almost continuously, and cemeteries at 'Athlit (Carmel) and Tell el-Far'a (Negeb) produced Iron Age III pottery and Persian objects. The Persians allowed a measure of local autonomy, and locally minted coins begin to appear in the 5th and are abundant by the 3rd century. Most are imitations of Attic drachmas, but some bear Hebrew–Aramaic inscriptions (*yehud*,

'Judah') similar to those found on the Jewish coin which shows also a male deity seated on a chariot holding a hawk (early 4th century BC; see *IBA*, fig. 96). See MONEY. Many jar handles of this period are stamped with inscriptions such as 'Judah' (*yhd*), Jerusalem (*yršlm*), or the enigmatic *mṣh* or *nmšt*. Greek influence steadily increased through the imports *via* their coastal trading colonies. Attic red-figured and, later, Ionian and Attic black-figured wares are increasingly found. Trade from Arabia flourished with the establishment of the 'Idumaean' kingdom. S Palestine was controlled by an Arab, Gashmu (Ne. vi. 1); the name of this 'king of Kedar' is inscribed on silver bowls, and it is possible that the Persian villa at Lachish, of a design similar to the Parthian palace at Nippur in Babylonia, was a centre of his administration. Persian silver vessels have been unearthed at Gezer and Sharuhen. Arabian carved limestone incense altars similar to those at Ḥureidha in the Hadramaut were found at Tell Jemmeh.

VI. THE HELLENISTIC–ROMAN PERIOD

When the Macedonian Alexander the Great won Palestine as part of the former Persian Empire in 332 BC, the country was yet further opened to Hellenistic influence. However, after his death internecine warfare between his generals retarded this development. Only isolated pottery and coins can be assigned with confidence to the ruling Lagides in 332–200 BC. Mareshah (Marisa) now took over control of Idumaea from Lachish, and here a carefully laid-out Greek town has been uncovered. The streets set at right angles and parallel to each other led near the city gate to a market square (*agora*), round three sides of which were shops. Near the city were tombs of Greek, Phoenician, and Idumaean traders (*c.* 250–200 BC).

The stern days in which the Maccabees fought for Jewish independence (165–37 BC) are attested by refugee camps and caves (Wadi Ḥabsa) and forts like that built at Gezer by Simon Maccabaeus. Traces of the northern line of forts said to have been created by Alexander Jannaeus (Jos., *BJ* vi. 9. 7) have been found near Tel Aviv, Jaffa, and Hazor. At Beth-zur, commanding the road from Hebron to Jerusalem, Judas (165–163 BC) had built a fort on top of an earlier Persian structure, and this in turn was later rebuilt by the general Bacchides. Shops, houses, fortifications, reservoirs, Rhodian stamped jar handles, and coins help to illustrate the life of these zealots, one of whom, John Hyrcanus (134–104 BC), destroyed the pagan Greek cities of Samaria and Marisa.

Herod I (the Great; 37–4 BC) encouraged the process of Hellenization, effacing all the earlier temples in his new constructions, of which, however, only parts of the retaining walls, the 'Tower of David' and the first wall of Jerusalem remain to show the typical massive masonry of his reign. The inscribed tomb of the Bene Hazir near the city may also be of this date. Herod also renovated historic sites by building walls at Machpelah (Hebron) and at Mamre. At Samaria he rebuilt part of the city-wall and gateway, reinforcing the ancient Israelite walls with round towers. The city was given a temple dedicated to

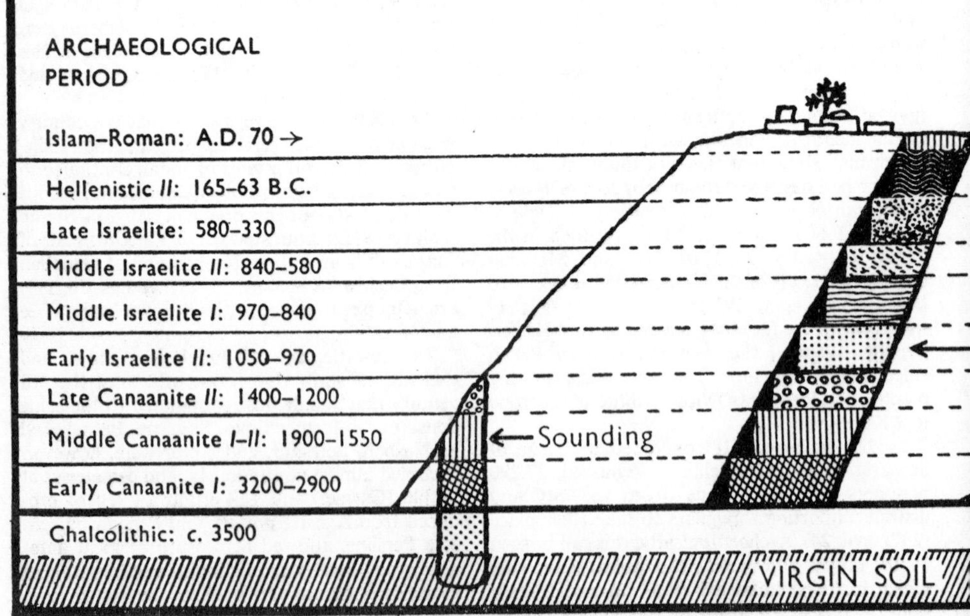

Fig. 12. Schematic drawing of an ancient Palestinian site showin

Augustus and a stadium, and renamed Sebaste. For his own use the king built a luxurious winter palace at Jericho (Wadi Qelt) and residences near Bethlehem (Herodium) and at Caesarea, which city, like Phasaelis and Antipatris, he embellished. His increasing fear of his enemies may be reflected in the massive fort he built at Masada, the lay-out of which is in striking agreement with the description given by Josephus (*BJ* xii. 8. 3). Little is known archaeologically of the time of Herod Agrippa who built the third wall of Jerusalem (*q.v.*) and whose sister Queen Bernice, according to her inscription, restored the buildings erected at Caesarea by Herod I.

The destruction of Jerusalem in AD 70 and the subsequent building by Hadrian of a Roman colony, Aelia Capitolina, on the ruined site makes difficult the identification of earlier remains, except for the Temple area. The presence of the Roman Tenth Legion among the garrison under Pilate is attested by a number of finds in the city (*e.g.* Qirya). A Greek inscription, found by Clermont-Ganneau in 1871, warns Gentiles against passing the balustrade into the inner Temple court on pain of death (*IBA*, p. 101), and this illustrates the words of Paul (Eph. ii. 13–19; Acts xxi. 28). Gabbatha (Gk. *Lithostrōton*, Jn. xix. 13) is identified with the 2,500-square-metre stone pavement beneath the Tower of Antonia, in which marks of a game played by the Roman soldiers can still be seen. The pools of Bethesda (Jn. v. 2) in the north-east section of the city and of Siloam (Jn. ix. 11), south of the Temple area, have now been identified. Sychar's well near Balatah (Shechem, Jn. iv. 5, 6) remains in use.

There is still much controversy over the location of the 'second wall' of Jerusalem, so the site of the crucifixion and sepulchre of our Lord remains uncertain. However, the type of tomb sealed by a 'cartwheel' stone is known from a number of Roman sites. Among more than two hundred burial chambers examined, many near Jerusalem, E. L. Sukenik in 1945 discovered ossuaries inscribed in Greek *Iēsous iou* and *Iēsous aloth*. Since these tombs are to be dated prior to AD 50, his description of these as 'the earliest records of Christianity' may be well founded, at least as far as extra-biblical evidence yet goes. The inscriptions, which he probably correctly suggested referred to Jesus, are perhaps prayers and provide evidence of the Church in Jerusalem in its first twenty years. Many other ossuaries bear Hebrew, Aramaic, or Greek names, including Simon, Lazarus, Judas, Ananias, Joseph, Miriam (Mary), Martha, Elisabeth, Salome, and Johanna, showing that such names were common in Jerusalem at this same period. Some with rarer names may possibly refer to the very persons named in the New Testament, but such identifications must remain tentative (*e.g.* Barsabas, Acts i. 23, xv. 22; and Sapphira, Acts v. 1). Some scholars believe that the inscriptions, and absence of the usual pagan accoutrements in these tombs, reflect a new belief in the after-life.

VII. EXPLORATION AND EXCAVATION

Interest in traditional biblical sites revived after the Reformation, and many wrote of their travels

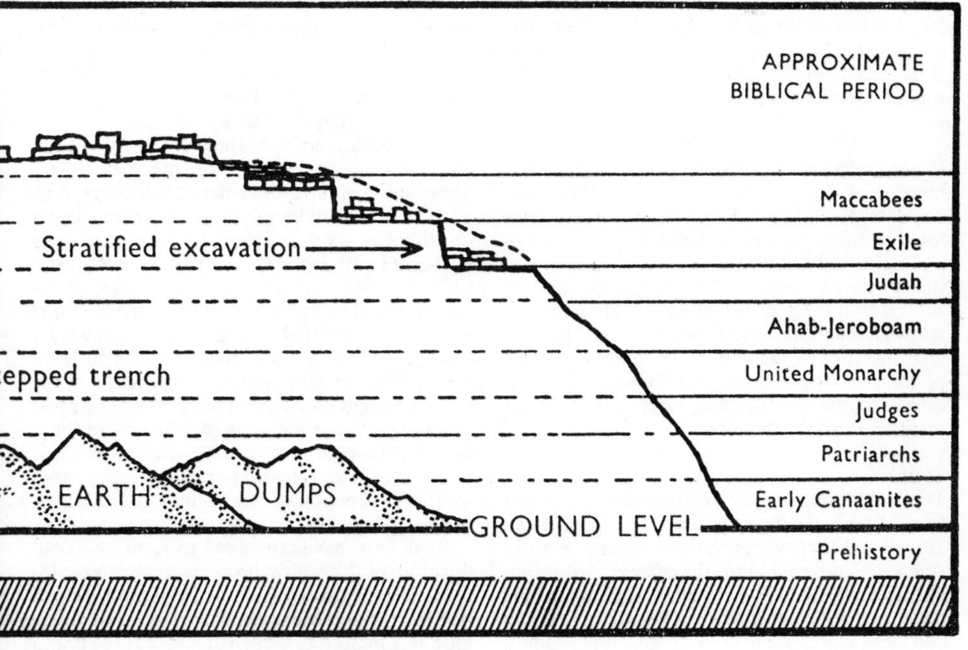

ethods of excavation and levels (strata) of occupation.

in Palestine. It was not, however, until 1838 that the Americans, Edward Robinson and Eli Smith, carried out the first planned surface exploration, identifying several ancient sites with places named in the Bible. The first excavation was undertaken by the Frenchman, De Saulcy, near Jerusalem in 1863, and this was followed by a series of surveys on behalf of the Palestine Exploration Fund in 1865–1914. The areas visited and mapped included Kadesh (Conder), Galilee and the Arabah (Kitchener), the desert of the Exodus (Palmer), and sites including Capernaum, Samaria, and Caesarea (Wilson). Interest centred on Jerusalem itself, where underground tunnelling revealed the foundations of walls, and rock levels and parts of the south wall and gates and Ophel were explored between 1867 and 1928. Following the excavation in 1890 by Sir Flinders Petrie of Tell el-Hesi, which established the first ceramic index and stratigraphical chronology based on comparisons with Egypt, many scientific expeditions led by American, British, French, German, and Israeli scholars have worked at a variety of sites, some of which are listed on pp. 72–76.

Surface surveys have in recent years been primarily conducted by the Israeli Department of Antiquities. Among the areas covered have been the Jordan valley–Galilee (*BIES*, XVIII, XIX), Israelite settlements of the time of the Judges in N Israel and Carmel. In the Shephelah Tell Najela has been identified with Eglon and Ras 'Abu Humeyd with the biblical Gittim (*IEJ*, IV, 1954, pp. 227 ff.). Tell Haror in the Negeb has been suggested as the site of Gerar and the ancient road from Tell 'Arad to Kadesh-barnea ('Eyn Qudeyrat) found to have been defended by Israelite forts. Glueck has shown that the Negeb supported a heavy population in the patriarchal (MB) age as well as in Israelite and Nabataean times (*Rivers in the Desert*, 1959).

VIII. CUNEIFORM INSCRIPTIONS

In the course of excavations in the Near East a number of archives have been discovered, the contents of which are of considerable importance for the understanding of the historical, cultural, and religious background of the Canaanites, and thus of the Hebrews as they entered the land. A summary of these principal groups of cuneiform texts is therefore given below. For Egyptian texts, see EGYPT, and for finds relating to later periods, see also PAPYRI AND OSTRACA. The few early Hebrew inscriptions have already been mentioned briefly (but see also WRITING).

a. Alalaḫ

The excavation of Tell el-'Atshana in N Syria (now Açana, Turkey) by Sir C. L. Woolley in 1937–9 and 1946–9 uncovered two main levels in which tablets were found; the palaces of (i) Iarimlim (level VII, *c.* 1900–1780 BC) and (ii) Niqmepa (level IV, 15th century BC; *cf.* Ras Shamra). The 456 texts, like those from Mari and Ras Shamra, and roughly contemporary with these two groups, have opened up a new field for study, which incidentally provides fresh contacts with biblical literature, since they are closer geographically and chronologically to the patriarchal age than the texts from Assyria (see Nuzi below), with which comparisons are frequently made.

Among the customs which can be studied afresh is that of the preferential status given to the son who could be elevated to the position of first-born in the family, thereby becoming entitled to a double share in the inheritance of the paternal estate. This practice, already attested in Assyria and Nuzi, is now seen to have been in use at Alalaḫ (AT.92) in a marriage contract between Iriḫalpa and the woman Naidu. 'If Naidu does not give birth to a son (then) the daughter of his brother Iwaššura shall be given (to Iriḫalpa as wife); . . . if (another wife) of Iriḫalpa gives birth to a son first and after that Naidu gives birth to a son, the son of Naidu alone shall be the first-born.' This custom of choosing a first-born and the father's right to disregard the law of primogeniture, already known from Nuzi and Ugarit, throw light on Abraham's relation with Isaac, and on the case of Manasseh and Ephraim (Gn. xlviii. 13–20), the repudiation of Reuben (Gn. xlix. 3, 4), and elevation of Joseph (xlviii. 22; 1 Ch. v. 2; *BASOR*, 156, pp. 38 ff.).

The Alalaḫ treaties include a number of agreements between sovereign states and provide an example of the method of dealing with fugitive slaves (AT.3). Thus in 1 Ki. ii. 39, 40 Shimei entered Philistinian territory to search for his two slaves and King Achish of Gath returned them on demand. This would imply a treaty with extradition rights probably made between Solomon and Gath after the experience of David there (1 Sa. xxvii. 5 ff.). It also throws light on the Deuteronomic provision prohibiting the extradition of fugitive (presumably Hebrew) slaves in Dt. xxiii. 15, 16 (*IEJ*, V, 1955, pp. 65–72).

The Alalaḫ practice of the exchange of villages (AT.456) perhaps to preserve inter-state boundaries along natural and defensible features, may be reflected in Solomon's 'gift' of twenty villages to Hiram of Tyre in return for wood and gold (1 Ki. ix. 10–14; *JTVI*, 1956, p. 124; *JBL*, LXXIX, 1960, pp. 59–60). The ceremony involved the slaughter of a sheep over which the participants declared 'If ever I take back what I have given you . . .' implying 'may the gods cut off my life', an idea paralleled frequently in the Old Testament oaths (*e.g.* 1 Sa. iii. 17). This same text indicates the presence of 'Hittites' in Syria in the 20th–19th centuries BC, and there is no reason why some should not be resident farther south in the period of Abraham (Gn. xxiii. 5, 7; *JTVI*, 1956, p. 124).

Ahab may have attempted to justify his confiscation of Naboth's property (1 Ki. xxi. 15) following the law (AT.17) whereby an evil-doer, or a man who rebels against the national god or king (*bēl mašiktim*, verse 10), came to be put to death and his property appropriated by the palace, which had to pay off any outstanding debts (*IEJ*, VI, 1956, p. 224).

The Alalaḫ tablets, of importance for the study of the Mitannian Akkadian dialect and Hurrian, also help in the understanding of Hebrew phrases. Thus, in the manumission of slaves the Heb. *mišneh* (Dt. xv. 18), taken as 'double', 'twice as much' by AV, is possibly the *mištannu* of Alalaḫ (AT.3) meaning 'equivalent', '*quid pro quo*'; and this sense helps in Je. xvi. 18, which, when given the former of these two interpretations, has been said to 'stigmatize God as unreasonable and unjust' (*HUCA*, XXIX, 1958, pp. 125, 126). The month *niggallim* (AT.51, *etc.*), a word also found in Old Assyrian, is closely related to the time 'you first put the sickle to the standing grain' (Dt. xvi. 19, RSV), and the occurrence of *ribbat* (AT.55–6 'ten thousand') shows that the Heb. *ribbô* (*e.g.* Jon. iv. 11) is not necessarily a late Aramaism as has been argued. In David's list of heroes it is said of Abishai (and Benaiah) that 'he attained [lit. 'entered'] not unto the (first) three' (2 Sa. xxiii. 19, 23; 1 Ch. xi. 21, 25). The Alalaḫ tablet (263) suggests that this does not refer to grading or appreciation, but was a scribal method used in accounting and simply implies the names were not included in the first group. The corvée (*masi*) was enforced at Alalaḫ (AT.246) as later in Israel (Heb. *mas*; Jos. xvii. 13). Since Alalaḫ, even in the earlier period (VII) already had a predominantly Hurrian population (see HORITES) the appearance there of such names as Anah, Aholibamah, Alian, Ajah, Dishon, and Ezer (Gn. xxxvi), 'Anath and Shamgar (Jdg. iii. 31), To'i (2 Sa. viii. 9), Agee (2 Sa. xxiii. 11), Eli-hepa (2 Sa. xxiii. 32), which can now be illustrated and explained from existing Hurrian personal names, is significant (*JTVI*, LXXXII, 1950, p. 6). Among the classes named in these texts a substantial proportion of the population can be shown to have been freeborn, householders and tenant-farmers. These were called *ḫupšu*, the equivalent of the Heb. *ḥopšî* (Ex. xxi. 5, *etc.*).

b. Amarna

In 1887 a peasant digging in the ruins of Tell el-Amarna, Egypt, found an archive of cuneiform tablets from which, with subsequent discoveries, about 350 documents have been recovered. These supply important information of the state of Palestine and Syria *c.* 1400–1360 BC. The frank personal despatches from Asiatic kings to the pharaohs Amenhotep III and Akhenaten give a vivid picture of the intrigues and inter-city strife which followed the weakening of Egyptian control shortly before the Israelites entered the land.

In S Syria, Abdi-ashirta and his son Aziru, though protesting their loyalty to their Egyptian overlords, were in reality increasing their own domains with the connivance of the Hittites of N Syria and thus preparing the way for the eventual conquest of all Syria by Suppiluliuma. Rib-Addi of Byblos, a loyalist who wrote fifty-three letters to the Egyptian court, describes the uncertainty and chaos which followed his unanswered pleas for military assistance. He reports the capture by Aziru of an adjacent town, where the Egyptian resident had been slain, and the attack on Byblos from which he was forced to flee. Similarly Laba'ya of Shechem, despite his protests of innocence (EA.254), was increasing his hold in the central hills in league with the semi-nomadic Habiru, who are frequently named in the texts, mainly as small armed bands (see HEBREWS). The activities of these Habiru are reported by many cities. When Laba'ya threatened Megiddo, its ruler, Biridiya, begged Egypt for help.

Abdi-hepa of Jerusalem makes frequent reports, complaining that Miliku of Gezer and others are engaged on raids. He cannot, therefore, understand why the pharaoh should allow Gezer, Lachish, and Ashkelon to escape from the duty of providing the Egyptian garrison with food when they have plenty. He himself has been robbed by Egyptian troops and warns the pharaoh that his tribute and slaves being sent to Egypt will probably not arrive, as Laba'ya and Miliku have planned an ambush (EA.287). The latter might be a ruse to avoid sending any gifts, for in another letter Shuwardata of Hebron warns the pharaoh that Abdi-hepa of Jerusalem is a rogue (EA.280).

In addition to the local historical evidence these letters are important for the wider implications of alliances between Egypt and the rulers of Mitanni and Babylon, often concluded, or supported, by marriages between the ruling families. Letters from Mitanni (Tushratta), being in Hurrian or containing Hurrian terms, have greatly advanced the understanding of that non-Semitic language (see HORITES). The presence of a Babylonian myth (Nergal and Ereshkigal) shows the influence of Babylonian, the *lingua franca* of the whole Ancient Near East at this period. This fact has been confirmed by the discovery in 1946 of a fragment of the Gilgamesh Epic (*c.* 1400 BC) at Megiddo.

Our knowledge of the political geography of Palestine at this time is helped by the naming, among others, of Ammuniru of Beirut, Abi-milki of Tyre, Akizzi of Qatna, Abdi-Tirši of Hazor, and other kings. Some of these kings and names can be correlated with the contemporary texts from Ugarit (see *Ras Shamra* below). Since the tablets are written in a dialect of Babylonian unfamiliar to the scribes, and contain a number of Canaanite glosses, they are also of importance for philological studies.

Since some have argued that the Habiru of these texts are to be identified with the Hebrews under Joshua, instead of being evidence of the state of the land prior to his conquest, the following aspects of the Amarna evidence should perhaps be stressed. The *ḫab/piru* (SA.GAZ) here, as indicated also by the Ras Shamra and Alalaḫ texts, were occupying the areas not strictly controlled by the larger towns; they operated usually in small numbers throughout Palestine from

Lachish and Syria, and do not appear as besiegers of cities. Moreover, these texts show a situation different from that under Joshua; Lachish and Gezer, far from being destroyed (Jos. x), are in active support of the Habiru. The names of rulers also differ, the king of Jerusalem at this time being named as Abdi-hepa.

c. Mari

During the excavation of Tell Ḥarīri, near the R. Euphrates and 7 miles from Abụ Kemal in SE Syria, from 1933 to 1960, A. Parrot uncovered a large area of the ancient city of Mari, including the temples of the god Dagon and the goddess Ishtar. Of more than 20,000 tablets found in the 18th-century BC palace of the ruler Zimri-Lim, a magnificent building of 300 rooms covering more than 15 acres, about a quarter were state letters. These texts are written in a Semitic dialect 'virtually identical' with that spoken by the Hebrew Patriarchs. They provide a wealth of evidence bearing on the geography, history, and religion of NW Mesopotamia in this period. The rival city-states held only a loose control over the intervening countryside, which was the dwelling-place of diverse groups of nomads and semi-nomads. One group, the Bene(TUR.MEŠ)-Iamina, 'sons of the right (south)', have been questionably compared with the biblical Benjamites. Again and again the reports tell of the incursion of the Habiru, a people mentioned also in the Ras Shamra, Alalaḫ, and later Amarna texts. In these clashes a term *dawīdum*, translated 'chief', has been compared with the name of David (*BA*, XI, p. 2), though other scholars believe it to be a word for 'defeat' (*JNES*, XVII, 1958, p. 130).

This was a time of intense diplomatic activity, arbitration, treaties, and the interchange of letters and gifts between rulers (*Iraq*, XVIII, 1956, pp. 68–110). Before Mari fell to Hammurabi of Babylon, whose date has been lowered following the discovery of these texts, one of Zimri-Lim's agents reported 'There is no king really powerful in himself. Some ten or fifteen kings go with Hammurabi of Babylon, as many with Rim-Sin of Larsa, as many with Ibal-piel of Eshnunna, as many with Amut-piel of Watanum and twenty with Iarimlim of Yamhad (Aleppo).' Among other kings named in these letters are Hammurabi king of Aleppo and a king of the same name ruling at Qatna (see HAMMURABI), and coalitions with rulers as far afield as Elam are thus shown to be possible (*cf.* Gn. xiv). However, the only Palestinian city named is Hazor, though a number of towns or villages in the region of Harran, where the temple of Sin was a centre of attraction for many Semites, are mentioned. The identification of such places as Naḫur, Til-Turaḫi, and Sarug (*cf.* Nahor, Terah, and Serug, Gn. xi. 23, 24) in the very area to which Abraham migrated is remarkable, though the relation of such place-names to the earlier persons cannot yet be defined.

In the Mari texts connected with the making of treaties or covenants reference is made to the 'killing of an ass'. The words (*ḫaiarum qatalum*) occur in Hebrew, and the idea seems to have been preserved by the Shechemites (the Bene Hamor, or 'Sons of an ass', of Jos. xxiv. 32) in their dealings with Jacob (Gn. xxxiii. 19, xxxiv. 1–3). Other aspects of covenant-making at Mari throw light on Old Testament practice (M. Noth, *Mélanges Isidore Lévy*, 1958, pp. 433–444). In contrast to the faith of the Patriarchs, divination was widely practised at Mari, the majority of texts following the Akkadian pattern of reports of the observation of the liver of sacrificial animals, astronomical and other data. The diviner's word was considered of especial importance in military affairs. Prophecy was also practised, the god having those whom he sent to proclaim his word. Letters tell of the arrival of a messenger who claims to have been sent by a god, sometimes called an 'answerer' (*apilum*), who has been compared with the prophets of Israel, though the latter are outstanding by comparison for the clarity, range, content, and purpose of their oracles. One report from Itur-Asdu to king Zimri-Lim tells of a dream revelation in the temple of Dagon at Tirqa. The message was not good, because the king had failed to report regularly to his god. 'If he had done so I would have delivered the sheikhs of the Benjamites into the hands of Zimri-Lim.' In this way too the king was told of the sacrifices the god required.

Another custom illustrated from these texts is that of the royal census, which at Mari, as in the Old Testament, is no mere routine mustering, but is linked with political reform, the granting of land and ritual. The terminology is strikingly parallel to the Hebrew. Thus the technical details refer to enrolment (*pqd*, 'called to account': *cf.* Ex. xxx. 13, 14, 'he who is entered among the enrolled'), purification (Heb. *kōper*, Mari *tebibtum*), and the occurrence of *nāśā' rô'š*, 'to take into account, take notice of' (AV 'lift up the head'). Many Hebrew phrases are illustrated by these texts, *e.g.* the use of *šipṭu*/*šipiṭum* at Mari for a disciplinary warning or measure, a term which in Hebrew (*šōpēṭ*) is often mistranslated 'judge' (*BASOR*, 149, 1958, pp. 17–25).

d. Nuzi

The excavations at Nuzi (Yorghan Tepe) and adjacent mounds near Kirkuk, Iraq, were commenced by the University of Pennsylvania (E. Chiera) in 1925 and carried on until 1931 with the co-operation of the Semitic Museum, Harvard and American Schools of Oriental Research. Although soundings reached virgin soil, the principal level of occupation uncovered was the 15th–14th centuries BC, when the town was under Hurrian domination (see HORITES). In the palace and private homes more than 20,000 clay tablets, in a Babylonian dialect in the cuneiform script, were found covering four or five generations. These included complete archives, among which those of Tehiptilla, prince Shilwateshup, and a successful business woman, Tulpunnaya, are the best known, and provide one of the most intimate pictures yet discovered of an ancient community. The remarkable parallels between the customs and social conditions of these peoples and the patriarchal narratives in Genesis have led some scholars to argue from this for a similar 15th-century date for Abraham and his sons; but there is evidence that many of these customs had been observed for some centuries, and that the Hurrians were already a virile part of the population of N Mesopotamia and Syria by the 18th century BC (see *Alalaḫ* above). These parallels provide useful background information to the patriarchal age, and are one of the external factors supporting the historicity of this part of Genesis.

Many of the documents (contracts, reports, and judicial decisions) relate to *exchange*, either permanent or temporary, of persons, goods, and land, the value being fixed at the rate of a half a mana of silver as equal to an ox, ass, or ten sheep. All transactions involving transfer of property were recorded after they had been witnessed, sealed, and 'proclaimed at the (town) gate' (Gn. xxiii. 10, 18).

Another large group of documents deals with *inheritance*. Normally the estate passed to the eldest son, who received a 'double portion' compared with the younger. Should a man (or woman) have no sons, he could adopt as a son a person from outside the family, even if he was a slave. Such an adopted son was expected to care for the man in his old age, to provide proper burial and the maintenance of religious rites (including the pouring of libations), and to continue the family name in return for the property. This may explain Abram's adoption of Eliezer as heir prior to the birth of Isaac (Gn. xv. 2–4). Such agreements were legally void if the adopter subsequently had a son of his own; the adoptee then took second place. At Nuzi this process of adoption was extended to become a fiction by which property, legally inalienable, might be sold.

A further way of ensuring an heir was the custom, known also from earlier Babylonian texts, whereby a childless wife would give her husband a substitute slave-wife to bear sons. Thus one contract relating the adoption by Shurihil of Shennima, son of Zigi, reads 'And Shurihil, as concerns Shennima, has given to Shennima a share of all these lands (and) his earnings of whatever their description. If Shurihil has a son of his own, he shall be the firstborn (with) a double share. He shall receive a double portion. Shennima shall then be second and shall receive according to his allocation of the inheritance. As long as Shurihil is alive, Shennima shall serve him; when Shurihil dies Shennima shall become heir. Further, Gilimninu has been given as wife to Shennima. If Gilimninu bears children, Shennima shall not take another wife; but if she does not bear, Gilimninu shall take a woman of the Lullu (a slave) as wife for Shennima. As for the concubine's offspring, Gilimninu may not send them away. . . . Yalampa has been given to Gilimninu as handmaid. . . . If Gilimninu bears children and Shennima takes another wife, her "bundle" she shall take up and she shall leave' (H.67). In similar fashion the childless Sarah gave Hagar to her husband (Gn. xvi. 3) and Rachel gave Bilhah to Jacob (Gn. xxx. 3). Sarah, despite the undertaking that Hagar's sons would be counted as hers (Gn. xvi. 2) and thus have a claim to the inheritance, sought to drive Hagar away (Gn. xxi. 10). Abraham acted against the contemporary custom only when given a special assurance from God that he should do so (verse 12).

Esau's *exchange of birthright* with Jacob is also paralleled in a Nuzi text (HV.99), in which three brothers draw up a 'document of brotherhood' concerning a plantation, whereby one gives his brother 'three sheep in exchange for his inheritance share'—a more valuable exchange than Jacob's 'bread and a mess of lentils' (Gn. xxv. 30–34). A similar power to exchange property, or an anticipated inheritance, is attested in earlier Assyrian and Babylonian texts.

These texts also throw light on the weight given to oral blessings and death-bed statements (Gn. xxvii. 29, 33, xlix. 8). At Nuzi a son who produced witnesses to corroborate the words of his dying father won his case at court. In another case an oral 'blessing' was upheld.

Some incidents in the life of Jacob also find parallels in these documents. Jacob's claim to have protected Laban's flock (Gn. xxxi. 38, 39) is of significance, since at Nuzi an owner won a lawsuit against his herdsmen for illegal slaughtering. This is a matter also covered by Ex. xxii. 1, 2 and the laws of Hammurabi (§ 262).

The possession of household-gods was of legal significance denoting the title of the holder to inheritance of the family property, the gods passing with the property. It may well be that Laban had no sons at the time his daughters became wives of Jacob (Gn. xxix), and Rachel's action in carrying off the 'gods' (Gn. xxxi. 30), unknown to Jacob (verse 19), may have been her attempt to secure for Jacob the inheritance he had lost by the subsequent birth of sons to Laban (verse 1). Laban's primary concern would seem to have been with the loss of these images (see TERAPHIM) rather than of his daughter and flocks.

The right of daughters to inherit property is attested in Nuzi texts, as in earlier Old Babylonian contracts (*cf.* Nu. xxvii. 8). At Nuzi slaves seem to have worked for a stated period of years to obtain their wives, a custom perhaps reflected in Jacob's case, though he may have been 'adopted' as Laban's son. An adopted son at Nuzi was given the daughter as bride (see above). Marriage contracts sometimes included a clause prohibiting the acquisition of other wives, a safeguard sought by Laban for Rachel (Gn. xxxi. 50).

Levirate marriage, which appears to have been implied in patriarchal times (Gn. xxxviii. 8; *cf.* Dt. xxv. 5–10), is known from Nuzi as well as Hittite and Assyrian contracts. A father requires that, if his son dies, his bride is to be married to another of his sons (*BA*, III, 1940, p. 10). Similarly a number of customs which appear in later Hebrew history are already found in the 15th century, the idea of periodic 'release' from obligation as to debts at certain times (Dt. xv); the shoe as a legal symbol being included in token payments (*e.g.* H.76). To take a person's sandal legally signified that one assumed rights over the whole person (Ru. iii. 12, iv. 1–7), and such an action must be exercised only with care. To oppress the poor was to sell him for a pair of shoes, a mere token payment (Am. ii. 6, viii. 4–6; 1 Sa. xii. 3, LXX). As a result of Nuzi references, 1 Sa. i. 24 is now seen to read 'a bullock, three years old'.

e. Ras Shamra (*Ugarit*)

Following up an accidental discovery made by a peasant at Minet el-Beida on the N Syrian coast near Latakia in 1928, C. F. A. Schaeffer excavated there and at nearby Ras Shamra (ancient Ugarit) for twenty-two seasons between 1929 and 1960. Among the many important finds by this French expedition have been the royal palaces, temples (including one dedicated to Baal), and administrative buildings dated from the early 14th century BC. Together with many fine objects, including ivories, weapons, statues, and stelae, were found many inscriptions in cuneiform (Sumerian, a local dialect of Babylonian and Hurrian), Egyptian and Hittite hieroglyphs, Cypriot, and in a hitherto unknown cuneiform alphabet (Ugaritic). This well reflects the cosmopolitan population at this busy seaport.

The Ugaritic alphabet employs a unique combination of wedges to form thirty letters, written like Akkadian from left to right, and must have been a local invention, since the letters peculiar to it are added at the end of the alphabet, which otherwise follows the same order as Hebrew (see fig. 237). Two inscriptions in this script found in Palestine, on a tablet at Beth-shemesh, and on a bronze knife from near Tabor, may show that this form of writing was widely used (see WRITING). Within eight months of the publication of the first fifty tablets by C. Virolleaud in 1930 he had deciphered the alphabet with the help of H. Bauer and E. Dhorme, though discussion continues on the relation of this NW Semitic dialect to 'Canaanite' and Hebrew. The importance of the 350 or more Ugaritic texts for biblical studies was quickly recognized, and few aspects of Old Testament studies are unaffected by these discoveries, which also give promise of further literary finds from Palestine.

The texts include a number of epics written on a series of tablets. Among these are those of the storm-god Baal and his sister or consort Anat, who rescues him from Mot, the god of death; of the deeds of King Keret, and of the death and revival of Dan(i)el's son Aqhat. These epics are believed to go back several centuries, since Baal (see also HADAD) had already by the 14th century displaced 'El, a remote and shadowy god, the father of gods and men and possessor of several wives, including Asherah and Astarte (*q.v.*), as head of the pantheon. From these texts 'Canaanite' religious beliefs and practices are becoming well known. Baal was god of the storms, controller of the rain and fertility, called 'Lord of heaven and earth' and 'the rider on the clouds' (*cf.* Is. xix. 1). Anat was similar to the Phoenician Ashtart, a goddess of war, love, and fertility. The Lady Asherah 'of the Sea' was perhaps a form of the Babylonian *Ašuratum*; she was chief goddess of Tyre, where she was known as *Qudšu*, 'Holy'. Her name was employed as a general term for goddess (pl. *'ašērôṯ*) and linked with Baal's in Jdg. iii. 7. The texts show the degrading results of the worship of these deities, with their emphasis on war and sensuous love, sacred prostitution, and the consequent social degradation. Other deities named include Reshep (Hab. iii. 5, AV 'burning coals') and Dagon (*q.v.*).

There is a similarity between the terminology of the elaborate Ugaritic ritual system and that in Leviticus. Thus the whole burnt-offering (Ugar. *kll*; Dt. xxxiii. 10), burnt- (*srp*), peace- (*šlmn*), trespass- (*'asm*), and tribute- or gift- (*mtn*) offerings and offerings made by fire (*'ešt*) are named, though their use differs from Old Testament spirit and practice (see SACRIFICE AND OFFERING). These epics, myths, and hymns have a distinct poetic style, with irregular metre, repetitions, and parallelisms, which have led Albright and his students to argue for a date of 13th–10th century BC or earlier for some Hebrew poetic passages, *e.g.* for the Songs of Miriam (Ex. xv; *JNES*, XIV, 1955, pp. 237–250), and Deborah (Jdg. v); the blessing of Moses (Dt. xxxiii; *JBL*, LXVII, 1948, pp. 191–210), and Pss. xxix, lviii (*HUCA*, XXIII, 1950–51, pp. 1–13). Many phrases which occur in Hebrew poetry are found in these texts; a few examples may be cited: 'flashing (*ysr*) his lightning to the earth', as Jb. xxxvii. 2 is to be read; 'the dew of heaven and the fat (*smn*) of the earth' (*cf.* Gn. xxvii. 28, 39); 'LTN the swift . . . the crooked serpent' is the Leviathan of Is. xxvii. 1; Jb. xxvi. 13. In this way the meaning and exegesis of a number of difficult Hebrew passages can be elucidated. The 'fields of offerings' of 2 Sa. i. 21 (AV) is rather the Ugaritic 'swelling of the deep', and the Ugaritic root *spsg*, 'glaze', helps to translate Pr. xxvi. 23 correctly as 'like glaze upon a potsherd'. The study of Ugaritic grammar and syntax, especially such prepositions and particles as *b*, *l*, *'el*, *k*(*ī*), has shown that many of the old emendations proposed for the *MT* are unnecessary.

In addition to the Ugaritic texts, which also include a number of letters, memoranda, and lists (*spr*), there are many tablets written in a Babylonian script and dialect. These include lexicographical texts, some providing Sumerian–Akkadian–Hurrian–Ugaritic equivalents of great importance for understanding these languages. The many royal letters, treaties, contracts, and administrative texts help towards the reconstruction of the history of Syria in the early 14th century BC. The study of these Babylonian texts is, like those from Alalaḫ and Mari, providing useful parallels to the patriarchal age. For example, the contract whereby Abdiya adopts Ana-Tešub (his grandson) as his son shows that this type of intra-family adoption was known and practised in Canaan, and hence the adoption by Jacob of Ephraim and Manasseh to the same basis of sonship as Reuben and Simeon (Gn. xlviii. 5) is not an isolated instance. Compare also the adoption of the sons of Machir by their grandfather Joseph (Gn. l. 23); Obed by his grandmother Naomi (Ru. iv. 16, 17) and, though much later, Esther by her cousin Mordecai recorded in Est. ii. 7 (*IEJ*, IX, 1959, pp. 180–183).

IX. OTHER INSCRIPTIONS (GREEK AND LATIN)

A number of inscriptions bear on the history of the early Church. A Roman imperial edict, said to have been found at Nazareth in 1878, is perhaps to be ascribed to Claudius. This orders the trial of anyone who 'has in any way extracted the buried or maliciously transferred them to another place . . . or has displaced the sealing or other stones'. If the proposed dating to *c.* AD 50 is correct, this may be part of the attempt by Claudius to settle the disturbances caused by Jews who opposed the early Christians who were 'fomenting a malady common to the world'. Claudius issued a number of decrees on this subject. One of his inscriptions at Delphi (Greece) describes Gallio as proconsul of Achaia in AD 51, thus giving a correlation with the ministry of Paul in Corinth (Acts xviii. 12). In Corinth also a door inscription—'Synagogue of the Hebrews'—may indicate the place where Paul preached (Acts xviii. 4). Excavations there revealed a text naming a benefactor, Erastus, probably the city-treasurer of Rom. xvi. 23; shops similar to those in which Paul worked (Acts xviii. 2, 3), and an inscription of 'Lucius the butcher', which probably marks the site of the 'meat-market' (*makellon*) to which Paul referred in 1 Cor. x. 25.

At Ephesus parts of the temple of Artemis, the 'Diana of the Ephesians', have been recovered together with the agora and open-air theatre capable of seating more than 25,000 persons. A votive text of Salutaris, dedicating a silver image of Artemis 'to be erected in the theatre during a full session of the *ecclesia*', shows that the full assembly met here as implied by Acts xix. 28–41. The historical trustworthiness of Luke has been attested by a number of inscriptions. The 'politarchs' of Thessalonica (Acts xvii. 6, 8) were magistrates and are named in five inscriptions from the city in the 1st century AD. Similarly Publius is correctly designated *prōtos* ('first man') or Governor of Malta (Acts xxviii. 7). Near Lystra inscriptions record the dedication to Zeus of a statue of Hermes by some Lycaonians, and near by was a stone altar for 'the Hearer of Prayer' (Zeus) and Hermes. This explains the local identification of Barnabas and Paul with Zeus (Jupiter) and Hermes (Mercury) respectively (Acts xiv. 11). Derbe, Paul's next stopping-place, was identified by Ballance in 1956 with Kaerti Hüyük near Karaman (*AS*, VII, 1957, pp. 147 ff.). Luke's earlier references to Quirinius as governor of Syria before the death of Herod I (Lk. ii. 2) and to Lysanias as tetrarch of Abilene (Lk. iii. 1) have likewise received inscriptional support (see LYSANIAS, QUIRINIUS).

For a summary of excavations outside Palestine, see EGYPT, ASSYRIA, BABYLONIA, SYRIA. By consulting the articles on the individual place-names (see, *e.g.*, List of Sites below) further archaeological details can be obtained. Similarly, certain aspects of biblical archaeology have been covered by articles on specific topics, *e.g.* ART, ARCHITECTURE, ARTS AND CRAFTS, *etc.* For the evidence provided by ancient coins, see MONEY. For early inscriptions on papyrus (*e.g.* Elephantine), see PAPYRI AND OSTRACA, WRITING.

BIBLIOGRAPHY. *General.* W. F. Albright, *The Archaeology of Palestine*², 1960; *Archaeology and the Religion of Israel*², 1956; A. G. Barrois, *Manuel d'Archéologie biblique*, I–II, 1939, 1953; I. J. Franken, *Outline of Palestinian Archaeology*, 1961; G. L. Harding, *The Antiquities of Jordan*, 1959; K. Kenyon, *Archaeology in the Holy Land*, 1960; G. E. Wright, *Biblical Archaeology*, 1957; S. Yeivin, *A Decade of Archaeology in Israel (1948–1958)*, 1960.

Illustrations. M. Avi-Yonah and A. Malamat, *Views of the Biblical World*, I–III, 1959–60; D. J. Wiseman, *Illustrations from Biblical Archaeology*, 1958.

Excavated Sites. Alalaḫ: D. J. Wiseman, *The Alalakh Tablets*, 1953; *JCS*, VIII, 1954, pp. 1–30; XII, 1958, pp. 124–129; XIII, 1959, pp. 19–33, 50–62; *cf. JAOS*, LXXIV, 1954, pp. 18 ff.; *JNES*, XIV, 1955, pp. 196 ff., and refs. in VIIIa above. *Amarna:* W. F. Albright in *ANET*, pp. 483–490; *BASOR*, nos. 86 ff.; C. J. Mullo Weir in *DOTT*, pp. 38–45; J. A. Knudtzon, *Die El-Amarna-Tafeln*, I–II, 1907, 1915. *Mari:* W. F. Albright in *ANET*, pp. 482, 483; G. E. Mendenhall, *BA*, XI, 1948, pp. 1–19; C. J. Gadd, *ExpT*, LXVI, 1954–5, pp. 174 ff., 195–198. *Texts:* G. Dossin *etc.*, *Archives Royales de Mari*, I–IX, 1941–60, and references VIIIc above. *Nuzi:* C. H. Gordon, 'Biblical Customs in the Nuzu Tablets', *BA*, III, 1940, and references. *Texts:* E. Chiera, *Publications of Baghdad School*, I–III, 1927–31; E. R. Lachemann, *etc.*, *Excavations at Nuzi*, I–VI, 1929–55. *Ras Shamra*: R. de Langhe, *Les Textes de Ras Shamra-Ugarit et leurs Rapports avec le Milieu biblique de l'Ancien Testament*, I–II, 1945; C. H. Gordon, *Ugaritic Literature*, 1949; G. R. Driver, *Canaanite Myths and Legends*, 1956; C. F. A. Schaeffer, *Ugaritica III*, 1956 (full references for excavations). *Texts:* C. Virolleaud in *Syria*, IX, 1930–XXXVIII, 1960; also *Le Palais Royal d'Ugarit*, II, 1957; *ib.*, III–IV; J. Nougayrol, 1955–6 (for Babylonian Texts); J. Gray, *The Legacy of Canaan*, 1957 and *DOTT*, pp. 118–133; H. L. Ginsberg, *ANET*, pp. 129–155. D.J.W.

LIST OF THE PRINCIPAL EXCAVATED SITES IN PALESTINE (ISRAEL AND JORDAN)

1 PLACE *Where a name is printed in capitals, see also separate article*	2 LOCATION *See map section at end of Dictionary*	3 EXCAVATED *Organization responsible and name of Director*	4 DATES	5 OCCUPATIONAL PERIODS, MAIN DISCOVERIES, ETC. *For abbreviations, see* ARCHAEOLOGY, *Section II above*	6 PUBLICATION *Abbreviations as in Palestine Exploration Fund Quarterly*
Abu Hawam	Nr. Carmel	DAP (R. W. Hamilton)	1932–3	LC II–MI I. IA III	*QDAP*, I–II
Abu Matar	SE of Beersheba	Centre Nat. de Récherche, France (J. Perrot)	1954	Chalcolith. (Subterranean dwellings)	*IEJ*, V–VI
AI	Et-Tel, 2 m. SE of Bethel	Rothschild Exp. (J. Marquet-Krause)	1933–5	Proto-Urban; EC (walls and temple)	J. Marquet-Krause, *Les Fouilles d'Ay*, 1949
ANATHOTH	'Anāta, 3 m. NE of Jerusalem	ASOR (A. Bergman)	1936	MI–Hellen. (Pottery)	*BASOR*, 62–3
ASHKELON	Ascalon, Sharon	PEF–BSAJ (J. Garstang)	1920–2	LC–EI I (Philistines); Roman	*PEQ*, 1921–4
'Athlit	SW of Carmel	DAP (C. N. Johns)	1930–3	EI–LI (Phoenician graves)	*QDAP*, I–VI
Beth-eglaim	Tell el-'Ajjūl, 4 m. SW of Gaza	BSA Egypt (F. Petrie)	1930–4	EC–MC (Pottery); MC (large city); Hyksos (fosse, cemetery, jewellery)	F. Petrie, *Ancient Gaza*, I–IV; K. Kenyon, *ADAJ*, III. W. F. Albright, *Chronology of a S Palestine City*, 1938; E. J. H. Mackay, *Ancient Gaza*, V, 1952
BETHEL	Beitin, NE of Rumallah	ASOR–Pittsburg–Xenia (W. F. Albright & J. L. Kelso)	1935–58	EC–MC (Hyksos); LC (destroyed by Israelites); Rom. (coins)	*BASOR*, 29, 55–58, 151
BETHLEHEM	5 m. S of Jerusalem	BM (E. W. Gardner)	1934–6	Paleolith.	*QDAP*, V, VI
		DAP (H. Richmond)	1935	Byzant. (Church of the Nativity)	*QDAP*, V
BETH-SHAN	Scythopolis; Tell el-Husn	Univ. Pennsylvania Mus. (A. Rowe)	1921–33	Chalcolith.; EC (level XI; Canaanite temples); levels VIII (= 1350 BC), VII (= 1300), VI (= 1150), V (= 1000); EI I; Hellen.-Byzant. Egypt. occupation	A. Rowe, *etc.*, *Beth-Shan*, I–IV, 1930; *PEQ*, 1927–9, 1931–3, 1934
Beth-She'arim	Sheikh Abreik	(B. Mazar, N. Avigad)	1936–40, 1955–9	Hellen. I–Rom. (catacombs); EI–Rom. (town)	B. Mazar, *Beth-She'arim*, 1957; N. Avigad, *IEJ*, V

1	2	3	4	5	6
Beth-shemesh	('Ain Shems) Tell er-Rumeileh, WSW of Jerusalem	PEF (D. Mackenzie) ASOR Pac. Sch. Relig. & Haverford (E. Crant)	1911–12 1928–31	MC. LC. MI II (Philistine pottery); Byzant. (monastery)	*APEF*, I–II; E. Grant, *Ain Shems*, I–IV, 1931; *QDAP*, III
Beth-yeraḥ	Khirbet Kerak, SW Galilee	IES (B. Mazar, M. Avi-Yonah)	1944–6, 1950–60	Chalcolith.–MC; LI–Rom. (camp); Islam	*IEJ*, II
Beth-zur	Khirbet et-Tubeiqeh, *c.* 5 m. N of Hebron	ASOR McCormick Sem. (O. R. Sellers, W. F. Albright)	1931, 1957	MC II (Hyksos); LC–IA I; Hellen. II (Maccabean fortress)	O. R. Sellers, *The Citadel of Beth-Zur*, 1933; *BA*, XXI; *BASOR*, 43, 51, 150
Capernaum	Tell Ḥûm, NW Galilee	Deutsche Orient-Gesellschaft (Kohl, Mader & Schneider)	1905–14	Synagogue (3rd century AD)	H. Kohl & C. Watzinger, *Antike Synagogen in Galilaea*, 1916
Carmel	Wadi el-Mughāra and vicinity	DAP (D. Garrod) BSAJ–Univ. Calif. (Th. McCown)	1922 1926–34	Paleolith. (animals)-Neolith.; EI (cemetery)	D. Garrod (I, 1937), T. D. McCown (II, 1939), *The Stone Age of Mount Carmel*; *PEQ*, 1938
Debir (?Kiriath-sepher)	Tell Beit Mirsim, SW of Hebron	ASOR. Pittsburg-Xenia (W. F. Albright & M. G. Kyle)	1926–32	EC III; LC II (Israelite capture); Israelite city; dye-vats (see Arts)	*AASOR*, XII–XIII, XVII, XXI–XXII
Dibon	Dhībân, 40 m. S of Amman	ASOR; DAJ	1930, 1950–7	EC; MI II (capital of Mesha); Nabataean	*BASOR*, 125, 133, 146
Dothan	Tell Dotha, 13 m. N of Samaria	Wheaton College (J. P. Free)	1953–60	Chalcolith.; EC–LC; EI–MI (city and gateway)	*BASOR*, 131, 135, 139, 143, 152, 156
Eglon	Tell el-Hesi; W of Lachish (wrongly identified as Lachish)	PEF (F. Petrie) PEF (F. J. Bliss)	1890 1891–3	EC–EI I (pottery sequence; weapons)	W. F. Petrie, *Tell el Hesy* (*Lachish*), 1891; F. J. Bliss, *Mound of Many Cities*, 1894
Ezion-geber	Tell el-Kheleifah, Aqabah	ASOR (N. Glueck)	1937–40	EI II (Solomon's refineries)	N. Glueck, *Other Side of Jordan*, 1940; *BASOR*, 71–72, 75, 79, 82
Gaza	(See also Beth-eglaim)	PEF (W. J. Phythian-Adams)	1911, 1914, 1920–22	Soundings	*PEQ*, 1910, 1920, 1923
Gerasa	Jerash	DAP Yale–ASOR	1920, 1928–34	Neolith.; EC (village); Hellen. (traces); Rom. (Decapolis) (Church, *etc.*)	E. G. Kraeling, *Gerasa, City of the Decapolis*, 1938
Gezer	Tell Abu Shusheh, 12 m. S of Lydda	PEF (R. A. S. Macalister)	1902–5, 1907–9	Chalcolith.; EI I; Rom.-Byzant.	R. A. S. Macalister, *Gezer*, I–III, 1912; *PEQ*, 1935; *QDAP*, IV

1	2	3	4	5	6
Ghassul (Teileilat G.)	3 m. E of Jordan, NE of Dead Sea	Pontifical Bib. Inst. (A. Mallon, R. Koeppel) .	1929–38	Chalcolith. (4 main levels: pottery, flints, simple copper axes)	A. Mallon, *etc. Teileiat Ghassul*, I–II, 1934–1940; *BASOR*, 130; *BIES*, XVIII
GIBEAH	Tell el-Fûl, 3 m. N of Jerusalem	ASOR (W. F. Albright)	1922, 1933	EC (village); EI I (citadel (Saul); Late(?) watch-tower)	*AASOR*, IV, XXXIV
GIBEON	El-Jīb, 8 m. N of Jerusalem	Univ. Mus. Philadelphia, Ch. Div. Sch. of Pacific (J. B. Pritchard)	1956–7	EC–MC; EI (pool and tunnel, 2 Sa. ii. 13); inscribed jar handles; wine cellars); Hellen. II (coins)	*BA*, XIX, XXIII; J. B. Pritchard, *Hebrew Inscriptions and Stamps from Gibeon*, 1959; *Univ. Mus. Penn. Bulletin*, XXI
Ḥadera	Sharon	Heb. Univ. (E. L. Sukenik)	1934–5	Chalcolith. (Ghassulian) ossuaries	*JPOS*, XVII
HAZOR	Tell el-Qedah (Waqqas), 5 m. SW of L. Huleh	Marston (J. Garstang)	1926–7	Sounding: EC–Hellen. MC II*a* (Hyksos city); LC II (city (temple) captured by Israelites); EI II (Solomon gateway; destroyed *c.* 730 BC)	*LAAA*, XIV; Y. Yadin, *Hazor*, I–II, 1959, 1960; *IEJ*, VI–IX
		Heb. Univ. Rothschild (Y. Yadin)	1955–8		
Jaffa		Israel DA (P. Guy)	1950	LI–Hellen. II-Rom. (Maccab. town; coins)	*IEJ*, IV
		Univ. Leeds (J. Bowman)	1955		
Jemmeh	6 m. SE of Gaza (misidentified as Gerar)	PEF (W. J. Phythian-Adams)	1921–2	Soundings: MI (fort); LC II–LI Stratification continuous	W. F. Petrie, *Gerar*, 1928
		BSA Egypt. (W. F. Petrie)	1926–7		
JERICHO (OT)	Tell es-Sulṭān, NE of Jerusalem	PEF. Deutsche Orientg. (E. Sellin)	1869, 1907, 1909	Mesolith.-Neolith.; LCI (traces only Joshua period)	E. Sellin, *etc. Jericho*, 1913. *LAAA*, XIX–XXII
		Liverpool Univ.–Marston (J. Garstang)	1930–6		J. Garstang, *Story of Jericho*, 1948
		BSAJ–PEF–B.Ac.–ASOR (K. Kenyon)	1952–8		K. Kenyon, *Jericho I*, 1960; *Digging up Jericho*, 1957; *PEQ*, 1951–7
JERICHO (NT)	Tulul Abu el-ʻAlayiq (Wadi Qelt), 1 m. W of Jericho	AASOR–Pittsburg-Xenia (J. L. Kelso, A. H. Detweiler)	1950–1	Herod's winter palace; Herod Archelaus' building	J. L. Kelso, J. B. Pritchard, *Excavations at New Testament Jericho* (*AASOR*, XXIX–XXX, XXXII–XXXIII)
JERUSALEM		PEF (C. Warren)	1864–7	Structures	C. Warren, *Survey of W Palestine and Jerusalem*; *id.*, *Underground Jerusalem*
		PEF (Clermont-Ganneau)	1873–4	Inscriptions	

1	2	3	4	5	6
JERUSALEM		PEF (F. J. Bliss, A. C. Dickie)	1894–7	South Wall	F. J. Bliss, *Excavations at Jerusalem*
		Parker Mission	1909–11	Tunnels (Virgin Fountain)	H. Vincent, *Jérusalem sous Terre*, 1911
		Rothschild (R. Weill)	1913–14	Ophel	R. Weill, *La cité de David*, I–II, 1920, 1947;
		PEF (R. A. S. Macalister)	1923–5, 1927–8	Ophel (Jebusite)	*APEF*, IV
		DAP (C. N. Johns)	1934–48	Maccab. (gateway); Hellen. (walls)	*APEF*, V
		DAP (R. W. Hamilton)	1937–8	North Wall	*QDAP*, X; *PEQ*, 1944
		IES (E. L. Sukenik, M. Dothan)	1956–60	Hellen. I (tombs)	*'Atiqot*, III
		BSAJ (K. Kenyon)	1961–	Old city	
KIR (Haraseth)	Kerak, Jordan	—	—	Sounding; IA II (city of Mesha of Moab; Crusader remains)	G. L. Harding, *Antiquities of Jordan*, 1959
LACHISH	Tell ed-Duweir, W of Hebron	Wellcome-Marston (J. Starkey)	1932–8	LC I–II (temples; earlier burials); MI II (main city, destroyed 588 BC; Hebrew letters); IA III–Hellen.	H. Torczyner, *Lachish I* (Letters), 1938; O. Tuffnell, *etc.*, *Lachish* II–IV, 1940–58
Madaba	SW of Amman, Jordan	ASOR (A. H. Detweiler)		LC II*b* (tombs); Maccab.–Byzant. (Mosaic map of Palestine, 6th century AD)	M. Avi-Yonah, *The Madaba Mosaic Map*, 1954
MARESHAH	Tell Sandaḥannah (Marisa) NW of Hebron	PEF (R. A. S. Macalister)	1898–1900	EI; Hellen. II (city; painted tombs); Rom. (villa)	R. A. S. Macalister, *Excavations in Palestine*, 1902; J. Peters-Thiersch, *Painted Tombs in the Necropolis of Marisa*, 1905; *RB*, 1922–5
		École Biblique, Jerusalem	1921–4		
Masada	W of Dead Sea	IDA–Heb. Univ.–IEJ (M. Avi-Yonah)	1955–6	Herodian fortress	*IEJ*, VII
MEGIDDO	Tell el-Mutesellim	Deutsche Orientges.	1903–5	EI I–MI II (levels I–V) completely cleared	G. Schumacher, C. Watzinger, *Tell el-Mutesellim I–II*, 1908; R. S. Lamon, *Megiddo I*, 1939; G. Loud, *Megiddo II*, 1948; *id.*, *Megiddo Ivories*, 1939; *BA*, XXIII
		Oriental Inst. Chicago (C. S. Fisher, *etc.*)	1925–39	Some earlier Canaanite discoveries. Ivories	
		IES (Y. Yadin)	1960	EI (gateway)	
MIZPAH	Tell en-Nasbeh, 8 m. N of Jerusalem	Pacific Sch. Relig. (W. F. Badé, *etc.*)	1926–35	EC I (burials); EI–MI (Philistine pottery; city gateway)	C. C. McCown, *Tell en-Nasbeh*, I–II, 1947; *BA*, X

1	2	3	4	5	6
Qasileh	El Khirbe; E of Tell Aviv	IES (B. Mazar)	1948–9	EI. Destroyed time David. Trade with Cyprus, Egypt, Ophir	*IEJ*, I
QUMRAN	ʻAin Feshkha, W of Dead Sea	DAJ–École Biblique Jerusalem (G. L. Harding, R. de Vaux)	1948–58	Community Centre *c.* 100 BC. Caves I–XI containing Biblical and Sectarian Scrolls	See DEAD SEA SCROLLS; also *QDAJ*, IV–V
RABBATH AMMON	Amman, Jordan (Philadelphia)	DAJ (G. L. Harding)	1949	Paleolith.-Chalcolith. EC–MC (tombs; pottery); MC–LC (Hyksos tomb); IA II; Hellen.-Rom. (theatre)	G. L. Harding, *Antiquities of Jordan*, 1959; *QDAJ*, I; *QDAP*, XIII–XIV
SAMARIA	Sebaste	Harvard Univ. (G. A. Reisner) & Heb. Univ.-PEF. BSAJ. Br. Acad. (J. W. Crowfoot)	1908–10, 1931–5	Proto-Urban. I (city; ivories–Ahab; Ostraca-Jeroboam II); Hellen. (fort); Rom. (temple)–Byzant.	J. W. Crowfoot, *etc.*, *Samaria-Sebaste*, I–III
SELA	Petra, E Arabah	Melchett Fund (C. & G. Horsfield). AASOR (W. F. Albright); DAJ–BSAJ (P. Parr, *etc.*)	1934, 1938, 1929, 1944–5, 1937, 1957–60	Chalcolith.–LC?; Hellen. I–II (Nabataean city and gateway; high place)	*AASOR*, XXXIV–V; *QDAP*, VII–IX; *QDAJ*, IV; *BASOR*, 151, 159; *BA*, XXIII
Sharuhen	Tell el-Farʻa, SE of Gaza	BSA Egypt. (W. F. Petrie)	1928–30	EI I (tombs; Philistine pottery); MC II (Hyksos); MI II–Phoenician colonists: LI (Persian vessels)	W. F. Petrie, *Beth-pelet* (*Tell Fara*), I–II, 1930, 1932
SHECHEM	Tell Balātah	Vienna Academy (E. Sellin)	1913–34	EC–LC. MC II (sanctuary; E Gate)	*QDAP*, I, V (full bibliography)
		Drew-McCormick–ASOR (G. Wright)	1956–60		*BA*, XX; *BASOR*, 144, 148
SHILOH	Khirbet Seilun, S of Samaria	Danish Pal. Exp. (A. Schmidt)	1926–9, 1932	MC. EI I (destroyed by Philistines). Hellen.–Islam (Byzant. mosaics)	*PEQ*, 1927; *JPOS*; *QDAP*, III
SUCCOTH	Tell Deirʻalla, R. Jabbok	Nederlands Inst. (H. Francken)	1961	MC–MI	*VT*, X
TAANACH	Tell Taʻannak, 5 m. SE of Megiddo	Vienna Academy (E. Sellin)	1902–4	EC–Hellen. LC (Port; tablets 15th century); IA I (citadel)	E. Sellin, *Tell Taʻannak*, 1904
TIRZAH	Tell Farʻa, NE of Shechem	École Biblique, Jerusalem (de Vaux)	1946–7, 1950–	Chalcolith. Proto-Urban (tombs) EC II. MI (abandoned for Samaria. Town walls). Re-occupation *c.* 700–600 BC	*RB*, LIV–LVI, LVIII–LIX, LXII, LXIV; *PEQ*, 1956

ARCHANGEL. See ANGEL.

ARCHELAUS. See HEROD.

ARCHER. See ARMY, ARMOUR AND WEAPONS.

ARCHIPPUS. 'Fellowsoldier' of Paul and Timothy (Phm. 2); the phrase implies previous service together (*cf.* Phil. ii. 25). He is addressed with Philemon and Apphia in a manner suggesting that he may have been their son. This does not necessarily exclude the early suggestion (*cf. Theodore of Mopsuestia*, ed. Swete, I, p. 311), based on the context of Col. iv. 17, and adopted with divergent conclusions by Lightfoot and Goodspeed, that the 'ministry' that the Colossians must exhort him to fulfil was exercised in nearby Laodicea; but the context does not demand, and may not support, this. Even if he ministered at Colossae, and the charge is to root out the heresy there (*cf.* W. G. Rollins, *JBL*, LXXVIII, 1959, pp. 277 f.), it is curious that the *church* is bidden to convey it. Even more dubious is Knox's suggestion that Archippus was host to the Colossian house-church, the owner of Onesimus, and the principal addressee of Philemon. The expressions in Col. iv. 17 imply the reception of a tradition, and can hardly be interpreted in terms of the release of Onesimus. The precise nature of the ministry is unknown, but perhaps Paul's old comrade-in-arms, while still linked with his home church, was again on missionary service. The solemn charge need not imply actual dereliction (*cf.* 2 Tim. iv. 5). See also PHILEMON, EPISTLE TO. A.F.W.

ARCHITECTURE.

I. IN THE OLD TESTAMENT

a. City defences

Since towns were essentially defensible localities within the walls of which the surrounding rural population could retreat in time of danger, they were usually located near water and at strategic sites. Thus they were set on a hill or 'on their ruin-mounds' (Jos. xi. 13, AV 'in their strength'). There was no systematic town-planning in Palestine before the Hellenistic period (at Marisa). Buildings conformed to the limited space available within the narrow streets and defence walls.

The higher part of the site was usually occupied by the citadel, which formed an inner defence in which were located the principal public buildings and, at Jerusalem, the Temple. This 'fortified area' (*bîrâ*) at Jerusalem (1 Ch. xxix. 1, 19, AV 'palace') and at Susa in Elam (Ne. i. 1; Est. i. 2), as in other ancient places, was a distinct quarter of the capital. This was the 'fastness' (*meṣūḏâ*) of Zion captured by David (1 Ch. xi. 5–7).

From early times the city was defended by a double or triple vertical wall (Jericho, Ai). At Beit Mirsim the 11-foot-thick wall was built of stones laid in rough courses and strengthened by towers. By the Middle Bronze Age II the outer face of the wall was battered or sloped, often with a stone glacis, the inner face being vertical, on a substructure of massive polygonal masonry (Jericho and Shechem). This plan, together with the double or triple gateway with four to six parallel piers or towers, as at Shechem and Megiddo, seems to have followed an earlier Syrian pattern.

The prosperous united Monarchy developed a typical Israelite fortification consisting of a massive structure of unhewn stones. The casemate walls at Beth-shemesh and Debir were formed by an outer (5-foot-thick) and inner (3-foot-thick) wall joined by cross walls. The same technique was used by Saul at his fortress-capital Gibeah (Tell el-Fûl). Solomon used carefully drafted stones in the walls of Megiddo and Gezer and at these two store-cities and at Hazor (1 Ki. ix. 15) the same royal architect-mason built identical gate-houses set in casemate walls, three chambers on each side with square towers in the 66-foot-long external walls (see fig. 102).

At Tell en-Nasbeh, where 20–26-foot-thick city walls were plastered, the 9th-century gateway (13 feet wide) opened into a courtyard where stone benches lined the walls. This was the place of justice (Dt. xxi. 19; Am. v. 15) and of the market (2 Ki. vii. 1). By the 7th century BC city gateways were built so as to provide only indirect access as an additional defence (see LACHISH, SAMARIA). At Tell Beit Mirsim the northern part of the gate-tower was designed with a courtyard off which were six paved rooms in which were built-in cupboards, wash-basins, and other conveniences for official travellers. At this city, as at others, there was a second smaller gateway for pedestrians and donkeys. See also FORTIFICATION AND SIEGECRAFT.

b. Public buildings

The taxation required to support the extensive building inaugurated by David itself led to the construction of 'store-cities'. At Beth-shemesh and Lachish the residence of local officials adjoined a building with exceptionally thick walls and long narrow rooms probably used for the storage of grain. The whole was raised on a platform with an earth-filled interior (105 feet long, later extended to 256 feet), perhaps the 'Millo' or 'filling' technique used by David at Jerusalem (2 Sa. v. 9; see also FOUNDATION, LACHISH). At Megiddo and Hazor large pillared buildings with paved courtyards, usually taken to be the stables for Solomon's chariot-horses, may well be public chancelleries and other offices rather than military establishments. Similar buildings have been excavated at Taanach, Eglon, and Gezer.

In Palestine a construction technique common in Syria (Alalaḫ) was employed; rough stone for the lower courses, aligned and bonded by carefully dressed corner-stones (*q.v.*), supported courses of wood interspersed with mud-brick (see fig. 227; *cf. PEQ*, XCII, 1960, pp. 57 ff.). In other buildings at Megiddo, Samaria, and Bethshan large stones, marginally drafted and with embossed or pecked centres, were laid regularly as headers and stretchers without mortar. The work is very precisely carried out and shows great architectural progress.

The large open courtyards of these buildings drained off into rock-hewn cisterns (as at Beth-shemesh in the earlier 14th–13th centuries), which were used both for washing purposes (1 Ki. xxii. 38, see SAMARIA) and as dungeons (Je. xxxviii. 6). Beneath other courtyards deep tunnels were cut to the nearest spring, those mined at Lachish (144 feet), Gibeon, Gezer, Megiddo, and Jerusalem (see SILOAM) being remarkable engineering feats.

A rock-hewn tomb at Kidron, Jerusalem, dated in the Monarchy, shows Egyptian influence, the walls (12 feet high) sloping slightly inwards, the overhanging cornice bearing a cavetto design.

c. Solomon's Temple

The first Temple was built by Hiram of Tyre *c.* 960 BC on a 'Syro-Phoenician' pattern, using white limestone trimmed at the quarries (1 Ki. v. 6). The architectural details are given in 1 Ki. vi (see fig. 206). The whole building measured *c.* 100 × 30 feet wide and was set on a 9-foot-high platform which was *c.* 7½ feet wider than the structure itself. The main approach was up ten steps, at the top of which was a pair of free-standing bronze pillars (*c.* 37½ feet high × 18 feet circum., see JACHIN AND BOAZ). Between these the entrance through high doors led into a vestibule or entrance porch (*'ûlām*, verse 3) measuring *c.* 33 × 15 feet, from which double doors (15 feet wide) led into the main room (*hêḵāl*; 45 feet high × 60 feet long × 30 feet wide). This was lit by high clerestory windows set below the ceiling and larger on the inside than outside (verse 9). The wooden pillars and pilasters were probably crowned with proto-Ionic capitals. The walls, floors, and doors of this 'Holy Place' were lined with wood overlaid, and in part inset, with gold upon the engraved and sculptured designs of palm-trees, cherubim, and guilloches or chains (2 Ch. iii. 5; Ezk. xli. 18; see ART). Beyond further steps a door led into the 'Holy of Holies' (*d^eḇîr*, 'oracle'), a room without windows, designed as a cube of *c.* 30 feet, which was the special abode of Yahweh (verse 13). This innermost room was dominated by the outspread wings (each *c.* 7½ feet) of the 15-foot-high gilded wooden cherubim over the mercy-seat.

Against the outside of the Temple three-storeyed store-chambers were built with separate entrances (verses 5–9). The whole was surrounded by a courtyard wall of three stone courses topped by a heavy wooden rail (see verse 36).

Solomon's Temple follows the general lay-out of temples found at Tainat (Syria, 9th century) and Hazor (*q.v.*).

d. Private houses

The 17th-century BC villa near Shechem follows a typical plan with its single entrance leading to an open inner courtyard, off which led rooms used by servants and for storage (*cf.* fig. 109). This basic lay-out was similar to that in use throughout the Ancient Near East (see D. J. Wiseman, *IBA*, pp. 22, 23). At Hazor ashlar steps led up to the second floor where the owners lived and on up to the flat roof, which was ideal for rest in the summer or for drying stores (Jos. ii. 6). The majority of dwellings had roofs thatched with straw and mud supported by 12–15-foot wooden beams, and were kept water-tight by periodical rolling with a heavy stone. Since the arch and vaulting was known from *c.* 3000 BC, it is likely that this was employed to support the flat roofs of large buildings which could stand a great weight (Jdg. xvi. 27). A parapet round the flat

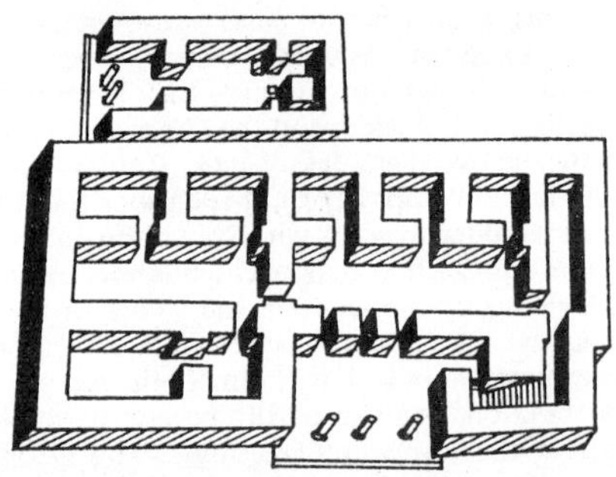

Fig. 13. The royal palace at Tell Tainat, Syria. The adjacent temple follows a ground plan similar to that adopted for Solomon's Temple. See also figs. 36, 61, 204.

roof was considered a necessary safety measure (Dt. xxii. 8). After the 12th century most houses had their own cisterns in the inner courtyard to collect rain-water from the roof.

After the 10th century the practice of erecting one or two rows of pillars along the axis of the main rooms became increasingly popular. These pillars were of stone or wood set on a stone plinth, and Samson may have dislodged two central pillars of this type to bring down the upper storeys of the house at Gaza (Jdg. xvi. 25–30). As well as supporting the upper floor, such pillars served to hold the rubble partition walls which subdivided the ground floor. See HOUSE and fig. 110.

A large Persian villa at Lachish (*c.* 400 BC) had a similar lay-out of courts, columned entrances, and barrel-vaulted ceilings to Parthian buildings at Nippur and showed Mesopotamian influences.

e. The inter-testamental period

The architecture of the Seleucid era is best represented by the mausoleum of the Tobiad family at 'Araq el-Emir, Jordan (see fig. 14). Huge drafted stones, ornate 'Corinthian' capitals, and a frieze of lions beneath the cornice show vigorous early Hellenistic influences. The continuation of Phoenician influences can be seen alongside outright Hellenistic introductions in the Maccabean period represented in discoveries made at Beth-zur and Marisa, where excavations have unearthed many buildings. At Samaria round towers were built on the line of the earlier Israelite casemate-wall. Outside Jerusalem a number of Maccabean tombs remain. 'The Tomb of Zacharias' has an 'Egyptian' pyramidal roof,

Fig. 14. Reconstruction of the façade of the Tobiad family mausoleum at Araq el-Emir, Jordan, c. 175 BC.

'Greek' capitals and pilasters with quarter columns at the corners hewn out of the rock. Such experimentation prepared the way for the introduction of finer Hellenistic buildings under Herod. D.J.W.

II. IN THE NEW TESTAMENT

a. Herod's Temple

This fine building, which dominated Jerusalem, was a show-piece built as a demonstration of magnificence and to further Herod's policy of patronage towards Judaism. Building was commenced in 20 or 19 BC and was substantially completed in forty-six years (Jn. ii. 20). It was not finally finished until AD 64. Mk. xiii. 1, 2 refers to the impression created by the great stonework of the foundations, and the grandeur of the whole. The building was totally destroyed in the siege of AD 70, and a complete description cannot be given. It can, however, be said that it was a triple structure—a lower court forming a fine terrace, having in the middle an inner court raised on a platform, and the shrine itself rising from this and crowning the whole. Sited magnificently as it was, it must have been a striking spectacle. Cloisters or porticos seem to have surrounded the outer court, a feature Greek rather than Hebrew in its architecture, and here Christ taught, and the early Christians assembled (Jn. x. 23; Acts iii. 11, v. 12). The open area became a market-place for sacrificial animals, and a money-mart for pilgrims, a corrupt commerce in which the hierarchy was no doubt involved (Jn. ii. 13–17, *et al.*). See fig. 15.

b. Jewish synagogues

At Capernaum an ancient floor beneath a 4th-century synagogue has been excavated. It may be the remains of the building (given by a Roman centurion) in which Christ preached (Lk. vii. 5). At Ain Duk 2 miles north-west of the site of ancient Jericho, a mosaic floor of uncertain date, but possibly 3rd century AD, is undoubtedly a synagogue relic. An inscription records the congregation's gratitude to the donor of the building, 'Benjamin, son of Joseph'. A door lintel from the Corinth synagogue (Acts xviii. 4), bearing the fragmentary inscription '. . . GOGEEBR. . .' enables the archaeologist to place the Corinth ghetto and its house of worship. In all these cases nothing is known of the architecture. See figs. 51, 199.

c. The remains of early Christian chapels

These are similarly indeterminate in the terms of this article. Two survive from the 4th century—that of Dura-Europos, and that which has been identified as a second-floor room in the recently excavated villa at Lullingstone in Kent.

d. The Palestinian house

In Palestine the dwellings of the poor probably differed little from those to be seen in remote Turkish or Syrian villages today. Poorer folk had little more than one or two rooms

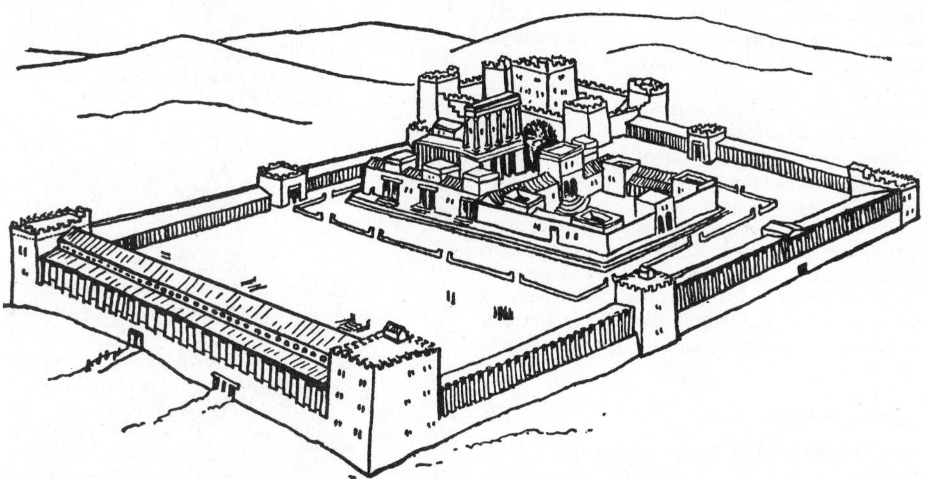

Fig. 15. A reconstruction of Herod's Temple. See also fig. 207 and *cf.* pl. XIV*b*.

(Lk. xi. 7). Privacy was difficult to find, and the poor man seeking quiet for prayer was bidden go into his storeroom (AV 'closet'), no doubt a small lean-to where vegetables, fruit, and grain were stored (Mt. vi. 6). The structure was simple, mainly lath-and-plaster, which thieves could 'break through' (Mt. vi. 19). Larger houses were built round a central courtyard, but this was not as invariable a feature as the flat roof which was common to all dwelling-places. Awnings were sometimes spread over this open, airy place, and guests or the inmates of the house could find restful comfort there (Acts x. 9). It was part of the flooring of such a roof-top (tiles or lath-and-plaster) which was removed by those who lowered the paralytic into the presence of Christ (Mk. ii. 4). The 'upper room' (Acts i. 13, ix. 37, 39, xx. 8) was either a second-storey room in a house with a court or a covered chamber on a flat roof, perhaps with an outer stairway. There is no definite evidence to connect this meeting-place with the guest chamber of the Last Supper, though in Acts i. 13 and in Mk. xiv. 15 and Lk. xxii. 12 the Vulgate uses *coenaculum*. See also HOUSE.

e. Architectural metaphor

The New Testament abounds in these. There are many references to the true foundation (see Mt. vii. 24–27; Lk. vi. 48, xiv. 29; Rom. xv. 20; 1 Cor. iii. 10–12; Eph. ii. 20; 1 Tim. vi. 19; 2 Tim. ii. 19; Heb. xi. 10). The *architektōn* of 1 Cor. iii. 10 was not a designer of blue-prints in the sense of our use of the derived term, but like the 'master-mason' of the medieval cathedral developed his plan as it proceeded and sometimes as his material dictated. The 'cornerstone' (1 Pet. ii. 7; *cf.* Ps. cxviii. 22 and Is. viii. 14) was the block at the corner of the foundation whose true shape and accurate laying determined the symmetry and lay-out of the whole structure. The integration of the upper structure is used metaphorically by Paul (1 Cor. iii. 9–16; Eph. ii. 20, 21). The former passage is poetical in its naming of 'gold, silver, and precious stones' as building material (*cf.* Rev. xxi. 18-21), but literal enough in its reference to 'wood, hay, stubble'. The wood is obvious. Hay is a thatch to form a foundation for mud plaster. Stubble is an essential ingredient of mud brick, cheap, sun-dried blocks for poor building such as may still be seen in Greece and the Middle East. E.M.B.

BIBLIOGRAPHY. W. F. Albright, *The Archaeology of Palestine*, 1960; Y. Yadin, 'New Light on Solomon's Megiddo', *BA*, XXIII, 1960, pp. 62–68; H. H. Frankfort, *The Art and Architecture of the Ancient Orient*, London, 1954; A. G. Barrois, *Manuel d'Archéologique biblique*, I, 1953, pp. 89–301.

ARCTURUS. See STARS.

AREOPAGUS (Gk. *Areios pagos*, 'the hill of Ares', the Greek god of war, corresponding to the Roman Mars).

1. A little hill north-west of the Acropolis in Athens, called 'Mars' hill' in Acts xvii. 22.

2. The Council of the Areopagus, so called because the hill of Ares was its original meeting-place. In New Testament times, except for investigating cases of homicide, it met in the 'Royal Porch' (*stoa basileios*) in the Athenian market-place (*agora*), and it was probably here that Paul was brought before the Areopagus (Acts xvii. 19) and not, as AV puts it, 'in the midst of Mars' hill' (verse 22). It was the most venerable institution in Athens, going back to legendary times, and, in spite of the curtailment of much of its ancient powers, it retained great prestige, and had special jurisdiction in matters of morals and religion. It was therefore natural that 'a setter forth of strange gods' (Acts xvii. 18) should be subjected to its adjudication.

The Areopagus address delivered by Paul on the occasion referred to (Acts xvii. 22–31) is a discourse on the true knowledge of God. Taking as his point of departure an altar-inscription 'To an unknown God' (see UNKNOWN GOD), he tells his audience that he has come to make known to them the God of whose nature they confess themselves ignorant. The true God is Creator and Lord of the universe; He does not inhabit material shrines; He is not dependent on the offerings of His creatures but bestows on them life and everything else that they need. He who is Creator of all things in general is Creator of mankind in particular; and so the speech goes on to make certain affirmations about man in relation to God. Man is one; the habitable zones of earth and the seasons of the year have been appointed for his advantage; God's purpose in these appointments is that men might seek and find Him, the more so because they are His offspring. While the wording and citations of the speech are Hellenistic, the emphases are thoroughly biblical. In the peroration Paul calls his hearers to repent and submit to the knowledge of God, since He is not only Creator of all but Judge of all; the pledge of His coming judgment has been given in His raising from the dead the Man empowered to execute that judgment. Hearing this reference to resurrection, the Areopagus dismissed Paul as unworthy of serious consideration.

BIBLIOGRAPHY. N. B. Stonehouse, *Paul before the Areopagus*, 1957; M. Dibelius, *Studies in the Acts of the Apostles*, 1956, pp. 26–83.

F.F.B.

ARETAS. The reference in 2 Cor. xi. 32 is to Aretas IV, Philopatris, the last and most famous Nabataean king of that name (*c.* 9 BC–AD 40). He was confirmed in the tenure of his client kingdom by Augustus, albeit somewhat reluctantly, for he had snatched it without permission. His daughter married Herod Antipas, but was divorced by him when he wanted to marry Herodias (Mk. vi. 17). Aretas declared war on Herod and defeated him in AD 28. Rome sided with Herod, but the punitive expedition which was eventually despatched under Vitellius, governor of Syria, had only reached Jerusalem when the Emperor's death in AD 37 caused it to be abandoned. According to Josephus (*Ant.* i. 12. 4), under Aretas, the Nabataean frontiers expanded from the Euphrates to the Red Sea. From 2 Cor. xi. 32 it seems probable, though very surprising, that Aretas had at some stage held Damascus, the old Syrian capital. It has usually been assumed that this would most probably have been under Gaius, whose policy it was to encourage client kingdoms. However, the B.M. Catalogue records a complete absence of Roman coinage minted at Damascus from the death of Augustus until the accession of Nero. Consequently it would seem that no conclusion can legitimately be drawn as to the date of Paul's conversion from the supposed date of Aretas' acquisition of Damascus after Tiberius' death in AD 37. He may have gained control of the town any time after AD 14. See also NABATAEANS.

E.M.B.G.

ARGOB. A district of Transjordan which was ruled over by Og, king of Bashan, before the Israelite conquest under Moses (Dt. iii. 3–5). It contained sixty strongly fortified, walled cities and many unwalled towns. The exact location of the area has been a matter of dispute. The view which had the support of Jewish tradition and derived additional weight from an unlikely etymology of Argob identified the region with the volcanic tract of land known as *el-Leja* (see TRACHONITIS). This view is no longer favoured. The name probably indicates a fertile area of arable land (*'argōḇ* probably from *regeḇ*, 'a clod'. *Cf.* Jb. xxi. 33, xxxviii. 38). Its westward extent is given as the border of the petty kingdoms of Geshur and Maacah (Dt. iii. 14). Some difficulty arises over the reference to the renaming of the cities of Argob, Havvoth-jair, by Jair the Manassite. In 1 Ki. iv. 13 the towns of Jair are located in Gilead (*cf.* Jdg. x. 3, 4; see HAVVOTH-JAIR).

J.C.J.W.

ARIEL (*'ᵃrî'ēl*, 'hearth of El (God)'). **1.** A name for the altar of burnt-offering described by Ezekiel (xliii. 15, 16). Several interpretations of this name have been given; 'altar-hearth' (RV); 'mount of God' or, less likely, 'Lion of God'. **2.** A name applied to Jerusalem (Is. xxix. 1, 2, 7) as the principal stronghold and centre of the worship of God (see 1 above). **3.** A Moabite whose sons were slain by Benaiah, one of David's warriors (2 Sa. xxiii. 20; 1 Ch. xi. 22). AV translates 'lionlike man' (see 1 above). **4.** A delegate sent by Ezra to Casiphia to bring men to accompany him to Jerusalem for the temple-ministry (Ezr. viii. 16).

D.J.W.

ARIMATHAEA. 'A city of the Jews', and home of Joseph (*q.v.*), in whose sepulchre the body of Jesus was laid (Mt. xxvii. 57; Mk. xv. 43; Lk. xxiii. 51; Jn. xix. 38). Identified by Eusebius and Jerome with Ramah or Ramathaim, the birth-place of Samuel (1 Sa. i. 19), the exact location of which is uncertain. See RAMAH.

J.W.M.

ARIOCH. 1. Name of the king of Ellasar, an ally of Chedorlaomer of Elam and Amraphel of Shinar, who warred against Sodom and Gomorrah (Gn. xiv. 1, 9). Although this person is unidentified, the name (*'aryôḵ*) can be compared with the Hurrian personal names Ari-aku and Ari-ukku commonly found in the texts of the second millennium BC. However, to equate him with Ariwuku, son of Zimrilim, of the Mari texts (Böhl), would imply a late date for Abraham.

2. Captain of Nebuchadrezzar's bodyguard (Dn. ii. 14, 15). He was commanded to slay the 'wise men' who had failed to interpret the royal dream but avoided this command by introducing Daniel to the king.

D.J.W.

ARISTARCHUS. All the references undoubtedly relate to the same person. The first, Acts xix. 29, describes him as already Paul's fellow-traveller when seized by the Ephesian mob (though it has been argued that this is proleptic). In Acts xx. 4 he accompanies Paul to Jerusalem, probably as an official Thessalonian delegate with the collection; and in Acts xxvii. 2 he is on Paul's ship from Caesarea. Ramsay argued that he could have travelled only as Paul's slave (*SPT*, pp. 315 f.), though Lightfoot's suggestion still deserves mention, that the manner of reference indicates that he was on his way home to Thessalonica. However (assuming a Roman origin for Colossians), he rejoined Paul, and became his 'fellow prisoner-of-war' (Col. iv. 10), possibly alternating with Epaphras in voluntary imprisonment (*cf.* Col. iv. 10–12 with Phm. 23, 24). On the 'Ephesian imprisonment' theory he will have gone home after the riot and the writing of Colossians (*cf.* G. S. Duncan, *St. Paul's Ephesian Ministry*, 1929, pp. 196, 237 ff.). His association with the collection has suggested an identification with the 'brother' of 2 Cor. viii. 18 (Zahn, *INT*, I, p. 320). The most natural reading of Col. iv. 10, 11 implies a Jewish origin.

A.F.W.

ARK. 1. The Ark of Noah (*tēḇâ*, probably from Egyp. *ḏb'.t*, 'chest, coffin', Gn. vi–ix; *kibōtos*, 'box, chest' in the New Testament) was evidently intended to be no more than a floating repository, measuring, if the cubit is taken at 18 inches (see WEIGHTS AND MEASURES), about 450 × 75 × 45 feet (vi. 15). It is possible to read *qānîm*, 'reeds', for *qinnîm*, 'nests', in vi. 14, without interfering with the consonantal text, giving the sense that the gopher wood components were bound together and caulked with reeds, and the whole then finished off with bitumen (*q.v.*). While the statement in vi. 16 (literally, 'thou shalt make it lower, second, and third') can be taken in the traditional sense as describing three storeys, it is also possible to understand it to indicate three layers of logs laid cross-wise, a view which would accord well with a construction of wood, reeds, and bitumen. The ark also had an opening (*peṯaḥ*) in the side, and a *ṣōhar*, a word not properly understood, but most commonly taken to mean an opening for light, running right round the vessel just below the roof.

2. The ark of Moses (*tēḇâ*, Ex. ii. 3–6) may perhaps be pictured as a miniature version of that of Noah, but only of sufficient size to take a small infant. It was made of reeds (*gōme'*, see PAPYRUS), and sealed with bitumen (*ḥēmār*) and pitch (*zepeṯ*, see BITUMEN), and from the fact that it was necessary to open it (Ex. ii. 6) it was apparently, as was probably Noah's Ark, completely closed in.

3. For the Ark of the Covenant, see next article.

BIBLIOGRAPHY. A. Heidel, *The Gilgamesh Epic and Old Testament Parallels*², 1949, pp. 232–237; E. Ullendorff, *VT*, IV, 1954, pp. 95, 96. T.C.M.

ARK OF THE COVENANT. Called also 'ark of the Lord', 'ark of God', 'ark of the covenant of the Lord' (Dt. x. 8), and 'ark of the testimony' (*'ēḏûṯ* = covenant-terms: see TESTIMONY). The ark was a rectangular box (*'ārôn*) made of acacia wood, and measured 2½ × 1½ × 1½ cubits (*i.e. c.* 4 × 2½ × 2½ feet; see WEIGHTS AND MEASURES). The whole was covered with gold and was carried on poles inserted in rings at the four lower corners. The lid, or 'mercy-seat', was a gold plate surrounded by two antithetically-placed cherubs with outspread wings.

The ark served (i) as receptacle for the two tablets of the Decalogue (Ex. xxv. 16, 21, xl. 20; Dt. x. 1–5) and also for the pot of manna and Aaron's rod (Heb. ix. 4, 5); (ii) as the meeting-place in the inner sanctuary where the Lord revealed His will to His servants (Moses: Ex. xxv. 22, xxx. 36; Aaron: Lv. xvi. 2; Joshua: Jos. vii. 6). Thus it served as the symbol of the divine presence guiding His people. The ark was made at Sinai by Bezaleel to the pattern given to Moses (Ex. xxv. 8 ff.). It was used as a depository for the written law (Dt. xxxi. 9; Jos. xxiv. 26) and played a significant part at the crossing of Jordan (Jos. iii–iv), the fall of Jericho (Jos. vi), and the ceremony of remembering the covenant at Mt. Ebal (Jos. viii. 30 ff.).

From Gilgal the ark was moved to Bethel (Jdg. ii. 1, xx. 27), but was taken to Shiloh in the time of the Judges (1 Sa. i. 3, iii. 3), remaining there till captured by the Philistines on the battle-field at Ebenezer (1 Sa. iv). Because its presence caused seven months of plagues, the Philistines returned it to Kiriath-jearim, where it remained for twenty years (2 Sa. v–vii. 2), except possibly for a temporary move to Saul's camp near Bethaven (1 Sa. xiv. 18—where, however, LXX indicates that the original reading was probably 'ephod').

David installed the ark in a tent at Jerusalem (2 Sa. vi), and would not remove it during Absalom's rebellion (2 Sa. xv. 24–29). It was placed in the Temple with great ceremony in the reign of Solomon (1 Ki. viii. 1 ff.), and re-sited in the sanctuary during Josiah's reforms (2 Ch. xxxv. 3) when Jeremiah anticipated an age without its presence (iii. 16). It was presumably lost during the destruction of Jerusalem by the Babylonians in 587 BC. There was no ark in the second Temple (Josephus, *BJ* v. 5).

Gold-overlaid wooden receptacles or portable shrines are known from the Ancient Near East in pre-Mosaic times. The ark is unique, however, as the repository of the covenant-tablets, *i.e.* documents bearing the 'covenant-stipulations' (*'ēḏûṯ*). K.A.K.

ARKITE. Gn. x. 17; 1 Ch. i. 15. A descendant of Ham through Canaan, and the eponymous ancestor of the inhabitants of a city in the Lebanon, modern Tell 'Arqa. The city is mentioned in Egyptian sources and in the Amarna letters, while Shalmaneser II and Tiglath-pileser III describe the city as rebellious. R.J.W.

ARM (*zᵉrōa'*, common throughout the Old Testament, with parallels in other Near Eastern languages, of the human arm or shoulder as a symbol of strength; paralleled, less frequently, in the New Testament by *brachiōn*).

The symbol of the arm outstretched, or made bare (much the same idea in view of Eastern dress), is used especially of the Lord to portray His mighty acts, referring often to the deliverance of Israel from Egypt (Ex. vi. 6, *etc.*), also to other acts of judgment or salvation evidenced or sought (Is. li. 9; Ezk. xx. 33). Thus, logically, the arm or arms of the Lord become the symbol of safe refuge (Dt. xxxiii. 27). The powerful arm of the Lord is contrasted with the puny arm of man, 'an arm of flesh' (2 Ch. xxxii. 8). The arms of the wicked are broken, or dried up (Ps. xxxvii. 17; Zc. xi. 17), but the Lord can strengthen the arms of those whom He chooses to enable them to do wonders (Ps. xviii. 34).

In Dn. xi. 22 the symbol is used of impersonal force, 'the arms of a flood'. The parallelism with 'hand' or 'right hand' is natural (Ps. xliv. 3). See HAND. B.O.B.

ARMAGEDDON. See HAR-MAGEDON.

ARMENIA. See ARARAT.

ARMLET. See ORNAMENTS.

ARMOUR AND WEAPONS. Both ideas are summed up in the general terms *kēlîm* (Gn. xxvii. 3; 1 Sa. xvii. 54) and Gk. *hopla* (LXX *passim*; 2 Cor. x. 4; *Testament of Levi* v. 3). The defensive aspect is emphasized in *maddîm* ('apparel', 1 Sa. xvii. 38) and the offensive in *nēšeq* ('weapons', 2 Ki. x. 2).

I. ARMOUR (DEFENSIVE)

a. Shield

All the nations of antiquity employed shields. The Israelites used two varieties. The large shield (*ṣinnâ*, also translated 'buckler' and 'target' in AV) was adapted to cover the whole body, being either oval or rectangular like a door (the Gk. *thyreos* is derived from *thyra*, a 'door'). This was carried by the heavy-armed infantry (2 Ch.

xiv. 8) and, in Goliath's case, there was a special shield-bearer (1 Sa. xvii. 7). The small shield (*māḡēn*, also translated 'buckler' in AV) was carried by archers, such as the Benjamites in King Asa's army (2 Ch. xiv. 8). Unfortunately the AV frequently confuses these two kinds of shield. Solomon's ornamental 'targets', or large shields, required about four times as much gold as the bucklers (1 Ki. x. 16, 17; see WEIGHTS AND MEASURES), which gives some idea of the difference in size. Normally they were constructed from wood or wicker-work overlaid with leather, for they could be burned (Ezk. xxxix. 9). The leather was oiled before battle, either to preserve it or to make it glisten (Is. xxi. 5). Occasionally bronze was the material used for construction (1 Ki. xiv. 27). See figs. 70, 94.

b. Helmet

In early times the helmet (*kôḇa'*) was apparently restricted to kings or prominent leaders. Thus King Saul provided David with his own helmet of bronze (1 Sa. xvii. 38). The Hittite helmets depicted on the walls of Karnak in Egypt are in the form of a skull-cap. By the time of Uzziah all the Hebrew soldiers were supplied with helmets (2 Ch. xxvi. 14), which were probably made of leather. This was the normal material until bronze came into common use: in the Seleucid period the rank and file were supplied with bronze helmets (1 Macc. vi. 35). Among the Romans and Greeks in Herodian times helmets of either substance were common. Paul uses the helmet figuratively for the Christian warrior (*perikephalaia*, Eph. vi. 17). See figs. 70, 103.

c. Coat of mail

Bronze for the leaders and leather for the soldiers was also the general rule in body-armour. Goliath was an exception because he was 'champion' of the Philistines; therefore he possessed mail-armour composed of bronze scales (1 Sa. xvii. 5). The *širyôn*, translated 'habergeon' in AV and 'coat of mail' in RV, was a cuirass, which protected not only the breast but also the back. It was part of the armour of Nehemiah's workers (Ne. iv. 16). The translations 'breastplate' and 'harness' in the AV are misleading. The 'harness' of Ahab was a cuirass, with leather flaps hanging at the waist-line (technically termed the 'tassets'); it is these that are meant when he is described as struck 'between the joints of the harness' (1 Ki. xxii. 34). Twice in Jeremiah (xlvi. 4, li. 3) the same word is translated 'brigandine'; this was an exceptionally light-armoured coat, consisting of small iron plates sewn on to a leather foundation. Is. xli. 6, 7 appears to refer to the smith's manufacture of scale armour; the 'nails' are probably the pins for fastening the scales. The discovery of armour-scales at Ras Shamra (Ugarit), Boghaz-köi, and Alalaḫ has at least shown that the use of such armour was already well known in the 15th century BC. At Nuzi many such plates have been found. The inscribed tablets from the palace also record armour for chariots and horses, but examples of this have been discovered only in Assyrian cities. Where greater flexibility was required, smaller plates were used, the shape always being rectangular, unlike the rounded armour-plates on Assyrian reliefs (see fig. 89). There were two different systems for securing them to the leather foundation: sometimes it was done vertically by a cord, sometimes horizontally.

The Greek equivalent was the *thōrax*, also used in 1 Macc. vi. 43 of the armour protecting war-elephants. Paul derived his 'breastplate of righteousness' (Eph. vi. 14) from the LXX of Is. lix. 17. For this section, see S. Smith, *Isaiah XL–LV*, 1944, pp. 160, 182; R. F. Storr, *Nuzi*, I, 1939, pp. 470 ff.

d. Greaves

Armour to protect the leg between the knee and the ankle is only once mentioned in Scripture (1 Sa. xvii. 6, *miṣḥâ*). Goliath wore greaves of bronze. It is possible that the Hebrew word may in fact mean a type of boot.

II. WEAPONS (OFFENSIVE)

a. Sword

The sword (*ḥereḇ*) is the most frequently mentioned weapon in the Bible. The straight blade was made of iron (1 Sa. xiii. 19) and was sometimes two-edged (Ps. cxlix. 6). It hung on the left

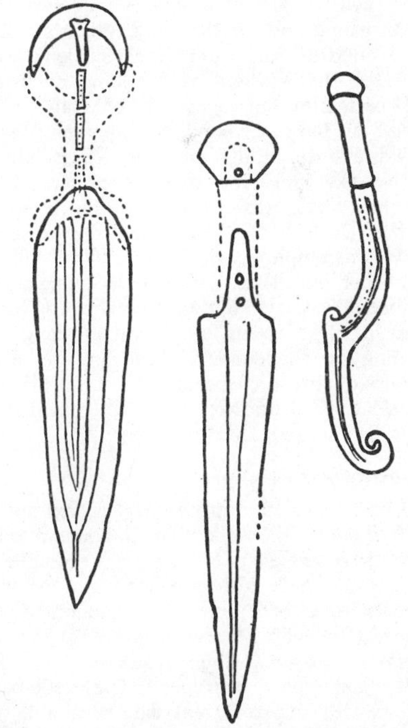

Fig. 16. *Left:* short and longer daggers with pointed leaf-shaped blades of a Hyksos type common in Palestine c. 2000–1500 BC. *Right:* a curved sword (sometimes misnamed 'scimitar') sharpened on both edges and in use in Palestine from c. 1800 BC (from Shechem).

side from a girdle (*ḥ^{a}gôrâ*) and was usually housed in a sheath (*ta'ar*; 2 Sa. xx. 8). Ehud's weapon, with its 18-inch blade, was really a dagger, though called a sword in RV (Jdg. iii. 16); being left-handed, he carried it slung by a girdle upon his right thigh. Daggers have been found at both Lachish and Megiddo, dating from the last phase of the Early Bronze Age. An example from Lachish, of the 17th century BC, carries an inscription which is one of the earliest attempts known at alphabetic writing. Philistine sword-furnaces have been discovered at Gerar. Sometimes the hilt was highly ornamented, especially among the Egyptians, Assyrians, and Babylonians.

In the New Testament *machaira* is the word usually employed (Mt. xxvi. 47). The *rhomphaia*, occurring, with one exception, only in Revelation, was a large, broad sword, used especially by the Thracians. The revolutionary Jewish assassins, the *sicarii*, carried short, slightly curved daggers under their clothing (Jos., *BJ* ii. 13. 3). In both Testaments the sword is frequently used figuratively for the judgment of war or for the Word of God (Ezk. xxi. 28; Eph. vi. 17). For useful references, see *Lachish IV*, 1958, pp. 74–79, 128.

b. Spear and javelin

The *ḥ^{a}nîṯ* was a spear with a wooden shaft and a metallic head of bronze or, in later times, of iron (1 Sa. xvii. 7). This weapon was employed both for thrusting and for throwing. When stuck in the ground at Saul's bolster (1 Sa. xxvi. 7) it indicated the quarters of the king, a custom still pertaining among Arab chieftains. The *rōmaḥ*, on the other hand, was apparently used only as a lance, though mistranslated 'javelin' in AV (Nu. xxv. 7). Heavy-armed troops carried this weapon, which was a feature of the Egyptian soldiery (Je. xlvi. 4). A lighter and shorter spear, *kîḏôn*, was employed as a javelin (Jos. viii. 18, RV). When not in use, it was carried slung across the back (1 Sa. xvii. 6, RV). Several words translated 'dart' in AV are of general meaning; depending on the context, they may be either missiles or thrusting spears (2 Sa. xviii. 14). The Gk. *longchē* of Jn. xix. 34 is the equivalent of *ḥ^{a}nîṯ*. See figs. 70, 164.

c. Bow and arrow

The bow (*qešeṯ*) and arrow (*ḥēṣ*) played an important part in the wars of Israel. Sometimes the bow had a single curve, sometimes a double. It was usually made with seasoned wood, or occasionally from horn, and was often mounted with bronze (Ps. xviii. 34, RV). The bow-string was commonly ox-gut and the arrows were of reed or light wood, tipped with metal. The battle-bows (Zc. ix. 10) were of great length; among the Egyptians they were 5 feet long. To string them, the lower end was held down by the foot, while the upper end was bent down to fasten the string in a notch (Je. l. 14). This explains the Hebrew expression to 'tread' the bow, which means to string it: thus archers are called in Hebrew 'bow-treaders'. Arrows are naturally called 'the sons of the quiver' (La. iii. 13, AVmg), as in many Oriental languages. Whether on foot or on horse-back, archers fulfilled an important function among the light-armed troops of antiquity. The Assyrians, Elamites, Egyptians, and Philistines

Fig. 17. Egyptian archers moving in to the attack. The one on the left uses his foot to hold his bow steady while he bends it in order to fix the string.

were exponents of this method of warfare. Among the Israelites, the tribes of Benjamin, Reuben, Gad, and Manasseh were especially famed for their bowmen (see 1 Ch. v. 18, xii. 2; 2 Ch. xiv. 8). Subsequently, Greek and Roman armies were often indebted to their archers for victory. See figs. 89, 228.

d. The sling

The *qela'* was carried chiefly by shepherds (*e.g.* David, 1 Sa. xvii. 40), to ward off wild beasts from their flocks, and to prevent the animals straying. It was commonly used also as a weapon of war in the Egyptian, Assyrian, and Babylonian armies. The Israelites also employed companies of slingers as an important element in their forces, among whom the ambidextrous Benjamites were renowned (1 Ch. xii. 2). The sling was made of leather, either plaited or a single strip, and was broadened in the middle to form a hollow for the missile. Both ends were held firmly in the hand as the loaded sling was whirled about the head, till one end was suddenly released. See fig. 194. Graphic metaphorical use of this is made in Je. x. 18. In 2 Ch. xxvi. 14, 15 Uzziah's 'slings to cast stones' were giant catapults.

e. The battle-axe

This weapon was frequently employed among the Hittites, Assyrians, Babylonians, and Elamites (R. M. Hyslop, *Iraq*, XI (Pt. I), 1949, pp. 90–125; XV (Pt. I), 1959, pp. 69–87). The only mention in Scripture is Je. li. 20, but the Heb. *mēp̄îṣ* (literally, 'scatterer') is really a club, probably studded with iron spikes. Herodotus (vii. 63) describes such a weapon as carried by Assyrian troops in Xerxes' army. J.W.C.

ARMY. Old Testament: *ḥayil*, of which the root meaning is 'strength' or 'force'; *'am*, 'people'; *ṣāḇā'*, 'host', 'warfare', 'service', *cf.* Assyr. *ṣâbu*, 'man', 'soldier', or Arab. *ṣābā*, 'to conceal oneself', or *saba*, 'to go forth'; *'îš milḥāmâ*, 'man of war'. New Testament: *strateuma, parembolē* and *stratopedon.*

a. Composition

As no regular Israelitish army was formed before the days of Saul, it said much for the military leaders of premonarchical days that they were able to muster men quickly for battle. To claim authority the leader would sometimes perform a heroic deed (Jdg. vi. 24–34), and then all able-bodied men would rally to his call, though sometimes there was not full response (Jdg. v. 16, 17). The nucleus of Saul's standing army consisted of permanent warriors privately selected. David followed this pattern, but by his time the force was considerably increased (2 Sa. xv. 18). The general levy, that is the non-professionals, was divided into thousands, hundreds, fifties, and tens, each section with its own commander; this probably dated from Moses' time (see Ex. xviii. 24–26). The term 'thousand', *'elep̄*, is not necessarily to be understood in a strictly numerical sense, and may even be as low as 200. It was a territorial term (Mi. v. 2) sometimes used for the chief towns of Judah. This may explain the very large numbers in 1 Sa. xi. 8. The bands, *geḏîḏ*, a name also used for a section of the army, were private marauding companies often of great use in the national army (Jdg. xi. 3). Those with new property, the newly married, and the faint-hearted were exempt from battle (Dt. xx. 1–9). Cavalry did not play a prominent part until the time of Solomon, as the hill-country was best suited to infantry. Also the law forbade the multiplying of horses (Dt. xvii. 16, *cf.* xx. 1). Solomon introduced horses and chariots on a large scale (1 Ki. x. 26, *cf.* 1 Ki. ix. 22), and his stables at Megiddo, where there was room for 900 horses, are famous (1 Ki. iv. 26, *cf.* 1 Ki. ix. 15, 19). See D. J. Wiseman, *Illustrations from Biblical Archaeology*, 1958, pp. 53 f. The archer was always prominent in battle and the bow is commonly represented on Assyrian and Egyptian monuments (Gn. xxi. 20, xlviii. 22; 2 Sa. i. 18; 2 Ch. xxxv. 23). Soldiers were maintained by booty, unless it was under the 'ban' (1 Sa. xxx. 24) (see WAR), by the produce of the land where they were encamped, and sometimes by regular pay (1 Ki. iv. 27).

b. Camp

The formation of the camp, *maḥaneh*, was all-important in warfare. It was probably in the shape of a circle or a square (Nu. ii), and was guarded constantly (Jdg. vii. 19), the soldiers sleeping in tents or booths (2 Sa. xi. 11). The whole camp was surrounded by a *ma'gāl* (1 Sa. xvii. 20, xxvi. 5), RVmg 'barricade'. During battle a remnant remained behind to guard the base (1 Sa. xxv. 13). See also ASSYRIA, BABYLONIA.

c. Roman army

The main divisions were the legion (*q.v.*), auxiliary cohorts, and *alae*, the latter two being mainly composed of provincial subjects, though Jews were exempt (Josephus, *Ant.* xiv. 10. 6). The auxiliary cohorts (Gk. *speira*, AV 'band') were sometimes referred to by distinctive epithets, *e.g.* Italian (Acts x. 1), Augustan (Acts xxvii. 1), and were divided into ten centuries of a hundred men, each commanded by a centurion, one of whom, Cornelius, was an important convert to the faith (Acts x). At Jewish festivals the force in Jerusalem was strengthened.

d. Spiritual armies

The meaning of the term *ṣāḇā'*, generally translated 'host', is uncertain, though it may well include the idea of a spiritual army in the 'heavenlies'. See HOST. Elisha showed his servant at Dothan an angelic host of chariots and horses (2 Ki. vi. 17, *cf.* 2 Ki. ii. 12), and Joshua was confronted with a theophanic angel who was 'captain of the host of the Lord' (Jos. v. 13–15; *cf.* Dn. viii. 11). In the final battle of good and evil Christ appears as leader of the 'armies in heaven' (Rev. xix. 14), defeating the armies of the beast and of the kings of the earth (Rev. xix. 19).

BIBLIOGRAPHY. See under WAR. J.A.B.

ARNON. A wadi running into the east side of the Dead Sea opposite En-gedi. This formed the southern border of Reubenite territory at the time of the settlement (Dt. iii. 12, 16), and previously marked the boundary between Moab to the south and Ammon to the north (Jdg. xi. 18, 19). The invading Hebrews crossed the Arnon from south to north, and this proved a turning-point in their career, for they took their first territorial possessions on the north side (Dt. ii. 24). However, the Moabite Stone (*q.v.*) (line 10) mentions Moabites living in Ataroth, which is to the north of the wadi, suggesting either incomplete conquest on the part of the settlers or later Moabite infiltration. The importance of the river is confirmed by the number of forts and bridges which are found there, the latter being mentioned by Isaiah (Is. xvi. 2). R.J.W.

AROER. 1. In Transjordan, on the north bank of the river Arnon (Wadi Môjib) overlooking its deep gorge (D. Baly, *The Geography of the Bible*, 1957, fig. 72 on p. 237), at modern 'Ara'ir (N. Glueck, *Explorations in Eastern Palestine*, I, (= *AASOR*, XIV), 1934, pp. 3, 49–51 with fig. 21a and Plate 11), about 14 miles east of the Dead Sea (Dt. ii. 36, iii. 12, iv. 48; Jos. xii. 2). It symbolized the southern limit, first, of the Amorite kingdom of Sihon, second, of the tribal territory of Reuben (Jos. xiii. 9, 16; Jdg. xi. 26 and probably 33) being the seat of a Reubenite family (1 Ch. v. 8), and third, of the Transjordanian conquests of Hazael of Damascus in Jehu's time (2 Ki. x. 33). About this time, Mesha, king of Moab, 'built Aroer and made the road by the Arnon' (Moabite Stone, line 26); Aroer remained Moabite down to Jeremiah's time (Je. xlviii. 18–20). In Nu. xxxii. 34 Gad apparently helped to repair newly conquered cities, including Aroer, before formal allotment of Reubenite and Gadite territories by Moses. In 2 Sa. xxiv. 5 probably read with RSV that Joab's census for David started from Aroer and the city in the valley *towards* Gad and on to Jazer. Isaiah (xvii. 1–3) prophesied against (Moabite-held) Aroer, alongside Damascus and Ephraim. The 'city that is in the valley' (Dt. ii. 36; Jos. xiii. 9, 16, all RV [but not xii. 2, see AV, RSV]; 2 Sa. xxiv. 5, RV) may be present Khirbet el-Medeiyineh some 7 miles south-east of Aroer (Simons, *Geographical and Topographical Texts of the Old Testament*, 1959, § 298, pp. 116, 117; for a description, see Glueck, *op. cit.*, p. 36, No. 93).

2. In Transjordan, 'before Rabbah' (Jos. xiii. 25, AV, RV, against RSV); could be modern eṣ-Ṣweiwînā, about 2 miles south-west of Rabbah (Glueck, *Explorations in Eastern Palestine*, III, (= *AASOR*, XVIII/XIX), 1939, pp. 247, 249; for a description see *ibid.*, pp. 168–170 and fig. 55). But the existence of this Aroer separate from (1) above is doubtful, as Jos. xiii. 25 might perhaps be rendered '. . . half the land of the Ammonites unto Aroer, which (land is/extends) towards/as far as Rabbah' (Glueck, *op. cit.*, p. 249).

3. In Negeb (southland) of Judah, 12 miles south-east of Beersheba, present Khirbet Ar'areh (N. Glueck, *Rivers in the Desert*, 1959, pp. 131–132, 184–185). Among the Judaeans receiving presents from David at Ziklag (1 Sa. xxx. 26–28) were 'them which were in Aroer'; among his mighty men were two sons of 'Hotham the Aroerite' (1 Ch. xi. 44). K.A.K.

ARPACHSHAD, ARPHAXAD (Heb. *'arpakšad*; LXX and New Testament *Arphaxad*). One of the sons of Shem (Gn. x. 22; 1 Ch. i. 17, 24), who was born two years after the flood (Gn. xi. 10). The *MT* states that he was the father of Shelah, who was born when he was thirty-five years old (Gn. x. 24, xi. 12; 1 Ch. i. 18, 24; LXX and Samaritan Pentateuch read 135), but some MSS of the LXX interpose a *Kainan* between Arpachshad and Shelah, and this has evidently been followed by Lk. iii. 36. Arpachshad lived for a total of 438 years (Gn. xi. 13; LXX gives 430, but the Samaritan Pentateuch agrees in the total in spite of disagreement on the component figures). Several theories about the identification of the name have been put forward, perhaps the commonest being that which would connect it with *Arrapḫu* of the cuneiform inscriptions, Gk. *Arrapachitis*, probably modern Kirkuk. Other theories would see the end of the name, *-kšad*, as a corruption from *keśed*, *kaśdîm*, 'Chaldeans' (*q.v.*), and therefore referring to S Mesopotamia. An Iranian etymology has also been suggested, in which connection it is to be noted that it is stated in the Apocrypha (Judith i. 1) that one Arphaxad (*cf.* LXX *Arphaxad*) ruled over the Medes in Ecbatana. This book is, however, largely fiction, and in the absence of a Hebrew original there is no guarantee that the name is the same. The name continues therefore to be unknown outside the Bible.

BIBLIOGRAPHY. J. Skinner, *ICC*, *Genesis*², 1930, pp. 205, 231, 233; W. F. Albright, *JBL*, XLIII, 1924, pp. 388, 389; W. Brandenstein, in *Sprachgeschichte und Wortbedeutung: Festschrift Albert Debrunner*, 1954, pp. 59–62; and for another theory G. Dossin, *Muséon*, XLVII, 1934, pp. 119–121. T.C.M.

ARPAD. A city which was first captured by the Assyrians in 754 BC in their efforts to control the route to Hamath and Damascus with which it was allied (Je. xlix. 23). It was sacked by Tiglath-pileser III after a two-year siege in 740 BC, and again by Sargon II in 720 BC. Its destruction strengthened Rabshakeh's boast to Jerusalem (2 Ki. xviii. 34, xix. 13; Is. xxxvi. 19, xxxvii. 13, AV 'Arphad'), and its fall symbolized the overwhelming power of Assyria (Is. x. 9). The ruins at Tell Rifa'ad *c.* 20 miles north-west of Aleppo were excavated in 1956 and 1960 (*Iraq*, XXIII, 1961). D.J.W.

ARROW. See ARMOUR AND WEAPONS, DIVINATION.

ART.

I. IN THE OLD TESTAMENT

a. The place of art in Hebrew life

There is little evidence, either in the Old Testament or from archaeological discoveries, upon which to build a picture of ancient Hebrew art. Throughout its long history Palestine was occupied by mixed peoples and cultures, and it is not easily possible to distinguish indigenous Jewish art before the Maccabean period from the Egyptian, Phoenician, Syrian, Mesopotamian, or later Hellenistic and Graeco-Roman importations, imitations, or influences. Moreover, although the second commandment, which forbade the making of 'any graven image or any likeness of anything that is in heaven . . . or . . . earth . . . or in the water . . .' (Ex. xx. 4), did not condemn art but the idolatry to which it might lead ('thou shalt not bow down thyself to them, nor serve them', verse 5), this was interpreted as precluding any representation of the human form. During the united Monarchy, however, other natural or stylized objects were allowed to be reproduced.

This does not mean that the Israelites were devoid of any appreciation of art (see also ARTS AND CRAFTS). They accepted fine Egyptian jewellery as gifts (Ex. xii. 35) and used gold and silver for fashioning a statue in the round (Ex. xxxii. 2–4); and they gave their fine possessions to make and decorate the Tabernacle. Bezaleel is an instance of a native Judaean endowed with artistic ability to design and execute the wood-carving, metal and jewellery-working, and embroidery required for this intricate operation (Ex. xxxv. 30–33). Moreover, the large task of building David's royal palace and Solomon's

Temple, though much dependent on Phoenician art and skill, was a work involving trained Israelite workers and the plans must have received royal approval (see ARCHITECTURE).

The hard circumstances of Israelite life did not encourage experimentation in representational art, and when craftsmen were employed by wealthy kings (1 Ki. xxii. 39) or citizens to beautify their homes with expensive artistic

Fig. 18. Bronze stand (half original size) from Megiddo (*c.* 1000 BC). The basins in Solomon's Temple rested on open-work modelled bronzes.

works it was condemned as an inappropriate luxury, mainly on the grounds of its expression of a self-interest which failed to put the adornment of God's house and work first (Am. iii. 15; Ps. xlv. 8; Hg. i. 4). It must always be remembered that the Hebrews, by their encouragement of sacred music, literature (both prose and poetry), and speech, set a high standard of 'artistic expression' which has profoundly influenced later art.

b. Design

From the earliest periods polychrome pottery and frescoes show geometric patterns and intricate designs of stylized dragons, figures, and birds (Ghassul, *c.* 3500 BC). In common with the nations surrounding Palestine this was followed by patterns built up of parallel lines or lattice work (*c.* 3100 BC). A lustrous red-and-black burnished ware (Khirbet Kerak, *c.* 2600–2400 BC) has been considered 'some of the most beautiful pottery ever made in Palestine' and was often elegantly ribbed and fluted and gracefully shaped. It is clear that the Canaanites did not depend entirely on outside sources of inspiration and produced many painted ornaments (Chalcolithic house-urns and Late Bronze Age I patterns, including the 'union jack' style). The 15th to the 13th centuries BC showed a decline in skill and artistic ability in Palestine and Syria which is but a reflection of widespread changes as in Mesopotamia. See fig. 171.

With the Monarchy a native repertory of designs can be clearly seen, but is perhaps indistinguishable from Syro-Phoenician art: human-headed lions (cherubim), winged griffins, palmettes, floral and arboreal patterns, 'Egyptian' type figures and symbols as well as birds and reptiles and a variety of animals (bulls, lions, *etc.*) and patterns (guilloche). These are found on the Temple decorations (1 Ki. vi. 18, 29) and on ivories from Samaria and Hazor, drawn on pots, and engraved on seals (*q.v.*).

c. Media

(i) *Painting*. Since the Egyptians and Amorites (*e.g.* the Investiture fresco from Mari) commonly painted scenes on plastered walls, it is possible that the Hebrews may have done so, though no surviving examples are yet known. Pigments have been found in excavations (see also Dyeing under ARTS AND CRAFTS) and red ochre (Heb. *šāšēr*) was used for painting on walls and wood (Je. xxii. 14; Ezk. xxiii. 14). Oholibah in the 6th century saw Chaldeans painted (*māšaḥ*, 'to smear, anoint') on a wall in vermilion (Ezk. xxiii. 14).

Fig. 19. A drawing of a Judaean king, 8th–7th centuries BC, from Ramat Rahel.

(ii) *Wood-carving*. Bezaleel and his assistant Aholiab directed the wood-cutting (*ḥ*ᵃ*rōšeṯ ʿēṣ*) for the Tabernacle, which included pillars with curved capitals (Ex. xxxvi. 38, xxxv. 33), and a horned altar recessed to take a grating (xxxviii. 2–4). See fig. 176. The Temple built by Solomon was roofed with pine with appliqué palmettes and guilloche borders (2 Ch. iii. 5) and panelled in cedar (1 Ki. vi. 15, 16). The walls and doors were sculptured in bas-relief with carvings (*miqlāʿôṯ*) of lotus buds and 'fleur-de-lis' or 'Prince-of-Wales' feathers' forming a triple flower (AV 'knops and open flowers'), palm designs, and representations of cherubim (1 Ki. vi. 18, 29). The doors of olive-wood had similar designs etched (*ḥāqâ*) and in intaglio work (verses 32–35); the whole, as so often with fine wood or ivory work, overlaid with gold. Since hard woods, such as almug (sandalwood) and ebony, had to be imported (1 Ki. x. 11), and skilled carvers were rare, the use of panelling (*sāp̄an*), elaborate woodwork, and carved windows (see fig. 24) was considered an extravagant display of wealth (Je. xxii. 14; Hg. i. 4). Ezekiel's Temple was conceived as having carved panels of two-faced cherubim alternating with palm-trees and young lions, the outer doors being veneered (*šᵉḥîp̄*) with wood (Ezk. xli. 16–26).

Elaborately carved furniture and other objects of wood, boxes, spoons, and vessels, have been found in the 'Amorite' tombs at Jericho (*q.v.*). Since ancient Egyptian wood-carving (*c.* 2000–500 BC) 'both on a large and miniature scale reached a standard not equalled in Europe until the Renaissance', something of this work must have been known to wealthy Hebrews. See also Carpenter under ARTS AND CRAFTS.

(iii) *Ivory-carving.* As early as 34th–33rd centuries BC (Abu Matar) ivory and bone was worked in Palestine to make precious objects, figurines, and furniture. It was incised (mostly in panels), sculptured in the round, or cut as open work, or relief. 'Canaanite' ivories include an ointment vase in female form with a hand-shaped (Lachish, 14th century BC) or Hathor-headed stopper (Hazor, 13th century BC), an unguent spoon shaped as a swimming lady catching a duck (Tell Beit Mirsim), and several pyxides show human figures. After a period of decline in the art, incised panels from Megiddo, probably of local workmanship in the 12th to 10th centuries, show lively scenes in one of which the king seated on a throne, which must have been similar to that later made for Solomon (2 Ch. ix. 17, 18), receives tribute (see fig. 114).

Ivories found at Samaria, of the time of Ahab, show the influence of Phoenician art with its Egyptian, Syro-Hittite, and Assyrian elements. They compare closely with contemporary ivories found at Arslan Tash (Syria) and Nimrud (Iraq), and may have been from the same 'school' or guild of craftsmen. Some are inlaid with gold, lapis-lazuli, coloured stones, and glass. Commonly recurring designs include the 'lotus' patterns and cherubim already noted in wood-carving and allied art; also panels with a woman's head (Astarte?) at a window (see fig. 24), couchant and suckling animals, and 'Egyptian' figures and symbols, especially the kneeling infant Horus. A matching cosmetic palette and jar from Hazor (8th century) bears a simple hatched pattern and is of Israelite manufacture.

(iv) *Sculpture.* A few sculptures from the 'Canaanite' period in Palestine have been recovered. The seated basalt figure of a Baal, the roughly engraved stele with its pair of upraised hands and the altars from Hazor, and the serpent-coiled goddess on a stele from Beit Mirsim (see figs. 16, 65) must be considered alongside the well-sculptured feet of a statue from Hazor (13th century BC) to show that good as well as moderate artists were at work there. A stone incense ladle in the form of a hand clasping a bowl from the same city (8th century) shows affinities with contemporary Assyrian art. The plaster-sculptured skulls from Jericho (*c.* 5000 BC), the clay face-masks of the same period, and the boulder in the Lachish water-shaft (9th century BC) worked into the likeness of a bearded man, show that the people of Palestine were never without an inventive spirit, but little has so far survived, and the work of their neighbours (*e.g.* the sculptured sarcophagus of Ahiram from Byblos) is better known. Volute capitals, forerunners of the Ionic type, found at Megiddo and Samaria, were probably similar to those used in the Temple (see also ARCHITECTURE). In the Maccabean period Hellenistic–Jewish ornamentalists of stone carved the fruits of the land (grapes, ethrog, and acanthus leaves), symbols which are also found on coins (*q.v.*).

A special guild of ossuary workers at Jerusalem has bequeathed us several chests engraved with six-pointed stars, rosettes, flowers, and even architectural designs (see fig. 46).

(v) *Engraving.* Cylinder, scarab, and stamp seals from Palestine bear typical 'Phoenician' motifs as found on ivories, though here the winged disc and winged scarab occur more frequently. The human figure is often engraved up to the Monarchy, and the inclusion of personal names seems to be more customary in Israel than among her neighbours. Pictorial representations are rare on Judaean seals, which may show a growing awareness of the religious prohibition (see section *a* above). See also SEAL.

(vi) *Metal-work.* There is every indication that the Hebrews were expert metal-workers, but little has survived. This impression is borne out by the miniature bronze stand from Megiddo in open-work style showing the invocation of a seated god (*c.* 1000 BC; see fig. 18). See ARTS AND CRAFTS. The bronze 'sea' of Solomon's Temple is computed to have weighed about 25 tons and have been of cast bronze 3 inches thick with a bowl 15 feet in diameter and 7½ feet high with a 'petalled' rim. The whole rested on the backs of twelve oxen separately cast and arranged in four supporting triads (1 Ki. vii. 23 ff.). It held about 10,000 gallons of water and must have been a remarkable technological achievement (see also JACHIN and BOAZ).

For other examples of art-work, see also EMBROIDERY, JEWELS, EGYPT, ASSYRIA, ARCHITECTURE.

BIBLIOGRAPHY. A. Reifenberg, *Ancient Hebrew Arts*, 1950; H. H. Frankfort, *The Art and Architecture of the Ancient Orient*, 1954. D.J.W.

II. IN THE NEW TESTAMENT

Art in New Testament times was in a post-classical phase. It was imitative and commercialized, and no great works come from the Hellenistic age. It tended to realism and overelaboration. It slipped into extravagance. The sculptured vine with gilded clusters 6 ft. long, which is said to have draped the doors of Herod's temple, might illustrate the latter fault.

If Jn. xv. 1 refers to this vine, some might find a trace of criticism in the Lord's homiletic use of it. In spite of the wealth of art which its theme has inspired from the days of the Catacombs until the Renaissance and today, the New Testament has singularly little to say about art. The Old Testament, in fact, set the pattern. When Abraham left Ur, his break with tradition was sharp. He left behind an artistic culture, and his westward progress brought him into touch with lands as rich in art. But everywhere glyptic art was preoccupied with the representation of deity, and Hebrew monotheism, which may be traced to Abraham, revolted against the 'graven image', and all attempts to set forth the divine in 'gold, or silver, or stone, graven by art or man's device'. In two contexts only is art clearly in view in the New Testament, and both contexts are hostile.

1. Acts xvii. 24 and 29. From where Paul stood on the knoll of the Areopagus, the Acropolis of Athens was in full view, covered with the finest works of Greek art and architecture from the classical age (see pl. XV*d*). He could see the frieze of the Parthenon, the famous 'Elgin marbles', the temple of the Wingless Victory, the Propylaea, the Erechtheum, and the vast statue of Athene Promachos. Steeped in Hebrew tradition, and in a world where the battle with base idolatry was still a burning memory, if not a still living issue, Paul was unable to see in such a pageant aught but the folly of idolatry.

2. Rev. ii. 13. Pausanias mentions a throne-like altar to Zeus on the Pergamenian acropolis. Part of it still exists. The altar commemorated a defeat of a Gallic invasion under the symbolic imagery of the conflict of the gods and the giants. The latter were shown as a brood of muscular Titans, with snake-like tails. John refers to the Christians in Pergamum as living 'where Satan's seat is', and none would fail to see the words as an apocalyptic reference to the great throne-like altar of Zeus. John's attitude coincides with that of Paul. The same John closed the canon of the New Testament with the words: 'Little children, keep yourselves from idols' (1 Jn. v. 21).

E.M.B.

ARTAXERXES (*'artaḥšastā'*, with variant vocalizations). **1.** Artaxerxes I (Longimanus), 464–424 BC. In his reign Ezra and Nehemiah came to Jerusalem, according to Ezr. vii. 1, Ne. ii. 1, *etc.* It has been argued that in the former case the Chronicler has confused him with Artaxerxes II (Mnemon), 404–359 BC, but there is no need to doubt the biblical record. (See J. Stafford Wright, *The Date of Ezra's Coming to Jerusalem*, 1958). See pl. XIc.

2. Ezr. iv. 7. This also is likely to be Artaxerxes I, and the date is shortly before Ne. i. 1 f., when the king reverses the edict of Ezr. iv. 21. (See also AHASUERUS.) Others (improbably) identify him with the pseudo-Smerdis, who reigned for a few months in 522–521 BC.

3. The LXX has Artaxerxes in place of Ahasuerus in Esther, and some believe that the king here is Artaxerxes II, 404–359 BC. (See ESTHER, BOOK OF.)

J.S.W.

ARTEMIS. See DIANA.

ARTS AND CRAFTS. Throughout their history the inhabitants of Palestine maintained the same basic trades as their neighbours and were able to make most of their artifacts by the use of clay, wood, and stone. Working with these materials was the task of any able-bodied peasant, supported by the women in the home spinning and weaving cloth and cooking. Contacts with countries which were more advanced technologically meant that the Hebrews were quick to learn and adapt for their own use more specialized crafts, and were thus probably never bereft of a few outstanding craftsmen, though few examples of their work have survived (see ARCHAEOLOGY).

There is evidence that the Israelites, while not of outstanding inventiveness or artistry, themselves appreciated good workmanship. The possession of such skill by the Judaean Bezaleel was considered a divine gift (Ex. xxxi. 3, xxxv. 31, xxviii. 3). Iron-working was learned from the Philistines (1 Sa. xiii. 20) and the secrets of dyeing from the Phoenicians, who supplied designers, foremen, and craftsmen to supplement the local labour force available for work on such major projects as the building of David's royal palace and the Temple at Jerusalem (see section III*c* below). In the 1st century BC the art of glass-making was similarly imported from Tyre.

I. TRADES AND TRADE GUILDS

For reasons of economy and supply the more skilled artisans lived in the larger towns and cities, usually working in special quarters as in the modern bazaar (*sūq*). This led to the organization of craft-unions or guilds called 'families' which were sometimes located at a town where their work was centred, as the scribes at Jabez (1 Ch. ii. 55) or dyers and weavers at Tell Beit Mirsim (Debir?; 1 Ch. iv. 21). At Jerusalem certain areas were allotted to the wood- and stone-workers (1 Ch. iv. 14; Ne. xi. 35); potters (Mt. xxvii. 7) and fullers (2 Ki. xviii. 17) had fields of their own outside the city walls. A guild member was called 'a son' of his craft (*e.g.* the goldsmiths in Ne. iii. 8, 31). By New Testament times the guilds were powerful political groups working under imperial licence. Demetrius led the guild of silversmiths at Ephesus (Acts xix. 24), and the designation of Alexander as coppersmith (Gk. *chalkeus*) implies his membership of such a union (2 Tim. iv. 14).

A general term (Heb. *ḥārāš*, 'one who cuts in, devises') is used both of craftsmen (AV 'artificers') in general (Ex. xxxviii. 25; 2 Sa. v. 11) or of a skilled worker in metal, whether copper (2 Sa. viii. 10; Is. xl. 19) or iron (Is. xliv. 12; 2 Ch. xxiv. 12). It includes those who prepared and refined the basic metal (Je. x. 9) and was also applied to wood-workers (Is. xliv. 13; 2 Ki. xii. 12), stonemasons (2 Sa. v. 11), engravers of gems (Ex. xxviii. 10), or those specially devoted to manufacturing idols (Is. xliv).

II. BASIC TOOLS

From prehistoric times in Palestine worked flint knives, scrapers, and hoes have been found, and these long continued in use for rough tools, for reaping-hooks, in which the flints are set in a semicircle of plaster, or for striking lights. Wooden implements and stone hammers and pestles were of early origin. With copper (from *c.* 4000 BC), bronze, and meteoric iron (*c.* 3300 BC) tools were soon developed to meet trade requirements (Gn. iv. 22). However, with the advent of iron-working (*c.* 1100 BC) tools were plentiful (1 Ki. vi. 7). Axe-heads, fitted on wooden handles, were used for felling trees (Dt. xix. 5), and knives (Gn. xxii. 6) for a variety of purposes, including eating (Pr. xxx. 14). Tools are sometimes mentioned under the collective Heb. *kᵉlî*, 'vessels, instruments', or *ḥereḇ*, which includes the sword, knife, or any sharp cutter. Iron axe-heads (2 Ki. vi. 5), saws (1 Ki. vii. 9), adzes, hoes, scrapers, chisels, awls, bow-drills, and nails (Je. x. 3) were in constant use and have left their traces on objects recovered by excavation. See fig. 22.

III. ARCHAEOLOGICAL EVIDENCE

a. The potter

Pottery first appears (at Jericho) *c.* 5000 BC, and until *c.* 3000 BC was hand-moulded; thereafter, as in Egypt and Sumer, it was wheel-made. The potter, whose work is described in Je. xviii. 3, 4, sat on a stone seat with his feet working a large stone or wooden wheel, set in a pit, which turned an upper stone on which the vessel was thrown. A potter's workshop, with its 'two stones' (verse 3), has been found at Lachish (*c.* 1200 BC). The smaller wheels of stone or clay which revolve in a socketed disc date from the time of the monarchy at Megiddo, Gezer, and Hazor (see fig. 20). The clay used for finer vessels or slips was prepared by treading out coarser clay in water with the feet (Is. xli. 25). Although Israelite pottery was mainly utilitarian in purpose, it often shows an independence of the forms and decorations used by her neighbours (see ART) and when fired the local clay turned red or reddish-brown. For the development and types of pottery in use, see POTTER and fig. 171. A number of kilns which may have been used by both potters and metal-workers have been discovered. Outside a potter's shop at Megiddo lay three U-shaped furnaces (8th–7th century BC). See FURNACE.

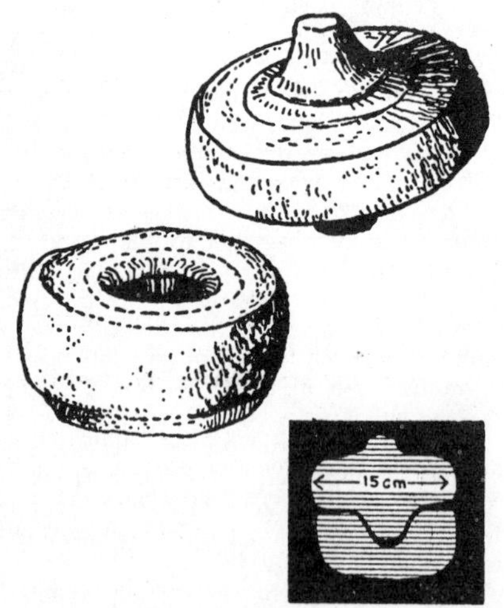

Fig. 20. A potter's wheel or bearings for foot-wheels. The lower stone was set in a pit while the upper bore a wooden collar to be turned by the potter's feet. Such potter's wheels have been found at Jericho, Megiddo, Gezer, Lachish, Hazor, and other Palestinian sites.

b. The builder

The manufacture of sun-dried bricks for use in building the ordinary dwelling was part of the seasonal work of the peasant, who covered his house with clay or thatch spread over roof timbers. Such buildings require constant attention. In a few cases bricks made in a mould were fired, and this was probably the potters' work (see BRICK, BRICK-KILN).

The Heb. *bānâ*, meaning 'to build' and 'to rebuild, to repair' and 'builder' (so AV), is used both of skilled and unskilled workmen (2 Ch. xxxiv. 11) who were needed for work on any large project which involved the labours of stonemasons, carpenters, and many porters and untrained men. Large buildings were both planned and constructed under the close supervision of a master-builder (Gk. *architektōn*; 1 Cor. iii. 10).

A site was first surveyed with a measuring-line consisting of a rope or cord (2 Sa. viii. 2; Zc. ii. 1), string (1 Ki. vii. 15), or twisted linen thread (Ezk. xl. 3) marked in cubits (1 Ki. vii. 15, 23). In Hellenistic times a reed rod marked in furlongs was similarly used (Rev. xi. 1, xxi. 15). More than one line might be used to mark out a site (2 Sa. viii. 2), the survey of which was recorded in plan and writing. The work of the surveyor was taken as a symbol of divine judgment (Is. xxviii. 17; Je. xxxi. 39).

The progress of the building was checked by the chief builder using a 'plumb-line', or cord weighted with lead or tin (*'ᵃnāḵ*; Am. vii. 7, 8), a stone (Zc. iv. 10), or any heavy object (Heb. *mišqeleṯ*, AV 'plummet'; 2 Ki. xxi. 13), to test any vertical structure. This was a symbol of testing the truth (Is. xxviii. 17). The metaphor of building is frequently used, for God as Builder establishes the nation (Ps. lxix. 35), the house of David (Ps. lxxxix. 4), and His city of Jerusalem (Ps. cxlvii. 2). So the Church is compared to a building (1 Cor. iii. 9; 1 Pet. ii. 4–6). Paul uses the word 'to build (up), edify' (Gk. *oikodomeō*) about twenty times. The believers are both built up (*epoikodomeō*) into Christ (Col. ii. 7) and exhorted to build themselves up in their faith (Jude 20).

c. The carpenter

Both Joseph (Mt. xiii. 55) and Jesus (Mk. vi. 3) followed the ancient trade of carpenter (Gk. *tektōn*). A skilled worker in wood (Heb. *ḥāraš 'ēṣîm*) undertook all the carpentry tasks required in building operations, making roof, door, window, and stair fittings. Of the furniture he constructed couches, beds, chairs, tables, and footstools. Examples of some of these and of finely

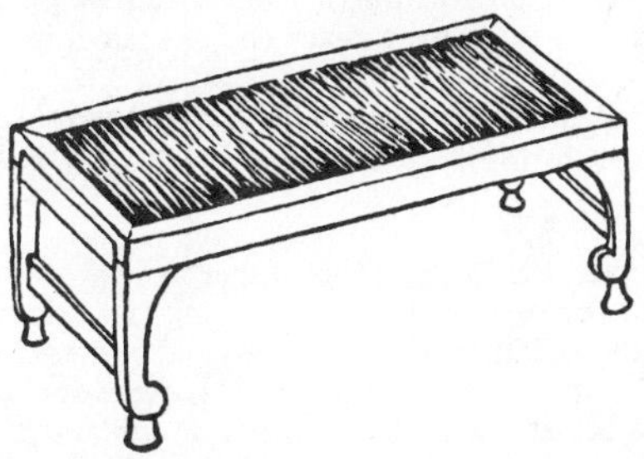

Fig. 21. Wooden stool from a Middle Bronze Age (early second millennium BC) tomb at Jericho.

carved bowls, spoons, and boxes have survived in the tombs at Jericho (*c.* 1800 BC). The same carpenter would manufacture agricultural implements, ploughs, yokes, threshing instruments (2 Sa. xxiv. 22) or boards (Is. xxviii. 27, 28), and irrigation machines. In the large cities groups of carpenters who made carts would, in time of war,

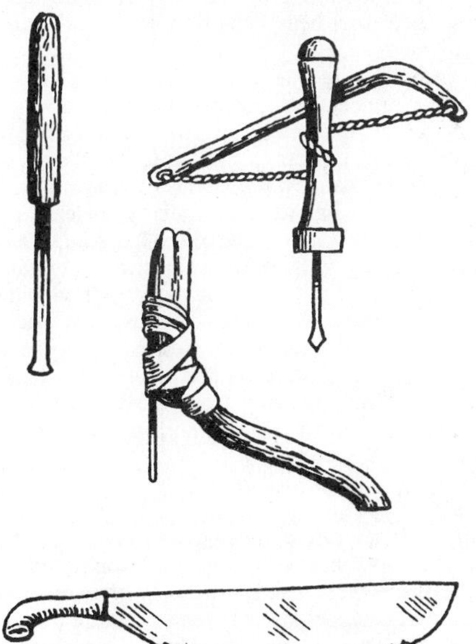

Fig. 22. A woodworker's tools. *Above:* copper chisel and a drill with copper bit turned by a bow with leather thong. *Centre:* an adze with a copper blade lashed to the wooden handle. *Below:* a saw. These (Egyptian) tools were of a type in general use from *c.* 2000 BC throughout the Near East.

build chariots (Ct. iii. 9). Ship-building seems to have remained a Phoenician monopoly centred at Tyre, where boats were constructed of local cypress with masts of cedar and oars of oak (Ezk. xxvii. 5, 6). See SHIPS and fig. 190. Some carpenters made idols (Is. xliv. 13–17). Though the Israelites undertook their own wood-working for the Tabernacle fitments (Ex. xxv), wood and experienced carpenters were supplied by agreement with Tyre for the construction of David's palace (2 Sa. v. 11) and the Temple built by Solomon. The same practice was followed for the later Temple (Ezr. iii. 7) and possibly for the repair of the Temple recorded in 2 Ch. xxiv. 12.

Wood-carving was undertaken by a few specialists (Ex. xxxi. 5, xxxv. 33), who may have also worked on bone and ivory. These worked the cherubim for the first Temple (1 Ki. vi. 33) and other *objets d'art* (see ART). For this hard woods, ebony, sandal- and boxwood, were imported, while the local woods, cedar, cypress, oak, ash (Is. xliv. 14), and acacia (AV 'shittim') were used for most joinery, the mulberry being commonly worked for agricultural implements (see TREES).

The carpenter's special tools included a marking tool (*śereḏ*, AV 'rule'), compass or dividers (*meḥûḡâ*), an adze (*maqṣu'â*—'a scraping instrument', AV 'plane', Is. xliv. 13), small chopper (*ma'aṣāḏ*), iron saw (some two-edged), and files (Je. x. 4), bow-drill and wooden mallet (*halmûṯ*, Jdg. v. 26, AV 'hammer') and hammer (*maqqāḇâ*, Is. xliv. 12) as well as the various chisels and awls, examples of which have been recovered (see fig. 22). Both nail and dowel joints can be seen on wooden objects from Middle Bronze Age and monarchy period sites.

d. The mason

Stone, being costly to transport and work, was considered an extravagance in a private house (Am. v. 11), and for the more important public buildings would be used only sparingly for essential constructional features (see CORNER-STONE, ARCHITECTURE). The local limestone being soft and not very durable, blocks of harder stones for the Temple and other splendid buildings were worked in the Lebanon prior to importation (1 Ki. vi. 7). The stonemason used many of the same tools as the carpenter, sawing the limestone (1 Ki. vii. 9) and trimming it with a pick or axe. In quarrying large blocks of stone wooden wedges were knocked in with wooden hammers and soaked until the stone cracked under the force of their expansion; a method commonly used in the Ancient Near East. Stone was broken by repeated pounding with a large metal forge-hammer (Heb. *paṭṭîš*). Such a hammer is used to describe the action of the divine Word (Je. xxiii. 29) and of mighty Babylon (Je. l. 23).

The mason also quarried out tombs in the natural caves in the hills or drove shafts into the hillside off which chambers were excavated (Is. xxii. 16). Particularly fine examples of such family mausolea have been found at Beth-shemesh (8th century) and round Jerusalem and Beth-shearim (1st century BC–2nd century AD). Deep silos or cisterns as cut at Jericho, Lachish, Megiddo, and Gibeon involved the removal of as much as half a million cubic yards of limestone by hand. There, and in the water tunnels cut by masons and miners, the marks of their adzes remain visible (see MINING, ARCHITECTURE, SILOAM).

In the Monarchy large stone pillar bases were cut, and from the tenth century BC pecked and marginally drafted masonry was used. By the Hellenistic period Herodian buildings at Jerusalem, Machpelah, and other sites show the use of immense blocks of stone so carefully dressed as to be aligned without mortar, and it is still impossible to insert a knife blade between the joins. Such careful work can also be seen at Megiddo in the 9th century BC. Masons' marks can be seen on a number of constructions such as the steps of the Capernaum synagogue. Masons were also employed to cut inscriptions on rock surfaces, and for this seem to have copied cursive inscriptions, for surviving examples at Shebna's tomb, the Siloam tunnel, and the Samaria fragment show no adaptation to the material (see WRITING). For finer engraving and work on small stones, see SEAL.

e. The smith

For centuries before the discovery of iron-working (*c.* 1200 BC) the Palestinians knew how to mine, smelt, refine, and work gold, silver, and copper. The development of Solomon's copper and iron mines and smelting-plants in the Wadi Arabah and Ezion-geber regions ushered in an economic and industrial revolution in Israel. Processes long used for other metals were adapted to mass production (see MINING AND METALS). Though large objects, such as the bronze pillars for Solomon's Temple, were cast in sand moulds near the mines (2 Ch. iv. 17), the ore, shaped into blocks, ingots or rings, or discs ('talents') was usually transported to the smiths' workshops. Here it was refined in a furnace (*q.v.*) to which the draught was forced through clay-pipes from the bellows (Heb. *mappuaḥ*, 'a blowing instrument'), usually a sewn goat- or sheep-skin. Thus a smith was commonly designated 'he who blows (the coals)', a title akin to the common Akkadian *nappāḫu* (Is. liv. 16). The molten metal was poured from ladles or buckets into stone or clay moulds or beaten on an anvil (Is. xli. 7, AV; Heb. *pa'amâ*, 'regular beating') with a forge-hammer. From this characteristic hammering and the flattening of thin metal by pounding (Is. xli. 7, AV 'smoothing') the coppersmith and iron-worker (*ḥāraš barzel*, Is. xliv. 12) were known as 'hammerers' and as those who made things firm and rigid (*masgēr*, AV 'locksmith') by jointing metal (*deḇeq*, Is. xli. 7, AV 'sodering') with solder, welding, and rivets. Objects found in excavations, such as the small bronze stand from Megiddo (see fig. 18), show a skill in fine *à jour* open-work which, if Israelite, indicates a technical ability as good as that of the contemporary Assyrians and Phoenicians.

The smiths manufactured a variety of metal vessels and implements, plough-blades, tips for ox-goads, forks, axle-trees, and axes, as well as the smaller pins, fibulae (from 10th century BC), images, figurines, and small instruments. The manufacture of knives, which were a close relation to daggers and swords, lance and spear-heads, and other weapons of war (see ARMOUR AND WEAPONS), reminds us how easily these same craftsmen could turn their hand to making implements for war or peace (Is. ii. 4; Joel iii. 10; Mi. iv. 3).

For the work of the related craft of the gold and silver smiths, see JEWELS AND PRECIOUS STONES.

f. The tanner

Leather, the treated skins of sheep and goats, was used for certain items of clothing (Lv. xiii. 48; Nu. xxxi. 20), including sandals and girdles (2 Ki. i. 8; Mt. iii. 4). The sewn skins were specially suitable at low cost for vessels or containers for water (Gn. xxi. 14), wine (Mt. ix. 17), or other liquids (Jdg. iv. 19). Sometimes the skins were sewn into true 'bottle' shapes. Leather was rarely used for tents (Ex. xxv. 5; Nu. iv. 6) but commonly for military articles, such as helmets, quivers, chariot fittings, slings, and shields, the latter well oiled to prevent cracking or the penetration of missiles (2 Sa. i. 21; Is. xxi. 5). Sandals of seal or porpoise skin (AV 'badgers' skin') were a sign of luxury (Ezk. xvi. 10), though it is likely that, as in Egypt and Assyria, fine leather was used for beds, chair covers, and other furnishings.

Since tanning was a malodorous task, it was usually undertaken outside a town and near abundant water. Peter's visit to Simon the tanner outside Joppa (Acts ix. 43, x. 6, 32) illustrates how far he had overcome his scruples against contact with what was ceremonially unclean. The usual process was to remove the hairs by smearing or soaking with lime or a substitute (*Periploca secamine*), and then to treat the sun-dried hides with sumach (*Acacia nilotica*) pods, pine or oak bark or leaves. Skins were sometimes dyed, and for fine pouches were tanned with mineral salt, usually alum, imported from the Dead Sea or Egypt, or treated like parchment (Gk. *membrana*; see WRITING).

g. The dyer

The ancient craft of dyeing was known to the Israelites at the Exodus, when skins used for the Tabernacle were dyed scarlet by the juices of crushed cochineal insects (*qermes*) found in oak-trees (Ex. xxvi. 1, 31, xxxvi. 8; Lv. xiv. 4). The black-purple or red-violet 'Tyrian' or 'Imperial' dye, prepared from the molluscs *Purpura* and *Murex* found on the E Mediterranean coast, was mainly a Phoenician monopoly and used for dyeing the highly priced garments which were a mark of rank and nobility (Jdg. viii. 26; Pr. xxxi. 22;

Lk. xvi. 19; Rev. xviii. 12, 16). The trade was attested in Ras Shamra texts (*c.* 1500 BC). This was also the 'purple' used in the tabernacle fabric (Ex. xxvi. 31, xxviii. 5), for the Temple veil, the 'blue, and purple, and crimson' being variants of the same dye (2 Ch. iii. 14), and for the garment put upon Jesus at His trial (Jn. xix. 2, 5). Native Israelites were taught the trade by Tyrian workmen at Solomon's request (2 Ch. ii. 7). Lydia traded in cloth similarly treated in Thyatira (Acts xvi. 14).

In Palestine yellow dyes were made from ground pomegranate rind, the Phoenicians also using safflower and turmeric. Blue was obtained from indigo plants (*Indigofera tinctoria*) imported

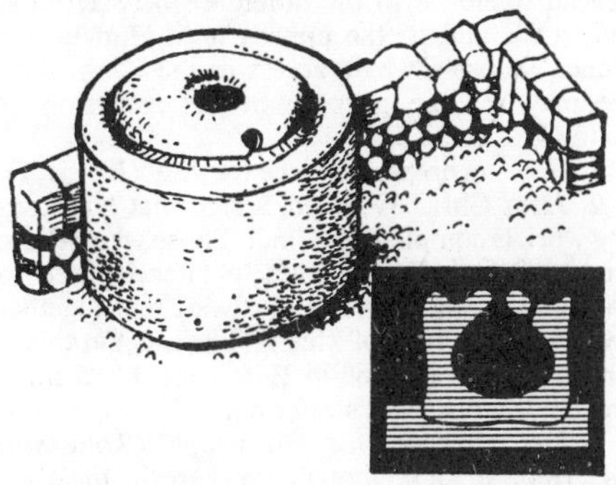

Fig. 23. Dye vat of the 7th century BC from Tell Beit Mirsim (Debir?)

from Syria or Egypt, where it had been originally transplanted from India. Woad was known after 300 BC. See also ART.

Tell Beit Mirsim (Debir?) on the edge of the Negeb was a town devoted to the weaving and dyeing industries. At least twenty dye-plants have been excavated, each of two or more stone vats (1½ feet) in a room 20 feet × 10 feet, with channels to catch splashed dyes. Potash and slaked lime were stood in the vats for two days before the dye was added. In some cases thread was dyed before weaving, but cloth would be steeped in the vat for a varying number of baths according to the depth of colour required. See fig. 23.

h. The fuller

The art of fulling, cleansing, and bleaching cloth was of importance because of the high cost of clothing and the need to cleanse the fibres of their natural oil or gums before dyeing. In some places the fuller was also the dyer.

It was customary for a fuller to work outside a town within reach of water in which clothes could be cleaned by treading them on a submerged stone. Hence the fuller was characteristically called a 'trampler' (Heb. *kāḇas*). At Jerusalem the locality outside the east wall where garments were spread to dry in the sun was called the 'fuller's field' (2 Ki. xviii. 17; Is. vii. 3, xxxvi. 2). Christ's garments at the transfiguration were described as brighter than it was possible for any fuller (Gk. *gnapheus*, 'cloth dresser') to whiten them (Mk. ix. 3).

For cleansing natron (nitre) was sometimes imported from Egypt, where, mixed with white clay, it was used as soap (Pr. xxv. 20; Je. ii. 22). Alkali was plentifully available in plant ash, and 'soap' (Heb. *bōrîṯ*, *kâlî*) was obtained by burning the soda plant (*Salsola kali*). The 'fullers' sope' of Mal. iii. 2 was probably 'cinders of *bōrîṯ*', since potassium and sodium nitrate do not seem to have been known in Syria or Palestine, though found in Babylonia.

For other crafts, see entries under ART, IVORY, SPINNING AND WEAVING, EMBROIDERY; for brewing, see MEALS; for glass-making, see GLASS; for other references to crafts, see MUSIC, EGYPT, ASSYRIA, and BABYLONIA.

BIBLIOGRAPHY. C. Singer (ed.), *A History of Technology*, I, 1958; G. E. Wright, *Biblical Archaeology*, 1957, pp. 191–198; R. J. Forbes, *Studies in Ancient Technology*, I–VI, 1955–8; A. Reifenberg, *Ancient Hebrew Arts*, 1950.

D.J.W.

ARVAD. The modern Ruād, an island 2 miles off the coast of Syria (anciently Phoenicia), and about 50 miles north of Byblos. It is mentioned only in Ezk. xxvii. 8, 11 and 1 Macc. xv. 23, though the Arvadites, its inhabitants, are referred to in Gn. x. 18; *cf.* 1 Ch. i. 16. The most northerly of the great Phoenician cities, it was independent until the 9th century BC, but subordinate to Tyre in the days of Ezekiel. In the Persian age it regained its former importance, and in the time of Alexander it controlled quite a large area of the mainland. R.F.H.

ASA. The third king of Judah after the disruption of the kingdom, Asa (*'āsā'*) reigned for forty-one years (1 Ki. xv. 9–24; 2 Ch. xiv–xvi). He began his reign with a partial reformation, abolishing cult prostitution and courageously deposing the queen-mother Maacah, whose image of the goddess Asherah he destroyed (1 Ki. xv. 13, RVmg). Certain high places—probably those of entirely pagan origin—he removed (2 Ch. xiv. 3), others were allowed to remain (1 Ki. xv. 14; 2 Ch. xv. 17). His appeal to Syria for help against the military threat of Baasha of Israel was an act of unbelief which received prophetic censure (2 Ch. xvi. 7 ff.). It was all the more inexcusable in view of his earlier great victory over the vast army of Zerah (*q.v.*) 'the Ethiopian'. J.C.J.W.

ASAHEL (*'ᵃśāh'ēl*, 'El performs', 'God is a doer'). **1.** Youngest son of Zeruiah, David's sister, and brother of Joab and Abishai. Renowned for his fleetness of foot, he was killed by Abner while pursuing him, which precipitated a blood-feud between Abner and his brothers (2 Sa. ii. 18–23, iii. 27, 30). He was one of 'the thirty' of David's mighty men (2 Sa. xxiii. 24; 1 Ch. xi. 26), and commanded the army for the fourth month (1 Ch. xxvii. 7). **2.** One of nine Levites who, with five princes and two priests, were sent by

Jehoshaphat throughout Judah teaching the law of the Lord (2 Ch. xvii. 8). **3.** One of those appointed to receive tithes and offerings in Hezekiah's reign (2 Ch. xxxi. 13). **4.** Father of Jonathan, an opponent of Ezra's policy regarding mixed marriages (Ezr. x. 15). J.G.G.N.

ASAPH. 1. A descendant of Gershom, son of Levi (1 Ch. vi. 39); nominated by the chief Levites as a leading singer, using cymbals, when the ark was brought to Jerusalem (1 Ch. xv. 17, 19). David made him leader of the choral worship (xvi. 4, 5). The 'sons of Asaph' remained the senior family of musicians until the Restoration (1 Ch. xxv; 2 Ch. xx. 14, xxxv. 15; Ezr. iii. 10; Ne. xi. 17, 22, xii. 35), primarily as singers and cymbalists. Asaph himself had a reputation as a seer, and was recognized as the author of psalms used when Hezekiah revived the Temple-worship (2 Ch. xxix. 30; *cf.* the traditional ascriptions of Ps. l, lxxiii–lxxxiii; *cf.* also the prophecy of Jahaziel, 2 Ch. xx. 14 ff.). It is not clear whether Asaph lived to see Solomon's Temple consecrated, or whether 2 Ch. v. 12 simply means 'the families of Asaph', *etc.*

2. Warden of forests in Palestine under Artaxerxes (Ne. ii. 8). J.P.U.L.

ASCENSION, THE. The story of the ascension of the Lord Jesus Christ is told in Acts i. 4–11. In Lk. xxiv. 51 the words 'and (was) carried up into heaven' are less well attested, as is also the description in Mk. xvi. 19. There is no alternative suggestion in the New Testament of any other termination to the post-resurrection appearances, and the fact of the ascension is always assumed in the frequent references to Christ at the right hand of God, and to His return from heaven. It would be unreasonable to suppose that Luke would be grossly mistaken or inventive about such an important fact so long as any of the apostles were alive to note what he had written. For other allusions to the ascension see Jn. vi. 62; Acts ii. 33, 34, iii. 21; Eph. iv. 8–10; 1 Thes. i. 10; Heb. iv. 14, ix. 24; 1 Pet. iii. 22; Rev. v. 6.

Objections are made to the story on the ground that it rests upon out-dated ideas of heaven as a place above our heads. Such objections are beside the point for the following reasons:

1. The act of ascension could have been an acted parable for the sake of the disciples who held this idea of heaven. Jesus thus indicated decisively that the period of post-resurrection appearances was now over, and that His return to heaven would inaugurate the era of the presence of the Holy Spirit in the Church. Such acted symbolism is perfectly natural.

2. The terms 'heaven' and 'the right hand of the Father' have some necessary meaning in relation to this earth, and this meaning can best be expressed with reference to 'above'. Thus Jesus lifted up His eyes to heaven when He prayed (Jn. xvii. 1; *cf.* 1 Tim. ii. 8), and taught us to pray, 'Our Father which art in heaven . . . Thy will be done in earth, as it is in heaven.' In one sense heaven is away from this earth, whatever may be its nature in terms of a different dimension. In passing from the earthly space-time to the heavenly state, Jesus was observed to move away from the earth, just as at His second coming He will be observed to move towards the earth. This doctrine of bodily absence is balanced in the New Testament by the doctrine of spiritual presence (see HOLY SPIRIT). Thus the Lord's Supper is in memory of One who is bodily absent 'till he come' (1 Cor. xi. 26), yet, as at all Christian gatherings, the risen Lord is spiritually present (Mt. xviii. 20).

The concept of God above on the throne has special reference to the difference between God and man, and to the approach to Him by the sinner, whose sin bars access to the King. Thus we may see the purpose of the ascension as follows:

1. 'I go to prepare a place for you' (Jn. xiv. 2).

2. Jesus Christ is seated, a sign that His atoning work is complete and final. Those who believe that as Priest He continues to offer Himself to the Father, say that one must not mix together the two metaphors of king and priest. Yet this is precisely what is done in Heb. x. 11–14 to show the finality of Christ's offering.

3. He intercedes for His people (Rom. viii. 34; Heb. vii. 25), though nowhere in the New Testament is He said to be offering Himself in heaven. The Greek word for intercede, *entynchanō*, has the thought of looking after someone's interests.

4. He is waiting until His enemies are subdued, and will return as the final act in the establishment of the kingdom of God (1 Cor. xv. 24–26). J.S.W.

ASENATH. Daughter of 'Potiphera priest of On' in Egypt, given in marriage to Joseph by Pharaoh (Gn. xli. 45) and so mother of Manasseh and Ephraim (Gn. xli. 50–52, xlvi. 20). The name Asenath (Heb. *'āsᵉnaṯ*) is good Egyptian, of the pattern *'I(w).s-n-X*, 'she belongs to X', X being a deity, a parent, or a pronoun referring to one of these. Three equally good possibilities would be: *'Iw.s-(n)-Nt*, 'she belongs to (the goddess) Neit', *'Iw.s-n-'t*, 'she belongs to (her) father', or *'Iw.s-n.t* (*t* for *ṯ*), 'she belongs to thee' (fem., either a goddess or the mother). Such names are well-attested in the Middle Kingdom and Hyksos periods (*c.* 2100–1600 BC) of Egyptian history, corresponding to the age of the Patriarchs and Joseph. See Kitchen, *The Joseph Narrative and its Egyptian Background.* K.A.K.

ASH. See TREES.

ASHDOD. Modern Esdud, 18 miles north-east of Gaza. Its early occupation was noted by Joshua (xi. 22) when it withstood attempts by Judah to conquer it and settle there (Jos. xiii. 3, xv. 46, 47). It was one of the principal ports and strongholds of the Philistines with a temple of

Dagon to which the ark was taken (1 Sa. v. 1 ff.). *Asdudu* was made subject to Assyria until its governor Aḫimiti revolted in 711 BC, when it was sacked by Sargon II. This calamity was noted by Amos (i. 8) and Isaiah (xx. 1). By the time of Jeremiah the city was weak (Je. xxv. 20) and gradually became more derelict (Zp. ii. 4; Zc. ix. 6). It was partially repopulated after the Exile (Ne. xiii. 23–24), but its continued idolatry provoked attacks by the Maccabees (1 Macc. v. 68, x. 84). As Azotus (Acts viii. 40) the city flourished after its restoration by Herod. Gabinius continued reconstruction work in the inner city, which was presented by Augustus to Salome, Herod's sister. D.J.W.

ASHER (Heb. *'āšēr*, 'happy, blessed'). **1.** Jacob's eighth son, his second by Leah's maid Zilpah (Gn. xxx. 13, xxxv. 26). Asher himself fathered four sons and a daughter (Gn. xlvi. 17; Nu. xxvi. 46; with descendants, 1 Ch. vii. 30–40). His descendants' prosperity was foreshadowed in Jacob's last blessing (Gn. xlix. 20). As an authentic north-western Semitic personal name Asher is attested at precisely Jacob's period, as that of a female servant (*c.* 1750 BC in an Egyptian papyrus list; see W. C. Hayes, *A Papyrus of the Late Middle Kingdom in the Brooklyn Museum*, 1955, pp. 88, 97, and especially W. F. Albright, *JAOS*, LXXIV, 1954, pp. 229, 231: *ỉšr*, *'šra*). This particular philological discovery rules out the commonly adduced equation of biblical Asher with the *ỉsr* in Egyptian texts of the 13th century BC as a Palestinian place-name: *ỉsr* would represent *'ṯr* not *'šr* (*cf.* Albright, *loc. cit.*). This, then, eliminates the consequent suggestion that the Egyptian *ỉsr* of 1300 BC (Sethos I) indicated an 'Asher'-settlement in Palestine prior to the Israelite invasion later in the 13th century BC.

2. An Israelite tribe descended from (1), and its territory. Consisting of five main families or clans (Nu. xxvi. 44–47), Asher shared the organization and fortunes of the tribes in the wilderness journeyings (Nu. i. 13, ii. 27, vii. 72, xiii. 13, *etc.*), and shared in Moses' blessing (Dt. xxxiii. 24). Asher's territory as assigned by Joshua was principally the Plain of Acre, the western slopes of the Galilaean hills behind it, and the coast from the tip of Carmel northwards to Tyre and Sidon (Jos. xix. 24–31, 34). On the south, Asher bordered on Manasseh, *ex*cluding certain border-cities (Jos. xvii. 10, 11; translate verse 11, 'Manasseh had *beside* Issachar and *beside* Asher . . . (various towns) . . .'). See Y. Kaufmann, *The Biblical Account of the Conquest of Palestine*, 1953, p. 38. (*Cf.* also HELKATH and IBLEAM.) In Asher the Gershonite Levites had four cities (1 Ch. vi. 62, 74, 75). However, the Asherites failed to expel the Canaanites, and merely occupied parts of their portion among them (Jdg. i. 31, 32). On topography and resources of Asher's portion, *cf.* D. Baly, *The Geography of the Bible*, 1957, pp. 128–131. In the judges' period Asher failed to help Deborah but rallied to Gideon's side (Jdg. v. 17, vi. 35, vii. 23). Asher provided warriors for David (1 Ch. xii. 36) and formed part of an administrative district of Solomon (1 Ki. iv. 16). After the fall of the northern kingdom some Asherites responded to Hezekiah's call to revive the Passover at Jerusalem (2 Ch. xxx. 11). In much later times the aged prophetess Anna, who rejoiced to see the infant Jesus, was of the tribe of Asher (Lk. ii. 36).

3. Possibly a town on the border of Manasseh and Ephraim, location uncertain (Jos. xvii. 7). K.A.K.

ASHERAH. A Canaanite mother-goddess mentioned in the Ras Shamra texts (*'aṯrt*) as a goddess of the sea and the consort of El, but associated in the Old Testament with Baal (*e.g.* Jdg. iii. 7). While the Old Testament sometimes refers to Asherah as a goddess (*e.g.* 1 Ki. xviii. 19; 2 Ki. xxiii. 4; 2 Ch. xv. 16), the name is used also of an image made for that goddess (*e.g.* 1 Ki. xv. 13) which consequently came to represent her. The Israelites were commanded to cut down (*e.g.* Ex. xxxiv. 13) or burn (Dt. xii. 3) the *asherim* of the Canaanites, and were likewise forbidden themselves to plant 'an Asherah of any kind of tree' beside God's altar (Dt. xvi. 21). From these references it appears that the object was of wood, and was presumably an image of some kind. A piece of carbonized wood about 4 ft. long, discovered in the Early Bronze Age shrine at Ai, has been interpreted as a possible asherah, but many scholars would now reject the view that the object was a post, and would give the translation 'Asherah-image' in all occurrences. In the AV the word is consistently translated 'grove' (*q.v.*).

BIBLIOGRAPHY. W. L. Reed, *The Asherah in the Old Testament*, 1949; J. B. Pritchard, *Palestinian Figurines in Relation to Certain Goddesses Known through Literature*, 1943, pp. 59–65; Millar Burrows, *What Mean These Stones?*, 1941, pp. 212, 213; W. F. Albright, *Archaeology and the Religion of Israel*[3], 1953, pp. 77–79; J. Marquet-Krause, *Les Fouilles de 'Ay (et-Tell) 1933–1935 . . .*, 1949, p. 18. T.C.M.

ASHES. This translates two Hebrew words. **1.** *'ēp̄er* (often parallel to *'āp̄ār*, 'dust' (*q.v.*), meaning 'product of burning'). It is used metaphorically signifying what is valueless (Is. xliv. 20) and loathsome (Jb. xxx. 19); misery (Ps. cii. 9; Je. vi. 26) and shame (2 Sa. xiii. 19); abasement before God (Gn. xviii. 27; Jb. xlii. 6) and contrition (Dn. ix. 3; Mt. xi. 21). It is also used ritually for purification (Nu. xix. 9, 10, 17; Heb. ix. 13); ashes as the residual product of a special sacrifice were kept to be used with running water to cleanse from pollution, and as a sign of fasting (Is. lviii. 5; Jon. iii. 6).

2. *dešen* meaning 'fatness'. AV translates 'ashes' when the word is used for fat residues from sacrifices (see Lv. vi. 10, 11; 1 Ki. xiii. 3, 5; *cf.* also Lv. i. 16, 'place of the ashes').

P.A.B.

ASHIMA. The god or idol of the people of Hamath (2 Ki. xvii. 30), which they made in the territory of Samaria, whence they had been deported by the Assyrians. Not known outside the Old Testament, though some have suggested identity with the Syrian Semios or the *'šm* of the Elephantine papyri. See A. Vincent, *La Religion des Judéo-Araméens d'Elephantine*, 1937, pp. 654 ff. T.C.M.

ASHKELON. Also called Askelon, Eshkalon (AV); modern *Asqalōn* on Palestinian coast between Jaffa and Gaza. The site has been occupied from Neolithic times till the 13th century AD (*IEJ*, V, p. 271). Ruled by a king in the Amarna age, this pre-Philistinian occupation is mentioned in Dt. ii. 23 and Egyp. execration texts. It was sacked by Rameses II in 1280 BC, and later captured by Judah (Jdg. i. 18). It became one of five principal Philistine cities (Jos. xiii. 3) and was always associated with Gaza, Ashdod, and Ekron (Am. i. 7, 8) and sometimes with Gath (2 Sa. i. 20). Tiglath-pileser III made *Asqalluna* a vassal-city of Assyria in 734 BC until it was sacked by Sennacherib after revolt. Ashkelon regained its independence from Assyria in 630 BC, but was sacked for resisting Nebuchadrezzar in 604 BC (Bab. Chronicle). Its king was slain and prisoners taken to Babylon (*Mélanges Dussaud*, II, 1939, p. 298). This event, predicted by Jeremiah (xlvii. 5–7) and Zephaniah (ii. 4–7), had a profound effect on Jerusalem, which was to suffer a similar fate a few years later (Je. lii. 4–11). Subordinated to Tyre in Persian times Ashkelon became a free Hellenistic city in 104 BC. It was captured by Jonathan (1 Macc. x. 86). Herod the Great embellished the city, which was his birthplace, and remains of this later period were excavated in 1921 (*PEQ*, 1921). D.J.W.

ASHKENAZ. A descendant of Noah through Japheth and Gomer (Gn. x. 3; 1 Ch. i. 6). Eponymous ancestor of the successive inhabitants of an area between the Black and Caspian Seas. *Ascanius* occurs as the name of a Mysian and Phrygian prince, while elsewhere these people are said to live in the district of *Ascania*. Cuneiform tablets tell of a tribe *Aš-ku-za*, the allies of the Mannai in their revolt against the Assyrians in the 7th century. This revolt is reflected in Je. li. 27. The Ashkenaz are to be identified with the *Skythai* (Scythians) mentioned by Herodotus (i. 103–107, iv. 1). See Schrader, *Keilinschriftliche Bibliothek*, II, pp. 129, 147; Schmidt, *EBi*, IV, pp. 4330 ff. R.J.W.

ASHTAROTH, ASHTORETH. 1. *'Aštōreṯ*, *'aštārôṯ*, a mother goddess with aspects as goddess of fertility, love, and war, known to the Israelites through the Canaanites (1 Ki. xi. 5). The name was common in one form or another, among many of the Semitic-speaking peoples of antiquity. In Mesopotamia Ištar was identified with the Sumerian mother goddess Inanna. The name occurs in the form *'ṯtrt* in the Ugaritic texts, and as *'štrt* in the (later) Phoenician inscriptions, transcribed in the Greek script as *Astartē*. It has been suggested that the Hebrew *'aštōreṯ* is an artificial form created from *'štrt*, by analogy with the vowel pattern of *bōšeṯ* 'shame', to show a fitting attitude among the Israelites to the goddess, whose cult as practised by the Canaanites was depraved in the extreme. *'Aštārôṯ* is the plural form of the name. The Israelites turned to the worship of Ashtoreth soon after arriving in the land (Jdg. ii. 13, x. 6); it was rife in the time of Samuel (1 Sa. vii. 3, 4, xii. 10) and was given royal sanction by Solomon (1 Ki. xi. 5; 2 Ki. xxiii. 13). After Saul had been killed by the Philistines, his armour was placed in the temple of Ashtaroth at Beth-shan (1 Sa. xxxi. 10), and the excavators of this site have suggested that the northern temple in level V there (see fig. 36) may have been the one in question, though this remains an inference. Numerous clay plaques depicting naked female images have been discovered in Palestinian sites of the Bronze and Iron Ages, and it is probable that some of these are representations of the goddess Ashtoreth-Astarte.

BIBLIOGRAPHY. J. B. Pritchard, *Palestinian Figurines in Relation to Certain Goddesses Known through Literature*, 1943, esp. pp. 65–72; W. F. Albright, *Mélanges Syriens . . . Dussaud*, I, 1939, pp. 107–120; *Archaeology and the Religion of Israel*, 1953, pp. 74 ff.; E. Dhorme, *Les Religions de Babylonie et d'Assyrie*², 1949, pp. 67 ff., 89 ff.; A. Rowe, *The Four Canaanite Temples of Beth-Shan*, Part I, 1940, pp. 31–34.

Fig. 24. Ivory panel showing the head of a woman in an Egyptian wig looking out of a recessed and carved window. This may represent the goddess Astarte or her votaress gazing unveiled from her chamber in the rôle of a sacred prostitute. From Khorsabad, 9th–8th centuries.

2. *'ašt^e^rôṯ ṣō'neḵā*, a phrase occurring four times (Dt. vii. 13, xxviii. 4, 18, 51), and rendered variously 'flocks of thy sheep' (AV) and 'young of thy flock' (RV, RSV). It may be that from her fertility aspect the name of Astarte was associated by the Canaanites with sheep-breeding, and came to mean 'ewe' or something similar, the word being later borrowed by the Israelites without the cultic overtones.

BIBLIOGRAPHY. W. F. Albright, *Archaeology and the Religion of Israel*, 1953, pp. 75, 220.

3. *'aštārôṯ*. A city, presumably a centre of the worship of the goddess Ashtaroth, which is probably to be identified with modern Tell Ashtarah some 20 miles to the east of the Sea of Galilee. The city, probably mentioned in the time of Abraham (see ASHTEROTH-KARNAIM), was later the capital of Og, king of Bashan (Dt. i. 4). It was in the territory allotted to Manasseh by Moses (Jos. xiii. 31), but, though Joshua conquered Og (Jos. ix. 10) and took Ashtaroth (Jos. xii. 4), it was evidently not held, for it remained among the territories yet to be possessed when Joshua was an old man (Jos. xiii. 12). It later became a levitical city (1 Ch. vi. 71; Jos. xxi. 27, *be'ešterâ*, possibly a contraction of *bêṯ 'aštārâ*, which appears in EVV as Beeshterah), and is only subsequently mentioned in the Bible as the home of Uzzia, one of David's mighty men (1 Ch. xi. 44). It is perhaps to be identified with the *'s'tm* (As(t)artum?) in the Egyp. execration texts of about the 19th century, and with more certainty with the *'strt* of the records of Tuthmosis III, the *aš-tar-te* of the Amarna Letters, and the *as-tar-tu* of the Assyrian inscriptions. A stylized representation of a city with crenellated towers and battlements standing on a mound below the name *as-tar-tu* is given on a bas-relief of Tiglath-pileser III which was discovered at Nimrud (BM 118908).

BIBLIOGRAPHY. N. Glueck, *AASOR*, XVIII–XIX, 1937–9, p. 265; F. M. Abel, *Géographie de la Palestine*, II, 1938, p. 255; W. F. Albright, *BASOR*, 83, 1941, p. 33; J. A. Knudtzon, *Die el-Amarna Tafeln*, I, 1907, pp. 726, 816, II, 1915, p. 1292; Honigman, *Reallexikon der Assyriologie*, I, 1932, p. 304; S. Smith, *Assyrian Sculptures in the British Museum: from Shalmaneser III to Sennacherib*, 1938, pl. IX.

T.C.M.

ASHTEROTH-KARNAIM. A city inhabited by the Rephaim, sacked by Chedorlaomer in the time of Abraham (Gn. xiv. 5). Some scholars interpret the name as 'Astarte of the Two Horns' and identify this goddess with representations in art of a female with two horns of which Palestinian examples have been found at Gezer and Beth-shan. It is more probable, however, that the name is to be taken as 'Ashteroth near Karnaim' and identified with the city of Ashteroth (*q.v.*), which lies in the vicinity of Karnaim (not mentioned in the Bible; *cf.* 1 Macc. v. 43, 44).

BIBLIOGRAPHY. F. M. Abel, *Géographie de la Palestine*, II, 1938, p. 255; D. Baly, *The Geography of the Bible*, 1957, pp. 221, 226; see also W. C. Graham and H. G. May, *Culture and Conscience: An Archaeological Study of the New Religious Past in Ancient Palestine*, 1936, pp. 161 162; May, *Material Remains of the Megiddo Cult*, 1935, p. 12.

T.C.M.

ASHURBANIPAL (Assyr. *Aššur-bān-apal*, 'Ashur has made a son'). He was created crown

Fig. 25. King Ashurbanipal shooting from the saddle with bow and arrow at leaping lions. Relief from Nineveh *c.* 650 BC. See also figs. 77, 137.

prince in May 672 BC by his father Esarhaddon whom he succeeded in 669 BC as king of Assyria. Early in his reign he warred against Egypt, where he captured Thebes in 663 BC (see NO-AMON; *cf.* Na. iii. 8), and to hold this distant land had to make a number of punitive raids against the Syrians, Phoenicians, and Arabs. He is probably the king who freed Manasseh from exile in Nineveh (2 Ch. xxxiii. 13) and thus had a vassal-king serving him in Judah. In 641 BC Ashurbanipal sacked Susa, capital of Elam (see SHUSHAN), and for this reason is thought to be the 'great and noble Osnappar (AV Asnappar)', whom the Samaritans claimed had brought Susanites and Elamites to their city (Ezr. iv. 9, 10). Since this is a reference in an Aramaic letter more than two hundred years after the event, the rendering of the Assyrian royal name as *'as(rb)npr* (LXX *Asennaphar*; Gk. (Luc.) interprets as Shalmaneser, *q.v.*) is not unlikely.

From 652 BC Ashurbanipal was at war with his twin-brother Šamaš-šum-ukin of Babylon and the Assyrian hold on Palestine weakened. The end of his reign is obscure for *c.* 631 BC he died or had his son Aššur-eṭil-ilāni as co-regent. Ashurbanipal is well known for his library of Akkadian literature collected at Nineveh (see ASSYRIA). D.J.W.

ASHURITES. The translation of *Ashuri* (2 Sa. ii. 9) by Ashurites, taking it as a gentilic collective, has raised problems. It seems clear that there is no connection with the Ashurites of Gn. xxv. 3. Some would read Asherites and connect it with Jdg. i. 32, since the Targum of Jonathan reads Beth-Asher. Some scholars would emend to Geshurites, for which support is found in the Syr. and Vulg. The objection to this reading is that Geshur had its own king Talmai (*cf.* 2 Sa. xiii. 37), whose daughter David had married (1 Ch. iii. 2). The LXX has *thasiri*, possibly due to the misreading of the *h* as a *t*.

The use, however, of the preposition *'el* in 2 Sa. ii. 9 with the names Gilead, Ashuri, and Jezreel rather indicates place-names, as this preposition can have the meaning of 'at'. The meaning would then be that we have here the names of three administrative centres. In the choice of such centres consideration would be given to geographical accessibility. In the case of Ashuri, otherwise unknown, this could have been the decisive factor. With the following three names the preposition *'al* is used, which is a common construction with 'people' in the phrase 'to reign over', thus, 'and over Ephraim, and over Benjamin, even over all Israel'. The use of the definite article with Ashuri, is not unusual with proper names (*cf.* Gilead), and there are other examples of place-names with the ending *i* (*e.g.* Edrei, Ophni; and Naphtali is used occasionally as a geographical name). If the three towns formed a triangle, then Ashuri would be the southern point with Jezreel north and Gilead east. Thus geographically an identification with Asher (Jos. xvii. 7) would not be impossible. W.J.M.

ASIA. To Greeks the name either of the continent or more commonly of the region in Asia Minor based on Ephesus. The latter embraced a number of Greek states which in the 3rd century BC fell under the control of the kings of Pergamum. In 133 BC the royal possessions were bequeathed to the Romans, and the area was subsequently organized as a province including the whole western coast of Asia Minor together with adjacent islands, and stretching inland as far as the Anatolian plateau. There was a galaxy of wealthy Greek states which suffered at first from Roman exploitation, but recovered in the New Testament period to become the most brilliant centres of Hellenism in the world. The Roman jurisdiction was exercised through nine or more assizes (*agoraioi*, Acts xix. 38) presided over by the senatorial proconsul or his legates (*anthypatoi*, *ibid.*). The Greek republics formed a confederation whose chief expression was the cult of Rome and Augustus established initially at Pergamum. It is not certain whether the 'chief of Asia' (*asiarchēs*, Acts xix. 31) were the ex-high priests of the cult or the members of the federal assembly. In either case they represent a pro-Roman political élite. (J. A. O. Larsen, *Representative Government in Greek and Roman Antiquity*, 1955, pp. 117–120.)

Christianity was established only in the administrative heart of the province at first. All three metropolitan centres, Pergamum, Smyrna, and Ephesus, had churches. Beyond that we know for certain of churches in only two of the nearer assize centres, Sardis in the Hermus valley (Thyatira and Philadelphia being important cities in the same region) and Laodicea (on the Lycus) at the head of the Maeander valley (with the smaller towns of Colossae and Hierapolis near by).

BIBLIOGRAPHY. Pliny, *Historia Naturalis*, v. 28–41; Strabo, xii–xiv; J. Keil, *CAH*, XI, pp. 580–589; *RAC*, II, pp. 740–749; A. H. M. Jones, *Cities of the Eastern Roman Provinces*, 1937, pp. 28–95; D. Magie, *Roman Rule in Asia Minor*, 2 vols., 1950. E.A.J.

ASIARCH. In Acts xix. 31 some of the Asiarchs (Gk. *asiarchēs*; AV 'certain of the chief of Asia'), described as friends of Paul, warn him not to risk his life by going into the Ephesian theatre during the riotous demonstration in honour of Artemis. The league (*koinon*) of cities of the province of Asia was administered by the Asiarchs, who were chosen annually from the wealthiest and most aristocratic citizens. From their ranks were drawn the honorary high priests of the provincial cult of 'Rome and the Emperor', established by the league with its headquarters at Pergamum in 29 BC. They are further mentioned by Strabo (*Geography*, xiv. 1. 42) and in inscriptions.

BIBLIOGRAPHY. L. R. Taylor, 'The Asiarchs', in Foakes-Jackson and Lake, *The Beginnings of Christianity*, V, 1933, pp. 256–262. F.F.B.

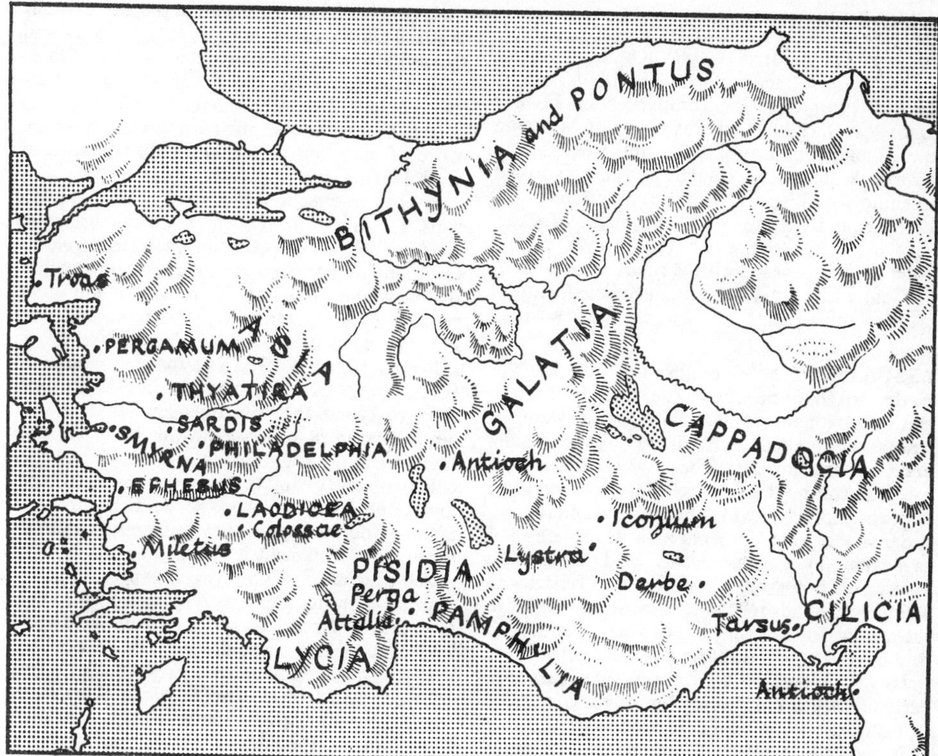

Fig. 26. Asia in New Testament Times. The seven churches to which letters are sent in Revelation ii, iii are shown in small capitals.

ASNAPPER. See Ashurbanipal.

ASP. See Serpent.

ASS. Two Hebrew words are thus rendered: *'āṯôn*, referring to its endurance, and *ḥᵃmôr* from the reddish coat of the most usual colour form. The latter is used much more frequently than the former, which is found mainly in the two incidents of Balaam's ass (Nu. xxii) and the asses of Kish (1 Sa. ix, x). The words cited refer only to the domesticated ass. In addition, two words are rendered 'wild ass'—*'ārōḏ* and *pere'*. The former is found both in the Aramaic form *'ᵃrād* (Dn. v. 21), and as Heb. *'ārôḏ* (Jb. xxxix. 5), and, while most translators render it 'wild ass', this is questioned by some. *Pere'* occurs nine times, and its translation as 'wild ass' in Jb. xxxix. 5–8 is well endorsed by the context. This species is known today as the onager (*Equus onager*), and it is still found in parts of Western and Central Asia.

The domestic ass is descended from the Nubian wild ass (*Equus asinus*), and it is thought to have been domesticated in Neolithic times in NE Africa. The first mention of asses is during Abram's stay in Egypt (Gn. xii. 16), and it is possible that they had not then been exported from Egypt into Asia. Asses were of vital importance to the poorer nomadic peoples and provided their basic transport, allowing an average journey of about 20 miles a day. A text from Mari also shows that as early as the 17th century BC it was considered improper for royalty to ride a horse rather than an ass. In the light of this, *cf.* Zc. ix. 9; Mt. xxi. 2 ff.

Some American scholars, including W. F. Albright, consider that the camel was not domesticated until after the patriarchal period and that the Hebrews in Genesis had only asses. Against this theory are the important facts that camels are depicted in drawings from Upper Egypt dated around 3000 BC, and that the Arabian camel has not been known as a wild animal within historic times, which suggests a much older date for its domestication (see Camel). G.C.

ASSASSINS. A term used by RV and RSV in Acts xxi. 38 to render the Gk. *sikarioi* (AV 'murderers'), who were followers of an Egyptian impostor (see Egyptian, The). The term was applied specially to groups of militant Jewish nationalists in the middle years of the 1st century AD who armed themselves with concealed daggers (Lat. *sicae*, whence *sicarii*, 'dagger-men') to despatch unawares men whom they regarded as enemies of the nation (Josephus, *BJ* ii. 13. 3; *Ant.* xx. 8. 5, 10). F.F.B.

ASSEMBLY. See CONGREGATION.

ASSOS. The modern Behram Köi, a seaport of Asia Minor directly north of the island of Lesbos. From here Paul embarked on his last journey to Jerusalem. It was a city of Mysia, in the Roman province of Asia, and was situated on a rock about 700 ft. high. Strabo says it had splendid fortifications, and communicated with its harbour by means of a long flight of steps. This harbour, from which Paul sailed, is now filled up and covered with gardens. The modern harbour exists beside it, being protected with an artificial mole. R.F.H.

ASSURANCE. 1. Grounds for certainty (a pledge, token, or proof). **2.** The state of certainty. Both Testaments depict faith as a state of assurance founded upon divinely given assurances. Apart, however, from Is. xxxii. 17 (where RV substitutes 'confidence'), the word itself appears in EVV only in the New Testament.

Sense **1** is found in Acts xvii. 31, where Paul says that by raising Jesus God has 'given assurance unto all men' (*pistis*, objectively adequate grounds for belief) that Jesus will judge the world. *Cf.* 2 Tim. iii. 14, where Timothy is told to continue in what he has 'been assured of' (passive of *pistoō*, render certain)—the assurance deriving in this case from Timothy's knowledge of his teachers and of the Scriptures.

Sense **2** is regularly expressed by the noun *plērophoria* (fulness of conviction and confidence), which EVV translate 'full assurance'. We read of the 'riches of the *plērophoria* of understanding' ('a wealth of assurance, such as understanding brings', *Arndt*) (Col. ii. 2); of approaching God with *plērophoria* of faith (Heb. x. 22); of maintaining *plērophoria* of hope (Heb. vi. 11); and of the gospel being preached 'in the Holy Ghost, and (in) much *plērophoria*'—*i.e.* with strong, Spirit-wrought conviction in both preacher and converts (1 Thes. i. 5). Paul uses the passive of the corresponding verb *plērophoreō* (lit., 'be filled full; be fully resolved', Ec. viii. 11, LXX; 'be fully satisfied', papyri (see *LAE*, p. 82)) to denote the state of being fully assured as to God's will (Rom. xiv. 5) and His ability to perform His promises (Rom. iv. 21). Another passive (*pepeismai*, 'I am persuaded') introduces Paul's conviction that God can guard him (2 Tim. i. 12), and that nothing can separate him from God's love (Rom. viii. 38 f.). This passive points to the fact that Christian assurance is not an expression of human optimism or presumption, but a persuasion from God. It is, indeed, just one facet of the gift of faith (*q.v.*; *cf.* Heb. xi. 1, RV). God's witness is its ground and God's Spirit its author.

Assured faith in the New Testament has a double object: first, God's revealed truth, viewed comprehensively as a promise of salvation in Christ; second, the believer's own interest in that promise. In both cases, the assurance is correlative to and derived from divine testimony.

1. God testifies to sinners that the gospel is His truth. This He does, both by the miracles and charismata which authenticated the apostles as His messengers (Heb. ii. 4), and by the Spirit-given illumination which enabled their hearers to recognize and receive their message 'not as the word of men, but as it is in truth, the word of God' (1 Thes. ii. 13, *cf.* i. 5).

2. God testifies to believers that they are His sons. The gift to them of the Spirit of Christ (see Acts ii. 38, v. 32; Gal. iii. 2) is itself God's testimony to them that He has received them into the messianic kingdom (Acts xv. 8), and that now they know Him savingly (1 Jn. iii. 24). This gift, the 'earnest (*q.v.*) of our inheritance' (Eph. i. 14), seals them as God's permanent possession (Eph. i. 13, iv. 30), and assures them that through Christ they are now His children and heirs. The Spirit witnesses to this by prompting them to call God 'Father' (Rom. viii. 15 f.; Gal. iv. 6) and giving them a sense of His fatherly love (Rom. v. 5). Hence the boldness and joy before God and men that everywhere characterize New Testament religion.

Self-deception is, however, a danger here, for strong persuasions of a saving relationship with God may be strong delusions of demonic origin. Inward assurance must therefore be checked by external moral and spiritual tests (*cf.* Tit. i. 16). John's Epistles deal directly with this. John specifies right belief about Christ, love to Christians, and righteous conduct as objective signs of being a child of God and knowing Him savingly (1 Jn. ii. 3–5, 29, iii. 9 f., 14, 18 f., iv. 7, v. 1, 4, 18). Those who find these signs in themselves may assure (lit., persuade) their hearts in the presence of God when a sense of guilt makes them doubt His favour (1 Jn. iii. 19). But absence of these signs shows that any assurance felt is delusive (1 Jn. i. 6, ii. 4, 9–11, 23, iii. 6–10, iv. 8, 20; 2 Jn. 9; 3 Jn. 11).

BIBLIOGRAPHY. L. Berkhof, *The Assurance of Faith*; and, among older works, W. Guthrie, *The Christian's Great Interest*. J.I.P.

ASSYRIA. The name of the ancient country whose inhabitants were called Assyrians. It lay in the upper Mesopotamian plain, bounded on the west by the Syrian desert, on the south by the Jebel Hamrin and Babylonia, and on the north and east by the Urarṭian (Armenian) and Persian hills (see fig. 27). The most fertile and densely populated part of Assyria lay east of the central river Tigris ('Hiddekel', Gn. ii. 14). The Heb. *'aššûr* (Assyr. *aššur*) is used both of this land and of its people. The term Assyria was sometimes applied to those territories which were subject to the control of its kings dwelling at Nineveh, Assur, and Calah, the principal cities. At the height of its power in the 8th–7th centuries BC, these territories included Media and S Anatolia, Cilicia, Syria, Palestine, Arabia, Egypt, Elam, and Babylonia.

In the Old Testament Asshur was considered the second son of Shem (Gn. x. 22) and was distinct from Ashuram (AV 'Asshurim'), an Arab tribe descended from Abraham and Keturah (Gn. xxv. 3), and from the Ashurites of 2 Sa. ii. 9 (where 'Asherites' or 'Geshur' is perhaps to be read; *cf.* Jdg. i. 31, 32). Assyria, which is always carefully distinguished from Babylonia, stands for the world power whose invasions of Israel and Judah were divinely permitted, though later it too suffered destruction for its godlessness. There are frequent references to the land (Is. vii. 18; Ho. xi. 5) and to the kings of Assyria (Is. viii. 4; 2 Ki. xv–xix).

I. HISTORY

a. Early history down to 900 BC

Assyria was inhabited from prehistoric times (*e.g.* Jarmo, *c.* 5000 BC) and pottery from the periods known as Hassuna, Samarra, Halaf, and 'Ubaid (*c.* 5000–3000 BC) has been found at a number of sites, including Assur, Nineveh, and Calah, which, according to Gn. x. 11, 12, were founded by immigrants from Babylonia. Although the origins of the Assyrians are still disputed, there can be no doubt that the Sumerians were present at Assur by 2900 BC and that Assyrian language and culture owes much to the southerners. At the same time there was a constant influx from the western deserts and influence from the non-semitic peoples of the northern hills.

The kings of Agade (see ACCAD), including Sargon, *c.* 2350 BC (see fig. 2) built in Assyria at Nineveh, and a building inscription of Amar-Su'en of Ur (*c.* 2040 BC) has been found at Assur. After the fall of Ur to Amorite invaders Assur, according to the Assyrian king list, was ruled by independent princes. These established trade connections with Cappadocia (*c.* 1920–1870 BC). Šamši-Adad I (1813–1781 BC) gradually increased his lands, his sons Yasmaḫ-Adad and Zimrilim ruling at Mari (see also ARCHAEOLOGY) until that city was captured by Hammurabi of Babylon. With the advent of the Mitanni and Hurrian groups in the Upper Euphrates the influence of Assyria declined, though it remained a prosperous agricultural community whose typical life and customs can be seen in the tablets recovered from Nuzi (see ARCHAEOLOGY). Under Ashur-uballiṭ I (1365–1330 BC) Assyria began to recover something of its former greatness. He entered into correspondence with Amenophis IV of Egypt whereupon Burnaburias II of Babylon objected, declaring him to be his vassal (Amarna letters). However, the decline of the Mitanni allowed the trade routes to the north to be reopened and in the reigns of Arik-den-ili (1319–1308 BC) and Adad-nirari I (1307–1275 BC) the territories as far west as Carchemish, lost since the days of Šamši-Adad, were recovered.

Shalmaneser I (1274–1245 BC) made constant expeditions against the tribes in the eastern hills and against new enemies in Urarṭu. He also sought to contain the Hurrian forces by campaigns in Hanigalbat to the north-west. He rebuilt Calah as a new capital. His son Tukulti-Ninuta I (1244–1208 BC) had to devote much of his attention to Babylonia, of which he was also king for seven years until murdered by his son Aššurnadinapli. Soon afterwards Babylonia became independent again and there was a revival of fortune for a while under Tiglath-pileser I (1115–1077 BC). He vigorously campaigned against the Muški (see MESHEK) and Subarian tribes, thrusting also as far as Lake Van in the north and to the Mediterranean, where he received tribute from Byblos, Sidon, and Arvad, and making expeditions as far as Tadmor (Palmyra) in his efforts to control the Aramaean (Aḫlame) tribes of the desert. It was the activities of these latter tribes which contained Assyria and left David and Solomon free to strike into Syria (Aram).

b. The Neo-Assyrian period (900–612 BC)

A new ruling family at Assur under Tukulti-Ninurta II (890–885 BC) began to take more vigorous military action against the tribes oppressing Assyria. His son, Ashurnasirpal II (885–860 BC), in a series of brilliant campaigns subdued the tribes on the Middle Euphrates, and reached the Lebanon and Philistia, where the coastal cities paid him tribute. He also sent expeditions into N Babylonia and the eastern hills. His reign marked the commencement of a sustained pressure by Assyria against the west which was to bring her into conflict with Israel. More than 50,000 prisoners were employed on the enlargement of Calah, where Ashurnasirpal built a new citadel, palace, and temples, and commenced work on the ziggurat. He employed artists to engrave sculptures in his audience chambers and skilled men to maintain botanical and zoological gardens and a park.

Ashurnasirpal's son Shalmaneser III (859–824 BC) continued his father's policy and greatly extended Assyria's frontiers, making himself the master from Urarṭu to the Persian Gulf and from Media to the Syrian coast and Cilicia (Tarsus). In 857 BC he captured Carchemish and his attack on Bit-Adini (see EDEN, GARDEN OF) alerted the major city-states to the south-west. Irhuleni of Hamath and Hadadezer of Damascus formed an anti-Assyrian coalition of ten kings who faced the Assyrian army in the indecisive battle of Qarqar in 853 BC. According to the Assyrian annals, 'Ahab the Israelite (*sirla'aia*)' supplied 2,000 chariots and 14,000 men on this occasion. Three years later Shalmaneser undertook a further series of operations directed mainly against Hadadezer (see BEN-HADAD). By 841 BC, Shalmaneser's eighteenth year, the coalition had split up, so that the full force of the Assyrian army could be directed against Hazael, who fought a rearguard action in the Anti-Lebanon mountains and withdrew into Damascus. When the siege of this city failed, Shalmaneser moved through the Hauran to the Nahr el-Kelb in the Lebanon and there received tribute from the rulers of Tyre, Sidon, and 'Jehu, son of Omri', an act not mentioned in the Old Testament but depicted on Shalmaneser's 'Black Obelisk' at

Nimrud. He had scenes from the other campaigns engraved on the gates of the temple at Imgur-Bel (Balawat). (These are now in the British Museum.)

Šamši-Adad V (823–810 BC) was obliged to initiate reprisal raids in Nairi to counteract the plots of the rebel Ispuini of Urarṭu, and also launched three campaigns against Babylonia and the fortress Der on the Elamite frontier. Šamši-Adad died young, and his influential widow Sammuramat (Semiramis) acted as regent until 805 BC, when their son Adad-nirari III was old enough to assume authority. Meanwhile the army undertook expeditions in the north and west, and Guzana (see GOZAN) was incorporated as an Assyrian province. Adad-nirari set out to support Hamath in 804 by attacking Damascus, where Hazael, son of Ben-hadad II—whom he called by his Aramaic title *Mari'*—was ruling. This gave Israel a respite from the attacks from Aram (2 Ki. xii. 17; 2 Ch. xxiv. 23 f.), and many rulers brought the Assyrian gifts in recognition of his aid. He claims that among those bringing tribute were 'Hatti (N Syria), Amurru (E Syria), Tyre, Sidon, Omri-land (Israel), Edom, and Philistia as far as the Mediterranean'. The Assyrian action seems to have enabled Joash to recover towns on his northern border which had previously been lost to Hazael (2 Ki. xiii. 25). Affairs at home appear to have been peaceful, for the Assyrian king built a new palace outside the citadel walls at Calah.

Shalmaneser IV (781–772 BC), though harassed by the Urarṭian Argistis I on his northern border, kept up the pressure against Damascus, and this doubtless helped Jeroboam II to extend the boundaries of Israel to the Beqa' (AV 'entering of Hamath', 2 Ki. xiv. 25–28). But Assyria was now being weakened by internal dissension, for the succession was uncertain, since Adad-nirari had died when young and childless. A notable defeat in the north was marked by that 'sign of ill omen', an eclipse of the sun, in 763 BC, a date of importance in Assyrian chronology. Once again the west was free to re-group to withstand further attacks, as indicated by the Aramaic treaty of Mati'el of Bit-Agusi (Arpad) with Barga'ayah.

The records of Tiglath-pileser III (745–727 BC) are fragmentary, and the order of events in his reign uncertain. He was, however, a strong ruler who set out to regain, and even extend, the territories which owed allegiance to the national god Ashur. Early in his reign he was proclaimed king of Babylon under his native name Pul(u) (2 Ki. xv. 19; 1 Ch. v. 26). In the north he fought Sardur II of Urarṭu, who was intriguing with the Syrian states. By relentless campaigning Tiglath-pileser defeated the rebels in the towns along the Anti-Taurus (Kashiari) mountains as far as Kummuḫ, organizing the subdued country in a series of provinces owing allegiance to the king. Arpad was besieged for three years (743–740 BC), and during this time Rezin of Damascus and other neighbouring rulers brought in their tribute. While Tiglath-pileser was absent in the northern hills in 738 a revolt was stimulated by 'Azriau of Yaudi' in league with Hamath. Yaudi was a small city-state in N Syria, though there is a possibility that the reference is to Azariah of Judah (*q.v.*). At this time Tiglath-pileser claims to have received tribute from Menahem (*Meniḫimmu*) of Samaria and Hiram of Tyre. This event is not mentioned in the Old Testament, which records a later payment. Then the amount of 50 shekels of silver extorted from the leading Israelites to meet this demand is to be compared with contemporary Assyrian contracts. Each man was, in effect, required to pay the equivalent value of a slave to avoid deportation (2 Ki. xv. 20).

Two years later a series of campaigns was undertaken which ended with the capture of Damascus in 732 BC. Tiglath-pileser, according to his annals, replaced Pekah, the murderer of Pekahiah, son of Menahem, by 'Ausi (Hoshea). *Cf.* 2 Ki. xv. 30. This was probably in 734 BC, when the Assyrians marched down the Phoenician coast and through 'the border of Israel' as far as Gaza, whose king, Hanunu, fled across the 'River of Egypt' (Wadi el-Arish; *Iraq*, XIII, 1951, pp. 21–24). This action in Palestine was at least in part a response to the appeal of *Iauḫazi* ((Jeho)Ahaz) of Judah, whose tribute is listed with that of Ammon, Moab, Ashkelon, and Edom, for help against Rezin of Damascus and Pekah of Israel (2 Ki. xvi. 5–9). Israel (*Bit-Humria*) was attacked, Hazor in Galilee destroyed (2 Ki. xv. 29; see ARCHAEOLOGY), and many prisoners taken into exile. Ahaz, too, paid dearly for this bid and had to accept religious obligations (2 Ki. xvi. 10 ff.), the imported altar being but one symbol of vassalage, another being an image of the king such as Tiglath-pileser set up in conquered Gaza.

Shalmaneser V (727–722 BC), son of Tiglath-pileser III, also warred in the west. When the Assyrian vassal Hoshea failed to pay his annual tribute after listening to overtures of help promised by Egypt (2 Ki. xvii. 4), Shalmaneser laid siege to Samaria (verse 5). After three years, according to the Babylonian Chronicle, 'he broke the resistance of the city of Shamara'in' (Samaria?) so 'the king of Assyria (who) took Samaria' (verse 6) and carried off the Israelites to exile in the Upper Euphrates and Media (see GOZAN) may be this same Assyrian king. However, since his successor Sargon II later claims the capture of Samaria in 722 BC as his own act, it may be that the unnamed king of verse 6 was Sargon, who could have been associated with Shalmaneser in the siege and could have completed the operation on the latter's death.

Sargon II (722–705 BC) was a vigorous leader like Tiglath-pileser III. He records that, when the citizens of Samaria were led by Iau-bi'di of Hamath to withhold their taxes, he removed 27,270 (or 27,290) people from the area of Samaria, 'with the gods in which they trusted'. The exact date of this exile, which broke Israel as an independent nation, cannot be determined as yet from Assyrian records. Hanunu of Gaza had returned from Egypt with military support so Sargon marched to Raphia, where, in the first clash between the armies of the two great nations, he defeated the Egyptians. Despite this, the Palestinian rulers and peoples still leaned on Egypt for support, and the history of this period is an essential background for the prophecies of Isaiah. In 715 Sargon intervened once more, sacking Ashdod and Gath and claiming to have 'subjugated Judah'; but there is no evidence in the Old Testament that he entered the land at this time. Sargon defeated Pisiris of Carchemish in 717 and campaigned in Cilicia. He also continued the Assyrian raids on the Mannai and tribes in the Lake Van area (714 BC) who were restless under Cimmerian pressure. In the south he invaded Elam, sacked Susa, and drove Marduk-apla-iddina II back into the marshland at the head of the Persian Gulf (see MERODACH-BALADAN). Sargon died before his new palace at Dur-Šarrukin (Khorsabad) could be completed.

The first years of Sennacherib (705–681 BC) were occupied in suppressing revolts which broke out on his father's death. While Crown prince he had been responsible for safeguarding the northern frontier, and this knowledge proved invaluable in his dealings with Urarṭu and Media, and in his military expeditions, which reached as far west as Cilicia, where Tarsus was captured in 698 BC. Marduk-apla-iddina seized the throne of Babylon (703–701 BC), and it required a concentrated military expedition to dislodge him. It was probably during these years that the Chaldean asked Hezekiah for help (2 Ki. xx. 12–19). Isaiah's disapproval of this alliance was justified, for by 689 BC the Assyrians had driven Merodach-baladan out of the country and sacked Babylon. A naval operation which was planned to cross the Gulf in pursuit of the rebel was called off on receipt of the news of his death in Elam. Moreover, in 701 BC Sennacherib had marched to Syria, besieged Sidon, and moved southwards to attack rebellious Ashkelon. It was probably at this time that the Assyrians successfully besieged Lachish (2 Ki. xviii. 13, 14), a victory depicted on the bas-reliefs in Sennacherib's palace at Nineveh (see fig. 127 for a drawing taken from these reliefs). The army next moved to meet the Egyptians at Eltekeh. During these moves in Judah, Hezekiah paid tribute (2 Ki. xviii. 14–16), an act which is recorded in the Assyrian annals. There is a divergence of opinion whether it was later in this same campaign and year that Sennacherib 'shut up Hezekiah the Judaean in Jerusalem as a bird in a cage' (see fig. 105), and demanded his surrender (2 Ki. xviii. 17–xix. 9). The text of 2 Ki. xix. 8 may support this view and, on any interpretation, the Assyrians raised the siege suddenly and withdrew (2 Ki. xix. 35; *cf.* Herodotus, ii. 141). Another view is that the siege of Jerusalem is to be connected with a later campaign, perhaps that against the Arabs in 686 BC, because verse 37 recounts the Assyrian king's death. But there is no evidence of the time which elapsed between the return to Nineveh and Sennacherib's assassination by his sons in the month Tebet 681 BC (Is. xxxvii. 37; 2 Ki. xix. 38; see also SENNACHERIB).

The Babylonian Chronicle states that Sennacherib was murdered by 'his son', though Esarhaddon, his younger son and successor, claimed to have pursued his rebel brothers, presumably the murderers, into S Armenia (for a fuller discussion of the seeming discrepancy between the Old Testament and Assyrian texts on the place and number of the assassins, see *DOTT*, pp. 70–73). Sennacherib, with his western Semitic wife Naqi'a-Zakutu, extensively rebuilt Nineveh, its palaces, gateways, and temples, and to ensure water-supplies aqueducts (Jerwan) and dams were built. This water was also used to irrigate large parks around the city. Prisoners from his campaigns, including Jews, were used on these projects (see Assyrian reliefs).

Esarhaddon (680–669 BC) had been designated Crown prince by his father two years before he came to the throne, and had served as viceroy in Babylon. When the S Babylonians rebelled, a single campaign sufficed to subdue them, and Na'id-Marduk was appointed as their new chief in 678. But a series of campaigns was needed to counteract the machinations of their neighbours, the Elamites. In the hills farther north also periodic raids kept the tribesmen of Zamua and the Median plain subject to Assyrian overlordship. The northern tribes were more restless, due to the plotting of Teušpa and the Cimmerians. Esarhaddon also came into conflict with the Scythian tribes (*Išguzai*).

In the west Esarhaddon continued his father's policy of exacting tribute from the city-states, including those in Cilicia and Syria. Baal of Tyre refused payment and was attacked, and Abdi-Milki was besieged in Sidon for three years from 676. This opposition to Assyrian domination was incited by Tirhakah and provoked a quick reaction. Esarhaddon increased the amount payable, collecting in addition wood, stone, and other supplies for his new palace at Calah (*q.v.*) and for his reconstruction of Babylon. It may have been in connection with the latter that Manasseh was taken there (2 Ch. xxxiii. 11). 'Manasseh (*Menasi*) of Judah' is named among those from whom Esarhaddon claimed tribute at this time. These included 'Baal of Tyre, Qauš-(Chemosh)-gabri of Edom, Muṣuri of Moab, Ṣili-Bel of Gaza, Metinti of Ashkelon, Ikausu of Ekron, Milki-ašapa of Gebal, . . . Aḫi-Milki of Ashdod as well as 10 kings of Cyprus (*Iadnana*)'.

With these states owing at least a nominal allegiance, the way was open to the fulfilment of Assyria's ambition to control the Egyptian Delta from which so much opposition was mounted. This was accomplished by a major expedition in 672 BC, which resulted in Assyrian governors being installed in Thebes and Memphis. In this same year Esarhaddon summoned his vassals to hear his declaration of Ashurbanipal as Crown prince of Assyria and Šamaš-šum-ukin as Crown prince of Babylonia. In this way he hoped to avoid disturbances similar to those which marked his own succession to the throne. Copies of the terms and oaths imposed at this ceremony are of interest as indicative of the 'covenant' form of relationship between a suzerain and his vassals. Many parallels can be drawn between this and Old Testament terminology (*Iraq*, XX, 1958). It shows that Manasseh, as all the other rulers, would have had to swear eternal allegiance to Ashur, the national god of his overlord (2 Ki. xxi. 2–7, 9). The end of Esarhaddon's reign saw the beginning of the very revolts these 'covenants' were designed to forestall. Pharaoh Tirhakah incited the native chiefs of Lower Egypt to break away. It was at Harran, while on his way to crush this insurrection, that Esarhaddon died and was succeeded by his sons as planned.

Ashurbanipal (669–*c.* 627 BC) immediately took up his father's unfinished task and marched against Tirhakah (*Tarqu*); but it required three hard campaigns and the sack of Thebes in 663 (Na. iii. 8, 'No') to regain control of Egypt. In his reign Assyria reached its greatest territorial extent. Punitive raids on the rebels in Tyre, Arvad, and Cilicia brought Assyria into contact with another rising power—Lydia, whose king Gyges sent emissaries to Nineveh seeking an alliance. The raids on the Arab tribes and the restoration of Manasseh of Judah, called *Minse* by Ashurbanipal, probably had the one aim of keeping the route open to Egypt. Nevertheless, Assyria was doomed to fall swiftly. The Medes were increasing their hold over neighbouring tribes and threatening the Assyrian homeland. By 652 BC Šamaš-šum-ukin had revolted and the resultant struggle with Babylonia, which restrained the army from needed operations farther afield, ended in the sack of the southern capital in 648 BC. This rebellion had been supported by Elam, so Ashurbanipal marched in to sack Susa (see SHUSHAN) in 639 and henceforth made it an Assyrian province. Free from the frequent incursions of the Assyrian army in support of its local officials and tax-collectors, the western city-states gradually loosed from Assyria, and in Judah this new-found freedom was to be reflected in the reforms initiated by Josiah. Once again Egypt was independent and intriguing in Palestine.

The date of Ashurbanipal's death is uncertain (*c.* 631–627 BC), and very few historical texts for this period have yet been found. The hordes of the Scythians (Umman-manda) began to dominate the Middle Euphrates area and Kyaxares the Mede besieged Nineveh. Ashurbanipal may have delegated power to his sons Aššur-eṭel-ilāni (632–628 BC) and Šin-šar-iškun (628–612 BC). Ashurbanipal himself was interested in the arts. He built extensively in Nineveh (*q.v.*), where in his palace and in the Nabu temple he collected libraries of tablets (see section III, Literature, below).

With the rise of Nabopolassar, the Chaldean (see CHALDAEA, CHALDEANS), the Assyrians were driven out of Babylonia in 625 BC. The Babylonians joined the Medes to capture Assur (614 BC) and in July/August 612 BC, as foretold by Nahum and Zephaniah, Nineveh fell to their attack. These campaigns are fully told in the Babylonian Chronicle. The walls were breached by floods (Na. i. 8; Xenophon, *Anabasis*, iii. 4) and Šin-šar-iškun (Sardanapalus) perished in the flames. For two years the government under Ashur-uballiṭ held out at Harran, but no help came from Egypt, Necho marching too late to prevent the city falling to the Babylonians and Scythians in 609 BC. Assyria ceased to exist and her territory was taken over by the Babylonians (see BABYLONIA).

In later years 'Assyria' formed part of the Persian, Hellenistic (Seleucid), and Parthian Empires, and during this time 'Assyria' (Persian *Athura*) continued to be used as a general geographical designation for her former homelands (Ezk. xvi. 28, xxiii. 5–23).

II. RELIGION

The Assyrian king acted as regent on earth for the national god Ashur, to whom he reported his activities regularly. Thus the Assyrian campaigns were conceived, at least in part, as a holy war against those who failed to avow his sovereignty, and were ruthlessly pursued in the event of rebellion. Ashur's primary temple was at the capital Assur, and various deities were thought to guard the interests of the other cities. Anu and Adad resided at Assur, having temples and associated ziggurats there, while Ishtar, goddess of war and love, was worshipped at Nineveh, though as 'Ishtar of Arbela' she also held sway at Erbil. Nabu, god of wisdom and patron of the sciences, had temples at both Nineveh and Calah (Nimrud), where there were libraries collected by royal officials and housed in part in the sacred buildings (see NEBO, and section III, Literature, below). Sin, the moon-god, and his priests and priestesses had a temple and cloisters at Ehulhul in Harran and were in close association with their counterpart in Ur. In general, divine consorts and less prominent deities had shrines within the major temples; thus at Calah, where the temples of Ninurta, god of war and hunting, Ishtar, and Nabu have been discovered, there were places for such deities as Shala, Gula, Ea, and Damkina. In most respects Assyrian religion differed little from that of its southern neighbour, whence it had been derived; for other details therefore see BABYLONIA. For the part played by religion in daily life, see the next section.

III. LITERATURE

The daily life and thought of the Assyrians is to be seen in the many hundreds of letters, economic and administrative documents, and literary texts found during excavations. Thus the early second millennium BC is illuminated by the letters from Mari and Shemshara and *c.* 1500, during the period of Hurrian influence, from Nuzi (see

ARCHAEOLOGY). The best-known period is, however, that of the Neo-Assyrian Empire, when many texts, including some copied from the Middle Assyrian period, enable a detailed reconstruction to be made of the administration and civil service. Thus the historical annals, recorded on clay prisms, cylinders, and tablets, though originally intended as introductions to inscriptions describing the king's building operations, can be supplemented by texts which record the royal requests to a deity (often Shamash) for oracles to guide in decisions concerning political and military affairs. A number of the letters and legal texts, as well as the annals, make reference to Israel, Judah, and the Western city-states (*DOTT*, pp. 46–75; *Iraq*, XVII, 1955, pp. 126–154).

Ashurbanipal, an educated man, created a library by importing or copying texts both from the existing royal archives at Nineveh, Assur, and Calah and from Babylonian religious centres. Thus, in 1852–3 in his palace at Nineveh and in the Nabu temple there, Layard and Rassam discovered 26,000 fragmentary tablets, representing about 10,000 different texts. This find and its subsequent publication laid the foundation for the study of the Semitic Assyrian language and of Babylonian, from which it differs mainly dialectally. The cuneiform script, employing six hundred or more signs as ideographs, syllables, or determinatives, was taken over from the earlier Sumerians. Assyro-Babylonian (Akkadian) now provides the major bulk of ancient Semitic inscriptions. Since some texts had interlinear Sumerian translations, this find has been of importance in the study of that non-Semitic tongue which survived, as did Latin in England, for religious purposes.

The discovery among the Nineveh (Kuyunjik) collection, now housed in the British Museum, of a Babylonian account of the flood (Gilgamesh XI), later published by George Smith in December 1872, proved a stimulus to further excavations, and much has been written with special reference to the bearing of these finds on the Old Testament. The library texts represent many scholarly handbooks, vocabularies, sign and word lists, and dictionaries. The mythological texts written in poetic form include the series of twelve tablets now called the 'Epic of Gilgamesh' which describes his quest for eternal life and the story he was told by Uta-napishtim of his own survival of the Flood in a specially constructed ship (see FLOOD). The Epic of Creation, called *enuma eliš* after the opening phrase, survives in several versions, principally that of the Old Babylonian exaltation of Marduk as the head of the pantheon. Other epics include the Descent of Ishtar into the underworld in search of her husband Tammuz. Contrary to many recent theories, no text describing the resurrection of Tammuz has yet been found. Legends, including that of Sargon of Agade, who was saved at birth by being placed in a reed basket on the river Euphrates until rescued by Ishtar, who brought him up to be king, have been compared with Old Testament incidents. These Akkadian literary texts also contain the legend of Etana, who flew to heaven on an eagle, and that of the plague god Era, who fought against Babylon. Wisdom literature includes the poem of the righteous sufferer (*Ludlul bēl nēmeqi*) or the so-called 'Babylonian Job', the Babylonian theodicy, precepts, and admonition, among which are counsels of wisdom, sayings, and dialogues of a pessimist and advice to a prince of the same *genre*, but not spirit, as Old Testament Wisdom literature. There are also collections of hymns, fables, popular sayings, parables, proverbs, and tales ('The poor man of Nippur') which are precursors of later literary forms.

In addition to the texts already mentioned, religious literature is well represented by tablets grouped in series of up to ninety with their number and title stated in a colophon. The majority are omens derived from the inspection of the liver or entrails of sacrificial animals, or the movements and features of men, animals, birds, objects, and planets. Closely allied to these texts are the carefully recorded observations which formed the basis of Akkadian science, especially medicine (prognosis and diagnosis), botany, geology, chemistry, mathematics, and law. For chronological purposes lists covering many of the years from *c.* 1100 to 612 BC gave the name of the eponym or *limmu*-official by whom each year was designated. These, together with the recorded king lists and astronomical data, provide a system of dating which is accurate to within a few years.

IV. ADMINISTRATION

The government derived from the person of the king who was also the religious leader and commander-in-chief. He exercised direct authority, although he also delegated local jurisdiction to provincial governors (see RAB-SHAKEH, RAB-SARIS) and district-governors who collected and forwarded tribute and taxes, usually paid in kind. They were supported by the expeditions of the Assyrian army, the nucleus of which was a highly trained and well-equipped regular force of chariots, siege-engineers, bowmen, spearmen, and slingers (see figs. 89, 228). Conquered territories were made vassal-subjects of the god Ashur on oath and forced to render both political and religious allegiance to Assyria (*Iraq*, XX, 1958). Offenders were punished by reprisals and invasion, which resulted in the loot and destruction of their cities, death to the rebel leaders, and slavery and exile for the skilled citizens. The remainder were subjected to the surveillance of pro-Assyrian deputies. This helps to explain both the attitude of the Hebrew prophets to Assyria and the fear of 'this cauldron boiling over from the north' (*cf.* Je. i. 13) by the small states of Israel and Judah.

V. ART

Many examples of Assyrian art, wall-paintings, sculptured bas-reliefs, statues and ornaments, cylinder seals, ivory carvings, as well as bronze and metal work, have been preserved following excavation. Some of the reliefs are of particular interest in that the stele and obelisk of Shalmaneser III from Nimrud mention Israel and portray Jehu (see plate VII*a*). Sennacherib, on his palace sculptures at Nineveh, depicts the siege of Lachish (see, for example, fig. 127) and the use of Judaean captives to work on his building projects; while the bronze gates at Balawat show the Assyrian army engaged in Syria and Phoenicia. Other reliefs of Ashurnasirpal II at Nimrud and Ashurbanipal in the 'Lion Hunt' from Nineveh are a pictorial source for the costume, customs, and military and civilian operations of the Assyrians from the 9th to the 7th centuries BC. (R. D. Barnett, *Assyrian Palace Reliefs*, 1959; H. H. Frankfort, *Art and Architecture of the Ancient Orient*, 1954.) See also SEAL, ART.

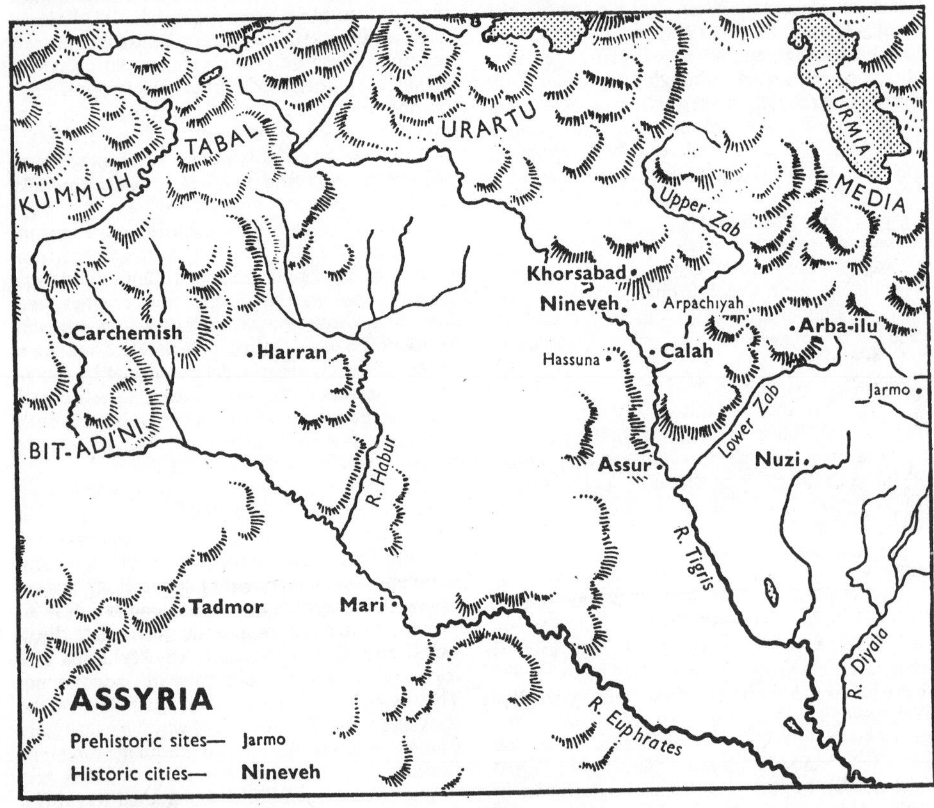

Fig. 27.

VI. EXCAVATIONS

Several early explorers reported the ruined cities of Mesopotamia and searched for the possible site of the biblical Nineveh, but it was not until 1820 that C. J. Rich planned the mounds of Kuyunjik and Nebi Yunus, opposite Mosul, which covered that city. In 1842 the Frenchman P. E. Botta commenced excavations there, but soon transferred his attentions to Khorsabad (1843–4), which he thought might be ancient Nineveh, and unearthed Sargon's palace there. In 1853–4 A. H. Layard and H. Rassam discovered Ashurbanipal's palace and many thousands of inscribed tablets at Kuyunjik at a site which was the scene of many British excavations till 1932 (see NINEVEH), while V. Place continued the work at Khorsabad (to be completed by the Oriental Institute of Chicago in 1929–35). Mr. (later Sir) A. Henry Layard cleared four palaces on the acropolis at Calah (Nimrud) in 1845–52 and was followed by Loftus (1854–5), who discovered many ivories, and by G. Smith (1873), in search for other parts of the flood tablet. Work at this site by the British School of Archaeology in Iraq (Mallowan and Oates) from 1949 to 1961 has continued to bring to light many important Assyrian buildings, ivories, and documents (*Iraq*, XII–XXIII). The thorough German excavations at Assur (Qal'at Sharqat) in 1903–14 by the Deutsche Orient-Gesellschaft (R. Koldewey and W. Andrae) also did much to elucidate Assyrian history. Other partially excavated Assyrian sites include Balawat (Imgur-Bel); Nebi Yunus (part of Nineveh), and Shibaniba (Tell Billah; 1846, 1930–1, *ASOR*; E. A. Speiser). The early periods are represented by the excavation of such sites as Arpaehiyah, Nineveh (early levels), Hassuna, Jarmo, and Tepe Gawra. For details of excavations and discoveries in 1842–1954, see S. A. Pallis, *The Antiquity of Iraq*, 1956, and for later work the journal *Iraq*. See also the separate articles on CALAH, NINEVEH.

BIBLIOGRAPHY. *History:* H. Schmökel, *Geschichte des alten Vorderasien*, 1957; 'The Assyrian Empire', *CAH*, III, 1925; S. Smith, *Early History of Assyria to 1000 BC*, 1928. *General:* A. Pallis, *The Antiquity of Iraq*, 1957; H. W. F. Saggs, *The Beginnings that were Babylon*, 1961. *Excavations:* M. E. L. Mallowan, *Twenty-Five Years of Mesopotamian Discovery*, 1956; and bibliography in the journals, *Iraq*, *Sumer*, *Archiv für Orientforschung*, *Orientalia*. D.J.W.

ASTROLOGY. See MAGIC AND SORCERY.

ASTRONOMY. See STARS.

ATAROTH ('*aṭārôṯ*, lit. 'crowns'). **1.** A city on the east of Jordan in Reubenite territory (Nu. xxxii. 3, 34), modern Khirbet 'Attarus; *cf.* ARNON. A city called Atroth occurs in Nu. xxxii. 35, but this may be an accidental repetition from the previous verse, or else should be taken with the following word, giving the otherwise unknown place-name Atroth-Shophan. **2.** A city in Ephraim, perhaps the same as Ataroth-Addar, Jos. xvi. 2, 5, 7, xviii. 13. **3.** 'Ataroth, the house of Joab' is mentioned in a Judaean genealogy (1 Ch. ii. 54). This may be understood as 'the crowns (scions, chiefs) of the house of Joab', a description of Bethlehem and Netophathi, whose names immediately precede. R.J.W.

ATHALIAH ('*aṯalyāhû*, 'Yahweh is exalted'). **1.** The daughter of Ahab, and the granddaughter of Omri (this is the meaning of 2 Ki. viii. 26). Her marriage with Jehoram, king of Judah, marked an alliance between north and south, and implied the superiority of Israel. The death of her son, Ahaziah, after a reign of one year, at the hand of Jehu, in the 'Prophetic Revolution' (2 Ki. viii. 25–x. 36), revealed her as 'that wicked woman' (2 Ch. xxiv. 7). To retain the power she had enjoyed as queen-mother, she 'destroyed all the seed royal' (2 Ki. xi. 1); and began to reign (*c.* 842 BC). For six years her authority was unchallenged, then the priest Jehoiada put the child Joash on the throne. She came out to meet her enemies, and was put to death outside the Temple.

2. A person named in the genealogy of Benjamin (1 Ch. viii. 26).

3. One of the exiles who returned from Babylon with Ezra (Ezr. viii. 7). M.G.

ATHENS. Acts xvii. 15–34; 1 Thes. iii. 1. After the Roman conquest Athens became a *civitas foederata*, entirely independent of the governor of Achaia, paying no taxes to Rome and with internal judicial autonomy. Of the three great university cities Athens, Tarsus, and Alexandria, Athens was the most famous. Philo the Alexandrian said that the Athenians were the keenest-sighted mentally of the Greeks. It was also famous for its temples, statues, and monuments. The first 168 pages of the Loeb edition of the *Description of Greece*, by Pausanias, written a century after Paul's visit, are a good tourists' guide to the antiquities of Athens. Though the Athenians were religious and eager to discuss religion, their spiritual level was not exceptionally high. Apollonius the philosopher, a contemporary of Paul, rebuked them for their lascivious jigs at the festival of Dionysus and for their love of human slaughter in the gladiatorial games, which the first-century Athenians, according to Philostratus, the biographer of Apollonius, took more delight in than the third-century Corinthians. See plate XV*d*. D.R.H.

ATONEMENT. The word 'atonement' is one of the few theological terms which derive basically from Anglo-Saxon. It means 'a making at one', and points to a process of bringing those who are estranged into a unity. The word occurs in the Old Testament to translate words from the *kpr* word group, and it is found once in the New Testament, rendering *katallagē* (which is better translated 'reconciliation'). Its use in theology is to denote the work of Christ in dealing with the problem posed by the sin of man, and in bringing sinners into right relation with God.

I. THE NEED FOR ATONEMENT

The need for atonement is brought about by three things, the universality of sin, the seriousness of sin, and man's inability to deal with sin. The first point is attested in many places: 'there is no man that sinneth not' (1 Ki. viii. 46); 'there is none that doeth good, no, not one' (Ps. xiv. 3); 'there is not a just man upon earth, that doeth good, and sinneth not' (Ec. vii. 20). Jesus told the rich young ruler, 'there is none good but one, that is, God' (Mk. x. 18), and Paul writes, 'all have sinned, and come short of the glory of God' (Rom. iii. 23). Much more could be cited.

The seriousness of sin is seen in passages which show God's aversion to it. Habakkuk prays 'Thou art of purer eyes than to behold evil, and canst not look on iniquity' (Hab. i. 13). Sin separates from God (Is. lix. 2; Pr. xv. 29). Jesus said of one sin, blasphemy against the Holy Spirit, that it will never be forgiven (Mk. iii. 29), and of Judas He said, 'good were it for that man if he had never been born' (Mk. xiv. 21). Before being saved men are 'alienated and enemies in (their) mind by wicked works' (Col. i. 21). There awaits the unrepentant sinner only 'a certain fearful looking for of judgment and fiery indignation, which shall devour the adversaries' (Heb. x. 27).

And man cannot deal with the situation. He is not able to keep his sin hidden (Nu. xxxii. 23), and he cannot cleanse himself of it (Pr. xx.

9). No deeds of law will ever enable man to stand before God justified (Rom. iii. 20; Gal. ii. 16). If he must depend on himself, then man will never be saved. Perhaps the most important evidence of this is the very fact of the atonement. If the Son of God came to earth to save men, then men were sinners and their plight serious indeed.

II. ATONEMENT IN THE OLD TESTAMENT

God and man, then, are hopelessly estranged by man's sin, and there is no way back from man's side. But God provides the way. In the Old Testament atonement is usually said to be obtained by the sacrifices, but it must never be forgotten that God says of atoning blood, 'I have given it to you upon the altar to make an atonement for your souls' (Lv. xvii. 11). Atonement is secured, not by any value inherent in the sacrificial victim, but because sacrifice is the divinely appointed way of securing atonement. The sacrifices point us to certain truths concerning atonement. Thus the victim must always be unblemished, which indicates the necessity for perfection. The victims cost something, for atonement is not cheap, and sin is never to be taken lightly. The death of the victim was the important thing. This is brought out partly in the allusions to blood (*q.v.*), partly in the general character of the rite itself, and partly in other references to atonement. There are several allusions to atonement, either effected or contemplated by means other than the cultus, and where these bear on the problem they point to death as the way. Thus in Ex. xxxii. 30–32 Moses seeks to make an atonement for the sin of the people, and he does so by asking God to blot him out of the book which He has written. Phinehas made an atonement by slaying certain transgressors (Nu. xxv. 6–8, 13). Other passages might be cited. It is clear that in the Old Testament it was recognized that death was the penalty for sin (Ezk. xviii. 20), but that God graciously permitted the death of a sacrificial victim to substitute for the death of the sinner. So clear is the connection that the writer of the Epistle to the Hebrews can sum it up by saying 'without shedding of blood is no remission' (Heb. ix. 22).

III. ATONEMENT IN THE NEW TESTAMENT

The New Testament takes the line that the sacrifices of old were not the root cause of the putting away of sins. Redemption is to be obtained even 'of the transgressions that were under the first testament' only by the death of Christ (Heb. ix. 15). The cross is absolutely central to the New Testament, and, indeed, to the whole Bible. All before leads up to it. All after looks back to it. Since it occupies the critical place, it is not surprising that there is a vast volume of teaching about it. The New Testament writers, writing from different standpoints, and with different emphases, give us a number of facets of the atonement. There is no repetition of a stereotyped line of teaching. Each writes as he sees. Some saw more and more deeply than others. But they did not see something different. In what follows we shall consider first of all what might be termed the common, basic teaching about the atonement, and then some of the information that we owe to one or other of the New Testament theologians.

a. It reveals God's love for men

All are agreed that the atonement proceeds from the love of God. It is not something wrung from a stern and unwilling Father, perfectly just, but perfectly inflexible, by a loving Son. The atonement shows us the love of the Father just as it does the love of the Son. Paul gives us the classic exposition of this when he says, 'God commendeth his own love toward us, in that, while we were yet sinners, Christ died for us' (Rom. v. 8, RV). In the best known text in the Bible we find that 'God so loved the world, that he gave his only begotten Son . . .' (Jn. iii. 16). In the Synoptic Gospels it is emphasized that the Son of man 'must' suffer (Mk. viii. 31, *etc.*). That is to say, the death of Christ was no accident: it was rooted in a compelling divine necessity. This we see also in our Lord's prayer in Gethsemane that the will of the Father be done (Mt. xxvi. 42). Similarly, in Hebrews we read that it was 'by the grace of God' that Christ tasted of death for us all (Heb. ii. 9). The thought is found throughout the New Testament, and we must bear it well in mind when we reflect on the manner of the atonement.

b. The sacrificial aspect of Christ's death

Another thought that is widespread is that the death of Christ is a death for sin. It is not simply that certain wicked men rose up against Him. It is not that His enemies conspired against Him and that He was not able to resist them. He 'was delivered for our offences' (Rom. iv. 25). He came specifically to die for our sins. His blood was shed 'for many for the remission of sins' (Mt. xxvi. 28). He 'purged our sins' (Heb. i. 3). He 'bare our sins in his own body on the tree' (1 Pet. ii. 24). He is 'the propitiation for our sins' (1 Jn. ii. 2). The cross of Christ will never be understood unless it is seen that thereon the Saviour was dealing with the sins of all mankind.

In doing this He fulfilled all that the old sacrifices had foreshadowed, and the New Testament writers love to think of His death as a sacrifice. Jesus Himself referred to His blood as 'blood of the covenant' (Mk. xiv. 24, RV), which points us to the sacrificial rites for its understanding. Indeed, much of the language used in the institution of the Holy Communion is sacrificial, pointing to the sacrifice to be accomplished on the cross. Paul tells us that Christ has 'loved us, and hath given himself for us an offering and a sacrifice to God' (Eph. v. 2). On occasion he can refer, not to sacrifice in general, but to a specific sacrifice, as in 1 Cor. v. 7, 'For even Christ our passover is sacrificed for us.' Peter speaks of 'the precious blood of Christ, as of a lamb without blemish and without spot' (1 Pet. i. 19), which indicates that in one aspect Christ's death was a sacrifice. And in John's Gospel we read the words of John the Baptist, 'Behold the Lamb of God, which taketh away the sin of the world' (Jn. i. 29). Sacrifice was practically the universal religious rite of the first century. Wherever men were and whatever their background, they would discern a sacrificial allusion. The New Testament writers made use of this, and employed sacrificial terminology to bring out what Christ had done for men. All that to which the sacrifices pointed, and more, He had fully accomplished by His death.

c. The representative nature of Christ's death

It is agreed by most students that Christ's death was vicarious. If in one sense He died 'for sin', in another He died 'for us'. But 'vicarious' is a term which may mean much or little. It is better to be more precise. Most scholars today accept the view that the death of Christ is representative. That is to say, it is not that Christ died and somehow the benefits of that death become available to men (did not even Anselm ask to whom more fittingly than to us could they be assigned?). It is rather that He died specifically for us. He was our representative as He hung on the cross. This is expressed succinctly in 2 Cor. v. 14, 'one died for all, then were all dead'. The death of the Representative counts as the death of those He represents. When Christ is spoken of as our 'advocate with the Father' (1 Jn. ii. 1) there is the plain thought of representation, and as the passage immediately goes on to deal with His death for sin it is relevant to our purpose. The Epistle to the Hebrews has as one of its major themes that of Christ as our great High Priest. The thought is repeated over and over. Now whatever else may be said about a High Priest, he represents men. The thought of representation may thus be said to be very strong in this Epistle.

d. Substitution taught in the New Testament

But can we say more? There is a marked disinclination among many modern scholars (though not by any means all) to use the older language of substitution. Nevertheless, this seems to be the teaching of the New Testament, and that not in one or two places only, but throughout. In the Synoptic Gospels there is the great ransom saying, 'the Son of man came not to be ministered unto, but to minister, and to give his life a ransom for many' (Mk. x. 45). Both the details ('ransom' has a substitutionary connotation, and *anti*, 'for', is the preposition of substitution), and the general thought of the passage (men should die, Christ dies instead, men no longer die) point to substitution. The same truth is indicated by passages which speak of Christ as the suffering Servant of Is. liii, for of Him it is said, 'he was wounded for our transgressions, he was bruised for our iniquities: the chastisement of our peace was upon him; and with his stripes we are healed . . . the Lord hath laid on him the iniquity of us all' (Is. liii. 5 f.). The shrinking of Christ in Gethsemane points in the same direction. He was courageous, and many far less worthy than He have faced death calmly. The agony seems to be inexplicable other than on the grounds disclosed by Paul, that God 'hath made him to be sin for us, who knew no sin' (2 Cor. v. 21). In His death He took our place, and His holy soul shrank from this identification with sinners. And it seems that no less than this gives meaning to the cry of dereliction, 'My God, my God, why hast thou forsaken me?' (Mk. xv. 34).

Paul tells us that Christ 'hath redeemed us from the curse of the law, being made a curse for us' (Gal. iii. 13). He bore our curse, which is but another way of saying substitution. The same thought lies behind Rom. iii. 21–26, where the apostle develops the thought that God's justice is manifested in the process whereby sin is forgiven, *i.e.* the cross. He is not saying, as some have thought, that God's righteousness is shown in the *fact* that sin is forgiven, but that it is shown in the *way* in which sin is forgiven. Atonement is not a matter of passing over sin as had been done aforetime (Rom. iii. 25, RV). The cross shows that God is just at the same time as it shows Him justifying believers. This must mean that God's justice is vindicated in the way sin is dealt with. And this seems another way of saying that Christ bore the penalty of men's sin. This is also the thought in passages dealing with sin-bearing as Heb. ix. 28; 1 Pet. ii. 24. The meaning of bearing sin is made clear by a number of Old Testament passages where the context shows that the bearing of penalty is meant. For example, in Ezk. xviii. 20 we read, 'The soul that sinneth, it shall die. The son shall not bear the iniquity of the father . . .', and in Nu. xiv. 34 the wilderness wanderings are described as a bearing of iniquities. Christ's bearing of our sin, then, means that He bore our penalty.

Substitution lies behind the statement in 1 Tim. ii. 6 that Christ gave Himself 'a ransom for all'. *Antilytron*, translated 'ransom', is a strong compound meaning 'substitute-ransom'. Grimm–Thayer define it as 'what is given in exchange for another as the price of his redemption'. It is impossible to empty the word of substitutionary associations. A similar thought lies behind John's recording of the cynical prophecy of Caiaphas, 'it is expedient for us, that one man should die for the people, and that the whole nation perish not' (Jn. xi. 50). For Caiaphas the words were sheer political expediency, but John sees in them a prophecy that Christ would die instead of the people.

This is a formidable body of evidence (and is not exhaustive). In the face of it it seems impossible to deny that substitution is one strand in the New Testament understanding of the work of Christ.

e. Other New Testament aspects of the atonement

Such are the main points attested throughout the New Testament. Other important truths are set forth in individual writers (which does not, of course, mean that they are any the less to be accepted; it is simply a method of classification). Thus Paul sees in the cross the way of deliverance. Men naturally are enslaved to sin (Rom. vi. 17, vii. 14). But in Christ men are free (Rom. vi. 14, 22). Similarly, through Christ men are delivered from the flesh, they 'have crucified the flesh' (Gal. v. 24), they 'do not war after the flesh' (2 Cor. x. 3), that flesh which 'lusteth against the Spirit' (Gal. v. 17), and which apart from Christ spells death (Rom. viii. 13). Men are under the wrath of God on account of their unrighteousness (Rom. i. 18), but Christ delivers from this, too. Believers are 'justified by his blood', and thus will 'be saved from wrath through him' (Rom. v. 9). The law (*i.e.* the Pentateuch, and hence the whole Jewish Scripture) may be regarded in many ways. But considered as a way of salvation it is disastrous. It shows a man his sin (Rom. vii. 7), and, entering into an unholy alliance with sin, slays him (Rom. vii. 9–11). The end result is that 'as many as are of the works of the law are under the curse' (Gal. iii. 10). But 'Christ hath redeemed us from the curse of the law' (Gal. iii. 13). Death to men of antiquity was a grim antagonist against whom none might prevail. But Paul sings a song of triumph in Christ who gives victory even over death (1 Cor. xv. 55–57). It is abundantly plain that Paul sees in Christ a mighty Deliverer.

The atonement has many positive aspects. It must suffice simply to mention such things as redemption, reconciliation, justification, adoption, and propitiation. These are great concepts and mean much to Paul. In some cases he is the first Christian of whom we have knowledge to make use of them. Clearly he thought of Christ as having wrought much for His people in His atoning death.

For the writer to the Hebrews the great thought is that of Christ as our great High Priest. He develops thoroughly the thought of the uniqueness and the finality of the offering made by Christ. Unlike the way established on Jewish altars and ministered by priests of the Aaronic line, the way established by Christ in His death is of permanent validity. It will never be altered. Christ has dealt fully with man's sin.

In the writings of John there is the thought of Christ as the special revelation of the Father. He is One sent by the Father, and all that He does must be interpreted in the light of this fact. So John sees Christ as winning a conflict against the darkness, as defeating the evil one. He has much to say about the working out of the purpose of God in Christ. He sees the true glory in the lowly cross whereon such a mighty work was done.

From all this it is abundantly apparent that the atonement is vast and deep. The New Testament writers strive with the inadequacy of language as they seek to present us with what this great divine act means. There is more to it by far than we have been able to indicate. But all the points we have made are important, and none is to be neglected. Nor are we to overlook the fact that the atonement represents more than something negative. We have been concerned to insist on the place of Christ's sacrifice of Himself in the putting away of sin. But that opens up the way to a new life in Christ. And that new life, the fruit of the atonement, is not to be thought of as an insignificant detail. It is that to which all the rest leads.

See also EXPIATION, FORGIVENESS, PROPITIATION, RECONCILIATION, REDEEMER, SACRIFICE.

BIBLIOGRAPHY. D. M. Baillie, *God was in Christ*; J. Denney, *The Death of Christ*; *The Christian Doctrine of Reconciliation*; Vincent Taylor, *The Atonement in New Testament Teaching*; G. Aulen, *Christus Victor*; S. Cave, *The Doctrine of the Work of Christ*; E. Brunner, *The Mediator*; K. Barth, *Church Dogmatics*, IV, i; *The Doctrine of Reconciliation*; J. S. Stewart, *A Man in Christ*; Anselm, *Cur Deus Homo*; Leon Morris, *The Apostolic Preaching of the Cross*.

L.M.

ATONEMENT, DAY OF (*yôm hakkippurîm*). On the tenth day of the seventh month (Tishri, September/October), Israel observed its most solemn holy day. All work was forbidden and a strict fast was enjoined on all of the people.

I. PURPOSE

The Day of Atonement served as a reminder that the daily, weekly, and monthly sacrifices made at the altar of burnt offering were not sufficient to atone for sin. Even at the altar of burnt offering the worshipper stood 'afar off', unable to approach the holy Presence of God, who was manifest between the cherubim in the Holy of Holies. On this one day in the year, atoning blood was brought into the Holy of Holies, the divine throne-room, by the high priest as the representative of the people.

The high priest made atonement for 'all the iniquities of the children of Israel and all their transgressions in all their sins'. Atonement was first made for the priests because the mediator between God and His people had to be ceremonially clean. The sanctuary was also cleansed, for it, too, was ceremonially defiled by the presence and ministration of sinful men.

II. ANCIENT OBSERVANCE

To prepare for the sacrifices of the day, the high priest put aside his official robes and dressed in a simple white garment. He then offered a bullock as a sin offering for himself and the priesthood. After filling his censer with live coals from the altar, the high priest entered the Holy of Holies, where he placed incense on the coals. The incense sent forth a cloud of smoke over the mercy seat, which served as a covering for the ark of the covenant. The high priest took some of the blood of the bullock and sprinkled it on the mercy seat and on the ground in front of the ark. In this way atonement was made for the priesthood.

The high priest next sacrificed a he-goat as a sin offering for the people. Some of the blood was taken into the Holy of Holies, and it was sprinkled there in the manner in which the sin offering for the priests had been sprinkled (Lv. xvi. 11–15).

After purifying the Holy Place and the altar of burnt offering with the mingled blood of the bullock and the goat (Lv. xvi. 18, 19) the high priest took a second goat, laid his hands upon its head, and confessed over it the sins of Israel. This goat, commonly called the scape goat (*i.e.* escape goat), was then driven into the desert, where it symbolically carried away the sins of the people (see AZAZEL).

The carcasses of the two burnt offerings—the bullock and the he-goat—were taken outside the city and burned. The day was concluded with additional sacrifices.

III. SIGNIFICANCE

The Epistle to the Hebrews interprets the ritual of the Day of Atonement as a type of the atoning work of Christ (Heb. ix, x). Jesus Himself is termed our 'great high priest', and the blood shed on Calvary is seen as typified in the blood of bulls and goats. Unlike the Old Testament priesthood, the sinless Christ did not have to make sacrifice for any sins of His own.

As the high priest of the Old Testament entered the Holy of Holies with the blood of his sacrificial victim, so Jesus entered heaven itself to appear before the Father on behalf of His people (Heb. ix. 11, 12).

The high priest had to offer sin offerings each year for his own sins and the sins of the people. This annual repetition of the sacrifices served as a reminder that perfect atonement had not yet been provided. Jesus, however, through His own blood effected eternal redemption for His people (Heb. ix. 12).

The Epistle to the Hebrews notes that the levitical offerings could only effect 'the cleansing of the flesh'. They ceremonially cleansed the sinner, but they could not bring about inward cleansing, the prerequisite for fellowship with God. The offerings served as a type and a prophecy of Jesus, who, through His better sacrifice, cleanses the conscience from dead works (Heb. ix. 13, 14).

The Old Testament tabernacle was designed, in part, to teach Israel that sin hindered access to the presence of God. Only the high priest, and he only once a year, could enter the Holy of Holies, and then 'not without blood' offered to atone for sins (Heb. ix. 7). Jesus, however, through a 'new and living way' has entered heaven itself, the true Holy of Holies, where He ever liveth to make intercession for His people. The believer need not stand afar off, as did the Israelite of old, but may now through Christ approach the very throne of grace.

In Heb. xiii. 11, 12 we are reminded that the flesh of the sin offering of the Day of Atonement was burned outside the camp of Israel. Jesus, also, suffered outside the gate of Jerusalem that He might redeem His people from sin.

IV. MODERN OBSERVANCE

In modern Jewish usage the Day of Atonement, *Yom Kippur*, is the last of the 'Ten Days of Penitence' which begin with *Rosh Hashanah*—the Jewish New Year's Day. This ten-day period is devoted to the spiritual exercises of penitence, prayer, and fasting in preparation for the most solemn day of the year, *Yom Kippur*. Although the sacrificial aspects of the Day of Atonement have not been in effect since the destruction of the Temple, Jews still observe the day by fasting and refraining from all types of work.

The shophar, or ram's horn, is blown to assemble the people for worship in the synagogue on the eve of *Yom Kippur*. At this time the impressive *Kol Nidre* ('all vows') service is chanted. The congregation penitently asks God to forgive them for breaking the vows which they were unable to fulfil.

Services are held on the next day from early morning until nightfall. At sunset the Day of Atonement is ended by a single blast of the shophar, after which the worshippers return to their homes. C.F.P.

ATTALIA, modern Andaliya (Adalia), at the mouth of the river Cataractes, was the chief port of Pamphylia. Founded by Attalus II of Pergamum (159–138 BC), it was bequeathed by Attalus III to Rome. Paul and Barnabas returned from their missionary journey through Attalia (Acts xiv. 25). There was another Attalia in northern Lydia. K.L.McK.

AUGURY. See DIVINATION.

AUGUSTAN BAND. See ARMY.

AUGUSTUS. An additional name adopted by Caesar Octavianus upon the regularization of his position in 27 BC, and apparently intended to signalize that moral authority in terms of which he defined his primacy in the Roman republic (*Res Gestae*, 34). It passed to his successors (see CAESAR) as a title of office rather than a name, and was hence translated into Greek (*sebastos*, 'His Reverence', Acts xxv. 21, 25) when referring to them, though transliterated when referring to him (Lk. ii. 1).

BIBLIOGRAPHY. F. Müller and K. Gross, *RAC*, I, pp. 993–1004. E.A.J.

AUTHORITY. The New Testament word is *exousia*, meaning rightful, actual, and unimpeded power to act, or to possess, control, use, or dispose of, something or somebody. Whereas *dynamis* means physical power simply, *exousia* properly signifies power that is in some sense lawful. *Exousia* may be used with the stress on either the rightfulness of power really held, or the reality of power rightfully possessed. In the latter case, EVV often translate it as 'power'. *Exousia* sometimes bears a general secular sense (*e.g.* in 1 Cor. vii. 37, of self-control; Acts v. 4, of disposing of one's income), but its significance is more commonly theological.

The uniform biblical conviction is that the only rightful power within creation is, ultimately, the Creator's. Such authority as men have is delegated to them by God, to whom they must answer for the way they use it. Because all authority is ultimately God's, submission to authority in all realms of life is a religious duty, part of God's service.

I. THE AUTHORITY OF GOD

God's authority is an aspect of His unalterable, universal, and eternal dominion over His world (for which see Ex. xv. 18; Pss. xxix. 10, xciii. 1 f., cxlvi. 10; Dn. iv. 34 f., *etc.*). This universal Kingship is distinct from (though basic to) the covenanted relationship between Himself and Israel by which Israel became His people and kingdom (*cf.* Ex. xix. 6), and so heirs of His blessing. His regal authority over mankind consists in His unchallengeable right and power to dispose of men as He pleases (compared by Paul to the potter's *exousia* over the clay, Rom. ix. 21; *cf.* Je. xviii. 6), plus His indisputable claim that men should be subject to Him and live for His glory. Throughout the Bible, the reality of God's authority is proved by the fact that all who ignore or flout this claim incur divine judgment. The royal Judge has the last word, and so His authority is vindicated.

In Old Testament times, God exercised authority over His people through the agency of prophets, priests, and kings, whose respective work it was to proclaim His messages (Je. i. 7 ff.), teach His laws (Dt. xxxi. 11; Mal. ii. 7), and rule in accordance with those laws (Dt. xvii. 18 ff.). So doing, they were to be respected as God's representatives, having authority from Him. Also, written Scripture was acknowledged as God-given and authoritative, both as instruction (*tôrâ*) to teach Israelites their King's mind (*cf.* Ps. cxix) and as the statute-book by which He ruled and judged them (*cf.* 2 Ki. xxii–xxiii).

II. THE AUTHORITY OF JESUS CHRIST

Jesus Christ's authority is also an aspect of kingship. It is both personal and official, for Jesus is both Son of God and Son of man (*i.e.* the messianic man: see JESUS CHRIST). As man and Messiah, His authority is real because delegated to Him by the God at whose command He does His work (Christ applauded the centurion for seeing this, Mt. viii. 9 f.). As the Son, His authority is real because He is Himself God. Authority to judge has been given Him, both that He may be honoured as the Son of God (for judgment is God's work), and also because He is the Son of man (for judgment is the Messiah's work) (Jn. v. 22 f., 27). In short, His authority is that of a divine Messiah: of a God-man, doing His Father's will in the double capacity of (*a*) human servant, in whom meet the saving offices of prophet, priest, and king, and (*b*) divine Son, co-creator and sharer in all the Father's works (Jn. v. 19 ff.).

This more-than-human authority of Jesus was manifested during His ministry in various ways, such as the finality and independence of His teaching (Mt. vii. 28 f.); His exorcizing power (Mk. i. 27); His mastery over storms (Lk. viii. 24 f.); His claiming to forgive sins (a thing which, as the bystanders rightly pointed out, only God can do) and, when challenged, proving His claim (Mk. ii. 5–12; *cf.* Mt. ix. 8). After His resurrection, He declared that He had been given 'all *exousia* in heaven and on earth'—a cosmic messianic dominion, to be exercised in such a way as effectively to bring the elect into His kingdom of salvation (Mt. xxviii. 18 ff.; Jn. xvii. 2, *cf.* Jn. xii. 31 ff., Acts v. 31, xviii. 9 f.). The New Testament proclaims the exalted Jesus as 'both Lord and Christ' (Acts ii. 36)—divine Ruler of all things, and Saviour-king of His people. The gospel is in the first instance a demand for assent to this estimate of His authority.

III. APOSTOLIC AUTHORITY

Apostolic authority is delegated messianic authority; for the apostles were Christ's commissioned witnesses, emissaries, and representatives (*cf.* Mt. x. 40; Jn. xvii. 18, xx. 21; Acts i. 8; 2 Cor. v. 20), given *exousia* by Him to found, build up, and regulate His universal Church (2 Cor. x. 8, xiii. 10; *cf.* Gal. ii. 7 ff.) (see APOSTLE). Accordingly, we find them giving orders and prescribing discipline in Christ's name, *i.e.* as His spokesmen and with His authority (1 Cor. v. 4; 2 Thes. iii. 6). They appointed deacons (Acts vi. 3, 6) and presbyters (Acts xiv. 23). They presented their teaching as Christ's truth, Spirit-given in both content and form of expression (1 Cor. ii. 9–13; *cf.* 1 Thes. ii. 13), a norm for faith (2 Thes. ii. 15; *cf.* Gal. i. 8) and behaviour (2 Thes. iii. 4, 6, 14). They expected their *ad hoc* rulings to be received as 'the commandment of the Lord' (1 Cor. xiv. 37). Because their authority depended on Christ's direct personal commission, they had, properly speaking, no successors; but each generation of Christians must show its continuity with the first generation, and its allegiance to Christ, by subjecting its own faith and life to the norm of teaching which Christ's appointed delegates provided and put on record for all time in the documents of the New Testament. Through the New Testament, apostolic *exousia* over the Church has been made a permanent reality.

IV. AUTHORITY DELEGATED TO MAN

Besides the Church, the Bible mentions two other spheres of delegated divine authority.

a. Marriage and the family

Men have authority over women (1 Cor. xi. 3; *cf.* 1 Tim. ii. 12) and parents over children (*cf.* 1 Tim. iii. 4, 12). Hence, wives must obey their husbands (Eph. v. 22; 1 Pet. iii. 1–6) and children their parents (Eph. vi. 1 ff.). This is God's order.

b. Civil government

Secular (Roman) governors are called *exousiai*, and described as God's servants to punish evildoers and encourage law-abiding citizens (Rom. xiii. 1–6). Christians are to regard the 'powers that be' as God-ordained (see Jn. xix. 11), and dutifully subject themselves to civil authority (Rom. xiii. 1; 1 Pet. ii. 13 f.; *cf.* Mt. xxii. 17–21) so far as is compatible with obedience to God's direct commands (Acts iv. 19, v. 29).

V. SATANIC POWER

The exercise of power by Satan and his hosts is sometimes termed *exousia* (*e.g.* Lk. xxii. 53; Col. i. 13). This indicates that, though Satan's power is usurped from God and hostile to Him, Satan holds it only by God's permission and as God's tool.

For *exousiai* as the title of a rank of angels, see ANGEL.

BIBLIOGRAPHY. *Arndt*; *MM*; *TWNT*, II, pp. 559 ff. (Foerster on *exousia*); T. Rees in *ISBE* and J. Denney in *DCG*, *s.v.* 'Authority'; N. Geldenhuys, *Supreme Authority*, 1953.

J.I.P.

AUTHORIZED VERSION. See ENGLISH VERSIONS.

AVEN. 1. Abbreviated (Ho. x. 8) for Beth-aven (*q.v.*), epithet of Bethel (Ho. iv. 15, *etc.*). **2.** In Am. i. 5, probably the Beqa' valley between Lebanon and Anti-lebanon in the Aramaean kingdom of Damascus. **3.** For Ezk. xxx. 17, see ON.

K.A.K.

AVENGER OF BLOOD (*gō'ēl haddām*, lit. 'redeemer of blood'). Even before the time of Moses, a basic feature of primitive life was the system of blood revenge for personal injury. It is mentioned with approval in Scripture as early as Gn. ix. 5. All members of the clan were regarded as being of one blood, but the chief responsibility for avenging shed blood devolved upon the victim's next-of-kin, who might under other circumstances be called on to redeem the property or person of a poor or captive relative (Lv. xxv. 25, 47–49; Ru. iv. 1 ff., though in the latter case other factors were involved also). The Mosaic penal code authorized the avenger to execute the murderer but no-one else (Dt. xxiv. 16; 2 Ki. xiv. 6; 2 Ch. xxv. 4), and made provision for accidental homicide. Blood revenge seems to have persisted into the reigns of David (2 Sa. xiv. 7, 8) and Jehoshaphat (2 Ch. xix. 10). See also KIN, KINSMAN, and CITIES OF REFUGE.

J.D.D.

AZARIAH (*'ᵃzaryāhû*, *'ᵃzaryâ*, 'Yahweh has helped'). **1.** One of Solomon's ministers, son of Zadok (1 Ki. iv. 2; *cf.* 1 Ch. vi. 9). **2.** Another of Solomon's ministers, son of Nathan; he was over the officers (1 Ki. iv. 5). **3.** Alternative name for King Uzziah (2 Ki. xiv. 21, *etc.*). Montgomery (*Kings*, *ICC*, p. 446) calls it the 'throne-name', Uzziah representing the popular or adopted name. **4, 5.** Son of Ethan (1 Ch. ii. 8) and son of Jehu (1 Ch. ii. 38) in the genealogical table of Judah.

6–8. Son of Johanan (1 Ch. vi. 10; *cf.* Ezr. vii. 3), son of Hilkiah (1 Ch. vi. 13, *cf.* ix. 11; Ezr. vii. 1) and son of Zephaniah (1 Ch. vi. 36) in the genealogical table of Levi. **9.** The prophet, son of Oded, who encouraged Asa in his reformation (2 Ch. xv. 1–8). **10, 11.** Two of Jehoshaphat's sons, slain by Jehoram on his accession (2 Ch. xxi. 2, 4). **12.** Scribal error for Ahaziah (2 Ch. xxii. 6).

13, 14. Two of the 'centurions' who helped to restore Joash (2 Ch. xxiii. 1). **15.** High priest who withstood Uzziah's attempt to offer incense in the Temple (2 Ch. xxvi. 16–20). **16.** An Ephraimite chief who supported the prophet Oded's plea for clemency (2 Ch. xxviii. 12). **17, 18.** Two Levites connected with Hezekiah's cleansing of the Temple (2 Ch. xxix. 12). **19.** A chief priest in Hezekiah's reign (2 Ch. xxxi. 10).

20. A workman repairing the city wall (Ne. iii. 23). **21.** One of Zerubbabel's companions (Ne. vii. 7; *cf.* Ezr. ii. 2—'Seraiah'). **22.** One who expounded the law after Ezra had read it (Ne. viii. 7). **23.** A priest who sealed the covenant with Nehemiah (Ne. x. 2; *cf.* Ne. xii. 33).

24. Son of Hoshaiah and supporter of Gedaliah, who later rejected Jeremiah's advice to remain in Palestine (Je. xliii. 2). Called Jezaniah in Je. xlii. 1 (*cf.* Je. xl. 8; 2 Ki. xxv. 23). **25.** Heb. name of Abed-nego (Dn. i. 6 f., 11, 19, ii. 17).

J.G.G.N.

AZAZEL. The word *'ᵃzāzēl* occurs only in the description of the day of atonement (Lv. xvi. 8, 10 (twice), 26). There are four possible interpretations. 1. The word denotes the 'scape-goat' and is to be explained as 'the goat (*'ēz*) that goes away (from *'āzal*)'. 2. It is used as an infinitive, 'in order to remove'; *cf.* Arab. *'azala* 'to remove'. 3. It means a desolate region (*cf.* Lv. xvi. 22). 4. It is the name of a demon haunting that region, derived from *'āzaz* 'to be strong' and *'ēl* 'God'.

Most scholars prefer the last possibility, as in verse 8 the name appears in parallelism to the name of the Lord. As a fallen angel Azazel is often mentioned in Enoch (vi. 6 onwards), but probably the author got his conception from Lv. xvi. The meaning of the ritual must be that sin in a symbolical way was removed from human society and brought to the region of death (*cf.* Mi. vii. 19). It is not implied that a sacrifice was presented to the demon (*cf.* Lv. xvii. 7).

BIBLIOGRAPHY. W. H. Gispen, 'Azazel', in *Orientalia Neerlandica*, 1948, pp. 156–161.

A. VAN S.

AZEKAH. A Judaean conurbation (Jos. xv. 35), lying in the low agricultural plains along the west coast, perhaps modern Tell ez-Zahariyeh. Joshua pursued the Amorites as far as Azekah on the day they attacked the newly settled Gibeonite group (Jos. x. 10, 11). In the days of Rehoboam it was a fortified border city (2 Ch. xi. 5 ff.), and in later times was one of the few strong points to resist the Babylonian incursion under Nebuchadrezzar (Je. xxxiv. 7). Azekah is mentioned, and its capture by Nebuchadrezzar probably implied, in one of the Lachish Letters (*DOTT*, pp. 216 f.).

R.J.W.

B

BAAL. The Hebrew word *ba'al* means 'master', 'possessor', or 'husband'. When the Israelites entered Canaan they found that every piece of land had its own deity, its 'owner'. There were thus many 'Baals'; the Hebrew plural *b^e'ālîm* appears in English as 'Baalim' (*e.g.* 1 Ki. xviii. 18). The gods of individual localities had appropriate surnames, *e.g.* Baal-peor (Nu. xxv. 3). But the word gradually became a proper name, to indicate the great fertility god of the Canaanites. (Similarly Marduk, the chief Babylonian deity, was called 'Bel', which became a proper name.) Some consider 'the Baal' to have been the sun-god, in view of the temple to him at Beth-shemesh ('house of the sun'); but the two are clearly distinguished in 2 Ki. xxiii. 5. The Baal cults affected and challenged the worship of Yahweh throughout Israelite history. The incident on Mount Carmel was the outstanding battle between the two; the particular Baal favoured by Ahab was Melqart, the seat of whose worship was at Tyre, Jezebel's home. The Baal rites not only involved the usual lascivious practices of fertility cults, but even such abominations as child sacrifice (*cf.* Je. xix. 5). The worship of Baal was often linked with that of the goddess Ashtoreth, and the use of the Asherah pole (see ASHERAH).

Fig. 28. Baal in his aspect of storm god, brandishing a club and resting a spear, with lightning or a sacred tree at upper end, on the ground. Limestone stele of the mid-second millennium BC from Ras Shamra, Ugarit.

Yahweh was the 'master', and 'husband', of the Israelites, and therefore they called Him 'Baal', in all innocence. But naturally this led to confusion of the worship of Yahweh with the Baal rituals, and it presently became essential to call Him by some different title, and *'îš*, another word meaning 'husband', was proposed (Ho. ii. 16). Once the title 'Baal' was no longer applied to Yahweh, personal names incorporating the word were likely to be misunderstood. So *bōšeṯ* ('shame') tended to replace *ba'al* in such names. Thus Esh-baal and Merib-baal (1 Ch. viii. 33 f.) are better known as Ish-bosheth (2 Sa. ii. 8) and Mephibosheth (2 Sa. ix. 6).

For reference to Ugaritic Baals, see note on Ras Shamra in the article on ARCHAEOLOGY. See also fig. 28.

The word Baal also occurs once or twice as a man's name and as a place-name (*cf.* 1 Ch. v. 5, iv. 33). D.F.P.

BAAL-BERITH (*ba'al b^erîṯ*, 'Lord of the covenant'). Only in Jdg. viii. 33, ix. 4; but *cf.* 'El-Berith', Jdg. ix. 46, RV, RSV. A Canaanite god with a shrine at Shechem. The Hebrew of Jdg. viii. 33 can hardly read (with some versions), 'They made a covenant with Baal, that he should be their god.' If Shechem was a federal community, Baal may have been the god of their federation (*b^erîṯ*). Otherwise he could be the god of the covenant between them and Israel, or simply of covenants. *Cf. Zeus Horkios, Deus Fidius.* G.W.G.

BAAL-GAD. The northern limit of Israelite conquest lying at the foot of and to the west of Mount Hermon (Jos. xi. 17, xxi. 7, xiii. 5). It may be Hasbeiyah (so F. M. Abel, *Géographie de la Palestine*, II, 1938, p. 258) or Tell Hauš (so *GTT*, 509), 12 miles farther north, both in the Wadi et-Teim. Archaeological evidence favours the latter. A.R.M.

BAAL-HAZOR. A mountain 3,333 feet high, 9 miles NNW of Bethel, modern Jebel el-'Aṣûr. Absalom gathered his half-brothers to this mountain, perhaps to a settlement of the same name at its foot, at sheep-shearing time and killed Amnon (2 Sa. xiii. 23). See OPHRAH. A.R.M.

BAAL-MEON, known also as Beth-baal-meon (Jos. xiii. 17), Beth-meon (Je. xlviii. 23), and Beon (Nu. xxxii. 3), was one of several towns built by the Reubenites in the territory of Sihon the Amorite (Nu. xxxii. 38). It was later captured by the Moabites and was still in their hands in the 6th century BC (Je. xlviii. 23; Ezk. xxv. 9). Today the site is known as Ma'in. See MOABITE STONE.

J.A.T.

BAAL-ZEBUB, BEELZEBUB. 1. In the Old Testament Baal-zebub ('lord of flies') was the god of Ekron, whom Ahaziah wished to consult, but he was prevented by Elijah's interruption (2 Ki. i. 1–6, 16). The name may have been a mocking Hebrew alteration of the Canaanite Baal-zebul, 'lord of the high place'. See BAAL.

2. In the New Testament. The Pharisees accused Jesus of casting out devils by 'Beelzebub the prince of the devils' (Mt. xii. 24–29; *cf.* Mt. x. 25; Mk. iii. 22; Lk. xi. 15–19). To this charge the Lord gave a most effective reply, in which He transferred the thought to 'Satan' and 'his kingdom'. Wherever Beelzebub is mentioned in the New Testament the Greek MSS have *Beelzeboul*, which most probably was the word originally used, while the Syriac and other Eastern MSS have Beelzebub.

G.T.M.

BAAL-ZEPHON ('Baal (lord) of the north'). The name of a place in the Egyptian East Delta near which the Israelites camped during their exodus (Ex. xiv. 2, 9; Nu. xxxiii. 7), deriving from the name of the Canaanite god Baal-Zephon. The 'waters of Baal' were in the general area of the Delta residence Pi-Ramessē (Tanis or Qantir) in the 13th century BC; a Phoen. letter of the 6th century BC alludes to 'Baal-Zephon and all the gods of Tahpanhes'. This has led to the suggestion that Tahpanhes, modern Tell Defneh some 27 miles SSW of Port Said, was earlier the Baal-Zephon of the 'waters of Baal' near Ra'amses and of the Israelite Exodus. Eissfeldt and Cazelles identify Baal-Zephon and Baal-Hasi (in Ugaritic; later Zeus Casios) and place the Egyptian Zephon/Casios at Ras Qasrun on the Mediterranean shore some 43 miles due east of Port Said, backed by Lake Serbonis. However, the deity Baal-Zephon/Casios was worshipped at various places in Lower Egypt, as far south as Memphis, which leaves several possibilities open. See also ENCAMPMENT BY THE SEA.

BIBLIOGRAPHY. Caminos, *Late-Egyptian Miscellanies*, 1954; N. Aimé-Giron, *Annales du Service des Antiquités de l'Égypte*, XL, 1940/41, pp. 433–460; W. F. Albright in *BASOR*, 109, 1948, pp. 15, 16, and in *Festschrift Alfred Bertholet*, 1950, pp. 1–14; *RB*, LXII, 1955, pp. 332 ff.

C.D.W.

BAASHA. The founder of the second brief dynasty of northern Israel (*c.* 900–880 BC). Though of humble origin (1 Ki. xvi. 2), Baasha usurped the throne following his assassination of Nadab, son of Jeroboam I, during the siege of the Philistine town of Gibbethon (1 Ki. xv. 27 ff.). His extermination of the entire house of Jeroboam fulfilled the prophecy of Ahijah (1 Ki. xvi. 5 ff.). Active hostility between Israel and Judah continued steadily throughout the twenty-four years of his reign (1 Ki. xv. 32). His provocative action in fortifying Ramah, 4 miles north of Jerusalem, prompted Asa's appeal for Syrian intervention. He continued the religious policy of Jeroboam and earned a stern prophetic rebuke (1 Ki. xvi. 1 ff.).

J.C.J.W.

BABEL (Heb. *Bāḇel*, 'gate of god'; see also BABYLON). The name of one of the chief cities founded by Nimrod in the land of Shinar (Sumer), ancient Babylonia. It is named with Erech and Accad (Gn. x. 10) and according to Babylonian tradition was founded by the god Marduk (see NIMROD) and destroyed by Sargon *c.* 2350 BC when he carried earth from it to found his new capital Agade (see ACCAD). The history of the building of the city and its lofty tower is given in Gn. xi. 1–11, where the name Babel is explained by popular etymology based on a similar Heb. root *bālal*, as 'confusion' or 'mixing'. Babel thus became a synonym for the confusion caused by language differences which was part of the divine punishment for the human pride displayed in the building.

There is as yet no archaeological evidence to confirm the existence of a city at Babylon prior to the Ist Dynasty (*c.* 1800 BC) but Babylonian tradition and a text of Sharkalisharri, king of Agade *c.* 2250 BC, mentioning his restoration of the temple-tower (*ziggurat*) at Babylon, implies the existence of an earlier sacred city on the site. Sargon's action would confirm this. The use of burnt clay for bricks and of bitumen (AV 'slime') for mortar (Gn. xi. 3) is attested from early times. The latter was probably floated down the Euphrates from Hit.

The 'Tower of Babel', an expression not found in the Old Testament, is commonly used to describe the tower (*miḡdōl*) intended to be a very high landmark associated with the city and its worshippers. It is generally assumed that, like the city, the tower was incomplete (verse 8), and that it was a staged temple tower or multi-storeyed *ziggurat* first developed in Babylonia in the early third millennium BC from the low temenos or platform supporting a shrine set up near the main city temples (as at Erech and 'Uqair). After Sharkalisharri the earliest reference to the *ziggurat* at Babylon is to its restoration by Esarhaddon in 681–665 BC. This was named in Sumerian 'Etemenanki'—'the Building of the Foundation-platform of Heaven and Earth' and associated with the temple of Marduk Esagila, 'the Building whose top is (in) heaven'. It is very probable that such a sacred edifice followed an earlier plan. The tower was severely damaged in the war of 652–648 BC but restored again by Nebuchadrezzar II (605–562 BC). It was this building, part of which was recovered by Koldewey in 1899, which was described by Herodotus on his visit *c.* 460 BC and is discussed in a cuneiform tablet dated 229 BC (Louvre, AO 6555). These enable an approximate picture of the later tower to be given. The base stage measured 295 × 295 feet and was 108 feet high. Above this were built five platforms, each 20–60 feet high but of diminishing area. The whole was crowned by a temple where the god was thought to descend for intercourse with mankind. Access was by ramps or stairways. For similar *ziggurats*, see ASSYRIA, BABYLONIA, UR, NIMRUD, ERECH, NINEVEH.

The *ziggurat* at Babylon was demolished by Xerxes in 472 BC, and though Alexander cleared the rubble prior to its restoration this was thwarted by his death. The bricks were subsequently removed by the local inhabitants, and today the site of Etemenanki is a pit (*Es-Saḥn*) as deep as the original construction was high.

Travellers of all ages have sought to locate the ruined tower of Babel. Some identify it with the site described above and others with the vitrified remains of a *ziggurat* still visible at Borsippa (mod. Birs Nimrūd) 7 miles SSW of Babylon, which is probably of Neo-Babylonian date. Yet others place the biblical tower at Dūr-Kurigalzu (Aqar Quf), west of Baghdad, a city which was, however, built *c.* 1400 BC. All that can certainly be said is that the Gn. xi account bears all the marks of a reliable historical account of buildings which can no longer be traced.

Some scholars associate Jacob's vision of a ladder and a 'gate of heaven' (Gn. xxviii. 11–18) with a *ziggurat* of the kind once built at Babel.

According to Gn. xi. 9, the intervention of Yahweh at the building of Babel led to the confusion of tongues and the subsequent dispersion of mankind, possibly in the days of Peleg (Gn. x. 25). See LANGUAGE, NATIONS, TABLE OF (Gn. x).

Babel, as Babylon throughout its history, became a symbol of the pride of man and his inevitable fall. See also BABYLON.

BIBLIOGRAPHY. A. Parrot, *The Tower of Babel*, 1955.

D.J.W.

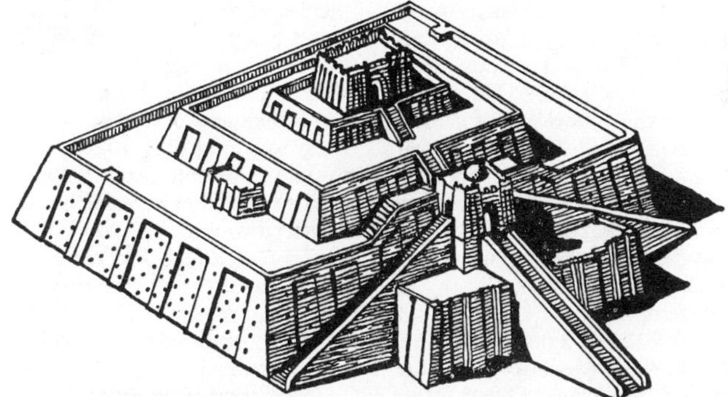

Fig. 29. A reconstruction of the temple-tower, or ziggurat, as built by Ur-Nammu, king of Ur, *c.* 2100 BC. The platforms were of different colours (black, red, blue), the temple at the top being covered with silver. The terraces were planted with trees, and this arrangement on the ziggurat at Babylon may have given rise to the idea of the 'hanging gardens' there.

BABYLON.

I. IN THE OLD TESTAMENT

The city on the river Euphrates (51 miles south of modern Baghdad, Iraq) which became the political and religious capital of Babylonia and of the empire and civilization based upon it.

a. Name

The Heb. *Bāḇel* is translated by EVV as Babylon (except Gn. x. 10, xi. 9, Babel) based on the Gk. *Babylon* (O. Pers. *Babiruš*). These are renderings of the Babylonian *bâb-ili*; pl. *bâb-ilāni*, which in its turn translates the earlier Sumerian name *kà-dingir-ra*, 'gate of god'. Other common names for the city in the Babylonian texts are *tin-tir* (*ki*), 'life of the trees', explained by them as 'seat of life' and *e-ki*, 'place of canals'. *Šešaḵ* of Je. xxv. 26, li. 41 is generally taken to be an '*atbash*' cypher rendering of Babel, but may be a rare occurrence of an old name *šeš-ki*.

b. Foundation

According to Gn. x. 10, Nimrod founded the city as his capital, while Babylonian religious tradition gives the credit to the god Marduk (see NIMROD). For the early history of the city, see BABEL.

c. History

Sargon I of Agade (*c.* 2350 BC) and his successor Sharkalisharri built temples for the gods Anunitum and Amal and restored the temple-tower. It is possible that their city of Agade was built on part of the ruins of the earlier city of Babylon. In the time of Shulgi of Ur (*c.* 2000 BC) Babylon was attacked and then ruled by governors (*patesi*) appointed from Ur. With the advent of the Semitic Ist Dynasty of Babylon under Sumu-abum the city walls were restored and Hammurabi and his successors enlarged the town, which flourished as capital of their realm until its overthrow by the Hittites *c.* 1595 BC. After a period under Kassite domination (see ASSYRIA and BABYLONIA) the city revolted and was attacked on several occasions, notably by Tiglath-pileser I of Assyria *c.* 1100 BC. Babylon repeatedly strove for its independence, and once a Chaldean ruler, Marduk-apla-iddina II (722–710, 703–702 BC), sent embassies to enlist the help of Judah (2 Ki. xx. 12–18). Isaiah's account of the fate of the city (Is. xiii) is very similarly worded to the account by Sargon II of Assyria of his sack of the place. In an attempt to remove the chief rebels, some of the leading citizens were deported to Samaria, where they introduced the worship of local Babylonian deities (2 Ki. xvii. 24–30). Despite this, there was another serious revolt against Sennacherib in 689 BC. His son, Esarhaddon, sought to restore the holy city to which he transported Manasseh as prisoner (2 Ch. xxxiii. 11). He made Babylon a vassal-city under a son, Šamaš-šum-ukin, who, however, quarrelled with his brother Ashurbanipal of Assyria. In the subsequent war of 652–648 BC Babylon was severely damaged by fire, and once again the Assyrians tried appointing a local chief, Kandalanu, as governor.

The decline of the Assyrian Empire enabled Nabopolassar, a Chaldean, to recover the city and found a new dynasty in 626 BC. His work of restoring the city was ably continued by his successors, especially his son, Nebuchadrezzar II, king of Babylonia (2 Ki. xxiv. 1), whose boast was of the great city he had rebuilt (Dn. iv. 30). It was to Babylon that the victorious Babylonian army brought the Jewish captives after the wars against Judah. Among these was Jehoiachin, whose captivity there is confirmed by inscriptions found in the ruins of Babylon itself. The plunder from the temple at Jerusalem, brought with the blinded king Zedekiah (2 Ki. xxv. 7–13), was stored in the main temple of the city, probably that of the god Marduk (2 Ch. xxxvi. 7). The city was later ruled by Amēl-Marduk (see EVIL-MERODACH) and was the place where Daniel served the last Chaldean ruler Belshazzar, co-regent of Nabonidus. See pl. VIIIa for the excavated site of the Ishtar Gate and pl. IX*a* for a model of the approach to it.

As predicted by Isaiah (xiv. 1–23, xxi. 1–10, xlvi. 1, 2, xlvii. 1–5) and Jeremiah (l–li), Babylon was to fall in its turn and be left a heap of ruins (see *d*). In October 539 the Persians under Cyrus entered the city and Belshazzar was slain (Dn. v. 30). The principal buildings were spared and the temples and their statues restored by royal decree. There is no extra-biblical record of the government of the city, which now became a subsidiary Persian capital (see DARIUS). The temple vessels were delivered to Sheshbazzar for restoration to Jerusalem, and the discovery of the record of this, probably in the record office at Babylon, in the reign of Darius I (Ezr. v. 16 ff.) was the cause of a further return of exiles rallied at Babylon by Ezra (viii. 1). Babylon, as of old, was the centre of a number of rebellions, by Nidintu-Bēl in 522 BC, and Araka (521 BC), and by Bel-shimanni and Shamash-eriba in 482 BC. In suppressing the latter, Xerxes destroyed the city (478 BC); although Alexander planned to restore it, he met his death there before work had progressed far, and with the founding of Seleucia on the river Tigris as the capital of the Seleucid rulers after the capture of Babylon in 312 BC, the city once again fell into disrepair and ruins, although, according to cuneiform texts, the temple of Bel there continued in existence at least until AD 75.

d. Exploration

Many early travellers since Herodotus of Halicarnassus *c.* 460 BC (*History*, i. 178–188) have left accounts of their visits to Babylon. Benjamin of Tudela (12th century), Rauwolf (1574), Niebuhr (1764), C. J. Rich (1811–21), and Ker Porter (1818) were among those who were followed by the more scientific explorers who made soundings and plans of the ruins. The preliminary work by Layard (1850) and Fresnel (1852) was succeeded by systematic excavation of the inner city by the Deutsche Orient-Gesellschaft under Koldewey (1899–1917) and more recently by Lenzen in 1956–8.

This work, combined with evidence of more than 10,000 inscribed texts, recovered from the site by natives digging for bricks, enables a fair picture of the city of Nebuchadrezzar's day to be reconstructed. The deep overlay of debris, the frequent destruction and rebuilding, together with the change in the course of the river Euphrates and a rise in the water-table, means that, excepting only a few parts of it, the city of the earlier period has as yet not been uncovered.

The site is now covered by a number of widely scattered mounds (see Plan). The largest, Qasr, covers the citadel, Merkes a city quarter; to the north Bāwil the northern or summer palace of Nebuchadrezzar; Amran ibn 'Ali the temple of Marduk; and Sahn the site of the *ziggurat* or temple-tower.

The city was surrounded by an intricate system of double walls, the outer range covering 17 miles, strong and large enough for chariots to pass upon the top, buttressed by defence towers, and pierced by eight gates. On the north side the massive Ishtar gates led to the sacred procession way leading south to the citadel to Esagila, the temple of Marduk, and the adjacent *ziggurat* Etemenanki. This paved roadway was 1,000 yards long with walls decorated with enamelled bricks showing 120 lions (symbol of Ishtar) and 575 *mušrušu*—dragons (Marduk) and bulls (Bel) ranged in alternate rows (see pl. IX*a*). This road turned west to cross the river Euphrates by a bridge which linked the New Town on the west bank with the ancient capital. The main palaces on which successive kings lavished attention are now represented by the complex of buildings in the citadel, among which the throne-room (52 × 17 m.) may have been in use in the time of Daniel. At the north-east angle of the palace are the remains of vaulted pillars thought by Koldewey to be supports for the terraced 'hanging gardens' built by Nebuchadrezzar for Amytis, his Median wife, as a reminder of her homeland.

For a description of the temple-tower of Babylon, see BABEL.

Many details of the city quarters and their temples, of which fifty-three are now known, have been recovered. Some of the names of these quarters were sometimes used on occasions to designate the city as a whole (Shuanna, Shushan, Tuba, Tintir, Kullab). The frequent destructions of the city left few of the contents of the temples *in situ*. The possession of the statue of Marduk,

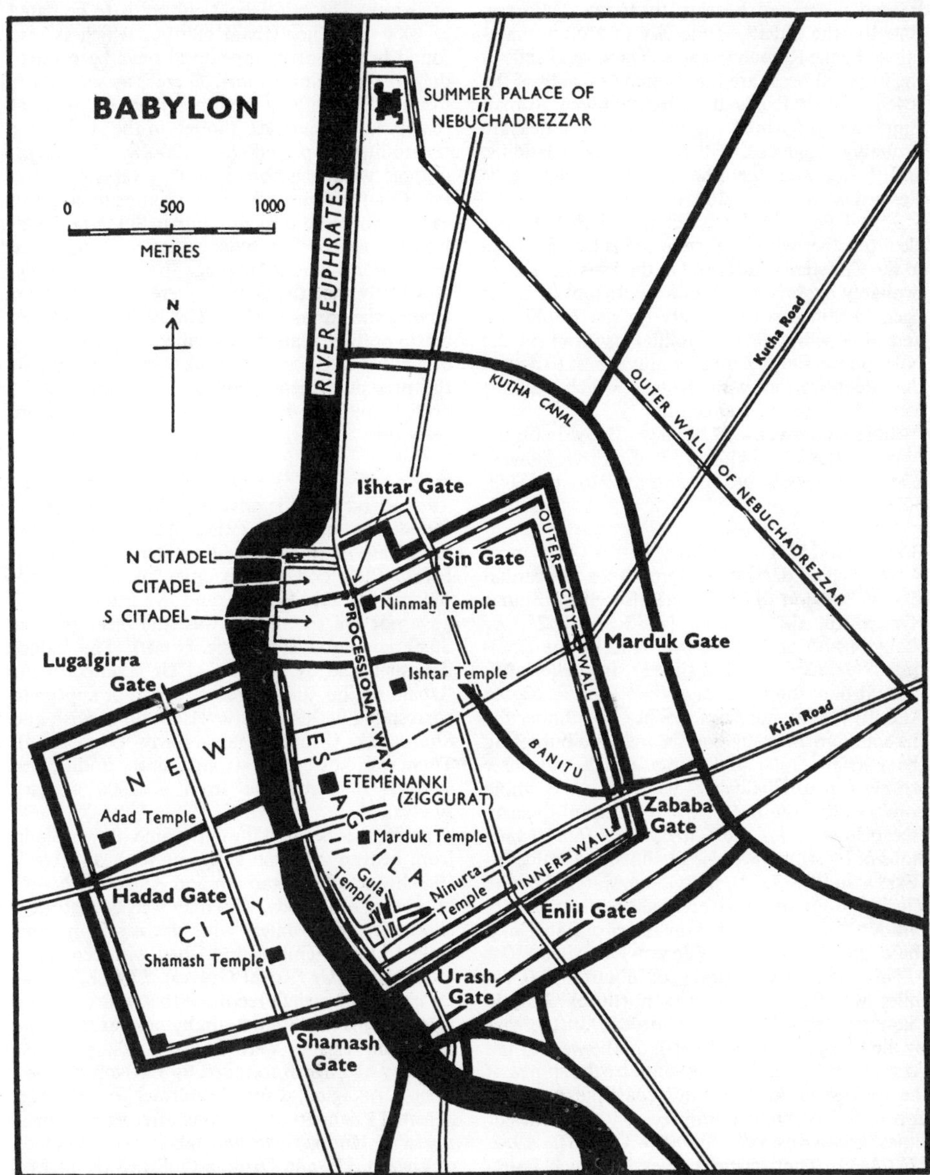

Fig. 30. Plan of Babylon at the time of Nebuchadrezzar II (605–582 BC).

housed in Esagila, was a mark of victory, and it was carried off to the conqueror's capital. For the religion and civilization of Babylon, see ASSYRIA and BABYLONIA.

BIBLIOGRAPHY. E. Unger, *Babylon, Die Heilige Stadt*, 1931; art. 'Babylon' in *Reallexikon der Assyriologie*, 1932, pp. 330–369; A. Parrot, *Babylon and the Old Testament*, 1958; O. E. Ravn, *Herodotus' Description of Babylon*, 1932; R. Koldewey, *The Excavations at Babylon*, 1914.

D.J.W.

II. IN THE NEW TESTAMENT

1. Babylon on the Euphrates, with special reference to the Babylonian Exile (Mt. i. 11, 12, 17 (2); Acts vii. 43).

2. In Rev. xiv. 8, xviii. 2, 'Fallen, fallen is

Babylon the great' (RV) is an echo of Is. xxi. 9 (*cf.* Je. li. 8), but refers no longer to the city on the Euphrates but to Rome, as is made plain by the mention of seven hills in Rev. xvii. 9 (*cf.* also Rev. xvi. 19, xvii. 5, xviii. 10, 21). The scarlet woman of Rev. xvii, enthroned upon the seven-headed beast and bearing the name 'Mystery, Babylon the Great', is the city of Rome, maintained by the Roman Empire. The seven heads of the imperial beast are interpreted not only of the seven hills of Rome but also of seven Roman Emperors—of whom the five already fallen are probably Augustus, Tiberius, Gaius, Claudius, and Nero, and the one currently reigning is Vespasian (Rev. xvii. 10).

3. In 1 Pet. v. 13, RV 'she that is in Babylon, elect together with you', who sends her greetings to the Christians addressed in the Epistle, is most probably a Christian church. 'Babylon' here has been identified with the city on the Euphrates, and also with a Roman military station on the Nile (on the site of Cairo); but it is best to accept the identification with Rome, which can be traced back to the 2nd century.

BIBLIOGRAPHY. G. T. Manley, 'Babylon on the Nile', *EQ*, XVI, 1944, pp. 138 ff.; E. G. Selwyn, *The First Epistle of St. Peter*, 1946, pp. 243, 303 ff. F.F.B.

BABYLONIA. The territory in SW Asia, now S Iraq, which derived its name from the capital city of Babylon (*q.v.*). It was also called Shinar (Gn. x. 10, xi. 2; Is. xi. 11; Jos. vii. 21, AV 'Babylonish') and, later, 'the land of the Chaldeans' (Je. xxiv. 5; Ezk. xii. 13). In earlier antiquity it bore the name of Akkad (Gn. x. 10, see ACCAD) for the northern reaches and Sumer for the southern alluvium and the marshes bordering the Persian Gulf; a territory which was later strictly called 'Chaldaea', a term for the whole country after the rise of the 'Chaldean' dynasty (see below). Thus the Babylonians (*b^e^nê bāḇēl*, 'sons of Babylon') are also qualified as Chaldeans (Ezk. xxiii. 15, 17, 23). Babylonia, watered by the Tigris and Euphrates rivers, was the probable site of Eden (Gn. ii. 14) and of the tower of Babel, and the country to which the Jews were exiled.

This small flat country of about 8,000 sq. miles was bounded on the north by Assyria (Samarra–Jebel Hamrîn as border), on the east by the Persian hills (see ELAM), on the west by the Arabian desert, and on the south by the shores of the Persian Gulf. The latter coastline does not appear to have changed appreciably since ancient times (*Geographical Journal*, CXVIII, 1952, pp. 24–39). The principal cities, of which Babylon, Erech, and Agade are the first mentioned in the Old Testament (Gn. x. 10), with Nippur, Ur, Eridu, and Lagash, were all located on or near the Euphrates. See fig. 31 below.

I. HISTORY

a. Pre-history

There is still much discussion regarding the relation of the earliest discoveries in southern Mesopotamia to those in the north. The earliest types of pottery from the lowest level at Eridu (levels XV–XVII) imply very early settlement, while the pottery which lay above it (Haji Muhammad) is of a type known from near Kish and Warka which has affinities with Halaf and Hassuna in the north. The pre-'Ubaid culture is to be dated *c.* 4000 BC. The 'Ubaid culture, which is also found in the north, appears to have been introduced by new immigrants. There is as yet no sure means of identifying the inhabitants of Sumer at this period as Semites, though in the succeeding 'Proto-literate period' (*c.* 3100–2800 BC) pictographic writing is found on clay tablets (Uruk, levels III–IV). Since the language appears to be an early non-Semitic agglutinative Sumerian, employing names for older cities and technical terms in a different language, probably Semitic, it is likely that the Semites were the earliest, or among the early, settlers. The highly developed art, in pottery, seals, and architecture, is generally attributed to the influx of the Sumerians, so that the present evidence points to the presence of both Semites and Sumerians in the land from early times.

b. The Early Dynastic period (*c. 2800–2500 BC*)

This period saw the advent of kingship and the foundation of great cities. According to the Sumerian king list, eight or ten kings ruled before the flood at the cities of Eridu, Badtibirra, Larak, Sippar, and Shuruppak. The governor of the latter was the hero of the Sumerian flood story (see NOAH). The 'flood' deposit found by Woolley at Ur is dated in the 'Ubaid period, and therefore does not appear to correspond with similar levels found at Kish and Shuruppak (Proto-literate—Early Dynastic I). There was, however, a strong literary tradition of a flood in Babylonia from *c.* 2000 BC (see FLOOD).

After the flood 'kingship came down again from heaven' and the rulers at Kish and Uruk (Erech) include Gilgamesh and Agga, the heroes of a series of legends, who may well be historical characters. City-states, with the economy controlled by the temple, flourished with centres at Uruk, Kish, Ur (Royal Graves), Lagash, and as far north as Mari. Often more than one powerful ruler sought to dominate Babylonia at the same time, and clashes were frequent. Thus the Ist Dynasty at Lagash founded by Ur-Nanše ended when Urukagina, a social reformer (*c.* 2375 BC), defeated Enannatum and soon afterwards Lugalzagesi of Umma, who had taken over the cities of Lagash, Ur, and Uruk, established the first or 'proto-' imperial domination of Sumer as far as the Mediterranean.

c. The Akkadians (*2371–2191 BC*)

A strong Semitic family founded a new city at Agade and about this time restored Babylon. This 'Akkadian' or Sargonid dynasty (2371–2191 BC), so called after the name of its founder Sargon (see fig. 2), developed a new technique of war with the bow and arrow and soon defeated the despot Lugalzagesi of Umma, Kish, and Uruk to gain the whole of Sumer. This king carried his arms to the Mediterranean and Anatolia (see SARGON). His widespread authority was maintained by his grandson Naram-Sin before the Gutians from the eastern hills overran northern Babylonia (2230–2120 BC) and kept their hold over the economy until defeated by a coalition led by Utuḫegal of Uruk. Their rule was, however, somewhat local and strongest east of the river Tigris. Lagash under its *patesi*, or ruler, Gudea (*c.* 2150 BC) remained independent and dominated Ur and the southern cities. Gudea gradually extended his territory and expeditions as far as Syria to win wood, precious stones, and metals, and so increased the prosperity of his city. The Sumerian renaissance or 'Golden Age' which followed was one of economic and artistic wealth.

d. IIIrd Dynasty of Ur (2113–2006 BC)

Following the reign of Utuḫegal of Uruk and Namaḫani, the son-in-law of Gudea, in Lagash, Ur once more became the centre of power. Ur-Nammu (2113–2096 BC) rebuilt the citadel with its ziggurat and temples (see UR and fig. 29) and in Uruk, Isin, and Nippur set up statues of himself in the temples which were controlled by his nominees. Gradually Ur extended its influence as far as Assur and the Diyala, and for a while his successors were accorded divine honours, depicted on their monuments and seals by the horned headgear of divinity (C. J. Gadd, *Ideas of Divine Rule in the Ancient Near East*, 1944). Similar honours appear to have been granted to Naram-Sin earlier. Many thousands of documents reveal the administration and religion of this period when Ur traded with places as far distant as India. The end came after severe famines, and the Sumerian rulers were displaced by invaders from Elam and Semitic semi-nomads from the western deserts. It is possible that the migration of Terah and Abraham (Gn. xi. 31) took place at this time of change in Ur's fortune (see PATRIARCHAL AGE).

e. The Amorites (1894–1595 BC)

The territories formerly controlled by Ur were divided up among the local chiefs at Assur, Mari on the Upper Euphrates, and Eshnunna. Independent rule was established by Ishbi-Irra in Isin and Naplanum in Larsa, thus dividing the loyalties of the previously united Sumerians. Then Kudurmabug of Yamutbal, east of the river Tigris, made his son Warad-Sin ruler of Larsa. He was followed by Rim-Sin, who took over Isin but failed to make headway against the growing power of Babylon, where a series of vigorous rulers in the Ist Amorite Dynasty (1894–1595 BC) held sway. The sixth of the line, Hammurabi (1792–1750 BC; see CHRONOLOGY OF THE OLD TESTAMENT; HAMMURABI), eventually defeated Rim-Sin and for the last decade of his reign ruled from the Persian Gulf to Mari, where he defeated Zimrilim, a Semite who had previously driven out Yasmaḫ-Adad, son of Shamshi-Adad I of Assyria. Despite this victory, Hammurabi was not as powerful as his namesake in Aleppo, and the Mari letters, which afford a remarkable insight into the diplomacy, trade, history, and religion of those days, show that he did not subdue Assyria, Eshnunna, or other cities in Babylonia (see ARCHAEOLOGY). The relations between Babylon, Elam, and the west at this time made possible a coalition such as that described in Gn. xiv. With the decline of Sumerian influence the increasing power of the Semites was emphasized by the public place given to Marduk as the national god (see MERODACH), and this encouraged Hammurabi to revise the laws of Babylon to accommodate both traditions. The text bearing this 'code' of 282 laws is based on the earlier reforms of Urukagina, Ur-Nammu, and Lipit-Ishtar.

f. The Kassites (1595–1174 BC)

Babylon, as often in its history, was to fall by sudden assault from the north. About 1595 BC the Hittite Mursili I raided the city and the Kassites ('Cossaeans') from the eastern hills gradually took over the country, later ruling from a new capital (Dur-Kurigalzu) built by Kurigalzu I (*c.* 1450 BC). In the centuries which followed Babylonia was weak, though independent except for brief periods when under direct Assyrian control (*e.g.* Tukulti-Ninurta I, 1234–1228 BC). Aramaean incursions were frequent, and these raids may well have left the Israelites free to settle into S Palestine and later to expand their borders under Solomon with little opposition from these desert peoples (see ASSYRIA). Periodically national heroes were able to maintain local control and trade, as when Nebuchadrezzar I (1124–1103 BC) defeated Elam, but soon Tiglath-pileser I re-established Assyrian overlordship.

g. Assyrian domination (745–626 BC)

About the time of Nabu-naṣir (Nabonassar), whose reign (747–735 BC) marked the beginning of a new era, there began a prolonged struggle for independence from Assyria. Tiglath-pileser III of Assyria proclaimed himself 'King of Sumer and Akkad', took the hands of Bel(= Marduk) and thus claimed the throne in Babylon in 745 BC, using his native name Pul(u) (1 Ch. v. 26). Fifteen years later he had to bring the Assyrian army to fight the rebel Ukin-zēr of Bît-Amukkani. He defeated him in Sapia and deported many prisoners. A rival sheikh, Marduk-apla-iddina II, of the southern district of Bît-Yakin, paid Tiglath-pileser tribute at this time (*Iraq*, XVII, 1953, pp. 44–50). However, the preoccupation with the siege of Samaria (*q.v.*) by Shalmaneser V (*q.v.*) and Sargon II in 726–722 gave Marduk-apla-iddina (Merodach-baladan, *q.v.*) his opportunity for intrigue. For ten years (721–710 BC) he held the throne in Babylon until the Assyrian army attacked Der, defeated Ḫumbanigaš of Elam, and occupied Babylon.

The Assyrian army moved south, but Merodach-baladan was retained as local ruler. It says much for Sargon's diplomacy that he kept him a loyal subject for the rest of his reign.

On Sargon's death in 705 BC, however, Merodach-baladan again plotted against his masters, and it is likely that it was he, rather than Hezekiah, who initiated the overtures for an alliance against Assyria (2 Ki. xx. 12–19; Is. xxxix). Isaiah's opposition was well founded, for the Babylonians themselves set their own citizen Marduk-zakir-šum on the throne in 703 BC. This freed Merodach-baladan's hand and he had himself proclaimed king of Babylon, though he lived in the more friendly city of Borsippa. Sennacherib marched against him, defeated the rebels and their Elamite supporters in battles at Kutha and Kish, and entered Babylon, where he set a pro-Assyrian, Bel-ibni, on the throne. Bît-Yakin was ravaged, but Merodach-baladan had already fled to Elam, where he died before Sennacherib was able to assemble a punitive naval force in 694 BC.

For a while Sennacherib's son Esarhaddon had special responsibilities as viceroy at Babylon, and when he came to the throne in 681 did much to repair the city's temples and to restore its fortunes. It may be in conjunction with this that he temporarily deported Manasseh there (2 Ch. xxxiii. 11). Since the Elamites continued to stir up the Babylonian tribes, Esarhaddon led a campaign into the 'sea-lands' in 678 BC and installed Na'id-Marduk as chief. In May 672 Esarhaddon made all his vassals swear to support his son Ashurbanipal as Crown prince of Assyria, and his son Šamaš-šum-ukin as Crown prince of Babylonia (*Iraq*, XX, 1958). On his death in 669 this arrangement came into force and worked well under the influence of the queen-mother. Nevertheless, by 652 BC the twin brother in Babylon was in open revolt against the central government, and his death followed the sack of Babylon in 648. Ashurbanipal struck at Elam also and captured Susa, from which prisoners were taken with Babylonian rebels to be settled in Samaria (Ezr. iv. 2; see ASHURBANIPAL). Kandalanu was made viceroy of Babylonia (648–627 BC), while Ashurbanipal kept direct control of the religious centre of Nippur. These preoccupations in the south diverted Assyrian attention from the west, and the city-states in Palestine were able to take steps towards independence (see JOSIAH). The end of Ashurbanipal's reign is obscure, but it appears to have coincided with the death of Kandalanu. In the interregnum which followed, the local tribes rallied to support the Chaldean Nabopolassar against the Assyrian Sin-šar-iškun.

Fig. 31.

h. The Neo-Babylonian (*Chaldean*) *period* (*626–539 BC*)

Nabopolassar, a governor of the 'sea-lands' (Persian Gulf), occupied the throne in Babylon on 22 November 626, and at once made peace with Elam. In the following year he defeated the

Assyrians at Sallat, and by 623 Der had broken from their yoke. The Babylonian Chronicle, the principal and reliable source for this period, is silent on the years 623–616 BC, by which time Nabopolassar had driven the Assyrians back along the rivers Euphrates and Tigris. In 614 the Medes joined the Babylonians to attack Assur, and the same allies, perhaps with Scythian support, captured Nineveh in the summer of 612 BC, the Babylonians pursuing the refugees westwards. Babylonian campaigns in Syria were followed by the assault on Harran in 609 and raids on the northern hill-tribes in 609–606 BC. Nabopolassar, now aged, entrusted the Babylonian army to his Crown prince Nebuchadrezzar, who fought the Egyptians at Kumuḫi and Quramati (Upper Euphrates).

In May–June 605 BC Nebuchadrezzar made a surprise attack on Carchemish, sacked the city, and annihilated the Egyptian army at Hamath. Thus the Babylonians now overran all Syria as far as the Egyptian border but do not appear to have entered the hill-country of Judah itself (2 Ki. xxiv. 7; Jos., *Ant.* x. 6; *cf.* Dn. i. 1). Jehoiakim, a vassal of Necho II, submitted to Nebuchadrezzar, who carried off hostages, including Daniel, to Babylon. While in Palestine, Nebuchadrezzar heard of the death of his father (15 August 605 BC) and immediately rode across the desert to 'take the hands of Bel', and thus officially claim the throne, on 6 September 605 BC.

In 604 BC Nebuchadrezzar received the tribute of 'all the kings of Hatti-land (Syro-Palestine)', among whom must have been Jehoiakim. Ashkelon, however, refused and was sacked, an event which had a profound effect on Judah (Je. xlvii. 5–7). An Aramaic letter appealing for help from the pharaoh against the advancing Babylonian army may be assigned to this time (*cf. DOTT*, pp. 251–255). In 601 the Babylonians fought the Egyptians, both sides sustaining heavy losses; the Babylonians remained at home to re-equip the army during the next year. It was probably as a result of this that Jehoiakim, contrary to the word of Jeremiah (Je. xxvii. 9–11), transferred his allegiance to Necho II after submitting to Babylon for three years (2 Ki. xxiv. 1).

In preparation for further campaigns the Babylonian army raided the Arab tribes in 599/8 (Je. xlix. 28–33). In the month Kislev in his seventh year (December 598) Nebuchadrezzar called out his army once more and, according to the Babylonian Chronicle, 'besieged the city of Judah, capturing it on the second day of Adar. He captured its king, appointed a ruler of his own choice and, having taken much spoil from the city, sent it back to Babylon' (BM 21946). The fall of Jerusalem on 16 March 597, the capture of Jehoiachin, the appointment of Mattaniah-Zedekiah, and the commencement of the Jewish Exile are thus recorded as in the biblical record (2 Ki. xxiv. 10–17; 2 Ch. xxxvi. 8–10).

In the following year Nebuchadrezzar appears to have marched against Elam (*cf.* Je. xlix. 34–38). The Babylonian Chronicle is missing from 595 BC, but further Babylonian operations against Judah when Zedekiah rebelled are recorded by Jeremiah (lii. 4 ff.; 2 Ki. xxv. 7). Jerusalem was destroyed in 587 BC and a further deportation effected in 581 (2 Ki. xxv. 8–21), leaving Judah a dependent province under Gedaliah (verses 22–26). A Babylonian text gives a glimpse of an invasion of Egypt in 568/7 BC (Je. xlvi). The exiled Jehoiachin, who is named in ration-tablets from Babylon (dated 595–570 BC), was favourably treated by Nebuchadrezzar's successor Amēl-Marduk (562–560 BC, see EVIL-MERODACH; 2 Ki. xxv. 27). This king was assassinated by Nebuchadrezzar's son-in-law Neriglissar (560–556 BC; see NERGAL-SHAREZER), who campaigned in Cilicia in an effort to stem the rising power of Lydia. His son, Labaši-Marduk, reigned only nine months before Nabonidus took the throne and immediately marched to Cilicia, where, according to Herodotus, he mediated between the Lydians and Medes. The latter now threatened Babylonia, from which Nabonidus was driven by the people's unwillingness to accept his reforms. He campaigned in Syria and N Arabia, where he lived at Tema for ten years while his son Belshazzar acted as co-regent in Babylon. About 544 his people and the kings of Arabia, Egypt, and the Medes being favourably disposed, Nabonidus returned to his capital (*AS*, VIII, 1958), but by this time the country was weak and divided.

i. The Achaemenids (539–332 BC)

Cyrus, who had taken over Media, Persia, and Elam, entered Babylon on 16 October 539 BC, following its capture by his general Gobryas. The course of the river Euphrates had been diverted at Opis to enable the invaders to penetrate the defences along the dried-up river-bed. Belshazzar and later Nabonidus were killed (Dn. v. 30). For a discussion of the problem of the identity of 'Darius the Mede' (Dn. v. 31, RSV), see DARIUS.

The rule of Cyrus in Babylon (539–530 BC) was just and favourable to the Jews, whose return from exile he encouraged (Ezr. i. 1–11; *cf.* Is. xliv. 24–28, xlv. 13; Mi. v). For a brief time his son Cambyses acted as co-regent until his father died fighting in the north-eastern hills. Cambyses' death (522 BC) brought insurgence, and pretenders seized the throne (*AJSL*, LVIII, 1941, pp. 341 ff.), until in December 522 Darius I restored law and order. During his reign (522–486 BC) he allowed the Jews to rebuild the Temple at Jerusalem under Zerubbabel (Ezr. iv. 5; Hg. i. 1; Zc. i. 1).

Henceforth Babylonia was ruled by Persian kings (see PERSIA); Xerxes (486–470 BC; see AHASUERUS), Artaxerxes I (464–423 BC) and Darius II (423–408 BC), who may be the 'Darius the Persian' so named in Ne. xii. 22 to distinguish him from 'Darius the Mede'.

Following the capture of Babylon, which he planned to rebuild, Alexander III (the Great) ruled the city (331–323 BC) and was followed by a

Hellenistic line; Philip Arrhidaeus (323–316 BC) and Alexander IV (316–312 BC). The country then passed in turn into the hands of the Seleucids (312–64 BC) and then of the Parthians (Arsacids) until its conquest by the Arabs in AD 641.

From the Neo-Babylonian period onwards there were a number of Jewish settlements in Babylonia, and after the fall of Jerusalem in AD 70 these became influential in the *diaspora* (see BABYLON, II).

II. RELIGION

From the third millennium BC onwards lists of the names of deities with their titles, epithets, and temples were compiled. Although in the final library version at Nineveh in the 7th century BC these numbered more than 2,500, many can be identified as earlier Sumerian deities assimilated by the Semites after the time of the Ist Dynasty of Babylon (*c.* 1800 BC), so that the actual number of deities worshipped in any one period was considerably less.

a. The Pantheon

The chief gods were Anu (Sumerian *An*) the heaven-god, with his principal temple É.anna at Uruk (see ERECH). He was the Semitic 'El, and his wife Innana, or Innin, was later confused with Ishtar. Similar syncretistic tendencies can be traced over Enlil, the air-god, whose attributes were later taken over by Bel (Baal) and Marduk (see MERODACH). His wife, called Ninlil or Ninhursag, was later identified also with Ishtar. The third deity of the supreme triad was Ea (Sum. *Enki*), 'lord of the deep waters', god of wisdom and thus especially favourable to mankind, to whom he revealed the means of learning the mind of the gods through divination, and for whom he interceded. His temple É.abzu was at Eridu, and his wife bore the names of Dam-gal, Nin-mah, or Damkina, the great wife of earth and heaven.

Among the other principal deities was the Semitic Ishtar, at first perhaps a male deity (*cf.* Arab. *'Athtar*). But later, by the assumption of the powers of Innana through the same process of syncretism, Ishtar became supremely the goddess of love and the heroine of war and was considered to be the daughter of Sin. Sin, the Babylonian moon-god (Sum. *su'en*) was worshipped with his wife Ningal in temples at Ur and Haran. He was said to be the son of Anu and Enlil. Shamash, whose wife Aya was also later considered to be a form of Ishtar, was the sun in his strength (Sum. *utu*), the son of Sin, the god of power, justice, and of war. His main temples (É.babbar, 'the House of the Sun') were at Sippar and Larsa, though like that of all the principal deities his worship was perpetuated in shrines in other cities.

Adad, of W Semitic origin, was the god of storms, the Canaanite-Aramaean Addu or Hadad (*q.v.*). Nergal and his wife Ereshkigal ruled the underworld, and thus he was the lord of plagues (Irra), fevers, and maladies. With the rise of the Amorites the worship of Marduk (Sum. *amar. utu*, 'the young bull of the sun'?), the eldest son of Enki, became paramount in Babylon. The Epic of Creation (*enuma eliš*) is an epic poem concerning the creation of the universe and of order restored by Marduk, whose fifty titles are given. Nabu, god of science and writing, had his temple (É.zida) in many cities (see NEBO, NINEVEH, CALAH). Many deities were of importance in certain localities. Thus Ashur (*an.šar*) became the national god of Assyria. Amurru (*mar.tu*, 'the west'), who is identified with Anu, Sin, and Adad, was a W Semitic deity as was Dagon (see DAGON). Dummuzi (see TAMMUZ) was a god of vegetation whose death, but not resurrection, forms the subject of an Ishtar myth. Ninurta was the Babylonian and Assyrian god of war and hunting (see NIMROD).

The upper world was peopled with Igigi-gods and the lower by Annunaki. The whole spiritual and material realm was regulated by divine laws (*me*), over a hundred of which are known, ranging from 'godship' to 'victory' and 'a musical instrument', *i.e.* cultural traits and complexes. The gods were immortal yet of limited power. The myths, in which but few of the principal deities figure, illustrate their anthropomorphic character and the conception of any object (*e.g.* a stone) being imbued with 'life'. Spirits and demons abound. The Sumerians sought by various theological devices to resolve the problems inherent in their polytheistic system. Thus the myths are primarily concerned with such questions as the origin of the universe, the foundation and government of the world, and the creation of man (see CREATION) and the search for immortality, as in the Epic of the Flood, and man's relationship to the spiritual world.

b. Priesthood

There were many classes of temple servants, with the king or ruler as the supreme pontiff at certain solemn festivals. In early Sumerian times the whole economy was centred on the temple, where the chief official (*ênû*) was 'the lord of the manor'. In the worship of Sin, the high-priestess (*entu*) was usually a royal princess. The chief priests (*maḫḫu*) had many priests (*šangu*), males of sound body and often married, to assist them. The chief liturgist (*urigallu*) was supported by a host of minor officials who had access to the temple (*ēreb bîti*). In the ceremonial, chanters, psalmists, dirge-singers, and musicians played a great part.

In man's approach to the god many specialists might play a rôle. The exorcist (*ašipu*) could remove the evil spirit or spell with the incantations or ritual prescribed in the texts (*šurpu*; *maqlu*) involving symbolic substitutions (*kuppuru*), purification by *mašmašu*-priests or by those who cleansed by water (*ramku*). There are many documents describing the action to be taken against evil spirits (*utukki limnuti*), demons of fate (*namtaru*), demons plaguing women (*lamaštu*), or taboos. The extensive medical literature of the early period was closely allied to religion, as was

1 PLACE *Where a name is in capitals, see also separate article*	2 LOCATION *See map section at end of Dictionary*	3 EXCAVATED *Organization responsible and name of Director**	4 DATES	5 OCCUPATIONAL PERIODS, MAIN DISCOVERIES, ETC. *For abbreviations, see* ARCHAEOLOGY, *Section II*	6 PUBLICATIONS *Abbreviations as in* Iraq
Adab	Bismāya, 48 m. SE of Diwaniyah	DOG (W. Andrae)	1903	Plan	*MDOG*, XVI, 1902–3
		Orient. Explor. Fund, Chicago (E. J. Banks)	1903–4	Temple, inscriptions, palace (Agade-Ur III)	E. J. Banks, *Bismya, or the Lost City of Abad*, 1912
Al 'Ubaid	4 m. NW of Ur	BM (H. R. Hall)	1919	'Ubaid temple terrace, reliefs, mosaics	H. R. Hall, *A Season's Work at Ur, Al-'Ubaid*, 1930
		BM (C. L. Woolley)	1923–4	Pottery, copper sculptures, inscriptions	C. L. Woolley, *Al-'Ubaid*, 1927
BABYLON	Bâbil Kasr, Amrân-ibn-Ali, 4 m. N of Hilla	BM (A. H. Layard)	1850	Buildings, *etc.*	A. H. Layard, *Discoveries in Nineveh and Babylon*, 1853
		French Expéd. scientifique (F. Fresnel)	1852	Buildings, *etc.*	J. Oppert, *Expédition scientifique en Mésopotamie*, 1863, 1859
		BM (H. Rassam)	1879–80, 1882	N. Bab. Achaemenian Tablets	H. Rassam, *Ashur and the Land of Nimrod*, 1897
		DOG (R. Koldewey)	1899–1917	Acropolis, Ishtar Gateway, temples, walls, private houses (N. Bab.)	R. Koldewey, *The Excavations at Babylon*, 1914 E. Unger, *Babylon*, 1931
		DOG (H. Lenzen)	1957	Greek theatre	*Sumer. Ausgrabungen der Deutsch. Or.-Gesell. in Babylon*, I–VIII, 1918–1957
Borsippa	Birs Nimrud, 7 m. SSW of Babylon	BM (A. H. Layard, *etc.*) (H. Rassam)	1850, 1854, 1880	Ziggurat, cylinder inscriptions, Ezida (N. Bab.); palace of Nebuchadrezzar II	H. Rassam, *Asshur and the land of Nimrod*, 1897
		DOG	1901–2	Ezida, city wall	R. Koldewey, *Die Tempel von Babylon und Borsippa*, 1911
Dēr	16 m. SW of Baghdad	BM (H. Rassam)	1880	Tablets	H. Rassam, *Ashur and the land of Nimrod*, 1897
		BM (E. A. W. Budge)	1890–1	Tablets	E. A. W. Budge, *By Nile and Tigris*, 1920
		Notgemeinschaft der Deutsch. Wiss. (W. Andrae)	1927	Plan of city	*Iraq*, I, 1934
		Iraq Dept. Antiq. (Taha Baqir)	1941	Tablets	*Sumer*, I, 1945
Dilbat	Tell Dailem, 18 m. SSE of Hilla	BM (H. Rassam)	1880	Persian period tablets (N. Bab.)	H. Rassam, *Asshur and the land of Nimrod*, 1897

* Abbr.: DOG = Deutsche Orient-Gesellschaft; BM = British Museum.

1	2	3	4	5	6
Drehem	Tell Duraihim (Puzurish-Dagan), 3 m. S of Nippur	Weld-Field Mus. Chicago (S. Langdon)	1924	Many tablets (Ur III)	
Dur-Kurigalzu	'Aqar Quf; 12 m. W of Baghdad	Iraq Dept. Antiq. (Taha Baqir)	1942–5	Kassite capital, ziggurat, temples, palace, tablets	Taha Baqir, *Excavations at 'Aqar Quf* (*Iraq*, Suppl. VIII), 1944–6
Erech	Uruk (Warka), 25 m. E of Samawa	Assyr. Excav. Fund (W. K. Loftus)	1850, 1854	Uruk: mosaics, temple, Parthian tombs	W. K. Loftus, *Travels and Researches in Chaldaea*, 1857
		DOG (J. Jordan, *etc.*)	1912–13	Anu-Antum (Seleucid): Parthian palace	J. Jordan, *Uruk-Warka*, 1928
		DOG (H. Lenzen)	1928–39, 1954–61	Archaic cuneiform texts, Eanna and ziggurat temples (18 levels) (Uruk–N. Bab.); Parthian temples	H. Lonzen, *Ausgrabungen . . . in Uruk-Warka*, I–VI
Eridu	Abu Shahrain, 24 m. SW of Nasiriyah	BM (J. E. Taylor)	1855	Plan of site	*JRAS*, XV, 1955
		BM (R. C. Thompson)	1918	Trial pits (pottery, iron implements)	R. C. Thompson, *BM Excavations at Abu Shahrain*, 1920
		BM (H. R. Hall)	1919	Ziggurat	H. R. Hall, *Season's Work at Ur . . . Eridu*, 1930
		Iraq. Dept. Antiq. (Naji al-Aṣil)	1946–9	Pottery, skulls, 17 temples (to 'Ubaid or earlier)	*Sumer*, III, 1947–VI, 1950
Eshnunna	Tell Asmar, 55 m. NE of Baghdad	Orient. Instit. Chicago (H. H. Frankfort)	1930–36	Isin period palace; pre-Sargon temples, cuneiform tablets, E. Dynastic statues	*Oriental Institute Publications*, XIX (1932), XVI–XX, XLIII (1940), XLIV (1939), LVIII (1942), LX (1943), LXIII (1952).
Harmal	Tell Abu Harmal (Diniktim), 1 m. E of Baghdad	BM (A. H. Layard)	1850	Old Bab. inscriptions and masonry, temple of Hani, tablets (incl. Code of Eshnunna)	*Sumer*, II, IV.
		Iraq. Dept. Antiq. (Taha Baqir)	1945, 1947–9		A. Goetze, *The Laws of Eshnunna*, 1956
Jemdat Nasr	15 m. NE of Hillah	Weld–Field Mus. Chicago (S. Langdon & L. C. Watelin)	1925–6	Jemdat Nasr palace, pottery, archaic texts	E. MacKay, *Report on Excavations at Jemdat Nasr*, 1931
					AJA, XXXIX, 1935; *JRAS*, 1932
Kish	Al Uḥaimir, 10 m. NE of Hillah	French Expéd. Scientifique (F. Fresnel)	1852	Building (N. Bab.), archaic temple	J. Oppert, *Expédition scientifique en Mesopotamie I*, 1863
		Ministère de l'Instr. publique (H. de Genouillac)	1912	Buildings (O. Bab. and N. Bab.), tablets	*Fouilles françaises d'El-Akhymer*, I–II, 1924–5
		Weld–Mus. Nat. Hist. Chicago (S. Langdon, *etc.*)	1923–33	Cemeteries (E. Dyn.), ziggurats, palace, temples	S. Langdon, E. MacKay, *etc.*, *Excavations at Kish*, I–IV, 1924–34
Kutalla	Tell Ṣifr, 25 m. NW of Nasiriyah	Assyr. Explor. Fund (W. K. Loftus)	1854	Buildings, tablets (O. Bab.)	W. K. Loftus, *Travels and Researches*, 1857
Kutha (Cuth)	Tell Ibrahīm, 20 m. NE of	BM (H. Rassam)	1881–2	Necropolis, tablets (N. Bab.)	H. Rassam, *Ashur and the land*

	2	3	4	5	6
Lagash	Tell-Lōh, 12 m. NE of Shatra	French Government, Louvre (De Sarzec, de Genouillac, A. Parrot)	1877–8, 1880–1900, 1903–9, 1929–33	Gudea statues, pottery, inscriptions (Uruk–Ur III)	A. Parrot, *Tello. Vingt Campagnes de fouilles*, 1948
Larsa	Senkereh, 25 m. WNW of Nasiriyah	Assyr. Explor. Fund (W. K. Loftus)	1854	Ziggurat, temple, tablets (Ur III–N. Bab.)	W. K. Loftus, *Travels and Researches in Chaldaea*, 1857
		Louvre (A. Parrot)	1932–4	Temple, palaces, inscriptions	A. Parrot, *Villes enfouies*, 1934
Nippur	Tell Nuffar, 6 m. NNW of 'Afak	BM (A. H. Layard)	1851	Late tombs	A. H. Layard, *Discoveries in Babylon*, 1853
		Babylon. Explor. Fund, Philadelphia (J. P. Peters, *etc.*)	1889–90, 1893–6, 1899–1900	Palace mound, temple site, many tablets (all periods, esp. Sum. lit. N. Bab.)	
		Orient. Inst. Chicago–Univ. Penn. (D. E. McCown, R. C. Haines)	1948–61	Early Dynastic temple, tablets	*Sumer*, V
Shuruppak	Tell Far'a, 35 m. NW of Shatra	Univ. Penn. (H. V. Hilprecht)	1900	Pre-Sargonid finds	H. V. Hilprecht, *Excavations in Assyria and Babylonia*, 1904
		DOG (R. Koldewey)	1902–3	Pottery (Jemdat Nasr); archaic tablets, seals, buildings	E. Heinrich, *Fara*, 1931
		Univ. Penn. (E. Schmidt)	1930–1	Archaic texts (Jemdat Nasr-Ur III)	E. Schmidt, *Excavations at Fara*, 1931
Sippar	Abu Habbah, 18 m. SE of Baghdad	BM (H. Rassam)	1881–2	Ziggurat, palace, tablets (O. Bab.–N. Bab.)	H. Rassam, *Asshur and the land of Nimrod*, 1897
		Ottoman Museum (V. Scheil)	1894	Private houses, tablets	V. Scheil, *Une saison de fouilles à Sippar*, 1902
		Notgemeinsch. der Deutsch. Wissen. (W. Andrae)	1927	Plan	*Iraq*, I, 1934
Umma	Tell Jōkha, 25 m. NNW of Shatra	DOG (W. Andrae)	1902	Many Ur III tablets, plan, buildings	*MDOG*, XVI, 1902–3
'Uqair	Tell 'Uqair, 24 m. NE of Babylon	Iraq Dept. Antiq. (S. Lloyd)	1940–1	Uruk–Jamdat Nasr pottery, mosaics, temple on platform	*JNES*, II, 1943
UR	Tell Muqayyar, 14 m. WSW of Nasiriyah	BM (J. E. Taylor)	1854	Foundation cyl. of ziggurat (N. Bab.)	*JRAS*, XV, 1855
		BM (R. C. Thompson)	1918	Trial trenches	
		BM (H. R. Hall)	1919	Eharsag temple	H. R. Hall, *A Season's Work at Ur*, 1930
		BM & Univ. Mus. Philad. (C. L. Woolley)	1922–34	Ziggurat (Ur III–N. Bab.); royal cemetery, flood pit, temenos, temples, palaces, and private houses	C. L. Woolley, *Excavations at Ur*, 1954; *id.*, *Ur Excavations*, I–VIII, 1934–62; C. J. Gadd (ed.), *Ur Excavations Texts*, I–VII, 1928–62

the astronomy or astrology of the later 'Chaldean' dynasty. The latter was based on the equation of deities with planets or stars (*e.g.* Nabu = Mercury), or with parts of the heavens ('The Way of Anu' = fixed stars; see STARS).

Others were engaged in ascertaining the will of the gods by omens from livers (the *baru*-priest or 'seer'), or by inquiry by oracle (*ša'ilu*), or by offering prayers. Many women, including sanctuary prostitutes, were attached to the temples, and local shrines where travellers prayed have been found at Ur (*Iraq*, XXII, 1960).

The regular service (*dullu*) included giving the gods something to eat and drink. Statues were dressed and ornamented and votive figures of worshippers placed near by. Sacrifices placed on altars were subsequently allocated, wholly or in part, to the priests. The gods had their own chairs, chariots, and boats for use in processions.

c. *Festivals*

Most temples, cities, and months had their own characteristic festivals. At Babylon and Assur a New Year festival (*zag.muk*) was performed originally in the autumn, but, after the Ist Dynasty of Babylon, in the spring. At Babylon this involved the temporary reduction of the king to the status of an ordinary citizen, after which he received afresh the symbols and authority of kingship. He 'took the hand of Bel' to lead that deity in the procession, and ceremonies included a 'sacred-marriage' and the deciding of the fates in the Festival House (*bît akîti*) outside the city, on which depended the prosperity of the realm. There is no reference to the recital of the Epic of Creation other than at Babylon or certain evidence as to the nature of the New Year festival outside that city. At Ur and Erech there were more frequent festivals.

III. EXPLORATION AND EXCAVATION

Many travellers, from the time of Herodotus in the 5th century BC, have described their journeys in Babylonia. From the 19th century AD interest in the location of Babylon and the 'Tower of Babel' was increased by the objects and drawings brought to Europe by travellers such as C. J. Rich (1811–25), Ker Porter (1818), and Costin and Flandin (1841). Excavation soon followed at Babylon, Erech, and Borsippa (Layard, Loftus), and the good results led to more scientific expeditions, notably at Kish, Babylon, Ur, Lagash, and Nippur from 1850 onwards. For details of the sites together with the date of their excavation, see the list given on pp. 125–127.

See also ASSYRIA for references to Babylonian Literature; BABYLON, UR, *etc.* for sites; CHALDAEA, SHINAR for specific periods of history.

BIBLIOGRAPHY. *General:* S. A. Pallis, *The Antiquity of Iraq*, 1956; H. W. F. Saggs, *The Beginnings that were Babylon*, 1961; S. N. Kramer, *History Begins at Sumer*, 1958. *History:* H. Schmökel, *Geschichte des alten Vorderasien*, 1957; *CAH*, I–III (1925; being revised); D. J. Wiseman, *Chronicles of Chaldaean Kings (626–556 BC)*, 1956. *Religion:* S. N. Kramer, *Mythologies of the Ancient World*, 1961; J. Bottéro, *La Religion babylonienne*, 1952. *Art:* H. H. Frankfort, *The Art and Architecture of the Ancient Orient*, 1954. D.J.W.

BACA, VALLEY OF (*'ēmeq habbāḵā'*, 'valley of the balsam tree'). Mentioned in Ps. lxxxiv. 6, this unlocated site had the reputation of being a waterless place. Reference is also made to balsam trees in 2 Sa. v. 23, 24 and 1 Ch. xiv. 14, 15 (see RVmg).

BADGERS' SKINS (Heb. *taḥaš*, probably from Egyp. *ṯḥś*, 'leather', and Arab. *tuḫasun*, 'dolphin'). Mentioned in AV as the upper covering of the tabernacle, *etc.* (Ex. xxv. 5, xxvi. 14, *etc.*, in all of which cases RSV has 'goatskins'), and as the material used in making sandals (Ezk. xvi. 10, where RV has 'sealskin', RVmg 'porpoiseskin', RSV 'leather'). LXX has *hyakinthos*, probably meaning 'skins with the colour of the hyacinth', the colour of which is difficult to ascertain because classical authors differ about it. The common opinion of modern scholars is that *taḥaš* means 'dolphin' or 'porpoise'.

The *taḥaš*-skin was precious in Old Testament times as is indicated by Ezk. xvi. 10, where it is mentioned along with embroidered cloth, fine linen, and silk. The skins are included among the gifts for the erecting of the sanctuary (Ex. xxv. 5); they were used with tanned rams' skins for the covering of the tent of the tabernacle and the ark (*e.g.* Nu. iv. 6). F.C.F.

BAG. In AV several different terms are translated by this word. 1. *kîs*. A bag or purse containing either money (Is. xlvi. 6; Pr. i. 14), or stones for weighing, which may be used deceitfully (Dt. xxv. 13; Mi. vi. 11). Modern Arabic uses the same word. 2. *ḥārîṭ*. This is a rare word which is also found in Arabic. It occurs in 2 Ki. v. 23 and also in Is. iii. 22. In the latter place RV renders 'satchels'; the reference is probably to a primitive form of ladies' handbag. The Arabic Bible uses *kîs* in both passages. 3. *keli hārō'îm* (1 Sa. xvii. 40, 49) and *yalqûṭ* (1 Sa. xvii. 40) are used synonymously for a shepherd's bag or scrip. (*Cf.* Mt. x. 10 and parallels where the Gk. has *pēra*.) In Gn. xlii. 25 *kelî* means sack (*q.v.*); the word is more commonly employed, however, for a utensil or vessel. 4. *ṣerôr* is sometimes rendered 'bag' (Jb. xiv. 17; Pr. vii. 20; Hg. i. 6), but can usually be translated 'bundle' (*e.g.* Gn. xlii. 35; Ct. i. 13).

5. Judas's 'moneybag', Gk. *glōssokomon* (Jn. xii. 6), is really a box or chest; the word is used in 2 Ch. xxiv. 8, 10, 11 (LXX) for the chest placed by Joash at the temple gate for the reception of the temple tax, and in Aquila's version of Ex. xxxvii. 1 and 1 Sa. vi. 19 for the ark of the covenant. It appears also as a loan-word in the Mishnah in the sense of 'bookcase' or 'coffin'. 6. Gk. *ballantion* (Lk. x. 4, xii. 33, *etc.*) is a bag proper. R.A.S.

BAHURIM. Modern Ras eṭ-Ṭmim, to the east of Mount Scopus, Jerusalem. Phaltiel, the husband of Michal, accompanied his wife as far as Bahurim when she went to David to become his wife (2 Sa. iii. 14–16). Shimei, a man of Bahurim, met and cursed David as he reached this locality in his flight from Jerusalem before Absalom (2 Sa. xvi. 5), and David's soldiers hid in a well in Bahurim when pursued by Absalom's men (2 Sa. xvii. 17–21). R.J.W.

BAKER, BAKING. See BREAD.

BALAAM. The name *Bil‘ām* occurs in Nu. xxii–xxiv fifty times; it is mentioned also in Nu. xxxi. 8, 16; Dt. xxiii. 4, 5; Jos. xiii. 22, xxiv. 9, 10; Ne. xiii. 2; Mi. vi. 5. In the Greek of the New Testament the name is written *Balaam* (2 Pet. ii. 15; Jude 11; Rev. ii. 14). Most scholars derive the name from the verb *bāla‘*, 'to swallow down', with *ām* suffix; *cf.* the rather frequent name *Bela‘*, and the place-names *Bela‘* and *Yibl^{e}‘ām* (written *Bil‘ām* in 1 Ch. vi. 70, LXX). In Arabic the word *bal‘am* means 'glutton'. Underlying the description 'Nicolaitans' in Rev. ii. 6, 15 there seems to be a Gk. translation (*Nikolaos*, 'conqueror of the nation') of *Bil‘am* conceived as a combination of *bāla‘* and *‘am* ('nation'). Albright, however, compares the Amorite name *Yabil‘ammu*: 'the (divine) uncle brings'.

Balaam's father is called Beor, but that is insufficient reason to identify him with Bela the son of Beor, a king in Edom (Gn. xxxvi. 32). He was living in Pethor (misunderstood in the Vulg. as 'the diviner') on the river Euphrates, probably the same as Pitru, 12 miles south of Carchemish. In Jos. xiii. 22 he is called a soothsayer, somebody who not only predicts the future but also influences it by his prediction.

Nu. xxii narrates how he was hired by Balak, king of Moab, in order to rob the Israelites of their strength by his curses (*cf.* the Egyptian execration texts, *ANET*, pp. 328, 329). Balak co-operated with the elders of Midian (xxii. 4, 7; *cf.* xxxi. 16; Jos. xiii. 22). Some scholars find two different threads of narration in Nu. xxii; but what may look to us like inconsistencies, especially in the Lord's behaviour, may agree quite well with a conception of God wherein rationalistic elements do not play such a preponderant rôle as in our theology. The problem of whether Balaam was a true prophet, and how a true prophet could act in the way he did, is also a product of modern rationalism. A person may be a true prophet at one time and a miserable deceiver at another (*cf.* Jn. xi. 49–52). The biblical narrator presented the oracles of Balaam in the form they could have had, without bothering, for one thing, about which language Balaam spoke.

The resemblances between these oracles and 2 Sa. xxiii. 1–7, and the explanation of Nu. xxiv. 17, 18 as an allusion to the expansion of Israel under David, point to the 10th century as the probable date of their written form. Albright assumes an oral tradition going back to the 12th century. If Asshur in xxiv. 22, 24 is to be identified with the Arabian tribe of that name (Gn. xxv. 18; Ps. lxxxiii. 8), there is no objection against an early date, and no reason to bring the oracles down to the 3rd century.

Notwithstanding Nu. xxiv. 25, Balaam afterwards sojourned with the Midianites, whom he advised to lure the Israelites into the cult of Baal-peor (Nu. xxxi. 16, *cf.* xxv). Together with the kings of Midian he was killed by the Israelites (Nu. xxxi. 8). In the New Testament his name is a symbol of avarice (2 Pet. ii. 15; Jude 11) and of participation in pagan cult and fornication (Rev. ii. 14).

BIBLIOGRAPHY. O. Eissfeldt, 'Die Komposition der Bileam-Erzählung', *ZAW*, LVII, 1939, pp. 212–241; W. F. Albright, 'The Oracles of Balaam', *JBL*, LXIII, 1944, pp. 207–233; A. H. van Zyl, *The Moabites*, 1960, pp. 10–12, 121–125.

A. VAN S.

BALAK. The king of Moab who employed Balaam (*q.v.*) to put a curse on the Israelites (Nu. xxii–xxiv).

BALANCE. See WEIGHTS AND MEASURES.

BALDNESS. See HAIR.

BALM (*ṣ^{e}rî, ṣ^{o}rî*; LXX *rhētinē*). This product of Gilead (*q.v.*), a somewhat vague geographical area, was exported to Egypt (Gn. xxxvii. 25, xliii. 11) and to Tyre (Ezk. xxvii. 17). Celebrated for healing properties (Je. xlvi. 11) and often used for cosmetic (*q.v.*) purposes, it was used also to symbolize deliverance from national distress (Je. viii. 22, li. 8). It was probably an aromatic gum or spice, but the original meaning of the word is not clear and it cannot now be identified with any plant in Gilead, despite the claims made for a similarly-named substance prepared by the monks of Jericho from the fruit of the *zaqqûm* (*Balanites aegyptiaca*). Some understand the *ṣ^{o}rî* of Gn. xxxvii. 25 to be *mastich* (RVmg 'mastic'), a product of the *Pistacia lentiscus* which, common in Palestine and used for healing purposes, is used by the Arabs in flavouring coffee and sweets, and as a chewing-gum. Classical authors applied the name 'balm' to what is now known as Mecca balsam, still imported into Egypt from Arabia. See SPICE. J.D.D.

BAMAH. The Hebrew for 'high place'. This form is retained in Ezk. xx. 29 because of the play upon the words *bā'* ('go'), *māh* ('what?'). See HIGH PLACE.

BAMOTH, BAMOTH-BAAL. Bamoth ('high places') is named as a stage on the Israelite journey in the neighbourhood of the river Arnon (Nu. xxi. 19 f.). As the journey led up to a *pisgah* (*q.v.*), 'ridge', the word may denote actual height. It might, however, be identical with Bamoth-baal, a city of Reuben in the tableland (Jos. xiii. 17) and with 'the high places (*bamoth*) of Baal' which Balaam ascended (Nu. xxii. 41), where the name denotes a sanctuary to Baal. See HIGH PLACE. G.T.M.

BAND. See ARMY.

BANK. See FORTIFICATION AND SIEGECRAFT (II*a*).

BANK, BANKER. There was no bank in Israel in the sense of an establishment for the custody of private money or the granting of commercial credit. For safe keeping a private person would either bury his valuables (Jos. vii. 21) or deposit them with a neighbour (Ex. xxii. 7). Commerce remained largely a royal monopoly (2 Sa. v. 11; 1 Ki. x. 14–29; *cf.* 2 Ch. xx. 35 ff.). The palace and the Temple were the repositories of the national wealth (1 Ki. xiv. 26); later private property also was deposited for safe keeping in temples (2 Macc. iii. 6, 10 ff.). A banking system existed in Babylonia in 2000 BC, but the Jews did not use it until the Exile. The money-changers in Mt. xxi. 12; Mk. xi. 15; Jn. ii. 14, 15 converted Roman money into orthodox coinage for the Temple half-shekel (Mt. xvii. 24). Mt. xxv. 27 (Lk. xix. 23) refers to a money-lender. A.E.W.

BANNER. 1. *degel*, meaning 'standard' or 'flag', is rendered 'banner' three times and 'standard' thirteen times in AV. In the wilderness each tribe

Fig. 32. Three Egyptian army banners, with (second from right) a 9th–8th-century Assyrian standard. The individual symbols were probably the distinctive signs of the unit carrying them.

was marked by its own banner (Nu. i. 52, ii. 2, 3, *etc.*). In Ps. xx. 5 the word is used for a flag of battle. In the Song of Solomon it is used figuratively by the Shulamite to denote the distinguished appearance of her beloved (Ct. v. 10 mg.), and by him in referring to her overpowering beauty (Ct. vi. 4, 10, *cf.* ii. 4).

2. *nēs*, meaning 'ensign', is rendered 'banner' and in several other ways in AV. It is usually employed to designate a rallying-standard. In Is. xi. 12 the Messiah is said to raise up such a standard, while in verse 10 He is Himself said to be one. Perhaps this latter reference is intended to be a link with Jehovah-nissi ('The Lord is my Banner') in Ex. xvii. 15. The RSV is probably correct in removing references to a banner in Is. x. 18 and lix. 19. G.W.G.

Fig. 33. Assyrian military standard bearing the figure of Ashur or Ninurta as the god of war.

BANQUET. The words so translated in AV include or actually stand for wine-drinking. They are *mišteh* (*e.g.* Est. v. 4 ff.; Dn. v. 10); *šāṭâ* (Est. vii. 1); *yayin* (Ct. ii. 4); and *potos* (1 Pet. iv. 3). The eastern custom of hospitality, which was of such intimate significance, assumed religious importance among the Jews, and the 'feast' or 'banquet' was often used in the Old Testament as an emblem for the happiness of the messianic kingdom (Is. xxv. 6; *cf.* Mt. viii. 11; Lk. xiv. 15 ff.). Since eating was frequently associated in the Old Testament with covenant-making (see Gn. xxvi. 28–31), it is not surprising that at the Last Supper our Lord, having combined the elements of 'covenant' and 'blood', should remind His disciples that this banquet was but a foretaste of the true messianic glory to come, made possible by His death (Mk. xiv. 25; *cf.* Rev. iii. 20). S.S.S.

BAPTISM.

I. BAPTISM AND THE COVENANT

If the doctrine of baptism is to be fully grasped, it must be seen as an integral part of God's single plan of salvation. Hence, we must first place baptism in the setting of the covenant. In this connection, we notice how the New Testament finds in baptism fundamental parallels with the three greatest Old Testament administrations of the covenant.

a. The parallel with the *Noahic* covenant is remarked in 1 Pet. iii. 18–22. The main contentions of this difficult passage are plain enough.

Noah and his family, secure in the ark, were tided over into a new world by the waters which overwhelmed the ungodly. They passed through the judgment unscathed, and the very mode of the judgment on sin, paradoxically, guaranteed their deliverance. In the same way the Christian passes through a judgment on sin, secure in Christ. As the waters of the flood pounded the ark, but could not harm those in it, so the judgment of God fell upon the Lord Jesus Christ, who died, the Just in place of, and so shielding, the unjust. Being thus brought 'to God', the Christian now lives in the sphere where the risen Christ reigns. The flood was the type; baptism is the antitype. Here is the Christian's passing into the new order, but not, as Peter warns, by baptism as such, which is powerless to cleanse the filth of the flesh. The power resides in the death and resurrection of Christ, appropriated by a personal appeal to God. Baptism therefore represents to us the establishing of the new covenant and our personal entering into the benefits of it.

b. The parallel with the *Abrahamic* covenant centres on circumcision (*q.v.*). There are two lines of New Testament teaching. First, the spiritual significance of circumcision is an abiding human need. Paul (Col. ii. 13) equates deadness in trespasses with uncircumcision, *i.e.* utter lack of acquaintance with the renewing work of God. The implication is that, if a man knew the reality of which circumcision is the sign, he would know a divine 'quickening', just as Abram was quickened into new life, and became the new man, Abraham (Gn. xvii). Consequently, Paul can say of Christians, who know the quickening work of God in Christ by the Holy Spirit, that they are 'the circumcision'—the reality has been fulfilled in them. Secondly, what circumcision was in the covenant of Abraham, baptism is to the Christian. This is hinted in the use of the word 'seal'. In Rom. iv. 11 circumcision is called a seal, and in 2 Cor. i. 21, 22, and Eph. i. 13, the same word probably refers to baptism, an interpretation based on the use of the word 'anointed' in 2 Cor. i. 21 (*cf.* Acts x. 38, referring to the baptism of Jesus), and on the order of words 'heard . . . believed . . . sealed' in Eph. i. 13 (*cf.* Acts xviii. 8: 'hearing believed, and were baptized'). The relationship between circumcision and baptism is, however, made explicit in Col. ii. 11, 12. Christians enjoy the reality which circumcision figured. This reality is called 'the circumcision of Christ'; it is spiritual, 'not made with hands'; of total effect, dealing with 'the body of the flesh'; and it took place through baptism, whereby they were brought into vital contact with the death and resurrection of Christ, personally appropriated 'through faith in the working of God'. Thus, once again, baptism stands at the entrance to the covenant, and is so taught as to display the unity of God's covenant dealings.

c. The parallel with the *Mosaic* covenant occurs in 1 Cor. x. Paul's underlying assumption is that the old covenant possessed sacraments parallel to those of the new. The Lord's Supper was prefigured in the drinking from the Rock (verse 4), and baptism in the cloud and the sea. Peter displayed baptism as the Christian's escape from judgment and transition into the kingdom of God; Paul, by linking it with circumcision, showed baptism as the entrance upon enjoyment of the powers of the new age; and now he issues a profound warning against resting on the outward sign. There must be a life of obedience. The Israelite baptism symbolized separation: the passage through the sea separated them from the Egyptians; the cloud separated them to God. But neither of these separations was displayed in their subsequent life, for they displeased God by disobedience and worldliness. This being so, the outward signs could not save them, and they perished in the wilderness. This, says Paul, is for our admonition. No matter how wonderful the truths of baptism, or how the New Testament associates sign and thing signified as though inevitably conjoined, there must be no leaning on the sign as such. It points back to the mighty acts of our saving God, and forward to a life of obedient faith. It is only in connection with the flood that the New Testament specifies the relation of type to antitype (1 Pet. iii. 21), but the treatment of the two other topics surely warrants the same expression. In the one covenant of God, now expressed finally, baptism fulfils all that was expressed by the earlier initiatory ministrations.

II. THE BLESSINGS ASSOCIATED WITH BAPTISM

John the Baptist called people to repent, promising remission of sins, and sealing the promise in his 'baptism of repentance unto the remission of sins' (Mt. iii. 2, 6; Mk. i. 4). He pointed forward to One who would baptize with the Holy Ghost, the token of whose advent was the visible descent of the Spirit (Jn. i. 30–34). At the baptism of the Lord Jesus water-baptism and Spirit-baptism are united, and therein is the pattern of New Testament baptismal blessings. The Holy Spirit is linked with baptism in Jn. iii. 5; Acts ii. 38, ix. 17, 18, x. 47; 1 Cor. xii. 13; 2 Cor. i. 22; Eph. i. 13; Tit. iii. 5. The Spirit is present at baptism, and it is He who accomplishes the spiritual operations of which the water is the sign and seal (*e.g.* 1 Cor. xii. 13; Tit. iii. 5); equally He is the gift promised (*e.g.* Acts ii. 38). The other leading idea in our Lord's baptism is that of Sonship. Following this, not only sonship itself (Gal. iii. 26, 27), but all the spiritual blessings necessary to sonship are associated with baptism: remission of sins (Acts ii. 38; Tit. iii. 5; Heb. x. 22); new birth and entrance to the kingdom (Jn. iii. 3, 5; Tit. iii. 5); designation for union with God, participation in the work of Christ, and incorporation into His body (Mt. xxviii. 19; Acts viii. 16, xix. 5; Rom. vi. 1–11; 1 Cor. xii. 13; Gal. iii. 27).

But these are all the blessings of the covenant, the fruits of the death and resurrection of the Lord Jesus, two events which constantly bracket

New Testament references to baptism. On the day of His baptism, He was publicly declared to be the covenant-maker: the words 'This is my beloved Son, in whom I am well-pleased' point back to the foretold King and Servant (Ps. ii. 7; Is. xlii. 1), two figures associated in the promised covenant (Is. lv. 3). The gift of the Spirit additionally recalls the covenant-maker of Is. lix. 21. When the Lord had established the covenant, He sealed the benefits to His followers by baptism.

But the blessings are not to be derived from baptism as such, but from the Lord. Consequently, we find that while the blessings are apparently conjoined to the rite, they are none the less enjoyed only through the activity of obedient faith following the rite. This is manifest in Rom. vi. 1–11. The topic is the obligation of the life of practical holiness. The apostle first says that baptism has effected a union with Christ in His death and resurrection, so that, for the Christian, there has taken place a death to sin, and a new life to righteousness (verse 4). He then tells how this death and life are to be enjoyed experimentally: by a daily reckoning of oneself dead and alive—*i.e.* by the activity of obedient and costly faith (verse 11). The blessings are not automatically operative in the Christian because of baptism. Baptism is rather the public testimony of God that these blessings have been secured for the believer. Baptism therefore points back to the work of God, and forward to the life of faith.

III. THE CANDIDATES FOR BAPTISM

All the baptized do not possess the thing signified as well as the sign (Acts viii. 21–23; *cf.* Jn. xiii. 10, 11, xv. 1–6). To whom, then, may baptism be administered? Clearly, not all candidates for baptism in New Testament times were publicly authenticated by God as was Cornelius (Acts x. 47), and the case of Simon (Acts viii. 13 ff.) shows the principle upon which the Church normally acted. God does not generally guide the Church by revelations of His secret counsels, but has committed the administration of the covenant rite to fallible human judgment. Man cannot read the heart of man, and must not presume to judge it. Baptism was administered to new converts who could give an intelligent profession of faith in the Lord Jesus Christ. The Lord Himself commanded this in His missionary charge (Mk. xvi. 16 if this evidence can be admitted; and *cf.* Mt. xxviii. 19).

In this practice, some discern an exclusive rule: baptism must be administered only to those who can give a personal testimony, whatever their antecedents. Others urge that, while all accounts of baptisms in the New Testament relate to adult believers, in no case has this adult grown up within the visible Church; all are converts from without. The attitude of the Church towards those born within its bounds must be decided on the basis of general scriptural principles relative to believers' families. In this matter, it is asserted, the Baptist and the Paedo-baptist are on an equal footing, as touching New Testament evidence. Each must put aside the records of individual baptisms as not covering the case in mind, and go rather to the sacramental and covenantal principles involved. The Paedo-baptist believes that the covenant signs, but not the covenant administration, have changed, and that baptism is for the children of the covenant exactly as circumcision was. He sees this position confirmed by the attitude of Christ (Mk. x. 13 ff.), the words of Peter (Acts ii. 39) and Paul (1 Cor. vii. 14). The Baptist baptizes believers on the ground of their testimony; the Paedo-baptist baptizes believers and the infants of believers on the ground (as he holds) of separate commands of God covering these two cases.

IV. THE MODE OF BAPTISM

On this matter also there is difference of opinion. On the one side, total immersion is held to be the order: it accords with the etymology of the verb *baptizō*; it suits New Testament practice (*e.g.* Acts viii. 38, 39); and it expresses the reality of burial with Christ (Rom. vi. 4). On the other side it is contended that, whatever its etymology, *baptizō*, as it is used in the New Testament, does not demand immersion, *e.g.* the 'baptism' of the Spirit is also described as a 'pouring out' (Acts ii. 33; *cf.* Is. xxxii. 15; Ezk. xxxvi. 25, 26); that examples such as Acts viii. 38, 39, pressed to mean immersion, would involve also the immersion of the baptizer; and that to insist on the symbolism of burial is to ignore the many other aspects of union with Christ which baptism proclaims—*e.g.* 'planted together' (Rom. vi. 5), or 'putting on' Christ (Gal. iii. 27).

BIBLIOGRAPHY. J. Calvin, *Institutes*, IV, 14–16; C. Hodge, *Systematic Theology*, III, pp. 526 ff.; O. Cullmann, *Baptism in the New Testament*, 1950; J. Warns, *Baptism*, 1957; A. Gilmore, *Christian Baptism*, 1959; G. W. H. Lampe, *The Seal of the Spirit*, 1951; J. Murray, *Christian Baptism*, 1952; G. W. Bromiley, *The Baptism of Infants*, 1955; P. Marcel, *The Biblical Doctrine of Infant Baptism*, 1953; R. E. O. White, *The Biblical Doctrine of Initiation*, 1960. J.A.M.

BARABBAS. A bandit (Jn. xviii. 40), arrested for homicidal political terrorism (Mk. xv. 7; Lk. xxiii. 18 f.). Mark's language could indicate a well-known incident, and the epithet 'notable' (Mt. xxvii. 16) some reputation as a species of hero. The priests, possibly taking up an initial demand from his supporters (*cf.* Mk. xv. 8), engineered a movement for his release to counter Pilate's intended offer of that of Jesus (Mt. xxvii. 20; Mk. xv. 11)—and Barabbas became an exemplification of the effects of substitutionary atonement.

The name is a patronymic ('son of Abba'). It occurs as 'Jesus Barabbas' (*cf.* 'Simon Barjonah') in some authorities at Mt. xxvii. 16 f., and Origen *in loc.* notes this reading as ancient. It adds pungency to Pilate's offer—'Jesus Barabbas or Jesus Christ?', but this tradition of Barabbas's name keeps dubious company in Syrian sources, and must remain uncertain. There is no textual warrant for introducing it, with Deissmann, into Mk. xv. 7.

BIBLIOGRAPHY. Deissmann in G. K. A. Bell and A. Deissmann, *Mysterium Christi*, pp. 12 ff. (for the text: *per contra*, *cf.* M. J. Lagrange, *S. Matthieu*, pp. 520 f.); H. A. Rigg, *JBL*, LXIV, 1945, pp. 417 ff. (a romance with footnotes); C. E. B. Cranfield, *St. Mark*, pp. 449 ff. (a sensitive reading of the incident). A.F.W.

BARACHIAH. See ZECHARIAH.

BARAK (*bārāq*, 'lightning'; *cf.* Carthaginian *Barca*). In Jdg. iv. 6 ff. the son of Abinoam, from Kedesh-naphtali, summoned by the prophetess Deborah to muster the tribes of Israel and lead them to battle against Sisera, commander-in-chief of the confederate Canaanite forces. He consented to act on condition that Deborah accompanied him, for which reason he was told that not he, but a woman, would have the honour of despatching Sisera. The details of his victory, when a sudden downpour flooded the river Kishon and immobilized Sisera's chariotry, are graphically depicted in the Song of Deborah (Jdg. v. 19–22). In Heb. xi. 32 Barak is listed among the 'elders' whose faith is attested in the sacred record. In 1 Sa. xii. 11 'Bedan' should perhaps be emended to 'Barak', following LXX and Syr. (so RSV). F.F.B.

BARBARIAN. To the Greeks, all non-Greek-speaking peoples were regarded as barbarians. The word originally meant nothing offensive, nor did it imply a lack of refinement. Luke, the Greek-speaking writer of the Acts, praises the 'barbarous people' of Melita for showing kindness to Paul (Acts xxviii. 2–4). Here he simply means 'foreigners' or 'natives'. They were probably of Phoenician origin. The word is used also of anyone speaking in a language not familiar to the listener. In 1 Cor. xiv. 11 it refers to speaking in unfamiliar, or unintelligible, tongues. Greeks and barbarians in Rom. i. 14 is a periphrasis for 'all peoples', 'all the world'. D.O.S.

BAR-JESUS ('son of Joshua' or 'son of Ishvah'). In Acts xiii. 6 ff. a magician and false prophet, attached to the court of Sergius Paulus, proconsul of Cyprus. He is given the alternative name Elymas in verse 8, possibly from a Semitic root meaning 'sage', 'wise man'. In the Western Text his names appear as Bariesouan and Hetoimas. He tried to dissuade Sergius Paulus from paying attention to Paul and Barnabas, but came off worse in an encounter with Paul. His temporary blinding may have been intended to have the same salutary effect as Paul's similar experience on the Damascus road. F.F.B.

BARLEY. An edible grain of the *Graminae* family, genus *Hordeum*. The cultivated varieties were possibly developed from the wild species *Hordeum spontaneum*, which still grows in Palestine. Barley formed the major part of the staple food in Palestine (Dt. viii. 8), particularly of the poorer classes (Ru. ii. 17; Ezk. iv. 9; Jn. vi. 9). It was used as fodder for horses and cattle (1 Ki. iv. 28). In Jdg. vii. 13 it apparently symbolizes a reformed Israel. Barley meal as a jealousy offering (Nu. v. 15) seems to indicate that basic integrity had been disrupted. D.C.

BARN. The AV rendering of four Heb. words, each of them used only once. They are: 1. *gōren*, 'an open threshing-floor' (Jb. xxxix. 12). RV renders 'threshing-floor' (see AGRICULTURE). 2. *m^e^gûrâ*, 'a granary' (Hg. ii. 19). 3. *'āṣām*, 'a storehouse' (Pr. iii. 10). 4. *mamm^e^gôrâ*, 'a repository' (Joel i. 17). We know little about these storing-places. Often a dry cistern in the ground was used, covered with a thick layer of earth. Grain could keep for years under such conditions. See also AGRICULTURE.

In the New Testament, Gk. *apothēkē*, 'a place for putting away', is used literally (Mt. vi. 26; Lk. xii. 18, 24), and metaphorically to signify heaven (Mt. xiii. 30). J.D.D.

BARNABAS. The cognomen of Joseph, a foremost early missionary. Luke (Acts iv. 36) interprets 'son of *paraklēsis*', 'one who consoles, or exhorts' (*cf.* 'son of peace' in Lk. x. 6). *Nabas* may reflect Aramaic *n^e^waḥah*, 'pacification', 'consolation' (the abnormal Greek transcription being eased by the contemporary soft pronunciation of *b*), or some derivative of the root *nb'*, 'to prophesy'. Strictly, this would be 'son of a prophet' or 'of prophecy', but exhortation was supremely a prophetic function (Acts xv. 32; 1 Cor. xiv. 3), and Luke is concerned, not to provide a scientific etymology, but to indicate the man's character. We find him engaged in *paraklēsis* in Acts xi. 23. Deissmann equates the name with *Barnebous* (Aramaic *Barn^e^bō*, 'son of Nebo') found in Syrian inscriptions; but Luke states that the apostles gave it, and they would hardly confer a name redolent of a pagan deity.

He came from a Jewish-Cypriot priestly family, but the Jerusalemite John Mark was his cousin (Col. iv. 10), and he himself an early member of the Jerusalem church, selling his property (in Cyprus?) for the common good (Acts iv. 36 ff.). Clement of Alexandria calls him one of the Seventy (*Hypot.* vii; *Stromateis* ii. 20. 116). The Western Text of Acts i. 23 confounds him with Joseph-Barsabas in the apostolic election; but later Luke (Acts xiv. 4, 14) and Paul (1 Cor. ix. 6, in context) regard him as an apostle (see APOSTLE).

'A good man,' says Luke, 'full of the Holy Spirit and of faith' (Acts xi. 24), and on at least four occasions his warm-heartedness and spiritual insight, and the apparently universal respect for him, had momentous results.

a. When the converted Saul arrived in Jerusalem only to discover that the Christians thought him a spy, it was Barnabas who introduced him to the 'pillar' apostles and convinced them of his conversion and sincerity (Acts ix. 27; *cf.* Gal. i. 18).

b. It was Barnabas who represented the apostles at Antioch when, for the first time, Gentiles had been evangelized in significant numbers, and where fellow-Cypriots had been prominent (Acts xi. 19 ff.). He saw the movement as a work of God—and as a fitting sphere for the forgotten Saul, whom he brought to share his labours. On their visiting Jerusalem with famine-relief, their call to Gentile missionary work was recognized (Gal. ii. 9. See also CHRONOLOGY OF THE NEW TESTAMENT). But Barnabas was not the man to withstand Peter to his face when he succumbed to Judaizing pressure: 'even Barnabas' temporarily broke table-fellowship with the Antiochene Gentiles (Gal. ii. 13).

c. Barnabas' third great contribution, however, showed him committed to full acceptance of Gentiles on faith in Christ (*cf.* Acts xiii. 46). The journey with Paul (Acts xiii, xiv), beginning in his own Cyprus, resulted in a chain of predominantly Gentile churches far into Asia Minor and a surging Jewish opposition.

For the Church and for Barnabas it was a milestone. Hitherto he had been leader, Paul his protégé. Luke's consistent order up to the departure from Cyprus is 'Barnabas and Saul'. Thereafter he usually says, 'Paul and Barnabas'. (Acts xiii. 43, 46, 50, xv. 2, twice, 22, 35. The order in xiv. 14 is probably due to the order of the deities.) This doubtless reflects the progress of events.

d. But Barnabas had another crucial task. Back at Antioch, the circumcision question became so acute that he and Paul were appointed to bring the matter before the Jerusalem Council. Their policy was triumphantly vindicated (Acts xv. 1–29). Significantly, Barnabas stands before Paul both in the account of the proceedings (verse 12) and in the Council's letter (verse 25, contrast 22); probably the words of the original apostolic representative in Antioch carried greater weight with many in the Council. Barnabas insisted on including Mark, who had previously deserted them, on a proposed second journey. Paul refused, and the itinerary was divided, Barnabas taking Cyprus (Acts xv. 36–40). Paul's later testimonies to Mark (*e.g.* 2 Tim. iv. 11) may mean that the latter greatly profited from working under his cousin. The close partnership was broken, but not the friendship. 'Whenever Paul mentions Barnabas, his words imply sympathy and respect' (Lightfoot on Gal. ii. 13). In principles and practice they were identical, and we shall never know how much Paul owed to Barnabas. When 1 Corinthians was written, Barnabas was still alive, and, like Paul and unlike most of their colleagues, supporting himself without drawing on the churches (1 Cor. ix. 6). After this, we hear only insubstantial traditions associating him with Rome and Alexandria.

His name was early attached to an anonymous letter of Alexandrian provenance, but there is nothing else to connect it with him (see PATRISTIC LITERATURE). The Epistle to the Hebrews has often been ascribed to him, at least from Tertullian's time (*cf.* Zahn, *INT*, II, pp. 301 ff.), and 1 Peter by A. C. McGiffert (*Christianity in the Apostolic Age*, 1897, pp. 593 ff.). There is a late Cypriot martyrology (see James, *ANT*, p. 470). The *Gospel of Barnabas* (ed. L. Ragg, 1907) is a medieval work in Muslim interest.

BIBLIOGRAPHY. A. Klostermann, *Probleme im Aposteltexte neu erörtert*, 1883; Deissmann, *BS*, pp. 307 ff.; H. J. Cadbury in *Amicitiae Corolla* (Rendel Harris Festschrift), 1933, pp. 45 ff.; *BC*, IV; Bruce, *Acts*, *passim*.

A.F.W.

BARREL. See VESSELS.

BARRENNESS. To be a wife without bearing children has always been regarded in the East, not only as a matter of regret, but as a reproach which could lead to divorce. This is the cause of Sarah's despairing laughter (Gn. xviii. 12), Hannah's silent prayer (1 Sa. i. 10 ff.), Rachel's passionate alternative of children or death (Gn. xxx. 1), and Elisabeth's cry that God had taken away her reproach (Lk. i. 25). The awfulness of the coming judgment on Jerusalem is emphasized by the incredible statement, 'Blessed are the barren . . .' (Lk. xxiii. 29). It was believed that the gift of children or the withholding of them indicated God's blessing or curse (Ex. xxiii. 26; Dt. vii. 14), as also did the barrenness or fruitfulness of the land (Ps. cvii. 33, 34). J.W.M.

BARTHOLOMEW (*bartholomaios*, 'son of Tolmai'). One of the Twelve; his name appears only in the lists of apostles (Mt. x. 3; Mk. iii. 18; Lk. vi. 14; Acts i. 13). From the 9th century many have identified him with Nathanael (*q.v.*), but the evidence for this is not conclusive.

BARTIMAEUS. A blind beggar who was healed by Jesus (Mk. x. 46–52). The name means 'Son of Timaeus' and may have been recorded by Mark because he was a well-known figure in the early Church. The incident took place on Jesus' last journey to Jerusalem as He left Jericho, and is found in the other Synoptic Gospels, though with a number of differences. In Mt. xx. 29–34 there are two blind men, while in Lk. xviii. 35–43 the healing takes place as Jesus is approaching Jericho. The story has been variously reconstructed, and it may be that Matthew and Mark refer to Old Jericho and Luke to New Jericho, which was to the south of it. The incident is remarkable for the persistence of Bartimaeus' faith in Jesus as the Messiah. R.E.N.

BARUCH (*bārûḵ*, 'blessed'). **1.** The son of Neriah (Je. xxxvi. 4), and brother of Seraiah, quartermaster to king Zedekiah (Je. li. 59). He was a faithful attendant on the prophet Jeremiah (xxxvi. 10), wrote his master's prophecies (xxxvi. 4, 32) and read them to the people (verses 14, 15). He acted as witness to the purchase by the imprisoned prophet of his family estate at Anathoth (Je. xxxii). Following the sack of Jerusalem, he is said to have resided with Jeremiah at Masphatha (Mizpah, Josephus, *Ant.* x. 9. 1) but after the murder of Gedaliah was arrested for influencing Jeremiah's departure (xliii. 3). He was taken with Jeremiah to Egypt (xliii. 6), where according to one tradition he and Jeremiah died (Jerome on Is. xxx. 6). Josephus, however, implies that they were both carried captive to Babylon after Nebuchadrezzar had invaded Egypt in 583 BC (*Ant.* x. 9. 7). Josephus also says that Baruch was of noble family (as Baruch i. 1). His association with Jeremiah resulted in his name being given to a number of apocryphal books, notably *The Apocalypse of Baruch*, a work probably of Hebrew or Aramaic origin of which Gk. (2nd century AD) and Syr. versions survive; *The Book of Baruch*, a deutero-canonical book found in LXX between Jeremiah and Lamentations, of which various VSS (Lat. and Gnostic) are known; and *The Rest of the Works of Baruch*. Jewish tradition (*Mid. Rabba* on Ct. v. 5) speaks of Baruch as Ezra's teacher.

2. A priest, son of Zabbai, who assisted Nehemiah in rebuilding work (Ne. iii. 20) and as witness to a covenant (x. 6).

3. Son of Col-hozeh, a Judaean, father of Maaseiah (Ne. xi. 5). D.J.W.

BARZILLAI ('Man of iron'). **1.** 'The Gileadite of Rogelim' (2 Sa. xvii. 27, *etc.*), a faithful follower of David. **2.** A relation of the above by marriage who took the family name (Ezr. ii. 61), and is called 'Jaddus' in 1 Esdras v. 38. **3.** 'The Meholathite', whose son Adriel married Saul's daughter Merab (1 Sa. xviii. 19; 2 Sa. xxi. 8, LXX and two Heb. MSS), or Michal (2 Sa. xxi. 8, *MT*). G.W.G.

BASHAN. A fertile region east of Jordan lying to the north of Gilead, from which it was divided by the river Yarmuk. The name, nearly always written with the article (*habbāšān*), had varying connotations. In the wide sense it was counted as extending northwards to Mt. Hermon and eastwards to Salecah (*q.v.*); and in the narrower sense it comprised roughly the area called today en-Nuqra. It included the cities of Ashtaroth, Golan, and Edrei (*q.v.*), and the regions of Argob and Havvoth-jair (*qq.v.*). At the time of the conquest Bashan was under the rule of Og, who had his capital at Ashtaroth. He was defeated by the Israelites at Edrei (Dt. i. 4, iii. 1–3) and the territory fell to the lot of Manasseh. It formed part of the dominions of David and Solomon, falling within the sixth administrative district of the latter (1 Ki. iv. 13). It was lost during the Syrian wars, but was regained by Jeroboam II (2 Ki. xiv. 25), only to be taken by Tiglath-pileser III (2 Ki. xv. 29), after which it formed part of the successive Assyrian, Babylonian, and Persian empires. Under the Persians it roughly coincided with the district of Qarnaim, and in the Greek period with that of Batanaea.

BIBLIOGRAPHY. G. A. Smith, *The Historical Geography of the Holy Land*, 11th edition, 1904, pp. 542, 548–553, 575 ff.; F. M. Abel, *Géographie de la Palestine*, I, 1933, pp. 274, 275.

T.C.M.

BASHEMATH. Probably from Semitic stem *bsm*, 'fragrant'. **1.** According to Gn. xxvi. 34, Esau married Bashemath, the daughter of Elon, the Hittite. According to Gn. xxxvi. 3, he was married to a certain Bashemath who was the daughter of Ishmael and the sister of Nebaioth. *Cf.* Gn. xxviii. 9, where she is called Mahalath, and Gn. xxxvi. 2, where Elon's daughter is called Adah. It is possible that both Mahalath and Adah were given the nickname Bashemath, 'fragrant', or else it is a scribal error (*cf.* some MSS of the LXX). **2.** Basmath, daughter of Solomon, married Ahimaaz of Naphtali (1 Ki. iv. 15).

BIBLIOGRAPHY. C-F. Jean, *Dictionnaire des Inscriptions Sémitiques de l'Ouest*, 1954.

F.C.F.

BASIN, BASON. See VESSELS.

BASKET. In AV the following Heb. words are translated 'basket'. 1. *dûḏ*, a round basket large enough to hold a human head (2 Ki. x. 7), but normally used for carrying figs, *etc.* (Je. xxiv. 1, 2; Ps. lxxxi. 6). 2. *ṭene'* (loan-word from Egyp. *dnyt*, 'basket'), used for storing produce (Dt. xxvi. 2, 4) parallel to kneading-trough (Dt. xxviii. 5, 17) as an item in the household. 3. *keᵉlûḇ*, which held fruit in Amos' vision (viii. 1) but was originally used for trapping birds, as in Je. v. 27 and the Canaanite letters from Amarna. 4. *sal*, a flat, open basket for carrying bread (unleavened, Ex. xxix. 3, 23, 32; Lv. viii. 2, 26, 31; Nu. vi. 15, 17, 19; Jdg. vi. 19). Pharaoh's baker dreamt he was carrying three full of white bread (Heb. *ḥōrî*, see BREAD) on his head (Gn. xl. 16; *cf.* D. J. Wiseman, *Illustrations from Biblical Archaeology*, 1958, fig. 28). 5. *salsillôṯ* (Je. vi. 9); but these are more probably branches or tendrils (RSV) which are being thoroughly plucked, rather than 'baskets'.

The distinction between the feeding of the four thousand and of the five thousand is emphasized by the Gospel writers' use of Gk. *kophinos* for basket in the former miracle (Mt. xiv. 20, xvi. 9; Mk. vi. 43, viii. 19; Lk. ix. 17; Jn. vi. 13), but Gk. *spyris* in the latter (Mt. xv. 37, xvi. 10; Mk. viii. 8, 20). Both words denote a hamper, *kophinos* appearing elsewhere in a Jewish context, and *spyris*, in which Paul was lowered from the wall of Damascus, being the larger (Acts ix. 25; parallel to Gk. *sarganē*, a plaited container, 2 Cor. xi. 33). A.R.M.

BAT. A reasonable translation of *'ᵃṭallēp̄* (Lv. xi. 19; Dt. xiv. 18), especially if the former is considered linked to Lv. xi. 20, which refers to fowls that creep, going on all fours. This is how a bat progresses on a flat surface.

Bats (*Chiroptera*) are regarded with considerable abhorrence. Many species are found abundantly throughout the Middle East, some of which roost communally in caves, either hanging from the roof or clustering in crevices. They would thus be easily accessible as food, and the insectivorous bats would be logically included in the list of meats forbidden to the Hebrews. G.C.

BATH. See WEIGHTS AND MEASURES.

BATH, BATHING (Heb. *rāḥaṣ*, 'to wash', 'to rub'; Gk. *louō, niptō* [distinguished in Jn. xiii. 10]). The heat and dust of Eastern lands make constant washing necessary for both health and refreshment. It is likely that the bathing in the Nile of Pharaoh's daughter (Ex. ii. 5) was typical of a nation whose priests, according to Herodotus (ii. 27), bathed four times a day. A host was expected to provide newly arrived travellers with water for their feet (Gn. xviii. 4, xix. 2; 1 Sa. xxv. 41; *cf.* Jn. xiii. 1–10; see also FOOT). Bathsheba was bathing when David first saw her (2 Sa. xi. 2); Naomi's words to Ruth (Ru. iii. 3) suggest that it was customary to bathe before calling on one of superior rank; and there is an obscure allusion to bathing in 1 Ki. xxii. 38.

Nevertheless, bathing as we know it is rarely mentioned in the Bible. Bodily cleanliness was, however, greatly furthered by the injunctions of the law, and most biblical allusions to washing are bound up with ceremonial occasions, for which aspect see CLEAN AND UNCLEAN. Reference is made to bathing for curative purposes (2 Ki. v. 14; *cf.* Jn. ix. 11), though here faith is a necessary part.

Josephus mentions hot springs at Tiberias, Gadara, *etc.*, about the beginning of the Christian era (*Ant.* xvii. 6. 5, xviii. 2. 3), and also public baths (xix. 7. 5), but there is no definite proof of the existence of the latter in Palestine before the Graeco-Roman age. J.D.D.

BATHSHEBA (called, in 1 Ch. iii. 5, 'Bathshua, daughter of Ammiel'). She was the daughter of Eliam (2 Sa. xi. 3), and, if he is the 'mighty man' of 2 Sa. xxiii. 34, granddaughter of Ahithophel. David took her while her husband, Uriah the Hittite, was in command of the army which was besieging Rabbah, the Ammonite capital. This led to Uriah's murder, Bathsheba's entry into the royal harem, and the rebuke by Nathan the prophet (2 Sa. xii). In David's old age Bathsheba allied with Nathan to secure Solomon's accession, and became queen-mother. She petitioned Solomon, on Adonijah's behalf, for Abishag, David's concubine (1 Ki. ii. 19–21). This was interpreted as a bid for the throne, and resulted in Adonijah's death. M.G.

BATTERING-RAM. See FORTIFICATION AND SIEGECRAFT (II*a*).

BAY-TREE. See TREES.

BDELLIUM. A precious substance found in the land of Havilah, near Eden (Gn. ii. 12), the colour of which was the same as that of manna (Nu. xi. 7); this identification of colour suggests bdellium to have been a well-known substance to the Hebrews. LXX suggests it to be a precious mineral by its use of the words *anthrax* and *krystallos* respectively in the two texts cited. Vulgate uses *bdellium*, which is the cognate of the Greek *bdellion*, but *bdellion* is not used to render *beḏōlaḥ* in the Old Testament. 'Pearl' has been suggested, but the exact denotation of the word is unknown. R.J.W.

BEANS. 2 Sa. xvii. 28 includes them in the food brought for David and his men. Ezk. iv. 9 refers to them as a substitute for corn meal in famine bread. Ezekiel's bread probably did not break the levitical law against mixing diverse kinds (see *ICC, ad loc.*). The Mishnah uses the same word with national adjective for Egyptian beans, as do the Greek writers with *kyamos*. The genus is determined, the species open to botanical controversy. The modern Arabic word has wide scope, including peanuts and other plants distinguished by adjective. R.A.S.

BEAR. The Syrian form of the widely-distributed brown bear is still found in parts of the Middle East (including Lebanon), though no longer within the actual area of Palestine, and it is clearly the *dōḇ* (Arab. *duḇ*). It is paler than the typical race and is usually referred to as the subspecies *Ursus arctos syriacus.* Like most bears other than the polar bear, it is omnivorous or vegetarian for most of the year, and its attacks on livestock, especially on sheep, would be most likely during winter when no wild fruits are available.

The term 'bear robbed of her whelps' (2 Sa. xvii. 8; Pr. xvii. 12) was presumably proverbial, as also the expression in Am. v. 19, 'as if a man did flee from a lion and a bear met him'. The bear was more feared than the lion because its strength was greater and its actions less predictable. See fig. 39. G.C.

BEARD. 1. *zāqān.* Israelites and their neighbours generally wore full round beards which they tended scrupulously. *Cf.* figs. 77, 100. The beard was a mark of vitality and of manly beauty (Ps. cxxxiii. 2; *cf.* 2 Sa. xix. 24); to shave or cover it was a sign of grief or mourning (Is. xv. 2; Je. xlviii. 37, *etc.*; *cf.* Lv. xix. 27, xxi. 5, enacted probably against idolatrous practices), or of leprosy (Lv. xiv. 9). To mutilate another's beard was to dishonour him (2 Sa. x. 4; Is. l. 6). Jeremiah criticizes those who shave their temples (Je. ix. 26, *etc.*). See also HAIR; BURIAL AND MOURNING.

2. The AV translation of Heb. *śāpām* (2 Sa. xix. 24), denoting the moustache. J.D.D.

BEAST. A word largely replaced in modern English usage by 'animal', in which sense it was widely used in the AV to translate a variety of terms. 1. *behēmâ*, 'animal, cattle', one of the most common Heb. words for 'animal' (*e.g.* Gn. vi. 7). See BEHEMOTH. 2. *ḥay*, 'alive, living', likewise used very commonly in the Old Testament for 'animal' (*e.g.* Gn. i. 24). Translated 'wild beasts' in 1 Sa. xvii. 46. 3. *be'îr*, 'beast, cattle', used of cattle in general (Ex. xxii. 5; Nu. xx. 8, 11), but in Gn. xlv. 17 of beasts of burden, perhaps asses. 4. *nep̄eš*, 'living being', 'life', *etc.*, used in Lv. xxiv. 18, first in the combination *nep̄eš-behēmâ*, but twice alone, *nep̄eš taḥaṯ nep̄eš*. The AV gives 'beast for beast' for the latter phrase, but the RV and RSV prefer 'life for life'. 5. *kirkārâ*, 'dromedary' (*q.v.*) is translated 'swift beasts' in the AV and RV of Is. lxvi. 20, but the RSV and RVmg give 'dromedaries'. 6. In the EVV of Pr. ix. 2, the phrase *ṭāḇeḥâ ṭiḇḥâ*, literally 'she has slaughtered her slaughtering', is rendered 'she has killed her beasts'.

7. *zōon*, 'living creature', used in the New Testament of animals in general (*e.g.* Heb. xiii. 11), and in particular of the four heavenly living creatures of the Apocalypse (Rev. iv. 6 ff.). Used in the LXX chiefly to translate *ḥay* and its cognates. 8. *thērion*, used, like (7), chiefly to translate *ḥay* and its cognates in the LXX, but having in the New Testament more emphasis on the brutal and bestial element; see BEAST (APOCALYPSE). Rendered in the AV of Mk. i. 13 and Acts x. 12 by 'wild beasts'. 9. *ktēnos*, 'beast, beast of burden', occurs only four times in the New Testament: Lk. x. 34; Acts xxiii. 24; 1 Cor. xv. 39; Rev. xviii. 13. Used in the LXX chiefly to translate *behēmâ*. T.C.M.

BEAST (APOCALYPSE). 1. The 'beast that cometh up out of the abyss' (Rev. xi. 7, RV) is the apocalyptic symbol of the last anti-Christian power (Rev. xiii. 1 ff., xvii. 3 ff., xix. 19 f.), portrayed as a composite picture of the four beasts of Dn. vii. 3 ff. His ten horns are borrowed from Daniel's fourth beast; his seven heads mark his derivation of authority from the dragon of Rev. xii. 3, and go back ultimately to Leviathan (*cf.* Ps. lxxiv. 14; Is. xxvii. 1); John reinterprets them once of the seven hills of Rome (Rev. xvii. 9), otherwise of seven Roman emperors. The beast is usually the persecuting empire, occasionally the final emperor, a reincarnation of one of the first seven, probably Nero. He claims divine honours, wages war on the saints, and is destroyed by Christ at His parousia (*cf.* 2 Thes. ii. 8).

2. The 'beast from the earth' (Rev. xiii. 11 ff.), also called the 'false prophet' (xvi. 13, xix. 20, xx. 10), is public relations officer of the former beast, persuades men to worship him, and ultimately shares his fate. The imperial cult in the province of Asia (see ASIARCH) evidently suggested some of his features to John. F.F.B.

BEATITUDES. See SERMON ON THE MOUNT.

BEAUTIFUL GATE. See TEMPLE.

BED. See HOUSE (v).

BEE. The name bee is correctly applied today to several families of the insect order *Hymenoptera*, and it includes solitary and bumble bees, as well as honey bees. The Hebrew word *deḇôrâ* probably covered an even larger range of insects of this order, but it is clear from their contexts that three out of four Old Testament occurrences of this word refer to the honey bee (see Jdg. xiv. 8; Ps. cxviii. 12; Dt. i. 44). The fourth passage using this word is a figurative one—Is. vii. 18, 'The Lord shall hiss . . . for the bee that is in the land of Assyria'. The verb *šāraq* ('hiss', AV) is rendered 'whistle' in RSV, and this is to be preferred. A tradition that the natives of Palestine called their bees by making a whistling or hissing sound suggests that *deḇôrâ* is the honey bee.

The very numerous references to honey (*q.v.*) in Old Testament and New Testament imply that it was common and widespread. It is likely that much of the honey was produced by wild bees nesting in hollow trees or in rocky holes, but from very early times bees have been encouraged to occupy simple hives of basket or earthenware. G.C.

BEELZEBUB. See BAAL-ZEBUB.

BEER (*be'ēr*, lit. 'a well', 'cistern', usually man-made). **1.** Nu. xxi. 16. A point on the itinerary of the wandering Hebrews, reached soon after leaving Arnon. This verse records an otherwise unknown story of the provision of water; an important event, for verse 18b suggests that Beer was in a desert place. The site is unknown. **2.** Jdg. ix. 21. The place to which Jotham fled after having denounced the *coup d'état* of his brother Abimelech. The site is unknown. R.J.W.

BEER-LAHAI-ROI. The name itself and certain elements of Gn. xvi. 13, 14, where it first appears, defy certain translation. As it stands, the name may mean 'The well of the living one who sees me' or 'The well of "He who sees me lives"'. However, it may be that the original place-name has suffered a degree of distortion in transmission, and the original is beyond our discovery. This is not the only proper name in the Old Testament to have suffered in this way. The exact site is not known, but Gn. xvi. 7, 14 places it towards the Egyptian border, to which country Hagar, the Egyptian maid, was fleeing from the wrath of Sarai her mistress. God appeared to Hagar here and announced the birth of Ishmael. Isaac passed through Beer-lahai-roi when waiting for Eliezer to bring him a wife from Mesopotamia (Gn. xxiv. 62), and settled there after the death of Abraham. R.J.W.

BEERSHEBA. The name given to an important well, and also to the local town and district (Gn. xxi. 14; Jos. xix. 2). The present town, 48 miles south-west of Jerusalem and approximately midway between the Mediterranean and the southern part of the Dead Sea, lies 2 miles west of what was probably the original site (now Tel-es-Seba) of the ancient town. There are several wells in the vicinity, the largest of which is 12¼ feet in diameter. The digging of this well involved cutting through 16 feet of solid rock. On one of the stones of the masonry lining the shaft, Conder found a date indicating that repairs had been carried out as late as the 12th century AD. At the time of his visit in 1874, it was 38 feet to the surface of the water.

The meaning of the name is given in Gn. xxi. 31, 'The well of the seven' (*viz.* lambs). The alternative interpretation, 'the well of the oath', arises through a misunderstanding of the use of the Hebrew word for 'therefore', which can refer only to an antecedent statement (Gn. xi. 9 is not really an exception), and a mistranslation of the Hebrew particle *kî* by 'because', whereas it here introduces an independent temporal clause and should be rendered 'when', or even 'then'. The antecedent statement tells *why* it was done; this clause, *when* it was done. (For a similar use of *kî*, *cf.* Gn. xxiv. 41; *cf.* König, *Heb. Syntax*, 387 h.) The explanation of the alleged second account of the naming of the well by Isaac (Gn. xxvi. 33) is given in verse 18 of chapter xxvi: 'And Isaac dug again the wells which had been dug in the days of Abraham, his father, and which the Philistines had filled in, and he gave to them names, according to the names which his father had given them.' Since the digging of a well was often a major achievement, filial respect alone would insist that the work of a great father would be thus remembered. In verse 33 the actual wording is: 'and he proclaimed it "Shibah".' The use here of the feminine of the numeral, may merely express the numerical group, roughly equivalent to: 'It, of the seven'.

Beersheba has many patriarchal associations. Abraham spent much time there (Gn. xxii. 19). It was probably a part of Palestine without an urban population, since the seasonal nature of the pasturage would not have been conducive to settled conditions. It was from here that he set out to offer up Isaac. Isaac was dwelling here when Jacob set out for Harran (Gn. xxviii. 10). On his way through to Joseph in Egypt, Jacob stopped here to offer sacrifices (Gn. xlvi. 1). In the division of the land it went to the tribe of Simeon (Jos. xix. 2).

In the familiar phrase 'from Dan even unto Beersheba' (Jdg. xx. 1 *et passim*) it denoted the southernmost place of the land. The town owed its importance to its position on the trade-route to Egypt.

The reference to it in Amos (v. 5 and viii. 14) indicates that it had become a centre for undesirable religious activities.

Beersheba and its villages (Heb. 'daughters') were resettled after the captivity (Ne. xi. 27).

The place referred to by Josephus (*BJ* ii. 573 and iii. 39), which Winckler wanted to identify with the Beersheba of the Old Testament, was a village in lower Galilee (Jos., *Life* v. 188).

For an account of the excavations that have been carried out in the neighbourhood of Beersheba, see Jean Perrot, 'Les Fouilles d'Abou Matar près de Beersheba', *Syria*, XXXIV, 1957.

BIBLIOGRAPHY. Zimmerli, *Geschichte u. Tradition von Beer-sheba im A.T.*, 1932. W.J.M.

BEESHTERAH. See ASHTAROTH (3).

BEETLE. See LOCUST.

BEGGAR. See ALMS, ALMSGIVING.

BEHEMOTH. Morphologically the plural of *b^e^hēmâ* (see BEAST (1)), occurring nine times in the Old Testament (Dt. xxxii. 24; Jb. xii. 7, xl. 15; Ps. xlix. 12, 20, l. 10, lxxiii. 22; Je. xii. 4; Hab. ii. 17), and in all but one of these occurrences 'beasts', 'animals', or 'cattle' is apparently the intended meaning. In Jb. xl. 15, however, the reference is so qualified in the following verses as to suggest some specific animal, and it is usual to take the plural here as having intensive force, 'great beast', and referring to the hippopotamus which seems to fit the description best. A derivation has been suggested from a hypothetical Egyptian *p'.iḥ.mw*, 'the ox of the water', but the fact that Egyptian has other words for hippopotamus renders this unlikely. While other theories have been put forward, the hippopotamus identification may be tentatively accepted in the present state of knowledge. The LXX renders the word here by *ktēnos* (see BEAST (9)).

BIBLIOGRAPHY. *BDB*, pp. 96, 97; S. R. Driver and G. B. Gray, *The Book of Job*, *ICC*, 1921, I, pp. 351–358; *KB*, p. 111; for another theory, see G. R. Driver in Z. V. Togan (ed.), *Proceedings of the Twenty Second Congress of Orientalists . . . Istanbul . . . 1951*, II, 1957, p. 113. T.C.M.

BEKAH, BEKA. See WEIGHTS AND MEASURES.

BEL. The name of the principal Babylonian deity whose overthrow was synonymous with the end of Babylon and its domination (Je. l. 2, li. 44). In this connection Bel is named with the god Nabu, who was considered his son (Is. xlvi. 1; see NEBO). Bel (Sumerian *en*, 'lord'; Heb. *Ba'al*) was one of the original Sumerian triad of deities, with Anu and Enki, his name being a title or epithet of the wind and storm god Enlil. When Marduk (see MERODACH) became the chief god of Babylon in the second millennium he was given the additional name of Bel. According to the apocryphal book Bel and the Dragon it was the image of Bel(-Marduk) that Daniel and his companions were asked to worship. D.J.W.

BELIAL. The sense of this word is generally clear from its context; 'son of' or 'man of' Belial clearly means a very wicked person. The word occurs in Ps. xviii. 4, parallel to the word 'death'; hence the RSV translation 'perdition'. In 2 Cor. vi. 15 Paul uses it as a synonym for Satan. The derivation is, however, obscure. The Hebrew text, with the Massoretic vowels, reads *b^e^lîya'al*, apparently from *b^e^lî* and *ya'al* ('without profit'), so meaning 'worthlessness'. Or the second part could conceivably derive from *'ālâ* ('to come up'), giving a sense 'ne'er-do-well'. But T. K. Cheyne links the word with the Babylonian goddess of vegetation, who may also have been goddess of the underworld; thus the word would have come into Hebrew as a synonym for Sheol, initially. C. F. Burney, however, ignores the Massoretic vowels, and reads a diminutive from the root *bāla'*, 'to swallow', translating it as 'engulfing ruin'. D.F.P.

BELL. Two Hebrew words are thus translated. 1. *pa'amôn* ('striking', 'beating'—of a clapper). Small gold bells, alternating with pomegranates of blue, purple, and scarlet stuff, were attached to the hem of the high priest's ephod (Ex. xxviii. 33, 34, xxxix. 25, 26), their ringing thus announcing his going into the sanctuary. Bells for religious purposes are known from Assyria, see B. Meissner, *Babylonien und Assyrien*, I, 1920, p. 268, and photograph, Abb. 142. Bells are also attested for personal adornment in Egypt, from at least the Bubastite period (*c.* 800 BC) to Roman and Coptic times, and were often attached to children to announce their whereabouts. See, with illustrations, Petrie, *Objects of Daily Use*, 1927, pp. 24, 57, 58, plates 18: 33–37 and 50: 292–305; Petrie, *Hyksos and Israelite Cities*, 1906, pp. 17, 18, plates 19A: E and 37A: bottom

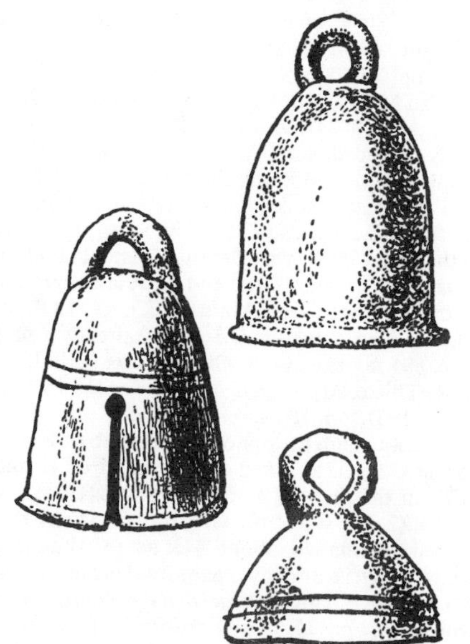

Fig. 34. Assyrian bells: part of horse trappings or ceremonial dress. From Calah (Nimrud), 8th–7th centuries BC.

2. Heb. *meṣillâ* ('tinkling'). These are little bells. In Zc. xiv. 20 they are part of the trappings of horses, prophesied to become 'holy unto the Lord' (and so inscribed). Little bells often appeared among horse-trappings in antiquity (Contenau, *Everyday Life in Babylon and Assyria*, 1954, p. 125); they can be seen at the necks of Assyrian war-horses in Grollenberg, *Shorter Atlas of the Bible*, 1959, p. 113, bottom photograph. K.A.K.

BELLOWS. See ARTS AND CRAFTS.

BELSHAZZAR. The ruler of Babylon who was killed at the time of its capture in 539 BC (Dn. v). Bēl-šar-uṣur ('Bel has protected the king(ship)') is named in Babylonian documents by his father Nabonidus, king of Babylon in 556–539 BC (BM 91125). Other texts give details of Belshazzar's administration and religious interests in Babylon and Sippar up to the fourteenth year of his father's reign. He was probably a grandson of Nebuchadrezzar II and, according to the Nabonidus Chronicle, his father 'entrusted the army and the kingship' to him *c.* 556 BC, while Nabonidus campaigned in central Arabia, where he eventually remained for ten years. Belshazzar ruled in Babylonia itself. It is possible that Daniel dated events by the years of this co-regency (Dn. vii. 1, viii. 1), though the official dating of documents continued to use the regnal years of Nabonidus himself. Since a Harran inscription (*AS*, VIII, 1958, pp. 35–92) gives ten years for the exile of Nabonidus, this would confirm other sources in implying that the 'king' who died in October 539 BC was Belshazzar (Dn. v. 30), whose father was captured on his subsequent return to the capital (Xenophon, *Cyropaedia*, vii. 5. 29–30, does not give names). Belshazzar (Aram. *Bēlša'ṣṣar*) is also called Balthasar (Gk. Baruch i. 11–12; Herodotus, i. 188) or Baltasar (Jos., *Ant.* x. 11. 4).

BIBLIOGRAPHY. R. P. Dougherty, *Nabonidus and Belshazzar*, Yale Oriental Series, XV, 1929. D.J.W.

BELTESHAZZAR (Heb. *bēlṭešа'aṣṣar*; Gk. *Baltasar*). The name given to Daniel in Babylon (Dn. i. 7, ii. 26, v. 12). The Heb. may be a transliteration of the common Babylonian name *Balaṭsu-uṣur* ('Protect his life'), in which the name of the deity invoked (Bēl?) is omitted (*cf.* ABEDNEGO). Such a name would be appropriate in the light of Daniel's later experiences. Those who consider from Dn. iv. 18 that the name of the deity must be contained in the name seek a form like Belit or *Belti-šar-uṣur* ('Belti, protect the king'), but the Heb. transliteration with *ṭ* renders this unlikely. See, however, BELSHAZZAR (*cf.* also SHAREZER). D.J.W.

BENAIAH (*benāyāhû*, *benāyâ*, 'Yahweh has built up'). **1.** Son of Jehoiada from Kabzeel in S Judah (2 Sa. xxiii. 20). Captain of David's foreign bodyguard (2 Sa. viii. 18, xx. 23), he commanded the host for the third month (1 Ch. xxvii. 5, 6). He was renowned among 'the thirty' of David's mighty men (2 Sa. xxiii. 20–23; 1 Ch. xi. 22–25), and probably accompanied David during Absalom's rebellion (2 Sa. xv. 18). He helped to thwart Adonijah and establish Solomon as king (1 Ki. i), and later executed Adonijah, Joab, and Shimei (1 Ki. ii. 25, 29 ff., 46), replacing Joab as commander-in-chief (1 Ki. ii. 35).

2. One of 'the thirty' of David's mighty men from Pirathon in Ephraim (2 Sa. xxiii. 30; 1 Ch. xi. 31), who commanded the host for the eleventh month (1 Ch. xxvii. 14).

Ten other persons bearing this name are known only from the following references: 1 Ch. iv. 36; 1 Ch. xv. 18, 20; 1 Ch. xv. 24, xvi. 6; 2 Ch. xx. 14; 2 Ch. xxxi. 13; Ezr. x. 25; Ezr. x. 30; Ezr. x. 35; Ezr. x. 43; Ezk. xi. 1, 13. J.G.G.N.

BEN-AMMI ('son of my kinship'). The name given to the child born of Lot's incestuous union with his younger daughter (Gn. xix. 38), from whom sprang the children of Ammon (*q.v.*). Moses recognized their kinship, through Lot, with the children of Israel; and so directed that they should not be disturbed in the land which had been 'given them for a possession' (Dt. ii. 19). Nevertheless, 'the children of Lot' in later times became their enemies (2 Ch. xx. 1; Ps. lxxxiii. 6–8). G.T.M.

BENE-BERAK. A town in the territory of Dan (Jos. xix. 45), identified with the modern el-Kheirîyeh (till recently Ibn Ibrâq), about 4 miles east of Jaffa. According to Sennacherib (quoted in L. H. Grollenberg, *Atlas of the Bible*, 1956, p. 89), it was one of the cities besieged and taken by him. J.D.D.

BENEDICTUS. The prophecy of Zacharias (Lk. i. 68–79), named from the first word in the Latin version, is one of six visions (Lk. i. 5–25, 26–38, ii. 1–20) and prophecies (Lk. i. 46–56, ii. 29–35) in the Lucan infancy narrative. It is a recurrent pattern in Hebrew prophecy to reflect upon or elaborate former revelations (*cf.* Ps. cv; Mi. iv. 4; Zc. iii. 10). In the New Testament the Revelation of John is a mosaic of Old Testament language and concepts. Likewise the Benedictus alludes to a number of passages in the Psalms and Isaiah.

The first division of the passage (Lk. i. 68–75), in parallelisms characteristic of Jewish poetry, extols God for His messianic deliverance and rejoices in its results. The second section (Lk. i. 76–79) describes the place which John will have in this mighty act of God. In the Benedictus Messiah's work is particularly a spiritual deliverance. Does this mean that Zacharias' thought has itself been paraphrased and interpreted in the light of the interpretation of the Old Testament by Christ and His apostles? Not necessarily. While the mass of Jews viewed the Messiah as a political Redeemer, His rôle as a religious or priestly Redeemer was not absent in Judaism (*cf.* K. Stendahl, *The Scrolls and the New Testament*, 1957, pp. 54–64). This would be central in the thoughts of a pious priest; therefore, it is quite in keeping with his personality and background that, 'filled with the Holy Ghost', Zacharias should utter this particular revelation. See also ANNUNCIATION. E.E.E.

BENEFACTOR. The Gk. *euergetēs* was used as a title by kings of Egypt (*e.g.* Ptolemy IX, 147–117 BC) and of Syria (*e.g.* Antiochus VII, 141–129 BC) and appears on their coins. It occurs also as a laudatory title on inscriptions of the 1st century AD, commemorating services rendered, *e.g.* to the people of Cos (A. Deissmann, *LAE*, 1927, p. 253). Such a title is no honour to any disciple of Jesus (Lk. xxii. 25). A.R.M.

BENE-JAAKAN. A camping-ground of the Israelites (Nu. xxxiii. 31 f.; Dt. x. 6, RV). The passage in Dt. x. 6, 7 is clearly an insertion, either a gloss by Moses himself (Hertz) or one of his younger companions. The author was evidently interested in the provision of water (see JOTBATH), for he prefaces the word with 'Beeroth', so that the RVmg renders 'the wells of the children of Jaakan'. G.T.M.

BEN-HADAD. Heb. form of Aramaic Bar- or Bir-Hadad, 'son of Hadad', name of either two or three rulers of the Aramaean kingdom of Damascus.

1. Ben-hadad I is called 'son of Tabrimmon, son of Hezion, king of Aram' in identical wording both in 1 Ki. xv. 18 and in his own (so-called) 'Melqart Stele' of *c.* 860 BC. For this stele, see Albright and Levi della Vida in *BASOR*, 87, 1942, pp. 23–29, and *BASOR*, 90, 1943, pp. 30–34; also M. Black in D. W. Thomas (ed.), *DOTT*, 1958, pp. 239–241 with plate 15. In his 15th year (35th of the divided Monarchy), King Asa of Judah vanquished Zerah the Ethiopian (*q.v.*) and held a great thanksgiving-feast in Jerusalem, inviting Israelites also (2 Ch. xiv. 9–xv); therefore in the 16th (36th) year, Baasha of Israel attacked Judah (2 Ch. xvi. 1–10), and so Asa sought aid from Ben-hadad I of Aram (1 Ki. xv. 18 ff., as above). Hence Ben-hadad I was already ruling by *c.* 895 BC, say about 900. For this period, see E. R. Thiele, *Mysterious Numbers of the Hebrew Kings*, 1951, pp. 58–60.

2. Ben-hadad, the opponent of Ahab (*c.* 874/3–853 BC), 1 Ki. xx, died by the hand of Hazael (*q.v.*) in the days of Joram (*c.* 852–841 BC) and Elisha (2 Ki. vi. 24 ff., viii. 7–15). Hazael succeeded Ben-hadad about 843 BC (Shalmaneser III of Assyria already mentions Hazael in 841 BC), see M. F. Unger, *Israel and the Aramaeans of Damascus*, p. 75. Two problems here arise. First, is the Ben-hadad of Ahab and Joram Asa's Ben-hadad I (implying a long but not unparalleled fifty-seven years' reign, *c.* 900–843 BC), or is he a separate Ben-hadad II? Albright (*op. cit.*) would identify them as a single Ben-hadad (I), but his only positive reason is a possible date about 850 BC (limits, *c.* 875–825 BC) for the Melqart Stele on the style of its script. But the most natural interpretation of 1 Ki. xx. 34 is that Omri had earlier been defeated by Ben-hadad I, father of a Ben-hadad II the contemporary of

Ahab; Albright's interpretation of this passage (*BASOR*, 87, p. 27) is distinctly forced, and non-mention by the Old Testament of an event like Omri's discomfiture is well paralleled by its similar omission of Jehu's paying tribute to Shalmaneser III. Secondly, Shalmaneser III's annals for 853 BC (Wiseman, in *DOTT*, p. 47) and for 845 BC (*ANET*, p. 280a; *ARAAB*, I, §§ 658, 659) call the king of Damascus ᵈIM-idri, probably to be read as Adad-idri ('Hadad-ezer'); this must be almost certainly another name for Ben-hadad (I/II), Ahab's contemporary; *cf.* Michel, *Welt des Orients*, I, 1947, p. 59, n. 14. If two Ben-hadads are admitted, 'I' may be dated roughly 900–860 BC, and 'II' about 860–843 BC.

Fig. 35. This stele, showing the god Melqart bearing his battle-axe, is inscribed on the lower part (not shown) with the name of Ben-hadad, king of Aram. *c.* 860 BC.

3. Ben-hadad III (or II), *c.* 796–770 BC, son of Hazael, continued his father's oppression of Israel (*temp.* Jehoahaz, *c.* 814/3–798 BC, 2 Ki. xiii. 22) into the reign of Jehoash (*c.* 798–782/1 BC), who, in fulfilment of Elisha's dying prophecy, was able successfully to repel Ben-hadad (2 Ki. xiii. 14–19, 25); this Aramaean king is also mentioned on the contemporary stele of Zakir, king of Hamath and Lu'ash, *cf.* Black, in *DOTT*, pp. 242–250. The unnamed 'deliverer' against Syria at this time (to Israel's benefit) may be a veiled reference to intervention by Adad-nirari III of Assyria against Aram; *cf.* W. Hallo, *BA*, XXIII, 1960, p. 42, n. 44, following H. Schmökel, *Geschichte des Alten Vorderasien*, 1957, p. 259, n. 4. Amos (i. 4) prophesied the destruction of the 'palaces of (Hazael and) Ben-hadad', and their memory is evoked by Jeremiah (xlix. 27) in his prophecy against the Damascus province.

BIBLIOGRAPHY. For these kings, see M. F. Unger, *Israel and the Aramaeans of Damascus*, 1957, chapters V–X; R. de Vaux, *RB*, XLIII, 1934, pp. 512–518; A. Jepsen, *Archiv für Orientforschung*, XIV, 1941–4, pp. 153 ff., and *ibid.*, XVI, 1952–3, pp. 315–317. See also ARAM and DAMASCUS.

K.A.K.

BENJAMIN. 1. The youngest son of the Patriarch Jacob, called *Binyāmîn* ('son of the right hand') by his father, though his mother Rachel, dying in childbirth, called him *Ben-'ônî* ('son of my sorrow'; Gn. xxxv. 18, 24, xlii. ff.). After Joseph's disappearance, he took first place in his father's affections as the surviving son of Rachel; this was an important factor in the eventual surrender of Joseph's brothers (Gn. xlii. 4, 38, xliv).

2. The tribe descended from Benjamin; Heb. *Binyāmîn*, as collective, or pl. *bᵉnê Binyāmîn*; also *bᵉnê yᵉmînî* (1 Sa. xxii. 7; Jdg. xix. 16) and sing. *ben yᵉmînî* or *ben hayyᵉmînî* (*cf.* 1 Sa. ix. 1, *'îš yᵉmînî*; ix. 4, *'ereṣ yᵉmînî*). A similar name *Binu* (or *Maru*) *yamina*, probably meaning 'sons of (dwellers in) the south', is found in the 18th-century BC Mari texts, and some scholars (*e.g.* Alt, Parrot) have sought here the antecedents of the biblical tribe; but the difference in time and origin makes such an identification very uncertain.

Much detail of Benjamite genealogies is available, though incomplete in any one place; ten families are enumerated in Gn. xlvi. 21, but the Chronicler names only three clans (1 Ch. vii. 6 ff.), of which Jediael does not appear as such in the Pentateuch. The pre-invasion reckoning of 'fathers' houses' is given in Nu. xxvi. 38 ff.; for further details, see 1 Ch. viii.

The tribe occupied a strip of land in the passes between Mt. Ephraim and the hills of Judah. The boundary with Judah is clearly defined (Jos. xviii. 15 ff., *cf.* xv. 5 ff.), and passed south of Jerusalem, which, however, remained in Jebusite hands until captured by David. The northern boundary as given in Jos. xviii. 11 ff. is less clear, though it corresponds with the southern border of Ephraim (xvi. 1–3). It passed south of Bethel (*cf.* Jdg. i. 22; 1 Ki. xii. 29); but at some period not only Bethel, but Ophrah to the north-east, was Benjamite (Jos. xviii. 23; *cf.* 2 Ch. xiii. 19; Ezr. ii. 28). In Jos. xviii. 21 ff. two groups of settlements are listed, eastern and central; westward expansion is indicated by references to Beeroth (2 Sa. iv. 2 f.) and Aijalon (1 Ch. viii. 13); Lod and Ono were occupied after the Exile (Ne. xi. 35). It is not clear whether the Hivite city of Kiriath-jearim, a mile south of Chephirah, was occupied early or late; Noth (*Josua*, p. 89) considers the identification with Ba'alah of Judah an erroneous gloss, but it is repeated (Jos. xv. 9, 60, xviii. 14; *cf.* Jdg. xviii. 12; 1 Ch. ii. 52, xiii. 6).

'Benjamin is a ravenous wolf'—so ran the ancient blessing of Jacob (Gn. xlix. 27). The tribe earned a high reputation for bravery and skill in war, and was noted for its slingers with their traditional left-handed action (Jdg. iii. 15, xx. 16; *cf.* 1 Ch. viii. 40). Ehud, who delivered Israel from the Moabites, was of Benjamin; so also was Saul, the first king (1 Sa. ix. 1); so were Queen Esther (Est. ii. 5) and the apostle Paul (Rom. xi. 1). Lying right in the path of Philistine expansion, the tribe played its chief part in Israelite history under Saul's leadership, and on the whole remained loyal to him, though a number came over to David in his exile (1 Ch. xii. 2–7, 29). Indeed, the feud was remembered long after (2 Sa. xvi. 5, xx. 1). Such clan loyalty was evident in their disastrous resistance to the national demand for justice in the matter of the Levite's concubine (Jdg. xx, xxi), many years before the Monarchy (xx. 26 f.).

With the capital established at Jerusalem, Benjamin was drawn much closer to Judah (1 Ch. viii. 28), and after the division Rehoboam retained its allegiance (1 Ki. xii. 21; 2 Ch. xi; note 1 Ki. xi. 32, 'for the sake of Jerusalem'). There were two 'Benjamin gates' in the city, one in the Temple (Je. xx. 2), the other perhaps the same as the 'sheep gate' in the north city wall (Je. xxxvii. 13; Zc. xiv. 10). Despite the varying fortunes of war (1 Ki. xv. 16 ff.; 2 Ki. xiv. 11 ff.), Benjamin remained part of Judah (*cf.* 2 Ki. xxiii. 8, 'Geba'). In the records of the Restoration settlement the distinction is confined to personal genealogy (*cf.* Ne. vii with xii. 7 ff.).

In the vision of Ezekiel the portion of Benjamin lies immediately south of the city (Ezk. xlviii. 22 f.).

3. A Benjamite of the clan Jediael (1 Ch. vii. 10). **4.** A Benjamite of the Restoration who took a foreign wife (Ezr. x. 32). Ne. iii. 23, xii. 34 may refer to the same person.

BIBLIOGRAPHY. *Mari texts:* M. Noth, *Geschichte und Altes Testament*, 'Mari und Israel', 1953, pp. 127–152; *JSS*, I, 1956, pp. 322–333; R. de Vaux, *RB*, LIII, 1946, p. 344; H. H. Rowley, *From Joseph to Joshua*, 1950, pp. 115 f.; W. F. Albright, *JBL*, LVIII, 1939, p. 102. *Topography: GTT*, pp. 164 ff., 170 ff. *General:* J. Bright, *History of Israel*, 1960, pp. 142, 189, 213–216; M. Noth, *History of Israel*, 1958, pp. 73 f., 146, 233. J.P.U.L.

BEN-SIRA. See APOCRYPHA.

BERACHAH (lit. 'blessing'). **1.** One of the warriors who joined David at Ziklag when he was in straits because of the enmity of Saul (1 Ch. xii. 1–3). **2.** A valley where Jehoshaphat and his people gave God thanks for the victory which they had gained over the Ammonites, Moabites, and Edomites (2 Ch. xx. 26). It is identified with Wadi Bereikūt between Jerusalem and Hebron, and west of Tekoa. The modern name suggests an earlier form which was pronounced slightly differently from that in the Hebrew text with the meaning 'water pool' (*berēḵâ*). R.J.W.

BERNICE. The eldest daughter of Herod Agrippa I, and sister of Drusilla, born in AD 28. Having been engaged, if not married, previously, she married at the age of thirteen her uncle Herod of Chalcis. Upon his death in AD 48, she began an incestuous relationship with her brother Herod Agrippa II (Juv., *Sat.* vi. 156 ff.), married Polemon king of Cilicia, deserted him, and returned to her brother, in whose company she heard Paul (Acts xxv. 13). She subsequently became the mistress both of Titus and Vespasian.

E.M.B.G.

BEROEA, BEREA. 1. The modern Verria, a city of southern Macedonia probably founded in the 5th century BC. In New Testament times it was evidently a prosperous centre with a Jewish colony. When Paul and Silas were smuggled out of Thessalonica to avoid Jewish opposition (Acts xvii. 5–11) they withdrew to Beroea, 50 miles away. Here they received a good hearing until the pursuit caught up with them. Beroea was the home of Sopater (Acts xx. 4). **2.** The Hellenistic name of Aleppo (2 Macc. xiii. 4).

BIBLIOGRAPHY. Strabo vii; *BC*, IV, pp. 188 f., 206 f. J.H.P.

BERYL. See JEWELS AND PRECIOUS STONES.

BETEN. One of the towns of Asher listed in Jos. xix. 25. Its location is uncertain. Eusebius' *Onomasticon*, calling it Bethseten, puts it 8 Roman miles east of Ptolemais (Acco). It may be the modern Abtûn, east of Mt. Carmel.

BETHABARA (probably from Heb. *bêṯ ʿᵃḇārâ*, 'house of (the) ford'). This place is read in many Gk. MSS at Jn. i. 28 for 'Bethany beyond Jordan' (see BETHANY): hence it is found in AV and RVmg. Origen preferred this reading while admitting that the majority of contemporary MSS were against him. He gives its etymology as 'house of preparation', which he associated with the Baptist's 'preparation'. In his day, he says, this place was shown as the place of John's baptism. It is probably the present Qasr el-Yehud, on the right bank of the Jordan, east of Jericho, where a monastery of St. John stands.

BIBLIOGRAPHY. F. M. Abel, *Géographie de la Palestine*, II, 1938, pp. 264, 265. J.N.B.

BETH-ANATH (*bêṯ ʿᵃnāṯ*, 'temple of Anat'). Perhaps modern el-Ba'neh 20 miles ESE of Hazor. The city was allotted to Naphtali (Jos. xix. 38), but was one from which the original inhabitants were not expelled, but made tributary (Jdg. i. 33). R.J.W.

BETH-ANOTH (*bêṯ ʿᵃnôṯ*, probably 'temple of Anat'). A conurbation (a city with its villages, Jos. xv. 59) which was allotted to Judah. Modern Beit 'Anûn 4 miles NNE of Hebron.

BETHANY. 1. A village (present population 726) on the farther side of the Mount of Olives, about 15 furlongs from Jerusalem on the road to Jericho. It is first mentioned in the Gospels, especially as the home of Jesus' beloved friends,

Mary, Martha, and Lazarus; hence the modern Arabic name 'el-'Azariyeh. Its most central rôle in the Gospel history is as the place of Jesus' anointing (Mk. xiv. 3–9). Outside the Gospels it figures largely in Christian itineraries, traditions, and legends.

2. The place where John baptized 'beyond the Jordan' (Jn. i. 28, RV). Its identification remains uncertain. Already by the time of Origen (*c.* AD 250) it was unknown (see his *Commentary on John*, VI, 40, p. 157, ed. Brooke). Origen preferred the reading Bethabara (*q.v.*), since this place was known in his day and, moreover, this choice might in his opinion be corroborated by allegory. 'Bethany', however, should be accepted as the more difficult reading. The mention of a place so soon unknown is frequently adduced as a token of knowledge of 1st-century Palestine by the evangelist or his source. J.N.B.

BETH-ARBEL. A city described (Ho. x. 14) as having been destroyed by Shalman (*q.v.*) in the 'day of battle'. The name is known only from this reference, so that the common identification with modern Irbid, probably the Arbela of Eusebius, some 18 miles south-east of the Sea of Galilee, remains uncertain.

BIBLIOGRAPHY. W. F. Albright, *BASOR*, 35, 1929, p. 10; G. L. Harding, *The Antiquities of Jordan*, 1959, pp. 54–56. T.C.M.

BETH-AVEN (*bêṯ 'āwen*, 'house of iniquity'). Near Ai (Jos. vii. 2) and to the east of Bethel. The site served as a boundary mark for Benjamin's allotment (Jos. xviii. 12). In Hosea (iv. 15, v. 8, x. 5) the name may be a derogatory synonym for Bethel, 'House of the (false) god'. R.J.W.

BETH-DAGON (*bêṯ-dāḡôn*, 'house of Dagon'). **1.** A city in the lowlands of Judah (Jos. xv. 41). *GTT* identifies with Khirbet Değūn, a Roman site 2 miles south-west of the modern Beit Dağān. This, however, is by no means certain; nor is there any evidence that Beth-dagon, despite its name, was a Philistine city. **2.** A city near the south-east boundary of Asher (Jos. xix. 27), not yet identified. J.D.D.

BETHEL. The modern Tell Beitīn on the watershed route 12 miles north of Jerusalem. Although traces of earlier occupation have been found, the city seems to have been established early in the Middle Bronze Age. During this period, Abram camped to the east of Bethel, where he built an altar to Yahweh (Gn. xii. 8). After his visit to Egypt, he returned to this site (Gn. xiii. 3). For Jacob, Bethel was the starting-point of his realization of God, who is for him 'God of Bethel' (Gn. xxxi. 13, xxxv. 7). As a result of his vision of Yahweh he named the place 'House of God' (Heb. *bêṯ-'ēl*) and set up a pillar (Heb. *maṣṣēḇâ*, see PILLAR) (Gn. xxviii. 11–22). He was summoned to Bethel on his return from Harran, and both built an altar and set up a pillar, reiterating the name he had given before (Gn. xxxv. 1–15). The site is perhaps Burġ Beitīn to the south-east of Tell Beitin, the 'shoulder of Luz' (Jos. xviii. 13, RSV).

At the beginning of the Late Bronze Age a strong city wall was built, and a prosperous period with well-built houses and Egyptian luxuries ensued. The gradual decline which followed was ended by a violent destruction of the city, the burnt débris lying 5 feet deep in places. On the evidence of potsherds found in this débris and of the different cultural nature of the following settlement, this destruction is assigned to the Israelite invasion in the latter part of the 13th century BC (Jos. xii. 16; Jdg. i. 22–26). Bethel was allotted to the Joseph tribes who captured it, particularly to Ephraim (1 Ch. vii. 28), and bordered the territory of Benjamin (Jos. xviii. 13). The Israelites soon resettled the town, calling it by the name Jacob had given to the scene of his vision instead of Luz (Jdg. i. 23). When it was necessary for Israel to punish Benjamin, the people sought advice on the conduct of the battle and worshipped at Bethel 'for the ark . . . was there' (Jdg. xx. 18–28, xxi. 1–4). It was a sanctuary too in the time of Samuel, who visited it annually (1 Sa. vii. 16, x. 3). The material remains of this period indicate an unsophisticated and insecure community. The settlement was twice burnt, possibly by the Philistines.

Under the early monarchy the city prospered, presently becoming the centre of Jeroboam's rival cult, condemned by a man of God from Judah (1 Ki. xii. 28–xiii. 32). The Judaean Abijah captured it (2 Ch. xiii. 19), and his son, Asa, may have destroyed it (2 Ch. xiv. 8). Elisha met a group of the 'sons of the prophets' from Bethel but also the mocking boys (2 Ki. ii. 3, 23). Amos condemned the rites of the Israelite royal sanctuary (Am. iv. 4, v. 5, 6, vii. 13; *cf.* Ho. x. 15, RV), and Jeremiah showed their futility (Je. xlviii. 13). The priest sent to instruct the Assyrian settlers in Samaria settled at Bethel (2 Ki. xvii. 28), and worship evidently continued there until Josiah took advantage of Assyrian weakness to invade Israel and destroy its sanctuaries. No traces of Jeroboam's shrine have been unearthed; it may well have been outside the city proper on the site of the patriarchal altars. In the 6th century BC the city was destroyed by fire. Returning exiles settled in Bethel (Ne. xi. 31), but their worship was centred on Jerusalem (Zc. vii. 2, RV). The city grew during the Hellenistic period until it was fortified by Bacchides *c.* 160 BC (1 Macc. ix. 50). When Vespasian captured it in AD 69, there was a short break before it was rebuilt as a Roman township. It continued to flourish until the Arab conquest. See also BETH-AVEN.

BIBLIOGRAPHY. For a summary of the excavations, see *BA*, XIX, 1956, pp. 36–43; *BASOR*, 151, 1958, pp. 3–8. A.R.M.

BETHESDA. A Jerusalem pool, with five porticos big enough to hold great numbers (Jn. v. 2 f.). The name is the Greek form of Aramaic *bêṯ ḥasdâ*, 'house of mercy'; but there are textual variants of the name, and indeed Bethzatha appears to be the best reading—the name of the northern quarter of Jerusalem. Excavations last century brought to light a five-porched pool in the north-east of the city, with a faded fresco making it clear that this is the site, according to early Christian tradition. This location has its supporters; but some have preferred the Virgin's Pool, to the south of the temple area. The word *probatikē*, usually translated 'Sheep [Gate]', must then be taken to mean 'place for watering sheep', for the Sheep Gate was in the northern part of Jerusalem. But the reading 'Bethzatha' clearly rules out this latter hypothesis. The 'copper scroll' from Qumran mentions a place *Bêṯ 'ešdāṯayin* (3Q 15, § 57), 'house (or 'place') of two outpourings', which might suggest a derivation *bêṯ 'ešdâ* ('house of outpouring') for Bethesda; the dual *'ešdāṯayin* is the more noteworthy because Eusebius and the Bordeaux pilgrim speak of 'twin pools' at Bethesda. D.F.P.

BETH-HARAN (Nu. xxxii. 36, to be identified with Beth-aram, Jos. xiii. 27). This site formed part of the allotment of Gad, and so lay on the east of the Jordan. It was probably a border strong-point which the Gadites built (Nu. xxxii. 36) or else an existing settlement which they fortified (Jos. xiii. 27) to protect themselves and their cattle. The settlement was in good pasture (Nu. xxxii. 1) but in the valley (Jos. xiii. 27), and so lacked the security of hill fastnesses which those who crossed the river enjoyed. Identified with modern Tell Iktanû 8 miles north-east of the mouth of the Jordan. R.J.W.

BETH-HORON. A Canaanite place-name meaning 'house of Hauron' (a Canaanite god of the underworld). Beth-horon the upper (Jos. xvi. 5) is modern Beit 'Ûr al-Fôqâ, 2,022 feet above sea-level, 11 miles north-west of Jerusalem, and Beth-horon the nether (Jos. xvi. 3) is Beit 'Ûr al-Taḥtâ, 1,210 feet above the sea and 1¾ miles farther north-west. These towns were built by Sherah, of the tribe of Ephraim (1 Ch. vii. 24). They were within the territory of this tribe, and one of them was assigned to the Levite family of Kohath (Jos. xxi. 22). They were rebuilt by Solomon (2 Ch. viii. 5) and fortified by the Jews after the Exile (Judith iv. 4, 5) and by Bacchides the Syrian general (1 Macc. ix. 50). They controlled the valley of Aijalon, up which went one of the most important ancient routes between the maritime plain and the hill-country. Therefore many armies passed by these towns in biblical times, *e.g.* the Amorites and the pursuing Israelites under Joshua (Jos. x. 10, 11), the Philistines (1 Sa. xiii. 18), and the Egyptian army of Shishak (according to his Karnak inscription), the Syrians under Seron (1 Macc. iii. 16, 24) and under Nicanor (1 Macc. vii. 39), both of whom Judas defeated at Beth-horon, and the Romans under Cestius (Jos., *BJ* ii. 19. 1).

Sanballat was a native of Beth-horon (Ne. ii. 10). Pseudo-Epiphanius, in *The Lives of the Prophets*, states that Daniel was born in Beth-horon the upper.

BIBLIOGRAPHY. E. Robinson, *Biblical Researches in Palestine*, II, 1874, pp. 250–253; G. A. Smith, *Historical Geography of the Holy Land*, 1931, pp. 248–250, 287–292; F. M. Abel, *Géographie de la Palestine*, II, 1938, pp. 274, 275.
J.T.

BETH-JESHIMOTH. Probably the modern Tell 'Adeimeh near the north-eastern shore of the Dead Sea, and near which is a Roman settlement whose Greek name was *Bēsimōth* (the modern Khirbet Sueimeh), clearly derived from the biblical name. This city was in the plains of Moab (Nu. xxxiii. 49), one of the final stopping-places of the Exodus, and was included by Moses in the inheritance of Reuben (Jos. xiii. 20). It is mentioned in Ezk. xxv. 9 as one of the important cities of the Moabites. R.F.H.

BETHLEHEM (*bêṯ leḥem*, 'house of bread' the latter word probably in the wider sense, 'food'). It has been suggested that the final word *leḥem* is Lakhmu, an Assyrian deity; but there is no evidence that this god was ever revered in Palestine. There are two towns of the name in the Old Testament, both today given the Arabic name Bayt Lahm, the exact equivalent of the Hebrew.

1. The famed city of David, as it came to be styled. It lies a few miles south of Jerusalem. Its earlier name was Ephrath (Gn. xxxv. 19), and it was known as Bethlehem Judah, or Bethlehem Ephrathah, to distinguish it from the other city of the same name. Rachel's tomb was near it; David's ancestors lived there; and the Messiah was destined to be born there. Jesus was accordingly born there, and the stories of the shepherds and the Magi centre upon it. The Roman emperor Hadrian devastated it in the second century AD, and the site of the nativity grotto was lost for two centuries; so the Church of the Nativity erected by Helena in the reign of Constantine may or may not mark the true site. The traditional tomb of Rachel outside the town is still pointed out; and so are the 'Shepherds' Fields'.

2. The second Bethlehem lay in Zebulunite territory (Jos. xix. 15); it is 7 miles north-west of Nazareth. Most scholars think the judge Ibzan (Jdg. xii. 8) was a resident of it, but ancient tradition favours Bethlehem Judah. D.F.P.

BETH-MARCABOTH (*bêṯ hammarkāḇôṯ*, 'house of chariots'). A part of the allotment to Simeon (Jos. xix. 5; 1 Ch. iv. 31). The site is uncertain but, being connected with Ziklag and Hormah, was probably a strong-point on the Judaean–Philistine border. The name suggests that the settlement may have been a Canaanite arsenal in the days of the conquest. The possession of chariots by the Canaanites prevented the unmounted Hebrew soldiers from entirely occupying the land (Jdg. i. 19). R.J.W.

BETH-NIMRAH. 'House of pure water' or 'House of leopard', a city in Gad (Nu. xxxii. 36), probably equalling Nimrah (Nu. xxxii. 3) and Nimrim (Is. xv. 6; Je. xlviii. 34). By Eusebius, called Betham-Naram and located 5 miles north of Livias. Possibly either modern Tell Nimrin beside the Wadi Shaîb or nearby Tell Bileibil, some 15 miles east of Jericho. G.W.G.

BETH-PEOR (lit. 'Temple of Peor'). A place in the hill country in the land of Moab (Jos. xiii. 20) or of the Amorites (Dt. iv. 46), to the east of Jordan, which was part of Reubenite territory. The historical framework of Deuteronomy describes the Hebrews gathering at Mt. Pisgah near to Beth-Peor to receive their final exhortation before going over into the promised land (Dt. iii. 29, iv. 44–46). Having repeated the law to the immigrants, Moses died, and was buried nearby (Dt. xxxiv. 5, 6). Beth-peor may be near, or even the same as, Peor, where Balaam later built seven altars (Nu. xxiii. 28). Nu. xxv. 1–5 mentions the worship of a god Baal Peor (Lord of Peor) by the Moabites. The site is uncertain. R.J.W.

BETHPHAGE (in Aram. 'place of young figs'). A village on the Mount of Olives. On or near the road from Jericho to Jerusalem and near Bethany (Mt. xxi. 1; Mk. xi. 1; Lk. xix. 29). Its site is unknown. J.W.M.

BETHSAIDA. A town on the north shores of Galilee, near the Jordan. The name is Aramaic, meaning 'house of fishing' (if *bêṯ ṣaydâ*) or else 'fisherman's house' (if *bêṯ ṣayyāḏâ*). Philip the tetrarch rebuilt it and gave it the name Julias, in honour of Julia the daughter of Augustus. Pliny and Jerome tell us that it was on the east of the Jordan, and there are two likely sites, al-Tell or Mas'adiya. (The two are close together, the latter being nearer the actual shore.) But in Mk. vi. 45 the disciples were sent from east of the Jordan to Bethsaida, towards Capernaum (*cf.* Jn. vi. 17); hence a second Bethsaida has been postulated west of the Jordan—perhaps to be located at 'Ayn al-Tabigha. This is also claimed to be Bethsaida 'of Galilee' (Jn. xii. 21), since the political division Galilee may not have extended east of the Jordan. But this is unlikely; 'Galilee' is not necessarily used in the technical sense. A suburb of Julias on the west bank may suit Mk. vi. 45 best; Capernaum was not many miles away. D.F.P.

BETH-SHEAN, BETH-SHAN. A city situated at the important junction of the Valley of Jezreel (*q.v.*) with the Jordan valley. The name occurs in the Bible as *bêṯ šᵉʾān* (Jos. xvii. 11, 16; Jdg. i. 27; 1 Ki. iv. 12; 1 Ch. vii. 29) and *bêṯ šan* (1 Sa. xxxi. 10, 12; 2 Sa. xxi. 12), but there is little doubt that both names refer to the same place. The name is preserved in the modern village of Beisân, adjacent to which stands Tell el-Ḥosn, the site of the ancient city, which was excavated under the direction of C. S. Fisher (1921–3), A. Rowe (1925–8), and G. M. Fitzgerald (1930–3).

Though a deep sounding was made, revealing settlements of the fourth millennium and an important Canaanite city of the Early Bronze Age, the main excavations were devoted to the nine upper levels which extended from the 14th century BC to Islamic times. During much of the earlier part of this period, Beth-shean was an Egyptian fortified outpost. Already in the 15th century Tuthmosis III mentions it as under his control (scarabs bearing his name were found there), and in the following century one of the Amarna letters speaks of reinforcements sent to garrison *bît-sa-a-ni* on behalf of Egypt. The earliest main level (IX) probably belongs to this century (the levels have been redated on the basis of pottery sequence, since the original dates of the excavators relied on less certain criteria), and in this an extensive temple dedicated to 'Mekal, the Lord (Ba'al) of Beth-shan' was uncovered, in which were found the remains of a sacrificed three-year-old bull (see SACRIFICE AND OFFERING).

Level VIII was comparatively unimportant, dating from about the end of the 14th century, but at this time Sethos (Seti) I was seeking to restore Egyptian control in Asia, which had been largely lost under the later kings of the XVIIIth Dynasty, and in his first year he retook Beth-shean. Two of his royal stelae have been found there, one of them recording that he had a clash near by with the '*pr.w* (see HEBREWS). Level VII (*c.* 13th century) contained a temple in which was found a stele depicting a goddess with a two-horned head-dress (see ASHTEROTH-KARNAIM), and in level VI a similar temple was uncovered. This level probably dates to the 12th century, the time of Rameses III, of whom a statue was found there, and the discovery in the city cemetery of anthropoid clay coffins characteristic of the Philistines (*q.v.*) suggests that these people were stationed as a mercenary garrison at Beth-shean by Rameses. It was not long before this that the Israelites had arrived in Palestine, and Manasseh, being allotted Beth-shean (Jos. xvii. 11), found it too formidable to take (Jos. xvii. 16; Jdg. i. 27), so that it remained in hostile hands until the time of David. Its importance at this time is suggested by the fact that the Bible refers to it as Beth-shan 'and her daughters' (*i.e.* dependent villages). It was still in Philistine hands at the time of Saul, for it was upon its walls that his body and those of his sons were hung, and from which the men of Jabesh-gilead recovered them (1 Sa. xxxi. 10, 12).

In level V (*c.* 11th century) two temples were uncovered, one (the southern) dedicated to the god Resheph and the other to the goddess Antit (see figs. 61 and 36), and Rowe has suggested that these are the temples of Dagon and Ashteroth in which Saul's head and armour were displayed by the Philistines (1 Ch. x. 10; 1 Sa. xxxi. 10). The city must have fallen finally to the Israelites in the time of David, and the excavations have revealed little material settlement (level IV) from then until the Hellenistic Period (level III). During this time it is mentioned with its environs ('all of Beth-shean', *kol-bêṯ šᵉ'ān*) as belonging to Solomon's fifth administrative district (1 Ki. iv. 12), and in the reign of Rehoboam (1 Ki. xiv. 25) Sheshonq (see SHISHAK) claimed it among his conquests. The city was refounded as the Hellenistic centre of Scythopolis, and this later became a part of the Decapolis (*q.v.*).

BIBLIOGRAPHY. A. Rowe, *Beth-shan*, I, *The Topography and History of Beth-shan*, 1930, II, i, *The Four Canaanite Temples of Beth-shan*, 1940; with which see G. E. Wright, *AJA*, XLV, 1941, pp. 483–485; G. M. Fitzgerald, *Beth-shan*, II, ii, 1930, III, 1931; C. C. McCown, *The Ladder of Progress in Palestine*, 1943, pp. 151–170; *ANET*, pp. 242, 249, 253; J. Knudtzon, *Die El-Amarna Tafeln*, I, 1907, pp. 874, 875, No. 289. 20; II, 1915, p. 1343; (= *ANET*, p. 489); W. F. Albright, 'The Smaller Beth-Shan Stele of Sethos I (1309–1290 B. C.)', *BASOR*, 125, 1952, pp. 24–32; G. Posener in J. Bottéro, *Le Problème des Habiru*, 1954, p. 168; (= *ANET*, p. 255); on anthropoid coffins, see G. E. Wright, *BA*, XXII, 1959, pp. 53–56, 65; *'Atiqot*, II, 1959, p. 169.

T.C.M.

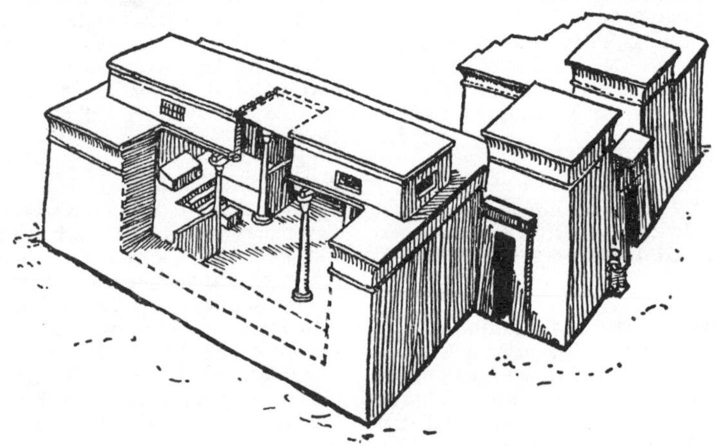

Fig. 36. A reconstruction of the 'northern temple' of level V at Beth-shan. Perhaps the house of Ashtaroth (I Sa. xxxi. 10) in which the Philistines placed Saul's armour after his death. The dotted line indicates walls cut away to show the interior. Dated *c.* 1000 BC. See also fig. 61.

BETH-SHEMESH (Heb. *bêṯ-šemeš*, 'house (temple) of the sun'), a name applied to four places in the Bible.

1. An important city of Judah (2 Ki. xiv. 11; 2 Ch. xxv. 21) on its northern border with Dan (Jos. xv. 10), situated in a west-facing valley of the hill-country some 15 miles west of Jerusalem and consequently commanding a route from the uplands to the coast plain. The site is probably to be identified with modern Tell er-Rumeileh, situated on the saddle of a hill spur to the west of the later settlement of 'Ain Shems. Excavations were conducted in 1911–12, and more extensively in 1928–32. The site was first settled near the end of the Early Bronze Age, some time before 2000 BC, and flourished as a strongly fortified Canaanite city throughout the Middle and Late Bronze Ages, reaching its zenith in the time of the Egyptian domination under the pharaohs of Dynasty XIX. Connections with the north are illuminated by the discovery in the Late Bronze Age levels of a clay tablet inscribed in the cuneiform alphabet of Ugarit (see 'Ras Shamra' in article ARCHAEOLOGY). The close of the Bronze Age is marked by quantities of Philistine (*q.v.*) pottery, showing that these people, who settled initially along the coast, also established themselves well inland, where they became the chief rivals of the newly-arrived Israelites. The city must have been taken by the Israelites in the period of the Judges, as it was set aside as a levitical city (Jos. xxi. 16; 1 Ch. vi. 59), and was certainly in their hands by the time of Samuel, as it was thither that the captured ark came when the Philistines released it (1 Sa. vi). It is probable that David strengthened this city in the later phases of his struggle with the Philistines, and it is likely that the casemate walls (see FORTIFICATION AND SIEGECRAFT) discovered there date from this period. There is evidence that the city was destroyed in the 10th century, probably at the hands of the Egyptian king Sheshonq, who invaded Judah in Rehoboam's fifth year (1 Ki. xiv. 25–28). About a century after this, Beth-shemesh was the scene of the great victory of Joash of Israel over Amaziah of Judah (2 Ki. xiv. 11–13; 2 Ch. xxv. 21–23). In the reign of Ahaz, Beth-shemesh was with other cities again taken by the Philistines (2 Ch. xxviii. 18), but they were driven out by Tiglath-pileser III, to whom Ahaz had appealed and of whom Judah now became a vassal. Life in the city during the period of the monarchy was illuminated by the discovery of a refinery for olive-oil and installations for copper-working, which last had already existed in the Bronze Age. The city was now in decline, however, and it was finally destroyed by Nebuchadrezzar in the 6th century BC.

It is probable that Ir-shemesh, 'city of the sun' (Jos. xix. 41), is to be equated with Beth-shemesh.

BIBLIOGRAPHY. D. Mackenzie, 'Excavations at Ain Shems', *Annual Report of the Palestine Exploration Fund*, I, 1911, pp. 41–94; II, 1912–13, pp. 1–100; E. Grant (and G. E. Wright), *Ain Shems Excavations*, I–V, 1931–9; E. Grant and G. A. Barton, *BASOR*, 52, 1933, pp. 3–6.

2. A city on the border of Issachar (Jos. xix. 22), from which the Canaanites were not driven out, but became tributary to the Israelites (Jdg. i. 33), perhaps to be identified with modern el-'Abēdîyeh, which commands a ford over the Jordan some 2 miles south of the Sea of Galilee.

BIBLIOGRAPHY. A. Saarisalo, *The Boundary between Issachar and Naphtali*, 1927, pp. 71–73, 119, 120.

3. A fortified city allotted to Naphtali (Jos. xix. 38), whose site is unknown, unless it is to be identified with (2).

4. A city in Egypt (Je. xliii. 13) probably to be identified with Heliopolis (which is here given in RSV)—On (*q.v.*). T.C.M.

BETH-SHITTAH (*bêṯ-šiṭṭâ*, 'house of (the) acacia'). A town near Abel-meholah, to which the Midianites fled from Gideon (Jdg. vii. 22). No definitive identification has yet been made.

BETH-ZUR (*bêṯ-ṣûr*). A city in Judah (Jos. xv. 58), not mentioned in the account of the conquest, but settled by the descendants of Caleb the son of Hezron (1 Ch. ii. 45; see CALEB). It was fortified by Rehoboam in the 10th century (2 Ch. xi. 7), was of some importance in the time of Nehemiah (iii. 16), and was a strategic fortified city during the Maccabean wars (1 Macc.).

The name is preserved at the site called Burj eṣ-Ṣur, but the ancient city is represented today by the neighbouring mound of Khirbet eṭ-Ṭubeiqah, about 4 miles north of Hebron. The site was identified in 1924, and in 1931 an American expedition under the direction of O. R. Sellers and W. F. Albright carried out preliminary excavations, which, due to the troubled times, were not resumed until 1957, when a further season was undertaken under Sellers.

There was little settlement on the site until Middle Bronze Age II (*c.* 19th–16th century BC), in the latter part of which the Hyksos dominated Palestine, and it is probably to them that a system of massive defensive walls on the slope of the mound is to be attributed. When the Egyptians finally expelled the Hyksos from Egypt and pursued them well into Palestine, Beth-zur was destroyed and largely abandoned, and it evidently remained so throughout the Late Bronze Age (*c.* 1550–1200 BC) and therefore offered no resistance to the armies of Joshua, as is indicated by its absence from the conquest narratives. The Israelites evidently settled there, for in the 12th and 11th centuries the city was flourishing, though the population seems to have declined towards the end of the 10th century. No certain evidence of Rehoboam's fortifications has come to light, so it may be that he re-used the Middle Bronze Age walls and only stationed a small garrison there. The site was occupied throughout the Monarchy, abandoned during the Exile and resettled in the Persian period, but its zenith of importance came during the Hellenistic period. It was then a garrison city commanding the Jerusalem–Hebron road at the boundary between Judaea and Idumaea, and figured prominently in the Maccabean wars. A

Fig. 37. Silver Jewish coin from Beth-zur inscribed 'Hezekiah', perhaps the friend of Ptolemy I (323–285 BC). Approximately 7 times actual size.

large fortress was uncovered on the summit, in which were found a great number of coins, including many of Antiochus IV Epiphanes, and several stamped Rhodian jar handles, indicating that it had been garrisoned by Greek troops. The fort had seen three main phases, the second probably due to Judas Maccabaeus, who fortified it after having defeated Antiochus' deputy Lysias there (1 Macc. iv. 26–34, 61), and the third probably to be ascribed to the Macedonian general Bacchides, who fortified it around 161 BC (1 Macc. ix. 52).

BIBLIOGRAPHY. O. R. Sellers, *The Citadel of Beth-zur*, 1933; 'The 1957 Campaign at Beth-zur', *BA*, XXI, 1958, pp. 71–76; W. F. Albright, *The Archaeology of Palestine*, revised edition, 1960, *passim*, esp. pp. 150–152; F. M. Abel, *Géographie de la Palestine*, II, 1938, p. 283; L. H. Grollenberg, *Atlas of the Bible*, 1947, p. 105. T.C.M.

BEULAH. When the Lord saves Zion, her land shall receive this symbolic name, meaning 'married' (Is. lxii. 4). Expressing the closeness of the relation between Zion and her sons (verse 5a), and the restoration of Zion to her God (verse 5b, *cf.* Is. xlix. 18, liv. 1–6; Ho. ii. 14–20; contrast Ho. i. 2), the name foretells the fertility of the messianic age. The Lord will be the *ba'al*,

Husband, Guarantor of fruitfulness, on the basis of righteousness (Is. lxii. 1, 2; Dt. xxviii. 1–14).

J.A.M.

BEZALEEL, BEZALEL (*b^{e}ṣal'ēl*, 'in the shadow [protection] of God'). **1.** A Judahite, of Hezron's family in Caleb's house, Uri's son, Hur's grandson; gifted by God as a skilled craftsman in wood, metal, and precious stones, and placed in charge of the making of the tabernacle; he also taught other workers. See Ex. xxxi. 1–11, xxxv. 30–35. **2.** A son of Pahath-moab, persuaded by Ezra to put away his foreign wife, Ezr. x. 30.

D.W.G.

BIBLE. Derived through Latin from Gk. *biblia* ('books'), the books which are acknowledged as canonical by the Christian Church. The earliest Christian use of *ta biblia* ('the books') in this sense is said to be *2 Clement* xiv. 2 (*c.* AD 150): 'the books and the apostles declare that the Church . . . has existed from the beginning'. *Cf.* Dn. ix. 2, RV, 'I Daniel understood by the books' (Heb. *bass^{e}pārîm*), where the reference is to the corpus of Old Testament prophetic writings. Gk. *biblion* (of which *biblia* is the plural) is a diminutive of *biblos*, which in practice denotes any kind of written document, but originally one written on papyrus (Gk. *byblos*; *cf.* the Phoen. port of Byblus, through which in antiquity papyrus was imported from Egypt).

A term synonymous with 'the Bible' is 'the writings' or 'the Scriptures' (Gk. *hai graphai, ta grammata*), frequently used in the New Testament to denote the Old Testament documents in whole or in part; *cf.* Mt. xxi. 42, 'did ye never read in the scriptures?' (*en tais graphais*); the parallel passage Mk. xii. 10 has the singular, referring to the particular text quoted, 'have ye not read this scripture?' (*tēn graphēn tautēn*); 2 Tim. iii. 15, RV, 'the sacred writings' (*ta hiera grammata*), verse 16, RV, 'every scripture inspired of God' (*pasa graphē theopneustos*). In 2 Pet. iii. 16 'all' the Epistles of Paul are included along with 'the other scriptures' (*tas loipas graphas*), by which the Old Testament writings and probably also the Gospels are meant.

The Old and New Testaments—the *tawrat* (from Heb. *tôrâ*) and the *injil* (from Gk. *euangelion*)—are acknowledged in the Qur'an (Sura 3) as earlier divine revelations. The Old Testament in Hebrew is the Jewish Bible. The Pentateuch in Hebrew is the Samaritan Bible.

I. CONTENT AND AUTHORITY

Among Christians, for whom the Old and New Testaments together constitute the Bible, there is not complete agreement on their content. Some branches of the Syriac Church do not include 2 Peter, 2 and 3 John, Jude, and Revelation in the New Testament. The Roman and Greek communions include a number of books in the Old Testament in addition to those which make up the Hebrew Bible; these additional books formed part of the Christian Septuagint. While they are included, along with one or two others, in the complete Protestant English Bible, the Church of England (like the Lutheran Church) follows Jerome in holding that they may be read 'for example of life and instruction of manners; but yet doth it not apply them to establish any doctrine' (Article VI). Other Reformed Churches accord them no canonical status at all. (See APOCRYPHA.) The Ethiopic Bible includes 1 Enoch and the book of Jubilees.

In the Roman, Greek, and other ancient communions the Bible, together with the living tradition of the Church, constitutes the ultimate authority. In the Churches of the Reformation, on the other hand, the Bible alone is the final court of appeal in matters of doctrine and practice. Thus Article VI of the Church of England affirms: 'Holy Scripture containeth all things necessary to salvation: so that whatsoever is not read therein, nor may be proved thereby, is not to be required of any man, that it should be believed as an article of the Faith, or be thought requisite or necessary to salvation.' To the same effect the *Westminster Confession of Faith* (i. 2) lists the thirty-nine books of the Old Testament and the twenty-seven of the New as 'all . . . given by inspiration of God, to be the rule of faith and life'.

II. THE TWO TESTAMENTS

The word 'testament' in the designations 'Old Testament' and 'New Testament', given to the two divisions of the Bible, goes back through Latin *testamentum* to Gk. *diathēkē*, which in most of its occurrences in the Greek Bible means 'covenant' rather than 'testament'. In Je. xxxi. 31 ff. a new covenant (Heb. *b^{e}rîṯ*, LXX *diathēkē*) is foretold which will supersede that which Yahweh made with Israel in the wilderness (*cf.* Ex. xxiv. 7 f.). 'In that he saith, A new covenant, he hath made the first old' (Heb. viii. 13). The New Testament writers see the fulfilment of the prophecy of the new covenant in the new order inaugurated by the work of Christ; His own words of institution (1 Cor. xi. 25) give the authority for this interpretation. The Old Testament books, then, are so called because of their close association with the history of the 'old covenant'; the New Testament books are so called because they are the foundation documents of the 'new covenant'. An approach to our common use of the term 'Old Testament' appears in 2 Cor. iii. 14, AV, 'in the reading of the old testament' (RV, RSV, '. . . the old covenant'), although Paul probably means the law, the basis of the old covenant, rather than the whole volume of Hebrew Scripture. The terms 'Old Testament' (*palaia diathēkē*) and 'New Testament' (*kainē diathēkē*) for the two collections of books came into general Christian use in the later part of the 2nd century; in the West, Tertullian rendered *diathēkē* into Latin now by *instrumentum* (a legal document) and now by *testamentum*; it was the latter word that survived—unfortunately, since the two parts of the Bible are not 'testaments' in the ordinary sense of the term.

III. THE OLD TESTAMENT

In the Hebrew Bible the books are arranged in three divisions—the Law (*tôrâ*), the Prophets (*n*^{e}*ḇî'îm*), and the Writings (*k*^{e}*ṯûḇîm*). The Law comprises the Pentateuch, the five 'books of Moses'. The Prophets fall into two subdivisions —the 'Former Prophets' (*n*^{e}*ḇî'îm rî'šônîm*), comprising Joshua, Judges, Samuel, and Kings, and the 'Latter Prophets' (*n*^{e}*ḇî'îm 'aḥ*^{a}*rônîm*), comprising Isaiah, Jeremiah, Ezekiel, and 'The Book of the Twelve Prophets'. The Writings contain the rest of the books—first, Psalms, Proverbs, and Job; then the five 'Scrolls' (*m*^{e}*ḡillôṯ*), namely Canticles, Ruth, Lamentations, Ecclesiastes, and Esther; and finally Daniel, Ezra-Nehemiah, and Chronicles. The total is traditionally reckoned as twenty-four, but these twenty-four correspond exactly to our common reckoning of thirty-nine, since in the latter reckoning the Minor Prophets are counted as twelve books, and Samuel, Kings, Chronicles, and Ezra-Nehemiah as two each. There were other ways of counting the same twenty-four books in antiquity: in one (attested by Josephus) the total was brought down to twenty-two; in another (known to Jerome) it was raised to twenty-seven.

The origin of the arrangement of books in the Hebrew Bible cannot be traced; the threefold division is frequently believed to correspond to the three stages in which the books received canonical recognition, but there is no direct evidence for this (see CANON OF THE OLD TESTAMENT).

In the LXX the books are arranged according to similarity of subject-matter. The Pentateuch is followed by the historical books, these are followed by the books of poetry and wisdom, and these by the prophets. It is this order which, in its essential features, is perpetuated (*via* the Vulgate) in most Christian editions of the Bible. In some respects this order is truer to chronological sequence than that of the Hebrew Bible; for example, Ruth appears immediately after Judges (since it records things which happened 'in the days when the judges judged'), and the work of the Chronicler appears in the order Chronicles, Ezra, Nehemiah.

The threefold division of the Hebrew Bible is reflected in the wording of Lk. xxiv. 44 ('the law of Moses . . . the prophets . . . the psalms'); more commonly the New Testament refers to 'the law and the prophets' (see Mt. v. 17, *etc.*) or 'Moses and the prophets' (Lk. xvi. 29, *etc.*).

The divine revelation which the Old Testament records was conveyed in two principal ways—by mighty works and prophetic words. These two modes of revelation are bound up indissolubly together. The acts of mercy and judgment by which the God of Israel made Himself known to His covenant-people would not have carried their proper message had they not been interpreted to them by the prophets—the 'spokesmen' of God who received and communicated His word. For example, the events of the Exodus would not have acquired their abiding significance for the Israelites if Moses had not told them that in these events the God of their fathers was acting for their deliverance, in accordance with His ancient promises, so that they might henceforth be His people and He their God. On the other hand, Moses' words would have been fruitless apart from their vindication in the events of the Exodus. We may compare the similarly significant rôle of Samuel at the time of the Philistine menace, of the great 8th-century prophets when Assyria was sweeping all before her, of Jeremiah and Ezekiel when the kingdom of Judah came to an end, and so forth.

This interplay of mighty work and prophetic word in the Old Testament explains why history and prophecy are so intermingled throughout its pages; it was no doubt some realization of this that led the Jews to include the chief historical books among the Prophets.

But not only do the Old Testament writings record this progressive twofold revelation of God; they record at the same time men's response to God's revelation—a response sometimes obedient, too often disobedient; expressed both in deeds and in words. In this Old Testament record of the response of those to whom the word of God came the New Testament finds practical instruction for Christians; of the Israelites' rebellion in the wilderness and the disasters which ensued Paul writes: 'these things happened unto them by way of example; and they were written for our admonition, upon whom the ends of the ages are come' (1 Cor. x. 11, RV).

As regards its place in the Christian Bible, the Old Testament is preparatory in character: what 'God . . . spake in time past unto the fathers by the prophets' waited for its completion in the word which 'in these last days' He has 'spoken unto us by his Son' (Heb. i. 1 f.). Yet the Old Testament was the Bible which the apostles and other preachers of the gospel in the earliest days of Christianity took with them when they proclaimed Jesus as the divinely sent Messiah, Lord, and Saviour: they found in it clear witness to Christ (Jn. v. 39) and a plain setting forth of the way of salvation through faith in Him (Rom. iii. 21; 2 Tim. iii. 15). For their use of the Old Testament they had the authority and example of Christ Himself; and the Church ever since has done well when it has followed the precedent set by Him and His apostles and recognized the Old Testament as Christian Scripture. 'What was indispensable to the Redeemer must always be indispensable to the redeemed' (G. A. Smith).

IV. THE NEW TESTAMENT

The New Testament stands to the Old in the relation of fulfilment to promise. If the Old Testament records what 'God . . . spake in time past unto the fathers by the prophets', the New

Testament records that final word which He spoke in His Son, in which all the earlier revelation was summed up, confirmed, and transcended. The mighty works of the Old Testament revelation culminate in the redemptive work of Christ; the words of the Old Testament prophets receive their fulfilment in Him. But He is not only God's crowning revelation to man; He is also man's perfect response to God—the High Priest as well as the Apostle of our confession (Heb. iii. 1). If the Old Testament records the witness of those who saw the day of Christ before it dawned, the New Testament records the witness of those who saw and heard Him in the days of His flesh, and who came to know and proclaim the significance of His coming more fully, by the power of His Spirit, after His rising from the dead.

The New Testament has been accepted by the great majority of Christians, for the past 1,600 years, as comprising twenty-seven books. These twenty-seven fall naturally into four divisions: (*a*) the four Gospels, (*b*) the Acts of the Apostles, (*c*) twenty-one letters written by apostles and 'apostolic men', (*d*) the Revelation. This order is not only logical, but roughly chronological so far as the subject-matter of the documents is concerned; it does not correspond, however, to the order in which they were written.

The first New Testament documents to be written were the earlier Epistles of Paul. These (together, possibly, with the Epistle of James) were written between AD 48 and 60, before even the earliest of the Gospels was written. The four Gospels belong to the decades between 60 and 100, and it is to these decades too that all (or nearly all) the other New Testament writings are to be ascribed. Whereas the writing of the Old Testament books was spread over a period of 1,000 years or more, the New Testament books were written within a century.

The New Testament writings were not gathered together in the form which we know immediately after they were penned. At first the individual Gospels had a local and independent existence in the constituencies for which they were originally composed. By the beginning of the 2nd century, however, they were brought together and began to circulate as a fourfold record (see GOSPELS). When this happened, Acts was detached from Luke, with which it had formed one work in two volumes, and embarked upon a separate but not unimportant career of its own (see ACTS).

Paul's letters were preserved at first by the communities or individuals to whom they were sent. But by the end of the 1st century there is evidence to suggest that his surviving correspondence began to be collected into a Pauline Corpus, which quickly circulated among the churches—first a shorter Corpus of ten Epistles and soon afterwards a longer one of thirteen, enlarged by the inclusion of the three Pastoral Epistles (*q.v.*). Within the Pauline Corpus the Epistles appear to have been arranged not in chronological order but in descending order of length. This principle may still be recognized in the order found in most editions of the New Testament today: the Epistles to churches come before the Epistles to individuals, and within these two subdivisions they are arranged so that the longest comes first and the shortest last. (The only departure from this scheme is that Galatians comes before Ephesians, although Ephesians is slightly the longer of the two.)

With the Gospel-collection and the Pauline Corpus, and Acts to serve as a link between the two, we have the beginnings of the New Testament Canon as we know it (see CANON OF THE NEW TESTAMENT). The early Church, which inherited the Hebrew Bible (or the Greek version of the LXX) as its sacred Scriptures, was not long in setting the new evangelic and apostolic writings alongside the Law and the Prophets, and in using them for the propagation and defence of the gospel and in Christian worship. Thus Justin Martyr, about the middle of the 2nd century, describes how Christians in their Sunday meetings read 'the memoirs of the apostles or the writings of the prophets' (*Apology* i. 67). It was natural, then, that when Christianity spread among people who spoke other languages than Greek, the New Testament should be translated from Greek into those languages for the benefit of new converts. There were Latin and Syriac versions of the New Testament by AD 200, and a Coptic one within the following century.

V. THE MESSAGE OF THE BIBLE

The Bible has played, and continues to play, a notable part in the history of civilization. Many languages have been reduced to writing for the first time in order that the Bible, in whole or in part, might be translated into them in written form. And this is but a minor sample of the civilizing mission of the Bible in the world.

This civilizing mission is the direct effect of the central message of the Bible. It may be thought surprising that one should speak of a central message in a collection of writings which reflects the history of civilization in the Near East over several millennia. But a central message there is, and it is the recognition of this that has led to the common treatment of the Bible as a book, and not simply a collection of books—just as the Greek plural *biblia* ('books') became the Latin singular *biblia* ('the book').

The Bible's central message is the story of salvation, and throughout both Testaments three strands in this unfolding story can be distinguished: the bringer of salvation, the way of salvation, and the heirs of salvation. This could be reworded in terms of the covenant idea by saying that the central message of the Bible is God's covenant with men, and that the strands are the mediator of the covenant, the basis of the covenant, and the covenant people. God Himself is the Saviour of His people; it is He who confirms His covenant-mercy with them. The bringer of salvation, the Mediator of the covenant, is Jesus Christ, the Son of God. The way of salvation, the basis of the covenant, is God's grace, calling forth from His people a response of faith and obedience. The heirs of salvation, the covenant people, are the Israel of God, the Church of God.

The continuity of the covenant people from the Old Testament to the New is obscured for the reader of the common English Bible because 'church' is an exclusively New Testament word, and he naturally thinks of it as something which began in the New Testament period. But the reader of the Greek Bible was confronted by no new word when he found *ekklēsia* in the New Testament; he had already met it in the LXX as one of the words used to denote Israel as the 'assembly' of Yahweh. To be sure, it has a new and fuller meaning in the New Testament. Jesus said 'I will build my church' (Mt. xvi. 18), for the old covenant people had to die with Him in order to rise with Him to new life—a new life in which national restrictions had disappeared. But He provides in Himself the vital continuity between the old Israel and the new, and His faithful followers were both the righteous remnant of the old and the nucleus of the new. The Servant Lord and His servant people bind the two Testaments together. (See CHURCH; ISRAEL OF GOD.)

The message of the Bible is God's message to man, communicated 'by divers portions and in divers manners' (Heb. i. 1, RV) and finally incarnated in Christ. Thus 'the authority of the holy scripture, for which it ought to be believed and obeyed, dependeth not upon the testimony of any man or church, but wholly upon God (who is truth itself), the author thereof; and therefore it is to be received, because it is the word of God' (*Westminster Confession of Faith*, i. 4).

See also BIBLICAL CRITICISM; CANON OF NEW TESTAMENT; CANON OF OLD TESTAMENT; ENGLISH VERSIONS; INSPIRATION; INTERPRETATION (BIBLICAL); LANGUAGE OF APOCRYPHA, OF OLD TESTAMENT, OF NEW TESTAMENT; REVELATION; SCRIPTURE; TEXT AND VERSIONS.

BIBLIOGRAPHY. B. F. Westcott, *The Bible in the Church*, 1896; T. W. Manson (ed.), *A Companion to the Bible*, 1939; N. H. Snaith, *The Distinctive Ideas of the Old Testament*, 1944; B. B. Warfield, *The Inspiration and Authority of the Bible*, 1948; A. Richardson and W. Schweitzer (eds.), *Biblical Authority for Today*, 1951; C. H. Dodd, *According to the Scriptures*, 1952; H. H. Rowley, *The Unity of the Bible*, 1953; F. F. Bruce, *The Books and the Parchments*, 1953; A. M. Chirgwin, *The Bible in World Evangelism*, 1954; J. Bright, *The Kingdom of God in Bible and Church*, 1955; J. K. S. Reid, *The Authority of the Bible*, 1957; E. J. Young, *Thy Word is Truth*, 1957; C. F. H. Henry (ed.), *Revelation and the Bible*, 1959; O. Weber, *Ground Plan of the Bible*, 1959.

F.F.B.

BIBLICAL CRITICISM is the application to the biblical writings of certain techniques which are used in the examination of many kinds of literature in order to establish as far as possible their original wording, the manner and date of their composition, their sources, authorship, and so forth.

I. TEXTUAL CRITICISM

Textual criticism is the discipline by which an attempt is made to restore the original wording of a document where this has been altered in the course of copying and recopying. Even with modern printing methods, where repeated revisions in proof by a number of readers reduce the chance of error to a minimum, it is not often that the printed form reproduces the original copy to the last detail. It was much easier for errors in copying to arise before the invention of printing, when each copy of a document had to be written out by hand. When the author's autograph survives, the copyists' errors can be corrected by reference to it. But when the autograph has disappeared, and the surviving copies differ from one another in various details, the original wording can be reconstructed only by dint of careful study and comparison of these copies. Questions about the scribal habits of this or that copyist, and the remoteness or nearness of this or that copy to the original, must be asked. The types of error most commonly made must be borne in mind. Textual criticism is not a technique that can be learned overnight; expertise in it comes with long study and practice, although some scholars in addition seem to have a special flair for divining the original text, even where the available copies are almost desperately corrupt.

Since no autograph of any book of the Bible has survived, textual criticism plays an important part in Bible study. The material on which textual critics of the Bible work includes not only manuscript copies of the books of the Bible in their original languages but also ancient translations into other languages and quotations of biblical passages by ancient authors. Since it is important to establish a reliable text before proceeding to further study, textual criticism used to be called 'lower criticism', as though it represented the lower and earlier courses in the structure of critical examination. For further details of biblical textual criticism, see TEXT AND VERSIONS.

II. LITERARY CRITICISM

To distinguish it from textual or 'lower' criticism, literary criticism of the documents was formerly known as 'higher' criticism, because it represented the upper courses of the critical structure, which could not be laid until the lower courses of textual criticism had been placed in position. The phrase 'higher criticism' was first applied to biblical literature by J. G. Eichhorn, in the preface to the second edition of his *Old Testament Introduction* (1787): 'I have been obliged to bestow the greatest amount of labour on a hitherto entirely unworked field, the investigation of the inner constitution of the individual books of the Old Testament by the aid of the higher criticism—a new name to no humanist.' By the 'inner constitution' of a book he meant its structure, including a study of the sources which were used by its author and the way in which these sources were utilized or combined by him. This last aspect of the study is commonly referred to as 'source criticism'. The literary criticism of documents includes also such questions as their date and authorship.

Source criticism can be pursued with greater certainty when a documentary source of a later work has survived along with the work which has drawn upon it. In the Old Testament this is the situation with regard to the books of Chronicles. Prominent among the sources of the Chronicler were the books of Samuel and Kings, and as these have survived we can reach fairly definite conclusions about the Chronicler's use of them. In the New Testament Mark's Gospel is usually believed to have been a principal source of the other two Synoptic Evangelists; here, too, the source survives alongside the later works which incorporated much of it, so that we can study the way in which Matthew and Luke used Mark.

Where the sources are no longer extant, source criticism is much more precarious. If, for example, our four Gospels in their separate form had disappeared, and we had to depend on Tatian's *Diatessaron*—a 2nd-century compilation which unstitched the contents of the Gospels and rewove them into a continuous narrative—it would have been impossible to reconstruct the four Gospels on its basis. We could certainly recognize that the *Diatessaron* was not a unitary work, and it would not be difficult to distinguish between the Johannine and Synoptic material embodied in it; but to disentangle the three Synoptic narratives would be impossible, the more so because of the considerable amount of material common to the three or to two of them. This is the kind of situation we are faced with in the source criticism of the Pentateuch. That a number of sources underlie the Pentateuch as we have it is generally agreed, but what these sources are, what their date and mutual relation may be, and how and when they were utilized in the final recension of the Pentateuch—these are questions on which scholars disagree, more today indeed than they did at the beginning of the 20th century.

The criteria for dating an ancient work are partly internal, partly external. If a work is quoted or otherwise alluded to by a reliable and dateable authority we conclude that it must have been composed earlier. It may refer to events which can be dated on the basis of other documents; thus some parts of the Old Testament can be dated because of their references to persons or incidents of Egyptian or Mesopotamian history. It may, of course, date itself; thus some of the prophetical books of the Old Testament indicate the actual year in which this or that oracle was uttered, or the reign or reigns within which a prophet prophesied. And as the history of the Ancient Near East is being reconstructed in ever-greater detail, it becomes increasingly possible to put an ancient work into its proper setting in the historical framework.

The predictive element in biblical prophecy, however, involves some modification of the common dating criteria. To interpret all fulfilled predictions as *vaticinia ex eventu* is quite uncritical. When we are trying to date a genuine piece of predictive prophecy, we shall regard it as earlier than the events it predicts, but not earlier than those which it refers to as having taken place, or presupposes as its historical background. On this basis we should date Nahum's prophecy before the fall of Nineveh in 612 BC, which it foretells, but later than the fall of Thebes in 663 BC, to which it refers as a past event (Na. iii. 8 f.). Just where within that half-century the prophecy should be located must be decided by a close examination of the wording and a reckoning of probabilities.

Basic to Old Testament literary criticism is the criticism of the Pentateuch. The continuous modern history of Pentateuchal criticism begins with the work of H. B. Witter (1711) and J. Astruc (1753), who distinguished two documentary sources in the earlier part of the Pentateuch, using as their criterion the alternating use of the divine names Yahweh and *'ᵉlōhîm*. J. G. Eichhorn (1780) correlated stylistic variations with the analysis based on the distribution of divine names. This preliminary stage in source criticism was followed by the analysis of the Pentateuch into a large number of smaller units (A. Geddes, 1792, and J. S. Vater, 1802–5). This, in turn, was followed by the 'supplementary hypothesis' (H. Ewald, 1843), which envisaged one basic document (the 'Elohist'), supplemented by a few shorter ones. H. Hupfeld (1853) distinguished two separate sources, both of which used the divine name *'ᵉlōhîm* in Genesis (the sources later known as P and E). These two, with the Yahwist (J) and Deuteronomic (D) sources, made up the four main sources ever since widely recognized in the documentary analysis of the Pentateuch.

To the purely literary analysis a new generation of critics (outstandingly J. Wellhausen, 1876–7) added a new criterion. The documentary sources were correlated with the religious history of Israel in so persuasive a manner that for long the Wellhausenist construction commanded the allegiance of a majority of Old Testament scholars. Vastly augmented knowledge of Near Eastern religious and literary history, especially for the period 2000–800 BC, has now increasingly exposed the weaknesses of Wellhausenism, but of the rival constructions that have been propounded none has received anything like the acceptance which Wellhausenism once enjoyed. (See PENTATEUCH.)

As for the New Testament, the dominant critical problem in Gospel study is the interrelation of the Synoptic Gospels. The most notable step forward here was taken when C. Lachmann (1835) showed that Mark was the earliest of the Synoptics and was drawn upon by the other two. Source criticism in the Fourth Gospel (*cf.* R. Bultmann, 1941) has never proved convincing; criticism of this Gospel has centred round its historical character, purpose, date, and authorship. (See GOSPELS; JOHN, GOSPEL OF.)

In the New Testament the criticism of the Pauline Epistles has played a more comparable part to that played by Pentateuchal criticism in the Old Testament. The Tübingen school of F. C. Baur (1831) and his colleagues related the Pauline Epistles to the early history of the Church, reconstructed on Hegelian principles like Wellhausen's presentation of the history of Israel. Paul (of whose Epistles only Romans, 1 and 2 Corinthians, and Galatians were held to be genuine) stood in sharp antithesis to the Judaizing Petrine party with regard to the way of salvation; later New Testament writings (notably Acts) reflect a synthesis of the two opposing positions. Even more radical was the criticism of W. C. van Manen (1890), who treated *all* the Pauline Epistles as pseudepigrapha. His position was generally rejected; the Tübingen position has been subjected to severe criticism (in England notably by J. B. Lightfoot, B. F. Westcott, and W. Sanday) and wholesale modification, but its influence can be traced in New Testament study to the present day. (See the protest in J. Munck, *Paul and the Salvation of Mankind*, 1959.)

III. FORM CRITICISM

While the main schools of biblical source criticism have been predominantly literary in their interest, others have insisted on the importance of determining the oral prehistory of the written sources, and of classifying the source material into its appropriate 'forms' or categories of narrative, utterance, *etc.*

In the Old Testament this approach has proved specially fruitful in the study of the Psalms; their classification according to their principal types (*Gattungen*), especially by H. Gunkel (1904), where each type is related to a characteristic life-setting, has done more for the understanding of the Psalter than anything else in the 20th century.

From Scandinavia in recent times has come a more radical challenge to the basic principles of classical Old Testament criticism in the 'traditio-historical method' of I. Engnell and the 'Uppsala school'. This method makes much more room for oral transmission alongside documentary sources, and emphasizes the great reliability of material orally transmitted.

In the New Testament form criticism has been intensively applied to the Gospels from 1919 onwards. By the classification of the Gospel material according to 'form' an attempt has been made to get behind the postulated documentary sources so as to envisage the state of the tradition in the pre-literary stage. Both narrative and sayings have been classified according to 'form'; but such classification throws little light on the historicity of any particular incident or utterance. The common association of form criticism with a very sceptical estimate of the historical trustworthiness of the Gospels is mostly due not to form criticism itself but to the theological outlook of many form critics. Much form criticism has endeavoured to establish the life-setting of the various units of the Gospel tradition, and this life-setting is usually discovered in the worship and witness of the early Church. But a life-setting of one kind in the early Church does not necessarily exclude an original life-setting in the ministry of Jesus. The form criticism of the Gospels reminds us of the inadequacy of literary analysis alone to account for their composition, and it underlines the fact that no stratum of Gospel tradition, however far back we press our investigation, portrays any other Jesus than the divinely-commissioned Messiah, the Son of God.

BIBLIOGRAPHY. W. R. Smith, *The Old Testament in the Jewish Church*^{2}, 1892; T. K. Cheyne, *Founders of Old Testament Criticism*, 1893; F. C. Grant (ed.), *Form Criticism*, 1934; E. B. Redlich, *Form Criticism*, 1939; A. Bentzen, *Introduction to the Old Testament*, 1948; H. H. Rowley (ed.), *The Old Testament and Modern Study*, 1951; A. H. McNeile, *An Introduction to the Study of the New Testament*^{2}, 1953; C. H. Dodd, *New Testament Studies*, 1953; J. Knox, *Criticism and Faith*, 1953; A. Souter, *Text and Canon of the New Testament*^{2}, 1954; W. B. Glover, *Evangelical Nonconformists and Higher Criticism in the Nineteenth Century*, 1954; W. Broomall, *Biblical Criticism*, 1957; P. E. Kahle, *The Cairo Geniza*^{2}, 1959; I. Engnell, 'Methodological Aspects of Old Testament Study', *VT* Supplements, VII, 1959, pp. 13 ff.

F.F.B.

BIBLICAL INTERPRETATION. See INTERPRETATION, BIBLICAL.

BILHAH. 1. A servant-girl in Laban's household, given to Rachel on her marriage; in her mistress' place she bore Dan and Naphtali to Jacob (Gn. xxix. 29 ff.). Theories which start from the assumption that the 'sons of Israel' never actually existed as one family must suppose 'sons of Bilhah' to have a special meaning; *e.g.* Steuernagel (followed by Burney, *Judges*, Introduction, pp. cvi f., cx n.) equates them with 'Canaanite tribes which amalgamated with Rachel tribes'. There is, however, no common factor in the records concerning Dan and Naphtali which would supply independent evidence for such a hypothesis.

2. A Simeonite settlement, perhaps Tulul el-Medbah near Kh. Mesas; = Balah (Jos. xix. 3). Abel, *Géographie*, II, p. 258, 'Ba'alah (2)'. 1 Ch. iv. 29.

J.P.U.L.

BINDING AND LOOSING (Aram. *'^{a}sar* and *š^{e}rā'*). These are technical terms describing things forbidden or permitted by decisions of the scribes. Their Gk. equivalents, *deō* and *lyō*, are applied to Peter in Mt. xvi. 19, where he seems to be regarded as an ideal Christian scribe, to whom the sacred keys of knowledge and discipline, misused by Jewish scribes (Lk. xi. 52), are entrusted. The terms are used in Mt. xviii. 18 in a context which defines the Church's power to excommunicate and reconcile the sinner. While Peter sometimes acts on behalf of the Church (Acts ii, v, x), he does not appropriate the power of binding and loosing exclusively to himself. Power to remit and retain sins is vested in the whole Spirit-filled community in Jn. xx. 23.

deō (alone) is used of a prisoner (Acts xii. 6), of Satan, of legal ties (Rom. vii. 2). *lyō* (alone) is used of laws relaxed (Mt. v. 19) and sins (Rev. i. 5).

BIBLIOGRAPHY. *HDB*; *Arndt*; B. T. D. Smith, *CBSC*, pp. 97, 98. Magical use: H. J. Cadbury, *JBL*, LVIII, 1939, pp. 243–249. D.H.T.

BIRDS OF THE BIBLE. Palestine is a land very rich in birds. It has a great range of habitats, varying from semi-tropical to true desert; moreover, one of the main migration routes from Africa into Europe and Western Asia runs from the northern point of the Red Sea through the whole length of Israel. The resident birds are therefore augmented by numerous migrants, and there is some movement in progress in almost every month.

This wealth of bird life makes it difficult to name with certainty some of the birds named in the Bible, and in some cases it is not always possible to state with certainty whether the Hebrew words refer to birds or other classes of animals (*e.g.*, see BITTERN). The precise study of animal life began only in the 19th century, and it was formerly usual to give names only to animals which were very obvious or of practical importance. Animals resembling each other in general appearance or usage would thus be called by the same or by similar names. These general principles apply to animal life as a whole. There is usually little difficulty in identifying animals mentioned several times in varying contexts likely to provide clues, but the correct translation of many names found only in the various lists of Leviticus and Deuteronomy will always be difficult. With the exception of 'hawk', which is also mentioned in Jb. xxxix. 26, the following birds are found only in these lists: cuckoo (*šaḥap̄*), hawk (*nēṣ*), night-hawk (*taḥmās*), cormorant (*šālāḵ*), glede (*rā'â*), lapwing (*dûḵîpeṯ*), osprey (*'ozniyyâ*), and swan (*tinšemeṯ*). It is very doubtful if these indicate even the major group to which each bird belongs, and Driver (1955) gives an interesting new list of translations.

Treatment here will be confined to the more important species of birds and those that can be named with some certainty.

Palestine is still rich in large birds of prey, and outside the main towns the traveller is likely to see some of them in the air almost every day.

Heb. *rāḥām* (Lv. xi. 18; Dt. xiv. 17), 'gier eagle' (AV), 'vulture' (RSV), rendered by Young as 'parti-coloured vulture', is likely to be the Egyptian vulture, a conspicuous black-and-white bird frequently seen scavenging on garbage tips.

Among several birds of prey forbidden as food (Lv. xi. 13) is the ossifrage or bone-breaker (Heb. *peres*). This accurately describes the lammergeier or bearded vulture, which drops bones from a height on to rocks in order to break them and get the marrow within.

Some true eagles are still found in, or travel through, Palestine: Heb. *nešer* is probably as much a generic term as the English word 'eagle'. It could include all large birds of prey, and the many references, most of them figurative, give few clues as to the species. Mi. i. 16, 'enlarge thy baldness as the eagle', clearly suggests the griffon vulture, whose pale down-covered head contrasts with the well-feathered heads of all eagles. Some authorities consider that in all cases *nešer* should be the griffon vulture, just as Gk. *aetos*, translated 'eagle' in Mt. xxiv. 28 ('there will the eagles be gathered together'), should be rendered 'griffon vulture'. This verse clearly describes the flocking of vultures to a carcass.

'Vulture'—Heb. *'ayyâ* (Jb. xxviii. 7), *dā'â* (Lv. xi. 14) and *dayyâ* (Dt. xiv. 13; Is. xxxiv. 15)—is probably the kite, of which both the black and the red species are common.

Owls are referred to sixteen times in the Old Testament, by five Heb. words. With one exception (see 'ostrich' below), the translation is probably correct, and several different species may be intended.

The white stork is one of the most striking migratory birds of Palestine, slowly travelling north, especially along the Jordan valley in March and April. Je. viii. 7, 'the stork in the heaven knoweth her appointed times', suggests that *ḥªsîḏâ* may well be the stork, though it could refer to several other large birds, including the kite and heron.

The crane is a bird of similar build to the white stork and is also a migrant. It is thought that in Is. xxxviii. 14 and Je. viii. 7 Heb. *'āḡûr* and *sûs* have become interchanged and that the former should be translated 'crane' and the latter 'swallow', from its note. Both are migrants, as Je. viii. 7 suggests. Another word, *dᵉrôr*, is translated 'swallow' in Ps. lxxxiv. 3 and Pr. xxvi. 2, and in the former it is implied that it nests within the temple buildings. This would be true of several species of swallow and also of the swift, a bird of similar build and habits, but unrelated to the swallow. At least four species of swallow, four species of martin, and three species of swift occur in Palestine.

Sparrows are associated with human habitations in many parts of the world, and the house sparrow so common in Palestine today is identical with the Western European form. This could well have been the bird to which our Lord referred (Mt. x. 29, *etc.*), though Gk. *strouthion* implies a group of assorted small birds such as were, and still are, killed and offered for sale in Palestine. In Pss. lxxxiv. 3 and cii. 7, Heb. *ṣippôr* is translated 'sparrow', but in the latter 'a sparrow alone

Fig. 38. Birds and animals of the Palestinian desert. Much of Palestine is desert enjoying only 2 or 3 inches of rain per annum. See the map showing physical regions on p. 924. The mallow (9), or saltwort (genus *Atriplex*), flowers after the infrequent rain storms in spring, and other plants such as juniper (4), or white broom (*Retama raetam*), draw water from deep down in the soil. The quail (2) is one of many species that pass over the desert on migration, while the griffon vulture (1) is always waiting for casualties. The Palestinian gazelle (3) lives on the desert edge, drinking only seldom, but the gecko (5), carpet viper (6), desert viper (8), and desert monitor (7) are typical of the dry, inhospitable country, where they are active mostly at night. See also figs. 39, 40, 90.

upon the house top' hardly suggests the sociable house sparrow, and it could refer to the blue rock thrush, a solitary bird which sometimes perches on houses.

The absence of any mention of the domestic fowl from the Old Testament is at first surprising, since there is some evidence that Assyria paid tribute to Egypt, in the form of hens, *c.* 1500 BC, and cocks are shown on seals of the 7th century BC (see fig. *115*). However, Homer (*c.* 9th century BC) does not refer to hens, though he mentions geese. Some authorities consider that the fatted fowl of 1 Ki. iv. 23 could be domestic fowls. The importation of peacocks (1 Ki. x. 22) suggests that Solomon had traffic with Ceylon or India, the original home of the domestic fowl, and he could therefore have introduced them.

The only mention of the hen in the New Testament is in Mt. xxiii. 37 and Lk. xiii. 34, where in one of our Lord's most poignant similes it is obvious that Gk. *ornis* is the domestic hen. The cock (*alēktor*) is mentioned in two incidents. In Mk. xiii. 35 Jesus mentioned the four night watches, including 'at the cockcrowing'. The crowing of the cock was thought to take place at set times, and in many countries the domestic cock was regarded as an alarm clock, but it would be unwise to read any specific hours into the incident of Peter and the cockcrowing, Mt. xxvi. 74, 75, *etc.*

The peacock is native to the jungles of the Indo-Malayan region. There is no independent evidence to confirm the identification *tukkiyyim*, though it is suggested that this word is derived from the Sinhalese *tokei*, peacock. This splendid bird had reached Athens by 450 BC, and had been kept on the island of Samos earlier still.

The quail, almost the smallest of the game birds, features in only one incident, Ex. xvi. 13, *etc.*, 'at even the quails (*śelāw*) came up, and covered the camp'. There has been speculation as to the correct translation, but the quail fits better than any other creature. Ps. lxxviii. 27, 'feathered fowls', confirms that *śelāw* were birds; they also belonged to one of the few groups regarded as clean. Quails are migrants, and at certain seasons travel in large flocks a few feet above the ground. Their migrations take them across the route followed after the Exodus.

The only other gallinaceous bird identifiable is the partridge: 1 Sa. xxvi. 20, 'as when one doth hunt a partridge in the mountains'. Heb. *qôrē'* is the rock partridge (*Alectoris graeca*), which is hunted regularly in many parts of the Middle East and south-east Europe. It is similar to the red-legged partridge (*A. rufa*). The significance of the proverb in Je. xvii. 11 is not clear.

Two members of the crow family can be seen very frequently in Palestine—the raven and the hooded crow. Heb. *'ôrēḇ* and Gk. *korax* are analogous to the English 'crow' in that they probably refer primarily to the raven but are also used of crows as a whole. Both raven and hooded crow are similar in appearance and habits to the British birds.

The ostrich finds mention in several passages, but it is likely that *baṯ ya'anâ* should be translated 'ostrich' and not 'owl' in eight passages. Jb. xxxix. 13–18 is clearly a description of the ostrich, a bird which once lived in the Middle East. Here also there is some textual confusion, for while *ḥasîḏâ* is elsewhere translated 'stork', it is here translated 'ostrich', but AVmg reads 'of the stork and ostrich' (verse 13). Heb. *ye'ēnîm* is also translated 'ostriches' in La. iv. 3, but a bird such as an ostrich may well have several native names.

'A pelican of the wilderness' (Ps. cii. 6) has been thought a contradiction, but wilderness does not always connote desert. A swamp could also be described in this way, and the swamps in the northern Jordan valley at some seasons are still the home of flocks of white pelicans.

Several species of doves and pigeons are found in Palestine, and there is some confusion of names (so the English wood-pigeon is also known as ring-dove). Heb. *yônâ* is usually translated 'dove', but in the sacrificial passages of Leviticus and Numbers it is always translated '(young) pigeon'. In the same verses is the *tôr*, turtle or turtle dove; this has the scientific generic name *Turtur*, from its call, and this can be identified with both the common turtle dove and the collared turtle dove, mostly the latter, which has long been domesticated with the name Barbary dove. Heb. *yônâ* is therefore the rock dove (*Columba livia*), which was domesticated in antiquity and has been used widely as a source of food and for message-carrying.

Speckled bird (*ṣāḇûa'*), Je. xii. 9, is considered by many authorities to be better rendered 'hyena' (*q.v.*).

BIBLIOGRAPHY. G. R Driver, 'Birds in the Old Testament', *PEQ*, LXXXVI, 1954, pp. 5 ff., LXXXVII, 1955, pp. 129 ff.; 'Once Again: Birds in the Bible', *PEQ*, XC, 1958, pp. 56 ff.; A. Parmelee, *All the Birds of the Bible*, 1960.

G.C.

BIRTHDAY. The day of birth and its anniversaries were usually a day of rejoicing and often of feasting. Only two such anniversaries are recorded in Scripture, that of Joseph's pharaoh (Gn. xl. 20) and that of Herod Antipas (Mt. xiv. 6; Mk. vi. 21). In Egypt, celebration of birthdays is mentioned at least as early as the 13th century BC, and probably goes back much earlier (Helck and Otto, *Kleines Wörterbuch der Ägyptologie*, 1956, p. 115, with textual references). Pharaoh's accession was likewise kept as a feast-day, as is indicated by a text of Amenophis II, *c.* 1440 BC (Helck, *JNES*, XIV, 1955, pp. 22–31); observation of the royal birthday is attested under Ptolemy V (*c.* 205–182 BC; Budge, *The Rosetta Stone*, 1951, p. 8). An amnesty on a royal birthday is mentioned in a wisdom-papyrus of the 4th/5th century BC (S. R. K. Glanville, *The Instructions of 'Onchsheshonqy*, I, 1955, p. 13).

K.A.K.

Fig. 39. Birds and animals of the Judaean hills. The hooded crow (2) is one of the commonest medium-sized birds of the countryside; the closely related raven (1) is chiefly found in the steeper, rocky areas. The heaps thrown up by the mole rat (5) are seen wherever the soil is deep enough, often among the spring-flowering anemones (6) and chamomile (8). For a note on these plants (*Anemone coronaria* and *Anthemis palaestina*) see PLANTS under 'Lily' (p. 1004). Sheep (10) are typical of the hill country, being led from one patch of grazing to another. Syrian bears (9) spend most time in the hills, coming down mainly in winter. About a dozen species of scorpion (7) are known in Palestine, each having its own habitat. The rock hyrax (4) (AV 'Coney') lives only where it can find crevices for safe hiding. A typical plant of this region is the hyssop (3) or thorny caper (*Capparis spinosa*). See also figs. 38, 40, 90.

BIRTHRIGHT. See FIRSTBORN.

BISHOP.

I. APPLICATION OF THE TERM

In classical Greek, both gods and men can be described as *episkopoi* or 'overseers' in a general and non-technical sense; inscriptions and papyri of wide distribution use the word to denote magistrates, who sometimes appear to have administered the revenues of heathen temples; Plutarch (*Numa*, 9) calls the Roman pontifex *episkopos* of the Vestal Virgins; and the word can apply also to philosophers, especially Cynics, when acting as spiritual directors. The LXX employs the same term to describe taskmasters or officers (Ne. xi. 9; Is. lx. 17), and *episkopē* in reference to a visitation of God (Gn. l. 24; *cf.* Lk. xix. 44). In the New Testament the name is applied pre-eminently to Christ (1 Pet. ii. 25), next to the apostolic office (Acts i. 20, quoting Ps. cix. 8), and finally to the leaders of a local congregation (Phil. i. 1).

II. QUALIFICATIONS AND FUNCTION

It is improbable that the Christian use of the term was directly copied from either pagan or Jewish sources; taken over as a generic description of responsible office, its meaning was defined in accordance with the qualifications demanded by the Church. These are listed in 1 Tim. iii. 1 ff. and Tit. i. 7 ff.: blameless moral character, teaching ability, a hospitable nature, patience, experience, sobriety, leadership, and complete integrity, or in other words, the qualities required in a good teacher, pastor, and administrator. It appears to be virtually certain that the terms 'bishop' and 'presbyter' are synonymous in the New Testament (see PRESBYTER), with the proviso that, while a bishop should be apt to teach, not all elders actually laboured in the word and doctrine (1 Tim. v. 17). In Acts xx. 17, 28 Paul describes the presbyters of Ephesus as *episkopoi*; he says that the Holy Ghost has made them overseers of the flock, and this might be thought to imply that only now in his absence are they to succeed to the episcopal duties which he himself has previously performed; but the usage elsewhere current is against this interpretation. Thus, in Tit. i. 5 Titus is enjoined to ordain elders, and immediately afterwards (verse 7), in obvious reference to the same persons, the qualifications of a bishop are described; again, the verb *episkopein* is used to describe the elders' function in 1 Pet. v. 2; and while 1 Tim. iii confines itself to bishops and deacons, the mention of elders in v. 17 suggests that the eldership is another name for the episcopate. There was a plurality of bishops in the single congregation at Philippi (Phil. i. 1), from which we may conclude that they acted in a corporate capacity as its governing body.

III. THE RISE OF MONARCHICAL EPISCOPACY

There is no trace in the New Testament of government by a single bishop; the position of James at Jerusalem (Acts xv. 13, xxi. 18; Gal. ii. 9, 12) was quite exceptional, and the result of his personal relationship to Christ; but influence is a different thing from office. Among the Apostolic Fathers, Ignatius is the only one who insists on monarchical episcopacy, and even he never states that this is of divine institution—an argument which would have been decisive, if it had been available for him to use. Jerome, commenting on Tit. i. 5, remarks that the supremacy of a single bishop arose 'by custom rather than by the Lord's actual appointment', as a means of preventing schisms in the Church (*cf. Ep.* 146). It seems most probable that monarchical episcopacy appeared in the local congregations when some gifted individual acquired a permanent chairmanship of the board of presbyter-bishops. Harnack thought that the elders were the ruling body, while the bishops and deacons were the liturgical leaders and administrators employed by them. Others have seen the origins of the later episcopate in the position held by Paul's lieutenants Timothy and Titus; but these men are never called bishops, and we meet them in letters of recall, which make no clear provision for the appointment of personal successors.

We do not know how bishops were at first instituted to their office; but the emphasis on popular election in Clement of Rome and the *Didache* suggests that this was an early practice; and it was doubtless followed by prayer and imposition of hands.

See also CHURCH GOVERNMENT, MINISTRY.

BIBLIOGRAPHY. See bibliography under MINISTRY. G.S.M.W.

BITHYNIA. A territory on the Asiatic side of the Bosporus, bequeathed by its last king to the Romans in 74 BC and subsequently administered with Pontus as a single province. The area was partitioned between a number of flourishing Greek republics. It early attracted the attention of Paul (Acts xvi. 7), though he apparently never fulfilled his ambition of preaching there. Others did so, however (1 Pet. i. 1), and by AD 111 there was a thoroughly well-established church, even extending to rural areas, which had excited a good deal of local opposition (Pliny, *Ep.* x. 96).

E.A.J.

BITTER HERBS (Heb. *m^erôrîm*; Gk. *pikrides*). A salad composed of herbs constituted part of the Passover ordinance (Ex. xii. 8; Nu. ix. 11), and ordinarily was eaten after the Passover lamb had been tasted. The bitter herbs were not named individually, but would include lettuce, endive, parsley, watercress, cucumber, and horseradish. Though *mêrôrîm* was used elsewhere of 'bitterness' (*cf.* La. iii. 15), the Passover herbs, being easily prepared, reminded the Israelites of their haste in leaving Egypt, not their bitter persecution there. R.K.H.

BITTERN. The Heb. word *qippōḏ* is mentioned three times in the AV with reference to a creature of waste places which was to have a part in God's judgment on Babylon (Is. xiv. 23), Idumaea (Is. xxxiv. 11, RV 'porcupine'), and Nineveh (Zp. ii. 14). More precise definition seems impossible. Some equate the root with the Arabic word for 'porcupine' (so LXX, Vulg.), but the context in Zephaniah appears to rule out this translation; others suggest vaguely some sort of lizard. *ISBE*, with perhaps unwarranted confidence, describes the creature as a nocturnal variety of heron whose strange booming note from waste and desert places disturbs the stillness of night, giving 'an idea of desolation which nothing but the wail of a hyena can equal'. G. R. Driver, after an interesting discussion of the various possibilities ('Birds in the Old Testament', *PEQ*, LXXXVII, 1955, pp. 129 ff.), suggests identification with the ruffed bustard, a shy bird found usually in more solitary places. A marsh bird bearing the name of bittern is common today around Lake Huleh, north of the Sea of Galilee. J.D.D.

BITUMEN. In the EVV of the Old Testament the Hebrew words *kōp̄er* (Gn. vi. 14) and *zep̄eṯ* (Ex. ii. 3; Is. xxxiv. 9) are rendered 'pitch', and *ḥēmār* (Gn. xi. 3, xiv. 10; Ex. ii. 3) 'slime', and the word 'bitumen' is not used. It would seem better, however, to render all three terms by 'bitumen', since, while pitch is strictly the product of a distillation process, bitumen, a natural derivative of crude petroleum, is found ready to hand in Mesopotamia and Palestine, and is therefore more probably the material referred to. The word *kōp̄er* is derived from Akkadian *kupru* (from *kapāru*, 'to smear'), and an outside origin for *zep̄eṯ* is suggested by its west and south Semitic cognates, while *ḥēmār* may be a native Hebrew word from the verb *ḥāmar*, 'to ferment, boil up'. In view of the diverse origins of the three terms, it seems probable that they all meant the same thing and that no scientific distinctions are to be observed. See ARK.

BIBLIOGRAPHY. R. J. Forbes, *Studies in Ancient Technology*, I, 1955, pp. 1–120.

T.C.M.

BLASPHEMY.

I. IN THE OLD TESTAMENT

Here the root meaning of the word is an act of effrontery in which the honour of God is insulted by man. The proper object of the verb is the name of God, which is cursed or reviled instead of being honoured. (Compare the common biblical and rabbinical phrase, 'Blessed art Thou, O Lord.') The penalty for the outrage of blasphemy is death by stoning (Lv. xxiv. 10–23; 1 Ki. xxi. 9 ff.; Acts vi. 11, vii. 58). In the first reference it is a half-caste Israelite who sins in this way; and, generally speaking, blasphemy is committed by pagans (2 Ki. xix. 6, 22 = Is. xxxvii. 6, 23; Ps. xliv. 16; Is. lii. 5; Ps. lxxiv. 10, 18), sometimes incited to it by the bad example and moral lapses of the Lord's people (2 Sa. xii. 14). It follows also that when God's people fall into idolatry they are regarded as committing the blasphemy of the heathen (Ezk. xx. 27; Is. lxv. 7). The name of Yahweh which it is Israel's peculiar destiny to hallow (see G. F. Moore, *Judaism*, II, 1927–30, p. 103) is profaned by the faithless and disobedient people.

II. IN THE NEW TESTAMENT

Here there is an extension of the meaning. God is blasphemed also in His representatives. So the word is used of Moses (Acts vi. 11); Paul (Rom. iii. 8; 1 Cor. iv. 12, x. 30); and especially the Lord Jesus, in His ministry of forgiveness (Mk. ii. 7 and parallels), at His trial (Mk. xiv. 61–64: see TRIAL OF JESUS), and at Calvary (Mt. xxvii. 39; Lk. xxiii. 39). Because these representatives embody the truth of God Himself (and our Lord in a unique way) an insulting word spoken against them and their teaching is really directed against the God in whose name they speak (so Mt. x. 40; Lk. x. 16). Saul of Tarsus fulminated against the early followers of Jesus and tried to compel them to blaspheme, *i.e.* to curse the saving name (Acts xxvi. 11), and thereby to renounce their baptismal vow in which they confessed that 'Jesus is Lord' (*cf.* 1 Cor. xii. 3; Jas. ii. 7). His misdirected zeal, however, was not simply against the Church, but against the Lord Himself (1 Tim. i. 13; *cf.* Acts ix. 4).

The term is also used, in a weaker sense, of slanderous language addressed to men (*e.g.* Mk. iii. 28, vii. 22; Eph. iv. 31; Col. iii. 8; Tit. iii. 2). Here the best translation is 'slander, abuse'. These verses condemn a prevalent vice; but their warning may be grounded in a theological as well as an ethical context if we remember James iii. 9. Men are not to be cursed because on them, as men, the 'formal' image of God is stamped and the human person is, in some sense, God's representative on earth (*cf.* Gn. ix. 6).

There are two problem texts. 2 Pet. ii. 10, 11 speaks of blasphemy against 'the glorious ones' (RSV) whom angels dare not revile. These are probably evil angelic powers against whom false teachers presumed to direct their insults (*cf.* Jude 8). The blasphemy against the Holy Spirit (Mt. xii. 32; Mk. iii. 29) carries with it the awful pronouncement that the sinner is 'guilty of an eternal sin' which cannot be forgiven. The verse is a solemn warning against persistent, deliberate rejection of the Spirit's call to salvation in Christ. Human unresponsiveness inevitably leads to a state of moral insensibility and to a confusion of moral issues wherein evil is embraced as though it were good ('Evil, be thou my Good'; *cf.* Is. v. 18–20; Jn. iii. 19). The example of this attitude is that of the Pharisees, who attributed Jesus' works of mercy to Satan. In such a frame of mind repentance is not possible to the hardened heart because the recognition of sin is no longer possible, and God's offer of mercy is in effect peremptorily refused. To be in this perilous condition is to cut oneself off from the source of forgiveness. Hebert adds a helpful pastoral note: 'People who are distressed in their souls for fear that they have committed the sin against the Holy Ghost should in most cases be told that their distress is proof that they have not committed that sin' (*TWB*, p. 32).

BIBLIOGRAPHY. *TWNT*, I, pp. 620 ff. (H. W. Beyer); *Arndt*, p. 142; *TWB*, pp. 32 f.; *Vocabulary of the Bible*, pp. 35 f. (C. Senft). R.P.M.

BLESSED. The most frequent Old Testament word is *bārûḵ*. When applied to God it has the sense of praise (Gn. ix. 26; 1 Ki. i. 48; Ps. xxviii. 6, *etc.*), and when used of man denotes a state of happiness (1 Sa. xxvi. 25; 1 Ki. ii. 45). *'Aš^{e}rê* ('how happy!', Ps. i. 1) is always used of men and has for its New Testament equivalent *makarios*. The latter is used in pagan Greek literature to describe the state of happiness and well-being such as the gods enjoy. In the New Testament it is given a strong spiritual content, as revealed in the Beatitudes (Mt. v. 3–11) and elsewhere (Lk. i. 45; Jn. xx. 29; Acts xx. 35; Jas. i. 12). The word seems also to contain a congratulatory element, as a note in *Weymouth's New Testament* suggests: 'People who are blessed may outwardly be much to be pitied, but from the higher and therefore truer standpoint they are to be envied, congratulated and imitated.' *Eulogētos* is used only of Christ and God (Rom. ix. 5; Eph. i. 3).

BIBLIOGRAPHY. J. Pedersen, *Israel: Its Life and Culture*, 1926. W.W.W.

BLESSING. The Old Testament word is *b^{e}rāḵâ*, and generally denotes a bestowal of good, usually conceived of as material (Dt. xi. 26; Pr. x. 22, xxviii. 20; Is. xix. 24, *etc.*). Often it is contrasted with the curse (Gn. xxvii. 12; Dt. xi. 26–28, xxiii. 5, xxviii. 2, xxxiii. 23), and sometimes is used of the formula of words which constitute a 'blessing' (Gn. xxvii. 36, 38, 41; Dt. xxxiii. 1). The New Testament word, *eulogia*, is used also in the latter sense (Jas. iii. 10), but in addition denotes both the spiritual good brought by the gospel (Rom. xv. 29; Eph. i. 3) and material blessings generally (Heb. vi. 7, xii. 17; 2 Cor. ix. 5, 'bounty').

W.W.W.

BLINDNESS. See DISEASE AND HEALING.

BLOOD. The point chiefly to be determined is whether 'blood' in biblical usage points basically to life or to death. There are those who hold that in the sacrificial system of the Old Testament 'blood' represents life liberated from the limitations of the body and set free for other purposes. The ceremonial manipulation of blood on this view represents the solemn presentation to God of life, life surrendered, dedicated, transformed. The death occupies a subordinate place or even no place at all. On this view 'the blood of Christ' would mean little more than 'the life of Christ'. The evidence, however, does not seem to support it.

In the first place there is the statistical evidence. Of the 362 passages in which the Hebrew word *dam* occurs in the Old Testament, 203 refer to death with violence. Only seven passages connect life and blood (seventeen refer to the eating of meat with blood). From this it is clear enough that death is the association most likely to be conjured up by the use of the term.

Then there is the lack of evidence adduced in support of the life theory. Exponents of this view regard it as self-evident from passages such as Lv. xvii. 11, 'the life of the flesh is in the blood'. But the scriptural passages can just as well be interpreted of life yielded up in death, as of life set free.

It is undeniable that in some places atonement is said to have been secured by death, *e.g.* Nu. xxxv. 33, 'for blood it defileth the land: and the land cannot be cleansed (lit. atoned) of the blood that is shed therein, but by the blood of him that shed it'. See also Ex. xxix. 33; Lv. x. 17.

The Old Testament, then, affords no grounds for the far-reaching statements that are sometimes made. Atonement is secured by the death of a victim rather than by its life. This carries over into the New Testament. There, as in the Old Testament, blood is more often used in the sense of death by violence than in any other sense. When we come to the blood of Christ there are some passages which indicate in the plainest possible fashion that death is meant. Such are the references to being 'justified by his blood' (Rom. v. 9; parallel to 'reconciled . . . by the death of his Son' in verse 10), 'the blood of his cross' (Col. i. 20), the reference to coming 'by water and blood' (1 Jn. v. 6), and others.

Sometimes the death of Christ is thought of as a sacrifice (*e.g.* the blood of the covenant). But a close examination of all these passages indicates that the term is used in the same way as in the Old Testament. That is to say, the sacrifices are still understood to be efficacious by virtue of the death of the victim. 'The blood of Christ' accordingly is to be understood of the atoning death of the Saviour. See also ATONEMENT.

BIBLIOGRAPHY. J. Behm, in *TWNT*; S. C. Gayford, *Sacrifice and Priesthood*[2], 1953; Leon Morris, *The Apostolic Preaching of the Cross*, 1955; F. J. Taylor, in *RTWB*; H. C. Trumbull, *The Blood Covenant*, 1887; A. M. Stibbs, *The Meaning of the Word 'Blood' in Scripture*, 1947. L.M.

BLOOD, AVENGER OF. See AVENGER OF BLOOD.

BLOOD, FIELD OF. See AKELDAMA.

BOANERGES. The name given by Jesus to the sons of Zebedee and recorded only in Mk. iii. 17. Its derivation is uncertain, but it is most likely to be the equivalent of the Hebrew *b^{e}nê regeš* ('sons of confusion or thunder') but might be from *b^{e}nê r^{e}ğaz* ('sons of wrath'; *cf.* Jb. xxxvii. 2). It is strange that *b^{e}nê* should be transliterated by *boanē-* in Gk.; some corruption has been suspected.

The title seems not to have been greatly used. It is variously seen to be appropriate in their

Fig. 40. Birds and animals of Upper Galilee. Compared with the rest of Palestine, Upper Galilee is green and well watered. See the map showing physical regions on p. 924. The chameleon (2) lives on such bushes as the rose (1; *Nerium oleander*, for which see p. 1006) which are green all the year. Wild boars (6) are found in the bulrush (papyrus) beds (5). Wild mint (8) grows in the moister places and water lilies (7) right in the water. The fallow deer (9) is an animal of the more wooded regions, but the fox (4) may be found over a wide range of country. The white stork (3) is Palestine's most conspicuous migrant, passing through in great numbers in spring and autumn. See also figs. 38, 39, 90.

fiery temper (Lk. ix. 54–56), which may have caused James' death (Acts xii. 2), and in the heavenly resonance of the Johannine writings.

R.E.N.

BOAR. The only occurrence of *ḥazîr*, tr. boar or swine, is in Ps. lxxx. 13. The wild boar is the species (*Sus scrofa*) from which the domestic pig is derived, and it is still common in suitable areas of the Middle East, where the food habits of both Jew and Muslim provide no incentive for control. Its main habitat is forest and reed beds, and it is likely that the first phrase of Ps. lxviii. 30 is more accurately rendered, as in AVmg and RSV, as '. . . the beasts that dwell among the reeds', *i.e.* wild boars. See fig. 40.

G.C.

BOAT. See SHIPS AND BOATS.

BOAZ. The hero of the book of Ruth, a wealthy landowner of Bethlehem, a benevolent farmer who had a concern for his workers' welfare and a sense of family responsibility. This led him to redeem Ruth, a widow of a distant relative, in place of her next-of-kin, under the levirate marriage law. He thus became the great-grandfather of David (Ru. iv. 17–22; *cf.* Mt. i. 5).

M.G.

BOAZ (PILLAR). See JACHIN AND BOAZ.

BODY. Several Hebrew words are translated 'body' in the AV, the principal one being *gewiyyâ*, which is used primarily of a 'corpse', though also of the living human body (Gn. xlvii. 18). Contrary to Greek philosophy and much modern thought, the emphasis in Hebrew is not on the body as distinct from the soul or spirit, although in Aramaic sections of Daniel, often regarded as late and influenced by Greek thought, there is a clearer distinction between body and spirit (vii. 15), where the word (*niḏneh*) is probably a loan-word from Persian.

The common Hebrew word for flesh (*bāśār*) comes nearest to presenting a distinction from spirit (Is. xxxi. 3), and may have influenced Paul in his theological use of the term (see FLESH). The usage of the term for 'heart' in Heb. could perhaps be said to come near to what we would mean by spirit (Ps. lxxxiv. 2), but it is significant that it is at the same time a physical organ (see HEART). It is noteworthy that much modern psychology is realizing the essential unity of the whole man.

On the other hand, in Hebrew thought there were no clearly defined physiologically unifying concepts, such as the nervous or circulatory systems, and the various organs are sometimes spoken of as having a seeming independence of action (Mt. v. 29, 30) (see EYE, HAND, LIP, *etc.*), though this is obviously synecdoche in certain passages, *e.g.* Dt. xxviii. 4, *beṭen* = 'belly', translated 'body' in AV. Likewise Is. li. 23, *gēwâ* = 'back'; La. iv. 7, *'eṣem* = 'bone'.

The New Testament usage of *sōma*, 'body', keeps close enough to the Hebrew to avoid the thought of Greek philosophy, which tends to castigate the body as evil, the prison of the soul or reason, which is good, though Paul does use 'body of sin' as a theological term parallel to 'flesh' indicating the locality of operation of sin. There is, however, a clearer distinction in the New Testament between body and soul or spirit (Mt. x. 28; 1 Thes. v. 23; Jas. ii. 26).

But nowhere in the Bible do we get a view of man as existing apart from the body, even after death in the future life, though there are evil disembodied spirits around, liable to enter a man (Lk. iv. 36, viii. 26 ff., *cf.* xxiv. 39). The clearly-enunciated belief in a physical resurrection found in the New Testament (1 Cor. xv. 42–52; 1 Thes. iv. 13–18), foreshadowed in the Old Testament (Dn. xii. 2), militates against any idea of man enduring apart from some bodily manifestation or form of expression, though this does not imply the regrouping of the selfsame material atoms (1 Cor. xv. 44). A passage which at first sight seems to suggest separation from the body (2 Cor. v. 1–8) is perhaps best explained by J. A. T. Robinson (*In the End God*, 1950) as referring not to death, but the parousia, thus not to the distinction between soul or spirit and body, but between the future resurrection body and the present mortal body.

The form of the resurrection body—the 'spiritual body' of 1 Cor. xv—can only be glimpsed from what we know of Christ's risen body, which left no corpse in the tomb, and, it seems, passed through the graveclothes (Lk. xxiv. 12, 31). The ascension of His body does not necessarily suppose movement to a certain locality known as heaven, but suggests the emergence of the body into the larger life beyond the inevitable space–time limitations of this life.

The metaphor of the Church as the Body of Christ (*q.v.*; 1 Cor. xii. 12 ff., *etc.*) develops the idea of the body as the essential form and means of expression of the person.

BIBLIOGRAPHY. E. C. Rust, *Nature and Man in Biblical Thought*, 1953; A. R. Johnson, *The Vitality of the Individual in the Thought of Ancient Israel*, 1949.

B.O.B.

BODY OF CHRIST. This phrase has a threefold use in the New Testament.

1. The human body of Jesus Christ, insisted on by the New Testament writers in the face of docetism as real (denial that Jesus Christ came in the flesh is 'of the antichrist', 1 Jn. iv. 2, 3). The reality of Christ's body is the proof of His true manhood. That the Son should take a human body is thus a fact essential for salvation (*cf.* Heb. ii. 14 ff.) and specifically for atonement (Heb. x. 20). The transformation (not relinquishment) of it at the resurrection is a guarantee and prototype of the resurrection body for believers (1 Cor. xv; Phil. iii. 21).

2. The bread at the Last Supper over which Christ spoke the words 'This is my body' (recorded in Mt. xxvi; Mk. xiv; Lk. xxii; 1 Cor. xi, *cf.* 1 Cor. x. 16). The words have been inter-

preted historically as meaning both 'This represents my sacrifice' and also 'This is myself'.

3. The exact phrase is used by Paul in 1 Cor. x. 16, xii. 27 as a description of a group of believers —*cf.* 'one body in Christ' (Rom. xii. 5) and 'body' in verses referring to a church, or to the Church, *i.e.* 1 Cor. x. 17, xii. 12; Eph. i. 23 (but see C. F. D. Moule, *Colossians*, p. 168), ii. 16, iv. 4, 12, 16, v. 23; Col. i. 18, 24, ii. 19, iii. 15. It should be noted that the phrase is 'body of Christ', not 'of Christians', and that it has visible, congregational, and also eschatological significance.

The image is developed in two distinct ways. In the Corinthian and Roman Epistles Paul speaks to a local church and there is no reference to the headship of Christ (indeed, the reference to the 'head' in 1 Cor. xii. 21 shows that this thought is not in Paul's mind at all). In the Ephesian and Colossian Epistles the whole Church is in view, and he speaks of Christ as the Head of the Body.

The origin of Paul's image has been sought in: (i) the communal participation in the Communion bread, representing the broken body (so Rawlinson, Thornton); (ii) Stoic conceptions (W. L. Knox, T. W. Manson); (iii) Christ's close identification with Christians (*e.g.* Acts ix. 4, 5; Col. i. 24).

The exegetical problem is to establish the amount of metaphor in the phrase. If it is literal, the Church is viewed as the extension of the incarnation; if metaphorical, believers are being instructed that Church unity depends upon Christ. The diverse developments of the thought in 1 Corinthians, on the one hand, and Colossians–Ephesians, on the other, would seem to rule out the possibility of the phrase being other than a metaphor.

BIBLIOGRAPHY. *Arndt*; 'Body' and 'Thank' in *RTWB*; *TWNT*; 'Eucharist' in *ODCC*; J. A. T. Robinson, *The Body*, 1953; E. Best, *One Body in Christ*, 1955. M.R.W.F.

BOIL, BOTCH (Heb. *šᵉḥîn*, 'burning'; *cf.* root in Arab., Aram., Eth., 'to be hot'). A generic term which the Old Testament uses to denote different kinds of localized inflammation. For the 'boils with blains' of the sixth plague (Ex. ix. 9 ff.), see PLAGUES OF EGYPT (sixth plague). In Lv. xiii. 18–24 boils are mentioned in association with what is there termed leprosy (*q.v.*), while the malignant boils which afflicted Job (ii. 7), of which various diagnoses have been made, may have been tubercular leprosy. 'The botch of Egypt', which extended from top to toe (Dt. xxviii. 27, 35), was probably one of the cutaneous diseases peculiar to Egypt (*cf.* Pliny, *NH* xxvi. 5); J. R. Bennett (*Diseases of the Bible*, pp. 64 f.) suggests an endemic boil or malignant pustule. Hezekiah's boil (2 Ki. xx. 7; Is. xxxviii. 21; see FIG) was most likely a carbuncle. See also DISEASE AND HEALING. J.D.D.

BONES (*'eṣem*, common in the Old Testament; *osteon*, in the New Testament only five times; with occasional alternatives to each). As the basic and most durable part of the human body, the bones are used to describe the deepest feelings, affections, and affiliations (Gn. xxix. 14; Jdg. ix. 2; Jb. ii. 5, xxx. 30; Ps. xlii. 10; Eph. v. 30), often with 'flesh' as a parallel. The decent burial of the bones, or corpse, was regarded as an important matter (Gn. l. 25; Heb. xi. 22; Ezk. xxxix. 15). Contact with them caused defilement (Nu. xix. 16); to burn men's bones on altars was a most effective way of deconsecrating them (2 Ki. xxiii. 20).

The bones preserved some of the vitality of the individual (2 Ki. xiii. 21), but dry bones less so (Ezk. xxxvii. 1, 2 and figuratively verse 11). To break or scatter the bones was utterly to defeat an enemy (Ps. liii. 5; Is. xxxviii. 13) and to burn them a sin (Am. ii. 1). B.O.B.

BONNET. In AV this translates two Hebrew words. 1. *miḡbā'ôṯ*, 'turbans' (Ex. xxviii. 40; Lv. viii. 13, *etc.*). 2. *pᵉ'ēr*, 'tires' (Is. iii. 20, RSV 'head-dress'; Ezk. xliv. 18, RSV 'linen turbans'). For a head-covering Israelites probably wore a folded square of cloth as a veil for protection against the sun, or wrapped it as a turban around the head. See also MITRE, DRESS. J.D.D.

BOOK. See WRITING.

BOOK OF LIFE (Heb. *sēper ḥayyîm*; Gk. *biblos* or *biblion zōēs*, 'the roll of the living').

1. It is used of natural life, Ps. lxix. 28, where 'let them be blotted out of the book of the living' means 'let them die'. *Cf.* Ex. xxxii. 32 f., where Moses prays to be blotted out of God's book if Israel is to be destroyed; Ps. cxxxix. 16 ('in thy book all my members were written'); Dn. xii. 1, where all the righteous who 'shall be found written in the book' will survive the eschatological tribulation.

2. In later Judaism and the New Testament it is used of the life of the age to come. Thus Is. iv. 3, where 'every one that is written among the living in Jerusalem' refers to natural life, is re-interpreted in the Targum as speaking of 'eternal life'. So in the New Testament the book of life is the roster of believers, *e.g.* Phil. iv. 3; Rev. iii. 5, xxii. 19, *etc.* At the last judgment everyone not enrolled in the book of life is consigned to the fiery lake (Rev. xx. 12, 15); this is the book of life of the slaughtered Lamb (Rev. xiii. 8, xxi. 27), in which the names of the elect have been inscribed 'from the foundation of the world' (xvii. 8). The same idea is expressed in Lk. x. 20, 'your names are written in heaven'; Acts xiii. 48, 'as many as were ordained (*i.e.* inscribed) to eternal life believed'. F.F.B.

BOOTH. A word sometimes used in the EVV to translate the Hebrew term *sukkâ*, a booth or rude temporary shelter made of woven boughs (Ne. viii. 14–17). This type of structure figured particularly in the annual Feast of Tabernacles (*q.v.*; Lv. xxiii. 34; Dt. xvi. 13, AV, RV 'tabernacles', RSV 'booths'), but was also used by armies in the

field (see PAVILION and TENT), and in agriculture as a shelter from the sun (see Jb. xxvii. 18; Jon. iv. 5); or for cattle (Gn. xxxiii. 17; see SUCCOTH).
T.C.M.

BOOTHS, FEAST OF. See TABERNACLES, FEAST OF.

BOTCH. The AV rendering of *šeḥîn* in Dt. xxviii. 27, 35; elsewhere rendered 'boil'. See BOIL and PLAGUES OF EGYPT (sixth plague).

BOTTLE. Glass bottles were used in Egypt, probably rarely in Palestine (see GLASS). The narrow-necked earthenware bottle, *baqbuq* (Je. xix. 1, 10), was onomatopoeically named from the gurgling of escaping liquid. In 1 Ki. xiv. 3 the same word is translated 'cruse'. Biblical bottles are usually skins of goat, sheep, or occasionally ox, gutted, tanned, and sewn, serviceable, but subject to wear and tear (*cf.* Jos. ix. 4; Mt. ix. 17, *etc.*). They were used for water, wine, milk, *etc.* Heb. *ḥēmeṯ*, *nō'ḏ*, *nēḇel*; Gk. *askos* are the common words.

In Ps. cxix. 83 the Psalmist likens the trials of his waiting to the smoke-blackening of the hanging wineskin. In Ps. lvi. 8 God is poetically urged to preserve the tears of His saint in a bottle. The bottles of heaven in Jb. xxxviii. 37 are the rain-clouds likened to vast water-skins.
R.A.S.

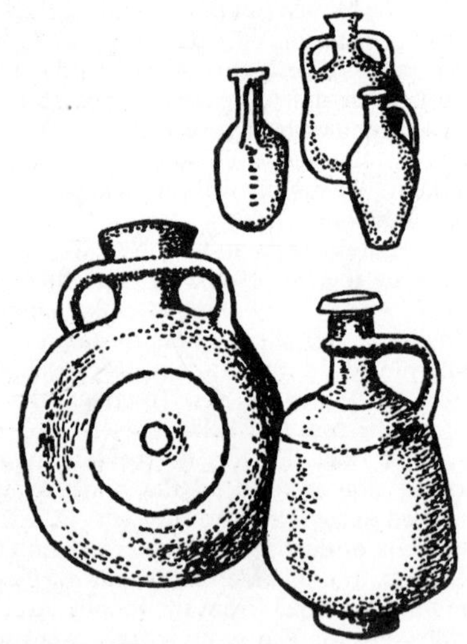

Fig. 41. Bottles from Lachish. 8th–7th centuries BC.

BOTTOMLESS PIT. See ABYSS.

BOW. See ARMOUR AND WEAPONS.

BOWELS (Heb. *mē'îm*; Gk. *splanchna*). The Hebrews had no clear idea of the physiology of the internal organs, and though 'bowels' refers primarily to the intestines, it is used in parallel with, or interchangeably for, the 'belly', 'womb', 'liver', or 'heart' (*qq.v.*), and may sometimes refer collectively to all the internal organs.

As well as the general physical usage, the psychical or symbolic usage is common, mainly in the New Testament. The bowels were conceived of as the seat of the deepest emotions, particularly compassion, from which comes the Gk. verb *splanchnizomai* (Lk. x. 33) to feel pity or compassion (Je. xxxi. 20; Phil. i. 8; 1 Jn. iii. 17; *cf.* *rāḥam* in Heb.; see WOMB).
B.O.B.

BOWL. See VESSEL.

BOX. 1. Heb. *paḵ*, 'flask', used as an oil container by Samuel when anointing Saul (1 Sa. x. 1, AV 'vial') and by one of the sons of the prophets

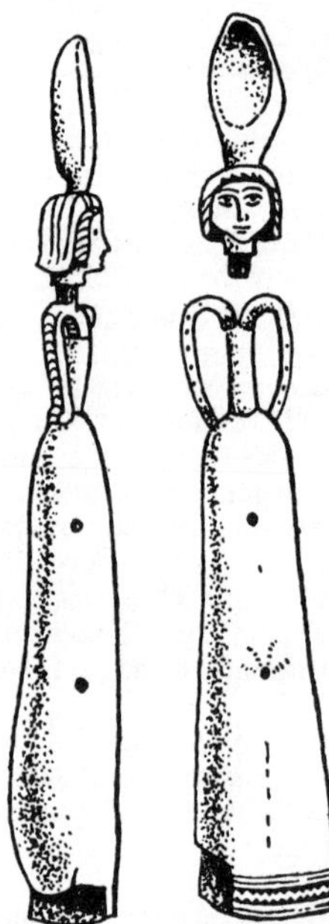

Fig. 42. Unguent vase of ivory with stopper pierced for contents to flow into bowl. 14th century BC from Lachish.

when anointing Jehu (2 Ki. ix. 1, 3). Narrow-necked juglets found on Iron Age sites may have been called *paḵ*, but the LXX *phakos*, lentil-shaped, suggests a lentoid flask with two handles, of similar date.

2. Gk. *alabastron*, a perfume bottle of alabaster. The woman at Simon the leper's house may have broken off the narrow neck (Mt. xxvi. 7; Mk. xiv. 3; *cf.* Lk. vii. 37). See BOTTLE.
A.R.M.

BOX-TREE. See TREES.

BOZEZ. See SENEH.

BOZRAH. 1. Bozrah in Moab is mentioned only in Je. xlviii. 24, and cannot be identified with any certainty. Grollenberg suggests Bezer, the levitical and refuge city (Dt. iv. 43; Jos. xxi. 36), 15 miles east of the point where the Jordan enters the Dead Sea. The *Westminster Historical Atlas*, however, prefers an identification with Bosora in the Hauran.

2. Bozrah in Edom (Gn. xxxvi. 33; Is. xxxiv. 6, lxiii. 1; Je. xlix. 13, 22; Am. i. 12; Mi. ii. 12) was the northernmost of the great Edomite cities, lying about 30 miles south of the Dead Sea. The overthrow of Bozrah, like that of Edom, is prophesied both as historical (Am. i. 12) and as symbolic of the Lord's final dealing with His enemies in the day of vengeance and salvation (Is. xxxiv. 6, lxiii. 1). J.A.M.

BRACELETS. See ORNAMENTS.

BRAMBLE. See THORN.

BRANCH. 1. The word is used in AV to represent various Heb. and Gk. words meaning sucker, sprout, twig, bough, palm-branch, *etc.* It occurs frequently in passages where Israel is spoken of under the figure of a tree, *e.g.* a vine (Ps. lxxx. 11; Ezk. xvii. 6; Na. ii. 2; *cf.* Jn. xv. 1 ff.) or a cedar (Ezk. xvii. 23) or an olive (Ho. xiv. 6; *cf.* Rom. xi. 16 ff.). Branches of trees, palm, myrtle, and willow were used ceremonially at the Feast of Tabernacles for making booths, *sukkôṯ* (Lv. xxiii. 40; Ne. viii. 15), and for carrying in procession with cries of Hosanna (*q.v.*; Ps. cxviii. 27, RSV; Mishnah, *Sukkah* iv). *Cf.* Jesus' triumphal entry into Jerusalem, Mt. xxi. 8; Mk. xi. 8; Jn. xii. 13.

2. Of special interest is the messianic use of the word (Heb. *ṣemaḥ*) for the scion of the family of David who would come to rule Israel in righteousness. Explicitly prophesied in Je. xxiii. 5, xxxiii. 15, the expression looks back to Is. iv. 2 (where, however, no personal Messiah is envisaged) and to Is. xi. 1 (where Heb. *nēṣer* is used). Zc. iii. 8, vi. 12 show that the title 'branch' was a recognized messianic term after the Exile. The idea of a Davidic Messiah is, however, much earlier than the language of this particular metaphor. See MESSIAH.

3. In Ex. xxv. 31 ff., xxxvii. 17 ff. the word is used of the golden candlestick in the tabernacle. The Heb. *qāneh* refers to the central shaft of the candlestick in xxv. 31, xxxvii. 17 (so RV), but in all other places to the six branches which stemmed from it, three on either side. J.B.Tr.

BRASS. See MINING AND METALS.

BRAZEN SERPENT. See SERPENT, BRAZEN.

BREAD. Bread was the all-important commodity of the Ancient East, and the price of grain is an infallible index to economic conditions at any given time. In the Old Babylonian period the grain of corn provided the basic unit for the system of weights, and cereal took the place of money in commerce. Hosea, even in his day, paid part of the price of his wife in grain.

While we possess much information about the price of grain, references to the price of bread are extremely rare. One reference from the Hammurabi period (18th century BC) gives 10 *še* (about a twentieth of a shekel) as the price of 4 *sila* bread. (B. Meissner, *Werenpreise in Babylonien*, p. 7.) In 2 Ki. vii. 1 the price quoted for cereal seems abnormally high, but it was doubtless considerably lower than in the preceding famine. In Rev. vi. 6 the prices describe graphically the grim conditions of famine.

Barley bread was probably the most widely used. The fact that barley was also fed to horses (1 Ki. iv. 28) does not necessarily imply that it was considered inferior, any more than is oats in our day. Wheat bread was more highly prized and was probably fairly common. Spelt was also used, but rye does not seem to have been cultivated. On occasions various cereals may have been mixed together and, as Ezk. iv. 9 indicates, even lentil and bean meal were added.

The general term for grain was *dāḡān*. After threshing and winnowing, the grain was either crushed in a mortar with a pestle or was ground in a mill by rubbing the upper stone to and fro on the nether millstone. This form of mill, and not the rotating type (quern), seems to have been the one in common use. Different kinds of flour were in use. The term for flour or meal in general was *qemaḥ*, and when necessary this was qualified by the addition of the name of the cereal (Nu. v. 15). What was probably a finer quality was called *sōleṯ* (*cf.* 1 Ki. iv. 22), but some scholars take this word to mean 'groats'. This was the meal used in the offerings (Ex. xxix. 40; Lv. ii. 5, *etc.*).

The word *qālî*, often translated 'parched corn', was probably roasted grains, which were eaten without further preparation.

The flour, mixed with water and seasoned with salt, was kneaded in a special trough. To this, leaven in the form of a small quantity of old fermented dough was added until the whole was leavened. Unleavened bread also was baked. Leaven was not used in the offerings made by fire (Lv. ii. 11, *etc.*), and its use was forbidden during Passover week. The baking was done either over a fire on heated stones or on a griddle, or in an oven. Leavened bread was usually in the form of round, flat loaves, and unleavened in the form of thin cakes. The form called *'uḡâ* was probably the griddle cake, since it required turning (Hos. vii. 8).

When bread was kept too long it became dry and crumbly (Jos. ix. 5 and 12). In Gilgamesh, XI, 225–229, there is an interesting reference to the deterioration of bread. See also FOOD.

That a commodity of such vital importance should leave its mark on language and symbolism is not surprising. From earliest times the word 'bread' was used for food in general (Gn. iii. 19 and Pr. vi. 8, where Heb. has 'bread'). Since it was the staple article of diet, it was called 'staff' of bread (Lv. xxvi. 26), which is probably the origin of our phrase 'staff of life'. Those who were responsible for bread were important officials, as in Egypt (Gn. xl. 1), and in Assyria a chief baker is honoured with an eponymy. Bread was early used in sacred meals (Gn. xiv. 18), and loaves were included in certain offerings (Lv. xxi. 6, *etc.*). Above all, it had a special place in the sanctuary as the shewbread, lit. 'bread of the presence'. The manna was later referred to as 'heavenly bread' (see Ps. cv. 40). Our Lord referred to Himself as the 'bread of God' and as the 'bread of life' (Jn. vi. 33 and 35), and He chose the bread of the Passover to be the symbolic memorial of His broken body. W.J.M.

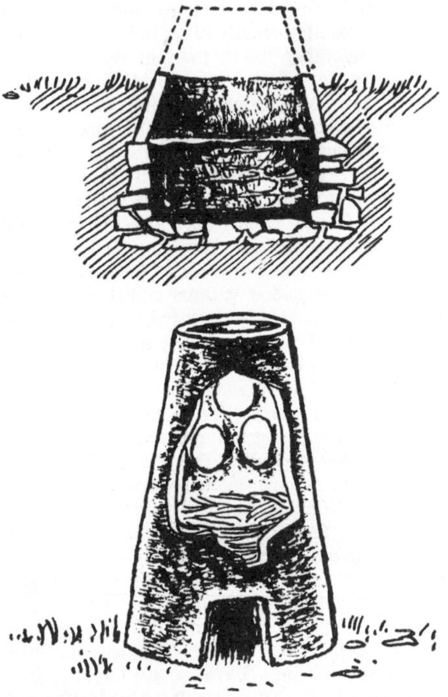

Fig. 43. Section (*above*) and cut-out model (*below*), of a bread oven as found at Megiddo. The flat round cakes of dough were placed to cook on the warm walls of the oven.

BREAKFAST. See MEALS.

BREAST. Four uses of the word may be distinguished. 1. Heb. *dad̲* or *šad̲* (Pr. v. 19; Jb. iii. 12, *etc.*); Gk. *mastos*, translated 'paps' in AV (Lk. xi. 27). 2. *šōd̲* (Is. lx. 16, lxvi. 11), symbolic of riches. 3. *ḥāzeh* (Ex. xxix. 26; Lv. viii. 29, *etc.*), the breast portion of an animal, often offered as a wave-offering. 4. Aram. *ḥᵃd̲î* (Dn. ii. 32), the chest, equivalent to the Gk. *stēthos* in the New Testament, where smiting upon the breast is a sign of anguish (Lk. xviii. 13), and leaning upon the breast a sign of affection (Jn. xiii. 25). The word 'bosom' (Mi. vii. 5; Jn. xiii. 23) presents a close parallel in this sense.

In Jb. xxi. 24 the Heb. '*ᵃṭîn* (AV 'breasts') is better translated 'pail' according to *BDB*.

B.O.B.

BREASTPLATE. See ARMOUR AND WEAPONS.

BREASTPLATE OF THE HIGH PRIEST. Heb. *ḥōšen*, interpretatively translated 'breastplate' (Ex. xxviii. 4, 15–30, xxxix. 8–21; *cf.* LXX, *peristēthion*, Ex. xxviii. 4), means, from Arab. cognates, 'beauty', pointing to its intrinsic loveliness and importance among the holy garments. Made of the same materials as the ephod (Ex. xxviii. 15), the breastplate was a square pouch (verse 16), with gold rings at the four corners (verses 23, 26). The lower rings were fastened by blue laces to rings above the girdle of the ephod (verse 28). On the breastplate were set twelve gems engraved with the names of the tribes (verses 17–21), and gold cords fastened the upper rings to the two similarly engraved gems on the shoulders of the ephod (verses 9–12, 22–25). Thus, symbolically, on the one hand the nation, in God's sight, rested on a high-priestly person and work; on the other hand, the priest carried continually into God's presence the people, as a loved responsibility (verse 29); and equally, as

Fig. 44. Part of a tomb-painting from Thebes, c. 1450 BC, showing men working under a taskmas
from a pond and placed in moulds to s

containing the oracular Urim and Thummim (verse 30)—hence the title 'breastplate of judgment' (verse 15; *cf.* the customary LXX, *logion tēs kriseōs*, 'oracle of judgment')—the breastplate symbolizes the priest as the announcer of God's will to man (*cf.* Mal. ii. 6, 7).

BIBLIOGRAPHY. Josephus, *Ant.* iii. 5; A. H. McNeile, *Exodus*, *WC*, 1908, on Ex. xxviii. 13 ff.

J.A.M.

BRETHREN OF THE LORD. Four men are described in the Gospels as 'brothers' of Jesus, *viz.* James, Joses, Simon, and Judas (Mt. xiii. 55; Mk. vi. 3). The native townsmen of Jesus expressed amazement that a brother of these men should possess such wisdom and such power (Mk. vi. 2, 3). On the other hand, Jesus contrasted His brothers and His mother, who were bound to Him by physical ties, with His disciples, who in virtue of their obedience to the will of His Father were regarded by Him as His spiritual 'brothers' and 'mother' (Mt. xii. 46–50). Three views have been held as to the nature of the relationship between these men and Jesus.

a. The 'brothers' were the younger children of Joseph and Mary. This view is supported by the *prima facie* meaning of 'firstborn' in Lk. ii. 7, and by the natural inference from Mt. i. 25 that after the birth of Jesus normal marital relations between Joseph and Mary followed. It was strongly advocated by Helvidius in the 4th century, but came to be regarded as heretical in the light of the doctrine, increasingly attractive as the ascetic movement developed, that Mary was always virgin. Since the Reformation it has been the view most commonly held by Protestants.

b. The 'brothers' were the children of Joseph by a former wife. This view, first promulgated in the 3rd century and defended by Epiphanius in the 4th, became the accepted doctrine of the Eastern Orthodox Church. It has no direct support from the New Testament. Its advocates have usually supposed, however, that the opposition of the brothers to Jesus during His earthly life was largely due to jealousy of the achievements of their younger half-brother.

c. The 'brothers' were the cousins of Jesus. This view, put forward by Jerome in defence of the doctrine of the perpetual virginity of the mother of Jesus, has remained the official teaching of the Roman Catholic Church. It is based on the following series of arbitrary assumptions: (i) that the correct interpretation of Jn. xix. 25 is that there were three, not four, women standing near the cross, *viz.* Mary the mother of Jesus, her sister identified with 'Mary of Clopas', and Mary of Magdala; (ii) that the second Mary in the Johannine passage is identical with the Mary described in Mk. xv. 40 as 'the mother of James the less and of Joses'; (iii) that this 'James the less' is the apostle called in Mk. iii. 18 'the son of Alphaeus'; (iv) that the second Mary in Jn. xix. 25 was married to Alphaeus. Why she should be described as 'of Clopas', which presumably means 'the wife of Clopas', Jerome admitted that he was ignorant. The theory would seem to demand either that Clopas is another name for Alphaeus, or that this Mary was married twice. By this ingenious but unconvincing exegesis Jerome reduced the number of men called James in the New Testament to two—the son of Zebedee, and James the Lord's brother, who was also an apostle and known as 'the less' to distinguish him from the son of Zebedee! It is probable that 'my brethren' in Mt. xxviii. 10 refers to a wider group than 'the brothers' already mentioned.

BIBLIOGRAPHY. See the excursus by J. B. Lightfoot 'The Brethren of the Lord' in *Saint Paul's Epistle to the Galatians*, and the introductions to the commentaries mentioned under JAMES, EPISTLE OF.

R.V.G.T.

BRICK. A lump of mud or clay, usually rectangular, sun-dried or kiln-baked ('burnt'); the commonest building material of the ancient biblical world. At first moulded by hand, bricks early began to be made ('struck') with open, rectangular, wooden moulds. The mud was mixed

aking bricks to renew the workshop at Karnak' of the god Amūn. The clay is mixed with water taken
e dried bricks are then built into a wall.

with sand, chopped straw, *etc*., the bricks struck off in long rows, and left to dry out; see D. J. Wiseman, *Illustrations from Biblical Archaeology*, 1959, pp. 42–45, figs. 36–38; Petrie, *Egyptian Architecture*, 1938, pp. 3–13; Lucas, *Ancient Egyptian Materials and Industries*³, 1948, pp. 43–45. Bricks often bore stamped impressions: in Egypt, the name of the pharaoh (see plate III*b*) or of the building they were used in; in Babylonia, also the king's name and dedication; *e.g*. Nebuchadrezzar (Wiseman, *op. cit*., p. 71, fig. 66), of whom five different stamps are known. For these and Nebuchadrezzar's brick-making techniques, see R. Koldewey, *Excavations at Babylon*, 1914, pp. 75–82 and figures.

Sun-dried brick was the universal building material of Mesopotamia, where kiln-baked bricks were often used for facings and pavements (*cf*. also Gn. xi. 3). In Egypt sun-dried brick was usual for all but the most important and permanent buildings (*i.e*. stone temples and tombs); kiln-baked bricks are almost unknown before Roman times. Various forms of bonding were practised.

Ex. v. 6–19 accurately reflects brick-making usage in ancient Egypt; straw or stubble was regularly used in the XIXth and XXth Dynasties (13th–12th centuries BC), as bricks so made proved much stronger. In contemporary papyri one official reports of his workmen, 'they are making their quota of bricks daily', while another complains, '. . . at Qenqenento, . . . there are neither men to make bricks nor straw in the neighbourhood'; *cf*. Caminos, *Late-Egyptian Miscellanies*, 1954, pp. 106, 188. The straw itself is not so much a binding-agent, but its chemical decay in the clay released an acid which (like glutamic or gallotannic acid) gave the clay greater plasticity for brick-making. This effect (but not, of course, the chemistry) was evidently a well-known one. See A. A. McRae in *Modern Science and Christian Faith*, 1948, pp. 215–219, after E. G. Acheson, *Transactions of the American Ceramic Society*, VI, 1904, p. 31; further comment and references in Lucas, *op. cit*., p. 44; and *cf*. also C. F. Nims, *BA*, XIII, 1950, pp. 21–28.

In Palestine sun-dried brick was also the norm; city and house walls were often of brick upon a stone foundation.

Wooden baulks were frequently incorporated into brickwork; in Egypt at least, this served to prevent warping as the mud-brick structure dried out, and to bind the whole (Petrie, *Egyptian Architecture*, p. 9). In Asia Minor, the Aegean, and N Syria such beams were commonly inserted on stone foundations under or in mud-brick or stone walls (R. Naumann, *Architektur Kleinasiens*, 1955, pp. 83–86, 88–104, and figs. 63–66, 72–89)—so in houses of 14th–13th centuries BC at Canaanite Ugarit (Schaeffer, *Ugaritica*, I, 1939, plate 19, with pp. 92–96 and fig. 90). This widespread and venerable use of brick upon wood over stone is apparently referred to in 1 Ki. vii. 12, vi. 36, as used by Solomon in buildings at Jerusalem. This technique was actually found at the Israelite Megiddo of Solomon or Ahab's day; Guy, *New Light from Armageddon*, Oriental Institute Communication No. 9, 1931, pp. 34–35; *cf*. building illustrated in Heaton, *Everyday Life in Old Testament Times*, 1956, fig. 106 opposite p. 207. See also H. C. Thomson, *PEQ*, XCII, 1960, pp. 57–63.

For 'burning incense upon bricks' (Is. lxv. 3), *cf*. mud-brick altars from a very early period at Megiddo, *ANEP*, p. 229, fig. 729. See also ARCHITECTURE and WALLS. K.A.K.

BRICK-KILN. Oven for baking mud bricks. In the biblical East sun-dried mud bricks were always the cheapest and commonest building material, but were not specially durable (*e.g*. in rainy weather). Burnt bricks were almost indestructible. They were used in Mesopotamia for facings, pavements, *etc*., in important buildings from very early times, but are hardly known in Palestine or Egypt before Roman times; see BRICK. Hence brick-kilns are regularly found in Mesopotamia but not by the Nile or Jordan. In the AV of 2 Sa. xii. 31; Je. xliii. 9; Na. iii. 14 the term *malbēn* is rendered 'brickkiln', but this seems to be incorrect. The *malbēn* is the rectangular, hollow wooden brick-mould for making ordinary sun-dried bricks in 2 Samuel and Nahum, and is used figuratively to describe the rectangular brick pavement in Tahpanhes in Jeremiah. See RSV. In 2 Sa. xii. 31 the meaning is that David put the Ammonites to hard labour (in the verb, reading *d* for *r*, very similar letters in Heb.), with saws, harrows, axes, and brick-moulds (*malkēn* is probably for *malbēn*, *MT* margin/Qᵉrê).

However, the 'fiery furnace' into which Daniel's three friends were cast as punishment (Dn. iii. 6, 11, 15, 19–23) was very likely a brick-kiln, one of those that must have supplied burnt bricks to Nebuchadrezzar's Babylon. The word used, *'attûn*, 'furnace', is probably identical with the Assyro-Babylonian word *utūnum*, 'furnace, kiln'. Outside of Daniel, Nebuchadrezzar's cruel punishment is attested not only in Je. xxix. 22 but also by actual inscriptions: in a Babylonian letter of *c*. 1800 BC and in an Assyrian court regulation of *c*. 1130 BC people were (or might be) thrown into a furnace as a punishment; see G. R. Driver, *Archiv für Orientforschung*, XVIII, 1957, p. 129, and E. F. Weidner, *ibid*., XVII, 1956, pp. 285–286. The practice is used as a comparison in Ps. xxi. 9. On the 'fiery furnace' being a brick-kiln, compare the reference to the flames of similar modern brick-kilns lighting up the sky near Babylon by R. Koldewey, *The Excavations at Babylon*, 1914, pp. 81–82. The brick-kilns of ancient Babylonia may have looked like the large pottery-kiln excavated in Nippur and pictured in B. Meissner, *Babylonien und Assyrien*, I, 1920, p. 234 and figs. 55, 56. K.A.K.

BRIDE, BRIDEGROOM. These two words are quite naturally complementary to each other (Jn. iii. 29a) and are found side by side in Is. lxii. 5;

Je. vii. 34, xvi. 9, xxv. 10, xxxiii. 11; Rev. xviii. 23. 'The voice of the bridegroom and the voice of the bride' in these references is parallel with 'the voice of mirth and gladness', and illustrates the rich concept of marital joy of which the Bible often speaks (*e.g.* Ps. cxxviii; Pr. and Ct.). Is. lxii. 5 extends this significance to include a comparison between human relationships and God's joy in His people Israel, who are regarded as His bride (*cf.* Is. liv. 6; Je. ii. 2, iii. 20; Ezk. xvi. 8, xxiii. 4; Ho. ii. 16 RVmg). This metaphor prepares the way for the New Testament allusions to the Church as the bride of Christ, especially in the Epistles (2 Cor. xi. 2; Eph. v. 25–27, 31 f.; *cf.* Rev. xix. 7, xxi. 2, xxii. 17). According to this picture the Lord Jesus is the divine Bridegroom who seeks His bride in love and enters into covenant relations with her.

Whether this allegory of Christ and the Church is derived from the teaching of Jesus or not is a debatable point. Some deny the allegorical interpretation of Mt. xxv. 1–12 on the ground that the Messiah is not represented in the Old Testament and in the rabbinical literature as a Bridegroom (so J. Jeremias, *TWNT*, IV, pp. 1094 f., and *The Parables of Jesus*, E.T. 1954, p. 46). But, on the other hand, there is the witness of Mk. ii. 19, 20 (*cf.* Mt. ix. 15; Lk. v. 34, 35), which shows that the term Bridegroom was used by the Lord as a messianic designation and corresponds to His use of the third person in speaking of Himself as 'the Son of man' (so V. Taylor, *The Gospel according to St. Mark*, 1952, *ad loc.*). This is further confirmed if the variant reading of Mt. xxv. 1, 'to meet the bridegroom and the bride', is accepted; and there is early and important attestation of it (see A. H. McNeile, *The Gospel according to St. Matthew*, 1915, *ad loc.*; F. C. Burkitt, *JTS*, 1929, pp. 267–270; T. W. Manson, *The Sayings of Jesus*, 1949, pp. 243 f., who makes an interesting and plausible suggestion to explain the identity of the bride). See also Jn. iii. 29b for John the Baptist as 'the friend of the bridegroom', *i.e.* the groomsman (Heb. *šôšᵉḇîn*), who acted as 'best man' (*cf.* 1 Macc. ix. 39). He was the agent for the bridegroom in arranging the marriage and played an important part in the wedding festivities, as did also the bridegroom's attendants, who are referred to in Mk. ii. 19 as 'the sons of the bridechamber'.

BIBLIOGRAPHY. For a full study of 'the bridal dignity of the Church', see C. Chavasse, *The Bride of Christ*, 1939. R.P.M.

BRIER. See THORN.

BRIMSTONE (Heb. *goprîṯ*, Gk. *theion*, 'sulphur'), a yellow crystalline solid, with medicinal and fumigating properties, which occurs in the natural state in regions of volcanic activity such as the valley of the Dead Sea (*cf.* Gn. xix. 24). The element burns readily in air, and is consequently frequently associated in the Bible with fire (*e.g.* Gn. xix. 24; Ps. xi. 6; Ezk. xxxviii. 22; Lk. xvii. 29; Rev. ix. 17, 18, xiv. 10, xix. 20, xx. 10, xxi. 8), and appears in figures of the burning wrath of God (Is. xxx. 33, xxxiv. 9; Rev. xiv. 10). The usual environment of its natural occurrence also led to the use of the word to indicate barrenness of land (Dt. xxix. 23; Jb. xviii. 15). That the substance was well known in the ancient world is suggested by the occurrence of cognates to *goprîṯ* in Akkadian, Aramaic, and Arabic. *Theion* occurs already in Homer, and is regularly used in the LXX to translate *goprîṯ*. 'Brimstone' was the form current in 1611 of a Middle English word, meaning 'burn(ing)-stone', which had appeared, for instance, in Wyclif's Bible as (among other spellings) 'brunston'. The word, though archaic in modern extra-biblical usage, has been retained by the RV and RSV.

BIBLIOGRAPHY. R. Campbell Thompson, *A Dictionary of Assyrian Chemistry and Geology*, 1936, pp. 38, 39; *KB*, p. 192. T.C.M.

BRONZE. See MINING AND METALS.

BROOCH. See ORNAMENTS.

BROOK. The word *naḥal* is used variously of a perennial stream, the flow of water, and the dried course of a river-bed. Apart from the Jordan itself, nearly all the perennial streams are left-bank tributaries of the Jordan fed by springs. Such is the Kishon (1 Ki. xviii. 40), the second largest river by volume, and the Jabbok, modern Zerka (Gn. xxxii. 22, 23). The brook in full spate is used metaphorically (*e.g.* Am. v. 24), while the ephemeral nature of the dried-up brook is also used (Jb. vi. 15). A severe drought will terminate the flow even of spring-fed brooks (*e.g.* 1 Ki. xvii. 2–7). Sometimes the stream-bed has a mantle of vegetation owing to the shallow water-table. Thus 'the brook of the willows' (Is. xv. 7) may describe the cover of oleander bushes and other vegetation. Frequent reference is made to a poetical word, *mayim*, 'water-brook', denoting the channel bed (Jb. xii. 15; Ps. xlii. 1; Is. viii. 7; Joel i. 20). See also EGYPT, RIVER OF. J.M.H.

BROOM. See PLANTS.

BROTHERLY LOVE. Gk. *philadelphia* (Rom. xii. 10; 1 Thes. iv. 9; Heb. xiii. 1; 1 Pet. i. 22; 2 Pet. i. 7) means, not figurative brother-*like* love, but the love of those united in the Christian brotherhood (*adelphotēs*, 1 Pet. ii. 17, v. 9; *cf.* the adjective *philadelphos*, 1 Pet. iii. 8). Outside Christian writings (*e.g.* 1 Macc. xii. 10, 17) *philadelphia* is used only of men of common descent. In the Old Testament, 'brother', like 'neighbour', meant 'fellow-Israelite' (Lv. xix. 17 f.; *cf.* Acts xiii. 26). Jesus widened the scope of love for fellow-men (Mt. v. 43–48; Lk. x. 27–37), but also, by calling His followers His own (Mk. iii. 33 ff.; Mt. xxviii. 10; Jn. xx. 17) and one another's (Mt. xxiii. 8; Lk. xxii. 32) brethren, and by the Johannine command to love one another (Jn. xiii. 34, xv. 12, 17), established the special love of fellow-Christians which *philadelphia* describes (*cf.* Rom. viii. 29).

This is shown in the common life of the Church (*cf. homothymadon*, 'with one accord, together', Acts i. 14, ii. 46, iv. 24, v. 12, xv. 25). It is an out-working of Christ's love (Eph. v. 1 f.) which it is natural to find among Christians (1 Thes. iv. 9 f.), but which must be increased (1 Thes. iv. 10) and deepened (Rom. xii. 10) so as to be lasting (Heb. xiii. 1), genuine (*anypokritos*, 1 Pet. i. 22; *cf.* Rom. xii. 9), and earnest (*ektenēs*, 1 Pet. i. 22; *cf.* iv. 8). It is shown in a common way of thinking (*to auto phronein*, Rom. xii. 16, xv. 5; 2 Cor. xiii. 11; Phil. iv. 2; *cf.* Gal. v. 10; Phil. ii. 2, 5, iii. 15) and living (*tō autō stoichein*, Phil. iii. 16), especially in hospitality (Heb. xiii. 1 f.; 1 Pet. iv. 8 f.) and help to needy Christians (Rom. xii. 9–13). It proves, to Christians themselves (1 Jn. iii. 14) and to the world (Jn. xiii. 35), the genuineness of their faith (1 Jn. ii. 9–11, iii. 10, iv. 7, 11, 20, v. 1).

Philadelphia cannot by definition be realized outside the 'household of faith', but it is associated with honouring (1 Pet. ii. 17) and doing good to (Gal. vi. 10) all. Its converse is not exclusiveness or indifference to those outside (*hoi exō*, Mk. iv. 11; 1 Cor. v. 12 f.; Col. iv. 5; 1 Thes. iv. 12), but the constraining, dividing, and still unconsummated love of Christ (2 Cor. v. 14; *cf.* Lk. xii. 50–53). See also LOVE, FAMILY, NEIGHBOUR.

BIBLIOGRAPHY. Sladeczek, 'Hē philadelphia nach den Schriften des h. Apostels Paulus', *Theologische Quartalschrift*, LXXVI, 1894, pp. 272–295; A. Nygren, *Agape and Eros*², 1953, pp. 153–155.

P.E.

BUCKLE. See ORNAMENTS.

BUCKLER. See ARMOUR AND WEAPONS.

BUILDER. See ARTS AND CRAFTS.

BUL. See CALENDAR.

BULL, BULLOCK. See CATTLE.

BULRUSH. See PAPYRI AND OSTRACA, I*a*(ii).

BURDEN. A noun used more than eighty times in AV to translate several Heb. and Gk. words. 1. Heb. *maśśā'*, 'thing lifted up', and other cognate words from the root *nāśā'*, 'he lifted up'. This word occurs most frequently, notably of prophetic utterances. See also ORACLE. 2. Heb. *sāḇal*, 'to bear a load' (in various derivative forms). 3. Heb. *yāhaḇ*, 'to give' (Ps. lv. 22 only). 4. Heb. *'ᵃḡuddâ*, 'bundle' (Is. lviii. 6 only). 5. Gk. *baros*, 'something heavy'. 6. Gk. *phortion*, 'something to be borne'. 7. Gk. *gomos*, 'the freight' of a ship (Acts xxi. 3 only).

Those terms which occur more than once vary little in meaning, and seem at times to be interchangeable. A burden is whatever renders body or mind uneasy (*e.g.* Zp. iii. 18); as much as one can bear (2 Ki. v. 17); government in church or state (Nu. xi. 17); prediction of heavy judgment (Is. xiii); labour, bondage, affliction, fear (Ps. lxxxi. 6; Ec. xii. 5; Mt. xx. 12); Christ's laws (Mt. xi. 30; Rev. ii. 24); God's ceremonial law and men's superstitious ceremonies (Mt. xxiii. 4; Acts xv. 28); men's infirmities (Gal. vi. 2).

J.D.D.

BURIAL AND MOURNING.

I. IN THE OLD TESTAMENT

a. The times of the Patriarchs

It was customary for successive generations to be buried in the family tomb (cave or rock-cut); thus Sarah (Gn. xxiii. 19), Abraham (Gn. xxv. 9), Isaac and Rebekah, Leah (Gn. xlix. 31), and Jacob (Gn. l. 13) were all buried in the cave of Machpelah, east of Hebron. Individual burial was sometimes necessitated by death at a distance from the family tomb; so Deborah near Bethel (Gn. xxxv. 8) and Rachel on the road to Ephrath (Gn. xxxv. 19, 20), their tombs being marked by an oak and a pillar respectively. Besides weeping, mourning already included rending one's garments and donning sackcloth (Gn. xxxvii. 34, 35), and might last for as long as seven days (Gn. l. 10). The embalming of Jacob and Joseph and the use of a coffin for Joseph in Egyptian fashion was exceptional (Gn. l. 2, 3, 26). Mummification required removal of the viscera for separate preservation, and desiccation of the body by packing in salt (not brine); thereafter the body was packed with impregnated linen and entirely wrapped in linen. Embalming and mourning usually took seventy days, but the period for embalming could be shorter, as for Jacob.

b. The Pentateuchal legislation

Prompt burial, including that of the bodies of hung criminals, was the norm (Dt. xxi. 22, 23). Contact with the dead and formal mourning brought ceremonial defilement. Mourning by weeping, rending the garments, and unbinding the hair was permitted to the Aaronic priests (Lv. xxi. 1–4), but not to the high priest (Lv. xxi. 10–11) or the Nazirite under vow (Nu. vi. 7). Expressly forbidden to priests (Lv. xxi. 5) and people (Lv. xix. 27–28; Dt. xiv. 1) were laceration ('cuttings in the flesh'), cutting the corners of the beard, baldness between the eyes, and 'rounding' (mutilation?) of the corner(s) of the head. Eating of tithes in mourning or offering them to the dead (Dt. xxvi. 14) was also forbidden. These were heathen, Canaanite practices. Women captured in war might mourn their parents for one month before marrying their captors (Dt. xxi. 11–13). The national leaders Aaron (Nu. xx. 28, 29; Dt. x. 6) and Moses (Dt. xxxiv. 5–8) were each accorded thirty days' national mourning after burial.

c. Israel in Palestine

(i) *Burial.* When possible, people were buried in the ancestral inheritance in a family tomb: so Gideon and Samson (Jdg. viii. 32, xvi. 31), Asahel and Ahithophel (2 Sa. ii. 32, xvii. 23), and eventually Saul (2 Sa. xxi. 12–14). Burial in one's 'house', as of Samuel (1 Sa. xxv. 1, *cf.*

xxviii. 3) and Joab (1 Ki. ii. 34) may merely mean the same, unless it was more literally under the house or yard floor. The body was borne to rest on a bier (2 Sa. iii. 31). Lack of proper burial was a great misfortune (1 Ki. xiii. 22; Je. xvi. 6). Tombs were usually outside the town; there is limited archaeological evidence for family tombs having an irregular rock-cut chamber (or chambers) with benches, reached by a short, sloping shaft blocked by a stone cut to fit over the entrance. The upstart treasurer Shebna drew Isaiah's condemnation in hewing himself an ambitious rock-tomb (Is. xxii. 15, 16; see SHEBNA). Pottery and other objects left with the dead became a pure formality during the Israelite period, by contrast with elaborate Canaanite funerary provision. Memorial pillars were sometimes erected in Israel as elsewhere in antiquity; 2 Sa. xviii. 18 is an anticipatory example. Outside Jerusalem was a tract of land set aside for 'the graves of the common people' (2 Ki. xxiii. 6; Je. xxvi. 23). This, doubtless, was for simple interments, and was paralleled by similar cemeteries at other towns.

The grave of an executed criminal or foe was sometimes marked by a heap of stones. Examples are the sinner Achan (Jos. vii. 26), rebellious Absalom (2 Sa. xviii. 17), the king of Ai, and the five Canaanite kings (Jos. viii. 29, x. 27). Cremation was not a Hebrew practice, but in difficult circumstances a corpse might be burnt and the remains buried pending proper burial in the ancestral tomb, as with Saul (1 Sa. xxxi. 12, 13) and probably envisaged in Am. vi. 10. For royal burials, see SEPULCHRE OF KINGS.

(ii) *Mourning*. In Palestine in the second and first millennia this included: (1) baldness of head and cutting the beard; (2) lacerating the body; (3) rending garments and wearing sackcloth; (4) scattering dust on the head and wallowing in ashes; and (5) weeping and lamentation. Not all of these were favoured by the law. (See section *b* above.) For Hebrew mourning, see the action of David (2 Sa. i. 11, 12, xiii. 31), the woman of Tekoah (2 Sa. xiv. 2), and note the allusions in the prophets (Is. iii. 24, xxii. 12; Je. vii. 29; Ezk. vii. 18; Joel i. 8; Am. viii. 10; Mi. i. 16). For Tyrian seafarers, Philistia and Moab, see Ezk. xxvii. 30, 32; Je. xlvii. 5; Is. xv. 2, 3 and Je. xlviii. 37.

Notable deaths sometimes occasioned poetic laments. So David lamented over Saul and Jonathan (2 Sa. i. 17–27) and Jeremiah and others over Josiah (2 Ch. xxxv. 25). For professional mourners, *cf.* Je. ix. 17, 18; Am. v. 16. After a funeral a breaking-fast meal was possibly given to mourners (Je. xvi. 7; *cf.* Ho. ix. 4). A 'great burning' sometimes marked the funeral of Judaean kings (2 Ch. xvi. 14, xxi. 19, 20; Je. xxxiv. 5).

Fig. 45. A boatload of professional mourners with hair and garments dishevelled, crossing the Nile while accompanying a mummy (not here shown) on its way to burial. Egyptian tomb painting, Thebes, 15th–14th centuries BC.

d. Non-funereal mourning

Mourning was associated with repentance or contrition (*e.g.* Ex. xxxiii. 4; Joel i. 13, ii. 12, 13; Ezr. ix. 3, 5) or took place because of misfortune (*e.g.* 2 Sa. xiii. 19, xv. 32; Jb. ii. 12, 13). There are also references to laceration, weeping, *etc.*, in pagan(izing) cult-practices. *Cf.* the actions of Baal's prophets on Mount Carmel (1 Ki. xviii. 28), and those of the men of Israel who came with oblations for God (Je. xli. 5). Ezekiel saw in a vision the women of Jerusalem weeping for the god Tammuz (Ezk. viii. 14); and Isaiah depicts pagan observances at graves being performed by the rebellious Israelites (Is. lxv. 4).

BIBLIOGRAPHY. For Canaanite tombs analogous to those used by the Patriarchs, see K. M.

Kenyon, *Digging up Jericho*, 1957, pp. 233–255. For laceration in Ugaritic (N Canaanite) epics, see *DOTT*, 1958, p. 130. K.A.K.

II. IN THE NEW TESTAMENT

Jewish practices in New Testament times differed little from those described in the Old Testament, though there are certain extra details given. The corpse was first washed (Acts ix. 37); it was then anointed (Mk. xvi. 1), wrapped in linen garments with spices enclosed (Jn. xix. 40), and finally the limbs were bound and the face covered with a napkin (Jn. xi. 44). The scene in Acts v. 6 may perhaps suggest that some young men's fraternity had the duty of seeing to such matters.

Weeping and wailing and beating the breast are, of course, typically Oriental, and are evidenced in the New Testament too. As in the Old Testament, professional mourners might be employed. Mt. ix. 23 refers specifically to flute players. It may be that Jesus did not much care for this noisy and professional mourning. He Himself, we read, wept quietly at the tomb of Lazarus (Jn. xi. 35). By this time the normal period of mourning was of seven days' duration (*cf.* Ecclus. xxii. 12). The actual interment, on the other hand, took place as soon as possible after death, normally on the same day.

Burial places and grounds were usually outside the city or town. Common burial grounds did exist (*cf.* Mt. xxvii. 7), but individual and family tombs were widely used. Some men, such as Joseph of Arimathaea, liked to prepare their burial place beforehand (*cf.* Mt. xxvii. 60). Coffins were not used to transport the dead to the place of burial; they were carried on simple biers (see Lk. vii. 12, 14).

Cremation was never a Jewish practice, but there were several types of burial place. There were ordinary graves in the earth, some unmarked (*cf.* Lk. xi. 44). Then there were rock-hewn tombs or caves, which might well have monuments or pillars erected over them. Family tombs often had a number of separate chambers. In these were fashioned ledges (*arcosolia*) or niches (*kôḵîm*) to accommodate the bodies. Here the bodies might be placed within receptacles, such as stone coffins or sarcophagi. Another practice of the New Testament period was to place bones in small stone coffers known as ossuaries—a custom perhaps borrowed and adapted from the Roman boxes to hold ashes after cremation. Thus, if a family tomb became over-filled, dry bones could be taken from the ledges and niches and placed in ossuaries. Ossuaries might house the bones of more than one person. These various receptacles usually bore designs and motifs of various types, although among the very orthodox Jews very little in the way of embellishment was permitted. Names were also frequently inscribed on ossuaries. The practice of adornment and embellishment of tombs appears to have been common in the time of Jesus, judging by His denunciation of the Pharisees in Mt. xxiii. 29. He made scathing reference also to the practice of whitewashing tombs (Mt. xxiii. 27). The purpose of this was doubtless to render them conspicuous (especially at night), thereby preventing passers-by from touching them accidentally and so incurring ritual defilement.

To prevent too easy access to tombs, in view of jackals and thieves, the doorways were firmly closed by hinged doors, or less commonly by large flat stones like millstones, which could, with difficulty, be rolled sideways from the tomb entrances.

Fig. 46. Stone ossuary, in which the bones of the dead were placed. Decorated with rosettes, flowers and an architectural feature of a colonnade; perhaps similar to that round the Temple, in Jerusalem. Palestine, 1st century BC.

There are a number of tombs in and around Jerusalem which date from within a century or two of the time of Christ, notably those of Absalom, Jehoshaphat, St. James, Zechariah, the Herod family, and 'the Kings' (most of these names are fictional, it should be added). An illustrated description of these, with further information on modes of burial, can be seen in A. Parrot, *Golgotha*, 1957, pp. 84–122. D.F.P.

BURNING BUSH. The call of Moses to be Israel's deliverer took place when he turned to see the marvel of the bush which burned and yet was not consumed (Ex. iii. 3). Like all such manifestations which the Bible records—*e.g.* the smoking-flashing oven (Gn. xv. 17) and the cloudy-fiery pillar (Ex. xiii. 21)—the burning bush is a self-revelation of God, and not, as some hold, of Israel in the furnace of affliction. The story commences by saying that 'the angel of the Lord showed himself' (verse 2); the Hebrew translated 'in a flame' more aptly signifies 'as' or 'in the mode of' a flame (verse 2); Moses (verse 6) 'was afraid to look upon God'; Dt. xxxiii. 16 speaks of 'him that dwelt in the bush'. The revelation thus conveyed may be summarized in the three words 'living', 'holy', and 'indwelling'. The bush is not consumed because the flame needs no fuel, being self-sufficient, alive in itself. Equally, and by a consistent symbolism (*e.g.* Gn. iii. 24; Ex. xix. 18), the flame is the unapproachable holiness of God (verse 5). And, thirdly, so as to reveal the sovereign grace of God who, though self-sufficient, freely chooses and empowers instruments of service, the flame in the bush declares that the living, holy God is the Indweller. Thus the revelation at the bush is the background of the promise of the divine presence to Moses (verse 12), of the implementation of the covenant with the fathers (ii. 24, iii. 6, vi. 5), of the divine Name (verse 14), and of the holy law of Sinai.

BIBLIOGRAPHY. G. A. Chadwick, *Exodus*, 1892, pp. 47 ff.; S. R. Driver, *Exodus*, 1911, on Ex. iii. 2; G. A. F. Knight, *The Christian Theology of the Old Testament*, 1959, pp. 46, 280. J.A.M.

BURNT-OFFERING. See SACRIFICE AND OFFERING.

BUSHEL. See WEIGHTS AND MEASURES.

BUTLER. See CUPBEARER.

BUTTER. See MILK.

BUZI. The father of Ezekiel (Ezk. i. 3). The Jewish tradition that he was Jeremiah must be firmly rejected, being based on an unwarranted supposition and fanciful etymology. He was a priest, probably a Zadokite and most likely of a more important priestly family, since his son was carried into captivity with Jehoiachin (2 Ki. xxiv. 14–16). H.L.E.

BYBLOS. See GEBAL.

C

CAB. See WEIGHTS AND MEASURES.

CABUL. The name of a border city in the tribal location of Asher (Jos. xix. 27), situated 10 miles north-east of Carmel. The ironic use in 1 Ki. ix. 13 probably rests on a popular etymology signifying 'as nothing' (Heb. *k^{e}bal*). J.A.M.

CAESAR. The name of a branch of the aristocratic family of the Julii which established an ascendancy over the Roman republic in the triumph of Augustus (31 BC) and kept it till Nero's death (AD 68). This hegemony (as it is nicely called in Lk. iii. 1) was an unsystematic compound of legal and social powers, novel to Roman tradition in its monopoly of leadership rather than its form or theory. It was not technically a monarchy. Its success produced so thorough a reorientation of government, however, that, on the elimination of the Caesarian family, their position was institutionalized and their name assumed by its incumbents.

One of the bases of a Caesar's power was his extended tenure of a provincial command embracing most of Rome's frontier forces. Judaea always fell within this area, hence Paul's appeal (Acts xxv. 10, 11) against the procurator, which would not have been possible where the governor was a fully competent proconsul and thus Caesar's equal. Hence also the Jewish custom of referring to Caesar as a king (Jn. xix. 12, 15). The dynastic family was from their point of view monarchical. Even where the technical powers were not in Caesarian hands, however, the same terminology occurs (Acts xvii. 7; 1 Pet. ii. 13, 17). The force of Hellenistic traditions of royal suzerainty over the republics, redirected through the universal oath of personal allegiance to the Caesarian house and their association in the imperial cult, nullified the strict Roman view of the Caesar's position. His quasi-monarchical rôle in any case simplified Rome's imperial task. But the cult of the Caesar came to pose an agonizing problem for Christians (Pliny, *Ep.* x. 96, 97, and perhaps Rev. xiii).

The Caesars referred to in the New Testament are, in the Gospels, Augustus (Lk. ii. 1), and elsewhere Tiberius, and in the Acts, Claudius (Acts xi. 28, xvii. 7, xviii. 2), and elsewhere Nero.

BIBLIOGRAPHY. Suetonius, *Lives of the Caesars*; Tacitus, *Annals*; *CAH*, X, XI; M. Hammond, *The Augustan Principate*, 1933; A. Heuss, *RAC*, II, pp. 822–826. E.A.J.

CAESAREA. This magnificent city, built by Herod the Great on the site of Strato's Tower, stood on the Mediterranean shore 23 miles south of Mt. Carmel and about 65 miles north-west of Jerusalem. Named in honour of the Roman Emperor Caesar Augustus, it was the Roman metropolis of Judaea and the official residence both of the Herodian kings and the Roman procurators. It stood on the great caravan route between Tyre and Egypt, and was thus a busy commercial centre for inland trade. But Caesarea was also a celebrated maritime trading-centre, due largely to the construction of elaborate stone breakwaters to the north and south of the harbour. The city was lavishly adorned with palaces, public buildings, and an enormous amphitheatre. One outstanding architectural feature was a huge temple dedicated to Caesar and Rome, and containing vast statues of the emperor. Traces of this ruin can still be seen at the south end of the site of Kaisarieh on the Plain of Sharon.

Fig. 47. Copper coin of Caesarea-on-the-Sea, c. AD 3–4 (?), showing (*obverse*) inverted anchor; (*reverse*) rudder-blade surrounded by the legend *Kaisareōn*, 'of the Caesareans'.

Like many of the Mediterranean communities of New Testament times, Caesarea had a mixed population, so that clashes between the Jews and other elements of the populace were inevitable. When Pilate was procurator of Judaea he occupied the governor's residence in Caesarea. Philip, the evangelist and deacon, brought Christianity to his home city, and subsequently entertained Paul and his companions (Acts xxi. 8). Paul departed from Caesarea on his way to Tarsus, having escaped his Jewish enemies in Damascus (Acts ix. 30). This city was also the abode of the centurion Cornelius and was the locale of his conversion (Acts x. 1, 24, xi. 11). At Caesarea Peter gained greater insight into the nature of the divine kingdom by realizing that God had disrupted the barriers between Gentile and Jewish believers (Acts x. 35), and had dispensed with such classifications as 'clean' and 'unclean'.

Paul made Caesarea his port of landing when returning from his second and third missionary journeys (Acts xviii. 22, xxi. 8). Paul's fateful decision to visit Jerusalem was made here also (Acts xxi. 13), and it was to Caesarea that he was sent for trial by Felix (Acts xxiii. 23–33) before being imprisoned for two years. Paul made his celebrated defence before Festus and Agrippa in Caesarea, and sailed from there in chains when sent by Festus to Rome on his own appeal (Acts xxv. 11). R.K.H.

CAESAREA PHILIPPI. A beautiful locality at the foot of Mt. Hermon, on the main source of the river Jordan, famed as the place of Peter's confession (Mt. xvi. 13 ff.). It may be the Old Testament Baal-Gad. Baal was the deity worshipped there in Old Testament times; the Greeks later substituted their god Pan, and the town took the name Paneas, the shrine itself being called Panion. When the Seleucid ruler Antiochus III wrested Palestine (together with the whole of Coelesyria) from the Ptolemies, Paneas was the scene of one of the decisive battles (200 BC). Herod the Great built a marble temple there to Augustus Caesar, who had given him the town; and Philip the tetrarch later in the same emperor's reign further adorned the town, renaming it Caesarea in the emperor's honour. The addition 'Philippi'—*i.e.* of Philip—was to distinguish it from the coastal Caesarea (*cf.* Acts viii. 40). Agrippa II then rebuilt the town in Nero's reign, and gave it another name, Neronias; but this name was soon forgotten. The town had a considerable history in Crusader times. Its ancient name persists as Banias today. There is a shrine there to the Muslim al-Khidr, equated with St. George. D.F.P.

CAESAR'S HOUSEHOLD. A Roman aristocrat's household (*oikia*, Lat. *familia*) was his staff of servants, primarily those held in slavery, but probably also including those manumitted and retaining obligations of clientship as his freedmen. Their duties were extremely specialized, and covered the full range of domestic service, professional duties (medicine, education, *etc.*), and business, literary, and secretarial assistance. In the case of the Caesars, their permanent political leadership made their household the equivalent of a modern civil service, providing the experts in most fields of state. Its servile origins, and the eastern responsibilities of the Caesars, made it largely Greek and Oriental in its composition. It is not therefore surprising to find it well represented in the Christian group at Rome.

BIBLIOGRAPHY. J. B. Lightfoot, *Philippians*, pp. 171–178; R. H. Barrow, *Slavery in the Roman Empire*, 1928; A. M. Duff, *Freedmen in the Early Roman Empire*[2], 1958. E.A.J.

CAIAPHAS (Mt. xxvi. 57; Jn. xi. 49; Acts iv. 6). Joseph, called Caiaphas, was high priest from roughly AD 18 to 36, when he was deposed by Vitellius, governor of Syria. He was son-in-law to Annas (Jn. xviii. 13), and seems to have worked in close co-operation with him. He was high priest at the trial of Jesus and during the persecutions described in the early chapters of Acts. D.R.H.

CAIN (*qayin*). **1.** The eldest son of Adam and Eve (Gn. iv. 1), at whose birth Eve said, 'I have gotten (*qānîṯî*) a man' (AV). Since this account is unlikely to have been originally couched in Heb., no judgment can be made on the validity of the pun, and nothing can be concluded from apparent etymologies of the name. He was an agriculturalist (Gn. iv. 2), unlike Abel (*q.v.*), who was a shepherd, and being 'of the evil one' (*ek tou ponērou*, 1 Jn. iii. 12) and out of harmony with God (Heb. xi. 4), his offering (*minḥâ*) was rejected (Gn. iv. 3–7) and he subsequently killed his brother (Gn. iv. 8). God punished him by sending him to become a wanderer, perhaps a nomad, in the land of Nod (*q.v.*) (Gn. iv. 9–16), and to protect him from being slain himself God set a 'mark' ('*ôṯ*, 'sign, token', *cf.* Gn. ix. 12, 13) 'for' (*le*) him. The nature of the 'mark' is unknown. Cain was the father of Enoch (*q.v.*). Parallels to the conflict between Cain and Abel have been drawn from Sumerian literature, where disputations concerning the relative merits of agriculture and herding are found, but in none of those known does the farmer kill the herdsman, and such a conflict probably only reflects the historical situation in Mesopotamia from Late Prehistoric times onwards (see NOMADS).

BIBLIOGRAPHY. S. N. Kramer, 'Sumerian Literature and the Bible', in *Analecta Biblica*, XII, 1959, p. 192; *History Begins at Sumer*, 1958, pp. 164–166, 185–192; *Sumerian Mythology*, 1944, pp. 49–51, 53, 54, 101–103; C. J. Gadd, *Teachers and Students in the Oldest Schools*, 1956, pp. 39 ff.; S. H. Hooke, 'Cain and Abel', in *The Siege Perilous*, 1956, pp. 66 ff.

2. The name of a town, written with the article (*haqqayin*), in the south of the territory allotted to Judah (Jos. xv. 57), and probably to be identified with modern Khirbet Yaqin to the south-east of Hebron. See A. Alt, *Palästinajahrbuch*, XXII, 1926, pp. 76, 77. T.C.M.

CAKE. See BREAD.

CALAH. A city founded by Asshur, a follower of Nimrod, moving from Shinar (Gn. x. 11). The Assyr. *Kalḫu* (mod. Nimrud) lies 24 miles south of Nineveh on the east bank of the river Tigris. The principal excavations there by Sir Henry Layard in 1845–8 and the British School of Archaeology in Iraq 1949–61 have traced the city's history from prehistoric to Hellenistic times. Soundings show early influences from the south before the main citadel (600 × 400 yards) was rebuilt by Shalmaneser I (*c.* 1250 BC) and again by Ashurnasirpal II in 879 BC. The city then covered an area of 16 square miles and had a population of about 60,000. It was from Calah that Shalmaneser III attacked Syria, and his Black Obelisk recording the submission of Jehu and stelae mentioning Ahab were originally set up in the main square. Inscriptions of Tiglath-pileser III and Sargon II mention their attacks on Israel and Judah launched from this Assyrian military capital. A list of Hebrew names written in Aramaic may attest the presence of captives settled here. Sargon II, conqueror of Samaria, stored his booty here. Esarhaddon subsequently built himself a palace here and recorded his treaties with conquered peoples on tablets set up in the Temple of Nabu. Many of the discoveries of sculptures, ivories, metal objects, and weapons, found in the citadel and barracks of 'Fort Shalmaneser' in the outer town illustrate the splendour of the booty taken from Syria and Palestine and the might of the Assyrian army. Calah fell to the Medes and Babylonians in 612 BC.

BIBLIOGRAPHY. M. E. L. Mallowan, *Nimrud and its Remains*, 1962; *Iraq*, XIII–XXI, 1952–9.

D.J.W.

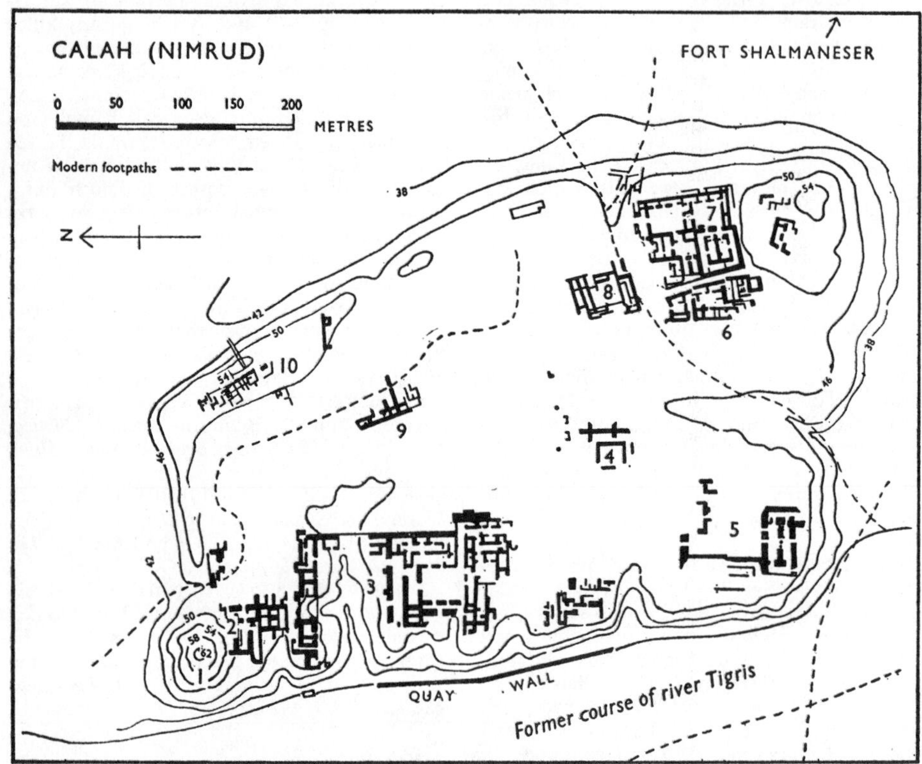

Fig. 48. *Key:* (1) Ziggurat (Temple Tower); (2) Temple of Ninusta; (3) Palace of Ashurnasirpal; (4) Centre Palace (Shalmaneser); (5) SW Palace (Esarhaddon); (6) The Burnt Palace; (7) Temple of Nabu; (8) Governor's Palace; (9) Administrative Building; (10) Private Houses.

CALAMUS. See REED.

CALDRON. See VESSELS.

CALEB. 1. Third son of Hezron son of Pharez; Jerahmeel's youngest brother (spelt Chelubai, 1 Ch. ii. 9, AV). From him, through Ephrathah, lines of descent are given in 1 Ch. ii. 18 ff. to Bezaleel, Moses' chief craftsman; ii. 24, to the town Tekoa (the text is uncertain, but may be read 'C. married E. the wife of Hezron his father, and she bore . . .'); ii. 50 ff., to the towns Q. Jearim, Bethlehem, Netophah, Zorah, Eshtaol, Bethgeder, and others (the Kenite families named in ii. 55 may be loosely connected).

2. 'Brother of Jerahmeel', possibly the same as (1), from whom descent was traced in the towns Ziph, Ma'on, and Beth-zur (the names Hebron and Tappuach also occur; 1 Ch. ii. 42 ff.). This list may refer in part to Caleb ben Jephunneh (see 'Achsah', verse 49).

3. Caleb ben Jephunneh, an outstanding leader of Judah, whose faithfulness in the reconnaissance from Kadesh won him exemption from the curse pronounced there; he directed the invasion of Judaea and settled at Hebron. Nabal of Carmel was his descendant. From Jos. xiv. 6, *etc.*, 1 Ch. iv. 13–15 we learn that he was a Kenizzite.

4. 'Brother of Shuah', spelt *Chelub*, 1 Ch. iv. 11 (EVV).

J.P.U.L.

CALENDAR.

I. IN THE OLD TESTAMENT

There is no precise Hebrew equivalent of the Lat. *calendarium*, the passage of the year being

TABLE SHOWING HEBREW CALENDAR

Month	Pre-exilic Name	Post-exile Name	Biblical Reference	Modern Equivalent	Season	Festivals
1	*'Aḇiḇ*	*Nīsān*	Ex. xii. 2; Ne. ii. 1	March–April	Spring Latter rains Barley harvest Flax harvest	14: Passover (Ex. xii. 18) 15–21: Unleavened Bread (Lv. xxiii. 6) 16: Firstfruits (Lv. xxiii. 10 f.)
2	*Ziw*	*'Iyyār*	1 Ki. vi. 1, 37	April–May	Dry season begins	14: Later Passover (Nu. ix. 10, 11)
3		*Sīwān*	Est. viii. 9	May–June	Early figs ripen	6: Pentecost (Lv. xxiii) Feast of Weeks Harvest
4		*Tammūz*	Ezk. viii. 14	June–July	Grape harvest	
5		*'Aḇ*		July–August	Olive harvest	
6		*Elūl*	Ne. vi. 15	August–September	Dates and summer figs	
7	*'Eṯānīm*	*Tišri*	1 Ki. viii. 2	September–October	Early rains	1: Trumpets (Nu. xxix. 1) 10: Day of Atonement (Lv. xvi. 29 ff.) 15–21: Tabernacles (Lv. xxiii. 34 ff.) 22: Solemn Assembly (Lv. xxiii. 36)
8	*Būl*	*Marḥešwān*	1 Ki. vi. 38	October–November	Ploughing Winter figs	
9		*Kislew*	Ne. i. 1	November–December	Sowing	25: Dedication (1 Macc. iv. 52 f.; Jn. x. 22)
10		*Ṭēḇēṯ*	Est. ii. 16	December–January	Rains (Snow on high ground)	
11		*Šᵉḇaṭ*	Zc. i. 7	January–February	Almond blossom	
12		*'ᵃḏār*	Ezr. vi. 15	February–March	Citrus fruit harvest	

generally marked by reference to the months, agricultural seasons, or the principal festivals.

a. The Year (Heb. *šānâ*—so named from the change or succession of the seasons) was at first reckoned to begin with the autumn (seventh) month of Tishri (Ex. xxiii. 16, xxxiv. 22), the time also of the commencement of the sabbatical year (Lv. xxv. 8–10). While in Egypt the Hebrews may have conformed to the solar year of 12 months, each of 30 days + 5 additional days, *i.e.* 365 days (Herodotus, ii. 4), but if so a change was made thereafter and the 'beginning of months' or first month of the year was fixed in the spring (Ex. xii. 2; Dt. xvi. 1, 6). Thereafter

Fig. 49. Hebrew Calendar from Gezer. Possibly a schoolboy's composition detailing the agricultural operations appropriate to each season. Tenth century BC.

the Hebrew year followed the West Semitic Calendar with a year of 12 lunar months (1 Ki. iv. 7; 1 Ch. xxvii. 1–15). It is not certain whether the commencement of the year in spring (Nisan) was for use only in the ritual, since there is some evidence for the year for civil purposes being sometimes reckoned from the autumn month of Tishri (see CHRONOLOGY OF THE OLD TESTAMENT).

b. The Month (see Table). The Hebrew calendar year was composed of lunar months, which began when the thin crescent of the new moon was first visible at sunset. The day of the new moon thus beginning was considered holy (see MOON). The month (Heb. *yeraḥ*—'moon') was reckoned to consist of 29/30 days and, since the lunar year was about 11 days less than the solar year, it was periodically necessary to intercalate a thirteenth month in order that new year's day should not fall before the spring of the year (March–April). No precise details are known of the method used by the Hebrews to accommodate the agricultural with the lunar calendar. They may have interposed a second Adar (twelfth month) or second Elul (sixth month) within the lunar cycle of 3, 6, 11, 14, 17, or 19 years.

The observation of the autumnal equinox, *i.e.* 'the going out of the year' (see Ex. xxiii. 16) and of the spring or vernal equinox, called 'the return of the year' (1 Ki. xx. 26; 2 Ch. xxxvi. 10) was important for controlling the calendar and consequently the festivals. Thus the year began with the new moon nearest to the vernal equinox when the sun was in Aries (Jos., *Ant.* iii. 8. 4), and the Passover on the fourteenth day of Nisan coincided with the first full moon (Ex. xii. 2–6).

The early month names were probably local Palestinian references to the seasons, and differ from the designation of the months named in texts from Syria (Ras-Shamra, Alalaḫ, Mari). *Abib*, 'ripening of corn' (Ex. xiii. 4); *Ziw* (AV Zif; 1 Ki. vi. 1, 37); *Ethanim* (1 Ki. viii. 2) and *Bul* (1 Ki. vi. 38) of uncertain meaning, are the only names extant from this period. At all periods the months were usually designated numerically; first, Ex. xii. 2; second, Gn. vii. 11; third, Ex. xix. 1; fourth, 2 Ki. xxv. 3; fifth, Nu. xxxiii. 38; sixth, 1 Ch. xxvii. 9; seventh, Gn. viii. 4; eighth, Zc. i. 1; ninth, Ezr. x. 9; tenth, Gn. viii. 5; eleventh, Dt. i. 3; twelfth, Est. iii. 7. In post-exilic times the month-names of the Babylonian calendar were followed (see Table).

c. The Seasons—the Agricultural Calendar. Although the Hebrews adopted a calendar based on lunar months, they also, as agriculturalists, commonly indicated time of year by the season rather than by the names or numeration of the months. Thus, the year which in Palestine divided approximately into the dry season (April–September) and the rainy season (October–March) could be again subdivided generally into 'seed-time' (November–December) and 'harvest' (April–June; Gn. viii. 22). More specific designations would indicate to the local inhabitants actual months, *e.g.* wheat (Gn. xxx. 14; Jdg. xv. 1) or barley harvest (2 Sa. xxi. 9; Ru. i. 22) denote March–April; the 'earing time' (Ex. xxxiv. 21) would be March; and 'the firstripe grapes' (Nu. xiii. 20) the month *Tammuz* (June–July). 'The first rains' (based on the old civil calendar beginning in *Tishri*) fell in September–October, and the 'latter rains' in March–April. The 'summer-fruit' (*qāyiṣ*) of August–September gave its name to the 'summer', also called the 'heat'. The months *Ṭebet* and *Šebaṭ* were the 'cold' months (see Table on p. 177 under heading 'Seasons').

With the above Old Testament references may be compared the agricultural calendar roughly written on stone, perhaps a palimpsest inscribed by a schoolboy in the 10th century BC, found at Gezer in 1908. The translation is uncertain, but it lists the agricultural operations for the twelve months of the year beginning with the autumn: 'Two months of storage. Two months of sowing. Two months of spring growth. Month of pulling flax. Month of barley harvest. Month when everything (else) is harvested. Two months of pruning (vines). Month of summer fruit' (*cf. DOTT*, pp. 201–203).

d. Other ways of accounting times and seasons are covered by general words for a specified 'time' or festival (*'iddān*, Dn. vii. 25; *mō'ēd*, Dn. xii. 7; *z^emān*, Ec. iii. 1; Ne. ii. 6), *cf.* Ps. civ. 27. See TIME. Historical events are normally dated by the regnal years of rulers or by synchronism with some memorable national event, *e.g.* the Exodus; the sojourn in Egypt (Ex. xii. 40); the construction of the first Temple (1 Ki. vi. 1); or the seventy-year Exile in Babylon (Ezk. xxxiii. 21); or the earthquake in the reign of Uzziah (Am. i. 1; Zc. xiv. 5). D.J.W.

II. BETWEEN THE TESTAMENTS

The 'year of the kingdom of the Greeks' (1 Macc. i. 10) is the Seleucid era, dating officially from the first day of the Macedonian month Dios (September/October) in 312 BC. This era is followed in 1 Maccabees, though in some of the sources used in that book (under the influence of the Babylonian reckoning of the beginning of the year from Nisan) the era is dated from March/April, 311 BC.

III. IN THE NEW TESTAMENT

Dates in the New Testament are occasionally reckoned by reference to Gentile rulers. The most elaborate example is in Lk. iii. 1 f., where the beginning of the ministry of John the Baptist is dated not only 'in the fifteenth year of the reign of Tiberius Caesar' (*i.e.* AD 27–8, according to the reckoning retained in the former Seleucid realm, where a new regnal year was held to start in September/October), but also by reference to rulers then in office, whether secular or sacerdotal, in Judaea and the neighbouring territories. *Cf.* datings by reference to the emperors Augustus (Lk. ii. 1) and Claudius (Acts xi. 28), the provincial governors Quirinius (Lk. ii. 2) and Gallio (Acts xviii. 12), and Herod, king of the Jews (Mt. ii. 1; Lk. i. 5).

For the most part, however, the New Testament writers measure time in terms of the current Jewish calendar (or calendars). The record is punctuated by reference to Jewish festivals and other sacred occasions. This is especially so in the Fourth Gospel; *cf.* Jn. ii. 13, 23 (Passover), v. 1 (perhaps the New Year), vi. 4 (Passover), vii. 2 (Tabernacles; in verse 37 'the last day, that great day of the feast' is the eighth day; *cf.* Lv. xxiii. 36; Nu. xxix. 35; Ne. viii. 18), x. 22 (Dedication, on 25th *Kislew*; *cf.* 1 Macc. iv. 59), xi. 55 ff. (Passover). *Cf.* also Mt. xxvi. 2; Mk. xiv. 1; Lk. xxii. 1 (Passover and Unleavened Bread); Acts ii. 1 (Pentecost), xii. 3 f. (Passover and Unleavened Bread), xviii. 21, AV (perhaps Passover), xx. 6 (Unleavened Bread), xx. 16 (Pentecost), xxvii. 9 (where 'the fast' is the Day of Atonement, about which time sailing in the Mediterranean came to an end for the winter); 1 Cor. xvi. 8 (Pentecost).

Among days of the week, the sabbath is frequently mentioned. The 'second-first sabbath' (Lk. vi. 1, RVmg) is probably a technical term whose meaning can no longer be determined with certainty. Friday is 'the preparation (Gk. *paraskeuē*), that is, the day before the sabbath (Gk. *prosabbaton*)' (Mk. xv. 42; *cf.* Jn. xix. 31); 'the preparation of the passover' (Jn. xix. 14) means 'Friday of Passover week' (Gk. *paraskeuē tou pascha*). The 'first day of the week' (Gk. *mia sabbatou* or *mia tōn sabbatōn*, *i.e.* one day after the sabbath) receives a new significance from its being the resurrection day; *cf.* (in addition to the resurrection narratives in the Gospels) Acts xx. 7; 1 Cor. xvi. 2; also 'the Lord's day' (Gk. *kyriakē hēmera*) in Rev. i. 10.

In general, the Jewish calendar in New Testament times (at least before AD 70) followed the Sadducean reckoning, since it was by that reckoning that the Temple services were regulated. Thus the day of Pentecost was reckoned as the fiftieth day after the presentation of the first harvested sheaf of barley, *i.e.* the fiftieth day (inclusive) from the first Sunday after Passover (*cf.* Lv. xxiii. 15 f.); hence it always fell on a Sunday, as it does in the Christian calendar. The Pharisaic reckoning, which became standard after AD 70, interpreted 'sabbath' in Lv. xxiii. 15 as the festival day of Unleavened Bread and not the weekly sabbath; in that case Pentecost always fell on the same day of the month (an important consideration for those in whose eyes it marked the anniversary of the law-giving) but not on the same day of the week.

Even more important than the minor calendrical differences between Sadducees and Pharisees was the cleavage between the Sadducees and Pharisees, on the one hand, and those, on the other hand, who followed the 'sectarian' calendar known from the Book of Jubilees and now also from the Qumran literature. If Jesus and His disciples followed this 'sectarian' calendar, that might explain how they kept the Passover before His arrest, while the chief priests and their associates did not keep it until after His crucifixion (Jn. xviii. 28).

BIBLIOGRAPHY. J. C. Dancy, *Commentary on I Maccabees*, 1954, pp. 48 ff.; N. Geldenhuys, *Commentary on Luke*, 1950, pp. 649 ff.; A. Jaubert, *La Date de la Cène*, 1957, and 'Jésus et le calendrier de Qumrân', *NTS*, VII, 1960–1, pp. 1 ff.; J. Finegan, *Light from the Ancient Past*[2], 1959, pp. 552 ff.; J. van Goudoever, *Biblical Calendars*, 1959; A. E. Guilding, *The Fourth Gospel and Jewish Worship*, 1960. F.F.B.

CALF, GOLDEN. 1. The golden image made after the Exodus by Aaron and the Israelites at Sinai while Moses was in the mountain. On finding that they were idolatrously worshipping it as God with sacrifices, feasting, and revelry, Moses destroyed it (Ex. xxxii. 4–8, 18–25, 35; Dt. ix. 16, 21; Ne. ix. 18; Ps. cvi. 19, 20; Acts vii. 41). This idol is sometimes thought to be the Egyptian Apis-bull of Memphis (see D. J. Wiseman, *Illustrations from Biblical Archaeology*, 1959, p. 39, fig. 33) or the Mnevis bull of Heliopolis, but these are too far away from Goshen to have been really familiar to the Hebrews. In fact, there were several not dissimilar bull-cults in the East Delta, much closer to the Hebrews in Goshen, which they could have aped later at Sinai. To the south-west of Goshen (Tumilat-area, see GOSHEN), in the 10th Lower Egyptian nome or province, called 'the Black Bull', there was an amalgam of Horus-worship and bull- or calf-cult; farther north and extending along the north-west of Goshen itself, the 11th Lower Egyptian nome also possessed a bull-cult linked with Horus-worship; other traces are known. (See E. Otto, *Beiträge zur Geschichte der Stierkulte in Aegypten*, 1938, pp. 6–8, 32, 33.) In Egypt, the bull or calf was symbol of fertility in nature, and of physical strength (*cf.* Otto, *op. cit.*, pp. 1, 2, 24 f., and *passim*), and, as elsewhere in the Near East, could even perhaps have had links with the worship of the host of heaven. (*Cf.* Wainwright, *JEA*, XIX, 1933, pp. 42–52, especially pp. 44–46. For certain reserves, see Otto, *op. cit.*, p. 7, n. 4. Perhaps *cf.* also Acts vii. 41, 42 in conjunction?)

In nearby Canaan, however, the bull or calf was the animal of Baal or Hadad, god(s) of storm, fertility, and vegetation, and, as in Egypt, symbolized fertility and strength. Bearing in mind the close links between Canaan and the Egyptian East Delta (see EGYPT; MOSES) and the presence of many Semites in the Delta besides the Israelites, it is possible to view the idolatry at Sinai as a blending of contemporary, popular bull- and calf-cults, Egyptian and Canaanite alike, with their emphasis on natural strength and fertility. In any case, it represented a reduction of the God of Israel (*cf.* 'feast to the Lord', Ex. xxxii. 5) to the status of an amoral (tending to immoral) nature-god like those of the surrounding nations, and meant that He could then all too easily be identified with the Baals. This God rejected, refusing to be identified with the god of the calf, hence condemning it as the worship of an 'other' god, and therefore idolatry (Ex. xxxii. 8).

2. At the division of the Hebrew kingdom, Israel's first king, Jeroboam I, wishing to counteract the great attraction of the Temple at Jerusalem in Judah, set up two golden calves, in Bethel and Dan, to be centres of Israel's worship of Yahweh (1 Ki. xii. 28–33; 2 Ki. xvii. 16; 2 Ch. xi. 14, 15, xiii. 8). In Syria–Palestine the gods Baal or Hadad were commonly thought of (and shown) as standing upon a bull or calf, emblem of their powers of fertility and strength (see *ANEP*, pp. 170, 179, figs. 500, 501, 531), and Jeroboam's action had the same disastrous implications as Aaron's golden calf: the reduction of Yahweh to a nature-god, and His subsequent identification with the Baals of Canaan. With this would go a shift in emphasis from righteousness, justice, and an exemplary moral standard to purely physical and material considerations, sliding easily into immorality with a religious backing, with social disintegration, and total loss of any sense of the divinely appointed mission of the chosen people in a darkened world. All this was bound up in the idolatry that was 'the sin of Jeroboam, son of Nebat'.

Jehu (2 Ki. x. 29) removed the more obvious and explicit Baal-worship in Israel, but not the calves of a Baalized Yahweh. Hosea (viii. 5, 6, xiii. 2) prophesied the coming end of such 'worship'. K.A.K.

CALL, CALLING. In the Old and New Testaments together there are some 700 occurrences of the word as verb, noun, or adjective. The principal Heb. root is *qr'*; in Gk. *kalein* (with its compounds, and derivatives *klētos*, 'called', and *klēsis*, 'calling'), *legein*, and *phōnein* are used. In both languages other verbs are occasionally rendered by parts of 'to call', *e.g.* *'mr* in Is. v. 20, and *chrēmatizein* in Rom. vii. 3.

I. IN THE OLD TESTAMENT

a. 'Call to', hence 'invite or summon (by name)' (Gn. iii. 9, *etc.*); 'invite an assembly' (La. i. 15). 'Call upon the name' is found from Gn. iv. 26 onwards ('then began men to call upon the name of the Lord'), and denotes claiming God's protection either by summoning assistance from one whose name (*i.e.* character) was known, or by calling oneself by the name of the Lord (*cf.* Gn. iv. 26 AVmg; Dt. xxviii. 10; Is. xliii. 7).

b. 'Give a name to' is found in such verses as Gn. i. 5 ('God called the light Day'). Those verses where God is the subject indicate the underlying unity of the two senses of *qr'*, thereby revealing its theological meaning. The first sense implies a call to serve God in some capacity and for some particular purpose (1 Sa. iii. 4; Is. xlix. 1). The meaning of the second sense is not simply to identify; it is both to describe (Gn. xvi. 11; *cf.* Mt. i. 21) and to indicate a relationship between God the nominator and His nominee, especially Israel. Is. xliii. 1 epitomizes God's call and naming of Israel to be His, separated from other nations, granted the work of bearing witness, and the privilege of the protection afforded by His name. God alone initiates this call, and only a minority (remnant) respond (*e.g.* Joel ii. 32).

II. IN THE NEW TESTAMENT

Here the same usages are found, and the call of God is now 'in Christ Jesus' (Phil. iii. 14). It is a summons to bear the name of Christian (1 Pet. iv. 16; Jas. ii. 7; Acts v. 41; Mt. xxviii. 19) and to belong to God in Christ (1 Pet. ii. 9). 'Call to' is found in Mk. ii. 17, *e.g.*, and 'give a name to' in Lk. i. 59. The present passive participle is in frequent use, as in Lk. vii. 11. Jesus called disciples and they followed Him (Mk. i. 20). The Epistles, especially Paul's, make clear the theological meaning of Christ's call. It comes from

God, through the gospel for salvation and holiness and faith (2 Thes. ii. 14) to God's kingdom (1 Thes. ii. 12), for fellowship (1 Cor. i. 9) and service (Gal. i. 15). Other writers impart this full meaning to God's call (*cf.* Heb. iii. 1, ix. 15; 1 Pet. ii. 21; 1 Jn. iii. 1 especially—'. . . that we should be called the sons of God'). Those who respond are 'called' (1 Cor. i. 24; Lightfoot translates 'believers'). Paul equates the call with the response (Rom. viii. 28 ff.) to emphasize God's unchanging purpose (Rom. ix. 11). The saying of Jesus in Mt. xxii. 14 distinguishes 'the called', those who hear, from 'the chosen', those who respond. Paul sees the call as effective.

Many commentators interpret 'calling' in 1 Cor. vii. 20 ff. as 'particular occupation'. Rather *klēsis* here means the divine calling of each man as a concrete historical event, *i.e.* as including in itself the outward circumstances in which it was received. Slavery as such is not incompatible with faith in Christ.

BIBLIOGRAPHY. *Arndt*; *BDB*; articles in *Baker's Dictionary of Theology*, *HDB*, *RTWB*, *TWNT*, and von Allmen's *Vocabulary of the Bible*.

M.R.W.F.

CALNEH, CALNO. 1. Calneh. The name of a city founded by Nimrod in the land of Shinar (Gn. x. 10). Since no city of this name is known in Babylonia, some scholars propose to point the Heb. *kullānâ*, 'all of them', as in Gn. xlii. 36; 1 Ki. vii. 37. This would then be a comprehensive clause to cover such ancient cities as Ur and Nippur (identified with Calneh in TB). Those who locate Shinar in N Mesopotamia equate this city with (2). (See *JNES*, III, 1944, p. 254.)

2. Calno (Kalno), Is. x. 9; Kalneh, Am. vi. 2 (LXX *pantes*, 'all', see (1)). A town Kullania mentioned in Assyr. tribute lists. Associated with Arpad. Modern Kullan Köy 16 km. south-east of Arpad (*AJSL*, LI, 1935, pp. 189–191).

D.J.W.

CALVARY. The name occurs once only in the AV, in Lk. xxiii. 33. The word comes from the Vulgate, where the Lat. *calvaria* translates the Gk. *kranion*; both words translate Aramaic *gulgoltâ*, the 'Golgotha' of Mt. xxvii. 33, meaning 'skull'. Three possible reasons for such a name have been propounded: because skulls were found there; because it was a place of execution; or because the site in some way resembled a skull. All we know of the site from Scripture is that it was outside Jerusalem, fairly conspicuous, probably not far from a city gate and a highway, and that a garden containing a tomb lay near by.

Two Jerusalem localities are today pointed out as the site of the Lord's cross and tomb; the one is the Church of Holy Sepulchre, the other Gordon's Calvary, commonly known as the Garden Tomb. Unfortunately it has always proved difficult to debate the question objectively; in some quarters the identification one accepts is almost the touchstone of one's orthodoxy. The Church of Holy Sepulchre marks the site of a temple to Venus which the Emperor Constantine removed, understanding that it stood over the sacred site. The tradition thus goes back at least to the 4th century. But in view of the operations and activities of Titus in the 1st century and Hadrian in the 2nd, the identification must still be viewed as precarious. Moreover, a problem is raised by the uncertainty about whether the wall of Jerusalem in the lifetime of Jesus included or excluded the place where the church stands. Josephus' details are too few for dogmatism about the line that the wall took; and Jerusalem is too built up for archaeologists to be able to get to grips with the problem.

The Garden Tomb was first pointed out in 1849; a rock formation there resembles a skull; and admittedly the site accords with the biblical data. But there is no tradition nor anything else to support its claim. The more ancient site is much more likely; but any identification must remain conjectural. D.F.P.

CAMEL (Heb. *gāmāl*; Gk. *kamēlos*). A desert quadruped, famous for its ability to cross desert regions through being able to carry within itself several days' water-supply. The Heb. term (like the popular use of the word 'camel' in English) does *not* distinguish between the two characteristic kinds of camel: the one-humped animal (*Camelus dromedarius*) or 'dromedary' of Arabia, and the two-humped beast (*Camelus bactrianus*) or Bactrian camel from north-east of Iran (Bactria, now in Turkmen and NW Afghanistan). In antiquity, both kinds are represented on the monuments.

In Scripture, camels are first mentioned in the days of the Patriarchs (*c.* 1900–1700 BC). They formed part of the livestock wealth of Abraham and Jacob (Gn. xii. 16, xxiv. 35, xxx. 43, xxxii. 7, 15) and also of Job (i. 3, 17, xlii. 12). On only two notable occasions are the Patriarchs actually shown using camels for transport: when Abraham's servant went to Mesopotamia to obtain a wife for Isaac (Gn. xxiv. 10 ff.), and when Jacob fled from Laban (Gn. xxxi. 17, 34)—neither an everyday event. Otherwise, camels are attributed only to the Ishmaelites/Midianites, desert traders, at this time (Gn. xxxvii. 25). This very modest utilization of camels in the patriarchal age corresponds well with the known rather limited use of camels in the early second millennium BC (see below).

In the 13th century BC the Egyptian beasts of burden smitten with disease included horses (the most valuable), asses (the most usual), and camels (a rarity), besides others (Ex. ix. 3); and in the law camels were forbidden as food (Lv. xi. 4; Dt. xiv. 7).

The mention of camels in the Pentateuch, especially in Genesis, has been often and persistently dismissed as anachronistic by some but stoutly defended by others. The truth appears to be as follows. From the 12th century BC the camel (and camel-nomadism) becomes a regular feature in the biblical world (other than Egypt, where it remains rare). Before this date, definite but very limited use was made of the camel. Though limited and imperfect, the extant evidence clearly indicates that the domesticated camel was known by 3000 BC, and continued in limited use as a slow-moving burden-carrier down through the second millennium BC, the ass being the main beast of burden.

Archaeological Evidence. From the evidence available, only a few items bearing on Genesis and Exodus can be cited here. First and foremost, a mention of the (domesticated) camel occurs in a cuneiform tablet from Alalaḫ in North Syria (18th century BC) as GAM.MAL; see Wiseman, *JCS*, XIII, 1959, p. 29 and Goetze, *ibid.*, p. 37, on text 269, line 59. Lambert (*BASOR*, 160, 1960, pp. 42, 43), however, disputes the Alalaḫ camel-reference, and instead produces evidence for knowledge of the camel in the Old Babylonian period (*c.* 19th century BC) in a text from Ugarit. Then there is the kneeling camel-figure from Byblos of similar date, Montet, *Byblos et l'Égypte*, 1928, p. 91 and plate 52, No. 179. Albright's objection (*JBL*, LXIV, 1945, p. 288) that it has no hump (hence not a camel) is ruled out because the figure is incomplete and has a socket by which a separately-fashioned hump and load were once fixed (this is also noted by R. de Vaux, *RB*, LVI, 1949, p. 9, notes 4, 5). A camel's jaw was found in a Middle Bronze Age tomb at Tell el-Fara' by Nablus (*c.* 1900–1550 BC), de Vaux, *op. cit.*, p. 9, note 8. Nor does this exhaust the evidence for the patriarchal period.

In the Egyptian Fayum province was found a camel-skull dated to the 'Pottery A' stage, *i.e.* within the period *c.* 2000–1400 BC, the period from the Patriarchs practically to Moses; see O. H. Little, *Bulletin de l'Institut d'Égypte*, XVIII, 1935–6, p. 215. From the Memphis region comes a figure of a camel with two water-jars (clear evidence of its domestication in Egypt) datable by associated archaeological material to about the 13th century BC, Petrie, *Gizeh and Rifeh*, 1907, p. 23 and plate 27. Albright (*JBL*, LXIV, 1945, pp. 287–288) wished to lower the date of this example; but as he fails to offer specific evidence of any kind in support of his contention, it must be dismissed. Palestine also affords some evidence of camels at this general period. Hence the references in Exodus, Leviticus, and Deuteronomy are no more objectionable than those in Genesis.

In the judges' period Israel was troubled by camel-riding Midianites (repelled by Gideon, Jdg. vi–viii) and others, *e.g.* the Hagarites (1 Ch. v. 21); likewise Saul and David fought camel-using Amalekites (1 Sa. xv. 3, xxvii. 9, xxx. 17). The Arabians made particular use of camels in peace and war—so did the Queen of Sheba (1 Ki. x. 2; 2 Ch. ix. 1) and the people of Kedar and 'Hazor' (Je. xlix. 29, 32). Hazael the Aramaean brought 40 camel-loads of gifts from king Ben-hadad to Elisha (2 Ki. viii. 9). *Cf.* the pictures of Assyrian, Arabian, and Aramaean camels cited at the end of this article. The Jews who returned to Judaea with Zerubbabel after the Exile had 435 camels (Ezr. ii. 67; Ne. vii. 69). In New Testament times camel's hair furnished clothing for John the Baptist (Mt. iii. 4; Mk. i. 6), while the camel featured in two of Christ's most striking word-pictures (Mt. xix. 24 = Lk. xviii. 25; Mt. xxiii. 24).

Fig. 50. Two Arabs on a camel. One urges on the animal with a stick. The other shoots with bow and arrow at pursuing Assyrian archers and spearmen. Relief from Nineveh *c.* 650 BC.

BIBLIOGRAPHY. For one-humped camels, see *ANEP*, p. 20, fig. 63, p. 52, fig. 170, p. 58, fig. 187,

p. 132, fig. 375 (Assyrian and Arabian ones), p. 59, fig. 188 (Aramaean). For two-humped camels, see *ANEP*, p. 122, fig. 355 = Wiseman, *Illustrations from Biblical Archaeology*, 1959, p. 57, fig. 51, for Assyrian times, and H. Frankfort, *Art and Architecture of the Ancient Orient*, 1954, plate 184B of Persian period.

Specially valuable for the camel in antiquity are the richly-documented studies by R. Walz, in *Zeitschrift der Deutschen Morgenländischen Gesellschaft*, 101, NS 26, 1951, pp. 29–51; *ibid.*, 104, NS 29, 1954, pp. 45–87; and in *Actes du IVe Congrès Internationale des Sciences Anthropologiques et Ethnologiques*, III, Vienna, 1956, pp. 190–204. More recent are: F. S. Bodenheimer, *Animal and Man in Bible Lands*, 1960, under 'camelides', and W. Dostal in F. Gabrieli, W. Dostal, G. Dossin, *etc.*, *L'antica società beduina*, ed. Gabrieli, 1959. K.A.K.

CAMP. See ARMY.

CAMPHIRE. See PLANTS.

CANA (Gk. *kana*, probably from Heb. *qānâ*, 'place of reeds'). A Galilaean village in the uplands west of the lake, mentioned in John's Gospel only. It was the scene of Jesus' first miracle (Jn. ii. 1, 11), the place where with a word He healed the nobleman's son who lay sick at Capernaum (iv. 46, 50), and the home of Nathanael (xxi. 2). Not definitely located, it has been identified by some with Kefr Kenna, about 4 miles NNE of Nazareth on the road to Tiberias. This site, where excavations have been made, is a likely place for the events of Jn. ii. 1–11, having ample water springs, and providing such shady fig-trees as that suggested in Jn. i. 48. Many modern scholars, however, prefer an identification with Khirbet Kānā, a ruined site 9 miles north of Nazareth, which local Arabs still call Cana of Galilee. J.D.D.

CANAAN. Son of Ham, grandson of Noah, who laid a curse upon him (Gn. ix. 18, 22–27). In Gn. x. 15–19 eleven groups who historically inhabited Phoenicia in particular and Syria–Palestine in general are listed as his descendants. See also the following article. K.A.K.

CANAAN, CANAANITES. A Semitic-speaking people and their territory, principally in Phoenicia. Their racial affinities are at present uncertain.

I. THE NAME

The name Canaan (Heb. *Kena'an*) of people and land derives from that of their forebear Canaan or Kna' (see previous article) according to both Gn. x. 15–18 and native Canaanite–Phoenician tradition as transmitted by Sanchuniathon and preserved by Philo of Byblos. *Kna'(an)* is the native name of the Canaanites–Phoenicians applied to them both in Greek sources and by the Phoenicians themselves (*e.g.* on coins; see W. F. Albright, p. 1, n. 1, in his paper, 'The Rôle of the Canaanites in the History of Civilization', in *Studies in the History of Culture Presented to Waldo G. Leland*, 1942, pp. 1–50; cited hereafter as *Leland Vol.*). The meaning of *Kn'(n)* is unknown. Outside the Bible, the name occurs both with and without the final *n*. This *n* could be either a final *n* of a common Semitic type, or else a Hurrian suffix (Albright, *op. cit.*, p. 25, n. 50). Among the Hurrians in Mesopotamia to the east, the term *Kna'(n)*, 'Canaan(ites)', was appropriately turned into an adjectival form (with Hurrian suffix *-aḫḫe* or *-ġġi*) and applied to the Canaanites' characteristic product (Speiser, *Language*, XII, 1936, p. 124), that of purple dye and cloth so dyed. *Kinaḫḫe(na)* means, then, in Hurrian, 'Kna'-ian dye' or 'dyed cloth'. (It is still not properly determined whether *kinaḫḫe* signifies red-purple or blue-purple. For the former, see Speiser, *AASOR*, XVI, 1936, pp. 121, 122 (but he is less positive in *Language*, *loc. cit.*); for the latter, see Goetze, *JCS*, X, 1956, p. 35, n. 36.)

II. EXTENT OF CANAAN

'Canaan' in both Scripture and external sources has threefold reference. First and fundamentally it indicates the land and inhabitants of the Syro-Palestinian coastland, especially Phoenicia proper. This is indicated within Gn. x. 15–19 by its detailed enumeration of Sidon 'the first-born', the Arkite (*q.v.*), the Sinite, the Zemarite and Hamath in the Orontes valley. Still more specific for the location of the Canaanites are Nu. xiii. 29; Jos. v. 1, xi. 3; Jdg. i. 27 ff., putting them on the coastlands and in the valleys and plains (including the Jordan valley), and Amorites and others in the hills. This division also underlies the detail of the lists of nations in Gn. xv. 18–21; Ex. iii. 8, 17; Dt. vii. 1, xx. 17, *etc.* This 'strict' use of 'Canaan(ites)' is also attested by external records of early date. Thus, for example, the inscription of Idrimi, king of Alalaḫ (15th century BC), mentions his flight to (the seaport of) Ammia in (coastal) Canaan (S. Smith, *The Statue of Idrimi*, 1949, pp. 72, 73).

Secondly, 'Canaan(ite)' can also cover by extension the hinterland and so Syria–Palestine in general. Thus, Gn. x. 15–19 includes also the Hittite, Jebusite, Amorite, Hivite, and Girgashite, explaining that 'the families of the Canaanite spread abroad' (verse 18); this wider area is defined as extending coastally from Sidon to Gaza, inland to the Dead Sea cities Sodom and Gomorrah and apparently back up north to Lasha (location uncertain). See also Gn. xii. 5, xiii. 12, or Nu. xiii. 17–21, xxxiv. 1, 2, with the following delimitation of West Palestinian boundaries; Jdg. iv. 2, 23, 24 calls Jabin (II) of Hazor titular 'king of Canaan'. This wider use is also encountered in early external sources. In their Amarna letters (14th century BC) kings of Babylon and elsewhere sometimes use 'Canaan' for Egypt's Syro-Palestinian territories generally. And the Egyptian Papyrus Anastasi IIIA (lines 5–6) and IV (16: line 4) of 13th century BC mention 'Canaanite slaves from Huru' (= Syria–

Palestine generally) (Caminos, *Late-Egyptian Miscellanies*, 1954, pp. 117, 200).

Thirdly, the term 'Canaanite' can bear the more restricted meaning of 'merchant, trafficker', trading being a most characteristic Canaanite occupation. In Scripture this meaning may be found in Jb. xli. 6; Is. xxiii. 8; Ezk. xvii. 4; Zp. i. 11 (see RVmg); the word *kn't* in Je. x. 17 is even used for 'wares, merchandise'. This use of 'Canaanite' for 'merchant' is a venerable one: a stele of the pharaoh Amenophis II (*c.* 1440 BC) lists among his Syrian captives '550 *maryannu* (= noble chariot-warriors), 240 of their wives, 640 *Kn'nw*, 232 sons of princes, 323 daughters of princes', among others (*ANET*, p. 246). From this, Maisler (*BASOR*, 102, 1946, p. 9) rightly draws the conclusion that the 640 *Kn'nw* (Canaaneans) found in such exalted company are of the merchant 'plutocracy of the coastal and the trading centres of Syria and Palestine'.

III. CANAANITES AND AMORITES

Alongside the specific, wider, and restricted uses of 'Canaan(ite)' noted above, 'Amorite(s)' (*q.v.*) also has both a specific and a wider reference. Specifically, the Amorites in Scripture are part of the hill-country population of Palestine (Nu. xiii. 29; Jos. v. 1, xi. 3). But in its wider use 'Amorite' tends to overlap directly the term 'Canaanite'. 'Amorite' comes in under 'Canaan' in Gn. x. 15, 16 for a start. Then, Israel is to conquer Canaan (= Palestine) in Nu. xiii. 17–21, *etc.*, and duly comes to dwell in the land of the Amorites, overcoming 'all the people' there, namely Amorites (Jos. xxiv. 15, 18). Abraham reaches, and is promised, Canaan (Gn. xii. 5, 7, xv. 7, 18), but occupation is delayed as 'the iniquity of the Amorites is not yet full' (Gn. xv. 16). Shechem is a Canaanite principality under a Hivite ruler (Gn. xii. 5, 6, xxxiv. 2, 30), but can be called 'Amorite' (Gn. xlviii. 22).

The documentary theory of literary criticism has frequently assayed to use these overlapping or double designations, Canaanites and Amorites (and other 'pairs'), as marks of different authorship (see *e.g.* S. R. Driver, *Introduction to the Literature of the Old Testament*[9], 1913, p. 119, or O. Eissfeldt, *Einleitung in das Alten Testament*, 1956, p. 217). But any such use of these terms does not accord with the external records which have no underlying 'hands', and it must therefore be questioned.

In the 18th century BC Amurru is part of Syria in the Alalaḫ tablets, while Amorite princes are mentioned in a Mari document in relation to Hazor in Palestine itself (*cf.* J.-R. Kupper, *Les Nomades en Mésopotamie au temps des Rois de Mari*, 1957, pp. 179, 180). As Hazor is the Canaanite city *par excellence* of North Palestine, the mingling of people and terms is already attested in Abraham's day. In the 14th/13th centuries BC the specific kingdom of Amurru of Abdi-aširta, Aziru, and their successors in the Lebanon mountain region secured a firm hold on a section of the Phoenician coast and its Canaanite seaports by conquest and alliance 'from Byblos to Ugarit' (Amarna Letter No. 98). This Amorite control in coastal Canaan is further attested by the Battle of Qadesh inscriptions of Rameses II (13th century BC) mentioning the timely arrival inland of a battle-force from a 'port in the land of Amurru' (see Gardiner, *Ancient Egyptian Onomastica*, I, 1947, pp. 188*–189*, and Gardiner, *The Kadesh Inscriptions of Ramesses II*, 1960, on this incident). This is further evidence for a contiguous use of Amor(ites) and Canaan(ites) in Moses' time. The use of these terms as the distinguishing marks of different literary hands is thus erroneous. In any case the situation reflected in the Pentateuch and Joshua by this usage was radically changed by the impact of the sea peoples at the end of the 13th century BC, after which date the emergence of that usage would be inexplicable. See also AMORITES.

IV. THE LANGUAGE

The definition of what is or is not 'Canaanite' is much controverted. Within the general group of the North-West Semitic languages and dialects, biblical Hebrew (*cf.* Is. xix. 18) and the West Semitic glosses and terms in the Amarna tablets can correctly be termed 'South Canaanite' along with Moabite and Phoenician. Separate but related are Aramaic and Ya'udic. Between these two groups comes Ugaritic. Some hold this latter to be a separate North-West Semitic language, others that it is Canaanite to be classed with Hebrew, *etc.* Ugaritic itself betrays historical development linguistically, and thus the Ugaritic of the 14th/13th centuries BC is closer to Hebrew than is the archaic language of the great epics (Albright, *BASOR*, 150, 1958, pp. 36–38). Hence it is provisionally possible to view North-West Semitic as including South Canaanite (Hebrew, *etc.*), North Canaanite (Ugaritic), and Aramaic. *Cf.* S. Moscati (*The Semites in Ancient History*, 1959, pp. 97–100), who (rather radically) would abolish 'Canaanite'; and J. Friedrich (*Scientia*, LXXXIV, 1949, pp. 220–223), on this question. The distinction between 'Canaanite' and 'Amorite' is almost illusory, and little more than dialectal. They differ in little more than the sibilants. See LANGUAGE OF THE OLD TESTAMENT.

V. CANAANITE HISTORY

The presence of Semitic-speaking people in Palestine in the third millennium BC is so far explicitly attested only by two Semitic placenames in a text of that age: *Ndi'* which contains the element *'il(u)*, 'god', and *'n..k..* which begins with *'ain*, 'spring, well', both these names occurring in an Egyptian tomb-scene of Vth/VIth Dynasty, *c.* 2400 BC.

However, the question as to whether these indicate the presence of Canaanites, and just when Canaanites appeared in Palestine, is a matter of dispute. It is certain that Canaanites and Amorites were well established in Syria–Palestine by 2000 BC.

Throughout the second millennium BC, Syria–Palestine was divided among a varying number of Canaanite/Amorite city-states. For the 19th/18th century BC, many names of places and rulers are recorded in the Egyptian execration texts. On the organization of some of the separate states in Palestine in this, the patriarchal period, see also A. van Selms, *Oudtestamentische Studiën*, XII, 1958 (*Studies on the Book of Genesis*), pp. 192–197.

During the period roughly 1500–1380 BC, these petty states were part of Egypt's Asiatic empire; in the 14th century BC the northern ones passed under Hittite suzerainty, while the southern ones remained nominally Egyptian. Early in the 13th century BC Egypt regained effectual control in Palestine and coastal Syria (the Hittites retaining north and inner Syria), but this control evaporated as time passed. Thus Israel in the late 13th century met Canaanite/Amorite, but not specifically Egyptian, opposition (except for Merenptah's abortive raid). The 'conquest' by Rameses III, *c.* 1180 BC, was a sweeping raid into upper Syria, mainly *via* the coast and principal routes, and was superficial.

At the end of the 13th century BC the sway of the Canaanite/Amorite city-states, now decadent, was shattered by political upheavals. The Israelites, under Joshua, entered West Palestine from across the Jordan, gaining control of the hill country first and defeating a series of Canaanite kings. The Iron Age Philistines (*q.v.*) established themselves in coastal Palestine and beyond. Meantime, the sea-peoples of the Egyptian records (including Philistines) had destroyed the Hittite Empire and swept through Syria and Palestine to be halted on the Egyptian border by Rameses III. Finally, Aramaean penetration of Syria swiftly increased inland in the century or so following. The result was that the Canaanites now ruled only in Phoenicia proper with its ports and in isolated principalities elsewhere. From the 12th century BC onwards, the former Bronze Age Canaanites in their new, restricted, circumstances emerged as the more-than-ever maritime Phoenicians of the first millennium BC, centred on the famous kingdom of Tyre and Sidon. See further under PHOENICIA, TYRE, SIDON. On the history of the Canaanites, especially as continuing as Phoenicians, see Albright, *Leland Vol.*, pp. 1–50.

VI. CANAANITE CULTURE

Our knowledge of this is derived from two main sources: firstly, literary, from the North Canaanite and Babylonian texts discovered at Ugarit (Ras Shamra, on the Syrian coast) with odd fragments elsewhere; and secondly, archaeological, in the sense of being derived from the excavated objects and remains from and of towns and cemeteries in Syria and Palestine.

a. Canaanite Society

Most of the Canaanite city-states were monarchies. The king had extensive powers of military appointment and conscription, of requisitioning lands and leasing them in return for services, of taxation, including tithes, customs-dues, real-estate tax, *etc.*, and of corvée to requisition the labour of his subjects for state purposes. This is directly reflected in Samuel's denunciation of a kingship like that of the nations round about (1 Sa. viii, *c.* 1050 BC), and clearly evident in the tablets from Alalaḫ (18th–15th centuries BC) and Ugarit (14th–13th centuries BC) (see I. Mendelsohn, *BASOR*, 143, 1956, pp. 17–22). Military, religious, and economic matters were under the king's direct oversight; the queen was an important personage sometimes appealed to by high officials; the court was elaborately organized in larger states like Ugarit.

The basic unit of society was the family. For the period of the 19th–15th centuries BC, the great North Canaanite epics from Ugarit (see *Literature*, below) betray the main features of family life (see A. van Selms, *Marriage and Family Life in Ugaritic Literature*, 1954). Further information is afforded by the tablets written in Babylonian for the 14th/13th centuries BC. Among larger social units, besides the obvious ones of towns with their associated villages (in Ugarit state, see Virolleaud, *Syria*, XXI, 1940, pp. 123–151, and *cf.* briefly, C. H. Gordon, *Ugaritic Literature*, p. 124), for which compare the assignment of towns with their villages ('suburbs') in Jos. xiii ff., one may note the widespread organization of guilds. These include primary producers (herdsmen, fowlers, butchers, and bakers), artisans (smiths, both copper (or bronze) smiths and silversmiths, potters, sculptors, and house-, boat-, and chariot-builders), and traders both local and long-distance. Priests and other cult-personnel (see below), also musicians, had guilds or groups; and there were several special classes of warriors. Several inscribed javelin- or spear-heads recently found in Palestine perhaps belonged to late-Canaanite mercenary troops of the 12th/11th centuries BC, the sort of people commanded by a Sisera or Jabin (Jdg. iv, *etc.*); these also illustrate the free use of early West Semitic alphabetic script in the Palestine of the judges. It has been suggested that in Canaanite society in 13th-century-BC Palestine there was a sharp class-distinction between upper-class patricians and lower-class, half-free serfs, the contrast with the relatively humble and homogeneous Israelites possibly being reflected in the excavated archaeological sites.

b. Literature

This is principally represented by the North Canaanite texts from Ugarit. These include long, but disordered and fragmentary, sections of the Baal Epic (deeds and fortunes of Baal or Hadad), which goes back linguistically to at least *c.* 2000 BC; the legend of Aqhat (vicissitudes of the only son of good king Dan'el) perhaps from *c.* 1800 BC; the story of King Keret (bereft of family, he gains a new wife virtually by conquest, and also incurs the wrath of the gods) perhaps about 16th century BC; and other fragments. All extant copies date from the 14th/13th centuries BC. The high-flown poetry of the early epics has clearly demonstrated the archaic flavour of much Hebrew Old Testament poetry in its vocabulary and turns of speech. For full translations of the epics, so important for early Canaanite religion, see C. H. Gordon, *Ugaritic Literature*, 1949, and G. R. Driver, *Canaanite Myths and Legends*, 1956. Selections are given in *ANET*, pp. 129–155, by H. L. Ginsberg, and in *DOTT* by J. Gray.

c. Religion

The Canaanites had an extensive pantheon, headed by El. More prominent in practice were Baal ('lord'), *i.e.* Hadad the storm-god (see BAAL), and Dagon, with temples in Ugarit and elsewhere (see DAGON). The goddesses Asherah, Astarte (Ashtaroth), and Anath—like Baal—had multi-coloured personalities and violent characters; they were goddesses of sex and war (see ANATH, ASHERAH, ASHTAROTH). Kothar-and-Hasis was artificer-god (*cf.* Vulcan), and other and lesser deities abounded.

Actual temples in Palestine include remains at Beth-shan, Megiddo, Lachish, Shechem, and especially Hazor (which had at least three), besides those in Syria at Qatna, Alalaḫ, or Ugarit. The Ugaritic texts mention a variety of animals sacrificed to the gods: cattle, sheep (rams and lambs), and birds (including doves)—plus, of course, libations. Animal-bones excavated in several Palestinian sites support this picture.

The title of high priest (*rb khnm*) is attested for Canaanite religion at Ugarit. That the *qdšm* of the Ugaritic texts were cult-prostitutes is very possible; at any rate, the *qdšm* were as much an integral part of Canaanite religion there as they were forbidden to Israel (Dt. xxiii. 17, 18, *etc.*; *cf.* RSV). Human sacrifice in second-millennium Canaanite religion has not yet been isolated archaeologically with any certainty. That Canaanite religion appealed to the bestial and material in human nature is clearly evidenced by the Ugaritic texts and in Egyptian texts of Semitic origin or inspiration; *cf.* Albright, *Archaeology and Religion of Israel*³, 1953, pp. 75–77, 158, 159, 197, n. 39; see also CALF, GOLDEN. When the full import of this is realized it will be the more evident that physically and spiritually the sophisticated crudities of decaying Canaanite culture, and emergent Israel with a unique mission could not coexist.

BIBLIOGRAPHY. Readers are referred to the works cited in the text. For discoveries at Ugarit see Schaeffer's reports in *Syria* since 1929, and the fully documented series of volumes, *Mission de Ras Shamra* by Schaeffer, Virolleaud and Nougayrol. See also ARCHAEOLOGY. K.A.K.

CANANAEAN (Gk. *Kananaios*, from Heb. and Aramaic *qannā'ī* or Aramaic *qan'ān*, 'zealot', 'zealous'). In Mt. x. 4; Mk. iii. 18 (RV and RSV rightly for AV 'Canaanite'), the surname of Simon, one of the Twelve. In Lk. vi. 15; Acts i. 13 he is called by the equivalent Greek term *Zēlōtēs*, 'zealot'. The presence of a Zealot (or past Zealot) among the apostles gives rise to interesting speculation; he may not, of course, have been a Zealot proper, but received the designation from Jesus or his fellow-apostles because of his temperament. The suggestion that Mark, followed by Matthew, used the Semitic form from prudential considerations is unlikely, since Luke, whose apologetic motives are patent, saw no reason against using the Greek form. See ZEALOT. F.F.B.

CANDACE. The name or, more properly, title of the Ethiopian queen whose minister was converted under the ministry of Philip (Acts viii. 27). For the extent of her kingdom, which probably centred in the region of Upper Nubia (Meroë) rather than in modern-day Ethiopia, see ETHIOPIA. Women rulers bearing this title during the Hellenistic period are well-attested in ancient literature, *e.g.* Pseudo-Callisthenes (iii. 18), Strabo (xvii. 820), Pliny (*Nat. Hist.* vi. 186).

BIBLIOGRAPHY. *Arndt*; E. Ullendorff in *NTS*, II, 1955, pp. 53–56. D.A.H.

CANDLE, -STICK. See LAMP.

CANE. See SWEET CANE.

CANKERWORM. See LOCUST.

CANNEH. The name of a settlement or town mentioned, with Harran (*q.v.*) and Eden (*q.v.*), as trading with Tyre (Ezk. xxvii. 23). The site is unknown, but the above association suggests the area of the middle Euphrates. T.C.M.

CANON OF THE OLD TESTAMENT.

I. NAME AND CONCEPTION

The Greek word *kanōn*, which is of Semitic origin (*cf.* Heb. *qāneh* in Ezk. xl. 3, *etc.*), originally meant measuring-instrument, and later it was used in the metaphorical sense of 'rule of action' as well. The word found its place in ecclesiastical parlance. At first it denoted the formulated creed, especially the symbol of baptism, or the Church's doctrine in general. It was used also to indicate church regulations of a varied nature, as well as simply in the meaning of 'list', 'series'. Not till the middle of the 4th century does it seem to be applied to the Bible. In Greek usage, 'canon' seems at first to have denoted only the *list* of holy writings, but in Latin it also became the name for the Scripture itself, thus indicating that the Scripture is the rule of action vested with divine authority. When we use the term 'Canon of the Old Testament' we thereby denote that the Old Testament is a closed collection of writings inspired by the Spirit of God, that they have a normative authority, and are held as the rule for our faith and life.

II. SELF-AUTHENTICATING CHARACTER

Under this heading we consider how the Canon of the Old Testament came into being, and how it came to be acknowledged.

The books of the Old Testament, like those of the New, were inspired by God. See INSPIRATION. But the Holy Spirit worked also in the hearts of God's people, so that they came to accept these books as the Word of God, and submitted to their divine authority. God's 'singular providence' extended over the origin of the separate books, as well as over their collection; it is because of this that the number of Old Testament books is what it is, no more and no less.

This is the fundamental truth concerning the Canon of the Old Testament and its origin. But it stands to reason that the mere ascertaining of this is not enough. In what has already been said it is implied that, when God brought the Canon into being, He used men as His instruments; human actions and human reflections have performed their functions in the whole process. Questions therefore arise. What is known to us of these human acts and considerations? When was the Canon or parts of it acknowledged as canonical? How was the collection of the holy writings effected? Who exercised an influence on the varied stages of its growth?

In what follows we shall mention what data are at our disposal to answer these questions. It should be observed at once, however, that these data are scarce, and that often we cannot draw definite conclusions from them. Historical investigation reveals only a little about the actions of synods or of other authoritative bodies with regard to the formation of the Old Testament Canon. This need not surprise us, for it was not necessary for such authoritative bodies to have any great share in its formation. The Bible derives its authority neither from ecclesiastical statements nor from any human authority.

The Bible is *autopistos*, 'self-authenticating', radiating its divine authority itself. By the inward testimony of the Holy Spirit, man receives an eye which enables him to catch this light. As the *Confessio Belgica*, art. 5, says: 'We believe without any doubt all that is implied in them; and not so much because the Church accepts them and regards them as such, but especially because the Holy Spirit gives us testimony in our hearts, that they come from God' (*cf. Westminster Confession*, I. 4, 5). Church councils and other authoritative bodies have come to conclusions regarding the Canon, and these judgments have, indeed, performed an important function in effecting the acknowledgment of the Canon. But it is not a Church council, nor any other human authority, that has canonized the books of the Bible or given them divine authority. The books possessed and also exercised divine authority before such bodies made their pronouncements; their divine authority was already acknowledged in larger or smaller circles. The Church councils did not give the books their divine authority, but simply recognized that they had it and exercised it.

III. ACKNOWLEDGMENT OF THE SEPARATE BOOKS

Here we shall discuss the data which the Old Testament itself presents with regard to the collection and acknowledgment of the books. In doing so we shall follow the order of the books in the Hebrew Bible. We should observe, incidentally, that the very existence of many of the individual books implies an antecedent work of collection. This becomes very clear, *inter alia*, with the book of Psalms (see *e.g.* lxxii. 20) and with the Proverbs (see *e.g.* xxv. 1).

a. The Law

As early as the Mosaic age, collections of laws were put into writing. As appears from Ex. xxiv. 4–7, Moses formed 'the book of the covenant' and the people acknowledged its divine authority. Dt. xxxi. 9–13 (see also verses 24 ff.) informs us that Moses took down 'this law', *i.e.* the essentials of Deuteronomy, and took measures to ensure that its divine authority would be acknowledged into the remote future. It is remarkable that it is already foretold here that the people will frequently fail to acknowledge this authority. Many testimonies show that, in the course of the history of Israel, the Mosaic Law was considered the divine rule for faith and life (*e.g.* Jos. i. 7, 8; 1 Ki. ii. 3; 2 Ki. xiv. 6, *etc.*). We do not know for certain when the Pentateuch was completed in full, but we may assume that from the beginning high authority was attached to it. It contained the laws which the Lord had given to Israel by Moses, and, in addition, the record of the beginning of Israel's history, *i.e.* the dealings of the Lord with His chosen people. Two remarks may be added:

1. In former times people did not deal with writings which were considered holy in the same way as we do now. In many books we find smaller or greater portions which are to be regarded as later additions. One law could be replaced by another because altered circumstances made it necessary (*cf.* Nu. xxvi. 52–56 with xxvii. 1–11 and xxxvi, and *cf.* Nu. xv. 22 ff. with Lv. iv). Nevertheless, we may assume that Israel was cautious in handling written texts containing Israel's history, or their laws. The additions and alterations will have been of a limited extent and will have been made by people qualified by their office to do so. In addition a remark of more general tenor may be made: the fact that Israel handled its holy writings cautiously appears from the manner in which the writers of the Old Testament used their sources. They did not work with them as modern authors do, but copied the parts they needed as literally as possible.

2. The Old Testament tells us that on two occasions Israel solemnly pledged itself to obey the book of the law which God had given by Moses, *viz.* during the reign of Josiah (2 Ki. xxii, xxiii; 2 Ch. xxxiv, xxxv; the 'book of the law' possibly means Deuteronomy) and during the lives of Ezra and Nehemiah (Ezr. vii. 6, 14; Ne.

viii–x; the 'book of the law' here may mean the whole Pentateuch).

b. The Prophets

Three factors in particular will have contributed to the acknowledgment of 'the former prophets' (Joshua, Judges, Samuel, Kings) as authorities. First, these books describe the dealings of the Lord with His chosen people. Secondly, they do so in the spirit of the Law and the Prophets. Thirdly, the authors will have been official persons in a more or less strict sense. It is interesting to read in Jos. xxiv. 26 that some later additions were made to 'the book of the covenant of God', which presumably is the book of the law mentioned in Dt. xxxi. 24 ff.

Because of their very nature, the writings of 'the latter prophets' (Isaiah, Jeremiah, Ezekiel, and the twelve 'Minor Prophets') were considered authoritative from their earliest beginning by smaller or larger circles. That their predictions of disaster were fulfilled in the Exile will no doubt have conduced to the extension of their authority. From the fact that one prophet sometimes quotes another it is clear that they ascribed authority to their predecessors. Indeed, more than once a prophet rebukes Israel because they have not listened to his predecessors (*cf.* Zc. i. 4 ff.; Ho. vi. 5; *etc.*). Is. xxxiv. 16 probably mentions the roll on which the prophecies of Isaiah were noted down as 'the book of the Lord'. Dn. ix. 2 speaks of 'the books', by which is evidently meant a collection of prophetic writings, including, among others, prophecies of Jeremiah. It is obvious from the context that divine authority is attributed to these prophetic writings.

c. The Writings

The third part of the Hebrew Canon contains books of differing character, and we have little knowledge of the considerations which led some of them to be regarded as holy writings. With regard to the Song of Solomon, it is often posited that it owes its place in the Canon to an allegoric exegesis which was applied to it. But this is to assert more than can be proved. In the first place, this assertion starts from a wrong conception of 'canonization' (see under II above). Secondly, even supposing Canticles was not completed before the Exile, it still contains old material (*e.g.* Ct. vi. 4). There is no reason to deny the possibility that already, in an early period, these songs of love, in which Solomon is one of the principal figures, were considered to a certain degree to be holy writ. Finally, the appeal to pronouncements in Jewish literature (*e.g.* in *Aboth de-Rabbi Nathan*, 1) is weak, if only for the fact that these pronouncements are of recent date.

We cannot be surprised at the Psalter's being regarded as a holy writing. Many of the psalms may have served as formularies for the sanctuary; David had an important share in writing the psalms; various psalms are prophetic in their tone (*e.g.* l, lxxxi, cx). With regard to the Wisdom books, to which belong Proverbs and Ecclesiastes and, to a certain extent, Job, we should bear in mind that wisdom, and especially the power to act as a teacher of wisdom, was regarded as an exceptional gift of God (*cf.* 1 Ki. iii. 28, iv. 29; Jb. xxxviii ff.; Ps. xlix. 1–4; Pr. viii; Ec. xii. 11, *etc.*). The fact that many proverbs came from Solomon has certainly contributed to the acknowledgment of the book of Proverbs. Similar observations as are made under (*b*) above can be made on the historical and prophetic books Ezra, Nehemiah, Ruth, Esther, Lamentations, Daniel. So, too, the two books of Chronicles, though in a different way from Kings, are written in the spirit of the Law and the Prophets.

Naturally what has just been said by no means answers all the questions which could arise. Let us go further into one of them. Why have the sources used for the writing of Chronicles not been taken up into the Canon? It is true that several books which existed during the time when the books of the Old Testament were written have been lost, *e.g.* 'the book of the wars of the Lord' (Nu. xxi. 14), 'the book of Jashar' (Jos. x. 13; 2 Sa. i. 18). But with regard to the sources of Chronicles this question presses all the more because these books still existed during the relatively recent time in which Chronicles was formed, and because they were written, at least partly, by prophets (*e.g.* 1 Ch. xxix. 29; 2 Ch. ix. 29, xxxii. 32). We shall have to assume that these books —or was it one book?—were superseded by Chronicles.

IV. THE CANON DURING THE TIMES OF EZRA AND NEHEMIAH

For a long time the idea widely prevailed that during Ezra's life the Canon of the Old Testament was completed, and that Ezra was the leading figure in this accomplishment. Besides the data already mentioned, given in Ezr. vii and Ne. viii–x, this opinion was founded on old testimonies. We may note especially the following.

Flavius Josephus records in AD 95 (*Contra Apionem*, i. 8) that in the Jewish holy writings the history of the origin of the world up to the reign of Artaxerxes I (465–425 BC) has been described. He then continues: 'All that has occurred from Artaxerxes' time towards the present time has also been described, but these books do not deserve the same trust as the previous ones, since the succession of the prophets was not accurately fixed'. By this statement Josephus probably means that during Ezra's life (the middle of 5th century BC) at least the historical books of the Old Testament had been completed.

The Talmud, which was completed about AD 500, but which contains many century-old Jewish traditions, gives an enumeration of the writers of the Old Testament books (*Baba Bathra*, 14b, 15a). It concludes by saying: 'Hezekiah and his men wrote Isaiah, Proverbs, Canticles and Ecclesiastes; the men of the great gathering wrote Ezekiel, the Twelve, Daniel, Esther; Ezra wrote his book and the genealogy of Chronicles except his own; Nehemiah completed it' (*viz.* the book of Ezra). We must note that the meaning of the expression 'the men of the great gathering' is not established, and opinions vary widely. Nowadays several scholars hold that the expression denotes the men who had returned from exile during the times of Zerubbabel and Ezra. The expression would then correspond to statements made in Ezk. xxxix. 27, 28, *etc.* (See, *e.g.*, E. Bickerman, 'Viri magnae congregationis', *RB*, LV, 1948, pp. 397–402.)

4 Ezra, a Jewish apocalyptic writing written about AD 100, relates that in the thirtieth year after the destruction of Jerusalem, *i.e.* 557 BC, Ezra stayed in Babylon. On his complaint that the law of the Lord had been burnt, he received the Holy Spirit and then in the course of forty days he dictated ninety-four books to five scribes. Then he received instructions to make known twenty-four books 'so that the worthy and unworthy man may read in them', but the remaining seventy he was to keep secret 'in order to surrender them to the wise among your people' (xiv. 18 ff.). We shall have to assume that the twenty-four books to which the writer refers are identical with the thirty-nine books of which, according to our counting, the Old Testament consists (see under section IX below). By the seventy books we shall have to understand apocalyptic and similar literature; a precise definition and enumeration is not possible.

In this context we may also refer to a piece of information given in 2 Maccabees. In a letter which purports to be written by the inhabitants of Jerusalem and Judaea to the Jews of Egypt we read: 'In the annals and memoirs concerning Nehemiah we are told the same things, and how, making a library, he gathered together the books about the kings and (the books) of the prophets and (the writings) of David, and letters from the kings concerning votive offerings (or sacrifices). Likewise Judas collected everything that had been scattered by the war which came over us, and we are in possession of this collection; so if you are in want of them, send men to carry them to you' (2 Macc. ii. 13–15). If the letter is authentic, it was written in 165 BC; but many deny its authenticity and date it in the 1st century BC. As to the books, the collection of which is attributed to Nehemiah, we shall have to think of a great part of the Old Testament. By the 'books about the kings' may be meant the so-called 'former prophets' (see under IX), 'the writings of David' will be the Psalms, and the 'letters from the kings concerning votive offerings' will be writings of the Persian kings as we find them in Ezr. vi. 3–12, vii. 12–26. The fact that the Law is not mentioned need not surprise us, as it had only recently been rehabilitated by Ezra. For the rest, it is evident that Nehemiah is not credited with the collection of all the books of the Old Testament. The size of the collection which Judas is said to have made can no longer be assessed; it may have comprised all the books of the Old Testament and other books as well.

What can now be concluded from all this? First, we have to go further into the data given in Ezr. vii and Ne. viii–x. In these places we are certainly not informed that at a certain moment Ezra and his people decreed that from that time onwards the 'book of the law' was to be considered a holy writing vested with divine authority. The book of the law had for long been credited with divine authority. It was 'the book of the law of Moses, which the Lord had commanded to Israel' (Ne. viii. 1). It was true that for a long time the people had paid little attention to this law; in Canaan the knowledge of it was even lost to a considerable extent (see, *e.g.*, Ne. viii. 14), just as was the case during the reigns of Manasseh and Amon (*cf.* 2 Ki. xxii). But the people acknowledged this as their own fault. They accepted the book of the law as a holy writing, not in virtue of any decree of Ezra and his assistants, but because its contents arrested their hearts.

For the reason that, at the time of Ezra, not all the books of the Old Testament had yet been written, it is impossible that the Canon could have been completed then, and the quotations from the Talmud and Josephus do not clearly state this Attention should be paid to the fact that neither of the two places quoted credits Ezra with a special task in the formation and completion of the Old Testament Canon. According to E. Bickerman, p. 398: 'Ezra is not even mentioned in any Jewish writing before the destruction of the second Temple, with the exception, of course, of the Bible story and the Greek paraphrases of it (1 Esdras).' Possibly, *Baba Bathra*, 14b, 15a means to say that Ezra and Nehemiah were the last to write books of the Old Testament; this tradition may have arisen from the fact that the Old Testament narrates the history of Israel until the time of Ezra and Nehemiah.

The story of 2 Esdras xiv is the first place where it is asserted that Ezra was the creator of the Old Testament Canon. We cannot attach any historical credibility to this story. We must admit that the author was aware of the problems of what had happened during the destruction of Jerusalem to the books of the Old Testament then already in existence, and of how post-exilic Israel retained or regained possession of them; but the solution he proposes for this problem is not acceptable.

Nevertheless, it is possible that a true tradition lies at the root of the story of 2 Esdras xiv, *viz.* that Ezra, or at least certain people during Ezra's lifetime, were engaged in the collection of Old Testament books. From Ezr. vii and Ne. viii–x it appears that Ezra exercised a special activity in connection with the Law, although we do not know exactly what this activity was; as for this, all kinds of questions may be asked, *e.g.* 'Did the Law reach its final completion through Ezra?' In addition, we cannot preclude the possibility that a historically reliable tradition lies at the root of the information given in 2 Macc. ii. 13.

On the strength of all that has been stated we presume that a considerable part of the Old Testament Canon was gathered together by Ezra and Nehemiah.

V. THE CANON FROM EZRA TO THE BEGINNING OF OUR ERA

About the history of the Jewish people during the centuries after Ezra and Nehemiah we know little. It is not surprising, therefore, that no records about the Canon have come down to us from that time either.

The prologue to Ecclesiasticus, written by the man who translated the book from Hebrew into Greek, begins thus: 'As many great things have been given us through the law and the prophets, and others that succeeded them, for which it is proper to praise Israel on account of their instruction and wisdom . . .' Later on the author speaks of 'the law and the prophecies and the rest of the books', and he tells us that Jesus Ben-Sira, his *pappos* (probably 'grandfather', possibly 'ancestor'), devoted himself to reading 'the law and the prophets and the other books of our fathers'. It is quite obvious from the prologue that both its writer and Ben-Sira himself knew the three parts (see under IX) of the Old Testament Canon, and attached high authority to them. It is not possible, however, to conclude with certainty from the prologue that the third part, 'the Writings', had been completed. It does appear from Ecclesiasticus, on the other hand, that Ben-Sira knew several books of 'the Writings'. Ben-Sira apparently lived in Palestine. It is usually assumed that his book was written in the first half of the 2nd century BC, and that the author of the prologue worked during the latter half of that century (although some have dated Ben-Sira about 300 BC and the writer of the prologue about 250–200 BC).

In the stories about the Maccabees the sacred books are repeatedly mentioned, *e.g.* 1 Macc. i. 56, 57 ('And the books of the law were burned with fire, after having been rent; and whenever a book of the covenant was found with someone, and if there was anybody adhering to the law, he was put to death according to the order of the king', *i.e.* Antiochus Epiphanes), iv. 30 (referring to the narrative in 1 Sa. xiv and xvii), vii. 41 (referring to 2 Ki. xix. 35), xii. 9 (in a letter to Sparta, Jonathan writes: 'We, as being in possession of the holy books'); 2 Macc. ii. 13–15 (see under IV), viii. 23 (before the battle Judas has the 'holy book' read, and gives as a rallying-cry 'Help from God'; perhaps the book was opened at some place chosen at will and in this way the rallying-cry was found; *cf.* also 1 Macc. iii. 48), xv. 9 (Judas encourages his men out of 'the law and the prophets'). It is clear that in those days the Jews had holy books to which they attached divine authority. It cannot be proved that there was already a complete Canon, although the expression 'the holy books' (1 Macc. xii. 9) may point in that direction.

VI. THE CANON OF THE OLD TESTAMENT IN THE NEW TESTAMENT

Upon the authority of the New Testament, it may be assumed that during our Lord's ministry, and when the New Testament books were coming into being, the Old Testament existed as a completed collection to which divine authority was attached. Repeatedly the Old Testament is referred to as 'the scriptures' (Mt. xxvi. 54; Jn. v. 39; Acts xvii. 2, *etc.*), indicating that the Old Testament was a well-known collection of writings, forming a unity. This applies equally to the expression 'the scripture', which sometimes denotes a definite place (Lk. iv. 21; Jn. xiii. 18, *etc.*) but more than once points to the Old Testament as a whole (Jn. ii. 22; Acts viii. 32, *etc.*). It is hardly necessary to prove that divine authority was attached to 'the scriptures' or 'the scripture' (see Mt. i. 22, v. 18; Jn. x. 35; Acts i. 16, *etc.*).

The degree to which the Old Testament books were considered a unity is indicated by the fact that for statements from the prophets or the Psalms we are referred to 'the law'. The expression 'the law', which is in fact an indication of the first part of the Old Testament Canon (see under IX), is used to denote the whole Canon of the Old Testament (*e.g.* Jn. x. 34; 1 Cor. xiv. 21).

In this connection we should pay attention to Christ's words in Mt. xxiii. 35; Lk. xi. 51. The murder of Abel is narrated in the first book of the Hebrew Canon, Genesis. The murder of the Zacharias here mentioned is narrated in the last book of the Hebrew Canon, Chronicles (see under IX). This may indicate that as early as that time the Canon finished with Chronicles; of course, this favours the view that the Canon comprised the same books then as now. No chronological order can be indicated by Jesus' words, for the murder of Urijah (Je. xxvi. 23) took place after the murder of Zacharias. *Cf.* further, Lk. xxiv. 44.

The name 'Old Testament' as an indication of the collection of the holy Scriptures already occurs in the New Testament, *viz.* 2 Cor. iii. 14 ('the reading of the old testament'). See BIBLE, II.

Naturally the fact that several books of the Old Testament (Esther, Ecclesiastes, Canticles, Ezra, Nehemiah, Obadiah, Nahum, Zephaniah) are not quoted in the New Testament certainly does not prove that they were not then reckoned as part of the Canon.

It is often alleged that, in the New Testament, parts of the Apocrypha and of the pseudepigrapha are quoted as authoritative. It is true that sometimes a quotation is given from 'the scripture' which cannot easily be traced in the Old Testament; but in these cases a non-canonical book from which the quotation may be taken cannot be found either. We may be encountering here a (perhaps traditional) combination of Old Testament pronouncements. Thus Jn. vii. 38 may refer to Is. lviii. 11 and Ezk. xxxvi. 25, 26; 1 Cor. ii. 9 to Is. lxiv. 4; *cf.* Ps. xxxi. 19. Another case is Jude 14, 15, where it is possible that Jude quotes 1 Enoch i. 9. This need not surprise us, since the New Testament also quotes pagan authors (Acts xvii. 28; 1 Cor. xv. 33). It is significant that Jude does not tell us that he quotes from 'the scripture'.

For the rest, we need not consider as precluded the possibility that both Jude 14, 15 and 1 Enoch i. 9 refer back to an oral tradition. (See Bruce M. Metzger, *An Introduction to the Apocrypha*, 1957, especially chapter xvi, 'The Apocrypha and the New Testament'.)

VII. THE CANON AMONG THE JEWS OF THE EARLY CENTURIES OF OUR ERA

a. More than once the suggestion has been made that the synod of Jabneh or Jamnia, said to have been held about AD 90, closed the Canon of the Old Testament and fixed the limits of the Canon. To speak about the 'synod of Jamnia' at all, however, is to beg the question (see, *e.g.*, G. F. Moore, *Judaism*, I[6], 1950, pp. 83 ff.; G. Lisowsky, *Jadajim*, 1956, pp. 9, 57). It is true, certainly, that in the teaching-house of Jamnia, about AD 70–100, certain discussions were held, and certain decisions were made concerning some books of the Old Testament; but similar discussions were held both before and after that period. One of the most important places informing us about this is the Mishnah tractate *Yadayim* iii. 5; see especially the interpretation which Lisowsky gives of it, *op. cit.* These discussions dealt chiefly with the question as to whether or not some books of the Old Testament (*e.g.* Esther, Proverbs, Ecclesiastes, Canticles, Ezekiel) 'soiled the hands', or had to be 'concealed'. In the discussions whether a book had to be 'concealed' or not, the canonicity at any rate will not have been at stake (see G. F. Moore, *ibid.*, pp. 246 f.). As regards the phrase 'soil the hands', the prevailing opinion is that it referred to the canonicity of the book in question (see, however, Menahem Haran, 'Problems of the Canonization of Scripture', *Tarbiz*, XXV, 1956, pp. 245–271). If indeed the canonicity of Esther, Ecclesiastes, and Canticles was disputed, we shall have to take the following view. On the whole these books were considered canonical. But with some, and probably with some Rabbis in particular, the question arose whether people were right in accepting their canonicity, as, *e.g.*, Luther in later centuries found it difficult to consider Esther as a canonical book. So the above-mentioned discussions started from the existing Canon.

In the context we have to revert to the testimonies of 2 Esdras and Josephus (see under section IV, above). As we have seen, the Canon, at any rate in its broad outline, had the same extent for the author of 2 Esdras as for the later Jews. The same applies to Josephus. He writes (*loc. cit.*): 'With us, one does not find innumerable books, mutually divergent and conflicting, but only twenty-two, comprising the whole past, and in which one is obliged to believe. As so much time is already passed now, yet no one of us has ever ventured to take anything away from them, or to add anything to them, or to make even the slightest alteration. From his very birth it is inbred in every Jew to consider them as writings given by God, to adhere to them and, if need be, gladly to die for them.'

We may presume that the twenty-two books mentioned by Josephus are identical with the thirty-nine books of which the Old Testament consists according to our reckoning (see under section IX, below). (For the sake of completeness we must observe that Josephus also uses books which we count among the Apocrypha, *e.g.* 1 Esdras and the additions to Esther.) These two testimonies gain force because the author of 2 Esdras and Josephus lived in diverse environments.

b. Here too we shall try to come to a conclusion. During the early centuries of our era, especially after the fall of Jerusalem in AD 70, the Jews took stock of their spiritual assets, in particular of what had come down to them as 'holy books'. It is not surprising that on reflection some of them raised objections to some of these books, *viz.* Ecclesiastes, Canticles, Esther. In consequence, the limits of the Canon were defined somewhat more clearly than hitherto. But the Canon of the Old Testament is not the creation of the Jews of the early centuries AD. The Jews did not create something new, nor did they intend to create something new. They only established in detail what was already accepted in substance.

c. One of the factors which induced the Jews to define the limits of the Canon more particularly was that, beside the holy writings, several other books had been written. Here the question arises as to why the Jews did not include in the Canon such books as Ecclesiasticus or 1 Maccabees. Everyone who accepts the thirty-nine books of our Old Testament as the Canon will find the ultimate reason in the fact that these books were not inspired. Various conjectures may be made concerning the human considerations which led to their omission, but a definite conclusion is hardly possible. One point may have been the time when a book came into being. In any case, it remains a curious phenomenon that, at least with the Palestinian Jews, there is nothing to indicate that they ever seriously considered bringing into the Canon any one of the books which we include in the Apocrypha or list among the pseudepigrapha.

At the present stage it is advisable not to draw any conclusions as to the origin of the Canon from the finds of Qumran (see DEAD SEA SCROLLS).

d. It is often presumed that the Jews of Alexandria, or more generally in the Greek *diaspora*, had a wider Canon, or rather a wider conception of the Canon, than the Jews in Palestine. Certainty on this is not available, but the following observations can be made. It is alleged that the Alexandrian Jews had a wider conception of the Canon because they had a wider conception of inspiration; see, however, P. Katz, 'The Old Testament Canon in Palestine and Alexandria', *ZNW*, XLVII, 1956, pp. 191–271, in particular pp. 209 ff.

The use that Philo makes of the Old Testament seems not to indicate that he ranks other books with the thirty-nine of our counting.

The LXX contains more books than our thirty-nine. However, we should be guarded in drawing our conclusions from this. The history of the origin and growth of the LXX is in many respects unknown to us. The oldest complete MSS of the LXX which we possess originate from Christian circles of the 4th century. These do contain 'the plus of the LXX'. But it is not permissible to draw from this fact alone our conclusions about the views held by the Greek Jews in the early part of our era (see under VIII). In addition, we should bear in mind that not all the MSS of the LXX contain the same books; rather, they reveal a considerable divergence. Finally one detail: it is noteworthy that, during the lifetime of the author of the prologue to Ecclesiasticus, 'the law, the prophecies and the other books' had already been translated into Greek, but this author clearly distinguishes between these three categories and the writing of Ben-Sira.

On the other hand, if the Greek Jews had distinguished as sharply between the canonical and non-canonical books as the Palestinian Jews did during the 1st century AD, would not the early Christian Church also have defined the limits more precisely than they did? There is this further fact: in his translation of Daniel, Theodotion includes the appendices ('the prayer of Azariah', *etc.*); it is possible that this translation originates from Jewish circles of the 2nd century AD.

VIII. THE CANON IN THE CHRISTIAN CHURCH

In his article, 'Zur Kanongeschichte des Alten Testaments' (*ZAW*, LXXI, 1959, pp. 114–136), A. Jepsen writes, and not without reason: 'The history of the Old Testament Canon in the Christian Church has not yet been written' (p. 125). We shall confine ourselves to the following remarks.

The main fact is that, following Christ and the apostles, the Church has, from the very beginning, accepted as canonical the same thirty-nine books of the Old Testament as are contained in our enumeration. There may have been some doubt about a few of them, but that was of little importance. This is the principal point, but there is more to be said. The young church in the Greek-speaking world repeatedly appealed not only to the books constituting the Jewish Canon but also to other books of Jewish origin. It is important to note here that the Greek-speaking Christians did not only appeal to what we call the Apocrypha, but also to other books, the pseudepigrapha, as well as to oral Jewish tradition. (See J. L. Koole, *De overname van het Oude Testament door de Christelijke kerk*, 1938, pp. 16–51, 149–151.)

The Greek-speaking Christians came upon many books of Jewish origin, so it is not surprising to find that they did not define the limits of the Canon in its details from the very beginning. The Jews in the Greek *diaspora* may not have done so either (see under VII*d*, above). Decisions such as those made in Jamnia were unknown to many Christians.

For that matter, Josephus, who generally will have been guided by the decisions of Jamnia, still made use of books that had not been accepted at Jamnia (see under section VII*a*, above).

It is, for the rest, certainly not true that the Church from the beginning acknowledged a wider Canon; in fact, when making up lists of canonical books, the Christians confined themselves in the main to the books of the Jewish Canon, as we see from the list of Melito of Sardis (*c.* AD 160), and those of Origen, Athanasius, Cyril of Jerusalem, and others (*cf.* the articles quoted from Katz and Jepsen).

For all that, the Church used the LXX (and the translations based on it), which comprised more writings than the Jewish Canon. When the LXX was published in book form the writings forming 'the plus of the LXX' entered into it, scattered among the writings that made up the Jewish Canon. This does not prove conclusively that the same authority was ascribed to every one of these books, but it certainly tended in that direction. Thus the books forming 'the plus of the LXX' came to acquire high authority, especially in the Western Church, which naturally had less frequent contact with Palestine than the Eastern Church. At the synods of the North African Church held at Hippo (AD 393) and Carthage (AD 397), in spite of the voices of Rufinus, Jerome, and others, 'the plus of the LXX' was taken up among the canonical books. On these synods Augustine exerted great influence. It is not at all surprising, therefore, that he made several statements in which he ascribed as much authority to 'the plus of the LXX' as to the books of the Hebrew Canon. On the other hand, there are statements of his, some of them made during the last years of his life, in which he positively distinguished between the authority of these two groups (see A. D. R. Polman, *De theologie van Augustinus*, I, 1955, pp. 198–208). In the following centuries 'the plus of the LXX' was as a rule accepted as canonical in the Western Church, although the opposite opinion also frequently found its defenders (see B. M. Metzger, *op. cit.*, p. 180, for important data about the attitude of several Roman Catholic scholars of the 16th century, before the Council of Trent). The Reformers reverted to the Hebrew Canon, or, to express it better, to the Canon of Christ and the apostles. Thus Calvin repeatedly pointed out that there is no unanimous verdict of tradition concerning the Apocrypha, and that the Apocrypha are definitely inferior to the canonical writings (see, *e.g.*, *Antidote to the Council of Trent*). Against the position of the Reformers, the Roman Catholic Church finally decreed in 1546 at the Council of Trent that Tobias, Judith, Wisdom, Ecclesiasticus, Baruch, 1 and 2 Maccabees were also to be accepted as canonical. Here it should be noted that the Roman Catholic Church also accepts as canonical the additions to the books of Esther, Baruch ('the letter of Jeremiah'), and Daniel ('the prayer of Azariah', 'the song of the three young men', 'the history of Susanna', 'Bel and the Dragon'). In the official edition of the Vulgate, which had been decided on by the Council of Trent but which was not issued before 1592, 1 and 2 Esdras and the Prayer of Manasseh were also inserted, but after the New Testament. That which is included in the Vulgate in addition to the books of the Hebrew Canon, Protestants usually call 'the Apocrypha' (*q.v.*).

For the development of the Canon in the Eastern Church, see B. M. Metzger, *ibid.*, pp. 192–195. Besides the books of the Hebrew Canon, the council of Jerusalem of 1672 accepted as canonical Wisdom, Judith, Tobit, Bel and the Dragon, 1, 2, 3, and 4 Maccabees, and Ecclesiasticus. Today there appears to be no unanimity on the subject of the Canon in the Greek Orthodox Church.

IX. DIVISION OF THE CANON OF THE OLD TESTAMENT; ORDER OF THE BOOKS

All kinds of arrangements of the books of the Canon have been handed down to us, the most important of them falling into two groups. One group is based on the division of Law, Prophets, Writings. *Baba Bathra*, 14b, first mentions the Law, the five books of Moses, and then continues: 'The rabbis taught that the order of the prophets is: Joshua, Judges, Samuel, Kings, Jeremiah, Ezekiel, Isaiah, the Twelve. The order of the Writings is thus: Ruth, Psalms, Job, Proverbs, Ecclesiastes, Canticles, Lamentations, Daniel, Esther, Ezra (= Ezra and Nehemiah), Chronicles'. Most Jewish traditions give a similar order, as also the printed Hebrew Bibles. Thus in the *Biblia Hebraica* edited by Kittel (third and subsequent editions) the order is as follows: Genesis, Exodus, Leviticus, Numbers, Deuteronomy, Joshua, Judges, Samuel, Kings, Isaiah, Jeremiah, Ezekiel, the Twelve, Psalms, Job, Proverbs, Ruth, Canticles, Ecclesiastes, Lamentations, Esther, Daniel, Ezra, Nehemiah, Chronicles. Concerning this we may make the following observations. First, in Jewish literature, there is repeatedly talk of twenty-four books. From the above enumerations we may deduce how they arrived at this number. The oldest place where this number occurs is 4 Ezra (see under IV). Secondly, the Prophets are usually divided into the 'Former Prophets' (Joshua–Kings) and the 'Latter Prophets' (Isaiah–the Twelve). Thirdly, in the order just given the five 'rolls', namely Ruth–Esther, have been put together.

In the other main group of arrangements that has come down to us the historic books come first (our Genesis–Esther), then follow the poetic and didactic books, which particularly refer to the present (our Job–Canticles), and finally there are the prophetic books, which especially deal with the future (our Isaiah–Malachi). With all kinds of variation this arrangement is found in the various MSS of the LXX, and, through the Vulgate, it has also come to be used by us; the Bibles translated into modern languages generally present this arrangement.

It is usually taken that the arrangement as given by *Baba Bathra* is essentially the original one, whereas the arrangement presented by the LXX is secondary. However, this is not undisputed. It is true that the division Law, Prophets, Writings, is old (see under V on the prologue to Ecclesiasticus, and *cf.* Lk. xxiv. 44; reference may also be made to several statements in the Talmud). But we must ask, 'What books are we to think of when the prologue to Ecclesiasticus and Lk. xxiv. 44 speak of "the Prophets"?' The question cannot be answered with certainty. Here reference may be made to the testimony of Josephus (*Contra Apionem*, i. 8). He speaks about twenty-two books and gives the following enumeration: the five books of Moses, thirteen books in which the prophets describe the history from Moses' death until the reign of the Persian king Artaxerxes, the successor to Xerxes, and four books containing hymns of praise to God, and regulations for the life of mankind. It is quite evident that Josephus reckoned among the prophetic books some that were usually classed among 'the Writings'. Did he do so under the influence of the Alexandrian Jews? Against this, however, is the fact that he greatly deviates from the order of the LXX.

Further, Josephus speaks of twenty-two books. This suggests that Judges and Ruth are reckoned to be one book, and so are Jeremiah and Lamentations. According to Origen, Epiphanius, and Jerome, the Jews were accustomed to reckon Ruth with Judges and Lamentations with Jeremiah. By having Judges followed by Ruth, and Jeremiah by Lamentations, the LXX has preserved an old Jewish tradition which may very well be of Palestinian origin.

Origen, who regularly associated with Jewish scholars in Palestine, gives an enumeration of the books that were considered canonical among the Jews (see Eus., *EH* vi. 25). The order in which he mentions the books shows great conformity to that of the LXX. Nevertheless, it cannot be said that he copied the order of the LXX, for the differences are too great. For one thing, the books forming the end of the Canon are Job and Esther. What induced Origen to use this order? The least that can be said is that this datum does not strengthen the opinion that during Origen's days the order given by *Baba Bathra* had absolute authority in Palestine. The testimonies of several Church fathers could be mentioned, from which a similar conclusion could be drawn (see the articles of Katz and Jepsen, already referred to).

From what has been said it is certainly not permissible to draw the conclusion that the division and order of the LXX is primary and that of *Baba Bathra* secondary. There are all kinds of statements in the Talmud and elsewhere that point in the direction of the division and order, not of the LXX, but of *Baba Bathra*. Even though these statements were noted down later, they will still contain old traditions. Mt. xxiii. 35 may also tell in favour of the age of the order as presented to us by *Baba Bathra* (see under section VI, above).

We conclude that in early times more than one division and order existed beside one another. In antiquity the books of the Old Testament were written down on separate rolls, and this procedure was not conducive to a fixed order becoming current.

These things are of greater importance than may appear. The following view is frequently put forward. First, the Law was accepted as canonical. Then, about 200 BC, it is said, the Canon of the Prophets was concluded. Later still, during the synod of Jamnia, the third part, 'the Writings', was concluded. But this creates the incorrect impression that about 200 BC, at least for the Palestinian Jews, 'the Prophets' were an established entity. This can be made concrete concerning one point. When dating the book of Daniel in the time of the Maccabees, an appeal is made to the fact that this book was included among 'the Writings', the argument being that it was written too late to have received a place among 'the Prophets'. From what has been said above, however, this argument is not valid. Indeed, it is possible that Daniel first had a place among 'the Prophets' and was only afterwards placed among 'the Writings'. This seems to be borne out by the testimony of Josephus (*cf.* also Mt. xxiv. 15). This change of place could have resulted from the consideration that the book of Daniel differs considerably in character from the other books of 'the Prophets'.

BIBLIOGRAPHY. See the Introductions to the Old Testament, *e.g.* G. Ch. Aalders, *Oud-Testamentissche Kanoniek*, 1952, pp. 27–66; O. Eissfeldt, *Einleitung in das Alte Testament*[2], 1956, pp. 691–710; A. Bentzen, *Introduction to the Old Testament*, 1948, I, pp. 20–41. See further, H. E. Ryle, *The Canon of the Old Testament*[2], 1904; W. Robertson Smith, *The Old Testament in the Jewish Church*[3], 1926; S. Zeitlin, *A Historical Study of the Canonization of the Hebrew Scriptures*, 1933; G. Ostborn, *Cult and Canon. A Study in the Canonization of the Old Testament*, 1950; J. L. Koole, *Het Probleem van de canonisatie van het Oude Testament*, 1955; E. J. Young, 'The Canon of the Old Testament' in C. F. H. Henry (ed.), *Revelation and the Bible*, 1958, pp. 153–185; H. B. Swete, *An Introduction to the Old Testament in Greek*, revised by R. R. Ottley, 1914; B. M. Metzger, *An Introduction to the Apocrypha*, 1957.

N.H.R.

CANON OF THE NEW TESTAMENT.

I. THE EARLIEST PERIOD

Biblical theology demands as its presupposition a fixed extent of biblical literature: this extent is traditionally fixed, since the era of the great theological controversies, in the Canon of the New Testament. 'Canon' is here the latinization of the Gk. *kanōn*, 'a reed', which, from the various uses of that plant for measuring and ruling, comes to mean a ruler, the line ruled, the column bounded by the line, and hence, the list written in the column. Canon is the list of books which the Church uses in public worship. *Kanōn* also means rule or standard: hence a secondary meaning of Canon is the list of books which the Church acknowledges as inspired Scripture, normative for faith and practice. Our understanding of inspiration requires, then, not only that we fix the text of Scripture and analyse the internal history of scriptural books but also that we trace as accurately as possible the growth of a concept of a canon and of the Canon itself.

In this investigation, especially of the earliest period, three matters must be distinguished clearly: the knowledge of a book evinced by a particular Father or source; the attitude towards such a book as an inspired Scripture on the part of the Father or source (which may be shown by introductory formulae such as 'It is written' or 'As the scripture says'); and the existence of the concept of a list or canon in which the quoted work figures (which will be shown, not only by actual lists but also by reference to 'the books' or 'the apostles', where a literary corpus is intended). This distinction has not always been made, with resultant confusion. Quotations, even in the earliest period, may be discovered; but whether quotation implies status as inspired Scripture is a further question for which precise criteria are frequently lacking. This being so, it is not surprising that a decision about the existence of any canonical list or concept of a canon often fails to find any direct evidence at all, and depends entirely upon inference.

The earliest point at which we can take up the investigation is in the data provided by the New Testament itself. The apostolic Church was not without Scripture—it looked for its doctrine to the Old Testament, usually in a Gk. dress, though some writers appear to have used the Heb. text. Apocrypha such as 1 Enoch were also used in some circles. Whether the term 'canonical' should be applied here is debatable, as the Jewish Canon was not yet fixed, at least *de jure*, and when it was it was moulded by anti-Christian controversy, in addition to other factors. In worship, the Church already used some of its own peculiar traditions: in the Lord's Supper the Lord's death was 'proclaimed' (1 Cor. xi. 26) probably in word (*sc.* the earliest Passion narrative) as well as in the symbols of the ordinance. The account of the Lord's Supper itself is regarded as derived 'from the Lord', a closely guarded tradition: we find this terminology too in places where ethical conduct is based on dominical utterance (*cf.* 1 Cor. vii. 10, 12, 25; Acts xx. 35). This is in the main oral material, a phrase which, as form-criticism has shown, is by no means intended to suggest imprecision of outline or content. Written repositories of Christian tradition are at best hypothetical in the earliest apostolic age; for although it has been proposed to find in the phrase 'according to the scriptures' (1 Cor. xv. 3, 4) a reference to documents at this early date, this has met with but little favour. In this material, then, whether oral or written, we find at the earliest stage a Church consciously preserving its traditions of the passion, resurrection, life (*cf.* Acts x. 36–40) and teaching of Jesus. Quite evidently, however, whatever was known and preserved by anyone did not exclude in his view the validity and value of traditions elsewhere preserved. The preservation is to a large extent unselfconscious in this 'prehistoric' stage of the development of Christian Scripture. It continues in the making of the Gospels, where two main streams are developed in independence of each other. It would appear that little escaped inclusion in these.

The epistolary material in the New Testament also possesses from the beginning a certain claim, if not to inspiration, at least to be an authoritative and adequate teaching on points of doctrine and conduct; yet it is as clear that no letter is written for other than specific recipients in a specific historical situation. The collection of a corpus of letters evidently post-dates the death of Paul: the Pauline Corpus is textually homogeneous and there is more weighty evidence for the suggestion, most thoroughly developed by E. J. Goodspeed, that its collection was a single act at a specific date (probably about AD 80–85), than for the earlier view of Harnack that the corpus grew slowly. The corpus from the start would enjoy high status as a body of authoritative Christian literature. Its impact upon the Church in the late 1st and early 2nd centuries is plain from the doctrine, language, and literary form of the literature of the period. There is no corresponding evidence for any such corpora of non-Pauline writings at so early a date; nor does the Acts seem to have been produced primarily as a teaching document. The Revelation of John, on the contrary, makes the clearest claim to direct inspiration of any New Testament document, and is the sole example in this literature of the utterances and visions of the prophets of the New Testament Church. Thus we have, in the New Testament itself, several clear instances of Christian material, even at the oral stage, viewed as authoritative and in some sense sacred: yet in no case does any writing explicitly or implicitly claim that it alone preserves tradition. There is no sense, at this stage, of a Canon of Scripture, a closed list to which addition may not be made. This would appear to be due to two factors: the existence of an oral tradition and the presence of apostles, apostolic disciples, and prophets, who were the foci and the interpreters of the dominical traditions.

II. THE APOSTOLIC FATHERS

The same factors are present in the age of the so-called Apostolic Fathers and are reflected in the data provided by them for Canon studies. As regards the Gospels, Clement (*First Epistle*, *c.* AD 90) quotes material akin to the Synoptics yet in a form not strictly identical with any particular Gospel; nor does he introduce the words with any formula of scriptural citation. John is unknown to him. Ignatius of Antioch (martyred *c.* AD 115) speaks frequently of 'the gospel': yet in all cases his words are patient of the interpretation that it is the message, not a document, of which he speaks. The frequent affinities with Matthew may indicate that this source was utilized, but other elucidations are possible. Whether John was known to him remains a matter of debate, in which the strongest case appears to be that it was not. Papias, fragmentarily preserved in Eusebius and elsewhere, gives us information on the Gospels, the precise import of which remains uncertain or controversial: he specifically asseverates his preference for the 'living and abiding voice', contrasted with the teaching of books. Polycarp of Smyrna's letter to the Philippians shows clear knowledge of Matthew and Luke. He is then the earliest unambiguous evidence for their use, but if, as is most likely, his letter is in fact the combination of two written at different times (*viz.* chapters 13 and 14 *c.* AD 115; the rest *c.* AD 135), this will not be so early as once was thought. The so-called *2 Clement* and the *Epistle of Barnabas* both date about AD 130. Both use much oral material, but attest the use of the Synoptics too; and each introduces one phrase from the Gospels with a formula of scriptural citation.

There is considerable and wide knowledge of the Pauline Corpus in the Apostolic Fathers: their language is strongly influenced by the apostle's words. Yet, highly valued as his letters evidently were, there is little introduction of quotations as scriptural. A number of passages suggest that a distinction was made in all Christian circles between the Old Testament and writings of Christian provenance. The Philadelphians judged the 'gospel' by the 'archives' (Ign. *Philad.* viii. 2): *2 Clement* speaks of 'the books (*biblia*) and the apostles' (xiv. 2), a contrast which is probably equivalent to 'Old and New Testaments'. Even where the gospel was highly prized (*e.g.* Ignatius or Papias), it is apparently in an oral rather than a written form. Barnabas is chiefly concerned to expound the Old Testament; the *Didache*, didactic and ethical material common to Jew and Christian. Along with material from the canonical Gospels or parallel to them, most of the Apostolic Fathers utilize what we anachronistically term 'apocryphal' or 'extra-canonical' material: it was evidently not so to them. We are still in a period when the New Testament writings are not clearly demarcated from other edifying material. This situation in fact continues yet further into the 2nd century, and may be seen in Justin Martyr and Tatian. Justin records that the 'memoirs of the apostles' called Gospels were read at Christian worship: his quotations and allusions, however, afford evidence that the extent of these was not identical with the four, but contained 'apocryphal' material. This same material was used by Tatian in his harmony of the Gospels known as the *Diatessaron*, or, as in one source, perhaps more accurately as *Diapente*.

III. INFLUENCE OF MARCION

It was towards the close of the 2nd century that awareness of the concept of a canon and scriptural status begins to reveal itself in the thought and activity of Christians. The challenge of heretical teachers, and especially the work of Marcion of Sinope, who broke with the Church in Rome about AD 150, but was probably active in Asia Minor for some years previously, was largely instrumental in stimulating this. Misinterpreter of Paul, Marcion preached a doctrine of two Gods: the Old Testament was the work of the Just God, the Creator, harsh judge of men: Jesus was the emissary of the Good (or Kind) God, higher than the Just, sent to free men from that God's bondage: crucified through the malice of the Just God, He passed on His gospel, first to the Twelve, who failed to keep it from corruption, and then to Paul, the sole preacher of it. Since Marcion rejected the Old Testament, according to this scheme, he felt the need of a distinctively Christian Scripture, and created a definite Canon of Scripture: *one* Gospel, which stood in some relation or other to our present Luke, and the ten Epistles of Paul (omitting Hebrews and the Pastorals), which constituted the *Apostolos*. The rapid growth of the major part of the New Testament Canon, which supervenes upon the age of Justin and Tatian, is directly due to the challenge of Marcion to the Church after his final breach with it. The imprint of Marcion remains upon that Canon: first in the Prologues found in some MSS prefaced to the Epistles and now known as the Marcionite Prologues, since that is undoubtedly their origin; secondly, in the Prologues to the Gospels, clearly anti-Marcionite in tone, found in some MSS, produced to balance the prefaced Epistles; thirdly, and more universally observable, in the overwhelming place occupied by Paul in the Catholic Canon, in spite of his relative neglect in the mid-2nd century. From these data it is plain that in creating a Canon, the champions of orthodoxy took over the Canon of Marcion as the basis of their own, redressing the balance by means of adaptation and addition to his material and introductory matter. About this same time, Acts comes out of oblivion: previously it is scarcely known or quoted; its irenical picture of the harmony of Paul and the Jerusalem church came into its own as the antidote to Marcion's Proto-Tübingen version of Church history.

IV. IRENAEUS TO EUSEBIUS

In the second half of the 2nd century, as has been intimated, clear evidence of the concept of a canon appears, although not all the books now included in the Canon are decided upon in any one church. Irenaeus of Lyons, in his work *Against the Heresies*, gives plain evidence that by his time the fourfold Gospel was axiomatic, comparable with the four corners of the earth and the four winds of heaven. Acts is quoted by him, sometimes explicitly, as Scripture. The Pauline Epistles, the Revelation, and some Catholic Epistles are regarded, although not often explicitly as Scripture, yet (especially in the two former cases) sufficiently highly to indicate that here is a primary source of doctrine and authority to which reference must be made in the context of controversy. Against the so-called esoteric knowledge of his opponents, Irenaeus stresses the traditions of the Church as apostolically derived. In these traditions, the Scriptures of the New Testament have their place. We know, however, that he definitely rejected Hebrews as non-Pauline.

Hippolytus of Rome, contemporary of Irenaeus, is known to us through writings only partially extant. He cites most New Testament books, speaking explicitly of two testaments and of a fourfold Gospel. Many critics are willing to ascribe to him the fragmentary list of canonical Scriptures preserved in Latin in a MS at Milan, known as the Muratorian Canon (after its first editor Ludovico Muratori). This ascription should not be taken as proved, however: the Latin is not necessarily a translation. A reference to the recent origin of the *Shepherd* of Hermas places it within the approximate dates AD 170–210. The extant part of the document gives a list of New Testament writings with some account of their origin and scope. Here again we meet a fourfold Gospel, acknowledgment of the Pauline Epistles, knowledge of some Catholic Epistles, the Acts of the Apostles and the Revelation of John; also included as canonical are the *Apocalypse of Peter* (there is no reference to any Petrine Epistle) and, rather surprisingly, the *Wisdom of Solomon*. The *Shepherd* is mentioned, but is not regarded as fit for use in public worship. The date of this document makes it highly significant, not only as witness to the existence at that time of a wide-embracing concept of the Canon but also of the marginal uncertainties, the omissions, and the inclusion of writings later rejected as apocryphal.

The state of affairs shown in these sources was widespread and continued into the 3rd century. Tertullian, Clement of Alexandria, and Origen all make wide use of the New Testament Scriptures, either in controversy, in doctrinal discussion, or in actual commentary upon the component books. The majority of books in the present Canon are known to them and given canonical status; but uncertainty remains in the case of Hebrews, some of the Catholic Epistles, and the Revelation of John. Uncanonical Gospels are cited, *agrapha* quoted as authentic words of the Lord, and some works of the Apostolic Fathers such as the *Epistle of Barnabas*, the *Shepherd*, and the *First Epistle of Clement* are cited as canonical or scriptural. We find great codices even of the 4th and 5th centuries which contain some of these latter: the Codex Sinaiticus includes Barnabas and Hermas; the Codex Alexandrinus includes the *First* and *Second Epistles of Clement*. Claromontanus contains a catalogue of canonical writings in which Hebrews is absent, and *Barnabas*, the *Shepherd*, the *Acts of Paul*, and the *Apocalypse of Peter* are included. In brief, the idea of a definite canon is fully established, and its main outline firmly fixed: the issue now is which books out of a certain number of marginal cases belong to it. The position in the Church in the 3rd century is well summarized by Eusebius (*EH* iii. 25). He distinguishes between acknowledged books (*homologoumena*), disputed books (*antilegomena*), and spurious books (*notha*). In the first class are placed the four Gospels, the Acts, the Epistles of Paul, 1 Peter, 1 John, and (according to some) the Revelation of John; in the second class he places (as 'disputed, nevertheless known to most') James, Jude, 2 Peter, 2 and 3 John; in the third class the *Acts of Paul*, the *Shepherd*, the *Apocalypse of Peter*, the *Epistle of Barnabas*, the *Didache*, the *Gospel according to the Hebrews*, and (according to others) the Revelation of John. These latter, Eusebius suggests, might well be in the second class were it not for the necessity of guarding against deliberate forgeries of Gospels and Acts under the name of apostles, made in a strictly heretical interest. As examples of these he names the Gospels of Thomas, Peter, and Matthias, and the Acts of Andrew and John. These 'ought to be reckoned not even among the spurious books but shunned as altogether wicked and impious'.

V. FIXATION OF THE CANON

The 4th century saw the fixation of the Canon within the limits to which we are accustomed, both in the Western and Eastern sectors of Christendom. In the East the definitive point is the Thirty-ninth Paschal Letter of Athanasius in AD 367. Here we find for the first time a New Testament of exact bounds as known to us. A clear line is drawn between works in the Canon which are described as the sole sources of religious instruction, and others which it is permitted to read, namely, the *Didache* and the *Shepherd*. Heretical apocrypha are said to be intentional forgeries for the purposes of deceit. In the West the Canon was fixed by conciliar decision at Carthage in 397, when a like list to that of Athanasius was agreed upon. About the same period a number of Latin authors showed interest in the bounds of the New Testament Canon: Priscillian in Spain, Rufinus of Aquileia in Gaul, Augustine in North Africa (whose views contributed to the decisions at Carthage), Innocent I, bishop of Rome, and the author of the pseudo-Gelasian Decree. All hold the same views.

VI. THE SYRIAC CANON

The development of the Canon in the Syriac-speaking churches was strikingly different. It is probable that the first Scripture known in these circles was, in addition to the Old Testament, the apocryphal *Gospel according to the Hebrews* which left its mark upon the *Diatessaron* when that took its place as the Gospel of Syriac Christianity. It is likely that Tatian introduced also the Pauline Epistles and perhaps even the Acts: these three are named as the Scriptures of the primitive Syriac church by the *Doctrine of Addai*, a 5th-century document which in its account of the beginnings of Christianity in Edessa mingles legend with trustworthy tradition. The next stage in the closer alignment of the Syriac Canon with the Greek was the production of the 'separated gospels' (*Evangelion da-Mepharreshe*) to take the place of the *Diatessaron*. This was by no means easily accomplished. The Peshitta (textually a partially corrected form of the *Evangelion da-Mepharreshe*) was produced at some time in the 4th century; it contains, in addition to the fourfold Gospel, the Paulines and the Acts, the Epistles of James, 1 Peter, and 1 John, *i.e.* the equivalent of the basic Canon accepted in the Greek churches about a century before. Two versions of the remaining books of the eventually accepted Canon were produced among the Syriac Monophysites: that of Philoxenos is probably extant in the so-called 'Pococke Epistles' and 'Crawford Apocalypse', while the later version of Thomas of Harkel also contains 2 Peter, 2 and 3 John, and Jude, and the version of Revelation published by de Dieu is almost certainly from this translation. Both show in their slavish imitation of Greek text and language, as well as in the mere fact of their production, the ever-increasing assimilation of Syriac Christianity to a Greek mode.

VII. RECAPITULATION

We may recapitulate by tracing the canonical fortunes of the individual books of the New Testament. The four Gospels circulated in relative independence until the formation of the fourfold Canon. Mark was apparently eclipsed by its two 'expansions', but not submerged. Luke, in spite of Marcion's patronage, does not seem to have encountered opposition. Matthew very early achieved that predominant place which it occupied till the modern era of scholarship. John was in rather different case, since in the late 2nd century there was considerable opposition to it, of which the so-called Alogoi and the Roman presbyter Gaius may serve as examples; this was no doubt due to some of the obscurities which still surround some aspects of its background, origin, and earliest circulation. Once accepted, its prestige continued to grow, and it proved of the highest value in the great doctrinal controversies and definitions. The Acts of the Apostles did not lend itself to liturgical or controversial use; it makes little appearance until after the time of Irenaeus; from then on it is firmly fixed as part of the Scriptures. The Pauline Corpus was securely established as Scripture from the earliest times. Marcion apparently rejected the Pastorals; otherwise we have no record of doubts concerning them, and already Polycarp holds them as authoritative. Hebrews, on the other hand, remained in dispute for several centuries. In the East, Pantaenus and Clement of Alexandria are known to have discussed the critical problems of its authorship; Origen solved the question by assuming that Pauline thought was here expressed by an anonymous author; Eusebius and some others report the doubts of the West, but after Origen the letter was accepted in the East. It is noteworthy that the letter takes pride of place after Romans in the 3rd-century Chester Beatty papyrus (p46). In the West doubts persisted from the earliest days: Irenaeus did not accept it as Pauline, Tertullian and other African sources pay it little regard, 'Ambrosiaster' wrote no commentary upon it, and in this was followed by Pelagius. The councils of Hippo and Carthage separate Hebrews from the rest of the Pauline Epistles in their canonical enumerations, and Jerome reported that in his day the opinion in Rome was still against authenticity. The matter was not considered settled until a century or so later. The corpus of the Catholic Epistles is evidently a late creation, post-dating the establishment of the essential structure of the Canon at the end of the 2nd century. Its exact constitution varies from church to church, and Father to Father. The First Epistle of John has a certain place from the time of Irenaeus: the Second and Third are but little quoted, and sometimes (as in the Muratorian Canon) we are uncertain whether both are being referred to. This may, of course, be due to their slenderness or apparent lack of theological import. The First Epistle of Peter, too, has a place only less secure (note, however, the ambiguities of the Muratorian Canon); the Second is still among the 'disputed books' in Eusebius' day. The status of James and Jude fluctuates according to church, age, and individual judgment. (We may note here how Jude and 2 Peter are grouped with a veritable pot-pourri of religious literature as one volume in a papyrus in the Bodmer collection.) For inclusion in this corpus there appear to have competed with all these such works as the *Shepherd*, *Barnabas*, the *Didache*, the Clementine 'correspondence', all of which seem to have been sporadically recognized and utilized as scriptural. The Revelation of John was twice opposed: once in the 2nd century because of its apparent support of the claims of Montanus to prophetic inspiration, once in the late 3rd century on critical grounds, by comparison with the Gospel of John, in the controversy of the Dionysii of Rome and Alexandria. Both kinds of doubt contributed to the continued mistrust with which it was viewed by the Gk. churches, and its very late acceptance in the Syriac and Armenian churches. In the West, on the contrary, it was very early accorded a high place; it was translated into Latin on at least three different occasions, and numerous commentaries were dedicated to it from the time of Victorinus of Pettau (martyred 304) onwards.

VIII. THE PRESENT POSITION

So the Canon of the New Testament grew and became fixed in that form in which we now know it. In the 16th century both Roman and Protestant Christianity, after debate, reaffirmed their adherence to the traditions, and the Roman Church has yet more recently emphasized its continued adherence. Conservative Protestantism, too, continues to use the Canon received by tradition, and even the representatives of liberal theology promulgate no contrary dogma. Doubtless, in the face of modern biblical research and the new acknowledgment of non-apostolic authorship which some scholars, at least, feel obliged to make concerning some of the New Testament documents, we need to understand afresh the factors and motives which underlie the historical processes here outlined. The inclusion of documents in the Canon is the Christian Church's recognition of the authority of these documents. There is no Canon in the earliest times because of the presence of apostles or their disciples, and because of the living oral traditions. In the mid-2nd century, the apostles are dead, but their memoirs and other monuments attest their message: at the same time heresy has arisen, and by its appeal either to theological theory or to new inspiration has necessitated a fresh appeal to orthodoxy's authority, and a closer definition of authoritative books. Thus the fourfold Gospel and the Pauline Corpus, already widely used, are declared to be scriptural, together with some other works with claims to apostolic authorship. Both doctrinal and scholarly discussion and development continue the process of recognition until, in the great era of the intellectual and ecclesiastical crystallization of Christianity, the Canon is completed. Three criteria were utilized, whether in the 2nd or the 4th century, to establish that the written documents are the true record of the voice and message of apostolic witness. First, attribution to apostles: this does not meet all cases; such Gospels as Mark and Luke were accepted as the works of close associates of the apostles. Secondly, ecclesiastical usage: that is, recognition by a leading church or by a majority of churches. By this were rejected many apocrypha, some perhaps innocuous and even containing authentic traditions of the words of Jesus, many more mere fabrications, but none known to be acknowledged by the majority of churches. Thirdly, congruence with the standards of sound doctrine: on this ground the Fourth Gospel is at first in doubt and at length accepted; or, to give a contrary case, the *Gospel of Peter* is banned by Serapion of Antioch because of its docetic tendencies in spite of its claim to apostolic title. Thus the history of the canonical development of the New Testament Scripture shows it to be a collection attributed to apostles or their disciples which in the view of the Church in the first four Christian centuries were justly thus attributed because they adequately declared and defined apostolic doctrine, and so had been or were considered to be fit for public lection at divine worship. When this is understood, with the gradual growth and variegated nature of the Canon, we can see why there were, and still are, problems and doubts about particular works there included. But taking these three criteria as adequate, orthodox Protestant Christianity today finds no reason to reject the decisions of earlier generations and accepts the New Testament as a full and authoritative record of divine revelation as declared from of old by men chosen, dedicated, and inspired.

BIBLIOGRAPHY. Th. Zahn, *Geschichte des neutestamentlichen Kanons*, 1888–92; J. Leipoldt, *Geschichte des neutestamentlichen Kanons*, 1907–8; M.-J. Lagrange, *Histoire ancienne du Canon du Nouveau Testament*, 1933; A. H. McNeile, *Introduction to the Study of the New Testament*[2], 1953; A. Wikenhauser, *New Testament Introduction*, Part I: the Canon of the New Testament; A. Souter, *The Text and Canon of the New Testament*[2], 1954; J. Knox, *Marcion and the New Testament*, 1942; E. C. Blackman, *Marcion and His Influence*, 1948; *The New Testament in the Apostolic Fathers*, 1905; J. N. Sanders, *The Fourth Gospel in the Early Church*, 1943; J. Hoh, *Die Lehre des heiligen Irenaeus ueber das Neue Testament*, 1919; W. Bauer, *Der Apostolos der Syrer*, 1903; W. Bauer, *Rechtgläubigkeit und Ketzerei im ältesten Christentum*, 1934. J.N.B.

CANTICLES. See SONG OF SOLOMON.

CAPERNAUM. A city on the north-west shore of the Sea of Galilee. Its name is clearly the Heb. *kᵉp̄ar naḥûm*, 'village of Nahum', made one word in Greek. Whether this is meant to be the prophet Nahum or not, it is impossible to say. Capernaum is not mentioned in the Old Testament, but it was an important city in the time of Christ. It housed a tax-collector; and the presence of a centurion (Mt. viii. 5) may well mean there was a Roman military post there. Jesus made it His headquarters for some time, and so it became known as 'his' city (Mt. ix. 1). He eventually condemned it for its lack of faith, and predicted its downfall. There are two possible sites, having the Arab. names Tell Hum and Khan Minya. There is less than 3 miles between them; Tell Hum is nearer the Jordan. Josephus was carried from Julias (*i.e.* Bethsaida) at the mouth of the Jordan to Capernaum (*Life* 72); but both sites are near enough to suit this story. The fountain of Capernaum (Jos., *BJ* iii. 10. 8) must be 'Ayn al-Tabigha; but this spring is almost exactly midway between Tell Hum and Khan Minya. Several scholars have favoured Khan Minya, but the present trend of opinion supports Tell Hum; this name appears to mean 'brown mound', but possibly 'Hum' is reminiscent of 'Nahum'. This is undoubtedly the site of a town of size and importance; and the evidence of early travellers such as Jerome supports this identification. A synagogue at Tell Hum dating from the early Christian centuries has been excavated and partially restored. Perhaps on the strength of this, the Israel Government has begged the question and labelled Tell Hum 'Kefar Nahum'.

D.F.P.

Fig. 51. Lintel from the gate of the synagogue courtyard at Tell Hum. This synagogue, of the 2nd or 3rd century AD, was an imposing structure of white limestone, facing southward (towards Jerusalem).

CAPHTOR (*kap̄tôr*). The home of the *kap̄tōrîm* (Dt. ii. 23), one of the peoples listed in the Table of Nations as descended, with Casluhim, whence went forth the Philistines (*q.v.*), from Mizraim (Gn. x. 14; 1 Ch. i. 12). Caphtor was the land from which the Philistines came (Je. xlvii. 4; Am. ix. 7), and it is presumably the Philistines, as erstwhile sojourners in Caphtor, who are referred to as Caphtorim in Dt. ii. 23. It is probable that the biblical name is to be identified with Ugaritic *kptr*, and *kap-ta-ra* in a school text from Assur which may well be a copy of one of second-millennium date. It is likewise held by many scholars that Egyptian *kftyw* is also to be connected with this group, all of which refer in all probability to Crete (*q.v.*). At its height in the second millennium, Minoan Crete controlled much of the Aegean area, and this would accord with the biblical description of Caphtor as an *'î*, a term which can mean both 'island' and 'coastland'. Western Asia was influenced in art and other ways by the Aegean, and this may explain the occurrence in the Bible of the term *kap̄tôr* as applying to an architectural feature, evidently a column capital, rendered in the AV by 'knop' (Ex. xxv. 31–36, xxxvii. 17–22) and 'lintel' (Am. ix. 1; Zp. ii. 14).

BIBLIOGRAPHY. A. H. Gardiner, *Ancient Egyptian Onomastica*, Text, I, 1947, pp. 201*–203*; C. H. Gordon, *The World of the Old Testament*, 1960, p. 293; *HUCA*, XXVI, 1955, pp. 52, 62; G. R. Driver, *Canaanite Myths and Legends*, 1956, p. 146; S. Smith, *Early History of Assyria*, 1928, p. 89. T.C.M.

CAPPADOCIA. A highland province, much of it around 3,000 feet, in the east of Asia Minor, bounded on the south by the chain of Mt. Taurus, east by the Euphrates and north by Pontus, but its actual limits are vague. It was constituted a Roman province by Tiberius, AD 17, on the death of Archelaus. In AD 70 Vespasian united it with Armenia Minor as one of the great frontier bulwarks of the empire. Under later emperors, especially Trajan, the size and importance of the province greatly increased. It produced large numbers of sheep and horses. The trade route between Central Asia and the Black Sea ports passed through it, and it was easily accessible from Tarsus through the Cilician

Gates. Jews from it were present at Jerusalem on the day of Pentecost (*q.v.*; Acts ii. 9). Some of the Dispersion to whom Peter wrote lived in Cappadocia (1 Pet. i. 1). J.W.M.

CAPTAIN. Seventeen different words, thirteen Heb. and four Gk., are translated 'captain' in the AV. Some of these terms are also translated 'officer', 'prince', 'ruler' (AV), and 'marshal' (RV). Three words mistranslated 'captain' are in 2 Ki. xi. 4, 19, RSV 'Carites'; Ezk. xxi. 22, RSV 'battering rams'; and Je. xiii. 21, RSV 'friends'. The Heb. word best translated 'captain', and the most military, is *śar* (419 times), meaning a leader of thousands, hundreds, or fifties (1 Sa. viii. 12), thus not denoting one particular rank. It can, however, mean chief in other spheres, *e.g.* butler (Gn. xl. 9), baker (Gn. xl. 16), tribes (Ps. lxviii. 27), priests (Ezr. viii. 29). *Rô'š*, head or chief (Nu. xiv. 4; 1 Ch. xi. 42), is translated 'captain' only ten times in AV, but is used many more times in a military sense. *Šālîš*, lit. 'third', denotes the third man in the chariot crew (2 Ki. ix. 25). *Peḥâ*, from the Assyrian *paḫâtu*, means governor (Dn. iii. 2, 3, 27). Other Heb. words include *qāṣîn*, 'a decider' (Jdg. xi. 6); *nāgîḏ* 'one who goes in front' (1 Sa. xiii. 14); *ba'al*, 'lord' (Je. xxxvii. 13). In the New Testament *chiliarchos*, almost always translated 'chief captain' in AV, means lit. 'a commander of a thousand men', but is generally used as a term for any military officer (Mk. vi. 21), especially a military tribune (Acts xxi. 31). The Temple employed police who were governed by *stratēgoi*, a levitical or priestly office. *Stratopedarchos*, once only (Acts xxviii. 16, absent from *WH*), is translated 'captain of the guard', and was probably the *princeps peregrinorum*, commander of the corps of imperial couriers. *Archēgos* (Acts iii. 15, v. 31; Heb. ii. 10, xii. 2) is best understood as 'author' or 'head'; its primary sense is 'pioneer', 'file-leader'. J.A.B.

CAPTIVITY. See ISRAEL.

CARAVAN. See TRADE.

CARBUNCLE. See JEWELS AND PRECIOUS STONES.

CARCHEMISH. A city (mod. Jerablus) which guarded the main ford across the river Euphrates 63 miles north-east of Aleppo. It is first mentioned in a text of the 18th century BC as an independent trade-centre (Mari, Alalaḫ), but was later claimed by the Egyptian Tuthmosis III. For many decades it was a Hittite fortress, until by 1110 BC it is named as ruled by an independent king Ini-Tešup. In 717 BC Sargon II defeated Pisiris, its king, and replaced him by an Assyrian governor. The sack of the city at this time is noted in Is. x. 9. In 609 BC Necho II of Egypt moved *via* Megiddo to recapture the city (2 Ch. xxxv. 20), which was made a base from which his army harassed the Babylonians. However, in May–June 605 BC Nebuchadrezzar II led the Babylonian forces who entered the city by surprise. The Egyptians were utterly defeated in hand-to-hand fighting in and around the city (Je. xlvi. 2) and pursued to Hamath. Details of this battle, which resulted in the Babylonian control of the west, are given in the Babylonian Chronicle.

Excavations in 1912 and 1914 uncovered Hittite sculptures, a lower palace area with an open palace (*bît-ḫilani*), and evidence of the battle and later Babylonian occupation.

BIBLIOGRAPHY. C. L. Woolley, *Carchemish*, I–III, 1914–52; D. J. Wiseman, *Chronicles of Chaldaean Kings*, 1956, pp. 20–26. D.J.W.

CARMEL (*karmel*, 'garden-land', 'fruitful land'). The word is used as a common noun in Hebrew with this meaning; examples are Is. xvi. 10; Je. iv. 26; 2 Ki. xix. 23 (RV, RSV); 2 Ch. xxvi. 10 (RV, RSV). It can even be used of fresh ears of grain, as in Lv. ii. 14, xxiii. 14. Thus, the limestone Carmel hills probably got their name from the luxuriant scrub and woodland that covered them. In the Old Testament two places bear this name.

1. A range of hills, some 30 miles long, extending from NW to SE, from Mediterranean (south shore of Bay of Acre) to the plain of Dothan. Strictly, Mt. Carmel is the main ridge (maximum height about 1,740 feet) at the north-west end, running some 12 miles inland from the sea, forming a border of Asher (Jos. xix. 26). This densely vegetated and little-inhabited region was a barrier pierced by two main passes, emerging at Jokneam and Megiddo, and a lesser one emerging at Taanach; between the first two, the hills are lower and more barren but have steep scarps. The main north–south road, however, passes by Carmel's hills through the plain of Dothan on the east. Carmel's luxuriant growth is reflected in Am. i. 2, ix. 3; Mi. vii. 14; Na. i. 4; also in Ct. vii. 5 in an apt simile for thick, bushy hair. The forbidding figure of Nebuchadrezzar of Babylon marching against Egypt is once compared with the rocky eminences of Carmel and Tabor (Je. xlvi. 18).

Joshua's vanquished foes included 'the king of Jokneam in Carmel' (Jos. xii. 22). It was here that Elijah in the name of his God challenged the prophets of Baal and Asherah, the deities promoted by Jezebel, and won a notable victory against them (1 Ki. xviii, xix. 1, 2). The text makes it obvious that it was Jezebel's gods that were thus discredited; as she came from Tyre, the Baal was almost certainly Baal-Melqart the chief god there. This god also penetrated Aram; see BEN-HADAD for the latter's stele to this deity. Baal was still worshipped on Carmel as 'Zeus Heliopolitēs Carmel' in AD 200 (Ap-Thomas, *PEQ*, XCII, 1960, p. 146; see BAAL). Alt considered this Baal as purely local, a view refuted by the biblical text, and Eissfeldt preferred Baal-shamêm who is less appropriate than Baal-Melqart (latter also advocated by de Vaux).

2. A town in Judah (Jos. xv. 55), at present-day Khirbet el-Karmil (var. Kermel or Kurmul), some 7½ miles (12 km.) south-south-east of Hebron, in a rolling, pastoral region (Baly, p. 164) ideal for the flocks that Nabal grazed there in David's time (1 Sa. xxv). His wife Abigail was a Carmelitess, and Hezro, one of David's warriors (2 Sa. xxiii. 35; 1 Ch. xi. 37) probably hailed from there. Saul passed that way on his return from the slaughter of the Amalekites (1 Sa. xv. 12).

BIBLIOGRAPHY. D. Baly, *Geography of the Bible*, 1957, pp. 88, 180–182, and map, p. 153, fig. 33. K.A.K.

CARPENTER. See ARTS AND CRAFTS.

CART, WAGON (*ʿᵃgālâ*, from the 'rolling' of wheels). Originally in Babylonia (Early Dynastic period) sledges were devised for carrying light loads, and these were soon adopted in Egypt and other flat countries. With the advent of the wheel,

Fig. 52. A Philistinian cart of a type in which this people transported their families and goods in migration. After a relief of Rameses III at Medinet Habu.

and the consequent increased mobility, carts early came into common use throughout Babylonia, Egypt (Gn. xlv. 19–21, xlvi. 5), and Palestine, especially in the south and low-lying Shephelah. However, in the hills their use was

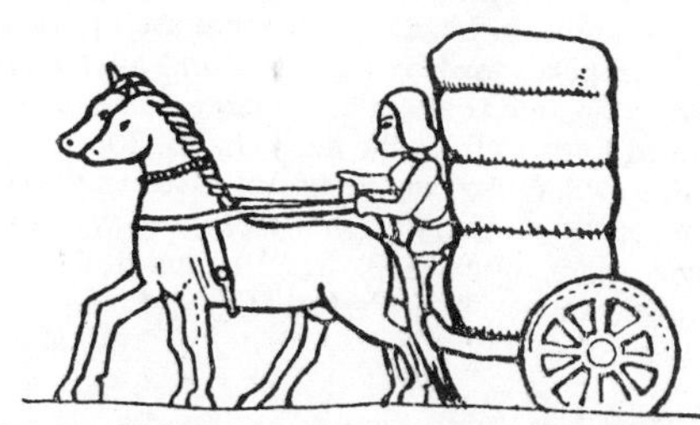

Fig. 53. Horse-drawn wagon of the 11th century BC from an obelisk of Ashurnasirpal I from Nineveh.

restricted to the main tracks (1 Sa. vi. 12), and they were not commonly used for long distances (Gn. xlv). They could carry one or two drivers with a light load, despite a general instability (1 Ch. xiii. 7). The main use was transporting the more bulky harvest in country districts (Am. ii. 13).

Such carts were made by carpenters of wood (1 Sa. vi. 7), and could therefore be dismantled and burned (verse 14; Ps. xlvi. 9, where AV wrongly has 'chariot'). Some were covered wagons (Nu. vii. 3). The two wheels, either solid or spoked, were sometimes equipped with a heavy metal tread (see Is. xxviii. 27, 28). These carts were drawn by two oxen (Nu. vii. 6, 7; 1 Sa. vi. 10) and are represented on Assyr. sculptures showing the fall of Lachish in 701 BC (British Museum; see also fig. 127). The figurative reference to a cart-rope in Is. v. 18 is now obscure. See also CHARIOT. D.J.W.

CASEMENT (*'ešnāḇ*, 'lattice', so RV, Pr. vii. 6). A lattice window through which a person inside the house could see without being seen (*cf.* Jdg. v. 28). See also HOUSE.

CASLUHIM. The name of a people descended from Mizraim, and from whose territory ('from thence') came the Philistines (*q.v.*; Gn. x. 14; 1 Ch. i. 12). Not known outside the Old Testament. The LXX reads *Chasmōnieim.* T.C.M.

CASSIA (*qiddâ*, Ex. xxx. 24; Ezk. xxvii. 19; *qᵉṣîʿôṯ*, Ps. xlv. 8). These two words, identified as similar in the Pesh. and the Targ., probably both refer to *Cassia lignea*, the inner bark of *Cinnamomum cassia*, a plant cultivated in East Asia and having a fragrant aromatic quality. The product was used in the 'holy anointing oil' of Ex. xxx. 24, and, like cinnamon (*q.v.*), was one of the perfumes used at Roman funerals. J.D.D.

CASTLE. Five different words are thus translated in the AV of the Old Testament. 1. *ṭîrâ* really means 'an enclosed group of tents' and is rightly translated 'encampment' or 'settlement' in the RV and RSV of Gn. xxv. 16; Nu. xxxi. 10; 1 Ch. vi. 54. It is incorrectly translated 'palace' in the AV of Ct. viii. 9; Ezk. xxv. 4. 2. *miḡdāl* (1 Ch. xxvii. 25). 3. *mᵉṣāḏ* (1 Ch. xi. 7), and 4. *mᵉṣûḏâ* (1 Ch. xi. 5) all refer to a tower or some similar edifice raised for defensive purposes. 5. *'armôn* (Pr. xviii. 19) has a wider significance and may be applied to any building of eminence, and so is frequently rendered 'palace' (*e.g.* in 1 Ki. xvi. 18; Ps. xlviii. 3). In the New Testament, 'castle' is always *parembolē* and occurs only in reference to the Roman fort of Antonia at Jerusalem (Acts xxi. 34, *etc.*). G.W.G.

CASTOR AND POLLUX (Gk. *dioskouroi*, lit. 'sons of Zeus'). The sign of the Alexandrian ship in which Paul sailed from Melita to Puteoli on his way to Rome (Acts xxviii. 11, AV). RV and RSV render 'The Twin Brothers'. According to Greek mythology they were the sons of Leda. They were worshipped especially at Sparta and were regarded as the special protectors of sailors. Their images were probably fastened one on either side of the bow of the vessel. J.W.M.

CATERPILLAR. See Locust.

CATHOLIC EPISTLES. During the course of the formation of the Canon of the New Testament the Epistles of James, 1 and 2 Peter, the Epistles of John, and Jude came to be grouped together and known as 'Catholic' (AV 'General'), because, with the exception of 2 and 3 John, they were addressed to a wider audience than a local church or individual. Clement of Alexandria speaks of the Epistle sent out by the Council at Jerusalem (Acts xv. 23) as 'the catholic Epistle of all the Apostles'; and Origen applies the term to the *Epistle of Barnabas*, as well as to the Epistles of John, Peter, and Jude. Later the word 'Catholic' was applied to Epistles which were accepted by the universal Church and were orthodox in doctrine; so it became synonymous with 'genuine' or 'canonical'. Thus with regard to other documents put forward in the name of Peter, Eusebius says 'we know nothing of them being handed down as catholic writings' (Eus., *EH* iii. 3). R.V.G.T.

CATTLE. Human wealth and the sacrificial worship of God centred largely around cattle, under both nomadic and agricultural conditions. Of the many words employed, *b*ᵉ*hēmâ*, 'beast', used as singular or collective, denotes the larger domestic animals—Gk. *ktēnos*. The plural may (Jb. xl. 15), but need not (*cf.* Ps. xlix. 12, 20) denote the hippopotamus. *šôr* is an ox or cow—the stalled or fattened ox was a symbol of luxury (Pr. xv. 17). *'*ᵃ*lāpîm* (plural only) is used for cattle in general. *b*ᵉ*'îr* has a normal, though not exclusive, reference to beasts of burden. *bāqār* is a generic word incapable of pluralization denoting 'cattlehood', frequently accompanied by a defining word. *'ēgel* is commonly used for calf or heifer. *par* is a bull, fem. *pārâ*. The latter is used for the spectacular red heifer ceremonial of Nu. xix. The New Testament references to cattle (Lk. xvii. 7; Jn. iv. 12) probably denote sheep and goats. *miqneh* (*e.g.* Gn. xiii. 2) means primarily wealth or possessions, derivatively cattle, the significant form of ancient Eastern wealth. A similar duality of meaning is found in the Arab. *m'āl*. *'Anšê miqneh* are herdsmen or nomads. Similarly, *m*ᵉ*lā'ḵâ* means occupation or property, derivatively cattle. R.A.S.

CAUDA, modern Gavdho (Gozzo), is an island off the south of Crete. Some ancient authorities call it Clauda (as in AV). Paul's ship was in the vicinity of Cape Matala when the wind changed from south to a strong ENE, and drove it some 23 miles before it came under the lee of Cauda, where the crew were at last able to make preparations to face the storm (Acts xxvii. 16. See Ships and Boats). K.L.McK.

CAUL. The AV translation of three Heb. words. 1. *š*ᵉ*ḇîmîm* (Is. iii. 18, RVmg 'networks', RSV 'headbands'). A kind of hair-net or head-veil worn by women in Isaiah's day, without which it was indecorous to be seen. 2. *yōṯereṯ* (Lv. iii. 4, *etc.*). Part of the liver usually associated in burnt offerings with the kidneys. See Liver. 3. *s*ᵉ*ḡôr* (Ho. xiii. 8; from *sāḡar*, 'to enclose', 'shut up'). The covering or 'mail-coat' of the heart, the pericardium, or perhaps the chest; thus the possible metaphorical meaning here of a hardened heart shut to the influence of God's grace. J.D.D.

CAVE. Except in Jb. xxx. 6, where *ḥôr*, 'hole', is used, the Heb. word usually rendered 'cave' is *m*ᵉ*'ārâ*. Natural caves are no rarity in Palestine, as nearly all the hill-country of Palestine west of the Jordan (except a basalt outcrop in S Galilee) is of limestone and chalk. Such caves were used as dwellings, hiding-places, and tombs from the earliest times.

a. Use as dwellings

A remarkable settlement of cave-dwellers of 34th/33rd centuries BC has been excavated at Tell Abu Matar, just south of Beersheba. Great caverns had been hollowed out as homes of several chambers linked by galleries for a prosperous community of cultivators and copperworkers. In much later days (early second millennium BC), Lot and his two daughters lodged in a cave after the fall of Sodom and Gomorrah (Gn. xix. 30), and David and his band frequented the great cave at Adullam (1 Sa. xxii. 1, xxiv).

b. Use as refuges

Joshua cornered five Canaanite kings who hid thus at Makkedah (Jos. x. 16 ff.). Israelites also hid in this way from Midianite (Jdg. vi. 2) and Philistine (1 Sa. xiii. 6) invaders. Elijah's friend Obadiah hid 100 prophets in caves 'by fifties' from the sword of Jezebel (1 Ki. xviii. 4, 13).

c. Use as tombs

This was a very common practice from prehistoric times onwards; see Burial and Mourning. Famous instances in Scripture are the cave at Machpelah used by Abraham and his family (Gn. xxiii, *etc.*), and that whence Jesus summoned Lazarus from the dead (Jn. xi. 38).

Bibliography. For the use of caves as dwellings see K. M. Kenyon, *Archaeology in the Holy Land*, 1960, pp. 77–80, fig. 10, and full preliminary reports by J. Perrot, *IEJ*, V, 1955, *etc.* K.A.K.

CEDAR. See Trees.

CEDRON. See Kidron.

CENCHREAE, the modern Kichries, a town near Corinth which served as outport for the city, handling its traffic with the Aegean and the Levant. Cenchreae had a church in which Phoebe served (Rom. xvi. 1, 2); this was perhaps a fruit of Paul's long stay in Corinth. Here the apostle shaved his head, in observance of a vow he had taken (Acts xviii. 18), prior to leaving for Ephesus. J.H.P.

CENSER. 1. *maḥtâ*, a copper vessel (the gold *maḥtôṯ* in 1 Ki. vii. 50; 2 Ch. iv. 22 are probably snuff-dishes; see SNUFFERS), for carrying live coals (hence 'firepans', Ex. xxvii. 3) and for burning incense (hence 'censer' of any kind, Nu. xvi. 6). 2. *miqṭereṯ* and 3. *libanōtos* are both 'incense-burner'. For archaeological literature, see Montgomery and Gehman, *ICC*, *Kings*, 1951, p. 184. 4. *Thymiatērion*, in LXX 2 Ch. xxvi. 19; Ezk. viii. 11 = *miqṭereṯ*. In Heb. ix. 4 it may have its other meaning 'incense-altar' (see B. F. Westcott, *The Epistle to the Hebrews*, 1903, pp. 248–250). D.W.G.

CENSUS (Lat. *census*, 'assessment', appearing as a loan-word in Gk. *kēnsos*, 'tribute money', Mt. xvii. 25, xxii. 17, 19; Mk. xii. 14; the general sense of the word, however, is represented by Gk. *apographē*, 'enrolment', AV 'taxing', Lk. ii. 2; Acts v. 37). Two Roman censuses are mentioned in the New Testament.

The census of Acts v. 37, which was marked by the insurrection led by Judas of Galilee, was held in AD 6. In that year Judaea was incorporated into the Roman provincial system, and a census was held in order to assess the amount of tribute which the new province should pay to the imperial exchequer. The census was conducted by P. Sulpicius Quirinius, at that time imperial legate of Syria. The suggestion that Israel should pay tribute to a pagan overlord was deemed intolerable by Judas, and by the party of the Zealots (*q.v.*), whose formation is to be dated from this time.

The census of Lk. ii. 1 ff., in the course of which Christ was born in Bethlehem, raises a number of problems. It is, however, widely agreed: (i) that such a census as Luke describes could have taken place in Judaea towards the end of Herod's reign (37–4 BC); (ii) that it could have formed part of an empire-wide enrolment, as Lk. ii. 1 indicates; (iii) that it could have involved the return of each householder to his domicile of origin, as Lk. ii. 3 states. (i) In Herod's later years Augustus treated him as a subject; all Judaea had to take an oath of loyalty to Augustus as well as to Herod (Jos., *Ant.* xvi. 9. 3, xvii. 2. 4). Compare the census imposed in AD 36 in the client-kingdom of Antiochus (Tacitus, *Annals* vi. 41). (ii) There is evidence of census activity in various parts of the Roman Empire between 11 and 8 BC; that for a census in Egypt in 10–9 BC (first of a series held every fourteen years) is practically certain. (iii) The custom described in Lk. ii. 3 (evidently as something familiar) is attested from Egypt in AD 104. On the further question whether Quirinius was governor of Syria at this time as well as on the occasion of the census of AD 6, see QUIRINIUS.

BIBLIOGRAPHY. W. M. Ramsay, 'The Augustan Census-System', in *The Bearing of Recent Discovery on the Trustworthiness of the New Testament*, 1915, pp. 255 ff. F.F.B.

CENTURION. See ARMY.

CEPHAS. See PETER.

CHAFF. The AV rendering of several biblical words. 1. Heb. *mōṣ*, the most common word, denotes worthless husks and broken straw blown away by the wind during the winnowing of grain (Jb. xxi. 18; Ps. i. 4, xxxv. 5; Is. xvii. 13, xxix. 5, xli. 15; Ho. xiii. 3; Zp. ii. 2). See also FAN. 2. Heb. *ḥᵃšaš*, 'hay', 'dry grass' (Is. v. 24, xxxiii. 11). 3. Heb. *teḇen*, 'straw' (Je. xxiii. 28), that which was withheld from the Israelites in the making of bricks (Ex. v. 7, 10). 4. Aram. *'ûr*, 'skin', 'chaff' (Dn. ii. 35). 5. Gk. *achyron*, 'chaff' (Mt. iii. 12; Lk. iii. 17).

In some of the above references it is applied figuratively in connection with superficial or wrong teaching, and with the inevitable fate of wrongdoers. See also AGRICULTURE. J.D.D.

CHAIN. See ORNAMENTS.

CHALCEDONY. See JEWELS AND PRECIOUS STONES.

CHALDAEA, CHALDEANS. The name of a land, and its inhabitants, in S Babylonia, later used to denote Babylonia as a whole. A semi-nomadic tribe occupying the deserts between N Arabia and the Persian Gulf (*cf.* Jb. i. 17) who early settled in the area occupying Ur 'of the Chaldees' (Gn. xi. 28; Acts vii. 4) and are distinct from the Aramaeans. The proposed derivation from Kesed (Gn. xxii. 22) is unsubstantiated. From at least the 10th century BC the land of *Kaldu* is named in the Assyr. annals to designate the 'Sea-land' of the earlier inscriptions. Ashurnasirpal II (883–859 BC) distinguished its peoples from the more northerly Babylonians, and Adad-nirari III (*c.* 810 BC) names several chiefs of the Chaldeans among his vassals. When Marduk-apla-iddina II, the chief of the Chaldean district of Bit-Yakin, seized the throne of Babylon in 721–710 and 703–702 BC he sought help from the west against Assyria (Is. xxxix; see MERODACH-BALADAN). The prophet Isaiah warned of the danger to Judah of supporting the Chaldean rebels (Is. xxiii. 13) and foresaw their defeat (xliii. 14), perhaps after the initial invasion by Sargon in 710 BC. Since Babylon was at this time under a Chaldean king 'Chaldean' is used as a synonym for Babylonian (Is. xiii. 19, xlvii. 1, 5, xlviii. 14, 20), a use later extended by Ezekiel to cover all the Babylonian dominions (xxiii. 23).

When Nabopolassar, a native Chaldean governor, came to the Babylonian throne in 626 BC he inaugurated a dynasty which made the name of Chaldean famous. Among his successors were Nebuchadrezzar, Amēl-Marduk (see EVIL-MERODACH), Nabonidus, and Belshazzar, 'king of the Chaldeans' (Dn. v. 30). The sturdy southerners provided strong contingents for the Babylonian army attacking Judah (2 Ki. xxiv–xxv).

In the time of Daniel the name was again used of Babylonia as a whole (Dn. iii. 8), and Darius the Mede ruled the kingdom of the 'Chaldeans' (ix. 1). The 'tongue of the Chaldeans' (Dn. i. 4) was, perhaps, a semitic Babylonian dialect, the name 'Chaldee' being, in modern times, wrongly applied to Aramaic. The prominence of the classes of priests who, at Babylon and other centres, maintained the ancient traditions of astrology and philosophy in the classical Babylonian languages led to the designation 'Chaldean' being applied both to priests (Dn. iii. 8), astrologers, and educated persons (Dn. ii. 10, iv. 7, v. 7, 11).

BIBLIOGRAPHY. D. J. Wiseman, *Chronicles of Chaldaean Kings*, 1956. D.J.W.

CHALKSTONES. An expression which is used once in the Old Testament (Is. xxvii. 9) as a figure of what must be done to idolatrous altars if forgiveness and restoration are to come. They are to be 'pulverized' as if they were made of gypsum or limestone. T.C.M.

CHAMBERLAIN. The English word denotes the guardian of the (royal) chamber; in eastern antiquity men who performed this function were regularly eunuchs, and therefore words for 'chamberlain' and 'eunuch' are to a large extent interchangeable. This is true of Heb. *sārîs* and Gk. *eunouchos* (it is from the latter word, literally meaning 'bed-keeper', that 'eunuch' is derived). See EUNUCH.

In Acts xii. 20 'the king's chamberlain' represents Gk. *ton epi tou koitōnos tou basileōs*, literally, 'him who was over the king's bedchamber'. In Rom. xvi. 23 Erastus, 'the chamberlain of the city' (AV), is the city treasurer (Gk. *oikonomos tēs poleōs*, *cf.* RV, RSV); a Corinthian inscription describes him as curator of public buildings. See ERASTUS. F.F.B.

CHAMELEON. Among the animal names included in lists of prohibited food (Lv. xi. 30) and occurring nowhere else is *kōaḥ*, generally translated chameleon. The chameleon (*Chamaeleo chamaeleon*) is found in the more wooded areas of Palestine, but it is small (usually under 6 inches) and not common. Some authorities consider that *kōaḥ* was the desert monitor, a powerful lizard reaching a length of 4 feet and found through much of Palestine. Monitor lizards are widely used as food in Africa, but their habit of eating carrion would logically ban them as food for the Hebrews. See figs. 40, 38. G.C.

CHAMOIS. Dt. xiv. 5 gives a list of animals allowed as food, which implies that they are cloven-hoofed ruminants. *Zemer* cannot be correctly translated chamois, for this alpine species was never found near Palestine. If *zemer* has as its root meaning 'the leaper', RSV is more correct with 'mountain sheep', usually called Barbary sheep, *Ammotragus lervia*, but the mouflon (*Ovis musimon*) might also have been included. G.C.

CHANGES OF RAIMENT. The word used for changes (*ḥ^a^lîpôṯ*) suggests not merely additional garments but also new ones, in contrast to those already worn. Such changes were highly valued; witness the stake involved in Samson's wager (Jdg. xiv. 12, 13). The number given indicated either the value of the prize or, in the case of a gift, the degree of honour accorded to the recipient. Thus Joseph gives extra changes to Benjamin (Gn. xlv. 22). Naaman brings ten for the prophet, while Gehazi is content to ask for two (2 Ki. v. 5, 22). H.M.C.

CHAPITER. See TEMPLE.

CHARIOT.

I. IN THE ANCIENT NEAR EAST

Heavy wheeled vehicles drawn by asses were used for war and ceremonial in southern Mesopotamia in the third millennium BC, as is shown by discoveries from Ur, Kish, and Tell Agrab. The true chariot, however, which was of light construction and was drawn by the swifter horse, did not appear until the second millennium. It is probable that the horse (*q.v.*) was introduced by the peoples of the south Russian steppe who precipitated many folk movements in the second

Fig. 54. Copper model of a chariot drawn by four onagers, of the Early Dynastic Period (*c.* 2500 BC) from Tell Agrab.

millennium, and the likelihood that the word for horse in many Ancient Near Eastern languages, including Heb. (*sûs*), was derived from an Indo-European original suggests that these people played an important part in its introduction. In the cuneiform inscriptions, 'horse' is commonly written with a logogram which signifies 'foreign ass', but the phonetic writing (*sisû*), which also occurs, is first found, significantly enough, in the 19th-century tablets from Kültepe in Asia Minor, indicating perhaps the linguistic influence of the forerunners of the northern nomads, who not long after entered the Near East in large numbers. Perhaps as a result of these early contacts, the northerners developed the light horse-drawn war-chariot, and when in the first half of the second millennium new peoples entered the ancient world, Hittites in Anatolia, Kassites in Mesopotamia, and Hyksos in Syro-Palestine and Egypt, they brought the chariot with them.

The foreign character of the chariot is emphasized by the fact that in many of the Semitic languages of the ancient world the word for chariot was formed from the root *rkb*, 'to ride', resulting, for instance, in Akkadian *narkabtu*, Ugaritic *mrkbt*, Heb. *merkāḇâ*, and the form was even adopted in New Kingdom Egypt (*mrkb.t*). In the second half of the second millennium, a class of society whose members were known as *mariannu* is attested at Alalaḫ, Ugarit, in the Amarna letters, and in New Kingdom Egypt. This indicated an individual of esteemed rank characterized particularly by the ownership of a chariot or wagon, and in many instances the best translation seems to be 'chariot warrior'. The word is usually considered of Indo-European origin (though some favour a Hurrian derivation), which would further illustrate the milieu of its introduction to the Near East. This is again emphasized by the treatise on horse-training by one Kikkuli of Mitanni, which was found in the cuneiform archives at Boghaz-Koi (see HITTITES). This work, written in Hurrian, contains a number of technical terms which are evidently Indo-European, the language-group of the rulers of Mitanni, who were among the newcomers disposing of horses and chariots in the second millennium.

By the second half of the second millennium the two great powers, the Hittites and the Egyptians, were fully equipped with horse-drawn chariots, as indeed were many of the small Aramaean and Canaanite city states of Syro-Palestine, and it was in this milieu that the Israelites found themselves on their conquest of Palestine. In the first millennium the Assyrians developed this engine as the basis of one of their principal arms, and indeed it became an essential element in plains warfare.

In general, the chariot was of very light construction, wood and leather being extensively employed, and only the necessary fittings being of bronze or iron. The car was usually open at the back, and fitments for shields and receptacles for spears and archers' equipment were disposed on the outside of the front or side panels. The wheels were generally six-spoked, but occasionally there were four, and some of the later Assyrian ones had eight. While the wheels usually stood about waist-high, a bas-relief of Ashurbanipal shows an eight-spoked one as high as a man, with a nail-studded tyre, probably of iron. The practice of fixing scythes to the wheels was probably not introduced until Persian times. There were usually two horses—though in the time of Ashurnasirpal II the Assyrians had a third, running at the side as a reserve, a practice subsequently abandoned—and these were yoked on either side of the pole, which curved upwards from the floor level of the car. The yoke, which had been developed for harnessing oxen, was unsuitable for horses, but the more practical horse-collar did not come into use until well into the Christian era.

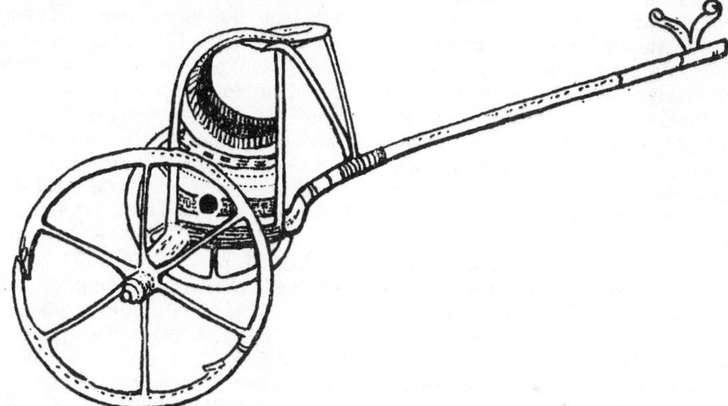

Fig. 55. A gold-overlaid state chariot of the pharaoh Tutankhamūn from his tomb at Thebes, c. 1340 BC.

The crew consisted of from two to four men. The Egyptians favoured two, a driver and a warrior, but the Assyrians added a third, the *šalšu rakbu*, 'third rider', who manipulated a shield to protect the others. This was the most usual number, and was also employed by the Hittites, but in the time of Ashurbanipal a fourth man was sometimes placed in the Assyrian vehicles.

The chariot was obviously of main service in campaigns on flat country, and could be a handicap in irregular terrain, as is shown on the Bronze Gates of Shalmaneser III, which depict the difficulties encountered in a campaign to the source of the Tigris.

II. IN THE OLD TESTAMENT

In company with the other Semitic-speaking peoples of antiquity, the Hebrews chiefly described the chariot by derivatives of *rkb*. The commonest form, used over a hundred times, is *reḵeḇ*; *merkāḇâ* is used some forty-four times; and *riḵbâ* (Ezk. xxvii. 20) and *r*ᵉ*ḵûḇ* (Ps. civ. 3) once each. The word *merkāḇ*, while used of chariot in 1 Ki. iv. 26, seems to have more the meaning of 'riding-seat' in Lv. xv. 9 (AV 'saddle') and Ct. iii. 10 (AV 'covering'). Also from *rkb* is formed *rakkāḇ*, 'charioteer', as used in 1 Ki. xxii. 34; 2 Ki. ix. 17 (EVV 'horseman' on account of 'horse' in verses 18, 19, but he could be a 'charioteer' on horseback); and 2 Ch. xviii. 33. Of the terms not formed from *rkb*, the commonest, *'ᵃgālâ*, probably usually signifies wagon or cart (*q.v.*), though in a poetic phrase in Ps. xlvi. 9 it seems to mean chariot. In Ezk. xxiii. 24 it is said of a warlike invasion that 'they shall come against thee with *hōṣen reḵeḇ* . . .' where *hōṣen* is a *hapax legomenon* of uncertain meaning. AV translates these terms as 'chariots, wagons', RV as 'weapons, chariots', and RSV as 'from the north with chariots'. The rendering of *reḵeḇ* as chariots rather than wagons is preferable. One other *hapax legomenon*, *'appiryôn* in Ct. iii. 9, is rendered 'chariot' by AV, but it is possible that this may mean 'palanquin' or 'litter', perhaps being an Iranian loan-word.

As one would expect, all the references to chariots in the Pentateuch concern the Egyptians. Joseph in his success came to own one (Gn. xli. 43, xlvi. 29, l. 9), and the fleeing Israelites were pursued with them (Ex. xiv; *cf.* Ex. xv. 4, 19; Dt. xi. 4). The only exception is Dt. xx. 1, and this looks forward to the things to be encountered during the conquest. While from the military point of view chariots were of little use in the hill country, and the Israelites who were without chariots seem to have taken this part of the land first, the 'chariots of iron' (*i.e.* with iron fittings) of the Canaanites of the plains (Jos. xvii. 16; Jdg. i. 19) and of the Philistines of the coast (1 Sa. xiii. 5) were a more formidable weapon. The excavations at Hazor (*q.v.*) have shown what a large number of chariots could have been accommodated in a city at this period (see Jos. xi and Jdg. iv, v). Chariots were looked upon as symbols of the worldly splendour of a king (*cf.* 1 Sa. viii. 11), but though David kept a hundred captured chariot-horses after one battle (2 Sa. viii. 4; *cf.* also 2 Sa. xv. 1), it was not till the time of Solomon that they were incorporated into the Israelite forces as a main arm. At this time the best horses were bred in Cilicia (*q.v.*) and the best chariots manufactured in Egypt, and Solomon established himself as a middleman in trading these (1 Ki. x. 28, 29). For his own army he established 'chariot cities' at Hazor, Megiddo, Gezer (*qq.v.*), and Jerusalem and reorganized his army to include 1,400 chariots (1 Ki. ix. 15–19, x. 26). The Israelite chariot carried three men, the third man, like his Assyrian counterpart, the *šalšu rakbu*, being called the *šālîš* (*e.g.* 1 Ki. ix. 22; AV renders variously as 'captain', 'lord', 'prince'). The division of the kingdom at Solomon's death was such that Israel kept most of the chariot forces, since Hazor, Megiddo, and Gezer were all in its territory, and most of the territory of Judah was hill country where chariots were of less use. In Israel Ahab had a very large chariot force, as is shown by the statement of Shalmaneser III that he brought 2,000 chariots to the battle of Qarqar (853 BC; Kurḫ Stele ii. 91), and it is probable that the stables uncovered at Megiddo, which have hitherto been ascribed to Solomon, are really due to him, Solomon's perhaps still lying buried in the mound (see MEGIDDO). This large force was reduced by the setbacks suffered in the Aramaean wars, and indeed it is stated that Jehoahaz was left with no more than ten chariots (2 Ki. xiii. 7). Samaria, as the capital, housed a chariot force, and it is illuminating that when the city fell to Sargon he took only fifty chariots (*Annals* 15), a clue to the declining forces of Israel. Judah was, of course, not entirely without chariots, as is shown by the fact that Josiah evidently had two personal ones at the battle of Megiddo (2 Ch. xxxv. 24), but they may have been limited to those of high rank.

III. IN THE NEW TESTAMENT

Chariots do not figure greatly in the New Testament, the best-known reference being to that in which the Ethiopian eunuch was evangelized by Philip (Acts viii). The word used here, *harma*, the common word for 'chariot' in Homer, occurs in the LXX usually for *reḵeḇ*. In the Apocalypse chariots are twice referred to, Rev. ix. 9 (*harma*), xviii. 13 (*rheda*).

BIBLIOGRAPHY. I. V. G. Childe, in Singer, Holmyard, and Hall (eds.), *A History of Technology*, 1954, pp. 724–728; S. Piggott, *Prehistoric India*, 1950, pp. 266, 267, 273–281; Lefèvre des Noëttes, *L'Attelage, le Cheval de Selle à travers les ages*, 1931; O. R. Gurney, *The Hittites*, 1952, pp. 104–106, 124, 125; E. Drioton and J. Vandier, *L'Égypte*³, 1952, pp. 555, 556; D. J. Wiseman, *The Alalakh Tablets*, 1953, p. 11; J. Gray, *The Legacy of Canaan*, 1957, pp. 7, 167, 168; C. J. Gadd, *The Assyrian Sculptures*, 1934, pp. 27, 28, 30–35; A. Salonen, *Die Landfahrzeuge des Alten Mesopotamien*, 1951; *Hippologica Accadica*, 1955, pp. 11–44.

II. R. de Vaux, *Les Institutions de l'Ancien Testament*, 1960, pp. 21–25, 432; Y. Yadin, *BA*, XXIII, 1960, pp. 62–68. T.C.M.

CHARISMATA. See SPIRITUAL GIFTS.

CHARITY. See LOVE.

CHARM. See AMULETS, MAGIC AND SORCERY.

CHEBAR. The name of a river in Babylonia, by which Jewish exiles were settled; the site of Ezekiel's visions (i. 1, 3, iii. 15, 23, x. 15, xliii. 3). The location is unknown, though Hilprecht proposed an identification with the *nāri kabari* ('great river'), a name used in a Babylonian text from Nippur for the Shaṭṭ-en-Nil canal running east of that city.

BIBLIOGRAPHY. E. Vogt, *Biblica*, XXXIX, 1958, pp. 211–216. D.J.W.

CHEDORLAOMER (Heb. *Keḏorlā'ōmer*; Gk. *Chodolla(o)gomor*). The king of Elam, leader of a coalition with Amraphel, Arioch and Tidal (*q.v.*), who marched against Sodom and Gomorrah, which had rebelled against him after twelve years as his vassals (Gn. xiv. 1–5). He was pursued by Abraham who slew him near Damascus (verse 15).

This ruler has not been certainly identified. An Elamite Kudur-KU.MAL is named in cuneiform texts (BM 34062, *etc.*) as the conqueror of Babylon. This name is now read Kutirnahuti (Sum. KU.MAL = *ḫunga* = Bab. *nāḫu*). Albright equates Chedorlaomer with this king (Kutir-Naḫḫunti I of Elam *c.* 1625 BC), but this implies both a late date for Abraham and a confusion of the final *r* with *d* (very similar in the Old Heb. script). The phonetic identification is possible (*Naḫundi* = W. Sem. *La'nd* = *La'mr*), but because the names of some early Elamite kings are unknown the equation must remain an open question. The political history of this period makes the presence of a coalition of Elamites and West Semites in the area feasible (see PATRIARCHAL AGE).

BIBLIOGRAPHY. W. F. Albright, *BASOR*, 88, 1942, pp. 33 ff. D.J.W.

CHEEK (Heb. *lᵉḥî*, of cheek or jaw of man or animal, also of jawbone (Jdg. xv. 15); Gk. *siagōn*). A blow on the cheek is indicative of ignominy or defeat (Jb. xvi. 10; Mt. v. 39), plucking or shaving off the beard more so (Is. l. 6; 1 Ch. xix. 4), and breaking the jaw-teeth was to render powerless (Jb. xxix. 17) B.O.B.

CHEESE. See FOOD, MEALS.

CHEMARIM. In the AV this word appears only in Zp. i. 4 as a proper name, but it also occurs in two other places in *MT*, Ho. x. 5; 2 Ki. xxiii. 5; where it is rendered 'priests' and 'idolatrous priests' respectively. A doubtful emendation of Ho. iv. 4 should be disregarded. The exact significance of the word is quite uncertain, a variety of etymologies having been offered. Some have suggested a comparison of Chemarim with Akkad. *kamāru*, 'to throw down', a reference to priests who prostrate themselves; others, referring to Syriac roots, suppose the word to derive from the presumed *black* robe of the priest, or from the *sad* demeanour of the ascetic. What is certain is that while the Old Testament uses the word in a pejorative sense, it is a neutral word for priest in Aramaic (*kumrā'*); indeed, it is used of the priests in restored Jerusalem in the Pesh. version of Is. lx. 6. This may suggest that the false religion in which the priests were engaged was of Syrian origin. R.J.W.

CHEMOSH (*kᵉmôš*), the god of the Moabites, the people of Chemosh (Nu. xxi. 29; Je. xlviii. 46). The sacrifice of children as a burnt offering was part of his worship (2 Ki. iii. 27). Solomon erected a high place for Chemosh in Jerusalem (1 Ki. xi. 7), but Josiah destroyed this (2 Ki. xxiii. 13). See MOAB, MOABITE STONE. J.A.T.

CHENOBOSKION (lit. 'goose-pasture'; Coptic *Sheneset*), an ancient town in Egypt, east of the Nile, *c.* 30 miles north of Luxor. Here one of the earliest Christian monasteries was founded by Pachomius, *c.* AD 320. Chenoboskion has acquired new fame because of the discovery in its vicinity, *c.* 1945, of a library of Gnostic literature (mainly Coptic translations from Gk.)—forty-eight or forty-nine documents in thirteen papyrus codices. They are commonly referred to as the Nag Hammadi documents, presumably because it was in Nag Hammadi, west of the river (the nearest modern town to the scene of the discovery), that the discovery was first reported. One of the codices was acquired by the Jung Institute in Zürich, whence it is called the Jung Codex; the others are now the property of the Coptic Museum in Cairo. At the time of writing only two of these documents have been published—*The Gospel of Truth*, contained in the Jung Codex, and *The Gospel of Thomas*, contained in one of the codices at Cairo. *The Gospel of Truth* is a speculative meditation on the Christian message, coming from the Valentinian school of Gnosticism, and quite probably the work of Valentinus himself (*c.* AD 150). *The Gospel of Thomas* is a collection of 114 sayings ascribed to Jesus, fragments of which (in Gk.) were found at Oxyrhynchus at the end of the 19th century and beginning of the 20th. The whole collection when published will make an invaluable contribution to our knowledge of Gnosticism.

BIBLIOGRAPHY. W. C. van Unnik, *Newly Discovered Gnostic Writings*, 1960; J. Doresse, *The Secret Books of the Egyptian Gnostics*, 1960.

F.F.B.

CHEPHIRAH. A Hivite fortress (Jos. ix. 17) on a spur 5 miles west of Gibeon, dominating the Wadi Qatneh, which leads down to Aijalon. It became Benjamite territory (Jos. xviii. 26); the Gola-list (Ezr. ii. 25; Ne. vii. 29) associates it with Q. Jearim, now Khirbet Kefireh. See Garstang, *Joshua–Judges*, pp. 166, 369.

J.P.U.L.

CHERETHITES (*kᵉrēṯî*). A people who were settled alongside the Philistines in southern Palestine (1 Sa. xxx. 14; Ezk. xxv. 16; Zp. ii. 5). In the reign of David they formed, with the Pelethites, his private bodyguard under the command of Benaiah the son of Jehoiada (2 Sa. viii. 18, xx. 23; 1 Ch. xviii. 17). They remained loyal to him through the rebellions of Absalom (2 Sa. xv. 18) and Sheba (2 Sa. xx. 7), and were present when Solomon was anointed for kingship (1 Ki. i. 38, 44), though the fact that they are never again mentioned after this suggests that their loyalty to David depended on the personal factor which ended with his death.

It seems reasonable to suppose that the Cherethites were Cretans and the Pelethites Philistines, the latter name being perhaps an analogic adaptation of *pᵉlištî* on the basis of *kᵉrēṯî*, together with assimilation of *š* to following *ṭ*, to form the easy phrase *hakkᵉrēṯî wᵉhappᵉlēṯî*, 'the Cherethites and the Pelethites'. This being so, the distinction between them was that though they both came from Crete, the Cherethites were native Cretans, whereas the Pelethites had only passed through the island in their travels from some other original homeland (see PHILISTINES).

It seems that mercenaries from the Aegean were now, as in later times, not uncommon, for though Jehoiada no longer employed the Cherethites and Pelethites, he did have Carian troops (2 Ki. xi. 4, 19; *kārî*, translated 'captains' in AV).

BIBLIOGRAPHY. A. H. Gardiner, *Ancient Egyptian Onomastica*, Text, I, 1947, p. 202*; J. A. Montgomery, *The Books of Kings*, *ICC*, 1951, pp. 85, 86; R. de Vaux, *Les Institutions de l'Ancien Testament*, I, 1958, p. 189, II, 1960, pp. 17–19. T.C.M.

CHERITH. A brook in Transjordan beside which Elijah hid from Jezebel at God's command (1 Ki. xvii. 3, 5). The form of words suggests that it was east of the Jordan, and therefore in Gilead, but the precise location is uncertain.

J.D.D.

CHERUBIM (*kᵉrûḇîm*). The plural of 'cherub', represented in the Old Testament as symbolic and celestial beings. In the book of Genesis they were assigned to guard the tree of life in Eden (Gn. iii. 24). A similar symbolic function was credited to the golden cherubim, which were placed at either end of the cover ('mercy seat') of the ark of the covenant (Ex. xxv. 18–22; *cf.* Heb. ix. 5), for they were thought of as protecting the sacred objects which the ark housed, and as providing, with their outstretched wings, a visible pedestal for the invisible throne of Yahweh (*cf.* 1 Sa. iv. 4; 2 Sa. vi. 2; 2 Ki. xix. 15; Ps. lxxx. 1, xcix. 1, *etc.*). In Ezk. x the chariot-throne of God, still upborne by cherubim, becomes mobile. Representations of those winged creatures were also embroidered on the curtains and veil of the tabernacle and on the walls of the Temple (Ex. xxvi. 31; 2 Ch. iii. 7).

Figures of cherubim formed part of the lavish decorations of Solomon's Temple (1 Ki. vi. 26 ff.). Two of these, carved in olivewood and overlaid with gold, dominated the inner sanctuary. They stood about 15 feet in height, with a total wingspread of similar dimensions, and when placed together they covered one entire wall. Cherubim were also carved in the form of a frieze around the wall of Solomon's Temple, and they appeared together with animal representations on decorative panels forming part of the base of the huge brass basin ('molten sea') which contained the water for ritual ablutions.

Allusions to these celestial beings occur occasionally in the Old Testament, especially in the poetical books, where they are symbolical representations of the storm-winds of heaven; thus in 2 Sa. xxii. 11 (Ps. xviii. 10) God was spoken of as riding upon a cherub (an expression which has as its parallel clause, 'he did fly upon the wings of the wind').

From the descriptions given in the Old Testament there is considerable doubt both as to the appearance and the essential nature of cherubim. They were generally represented as winged creatures having feet and hands. In Ezekiel's vision of the restored Jerusalem the carved likenesses of cherubim had two faces, one of a man and the other of a young lion (Ezk. xli. 18 f.), whereas in those seen in his vision of the divine glory, each of the cherubim had four faces and four wings (Ezk. x. 21). To what extent they were thought to be possessed of moral and ethical

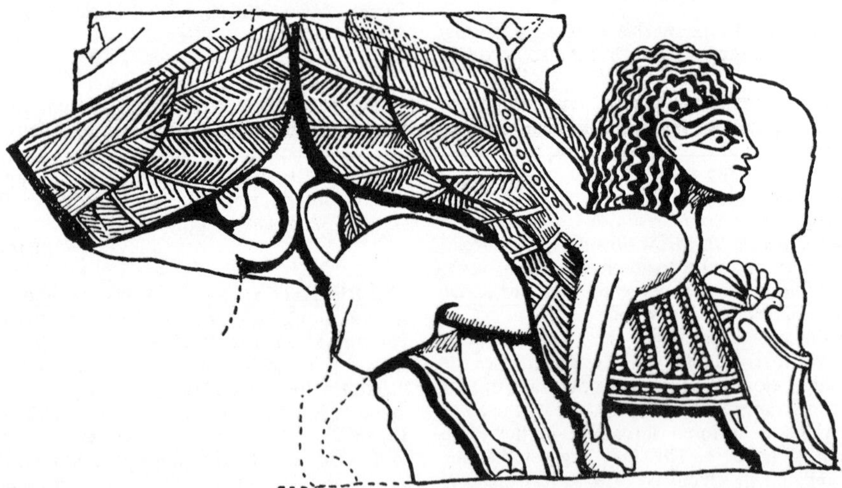

Fig. 56. Part of a thick ivory panel, found at Nimrud, showing two winged and skirted sphinxes back to back. These are the 'cherubim' of the Old Testament (Ex. xxv. 20). Original $3\frac{1}{4}$ inches high.

qualities is unknown. They were invariably in close association with God, and were accorded an elevated, ethereal position.

Archaeological discoveries in Palestine have brought to light some ancient representations of cherubim. At Samaria some ivory panels depicted a composite figure with a human face, an animal body with four legs, and two elaborate and conspicuous wings. The appearance of the face suggests a degree of Hittite influence. Excavations at the ancient Phoenician city of Gebal (the Gk. Byblos) have revealed a carved representation of two cherubim supporting the throne of Hiram king of Gebal, who reigned *c.* 1200 BC. These figures were in general accord with their counterparts from Samaria.

Symbolic winged creatures were a prominent feature alike of Ancient Near Eastern mythology and architecture. Representations of this kind were a common feature of Egyptian animism, while in Mesopotamia, winged lions and bulls guarded all buildings of any importance. The Hittites popularized the griffin, a highly composite creature consisting of the body of a lion with the head and wings of an eagle, and in general appearance resembling a sphinx.

BIBLIOGRAPHY. *ICC*, *Genesis*, pp. 89 f., *Ezekiel*, pp. 112–114, *Revelation*, I, pp. 118–127; art. 'Cherub' in *JewE*; art. 'Cherubim' in *HDB* and *DAC*; H. Heppe, *Reformed Dogmatics*, E.T., 1950.

See figs. 56, 167. R.K.H.

CHESNUT. See TREES.

CHESULLOTH (Jos. xix. 18). A town of Issachar near the border of Zebulun, and evidently the Chisloth-tabor of Jos. xix. 12. Generally identified with the ruins north of Iksâl, about 2 miles south-east of Nazareth. J.D.D.

CHILD, CHILDREN. See FAMILY.

CHILDREN OF GOD. See SONS OF GOD.

CHINNERETH, CHINNEROTH, CINNEROTH, GENNESARET. 1. In 1 Ki. xv. 20 and elsewhere, a small triangular plain on the north-western shore of the Sea of Galilee (*q.v.*), also referred to as the Sea of Chinnereth (Nu. xxxiv. 11, *etc.*) or the lake of Gennesaret (Lk. v. 1). Some see a similarity between the shape of the lake and that of a harp (*kinnor*) and derive the name from this Hebrew word.

2. A city of Naphtali (Jos. xix. 35) in the plain of Chinnereth, probably the modern Khirbet el-'Oreimeh. R.F.H.

CHIOS. One of the larger Aegean islands off the west coast of Asia Minor, this was a free city-state under the Roman Empire until Vespasian's day. Paul's ship on the way from Troas to Patara anchored for a night near the island (Acts xx. 15). J.D.D.

CHISLEV. The ninth month in the Hebrew calendar (Ne. i. 1). See CALENDAR.

CHISLOTH-TABOR. See CHESULLOTH.

CHITTIM. See KITTIM.

CHIUN (*kiyyûn*) occurs once only in the Old Testament (Am. v. 26). Some scholars have thought that it is a common name, meaning 'pedestal' or 'image-stand' (see W. R. Harper, *ICC*, *Amos*, 1910, pp. 139 f.). Vulg. similarly has *imaginem*, RVmg 'shrine'. Most, however, believe that the Massoretes have substituted the vowel points of *šiqqûṣ* (= 'detestable thing') for the vowel points of an original *kaiwan* or *kewan* = Assyrian *kaiwanu*, a name of Ninib, god of the planet Saturn. The LXX translation *Rhaiphan* seems to support this view; see REPHAN and SICCUTH. D.W.G.

CHLOE. Greek female name, signifying 'verdant', especially appropriated to Demeter.

'Chloe's people' told Paul of the Corinthians' schisms (1 Cor. i. 11) and perhaps other items in 1 Cor. i–vi. That the tactful Paul names his informants suggests they were not Corinthian. Possibly they were Christian slaves of an Ephesian lady visiting Corinth. Whether Chloe was herself a Christian is unknown.

F. R. M. Hitchcock (*JTS*, XXV, 1924, pp. 163 ff.) argues that a pagan body, associated with the Demeter-cult, is intended. A.F.W.

CHORAZIN. A town on the Sea of Galilee associated with the Lord's preaching and miracles, but which He denounced because it did not repent (Mt. xi. 21; Lk. x. 13). Now identified with Kerazeh, 2½ miles north of Capernaum (Tell Hum?), the black basalt ruins of its synagogue can still be seen. J.W.M.

CHRIST. See JESUS CHRIST, MESSIAH.

CHRISTIAN. The three occurrences (Acts xi. 26, xxvi. 28; 1 Pet. iv. 16) all imply that it was a generally recognized title in the New Testament period, though it is evident that there were other names which Christians themselves used, and perhaps preferred (*cf.* H. J. Cadbury, *BC*, V, 1933, pp. 375 ff.).

a. Origin of the name

The formation seems to be Latin, where plural nouns ending in *-iani* may denote the soldiers of a particular general (*e.g. Galbiani*, Galba's men, Tacitus, *Hist.* i. 51), and hence partisans of an individual. Both elements are combined in the quasi-military *Augustiani* (see below). In the late 1st century AD at least, *Caesariani* was used of Caesar's slaves and clients, and in the Gospels we meet the *Herodianoi*, who may have been partisans or clients of Herod (see HERODIANS).

Christian(o)i, therefore, may have originally been thought of as 'soldiers of Christus' (Souter), or 'the household of Christus' (Bickerman), or 'the partisans of Christus' (Peterson). H. B. Mattingley has recently given an ingenious turn to the latter interpretation by suggesting that

Christiani, by an Antiochene joke, was modelled on *Augustiani*, the organized brigade of chanting devotees who led the public adulation of Nero Augustus; both the enthusiasm of the believers and the ludicrous homage of the imperial cheer-leaders being satirized by the implicit comparison with each other. But the name 'Christian' may well be older than the institution of the *Augustiani.*

b. Place and period of origin

Luke, who clearly knew the church there well, places the first use of the name at Syrian Antioch (Acts xi. 26). The Latinizing form is no obstacle to this. The context describes events of the forties of the 1st century AD, and Peterson has argued that the contemporary persecution by Herod Agrippa I (Acts xii. 1) evoked the name *Christian(o)i* as a parallel to their foes, the *Herodian(o)i*. If *Augustiani* be the model, the title cannot have been coined before AD 59, and Acts xi. 26 cannot be taken as implying any date for the title. There is, however, good reason to associate the occasion with what precedes, for Luke has just shown Antioch as the first church with a significant pure-Gentile, ex-pagan element: that is, the first place where pagans would see Christianity as something other than a Jewish sect. Appropriate names for the converts would not be long in coming.

At any rate, 'Christian' was well established in the sixties. The 'smart' Herod Agrippa II (Acts xxvi. 28) uses it, doubtless satirically, to Paul (Mattingley: 'In a moment you'll be persuading me to enroll as a *Christianus*'). Peter, probably from Rome just before the Neronian persecution, warns 'the elect' in parts of Asia Minor that no-one should be ashamed if called on to suffer as a Christian (1 Pet. iv. 16—this need not imply a formal charge in a law-court); and Nero, according to Tacitus (*Ann.* xv. 44), trumped up a charge against a sect 'whom the common people *were calling* (*appellabat*—the tense is significant) Christians'.

c. The source of the name

Chrēmatisai (AV 'were called') in Acts xi. 26 is variously interpreted. Bickerman, translating it 'styled themselves', holds that 'Christian' was a name invented in the Antiochene church. His translation is possible, but not necessary, and it is more likely that Antiochene pagans coined the word. Certainly elsewhere, it is non-Christians who use the title—Agrippa, the accusers in 1 Peter, the 'common people' in Tacitus. *Chrēmatisai* is frequently translated 'were publicly called', referring to official action in registering the new sect under the name 'Christians'. (Registration would easily account for a Latin title.) But the verb could be used more loosely, and perhaps Luke means no more than that the name came into popular use in the first city where a distinctive name became necessary. From this it might early and easily pass into official and universal use.

d. Subsequent use

If 'Christian' was originally a nickname, it was, like 'Methodist' later on, adopted by the recipients. Increasingly, believers would have to answer the question 'Are you a Christian?', and there was no shame in accepting what was intended as a term of opprobrium when it contained the very name of the Redeemer (1 Pet. iv. 16). And it had a certain appropriateness: it concentrated attention on the fact that the distinctive element in this new religion was that it was centred in the Person, Christ; and if the name *Christos* was unintelligible to most pagans, and they sometimes confused it with the common name *Chrēstos*, meaning 'good, kind', it was a *paranomasia* which could be turned to good effect. And so, in the earliest 2nd-century literature, the name is employed without question by the Christian bishop Ignatius (in Antioch) and the pagan governor Pliny (in the area addressed in 1 Peter).

BIBLIOGRAPHY. Zahn, *INT*, II, 1909, pp. 191 ff.; E. Peterson in *Miscellanea G. Mercati*, I, 1946, pp. 355 ff.; E. J. Bickerman, *HTR*, XLII, 1949, pp. 109 ff.; H. B. Mattingley, *JTS* (NS), IX, 1958, pp. 26 ff. A.F.W.

CHRISTOLOGY. See JESUS CHRIST, INCARNATION.

CHRONICLES, BOOKS OF.

I. OUTLINE OF CONTENTS

1 Chronicles

a. Genealogies, i. 1–ix. 44

Adam to Noah, i. 1–4; Noah's sons to Jacob and Esau, i. 5–54; the sons of Jacob: (i) Judah and the royal line, ii. 1–iv. 23; (ii) the other tribes, iv. 24–viii. 40; (iii) Levi, vi. 1–81; returned exiles and allocation of temple duties, ix. 1–34; Saul, ix. 35–44.

b. The acts of David, x. 1–xxix. 30

(i) *David made king.* Death of Saul, x. 1–14; David crowned, xi. 1–3; capture of Jerusalem, xi. 4–9; David's chief supporters and 'mighty men', xi. 10–47; before his coronation, xii. 1–22; after his coronation, xii. 23–40.

(ii) *David's religious acts.* Abortive attempt to bring in the ark, xiii. 1–14; guidance in battle, xiv. 1–17; the bringing in of the ark, xv. 1–29; dedication of the ark, xvi. 1–43; the promise to David's line, xvii. 1–27.

(iii) *Victories abroad.* Philistines, Moab, Zobah, Syria, Edom, xviii. 1–17; Ammon, xix. 1–xx. 3; Philistines, xx. 4–8.

(iv) *Organization at home.* The census, xxi. 1–30; preparation for the Temple, xxii. 1–19; priests and Levites, xxiii. 1–xxvi. 28; other officials, xxvi. 29–xxvii. 34.

(v) *David's farewell.* To the leaders, xxviii. 1–8; to Solomon, xxviii. 9–21; to all the people, xxix. 1–5; dedication of the gifts, xxix. 6–21; David and Solomon, xxix. 22–30.

2 Chronicles

a. The reign of Solomon, i. 1–ix. 31

His establishment in the kingdom, i. 1–17; the building of the Temple, ii. 1–v. 1; the bringing in of the ark, v. 2–14; dedication and prayer, vi. 1–vii. 22; Solomon's glory at home and abroad, viii. 1–ix. 31.

b. The kings of Judah, x. 1–xxxvi. 23

Rehoboam, x. 1–xii. 16; Abijah, xiii. 1–22; Asa and his reforms, xiv. 1–xvi. 14; Jehoshaphat and his reforms, xvii. 1–xx. 37; Jehoram, xxi. 1–20; Ahaziah, xxii. 1–9; Athaliah usurps the throne, xxii. 10–12; Joash and his reforms, xxiii. 1–xxiv. 27; Amaziah, xxv. 1–28; Uzziah, xxvi. 1–23; Jotham, xxvii. 1–9; Ahaz, xxviii. 1–27.

Hezekiah, his reforms, and miraculous deliverance, xxix. 1–xxxii. 33; Manasseh, xxxiii. 1–20; Amon, xxxiii. 21–25; Josiah and his reforms, xxxiv. 1–xxxv. 27; Jehoahaz, xxxvi. 1–4; Jehoiakim, xxxvi. 5–8; Jehoiachin, xxxvi. 9, 10; Zedekiah, xxxvi. 11–21.

c. Epilogue

The Exile and return, xxxvi. 22, 23.

II. AUTHORSHIP AND DATE

According to Jewish tradition the books of Chronicles were written by Ezra. Some arguments in favour of this view were given by W. F. Albright in *JBL*, XL, 1921, pp. 104–124, and there is no reason why the date should be put later than the last part of the 5th century BC. The link between the end of Chronicles and the beginning of Ezra, and also the general standpoint of the books, suggest that Chronicles–Ezra–Nehemiah were intended to form one work.

Those who date Ezra's coming to Jerusalem after 400 BC (see EZRA) naturally date the total work later. Additional evidence for a date well down in the 4th century is sought in names in genealogical lists. Thus 1 Ch. iii. 19–24 gives the names of Zerubbabel's descendants to the sixth generation (LXX to the eleventh), and Zerubbabel's date is 520 BC. The list of high priests in Ne. xii. 22 continues to Jaddua, who, according to Josephus, lived in the time of Alexander the Great, whose death occurred in 323 BC. These facts have been disputed (*e.g.* by E. J. Young, *Introduction to the Old Testament*, p. 383), but, if true, they do not overthrow an earlier date for the books in general, since copyists would tend to make marginal notes to bring important lists up to date.

III. SOURCES OF THE BOOK

The Chronicler refers to various writings that contain further information about the history. Although he does not say that he is using them himself, it would be a fair deduction that he has done so. These records fall into two groups.

a. A book referred to as 'the book of the kings of Judah and Israel' (2 Ch. xvi. 11, xxv. 26, xxviii. 26, xxxii. 32); 'the book of the kings of Israel and Judah' (2 Ch. xxvii. 7, xxxv. 27, xxxvi. 8); 'the book of the kings of Israel' (2 Ch. xx. 34); 'the acts of the kings of Israel' (2 Ch. xxxiii. 18, RV). The general similarity of the titles suggests that a single set of records is referred to, and the probability is that there is a further reference to this book in 2 Ch. xxiv. 27, in the words 'the story (*midrash*) of the book of the kings'. These records could be the official annals of the kings that are also referred to frequently in our books of 1 and 2 Kings (1 Ki. xiv. 19, *etc.*). The Chronicler probably had direct access to these annals, in addition to the extracts that had already been made from them by the writers of Kings, and some of his additional information must have come from them.

b. Writings associated with certain prophets. For David's reign the words of Samuel, Nathan, and Gad (1 Ch. xxix. 29); for Solomon the words of Nathan, the prophecy of Ahijah, and the visions of Iddo (2 Ch. ix. 29); for Rehoboam the words of Shemaiah and Iddo (2 Ch. xii. 15); for Abijah the story (*midrash*) of Iddo (2 Ch. xiii. 22); for Jehoshaphat the words of Jehu (2 Ch. xx. 34); for Manasseh the words of Hozai (2 Ch. xxxiii. 19, AVmg), where the LXX translates 'seers' from the reading *ḥōzîm*. In addition there are two references to Isaiah. He is said to have written the acts of Uzziah, first and last (2 Ch. xxvi. 22). Also the rest of the acts of Hezekiah are said to be written in the vision of Isaiah in the book of the kings of Judah and Israel (2 Ch. xxxii. 32, RV). This last phrase may be linked with what is said of the words of Jehu in 2 Ch. xx. 34, that they are taken up (*hō'ᵃlâ*) into the book of the kings of Israel. All this suggests that prophets wrote records of their times, presumably in the form of God-given characterizations of the kings and moral and spiritual interpretations of the history. They may well have been responsible for those sections in the history that are in the style of Deuteronomy.

In addition to these named sources, we must assume that the Chronicler had access to temple records, lists, and genealogies, and that the information that he supplies about priests, Levites, and temple organization is not fictitious but drawn from documents that had been handed down in a similar way to the official annals.

IV. THE STANDPOINT OF THE CHRONICLER

The Chronicler intends his history to be supplementary to other records that already existed. His interests lie in the rise and fall of the Davidic monarchy, the Temple and its cultus, and the priests and Levites who served the Temple. The human stories of David's family troubles are omitted, but much is said of David's arrangements for the cultus, following on the laws of Moses in the so-called priestly code. An ecclesiastical historian naturally includes much fresh information that is omitted by historians writing from other points of view.

There are certain differences between statements in Chronicles and parallel statements in Samuel and Kings. In some places our text of Chronicles preserves a reading that has been corrupted in Samuel–Kings. Thus 1 Ch. xx. 5 is more likely to be correct concerning the death of the brother of Goliath than is 2 Sa. xxi. 19, which, as the commentaries show, contains two clear textual corruptions in addition. In other places the Chronicler draws on additional information. Thus the larger amount of money paid by David in 1 Ch. xxi. 25, as compared with 2 Sa. xxiv. 24, would represent the final amount that the temple records showed to have been paid for the whole temple site, as compared with the immediate sum paid for the threshing-floor and the oxen. There are some big variations in figures, but we know from similar variations in the LXX how difficult it was to transmit figures accurately in copying MSS. There is also room for further investigation of the significance of the consonants *'lp*, translated 'thousands', since they may in places indicate units of various sizes, or leaders of units. (See R. E. D. Clark, 'The Large Numbers of the Old Testament', *JTVI*, LXXXVII, 1955.) Some other points of difference will be noted under individual entries in the Dictionary, and may also be found in E. J. Young, *Introduction to the Old Testament*, 1949, pp. 381 ff. J.S.W.

CHRONOLOGY OF THE OLD TESTAMENT. The aim of such a chronology is to determine the correct dates of events and persons in the Old Testament as precisely as possible, that we may better understand their significance.

I. SOURCES AND METHODS OF CHRONOLOGY

a. Older method

Until about a century ago Old Testament dates were calculated almost entirely from the biblical statements (so Ussher). Two difficulties beset this approach. Firstly, the Old Testament does not provide all the details needed for this task, and some sequences of events may be concurrent rather than consecutive. Secondly, the ancient versions, *e.g.* the LXX, sometimes offer variant figures. Hence schemes of this kind are subject to much uncertainty.

b. Present methods

Modern scholars try to correlate data culled both from the Bible and from archaeological sources, in order to obtain absolute dates for the Hebrews and for their neighbours. From *c.* 620 BC, a framework is provided by the Canon of Ptolemy and other classical sources (*e.g.* Manetho, Berossus) which can be completed and corrected in detail from contemporary Babylonian tablets and Egyptian papyri, *etc.*, for the two great riverine states. The margin of error almost never exceeds a year, and in some cases is reduced to a week within a month, or even to nil.

Good dates from *c.* 1400 BC onwards are available, based on Mesopotamian data. The Assyrians each year appointed an official to be *limmu* or eponym, his name being given to his year of office. They kept lists of these names and often noted down events under each year, *e.g.* a king's accession or a campaign abroad. Thus, if any one year can be dated by our reckoning, the whole series is fixed. An eclipse of the sun in the year of the eponym Bur-Sagale is that of 15 June 763 BC, thus fixing a whole series of years and events from 892 to 648 BC, with material reaching back to 911 BC. Alongside these *limmu*-lists, king-lists giving names and reigns take Assyrian history back to nearly 2000 BC, with a maximum error of about a century then, which narrows to about a decade from *c.* 1400 BC until *c.* 1100 BC. Babylonian king-lists and 'synchronous histories' narrating contacts between Assyrian and Babylonian kings help to establish the history of the two kingdoms between *c.* 1400 BC and *c.* 800 BC. Finally, the scattered information from contemporary tablets and annals of various reigns provides first-hand evidence for some periods.

Good dates from *c.* 1200 BC back to *c.* 2100 BC can be obtained from Egyptian sources. These include king-lists, year-dates on contemporary monuments, cross-checks with Mesopotamia and elsewhere, and a few astronomical phenomena dated exactly in certain reigns. By this means, the XIth and XIIth Dynasties can be dated to *c.* 2134–1786 BC, and the XVIIIth to XXth Dynasties to *c.* 1570–1085 BC, each within a maximum error of some 4 to 10 years; the XIIIth to XVIIth Dynasties fit in between these two groups with a maximum error of about 15 or 20 years in their middle. Mesopotamian dates during 2000–1500 BC depend largely on the date assignable to Hammurabi of Babylon: at present it varies within the period 1850–1700 BC, the date 1792–1750 BC (S. Smith) being as good as any.

Between 3000 and 2000 BC all Near Eastern dates are subject to greater uncertainty, of up to two centuries, largely because they are inadequately linked to later dates. Before 3000 BC, all dates are reasoned estimates only, and are subject to several centuries' margin of error, increasing with distance in time. The 'Carbon-14' method of computing the dates of organic matter from antiquity is of most service for the period before 3000 BC, and such dates carry a margin of error of $\pm$ 250 years. Hence this method is of little use to biblical chronology; the possible sources of error in the method itself scientifically, and in contamination of dating-samples to be treated, require that 'Carbon-14' dates must still be treated with reserve.

Such a framework for Mesopotamia and Egypt helps to fix the dates of Palestinian discoveries and of events and people in the Bible; thus the story of the Heb. kingdoms affords cross-links with Assyria and Babylonia. The successive levels of human occupation discerned by archaeologists in the town-mounds ('tells') of ancient Palestine often contain datable objects which link a series of such levels to corresponding dates in Egyptian history down to the 12th century BC. Thereafter, the changes of occupation can sometimes be linked directly with Israelite history, as at Samaria, Hazor, and Lachish (see ARCHAEOLOGY). Israelite dates can be fixed within a margin of error of about 10 years in Solomon's day, narrowing to almost nil by the time of the fall of Jerusalem. The margins of error alluded to arise from slight differences in names or figures in parallel king-lists, actual breakage in such lists, reigns of yet unknown duration, and the limitations of certain astronomical data. They can be eliminated only by future discovery of more detailed data.

Further complications in chronology stem from the different modes of calendaric reckoning used by the ancients in counting the regnal years of their monarchs. By the accession-year system, that part of a civil year elapsing between a king's accession and the next New Year's day was reckoned not as his first year, but as an 'accession-year' (that year being credited to the previous ruler), and his first regnal year was counted from the first New Year's day. But by the non-accession-year system of reckoning, that part of the civil year between a king's accession and the next New Year's day was credited to him as his first regnal 'year', his second being counted from the first New Year's day. The type of reckoning used, by whom, of whom, and when, is especially important for right understanding of the chronological data in Kings and Chronicles.

II. PRIMEVAL ANTIQUITY BEFORE ABRAHAM

The creation is sufficiently dated by that immortal phrase, 'in the beginning . . .', so distant is it. The period from Adam to Abraham is spanned by genealogies in the midst of which occurs the flood. However, attempts to use this information to obtain dates for the period from Adam to Abraham are hindered by lack of certainty over the right interpretation. A literal Western interpretation of the figures as they stand yields too low a date for events recorded, *e.g.* the flood. Thus, if, for example, Abraham's birth be set at about 2000 BC (the earliest likely period), the figures in Gn. xi. 10–26 would then yield a date for the flood just after 2300 BC—a date so late that it would fall some centuries *after* Sir Leonard Woolley's flood-level at Ur, itself of too late a date to be the flood of either the Heb. or Bab. records. Similar difficulties arise if Adam's date be further calculated in this way from Gn. v on the same basis.

Hence an attempted interpretation must be sought along other lines. Ancient Near Eastern documents must be understood in the first place as their writers and readers understood them. In the case of genealogies, this involves the possibility of abbreviation by omission of some names in a series. The main object of the genealogies in Gn. v and xi is apparently not so much to provide a full chronology as to supply a link from earliest man to the great crisis of the flood and then from the flood down through the line of Shem to Abraham, forefather of the Hebrew nation. The abbreviation of a genealogy by omission does not affect its value ideologically as a link, as could be readily demonstrated from analogous Ancient Near Eastern sources. Hence genealogies, including those of Gn. v and xi, must always be used with great restraint whenever it appears that they are open to more than one interpretation. See GENEALOGY, GENERATION.

III. DATES BEFORE THE MONARCHY

a. The Patriarchs

Three lines of approach can be used for dating the Patriarchs: mention of external events in their time, statements of time elapsed between their day and some later point in history, and the evidence of period discernible in the social conditions in which they lived.

The only two striking external events recorded are the raid of the four kings against five in Gn. xiv (see AMRAPHEL, ARIOCH, CHEDORLAOMER) and the destruction of the cities of the plain in Gn. xix (see PLAIN, CITIES OF THE), both falling in Abraham's lifetime.

None of the kings in Gn. xiv has yet been safely identified with a particular individual in the second millennium BC, but the names can be identified with known names of that general period, especially 1900 to 1500 BC. Power-alliances formed by rival groups of kings in Mesopotamia and Syria are particularly typical of the period 2000–1700 BC: a famous letter from Mari on the middle Euphrates says of this period, 'there is no king who of himself is the strongest: ten or fifteen kings follow Hammurabi of Babylon, the same number follow Rim-Sin of Larsa, the same number follow Ibal-pi-El of Eshnunna, the same number follow Amut-pi-El of Qatna, and twenty kings follow Yarim-Lim of Yamkhad.' In this period also, Elam was one of several prominent kingdoms.

Glueck has endeavoured to date the campaign of Gn. xiv from its supposed archaeological results: he claims that the line of city-settlements along the later 'King's Highway' was clearly occupied at the start of the second millennium (until the 19th century BC, on modern dating), but that soon thereafter the area suddenly ceased to be occupied, except for roving nomads, until about 1300 BC, when the Iron Age kingdoms of Edom, Moab, and Ammon were effectually founded.

Similar reasoning has been applied to the date of the fall of the cities of the plain; although their actual remains appear now to be beyond recovery (probably being under the Dead Sea), an open-air shrine on the plateau above apparently shows a history paralleled by that of the Highway cities, its use ceasing about the 19th century BC.

This picture of an occupational gap between the 19th and 13th centuries BC has been criticized by Lankester Harding in the light of certain recent finds in Transjordan, including Middle Bronze tombs and an important Middle and Late

Bronze temple. However, the views of neither Glueck nor Harding need be pressed to extremes; in all probability the view of a reduced density of population between the 19th and 13th centuries is true generally and of the Highway cities in particular, while at certain isolated points occupation may have been continuous.

Two main statements link the day of the Patriarchs with later times. In Gn. xv. 13–16 Abraham is forewarned that his descendants will dwell in a land not theirs for some four centuries. The 'fourth generation' of verse 16 is difficult; if a 'generation' be equated with a century (*cf.* Ex. vi. 16–20), this usage would be unique. A possible but dubious alternative is to see in verse 16 a prophetic allusion to Joseph's journey to Canaan to bury Jacob (Joseph being in the 'fourth generation' if Abraham is the first). The entry of Jacob into Egypt (Gn. xlvi. 6, 7) was the starting-point of the general four centuries of Gn. xv. 13 as well as of the more specific 430 years of Ex. xii. 40. The Hebrew *MT* form of Ex. xii. 40, giving Israel 430 years in Egypt, is to be preferred to the LXX variant, which makes the 430 years cover the sojournings in both Canaan and Egypt, because Ex. xii. 41 clearly implies that the 'selfsame day', after 430 years, on which Israel went forth from Egypt was the anniversary of that distant day when the Patriarch Israel and his family had entered Egypt. Hence an interval of 430 years from Jacob's entry till Moses and Israel's departure seems assured. The genealogy of Ex. vi. 16–20, which can hardly cover the 430 years if taken 'literally' Westernwise, is open to the same possibility of selectivity as those of Gn. v and xi, and so need raise no essential difficulty. Three points are worthy of reflection. First, although Moses is apparently in the fourth generation from the Patriarch Jacob through Levi, Kohath, and Amram (Ex. vi. 20; 1 Ch. vi. 1–3), yet Moses' contemporary Bezaleel is in the seventh generation from Jacob through Judah, Perez, Hezron, Caleb, Hur, and Uri (1 Ch. ii. 18–20), and his younger contemporary Joshua is in the twelfth generation from Jacob through Joseph, Ephraim, Beriah, Rephah, Resheph, Telah, Tahan, Laadan, Ammihud, Elishama, and Nun (1 Ch. vii. 23–27). Hence there is a possibility that Moses' genealogy is abbreviated by comparison with those of Joshua and even Bezaleel. Secondly, Moses' 'father' Amram and his brothers gave rise to the clans of Amramites, Izharites, *etc.*, who already numbered 8,600 male members alone within a year of the Exodus (Nu. iii. 27, 28), an unlikely situation unless Amram and his brothers themselves flourished distinctly earlier than Moses. Thirdly, the wording that by Amram Jochebed 'bare' Moses, Aaron, and Miriam (Ex. vi. 20; Nu. xxvi. 59), like 'begat' in Gn. v and xi, need not imply immediate parenthood but also simply descent. Compare Gn. xlvi. 18, where the preceding verses show that great-grandsons of Zilpah are included among 'these she bare unto Jacob'. On these three points, see also J. D. Davis, ed. H. S. Gehman, *The Westminster Dictionary of the Bible*, 1944, p. 153. For the date of the Exodus occurring on independent grounds 430 years after a late-18th-century date for Jacob, see below.

The social conditions reflected in the patriarchal narratives afford no close dating, but fit in with the general date obtainable from Gn. xiv and xix and from the use of the 430-year figure to the Exodus. Thus the social customs of adoption and inheritance in Gn. xv, xvi, xxi, *etc.*, show close affinity with those observable in cuneiform documents from Ur and Nuzi, ranging in date from the 18th to 15th centuries BC.

The great freedom to travel long distances—witness Abraham's path including Ur and Egypt—is prominent in this general age: compare envoys from Babylon passing Mari to and from Hazor in Palestine. For power-alliances at this time, see above. In the 20th and 19th centuries BC in particular, the Negeb ('the South') of the later Judaea supported seasonal occupation, as illustrated by Abraham's periodic journeys into 'the South'. The general result, bearing in mind the traditional figures for the lives, births, and deaths of the Patriarchs, is to put Abraham at about 2000–1850, Isaac about 1900–1750, Jacob about 1800–1700, and Joseph about 1750–1650; these dates are deliberately given as round figures to allow for any later adjustment. They suit the limited but suggestive archaeological evidence, as well as a plausible interpretation of the biblical data.

A date for the entry of Jacob and his family into Egypt at roughly 1700 BC would put this event and Joseph's ministry in the Hyksos period of Egyptian history, during which rulers of Semitic stock posed as pharaohs of Egypt; the peculiar blend of Egyptian and Semitic elements in Gn. xxxvii. 1 would agree with this (see JOSEPH).

b. The Exodus and Conquest

(For alternative Egyptian dates in this section, see the Chronological Tables.) The next contact between Israel and her neighbours occurs in Ex. i. 11, when the Hebrews were building the cities Pithom and Ra'amses in Moses' time. Ra'amses was Egypt's Delta capital named after, and largely built by, Rameses II (*c.* 1290–1224 BC) superseding the work of his father Sethos I (*c.* 1302–1290 BC); this is true of both Tanis and Qantir, the likeliest sites for Ra'amses. Rameses I (*c.* 1303–1302 BC) reigned for just over a year, and so does not come into consideration. Before Sethos I and Rameses II, no pharaoh had built a Delta capital since the Hyksos period (Joseph's day); the city Ra'amses is thus truly an original work of these two kings, and not merely renamed or appropriated by them from some earlier ruler, as is sometimes suggested. Hence, on this bit of evidence, the Exodus must fall after 1300 BC and preferably after 1290 BC (accession of Rameses II). A lower limit for the date of the Exodus is probably indicated by the so-called Israel Stele, a triumphal inscription of Merenptah dated to his 5th year (*c.* 1220 BC), which mentions the defeat of various cities and peoples in Palestine, including Israel. Some deny that Merenptah ever invaded Palestine; for Drioton, *La Bible et l'Orient*, 1955, pp. 43–46, the Palestinian peoples were merely overawed by Merenptah's great victory in Libya, which his stele principally commemorates; and the mention of Israel would be an allusion to the Hebrews disappearing into the wilderness to, as the Egyptians would think, certain death. See further, C. de Wit, *The Date and Route of the Exodus*, 1960. The Exodus would then fall in the first five years of Merenptah (*c.* 1224–1220 BC). However, this view is open to certain objections. An inscription of Merenptah in a temple at Amada in Nubia in strictly parallel clauses names him as 'Binder of Gezer' and 'Seizer of Libya'. 'Seizer of Libya' refers beyond all doubt to Merenptah's great Libyan victory in his 5th year, recounted at length in the Israel Stele. Hence the very specific, strictly parallel, title 'Binder of Gezer' must refer to successful intervention by Merenptah in Palestine, even if of limited scope. With this would agree the plain meaning of the Israel Stele's references to Ascalon, Gezer, Yenoam, Israel, and Khuru as 'conquered', 'bound', 'annihilated', 'her crops are not', and 'widowed' respectively. Then, the reference to 'Israel, her crops (= lit. 'seed') are not' may reflect the Egyptians' practice of sometimes burning the growing crops of their foes—applicable to Israel beginning to settle in Palestine, but *not* to Israel going forth into the wilderness. Hence, on the likelier interpretation of the Israel Stele here upheld, Israel must have entered Palestine before 1220 BC, and the Exodus 40 years earlier would therefore fall before 1260 BC. The probable date of the Exodus is thus narrowed down to the period 1290–1260 BC. A good average date for the Exodus and wanderings would thus be roughly the period 1280–1240 BC. For views which postulate more than one Exodus, or that some tribes never entered Egypt, there is not a scrap of objective external evidence, and the biblical traditions are clearly against such suggestions.

The figure of 40 years for the wilderness travels of the Hebrews is often too easily dismissed as a round figure which might mean anything. This particular 40-year period is to be taken seriously as it stands, on the following evidence. Israel took a year and a fraction in going from Ra'amses to Kadesh-barnea (they left Ra'amses on the 15th day of the 'first month', Nu. xxxiii. 3) leaving Mt. Sinai on the 20th day of the second month of the second year, Nu. x. 11. To this period, add at least: 3 days, Nu. x. 33; perhaps a further month, Nu. xi. 21; and 7 days, Nu. xii. 15; total, one year and 2½ months' travel; then the subsequent 38 years from Kadesh-barnea to crossing the brook Zered (Dt. ii. 14 and Nu. xxi. 12), Moses addressing Israel in the plains of Moab in the eleventh month of the 40th year (Dt. i. 3). The function of the 40 years in replacing one generation (rebellious) by another is clearly stated in Dt. ii. 14.

The statement that Hebron was founded 7 years before Zoan in Egypt (Nu. xiii. 22) is sometimes linked with the contemporary Era of Tanis (Zoan) in Egypt, covering 400 years from approximately 1720/1700 to about 1320/1300 BC. This Era would then run parallel to the 430 years of Hebrew tradition. This idea, however, is interesting rather than convincing.

The Palestinian evidence agrees in general terms with the Egyptian data. Even allowing for some settlements flourishing earlier (*e.g.* Lankester Harding's temple site at Amman), intensive occupation of the Iron Age kingdoms of Edom and Moab ringed by powerful border forts or blockhouses dates principally from about 1300 BC onwards. Hence these kingdoms could hardly have effectively opposed Israel (as in Nu. xx) before *c.* 1300 BC. Thus again the Exodus is better dated after 1300 BC than before it.

Various Palestinian city-sites show evidence of clear destruction in the second half of the 13th century BC, which would agree with the onset of the Israelites placed at roughly 1240 BC onward. Such sites are Tell Beit Mirsim (possibly biblical Debir/Kiriath-sepher), Lachish, Bethel, and Hazor. Two sites only have given rise to controversy: Jericho and Ai.

At Jericho the broad truth seems to be that Joshua and Israel did their work so well that Jericho's ruins lay open to the ravages of nature and of man for five centuries until Ahab's day (*cf.* 1 Ki. xvi. 34), so that the Late Bronze Age levels, lying uppermost, were almost entirely denuded, even earlier levels being distinctly affected. Thus on some parts of the mound the uppermost levels that remain date as far back as the Early Bronze Age (third millennium BC), but the evidence from other parts and the tombs demonstrates clearly the existence of a large Middle Bronze Age settlement subsequently much denuded by erosion. The exceedingly scanty relics of Late Bronze Age Jericho (*i.e.* of Joshua's age) are so few simply because they were exposed to erosion for an even longer period, from Joshua until Ahab's reign; and any areas not occupied by the Iron Age settlement of Ahab's time and after have been subject to erosion right down to the present day. Hence the nearly total loss of Late Bronze Jericho of the 14th century BC and the likelihood of the total loss of any settlement of the 13th century BC.

The walls attributed to the Late Bronze Age by Garstang prove, on fuller examination, to belong to the Early Bronze Age, *c.* 2300 BC, and so cease to be relevant to Joshua's victory. The apparent cessation of Egyptian kings' scarabs at Jericho with those of Amenophis III (died *c.* 1353 BC) does not of itself prove that Jericho fell then, but merely witnesses to the temporary eclipse of direct Egyptian influence in Palestine in the time of that king and his immediate successors, known also from other sources. Of Mycenaean pottery (commonly imported into Syria–Palestine in the 14th and 13th centuries BC), a paucity at Jericho likewise does not prove that Jericho fell earlier in the 14th century rather than well on in the 13th. The fact has been overlooked hitherto that these imported vessels are sometimes very rare on inland Syro-Palestinian sites at the same time as they are common in other settlements at, or readily accessible from, the coast. Thus the equally inland town of Hama in Syria is known to have been occupied during the 13th century BC, but it yielded only two late Mycenaean potsherds—which is less than even the few from Jericho; for Hama, see G. Hanfmann, review of P. J. Riis, 'Hama II', pt. III, in *JNES*, XII, 1953, pp. 206–207. The net result of all this is that a 13th-century Israelite conquest of Jericho cannot be formally proven on the present archaeological evidence, but neither is it precluded thereby (see also JERICHO).

Ai presents a problem demanding further field-research; the parts of the mound of Et-Tell so far excavated ceased to be occupied about 2300 BC. The answer may be that a Late Bronze settlement is still to be located in the neighbourhood, but certainty is at present unattainable (see AI).

The Habiru/Apiru, known from the Tell el-Amarna tablets to have been active in Palestine about 1350 BC, are sometimes equated with the invading Israelites ('Hebrews') under Joshua. But 1350 BC is too early a date for the conquest, as already shown above. Further, the term Habiru/Apiru is applied to many other people besides the biblical Hebrews in documents ranging in date from 1800 to 1150 BC and in space as far afield as Mesopotamia, Egypt, Syria, and Asia Minor. The Israelites may well have been reckoned as Habiru/Apiru, but obviously they cannot be identified with any given group of these without additional evidence.

c. From Joshua until David's accession

This period presents a problem in detail which cannot be finally solved without more information. If the 40 years of the Exodus journeyings, the 40 years of David's reign, and the first three of Solomon's be subtracted from the total of 480 years from the Exodus to Solomon's 4th year (1 Ki. vi. 1) a figure of about 397 years is obtained for Joshua, the elders, the judges, and Saul. The archaeological evidence indicates roughly 1240 BC for the start of the conquest (see above), giving only some 230 years to 1010 BC, the probable date of David's accession. However, the actual total of recorded periods in Joshua, Judges, and Samuel amounts neither to 397 nor to 230 years, but to $470 + x + y + z$ years, where x stands for the time of Joshua and the elders, y for the number of years beyond 20 that Samuel was judge, and z for the reign of Saul, all unknown figures. But the main outline of the problem need not be difficult to handle in principle, if viewed against the background of normal Ancient Oriental modes of reckoning, which alone are relevant. It is nowhere explicitly stated that either the 397 years obtained from using 1 Ki. vi. 1 or the 470 plus unknown years of Joshua–Samuel must all be reckoned consecutively, nor need this be assumed. Certain groups of judges and oppressions are clearly stated to be successive ('and after him . . .'), but this is not said of all: at least three main groups can be partly contemporary. So between the evidently consecutive 230 years obtained archaeologically and the possibly partly-concurrent 470-plus-unknown years recorded, the difference of some 240-plus-unknown years can readily be absorbed. The 397 years in turn would then be simply a selection on some principle not yet clear (such as omission of oppressions or something similar) from the greater number of the 470-plus-unknown total years available.

In Near Eastern works involving chronology, it is important to realize that ancient scribes did not draw up synchronistic lists as is done today. They simply listed each series of rulers and reigns separately, in succession on the papyrus or tablet. Synchronisms were to be derived from special historiographical works, not the king-lists or narratives serving other purposes. An excellent example of this is the Turin Papyrus of Kings from Egypt. It lists at great length all five Dynasties XIII to XVII in successive groups, totalling originally over 150 rulers and their reigns accounting for at least 450 years. However, it is known from other sources that all five Dynasties, the 150-odd rulers and 450-odd regnal years alike, must all fit inside the 216 years from *c.* 1786 to *c.* 1570 BC: rarely less than two series, and sometimes three series, of rulers are known to have reigned contemporaneously. The lack of cross-references between contemporaries (*e.g.* among the judges) is paralleled by similar lack of such references for most of the period of Egyptian history just cited.

A similar situation can be discerned in the king-lists and history of the Sumerian and Old Babylonian city-states of Mesopotamia. Hence, there is no reason why such methods should not apply in a work like the book of Judges. It must be stressed that in no case, biblical or extra-biblical, is it a question of inaccuracy, but of the methods current in antiquity. All the figures may be correct in themselves—it is their interpretation which needs care. Selective use of data by omission, as suggested above for the origin of the 397 (of 480) years is known from both Egyptian lists and Mesopotamian annals, as well as elsewhere. The biblical figures and archaeological data together begin to make sense when the relevant ancient practices are borne in mind; any final solution in detail requires much fuller information.

IV. THE HEBREW MONARCHIES

a. The United Monarchy

That David's reign actually lasted 40 years is shown by its being a compound figure: 7 years at Hebron, 33 at Jerusalem (1 Ki. ii. 11). Solomon's reign of 40 years began with a brief co-regency with his father of perhaps only a few months; *cf.* 1 Ki. i. 37–ii. 11; 1 Ch. xxviii. 5, xxix. 20–23, 26–28. As Solomon's reign appears to have ended *c.* 931/30 BC, he acceded *c.* 971/70 BC, and David at *c.* 1011/10 BC.

The reign of Saul can only be estimated, as something has happened in the Hebrew text of 1 Sa. xiii. 1; but the 40 years of Acts xiii. 21 must be about right, because Saul's fourth son, Ishbosheth, was not less than 35 years old at Saul's death (dying at 42, not more than 7 years later, 2 Sa. ii. 10). Hence if Jonathan the eldest was about 40 at death, Saul could not be much less than 60 at death. If he became king shortly after being anointed as a 'young man' (1 Sa. ix. 2, x. 1, 17 ff.), he probably would not be younger than 20 or much older than 30, so practically guaranteeing him a reign of 30 or 40 years. Thus if taken at a middle figure of about 25 years old at accession with a reign of at least 35 years, the biological data suit, and likewise Acts xiii. 21 as a figure either round or exact. Saul's accession is thus perhaps not far removed from about 1045 or 1050 BC.

b. The Divided Monarchy

(i) *To the fall of Samaria.* From comparison of the Assyrian *limmu* or eponym lists, king-lists and historical texts, the date 853 BC can be fixed for the battle of Qarqar, the death of Ahab and accession of Ahaziah in Israel; and likewise Jehu's accession at Joram's death in 841 BC. The intervening reigns of Ahaziah and Joram exactly fill this interval if reckoned according to the customary methods of regnal counting. Similar careful reckoning by ancient methods gives complete harmony of figures for the reigns of both kingdoms back to the accessions of Rehoboam in Judah and Jeroboam in Israel in the year 931/30 BC. Hence the dates given above for the United Monarchy.

Likewise the dates of both sets of kings can be worked out down to the fall of Samaria not later than 722 BC. This has been clearly shown by E. R. Thiele, *Mysterious Numbers of the Hebrew Kings*, 1951. It is possible to demonstrate, as he has done, co-regencies between Asa and Jehoshaphat, Jehoshaphat and Jehoram, Amaziah and Azariah (Uzziah), Azariah and Jotham, and Jotham and Ahaz. However, Thiele's objections to the synchronisms of 2 Ki. xvii. 1 (12th year of Ahaz equated with accession of Hoshea in Israel), 2 Ki. xviii. 1 (3rd year of Hoshea with accession of Hezekiah of Judah), and 2 Ki. xviii. 9, 10 (equating Hezekiah's 4th and 6th years with Hoshea's 7th and 9th), are invalid. Thiele took these for years of sole reign, 12/13 years in error. However, the truth appears to be that in fact these four references simply continue the system of co-regencies: Ahaz was co-regent with Jotham 12 years, and Hezekiah with Ahaz. This practice of co-regencies in Judah must have contributed notably to the stability of that kingdom; David and Solomon had thus set a valuable precedent.

(ii) *Judah to the fall of Jerusalem.* From Hezekiah's reign until that of Jehoiachin, dates can still be worked out to the year, culminating in that of the Babylonian capture of Jerusalem in 597 BC, precisely dated to 15/16 March (second of Adar) 597 by the recently published Babylonian chronicle tablets covering this period. But from this point to the final fall of Jerusalem, some uncertainty reigns over the precise mode of reckoning of the Hebrew civil year and of the various regnal years of Zedekiah and Nebuchadrezzar in 2 Kings and Jeremiah. Consequently two different dates are current for the fall of Jerusalem: 587 and 586 BC. The date 587 is here preferred, with Wiseman and Albright (against Thiele for 586).

V. THE EXILE AND AFTER

Most of the dates in the reigns of Babylonian and Persian kings mentioned in biblical passages dealing with this period can be determined accurately. For over half a century, opinions have been divided over the relative order of Ezra and Nehemiah at Jerusalem. The biblical order of events which makes Ezra reach Jerusalem in 458 BC and Nehemiah arrive there in 445 is perfectly consistent under close scrutiny (*cf.* Stafford Wright). See EZRA, NEHEMIAH.

The Inter-Testamental period is reasonably clear; for the main dates, see the chronological table.

BIBLIOGRAPHY. *Near Eastern chronology*: T. Jacobsen, *The Sumerian King List*, 1939—deals with the early Mesopotamian rulers; R. A. Parker and W. H. Dubberstein, *Babylonian Chronology 626 BC–AD 75*, 1956—full dates for Babylonian, Persian, and later kings for 626 BC–AD 75, and tables to work out day and month dates in much of that period; A. Parrot, *Archéologie Mésopotamienne*, II, 1953—Pt. Two: II deals with Hammurabi and related problems, and discusses the Assyrian king-lists; Vol. III will contain full chronological outlines (not yet published); S. Smith, *Alalakh and Chronology*, 1940—deals with Hammurabi and critical use of Assyro-Babylonian king-lists; E. R. Thiele, *Mysterious Numbers of the Hebrew Kings*, 1951—full discussion of dates of the Divided Monarchy (slightly corrected above), with outline of basic chronological sources and study of Hebrew-Assyrian contacts; for additions to Israelite dates and corrections to Thiele, see K. A. Kitchen, *Hittite Hieroglyphs, Aramaeans and Hebrew Traditions* (forthcoming); A. Ungnad, *Eponymen* in E. Ebeling and B. Meissner, *Reallexikon der Assyriologie*, II, 1938, pp. 412–457—full statement and texts of the Assyrian eponym-lists.

Egypt: É. Drioton and J. Vandier, *L'Égypte* (Coll. *Clio*, I: 2), 1952—standard source of reference for Egyptian history and chronology; Sir A. H. Gardiner, in *JEA*, XXXI, 1945, pp. 11–28—Egyptian regnal and civil years; R. A. Parker, *The Calendars of Ancient Egypt*, 1950—standard work; R. A. Parker in *JNES*, XVI,

CHRONOLOGICAL OUTLINE: OLD TESTAMENT

Special Note.
All dates are best taken as '*about* BC', as the possible variation can run to a century or more in 2000 BC, down to a decade by 1000 BC. Most of the dates for the Hebrew monarchies are quoted in double form, *e.g.* Asa, 911/10–870/69 BC, and Baasha, 909/8–886/5 BC, because the Hebrew year does not coincide with the January to December of our civil year. Apparent variations from biblical lengths of reign are not real but stem from the kinds of regnal-year reckoning then in use.

For other Near Eastern rulers, space and scope forbid any attempt to set forth here the vast amount of documentation and reasoning which underlie the dates given in the subjoined tables. From *c.* 900 BC onward, Assyrian, Babylonian, and Persian dates are nearly all very closely fixed. Dates for Aramaean kings, *e.g.* of Zobah and Damascus, are approximations based on the Old Testament and Assyr. references and rare inscriptions from Syria itself. Dates for the Phoenicians Hiram I and Ethbaal I (father of Jezebel) are based on synchronisms and regnal years derived from the Old Testament references and Josephus, *Against Apion*, i. 116–126.

The two sets of dates given for later XVIIIth and the XIXth Dynasties of Egypt depend on the two possible dates offered by lunar data for the accession of Rameses II, *i.e.* 1304 and 1290 BC. At present neither Egyptian nor related Near Eastern data are sufficiently free of gaps and uncertainties to enable a final choice to be made between these two possible dates.

EGYPT	OLD TESTAMENT	PALESTINIAN ARCHAEOLOGY	MESOPOTAMIA
Middle Kingdom			
2134–1991: XIth Dynasty	Before 2000: Events of Gn. i–xi	2200–1950: Intermediate Bronze Age	? 1894–1595: Ist Dynasty of Babylon
1991–1786: XIIth Dynasty		1950–1550: Middle Bronze Age	? 1792–1750: Hammurabi
1710?–1570: Hyksos rule in Egypt	2000–1850: Abraham*		
	1900–1750: Isaac*		
	1800–1700: Jacob*		
	1750–1650: Joseph*		
New Kingdom (Empire)			
1570–1303 (or –1319): XVIIIth Dynasty, incl.:		1550–1400: Late Bronze Age I	
1490–1437: Tuthmosis III (or 1515–1462)			
1390–1353: Amenophis III (or 1405–1368)	Israel in Egypt	1400–1300: Late Bronze Age IIa	
1361–1345: Amenophis IV/ Akhenaten (or 1376–1360)			
1303–1200? (or 1319–1214?): XIXth Dynasty, incl.:		1300–1200: Late Bronze Age IIb	
1303–1302: Rameses I (or 1319–1318)			
1302–1290: Sethos I (or 1318–1304)			

* Only round figures given to indicate *general* date.

EGYPT	OLD TESTAMENT	PALESTINIAN ARCHAEOLOGY		MESOPOTAMIA
New Kingdom (Empire) 1290–1224: Rameses II (or 1304–1238) 1224–1215: Merenptah (or 1238–1229) 1220: 'Israel Stele' (or 1234) 1200?–1193?: Interregnum (or 1214?–1193?) 1193?–1085: XXth Dynasty, *i.e.* Setnakht and Rameses III–XI	1280 (approx.): The Exodus 1240 (approx.): Israel crosses the Jordan 1220?–1050/45?: Period of the judges 1125?: Deborah and Barak 1115?–1075?: Eli's judgeship 1075?–1035?: Samuel, judge and prophet	1200–970: Iron Age I		
EGYPT	**UNITED MONARCHY**	**ARAM (and PHOENICIA)**		
Late Period 1085–945: XXIst Dynasty, incl.: Psusennes I Amenemope Siamūn Psusennes II 945–716: XXIInd Dynasty, incl.: 945–924: Sheshonq I (Shishak)	1050/45?–1011/10: Saul 1011/10–971/70 David 971/70–931/30: Solomon	? 990–965: Hadad/r-ezer of Zobah. *c.* 980: Toi of Hamath (979/78–945/44: Hiram I of Tyre) 970–580: Iron Age II		
EGYPT	**JUDAH**	**ISRAEL**	**DAMASCUS (and TYRE)**	**ASSYRIA**
924–889: Osorkon I 889–867: Takeloth I	931/30–913: Rehoboam 925: Sheshonq I's (Shishak) invasion of Palestine 913–911/10: Abijam 911/10–870/69: Asa	931/30–910/09: Jeroboam I 910/09–909/08: Nadab 909/08–886/85: Baasha 886/85–885/84: Elah 885/84: Zimri 885/84–880: Tibni	? 955–925: Rezon ? 925–915: Hezion ? 915–900: Tabrimmon ? 900–860?: Ben-hadad I, son of Tabrimmon 898/97–866/65: Ethbaal I of Tyre	

EGYPT	JUDAH	ISRAEL	DAMASCUS (and TYRE)	ASSYRIA
		885/84–874/73: Omri		883–859: Ashurnasirpal II
867–839: Osorkon II	870/69–848: Jehoshaphat (Co-regent from 873/72)	874/73–853: Ahab	**Either** ? 860–843: Ben-hadad II, Assyrian Hadadidri, contemporary of Ahab	859–824: Shalmaneser III 853: Battle of Qarqar
	848–841: Jehoram (Co-regent from 853)	853–852: Ahaziah 852–841: Joram	**or:** ? 900–843: Ben-hadad I, son of Tabrimmon, Assyrian Hadadidri, contemporary of Ahab 843–796: Hazael	
763–727: Sheshonq IV	841–835: Athaliah 835–796: Joash 796–767: Amaziah 767–740/39: Azariah (Uzziah) (Co-regent from 791/90)	841–814/13: Jehu 814/13–798: Jehoahaz 798–782/81: Jehoash 782/81–753: Jeroboam II (Co-regent from 793/92) 753–752: Zachariah 752: Shallum 752–742/41: Menahem 742/41–740/39: Pekahiah	796–770: Ben-hadad III/II ? 770–750: Dominance of Jeroboam II of Israel ? 750–732: Rezin	745–727: Tiglath-pileser III
	740/39–732/31: Jotham (Co-regent from 750) 732/31–716/15: Ahaz (Co-regent from 744/43; senior partner from 735)	740/39–732/31: Pekah (Counted his years from 752) 732/31–723/22: Hoshea	732: Fall of Damascus to Tiglath-pileser III	
727?–716: Osorkon IV 715–664: XXVth Dynasty 715–702: Shabako ('Shabaka') 702–690: Shebitku ('Shabataka') 690–664: Taharqa ('Tirhakah') 664–657: Tanwetamani ('Tanutamen') 664–525: XXVIth Dynasty 664–610: Psammetichus I 610–595: Necho II	716/15–687/86: Hezekiah (Co-regent from 729) 687/86–642/41: Manasseh (Co-regent from 696/95) 642/41–640/39: Amon 640/39–609: Josiah 609: Jehoahaz	722: Fall of Samaria		727–722: Shalmaneser V 722–705: Sargon II 705–681: Sennacherib 681–669: Esarhaddon 669–627: Ashurbanipal 612: Fall of Nineveh 609/08: End of Assyria
				BABYLON
605	609–597: Jehoiakim 605: Battle of Carchemish: Daniel and his friends are taken to Babylon			626–605: Nabopolassar 605–562: Nebuchadrezzar II

EGYPT	JUDAH	ASSYRIA
595–589: Psammetichus II 589–570: Apries (Hophra) 570–525: Amasis (Ahmose II)	597: Jehoiachin 597: 2 Adar (15/16 March), Jerusalem taken by Nebuchadrezzar II. Many Jews exiled, including Jehoiachin and Ezekiel 597–587: Zedekiah 587: Fall of Jerusalem. More Jews into exile (550–330: Iron Age III)	595–570: Ration-tablets of Jehoiachin at Babylon, 10th to 35th years of Nebuchadrezzar II 562–560: Amēl-Marduk (Evil-Merodach) 562: Captive Jehoiachin favoured by Amēl-Marduk 560–556: Neriglissar 556: Labashi-Marduk 556–539: Nabonidus. (Belshazzar usually acting in Babylon) 539: Fall of Babylon

THE JEWS	PERSIAN EMPIRE
538: Zerubbabel, Sheshbazzar and others return to Jerusalem 537: Rebuilding of the Temple begun	539–530: Cyrus
	530–522: Cambyses 522–486: Darius I
520: Temple-rebuilding resumed 516: Temple completed, 3 Adar (10 March)	
	486–465/64: Xerxes I (Ahasuerus)
458: Ezra goes to Jerusalem 445–433: Nehemiah at Jerusalem	464–423: Artaxerxes I
	423–404: Darius II Nothus 404–359: Artaxerxes II Mnemon 359/58–338/37: Artaxerxes III Ochus 338/37–336/35: Arses 336/35–331: Darius III Codomannus 331–323: Alexander of Macedon

THE INTERTESTAMENTAL PERIOD

EGYPT	SYRIA
323/04–285: Ptolemy I Soter 320: Judaea annexed by Ptolemy I 285–247: Ptolemy II Philadelphus 247–222: Ptolemy III Euergetes 222–205: Ptolemy IV Philopator 205–182: Ptolemy V Epiphanes 198: Palestine passes from Egyptian to Syrian rule till 63 BC	312–281: Seleucus I Nicator 281–261: Antiochus I Soter 261–246: Antiochus II Theos 246–226/25: Seleucus II 226/25–223: Seleucus III Soter 223–187: Antiochus III the Great
JUDAEA	
167–40: Maccabees/Hasmoneans in Judaea 167: Mattathias inspires revolt at Modin 166–161: Judas Maccabaeus 160–143: Jonathan Maccabaeus 143–135: Simon Maccabaeus 135–104: John Hyrcanus I 104/03: Aristobulus I 103–76: Alexander Jannaeus 76–67: Queen Salome Alexandra and Hyrcanus II 67–40: Hyrcanus II and Aristobulus II 63: Pompey establishes Roman protectorate 40: Herod appointed king of Judaea by Rome 37–4: Herod 150 BC–AD 70: General period of the Dead Sea scrolls	187–175: Seleucus IV 175–163: Antiochus IV Epiphanes 163–162: Antiochus V 162–150: Demetrius I 139/38–129: Antiochus VII Sidetes

1957, pp. 39–43—on dates of Tuthmosis III, Dynasty XVIII and Rameses II, Dynasty XIX; W. G. Waddell, *Manetho*, 1948—standard work; R. J. Williams, in *DOTT*, pp. 137–141—gives the Israel Stele.

Palestine: W. F. Albright, *Archaeology of Palestine*, 1956—a very convenient outline of its subject; N. Glueck, *Rivers in the Desert*, 1959—a popular summary of his work on 20th century BC seasonal occupation of the Negeb, continuing his reports in *BASOR*, Nos. 131, 137, 138, 142, 145, 149, 150, 152, and 155; N. Glueck, *The Other Side of the Jordan*, 1940—on the question of Middle Bronze and Iron Age settlements in Transjordan, concerning the dates of Abraham and the Exodus; G. L. Harding in *PEQ*, XC, 1958, pp. 10–12—against Glueck on Transjordanian settlement; H. H. Rowley, 'The Chronological Order of Ezra and Nehemiah', in *The Servant of the Lord and Other Essays on the Old Testament*, 1952, pp. 129 ff.; J. S. Wright, *The Building of the Second Temple*, 1958—for the post-exilic dates; J. S. Wright, *The Date of Ezra's Coming to Jerusalem*[2], 1958.

The fall of Judah: D. J. Wiseman, *Chronicles of Chaldaean Kings (626–556 BC)*, 1956—fundamental for its period; compare the following: W. F. Albright in *BASOR*, 143, 1956, pp. 28–33; E. R. Thiele, *ibid.*, pp. 22–27; H. Tadmor, in *JNES*, XV, 1956, pp. 226–230.

K.A.K. and T.C.M.

CHRONOLOGY OF THE NEW TESTAMENT. The early Christians were little interested in chronology, and the scantiness of data in the New Testament writings and uncertainties as to the interpretation of most of the data which they do provide make New Testament chronology a thorny subject. It is, moreover, an unfinished subject, since light may yet arise from unexpected quarters. At present we can at most points merely weigh probabilities and say on which side the balance seems to be weighted.

I. CHRONOLOGY OF THE LIFE OF JESUS

a. His birth

The birth of Jesus took place before the death of Herod the Great (Mt. ii. 1; Lk. i. 5), therefore not later than 4 BC (Jos., *Ant.* xvii. 191, xiv. 389, 487).

According to Lk. ii. 1–7, Jesus was born at the time of an enrolment made when Quirinius was governor of Syria. Now Quirinius cannot have governed Syria until after his consulship in 12 BC, and there is no record in Josephus or the Roman historians of his having done so in the interval 11–4 BC. But he was governor of Syria in AD 6/7 and made then the enrolment of Judaea which occasioned the revolt of Judas the Galilaean (Jos., *Ant.* xviii. 1 ff.). This suggests that in Lk. ii. 2 the enrolment made at the time of Jesus' birth has been confused with this later and better known enrolment. It is possible, however, that Quirinius governed Syria from 11 BC to the coming of Titius as its governor in 9 BC (so, *e.g.*, Marsh, *Founding of the Roman Empire*, p. 246, n. 1), and that Augustus decided to make an enrolment after consultation with Herod when the latter visited him in 12 BC. Jesus' birth may thus have taken place in 11 BC. Attempts to determine its month and day have had no real results.

Halley's comet seen in 12 BC was a brilliant spectacle well fitted to be the harbinger of Him who was to be the Light of the world. But in antiquity comets were usually regarded as portents of evil. The Italian astronomer Argentieri's conclusion that this comet was the star of the Magi rests on two questionable assumptions, that Jesus was born on a Sunday and that he was born on 25 December.

Recognizing that the word translated 'star' in Mt. ii denotes only a single star, adherents of the well-known Saturn–Jupiter conjunction theory of the star of the Magi have separated into two schools, the one maintaining that *the* star of Israel was Saturn (so Gerhardt, *Das Stern des Messias*) and the other that it was Jupiter (so Voigt, *Die Geschichte Jesu und die Astrologie*). But it seems unlikely that a conjunction of these two planets would have signified to Eastern astrologers the birth of a king.

b. The commencement of His ministry

Between the birth of Jesus and the commencement of His ministry there was a period of 'about thirty years'. So Lk. iii. 23 as rendered in the RV. But the commencement referred to there may not be that of the ministry, and it is not known what amplitude the 'about' allows. The assertion, 'Thou art not yet fifty years old' (Jn. viii. 57), suggests that in the course of His ministry Jesus was in His forties, and according to Irenaeus there was a tradition to that effect among the Asian elders.

Jesus began His ministry after John the Baptist had begun his, therefore not earlier than the 15th year of the reign of Tiberius (Lk. iii. 1). For sound reasons the view that this year is reckoned from the time when Tiberius became co-regent with Augustus is now generally abandoned. Since Augustus died on 19 August 14, the second year of Tiberius' reign began on 1 October 14 in the Syrian calendar, on 1 Nisan 15 in the Jewish calendar. Consequently in Lk. iii. 1 the fifteenth year of his reign means either 27 (1 Oct.)–28, or 28 (1 Nisan)–29. The latter is the more likely, for here Luke appears to use a source derived from a Baptist circle, and in many early writings, pagan, Jewish, and Christian, Tiberius' 15th year comprises part of 29.

Lk. iii. 21 indicates that there was some time between the call of the Baptist and the baptism of Jesus, but its length cannot be determined. The baptism of Jesus was followed by the forty days in the wilderness, the call of the first disciples, the marriage in Cana, and a brief stay in Capernaum. After these happenings, which occupied at least two months, Jesus went to

Jerusalem for the first Passover of His ministry (Jn. ii. 13). Its date may appear to be given by the statement of the Jews, 'Forty and six years was this temple in building' (Jn. ii. 20), taken with the statement of Jos., *Ant*. xv. 380, that Herod in the eighteenth year of his reign (20/19 BC) 'undertook to build' this Temple. But he assembled much material before building commenced, and the time thus spent may not be included in the forty-six years. Moreover, the statement of the Jews implies perhaps that the building had already been completed some time before this Passover.

c. The end of His ministry

Jesus was crucified when Pontius Pilate was procurator of Judaea (all four Gospels, Tac., *Ann*. xv. 44, and possibly Jos., *Ant*. xviii. 63 f.), therefore in one of the years 26–36. Various attempts have been made to determine which of these is the most likely.

(i) From Lk. xiii. 1 and xxiii. 12 it may be inferred that Pilate had already been procurator for some time before the crucifixion, and therefore that it can hardly have taken place so early as 26 or 27.

(ii) In many early authorities the crucifixion is assigned to the consulship of the Gemini, *i.e.* to 29. But this dating was by no means accepted everywhere throughout the early Church; and there is no proof that, as some think, it embodies a reliable tradition. The writers who give it, of whom Tertullian is the earliest, belong mainly to the Latin West. The 25th of March, the month-date of the crucifixion given by Hippolytus, Tertullian, and many others, was a Friday in 29; but the crucifixion took place at the time of the Paschal full moon, and in 29 that moon was almost certainly in April.

(iii) When Pilate was procurator he offended the Jews by setting up a votive shield in the palace at Jerusalem. Herod Antipas took a leading part in furthering a request to Tiberius for its removal. This, some scholars maintain, explains the enmity referred to in Lk. xxiii. 12. Tiberius granted the request; and this, the same scholars maintain, he cannot have done so long as he was under the influence of his confidant Sejanus, an arch-enemy of the Jews. The crucifixion, it is concluded, must have taken place after the death of Sejanus in October 31, therefore not earlier than 32. But the enmity may equally well have been occasioned by the slaughter mentioned in Lk. xiii. 1 or by some dispute about which history is silent.

(iv) Keim, in his *Geschichte Jesu von Nazara*, E.T., Vol. II, pp. 379 ff., determines 'the great year in the world's history' in dependence on the statement of Josephus (*Ant*. xviii. 116) that the defeat of Antipas by Aretas in 36 was considered by some to have come 'from God, and that very justly, as a punishment of what he did against John, that was called the Baptist'. The execution of John, Keim concludes, must have taken place but two years previously, in 34, and the crucifixion in 35. But punishment does not always follow hard on the heels of crime; and while the origin of the hostility between Antipas and Aretas may well have been the divorce by the former of the daughter of the latter, there are indications in Josephus that there was an interval between the divorce and the war of 36.

(v) Of attempts to determine the year of the crucifixion the most fruitful is that made with the help of astronomy. According to all four Gospels, the crucifixion took place on a Friday; but whereas in the Synoptics that Friday is 15 Nisan, in John it is 14 Nisan. The problem then that has to be solved with the help of astronomy is that of determining in which of the years 26–36 the 14th and 15th Nisan fell on a Friday. But since in New Testament times the Jewish month was lunar and the time of its commencement was determined by observation of the new moon, this problem is basically that of determining when the new moon became visible. Studying this problem, Fotheringham and Schoch have each arrived at a formula by applying which they find that 15 Nisan was a Friday only in 27 and 14 Nisan a Friday only in 30 and 33. Since as the year of the crucifixion 27 is out of the question, the choice lies between 30 (7 April) and 33 (3 April).

In the Synoptic chronology of passion week events are assigned to 15 Nisan which are unlikely on that day of holy convocation. The Johannine chronology of that week certainly seems to be in itself the more probable, and until at least the beginning of the 3rd century it appears to have been the more generally accepted throughout the Church. Attempts to reconcile the Gospels on this matter have not secured general consent, and discussion of the problem continues. But it is noteworthy that the calculations of the astronomers do not point to a year for the crucifixion that can on other grounds be accepted in which 14 Nisan was a Thursday.

d. The length of His ministry

To know the length of Jesus' ministry is more important than to know when it began or ended. There are three principal theories as to its length.

(i) *The one-year theory*. Its first supporters considered it a strong confirmation of it that Jesus had applied to Himself the Isaianic passage which foretells 'the acceptable year of the Lord' (Is. lxi. 2; Lk. iv. 19). The theory was widely accepted in the ante-Nicene period. Renewed interest in it dates from the 17th century. Among challenging presentations of it are those of van Bebber, *Zur Chronologie des Lebens Jesu*, 1898, and Belser in contributions to the *Biblische Zeitschrift*, I, 1903, II, 1904.

(ii) *The two-year theory*. Its supporters, of whom one of the earliest was Apollinaris of Laodicea, maintain that in the interval from Jesus' baptism to His crucifixion the only Passovers were the three explicitly mentioned in Jn. (ii. 13, vi. 4, xi. 55). Little, if at all, in favour in the Middle Ages, this theory now commands a large following.

(iii) *The three-year theory*. Its earliest known supporter was Melito of Sardis. But its wide acceptance in post-Nicene times and throughout the Middle Ages must be put down mainly to the influence of Eusebius. He rejected the literal interpretation of the word 'year' in the phrase 'the acceptable year of the Lord' and showed convincingly that only a ministry of fully three years satisfied the requirements of the Fourth Gospel. In our time this theory also commands a large following.

Because of the Passover of Jn. vi. 4, a verse that has excellent manuscript authority, the one-year theory must be rejected. That a decision may be made between the two- and the three-year theories, the interval between the Passovers of Jn. ii. 13 and vi. 4 must be carefully examined.

Since ordinarily there were six months between seedtime and harvest, the words 'There are yet four months, and then cometh harvest' (Jn. iv. 35) cannot be a proverbial saying, but must relate to the circumstances obtaining at the time when they were spoken. Jesus' return to Galilee mentioned in Jn. iv. 43 must then have taken place in winter. That the unnamed feast of Jn. v. 1 was Purim, as, following Kepler, many supporters of the two-year theory have maintained, is unlikely. Purim was observed in February/March, therefore soon after Jesus' return. But the words 'after these things' (Jn. v. 1, RV) indicate that there was a considerable interval between His return and His next visit to Jerusalem. The unnamed feast is more likely to have been the following Passover in March/April or the following Pentecost or Tabernacles. Certain supporters of the two-year theory, while agreeing that it was the following Passover, identify the latter with the Passover of Jn. vi. 4, some maintaining that in Jn. vi. 4 'nigh' means 'just past' and others that Jn. vi should be read immediately before Jn. v. But 'nigh' in Jn. vi. 4 cannot mean 'just past', since, as is clear from the words 'after these things' in Jn. vi. 1, there was a considerable interval between the events of Jn. v and those of Jn. vi. There is, moreover, no textual evidence in support of the proposed rearrangement of chapters. It would appear, therefore, that there was a Passover between those of Jn. ii. 13 and vi. 4 and consequently that the duration of Jesus' ministry was fully three years.

According to the first of the above-mentioned theories, the first and last Passovers of Jesus' ministry were those of 29 and 30, according to the second those of 28 and 30, according to the third those of 30 and 33.

II. THE CHRONOLOGY OF THE APOSTOLIC AGE

a. From Pentecost to the conversion of Paul

When, three years after his conversion (Gal. i. 18), Paul escaped from Damascus, an official there, 'the ethnarch of king Aretas', 'guarded the city of the Damascenes' to seize him (2 Cor. xi. 32 f.). According to some, this official was the sheikh of a band of Arabs, subjects of Aretas, encamped outside the city walls. But Paul's reference to him suggests an official who acted within the city. According to others, Damascus was under direct Roman administration, and this official was the representative of the Arab community resident within it (*cf.* the ethnarch of the Jews in Alexandria, Jos., *Ant.* xiv. 117). But this representative would not have had power to guard the city. At this time, then, Aretas apparently possessed Damascus, and this official was his viceroy there. Coins show that Damascus was in Roman hands until 33. When in 37 Vitellius the governor of Syria marched against Aretas, he proceeded not to Damascus but southwards towards Petra. That he would not have done unless Damascus had still been in Roman hands. Aretas, who died in 40, must then have obtained possession of Damascus between 37 and 40, and Paul's conversion must be dated between 34 and 37.

There are no clear indications that the interval under consideration was long. The stoning of Stephen was, some have urged, an illegal act on which the Jews would not have ventured during Pilate's procuratorship, and consequently must be dated not earlier than 36. But no-one can say when such an outburst of fanaticism may not take place. Others have noted that before Paul's conversion Christianity had spread to Damascus. But as yet there were apparently no organized Christian communities outside Jerusalem. Rapid advance in those early pentecostal days is likely; and while a tradition preserved in Irenaeus and in the *Ascension of Isaiah* that this interval was one of eighteen months may be of doubtful value, Paul's conversion seems more likely in 34 or 35 than in 36 or 37.

b. From Paul's first post-conversion visit to Jerusalem to the famine-relief visit

In 37 or 38 Paul visited Jerusalem for the first time since his conversion, stayed fifteen days and then, departing for Syria and Cilicia, stayed there until called by Barnabas to assist him in Antioch. A year later the two paid the famine-relief visit to Jerusalem of Acts xi. 29 f. and xii. 25.

Since in Acts xii. 1–24 Luke breaks away from his account of this visit that he may bring his history of the Church in Jerusalem up to the time of it, it follows that he dates it after the death of Agrippa I. Particulars given in Josephus indicate that he died in 44, perhaps before 1 Nisan. His persecution of the Church, which took place at a Passover season, may then be dated 43, but perhaps not earlier, there having apparently been no long time between it and his death.

The famine predicted by Agabus befell Judaea when Tiberius Alexander was procurator (46–48). Conditions were at their worst in the year following the one in which the harvest had failed and immediately before the new harvest was cut. Just then Helena, Queen of Adiabene, came to Jerusalem and fetched its inhabitants corn from

Egypt. As papyri show, famine conditions obtained in Egypt in the second half of 45. Helena's servants are not then likely to have found corn there until, at the earliest, after the harvest there of 46. The bad harvest in Palestine must then have been that of 46 or that of 47. The collection made in Antioch is likely to have been forwarded only when the Judaean Christians began to feel the need of it, therefore towards the end of 45 or 46. The earlier of these dates makes slightly larger room for subsequent events, and is to be preferred.

c. The first missionary journey

Returning to Antioch, Paul and Barnabas soon afterwards, probably early in 46, began the first missionary journey. Sailing to Salamis in Cyprus, they crossed the island to Paphos, where they met Sergius Paulus the proconsul. That he is the Sergius Paulus whom Pliny names in his *Historia Naturalis* as one of his authorities, is uncertain. An inscription in Rome mentions one L. Sergius Paullus as a curator of the Tiber in the reign of Claudius, but that he subsequently governed Cyprus is not known. An inscription found at Soloi in Cyprus ends with the date 'year 13, month Demarchousios 25', but has as postscript the statement, 'He [the Apollonius of the inscription] also revised the senate when Paulus was proconsul.' This Paulus may possibly be the Paulus of the Acts. But Apollonius may not have revised the senate in year 13; moreover, what 'year 13' itself means is also uncertain. Whilst another inscription shows that the year of Paulus' proconsulship was neither 51 nor 52, it is not possible with the information which inscriptions at present provide to determine that year precisely.

In advancing westwards from Salamis the missionaries are likely to have preached in the towns to which they came. They may then have reached Paphos by autumn and, crossing to Perga, have begun their mission in Pisidia and Lycaonia before winter set in. Since a twelvemonth seems sufficient time for that mission, their return to Antioch may be put in autumn 47.

d. The Apostolic Council

Early in 48, fourteen years after his conversion, Paul with Barnabas attended the Apostolic Council of Acts xv.

Some identify this Council with the conference of Gal. ii. 1–10, feeling that the objection that in Galatians Paul cannot have left the Jerusalem visit of Acts xi. 30 unmentioned is not valid, since he adduces the visit of Gal. i. 18 for one reason and that of Gal. ii. 1 for another. To show that he was 'an apostle, not of men, neither by man' he states that he had no contact with the apostles until three years after his conversion. His purpose in mentioning a later visit to Jerusalem is to assure the Galatians that his apostleship to the Gentiles was then recognized by the leaders of the Church. But see COUNCIL, JERUSALEM, and GALATIANS, EPISTLE TO THE.

Some put the visit of Acts xi. 30 before Agrippa's persecution of the Church and maintain that the Council of Acts xv (= Gal. ii. 1–10) took place then. But that is chronologically difficult, since Paul's conversion must then be dated not later than 30. Others hold that the Council took place after the first missionary journey, but that it was then, and not earlier, that the famine-relief collection made in Antioch was carried to Jerusalem. Luke, it is assumed, had two accounts of this visit, originating one in Antioch and one in Jerusalem, and thought wrongly that they referred to different visits. More recently J. Knox, in his *Chapters in a Life of Paul*, has placed the Apostolic Council between the second and the third missionary journeys.

e. The second missionary journey

Paul began his second journey apparently late in spring 48. After visiting the churches in Syria and Cilicia and those already founded in Asia Minor, he entered a new field, 'the region of Phrygia and Galatia' (Acts xvi. 6, RV). No account is given of his missionary work there. But it must have included the founding of the churches to which the Epistle to the Galatians was later addressed, for according to the view everywhere entertained until the 19th century, and which seems still to have the weight of evidence on its side, these churches were in Galatia in the ethnographical sense. The founding of them may have occupied Paul until early in 49. The mission which followed in Macedonia and Achaia ended shortly after the Gallio episode (Acts xviii. 12–17), the time of which can with the help of an inscription be set within narrow limits. In this inscription, a rescript of Claudius to the Delphians dated to his '26th imperatorial acclamation', Gallio is mentioned as proconsul. Now inscriptions (*CIL*, iii. 476 and vi. 1256) show that Claudius was acclaimed for the twenty-third time on a date later than 25 January 51 and for the twenty-seventh time before 1 August 52. This makes it very probable that he was acclaimed for the 26th time, and consequently that the rescript was written, in the first half of 52. But before then Gallio had investigated the boundary question with which it is concerned and had corresponded with Claudius about it. The rescript must then belong to the second half of Gallio's year as proconsul, and that year must have begun in summer 51. Verse 12 indicates that Gallio had been in office for some time before the Jews acted. But they are not likely to have waited for more than, say, a couple of months. Since Paul had been in Corinth for eighteen months before this episode, he must have arrived there early in 50; and since after it he tarried in Corinth 'yet many days' (Acts xviii. 18, RV), an expression which here cannot denote more than one or two months, he may have returned to Syria before winter 51/52.

On arrival in Corinth Paul found Aquila and Priscilla lately come from Rome because Claudius had ordered all Jews to leave the city.

CHRONOLOGICAL OUTLINE: NEW TESTAMENT

THE ROMAN EMPIRE	PALESTINE	THE LIFE OF CHRIST AND THE APOSTOLIC AGE
27 BC–AD 14: Caesar Augustus	37–4 BC: Herod the Great, king of Judaea	8/7 BC?: Birth of Jesus
AD 14–37: Tiberius	4 BC–AD 6: Archelaus, Ethnarch of Judaea	AD 29?: Baptism of Jesus
AD 37–41: Caligula	4 BC–AD 39: Herod Antipas, Tetrarch of Galilee	AD 30: (Passover) Jesus in Jerusalem (Jn. ii. 13)
	4 BC–AD 34: Herod Philip, Tetrarch of Ituraea	AD 30/31 (December/January): Jesus in Samaria (Jn. iv. 35)
	AD 26–36: Pontius Pilate, Roman Procurator	AD 31 (Feast of Tabernacles): Jesus in Jerusalem (Jn. v. 1)
		AD 32 (Passover): Feeding of the Five Thousand (Jn. vi. 4)
		AD 32 (Feast of Tabernacles): Jesus in Jerusalem (Jn. vii. 2)
		AD 32 (Feast of Dedication): Jesus in Jerusalem (Jn. x. 22)
		AD 33 (Passover): Crucifixion and Resurrection
		AD 34 or 35: Paul's conversion
AD 41–54: Claudius		AD 37 or 38: Paul's first visit to Jerusalem
	AD 41–44: Herod Agrippa I, king of Judaea	AD 45 or 46: Famine collection in Antioch
		AD 46–47: First Missionary Journey
		AD 48: Apostolic Council in Jerusalem
		AD 48–51: Second Missionary Journey
	AD 50–*c.* 93: Herod Agrippa II, Tetrarch of Northern Territory	AD 50: Paul reaches Corinth
	AD *c.* 52–*c.* 60: Felix, Roman Procurator	AD 53: Third Missionary Journey begins
AD 54–68: Nero		AD 54–57: Paul's Stay in Ephesus
		AD 57: Departure for Troas
		AD 58: Meeting with Titus in Europe
		AD 58–59: Paul in Macedonia and Achaia (and Illyria?)
		AD 59: Paul returns to Jerusalem
	AD *c.* 60–62: Festus, Roman Procurator	AD 59–61: Imprisonment in Caesarea
		AD 61: Appeal to Caesar and departure for Rome
		AD 62: Arrival in Rome
		AD 62–64: Imprisonment in Rome
AD 68–69: Galba		AD 62?: Martyrdom of James, the Lord's brother
AD 69: Otho		
AD 69: Vitellius		
AD 69–79: Vespasian		AD 70: Fall of Jerusalem
AD 79–81: Titus		
AD 81–96: Domitian		AD 81–96: Persecutions under Domitian
		AD *c.* 100: Death of John

Orosius puts this expulsion order in Claudius' ninth year, 49 (25 January)–50. While there is uncertainty as to where Orosius found this date, it may rest on good authority. It accords well with the conclusion that Paul reached Corinth early in 50.

f. From the beginning of Paul's third missionary journey to his arrival in Rome

Paul's third journey can hardly have begun earlier than 52; and since it included a three years' stay in Ephesus (Acts xx. 31) and three months spent in Greece (Acts xx. 3), its end must be dated 55 at the earliest. The coming of Festus as procurator in place of Felix two years later (Acts xxiv. 27) must then be dated 57 at the earliest. Since Festus' successor was in Palestine by Tabernacles 62 (Jos., *BJ* vi. 300 ff.), Festus, who died in office, must have arrived by 61 at the latest. Of these possible years 57–61, most scholars reject 57 and 58 as too early and, adopting 59 or 60, put Paul's arrival in Rome in 60 or 61.

But, when procurator, Festus permitted an embassy to carry a request to Rome, and there it was granted them 'to gratify Poppaea, Nero's wife' (Jos., *Ant.* xx. 195). Since Nero married Poppaea in May 62, Festus may still have been alive in April; and since the few events of his procuratorship need have occupied but a short time, he may have succeeded Felix in 61.

Paul's return from Corinth to Syria was perhaps occasioned by sickness, and he may not have commenced his third journey until 53. Returning to the region of Phrygia and Galatia, he entered it this time by way of Galatia (Acts xviii. 23) and, after what from Acts xix. 1 appears to have been a considerable mission in central Asia Minor, came to Ephesus, probably in autumn 54. In 57, after the riot there, he left for Troas. Crossing to Europe early in 58, he met Titus, who relieved him of anxiety about the Corinthian Church. He then laboured in Macedonia and Achaia and possibly in Illyria (Rom. xv. 19) and returned to Jerusalem in 59. In 61, after two years' imprisonment in Caesarea, he appealed to Caesar and in the autumn (Acts xxvii. 9) sailed for Rome, arriving there in 62.

Noting that, according to Josephus, Felix on returning to Rome escaped punishment for his misdoings in Palestine thanks to the intervention of his brother Pallas, 'who was then had in the greatest honour by him (Nero)' and that, according to Tacitus, Nero removed Pallas from office soon after his accession, noting also that in the *Chronicle* of Eusebius (Hieronymian version) the coming of Festus as procurator is put in Nero's second year, and regarding the period of two years of Acts xxiv. 27 as that of Felix's procuratorship, certain scholars maintain that Festus succeeded Felix in 55 or 56. Objections to this 'ante-dated' chronology are that it allows scant room for the happenings of Paul's third journey, that it assumes the less natural interpretation of Acts xxiv. 27, and that Josephus himself puts the events of Felix's procuratorship in Nero's reign.

g. From Paul's arrival in Rome to the end of the apostolic age

For at least two years, *i.e.* until 64, the year of the Neronian persecution, Paul remained a prisoner in Rome. As to what befell him then nothing is known with certainty.

Peter was miraculously delivered out of the hands of Agrippa (Acts xii. 3 ff.). Later he attended the Apostolic Council and later still visited Antioch (Gal. ii. 11 ff.). Reference to a Cephas party in Corinth (1 Cor. i. 12) affords no absolute proof that Peter came there. According to most scholars, there is sufficient evidence that eventually he came to Rome; but that has been denied, notably by Merrill, *Essays in Early Christian History*, 1924, pp. 267 ff.

James the Lord's brother was stoned to death in 62 according to Jos., *Ant.* xx. 200, which passage may, however, be an interpolation. Shortly before the Jewish War (66–70) the Jerusalem Christians fled to Pella. What persecutions of Christians there were in Domitian's reign (81–96) were due apparently to personal enmity or popular fury and not to state action. There is but little evidence that the apostle John suffered martyrdom along with his brother James (Acts xii. 2). That, as Irenaeus (*Adv. Haer.* II. xxii. 5) records, he lived on to the time of Trajan is much more likely. His death (*c.* 100) marks the end of the apostolic age.

BIBLIOGRAPHY. Ginzel, *Handbuch der mathematischen und technischen Chronologie*, 1906–1914; Cavaignac, *Chronologie*, 1925; Neugebauer, *Astronomische Chronologie*, 1929; U. Holzmeister, *Chronologia Vitae Christi*, 1933; J. K. Fotheringham, 'The Evidence of Astronomy and Technical Chronology for the Date of the Crucifixion' in *JTS*, XXXV, 1934, 146 ff.; E. F. Sutcliffe, *A Two Year Public Ministry*, 1938; G. Ogg, *The Chronology of the Public Ministry of Jesus*, 1940; L. Girard, *Le Cadre chronologique du Ministère de Jésus*, 1953; A. Jaubert, *La Date de la Cène*, 1957; D. Plooij, *De Chronologie van het Leven van Paulus*, 1918; U. Holzmeister, *Historia Aetatis Novi Testamenti*, 1938; J. Dupont, *Les Problèmes du Livre des Actes*, 1950; G. B. Caird, *The Apostolic Age*, 1955, Appendix A. G.O.

CHRYSOLITE, -PRASE. See JEWELS AND PRECIOUS STONES.

CHURCH.

I. MEANING

The English word 'church' is derived from the Gk. adjective *kyriakos* as used in some such phrase as *kyriakon dōma* or *kyriakē oikia*, meaning 'the Lord's house', *i.e.* a Christian place of worship. 'Church' in the New Testament, however, renders Gk. *ekklēsia*, which mostly means a local congregation of Christians and never a building. (Tyndale, who uniformly translated *ekklēsia* as 'congregation', used 'churches' in

Acts xix. 37 for heathen temples; this rendering remained in the AV, which at the same time fully replaced 'congregation' with 'church'.) Although we often speak of these congregations collectively as the New Testament Church or the Early Church, no New Testament writer uses *ekklēsia* in this collective way. An *ekklēsia* was a meeting or assembly. Its commonest use was for the public assembly of citizens duly summoned, which was a feature of all the cities outside Judaea where the gospel was planted (*e.g.* Acts xix. 39). *Ekklēsia* was also used among the Jews (LXX) for the 'congregation of Israel' which was constituted at Sinai and assembled before the Lord at the annual feasts in the persons of its representative males (Acts vii. 38). Whether the Christian use of *ekklēsia* was first adopted from Gentile or Jewish usage—the point is disputed—it certainly implied 'meeting' rather than 'organization' or 'society'. Locality was essential to its character. The local *ekklēsia* was not thought of as part of some world-wide *ekklēsia*, which would have been a contradiction in terms. The reference in the best texts of Acts ix. 31 to the church 'throughout all Judaea and Galilee and Samaria' is not an exception. Since this verse concludes the pericope describing the scattering of the Jerusalem church (viii. 1), it seems right to take *ekklēsia* here to be the Jerusalem church so spread as to occupy the territory of 'the ancient Ecclesia which had its home in the whole land of Israel' (Hort, *The Christian Ecclesia*, p. 46).

While there might be as many churches as there were cities or even households, yet the New Testament recognized only one *ekklēsia* without finding it necessary to explain the relationship between the one and the many. The one was not an amalgamation or federation of the many. It was a 'heavenly' reality belonging not to the form of this world but to the realm of resurrection glory where Christ is exalted at the right hand of God (Eph. i. 20–23; Heb. ii. 12, xii. 23). Yet since the local *ekklēsia* was gathered together in Christ's name and had Him in its midst (Mt. xviii. 20), it tasted the powers of the age to come and was the firstfruits of that eschatological *ekklēsia*. So the individual local church was called 'the church of God, which he hath purchased with his own blood' (Acts xx. 28; *cf.* 1 Cor. i. 2; 1 Pet. v. 2; 1 Cor. xii. 27).

II. THE CHURCH AT JERUSALEM

The church in the Christian sense appeared first in Jerusalem after the ascension of Jesus. It was made up of the predominantly Galilaean band of Jesus' disciples together with those who responded to the preaching of the apostles in Jerusalem. While, to judge from Acts, the new community did not at once use *ekklēsia* to describe itself, it saw itself as the elect remnant of Israel destined to find salvation in Zion (Joel ii. 32; Acts ii. 17 ff.) and as the restored tabernacle of David which Jesus Himself had promised to build (Acts xv. 16; Mt. xvi. 18). Jerusalem was thus the divinely-appointed locale for those who awaited 'the times of restitution of all things' (Acts iii. 21). Externally, the group of baptized believers had the character of a sect (Gk. *haeresis*) within Judaism. It was called 'the sect of the Nazarenes' by a professional orator (Acts xxiv. 5, 14, *cf.* xxviii. 22), while its own adherents called their distinctive faith 'The Way'. It was more or less tolerated by Judaism throughout the thirty-odd years of its life in Judaea, except when the Jewish authorities were disturbed by its fraternization with Gentile churches abroad. But the essentially Jewish character of the Jerusalem church should be noted. Its members accepted the obligations of the law and the worship of the Temple. Their distinctive belief was that Jesus of Nazareth was Israel's Messiah, that God Himself had vindicated this by raising Him from the dead after He had suffered for Israel's redemption, and that the 'great and terrible day of the Lord' was even now upon them and would culminate in a final manifestation of Messiah in judgment and glory. Their distinctive practices included a baptism in the name of Jesus, regular attendance at instruction given by the apostles, and 'fellowship' on a household basis which Luke described as being 'in breaking of bread, and in prayers' (Acts ii. 41–46). The first leadership of the church was by the twelve (Galilaean) apostles, especially Peter and John, but soon gave way to that of elders in the regular Jewish manner, with James the brother of Jesus as president (Gal. ii. 9; Acts xv. 6 ff.). The latter's presidency extended through most of the life of the Jerusalem church, possibly from as early as the thirties (Gal. i. 19; *cf.* Acts xii. 17) until his execution *c.* AD 62. It may well have been associated with the church's messianic conceptions. 'The Throne of David' was a much more literal hope among believing Jews than we commonly realize, and James was also 'of the house and lineage of David'. Was he thought of as a legitimate Protector or Prince Regent pending the return of Messiah in person? Eusebius reports that a cousin of Jesus, Simeon son of Clopas, succeeded James as president, and that Vespasian, after the capture of Jerusalem in AD 70, is said to have ordered a search to be made for all who were of the family of David, that there might be left among the Jews no-one of the royal family (*EH* iii. 11, 12).

The church became large (Acts xxi. 20) and included even priests and Pharisees in its membership (vi. 7, xv. 5). At the outset it included also many Hellenists, Greek-speaking Jews of the Dispersion who came as pilgrims to feasts or for various reasons were staying in Jerusalem. Such Jews were often more wealthy than those of Jerusalem, and displayed piety by bringing 'alms to their nation' (*cf.* Acts xxiv. 17). When the church adopted the practice of mutual support, a typical benefactor was the Cypriot Barnabas (Acts iv. 34–37), and when a committee was needed to administer the relief the seven appointed were, to judge by their names, Hellenists (vi. 5). It was apparently through this

Hellenist element that the gospel overflowed the narrow limits of Judaistic Christianity and created fresh streams in alien territories. Stephen, one of the Seven, came into debate in a Hellenist synagogue in Jerusalem (of which Saul of Tarsus was possibly a member) and was charged before the Sanhedrin with blaspheming the Temple and the Mosaic law. His defence certainly shows a liberal attitude towards the inviolability of the Temple, and the persecution which followed his death may have been directed against this sort of tendency among Hellenist believers rather than against the law-abiding Christianity of the apostles who remained in Jerusalem when others were 'scattered abroad'. Philip, another of the Seven, took the gospel to Samaria and, after baptizing a foreign eunuch near the old Philistine city of Gaza, went preaching up the coast till he came to the largely pagan Caesarea, where soon afterwards Peter found himself admitting uncircumcised Gentiles to baptism. Significantly it was Hellenists who went from Jerusalem to Antioch and there preached to Gentiles without any stipulation about the Mosaic law. After Stephen, the Hellenistic element in the Jerusalem church seemed to disappear and its Judaic character to prevail. Some of its members disapproved of the gospel's being offered to Gentiles without obligation to keep the law and went off to press their point of view in the new churches (Acts xv. 1; Gal. ii. 12, vi. 12 f.). Officially, however, the Jerusalem church gave its approval not only to Philip's mission in Samaria and the baptism of Cornelius at Caesarea, but to the policy of the new church at Antioch and its missionaries. In *c.* AD 49 the Jerusalem church was formally asked what should be demanded of 'them which from among the Gentiles turn to God'. It was determined that, while Jewish believers would, of course, continue to circumcise their children and keep the whole law, these requirements should not be laid on Gentile believers, although the latter should be asked to make certain concessions to Jewish scruples which would make table-fellowship between the two groups easier, and to keep the law concerning sexual purity (Acts xv. 20, 29, xxi. 21–25). The proceedings reflect the primacy of Jerusalem in matters of faith and morals. Indeed, throughout the first generation it was 'the church' *par excellence* (see Acts xviii. 22, where the Jerusalem church is meant). This is noticeable in the attitude of Paul (Gal. i. 13; Phil. iii. 6), who impressed it on his churches (Rom. xv. 27). His final visit to Jerusalem *c.* AD 57 was in recognition of this spiritual primacy. He was greeted by 'James and all the elders' and reminded that the many members of the church were 'all zealous for the law'. Its scrupulosity, however, did not save it from suspicion of disloyalty to Jewish national hopes. James 'the Just' was judicially murdered at the instigation of the high priest *c.* AD 62. When the war with Rome broke out in AD 66 the church came to an end. Its members betook themselves, says Eusebius, to Pella in Transjordan (*EH* iii. 5). Thereafter they divided into two groups: the Nazarenes, who, keeping the law themselves, had a tolerant attitude towards their Gentile fellow-believers, and the Ebionites, who inherited the Judaizing view of obligation to the law. Later Christians listed the Ebionites among the heretics.

III. THE CHURCH AT ANTIOCH

It is easy to understand that for the Jerusalem church to describe itself as the *ekklēsia* was in keeping with its claim to be the restored remnant of Israel, the true 'congregation of the Lord'. What Acts does not explain is how, right outside the territory of Israel, there should appear a mixed Jewish and Gentile group to be called 'the *ekklēsia* which is at Antioch' (see Acts xiii. 1). Yet it was so. Antioch, not Jerusalem, was the model of the 'new church' which was to appear all over the world. It was founded by Hellenist Jews. Here believers were first dubbed *christianoi*, 'Christ-men', by their Gentile neighbours (Acts xi. 26). Antioch became the springboard for the expansion of the gospel throughout the Levant. The key figure at first was Barnabas, himself perhaps a Hellenist but enjoying the full confidence of the Jerusalem leaders who sent him to investigate. He is first named among the 'prophets and teachers' who are the only functionaries we know to have been in this church. He brought Saul the converted Pharisee from Tarsus—an interesting solvent for the ferment! Barnabas also led two missionary expeditions to his own country of Cyprus, and with Paul made the first incursions into Asia Minor. There were important links between Antioch and Jerusalem. Prophets from Jerusalem came up and ministered (Acts xi. 27), as did Peter himself and delegates from James (Gal. ii. 11, 12), not to mention the Pharisaic visitors of Acts xv. 1. In return, Antioch expressed its fellowship with Jerusalem by sending relief in time of famine (Acts xi. 29) and later looked to the Jerusalem church to provide a solution to the legal controversy. The prophetic leadership of the church included an African called Symeon, Lucius of Cyrene, and a member of Herod Antipas's entourage. The author of Acts has been claimed as a native of Antioch (Anti-Marcionite Prologues). But the greatest fame of the church at Antioch was that it 'recommended' Barnabas and Saul 'to the grace of God for the work which they fulfilled' (Acts xiv. 26).

IV. PAULINE CHURCHES

While Paul and Barnabas were clearly not the only missionaries of the first generation, we know next to nothing about the labours of others, including the twelve apostles themselves. Paul, however, claimed to have preached the gospel 'from Jerusalem and round about unto Illyricum' (Rom. xv. 19), and we know that he founded churches on the Antiochene pattern in the southern provinces of Asia Minor, in Macedonia and Greece, in western Asia, where he made Ephesus his base, and, by inference from the Epistle to Titus, in Crete. Whether he founded churches in Spain (Rom. xv. 24) is unknown. Everywhere he made cities his centre, whence he (or his associates) reached other cities of the province (Acts xix. 10; Col. i. 7). Where possible, the Jewish synagogue was the jumping-off point, Paul preaching there as a Rabbi as long as he was given opportunity. In time, however, a separate *ekklēsia*—the word must sometimes have had the flavour of *synagōgē* (*cf.* James ii. 2, RV)—of Jewish and Gentile converts came into being, each with its own elders appointed by the apostle or his delegate from among the responsible senior believers. The household played an important rôle in the development of these churches (see FAMILY). The Old Testament in Greek was the sacred Scripture of all these churches, and the key to its interpretation was indicated in certain selected passages together with a clearly defined summary of the gospel itself (1 Cor. xv. 1–4). Other 'traditions' concerning Jesus' ministry and teaching were laid on every church (1 Cor. xi. 2, 23–25, vii. 17, xi. 16; 2 Thes. ii. 15), with fixed patterns of ethical instruction in regard to social and political obligation. It is unknown who regularly baptized or presided at the Lord's Supper, though both ordinances were kept. How frequently or on what days the church assembled is also unknown, though a meeting to break bread on the first day of the week at night is attested for Troas (Acts xx. 7). The first day could not have been observed as a sabbath, however, since it was not a holiday, and Paul would have no binding rules about keeping days unto the Lord (Rom. xiv. 5). Jewish members must have observed many customs not joined in by their Gentile brethren. The fullest evidence for what took place when the church actually assembled is 1 Cor. xi–xiv. There was no organizational link between Paul's churches, though there were natural affinities between churches in the same province (Col. iv. 15, 16; 1 Thes. iv. 10). All were expected to submit to Paul's authority in matters of the faith, but this was spiritual and admonitory, not coercive (2 Cor. x. 8, xiii. 10). Local administration and discipline was autonomous (2 Cor. ii. 5–10). No church had superiority over any other, though all acknowledged Jerusalem as the source of 'spiritual blessings' (Rom. xv. 27, RSV), and the collection for the saints there was a token of this acknowledgment.

V. OTHER CHURCHES

The origin of other churches mentioned in the New Testament is a matter of inference. There was a well-established church of Jewish and Gentile membership in Rome by *c.* AD 56 when Paul wrote his Epistle to it. We have no knowledge of its origins. 'Visitors from Rome, both Jews and proselytes' were present at Pentecost (Acts ii. 10, RSV), and among greetings in Rom. xvi is one to two 'of note among the apostles', Andronicus and Junias, kinsmen of Paul's who were converted before him. Is this a complimentary reference to their having brought the gospel to Rome? 'Brethren' came to meet Paul and his party when they went to Rome, but our knowledge of the church there, its composition and its status, is problematical (see ROME).

The address of 1 Peter shows that there was a group of churches scattered along the south coast of the Black Sea and its hinterland ('Pontus, Galatia, Cappadocia, Asia, and Bithynia') of either Jewish or Jewish–Gentile membership. These are the parts which Paul was prevented from entering (Acts xvi. 6, 7), which may imply that they were the scene of another man's foundation, perhaps Peter's himself. But we learn nothing distinctive of these churches from the Epistle. Oversight and responsibility for 'feeding the flock' in each place was exercised by elders (1 Pet. v. 1, 2).

This exhausts our knowledge of the founding of particular churches in New Testament times. A little more about the western Asian churches emerges from the Apocalypse. It is thought that churches must surely have been founded at least in Alexandria, and in Mesopotamia, if not farther east, within the first century, but of this there is no certain evidence.

Of the life and organization of the churches generally, we know very little, except for Jerusalem, which was not typical. Yet what we know makes us confident that their unity lay in the gospel itself, acceptance of the Old Testament Scriptures, and acknowledgment of Jesus as 'Lord and Christ'. Differences of organization, forms of ministry, moulds of thought, and levels of moral and spiritual achievement were probably greater than we commonly realize. No one New Testament church, nor all the churches together—though they formed no visible unity —exercises any authority over our faith today. This divine authority belongs only to the apostolic gospel as contained in the whole of the Scriptures.

BIBLIOGRAPHY. F. J. A. Hort, *The Christian Ecclesia*, 1897; R. Newton Flew, *Jesus and His Church*, 1938; W. L. Knox, *St. Paul and the Church of Jerusalem*, 1925; Jackson and Lake, *The Beginnings of Christianity*, 1920; Hans Lietzmann, *The Beginnings of the Christian Church*, 1937; F. F. Bruce, *The Acts of the Apostles*, 1950, *The Spreading Flame*, 1958; Dom Gregory Dix, *Jew and Greek*, 1953.

D.W.B.R.

CHURCH GOVERNMENT. The New Testament provides no detailed code of regulations for the government of the Church, and the very idea of such a code might seem repugnant to the liberty of the gospel dispensation; but Christ left behind Him a body of leaders in the apostles whom He Himself had chosen, and He also gave them a few general principles for the exercise of their ruling function.

I. THE TWELVE

The Twelve were chosen that they might be with Christ (Mk. iii. 14), and this personal association qualified them to act as His witnesses (Acts i. 8); they were from the first endowed with power over unclean spirits and diseases (Mt. x. 1), and this power was renewed and increased, in a more general form, when the promise of the Father (Lk. xxiv. 49) came upon them in the gift of the Holy Ghost (Acts i. 8); on their first mission they were sent forth to preach (Mk. iii. 14), and in the great commission they were instructed to teach all nations (Mt. xxviii. 19). They thus received Christ's authority to evangelize at large.

But they were also promised a more specific function as judges and rulers of God's people (Mt. xix. 28; Lk. xxii. 29, 30), with power to bind and to loose (Mt. xviii. 18), to remit and to retain sins (Jn. xx. 23). Such language gave rise to the conception of the keys, traditionally defined in both mediaeval and Reformed theology as: (*a*) the key of doctrine, to teach what conduct is forbidden and what permitted (this is the technical meaning of binding and loosing in Jewish legal phraseology), and (*b*) the key of discipline, to excommunicate the unworthy and reconcile the contrite, by declaring God's forgiveness through the remission of sins in Christ alone.

Peter received these powers first (Mt. xvi. 18, 19), as he also received the pastoral commission to feed Christ's flock (Jn. xxi. 15), but he did so in a representative, rather than in a personal, capacity; for when the commission is repeated in Mt. xviii. 18, authority to exercise the ministry of reconciliation is vested in the body of disciples as a whole, and it is the faithful congregation, rather than any individual, which acts in Christ's name to open the kingdom to believers and to close it against unbelief. None the less, this authoritative function is primarily exercised by preachers of the word, and the process of sifting, of conversion and rejection, is seen at work from Peter's first sermon onwards (Acts ii. 37–41). When Peter confessed Christ, his faith was typical of the rock-like foundation on which the Church is built (Mt. xvi. 18), but in fact the foundations of the heavenly Jerusalem contain the names of all of the apostles (Rev. xxi. 14); these acted as a body in the early days of the Church, and the idea that Peter exercised any constant primacy among them is refuted, partly by the leading position occupied by James in the Jerusalem Council (Acts xv. 13, 19), and partly by the fact that Paul withstood Peter to the face (Gal. ii. 11). It was in a corporate capacity that the apostles provided leadership for the primitive Church; and that leadership was effective both in mercy (Acts ii. 42) and in judgment (Acts v. 1–11). They exercised a general authority over every congregation, sending two of their number to supervise new developments in Samaria (Acts viii. 14), and deciding with the elders on a common policy for the admission of Gentiles (Acts xv), while Paul's 'care of all the churches' (2 Cor. xi. 28) is illustrated both by the number of his missionary journeys and by the extent of his correspondence.

II. AFTER THE ASCENSION

Their first step, immediately after Christ's ascension, was to fill the vacancy left by the defection of Judas, and this they did by means of a direct appeal to God (Acts i. 24–26). Others were later reckoned in the number of apostles (Rom. xvi. 7; 1 Cor. ix. 5, 6; Gal. i. 19), but the qualifications of being an eye-witness of the resurrection (Acts i. 22), and of having been in some way personally commissioned by Christ (Rom. i. 1, 5), were not such as could be extended indefinitely. When the pressure of work increased, they appointed seven assistants (Acts vi. 1–6), elected by the people and ordained by the apostles, to administer the Church's charity; these seven have been regarded as deacons from the time of Irenaeus onwards, but Philip, the only one whose later history is clearly known to us, became an evangelist (Acts xxi. 8) with an unrestricted mission to preach the gospel. Church-officers with a distinctive name are first found in the elders of Jerusalem, who received gifts (Acts xi. 30) and took part in Council (Acts xv. 6). This office (see PRESBYTER) was probably copied from the eldership of the Jewish synagogue; the Church is itself called a synagogue in Jas. ii. 2, and Jewish elders, who seem to have been ordained by imposition of hands, were responsible for maintaining discipline, with power to excommunicate breakers of the law. But the Christian eldership, as a gospel ministry, acquired added pastoral (Jas. v. 14; 1 Pet. v. 1–3) and preaching (1 Tim. v. 17) duties. Elders were ordained for all the Asian churches by Paul and Barnabas (Acts xiv. 23), while Titus was enjoined to do the same for Crete (Tit. i. 5); and although the disturbances at Corinth may suggest that a more complete democracy prevailed in that congregation (*cf.* 1 Cor. xiv. 26), the general pattern of Church government in the apostolic age would seem to be a board of elders or pastors, possibly augmented by prophets and teachers, ruling each of the local congregations, with deacons to help in administration, and with a general superintendence of the entire Church provided by apostles and evangelists. There is nothing in this system which corresponds exactly to the modern diocesan episcopate; bishops (*q.v.*), when they are mentioned (Phil. i. 1), form a board of local congregational officers, and the position occupied by Timothy and Titus is that of Paul's personal lieutenants in his missionary work. It seems most likely that one elder acquired a permanent chairmanship of the board, and that he was then specially designated with the title of bishop; but even when the monarchical bishop appears in the letters of Ignatius, he is still the pastor of a single congregation. New Testament terminology is much more fluid; instead of anything resembling a hierarchy, we meet with such vague descriptions as 'he that ruleth', those which 'are over you in the Lord' (*proïstamenoi*, 'presidents'; Rom. xii. 8; 1 Thes. v. 12) or 'them which have the rule over you' (*hēgoumenoi*, 'guides'; Heb. xiii. 7, 17, 24). The angels of the churches in Rev. ii, iii have sometimes been regarded as actual bishops, but they are most probably personifications of their respective communities. Those in responsible positions are entitled to honour (1 Thes. v. 12, 13), maintenance (1 Cor. ix. 14), and freedom from trifling accusations (1 Tim. v. 19).

III. GENERAL PRINCIPLES

Five general principles can be deduced from the New Testament teaching as a whole: (*a*) all authority is derived from Christ and exercised in His name and Spirit; (*b*) Christ's humility provides the pattern for Christian service (Mt. xx. 26–28); (*c*) government is collegiate rather than hierarchical (Mt. xviii. 19, xxiii. 8; Acts xv. 28); (*d*) teaching and ruling are closely associated functions (1 Thes. v. 12); (*e*) administrative assistants are required to help the preachers of the word (Acts vi. 2, 3). See also MINISTRY and bibliography there cited. G.S.M.W.

CILICIA. A region in South-East Asia Minor. The western part, known as Tracheia, was a wild plateau of the Taurus range, the home of pirates and robbers from prehistoric to Roman times. The eastern part, known as Cilicia Pedias, was a fertile plain between Mts. Amanus, Taurus, and the sea; and the vital trade route between Syria and Asia Minor lay through its twin majestic passes, the Cilician Gates and the Syrian Gates. Cilicia was officially made a province in 103 BC, but effective rule began only after Pompey's pirate drive in 67 BC. Cicero was governor here in 51 BC. The province apparently disappeared under the Early Empire, Augustus ceding Tracheia partly to the native dynasty and partly to the adjacent client kingdoms of Galatia and Cappadocia. Pedias, which consists of sixteen semi-autonomous cities, of which Tarsus was the most outstanding, was administered by Syria until AD 72, when Vespasian re-combined both regions into the single province of Cilicia (Suet., *Vesp.* 8). Thus Paul, its most distinguished citizen, and Luke, both writing before AD 72, are strictly correct in combining Cilicia (*i.e.* Pedias) with Syria (Gal. i. 21; Acts xv. 23, 41; see Note 'Syria and Cilicia' by E. M. B. Green in *ExpT*, Nov. 1959, and authorities quoted there).

E.M.B.G.

CINNAMON (Heb. *qinnāmôn*; Gk. *kinnamōmon*). Almost certainly the product of *Cinnamomum zeylanicum*, a plant of the laurel family cultivated in Ceylon and Java. Used as one of the perfumes of the 'holy anointing oil' (Ex. xxx. 23), and for beds (Pr. vii. 17), it was highly prized in Solomon's day (Ct. iv. 14), and was listed as one of the valuable commodities of 'Babylon the Great' (Rev. xviii. 13). See also CASSIA.

J.D.D.

CIRCUMCISION.

I. IN THE OLD TESTAMENT

The Old Testament gives a coherent account of the origin and practice of circumcision in Israel.

a. Origin

It is alleged that Ex. iv. 24 ff. and Jos. v. 2 ff., along with Gn. xvii, offer three different accounts of the origin of the rite, but, in fact, Ex. iv. 24 ff. makes no pretence at explaining the origin of the practice, and Jos. v. 2 ff. states that those who left Egypt were circumcised. Gn. xvii therefore remains as the sole biblical account of the origin of Israelite circumcision. It was integrated into the Mosaic system in connection with the Passover (Ex. xii. 44), and apparently continued throughout the Old Testament. It is a foundation feature of New Testament Judaism, and occasioned the Judaistic controversies of the apostolic period. The Jews in the New Testament had so associated circumcision with Moses that they had virtually forgotten its more fundamental association with Abraham (Acts xv. 1, 5, xxi. 21; Gal. v. 2, 3). Our Lord had to remind them that it antedated Moses (Jn. vii. 22); Paul is emphatic that it was the current understanding of the Mosaic connection which was obnoxious to Christianity (Gal. v. 2, 3, 11, *etc.*), and constantly brings his readers back to Abraham (Rom. iv. 11, xv. 8, *etc.*).

b. Significance of the practice

Gn. xvii shows circumcision as firstly a spiritual, and only secondarily a national, sign. That it is national, signifying membership of the Israelite nation, is not to be denied and is, indeed, as clear in Gn. xxxiv as ever it became after Moses (*cf.* Jdg. xiv. 3), but this is a by-product of the identification of the Israelite Church with the Israelite nation in the Old Testament, and circumcision belonged primarily to the Church. In Gn. xvii. 10, 11, 13, 14 circumcision is identified with the covenant made with Abraham (*cf.* Acts vii. 8); that is to say, circumcision signifies the gracious movement of God to man, and only derivatively, as we shall see, the consecration of man to God. This truth underlies Jos. v. 2 ff.: while the nation walked in the wilderness under God's displeasure (*cf.* Nu. xiv. 34, RVmg), the covenant was, as it were, in abeyance, and circumcision lapsed. Or again, when Moses spoke of possessing 'uncircumcised lips' (Ex. vi. 12, 30; *cf.* Je. vi. 10), only the gift of God's word can remedy it. Further, the New Testament speaks of circumcision as a 'seal' (Rom. iv. 11) upon God's gift of righteousness; also, the Lord Jesus is a minister of circumcision 'for the truth of God, that he might confirm the promises given unto the fathers' (Rom. xv. 8). Circumcision, therefore, is the token of that work of grace whereby God chooses out and marks men for His own.

The covenant of circumcision operates on the principle of the spiritual union of the household in its head. The covenant is 'between me and thee and thy seed after thee' (Gn. xvii. 7), and verses 26, 27 notably express the same truth: 'Abraham . . . Ishmael . . . and all the men of his house . . . were circumcised with him.' It was in this way that infant circumcision became the practice of most people in Israel—a practice which focused attention on the spiritual nature of the rite, whereas the deferring of circumcision to puberty or later adolescence inevitably makes it of primarily social importance, the entrance upon the privileges and duties of adult tribal membership.

Those who thus became members of the covenant were expected to show it outwardly by obedience to God's law, expressed to Abram in its most general form, 'Walk (thou) before me, and be thou perfect' (Gn. xvii. 1). The relation between circumcision and obedience remains a biblical constant (Je. iv. 4; Rom. ii. 25–29; *cf.* Acts xv. 5; Gal. v. 3). In this respect, circumcision involves the idea of consecration to God, but not as its essence. The blood which is shed in circumcision does not express the desperate lengths to which a man must go in self-consecration, but the costly demand which God makes of those whom He calls to Himself and marks with the sign of His covenant.

This response of obedience was not always forthcoming, and, though sign and thing signified are identified in Gn. xvii. 10, 13, 14, the Bible candidly allows that it is possible to possess the sign and nothing more, in which case it is spiritually defunct and, indeed, condemnatory (Rom. ii. 27). The Old Testament plainly teaches this, as it calls for the reality appropriate to the sign (Dt. x. 16; Je. iv. 4), warns that in the absence of the reality the sign is nothing (Je. ix. 25), and foresees the circumcising of the heart by God (Dt. xxx. 6).

II. IN THE NEW TESTAMENT

The New Testament is unequivocal: without obedience, circumcision becomes uncircumcision (Rom. ii. 25–29); the outward sign fades into insignificance when compared with the realities of keeping the commandments (1 Cor. vii. 18, 19), faith working by love (Gal. v. 6), and a new creation (Gal. vi. 15). Nevertheless, the Christian is not at liberty to scorn the sign. Although, in so far as it expressed salvation by works of law, the Christian must shun it (Gal. v. 2 ff.), yet in its inner meaning he needs it (Col. ii. 13; *cf.* Is. lii. 1). Consequently, there is a 'circumcision of Christ', the 'putting off (of) the body (and not only part) of the . . . flesh', a spiritual transaction not made with hands, a relation to Christ in His death and resurrection, sealed by the initiatory ordinance of the new covenant (Col. ii. 11, 12). Christians, as a result, 'are the circumcision' (Phil. iii. 3).

BIBLIOGRAPHY. L. Koehler, *Hebrew Man*, 1956, pp. 37 ff.; G. A. F. Knight, *A Christian Theology of the Old Testament*, 1959, pp. 238 f.; S. R. Driver, *The Book of Genesis*, *WC*, 1905, on Gn. xvii. 1 ff., and Additional Note on p. 189; C. Hodge, *Systematic Theology*, III, 1873, pp. 552 ff.; P. Marcel, *The Biblical Doctrine of Infant Baptism*, 1953, pp. 82 ff. J.A.M.

CISTERN (*bôr* or *bō'r*, from *bā'ar*, 'to dig or bore'), a subterranean reservoir for storing water which was collected from rainfall or from a spring. In contrast, the cylindrical well (*be'ēr*) received water from percolation through its walls. However, the term *bôr* is translated 'well' or 'pit' many times and 'cistern' only five times in the AV and ten times in the RV. Many cisterns are found in Palestine, where rainfall is scarce from May to September. They are usually pear-shaped with a small opening at the top which can be sealed to prevent accidents (Ex. xxi. 33, 34) and unauthorized use. Both Joseph (Gn. xxxvii. 22) and Jeremiah (Je. xxxviii. 6) nearly perished in such pits (*cf.* Zc. ix. 11). Most homes in Jerusalem had private cisterns (2 Ki. xviii. 31; *cf.* Pr. v. 15); but there were also huge public cisterns, one in the temple area having a capacity of over two million gallons. By 1200 BC cisterns were cemented, thus permitting large settlements in the barren Negeb region (*cf.* 2 Ch. xxvi. 10), especially in Nabataean and Byzantine times (Nelson Glueck, *Rivers in the Desert*, 1959, p. 94). See also DUNGEON, PIT, WELL. J.C.W.

CITIES OF REFUGE. These were places of asylum mentioned principally in Nu. xxxv. 9–34 and Jos. xx. 1–9 (where they are named). They are also mentioned in Nu. xxxv. 6; Jos. xxi. 13, 21, 27, 32, 38; 1 Ch. vi. 57, 67. From these it appears that they were among the cities of the Levites. Dt. iv. 41–43, xix. 1–13 deal with the institution indicated by this name (*cf.* Ex. xxi. 12–14).

In Israel's public life the law of retribution was to be applied, and is, moreover, specified in the *lex talionis* (see Ex. xxi. 23–25, *etc.*) which particularly applied in cases of bloodshed (see Gn. ix. 5 f.; Ex. xxi. 12; Lv. xxiv. 17, *etc.*; *cf.* also Dt. xxi. 1–9). In ancient Israel at least, the duty of punishing the slayer rested upon the *gō'ēl*, the nearest male relative. A distinction was made between slaying a man purposely or unawares. The wilful murderer was to be killed, while the unintentional murderer could find asylum in one of the cities of refuge. It may be said that the institution of the cities of refuge mainly served to prevent excesses which might develop from the execution of what is usually called the 'blood-feud'.

In 'the book of the covenant', Israel's oldest collection of laws, there is already a stipulation concerning this matter (Ex. xxi. 12–14). Perhaps the tendency of this regulation can be described as follows. Israel knew the ancient practice, which also prevailed among other nations, of regarding the altar or the sanctuary as an asylum. Here it is stipulated that the wilful slayer shall not find a refuge near the altar, though the unintentional slayer may do so. But the altar may be at a great distance, and, moreover, he cannot stay permanently near the altar, in the sanctuary. So the

Lord announces that He will make further provisions for this matter. The curious expression 'God delivered him into his hand' has been interpreted in the sense that the unintentional murderer is an instrument of God, and accordingly it is only natural that God should look after his protection. Examples of the altar as an asylum in Israel occur in 1 Ki. i. 50–53, ii. 28–34, while expressions such as those used in Ps. xxvii. 4–6, lxi. 4; Ob. 17 show that this practice was well known in Israel.

There are characteristic differences between the two principal groups of regulations concerning the cities of refuge, Nu. xxxv. 9 ff.; Dt. xix. 1 ff. (*cf.* Dt. iv. 41–43). As to the regulations of Nu. xxxv, which were also given in the plains of Moab (verse 1), we should note the following. The term 'cities of refuge, cities where a person is received (?)' is used. In due course Israel is to appoint three cities on the east side of Jordan, and three cities on the west side (verses 13 ff.), which cities are to be among the cities of the Levites (verse 6). The 'congregation' is to pronounce the final judgment (verses 12, 24). (During the wanderings through the desert this body made decisions in such cases. Here no further stipulation is made as to what body is to act in a similar capacity once Israel had settled in Canaan.) In verses 16–23 criteria are given to define accurately whether one has to do with intentional or unintentional murder. The unintentional slayer is to remain in the city until the death of the high priest (verses 25, 28, 32). In this connection the stay receives the character of an exile, of penance (verses 28, 32). Note also the stipulations of verses 30–32, with the important motivation, given in verses 33 f.

Dt. iv. 41–43 narrates how 'Moses severed three cities on this side Jordan toward the sunrising' (see below). Dt. xix. 1 ff. stipulates that, after the conquest of Canaan, three cities of refuge shall be appointed on the west side of Jordan, and another three in case of a further extension of Israel's territory (the last regulation was apparently never carried out). It is emphasized that the Israelites should take care that a slayer who killed ignorantly was within easy reach of a city of refuge (verses 3, 6 ff.). To indicate the difference between a wilful and unintentional murder, an example is given in verse 5. The elders of the slayer's dwelling-place are to make the final decision (verse 12).

According to Jos. xx, the following cities of refuge were appointed during Joshua's lifetime: Kedesh, Shechem, Kiriath-arba (= Hebron), Bezer, Ramoth, and Golan. Jos. xx assumes as known both the regulations of Nu. xxxv and of Dt. xix. A new feature here is that the elders of the cities of refuge also have a responsibility (verses 4, 5).

Nothing is known about the putting into practice of the right of asylum. Except for 1 Ki. i. 50–53, ii. 28–34, it is not mentioned, which *per se* need not surprise us. It is possible that, as the central authority established itself more firmly the right of asylum decreased in significance.

Concerning the dating of these passages and the historicity of the facts they contain, many scholars hold them to be the result of a development, as follows. Originally the sanctuary was the asylum. In the 7th century BC the authors of Deuteronomy aimed at the centralization of the cult. In this connection they secularized the right of asylum, and replaced the sanctuaries by a few cities and superseded the priests by the elders. Nu. xxxv contains a project dating from the exilic or post-exilic time which was never carried out. Jos. xx dates from an even later period.

But there seems to be no reason why we should not accept that the regulations in question date, at least in essence, from Moses' time, and that, indeed, Moses and Joshua appointed the cities mentioned as cities of refuge. It is obvious that this cannot be discussed as an isolated question, for it is closely connected with the dating of sources (see, *e.g.*, PENTATEUCH). Suffice it to say here that only in ancient times did these six cities belong to Israel's territory, Golan already being lost shortly after Solomon's death, and Bezer about 850 BC (according to the Moabite Stone, *etc.*). So it is no wonder that among those who accept, in broad outline, the view stated above, there are some scholars who consider Jos. xx. 7–9a as a relatively old tradition. It should then date from Solomon's time (see Nicolsky, de Vaux, and others).

Two questions remain for discussion. First, why was the unintentional slayer to remain in the city of refuge till the death of the high priest? One answer given is that his guilt devolved upon the high priest and was atoned for by the (untimely) death of the high priest. A similar view occurs already in the Talmud (*Makkoth* iib) and is still defended, among others by Nicolsky and Greenberg. This view has something attractive about it (*cf.* Ex. xxviii. 36–38), but is still questionable. It is better to take the view that by the death of the high priest a definite period was concluded.

Secondly, can it be stated with regard to the unintentional slayer that justice gave way to mercy? Probably the best thing to say is that the question cannot be answered, because the Old Testament does not distinguish between mercy and justice in the way we do. But the pronouncement that the decrees which the Lord gave to Israel were good and just (Dt. iv. 6 ff., *etc.*) certainly applies to the regulations concerning the cities of refuge. The answer to these two questions affects the extent to which we are to regard the regulations about the cities of refuge as Christological.

For the opinions of later Judaism on these regulations, see the Mishnah tractate *Makkoth* ii, and the tractate in the Talmud associated with it (*cf.* also Löhr, p. 34).

BIBLIOGRAPHY. N. M. Nicolsky, 'Das Asylrecht in Israel', *ZAW*, XLVIII, 1930, pp. 146–175; M. Löhr, *Das Asylwesen im Alten Testament*, 1930; M. David, 'Die Bestimmungen über die Asylstädte in Josua xx', *Oudtestamentische*

Studiën, IX, 1951, pp. 30–48; R. de Vaux, *Les Institutions de l'Ancien Testament*, I, 1958, pp. 247–250; M. Greenberg, 'The Biblical Conception of Asylum', *JBL*, LXXVIII, 1959, pp. 125–132. N.H.R.

CITY.

I. IN THE OLD TESTAMENT

The word *'îr* occurs 1,090 times in the Old Testament and describes a wide variety of permanent settlements. It does not appear to have regard to size or rights (*cf.* Gn. iv. 17, xix. 29, xxiv. 10; Ex. i. 11; Lv. xxv. 29, 31; 1 Sa. xv. 5, xx. 6; 2 Ki. xvii. 6; Je. li. 42, 43, 58; Jon. iii. 3; Na. iii. 1).

There are other words used in the Bible for city. Of the Hebrew words we note *qiryâ* (Ezr. iv. 10), *qiryā'* (Ezr. iv. 15, *etc.*), *qereṯ* (Jb. xxix. 7; Pr. viii. 3, ix. 3, *etc.*), *ša'ar*, literally 'gate', but used frequently for city or town in Deuteronomy (v. 14, xii. 15, xiv. 27, 28).

A city was either walled or unwalled. The spies that Moses sent to Canaan were told to report on this point (Nu. xiii. 19, 28). In their report they spoke of cities which were 'walled and very great' (*cf.* Dt. i. 28, 'walled up to heaven'). Many of the Canaanite cities which the Israelites encountered at the time of the conquest were in fact walled as a study of Jos. i–xi will show. In the case of Jericho a good deal is made of the walls (Jos. ii. 15, vi. 20). Modern excavation of several ancient cities gives information about the precise nature of the walls and the area enclosed. Excavation reports for specific cities should be consulted in each case (see the list of excavated sites inserted under ARCHAEOLOGY).

The word *ḥāṣēr* seems to be used specifically for the open village in distinction from *'îr*, which was probably enclosed in most cases, at least in some way (Gn. xxv. 16; Ex. viii. 13; Jos. xiii. 23). In order to be specific, a city defended by solid structures was called *'îr mibṣar*, a fortified city (Je. xxxiv. 7).

In any case, there was a central area where commerce and law were transacted, and round about were the 'suburbs' (*migrāš*, 'pasture grounds'), where farming was carried on (Nu. xxxv. 2; Jos. xiv. 4; 1 Ch. v. 16, vi. 55; Ezk. xlviii. 15, 17). There seem to have been villages as well in the general neighbourhood of the bigger towns, which were described as 'daughters', *bānôṯ*, and which were probably unwalled (Nu. xxi. 25, xxxii. 42; 2 Ch. xxviii. 18; Ne. xi. 25–31). Where the central city was walled it was the place of shelter for the entire surrounding population in times of danger (see FORTIFICATION AND SIEGECRAFT). In pre-Israelite times many of these areas with their walled city were small city states ruled by a 'king', *meleḵ*, and owing allegiance to some great power such as Egypt.

There are numerous references to non-Israelite cities in the Old Testament, among the most famous being Pithom and Ra'amses, the store-cities of the pharaoh (Ex. i. 11), the cities of the Philistines, which were really city states of the Greek type (1 Sa. vi. 17, 18), Damascus, the Syrian capital, Nineveh, 'an exceeding great city of three days journey' (Jon. iii. 3), Babylon the great (Dn. iv. 30; Je. li. 37, 43, 58), Susa (Shushan), the capital of Persia (Est. i. 2). Excavation and general archaeological research have given us a good deal of significant information about some of these cities. Thus Nineveh was a great walled city of nearly 10 miles circumference, but in the neighbourhood were two other Assyrian cities, Khorsabad and Nimrud, both of some size. In addition, there were numerous villages in the area. The extent of the city that was in the mind of the writer may not be quite clear today, but there is good reason to think of 'an exceeding great city'. Again Babylon was a remarkable city with great fortifications and palaces (see BABYLON, NINEVEH, and figs. 30, 152).

Inside the walls of the city would be found the houses of the citizens, possibly the large houses of the nobles, and even a palace (*q.v.*). Excavations in Palestine have given a good idea of the lay-out of these cities. The gate (*q.v.*) of the city was the place of commerce and law, and here the judges sat to give their decisions (Gn. xix. 1; 2 Sa. xv. 2–6; 1 Ki. xxii. 10; Am. v. 10, 12, 15). The number of gates varied. In Jericho there seems to have been only one gate, but in other cities there were several. The ideal city of Ezekiel had twelve gates (Ezk. xlviii. 30–35; *cf.* Rev. xxi. 12, 13).

Sometimes cities had a specific purpose. The Egyptian cities of Pithom and Ra'amses were store cities (Ex. i. 11) or 'treasure' cities. Solomon had cities for 'chariots and for horsemen' (1 Ki. iv. 26, ix. 19) as well as cities for stores. We judge that these were for defence and for grain storage. Excavations at Megiddo were particularly instructive in this regard, for they revealed that this town had at one time a huge grain storage bin of some 13,000 bushels capacity, and in Solomon's day had stables for 450 horses (see MEGIDDO).

At times cities were used in bargaining between states, and when treaties were drawn up and boundaries were adjusted there was often a transfer of cities from one state to another (1 Ki. ix. 10–14, xx. 34). At times also, cities formed part of a marriage dowry (1 Ki. ix. 16). Again, people of neighbouring states were always anxious to gain access to the markets of their neighbours and to 'make streets' in their cities (1 Ki. xx. 34), where trade could be carried on.

In any discussion of the term city in reference to the Bible Jerusalem should receive a special place, for among the cities of Israel Jerusalem predominated as the seat of the house of David and the centre of the religious life of the nation. It is termed the 'city of David' and the 'city of God', terms which have a close association with the pre-exilic worship of Israel and her king which is reflected in many of the psalms. The word did not of necessity, however, carry these overtones, and this is in marked contrast with the Greek term *polis*, which though of like etymology came to carry with it by implication the political and legislative concepts which were developed in the Greek states. *Polis* means 'state' or 'body politic' rather than merely 'city': it dominated Greek political thinking and became the normal word for city (with or without political overtones) in Hellenistic Greek. As such it translates *'îr* in the LXX: in this Hebrew setting it becomes again quite apolitical; the same is true of the word in the usage of Josephus. Philo is the only Jewish writer who, in his use of 'city', emphasizes men rather than walls; he expounds Adam, Abraham, and others of the Patriarchs, as citizens of the true city, *i.e.* the world of ideas in which they move and are at home. In this, as is his wont, he uses Greek concepts to explain and commend biblical, and like many liberals he is faithful more to the non-biblical by which he seeks to persuade than to the biblical which he claims to expound.

II. IN THE NEW TESTAMENT

In the New Testament *polis* is frequently found. In the Gospels it bears the extended and non-political sense of village, *etc.*, which is germane to the Jewish background of Jesus' ministry. In Acts it is used of various Hellenistic cities of Asia Minor and Europe but bears no reference to their political structure. In Rom. xvi. 23 we find the treasurer or steward of Corinth in fellowship with the Christian Church (the term is known from inscriptions): apart from Paul's boast in Acts xxi. 39, this is practically the only place in the New Testament where we find even the most distant allusion to the political structure of the city. It may be tempting, however, to see in the words of Acts xv. 28 *edoxen tō pneumati tō hagiō kai hēmin*, a phrase framed upon the civic formulary *edoxen tē boulē kai tō dēmō*. Even so, however attractive and suggestive the idea that here the Holy Spirit takes the place of the council and the apostles the assembly of citizens, it is quite clear that neither the apostles nor Luke are concerned to press the analogy.

The verb *politeuomai* means in the New Testament simply 'to live one's life, to conduct oneself' (Acts xxiii. 1; Phil. i. 27). The noun *politeia*, 'commonwealth' or 'body politic', is used with reference to the rights and privileges of Israel (Eph. ii. 12). *Politeuma* is used in Phil. iii. 20, where some seek to find in it the technical use as 'colony', and to translate the verse 'we are a colony of heaven' (so appropriate to Philippi). To render it thus, however, involves turning the sentence about, and the suggestion must be rejected. We find here either the less specific 'citizenship' (*cf.* Philo, *Concerning the Confusion of Tongues* 78; *Epistle to Diognetus* v. 9) or the very general 'way of life' (as AV 'conversation'), in which case *cf.* 2 Cor. iv. 18.

Jerusalem still possesses for the New Testament writers the title 'holy city' and ranks high in the esteem of Jesus as the city of the great King (Mt. v. 35). It remained until AD 70 a centre of Christian influence and a focus of esteem. Yet it is spoken of also as a city of sinful men who have persecuted and slain the prophets, over which Jesus weeps as He sees the approach of its doom. This spiritual ambivalence strikes us in Revelation. Jerusalem is the beloved city (xx. 9), object of God's promises, centre of the millennial reign; but in chapter xi the holy city is Sodom and Egypt where the Lord was crucified, and even the great city, a term normally reserved for the hybristic adversary of God (see chapters xvi–xviii), of which Jerusalem in that hour was the locus and type. We may compare Paul's contrast of two Jerusalems in Gal. iv. 24–26.

For the writer to the Hebrews and his addressees (whoever and however Hebrew either were), the emphasis lies upon the heavenly Jerusalem. It is their goal, the vision of which sustained the saints of old in their quest. In the coming of the Son it was given at length for a Man to sit down by God, to His brethren to come to the city of the living God, and to the just men to be at last made perfect (xii. 22, 23, xi. 40). But it is yet to come in its fulness, in that end which the writer so eagerly awaits. There are affinities here with Philo (*e.g. loc. cit. supra*), but Hebrews remains true to the kerygmatic points of crisis, the first and second comings of Jesus.

Heavenly Jerusalem, New Jerusalem, forms the subject of Rev. xxi, xxii. As recent study of Revelation has revealed and emphasized, a number of sources are laid under contribution for the description. In the first place, for the plan of the city, Ezk. xl–xlviii is of predominant importance, and, for the benefits and blessings of that place and state, prophecies, especially of Isaiah and Zechariah, provide much of the language. Such hopes are also to be found widely in Jewish apocalyptic writing. Secondly, since the comparative work of the religio-historical school of exegetes, the relation of the description to the astronomy and astrology of antiquity has tended to be stressed. The twelve precious stones of the foundation are well-known counterparts of the twelve Zodiacal signs: the intermingled stones and pearls reflect the starry heavens above, and both street and stream the Milky Way: the cubic dimensions of the city and its vast size are patterned on the vastness of space. Even the heavenly wall has its origin in the pillars of the sky. Thirdly, numerous parallels may also be drawn between this description and that of Hellenistic cities (and Babylon, their possible pattern) in Greek geographers and orators. In these courses we find a tetragonal plan, a central street, praise of a river flanked by avenues or dotted with wooded islets, visions of cities adorned with fine trees and rendered salubrious by natural situation and flora. Yet there is one marked contrast. There were many temples in Hellenistic cities; there are none, nor any need of one, in the new Jerusalem. No one source necessarily excludes the others; the recognition of all brings out the spiritual meaning of this vision. In the appointed end, when God is All in All, we find the fulfilment of Israel's hopes, the realization of God's promises to her; the manifestation, in a city which has the glory of God, of the reality already declared by the heavens and the firmament; and the answer to all aesthetic yearnings and national aspirations in the place to which the kings of the earth bring their glory. Of this city the reborn are citizens, and to it all pilgrims of faith tend. The city is also described as the Lamb's bride; it is in another aspect His Church for which He died, the pattern and goal of all human society. In the last analysis this chief of scriptural cities is men, not walls: just men made perfect, the city of the living God.

BIBLIOGRAPHY. R. de Vaux, *Les Institutions de l'Ancien Testament*, II, 1960, pp. 32 ff.; M. du Buit, *Géographie de la Terre Sainte*, 1958; R. S. Lamon and G. M. Shipton, *Megiddo I*, 1939; G. Loud, *Megiddo II*, 1948, pp. 46–57; R. de Vaux, articles on excavations at Tell el-Far'a in *Revue Biblique*, 1947–52; *TWB s.v.*; D. H. McQueen, *The Expositor* (Ninth Series), II, 1924, pp. 221–226; R. Knopf and G. Heinrici, *Festschrift*, 1914, pp. 213–219; Bousset and Charles, commentaries on *Revelation* on *loc. cit.*

J.A.T.
J.N.B.

CLAUDA. See CAUDA.

CLAUDIA. A Roman Christian, greeting Timothy (2 Tim. iv. 21); in some imaginative reconstructions the wife of Pudens (*q.v.*), and even, on the bad authority of *Apostolic Constitutions* vii. 2. 6, mother of Linus (*q.v.*). Alford, *in loc.*, identifies Timothy's friend with the British Claudia, whose marriage with one Pudens is celebrated by Martial (*cf. Epig.* iv. 13 with xi. 53), and with the hypothetical Claudia of a putative Pudens in a Chichester inscription (*CIL*, vii. 11). Martial, however, came to Rome only in AD 66, and implies scarcely Christian proclivities of his Pudens. Another Pudens and Claudia appear in *CIL*, vi. 15066; but Claudia is a very common contemporary name.

BIBLIOGRAPHY. J. B. Lightfoot, *Clement*, I, pp. 76 ff.; G. Edmundson, *The Church in Rome*, 1913, pp. 244 ff.

A.F.W.

CLAUDIUS. Roman Caesar from AD 41 to 54. He is supposed, on inconclusive grounds in each case, to have taken three different measures to deal with Christianity. (*a*) He expelled Jews from Rome for rioting at the instigation of Chrestus (Suetonius, *Claudius* 25). This is presumably the incident referred to in Acts xviii. 2. Chrestus is either a personal name or a variant of Christus. Suetonius assumes the former, and was, moreover, capable of recognizing Christianity. Even if he was wrong, it need not refer to *Christian* messianism. Neither Paul's welcome in Rome nor the Epistle to the Romans suggests any history of conflict between Jews and Christians there. (*b*) Claudius reprimanded Jewish agitators imported into Alexandria from Syria (H. I. Bell, *Jews and Christians in Egypt*, 1924). Apollos's defective knowledge of Christianity, however, suggests that these were not Christians. (*c*) A Caesarian decree (*JRS*, XXII, 1932, pp. 184 ff.),

Fig. 57. Sardonyx cameo showing the Emperor Claudius, wearing the laurel wreath for which Julius Caesar had set the fashion.

perhaps of Claudius, punished tomb robbery and was apparently published in Galilee. Whether or not this refers to the resurrection is likely to remain a moot point.

BIBLIOGRAPHY. W. den Boer, *RAC*, III, pp. 179–181.

E.A.J.

CLAUDIUS LYSIAS. In Acts xxi. 31 ff. the military tribune (Gk. *chiliarchos*, 'captain of a thousand'; AV, RV 'chief captain'; RSV 'tribune of the cohort') in command of the Roman garrison of the Fortress of Antonia in Jerusalem, who took Paul into custody. He had acquired his Roman citizenship by purchase (Acts xxii. 28); his *nomen* Claudius suggests that he had bought it in the principate of Claudius, when Roman citizenship became increasingly available for cash down. His *cognomen* Lysias implies that he was of Greek birth. His letter to Felix about Paul (Acts xxiii. 26–30) subtly rearranges the facts so as to place his own behaviour in the most favourable light.

F.F.B.

CLAY. See ARTS AND CRAFTS.

CLEAN AND UNCLEAN. A number of terms express cleanness and uncleanness in the Old Testament and New Testament. The Hebrew *ṭum'â* ('uncleanness') occurs twenty-six times, whereas the adjective *ṭāmē'* ('unclean') is found seventy-two times. Other words appear less frequently. The Greek *akatharsia* ('uncleanness') and *akathartos* ('unclean') occur forty-one times. Other terms are found less often. The concept of cleanness is conveyed by the Heb. *ṭāhōr*, *bārār*, and synonyms; the New Testament employs *katharos* almost exclusively. In the biblical words for 'clean', the physical, ritual, and ethical usages overlap.

I. CLEANLINESS HIGHLY REGARDED

Bodily cleanliness was esteemed highly and practised in Bible lands. Herodotus (ii. 27) stated that Egyptian priests bathed twice each day and twice each night. In Israel physical cleanness rendered a man ready to approach God, if his motive was proper. As early as the age of Noah the distinction between clean and unclean obtained. Gn. vii. 2 records: 'Of every clean beast thou shalt take to thee by sevens, the male and his female: and of beasts that are not clean by two, the male and his female.' The early references in Genesis to clean and unclean animals appear to have in mind the question of whether these animals were intended for sacrifice or not. Gn. ix. 3 is explicit that 'every moving thing that liveth shall be meat for you'. The regulations in Lv. xi and Dt. xiv make the distinction as a basis for food laws. It is stated: 'This is the law of the beasts, and of the fowl, and of every living creature that moveth in the waters, and of every creature that creepeth upon the earth: to make a difference between the unclean and the clean, and between the beast that may be eaten and the beast that may not be eaten' (Lv. xi. 46, 47).

II. IN EARLIEST TIMES

In patriarchal times and in the era of the monarchy in Israel the differentiation is found. Compare Gn. xxxi. 35 (the case of Rachel with the household gods of her father, Laban) and 1 Sa. xx. 26 (the incident of David's absence from the table of King Saul). Unfortunately, some writers have largely misunderstood the important distinctions here, because they have related all Old Testament regulations of this character to alleged originally superstitious taboos. (*Cf.* A. S. Peake, *HDB*, IV, pp. 825 ff.)

III. UNDER THE PROPHETS

The prophets, whose high ethical standards have been acclaimed on every hand, spoke of uncleanness also. Isaiah, envisioning the future age of righteousness, predicted that the way of holiness would not be traversed by the unclean (xxxv. 8); again, he called upon Jerusalem to gird on her strength, for the uncircumcised and the unclean would no longer trouble her in the hour of her glory (lii. 1). The plea is further made by the evangelical prophet for those in holy service to avoid any unclean thing, and to be clean in the handling of the sacred vessels of the Lord (lii. 11). Hosea, the prophet of the heartbroken love of God, warned his people that the northern kingdom would not only return to Egypt, but would eat the unclean in Assyria (ix. 3). Amos, the unparalleled champion of the righteousness of God, in response to coercion which would muzzle his prophetic testimony, foretold that Amaziah of Bethel would experience the hand of God heavily upon him in his immediate family, and would himself die in a polluted land (vii. 17). The priestly Ezekiel expressed in various ways the loathing he felt for the pollution of his people, and his own abhorrence for the manner in which he was called upon to portray it dramatically before them (iv. 14).

IV. THE MOSAIC LAW

The law of Moses made clear distinctions between clean and unclean, the holy and unholy (Lv. x. 10). Uncleanness was primarily ceremonial defilement, not moral, unless done wilfully. It kept a man from the service of the sanctuary and from fellowship with his co-religionists. Ceremonial defilement was contracted in several ways, and provision was made for cleansing.

a. Contact with a dead body rendered the individual unclean (Nu. xix. 11–22). The human corpse was the most defiling according to Old Testament regulations. In all probability it epitomized for the people of God the full gravity and ultimate consequences of sin.

b. Leprosy, whether in a person, clothing, or a house, was polluting (Lv. xiii, xiv).

c. Natural (those connected with the functions of reproduction) and unnatural issues were defiling to the observant Israelite (Lv. xii, xv).

d. Eating the flesh of an unclean bird, fish, or animal made one unclean. Lv. xi and Dt. xiv contain extended lists of the clean and unclean. Beasts of prey were considered unclean, because they consumed the blood and flesh of their victims. Unclean birds for the most part were birds of prey or those which fed on carrion. Fish without fins and scales were unclean. It is thought that their serpent-like appearance accounts for the prohibition against them. Eating of flesh of animals torn to pieces or violently slain was a source of uncleanness (Ex. xxii. 31; Lv. xvii. 15; Acts xv. 20, 29). Eating of blood was forbidden from earliest times (Gn. ix. 4).

e. Physical impairments were considered like uncleanness in their power to exclude from approach to the altar. The regulations are given explicitly for the sons of Aaron, the ministering priests in the sanctuary (Lv. xxi. 16–24). Finally, unpunished murder (Dt. xxi. 1–9) and especially idolatry (Ho. vi. 10) rendered the land unclean. The former struck at the image of God (Gn. ix. 6), whereas the latter was a violation of the spiritual worship due to God (Ex. xx. 4).

V. IN POST-EXILIC TIMES

The scribes of post-exilic times and the Pharisees of the New Testament period enlarged artificially the distinction between clean and unclean (Mk. vii. 2, 4). An elaborate and burdensome system developed therefrom. For example, a canonical book rendered the hands unclean; a non-canonical book did not. The largest of the six divisions of the Mishnah (*q.v.*) dealt with the subject of purifications. The multiplied regulations give validity to the observation of our Lord: 'Full well ye reject the commandment of

God, that ye may keep your own tradition' (Mk. vii. 9).

VI. THE NECESSITY AND FORM OF PURIFICATION

Israel was to be holy (Lv. xi. 44, 45) and separate from all uncleanness. Ceremonial uncleanness spoke of sin. Bodily cleanliness was required in their society. Laws of cleanliness were followed by the observant in their approach to God. The clean person is the one who can approach God in worship. See Ex. xix. 10 f., xxx. 18–21; Jos. iii. 5. In religious usage the clean denoted that which did not defile ceremonially. The term was employed of beasts (Gn. vii. 2), places (Lv. iv. 12), objects (Is. lxvi. 20), or persons who were not ceremonially (ritually) defiled (1 Sa. xx. 26; Ezk. xxxvi. 25). Ethical cleanness or purity is in view in Pss. xix. 9, li. 7, 10. A rare usage in the sense of 'blameless' or 'guiltless' is found in Acts xviii. 6.

The usual mode of purification was bathing of the body and washing of the clothes (Lv. xv. 8, 10, 11). Cleansing from an issue called for a special cleansing (Lv. xv. 19), also childbirth (Lv. xii. 2, 8; Lk. ii. 24), leprosy (Lv. xiv), contact with a corpse (Nu. xix; for a Nazirite, Nu. vi. 9–12). Cleansing may be physical (Je. iv. 11; Mt. viii. 3); ritual, by a sin-offering (Ex. xxix. 36), to expiate sin (Nu. xxxv. 33), to remove ceremonial defilement (Lv. xii. 7; Mk. i. 44); ethical, either by man's removal of the uncleanness or sin (Ps. cxix. 9; Jas. iv. 8), or by God's removal of the guilt (Ezk. xxiv. 13; Jn. xv. 2). Ritual cleansing was effected by water, fire, or the ashes of a red heifer. Psalm li. 7 is a good example of the ceremonial as a figure of the ethical or spiritual. David prayed: 'Purge me with hyssop, and I shall be clean: wash me, and I shall be whiter than snow.'

VII. THE NEW TESTAMENT VIEW

In His teachings Christ emphasized moral, rather than ceremonial, purity (Mk. vii. 1–23). His strongest denunciations were against those who elevated the ritual and external over the moral and ethical. What is important is not ceremonial, but moral, defilement. A careful reading of certain New Testament texts will give indications of the customs of the Jews regarding cleanness and defilement. Mark vii. 3, 4 is a concise statement of the regulations concerning washing of hands, defilement contracted in the market-place, and cleansing of utensils. John ii. 6 touches upon the method of purifying upon entering a household, and John iii. 25 indicates that the matter of cleansing was a ready subject for disputation. Strict regulations governed purification for the Feast of the Passover; these are alluded to in John xi. 55 and xviii. 28. The leper once cleansed was enjoined to offer for his cleansing what the law of Moses required (Mk. i. 44). In order to allay the opposition against him and procure for himself a readier acceptance in his message, Paul underwent the rite of purification in the Temple in Jerusalem (Acts xxi. 26). This puzzling behaviour must be evaluated in the light of the truth that Christ repealed all the levitical regulations on unclean meats and practices (Mt. xv. 1–20 and Mk. vii. 6–23), in the light of which Peter was commanded to act (Acts x. 13 ff.), and Paul promulgated his precepts for Christian conduct in his Epistles (Rom. xiv. 14, 20; 1 Cor. vi. 13; Col. ii. 16, 20–22; Tit. i. 15).

As is to be expected, the Gospels have most to say of the distinction between clean and unclean. Purification is treated in the Gospels under several categories. It is seen in relation to leprosy (Mt. viii. 2; Mk. i. 44; Lk. v. 14, xvii. 11–19). The word used in this connection is *katharizein*, but in Luke xvii. 15 (the case of the ten lepers) *iasthai* ('to heal') is employed. The cleansing of the leper had two parts: (*a*) the ritual with the two birds (Lv. xiv); and (*b*) the ceremony eight days later. In regard to food there was the ritualistic washing of the hands (Mt. xv. 1–20; Mk. vii. 1–23; Jn. ii. 6, iii. 25). As already indicated, there was a purification in connection with the Passover (Jn. xi. 55, xviii. 28). There had to be a thoroughgoing removal of all leaven from the home (Ex. xii. 15, 19, 20, xiii. 7). Finally, following childbirth an offering was brought at the termination of the period of uncleanness, that is, forty days for a male child and eighty for a girl (Lk. ii. 22).

VIII. CONCLUSION

Some have supposed that the laws regulating clean and unclean not only had the effect of hindering social and religious intercourse with the heathen, especially in the matter of eating, but were originally given to accomplish this purpose. Moore feels there is neither internal nor external evidence to support this position (*Judaism*, Vol. I, p. 21). He reasons thus: 'They were ancient customs, the origin and reason of which had long since been forgotten. Some of them are found among other Semites, or more widely; some were, so far as we know, peculiar to Israel; but as a whole, or we may say, as a system, they were the distinctive customs which the Jews had inherited from their ancestors with a religious sanction in the two categories of holy and polluted. Other peoples had their own, some of them for all classes, some, as among the Jews, specifically for the priests, and these systems also were distinctive' (*op. cit.*, pp. 21, 22).

In the discussion of the far-reaching rules which differentiate between clean and unclean among animals, fowl, and fish, various reasons have been given for these laws. The traditional and most obvious reason is the religious or spiritual: 'ye shall be holy men unto me' (Ex. xxii. 31). Another explanation is the hygienic. It was espoused by Maimonides, the great Jewish philosopher of the Middle Ages in Spain, and other notable scholars. The argument was that scaleless fish and the swine produce diseases. Still another interpretation was the psychological. The forbidden animals appeared either loathsome or begat a spirit of cruelty in those who ate them. A fourth reason is the dualistic. The

Israelites, like the Persians, are said to have assigned all unclean animals to an evil power. Another explanation is the national, which holds that the Israelites were surrounded with such prohibitions in order to keep them separate from all other nations. Opponents of this view have pointed out that the animals forbidden in the law of Moses are practically the same as those proscribed in the Hindu, Babylonian, and Egyptian religions.

The most popular theory in critical circles is that advanced by W. Robertson Smith (*The Religion of the Semites*, p. 270). Köhler states it succinctly, 'In view of the fact that almost every primitive tribe holds certain animals to be tabooed, the contention is that the forbidden or tabooed animal was originally regarded and worshipped as the totem of the clan; but the facts adduced do not sufficiently support the theory, especially in regard to the Semites, to allow it to be more than an ingenious conjecture . . .' (*JE*, IV, p. 599). If the scriptural data are allowed their normal force, the spiritual and national explanations are the correct ones.

BIBLIOGRAPHY. A. C. Zenos, 'Pure, Purity, Purification', *Standard Bible Dictionary*, pp. 719–721; G. A. Simcox, 'Clean and Unclean, Holy and Profane', *EB*, I, pp. 836–848; J. Hastings, 'Clean', *HDB*, I, p. 448; R. Bruce Taylor, 'Purification', *DCG*, II, pp. 457, 458; P. W. Crannell, 'Clean' and 'Cleanse', *ISBE*, I, pp. 667, 668; 'Uncleanness', *Westminster Dictionary*, p. 617; A. S. Peake, 'Unclean, Uncleanness', *HDB*, IV, pp. 825–834; Charles B. Williams, 'Uncleanness', *ISBE*, V, pp. 3035–3037; *JewE*, IV, pp. 110–113 and 596–600; George F. Moore, *Judaism*, I and II, 1927. C.L.F.

CLEMENT. A Philippian Christian mentioned in Phil. iv. 3. It is uncertain whether the reference means that the 'true yoke-fellow' addressed by Paul is asked to assist Clement as well as Euodia and Syntyche; or that Clement as well as Euodia and Syntyche laboured with Paul in the work of the gospel. AV appears to adopt the former interpretation and RSV the latter. Some of the early Fathers identified him with Clement, the bishop of Rome at the close of the 1st century; but as the date of Clement of Rome's death is uncertain, and the name was a common one, this also must be regarded as uncertain. R.V.G.T.

CLEOPAS (a contracted form of *Cleopatros*). One of the two disciples accosted by the risen Jesus on the afternoon of the first Easter Day as they were returning to their home at Emmaus (see Lk. xxiv. 18). When Jesus questioned them about the subject of their anxious conversation, Cleopas replied, 'Are you the only visitor to Jerusalem who does not know the things that have happened there in these days?' (See also CLEOPHAS.) R.V.G.T.

CLEOPHAS ('Clopas' in AVmg, RV, and RSV) is mentioned in Jn. xix. 25, where one of the women who stood near the cross is said to have been Mary *hē tou Klōpa*, an expression which could mean either the daughter, the wife, or the mother of Clopas. AV adopts the rendering 'wife'. The view that Cleophas was the father of the apostle described in the lists of the apostles as 'James, the son of Alphaeus' rests on the assumption that Cleophas and Alphaeus are renderings of the same Hebrew word—pronounced differently. In the early Latin and Syriac versions the Cleopas of Lk. xxiv. 18, was confused with the Clopas of Jn. xix. 25, but it is probable that they were two different people with two distinct names, as *eo* was usually contracted into *ou* and not into *ō*. R.V.G.T.

CLOUD. The regularity of the seasons in the Mediterranean area gives climatic significance to the appearance of clouds. But apart from the direction of wind influencing the weather and the colour of the evening sky, there is little evidence that the Hebrews understood the meteorological signs.

Clouds were well recognized as an indication of moisture. During the rainy season in the winter half-year, air-streams bringing rainfall are associated with cumulus clouds rising from the Mediterranean sea—'a cloud rising in the west' (Lk. xii. 54). Hence Gehazi was told to look seawards for the first indication that the spell of drought was to be broken (1 Ki. xviii. 44). Towards the end of the rainy season in April–May 'clouds of the latter rain' (Pr. xvi. 15) describe the king's favour, since they provide the necessary moisture to swell the ripening ears of grain. Contrasted are the high cirrus 'clouds without water' (Pr. xvi. 15; Is. xviii. 4, xxv. 5; Jude 12), which draw in desert air from the south-east and east, called Sirocco or Khamsīn, in association with depressions. The clouds and wind without rain (Pr. xxv. 14), the 'heat by the shadow of a cloud' (Is. xxv. 5), and subsequently the 'sky of brass' (Dt. xxviii. 23) vividly describe these dust-storms.

Clouds brought by sea-breezes readily dissolve as the hot, dry air of the interior is encountered. Thus the 'morning cloud' (Ho. vi. 4) is symbolic of transitory things, of human prosperity (Jb. xxx. 15), and of human life (Jb. vii. 9). It is also a text on the reality of divine forgiveness (Is. xliv. 22).

The usual luminosity of the Palestinian sky emphasizes that clouds cover and obscure (Ezk. xxxii. 7), and the joy of 'a morning without clouds in spring-time' (2 Sa. xxiii. 4) is vividly described. Like the cloud which hides the sun, divine favour or a supplication may be intercepted (La. ii. 1, iii. 44). Job prays that a cloud may rest upon the day of his birth (Jb. iii. 5).

The cloud frequently means the whole circle of the sky; *cf.* 'the bow in the cloud' (Gn. ix. 14). It represents the sphere of partial knowledge and hidden glory where God has a mysterious purpose in their motions (Jb. xxxvi. 29, xxxvii. 16, xxxviii. 37; Ps. lxxviii. 23). Thus too a cloud closes the scene of the incarnation (Acts i. 9), the transfiguration (Mt. xvii. 5; Mk. ix. 7; Lk. ix. 34), and clouds herald the second advent (Rev. i. 7). To the Israelites the cloud of God's presence was intimately related to their religious symbolism (Ex. xiii. 21, xl. 34; 1 Ki. viii. 10).

The clouds of Mk. xiv. 62, *etc.*, may refer to the ascension rather than the parousia.

J.M.H.

CNIDUS. A city of Caria in South-West Asia Minor, where Paul's ship changed course on its way to Rome (Acts xxvii. 7). Cnidus had Jewish inhabitants as early as the 2nd century BC (1 Macc. xv. 23), and had the status of free city.

J.D.D.

COAL. In the Old Testament (*MT*) there are five words rendered 'coal'. 1. *gaḥeleṯ* (*e.g.* Pr. xxvi. 21) means burning, as opposed to unlit, fuel; it is metaphorically employed in 2 Sa. xiv. 7, xxii. 9, 13. 2. *peḥām* (*e.g.* Pr. xxvi. 21; Is. xliv. 12) is used indifferently of unlit and burning fuel. 3. *riṣpâ* (*e.g.* Is. vi. 6; 1 Ki. xix. 6) means a flat stone girdle (*cf.* Arab. *raḍf*, *raḍafa*). 4. *rešep̄* (*e.g.* Ct. viii. 6) means 'burning coals'; it should perhaps be rendered 'fiery pestilence' in Hab. iii. 5. 5. *šeḥôr* (*e.g.* La. iv. 8) is literally 'blackness'.

In the New Testament the word *anthrax*, 'coal', occurs once (Rom. xii. 20) as a metaphor for feelings of shame, but elsewhere *anthrakia*, 'a heap of burning fuel', is used. See also FUEL.

R.J.W.

COCK. See BIRDS OF THE BIBLE.

COCKATRICE. See SERPENT.

COCKLE (*bo'šâ* = 'stinking weeds', AVmg; 'noisome weeds', RVmg). Referred to by Job while defending his integrity (xxxi. 38–40), this sturdy plant, *agrostemma githago*, common in Palestine and Syria, is a weed often found among wheat and barley crops.

J.D.D.

COELESYRIA (Gk. *koilē syria*, 'hollow Syria'), 1 Esdras ii. 17, *etc.*; 2 Macc. iii. 5, *etc.*, the valley lying between the Lebanon and Antilebanon ranges, modern El-Biqa' (*cf.* *biq'aṯ 'āwen*, 'the valley of Aven', Am. i. 5, RV). As a political region under the Ptolemaic and Seleucid Empires it frequently embraces a wider area, sometimes stretching as far north as Damascus and including Phoenicia to the west or Judaea to the south. From 312 to 198 BC it formed part of the Ptolemaic Empire, but fell to the Seleucids in consequence of the battle of Panion in the latter year. Coelesyria was an administrative division of the province of Syria after the Roman occupation (64 BC). Herod was appointed military prefect of Coelesyria by Sextus Caesar in 47 BC and again by Cassius in 43 BC.

F.F.B.

COINS. See MONEY.

COLLEGE (Heb. *mišneh*, 'second part', 'place of repetition'). The RV more correctly renders the word (2 Ki. xxii. 14 = 2 Ch. xxxiv. 22) as 'second quarter'—*i.e.* a quarter of the city lying to the north (*cf.* Zp. i. 10). Another possible reference is found in Ne. xi. 9, where the original could be read as 'over the second part of the city'. The rendering 'college' may be connected with the Targum of Jonathan on 2 Ki. xxii. 14, 'house of instruction'.

BIBLIOGRAPHY. J. Simons, 'The Wall of Manasseh and the "Mišneh" of Jerusalem', *Oudtestamentische Studiën*, VII, 1950, pp. 179–200.

J.D.D.

COLONY. A corporation of Roman citizens settled in foreign parts and enjoying local self-government. The objective was sometimes strategic, more often the rehabilitation of veterans or the unemployed, probably never economic or cultural romanization. In the East colonies were rare, and often composed of Gk.-speaking citizens in any case. The practice even grew up of conferring colonial status on Gk. republics for honorific reasons. The self-conscious Romanism at Philippi (Acts xvi. 12) was probably therefore exceptional, and none of the other colonies mentioned in the New Testament is noticed as such (Corinth, Syracuse, Troas, Pisidian Antioch, Lystra, Ptolemais, and possibly Iconium). Prominent in the affairs of most foreign states, however, was an association (*conventus*) of resident Roman citizens. The 'strangers of Rome' at Jerusalem (Acts ii. 10) are an example of this.

BIBLIOGRAPHY. A. H. M. Jones, *The Greek City from Alexander to Justinian*, 1940, pp. 61–84; A. N. Sherwin-White, *The Roman Citizenship*, 1939.

E.A.J.

COLOSSAE. A city in the Roman province of Asia, in the west of what is now Asiatic Turkey. It was situated about 10 miles farther up the Lycus valley from Laodicea (*q.v.*), on the main road from Ephesus to the east. It was originally the point at which the road to Sardis and Pergamum branched off, and was an important city in the Lydian kingdom and later in the Pergamene kingdom. But under the Romans its importance waned, partly because the road to Pergamum was resited farther west, and Laodicea became the larger and more prosperous city. The site is now uninhabited; it lies 10 miles east of the town of Denizli.

Like the rest of the Lycus valley, the gospel probably reached Colossae while Paul was living at Ephesus (Acts xix. 10), perhaps through Epaphras, who was a Colossian (Col. i. 7, iv. 12, 13). Paul apparently had not visited it when he wrote his letter (Col. i. 4, ii. 1), though his desire to do so (Phm. 22) may have been met at a later date. Philemon (Phm. 1) and his slave Onesimus (Col. iv. 9; Phm. 10) were among the other members of the early Colossian church. The mixture of Jewish, Greek, and Phrygian elements in the population of the city was probably found also in the church: it would have been fertile ground for the type of speculative heresy which Paul's letter was designed to counter.

E.M.B.G.

COLOSSIANS, EPISTLE TO THE.

I. OUTLINE OF CONTENTS

a. i. 1, 2. Address.
b. i. 3–8. Thanksgiving for the faith and love of the Colossian Christians, and for the fruit of the preaching of the gospel among them.
c. i. 9–12. Prayer for their growth in understanding, and consequently in good works.
d. i. 13–23. The glory and greatness of Christ, the Image of God, His Agent in the creation of all things, the Head of the Church, the One who by His cross reconciled all things to Himself.
e. i. 24–ii. 3. Paul's labours and sufferings in making known the mystery of Christ, and in seeking to present every man perfect in Christ.
f. ii. 4–iii. 4. The specific warning against the false teaching, and the apostle's answer to it.
g. iii. 5–18. The sins of the old life to be put off, and the virtues of the new to be put on with Christ.
h. iii. 19–iv. 1. Instructions concerning conduct to wives and husbands, children and parents, servants and masters.
i. iv. 2–6. Exhortation to prayer and wisdom of speech.
j. iv. 7–18. Personal messages.

II. AUTHORSHIP

No doubts about the genuineness of Colossians were expressed until the Tübingen school in the 19th century rejected the Pauline authorship of this and other letters on the basis of supposed Gnostic ideas present in them. Such arguments are no longer considered seriously. More serious are the arguments based on the vocabulary, style, and doctrine of this letter as compared with other Pauline letters, but these are not sufficiently strong to have led many scholars to reject the Pauline authorship (see *ICC*, pp. l–lix). The marked similarity to Ephesians has led a few to argue for the genuineness of that letter and against that of Colossians, but the evidence has almost always been taken overwhelmingly to indicate the priority of Colossians. (See EPHESIANS.) The connection of Colossians with the letter to Philemon and the nature of that letter are such that it stands virtually as Paul's 'signature' to Colossians.

III. TIME AND PLACE OF WRITING

There is little doubt that this letter was written by Paul from Rome at the time of the imprisonment referred to in Acts xxviii. 30 f. Alternative suggestions have been made, that it was written at the time of (*a*) his Caesarean imprisonment, or (*b*) an imprisonment in Ephesus. Both present serious difficulties, whereas there is no difficulty urged against the Roman origin of the letter that has not been adequately met. There is no place more likely than Rome to which the fugitive Onesimus would go, and the contents and personal references of the letter would seem to be more suited to Paul's Roman imprisonment than to any other. A date of AD 61 therefore seems likely.

IV. DESTINATION OF THE EPISTLE

Colossae was a city of Phrygia in the Roman province of Asia, situated, like Hierapolis and Laodicea, in the valley of the river Lycus. Its former importance was diminished by New Testament times, and was further reduced by a disastrous earthquake in the reign of Nero. Paul did not found the church there, nor had he visited it when he wrote this letter (i. 4, 7–9, ii. 1). On his second missionary journey he passed to the north of the Lycus valley (Acts xvi. 6–8). On his third journey Ephesus was for three years the centre of his labours (Acts xix. 1–20, xx. 31), and it is most likely that at this time the gospel reached Colossae through the agency of the Colossian Epaphras (i. 7, iv. 12). Most of the Christians there were Gentiles (i. 27, ii. 13), but from the time of Antiochus the Great there had been considerable and influential settlements of Jews in the neighbourhood.

V. REASON FOR THE EPISTLE

Two matters brought the church in Colossae especially before Paul, and occasioned the writing of this letter. First, he was writing and sending a messenger to Philemon in Colossae in connection with his runaway, but now converted, slave Onesimus (iv. 7–9; Phm.). Secondly, Epaphras had brought to Paul a report of the church in Colossae which included many encouraging things (i. 4–8), but also disquieting news of the false teaching that threatened to lead its members away from the truth of Christ.

VI. THE FALSE TEACHING

In his characteristic manner Paul meets the challenge confronting the Colossian church by positive teaching rather than by point-by-point refutation. Thus we do not know fully what it involved, but we may infer three things:

1. It gave an important place to the powers of the spirit world to the detriment of the place given to Christ. In ii. 18 he speaks of 'worshipping of angels', and other references to the relation of the spiritual creation to Christ (i. 16, 20, ii. 15) appear to have similar significance.

2. Great importance was attached to outward observances, such as feasts and fasts, new moons and sabbaths (ii. 16 f.), and probably also circumcision (ii. 11). These were presented proudly as the true way of self-discipline and the subjection of the flesh (ii. 20 ff.).

3. The teachers boasted that they possessed a higher philosophy. This is clear from ii. 4, 8, 18; and we may assume also that Paul, in his frequent use of the terms 'knowledge' (*gnōsis* and *epignōsis*), 'wisdom' (*sophia*), 'understanding' (*synesis*), and 'mystery' (*mystērion*), was countering such a view.

Some (*e.g.* Hort and Peake) have maintained that Jewish teaching could sufficiently account for all these different elements; Lightfoot argued that the false teaching was that of the Essenes, but we have no knowledge of the Essenes outside Palestine before AD 70. Others have identified the Colossian heresy with one of the Gnostic schools known to us from 2nd-century writers. We may not label it precisely, and the prevailing syncretism in religion and philosophy makes it unlikely that it was purely Jewish in origin. We would probably be as accurate as is possible in calling it a Judaistic form of Gnosticism.

Paul deals with these three errors as follows:

1. It is a misguided humility, he tells the Colossians, that exalts angels, and emphasizes the functions of the spirit powers of good and the fear of the principalities of evil; Christ is the Creator and Lord of all things in heaven and on earth, and the Vanquisher of all evil powers (i. 15 ff., ii. 9 ff.). All the fullness (*plērōma*) of the Godhead is in Christ. (Here, too, Paul was probably taking and putting to a Christian use one of the keywords in the false teaching.)

2. The way of holiness is not by an asceticism that promotes only spiritual pride, nor by self-centred efforts to control the passions, but by putting on Christ, setting one's affections on Him, and so stripping off all that is contrary to His will (ii. 20 ff., iii. 1 ff.).

3. The true wisdom is not a man-made philosophy (ii. 8), but the 'mystery' (revealed secret) of God in Christ, who indwells all who receive Him (i. 27), without distinction of persons (iii. 10 f.).

BIBLIOGRAPHY. J. B. Lightfoot, *St. Paul's Epistles to the Colossians and to Philemon*, 1875; H. C. G. Moule, 'The Epistles to Colossians and to Philemon', *CBSC*, 1893; T. K. Abbott, 'The Epistles to Ephesians and to the Colossians', *ICC*, 1897; A. S. Peake on Colossians in *EGT*; E. F. Scott, 'The Epistles of Paul to the Colossians, to Philemon, and to the Ephesians', *MNT*, 1930; C. F. D. Moule, 'The Epistles to the Colossians and to Philemon', *CGT*, 1957; 'Colossians' in Simpson and Bruce, *The Epistles of Paul to the Ephesians and to the Colossians*, *NLC*, 1957. F.F.

COLOURS. Colour-adjectives appear but sparsely in Old Testament and New Testament alike, for a variety of reasons. The first reason is specific: the Bible, being the account of God's dealings with a nation, and not the subjective record of a nation's aesthetic experience, is sparing in descriptive writing of the kind that involves extensive and precise use of adjectives of colour. Even where nature, animate or inanimate, is described in the Old Testament (as frequently in the Pentateuch, Job, and Psalms), it is nature in its more awe-inspiring aspects, as fitting reflection of nature's Creator.

The second reason is more general and linguistic: biblical Hebrew did not possess a complex and highly-developed colour vocabulary, such as exists in most modern Indo-European languages today. Thus, close definition of colour would have been difficult if not impossible, unless by the use of simile or metaphor. But this reason, which seems at first sight to be purely linguistic, turns out to be psychological, after all; for it is an axiom of linguistics that any culture, no matter how primitive, develops that vocabulary which is perfectly adequate to express its thought and desires. This linguistic paucity, then, corresponds to a lack of interest in colour as an aesthetic experience on the part of the Hebrew people; their practical concern was more with the nature of the material of which the article was made, by virtue of which it was a particular colour. Indeed, many of their colour-words were descriptive of origin rather than shade; *'argāmān*, for instance, is reddish-purple cloth, usually woollen. It is a borrowed word, and probably means 'tribute'. Other similar words contain a reference to the *murex*, the shellfish from whose juice the costly dye was obtained. In consequence, one clothed in purple is not to the Hebrew primarily a beautiful object. He is a king, or wealthy man; just as one in sackcloth is not primarily an ugly object, but a beggar or a mourner. This approach makes easy the symbolic use of colour, which appears spasmodically in the Old Testament and fully developed in the Apocalypse.

The New Testament writers were, of course, fully equipped with the extensive and flexible Greek colour-vocabulary; but they were, by virtue of their subject, concerned with colour as such even less than the writers of the Old Testament. In any case, fixity of shade, and therefore exact precision of terminology, had to wait until the advent of purely chemical dyes, which are easier to control, and the consequent development of colour-charts. In common with other ancient peoples, the Greeks were much more impressed by the contrast between light and shade than that between different colours. In other words, they tended to see and describe all colours as gradations between black and white. To compensate, they had a remarkably rich vocabulary to describe degrees of refracted light. When this is realized, many imagined Bible problems disappear; the fields of Jn. iv. 35, are not 'white already to harvest' but 'gleaming'; Ex. xxv. 4 groups 'blue, and purple, and scarlet' together, not only as all alike being symbols of richness, but because to the writer they were akin, perhaps scarcely differentiated, as being 'dark', not 'light', colours, similarly produced, and all alike being colours of textiles, *i.e.* artefacts and not natural objects.

For Joseph's coat of many colours, see JOSEPH.

BIBLIOGRAPHY. Platt, *CQ*, 1935; A. E. Kober, *The Use of Color Terms in the Greek Poets*, 1932, for discussion of the ancient attitude to colour, as reflected in Greek colour-vocabulary. A.C.

COLT. When this word appears in the English Bible the reference is to the young ass or (Gn. xxxii. 15 only) to the young camel (*qq.v.*).

COMFORTER. See Advocate.

COMING OF CHRIST. See Eschatology.

COMMANDMENTS. See Ten Commandments.

COMMERCE. See Trade and Commerce.

COMMUNION. In the New Testament the basic term, translated variously as 'communion', 'fellowship', 'communicate', 'partake', 'contribution', 'common' (in the sense of the Latin *communis*), stems from the Greek root *koin-*. There are two adjectives, *koinōnos* (found ten times) and *synkoinōnos* (found four times), which are used as nouns also; and two verbs *koinōneō* (eight times) and *synkoinōneō* (three times); and the noun *koinōnia* (twenty times).

The fundamental connotation of the root *koin-* is that of sharing in something (genitive) with someone (dative); or the simple cases may be replaced by a prepositional phrase. In both constructions nouns may be replaced by prepositions. Very rarely it may mean 'to give a share in' something; the most characteristic New Testament usage is that which employs *koin-* with the genitive of the thing (or person) shared. There is also another New Testament use in which the term is found actively of a 'willingness to give a share'; hence the meaning 'generosity'. A third meaning emerges from the first use, with the sense of 'sharing' or 'fellowship' (which arises out of a common sharing of something). The results of the recent linguistic researches of such scholars as H. Seesemann and A. R. George may be stated in the latter's words: 'The important thing is that these words (belonging to the *koin-* family) refer primarily, though not invariably, to participation in something rather than to association with others: and there is often a genitive to indicate that in which one participates or shares' (A. R. George, *Communion with God in the New Testament*, p. 133). From this ground-plan of the word, the New Testament passages may be divided into three classes, according to whether the predominant idea is (*a*) having a share; (*b*) giving a share; or (*c*) sharing.

a. 'Having a share'

Under this heading we may classify, first of all, the adjectives which are used to describe partners in some common enterprise, *e.g.* Christian work (2 Cor. viii. 23), or secular business (Lk. v. 10); also those who share in a common experience (*e.g.* persecution, Heb. x. 33; Rev. i. 9; suffering, 2 Cor. i. 7; worship, 1 Cor. x. 18; murder, Mt. xxiii. 30; the compact with demons in pagan cult worship, 1 Cor. x. 20). Then it is used similarly of those who enjoy certain privileges in common, *e.g.* Rom. xi. 17; 1 Cor. ix. 23. References to a common sharing in direct spiritual realities are Phil. i. 7, RV; 1 Pet. v. 1; and 2 Pet. i. 4, although in the first text the 'grace' in question may be that of apostleship in which both the apostle and church share, and of which Paul writes in Rom. i. 5; Eph. iii. 2, 8.

The verb *koinōneō* and its cognate form, which adds the prefix *syn* meaning 'together with', occur in eleven passages in the New Testament; but some of these will fall more naturally under section (*b*), *i.e.* they will lend themselves best to the translation 'generosity'. But under this heading we may note Rom. xv. 27; Eph. v. 11; 1 Tim. v. 22; 2 Jn. 11; Rev. xviii. 4; Phil. iv. 14; Heb. ii. 14.

The noun is found to denote the corporate Christian life with the thought that believers share together in certain objective realities (*cf.* E. Lohmeyer, *Der Brief an die Philipper*, 1956, p. 17, who denies that it is ever found in Paul's writing in the sense of a bond joining Christians together, but always with the meaning of participation in an object outside the believer's subjective experience). These references are most notably: (i) 1 Cor. x. 16 (RVmg 'participation in the blood and body of Christ'); (ii) 1 Cor. i. 9, where Anderson Scott's view aims at seeing *koinōnia* as a designation of the Church; but his interpretation here and elsewhere is being increasingly abandoned in favour of the objective sense of the genitive (or, with Deissmann, the 'mystical genitive' or 'genitive of fellowship'). So the best translation of a difficult verse is 'fellowship with his Son, Jesus Christ our Lord' whether in the sense of 'sharing in' or 'sharing with' Him; (iii) Phil. ii. 1, where the issue is to decide between a subjective genitive ('any fellowship wrought by the Spirit': so Anderson Scott, *Christianity According to St Paul*, 1927, pp. 160 ff.), or an objective genitive ('fellowship with the Spirit', 'participation in the Spirit': so convincingly Seesemann); (iv) 2 Cor. xiii. 14, where again the choice is between *koinōnia* as fellowship which is created by the Holy Spirit and fellowship as participation in the Holy Spirit, a translation (*cf.* RSVmg) which is much in favour since Seesemann's discussion in 1933; (v) 2 Cor. viii. 4, 'participation in the ministry to the saints'; and (vi) Phil. iii. 10, where the genitive is clearly objective, meaning that Paul's 'own actual sufferings are a real participation in Christ's sufferings, suffered by virtue of his communion with Christ' (A. R. George, *op. cit.*, p. 184; *cf.* R. P. Martin, *Philippians* in *TNTC*, pp. 49, 50).

b. 'Giving a share'

The main texts which support the interpretation of *koinōnia* as 'giving a share' are 2 Cor. ix. 13, 'the liberality of your contribution unto them and unto all'. 'Your contribution' represents the Greek *tēs koinōnias*, for which Seesemann proposes the translation *Mitteilsamkeit*, *i.e.*, in this context, generosity. This same rendering may be suggested also for Phil. i. 5 in which case the object of Paul's gratitude to God is the generosity of the Philippian Christians in their support of the apostolic ministry for the progress of the gospel. Similarly, the same translation clarifies Phm. 6.

Another reference under this heading is Rom. xv. 26, which indicates that *koinōnia* can take on a concrete form as a generosity which clothes itself in practical action, and is so applied to the collection for the saints of the Jerusalem church in their poverty-stricken condition (*cf.* 2 Cor. viii. 4). In this light we may consider, finally, Acts ii. 42, although A. R. George rules out the meaning of 'almsgiving', 'generosity'. Other views which have been offered to explain this reference are an allusion to the Lord's Supper, *q.v.* (*cf.* C. H. Dodd, *The Johannine Epistles*, 1946, p. 7); a technical expression for having a community of goods as in Acts ii. 44, iv. 32, as C. E. B. Cranfield takes it in *A Theological Wordbook of the Bible*, 1950, p. 82; Anderson Scott's view that the term *hē koinōnia* (= the fellowship) is the translation of a special word *ḥ*[a]*ḇûrâ* meaning a religious society within Judaism; a recent proposal of J. Jeremias that Acts ii. 42 lists, in its four notes of the Church's corporate life, the liturgical sequence of early Christian worship, in which case *koinōnia* is an allusion to the offering (*The Eucharistic Words of Jesus*, E.T., 1955, p. 83, note 3); and the view that *koinōnia* describes the inward spiritual bond which joined the early Jerusalem brotherhood and which expresses itself in the outward acts of a pooling of material resources (*cf.* L. S. Thornton, *The Common Life in the Body of Christ*, 1942, p. 451). See, further, R. N. Flew, *Jesus and His Church*[2], 1943, pp. 109, 110.

c. 'Sharing'

Under this heading there are only three possible occurrences where *koinōnia* is used absolutely or with the preposition *meta* (with). These are Acts ii. 42; Gal. ii. 9; and 1 Jn. i. 3 ff.

BIBLIOGRAPHY. The most important treatment of the *koin-* group of words in the New Testament is that by H. Seesemann, *Der Begriff KOINŌNIA im Neuen Testament*, *ZNTW*, Beiheft 14, 1933. His conclusions are utilized by most subsequent writers on this theme, especially A. R. George, *Communion with God in the New Testament*, 1953, who provides a full discussion of most of the controverted passages to which allusion has been made above. He gives also a complete bibliography, to which may be added the most recent contribution to the subject, namely, J. G. Davies, *Members One of Another, Aspects of Koinōnia*, 1958.

See also LORD'S SUPPER.

R.P.M.

COMPASSION. In the Bible it is a divine as well as a human quality. In the AV and RV the word is used about ten times to translate the Heb. *ḥāmal* and *raḥ*[a]*mîm* which are, however, more frequently rendered by 'pity' or 'spare' and 'mercy' respectively. Thus compassion, pity, and mercy can be regarded as synonyms. In the New Testament the most frequent words are *eleeō* (and cognate forms), translated by 'have compassion', 'have mercy', and 'have pity', and *eleos*, which is always translated 'mercy'. *Oikteirō* is found twice and translated 'have compassion' and *oiktirmōn* three times with the meaning 'merciful' and 'of tender mercy'.

The prophets and other men of God were deeply aware of the wonder of God's mercy to sinful men. They taught that anyone who had experienced this would feel it his duty to have compassion on his fellows, especially 'the fatherless, the widow, and the stranger' (frequently named together as in Dt. x. 18, xiv. 29, xvi. 11, xxiv. 19; Je. xxii. 3, *etc.*) and also on the poor and the afflicted (Ps. cxlvi. 9; Jb. vi. 14; Pr. xix. 17; Zc. vii. 9, 10; Mi. vi. 8). There is no doubt from the frequent references in Deuteronomy that God expected His people to show compassion not only to each other but to foreigners who lived among them. Through the teaching of our Lord Jesus Christ, especially in the parable of the good Samaritan, it is clear that compassion is to be shown by His disciples to anyone who needs their help. It is to be like His, not only in being without respect of persons, but also in that it is expressed in deeds (1 Jn. iii. 17) which may involve personal sacrifice. See MERCY, POVERTY.

J.W.M.

CONCISION. By this deliberately offensive word (*katatomē*, Phil. iii. 2), Paul is not defaming circumcision, but condemning those who, without regard for spiritual truth, would enforce circumcision on Christians (*cf.* Gal. v. 12). The cognate verb (*katatemnō*) is used (Lv. xxi. 5, LXX) of forbidden heathen mutilations. To Christians, who are 'the circumcision' (Phil. iii. 3), the enforcement of the outmoded sign is tantamount to a heathenish gashing of the body.

J.A.M.

CONCUBINE. A secondary wife acquired by purchase or as a war captive, and allowed in a polygamous society such as existed in the Middle East in biblical times. The codes of Hammurabi, *etc.*, illustrate the non-Israelite background of this practice. Where marriages produced no heir, wives presented a slave concubine to their husbands in order to raise an heir (Gn. xvi. 2, 3). Handmaidens, given as a marriage gift, were often concubines (*e.g.* Zilpah in Gn. xxix. 24 and Bilhah in Gn. xxix. 29). Concubines were protected under Mosaic law (Ex. xxi. 7–11; Dt. xxi. 10–14), though they were distinguished from wives (Jdg. viii. 31) and were more easily divorced (Gn. xxi. 10–14). Kings such as Solomon went to excess in plurality of wives and concubines, and later prophets encouraged monogamy (Mal. ii. 14 ff.). The ideal woman of Pr. xxxi lived in a monogamous society.

By New Testament times monogamy was regularly practised among the Jews and is enjoined by Jesus and New Testament writers.

J.A.T.

CONEY. The meaning of the word coney has been confused by its popular Eng. usage for 'rabbit'. Heb. *šāpān* is clearly identifiable from its four Old Testament occurrences (Lv. xi. 5; Dt. xiv. 7; Ps. civ. 18; Pr. xxx. 26) as the Syrian rock hyrax, sometimes referred to as the rock coney. It belongs to a small order most nearly related to elephants, and is about the size of the Alpine marmot. It is entirely vegetarian and lives in rocky country. See fig. 39. G.C.

CONFECTION. See COSMETICS AND PERFUMERY.

CONFESSION. The word to 'confess' in both the Heb. and the Gk. (*yāḏâ* and *homologein*) has, as in English, a twofold reference. There is confession of faith and confession of sin. On the one hand, confession means to declare publicly a personal relationship with and allegiance to God. It is an act of open joyful commitment made to God in the presence of the world, by which a congregation or individuals bind themselves in loyalty to God or Jesus Christ. It is an avowal of faith which can have eternal eschatological consequences. On the other hand, it means to acknowledge sin and guilt in the light of God's revelation, and is thus generally an outward sign of repentance and faith. It may or may not be followed by forgiveness (Jos. vii. 19; Lv. xxvi. 40; Ps. xxxii. 5; Mt. xxvii. 4; 1 Jn. i. 9).

I. IN THE OLD TESTAMENT

In the Old Testament confession frequently has the character of praise, where the believer in gratitude declares what God has done redemptively for Israel or his own soul. The noun (*tôḏâ*) may thus mean confession, thanksgiving, praise, or even be used for a company of people singing songs of praise. Such acknowledgment of God's mighty acts of mercy and deliverance is consequently closely related to the confession of sin. Both aspects of confession form an integral part of prayer and true worship (Gn. xxxii. 9–11; 1 Ki. viii. 35; 2 Ch. vi. 26; Ne. i. 4–11, ix; Jb. xxxiii. 26–28; Pss. xxii, xxxii, li, cxvi; Dn. ix). Confession can lead the believer to pledge himself anew to God, to sing hymns of praise, to offer joyful sacrifice, and can give him a desire to tell others of God's mercy and to identify himself with the worshipping congregation in the house of God at Jerusalem.

II. IN THE NEW TESTAMENT

In the New Testament the Gk. word to 'confess' has the generic meaning of acknowledging something to be the case in agreement with others; it is primarily used with reference to faith in Christ. It gathers up the Old Testament aspects of thanksgiving and joyful praise, as well as of willing submission, as in Mt. xi. 25; Rom. xv. 9; Heb. xiii. 15. In this it follows the LXX usage of the word, as in Pss. xlii. 6, xliii. 4, 5; Gn. xxix. 34. It means, however, more than mental assent. It implies a decision to pledge oneself in loyalty to Jesus Christ as Lord in response to the work of the Holy Spirit.

To confess Jesus Christ is to acknowledge Him as the Messiah (Mt. xvi. 16; Mk. viii. 29; Jn. i. 41, ix. 22), as the Son of God (Mt. viii. 29; Jn. i. 34, 49; 1 Jn. iv. 15), that He came in the flesh (1 Jn. iv. 2; 2 Jn. 7), and that He is Lord, primarily on the ground of the resurrection and ascension (Rom. x. 9; 1 Cor. xii. 3; Phil. ii. 11).

Confession of Jesus Christ is linked intimately with the confession of sins. To confess Christ is to confess that He 'died for our sins', and conversely to confess one's sins in real repentance is to look to Christ for forgiveness (1 Jn. i. 5–10). In preparation for the coming of Christ, John the Baptist summoned people to confess their sins, and confession was a constant element in the ministry both of our Lord and of the apostles (Mt. iii. 6, vi. 12; Lk. v. 8, xv. 21, xviii. 13, xix. 8; Jn. xx. 23; Jas. v. 16).

Although addressed to God, confession of faith in Jesus Christ should be made openly 'before men' (Mt. x. 32; Lk. xii. 8; 1 Tim. vi. 12), by word of mouth (Rom. x. 9; Phil. ii. 11), and may be costly (Mt. x. 32–39; Jn. ix. 22, xii. 42). It is the opposite of 'denying' the Lord. Confession of sin is likewise primarily addressed to God, but may also be made before men, for example, in corporate confession by a congregation or its representative in public prayer. Where the confession is for the benefit of the Church or of others, an individual may openly confess sins in the presence of the Church or of other believers (Acts xix. 18; Jas. v. 16), but this should never be unedifying (Eph. v. 12). True repentance may require an acknowledgment of guilt to a brother (Mt. v. 23, 24), but there is no suggestion that confession of private sin must be made to an individual presbyter.

Confession of Jesus Christ is the work of the Holy Spirit, and as such is the mark of the true Church, the Body of Christ (Mt. x. 20, xvi. 16–19; 1 Cor. xii. 3). For this reason it accompanies baptism (Acts viii. 37, x. 44–48), out of which practice emerged some of the earliest creeds and confessions of the Church, which acquired added significance with the rise of error and false doctrine (1 Jn. iv. 2; 2 Jn. 7).

The perfect pattern of confession is given to us in Jesus Christ Himself, who witnessed a good confession before Pontius Pilate (1 Tim. vi. 12, 13). He confessed that He is the Christ (Mk. xiv. 62) and that He is a King (Jn. xviii. 36). His confession was before men, over against the false witness of His enemies (Mk. xiv. 56) and the denial of a disciple (Mk. xiv. 68), and was infinitely costly, with eternal consequences for all men. The Church in her confession identifies herself 'before many witnesses' with the 'good confession' of her crucified and risen Saviour. Her confession (of faith and of sin) is a sign that the old man is 'dead with Christ' and that she is possessed by her Lord, whom she is commissioned to serve.

Confession in the New Testament (like denial of Christ) has an eschatological perspective, leading either to judgment or salvation, because it is the outward manifestation of faith or lack of it. Christ will one day confess before the Father those who confess Him today, and deny those who deny Him (Mt. x. 32, 33; Lk. xii. 8; 2 Tim. ii. 11–13). Confession with the mouth is made to salvation (Rom. x. 9, 10, 13; 2 Cor. iv. 13, 14), and our confessions today are a foretaste of the Church's confessions of the last day, when every tongue shall confess that Jesus Christ is Lord (Rom. xiv. 11, 12; Phil. ii. 11; Rev. iv. 11, v. 12, vii. 10). J.B.T.

CONFIRMATION. Two main uses of this word can be cited.

1. Gk. *bebaiōsis* (Phil. i. 7; Heb. vi. 16) is thus rendered, meaning 'a making firm' and 'a valid ratification', respectively. In the Old Testament seven Heb. roots are rendered 'confirm', meaning either physical or moral strengthening or legal validation (*e.g.* Is. xxxv. 3; Est. ix. 32). In the New Testament four Gk. verbs are similarly used. These are as follows: 1. *bebaioun*; *e.g.* Rom. xv. 8, 'confirm the promises'. 2. *kyroun*, used of a covenant (Gal. iii. 15), and of a personal attitude (2 Cor. ii. 8—AV 'confirm your love'; RSV 'reaffirm your love'; *Arndt*, 'affirm' or 'reaffirm'). 3. *mesiteuein*, *e.g.* Heb. vi. 17 (AV 'confirm', RV, RSV 'interpose with an oath') where the meaning is that a promise is guaranteed because God is acting as Mediator. 4. *epistērizein* is Luke's word in Acts for the strengthening effect of an apostolic mission on fellow-Christians (xi. 2, Western Text), on the souls of the disciples (xiv. 22), on the churches (xv. 41). It is used absolutely in xv. 32.

2. The ecclesiastical rite known as 'confirmation', or 'laying on of hands', is not traced to these verses, where Luke speaks only of the consolidating effect on faith of the apostolic presence and preaching, but, presumably, to such passages as Acts viii. 14–17, xix. 1–6, where laying on of hands precedes a spectacular descent of the Holy Spirit upon previously baptized persons. Two observations may be made. In the first place, in these verses in Acts the gift of the Spirit is associated primarily with baptism, not with a subsequent and separate rite of 'laying on of hands' (*cf.* Heb. vi. 2). Secondly, Acts shows no constant sequence. Thus, laying on of hands may precede baptism, and be performed by one not an apostle (ix. 17 ff.); in Acts vi. 6, xiii. 3 it is associated, not with baptism, but with special tasks to be done (*cf.* Nu. xxvii. 18, 20, 23) in connection with the missionary activity of the Church. On the rite of 'confirmation', see bibliography in *ODCC*. M.R.W.F.

CONGREGATION, SOLEMN ASSEMBLY. The noun 'congregation' is used in AV to render six Heb. words, one of which is also translated 'assembly' in various places.

1. *mô'ēḏ* and *'ēḏâ* come from the root *yā'aḏ*, 'to appoint, assign, designate'. *mô'ēḏ* means an appointed time or place, or meeting, and occurs 223 times (*e.g.* Gn. xviii. 14; Ho. ix. 5). In its most frequent use *'ōhel mô'ēḏ* means the 'tent of meeting', AV 'tabernacle of the congregation'—a translation which fails to convey the sense of 'due appointment' (*e.g.* Ex. xxvii. 21). In Is. xiv. 13 *mô'ēḏ* is used for 'mount of the congregation'. See *BDB*. *'ēḏâ* occurs 149 times (never in Deuteronomy), and means a company of people assembled together by appointment (*e.g.* Ex. xvi. 1, 2, where the congregation of Israel are assembled by God for the purpose of journeying from Egypt to Canaan).

2. *qāhāl* occurs 123 times, and comes from a root meaning 'assemble together', whether for war (*e.g.* 2 Sa. xx. 14), rebellion (Nu. xvi. 3), or a religious purpose (*e.g.* Nu. x. 7). It is used in Dt. v. 22, where all Israel is assembled to hear the words of God, and in Dt. xxiii. 3, where solemn statements of excommunication are being made. On the distinction between *'ēḏâ* and *qāhāl*, see *HDB*, *RTWB*, and especially *TWNT* (*ekklēsia*). It is apparent that *'ēḏâ*, the older word, is in frequent use in Exodus and Numbers, and bears an almost technical sense of 'those gathered together' (for a specific purpose), but that *qāhāl*, preferred by Deuteronomy and later writers, came to mean 'all Israel gathered together by God as a theocratic state'.

3. The rare word *'aṣereṯ*, from a root meaning 'restrain' or 'confine', is rendered 'solemn assembly' (*e.g.* Is. i. 13; Ne. viii. 18; Am. v. 21) in connection with high festivals, *e.g.* Unleavened Bread, Tabernacles (Dt. xvi. 8; Lv. xxiii. 36). This word, translated as *panēgyris*, lies behind 'general assembly' in Heb. xii. 23.

4. In the LXX *ekklēsia* was usually employed to translate *qāhāl*, sometimes for *'ēḏâ*, for which *synagōgē* was also used. In the New Testament *ekklēsia* is normally rendered 'church', though Luke uses it in its classical sense in Acts xix. 39 of a summoned political assembly, and as a gathering in Acts xix. 32, 41. In Acts xiii. 43 *synagōgē* is rendered 'congregation' by the AV (RV and RSV correctly 'synagogue'); its use in Jas. ii. 2 indicates a Jewish-Christian meeting. Since *synagōgē*, like 'church' in English, had come to mean both the gathering and the building, and since the Christians no longer met in synagogues, they chose *ekklēsia* to describe themselves. M.R.W.F.

CONSCIENCE. The etymology of the Gk. word *syneidēsis* (as of its Lat. equivalent, *conscientia*) suggests that its proper meaning is 'co-knowledge' or, in C. J. Vaughan's phrase, the faculty of 'fellow-knowledge with oneself' (*Romans*, 1880, p. 40). Conscience, in other words, implies more than simply 'consciousness' or 'awareness', since it includes also judgment (in biblical terms a precisely moral judgment) upon a conscious act.

a. Background

The term *syneidēsis* is almost completely absent from the LXX, and if the concept which it denotes is not to be regarded as a New Testament invention (*cf.* the new meaning given in the New Testament to the term *agapē*), its origin must be sought in a nexus of Hellenistic and not Hebraic ideas. Against the weight of scholarship that opts for a Stoic origin of the term, including Denney (*Romans* in *EGT*), Dodd (*Romans* in *MNT*), and

Moffatt (on 1 Cor. viii. 7 ff. in *MNT*), stands the thesis of C. A. Pierce (in *Conscience in the New Testament*, 1955, pp. 13 ff.), who describes this suggestion as a 'fallacy'. He is much more ready to see the *fons et origo* of the Pauline use of the term *syneidēsis* in non-philosophical, popular Greek thought, and he comes to the conclusion that the word belongs to a group of words and phrases that recurs 'throughout the range of Greek writing as a whole . . . from the sixth century B.C. to the seventh century A.D.' (*ibid.*, pp. 16 f. In his *Gnosis*, 1949, Dom Jacques Dupont had already suggested that *syneidēsis* was a term taken over from 'la philosophie morale populaire' into the New Testament, and there reinterpreted; p. 267). The foundation word of this group is *synoida*, which occurs rarely in the New Testament, and means 'I know in common with', derivatively 'I bear witness' (Acts v. 2), or, as it is used in the particular construction *hautō syneidenai*, something akin to 'sharing knowledge with oneself' (1 Cor. iv. 4). But, according to Pierce, the differences that exist between the term *syneidēsis* as found in Greek thought and as used by the writers of the New Testament are less a matter of content than of emphasis, and are to be accounted for by the altogether new and richer biblical setting. It is, he says (*op. cit.*, p. 106), against the background of the 'idea of God, holy and righteous, creator and judge, as well as redeemer and quickener', that the New Testament use of 'conscience' must be considered.

b. Meaning

We cannot, however, escape the fact that in the New Testament there emerges a concept denoted by the word *syneidēsis* developed beyond, if not different from, anything that had gone before. For Greek philosophy and the Old Testament alike, reference was made to the state or to the law for the judgment of action. Compare, however, such an instance as 1 Sa. xxiv. 5, where 'heart', in the phrase 'David's heart smote him', plays the part of conscience. This actually conforms to the normative meaning of 'conscience' found in popular Greek, as the pain suffered by man as man, when by his actions begun or completed he 'transgresses the moral limits of his nature' (Pierce, *op. cit.*, p. 54; the effect of 'conscience' in this sense is illustrated, though the actual word does not occur, by the action of Adam and Eve in Gn. iii. 8). The one occurrence of *syneidēsis* in the LXX is in Ec. x. 20: 'Curse not the king in thy conscience (*en syneidēsei sou*)', where AV (followed by RV, RSV) has 'in thy thought'. This use does not conform to the pattern just noted, however, and it is only at Wisdom xvii. 11, the one clear Apocryphal appearance of the term (in its absolute form), that we find emerging a use which looks forward to the New Testament setting.

c. New Testament

Syneidēsis is often used in the Pauline letters, as well as in Hebrews, 1 Peter and two (Pauline) speeches in Acts. The word also occurs in the phrase 'convicted by their own conscience' in Jn. viii. 9, though this is rejected as a gloss by RV, RSV, and NEB (indeed, the whole *pericope de adultera*, viii. 1–11, is omitted in the best MSS, though probably more on the grounds of misplacement than of falsity). Even so, as the term is used in this passage it bears all the marks of 'the final Pauline doctrine in Romans' (Pierce, *op. cit.*, p. 105). It is this we must investigate.

The *locus classicus* for the Pauline use of *syneidēsis* is, of course, Rom. ii. 14 f. The implication of this passage is that God's general revelation of Himself as good and demanding goodness faces all men with moral responsibility. For the Jews the divine demands were made explicit in the Sinaitic Code, while the Gentiles perform 'by nature' what the law requires. But the recognition of their holy obligations, whether by Jew or Gentile, is something individually apprehended (the law is 'written in their hearts', verse 15) and, according to personal response, morally judged (for 'their conscience also bears witness' with the understanding of their heart, *ibid.*, RSV). And although 'conscience' belongs to all men, and is the means by which they appreciate actively the divine character and will, since it also 'presents man as his own judge' (B. F. Westcott, *Hebrews*, 1889, note on Heb. ix. 9, p. 293), it may be regarded as simultaneously a power 'apart' from man himself (*cf.* Rom. ix. 1).

It is just here that we can see the characteristic Pauline content of *syneidēsis* beginning to clarify. It is the contention of C. A. Pierce (*op. cit.*, pp. 66 ff.) that Paul was forced to find a place for 'the catchword of Corinth' in his 'comprehensive scheme', since it was forced upon him by Gentile controversialists. Whether or not Paul regarded it as the negative attribute that Pierce suggests, the fact remains that 'conscience' in its Pauline setting means again the pain suffered by man when he has done wrong (see Rom. xiii. 5, where Paul urges 'subjection' for the sake of *syneidēsis* as well as *orgē*—the personal and the social manifestations of the judgment of God). It is from this that man is delivered by dying to sin through incorporation into Christ (*cf.* Rom. vii. 15 and viii. 2). At the same time it is possible for man's conscience, the faculty by which he apprehends the moral demands of God, and which causes him pain when he falls short of those demands, to be inadequately disciplined and informed (1 Cor. viii. 7), to become weakened (1 Cor. viii. 12) and even defiled (viii. 7; *cf.* Tit. i. 15), and to become seared and ultimately insensible (1 Tim. iv. 2). For this reason it is essential for the conscience to be properly educated, and indeed *informed*, by the Holy Spirit. This is why 'conscience' and 'faith' cannot be separated. By repentance and faith man is delivered from conscience as 'pain'; but faith is also the means by which his conscience is 'quickened and informed' (Pierce, *op. cit.*, p. 110). To walk 'in newness of life' (Rom. vi. 4) implies a living, growing faith, through which the

Christian is open to the influence of the Holy Spirit (Rom. viii. 14), and this in turn is the guarantee of a 'good conscience' (1 Pet. iii. 16).

We must finally mention the use of this term in the Epistle to the Hebrews, where the writer introduces it in both of the major relations already noted. Under the terms of the old covenant, 'conscience' frustrated access to God Himself (ix. 9), though deliverance has been made possible by the work of Christ under the terms of the new covenant (ix. 14), and by the appropriation of the benefits of Christ's death through Christian initiation (x. 22; *cf.* 1 Pet. iii. 21). In terms of growth in the Christian life, therefore, the worshipper's conscience may be described as 'good' in the sense discussed above (Heb. xiii. 18; note the use of *peithometha*).

To summarize, we can see the function of 'conscience' as it appears in the New Testament, following two main lines of development: it is the means of moral judgment, painful and absolute since the judgment is in fact divine, upon the actions of an individual completed or begun; and it also acts as a witness and a guide in both the negative and the positive aspects of the individual's sanctification (see O. Hallesby, *Conscience*, 1950, p. 82 and chapter X).

BIBLIOGRAPHY. J. Dupont, *Gnosis*, 1949, and 'Syneidesis' in *Studia Hellenistica*, 1949, pp. 119–153 (for origins); O. Hallesby, *Conscience* (tr. C. J. Carlsen), 1950; C. A. Pierce, *Conscience in the New Testament*, 1955. S.S.S.

CONTENTMENT. The noun 'contentment' occurs only once in AV (1 Tim. vi. 6), but its Gk. equivalent *autarkeia* appears also in 2 Cor. ix. 8 as 'sufficiency'; the adjective *autarkēs* in Phil. iv. 11 and the verb in Lk. iii. 14; 1 Tim. vi. 8; Heb. xiii. 5; 3 Jn. 10; see also 2 Cor. xii. 9, 'is sufficient'. *Autarkeia* denotes freedom from reliance upon others, whether other persons or other things; hence the satisfaction of one's needs (2 Cor. ix. 8) or the control of one's desires (1 Tim. vi. 6, 8). It is not a passive acceptance of the *status quo*, but the positive assurance that God has supplied one's needs, and the consequent release from unnecessary desire. The Christian can be 'self-contained' because he has been satisfied by the grace of God (2 Cor. xii. 9). The Christian spirit of contentment follows the fundamental commandment of Ex. xx. 17 against covetousness, the precepts of Pr. xv. 17, xvii. 1, the exhortations of the prophets against avarice (*e.g.* Mi. ii. 2), and supremely the example and teaching of Jesus, who rebuked the discontent which grasps at material possessions to the neglect of God (Lk. xii. 13–21) and who commended such confidence in our Father in heaven as will dispel all anxiety concerning physical supplies (Mt. vi. 25–32). In the Old Testament the phrase 'be content' (from Heb. *yā'al*) indicates pleasure or willingness to do a certain action, usually one which has been requested by another person, *e.g.* Ex. ii. 21; Jdg. xvii. 11; 2 Ki. v. 23.

J.C.C.

CONVERSATION. In AV the word always has the meaning 'behaviour', 'conduct', 'manner of life'.

In the Old Testament the word appears twice only (Pss. xxxvii. 14 and l. 23), translating Heb. *dereḵ*, 'way', signifying the course one travels—a familiar form of speech in eastern lands.

In the New Testament it appears eighteen times, involving the following three groups of Gk. words. *Anastrophē*, meaning 'behaviour', literally 'a turning up and down' (*e.g.* in Gal. i. 13; 1 Pet. i. 15); and *anastrephesthai*, 'to behave oneself' (2 Cor. i. 12; Eph. ii. 3). *Politeuma*, meaning 'citizenship' (Phil. iii. 20), or 'commonwealth' (correctly rendered thus in Eph. ii. 12); and *politeuesthai*, 'to act as citizen' (Phil. i. 27). *Tropos*, meaning 'manner', or 'character', literally 'turning' (*cf.* Heb. xiii. 5, where RVmg translates 'turn of mind').

HDB suggests that the archaic English rendering of the first of the above groups tends to obscure the very marked emphasis on conduct in New Testament teaching. The actual word 'conduct' remarkably does not figure in AV, and occurs once only in RV (to render *agōgē* in 2 Tim. iii. 10), though the RV marginal readings and those of other EVV often convey more adequately the present-day meaning.

The New Testament words for the modern 'to converse' (*homileō* and *synomileō*) are found respectively in Lk. xxiv. 14, 15 and Acts x. 27.

J.D.D.

CONVERSION.

I. MEANING OF THE WORD

A turning, or returning, to God. The chief words for expressing this idea are, in the Old Testament, *šûḇ* (translated in EVV 'turn' or 'return'), and, in the New Testament, *strephomai* (Mt. xviii. 3; Jn. xii. 40: the middle voice expresses the reflexive quality of the action, *cf.* the French 'se convertir'), *epistrephō* (regularly used in LXX to render *šûḇ*), and (in Acts xv. 3 only) the cognate noun *epistrophē*. Despite the AV of Mt. xiii. 15, xviii. 3; Mk. iv. 12; Lk. xxii. 32; Jn. xii. 40; Acts iii. 19, xxviii. 27 (all changed to 'turn' or 'turn again' in RV), *epistrephō* is not used in the New Testament in the passive voice. *Šûḇ* and *epistrephō* can be used transitively as well as intransitively: in the Old Testament God is said to turn men to Himself (fifteen times), in the New Testament preachers are spoken of as turning men to God (Lk. i. 16 f., echoing Mal. iv. 5, 6; Jas. v. 19 f.; probably Acts xxvi. 18). The basic meaning which the *strephō* word-group, like *šûḇ*, expresses is to turn *back* (*re*turn: so Lk. ii. 39; Acts vii. 39) or turn *round* (*about* turn: so Rev. i. 12). The theological meaning of these terms represents a transference of this idea into the realm of man's relationship with God.

II. OLD TESTAMENT USAGE

The Old Testament speaks mostly of national conversions, once of a pagan community (Nineveh: Jon. iii. 7–10), otherwise of Israel; though there are also a few references to, and examples of, individual conversions (*cf.* Ps. li. 13, and the accounts of Naaman, 2 Ki. v; Josiah, 2 Ki. xxiii. 25; Manasseh, 2 Ch. xxxiii. 12 f.), together with prophecies of world-wide conversions (*cf.* Ps. xxii. 27). Conversion in the Old Testament means, simply, turning to Yahweh, Israel's covenant God. For Israelites, members of the covenant community by right of birth, conversion meant turning to 'Yahweh *thy God*' (Dt. iv. 30, xxx. 2, 10) in wholehearted sincerity after a period of disloyalty to the terms of the covenant. Conversion in Israel was thus essentially the returning of backsliders to God. The reason why individuals, or the community, needed to '(re)turn to the Lord' was that they had turned away from Him and strayed out of His paths. Hence national acts of returning to God were frequently marked by leader and people 'making a covenant', *i.e.* making together a fresh solemn profession that henceforth they would be wholly loyal to God's covenant, to which they had sat loose in the past (so under Joshua, Jos. xxiv. 25; Jehoiada, 2 Ki. xi. 17; Asa, 2 Ch. xv. 12; Hezekiah, 2 Ch. xxix. 10; Josiah, 2 Ch. xxxiv. 31). The theological basis for these public professions of conversion lay in the doctrine of the covenant. God's covenant with Israel was an abiding relationship; lapses into idolatry and sin exposed Israel to covenant chastisement (*cf.* Am. iii. 2), but could not destroy the covenant; and if Israel turned again to Yahweh, He would return to them in blessing (*cf.* Zc. i. 3) and the nation would be restored and healed (Dt. iv. 23–31, xxix–xxx. 10; Is. vi. 10).

The Old Testament stresses, however, that there is more to conversion than outward signs of sorrow and reformation of manners. A true turning to God under any circumstances will involve inward self-humbling, a real change of heart, and a sincere seeking after the Lord (Dt. iv. 29 f., xxx. 2, 10; Is. vi. 9 f.; Je. xxiv. 7), and will be accompanied by a new clarity of knowledge of His being and His ways (Je. xxiv. 7; *cf.* 2 Ki. v. 15; 2 Ch. xxxiii. 13).

III. NEW TESTAMENT USAGE

In the New Testament, *epistrephō* is only once used of the return to Christ of a Christian who has lapsed into sin (Peter: Lk. xxii. 32). Elsewhere, backsliders are exhorted, not to conversion, but to repentance (Rev. ii. 5, 16, 21 f.; iii. 3, 19), and the conversion-words refer only to that decisive turning to God whereby, through faith in Christ, a sinner, Jew or Gentile, secures present entry into the eschatological kingdom of God and receives the eschatological blessing of forgiveness of sins (Mt. xviii. 3; Acts iii. 19, xxvi. 18). This conversion secures the salvation which Christ has brought. It is a once-for-all, unrepeatable event, as the habitual use of the aorist in the oblique moods of the verbs indicates. It is described as a turning from the darkness of idolatry, sin, and the rule of Satan, to worship and serve the true God (Acts xiv. 15, xxvi. 18; 1 Thes. i. 9) and His Son Jesus Christ (1 Pet. ii. 25). It consists of an exercise of repentance and faith, which Christ and Paul link together as summing up between them the moral demand of the gospel (Mk. i. 15; Acts xx. 21). Repentance means a change of mind and heart towards God; faith means belief of His word and trust in His Christ; conversion covers both. Thus we find both repentance and faith linked with conversion, as the narrower with the wider concept (repentance and conversion, Acts iii. 19, xxvi. 20; faith and conversion, Acts xi. 21).

Though the New Testament records a number of conversion experiences, some more violent and dramatic (*e.g.* that of Paul, Acts ix. 5 ff.; of Cornelius, Acts x. 44 ff., *cf.* xv. 7 ff.; of the Philippian jailer, Acts xvi. 29 ff.), some more quiet and unspectacular (*e.g.* that of the eunuch, Acts viii. 30 ff.; of Lydia, Acts xvi. 14), the writers show no interest in the psychology of conversion as such. Luke makes space for three accounts of the conversions of Paul and of Cornelius (Acts x. 5 ff., xxii. 6 ff., xxvi. 12 ff., and x. 44 ff., xi. 15 ff., xv. 7 ff.) because of the supreme significance of these events in early Church history, not for any separate interest in the manifestations that accompanied them. The writers think of conversion dynamically—not as an experience, something one feels, but as an action, something one does—and they interpret it theologically, in terms of the gospel to which the convert assents and responds. Theologically, conversion means committing oneself to that union with Christ which baptism symbolizes: union with Him in death, which brings freedom from the penalty and dominion of sin, and union with Him in resurrection from death, to live to God through Him and walk with Him in newness of life through the power of the indwelling Holy Spirit. Christian conversion is commitment to Jesus Christ as divine Lord and Saviour, and this commitment means reckoning union with Christ to be a fact and living accordingly. (See Rom. vi. 1–14; Col. ii. 10–12, 20 ff., iii. 1 ff.)

IV. GENERAL CONCLUSION

Turning to God under any circumstances is, psychologically regarded, man's own act, deliberately considered, freely chosen and spontaneously performed. Yet the Bible makes it clear that it is also, in a more fundamental sense, God's work in him. The Old Testament says that sinners turn to God only when themselves turned by God (Je. xxxi. 18 f.; La. v. 21). The New Testament teaches that when men will and work for the furthering of God's will in regard to their salvation it is God's working in them that makes them do so (Phil. ii. 12 f.). Also, it describes the initial conversion of unbelievers to God as the result of a divine work in them in which, by its very nature, they could play no part, since it is essentially a curing of the spiritual impotence which has precluded their turning to God hitherto: a raising from death (Eph. ii. 1 ff.), a new birth (Jn. iii. 1 ff.), an opening of the heart (Acts

xvi. 14), an opening and enlightening of blinded eyes (2 Cor. iv. 4–6), and the giving of an understanding (1 Jn. v. 20). Man responds to the gospel only because God has first worked in him in this way. Furthermore, the accounts of Paul's conversion and various references to the power and conviction imparted by the Spirit to the converting word (*cf.* Jn. xvi. 8; 1 Cor. ii. 4 f.; 1 Thes. i. 5) show that God draws men to Himself under a strong, indeed overwhelming, sense of divine constraint. Thus, the AV's habit of rendering the active verb 'turn' by the interpretative passive, 'be converted', though bad translation, is good biblical theology.

See FAITH; REGENERATION; REPENTANCE.

J.I.P.

CONVOCATION. See CONGREGATION.

COOKING AND COOKING UTENSILS. See HOUSE, VESSELS.

COPPER. See MINING AND METALS.

COPPERSMITH. See ARTS AND CRAFTS.

COR (KOR). See WEIGHTS AND MEASURES.

CORAL. See JEWELS AND PRECIOUS STONES.

CORBAN. See SACRIFICE AND OFFERING (O.T.), I.

CORD, ROPE. A number of Heb. words and one Gk. word are thus rendered in the AV. 1. *ḥeḇel* is the most common and it is the usual word for rope, being translated 'cord' in Jos. ii. 15, *etc.*, 'line' in Mi. ii. 5, *etc.*, 'ropes' in 1 Ki. xx. 31, and 'tacklings' in Is. xxxiii. 23. Some consider it is related etymologically to the English 'cable'. 2. *'aḇōṯ*, lit. 'something intertwined', is also common and is rendered 'band' in Jb. xxxix. 10, *etc.*, 'cords' in Jdg. xv. 13, 14, and in Ps. cxviii. 27, *etc.*, and 'cart rope' in Is. v. 18. 3. *yeṯer*, the third general word, is variously rendered in Jdg. xvi. 7, Jb. xxx. 11, and Ps. xi. 2. Rope was normally made of twisted hair or strips of skin. 4. *mêṯār* (Ex. xxxv. 18, *etc.*) is a tent-cord. 5. *ḥûṭ* (Ec. iv. 12) is thread.

6. The only word employed in the New Testament is *schoinion*, 'bulrush rope', which is rendered 'cord' in Jn. ii. 15 and 'ropes' in Acts xxvii. 32.

G.W.G.

CORIANDER (*gaḏ*, Ex. xvi. 31; Nu. xi. 7). Indigenous to the Mediterranean area, this umbelliferous plant (*Coriandrum sativum*) is known to have been used as early as 1550 BC for culinary and medicinal purposes. Its aromatic seed, grey-yellow in colour, is about twice the size of a hemp seed. See MANNA.

J.D.D.

CORINTH. A city of Greece at the western end of the isthmus between central Greece and the Peloponnesus, in control of trade routes between northern Greece and the Peloponnese, and across the isthmus. The latter was particularly important because much trade was taken across the isthmus rather than round the stormy southern promontories of the Peloponnese. There were two harbours, Lechaeum 1½ miles west of the Corinthian Gulf, connected with the city by long walls; and Cenchreae 8½ miles east on the Saronic Gulf. Corinth thus became a flourishing centre of trade, as well as of industry, particularly ceramics. The town is dominated by the Acrocorinth (1,857 feet), a steep, flat-topped rock surmounted by the acropolis, which in ancient times contained, *inter alia*, a temple of Aphrodite, goddess of love, whose service gave rise to the city's proverbial immorality, notorious already by the time of Aristophanes (Strabo, 378; Athenaeus, 573).

From the late 4th century until 196 BC Corinth was held mainly by the Macedonians; but in that year it was liberated, with the rest of Greece, by T. Quintius Flamininus, and joined the Achaean League. After a period of opposition to Rome, and social revolution under the dictator Critolaus, the city was, in 146 BC, razed to the ground by the consul, L. Mummius, and its inhabitants sold into slavery.

In 46 BC Corinth was rebuilt by Caesar and began to recover its prosperity. Augustus made it the capital of the new province of Achaea, now detached from Macedonia and ruled by a separate proconsular governor.

Paul's eighteen months' stay in Corinth in his second missionary journey (Acts xviii. 1–18) has been dated by an inscription from Delphi which shows that Gallio came to Corinth as proconsul in AD 51 or 52 (Acts xviii. 12–17; see PAUL, section II). His *bēma*, or judgment seat (Acts xviii. 12), has also been identified, as has the *macellum* or meat-market (the 'shambles' of 1 Cor. x. 25, AV). An inscription near the theatre mentions an aedile Erastus, who has been identified with the treasurer of Rom. xvi. 23. See ERASTUS.

BIBLIOGRAPHY. Strabo, 378–382; Pausanias, ii. 1–4; Athenaeus, 573; *Corinth I–VIII* (Princeton University Press), 1951 onwards; *EBr. s.v.* 'Corinth' (with older bibliography); Excavation reports annually from 1896 to *A.J.Arch.*, *J.H.S.*, *Hesperia*; J. G. O'Neill, *Ancient Corinth*, 1930; H. G. Payne, *Necrocorinthia*, 1931; H. J. Cadbury, *JBL*, LIII, 1934, pp. 134 ff.; O. Broneer, *BA*, XIV, 1951, pp. 78 ff. Fine plates may be seen in van der Heyden and Scullard, *Atlas of the Classical World*, 1959, pp. 43 f.

J.H.H.

CORINTHIANS, EPISTLES TO THE.

I. OUTLINE OF CONTENTS

1 Corinthians

a. Greeting and exordium (i. 1–9).

b. Party divisions; Paul's teaching compared with that of Apollos (i. 10–iv. 21).

c. A case of unchastity (v. 1–13).

d. The undesirability of going before heathen tribunals; further warning against impurity (vi. 1–20).

e. Discussion about marriage (vii. 1–40).

f. The question of meats offered to idols; Paul's

practical interpretation of his apostolic office (viii. 1–xi. 1).

g. The correction of irregularities in meetings for worship; the head-covering of women; love feasts; the Lord's Supper (xi. 2–34).

h. Spiritual gifts (xii. 1–31; xiv. 1–40).

i. The true ideal: Christian love (xiii. 1–13).

j. The correct Christian teaching about the resurrection of the dead (xv. 1–58).

k. Instructions about the collection for Jerusalem; miscellaneous remarks; final greetings (xvi. 1–24).

2 Corinthians

a. Troubles and sufferings before the return of Titus (i. 1–14).

b. First plan of coming; defence against fickleness (i. 15–ii. 1).

c. Satisfaction at having changed plan; time for repentance of incestuous offender; need now for sympathy and pardon (ii. 2–11).

d. Mention of meeting with Titus brings back the exultant joy of that moment, and fills Paul with a sense of the vital issues hanging on his words (ii. 12–17).

e. The credentials of effective preaching; the new covenant which he preaches; the old and the new contrasted, with an eye to the Judaizers (iii. 1–18).

f. His heavy responsibility; his fitness and unfitness; his reliance on Christ (iv. 1–18).

g. The life after death when the spirit shall be free from the flesh (v. 1–9).

h. Paul urges the fear of judgment so that men can assess aright the urgency of the message of reconciliation (v. 10–21).

i. A plea to his hearers to give Christ the supreme place in their hearts (vi. 1–18).

j. Commendation of those who had stood out against impurity (vii. 1–16).

k. Arrangements for the collection for poor Christians in Jerusalem (viii. 1–ix. 15).

l. Final vindication of his apostolic authority (x. 1–18).

m. Accusation and self-defence against the Judaizers (xi. 1–29).

n. Even his infirmities were a ground of confidence and strength (xi. 30–xii. 8).

o. His projected visit, with the possibility that he may have to discipline offenders, but expressing the hope that they may be restored without such drastic treatment; Paul ends with words of peace and blessing (xii. 19–xiii. 14).

II. THE CHURCH AT CORINTH

a. Its foundation

An outline of the early history of the Corinthian church is provided in Acts xviii. In or about AD 50 Paul moved, alone, so far as we are told, from Macedonia, through the rather stony ground of Athens, into the livelier air of Corinth. He was anything but confident (1 Cor. ii. 3). He stayed with a Jewish couple, Aquila and Prisca (*q.v.*), probably already Christians and recently expelled from Rome. The first Corinthian church thus came about in Aquila's household. Paul, however, as his right and custom was, began regular synagogue preaching, bringing conviction of the Messiahship of Jesus to members of the Jewish community and to the fringe of interested Gentiles. An accession of strength to the Christian party in the arrival of Silas and Timothy, with good news from Macedonia (*cf.* 1 Thes. iii. 6), brought renewed strength to Paul's preaching. This provoked fierce opposition from the Jewish community, culminating in a breach between Paul and the synagogue. Henceforth his Corinthian ministry was predominantly Gentile; but his first centre was next door to the hostile synagogue, in the house of a Gentile God-fearer, Titius Justus. Probably, as in other places, the God-fearers as a whole adhered to the gospel, but so did some Jews by birth, including the high synagogue official Crispus (*cf.* 1 Cor. i. 14), perhaps followed by his colleague or successor Sosthenes (*q.v.*). Many townsmen now came to faith and were baptized—but not by Paul (1 Cor. i. 14).

The situation must have had both dangers and difficulties. Paul's state of mind when his Corinthian preaching began has already been mentioned. At some time Aquila and Prisca risked death for Paul's sake (Rom. xvi. 3), and it was perhaps while he was their guest at Corinth. Some acute distress may underlie the vision (Acts xviii. 9 ff.) assuring him of divine protection and of the large number that God had in Corinth. Matters came to a head when the Jews brought him into the proconsular court; but when Gallio ruled that the dispute was outside his jurisdiction (and connived at a spirited display of anti-Semitism by the bystanders), it was clear that for the moment there was nothing to fear from the civil power, and that Jewish spite could not overstep the law.

Paul's stay in Corinth lasted the (for him) unusually long period of eighteen months (Acts xviii. 11). When he left he took Aquila and Prisca with him; but in Ephesus the couple were of great spiritual benefit to another Christian Rabbi, Apollos, who moved on to Corinth and clearly made a deep impression. That he saw fresh conversions in the Jewish community may be implied in Acts xviii. 28; Paul's language may also suggest a deeper ministry of instruction (1 Cor. iii. 6). Other teachers followed. There was a Cephas party at Corinth (1 Cor. i. 12); this need not imply a personal visit from Peter, but it may have been formed by Jewish teachers from the older churches. Certainly the false apostles so vehemently attacked in 2 Cor. xi were Jewish, and presumed on that fact (*cf.* verse 22). Corinth had no shortage of 'instructors in Christ' (1 Cor. iv. 15).

b. Its composition

Corinth would, then, seem to have been a fairly large church (Acts xviii. 8, 10), and free from imminent danger of persecution: indeed, the Corinthians enjoyed more security than the apostle (1 Cor. iv. 9 ff.). It had some Jews in its membership, but it was predominantly Gentile and ex-pagan in character, with a significant proportion of members from vicious backgrounds (1 Cor. vi. 11). Judaizing tendencies, the bane of churches where members had been trained through the synagogue, seem not to have been a major issue in Corinth: they are present (*e.g.* 1 Cor. xii. 18) but incidental; and the Judaistic pseudo-apostles of 2 Corinthians with their 'other gospel' seem more concerned to blacken Paul's character than to secure conformity to the Torah. On the other hand, pagan habits (1 Cor. vi. 15), pagan clubs (1 Cor. viii, x), meals in pagan houses (1 Cor. x. 27 ff.), things which were part of the ABC for proselytes and God-fearers, receive extended treatment.

Socially, the church covered a wide range: what contact would the wealthy city-treasurer Erastus (*q.v.*) ordinarily have with the refugee Jewish saddler Aquila, or the domestic slaves of a visiting lady? (see CHLOE). However, the line between the haves and the have-nots could be drawn across the fellowship meal-table (1 Cor. xi. 21 f.). Although the majority were not of high birth or education (1 Cor. i. 26), there was an air of social and intellectual pretension about the church (*cf.* E. A. Judge, *The Social Pattern of Christian Groups in the First Century*, 1960, pp. 49–61). They delighted in cheap rhetoric (1 Cor. i. 20 ff., ii. 1 ff.), made comparisons between their teachers on a false basis (1 Cor. iii. 4 ff.), assumed airs of comfortable superiority (1 Cor. iv. 10 ff.), and modified some of Paul's 'cruder' doctrines to make them more acceptable to contemporary educated men (1 Cor. xv. 12).

The proneness of the Corinthians to faction and division (*e.g.* 1 Cor. iii. 3, xi. 18 f.; 2 Cor. xii. 20) may be associated with this. Parties assumed the names of the various teachers as battle-cries (1 Cor. i. 12). A case between members was being dragged through the pagan courts (1 Cor. vi. 1, 6). Opposite perversions were represented side by side: incest could be countenanced (1 Cor. v. 1), while some denied that married life could be holy (1 Cor. vii). How far any of these divisions represented pre-existing social and communal rivalries and antipathies in a large and diverse community, now put forward in a Christianized form in the church which united them, cannot now be said. Certainly Paul never suggests that the divisions concerned central doctrine. Rather were the Corinthians behaving 'just like men of the world' (1 Cor. iii. 3, Phillips)—surrendering to traditional tensions and feeding prejudice, envy, and hatred.

c. Its world of thought

Paul mentions the Corinthians' notable endowments in spiritual gifts (1 Cor. i. 5 f.). They delighted in the more spectacular of these, notably tongues, and allowed them unlimited indulgence (1 Cor. xii, xiii. 1, 8, xiv. 2 ff.). This gave rein to their besetting factiousness, conceit, and self-assertion, and scenes of confusion, useless to believers and distressing to outsiders, could result (1 Cor. xiv. 9 ff., 16, 23 ff.). Ecstasy was a recognized phenomenon in non-Christian, Graeco-Oriental religion, and the Corinthian delight in it was probably in part a 'carry-over'. Even blasphemous and Christ-dishonouring words could be spoken in ecstasy (1 Cor. xii. 2 f.). Women, perhaps more subject to abnormal psychical experiences than men, were taking an unrestricted part (1 Cor. xiv. 34 ff.).

More sophisticated Hellenistic elements in Corinthian Christianity were capable, if unchecked, of leading into the several forms of later Gnosticism (*q.v.*). Salvation was seen in terms of wisdom, in the possession of the secret of the universe (1 Cor. i. 19 ff., ii. 1 ff.). The Christian's key-word was said to be 'knowledge' (1 Cor. viii. 1). The gospel's centre of gravity was thus shifted away from the historical events of the cross and resurrection, and its essential 'otherness' from all human systems diluted.

The Greek and pagan background of the members had also conditioned them to the influence of the idea of the inherent evil of matter. This, rather than Paul's practical considerations (1 Cor. vii. 32 f.), would raise the question of whether marriage was desirable for saints, its physical aspect being particularly suspect (1 Cor. vii. 5, 37). Perhaps those who were given to sexual licence (1 Cor. vi. 16) justified themselves, like their 2nd-century successors, from the same premises; the gospel had liberated them from the evil power of matter. They were free, and consequently beyond reach of harm. The same pervasive principle underlies the modification of the resurrection hope asserted by some Corinthians (1 Cor. xv. 2). Greek thought was accustomed to the idea of the immortality of the soul: the Hebraic doctrine of the resurrection of the body was too 'materialistic' for them. The Corinthians were in danger of refining it away.

Some Corinthian attitudes to pagan sacrifice and club meals were also probably affected by Greek rationalism. Some had imbibed a scepticism, now reinforced by Christian faith, which held that 'an idol is nothing' (1 Cor. viii. 4); but they were prepared to maintain the sacrifice and the forms of pagan worship for their social value and significance (1 Cor. viii. 10). But there were others in the church, nourished in superstition and immature in faith. Their faith in Christ was real, but so, to them, were the demons (1 Cor. viii. 8 ff.). (On this section, see J. Denney, *The Expositor*, VII, 5, 1908, pp. 289 ff.)

There have been differing analyses of the thought-world of Corinthian Christianity: among those which at least deserve notice is that of Schlatter, who sees most of the perversions Paul notes as due to the 'Christ-party' (*cf.* 1 Cor. i. 12 with 2 Cor. x. 7), formed, he believes, by the Judaic false apostles of 2 Corinthians, and based on a mutilated version of Johannine expressions: pressing statements of the type of 1 Jn. iii. 9 and neglecting such as 1 Jn. i. 5, 6 (*The Church in New Testament Period*, E.T., 1955, chapter XX). But we have not really sufficient evidence to decide the relationship of the various parties to the perversions, and we must not assume too much unity or consistency in the Corinthian phenomena. The peculiarities of Christian faith, expression, worship, and morality show the pressures of varied cultural and environmental factors in a prosperous pagan city connected with both Greece and the Orient, and a church embracing different classes and religious backgrounds and levels of Christian attainment. The situation was complicated by half-understood Christian doctrines, served up with pretentious rhetoric, and irresponsible use of such slogans as 'Knowledge' (1 Cor. viii. 1) and 'Liberty' (1 Cor. viii. 9). And ever at hand were the world, the flesh, and the devil, in a characteristically yeasty Corinthian form.

And yet the Corinthians supplied abundant encouragement to Paul. At the most crucial period in their relations he could 'boast' to Titus that they would certainly respond aright, and both felt the confidence abundantly justified (2 Cor. vii. 14–16). Despite their dangerous statements on the resurrection, their faith still stood in Christ crucified and risen as preached by the apostles (1 Cor. xv. 1 f.). They were not yet so Greek and cultured as to refine away the Lord's return (1 Cor. i. 7). In 1 Corinthians it is only tendencies, albeit perilous tendencies, with which Paul has to wrestle. The disease is not so desperate as the 'other gospel' in Galatia. In 2 Corinthians there seems to be danger of the 'other gospel' being received by the Corinthians from a 'super-apostle' (2 Cor. xi. 4 f.), but the same letter is full of tender confidence in the Corinthians' essential loyalty.

III. THE RELATIONS OF PAUL AND THE CORINTHIANS

Despite the succession of teachers at Corinth, Paul stood in a peculiar relationship to the church there (*cf.* 1 Cor. iii. 10, iv. 15). His intense love for them is witnessed in every page of 2 Corinthians, and involved him in an agony of distress while he was unsure of their reactions (*e.g.* 2 Cor. vii. 3–5, xii. 15). It dictates the very vehemence of his reproaches (*e.g.* 2 Cor. vii. 8 ff., xi. 2). The Corinthians are the proofs of his apostolic commission (1 Cor. ix. 2), his letters testimonial from Christ (2 Cor. iii. 1 ff.).

There is less clarity on the scriptural allusions to Paul's connections by letter and visit, and, in view of the wide diversity of opinion on these, it seems best to collect the principal data.

a. Data from Acts

Paul left Corinth, with Prisca and Aquila, in (probably) AD 52 (Acts xviii. 18 ff.). For most of the succeeding two years he was at Ephesus, but he was apparently absent when Aquila (?) wrote a letter of commendation to Corinth for Apollos (Acts xviii. 27). In Ephesus he decided to go to Jerusalem but to return through Macedonia and Achaia (Corinth was in the latter province), and, as a first step, sent Timothy and Erastus in that direction (Acts xix. 21 f.). It was some time later, after the riot, that he followed, and spent three months in Achaia (Acts xx. 2, 3). It may be added that it is quite in Luke's manner to pass over quite considerable events in silence (*cf.* 2 Cor. xi. 24 ff.).

b. Data from 1 Corinthians

There is no hint of any visit other than the first; but a pastoral letter, warning of moral contagion, had been written (v. 9—some, improbably, translate 'I *write* in (this) epistle'). 'Chloe's people' brought news, not uniformly good, from Corinth (i. 11), and, to Paul's delight, his old friend Stephanas arrived (xvi. 17 f., *cf.* i. 16, xvi. 15) with others, bringing a 'little bit of Corinth' (Morris on xvi. 17) with them. It may be conjectured that they brought an official letter from the church: at any rate it is certain that 1 Corinthians is in part a reply to a letter (see below). Paul has failed to persuade Apollos to return at once to Corinth (xvi. 12), but Timothy is evidently on his way thither with 'the brethren' (xvi. 10 f.). The collection for Jerusalem is a familiar idea to the Corinthians, but has not yet been gathered (xvi. 1 ff.). Paul is coming 'shortly' (iv. 19), having decided not to call on his intended journey to Macedonia, and hopes to spend some time, perhaps a winter, with them, and possibly to sail with their delegates for Jerusalem; but meanwhile, work detains him in Ephesus till Pentecost (about early May).

c. Data from 2 Corinthians

Timothy is with Paul (i. 1), evidently in Macedonia: there is no mention of his intended mission of 1 Cor. xvi. 10 (*cf.* Acts xix. 22). Paul seems to be defending himself from a charge of light promises, in that he had failed to make a visit on his way *to and from* Macedonia (contrast 1 Cor. xvi. 7): he had thus changed his plan twice (2 Cor. i. 15 ff.). He asserts, however, that the reason was to spare the Corinthians 'another painful visit' (ii. 1—so RSV, NEB, probably correctly). He had written to them a sharp letter which cost him much distress (ii. 3 f.) and which he even at one time regretted having sent (vii. 8); but the effect was godly sorrow on the part of the Corinthians and punishment—in which he desires moderation—of the principal offender who called forth Paul's severity (ii. 5–11, vii. 9–12). Titus brought this good news (vii. 6). But in waiting for him Paul was in such agony to hear the result that he left an open field in Troas (ii. 12 f.) in hopes of meeting him in Macedonia. No peace awaited him there, however; to the external difficulties of the work was added fears about the Corinthians (vii. 5), until God brought sweet relief through Titus.

The collection has still not been taken up (viii, ix, *passim*), but the church was ready for it 'a year ago' (ix. 2). Titus will attend to this (viii. 6), and other tried and eminent brethren will assist him (viii. 16–23, *cf.* xii. 18, best translated 'I am asking Titus, and I am sending the brother along with him'—see Menzies and Tasker *in loc.*). Paul himself is now coming for the third time (xii. 14, xiii. 1): severe warnings given on his second visit (xiii. 2, RV) or, just possibly, *as if* on his second visit (*cf.* RVmg) will be implemented if the Corinthians remain obdurate.

The order of events seems reasonably clear up to the sending of 1 Corinthians. Thereafter, we must submit to some uncertainty.

d. How many letters?

It has been frequently assumed that the letter referred to in 2 Cor. ii, vii, is 1 Corinthians. The guilty person would be the incestuous man of 1 Cor. v and he 'that suffered wrong' (2 Cor. vii. 12) his father. (*Cf.* Zahn, *INT*, I, pp. 307 ff., for a good statement of this position.) But it may be questioned if the torments reflected in 2 Cor. ii. 4, vii. 8, and the motivation implied in 2 Cor. ii. 9 (where the context relates *wholly* to the offender) are appropriate to the general tone and contents of 1 Corinthians, and from 2 Cor. ii it looks as if the offence in question could be taken as against Paul personally. It would seem probable, then, that 2 Corinthians refers to a 'severe letter' sent *after* 1 Corinthians, dealing with one urgent matter. Its bearer was doubtless Titus, who brought back the news of its reception.

e. How many visits?

2 Cor. xii. 14, xiii. 1 can be taken to mean 'I am ready to come for the third time', implying a journey once intended and forborne; but it is most natural to read them, and 2 Cor. xiii. 2, as implying two completed visits. Acts mentions only one: and 1 Corinthians conveys no hint of Lightfoot's suggestion of a second visit before its composition. Further, 2 Cor. ii. 1, as we have seen, seems to say that Paul wanted to spare the Corinthians another painful visit. The visit of Acts xviii was not painful: another must therefore have been paid.

f. The 'painful visit' and the 'severe letter'

It thus seems likely that Paul visited Corinth from Ephesus sometime after 1 Corinthians was sent, and perhaps because the latter had not sufficiently improved the situation. The visit was neither protracted nor pleasant, nor could Paul feel satisfied with its outcome. He left, promising to return (2 Cor. i. 16); but, to avoid another and even more painful scene (2 Cor. i. 23, ii. 3, xiii. 2), and to give the Corinthians one more chance of submission (2 Cor. ii. 9), he postponed this, and returned to Asia (where he was in danger of his life, 2 Cor. i. 8 ff.), writing a very sharp letter to bring them to their senses. When 2 Corinthians is written, the worst is over: the projected third visit, though it will be painful for those who resist (2 Cor. x. 6–11, xiii. 1 f.), can be talked of cheerfully, and the collection, for which Paul had made provisional arrangements in projecting his visit in 1 Cor. xvi. 3, 4, could now be concluded against this visit.

As to the sense in which the intermediate visit was painful, we can say little. It is frequently suggested that Paul had a painful collapse in the face of those who resisted his authority, and of one man in particular, which provoked taunts such as those reflected in 2 Cor. x. 1, 10, xi. 6. Had this been the case, however, the reasons given for delaying the third visit would surely have carried little conviction, and there would have been little ground for the 'boasting' to Titus. The indications are that the visit was painful for the Corinthians as well as for Paul. Perhaps there was some dread sign, of which there may be hints in 1 Cor. v. 4 f., xi. 30. Even after this the Corinthians remained refractory, and Paul might well shrink from the thought of what he might be compelled to enforce if he returned. (*Cf.* R. Mackintosh, *The Expositor*, VII, 6, 1908, pp. 226 ff.)

g. The end of the affair

The above assumes the unity of our 2 Corinthians, and would need slight modification were 2 Cor. x–xiii part of the 'severe letter', as some argue (see below). On the same assumption, we may see that even after the 'severe letter' had brought repentance, opposition to Paul remained in some quarters in Corinth, the 'super-apostles' were dangerously influential, and a blighting alternative gospel might at least be given houseroom there (2 Cor. xi. 4). But the visit which is the subject of 2 Corinthians was paid at last (Acts xx. 2 ff.), and the collection was taken (Rom. xv. 26). The Epistle to the Romans, written during this third visit, provides the signs of a happy ending. After long frustrations and delays, Paul can now look for the fulfilment of his cherished hope—to preach in Rome and beyond it (Rom. i. 10, 13, 15, xv. 28). The Corinthian affair is over.

IV. THE CORINTHIAN CORRESPONDENCE

We can thus trace the following items in the correspondence between Paul and the Corinthians:

a. Paul's 'previous letter'

This contained (at least) instructions, not fully comprehended at Corinth, about not receiving evil-doers (1 Cor. v. 9 f.). Some have thought part may be preserved in 2 Cor. vi. 14–vii. 1, which, as it stands, is a long parenthesis in an otherwise connected flow of language.

b. The Corinthians' letter to Paul

Some idea of its contents may be deduced from Paul's allusions to it in 1 Corinthians; indeed, some points in that Epistle might be clearer if we could be certain what the Corinthian questions were.

One question concerned the lawfulness, or at least the Christian dignity, of marriage (vii. 1), and subordinate issues included re-marriage (vii. 8), mixed marriages (vii. 12), and virgins (*q.v.*)—whether of marriageable daughters or not is hard to say (vii. 25, *cf.* RV). Another question was the attitude to be adopted towards pagan sacrifice, apparently including the statement 'we have knowledge' (*sc.* of the nothingness of the heathen deities—viii. 1). At one point the Corinthians evidently said that they remembered Paul and observed what he had taught (xi. 2), to which statement Paul contrasts the unsuitable rôles they were now giving to women (xi. 3) and the disgraceful scenes which at times marred their public worship (xi. 17). Minor questions on the sacrament—if, indeed, the Corinthians raised these—could await Paul's arrival (xi. 34). The Corinthians did, however, ask something about spiritual gifts, probably about testing ecstatic utterances (xii. 1). There is nothing to show whether they mentioned the novel interpretation of the resurrection (xv. 12), but apparently they asked for details about the collection arrangements (xvi. 1).

c. 1 Corinthians

There is no real case for questioning the unity of 1 Corinthians. Attempts at dividing it into two or more letters, based on alleged differences in the travelling arrangements and the teaching on pagan sacrifices (*cf.* J. Héring, *1 Corinthiens*, 1948) savour of hypercriticism. The date cannot be decided; but xvi. 8 may suggest that it was written in the spring, or late winter, and general considerations show that the Ephesian residence ended in the late fifties. About AD 55 will not, therefore, be far out.

d. The 'severe letter'

This letter, or part of it, has often been detected in 2 Cor. x–xiii. The principal arguments in favour of this are: (i) The early chapters of 2 Corinthians breathe relief and thanksgiving and tender appeal. Why should Paul turn suddenly to biting sarcasm and violent denunciation? (ii) 2 Cor. x–xiii attacks interlopers who are not in evidence in i–ix: it is suggested, because they have by this time departed. (iii) Some passages in x–xiii (*e.g.* x. 6, xiii. 2, 10) are held to refer to matters as future which passages in i–ix (i. 23, ii. 3, 9) refer to in the past.

The implication is that the four last chapters of 2 Corinthians were written *before* the early ones. Whatever the attractions of this view, there is much against it: (i) There is no suggestion whatever of manuscript disturbance. (ii) Paul's general confidence in the Corinthians and his relief at their recent justification of it is not incompatible with the sharpest language about a poisonous minority whose influence could yet corrupt the church. The minority is not unnoticed in the earlier chapters, and its innuendoes can be sensed in i. 17 ff., ii. 17, iii. 1, iv. 2, 5, v. 12 ff. (iii) The parallels in language between chapters i, ii and x–xiii mentioned above can simply mean that the severe letter was sent to avoid an unpleasant visit. If this were the case, it seems strange that the severe letter should speak as if a *third* visit were imminent (xii. 14, xiii. 1 f.). (iv) It is assumed in xii. 18 (best read with epistolary aorists, 'I am desiring Titus to go to you', *etc.*) that Titus is well known at Corinth: which is natural enough if he had already taken the severe letter. Reference is made to this same mission of Titus and 'the brother' in the early chapters (viii. 16 ff.). (v) The sneers about the contrast of Paul's fierce letters and his miserable presence (x. 9 ff.) sound more like the verjuice of opponents defeated by the effect of the severe letter on the church (Titus would have heard them) than remarks picked up in Corinth during the painful visit and before the severe letter was sent.

2 Corinthians makes good sense if read as a unity, and the case for placing x–xiii before i–ix has not yet been established. On the whole question, see J. H. Kennedy, *The Second and Third Epistles to the Corinthians*, and K. Lake, *The Earlier Epistles of Paul*, 1927, pp. 144 ff., and *per contra*, R. V. G. Tasker, *ExpT*, XLVII, 1935–6, pp. 55–58 (and the commentaries of Menzies and Tasker).

e. 2 Corinthians

This was clearly written from Macedonia, where Paul met Titus (ii. 13). Since the Macedonians were told that the Corinthians were ready with their quota for Jerusalem 'a year ago' (viii. 10, ix. 2), and since, after three months in Achaia, Paul left Macedonia by April at latest (*cf.* Acts xx. 3, 6), we may conclude that 2 Corinthians was written in the autumn of the year following that in which 1 Corinthians was written.

f. Authenticity of the letters

This is hardly in doubt, whatever views are held on the unity of 2 Corinthians. No more ardently personal letter than 2 Corinthians was ever written. As for 1 Corinthians, a writer as early as Ignatius knows it 'almost by heart' (*The New Testament in the Apostolic Fathers*, p. 67).

BIBLIOGRAPHY. For the treatment of specific themes in the Epistles the reader is referred to the articles ATONEMENT, COMMUNION, IDOLS (MEATS OFFERED TO), MARRIAGE, PREACHING, RESURRECTION, SPIRITUAL GIFTS, and the various commentaries. Among the best of these in English are: *On 1 Corinthians:* Calvin; C. Hodge, 1857, re-issue 1953 (theological); T. C. Edwards, 1885 (Greek text, learned and stimulating); J. A. Beet, 1889; A. Robertson and A. Plummer, *ICC*, 1911 (Greek text); R. St. J. Parry, *CGT*, 1916; F. W. Grosheide, 1954; L. Morris, *TNTC*, 1958.

On 2 Corinthians: Calvin; C. Hodge, 1859, re-issue 1953; J. A. Beet, 1889; J. Denney, *EB*, 1894 (a stirring exposition); A. Menzies, 1912 (better on history and criticism than theology); A. Plummer, *ICC*, 1915 (Greek text: see also his smaller commentary in *CGT*); R. V. G. Tasker, *TNTC*, 1958.

The learned French Roman Catholic commentaries by E. B. Allo (1 Corinthians, 1935, 2 Corinthians, 1937) contain much of value. The German radical H. Lietzmann, *An die Korinther*, 1933, has also been influential. A.F.W.

CORMORANT. See Birds of the Bible.

CORN. The most common Old Testament words are: 1. *dāḡān*, wheat (fully-developed grain). 2. *bar*, grain of any kind standing in the open field (hence *bar* means also 'open country'). 3. *šeḇer*, corn, victuals, *i.e.* broken, crushed corn.

The tendency is, however, to regard 'corn' as an inclusive term to denote cereal grains. See Barley, Beans, Fitches, Lentils, Millet, Pulse, Rye, Wheat.

'A corn' (Gk. *kokkos*, 'kernel, grain') of wheat is mentioned in Jn. xii. 24. J.D.D.

CORNELIUS. In Acts x. 1 ff. a Roman centurion of Caesarea in Palestine, one of the class of Gentiles known as 'God-fearers' because of their attachment to Jewish religious practices, such as almsgiving and prayer, for which Cornelius receives special mention. Cornelius was a common *nomen* in the Roman world ever since Publius Cornelius Sulla in 82 BC liberated 10,000 slaves and enrolled them in his own *gens Cornelia*. The Cornelius of Acts is specially notable as the first Gentile convert to Christianity. As he and his household and friends listened to Peter's preaching, they believed and received the Holy Spirit, whereupon they were baptized at Peter's command. The importance of this occasion in Luke's eyes is emphasized by repetition (*cf.* Acts xi. 1–18, xv. 7, 14). The 'Italian band' to which Cornelius belonged was an auxiliary cohort of Roman citizens, whose presence in Syria in the 1st century AD is inscriptionally attested. F.F.B.

CORNERSTONE. Two passages deserve special comment. The first is Ps. cxviii. 22, 'the stone which the builders rejected is become the head of the corner' (Heb. *rō'š pinnâ*, LXX *kephalē gōnias*). In its context the phrase expressed the psalmist's sense of triumph that God had exalted him over his enemies to a place of high honour, but in its liturgical setting in the Feast of Tabernacles the idea of national rather than personal deliverance became predominant. A messianic passage in rabbinic exegesis, it was used by Christ of Himself in Mt. xxi. 42; Mk. xii. 10; Lk. xx. 17; and by Peter of Him in Acts iv. 11 and 1 Pet. ii. 7, thus explaining His rejection by the Jews and His divine exaltation as Head of the Church. It also underlies Eph. ii. 20 (Gk. *akrogōniaios*, *sc. lithos*), where Paul depicts the stones of the new Temple as compacted together by Christ, just as the head cornerstone holds together at the top of the joint two walls which might otherwise fall apart.

The second passage (Is. xxviii. 16) probably refers to the massive stonework of the Temple, symbolizing Yahweh's abiding presence amid His people. It is quoted, in conjunction with Is. viii. 14, in Rom. ix. 33 and in 1 Pet. ii. 6, where the stone is interpreted messianically of Christ as the stumbling-block to the unbeliever but as the unifying force among God's believing people.

Of other occurrences, Je. li. 26 is literal of stone for building; Jb. xxxviii. 6 refers to the substructure of the created world; Zc. x. 4 uses 'corner' metaphorically for 'ruler' (*cf.* Jdg. xx. 2; 1 Sa. xiv. 38) and is given a messianic interpretation in the Targum; Ps. cxliv. 12 (Heb. *zāwiyyōṯ*) probably refers to the beautifully carved corner-pillars of a palace.

Bibliography. E. E. LeBas, 'Was the Corner-Stone of Scripture a Pyramidion?', *PEQ*, LXXXII, 1946; S. H. Hooke, 'The Corner-Stone of Scripture' in *The Siege Perilous*, 1956, pp. 235 ff. J.B.Tr.

CORNET. See Music and Musical Instruments.

CORRUPTION (Gk. *phthora*, *diaphthora*) in EVV, and especially AV, usually connotes the transience of the present world order. In Rom. viii. 21 it is used of the liability of the material universe to change and decay; contrast the 'incorruptible' (Gk. *aphthartos*) inheritance reserved for believers (1 Pet. i. 4). In 1 Cor. xv. 42 ff. it denotes the liability of the 'natural' body to death and dissolution; 'corruptible' (Gk. *phthartos*) is practically equivalent to 'mortal' (Gk. *thnētos*), as 'incorruption' (Gk. *aphtharsia*), predicated of the 'spiritual' body, is a synonym of 'immortality' (Gk. *athanasia*). In Acts ii. 27 ff., xiii. 35 ff. 'corruption' (in the sense of decomposition) is the rendering of Gk. *diaphthora*, quoted from Ps. xvi. 10, LXX, for *MT šaḥaṯ* (RSV 'the Pit'), parallel to Sheol. As a messianic 'testimony' Ps. xvi. 10 in LXX lends itself even better than *MT* to the case of Jesus, whose body, being raised from death, 'saw no corruption' (Acts xiii. 37). See Death, Hell, Immortality, Pit.

Bibliography. E. F. Sutcliffe, *The Old Testament and the Future Life*, 1946, pp. 76–81.

F.F.B.

COS, COOS (Acts xxi. 1). A massive and mountainous island, one of the Sporades group, off the south-west coast of Asia Minor, near Halicarnassus. It was colonized at an early period by Dorian Greeks, and achieved fame as the site of the medical school founded in the 5th century BC by Hippocrates, and again as a literary centre, the home of Philetas and Theocritus, in the 3rd century BC. It was also noted for fine weaving.

The Romans made Cos a free state in the province of Asia, and the Emperor Claudius, influenced by his Coan physician, conferred on it immunity from taxes. Herod the Great was a benefactor of the people of Cos. K.L.McK.

COSMETICS AND PERFUMERY.

I. INTRODUCTORY

a. Scope

By cosmetics is here understood that wide range of concoctions from pulverized minerals, vegetable oils and extracts, and animal fats which has been used from earliest times to beautify, improve, or restore personal appearance ('visual' cosmetics) or to produce pleasing fragrances ('odoriferous' cosmetics).

b. Cosmetic vessels and appliances

In Scripture, little is said of the boxes, phials, flasks, spoons, and other cosmetic trinkets known from archaeology. Besides the 'perfume boxes' of Is. iii. 20, RV, RSV, a rendering the accuracy of which has been questioned, there is the well-known flask of precious ointment or spikenard with which the repentant woman anointed Christ's head (Lk. vii. 37; *cf.* Mt. xxvi. 7; Mk. xiv. 3). But Israelite town-sites in Palestine have produced many little patterned cosmetic-bowls;

Fig. 58. Israelite ivory cosmetic palette, the handle formed by a 'tree of life' design; the reverse of the palette is in the form of a woman's face. From Hazor, 8th century BC.

at most periods the tiny handled pottery vessels probably served for scent-bottles, while from 14th/13th-century BC Lachish comes a superb ivory ointment-flask. Egyptian ladies of rank favoured elaborate ivory cosmetic-spoons featuring lotuses, maidens, ducks, *etc.*, in shape, and these were sometimes used in Palestine too. For eye-paint there were many little boxes and tubes, and the paint was commonly applied with a little stick (*spatula*) of wood or bronze. Egypt has yielded scores of such pots and spatulae. See also MIRROR.

c. Hygiene

Throughout the biblical East, oil to anoint the body, with the object of soothing the sun-dried skin, was almost as essential as food and drink. This use of oil was customary except in mourning; see Dt. xxviii. 40 (its loss, a curse); Ru. iii. 3; 2 Sa. xii. 20 (*cf.* Mt. vi. 17). A striking example is the clothing, feeding, and anointing of the repatriated troops of King Ahaz (*c.* 730 BC), described in 2 Ch. xxviii. 15. Those with a passion for luxury, however, made free with expensive ointments (Am. vi. 6), a sure way to empty one's purse (Pr. xxi. 17).

External sources corroborate the biblical picture. In Ramesside Egypt (13th century BC) one papyrus mentions 600 *hin* of 'anointing-oil' for a gang of workmen; other workmen are given 'ointment to anoint them, three times in the month', or 'their corn-ration and their ointment' (see Caminos, *Late Egyptian Miscellanies*, 1954, pp. 307, 308, 312, 470). The same situation held true in Mesopotamia from at least the 18th century BC onwards. Oriental cosmetics, it must be remembered, were as much used for utilitarian as for decorative purposes. (See the oil-distribution texts from Mari, J. Bottéro, *Archives Royales de Mari*, VII, texts 5–85.)

II. PERFUMERS AND PERFUME-MAKING

In 1 Sa. viii. 13 Samuel pictures a typical king 'like all the nations round about' as requiring the services of 'perfumers (RVmg, RSV) and cooks and bakers'. Three aspects of this passage find illumination in external sources: the existence of palace perfumeries, the association of cosmetics-manufacture and cooking, and the basic (Heb.) term *rqḥ*.

a. Royal perfumeries

The great palace at Mari on the middle Euphrates (18th century BC) had its own perfumery, the *bīt-raqqi*, which had to supply large quantities of various ointments for the king's dignitaries and soldiers, and the perfumes which were required for bodily use, for ritual, festivals, and royal banquets. (See J. Bottéro, *Archives Royales de Mari*, VII, 1957, *Textes Économiques et Administratifs*, pp. 3–27 (texts 5–85), 176–183 (the various oils), 183–184 (large quantities), 274, n. 2, and p. 360 (*bīt-raqqi*).)

b. Methods of manufacture associated with cooking

The implication of 1 Sa. viii. 13, which groups together perfumers (AV 'confectionaries'), cooks, and bakers, also corresponds to ancient usage. The techniques of the perfumer were closely related to cooking. The perfume of flowers, *etc.*, could be extracted and 'fixed' by three processes. First is *enfleurage*: steeping the flowers in fat and continually changing them. Second is *maceration*: dipping the flowers, *etc.*, into hot fats or oils at 65° C (150° F). This was most widespread and closest to cooking. Third is *expressing*: squeezing out the scent-bearing juices by compressing flowers, *etc.*, in a bag. Oil of myrrh and other gum-resins were obtained by heating the substance concerned in a greasy-type 'fixative' oil/fat (plus water to avoid scent-evaporation); the perfume-essence of the myrrh or other 'resin' was thereby transferred to the greasy oil/fat which could then be strained off as liquid perfume. For these processes, see R. J. Forbes, *Studies in Ancient Technology*, III, 1955, pp. 9, 10, and references, and A. Lucas, *JEA*, XXIII, 1937, pp. 29, 30, 32, 33. The North Canaanite texts of Ugarit mention 'oil of the perfumer' (*šmn rqḥ*; see Gordon, *Ugaritic Literature*, 1949, p. 130) and items such as '10 logs of oil', '3 logs of perfume' (*ṯlṯ lg rqḥ*; see Gordon, *Ugaritic Manual*, III, 1955, p. 284, No. 1007—14th/13th century BC; the same measure (log) is used in Lv. xiv. 10, 12, 15, 21, 24 (see WEIGHTS AND MEASURES)).

These processes, so akin to cooking with fats, *etc.*, are sometimes pictured in Egyptian tomb-paintings of the 15th century BC, showing people pouring and stirring the mixture in heated pans, or moulding incense into fancy shapes. Typical examples will be found in Davies, *JEA*, XXVI, 1940, plate 22 with p. 133, and Forbes, *op. cit.*, p. 13 and fig. 1. The cookery aspect of perfumery is also directly reflected in an Egyptian term for 'perfumer', *ps-sgnn*, lit. 'cooker of ointment', and by the use of fire in the elaborate cosmetics-recipes from Assyria (on which see E. Ebeling, *Parfümrezepte und Kultische Texte aus Assur*, 1950).

c. The rqḥ terminology

The ordinary participle *roqeaḥ* is used for 'perfumer' in Ex. xxx. 25, 35 (AV 'compound', 'confection'), xxxvii. 29, and also in 1 Ch. ix. 30, where it refers to priests commissioned by David and Saul to make perfumes for the tabernacle. It also occurs in Ec. x. 1, where it is identical with Ugaritic *šmn rqḥ* quoted above. *Raqqāḥ*, fem. *raqqāḥâ*, is the noun-form for 'professional perfumer'; the latter is found in 1 Sa. viii. 13 (AV 'confectionaries'), the former occurs in Ne. iii. 8, 'Hananiah, a member (lit. 'son') of the perfumers' (guild)'. (*Cf.* Mendelsohn, *BASOR*, 80, 1940, p. 18.) Of words for 'perfume' itself, *rōqaḥ* occurs in Ex. xxx. 25, 35; *riqqûaḥ*, 'unguents', in Is. lvii. 9; *reqaḥ*, of spiced wine in Ct. viii. 2 (see FOOD); *merqaḥ*, 'perfume' or 'fragrance' (RSV), in Ct. v. 13; *meruqqāḥîm* is verbal passive in 'compounded with the perfumery of the artificer' in 2 Ch. xvi. 14; *mirqaḥaṯ* is 'ointment, perfumery' in 'makers of ointment', 1 Ch. ix. 30, and in 'an ointment, a perfume of the perfumer's art', Ex. xxx. 25; finally, *merqāḥâ*, '(pot of) ointment' in Jb. xli. 31, and perhaps in an imperative, 'spice the spicery', in a cooking context (?spiced meat), in Ezk. xxiv. 10 (difficult).

III. 'VISUAL' COSMETICS

a. 'Painting' of face and body

From the earliest times, ancient Oriental womenfolk used to paint round their eyes and darken their eyebrows with mineral pastes which were usually black. At first this was largely medicinal in aim (to protect the eyes from strong sunglare), but it speedily became principally a feminine fashion, giving an enlarged and intense appearance to the eyes. This is attested in Egypt, Palestine, and Mesopotamia.

In 841 BC Queen Jezebel is said to have used such cosmetics. 2 Ki. ix. 30 indicates that she 'treated her eyes with eye-paint (*pûḵ*) and adorned her head' before going to the window whence she was thrown to her death at Jehu's word. Over two centuries later two Heb. prophets pictured their idolatrous nation, faithless to God, as a woman made up for illegitimate lovers. Jeremiah (iv. 30) says 'you enlarge your eyes with eye-paint (*pûḵ*)', while Ezekiel (xxiii. 40) alleges 'you painted (*kāḥal*) your eyes . . .'. Note also Keren-happuch, the name of Job's third daughter (xlii. 14), 'horn of eye-paint'—*i.e.* source of beauty. Such eye-paint was prepared by grinding the mineral concerned to a fine powder and mixing it with water or gum to form a paste that could be kept in a receptacle and applied to the face with the finger or a spatula (see I*b*, above).

The minerals used require some comment. In Roman times an antimony compound was used in eye-preparations; the Lat. for antimony sulphide and then antimony itself is *stibium*. Unfortunately this has led to ancient Oriental eye-paints being generally dubbed antimony or stibium—in large measure, wrongly so. In Egypt green malachite was quickly superseded by black eye-paint (Egyp. *msdmt*). Analysis of many excavated samples has shown that this consisted principally of *galena* (lead sulphide), never of antimony except as an accidental impurity. (See A. Lucas, *Ancient Egyptian Materials and Industries*[3], 1948, pp. 99–104 and *cf.* pp. 222–228.) In Mesopotamia the Babylonians called their black eye-paint *guḫlu*, alleged to be either galena or antimony/stibium. (For the former, see Forbes, *Studies in Ancient Technology*, III, p. 18, who adduces no evidence for his case; for the latter, see R. C. Thompson, *Dictionary of Assyrian Chemistry and Geology*, 1936, pp. 49–51, where the evidence produced is irrelevant—but his 'needles of "lead"' would suit galena better than antimony.) *Guḫlu* is same as Heb. *kāḥal*, 'to paint (eyes)', and passed into Arabic as *kohl*, 'eye-paint'. Modern Arab. *kohl* is often just moistened soot; it can include galena but not antimony (*cf.* Lucas, *op. cit.*, p. 101). Hence Heb. *pûḵ*, 'eye-paint', was very likely galena rather than antimony. Thus, the *'aḇnê pûḵ* in the temple treasures (1 Ch. xxix. 2) would be 'lumps of galena'. The use of *pûḵ* in Is. liv. 11 (AV 'fair colours', RSV 'antimony'), may presuppose the employment of (powdered) galena as part of an (dark-tinted) adhesive (*e.g.* resin) for setting gem-stones. For resin plus powdered minerals in tinted adhesives for setting jewellery, *etc.*, see Lucas, *op. cit.*, pp. 12, 13.

In Egypt red ochre (red oxide of iron), often found in tombs, may have served as a rouge for colouring the cheeks (Lucas, *op. cit.*, p. 104). Egyptian ladies also used powder-puffs (Forbes, *op. cit.*, p. 20 and fig. 4) and lipstick (see the lively picture reproduced in *ANEP*, p. 23, fig. 78!).

In antiquity the leaves of the fragrant henna-plant (see IV, below) were crushed to provide a red dye for feet, hands, nails, and hair (Lucas, *op. cit.*, p. 107). In Mesopotamia the Sumerians used for face-powder yellow ochre, quaintly called 'golden clay' or 'face bloom'; the Babylonians commonly used red ochre (Forbes, *op. cit.*, p. 20). Similar fads doubtless pleased coquettish Hebrew ladies like those of Is. iii. 18–26.

b. Hairdressing and restoratives

Hair-styles were part of Ancient Near Eastern fashions. In Egypt skilled hairdressers attended to the coiffure (and wigs) of the great. For reproductions of these hairdressers and details of the hair-styles and the hair-pins used, see *ANEP*, p. 23, figs. 76, 77, and refs. on p. 259, and also E. Riefstahl, *JNES*, XV, 1956, pp. 10–17 with plates 8–14. Mesopotamia also had its fashions in hair-dressing (*cf.* B. Meissner, *Babylonien und Assyrien*, I, 1920, pp. 410, 411; *Revue d'Assyriologie*, XLVIII, 1934, pp. 113–129, 169–177, XLIX, pp. 9 ff.). Canaan and Israel, too, provide examples of a variety of coiffures with curls long or short (see G. E. Wright, *Biblical Archaeology*, 1957, p. 191 and figs. 136, 137, 72). In this connection notice Isaiah's jibe (iii. 24) and Jezebel's adorning her head (2 Ki. ix. 30). Ornate combs were popular (see, *e.g.*, *ANEP*, p. 21, fig. 67). Men in the Semitic world (in contrast to Egypt) rejoiced in fine beards and took care over their hair—witness Samson's seven locks (Jdg. xvi. 13, 19). Barbers and razors are well-known in the Old Testament (*e.g.* Ezk. v. 1, *etc.*) and in the Ancient Orient alike (*ANEP*, p. 24, figs. 80–83). Restoratives to repair the ravages of age were eagerly sought. Recipes found in the Egyptian medical papyri include one hopefully entitled 'Book of Transforming an Old Man into a Youth'; several were devoted to improving the complexion (see the renderings in Forbes, *op. cit.*, pp. 15–17).

IV. 'ODORIFEROUS' COSMETICS IN PERSONAL USE

a. Perfumery in the Song of Songs

'Ointment' is simply *šemen* (*ṭôb*) (i. 3, iv. 10); *rēaḥ*, 'fragrance', applies to man-made ointments (i. 3) and nature's scents (ii. 13) alike. Spikenard or nard (i. 12, iv. 13–14) is here very likely to be the same as the *lardu* of Assyro-Babylonian inscriptions, the root of the gingergrass *Cymbopogon schoenanthus* imported perhaps from Arabia (see R. C. Thompson, *Dictionary of Assyrian Botany*, 1949, p. 17). But the New Testament *nardos pistikē*, 'precious (spike)nard' (Mk. xiv. 3; Jn. xii. 3), is probably the *Nardostachys jatamansi* of India (Himalayas), a very expensive import for Roman Palestine. 'Bether' (Ct. ii. 17) is either a place-name or 'cleft mountains', rather than a spice. For myrrh (i. 13, iii. 6, iv. 6, v. 1) and liquid myrrh, *mōr 'ōḇēr* (v. 5, 13), see V*a*, below; for frankincense, see V*b*, below. The expressions 'mountain(s), hill, of myrrh, frankincense, spices' (iv. 6, viii. 14) may perhaps allude to the terraces (mentioned also by Egyptian texts) on which the producing trees grew.

In i. 14, iv. 13 *kōp̄er* may be the henna-plant with fragrant flowers whose leaves when crushed yield a red dye; see on henna, Lucas, *Ancient Egyptian Materials, etc.*, pp. 107, 355–357. 'Perfumed' in iii. 6 is *meqoṭṭereṯ*, same root as *qeṭōreṯ*, 'incense'; as for 'powders of the merchant', see the powder-puff reference at the end of III*a*, above. In iv. 14 *karkōm* is usually rendered as saffron; it could be either or both of saffron-crocus and turmeric, which yield a yellow dye (Thompson, *op. cit.*, pp. 160, 161, and refs. on Assyrian *azupiranu* and *kurkanu* for these). For calamus and cinnamon, see V*a*, below; on aloes, see ALOES. The verses v. 13, vi. 2 allude to beds of spices, *bōśem*, perhaps here specifically balm of Gilead, as opposed to its more general meaning of spices. For mandrakes (vii. 13), see MANDRAKE. 'Spiced wine' (viii. 2) is known elsewhere in the Ancient East; see FOOD.

b. Other references

Bōśem, 'perfume', in Is. iii. 24 is a general term in Scripture for spices; *cf.* the gifts of the Queen of Sheba (1 Ki. x. 2, 10), the treasures of Hezekiah (2 Ki. xx. 13), and the references in the Song of Solomon (iv. 10, 14, 16, viii. 14). Cleansing and beautifying of the body is apparently implied in the term *tamruq* used in Est. ii. 3 (AV, RV 'purifications'; RSV 'ointments'), when Esther and others were preparing for King Ahasuerus. The 'perfume' of Pr. xxvii. 9 is *qeṭōreṯ* ('incense'). The 'precious ointment' of Ec. vii. 1 (as of Ct. i. 3) is *šemen ṭôb*, exactly the term *šamnu ṭâbu* already used by a dignitary in a Mari tablet of the 18th century BC who requests it to rub himself with (C. F. Jean, *Archiv Orientální*, 17: 1, 1949, p. 329, A179, l. 6). Perfumes were put on clothes (Ps. xlv. 8), sprinkled on couches (Pr. vii. 17), and precious oil (*šemen ṭôb* again) was poured upon the head, as in Aaron's anointing (Ps. cxxxiii). Perfumes or spices were burnt at the funerals of the great (2 Ch. xvi. 14). For Gn. xxxvii. 25, see SPICES, BALM, MYRRH, JOSEPH.

V. SACRED PERFUMERY

a. The holy anointing oil

For anointing the tabernacle and its furnishings, and the Aaronic priests at induction, not for profane use (Ex. xxx. 22–33). Several of its constituents can be identified. Myrrh, Heb. *mōr*, is a fragrant gum-resin of the tree-species *balsamodendron* and *commiphora* of South Arabia and Somaliland. Its fragrance resides in the 7–8% content of volatile oil. It is this essence that could be incorporated into a liquid perfume by heating with fixative oil/fat and straining off (see II*b*, above). Besides the 'liquid myrrh' of Ct. v. 5, 13, this liquid myrrh-perfume may be what is meant by 'flowing' or 'liquid myrrh' (*mor-derôr*) in Ex. xxx. 23 (RV, RSV), and is probably the *šmn mr* of 14th–13th-century BC Canaanite texts from Ugarit (Gordon, *Ugaritic Literature*, 1949,

p. 130: texts 12 + 97, 11. 2, 8, 15 and 120, l. 15) and of the contemporary Amarna Letter No. 25, IV:51 (*šaman murri*); the Heb. word *mōr* is therefore early, not 'late' as is wrongly stated in *BDB*, p. 600b. Egyptian *'ntyw*, 'myrrh', was also used in this liquid form, for anointing and medicine (refs., Erman and Grapow, *Wörterbuch der Aegyptischen Sprache*, I, p. 206: 7). It is this kind of liquid myrrh that is the true *stacte* (Lucas, *JEA*, XXIII, 1937, pp. 29–33; Thompson, *Dictionary of Assyrian Botany*, p. 340).

The precise identity of the 'sweet cinnamon', *qinnmon beśem* (Ex. xxx. 23, *cf.* Pr. vii. 17, Ct. iv. 14) is uncertain. There is no formal evidence that this term represents the *Cinnamomum zeylanicum*, native to Ceylon; other plants with aromatic bark or wood in this cinnamon/cassia group are possible (*cf.* Thompson, *op. cit.*, pp. 189–190). That the Egyp. *t'i-šps*-wood is cinnamon (Forbes, *Studies in Ancient Technology*, III, p. 8, Table II, and Lucas, *op. cit.*, p. 354, by implication) is wholly uncertain. See also Cassia below. For fragrant cosmetic woods in Egypt (samples), see Lucas, p. 119; Shamshi-Adad I of Assyria also sought them (G. Dossin, *Archives Royales de Mari*, I, No. 88, 11. 27–30—*iṣu riqu*).

The 'sweet calamus' (Ex. xxx. 23, AV, RV) or 'aromatic cane' (RSV) is Heb. *qᵉnēh-bōśem*, and its identity with the 'sweet cane from a far country' (Je. vi. 20, and also the 'calamus' of Ezk. xxvii. 19), *qāneh haṭṭôb*, is not certain. The latter, however, is very likely the *qanu ṭâbu* of Assyro-Babylonian texts, from 18th century BC onwards (for that of Mari, see C. F. Jean, *Archiv Orientální*, 17: 1, 1949, p. 328). And this is probably the *Acorus calamus* having an aromatic rhizome or stem-root; see Thompson, *op. cit.*, pp. 20, 21. In New Kingdom Egypt, 15th–12th centuries BC, the scented *ḳnn*-plant is identified as *Acorus calamus* (G. Jéquier, *Bulletin de l'Institut Français d'Archéologie Orientale*, XIX, 1922, pp. 44, 45, 259 and n. 3; Caminos, *Late-Egyptian Miscellanies*, 1954, p. 209—*ḳnnl*-oil). Actual plant stalks in a pot labelled 'perfume' or similar were found in Tutankhamūn's tomb, *c.* 1340 BC (Lucas, p. 119). The '50 talents of reeds' in an Ugarit tablet (Gordon, *Ugaritic Literature*, p. 130, text 120: 9–10) among other aromatics might be sweet cane, but hardly cinnamon (Sukenik, *Tarbiz*, XVIII, 1947, p. 126; see Gordon, *Ugaritic Manual*, III, 1955, p. 320, No. 1698).

Finally, there is cassia, which translates Heb. *qiddâ* in Ex. xxx. 24 and Ezk. xxvii. 19. Whatever the real identity of this might be, it is very possible that *qiddâ* is the same as Egyptian *ḳdt* in Papyrus Harris I of *c.* 1160 BC (so Forbes, *op. cit.*, p. 8, Table II). The other Heb. term often rendered 'cassia'—*qᵉṣî'āh*—is obscurer still. However, if in meaning this term is parallel to Arabic *salīḫāh*, 'peeled', and this in turn to Assyro-Babylonian *kasi ṣiri* (as Thompson, *op. cit.*, p. 191, would suggest), then it might well be Assyr. *qulqullânu*, modern Arabic *qulqul*, the *Cassia tora* (Thompson, *op. cit.*, pp. 188–192). *Cf.* name of Job's second daughter (Jb. xlii. 14). See also CASSIA.

b. The sacred incense

For the significance of incense, see INCENSE. Only its make-up is dealt with here. The general Heb. word for incense (which also appears as 'smoke', and 'perfume' at times) is *qᵉṭoreṯ*, known as a loan-word in Egyp. from the 1?th century BC (Erman and Grapow, *Wörterbuch d. Aeg. Sprache*, V, p. 82: 3); other forms from the root *qṭr* occur. In the sacred incense of Ex. xxx. 34–38 the last two constituents are easiest to identify. One of these, Heb. *ḥelbᵉnāh*, is pretty certainly galbanum, *Ferula galbaniflua* Boiss., growing in Persia and known in Mesopotamia (Babylonian *buluḫḫum*) from the third millennium BC onwards. (See Thompson, *op. cit.*, pp. 342–344; W. von Soden, *Akkadisches Handwörterbuch*, Lieferung 2, 1959, p. 101 and refs.)

Frankincense, Heb. *lᵉḇonāh* ('white'), is named from its appearance as whitest of the gum-resins used for incense; it comes from the genus of trees *Boswellia* of South Arabia and Somaliland, and is the classical olibanum. The Egyptian queen Hatshepsut apparently had such trees brought to Egypt *c.* 1490 BC, and small balls of frankincense were found in Tutankhamūn's tomb (*c.* 1340 BC). See Lucas, *Ancient Egyptian Materials, etc.*, pp. 111–113. *Naṭap̄*, 'drops', is given as *stacte* in LXX, but for true stacte see *va* above on myrrh. The name suggests a natural exudation and suitable for incense—perhaps a storax (*cf.* on these, Lucas, *op. cit.*, p. 116; Thompson, *op. cit.*, pp. 340–342) or else balm of Gilead, *opobalsamum, etc.*, on which see Thompson, pp. 363, 364. The last term, *šᵉḥēleṯ*, is quite uncertain; LXX renders as *onyx*, hence English versions' onycha —part of a mollusc giving an odour when burnt (Black and Cheyne, *Encyclopaedia Biblica*, under ONYCHA). But it might just conceivably be a plant-product, *šiḫiltu* in Assyrian medicine (Aramaic *šiḫlâ*), Thompson, *Dictionary of Assyrian Chemistry*, 1936, p. 73 and n. 1; but hardly Assyrian *saḫlê*, 'cress' (for which see Thompson, *Dictionary of Assyrian Botany*, 1949, pp. 55–61). But *šḫlt* in Ugarit-text 12 + 97 among aromatics and foodstuff (Gordon, *Ugaritic Literature*, p. 130, l. 4; *Ugaritic Manual*, III, p. 327, No. 1815) could very well be Heb. *šᵉḥēleṯ* and even Assyr. *šiḫiltu* and Aramaic *šiḫlâ* already mentioned. None of these are Assyr. *saḫullatu*, because this latter must be read as *ḫullatu* (Thompson, *op. cit.*, p. 69). To attempt any closer solution would be too hazardous at present.

For an attempt to reconstitute the sacred incense of Ex. xxx, see *Progress*, Vol. 47, No. 264, 1959–60, pp. 203–209 with specimen. K.A.K.

COUCH. See HOUSE.

COULTER. The translation in 1 Sa. xiii. 20 f. of the Hebrew *'ēṯ*, more correctly rendered elsewhere in Scripture as 'plowshare'. See AGRICULTURE. J.D.D.

COUNCIL. In the Old Testament (AV) the word appears once only, as a translation of Heb. *riḡmâ* (Ps. lxviii. 27) in referring to 'the princes of Judah and their council', a general word which could be rendered 'company' (so AVmg) or 'throng' (RSV). The similar word 'counsel' is used in Je. xxiii. 18, 22, AV (RV, RSV 'council'), of the privy council (Heb. *sôḏ*) of Yahweh (*cf.* 1 Ki. xxii. 19 ff.; Jb. i. 6 ff., ii. 1 ff.), where His decrees are announced; true prophets have access to this council and so have foreknowledge of those decrees.

In the New Testament two Gk. words are used. *Symboulion* denotes a consultation of people (Mt. xii. 14), or the provincial governor's advisory board (Acts xxv. 12). *Synedrion*, 'a sitting together', is used most frequently with reference to the Sanhedrin (*q.v.*), the supreme court of the Jews, but sometimes also to lesser courts (*e.g.* Mt. x. 17; Mk. xiii. 9), of which Jerusalem had two and each Palestinian town one. J.D.D.

COUNCIL, JERUSALEM. The Council of Jerusalem is the name commonly given to the meeting convened between delegates from the Church of Antioch (led by Paul and Barnabas) and the apostles and elders of the Church of Jerusalem, to discuss problems arising from the large influx of Gentile converts into the Church (Acts xv. 2–29). Many commentators identify this meeting with the one described in Gal. ii. 1–10; the view taken here, however, is that in Gal. ii. 1–10 Paul refers to a private meeting which he and Barnabas had with James the Just, Peter, and John (probably on the occasion of their famine-relief visit to Jerusalem mentioned in Acts xi. 30), at which the Jerusalem leaders recognized the vocation and status of Paul and Barnabas as apostles to the Gentiles. For the other view see CHRONOLOGY OF THE NEW TESTAMENT, Section II*d*.

I. THE OCCASION

The rapid progress of the gospel among Gentiles in Antioch (Acts xi. 19 ff.) and in Cyprus and Asia Minor (Acts xiii. 4–xiv. 26) presented the conservative Jewish believers in Judaea with a serious problem. The apostles had acquiesced in Peter's evangelization of the household in Caesarea because it was attended by evident marks of divine approval (Acts x. 1–xi. 18), but if the spread of the gospel among Gentiles continued on the present scale there would soon be more Gentiles than Jews in the Church, with a consequent threat to the maintenance of Christian moral standards. To this problem many Jewish Christians had a simple solution. Let the Gentile converts be admitted to the Church in the same way as Gentile proselytes were admitted into the commonwealth of Israel: let them be circumcised and accept the obligation to keep the Jewish law.

Thus far these conditions had not been imposed on Gentile converts. No word appears to have been said about circumcision to Cornelius and his household, and when Titus, a Gentile Christian, visited Jerusalem with Paul and Barnabas on an earlier occasion the question of circumcising him was not even aired (Gal. ii. 3). Now, however, some zealots for the law in the Jerusalem church decided to press upon the Gentile Christians of Antioch and her daughter-churches the necessity of taking upon themselves the yoke of the law. Their pressure proved so persuasive in the recently-founded churches of Galatia that Paul had to send these churches the urgent protest which we know as his Epistle to the Galatians (*q.v.*). In Antioch itself they caused such controversy that the leaders of the church there decided to have the whole question ventilated and settled at the highest level. Accordingly, the Council of Jerusalem was convened (*c.* AD 48).

II. THE MAIN QUESTION SETTLED

The debate was opened by the Pharisaic party in the Jerusalem church, who insisted that the Gentile converts must be circumcised and required to keep the law. After much disputing, Peter reminded the Council that God had already shown His will in the matter by giving the Holy Spirit to Cornelius and his household on the ground of their faith alone. Paul and Barnabas supported Peter's argument by telling how God had similarly blessed large numbers of believing Gentiles through their ministry. Then James the Just, leader of the Jerusalem church, summed up the debate and expressed his judgment that no conditions should be imposed on the Gentile converts beyond the condition of faith in Christ with which God had clearly shown Himself to be satisfied. The Gentile cities, he said, had no lack of witnesses to the Mosaic law; but the entry of Gentiles into the Church of the Messiah was the fulfilment of the promise that David's fallen tent would be set up again and his sovereignty be re-established over Gentile nations (Am. ix. 11 f.).

III. A PRACTICAL ISSUE DECIDED

Once the main question of principle was settled in a way which must have given complete satisfaction to the Antiochene delegation, a practical matter remained to be dealt with, affecting the day-to-day fellowship between Jewish and Gentile converts where there were mixed communities. It would be a sign of grace and courtesy if Gentile Christians respected certain Jewish scruples. Hence, at James's suggestion, the letter in which the Jerusalem leaders conveyed their findings to the Gentile churches included a request to them to abstain from certain kinds of food which their brethren of Jewish stock would find offensive, and to conform to the Jewish code of relations between the sexes. Without such concessions from Gentile Christians, there would have been grave practical difficulties in the way of their enjoying unrestrained table-fellowship with Jewish Christians. (When it is remembered that in those days the Lord's Supper was regularly taken in the course of a general fellowship meal, the importance of this consideration will be realized.) There is no real substance in the objection that Paul would not have agreed to communicate these conditions to his Gentile converts (as he is said to have done in Acts xvi. 4). Where basic principles were not compromised, Paul was the most conciliatory of men, and he repeatedly urges on his converts this very duty of respecting the scruples of others in such matters (*cf.* Rom. xiv. 1 ff.; 1 Cor. viii. 1 ff.).

After a generation or two, the situation which called forth the Jerusalem Council and the apostolic letter of Acts xv. 23–29 disappeared, and the Western Text of Acts adapts the letter to a new situation by altering its requirements in a more purely ethical direction—requiring abstention from idolatry, bloodshed, and fornication. But the requirements in their original form were observed by Christians in Gaul and North Africa late in the 2nd century, and were incorporated by Alfred the Great in his English law-code towards the end of the 9th century.

BIBLIOGRAPHY. W. L. Knox, *The Acts of the Apostles*, 1948, pp. 40 ff.; C. S. C. Williams, *The Acts of the Apostles*, 1957, pp. 177 ff. F.F.B.

COUNSELLOR (Heb. *yôʿēṣ*, 'one who gives advice or counsel'). The basic idea appears in Pr. xxiv. 6b. The word is used as a designation of the Messiah in Is. ix. 6, where in respect to the giving of counsel He is said to be a wonder (*pele'*). This attribute is applied to Him in order to emphasize His ability wisely to administer the government which is placed upon His shoulders so as by means of justice and righteousness to achieve and to maintain everlasting peace.

E.J.Y.

COURAGE. The Heb. word *ḥāzaq* means literally 'to show oneself strong'. Other words, *e.g.* *rûaḥ*, 'spirit' (Jos. ii. 11), *lēḇāḇ*, 'the heart' (Dn. xi. 25), and *'āmaṣ*, 'to be quick' or 'alert', exhibit the basic attitude from which courage flows. Courage is, therefore, a quality of the mind, and, as such, finds a place among the cardinal virtues (Wisdom viii. 7). Its opposite, cowardice, is found among the mortal sins (Ecclus. ii. 12, 13). The quality can be seen only in its manifestations and especially, in the Old Testament, on the battlefield (Judges, Samuel, Chronicles). The moral idea is not entirely absent. Those who are objects of God's special care are to 'fear not' (Is. xli. 13, 14; Je. i. 8; Ezk. ii. 6).

The absence of the word from the New Testament is striking. The noun *tharsos* occurs only once (Acts xxviii. 15). The ideal for the Christian is not the Stoic *aretē* (virtue), but a quality of life based on faith in the present Christ. Here is no 'grin and bear it' attitude, but a more than natural one which sees an occasion for victory in every opposition (*cf.* 1 Cor. xvi. 9).

H.D.McD.

COURT. A word used in the AV to translate five different words. 1. *ḥāṣēr* (*ḥāṣîr*, Is. xxxiv. 13), 'an enclosure or court', as found in a private house (2 Sa. xvii. 18) or a palace (1 Ki. vii. 8), or in a garden (Est. i. 5). It is very commonly used of the court of the tabernacle (*q.v.*; *e.g.* Ex. xxvii, xxxv, xxxviii); of the main courts, the Inner (*heḥāṣēr happenîmîṯ*, *e.g.* 1 Ki. vi. 36) and the Outer (*heḥāṣēr haḥîṣōnâ*, *e.g.* Ezk. x. 5) of the Temple of Solomon; and the courts of the Temple in the vision of Ezekiel (Ezk. xl–xlvi). See 4 below, and TEMPLE.

2. *ʿazārâ*, a word of rare occurrence, and therefore uncertain meaning, but evidently used in the sense of 'court' and so translated in 2 Ch. iv. 9, vi. 13. 3. *bayiṯ*, 'house', rendered '(king's) court' in AV of Am. vii. 13 (*bêṯ mamlāḵâ*), but RV and RSV give variant translations. 4. *'îr*, 'city' in 2 Ki. xx. 4, and so translated in RV, but AV and RSV follow some MSS, the *Qerē*, and the Ancient Versions in reading (*ḥa*)*ṣer*, 'court' (see (1) above). 5. *aulē*, an open enclosure, once (Rev. xi. 2) translated 'court' (see PALACE).

In Herod's Temple, which is not systematically described in the Bible, there were four courts, those of the Gentiles, the Women, the Men (Israel), and the Priests, in ascending order of exclusiveness (see TEMPLE and fig. 15). See also ARCHITECTURE.

T.C.M.

COUSIN. The AV rendering in Lk. i. 36 and i. 58 (plural) of Gk. *syngenēs*, 'one of the same race'. Because of the modern restricted use of the Eng. word 'cousin', a more accurate translation would be 'kinswoman' (so RV, RSV). See KIN. In Col. iv. 10 *anepsios* ('sister's son' in AV) means 'cousin' (so RV, RSV).

COVENANT. In Heb. 'covenant' is designated by the term *berîṯ* and the making of a covenant by *kāraṯ berîṯ*. In Gk. the term is *diathēkē* and the corresponding verb is *diatithēmi* (*cf.* Acts iii. 25; Heb. viii. 10, ix. 16, x. 16).

I. THE PRE-DILUVIAN NOAHIC COVENANT

The first occurrence of the term in Scripture is Gn. vi. 18, where the reference is to the pre-diluvian Noahic covenant. In this brief reference we have already an intimation of what a covenant is. The thought is as far removed as can be from that of compact, contract, or agreement between God and Noah. God announces to Noah that He will establish His covenant with him. It is a sovereign dispensing of grace on God's part, and the security arises from the action of God. It is God's covenant, and He establishes it. Flowing from this dispensation to Noah there are corresponding obligations. Noah and his family were to come into the ark and he was to bring with him the specified number of animals and birds and creeping things (Gn. vi. 18b–21). Thus there is no conflict between sovereign administration of grace and ensuing obligation.

II. THE POST-DILUVIAN NOAHIC COVENANT

This is recorded in Gn. ix. 9–17, and shows us more clearly than any other instance what the essential nature of a covenant is, and it advises us again how alien to the covenant-concept is any notion of compact or contract between two parties. The thought of bilateral agreement is wholly excluded. The keynote here is: 'And I, behold I, am establishing my covenant with you' (see Gn. ix. 9). The salient features should be noted.

a. It is conceived and established by God Himself.

b. It is universal in its scope; it embraces not only Noah but his seed after him and every living creature. The scope demonstrates that the grace bestowed is not dependent upon intelligent understanding or favourable response on the part of the beneficiaries.

c. This covenant is unconditional; no commandment or requirement is appended which could be construed as the condition upon which the grace bestowed is contingent. In fact, there is no ensuing obligation for Noah and his seed which could be regarded as the means through which the grace promised is to be realized. Hence the thought of breaking the covenant is irrelevant.

d. The divine monergism is intensely exhibited in this covenant; there is no human contribution to the agency by which the promises are fulfilled. The sign does not even take the form of an ordinance to be performed by man at the divine behest. The bow in the cloud is for the purpose of attesting the faithfulness of God and, in anthropomorphic terms, is to bring to God's remembrance His covenant promise. It is not a sign over which men exercise any control.

e. The covenant is everlasting. The perpetuity is correlative with the unilateral character and with the divine monergism. No uncertainty or mutability can belong to God's unconditional promise.

The covenant is, therefore, a sovereign administration of grace and forbearance, divine in its origin, disclosure, confirmation, and fulfilment.

III. THE ABRAHAMIC COVENANT

The Noahic covenants provide us with the concept of sovereign dispensation on God's part. When we study the Abrahamic covenant we find no deviation from this governing definition. But we do discover new features. Hence it is necessary to take account of the generic characteristics and the specific.

a. Generic features

(i) Promises were given. The three expressly mentioned in connection with the covenant are the possession of the land of Canaan, the multiplying of Abraham's seed, and the promise that God would be a God to him and his seed after him (Gn. xv. 8, 18, xvii. 6–8). But we cannot exclude the promise that in him and his seed all the nations of the earth would be blessed (Gn. xii. 3; *cf.* Acts iii. 25). (ii) Divine monergism is distinctly in the forefront (Gn. xv. 18, xvii. 1–8). (iii) Perpetuity is emphasized as much as in the postdiluvian Noahic (Gn. xvii. 7, 8, 19). (iv) Confirmation is given by a sanction which is irrevocable in its import (Gn. xv. 9–17). These features indicate that the covenant is divinely devised, administered, confirmed, and executed.

b. Specific features

(i) The promises have specific character; they are soteric in their intent and effect, having their centre in the promise that God will be the God of Abraham and his seed (Gn. xvii. 7, 8). (ii) In scope the covenant is particularistic to the extent of excluding Ishmael (Gn. xvii. 18–21). All nations are to be blessed in Abraham's seed. But it is not a covenant with all flesh as in Gn. ix. 9–17. It is not a covenant that is to yield its benefits to all indiscriminately. (iii) The sanction by which it is confirmed is one of peculiar solemnity (Gn. xv. 9–17). This is of the nature of a self-maledictory oath on the part of God (*cf.* Je. xxxiv. 18–20; *ANET*, pp. 353 f.). Nothing could more effectively certify the security and immutability of the promise of the inheritance of the land of Canaan. And the other promises of the covenant, since they are so closely bound up with this particular promise, must be regarded as guaranteed by the same sanction. (iv) In this case the necessity of keeping the covenant devolves upon Abraham and his seed (Gn. xvii. 10–14). The person failing to comply with the requirement breaks the covenant and is cut off from the people. This feature is co-ordinate with the added richness of the covenant promises and blessings in distinction from those of the Noahic. The intense spirituality of the relation constituted demands consecration on the part of those embraced in the covenant. And the particularism likewise is correlative with the keeping. A covenant that yields its blessings to all indiscriminately cannot be kept or broken. (v) The sign of the covenant is circumcision, and therefore an ordinance to be observed by men (Gn. xvii. 11). Circumcision is the sign or seal of the covenant in the highest reaches of its spirituality; it is even called the covenant (Gn. xvii. 10). Circumcision signifies the purification (*cf.* Ex. vi. 12, 30; Lv. xix. 23, xxvi. 41; Dt. x. 16, xxx. 6; Je. iv. 4, vi. 10, ix. 25) indispensable to that communion with God which is the central blessing of the covenant (Gn. xvii. 7).

The emphasis which falls upon the unilateral character of the covenant as a dispensation of grace on God's part and the obligation devolving upon men to keep the covenant might appear to be incompatible. Careful consideration, however, shows that these are complementary. In the Abrahamic covenant we have grace on the highest level because it contemplates the apex of spiritual relationship. The greater the grace, the more accentuated becomes the sovereignty of the bestowal. But, likewise, the greater the grace and the more intimate the relation constituted, the more intensified become the demands of that relationship. The necessity of keeping the covenant is the expression of the spirituality involved. Keeping is the condition of continuance in this grace and of its consummating fruition;

it is the reciprocal response apart from which communion with God is impossible.

IV. THE MOSAIC COVENANT

This was made with Israel as a people who had been sovereignly chosen in love unto redemption and adoption. The elements of this proposition and the evidence in support of each should be noted. Israel was sovereignly chosen (Ex. ii. 25; Dt. iv. 37, vii. 6–8, viii. 17, 18, ix. 4–6, xiv. 2; Ho. xiii. 5; Am. iii. 2). The covenant was made with a redeemed people (Ex. vi. 6–8, xv. 13, xx. 2; Dt. vii. 8, ix. 26, xiii. 5, xxi. 8). Israel had been adopted into a filial relation to God (Ex. iv. 22, 23; Dt. viii. 5, xiv. 1, xxxii. 6; 1 Ch. xxix. 10; Is. lxiii. 16, lxiv. 8; Je. iii. 19, xxxi. 9; Ho. xi. 1; Mal. i. 6, ii. 10).

Of equal significance for the interpretation of the Mosaic covenant is the fact that it was made with Israel in pursuance and fulfilment of the Abrahamic covenant (Ex. ii. 24, iii. 16, vi. 4–8; Pss. cv. 8–12, 42–45, cvi. 45).

These facts conspire to show that the Mosaic covenant is not to be construed in a way that would place it in sharp contrast with the Abrahamic and indicate that the same concept of sovereign administration of grace rules in this case as in the earlier covenants. This construction is confirmed by other considerations. The spiritual relationship which is at the centre of the Abrahamic covenant is also at the centre of the Mosaic. 'And I will take you to me for a people, and I will be to you a God: and ye shall know that I am the Lord your God' (Ex. vi. 7; *cf.* Dt. xxix. 13). Like the other covenants, sovereign dispensation occupies the forefront (Ex. xix. 5–8, xxiv. 3, 4; Dt. iv. 13, 14).

The feature which has influenced interpreters to construe the Mosaic covenant in legalistic terms is the fact that the necessity of keeping the covenant is given such prominence in connection with the dispensing of the covenant and that the people entered into solemn engagement to be obedient (Ex. xix. 5, 6, xxiv. 7, 8). That the demand for obedience and the keeping of the covenant does not place the Mosaic in a different category and does not make it a conditional covenant of works is demonstrated by several considerations.

a. As found already, the necessity of keeping the covenant is as patent in the Abrahamic as in the Mosaic (*cf.* Gn. xvii. 9–14, xviii. 18, 19). If this condition interferes with the gracious character of the Mosaic, it must have the same effect in the Abrahamic.

b. Since the covenant contemplated no less intimate a relationship than that of being the adopted people of God, then it is inconceivable that the demands of God's holiness should not come to expression as governing and regulating that fellowship and as conditioning the continued enjoyment of its privileges. This principle is frequently asserted (Dt. vi. 4–15; Lv. xi. 44, 45, xx. 7, 26, xxi. 8). It is summed up in Lv. xix. 2, 'Ye shall be holy: for I the Lord your God am holy' (*cf.* 1 Pet. i. 15; Heb. xii. 14). And the holiness demanded by the covenant fellowship is expressed concretely in obedience to God's commandments.

c. Holiness was an integral aspect of the covenant blessing. Israel had been redeemed to be a holy people, that is, separated unto the Lord.

d. Holiness, concretely illustrated in obedience, was the means through which the covenant relationship continued to bestow its blessings and proceeded to its fruition. Both negatively and positively this is the burden of Lv. xxvi.

e. It is a mistake to read Ex. xix. 5, 6, xxiv. 7, 8 as if the making of the covenant had to wait for the promise of obedience on the part of the people. In the keeping of the covenant and in obeying God's voice the covenant is conceived of as dispensed, as in operation, and as constituting a certain relation. What is conditioned upon obedience is the enjoyment of the blessing which the covenant contemplates. And the promise of obedience (Ex. xxiv. 7) was the only proper response on the part of the people to the grace which the covenant disclosed. The demand for obedience in the Mosaic covenant is identical in principle with the same demand in the new covenant. Believers do not continue in the grace which the covenant dispenses irrespective of perseverance and obedience. These are indeed blessings of the new covenant, but they are also the means through which the covenant favour and fellowship go on to consummating fruition (*cf.* Rom. xi. 22; Col. i. 23; Heb. iii. 6, 14; 1 Pet. i. 5). The failure to construe the demand for obedience in the Mosaic covenant as in principle identical with the same demand under the gospel arises from misconception as to the relations of law and grace in the new covenant.

V. THE DAVIDIC COVENANT

This is enunciated in such passages as Pss. lxxxix. 3, 4, 26–37, cxxxii. 11–18. Although the term covenant is not used in 2 Sa. vii. 12–17, it is apparent from the other relevant passages that this is the basic annunciation to David of the covenant concerned. These references show that no covenant administration expresses more plainly the concept of sovereign dispensation of grace. The most patent features are the security, determinateness, and immutability of the promises given (*cf.* Ps. lxxxix. 3; 2 Sa. xxiii. 5).

The Davidic covenant is messianic in its ultimate reference (*cf.* Is. xlii. 1, 6, xlix. 8, lv. 3, 4; Mal. iii. 1; Lk. i. 32, 33; Acts ii. 30–36). The striking feature of the Isaianic passages is that the Servant of the Lord is given to be a covenant of the people. The Messiah is Himself the covenant because the blessings and provisions of God's covenant with the people of God are to such an extent bound up with the Messiah that He is Himself the embodiment of these blessings and of the presence of the Lord with His people which the covenant ensures. No consideration certifies the grandeur of the covenant conception, the richness of its grace, the security of its provisions, and the assurance of its promises more than the fact that Christ Himself is the angel of the covenant and is given as the covenant of the people. What could disclose more effectively the sovereign grace of which covenant is the epitome than that He in whom the promises of God are yea and amen should be given as a covenant?

VI. THE NEW COVENANT

This is the covenant of the fulness of the time, of the consummation of the ages (*cf.* Gal. iv. 4; Heb. ix. 26), and is, for this reason, the everlasting covenant (*cf.* Heb. xiii. 20, xii. 28). It is everlasting not for the purpose of negating the perpetuity which belongs essentially to the covenant grace exemplified in the older covenants but because it brings that grace to its fullest exhibition and bestowal; it is God's covenant relationship on the highest level of achievement. And it is everlasting because it is not to be displaced by any other more complete realization of what covenant grace embodies. Covenant grace has now attained the finale of its revelation. Consummated bliss for the people of God will be in pursuance of the new covenant. It could not be otherwise. For the new covenant is correlative with the grace which Christ is and brings.

The New Testament data bear out these conclusions. Certain references clearly establish the recognition of continuity in the history of covenant administration. Gal. iii. 17–22 is explicitly concerned with the relation of the Mosaic to the Abrahamic. Several facts are apparent. The Mosaic did not make void the Abrahamic; the promise of the latter is not brought to nought. The Mosaic was an addition, not a suspension, an addition subserving the interests of the promise which found its focal point in the seed that was to come. The Mosaic was not against the promissory character of the Abrahamic; it was not governed by or directed to an antithetical principle. The Mosaic did not propound a law-method of justification—the Mosaic revelation is included in that Scripture which provides for the method of faith. The Mosaic is, therefore, for these reasons, to be construed as supplementing the Abrahamic and organized upon the same principles of promise and faith.

Lk. i. 72 shows that Zacharias saw in the redemptive events which form the subject of his thanksgiving the fulfilment of the Abrahamic covenant, and Paul finds in Christ as the promised seed the fulfilment of the promises made to Abraham and to his seed, promises which are to be identified with the covenant (Gal. iii. 15, 16).

When our Lord said that His blood was the blood of the covenant shed for the remission of sins and that the cup of the Last Supper was the new covenant in His blood (Mt. xxvi. 28; Mk. xiv. 24; Lk. xxii. 20; 1 Cor. xi. 25), the new covenant will have to be regarded as referring to the grace secured and the relationship established by the blood which He shed. The covenant is the sum-total of the grace, blessing, truth, and relationship comprised in that redemption which was secured by Jesus' blood.

In 2 Cor. iii. 6–18 Paul reflects on some of the characteristic benefits ministered by the new covenant; it ministers the Spirit as the Spirit of life; it is the ministration of righteousness and of liberty, and, above all, of the transfiguration by which we are conformed to the image of the Lord Himself. These are the highest of blessings, culminating in what is the crown and goal of redemptive accomplishment.

In Heb. ix. 16, 17 the writer uses the testamentary notion of a last will. This is an exceptional use of the term for covenant. But it is introduced at this point for the purpose of emphasizing the definitive effectiveness of the death of Christ in securing and ensuring the benefits of the covenant. There is no more possibility of voiding the effective application of the blessings of the covenant than there is of making void the provisions of a last will and testament after the testator has died. Here we have the most express witness to the fact that the new covenant is to be interpreted as a unilateral disposition and, therefore, totally foreign to the idea of mutual contract.

The foregoing summary review of the evidence shows that in Scripture God's covenants with men are always sovereign administrations of grace and of promise. This central concept is applied, however, to different circumstances and conditions, and thus the precise character of the grace and promise is determined by the historical situation in view. From the time of Abraham the covenants are specifically redemptive in content and purpose. This does not mean that redemptive grace began with Abraham, nor does it mean that the Noahic covenants had no redemptive reference. Even the post-diluvian, though not redemptive in itself, can be understood only in the broader context of God's redemptive purposes respecting mankind and in its relation to Noah as a man of God. But it is with the Abrahamic that specifically redemptive grace and promise are administered in the form of covenant, and covenant grace is redemptive at its core. Beginning with Abraham, the successive covenants are coeval with the successive epochs in the progressive unfolding of God's redemptive will and purpose. Not only are they coeval, they are also correlative. Covenant revelation and redemptive accomplishment are virtually identical. There is, therefore, progressive enrichment of the successive covenants. This enrichment, however, is not a retraction of or deviation from the central and governing features of covenant. The enrichment is a fuller development of what is present from the outset. So the apex of grace and relationship achieved in redemption does not go beyond the ambit of covenant. The climax of redemption is the climax of covenant administration, and sovereign grace reaches the zenith of its manifestation and realization. At the centre of all the covenants of redemptive grace was the promise,

'I will be your God, and ye shall be my people.' In this respect also the new covenant brings this relationship to the highest level of achievement, and there will be no further expansion or enrichment than that which the new covenant provides. Christ's blood secured its provisions; Christ is its mediator and surety. And He is the covenant. Nothing more ultimate is conceivable.

BIBLIOGRAPHY. G. Vos, *Biblical Theology: Old and New Testaments*, 1948; 'Hebrews, the Epistle of the Diatheke' in *PTR*, XIII, pp. 587–632, XIV, pp. 1–61; G. A. Mendenhall, *Law and Covenant in Israel and the Ancient Near East*, 1955; J. Murray, *The Covenant of Grace*, 1954; R. Campbell, *Israel and the New Covenant*, 1954; Meredith G. Kline, 'The Two Tables of the Covenant' in *WTJ*, XXII, 2, pp. 123–146, 'Dynastic Covenant', XXIII, 1, pp. 1–15.

J.M.

COVENANT, BOOK OF THE. In Ex. xxiv. 7 'the book of the covenant' (*sēper habberît*) is read by Moses as the basis of Yahweh's covenant with Israel, at its ratification at the foot of Sinai. Probably this 'book' was the Decalogue of Ex. xx. 2–17. It has, however, become customary to give the designation 'The Book of the Covenant' to Ex. xx. 22–xxiii. 33 (which may at one time have occupied a later position in the record). In 2 Ki. xxiii. 2, 21; 2 Ch. xxxiv. 30 'the book of the covenant' is the Deuteronomic law. (See DEUTERONOMY.)

Here we are concerned with Ex. xx. 22–xxiii. 33, conventionally called 'The Book of the Covenant' and in any case the oldest extant codification of Israelite law. It comprises 'judgments' (*mišpāṭîm*, 'precedents') and 'statutes' (*dᵉḇārîm*, lit. 'words'). The 'judgments' take the form of case-laws: 'If a man do so-and-so, he shall pay so much.' The 'statutes' take the categorical or 'apodictic' form: 'Thou shalt (not) do so-and-so.' Intermediate between those types are the participial laws (so called because they are expressed by means of the Hebrew participle), of the type: 'He that doeth so-and-so shall surely be put to death.' This type frequently replaces the 'If a man . . .' type when the death penalty is prescribed.

The principle on which the laws in this code are arranged does not lie on the surface, but it has been persuasively argued that each section falls within the scope of one of the Ten Commandments: the code could thus be described as 'a running midrash to the decalogue' (E. Robertson, *The Old Testament Problem*, 1950, p. 95; *cf.* A. E. Guilding, 'Notes on the Hebrew Law Codes', *JTS*, XLIX, 1948, pp. 43 ff.).

I. CULTIC REGULATIONS

The code begins with two cultic regulations: the making of gods of silver or gold is forbidden (Ex. xx. 22 f.) and an 'altar of earth' is prescribed (xx. 24–26), neither manufactured of hewn stones nor approached by steps, like the more elaborate altars of Israel's neighbours.

II. JUDGMENTS

There follows a series of case-laws (xxi. 1–xxii. 17). These cover such civil and criminal cases as the treatment of Hebrew slaves (xxi. 2–6), the sale of one's daughter into slavery (xxi. 7–11), murder and manslaughter (xxi. 12–14), injury to parents (xxi. 15, 17), kidnapping (xxi. 16), assault and battery (xxi. 18–27, incorporating the *lex talionis*, xxi. 23–25), a goring ox (xxi. 28–32), accidents to animals (xxi. 33 f.), killing of one ox by another (xxi. 35 f.), theft (xxii. 1–4), damage to crops (xxii. 5 f.), deposits and loans (xxii. 7–15), seduction (xxii. 16 f.).

It is this section of the code that presents affinities with the other ancient law-codes of the Near East—those of Ur-nammu of Ur, Lipit-ishtar of Isin, Bilalama (?) of Eshnunna, and Hammurabi of Babylon, for example. These are constructed on the same general lines as the Israelite case-law. The Hittite code, too, in several points of detail and arrangement, shows resemblances to these Israelite laws, although the general outlook of the Hittite code differs from that of other Near Eastern codes, reflecting the Indo-European principle of compensation for injury done rather than the Semitic insistence on *talio* (retaliatory punishment).

While the Israelite case-laws are comparable to these other codes, they reflect a simpler way of life. A settled agricultural community is presumed, and people live in houses, but there is nothing of the rather elaborate urban organization or social stratification of Hammurabi's code. Full-grown men in the Israelite community are either citizens or serfs, whereas in Hammurabi's code the punishment for physical injury, for example, is graduated according as the injured person is a superior, an equal, a 'vassal' or a serf. If the case-laws of Ex. xxi. 1–xxii. 17 were derived from a Canaanite code, we should expect the city-state culture of Canaan to be more clearly reflected.

A life-setting in the early days of agricultural settlement in Israel suggests itself, and we may recall that such settlement began before the crossing of the Jordan—if not at Kadesh-barnea, then certainly in Transjordan, where the conquered kingdoms of Sihon and Og, with their cities, were occupied by Israelites (Nu. xxi. 25, 35).

In Ex. xviii we have a picture of Israelite case-law in formation; Moses and his assistants adjudicate on cases which are submitted to them. With this we may associate the alternative name of Kadesh given in Gn. xiv. 7, En-mishpat, *i.e.* the spring where judgment is given.

III. STATUTES

The 'apodictic' laws which constitute the remaining part of the code have the form of directions (*tôrâ*) given by God through one of His spokesmen (*cf.* the function of the priest in Mal. ii. 7), preferably at a sanctuary—in the first instance, through Moses at Sinai or Kadesh. They have no parallel in the ancient law-codes of Western Asia, but it has been pointed out that they have close stylistic affinities with Ancient Near Eastern treaties, especially treaties in which a superior imposes conditions on a vassal. The Decalogue, which is also couched in this apodictic style, is the constitution of the covenant established by Yahweh with Israel; the other apodictic laws are corollaries to the basic covenant-law. Many of the statutes of Ex. xxii. 18–xxiii. 33 are concerned with what we should call religious practice, *e.g.* the offering of firstfruits (xxii. 29 f., xxiii. 19a), sabbatical years and days (xxiii. 10–12), the three pilgrimage festivals (xxiii. 14–17). In xxiii. 15 we find the beginning of a re-interpretation of these festivals to commemorate events in Israel's redemptive history. Ex. xxiii. 10–19 has been regarded as a self-contained ritual code (compare the so-called 'Kenite' code of xxxiv. 17–26). But the statutes also include ethical and humanitarian injunctions, protecting those who have no natural protector (xxii. 21–24), forbidding excessive severity to debtors (xxii. 25–27), insisting on judicial impartiality, especially where one of the litigants is an alien who might feel himself at a disadvantage (xxiii. 6–9). We should remember that the Israelites knew no such clear-cut distinction between civil and religious law as we take for granted today.

IV. CONCLUSION

The code ends with Yahweh's assurance of success and prosperity to Israel if His covenant-law is obeyed, accompanied by a solemn warning against fraternization with the Canaanites.

While the 'statutes' take the form of direct utterances of God, the 'judgments' also derive their authority from Him (Ex. xviii. 19, xxi. 1).

BIBLIOGRAPHY. H. Cazelles, *Études sur le Code de l'Alliance*, 1946; G. E. Mendenhall, *Law and Covenant in Israel and the Ancient Near East*, 1955. F.F.B.

COVETOUSNESS. The Hebrews visualized the soul as full of vigorous desires which urged it to extend its influence over other persons and things. There was *ḥāmaḏ*, the desire for a neighbour's possessions (Dt. v. 21; Mi. ii. 2), *beṣa'*, the desire for dishonest gain (Pr. xxviii. 16; Je. vi. 13), and *'āwâ*, selfish desire (Pr. xxi. 26). These are all rendered in AV by 'covetousness'. The Old Testament places covetousness under a ban (Ex. xx. 17), and Achan is stoned for the crime in Jos. vii. 16–26.

Gk. *epithymia* expresses any intense desire, which if misdirected may be concentrated on money, as in Acts xx. 33; 1 Tim. vi. 9; Rom. vii. 7. Gk. *pleonexia* generally expresses ruthless self-assertion, 2 Cor. ii. 11, vii. 2, which is applied to possessions in Lk. xii. 15, and repudiated by Christ in Mk. vii. 22. The word is often associated with immorality in lists of vices (Eph. iv. 19; *cf.* Philo), and, being in essence the worship of self, is characterized as the ultimate idolatry in Eph. v. 5 and Col. iii. 5. It can be rendered 'avarice' in 2 Cor. ix. 5 and 2 Pet. ii. 3. Gk. *zēlos* is used to inculcate an intense desire for spiritual gifts in 1 Cor. xii. 31; but it describes a very sordid carnal strife in Jas. iv. 2. D.H.T.

CRAFTS. See ARTS AND CRAFTS.

CRANE. See BIRDS OF THE BIBLE.

CREATION.

I. THE BIBLICAL DOCTRINE

This must not be confused or identified with any scientific theory of origins. The purpose of the biblical doctrine, in contrast to that of scientific investigation, is ethical and religious. Reference to the doctrine in Scripture is widespread in both the Old Testament and the New Testament, and is not confined to the opening chapters of Genesis. The following references may be noted: in the prophets, Is. xl. 26, 28, xlii. 5, xlv. 18; Je. x. 12–16; Am. iv. 13; in the Psalms, xxxiii. 6, 9, xc. 2, cii. 25; also Jb. xxxviii. 4 ff.; Ne. ix. 6; and in the New Testament, Jn. i. 1 ff.; Acts xvii. 24; Rom. i. 20, 25, xi. 36; Col. i. 16; Heb. i. 2, xi. 3; Rev. iv. 11, x. 6.

A necessary starting-point for any consideration of the doctrine is Heb. xi. 3, 'Through faith we understand that the worlds were framed by the word of God.' This means that the biblical doctrine of creation is based on divine revelation and understood only from the standpoint of faith. It is this that sharply distinguishes the biblical approach from the scientific. The work of creation, no less than the mystery of redemption, is hidden from man and can be perceived only by faith.

The work of creation is variously attributed to all three persons of the Trinity: to the Father, as in Gn. i. 1; Is. xliv. 24, xlv. 12; Ps. xxxiii. 6; to the Son, as in Jn. i. 3, 10; Col. i. 16; to the Holy Spirit, as in Gn. i. 2; Jb. xxvi. 13. This is not to be taken to mean that different parts of creation are attributed to different persons within the Trinity, but rather that the whole is the work of the triune God.

The words in Heb. xi. 3, 'things which are seen were not made of things which do appear', taken with Gn. i. 1, 'in the beginning God created the heaven and the earth', indicate that the worlds were not made out of any pre-existent material, but out of nothing by the divine Word, in the sense that prior to the divine creative fiat there was no other kind of existence. This *creatio ex nihilo* has important theological implications, for among other things it precludes the idea that matter is eternal (Gn. i. 1 indicates that it had a beginning) or that there can be any kind of dualism in the universe in which another kind of existence or power stands over against God and outside His control. Likewise it indicates that God is distinct from His creation, and it is not, as Pantheism maintains, a phenomenal, or external, manifestation of the Absolute.

At the same time, however, it is clear that the idea of primary creation contained in the formula *creatio ex nihilo* does not exhaust the biblical teaching on the subject. Man was not created *ex nihilo*, but out of the dust of the ground (Gn. ii. 7) and the beasts of the field and the fowls of the air were formed out of the ground (Gn. ii. 19). This has been called secondary creation, a creative activity making use of already created materials, and stands alongside primary creation as part of the biblical testimony.

Statements such as Eph. iv. 6, 'One God . . . above all, and through all, and in you all' indicate that God stands in a relationship of both transcendence and immanence to the created order. In that He is 'above all' and 'over all' (Rom. ix. 5), He is the transcendent God, and independent of His creation, self-existent and self-sufficient. Thus creation must be understood as a free act of God determined only by His sovereign will, and in no way a necessary act. He did not need to create the universe (see Acts xvii. 25). He chose to do so. It is necessary to make this distinction, for only thus can He be God the Lord, the unconditioned, transcendent One. On the other hand, in that He is 'through all, and in you all', He is immanent in His creation (though distinct from it), and it is entirely dependent on His power for its continued existence. 'By him [*en autō*] all things consist' (Col. i. 17) and 'in him we live, and move, and have our being' (Acts xvii. 28).

The words 'by reason of thy will they existed and were created' (Rev. iv. 11, RV, RSV), *cf.* 'created by him, and for him' (Col. i. 16), indicate the purpose and goal of creation. God created the world 'for the manifestation of the glory of His eternal power, wisdom and goodness' (Westminster Confession). Creation, in other words, is theocentric, and intended to display the glory of God; to be, as Calvin says, 'the theatre of His glory'. J.P.

II. THE GENESIS ACCOUNT

The basic Genesis account of creation is Gn. i. 1–ii. 4a. It is a lofty, dignified statement devoid of those coarser elements that are to be found in the non-biblical creation stories (see section III, below). This chapter makes a series of assertions about how the visible world came into being. Its form is that of a simple eye-witness account and no attempt is made to introduce subtleties of a kind which would be appreciated by modern scientific knowledge. Even granting the fact of revelation, a simple phenomenological creation story would describe the origin of only those elements in the world around that were visible to the naked eye. To the degree that Gn. i deals with simple observable phenomena, it is parallel to many other creation stories, for all such stories will have to deal with the earth, sea, sky, sun, moon and stars, animals, and man.

The fact of inspiration preserved the writer of Gn. i from the language and crudities of contemporary polytheism, but the writer remained an ordinary man who used his eyes to good advantage as he sought to describe the way in which God brought this world into being. Comparison of the biblical creation story with the Babylonian story does give a number of parallels, but the external relationship between the two is not clear. It cannot, however, be one of simple borrowing, for there is a depth and dignity in Gn. i that is not to be found in the Babylonian story. A. Heidel, *The Babylonian Genesis*, chapter III, gives a full discussion of the relation between the two stories.

a. Things created

Taking Gn. i as a simple phenomenological account, then, the first item concerns the creation of light. It must be one of the simplest of all human observations, that day and night occur in regular sequence, and that light is an indispensable necessity for all life and growth. 'Who caused this to be so?' asks the author of Gn. i. The answer is, God did (verses 3–5). A second simple observation is that not merely are there waters below, which form the seas and the underground springs, but there are waters above which provide the source of rain. Between the two is the firmament (*rāqîa*', something beaten out). Who caused this to be so? God did (verses 6–8). Again, it is a matter of common experience that seas and land-masses are distributed in specific areas of the earth's surface (verses 9, 10). That too is God's doing. Then, the earth has produced vegetation of many kinds (verses 11–13). That too is God's handiwork. There are no subtleties of botanical distinction, but the writer knows only three broad groupings of plant life, grass (*deše*', young, new, vegetation), herb (*'ēśeḇ*, plants) yielding seed after its kind, and trees (*'ēṣ*) yielding fruit whose seed is in itself. Presumably the writer felt that this simple classification covered all cases. The next observation is that heavenly bodies are set in the firmament, sun, moon, stars (verses 14–19). It was God who placed them there to mark off times and seasons. It would be altogether too subtle to expect the writer to distinguish meteors, planets, nebulae, *etc.* Turning to the spheres in which living creatures are to be found, the writer observes that the waters brought forth 'the moving creature that hath life' (verse 20, *šereṣ*, swarming things, small animals to be found in large numbers, *cf.* RSV 'swarms of living creatures'), and great whales (sea monsters) and every living creature that moves (verse 21, *tannîn*, sea monster, serpent). There is no attempt to make fine distinctions between the various species of sea animals in the zoological sense. It suffices to say that God made the animals of the sea, both small and great. God also made the birds that fly in the firmament (verses 20, 21, 22, *'ôp̄*). The term *'ôp̄* covers all varieties of birds. Whence came the multitudes of creatures that people the earth? God made these too. Then again, the earth brought forth living creatures (verses 24, 25, *nep̄eš ḥayyâ*), which are classified by the writer as cattle (*b^e^hēmâ*, animals), creeping things (verses 24, 25, *remeś*), and beasts of the earth (verses 24, 25, *ḥayyâ*). Zoological distinctions are not to be found here either. The writer was evidently persuaded that his simple classification covered all the main types of terrestrial life sufficiently for his purpose. Finally, God made man (verses 26, 27, *'āḏām*) in His own image and likeness, a phrase that is immediately defined as having dominion over the denizens of earth, sea, and firmament (verses 26, 28). And God created (*bārā'*) man composite, male and female (verse 27, *zāḵār* and *nᵉqēḇâ*).

b. Chronology of events

Close examination of this chapter will reveal a schematic presentation in which the creative acts are compressed into a pattern of six days, there being eight creative acts introduced by the words *And God said.* The scheme can best be understood from a simple table.

The emphasis in the chapter is on what God said (verses 3, 6, 9, 11, 14, 20, 24, 26). It is the divine creative word that brings order out of chaos, light out of darkness, life out of death. More weight should be given to the word 'said' (*'āmar*), than to the words 'create' or 'make', for creation is asserted to be the product of God's personal will. It is true that the word 'create' (*bārā'*) is used of the heavens and the earth (verse 1), of the great sea monsters and living creatures (verse 21) and of man (verse 27), and that this verb is used exclusively elsewhere in the Old Testament for divine activity. But in Gn. i other words are used as well. Thus 'made' (*'āśâ*) is used of the firmament (verse 7), the luminaries (verse 16), the beasts, cattle, and creeping things (verse 25), and of man (verse 26). Again, the divine activity is described under the jussive form of the verb in several places: 'let . . . be' (verses 3, 6, 14, 15), 'let . . . be gathered' (verse 9), 'let . . . bring forth' (verses 11, 20, 24). In the interests of variety the writer has gathered a range of verbs which together stress the divine activity. But the essential activity springs from the Word of God ('God said').

Creative Acts (God said)	*Day No.*	*Elements*	*Creative Acts (God said)*	*Day No.*	*Elements*
1. verse 3	1	Light	5. verse 14	4	Luminaries
2. verse 6	2	Firmament	6. verse 20	5	Birds
3. verse 9	3	Seas	7. verse 24	6	Fishes
4. verse 11		Land and Vegetation	8. verse 26		Animals and Man

If we insist on a strict chronology of events here we become troubled by the appearance of the luminaries on the fourth day. This problem is avoided if we treat Gn. i like some other passages in the Bible which are concerned with great facts but not with chronology (*cf.* the temptation narratives in Mt. iv and Lk. iv which stress the *fact* of the temptations but give different orders; see also Ps. lxxviii. 13, 15, 24, which stress the *fact* of God's care for the liberated people of Israel, but place the manna incident after the smiting of the rock, contrary to Exodus). If the writer of Gn. i is concerned to stress the *fact* of creation and is not particularly concerned with the chronological sequence of events, we avoid a number of difficulties.

There is a reasonably consistent scheme in the arrangement of the material. The first three days are preparatory. The giving of light and the preparation of firmament, seas, land, and vegetation, are preliminary to the setting of inhabitants in a prepared home. Birds people the firmament, fishes the seas, animals and man the land. Days 1 and 4 do not quite follow the scheme, but there is some sort of correlation. Days 3 and 6 each have two creative acts. The seventh day lies outside the scheme and tells of God's rest of enjoyment when His work was completed, the pattern for rest for His creation, one day in seven.

Something is lost if in interpreting this chapter we press the exegesis to unnecessary limits. The whole is poetic and does not yield to close scientific correlations.

c. The meaning of 'day'

Again, the word 'day' has occasioned difficulty. In the Bible this word has several meanings. In its simplest form it means a day of twenty-four hours. But it is used of a time of divine judgment ('day of the Lord', Is. ii. 12 f.), an indefinite period of time ('day of temptation', Ps. xcv. 8), a long period of (say) 1,000 years (Ps. xc. 4). On the view that a day is twenty-four hours, some have insisted that the creation was carried out in six days literally. This does not agree with the facts of geology, nor does it allow for the use of poetic, symbolic, or schematic arrangements, in biblical literature. Others have argued that a day represents a long period, and have sought to find a correlation with the geological records, a view which is tied too closely to the current scientific theories, and these are notoriously prone to change. If we allow that Gn. i has an artificial literary structure and is not concerned to provide a picture of chronological sequence but only to assert the fact that God made everything, we avoid these speculations.

A related problem is how to interpret the phrase 'evening and morning'. It is possible that we do not know what the writer meant. Among suggestions offered are the following: it refers to the Jewish system of reckoning the day from sunset to sunset, that is from evening, *via* morning, to the next evening; or, '*evening*' marks the completion of a period whose *terminus a quo* was the morning which dawned with the creation of light, while the 'morning' that follows marks the beginning of the new day and the end of the night section of the old day. These views are the exact opposite of each other, and suggest that the meaning is not clear.

Some writers have sought to overcome the difficulty of the six days by suggesting that creation was revealed to the writer in six days, rather than carried out in six days. Six visions of the divine activity were granted to the author, in each of which one aspect of God's creative work was dealt with. Each of the visions was cast into precisely the same form commencing with the words 'And God said ——' and concluding with 'And the evening and the morning were the —— day'. It is argued that the six blocks of material may have been written down on six similar tablets with a similar structure and a similar colophon to conclude each. The view is an interesting one, but is really a variant of the idea that in Gn. i we have to do with a literary composition arranged in an artificial way in order to teach the lesson that it was God who made all things. No comment is made about the divine method of working.

d. Genesis i and Science

Questions of the relation of Gn. i to the geological and biological sciences have been approached in many ways. The Concordist view has sought to find a more or less exact correlation between science and the Bible. Parallels have been drawn between the geological strata and statements in Genesis in a chronological sequence. Some have insisted that the phrase 'after its kind' is a complete refutation of the theory of evolution. It is not, however, at all clear what the Hebrew word 'kind' (*mîn*) means, except as a general observation that God so made creatures that they reproduced in their families. But if the Hebrew word is not understood, it is also true to say that the biological groupings are not at all finally decided. Let it be agreed that the Bible is asserting that, however life came into being, God lay behind the process, then the chapter neither affirms nor denies the theory of evolution, or any theory for that matter.

The second verse of the chapter has been made the ground for the theory of a gap in the world's history. It is asserted that the translation should be: 'and the earth *became* without form and void'. That is, it was created perfect, something happened, and it became disordered. Subsequently God re-created it by refashioning the chaos. The gap in time allows in this view for the long geological ages before the calamity. The original creative act is said to belong to the dateless past and to give scope for the geological eras. It should be said that there is neither geological evidence for this, nor is this translation at all likely. This phrase in Hebrew normally means 'and it was', not 'and it became'.

Many writers have sought to find a second creation story in Gn. ii which is said to have a different chronological order from that in Gn. i. Such a view is not necessary if we regard Gn. ii as part of the fuller narrative Gn. ii and iii, in which Gn. ii merely forms an introduction to the temptation story, and provides the setting without any attempt to give a creation story, and certainly not to give any sort of chronological sequence of events.

It ought to be asserted finally, that while there is still a good deal of discussion about the exact significance of Gn. i, all must agree that the one central assertion of the chapter is that God made all that constitutes this universe in which we live. If we assert this on the simple observational level, the nature of the passage is such as to enable an easy extension to those areas which cannot be seen by the naked eye. J.A.T.

III. ANCIENT NEAR-EASTERN THEORIES

No myth has yet been found which explicitly refers to the creation of the universe, and those concerned with the organization of the universe and its cultural processes, the creation of man and the establishment of civilization are marked by polytheism and the struggles of deities for supremacy in marked contrast to the Hebrew monotheism of Gn. i, ii. Most of these tales form part of other texts and the views of these early peoples have to be gleaned from religious writings which, though dated to the first part of the second millennium BC, may well go back to earlier sources.

a. Sumer and Akkad

There are a number of creation stories linked with the supremacy ascribed to various ancient cities and the deity conceived to have first dwelt there. Thus Nippur was thought to have been inhabited only by gods prior to the creation of mankind. Enki, the god of the deep and of wisdom, first chose Sumer and then set about founding neighbouring territories, including the paradise Dilmun. He first appointed the rivers, marshes, and fishes, and then the sea and the rain. Next, earth's cultural requirements are met by the provision of grain and green growth, the pickaxe and the brick-mould. The high hills are covered with vegetation and cattle and sheep fill the folds.

Another myth tells of the paradise Dilmun in which the mother-goddess Ninhursag produces offspring without pain or travail, though Enki, after eating plants, is cursed and falls sick until cured by a specially created goddess *Nin.ti*, whose name means 'the lady of the rib' and 'the lady who makes live' (see EVE).

Another myth of Enki and Ninhursag concerns the creation of man from clay. This followed a battle in which Enki led the host of the good against Nammu, the primeval sea. Then with the aid of Nin-mah, the earth-mother-goddess, he creates frail man.

The best known of the creation-myths is a later Babylonian adaptation of the Sumerian cosmogony called *enuma eliš* from its initial words 'when on high the heavens were not named and earth below had not been called by name'. Tiamat (*cf.* Heb. *teḥōm*, the deep) and Apsu (the sweet-water) existed, but after other gods were born Apsu tried to do away with them because of their noise. One of the gods Ea, the Sumerian Enki, killed Apsu; then Tiamat, bent on revenge, was herself killed by Ea's son Marduk, the god of Babylon in whose honour the poem was composed. Marduk used the two halves of Tiamat to create the firmament of heaven and earth. He then set in order the stars, sun, and moon, and lastly, to free the gods from menial tasks Marduk, with the help of Ea, created mankind from the clay mingled with the blood of Kingu, the rebel god who had led Tiamat's forces.

Other creation epics differ in detail. One tells how when 'all lands were sea' the gods were created and the city of Babylon built. Marduk therefore made a reed mat over the waters on which he and the mother-goddess Aruru created man. There followed the creation of beasts, rivers, green herbs, lands, and domesticated animals. Yet another myth ascribes the creation of the heavens to Anu and of the earth to Ea. Here again when the land, and the gods thought necessary to its order, had provided a temple and its supplies of offerings man was created to serve the gods.

b. Egypt

Among a number of allusions to creation one, dated *c.* 2350 BC, describes the act of the god Atum who brought forth gods on a primeval hill above the waters of Chaos. Atum 'who came into being by himself' next brought the world into order and out of the dark deep assigned places and functions to the other deities, including Osiris. The theologians of Memphis, as of Thebes, had their way of justifying the emergence of their city and god. For them it was the god Ptah who conceived the creation and brought it into being by his commanding word, an early reflection, found also in the Sumerian texts, of the *Logos* doctrine. Another myth ascribes to the sun-god Rē' the victory over the underworld Apophis. According to this version, mankind was created from Rē''s tears, all men being created equal in opportunity to enjoy the basic necessities of life.

It will be seen that throughout the Ancient Near East there was a conception of a primary watery emptiness (rather than chaos) and darkness; that creation was a divine act *ex nihilo* and that man was made by direct divine intervention for the service of the gods. The Hebrew account, with its clarity and monotheism, stands out unique; there are no struggles between deities or attempts to exalt any special city or race.

D.J.W.

c. Ancient Greece

To the Greeks in general the gods they worshipped were not responsible for the creation of the world, but rather were beings created, or begotten, by vaguely conceived deities or forces which they replaced. Hesiod, in his *Theogony*, says that first of all Chaos came into being, then Earth, who, impregnated by Heaven, became the great mother of all. In fact, rather than creation there is an automatic development, mainly by procreation, from undefined beginnings. There are many variations in detail, and the philosophers rationalized them in various ways. The Epicureans attributed all to chance combinations of atoms, and the pantheistic Stoics conceived of a *logos*, or impersonal world-principle (see EPICUREANS, STOICS, LOGOS).

Of particular interest is the Orphic myth, although it was probably accepted by comparatively few, for some have seen in Orphism significant parallels with Christianity. In this the great creator is Phanes, who emerged from an egg, and after creating the universe and the men of the Golden Age retired into obscurity until his great-grandson Zeus swallowed him and all his creation and subsequently re-created the existing world. The men of the present race arose from the blasted remains of the Titans who had killed and eaten Dionysus son of Zeus, and so have in them elements both of evil and of the divine. Dionysus was restored to life by Zeus, and was often identified with Phanes.

K.L.McK.

BIBLIOGRAPHY. *The Biblical Doctrine:* C. Hodge, *Systematic Theology*, I, 1878, pp. 553 ff.; S. Harris, *God the Creator and Lord of All*, I, 1897, pp. 463–518; J.-J. von Allmen, *Vocabulary of the Bible*, 1957 (*s.v.* 'Creation'). *The Genesis account:* F. Delitzsch, *Commentary on Genesis*, E.T., 1888; P. J. Wiseman, *Creation Revealed in Six Days*, 1948; A. Heidel, *The Babylonian Genesis*, 1950, pp. 82–140; W. J. Beasley, *Creation's Amazing Architect*, 1953, for a typical Concordist treatment; N. H. Ridderbos, *Is There a Conflict between Genesis i and Natural Science?*, 1957. *Non-biblical views:* see *ANET*, pp. 1–9; S. N. Kramer, *Mythologies of the Ancient World*, 1961, for details of Sumerian and other traditions; and A. Heidel, *op. cit.*, for a discussion of their relation to Genesis. See also W. K. C. Guthrie, *Orpheus and Greek Religion*, 1935, pp. 79 ff.

CREATURES. 1. AV tr. of *nepeš ḥayyâ*, which emphasizes sentience, vitality, rather than createdness. The term embraces 'all flesh that is upon the earth' (Gn. ix. 16)—though elsewhere man is distinguished (Gn. ii. 19)—and includes celestial creatures (Ezk. i; *ḥayyim* alone).

2. AV tr. of *ktisis*, *ktisma*, which etymologically mean 'act of creation', 'created thing'. But usage emphasizes the continuing relationship of every creature with God: His scrutiny, Heb. iv. 13; His control, Rom. viii. 39; His ultimate purposes,

Rom. viii. 19–21; and the response of worship from heaven and earth, Rev. v. 13. Man is distinguished by his idolatrous abuse of other creatures, Rom. i. 25, and by his privilege of new creation in Christ, the Firstborn, Col. i. 15; 2 Cor. v. 17; Gal. vi. 15; Jas. i. 18. P.A.B.

CREED. It is clear that a full-scale creed in the sense in which J. N. D. Kelly defines it ('a fixed formula summarizing the essential articles of the Christian religion and enjoying the sanction of ecclesiastical authority', *Early Christian Creeds*, 1950, p. 1) is not found in the New Testament. The so-called 'Apostles' Creed' does not go back to apostolic times. Yet recent investigation in the field of symbolic theology will not postpone the Church's creed-making to the 2nd and subsequent centuries. There are clear indications that what appear as credal fragments, set in the context of the Church's missionary preaching, cultic worship, and defence against paganism, are already detectable in the New Testament. Let us examine some representative examples of these confessional forms with the help of the 'twelve criteria of Creedal Formulae in the New Testament' which E. Stauffer, *New Testament Theology*, E.T., 1955, Appendix III, has drawn up.

a. Missionary preaching

There is evidence that in the primitive Church there was a corpus of distinctive Christian teaching held as a sacred deposit from God (see Acts ii. 42; Rom. vi. 17; Eph. iv. 5; Phil. ii. 16; Col. ii. 7; 2 Thes. ii. 15; and especially in the Pastoral Epistles, 1 Tim. iv. 6, vi. 20; 2 Tim. i. 13, 14, iv. 3; Tit. i. 9). This body of doctrinal and catechetical instruction, variously known as 'the apostles' teaching', 'the word of life', 'the pattern of doctrine', the apostolic 'traditions', 'the deposit', the 'sound words', formed the basis of Christian ministry, and was to be held firm (Jude 3; and especially in Heb. iii. 1, iv. 14, x. 23), handed on to other believers as the apostolic men themselves had received it (see 1 Cor. xi. 23 ff., xv. 3, where the verbs, 'received', 'delivered', are technical terms for the transmission of authoritative teaching, *cf.* Mishnah, *Aboth* i. 1, Danby's edition, p. 446), and utilized in the public proclamation of the gospel. In fact, the term 'gospel' designates the same web of truth, the *Heilsgeschichte*, which proclaims God's redeeming mercy in Christ to men (Rom. ii. 16, xvi. 25; 1 Cor. xv. 1 ff.).

b. Cultic worship

Under this heading the cultic and liturgical acts of the Church as a worshipping community may be shown to reveal credal elements, *e.g.* in baptism (Acts viii. 37 according to the Western Text; Rom. x. 9: see J. Crehan, *Early Christian Baptism and the Creed*, 1950); in the worshipping life of the Church, especially in the Eucharist, with which are associated ceremonial declarations of faith, hymnic compositions, liturgical prayers, and devotional exclamations (as in 1 Cor. xii. 3, xvi. 22, which is probably the earliest example of corporate prayer, *Marānā thā*, 'Our Lord, come!' and Phil. ii. 5–11, on which *cf.* R. P. Martin, *An Early Christian Confession*, 1960, pp. 7 ff.); and in exorcism for which formulae used in the casting out of evil spirits (*e.g.* Acts xvi. 18, xix. 13) came into prominence, as in the Jewish practice (*cf.* Stauffer, *op. cit.*, p. 323, n. 787).

c. Cullmann's theory of formulation

O. Cullmann, *The Earliest Christian Confessions*, E.T., 1949, pp. 25 ff., has set forth the theory that the formulation of early creeds was controlled partly by the polemical needs of the Church in the pagan world. When arraigned before the magistrates and required to attest their allegiance, the Christians' reply would be 'Jesus Christ is Lord'; and thus a credal form was shaped and systematized.

The New Testament 'creeds' range in scope from the simple confession, 'Jesus is Lord', to implicit Trinitarian formulations, as in the apostolic benediction of 2 Cor. xiii. 14 and such references as Mt. xxviii. 19 (on which, see P. W. Evans' Tyndale monograph, *Sacraments in the New Testament*, London, 1947); 1 Cor. xii. 4 ff.; 2 Cor. i. 21 ff.; 1 Pet. i. 2; but excepting the interpolated 1 Jn. v. 7 f. There are binitarian creeds which associate the Father and the Son, as in 1 Cor. viii. 6 (which may be a Christianized version of the Jewish credo known as the *Shema*', based on Dt. vi. 4 ff.); 1 Tim. ii. 5 f., vi. 13 f.; 2 Tim. iv. 1. The main type, however, is the Christological formula with such detailed summaries as in 1 Cor. xv. 3 ff.; Rom. i. 3, viii. 34; Phil. ii. 5–11; 2 Tim. ii. 8; 1 Tim. iii. 16 (on which, see H. A. Blair, *A Creed before the Creeds*, 1955); and 1 Pet. iii. 18 ff. (on which, see R. Bultmann, *Coniectanea Neotestamentica*, xi, 1949, pp. 1–14). R.P.M.

CREEPING THINGS. A phrase used in the EVV to translate two Hebrew terms which are used particularly in the creation (*q.v.*) narrative.

1. *remeś*, from the verb *rāmaś*, 'to creep, move', and having, with *rōmēś*, the participle of that verb, the meaning 'creeping or moving thing'. It is apparently applied to all animals in Gn. ix. 3, but is sometimes used of sea (Gn. i. 21; Ps. civ. 25) or land (Gn. i. 24, 25, vi. 20, vii. 8, 14, 21, 23) creatures exclusively, and in 1 Ki. iv. 33 and Ezk. xxxviii. 20 it is distinguished from beasts (*b*e*hēmâ*), fowls (*'ôp̄*), and fishes (*dāḡ*). Though some commentators have argued that in the creation account it refers to reptiles, it is unlikely to correspond exactly to any modern scientific category, referring rather to all creatures which appear to the observer to move close to the ground.

2. *šereṣ*, from the verb *šāraṣ*, 'to swarm, teem', and meaning 'swarming thing', translated in the AV as 'creeping thing' (Gn. vii. 21; Lv. v. 2, xi. 21, 23, 29, 41–44, xxii. 5; Dt. xiv. 19) and 'moving creature' (Gn. i. 20; see CREATION). It could be

applied to water (Gn. i. 20; Lv. xi. 10) and land (Gn. viii. 21) creatures, and in Lv. xi. 29 is specifically defined as including weasels, mice, and lizards. In short *šereṣ*, like *remeś*, seems to refer to creatures which appear to move close to the ground, with a range of possibilities according to the context.

In the New Testament the word *herpeton*, derived from *herpō*, 'to creep, crawl' (not in the Bible), and therefore meaning 'creeping thing', is used four times (Acts x. 12, xi. 6; Rom. i. 23; Jas. iii. 7), probably meaning 'reptile' in each case. In the LXX it is used chiefly as a translation for *remeś* and *šereṣ*. T.C.M.

CRESCENS. Companion of Paul (2 Tim. iv. 10) on service in 'Galatia'. Elsewhere Paul uses this term of Anatolian Galatia, but here it could equally designate European Gaul, as most ancient commentators and some MSS interpret it. If so, with the contiguous reference to Titus's Dalmatian mission, it may point to a concerted penetration of the West by associates of the imprisoned Paul. The name is Latin, and infrequent in Greek.

BIBLIOGRAPHY. Zahn, *INT*, II, pp. 25 f.

A.F.W.

CRESCENTS. See AMULETS, ORNAMENTS.

CRETE. A mainly mountainous island in the Mediterranean lying across the southern end of the Aegean. It is about 156 miles long, and its breadth varies from 35 miles to 7 miles. It is not mentioned by name in the Old Testament, but it is probable that the Cherethites (*q.v.*), who formed part of David's bodyguard, came from it, and the place-name Caphtor (*q.v.*) probably referred to the island and the adjacent coastlands which fell within its dominion during the second millennium BC. In the New Testament Cretans (*Krētes*) are mentioned among those present at Pentecost (Acts ii. 11), and later the island (*Krētē*) is named in the account of Paul's journey to Rome (Acts xxvii. 7–13, 21). His ship sailed past Salmone at the eastern end and put into a port called Fair Havens near Lasea in the centre of the south coast, and Paul advised wintering there. He was overruled, however. The ship set out to coast round to a better wintering-berth at Phenice in the south-west, but a heavy wind sprang up, driving them out to sea, and finally to Malta. After his imprisonment at Rome Paul evidently revisited Crete, for he left Titus (*q.v.*) there to carry on the work. The unflattering description of the Cretans in Tit. i. 12 is a quotation from Epimenides of Crete (quoted also in Acts xvii. 28a).

Our knowledge of the island's history is derived chiefly from archaeology. There were neolithic settlements on it in the fourth and third millennia BC, but it was in the Bronze Age that a powerful civilization was achieved. This was centred upon Knossos, a site excavated over many years by Sir Arthur Evans. The Early Bronze Age (Early Minoan I–III, *c.* 2600–2000 BC) was a period of gradual commercial expansion, which was continued during the Middle Bronze Age (Middle Minoan I–III, *c.* 2000–1600 BC). In this latter period writing (on clay and copper tablets) was in use, first of all in the form of a pictographic script (*c.* 2000–1650 BC) and then in a simplified form, known as Linear A (*c.* 1750–1450 BC). Neither of these scripts has been positively deciphered, though C. H. Gordon believes that Linear A was used to write Akkadian, a suggestion which has not been widely accepted.

The peak of Cretan civilization was reached in the early part of the Late Bronze Age (Late Minoan I(–II), *c.* 1600–1400 BC). The Linear A script continued in use during part of this period, but a third script, Linear B, appeared at Knossos alone (Late Minoan II, known only from Knossos). This was deciphered finally in 1953 by M. Ventris, and found to be couched in an archaic form of Greek, suggesting that the Late Minoan II period at Knossos was due to an enclave of Greek-speaking invaders. Similar tablets have also been found at Mycenae and Pylos on the mainland of Greece, where the script continued to be used after the decline of Minoan civilization, a decline which was accelerated by the violent destruction, perhaps by pirates, of most of the towns in Crete, around 1400 BC. This decline continued through the last phases of the Bronze Age (Late Minoan III, *c.* 1400–1125 BC). Towards the end of this period Dorian Greeks came to the island and ushered in the Iron Age.

Discoveries in Egypt, and at such sites as Ras Shamra (*cf.* the name of king *krt* in the cuneiform tablets), Byblos and Atchana (Alalaḫ) in Syria, show that Cretan commerce had extended to western Asia by the Middle Minoan II period (first quarter of the second millennium), and from this time on the folk-movements in which the Philistines (*q.v.*) played a part and which culminated in the invasions of the 'Sea Peoples' in the 14th century, were taking place. Throughout the Iron Age the island was divided among a number of feuding city states, until it was subdued by Rome in 67 BC.

BIBLIOGRAPHY. J. D. S. Pendlebury, *The Archaeology of Crete*, 1939; R. W. Hutchinson, *Prehistoric Crete*, 1961; H. J. Kantor, *The Aegean and the Orient in the Second Millennium BC*, 1947; J. Chadwick, *The Decipherment of Linear B*, 1958; C. H. Gordon, *HUCA*, XXVI, 1955, pp. 43–108; *JNES*, XVII, 1958, pp. 245–255.

T.C.M.

CRICKET. See LOCUST.

CRIME AND PUNISHMENT. Crime and punishment can be taken either in the juridical or in the religious sense, the latter in one way closely related to the former. We have thus to investigate the meaning of both to get a clear conception of our subject. The combination of crime and punishment in a strictly legal sense raises questions. The clear-cut distinction between criminal and civil offences of modern times is not present in Old Testament and Near Eastern jurisprudence. Every offence was committed, in the first place, against a certain person or community, and the only way to put the wrong right was to compensate the injured or wronged person.

Jurisprudence was also connected all over the Near East with the divine. The god sanctioned the laws of a community. This is, *e.g.*, evident from the prologue of the laws of Ur-Nammu, where Nanna, the Sumerian moon god, is mentioned; there is the famous law code of Hammurabi with the well-known stele presenting the god Shamash and Hammurabi in front of him receiving the symbols of authority and justice. In a very special sense this is also true of the Old Testament. The promulgation of laws is closely connected with the forming of the covenant. This can now be paralleled by certain treaties like the treaty between Ir-IM of Tunip and Niqmepa of Alalaḫ, where a covenant is made, with certain mutual obligations couched in the typical form of Near Eastern jurisprudence. This is, however, only a formal parallel. The Old Testament tradition takes the promulgation back to the origin of the covenant at Sinai, giving every law the sanction of the Lord.

For our purpose it is preferable to sketch the meaning and background of crime and punishment separately.

I. CRIME

a. Etymology

There is a close affinity between crime, guilt, and punishment. This is evident from the Heb. word *'āwōn*, encountered fifty-five times as 'offence' or 'crime', 159 times as 'guilt', and seven times as 'punishment'. The basic meaning of crime is to act in a consciously crooked or wrong way. The word *reša'* means guilt and crime, and refers to the way of life of an irreligious person. The Heb. word in verb form, *šāğâ*, gives the meaning to act wrongly in ignorance. Another Heb. word, *peša'*, has the emphatic meaning rebellion or revolt. The common word for an offence, crime, or sin is the verb *ḥāṭā'*, and noun *ḥēṭ'*. It has the double connotation of an offence against human beings (*e.g.* Gn. xli. 9); and sin against God (*e.g.* Dt. xix. 15). The basic meaning of the word was presumably 'to miss something', 'to err'; and this meaning was carried over to the sphere of offences against humanity and the deity. The whole idea of sin in the Old and New Testament (Gk. *hamartia* is a direct translation of *ḥēṭ'*) is built up around this word.

In the Gk. New Testament the most important words connected with crime are *hamartia, hamartēma, asebeia, adikia, parakoē, anomia, paranomia, paraptōma. Hamartia* and *hamartēma* mean to 'miss a mark', thus closely bound in meaning to the Heb. *ḥēṭ'*, denoting sin. *Asebeia* and *adikia* mean to be actively irreligious and to be deliberately against God, a type of conduct usually regarded in the Old Testament as the impious way of living, and described by *rāšā'*. *Parakoē* means to be actively disobedient; the Old Testament calls disobedience a refusing to hear (*lō' šāma'*, *e.g.* in Je. xi. 10, xxxv. 17). It denotes an action against the law, like *paranomia.* The nearest parallel in the Old Testament is *'āwōn.* It is interesting to note that no technical terminology was used in biblical times to describe a transgression of law. The Near Eastern jurisprudence has not developed theoretical legal terminology. *Parabasis* means literally to transgress, to transgress the existing laws with individual acts, *e.g.* Rom. iv. 15. *Paraptōma* is a less rigorous word than all those already discussed. It has the meaning of sin not of the worst enormity. 'Fault' comes nearest to the meaning, *e.g.* Gal. vi. 1.

b. The treatment of offences

Legal decisions in Near Eastern civil and criminal law were made to protect individuals and the community against injustice. It is obvious from the general casuistic style of Near Eastern jurisprudence that the codified laws as found in the laws of Ur-Nammu, of the city of Eshnunna, of Hammurabi, of the Middle Assyrian times, as well as of certain laws from the Covenant Code and other parts of the Pentateuch, must be regarded as decisions by famous kings, officials, or elders, and not as a theoretical legal system built up by judges and sages. Every stipulation in the casuistic legal material is made to protect certain rights and to restore by compensation the damage done. For example, negligence in not properly looking after a goring ox was regarded as a crime when that ox gored a man, a slave, or someone else's ox, *e.g.* Ex. xxi. 28–32, 35, 36, Laws of Eshnunna §§53–55. According to Exodus, when negligence causes the death of a free person, the negligent person is punished by death. In all other cases fixed compensation in kind or in shekels must be paid. Even in criminal offences, such as rape or theft, the guilty person must compensate the victim. For the rape of a young girl, the Old Testament prescribes fixed compensation to the amount of the normal bride-price. This shows that the value of the girl is diminished in a way which makes it impossible for her father, who has the legal right over her, to give her to another person for the usual bride-price. The guilty person, then, has to compensate the father for his loss, *e.g.* Ex. xxii. 16, 17. This is true of all codified laws of the Near East, where in some cases further stipulations are inserted to cover various situations, *e.g.* in a special sense in the Middle Assyrian laws.

There is, however, one type of law, which A. Alt in 1934 considered as quite foreign to anything discovered outside the Israelite world, namely apodictic law. The publication in 1958, however, of 'covenant' forms using a similar apodictic method in Assyr. times may show that such legal phraseology in the second person was not unknown elsewhere in the Ancient Near East. What is unique in the Old Testament legislation is that the laws in apodictic style are direct commands from the Lord to His people. The Ten Commandments, for example, are typical of this kind of law. 'Thou shalt not kill' (Ex. xx. 13) is given as a direct command by God to His people at Sinai, according to the reliable Old Testament tradition. These laws originated in the sacred sphere of the Lord, and came as part of the Israelite religion right at the beginning of their nationhood when the covenant between God and His people was made. From the Old Testament tradition it is also obvious that the casuistic laws were regarded as laws sanctioned by God. The whole corpus of legal material is immediately regarded as divinely inspired. These laws, promulgated with the covenant at Sinai, were there to bind the people to God and to unite the various tribes and individuals. Any transgression against a fellow-Israelite is a transgression against God.

c. A distinction made

The Old Testament as well as the New Testament makes a distinction between a mere transgression and a crooked and sinful life. The way of life was regarded as very important, especially in the Wisdom literature. The existence of the wicked is described in detail, *e.g.* in Psalm i, which is strongly connected with the Wisdom material of the Old Testament. This psalm gives expression to wickedness and crime as the way of life of the ungodly, the sinners, and the scornful. The life of these groups is a denial of the law of God. This kind of ungodly life means rebellion against God, and this is closely linked with all kinds of unrighteous deeds against other people. The clearest representation of this attitude is present in the writings of the prophets around 600 BC, and is especially stressed by Jeremiah. Crime against fellow-men is always regarded as crime against the Lord. A deep religious interpretation is thus attached to crime and transgression.

d. The New Testament interpretation

It is precisely this religious interpretation which predominates in the New Testament. Every transgression is taken as an offence against God. Paul's conception in Rom. vii is that the law brings knowledge of sin, but cannot take it away; it even quickens the consciousness of sin and makes transgressions abound (vii. 7–11). Law is, however, not sin, but is intended to restrain transgression by ordaining penalties. By knowing the law, our sinful nature (*hamartia*) is provoked and entices us to individual sinful acts (*parabasis*). The sinful nature, the sinful way of life, is expressed by Paul in terms of the flesh (*sarx*); to describe the life saved by Christ, the word 'spiritual' (*pneuma*) is used. Every life which is not saved by Christ is sinful in nature, and thus culpable, and has to be punished by God.

II. PUNISHMENT

a. Etymology

Among the more important biblical words connected with punishment, the stem *šlm* has the meaning 'to compensate', or 'to restore the balance'. This word has a specific legal connotation, as is also evident from certain Amarna Letters. The stem *ykḥ* has a legal meaning 'to punish', *e.g.* in Gn. xxxi. 37; Jb. ix. 33, xvi. 21, but in numerous other places has the more usual meaning 'to reprove'. The stem *ysr* is more widely used in the sense of punishment. It is interesting to note that in Ugaritic (Canaanite cuneiform) this word is present in the sense of instruction, as also in Heb. The noun *mûsār* is also used; this stem is thus linked up with an education background and not primarily with legal punishment. It is corrective punishment, as is the punishment inflicted by a father on his son. A strong word, used with the Lord as subject, is the stem *nqm*. Mendenhall pointed out that this, in the light of cuneiform material from Mari, means to vindicate. Vindication in the sense of punishment inflicted by God on the wicked is present, for example, in Nahum.

It is an interesting feature that in the New Testament, where the concept of divine punishment is fully realized, words with this connotation are used in only seven places. It is evident that *dikē*, the common word for judgment, may also have the secondary meaning 'punishment', much the same as the Heb. *mišpāṭ*. The only words with the clear meaning of punishment are *timōria* and *kolasis*. In classical Gk. the former has a vindicative character, very much like *nqm* in Heb. But in *koinē* and in New Testament Gk. this meaning is hardly found. The term became synonymous with *kolasis*, the ordinary word for punishment, *e.g.* Mt. xxv. 46; Acts iv. 21, xxii. 5, xxvi. 11; Heb. x. 29; 2 Pet. ii. 9; 1 Jn. iv. 18. In Matthew *kolasis* is used for the final punishment, in contrast to eternal life. The same meaning for the final judgment is present in 2 Peter, where the punishment is connected with the eschatological day of judgment, a later development from the Old Testament conception of the Day of the Lord.

b. The practice of blood revenge

Every crime or transgression must be punished, according to the common legal principles of the Near East. Primarily, this punishment was inflicted in the more primitive nomadic or semi-nomadic society by the victim or his relations, *e.g.* a common Semitic legal procedure is that a murderer must be punished by death by the dead person's nearest relations (see AVENGER OF BLOOD). This is still Islamic law. We have numerous examples of blood revenge in the Old Testament, *e.g.* Ex. xxi. 23–25, xxii. 2, 3. This is called *ius talionis*. The common formula of the *ius talionis* can not only be traced back to the Old Babylonian Code of Hammurabi but is also present in a much later votive tablet discovered at Marseilles. It is the very basis of the Islamic law of 'deliberate homicide'.

c. The dispensing of justice

Decisions on various cases were made by judges or elders, usually in the city gate. Their activity is not to be confused with the modern conception of judge. These judges were arbitrators between two parties (the Heb. word *šāpaṭ* means in some cases 'to decide between two parties'). This rôle of arbitration was not only played by elders and officials but also by the king himself, *cf.*, *e.g.*, the decision made by David in favour of the woman of Tekoa (2 Sa. xiv), and the wise decision of Solomon (1 Ki. iii. 16 ff.). But it is also clear that in nomadic and semi-nomadic society retribution was in some cases inflicted without the help of an arbitrator, *e.g.* in case of murder, where the common law of blood revenge took place. On the other hand, in modern Bedouin society people travel long distances to a famous judge to get his decision on a case.

Both in civil and criminal offences the judge gave decisions designed to maintain 'social equilibrium'. When a bodily injury was inflicted, or damage done to a neighbour's property (which was taken in a much broader sense than our modern one, so that his wife, children, and slaves, for example, were also included), the loss was restored by fixed compensation. It is, however, incorrect to suggest that in all cases only the value of the damage was paid; *e.g.* a thief had to compensate for stolen property such as cattle and sheep with five times its value in the former, and four times in the latter, case (*cf.* Ex. xxii. 1). This was probably used as a kind of deterrent against theft.

d. God as Judge

It is a fact that God is regarded in the Bible as the supreme Judge. This conception is not alien to the Ancient Near East, *e.g.* in a very important cuneiform tablet of Mari, the god Shamash is described as judge of gods and men. Very early in the history of Israel God was regarded as Creator of all things. This makes Him the Possessor of His creation. Any damage done to His creation is a direct act of rebellion against Himself.

From a legal standpoint this gives Him the right to punish. On the other hand, laws were made and sanctioned by God to protect His creation. His own commands put Him under the compulsion to punish any transgression of them. Some places in the Old Testament give the impression that the punishment decided on by the elders or officials was sufficient. On the other hand, it is evident that people who get away without human punishment are punished by God, some of them by a violent death, others by great damage (*cf.* Nu. xvi). The idea shifted from punishment during a man's lifetime to the Day of the Lord, with a final judgment where everybody shall be judged according to his deeds. The idea of a judgment after death is present also in the Egyptian conception of death. A deceased person is weighed over against the goddess Maat and receives his due according to his weight. The biblical conception does not only refer to judgment after death but also to a final judgment at the eschatological end of days. This idea is fully developed in the New Testament in the eschatological parts of the Gospels, in parts of Paul's Epistles, in 2 Peter, and in Revelation (*e.g.* Mt. xxiv, xxv; Mk. xiii; Lk. xxi; 1 Thes. v; 2 Thes. ii; 2 Pet. iii; Rev. xx–xxii). See ESCHATOLOGY.

III. CONCLUSION

It is evident that crime and punishment were not only bound up with ordinary jurisprudence but also with the divine. A crime against a human being or his property is a crime against God, and must be punished either by the authorities or by God. A transgression of religious stipulations must likewise be punished by God. A wicked way of life is rejected by God and punished.

BIBLIOGRAPHY. A. Alt, *Die Ursprünge des israelitischen Rechts*, 1934; G. Mendenhall, *Law and Covenant in Israel and the Ancient Near East*, 1955; H. Cazelles, *Études sur le code de l'alliance*, 1946; M. Noth, *Die Gesetze im Pentateuch*, 1940; R. C. Trench, *The Synonyms of the New Testament*, 1901; G. B. Stevens, *The Theology of the New Testament*, 1931; W. Eichrodt, *Theologie des Alten Testaments*, 1948; F. C. Fensham, *The mišpāṭîm in the Covenant Code* (typed dissertation), 1958. F.C.F.

CRIMSON. The AV rendering of three different Heb. words. 1. *šānî* (Je. iv. 30), which in RV and all other occurrences of the term is translated 'scarlet'. 2. *karmîl* (2 Ch. ii. 7, 14, iii. 14), a word later substituted for (1) above. 3. *tôlā'* (Is. i. 18), but 'scarlet' in La. iv. 5. Elsewhere this word is translated 'worm' (*q.v.*), the *Ciccus ilicis*, called in Heb. the 'scarlet worm'.

No clear distinction seems to have been made between 'scarlet' and 'crimson'. See COLOURS. J.D.D.

CRISPUS. *Archisynagōgos* (see SYNAGOGUE) at Corinth. His conversion, with his family, was significant, most Corinthian Jews being bitterly hostile (Acts xviii. 5–8); hence, perhaps, his baptism by Paul himself (1 Cor. i. 14). *Acts of Pilate* ii. 4 probably intends him.

The name (meaning 'curly') is Lat., but is used elsewhere by Jews (*cf.* TJ *Yebhamoth* ii. 3, xii. 2, Lightfoot, *HHT* in 1 Cor. i. 14). Pesh., Goth. (*v.l.*) read 'Crispus' for 'Crescens' in 2 Tim. iv. 10. A.F.W.

CRITICISM, BIBLICAL. See BIBLICAL CRITICISM.

CROCODILE. The word 'crocodile' is not used in the AV, but is generally thought to be the reptile described in Jb. xli under the name 'leviathan' (*q.v.*). In Lv. xi. 30 the RV and RSV use the word 'land-crocodile' where the AV has 'chameleon' (*kōaḥ*). This verse and the one preceding contain a list of creeping things which were to be regarded as unclean by the Israelite. Among them is a reptile (*ṣāḇ*) translated in the AV 'tortoise'. The LXX renders *krokodeilos chersaios*, 'land-crocodile', and the creature is evidently a member of the lizard family. The RV and RSV translate 'great lizard'. The other creatures mentioned in the passage are probably some of the many different varieties of lizard which abound in Palestine. D.G.S.

CROSS. The Gk. word for 'cross' (*stauros*, verb *stauroō*) means primarily an upright stake or beam, and secondarily a stake used as an instrument for punishment and execution. It is used in this latter sense in the New Testament. The noun occurs twenty-eight times and the verb forty-six. The crucifixion of live criminals did not occur in the Old Testament (*stauroō* in the LXX of Est. vii. 10 is the Heb. *tālâ*, meaning 'to hang'). Execution was by stoning. However, dead bodies were occasionally hung on a tree as a warning (Dt. xxi. 22, 23; Jos. x. 26). Such a body was regarded as accursed (hence Gal. iii. 13) and had to be removed and buried before night came (*cf.* Jn. xix. 31). This practice accounts for the New Testament reference to Christ's cross as a 'tree' (Acts v. 30, x. 39, xiii. 29; 1 Pet. ii. 24), a symbol of humiliation.

Crucifixion was practised by the Phoenicians and Carthaginians and later used extensively by the Romans. Only slaves, provincials, and the lowest types of criminals were crucified, but rarely Roman citizens. Thus tradition, which says that Peter, like Jesus, was crucified, but Paul beheaded, is in line with ancient practice.

Apart from the single upright post (*crux simplex*) on which the victim was tied or impaled, there were three types of cross. The *crux commissa* (St. Anthony's cross) was shaped like a capital T, thought by some to be derived from the symbol of the god Tammuz, the letter *tau*; the *crux decussata* (St. Andrew's cross) was shaped like the letter X; the *crux immissa* was the familiar two beams †, held by tradition to be the shape of the cross on which our Lord died (Irenaeus, *Haer.* ii. 24. 4). This is strengthened by the references in the four Gospels (Mt. xxvii. 37; Mk. xv. 26; Lk. xxiii. 38; Jn. xix. 19–22) to the title nailed to the cross of Christ over His head.

After a criminal's condemnation he was made to carry the cross-beam (*patibulum*) to the scene of his torture and death, always outside the city, while a herald carried in front of him the 'title', the written accusation. It was this *patibulum*, not the whole cross, which Jesus was too weak to carry, and which was borne by Simon the Cyrenian. The condemned man was stripped naked, laid on the ground with the cross-beam under his shoulders, and his hands tied or nailed (Jn. xx. 25) to it. This cross-bar was then lifted and secured to the upright post, so that the victim's feet, which were then tied, were just clear of the ground, not high up as so often depicted. The main weight of the body was usually borne by a projecting peg (*sedile*), astride which the victim sat. There the condemned man was left to die of hunger and exhaustion. Death was sometimes hastened by the *crurifragium*, breaking of the legs, as in the case of the two thieves, but not done in our Lord's case, because He was already dead. However, a spear was thrust into His side to make sure of death, so that the body could be removed, as the Jews demanded, before the sabbath (Jn. xix. 31 ff.).

Contemporary writers describe it as a most painful form of death (see CRUCIFIXION). The Gospels, however, give no detailed description of our Lord's physical sufferings, but simply and reverently say 'they crucified him'. According to Mt. xxvii. 34, our Lord refused any form of alleviation for His sufferings, doubtless that He might preserve clarity of mind to the end, in doing His Father's will. Hence the fact that He was able to comfort the dying thief, and pronounce the rest of the seven wonderful words from the cross.

The New Testament writers' interest in the cross is neither archaeological nor historical, but Christological. They are concerned with the eternal, cosmic, soteriological significance of what happened once for all in the death of Jesus Christ, the Son of God, on the cross. Theologically, the word 'cross' was used as a summary description of the gospel of salvation, that Jesus Christ 'died for our sins'. So the 'preaching of the gospel' is 'the word of the cross', 'the preaching of Christ crucified' (1 Cor. i. 17 ff.). So the apostle glories 'in the cross of our Lord Jesus Christ', and speaks of suffering persecution 'for the cross of Christ'. Clearly the word 'cross' here stands for the whole glad announcement of our redemption through the atoning death of Jesus Christ.

'The word of the cross' is also 'the word of reconciliation' (2 Cor. v. 19). This theme emerges clearly in the Epistles to the Ephesians and Colossians. It is 'through the cross' that God has reconciled Jews and Gentiles, abolishing the middle wall of partition, the law of commandments (Eph. ii. 14–16). It is 'through the blood of his cross' that God has made peace, in reconciling all things to himself' (Col. i. 20 ff.). This reconciliation is at once personal and cosmic. It comes because Christ has set aside the bond which stood against us with its legal demands, 'nailing it to his cross' (Col. ii. 14).

The cross, in the New Testament, is a symbol of shame and humiliation, as well as of God's wisdom and glory revealed through it. Rome used it not only as an instrument of torture and execution but also as a shameful pillory reserved for the worst and lowest. To the Jews it was a sign of being accursed (Dt. xxi. 23; Gal. iii. 13). This was the death Jesus died, and for which the crowd clamoured. He 'endured the cross, despising the shame' (Heb. xii. 2). The lowest rung in the ladder of our Lord's humiliation was that He endured 'even the death of the cross' (Phil. ii. 8). For this reason it was a 'stumblingblock' to the Jews (1 Cor. i. 23; *cf.* Gal. v. 11). The shameful spectacle of a victim carrying a *patibulum* was so familiar to His hearers, that Jesus three times spoke of the road of discipleship as that of cross-bearing (Mt. x. 38; Mk. viii. 34; Lk. xiv. 27).

Further, the cross is the symbol of our union with Christ, not simply in virtue of our following His example, but in virtue of what He has done for us and in us. In His substitutionary death for us on the cross, we died 'in him' (*cf.* 2 Cor. v. 14), and 'our old man is crucified with him', that by His indwelling Spirit we might walk in newness of life (Rom. vi. 4 ff.; Gal. ii. 20, v. 24 ff., vi. 14), abiding 'in him'. See RECONCILIATION; ATONEMENT. J.B.T.

Fig. 59. Types of royal headdress. *Left to right:* Egyptian double crown (Rameses III); Babylonian crown (Marduk, 7th–6th centuries BC); and Persian crown (Darius, 6th century BC). For an Assyrian crown see fig. 77.

CROWN. A distinctive head-dress, often ornate, worn by kings and other exalted persons.

I. IN THE OLD TESTAMENT

The high priest's crown was a gold plate inscribed 'Holy unto the Lord', fastened to his mitre or turban by blue cord, this being an emblem of consecration (Ex. xxix. 6, xxxix. 30; Lv. viii. 9, xxi. 12). After the Exile, in 520 BC, Zechariah (vi. 11–14) was commanded by God to make gold and silver crowns and to place them on the head of Joshua the high priest, these being (later) laid up in the Temple as emblems of God's favour. They may have been combined in one double crown, uniting priestly and regal offices in one person.

Among royal crowns, David's gold crown was an emblem of his God-given kingship (Ps. xxi. 3, *cf.* cxxxii. 18; withdrawal of God's gift—and crown—*cf.* Ps. lxxxix. 39; Ezk. xxi. 25, 26). Joash's actual coronation is recorded (2 Ki. xi. 12; 2 Ch. xxiii. 11). David captured the gold, stone-inset crown of the king (or god Milcom) of Ammon, which weighed a talent (2 Sa. xii. 30; 1 Ch. xx. 2—RV, RSV, and mgs). For crown set with stones, *cf.* Zc. ix. 16. The great royal crown of Vashti, Ahasuerus' queen (Est. i. 11), came to Esther's head (ii. 17), and the royal apparel with which Mordecai eventually was honoured included a gold crown (Est. vi. 8, viii. 15).

Besides being the mark of royalty (Pr. xxvii. 24), a crown became metaphorical of glory (Jb. xix. 9; Is. xxviii. 5, lxii. 3; Je. xiii. 18; La. v. 16; Pr. iv. 9, xii. 4, xiv. 24, xvi. 31, xvii. 6), and sometimes, less happily, of pride (Jb. xxxi. 36; Is. xxviii. 1, 3).

The Bible world offers many examples of a variety of crowns. In Egypt the king and the gods wore a variety of tall and elaborate crowns of varying significance as well as a simple gold circlet or diadem. Most characteristic is the great Double Crown of Upper and Lower Egypt combined, incorporating the red crown of Lower Egypt (flat cap, with spiral at front and tall projection at rear) and above it the white crown of Upper Egypt (tall and conical with a knob at the top); see Wiseman, *Illustrations from Biblical Archaeology*, 1959, p. 41, fig. 35. Pharaoh's diadems were always fronted by the *uraeus* or royal cobra.

In Mesopotamia the Assyr. kings wore a truncated conical cap adorned with bands of coloured embroidery or precious stones; *cf.* Wiseman, *op. cit.*, p. 65, fig. 59. The kings of Babylon wore a curving mitre ending in a point; see H. Frankfort, *Art and Architecture of the Ancient Orient*, 1954, plate 120.

Palestinian excavations have yielded a series of circlets or diadems; for one of strip gold patterned with dots, see Petrie, *Ancient Gaza III*, 1933, plates 14: 6, 15. See also for further examples, K. Galling, *Biblisches Reallexikon*, 1937, cols. 125–128 and figures. K.A.K.

II. IN THE NEW TESTAMENT

There are two words to be considered. The more important is *stephanos*, which denotes properly a chaplet or a circlet. It is used of Christ's crown of thorns. 'Thorns' are no more specific in Gk. than in English, so that it is impossible to be sure just what plant was used. What is clear is that this 'crown' was a mocking symbol of royalty, perhaps also of divinity (see H. St. J. Hart, *JTS*, NS, III, pp. 66–75). But though the *stephanos* might denote a crown of royalty (Rev. vi. 2, *etc.*), its more usual use was for the laurel wreath awarded to the victor at the Games or for a festive garland used on occasions of rejoicing. These uses underlie most of the New Testament references. Thus Paul reminds the Corinthians that athletes strive 'to obtain a corruptible crown' and he adds, 'but we an incorruptible' (1 Cor. ix. 25). It is important that the seeker after the crown 'strive lawfully' (2 Tim. ii. 5). Sometimes the Christian's crown is here and now, as when Paul thinks of his converts as his crown (Phil. iv. 1; 1 Thes. ii. 19). More usually it is in the hereafter, as the 'crown of righteousness, which the Lord, the righteous judge, shall give me at that day' (2 Tim. iv. 8). There are references also to a 'crown of life' (Jas. i. 12; Rev. ii. 10), and to 'a crown of glory that fadeth not away' (1 Pet. v. 4). The crown may be lost, for Christians are exhorted to hold fast lest it be taken from them (Rev. iii. 11). God has crowned man 'with glory and honour' (Heb. ii. 7), and Jesus was crowned likewise, 'that he by the grace of God should taste death for every man' (Heb. ii. 9).

Diadēma is not frequent (Rev. xii. 3, xiii. 1, xix. 12). In the New Testament it is always a symbol of royalty or honour. L.M.

CRUCIFIXION. From the Lat. *cruci figo*, 'I fasten to a cross'. In the New Testament the verb *stauroō*, 'I impale', from the noun *stauros*, 'stake', is used.

I. ITS HISTORY

The *stauros* was originally a pointed stake used in fortifications, and in its earliest uses as an instrument of torture or punishment the sufferer was either bound to this stake, from which he hung by his arms (Livy, xxvi. 13, xxviii. 29), or else impaled with the stake thrust through his chest or driven longitudinally through the back or privy parts and coming out of the mouth (Seneca, *Epistulae* xiv; *De Consolatione ad Marciam* xx: the latter reference stresses the variations of this torture that were devised). As a variation a cross-piece (*patibulum*) was added, to which a person could be bound or nailed: the invention of this cruel practice is traditionally ascribed to Semiramis, though it is also regarded as originally a Phoenician practice. There is evidence of its use in Persia in the 6th and 5th centuries BC (Herodotus, iii. 125, iv. 43; Ezr. vi. 11, where Jos., *Ant*. xi. 1. 3, 4. 6, indicates that by hanging crucifixion is meant, as also possibly in Est. vii. 10); in Egypt in the 5th century (Thucydides, i. 110; Herodotus, iii. 159; some think that Gn. xl. 19 refers to crucifixion, but if it does, then in that case the body was crucified only after beheading); in Carthage during the Punic Wars (Valerius Maximus, ii. 7; Silius Italicus, ii. 344); in India (Diodorus Siculus, ii. 18); in Scythia (Diodorus Siculus, ii. 44); and among the Assyrians (Diodorus Siculus, ii. 1) and Germans (Tacitus, *Germania* xii). The Greeks and Romans adopted it from the Phoenicians: Livy (i. 26) ascribes its introduction to the earliest kings, while Cicero, who stresses its extreme cruelty (*In Verrem* v. 66), ascribes it to Tarquinius Superbus (*pro Rabirio* iv). This punishment was reserved for slaves (Juvenal, *Satires* vi. 219; *cf.* Tacitus, *Histories* iv. 11—*servile supplicium*), and citizens were exempt from it (Cicero, *In Verrem* ii. 1. 3, 4). It was finally abolished in the Roman Empire by Constantine in 315.

Among the Jews hanging or crucifixion appears to have been carried out only after death for the purposes of exposure (Dt. xxi. 22, 23): according to the Talmudic *Tractate on the Sanhedrin and Criminal Jurisprudence* (vi. 4), this treatment was meted out only to those guilty of idolatry and blasphemy. However, in his excesses of 167–166 BC Antiochus Epiphanes crucified those who refused to disregard the old religion (Jos., *Ant*. xii. 5. 4), and the Maccabean king Alexander Jannaeus after an insurrection *c*. 88 BC crucified 800 leading Pharisees (Jos., *Ant*. xiii. 14. 2; *Wars* i. 4. 6, 5. 3). In 4 BC the Roman general Varus is reported to have crucified 2,000 insurgents (Jos., *Ant*. xvii. 10. 10), and it was the crucifixion of 3,600 Jews, including those of equestrian rank, by Florus in AD 66 which precipitated the rebellion (Jos., *Wars* ii. 14. 9). During the siege of Jerusalem by Titus (AD 70) so many were crucified that there was a shortage both of wood and of room for the crosses.

II. ITS METHOD

Three kinds of cross are known to ancient writers: the *crux decussata* or St. Andrew's cross (X), the *crux commissa* or St. Anthony's cross (T), and the *crux immissa*, or Latin cross (†). The Greek cross, where the cross-piece is about in the middle of, and of the same length as, the upright, is of later date. The fact that the superscription was affixed above the head of Jesus (Mt. xxvii. 37; Lk. xxiii. 38) would indicate that He suffered on the *crux immissa*, which tradition has made the Christian symbol. After sentence had been passed, it was the custom for the victim to be scourged with the *flagellum*, a whip of leather thongs with small pieces of metal or bone tied to them: in the case of Jesus Pilate may have carried this out first, hoping to move the crowd to pity (Jn. xix. 1; *cf.* Lk. xxiii. 16, 22); in this case *phragellōsas* in Mt. xxvii. 26; Mk. xv. 15 would be a reference in retrospect, as it is unlikely that the human frame could have survived two such dreadful scourgings.

Crucifixion was carried out outside the city (Cicero, *In Verrem* v. 66; Heb. xiii. 12; *cf.* 1 Ki. xxi. 13; Acts vii. 58), and the sufferer carried his cross, probably just the *patibulum*, otherwise called the *antenna*, with the superscription (*q.v.*) either hung about his neck or borne in front by a herald. In Judaea before the execution wine drugged with myrrh was provided for the condemned by an association of Jewish women obedient to Pr. xxxi. 6.

It seems most likely that the hands were nailed, first the right and then the left, to the antenna with the sharp nails (*clavi trabales*) while the sufferer lay on the ground, and then the whole was drawn up by ropes and affixed to the upright: to have nailed a person to an upright cross, or to have nailed him on the ground and then lifted up the whole frame and dropped it into a socket would seem unnecessarily difficult and awkward manoeuvres. Authorities differ as to whether each foot was nailed separately or one nail secured both: there was no foot-rest, but a *pēgma* (Gk.), *cornu*, or *sedile* (Lat.), supported the weight of the body to prevent it from tearing the hands free. The fact that Jesus spoke with the bystanders and a sponge on a hyssop-stalk was proffered to Him (Jn. xix. 29) suggests that the sufferer's feet were not more than a foot or two above the ground.

Death by this method was usually quite protracted, rarely supervening before thirty-six hours, and on occasion taking as long as nine days: so the centurion and four soldiers were left as a guard to prevent a rescue (Mt. xxvii. 54; Jn. xix. 23). The pain was obviously intense, as the whole body was strained, while the hands and feet, which are a mass of nerves and tendons, would lose little blood. After a while, the arteries of head and stomach would be surcharged with blood, causing a throbbing headache, and eventually traumatic fever and tetanus would set in. When for any reason it was proposed to put the sufferer out of his misery before the end, as if to compensate for the abbreviated suffering, the legs were shattered with blows from a club or hammer (Gk. *skelokopia*, Lat. *crurifragium*, *cf.* Jn. xix. 31–37) and the *coup de grâce* was dealt with a sword or lance, usually in the side (*percussio* or *perforatio sub alas*). See CROSS.

BIBLIOGRAPHY. J. Pearson, *Exposition of the Creed*, 1870, *v. sub* 'was crucified'; A. Edersheim, *The Life and Times of Jesus the Messiah*, 1906, II, pp. 582 ff.; J. Blinzler, *The Trial of Jesus*, 1959, pp. 246 ff.; W. Barclay, *Crucified and Crowned*, 1961, pp. 79–90. D.H.W.

CRUSE. See VESSELS.

CRYSTAL. See JEWELS AND PRECIOUS STONES.

CUBIT. See WEIGHTS AND MEASURES.

CUCKOO. See BIRDS OF THE BIBLE.

CUCUMBER (Heb. *qiššu'îm*). One of the articles of food which made the discontented Israelites, wandering in the wilderness of Paran, hanker after the pleasures of Egypt (Nu. xi. 5). We have no clear data by which to identify the plant. It could be *Cucumis chate*, now regarded as a variety of melon, or *Cucumis sativus*, the common cucumber, which, indigenous to NW India, seems to have reached the Mediterranean area in early times.

The 'lodge' referred to in Is. i. 8 as being in 'a garden of cucumbers' (Heb. *miqšâ*) was a crude wooden hut on four poles. It sheltered the watchman who protected the plants, but after the season was over it was abandoned and allowed to disintegrate, presenting a picture of desolation.

J.D.D.

CUMMIN (Heb. *kammōn*; Gk. *kyminon*). An aromatic seed from *Cuminum cyminum*, a plant indigenous to W Asia and cultivated from the earliest times. Resembling the caraway in flavour and appearance, it is used to flavour dishes, particularly during fasts, and is said to have medicinal properties. The plant is still beaten with rods, to preserve the small soft seeds (Is. xxviii. 27). The scribes and Pharisees, scrupulously paying tithes of cummin, were charged by Jesus with neglecting weightier matters (Mt. xxiii. 23). J.D.D.

CUP. The ancient cup was a bowl, wider and shallower than the normal teacup. While usually made of pottery, it was sometimes of metal (Je. li. 7).

1. Heb. *kôs*, commonly used for a drinking-vessel, whether Pharaoh's (Gn. xl. 11) or a poor man's (2 Sa. xii. 3). This could be of a size to hold in the hand or might be larger (Ezk. xxiii. 32), with a rim (1 Ki. vii. 26). In Solomon's court they were made of gold. 2. Heb. *gāḇîa'*. This is the name given to Joseph's silver divining cup (Gn. xliv. 2 ff.) and to the bowls of the golden candlestick in the tabernacle, which were formed like almond blossom (Ex. xxv. 31 ff.). In Je. xxxv. 5 (AV 'pots') it is used for a pitcher. It may mean simply a 'swollen' vessel. 3. Heb. *sap̄*. At the Passover the blood was held in this bowl (Ex. xii. 22, AV 'bason'). It was also a household vessel, appearing among equipment given to David (possibly of metal, contrasted with earthenware, 2 Sa. xvii. 28) and as a large wine bowl (Zc. xii. 2). 4. Heb. *qubba'aṯ* (Is. li. 17, 22) was evidently a large wine vessel, explained as *kôs*. 5. Heb. *'aggān*. This was the common name for a large bowl in the ancient Semitic world used in sacred rites (Ex. xxiv. 6) or for serving wine at a banquet (Ct. vii. 2). With the storage jar, it could be hung from a peg (Is. xxii. 24). 6. For Heb. *qaśwâ* (1 Ch. xxviii. 17, AV 'cup'), see PITCHER.

In the New Testament Gk. *potērion* denotes a drinking-vessel of any sort. Pottery continued in common use (Mk. vii. 4), but the rich were now able to possess glass as well as metal cups, which were normally goblet-shaped, *cf.* the chalice depicted on coins of the first revolt (see *IBA*, p. 89). The cup used at the Last Supper was probably an earthenware bowl, sufficiently large for all to share (Mt. xxvi. 27).

Throughout the Bible, cup is used figuratively as containing the share of blessings or disasters allotted to a man or nation or his divinely appointed fate (Pss. xvi. 5, cxvi. 13; Is. li. 17; Mt. xxvi. 39 ff.; Jn. xviii. 11). See LORD'S SUPPER.

A.R.M.

CUPBEARER (Heb. *mašqeh*, 'one giving to drink'). The 'butler' of Joseph's pharaoh (Gn. xl. 1 ff.) both in Heb. and by function was the king's cupbearer. His office as depicted in Gn. xl corresponds in part to the (wider) Egyp. *wdpw* of early times and especially the Middle Kingdom period (broadly, *c.* 2000–1600 BC, *cf.* Joseph *c.* 1700 BC), and exactly to the later term *wb'*, 'cupbearer', of New Kingdom times (*c.* 1600–1100 BC), which includes Moses' day. See Sir

Fig. 60. King Ur-Nanshe of Lagash, in Sumer, drinking from a goblet. He is served by his cupbearer who stands behind him. *c.* 2500 BC.

A. H. Gardiner, *Ancient Egyptian Onomastica*, I, Oxford, 1947, pp. 43*, 44* on No. 122 (*wb'*), and J. Vergote, *Joseph en Égypte*, 1959, pp. 35–40 (esp. p. 36). The Egyptian cupbearers, *wb'*, were often called *w'b- 'wy*, 'pure of hands', and in the 13th century BC one such cupbearer is actually entitled *wb' dp irp*, 'cupbearer (or, butler) who tastes the wine', Caminos, *Late-Egyptian Miscellanies*, 1954, p. 498. These officials (often foreigners) became in many cases confidants and favourites of the king and wielded political influence; this is very evident in XXth-Dynasty Egypt (12th century BC), and *cf.* Nehemiah. The (lesser) cupbearers of high Egyptian dignitaries are sometimes shown serving wine in the tomb-paintings.

Cupbearers were part of Solomon's glittering court that so impressed the queen of Sheba (1 Ki. x. 5; 2 Ch. ix. 4); for a somewhat earlier cupbearer at a Palestinian court (Canaanite), see left end of the Megiddo ivory illustrated in Heaton, *Everyday Life in Old Testament Times*, 1956, p. 164, fig. 80, or Albright, *Archaeology of Palestine*, 1960, p. 123, fig. 31.

Nehemiah (i. 11) was cupbearer to Artaxerxes. I of Persia (*c.* 464–423 BC) and, like his earlier colleagues in Egypt, enjoyed royal trust and favour, and had access to the royal ear. For a picture of an Assyr. cupbearer, see H. Frankfort, *Art and Architecture of the Ancient Orient*, 1954, plate 89.

K.A.K.

CURSE. The main biblical vocabulary of the curse consists of the Heb. synonyms *'ārar*, *qālal*, and *'ālâ*, corresponding to the Gk. *kataraomai*, *katara*, and *epikataratos*; and the Heb. *heḥ[e]rîm* and *ḥērem*, corresponding to the Gk. *anathematizō* and *anathema*.

The basic meaning of the first group is malediction. A man may utter a curse, desiring another's hurt (Jb. xxxi. 30; Gn. xii. 3); or in confirmation of his own promise (Gn. xxiv. 41, xxvi. 28; Ne. x. 29); or as a pledge of the truth of his testimony in law (1 Ki. viii. 31; *cf.* Ex. xxii. 11). When God pronounces a curse, it is, firstly, a denunciation of sin (Nu. v. 21, 23; Dt. xxix. 19, 20). Secondly, the curse is God's judgment on sin (Nu. v. 22, 24, 27; Is. xxiv. 6). And thirdly, the person who is suffering the consequences of sin by the judgment of God is called a curse (Nu. v. 21, 27; Je. xxix. 18).

However, for the Hebrew, just as a word was not a mere sound on the lips but an agent sent forth, so the spoken curse was an active agent for hurt. Behind the word stands the soul that created it. Thus, a word which is backed by no spiritual capacity of accomplishment is a mere 'word of the lip' (2 Ki. xviii. 20 RVmg), but when the soul is powerful the word is clothed in that power (Ec. viii. 4; 1 Ch. xxi. 4). The potency of the word is seen in some of our Lord's healing miracles (Mt. viii. 8, 16; *cf.* Ps. cvii. 20), and in His cursing of the barren fig-tree (Mk. xi. 14, 20, 21). In Zc. v. 1–4 the curse, representing the law of God, itself flies through the land, discerns sinners, and purges them out. A curse is as substantial a danger to the deaf man as is a stumbling-block to the blind, for he cannot take 'evasive action' by appeal to the more potent 'blessing' of Yahweh (Lv. xix. 14; Ps. cix. 28; contrast Rom. xii. 14). The rehearsing of the blessings and curses on Mts. Gerizim and Ebal (Dt. xxvii. 11 ff.; Jos. viii. 33) reveals the same dynamic view of the curse. On the borders of Canaan, Moses set before the people 'life and death, the blessing and the curse' (see Dt. xxx. 19). The first national act on entering the land is to set these two in motion: the blessing which will 'overtake' the obedient, and the curse which will 'overtake' the disobedient (Dt. xxviii. 2, 15). Between these two poles the national life moves.

It is because of the relation between obedience and blessing, disobedience and cursing (Dt. xi. 26–28; Is. i. 19, 20) that Dt. xxix. 12, for example, can speak of God's covenant as His 'curse', and Zc. v. 3 can call the Decalogue the 'curse'. The word of God's grace and the wòrd of God's wrath are the same word: the word which promises life is but a savour of death and judgment to the rebel, and therefore a curse. Paul uses this truth to expound the doctrine of redemption. The law is a curse to those who fail to obey it (Gal. iii. 10), but Christ redeemed us by becoming a curse for us (Gal. iii. 13), and the very means of His death itself proves that He took our place, for 'cursed is every one that hangeth on a tree'. This quotation from Dt. xxi. 23, where 'a curse of God' (see RVmg) means 'under God's curse', displays the curse of God against sin falling on the Lord Jesus Christ, who thus became a curse for us.

The Heb. root *ḥāram* means 'to seclude from society' (Koehler, *Lexicon, s.v.*). This is borne out by Old Testament usage. In general, the word applies to things open to human use but deliberately rendered unavailable to man. (*a*) Lv. xxvii. 29 (AV 'devoted') likely refers to capital punishment: the death penalty cannot be evaded. (*b*) In Ezk. xliv. 29; Nu. xviii. 14 offerings to God are called *ḥērem*, set apart for exclusively religious purposes. Lv. xxvii. 21 ff. parallels *ḥērem* with *qōḏeš* ('holiness') in order to express two sides of the same transaction: man sets something utterly apart for God (*ḥērem*), God accepts it and marks it as His own (*qōḏeš*), whereupon it becomes irredeemable by man. (*c*) Characteristically, the word is used of 'utter destruction'. Sometimes the implied reason is the wrath of God (*e.g.* Is. xxxiv. 5), but more often it is in order to remove a potential contagion for Israel's sake (Dt. vii. 26, xx. 17). Any contact with such a 'devoted thing' involved implication in its contagion, and share in its fate (Jos. vi. 18, vii. 1, 12, xxii. 20; 1 Sa. xv. 23; 1 Ki. xx. 42). However, while Achan involved himself and his house in the destruction of Jericho, Rahab, by identifying herself with Israel, escaped the curse and saved her house also (Jos. vi. 21–24, viii. 26, 27; Jdg. xxi. 11). (*d*) Spiritually, *ḥērem* is the judgment of God against impenitent sinners (Mal. iv. 6), and it is here that the impossibility of redeeming the *ḥērem* is clearly seen, *cf.* the New Testament, *anathema*, Gal. i. 8–9; 1 Cor. xvi. 22; Rom. ix. 3, *etc.*

BIBLIOGRAPHY. J. Pedersen, *Israel I and II, III and IV passim*, 1926, 1940; *HDB* art., 'Curse'; J-J. von Allmen, *Vocabulary of the Bible*, 1958, *s.v.* 'Curse'; J. B. Lightfoot, *Galatians*, 1880, on iii. 10, 13, and pp. 152–154. J.A.M.

CUSH. 1. Classed under Ham, and father of the hunter Nimrod (Gn. x. 6–8; 1 Ch. i. 8–10).

2. A region encompassed by the river Gihon (Gn. ii. 13); probably in W Asia and unrelated to (4) below.

3. A Benjamite, some utterance of whom occasioned a psalm (vii) of David seeking deliverance and justice.

4. The region south of Egypt, *i.e.* Nubia or N Sudan, the 'Ethiopia' of classical writers (not modern Abyssinia). The name Cush in both Heb. and Assyr. derives from Egyp. *Kš* (earlier *K'š*, *K'š*), 'Kush'. Originally only the name of a district somewhere between the second and third cataracts of the Nile *c.* 2000 BC, 'Kush' quickly became also a general term for Nubia among the Egyptians, which wider use the Hebrews, Assyrians, and others then took over (G. Posener, in *Kush*, 6, 1958, pp. 39–68).

In 2 Ch. xxi. 16 the Arabians are 'near' the Ethiopians—*i.e.* just across the Red Sea from them; Syene or Seveneh (modern Aswan) was the frontier of Egypt and Ethiopia in the first millennium BC (Ezk. xxix. 10, RVmg, RSV). The far-removed location of Cush/Ethiopia gives point to Pss. lxviii. 31, lxxxvii. 4; Ezk. xxix. 10, RVmg, RSV; Zp. ii. 12, iii. 10; and perhaps Am. ix. 7; it is one limit of Ahasuerus' (Xerxes) vast Persian Empire (Est. i. 1, viii. 9), as texts of Xerxes' time also indicate. Ethiopian contingents featured in the armies of Shishak (*q.v.*) against Rehoboam (2 Ch. xii. 3) and of Zerah (*q.v.*) against Asa (2 Ch. xiv. 9, 12, 13, xvi. 8). Later, throughout Isaiah (xi. 11, xviii. 1 ff. (preceding Egypt, xix. 1 ff.), xx. 3–5, and xliii. 3, xlv. 14), Egypt and Ethiopia are closely linked—for in the prophet Isaiah's time the 'Ethiopian' XXVth Dynasty ruled over both; so, *e.g.*, King Tirhakah (*q.v.*), Is. xxxvii. 9 (=2 Ki. xix. 9), *cf.* xxxvi. 6, *etc.* Na. iii. 9 also reflects this. But later still, from *c.* 660 BC onwards, the fortunes (and thrones) of Egypt and Ethiopia became separate again, and Ezekiel (xxx. 4, 5, 9) proclaims Egypt's impending fate as a warning to Ethiopia; in Je. xlvi. 9, likewise, the Ethiopians are merely mercenaries in the Egyptian forces again as in the days of Shishak. The 'topaz' (*q.v.*) came from this land (Jb. xxviii. 19) of unchangeably dark skins (Je. xiii. 23), as did Ebed-melech at the Judaean court (Je. xxxviii. 7 ff., xxxix. 15 ff.), and Queen Candace's minister (Acts viii. 27). The runner who bore news of Absalom's death to David was a 'Cushite' (2 Sa. xviii. 21, 23, 31, 32, RV, RSV). Ethiopia recurs in the prophecies of Ezk. xxxviii. 5 and Dn. xi. 43. On Nu. xii. 1, see ETHIOPIAN WOMAN. K.A.K.

CUSHAN-RISHATHAIM. The king of Aram-Naharaim (E Syria—see ARAM) who subjugated Israel for eight years until their deliverance by Othniel (Jdg. iii. 8–10). Both Heb. and Gk. versions take it as an unfamiliar composite personal name otherwise unknown. Various attempts have been made to identify this name, which may be related to Cushan, an archaic term for the Midianites (Hab. iii. 7) who, as nomads, reached Syria, where there is a place *Qsnrm* (Kushan-rōm). Cushan-Rishathaim may also be related to the Kušu of Egyp. execration texts but not to the Kassites, who did not move southwest of the Euphrates. He may be the Syrian Iršu who ruled Egypt for eight years from 1205 to 1197 BC. (*JNES*, XIII, 1954, pp. 231–242.)

D.J.W.

CUTH, CUTHAH. An ancient city in Babylonia (Akkad. *kûtu* from Sumer. *gu-du-a*), the seat of the god Nergal, whose inhabitants were deported by Sargon to repopulate Samaria (2 Ki. xvii. 24, 30). The site, represented today by the mound called Tell Ibrâhîm, was briefly excavated in 1881–2 by Hormuzd Rassam, who noted that it had at one time been a very extensive city.

BIBLIOGRAPHY. H. Rassam, *Asshur and the Land of Nimrod*, 1897, pp. 396, 409–411.

T.C.M.

CUTTINGS IN THE FLESH. See BURIAL AND MOURNING.

CYMBAL. See MUSIC AND MUSICAL INSTRUMENTS.

CYPRESS. See TREES.

CYPRUS. The island of Cyprus, some 140 miles long, and 60 miles wide at its broadest, lies in the eastern Mediterranean some 60 miles west of the coast of Syria and about the same distance from the Turkish coast.

Cyprus is not mentioned by that name in the Old Testament, where it is probably referred to as Elishah (*q.v.*); the people called Kittim (*q.v.*) in Gn. x may also have settled there at a later period. In the New Testament the island is named *Kypros* in the Acts. Barnabas was a native of it (iv. 36), as were some of the other early disciples, and the church in the island was further augmented by refugees from the first persecution (Acts xi. 19, 20, xxi. 16). Paul and Barnabas travelled across the island from Salamis to Paphos at the beginning of their first missionary journey (Acts xiii. 4–13). See map 17. It was at Paphos that they encountered Bar-jesus (*q.v.*), the sorcerer, and the 'deputy' (*anthypatos*, 'proconsul'), Sergius Paulus. Paul did not visit the island on his second missionary journey, but Barnabas went there separately with Mark (Acts xv. 39). When returning from his third journey, Paul's ship passed it to the south-west (Acts xxi. 3), and on the voyage to Rome contrary winds prevented him from landing (Acts xxvii. 4). There is no other mention of the island in the Bible, but the church there continued to flourish, sending three bishops to the Council of Nicaea in AD 325.

There are traces of neolithic settlement on the island, and its Bronze Age culture shows evidence of contacts with Asia Minor and Syria. In the 15th century BC the Minoan civilization of Crete (*q.v.*) extended to Cyprus, and in the following century there is evidence of colonization by the Mycenaeans, who were succeeding to the Cretan power on the Greek mainland. It was probably in this century that the copper mines, which in Roman times became famous enough for the metal to be named after the island (Lat. *cyprium*), first came into extensive use, and as a result of this Cyprus appears frequently in the records of the surrounding nations (see ELISHAH) at this period. In spite of outside influence, the basic Minoan-Mycenaean culture remained dominant, being evidenced particularly by the so-called Cypro-Minoan inscriptions (two early collections 15th and 12th centuries BC), which show close affinities with the Cretan Linear scripts. This script was still found in use in the late first millennium, together with the dialect of Greek most closely related to that in the Minoan Linear B Tablets, Arcadian, which had presumably been superseded in southern Greece and Crete by Doric.

Cyprus lay in the path of the 'Sea Peoples', and excavations at Enkomi and Sinda have revealed a late type of Mycenaean pottery from which the so-called 'Philistine' (*q.v.*) pottery of Palestine was clearly a development. In the 9th or 8th century Phoenicians settled on the island and later a number of bilingual inscriptions occur (*c.* 600–200 BC), of Phoenician and Greek severally with the Cypro-Minoan, now called classical Cypriot, script which was still in use at this time. That the Phoenicians did not gain much power is shown by an account of tribute to Esarhaddon in 672 BC, when only one Phoenician, as opposed to nine Greek kings, is mentioned (tribute had also been paid to Sargon in 709). In the 6th century Egypt dominated the island until it became part of the Persian Empire under Cambyses in 525. In 333 BC it submitted to Alexander, and after a brief period under Antigonus it passed to the Ptolemies. It was made a Roman province in 58 BC, and after various changes it became a Senatorial province in 27 BC, from which time it was governed by a proconsul (Gk. *anthypatos*; *cf.* Acts xiii. 7).

BIBLIOGRAPHY. S. Casson, *Ancient Cyprus*, 1937; Sir G. F. Hill, *A History of Cyprus*, 1940; for later articles, see L. Van den Berghe and H. F. Mussche, *Bibliographie Analytique de l'Assyriologie et de l'Archéologie du Proche Orient*, I, A, 1956, pp. 38–43; II, A, 1960, pp. 51–56.

T.C.M.

CYRENE. A port in N Africa, of Dorian foundation, rich in corn, silphium, wool, and dates. It became part of the Ptolemaic Empire in the 3rd century BC, and was bequeathed to Rome in 96 BC, becoming a province in 74 BC. Josephus quotes Strabo as stating that Cyrene encouraged Jewish settlement, and that the Jews formed one of the four recognized classes of the state (*Ant.* xiv. 7. 2). Josephus mentions also a Jewish rising there in Sulla's time, and Dio Cassius (lxviii) another in Trajan's. To this Jewish community belonged Simon the cross-bearer (Mk. xv. 21 and parallels), some of the missionaries to Antioch (Acts xi. 20), and the Antiochene teacher Lucius (*q.v.*). It was also represented in the Pentecost crowd (Acts ii. 10) and evidently had its own (or a shared) synagogue in Jerusalem (Acts vi. 9).

BIBLIOGRAPHY. P. Romanelli, *La Cirenaica Romana*, 1943; A. Rowe, D. Buttle, and J. Gray, *Cyrenaican Expeditions of the University of Manchester*, 1956; J. Reynolds, *JTS*, XI, 1960, pp. 284 ff.

J.H.H.

CYRENIUS. See QUIRINIUS.

CYRUS (Heb. *kôreš*; Old Persian *Kuruš*; Bab. *Kurašu*; Gk. *Kyros*). The king of Persia whom Isaiah foresaw as responsible for the restoration of the Temple at Jerusalem (xliv. 28) and as the 'Messiah'—deliverer of the Jews from exile in Babylon. He was an instrument of God's plan for His people (xlv. 1). In his first year as king of Babylon, after its capture in 539 BC, Cyrus gave orders for the rebuilding of the Temple (2 Ch. xxxvi. 22, 23; Ezr. i. 2, v. 13, vi. 3), then returned the temple vessels (Ezr. i. 7) and provided funds for rehabilitation work in Judah (Ezr. iii. 7).

The early history of Cyrus II ('the Great') remains obscure. He was a descendant of Teispes, grandson of Cyrus I and son of an Achaemenian Cambyses, king of Anshan (Elam). According to Herodotus (i. 107), his mother was Mandane, daughter of Astyages, king of Media. Ctesias, however, claims that his relationship with Astyages was due to marriage with his daughter Amytis. On his father's death Cyrus ruled Anshan, but soon incorporated the province of Parsua (Persia). By 550 BC he had defeated Astyages and become 'king of the Medes', a title ascribed to him by the Babylonian Nabonidus (*AS*, VIII, 1958, p. 77). He conquered Croesus and his kingdom of Lydia, and in 549 marched through Assyria. A few years later he was already threatening Babylonia, but it was not until 16 October 539 that the Persians with Gobryas entered Babylon, having diverted the river and thus been able to penetrate the city along the dried-up river bed to effect a surprise (Bab. Chronicle; Herodotus, i. 189–191; *cf.* Dn. v. 30). Seventeen days later Cyrus himself entered the city amid scenes of jubilation.

Cyrus' own inscriptions bear out the Old Testament view of a sympathetic ruler. He claims to have 'gathered together all the inhabitants (who were exiles) and returned them to their homes' and in the same decree to have restored deities to their renovated temples (see Cyrus Cylinder, *ANET* 315; Ezr. vi. 1 ff.). The Jews, having no images, were allowed to restore their Temple and its fittings (Ezr. vi. 3). During the first three years of the rule of Cyrus in Babylonia Daniel prospered (Dn. i. 21, vi. 28, x. 1), but then, according to Josephus (*Ant.* x. 11. 4), was removed to Media or more probably to Susa the Persian (Anshan) capital (Dn. viii. 2). For the theory that Cyrus might also have been called 'Darius the Mede', see DARIUS. In Babylonia Cyrus was succeeded in 530 BC by his son Cambyses (II) who had been also for a while his co-regent. D.J.W.

D

DABERATH. A levitical city of Issachar (1 Ch. vi. 72; Jos. xxi. 28, where AV has 'Dabareh'), probably on the border of Zebulun (Jos. xix. 12). It is usually identified with the ruins near the modern village of Dabûriyeh, at the western foot of Mt. Tabor. (See DEBORAH.) J.D.D.

DAGGER. See ARMOUR AND WEAPONS.

DAGON. In the Old Testament Dagon is a principal deity of the Philistines worshipped in Samson's time at Gaza (Jdg. xvi. 21–23), at Ashdod (to Maccabean days, 1 Macc. x. 83–85, xi. 4) and at Beth-shan in the days of Saul and David (1 Sa. v. 2–7; 1 Ch. x. 10 with 1 Sa. xxxi. 10). The true origin of this god's name is lost in antiquity, and even his precise nature is uncertain. The common idea that he was a fish-deity appears to have no foundation in fact; being adumbrated in Jerome (*BDB*, p. 1121) and first clearly expressed by Kimhi in the 13th century AD (Schmökel), influenced solely by the outward similarity between 'Dagon' and Heb. *dāḡ*, 'fish'. The fish-tailed divinity on coins from Arvad and Ascalon is linked with Atargitis and has no stated connection with Dagon (Dhorme and Dussaud). The common Heb. word *dāḡān*, 'grain, corn' (*BDB*, p. 186) may perhaps itself be derived from the name of the god Dagon or Dagan; it is thus possible that he was a vegetation or grain god (*cf.* Albright, *Archaeology and the Religion of Israel*[3], 1953, pp. 74, and 220, n. 15).

From at least 2500 BC onwards, Dagan received worship throughout Mesopotamia, especially in the Middle-Euphrates region, in which, at Mari, he had a temple (18th century BC) adorned with bronze lions (see illustration in A. Champdor, *Babylon*, 1959). Many personal names were compounded with Dagan. In the 14th century BC and earlier, Dagon had a temple at Ugarit in N Phoenicia, identified as his by two stelae dedicated in it to his name; these are pictured in *Syria*, XVI, 1935, plate 31: 1, 2, opposite p. 156, and last translated by Albright, *op. cit.*, p. 203, n. 30. This temple had a forecourt (?), an antechamber, and probably a tower (plan in Schaeffer, *The Cuneiform Texts of Ras Shamra-Ugarit*, 1939, plate 39), the whole probably taking the form of the model illustrated by Sir C. L. Woolley (*A Forgotten Kingdom*, 1953, p. 57, fig. 9). In the Ugaritic (N Canaanite) texts Dagon is father of Baal. At Beth-shan, one temple discovered may be that of 1 Ch. x. 10 (see A. Rowe, *Four Canaanite Temples of Beth Shan*, I, 1940, pp. 22–24. For reconstruction see fig. 61). That Dagon had other shrines in Palestine is indicated by two settlements each called Beth-Dagon (Jos. xv. 41, xix. 27) in the territories of Judah and Asher. Already, Rameses II mentions a B(e)th-

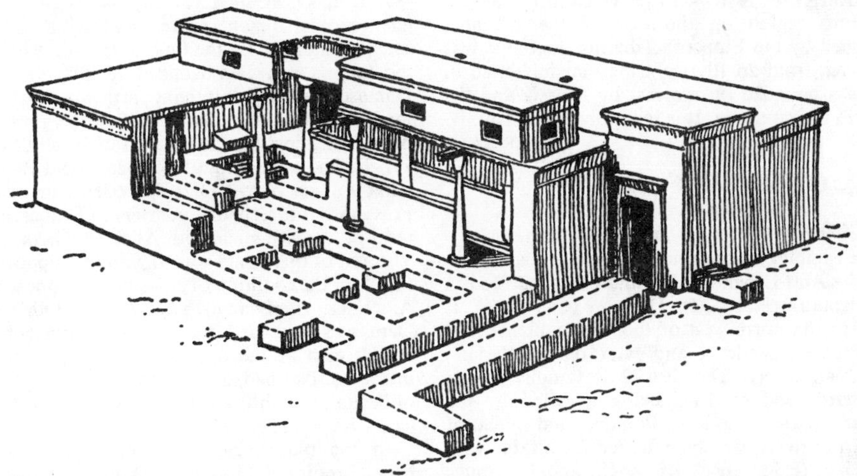

Fig. 61. A reconstruction of the 'southern temple' built for Rameses III at Beth-shan. This is possibly the temple of Dagon in use during the reign of David. The dotted lines indicate walls cut away to show the interior.

D(a)g(o)n in his Palestinian lists (*c.* 1270 BC), and Sennacherib a Bit-Dagannu in 701 BC.

BIBLIOGRAPHY. H. Schmökel, *Der Gott Dagan*, 1928, and in Ebeling and Meissner (eds.), *Reallexikon der Assyriologie*, II, 1938, pp. 99–101; Dhorme and Dussaud, *Les Religions de Babylonie et d'Assyrie . . . des Hittites . . . Phéniciens, etc.*, 1949, pp. 165–167, 173, 364, 365, 371, 395, 396. For Mari material, see J. R. Kupper, *Les Nomades en Mésopotamie au temps des Rois de Mari*, 1957, pp. 69–71. K.A.K.

DALMANUTHA. In Mk. viii. 10 a district on the coast of the Lake of Galilee, to which Jesus and His disciples crossed after the feeding of the four thousand. It has never been satisfactorily identified. (Magadan (RV, RSV), in the parallel passage, Mt. xv. 39, is equally unknown.) Various emendations have been proposed (including F. C. Burkitt's suggestion that it represents a corruption of Tiberias combined with its earlier name Amathus), but it is best to keep the attested reading and await further light. F.F.B.

DALMATIA. A Roman province in the mountainous region on the east of the Adriatic, formed by the Emperor Tiberius. Its name was derived from an Illyrian tribe that inhabited it. It was bounded on the east by Moesia and the north by Pannonia. It is mentioned in 2 Tim. iv. 10. B.F.C.A.

DAMASCUS.

a. Location

The capital city of Syria (Is. vii. 8) situated east of the Anti-Lebanon Mts. and overshadowed in the south-west by Mt. Hermon (Ct. vii. 4). It lies in the north-west of the Ghuta plain 2,300 feet above sea-level and west of the Syrian–Arabian desert. The district is famous for its orchards and gardens, being irrigated by the clear Abana (modern Barada) and adjacent Pharpar rivers, which compared favourably with the slower Jordan (2 Ki. v. 12) and Euphrates rivers (Is. viii. 5–8). It is a natural communications centre, linking the caravan route to the Mediterranean coast (*c.* 65 miles to the east) through Tyre (Ezk. xxvii. 18) to Egypt with the tracks east across the desert to Assyria and Babylonia, south to Arabia, and north to Aleppo (see map 2). The city was of special importance as head of an Aramaean state in the 10th–8th centuries BC (see ARAMAEANS, SYRIA).

The modern city covers an area about two by one miles along the Barada river, with one of the ancient streets running NE to SW through it called Straight Street (*Darb al-mustaqim*) or Long Street (*Sūq al-Tawilēh*) as in Acts ix. 11. The great mosque built in the 8th century AD is said to cover the site of the temple of Rimmon (2 Ki. v. 18).

b. Name

The meaning of Damascus (Gk. *Damaskos*; Heb. *Dammeseq*; Aram. *Darmeseq*; 1 Ch. xviii. 5; 2 Ch. xxviii. 5) is unknown. The *'aram darmeseq* of 1 Ch. xviii. 6 corresponds to the modern (*Dimašk-)eš-šām* as 'Damascus of the North (Syria)'. The name is found in Egyp. *Tjmšqw* (Tuthmosis III) and Amarna Letters (14th century) and cuneiform inscriptions as *Dimašqi*. Other names in the latter texts are *ša imerišu* (perhaps 'caravan city') and *Bīt-Haza'-ili* ('House of Hazael') in the 8th century BC (*DOTT*, p. 57).

c. History

Damascus appears to have been occupied from prehistoric times. In the second millennium BC it was a well-known city near which Abraham defeated a coalition of kings (Gn. xiv. 15). It is possible that his servant Eliezer was from this city (Gn. xv. 2; Syr. and vss). David captured and garrisoned Damascus after his defeat of the troops it had contributed in support of Hadadezer of Hobah (2 Sa. viii. 5 f.; 1 Ch. xviii. 5). Rezon of Hobah, who escaped from this battle, later entered the city which was made the capital of a newly formed Aramaean city-state of Aram (Syria; 1 Ki. xi. 24). The city increased its influence under Rezon's successors Hezion and his son Tabrimmon. By the time of the accession of the latter's son Ben-hadad I (*c.* 900–860 BC) Damascus was the dominant partner in the treaty made by Asa of Judah to offset the pressure brought against him by Baasha of Israel (2 Ch. xvi. 2). The same king (if not Ben-hadad II—see CHRONOLOGY OF THE OLD TESTAMENT) made the provision of merchants' quarters in Damascus a term of a treaty made with Ahab (1 Ki. xx. 34). The aim of this treaty was to gain the support of Israel for the coalition of city-states to oppose the Assyrians. Ben-hadad (Assyr. Adad-idri) of Damascus provided the largest contingent of 20,000 men at the indecisive battle of Qarqar in 853 BC. Ben-hadad may be the unnamed 'king of Aram', in fighting whom Ahab met his death (see 1 Ki. xxii. 29–36).

In the plain near Damascus the prophet Elijah anointed Hazael, a Damascene noble, as the future king of Syria (1 Ki. xix. 15), and Elisha, who had healed the general Naaman of Damascus, was invited there by Hazael to advise on Ben-hadad's health (2 Ki. viii. 7). In 843 BC Hazael had to face renewed attacks by the Assyrians under Shalmaneser III. For a time he held the pass leading through the Lebanon Mts., but having lost 16,000 men, 1,121 chariots, and 470 cavalry was forced to retreat within Damascus, where he successfully withstood a siege. The Assyrians fired orchards and plantations round the city before they withdrew (*DOTT*, p. 48). In 805–803 BC Adad-nirari III led fresh Assyrian attacks on Hazael and Damascus. A further campaign in 797 BC by Shalmaneser IV so weakened Damascus that J(eh)oash of Israel was able to recover towns on his northern border previously lost to Hazael (2 Ki. xiii. 25).

Under Rezin (Assyr. *Raḫi/ṣunnu*) Aram again oppressed Judah (2 Ki. xvi. 6), and in 739 was, with Menahem of Israel, a vassal of Tiglath-pileser III of Assyria. Soon thereafter Rezin revolted, captured Elath, and took many Judaeans captive to Damascus (2 Ch. xxviii. 5). Ahaz of Judah thereupon appealed for help to Assyria who responded by launching a series of punitive raids in 734–732 BC, which culminated in the capture of Damascus, as prophesied by Isaiah (xvii. 1) and Amos (i. 4, 5), and the death of Rezin. The spoiling of the city (Is. viii. 4), the deportation of its inhabitants to Kir (2 Ki. xvi. 9), and its destruction were cited as an object lesson to Judah (Is. x. 9 ff.). In return for this assistance Ahaz was summoned to pay tribute to the Assyrian king at Damascus, where he saw and copied the altar (2 Ki. xvi. 10–12) which led to the worship of Syrian deities within the Temple at Jerusalem (2 Ch. xxviii. 23). Damascus was reduced to a subsidiary city within the Assyrian province of Hamath and henceforth lost its political, but not completely its economic, influence (*cf.* Ezk. xxvii. 18). Judaean merchants continued to reside in the city, and the border of Damascus was considered the boundary of the ideal Jewish state (Ezk. xlvii. 16–18, xlviii. 1; Zc. ix. 1).

In the Seleucid period Damascus lost its position as capital, and thus much trade, to Antioch though it was restored as capital of Coelesyria under Antiochus IX in 111 BC. The Nabataean Aretas won the city in 85 BC, but lost control to Tigranes of Armenia. Damascus was a Roman city from 64 BC to AD 33.

By the time of Paul's conversion the city was governed by an ethnarch appointed by Aretas IV (9 BC–AD 40), who had defeated his son-in-law Herod Antipas (2 Cor. xi. 32, 33). The city had many synagogues (Acts ix. 2; Jos., *BJ* ii. 20) and in these, after being led to the house of Judas in Straight Street (ix. 10–12) where he was visited by Ananias, Paul first preached. Opposition forced Paul to escape over the city wall (ix. 19–27) but he returned to the city after a period spent in nearby Arabia (Gal. i. 17). Damascus continued to be subsidiary to Antioch, both politically and economically, until it was reclaimed by the Arab conquest of AD 634.

BIBLIOGRAPHY. M. F. Unger, *Israel and the Aramaeans of Damascus*, 1957; A. Jepsen, 'Israel und Damaskus' in *Archiv für Orientforschung*, XIV, 1942, pp. 153–172. D.J.W.

DAMNATION. See ESCHATOLOGY.

DAN (Heb. *dān*, commonly treated as active participle of *dîn*, 'to judge'). **1.** One of the twelve sons of Jacob, the elder of the two sons borne to him by Rachel's maidservant Bilhah (Gn. xxx. 1–6), eponymous ancestor of the tribe of Dan.

2. One of the twelve tribes of Israel. Its first settlement lay between the territories of Ephraim, Benjamin, and Judah (Jos. xix. 40 ff.). Pressed back into the hill-country by the Amorites, who themselves were being pressed from the west by the Philistines and other sea peoples who had occupied the Mediterranean seaboard, the majority of the Danites migrated northward to find a new home near the source of the Jordan (Jos. xix. 47; Jdg. i. 34, xviii. 1 ff.). Some members of the tribe, however, remained in their earlier settlement, with the Philistines as their western neighbours; it is in this region that the stories of Samson, a Danite hero, have their setting (Jdg. xiii. 1 ff.). It is probably the remnant of the tribe that stayed in its first home that is described in Deborah's song (Jdg. v. 17) as remaining 'in ships'—however we are to understand the 'ships' (various uncertain emendations have been suggested). This southern remnant appears to have been absorbed ultimately in Judah; the northern Danites were deported by Tiglath-pileser III in 732 BC (2 Ki. xv. 29). The aggressive qualities of the Danites are celebrated in the benedictions of Gn. xlix. 16 f. and Dt. xxxiii. 22.

Dan is missing from the list of tribes in Rev. vii. 5–8, either intentionally or by a primitive corruption. Irenaeus (*Adv. Haer.* v. 30. 2) explains the omission by saying that antichrist is to come from the tribe of Dan—a belief which he bases on Je. viii. 16, LXX ('from Dan shall we hear the noise of his swift horses').

3. A city in the northern Danite territory, modern Tell el-Qadi, near one of the sources of Jordan. Its earlier name was Laish (Jdg. xviii. 29; called Leshem in Jos. xix. 47), appearing as Lus(i) in Egyptian texts of *c.* 1850–1825 BC. It was the most northerly Israelite city, hence the phrase 'from Dan to Beersheba' (*e.g.* Jdg. xx. 1). The shrine established here under the priesthood of Moses' grandson Jonathan and his descendants (Jdg. xviii. 30) was elevated (along with Bethel) to the status of a national sanctuary by Jeroboam I (1 Ki. xii. 29 f.), and so remained until 'the captivity of the land' under Tiglath-pileser III.

BIBLIOGRAPHY. H. H. Rowley, 'The Danite Migration to Laish', *ExpT*, LI, 1939–40, pp. 466–471. F.F.B.

DANCE. The Old Testament makes occasional reference to dancing as a source of amusement only (*e.g.* Ex. xxxii. 19; Ec. iii. 4), but usually behind the activity is some form of religious significance. Groups of women engaged in it on occasions of national celebration, such as after the crossing of the Red Sea (Ex. xv. 20), after military victories (1 Sa. xviii. 6), and at religious festivals (Jdg. xxi. 19–21). Less frequently, men also are recorded as having danced (*e.g.* 2 Sa. vi. 14).

In New Testament times the Greek custom of employing professional women dancers was followed in the case of Salome at Herod's birthday feast (Mk. vi. 21, 22); there was dancing at the prodigal son's homecoming festivities (Lk. xv. 25); and it was such a common part of daily life that it entered into children's games (Mt. xi. 17; Lk. vii. 32; *cf.* Jb. xxi. 11).

For a comprehensive treatment, see the corresponding article in *EBi*. See also fig. 62. J.D.D.

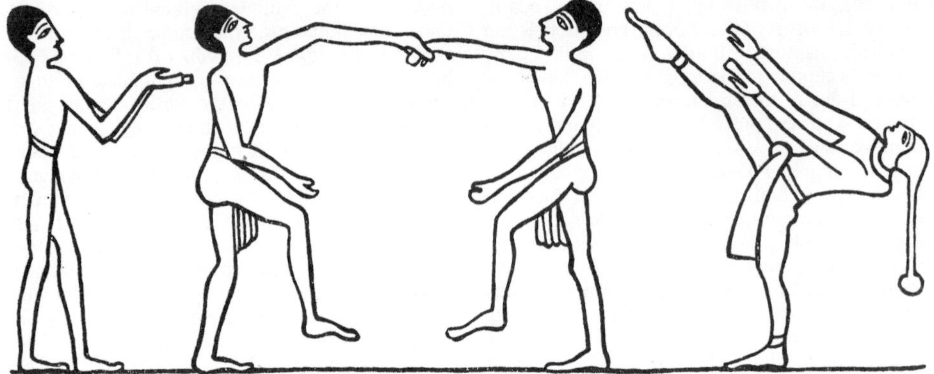

Fig. 62. Dancing-scenes of the Old Kingdom from Giza (*left*) and Sakkara (*right*) in Egypt.

DANIEL (*dāniyyē'l, dāni'ēl*, 'God is my judge'). **1.** Second son of David (1 Ch. iii. 1) and Abigail, called also 'Chileab' (AVmg). Although older than his brothers Absalom and Adonijah, nothing more is recorded of him, suggesting that he died young. **2.** A descendant of Ithamar, who accompanied Ezra (viii. 2) and was a signatory to the covenant (Ne. x. 1, 6). **3.** A man of extraordinary wisdom and righteousness whose name is coupled with Noah and Job (Ezk. xiv. 14, 20), and who is mentioned again in xxviii. 3. Perhaps identical with the Ugaritic *Dan'el*, or else with (4) below.

4. The fourth of the so-called 'greater' prophets, of whose early career nothing is known except for what we are told in the book which bears his name. An Israelite of royal or noble descent (*cf.* Jos., *Ant.* x. 10. 1), he was carried captive to Babylon by Nebuchadrezzar in the third year of Jehoiakim, and with various companions trained for the king's service (Dn. i. 1–6). Following a custom of the time, he was given (verse 7) the Babylonian name of Belteshazzar (*q.v.*). He gained a reputation first as an interpreter of other men's visions (chapters ii–v), then of his own, in which he predicted the future triumph of the messianic kingdom (chapters vii–xii).

Renowned for sagacity, he successfully occupied leading governmental posts under Nebuchadrezzar, Belshazzar, and Darius. His last recorded vision was on the banks of the Tigris in the third year of Cyrus. *EBr* (14th ed., VII, p. 28) quotes a late rabbinical tradition (*Midrash Šir ha-širim*, vii. 8) as saying that Daniel returned to Jerusalem among the exiles freed by the royal edict, and adds: 'The Jewish traveller Benjamin of Tudela (12th century AD) was shown his tomb in Susa, and notices of this tomb are found as early as the 6th century.' There is, however, no clear evidence that Daniel was buried at Susa.

There is a brief reference to 'Daniel the prophet' in Mt. xxiv. 15 (= Mk. xiii. 14).

See DANIEL, BOOK OF. J.D.D.

DANIEL, BOOK OF.

I. OUTLINE OF CONTENTS

Chapters i–vi are largely historical in content, with Daniel speaking of himself in the third person. Chapter i records his being carried away captive from Judah to Babylon and his subsequent rise to power. In the next five chapters he is seen serving as chief minister and interpreter of dreams to a number of Gentile kings. The visions of chapters ii, iv, and v are given to the Babylonian kings, Nebuchadrezzar and Belshazzar, and reveal the destiny of Gentile kings and kingdoms. At the end of chapter v the capture of Babylon by Darius the Mede is briefly mentioned. This is followed by an account of Daniel's continued influence and the plot against his life. This historical section ends with his miraculous deliverance and a brief note to the effect that 'he prospered in the reign of Darius, and in the reign of Cyrus the Persian'.

In chapters vii–xii the historical background almost fades from sight as Daniel himself, speaking now in the first person, becomes the recipient of visions which emphasize the destiny of Israel in relation to Gentile kingdoms.

II. AUTHORSHIP AND DATE

Modern critical scholarship is practically unanimous in its rejection of the book as a 6th-century BC document written by Daniel, in spite of the testimony of the book itself and the statement of our Lord that the abomination of desolation was 'spoken of by Daniel the prophet' (Mt. xxiv. 15). Critics claim that the book was compiled by an unknown author about 165 BC, because it contains prophecies of post-Babylonian kings and wars which supposedly become increasingly accurate as they approach that date (xi. 2–35). It is further claimed that the book was written to encourage faithful Jews in their conflict with Antiochus Epiphanes (*cf.* 1 Macc. ii. 59, 60) and that it was enthusiastically received by them as being genuine and authentic and was immediately placed in the Hebrew Canon.

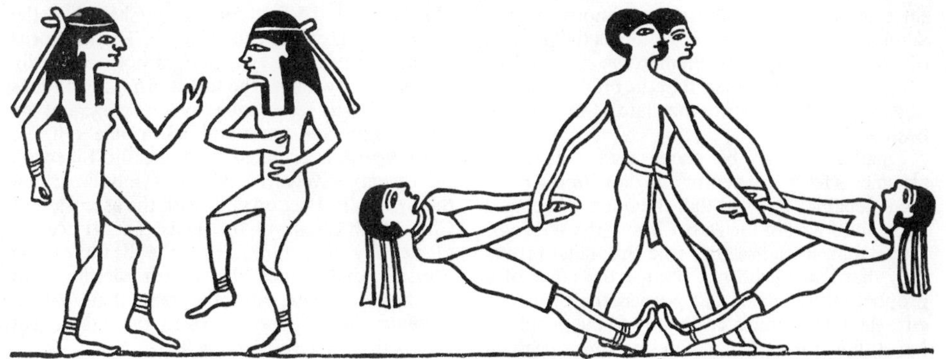

Fig. 63. Egyptian dancers of the New Kingdom from Qurnah (*left*), and of the Middle Kingdom from Beni Hassan (*right*).

In addition to its doubtful implications with regard to predictive prophecy, this critical view must be rejected for the following reasons.

1. The assumption that the author placed Darius I before Cyrus and made Xerxes the father of Darius I (*cf.* vi. 28, ix. 1) ignores the fact that Daniel is speaking of Darius the Mede, a governor under Cyrus whose father had the same name as the later Persian king. Critics do not question the fact that the author was an extremely brilliant Jew (*cf.* R. H. Pfeiffer, *Introduction to the Old Testament*, 1948, p. 776). But no intelligent Jew of the 2nd century BC could have committed such historical blunders as the critics suppose, with Ezra iv. 5, 6 before him, especially since he puts Xerxes as the fourth king after Cyrus in Daniel xi. 2 (*cf.* A. A. Bevan, *A Short Commentary on the Book of Daniel*, 1892, p. 109).

2. If the book were as full of serious historical blunders as the critics claim (*cf.* H. H. Rowley, *Darius the Mede and the Four World Empires of the Book of Daniel*, 1935, pp. 54–60), Jews of the Maccabean period would never have accepted it as canonical. Educated Palestinians of that era had access to the writings of Herodotus, Ctesias, Berossus, Menander, and other ancient historians whose works have long since been lost to us, and they were well acquainted with the names of Cyrus and his successors on the throne of Persia —yet they saw no historical blunders in the Book of Daniel, while rejecting such works as 1 Maccabees as being unworthy of the Canon (*cf.* R. D. Wilson, *Studies in the Book of Daniel*, 1917, p. 149).

3. The recent discovery of manuscript fragments of the Book of Daniel in Cave I and Cave IV of Wadi Qumran showing the Hebrew–Aramaic and Aramaic–Hebrew transition points in the text has called into serious question the possibility of a Maccabean date for the book (*cf.* W. S. LaSor, *Amazing Dead Sea Scrolls*, 1956, pp. 42–44).

4. The author gives evidence of having a more accurate knowledge of Neo-Babylonian and early Achaemenid Persian history than any known historian since the 6th century BC. Regarding Daniel iv, Robert H. Pfeiffer wrote: 'We shall presumably never know how our author learned that the new Babylon was the creation of Nebuchadnezzar (4:30), as the excavations have proved' (*op. cit.*, p. 758). Regarding Daniel v, the portrayal of Belshazzar as co-king of Babylon under Nabonidus has been brilliantly vindicated by archaeological discoveries (*cf.* R. P. Dougherty, *Nabonidus and Belshazzar*, 1929; and J. Finegan, *Light From the Ancient Past*[2], 1959, p. 228). Regarding Daniel vi, recent studies have shown that Darius the Mede corresponds remarkably well with what is known from the Nabonidus Chronicle and numerous other contemporary cuneiform documents of Gubaru, whom Cyrus appointed as 'the Governor of Babylon and the Region beyond the River'. It is no longer possible to attribute to the author the false concept of an independent Median kingdom between the fall of Babylon and the rise of Cyrus (*cf.* J. C. Whitcomb, *Darius the Mede*, 1959. For an alternative view, see also DARIUS). Again, the author knew enough of 6th-century BC customs to represent Nebuchadrezzar as being able to make and alter the laws of Babylon with absolute sovereignty (Dn. ii. 12, 13, 46), while depicting Darius the Mede as being helpless to change the laws of the Medes and Persians (vi. 8, 9). Also, he accurately represented the change from punishment by fire under the Babylonians (Dn. iii) to punishment by the lions' den under the Persians (Dn. vi), since fire was sacred to the Zoroastrians (*cf.* A. T. Olmstead, *The History of the Persian Empire*, 1948, p. 473).

On the basis of a careful comparison of the cuneiform evidence concerning Belshazzar with the statements of the fifth chapter of Daniel, R. P. Dougherty concluded that 'the view that the fifth chapter of Daniel originated in the Maccabean age is discredited' (*op. cit.*, p. 200). But the same conclusion must be reached concerning the fourth and sixth chapters of Daniel as well, as we have pointed out above. Therefore, since the critics are almost unanimous in their admission that the Book of Daniel is the product of one author (*cf.* R. H. Pfeiffer, *op. cit.*, pp. 761, 762), we may safely assert that the book could not possibly have been written as late as the Maccabean age.

Finally, it must be stated that the classic arguments for a 2nd-century BC date for the book are untenable. The fact that the book was placed in the third part of the Heb. Canon (the Writings) rather than in the second (the Prophets) proves only that Daniel did not occupy the office of a prophet, although he did possess the prophetic gift. He did not minister directly to the people of Israel, but was rather a statesman in a heathen court like Joseph (*cf.* E. J. Young, *The Prophecy of Daniel*, 1949, p. 20).

Again, the failure of Ben Sira, the author of Ecclesiasticus (180 BC), to mention Daniel among the famous men of the past certainly does not prove that he knew nothing of Daniel. This is evident from the fact that he also failed to mention Job, all the judges (except Samuel), Asa, Jehoshaphat, Mordecai, and even Ezra (Ecclus. xliv–xlix).

The presence of three Gk. names for musical instruments (translated 'harp', 'sackbut', and 'psaltery' in iii. 5, 10), another of the arguments for a late date, no longer constitutes a serious problem, for it has become increasingly clear that Gk. culture penetrated the Near East long before the time of Nebuchadrezzar (*cf.* W. F. Albright, *From Stone Age to Christianity*², 1957, p. 337). Persian loan words for technical terms are likewise consistent with an early date. The Aramaic of Daniel (ii. 4b–vii. 28) closely resembles that of Ezra (iv. 7–vi. 18, vii. 12–26) and the 5th-century BC Elephantine papyri, while the Hebrew of Daniel resembles that of Ezekiel, Haggai, Ezra and Chronicles more than that of Ecclesiasticus (180 BC).

III. THE PROPHECIES OF DANIEL

This important apocalyptic book provides the basic framework for Jewish and Gentile history from the time of Nebuchadrezzar to the second advent of Christ. An understanding of its prophecies is essential to the proper interpretation of the Olivet discourse of Christ (Mt. xxiv, xxv; Lk. xxi), Paul's doctrine of the man of sin (2 Thes. ii), and the book of Revelation. The book is also of great importance theologically for its doctrines of angels and the resurrection.

Among those who take the conservative view of the date and authorship of the book, there are two main schools of thought today concerning the interpretation of the prophecies it contains. On the one hand, some commentators interpret Daniel's prophecies of the great image (ii. 31–49), the four beasts (vii. 2–27), and the seventy weeks (ix. 24–27) as culminating in the first coming of Christ and related events, for they find in the Church, the new Israel, the fulfilment of God's promises to the Jews, the old Israel. Thus, the stone which strikes the image (ii. 34, 35) points to the first coming of Christ and the subsequent growth of the Church. The ten horns of the fourth beast (vii. 24) are not necessarily contemporary kings; the little horn (vii. 24) does not necessarily represent a human being; and the phrase 'time and times and half a time' (vii. 25, RV) is to be interpreted symbolically. Likewise, the seventy sevens (ix. 24) are symbolical; and this symbolical period ends with the ascension of Christ with all six of the goals (ix. 24) accomplished by that time. It is the death of the Messiah that causes the Jewish sacrifice and oblation to cease, and the 'one that maketh desolate' (ix. 27, RV) refers to the subsequent destruction of Jerusalem by Titus.

Other commentators, however (including the author), interpret these prophecies as culminating in the second advent of Christ, with the nation of Israel prominent once again in God's dealings with the human race. Accordingly, the great image of Daniel ii represents the Satan-dominated 'kingdom of the world' (Rev. xi. 15, RV) in the form of Babylon, Medo-Persia, Greece, and Rome, with Rome continuing in some form to the end of this age. This godless empire finally culminates in ten contemporaneous kings (ii. 41–44, *cf.* vii. 24; Rev. xvii. 12) who are destroyed by Christ at His second coming (ii. 45). Christ then establishes His kingdom on earth (*cf.* Mt. vi. 10; Rev. xx. 1–6), which becomes 'a great mountain' and fills 'the whole earth' (ii. 35).

Daniel vii depicts the same four monarchies as wild beasts, the fourth (Rome) producing ten horns which correspond to the toes of the image (vii. 7). There is an advance over the second chapter, however, in that the antichrist is now introduced as an eleventh horn who plucks up three of the others and persecutes the saints for 'a time and times and half a time' (vii. 25, RV). That this phrase means three and a half years may be seen by a comparison of Rev. xii. 14 with xii. 6 and xiii. 5. The destruction of the antichrist, in whom the power of the four monarchies and the ten kings is finally concentrated (Rev. xiii. 1, 2, xvii. 7–17; *cf.* Dn. ii. 35) is accomplished by 'one like unto a son of man' (Dn. vii. 13, RV) who comes 'with the clouds of heaven' (*cf.* Mt. xxvi. 64; Rev. xix. 11 ff.).

The 'little horn' of Dn. viii. 9 ff. is not to be identified with that of vii. 24 ff. (the antichrist), for he does not emerge from the fourth monarchy but from a division of the third. Historically, the little horn of Dn. viii was Antiochus Epiphanes, the Seleucid persecutor of Israel (viii. 9–14). Prophetically, in the author's personal view, this little horn represents the eschatological king of the north who opposes the antichrist (viii. 17–26, *cf.* xi. 40–45).

The prophecy of the seventy weeks (ix. 24–27) is felt to be of crucial importance for biblical eschatology. The writer believes that the seventy sevens of years are to be reckoned from the decree of Artaxerxes I to rebuild Jerusalem in 444 BC (Ne. ii. 1–8) and terminate with the establishment of the millennial kingdom (ix. 24). It seems clear that a gap or hiatus separates the end of the sixty-ninth week from the beginning of the seventieth (ix. 26), for Christ placed the abomination of desolation at the very end of the present age (Mt. xxiv. 15 in context; *cf.* Dn. ix. 27). Such prophetic gaps are not uncommon in the Old Testament (*e.g.* Is. lxi. 2; *cf.* Lk. iv. 16–21). Thus, the seventieth week, according to premillennial interpreters, is a seven-year period immediately preceding the second advent of Christ, during which time antichrist rises to world dominion and persecutes the saints.

Daniel xi. 2 ff. foretells the rise of four Persian kings (the fourth being Xerxes); Alexander the Great; and various Seleucid and Ptolemaic kings culminating in Antiochus Epiphanes (xi. 21–32), whose atrocities provoked the Maccabean wars (xi. 32b–35). Verse 35b is regarded as providing the transition to eschatological times. First the antichrist comes into view (xi. 36–39); and then the final king of the north, who, according to some premillennial scholars, will crush temporarily both the antichrist and the king of the south before being destroyed supernaturally on the mountains of Israel (xi. 40–45; *cf.* Joel ii. 20; Ezk. xxxix. 4, 17). In the meantime, antichrist will have recovered from his fatal blow to begin his period of world dominion (Dn. xi. 44; *cf.* Rev. xiii. 3, xvii. 8).

The great tribulation, which lasts three and a half years (Dn. vii. 25; *cf.* Mt. xxiv. 21), begins with the victory of the archangel Michael over Satan's heavenly armies (Dn. xii. 1; *cf.* Rev. xii. 7 ff.), and ends with the bodily resurrection of tribulation saints (Dn. xii. 2, 3; *cf.* Rev. vii. 9–14). Although the tribulation period lasts only 1,260 days (Rev. xii. 6), an additional thirty days seem to be required for the cleansing and restoration of the Temple (Dn. xii. 11), and yet another forty-five days before the full blessedness of the millennial kingdom is experienced (xii. 12).

BIBLIOGRAPHY. R. D. Wilson, *Studies in the Book of Daniel*, I, 1917, II, 1938; J. A. Montgomery, *The Book of Daniel, ICC*, 1927; R. P. Dougherty, *Nabonidus and Belshazzar*, 1929; H. H. Rowley, *Darius the Mede and the Four World Empires in the Book of Daniel*, 1935; C. Lattey, *The Book of Daniel*, 1948; E. J. Young, *The Prophecy of Daniel*, 1949, and *The Messianic Prophecies of Daniel*, 1954; H. C. Leupold, *Exposition of Daniel*, 1949; R. D. Culver, *Daniel and the Latter Days*, 1954; E. W. Heaton, *The Book of Daniel*, 1956; J. C. Whitcomb Jr., *Darius the Mede*, 1959. J.C.W.

DAN-JAAN. A place mentioned in 2 Sa. xxiv. 6 on the route followed by Joab and his companions in compiling the census ordered by David. Aroer, to the east of the Dead Sea, was the starting-point, and they camped south of the city in the valley of the Gadites (the Arnon Basin). Then they proceeded northwards to Jazer and on through Gilead and other territory to Dan-jaan and its environs, and to Sidon (most probably the territorial boundary is meant), and set out southwards past an outpost in the province of Tyre, ending up in Beersheba. As Beersheba is also mentioned in David's instruction along with Dan (verse 2), some scholars would identify Dan-jaan with the well-known Dan. More probably it was a northern town in the district of Dan. Among the different readings given by the LXX, Dan-jaar is found, which might be translated 'Dan of the Woods'. Another LXX reading 'and from Dan, they turned round to Sidon', seems indefensible. The epithet *Jaan* might well be a personal name (*cf.* 1 Ch. v. 12 for a possible cognate, and the Ugaritic *yʿrn* in C. H. Gordon's *Manual*, p. 274). W.J.M.

DARIC. See MONEY.

DARIUS (Heb. *Dārᵉyāweš*; Old Persian, *Darayavauš*; Gk. *Dareios*).

1. Darius the Mede, son of Ahasuerus (Xerxes; Dn. vi. 1, xi. 1), received the government on the death of Belshazzar (v. 30, 31), being made king of the Chaldeans (ix. 1) at the age of sixty-two (v. 31). He bore the title of 'king' (vi. 6, 9, 25) and the years were marked by his reign (xi. 1). He appointed 120 subordinate governors under three presidents, of whom one was Daniel (vi. 2), who prospered in his reign (vi. 28). Darius was a contemporary of Cyrus. According to Jos. (*Ant.* x. 11. 4), Daniel was removed by Darius to Media.

Since Darius the Mede is not mentioned by name outside the book of Daniel, and the contemporary cuneiform inscriptions reckon no king of Babylon between Nabonidus (and Belshazzar) and the accession of Cyrus, his historicity has been denied and the Old Testament account of this reign considered a conflation of confused traditions (H. H. Rowley, *Darius the Mede*, 1935). On the other hand, the narrative has all the appearance of genuine historical writing, and in the absence of many historical records of this period there is no reason why the history should not be accepted.

There have been many attempts to identify Darius with persons mentioned in the Babylonian texts. The two most reasonable hypotheses are the identification of Darius with (*a*) Gubaru, and (*b*) Cyrus. Gubaru was governor of Babylon and of the region beyond the river (Euphrates). There is, however, no specific evidence that he was a Mede, called king, named Darius, a son of Ahasuerus, or aged about sixty. Cyrus, who was related to the Medes, was called 'king of the Medes' and is known to have been about sixty-two years old on becoming king of Babylon. According to the inscriptions, he appointed many subordinate officials, and documents were dated by his regnal years. This theory requires that Dn. vi. 28 be translated '. . . in the reign of Darius, *even* in the reign of Cyrus the Persian' as an explanation by the writer of the use of sources using two names for the one person. The weakness of this theory lies in the fact that Cyrus is nowhere named son of Ahasuerus (but this might be a term used only of royal persons) or as 'of the seed of a Mede'. See CYRUS.

2. Darius I, son of Hystaspes, who was king of Persia and of Babylon, where he succeeded Cambyses (after two usurpers had been displaced), and ruled 521–486 BC. He enabled the returned Jews to rebuild the Temple at Jerusalem with Jeshua and Zerubbabel (Ezr. iv. 5; Hg. i. 1; Zc. i. 1).

Fig. 64. Darius I (521–486 BC) sits on an elaborate throne, probably of metal, with a matching footstool, holding a long sceptre or staff. From a limestone Palace relief, Susa.

3. Darius II (Nothus), who ruled Persia and Babylon (423–408 BC), called 'Darius the Persian' in Ne. xii. 22, perhaps to distinguish him from 'Darius the Mede'. Since the father of Jaddua the high priest is mentioned in an Elephantine papyrus *c.* 400 BC, there is no need to assume that this Jaddua was the high priest who met Alexander in 332 BC and that the Darius here meant is Darius III (Codomanus), who reigned *c.* 336–331 BC.

BIBLIOGRAPHY. J. C. Whitcomb, *Darius the Mede*, 1959. D.J.W.

DARKNESS. See LIGHT.

DART. See ARMOUR AND WEAPONS.

DATHAN (*dāṯān*, 'fount'?). A Reubenite, son of Eliab. Nu. xvi. 1–35 tells how, with his brother, Abiram, and Korah, a Levite, he rebelled against Moses. See KORAH.

DAUGHTER. See FAMILY.

DAVID (*dāwiḏ*, sometimes *dāwîḏ*; root and meaning doubtful, but see *BDB in loc.*; the equation with a supposed Old Bab. (Mari) *dawîdum*, 'chief', is now doubted (*JNES*, XVII, 1958, p. 130; *VT Suppl.* VII, 1960, pp. 165 ff.); *cf.* Laesoe, *Shemsharah Tablets*, p. 56). The youngest son of Jesse, of the tribe of Judah, and second king of Israel. In Scripture the name is his alone, typifying the unique place he has as ancestor, forerunner, and foreshadower of the Lord Jesus Christ—'great David's greater son'. There are fifty-eight New Testament references to David, including the oft-repeated title given to Jesus—'Son of David'. Paul states that Jesus is 'of the seed of David according to the flesh' (Rom. i. 3), while Jesus Himself is recorded by John as saying 'I am the root and the offspring of David' (Rev. xxii. 16).

When we return to the Old Testament to find who this is who occupies a position of such prominence in the lineage of our Lord and the purposes of God, the material is abundant and rich. The story of David is found between 1 Sa. xvi and 1 Ki. ii, with much of the material paralleled in 1 Ch. ii–xxix.

I. FAMILY BACKGROUND

Great-grandson of Ruth and Boaz, David was the youngest of eight brothers (1 Sa. xvii. 12 ff.) and was brought up to be a shepherd. In this occupation he learned the courage which was later to be evidenced in battle (1 Sa. xvii. 34, 35) and the tenderness and care for his flock which he was later to sing of as the attributes of his God. Like Joseph, he suffered from the ill-will and jealousy of his older brothers, perhaps because of the talents with which God had endowed him (1 Sa. xvii. 28). Modest about his ancestry (1 Sa. xviii. 18), David was to father a line of notable descendants, as the genealogy of our Lord in Matthew's Gospel shows (Mt. i. 1–17).

II. ANOINTING AND FRIENDSHIP WITH SAUL

When God rejected Saul from the kingship of Israel, David was revealed as his successor to Samuel, who anointed him, without any ostentation, at Bethlehem (1 Sa. xvi. 1–13). One of the results of Saul's rejection was the departure of the Spirit of God from him, with a consequent depression of his own spirit, which at times seems to have approached madness. There is an awesome revelation of divine purpose in the providence by which David, who is to replace Saul in the favour and plan of God, is selected to minister to the fallen king's melancholy (1 Sa. xvi. 17–21). So the lives of these two were brought together, the stricken giant and the rising stripling. At first all went well. Saul was pleased with the youth, whose musical skill was to give us part of our richest devotional heritage, and appointed him his armour-bearer. Then the well-known incident involving Goliath, the Philistine champion, changed everything (1 Sa. xvii). David's agility and skill with the sling outdid the strength of the ponderous giant, whose slaughter was the signal for an Israelite repulsion of the Philistine force. The way was clear for David to reap the reward promised by Saul—the hand of the king's daughter in marriage, and freedom for his father's family from taxation; but a new factor changed the course of events—the king's jealousy of the new champion of Israel. As David returned from the slaying of Goliath, the women of Israel greeted him, singing, 'Saul hath slain his thousands, and David his ten thousands'. Saul, unlike his son Jonathan (*q.v.*) in a similar situation, resented this and, we are told, 'eyed David from that day and forward' (1 Sa. xviii. 7, 9).

III. THE HOSTILITY OF SAUL

Saul's dealings with David declined progressively in amity, and we find the young national hero escaping a savage attack on his life by the king, reduced in military honour, cheated of his promised bride, and married to Saul's other daughter, Michal, after a marriage settlement which was meant to cause David's death (1 Sa. xviii. 25). It would appear from 1 Sa. xxiv. 9 that there was a group at Saul's court which deliberately fomented trouble between Saul and David, and the situation deteriorated steadily. Another abortive attempt by Saul at slaying David with his spear was followed by an attempted arrest, foiled only by a stratagem of Michal, David's wife (1 Sa. xix. 8–17). A marked feature of this period in David's life is the way in which Saul's two children, Jonathan and Michal, allied themselves with David and against their own father.

IV. FLIGHT FROM SAUL

The next stages in the story of David are marked by a constant flight from the relentless pursuit of Saul. No resting-place is safe for long; prophet, priest, national enemy—none can give him shelter, and those who help him are cruelly punished by the rage-maddened king (1 Sa. xxii. 6–19). After a narrow escape from destruction by the Philistine war-lords, David eventually established the Adullam band, at first a heterogeneous collection of fugitives, but later an armed task-force which harried the foreign invaders, protected the crops and flocks of outlying Israelite communities, and lived off the generosity of the latter. The churlish refusal of one of these wealthy sheep-farmers, Nabal, to recognize any indebtedness to David is recorded in 1 Sa. xxv, and is interesting in introducing Abigail, later to become one of David's wives. Chapters xxiv and xxvi of the same book record two instances when David spared the life of Saul, out of mingled piety and magnanimity. Eventually David, quite unable to curb the hostility of Saul, came to terms with the Philistine king, Achish of Gath, and was granted the frontier town of Ziklag in return for the occasional use of his warrior band. When the Philistines went out in force against Saul, however, the war-lords demurred at David's presence in their ranks, fearing a last-minute change of loyalty, so he was spared the tragedy of Gilboa, which he later mourned in one of the loveliest elegies extant (2 Sa. i. 19–27).

V. KING IN HEBRON

Once Saul was dead, David sought the will of God and was guided to return to Judah, his own tribal region. Here his fellow-tribesmen anointed him king, and he took up royal residence in Hebron. He was then thirty years old, and he reigned in Hebron for seven and a half years. The first two years of this period were occupied by civil war between the supporters of David, and the old courtiers of Saul, who had set up Saul's son Eshbaal (Ishbosheth) as king in Mahanaim. It may be doubted whether Eshbaal was more than a puppet, manipulated by Saul's faithful captain, Abner. With the death of these two by assassination, organized opposition to David came to an end, and he was anointed king over the twelve tribes of Israel in Hebron, from which he was soon to transfer his capital to Jerusalem (2 Sa. iii–v).

VI. KING IN JERUSALEM

Now began the most successful period in David's long reign, which was to last for another thirty-three years. By a happy combination of personal bravery and skilled generalship he led the Israelites in such a systematic and decisive subjugation of their enemies—Philistines, Canaanites, Moabites, Ammonites, Aramaeans, Edomites, and Amalekites—that his name would have been recorded in history quite apart from his significance in the divine plan of redemption. The contemporary weakness of the powers in the Nile and Euphrates valleys enabled him, by conquest and alliance, to extend his sphere of influence from the Egyptian frontier and the Gulf of Aqabah to the upper Euphrates. Conquering the supposedly impregnable Jebusite citadel of Jerusalem, he made it his capital, whence he bestrode the two major divisions of his kingdom, later to become the divided kingdoms of Judah and Israel. A palace was built, highways opened, trade routes restored, and the material prosperity of the kingdom secured. This, however, could never be the sole, nor yet the main, ambition of 'a man after Yahweh's own heart', and we soon see evidence of David's religious zeal. He brought back the ark of the covenant from Kiriath-jearim and placed it in a special tabernacle prepared for it in Jerusalem. It was during the return of the ark that the incident occurred which led to the death of Uzzah (2 Sa. vi. 6–8). Much of the religious organization which was to enrich the later temple worship owes its origin to the arrangements for the service of the tabernacle made by David at this time. In addition to its strategic and political importance, Jerusalem thus acquired the even greater religious significance, with which its name has been associated ever since.

It is all the more to be wondered at and remembered in godly fear, that it was in this period of outward prosperity and apparent religious fervour that David committed the sin referred to in Scripture as 'the matter of Uriah the Hittite' (2 Sa. xi). The significance and importance of this sin, both for its intrinsic heinousness and for its consequences in the whole ensuing history of Israel, cannot be overestimated. David repented deeply, but the deed was done, and stands as a demonstration of how sin spoils God's purpose for His children. The poignant cry of anguish with which he greeted the news of Absalom's death (see ABSALOM) was only a feeble echo of the heart's agony which knew that death, and many more, to be but part of the reaping of the harvest of lust and deceit sown by him so many years before.

Absalom's rebellion, in which the northern kingdom remained loyal to David, was soon followed by a revolt on the part of the northern kingdom, led by Sheba, a Benjamite. This revolt, like Absalom's, was crushed by Joab. David's dying days were marred by the scheming of Adonijah and Solomon for his throne, and by the realization that the legacy of internecine bloodshed foretold by Nathan (*q.v.*) had still to be spent.

In addition to David's standing army, led by his kinsman Joab, he had a personal bodyguard recruited mainly from warriors of Philistine stock, whose loyalty to him never wavered. There is abundant evidence in the historical writings to which reference has already been made of David's skill in composing odes and elegies (see 2 Sa. i. 19–27, iii. 33, 34, xxii, xxiii. 1–7). An early tradition describes him as 'the sweet psalmist of Israel' (2 Sa. xxiii. 1), while later Old Testament writings refer to his direction of the musical worship of Israel, his invention of and skill in playing musical instruments, and his composition (Ne. xii. 24, 36, 45, 46; Am. vi. 5). Seventy-three of the psalms in the Bible are recorded as 'David's', some of them in ways which clearly imply authorship. Most convincingly of all, our Lord Himself spoke of David's authorship of at least one psalm (Lk. xx. 42), using a quotation from it to make plain the nature of His Messiahship.

VII. CHARACTER

The Bible nowhere glosses over the sins or character defects of the children of God. 'Whatsoever things were written aforetime were written for our learning' (Rom. xv. 4). It is part of the task of Scripture to warn by example, as well as to encourage. The sin of David in the matter of Uriah the Hittite is a cardinal instance of this. Let this blot be seen for what it is—a stain on a character otherwise fair and wondrously to the glory of God. It is true that there are elements in the experience of David which seem foreign and even repugnant to the child of the new covenant. Yet 'he . . . served his own generation by the will of God' (Acts xiii. 36), and in that generation he stood out as a bright and shining light for the God of Israel. His accomplishments were many and varied; man of action, poet, tender lover, generous foe, stern dispenser of justice, loyal friend, he was all that men find wholesome and admirable in man, and this by the will of God, who made him and shaped him for his destiny. It is to David, not to Saul, that the Jews look back with pride and affection as the establisher of their kingdom, and it is in David that the more far-sighted of them saw the kingly ideal beyond which their minds could not reach, in the image of which they looked for a coming Messiah, who should deliver his people and sit upon the throne of David for ever. That this was not idealistic nonsense, still less idolatry, is indicated by the New Testament endorsement of the excellences of David, of whose seed Messiah indeed came, after the flesh.

BIBLIOGRAPHY. G. de S. Barrow, *David: Shepherd, Poet, Warrior, King*, 1946; A. C. Welch, *Kings and Prophets of Israel*, 1952, pp. 80 ff. For a concise estimate of the 'Davidic' psalms, see N. H. Snaith, *The Psalms, A Short Introduction*, 1945, where Ewald's rearrangement is cited with approval. For an important and interesting appraisal of David's official rôle as divine representative and the significance of Jerusalem in the religious life of the monarchy, see A. R. Johnson, *Sacral Kingship in Ancient Israel*, 1955. T.H.J.

DAVID, CITY OF. See JERUSALEM.

DAY. See CALENDAR.

DAY OF THE LORD. This expression forms part of the eschatology of the Bible (see ESCHATOLOGY). It has various equivalents, such as 'the day', 'in that day'. In this article we consider the uses of the actual phrase. Am. v. 18–20, the earliest use, shows that the phrase was already a standard one in popular phraseology. To the people it meant the day when Yahweh would intervene to put Israel at the head of the nations, irrespective of Israel's faithfulness to Him. Amos declares that the Day means judgment for Israel. So also in Is. ii. 12 f.; Ezk. xiii. 5; Joel i. 15, ii. 1, 11; Zp. i. 7, 14; Zc. xiv. 1.

Other prophets, conscious of the sins of other nations as well as of Israel, declare that the Day will come on individual nations as a punishment for their brutalities, *e.g.* Babylon, Is. xiii. 6, 9; Egypt, Je. xlvi. 10; Edom, Ob. 15; many nations, Joel ii. 31, iii. 14; Ob. 15.

The Day of the Lord is thus the occasion when Yahweh actively intervenes to punish sin that has come to a climax. This punishment may come through an invasion (Am. v, vi; Is. xiii; Ezk. xiii. 5), or through some natural disaster, such as a locust invasion (Joel i, ii). All lesser interventions come to a head in the actual coming of the Lord Himself. At this Day there are truly repentant believers who are saved (Joel ii. 28–32), while those who remain enemies of the Lord, whether Jews or Gentiles, are punished. There are also physical effects on the world of nature (Is. ii).

In the New Testament the Day of the Lord is the second coming of Christ, and the phrase 'the day of Jesus Christ', or an equivalent, occurs in 1 Cor. i. 8, v. 5; Phil. i. 6, 10, ii. 16; 2 Thes. ii. 2 (AV). The coming is unexpected (1 Thes. v. 2; 2 Pet. iii. 10), yet certain signs must occur first, and these should be discerned by Christians (2 Thes. ii. 2 f.). Physical effects on the world of nature accompany the Day (2 Pet. iii. 12 f.).

J.S.W.

DAY'S JOURNEY (Nu. xi. 31; 1 Ki. xix. 4; Jon. iii. 4; Lk. ii. 44). In the East distances were commonly considered in terms of hours and days. Thus a day's journey might be reckoned as 7–8 hours (perhaps 20–30 miles), but it was a somewhat indefinite expression appropriate to a country where roads and other factors vary greatly. It should not be confused with a sabbath day's journey, for which see WEIGHTS AND MEASURES.

J.D.D.

DAYSMAN (Heb. *yāḵaḥ*, 'to reason, argue, decide')—one who arbitrates, an umpire (so RVmg). Following the eastern practice, the daysman laid his hands on the heads of the disagreeing parties, thus stressing both his judicial function and his desire to give an impartial verdict. Job (ix. 33) declares that no man is worthy to question the purposes of (literally 'lay his hands on') God. Tyndale renders Ex. xxi. 22, 'He shall paye as the dayesmen appoynte him' (AV '. . . as the judges determine').

The New Testament rendering, 'man's judgment' (1 Cor. iv. 3, translating Gk. *anthrōpinē hēmera*) is literally 'man's day', signifying the day fixed for a trial.

J.D.D.

DAYSPRING (Heb. *šaḥar*, 'dawn'; Gk. *anatolē*, 'uprising', elsewhere in AV 'east'). The 'place' of the dayspring (Jb. xxxviii. 12) is the daily-changing point of the horizon at which the sun comes up. The Gk. (Lk. i. 78) presents difficulties of interpretation, but could intend a comparison of the Messiah with the rising of the sun. See discussion in A. R. C. Leaney, *The Gospel according to St. Luke*, 1958, pp. 90, 91.

J.D.D.

DEACON. AV renders 'deacon' only at Phil. i. 1 and four times in 1 Tim. iii; but the Gk. word thus represented, *diakonos* (generally in AV 'minister' or 'servant'), occurs some thirty times in the New Testament, and the cognates *diakoneō* (to 'minister') and *diakonia* ('ministry') occur between them a further seventy times. In the majority of the hundred occurrences of the words there is no trace of a technical meaning relating to specialized functions in the Church; in a few it is necessary to consider how far *diakonos* and its cognates have acquired such a connotation.

I. DERIVATION

Basically, *diakonos* is a servant, and often a table-servant, or waiter. In Hellenistic times it came also to represent certain cult and temple officials (see examples in *MM*), foreshadowing the Christian technical use. The more general sense is common in the New Testament, whether for royal servants (Mt. xxii. 13) or for a servant of God (1 Thes. iii. 2, TR). In a single passage Paul describes Epaphras as a 'deacon' of Christ and himself as a 'deacon' of the gospel and of the Church (Col. i. 7, 23, 25). Others exercise a *diakonia* towards Paul (Acts xix. 22; *cf.* Phm. 13 and perhaps Col. iv. 7; Eph. vi. 21), the context showing that they are his assistants in evangelistic work. To find here the origin of the later idea of the bishop with his deacon is straining language. In other words, *diakonia* is here being applied especially to preaching and pastoral work.

In the New Testament, however, the word never quite loses its connection with the supply of material needs and service (*cf.*, *e.g.*, Rom. xv. 25 in context; 2 Cor. viii. 4). A waiter is a *diakonos* still (Jn. ii. 5, 9); the table-waiting of Martha (Lk. x. 40) and of Peter's mother-in-law (Mk. i. 31) is *diakonia*. It is in this light that we are to see Christ's insistence that His coming was in order to minister (Mk. x. 45): significantly this claim is set in Lk. xxii. 26 f. in the context of table-service. The Lord is the Deacon *par excellence*, the table-waiter of His people. And, as these passages show, 'deaconship' in this sense is a mark of His whole Church.

II. THE NEW TESTAMENT DIACONATE

As we have seen, there was contemporary analogy for 'deacons' as cult officials. When, therefore, we find the Church greeted 'with bishops and deacons' (Phil. i. 1) it is natural to see a reference to two particular classes within the Church. It is true that Hort can see rather the 'ruling' and the 'serving' elements together making up the Church, but it is doubtful if this could be applied to 1 Tim. iii, where a list of qualifications for bishops is immediately followed by a parallel list for deacons: sobriety, straightforwardness, freedom from excess and greed, probity. These would be particularly appropriate for those with responsibilities in finance and administration, and the prominence of social service in the early Church would make *diakonos* an especially suitable word for such people—the more so since the love feast, involving literal table-service, was a regular agency of charity. While *diakonia* is a mark of the whole Church, it is also a special gift—parallel with prophecy and government, but distinct from generous giving—to be exercised by those who possess it (Rom. xii. 17; 1 Pet. iv. 11). And while any servant of Christ is rightly called a 'deacon', the term may be particularly applied to those who minister, like Phebe (Rom. xvi. 1), in the ways mentioned. But whether the diaconate existed universally under this name, or whether, for instance, the 'helps' at Corinth (1 Cor. xii. 28) were equivalent to the 'deacons' at Philippi, remains uncertain. There is little to suggest that in New Testament times the term 'deacon' is ever more than semi-technical, or that it has any connection with the Jewish *ḥazzān* (see SYNAGOGUE). Significantly, immediately after listing the qualifications for deacons, Paul returns to the general sense of the word in exhorting Timothy himself (1 Tim. iv. 6. *Cf.* also 1 Pet. iv. 10 with iv. 11).

The account in Acts vi of the appointment by the Jerusalem church of seven approved men to supervise the administration of the widows' fund is commonly taken as the formal institution of the diaconate. It is doubtful if this has much basis in language. Leaving aside unprovable theories which see the Seven as but the Hellenistic counterpart of the Twelve, we may note, first, that the Seven are never called 'deacons', and secondly, that while the cognate words are used they apply equally to the *diakonia* of the Word exercised by the Twelve (verse 4) and to that of the tables (whether for meals or money) exercised by the Seven (verse 2). Laying on of hands is too common in Acts to be seen as a special milestone here (see ORDINATION), and the careers of Stephen and Philip show that the Seven were not confined to table-service.

There is, however, weight in Lightfoot's argument that the position Luke gives to the incident reflects his view of its high significance. It is 'one of those representative facts of which the earlier part of his narrative is almost wholly made up'. (*Philippians*[5], p. 188.) The significance lies, however, not in the institution of an order in the ministerial hierarchy, but as the first example of that delegation of administrative and social responsibilities to those of appropriate character and gifts, which was to become typical of the Gentile churches, and the recognition of such duties as part of the ministry of Christ.

Ecclesiastical usage institutionalized and narrowed the New Testament conception. Early non-canonical literature recognizes a class of deacons without specifying their functions (*cf. 1 Clement* xlii; Ignatius, *Magn.* ii. 1; *Trall.* ii. 3, vii. 3). Later literature shows the deacons undertaking functions such as attending the sick, which must have been part of Christian *diakonia* in apostolic times; but their duties in the Eucharist (*via* table-service at the communal meal?), and personal relationship with the monarchical bishop, become increasingly prominent. The occasional limitation of the diaconate to seven is probably due to deliberate archaizing.

BIBLIOGRAPHY. H. W. Beyer in *TWNT*; J. B. Lightfoot, *The Christian Ministry* (= *Philippians*[5], pp. 181 ff.); F. J. A. Hort, *The Christian Ecclesia*, 1897, pp. 198 ff.; A. M. Farrer in *The Apostolic Ministry*, ed. K. E. Kirk, 1946, especially pp. 142 ff.; B. Reicke, *Diakonie, Festfreude und Zelos*, 1951, pp. 9 ff.

A.F.W.

DEACONESS. Phebe was *diakonos* of the church at Cenchreae (Rom. xvi. 1): a title rendered by AV 'servant', but by RVmg, RSV, with greater probability, 'deaconess'.

Greek Fathers regularly read 1 Tim. iii. 11 as 'Even so must *women* be grave, *etc.*', taking the qualities which follow as the requirements for women deacons rather than for deacon's wives. This gives a better sequence than AV, and perhaps more appropriateness: Theodore of Mopsuestia tellingly interprets 'not slanderers' as 'not babbling confidences received in their ministry' (ed. Swete, II, p. 128).

About AD 111 Pliny, Governor of Bithynia, reports that he has questioned under torture two maidservants who were called deaconesses (*ministrae*) concerning Christian rites (*Ep.* xcvi). 'Maidservant' here may denote their secular position, or their function in the Christian community: Pliny was doubtless looking for evidence of cannibalism.

Thereafter there seems no clear literary notice of deaconesses before the 3rd century *Didascalia.* Some have therefore doubted the existence of such an office in New Testament times. But, meticulous as early Christians were in observing the proprieties, many functions allotted to deaconesses in later literature (*e.g.* visiting women in pagan households) would also apply in apostolic times. The appointment of deaconesses, then, is *a priori* likely: and Lk. viii. 2 f. may be deeply significant. Their duties would be precisely analogous to those of deacons: they were, as our two New Testament passages suggest, simply 'female deacons'. (The later special word *diakonissa* would develop as the deacon's distinctive functions became liturgical.)

BIBLIOGRAPHY. Essays by C. H. Turner and W. Collins in *The Ministry of Women*, 1919.

A.F.W.

DEAD SEA. Old Testament: 'Salt Sea' (Gn. xiv. 3), 'Eastern Sea' (Ezk. xlvii. 18), 'Sea of the Arabah' (Dt. iv. 49); classical: *Asphaltites*, later 'Dead Sea'; Arabic: 'Sea of Lot'.

The great rift valley reaches its deepest point at the Dead Sea basin. The surface of the water is on average 1,280 feet below sea-level, and the deepest point of the bed some 1,300 feet lower still. The Sea is about 48 miles long and stretches from the sheer cliffs of Moab some 6 or 9 miles across to the hills of Judah. On this western side is a narrow shore bounded by many terraces, the remains of earlier beaches. Except for a few springs (*e.g.* 'Ain Feshkha and Engedi, *cf.* Ct. i. 14), the Judaean coast is arid and bare. Four main streams feed the Sea from the east: the Mojin (Arnon), Zerqa Ma'in, Kerak, and the Zered. The rate of evaporation is so great (temperature reaches 110° in summer) that the inflow of these waters and the Jordan serves only to keep the sea-level constant. The annual rainfall is about 2 inches. Luxuriant vegetation is to be found where the rivers flow in or where there are fresh-water springs. The oases around the

Kerak and the Zered delta show how fertile this basin could be (*cf.* Gn. xiii. 10), as Ezekiel saw in his vision of a river of pure water flowing from Jerusalem to sweeten the Salt Sea (Ezk. xlvii. 8–12).

Until the mid-19th century it was possible to ford the sea from Lisan ('tongue'), a peninsula which projects from beside the Kerak, to within 2 miles of the opposite shore. Traces of a Roman road remain. Masada, an almost impregnable fortress built by the Maccabees and by Herod, guarded this road on the edge of Judaea. South of the Lisan, the sea is very shallow, gradually disappearing into the salty marsh (Zp. ii. 9) called the Sebkha.

The concentrated chemical deposits (salt, potash, magnesium, and calcium chlorides and bromide, 25 per cent of the water), which give the Dead Sea its buoyancy and its fatal effects on fish, may well have been ignited during an earthquake and caused the rain of brimstone and fire destroying Sodom and Gomorrah. Lot's wife, stopping to look back, was overwhelmed by the falling salt, while her family, hastening on, escaped (Gn. xix. 15–28). Archaeological evidence suggests a break of several centuries in the sedentary occupation from early in the second millennium BC. A hill of salt (*Jebel Usdum*, Mt. Sodom) at the south-west corner is eroded into strange forms, including pillars which are shown as 'Lot's Wife' by local Arabs (*cf.* Wisdom x. 7). Salt was obtained from the shore (Ezk. xlvii. 11), and the Nabataeans traded in the bitumen which floats on the surface (see P. C. Hammond, *BA*, XXII, 1959, pp. 40–48). Throughout the Old Testament period the sea acted as a barrier between Judah and Moab and Edom (*cf.* 2 Ch. xx. 1–30), although it may have been used by small trading boats, as it was in Roman times. See also PLAIN, CITIES OF; PATRIARCHAL AGE; ARCHAEOLOGY; JORDAN; ARABAH; DEAD SEA SCROLLS.

BIBLIOGRAPHY. G. A. Smith, *Historical Geography of the Holy Land*, 1931, pp. 499–516; D. Baly, *The Geography of the Bible*, 1958, pp. 202–210.

A.R.M.

DEAD SEA SCROLLS, a popular name given to collections of manuscript material found in a number of regions west of the Dead Sea in 1947 and the years following. They fall for the most part into three groups which have no relation one with another.

I. QUMRAN TEXTS

Most important of the Dead Sea Scrolls are those which have been discovered since 1947 in eleven caves in and around the Wadi Qumran, north-west of the Dead Sea. The manuscript contents of these caves are, in the main, all that remains of the library of a Jewish community which had its headquarters in the neighbouring building complex now called Khirbet Qumran. The community appears to have occupied this place during the two centuries preceding AD 70 (with a break of thirty years between *c.* 34 and 4 BC).

This community, in all probability a branch of the Essenes (*q.v.*), arose among the pious Jews (*ḥ^asîḏîm*) who maintained their covenant-loyalty unblemished under the persecution in the days of Antiochus Epiphanes (175–163 BC). They could not accept as the will of God the ensuing settlement which gave the high priesthood as well as the chief civil and military power to the Hasmonean dynasty. Under the leadership of one whom they called the 'Teacher of Righteousness' they withdrew to the wilderness of Judaea, where they organized themselves as the righteous remnant of Israel, 'a people prepared for the Lord'. They expected the early arrival of the new age which would bring the present 'epoch of wickedness' to an end. They endeavoured, by diligent study and practice of the law, to win divine favour for themselves and expiate the errors of their misguided fellow-Israelites; they also expected to be the executors of divine judgment on the ungodly at the end-time.

The end-time, they believed, would be marked by the rise of three figures foretold in Old Testament prophecy—the prophet like Moses of Dt. xviii. 15 ff., the Davidic Messiah, and a great priest of Aaron's line. This priest would be head of state in the new age, taking precedence even over the Davidic Messiah. The Davidic Messiah would be a warrior-prince, leading the faithful hosts of Israel to annihilating victory over the 'sons of darkness' (chief among whom were the Gentile forces of the Kittim, probably the Romans). The prophet would communicate the will of God to His people at the end of the age, as Moses had done at the beginning of their history.

The men of Qumran refused to acknowledge the high priests of Jerusalem during the 'epoch of wickedness', partly because they did not belong to the legitimate house of Zadok (deposed under Antiochus Epiphanes) and partly because they were morally unfit for their sacred office. One of them, evidently a Hasmonean priest-king, is described as the 'Wicked Priest' *par excellence*, because of the violent hostility which he showed to the Teacher of Righteousness and his followers. The community preserved in its own ranks the framework of Zadokite priests and Levites, ready to restore a worthy sacrificial worship in the purified Temple of the New Jerusalem (which was no heavenly city, but the old Jerusalem renewed).

The community library, of which some 500 documents have been identified (the great majority in a sadly fragmentary condition), comprised biblical and non-biblical writings. About one hundred of the scrolls are books of the Old Testament in Heb.; among these all the Old Testament books are represented (some of them several times over), with the exception of Esther. Whether this exception is significant or accidental is difficult to say. These biblical manuscripts date from the last few centuries BC and the earlier part of the 1st century AD. They exhibit at least three distinct text-types of Hebrew Scripture—the proto-Massoretic type (probably of Babylonian provenance) from which the received Hebrew text is descended; the text underlying the LXX (probably of Egyptian provenance); and a text (probably of Palestinian provenance) closely related to the Samaritan Pentateuch. Some exhibit a mixed type of text; *e.g.* Cave IV has yielded a manuscript of Numbers (4Q Num.[b]) whose text is midway between the Samaritan and LXX types, and one of Samuel (4Q Sam.[b]) which has been thought to exhibit a text superior to *MT* and LXX alike. Another manuscript of Samuel from the same cave (4Q Sam.[a]) is of special interest; it exhibits a text not only very close to that underlying LXX but also standing closer than *MT* does to the text of Samuel used by the Chronicler. The discovery of these biblical manuscripts has reduced by 1,000 years and more the gap separating the time of writing from the oldest surviving copies, and has made immense contributions to the textual history of the Old Testament. (See TEXT AND VERSIONS.)

Some LXX fragments have also been found in the Qumran caves, and some targumic literature —notably an Aramaic targum of Job from Cave XI. A few books of the Apocrypha have also been identified, including Tobit (in Aramaic and Heb.), Ecclesiasticus (in Heb.), and the Epistle of Jeremiah (in Gk.), not to mention 1 Enoch (in Aramaic) and Jubilees (in Heb.).

The non-biblical scrolls, taken in conjunction with the evidence provided by the excavation of Khirbet Qumran and a subsidiary building near 'Ain Feshkha, a couple of miles farther south, give us welcome information about the beliefs and practices of the community. We must bear in mind, of course, that not every book in a community's library reflects the community's ideas and behaviour. But much of the Qumran literature presents a self-consistent picture on which we can reasonably rely for some conception of life at Qumran.

The Qumran community practised rigorous self-discipline. Entrance into the community was hedged about by strict conditions, including a testing novitiate. Their interpretation of the law was severe, more so than that of the severest Pharisaic school. Indeed, it is probably the Pharisees who are referred to in the Qumran literature as 'seekers after smooth things' (*cf.* Is. xxx. 10). The men of Qumran had regular ceremonial ablutions, they held fellowship meals, admission to which was closely guarded, they followed a calendar similar to that prescribed in the book of Jubilees. They interpreted the hope of Israel in apocalyptic terms, and believed that they themselves had an important part to play in the realization of that hope. They interpreted prophetic Scripture as referring to persons and events of their own days and the days which lay immediately before them. This interpretation finds clearest expression in the biblical commentaries (*p*ᵉ*šārîm*), several of which have been recovered from the Qumran caves. According to the Qumran exegetes, the prophets knew by revelation what God was going to do at the end-time, but they did not know when the end-time would come. This additional revelation was given by God to the Teacher of Righteousness, who communicated it to his disciples. They had accordingly an insight into the meaning of the prophetical oracles which was denied to other Jews, and they were conscious of the favour which God had bestowed on them by initiating them into the mysteries of His purpose and the time and manner of its fulfilment.

The expectations of the Qumran community, however, were not fulfilled in the way for which they had looked. They appear to have abandoned their headquarters during the war of AD 66–73; it was probably at that time that their books were stored for safety in the surrounding caves. What happened to the members of the community is obscure, but it seems likely that some at least of them made common cause with the refugee Church of Jerusalem.

Resemblances have been traced between the Qumran community and the early Church in regard to their eschatological outlook, remnant consciousness, biblical exegesis, and religious practices. But there are important differences to set against these resemblances. Their ceremonial ablutions and fellowship meals did not have the sacramental significance of Christian baptism and the Eucharist. The early Christians, like Jesus Himself, mixed freely with their fellows in the common ways of life, instead of forming ascetic communities in the wilderness. The New Testament presents Jesus as Prophet, Priest, and Prince of the house of David in His single person, instead of distributing these offices among three distinct figures, as was done in Qumran eschatology. And indeed it is Jesus in every respect who gives Christianity its uniqueness. The Teacher of Righteousness was no doubt a great leader and teacher, but he was no Messiah or Saviour, not even in his followers' eyes. Jesus was to the early Christians all that the Teacher of Righteousness was to the Qumran community, and much more —Messiah and Saviour, Servant of the Lord, and Son of man. When the Teacher of Righteousness died (or, in Qumran idiom, 'was gathered in'—an expression which suggests natural death), his followers *may* have expected him to rise from the dead, although this is doubtful. But it is certain that he never did rise from the dead, and in fact none of his followers appears to have claimed that he did so.

The copper scroll from Cave III has probably nothing to do with the Qumran community. It is more probable that it belonged to a Zealot band which was based on Qumran during the war of AD 66–73; it appears to contain (in code) an inventory of temple treasure, divided into sixty-one *caches* in Jerusalem and the district east and south of it.

II. TEXTS OF THE BAR-KOKHBA WAR

In caves in the Wadi Murabba'at, about 11 miles south of Qumran, a quantity of manuscript material was found around 1952. Most of this belonged to the period when these caves were occupied by an outpost of the army of Bar-kokhba, leader of the second Jewish revolt against Rome (AD 132–5). The documents included letters written to Bar-kokhba, and two letters written by him, from which it appeared that his proper patronymic was Ben-Kosebah; he calls himself 'Simeon Ben-Kosebah, prince of Israel'. (The title Bar-kokhba, 'son of the star', was due to Rabbi Akiba's hailing him as the 'star' of Nu. xxiv. 17, in other words the Davidic Messiah.) Many fragmentary biblical manuscripts of this period were found in the caves, all of them exhibiting a 'proto-Massoretic' type of text.

About the same time as the Murabba'at caves were explored, further manuscripts of the Bar-kokhba period were discovered in unidentified caves in the vicinity. These included fragments of Heb. Scripture and a fragmentary copy of a Gk. version of the Minor Prophets, showing a text similar to that used by Justin Martyr (*c.* AD 150). This version has been tentatively identified with Origen's *Quinta.*

Still more recently, similar discoveries have been made in Israeli territory, farther south along the west shore of the Dead Sea. Here too were caves which were used as headquarters by contingents of Bar-kokhba's guerrilla forces. The documents found in them included two scroll fragments inscribed with Ex. xiii. 1–16 and a small fragment containing parts of seven lines of Ps. xv.

III. KHIRBET MIRD

From the ruined site of Khirbet Mird (formerly a Christian monastery), north of the Kidron valley, manuscripts of great interest were unearthed about 1950 by members of the Ta'amire tribe of Bedouin (the same tribe as was responsible for the earliest Qumran discoveries). These were of much later date than the manuscripts found at Qumran and Murabba'at. They include papyrus fragments of private letters in Arabic from the 7th and 8th centuries, a Syr. letter on papyrus written by a Christian monk, a fragment of the *Andromache* of Euripides, and a number of biblical texts in Gk. and Palestinian Syriac. The Gk. biblical texts included fragments of uncial codices of Wisdom, Mark, John, and Acts, to be dated between the 5th and 8th centuries; those in Palestinian Syriac (many of which were palimpsests) included fragments of Joshua, Luke, John, Acts, and Colossians.

BIBLIOGRAPHY. M. Burrows, *The Dead Sea Scrolls*, 1955, and *More Light on the Dead Sea Scrolls*, 1958; F. M. Cross, *The Ancient Library of Qumran and Modern Biblical Studies*, 1958; T. H. Gaster, *The Scriptures of the Dead Sea Sect*, 1957; J. T. Milik, *Ten Years of Discovery in the Wilderness of Judaea*, 1959; E. F. Sutcliffe, *The Monks of Qumran*, 1960; J. M. Allegro, *The Dead Sea Scrolls*, 1956; *The People of the Dead Sea Scrolls*, 1959; *The Treasure of the Copper Scroll*, 1960; F. F. Bruce, *Second Thoughts on the Dead Sea Scrolls*, 1956, *The Teacher of Righteousness in the Qumran Texts*, 1957, and *Biblical Exegesis in the Qumran Texts*, 1960. F.F.B.

DEAFNESS. See DISEASE AND HEALING.

DEATH. From one point of view death is the most natural of things: 'it is appointed unto men once to die' (Heb. ix. 27). It may be accepted without rebellion: 'Let us also go, that we may die with him' (Jn. xi. 16). From another, it is the most unnatural of things. It is the penalty for sin (Rom. vi. 23), and it is to be feared as such. Both points of view are to be found in the Bible, and neither should be overlooked. Death is a biological necessity, but men do not die simply as the animals die.

I. PHYSICAL DEATH

Death seems to be necessary for bodies constituted as ours are. Physical decay and ultimate dissolution are inescapable. Yet the Bible speaks of death as the result of sin. God said to Adam, 'in the day that thou eatest thereof thou shalt surely die' (Gn. ii. 17). Paul tells us that 'by one man sin entered into the world, and death by sin' (Rom. v. 12), and again that 'the wages of sin is death' (Rom. vi. 23). Yet when we look more closely into the matter we see that Adam did not die physically on the day that he disobeyed God. And in Romans v and vi Paul is contrasting the death that came about through Adam's sin with the life that Christ brings men. Now the possession of eternal life does not cancel out physical death. It is opposed to a spiritual state, not to a physical event. The inference that we draw from all this is that that death which is the result of sin is more than bodily death.

But with this we must take the other thought that the Scriptural passages which connect sin and death do not qualify death. We would not understand from them that something other than the usual meaning attached to the word. Perhaps we should understand that mortality was the result of Adam's sin, and that the penalty includes both physical and spiritual aspects. But we do not know enough about Adam's pre-fallen condition to say anything about it. If his body was like ours, then it was mortal. If it was not, we have no means of knowing what it was like, and whether it was mortal or not.

It seems better to understand death as something that involves the whole man. Man does not die as a body. He dies as a man, in the totality of his being. He dies as a spiritual and physical being. And the Bible does not put a sharp line of demarcation between the two aspects. Physical death, then, is a fit symbol of, and expression of, and unity with, the deeper death that sin inevitably brings.

II. SPIRITUAL DEATH

That death is a divine penalty. We have already noticed that Rom. vi. 23 regards death as 'the wages' of sin, *i.e.* as the due reward for sin. Paul can speak of certain sinners who know 'the judgment of God, that they which commit such things are worthy of death' (Rom. i. 32). It is the thought of God's decree that underlies John's reference to the 'sin unto death' (1 Jn. v. 16). This is a very important truth. It enables us to see the full horror of death. And at the same time, paradoxically, it gives us hope. Men are not caught up in a web woven by blind fate, so that, once having sinned, nothing can ever be done about it. God is over the whole process, and if He has decreed that death is the penalty of sin He has also determined to give life eternal to sinful men.

Sometimes the New Testament emphasizes the serious consequences of sin by referring to 'the second death' (Jude 12; Rev. ii. 11, *etc.*). This is a rabbinic expression which signifies eternal perdition. It is to be understood along with passages wherein our Lord spoke of 'everlasting fire, prepared for the devil and his angels' (Mt. xxv. 41), 'everlasting punishment' (set in contrast to 'life eternal', Mt. xxv. 46), and the like. The final state of impenitent man is variously described as death, punishment, being lost, *etc.* Obviously it would be unwise to equate it with any one of them. But equally obviously on the Bible view it is a state to be regarded with horror.

Sometimes the objection is made that this is inconsistent with the view of God as a loving God. There is a profound mystery here, but at least it can be said that the objection, as commonly stated, overlooks the fact that death is a state as well as an event. 'The mind of the flesh is death,' writes Paul (Rom. viii. 6, RV). He does not say that the mind of the flesh will cause death. He says that it *is* death. He adds that it 'is enmity against God: for it is not subject to the law of God, neither indeed can be'. The same truth is put in a different way when John tells us that 'he that loveth not his brother abideth in death' (1 Jn. iii. 14). When we have grasped the truth that death is a state, we see the impossibility of the impenitent being saved. Salvation for such is a contradiction in terms. For salvation a man must pass from death into life (Jn. v. 24).

III. VICTORY OVER DEATH

An interesting feature of New Testament teaching on death is that the emphasis is on life. If we look up a concordance we will find that in most places *nekros* is used of resurrection from the dead or the like. The Scripture faces death, as it faces all reality. But its interest is in life, and death is treated more or less incidentally, as that from which men are saved. Christ took upon Him our nature 'that through death he might destroy him that had the power of death, that is, the devil' (Heb. ii. 14). The devil's power is always regarded as subject to God's overruling (Jb. ii. 6; Lk. xii. 5, *etc.*). He is no absolute disposer of death. Nevertheless death, the negation of life, is his proper sphere. And Christ came to put an end to death. It was through death, as the Hebrews passage indicates, that He defeated Satan. It was through death that He put away our sin. 'In that he died, he died unto sin once' (Rom. vi. 10). Apart from Christ, death is the supreme enemy, the symbol of our alienation from God, the ultimate horror. But Christ has used death to deliver men from death. He died that men may live. It is significant that the New Testament can speak of believers as 'sleeping' rather than as 'dying' (*e.g.* 1 Thes. iv. 14). Jesus bore the full horror of death. Therefore for those who are 'in Christ' death has been transformed so that it is no more than sleep.

The extent of the victory over death that Christ won is indicated by His resurrection. 'Christ being raised from the dead dieth no more; death hath no more dominion over him' (Rom. vi. 9). The resurrection is the great triumphal event, and the whole of the New Testament note of victory originates here. Christ is 'the Prince of life' (Acts iii. 15), 'Lord both of the dead and living' (Rom. xiv. 9), 'the Word of life' (1 Jn. i. 1). His victory over death is complete. And His victory is made available to His people. Death's destruction is certain (1 Cor. xv. 26, 54 ff.; Rev. xxi. 4). The second death has no power over the believer (Rev. ii. 11, xx. 6). In keeping with this the New Testament understands eternal life not as the immortality of the soul, but in terms of the resurrection of the body. Nothing could more graphically illustrate the finality and the completeness of death's defeat.

Not only is there a glorious future, there is a glorious present. The believer has already passed out of death and into life (Jn. v. 24; 1 Jn. iii. 14). He is 'free from the law of sin and death' (Rom. viii. 2). Death cannot separate him from God (Rom. viii. 38 f.). Jesus said, 'If a man keep my saying, he shall never see death' (Jn. viii. 51). Such words do not deny the reality of biological death. Rather they point us to the truth that the death of Jesus means that the believer has passed altogether out of the state which is death. He is brought into a new state, which is aptly characterized as life. He will in due course pass through the gateway we call death. But the sting has been drawn. The death of Jesus means victory over death for His followers.

BIBLIOGRAPHY. C. S. Lewis, *Miracles*, 1947, pp. 150 ff.; C. Ryder Smith, *The Bible Doctrine of Salvation*, 1941, *passim*; Leon Morris, *The Wages of Sin*, 1955. L.M.

DEBIR. 1. A city of the Judaean Hills, once called Kiriath-sepher (perhaps K. Sopher, 'scribe town', as LXX suggests; but the Hebrew may not preserve accurately the Canaanite vocalization or meaning; see Moore, *ICC*, *ad* Jdg. i. 11). Held by Anakim before the invasion, then by Kenizzites; unmentioned in later history.

Formerly identified with Dhahiriya (Abel, *Géographie*, II, pp. 303, 422), but soundings showed no trace of a Canaanite stronghold (*BASOR*, 47, 1932, p. 16). In 1924 Albright proposed Tell Beit Mirsim (142096), 12 miles south-west of Hebron; excavations revealed a Hyksos city covering 9 acres, followed by a prosperous Late Bronze occupation, destroyed and soon resettled with a poorer culture devoid for a time of foreign influence; this is taken to represent the Kenizzite conquerors. The position, while not dominating, is near an ancient route into the hills. Israelite levels contained Astarte figurines and evidence of woollen industry. Noth (*JPOS*, XV, 1935, p. 48), arguing for a less important site nearer Hebron, suggests Kh. Terrameh, which according to Wright (*JNES*, V, p. 110 n.) lacks pre-Hellenistic remains; see *GTT*, p. 15; *JPOS*, IV, 1924, p. 135; *PEQ*, 1931, p. 175; *BASOR*, 15, 1924, 39, 1930; Garstang, *Joshua*, pp. 210 ff.

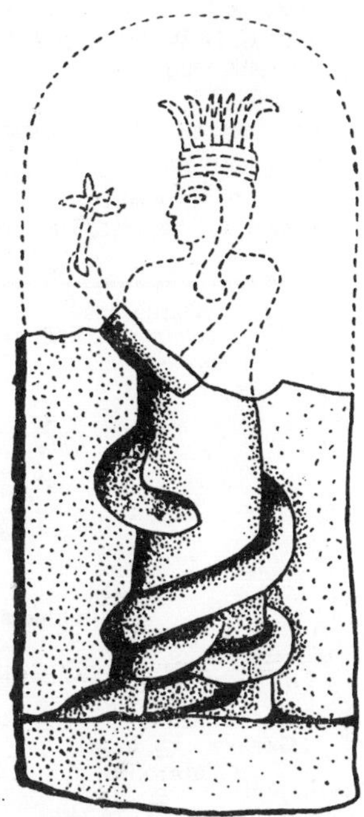

Fig. 65. A reconstruction of a stele found at Debir showing a serpent goddess.

2. A point on the north border of Judah; the name survives at Tugret ed Debr, 2 miles west of Ma'ale 'Adummim. 'Gilgal', Jos. xv. 7, is Geliloth of Jos. xviii. 17.

3. On the boundary of Gad near Mahanaim; *MT Lidebir* (Jos. xiii. 26); possibly Umm ed Debar, 10 miles south of Lake Tiberias (Abel, *Géographie*, II, p. 304). J.P.U.L.

DEBORAH (Heb. *d^e^bôrâ*, 'bee'). **1.** Rebekah's nurse, whose death at Bethel is recorded in Gn. xxxv. 8; the tree beneath which she was buried was known as Allon-bacuth, 'the oak (or terebinth) of weeping'.

2. A prophetess who appears in the list of judges of Israel (*c.* 1125 BC). According to Jdg. iv. 4 ff., she had her headquarters under 'the palm tree of Deborah' between Ramah and Bethel, and was consulted there by Israelites from various tribes who wished to have their disputes settled—either disputes which proved too intractable for their local judges or intertribal disputes. She was thus a judge in the ordinary, non-military sense of the word, and it was probably because of her judicial and charismatic renown that the Israelites had recourse to her in the straits to which they were reduced under Sisera's oppression. She commanded Barak (*q.v.*) to take the field as Israelite commander-in-chief against Sisera, and consented to accompany him at his insistence; the result was the crushing defeat of Sisera at the battle of Kishon (Jdg. iv. 15, v. 19 ff.).

She is called (Jdg. iv. 4) the wife of Lappidoth (lit. 'torches'), and she is described (Jdg. v. 7) as 'a mother in Israel'. It has been argued that this last phrase means 'a metropolis in Israel' (*cf.* 2 Sa. xx. 19), and that the reference is to the city of Daberath (Jos. xxi. 28; 1 Ch. vi. 72), modern Debûriyeh at the west foot of Mt. Tabor; but there is nothing in the narrative or in the poem to prepare us for the prominence which would thus suddenly be given to such an obscure place.

The song of Deborah (Jdg. v. 2–31a) has been preserved from the 12th century BC with its language practically unmodernized, and is thus one of the most archaic passages in the Old Testament. It was evidently composed on the morrow of the victory which it celebrates, and is an important source of information on tribal relations in Israel at the time. It may be divided into eight sections: an exordium of praise (verses 2, 3); the invocation of Yahweh (verses 4, 5); the desolation under the oppressors (verses 6–8); the mustering of the tribes (verses 9–18); the battle of Kishon (verses 19–23); the death of Sisera (verses 24–27); the description of Sisera's mother awaiting his return (verses 28–30); and the epilogue (verse 31a). It is from the song, rather than from the prose narrative of chapter iv, that we learn what precisely brought about Sisera's defeat: a cloudburst flooded the watercourse of Kishon and swept away the Canaanite chariotry (v. 21), throwing the army into confusion and making it an easy prey for Barak's men.

The vivid and moving description of Sisera's mother (verses 28 ff.) has been felt to confirm the feminine authorship of the song; if it betrays sympathy of a sort, it is not a compassionate sympathy.

Deborah is apostrophized in the song not only in verse 12 but probably also in verse 7, where the repeated Heb. *qamtî* may be understood not as the normal first person singular ('I arose') but as an archaic second person singular ('thou didst arise'). F.F.B.

DEBT, DEBTOR.

a. Lending, loan

Loans in Israel were not commercial but charitable, granted not to enable a trader to set up or expand a business but to tide a peasant farmer over a period of poverty. Since the economy remained predominantly agricultural up to the end of the monarchy, there developed no counterpart to the commercial loan system already existing in Babylonia in 2000 BC. Hence the legislation contains not mercantile regulations but exhortations to neighbourliness. The same outlook persists in Ecclus. xxix. The background changes in the New Testament. The debtors in the parable of the unjust steward (Lk. xvi. 1–8) are either tenants who pay rent in kind or merchants who have goods on credit. The description of sins as debts (Mt. vi. 12) is a Jewish commonplace which Jesus employs, not to characterize the relationship between God and man as one between creditor and debtor, but to proclaim the grace and enjoin the duty of forgiveness (Lk. vii. 41 f.; Mt. xviii. 21–27).

b. Interest, usury

The word 'usury' in the AV has not the modern sense of exorbitant interest. The complaint in the Old Testament is not that interest is excessive but that it is charged at all. All three Codes (Ex. xxii. 25, JE; Dt. xxiii. 19 f., D; Lv. xxv. 35 ff., H) forbid it as an unbrotherly exploitation of a fellow-Israelite's misfortune. Dt. xxiii. 20 (*cf.* xv. 1–8) allows that a foreigner may be charged. Interest is mentioned as an established practice in the Code of Hammurabi and earlier Babylonian laws. The word *nešeḵ* (lit. 'something bitten off') probably denotes simply rapacious exaction from a debtor, though the play on the word *nôšeḵîm* in Hab. ii. 7 RVmg (meaning both 'payers of interest' and 'biters') may imply a sum which eats away the savings set aside for repayment. The synonym *tarbiṯ* ('increase') and the Gk. *tokos* ('offspring') take the more modern view of interest as a growth upon principal. In keeping with a changed economy, Jesus approves of investment to earn income (Mt. xxv. 27; Lk. xix. 23) but retains the traditional distrust of any charge on a private loan (Lk. vi. 31 ff.).

c. Pledge, surety

Security took the form of a pledge of some personal effect for a small temporary loan (Dt. xxiv. 10; Jb. xxiv. 3), the mortgage of real estate (Ne. v), or the surety of a guarantor (Pr. vi. 1–5; Ecclus. viii. 13, xxix. 14–20). Where there was no security to forfeit debtors could be sold into slavery (Ex. xxii. 3; 2 Ki. iv. 1; Am. ii. 6, viii. 6, *etc.*). The laws are framed to mitigate the severity of custom. Restrictions are laid on the range of pledgeable items and conditions of borrowing (Dt. xxiv). By a sort of 'Statute of Limitations' all debts were to be cancelled every seventh year (Dt. xv. 1 ff., only Deuteronomy mentions debts in connection with the year of Jubilee), and Israelites giving service in discharge of debts to be released (Lv. xxv. 39–55, H). This legislation seems not to have been observed historically. Elisha helps the widow in 2 Ki. iv. 1–7 not by invoking the law but by working a miracle. Nehemiah v makes no appeal to Deuteronomy xv (though *cf.* Ne. x. 31 and Je. xxxiv. 13 f.). In the Judaistic period Hillel invented a system for legal evasion of Deuteronomy xv, the purpose of which was not to frustrate or circumvent the law but to adapt it to a commercial economy.

BIBLIOGRAPHY. C. H. W. Johns, *Babylonian and Assyrian Laws*, 1904, chapter xxiii. A.E.W.

DECALOGUE. See TEN COMMANDMENTS.

DECAPOLIS. A large territory south of the Sea of Galilee, mainly to the east of Jordan, but including Beth-shean to the west. The Greeks had

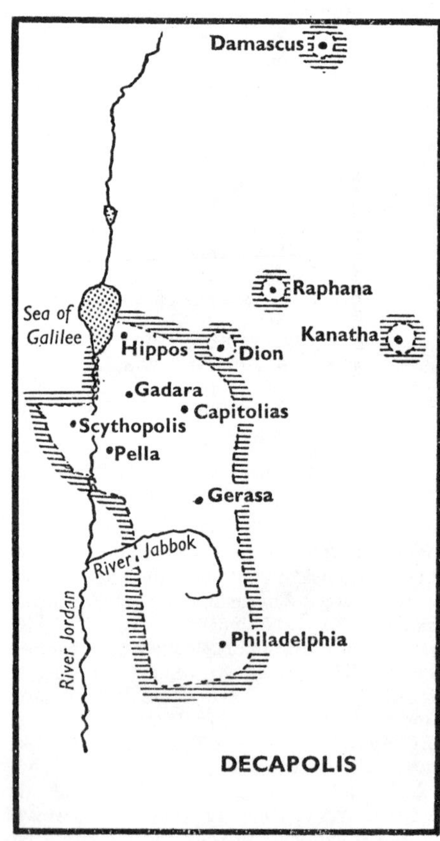

Fig. 66. The approximate extent of the territory of Decapolis in New Testament times.

occupied towns like Gadara and Philadelphia as early as 200 BC. In 63 BC Pompey liberated Hippos, Scythopolis, and Pella from the Jews. He annexed the cities to the province of Syria, but gave them municipal freedom. About AD 1 they formed a league for trade and mutual defence against Semitic tribes. Pliny named the ten original members as Scythopolis, Pella, Dion, Gerasa, Philadelphia, Gadara, Raphana, Kanatha, Hippos, and Damascus. Ptolemy included other towns south of Damascus in a list of eighteen cities in the 2nd century AD.

Inhabitants of Decapolis joined the great crowds which followed Christ in Mt. iv. 25. He landed in the territory at Gerasa (Mk. v. 1; Origen reads Gergesa, a site on the cliff). The presence of so many swine suggests a predominantly Gentile population who, on suffering economic loss through the miracle, requested Christ's departure, despite the demoniac's testimony. Christ revisited Decapolis when making an unusual detour through the Hippos area on a journey from Sidon to the eastern shore of Galilee (Mk. vii. 31). The Jewish Church retired to Pella before the war of AD 70.

BIBLIOGRAPHY. *DCG*; G. A. Smith, *Historical Geography of the Holy Land*, 1931, pp. 595–608; Pliny, *Hist. Nat*. v. 18. 74. D.H.T.

DECEIT. From Heb. root *rāmâ*, meaning treachery or guile (Ps. xxxiv. 13). It is used of a witness, of balances, and of a bow (Ps. lxxviii. 57). It is expressed by several Gk. words, *e.g. planē*, 'error', Eph. iv. 14; *dolos*, 'cunning', 'treachery', Rom. i. 29; Mk. vii. 22; *apatē*, 'beguiling pleasure', Mt. xiii. 22; Heb. iii. 13; Col. ii. 8. Since the devil is the arch-deceiver (Rev. xx. 10) his children are described as 'full of deceit', *e.g.* Elymas, Acts xiii. 10. Conversely, in Christ's mouth there is no deceit (1 Pet. ii. 22) and in the true Israelite Nathanael no guile, Jn. i. 47.

BIBLIOGRAPHY. *Arndt*; *MM*; *HDB*. D.H.T.

DECISION, VALLEY OF. Mentioned in Joel iii. 14 as the place of God's judgment on the nations, the 'valley of decision' is also called (verses 2, 12) 'the valley of Jehoshaphat'. While verse 16 suggests proximity to Zion, the identical phrase in Am. i. 2 prohibits a hasty conclusion. 'Jehoshaphat', meaning 'Yahweh judges', may be symbolic rather than topographic. 2 Ch. xx would explain the symbolism: in the valley of Berachah, 15 miles south of Jerusalem, king Jehoshaphat observed Yahweh's victory over heathen nations, a microcosm of the Day of Yahweh. However, from the 4th century AD onwards the name 'valley of Jehoshaphat' has been given to the valley between the Temple Hill and the Mount of Olives. J.A.M.

DECREE. In the AV the term occurs frequently in Esther, Ezra, and Daniel as a translation of different Heb. and Aram. words for royal decrees. RV often differentiates between them, using 'interdict' in Dn. vi. 8, 'law' in Dn. ii. 9, and 'decree' in Ezr. v. 13. God, as King of the earth, is said in the Old Testament to make decrees (Dn. iv. 24; Ps. ii. 7), and the world is controlled by them: there is one for the rain, Jb. xxviii. 26, and one for the sea, Pr. viii. 29, where we should speak of laws of nature. The Heb. *ḥōq*, 'ordinance' (Ps. cxix. 5, 8, 12, *etc.*), is the nearest biblical approach to the 'decrees of God' spoken of by theologians.

In the New Testament the Gk. *dogma* describes special decrees of the Roman Senate in Lk. ii. 1 and Acts xvii. 7. In Acts xvi. 4 it is used of the findings of the Jerusalem Council: *cf.* Gk. usage for authoritative decisions of groups of philosophers. In Eph. ii. 15 and Col. ii. 14, 20 it refers to Jewish enactments.

BIBLIOGRAPHY. *Arndt*; *HDB*; *MM*. D.H.T.

DEDAN. 1. A son of Raamah, grandson of Cush, and great-grandson of Ham (Gn. x. 7; 1 Ch. i. 9).

2. A son of Jokshan, and grandson of Abraham by his concubine Keturah (Gn. xxv. 3; 1 Ch. i. 32).

3. Dedan (the place) and the Dedanites refer to commercial peoples mentioned in the prophets, usually in condemnation. There is, however, some obscurity about the biblical passages where Dedan is mentioned (Is. xxi. 13; Je. xxv. 23, xlix. 8; Ezk. xxv. 13, xxvii. 15, 20, xxxviii. 13). The well-known Dedan (modern Al-'ulā), 70 miles south-west of Taima' (A. Musil, *Arabia Deserta*, p. 519), fulfils the requirement of being 'south of Edom'. In the time of Jeremiah and Ezekiel it was a flourishing caravan city, as is now known from cuneiform inscriptions. For further discussion, see *GTT*, pp. 21, 23–25. J.G.G.N.

DEDICATION. The term is used in the Old Testament almost exclusively of the consecration of things, *e.g.* the altar (Nu. vii. 10), silver and gold (2 Sa. viii. 11). Three Hebrew words are used: *ḥ[a]nukkâ*, 'consecration'; *qōdeš*, 'a thing separated, hallowed'; *ḥērem*, 'a thing devoted to God'. For a discussion of the meaning of this last term, see CURSE. For Feast of Dedication, see next article. D.G.S.

DEDICATION, FEAST OF (*ho engkainismos tou thysiastēriou*, 1 Macc. iv. 47–59; *ta engkainia*, Jn. x. 22). Held on 25 Kislew, and lasting eight days, it commemorated the cleansing of the Temple and altar by Judas Maccabaeus in 165 or 164 BC, three years to the day after their defilement by Antiochus Epiphanes. Its resemblance in mode of celebration to the Feast of Tabernacles (2 Macc. x. 6) was deliberate, though, unlike the great feasts, it might be celebrated outside Jerusalem. The prominent feature of illuminations gave it the name, Feast of Lights (Jn. ix. 5). The sole New Testament reference (Jn. x. 22) indicates the season of the year.

T.H.J.

DEER. See HART, and fig. 40.

DEFILEMENT. See CLEAN AND UNCLEAN.

DEGREES (*ma'[a]lôṯ*, from *ma'[a]lâ*, 'a going up', 'ascent', *cf.* Lat. *gradus*; Gk. *bathmos*, 'a step' (so LXX), 'ascent'). That the shadow should go back ten degrees was the sign by which the Lord confirmed to Hezekiah his recovery from mortal illness (2 Ki. xx. 8–11; *cf.* Is. xxxviii. 8). Josephus suggested that the stairs of the king's palace may have constituted a type of sun-dial, but for a detailed discussion of the whole incident and possible interpretations, see C. F. Keil, *The Books of the Kings*, n.d., pp. 463–465.

The word is found also in the titles of Ps. cxx–cxxxiv, which are called Songs of Degrees (RSV 'ascents') and said to have been sung by processions of pilgrims while ascending Mt. Zion during the great Temple festivals. See PSALMS.

The term occurs once only in the New Testament (1 Tim. iii. 13), where the Gk. word denotes 'good standing'. According to *Arndt*, a technical term of the mysteries may be involved here, implying a 'step' in the soul's journey heavenward. J.D.D.

DEHAITES, DEHAVITES. A name occurring in an Aramaic list (Ezr. iv. 9) prepared for Artaxerxes, which enumerates the various peoples who had been settled in Samaria by Ashurbanipal (*q.v.*). The name (*Keṯîḇ*: *dehāwē*'; *Qerē*: *dehāyē*') falls in the list between the Shushanchites (see SHUSHAN) and the Elamites, and from the facts that Susa was in Elam, and that no satisfactory identification for *dehāwē*' has been found in extra-biblical sources, it has been plausibly suggested that it be read *dî-hû*' (or Targ. *dihû*'), 'that is' (with Codex Vaticanus *hoi eisin*), which would result in the rendering, 'the Susians, that is the Elamites'.

BIBLIOGRAPHY. G. Hoffmann, *ZA*, II, 1887, p. 54. T.C.M.

DELILAH. See SAMSON.

DELIVERANCE. See SALVATION, REDEMPTION.

DELUGE. See FLOOD.

DEMAS. A co-worker of Paul in the first imprisonment, sending greetings in Phm. 24 and Col. iv. 14. In the latter he alone is mentioned without commendation. There follows the pathetic notice of his desertion in the second imprisonment (2 Tim. iv. 10; Parry neatly renders 'left me in the lurch'). Paul's words suggest that personal interests, not cowardice, took him to Thessalonica: perhaps he was a Thessalonian. The name is not uncommon; it may be a pet-form of Demetrius. Dom John Chapman (*JTS*, V, 1904, pp. 364 ff.) argued that Demas, restored, is the Demetrius of 3 Jn. 12; but this is as conjectural as the ugly portrait of Demas in the *Acts of Paul and Thecla*. A.F.W.

DEMETRIUS was a common Gk. name, and two people bearing it are mentioned in the New Testament. **1.** A Christian whose witness is commended in 3 Jn. 12. **2.** The silversmith of Ephesus, who stirred up a riot against Paul (Acts xix. 24, 38).

Conjectures have been made identifying the two (J. V. Bartlet, *JTS*, VI, 1905, pp. 208 f., 215), while Dom J. Chapman (*JTS*, V, 1904, pp. 364 ff.) would identify (1) above with Demas, the companion of Paul (Col. iv. 14; Phm. 24; 2 Tim. iv. 10). D.H.W.

DEMON. See DEVIL, POSSESSION.

Fig. 67. Terracotta head of a Babylonian demon. 7th–6th centuries BC.

DEMONIAC. See POSSESSION.

DENARIUS. See MONEY.

DEPUTY. In the Old Testament, two words are used: Heb. *niṣṣāḇ*, 'one set up', used in 1 Ki. xxii. 47 of the viceroy or regent who administered Edom when it was tributary to Judah in Jehoshaphat's reign; and Heb. *peḥâ*, in Est. viii. 9, ix. 3 (AV); see GOVERNOR.

In the New Testament, AV rendering of Gk. *anthypatos* (Acts xiii. 7, 8, 12, xix. 38) and *anthypateuō* ('was the deputy', Acts xviii. 12); see PROCONSUL. F.F.B.

DERBE (Lycaonian *delbeia*, 'juniper'). In Acts xiv. 6 ff. a city of the Lycaonian region of Roman Galatia, the most easterly place visited by Paul and Barnabas when they founded the churches of S Galatia. (Progress farther east would have taken them beyond the Roman province into the client-kingdom of Antiochus.) Paul and Silas visited it on their westward journey through Asia Minor (Acts xvi. 1). Paul's fellow-traveller Gaius came from Derbe (Acts xx. 4; the Western Text brings him from Doberus in Macedonia). The site of Derbe was identified in 1956 by M. Ballance at Kerti Hüyük, 13 miles NNE of Karaman (Laranda), some 60 miles from Lystra (whence Acts xiv. 20b must evidently be translated: 'and on the morrow he set out with Barnabas for Derbe').

BIBLIOGRAPHY. M. Ballance, 'The Site of Derbe: A New Inscription', *Anatolian Studies*, VII, 1957, pp. 147 ff. F.F.B.

DESCENT INTO HADES. Although the doctrine of the descent of Christ into hell is firmly embedded in the early Christian creeds (it first appears in 4th-century Arian formularies), its place in Scripture is in fact circumferential. It receives explicit mention possibly twice (1 Pet. iii. 19, iv. 6), and is indirectly referred to in only two other places (Acts ii. 27 and Rom. x. 7), where it is hinted at by the reinterpretation of Old Testament passages—Psalm xvi in the case of Acts, and Deuteronomy xxx. It is doubtful whether we are right to press for a reference to the *descensus ad inferos* in Eph. iv. 9 f., since the comprehensive movement in these verses is best understood as forming a parallel to that in the 'kenotic' passage Phil. ii. 6 ff.

The references in the two Petrine passages are more direct, but by no means clear. The context of the first (1 Pet. iii. 19) is the congruent suffering of Christ (the climax of which was His death) and the Christian. It was after His passion and 'in spirit' (*pneumati*) that the Lord 'preached' (the technical term *ekēryxen*) to the 'spirits in prison' (*q.v.*). As Victor, and no longer Victim, Christ proclaims His triumph (*kēryssein* is to be distinguished from *euangelizein*, iv. 6) inclusively.

In 1 Pet. iv. 6 the thought of preaching the good news to the 'dead' arises from a consideration of the painfulness as well as the glory of being dead to sin. This, says Peter, may well involve suffering for Christ's sake, as Christ suffered for ours (iv. 1 f.). It was this gospel that judged the 'dead', and gave them the opportunity of sharing God's eternal life (verse 6). This may well refer to Christians who have heard the gospel while alive, and died before the Lord's return (so E. G. Selwyn and A. M. Stibbs). Others interpret 'the dead' as meaning those who are spiritually dead, and a third view connects this verse with iii. 19, and sees in it a further reference to the 'spirits in prison'. In this case the thought of judgment (= death, here) is subordinate to that of life (the fulness of God's life, denoted by *zōsi*, as opposed to the transitoriness of man's life, implied in iv. 2 by the verb *bioō*, similarly translated).

The interval between the death and the resurrection of Christ cannot be regarded as without significance. But the event claimed by Christians as taking place then, whether or not Peter has it in mind in these two passages, is more a matter of theology than chronology. Then the *meaning* becomes more important than the manner, and we can understand the *descensus* as a part of the triumphant activity of Christ, who is Lord of hell as well as of heaven (*cf.* Rev. i. 18 and Phil. ii. 10), and who thus completes His involvement in every conceivable area of experience.

BIBLIOGRAPHY. See the commentaries on 1 Peter, in particular those by E. G. Selwyn, 1946; C. E. B. Cranfield, 1950 (and with 2 Peter and Jude in the *Torch Commentaries* series, 1960); and A. M. Stibbs, 1959. See also C. E. B. Cranfield, 'The Interpretation of 1 Peter iii. 19 and iv. 6', *ExpT*, LXIX, 12, pp. 369 ff. and bibliography there cited. S.S.S.

DESERT. See WILDERNESS.

DESIRE. In their numerous references to 'desire' the Old and New Testaments provide many acute and incisive psychological insights. Indeed both by the diversity of the vocabulary of 'desire', and the manner of handling it, the Bible makes plain an important part of its doctrine of man.

In the Old Testament 'desire' means much more than merely 'to long for', 'to ask for', or 'to demand'. In Heb. psychology the whole personality was involved in desire. Hence 'desire' could easily become 'covetousness', leading to 'envy' and 'jealousy', *etc.* Among the Hebrews 'desire' was the request which the *nep̄eš* (the 'soul' or 'self') made of the personality (Dt. xiv. 26, RV). 'Desire' was the inclination of the *nep̄eš* (2 Sa. iii. 21). And when the whole 'soul' lay behind an inclination or desire that was sinful then the soul, it was said, 'lusted a lust' (see Nu. xi. 4, 6). It was against this kind of covetousness that the tenth commandment was directed (Ex. xx. 17), because when such sinful desire was given free rein the well-being of the whole community was endangered (Je. vi. 13–15).

In the New Testament sinful desire is stimulated by the will to get rich (1 Tim. vi. 9); so much so that it is equated with 'the love of money' (verse 10). But it may also manifest itself in illicit sexual desire (Mt. v. 28), or in what Paul describes as 'the desires of the flesh and of the thoughts' (Eph. ii. 3, RVmg). The New Testament testifies also to what is an observable fact in human experience: that if these sinful desires are gratified instead of crucified they become a consuming fire (Col. iii. 5 f.). On the other hand, where God is the object of the soul's desire (Rom. x. 2a), and His best gifts (1 Cor. xii. 31), the body becomes the instrument of righteousness (Rom. vi. 12 f.). J.G.S.S.T.

DEUTERONOMY, BOOK OF. The word is derived from the LXX *deuteronomion* (Vulg. *deuteronomium*), 'repetition of the law', which is based upon a mistaken understanding of the words 'copy of this law' in Dt. xvii. 18.

I. OUTLINE OF CONTENTS

The book falls naturally into three sections.

a. i. 1–xi. 32. Discourses by Moses, of a prefatory character, with small elements of narrative. In i. 6–iii. 29 Moses rehearses the course of their journeyings from leaving Horeb to the valley where their camp was pitched. In iv. 1–40 he addresses exhortations and warnings to the coming generation. Moses also selects three cities of refuge, and the narrator gives a detailed geographical statement of the place where the words following were spoken (iv. 41–49). Chapters v–xi form a continuous discourse by Moses, beginning with a rehearsal of the Decalogue, and leading up to the legislation which follows.

b. xii. 1–xxvi. 19. The legislation which Moses put before the people (see below).

c. xxvii. 1–xxxiv. 12. A supplement, consisting of narrative and discourse, leading up to Moses' death. Chapter xxvii contains instructions for recording the law on stone, and for a solemn covenant, after the crossing of Jordan. Chapter xxviii follows with blessings upon obedience and curses on disobedience. In chapters xxix, xxx Moses binds the people in a covenant to serve Yahweh their God, and Him alone (xxix. 1, 10).

In chapter xxxi Joshua appears on the scene, and the narrator tells how Moses exhorts and commissions Joshua, and how together they teach the people a 'song' (xxxi, xxxii. 1–47). The book closes with an account of Moses' death (xxxii. 48–52, xxxiv. 1–8), Moses' blessing on the tribes 'before he died', and the people's obedience to Joshua his successor (xxxiv. 9–12).

II. AUTHORSHIP AND DATE

Since the time of Wellhausen, the date of Deuteronomy has been under constant discussion. Wellhausen himself put forward the theory that the author of the book (which he limited to the 'nucleus' of chapters xii–xxvi) was a prophet who compiled it in 622 BC. His object was a reform in religious practice, and in particular to abolish the 'high places' (*bāmôṯ*) and centralize worship in Jerusalem. He therefore hid it in the Temple that it might be 'discovered', as it was, by Hilkiah, the reforms of 2 Ki. xxii, xxiii being the consequence.

S. R. Driver adopted this view in its main outline, but considered chapters v–xi, and probably more, to be part of the book. In order to avoid the suggestion of fraud, he pushed the date back to *c*. 640 BC. The same theory has been accepted by H. H. Rowley, but he prefers a date *c*. 680 BC, and suggests that the author may have been a follower of Isaiah. On the other hand, some (Kennett, Hölscher) regarded it as post-exilic. They argued that Dt. xvii. 15 could never have been written while a prince of the house of David was seated firmly on the throne; that many of the laws would have been sheer anachronisms during the later monarchy, and provisions such as those of chapters xiii and xx utterly incapable of being carried into execution. Earlier dates suggested have been 701 BC or earlier (von Rad), the reign of Hezekiah (Westphal, Hempel), or the pre-prophetic period (A. C. Welch).

A more conservative view was put forward by E. Robertson, namely that the book was compiled by Samuel from Mosaic material, some of it in writing. A study of the arguments used by these different scholars shows that to a large extent they cancel one another out; none of them has a firm foundation.

Anything *less* like a programme of reform composed by a disciple of Isaiah in the early days of Manasseh's reign it is difficult to imagine. If the author's aim is to abolish the high places, why does he never mention them? If he wanted to centralize worship in Jerusalem, why not make it clear? Jerusalem is neither mentioned nor hinted at.

Those days were days of tragedy, following on the fall of the northern kingdom, and the accession of an idolatrous king to the throne of Judah. But they cast no shadow on this book: its tone is that of undiluted optimism. It is difficult to find any trace of Isaiah's influence, either in outlook or phrase. There is no doctrine of a 'remnant', but an appeal to 'all Israel'; no use of the prophetic formula 'thus saith the LORD', and no use of Isaiah's favourite title, 'the Holy One of Israel'. Finally, are we to believe that a preacher of great oratorical and spiritual power was afraid to proclaim his message openly, but preferred to remain unknown, to write it in a book, and hide it in the Temple?

On the other hand, the reasons for accepting the Mosaic authorship are peculiarly strong. An unbroken line of tradition assigns the authorship to Moses; this was accepted by our Lord Himself (Mt. xix. 8) and generally by the New Testament writers.

In chapter xxxi the narrator tells us that Moses wrote 'this law' in a book and gave it to the priests, commanding them to read it to the people (xxxi. 9–13). He furthermore commanded that 'the book of the law' be placed by the side of the ark of the covenant for a witness (xxxi. 24–26). It is in close accord with this that we read in xvii. 18 f. that the future ruler is to make a copy or duplicate of the book from that in the possession of the priests. It would appear from this that the book which Moses wrote did not contain chapters xxxi–xxxiv; indeed, the last two chapters were evidently added after his death.

The simplest and most probable interpretation is that Moses 'wrote' the legislation itself, namely chapters xii–xxvi, and that the discourses and closing chapters were recorded and added later. Thus the 'book' came to mean the whole book of Deuteronomy.

There is no adequate reason for assigning the narrator of chapters xxxi–xxxiv a date later than the time immediately following Moses' death. He might have been Eleazar or one of his companions. He writes as one who witnessed the events he describes. The accurate detail of the geographical material, and the nature of the laws, witness to its being a document contemporary with the events it describes (see also the following section).

References to experiences which must have deeply stirred Moses' feelings crop up sometimes unexpectedly, such as 'the house of bondage' (v. 6, *etc*.), the recalling of the dastardly attack by Amalek (xxv. 17 ff.), the burden of judgment (i. 9–18), the murmurings of the people (ix. 22), the material of which the ark was made (x. 3), the enemies they had overcome. The references to Aaron (ix. 20 f., x. 6 f., xxxii. 50 f.) and Miriam

(xxiv. 9) spring as naturally from Moses' lips as they would be strange if merely inventions of a 7th-century prophet. We may rest content in the assurance that we have here a true and trustworthy record of what Moses said and wrote.

III. CIRCUMSTANCES AND PLACE OF WRITING

The background of time, place, and circumstances is plainly stated. The discourses and events belong to the last month of the forty years of wandering which were imposed upon the people for their unbelief (i. 3, 35, ii. 14). They come to an end with events leading up to Moses' death.

The book contains much geographical detail, particularly in the opening and closing chapters. It is to be observed that Palestine is always viewed *from the outside*. The minute accuracy of the description of the land of Moab and the journey to it is a striking feature (see chapters ii, iii, and note i. 2).

There is a certain obscurity about the places named in Deuteronomy i. 1 (see DIZAHAB). They may indicate that some of the words of Moses were spoken before arriving at the place so carefully defined in iii. 29 and iv. 44–49. This was an upland 'valley', or ravine (*gāy*'). From the camp could be seen a temple (*bêṯ*) of the pagan god Peor, a name of bitter memory (Nu. xxv; Dt. iii. 29, iv. 46). From there, looking westward, the mountains of Ebal and Gerizim could be seen against the horizon (xi. 29, 30). High above the camp was the ridge or *pisgâ* (xxxiv. 1) from which a clear view of the land can be obtained. At Moses' side were elders and priests (xxvii. 1, 9), and his faithful minister Joshua was close at hand (i. 38). Those whom Moses addressed were mainly young, although a considerable number (Nu. xiv. 29) would have vivid memories of a childhood spent in bondage, and the wonders of their deliverance. Sometimes he speaks more directly to the latter, sometimes to the former. Moses looks to the future with optimism; our God is ever a 'God of hope' (Rom. xv. 13). The people will certainly cross over Jordan and inherit the land on the other side (iii. 28, xii. 10). The two most frequently recurring phrases in the book are 'go in and possess' (thirty-five times) and 'the land which the Lord thy God giveth thee' (thirty-four times). But there is no minimizing of the difficulties; there will be hard fighting to be done (chapter xx) and the temptations to idolatry will be severe (chapter xiii). Hence the emotion with which Moses urges them to 'cleave' unto Yahweh their God (xiii. 3, 4) with all their 'heart and . . . soul', and to 'beware lest they forget' all His mercies.

The laws laid down in chapters xii–xxvi exactly correspond to this background, as to no other.

IV. THE LEGISLATION

The laws contained in chapters xii–xxvi are described in the opening verse as statutes and judgments; in xxvi. 17 the word 'commandments' is added. These three words may serve as a convenient means for classifying the laws into three groups.

a. Judgments

In this connection the word is capable of strict definition. A judgment is a rule or law laid down by authority or settled by ancient custom, by which a judge must be guided in certain specified cases. Typical examples can be seen in the judgments of Exodus xxi. It is important to realize that many of these can be found in similar, even identical terms, in the Code of Hammurabi and other Semitic codes belonging to a period centuries earlier than Moses. This shows that Moses was divinely guided to include these well-established laws of public order among those which he wrote down for use in the promised land.

b. Statutes

The word 'statute' (*ḥōq*) is derived from a root meaning to engrave or inscribe. Hence it comes to mean a permanent rule of conduct. It differs from the judgment, in that whereas in the latter the appeal is to the judge, in the former it is to the conscience and to God. A distinction between them is drawn in 1 Ki. vi. 12, where Solomon is bidden to 'walk in' the statutes of God, and to 'execute' His judgments. They are usually couched in the second person; they are moral precepts, and so constitute a divine rule of life, and, being such, have no place in other Semitic codes. Some of them deal with religious institutions, feasts (Dt. xvi. 1–17), or offerings (xii. 5–28). They include also laws of justice, purity (*e.g.* xvi. 19, xxiii. 17), kindness and clemency (xxiii. 15, 24). While some apply to conditions now obsolete, others are as valid today as when they were written, and all are worthy of our careful study.

c. Commandments

While the word 'commandments' can be applied to any sort of command, it is convenient for our present purpose to limit its use here to those commands which are not of permanent obligation, but can be fulfilled once and for all, such as the destruction of pagan shrines (xii. 2), the appointment of judges and officers (xvi. 18), and the establishment of the cities of refuge (xix. 1–13).

The legislation is transfused with a wonderful warmth of religious feeling: the name Yahweh occurs 189 times. While Moses is setting forth rules whereby truth and justice may be established among the people, he is at the same time striving to bind them to Yahweh their God, in obedience and love.

V. LATER REFERENCES

There can be little doubt that the 'book of the law' found by Hilkiah in the Temple was, or contained, the book of Deuteronomy; and the same applies to the book which Ezra read (Ne. viii. 1). Long before this Jehoshaphat had sent Levites to the fenced cities of Judah to teach from 'the book of the law of the LORD' (2 Ch. xvii. 8 f.). Earlier still this was the book which David charged Solomon to observe (1 Ki. ii. 3). Joshua fulfilled in Shechem the command to inscribe the law on stones (Jos. viii. 30–35, *cf.* i. 8, xxiv. 26). More important is the use our Lord made of it. In His temptation He three times quoted it as authoritative Scripture (Mt. iv. 4, 7, 10; Dt. viii. 3, vi. 16, 13). He cited it also in reply to the lawyer's question (Mk. xii. 29; Dt. vi. 4). It was evidently very familiar to Him.

Moses' words concerning a future prophet (Dt. xviii. 15) were interpreted by Peter and by Stephen as predictions of Jesus Christ (Acts iii. 22, vii. 37); and there are other citations from it in the New Testament. Paul, following Moses' example, taught the need of true heart religion, and applied Dt. xxx. 11–14 to faith in Jesus Christ (Rom. x. 6–8). See also Gal. iii. 10, 13; Heb. x. 28.

Of Deuteronomy Jesus Christ said, 'It is written'; and we may gratefully add, 'for our learning' (Rom. xv. 4).

BIBLIOGRAPHY. S. R. Driver, *Deuteronomy*, *ICC*, 1902; J. H. Hertz, *The Pentateuch and Haftorahs*, V, 1936; G. T. Manley, *The Book of the Law*, 1957; A. C. Welch, *The Code of Deuteronomy*, 1924; *id.*, *Deuteronomy: The Framework to the Code*, 1932; G. von Rad, *Studies in Deuteronomy*, 1953; M. G. Kline, 'Dynastic Covenant', *WTJ*, XXIII, 1960–1, pp. 1 ff.; E. Robertson, *The Old Testament Problem*, 1950.

G.T.M.

DEVIL.

I. IN THE OLD TESTAMENT

In the Old Testament there are references to devils under the names *śā'îr* (Lv. xvii. 7; 2 Ch. xi. 15) and *šēḏ* (Dt. xxxii. 17; Ps. cvi. 37). The former term means 'hairy one', and points to the demon as a satyr. The latter is of uncertain meaning, though it is evidently connected with a similar Assyr. word. In such passages there is the thought that the deities who were served from time to time by Israel are no true gods, but are really devils (*cf.* 1 Cor. x. 19 f.). But the subject is not one of great interest in the Old Testament, and the relevant passages are few.

II. IN THE GOSPELS

It is otherwise when we turn to the Gospels. There are many references there to devils. The usual designation is *daimonion*, a diminutive of *daimōn*, which is found in Mt. viii. 31, but apparently with no difference of meaning (the parallel accounts use *daimonion*). In the classics *daimōn* is frequently used in a good sense, of a god or of the divine power. But in the New Testament *daimōn* and *daimonion* always refer to spiritual beings hostile to God and men. Beelzebub (or Beezeboul) is their 'prince' (Mk. iii. 22), so that they may be regarded as his agents. This is the sting behind the accusation that Jesus had 'a devil' (Jn. vii. 20, x. 20). Those who opposed His ministry tried to link Him with the very forces of evil, instead of recognizing His divine origin.

In the Gospels there are many references to people possessed by devils. A variety of effects results, such as dumbness (Lk. xi. 14), epilepsy (Mk. ix. 17 f.), a refusal to wear clothing, and a living among the tombs (Lk. viii. 27). It is often said in modern times that devil-possession was simply the way people had in the 1st century of referring to conditions that we today would call sickness or madness. The Gospel accounts, however, distinguish between sickness and possession by devils. For example, in Mt. iv. 24 we read of 'sick people that were taken with divers diseases and torments, and those which were possessed with devils, and those which were lunatick, and those that had the palsy'. None of these classes appears to be identical with the others.

Neither in the Old Testament nor in the Acts and Epistles do we find many references to demon-possession. (The incident of Acts xix. 13 ff. is exceptional.) It apparently was a phenomenon especially associated with the earthly ministry of our Lord. It should surely be interpreted as an outburst of demoniacal opposition to the work of Jesus.

The Gospels picture Jesus as in continual conflict with evil spirits. To cast out such beings from men was not easy. His opponents recognized both that He did this, and also that it required a power greater than human. Therefore they attributed His success to the indwelling of Satan (Lk. xi. 15), exposing themselves to the counter that this would spell ruin in the kingdom of the evil one (Lk. xi. 17 f.). Jesus' power was that of 'the Spirit of God' (Mt. xii. 28) or, as Luke expresses it, 'if I with the finger of God cast out devils . . .' (Lk. xi. 20).

The victory that Jesus won over demons He shared with His followers. When He sent out the Twelve He 'gave them power and authority over all devils, and to cure diseases' (Lk. ix. 1). Again, the seventy could report when they returned from their mission, 'Lord, even the devils are subject unto us through thy name' (Lk. x. 17). Others than Jesus' immediate disciples might use His name to cast out devils, a fact which caused perturbation to some of the inner circle, but not to the Master (Mk. ix. 38 f.).

III. OTHER NEW TESTAMENT REFERENCES

After the Gospels there are few references to devils. In 1 Cor. x. 20 f. Paul is concerned with idol worship, and regards idols as in reality demons, a use we see again in Rev. ix. 20. There is an interesting passage in Jas. ii. 19, 'the devils also believe, and tremble'. It reminds us of Gospel passages in which the devils recognized Jesus for what He was (Mk. i. 24, iii. 11, *etc.*).

There seems no reason *a priori* why we should reject the whole concept of demon-possession. When the Gospels give us good evidence that it did take place it is best to accept this.

See also EVIL SPIRITS; POSSESSION; SATAN.

BIBLIOGRAPHY. N. Geldenhuys, *Commentary*

on Luke's Gospel, pp. 174 f.; J. M. Ross, *ExpT*, LXVI, 1954–5, pp. 58–61; E. Langton, *Essentials of Demonology*, 1949. L.M.

DEVOTED THING. See Curse.

DEW. The Heb. *ṭal*, 'sprinkled moisture', is referred to indiscriminately for dew and night mist. As the effects upon plants of dew (*i.e.* condensation of water vapour on a cooled surface), and of mist (*i.e.* condensation in the air), are not yet understood, the difference is perhaps irrelevant. Moist air drawn in from the sea is largely responsible for dew-fall in western Palestine, especially in the districts near the coast and on the western slopes of the mountains, though it does not occur in summer in the Jordan valley south of Beisan and on the western uplands of Transjordan (fig. 157). According to Ashbel, the number of yearly dew-nights varies from 250 on the sandy soil of Gaza and the high slopes of Mt. Carmel to 100–150 days in the Judaean Highlands, dropping rapidly eastwards in the Jordan trough. The maximum dew occurs in the beneficial summer months when the plants need moisture most. Duvdevani has experimented with two types of condensation, 'Downward dew' is characteristic of summer in areas of loose soil, *i.e.* with good soil-cooling conditions. 'Upward dew' results from the condensation of water vapour from damp soil, and is therefore more frequent in the winter season. This may be the explanation of Gideon's signs (Jdg. vi. 36–40). In his first experience so heavy was the night mist or dew, that he wrung out from the fleece a bowl full of water, while the hard-baked earth of the threshing-floor was dry. In the second experience the fleece was dry, while the earth, perhaps the disturbed soil in the edge of the threshing-floor, produced conditions for 'upward dew' from the soil, inadequate to moisten the fleece.

Scriptural references show that, though dew-fall is mysterious, its incidence is well known. 'Who hath begotten the drops of dew?' says the Lord as He answers Job (xxxviii. 28), and its origin is considered heavenly (Gn. xxvii. 28; Dt. xxxiii. 28; Hg. i. 10; Zc. viii. 12). It falls suddenly (2 Sa. xvii. 12), gently (Dt. xxxii. 2), lies all night (Jb. xxix. 19), and exposure to it is discomforting (Ct. v. 2; Dn. iv. 15, 23, 25, 33), but it quickly evaporates in the morning (Jb. vii. 9; Ho. vi. 4). Dew is to be expected in the hot summer weather of harvest (Is. xviii. 4; *cf.* Ho. xiv. 5; Mi. v. 7).

Dew is beneficial to summer crops. This has been proved conclusively by agronomical field-studies made since 1937. The ancients therefore were not exaggerating it as a source of blessing. Dew is sufficiently copious to permit dry-farming in the absence of rain (Ecclus. xviii. 16, xliii. 22). It allows geophytes to be cultivated in the Negeb and aids the vine harvest; hence the prayer, 'May God give you of the dew of heaven, and of the fatness of the earth, and plenty of grain and wine' (Gn. xxvii. 28, RSV; *cf.* Dt. xxxiii. 28). The absence of dew was therefore a cause of severe plight (Hg. i. 10; *cf.* Jb. xxix. 19; Zc. viii. 12), intensifying the drought in the absence of rain (1 Ki. xvii. 1; *cf.* 2 Sa. i. 21). Its preciousness is therefore taken up as an emblem of resurrection; 'a dew of lights is thy dew, and to life shall the earth bring the shades' (Is. xxvi. 19). From this prophecy was based the talmudic phrase 'the dew of resurrection'.

The passage in Ps. cxxxiii. 3 appears to state that the dew of Hermon comes down on the mountain of Zion. This is incapable of a geographical interpretation. It may be a proverbial expression for plentiful dew, since Hermon receives a maximum amount (fig. 157). In consequence of the heavy dew on Hermon and Mt. Carmel, the soft, friable limestone rapidly disintegrates and the soil is frequently replenished. Thus, these mountains have been symbolic of fertility.

Bibliography. D. Ashbel, *Bio-climatic Atlas of Israel*, 1950, pp. 51–55; S. Duvdevani, 'Dew observations and their significances', *Proc. United Nations Scientific Conference in the Conservation and Utilization of Resources*, 1949, 4, p. 45. J.M.H.

DIADEM. See Crown.

DIAL. See Degrees.

DIAMOND. See Jewels and Precious Stones.

DIANA. This was the Lat. name of the goddess identified with the Gk. Artemis of classical mythology. Daughter of Jupiter and Latona, she was twin sister of Apollo, and horror at the pains her mother endured at her birth is supposed to have made her averse to marriage. She was goddess of the moon and of hunting, and is generally portrayed as a huntress, with dogs in attendance. Her temple at Ephesus was one of the seven wonders of the world, and here worship of the 'virgin goddess' appears to have been fused with some kind of fertility-cult of the mother-goddess of Asia Minor. The temple was supported on 100 massive columns, some of which were sculptured. Tradition claims that her image fell there from the sky (Acts xix. 35), and is thought to refer to a meteorite; Pliny tells of a huge stone above the entrance, said to have been placed there by Diana herself. Her worship was conducted by eunuch priests, called *megabyzoi* (Strabo, xiv. 1. 23), and archaeologists have discovered statues depicting her with many breasts. The silversmiths who made small votary shrines, portraying the goddess in a recess with her lions in attendance, or possibly souvenir models of the temple, caused the riot when Paul was ministering there (Acts xix. 23–xx. 1). Their cry of 'Great is Diana of the Ephesians' (Acts xix. 28, 34) is attested by inscriptions from Ephesus which call her 'Artemis the Great' (*CIG*, 2963c; *Greek Inscriptions in the British Museum*, iii, 1890, 481. 324). See fig. 79.

See also DEMETRIUS, EPHESUS; Conybeare and Howson, *Life and Epistles of St. Paul*, 1901, chapter xvi. D.H.W.

DIASPORA. See DISPERSION.

DIBLATH, DIBLAH. Occurring only in Ezk. vi. 14, no place of this name has been identified, and it is probably a scribal error for Riblah (*q.v.*).

DIBON. 1. A town in Judah, occupied after the Exile (Ne. xi. 25) but not identifiable today.

2. Dibon (*dîḇôn*) of Moab, marked by the modern village of Dhiban, to the east of the Dead Sea and 4 miles north of the river Arnon. Originally it belonged to Moab, but it was captured by Sihon, king of the Amorites, in pre-Israelite times (Nu. xxi. 26). The Israelites took it at the time of the Exodus (Nu. xxi. 30), and it was given to the tribes of Reuben and Gad (Nu. xxxii. 2, 3). Gad built Dibon, however, and hence it is called Dibon Gad (Nu. xxxii. 34), although in Jos. xiii. 15 ff. it is reckoned to Reuben. It is probably one of the halting-places on the Exodus journey, and is referred to in Nu. xxxiii. 45, 46. Israel lost it later, it was regained by Omri, and lost again to Mesha, king of Moab, who speaks of it on the Mesha Stone, lines 21 and 28 (see MOABITE STONE). Isaiah and Jeremiah knew it as a Moabite town (Is. xv. 2; Je. xlviii. 18, 22).

Important excavations were commenced here by the American Schools of Oriental Research in 1950 and show occupation from Early Bronze to Arab times with a gap in occupation from *c.* 1850 to 1300 BC.

BIBLIOGRAPHY. F. M. Abel, *Géographie de la Palestine*, 1933, II, pp. 304–305; W. H. Morton, *BASOR*, 140, 1955; A. D. Tushingham, 'Excavations at Dibon in Moab 1952–1953', *BASOR*, 133, 1954; F. V. Winnett, 'Excavations at Dibon in Moab 1950–1951', *BASOR*, 125, 1952.

J.A.T.

DIDRACHMON. See MONEY.

DIDYMUS. See THOMAS.

DILL. See PLANTS.

DINAH (*dînâ*, 'judgment' or 'judged'). Daughter of Jacob by Leah (Gn. xxx. 21, xlvi. 15). While Jacob was encamped near Shechem, Dinah went out to visit the local womenfolk (Gn. xxxiv); however, Shechem, son of Hamor, Hivite prince of Shechem, was attracted to her, apparently forced himself upon her, and then sought her in marriage from Jacob. But Jacob's sons were indignant; they stipulated circumcision of the Shechemites before any marriage could be agreed to. Then Simeon and Levi (obviously with their retainers) caught the Shechemites off guard and slaughtered them treacherously. This deed was disapproved of (Gn. xxxiv. 30) and denounced (Gn. xlix. 5–7) by Jacob. The recording of sad incidents of this kind involving womenfolk is noted as a mark of early (pre-Solomonic) date for such narratives by C. H. Gordon, *Hebrew Union College Annual*, XXVI, 1955, p. 80.

K.A.K.

DIONYSIUS THE AREOPAGITE. A member of the aristocratic council of Athens (see AREOPAGUS); one of Paul's few Athenian converts (Acts xvii. 34). A 2nd-century tradition (Dionysius of Corinth in Eusebius, *EH* iii. 4, iv. 23), that he was the first bishop of Athens may rest only on this passage. A body of much later mystical writings was long accepted as his and exercised a very strong influence in the Middle Ages (see partial English tr. by C. E. Rolt; R. Roques, 'Dionysius Areopagitica' in *RAC* for recent study). Other speculations about Dionysius, possibly related to the pagan Dionysos cult, are traced by Rendel Harris, *Annotators of the Codex Bezae*, 1901, pp. 76 ff. A.F.W.

DIOSCURI. See CASTOR AND POLLUX.

DIOTREPHES. A refractory person of overweening ambition who would not recognize the Elder, publicly attacked him, forbade the reception of his adherents, and, whether by formal excommunication or physical violence, excluded those who did receive them. Though the Elder's personal intervention would eventually be decisive, the effect of his letters could be annulled by the present influence of Diotrephes (3 Jn. 9, 10). It is not clear whether this was in virtue of a regular office (*e.g.* as an early monarchical bishop —*cf.* Zahn, *INT*, III, pp. 374 ff.) or by dominance of personality among his peers (*cf.* J. V. Bartlet, *JTS*, VI, 1905, pp. 204 ff.). For other imaginative reconstructions, *cf.* J. Chapman, *JTS*, V, 1904, pp. 357 ff., 517 ff.; B. H. Streeter, *The Primitive Church*, 1929, pp. 83 ff. A.F.W.

DISCIPLE (Heb. *limmûḏ*; Gk. *mathētēs*; Lat. *discipulus*—'pupil', 'learner').

In the English Old Testament the term appears once only (Is. viii. 16), but the same Hebrew word is translated 'learned' in Is. l. 4 and 'taught' in Is. liv. 13. 'Scholar' (1 Ch. xxv. 8) is from the same root. The teacher–pupil relationship was a common feature of the ancient world, where Greek philosophers and Jewish Rabbis gathered around them groups of apprentices or learners.

In New Testament times a similar practice still obtained, and the word signified broadly those who accepted the teachings of others—*e.g.* of John the Baptist (Mt. ix. 14; Jn. i. 35), of the Pharisees (Mk. ii. 18; Lk. v. 33), and of Moses (Jn. ix. 28). Its most common use was in denoting the adherents of Jesus: either in a general sense (as in Mt. x. 42; Lk. vi. 17; Jn. vi. 66), or with special reference to the Twelve (Mt. x. 1, xi. 1) who forsook all to follow Him. See APOSTLE. Apart from the Gospels, the only other New Testament occurrences of the term are in Acts, where it describes believers, those who confess Jesus as the Christ (vi. 1, 2, 7, ix. 36 [fem.

mathētria], xi. 26). The verbal form, *mathēteuō*, 'to be, become, or make a disciple (of)', is found in Mt. xxvii. 57, xxviii. 19 (RV, AVmg). J.D.D.

DISEASE AND HEALING.

I. THE PHENOMENA OF DISEASE IN THE BIBLE

a. The terms used

Disease and suffering, and attempts to relieve them, have been essential attendants of human life ever since the dawn of history. The Bible presents a view of man in all his experiences, and hence there are frequent mentions of the illnesses of individuals and of the epidemics of communities, and of attempts to prevent or remedy them, just as there are accounts of all other major human experiences. The words used for disease and healing, and their cognates, both in Hebrew and Greek, are mostly typical everyday words. *Ḥālâ* is used for 'to be sick' (nouns *ḥ^oli* and *maḥ^alâ*), and also *madweh* (Dt. vii. 15, xxviii. 61) and *dāḇār* (Ps. xli. 8) meaning 'a matter' (*i.e.* evil matter). In the New Testament disease is called *astheneia* (weakness), *malakia* (misfortune), *nosēma* and *nosos* (more specifically and medically 'disease'); verbs used are *astheneō* and *kakōs echein*, and in one verse (Jas. v. 15), *kamnō*. *Arrhōstos* ('not robust') is used in one place (Mk. vi. 13). In the Old Testament *rāpā'* (to heal) is most commonly used for healing, and is also used for 'physician' in Gn. l. 2 (twice); 2 Ch. xvi. 12; Jb. xiii. 4; Je. viii. 22. Other Old Testament terms include *ḥāyâ* (revive) and *šûḇ* (restore). In the New Testament the intransitive verbs *ischyō* (be strong) and *hygiainō* (more specifically 'be healthy') are used, and for healing (transitive) *sōzō* and *diasōzō* (save) are used non-specifically (though they are used in this way by other writers, including Hippocrates). *Stereoō* (set up, make strong) is used in Acts iii. 16. Specifically medical words for healing are *therapeuō*, *iaomai*, and *apokathistēmi*. There does not seem to be any special significance about the use of *sōzō*; and the translation of all these words in AV, *e.g.* 'save', 'restore', 'make well', 'make whole', are indiscriminate uses of the contemporary English of the translators. The noun *holoklēria* (AV 'perfect soundness') is used in Acts iii. 16 and it may have reference to active rehabilitation as well as physical restoration. In some places, *e.g.* Is. liii. 5 (*cf.* 1 Pet. ii. 24), words with the specific meaning of 'healing' are used with a purely spiritual connotation. Similar instances are Is. vi. 10 (*cf.* Acts xxviii. 27) and Mt. xiii. 15.

b. Biblical descriptions of disease

These are 'phenomenal', that is, they are couched in the terms of the lay observer. An exception to this is the phenomenon of demon possession, where a spiritual explanation is given. Some diseases are identifiable in terms of modern scientific pathology; but some descriptions are vague (*e.g.* 'lameness', 'palsy', 'fever', 'issue'), and some of the terms used in the AV are actually misleading, *e.g.* 'scurvy', 'emerods' (*q.v.*; 1 Sa. v, vi), 'boil', 'scab', 'botch' (Dt. xxviii. 27), 'blain'. In the course of time diseases appear and disappear or, if they persist, may change their natural history. This is particularly true of diseases of microbiological origin. 'Plague' refers to any epidemic disease and is not the equivalent of the modern infection with *Pasteurella pestis*. Others may be unchanged for centuries, *e.g.* blindness from the virus disease trachoma is still very common in the Middle East, and was probably even more common in biblical times. Sometimes a particular manifestation is mentioned, *e.g.* the dropsical man (Lk. xiv. 2), Gk. *hydrōpikos*, whose dropsy may have been caused by one of several different conditions. There is one well-known case, Paul's 'thorn in the flesh' (2 Cor. xii. 7–10), where it is difficult to make a diagnosis; none of the several explanations of this which have been given, such as malaria, ophthalmia, epilepsy, *etc.*, is entirely satisfactory. Those disorders which are healed miraculously, especially those recorded in the Gospels, are fairly certainly cases of organic disease; *e.g.* in the man 'blind from his birth' (Jn. ix. 1) the blindness cannot have been psychogenic, because it was congenital.

c. Mental disorder

This is also treated by the same kind of lay description as physical disorder, and in two major cases it is possible to describe the situation as seen in the light of modern psychiatry. Saul (1 Sa. *passim*) was a man who was gifted but in some respects inadequate, *e.g.* he was much at the mercy of other people's opinions; he was subject to moods of recurrent depression, and, in later life, had the paranoid ideas and irritability characteristic of depression in older patients, though homicidal tendencies such as he had are uncommon. His suicide is unimportant, and that of a defeated warrior rather than a depressed neurotic. (See also SAUL.) Nebuchadrezzar, active and irascible, had a hypomanic personality, *i.e.* an inherited liability to develop a manic-depressive psychosis. His illness (Dn. iv. 28–37) was long-lasting and occurred when he was perhaps in his fifties. He was conscious, but totally incapable of government. There was no evidence of organic disorder. There was some perversion of appetite. He recovered from it completely (v. 36) in the end, and it would be described today as involutional melancholia. (See also NEBUCHADREZZAR.) There is a depressive content in some psalms, *e.g.* cii, but often with a note of triumph at the end.

d. Demon possession

The singular phenomenon of demon possession, rarely paralleled since apostolic times, is clearly something *sui generis*. It is recorded as having occurred at the time of Christ more frequently than at any other time. (The account of Saul, 'an evil spirit from the Lord troubled him', in 1 Sa. xvi. 14, 15, is probably to be regarded as a statement of his mental disorder rather than as a theological explanation of its origin.) Those who were 'demon possessed' (Gk. *daimonizomenos* = 'demonized') could be used as a mouthpiece by the possessing spirit; they often had physical manifestations resembling epilepsy, and above all were sensitive to the name of Christ. However, demon possession is definitely *not* synonymous either with epilepsy or with mental disorder in general, and is clearly distinguished by the synoptists and in Acts (v. 16) from the general run of disease. The best authenticated modern cases seem to be those described by missionaries in China from about 1850 onwards. There is no good reason to doubt the biblical view of it as a 'possession' by an evil spiritual being of the personality and body of the person concerned. See also DEVIL.

e. Leprosy

The disease of *ṣāra'aṭ*, translated 'leprosy', is described in detail in Lv. xiii, but the description could, and probably did, embrace other skin diseases. Probably a variety of the latter conditions, particularly infectious ones, were diagnosed as *ṣāra'aṭ*. The term itself is also applied to clothes and to houses (Lv. xiv. 55) and seems to have been used quite generally to describe something which was ceremonially unclean. When a leper was 'cleansed', and pronounced so by the priest, it is likely that the condition was a self-limiting one, and not what would now be termed leprosy, *i.e.* an illness caused by a specific bacterium. This in no way detracts from the significance or validity of the biblical account, because the word *ṣāra'aṭ* is a purely phenomenal one, and typical of the thought and concepts of the time, which, of course, had no bacteriological basis. In the Septuagint *ṣāra'aṭ* is translated *lepra*, and in the New Testament *lepra* is also used. There was certainly true leprosy in the Near East in New Testament times.

II. THE BIBLICAL OUTLOOK ON DISEASE

a. The causes of human suffering

The topics of suffering and disease, in the Bible, are closely bound up with the questions of the nature and origin of evil itself. Suffering is a human experience, with diverse causes, and is one of the results of human sin. In the case of suffering from disease, the direct connection is not usually obvious, though sometimes the illness is directly connected. From the account of the fall of man in Genesis it is clear that soon afterwards man knew insecurity, fear, and pain (Gn. iii. 16, 17). Here *'iṣṣāḇôn* (AV 'sorrow') is better rendered 'pain', and then mental anguish (Gn. iv. 13). The direct connection between sin and suffering becomes rapidly more complex, but nations which obey God were, in general, promised freedom from disease (Ex. xv. 25, 26; Lv. xxvi. 14–16; Dt. vii. 12–16, xxviii, especially 22, 27, 58–61). On the other hand, pestilence is one of the three sore judgments on the people of God (Je. xxiv. 10, xxxii. 24; Ezk. xiv. 21) and on other nations, *e.g.* Philistines (1 Sa. v. 6) and Assyrians (2 Ki. xix. 35). There are passages such as Ps. cxix. 67, where the sinner himself is involved, and the case of the impotent man healed (Jn. v. 1–16), where his own fault is perhaps implied (v. 14). David's sin involved the afflictions of others (2 Sa. xxiv. 15–17). On the whole, human suffering, from disease or from any other cause, is the effect on the individual of the spiritual malaise of the human society of which he is an integral part. In the book of Job (especially chapter i) something is seen of the activity of Satan. This is also apparent in Acts x. 38, where the sick are spoken of as 'all that were oppressed of the devil', and in the suggestive parable of the wheat and tares ('An enemy hath done this', Mt. xiii. 28). Again, Christ Himself spoke of 'this woman, whom Satan hath bound . . .' (Lk. xiii. 16).

God does not stand by helplessly, however. Suffering is sometimes used punitively. At times, as mentioned above, this may be on a national scale. Or it may be applied to individuals, as in the cases of Moses (Ex. iv. 24), Miriam (Nu. xii. 10), Uzziah (2 Ch. xxvi. 16–21), Jeroboam (2 Ch. xiii. 20), Gehazi (2 Ki. v. 25–27), Ananias and Sapphira (Acts v. 5, 10), Herod (Acts xii. 21–23), and Elymas (Acts xiii. 11). Much more detail is given when suffering is used constructively (Heb. xii. 6–11), as in the case of Jacob, who, after a real physical injury miraculously inflicted, learnt to depend upon God, and matured spiritually to fulfil his new name of Israel (Gn. xxxii. 24–32). Hezekiah's illness demonstrated his faith in God, and is probably in this category (2 Ki. xx. 1–7). The book of Job shows that the real issue is a man's relationship to God rather than his attitude to his own suffering. It is the principal Old Testament refutation of the view, put forward with great skill by Job's 'comforters', that there is an inevitable link between individual sin and individual suffering. After disposing of the view, which is only partially true, that the reason for the existence of suffering is disciplinary, it leads to the sublime picture of Job both comforted, vindicated, and blessed. It is important to realize that the biblical picture is not a mere dualism (see DUALISM). Rather, suffering is presented in the light of eternity and in relation to a God who is sovereign, but who is nevertheless forbearing in His dealings with the world because of His love for men (2 Pet. iii. 9). Conscious of the sorrow and pain round about them, the New Testament writers look forward to the final consummation when suffering shall be no more (Rom. viii. 18; Rev. xxi. 4).

This conception is different from the Greek conception of the body as something inherently evil, and the spirit as something inherently good. The biblical conception of the transience yet nobility of the body is best seen in 2 Corinthians, especially in v. 1–10 (*cf.* also 1 Cor. vi. 15). It is an integral part of the complex of the individual through which the personality is expressed.

b. The treatment of disease

The therapeutics of the Bible are those of the time, and are described in general terms, *e.g.* Pr. xvii. 22; Je. xlvi. 11. Local applications are frequently referred to for sores (Is. i. 6; Je. viii. 22, li. 8), and a 'poultice of figs' is recommended by Isaiah for Hezekiah's boil (Is. xxxviii. 21). The good Samaritan used wine and oil as a local treatment (Lk. x. 34). Such treatment is often ineffective, however, as in the case of the woman with the issue of blood (Mk. v. 26), or conditions are apparently intrinsically incurable, as in the case of Mephibosheth (2 Sa. iv. 4). In Dt. xxviii. 27 there is a note of despair about some illnesses. It is not surprising that treatment is sometimes bound up with superstition, such as the attempt by Leah and Rachel to use mandrakes to increase sexual desire in infertility (Gn. xxx. 14–16). Wine is twice mentioned as a medicament and stimulant (Pr. xxxi. 6; 1 Tim. v. 23).

The word physician is rarely used, but implies much the same as 'doctor' in English today (Heb. *rāpā'*, *e.g.* Ex. xv. 26; Je. viii. 22; Gk. *iatros*, Mk. v. 26; Lk. viii. 43). Asa is condemned (2 Ch. xvi. 12) for consulting 'physicians', but these may have been pagan, magically minded, and worthless, and not really deserving the name of physician. The point of the condemnation is that he 'sought not to the Lord'. Job condemns his comforters as 'physicians of no value' (Jb. xiii. 4). In the New Testament physicians are twice mentioned proverbially by Christ (Lk. iv. 23, v. 31). They are mentioned in the incident of the woman who had an issue of blood (Lk. viii. 43). Luke is referred to by Paul as 'the beloved physician' (Col. iv. 14).

The Jewish religion differed from many pagan ones in that there was almost no confusion between the offices of priest and physician. Declaration of diagnosis of, and freedom from, leprosy is an exception (Lv. xiii. 9–17; Lk. xvii. 14). Prophets were consulted about prognosis (see, *e.g.*, 1 Ki. xiv. 1–13; 2 Ki. i. 1–4, viii. 9; Is. xxxviii. 1, 21). A primitive form of bone-setting is mentioned in Ezk. xxx. 21. Midwifery was in the hands of women, who had probably considerable experience, perhaps little skill, and certainly no training (Gn. xxxviii. 27–30; Ex. i. 15–21; Ezk. xvi. 4, 5). It is remarkable that medical practice changed so little in its essentials over the centuries during which the events described in the Bible occurred that it is possible to speak of the whole time as though it were a relatively circumscribed period, and there was scarcely any element in it which could be dignified with the name of science.

c. Hygiene and sanitation

One respect in which Jewish medicine was better than that of contemporary peoples was the remarkable sanitary code of the Israelites in Moses' time. Rendle Short gives an excellent short account of this (*The Bible and Modern Medicine*, pp. 37–46). Although generally referred to as a code, the details are, in fact, scattered through the Pentateuch. The Jews, as a nation, might not have survived their time in the wilderness, or the many other vicissitudes through which they passed, without the sanitary code. It deals with public hygiene, water supply, sewage disposal, inspection and selection of food, and control of infectious disease. The most interesting thing about it is that it implies a knowledge which the Jews did not possess beforehand and which in the circumstances of the Exodus and the wilderness wanderings they could scarcely have discovered for themselves, *e.g.* the prohibition, as food, of pigs and of animals which had died natural deaths, the burial of excreta, *etc.*, and the contagious nature of some diseases. The ultimate origin of the word 'quarantine' is the Jewish use of the period of forty days of segregation from patients with certain diseases (Lv. xii. 1–4) adopted by the Italians in the 14th century because of the relative immunity of Jews from certain plagues.

In a number of respects the biblical outlook on the sick, and on health in general, has a bearing on modern medical practice, and is perhaps more up-to-date than is generally realized. The story

Fig. 68. A Syrian settler in Egypt whose leg shows deformation typical of infantile paralysis. Stele of c. 13th century BC.

of the good Samaritan (Lk. x. 30–37) presents an ideal of care which has always inspired the profession, and typifies selflessness and after-care. There is more than a little in the Bible about what might be called 'the medicine of the family', the ideal of marriage among the Jews being a high one. The instructions to members of families in Eph. v. 22–vi. 4, if obeyed, would be excellent preventive psychiatry. The words for health are infrequently used in the Old Testament, and then always figuratively (*e.g.* Je. xxx. 17, xxxiii. 6; Ps. xlii. 11; Pr. xii. 18). 'Health' is used once in the AV of the New Testament, to mean general well-being, and is here a translation of *sōtēria* (salvation), Acts xxvii. 34. *Holoklēria* (AV 'perfect soundness', Acts iii. 16) is referred to above.

III. MIRACLES OF HEALING

In its simplest sense the word healing means the restoration to normal of a patient suffering from a remediable disorder, organic, or psychological, or both. It may also be used for the spontaneous improvement without major medical intervention which occurs in most illnesses anyway. It includes the improvement in a patient's outlook on his condition even if no physical amelioration is possible, and even a correction of a patient's misconception of the nature of his illness. In psychological disorders the term is used to describe an improved mental state. It is important that these different facets of the meaning of the word be realized, because the biblical miracles of healing (apart from cases of demon possession) show healing in its primary medical sense of the restoration to normal in cases of organic disease. Any cases claimed as present-day miracles must show comparably outstanding cases of the healing of organic disorders. Changes in spiritual outlook, an improved acceptance of an organically incurable condition, or the natural and spontaneous remission of disease, are all continually occurring, but do not partake of the miraculous, in the strict theological sense of 'a striking interposition of divine power by which the operations of the ordinary course of nature are overruled, suspended or modified' (*Chambers' Encyclopaedia*, art. 'Miracle'). There are, of course, natural recoveries from illness, as well as miracles, recorded in the Bible, and in fact probably most recoveries other than the miraculous ones were natural, because of the almost complete ineffectiveness of therapy in ancient times.

a. Miraculous healing in the Old Testament

Even if medical means were also used, recovery in the Old Testament is generally attributed to the intervention of God, *e.g.* the recovery of Moses (Ex. iv. 24–26) from the illness associated with his disobedience over his son's circumcision is given an entirely spiritual significance. The healing of Miriam's leprosy (Nu. xii. 1–15) and of Naaman, through Elisha (2 Ki. v. 8–14), appear to be miraculous. The healing of Jeroboam's suddenly paralysed hand (1 Ki. xiii. 4–6) and the raising from the dead of the son of the widow of Zarephath by Elijah (1 Ki. xvii. 17–24) and of the son of the Shunammite woman by Elisha (2 Ki. iv. 1–37) are clearly miraculous. This boy's illness has been attributed to sunstroke; but it could equally well have been a fulminating encephalitis or a subarachnoid haemorrhage. (The Jews were conscious of the effects of the sun (see Ps. cxxi. 6), and a case of sunstroke is reported in the Apocrypha, Judith viii. 2, 3.) The recovery of the Israelites bitten by the serpents when they looked on the brazen serpent is miraculous also, though individuals are not specified (Nu. xxi. 6–9). The salvation of the Israelites from the later plagues in Egypt is a curious example of what might be termed a 'prophylactic miracle', *i.e.* for them disease was miraculously prevented rather than miraculously healed. The recovery of Hezekiah (2 Ki. xx. 1–11) was probably natural, though it is attributed directly to God (verse 8) and is accompanied by a nature miracle (verses 9–11); the illness was probably a severe carbuncle.

Miraculous healing, even counting raising from the dead, is unusual in the Old Testament, and the few cases seem to cluster about the two critical times of the Exodus and the ministry of Elijah and Elisha. See Ex. vii. 10–12 for nature miracles performed by Moses and Aaron. The miracles apparently performed by the Egyptian sorcerers (Ex. vii. 22) were probably counterfeits, as they could not cope with the plague of boils (Ex. ix. 11). See also MIRACLES.

b. Miraculous healing in the Gospels

Our Lord's miracles of healing are reported by the synoptists as groups (*e.g.* Lk. iv. 40, 41) and, in greater detail and more specifically, as individual cases. Demon possession is clearly distinguished from other forms of disease (*e.g.* Mk. i. 32–34, where *kakōs echein* is separate from *daimonizomenos*). People came to Him in large numbers (Mt. iv. 23, 24) and were all healed (Lk. iv. 40). Doubtless cases of mental as well as of physical illness were included, and on one occasion our Lord even restored a severed part of the body (Lk. xxii. 50, 51). At the same time, these recorded instances can represent only a small fraction of those ill in the country at this time.

In the combined narrative of the four Gospels there are about two dozen stories of the healing of individuals or of small groups. Some were healed at a distance, some with a word but without physical contact, some with physical contact, and some with physical contact and 'means', *i.e.* the use of clay made from spittle, which was a popular remedy of the time for blindness (Mk. viii. 23; Jn. ix. 6) and deafness (Mk. vii. 32–35). This may have been to aid the patient's faith, or to demonstrate that God does not exclude the use of means, or both. (The realization of the connection between deafness and dumbness in this latter case is interesting.)

The individual case-reports refer to illnesses which are predominantly organic. Healing is instantaneous, or almost so; it occurs in cases where recovery is unlikely or problematical, and there appears to be immediate restoration to health with no convalescence or rehabilitation, and no relapse.

Luke's Gospel is the only one to give the story of the good Samaritan. It also includes three miracles of healing not recorded by the other evangelists. These are the raising of the son of the widow of Nain (vii. 11–16), the healing of the woman 'bowed together' (xiii. 11–16), and the healing of Malchus' ear (xxii. 50, 51). More details of cases are given, and the writer uses the more technical *iaomai* for healing, rather than the non-technical words.

The fourth evangelist, unlike the synoptists, never refers to healing of people in large numbers, nor to demon possession (though demons are referred to, and the word *daimonizomenos* is used, Jn. x. 21). In addition to the raising of Lazarus from the dead, only three cases are described. These are the healing of the nobleman's son of a serious febrile condition (iv. 46–54), the man paralysed thirty-eight years (v. 1–16), and the man born blind (ix. 1–14). The accounts are well documented, and all describe cases of apparently organic disorder instantly or almost instantly healed. The raising of Lazarus after four days (xi. 1–44) is no less miraculous, and the suggestion which has been made that this is no more remarkable than recovery after a few seconds' stoppage of the heartbeat during a surgical operation makes nonsense in the light of modern physiology. These miracles of healing in John's Gospel are not only mighty works (*dynameis*) but also signs (*sēmeia*). They demonstrate that Christ's miracles of healing have not only an individual, local, contemporary physical significance but a general, eternal, and spiritual meaning also. For example, in the case of the man born blind, the point is made that individual sickness is not necessarily attributable to individual sin. (In the case of the man sick of the palsy it is difficult to connect sickness and sin; *e.g.* syphilis seems to have been unknown at that time; his absolution by Christ does not necessarily imply a man whose illness was caused by sin.)

c. Miraculous healing in apostolic times

While the promise of healing powers in Mk. xvi. 18 is probably to be dismissed as being no part of the true text, Christ had commissioned the Twelve (Mt. x. 1) and the Seventy (Lk. x. 9). The Twelve were evidently commissioned for life, while the mission of the Seventy seems to have ended when they reported back (Lk. x. 17–20). In Acts there are several accounts of individual miracles, which have much the same character as those performed by Christ. The lame man in Jerusalem (iii. 1–11) and the one at Lystra (xiv. 8–10), the paralytic (ix. 33, 34), and Publius' father's dysentery ('bloody flux', AV, xxviii. 8) are individual cases, and there are a few reports of multiple healings, including that in v. 15, 16 and the unique case of the use of clothing taken from Paul (xix. 11, 12). Two people were raised from the dead (Dorcas, ix. 36–41, and Eutychus, xx. 9 f.) and demons were cast out on two occasions (v. 16 and xvi. 16–18). The author distinguishes between demon possession and other illness (v. 16).

Cases of illness among Christians in apostolic times are mentioned. The fact that they occur indicates that the apostolic commission to heal could not be used indiscriminately to keep themselves or their friends free from illness. Timothy had a gastric complaint (1 Tim. v. 23). Trophimus was too ill to accompany Paul from Miletus (2 Tim. iv. 20). Epaphroditus was gravely ill (Phil. ii. 30), and his recovery is attributed to the mercy of God (Phil. ii. 27). Most striking of all is Paul's enigmatic 'thorn in the flesh' (*skolops tē sarki*), which has been variously identified (most often as a chronic eye disease), but by few convincingly and by none conclusively. Its spiritual significance far exceeds its importance as an exercise in diagnosis. Paul gives three reasons (2 Cor. xii. 7–10) for it; 'to keep his feet on the ground' (v. 7), to enable him to be spiritually powerful (v. 9), and as a personal service to Christ (v. 10, 'for Christ's sake'). There is perhaps more resemblance between this 'thorn' and Jacob's shrunken sinew than has been realized.

The classical passage on prayer for the sick (Jas. v. 13–20) has suffered from two misinterpretations: that which finds in it authority for the institution of anointing those who are *in extremis*, and that which regards it as a promise that all who are sick and who are prayed over in faith will recover. The oil may have been used as was Christ's clay or spittle (see above) to reinforce faith, and may in some cases even have been medicinal. For a full discussion R. V. G. Tasker's Commentary on the Epistle (*TNTC*) should be consulted. The important points are that the outlook in the passage is spiritual (*i.e.* the matter is referred to God), the distress of the individual is made the concern of the Church, and what is said neither excludes nor condemns the use by doctors of the normal means of healing available at any particular time and place. The whole of this passage is really concerned with the power of prayer.

IV. THE SIGNIFICANCE OF THE MIRACLES OF HEALING

The miracles of healing reported in the Old Testament and in Acts are few compared with those of Christ reported in the Gospels. In general, it is true to say that the significance of the miracles of healing is not fundamentally different from that of other miracles. In the Old Testament miracles are more frequently nature miracles than miracles concerning the individual, while in the New Testament there are more recorded which affect individuals, such as the miracles of healing. Both display the power of God over evil and its effects. But the most important feature of miracles is their connection with revelation. 'Miracles do not appear on the page of Scripture vagrantly, here, there, and elsewhere indifferently, without assignable reason. They belong to revelation periods . . .' (Warfield, *op. cit.*, p. 191). Matthew connects Christ's healing miracles with the prophecy of Is. liii. 4 (Mt. viii. 17), and Christ Himself referred to them as evidence of the validity of His claims to be Messiah (Lk. vii. 22; Jn. x. 37, 38). They are spoken of as attesting Him (*apodeiknymi*, lit. 'point away to') in Acts ii. 22, in their threefold nature as wonders (*terata*), signs (*sēmeia*), and mighty works (*dynameis*). This explains, at least in part, why even Christ's miracles of healing were not indiscriminate and universal. Our Lord's reference to the 'greater works' which the apostles were to do (Jn. xiv. 12) must, of course, refer to the scope of the influence of their work, not its actual nature, for even when men were raised from the dead, these were not greater works than His. (See commentaries of Temple and of Westcott on this verse.) The *charismata* of 1 Cor. xii include both the gift of healing and the gift of speaking with tongues. Both seem to have been transitory, and this chapter must be read in the light of 1 Cor. xiii.

V. HEALING AFTER APOSTOLIC TIMES

This is, strictly, outside the scope of this article, but is relevant in that certain texts are quoted in favour of there being a possibility, and more, of miraculous healing mediated by Christians at the present day (*cf.* Jn. xiv. 12, above). However, there must be considerable caution in equating personal commands by Christ to the apostles with those which are generally binding upon Christians today. Such views are out of keeping with the general view of miracles as instruments and accompaniments of revelation. Great care must be exercised in avoiding the magical in a search for the miraculous. The ecclesiastical miracles of patristic times, often posthumously attributed, sometimes became absurd. It has also been shown that the frequently quoted passages in Irenaeus, Tertullian, and Justin Martyr which purport to show that miracles of healing continued well into the 3rd century will not in fact bear that interpretation. Post-apostolic claims should therefore be treated with extreme care. But this cautious attitude should not be confused with modern materialistic unbelief and scepticism.

BIBLIOGRAPHY. A. Edersheim, *The Life and Times of Jesus the Messiah*[12], 1906, Appendix XVI; V. Edmunds and C. G. Scorer, *Some Thoughts on Faith Healing*, 1956 (Report of a medical study group); H. W. Frost, *Miraculous Healing*, 1951; J. N. Geldenhuys, *Commentary on the Gospel of St. Luke*, 1950 (note on demon possession, pp. 174–175); J. S. McEwen, *SJT*, VII, 1954, pp. 133–152 (deals with miracles in patristic times); A. Rendle Short, *The Bible and Modern Medicine*, 1953 (brief but very helpful); R. V. G. Tasker, *The General Epistle of James*, 1956, pp. 126–133 (on Jas. v. 13–20); W. Temple, *Readings in St. John's Gospel*, 1943; B. B. Warfield, *Miracles: Yesterday and Today, True and False*, 1954 (reprint of *Counterfeit Miracles*, 1918; scholarly, exhaustive, and extremely valuable); A. P. Waterson, 'Faith Healing and Faith Healers', *Theology*, LX, 1957, pp. 8–16; L. Weatherhead, *Psychology, Religion and Healing*[2], 1957 (chapters on demon possession, Christian Science, and Lourdes; pp. 96–108, 147–159, 160–200); B. F. Westcott, *The Gospel according to St. John*, 1908; R. G. Cochrane, *Biblical Leprosy*, 1961. A.P.W.

DISPERSION. The term 'Dispersion' (Gk. *diaspora*) can denote either the Jews scattered in the non-Jewish world (as in Jn. vii. 35) or the places in which they reside (as in Judith v. 19).

I. ORIGINS

It is difficult to know how early the voluntary dispersion of Israel began; there are hints of an early 'colony' in Damascus (1 Ki. xx. 34), and Solomon's expansionist policies may well have led to earlier commercial outposts. But the conquering kings of Assyria and Babylonia introduced a new factor, the compulsory transplantation of sections of the population to other parts of their Empire (2 Ki. xv. 29, xvii. 6, xxiv. 14 ff., xxv. 11 ff.). Involved in this policy was the removal of the classes providing the natural leadership and the skilled craftsmen. Many of these transplanted groups, especially from the northern kingdom, probably lost their national and religious identity, but the Judaean community in Babylon had a rich prophetic ministry, learned to retain the worship of the God of Israel without Temple or sacrifice, and produced the purposeful men who returned to rebuild Jerusalem. Only a portion, however, returned under Cyrus; a sizeable and intensely self-conscious Jewish community remained in mediaeval times, with its own recension of the Talmud.

II. EXTENT

The Israelites abroad were not forgotten at home, and prophetic pictures of God's gracious intervention in the last times include the happy restoration of 'the dispersed of Israel' (*e.g.* Is. xi. 12; Zp. iii. 10; *cf.* also Ps. cxlvii. 2, where LXX significantly renders 'the *diasporas* of Israel'). The area of the prophets' visions is often much wider than the Assyrian and Babylonian Empires. In other words, another dispersion—probably originally voluntary, but reinforced, as Je. xliii. 7, xliv. 1 shows, by refugees—had already begun. Jews were settling in Egypt and beyond, and in less-known areas. Some rather lurid light is cast on what the communities in Egypt could be like by the Aramaic papyri found at Elephantine (see PAPYRI, SEVENEH) as distant as the First Cataract, from a Jewish trading-community with its own altar and idiosyncrasies.

With Alexander the Great's conquests a new era of the Dispersion begins: a steadily increasing stream of Jewish immigrants is noticed in the most diverse places. In the 1st century AD Philo numbered the Jews in Egypt at a million (*In Flaccum*, VI). Strabo the geographer, somewhat earlier, notes the number and status of the Jews in Cyrene, adding: 'This people has already made its way into every city, and it is not easy to find any place in the habitable world which has not received this nation and in which it has not made its power felt' (quoted by Jos., *Ant.* xiv. 7. 2, Loeb edition).

Of the general truth of Strabo's estimate there is abundant evidence. Syria had large Jewish 'colonies'. Juster listed seventy-one cities in Asia Minor which the Dispersion affected: the list could doubtless be augmented today. Roman writers such as Horace testify in no friendly fashion to the presence and habits of Jews in the capital. As early as 139 BC there was an expulsion of the Jews from Rome: the edict mentioned in Acts xviii. 2 had several precedents. But somehow the Jews always came back. For all their unpopularity—barely concealed in the speeches of the governors Pilate and Gallio, quite evident in the mob-cries of Philippi (Acts xvi. 20) and Ephesus (Acts xix. 34)—the Jews established themselves as a kind of universal exception. Their social exclusiveness, their incomprehensible taboos, and their uncompromising religion were all tolerated. They alone might be exempted from 'official' sacrifices, and (since they would not march on the sabbath) from military service. Under Seleucids, Ptolemies, and Romans alike, the Dispersion, with much patent dislike to face, and occasionally outbreaks of savage violence, enjoyed, in the main, peace and prosperity.

The spread of the Dispersion was not confined to the Roman Empire: it was prominent in the Persian sphere of influence too, as the account of the Pentecost crowd illustrates (Acts ii. 9–11). Josephus has revealing stories of Jewish freebooters of Fra Diavolo stature in Parthia (*Ant.* xviii. 9. 1 ff.), and of the conversion and circumcision of the king of the buffer state of Adiabene (*Ant.* xx. 2. 1 ff.).

III. CHARACTERISTICS

The oddities of Elephantine are not typical of later Dispersion Judaism. The life of most of these communities lay in the law and the synagogue, though it may be noted that the refugee Zadokite high priest Onias set up a temple at Leontopolis in Egypt, in the 2nd century BC, on the basis of Is. xix. 18 ff., and said that most of the Egyptian Jews had temples 'contrary to what is proper' (*Ant.* xiii. 3. 1). But in the nature of things they could not live exactly as the Jews in Palestine. The westward Dispersion had to live in the Greek world, and it had to speak Greek. One major result of this was the translation of the sacred books into Greek, the Septuagint (see TEXT AND VERSIONS). The legends about its origin at least bear witness to the missionary spirit of Hellenistic Judaism. Although it may be misleading to generalize from Alexandria, we can see there a prosperous and educated Jewish community seeking to make intellectual contact with an established Greek culture. The 'de-Messianized' but otherwise orthodox Judaism of the Book of Wisdom and Philo are characteristic products. There is evidence also of Jewish missionary apologetic directed to pagans of Greek education, and of codes of instruction for pagan converts. There is perhaps a slightly satirical commentary on Diaspora Judaism's understanding of its mission in Rom. ii. 17–24.

Hellenistic Jewish culture was faithful to law and nation (*cf.* Phil. iii. 5, 6—the confession of a Jew of the Dispersion). The communities paid the half-shekel temple tax, and maintained contact with each other and with Jerusalem (*cf.* Acts xxviii. 21 f.). The devout visited Jerusalem for the great feasts when possible (Acts ii. 5 ff., viii. 27) and often had closer ties with the mother-country. But so different had the cultural atmosphere become that the Dispersion communities had their own synagogues there (*cf.* Acts vi. 9). It is possible that Stephen learned some of his radicalism about the Temple from Diaspora Judaism in pre-conversion days.

Notwithstanding Jewish unpopularity, it is clear that Judaism strongly attracted many Gentiles. The simple but majestic worship of one God, the lofty ethics, the generally high standards of family life, brought many, including people of rank, to the synagogues. The necessity of circumcision probably held back many men from becoming full proselytes, but numbers remained in attendance as 'God-fearers' (see PROSELYTE). Thus we regularly find Gentiles in the synagogues during Paul's missionary journeys (*cf.* Acts xiii. 43 ff., xiv. 1, xvii. 4, xviii. 4 ff.).

A less happy aspect of the attraction of Judaism was the widespread belief, to which many sources testify, that Jews possessed special magical powers and that their sacred words were particularly efficacious in incantations. Undoubtedly unscrupulous Jews traded on this reputation, and we meet one such in Acts xiii. 6 ff. It is likely, too, that there was a fringe of Jewish syncretistic and sectarian teaching which dealt in the mystery and occult so fascinating to the Hellenistic world. Some pagan cults—such as the Sabazios cult in Phrygia—eagerly scattered Judaic ingredients into their exotically flavoured religious pot-pourri; but, however important these may be for the history of Christian heresy (see GNOSTICISM), there is little evidence that they were in themselves representative of and significant for Dispersion Judaism as a whole. As might be expected, archaeological study reveals considerable formal differences, and differing degrees of cultural exclusiveness, at various times and places; but nothing indicates that there was any major indecision in Diaspora Judaism as to the uniqueness of Israel's God, His revelation in the Torah, and His people.

IV. RELATION TO CHRISTIANITY

The influence of the Dispersion in preparing the way for the gospel is beyond doubt. The synagogues stretched over the greater part of the known world were the stepping-stones of the early missionaries. Acts shows Paul, the self-confessed apostle to the Gentiles, regularly opening his evangelistic work by synagogue preaching.

Almost as regularly a division follows, the majority of Israelites by birth refusing the proffered Messiah, the Gentiles (*i.e.* the proselytes and God-fearers) receiving Him joyfully. Representative converts, such as Cornelius and the Ethiopian eunuch, had first been proselytes or God-fearers. Clearly the God-fearers—children of the Dispersion—are a vital factor in early Church history. They came to faith with some previous knowledge of God and the Scriptures, and already watchful of idolatry and immorality.

The LXX also performed a missionary service beyond its effect on those Gentiles in contact with synagogues; and more than one Christian Father testifies that the reading of the LXX played a vital part in his conversion.

An apparent confusion in some pagan writers makes it difficult to tell whether Judaism or Christianity is alluded to. This may be due to the fact that so often a Christian community arose within the bosom of Diaspora Judaism: and to an ignorant or indifferent pagan, even if he believed the horror stories about Christian arson and cannibalism, the attitude of converts towards many traditional practices might seem to be Jewish. On the other hand, the Jewish influences on many leading converts helps to explain why 'Judaizing' was such a peril in the apostolic Church.

It is interesting that Peter and James, both Palestinian Jews, address Christians as 'the Dispersion' (Jas. i. 1; 1 Pet. i. 1; see RV). Like the members of the old dispersion, they are 'sojourners' where they live; they enjoy a solidarity unknown to the heathen; and they owe a transcendent loyalty to Jerusalem which is above.

BIBLIOGRAPHY. J. Juster, *Les Juifs dans l'Empire Romain*, 1914; A. Causse, *Les Dispersés d'Israel*, 1929; E. Schürer, *History of the Jewish People*, 1905, *etc.*, II, 2, pp. 219 ff.; *BC*, I, pp. 137 ff.; E. R. Goodenough, *Jewish Symbols in the Greco-Roman period*, 8 vols. to date (relation to pagan symbolism); R. McL. Wilson, *The Gnostic Problem*, 1958. A.F.W.

DISTAFF. See SPINNING AND WEAVING.

DIVES. See LAZARUS.

DIVINATION. The usual word translated 'divination' and 'diviner' is the root *qsm*. The root *nḥš* is used in Gn. xliv. 5, 15, and elsewhere this is translated 'enchanter', 'enchantment', 'use enchantments'. The root *'nn* is sometimes coupled with the former words, and is translated 'observe times' (RV 'practise augury'), and twice 'soothsayings'.

Divination is roughly the attempt to discern events that are distant in time or space, and that consequently cannot be perceived by normal means. A similar definition could be given for the seership aspect of prophecy, as exercised in, *e.g.*, 1 Sa. ix. 6–10. Hence the term could be used occasionally in a good sense, as we might speak of a prophet having clairvoyant gifts without thereby approving all forms of clairvoyance. Thus Balaam is a diviner as well as being inspired of God (Nu. xxii. 7, xxiv. 1). The divination condemned in Ezk. xiii. 6, 7 is specified as 'lying'. In Mi. iii. 6, 7, 11 divining is a function of the prophets, though here also they have prostituted their gift; *cf.* Zc. x. 2. In Pr. xvi. 10 *qesem* ('divine sentence') is used of the divine guidance given through the king.

Apart from these general uses, divination is condemned, except for two passages noted below. God's people are forbidden to use divination and enchantments as the pagan world did (Lv. xix. 26; Dt. xviii. 9–14), and 2 Ki. xvii. 17, xxi. 6 record their disobedience. Pagan diviners are mentioned in 1 Sa. vi. 2; Is. xliv. 25; Ezk. xxi. 22.

Divination may take many forms. One can make two broad divisions, namely, internal and mechanical: the former is either the trance inspiration of the shaman type or direct second sight; the latter makes use of technical means, such as sand, sticks, entrails of a sacrifice, or in modern times tea-leaves. These divisions cannot be pressed, since the objects may release the clairvoyant faculty, as with crystal-gazing. Balaam may have released his powers in this way (Nu. xxiv. 1).

The following forms are mentioned in the Bible.

a. Rhabdomancy. Ezk. xxi. 21. Sticks or arrows were thrown into the air, and omens were deduced from their position when they fell. Ho. iv. 12 could also be a reference to this.

b. Hepatoscopy. Ezk. xxi. 21. Examination of the liver or other entrails of a sacrifice was supposed to give guidance. Probably shapes and markings were classified, and the priest interpreted them. See fig. 135.

c. Teraphim (*q.v.*). Associated with divination in 1 Sa. xv. 23; Ezk. xxi. 21; Zc. x. 2 (RV in each case). If the teraphim were images of dead ancestors, the divination was probably a form of spiritualism.

d. Necromancy, or the consultation of the departed. This is associated with divination in Dt. xviii. 11; 1 Sa. xxviii. 8; 2 Ki. xxi. 6, and is condemned in the Law (Lv. xix. 31, xx. 6), the Prophets (Is. viii. 19, 20), and the historical books (1 Ch. x. 13). The medium was spoken of as having an *'ôḇ*, translated 'a familiar spirit', or in modern terms 'a control'. The term is associated with *yid'ônî*, probably from the root *yāḏa'*, 'know', and presumably refers to the supernatural knowledge claimed by the spirit and in a secondary sense by its owner. This word is uniformly translated 'wizard' in the AV. The only use of the term 'necromancer' in the AV is Dt. xviii. 11, where the Heb. means literally 'one who inquires of the dead'.

e. Astrology draws conclusions from the position of the sun, moon, and planets in relation to the zodiac and to one another. While not condemned, astrology is belittled in Is. xlvii. 13 and Je. x. 2. The exact meaning of the word *'aššāp̄*, translated 'astrologer' in Dn. i. 20, *etc.*, is uncertain. There is no proof that the wise men who came to the infant Jesus were astrologers, since the star is spoken of as though it had an unusual course, such as a comet has (Mt. ii. 9).

f. Hydromancy, or divination through water. Here forms and pictures appear in the water in a bowl, as also in crystal-gazing. The gleam of the water induces a state of light trance, and the visions are subjective. The only reference to this in the Bible is Gn. xliv. 5, 15, where it might appear that Joseph used his silver cup for this purpose. But one cannot say how much credence to give to a statement that comes in a section where Joseph and his steward are deliberately deceiving his brethren.

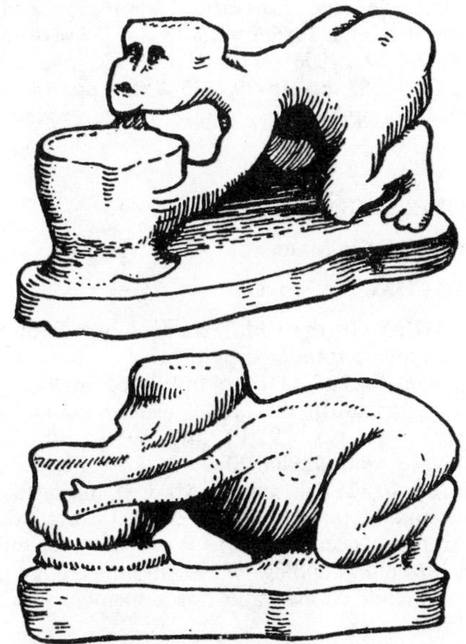

Fig. 69. Two Egyptian statuettes each showing a kneeling figure with chin resting on the rim of a bowl clasped in the arms. These may possibly represent cup-divination, *i.e.* observing portents from the configurations of drops of oil on water in the bowl. Probably Middle Kingdom, 19th–18th centuries BC.

g. Lots. In the Old Testament the lot was cast to discover God's will for the allocation of territory (Jos. xviii, xix, *etc.*), the choice of the goat to be sacrificed on the Day of Atonement (Lv. xvi), the detection of a guilty person (Jos. vii. 14; Jon. i. 7), the allocation of temple duties (1 Ch. xxiv. 5), the discovery of a lucky day by Haman (Est. iii. 7). In the New Testament Christ's clothes were allocated by lot (Mt. xxvii. 35). The last occasion in the Bible on which the lot is used to divine the will of God is in the choice of Matthias (Acts i. 15–26), and there may be a significance in that this is before Pentecost. (See also URIM AND THUMMIM.)

h. Dreams are often counted as a means of divination, but in the Bible there is no instance of a person's deliberately asking for guidance or supernatural knowledge through dreams, except perhaps the false prophets in Je. xxiii. 25–27. The spontaneous dream, however, is often a means of divine guidance. (See DREAM.)

The only use of the term 'divination' in the AV of the New Testament is Acts xvi. 16, where a girl has a spirit of divination. The Gk. here is *pythōn.* The famous Delphic oracle was in the district of Pytho, and the term evidently was used loosely for anyone supernaturally inspired, as was the priestess at Delphi.

See also MAGIC AND SORCERY.

J.S.W.

DIVORCE. See MARRIAGE.

DI-ZAHAB. One of the four names in Dt. i. 1 describing the place, or places, where Moses spoke the words which follow. These names have puzzled everybody. Di-zahab means 'place of gold', and the LXX boldly translated it *katachrysea.* The name is not found elsewhere and testifies to the early date when it was written (see HAZEROTH). G.T.M.

DOCTRINE. In the Old Testament the word occurs chiefly as a translation of *leqaḥ*, meaning 'what is received' (Dt. xxxii. 2; Jb. xi. 4; Pr. iv. 2; Is. xxix. 24). The idea of a body of revealed teaching is chiefly expressed by *tôrâ*, which occurs 216 times and is rendered as 'law'.

In the New Testament two words are used. *Didaskalia* means both the act and the content of teaching. It is used of the Pharisees' teaching (Mt. xv. 9; Mk. vii. 7). Apart from one instance in Colossians and one in Ephesians, it is otherwise confined to the Pastoral Epistles (and seems to refer often to some body of teaching used as a standard of orthodoxy). *Didachē* is used in more parts of the New Testament. It too can mean either the act or the content of teaching. It occurs of the teaching of Jesus (Mt. vii. 28, *etc.*) which He claimed to be divine (Jn. vii. 16, 17). After Pentecost Christian doctrine began to be formulated (Acts ii. 42) as the instruction given to those who had responded to the *kērygma* (Rom. vi. 17). There were some in the Church whose official function was to teach this to new converts (*e.g.* 1 Cor. xii. 28, 29). For the content of the *didachē*, see E. G. Selwyn, *The First Epistle of St. Peter*, 1946, Essay II. R.E.N.

DODANIM. The name of a people descended from Javan, son of Japheth, mentioned twice in the Old Testament (Gn. x. 4: Heb. *dōḏānîm*, LXX *Rhodioi*; 1 Ch. i. 7: Heb. *rôḏānîm*, LXX *Rhodioi*). The Genesis reference is probably to be read (with the Samaritan Pentateuch) *rōḏānîm* (*d* and *r* are readily confused in both the old and the 'square' Heb. scripts), referring to the inhabitants of the island of Rhodes. See E. Dhorme, *Syria*, XIII, 1932, pp. 48, 49. T.C.M.

DOG. The contempt and disgust with which the dog is regarded in the Old Testament cannot easily be understood by Western people, to whom the dog is a companion and an auxiliary. In many parts of the East the dog is still basically a scavenger, and although it played a very useful part in disposing of refuse, it was by its very nature unclean and a potential carrier of disease, and therefore could not be touched without defilement. Heb. *keleḇ* and Gk. *kyōn* are without doubt the semi-wild dog which roamed outside the walls waiting for dead bodies or rubbish to be thrown out. Dogs were differently regarded in Egypt, where they were used for hunting and also held in reverence.

A second Gk. word, the diminutive *kynarion*, is used in the incident of the Syrophoenician woman (Mt. xv. 26, 27; Mk. vii. 27, 28). The context suggests that this was a pet dog allowed to live about the house.

The 'dogs' of Phil. iii. 2 are Judaizing intruders who disturb the peace of the Church; the 'dogs' who are excluded from the new Jerusalem in Rev. xxii. 15 are people of unclean lives. G.C.

DOOR, DOORKEEPER. See HOUSE.

DOR. A city whose king joined with Jabin, king of Hazor, in his fight against Israel and shared in his defeat (Jos. xi. 1, 2, xii. 23). Though on the borders of Asher, it was given to Manasseh, who failed to drive out the Canaanite inhabitants (Jdg. i. 27). See also 1 Ki. iv. 11; 1 Ch. vii. 29. It is associated with, but distinguished from, En-dor (Jos. xvii. 11). It is mentioned as 'a town of the Tjeker' in the Wen-Amon Story, 11th century BC (*ANET*, p. 26). In Graeco-Roman times it was called Dora; according to Josephus (*Ant.* v. 1. 22, viii. 2. 3; *Ap.* ii. 10) it was on the Mediterranean coast, near Carmel. Mod. El-Burj, north of Tanturah. G.T.M.

DORCAS, or Tabitha ('gazelle'), was renowned for charity in the church at Joppa (Acts ix. 36). When she died they sent two members to Lydda for the apostle Peter. He came immediately, and following Jesus' example, excluded the mourners. Then he knelt and prayed, and fulfilled his divine commission (Mt. x. 8). She is the only woman disciple so called (*mathētria*) in the New Testament. M.G.

DOTHAN. The fertile plain of Dothan separates the hills of Samaria from the Carmel range. It provides an easy pass for travellers from Beth-shan and Gilead on their way to Egypt. This was the route of the Ishmaelites who carried Joseph into Egypt. The good pasturage had attracted Jacob's sons from Shechem, 20 miles to the south. Near the town (now *tell dōṯā*) are rectangular cisterns about 10 feet deep similar to the pit into which Joseph was put (Gn. xxxvii. 17 ff.). Elisha led the Syrian force, which had been sent to capture him, along the hill road to Samaria, 10 miles south. His servant was encouraged by a vision of heavenly forces arrayed on the hill to the east of the town (2 Ki. vi. 13–23).

Excavations since 1953 have revealed a continuous occupation from the Early Bronze Age until the time of the Assyrian invasions (*c.* 725 BC). The prosperous town of the second millennium was defended by strong walls but has not yet been investigated. Thothmes III lists Dothan among his conquests (*c.* 1480 BC). It was probably one of the towns which was absorbed by the Israelites, but not actually conquered (*cf.* Jdg. i. 27). Areas of the Iron Age town which have been cleared show the narrow streets and small houses with storage-pits and bread-ovens of Elisha's day. Among the finds are fifteen pieces of silver in a pottery box representing an individual's savings. There was also a Hellenistic settlement (*cf.* Judith iv. 6, vii. 3).

BIBLIOGRAPHY. Excavation reports by J. P. Free, *BA*, XIX, 1956, pp. 43–48, 1953–5 seasons; *BASOR*, 143, 1956, pp. 11–17, 152, 1958, pp. 10–18, 131, 1953, pp. 16–29, 135, 1954, pp. 14–20, 139, 1955, pp. 3–9. A.R.M.

DOUBT. See UNBELIEF.

DOVE. See BIRDS OF THE BIBLE.

DOWRY. See MARRIAGE.

DRACHM. See MONEY.

DRAGON. In the Old Testament two Hebrew words are so translated by the AV.

1. *tan*, 'jackal' (and so translated in RV). It always occurs in the plural, usually masculine (*tannîm*: Jb. xxx. 29; Ps. xliv. 19; Is. xiii. 22, xxxiv. 13, xxxv. 7, xliii. 20; Je. ix. 11, x. 22, xiv. 6, xlix. 33, li. 37; Ezk. xxix. 3; Mi. i. 8), but once in the feminine (*tannôṯ*: Mal. i. 3). In La. iv. 3 the form *tannîn* occurs, but this is probably *tan* with the rare plural ending *-în* (nunation, as found in the Moabite Stone), and not a member of (2) below.

2. *tannîn*. A word of uncertain meaning, probably unrelated to *tan*. It is translated in AV by 'dragon', 'whale' (Gn. i. 21; Jb. vii. 12) and 'serpent' (Ex. vii. 9, 10, 12), this last being a satisfactory rendering in the Exodus passage, and it also seems to be the sense in Dt. xxxii. 33 and Ps. xci. 13; and possibly in Ne. ii. 13. The other occurrences are less easy to define. In Gn. i. 21 evidently large sea-creatures such as the whale are intended, and this may be the meaning of Jb. vii. 12 and Ps. cxlviii. 7, though, on the basis of an Arabic cognate, 'water spout' is suggested by some (*e.g.* RVmg for the latter). In Ps. lxxiv. 13; Is. xxvii. 1 and li. 9, the crocodile may be intended, and the association with Egypt suggests the same possibility in Ezk. xxix. 3, xxxii. 2, and even Je. li. 34. None of these meanings can be certain, and in view of the New Testament (see below) the term may in some contexts refer to an apocalyptic creature of some kind.

In the New Testament *drakōn*, 'dragon', a word for an apocalyptic monster, is used figuratively of Satan in Rev. xii, xiii, xvi, and xx. The word is used in the LXX chiefly for *tannîn*.

BIBLIOGRAPHY. G. R. Driver in Z. V. Togan

(ed.), *Proceedings of the Twenty-Second Congress of Orientalists . . . Istanbul . . ., 1951*, II, 1957, pp. 114, 115; A. Heidel, *The Babylonian Genesis*[2], 1951, pp. 102–105. T.C.M.

DREAM. If one compares the 'dream' literature of the Babylonians and the Egyptians with the references to dreams in the Old Testament one is impressed by the Hebrews' lack of preoccupation with this phenomenon. Nor is the religious significance of the dreams that are recorded in the Old Testament at all prominent. Indeed, dreams are said to derive from the activities in which the dreamer has been immersed during the day (Ec. v. 3). However, the Old Testament recognizes that, whatever the origin of a dream, it may become a means by which God communicates with men, be they Israelites (1 Ki. iii. 5) or non-Israelites (Gn. xx. 3 ff.).

Dreams recorded in Scripture are of two kinds. Firstly, there are those consisting of the ordinary dream phenomena in which the sleeper 'sees' a connected series of images which correspond to events in everyday life (Gn. xl. 9–17, xli. 1–7). Secondly, there are dreams which communicate to the sleeper a message from God (Gn. xx. 3–7; 1 Ki. iii. 5–15; Mt. i. 20–24; Acts xviii. 9 f.). However, on occasion a vision and an accompanying communication were received simultaneously (Acts xvi. 9).

In common with contemporary peoples the Hebrews sought an explanation of their dream-experiences. But in the matter of the interpretation of dreams the Bible distinguishes between the dream-phenomena reported by non-Israelites and by Israelites. Gentiles such as Pharaoh (Gn. xli. 15 ff.) and his high-ranking officers (xl. 12 f., 18 f.) require Joseph to explain their dreams, and Nebuchadrezzar needs Daniel (Dn. ii. 17 ff.). On occasion God Himself speaks and so renders human intervention unnecessary (Gn. xx. 3 ff., xxxi. 24; Mt. ii. 12). But when the members of the covenant community dream, the interpretation accompanies the dream (Gn. xxxvii. 5–10; Acts xvi. 9 f.).

This subject is important for the Old Testament view of prophecy. Among the Hebrews there was a close association between dreams and the function of the prophet. The *locus classicus* is Dt. xiii. 1–5, but 1 Sa. ix. 9 remarks that 'a Prophet was beforetime called a Seer'. If 'seer' means a man of visions, then it supports Dt. xiii. 1, 3, 5, where the prophet is mentioned along with the dreamer without betraying any sense of incongruity. The close connection in Hebrew thought between dreaming and prophesying is again revealed in Je. xxiii. 25, 32. It is also clear that in the days of Samuel and Saul it was commonly believed that the Lord spoke through dreams as well as by Urim and prophets (1 Sa. xxviii. 6).

However, a revelation through dream-phenomena was thought of as being inferior to a revelation that was received by the prophet from the Lord at first hand. That is the conclusion which Nu. xii. 6–8 forces upon us. Jeremiah uses this same kind of distinction in his attempts to discredit the 'revelations' of the false prophets of his own day (xxiii. 25, 32). Jeremiah is not denying that God speaks through dreams but he is claiming that the Word of the Lord which came to the authentic prophet in his communion with God was infinitely superior to any 'revelation' that may have come through dreams. The first was a hammer and a fire (xxiii. 29) while the other was straw (verse 28).

BIBLIOGRAPHY. E. L. Ehrlich, *Der Traum im Alten Testament*, 1953; A. L. Oppenheim, *The Interpretation of Dreams in the Ancient Near East*, 1957. J.G.S.S.T.

DRESS. The Old Testament does not give us a detailed description of the various kinds of dress which were worn in Palestine. However, the Egyp., Bab., and Hittite monuments enable us to get a good idea of the general dress. In the tomb of Khnumhotep at Beni-Hassan (Egypt) we find a procession of Asiatics who arrive in Egypt with eyepaint (*ANEP*, fig. 3). They are all dressed in vividly coloured garments, and this gives a clue as to how Abraham and other nomads were clad in about the XIIth Egyptian Dynasty. See fig. 70*a* (12, 13) and also fig. 201.

According to Gn. iii. 7, 21 the origin of dress is associated with the sense of shame. It is a shame to be naked (Gn. ix. 22, 23) and this is especially the fate of prisoners and fugitives (Is. xx. 4; Am. ii. 16; Mk. xiv. 52). Children, however, used to run naked up to puberty.

The most important garments seem to have been a kind of loin- or waist-cloth, a long or short shirt or robe, an upper garment, and a cloak, not to speak of the belt, headdress, veil, and sandals.

a. Men's dress

We find but few mentions of a loin- or waist-cloth (*'ēzôr*) reaching from the waist to the knee. This was a common dress during the Bronze II and III ages, but it disappears as a civilian dress during Bronze III, although remaining as a military dress (Ezk. xxiii. 15; Is. v. 27). Almost as primitive is an animal skin and the hairy cloak or mantle (Zc. xiii. 4; 2 Ki. i. 8; Mt. iii. 4), which was worn only by prophets and poor people (Ecclus. xl. 4) or for penitence. Covering of the hips and thighs was required only of priests (Ex. xxviii. 42, xxxix. 28). Otherwise these breeches were unknown in the Old Testament and in the Ancient Near East, except among the Persians, who knew the *šalwâr*. The exact meaning of the *sarbâl* of Dn. iii. 21, 27 is unknown.

The ordinary shirt, which becomes predominant in Bronze III and is the normal dress in the Iron Age, is mentioned in the Bible as *kuttōneṯ* (Gk. *chitôn*), which seems to have been made of linen or wool. It is worn next to the skin and reaches down to the knees or to the ankles. It is made with or without sleeves, short or long (see Benzinger, *Hebr. Arch.*, figs. 59, 60; Marston, *The Bible Comes Alive*, plate 15, bottom). For

Fig. 70*a*. Dress in biblical times. Many of these illustrations are taken from royal monuments which tend to depict only important personages in detail. The ordinary dress of the peasant varied little throughout the period of biblical history. 1. Sumerian charioteer wearing a fleece. 2. Dress of a Babylonian citizen of Abraham's time. 3. Babylonian king, *c*. 1050 BC. 4. A soldier from NW Syria, *c*. 750 BC. 5. An Egyptian nobleman wearing a simple kilt and a collar. 6, 7, 8. A pharaoh, a prince, and a noblewoman of Egypt, *c*. 1150 BC. 9. Egyptian soldiers. 10. Slaves in Egypt. 11. Philistine warriors with plumed helmets. 12, 13. Nomads from Palestine of the time of the Patriarchs. 14. A Syrian bringing tribute to Egypt.

Fig. 70*b*. Dress in biblical times (continued). 1, 3, 4. Judaeans as depicted on the sculptures of Sennacherib's capture of Lachish; 3 and 4 wear simple tunics and the woman a long wimple. 2. A bearer of tribute from Jehu of Israel to the king of Assyria, *c*. 850 BC (*cf*. pl. VII*a*). 5, 6. Assyrian archers; 5 is wearing a jerkin of scale armour. 7, 8. Assyrian king and queen wearing richly embroidered clothes. 9. Darius of Persia. 10. An Elamite archer-spearman. 11, 12. Man and woman of the Hellenistic period wearing the *himation*. 13. A Roman citizen wearing a *toga* over his *tunica*. 14. Roman soldiers, one of them carrying a standard.

work or while running, this shirt was pulled up (Ex. xii. 11; 2 Ki. iv. 29). The Bible also mentions a *kuttōneṯ passîm*, which was a special kind of garment (Gn. xxxvii. 3, 23, 32), and was worn also by princes (2 Sa. xiii. 18, 19). It was possibly a highly coloured garment, a kind of plaid twisted round the body, as is shown by the Syrian ambassadors to Tutankhamūn (see *ANEP*, fig. 52). The shirt, presumably worn underneath it, is possibly the *sāḏin* (Jdg. xiv. 12; Pr. xxxi. 24; Is. iii. 23; LXX *sindōn*), but might include in this class of garments the *m*[e]*'îl*, regularly torn as a sign of mourning (Ezr. ix. 3; Jb. i. 20, ii. 12), and worn by men of importance, *e.g.* Jonathan (1 Sa. xviii. 4), Samuel (1 Sa. ii. 19, xv. 27, xxviii. 14), Saul (1 Sa. xxiv. 4, 11), Job and his friends (Jb. i. 20, ii. 12), and Ezra (Ezr. ix. 3).

The ordinary mantle is generally called *śimlâ*. It can be identified with the '*abâye* of the modern *fellahin* (Benzinger, *Hebr. Arch.*, fig. 73). This is a more or less square piece of cloth, which is sometimes thrown over one shoulder or, as now, over both shoulders. There are openings for the arms at the sides. This cloak, which everybody possessed, could not be given in loan, as it was used at night as a covering (Ex. xxii. 25, 26; Dt. xxiv. 13). It was generally taken off for work (Mt. xxiv. 18; Mk. x. 50). It was also used to carry all kinds of objects (see Ex. xii. 34; Jdg. viii. 25; 2 Ki. iv. 39; Hg. ii. 12).

Another cloak was called *'addereṯ*, which it is not easy to describe. It was sometimes made of a costly material (Jos. vii. 21, 24) and was worn by the king (Jon. iii. 6) and by prophets (1 Ki. xix. 13, 19; 2 Ki. ii. 13, 14), where it was possibly made from animal's skin. It was not in general use, and the word does not appear in late Hebrew.

Notable men and women wore in later times the *ṣānîp̄* (Is. iii. 23, lxii. 3), which was a piece of cloth twisted round the head.

The poor people generally went about barefoot, but the sandal was known (Dt. xxv. 10; Am. ii. 6, viii. 6). The soles (*n*[e]*'ālîm*) were of leather or wood and tied with thongs (*ś*[e]*rôḵ*) (Gn. xiv. 23; Is. v. 27; Mk. i. 7; Lk. iii. 16). These were taken off inside the house.

b. Women's dress

The dress of women was very much the same as that for men. But the difference must have been sufficiently noticeable, because it was forbidden for men to wear women's clothes, and vice-versa (Dt. xxii. 5). The difference has to be sought in finer material, more colours, and the use of a veil and a kind of headcloth (*miṭpaḥaṯ*: Is. iii. 22), which could be used to carry loads (see Benzinger, *Hebr. Arch.*, fig. 59, or Marston, *loc. cit.*). The most common dresses for the Israelite women are the *kuttōneṯ* and the *śimlâ*. The fine underwear *saḏîn* is also worn by women (Pr. xxxi. 24; Is. iii. 23). For feasts, women wore a more costly attire (1 Tim. ii. 9). Hip and thigh clothing was not worn. A long train or veil was used by ladies of rank (Is. xlvii. 2; Na. iii. 5). Articles mentioned in the catalogue of Is. iii. 18 ff. cannot now be more particularly identified.

c. Dress for special occasions

Festive attire was distinctive from ordinary dress only in that the material was more costly (Gn. xxvii. 15; Mt. xxii. 11, 12; Lk. xv. 22). The colour was preferably white (Ec. ix. 8; Mk. ix. 3; Rev. iii. 4). Tissues of byssus, scarlet, and purple were much appreciated (Pr. xxxi. 22; Ecclus. vi. 30; Je. iv. 30). Women liked to adorn their clothes with gold and silver (2 Sa. i. 24; Ps. xlv. 9, 14, 15; Ezk. xvi. 10, 13, xxvii. 7).

Dress for mourning and penitence (*śaq*) was probably some kind of haircloth similar to the mantle of the prophets. This was worn with a belt and sometimes on the naked body (Gn. xxxvii. 34; 2 Sa. iii. 31; 1 Ki. xxi. 27; 2 Ki. vi. 30).

d. Dress of priests

The oldest sacred dress seems to have been the *'ēp̄ôḏ baḏ*, probably a simple loin-cloth (2 Sa. vi. 14, 20). The priests of Nob were known as men who wore the 'linen ephod' (1 Sa. xxii. 18). Samuel (1 Sa. ii. 18) and David (2 Sa. vi. 14) wore a simple linen ephod. This ordinary ephod has to be distinguished from the ephod of the high priest made of costly material (byssus = *šēš*), worked with gold, purple, scarlet, or the like. This part of the dress reached from the breast down to the hips. It was held in place by two shoulder-bands and was tied round the waist (Ex. xxxix. 1–26). There is also mention of an ephod which was used for the oracles. This was hung in the Temple (1 Sa. xxi. 9). The ordinary priests wore during the liturgical service a cloth which covered the hips and thighs (Ex. xxviii. 42, 43; Lv. xvi. 4) and a long embroidered linen tunic with sleeves (Ex. xxviii. 40, xxxix. 27), also an elaborately worked belt of twined linen, blue, purple, and scarlet stuff (Ex. xxviii. 40, xxxix. 29). (See Nötscher, *Bibl. Alterumskunde*, 1940, fig. 109.) They had also a kind of turban called *miṣnep̄eṯ* (Ex. xxviii. 4, 37, 39, xxix. 6, xxxix. 28). As in Egypt and Babylon, it was forbidden for priests to wear woollen clothes (Ezk. xliv. 17). They were not allowed to wear sandals in the Temple (Ex. iii. 5, xxix. 20).

BIBLIOGRAPHY. In general, see the following. M. G. Houston, *Ancient Egyptian and Persian Costume and Decoration*[2], 1954; *ANEP*, figs. 1–66 and *passim*; H. F. Lutz, *Textiles and Customs among the People of the Ancient Near East*, 1923. Near East with special reference to the Old Testament, I. Benzinger, *Hebräische Archäologie*[3], 1927, pp. 72–89. Egyptian material in A. Erman, *Life in Ancient Egypt*, 1894 (old but useful), pp. 200–233, and M. A. Murray, *The Splendour that was Egypt*, 1949, pp. 120–122. All these works are profusely illustrated. C.D.W.

DRINK. See MEALS; WINE AND STRONG DRINK.

DROMEDARY. See CAMEL.

DROPSY (Gk. *hydrōpikos*, 'full of water', Lk. xiv. 2). Dropsy is strictly not a disease in itself, but rather a sign of disease of the heart, kidneys, or liver. See DISEASE AND HEALING.

DRUNKENNESS. See WINE AND STRONG DRINK.

DRUSILLA. Born in AD 38 (Jos., *Ant.* xix. 9. 1), the youngest daughter of Herod Agrippa I, and sister of Agrippa II, who gave her in marriage to a Syrian petty king, Azizus of Emesa. The procurator Felix (*q.v.*), abetted by the Cypriot magician Atomos (whom some, following an inferior text of Josephus (*Ant.* xx. 7. 2), connect with the 'Elymas' of Acts xiii. 8), persuaded her to desert Azizus, and to marry him.

The Western Text records that it was Drusilla, not her husband, who wanted to meet Paul (AD 57), but it seems doubtful whether in this sophisticated Jewish teen-ager the apostle would find a receptive listener to his discourse on 'righteousness, temperance, and judgment to come' (Acts xxiv. 24, 25). See HEROD. J.D.D.

DUALISM. Several characteristic themes of biblical doctrine can be better understood if considered against their background of dualistic thought. The word 'dualism' has been variously used in the history of theology and philosophy, but the basic conception is that of a distinction between two principles as independent of one another and in some instances opposed to one another. Thus in theology God is set over against some spiritual principle of evil or the material world, in philosophy spirit over against matter, in psychology soul or mind over against body.

I. GOD AND THE POWERS OF EVIL

The first use of the term 'dualism' was in Hyde's *Historia Religionis Veterum Persarum*, published in 1700. Although it is matter for dispute among experts whether Persian religion as a whole should be described as dualistic, it is clear that at some periods of Mazdaeism there existed a belief in a being evil by his own nature and the author of evil, who does not owe his origin to the creator of good but exists independently of him. This being brought into existence creatures opposed to those created by the good spirit.

With these views the Israelites certainly came in contact through Persian influences on them, but any such belief in the existence of evil from eternity and its creative power, even if modified by a belief in the ultimate victory of good, was unacceptable to the biblical writers. Satan and all the powers of evil are subordinated to God, not only in His final victory but also in their present activity and in their very being as fallen creatures of His (*cf.* especially Jb. i, ii; Col. i. 16, 17).

II. GOD AND THE WORLD

Many ancient cosmogonies picture God or the gods as imposing order and form on a formless but pre-existent matter. However malleable to the divine hand, matter which is not itself created by God necessarily imposes a limit on the divine operation, assimilating it to the creative activity of man, who always has to deal with a given material.

In the biblical conception of creation, although God and the world are kept very clearly distinct and Pantheism is rigorously avoided, the world is regarded as owing not only its form but also its very being to God (Heb. xi. 3; *cf.* 2 Macc. vii. 28).

III. SPIRIT AND MATTER

Dualism finds more philosophical expression in the making of an absolute distinction between spirit and matter, coupled with a considerable tendency to regard spirit as good and matter as positively evil or at best an encumbrance to spirit.

This moral depreciation of matter as contrasted with spirit is contrary to the Christian doctrine of creation and the biblical understanding of sin. The situation is both better and worse than dualism portrays it. On the one hand, matter is not inherently evil; the Creator saw all that He had made as good (Gn. i. 31); on the other hand, the evil consequences of rebellion against God affect not only the material but also the spiritual realm. There are spiritual hosts of wickedness in heavenly places (Eph. vi. 12), and the most heinous sins are spiritual. Nor does the Bible altogether accept the metaphysical distinction of spirit and matter. Hebrew dynamism sees the world less in terms of static substance than of a constant activity of divine providence which as readily uses material agencies as it does purely spiritual powers. Thus modern scientific concepts of the inter-relation of energy and matter are more akin to the biblical outlook than is a Platonist or idealist dualism. 'God is spirit' (Jn. iv. 24, RVmg); but 'the Word was made flesh' (Jn. i. 14).

IV. SOUL AND BODY

A particular instance of the Heb. avoidance of dualism is the biblical doctrine of man. Greek thought, and in consequence many Hellenizing Jewish and Christian sages, regarded the body as a prison-house of the soul: *sōma sēma*, 'the body is a tomb'. The aim of the sage was to achieve deliverance from all that is bodily and thus liberate the soul. But to the Bible man is not a soul in a body but a body/soul unity; so true is this that even in the resurrection, although flesh and blood cannot inherit the kingdom of God, we shall still have bodies (1 Cor. xv. 35 ff.).

M.H.C.

DUKE (Heb. *'allûp̄*, ? leader of an *'elep̄*, 'thousand'). Title of the sons of Seir the Horite (Gn. xxxvi. 20–30), of Esau's grandsons by Adah and Basemath and his sons by Aholibamah (Gn. xxxvi. 1–19), and of Esau's later(?) descendants (Gn. xxxvi. 40–43; 1 Ch. i. 51–54). Characteristic title of tribal chiefs of Edom down to Moses' time (Ex. xv. 15), and known also in Ugaritic about then. In Jos. xiii. 21, 'dukes' of AV represents Heb. *nāsîḵ*, *i.e.* 'princes' of Sihon. K.A.K.

DULCIMER. See MUSIC AND MUSICAL INSTRUMENTS.

DUMAH. 1. Son of Ishmael and founder of an Arab community (Gn. xxv. 14; 1 Ch. i. 30). These descendants gave their name to Dumah, capital of a district known as the Ǧawf, about halfway across N Arabia between Palestine and S Babylonia. Dumah is modern Arabic Dûmat-al-Ǧandal, and the Adummatu of Assyrian and Babylonian royal inscriptions in the 7th to 6th centuries BC (references in Ebeling and Meissner, *Reallexikon der Assyriologie*, I, 1932, pp. 39, 40).

2. The name is apparently used figuratively of that nearer semi-desert land, Edom (Seir), in a brief oracle of Isaiah (xxi. 11, 12).

3. A township in Judah (Jos. xv. 52), usually identified with the present ed-Dômeh or ed-Dûmah, some 11 miles south-west of Hebron. The name Rumah in 2 Ki. xxiii. 36 might conceivably be for Dumah in Judah; see *GTT*, § 963, p. 368. K.A.K.

DUMBNESS. See DISEASE AND HEALING.

DUNG. The word is used in the AV to translate various Heb. words. Heb. *'aśpōṯ*, usually rendered 'dunghill', is probably a refuse-tip, rubbish-dump, or ash-heap, and is used as a simile to convey the haunt of the destitute (1 Sa. ii. 8; Ps. cxiii. 7; La. iv. 5); *cf.* also Lk. xiv. 35. Jerusalem's Dung Gate (the same word) in Ne. ii. 13, iii. 13, 14, xii. 31, may be the gate by which refuse was taken out of the city; see JERUSALEM. A grimmer comparison was of unburied corpses (perishing) as dung (*dōmen*) in the fields (2 Ki. ix. 37, Jezebel; Je. viii. 2, ix. 22, xvi. 4, xxv. 33; *cf.* Jb. xx. 7; Zp. i. 17). Disobedient priests are once threatened that the dung of their sacrifices (*i.e.* that which is unclean, *cf.* Ex. xxix. 14; Lv. iv. 11, viii. 17, *etc.*) will be spread upon their faces and they removed with it (Mal. ii. 3). Jehu turned a temple of Baal into a latrine (2 Ki. x. 27). Utter privation under siege was pictured as eating dung (2 Ki. xviii. 27). The 'dunghills' (*n*ᵉ*wālî*/*û*) of Ezr. vi. 11; Dn. ii. 5, iii. 29, should probably be 'ruin-heaps'.

Animal-dung had of old two main uses: for fuel and for manure. As fuel, it would often be mixed with straw (*cf.* Is. xxv. 10) and dried; it was then suitable for heating the simple 'bread ovens' of clay or stones used in Palestine, human dung being so used only exceptionally (Ezk. iv. 12–15) and often burnt up (*cf.* the simile of 1 Ki. xiv. 10, RSV). When Ben-hadad II closely besieged Samaria, poor food and fuel (doves' dung) sold at inflated prices (2 Ki. vi. 25). For dung as fuel into modern times, see Doughty, *Travels in Arabia Deserta*.

Ps. lxxxiii. 10 may refer to manuring the ground, while Lk. xiii. 8 with reference to the fig-tree certainly does. In a powerful metaphor Paul counted all things as dung or refuse, in comparison with the 'excellency' of gaining Christ (Phil. iii. 8). K.A.K.

DURA (Aram. *Dûrā'*; LXX *Deeira*). The place in the administrative district of Babylon where King Nebuchadrezzar set up an image for all to worship (Dn. iii. 1). Possibly Tell Dēr (16 miles south-west of Baghdad), though there are several Bab. places named Dūru. Oppert reported structures SSE of Babylon at 'Doura' (*Expédition scientifique en Mésopotamie*, I, 1862, pp. 238–240). Pinches (*ISBE*) proposed the general interpretation of 'the plain of the Wall' (Bab. *dūru*), part of the outer defences of the city. For the name Dura, *cf.* Dura (Europos); Old Bab. *Da-ma-ra* (*Orientalia*, 1952, p. 275, n. 1). D.J.W.

DUST. *'āḇāq*, *'āpār*, dust of the earth, is used literally and in similes to express: multitude, Gn. xiii. 16; Is. xxix. 5; smallness, Dt. ix. 21; 2 Ki. xiii. 7; poverty, 1 Sa. ii. 8; abasement, Gn. xviii. 27 (*cf.* ASHES); dust on the head as a sign of sorrow, Jb. ii. 12; Rev. xviii. 19; contrition, Jos. vii. 6.

Man's lowliness is emphasized by his being taken from the dust, Gn. ii. 7; Jb. iv. 19; Ps. ciii. 14; and by his ultimate return to dust, Gn. iii. 19; Jb. xvii. 16. The serpent is sentenced to 'eat dust', Gn. iii. 14; and warning of judgment is conveyed by shaking the dust off the feet, Mt. x. 14, 15; Acts xiii. 51. P.A.B.

DWARF (*daq*, 'thin', 'small'). Used to denote one of the physical disabilities which precluded a man from officiating as a priest (Lv. xxi. 20), the exact meaning of the Hebrew word is not clear. The same word is used of the lean kine and blasted ears in Pharaoh's dream (Gn. xli. 3, 23), and the reference may simply be to a withered person. Dwarfs in the Ancient Near East were always thought to be possessed of special (frequently magical) powers. J.D.D.

DYEING. See ARTS AND CRAFTS.

DYSENTERY. The RV rendering of Gk. *dysenteria* (AV 'bloody flux'), the infectious disease of which Paul healed the father of Publius (Acts xxviii. 8). It has been suggested that the 'incurable disease' of the bowels with which the Lord afflicted Jehoram was a chronic amoebic dysentery (2 Ch. xxi. 15, 18, 19). See also DISEASE AND HEALING.

E

EAGLE. See Birds of the Bible.

EAR. 1. In the Old Testament *'ôzen*, possibly derived from a root meaning 'pointed', is used of the ears of animals (Am. iii. 12), and more frequently of man. There are parallels to this word in other Near Eastern languages. The denominative verb *'āzan* (in the Hiph'îl) means 'to give ear', 'to hear'. In the New Testament *ous* is commonly used. Occasionally (*e.g.* Acts xvii. 20) *akoē*, from *akouō*, 'to hear', is also found. In the incident of the cutting off of the ear, recorded in Mt. xxvi. 51 and parallels, the word is *ōtion* meaning particularly the external lobe.

While New Testament concepts envisage the interdependence of the body members (1 Cor. xii. 16), the Old Testament views them more as semi-independent organs (see Body). This is clear in the case of the ear, which God planted (Ps. xciv. 9), or dug (Ps. xl. 6, Heb.), and which not only hears but attends (Ne. i. 6), tries words (Jb. xxxiv. 3), and can be stopped from hearing (Is. xxxiii. 15) or made heavy, rendering hearing difficult (Is. vi. 10). God is spoken of also as having ears in the same way (Is. lix. 1), different from the unhearing ears of the idols (Ps. cxxxv. 17). The ears must be used aright to get the true meaning of words (Mt. xi. 15).

There are two Old Testament customs which focus attention on the ear especially. The one was the rite of confirming a Hebrew slave in perpetual, voluntary service, by nailing his ear to his master's door. The other was the putting of the blood of the sacrifice upon the right ear, thumb, and toe of the priest (Lv. viii. 23, 24). Both probably have reference to securing obedience. To 'open the ear' is used in Heb. as a figurative expression for revealing (*e.g.* Is. l. 5).

2. An ear of grain. This would be of barley in the Old Testament, of corn in the New Testament. The Hebrew word *'āḇîḇ* gives rise to the name for the first month, the month of the Passover, at the time of the barley harvest (Ex. xxiii. 15).

3. The verb 'to ear' (*e.g.* Ex. xxxiv. 21, AV) is an old English term, now obsolete, meaning 'to plough' (*cf.* Latin *aro*). B.O.B.

EARNEST (Gk. *arrabōn*, a Semitic loan-word; Heb. *'ērāḇôn*; Lat. *arrha*, *arr(h)abo*). This is a commercial term, probably brought west by Phoenician traders. It means, strictly, the first instalment of a gift or payment, put down as a pledge that the rest will follow later (*cf.* the down-payment in modern hire-purchase). Paying the earnest makes obligatory payment of the remainder.

In this sense Paul calls the gift of the Spirit an earnest of the Christian's inheritance (Eph. i. 14; 2 Cor. i. 22, v. 5)—a guarantee, foretaste, and first instalment of coming glory.

More generally, an *arrabōn* is any pledge or deposit, of whatever sort, given in token that a larger payment will later be made; so in LXX, Gn. xxxviii. 17, 18, 20, rendering *'ērāḇôn*.

J.I.P.

EARRING. See Ornaments.

EARTH. 1. The physical world in which man lives, as opposed to the heavens, *e.g.* Gn. i. 1; Dt. xxxi. 28; Ps. lxviii. 8; Dn. vi. 27, *etc.* (Heb. *'ereṣ* or Aram. *'ara'*). This word is ambiguous in so far as it sometimes expresses this wider meaning of 'earth' (*i.e.* so far as the Hebrews knew it) and sometimes only 'land', a more restricted area. In the accounts of the Flood (Gn. vi–ix) and of the division of speech (Gn. xi. 1) each meaning has its advocates. This ambivalence is not peculiar to Hebrew; suffice it to mention the Egyptian word *ta'*, which likewise means land (as in 'conqueror of all lands') and earth ('ye who are upon earth', *i.e.* the living). See also World.

2. Dry land as opposed to the sea, Gn. i. 10, *etc.* (Heb. *'ereṣ*; also *yabbešeṯ*, 'dry land' in Dn. ii. 10). Phrases such as 'pillars of the earth', 'foundations of the earth' (1 Sa. ii. 8; Jb. ix. 6; Ps. cii. 25; Is. xlviii. 13) are simply poetic expressions from early Semitic which do not imply a doctrine of a table-like surface upon supports. The 'waters under the earth' (Ex. xx. 4) are probably subterranean springs and pools and, as the main source of water in Palestine, are referred to in poetic passages such as Pss. xxiv. 2, cxxxvi. 6; *cf.* Gn. viii. 2.

3. The ground-surface, the soil which supports vegetation and so all life, *e.g.* Gn. i. 11, 12; Dt. xxvi. 2 (both *'ereṣ* and *'adāmâ* are so used). Soil served for temporary altars (Ex. xx. 24); the Aramaean Naaman took Israelite soil on which to worship Israel's God (2 Ki. v. 17). Torn clothes and the placing of earth on the head were tokens of mourning (2 Sa. i. 2, xv. 32).

4. In passages such as Gn. xi. 1; Ps. xcviii. 9; La. ii. 15, the word comes to mean, by transference, the inhabitants of the earth or part of it. See also World. In the New Testament Gk. *gē* is variously translated, generally 'earth', and appears with all these four meanings. For (1) see, *e.g.*, Mt. vi. 10 and note the restricted use in Jn. iii. 22, 'land of Judaea'; for (2) see Acts iv. 24

and *cf.* Mk. iv. 1; for (3) see Mt. xxv. 18, 25 and *cf.* Mt. x. 29; for (4) see Rev. xiii. 3 (AV 'world').

K.A.K.

EARTHQUAKE. Earthquakes have been the *alter ego* of Palestine consequent on its geological structure (see PALESTINE). In the biblical record earthquakes or their associated phenomena are recorded at various periods; at Mt. Sinai on the giving of the law (Ex. xix. 18), in the days of Saul (1 Sa. xiv. 15), Elijah (1 Ki. xix. 11), Uzziah (Am. i. 1; Zc. xiv. 5), and Paul and Silas (Acts xvi. 26). An earthquake associated with crustal fissures destroyed Korah and his companions (Nu. xvi. 31), and a similar event may have been associated with the destruction of Sodom and Gomorrah (see Am. iv. 11). The earthquake at the crucifixion is described in Mt. xxvii. 51 f. with miraculous manifestations.

Poetic and prophetic imagery makes use of this terrible form of natural calamity: Jdg. v. 4; Pss. xviii. 7, xxix. 6, xcvii. 4, cxiv. 4; Is. xxix. 6; Ezk. xxxviii. 19 f.; Joel ii. 10, iii. 16; Am. viii. 8; Na. i. 5; Hab. iii. 6; Zc. xiv. 4; Rev. vi. 12, viii. 5, xi. 13, xvi. 18.

BIBLIOGRAPHY. For a list of earthquakes in the Christian era, see Prof. E. Hull, art. 'Earthquake' in *HDB*. J.M.H.

EAST. A bearing indicated in the Old Testament by the phrase *mizraḥ-šemeš*, 'rising of the sun' (*e.g.* Nu. xxi. 11; Jdg. xi. 18), or more frequently by *mizrāḥ*, 'rising', alone (*e.g.* Jos. iv. 19), and once (Ps. lxxv. 6) by *môṣā'*, 'going forth', alone. In the New Testament the same usage is found with *anatolē*, 'rising' (*e.g.* in Mt. ii. 1). The rising of the luminaries gave the ancient peoples their standard of direction, so the term *qeḏem*, 'front', or some variation of the root *qdm*, was thus frequently employed to designate the east. The word *qdm* is attested from about 2000 BC as a loan-word in the Egyptian 'Story of Sinuhe' and from the 14th century in the Ugaritic texts.

T.C.M.

EAST, CHILDREN OF THE (Heb. *benê-qeḏem*). A general term applied to various peoples living to the east (and north-east, Gn. xxix. 1) of Canaan, and used in association with such neighbours as the Midianites, Amalekites (Jdg. vi. 3), Moabites, Ammonites (Ezk. xxv. 10), and Kedarites (Je. xlix. 28). Sometimes nomadic peoples are indicated (see NOMADS) (Ezk. xxv. 4), but the term could evidently also apply to the inhabitants of Mesopotamia (1 Ki. iv. 30), and the patriarch Job is described (i. 3) as one of the *bᵉnê-qeḏem*. (See EAST, KADMONITES.)

BIBLIOGRAPHY. A. Musil, *Arabia Deserta*, 1927, pp. 494 ff.; P. K. Hitti, *History of the Arabs*, 1956, p. 43. T.C.M.

EASTER, a word used in the Germanic languages to denote the festival of the vernal equinox, and subsequently, with the coming of Christianity, to denote the anniversary of the resurrection of Christ (which in Gk. and Romance tongues is denoted by *pascha*, 'Passover', and its derivatives). Tyndale, Coverdale, and others give 'Easter' as a rendering of *pascha*, and one example survives in AV, at Acts xii. 4 ('after Easter', where RV and RSV have 'after the Passover'; similarly NEB).

In the 2nd century AD and later there was considerable diversity and debate over the dating of the Christian Easter; the churches of Asia Minor for long followed the 'quartodeciman' reckoning, by which it was observed regularly on the 14th of Nisan, while those of Rome and elsewhere followed a calendar which commemorated the passion year by year on a Friday and the resurrection on a Sunday. The latter mode prevailed. F.F.B.

EAST SEA. See DEAD SEA.

EBAL (OBAL). 1. A 'son' of Joktan (Gn. x. 28; 1 Ch. i. 22); one of the Semitic families which inhabited South Arabia. **2.** A descendant of Esau (Gn. xxxvi. 23).

EBAL, MOUNT. The northern, and higher, of two mountains which overshadowed Shechem, the modern Nablus. It lies north of the Vale of Shechem, 1,402 feet above the valley and 3,077 feet above sea-level. The space between Ebal and its neighbour Gerizim, south of the vale, provides a natural amphitheatre with wonderful acoustic properties. At the close of his discourse in Dt. v–xi Moses points to the two mountains on the western horizon beyond Gilgal and Moreh (Shechem) and announces that when they have entered the land a blessing shall be set on Gerizim and a curse on Ebal.

After the laws of Dt. xii–xxvi the narrative is resumed, and Moses gives detailed directions. First, great stones were to be set up, covered with cement, and the law inscribed upon them. After this an altar of unhewn stones was to be erected and sacrifices offered (Dt. xxvii. 1–8).

In a further address (Dt. xxvii. 9–xxviii. 68) Moses ordered that six tribes should stand on Gerizim to pronounce blessing on obedience and six should stand on Ebal to lay curses on disobedience (xxvii. 9–13). Following upon this, the Levites shall call down curses on the tribes for sins against God or man, many of which could be done in secret (xxvii. 15–26). By their response of 'Amen', the people are to condemn such practices openly. After victories in the centre of Palestine, Joshua gathered the people at Shechem, where these ceremonies were duly performed (Jos. viii. 30–35). G.T.M.

EBED-MELECH (*'eḇeḏ-meleḵ*—a common name = 'servant of the king'). Ethiopian servant of Zedekiah who rescued Jeremiah from a dungeon (Je. xxxviii. 7–13), and for this his life was to be spared at the sack of Jerusalem (Je. xxxix. 15–18). D.J.W.

EBENEZER (Heb. *'eben 'ēzer*, 'stone of help').

1. The site of the dual defeat of Israel at the hands of the Philistines near Aphek in the north of Sharon. The sons of Eli were slain, the ark taken (1 Sa. iv. 1–22), and a period of Philistine overlordship begun which continued until the days of national reinvigoration under the monarchy.

2. The name of the stone which Samuel erected between Mizpah and Shen some years after this battle, to commemorate his victory over the Philistines (1 Sa. vii. 12). The stone was probably given the same name as the site of Israel's earlier defeat in order to encourage the impression that that defeat had now been reversed. The exact site of the stone is unknown. R.J.W.

EBER. 1. The son of Salah or Shelah (1 Ch. i. 18, 19, 25) and great-grandson of Shem who, when aged thirty-four, became father of Peleg (Gn. xi. 16) and later of other sons and daughters, one of whom was Joktan (Gn. x. 21, 25). He lived 464 years according to Gn. xi. 16, 17.

His name, Heb. *'ēber* (Gk. *Heber*), meaning 'one who passes over', is the same as the word Hebrew (Ḫabiru) and as such was later used to designate the wandering Semitic semi-nomads. His sons lived at a time when there was a 'division' (see BABEL), perhaps between those who were 'Arabs' (probably by metathesis the same as, or a dialectal variant for, *'ēber*) under Joktan and those who lived semi-sedentary lives on irrigated land (Akkad. *palgu*) under Peleg. The name Eber appears to be used as a poetic description of Israel in Nu. xxiv. 24.

2. A Gadite family (1 Ch. v. 13). **3.** Two Benjamites (1 Ch. viii. 12, 22). **4.** The head of a priestly family of Amok who returned to Jerusalem from Babylonia with Zerubbabel (Ne. xii. 20). D.J.W.

EBONY (Heb. *hobnim*; Egyp. *hbny*). The black heart-wood of *Diospyros ebenum* which, according to most modern authorities, was imported into Palestine/Syria from Sudan/Ethiopia, where it is abundant (not all Ethiopian ebony, however, is jet-black). This close-grained wood (mentioned in Ezk. xxvii. 15) was extensively used in ancient times in the manufacture of fine furniture, valuable vessels, sceptres, and idols. See A. Lucas, *Ancient Egyptian Materials*[3], 1948, pp. 498 ff. J.D.D.

ECCLESIASTES, BOOK OF. The writer calls himself *qōheleṯ*. The feminine ending probably denotes an office that is held, in this instance the office of a caller of assemblies. Hence 'Preacher' or 'Teacher' is a reasonable translation.

I. OUTLINE OF CONTENTS

The theme of the book is a search for the key to the meaning of life. The Preacher examines life from all angles to see where satisfaction can be found. He finds that God alone holds the key, and He must be trusted. Meanwhile we are to take life day by day from His hand, and glorify Him in the ordinary things.

Within this general framework Ecclesiastes falls into two main divisions of thought, (*a*) 'the futility of life', and (*b*) 'the answer of practical faith'. These run concurrently through its chapters. In the outline below, those passages belonging to the first category are printed in roman type, and those belonging to the second in italic.

i. 1, 2. The theme of futility stated.

i. 3–11. Nature is a closed system, and history a mere succession of events.

i. 12–18. Wisdom discourages man.

ii. 1–11. Pleasure leaves him unsatisfied.

ii. 12–23. Wisdom is to be rated above such things, but death defeats the wise and foolish alike.

ii. 24–26. *Take life day by day from God, and glorify Him in ordinary things.*

iii. 1–15. *Live step by step and remember that God alone knows the whole plan.*

iii. 16. The problem of injustice.

iii. 17. *God will judge all.*

iii. 18–21. Man dies like the beasts.

iii. 22. *God must therefore be glorified in this life.*

iv. 1–5. The problems of oppression and envy.

iv. 6. *Quietness of spirit is therefore to be sought.*

iv. 7, 8. The lonely miser.

iv. 9–12. *The blessing of friendship.*

iv. 13–16. The failure of kings.

v. 1–7. *The nature of the true worshipper.*

v. 8, 9. Oppressive officialdom.

v. 10–vi. 12. Money brings many evils.

v. 18–20. *Be content with what God gives.*

vii. 1–29. *Practical wisdom, involving the fear of God, is a guide for life.*

viii. 1–7. *Man must submit to God's commands even though the future is hidden.*

viii. 8–ix. 3. The problem of death, which comes to good and bad alike.

ix. 4–10. *Since death is universal, use life energetically while its powers remain.*

ix. 11, 12. *But do not be proud of natural talents.*

ix. 13–x. 20. *More proverbs for practical living.*

xi. 1–8. *Since the future cannot be known, man must co-operate sensibly with the natural laws that are known.*

xi. 9–xii. 8. *Remember God in youth, for old age weakens the faculties.*

xii. 9–12. *Listen to wise words.*

To summarize its contents, the book constitutes an exhortation to live a God-fearing life, realizing that one day account must be rendered to Him.

II. AUTHORSHIP AND DATE

Although the writer says that he was king over Israel (i. 12), and speaks as though he were Solomon, he nowhere says that he is Solomon. The style of the Heb. is later than Solomon's time. If Solomon was the author, the book underwent a later modernization of language. Otherwise a later writer may have taken up a comment on life that had been made by Solomon, 'Vanity of vanities, all is vanity,' and used this as a text to show why even a wise and wealthy king should say such a thing. We cannot tell at what date the book received its present form, since there are no clear historical allusions in it. About 200 BC is commonly suggested.

III. INTERPRETATION

(See the outline of contents above.) The interpretation is partially bound up with the question of the unity of the book. Those who reject the unity hold that there is an original nucleus by a sceptical writer who queried God's hand in the world. This was worked over by one or more writers, one at least trying to redress the balance on the side of orthodoxy (*e.g.* ii. 26, iii. 14, *etc.*), and another possibly inserting the Epicurean passages (*e.g.* ii. 24–26, iii. 12–15, *etc.*). It would, however, be strange if an orthodox writer thought it worthwhile to salvage what was fundamentally a book of scepticism. Moreover, why should a sceptic be commended as wise (xii. 9)?

If the book is a unity, some take it as the musings of the natural man. The Preacher gives up the problems of God and man, but holds that it is best to live a quiet and normal life, avoiding dangerous extremes (*e.g.* Bentzen, *Introduction to the Old Testament*, II, p. 191). The closing summary in xii. 13, 14 suggests that the book is not primarily sceptical, and that the so-called Epicurean passages are not intended in the Epicurean sense. Life is a riddle, for which the Preacher tries to find the key. The meaning of life is not to be found in the acquisition of knowledge, money, sensual pleasures, oppression, religious profession, or folly. Either these things prove empty or something happens against which they are helpless. Even God's hand at times is inscrutable. Man is so made that he must always try to make sense of the universe, since God has set eternity in his heart; yet God alone knows the whole pattern (iii. 11, RVmg). Therefore the plan for man is to take his life each day from the hand of God, and enjoy it from Him and for Him. This theme should be compared with what Paul says about the vanity of the world in Rom. viii. 20–25, 28.

BIBLIOGRAPHY. C. H. H. Wright, *The Book of Koheleth*, 1883; H. Ranston, *Ecclesiastes and the Early Greek Wisdom Literature*, 1925; G. S. Hendry, 'Ecclesiastes' in *The New Bible Commentary*, 1953; J. Paterson, *The Book that is Alive*, 1954, pp. 129–150.

J.S.W.

ECCLESIASTICUS. See APOCRYPHA.

ECLIPSE. See SUN.

ED. It is related in Jos. xxii that when the two and a half tribes left Shiloh to take up their possessions east of Jordan, they set up a 'great altar' (10) on the banks of the river, not for sacrifice, but as a 'witness' (Heb. *'ēḏ*). Fearing a schism, their brethren sent Phinehas and ten princes to protest (13, 14), but they were satisfied that, on the contrary, it was to bear witness to their loyalty to Yahweh (29). In verse 34 the word 'Ed' occurs only once, but the AV correctly gives the sense. G.T.M.

EDEN. 1. The name of the Levite(s) who shared in Hezekiah's reforms (2 Ch. xxix. 12, xxxi. 15).

2. A place that traded with Tyre, associated with Harran and Canneh (Ezk. xxvii. 23). This Eden and its people are identical with the Beth-eden (House of Eden) of Am. i. 5 and the 'children' of Eden of 2 Ki. xix. 12; Is. xxxvii. 12—and these comprise the Assyrian province (and former kingdom) of Bît-Adini between Harran and the Euphrates at Carchemish. See further on TELASSAR; EDEN, HOUSE OF, and literature there cited. K.A.K.

EDEN, CHILDREN OF. See TELASSAR.

EDEN, GARDEN OF. The place which God made for Adam to live in, and from which Adam and Eve were driven after the fall.

I. THE NAME

The *MT* states that God planted a garden in Eden (*gan-beʿēḏen*; Gn. ii. 8), which indicates that the garden was not co-extensive with Eden, but must have been an enclosed area within it. The LXX and Vulg. and subsequent commentators have noted that to a Hebrew-speaker the name *'ēḏen* would suggest the homophonous root meaning 'delight'; but many scholars now hold that Eden is not a proper name, but a common noun from the Sumerian *edin*, 'plain, steppe', borrowed either direct from Sumerian, or *via* Akkadian (*edinu*), the garden thus being situated in a plain, or flat region. From its situation in Eden the garden came to be called the 'garden of Eden' (*gan-'ēḏen*; Gn. ii. 15, iii. 23, 24; Ezk. xxxvi. 35; Joel ii. 3), but it was also referred to as the 'garden of God' (*gan-'elōhîm*, Ezk. xxviii. 13, xxxi. 9) and the 'garden of the Lord' (*gan-YHWH*, Is. li. 3). In Gn. ii. 8 ff. the word *gan*, 'garden', and in Is. li. 3 *'ēḏen* itself, is rendered *paradeisos*, by the LXX, this being a loan-word from Old Persian (Avestan) *pairidaēza*, 'enclosure', which came to mean 'park, pleasure ground', and from this usage came English 'paradise' (*q.v.*) for the Garden of Eden.

II. THE RIVERS

A river came from Eden, or the plain, and watered the garden, and from thence it was parted and became four heads (*rā'šîm*, Gn. ii. 10). The word *rō'š*, 'head, top, beginning', is interpreted variously by scholars to mean either the beginning of a branch, as in a delta, going down stream, or the beginning or junction of a tributary, going upstream. Either interpretation is possible, though the latter is perhaps the more probable. The names of the four tributaries or mouths, which were evidently outside the garden, are given as *pîšôn* (Gn. ii. 11), *gîḥôn* (ii. 13), *ḥiddeqel* (ii. 14), and *perāṯ* (ii. 14). The last two are identified, without dissent, with the Tigris and Euphrates respectively (*qq.v.*), but the identifications for the Pishon and Gihon are almost as diverse as they are numerous, ranging from the Nile and Indus to tributaries of the Tigris in Mesopotamia. Sufficient data are not available to make it possible to identify either of these two rivers with certainty.

Gn. ii. 6 states that 'there went up a mist (*'ēḏ*) from the earth, and watered the whole face of the ground'. It is possible that *'ēḏ* corresponds to Akkadian *edû*, itself a loan-word from Sumerian *id*, 'river', indicating that a river went up or overflowed upon the ground and provided natural irrigation. It seems reasonable to understand this as relating to the inside of the garden.

III. THE CONTENTS OF THE GARDEN

If the statement in Gn. ii. 5, 6 may be taken to indicate what did subsequently take place within the garden, an area of arable land (*śāḏeh*, AV 'field') to be tilled by Adam may be postulated. On this were to grow plants (*śîaḥ*) and herbs (*'ēśeḇ*), perhaps to be understood as shrubs and cereals respectively. There were also trees of every kind, both beautiful and fruit-bearing (Gn. ii. 9), and two in particular in the middle of the garden, the tree of life, to eat from which would make a man live for ever (Gn. iii. 22), and the tree of knowledge of good and evil, from which man was specifically forbidden to eat (Gn. ii. 17, iii. 3). Many views of the meaning of 'the knowledge of good and evil' in this context have been put forward. One of the most common would see it as the knowledge of right and wrong, but it is difficult to suppose that Adam did not already possess this, and that, if he did not, he was forbidden to acquire it. Others would connect it with the worldly knowledge that comes to man with maturity, and which can be put to either a good or bad use. Another view would take the expression 'good and evil' as an example of a figure of speech whereby an autonymic pair signifies totality, meaning therefore 'everything' and in the context universal knowledge. Against this is the fact that Adam, having eaten of the tree, did not gain universal knowledge. Yet another view would see this as a quite ordinary tree, which was selected by God to provide an ethical test for the man, who 'would acquire an experiential knowledge of good or evil according as he was stedfast in obedience or fell away into disobedience' (*NBC*, pp. 78, 79). See FALL, TEMPTATION. There were also animals in the garden, cattle (*behēmâ*, see BEAST, § 1), and beasts of the field (Gn. ii. 19, 20), by which may perhaps be understood those animals which were suitable for domestication. There were also birds.

IV. THE NEIGHBOURING TERRITORIES

Three territories are named in connection with the rivers. The Tigris is said to have gone 'toward the east of Assyria' (*qiḏmaṯ 'aššûr*, literally 'in front of *'aššûr*'; Gn. ii. 14) an expression which could also mean 'between *'aššûr* and the spectator'. The name *'aššûr* could refer either to the state of Assyria, which first began to emerge in the early second millennium BC, or the city of Assur, modern Qal'at Sharqât on the west bank of the Tigris, the earliest capital of Assyria, which was flourishing, as excavations have shown, in the early third millennium BC. Since even at its smallest extent Assyria probably lay on both sides of the Tigris, it is probable that the city is meant and that the phrase correctly states that the Tigris ran to the east of Assur. Secondly, the river Gihon is described as winding through (*sāḇaḇ*) 'the whole land of Cush' (*kûš*, Gn. ii. 13). Cush in the Bible usually signifies Ethiopia, and has commonly been taken in this passage (*e.g.* AV) to have that meaning; but there was also a region to the east of the Tigris, from which the Kassites descended in the second millennium, which had this name, and this may be the meaning in this passage (see CUSH). Thirdly, the Pishon is described as winding through the whole land of Havilah (*q.v.*; Gn. ii. 11). Various products of this place are named: gold, bdellium (*q.v.*), and *šōham*-stone (Gn. ii. 11, 12), the latter being translated 'onyx' (*q.v.*) in the EVV, but being of uncertain meaning. Since bdellium is usually taken to indicate an aromatic gum, a characteristic product of Arabia, and the two other biblical usages of the name Havilah (*q.v.*) also refer to parts of Arabia, it is most often taken in this context to refer to some part of that peninsula.

V. THE LOCATION OF THE GARDEN OF EDEN

Theories as to the location of the garden of Eden are numerous. That most commonly held, by Calvin, for instance, and in more recent times by Friedrich Delitzsch and others, is the view that the garden lay somewhere in southern Mesopotamia, the Pishon and Gihon being either canals connecting the Tigris and Euphrates, tributaries joining these, or in one theory the Pishon being the body of water from the Persian Gulf to the Red Sea, compassing the Arabian peninsula. These theories assume that the four 'heads' of Gn. ii. 10 are tributaries which unite in one main stream, which then joins the Persian Gulf; but another group of theories takes 'heads' to refer to branches spreading out from a supposed original common source, and seeks to locate the garden in the region of Armenia, where both the Tigris and Euphrates take their rise. The Pishon and Gihon are then identified with various smaller rivers of Armenia and Trans-Caucasia, and in some theories by extension, assuming an ignorance of true geography in the author, with such other rivers as the Indus and even Ganges.

The expression 'eastward in Eden' (Gn. ii. 8), literally 'in Eden from in front', could mean either that the garden was in the eastern part of Eden or that Eden was in the east from the narrator's point of view, and some commentators have taken it as 'in Eden in old times', but in either case, in the absence of certainty as to the meaning of the other indications of locality, this information cannot narrow it down further.

In view of the possibility that, if the Deluge was as universal as the Bible account suggests, the geographical features which would assist in an identification of the site of Eden would have been altered, the site of Eden remains unknown.

VI. DILMUN

Among the Sumerian literary texts discovered fifty years ago at Nippur in southern Babylonia, one was discovered which described a place called Dilmun, a pleasant place, in which neither sickness nor death were known. At first it had no fresh water, but Enki the water-god ordered the sun-god to remedy this, and, this being done, various other events took place, in the course of which the goddess Ninti (see EVE) is mentioned. In later times the Babylonians adopted the name and idea of Dilmun and called it the 'land of the living', the home of their immortals. Certain similarities between this Sumerian notion of an earthly paradise and the biblical Eden emerge, and some scholars therefore conclude that the Genesis account is dependent upon the Sumerian. But an equally possible explanation is that both accounts refer to a real place, the Sumerian version having collected mythological accretions in the course of transmission.

BIBLIOGRAPHY. S. R. Driver, *The Book of Genesis*[8], 1911, pp. 57–60; J. Skinner, *Genesis*[2], *ICC*, 1930, pp. 62–66; W. F. Albright, 'The Location of the Garden of Eden', *AJSL*, XXXIX, 1922, pp. 15–31; E. A. Speiser, 'The Rivers of Paradise', *Festschrift Johannes Friedrich*, 1959, pp. 473–485; M. G. Kline, 'Because It Had Not Rained', *WTJ*, XX, 1957–8, pp. 146 ff. On VI, S. N. Kramer, *History Begins at Sumer*, 1956, pp. 193–199. T.C.M.

EDEN, HOUSE OF (*bêṯ ʿeḏen*, Am. i. 5; sometimes written *bᵉnê ʿeḏen*, 2 Ki. xix. 12; Is. xxxvii. 12, which may be a contraction of *bᵉnê bêṯ ʿeḏen*, 'children of the house of Eden'). It is probably referred to in Ezk. xxvii. 23 as one of the places trading with Tyre, and its association with Gozan and Harran suggests a location on the middle Euphrates.

It is very probably to be identified with the Aramaean state of Bît-Adini which lay between the river Baliḫ and the Euphrates, and blocked the path of the Assyrian expansion to N Syria. Under these circumstances it could not last long, and its main city Til Barsip, modern Tell Aḥmar, on the east bank of the Euphrates, was taken by Shalmaneser III, and in 855 BC the state became an Assyrian province. It is presumably to this conquest that both Amos and Rabshakeh referred over a century later.

BIBLIOGRAPHY. Honigmann, *Reallexikon der Assyriologie*, II, 1933–8, pp. 33, 34; E. Forrer, *Die Provinzeinteilung des assyrischen Reiches*, 1920, pp. 12 f., 25 f.; F. Thureau Dangin and M. Dunand, *Til Barsib*, 1936; W. W. Hallo, *BA*, XXIII, 1960, pp. 38, 39. T.C.M.

EDER, EDAR (Heb. *ʿēḏer*, 'flock'). **1.** The place of Israel's encampment between Bethlehem and Hebron, Gn. xxxv. 21. In Mi. iv. 8 'tower of Eder' (AV 'tower of the flock') was probably the site of a watchtower erected against sheep thieves. **2.** A town to the south of Judah near to the Edomite border; perhaps modern Khirbet el-ʿAdar 5 miles to the south of Gaza (Jos. xv. 21). **3.** A Levite of David's time. A member of the house of Merari and a son of Muhi, 1 Ch. xxiii. 23, xxiv. 30. **4.** A Benjamite, and son of Beriah, 1 Ch. viii. 15. R.J.W.

EDOM, EDOMITES. The term Edom (*'ᵉḏôm*) denotes either the name of Esau, given in memory of the red pottage for which he exchanged his birthright (Gn. xxv. 30, xxxvi. 1, 8, 19), or the Edomites collectively (Nu. xx. 18, 20, 21; Am. i. 6, 11, ix. 12; Mal. i. 4), or the land occupied by Esau's descendants, formerly the land of Seir (Gn. xxxii. 3, xxxvi. 20, 21, 30; Nu. xxiv. 18). It stretched from the Wadi Zered to the Gulf of Aqabah for about 100 miles, and extended to both sides of the Arabah or wilderness of Edom (2 Ki. iii. 8, 20), the great depression connecting the Dead Sea to the Red Sea (Gn. xiv. 6; Dt. ii. 1, 12; Jos. xv. 1; Jdg. xi. 17, 18; 1 Ki. ix. 26, *etc.*). It is a rugged, mountainous area, with peaks rising to 3,500 feet. While not a fertile land, there are good cultivable areas (Nu. xx. 17, 19). In Bible times the king's highway passed along the eastern plateau (Nu. xx. 14–18). The capital, Sela, lay on a small plateau behind Petra (see SELA). Other important towns were Bozrah and Teman.

The Edomites (*'ᵉḏôm*, *'ᵃḏômîm*) were descendants of Edom (Esau, Gn. xxxvi. 1–17). Modern archaeology has shown that the land was occupied before Esau's time. We conclude that Esau's descendants migrated to that land and in time became the dominant group incorporating the original Horites (Gn. xiv. 6) and others into their number. After *c.* 1850 BC there was a break in the culture of Edom till just before *c.* 1300 BC and the land was occupied by nomads.

Esau had already occupied Edom when Jacob returned from Harran (Gn. xxxii. 3, xxxvi. 6–8; Dt. ii. 4, 5; Jos. xxiv. 4). Tribal chiefs (AV 'dukes') emerged here quite early (Gn. xxxvi. 15–19, 40–43; 1 Ch. i. 51–54), and the Edomites had kings 'before there reigned any king over the children of Israel' (Gn. xxxvi. 31–39; 1 Ch. i. 43–51).

At the time of the Exodus, Israel sought permission to travel by the king's highway, but the request was refused (Nu. xx. 14–21, xxi. 4; Jdg. xi. 17, 18). Notwithstanding this discourtesy, Israel was forbidden to abhor his Edomite brother (Dt. xxiii. 7, 8). In those days Balaam predicted the conquest of Edom (Nu. xxiv. 18).

Joshua allotted the territory of Judah up to the borders of Edom (Jos. xv. 1, 21), but did not encroach on their lands. Two centuries later King Saul was fighting the Edomites (1 Sa. xiv. 47) although some of them were in his service (1 Sa. xxi. 7, xxii. 9, 18). David conquered Edom and put garrisons throughout the land (2 Sa. viii. 13, 14. Emend *'ᵃrām* in verse 13 to *'ᵉdôm* because of a scribal confusion of *resh* 'r' and *daleth* 'd'. *Cf.* 1 Ch. xviii. 13). There was considerable slaughter of the Edomites at this time (2 Sa. viii. 13), and 1 Ki. xi. 15, 16 speaks of Joab, David's commander, remaining in Edom for six months 'until he had cut off every male in Edom'. Some must have escaped, for Hadad, a royal prince, fled to Egypt and later became a trouble to Solomon (1 Ki. xi. 14–22). This conquest of Edom enabled Solomon to build a port at Ezion-Geber, and to exploit the copper-mines in the region, as excavation clearly shows (1 Ki. ix. 26–28).

In Jehoshaphat's time the Edomites joined the Ammonites and Moabites in a raid on Judah (2 Ch. xx. 1), but the allies fell to fighting one another (verses 22, 23). Jehoshaphat endeavoured to use the port at Ezion-Geber, but his ships were wrecked (1 Ki. xxii. 48). At this time Edom was ruled by a deputy, who acted as king (1 Ki. xxii. 47). This 'king' acknowledged the supremacy of Judah and joined the Judah–Israel coalition in an attack on Mesha, king of Moab (2 Ki. iii. 4–27).

Under Joram (Jehoram), Edom rebelled, but, although Joram defeated them in battle, he could not reduce them to subjection (2 Ki. viii. 20–22; 2 Ch. xxi. 8–10), and Edom had a respite of some forty years.

Amaziah later invaded Edom, slew 10,000 Edomites in the Valley of Salt, captured Sela their capital, and sent 10,000 more to their death by casting them from the top of Sela (2 Ki. xiv. 7; 2 Ch. xxv. 11, 12). Uzziah, his successor, restored the port at Elath (2 Ki. xiv. 22), but under Ahaz, when Judah was being attacked by Pekah and Rezin, the Edomites invaded Judah and carried off captives (2 Ch. xxviii. 17). The port of Elath was lost once again. (Read 'Edom' for 'Aram' in 2 Ki. xvi. 6.) Judah never again recovered Edom. Assyr. inscriptions show that Edom became a vassal-state of Assyria after *c.* 736 BC.

After the fall of Judah, Edom rejoiced (Ps. cxxxvii. 7). The prophets foretold judgment on Edom for her bitter hatred (Je. xlix. 7–22; La. iv. 21, 22; Ezk. xxv. 12–14, xxxv. 15; Joel iii. 19; Am. ix. 12; Ob. 10 ff.). Some Edomites pressed into southern Judah and settled to the south of Hebron (see IDUMAEA). Edom proper fell into Arab hands during the 5th century BC, and in the 3rd century BC was overrun by the Nabataeans. Through these centuries yet other Edomites fled to Judah. Judas Maccabaeus later subdued them (1 Macc. v. 65), and John Hyrcanus compelled them to be circumcised and incorporated into the Jewish people. The Herods were of general Edomite stock.

BIBLIOGRAPHY. Nelson Glueck, *The Other Side of Jordan*, New Haven, 1940; *id.*, *AASOR*, 15, 18–19, which deal largely with Edom; *id.*, various articles in *BASOR*, 71, 72, 75, 76, 79, 80, 82, 84, 85; F. M. Abel, *Géographie de la Palestine*, 1933, II, pp. 281–285; M. Du Buit, *Géographie de la Terre Sainte*, 1958, pp. 143–144; D. Baly, *The Geography of the Bible*, 1958, Cp. 19. J.A.T.

EDREI. 1. A principal city of the Amorite kingdom of Og, Dt. i. 4 (LXX 'and in Edrei'; *cf.* S. R. Driver, *ICC*, *Deuteronomy*, *ad loc.*); Jos. xii. 4, xiii. 12, 31. Identified with Der'a, 15 miles ENE of Irbid, dating from Early Bronze, overlooking the uplands between Gilead and Hermon. Here the Israelites defeated the Amorites in a pitched battle (Nu. xxi. 33; Dt. iii. 1). Dt. iii. 10 suggests that its territory was the northern limit of Israelite penetration at that time. See Abel, *Géographie*, II, p. 310.

2. A place in Naphtali, probably south of Kedesh (Jos. xix. 37). J.P.U.L.

EDUCATION. The child has always been of paramount importance in Judaism, as the Mishnah and Talmud show clearly in several passages.

Fig. 71. Attic vase painting, c. 440 BC, showing a seated youth studying the alphabet.

For that matter, Jesus certainly taught the value of children, in His kindly treatment of them, as well as in His instruction regarding them. Because of this, there are a number of source-books for the study of education in the biblical period to be found in the Old Testament, the Apocrypha, and the Mishnah; *viz.* Proverbs, Ecclesiasticus, Wisdom of Solomon, and *Pirqe Aboth*, quite apart from useful allusions in other books. On the other hand, actual details of schooling are few; it is strange that the very word 'school' (*q.v.*) occurs but once in Scripture, and then refers merely to a lecture room borrowed by Paul (Acts xix. 9), not to any Jewish or Christian school.

I. EARLY LINKS WITH RELIGION

Three events stand out in the history of Jewish education. They centre on three persons, Ezra, Simon ben-Shetaḥ, and Joshua ben-Gamala. It was Ezra who established Scripture (such as it was at the time) as the basis for schooling; and his successors went on to make the synagogue a place of instruction as well as a place of worship. Simon ben-Shetaḥ enacted, in about 75 BC, that elementary schooling should be compulsory. Joshua ben-Gamala improved existing organization, appointing teachers in every province and town, a century later. But otherwise it is not easy to date innovations. Even the origins of the synagogue are obscure, though the Exile is a likely time for their rise. Schürer doubts the historicity of Simon ben-Shetaḥ's enactment, though most scholars accept it. In any case, Simon did not institute the elementary school, but merely extended its use. Simon and Joshua in no way interfered with existing trends and methods, and indeed Ezra only made more definite the previous linking of religion with everyday life. So it will prove better to divide the topic by subject rather than date, since none of the three men made sweeping changes.

II. THE DEVELOPMENT OF SCHOOLS

The place of learning was exclusively the home in the earliest period, and the tutors were the parents; and teaching in the home continued to play an important part in the whole of the biblical period. As it developed, the synagogue became the place of instruction. Indeed, the New Testament and Philo support Schürer's view that the synagogue's purpose was primarily instructional, and only then devotional; the synagogue ministry of Jesus consisted in 'teaching' (*cf.* Mt. iv. 23). The young were trained in either the synagogue itself or an adjoining building. At a later stage the teacher sometimes taught in his own house, as is evidenced by the Aramaic phrase for 'school', *bêṯ sāp̄ᵉrâ*, literally 'teacher's house'. The temple porticoes, too, proved very useful for Rabbis, and Jesus did much of His teaching there (*cf.* Mt. xxvi. 55). By Mishnaic times, eminent Rabbis had their own schools for higher learning. This feature probably started in the time of Hillel and Shammai, the famed 1st-century BC Rabbis. An elementary school was called *bêṯ has-sēp̄er*, 'house of the book', while a college for higher education was known as *bêṯ miḏrāš*, 'house of study'.

III. TEACHING AS A PROFESSION

The first tutors were the parents, as we have seen, except in the case of royal children (*cf.* 2 Ki. x. 1). The importance of this rôle is stressed here and there in the Pentateuch, *e.g.* Dt. iv. 9. Even as late as the Talmud, it was still the parent's responsibility to inculcate the law, to teach a trade, and to get his son married. After the period of Ezra, there arose a new profession, that of the scribe (*sōp̄ēr*), the teacher in the synagogue. The scribes were to change their character by New Testament times, however. The 'wise', or 'sages', seem to have been a different guild from the scribes, but their exact nature and function are obscure. The 'sage' (*ḥāḵām*) is, of course, frequently mentioned in Proverbs and later wisdom literature. By the New Testament period, there were three grades of teacher, the *ḥāḵām*, the *sōp̄ēr*, and the *ḥazzān* ('officer'), in descending order. Nicodemus was presumably of the highest grade, the 'doctors of the law' (Lk. v. 17, where the Gk. term is *nomodidaskalos*) of the lowest. The generic term 'teacher' (Heb. *mᵉlammēḏ*; Aram. *sāp̄ᵉrâ*) was usually applied to the lowest grade. But the honorific titles given to teachers (Rabbi, *etc.*) indicate the respect in which they were held. Ideally, they were not to be paid for teaching, but frequently a polite fiction granted them remuneration for time spent instead of services rendered. Ecclus. xxxviii. 24 f. considers manual labour beneath a teacher's dignity; besides, leisure is a necessary adjunct to his task. But later on there were many Rabbis who learnt a trade. Paul's views can be seen in 1 Cor. ix. 3 ff. The Talmud gives stringent rulings about the qualifications of teachers; it is interesting that none of them are academic—they are all moral, except those that prescribe that he must be male and married.

IV. THE SCOPE OF EDUCATION

This was not wide in the early period. The child would learn ordinary moral instruction from his mother, and a trade, usually agricultural, plus some religious and ritual knowledge, from his father. The interplay of religion and agricultural life would have been self-evident at every festival (*cf.* Lv. xxiii, *passim*). The festivals also taught religious history (*cf.* Ex. xiii. 8). So even at the earliest period everyday life and religious belief and practice were inseparable. This was the more so in the synagogue, where Scripture became the sole authority for both belief and daily conduct. Life, indeed, was itself considered a 'discipline' (Heb. *mûsār*, a frequent word in Proverbs). Education, then, was and remained religious and ethical, with Pr. i. 7 its motto. To read was essential for the study of Scripture; writing was perhaps less important, although it was known as early as Jdg. viii. 14 (RVmg). Basic arithmetic was taught. Languages were not taught *per se*, but note that, as Aramaic became the vernacular, study of the Heb. Scriptures became a linguistic exercise.

Girls' education was wholly in their mothers' hands. They learnt the domestic arts, simple moral and ethical instruction, and they were taught to read in order to become acquainted with the law. Their education was considered important, however, and they were even encouraged to learn a foreign language. King Lemuel's mother apparently proved an able teacher to him (Pr. xxxi. 1); this chapter also shows the character of the ideal woman.

V. METHODS AND AIMS

Methods of instruction were largely by repetition; the Heb. verb *šānâ*, 'repeat', came to mean both 'learn' and 'teach'. Mnemonic devices such as acrostics were therefore employed. Scripture was the textbook, but that other books were not unknown is evidenced by Ec. xii. 12. The value of rebuke was known (Pr. xvii. 10), but an emphasis on corporal chastisement is to be found in Proverbs and Ecclesiasticus. But discipline was much milder in Mishnaic times.

Until comparatively late times, it was customary for the pupil to sit on the ground at his teacher's feet, as did Paul at Gamaliel's (Acts xxii. 3). The bench (*sapsāl*) was a later invention.

Jewish education's whole function was to make the Jew holy, and separate from his neighbours, and to transform the religious into the practical. Such, then, was normal Jewish education; but undoubtedly there were schools after a Gk. pattern, especially in the closing centuries BC, and indeed Ecclesiasticus may have been written to combat deficiencies in such non-Jewish instruction. Hellenistic schools were found even in Palestine, but of course more frequently among Jewish communities elsewhere, notably in Alexandria.

In the infant Church child and parent were told how to behave towards one another (Eph. vi. 1, 4). Church officers had to know how to rule their own children. There were no Christian schools in early days; for one thing, the Church was too poor to finance them. But the children were included in the Church fellowship, and doubtless received their training there as well as in the home. See also WRITING.

BIBLIOGRAPHY. W. Barclay, *Educational Ideals in the Ancient World*, 1959, chapters I, VI; E. Schürer, *The Jewish People in the Time of Jesus Christ*, 1905, *passim*; articles on 'Education' in *EBi* and *HDB*. D.F.P.

EGLON. 1. A city near Lachish, eventually occupied by Judah (Jos. xv. 39). Under the Canaanite king Debir it was in the southern confederacy against Joshua (Jos. x. 3). Kh. Ajlan, 2 miles NNW of Tell el-Hesi (G. A. Smith, map), is too insignificant; and with Lachish fixed at Tell ed-Duweir, W. F. Albright identified Eglon with Tell el-Hesi, formerly thought to be Lachish (*BASOR*, 17, 1925, p. 7; Abel, *Géographie*, II, p. 311). It may still be argued from Jos. xii. 12 that Eglon was not north of Lachish; Tell en-Nejileh which is nearer the hills, originally suggested by Petrie, is not impossible: Elliger (*Palästinajahrbuch*, XXX, 1934, p. 67) favours Tell beit Mirsim.

2. The king of Moab, who occupied territory west of Jordan early in the period of the Judges, and was assassinated by Ehud (Jdg. iii. 12 ff.).

J.P.U.L.

EGYPT. The ancient kingdom and modern republic in the north-eastern corner of Africa and linked with W Asia by the Sinai isthmus.

I. NAME

a. Egypt

The word 'Egypt' derives from the Gk. *Aigyptos*, Lat. *Aegyptus*. This term itself is probably a transcript of the Egyp. *Ḥ(wt)-k'-Pt(ḥ)*, pronounced roughly *Ha-ku-ptah, as is shown by the cuneiform transcript *Ḫikuptaḫ* in the Amarna letters, *c.* 1360 BC. 'Hakuptah' is one of the names of Memphis, the old Egyptian capital on the west bank of the Nile just above Cairo (which eventually replaced it). This origin of the name 'Egypt' was first propounded by Brugsch in 1857 and latterly by Sir Alan Gardiner. If this explanation is correct, then the name of the city must have been used *pars pro toto* for Egypt generally besides Memphis by the Greeks, rather as today Cairo and Egypt are both *Miṣr* in Arabic. It is very doubtful indeed whether the place-name *ḥk(q)pt* in the Ugaritic (N Canaanite) texts is also to be identified with Egyptian 'Hakuptah' as Virolleaud thought. Rather, *ḥk(q)pt* may be in Crete.

b. Mizraim

The regular Heb. (and common Semitic) word for Egypt is *miṣrayim*. The word first occurs in external sources in the 14th century BC: as *mṣrm* in the Ugaritic (N Canaanite) texts and as *miṣri* in the Amarna letters. In the first millennium BC, the Assyro-Babylonian texts refer to *Muṣur* or *Muṣri*; unfortunately they use this term ambiguously: for Egypt on the one hand, for a region in N Syria/S Asia Minor on the other, and (very doubtfully) for part of N Arabia (see literature cited by Oppenheim in *ANET*, p. 279, n. 9). For the doubtful possibility of the N Syrian *Muṣri* being intended in 1 Ki. x. 28, see MIZRAIM. The term *Muṣri* is thought to mean 'march(es)', borderlands, and so to be applicable to any fringe-land (Egyptian, Syrian, or Arabian; *cf.* Oppenheim, *loc. cit.*). However true from an Assyr. military point of view, this explanation is hardly adequate to account for the Heb./Canaanite form *miṣrayim*/*mṣrm* of the second millennium, or for its use. That *miṣrayim* is a dual form reflecting the duality of Egypt (see II, 'Natural Features and Geography', below) is possible but quite uncertain. Spiegelberg, in *Recueil de Travaux*, XXI, 1899, pp. 39–41, sought to derive *mṣr* from Egyp. *(ỉ)mḏr*, '(fortification-) walls', referring to the guard-forts on Egypt's Asiatic frontier from *c.* 2000 BC onwards, the first feature of the country to be encountered by visiting Semites from that time. The fact that the term might be assimilated to Semitic *māṣôr*, 'fortress', adds weight to this. However, a final and complete explanation of *miṣrayim* cannot be offered at present.

c. 'Egypt' in Egyptian

Among the Egyptians' own names for their homeland, the commonest were: *Kmt* ('Kemyt'), 'the black land' (referring to the rich, black soil), *t'wy* ('tawy'), 'the two lands' (of the Upper Egyptian valley and Lower Egyptian delta), and *T'-mr'ỉ* ('To-meri'), 'Egypt', the exact literal meaning of which is uncertain.

II. NATURAL FEATURES AND GEOGRAPHY

a. General

The present political unit 'Egypt' is roughly a square, extending from the Mediterranean coast of Africa in the north to the line of 22° N latitude (some 670 miles from north to south), and from the Red Sea in the east across to the line of 25° E longitude in the west, with a total surface-area of roughly 386,200 square miles. However, of this whole area, 96% is desert and only 4% usable land; and 99% of Egypt's population live in that 4% of viable land.

The real Egypt is the land reached by the Nile, being Herodotus' oft-quoted 'gift of the Nile'. Egypt is in a 'temperate zone' desert-belt having a warm, rainless climate: in a year Alexandria has barely 7½ inches of rain, Cairo just over 1 inch, and Aswan virtually nil. For life-giving water, Egypt depends wholly on the Nile.

b. The two Egypts

Historically ancient Egypt consists of the long, narrow Nile valley from the first cataract at Aswan (not from the second, as today) to the Memphis/Cairo district, plus the broad, flat triangle (hence its name) of the Delta from Cairo to the sea. The contrast of valley and delta enforce a dual nature upon Egypt.

(i) *Upper Egypt.* Bounded on either side by cliffs (limestone to the north and sandstone to the south of Esna some 330 miles south of Cairo), the valley is never more than about 12 miles wide and sometimes narrows to a few hundred yards (as at Gebel Silsileh). At its annual inundation the Nile deposited fresh silt upon the land beyond its banks each year until the Aswan barrage halted deposition in modern times. As far as the waters reach, green plants can grow; immediately beyond, all is desert up to the cliffs. See further under NILE.

(ii) *Lower Egypt.* Some 12½ miles north of Cairo, the Nile divides into two main branches. The northern branch reaches the sea at Rosetta, and the eastern at Damietta about 90 miles away; from Cairo to the sea is roughly 100 miles. Between the two great arms of the Nile, and over a considerable area beyond them to the east and west, stretches the flat, swampy Delta-land, entirely composed of multi-millennial deposits of river-borne alluvium, and intersected by canals and drainage-channels. Lower Egypt has, from antiquity, always included the northernmost part of the Nile valley from just south of Memphis/Cairo, in addition to the Delta proper. In ancient times tradition held that the Nile had seven mouths on the Delta coast (Herodotus), but only three are recognized as important in ancient Egyptian sources.

(iii) *The effect of duality.* The contrast between these two regions deeply influenced the Egyptian people, history, and institutions. When the prehistoric kingdoms of Upper and Lower Egypt were united under one king at the start of their history the ultra-conservative Egyptians retained the dual nature of the kingdom in the title assumed by each pharaoh: 'King of Upper and Lower Egypt' and 'Lord of the *Two* Lands'. In periods of political weakness, Egypt regularly tended to fall back into her two natural divisions.

c. The Egypt of antiquity

The Nile valley has been habitable for only 6,000 years or so. During long ages before that time, the huge river carried out a continual process of alternate erosion and deposition in its own valley, ultimately flowing into a bay of the sea which later filled up with alluvium to form the Delta. Not till these processes had ceased, and much alluvium had been deposited in the valley, could settlers come and begin the work of swamp-clearing, cultivation, irrigation, and drainage.

To the west of the Nile valley stretches the Sahara, a flat, rocky desert of drifted sand, and parallel with the valley a series of oases—great natural depressions, where cultivation and habitation are made possible by a supply of artesian water. Close to, and directly linked with, the Nile valley by a natural channel is the Fayum depression, the Lake Moeris region of the ancients. From the XIIth Dynasty onwards this served as a flood-escape basin and reservoir for inundations of the Nile. Between the Nile valley and Red Sea on the east is the Arabian desert, a mountainous and broken terrain with some mineral wealth: gold, ornamental stone, including alabaster, breccia, and diorite. Across the Gulf of Suez is the rocky peninsula of Sinai (*q.v.*).

Egypt was thus sufficiently isolated between her deserts to develop her own individual culture; but, at the same time, access from the east by either the Sinai isthmus or Red Sea and Wadi Ḥammamat, and from the north and south by way of the Nile was direct enough for her to receive (and give) external stimulus.

The ancient geography of pharaonic Egypt is a subject of considerable complexity. The historic nomes or provinces first clearly emerge in the Old Kingdom (IVth Dynasty) in the third millennium BC, but not a few probably originated much earlier as territories of what were originally separate little communities in prehistory. There were reckoned twenty-two of these nomes for Upper Egypt and twenty for Lower Egypt in the main enumeration that was traditional by Graeco-Roman times, when geographical records are fullest.

III. PEOPLE AND LANGUAGE

a. People

The earliest evidences of human activity in Egypt are flint tools of the Palaeolithic age from the Nile terraces. But the first real Egyptians who settled as agriculturists in the Nile valley (and of whom physical remains survive) are those labelled as Taso-Badarians, the first predynastic (prehistoric) culture. They appear to be of African origin, together with the two successive prehistoric culture-phases, best called Naqada I and II, ending about 3000 BC or shortly thereafter. However, just prior to (and during) Egypt's abrupt emergence into history with the founding of a literate pharaonic monarchy, there is slight evidence for infiltration of new people from outside Egypt; they show differing physical characteristics and are found mainly in N Egypt. This is the so-called Giza or dynastic race, perhaps of Asiatic origin. Their ascendancy over, and fusion with, the older predynastic people is thought to have promoted the sudden flowering of the characteristic Egyptian historic culture, but this is still rather speculative. (See W. B. Emery, *Saqqara and the Dynastic Race*, 1952.) Modern Egyptians are in direct descent from the people of ancient Egypt.

b. Language

The ancient Egyptian language is of mixed origin and has had a very long history. It is usually called 'Hamito-Semitic', and was basically a Hamitic tongue (*i.e.* related to the Libyco-Berber languages of N Africa) swamped at an early epoch (in prehistory) by a Semitic language. Much Egyptian vocabulary is directly cognate with Semitic, and there are analogies in syntax. Lack of early written matter hinders proper comparison with Hamitic. On the affinities of the Egyptian language, see Gardiner, *Egyptian Grammar*, § 3, and (in more detail) G. Lefebvre, *Chronique d'Égypte*, XI, No. 22, 1936, pp. 266–292.

In the history of the Egyptian language, five main stages may conveniently be distinguished in the written documents. The first of these stages was *Old Egyptian*, an archaic and terse form, used during Dynasties I–VIII in the third millennium BC. The second, *Middle Egyptian*, was perhaps the vernacular of Dynasties IX–XI (2200–2000 BC) and was used universally for written records during the Middle Kingdom and early New Kingdom (to *c.* 1300 BC), and continued in use in official texts, in a slightly modified form, as late as Graeco-Roman days. This is the language of the great body of Egyptian classical literature (see 'Literature' below). The third stage, *Late Egyptian*, was the popular speech of the New Kingdom and after (16th–8th centuries BC), but was already coming into popular use two centuries before this time (1800–1600). It is also the language of documents and New Kingdom literature and official texts from Dynasty XIX onwards. Old, Middle, and Late Egyptian were written in hieroglyphic and hieratic scripts (see WRITING). *Demotic*, the fourth stage, is really the name of a script, and is the name applied to the still more evolved form of Egyptian current in documents dating from the 8th century BC to Roman times. Fifthly comes *Coptic*, the last stage of Egyptian, and the native language of Roman-Byzantine Egypt. This has several dialect forms and was turned into a literary medium by Egyptian Christians or Copts. It was written, not in Egyptian script, but in the Coptic alphabet, which is composed of the Greek alphabet plus seven extra characters taken over from the old Demotic script to cover sounds which do not exist in Gk. Coptic has survived as the purely liturgical language of the Coptic (Egyptian) Church down to modern times, its use being equivalent to that of Latin in the Roman Catholic Church. At all periods, foreign loanwords are to be found in Egyptian; these are, for the most part, Semitic in early Egyptian, and Gk. in Coptic.

IV. HISTORY

Space allows only the briefest possible treatment of Egypt's long history here. Attention is therefore concentrated on salient features, and on those periods of direct relevance to biblical studies. For further detail, see the classified Bibliography at the end of the article.

a. Egyptian chronology

The Egyptian priest Manetho (3rd century BC) wrote a history of Egypt, in which he listed the kings of Egypt in thirty Dynasties (later, thirty-one), a usage so convenient that it is retained today. Only a king-list and brief quotations from this work have survived, however, and even these are often badly transmitted; but this does at least provide a framework. (See W. G. Waddell, *Manetho*, 1940, for full text and translation; a recent evaluation is H. W. Helck, *Untersuchungen zu Manetho und den Ägyptischen Königslisten*, 1956.) The Egyptians themselves had kept annals and king-lists; little ivory tablets were used for this purpose in Dynasties I and II, while the annals of Dynasties I to VI were summarized on a large tablet now known as the Palermo Stone (*c.* 2400 BC). Several king-lists come from the New Kingdom, the most remarkable being the Turin Papyrus, which lists nearly all of Egypt's rulers from earliest times, apparently, to its own day (?Rameses II). Then there are the numerous contemporary inscriptions of many pharaohs (often bearing regnal year-dates) and of their officials, including genealogies. There are synchronisms with kings of Western Asia, permitting links with Near Eastern chronology. Finally, mentions of lunar dates and risings of the Dog-Star Sothis/Sirius in Egyptian texts afford limited astronomical control of Egyptian dates in the Middle and New Kingdoms. Bibliography on all these difficult questions will be found in the historical works cited below. For Egyptian dates most relevant to biblical history, see the table of dates in CHRONOLOGY OF THE OLD TESTAMENT, to which the following is complementary. The major periods of Egyptian history are are set out in the table on p. 340.

b. Egypt before 2000 BC

(i) *Predynastic Egypt*. During the three successive phases of predynastic settlement the foundations for historic Egypt were laid. Communities grew up having villages, local shrines, and belief in an after-life (evidenced by burial-customs). Copper was a rarity till near the end of the period. In Badarian and Naqada I periods contact was apparently made with S Arabia, Iran, and Mesopotamia *via* Wadi Hammamat and the Red Sea. At some time in the Predynastic period Hamitic Egyptian was swamped by a Semitic language (possibly pointing to Asiatic immigrants), which consequently crystallized into the Old Egyptian of the historic epoch. In the final prehistoric phase (Naqada II) definite contact with Sumerian Mesopotamia existed, and, on the eve of the union of the prehistoric kingdoms of Upper and Lower Egypt to form the single state of pharaonic Egypt, Mesopotamian influences and ideas were so strong as to leave their mark on formative Egyptian culture (*cf.* H. Frankfort, *Birth of Civilisation in the Near East*, 1951, pp. 100–111). It is at this point that hieroglyphic writing appears, Egyptian art assumes its characteristic forms, and monumental architecture begins.

(ii) *Archaic Egypt.* The first pharaoh of all Egypt was apparently Narmer of Upper Egypt, who conquered the rival Delta kingdom; he was perhaps the Menes of later tradition, and certainly the founder of Dynasty I. Egyptian culture advanced and matured rapidly during these first two Dynasties. Main state events that marked each year were put on ivory tablets (first annals). A strong, centralized administration was created, in which each department maintained two separate bureaux to deal with the affairs of Upper and Lower Egypt.

(iii) *Old Kingdom.* In Dynasties III–VI, Egypt reached a peak of prosperity, splendour, and cultural achievement. King Djoser's step-pyramid and its attendant buildings is the first major structure of cut stone in history (*c.* 2650 BC); its architect was probably Imhotep, who stood at the head of the long line of Egypt's sages as author of an 'Instruction' (*i.e.* a wisdom book). In Dynasty IV the pharaoh was absolute master, not in theory only (as was always the case) but also in fact, as never occurred before or after. Next in authority to the divine king stood the vizier, and beneath him the heads of the various branches of administration (treasury, agriculture, judiciary, *etc.*). At first members of the royal family held these offices. During this period material culture reached high levels in architecture (culminating in the Great Pyramid of Kheops, Dynasty IV), sculpture, and painted relief, as well as in furnishings and jewellery. In Dynasty V the power of the kings weakened economically, and the priesthood of the sun-god Rē stood behind the throne. In Dynasty VI the Egyptians were actively exploring and trading in Nubia (later Cush). Meanwhile the decline in the king's power continued, the provincial governors becoming hereditary landed barons and increasingly independent of the central government at Memphis. This situation reached its climax late in the ninety-four years' reign of Pepi II, by whose death Egypt had become a collection of petty princedoms. The literature of the time included several wisdom-books: those of Imhotep, Hardidief (?Kairos), to Kagemni, and, of especial note, that of Ptah-hotep.

(iv) *First Intermediate Period.* This period saw the culmination of trends noted in the section above. In the Delta, where the established order was overthrown, this was a time of social up-

Prehistory	Down to *c.* 3000 BC.
4th millennium BC	Three successive predynastic cultures. *Tasian and Badarian*: first agriculturalists. *Naqada I*: merges into *Naqada II*: emergence of separate kingdoms of Upper and Lower Egypt by end of this period.
3rd millennium BC	*Archaic Period (Protodynastic)*: Dynasties I, II, *c.* 2850–2650 BC. *Old Kingdom, or pyramid age*: Dynasties III–VI, *c.* 2650–2200 BC. First great flowering of Egyptian culture. *First Intermediate Period*: Dynasties VII–XI, *c.* 2200–2050 BC.
2nd millennium BC	*Middle Kingdom*: Dynasties XI, XII, *c.* 2134–1786 BC. Second great age of Egyptian culture. *Second Intermediate Period*: Dynasties XIII–XVII, includes the Hyksos, *c.* 1786–1570 BC. *New Kingdom or Empire*: Dynasties XVIII–XX, *c.* 1570–1085 BC. Third great period in Egyptian civilization.
1st millennium BC	*Late Period*: Dynasties XXI–XXXI, *c.* 1085–332 BC. Long period of decay interspersed with occasional brief periods of recovery. *Hellenistic Egypt*: Alexander the Great and the Ptolemies, *c.* 332–30 BC.
1st millennium AD	*Roman and Byzantine Epochs*: Egypt (Coptic) becomes part of Christendom, *c.* 30 BC–AD 641. This is followed by the Islamic epoch lasting to the present day.

heaval (revolution) and of Asiatic infiltration. For a time, VIIIth Dynasty pharaohs at Memphis kept a show of authority over the Upper Egyptian local princes (who were, nonetheless, virtually independent). New kings in Middle-Egypt (Dynasties IX and X) then took over and sought to restore order in the Delta. But eventually they quarrelled with the princes of Thebes in the southern section of Upper Egypt, and these then declared their independence (Dynasty XI) and eventually vanquished their northern rivals, reuniting Egypt under one strong sceptre (that of the Intef and Mentuhotep kings). The disturbances of this troubled epoch shattered the bland self-confidence of Old Kingdom Egypt and called forth a series of pessimistic writings that are among the finest and most remarkable in Egyptian literature (see Literature, below). Ancient royal funerary usages that had passed to the great nobles passed on further into the possession of all Egyptians of sufficiently comfortable means, as from this epoch.

c. The Middle Kingdom and Second Intermediate Period

(i) *Middle Kingdom.* Eventually the XIth Dynasty ended in confusion, and the vacant throne went to Amenemhat I, founder of Dynasty XII, the strong man of his time. He and his Dynasty (*c.* 1991 BC) were alike remarkable. Elected to an unstable throne by fellow-nobles jealous for their local autonomy, Amenemhat I sought to rehabilitate the kingship by a programme of material reform announced and justified in literary works produced as royal propaganda (see G. Posener, *Littérature et Politique dans l'Égypte de la XIIe Dynastie*, 1956). He therein proclaimed himself the (political) saviour of Egypt. He accordingly rebuilt the administration, settled land-disputes, promoted Egypt's agricultural prosperity (using the Fayum basin as a natural Nile-overflow catchment), and secured the frontiers, placing a series of forts on the Asiatic border. The administration was no longer at XIth-Dynasty Thebes, which was too far south, but moved back to the strategically far superior area of Memphis, to Ithet-Tawy, a centre specifically built for the purpose. The policies so well begun by Amenemhat I were worthily continued by most of his seven successors (three Sesostris, three more Amenemhat, and a queen). Sesostris I, and especially III, thoroughly subdued Nubia (Cush), to the 2nd cataract, building a series of massive forts (almost mediaeval castles!). Sesostris III also raided into Palestine, as far as Shechem ('Sekmem'). The extent of Egyptian influence in Palestine, Phoenicia, and S Syria in Dynasty XII is indicated by the execration texts (19th century BC) which record the names for magical cursing of possibly-hostile Semitic princes and their districts, besides Nubians and Egyptians. (See Albright, *JPOS*, VIII, 1928, pp. 223–256; *BASOR*, 81, 1941, pp. 16–21, and *BASOR*, 83, 1941, pp. 30–36.)

Internally, the restoration of royal power under Sesostris III is marked by the disappearance of the great landed local princes, who were presumably replaced by 'civil service' royal officials of the central authority. Art and architecture again flourished. This was the golden age of Egypt's classical literature, especially short stories (see Literature, below). This well-organized XIIth-Dynasty Egypt, careful of its Asiatic frontier, was in all probability the Egypt of Abraham. The charge which pharaoh gave to

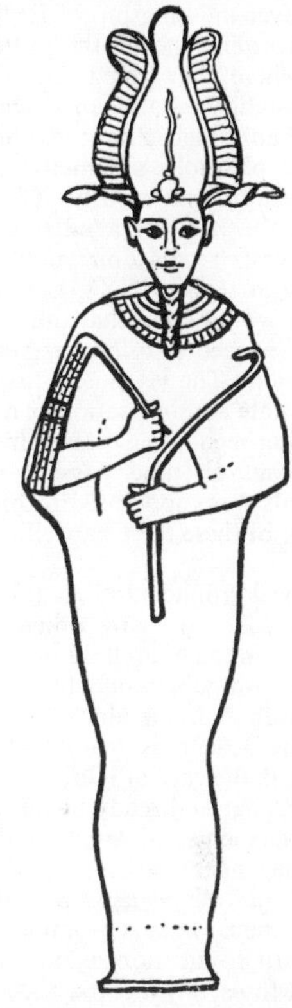

Fig. 72. A bronze statuette of Osiris, 7½ inches high. As the god who rules the realm of the dead, he is mummiform and holds the royal sceptres of crook and flail.

his men concerning Abraham (Gn. xii. 20) when he left Egypt is exactly paralleled (in reverse) by that given with regard to the returning Egyptian exile Sinuhe (*ANET*, p. 21, lines 240–250) and, pictorially, by the group of thirty-seven Asiatics visiting Egypt, shown in a famous tomb-scene at Beni-Hasan (see, *e.g.*, *IBA*, fig. 25, pp. 28–29). Amūn of Thebes, fused with the sun-god as Amen-Rē, had become chief national god; but in Osiris resided most of the Egyptians' hopes of the after-life.

(ii) *Second Intermediate Period and Hyksos.* For barely a century after 1786 BC (*i.e.* the end of Dynasty XII), a new line of kings, the XIIIth Dynasty, held sway over almost the whole of Egypt, still ruling from the Memphite centre

Ithet-Tawy. For the most part their reigns were brief and they followed one another in quick succession, so that a vizier might thus serve several kings. Deprived of settled, firm, personal royal control, the dependent machinery of state inevitably began to run down. At this time many Semitic slaves were to be found in Egypt, even as far south as Thebes (see JOSEPH), and eventually Semitic chiefs (Egyp. 'chiefs of foreign lands' *ḥḳ'w-ḫ'swt* = Hyksos) gained prominence in Lower Egypt and then (perhaps by a swift *coup d'état*) took over the kingship of Egypt at Ithet-Tawy itself (forming the XVth–XVIth 'Hyksos' Dynasties), where they ruled for roughly 140 years. They established also an E Delta capital, Avaris (? = Tanis, Heb. Zoan; *cf.* Nu. xiii. 22?). These Semitic pharaohs assumed the full rank and style of traditional royalty. That they had conquered at the head of a pillaging horde as Manetho suggests seems quite unlikely (see T. Säve-Söderbergh, *JEA*, XXXVII, 1951, pp. 53–71), though it would seem that the native Egyptian line was reduced to a local tributary line in the Theban south. The Hyksos at first took over the Egyptian state administration as a going concern, employing regular Egyptian officials of the old régime; but as time passed, naturalized Semitic officials were appointed to high administrative office; of these the Chancellor Ḥūr is the best-known.

Into this background, Joseph (Gn. xxxvii-l) fits perfectly. Like so many others, he was a Semitic servant in the household of an important Egyptian. The royal court is punctiliously Egyptian in etiquette (Gn. xli. 14, xliii. 32; *cf.* JOSEPH), yet the Semite Joseph is readily appointed to high office (as in the case of Ḥūr, perhaps, a little later). The peculiar and ready blend of Egyptian and Semitic elements mirrored in the Joseph-narrative (independent of its being a Heb. story set in Egypt) fits the Hyksos period perfectly. Furthermore, the E Delta is prominent under the Hyksos (Avaris), but not again in Egyptian history until Moses' day (*i.e.* the XIXth Dynasty, or, at the earliest, the very end of the XVIIIth). For some background points, see JOSEPH; on his date, see CHRONOLOGY OF THE OLD TESTAMENT.

Eventually a line of princes at Thebes clashed with their Hyksos overlords in the north; king Kamose took all Egypt from Apopi III ('Awoserrē) except for Avaris in NE Delta, according to his recently discovered historical stele (see most recently, T. Säve-Söderbergh, *Kush*, IV, 1956, pp. 54–61). Finally, Kamose's successor Ahmose I (founder of the XVIIIth Dynasty and the New Kingdom) expelled the Hyksos régime and its immediate adherents (Egyp. as well as Asiatic) from Egypt and worsted them in Palestine. The most recent outline of this period's history and culture (illustrated) is in W. C. Hayes, *Scepter of Egypt*, II, 1959, pp. 3–41.

d. New Kingdom—the Empire

The next five centuries, from *c.* 1570 to *c.* 1085 BC, witnessed the pinnacle of Egypt's political power and influence and the age of her greatest outward grandeur and luxury, but also, by their end, the breakdown of the old Egyptian spirit, and the beginning of that dilution, degeneration, fossilization, and eventual dissolution of Egyptian life and civilization which came about during the Late Period. Whereas the speed of the process varies from century to century, the general downward direction never changed, and reached its nadir in Roman times.

(i) *Dynasty XVIII.* The first kings of this line (except Tuthmosis I) were apparently content to expel the Hyksos and to rule Egypt and Nubia in the old XIIth-Dynasty tradition. But after the death of his aunt, the Queen-regnant Hatshepsut, the energetic Tuthmosis III took up the embryo policy of his grandfather Tuthmosis I, aiming to conquer Palestine–Syria and set the national boundary as far from Egypt proper as possible, in order to avoid any repetition of the Hyksos dominion. This imperial policy Tuthmosis III executed in seventeen Syrian campaigns, following out a consistent strategy of conquest, organization, and consolidation, in order to establish Egyptian rule in Palestine, Phoenicia, and much of N Syria as far as the Euphrates. The princes of the Canaanite/Amorite city-states were reduced to tribute-paying vassals. This structure lasted almost a century till late into the reign of Amenophis III (*c.* 1360 BC); for this brief spell, Egypt was the paramount power in the Ancient Near East.

Within Egypt there was much greater 'professionalism' than ever before; in earlier days officials could be appointed to a succession of quite different jobs in the course of their careers. But now, besides the bureaucracy of regular scribes, the standing army had professional officers who formed an élite around the person of the warrior-pharaoh; the great gods were served by priesthoods more professionally organized than ever before. Easily foremost among the latter was the priesthood of Amūn or Amen-Rē at Thebes, state god of Empire, to whom accrued incredible wealth in lands and *mobilia*, and great economic power thereby. The pharaohs began to sense this danger to their own power in the state, and sought to combat it—at first, by appointing their own trusted nominees to the high-priesthood of Amūn and by tactfully playing off his priests against the rival priesthoods of Ptah of Memphis and Rē' of Heliopolis. Nor was Thebes sole capital at this time: Memphis in the north was more convenient administratively (especially for Asia), and Amenophis II had been 'born at Memphis' (scarab, Petrie, *Scarabs and Cylinders*, 1917, plate 30: 1). Amenophis III showed particular predilection for Aten, the sun-god manifest in the solar disc, while seeking to curb priestly ambition and still officially honouring Amūn. But his son Amenophis IV broke completely with Amūn and then with almost all the old gods, proscribing their worship and excising their very names from the monuments. Amenophis IV proclaimed the sole worship of Aten, changed his own name to Akhenaten, and moved to his own newly created capital-city in Middle-Egypt (Akhet-Aten, the modern Tell el-Amarna). Only he and the royal family worshipped Aten directly; ordinary men worshipped Aten in the person of the divine pharaoh Akhenaten himself (see Religion, below).

Meantime, Egypt's hold on Syria–Palestine slackened somewhat. The petty princes there were free to fight each other in pursuit of personal ambition, denouncing each other to the pharaoh and seeking military aid from him to further their own designs. The correspondence from which we gain this information is the famous Amarna Letters, written in Bab. diplomatic cuneiform on clay tablets. Egypt's N Syrian ally, the Mitanni kingdom, was worsted (and then largely absorbed) by the redoubtable Hittite king Suppiluliuma who thus became overlord of the various N Syrian states. At home, Akhenaten eventually had to compromise with the opposing forces, and within two or three years of his death Thebes was again titular capital under Tutankhamūn and Ay. Amūn's worship, wealth, and renown were fully restored.

The main challenge to the power of the pharaoh now lay, not in the priesthood, but in the army, and it was from amongst the high officers close to the throne that the next ruler came. General Haremhab now assumed control and began to set the affairs of Egypt to rights again. At his death the throne passed to his colleague Paramessu, who, as Rameses I, founded Dynasty XIX and reigned for one year.

(ii) *Dynasty XIX.* Roughly 1300–1200 BC. Following Haremhab's internal restoration of Egypt, Sethos I (son of Rameses I) felt able to reassert Egyptian authority in Syria. His clash with the Hittites was not unsuccessful and the two powers made a treaty. Sethos began a large building programme in the NE Delta (the first since Hyksos times) and had a residence there. He may have founded the Delta capital so largely built by his son Rameses II, who named it after himself, 'Pi-Ramessē', 'House of Rameses' (the Raamses of Ex. i. 11). Rameses II posed as the imperial pharaoh *par excellence*, dazzling later generations to such an extent that nine later kings took his name (Rameses III–XI). Besides the Delta residence, this king undertook extensive building throughout all Egypt and Nubia during his long reign of sixty-six years. In Syria he campaigned (usually against the Hittites) for twenty years (the pyrrhic victory of the Battle of Qadesh being his most famous conflict) until, wearied of the struggle, and with other foes to face, he and his Hittite contemporary Hattusil III finally signed a treaty of (as it proved) lasting peace between them. During the remainder of Rameses' long reign of outward magnificence, Egypt's power at home and abroad steadily declined. His successor Merenptah made one brief raid into Palestine (his capture of Gezer is attested by an inscription at Amada independent of the famous Israel Stele), apparently brushing with a few Israelites among others, and had to beat off a dangerous invasion (that of the 'Sea Peoples') from Libya. His successors were ineffective; when the last one died, leaving the throne vacant (*c.* 1200 BC), Egypt lapsed into anarchy, and a Syrian opportunist briefly seized power.

The first half of Dynasty XIX apparently witnessed the Israelite oppression and Exodus (see CHRONOLOGY OF THE OLD TESTAMENT). The restoration of firm order under Haremhab and the great impetus given to building activity in the E Delta by both Sethos I and Rameses II, with the consequent need of a large and economic labour-force, set the background for the Heb. oppression which culminated in the work on Pithom and Ra'amses described in Ex. i. 8–11. Ra'amses was the great Delta-residence of the pharaoh, and Pithom a township in the Wadi Tumilat (see RA'AMSES, PITHOM). Ex. i. 12–22 gives some details of the conditions of this slavery, and for background to the Hebrews' brick-making, see BRICK, MOSES.

As for the early life of Moses, there is nothing either exceptional or incredible in a W Semite's being brought up in Egyptian court circles, perhaps in a *harim* in a Delta pleasure-residence, the pharaohs having several such scattered *harims* (*cf.* Yoyotte in Posener, *Dictionnaire de la Civilisation Égyptienne*, 1959, p. 126). Examples of this are close to hand. Mery-Rē, an attendant of Tuthmosis III (*c.* 1470 BC), was son of one Pa-Amurri ('the Amorite') and his wife Keren (*cf.* 'Keren-happuch', Job's daughter). (See Janssen, *Chronique d'Égypte*, XXVI, No. 51, 1951, p. 53.) At least from the reign of Rameses II onwards, Asiatics were brought up in royal *harims*, with the purpose of holding office (see Sauneron and Yoyotte, *Revue d'Égyptologie*, VII, 1950, pp. 67–70). In the late XVIIIth Dynasty(?), at Memphis, one Siribakhani was priest of (Egyptian) Amūn and (Semitic) Baal and Astarte (Ashtaroth) (see Janssen, *op. cit.*, p. 54 and refs.). In year 42 of Rameses II, his twenty-third son, Si-Mentu, is mentioned as being married to the daughter of the Syrian sea-captain Ben-'Anath (*Recueil de Travaux*, XVI, 1894, p. 64). In fact, Rameses II's eldest daughter bore the completely Semitic name Bint-'Anath (*cf.* Petrie, *History of Egypt*, III, 1905, pp. 37, 87 and fig. 35). The thoroughly Semitic Ben-'Ozen from Ṣûr-Bāšān ('Rock of Bashan') was royal cupbearer (*wb'-nsw*) to Merenptah (Janssen, *op. cit.*, pp. 54–57 and fig. 11), and another Semitic cupbearer of his was called Pen-Ḥaṣu[ri], ('he of Hazor') (*cf.* Sauneron and Yoyotte, *op. cit.*, p. 68, n. 6). Note too that it was a Syrian (*Ḥuru*) opportunist who briefly seized the power at the end of Dynasty XIX. Finally, on a lower level, an Egyptian of *c.* 1170 BC scolds his son for going so far as to join in blood-brotherhood with Asiatics in the Delta (J. Černý, *JNES*, XIV, 1955, pp. 161 ff.). Hence the Egyptian training and upbringing of Moses in Ex. ii is entirely credible; the onus of proof lies upon any who would discredit the account. A further implication is that Moses would have an Egyptian education (*cf.* the second instance cited above), one of the best available in his day. See further under MOSES. For the magicians, see MAGIC AND SORCERY; and for the plagues, PLAGUES OF EGYPT. For the flight of fugitives (comparable to that of Moses in Ex. ii. 15), *cf.* the flight of two runaway slaves in Papyrus Anastasi V (*ANET*, p. 259) and clauses on the extradition of fugitives in the treaty between Rameses II and the Hittites (*ANET*, pp. 200, 203). For movements of peoples or large groups, see the Hittite example quoted in the article on EXODUS, and for the number of Israelites at the Exodus, see WILDERNESS OF WANDERING. Between Egypt and Canaan at this period there was constant coming and going (*cf.* the frontier-reports in *ANET*, pp. 258–259). The age of the XIXth Dynasty was the most cosmopolitan in Egyptian history. More than in Dynasty XVIII, Hebrew–Canaanitic loan-words penetrated Egyptian language and literature by the score, and Egyptian officials proudly showed off their knowledge of the Canaanite tongue (Papyrus Anastasi I, see *ANET*, p. 477b). Semitic deities (Baal, Anath, Resheph, Astarte, or Ashtaroth) were accepted in Egypt and even had temples there. Thus the Hebrews could hardly fail to hear something of the land of Canaan, and Canaanites with their customs were before their eyes, before they had even stirred from Egypt; the knowledge of such matters displayed in the Pentateuch does not imply a date of writing after the Israelite invasion of Canaan, as is so often erroneously surmised.

(iii) *Dynasty XX.* In due course, a prince Setnakht expelled the Syrian adventurer, restored order, and founded a new dynasty. His son Rameses III was Egypt's last great imperial pharaoh. In the first decade of his reign (*c.* 1190–1180 BC) great folk-movements in the E Mediterranean basin swept away the Hittite empire in Asia Minor, entirely disrupted the traditional Canaanite–Amorite city-states of Syria–Palestine, and threatened Egypt with invasion from both Libya and Palestine. These attacks Rameses III beat off in three desperate campaigns, and he even briefly carried Egyp. arms into Syria and obtained fairly nominal suzerainty of Palestine (*via* the lowlands and main routes). In Egypt he continued the tradition of erecting great buildings, and for a time Egypt prospered again. But his life ended in a *harim*-conspiracy, and since his successors Rameses IV–XI were for the most part ineffective personally, the machinery of state became increasingly inefficient and corrupt, and chronic inflation upset the economy, causing great hardship for the common people. The famous robberies of the royal tombs at Thebes reached their peak at this time. The high priests of Amūn at Thebes grew increasingly independent of the king until an army *coup d'état* there brought the General Herihor into the high-priestly office. He then ruled Upper Egypt from Thebes, with a prince Nesubanebded governing the Delta, and Rameses XI still remaining king of Egypt. With his death the Empire was ended.

The archaeological remains of the New Kingdom period are particularly numerous and instructive as to the conditions of life during this general epoch. The splendid paintings of daily and official life in the tomb-chapels of the nobles in the cliffs of Thebes deserve special mention in this connection. For bibliography, see that given at the end of this article.

e. Late-Period Egypt and Israelite History

From now on, Egypt's story is one of a decline, halted at intervals, but then only briefly, by occasional kings of outstanding character. But the memory of Egypt's past greatness lingered on far beyond her own borders, and served Israel and Judah ill when they were foolish enough to depend on the 'bruised reed'. During most of the Late Period, Egyp. historical sources are extremely scanty, and the details of Egyp. internal history from 1085 to 664 BC are still a battle-ground for differing interpretations. However, it is just possible to follow out the main trends in Egyp. foreign policy in Asia by combining Old Testament data and Assyro-Bab. sources with the extant Egyptian evidence.

(i) *Dynasty XXI and the united monarchy.* Late in the reign of Rameses XI (as we have already mentioned) an arrangement was reached whereby the General Herihor (now also High Priest of Amūn) ruled Upper Egypt and the prince Nesubanebded I (Smendes) ruled Lower Egypt; this was styled, politically, as a 'renaissance' (*wḥm-mswt*). (See H. Kees, *Herihor und die Aufrichtung des Thebanischen Gottesstaates*, being the *Nachrichten v. d. Gesellschaft der Wissenschaften*, Göttingen (Phil.-Hist. Kl., Fachgr. I), NF, Vol. II, No. 1, 1936.) At the death of Rameses XI (*c.* 1085 BC), by a further mutual arrangement, Smendes at Tanis became pharaoh, the succession being secured for his descendants (Dynasty XXI), while, in return, Herihor's successors at Thebes were confirmed in the hereditary high-priesthood of Amūn, and in the rule of Upper Egypt under the Tanite pharaohs. So in Dynasty XXI, one half of Egypt ruled the whole only by gracious permission of the other half!

These peculiar circumstances help to explain the modest foreign policy of this Dynasty in Asia: a policy of friendship and alliance with neighbouring Palestinian states, military action being restricted to 'police' action to safeguard the frontier in the south-west corner of Palestine nearest the Egyptian border. Commercial motives would also be strong, as Tanis was a great port. All this links up with contemporary Old Testament references.

When King David conquered Edom, Hadad the infant Edomite heir was taken to Egypt for safety. There he found a welcome so favourable that, when he was grown up, he gained a royal wife (1 Ki. xi. 18–22). A clear example of XXIst Dynasty foreign policy occurs early in Solomon's reign (see PHARAOH). A pharaoh 'smote Gezer' and gave it as dowry with his daughter's hand in marriage-alliance with Solomon (1 Ki. ix. 16; *cf.* iii. 1, vii. 8, ix. 24, xi. 1). The combination of 'police' action in SW Palestine (Gezer) and alliance with the powerful Israelite state gave Egypt security on her Asiatic frontier and doubtless brought economic gain to both states. At Tanis was found a damaged triumphal relief-scene of the Pharaoh Siamūn smiting a foreigner —apparently a Philistine, to judge by the Aegean-type axe in his hand. This very specific detail very strongly suggests that it was Siamūn who conducted a 'police' action in Philistia (reaching Canaanite Gezer) and became Solomon's ally. (For this scene, see most recently P. Montet, *L'Égypte et la Bible*, 1959, p. 40, fig. 5 [to appear in English].)

(ii) *The Libyan Dynasties and the divided monarchy*. 1. Shishak. When the last Tanite king died in 945 BC a powerful Libyan tribal chief (? of Bubastis/Pi-beseth) acceded to the throne peacefully as Sheshonq I (biblical Shishak), thereby founding Dynasty XXII. For two centuries preceding this, Libyans had been constantly infiltrating into Egypt to swell the numbers of their countrymen already serving there as mercenaries. Some Libyans became powerful provincial governors; and it was as chief one of these, and allied by marriage to the Tanite royal house, that Sheshonq gained his throne. (*Cf.* Kees, *Priestertum im Ägyptischen Staat*, 1953, pp. 172–185.) Sheshonq rapidly brought all Egypt under his effective rule, installing his own son as non-hereditary high priest of Amūn in Thebes and so ending the semi-independence of the Theban priest-princedom in Upper Egypt. While consolidating Egypt internally under his rule, Sheshonq I began a new and aggressive Asiatic foreign policy. He viewed Solomon's Israel not as an ally but as a political and commercial rival on his north-east frontier, and therefore worked for the break-up of the Heb. kingdom. While Solomon lived, Sheshonq shrewdly took no action apart from harbouring political refugees, notably Jeroboam son of Nebat (1 Ki. xi. 29–40). At Solomon's death Jeroboam's return to Palestine precipitated the division of the kingdom into the two lesser realms of Rehoboam and Jeroboam. Soon after, in Rehoboam's 'fifth year', 925 BC (1 Ki. xiv. 25, 26; 2 Ch. xii. 2–12), and apparently on pretext of a Bedouin border incident (stele-fragment, Grdseloff, *Revue de l'Histoire Juive en Égypte*, 1, 1947, pp. 95–97), Shishak invaded Palestine, subduing Israel as well as Judah as is shown by the discovery of a stele of his at Megiddo (C. S. Fisher, *The Excavation of Armageddon*, 1929, p. 13 and fig.). Many biblical place-names occur in the list attached to the triumphal relief subsequently sculptured by Shishak on the temple of Amūn (Karnak) in Thebes (see *ANEP*, p. 118 and fig. 349, and on this campaign further bibliography under SHISHAK). See also SUKKIIM. Sheshonq's purpose was limited and definite: to gain political and commercial security by subduing his immediate neighbour. He made no attempt to revive the Empire of Tuthmosis or Rameses.

2. Zerah. It would appear from 2 Ch. xiv. 9–15, xvi. 8, that Sheshonq's successor Osorkon I sought to emulate his father's Palestinian success but was too lazy to go himself. Instead, he apparently sent as general Zerah the Ethiopian, who was soundly defeated by Asa of Judah *c.* 897 BC; see ZERAH. This defeat spelt the end of Egypt's aggressive policy in Asia. However, again like Sheshonq I, Osorkon I maintained relations with Byblos in Phoenicia, where statues of both pharaohs were found (*Syria*, V, 1924, pp. 145–147 and plate 42; *Syria*, VI, 1925, pp. 101–117 and plate 25).

3. Egypt and Ahab's dynasty. Osorkon I's successor, Takeloth I, was apparently a nonentity who allowed the royal power to slip through his incompetent fingers. Thus the next king, Osorkon II, inherited an Egypt whose unity was already menaced: the local Libyan provincial governors were becoming increasingly independent, and separatist tendencies appeared in Thebes, affecting Upper Egypt, despite the best efforts of the new ruler. Hence, he apparently returned to the old 'modest' foreign policy of (similarly-weak) Dynasty XXI, that of alliance with his Palestinian neighbours. This is hinted at by the discovery, in Omri and Ahab's palace at Samaria, of an alabaster vase of Osorkon II, such as the pharaohs included in their diplomatic presents to fellow-rulers (illustrated in Reisner, *etc.*, *Harvard Excavations at Samaria*, I, 1924, fig. on p. 247). This suggests that Omri or Ahab had links with Egypt as well as Tyre (*cf.* Ahab's marriage with Jezebel). Osorkon II also presented a statue at Byblos (Dunand, *Fouilles de Byblos*, I, pp. 115–116 and plate 43).

4. Hoshea and 'So king of Egypt'. The 'modest' policy revived by Osorkon II was doubtless continued by his ever-weaker successors, under whom Egypt progressively fell apart into its constituent local provinces with kings reigning in Thebes (Dynasty XXIII) alongside the main, parent XXIInd Dynasty at Tanis/Zoan. Prior to this dual rule (perhaps mutually agreed), the Egyp. state was rocked by bitter civil wars centred on Thebes (*cf.* R. A. Caminos, *The Chronicle of Prince Osorkon*, 1958), and could hardly have supported any different external policy.

All this indicates why Israel's last king, Hoshea, turned so readily for help against Assyria to 'So king of Egypt' in 725/4 BC (2 Ki. xvii. 4), and how very misplaced was his trust in an Egypt so weak and divided. No help came to save Samaria from its fall. The identity of 'So' has long been obscure. He is not Shabaka the Ethiopian pharaoh who comes rather later, nor is he the 'Sib'e, *turtan* (C.-in-C.) of Egypt' whom Sargon of Assyria mentions, because Sib'e must now be read as Re'e. 'So' is, then, either Osorkon IV, last pharaoh of Dynasty XXII/XXIII, *c.* 727–716 BC, or a Heb. transcript for 'the vizier of the king of Egypt' (the latter being still Osorkon IV). See So. The real power in Lower Egypt was wielded by Tafnekht and his successor Bekenrenef (Dynasty XXIV) from Sais in the W Delta; so powerless was Osorkon IV that in 716 BC he bought off Sargon of Assyria at the borders of Egypt with a gift of twelve horses (Tadmor, *JCS*, XII, 1958, pp. 77–78).

(iii) *Ethiopia—the 'bruised reed'*. In Nubia (Cush) there had meantime arisen a kingdom ruled by princes who were thoroughly Egyptian in culture. Of these, Kashta and Piankhy laid claim to a protectorate over Upper Egypt, being worshippers of Amūn of Thebes. In one campaign, Piankhy subdued Tafnekht of Lower Egypt to keep Thebes safe, but promptly returned to Nubia.

However, his successor Shabaka (*c.* 716–702 BC) promptly reconquered Egypt, eliminating Bekenrenef by 715 BC. Shabaka was a friendly neutral towards Assyria; in 712 he extradited a fugitive at Sargon II's request, and sealings of Shabaka (possibly from diplomatic documents) were found at Nineveh. Doubtless, Shabaka had enough to do inside Egypt without meddling abroad; but unfortunately his successors in this Dynasty (the XXVth) were less wise. When Sennacherib of Assyria attacked Hezekiah of Judah in 701 BC the rash new Ethiopian pharaoh Shebitku sent his equally young and inexperienced brother Tirhakah to oppose Assyria (2 Ki. xix. 9; Is. xxxvii. 9), resulting in dire defeat for Egypt. See TIRHAKAH, SENNACHERIB. The Ethiopian pharaohs had no appreciation of Assyria's superior strength—after this setback, Tirhakah was defeated twice more by Assyria (*c.* 671 and 666/5, as king) and Tanutamen once —and their incompetent interference in Palestinian affairs was disastrous for Egypt and Palestine alike. They were most certainly the 'bruised reed' of the Assyrian king's jibe (2 Ki. xviii. 21; Is. xxxvi. 6). Exasperated by this stubborn meddling, Ashurbanipal in 664/3 BC finally sacked the ancient holy city Thebes, pillaging fourteen centuries of temple treasures. No more vivid comparison than the downfall of this city could the prophet Nahum find (iii. 8–10) when proclaiming the oncoming ruin of Nineveh in its turn. However, Assyria could not occupy Egypt, and left only key garrisons.

(iv) *Egypt, Judah, and Babylon*. In a now disorganized Egypt, the astute local prince of Sais (W Delta) managed with great skill to unite all Egypt under his sceptre. This was Psammetichus I, who thereby established the XXVIth (or Saite) Dynasty. He and his successors restored Egypt's internal unity and prosperity. They built up an effective army round a hard core of Gk. mercenaries, greatly enhanced trade by encouraging Gk. merchants, and founded strong fleets on the Mediterranean and Red Seas. But, as if in compensation for the lack of real, inner vitality, inspiration was sought in Egypt's past glories; ancient art was copied and archaic titles were artificially brought back into fashion.

Externally, this dynasty (except for the headstrong Hophra) practised as far as possible a policy of the balance of powers in W Asia. Thus, Psammetichus I did not attack Assyria but remained her ally against the reviving power of Babylon. So, too, Necho II (610–595 BC) was marching to help a reduced Assyria (2 Ki. xxiii. 29; RSV gives correct translation here) against Babylon, when Josiah of Judah sealed Assyria's fate by delaying Necho at Megiddo at the cost of his own life. Egypt considered herself heir to Assyria's Palestinian possessions, but her forces were signally defeated at Carchemish in 605 BC so that all Syria–Palestine fell to Babylon (Je. xlvi. 2). Jehoiakim of Judah thus exchanged Egyp. for Bab. vassalage for three years. But as the recently-published Bab. chronicle-tablets reveal, Egypt and Babylon clashed in open conflict in 601 BC with heavy losses on both sides; Nebuchadrezzar then remained eighteen months in Babylonia to refit his army. At this point Jehoiakim of Judah rebelled (2 Ki. xxiv. 1 f.), doubtless hoping for Egyptian aid. None came; Necho now wisely kept neutral. So Nebuchadrezzar was not molested in his capture of Jerusalem in 597 BC. Psammetichus II maintained the peace; his state visit to Byblos was linked rather with Egypt's acknowledged commercial than other interests in Phoenicia. He fought only in Nubia. But Hophra (589–570 BC; the Apries of the Greeks) foolishly cast dynastic restraint aside, and marched to support Zedekiah in his revolt against Babylon (Ezk. xvii. 11–21; Je. xxxvii. 5), but returned in haste to Egypt when Nebuchadrezzar temporarily raised his (second) siege of Jerusalem to repulse him—leaving Jerusalem to perish at the Babylonian's hand in 587 BC. After other disasters (see HOPHRA), Hophra was finally supplanted in 570 BC by Ahmose II (Amasis, 570–526 BC). As earlier prophesied by Jeremiah (xlvi. 13 ff.), Nebuchadrezzar now marched against Egypt (as referred to in a damaged Bab. tablet), doubtless to prevent any recurrence of interference from that direction. He and Ahmose must have reached some understanding, for henceforth till both were swallowed up by Medo-Persia, Egypt and Babylon were allies against the growing menace of Media. But in 525 BC Egypt followed her allies into Persian dominion, under Cambyses. On this period, see further under ASSYRIA AND BABYLONIA.

(v) *The base kingdom*. At first Persian rule in Egypt (Darius I) was fair and firm; but repeated Egyptian rebellions brought about a harshening of Persian policy. The Egyptians manufactured anti-Persian propaganda that went down well in Greece (*cf.* Herodotus); they shared a common foe. Briefly, during *c.* 400–341 BC, Egypt's last native pharaohs (Dynasties XXVIII–XXX) regained a precarious independence until they were overwhelmed by Persia to whom they remained subject for just nine years, until Alexander entered Egypt as 'liberator' in 332 BC. (See Kienitz, in Bibliography, and G. Posener, *La Première*

Domination Perse en Égypte, 1936.) Thereafter, Egypt was first a Hellenistic monarchy under the Ptolemies (see PTOLEMY), and then fell under the heel of Rome and Byzantium. From the 3rd century AD, Egypt was a predominantly Christian land with its own, eventually schismatic (Coptic) church. In AD 641/2 the Islamic conquest heralded the mediaeval and modern epochs.

V. LITERATURE

Ancient Egypt was the first nation to produce fine literature for its own sake, over and above the functional and religious literature so common also in other lands. Some Egyptian works strive after literary style, others are of the simplest structure. Most Egyptian literature (omitting the great body of formal texts on stone, *etc.*) has come down to us in papyri, or, fragmentarily, in ostraca (see PAPYRI AND OSTRACA; WRITING).

a. Scope of Egyptian Literature

(i) *Third millennium* BC. Religious and wisdom-literature are the best-known products of the Old Kingdom and 1st Intermediate Period. The great sages Imhotep, Hardidief, [?Kairos] to Kagemni, and Ptahhotep produced 'Instructions' or 'Teachings' (Egyp. *sb'yt*), written collections of shrewd maxims for wise conduct of everyday life, especially for young men hopeful of high office, so beginning a very long tradition in Egypt. The best-preserved is that of Ptahhotep; latest edition, Z. Žába, *Les Maximes de Ptahhotep*, 1956. For the Pyramid Texts and Memphite Theology, see Religion, below.

In the 1st Intermediate Period, the collapse of Egyptian society and the old order are vividly pictured in the *Admonitions of Ipuwer*, while the *Dispute of a Man Tired of Life with his Soul* reflects the agony of this period in terms of a personal conflict which brings man to the brink of suicide, culminating in four moving poems in praise of death (latest rendering, R. O. Faulkner, *JEA*, XLII, 1956, pp. 21–40, and part in *DOTT*, pp. 162–167). The *Instruction for King Merikarē* shows remarkable regard for right dealing in matters of state, while the *Eloquent Peasant*'s nine rhetorical speeches within a narrative prose prologue and epilogue (*cf.* Job) call for social justice.

(ii) *Early second millennium* BC. In the Middle Kingdom, stories and propaganda-works are outstanding. Finest of the works in the first category is the *Biography of Sinuhē*, an Egyptian who spent long years of exile in Palestine, becoming a chief there before his honourable recall to Egypt. The *Shipwrecked Sailor* is a nautical fantasy. Among the propaganda, the *Prophecy of Neferty* ('*Neferrohu*' of older books) is a pseudo-prophecy to announce Amenemhat I as saviour of Egypt and declare his programme (*cf.* History, above). On prediction in Egypt, see Kitchen, *Tyndale House Bulletin*, V/VI, 1960, pp. 6–7 and refs. Two loyalist 'Instructions', *Sehetepibrē* and *A Man to his Son*, were intended to identify the good life with loyalty to the throne in the minds of the ruling and labouring classes respectively. The poetry of the *Hymns to Sesostris III* apparently also expresses that loyalty. For administrators in training, the *Instruction of Khety son of Duauf* or *Satire of the Trades* points out the advantages of the scribal profession over all other (manual) occupations by painting these in dark colours. For tales of magicians, see MAGIC AND SORCERY (Egyptian).

(iii) *Late second millennium* BC. During this period the Empire produced further stories, including delightful fairy-tales (*e.g. The Foredoomed Prince*; *Tale of the Two Brothers*), historical adventure (*The Capture of Joppa*, a precursor of *Alibaba and the Forty Thieves*), and biographical reports such as the *Misadventures of Wenamūn*, who was sent to Lebanon for cedarwood in the ill-starred days of Rameses XI. Poetry excelled in three forms: lyric, royal, and religious. Under the first head come some charming love-poems, in general style heralding the tender cadences of the Song of Songs. The Empire pharaohs commemorated their victories with triumph-hymns, the finest being those of Tuthmosis III, Amenophis III, Rameses II, and Merenptah (Israel Stele). For hymns to the gods, see Religion, below. Though less prominent, wisdom is still well represented; besides the 'Instructions' of Ani and Amennakhte, there is a remarkable ode on the Immortality of Writing. Amenemope's wisdom is probably later, see *b* (i), 2 below. The theme of the Satire of the Trades was further developed.

(iv) *First millennium* BC. Very little new Egyptian literature is known from this epoch so far. Amenemope dates to not later than *c.* 950 BC, see below. In Demotic the 'Instruction' of 'Onchsheshonqy dates to the last centuries BC, and the *Stories of the High Priests of Memphis* (magicians) to the first centuries AD. Most Coptic (Christian) literature is translated from Gk. church literature, Shenoute being the only outstanding native Christian writer.

b. Egyptian Literature and the Old Testament

The very incomplete survey given above will serve to emphasize the quantity, richness, and variety of early Egyptian literature; besides the additional matter under Religion below, there is a whole body of historical, business, and formal texts. Egypt is but one of the Bible lands; the others, too, offer a wealth of writings—see ASSYRIA and BABYLONIA, CANAAN, HITTITES. The relevance of such literatures is twofold: firstly, with regard to questions of direct contact with the Heb. writings; and secondly, in so far as they provide dated, first-hand comparative and contemporary material for objective control of Old Testament literary forms and types of literary criticism.

(i) *Questions of Direct Contact.* 1. Gn. xxxix; Ps. civ. In times past the incident of Potiphar's unfaithful wife in Gn. xxxix has occasionally been stated to be based on a similar incident in the mythical *Tale of Two Brothers*. But an unfaithful wife is the only common point; the *Tale* is designedly a work of pure fantasy (for example, the hero is changed into a bull, a persea-tree, *etc.*), whereas the Joseph-narrative is biography, touching actuality at every point. Unfortunately, unfaithful wives are not mere myth, either in Egypt or elsewhere (see an incidental Egyptian instance in *JNES*, XIV, 1955, p. 163).

Egyptologists today do not usually consider that Akhenaten's 'Hymn to Aten' inspired parts of Ps. civ as Breasted once thought (*cf.* Breasted, *Dawn of Conscience*, 1933, pp. 366–370). The same universalism and adoration of the deity as creator and sustainer occurs in hymns to Amūn both before and after the Aten hymn in date, which could carry these concepts down to the age of Heb. psalmody (so, *e.g.* Wilson, *Burden of Egypt*/*Culture of Ancient Egypt*, pp. 224–229). But even this tenuous link-up can carry no weight, for the same universalism occurs just as early in W Asia (*cf.* the examples given in Albright, *From Stone Age to Christianity*, 1957 ed., pp. 12, 13, 213–223) and is therefore too generally diffused to allow of its being made a criterion to prove direct relationship. The same point might be made with regard to the so-called penitential psalms of the Theban necropolis-workers of Dynasty XIX. A sense of shortcoming or sin is not peculiar to Egypt (and is even, in fact, quite atypical there); and the Egyp. psalms should be compared with the confession of man's sinfulness made by the Hittite king, Mursil II (*ANET*, p. 395b), and with the Babylonian penitential odes. The latter again show the wide diffusion of a general concept (although it may have different local emphases); and they cannot be used to establish direct relationship (*cf.* G. R. Driver, *The Psalmists*, ed. D. C. Simpson, 1926, pp. 109–175, especially 171–175).

2. The Wisdom of Amenemope and Proverbs. Impressed by the close verbal resemblances between various passages in the Egyptian 'Instruction' of Amenemope (*c.* 1100–950 BC, see below) and the 'words of the wise' (Pr. xxii. 17–xxiv. 22) quoted by Solomon (equating the 'my knowledge' of xxii. 17 with that of Solomon from x. 1), many have assumed, following Erman, that Proverbs was debtor to Amenemope; only Kevin and McGlinchey ventured to take the opposite view. Others, with Oesterley, *Wisdom of Egypt and the Old Testament*, 1927, doubted the justice of a view at either extreme, considering that perhaps both Amenemope and Proverbs had drawn upon a common fund of Ancient Oriental proverbial lore, and specifically upon an older Heb. work. The alleged dependence of Proverbs upon Amenemope is still the common view (*e.g.* Montet, *L'Égypte et la Bible*, 1959, pp. 113, 127), but is far from being definitive. Most recently, the late É. Drioton, the distinguished French Egyptologist, in two very important studies, has given detailed reasons for believing that the work of Amenemope is throughout a rather literal rendering into Egyptian of a Hebrew proverbial work upon which Proverbs also (independently) drew. Drioton took up Griffith's observations (*JEA*, XII, 1926, p. 193) on the difficult language of Amenemope (the artificial modes of expression, rare words, and idioms, *etc.*, used) and he claims that the abnormalities in vocabulary and syntax directly reflect *Semitic* usages, rendered too literally into Egyp. He cites words and prepositions used with meanings which are rare in Egyp. but common in Heb.; grammatical and syntactical solecisms in Egyp. that are good Heb.; and cruces which are almost meaningless in Egyp. but make excellent Heb. when turned word for word into that language. Certain specifically Egyp. points suggest that the author of the Heb. original translated by Amenemope lived in Egypt. See on this, É. Drioton, *Mélanges Bibliques* (André Robert), 1957, pp. 254–280, and in *Sacra Pagina*, I, 1959, pp. 229–241; he planned a further, larger work. Some details apart, Drioton's thesis will be difficult to controvert, and is of the first importance for Old Testament studies, Two other points require note. First, with regard to date, Plumley (*DOTT*, p. 173) mentions an unpublished Cairo ostracon of Amenemope that 'can be dated with some certainty to the latter half of the Twenty-first Dynasty'. Therefore the Egyp. Amenemope cannot be any later than 945 BC (= end of Dynasty XXI), and Drioton's Heb. original *must* be earlier still. In other words, the Heb. Words of the Wise were in existence by Solomon's reign (perhaps even earlier) and could therefore have been used by him in the 10th century BC. The second point concerns the word *šilšôm*, found in Pr. xxii. 20, which Erman and others render as 'thirty', making Proverbs imitate the 'thirty chapters' of Amenemope. It is in order to remark that Pr. xxii. 17–xxiv. 22 contains not thirty but thirty-three admonitions, and the simplest interpretation of *šlšwm* is to take it as elliptical for *'eṯmôl šilšôm*, 'formerly', 'already', and to render the clause simply as, 'Have I not written for thee, already, in/with counsels of knowledge?'.

(ii) *Literary usage and Old Testament criticism.* It is singularly unfortunate that the conventional methods of Old Testament literary criticism (see also BIBLICAL CRITICISM) have been formulated and developed, over the last century in particular, without any but the most superficial reference to the actual characteristics of the contemporary literature of the Bible world, alongside which the Hebrew writings came into existence and with the literary phenomena of which they present very considerable external, formal similarities. The application of such external and tangibly objective controls cannot fail to have drastic consequences for these methods of literary criticism. Only a sample can be given here; the full weight of evidence must await its definitive publication. While Egyp. texts are a specially fruitful source of such external control-data, Mesopotamian, North Canaanite (Ugaritic), Hittite, and other literatures provide valuable confirmation.

1. Major changes of general style. In Pentateuchal criticism it has long been customary to divide the whole into separate documents or 'hands'. These consist of flowing narrative, 'J' and 'E'; dry, statistical data and headings, 'P'; and specific 'blocks', *e.g.* the sacred law, 'H'. But the practice of Old Testament criticism in attributing these characteristics to different 'hands' or documents becomes a manifest absurdity when applied to other ancient Oriental writings that display precisely similar phenomena. One instance must suffice here. The biography of the Egyp. General Uni (Dynasty VI, *c.* 2300 BC) contains flowing narrative where his various employments and his warfare in Palestine are the subject ('J', 'E'?), while at intervals he makes varying use of two stereotyped refrains to indicate the king's recognition of his successive accomplishments ('P_1', 'P_2'?), and he further throws in for good measure the victory-hymn which he and his army chanted during their return from Palestine ('H', hymnal source?). Dozens of Egyp. and other texts in the last three millennia BC show the same wide variety in literary form. In Uni's biography, carved in stone at his own order, there can be no question of the final form having been developed through a number of documents in its literary prehistory; its events fall within the adult career of one man, and the work was conceived, composed, written, and carved within months, weeks, or even less. There can be no 'hands' behind its style, which merely varies with the subjects in view and the question of fitting treatment. For precisely the same points (and reactions) from the N Canaanite (Ugaritic) epics and the Mesopotamian story of Gilgamesh, see briefly C. H. Gordon, *Ugaritic Literature*, 1949, p. 6, in *Hebrew Union College Annual*, XXVI, 1955, p. 67, § 47, and his remarks in *Christianity Today*, IV, 1959, pp. 131–134.

2. Criteria or 'markers'. In outlining the extent and distribution of documents or 'hands' in the Pentateuch, *etc.*, the 'markers' used include double names for the Deity (YHWH/Elohim), for persons (*e.g.* Jethro/Reuel), and groups (*e.g.* Amorites/Canaanites), places (*e.g.* Sinai/Horeb), and (para-)synonyms (*e.g.* *'āmâ/šip̄ḥâ*, 'bondmaid/handmaid'). But these are just as misleading. As far as multiple divine names are concerned the stele of Ikhernofret (*c.* 1800 BC) offers *four* different names and epithets of the god Osiris, both singly and in combination (*cf.* YHWH-Elohim combined); and for Ugaritic examples, see Gordon. Egyptian examples of variant personal names are legion; suffice it to mention the officer Sebekkhu, who is also called Djaa; and with regard to groups, *cf.* the use of three separate terms in his Manchester Museum stele (*c.* 1800 BC)—*Mntyw-Stt* (Asian bedouin), *Rtnw* (Syrians), and *'Amw* (Asiatics)—for the same Palestinian foe fought by him under Sesostris III. For dual place-names, compare the two terms for Egypt (*Kmt*; *T'-mri*) and three for Memphis (*Mn-nfr*; *'Inb-ḥḏ*; *'Inb*) used in Merenptah's triumph-hymn on his 'Israel Stele'; and for parasynonyms, *cf.* the five different terms for ships and boats, in the new historical stele of King Kamose (*c.* 1580 BC), and so on, *ad infinitum*. All the examples given above are from monumental texts with no literary prehistory extending beyond months or days; the possibilities of 'hands' and documents are totally excluded. But the long-transmitted literary works on papyrus or ostraca reveal the same features, requiring the same interpretation. So also do other Near Eastern texts of which one example must suffice: two terms for 'envoy', 'messenger', *rakbu*, *mar-šipri*, are used by Ashurbanipal of Assyria (*c.* 650 BC) in his report of his relations with Gyges of Lydia.

So-called 'advanced' concepts are in no better case. The personification of Wisdom in Pr. i–ix has often been considered an 'advanced' (therefore, post-exilic) concept, to be paralleled from Gk. This is wholly fallacious, as just such a form of personification is native to the entire biblical East from the third millennium BC onwards (see Kitchen, *Tyndale House Bulletin*, V/VI, 1960, pp. 4–6, with examples and references).

3. Other critical methods are open to analogous objections and for the same reason: *i.e.* that they make no detailed consideration of ancient literary phenomena. For argument against the arbitrary atomization of prophetical books into mere fragments and scattered little impulsive utterances of a rigidly classified type (as required by *Gattungsforschung*), note the just strictures of S. Smith (*Isaiah XL–LV*, 1944, pp. 6–16), and his adduction of long sequences in Bab. oracles (p. 8, n. 47); and compare also the long tirades in the *Admonitions of Ipuwer* from Egypt as early as 2200 BC (disproving the erroneous shibboleth that what is 'early' must be short). The oral-traditionist school are on little sounder footing. They have failed entirely to distinguish between the complementary functions of written transmission (*i.e.* down through time) and oral dissemination (*i.e.* making it known over a wide area to contemporaries), and have confused the two as 'oral tradition', wrongly overstressing the oral element in Near Eastern transmission.

4. Textual methods and literary criticism. The famous literary works of ancient Egypt, *Sinuhe*, *Ptahhotep*, and others, offer instructive information on reliable transmission and the occasional revision of ancient texts. In Egypt, as in Mesopotamia, there were traditions of accurate copying. One religious papyrus of *c.* 1400 BC is docketed thus: '[The book] is complete from beginning to end as was found in writing, having been copied, revised, compared and verified sign by sign' (refs. in J. Černý, *Paper and Books in Ancient Egypt*, 1952, p. 25 and n. 131). There is no warrant for believing that pious Hebrews would be any more careless with their sacred literature.

Occasional revision of the grammar and/or spelling of an ancient text, the better to preserve its meaning, is well-attested, both in whole works and in isolated passages. Thus, the famous 'Instruction' of Ptahhotep, originally composed in terse Old Egyptian (*c.* 2400 BC), has been given Middle-Egyptian grammatical revision almost throughout (*c.* 1900 BC). But the Middle-Egyptian form of the 'received text' dates that

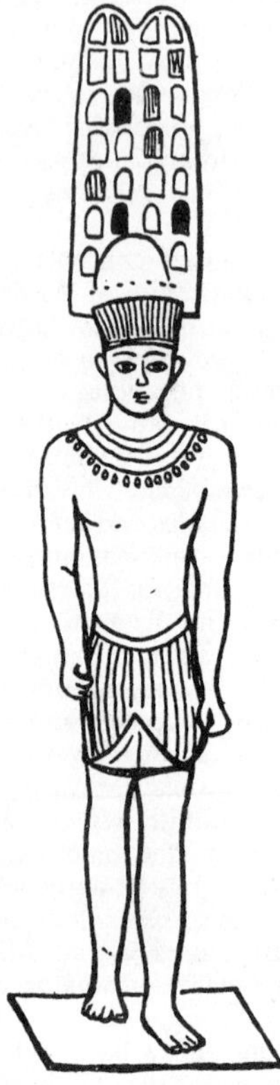

Fig. 73. A statuette (approx. 13 inches high) of Amūn or Amen-Rē, king of the gods, wearing royal kilt, broad collar and tall plumes.

text-form only, and not the original work. In fact, there are clear textual indications of the work's Old Kingdom date (see G. Fecht, *Die Habgierige und die Maat in der Lehre des Ptahhotep*, 1958, pp. 49 f.). In *Sinuhe*, indisputably a XIIth-Dynasty work (MSS of nearly 1800 BC), a Ramesside copy (Ashmolean Ostracon, 13th century BC) substitutes a Late-Egyptian negative *bw* for Middle-Egyptian *n* in one passage, and a Late-Egyptian loan-word *ym*, 'sea', for Middle-Egyptian *nwy*, 'waterflood', in another. These 'late words' date only that particular MS of Sinuhe, not its original composition. The full importance of such text-methods for Old Testament studies is still not appreciated. Similar occasional 'late words' in Heb. writings may be equally irrelevant as arguments against an earlier date of composition. And criticisms of theories of spelling-revision, such as those made by H. H. Rowley (*The Aramaic of the Old Testament*, 1929, pp. 23, 33, 155) against R. D. Wilson in the matter of Daniel, are therefore precarious.

Finally, it is a well-known phenomenon for a word to appear sporadically in early Egyp. texts (*e.g.* in the Pyramid Texts of *c.* 2400 BC), to 'disappear' for some time, and then to recur (often in much more common usage) very much later, especially in texts of the Graeco-Roman age. In Old Testament studies the similar occurrence, in Heb. books and passages which claim, explicitly or implicitly, to be early, of words that are rare until a very late date (*e.g.* in the Mishnah) is often made a reason for down-dating them, and the possibility that these same passages actually offer precious evidence for the earliest use of such words is usually either overlooked or dismissed. But in Egypt, in precisely similar circumstances, the VIth-Dynasty pyramids of *c.* 2400 BC cannot be down-dated two millennia to the Graeco-Roman epoch merely because words in their inscriptions never recur till that later period!

Enough has been said to indicate the vital importance of this specialized but fascinating Egyp. (and other Oriental) literary matter for a stricter control of method in Old Testament

Fig. 74. A bronze statuette of the royal god Horus represented as a hawk wearing the double crown of Upper and Lower Egypt. Approx. 11 inches high.

literary criticism. Presentation of the full weight of evidence must await future detailed publication. Where such critical methods are so obviously inapplicable to texts of the biblical period coming from among Israel's closest neighbours, the most serious doubts and misgivings concerning the validity of a vast amount of current Old Testament literary criticism cannot but be raised; and raised, moreover, on purely literary grounds well supported by tangibly objective data, without any recourse to theological predispositions or considerations.

VI. RELIGION

a. The gods and theology

Egyptian religion was never a unitary whole. There were always local gods up and down the land, among whom were Ptah, artificer-god of Memphis; Thoth, god of learning and the moon at Hermopolis; Amūn 'the hidden', god of Thebes, who overshadowed the war-god Mentu there and became state god of second-millennium Egypt; Hathor, goddess of joy at Dendera; and many more. Then there were the cosmic gods: first and foremost Rē' or Atum the sun-god, whose daughter Ma'et personified Truth, Justice, Right, and the cosmic order; then Nūt the sky-goddess and Shu, Geb, and Nu, the gods of air, earth, and the primordial waters respectively. The nearest thing to a truly national religion was the cult of Osiris and his cycle (with his wife, Isis, and son, Horus). The story of Osiris had great human appeal: the good king murdered by his wicked brother Seth, becoming ruler of the realm of the dead and triumphing in the person of his posthumous son and avenger Horus, who, with the support of his mother Isis, gained his father's kingship on earth. The Egyptian could identify himself with Osiris the revivified in his kingdom of the hereafter; Osiris's other aspect, as a god of vegetation, linking with the annual rise of the Nile and consequent rebirth of life, combined powerfully with his funerary aspect in Egyptian aspirations. See figs. 72, 73, 74, 75.

The place of chief god varied with political changes at successive periods. Ptah of Memphis under the first kings was supplanted by Rē' the sun-god in Dynasty V. Thereafter Osiris steadily gained nearly universal adherence among all classes of Egyptians, especially from the Middle Kingdom onwards, but at that time Amūn of Thebes, the XIIth Dynasty's patron, became state god, reaching the peak of his fame under the Empire. However, it was Osiris, with his wife Isis and son Horus, who dominated later religion. The various local and other deities had their own theological and cosmogonic systems attached to them; these were never really amalgamated or reconciled (they were, in any case, mutually incompatible), but existed side by side in complementary fashion. Their individual content cannot be given here; for further detail, see the books cited below, and translations in *ANET*.

The Aten, made so prominent by the 'heretic pharaoh' Akhenaten, was merely the sun-god manifest in the solar disc, whose rays gave life to all creatures. The king worshipped Aten, and the Egyptians the king, giving Atenism a personal focus. The other gods were proscribed, but recognized as entities, as is evident from the erasure of their names in order to destroy them magically. The result was an imperfect 'monotheism'. There was no ethical quality in Atenism; even the great Hymn expresses nothing more than Aten's general benevolence in creating and sustaining life; this faith had no bearing on Akhenaten's marrying his own daughter. It is clear that no origin for Mosaic monotheism can be found here.

b. Egyptian worship

Egyptian worship was a complete contrast to Hebrew worship in particular, and to Semitic in general. The temple was isolated within its own high-walled estate. The New Kingdom ones had at least one great towered gateway ('pylons') and open court; within was a pillared hall, and sanctuaries and cult-apparatus storerooms in the increasing gloom beyond. Only the officiating priesthood worshipped in such temples; and it was only when the god went forth in glittering procession on great festivals that the populace actively shared in honouring the great gods. Apart from this, they sought their solace in household and lesser gods. The cult of the great gods followed one general pattern, the god being treated just like an earthly king. He was awakened from sleep each morning with a hymn, was washed and dressed (*i.e.* his image), and breakfasted (morning offering), did a morning's business, and had midday and evening meals (corresponding offerings) before retiring for the night. The contrast could hardly be greater between the ever-vigilant, self-sufficient God of Israel with His didactic sacrificial system, symbolizing the need and means of atonement to deal with human sin, and of peace-offerings in fellowship at tabernacle or temple, and those earthly Egyp. deities of nature. For Egyp. temple-worship, *cf.* H. W. Fairman, *Bulletin of the John Rylands Library*, XXXVII, 1954, pp. 165–203.

c. The king

Pharaoh himself was one of the gods, and a central figure in his subjects' lives. Each reigning king was at once the incarnate Horus, falcon sky-god, and Horus (originally a separate person) the rightful heir upon the throne of his father Osiris. Egypt's well-being was directly associated with that of the king; his fundamental duty was to maintain *ma'at*, not merely justice but the inherently perfect cosmic order established by Rē' in the beginning. Each king was successor to the whole line of royal ancestors, stretching back beyond the historic human dynasties and the rule of the demi-gods to the dynasty of the gods themselves upon earth, and at death each king joined that august company—each pharaoh could re-echo the claim of the Egyptians in Is. xix. 11, 'I am the son of the wise, the son of ancient kings.' On the king, see H. W. Fairman in S. H. Hooke, ed., *Myth, Ritual and Kingship*, 1958, pp. 74–104.

d. Religious literature

To the third millennium BC belong the Pyramid Texts (so-called from their being inscribed in

VIth-Dynasty pyramids), a large body of 'spells', apparently forming incredibly intricate royal funerary rituals, and also the Memphite Theology, which glorifies the god Ptah as first cause, conceiving in the mind ('heart') and creating by the word of power ('tongue') (a distant herald of the *logos*-concept of John's Gospel (i. 1 ff.) transformed through Christ). At all times there are hymns and prayers to the gods, usually full of mythological allusions. In the Empire certain hymns to Amūn, and Akhenaten's famous Aten-hymn, remarkably illustrate the universalism of the day; see Literature, *b* (i) 1, above. Epics of the gods which at present remain to us exist only in excerpts. A ribald part of the Osiris-cycle survives in the *Contendings of Horus and Seth*. The Coffin Texts of the Middle Kingdom (usually painted inside coffins at that time) and the 'Book of the Dead' of the Empire and Late Period are nothing more than collections of magical spells to protect and benefit the deceased in the after-life; special guide-books to 'infernal' geography were inscribed on the tomb-walls of Empire pharaohs. On magical literature, *cf.* MAGIC AND SORCERY. See *ANET* for translations from religious texts.

Fig. 75. The goddess Hathor represented as a woman wearing a large wig. She has cows' ears. A sculptured capital in red granite 6 feet 6 inches high.

e. Funerary beliefs

The Egyptians' elaborate beliefs about the after-life found expression in the concrete, material terms of a more-glorious, other-worldly Egypt ruled by Osiris. Alternative hereafters included accompanying the sun-god Rē' on his daily voyage across the sky and through the under-world, or dwelling with the stars. The body was a material attachment for the soul; mummification was simply an artificial means of preserving the body to this end, when tombs early became too elaborate for the sun's rays to desiccate the body naturally, as it did in prehistory's shallow graves. Objects in tombs left for the use of the dead usually attracted robbers. Egyptian concern over death was not morbid; this cheerful, pragmatic, materialistic people simply sought to take the good things of this world with them, using magical means so to do. The tomb was the deceased's eternal physical dwelling. The pyramids were simply royal tombs whose shape was modelled on that of the sacred stone of the sun-god Rē' at Heliopolis (see I. E. S. Edwards, *The Pyramids of Egypt*, 1947). The Empire pharaohs' secret rock-hewn tombs in the Valley of Kings at Thebes were planned to foil the robbers, but failed, like the pyramids they replaced.

BIBLIOGRAPHY. *General.* Popular introductions to ancient Egypt are: L. Cottrell, *The Lost Pharaohs*, 1950, and *Life under the Pharaohs*, 1955; P. Montet, *Everyday Life in Egypt in the Days of Ramesses the Great*, 1958; Egyptian culture is summarized and contrasted with other Oriental cultures in S. Moscati, *The Face of the Ancient Orient*, 1960. Very useful is S. R. K. Glanville (ed.), *The Legacy of Egypt*, 1942; up-to-date and well-illustrated is Hayes, *Scepter of Egypt*, I, II, 1953, 1960. In French, G. Posener, S. Sauneron, and J. Yoyotte, *Dictionnaire de la Civilisation Égyptienne*, 1959, is packed with information and dozens of vivid little illustrations in colour as well as in black and white. A standard work is H. Kees, *Ägypten*, 1933, being part 1 of the *Kulturgeschichte des Alten Orients* in the *Handbuch der Altertumswissenschaft* series; also H. Kees, *Ancient Egypt, a Cultural Topography*, 1961, is useful and reliable. Full bibliography is obtainable from: I. A. Pratt, *Ancient Egypt*, 1925, and her *Ancient Egypt (1925–41)*, 1942, for nearly everything pre-war; W. Federn, eight lists in *Orientalia*, XVII, 1948, XVIII, 1949, and XIX, 1950, for the years 1939–47; and J. M. A. Janssen, *Annual Egyptological Bibliography*, 1948 ff., for 1947 onwards. Also Porter-Moss, *Topographical Bibliography*, 7 vols.

Origin of name. Brugsch, *Geographische Inschriften*, I, 1857, p. 83; A. Gardiner, *Ancient Egyptian Onomastica*, II, 1947, pp. 124*, 211*; Virolleaud in *Syria*, XXX, 1953, pp. 192, 193, *La Déesse Anat*, 1938, pp. 88 ff., *Palais Royal d'Ugarit*, II, 1957, pp. 34, 113, 114; C. H. Gordon, *Ugaritic Manual*, III, pp. 290 f., 356 and *Ugaritic Literature*, p. 23, n. 1.

Geography. Very valuable for the physical structure and geography of Egypt is J. Ball, *Contributions to the Geography of Egypt*, 1939. For modern statistics, see survey in *The Middle East, 1958*, or *Chambers' Encyclopaedia*, 1959 ed., V, pp. 9–11, and *EBr*, 1955 ed., VIII, pp. 33–35. Much information is contained in *Baedeker's Egypt*, 1929. The deserts find some description in A. E. P. Weigall, *Travels in the Upper Egyptian Deserts*, 1909. On the early state and settlement of the Nile valley, see now K. W. Butzer, *Studien zum vor- und frühgeschichtlichen Landschaftswandel der Sahara*, I/II and III, 1959, being *Abhandlungen* (*Math.-Naturwiss. Kl.*), *Jahrgang 1958*, Nos. 1 and 2, of the Akademie der Wissenschaften und der Literatur, Mainz. For ancient Egyptian geography, a mine of information is (Sir) Alan Gardiner's *Ancient Egyptian Onomastica*, 3 vols., 1947, with good discussions and references to literature. A massive hieroglyphic repertoire is H. Gauthier, *Dictionnaire des Noms Géographiques*, 7 vols., 1925–31. Most recent is P. Montet, *Géographie de l'Égypte Ancienne, I: Basse Égypte*, 1957. See also the articles on EGYPT, RIVER OF, HANES, MEMPHIS, NAPHTUHIM, NILE, NO, ON, PATHROS, PI-BESETH, RA'AMSES, ZOAN, *etc.*

Language. For details of, and bibliography on, the Egyp. language, see Sir A. H. Gardiner, *Egyptian Grammar*[3], 1957. For Coptic, see W. C. Till, *Koptische Grammatik*, 1955, and A. Mallon, *Grammaire Copte*, 1956, for full bibliography; in English, *cf.* J. M. Plumley, *Introductory Coptic Grammar*, 1948.

History. The standard work is É. Drioton and J. Vandier, *L'Égypte* (Collection '*Clio*')[3], 1952, with full discussions and bibliography. A valuable, if personal, survey is J. A. Wilson, *The Burden of Egypt*, 1951, reprinted as a paperback, *The Culture of Ancient Egypt*, 1956. J. H. Breasted's highly readable *History of Egypt*, various dates, is now out of date, as is H. R. Hall's *Ancient History of the Near East*. G. Steindorff and K. C. Seele, *When Egypt Ruled the East*, 1957 edn., is a popular survey of the New Kingdom period only (*c.* 1600–1100 BC). A fine background book, based upon the Egyp. collections of the Metropolitan Museum of Art, New York, is W. C. Hayes, *The Scepter of Egypt*, 2 vols. to date, 1953, 1959 (earliest times to 1085 BC; 3rd vol. for the first millennium in preparation). See now also Sir Alan Gardiner, *Egypt of the Pharaohs*, 1961; and the *Cambridge Ancient History*, a completely rewritten, new edition of Vols. I and II, 1961 ff.

On Egyp. historical writings, see L. Bull in R. C. Dentan (ed.), *The Idea of History in the Ancient Near East*, 1955, pp. 3–34; C. de Wit, *EQ*, XXVIII, 1956, pp. 158–169.

On rival Egyp. priesthoods, see H. Kees, *Das Priestertum im Ägyptischen Staat*, 1953, pp. 78–88 and 62–69, also *Nachträge*, 1958; see also J. A. Wilson, *Burden of Egypt/Culture of Ancient Egypt*, chapter ix.

On Egypt under Persian dominion, see F. K. Kienitz, *Die Politische Geschichte Ägyptens, vom 7. bis zum 4. Jahrhundert vor der Zeitwende*, 1953. For the Babylonian chronicle-tablets, see D. J. Wiseman, *Chronicles of Chaldaean Kings*, 1956. For a small but very important correction of Egyptian XXVIth Dynasty dates, see R. A. Parker, *Mitteilungen des Deutschen Archäologischen Instituts, Kairo Abteilung*, XV, 1957, pp. 208–212.

For Graeco-Roman Egypt, see *Cambridge Ancient History*, later volumes; Sir H. I. Bell, *Egypt from Alexander the Great to the Arab Conquest*, 1948, and his *Cults and Creeds in Graeco-Roman Egypt*, 1953 and later edns.; W. H. Worrell, *A Short Account of the Copts*, 1945.

Literature. For literary works and historical texts respectively, the basic corpuses of translations are still Erman and Blackman, *Literature of the Ancient Egyptians*, 1927, and Breasted, *Ancient Records of Egypt*, 5 vols., 1906/7. Considerable but abbreviated selections appear in *ANET*. The stories are given well in G. Lefebvre, *Romans et Contes Égyptiens*, 1949. Brilliant work in listing, identifying, and restoring Egyp. literature is Posener's *Récherches Littéraires*, I–VI, in the *Revue d'Égyptologie*, VI–XI (1949–57). Still valuable in its field is T. E. Peet, *A Comparative Study of the Literatures of Egypt, Palestine and Mesopotamia*, 1931.

Religion. For Egyptian religion, a convenient outline in English is J. Černý, *Ancient Egyptian Religion*, 1952; fuller detail and bibliography in J. Vandier, *La Religion Égyptienne*, 1949; H. Kees, *Der Götterglaube im alten Ägypten*, 1956, is good; *cf.* also R. T. Rundle Clark, *Myth and Symbol in Ancient Egypt*, 1959. K.A.K.

EGYPT, RIVER OF. The correct identification of 'River of Egypt' is still uncertain; several distinct Heb. terms must be carefully distinguished. *y*e*'ôr miṣrayim*, 'river (= Nile) of Egypt', refers exclusively to the Nile proper: its seasonal rise and fall being mentioned in Am. viii. 8, and its upper Egyptian reaches in Is. vii. 18 (plural); see also NILE. The term *n*e*har miṣrayim*, '(flowing) river of Egypt', occurs once only (Gn. xv. 18), where by general definition the promised land lies between the two great rivers, Nile and Euphrates. These two terms (*y*e*'ôr/n*e*har miṣrayim*) are wholly separate from, and irrelevant to, the so-called 'river of Egypt' proper, the *naḥal miṣrayim* or 'torrent-wadi of Egypt'. The identification of this term, however, is bound up with that of Shihor (*q.v.*), as will be evident from what now follows. In the Old Testament it is clear that Shihor is a part of the Nile; see the parallelism of Shihor and *y*e*'ôr* (Nile) in Is. xxiii. 3, and Shihor as Egypt's Nile corresponding to Assyria's great river (Euphrates) in Je. ii. 18. Shihor is the extreme south-western limit of territory yet to be occupied in Jos. xiii. 3 and from which Israelites could come to welcome the ark into Jerusalem in 1 Ch. xiii. 5, and Jos. xiii. 3 specifies it as 'before Egypt'. Hence Shihor is the lowest reaches of the easternmost of the Nile's ancient branches (the Pelusiac), flowing into the Mediterranean just east of Pelusium (Tell Farameh). This term Shihor is by origin Egyp. *š-ḥr*, 'waters of Horus'; the Egyptian references agree with the biblical location in so far as they mention Shihor's producing salt and rushes for the not-distant Delta-capital Pi-Ramessē (Tanis or Qantir) and as the 'river' of the 14th Lower-Egyptian nome (province); see Caminos, *Late-Egyptian Miscellanies*, 1954, pp. 74, 78 (his

Menzalah-identification is erroneous), and especially Gardiner, *JEA*, V, 1918, pp. 251, 252.

The real question is whether or not the *naḥal miṣrayim*, 'river (torrent-wadi) of Egypt', is the same as the Shihor, easternmost branch of the Nile.

Against the identification stands the fact that elsewhere in Scripture the Nile is never referred to as a *naḥal*. The river of Is. xi. 15 is often taken to be the Euphrates (note the Assyro-Egyp. context here, especially verse 16), and the threat to smite it into seven *neḥālîm*, wadis traversable on foot, represents a transformation of (not the normal description for) the river concerned, whether Nile or Euphrates.

If the 'wadi of Egypt' is not the Nile, the best alternative is the Wadi el-'Arish, which runs north out of Sinai to the Mediterranean about 90 miles east of Egypt proper (Suez Canal) and some 50 miles west of Gaza in Palestine. In defence of this identification can be argued a perceptible change of terrain west and east from El-'Arish. Westward to Egypt there is only barren desert and slight scrub; eastward there are meadows and arable land (Gardiner, *JEA*, VI, 1920, p. 115). Hence Wadi el-'Arish would be a practical boundary, including the usable land and excluding mere desert, in the specific delimitations of Nu. xxxiv. 5 and Jos. xv. 4, 47 (*cf.* also Ezk. xlvii. 19, xlviii. 28). This is then simply echoed in 1 Ki. viii. 65 (= 2 Ch. vii. 8), 2 Ki. xxiv. 7, and Is. xxvii. 12. Jos. xiii. 3 and 1 Ch. xiii. 5 would then indicate the uttermost south-west limit (Shihor) of Israelite activity (*cf.* above). Sargon II and Esarhaddon of Assyria also mention the Wadi or Brook of Egypt in their texts. In 716 BC Sargon reached the 'Brook (or Wadi) of Egypt' (*naḥal muṣur*), 'opened the sealed harbour of Egypt' mingling Assyrians and Egyptians for trade purposes, and mentioning 'the border of the City of the Brook of Egypt', where he appointed a governor. Alarmed by the Assyr. activity, the shadow-pharaoh Osorkon IV sent a diplomatic present of '12 big horses' to Sargon (H. Tadmor, *JCS*, XII, 1958, pp. 34, 78). All this fits well with *naḥal muṣur* being Wadi el-'Arish and the 'City' there being the settlement El-'Arish, Assyr. *Arzâ* (Tadmor, p. 78, note 194, with further bibliography on 'River of Egypt').

One or two points apparently favouring the alternative view, *viz.* that the 'Wadi of Egypt' is the Shihor/Pelusiac Nile-arm, must, however, not be overlooked. Many are inclined to equate precisely the terms of Jos. xiii. 3, Shihor, and Nu. xxxiv. 5, Jos. xv. 4, 47 (likewise 1 Ki. viii. 65 and 1 Ch. xiii. 5), *naḥal miṣrayim*, making Wadi of Egypt another name of the Shihor-Nile. But this would make no allowance for different nuances in the Scripture texts concerned as outlined above. Further, it is true that Sargon II could well have reached the Pelusiac (easternmost) arm of the Nile; his 'City' there would then be Pelusium—which would most certainly alarm Osorkon IV. But the 'City' is certainly the Arza(ni) of Esarhaddon's inscriptions (*ANET*, pp. 290–292, *passim*) which corresponds well to 'Arish but not Pelusium (Egyp. *sìnw*, *swn*). Finally, Egyptians of the XIXth Dynasty evidently regarded the Pelusiac area as *de facto* the edge of Egypt proper: in Papyrus Anastasi III, 1: 10, Ḫuru (Palestine generally) extends 'from Silē to 'Upa (= Damascus)'; Silē ('Thel') is modern Qantara a few miles south and east of the former Pelusiac Nile-arm (Caminos, *Late-Egyptian Miscellanies*, pp. 69, 73 and refs.). But this proves nothing about Israel's boundaries; as already mentioned, from Qantara to 'Arish is a desolate no-man's-land. In any case, XIXth-Dynasty Egypt did assert authority and maintain wells across the entire coast-strip, Qantara–'Arish–Gaza, see Gardiner, *JEA*, VI, 1920, pp. 99–116, on the military road here. The Shihor/Nile identification of the Wadi of Egypt has most recently been advocated by H. Bar-Deroma, *PEQ*, XCII, 1960, pp. 37–56, but he takes no account of the contemporary Egyp. and Assyr. sources, the post-biblical matter cited being imprecise and of too late a date. The subject is not closed, but Wadi el-'Arish is more likely to be the 'River (Wadi) of Egypt' than is the E Nile on present evidence. K.A.K.

EGYPTIAN, THE. In Acts xxi. 38 an agitator for whom the Roman officer commanding the fortress of Antonia mistook Paul when the latter was set upon in the Temple precincts. According to Josephus (*BJ* ii. 13. 4 f.; *Ant.* xx. 8. 6), this Egyptian came to Jerusalem *c.* AD 54, claiming to be a prophet, and led a great multitude to the Mount of Olives, promising that, at his command, the city walls would collapse before them. Soldiers sent by Felix dispersed his followers, with some bloodshed; the Egyptian escaped. See ASSASSINS. F.F.B.

EGYPTIAN VERSIONS. See TEXT AND VERSIONS.

EHUD. A Benjamite name (1 Ch. vii. 10, viii. 6; Jdg. iii. 15). Ehud, the son of Gera, led the revolt against the Moabite occupation of eastern Benjamin (Jdg. iii); gaining a private audience of King Eglon, he killed him in his own apartments, and gathered Israelites to take advantage of the confusion into which the Moabites were thrown. His left-handedness was doubtless useful in taking Eglon unawares. The Heb. phrase 'deformed (lit. 'bound') in his right hand' is idiomatic; *cf.* xx. 16.

BIBLIOGRAPHY. Moore, *ICC*, *Judges*, pp. 89–104. J.P.U.L.

EKRON. One of the five principal Philistine cities, and a place of some size and importance, having villages dependent upon it (Jos. xv. 45, 46). Recent surveys suggest that it is to be identified with modern Khirbet al-Muqanna', which has hitherto been commonly equated with Eltekeh (*q.v.*). Surface explorations in 1957 showed the site to have been occupied in the

Early Bronze Age but evidently not again until the Early Iron Age. The peak period, when the walled city occupied an area of some 40 acres, making it in fact the largest Iron Age settlement yet found in Palestine, was characterized by typical Philistine pottery. The tell has a projection at the north-eastern corner which perhaps represents the acropolis, and on the southern slopes a double wall with gates and towers has been traced. In the allotment of territories Ekron was placed on the border between Judah and Dan (Jos. xv. 11, 45, 46, xix. 43), but at the death of Joshua it remained to be possessed. It was finally taken by Judah (Jdg. i. 18), but must have been recaptured by the Philistines, for the ark was taken there when it was removed from Gath (1 Sa. v. 10), and it was from there that it was despatched to Beth-shemesh on the cow-drawn cart (1 Sa. vi). It appears that Ekron was again temporarily in Israelite hands in the time of Samuel (1 Sa. vii. 14), but the Philistines had retaken it by Saul's time (1 Sa. xvii. 52), and it was still held by them in the time of Amos (i. 8). In 701 BC Padi the ruler of Ekron, a vassal of the Assyrians, was expelled by certain Ekronites and held captive by Hezekiah in Jerusalem, but Sennacherib, in his campaign of that year, retook Ekron (*am-qar-ru-na*) and restored Padi (Taylor Prism ii. 69–iii. 11; Chicago Prism ii. 73–iii. 17). The city is mentioned in the Annals of Esarhaddon as tributary, but was still at that time regarded as a Philistine city from the ethnic point of view (Je. xxv. 20; Zp. ii. 4; Zc. ix. 5, 7). The Bible is not concerned with the subsequent history of the city, though the name of the city god, Baal-zebub (*q.v.*) (2 Ki. i. 2, 3), is familiar from the New Testament.

BIBLIOGRAPHY. J. Naveh, *IEJ*, VIII, 1958, pp. 87–100, 165–170; Y. Aharoni, *PEQ*, XC, 1958, pp. 27–31; Honigmann, *Reallexikon der Assyriologie*, I, 1932, p. 99; D. D. Luckenbill, *The Annals of Sennacherib*, 1924, pp. 31, 32; R. Campbell Thompson, *The Prisms of Esarhaddon and Ashurbanipal*, 1931, p. 25 (col. v, l. 58).

T.C.M.

EL. See GOD, NAMES OF.

ELAH (*'ēlâ*, 'terebinth'). **1.** A tribal prince of Edom (Gn. xxxvi. 41; 1 Ch. i. 52). He may have been the chief of the district of Elah, which was possibly the sea-port of Elath. **2.** Son of Baasha, and king of Israel for two years until he was assassinated by Zimri during a drunken orgy in the house of Arza, his steward (1 Ki. xvi. 6–14). **3.** Father of Hoshea, the last king of Israel (2 Ki. xv. 30, xvii. 1, xviii. 1, 9). **4.** Second son of Caleb, who was with Joshua one of the only survivors of the wilderness journey (1 Ch. iv. 15). **5.** A Benjamite who dwelt at Jerusalem after the Exile (1 Ch. ix. 8). His name is one of those omitted in the parallel list in Ne. xi.

J.G.G.N.

ELAH (Heb. *'ēlâ*, 'terebinth'). A valley used by the Philistines to gain access to Central Palestine. It was the scene of David's victory over Goliath (1 Sa. xvii. 2, xxi. 9), and is generally identified with the modern Wadi es-Sant, 11 miles south-west of Jerusalem.

J.D.D.

ELAM, ELAMITES. The ancient name for the plain of Khuzistan, watered by the Kerkh river, which joins the Tigris just north of the Persian Gulf. Civilization in this area is as old as, and closely connected with, the cultures of lower Mesopotamia. A local pictographic script appeared very soon after the invention of writing (*q.v.*) in Babylonia. The reference to Elam as a son of Shem (Gn. x. 22) may well reflect the presence of early Semites in this area, and there is archaeological evidence in the time of Sargon I (*c.* 2350 BC) and his successors of their influence on the local culture. Rock sculptures depict typical Akkadian figures and bear Akkadian inscriptions, although carved for Elamite rulers. The mountainous region to the north and east was known as Anshan and, from an early period, formed a part of Elam. Sumerian and Semitic plainsmen looked upon these ranges as the abode of evil spirits, and early epics describe the terrors they held for those who crossed them in search of the mineral wealth of states beyond (see S. N. Kramer, *History Begins at Sumer*, 1958, pp. 57 ff., 230 ff.).

Its control of the trade routes to the Iranian plateau, and to the south-east, made Elam the object of constant attacks from the plains of Mesopotamia. These in turn offered great wealth to any conqueror. A strong Elamite dynasty arose about 2000 BC and gained control of several cities in Babylonia, destroying the power of the Sumerian rulers of Ur and sacking that city (see *ANET*, pp. 455 ff., 480 f.). To this period of Elamite supremacy must Chedorlaomer (*q.v.*) most probably be assigned (Gn. xiv. 1). Hammurabi of Babylon drove the Elamites out *c.* 1760 BC, but the 'Amorite' dynasty, to which he belonged, fell before Hittite and Elamite attacks *c.* 1625 BC. Invasions of Kassites from the central Zagros mountains (see ASSYRIA and BABYLONIA) drove the Elamites back to Susa, until a resurgence of power enabled them to conquer and rule Babylon for several centuries (*c.* 1300–1120 BC). Among trophies taken to Susa at this time was the famous Law stele of Hammurabi. Elamite history is obscure from *c.* 1000 BC until the campaigns of Sargon of Assyria (*c.* 721–705 BC). Sennacherib and Ashurbanipal subjected the Elamites and deported some of them to Samaria, taking Israelites to Elam (Ezr. iv. 9; Is. xi. 11).

After the collapse of Assyria (*q.v.*), Elam was annexed by the Indo-Europeans, who had gradually gained power in Iran following their invasions *c.* 1000 BC. Teispes (*c.* 675–640 BC), ancestor of Cyrus, bore the title 'king of Anshan' and Susa eventually became one of the three chief cities of the Medo-Persian Empire.

Elam is called upon by Isaiah to crush Babylon (Is. xxi. 2) and this was carried out (*cf.* Dn. viii. 2). Yet Elam will be crushed in turn, even the famous archers defeated (Je. xxv. 25, xlix. 34–39; *cf.* Is. xxii. 6; Ezk. xxxii. 24). The crowd at Pentecost (Acts ii. 9) contained men from as far away as Elam, presumably members of the Aramaic-speaking Jewish communities who had remained in exile.

See also ARCHAEOLOGY, MEDES, PERSIANS, SUSA.

BIBLIOGRAPHY. R. Ghirshman, *Iran*, 1954; L. van den Berghe, *Archéologie de l'Iran Ancien*, 1959. A.R.M.

ELATH (ELOTH), EZION-GEBER. Settlement(s) at the north end of present-day Gulf of Aqabah. First mentioned as a stopping-place during Israel's wilderness journeyings (Nu. xxxiii. 35, 36; Dt. ii. 8) in the 13th century BC. Elath and/or Ezion-Geber was then probably little more than wells and palm-groves near present-day Aqabah, which has always been the normal settlement-site in this district.

Solomon (*c.* 960 BC) developed Ezion-Geber as a copper- and iron-smelting refinery, strongly-walled, about 2½ miles west of Aqabah (old Elath); this entirely new site (Tell el-Kheleifeh) stood squarely in the path of the north winds which, howling down the Arabah rift-valley, were utilized for the furnaces (Ezion-Geber, phase I). Ezion-Geber/Elath served also as the terminal port for Solomon's Red Sea trading-fleet to Ophir and Arabia (1 Ki. ix. 26; 2 Ch. viii. 17); some time after his reign, Ezion-Geber was burnt down and eventually rebuilt (phase II) in the 9th century BC, probably by Jehoshaphat of Judah (*c.* 860 BC), whose fleet, doubtless imitating Solomon's, was wrecked (1 Ki. xxii. 48; 2 Ch. xx. 36, 37), probably on the rocks there, by the strong winds of this region. Under Jehoram of Judah (*c.* 848 BC), Edom revolted (2 Ki. viii. 21, 22), cutting off, burning, and re-occupying Ezion-Geber. Some sixty years later Uzziah (Azariah) of Judah (*c.* 780 BC) recovered Ezion-Geber from the Edomites (2 Ki. xiv. 22; 2 Ch. xxvi. 2), and rebuilt it as Elath (phase III). A seal of his successor Jotham was found in this rebuilt Elath. However, Rezin of Aram (Syria) took Elath from Ahaz of Judah (*c.* 730 BC), letting it revert to (? allied) Edomite control (2 Ki. xvi. 6; but in verse 6b, for 'the Syrians came . . . and dwelt', AV, RV, read 'the Edomites came', *etc.*, RSV, changing a single *r* to a closely-similar *d*).

During the 7th–4th centuries BC (phases IV and V), Elath remained Edomite; several 7th-century BC sealings of the obviously Edomite 'Qos'anal, servant of the king' (of Edom) were discovered in 'Edomized' Elath. Under Persian rule, trade through Elath to Arabia still flourished, as evidenced by the discovery of 5th- and 4th-century BC Aramaic ostraca (including wine receipts), and even fine Attic pottery in transhipment from Greece for Arabia. When the Nabataeans supplanted the Edomites, Elath was restricted to the site of present-day Aqabah, becoming known as Aila under the Nabataeans and Romans.

BIBLIOGRAPHY. For Nelson Glueck's excavations at Ezion-Geber, see reports in *BASOR*, 71, 1938, pp. 3–18; 72, 1938, pp. 2–13; 75, 1939, pp. 8–22; Glueck, *The Other Side of the Jordan*, 1940, pp. 89–113; *BASOR*, 79, 1940, pp. 1–18. Reconstruction of ancient Ezion-Geber in Glueck, *The River Jordan*, 1946, p. 142, fig. 75. For the seals and ostraca, see Glueck, Albright, Torrey, Rosenthal, and Sukenik in *BASOR*, 71, 72, 1938; 75 (already cited), 79, 1940, pp. 27, 28; 80, 1940, pp. 3–10; 82, 1941, pp. 3–17; 85, 1942, pp. 8, 9. On state slavery at Ezion-Geber, see Mendelsohn, *BASOR*, 85, 1942, pp. 14–17. K.A.K.

ELDAD (Heb. 'God has loved'). An Israelite elder, associated with Medad in Nu. xi. 26, 27; perhaps to be identified with Elidad (Nu. xxxiv. 21). He was one of the two Israelites who failed to appear at the tabernacle of the congregation when summoned there with the seventy elders by Moses. He and Medad nevertheless shared in the gift of prophecy which the other elders received from Yahweh. Far from forbidding this apparently irregular display of divine power, Moses rejoiced and wished that all Yahweh's people might become prophets. For the ecstatic nature of their prophesying, see PROPHECY. J.B.Tr.

ELDER. In most civilizations authority has been vested in those who by reason of age or experience have been thought best qualified to rule. It is not surprising therefore that the leaders in many ancient communities have borne a title derived from a root meaning 'old age'. In this respect the Heb. 'elder' (*zāqēn*) stands side by side with the Homeric *gerontes*, the Spartan *presbys*, the Roman *senatus*, and the Arab *sheikh*.

In the Pentateuch elders are referred to among the Egyptians (Gn. l. 7) and the Moabites and Midianites (Nu. xxii. 7), as well as among the Israelites. In Ex. iii. 16 the Israelites are represented as having had elders from the time of the Egyp. captivity, and it is with them that Moses is commanded to collaborate in his bid for freedom. They were probably the heads of families in the first instance, but Ex. xxiv. 1 gives a fixed number of seventy. It was upon this inner circle of seventy elders that Yahweh poured out the spirit in order that they should share the government of the people with Moses (Nu. xi. 25).

After the wilderness period every city seems to have had its own ruling body of elders whose duties, according to Deuteronomic legislation, included acting as judges in apprehending murderers (Dt. xix. 12), conducting inquests (Dt. xxi. 2), and settling matrimonial disputes (Dt. xxii. 15, xxv. 7). If theirs was a city of refuge they also heard pleas for asylum (Jos. xx. 4, but see also Nu. xxxv. 24). Their numbers varied, Succoth having seventy-seven (Jdg. viii. 14), and they are associated with other civil officials, *e.g.* heads of tribes (Dt. v. 23, xxix. 10) and officers and judges (Jos. viii. 33). Maybe the term 'elders' was a general word for the ruling body and included some of these officials.

The national body of 'elders of Israel' still exercised considerable influence under the monarchy as the chieftains of the people, having first agitated for the appointment of a king (1 Sa. viii. 4 f.) and having finally accepted David (2 Sa. v. 3). Their position and influence were recognized by Solomon (1 Ki. viii. 1, 3), Ahab (1 Ki. xx. 7), Jezebel (1 Ki. xxi. 8), Jehu (2 Ki. x. 1), Hezekiah (2 Ki. xix. 2), and Josiah (2 Ki. xxiii. 1). Ezekiel in captivity dealt with them (Ezk. viii. 1, xiv. 1, xx. 1), and they appear also in Ezra's time and in the Gk. period. While their authority was originally civil, by New Testament times the 'elders of the people' (*presbyteroi tou laou*) shared with the chief priests the power of determining religious affairs and, if necessary, of expulsion from the synagogue.

See also SANHEDRIN, SYNAGOGUE, and (for use in the New Testament) PRESBYTER. J.B.TR.

ELEALEH (Heb. *'el'ālēh*, 'God is exalted'). A town east of Jordan always mentioned in conjunction with Heshbon. Conquered by Gad and Reuben (Nu. xxxii. 3), rebuilt by the latter tribe (xxxii. 37), and later Moabite, it was the subject of prophetic warnings (Is. xv. 4, xvi. 9; Je. xlviii. 34). Identified with the modern el-'Al, 1 mile north of Heshbon. J.D.D.

ELEAZAR (*'el'āzār*, 'God is helper'). Third son of Aaron and Elisheba (Ex. vi. 23; Nu. iii. 2), and husband of one of the daughters of Putiel, who bore him Phinehas (Ex. vi. 25). The life of Eleazar is of special interest in showing the nature of the Israelite priesthood in the days of the theocracy.

Aaron and his four sons were all consecrated to the service of the Lord (Lv. ix); and after the death of Nadab and Abihu, Aaron and his two remaining sons, Eleazar and Ithamar, continued to exercise priestly functions (Nu. iii. 2–4). Eleazar was set over the Levites (Nu. iii. 32), and to him was assigned the care of the sanctuary, and other priestly offices (Nu. iv. 16, xvi. 37, 39, xix. 3 f.).

The death of Aaron is recorded in detail in Nu. xx. The Israelites had left Kadesh and were on their way to the land of promise, and had reached Mt. Hor. There took place his 'chastisement' (see Dt. xxxii. 50 f., and MOSERA); as God directed, Moses, Aaron, and Eleazar ascended the mount together, Moses divested Aaron of his priestly garments and placed them on Eleazar. 'There Aaron died . . . and Eleazar his son ministered in the priest's office in his stead' (Dt. x. 6).

The relationship between Joshua and Eleazar is shown in Nu. xxvii. 15–23, where Moses gives Joshua 'a charge' (*cf.* Dt. xxxi. 14); he sets him 'before Eleazar the priest', who is to be his counsellor, by the divine oracle, as to his going out and his coming in.

The functions of the priest were not confined to the service of the tabernacle. Eleazar assisted Moses in the numbering of the people (Nu. xxvi. 1, 3, 63), and later in the important matter of dividing the land (Nu. xxxii. 2 ff., xxxiv. 17), a task executed later by Joshua and Eleazar (Jos. xiv. 1, xix. 51).

When a question of female inheritance arose, this was brought before Moses and Eleazar for decision (Nu. xxvii. 2), and Eleazar with Joshua carried it into effect (Jos. xvii. 4). When Moses sent the people to war against the Midianites, Phinehas, Eleazar's son, went with them (*cf.* Dt. xx. 2) and Eleazar was with Moses. When he received the spoil Eleazar was by his side (Nu. xxxi. 6, 12).

The book of Joshua closes with a brief statement of Eleazar's death and burial (Jos. xxiv. 33). G.T.M.

ELECTION. The act of choice whereby God picks an individual or group out of a larger company for a purpose or destiny of His own appointment. The main Old Testament word for this is the verb *bāḥar*, which expresses the idea of deliberately selecting someone or something after carefully considering the alternatives (*e.g.* slingstones, 1 Sa. xvii. 40; a place of refuge, Dt. xxiii. 16; a wife, Gn. vi. 2; good rather than evil, Is. vii. 15 f.; life rather than death, Dt. xxx. 19 f.; the service of God rather than of idols, Jos. xxiv. 22). The word implies a decided preference for, sometimes positive pleasure in, the object chosen (*cf.*, *e.g.*, Is. i. 29). In LXX and the New Testament the corresponding verb is *eklegomai*. *Eklegō* is commonly active in classical Gk., but the biblical writers always use it in the middle voice, with reflexive overtones: it thus means 'choose out for oneself'. *Haireomai* is used synonymously of God's choice in 2 Thes. ii. 13, as in Dt. xxvi. 18, LXX. The cognate adjectives are *bāḥîr* and *eklektos*, translated 'elect' or 'chosen'; the New Testament also uses the noun *eklogē*, 'election'. The Heb. verb *yāḏa'*, 'know', which is used of various acts of knowing that, in idea at least, imply and express affection (*e.g.* relations between the sexes, and the believer's acknowledgment of God), is used to denote God's election (*i.e.* His taking cognizance of persons in love) in Gn. xviii. 19 (see RV); Am. iii. 2; Ho. xiii. 5. The Gk. *proginōskō*, 'foreknow', is similarly used in Rom. viii. 29, xi. 2 to mean 'forelove' (*cf.* also the use of *ginōskō* in 1 Cor. viii. 3 and Gal. iv. 9).

I. OLD TESTAMENT USAGE

Israelite faith was founded on the belief that Israel was God's chosen people. His choice of her had been made by means of two connected and complementary acts. (*a*) He chose Abraham and his seed, by taking Abraham out of Ur and bringing him to the promised land of Canaan, making there an everlasting covenant with him and his descendants, and promising him that his seed should be a blessing to all the earth (Gn. xi. 31–xii. 7, xv, xvii, xxii. 15–18; Ne. ix. 7; Is. xli. 8).

(*b*) He chose Abraham's seed by redeeming them from slavery in Egypt, bringing them out of bondage under Moses, renewing the Abrahamic covenant with them in an amplified form at Sinai, and setting them in the promised land as their national home (Ex. iii. 6–10; Dt. vi. 21–23; Ps. cv). Each of these acts of choice is also described as God's call, *i.e.* a sovereign utterance of words and disposal of events by which God summoned, in the one case, Abraham, and in the other, Abraham's seed, to acknowledge Him as their God and live to Him as His people (Is. li. 2; Ho. xi. 1; see CALL). Israelite faith looked back to these two acts as having created the nation (*cf.* Is. xliii. 1; Acts xiii. 17).

The meaning of Israel's election appears from the following facts:

a. Its *source* was God's free omnipotent love. Moses' speeches in Deuteronomy stress this. When He chose Israel, God 'set his love on' Israel (Dt. vii. 7, xxiii. 5): why? Not because Israel first chose Him, nor because Israel deserved His favour. Israel was in fact the reverse of attractive, being neither numerous nor righteous, but feeble, small, and rebellious (Dt. vii. 7, ix. 4–6). God's love to Israel was spontaneous and free, exercised in defiance of demerit, having no cause save His own good pleasure. He made it His delight and satisfaction to do Israel good (Dt. xxviii. 63, *cf.* xxx. 9) simply because He resolved to do so. It was true that in delivering Israel from Egypt He was keeping a promise made to the Patriarchs (Dt. vii. 8), and there was a necessity of the divine character in that, for it is God's nature always to be faithful to His promises (*cf.* Nu. xxiii. 19; 2 Tim. ii. 13); but the making of this promise had itself been an act of free unmerited love, for the Patriarchs were themselves sinners (as Genesis is at pains to show), and God chose Abraham, the first recipient of the promise, out of idolatry (Jos. xxiv. 2 f.). Here too, therefore, the cause of election must be sought, not in man, but in God.

God is King in His world, and His love is omnipotent. Accordingly, He implemented His choice of Israel by means of a miraculous deliverance (by 'a mighty hand', Dt. vii. 8, *etc.*) out of a state of helpless captivity. Ezk. xvi. 3–6 dwells on Israel's pitiable condition when God chose her; Ps. cxxxv. 4–12 extols His display of sovereignty in bringing His chosen people out of bondage into the promised land.

b. The *goal* of Israel's election was, proximately, the blessing and salvation of the people through God's separating them for Himself (Ps. xxxiii. 12), and, ultimately, God's own glory through Israel's showing forth His praise to the world (Is. xliii. 20 f.; *cf.* Pss. lxxix. 13, xcvi. 1–10), and bearing witness of the great things He had done (Is. xliii. 10–12, xliv. 8). Israel's election involved separation. By it, God made Israel a holy people, *i.e.* one set apart for Himself (Dt. vii. 6; Lv. xx. 26b). He took them as His inheritance (Dt. iv. 20, xxxii. 9–12) and treasure (Ex. xix. 5; Ps. cxxxv. 4), promising to protect and prosper them (Dt. xxviii. 1–14), and to dwell with them (Lv. xxvi. 11 f.). Election made them His people, and Him their God, in covenant together. It had in view living communion between them and Him. Their destiny, as His chosen people, was to enjoy His manifested presence in their midst and to receive the multitude of good gifts which He promised to shower upon them. Their election was thus an act of blessing which was the fount of all other blessings. Hence the prophets express the hope that God would restore His people and presence to Jerusalem after the Exile, and re-establish conditions of blessing there, by saying that God will again 'choose' Israel and Jerusalem (Is. xiv. 1; Zc. i. 17, ii. 12, *cf.* iii. 2).

c. The *religious and ethical obligations* created by Israel's election were far-reaching. Election, and the covenant relationship based on it, which distinguished Israel from all other nations, was a motive to grateful praise (Ps. cxlvii. 19 f.), loyal keeping of God's law (Lv. xviii. 4 f.) and resolute non-conformity to the idolatry and wrongdoing of the unelected world (Lv. xviii. 2 f., xx. 22 f.; Dt. xiv. 1 f.; Ezk. xx. 5–7, *etc.*). Also, it gave Israel grounds for unfaltering hope and trust in God in times of distress and discouragement (*cf.* Is. xli. 8–14, xliv. 1 f.; Hg. ii. 23; Ps. cvi. 4 f.). Irreligious Israelites, however, were betrayed by the thought of the national election into complacently despising other nations, and assuming that they could always rely on God for protection and preferential treatment, no matter what their own lives were like (*cf.* Mi. iii. 11; Je. v. 12). It was this delusion, and in particular the idea that Jerusalem, as the city of God, was inviolable, that the false prophets fostered in the days before the Exile (Je. vii. 1–15, xxiii. 9 ff.; Ezk. xiii). In fact, however, as God had made plain from the first (Lv. xxvi. 14 ff.; Dt. xxviii. 15 ff.), national election implied a strict judgment of national sins (Am. iii. 2). The Exile proved that God's threats had not been idle.

d. Within the chosen people, *God chose individuals for specific tasks* designed to further the purpose of the national election—*i.e.* Israel's own enjoyment of God's blessing, and, ultimately, the blessing of the world. God chose Moses (Ps. cvi. 23), Aaron (Ps. cv. 26), the priests (Dt. xviii. 5), the prophets (*cf.* Je. i. 5), the kings (1 Sa. x. 24; 2 Sa. vi. 21; 1 Ch. xxviii. 5), and the Servant-Saviour of Isaiah's prophecy ('mine elect', Is. xlii. 1, *cf.* xlix. 1, 5), who suffers persecution (Is. l. 5 ff.), dies for sins (Is. liii), and brings the Gentiles light (Is. xlii. 1–7, xlix. 6). God's use of Assyria and 'my servant' Nebuchadrezzar as His scourges (Is. vii. 18 ff., x. 5 ff.; Je. xxv. 9, xxvii. 6, xliii. 10), and of Cyrus, a man ignorant of God, as a benefactor to the chosen people (Is. xlv. 4), is termed by H. H. Rowley 'election without covenant' (*The Biblical Doctrine of Election*, 1950, chapter V), but the phrase is improper; the Bible always reserves the vocabulary of election for the covenant people and covenant functionaries drawn from Israel's own ranks.

e. The promised blessings of election were *forfeited through unbelief and disobedience.* The prophets, facing widespread hypocrisy, insisted that God would reject the ungodly among His people (Je. vi. 30, vii. 29). Isaiah foretold that only a faithful remnant would live to enjoy the golden age that was to follow the inevitable judgment on Israel's sins (Is. x. 20–22, iv. 3, xxvii. 6, xxxvii. 31 f.). Jeremiah and Ezekiel, living in the time of that judgment, looked for a day when God, as part of His work of restoration, would regenerate such of His people as He had spared, and ensure their covenant faithfulness for the future by giving each of them a new heart (Je. xxxi. 31 ff., xxxii. 39 f.; Ezk. xi. 19 f., xxxvi. 25 ff.). These prophecies, with their focus on individual piety, pointed to an individualizing of the concept of election (*cf.* Ps. lxv. 4): they gave grounds for distinguishing between election to privilege and election to life, and for concluding that, while God had chosen the whole nation for the privilege of living under the covenant, He had chosen only some of them (those made faithful by regeneration) to inherit the riches of the relationship to Himself which the covenant held out, while the rest forfeited those riches by their unbelief. The New Testament teaching about election assumes these distinctions; see especially Rom. ix.

II. NEW TESTAMENT USAGE

The New Testament announces the extension of God's covenant-promises to the Gentile world and the transference of covenant-privileges from the lineal seed of Abraham to a predominantly Gentile body (*cf.* Mt. xxi. 43) consisting of all who had become Abraham's true seed and God's true Israel through faith in Christ (Rom. iv. 9–18, ix. 6 f.; Gal. iii. 14 ff., 29, vi. 16; Eph. ii. 11 ff., iii. 6–8). The unbelieving natural branches were broken off from God's olive-tree (the elect community, sprung from the Patriarchs), and wild olive branches (believing Gentiles) were ingrafted in their place (Rom. xi. 16–24). Faithless Israel was rejected and judged, and the international Christian Church took Israel's place as God's chosen nation, living in the world as His people and worshipping and proclaiming Him as their God.

The New Testament presents the idea of election in the following forms:

a. Jesus is hailed as God's elect one by the Father Himself (Lk. ix. 35, reading *eklelegmenos*, an echo of Is. xlii. 1), and probably by John the Baptist (Jn. i. 34, if *eklektos* is the right reading; see Barrett *ad loc.*). The sneer of Lk. xxiii. 35 shows that 'the elect one' was used as a messianic designation in Christ's day (as it is in the Book of Enoch, xl. 5, xlv. 3–5, *etc.*). In 1 Pet. ii. 4, 6 Christ is called God's elect corner-stone; this echoes Is. xxviii. 16, LXX. In reference to Christ, the designation 'points to the unique and distinctive office with which he is invested and to the peculiar delight which God the Father takes in him' (J. Murray in *Baker's Dictionary of Theology*, 1960, p. 179).

b. The adjective 'elect' denotes the Christian community in its character as the chosen people of God, in contrast with the rest of mankind. This usage simply echoes the Old Testament. The church is 'an elect race' (1 Pet. ii. 9, quoting Is. xliii. 20; *cf.* also 2 Jn. 1, 13), having the privileges of access to God and the responsibilities of praising and proclaiming Him, and faithfully guarding His truth, which Israel had had before. As in the case of Israel, God had magnified His mercy by choosing poor and undistinguished persons for this momentous destiny (1 Cor. i. 27 ff.; Jas. ii. 5; *cf.* Dt. vii. 7, ix. 6); and, as before, God's gracious choice and call had created a people—His people—which had no existence as a people before (1 Pet. ii. 10; Rom. ix. 25 f., citing Ho. i. 10, ii. 23).

In the Synoptics Christ refers to the *eklektoi* (pl.) in various eschatological contexts. They are those whom God accepts, and will accept, because they have responded to the gospel invitation and come to the wedding-feast stripped of self-righteousness and clad in the wedding-garment provided by the host, *i.e.* trusting in God's mercy (Mt. xxii. 14). God will vindicate them (Lk. xviii. 7) and keep them through coming tribulation and peril (Mk. xiii. 20, 22), for they are the objects of His special care.

c. Eklegomai is used of Christ's choice of His apostles (Lk. vi. 13; *cf.* Acts i. 24, ix. 15) and the Church's choice of deacons (Acts vi. 5) and delegates (Acts xv. 22, 25). This is election to special service from among the ranks of the elect community, as in the Old Testament. Christ's choosing of the Twelve for apostolic office involved the choosing of them out of the world to enjoy salvation (*cf.* Jn. xv. 16, 19), except in the case of Judas (*cf.* Jn. xiii. 18).

III. THEOLOGICAL DEVELOPMENT IN THE NEW TESTAMENT

The complete theological development of the idea of election is found in Paul's Epistles (see especially Rom. viii. 28–xi. 36; Eph. i. 3–14; 1 Thes. i. 2–10; 2 Thes. ii. 13, 14; 2 Tim. i. 9–10). Paul presents divine election as a gracious, sovereign, eternal choice of individual sinners to be saved and glorified in and through Christ.

a. Election is a *gracious* choice. 'The election of grace' (Rom. xi. 5; *cf.* 2 Tim. i. 9) is an act of undeserved favour freely shown towards members of a fallen race to which God owed nothing but wrath (Rom. i. 18 ff.). And not only does God choose sinners to save (*cf.* Rom. iv. 5, v. 6–8; Eph. ii. 1–9); He chooses to save them in a way which exalts His grace by magnifying their sinfulness. He shuts up His elect, both Jew and Gentile, in a state of disobedience and unbelief, so that they display their true character as sinners, and stand out in history confessed as unbelievers, before He shows them His mercy (Rom. xi. 30–32: the Gentiles, ix. 30, x. 20; the Jews, x. 19, 21,

xi. 11, 25 f. ['so' in verse 26 means 'through the coming in of the Gentiles']). Thus the outworking of election further exhibits the gratuitousness of grace.

b. Election is a *sovereign* choice, prompted by God's own good pleasure alone (Eph. i. 5, 9), and not by any works of man, accomplished or foreseen (Rom. ix. 11), or any human efforts to win God's favour (Rom. ix. 15–18). Such efforts would in any case be vain, for however high sinners aspire and however fast they run, they still in reality only sin (Rom. viii. 7 f.). God in sovereign freedom treats some sinners as they deserve, hardening (Rom. ix. 18, xi. 7–10, *cf.* i. 28; 1 Thes. ii. 15 f.) and destroying them (Rom. ix. 21 f.); but He selects others to be 'vessels of mercy', receiving 'the riches of His glory' (Rom. ix. 23). This discrimination involves no injustice, for the Creator owes mercy to none, and has a right to do as He pleases with His rebellious creatures (Rom. ix. 14–21). The wonder is not that He withholds mercy from some, but that He should be gracious to any. God's purpose of sovereign discrimination between sinner and sinner appeared as early as His limitation of the Abrahamic promise to Isaac's line and His setting of Jacob over Esau (Rom. ix. 7–13). It was true from the first that 'they are not all Israel, which are of Israel' (Rom. ix. 6), and that those Israelites who actually enjoyed the salvation promised to the chosen people were only 'a remnant according to the election of grace' (Rom. xi. 5, ix. 27–29). And it remains true, according to Paul, that it is God's sovereign election alone that explains why, when the gospel is preached, some do in fact respond to it. The unbelief of the rest requires no special explanation, for no sinner, left to himself, can believe (1 Cor. ii. 14); but the phenomenon of faith needs explaining. Paul's explanation is that God by His Spirit causes the elect to believe, so that when men come to a true and active faith in Christ it proves their election to be a reality (1 Thes. i. 4 ff.; Tit. i. 1; *cf.* Acts xiii. 48).

c. Election is an *eternal* choice. God chose us, says Paul, 'before the foundation of the world' (Eph. i. 4; 2 Thes. ii. 13; 2 Tim. i. 9). This choice was an act of predestination (Eph. i. 5, 11), a part of God's eternal purpose (Eph. i. 9), an exercise of loving foreknowledge whereby God determined to save those whom He foreknew (Rom. viii. 29 f.; *cf.* 1 Pet. i. 2). Whereas the Old Testament, dealing with the national election to privilege, equates God's choosing with His calling, Paul, dealing with personal election to salvation, distinguishes the choice from the call, and speaks of God's calling (by which he means a summons to faith which effectively evokes a response) as a stage in the temporal execution of an eternal purpose of love (Rom. viii. 30, ix. 23 f.; 2 Thes. ii. 13 f.; 2 Tim. i. 9). Paul stresses that election is eternal in order to assure his readers that it is immutable, and nothing that happens in time can shake God's resolve to save them.

d. Election is a choice of individual sinners to be saved *in and through Christ*. Election is 'in Christ' (see Eph. i. 4), the incarnate Son, whose historical appearing and mediation were themselves included in God's eternal plan (1 Pet. i. 20; Acts ii. 23). Election in Christ means, first, that the goal of election is that God's chosen should bear Christ's image and share His glory (Rom. viii. 29, *cf.* verse 17; 2 Thes. ii. 14). They are chosen for holiness (which means Christlikeness in all their conduct) in this life (Eph. i. 4), and glorification (which means Christlikeness in all their being, *cf.* 2 Cor. iii. 18; Phil. iii. 21) in the life to come. Election in Christ means, second, that the elect are to be redeemed from the guilt and stain of sin by Christ, through His atoning death and the gift of His Spirit (Eph. v. 25–27; 2 Thes. ii. 13; *cf.* 1 Pet. i. 2). As He Himself said, the Father has given Him a certain number of persons to save, and He has undertaken to do everything necessary to bring them all to eternal glory (Jn. vi. 37–45, x. 14–16, 27–30, xvii. 2, 6, 9 ff., 24). Election in Christ means, third, that the means whereby the blessings of election are brought to the elect is union with Christ—His union with them representatively, as the last Adam, and vitally, as the life-giver, indwelling them by His Spirit, and their union with Him by faith.

IV. SIGNIFICANCE OF ELECTION FOR THE BELIEVER

Paul finds in the believer's knowledge of his election a threefold religious significance.

a. It shows him that his salvation, first to last, is all of God, a fruit of sovereign discriminating mercy. The redemption which he finds in Christ alone and receives by faith alone has its source, not in any personal qualification, but in grace alone—the grace of election. Every spiritual blessing flows to him from God's electing decree (Eph. i. 3 ff.). The knowledge of his election, therefore, should teach him to glory in God, and God only (1 Cor. i. 31), and to give Him the praise that is His due (Rom. xi. 36). The ultimate end of election is that God should be praised (Eph. i. 6, 12, 14), and the thought of election should drive ransomed sinners to incessant doxologies and thanksgivings, as it does Paul (Rom. xi. 33 ff.; Eph. i. 3 ff.; 1 Thes. i. 3 ff.; 2 Thes. ii. 13 ff.). What God has revealed about election is to Paul a theme, not for argument, but for worship.

b. It assures the believer of his eternal security, and removes all grounds for fear and despondency. If he is in grace now he is in grace for ever. Nothing can affect his justified status (Rom. viii. 33 f.); nothing can cut him off from God's love in Christ (Rom. viii. 35–39). He will never be safer than he is, for he is already as safe as he can be. This is precious knowledge; hence the desirability of making sure that one's election is a fact (*cf.* 2 Pet. i. 10).

c. It spurs the believer to ethical endeavour. So far from sanctioning licence (*cf.* Eph. v. 5 f.) or presumption (*cf.* Rom. xi. 19–22), the knowledge of one's election and the benefits that flow from it is the supreme incentive to humble, joyful, thankful love, the mainspring of sanctifying gratitude (Col. iii. 12–17).

See also PREDESTINATION.

BIBLIOGRAPHY. *Arndt*; Quell and Schrenk in *TWNT*, IV, pp. 147–197; T. Nicol in *HDAC*; J. Orr in *HDB* (1 vol.); C. Hodge, *Systematic Theology*, II, pp. 331–353; H. H. Rowley, *The Biblical Doctrine of Election*, 1950; G. C. Berkouwer, *Divine Election*, 1960. J.I.P.

ELECT LADY. 2 John is addressed to 'the elect lady' (*eklektē kyria*). This may signify an individual, either unnamed, or named Electa, or Kyria, or Electa Kyria. There are fairly convincing objections to each of these suggestions. Further, the absence of personal allusions, the almost unvarying use of the plural, the contents of the letter, and the concluding 'The children of thy elect sister greet thee' combine to make it likely that the Epistle is addressed to a church. No parallel is known, but this seems to be the least difficult explanation. L.M.

EL ELYON. See GOD, NAMES OF.

ELEMENTS. *Stoicheia*, translated 'elements' in Gal. iv. 3, 9; 2 Pet. iii. 10, 12 (AV); Col. ii. 8, 20 (AVmg; AV 'rudiments'), is the neuter plural of the adjective *stoicheios*, which means 'standing in a row', 'an element in a series'. Hence *stoicheia* is used: (1) for the letters of the alphabet, or rather the elementary sounds for which they stand. From this use comes the meaning 'rudiments', 'the ABC' of any subject; it is thus used in Heb. v. 12. (2) It may also mean the component parts of physical bodies. In particular, the Stoics used the term for the four elements: earth, water, air, fire. (3) There is evidence in Christian writers from the middle of the 2nd century AD for the use of *stoicheia* in an astronomical sense for the heavenly bodies (*cf.* Justin Martyr, *Apol.* ii. 5. 2). (4) Evidence from the Orphic hymns and the *Hermetica*, coupled with modern Gk. usage, shows that *stoicheia* later came to mean 'angels', 'spirits' ('elemental spirits', Gal. iv. 3, 9; Col. ii. 8, RSV). But it is not established that it was thus used as early as the 1st century AD; alleged early instances are either of doubtful meaning or of doubtful date. Jewish writers associate spirits or angels with various physical objects (*cf.* 1 Enoch lx. 11–21; Jubilees ii. 2) but do not call them *stoicheia* (of 2 Enoch xvi. 7, sometimes cited for this, we do not have the Gk. text).

Critics have suggested all four senses for the Pauline passages. (2) agrees with the preoccupation with regulations about material things in Col. ii. 21, and the reference to philosophy in ii. 8. (3) agrees with the mention of calendar observances in Gal. iv. 10. (4) agrees with the reference to false gods in Gal. iv. 8 and to angels in Col. ii. 18. Paul seems to apply his remarks equally to the Jewish and Gentile worlds, but this offers no criterion for his meaning. The Jews paid great attention to physical things and astronomy in the law and believed in the mediation of angels (*cf.* Gal. iii. 19, i. 8); the Gentiles concerned themselves with the elements and with astronomy in their philosophy and worshipped false gods, whom Paul identifies with demons (1 Cor. x. 20). Perhaps the best interpretation on these lines combines senses (2) and (3) in the fashion of the Sibylline oracles (ii. 206, viii. 337). Sense (1), 'the ABC of religion', accords well with the general context in Galatians, with its insistence that Paul's converts should not turn back to a system meant for the 'childhood' of religion, but this gives a strained sense to the genitive 'of the world', which must be taken to mean 'favoured by the world' or 'characteristic of the world'. The question has been in dispute since the Patristic period, and must be left open unless more evidence comes to light.

In 2 Pet. iii the mention of *stoicheia* between 'heaven' and 'earth' in verse 10 strongly suggests sense (2). Those who favour sense (4) in Paul have argued for it here also, pointing to the Testament of Levi iv. 1; 1 Enoch lxviii. 2 for references to spirits being dissolved in fire.

BIBLIOGRAPHY. H. N. Ridderbos, *Commentary on Galatians*, 1953, p. 153, n. 5; F. F. Bruce, *Commentary on Colossians*, 1957, p. 231. M.H.C.

ELEPHANT. Not directly mentioned in Scripture. A word for ivory (*q.v.*) used only in 1 Ki. x. 22 and 2 Ch. ix. 21, *šenhabbîm* may mean literally 'tooth (= tusk) of elephants'; *habbîm* (pl.) might then derive from Egyp. *'bw*, 'elephant'. In intertestamental times elephants were used in rival armies of Ptolemies and Seleucids (1 Macc. i. 17, iii. 34, vi. 34, 37; 2 Macc. xiv. 12; 3 Macc. v. 2). Elephants, according to Assyrian records, were plentiful in Syria and hunted by trapping in pits. K.A.K.

ELEPHANTINE. See PAPYRI AND OSTRACA.

ELHANAN. 1. In 2 Sa. xxi. 19, RV, we read that Elhanan the son of Jaare-oregim slew Goliath the Gittite. When this is compared with 1 Ch. xx. 5, where we read, 'Elhanan the son of Jair slew Lahmi the brother of Goliath the Gittite', it is apparent from the setting and the names used that the two verses refer to the same event.

The solution favoured by A. F. Kirkpatrick in *CBSC* and A. M. Renwick in *NBC* is that in 2 Samuel we have an interesting example of how easily corruption may slip into the text.

Jaare is the same as Jair with the two final letters reversed. The word *'ōreḡîm* is the Heb. for 'weavers' and has slipped in by careless copying, duplicating the place where EVV translate 'weavers'. The Heb. words for 'Bethlehemite' and 'Lahmi the brother' are so similar as to make it almost certain that one is the corruption of the other. We should therefore regard 1 Ch. xx. 5 as the original and true reading. An alternative solution is to regard Elhanan as David's original name.

2. In 2 Sa. xxiii. 24 and 1 Ch. xi. 26 Elhanan, the son of Dodo, is named as one of David's mighty men. This is probably a different person. G.T.M.

ELI. The story of Eli is told in 1 Sa. i–iv. He was 'the priest' in 'the house of the Lord' at Shiloh (1 Sa. i. 3, 7, 9). This 'house' must have been the tabernacle (Jos. xviii. 1; Jdg. xviii. 31), perhaps with some additional structure; and here was the ark (1 Sa. iv. 3). Eli's ancestry is not given, but by comparing 1 Ki. ii. 27 with 1 Ch. xxiv. 3 we deduce that Phinehas, his son, and therefore Eli himself, was a descendant of Ithamar, the youngest son of Aaron. We have no information as to how the priesthood passed from the line of Eleazar (1 Ch. vi. 4–15); but the Samaritan tradition that it was seized from Uzzi when a child must be rejected as due to racial bias. (See E. Robertson, *The Old Testament Problem*, 1950, p. 176.)

From 1 Sa. xiv. 3 and xxii. 9 ff. it appears that Eli's descendants, through Phinehas and his son Ahitub, continued to exercise the priesthood for a time at Nob.

Because of the scandalous conduct of Eli's sons, ineffectively rebuked by their father, a man of God came to pronounce a doom upon them and their descendants (1 Sa. ii. 27–36). This was confirmed by a revelation to the child Samuel (iii. 11–14). It was partially fulfilled in the death of Hophni and Phinehas (1 Sa. iv. 11) and the ruthless murder of the priests in Nob (1 Sa. xxii. 9–20). But Abiathar escaped and shared with Zadok the priesthood under David (2 Sa. xix. 11). But from this he was degraded by Solomon, in further fulfilment of the ancient prophecy (1 Ki. ii. 26 f.).

Eli 'had judged Israel forty years' (1 Sa. iv. 18), a testimony to the service he rendered to his people. But it was marred by the sinful sacrilege of his sons, and by his failure to eject them from their sacred office. G.T.M.

ELIAB. 'God is father', a common Old Testament name. **1.** A son of Helon, prince and representative of Zebulun (Nu. i. 9, ii. 7, *etc.*). **2.** A Reubenite, the son of Pallu and father of Dathan, Abiram, and Nemuel (Nu. xxvi. 8, 9). **3.** The eldest son of Jesse and brother of David (1 Sa. xvi. 5 ff., *etc.*), father of Abihail (2 Ch. xi. 18), and called 'Elihu' in 1 Ch. xxvii. 18. **4.** A Gadite warrior and companion of David (1 Ch. xii. 9). **5.** A levitical musician of the time of David (1 Ch. xv. 18 ff.). **6.** An ancestor of Samuel (1 Ch. vi. 27), also called Eliel (1 Ch. vi. 34) and Elihu (1 Sa. i. 1). G.W.G.

ELIAKIM (Heb. *'el-yāqîm*, 'God establishes'?; Gk. *Eliakeim*). The name of at least five different individuals. Two were ancestors of our Lord (Mt. i. 13; Lk. iii. 30); one was a priest, a contemporary of Nehemiah (Ne. xii. 41). Eliakim was also the one whom Pharaoh-necho made king after Josiah and whose name he changed to Jehoiakim (2 Ki. xxiii. 34; 2 Ch. xxxvi. 4).

The most prominent individual to bear this name was the son of Hilkiah, who was appointed steward in place of the deposed Shebna (Is. xxii. 20 ff.). Since the time of Solomon (1 Ki. iv. 6) this office had existed both in the northern and southern kingdoms (1 Ki. xvi. 9, xviii. 3; 2 Ki. x. 5), and was apparently even exercised by Jotham after Uzziah's leprosy (2 Ki. xv. 5).

Fig. 76. Scaraboid seal inscribed 'belonging to Eliakim, intendant of Joiachin' (*l'lyqm n'r ywkn*). Three examples of this seal have been found at Tell Beit Mirsim and Beth-shemesh.

When Sennacherib besieged Jerusalem Eliakim went to talk with the Rabshakeh (2 Ki. xviii. 18, 26, 27; Is. xxxvi. 3, 11, 22), and Hezekiah then sent him to bear the news to Isaiah (2 Ki. xix. 2; Is. xxxvii. 2). Eliakim appears also as 'servant of Jehoiachin' (*n'r ywkn*) on three seal-impressions of the 6th century BC (see fig. 76). E.J.Y.

ELIASHIB. There are several people with this name in the Old Testament: a descendant of David (1 Ch. iii. 24); a priest in the time of David (1 Ch. xxiv. 12); a singer (Ezr. x. 24); a son of Zattu (Ezr. x. 27); a son of Bani (Ezr. x. 36).

The most important was the high priest in the time of Nehemiah. He is first mentioned in Ezr. x. 6 as the father of Johanan, but is not here called high priest. Josephus says that Eliashib's father, Joiakim, was high priest when Ezra came to Jerusalem in 458 BC (*Ant.* xi. 5. 5). When Nehemiah came in 445 BC Eliashib was high priest, and took part in the building of the city walls (Ne. iii. 1, 20, 21). Later he compromised, and formed a marriage alliance with Tobiah (Ne. xiii. 4) and gave him a room in the temple precincts (Ne. xiii. 5). One of his grandsons married Sanballat's daughter (Ne. xiii. 28). His genealogy is given in Ne. xii. 10, 11. J.S.W.

ELIEZER (*'ᵉlî'ezer*, 'God is (my?) help'). A name scattered right through biblical history.

1. Eliezer the Damascene, Abraham's chief servant, and his adopted heir before the birth of Ishmael and Isaac (Gn. xv. 2, 3). The custom whereby a childless couple could adopt someone from outside as an heir is very well attested during *c.* 2000–1500 BC; such an adoptive heir had to take second place to any subsequent first-born son. See also, D. J. Wiseman, *IBA*, 1959, pp. 25, 26. For these customs in Ur, *c.* 1800 BC, see Wiseman, *JTVI*, LXXXVIII, 1956, p. 124. For these customs well illustrated in the Nuzi tablets, see C. H. Gordon, *BA*, III, 1940, pp. 1–12; translations of typical ones will be found in Speiser, *AASOR*, X, 1930, texts H 60, H 67, pp. 30, 32, *etc*.

2. Second son of Moses, named Eliezer in allusion to Moses' escaping the sword of Pharaoh (Ex. xviii. 4; 1 Ch. xxiii. 15). Eliezer had only one son, Rehabiah, but the latter had many descendants, of whom one (Shelomith) became treasurer of David's dedicated things (1 Ch. xxiii. 17, 18, xxvi. 25, 26). **3.** Grandson of Benjamin, and progenitor of a later Benjamite clan (1 Ch. vii. 8).

4. One of the seven priests who sounded the trumpets before the ark when David brought it into Jerusalem (1 Ch. xv. 24). **5.** Eliezer son of Zichri, tribal ruler of Reuben under David (1 Ch. xxvii. 16). **6.** The prophet who prophesied to King Jehoshaphat of Judah that his fleet of vessels at Ezion-geber would be wrecked in punishment for his alliance with the wicked King Ahaziah of Israel (2 Ch. xx. 35–37).

7. One of eleven men commissioned by Ezra to seek out Levites for the return to Jerusalem in 458 BC (Ezr. viii. 16 ff.). **8–10.** Three men, including a priest and a Levite, who had taken alien wives (Ezr. x. 18, 23, 31). **11.** An Eliezer appears in Christ's earthly lineage as given by Luke (iii. 29). K.A.K.

ELIHU ('*ᵉlîhû*, 'My God is He'). **1.** An Ephraimite, Samuel's paternal great-grandfather (1 Sa. i. 1), whose name seems to occur as Eliab in 1 Ch. vi. 27 and as Eliel in 1 Ch. vi. 34. **2.** One of the captains of Manasseh, who deserted to David just before the battle of Ziklag (1 Ch. xii. 20). **3.** A Korahite, member of the gate-keepers, grandson of Obed-edom, and son of Shemaiah (1 Ch. xxvi. 7). **4.** A chief officer of Judah, brother (or near relative) of David (1 Ch. xxvii. 18), perhaps identical with Eliab (1 Sa. xvi. 6). **5.** Job's young friend, son of Barachel, a Buzite of the family of Ram (Jb. xxxii. 2, 4–6, xxxiv. 1, xxxv. 1, xxxvi. 1). D.A.H.

ELIJAH. The 9th-century prophet of Israel. His name appears in the Heb. Old Testament as '*ēlîyyâhû* and '*ēlîyyâ*, in the Gk. Old Testament as *Ēleiou*, and in the New Testament as *Ēleias*. The name means 'Yah is El' or 'Yahweh is God'.

Apart from the reference to Elijah in 1 Ki. xvii. 1 as 'the Tishbite, who was of the inhabitants of Gilead', no information about his background is available. Even this reference is obscure. The *MT* suggests that while Elijah resided in Gilead (*mittōšāḇê gilᵉ'āḏ*) his birthplace was elsewhere (perhaps Tishbe of Naphtali). The LXX reads *ek thesbōn tēs galaad*, thus indicating a Tishbe of Gilead. Josephus seems to concur (*Ant*. viii. 13. 2). This has traditionally been identified with a site about 13 kilometres north of the Jabbok (see GILEAD).

Elijah's prophetic ministry is recorded in 1 Ki. xvii–xix, xxi; 2 Ki. i, ii. These narratives are written in the purest classical Heb. 'of a type which can hardly be later than the 8th century' (W. F. Albright, *From the Stone Age to Christianity*, p. 307). They could not have enjoyed an existence for long in oral form. They describe his ministry to the northern kingdom during the Omrid Dynasty (see OMRI). Elijah was contemporary with Ahab and Ahaziah, and from the position of the translation narrative (2 Ki. ii) and the answer to Jehoshaphat's question in 2 Ki. iii. 11, we conclude that his translation probably occurred about the time of the accession to the throne of Jehoram of Israel. The difficulty presented to this conclusion by 2 Ch. xxi. 12–15 can possibly be resolved either by interpreting the much-controverted 2 Ki. viii. 16 to teach a co-regency of Jehoshaphat and Jehoram, kings of Judah (see CHRONOLOGY OF THE OLD TESTAMENT), or by regarding the letter as a prophetic oracle written prior to his translation.

The Elijah cycle presents six episodes in the life of the prophet: his prediction of drought and his subsequent flight, the Mt. Carmel contest, the flight to Horeb, the Naboth incident, the oracle about Ahaziah, and his translation. Except for the last, they are all basically concerned with the clash between the worship of Yahweh and Baal (see GOD and BAAL). The Baal in these stories is Baal-Melqart, the official protective deity of Tyre. Ahab fostered this Phoenician variant of the nature-religion of Canaan (see ARCHAEOLOGY) after his marriage with the Tyrian princess Jezebel (1 Ki. xvi. 30–33), but it was Jezebel who was chiefly responsible for the systematic extermination of Yahweh worship and the propagation of the Baal cult in Israel (1 Ki. xviii. 4, 13, 19, xix. 10, 14).

Elijah appears in the first episode (1 Ki. xvii) without introduction, and after the delivery of the oracle to Ahab announcing a drought he retires beyond Ahab's jurisdiction first to the wadi Cherith on the east of Jordan and then to Zarephath (modern Sarafend below Sidon still preserves the name and overlooks what remains of this ancient Mediterranean sea-port). Elijah was miraculously sustained in both places, and while at Zarephath he performed a miracle of healing (1 Ki. xvii. 17–24).

The second episode, three years later (1 Ki. xviii. 1; *cf*. Lk. iv. 25; Jas. v. 17 which follow Jewish tradition), recounts the break in the drought following the overthrow of organized Baal worship on Mt. Carmel. The drought imposed and withdrawn at Yahweh's word was a challenge to Baal's sovereignty over nature. 1 Ki. xvii had depicted Elijah in the very stronghold of Baal-Melqart sustained by Yahweh while the country languishes (1 Ki. xvii. 12; *cf*. Jos., *Ant*. viii. 13. 2). 1 Ki. xviii brings the challenge into the open, and Yahweh's supremacy is spectacularly demonstrated. That Baal worship was certainly not exterminated at Mt. Carmel is seen from later references (*e.g*. 2 Ki. x. 18–21). For the presence of an altar of Yahweh on Mt.

Carmel, see ALTAR. Keil suggests that this was probably built by pious Yahweh worshippers after the division in the kingdom. Some commentators omit 1 Ki. xviii. 30b altogether, while others omit verses 31 and 32a.

The third episode (1 Ki. xix) describing Elijah's flight to Horeb (see SINAI) to avoid Jezebel's wrath is particularly significant. Horeb was the sacred mountain where the covenant God of Moses had made Himself known, and Elijah's return to this place represents the return of a loyal but disheartened prophet to the very source of the faith for which he had contended. The closing commission in 1 Ki. xix. 15–18 seems to have been only partially discharged by Elijah. The accession of Hazael and Jehu to the thrones of Syria and Israel respectively is recorded in the Elisha cycle (see ELISHA).

The Naboth incident (1 Ki. xxi) illustrates and vindicates the principle embedded in the religious consciousness of Israel, that land owned by an Israelite family or clan was understood as a gift from Yahweh, and that failure to recognize this and respect the rights of the individual and family within the covenant community would issue in judgment. Elijah emerges as a champion of the strong ethical demands of the Mosaic faith so significantly lacking in the Baal cult.

The fifth episode in 2 Ki. i continues to illustrate the Yahweh–Baal clash. Ahaziah's dependence upon the life-god of Syria, Baal-zebub (Baal-zebul of Ras Shamra texts, *cf.* Mt. x. 25 RVmg; Baal-zebub, meaning 'Lord of Flies', was probably a way of ridiculing the Syrian deity), evokes the judgment of God (2 Ki. i. 6, 16). A judgment of fire also falls on those who endeavoured to resist the word of Yahweh by harming His prophet (2 Ki. i. 9–15). The translation of Elijah in a whirlwind (*s*[e]*'ārâ*) brings to a dramatic close his spectacular prophetic career. The exclamation of Elisha (2 Ki. ii. 12) is repeated in 2 Ki. xiii. 14 with reference to Elisha.

Two observations may be made about the importance of Elijah. First, he stands in the Old Testament tradition of ecstatic prophecy coming through from the days of Samuel and he is also a forerunner of the 8th-century rhapsodists or writing prophets (see PROPHET). His link with the earlier tradition is seen in that he is first of all a man of action and his Spirit-determined movements defy human anticipation (1 Ki. xviii. 12). In the background of the Elijah pericope the prophetic schools of Samuel's day continue to exist (1 Ki. xviii. 4, 13; 2 Ki. ii. 3, 5, 7). His link with the later prophets lies in his constant endeavour to recall his people to the religion of Moses, both in worshipping Yahweh alone as well as in proclaiming Mosaic standards of righteousness in the community. In both these respects he anticipates the more fully developed oracles of Amos and Hosea. This advocacy of the Mosaic faith by Elijah is supported by several details which suggest a parallel between Elijah and Moses. Elijah's return to Horeb is obvious enough, but there is also the fact that Elijah is accompanied and succeeded by Elisha as Moses was by Joshua. This parallel is quite striking. Not only has the death of Moses an air of mystery attaching to it (Dt. xxxiv. 6) but his successor secured the allegiance of Israel by participating in the same spirit as Moses and demonstrated his fitness for office by a miraculous river crossing (Dt. xxxiv. 9; Jos. iv. 14). The translation narrative (2 Ki. ii) reproduces this pattern fairly precisely. The fact also that God answers Elijah by fire on two occasions (1 Ki. xviii. 38; 2 Ki. i. 10, 12) seems to look back to the exhibition of God's presence and judgment in fire in the Exodus narratives (*e.g.* Ex. xiii. 21, xix. 18, xxiv. 17; Nu. xi. 1, xvi. 35). Little wonder that in Jewish Haggadic thought (see TALMUD) Elijah was viewed as the counterpart to Moses.

Second, his ministry is spoken of as being revived 'before the coming of the great and dreadful day of the Lord' (Mal. iv. 5, 6). This theme is a popular one in the Jewish Mishnah (see TALMUD AND MIDRASH) and was a common topic of discussion during the ministry of Jesus (Mk. viii. 28). Jesus indicated that the Malachi prophecy had reference to the ministry of John the Baptist (Mt. xi. 14, xvii. 12 f.; see JOHN THE BAPTIST). Elijah reappears in person on the mount of transfiguration (Mk. ix. 4) and he is referred to elsewhere in the New Testament in Lk. iv. 25, 26; Rom. xi. 2–4; Jas. v. 17, 18.

Three other men of the same name also appear in the Old Testament, the first being a Benjamite priest (1 Ch. viii. 27; Heb. *'ēlîyyâ*), and the second and third a priest and a layman respectively, who married foreign wives (Ezr. x. 21, 26; Heb. *'ēlîyyâ*).

BIBLIOGRAPHY. E. Fohrer, *Elia*, 1957; H. H. Rowley, 'Elijah on Mount Carmel', *BJRL*, XLIII, 1960–1, pp. 190 ff.; J. A. Montgomery and H. S. Gehman, *A Critical and Exegetical Commentary on the Books of Kings*, 1951; F. James, *Personalities of the Old Testament*, 1939, chapter ix.

B.L.S.

ELIM (Heb. 'terebinths' or 'oaks'). Second stopping-place of the Israelites after their crossing of the Re(e)d Sea from Egypt. Beyond the wilderness of Shur (*q.v.*), east of the modern Suez canal, they first encamped at Marah in the wilderness of Etham not far away (because named after Etham in easternmost Delta), and thence reached Elim with its twelve springs and seventy palm-trees. After this the Israelites went on 'and pitched by the Red Sea', before eventually reaching the wilderness of Sin (*q.v.*), Ex. xv. 27, xvi. 1; Nu. xxxiii. 9, 10.

By putting the stop at Elim shortly after the escape from Egypt and passage of its desert edge (Shur), and before a stop by the Red Sea prior to reaching the wilderness of Sin, the biblical references suggest that Elim is situated on the west side of the Sinai peninsula, facing on to the Gulf of Suez. Any closer location is still not certain, but a plausible suggestion of long standing is Wadi Gharandel (or, Ghurundel), a well-known watering-place with tamarisks and palms, some 40 or so miles SSE of Suez along the west side of Sinai. See also SINAI and WILDERNESS OF WANDERING.

BIBLIOGRAPHY. See E. Robinson, *Biblical Researches in Palestine*, I, 1841, pp. 99, 100, 105, 106, and map at end; A. P. Stanley, *Sinai and Palestine*, 1887, pp. 37, 38; among recent works, Wright and Filson, *Westminster Historical Atlas to the Bible*, 1956, pp. 38, 39 and plate V.

K.A.K.

ELISABETH (from Heb. *'ᵉlišeḇa'*, 'God is (my) oath'). The wife of Zacharias (*q.v.*) the priest, and mother of John the Baptist (Lk. i. 5 ff.). Herself of priestly descent, Elisabeth is described in the AV as a 'cousin' (more accurately, 'kinswoman') of the Virgin Mary (Lk. i. 36), to whom she addressed the remarkable words of Lk. i. 42–45.

J.D.D.

ELISHA. The 9th-century prophet of Israel. His name appears in the Heb. Old Testament as *'ᵉlîšā'*, in the Gk. Old Testament as *Eleisaie*, and in the New Testament as *Elisaios*. The name means 'God is salvation'. His father's name was Shaphat.

All that can be known about Elisha's background is found in 1 Ki. xix. 16, 19–21. We are not told his age or his birthplace, but we may assume that he was a native of Abel-meholah (Tell Abū Sifri?) in the Jordan valley and was still only young when Elijah sought him out. That he was the son of a family of some means also seems clear.

His ministry, if we date it from his call, extended through the reigns of Ahab, Ahaziah, Jehoram, Jehu, Jehoahaz, and Jehoash, a period of more than fifty years. The narratives of Elisha's ministry are recorded in 1 Ki. xix; 2 Ki. ii–ix, xiii, and comprise a series of some eighteen episodes. It is not possible to be certain of their chronological order throughout because of obvious breaks in the sequence of events (*e.g.*, *cf.* 2 Ki. vi. 23 with vi. 24; v. 27 with viii. 4, 5; xiii. 13 with xiii. 14 ff.). These episodes do not betray the same tension between Yahweh and Baal worship as those of the Elijah cycle (see ELIJAH). It is a ministry conducted at the head of the prophetic schools which consists of a display of signs and wonders both at a personal as well as a national level. Elisha emerges as a kind of seer in the tradition of Samuel to whom peasants and kings alike turn for help.

Examining these episodes in their biblical order, we may make the following observations. (1) Elisha's call (1 Ki. xix. 19–21) was not so much an anointing (*cf.* 1 Ki. xix. 16) as an ordination by investiture with Elijah's prophetic mantle. Until Elijah's translation Elisha remained his servant (1 Ki. xix. 21; 2 Ki. iii. 11). (2) 2 Ki. ii. 1–18 recounts Elisha's assumption of the rôle of his master. The double portion of the spirit upon Elisha recalls the language and thought of Dt. xxi. 17 while the whole episode is reminiscent of the replacement of Moses by Joshua as leader of Israel (see ELIJAH). (3) The healing of the injurious waters in 2 Ki. ii. 19–22 also finds a parallel in the events of the Exodus (Ex. xv. 22–25). (4) The incident in 2 Ki. ii. 23–25 must be understood as a judgment upon the deliberate mockery of the new head of the school of Yahweh's prophets. Some scholars incline to the view that Elisha's baldness was a prophetic tonsure.

(5) The story of Elisha's part in the campaign of the three kings against Moab (2 Ki. iii. 1–27; see MOAB) records his request for music when receiving an oracle from Yahweh (verse 15). There is a strong suggestion of ecstatic prophecy here as in 1 Sa. x. 5–13 (*cf.* 1 Ch. xxv. 1). (6) 2 Ki. iv. 1–7 is parallel to Elijah's miracle in 1 Ki. xvii. 8–16 and introduces (7) the longer story of Elisha's dealings with the Shunammite woman (2 Ki. iv. 8–37), which has many points of similarity with 1 Ki. xvii. 8–24. (8) 2 Ki. iv. 38–41 and (9) iv. 42–44 occur at sessions with the fraternity of prophets at Gilgal, probably during the famine referred to in 2 Ki. viii. 1. The second of these miracles anticipates the miracle of Jesus recorded in Mk. vi. 35–44.

(10) The Naaman story (2 Ki. v. 1–27) cannot be dated with accuracy. It must have occurred during one of the temporary lulls in hostilities between Israel and Syria. The editorial comment in verse 1 ascribing the Syrian's victories to Yahweh should be compared with Am. ix. 7. This cosmic view of Yahweh is recognized by Naaman (verse 15), and his request for Israelite soil (verse 17) need not necessarily imply that he believed Yahweh's influence to be confined to Israelite territory. See NAAMAN. Of Elisha's *pax tecum* (verse 19) Ellison says, 'If the vast majority of Israelites indulged in a debased worship of Jehovah in which room for minor deities could be found, no blame could be laid on a Syrian who did not rise to the heights of monotheism in a moment' (*NBC*). See RIMMON.

(11) 2 Ki. vi. 1–7 recounts a miraculous feat of Elisha and incidentally casts light on the size and habitations of prophetic fraternities (*cf.* 2 Ki. iv. 38–44). (12) 2 Ki. vi. 8–23 and (13) vi. 24–vii. 20 depict Elisha as a counsellor of kings and a deliverer of the nation from national disaster (*cf.* 2 Ki. iii. 1–27). The second of these episodes is said to involve Ben-hadad of Aram and 'the king of Israel'. This is unfortunately obscure. See BEN-HADAD. (14) 2 Ki. viii. 1–6 clearly belongs before v. 1–27. It is a continuation of the Shunammite story (2 Ki. iv. 8–37).

(15) 2 Ki. viii. 7–15, (16) ix. 1–13, and (17) xiii. 14–19 all depict Elisha involved in affairs of state. The first of these describes the ascent of Hazael to the throne (*cf.* 1 Ki. xix. 15). See HAZAEL. Elisha's reply (verse 10) may be understood to mean that the king would recover from his sickness but would die for other reasons, or it may have been the prophet's spontaneous reply that had to be corrected by a vision from Yahweh (*cf.*

2 Sa. vii. 1–17; 2 Ki. iv. 26–36). The anointing of Jehu discharged the last of the tasks committed to Elijah (1 Ki. xix. 15, 16) and precipitated the predicted overthrow of the Omrid Dynasty (1 Ki. xxi. 21–24). This prophetic-inspired revolt is in contrast to the corresponding priestly revolt in the south that removed Athaliah from the throne (2 Ki. xi). From 2 Ki. xiii. 14–19 and (18) xiii. 20, 21 Elisha's age has been estimated at eighty-five to ninety years. He appears as a favourite of the king, who realizes his political value (verse 14). Sympathetic or mimetic actions accompanying prophetic oracles are not uncommon in the Old Testament.

Although Elisha is a prophet of the 9th century and belongs to the prophetic tradition which produced the 8th-century rhapsodists or writing prophets (see PROPHECY), he has more affinities with the ecstatic prophets of the 11th century. He is very like Samuel, with gifts of knowledge and foresight and a capacity to work miracles. He figures at the head of the prophetic schools and is in frequent demand because of his singular gifts. Although he is spoken of as having a home in Samaria (2 Ki. vi. 32), he is, like Samuel, constantly moving about the land and enjoys an easy access into royal courts and peasant dwellings. While his relation to Elijah is certainly suggestive of the relationship between Joshua and Moses (see ELIJAH), the fact that Elijah's ministry is reproduced in John the Baptist (see ELIJAH) and Elisha's directly anticipates the miracle-aspect of the ministry of Jesus is even more significant. Elisha is only once referred to in the New Testament—in Lk. iv. 27.

BIBLIOGRAPHY. R. S. Wallace, *Elijah and Elisha*, 1957; J. A. Montgomery and H. S. Gehman, *A Critical and Exegetical Commentary on the Books of Kings*, 1951; F. James, *Personalities of the Old Testament*, 1939, chapter x. B.L.S.

ELISHAH. The eldest son of Javan (*q.v.*) (Gn. x. 4 = 1 Ch. i. 7), whose name was later applied to his descendants, who inhabited a maritime region (*'iyyê*, 'isles' or 'coastlands') which traded purple (*q.v.*) to Tyre (Ezk. xxvii. 7). It is very probable that the biblical name *'elîšâ* (LXX *Elisa*) is to be equated with Alašia of the extra-biblical sources. This name occurs in the Egyptian and cuneiform (Boghaz-Koi, Alalaḫ, Ugarit) inscriptions, and it was the source of eight of the Amarna letters (*q.v.*), in which it usually occurs in the form *a-la-ši-ia*. These texts indicate that Alašia was an exporter of copper, and it is possible, though not universally accepted, that it is to be identified with the site of Enkomi on the east coast of Cyprus, where excavations under C. F. A. Schaeffer have revealed an important trading-centre of the Late Bronze Age. The name Alašia would also apply to the area under the political domination of the city, and may at times have included outposts on the Phoenician coast.

BIBLIOGRAPHY. R. Dussaud in C. F. A. Schaeffer, *Enkomi-Alasia*, 1952, pp. 1–10; *AS*, VI, 1956, pp. 63–65. T.C.M.

ELLASAR. The city or kingdom ruled by Arioch, an ally of Chedorlaomer (*q.v.*) king of Elam, who attacked Sodom and captured Lot, Abraham's nephew (Gn. xiv. 1, 9). The identification with Larsa (modern Senkereh), *c.* 28 miles north-east of Ur, Babylonia, rests on the equation of the name of its king, formerly read as Eri-aku, with Arioch. The Eri-aku of the cuneiform text is now, however, more correctly read Warad-Sin. Those who look for the location of Ellasar in N Mesopotamia suggest the town of Ilanzura, between Carchemish and Harran, mentioned in the Mari texts. See ARIOCH. D.J.W.

ELOHIM. See GOD, NAMES OF.

ELOI, ELOI, LAMA SABACHTHANI. Occurs in Mk. xv. 34 and in a slightly different form in Mt. xxvii. 46. It is one of the Lord's sayings on the cross, and is a quotation from Ps. xxii. 1. The form 'Eli' would be more likely to give rise to the confusion with Elijah, and the form in Matthew is thus more likely to be original. Our Lord uses the Aramaic, almost exactly the form of the Targum.

The difficulty of accounting for this saying is the strongest argument for its authenticity. Inadequate explanations are that it reflects the intensity of the Lord's human feeling, that it reveals the disappointment of His hope that in His extremity the Father would usher in the new age, or that He was merely reciting the Psalm as an act of devotion. It can be understood only in the light of the New Testament doctrine of the atonement, according to which Christ identified Himself with sinful man and endured separation from God (*cf.* Phil. ii. 8; 2 Cor. v. 21). It is a mystery we cannot fathom.

BIBLIOGRAPHY. A. H. McNeile, *The Gospel according to St. Matthew*, 1915, *ad loc.*; D. H. C. Read, 'The Cry of Dereliction', in *ExpT*, LXVIII, June 1957, pp. 260 ff. A.G.

ELON (Heb. *'ēlôn*, *'êlôn*). **1.** A Hittite of Canaan; Gn. xxvi. 34, *cf.* xxxvi. 2. **2.** Head of a family of Zebulun; Gn. xlvi. 14; Nu. xxvi. 26; *cf.* Nu. i. 9, *etc.* ('Helon'). **3.** A Zebulonite judge of Israel; Jdg. xii. 11, 12.

4. A southern Danite town; Jos. xix. 43, perhaps also 1 Ki. iv. 9. Simons (*GTT*, p. 349) suggests Kh. Wadi 'Alin, a mile east of Beth-shemesh. **5.** Near Zaanannim in Naphtali, Jos. xix. 33; perhaps 'the terebinth in Zaanannim'. J.P.U.L.

ELPARAN. See PARAN.

EL SHADDAI. See GOD, NAMES OF.

ELTEKEH. A city in Palestine allotted to the tribe of Dan (Jos. xix. 44) and later made a levitical city (Jos. xxi. 23). Sennacherib mentions it (Altakū) together with Timnā among his conquests in his annals for 701/700 BC (Chicago Cylinder iii. 6; Taylor Cylinder ii. 82, 83). It has been identified by some with mod. Khirbet el-

Muqanna' about 25 miles west of Jerusalem (so Albright; but see EKRON).

BIBLIOGRAPHY. D. D. Luckenbill, *The Annals of Sennacherib*, 1924, p. 32; W. F. Albright, *BASOR*, 15, 1924, p. 8. T.C.M.

ELYMAS. See BAR-JESUS.

EMBALMING. See BURIAL AND MOURNING.

EMBROIDERY. The ornamentation of cloth falls into two main classes.

1. Plaited or chequered work (*tašbēṣ*) decorated the high priest's tunic (Ex. xxviii. 4). This may have been produced by the introduction of threads between the outer and inner layers of material, stitched to form the pattern (*HDB*). Similar chequered work inwrought with gold was fit clothing for a princess (Ps. xlv. 13). It is possible to read in this verse *p^{e}nînîm*, 'pearls', for *p^{e}nîmâ*, 'within the house', giving the sense of pearls in plaited settings of gold thread, which would be parallel to the use of gems and gold thread on the shoulders of the ephod (Ex. xxviii. 11, 12).

2. In contrast the ephod, girdle and breastplate of the high priest (Ex. xxviii. 6, 8, 15), the garments of plaited work (*bigᵉḏê-śᵉrāḏ*, Ex. xxxix. 1) for those who served in the sanctuary, and the tabernacle curtains and veil (Ex. xxvi. 1, 31) were worked in coloured embroidery (*riqmâ*) at times combined with gold thread. The word seldom occurs without specific reference to the colours used in the variegated work. By an extended use it is applied to the feathers of an eagle (Ezk. xvii. 3) and to stones prepared by David for the Temple (1 Ch. xxix. 2). Even the formation of the human embryo is thus described (Ps. cxxxix. 15).

Fig. 77. Detail of the crown and embroidered cloak worn by Ashurbanipal, king of Assyria, 669–c. 627 BC. Relief from Nineveh. See also figs. 25, 70*b* (7, 8), 164.

The thread of gold was produced by cutting thin plates of beaten gold in' .vires (Ex. xxxix. 3). These, together with the coloured strands, may have been woven in on the loom. The view that they would more probably have been sewn with a needle on the finished cloth is expressed by

T. G. Pinches (*EBi*) on the assumption that the design of cherubim was too complex for a weaver of that time. Where the design was of an elaborate kind the embroidery was the work of the 'inventive workman' (*ma'ᵃśēh ḥōšēḇ*, Ex. xxvi. 1). Appliqué work was probably used to adorn the skirt of the priestly robe with coloured pomegranates in between which were attached bells of gold (Ex. xxviii. 33). See also ARTS AND CRAFTS.

G.I.E.

EMERALD. See JEWELS AND PRECIOUS STONES.

EMERODS. An incurable disease to be inflicted on those who broke the divine covenant (Dt. xxviii. 27). It thus plagued the people of Ashdod and district when they captured the ark (1 Sa. v. 6). It resulted in 'haemorrhoids' or 'emerods' (AV; Heb. *'ᵉpōlîm*), affecting both old and young in the genital organs (verse 9).

These symptoms and the association with rodents (AV 'mice', 1 Sa. vi. 4, 5) supports the identification with bubonic plague. The *Bacillus pestis* infection spreads through fleas from dead rats. Enlarged lymphatic glands, sometimes with petechial haemorrhages, result. The disease is attested in the ancient Near East with 70% fatalities within a week. The offering to an offended deity of plague-buboes (*ṭᵉḥōrîm*, 'tumours', an explanation of emerods given in 1 Sa. vi. 11, 17, which is followed by *MT Qᵉrē* in all occurrences of *'ᵉpōlîm*) would be in accordance with customs known from antiquity. See DISEASE AND HEALING.

D.J.W.

EMIM. Early inhabitants of Moab, who were smitten in the plain of Kiriathaim (*q.v.*) by Chedorlaomer in the time of Abraham (Gn. xiv. 5). They were described by Moses as a great and numerous people, to be compared in stature to the Anakim (*q.v.*; Dt. ii. 10). They were evidently considered to belong to the peoples known as Rephaim (*q.v.*), but were called *'êmîm*, 'terrifying beings', by the Moabites who followed them in the area (Dt. ii. 11). They are unknown outside the Bible. See GIANT.

T.C.M.

EMMANUEL. See IMMANUEL.

EMMAUS. A village 60 furlongs from Jerusalem, to which two disciples were going when Jesus appeared to them after His resurrection (Lk. xxiv. 13). Luke did not specify the direction from the city, and the site is uncertain. Some identify with the Emmaus 'in the plain country' where in 166 BC Judas Maccabaeus defeated Gorgias (1 Macc. iii. 40, iv. 1–15), and which was renamed Nicopolis by Heliogabalus in the 3rd century. This is the modern 'Amwas, some 19 miles from Jerusalem on the road to Ramleh. It cannot be equated with Luke's village unless we take a variant reading (Codex Sinaiticus) and substitute '160' for Luke's '60' furlongs or stadia. This, however, involves a round trip of some 40 miles, a distance difficult to reconcile with the biblical narrative. See *Arndt* for fuller discussion of possible location.

J.D.D.

ENCAMPMENT BY THE SEA. The place where the Israelites camped by the sea and made the crossing (Ex. xiii. 18, xiv. 2) has been the subject of much controversy during the last hundred years. The question is inseparable from that of the location of such place-names as Baal-Zephon, Etham, Migdol, Pihahiroth, Sea of Reeds, and Succoth (*q.v.*).

Two main traditions have grown up around the route of the Exodus out of Egypt: the 'Southern' theory favouring a route from the Wadi Tumilat region south-east to the Suez area, and the 'Northern' theory advocating a crossing near Lake Menzaleh to south of Port Said. See fig. 80.

The southern theory was foreshadowed by Josephus (*Ant.* ii. 15. 1), who considered the Israelites to have started from Latopolis (= Egyp. Babylon, Old Cairo) to a Baal-Zephon on the Red Sea; Pierre Diacre and Antonin de Plaisance had a tradition of the Hebrews passing Clysma near the present-day Suez. Among moderns, Lepsius, Mallon, Bourdon (with a crossing at Clysma), Cazelles, and Montet favoured this view.

The northern route was championed by Brugsch, identifying the Sea of Reeds, *yam-sûp̄*, with Egyp. *p'-ṯwf* and placing it in Lake Serbonis on the Mediterranean shore with Baal-Zephon at Ras Qasrun there. But this hardly agrees with the biblical account, in which God forbade Israel to go by 'the way of the land of the Philistines' (Ex. xiii. 17, 18). Gardiner next espoused the northern route (*JEA*, V, 1918, pp. 261–269; *Recueil Champollion*, 1922, pp. 203–215), likewise O. Eissfeldt and N. Aimé-Giron, the former identifying Casios and Baal-Zephon on the Mediterranean shore and the latter equating Baal-Zephon with Tahpanhes (Phoenician papyrus). For Albright, see below.

Most recently, H. Cazelles has well summed up the whole problem and the views expressed on it. He considers that later tradition from the LXX onward (note the LXX's *thalassa erythra*, 'Red Sea') speaks for a southern route, but that study of the names in the Heb. text suggests that this latter indicates a northern route by the Mediterranean; according to Cazelles, these northern locations were due to an editor of J and E documents who (like Manetho and Josephus) associated the Hebrew Exodus with the expulsion of the Hyksos from Egypt. However, this is purely speculative.

Finally, there is an entirely different suggestion by Albright (*BASOR*, 109, 1948, pp. 15, 16). He places Ra'amses at Tanis in the north, brings the Israelites south-east past the places in the Wadi Tumilat (Pithom at Retabeh, Succoth at Tell el-Maskhutah) and then sharply back up north again (*cf.* 'that they turn back', Ex. xiv. 2) by the Bitter Lakes to the region of a Baal-Zephon located at later Tahpanhes (Defneh); Migdol is then Tell el-Her just south of Pelusium, with the Sea of Reeds (*yam-sûp̄*) in this general area. Having thus left Egypt proper, the Israelites would then flee to the south-east into the Sinai peninsula, so that Albright's route in its end-result becomes a 'southern' one (*i.e.* he does not take Israel by the forbidden way of the Philistines). Noth's reserves (*Festschrift Otto Eissfeldt*, 1947, pp. 181–190) are largely based on literary-critical considerations of doubtful relevance. As will be evident, the route of the Exodus is still a very live issue.

BIBLIOGRAPHY. N. Aimé-Giron, *Annales du Service des Antiquités de l'Égypte*, XL, 1940–1, pp. 433–460; Bourdon, *RB*, XLI, 1932, pp. 370–382, 538–549; H. Cazelles, *RB*, LXII, 1955, pp. 321–364; O. Eissfeldt, *Baal-Zaphon, Zeus Casios und der Durchzug der Israeliten durch das Meer*, 1932; Lepsius, *Zeitschrift für Aegyptische Sprache*, XXI, 1883, pp. 41–53; Mallon, 'Les Hébreux en Égypte', *Orientalia*, III, 1921; Montet, *Géographie de l'Égypte Ancienne*, I, 1957, pp. 218, 219, and *L'Égypte et la Bible*, 1959, pp. 59–63.

See also H. H. Rowley, *From Joseph to Joshua*, 1950, for much background matter and bibliography, and C. de Wit, *The Date and Route of the Exodus*, 1960, for more specifically Egyptian aspects and later references. C.D.W.

ENCHANTMENT. See MAGIC AND SORCERY.

ENDOR. Modern 'En-dûr 4 miles south of Mt. Tabor. The town was assigned to Manasseh, but was never wrested from Canaanite possession (Jos. xvii. 11, 12). The witch of Endor, of whom Saul inquired before his last battle (1 Sa. xxviii. 7), was probably from this Canaanite stock, for an attempt had been made to do away with such practices among the Hebrews (1 Sa. xxviii. 3).

R.J.W.

EN-EGLAIM (*'ên-'eḡlayim*, 'spring of the two calves'). A place mentioned once only (Ezk. xlvii. 10) as lying on the shore of the Dead Sea. Though the site is unknown, the reference to En-gedi (*q.v.*) suggests a location somewhere in the north-western sector. This site is distinct from Eglaim (*'eḡlayim*, Is. xv. 8), a town in Moab.

BIBLIOGRAPHY. *GTT*, pp. 459, 460; W. R. Farmer, *BA*, XIX, 1956, pp. 19–21. T.C.M.

EN-GANNIM (*'ên-gannîm*, 'spring of gardens'). **1.** A part of the inheritance of Judah (Jos. xv. 34); perhaps modern Beit-jemâl, midway between Jerusalem and Ashkelon, and near Beth-shemesh.

2. A city of Issachar (Jos. xix. 21, xxi. 29); modern Jenin, 10 miles south-east of Megiddo.

R.J.W.

EN-GEDI (*'ên-geḏî*, 'spring of the goat'). A fresh-water spring on the west of the Dead Sea, bearing the same name in modern times. The spring was allotted to Judah at the conquest (Jos. xv. 62). The fertility of the area in the midst of such barren country made it an ideal place for an outlaw, for food (Ct. i. 14) and hiding-places (1 Sa. xxiii. 29, xxiv. 1 ff.) were readily available.

R.J.W.

ENGLISH VERSIONS OF THE BIBLE.

I. ANGLO-SAXON VERSIONS

The history of versions of the Bible in English has its beginnings in challenging obscurity and uncertainty in the Anglo-Saxon period of the English language. The Venerable Bede has supplied a fascinating account (*Ecclesiastical History*, IV, chapter 24) of a heavenly endowment granted to the herdsman Cædmon in the latter part of the 7th century AD, which enabled him to sing in English verse the substance and the themes of Scripture. Cædmon was followed, according to Bede's testimony, by others who endeavoured to write religious verse. Although Bede does not quote any of Cædmon's poetry *verbatim*, he gives us the sense of the initial verses attributed to him, verses of stirring freshness and exaltation. Surviving Anglo-Saxon metrical treatments or paraphrases of biblical materials, whether or not they are to be connected with Cædmon, witness to an important means of disseminating knowledge of the Scriptures in that period.

To Bede himself has been attributed the translation of the Gospel according to John. His follower Cuthbert, in a letter on the death of his 'father and master', relates that Bede completed his translation of the Fourth Gospel on the day of his death at the virtual moment of his departure. If Bede did translate the entire Bible or the greater part of it into English, as certain evidence might indicate, his work has regrettably not survived.

Aldhelm (640–709) has been credited with a translation of the Psalms and indeed of much, if not all, of the Bible into English; but no extant MS can with certainty be said to represent his work. The Vespasian Psalter, the oldest surviving Latin text of the Psalms with a gloss or interlinear translation of the individual words into Anglo-Saxon, cannot with any assurance be held to contain Aldhelm's work. This manuscript of the Psalter was succeeded by a considerable number of others with Anglo-Saxon glosses.

King Alfred the Great (849–901) introduced his *Code of Saxon Laws* with an abbreviated and rearranged English rendering of the Ten Commandments and portions in English of Ex. xxi–xxiii and Acts xv. William of Malmesbury says that Alfred was at work on an English translation of the Psalms at the time of his death. There has been disagreement as to whether Alfred's work is represented by the prose rendering in English of the first fifty psalms in the Paris Psalter. His translation of Gregory's *De cura pastorali* involved, of course, translation of the Scripture references in the text.

Ælfric, an abbot at about the beginning of the

11th century, made translations or paraphrases of extensive parts of the Old Testament text.

Two manuscripts of the Gospels in Latin with an Anglo-Saxon gloss have survived. One of them is the famous Lindisfarne Gospels *c.* 700 with a gloss made *c.* 950. The other manuscript is the Rushworth Gospels, whose gloss is very much dependent on that of the Lindisfarne MS in Mark, Luke, and John.

A noteworthy development in the Anglo-Saxon period was the competent translation of the four Gospels into a continuous English text, a text which is represented by six extant MSS.

II. MIDDLE ENGLISH VERSIONS

The development of a literature in Middle English begins in the closing part of the 12th century. About 1300 a metrical version of the Psalter appeared; it was followed by prose translations, one of which was the work of Richard Rolle of Hampole. Portions of the New Testament were also translated. The distinguishing achievement of the Middle English period, however, was the translation work associated with Wyclif (*c.* 1320–84) and the movement he represented. An earlier Wyclifite version was produced in the latter part of the 14th century *c.* 1380–3, a substantial portion of which was made by Nicholas of Hereford (from Genesis to Baruch iii. 20) and the rest, including the New Testament, has been thought by some to have been made by Wyclif himself. Whatever may have been Wyclif's part in the actual work of translation, his zeal for the Scriptures and for making them accessible to the people in the English language must be credited with giving the impetus to this highly influential version. It was made from a Latin base and it clung to the original with some damage to English idiom and clarity, but it was a commendable new effort addressed to the needs of the present and facing towards the future. It was soon followed by a translation in smoother style which was quite probably made by John Purvey, a follower of Wyclif, with the assistance of others. The principles and procedures which were followed by Purvey were in many respects exemplary, and his revision was very influential. It was indeed finally superseded by the work of Tyndale and Coverdale in the 16th century, but its influence has been perpetuated through its successors.

III. WILLIAM TYNDALE

William Tyndale was the first to translate the New Testament directly from Greek into English. He received his M.A. degree at Oxford in 1515, the year before the appearance of Erasmus' Greek New Testament, the first printed New Testament in Greek actually to be published. Tyndale may have studied Greek at Cambridge. His zeal for making the Scriptures available in the vernacular is indicated in the story of his encounter with a 'learned man' who expressed the judgment that we might better be without the laws of God than without those of the Pope. To him Tyndale expressed defiance of the Pope and his laws and said that if God would spare his life he would cause a ploughboy to know more of the Scripture than his learned adversary did. Finding England uncongenial to his desire to lay the New Testament plainly before the eyes of the people in their native language, he went to Hamburg. He was never to return to the land which was to enter into his labours and to be enriched by his benefaction.

Tyndale now completed his translation of the New Testament, making use of the 1519 and 1522 editions of Erasmus' Greek New Testament. He consulted also Erasmus' Latin translation, Luther's German text, and the Latin Vulgate. The printing of his New Testament was begun in 1525 in Cologne, but opposition forced him to flee to Worms with the sheets that had been printed. There before long (in 1525 or 1526) two editions were completed (one quarto, the other octavo) of 3,000 copies each. Virulent official opposition in England was so very successful in destroying copies of early issues of Tyndale's New Testament that there are only minimal remains today. Revised editions appeared in 1534 and 1535. Tyndale's New Testament, despite the opposition to it, could not be destroyed. The first printed English New Testament, the first made from the Greek, opened a new period in the history of the English Bible and made an ineradicable contribution to the English Bibles yet to come. The influence of the wording and structure of Tyndale's New Testament on the Authorized Version is immense, and the latter provides a continuing tribute to the simplicity, freshness, vitality, and felicity of his work. Tyndale also published a translation of the Pentateuch in 1530, of Jonah in 1531, and of selections from the Old Testa-

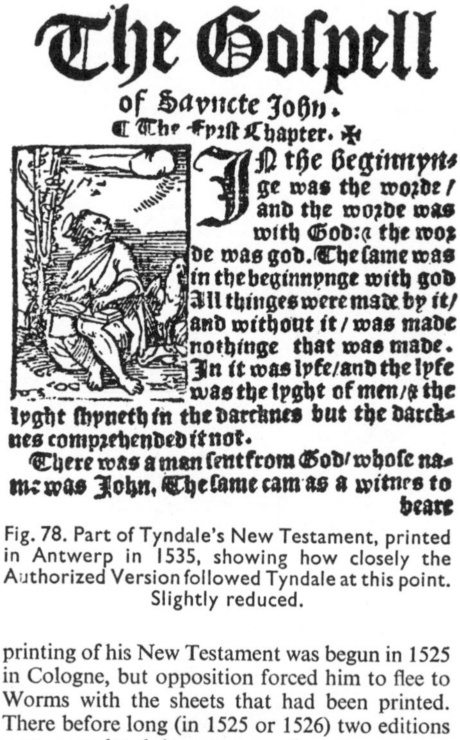

The Gospell
of Sayncte John.
The Fyrst Chapter.

In the beginnynge was the worde / and the worde was with God: & the worde was god. The same was in the beginnynge with god All thinges were made by it / and without it / was made nothinge that was made. In it was lyfe / and the lyfe was the lyght of men / & the lyght shyneth in the darcknes but the darcknes comprehended it not.

There was a man sent from God / whose name was John. The same cam as a witnes to beare

Fig. 78. Part of Tyndale's New Testament, printed in Antwerp in 1535, showing how closely the Authorized Version followed Tyndale at this point. Slightly reduced.

ment (published with his edition of the New Testament in 1534). An edition of the Pentateuch with a revised translation of Genesis was printed in 1534. There is good authority for believing that Tyndale translated an extensive additional section of the Old Testament text, but before he could complete his translation of the Bible he suffered a martyr's death. In his Old Testament work he used the Hebrew text. Among other works available to him were Luther's German translation, the Latin Vulgate, and a Latin rendering by Pagninus. Like his version of the New Testament, Tyndale's faithful and vivid translation of books of the Old Testament has been exceedingly influential. His dying prayer was that the Lord would open the eyes of the King of England.

George Joye also had a significant part in the development of the English Bible in Tyndale's day. He graduated from Cambridge in 1513, was later influenced by Lutheran doctrine, and found it necessary to seek refuge abroad *c.* 1527. He may have published a version of the Psalter in 1530, a version different from that which he published in 1534. He also published English translations of Isaiah (1531), of Jeremiah, Lamentations, and the Song of Moses at the Red Sea (1534), a revision of Tyndale's New Testament (1534) without Tyndale's authorization and with changes of which Tyndale did not approve. A source of disturbance to Tyndale was Joye's employment at times, in the interests of his own views, of an unjustifiable substitution for the term 'resurrection'. After Tyndale had issued his own revision of his New Testament in 1534, with selections from the Old Testament, Joye published another edition of his New Testament, together with selections from the Old Testament. He may also have published translations of Proverbs and Ecclesiastes. (See C. C. Butterworth, *The Literary Lineage of the King James Bible*, 1941, pp. 87 ff.)

IV. MILES COVERDALE

The first really notable name in the history of English Bible translation and revision in the period from Tyndale to the appearance of the Authorized Version is that of Miles Coverdale, whose work benefited from an altered royal and ecclesiastical attitude. In 1535 Coverdale published a translation (which he had prepared on the Continent) of the entire Bible, the first full Bible to be printed in English. This version was given a dedication to Henry VIII. It was made from the German and Latin with the aid, it would appear, of the Latin Vulgate and of the versions of Pagninus, Luther, Zwingli and Leo Juda, and of the translations made by Tyndale. A folio edition and a quarto edition appeared in 1537. The quarto edition asserts on its title-page that it was set forth with the King's most gracious licence. In 1538 Coverdale published an edition of the Latin Vulgate New Testament with an English translation in parallel columns. Coverdale's capacity for beautiful rhythm and phrasing have made an enduring contribution to the great tradition of English Bible translation.

V. THE MATTHEW BIBLE

In 1537 there appeared a Bible whose title-page asserts that it was truly and purely translated into English by Thomas Matthew. This Bible has often been regarded as the work of one of Tyndale's followers, John Rogers, who regarded it as inexpedient to send it forth under his own name. It was virtually a compilation of Tyndale's and Coverdale's work with minor alterations. The New Testament and the Pentateuch sections are Tyndale's. The section from Joshua to 2 Chronicles appears to be taken from a previously unpublished translation made by Tyndale. The sections from Ezra to Malachi and the Apocrypha were taken from Coverdale. The Prayer of Manasses was translated from Olivetan's French Bible of 1535. The text of this Bible was intelligently edited. It was a fact of remarkable irony that a Bible which was substantially the work of Tyndale, who had been opposed by Henry VIII and the Church, could now be dedicated to Henry and set forth with his most gracious licence! On the solicitation of Cranmer, the Archbishop of Canterbury, Thomas Cromwell secured Henry's authorization that this Bible would be allowed by his authority to be bought and read within the realm.

VI. TAVERNER'S BIBLE

Richard Taverner published in 1539 a revision of Matthew's Bible which introduced a number of improvements indicating some scholarly competence. It was not without influence on future versions, but has not generally been regarded as occupying a place in the main line of English versions of the Bible.

VII. THE GREAT BIBLE

In 1539 there appeared a Bible which was to exercise enormous influence on England and on the subsequent history of the English Bible. It was prepared by Coverdale on the invitation of Thomas Cromwell, and has therefore been called Cromwell's Bible. Because of its large size it has also been called the Great Bible. The second edition of April 1540 and later editions had a preface by Archbishop Cranmer, and consequently the version has frequently been referred to as Cranmer's Bible. But regardless of its multiple designations, this Bible is really a revision of Matthew's Bible. In revising the New Testament text Coverdale made use of Erasmus' Latin version and the Vulgate, and Munster's close Latin translation of the Hebrew, issued in 1534–5, in his work on the Old Testament. The Great Bible was authorized for distribution among the people and for the use of every church. When the opponents of the translation were unable to show him any heresies in it, Henry VIII said that if it were without heresies, 'let it go abroad among our people'. The title-page of the revised version of April 1540 declared that it was the Bible appointed 'to the use of the churches', and in 1541 there was a royal proclamation, decreeing that it should be placed in every church. Copies were obtained for the churches; people collected around them, and even disturbed church services with their reading and discussions. Three editions appeared in 1540 and three more in 1541. The Psalter of the Great Bible has been perpetuated in the Book of Common Prayer.

VIII. THE GENEVA BIBLE

In the last years of Henry VIII no new editions of the English Bible were produced, and the official attitude towards the use of the Scriptures changed. The Great Bible was not banned, as were Tyndale's and Coverdale's Bibles, but its use was limited. The new attitude was carried over into the field of Primers, which contained selections from the Scriptures. In 1545 a revised Primer, frequently referred to as the Primer of Henry VIII, was published, and the use of any other was forbidden. In the reign of Edward VI the climate again became favourable to the development and use of the Bible in English. Many editions of the older translations were published, but practically no new work was done. Sir John Cheke did prepare an independent translation of Matthew and the beginning of Mark made from the Greek in a style designed to be intelligible to the less cultured, which tried to avoid words of non-English origin, but his work was not in fact published until 1843.

The reign of Mary Tudor was of a quite different character from that of Edward. Bibles were taken from churches, and many Protestants suffered martyrdom. Some fled to the Continent. A group of such men in Geneva was responsible for the production of the Geneva Bible. First, however, a Geneva New Testament was published in 1557, prepared, it would seem, by William Whittingham. This New Testament was in roman type and employed the verse divisions which Stephanus had introduced into the fourth edition of his Greek New Testament in 1551. Italics were used to distinguish words introduced by the translator to clarify the meaning. Whittingham seems to have used as the foundation text for his praiseworthy revision a recently published edition of Tyndale's New Testament. He introduced changes suggested by Beza's Latin version of the Greek New Testament of 1556.

In 1558 Elizabeth's reign began, and again the official attitude towards the use of the Bible and towards its translators changed. Whittingham and others nevertheless continued in Geneva until they had completed the version of the Bible on which they had been working. In 1559 an edition of the Psalms was published. In 1560 the exceedingly important Geneva Bible appeared. It was dedicated to Elizabeth. It made an enormous contribution to the Authorized Version, and achieved a dominant popularity in the period 1570–1620. A very scholarly work, it drew upon the unique competence and assistance of the great and devoted men who were in Geneva at the time, and upon works in different languages which were available there. The Old Testament section was a painstaking revision of that of the Great Bible with careful attention to the Hebrew; and for the New Testament it drew upon the Whittingham 1557 edition. Because of its use of 'breeches' in Genesis iii. 7 (a reading which, however, was not new), it became known as the 'Breeches Bible'. Verse divisions were employed throughout the entire Bible.

IX. THE BISHOPS' BIBLE

The Geneva Bible was more accurate than the Great Bible, but official endorsement was not transferred to it. Instead, the Archbishop of Canterbury, Matthew Parker, promoted a revision of the Great Bible, with much of the work done by bishops. This revision, of varying merit, and at points considerably influenced by the Geneva Bible, was published in a folio edition in 1568. It came to be known as the Bishops' Bible, and received ecclesiastical authorization. A slightly revised quarto edition appeared in 1569. A folio edition with an extensive revision of the New Testament section was published in 1572. The Prayer Book version of the Psalms and the Bishops' Bible Psalter were published in this edition in parallel columns. In following editions, except for that of 1585, only the Prayer Book Psalter was included. The 1572 revision had a substantial influence on the Authorized Version.

X. THE RHEIMS–DOUAY VERSION

Roman Catholics, who during the reign of Elizabeth I had found refuge on the Continent, in 1582 brought forth in Rheims a New Testament which they hoped would counteract the influence of Protestant translations. This was the work of Gregory Martin, William Allen, and others of the English College in Rheims. Their reason for addressing themselves to this task was not that which actuated Protestant translators (*i.e.* a zealous desire to make the Word of God accessible to all men in the vernacular), for in their preface they held that, on the contrary, the translation of the Bible into the 'vulgar tongues' was not an absolute necessity, or even necessarily profitable. They made their position quite clear in the following words: 'Which translation we do not for all that publish, upon erroneous opinion of necessity, that the holy Scriptures should always be in our mother tongue, or that they ought, or were ordained by God, to be read indifferently of all, or could be easily understood of every one that readeth or heareth them in a known language: or that they were not often through man's malice or infirmity, pernicious and much hurtful to many: or that we generally and absolutely deemed it more convenient in itself, and more agreeable to God's word and honour or edification of the faithful, to have them turned into vulgar tongues, than to be kept and studied only in the ecclesiastical learned languages: Not for these nor any such like causes do we translate this sacred book, but upon special consideration of the present time, state, and condition of our country, unto which, divers things are either necessary, or profitable and medicinable now, that otherwise in the peace of the Church were neither much requisite, nor perchance wholly tolerable . . .' (A. W. Pollard, *Records of the English Bible*, 1911, pp. 301, 302). They based their translation on a Lat. Vulgate basic text, but did give attention to the Greek, as is evidenced by their treatment of the definite article. They gave some attention also to previous works in English. The style of their translation is Latinate. Of set purpose they retained certain Latin words and followed their basic text closely, even, at times, to the point of sacrifice of intelligibility. For all this, they did provide a glossary to assist the English reader, and their work served to broaden the word-base on which the Authorized Version was constructed. The Old Testament, however, was not published until 1609–10 at Douai, which was too late to exert much, if any, influence on the Authorized Version. In style it was similar to the Rheims New Testament.

XI. THE AUTHORIZED VERSION

At the Hampton Court Conference in 1604 a proposal was made by Dr. John Reynolds, a Puritan and president of Corpus Christi College, Oxford, that a new translation of the Bible be made. This proposal, although not favoured by a majority of those present, did appeal to King James I, and resulted ultimately in the production of the Authorized Version. The king wished to have a uniform translation made by the finest scholars in the two English universities, a translation to be reviewed by the bishops and the most learned men in the Church, afterwards presented to the Privy Council, and finally ratified by his authority.

James appointed fifty-four learned men for the work of translation. The translators were divided into six companies, two of which met at Westminster, two at Cambridge, and two at Oxford. One of the Westminster companies was assigned Genesis to 2 Kings, the other the Epistles of the New Testament; one of the Cambridge companies was assigned 1 Chronicles to the Song of Solomon, the other the Apocryphal Books; one of the Oxford companies was given Isaiah to Malachi, the other the Gospels, Acts and Revelation. Certain rules were provided for the guidance of the various committees, not all of which, however, may have been observed. Among other things, the revisers were to follow the Bishops' Bible, and were to modify it as slightly as the 'truth of the original' or emphasis required; they were to retain the old ecclesiastical terms such as 'church'; marginal notes were to be avoided except for certain non-controversial uses. Each man in a company was to translate independently, and then all were to discuss their private efforts and determine what was most acceptable. On completing a book a company was to send the text to the other companies for their consideration. If any company should not be satisfied with anything in the translation referred to it, it was to send back information about its objections and the reasons for them. Unresolved disagreements between companies were to be discussed at a meeting to be held on the completion of the entire work. The assistance of qualified persons was to be sought. Translations which were to be used instead of the Bishops' Bible if they conformed more truly to the text were those of Tyndale, Coverdale, Matthew, Whitchurch (the Great Bible), and also the Geneva Bible. Words introduced to complete the meaning were to be printed in a different type from other words.

Further information about the principles and practices which were followed by the revisers is furnished in the preface, 'The Translators to the Reader'. The Scriptures are there acknowledged to be high and divine, full and perfect; and their translation into the vernacular is shown to be necessary. The revisers appreciate the excellent translation work that has been done before. They never designed to make a new translation or to change a bad one into a good one, but their aim was 'to make a good one better, or out of many good ones, one principal good one, not justly to be excepted against' (Pollard, *op. cit.*, p. 369). They sought not praise, but the truth; their trust was in Him who has the key of David.

They worked from the Hebrew text of the Old Testament and from the Greek text of the New Testament. They did not work with undue haste or hesitate to revise what they had done; but brought back to the anvil that which they had hammered. They consulted translators or commentators in various languages. When the text was not clear, they took account of diversity of signification and sense in the margin. They did not bind themselves to a uniformity of phrasing or an identity of words, but felt free to use synonyms. They avoided the obscurity of the Douay Bible with its Latinate vocabulary. Their desire was that the Bible speak like itself, that it be understood 'euen of the very vulgar'.

When the various companies had completed their work twelve representatives chosen from among them all revised the entire translation. After some further touching up the version was ready for publication. There is no record of official ecclesiastical or royal authorization, but the words 'appointed to be read in Churches' appeared on the title-page of the first edition. Whether there was official formal authorization or not, the version immediately displaced the Bishops' Bible in the churches and in time gained a victory over the Geneva Bible in popular favour, although the latter continued in use privately for a long while. The Authorized Version has never since lost its pre-eminence. It gathered to itself the virtues of the long and brilliant royal line of English Bible translations; it united high scholarship with Christian devotion and piety. It came into being at a time when the English language was vigorous and young, and its scholars had a remarkable mastery of the instrument which Providence had prepared for them. Their version has justifiably been called 'the noblest monument of English prose'. The stylistic dependence of the Authorized Version on its predecessors has been sharply brought out by C. C. Butterworth in his work on *The Literary Lineage of the King James Bible*, 1941. Butterworth estimates in a study of selected passages that the Authorized Version is indebted to the earlier English translations of the Bible for about 60 per cent of its text (pp. 230 f.). The chief contributors to the form adopted in the Authorized Version were the Geneva Bible and the Geneva New Testament (about 19 per cent), and Tyndale's translations, including the Matthew Bible (about 18 per cent).

XII. FROM THE AUTHORIZED TO THE REVISED VERSION

It may be thought that with the appearance of the Authorized Version the high point in the history of the English Bible was attained and that all else is anti-climactic. But the story of the English Bible after 1611 must not be neglected In the case of the Authorized Version itself, change and revision of an unofficial kind were introduced through the years. More than three hundred changes are found in the 1613 edition. Very extensive modifications were introduced in editions published in the 18th century. Private translations were also made. Henry Ainsworth from 1616 to 1623 published translations of the Pentateuch and the Song of Solomon, and his translation of these books and of the Psalms was published after his death. His work was animated by a desire for accurate rendering. Paraphrases became fairly numerous. Richard Baxter in 1685 issued a *New Testament with a Paraphrase and Notes*; Henry Hammond in 1653 published a *New Testament with a Paraphrase and Annotations*; and Abraham Woodhead, Richard Allestry, and Obadiah Walker published in 1675 *A Paraphrase and Annotations upon all the Epistles of St. Paul.* This paraphrase was subsequently revised. Daniel Whitby in 1703 published a *Paraphrase and Commentary on the New Testament*, in which he used the Authorized Version and put explanations of the text in brackets. Edward Wells in 1718 issued a revision of the Authorized Version of the New Testament, *The Common Translation Corrected, with a Paraphrase and Notes*; and in 1724 a correction of the Old Testament text. John Guyse from 1739 to 1752 published an *Exposition of the New Testament in the Form of a Paraphrase.* Samuel Clarke published in 1701–2 *Paraphrases of the Gospels.* Thomas Pyle in 1725 issued his *Paraphrase of the Acts and Epistles, in the manner of Dr. Clarke* and in 1717–25 his *Paraphrase on the Historical Books of the Old Testament*, and in 1735 his *Paraphrase on the Revelation of St. John.* In 1837 Edward Barlee's version of the Epistles marks, perhaps, the end of a succession of revisions which incorporated paraphrastic material within brackets.

A number of significant contributions were made in the 18th century. William Mace published in 1729 a New Testament in Greek and English in which he attempted to take into account 'the most Authentic Manuscripts' and to use the accepted colloquial style of his day. His style is quite dated and is naturally inferior to that of the Authorized Version. Translations made in the 18th century by Philip Doddridge (*Family Expositor, or, a Paraphrase and Version of the New Testament*), George Campbell (*Translation of the Gospels*), and James Macknight (*A New Literal Translation of all the Apostolical Epistles*) were utilized in a New Testament published in 1818. (The Gospels were taken from Campbell's work, the Acts and Revelation from Doddridge's, and the Epistles from Macknight's.) In 1745 William Whiston published his *Primitive New Testament*, which uses the text of the Authorized Version, but modifies it in the interest of readings found in Codex Bezae (for the Gospels and Acts), Codex Claromontanus (for the Epistles of Paul), and Codex Alexandrinus (for the other Epistles and Revelation). John Wesley published in 1755 a revision of the Authorized Version. Richard Wynne issued in 1764 *The New Testament, carefully collated with the Greek, corrected, divided and printed according to the subjects treated of.* Wynne sought to find a middle course between a literal rendering and loose paraphrase. Anthony Purver, a member of the Society of Friends, worked for thirty years on the translation of the Bible which he published in 1764. One of the most noteworthy of 18th-century efforts was that of E. Harwood, who published in 1768 his *Liberal Translation of the New Testament.* His use of an 'elegant', literary, paraphrastic 18th-century style makes his work a literary novelty.

John Worsley made an effort to translate the New Testament from the Greek into the 'Present Idiom of the English Tongue'. He wished to remove from the text obsolete and hardly intelligible words, and to bring the translation closer to the original. His translation was published posthumously in 1770. Other versions which were published (or printed) in the late 18th century were those of Gilbert Wakefield, W. H. Roberts, Thomas Haweis, William Newcome, who utilized Griesbach's Greek text of 1774–5, Nathaniel Scarlett, assisted by certain other 'men of piety and literature' (whose translation allows itself the freedom of arranging material in the form of a drama), and 'J. M. Ray'.

The 19th century brought forth translations of the Epistles of Paul by the Unitarians Thomas Belsham (1822) and Charles Eyre (1832), and of the entire New Testament by the Unitarian Samuel Sharpe (1840) from J. J. Griesbach's Greek text. In 1865 Sharpe published a revised text of the Authorized Version of the Old Testament. Rodolphus Dickinson in 1833 with indifferent success published a New Testament in which he attempted to improve on the style of the Authorized Version. Among the literal translations of the 19th century, mention should be made of that of Robert Young in 1862. New textual information continued to be reflected in the English versions. 'Herman Heinfetter' made use of the Vatican MS; G. W. Braineld took into account the texts of Griesbach, Lachmann, Tischendorf, Alford, and Tregelles in his translation of the Gospels (1863); Robert Ainslie used the Authorized Version in 1869, but modified it in the interest of readings favoured by Tischendorf; Samuel Davidson published in 1875 a translation of the New Testament from the text of Tischendorf; and J. B. Rotherham translated the New Testament from the text of Tregelles (1872).

Andrew Norton's new translation of the Gospels (1855) and Leicester Ambrose Sawyer's translation of the New Testament (1858) were efforts to use the style of their day. They have been credited with introducing the succession of the 'modern-speech' versions of the 20th century (Pope, *English Versions of the Bible*, pp. 546 f.). Various private revisions of the Authorized Version were published in the 19th century.

XIII. ROMAN CATHOLIC VERSIONS IN THE 18TH AND 19TH CENTURIES

In the 18th century a number of Roman Catholic efforts were made to provide an improved English version. Cornelius Nary published in 1718 and 1719 a New Testament translated from the Latin Vulgate with attention given to the Greek and Hebrew idiom, in which he attempted to use intelligible, idiomatic English. Robert Witham also desired to make the text of the English New Testament intelligible to the contemporary reader. His version, translated from the Latin Vulgate, was published in 1730. In 1738 the fifth and lightly revised edition of the Rhemish New Testament appeared, more than a century after the fourth edition (1633). Richard Challoner, who has been credited with some of the editorial work on this fifth edition, later published two revisions of the Douay Old Testament and five of the New Testament (1749–72), and provided a simpler, more idiomatic type of text in general use among English-speaking Roman Catholics until at least 1941. He did not refuse to follow the Authorized Version when he approved its readings. The revisions made by Bernard MacMahon 1783–1810 had a noteworthy influence, especially in Ireland. Bishop Francis Patrick Kenrick from 1849 to 1860 published a revised text of the Rheims–Douay version with annotations.

XIV. THE REVISED VERSION

Conviction that a revision of the Authorized Version had become necessary came to formal ecclesiastical expression in 1870, and a revision of the Authorized Version was undertaken by the Convocation of Canterbury of the Church of England. Distinguished scholars, not all of whom were members of the Church of England, participated in the project. (See Westcott, *A General View of the History of the English Bible*, 1927, pp. 324 f.) Two companies were formed, one to revise the Authorized Version of the Old Testament, the other to do the same for the New Testament. Among the general principles adopted, it was agreed that as few changes as possible were to be made in the text of the Authorized Version consistent with faithfulness; that such changes as were introduced should be expressed in the language of the Authorized Version and its predecessors; that each company should go over the text twice; that no alteration of the text should be adopted on the second consideration or revision without the agreement of two-thirds of the members present, although a simple majority would suffice on the first consideration. The initial meeting of the New Testament Company was held on 22 June 1870, in the Jerusalem Chamber of Westminster Abbey. This opening session was preceded by a communion service conducted by the Dean of Westminster in the Henry VII Chapel. Among those who were admitted to the Lord's table was a Unitarian member of the company. Strong protest was naturally aroused. From this inauspicious beginning the company entered upon more than ten years of labour, meeting for four days every month (except in August and September). The work on the New Testament was completed on 11 November 1880. The Old Testament Company held its first meeting on 30 June 1870, and thereafter met for ten days every two months (except August and September) for about fourteen years. The Old Testament was completed on 20 June 1884. The assistance of American biblical scholars was sought; and two American companies, one for the Old Testament and one for the New, were formed. The American revisers came from various religious bodies, including the Unitarian. There was an effective exchange of views between the American and British companies. The regular procedure was for the British companies to send on to the American companies the texts which had passed the first revision, and the American companies informed the British companies of their views in time for consideration on the second revision. The British companies were well advanced when the American companies began their work. The Synoptic Gospels had been revised once; the Pentateuch had been revised twice. Exclusive copyright was given to the University Presses of Oxford and Cambridge; the American companies agreed not to publish an edition embodying their distinctive readings for fourteen years after the publication of the English Revised Version; the University Presses promised to publish during that period an appendix listing readings preferred by the American companies which had not been accepted by the British revisers. On 17 May 1881 the Revised Version of the New Testament was published in England, and the whole Bible was published on 19 May 1885. It was the fruit of much scholarship and labour. The influence of the textual theories of Westcott and Hort was manifest in the New Testament; the Old Testament characteristically followed the Massoretic Text, and much effort was made to represent the original faithfully and accurately even over details. Where possible the revisers attempted consistently to represent a given word in the original by a given English word. Because of its accuracy the Revised Version has proved very valuable for study purposes. Its style, however, has not generally been adjudged as felicitous as that of the Authorized Version; it has been accused of being often unnecessarily disruptive of the text of the Authorized Version; and the Bible-reading public, accustomed to the incomparable music of the Authorized Version, has not granted to the Revised Version a place of pre-eminence. In 1901 the preferences of the American companies and other preferences supported by the surviving members of the committee were embodied in the text of an 'American Standard Edition' of the Revised Bible. Among the changes which were introduced the substitution of 'Jehovah' for 'Lord' and 'God' (in small capitals) was rightly expected to be unwelcome to many. A very unfortunate note on a Gk. word for 'worship' was introduced in the New Testament, and at Jn. ix. 38 it took a form which called forth most necessary objection.

XV. SINCE THE REVISED VERSION

The Revised Versions did not succeed in displacing the Authorized Version in the affections of the majority of Bible-readers, and they were furthermore unable to satisfy all of those who were persuaded of the need and desirability of revision. Since 1881 there has been an unceasing flow of translations, or revisions of translations, of the New Testament, or the entire Bible, or of parts of the Bible. In the case of the New Testament the influence of the Greek text or of the theories of Westcott and Hort has been strongly felt. The realization that the Greek of the New Testament was in the main the popular, vernacular Greek of the 1st century and not the literary Greek of that time has encouraged translators to undertake versions in 'everyday English'. Much of the translation work since 1881 has been arid and undistinguished stylistically and has offered the Authorized Version no competition in the matter of felicity and grace of expression.

Several of the versions or revisions which have appeared since the time of the English Revised Version might be given brief mention. Among the pioneers in the translation of the Scriptures into modern English was Ferrar Fenton, who published a translation of Romans 'direct from the original Greek into modern English' in 1882 and a translation of the Epistles of Paul in 1883. His New Testament translated into 'current English' appeared in 1895 and his *Bible in Modern English* in 1903. *The Twentieth Century New Testament*, the work of about twenty persons, was published from 1898 to 1901, and was subsequently issued in revised form. *The Modern Speech New Testament*, R. F. Weymouth's much-used translation from the text of his *Resultant Greek Testament*, was posthumously published in 1903, with Ernest Hampden-Cook as editor. James Moffatt issued *The Historical New Testament* in 1901, in which he attempted to arrange the writings of the New Testament in a conjectured order of 'literary growth' and date of composition. In 1913 his new translation of the New Testament appeared. Its textual basis was mainly von Soden's Greek text. The clearly erroneous reading of the Sinaitic MS of the Old Syr. Version is followed at Mt. i. 16, and the reader is not assisted by any textual note (see J. G. Machen, *The Virgin Birth of Christ*, 1930, pp. 176 ff.). Moffatt's translation of the Old Testament, in which he takes undue liberty in handling textual matters, was published in 1924. E. J. Goodspeed's 'American' translation of the New Testament, based on the Greek text of Westcott and Hort and intended to be expressed in popular American idiom, appeared in 1923, and the 'American' translation of the Old Testament, prepared by A. R. Gordon, T. J. Meek, Leroy Waterman, and J. M. Powis Smith, appeared in 1927. Among other translations which should be mentioned are W. G. Ballantine's *Riverside New Testament*, (1923); Helen B. Montgomery's *Centenary Translation of the New Testament* (1924); C. B. Williams' translation of the New Testament 'in the language of the people' (1937), a version which attempts a precise rendering of Gk. verbal forms; *The New Testament in Basic English* (1941) and *The Bible in Basic English* (1949); Gerrit Verkuyl's *Berkeley Version of the New Testament* (1945) and the Berkeley Version of the entire Bible (1959), the Old Testament section of which was prepared by a sizeable staff of translators, with Gerrit Verkuyl as editor-in-chief; J. B. Phillips' translation of the New Testament (1947–57; one-volume edition, 1958), translations which are at times quite free and paraphrastic with considerable loss of the force of the Greek original; *The Letchworth Version* [of the New Testament] *in Modern English*, by T. F. Ford and R. E. Ford (1948), a remarkably successful light revision of the Authorized Version which conserves much of the stylistic beauty of its original; *The New World Translation of the Christian Greek Scriptures* (1950), a version prepared by the Jehovah's Witnesses; C. K. Williams' translation of the New Testament into a limited-vocabulary 'Plain English' (1952); H. J. Schonfield's *Authentic New Testament* (1955); Kenneth S. Wuest's *Expanded Translation of the Greek New Testament* (1956–9); and the *Amplified New Testament* (1958).

Several Roman Catholic translations of special interest have appeared. The New Testament section of *The Westminster Version of the Sacred Scriptures*, which was completed in 1935 (1913–35), was translated from the Greek by various men working on individual assignments under general editors. It employs a solemn or 'biblical' style with archaic forms. J. A. Carey issued a revision of the Challoner–Rheims New Testament in 1935. F. A. Spencer's translation of the New Testament from the Greek was published in 1937. Monsignor R. A. Knox published in 1945 a trial edition of a translation of the New Testament from the Vulgate and a slightly modified definitive edition in 1945, which was 'authorized by the Archbishops and Bishops of England and Wales'. It was accorded an official status along with the Rhemish version. Knox's translation of the Old Testament from the Latin Vulgate was published in 1949 in two volumes 'for private use only'. A revision appeared in 1955 with hierarchical authorization. The translation of the New Testament by James A. Kleist and Joseph L. Lilly (1954) was made from the Greek. Kleist translated the Gospels from the text of Bover; Lilly translated the rest of the New Testament.

A large amount of attention in recent decades has been paid to two works which claim to be revisions, the Confraternity Roman Catholic version and the Revised Standard Version. In 1941 there was published in the United States a revision of the Challoner–Rheims version of the New Testament, prepared under the supervision of the Confraternity of Christian Doctrine by a large number of scholars. It was not bound to the official Clementine text of the Lat. Vulgate, but its revisers were free to take account of critical editions. As a consequence its basic text is closer than is the Clementine Vulgate to the original Greek. An effort was made to read the Latin in the light of the Greek and to take account of the Semitic background of the Greek text. The Confraternity revisers succeeded in commendable measure in producing a version of clarity, simplicity, and contemporary style. A desire for accuracy in translation is evidenced. The first book of the Confraternity edition of the Old Testament, a translation of Genesis from the Hebrew, was published in 1948.

A committee-revision of the American Revised Version, authorized by the International Council of Religious Education, was published in 1946 (New Testament) and in 1952 (entire Bible). This 'Revised Standard Version' differs considerably in important respects from the Authorized and Revised Versions. It lacks their confidence in the Massoretic Hebrew text, and in places it indulges in what this author regards as unjustified conjecture; it allows itself more freedom in rendering its text than did the AV and RV.

March 1961 saw the publication of the New Testament part of a completely new version, the *New English Bible*, on which representatives of the larger British Churches (apart from the Roman Catholic Church), of the Oxford and Cambridge University Presses, and of the British and Foreign Bible Society and National Bible Society of Scotland have been engaged for fifteen years. The Old Testament and Apocrypha will follow later. In addition to panels of translators for the different parts of the work, this version is submitted to a panel of literary advisors, who scrutinize the work of the translators with an eye to good English style.

The history of the English versions of the Bible did not end with the Authorized Version. Nothing has, it is true, succeeded in displacing it so far from its regnant position, but the efforts of many labourers since 1611 have not been without profit. The fruits of advancing knowledge and scholarship have been reflected in many translations which have been available for discriminating use alongside of the enduring embodiment of a great tradition, that 'noblest monument of English prose'.

BIBLIOGRAPHY. F. F. Bruce, *The Books and the Parchments*, 1950, *The English Bible*, 1961; C. C. Butterworth, *The English Primers (1529–1545)*, 1953, *The Literary Lineage of the King James Bible*, 1941; J. I. Mombert, *A Hand-Book of the English Versions of the Bible* [*c.* 1883]; W. F. Moulton, *The History of the English Bible*[5], 1911; J. H. Penniman, *A Book about the English Bible*, 1919; A. W. Pollard, *Records of the English Bible*, 1911; H. Pope, *English Versions of the Bible*, revised and amplified by Sebastian Bullough, 1952; H. W. Robinson (ed.), *The Bible in its Ancient and English Versions*, 1940; P. M. Simms, *The Bible in America*, 1936; and B. F. Westcott, *A General View of the History of the English Bible*, third edition revised by W. A. Wright, 1927. J.H.S.

EN-HADDAH. 'Sharp spring', the name of a place which fell to the lot of Issachar (Jos. xix. 21). Suggested identifications have been made (see *GTT*, p. 185), but the site has not been definitely identified. T.C.M.

EN-HAKKORE (Heb. *'ên-haqqôrē'*). The spring in Lehi from which Samson refreshed himself after slaughtering the Philistines with the jawbone of an ass (Jdg. xv. 19). None of the places mentioned in the story has been identified. Enhakkore could mean 'the spring of the partridge' (*cf.* En-gedi, 'the spring of the goat'), but Jdg. xv gives a coherent account of the origin of the name, indicating that it means 'the spring of him who called'. J.A.M.

EN-HAZOR. The name of a place which fell to the lot of Naphtali (Jos. xix. 37). The site is unknown, though suggestions have been made (see *GTT*, p. 198). It is distinct from Hazor (*q.v.*). T.C.M.

EN-MISHPAT. See KADESH-BARNEA.

ENOCH. 1. The eldest son of Cain (Gn. iv. 17) after whom a city was named.

2. Son of Jared and father of Methuselah (Gn. v. 18, 21), a member of the line of descent through Seth by which the knowledge of God was preserved. He was characterized by outstanding devotion. The expression he 'walked with God' (Gn. v. 24) is used only of Enoch and Noah

(Gn. vi. 9) in the early chapters of Genesis. He lived 365 years, and is one of the two men in the Old Testament who were taken up bodily into the presence of God without dying (*cf.* Elijah in 2 Ki. ii. 1–11). These two translations provide glimpses in the Old Testament that God is the God of the living (Lk. xx. 38) and that Sheol is not the final answer to the fate of the righteous. Enoch is named in Lk. iii. 37. Hebrews attributes his translation to his outstanding faith (Heb. xi. 5). Jude quotes a saying from Enoch about the coming of the Lord with myriads of His saints (Jude 14).

Because Enoch was taken up bodily to heaven, his name became in later Judaism the centre of a large apocalyptic tradition in which he relates secrets of the heavens and of the future which he had seen in visions and journeys through the heavens. Three books bear the name of Enoch, one of which goes back to the first two centuries BC and is of great importance for an understanding of New Testament backgrounds. The quotation in Jude appears in 1 Enoch i. 9. G.E.L.

ENOCH, BOOKS OF. See PSEUDEPIGRAPHA.

ENOSH. The son of Seth and the father of Kenan (Gn. iv. 26, v. 6–11; 1 Ch. i. 1; Lk. iii. 38). Apart from his genealogical position, the only information given about him is his life-span, which is recorded as 905 years, and the statement that in his time men began to call upon the name of Yahweh. The name is the same as a Heb. word which occurs some forty-two times in the Old Testament as meaning 'man'; *cf.* Adam (*q.v.*). R.F.H.

EN-RIMMON (*'ên-rimmôn*, 'spring of the pomegranate'). A village in Judah reoccupied after the Exile, Ne. xi. 29. Either it was formed by the coalescing of two separate villages Ain and Rimmon, or more probably, reading Jos. xv. 32, xix. 7; 1 Ch. iv. 32 all as En-rimmon, it was always a single town, originally in Judah's inheritance (Jos. xv. 32), but soon transferred to Simeon (Jos. xix. 7). It has been identified with Umm er-Ramāmîn, 9 miles north of Beersheba. M.A.M.

EN-ROGEL (*'ên-rōḡēl*, 'well of the fuller'). A water source just outside Jerusalem, some 200 yards south of the confluence of the Valley of Hinnom and the Kidron valley. It is known today as Job's well. The well marked a point on the northern boundary of Judah (Jos. xv. 7) before David captured Jerusalem (2 Sa. v. 6 ff.). The narrative of Adonijah's abortive attempt to gain the throne in David's old age suggests the site had cultic associations (1 Ki. i. 9 ff.). R.J.W.

EN-SHEMESH (*'ên-šemeš*, 'spring of the sun'). A point on the Judah–Benjamin border 2½ miles from Jerusalem, below Olivet, and just south of the Jericho road; modern 'Ain Haud.

ENSIGN. See BANNER.

ENVY. A grudging regard for the advantages seen to be enjoyed by others—*cf.* Lat. *invidia* from *invideo*, 'to look closely at', then 'to look with malicious intent' (see 1 Sa. xviii. 9). The Heb. *qin'â* means originally a burning, then the colour produced in the face by a deep emotion, thus ardour, zeal, jealousy. RV substitutes 'jealousy' for 'envy' in Jb. v. 2; Pr. xxvii. 4; Acts vii. 9; 1 Cor. iii. 3, *etc.* But they are not synonymous. Jealousy makes us fear to lose what we possess, envy creates sorrow that others have what we have not. The word *qin'â* is used to express Rachel's envy for her sister (Gn. xxx. 1, *cf.* 'envied', Gn. xxxvii. 11; 'zeal', Nu. xxv. 11, *etc.*). Its evils are depicted especially in the book of Proverbs: thus the question in xxvii. 4: 'Who is able to stand before envy?' (RV 'jealousy'). The New Testament *zēlos* is usually translated in a good sense as 'zeal' as well as in a bad sense as 'envy' (*cf.* Jn. ii. 17; Col. iv. 13: note also its reference to God, 2 Ki. xix. 31; Is. ix. 7, xxxvii. 32, *etc.*). The word *phthonos* always appears in a bad sense except in the difficult verse Jas. iv. 5, which should be translated as in RVmg. (A comparable sentiment is expressed in the Qumran *Manual of Discipline*, iv. 16–18.) *Phthonos* is characteristic of the unredeemed life (Rom. i. 29; Gal. v. 21; 1 Tim. vi. 4; Tit. iii. 3). It was the spirit which crucified our Lord (Mt. xxvii. 18; Mk. xv. 10). Envy, *zēlos*, as inconsiderate zeal, is to be avoided by Christians (Rom. xiii. 13; 2 Cor. xii. 20; Jas. iii. 14, 16). H.D.McD.

EPAPHRAS. In Col. i. 7, iv. 12; Phm. 23, one of Paul's friends and associates, called by him his 'fellowslave' and 'fellowprisoner'. The name is abbreviated from Epaphroditus, but Epaphras is probably not to be identified with the Epaphroditus of Phil. ii. 25, iv. 18 (as T. R. Glover does, *Paul of Tarsus*, 1925, p. 179). We gather that Epaphras evangelized the cities of the Lycus valley in Phrygia under Paul's direction during the latter's Ephesian ministry, and founded the churches of Colossae, Hierapolis, and Laodicea. Later he visited Paul during his Roman captivity, and it was his news of conditions in the churches of the Lycus valley that moved Paul to write the Epistle to the Colossians.

BIBLIOGRAPHY. J. B. Lightfoot, *St. Paul's Epistles to the Colossians and to Philemon*, 1879, pp. 29 ff. F.F.B.

EPAPHRODITUS. A Macedonian Christian from Philippi. There are no grounds for identifying him with Epaphras of Col. i. 7, iv. 12, or Phm. 23. His name means 'comely' or 'charming'. Paul calls him 'your messenger' (*hymōn apostolon*, Phil. ii. 25), where the word used is one more frequently translated elsewhere as 'apostle'. This does not mean that Epaphroditus held any office in the Philippian church; he was simply a messenger (*cf.* 2 Cor. viii. 23) who brought the gift from the church to Paul in prison at Rome. He became seriously ill, possibly as a result of over-exerting himself in journeying from Philippi to Rome, or in serving Paul at Rome. The AV says 'he regarded not his life' (see Phil. ii. 30), but RSV more correctly 'risking his life'. The word used is *paraboleusamenos*, 'having gambled with his life', from *paraboleuesthai* 'to throw down a stake, to make a venture'.

BIBLIOGRAPHY. J. Agar Beet, 'Epaphroditus and the gift from Philippi', *The Expositor*, 3rd Series, XLIX, 1889. D.O.S.

EPHAH. See WEIGHTS AND MEASURES.

EPHESIANS, EPISTLE TO THE.

I. OUTLINE OF CONTENTS

This letter, in its form less restricted by particular controversial or pastoral needs than any other New Testament letter, stands as a wonderful declaration of the eternal purpose of God in Christ wrought out in His Church (chapters i–iii), and of the practical consequences for the Christian of that purpose (chapters iv–vi).

a. God's eternal purposes for man in Christ, i. 1–iii. 21

i. 1, 2. Greeting.

i. 3–14. Praise for all the spiritual blessings that come to men in Christ.

i. 15–23. Thanksgiving for the readers' faith, and prayer for their experience of the wisdom and power of God.

ii. 1–10. God's purpose to raise men from the death of sin to new life in Christ.

ii. 11–22. His purpose to reconcile men not only to Himself, but to one another—in particular to bring Jews and Gentiles together into the one people of God.

iii. 1–13. The glory of the apostle's calling to preach the gospel to the Gentiles.

iii. 14–21. A second prayer, for the knowledge of the love of Christ and His indwelling fulness; and a doxology.

b. Practical consequences, iv. 1–vi. 24

iv. 1–16. Exhortation to walk worthily, and to work to build up the one body of Christ.

iv. 17–32. The old life of ignorance, lust, and unrighteousness must be put off, the new life of holiness put on.

v. 1–21. A further call to live in love and purity, as children of light, full of praise and usefulness.

v. 22–33. Instructions to wives and husbands, based on the analogy of the relationship between Christ and His Church.

vi. 1–9. Instructions to children and parents, servants and masters.

vi. 10–20. Summons to Christian conflict in the armour of God and in His strength.

vi. 21–24. Concluding personal message.

II. AUTHORSHIP

There is abundant early evidence (perhaps going back to AD 95) of the use of this letter, and from the end of the 2nd century we read of its unquestioned acceptance as the letter of Paul that it claims to be (i. 1, iii. 1). In the last hundred years, however, the traditional authorship has been seriously questioned. It is impossible to do justice here to the arguments against Pauline authorship, or to attempt to answer them (they are expressed most fully in C. L. Mitton, *The Epistle to the Ephesians*, 1951). The case for the Pauline authorship is set forward in other books listed below (see also D. Guthrie, *New Testament Introduction: The Pauline Epistles*, 1961). We may summarize the arguments against Pauline authorship thus.

1. It is argued that this is not a real letter addressed to a particular situation like all the others we know as Paul's. It is more lyrical in style, full of participles and relatives, distinctive in its piling up of similar or related expressions. For the Pauline authorship it is argued that the absence of controversy accounts for the difference; we have here not the reasoned argument necessary in the other letters, but 'a prophetic declaration of incontrovertible, patent facts' (Dodd).

2. It is pointed out that there are forty-two words not otherwise used in the New Testament, and forty-four more not used elsewhere by Paul. This argument can be assessed only by comparison with other Epistles, and by examining the words themselves. In the view of many the nature of the subject-matter sufficiently accounts for them.

3. It is urged that nowhere in Paul's writings have we such great stress on the Church and so little eschatology. Yet satisfying reasons can be given for the difference of emphasis, and in particular for the great exposition here of the part of the Church in the eternal purpose of God.

4. It is argued that certain features and expressions are indicative of a later date or another hand than of the apostles, *e.g.* the reference to the 'holy apostles and prophets' (iii. 5, *cf.* ii. 20), the treatment of the Gentile question, and the self-abasement of iii. 8. Each individual objection may be answered, though those who oppose the Pauline authorship urge the cumulative effect of all the objections rather than the force of any particular one.

5. Other arguments are based on a comparison of Ephesians with other New Testament writings. This letter has more in common with non-Pauline writings (especially Luke and Acts, 1 Peter and the Johannine writings) than any other letter of the Pauline Corpus. (See J. Moffatt, *An Introduction to the Literature of the New Testament*[3], 1918, pp. 373 ff., and C. L. Mitton, *op. cit.*, pp. 170 ff.) Sometimes the resemblances in thought and expression are very striking, but rarely such as make literary dependence probable. They witness rather to a large common vocabulary, and perhaps also to a similar formalizing of teaching and belief in the early Church in different places. (See E. G. Selwyn, *The First Epistle of St. Peter*, 1946, pp. 363–466.)

Most significant, however, is the similarity in content, expression, and even order of subject-matter between this letter and Colossians. It is almost universally accepted that Colossians is prior to Ephesians—Ephesians has the doctrine and exhortation of Colossians, only developed further. With the possible exception of vi. 21 f., and Col. iv. 7 f., there is no evidence of direct copying; but in Ephesians the same expressions are often used with a slightly different connotation; one passage in one letter resembles two in the other; one passage in Ephesians has a parallel in Colossians and also in another Pauline letter. To some these phenomena are the strongest arguments for the work of an imitator; in the view of others they make the traditional authorship more sure.

III. DESTINATION

Although the great majority of MSS and all the early VSS have the words 'at Ephesus' in i. 1, the 4th-century codices Vaticanus and Sinaiticus, the important corrector of the cursive 424, the cursive 1739, and papyrus 46 (dated AD 200) omit these words. Tertullian probably, Origen certainly, did not have them. Basil said they were lacking in the oldest MSS known to him. The heretic Marcion called this letter 'to the Laodiceans'. This small but very weighty evidence is supported by the evidence of the contents of the letter. It is difficult to explain such verses as i. 15, iii. 2, iv. 21, and the complete absence of personal greetings, if this were a letter addressed by Paul to Christians among whom he had laboured three years (Acts xix, and xx. 31). Yet it seems to have been addressed to a specific circle of Christians (i. 15 ff., vi. 21). The most likely interpretation of all the evidence is that it was sent to a group of churches in Asia Minor (of which Ephesus was greatest). Either one copy was sent to each in turn, the place-name being inserted in reading; or there may have been several copies with different addresses. It is very likely also, though by no means certain, that 'Ephesians' is in fact the letter referred to in Col. iv. 16 as that '*from* Laodicea'.

IV. CONCLUSION

To many the arguments against Pauline authorship have carried conviction. A situation has been supposed towards the end of the 1st century in which someone with a great desire to commend the teaching of the apostle collected his writings, and then in his name wrote this 'letter' as a comprehensive statement of his doctrine to form an introduction to the others. There could have been such a situation and such a person as this. Yet, as Scott puts it, the Epistle 'is everywhere marked by a grandeur and originality of thought which seems utterly beyond the reach of any mere imitator' (*MNT*, p. 136). The cumulative force of the arguments cannot be regarded as strong enough to disprove the Pauline authorship. The similarities to Colossians (and to other letters), and the differences, seem most naturally accounted for by supposing that Paul wrote Colossians to meet the particular needs of that church. Then shortly afterwards (on date and place of writing, see COLOSSIANS), before his messenger had left with Colossians and Philemon, he fulfilled his desire to express, in a form suitable for all who might read it, the glory of the purpose of God in Christ, and the responsibility of the Church to make known that purpose by proclamation and by living in unity, love, and purity.

BIBLIOGRAPHY. F. J. A. Hort, *Prolegomena to St. Paul's Epistles to the Romans and the Ephesians*, 1895; J. A. Robinson, *St. Paul's Epistle to the Ephesians*, 1904; E. Percy, *Probleme der Kolosser- und Epheserbriefe*, 1946; F. L. Cross (ed.), *Studies in Ephesians*, 1956; *ICC* and *MNT* as under COLOSSIANS. F.F.

EPHESUS. The most important city in the Roman province of Asia, on the west coast of what is now Asiatic Turkey. It was situated at the mouth of the Caÿster River between the mountain ranges of Koressos and the sea. A magnificent road 70 feet wide and lined with columns ran down through the city to the fine harbour, which served both as a great export centre at the end of the Asiatic caravan-route and also as a natural landing-point from Rome. The city, now uninhabited, is still being excavated and is probably the most extensive and impressive ruin of Asia Minor. The sea is now some 7 miles away, owing to the silting-up process which has been at work for centuries. The harbour had to undergo extensive clearing operations under Domitian; is that, perhaps, why Paul had to stop at Miletus (Acts xx. 15)? The main part of the city, with its theatre, baths, libraries, agora, and marble-paved streets, lay between the Koressos ridge and the Caÿster, but the temple for which it was famed lay 1½ miles to the north-east. This site was originally sacred to the worship of the Anatolian fertility goddess, then to that of Artemis or Diana; Justinian built a church to St. John on this spot (hence its modern name Ayasoluk—a corruption of *hagios theologos*), which was itself succeeded by a Persian mosque.

The original Anatolian settlement was augmented in the 12th century BC by Ionian colonists, and a joint city was set up. The goddess of Ephesus took on a Greek name, Artemis, but clearly retained her primitive characteristics, for she is always represented as a many-breasted figure. In 560 BC Ephesus was conquered by Croesus, and owed some of its future artistic glories to his munificence. But in 557 the city was captured by the Persians, and thereafter it had a chequered history until 133 BC, when it formed part of the kingdom of Pergamum which Attalus III bequeathed to Rome. Pergamum remained the titular capital of the ensuing province of Asia, but Ephesus continued to be the most important city. It occupied a vast area, and its population has been calculated at one-third of a million. The fine theatre built into Mt. Pion in the centre of the city is enormous. Estimates of its capacity vary between 25,000 and 50,000.

The religious as well as the commercial eminence of the city increased under Roman rule. The emperor cult, encouraged by the Julio-Claudians, was not neglected at Ephesus, and temples were built to Claudius, Hadrian, and Severus. Coins and inscriptions show that the city prided itself on being *neōkoros*, temple warden, both of Artemis (Acts xix. 35) and of the emperors. The function of the commune of Asia was primarily to foster the imperial cult, and it is interesting that some of their officers (*asiarchoi*, Acts xix. 31) should have been friends of Paul, who was, of course, strongly opposed to emperor worship. The temple of Diana itself was rebuilt after a great fire in 365 BC and ranked as one of the wonders of the world until its destruction by the Goths in AD 260. After years of patient search J. T. Wood in 1870 uncovered its remains in the marsh at the foot of Mt. Ayasoluk. It was four times the size of the Parthenon at Athens, and was adorned with works of art by such masters as Phidias, Praxiteles, and Apelles. The temple contained an image of the goddess Artemis which, it was claimed, was fallen from heaven (*cf.* Acts xix. 35). Indeed, it may well have been a meteorite originally. Silver coins from many different countries show the validity of the claim that the goddess of Ephesus was revered all over the world (Acts xix. 27). They bear the inscription *Diana Ephesia* (*cf.* Acts xix. 34).

Fig. 79. Coin of Ephesus, belonging to the Roman period, showing the many-breasted goddess Diana enshrined within her temple.

There was a large colony of Jews at Ephesus, and they enjoyed a privileged position under the early empire (Jos., *Ant.* xiv. 10. 12, 25). Christianity probably came to Ephesus with Aquila and Priscilla in *c.* AD 52 when Paul made a short visit there on his second missionary journey (Acts xviii. 18, 19) and left them there. His third missionary journey had Ephesus as its goal, and he stayed there for over two years (Acts xix. 8, 10), attracted, no doubt, by its strategic importance as a commercial, political, and religious centre. Towards the end of his stay the spread of Christianity, which refused syncretism, steadily began to incur the hostility of vested religious interests. It began to affect not only the magic cults which flourished there (Acts xix. 13 ff.—a certain kind of magic formula was actually called *Ephesia grammata*) but also the worship of Diana (Acts xix. 27), where it caused a sharp falling off in the sale of votive figurines and cult objects which formed part of Ephesus' prosperity. There followed the celebrated riot described in Acts xix. Inscriptions show that the *grammateus* who gained control of the assembly on this occasion was no mere 'townclerk' (AV), but the leading civic official in the city, directly responsible to the Roman authorities for such breaches of the peace as illicit assembly (xix. 40). It has been suggested that his assertion 'there are proconsuls' (xix. 38) if it is not a generalizing plural, may fix the date of the happening with some precision. For in the autumn of AD 54 the proconsul, M. Julius Silvanus, was poisoned by two emissaries from Nero (Tacitus, *Annals* xiii. 1), Helius and Celer, who acted as proconsuls until Silvanus' successor arrived in the early summer of AD 55.

Luke furnishes us with little information as to the details of Paul's stay in Ephesus. During this period Christianity spread to the churches of the Lycus Valley (see Col. i. 7, ii. 1). It was Paul's headquarters during the Corinthian correspondence (1 Cor. xvi. 8), and he may have fought with wild beasts here if 1 Cor. xv. 32 is to be taken literally. However, as there is no amphitheatre at Ephesus and as Paul was a Roman citizen, a metaphorical allusion is probable. G. S. Duncan (*St. Paul's Ephesian Ministry*, 1929) has maintained that Paul was imprisoned three times at Ephesus, and that all the captivity Epistles were written from there and not from Rome. He is followed by E. J. Goodspeed (*History of Early Christian Literature*, 1942) and C. L. Mitton (*Formation of the Pauline Corpus*, 1955), who further regard Ephesus as the probable location of the Pauline Corpus of letters. *Per contra*, see C. H. Dodd, *BJRL*, XXIV, 1934, pp. 72 ff.

After Paul's departure, Timothy was left at Ephesus (1 Tim. i. 3) and soon had to deal with false teaching (Acts xx. 29, 30; 2 Tim. iv. 3, *etc.*). It is thought by many that Romans xvi was originally addressed by Paul to Ephesus. However that may be, the city soon became the headquarters of a John who had jurisdiction over the seven leading churches of Asia Minor addressed in the Apocalypse. The identity of this John is vigorously disputed, but at all events at the time of writing Revelation the Ephesian church (Rev. ii. 1–7) presents much the same picture as in Acts; it is addressed first of the seven because of its importance and its position at the head (to one coming from Patmos) of the circular road joining the seven cities; it is flourishing, it is troubled by false teachers, and it has lost some of its first love. The promise of 'eating of the tree of life' is probably an oblique reference to the date tree, sacred to Artemis, which figures on Ephesian coins.

According to Irenaeus and Eusebius, Ephesus became the home of John the apostle, and they record a few incidents during his residence here. A generation later Ignatius wrote of it in glowing terms (*Ephesians*, 11), and it remained the seat of a long line of Eastern bishops. The third General Council took place here in AD 431 to condemn Nestorian Christology, and sat in the double church of St. Mary, the ruins of which are still to be seen. Soon afterwards the city declined, probably owing to malaria; its fine sculptures were removed elsewhere, notably Constantinople, and in the 14th century the Turks carried off its remaining inhabitants.

BIBLIOGRAPHY. W. M. Ramsay, *The Letters to the Seven Churches*, 1909, and *The Historical Geography of Asia Minor*, 1890; J. T. Wood, *Modern Discoveries on the Site of Ancient Ephesus*, 1890; A. H. M. Jones, *Eastern Cities of the Roman Empire*; D. G. Hogarth, *Excavations at Ephesus: the Archaic Artemisia*. [Pauly-Wissowa *s.v. Ephesos*.] On recent excavations, see M. J. Mellink, *AJA*, 1958, pp. 91–104, and also *Forschungen in Ephesos*, III, 1923–53. E.M.B.G.

EPHOD. See DRESS.

EPHPHATHA. The actual word addressed by Jesus to the deaf man (Mk. vii. 34). It is an Aramaic imperative transliterated into Greek, and the evangelist adds the translation (in Greek), 'be opened'. The Aramaic verb used is *p^{e}ṯaḥ*, 'to open'; it is not certain whether the simple passive (ethpeel) or intensive passive (ethpaal) was employed. The former form would be *'eṯp^{e}ṯaḥ*, the latter *'eṯpattaḥ*. It seems that in either case the *ṯ* was assimilated to the *p*; this is a regular feature of later Aramaic and its dialects (*e.g.* Syriac). A few manuscripts have the transliteration *ephphetha*; this would certainly indicate the simple passive form. D.F.P.

EPHRAIM. The second son of Joseph, born to him by Asenath, the daughter of Potipherah, before the years of famine came (Gn. xli. 50–52). The sick Jacob acknowledged the two sons of Joseph (Gn. xlviii. 5), blessing Ephraim with his right hand and Manasseh with his left (verses 13, 14), thus signifying that Ephraim would become the greater people (verse 19).

That Ephraim did become a great tribe is shown by the census lists (Nu. i. 33, 40,500, and Nu. xxvi. 37, 32,500). In the order of the tribes the standard of Ephraim's camp was on the west side (Nu. ii. 18). From the tribe of Ephraim Elishama was to stand with Moses (Nu. i. 10), and Joshua the son of Nun, one of the spies, was descended from Ephraim (Nu. xiii. 8). He was chosen with Eleazar the priest to divide the land (Nu. xxxiv. 17). Ephraim is also included in the blessing of Moses.

Under the valiant leadership of Joshua, Ephraim with the other tribes received her inheritance, which is described in Jos. xvi. The territory may be roughly identified as follows. Proceeding west from Gilgal we come to Bethel, then to lower Beth-horon, west to Gezer, then north to Lod and westward towards the sea, north to the Kanah river and then east to Tappuah, Janobah, Taanath-shiloh to Ataroth, then south to Nasrath and Gilgal.

From the beginning the tribe of Ephraim occupied a position of prestige and significance. It complained to Gideon that he had not called it to fight against the Midianites. His reply reveals the superior position of Ephraim. 'Is not the gleaning of the grapes of Ephraim better than the vintage of Abi-ezer?' (Jdg. viii. 2). The men of Ephraim complained again to Jephthah, and this led to war between the Ephraimites and the Gileadites.

The prestige of Ephraim kept it from looking with favour upon Judah. After the death of Saul, Abner, Saul's captain, made Ishbosheth king over the northern tribes, including Ephraim. He reigned for two years, but Judah followed David (2 Sa. ii. 8 ff.).

Later David learned that Israel followed after Absalom. The northern tribes never did desire to yield to David's reign, but David grew continually greater and stronger. Under Solomon the southern kingdom reached the pinnacle of splendour and prosperity. Nevertheless, even at this time, there was discontent in the north (1 Ki. xi. 26 ff.).

Rehoboam's folly provided the necessary pretext, and the north apostatized, renouncing all claim to the promises made to David (1 Ki. xii. 16). Nevertheless, God continued to send His prophets to the northern kingdom, and one of the characteristics of the messianic kingdom is to be the healing of the tragic schism introduced by Jeroboam the son of Nebat (*cf.* Ho. i. 11). E.J.Y.

EPHRAIM (geographical). The boundaries of Ephraim are recorded in Jos. xvi, and with Manasseh in Jos. xvii. Only some of the main topographical features of these boundaries have so far been determined beyond dispute; most of the places mentioned cannot be precisely located at present.

The southern boundary of Ephraim is most clearly expressed in Jos. xvi. 1–3, where, however, it is given as the (southern) boundary of 'the children of Joseph', *i.e.* Ephraim-Manasseh. But as Manasseh was situated wholly to the north and north-east of Ephraim, this boundary is, in practice, that of Ephraim. It ran (east to west) up from the Jordan and Jericho inland to Bethel (Beitin, about 10 miles north of Jerusalem), Luz (?near by), and Ataroth (site uncertain), then *via* the border of Beth-horon the nether to Gezer —well-known site—and the Mediterranean seacoast (Jos. xvi. 1–3). Verse 5 is difficult, but may perhaps further define part of this southern boundary.

The northern boundary from a point Michmetha(t)h (xvi. 6) 'before Shechem' (xvii. 7) turned westward; its course in that direction ran from Tappuah (location still disputed) to and along the brook of Qanah (perhaps the present Wadi Qānah, which joins Wadi Aujah, and reaches the Mediterranean about 4 miles north of Joppa) to the sea (xvi. 8). Eastward from Michmetha(t)h, the border turned by Taanath-shiloh (southward) along the east of Janoah to (another) Ataroth, Naarah, and back to Jericho and the Jordan (xvi. 6, 7). On the north, Shechem apparently fell within Ephraim's share, to judge from the levitical city-lists (Jos. xxi. 20, 21; 1 Ch. vi. 67).

The region in central west Palestine that fell to Ephraim is mainly relatively high hill-country with better rainfall than Judaea and some good soils; hence some biblical references to the fruitfulness of the Ephraim district. The Ephraimites had direct but not over-easy access to the great north–south trunk road through the western plain.

BIBLIOGRAPHY. D. Baly, *The Geography of the Bible*, 1957, pp. 170–176; J. Simons, *The Geographical and Topographical Texts of the Old Testament*, 1959, pp. 158–169; Y. Kaufmann, *The Biblical Account of the Conquest of Palestine*, 1953, pp. 28–36; and E. Jenni, *Zeitschrift des Deutschen Palästina-Vereins*, LXXIV, 1958, pp. 35–40, with some detailed bibliography. Also F. M. Abel, *Géographie de la Palestine*, I–II, 1933–8. K.A.K.

EPHRATH. 1. The ancient name of Bethlehem-Judah (*q.v.*), which occurs in all cases but one (Gn. xlviii. 7, *'eprāṯ*) in the form *'eprāṯâ*. Rachel was buried on the route there from Bethel (Gn. xxxv. 16, 19, xlviii. 7; *cf.* 1 Sa. x. 2); it was the home of Naomi's family (Ru. iv. 11), who are described as Ephrathites (*'eprāṯî*, Ru. i. 2), of Ruth's descendant David (1 Sa. xvii. 12; *cf.* Ps. cxxxii. 6), and of the Messiah, as foretold in Mi. v. 2.

2. The gentilic *'eprāṯî* is applied three times to Ephraimites (Jdg. xii. 5; 1 Sa. i. 1; 1 Ki. xi. 26).

3. The second wife of Caleb the son of Hezron (1 Ch. ii. 19, 50, iv. 4, *cf.* ii. 24). T.C.M.

EPHRON. 1. Name of the son of Zohar, a 'son of Heth' (Hittite or Syrian) from whom Abraham purchased the cave of Machpelah as a burial place for Sarah (Gn. xxiii. 8, xxv. 9, xlix. 30). For the name *cf.* Apran (Alalaḫ). **2.** A hill or hilly area between Nephtoah and Kiriath-jearim (*q.v.*) by which the border of Judah is described (Jos. xv. 9). **3.** A place near Bethel captured by Abijah (2 Ch. xiii. 19, RV). The *MT* with some MSS here reads 'Ephraim' (so AV, *cf.* 2 Sa. xiii. 23) or Ophrah (Jos. xviii. 23). **4.** A city in Transjordan, between Carmion (Ashtoreth-karnaim) and Scythopolis (Beisan), captured by Judas Maccabaeus (1 Macc. v. 41; 2 Macc. xii. 27). Probably the modern et-Taiyibeh, south-east of the Lake of Galilee. D.J.W.

EPICUREANS. Some of the philosophers whom Paul encountered at Athens (Acts xvii. 18) were of this school, whose best-known disciple is the Roman poet Lucretius. The founder, Epicurus, was born in 341 BC on the island of Samos. His early studies under Nausiphanes, a disciple of Democritus, taught him to regard the world as the result of the random motion and combination of atomic particles. He lived for a time in exile and poverty. Gradually he gathered round him a circle of friends and began to teach his distinctive doctrines. In 306 he established himself in Athens at the famous 'Garden' which became the headquarters of the school. He died in 270 after great suffering from an internal complaint, but in peace of mind.

The founder's experiences, coupled with the general uncertainty of life in the last centuries before Christ, gave a special stamp to the Epicurean teachings. The whole system has a practical end in view, the achievement of happiness by serene detachment. Democritean atomism banished all fear of divine intervention in life or punishment after death; the gods follow to perfection the life of serene detachment and will have nothing to do with human existence, and death brings a final dispersion of our constituent atoms.

The Epicureans found contentment in limiting desire and in the joys and solaces of friendship. The pursuit of extravagant pleasure which gives to 'epicure' its modern connotation was a late perversion of their quest for happiness.

It is easy to see why the Epicureans found Paul's teaching about the resurrection strange and unpalatable. Jewish Rabbis use the word *apiqôrôs* to mean one who denies life after death, and later as a synonym for 'infidel'.

BIBLIOGRAPHY. Usener, *Epicurea*, 1887; A. J. Festugière, *Epicurus and his Gods*, E.T. 1955; N. W. de Witt, *Epicurus and his Philosophy*, 1954.

M.H.C.

EPILEPSY. See DISEASE AND HEALING (Section Id), POSSESSION.

EPISTLE. Gk. *epistolē* and Lat. *epistula* represent a letter of any kind: originally simply a written communication between persons apart, whether personal and private or official. In this sense epistles are a part of the heritage of all literate peoples, and examples are to be found in the Old Testament (2 Sa. xi; 1 Ki. xxi; 2 Ki. v, x, xx; 2 Ch. xxx, xxxii; Ezr. iv, v, vii; Ne. ii, vi; Est. i, iii, viii, ix; Is. xxxvii, xxxix; Je. xxix) and in the Greek papyri from Egypt (*cf.* all the large published collections of papyri, *passim*, and especially the Zenon correspondence). Such a letter was described by Demetrius, *Typoi epistolikoi* (1st century BC), as a written conversation, while Demetrius, *On Style* iii. 223 ff., quotes Artemon, the ancient collector of Aristotle's letters, as calling it half a dialogue.

But the earliest collections of Greek letters generally regarded as genuine, in part at least, those of Isocrates and Plato, already show a tendency to use letters, or the letter-form, for larger purposes than mere private or official communication; so that among Isocrates' letters (368–338 BC) some are sent speeches, or introductions to speeches, and Plato's Seventh Letter (*c.* 354 BC) is a refutation of popular misconceptions about his philosophy and conduct. In both cases the letters aim at other readers than those addressed, and are thus a form of publication. Compare here present-day letters 'to the Editor of *The Times*'.

Despite a feeling often hinted at, and sometimes expressed, that such letters have neither the size nor the subject-matter of true letters, but are rather 'writings with "greetings" added' (Demetrius, *On Style, loc. cit.*), the epistolary form continued to be used for philosophical, scientific, and literary publication (*e.g.* Epicurus, *Epistles*, and the three literary letters of Dionysius of Halicarnassus). The theory and practice of letter-writing came to be treated by the teachers of rhetoric (*e.g.* Demetrius, *On Style*; *id.*, *Typoi epistolikoi*), and letter-writing in the characters of famous men formed part of the rhetorical school exercise of *prosōpopoeia*. The growth in Hellenistic and Roman times of collections of fictitious letters may be attributed to such exercises, and to the eagerness of the great libraries to buy additional works, especially of famous men.

G. A. Deissmann, confronted by the simplicity of most letters in the papyri, maintained a sharp distinction between 'genuine letters' as personal, direct, transient, and un-literary, and 'epistles' as impersonal, aimed at a reading public and permanence, and literary. Feeling an undeniable similarity between certain elements in the New Testament Epistles and the papyri, he classed most of Paul's Epistles and 2 and 3 John as letters, Hebrews, James, 1 and 2 Peter, Jude, and Revelation as epistles, and 1 John as a *diatribē* (*LAE*[3], ch. iii, pp. 148–251). But the distinction cannot be so sharply maintained, as there are different degrees of 'literariness', sorts and sizes of 'public', and kinds of publication.

Of the Pauline letters to churches, those to the Corinthians, Galatians, Philippians, and Thessalonians contain most personal elements, Romans fewer, and Ephesians and Colossians least of all. Galatians and Ephesians are composed on a rhetorical plan, and all of them have considerable rhetorical elements. In the Pastoral Epistles the personal references are fairly numerous and rhetorical elements comparatively few. Philemon, rightly regarded by Deissmann as the most personal letter in the New Testament, and compared to British Museum Papyrus 417, is nevertheless very cleverly written and contains rhetorical elements noticeable especially when considered beside Isocrates, *Ep.* viii, and Demetrius, *Typoi epistolikoi* 12. Hebrews is the most artistic literary writing in the New Testament, being composed from beginning to end on the pattern of *proem, thesis, diēgēsis, apodeixis, epilogue*, laid down by Greek rhetoricians, and is written in rhythmic, periodic prose. In James, 1 and 2 Peter, and Jude there are very few personal references; all are literary, especially 1 Peter; and 2 Peter and Jude are definitely rhetorical. 2 and 3 John appear as private communications, while 1 John is not, as we have it, in letter-form at all. Thus most of the New Testament Epistles show a greater or smaller affinity with preaching; some may be classed as sent sermons, while in others the letter-elements are a mere literary form.

BIBLIOGRAPHY. *LAE*[4], 1927, pp. 146 ff.; R. Hercher, *Epistolographi Graeci*, 1873; J. Sykutris, *Epistolographie*, in Pauly-Wissowa-Kroll *RE*, Supplementband 5, pp. 185–220; V. Weichert (ed.), *Demetrii et Libanii qui feruntur Typoi Epistolikoi et Epistolimaioi Characteres* (Teubner), 1910; O. Roller, *Das Formular der Paulinischen Briefe*, 1933; M. Dibelius, *A Fresh Approach to the New Testament and Early Christian Literature*, E.T., 1936, pp. 137–171, 185–189, 194–197, 205–213, 226–234. J.H.H.

ERASTUS. 1. An assistant of Paul, who shared Timothy's mission to Macedonia to allow Paul to continue working from Ephesus (Acts xix. 22). The mission may have been directed ultimately to Corinth (*cf.* 1 Cor. iv. 17), and Erastus been one of the 'brethren' of 2 Cor. viii; but certainty is impossible. Undoubtedly, however, he is the Erastus mentioned as staying at Corinth in 2 Tim. iv. 20.

2. City-treasurer (not 'chamberlain' as AV) of Corinth, sending greetings in Rom. xvi. 23 (see also QUARTUS). A Latin inscription found at Corinth states, 'Erastus laid this pavement at his own expense, in appreciation of his appointment as aedile'. Many (*e.g.* Broneer) accept the identification with the Christian city treasurer.

Some further identify (1) and (2): G. S. Duncan, for example, suggests that 2 Tim. iv. 20 indicates that Erastus, unlike Timothy, completed the journey to Corinth, where he became treasurer a year or so later (*St. Paul's Ephesian Ministry*, pp. 79 ff.); but such a rapid rise to power is most unlikely, and the name is quite common.

BIBLIOGRAPHY. H. J. Cadbury, *JBL*, L, 1931, pp. 42 ff.; O. Broneer, *BA*, XIV, 1951, pp. 78 ff., especially p. 94. A.F.W.

ERECH. An ancient city of Mesopotamia mentioned in the Table of Nations (Gn. x. 10) as one of the possessions of Nimrod in the land of Shinar (*q.v.*). Known to the Sumerians as *Unu(g)* and to the Akkadians as *Uruk*, it was one of the great cities of Sumerian times. It is named in the Sumerian king list as the seat of the IInd Dynasty after the flood, one of whose kings was Gilgamesh, who later became one of the great heroes of Sumerian legend. Though the city continued in occupation during later periods (Gk. *Orchoē*), it never surpassed its early importance. Uruk is represented today by the group of mounds known to the Arabs as *Warka*, which lies in S Babylonia some 40 miles north-west of

Ur and 4 miles east of the present course of the Euphrates (*q.v.*). While the site was investigated over a century ago by W. K. Loftus (*Travels and Researches in Chaldaea and Susiana*, 1857), the principal excavations have been conducted by a series of German expeditions in 1912–13, 1928–39, and 1954–60. The results are of outstanding importance for the early history of Mesopotamia. Prehistoric remains of the Ubaid Period (see MESOPOTAMIA) were followed by monumental architecture and stone sculpture of the Late Prehistoric Period which richly illustrate the material culture of Mesopotamia at the beginning of history. It was in these levels, dating from the fourth millennium BC, that the earliest inscriptions so far known were found. These are in the form of clay tablets, and, though the signs are only pictographic, it is probable that the language behind them was Sumerian.

BIBLIOGRAPHY. R. North, 'Status of the Warka Excavations', *Orientalia*, NS XXVI, 1957, pp. 185–256. T.C.M.

ESAIAS. See ISAIAH.

ESARHADDON (Heb. *'esarhaddōn*; Assyr. *Aššur-aḫ-iddin*, 'Ashur has given a brother') was king of Assyria 681–669 BC. He succeeded his father Sennacherib who was murdered in Tebet in 681 BC (2 Ki. xix. 37; Is. xxxvii. 38). His first act was to pursue the murderers as far as Hanigalbat (S Armenia) and to quash the rebellion in Nineveh, which lasted six weeks. There is little support for the theory that Esarhaddon was the head of a pro-Babylonian faction or 'the son' mentioned in the Bab. Chronicle as the murderer (*DOTT*, pp. 70–73). His own inscriptions tell how he had been made crown-prince by his father earlier in the year, and though he had been viceroy in Babylon his attention to that religious centre was merely in keeping with his predecessor's care for the ancient shrines. His early military operations were designed to safeguard the northern frontier and trade-routes against the warlike Ṭeušpa and the incursions of the Cimmerians, whom he defeated (see GOMER). In the south the Elamites, who had been defeated by his father, once more stirred up the tribes of S Babylonia, and Esarhaddon was forced to undertake a series of campaigns against the 'sea-lands' where he installed Na'id-Marduk as the local sheikh in 678 BC. His clashes with Elam and the Babylonians resulted in the deportation of many captives, some of whom were settled in Samaria (Ezr. iv. 2).

In the west Esarhaddon continued his father's policy. He exacted heavy tribute from the kings of Syria and Palestine, listing Manasseh (*Menasi*) of Judah (Yaudi) after Mati-ilu of Tyre, with whom he concluded a treaty, having failed to isolate and thus subdue the port. The rulers of Edom, Moab, and Ammon were made vassals after a series of raids on their territory in which he sought to counter the influence of Tirhakah of Egypt, who had incited a number of the Philistine cities to revolt. Esarhaddon sacked Sidon in 676 BC, after a three-year siege, and incorporated part of its territory into an extended Assyrian province (probably including Samaria). Some of the refugees from the city were housed in a new town, Kar-Esarhaddon, built near by. About this time Gaza and Ashkelon were counted among his vassals.

The subordinate kingdoms in Syria and Palestine were called upon to provide materials for Esarhaddon's building operations in Assyria and in Babylon, which he now sought to revive after earlier changes of fortune (see MERODACH-BALADAN; SENNACHERIB). This may explain the temporary detention of Manasseh in Babylon (2 Ch. xxxiii. 11). Assyrian letters referring to tribute in silver received from Judah, Moab, and Edom may be assigned to this time.

In May 672 BC Esarhaddon brought all the vassal-kings together to acknowledge the arrangements he proposed to ensure a succession to the throne less disturbed than in his own experience. Ashurbanipal (see OSNAPPAR) was declared to be the crown-prince or heir to Assyria and Šamaš-šum-ukin to Babylonia. Copies of the treaty imposed on the Median city-chiefs on this occasion, found at Calah (Nimrud), show the provisions to which all, including Manasseh, had to assent. They declared their loyalty to the Assyrian national god Ashur and their willingness to serve Assyria for ever. History tells how soon all the client kings broke their oaths.

Having gained control of the west, Esarhaddon invaded Egypt, defeated Tirhakah, besieged Memphis, and counted the land as an Assyrian dependency under Necho. When the victorious army was withdrawn, local intrigues developed into open revolt. While Esarhaddon was on his way to deal with this in 669 BC he died at Harran, leaving five surviving sons and one daughter. His mother, the forceful wife of Sennacherib (Naqi'a-Zakutu), also survived him.

BIBLIOGRAPHY. R. Borger, *Die Inschriften Asarhaddons Königs von Assyrien*, 1956; D. J. Wiseman, *The Vassal-Treaties of Esarhaddon*, 1958. D.J.W.

ESAU. Esau was the elder of Isaac's twin sons (Gn. xxv. 21–26). His relations with Jacob his brother are the subject of the well-known stories in Gn. xxv. 27–34, xxvii. 1 ff., xxxii. 3–12, xxxiii. 1–16. Esau was his father's favourite son, and it was Isaac's intention to impart to him the blessing that was the eldest son's right (Gn. xxvii. 1 ff.). However, the supremacy of Jacob over his older brother, foreshadowed before, and at the moment of, their birth (Gn. xxv. 21–26), and eventually confirmed unwittingly by the aged Isaac (Gn. xxvii. 22–29, 33–37), was finally established.

It was from this duplicity on the part of Jacob, the ancestor of the Israelites, that there stemmed the deep-rooted animosity that dominated Israel's relations with Edom, of whom Esau was the ancestor. Instances of this antagonism between the Israelites and the Edomites occur in the Old Testament (*e.g.* Nu. xx. 18–21; 1 Ki. xi. 14 ff.; Ps. cxxxvii. 7).

The chief importance of the biblical references to Esau lies in the theological significance given to his rejection, in spite of the right of succession being his by virtue of primogeniture. The biblical explanation is that the Lord hated Esau and loved Jacob (Mal. i. 2 f.; Rom. ix. 13). Esau symbolizes those whom God has not elected; Jacob typifies those whom God has chosen.

But the ground of this election was not any difference in the lives and characters of Jacob and Esau. Jacob was chosen before he and his brother were born. And even God's 'hate' and 'love' could not be the ground of divine election, otherwise God's choice would depend on caprice or whim. God has exercised His sovereign will in the free exercise of His elective grace, the moral purpose of which He was the sole Originator. See also ELECTION.

In Heb. xii. 16 f. Esau symbolizes those who abandon their hope of glory for the sake of the things that are seen and are not eternal.

J.G.S.S.T.

ESCHATOLOGY (Gk. *eschatos*, 'last', and *logos*, 'subject', hence 'the doctrine of the last things'). Biblical eschatology is concerned not only with the destiny of the individual but also with history. This is due to the particular character of biblical revelation. God does not only reveal Himself by means of inspired men, but also in and through the events of redemptive history (*Heilsgeschichte*), the most important of which are the advent and life of His Son, Jesus Christ. Furthermore, the content of this revelation is not limited to truths about the character and purposes of God, but includes also His redemptive acts in history, and the inspired Word of God which interprets the meaning of those acts. Since God is the Lord of history, the consummation of God's redemptive work will include the redemption of history itself.

I. THE OLD TESTAMENT PERSPECTIVE

The prophets look forward to the day when the God of Israel who has repeatedly visited His people in history will finally visit them to judge the wicked, redeem the righteous, and purge the earth of all evil. 'The day of the Lord' and the abbreviated phrase 'in that day' designate this divine visitation and emphasize its quality rather than the time of its occurrence. Therefore 'the day of the Lord' denotes both divine visitations in history (Am. v. 18; Joel i. 15) and also the final eschatological visitation (Joel iii. 14, 18; Zp. iii. 11, 16; Zc. xiv. 9). 'In the last days' God will come to establish His kingdom (Is. ii. 2–4; Ho. iii. 5).

Several messianic personages appear in the Old Testament hope: a Davidic king (Is. ix. 6, 7, xi. 1 ff.; Je. xxiii. 5, 6), a heavenly Son of man (Dn. vii. 13, 14), and a suffering servant (Is. liii); but often it is God Himself who will come to redeem His people (Is. xxvi. 21; Joel iii. 16; Zc. xiv. 5; Mal. iii. 1, 2).

II. THE NEW TESTAMENT PERSPECTIVE

The New Testament sees in the incarnation of Christ the fulfilment of the Old Testament hope, and in His second coming the consummation of that hope. What the Old Testament anticipates in one day of visitation is in the New Testament accomplished in two days. Fulfilment and consummation are two parts of a single redemptive work. While the note of fulfilment is frequently sounded (Lk. iv. 18–21; Mt. xi. 4, 5, xiii. 16, 17; Lk. x. 23, 24), the consummation remains future. Therefore the historical work of Christ is an eschatological work and the blessings He has conferred are eschatological blessings. There is a 'realized' eschatology in the New Testament.

The life, death and resurrection of Christ inaugurated the messianic fulfilment, although in a form not previously anticipated. 'The last days', which would witness the establishment of the kingdom of God (Is. ii. 2–4; Ho. iii. 5), are now here (Heb. i. 2). The eschatological promise of the outpouring of the Spirit (Joel ii. 28; Ezk. xxxvi. 27) has occurred in these last days (Acts ii. 16, 17). However, the age to come is still regarded as the time of the consummation of God's kingdom (Mk. x. 25, 30), and remains throughout the New Testament an object of hope (Mt. xii. 32; Lk. xx. 35; Jn. xii. 25; Eph. i. 21), even though its powers may be experienced in measure here and now (Heb. vi. 5). The day of consummation is necessary to bring the fulness of the eschatological blessings now experienced in part. Thus the events attending the second coming of Christ do not represent something new. What Christ accomplished by His death and resurrection will be brought to consummation by His coming in glory.

III. THE PRECEDING EVENTS

The time of fulfilment has occurred within the old age. Therefore we live between the ages in a time of tension and conflict. The 'children of the kingdom' (Mt. xiii. 38) still live in the evil age (Gal. i. 4) of darkness, mortality, and of Satan's power (Eph. ii. 2, 3). While the sovereign God is 'King of the ages' (Rev. xv. 3, RV, RSV), He has permitted Satan to exercise such an influence that he is designated 'the god of this world' (2 Cor. iv. 4). Although Christ, by His death and resurrection, has broken the power of Satan (Jn. xii. 31; Heb. ii. 14), as long as this age lasts he will continue to oppose God's redemptive purposes and to persecute the people of God. Behind the events of human history during this age is a spiritual struggle between demonic evil and the kingdom of God (Rev. xii). God's people in this age are an eschatological people because they have been transferred out of the realm of darkness into the kingdom of Christ (Col. i. 13). They have experienced a transforming power by virtue of which they are no longer under the domination of this age (Rom. xii. 2), and they live in constant hope of the consummation (Rom. v. 2, viii. 18; Eph. iv. 4; Col. i. 5, 27). Nevertheless, because they still live in the old age, they are in principle a martyr-church and must expect tribulation (Mt. xiii. 21; Jn. xvi. 33; Acts xiv. 22; Rom. xii. 12) and satanic opposition (2 Cor. xi. 14, xii. 7; Eph. vi. 11, 12; 1 Pet. v. 8).

Satan's age-long opposition to the kingdom of God will be climaxed in the appearance of an eschatological personage described in various terms as the 'abomination of desolation' (*q.v.*) (Mt. xxiv. 15; *cf.* Dn. xi. 31, xii. 11), the 'man of lawlessness' (2 Thes. ii. 3, RSV, RVmg; *cf.* ANTICHRIST), and the 'beast' (Rev. xiii. 1; see BEAST (APOCALYPSE)). He will be satanically inspired and empowered to do wonderful signs (2 Thes. ii. 9; Rev. xiii. 3, 13) to captivate the admiration of men. He will be a political ruler who will use religion to serve his blasphemous end of claiming the worship of men in the stead of God (2 Thes. ii. 4; Rev. xiii. 8, 12). He will demand the total allegiance of his subjects—religious as well as political—and will use economic sanctions to compel submission (Rev. xiii. 16, 17).

Against those who do not submit, antichrist will direct fierce persecution (Mt. xxiv. 21; Rev. xiii. 7). So intense will be this 'great tribulation' (Mt. xxiv. 21) that God will intervene to shorten the days (Mt. xxiv. 22) for the sake of the elect. Those who stand steadfast in their faith in Christ, refusing to worship the beast, will be triumphant over the beast even in death and martyrdom (Rev. xv. 2).

The appearance of antichrist and the persecution of the saints is only the final attack of Satan against God's people. Antichrist is foreshadowed in several critical points in redemptive history: in the persecutions of Antiochus Epiphanes in 168 BC (Dn. viii), in the destruction of the Jewish state by Rome (Dn. ix. 26b; Lk. xxi. 20–24), and in the early persecution of the Church (Rev. xiii). Antichrist is an eschatological principle which appears both at the end time and throughout history (1 Jn. ii. 18, 22, iv. 3). This tension between eschatology and history is one of the most important phenomena in biblical eschatology.

This time of tribulation will witness also the beginnings of the divine judgment upon Satan and his followers. Revelation describes these judgments in symbolical terms, as seven trumpets (Rev. viii–ix) and seven bowls (Rev. xvi). These judgments will consist of plagues and disasters manifesting God's wrath (Rev. xv. 1, 7, xvi. 19) and will be directed against the beast and his worshippers (Rev. xiv. 9, 10, xvi. 2, 10). Before the onset of these judgments, God will seal His people (Rev. vii. 1–8), who will be protected from God's wrath (Rev. ix. 4) and will be preserved intact in the terrible conflict with satanic power, even though they suffer martyrdom (Rev. vii. 9–17). Many scholars see two different groups of God's people pictured in Rev. vii: the literal twelve tribes of Israel and the innumerable multitude of the Church. But since the twelve tribes listed in vii. 1–8 are nowhere else found in Scripture (Dan is omitted in Rev. vii but included in Ezk. xlviii. 1), it is best to interpret this vision as a symbolic prophecy of the spiritual preservation of the Church, the true Israel (Rev. ii. 9).

IV. THE COMING OF CHRIST

The Day of the Lord will bring the brief rule of antichrist to its end (2 Thes. ii. 2, RV, RSV). In the New Testament the Day of the Lord is a comprehensive term designating all the events which will attend the consummation. The expression takes different forms: the 'day of the Lord' (Acts ii. 20; 1 Thes. v. 2; 2 Thes. ii. 2, RV, RSV; 2 Pet. iii. 10), the 'day of the Lord Jesus' (1 Cor. v. 5; 2 Cor. i. 14), the 'day of our Lord Jesus Christ' (1 Cor. i. 8), the 'day of Jesus Christ' (Phil. i. 6), the 'day of Christ' (Phil. i. 10, ii. 16), the 'day of God' (2 Pet. iii. 12), and 'that day' (Mt. vii. 22, xxiv. 36, xxvi. 29; Lk. x. 12; 2 Thes. i. 10; 2 Tim. i. 18; *etc.*) or 'the last day' (Jn. vi. 39, 40, 44, 54, xi. 24, xii. 48).

The return of Christ, which may properly be called His 'second coming' (Heb. ix. 28), is represented by several important words. *Parousia* means 'presence' or 'arrival' (1 Cor. xvi. 17; 2 Cor. vii. 7) and was used in Hellenistic Greek to designate the visit of a ruler. The same Jesus who ascended to heaven will again visit the earth in personal presence (Acts i. 11) at the end of the age (Mt. xxiv. 3) in power and glory (Mt. xxiv. 27) to destroy antichrist and evil (2 Thes. ii. 8), to raise the righteous dead (1 Cor. xv. 23), and to gather the redeemed (Mt. xxiv. 31; 2 Thes. ii. 1; *cf.* also Mt. xxiv. 37, 39; 1 Thes. ii. 19, iii. 13, iv. 15, v. 23; Jas. v. 7, 8; 2 Pet. i. 16; 1 Jn. ii. 28). His return will also be an *apokalypsis*, an 'unveiling' or 'disclosure', when the power and glory which are now His by virtue of His exaltation and heavenly session (Phil. ii. 9; Eph. i. 20–23; Heb. i. 3, ii. 9) will be disclosed to the world (1 Pet. iv. 13). Christ is now reigning as Lord at God's right hand (Heb. i. 3, xii. 2; 1 Cor. xv. 25), sharing God's throne (Rev. iii. 21), but His reign is invisible to the world. It will, however, be made visible by His *apokalypsis* (1 Cor. i. 7; 2 Thes. i. 7; 1 Pet. i. 7, 13). Thus the second coming of Christ is inseparable from His ascension and heavenly session, for it discloses His present lordship to the world.

The third word, *epiphaneia*, 'appearing', designates the visibility of His return (2 Thes. ii. 8; 1 Tim. vi. 14; 2 Tim. iv. 1, 8; Tit. ii. 13).

V. THE RESURRECTION

At the return of Christ will occur the resurrection of 'the dead in Christ' (1 Thes. iv. 16). The resurrection of the dead was anticipated in a few places in the Old Testament (Is. xxv. 8, xxvi. 19; Dn. xii. 2; Ezk. xxxvii also reflects belief in resurrection). Belief in the resurrection is rooted in confidence that God is the living God and therefore will not abandon His people to death (Mt. xxii. 32). While the New Testament expresses the fact of resurrection for all men (Jn. v.

28, 29; Acts xxiv. 15; Rev. xx. 12, 13), its emphasis is upon resurrection as a fruit of redemption. Resurrection life is an eschatological blessing enjoyed by the redeemed (Col. ii. 12, 13). By His resurrection, Christ abolished death, and brought life and immortality to light (2 Tim. i. 10). Christ's resurrection was not merely the restoration of a dead body to life; it was the first stage of the eschatological resurrection of the last day. His resurrection is the 'firstfruits', the beginning of the eschatological harvest (1 Cor. xv. 23). Because the resurrection already has begun, believers share Christ's resurrection life (Eph. ii. 5, 6; Rom. vi. 4; Phil. iii. 10; Col. iii. 1–3). The resurrection of those in Christ is therefore guaranteed by the fact of His resurrection (1 Cor. xv. 12–20), and will be the second stage of the eschatological harvest (1 Cor. xv. 23).

The nature of the resurrection body transcends present experience (1 Cor. xv. 35–57). The essential ideas are that it will be a real body (38–42) which stands in a relationship of continuity with the 'natural' body (36, 37) but which is yet different, not a body of 'flesh and blood' (50). Paul can only describe the resurrection body in terms of incorruption, glory, and power (42, 43). A 'spiritual' body (44) does not mean a body made of spirit but one completely vitalized and transformed by the Spirit of life. The resurrection body does not belong to a *wholly* other order of existence; it is the present body redeemed (Rom. viii. 23) when mortality is swallowed up in life (2 Cor. v. 4).

Believers who are living at the return of Christ will be transformed without passing through death (1 Cor. xv. 51, 52; 1 Thes. iv. 17). This 'rapture' or being 'caught up (Lat. *rapiemur*) . . . to meet the Lord in the air' (1 Thes. iv. 17) is Paul's way of describing the experience of transition into the new redeemed order of resurrection life without passing through death. See also RESURRECTION.

VI. THE STATE OF THE DEAD

The biblical view of man demands the resurrection of the body as the goal of individual eschatology. Man does not consist of separate parts—body, soul, and spirit. Rather, these terms are different aspects of a single dynamic person. Therefore the life of the age to come requires the resurrection and redemption of the body. Both life and death concern the whole man. This is illustrated by the teaching on immortality. Immortality in Scripture does not mean endless existence but freedom from death (1 Cor. xv. 53; 1 Tim. vi. 16) and from corruption (Rom. ii. 7; 2 Tim. i. 10). God alone is free from death (1 Tim. vi. 16); but Christ has won life and incorruption for men (2 Tim. i. 10), and they will exchange mortality for immortality at the resurrection (1 Cor. xv. 53, 54).

The Bible has little to say about the state of the dead. However, even in the Old Testament, man does not cease to exist at death, but his soul descends to 'Sheol' (translated 'grave', 'hell', or 'pit' in AV). Sheol is pictured as a place beneath (Ps. lxxxvi. 13; Pr. xv. 24; Ezk. xxvi. 20), a region of darkness (Jb. x. 22), the land of silence (Pss. lxxxviii. 12, xciv. 17, cxv. 17). Here the dead, who are gathered in tribes (Ezk. xxxii. 17–32), receive the dying (Is. xiv. 9, 10). Sheol is not so much a place as the state of the dead. It is not non-existence; but it is not life, for life can be enjoyed only in the presence of God (Ps. xvi. 10, 11). Sheol is the Old Testament manner of asserting that death does not terminate existence. In a few places God gives the added revelation, later enlarged in the New Testament, that since He is the living God, He will not abandon His people to Sheol, but will bring them into the enjoyment of life in His presence (Ps. xvi. 9–11, xlix. 15, lxxiii. 24; Jb. xix. 25, 26). Enoch and Elijah were translated into the presence of God without seeing Sheol (Gn. v. 24; 2 Ki. ii. 11).

'Hades', translated 'hell' (Mt. xi. 23, xvi. 18; Lk. x. 15, xvi. 23; Acts ii. 27, 31; Rev. i. 18, vi. 8, xx. 13, 14) and 'grave' (1 Cor. xv. 55, Received Text), is the New Testament equivalent of Sheol. Probably the story of Dives and Lazarus (Lk. xvi), like the story of the unjust steward in the same chapter (Lk. xvi. 1–9), is a parable which made use of current Jewish thinking and is not intended to teach anything about the state of the dead. Peter speaks of the unrighteous dead as spirits in prison (1 Pet. iii. 19). See also HELL and section x below.

The revelation that death does not end human existence is enlarged in the New Testament. The natural metaphor of sleep is frequently used of the dead (Mt. xxvii. 52; 1 Cor. xi. 30; 1 Thes. iv. 13), and some see more than a metaphor in this terminology (O. Cullmann, *Immortality*, 1958). However, there are a few glimpses that the redeemed are with Christ after death (Lk. xxiii. 43; Phil. i. 23) and that their spirits are made perfect (Heb. xii. 23). Paul shrinks from death because it seems to be a state of disembodied nakedness (2 Cor. v. 3) and longs for the resurrection body (verse 4). However, his natural fear of death is overcome by the confidence that to be absent from the body means to be present with the Lord (verse 8), and therefore, even though he has no knowledge about the state of the soul after death, it is more desirable than earthly existence. The goal is the redemption of the total man, including the body. Sayings about 'the salvation of your souls' (1 Pet. i. 9; Jas. i. 21) do not anticipate a salvation of the soul apart from the body, for soul as in Mt. xvi. 25 designates man's real life without special reference to his body (*cf.* Acts xxvii. 10).

VII. JUDGMENT

'It is appointed unto men once to die, but after this the judgment' (Heb. ix. 27). The Bible represents God as ruler of men, lawgiver, and final judge (Jas. iv. 12, RV, RSV). Sometimes God is the Judge (Heb. xii. 23), sometimes Christ (2 Tim. iv. 8; Acts x. 42). God 'will judge the world in righteousness by that man whom he hath ordained' (Acts xvii. 31). The judgment-seat of God (Rom. xiv. 10, RV, RSV) and the judgment-seat of Christ (2 Cor. v. 10) are interchangeable terms.

It is impossible to identify a series of distinct and separate judgments. The Bible is concerned with the fact of judgment, not with a timetable. Our Lord's prophecy of the judgment of the nations is an extended simile based on the daily experience of separating the mixed flocks of sheep and goats. Jesus was about to send His 'brethren', *i.e.* His disciples and representatives (Mt. xii. 48–50, xxiii. 8), into the world, and the final destiny of men (xxv. 46) will be determined by the way they receive and treat His emissaries, for 'he that receiveth you receiveth me' (Mt. x. 40). This parable can be used neither to settle the millennial question nor to prove salvation by good works.

The final judgment will rest on two issues: works and faith in Christ (Rev. xx. 13–15). Judgment will be in accordance with light. Those who have not had the law of Moses will be judged without law (Rom. ii. 12); they have the light of general revelation (Rom. i. 20) and the law written in the heart (Rom. ii. 15). Those who 'by patient continuance in well-doing seek for glory and honour and immortality' will be rewarded with eternal life; those who have not obeyed the truth but have obeyed unrighteousness will suffer wrath (Rom. ii. 6–8). Again, those who have had the law of Moses will be judged by the law (Rom. ii. 12). The basic principle of judgment is the justice of God (Gn. xviii. 25; Rom. iii. 3, 4).

However, men have not lived up to the light God has given them, and therefore stand under condemnation. The Gentiles have perverted the light of general revelation (Rom. i. 21 ff.) and the Jews have failed to fulfil the law (Gal. iii. 10–12). Since God in His mercy has provided a way of salvation by the redeeming work of Christ, the final basis of judgment is relation to Christ. This is one meaning of the 'book of life' (Rev. xx. 15; *cf.* Lk. x. 20; Phil. iv. 3; Rev. iii. 5, xiii. 8).

Jesus taught that the destiny of men rested upon their attitude towards Himself (Mt. x. 32, 33, xi. 21–24; Mk. viii. 38). This is the heart of the gospel: salvation, which is primarily eschatological (Rom. xiii. 11; 1 Thes. v. 8, 9) and includes escape from God's condemnation in the day of judgment (Jn. v. 24), is God's gift to be received by faith in Jesus Christ (Acts iv. 12, xvi. 30, 31) and submission to His lordship (Rom. x. 9).

A further aspect of the realized eschatology of the Bible is seen in the fact that this judgment, which belongs to the last day, has essentially already taken place in history. The unbeliever stands under condemnation; the judgment has really taken place, even though the penalty has not yet been enforced (Jn. iii. 18). The believer will not experience condemnation, for he has already passed from death (the condemnation) to life (Jn. v. 24).

The Pauline teaching about justification embodies the same truth. Justification is an eschatological truth. It means acquittal from the guilt of sin by a favourable decision of the Judge on the last day. The opposite of justification is condemnation by the Judge (Mt. xii. 37; Rom. viii. 33, 34; *cf. TWNT*, II, pp. 210 f., 221). Yet because of the death of Christ, the justification of believers has already taken place (Rom. iii. 21–26, v. 1). Because of present justification, we shall be saved from wrath in the day of judgment (Rom. v. 9).

Nevertheless, judgment remains an eschatological fact, even for believers. The righteousness we hope for (Gal. v. 5) is acquittal in the final judgment (*TWNT*, II, pp. 210 f.). 'We must all appear before the judgment seat of Christ' (2 Cor. v. 10; *cf.* also Mt. xii. 36), which is also the judgment-seat of God (Rom. xiv. 10, RV, RSV). However, because of the redemption in Christ, the day of judgment has lost its terror for the man in Christ (1 Jn. iv. 17).

VIII. THE KINGDOM OF GOD

The kingdom of God means first the reign of God and second the realm in which His reign is enjoyed. The final goal will be realized only in the age to come. Negatively, this means the destruction of God's enemies: Satan, sin, and death (Rev. xx. 10, 14, 15). Positively, it means the enjoyment by the redeemed of perfected fellowship with God and the full measure of divine blessings (Rev. xxi. 3–8), which are summed up by the expression 'eternal life'. Thus eternal life and the kingdom of God are sometimes interchangeable expressions (Mt. xxv. 34, 46; Mk. x. 17, 24). 'The kingdom of God' in the Synoptic Gospels and 'eternal life' in John are synonymous concepts (W. F. Howard, *Christianity according to St. John*, 1946, p. 112).

God's kingdom is not established in a single eschatological act but in at least two, probably three, stages (see next section). By His incarnation, Christ 'bound' (Mt. xii. 29) or 'destroyed' Satan (Heb. ii. 14). He 'abolished death' and 'brought life and immortality to light' (2 Tim. i. 10). This initial victory over Satan and death is the work of God's kingdom, of God's redemptive reign in Christ. Thus the kingdom of God, which is still future (Mt. xiii. 43; 1 Cor. vi. 9; Rev. xii. 10), is said to have come near (Mt. iv. 17) or to have come (Mt. xii. 28), and it has therefore brought a present realm of blessing (Col. i. 13). The kingdom of God comes in several redemptive acts.

The final accomplishment of God's kingdom will include a redeemed earth. In the Old Testament this new order is sometimes described as though it were strictly continuous with the present order (Mi. iv. 1–5; Is. xi. 1–9); sometimes it arises out of a catastrophic judgment which falls on the old order (Is. xiii. 9–13, xxiv–xxvi). Once the new order is spoken of as 'new heavens and a new earth' (Is. lxv. 17, lxvi. 22), but this new creation is still earthly existence.

This expectation continues in the New Testament and is analogous to the teaching of resurrection: there is both continuity and discontinuity between the new and the old orders. Creation will share man's deliverance from the curse of sin (Rom. viii. 21). God's judgment will fall upon a sin-cursed earth and the present order will be shaken (Mt. xxiv. 29; Rev. vi. 12–17) and dissolved (2 Pet. iii. 10). Out of judgment will emerge 'new heavens and a new earth, wherein dwelleth righteousness' (2 Pet. iii. 13). On this new, redeemed earth the people of God will dwell in redeemed bodies enjoying perfect fellowship with God (Rev. xxi. 1–8). The final reconciliation is now accomplished (Col. i. 20; Eph. i. 10); the prayer is answered, 'Thy kingdom come. Thy will be done in earth, as it is in heaven' (Mt. vi. 10). See also KINGDOM OF GOD.

IX. MILLENNIALISM

The Revelation pictures the victory of God's kingdom over Satan occurring in two future stages. Satan, who has already been 'bound' by Christ (Mt. xii. 29), will be further curbed before his final destruction in the lake of fire (Rev. xx. 10). At the *parousia* he will be 'bound' and 'imprisoned' that he may not deceive the nations (Rev. xx. 1–3). Christ will reign with His resurrected saints for a thousand years (Rev. xx. 4) over the earth (Rev. v. 10, RSV; *cf.* Mt. xix. 28; 2 Tim. ii. 12. *Cf.* O. Cullmann, in *The Early Church*, 1956, pp. 112 ff.). This view is called 'millennialism' or 'pre-millennialism'. 'Chiliasm' designates the same view, but this word has usually been used of views which over-emphasize the materialistic side of the millennium.

Thus understood, the millennium is an extension of the present reign of Christ. This view is supported in 1 Cor. xv. 23–28, where there are three stages in the victory of God's kingdom: the resurrection of Christ, His *parousia*, and the *telos* or end (*cf.* C. T. Craig, *IB*, X, 237 ff.).

Christ is now Lord, enthroned at God's right hand; but His reign is not manifested to the world. The age to come will no longer be the time of Christ's reign, for He will then turn over His kingdom to the Father (1 Cor. xv. 24, 28). Strictly speaking, we might distinguish between the kingdom of Christ in the Church age and millennium and the kingdom of God in the age to come (see O. Cullmann, *op. cit.*, pp. 109 ff.), although the scriptural terminology does not support this distinction. The kingdom of Christ is the kingdom of God (Col. i. 13, iv. 11; Eph. v. 5).

'Dispensationalism' is a variant form of millennialism and ought not to be confused with it. Dispensationalism teaches that the millennium is not a stage in the redemptive work of Christ but the fulfilment of the theocratic promises to Israel. The prophecies of the restoration of Israel as a nation to her land with a literal throne, literal Davidic king, literal temple, and literal sacrificial system will be fulfilled *au pied de la lettre* (see John F. Walvoord, *The Millennial Kingdom*, 1959).

Many expositors feel that the idea of a millennium cannot be fitted into biblical eschatology. The binding of Satan in Rev. xx. 1–4 is therefore identified with that accomplished by the incarnation (Mt. xii. 28, 29), and the 'first resurrection' and the reign of the saints with Christ is either the new life in Christ (Eph. ii. 5; Jn. v. 25) or the victory of the martyred saints in heaven (*cf.* G. E. Ladd, *Crucial Questions about the Kingdom of God*, 1952, pp. 141 ff.). In either case the thousand years is a symbol of the Church age. The *parousia* will immediately usher in the consummation, final judgment, and the new heavens and earth. This view is called 'amillennialism'.

Another view holds that apocalyptic language is symbolic of God's working in history, and that the kingdom of God is to be realized in this age by the preaching of the gospel. The missionary task of the church includes the Christianizing of society (see Loraine Boettner, *The Millennium*, 1958). Because this view does not look for the *parousia* until after this 'golden age', it is called 'post-millennialism'.

X. HELL

The final destiny of the redeemed is the new earth; the final destiny of the wicked is Gehenna. This word, translated 'hell' in AV, is derived from the Heb. *gê-hinnōm*, the 'valley of Hinnom', which was situated outside Jerusalem, where children had been sacrificed by fire to Molech (2 Ch. xxviii. 3, xxxiii. 6). It became a prophetic symbol for judgment (Je. vii. 31, 32) and later for final punishment. God has power to cast both body and soul into hell (Lk. xii. 5; Mt. x. 28; *cf.* Mt. v. 29, 30). It is a place of unquenchable (Mk. ix. 43) or eternal (Mt. xviii. 8) fire. Revelation pictures the final punishment as a lake of fire and brimstone (Rev. xx. 10), which will be the fate of the beast, the devil, and the unsaved (Rev. xx. 15). That this is metaphorical language is shown by the fact that death and hades are also cast into this lake of fire. 'This is the second death' (Rev. xx. 14). Our Lord spoke of final punishment in terms of fire (Mt. xiii. 42, 50, xxv. 41) or of darkness (Mt. viii. 12, xxii. 13, xxv. 30; *cf.* 2 Pet. ii. 17; Jude 13). While both fire and darkness are symbolic of punishment, they describe a fearful reality of banishment from the presence and blessings of God in Christ (Mt. vii. 23, xxv. 41; 2 Thes. i. 9). Some scholars find an ultimate universal salvation in the New Testament (E. Stauffer, *New Testament Theology*, 1955, chapter 57), but this can be done only by overlooking these sayings about Gehenna which are found in the teachings of our Lord as well as in the Revelation.

BIBLIOGRAPHY. G. R. Beasley-Murray, *Jesus and the Future*, 1954; E. Brunner, *Eternal Hope*, 1954; O. Cullmann, 'The Return of Christ' in *The Early Church*, ed. A. J. B. Higgins, 1956; W. D. Davies and D. Daube (eds.), *The Background of the New Testament and its Eschatology*, 1956; C. H. Dodd, *The Coming of Christ*, 1951;

J. E. Fison, *The Christian Hope*, 1954; H. A. Guy, *The New Testament Doctrine of the 'Last Things'*, 1948; H. A. A. Kennedy, *St. Paul's Conception of the Last Things*, 1904; G. E. Ladd, *Crucial Questions about the Kingdom of God*, 1952; W. Manson *et al.*, *Eschatology*, 1952; H. H. Rowley, *The Relevance of Apocalyptic*, 1947 (this contains extensive bibliographies); C. Ryder Smith, *The Bible Doctrine of the Hereafter*, 1958; A. N. Wilder, *Eschatology and Ethics in the Teaching of Jesus*, 1950; G. Vos, *The Pauline Eschatology*, 1952 (re-issue); A. Hughes, *A New Heaven and a New Earth*, 1958; W. Strawson, *Jesus and the Future Life*, 1959; R. Summers, *The Life Beyond*, 1959. G.E.L.

ESDRAELON. The Greek form of the name Jezreel (*q.v.*). However, the Greek and Hebrew names really apply to two distinct but adjacent lowlands, even though in some modern works the term Jezreel is loosely extended to cover both regions. The vale of Jezreel proper is the valley that slopes down from the town of Jezreel to Beth-shan overlooking the Jordan rift-valley, with Galilee to the north and Mt. Gilboa to the south. See JEZREEL.

Esdraelon is the triangular alluvial plain bounded along its south-west side by the Carmel range from Jokneam to Ibleam and Engannim (modern Jenin), along its north side by a line from Jokneam to the hills of Nazareth, and on the east by a line thence back down to Ibleam and Engannim. On the east, Jezreel guards the entry to its own valley, while in the west the south-westernmost spur of hills from Galilee leaves only a small gap by which the river Kishon flows out into the plain of Acre after crossing the Esdraelon plain. At the foot of the north-east-facing slopes of Carmel the important towns of Jokneam, Megiddo, Taanach, and Ibleam (*qq.v.*) controlled the main passes and north–south routes through W Palestine, while these and Jezreel (town) also controlled the important route running east–west from the Jordan valley to the Mediterranean coast, the only one unimpeded by ranges of hills. Esdraelon was a marshy region, important mainly for these roads; the vale of Jezreel was agriculturally valuable as well as being strategically placed. For geographical background, see D. Baly, *Geography of the Bible*, 1957, pp. 38, 148–154. K.A.K.

ESDRAS. See APOCRYPHA, EZRA.

ESHCOL. 1. Brother of Mamre and Aner, who were 'confederates' with Abraham when in Hebron, and joined with his company in the rescue of Lot (Gn. xiv. 13–24).

2. The valley or wadi a few miles north of Hebron where the spies sent forth by Moses gathered a huge cluster (Heb. *'eškōl*) of grapes, typical of the fruitfulness of the land (Nu. xiii. 23, 24, xxxii. 9; Dt. i. 24). The vineyards in this region are still famous for the quality of their grapes. G.T.M.

ESHTAOL, ESHTAOLITES. A city on the border of Dan in the lowland to the west of Jerusalem, frequently associated with Zorah (Jos. xv. 33, RV, xix. 41). It was here that Samson, when young, was first moved by the Spirit of the Lord (Jdg. xiii. 24, 25) and at last was buried (xvi. 31). From Eshtaol and Zorah six hundred Danites set out on the adventure recorded in Jdg. xviii (1, 2, 11, 12) which ended in their settlement in Laish. The Eshtaolites are listed among the posterity of Caleb in 1 Ch. ii. 53. The name Eshtaol (*'eštā'ōl*, from the root *šā'al*, 'ask') may indicate the site of an ancient oracle. G.T.M.

ESSENES (Gk. *Essēnoi*, *Essaioi*, *Ōssaioi*, most probably from Aramaic *'āsên*, *'āsayyâ*, plural of *'āsê*, *'āsyâ*, 'healer'; *cf.* Philo's *Therapeutai*), a Jewish religious community which flourished in the 1st century BC and 1st century AD, the third of the Jewish 'philosophies' or schools of thought enumerated by Josephus (*BJ* ii. 8. 2–13; *cf. Ant.* xviii. 1. 5). Apart from Josephus, we have two accounts of them from his older Jewish contemporary Philo of Alexandria (*Quod omnis probus* 75–91; *Hypothetica ap.* Euseb., *Praep. Ev.* viii. 2), and one from the elder Pliny (*Nat. Hist.* v. 17). A later account in Hippolytus (*Refut.* ix. 20. 13–23) follows Josephus in the main, but includes some information apparently derived from independent sources.

Philo's description of the Essenes is intended to illustrate his thesis that only the truly good man is truly free. He estimates their numbers at about 4,000, and tells how they live in villages, working hard at agriculture and similar pursuits, devoting much time to the communal study of moral and religious questions, including the interpretation of the sacred books. They pay scrupulous attention to ceremonial purity, he says; they hold all their property in common, abstain from animal sacrifice, practise celibacy, keep no slaves, make provision for those of their number who are prevented from working by sickness or old age, swear no oaths, take no part in military or commercial activity, and in general cultivate all the virtues.

Pliny's account comes in the course of his description of the Dead Sea. He describes the Essenes as living on its west side, above Engedi. They have lived there for countless generations, he says, renouncing both women and money; yet their numbers have been continually maintained, because so many regularly come to join their solitary existence through sheer weariness of ordinary life. Pliny writes between AD 73 and 79, but he is probably dependent for his knowledge of the Essenes on earlier writers, such as Alexander Polyhistor (1st century BC).

The accounts in Philo and Pliny are idealized and marked by rhetorical exaggeration. Those in Josephus (when all due allowances are made for this author's tendency to modify historical truth for his private ends) strike one as being factual and based on first-hand knowledge. According to Josephus, the Essenes were to be found in all the cities of Judaea, including Jerusalem. They practised hospitality; an Essene from a distance would be treated as a brother by any fellow-Essene to whose house he came. But much of Josephus's description implies a community life such as could not be followed by city-dwellers; it is likely that the fully initiated Essenes lived in separate communities, while they had attached to their order associate members who lived in cities and followed the ordinary ways of life.

Josephus gives us a fairly detailed account of the Essenes' initiation procedure. This involved a three years' novitiate. At the end of the first year the novice (who had already worn the white habit of the order) was admitted to the ritual purification in water, but two further years had to elapse before he was admitted to share the common meal. This was evidently the token of full membership. Before finally passing from the novitiate to full membership the candidate was required to swear a succession of solemn oaths.

This account bears a general resemblance to the rules for admission to the Qumran community as detailed in 1QS, although it differs in a number of particulars; for example, 1QS lays down a novitiate of two years, not three.

The Essene's day, according to Josephus, began before sunrise with morning prayers, addressed to the sun, 'as though entreating him to rise'. Then he betook himself to his allotted task, under the direction of his overseer, and worked at it until noon. At noon the members bathed and partook of a simple meal in common; they then resumed their working clothes and continued at their appointed tasks till evening, when they assembled for another meal.

Hippolytus has nothing to say about the Essenes' morning address to the sun: according to him 'they continue in prayer from early dawn and speak no word until they have sung a hymn of praise to God'. The practice described by Josephus may have been that of the Sampsaeans, a group perhaps associated with the Essenes, who acquired their name (*cf.* Heb. *šemeš*, 'sun') from acts of homage paid to the sun as a manifestation of divinity. The term Essenes, in fact, was used at times to cover a fairly wide range of Jewish sectarian bodies that drew aside from the main stream of Jewish life. One of these, almost certainly, was the Qumran community; there may have been several more of which we know as little as we knew of the Qumran community before the discoveries of 1947 and the following years (see DEAD SEA SCROLLS, QUMRAN. See fig. 173).

Once it is established that the Qumran community was a community of Essenes (perhaps of those Essenes whom Josephus distinguishes from the rest because they did not abstain from marriage), the Qumran literature must take its place above all other accounts of the Essenes which have come down to us from antiquity because it comes from within the Essene ranks. It will then be proper to check the statements of ancient authors by the Qumran texts, and not *vice versa*.

BIBLIOGRAPHY. C. D. Ginsburg, *The Essenes*, 1864, reprinted 1955; J. B. Lightfoot, 'On Some Points connected with the Essenes' in *The Epistle to the Colossians*, 1879, pp. 348–419; D. Howlett, *The Essenes and Christianity*, 1957; H. Sérouya, *Les Esséniens*, 1959; A. Dupont-Sommer, *Essene Writings from Qumran*, E.T., 1961; H. Kosmala, *Hebräer-Essener-Christen*, 1959; G. Vermes, 'The Etymology of "Essenes"', *Revue de Qumran*, II, 1960, pp. 427–443.

F.F.B.

ESTHER. According to Est. ii. 7, Esther's Jewish name was Hadassah (Myrtle). The name Esther may be the equivalent of the Persian *stara* ('star'), though some find a link with the Babylonian goddess, Ishtar.

Esther married Ahasuerus, or Xerxes (486–465 BC). Herodotus (vii. 114, ix. 108 f.) says that Xerxes' wife was Amestris. It is unlikely that she is to be identified with Esther. Hence Esther may have been a second wife, who was a favourite for a time. This might be implied by the closing words of Est. iv. 11, though ii. 17 suggests something more than this. Alternatively, Amestris may have succeeded Esther as queen after Esther's death. The first reference in Herodotus is to Amestris's old age, and hence undated. The second, which Herodotus dates shortly after the expedition to Greece, might belong to a later date.

Although Esther was a brave woman, who risked her life to save the Jews (iv. 11–17), the Bible does not commend her encouragement of the Jews to massacre their enemies in ix. Here she was the child of her age. Amestris also was guilty of acts of brutality.

See also the following article. J.S.W.

ESTHER, BOOK OF. This book tells how Esther, a Jewess, became the wife of a Persian king, and was able to prevent the wholesale massacre of the Jewish race within the Persian Empire.

I. OUTLINE OF CONTENTS

a. i. 1–22. Ahasuerus deposes his wife, Vashti, for refusing to appear at his banquet.

b. ii. 1–18. Esther, the cousin of Mordecai, a Jew, is chosen in Vashti's place.

c. ii. 19–23. Mordecai tells Esther of a plot to kill the king.

d. iii. 1–15. Mordecai refuses to bow to Haman, the king's favourite, who thereupon plans to massacre the Jews on a fixed date.

e. iv. 1–17. Mordecai persuades Esther to intercede with the king.

f. v. 1–14. Esther invites the king and Haman to a banquet.

g. vi. 1–14. The king makes Haman honour Mordecai publicly as a reward for revealing the plot against him.

h. vii. 1–10. At a second banquet Esther reveals Haman's plan to massacre the Jews, and Haman is hanged on the gallows that he had prepared for Mordecai.

i. viii. 1–17. Since the edict for the massacre cannot be revoked, the king sends a second edict allowing the Jews to defend themselves.

j. ix. 1–19. The Jews take advantage of this to kill their enemies.

k. ix. 20–32. The deliverance is commemorated at the feast of Purim.

l. x. 1–3. Mordecai is put in a position of authority.

II. AUTHORSHIP AND DATE

The book was written some time after the death of Ahasuerus (i. 1), which would be after 465 BC if Ahasuerus is identified with Xerxes. Some Jews regarded Mordecai as the author, and the references in ix. 20, 32 could suggest this. Much of the contents may have been inserted in the annals of the king, as mentioned in x. 2 and perhaps vi. 1, and this would account for the omission of the name of God, although the reference to fasting for Esther in iv. 16 certainly implies prayer, and the doctrine of providence is stated in iv. 14.

It should be noted that the Gk. versions of Esther contain 107 extra verses, which include references to God by name. These are collected together in the Apocrypha of our English Version, and are numbered as though they followed x. 3. In fact, their order in the Greek is as follows: xi. 2–xii. 6, i. 1–iii. 13, xiii. 1–7, iii. 14–iv. 17, xiii. 8–xv. 16, v. 1–viii. 12, xvi. 1–24, viii. 13–x. 3, x. 4–xi. 1. The date given in xi. 1 is 114 BC, and could be the date when the Gk. translation or expanded version was made.

III. AUTHENTICITY

Although some, such as Pfeiffer, regard the book as entire fiction, other commentators would agree with the verdict of H. H. Rowley that the author 'seems to have had access to some good sources of information on things Persian, and the nucleus of his story may be older than his book' (*Growth of the Old Testament*, p. 155). The story as such has not been confirmed by any Persian records, and it is often supposed that it cannot be fitted into what is known of Persian history.

King Ahasuerus is usually identified with Xerxes (486–465 BC), though a few, *e.g.* J. Hoschander and A. T. Olmstead, have identified him with Artaxerxes II (404–359 BC). If he is Xerxes we have an explanation of the strange gap between the third year in i. 3 and the seventh year of ii. 16, since between 483 and 480 BC he was planning and carrying out his disastrous invasion of Greece. Herodotus (vii. 114, ix. 108 f.) gives the name of Xerxes' wife as Amestris, but we do not know from secular historians whether or not he had more than one wife. Although, according to Herodotus (iii. 84), the Persian king was supposed to choose his wife from one of the seven noble families (*cf.* Est. i. 14), rules of this kind can generally be evaded. Xerxes had no scruples about taking any women that he chose.

The author is alleged to be hopelessly in error in ii. 5, 6, when he describes Mordecai as having been taken captive in 597 BC. By this time he would have been over 120. On the principle that a translation that makes sense is preferable to one that makes nonsense, we may refer the word 'who' in verse 6 to Mordecai's great-grandfather, Kish, as the Hebrew allows us to do.

Other supposed improbabilities are largely a matter of subjective opinion. Thus, would Haman have attempted the massacre of all the Jewish race simply because one man defied him, and would the king have permitted it? And would Haman have fixed a date for the massacre so far ahead? Such criticism shows a strange ignorance of human nature. Massacres and wars have been sparked off many times through the injured pride of one or two individuals. Persian kings also were easily swayed by their favourites, and in this case Haman represents the Jews as traitors (iii. 8). Haman is depicted as a thoroughly superstitious man, and the day of the massacre was chosen because the casting of lots indicated that it would be a lucky day (iii. 7). The gallows 83 feet high (vii. 9) would be the typically extravagant display of a thwarted man in power, while the £2½ million offered as a bribe to the king in iii. 9 is hardly to be taken seriously; what the king would understand was that a large proportion of Jewish property would be put in the royal treasuries, and with Oriental politeness he replies that Haman may keep it for himself (iii. 11): both parties would understand that, so long as the king received a substantial share of the spoil, he would turn a blind eye to whatever Haman took for himself.

One strange interpretation of the book demands brief notice. This is the mythological origin postulated by Zimmern and Jensen. Esther is the goddess, Ishtar; Mordecai is Marduk; Haman is the Elamite deity, Humman; Vashti is Mashti, an Elamite goddess. The story may have concerned a conflict between Babylonian and Elamite gods. It would be strange if the Jews had made use of a polytheistic tale, or cultic ceremony, to account for a Jewish festival; even if Purim could be shown to have been originally a pagan ceremony (see PURIM), a whole new story must have been written round it, and in this story it is unlikely that the names of gods and goddesses would have been retained. It might still be true that the names of the characters in the Book of Esther have some connection with the names of gods and goddesses, since there are other examples of Jews being given extra names that probably contain the names of some god or goddess, *e.g.* Dn. i. 7; Ezr. i. 8. Moreover there is another Mordecai mentioned in Ezr. ii. 2. Esther is said to be a second name in ii. 7. (See ESTHER, HAMAN, MORDECAI.)

BIBLIOGRAPHY. L. B. Paton, *Esther*, *ICC*, 1908; J. Hoschander, *The Book of Esther in the*

Light of History, 1923; B. W. Anderson, *The Book of Esther*, Introduction and Exegesis, in *IB*, III, 1951. J.S.W.

ETAM. 1. A place in the hill-country of Judah, rebuilt by Rehoboam (2 Ch. xi. 6), probably referred to in 1 Ch. iv. 3, and in the LXX of Jos. xv. 59 (*Aitan*). The site is usually identified with modern Khirbet el-Ḫoḫ, some 6½ miles SSW of Jerusalem. **2.** A village in the territory of Simeon (1 Ch. iv. 32). The site is unknown, though some scholars would equate the place with (1) above. **3.** The cave (*s*e*'îp̄ sela'*, 'cleft of rock') where Samson took refuge from the Philistines (Jdg. xv. 8, 11). The site is unknown, but must be in W Judah.

BIBLIOGRAPHY. L. Köhler and W. Baumgartner, *Lexicon in Veteris Testamenti Libros*, 1953, p. 699; F. M. Abel, *Géographie de la Palestine*, II, 1938, p. 321. T.C.M.

ETERNAL LIFE. See ESCHATOLOGY.

ETERNITY. See TIME.

ETHAM. Camp of the Israelites somewhere on the isthmus of Suez (Ex. xiii. 20; Nu. xxxiii. 6, 7), about whose precise location scholars differ. Müller suggested a connection with the name of the Egyp. god Atum; Naville proposed Edom; Clédat, Gauthier, Bourdon, Lagrange, Abel, and Montet would connect it with the Old Egyp. word for 'fort' (*ḫtm*), a name which was given to several places; but none of these suggestions seem very likely. The Old Egyp. *ḫtm* seems rather to designate the frontier-city of Sile. (See ENCAMPMENT BY THE SEA.) C.D.W.

ETHAN (Heb. *'êṯān*, 'enduring', 'ancient'). A wise man in the time of Solomon, known as 'the Ezrahite', of the line of Judah, referred to in 1 Ki. iv. 31, in the title of Ps. lxxxix, and perhaps in 1 Ch. ii. 6, if 'Zerah' is regarded as a form of 'Ezrah'.

Two other men called Ethan are mentioned briefly—in 1 Ch. vi. 42 (perhaps identical with Jeduthun, *q.v.*), and 1 Ch. vi. 44, xv. 17.

J.D.D.

ETHICS, BIBLICAL. The term 'ethics' is derived from the Gk. word *ethos* or *ēthos*. In English the word 'manners' has been used to denote conduct or practice and this use corresponds to the meaning of the Gk. term in 1 Cor. xv. 33, 'good manners' (*ēthē chrēsta*). Ethics refers, therefore, to the manner of life or of conduct. In the New Testament the term used to denote manner of life is, more characteristically, *anastrophē* (see CONVERSATION) and its corresponding verb (*cf.* 2 Pet. iii. 11). Biblical ethics is concerned with the manner of life which the Bible prescribes and approves. According to Scripture, however, conduct or 'manners' can never be dissociated from the dispositional complex which comes to expression in observable behaviour. The ethic which the Bible requires is concerned with the heart of man, for 'out of it are the issues of life', and as a man 'thinketh in his heart, so is he' (*cf.* Pr. iv. 23, xxiii. 7; Mk. vii. 18–21; Lk. xvi. 15; Heb. iv. 12). The commandments of God are often in terms of the overt action required or prohibited. But we are not to suppose that these commands have respect merely to action (*cf.* Mt. v. 28; Rom. xiii. 9, 10).

I. THE UNITY

It could easily be averred that there is no basic unity to the ethic which the Bible prescribes and which is exemplified in the various eras of biblical history. In dealing with this question several observations and distinctions have to be made. (*a*) We must make allowance for the fact and significance of progressive revelation. God progressively revealed His will to men. Hence in the earlier periods of the history of revelation the rule of conduct was not as fully revealed as it was in later periods. Revelation, as it respects this world's history, has reached its finale in the New Testament, focused particularly in the coming and accomplishment of Christ. We have in these last days the fulness of revelation and of the grace to bring the revelation of God's will to its richest fruitage. To whom so much is given, of them more is required. This explains why certain practices of the saints in the Old Testament, clearly inconsistent with New Testament ethics, were tolerated and not visited with ecclesiastical and civil penalties in the Old Testament period. (*b*) The actual practice of the saints is not to be equated with the biblical ethic; the latter refers to what God requires, not to the shortcomings or attainments of men. (*c*) The fall of man materially affected the content of the ethic governing man's conduct. New provisions were necessary to deal with the radically altered situation which sin created. For example, by reason of sin and the resulting shame clothing is an institution that would have no necessary relevance in a sinless state (*cf.* Gn. ii. 25, iii. 21). And the various penal sanctions arose from the presence of sin. The unity of the biblical ethic takes full account of the exigencies created by sin and guilt. (*d*) We must distinguish between permission and sanction, tolerance and approval when we are dealing with practices prevalent in the Old Testament periods. Our Lord clearly enunciates this distinction in connection with the divorce permitted by Moses (Dt. xxiv. 1–4). Moses, he says, permitted divorce, 'but from the beginning it was not so' (Mt. xix. 8). The original ordinance of Gn. ii. 24, appealed to by Jesus (Mt. xix. 5), did not provide for such divorce, and we are not by any means to infer that the institution of Gn. ii. 24 had been suspended or abrogated. This passage likewise bears upon the question of polygamy, and the same distinction must be applied. (*e*) Redemption was brought to bear upon the history of mankind. Just as the situation created by sin required new regulative provisions, so redemption introduces institutions deeply affecting human conduct which would have no relevance in a sinless state.

There is, however, a unity characterizing the biblical ethic throughout all the periods of human history. The creation ordinances are clearly set forth in Gn. i and ii. These are the ordinances of procreation, of replenishing the earth, of subduing it, of exercising dominion (Gn. i. 28), of the sabbath (Gn. ii. 2, 3), of labour (Gn. ii. 15), of marriage, and of monogamy (Gn. ii. 23, 24). It is obvious that the prohibition to eat of the tree of the knowledge of good and evil, however important for Adam and Eve and for the whole human race, is in a different category; it could have relevance only in the original state of integrity and may be distinguished as the probation ordinance. When we examine these creation ordinances we see how relevant they are to man's basic instincts and to the interests that lay closest to his heart, how inclusive they are of the occupations which would have engaged man's thought and action, and how they complement and condition one another. They touch upon every area of life and behaviour. We might think that the change caused by the entrance of sin and its resulting miseries would require the abrogation or at least modification of these ordinances. But this is not the case. The sanctity of these ordinances is preserved, and their abiding relevance and obligation are plainly established in the subsequent history of revelation (*cf.* Gn. iii. 16, 19, iv. 1, 2, 17, 25, v. 1–3, ix. 7, xi. 1–8). The Ten Commandments furnish the core of the biblical ethic. But it can readily be seen how intimate are the points of contact between the Decalogue and the creation ordinances. While conditions and circumstances have been revolutionized by sin, the basic structure of this earth and of man's life in it has not been destroyed.

This unity we should expect to be the case on general principles. Man was created in the image of God. The fundamental norm regulative of man's obligation must, therefore, be likeness to God in those respects that are appropriate to man's creaturehood. The law of God for man is simply God's perfection coming to expression for the regulation of thought and conduct consonant with that perfection. Since God does not change, and since the obligation to God cannot be abrogated, any radical change in the ethical imperative is inconceivable.

II. THE CONTENT

The content of the biblical ethic is the sum-total of the revelatory data set forth in the Scripture bearing upon human behaviour. This sum-total comprises great variety. It includes the record of wrong-doing and the divine disapproval thereupon, as well as the commandments and the record of well-doing with the attendant approbation. The manifoldness of the biblical witness is, therefore, apparent, and even cursory exposition would require volumes. This complexity proceeds from the complexity of human life and the numberless variety of the situations in which men find themselves. The grandeur of the biblical revelation is that by its richness and fulness it is adequate to every situation in which we are placed. Scripture is directed 'to the instruction which is in righteousness, that the man of God may be perfect, thoroughly furnished unto every good work' (see 2 Tim. iii. 16 f.).

But though there is this manifold diversity, it is equally clear that the Bible provides us with a summary of what is normative for thought, life, and behaviour. The biblical witness, as it bears on the complexity of life and on the wide range of divine obligation, organizes itself around a central core of ethical principles. These are the Ten Commandments. As promulgated at Sinai, they were the concrete and practical form of enunciating principles which did not then for the first time come to have relevance. We have explicit evidence of their obligation and sanction prior to Sinai (*cf.* Gn. ii. 2, 3; Ex. xvi. 22, 23; Gn. iv. 10–12, 23, 24, vi. 11, ix. 5, 6, xxvi. 9, 10, xxxix. 9). As they did not begin to have relevance at Sinai, so they did not cease to have relevance when the Mosaic economy passed away. Our Lord Himself when He promulgated the law of His kingdom said, 'Think not that I am come to destroy the law, or the prophets' (Mt. v. 17), and in the subsequent discourse indicates how this statement bears upon the Decalogue. He proceeds to interpret and apply several of these commandments and vindicates their sanctity in the kingdom which He came to establish (Mt. v. 21–26, 27, 28, 33–37). Paul likewise, when he is dealing with the practical details of the believer's obligation, illustrates the law that love fulfils by quoting five of these commandments (Rom. xiii. 9). And James, characteristically jealous for the good works which are the fruits and proofs of faith and insistent upon the necessity of having regard for the law of God in its entirety, says: 'For whosoever shall keep the whole law, and yet offend in one point, he is guilty of all. For he that said, Do not commit adultery, said also, Do not kill' (Jas. ii. 10, 11). We have in these commandments an index to what James meant by the law of liberty as the criterion of good and the norm of judgment (*cf.* ii. 12).

The Ten Commandments are concerned with the most fundamental of our relationships, first to God and then to our fellow-men. No summary could be more inclusive. They enunciate the basic sanctities governing belief, worship, and life—the sanctity of God's being, of His worship, of His name, of His day as the day of rest and worship, the sanctity of parental honour, of life, of sex, of property, of truth, and of contentment with our lot. That these commandments govern behaviour in the sphere of redemption is inscribed on the occasion of their promulgation at Sinai. Their sanction is enforced by their preface: 'I am the Lord thy God, which have brought thee out of the land of Egypt, out of the house of bondage' (Ex. xx. 2). How much greater the enforcement derived from the redemption of which the Exodus was but the type.

III. THE MOTIVE

Confusion has often arisen with reference to the word of Christ that upon two commandments hang all the law and the prophets (Mt. xxii. 37–40; Mk. xii. 30, 31; Lk. x. 27; *cf.* Dt. vi. 5) and the word of Paul that 'love is the fulfilling of the law' (Rom. xiii. 10). Such texts have been interpreted to mean that in the Christian ethic love takes the place of law. There must be no gainsaying of Jesus' words or of Paul's statement. The place of love must be fully appreciated. But love must not be equated with law nor construed as dispensing with it.

In the words of Jesus and of Paul there is an obvious distinction between love and the law that hangs on it and between love and the law which it fulfils. Love is not itself the law. Hence there is content to the law that is not defined by love itself. And Paul makes clear what he means by law as distinct from love by quoting in the preceding context several precepts of the Decalogue (Rom. xiii. 9). Thus we may not speak of the law of love if we mean that love is itself the law.

Love is the fulfilment of the law because it constrains to compliance with and performance of that which the law prescribes. Love is both emotive and motive. Since love is emotive, it creates affinity with and affection for the object. The fulfilment which it constrains is, therefore, not coerced or unwilling compliance but that of cheerful and willing obedience. Apart from this constraining and impelling love, there is no fulfilment of the law. Fulfilment is obedience, and obedience always implies the hearty consent of heart and will. When love is all-pervasive, then the fulfilment of the law is complete. This is the witness of Scripture throughout. The supreme example is our Lord (*cf.* Ps. xl. 8; Jn. iv. 34). Psalmist and apostle confess the same (Ps. cxix. 97; Rom. vii. 22).

Sin is enmity against God, and enmity is the opposite of love. Since all have sinned, only by the forces of redemption can this love be generated in the heart of man. It is from the flame of God's love manifested in the gift of His Son that love in our hearts can be ignited. This is the import of the Scripture, 'We love him, because he first loved us' (1 Jn. iv. 19), and the preceding verses (7–18) unfold the sequence. Herein lies the motive power of love. When the love of God towards us is shed abroad in our hearts (*cf.* Rom. v. 5), then love to Him captivates our hearts and impels to godliness. The constraints of love and mercy only the forgiven know.

IV. THE PRINCIPLE

The governing principle of ethics may be stated in various ways.

a. It is likeness to God. The ultimate goal of the ethical process is conformity to the image of God's Son (Rom. viii. 29; 2 Cor. iii. 18; Phil. iii. 21). If this is the goal it must constantly be regulative in all behaviour. Our Lord's example is for this reason, as well as others, supremely normative. Jesus was holy, harmless, undefiled, and separate from sinners, and in no other way could we be brought face to face with the demands of holiness and truth than as His example confronts us. Even the unique and transcendent accomplishments of His commitment are adduced as furnishing us with an example that we should follow in His steps (*cf.* Mt. xx. 25–28; Mk. x. 42–45; Phil. ii. 6–8; 1 Pet. ii. 21–24), not because we follow Him in the discharge of these unique undertakings but because His unreserved devotion to the Father's will in His distinctive task is to be the example for us in the vocation that is ours. This conformity or likeness to Christ is, however, also conformity to God's image. Christ is the image of God. This is why likeness to the Father is presented as the norm of the believer's behaviour. This is Jesus' own summation of the law of His kingdom: 'Be ye therefore perfect, even as your Father which is in heaven is perfect' (Mt. v. 48). As creatures made in God's image we are bound to nothing less than perfection conformable to the Father's own as the norm and goal of ethical demand. It is likeness to the Father that John has in mind when he says: 'every man that hath this hope in him purifieth himself, even as he is pure' (1 Jn. iii. 3).

b. It is obedience to God's commandments. This principle was written on man's relation to God from the beginning; the prohibition of Eden (Gn. ii. 17) epitomized it; the interrogation of Adam after the fall placed it in sharp focus (Gn. iii. 11); the curse upon Adam registered its sanction (Gn. iii. 17). Redemptive revelation takes the form of covenant administration, and obeying God's voice and precept is the reciprocal response (*cf.* Gn. xvii. 10; Ex. xix. 5, xx. 1–17, xxiv. 7). Our Lord Himself confirmed this same principle when He said, 'If ye love me, keep my commandments' (Jn. xiv. 15). And John, who knew His Lord's will, reiterated the same: 'And hereby we do know that we know him, if we keep his commandments' (1 Jn. ii. 3; *cf.* Rom. vi. 16, 17; 2 Cor. x. 5; Heb. v. 9).

c. It is to be well-pleasing to God. No consideration looms higher in the thought of the sanctified than the necessity of being and doing what meets with God's approval. Enoch walked with God, and the tribute accorded to him was that he was well-pleasing to God (Heb. xi. 5). Paul's practical application of the teaching of his major Epistle begins with the enunciation of this canon (Rom. xii. 1, 2). He defends his own behaviour by appeal to it as the directing principle of his life (1 Thes. ii. 4; *cf.* Gal. i. 10; 1 Thes. iv. 1). The lordship of Christ is bound up with this principle. Christ died and rose again 'that he might be Lord both of the dead and living' (Rom. xiv. 9; *cf.* Phil. ii. 9–11). The service of Christ as Lord is the guarantee of our being acceptable to God (Rom. xiv. 18). Benediction can implore no greater benefit than to be made perfect in every good work to do God's will, and this is defined as the 'working in (us) that which is well-pleasing in his sight through Jesus Christ' (Heb. xiii. 21).

From whatever angle this question is viewed, it is reducible to the insistence that jealousy for compliance with and conformity to the revealed will of God is the governing principle of life set forth in Scripture.

V. THE DYNAMIC

The total impotence of fallen human nature is emblazoned on the testimony of the Bible. 'They that are in the flesh cannot please God' (Rom. viii. 8). The only hope of realizing the demands of the biblical ethic resides in the provisions of redemption, and only those brought within the ambit of redemption are the partakers of these provisions. Many factors are comprised in this provision. A few call for particular attention.

a. It is the relation a believer sustains to the death and resurrection of Christ that ensures the newness of life which the biblical ethic demands. The believer died with Christ and rose with Him to newness of life (*cf.* Rom. vi. 1–10; 2 Cor. v. 14, 15; Eph. ii. 1–7; Col. iii. 1–4; 1 Pet. iv. 1–4). There is definitive breach with sin in its defilement and power involved in this union, and there is definitive commitment to righteousness and holiness (*cf.* Rom. vi. 14–18). But the virtue derived from Christ's death and resurrection is abiding; it resides in Christ to whom believers are united. It is this virtue, emanating from Christ as the risen and ascended Lord, that is the continuous dynamic in bringing ethical demand to fruitful result. Abiding communion with Christ and communication from Him are the guarantees of willing and doing for God's good pleasure.

b. The resurrection of Christ is closely related to the work of the Holy Spirit (*cf.* Jn. xiv. 16, 17, 26, xv. 26, xvi. 7; Acts ii. 32, 33). Christ by the resurrection is made life-giving Spirit (1 Cor. xv. 45), and He is the Lord of the Spirit (2 Cor. iii. 18). The dynamic of the biblical ethic is, therefore, the Holy Spirit as the Spirit of Christ. The newness of life which is after the pattern of Jesus' resurrection is the 'newness of the Spirit' (see Rom. vii. 6). The sons of God are led of the Spirit (Rom. viii. 14), they walk by the Spirit (Gal. v. 16, 25), their virtues are the fruit of the Spirit (Gal. v. 22–24), the love which is the fulfilment of the law is the love of the Spirit (Rom. xv. 30). The believer is indwelt and controlled by the Spirit (*cf.* 1 Cor. ii. 15) and, since the Holy Spirit is the Spirit of truth (Jn. xiv. 17; 1 Jn. v. 6) and of love, His abiding presence brings truth to realization and love to effective exercise.

c. As the illumination, leading, and power of the Holy Spirit are brought to bear upon the consciousness of the believer, no reaction affects ethical behaviour more deeply than the fear of God. The commandment to love the Lord with all the heart and soul and mind is the first and great commandment (Mt. xxii. 37, 38). It is first and greatest because God is great. And the greatness of God is His majesty, reflected in the human consciousness in reverential awe. This fear of God is the soul of godliness, and consists in the profound apprehension of His majesty, the all-pervasive sense of His presence, and the constant awareness that in every detail of life His good pleasure is our paramount concern. This is the constraining force, and love is mere sentiment except as it is conditioned by the sense of God's greatness. Love must be informed by truth, and the fear of God is the beginning of knowledge and wisdom (Ps. cxi. 10; Pr. i. 7, ix. 10).

Of the ethic which Scripture demands and approves, faith in God is the fountain, love to God the impelling motive, the law of God the directing principle, and the glory of God the governing aim. These, in brief, are the criteria, and they interpenetrate one another.

BIBLIOGRAPHY. P. Fairbairn, *The Revelation of Law in Scripture*, 1957; J. H. Thornwell, *Discourses on Truth, Collected Writings*, II, 1886; R. S. Candlish, *The Christian's Sacrifice and Service of Praise*, 1867; C. A. A. Scott, *New Testament Ethics*, 1930; C. F. H. Henry, *Christian Personal Ethics*, 1957; J. Murray, *Principles of Conduct*, 1957; C. A. Pierce, *Conscience in the New Testament*, 1955; H. Martensen, *Christian Ethics*, 1882, 1888; C. B. Eavey, *Practical Christian Ethics*, 1959; D. Bonhoeffer, *Ethics*, 1955; E. Brunner, *The Divine Imperative*, 1937; A. Nygren, *Agape and Eros*, 1953; S. Cave, *The Christian Way*, 1949; C. H. Dodd, *Gospel and Law*, 1951; W. Elert, *The Christian Ethos*, 1957; T. W. Manson, *Ethics and the Gospel*, 1960; K. E. Kirk, *Conscience and its Problems*, 1948. J.M.

ETHIOPIA. Settled by the descendants of Cush (*q.v.*; Gn. x. 6), biblical Ethiopia (Gk. *Aithiōps*, 'burnt face', *cf.* Je. xiii. 23) is part of the kingdom of Nubia stretching from Aswan (see SEVENEH) southward to the junction of the Nile near modern Khartoum. Invaded in prehistoric times by Hamites from Arabia and Asia, Ethiopia was dominated by Egypt for nearly 500 years beginning with Dynasty XVIII (*c.* 1500 BC) and was governed by a viceroy ('King's Son of Kush') who ruled the African Empire, controlled the army in Africa, and managed the Nubian gold mines.

During the 9th century the Ethiopians, whose capital was Napata near the fourth cataract, engaged in at least one foray into Palestine, only to suffer defeat at Asa's hand (2 Ch. xiv. 9–15). Ethiopia's heyday began about 720 BC when Pi-ankhi took advantage of Egypt's internal strife and became the first conqueror of that land in a millennium. For about sixty years Ethiopian rulers (Dynasty XXV) controlled the Nile Valley. One of them, Tirhakah, seems to have been Hezekiah's ally and attempted to forestall Sennacherib's invasion (2 Ki. xix. 9; Is. xxxvii. 9; J. Bright, *History of Israel*, 1959, pp. 282 ff., discusses the chronological problems in this narrative). Na. iii. 9 alludes to the glory of this period: 'Ethiopia was her (Egypt's) strength.'

Invasions by Esarhaddon and Ashurbanipal reduced the Ethiopian–Egyptian kingdom to tributary status; the destruction of Thebes (*c.* 663 BC; Na. iii. 8–10) brought a total eclipse, fulfilling Isaiah's prophetic symbolism (xx. 2–6).

Ethiopian troops fought vainly in Pharaoh-Necho's army at Carchemish (605 BC; Je. xlvi. 9). Cambyses' conquest of Egypt brought Ethiopia under Persian sway; Est. i. 1, viii. 9 name Ethiopia as the most remote Persian province to the south-west, while biblical writers sometimes use her to symbolize the unlimited extent of God's sovereignty (Ps. lxxxvii. 4; Ezk. xxx. 4 ff.; Am. ix. 7; Zp. ii. 12). 'Beyond the rivers of Ethiopia' (Is. xviii. 1; Zp. iii. 10) may refer to N Abyssinia, where Jewish colonists had apparently settled along with other Semites from S Arabia. The Chronicler is cognizant of this close relationship between Ethiopia and S Arabia (2 Ch. xxi. 16).

In Acts viii. 27 Ethiopia refers to the Nilotic kingdom of Candace, who ruled at Meroë, where the capital had been moved during the Persian period. Modern Ethiopians (Abyssinians) have appropriated biblical references to Ethiopia and consider the Ethiopian eunuch's (*q.v.*) conversion to be a fulfilment of Ps. lxviii. 31.

BIBLIOGRAPHY. E. A. W. Budge, *History of Ethiopia*, 1928; E. Ullendorff, *The Ethiopians*, 1960; J. Wilson, *The Burden of Egypt*, 1951.

D.A.H.

ETHIOPIAN EUNUCH. A high official (*dynastēs*), royal treasurer in the court of Ethiopia's Queen Candace (*q.v.*), converted under Philip's ministry (Acts viii. 26–40). It was not unusual in antiquity for eunuchs, who were customarily harem attendants, to rise to positions of influence. (See EUNUCH.)

Barred from active participation in the Jewish rites by his race and his emasculation (Dt. xxiii. 1), he may have been a proselyte of the gate. His acquaintance with Judaism and the Old Testament (the quotation from Is. liii seems to be from the LXX) is not completely unexpected in light of Jewish settlements in Upper Egypt and the considerable impact made by Jewish life and thought on the Ethiopians. (See ETHIOPIA.) His zeal in studying the Scriptures, his ready reception of the gospel and baptism mark him as one of the outstanding converts in Acts, even if his confession (Acts viii. 37) is not supported in the better MSS. Ethiopian tradition claims him as his country's first evangelist.

D.A.H.

ETHIOPIAN WOMAN. Married by Moses, whom Aaron and Miriam then criticized (Nu. xii. 1). As the last mention of Zipporah is just after the defeat of Amalek (Ex. xvii) when Jethro returned her to Moses (Ex. xviii), it is possible that she subsequently died, Moses then taking this 'Cushite woman' as his second wife, unless Moses then had two wives. 'Cushite' is usually taken as 'Ethiopian' (*cf.* CUSH, ETHIOPIA); if so, she probably left Egypt among the Israelites and their sympathizers. It is also, perhaps, possible to derive 'Cushite' from Kushu and Heb. Cushan, associated with Midian (Hab. iii. 7); if so, this woman might be of allied stock to Jethro and Zipporah.

K.A.K.

ETHNARCH (AV 'governor', 2 Cor. xi. 32). An officer in charge of Damascus with a garrison under Aretas IV, king of Arabia Petraea (9 BC–AD 40), who was encouraged by the Jews to arrest Paul after his conversion (*cf.* Acts ix. 24, 25). Damascus in 64 BC became part of the Roman province of Syria. At this time (*c.* AD 33) it was temporarily under Aretas, perhaps as the gift of Caligula.

The title is used by Josephus for subordinate rulers, particularly of peoples under foreign control, *e.g.* the Jews in Alexandria (*Ant.* xiv. 7. 2); *cf.* Hohlwein, *L'Égypte Romaine*, p. 207.

B.F.H.

EUCHARIST. See LORD'S SUPPER.

EUNICE. Timothy's mother, a woman of notable faith (2 Tim. i. 5). She was Jewish (Acts xvi. 1) and pious, for Timothy's biblical instruction had begun early (2 Tim. iii. 15), but her husband was a Gentile and her son uncircumcised (Acts xvi. 3). In view of Jewish intermarriage with leading Phrygian families (Ramsay, *BRD*, p. 357; *cf. CBP*, II, pp. 667 ff.), such things may represent her family's social climbing, not personal declension. Some Latin MSS of Acts xvi. 1, and Origen in Rom. xvi. 21, call her a widow, and *hypērchen* in Acts xvi. 3 might support this. She lived at Derbe or Lystra: linguistically a case can be made for either (*cf. BC*, iv, pp. 184, 254). Her name is Greek, and does not seem common.

It is sometimes suggested that Paul refers to Jewish faith, but the most natural interpretation of 2 Tim. i. 5 (and of Acts xvi. 1) is that Christian faith 'dwelt' (aorist, perhaps alluding to the event of conversion, doubtless in Paul's first missionary journey) 'first' in Lois (*q.v.*) and herself (*i.e.* antecedent to Timothy's conversion).

A.F.W.

EUNUCH (Heb. *sārîs*). The derivation of the Old Testament word is uncertain, but is thought to be derived from an Assyr. term meaning, 'He who is head (to the king)'. (So Jensen (*ZA*, VII, 1892, 174 A.1), and Zimmern (*ZDMG*, LIII, 1899, 116 A.2); accepted by S. R. Driver and L. Koehler in their lexicons; see further note by the latter in his *Supplement*, p. 219.) The primary meaning is 'court officer'. In Hebrew a secondary meaning is found, namely, a 'castrate' or 'eunuch'. From Herodotus we learn that 'in eastern countries eunuchs are valued as being specially trustworthy in every way' (viii. 105, tr. Selingcourt). Such persons were frequently employed by eastern rulers as officers of the household. Hence, in the Old Testament it is sometimes difficult to know which of the two meanings is intended or whether both are implied. Potiphar (Gn. xxxix. 1), who was married (verse 7), is called a *sārîs* (LXX *eunouchos*): the meaning 'court officer' may be best here. In Is. lvi. 3 the meaning 'castrate' is obvious. In Ne. i. 11, 'I was the king's cupbearer', some copies of the LXX have *eunouchos*; but this is probably a slip for *oinochoos*, as Rahlfs in *Septuaginta* (I, p. 923) has seen. The 'castrate' was to be excluded from the assembly of the Lord (Dt. xxiii. 1). There is no necessity to assume, as Josephus seems to do (*Ant.* x. 10. 1), that Daniel and his companions were 'castrates', for they were 'without blemish' (see Dn. i. 4).

In the New Testament the word *eunouchos* is used, and may be derived from *eunēn echō* ('to keep the bed'). Like its counterpart *sārîs*, it need not denote strictly a castrate. In Acts viii. 27 both meanings may be intended; in Mt. xix. 12 the meaning 'castrate' is beyond doubt. In this last passage three classes of eunuch are mentioned, namely, born eunuchs, man-made eunuchs, and spiritual eunuchs. The last class includes all those who have sacrificed legitimate, natural desires for the sake of the kingdom of heaven. Origen, misinterpreting in a literal sense the above passage, mutilated himself.

Judaism knew only two classes of eunuch: man-made (*sārîs 'āḏām*) and natural (*sārîs ḥammâ*), thus the Mishnah (*Zab.* ii. 1). This last term *sārîs ḥammâ* or 'eunuch of the sun' is explained by Jastrow, *Dictionary of Babylonian Talmud, etc.*, I, p. 476, to mean 'a eunuch from the time of seeing the sun', in other words, a eunuch who is born so. See CHAMBERLAIN.

R.J.A.S.

EUODIA. This RV rendering is to be preferred to the AV's 'Euodias' (Phil. iv. 2), for the reference is to a woman rather than a man. Paul beseeches her and Syntyche to be reconciled. Probably, as Lightfoot suggests, they were deaconesses at Philippi. J.D.D.

EUPHRATES. The largest river in W Asia, and on this account generally referred to as *hannāhār*, 'the river', in the Old Testament (*e.g.* Dt. xi. 24). It is sometimes mentioned by name, however, the Heb. form being *p[e]rāṯ* (*e.g.* Gn. ii. 14, xv. 18) derived from Akkadian *purattu*, which represents Sumerian *buranun*, and the New Testament form *Euphratēs* (Rev. ix. 14, xvi. 12). The Euphrates takes its source in two main affluents in E Turkey, the Murad-Su, which rises near Lake Van, and the Kara-Su, which rises near Erzerum, and runs, joined only by the Ḫâbûr (see HABOR), for over 1,200 miles to the Persian Gulf. From low water in September it rises by degrees throughout the winter to some 8 feet higher by May, and then declines again until September, thus enjoying a milder régime than the Tigris (*q.v.*). In the alluvial plain of Babylonia (see MESOPOTAMIA) its course has shifted to the west since ancient times, when most of the important cities, now some miles to the east of it, lay on or near its banks. This is illustrated by the fact that the Sumerians wrote its name ideographically as 'river of Sippar', a city whose ruins lie today some 4 miles to the east (see SEPHARVAIM). In addition to the many important cities, including Babylon, which lay on its banks in the southern plain, the city of Mari (*q.v.*) was situated on its middle course, not far from the junction with the Ḫâbûr, and the strategic crossing-place from N Mesopotamia to N Syria was commanded by the fortress city of Carchemish (*q.v.*).

BIBLIOGRAPHY. S. A. Pallis, *The Antiquity of Iraq*, 1956, pp. 4–7. T.C.M.

EURAQUILO. See EUROCLYDON.

EUROCLYDON (RV 'Euraquilo') is the name given to the typhonic storm described at Paul's shipwreck (Acts xxvii. 14). The latter is probably a more accurate rendering, derived from 'Euros' the south-east or east wind and 'Aquilo' the north-east wind, fitly describing the source of the wind as ENE. The term used today by the Maltese sailors is the 'gregale', a southerly wind which shifts to become a violent northerly wind with accompanying rain squalls, common in the south central Mediterranean in the cool season. Five types of gregale have been recognized by meteorologists, all associated with the occurrence of depressions over Libya or the Gulf of Gabes, inducing a strong air-flow from Greece. The intensity of the storm is related to the steepness of the barometric gradient.

BIBLIOGRAPHY. J. Smith, *Voyage and Shipwreck of St. Paul*[4], 1880, pp. 287–291. J.M.H.

EUTYCHUS ('Lucky', a common Greek name). A young man from Troas who fell from an upstairs window-seat during Paul's protracted nocturnal address there (Acts xx. 7–12). H. J. Cadbury (*Book of Acts in History*, pp. 8 ff.) points out a similar fatal accident in *Oxyrhynchus Papyri*, III. 475. Luke's words suggest an increasing and eventually irresistible drowsiness, perhaps—since verse 8 seems related to the incident—induced by the numerous lamps or, less probably, in spite of them.

The miraculous nature of the outcome has been questioned, Paul's words in verse 10 being applied to diagnosis, not healing. However, verse 9 shows that Luke was himself sure that Eutychus died. 'His life' would then be 'in him' from the moment of Paul's embrace (*cf.* 2 Ki. iv. 34). On Paul's departure next morning, Eutychus was recovered (verse 12: according to the Western Text he joined the farewell party). Seen as an eye-witness account by Luke, the story is vivid and the broken sequence intelligible. The assumption that 'a current anecdote had come to be applied to Paul, that Luke found it in this form and introduced it into his narrative' (Dibelius) creates obscurities.

BIBLIOGRAPHY. W. M. Ramsay, *St. Paul the Traveller and Roman Citizen*, pp. 290 f.; M. Dibelius, *Studies in the Acts of the Apostles*, E.T., 1956, pp. 17 ff. A.F.W.

EVANGELIST. The word translated in the New Testament 'evangelist' is a noun from the verb *euangelizomai* 'to announce the good news', and usually translated in our English Bibles as 'preach the gospel'. (The New Testament term echoes Heb. *m*^{e}*ḇaśśēr*, *m*^{e}*ḇaśśereṯ*, in Is. xl. 9, lii. 7.) The verb is very common in the New Testament, and is applied to God (Gal. iii. 8), to our Lord (Lk. xx. 1), and to ordinary church members (Acts viii. 4), as well as to apostles on their missionary journeys. The noun 'evangelist' occurs three times only in the New Testament. Timothy (2 Tim. iv. 5) is exhorted by Paul to do the work of an evangelist; that is to say, make known the facts of the gospel. Timothy had accompanied the apostle on his missionary journeys. But it is plain from the injunctions given to him in the two letters addressed to him that his work when the apostle wrote was very largely local and pastoral. That he is enjoined to do the work of an evangelist shows that a man who was an evangelist could also be a pastor and teacher.

In Acts xxi. 8 Philip is described as 'the evangelist'. Philip had been chosen as one of the Seven in Acts vi, and after the persecution of Stephen he was prominent in preaching the gospel in unevangelized parts (*e.g.* Acts viii. 5, 12, 35, 40). Though an evangelist, he was not included among the apostles (Acts viii. 14). A similar distinction is made between Timothy and the apostles in 2 Cor. i. 1 and Col. i. 1. It will be seen, then, that though apostles were evangelists, not all evangelists were apostles. This distinction is confirmed in Eph. iv. 11, where the office of 'evangelist' is mentioned after 'apostle' and 'prophet', and before 'pastor' and 'teacher'. From this passage it is plain that the gift of evangelist was a distinct gift within the Christian Church; and although all Christians doubtless performed this sacred task, as opportunity was given to them, there were some who were pre-eminently called and endowed by the Holy Spirit for this task.

Later in the history of the Church the term 'evangelist' was used for a writer of one of the four Gospels. D.B.K.

EVE. The first woman, wife of Adam (*q.v.*), and mother of Cain, Abel, and Seth (Gn. iv. 1, 2, 25). When He had made Adam, God resolved to provide 'an help meet for him' (*'ēzer k*^{e}*neḡdô*, Gn. ii. 18, 20, literally 'a helper as in front of him', *i.e.* 'a helper corresponding to him'), so He caused him to sleep and, taking one of his ribs (*ṣēlā'*, Gn. ii. 21), made (*bānâ*, Gn. ii. 22, a word normally meaning 'to build') it into a woman (*l*^{e}*'iššâ*). See CREATION. Adam, recognizing his close relationship, declared that she should be called 'Woman (*'iššâ*), because she was taken out of (*min*; *cf.* 1 Cor. xi. 8, *ek*) Man (*'îš*)' (Gn. ii. 23). Some scholars consider that *'îš* and *'iššâ* are etymologically distinct, but this need not be material, as it is possible that the account was originally in a language other than Hebrew, the formal similarity between the words being all that was necessary, as indeed is the case with EVV 'man' and '*wo*man'.

Eve was the instrument of the serpent in causing Adam to eat the forbidden fruit (see FALL), and as a result God condemned her to bear children in pain, and to be ruled over (*māšal b*^{e}) by Adam (Gn. iii. 16). Adam then called her 'Eve (*ḥawwâ*, Gn. iii. 20); because she was the mother of all living (*ḥay*)'. Many theories have been put forward as to the name *ḥawwâ*. Some would see it as an archaic form of *ḥayyâ*, 'living thing' (the LXX takes this view, translating it in Gn. iii. 20 by *zōē*, 'life'), others note a similarity with Aramaic *ḥiwyā'*, 'serpent', with which is connected a Phoenician (possibly serpent) deity *ḥwt*, but as with *'îš* and *'iššâ* nothing beyond a formal assonance appears to be required by the text. The name *ḥawwâ* occurs twice only in the Old Testament (Gn. iii. 20, iv. 1), the word 'woman' being more commonly used. In the LXX and New Testament it appears as *Heua* (*Eua* in some MSS), which passes to *Heva* in the Vulgate, and thence to *Eve* in the EVV.

A sidelight on the biblical statements about Eve is found in a Sumerian myth concerning the god Enki. In this Enki finds himself suffering from a series of ailments, to deal with each of which the goddess Ninḫursag produces a special goddess. Thus, when he says 'My rib (*ti*; written with a logogram, one of whose Akkadian values was *ṣîlu*, 'side, rib') hurts me', she replies that she has caused a goddess *Nin-ti* 'Lady of the rib' to be born for him. But Sumerian *Nin-ti* can equally mean 'Lady who makes live'. It may be that this reflects in some way a common original narrative with the Genesis account.

BIBLIOGRAPHY. *KB*, pp. 280, 281; G. J. Spurrell, *Notes on the Text of the Book of Genesis*[2], 1896, p. 45; Z. S. Harris, *A Grammar of the Phoenician Language*, 1936, p. 101; S. N. Kramer, *Enki and Ninḫursag. A Sumerian Paradise Myth* (*BASOR* Supplementary Studies 1), 1945, pp. 8, 9; *From the Tablets of Sumer* (American edition), 1956, pp. 170, 171 = *History Begins at Sumer*, 1958, pp. 195, 196. T.C.M.

EVIL. The opposite of good (Heb. *ra'*; Gk. *kakos*, *ponēros*, *phaulos*). Evil has a broader meaning than sin (see SIN). The Heb. word comes from a root meaning 'to spoil', 'to break in pieces': being broken and so made worthless. It is essentially what is unpleasant, disagreeable, offensive. The word binds together the evil deed and its consequences. In the New Testament *kakos* and *ponēros* mean respectively the quality of evil in its essential character, and its hurtful effects or influence. It is used in both physical and moral senses. While these aspects are different, there is frequently a close relationship between them. Much physical evil is due to moral evil: suffering and sin are not necessarily connected in individual cases, but human selfishness and sin explain much of the world's ills. Though all evil must be punished, not all physical ill is a punishment of wrongdoing (Lk. xiii. 2, 4; Jn. ix. 3; *cf.* Job).

I. PHYSICAL EVIL

The prophets regarded God as the ultimate Cause of evil, as expressed in pain, suffering, or disaster. In His sovereignty He tolerates evil in the universe, though He overrules and uses it in His administration of the world. It is used to punish individual and national wickedness (Is. xlv. 7; La. iii. 38; Am. iii. 6). The world must be marked by regulation and order to be the scene of man's moral life; otherwise there would be chaos. When men violate the basic laws of God they experience the repercussions of their actions, which may be in penal or retributive affliction (Mt. ix. 2, xxiii. 35; Jn. v. 14; Acts v. 5, xiii. 11). Divine 'vengeance' in the form of pain or sorrow does not imply evil passions in God. Pain may awaken an evil man to reality; till then 'he is enclosed in illusion' (C. S. Lewis, *The Problem of Pain*, p. 83). Nature's present 'vanity' (profitlessness, Rom. viii. 19–23) is its mark of evil, the earth being under a curse (Gn. iii. 17, 18). Christian suffering, whether trouble or persecution, is divinely permitted for purposes of spiritual blessing (Jas. i. 2–4; 1 Pet. i. 7; *etc.*). It is chastening, not penal; nor can it separate from the love of God (Rom. viii. 38, 39); it prepares for glory (Rom. viii. 18; 2 Cor. iv. 16–18; Eph. iii. 13; Rev. vii. 14). Suffering and sorrow create sympathy and kindness in men, bringing them into fellowship with God's purpose to overcome evil.

II. MORAL EVIL

God is separate from all evil and is in no way responsible for it. Moral evil arises from man's sinful inclinations (Jas. i. 13–15). Israel repeatedly 'did evil' and suffered its consequences (Jdg. ii. 11; 1 Ki. xi. 6, *etc.*). Behind all history is a spiritual conflict with evil powers (Eph. vi. 10–17; Rev. xii. 7–12), 'the evil one' being the very embodiment of wickedness (Mt. v. 37, vi. 13, xiii. 19, 38; Jn. xvii. 15; Eph. vi. 16; 2 Thes. iii. 3; 1 Jn. ii. 13, 14, iii. 12, v. 18, 19, RV). Satan's power is under divine control (*cf.* Jb. i, ii), and will finally be broken (Heb. ii. 14; Rev. xii. 9–11).

God is against evil, but its existence is often a stumbling-block to belief in a God of love. It can only be attributed to the abuse of free-will on the part of created beings, angelic and human. God's whole saving activity is directed to deal with evil. In His life, Christ combated its manifestations of pain and sorrow (Mt. viii. 16, 17); but the cross is God's final answer to the problem of evil. His love was supremely demonstrated there (Rom. v. 8, viii. 32) in the identification of the Lord with the suffering world as the Sin-bearer. The moral change effected in men by the gospel is evidence of the reality of Christ's triumph over all evil powers (Col. ii. 15; 1 Jn. iii. 8), and therefore of the final victory of God. Evil will be eliminated from the universe, and the creation will share redeemed man's glorious destiny. Both physical and moral evil will be banished eternally (Rev. xxi. 1–8).

BIBLIOGRAPHY. C. S. Lewis, *The Problem of Pain*, 1940; C. E. M. Joad, *God and Evil*, 1943; J. S. Whale, *The Christian Answer to the Problem of Evil*, 1936; James Orr, *The Christian View of God and the World*, 1897. G.C.D.H.

EVIL-MERODACH. The king of Babylon who released Jehoiachin of Judah from imprisonment in the first year of his reign (Je. lii. 31; 2 Ki. xxv. 27–30). Amēl-Marduk ('The man is Marduk') succeeded his father Nebuchadrezzar II in the early days of October 562 BC. According to Josephus (from Berossus), he ruled 'lawlessly and wantonly', but the only allusions to him extant are in administrative tablets. He was killed *c.* 7–13 August 560 BC in a plot led by his brother-in-law Neriglissar (see NERGAL-SHAREZER). See also JEHOIACHIN. D.J.W.

EVIL SPEAKING may be defined as slander, calumny, or defamation. This may be done by spreading false reports (Pr. xii. 17, xiv. 5, 25) or by reporting truth maliciously, *i.e.* talebearing (Lv. xix. 16; Pr. xxvi. 20).

Evil speaking is prohibited in Ps. xxxiv. 13; Pr. xxiv. 28; Eph. iv. 31; Jas. iv. 11; 1 Pet. iii. 10. It disqualifies a person from God's favour (Ps. xv. 3) and from office in the church (1 Tim. iii. 8; Tit. ii. 3). When a Christian is slandered he must patiently bear it (1 Pet. iii. 9) even as Christ did (1 Pet. ii. 23).

The ninth commandment forbids false witness (Ex. xx. 16; Dt. v. 20; *cf.* Ex. xxiii. 1). To avoid the evil of false accusation more than one witness was required in courts of law (Nu. xxxv. 30; Dt. xvii. 6, xix. 15–21). M.R.G.

EVIL SPIRITS. The term 'evil (*ponēra*) spirit(s)' is found in but half a dozen passages (Matthew, Luke, Acts). There are twenty-three references to 'unclean (*akatharta*) spirits' (Gospels, Acts, Revelation), and these appear to be much the same. Thus in Lk. xi. 24 'the unclean spirit' goes out of a man, but when he returns it is with 'seven other spirits more wicked than himself' (verse 26). Similarly, 'unclean spirits' and 'devils' are interchangeable terms, for both are applied to the Gadarene demoniac (Lk. viii. 27, 29).

These beings appear to have been regarded in more than one light. They might cause physical disability (Mk. i. 23, vii. 25). Indeed, on most occasions in the New Testament when they are mentioned it is in such cases. There appears to have been nothing moral involved, for the sufferer was not excluded from places of worship, such as the synagogue. The idea would appear to be that the spirit was evil (or unclean) in that it produced baleful effects. But the sufferer was not regarded as especially evil or as polluted in any way. Yet the spirit itself was not to be regarded in neutral fashion. Everywhere it was to be resisted and defeated. Sometimes we read of Jesus as doing this in person (Mk. v. 8; Lk. vi. 18), sometimes of such power being delegated to His followers (Mt. x. 1) or being exercised by them (Acts v. 16, viii. 7). The spirits are apparently part of Satan's forces, and accordingly are reckoned as enemies of God and of men.

Sometimes it is clear that the spirits are concerned with moral evil. This is so in the case of the 'unclean spirit' who goes out of a man and returns with others more wicked than himself (Mt. xii. 43–45). The story indicates the impossibility of a man's bringing about a moral reformation by expelling the demons within. There must also be the entry of the Spirit of God. But for our present purpose it is sufficient to notice that the spirits are evil and may bring about evil. The evil spirits 'like frogs' of Rev. xvi. 13 are also thought of as working evil as they gather the forces of wickedness for the great final battle.

Such passages indicate that on the biblical view evil is not merely impersonal. It is led by Satan, and, just as there are subordinate powers of good, the angels, so there are subordinate powers of evil. Their appearance is mostly concerned with the incarnation (with a resurgence in the last days) as they oppose the work of Christ. See further SATAN, DEVIL, POSSESSION. L.M.

EXALTATION. See ASCENSION, GLORY.

EXCOMMUNICATION. Mt. xviii. 15–18; 1 Cor. v; 2 Cor. ii. 5–11; Tit. iii. 10. The exclusion of a member from the Church due to a serious (or aggravation, through stubbornness, of a less serious) offence. It is the final step in the negative side of normal discipline—there is also Anathema and delivering over to Satan (*q.v.*). When educative discipline (*disciplina*) fails to prevent offences, repressive discipline is used to remove them. The *gradus admonitionis* leading up to excommunication are private remonstrance (incumbent on all, Lv. xix. 17), then, if that proves ineffective, remonstrance with the aid of witnesses; finally, the offender should be dealt with by the Church, presumably through its duly-elected representatives, following the Jewish pattern. The apostle puts this responsibility upon the local church (1 Cor. v. 4–13). If the offender still shows no repentance he is to be excommunicated. 'Let him be unto thee as the Gentile and the publican.'

Some critics (*e.g.* Bultmann, T. W. Manson) make this 'quasi-legal' procedure a later development of the Church, from rabbinic sources. But then it is hard to see why Paul reproved the Corinthians so sharply for neglecting it. And our Lord's condemnation of these sources would be fresh in their minds (Mt. xxiii. 13 ff.). The opprobrious sense of 'Gentile and publican' has been said to show a Jewish-Christian origin, *c.* AD 50. This is, at least, doubtful. Ultimately, it is a question of 'the historical validity of the Gospel record and of the origins of Christianity itself, and this question it is impossible to ignore' (T. W. Manson, *Jesus the Messiah*, 1952, p. 26). The mind of the early Church is the mind of the Lord.

Public, notorious faults are to be rebuked publicly (1 Tim. v. 20; Gal. ii. 11, 14). Very serious offences merit immediate excommunication (1 Cor. v. 3). It is also noteworthy, however, that no amount of excommunication will produce a perfect Church, for it has to ignore secret sins and hypocrisy. Also, the oil of leniency has to be mixed with the vinegar of severity: 'We judge that it pertains unto sound doctrine . . . to attemper our life and opinion, so that we both endure dogs in the Church, for the sake of the peace of the Church, and, where the peace of the Church is safe, give not what is holy unto dogs . . . that we neither grow listless under the name of patience, nor be cruel under the pretext of diligence' (Augustine, *Short Treatises*, 1884, p. 43).

The aims involved are, first, to promote the glory of God, that His name be not blasphemed owing to manifest evil in the Church; second, to prevent the evil from spreading to other members (1 Cor. v. 6); and third, to bring about true repentance in the offender. Here the ultimate aim is seen to be redemptive (Calvin, *Institutes*, iv. 12. 5).

Excommunication implies that we suspend convivial intercourse with the offender, though not ceasing to pray for his recovery; and though he is excluded from the benefits of the sacraments, he will be encouraged to attend the preaching of the Word. R.N.C.

EXILE. See ISRAEL.

EXODUS. This event marked the birth of Israel as a nation and—through the immediately-following covenant at Sinai—as a theocracy.

I. THE EVENT ITSELF

After the Hebrews' residence in the Egyptian E Delta for 430 years (Ex. xii. 40, 41) culminating in enslavement in Egyptian state-corvée in the XVIIIth and XIXth Dynasties, God commissioned Moses, with Aaron as his mouthpiece, to lead out the Hebrew slaves, tribal descendants of Abraham, Isaac, and Jacob, from Egypt to become a nation in Palestine, the land of promise (Ex. iii, iv). Despite the hostility and temporal power of the pharaoh and, later, Israel's own faithlessness, this duly came to pass (Jos. xxiv).

That a large group of subject people should go out from a major state is neither impossible nor unparalleled in antiquity. In the late 15th century BC people of some 14 'lands', 'mountain-regions', and townships apparently decamped from their habitats within the Hittite kingdom, and transferred themselves to the land of Isuwa (Treaty-prologue of Suppiluliuma and 'Mattiwaza', Weidner, *Politische Dokumente aus Kleinasien*, 1923, p. 5), only later to be brought back by the powerful Hittite king Suppiluliuma. However, pharaoh's attempts to retain, and then to recapture, the Hebrews were rendered utterly futile by God's marshalling against him the powers of nature in nine plagues and a supernatural punishment in the tenth, and by swamping his pursuing chariotry in the Re(e)d Sea. The calling-out of a nation in this way specifically to serve a God, and live out a covenant directly with their God, is unique. The peoples who fled to Isuwa doubtless also considered themselves oppressed, but had no positive commission or divine calling to some high destiny.

Specific aspects of the Exodus are more appropriately dealt with in other articles as follows: For *date* of the Exodus, see CHRONOLOGY OF THE OLD TESTAMENT. For *route* of the Exodus, see fig. 80; see also on Egyptian sites ENCAMPMENT BY THE SEA, BAAL-ZEPHON, PITHOM, RA'AMSES, SUCCOTH, MIGDOL, *etc.*, and on the Sinaitic journeyings, WILDERNESS OF THE WANDERING, SINAI, and individual places—ELIM, REPHIDIM, *etc.* For the Egyptian background to the oppression and conditions attending on the Exodus, see EGYPT (History), MOSES, and PLAGUES OF EGYPT.

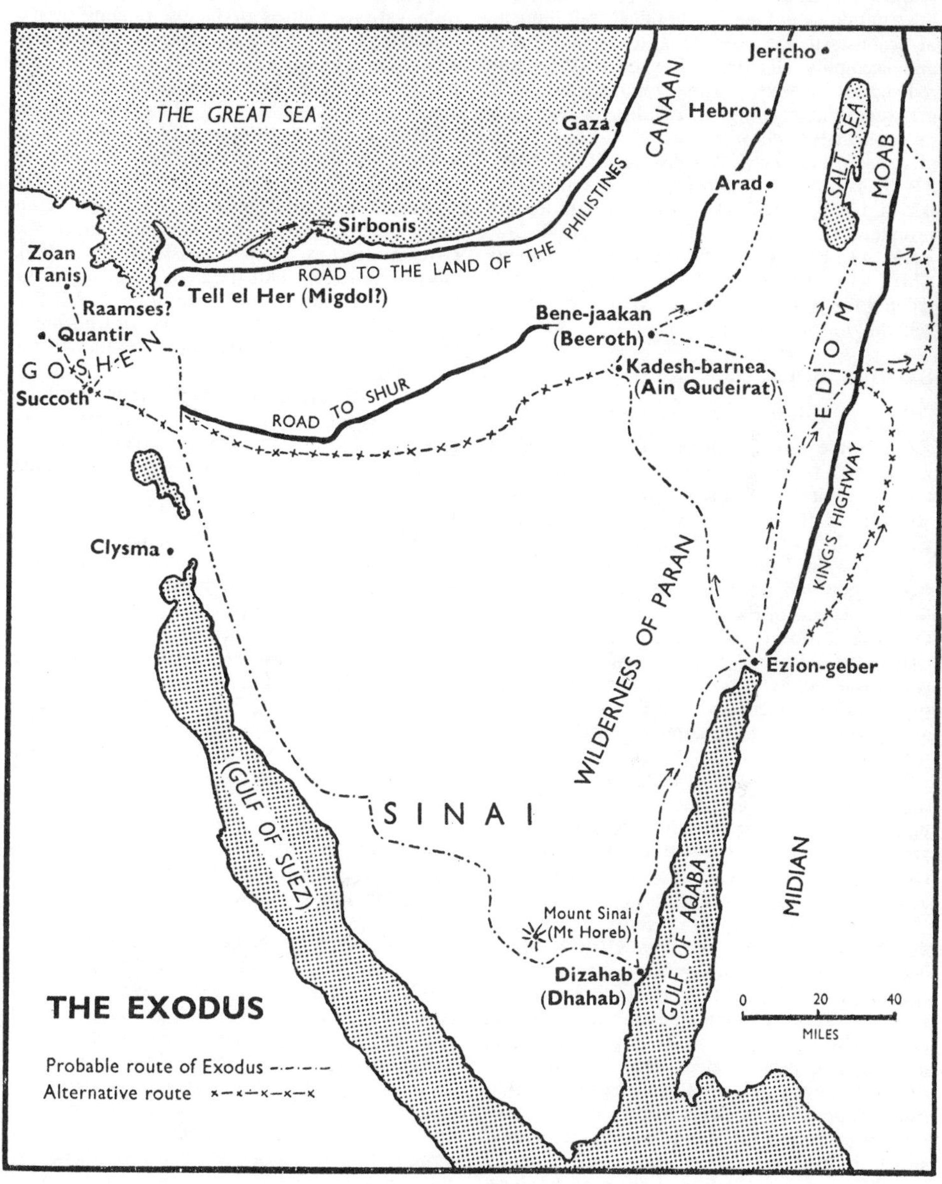

Fig. 80.

II. THE EXODUS IN LATER HISTORY

Repeatedly in later generations, the prophets in exhorting Israel to return to her God and the psalmists in their meditations hark back to this Exodus—to God's redeeming grace in summoning a nation from Egyptian bondage in fulfilment of promises to the Patriarchs, to serve Himself and exemplify His truth. For them, the great redemption is ever to be remembered with gratitude and response in obedience. See such passages as the following: historical books, Jdg. vi. 8, 9, 13; 1 Sa. xii. 6, 8; 1 Ki. viii. 51; 2 Ch. vii. 22; Ne. ix. 9 ff. For Psalms, *cf.* Pss. lxxvii. 14–20, lxxviii. 12–55, lxxx. 8, cvi. 7–12, cxiv. Among the prophets, see Ho. xi. 1; Je. vii. 21–24, xi. 1–8, xxxiv. 13; Dn. ix. 15. In the New Testament Christ accomplished the final 'Exodus', the full redemption (*cf.* Heb. xiii. 13 and elsewhere generally). K.A.K.

EXODUS, BOOK OF.

I. OUTLINE OF CONTENTS

Exodus (the latinized form of LXX *exodos*, 'a going out') is the second section of the Pentateuch, and deals with the fortunes of Israel subsequent to the propitious times of Joseph's governorship. It records the two great culminating points in Israel's history: the deliverance from Egypt and the giving of the law. Henceforth the events of Exodus hold a central place in God's revelation of Himself to His people, not only in the old but also in the new covenant, in which the Passover lamb provides the type for our Lord's sacrifice, and the Passover Feast is adapted to serve as the commemoration of our redemption.

The events leading up to and following Israel's flight from Egypt form the main theme of the book. The chronological setting is given only in general terms, consistent with the Hebrew treatment of history as a sequence of events and not as a series of dates.

The book, after giving a short genealogical note to effect the transition from Genesis, begins with an account of the disquiet on the part of the Egyptians at the great numerical increase of the Israelites. To counteract what was considered to be a growing menace, two, or possibly three, decrees were promulgated. The first subjected them to forced labour under Egyptian taskmasters, probably both to meet a current need for a large labour force and to keep them under strict observation. The second would seem to have been an intensification of this hard bondage, probably with the intention of reducing their leisure, and thus their opportunities for mischief, to a minimum. The third aimed at checking any further increase in the population by the extermination of all new-born male infants. The boys rather than the girls would be chosen, as they would be regarded as potential instigators of revolt. It is this last decree that furnishes the background of the account of the birth and upbringing of Moses, the second great figure in Jewish history, at the Egyptian court.

II. AUTHORSHIP

The leading critical schools see in Exodus a composition of diverse elements, originating from various sources or hands, ranging over a period from the 8th century until the 2nd century BC (A. H. McNeile, *Exodus*, p. ii). See PENTATEUCH, section II. The hypothetical documents are given the symbols of J (passages in which *YHWH* occurs), E (Elohim), D (Deuteronomic school), P (Priestly school), and R (various redactors). To these have been added L (lay source, O. Eissfeldt, *Einleitung in das Alte Testament*, p. 230), and B (*Bundesbuch*, book of the covenant, Ex. xx. 22–xxiii. 33, Eissfeldt, p. 253). According to Eissfeldt (p. 289), the order of the growth of Exodus would seem to be: L J E B P R^J R^E R^B R^P, where R is the redactor who added the source denoted by the superior letter to the corpus (pp. 287 ff.).

In the opinion of Eissfeldt the 'pious' attitude of the redactors towards their material, considered from the literary and aesthetic points of view, was a disadvantage, as this 'piety' prevented them from fashioning out of their materials a new and higher literary unity (p. 170). This would indeed have been remarkable restraint in view of the magnitude of the literary reconstruction they were undertaking without an apparent qualm. McNeile, however, says bluntly: 'Since in all ages of Israelite history every civil and religious institution was referred to Moses, every successive age found it necessary to manipulate the records' (*op. cit.*, p. ix). Again, according to McNeile it was the aim of the priestly writers 'to systematize traditions and often to supplement them, under the dominance of religious ideas' (*op. cit.*, p. lxxix), and that 'the narrators enriched the narratives from their own imagination', and 'the traditions acquired a miraculous element in the centuries that intervened between the events and the times of the several writers' (p. cxii).

About Moses, McNeile says: 'Vague traditions of the founder of the national religion were orally handed down, . . . legendary details would gather round his life' (p. cviii). He continues: 'It may be confidently asserted that Moses would not commit to writing a series of moral precepts'; and 'It is impossible to say of any particular detail that it derived from Moses himself' (p. cxvii). About the Tabernacle this same author says: 'the historicity is unhesitatingly denied by all who accept the main principles of historical and literary criticism' (p. cxviii). The reason given for this last piece of scepticism is the mention of the tent of audience in xxxiii. 7, alleged to be identical with the Tabernacle. It is, however, clear that the reference here is to the practice obtaining in the period preceding the erection of the Tabernacle, the purpose of which was to be a sanctuary, symbolizing God's presence in their midst (xxv. 8). S. R. Driver thinks that customs and rites 'are antedated and represented as having been already propounded and put in force in the Mosaic age' (*Exodus*, p. lxv).

If these views had any objective validity the narratives in Exodus would cease to be of historical value. The theories are in the nature of the case not amenable to proof. As Eissfeldt says: '. . . the whole criticism of the Pentateuch is a hypothesis, granted resting on very weighty arguments' (*Einleitung*, p. 288).

It is strange that P, written from a priestly point of view, does so little to enhance the priesthood. It is Moses, the political leader, who remains the great hero, while the one who allows the people to fall into idolatry is Aaron, the priest, whom Moses rebukes and reinstates. This was not the only lapse on the part of Aaron. If the whole of the materials was arranged to give an ideal picture of the theocracy, as it was supposed to have existed in the Mosaic age (Driver, *op. cit.*, p. xii), then the project, in the light of the stubbornness and intractability of the people, singularly miscarried.

Literary criticism in general would now look on it as a truism that a literary work contains sources, and would never view these as evidence of multiple authorship (*e.g.*, *cf.* J. L. Lowes, *The Road to Xanadu*). It is now also taken to be axiomatic that style is dictated largely by subject-matter, not by idiosyncratic vocabularies. The comparison of the alleged composite nature of the Pentateuch with the writings of Arabic historians, who are simply marshalling their witnesses, is not applicable to the literature of the ancient Semitic East (A. T. Chapman, *Introduction to the Pentateuch*, 1911).

The application of the dissecting criteria to documents of indisputable unitary authorship shows them to be worthless (*cf.* EGYPT, *sub* Egyptian Literature and the Old Testament). The selection of criteria was arbitrary, and other possible selections would give radically different results. A key passage as the justification of documentary fragmentation is Ex. vi. 3, where, it is claimed, the introduction of *YHWH* is stated to be an innovation. The great stress here laid on the continuity of identity with the God of the Patriarchs hardly indicates a new departure. There are two possible interpretations of this verse. 'Name' here can refer not to an appellation, but can stand for 'honour' and 'character', as it often does in Semitics generally. Or the sentence could be taken as an elliptical interrogative: 'for did I not let my name, *YHWH*, be known to them?' At least the 'and also' of the next verse followed by a positive implies a preceding positive (W. J. Martin, *Stylistic Criteria and the Analysis of the Pentateuch*, 1955, pp. 17 f.).

The Jewish view from the time of Joshua (viii. 34 f.), subscribed to by our Lord, and accepted by the Christian Church, held that Exodus was the work of Moses. From internal evidence this is also the impression given by the book itself. No objective philological evidence has been produced for the rejection of this view. If editing took place, one would expect it to be confined to such things as the modernization of geographical names. This done honestly in the interests of clarity would be far removed from inserting into documents extensive interpolations, and representing them as compositions of the Mosaic age. The Mosaic authorship would imply a date probably in the 13th century BC.

III. THE TEXT

The text of Exodus is remarkably free from transcriptional errors. Letters on occasion have dropped out. There are a few examples of dittography (*e.g.* possibly of *sammîm*, 'spices', in xxx. 34). Haplography (writing only once that which occurs twice) appears, *e.g.*, in xix. 12, where an *m* (= 'from') has been omitted. In xi. 1 a marginal note may have found its way into the text: 'when his sending away is final'. In xx. 18, apparently through the omission of a *y*, 'fear' has become 'saw'. In xxxiv. 19 the Hebrew definite article *h* has become *t*. In xxiii. 3, through the misreading of *g* as *w*, 'great' has become 'poor' (*cf.* Lv. xix. 15). In xvii. 16 the letters *k* and *s* have apparently been transposed: read probably: 'For he said: power is with the banner of the Lord'. In xxiii. 5 *b* seems to have replaced *r*, changing 'help' into 'forsake'; the reading is possibly: 'and thou shalt refrain from abandoning it, thou shalt surely give him your help'. One could read the text as it stands: 'and thou shalt refrain from abandoning it, thou shalt surely along with him free it'.

The magnitude of the numbers seems to some to present difficulties. The transmission of numbers is especially exposed to error. In any consideration of the large number of people involved and the problem of providing for them, it should be borne in mind that these were not an urbanized people, but men and women whose manner of life made them well able to fend for themselves. See also PENTATEUCH.

BIBLIOGRAPHY. A. H. McNeile, *The Book of Exodus*, *WC*, 1917; S. R. Driver, *The Book of Exodus*, 1918; E. J. Young, *Introduction to the Old Testament*, 1954; O. Eissfeldt, *Einleitung in das Alte Testament*, 1956. W.J.M.

EXORCISM. See MAGIC AND SORCERY.

EXPIATION. This term does not occur in AV, but it is found in some modern translations in place of 'propitiation' (*q.v.*). Objection is made to 'propitiation' on the ground that it means the appeasement of an angry God, an idea not found in Scripture. Therefore expiation is substituted for it. But the matter is not so simple. Expiation properly has a thing as its object. We may expiate a crime, or a sin. Propitiation is a personal word. We propitiate a person rather than a sin (though we should not overlook the fact that in the Bible 'propitiate' is occasionally found with sin as the object, the meaning being 'to make propitiation with respect to sin'). If we are to think of our relationship to God as basically personal we cannot afford to dispense with the concept of propitiation. Those who advocate the use of expiation must face questions like: Why should sin be expiated? What are the consequences if no expiation takes place? Is the hand of God in those consequences? Expiation is a valuable word only if we can confidently answer 'No' to the last question. If sin is a thing, and can be dealt with as a thing, blotted out, cast from us, and the like, then we may properly talk of expiation. But if sin affects man's relationship with God, if the relationship with God is the primary thing, then it is difficult to see how expiation is adequate. Once we bring in the category of the personal we need some such term as propitiation.

It seems, then, that, despite the confident claims of some, expiation is not the solution to our difficulties. The ideas expressed in the words usually translated 'propitiation' are not adequately safeguarded by the use of the term 'expiation'. See also PROPITIATION. L.M.

EYE. The Heb. word for eye, *'ayin*, with parallels in other Near Eastern languages, is used of the physical organ of man (Gn. iii. 6) or beast (xxx. 41), of God anthropomorphically (Ps. xxxiii. 18), and also of objects (Ezk. i. 18; *cf.* Rev. iv. 6). The Gk. word *ophthalmos* has familiar derivatives in English.

In Hebrew the physical organs are construed as acting semi-independently and possessing also psychical and moral qualities. (See BODY, EAR, *etc.*). Thus the eye not only has sight but is proud (Is. v. 15), has pity (Dt. vii. 16), sleep (Gn. xxxi. 40), desire (Ezk. xxiv. 16), *etc.*, and, while Paul emphasizes the interdependence of the physical organs (1 Cor. xii. 16 f.), Mt. v. 29 preserves the Hebraic notion of the almost self-contained function of the organ. Compare the phrase 'an evil eye' (Pr. xxiii. 6; Mt. vi. 23).

The practice of putting out the eyes of a defeated enemy was common in the East (Jdg. xvi. 21; 2 Ki. xxv. 7).

The phrase 'the eye of the Lord is upon them' (Ps. xxxiii. 18) is significant of God's watchful care (*cf.* i. 6).

Other phrases are: 'eye for eye' (Lv. xxiv. 20); 'face to face', literally 'eye to eye' (Nu. xiv. 14); 'before their eyes', *i.e.* in full view (Gn. xlii. 24; *cf.* Je. xxxii. 12); and 'between thine eyes', *i.e.* on the forehead (Ex. xiii. 9), of the phylactery.

Derived usages are: 'visible surface' (see Ex. x. 5), and 'colour' (see Ezk. i. 4; Pr. xxiii. 31).

B.O.B.

EZEKIEL (Heb. *y^eḥezqē'l*, 'God strengthens'). The name is found in approximately its Heb. form in 1 Ch. xxiv. 16 for the head of one of the priestly orders.

Ezekiel, the son of Buzi (*q.v.*), was deported to Babylonia, almost certainly with Jehoiachin in 597 BC (2 Ki. xxiv. 14–17). He was settled in the village of Tel-abib by the river Chebar (*q.v.*). Five years later he received his call as prophet (Ezk. i. 2), possibly at the age of thirty (i. 1), though this interpretation is denied by many without offering a more satisfactory one. He lived for at least another twenty-two years (xxix. 17).

We have little information about his life. Though he possessed detailed knowledge of the Jerusalem Temple and its cultus, there is no evidence he had served in it. His thought, more than that of any other prophet, is influenced by priestly symbolism. His first prophecies were badly received (iii. 25), but we soon find him in an honoured position (viii. 1, xiv. 1, xx. 1), due possibly to his family rank; the majority hardly took his message very seriously (xxxiii. 30–32—AV is misleading in verse 30). His wife died suddenly the day Nebuchadrezzar invested Jerusalem (xxiv. 1, 2, 15–18); there is no mention of children.

H. Klostermann, *Theologische Studien und Kritiken*, 1877, tried on the basis of such passages as iii. 23–iv. 8 to show that he suffered from an organic nervous disease, which he called catalepsy. Though popular for a time, the view is today accepted by few. Considerable controversy exists as to how Ezekiel's symbolic actions are to be interpreted. Some, *e.g.* A. B. Davidson, *Ezekiel* (*CBSC*), p. xxx, and J. Skinner, *HDB*, I, p. 817a, have held they took place purely in the prophet's mind. More usual is the conception that, though they were carried out, in our understanding of them we must allow for a metaphorical element inconsistent with a purely literal interpretation. See also the following article.

H.L.E.

EZEKIEL, BOOK OF.

I. STRUCTURE AND CONTENTS

The indications of date (i. 2, iii. 16, viii. 1, xx. 1, xxiv. 1–xxvi. 1, xxix. 1, 17, xxx. 20, xxxi. 1, xxxii. 1, 17–xxxiii. 21, xl. 1) apart from those in chapters xxv–xxxii form a coherent series marking major developments in Ezekiel's message (see previous article). It is reasonable to infer that chapters xxv–xxxii were inserted in their present position on analogy with Is. xiii–xxvii to mark the division between the two main phases of Ezekiel's activity. In chapters i–xxiv he is the prophet of inexorable doom, interpreting coming events to the remnant in exile (not to Jerusalem!) to prepare them for their future rôle. Chapters xxxiii–xxxix give an outline of the message by which he tried to build up the exiles as the people of God. The long interval between xxxiii. 21 and xl. 1 (some thirteen years), the striking change in style, and the fact that Josephus writes of Ezekiel's two books (*Ant.* x. 5. 1) suggest that chapters xl–xlviii represent a separate, though allied, group of prophecies beside chapters xxxiii–xxxix.

II. AUTHORSHIP AND DATE

Ezekiel has an unquestioned place in Ben Sira's list at the beginning of the 2nd century BC (Ecclus. xlix. 8), but there was a move in the 1st century AD to have the book withdrawn from public use. For this there were three reasons. Some felt chapter xvi too repugnant for public reading; chapter i and parallels were used in dangerous theosophical speculations (some thought they were the key to the mysteries of creation); above all, numerous details in chapters xl–xlviii were considered contradictory to the law of Moses, already considered immutable. The labours of Hananiah ben Hezekiah, which resolved the apparent discrepancies, guaranteed for Ezekiel a public position in the Pharisaic canon.

This position was seldom challenged, and J. Skinner could say in 1898 (*HDB*, I, p. 817a), 'The Book of Ezekiel (save for a somewhat corrupt text) exists in the form in which it left the hand of its author. . . . Neither the unity nor the authenticity of Ezekiel has been questioned by more than a very small minority of scholars. Not only does it bear the stamp of a single mind in its phraseology, its imagery, and its mode of thought, but it is arranged on a plan so perspicuous and so comprehensive that the evidence of literary design in the composition becomes altogether irresistible.'

In spite of the cogency of these arguments the position began to change in 1924; attacks on the unity and authenticity of *Ezekiel* may be divided into three groups, which tend to overlap.

a. The date of composition

C. C. Torrey saw in it a pseudepigraph, written about 230 BC, describing the abominations of Manasseh's reign; an editor gave it its present form not later than 200 BC. M. Burrows reached a similar date by linguistic evidence. L. E. Browne advocated a date during the time of Alexander the Great. J. Smith, on the other hand, regarded Ezekiel as a northern Israelite deported in 734 BC, who prophesied to his fellow exiles until he returned to Jerusalem in 691 BC, where he gave the bulk of his oracles. Such views have won very little favour.

b. The place of prophecy

Though Torrey's dating has had little acceptance, many have followed him in seeing the bulk of the book as Palestinian. It is widely believed that, whether or not Ezekiel was deported in 597 BC, he was prophesying in or near Jerusalem until its destruction in 586 BC. Perhaps the best presentation of this view is by Pfeiffer, *Introduction to the Old Testament*, 1948, pp. 535–543. The main justification for this interpretation is the traditional misinterpretation of Ezekiel's oracles before 586 BC as addressed to doomed Jerusalem. Its great weakness is the very extensive rearrangement of the text involved, and the absence of any adequate motivation for the distortion of Ezekiel's actual activity.

c. The unity of the book

Basing himself mainly on the contrast between Ezekiel's poetry and prose, G. Hölscher attributed to him only 170 verses (mostly poetry) of the total 1,273, the rest coming from a levitical editor between 500 and 450 BC. W. A. Irwin reached similar results by other methods, attributing some 250 verses to Ezekiel. Many deny chapters xl–xlviii to him. Their arguments are a challenge to profounder exegesis, but they have failed to carry conviction with the majority, though editorial insertions are increasingly recognized.

It seems fair to say that the intensive critical studies of thirty-five years have largely cancelled themselves out. They have led to a deeper understanding of many aspects of the book, but have left the general position much as it was before 1924.

III. THE TEXT

Many *hapax legomena* and technical expressions and obscurity in the symbolical language have led scribes into frequent error. The LXX can often be used to correct the Hebrew, but it must be used with extreme care. There is an interesting comparison of the Hebrew and Greek in Cooke, *Ezekiel, ICC*, pp. xl–xlvii.

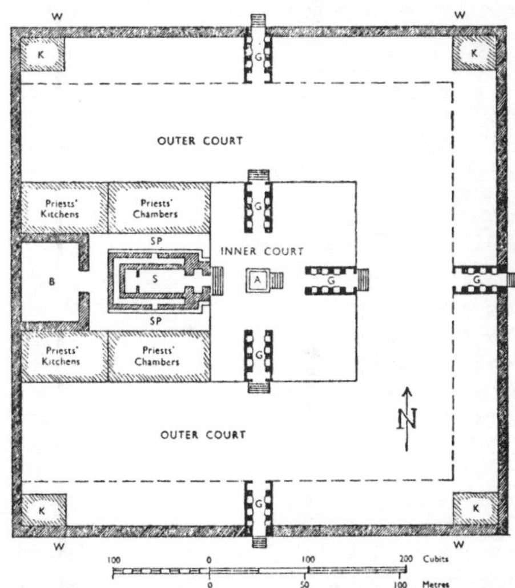

Fig. 81. Plan of Ezekiel's Temple. *Key:* A. Altar; B. Building mentioned in xli. 12; G. Gatehouses; K. Kitchens; S. The Sanctuary; S.P. The 'separate place' of xli. 12–14; W. The surrounding wall.

IV. THE RELIGIOUS TEACHING OF THE BOOK

To understand the book correctly we must grasp that, like all the writings of the prophets, it is not a manual of theology; it is the word of God to a battered remnant in exile experiencing what the theologians of the time had considered impossible. If Ezekiel by his symbolism seems to stress the transcendence of God, it is to make clear that His omnipotence cannot be limited by the failure of His people. This leads to the most unsparing exposure of Israel's history and religion in the Old Testament (xvi, xx, xxiii).

The promise of restoration is no longer bound to the prior repentance of the people, but is an act of God's grace which leads to repentance (xxxvi. 16–32). Because all is of God's grace, the relationship of the individual to God depends neither on his heredity nor his own past (xviii, xxxiii. 10–20). Many have deduced from xl–xlviii a picture of Ezekiel as a narrow, priestly ritualist, but this comes from failure to recognize the essentially eschatological character of these chapters. In the symbolism of exact conformity to divine plan and law we are shown God's people ultimately conforming perfectly to His purposes.

BIBLIOGRAPHY. G. Hölscher, *Hesekiel: Der Dichter und das Buch*, 1924; M. Burrows, *The Literary Relations of Ezekiel*, 1925; C. C. Torrey, *Pseudo-Ezekiel and the Original Prophecy*, 1930; G. A. Cooke, *The Book of Ezekiel, ICC*, 1936; W. A. Irwin, *The Problem of Ezekiel*, 1943, 'Ezekiel Research since 1943', *VT*, III, 1953, pp. 54–66; H. L. Ellison, *Ezekiel, The Man and His Message*, 1951; G. Fohrer and K. Galling, *Ezechiel*, 1955. H.L.E.

EZEL. The agreed rendezvous of David and Jonathan, occurring in 1 Sa. xx. 19 only. The word 'Ezel' in the phrase 'the stone Ezel' (AV and RV) is sometimes taken to mean 'departure', but the RVmg and the RSV, following the LXX, read 'this mound' and 'yonder stone heap' respectively, and assume corruption in the Heb. text. See also the RSV text and margin of 1 Sa. xx. 41. G.W.G.

EZION-GEBER. See ELATH.

EZRA. According to the record in Ezr. vii, Ezra was sent to Jerusalem by Artaxerxes I in 458 BC. It would seem probable that he held a position in Persia comparable to Secretary of State for Jewish affairs. His task was to enforce the uniform observance of the Jewish law, and to this end he had authority to make appointments within the Jewish state. A large company of exiles came with him, and he brought valuable gifts for the Temple from the king and the exiled Jews. He was asked to deal with the problem of mixed marriages, and, after fasting and prayer, he and a chosen committee blacklisted the guilty and induced some at least to put away their pagan wives (x. 19).

After this we do not hear of Ezra until he reads the law publicly in Ne. viii. This was in 444 BC. Since he had been sent by the king on a temporary mission, he presumably returned with his report, but was sent back again on a similar mission when the walls of the city were completed. Nehemiah, in part of his memoirs in xii. 36 ff., records that he himself led one party round the walls on the occasion of their dedication, while Ezra led the other.

Largely on the strength of three passages, many have held that Ezra did not come to Jerusalem until the time of Artaxerxes II, *i.e.* in 398 BC, long after the time of Nehemiah.

a. Ezr. ix. 9 speaks of a city wall, whereas the wall was not built until Nehemiah's time. But Ezr. iv. 12 shows that a wall of some sort was being built in the reign of Artaxerxes I, and its destruction is probably referred to in iv. 23 and Ne. i. 3. Ezra is rejoicing in faith at the work which has progressed so far.

b. Ezr. x. 1 speaks of a very great congregation in Jerusalem, whereas Ne. vii. 4 says that only a few people lived in the city. But the context of Ezr. x shows that the congregation was drawn from all around Jerusalem, *e.g.* x. 7, whereas Ne. vii is concerned with actual dwelling-houses in the city.

c. Ezr. x. 6 speaks of Jehohanan (or Johanan) the son of Eliashib as Ezra's contemporary. We know from Ne. xii. 22, 23 that Johanan was the grandson of Eliashib, and from the Elephantine papyri that Johanan was high priest in 408 BC. But Johanan was a common name, and it is reasonable to think that Eliashib had a son named Johanan, and also another son, Joiada, who in turn had a son, Johanan, who became high priest. Ezr. x. 6 does not say that Johanan was high priest in Ezra's day.

As against the idea that the writer of Ezra and Nehemiah confused Artaxerxes I and II (which this theory of the priority of Nehemiah demands), a writer even as late as 330 BC could not have confused the order of the two men. If Ezra really came in 398 BC, a few of the writer's contemporaries would have remembered him, and many would have been told of him by their parents; whereas no-one would have remembered Nehemiah. Thus the writer could not have put Ezra back before Nehemiah by accident, and no-one has suggested any reason for his doing so deliberately. (See J. Stafford Wright, *The Date of Ezra's Coming to Jerusalem*, 1958; H. H. Rowley, 'The Chronological Order of Ezra and Nehemiah' in *The Servant of the Lord and Other Essays*, 1952, pp. 129 ff.)

It should be noted that Ezra attained a great reputation among the Jews in post-biblical times. In 2 Esdras xiv he is said to have been inspired of God to re-write the law, which had been destroyed in the Exile, and a number of other books. See also the following article.

BIBLIOGRAPHY. H. H. Schaeder, *Esra der Schreiber*, 1930. J.S.W.

EZRA, BOOK OF.

I. OUTLINE OF CONTENTS

a. i. 1–11. Cyrus permits the Jews to return from exile under Sheshbazzar. 537 BC.

b. ii. 1–70. The register of those who returned.

c. iii. 1–13. The altar is set up and the Temple foundations laid. 536 BC.

d. iv. 1–5, 24. Enemies hinder the work until the time of Darius.

e. iv. 6–23. Further opposition to the building of the city walls in the reign of Ahasuerus (Xerxes, 485–465 BC) and Artaxerxes (464–424 BC), resulting in a decree to stop the building altogether.

f. v. 1–vi. 22. Renewal of the Temple building through the prophecies of Haggai and Zechariah. In spite of protests to Darius the work is completed. 520–516 BC.

g. vii. 1–28. Ezra is sent from Persia to enforce the law. 458 BC.

h. viii. 1–36. Ezra's journey and safe arrival.

i. ix. 1–x. 44. Ezra and the Jews deal with the problem of mixed marriages.

In this outline it is assumed that the author has collected examples of opposition together in iv. 6–23. There are those who think that Ahasuerus in verse 6 is Cambyses (529–522 BC) and Artaxerxes in verse 7 is the usurper Gaumata, or Pseudo-Smerdis, who reigned for a few months in 522–521 BC. But the subject-matter of verses 7–23 is the walls and not the Temple, and it is probable that the damage referred to in verse 23 is that which is referred to in Ne. i. 3.

II. AUTHORSHIP AND DATE

See the general note under CHRONICLES, of which it is probable that Ezra and Nehemiah formed part. Traditionally the author is Ezra himself, but some bring the date down to about 330 BC. Whether or not Ezra was the final compiler, vii–ix would appear to be from his hand, much of this section being in the first person singular. The account in i–vi is compiled from records, including decrees (i. 2–4, vi. 3–12), genealogies and name lists (ii), and letters (iv. 7–22, v. 6–17). There are two sections which have been preserved in Aramaic (iv. 8–vi. 18, vii. 12–26). Aramaic was the diplomatic language of the day, and was suitable for the section dealing with the coming and going of letters and decrees between Palestine and Persia.

III. CREDIBILITY

The documents that are found in Ezra present no great difficulties of harmonization with one another and with what is known from secular history. We may note the following.

a. The decree of Cyrus (i), acknowledging Jehovah, is in harmony with Cyrus's favourable references to Babylonian deities in contemporary records. This is a public decree, written in terms that would appeal to the Jews. The formal decree in vi. 3–5 is filed in the records, and gives the maximum size of the Temple for which the king was prepared to give a grant.

b. Sheshbazzar and Zerubbabel are unlikely to be the same person, since in v. 14–16 Sheshbazzar is referred to as one who is no longer alive, whereas Zerubbabel was then engaged in building the Temple. Sheshbazzar was the official leader, but Zerubbabel was the active enthusiast, both in 536 and 520 BC.

c. It is pointed out that from Haggai ii. 18 we learn that the foundation of the Temple was laid in 520 BC, whereas Ezr. iii. 10 indicates that it was laid in 536 BC. In actual fact so little was done in the intervening period that it is likely that the revival would begin with a fresh foundation ceremony. Records show that in important buildings there was more than one official foundation stone.

d. The date of the coming of Ezra is bound up with the Book of Nehemiah, and is considered separately under the entry EZRA, above. See also NEHEMIAH.

IV. THE BOOK OF EZRA AND 1 ESDRAS

Esdras is the Gk. equivalent of Ezra, and our Apocrypha contains in 1 Esdras, a book that is very similar to Ezra, though with certain striking differences. It runs from 2 Ch. xxxv. 1 to the end of Ezra, after which it adds Ne. viii. 1–12. Its history is confused. Thus Cyrus permits the return under Sheshbazzar, while Darius commissions Zerubbabel to go and build the Temple and the city; yet v. 70–73 says that Zerubbabel was working in Judah 'all the time that Cyrus lived'. Thus, while it may be useful to compare the two versions, Ezra is undoubtedly the more reliable. The famous story of the three guardsmen comes in 1 Esdras iii.

BIBLIOGRAPHY. J. Stafford Wright, *The Building of the Second Temple*, 1958; L. W. Batten, *Ezra and Nehemiah*, *ICC*, 1913; A. C. Welch, *Post-Exilic Judaism*, 1935; L. E. Browne, *Early Judaism*, 1920.

J.S.W.

F

FABLE. This word is a transliteration of the Lat. *fabula*, derived from *fari* 'to speak'. It is most commonly used to describe a picturesque, but fictitious, story, often satirical in character, told to bring home to the hearer a salutary, if unwelcome, truth. Thus Jotham's story of the king-tree (Jdg. ix) and Jehoash's story of the thistle and the cedars (2 Ki. xiv. 9) are in the strict sense 'fables', though they are not described as such. The former is a satire on the folly of choosing an unfit king, and the latter a rebuke of Amaziah for his presumption.

In the New Testament, 'fable' in AV translates *mythos*. The latter is used to describe a narrative which is not only fabulous in the sense of being fictitious but also deceptive because it is invented by a false teacher with the purpose of deflecting those who hear it from revealed truth. The 'fables' mentioned in 1 Tim. i. 4 were probably legends based on Old Testament narratives, for they are described in Tit. i. 14 as 'Jewish'. Such fables are ridiculed in 1 Tim. iv. 7 by the epithets 'profane and old wives'': they were godless because they were not based on divine revelation; and they were fit only for old women (see R. St. J. Parry, *The Pastoral Epistles*, pp. lxxxiv, lxxxv). In 2 Pet. i. 16 the author refers to 'cunningly devised fables' not followed by genuine Christian teachers. These fanciful stories, possibly the work of the early Gnostic teachers who produced the Apocryphal Gospels, are here contrasted with the true account of the transfiguration of Christ transmitted by Peter.

R.V.G.T.

FACE. The English word usually translates Heb. *pānîm* or Gk. *prosōpon*. The Heb. word is used in many English senses—of the faces of people and animals, and metaphorically of the sky; it could refer to the front of something, or its outward appearance. Then the 'face' of a person became synonymous with his 'presence', and the Heb. *lip̄ᵉnê* (literally 'to the face of', and so 'to the presence of', and 'in front of') is a very common preposition.

The face, of course, gives visible indication of inward emotions, and a variety of adjectives accompany the word in Scripture, such as 'sad', 'tearful', 'ashamed', or 'pale'. The face could change colour, darkening or blushing.

Modesty or reverence demanded the veiling of the face, as did Rebekah before Isaac. God's face might not be seen by man for fear of death (Ex. xxxiii. 20); in Isaiah's vision, seraphim veiled the Almighty's face. It was a sign of humility to bow the face to the ground; and falling on the face betokened great fear. Utter contempt, on the other hand, could be shown by spitting in somebody's face. Metaphorically, determination could be shown by 'setting' one's face—note the graphic phrase of Is. l. 7, denoting unswerving purpose. Determined opposition was made by withstanding someone to his face. Intimacy and understanding were conveyed by the phrase 'face to face'. This phrase has, of course, passed into English, as has also 'his face fell' (Gn. iv. 5).

The face of the dead was covered (Jn. xi. 44), and so this action to Haman made it clear that he was doomed (Est. vii. 8).

When a man prostrated himself to make a request, his superior would raise the supplicant's head as a sign that the favour would be granted. To lift someone's face thus meant primarily to grant a favour (*cf.* Gn. xix. 21), and then to make a favourite of (Dt. x. 17). This concept is also found in New Testament Greek, in the words *prosōpolēptēs* ('respecter of persons'; literally, 'face-taker') and *prosōpolēpsia*, the abstract noun (*cf.* Acts x. 34; Rom. ii. 11).

D.F.P.

FAIR HAVENS, modern Kaloi Limenes, a small bay on the south coast of Crete, a few miles east of Cape Matala. Although protected by small islands, it is too open to be an ideal winter harbour (Acts xxvii. 8), but it would be the last place Paul's ship could stay to avoid the north-west wind, as the coast swings north beyond Cape Matala.

K.L.McK.

FAITH.

I. IN THE OLD TESTAMENT

In the Old Testament the word 'faith' is found twice only, in Dt. xxxii. 20, 'a very froward generation, children in whom is no faith (*'ēmun*)', and in Hab. ii. 4, 'the just shall live by his faith (*'ᵉmûnâ*)'. Even here most scholars think the meaning is 'faithfulness' rather than 'faith' (though as faithfulness arises only out of a right attitude to God, faith in our sense is presupposed). This does not, however, mean that faith is unimportant in the Old Testament, for the idea, if not the word, is frequent. It is usually expressed by verbs such as 'believe', 'trust', or 'hope', and such abound.

We may begin with such a passage as Ps. xxvi. 1, 'Judge me, O Lord; for I have walked in mine integrity: I have trusted also in the Lord.' It is often said that the Old Testament looks for men to be saved on the basis of their deeds, but this passage puts the matter in its right perspective.

The Psalmist does indeed appeal to his 'integrity', but this does not mean that he trusts in himself or his deeds. His trust is in God. His 'integrity' is the evidence of his trust in God. The Old Testament is a big book, and the truths about salvation are stated in various ways. The writers do not always make the distinctions that we, with the New Testament in our hands, might wish. But close examination will reveal that in the Old Testament, as in the New, the basic demand is for a right attitude to God, *i.e.* for faith. *Cf.* Ps. xxxvii. 3 ff., 'Trust in the Lord, and do good . . . Delight thyself also in the Lord; and he shall give thee the desires of thine heart. Commit thy way unto the Lord; trust also in him; and he shall bring it to pass.' Here there is no question but that the Psalmist is looking for an upright life. But there is no question either, that basically he is advocating an attitude. He calls on men to put their trust in the Lord, which is only another way of telling them to live by faith. Sometimes men are urged to trust the Word of God (Ps. cxix. 42), but more usually it is faith in God Himself that is sought. 'Trust in the Lord with all thine heart; and lean not unto thine own understanding' (Pr. iii. 5).

The latter part of this verse frowns upon trust in one's own powers, and this thought is frequent. 'He that trusteth in his own heart is a fool' (Pr. xxviii. 26). A man may not trust to his own righteousness (Ezk. xxxiii. 13). Ephraim is castigated for trusting 'in thy way, in the multitude of thy mighty men' (Ho. x. 13). Trust in idols is often denounced (Is. xlii. 17; Hab. ii. 18). Jeremiah warns against confidence in anything human, 'Cursed be the man that trusteth in man, and maketh flesh his arm, and whose heart departeth from the Lord' (Je. xvii. 5). The list of things not to be trusted in might be multiplied, and it is the more impressive alongside the even more lengthy list of passages urging trust in the Lord. It is clear that the men of the Old Testament thought of the Lord as the one worthy object of trust. They put not their trust in anything they did, or that other men did, or that the gods did. Their trust was in the Lord alone. Sometimes this is picturesquely expressed. Thus He is 'my rock, and my fortress, and my deliverer; my God, my strength, in whom I will trust; my buckler, and the horn of my salvation, and my high tower' (Ps. xviii. 2). Faith may be confidently rested in a God like that.

Special mention must be made of Abraham. His whole life gives evidence of a spirit of trustfulness, of a deep faith. Of him it is recorded that 'he believed in the Lord; and he counted it to him for righteousness' (Gn. xv. 6). This text is taken up by New Testament writers, and the fundamental truth it expresses developed more fully.

II. IN THE NEW TESTAMENT

a. General use of the word

In the New Testament faith is exceedingly prominent. The noun *pistis* and the verb *pisteuō* both occur more than 240 times, while the adjective *pistos* is found sixty-seven times. This stress on faith is to be seen against the background of the saving work of God in Christ. Central to the New Testament is the thought that God sent His Son to be the Saviour of the world. Christ accomplished man's salvation by dying an atoning death on Calvary's cross. Faith is the attitude whereby a man abandons all reliance in his own efforts to obtain salvation, be they deeds of piety, of ethical goodness, or anything else. It is the attitude of complete trust in Christ, of reliance on Him alone for all that salvation means. When the Philippian jailer asked, 'Sirs, what must I do to be saved?', Paul and Silas answered without hesitation, 'Believe on the Lord Jesus Christ, and thou shalt be saved' (Acts xvi. 30 f.). It is 'whosoever believeth in him' that does not perish, but has everlasting life (Jn. iii. 16). Faith is the one way by which men receive salvation.

The verb *pisteuō* is often followed by 'that', indicating that faith is concerned with facts. This is important, as Jesus made clear to the Jews, 'for if ye believe not that I am he, ye shall die in your sins' (Jn. viii. 24). But it is not all-important. James tells us that the devils believe 'that there is one God', but this 'faith' does not profit them (Jas. ii. 19). *Pisteuō* may be followed by the simple dative, when the meaning is that of giving credence to, of accepting as true, what someone says. Thus Jesus reminds the Jews that 'John came . . . in the way of righteousness, and ye believed him not' (Mt. xxi. 32). There is no question here of faith in the sense of trust. The Jews simply did not believe what John said. This may be so also with respect to Jesus, as in Jn. viii. 45, 'ye believe me not', or the next verse, 'if I say the truth, why do ye not believe me?' Yet it must not be forgotten that there is an intellectual content to faith. Consequently this construction is sometimes used where saving faith is in mind, as in Jn. v. 24, 'He that heareth my word, and believeth him (not 'on him', as AV) that sent me, hath everlasting life.' The man who really believes God will, of course, act on that belief. In other words, a genuine belief that what God has revealed is true will issue in a true faith.

The characteristic construction for saving faith is that wherein the verb *pisteuō* is followed by the preposition *eis*. Literally this means to believe 'into'. It denotes a faith which, so to speak, takes a man out of himself, and puts him into Christ (*cf.* the expression frequently used of Christians, being 'in Christ'). This experience may also be referred to with the term 'faith-union with Christ'. It denotes not simply a belief that carries an intellectual assent, but one wherein the believer cleaves to his Saviour with all his heart. The man who believes in this sense abides in Christ and Christ in him (Jn. xv. 4). Faith is not accepting certain things as true, but trusting a Person, and that Person Christ.

Sometimes *pisteuō* is followed by *epi*, 'upon'. Faith has a firm basis. We see this construction in Acts ix. 42, where, when the raising of Tabitha was known, 'many believed in the Lord'. The people had seen what Christ could do, and they rested their faith 'on' Him. Sometimes faith rests on the Father, as when Paul speaks of believing 'on him that raised up Jesus our Lord from the dead' (Rom. iv. 24).

Very characteristic of the New Testament is the absolute use of the verb. When Jesus stayed with the Samaritans many of them 'believed because of his own word' (Jn. iv. 41). There is no need to add what they believed, or in whom they believed. Faith is so central to Christianity that one may speak of 'believing' without the necessity for further clarification. Christians are simply 'believers'. This use extends throughout the New Testament, and is not confined to any particular writer. We may fairly conclude that faith is fundamental.

The tenses of the verb *pisteuō* are also instructive. The aorist tense points to a single act in past time and indicates the determinative character of faith. When a man comes to believe he commits himself decisively to Christ. The present tense has the idea of continuity. Faith is not a passing phase. It is a continuing attitude. The perfect tense combines both ideas. It speaks of a present faith which is continuous with a past act of belief. The man who believes enters into a permanent state. Perhaps we should notice here that the noun 'faith' sometimes has the article 'the faith', *i.e.* the whole body of Christian teaching, as when Paul speaks of the Colossians as being 'stablished in the faith', adding 'as ye have been taught' (Col. ii. 7).

b. Particular uses of the word

(i) In the Synoptic Gospels faith is often connected with healing, as when Jesus said to the woman who touched His garment in the crowd, 'Daughter, be of good comfort; thy faith hath made thee whole' (Mt. ix. 22). But these Gospels are also concerned with faith in a wider sense. Mark, for example, records for us the words of the Lord Jesus, 'all things are possible to him that believeth' (Mk. ix. 23). Similarly, the Lord speaks of the great results of having 'faith as a grain of mustard seed' (Mt. xvii. 20; Lk. xvii. 6). It is clear that our Lord called for faith in Himself personally. The characteristic Christian demand for faith in Christ rests ultimately on His own requirement.

(ii) In the Fourth Gospel faith occupies a very prominent place, the verb *pisteuō* being found ninety-eight times. Curiously the noun *pistis*, 'faith', is never used. This is possibly due to its use in circles of a Gnostic type. There are indications that John had such opponents in mind, and it may be that he wanted to avoid using a term of which they were very fond. Or he may have preferred the more dynamic meaning conveyed by the verb. Whatever his reason, he uses the verb *pisteuō* more often than any other writer in the New Testament, three times as often, in fact, as the first three Gospels put together. His characteristic construction is that with the preposition *eis*, 'to believe into', 'to believe on'. The important thing is the connection between the believer and the Christ. Accordingly, John speaks again and again of believing in Him or of believing 'in the name' of Christ (*e.g.* Jn. iii. 18). The 'name', for men of antiquity, was a way of summing up the whole personality. It stood for all that the man was. Believing on the name of Christ, then, means believing in all that He is essentially in Himself. Jn. iii. 18 also says, 'He that believeth on him is not condemned: but he that believeth not is condemned already.' It is characteristic of Johannine teaching that eternal issues are decided here and now. Faith does not simply give men assurance of everlasting life at some unspecified time in the future. It gives them everlasting life here and now. He that believeth on the Son 'hath' everlasting life (iii. 36, *cf.* v. 24, *etc.*).

(iii) In Acts, with its story of vigorous missionary advance, it is not surprising that the characteristic expression is the use of the aorist tense, to indicate the act of decision. Luke records many occasions wherein people came to put their trust in Christ. Other constructions are found, and both the continuing state and the permanent results of belief find mention. But decision is the characteristic thing.

(iv) For Paul, faith is the typical Christian attitude. He does not share John's antipathy to the noun, but uses it more than twice as often as he uses the verb. It occurs in connection with some of his leading ideas. Thus in Rom. i. 16 he speaks of the gospel as 'the power of God unto salvation to every one that believeth'. It means a great deal to Paul that Christianity is more than a system of good advice. It not only tells men what they ought to do, but gives them power to do it. Again and again Paul contrasts mere words with power, always with a view to emphasizing that the power of the Holy Spirit of God is seen in the lives of Christians. This power becomes available to a man only when he believes. There is no substitute for faith.

Much of Paul's controversial writing centres round the dispute with the Judaizers. These men insisted that it was not enough for Christians to be baptized. They must also be circumcised, and, being thus admitted to Judaism, endeavour to keep the whole of the Mosaic law. They made obedience to the law a necessary pre-condition of salvation, at least in the fullest sense of that term. Paul will have none of this. He insists that men can do nothing, nothing at all, to bring about their salvation. All has been done by Christ, and no man can add anything to the perfection of Christ's finished work. So it is that Paul insists that men are justified (see JUSTIFICATION) 'by faith' (Rom. v. 1). The doctrine of justification by faith lies at the very heart of Paul's message. Whether with this terminology or not, he is always putting the idea forward. He vigorously combats any idea of the efficacy of good deeds. 'Knowing that a man is not justified by the works of the law', he writes to the Galatians, 'but by the faith of Jesus Christ, even we have believed in Jesus Christ, that we might be justified by the faith of Christ, and not by the works of the law.' He adds resoundingly 'for by the works of the law shall no flesh be justified' (Gal. ii. 16). Clearly, for Paul, faith means the abandonment of all reliance on one's ability to merit salvation. It is a trustful acceptance of God's gift in Christ, a reliance on Christ, Christ alone, for all that salvation means.

Another outstanding feature of Pauline theology is the very large place the apostle gives to the work of the Holy Spirit. He thinks of all Christians as indwelt by the Spirit (Rom. viii. 9, 14), and he connects this too with faith. Thus he writes to the Ephesians concerning Christ 'in whom also after that ye believed, ye were sealed with that holy Spirit of promise, which is the earnest of our inheritance' (Eph. i. 13 f.). Sealing represented the mark of ownership, a metaphor readily understood in an age when many could not read. The Spirit within believers is God's mark of ownership, and this mark is put on men only as they believe. The passage we have quoted goes on to speak of the Spirit as 'the earnest of our inheritance'. Paul employs here a word which in the 1st century meant a down-payment, *i.e.* a payment which at one and the same time was part of the agreed price and the guarantee that the remainder would be forthcoming. Thus when a man believes he receives the Holy Spirit as part of the life in the age to come, and as an assurance that the remainder will infallibly follow.

(v) The writer of the Epistle to the Hebrews sees that faith has always been a characteristic of the people of God. In his great portrait gallery in Heb. xi he reviews the worthies of the past, showing how one by one they illustrate the great theme that 'without faith it is impossible to please' God (Heb. xi. 6). He is particularly interested in the opposition of faith to sight. Faith is 'the substance of things hoped for, the evidence of things not seen' (Heb. xi. 1). He emphasizes the point that men who had nothing in the way of outward evidence to support them nevertheless retained a firm hold on the promises of God. In other words, they walked by faith, not by sight.

(vi) Of the other writers in the New Testament we must notice James, for he has often been held to be in opposition to Paul in this matter. Where Paul insists that a man is justified by faith and not by works James maintains 'that by works a man is justified, and not by faith only' (Jas. ii. 24). There is no more than a verbal contradiction, however. The kind of 'faith' that James is opposing is not that warm personal trust in a living Saviour of which Paul speaks. It is a faith which James himself describes: 'Thou believest that there is one God; thou doest well: the devils also believe, and tremble' (Jas. ii. 19). He has in mind an intellectual assent to certain truths, an assent which is not backed up by a life lived in accordance with those truths (Jas. ii. 15 f.). So far is James from opposing faith in the full sense that he everywhere presupposes it. Right at the beginning of his Epistle he speaks naturally of 'the trying of your faith' (Jas. i. 3), and he exhorts his readers to 'have not the faith of our Lord Jesus Christ, the Lord of glory, with respect of persons' (Jas. ii. 1). He criticizes a wrong faith but assumes that everyone will recognize the need for a right faith. Moreover, by 'works' James does not mean what Paul means by that term. Paul thinks of obedience to the commands of the law regarded as a system whereby a man may merit salvation. For James the law is 'the law of liberty' (Jas. ii. 12). His 'works' look uncommonly like 'the fruit of the Spirit' of which Paul speaks. They are warm deeds of love springing from a right attitude to God. They are the fruits of faith. What James objects to is the claim that faith is there when there is no fruit to attest it.

Faith is clearly one of the most important concepts in the whole New Testament. Everywhere it is required and its importance insisted upon. Faith means abandoning all trust in one's own resources. Faith means casting oneself unreservedly on the mercy of God. Faith means laying hold on the promises of God in Christ, relying entirely on the finished work of Christ for salvation, and on the power of the indwelling Holy Spirit of God for daily strength. Faith implies complete reliance on God and full obedience to God.

BIBLIOGRAPHY. H. F. Lovell Cocks, *By Faith Alone*, 1943; W. F. Howard, *Christianity according to St. John*, 1943; B. B. Warfield in *HDB*; W. A. Whitehouse in *RTWB*; J. G. Machen, *What Is Faith?*, 1925. L.M.

FALCON. See BIRDS OF THE BIBLE.

FALL.

I. THE BIBLICAL ACCOUNT

The story of the fall of man, given in Gn. iii, describes how mankind's first parents, when tempted by the serpent, disobeyed God's express command by eating of the fruit of the tree of the knowledge of good and evil. The essence of all sin is displayed in this first sin: having been tempted to doubt God's word ('Yea, hath God said . . .?'), man is led on to disbelieve it ('Ye shall not surely die'), and then to disobey it (they 'did eat'). Sin is man's rebellion against the authority of God, and pride in his own supposed self-adequacy ('Ye shall be as God'). The consequences of sin are twofold: first, awareness of guilt and immediate separation from God (they 'hid themselves'), with whom hitherto there had been unimpaired daily fellowship; and secondly, the sentence of the curse, decreeing toil, sorrow, and death for man himself, and in addition inevitably involving the whole of the created order, of which man is the crown.

II. THE EFFECT ON MAN

Man henceforth is a perverted creature. In revolting against the purpose of his being, which is to live and act entirely to the glory of his sovereign and beneficent Creator and to fulfil His will, he ceases to be truly man. His true manhood consists in conformity to the image of God in which he was created. This image of God is manifested in man's original capacity for communion with his Creator; in his enjoyment exclusively of what is good; in his rationality which makes it possible for him alone of all creatures to hear and respond to the Word of God; in his knowledge of the truth and in the freedom which that knowledge ensures; and in government, as the head of God's creation, in obedience to the mandate to have dominion over every living thing and to subdue the earth.

Yet, rebel as he will against the image of God with which he has been stamped, man cannot efface it, because it is part of his very constitution as man. It is evident, for example, in his pursuit of scientific knowledge, in his harnessing of the forces of nature, and in his development of culture, art, and civilization. But at the same time the efforts of fallen man are cursed with frustration. This frustration is itself a proof of the perversity of the human heart. Thus history shows that the very discoveries and advances which have promised most good to mankind have through misuse brought great evils in their train. The man who does not love God does not love his fellow-men. He is driven by selfish motives. The image of Satan, the great hater of God and man, is superimposed upon him. The result of the fall is that man now knows good *and evil*.

The psychological and ethical effects of the fall are nowhere more graphically described than by Paul in Rom. i. 18 ff. All men, however ungodly and unrighteous they may be, *know* the truth about God and themselves; but they wickedly *suppress* this truth (verse 18). It is, however, an inescapable truth, for the fact of the 'eternal power and Godhead' of the Creator is both manifested within them, by their very constitution as God's creatures made in His image, and also manifested all around them in the whole created order of the universe which bears eloquent testimony to its origin as God's handiwork (verses 19 f.; *cf.* Ps. xix. 1 ff.). Basically, therefore, man's state is not one of ignorance but of knowledge. His condemnation is that he loves darkness rather than light. His refusal to glorify God as God and his ingratitude lead him into intellectual vanity and futility. Arrogantly professing himself to be wise, he in fact becomes a fool (Rom. i. 21 f.). Having wilfully cut himself adrift from the Creator in whom alone the meaning of his existence is to be found, he must seek that meaning elsewhere, for his creaturely finitude makes it impossible for him to cease from being a religious creature. And his search becomes ever more foolish and degrading. It carries him into the gross irrationality of superstition and idolatry, into vileness and unnatural vice, and into all those evils, social and international, which give rise to the hatreds and miseries that disfigure our world. The fall has, in brief, overthrown the true dignity of man (verses 23 ff.).

III. THE BIBLICAL DOCTRINE

It will be seen that the scriptural doctrine of the fall altogether contradicts the popular modern view of man as a being who, by a slow evolutionary development, has succeeded in rising from the primeval fear and groping ignorance of a humble origin to proud heights of religious sensitivity and insight. The Bible does not portray man as risen, but as fallen, and in the most desperate of situations. It is only against this background that God's saving action in Christ takes on its proper significance. Through the grateful appropriation by faith of Christ's atoning work, what was forfeited by the fall is restored to man: his true and intended dignity is recovered, the purpose of life recaptured, the image of God restored, and the way into the paradise of intimate communion with God reopened.

IV. ITS HISTORICAL DEVELOPMENT

In the history of the Church the classic controversy concerning the nature of the fall and its effects is that waged by Augustine at the beginning of the 5th century against the advocates of the Pelagian heresy. The latter taught that Adam's sin affected only himself and not the human race as a whole, that every individual is born free from sin and capable in his own power of living a sinless life, and that there had even been persons who had succeeded in doing so. The controversy and its implications may be studied with profit in Augustine's anti-Pelagian writings. Pelagianism, with its affirmation of the total ability of man, came to the fore again in the Socinianism of the 16th and 17th centuries, and continues under the guise of modern humanistic religion.

A halfway position is taken by the Roman Catholic Church, which teaches that what man lost through the fall was a supernatural gift of original righteousness that did not belong properly to his being as man but was something extra added by God (*donum superadditum*), with the consequence that the fall left man in his natural state as created (*in puris naturalibus*): he has suffered a negative rather than a positive evil; deprivation rather than depravation. This teaching opens the door for the affirmation of the ability and indeed necessity of unregenerate man to contribute by his works towards the achievement of his salvation (semi-Pelagianism, synergism), which is characteristic of the Roman Catholic theology of man and grace. For a Roman Catholic view, see H. J. Richards, 'The Creation and Fall', in *Scripture*, VIII, 1956, pp. 109–115.

Although retaining the conception of man as a fallen being, contemporary liberal theology denies the historicity of the event of the fall. Every man, it is said, is his own Adam. Similarly, certain forms of modern existentialist philosophy, which is essentially a repudiation of historical objectivism, are willing to make use of the term 'fallenness' to describe the subjective state in which man pessimistically finds himself. A floating concept, however, which is unrelated to historical event explains nothing. But the New Testament certainly understands the fall as a definite event in human history—an event, moreover, of such critical consequences for the whole human race that it stands side by side with and explains the other great crucial event of history, namely the coming of Christ to save the world (see Rom. v. 12 ff.; 1 Cor. xv. 21 f.). Mankind, together with the rest of the created order, awaits a third and conclusive event of history, namely the second advent of Christ at the end of this age, when the effects of the fall will be finally abolished, unbelievers eternally judged, and the renewed creation, the new heavens and new earth wherein righteousness dwells, be established in accordance with almighty God's immutable purposes (see Acts iii. 20 f.; Rom. viii. 19 ff.; 2 Pet. iii. 13; Rev. xxi, xxii). Thus by God's grace all that was lost in Adam, and much more than that, is restored in Christ. See also SIN.

BIBLIOGRAPHY. N. P. Williams, *The Ideas of the Fall and of Original Sin*, 1927; J. G. Machen, *The Christian View of Man*, 1937, chapter XIV.

P.E.H.

FALLOW DEER (Heb. *yaḥmûr*, 'brown goat', 'gazelle'). This is mentioned among the clean animals in Dt. xiv. 5, and among the game available at Solomon's table in 1 Ki. iv. 23. It is, however, a mistranslation; RV and RSV correctly render it 'roebuck' (*q.v.*) in each case. J.D.D.

FALSEHOOD. See LIE.

FAMILIAR SPIRIT. See DIVINATION.

FAMILY, HOUSEHOLD.

I. IN THE OLD TESTAMENT

There is no word in the Old Testament which corresponds precisely to modern English 'family', as consisting of father, mother, and children. The closest approximation is found in the word *bêṯ* ('house'), which, from signifying the group of people, probably came to refer to the dwelling (AV translates as 'family' in 1 Ch. xiii. 14; 2 Ch. xxxv. 5, 12; Ps. lxviii. 6). In the Bible the term could be used not only of those sheltering under the same roof (Ex. xii. 4) but also of much larger groups, as for instance the 'house of Israel' (Is. v. 7), which included the whole nation. Perhaps a closer equivalent to English 'family' is found in the phrase *bêṯ 'āḇ*, 'father's house'. The term most frequently translated 'family' in the EVV is *mišpāḥâ*, which had more the meaning of 'clan' than the smaller 'family', being applied for instance to 600 Danites from two villages (Jdg. xviii. 11).

Some idea of the relation of these two terms can be gained from the account in Jos. vii. 16–18 of the detection of Achan after the failure to capture Ai. The search was first narrowed to the 'tribe' (*šēḇeṭ*) of Judah, then to the clan (*mišpāḥâ*, AV 'family') of the Zarhites, and finally to the 'household' (*bêṯ*) of Zabdi. The fact that Achan was a married man with children of his own (vii. 24), but was still counted as a member of the *bêṯ* of his grandfather Zabdi, shows the extent of this term. Conceptually the members of a tribe can be pictured as a cone, with the founding ancestor at the apex and the living generation at the base. The term *šēḇeṭ*, 'staff', perhaps in reference to the staff, signifying the authority, of the founding ancestor, applied to the whole tribe; *mišpāḥâ* referred to a smaller division lower down in the cone; and the term *bêṯ* could apply to a yet smaller division, though its application depended upon its context, for if qualified by the name of the founding ancestor it could refer to the whole tribe. In each case the terms could indicate simply the base of the relevant cone, *i.e.* the living members of the group; or the entire volume of the cone, *i.e.* the members past and present, living and dead.

a. Determination of mates

In the choice of mates certain close relatives both by blood and marriage were excluded (Lv. xviii. 6–18; Dt. xxvii. 20–23), but outside these prohibited degrees marriage with kin was preferred, as is shown by the marriages of Isaac with Rebekah (Gn. xxiv. 4), Jacob with Rachel and Leah (Gn. xxviii. 2, xxix. 19), and Manoah's wish concerning Samson (Jdg. xiv. 3). On the other hand, marriages with foreigners, Hittite (Gn. xxvi. 34), Egyptian (Gn. xli. 45), Midianite (Ex. ii. 21), Moabite (Ruth i. 4), Zidonian (1 Ki. xvi. 31), and others, did take place (see MARRIAGE). A special case where the mate is determined is found in the levirate marriage law (see MARRIAGE), whereby if a married man died childless his next brother was obliged to marry the widow, and raise up children to perpetuate the name of the deceased.

b. Methods of acquiring a wife

In most cases the choice of a mate and subsequent arrangements for marriage were made by the parents of the partners concerned, as is shown by the fact that, though Samson was attracted by the Timnathite, he applied to his parents to make the arrangements. The usual method of acquiring a wife was by purchase, though this is not an altogether satisfactory term, since the 'bride-price' (*mōhar*; Gn. xxxiv. 12; Ex. xxii. 16; 1 Sa. xviii. 25), though it was a payment made by the man to the bride's father, was more in the nature of a compensation to the family for the loss of a valued member than an outright cash purchase (see BRIDE). Service could be given instead of payment, as in the case of Jacob, who served Laban fourteen years for Rachel and Leah, but this practice was not common during the Monarchy. Unorthodox means of acquiring a wife, which did not always involve the parents, included capture in war (Dt. xxi. 10–14) or in raids (Jdg. xxi), or seduction, in which case the seducer was obliged to marry the violated maiden (Ex. xxii. 16; *cf.* Gn. xxxiv. 1–4).

c. Residence

Israelite marriage was patrilocal; the woman left her father's house and went to live with her husband. In patriarchal times this would often have involved going to live in the same group, *bêṯ* or *mišpāḥâ*, as her husband's father and brothers, but in the time of the Monarchy the son on marriage probably left home to set up his own *bêṯ*, as is suggested by the smallness of many of the private houses uncovered in excavations. Three cases are sometimes quoted as evidence for matrilocal residence, Jacob, Gideon (Jdg. viii. 31, ix. 1, 2), and Samson, but such an interpretation is not necessary. Jacob lived in Laban's 'house' only while he was working in return for his wives, and it was the manner rather than the fact of his departure which aroused Laban's ill-will (Gn. xxxi. 26–28). Gideon did not himself live with the woman in question, and she was in any case not more than a concubine. The same is true of Samson and the Timnathite, whom he only visited, and did not live with.

d. Number of mates

While at the creation monogamy seemed to have been intended, by the time of the patriarchal age polygamy (polygyny not polyandry) is found. At first Abraham had but one wife, Sarah, but when she proved barren he followed the custom of the time in having children by her handmaid Hagar (Gn. xvi. 1, 2), and he took Keturah as a wife after the death of Sarah (Gn. xxv. 1). In subsequent generations more wives were taken, Jacob having two and their two handmaids. The possession of two wives was evidently assumed in the Mosaic legislation (Dt. xxi. 15), and under the Judges and the Monarchy there was still less restraint, and the economic factor imposed the only limit (see MARRIAGE). That this was not God's plan is shown by the prophetic representation of Israel as the sole bride of God (Is. l. 1, liv. 6, 7, lxii. 4, 5; Je. ii. 2; Ezk. xvi; Ho. ii. 4 f.). In addition to wives and the maidservants of wives, those who could afford them had concubines (*q.v.*), and children born by these could be accorded equal status with true sons, if the father was so minded.

e. Husband and wife

In addition to the terms *'îš* and *'iššâ*, 'man' and 'woman', which also served for 'husband' and 'wife', the husband was the *ba'al*, 'master', and *'āḏôn*, 'lord', of the wife, which illustrates the legal and normally practical relative positions of the two (see MARRIAGE). Until her marriage a woman was subject to her father, and after marriage to her husband, and to each she was a chattel. A man could divorce his wife, but probably not she him; she did not inherit his property, which went to his sons; and she might have to get along with other wives. On the other hand, in practice there was great variation in accordance with personality and strength of character, and that some women came to public prominence is shown by the cases of Deborah (Jdg. iv–v), Athaliah (2 Ki. xi), Huldah (2 Ki. xxii. 14 f.), and Esther. The duties of the wife included first of all the bearing and care of children, and such household tasks as cooking, in addition to helping the husband in the fields when opportunity offered (see WOMAN). Fidelity was important in both parties, and there was strict provision in the law for the punishment of adultery. The most important function of the wife was the bearing of children, and to be barren was a source of shame (see BARRENNESS).

f. Parents and children

The four terms, 'father' (*'āḇ*), 'mother' (*'ēm*), 'son' (*bēn*), and 'daughter' (*baṯ*), have cognates in most of the Semitic languages and were in such frequent use in Old Testament times that they are irregular in grammatical inflexion. The greatest wish of man and wife was for many children (Ps. cxxvii. 3–5), but especially for sons, as is clearly shown in the history of Abraham and his dealings with God, from whom they came. The eldest son occupied a special position, and on his father's death he inherited a double portion and became head of the family. Sometimes, however, a father would show special favour to his youngest son, as did Jacob for Joseph and then Benjamin. A daughter did not inherit from her father unless there were no sons (*cf.*, however, Jb. xlii. 13–15; see also INHERITANCE).

In ancient Mesopotamia, particularly as evidenced in the Nuzi documents, the practice of adoption by childless people of someone to take the place of a son is well attested (see ARCHAEOLOGY (Nuzi) and PATRIARCHAL AGE), and it was in keeping with this practice that Abraham considered making one of his servants his heir (Gn. xv. 3; see ABRAHAM). There is, however, no specific legislation concerning this matter of adoption in the Old Testament. Such cases as are reported are either in a foreign setting (as for instance the case quoted above, Moses by Pharaoh's daughter (Ex. ii. 10) and Esther by Mordecai (Est. ii. 7, 15)) or else are not cases of full adoption, as the adoptees were already descendants of the adopters, as in the cases of Jacob and Joseph's sons (Gn. xlviii. 5, 12), and Naomi and the child of Ruth (Ru. iv. 16, 17). (See ADOPTION.) When they were very small all children were looked after by the mother, but as the boys grew older they were taught to share their father's work, so that in general the father governed the education of the son, and the mother that of the daughter (see EDUCATION). That to the children the mother was as worthy of honour as the father is shown by the fifth commandment (Ex. xx. 12).

g. Other kinsfolk

The terms 'brother' (*'aḥ*) and 'sister' (*'āḥôṯ*) could be applied not only to children of the same parents but to half siblings either by a different father or mother, and the restrictions on sexual intercourse between full siblings applied also to these (Lv. xviii. 9, 11; Dt. xxvii. 22). Often of particular importance to children were their uncles and aunts, especially the mother's brother to the son, and the father's sister to the daughter. These are usually designated by the appropriate combination of terms such as *'ᵃḥôṯ-'āḇ*, 'father's sister', but sometimes described by the words *dôḏ*, 'uncle' (*q.v.*), and *dôḏâ*, 'aunt'. A woman would refer to her husband's father and mother by the special terms *ḥām* (*e.g.* Gn. xxxviii. 13, 25; 1 Sa. iv. 19, 21) and *ḥāmôṯ* (*e.g.* Ru. i. 14), and it may be that *ḥōṯēn* (*e.g.* Ex. iii. 1, iv. 18) and *ḥōṯeneṯ* (Dt. xxvii. 23) were corresponding terms used by the man of his wife's mother and father, though the limited contexts in which these terms occur make this uncertain.

h. Solidarity of kin

Two main factors made for solidarity in patriarchal times, common blood or descent, and common habitation and legal obligations according to customs and law, and though after the settlement in the land the tendency for families to divide weakened these, they continued to be of importance throughout Old Testament times. The community of interests among the members of the household, clan, and tribe was also a source of unity within these groups, and under their heads. One of the outgrowths of this unity was the right of each member of a group to protection by that group, and indeed the obligations on the group to provide certain services. Outstanding among these was that of the *gō'ēl*, whose obligations might extend from marrying the widow of a kinsman (Ru. ii. 20, iii. 12, iv) to redeeming a kinsman from slavery into which he had sold himself to pay a debt (see also AVENGER OF BLOOD).

BIBLIOGRAPHY. R. de Vaux, *Les Institutions de l'Ancien Testament*, I, 1958, pp. 37–100, 321–325; A. G. Barrois, *Manuel d'Archéologie biblique*, II, 1953, pp. 1–36. T.C.M.

II. IN THE NEW TESTAMENT

Family (Gk. *patria*) is mentioned as such only three times, although the related idea of 'house' or 'household' (Gk. *oikos*, *oikia*) is more frequent. *Patria* ('lineage, descent', *LSJ*) signifies the historical origin of a household, *i.e.* its 'patriarch', rather than its present head. A family might be a tribe or even a nation. In Acts iii. 25 the promise to Abraham is quoted in the form, 'in thy seed shall all the families (*patriai*) of the earth be blessed' (RV). The LXX has 'tribes' (*phylai*) in the original promise (Gn. xii. 3) and 'nations' (*ethnē*) when the promise is recalled in Gn. xviii. 18 and xxii. 18. Joseph was 'of the house and lineage (*patria*) of David' (Lk. ii. 4), where the patronymic is the vital point. As this verse shows, 'house' (*oikos*) can be used in the same sense (*cf.* Lk. i. 27). Thus also 'the house of Israel' (Mt. x. 6, xv. 24; Acts ii. 36, vii. 42, *etc.*) and 'the house of Jacob' (Lk i. 33).

The prominence of paternity is well seen in the third occurrence of *patria*, Eph. iii. 14, 15: 'For this cause I bow my knees unto the Father, from whom every family in heaven and on earth is named' (RV). This means that, just as every *patria* implies a *patēr* ('father'), so behind them all stands the universal fatherhood of God whence the whole scheme of ordered relationships is derived. Elsewhere we meet the more restricted concept of the fatherhood of God in relation to the household of the faithful.

The word 'household', where it is not simply a synonym for 'family', is a unit of society which meets us everywhere in the Roman and Hellenistic, as well as the Jewish, world of the 1st century. It consisted not only of the lord (Gk. *kyrios*), master (Gk. *despotēs*) or paterfamilias, his wife, children, and slaves, but also of various dependants, such as servants, employees, and even 'clients' (*e.g.* freedmen or friends) who voluntarily joined themselves to a household for the sake of mutual benefits (see CAESAR'S HOUSEHOLD). The Gospels abound with allusions to the household and its character (*e.g.* Mt. xxi. 33 ff.). The household was an important factor in the growth and stability of the Church. Already among the Jews the household was the context of such religious exercises as the Passover, a weekly sacred meal, prayers, and instruction (see EDUCATION). Luke states that 'the breaking of the bread' (which he does not further identify) took place in the Jerusalem church 'by households' (see Acts ii. 46). This phrase, *kat' oikon*, occurs in papyri in contrast to the phrase 'by individuals' (*kata prosōpon*—see *MM*).

In Hellenistic cities the rôle of the household in the establishment of churches was no less important. The first accession of Gentiles was the entire household of Cornelius at Caesarea, comprising household servants, a batman, kinsmen, and near friends (Acts x. 7, 24). When Paul crossed to Europe, the Church was planted at Philippi with the baptism of Lydia's household and that of the jailer (Acts xvi. 15, 31–34). At Corinth 'the firstfruits of Achaia' was the household of Stephanas (1 Cor. xvi. 15), which, in common, probably, with the households of Crispus the ruler of the synagogue and the hospitable Gaius (Acts xviii. 8; 1 Cor. i. 14–16; Rom. xvi. 23), was baptized by Paul himself. Other Christian households mentioned by name are those of Prisca and Aquila (at Ephesus, 1 Cor. xvi. 19; and perhaps Rome, Rom. xvi. 5), Onesiphorus (at Ephesus, 2 Tim. i. 16, iv. 19), Philemon (at Colossae, Phm. 1, 2), Nymphas or Nympha (at Laodicea, Col. iv. 15), Asyncritus and Philologus (at Rome (?), Rom. xvi. 14, 15).

In the Jerusalem church households were apparently instructed as units (Acts v. 42), and this was also Paul's custom, as he reminded the Ephesian elders (Acts xx. 20). A regular catechesis existed setting forth the mutual duties of members of a Christian household: wives and husbands, children and fathers, servants and masters. See Col. iii. 18–iv. 1; Eph. v. 22–vi. 9; 1 Pet. ii. 18–iii. 7.

Reference is made to the church in the house of Prisca and Aquila (Rom. xvi. 5 and 1 Cor. xvi. 19), of Nymphas (Col. iv. 15) and of Philemon (or was it Archippus?) (Phm. 2). This means either that the household was regarded as an *ekklēsia* (see CHURCH) in itself, or that the church in a given locality met within the scope of one household's hospitality (see above, 'by households'). When Gaius is spoken of as host of 'the whole church' (Rom. xvi. 23), the existence of other household churches in Corinth is perhaps implied, with the suggestion that on occasion, presumably for the Lord's Supper (1 Cor. xi. 18–22), they all came together 'as a church'. It is, however, not unimportant to note that both baptism and the Lord's Supper in certain situations took place within a household, not to mention instruction of wife and children (1 Cor. xiv. 35; Eph. vi. 4), and that it was from the ranks of proved heads of households that overseers (bishops) as well as deacons for the church were drawn (1 Tim. iii. 2–7, 12).

It is not surprising that the Church itself should be thought of as the household of God (Eph. ii. 19, where the figure is combined with that of the sacred republic) or the household of faith (Gal. vi. 10). The description of believers as adopted sons (Rom. viii. 15–17) or as servants and stewards (1 Cor. ix. 17, RV; 1 Pet. iv. 10) implies this figure. Paul sees himself as a servant of Jesus Christ, a steward set to perform a particular ministry (Rom. i. 1; 1 Cor. iv. 1). In a related picture the writer to the Hebrews depicts Moses as a faithful head steward in God's household, foreshadowing Christ as the son and heir (*cf.* Gal. iii. 23–iv. 7) of the household of God, 'whose house', says the writer, 'are we, if we hold fast the confidence and the rejoicing of the hope firm unto the end' (Heb. iii. 1–6).

BIBLIOGRAPHY. Schrenk, *TWNT*, V, p. 1018; Selwyn, *1 Peter*, 1946, Essay II, p. 363; E. A. Judge, *The Social Pattern of the Christian Groups in the First Century*, 1960. D.W.B.R.

FAMINE. The Bible does not always indicate the moral and spiritual significance of the famines it records. Those, for example, of Gn. xii. 10, xxvi. 1; Acts xi. 28, *etc.*, are simply stated as historical facts. But famines, like every other event in nature or history, are elsewhere integrated into the characteristic biblical doctrine of the divine providence, *e.g.* Am. iv. 6; Rev. vi. 8. Canaanite religion deified natural processes, and sought to control these non-moral forces by the practice of sympathetic magic, but Israel possessed a different key to prosperity. Yahweh, as Creator, possessed and controlled the 'forces' of nature, the seasons in their order, and the material foundation of man's life on earth (*e.g.* Ps. civ). The exercise of this power by the holy God directly corresponds to the relationship existing between Him and man at any given time. Thus, at the one end of the scale the 'messianic day', when perfect accord between God and His people exists, is marked by unprecedented fertility of the earth (*e.g.* Is. iv. 2, xli. 19; Ho. ii. 21, 22; Am. ix. 13). On the other hand, the fruits of nature are withdrawn in times of disobedience, when the relationship of God and man is dislocated. Thus the curse on the soil was one of the foremost and immediate results of the fall (Gn.

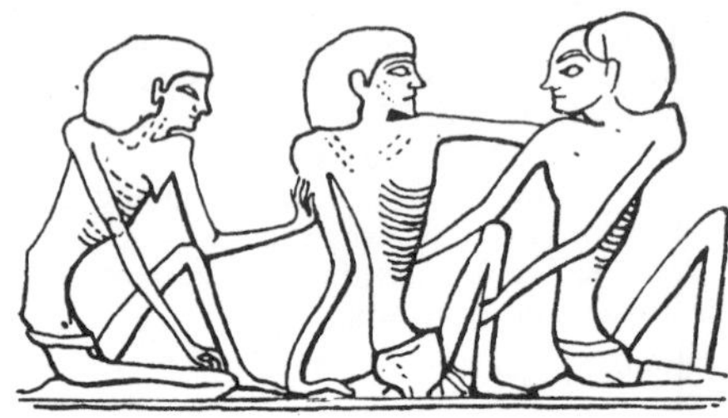

Fig. 82. A woman and two men (possibly Semites) from a large group apparently dying of hunger in a famine. Bas-relief from pyramid-causeway of King Unis, Saqqara, c. 2400 BC.

iii. 17, 18), and God used famines throughout Israel's history as indications of His displeasure, and as warnings to repent (*e.g.* 1 Ki. xvii. 1, xviii. 17, 18; Hg. i. 6, 9–11, ii. 16, 17). Obedience and prosperity (Ps. i. 1–3; Pr. iii. 7–10; Is. i. 19), disobedience and want (Lv. xxvi. 14–16) are biblical inseparables. The law is given classic expression in Dt. xxviii, and poetic illustration in Je. xiv. On specific famines in the biblical East, see JOSEPH. J.A.M.

FAN (Heb. *mizreh*, 'fan'; Heb. *zārâ*, 'to scatter', 'to winnow'; Gk. *ptyon*, 'fan'). A long wooden fork used by threshers to toss grain into the air so that the chaff is blown away (*e.g.* Is. xxx. 24; Je. xv. 7), a method still found in some remote areas of the Middle East. Thus John the Baptist employed an easily understood figure of speech in depicting Christ as the great Winnower who would separate evil from good (Mt. iii. 12; Lk. iii. 17). See also AGRICULTURE. J.D.D.

FARMING. See AGRICULTURE.

FARTHING. See MONEY.

FASTING. Fasting in the Bible generally means going without all food and drink for a period (*e.g.* Est. iv. 16), and not merely refraining from certain foods.

I. IN THE OLD TESTAMENT

The Heb. words are *ṣûm* (verb) and *ṣôm* (noun). The phrase *'innâ napšô* ('to afflict the soul') also refers to fasting. First, there were certain annual fasts. Thus the Hebrews fasted on the Day of Atonement (Lv. xvi. 29, 31, xxiii. 27–32; Nu. xxix. 7). After the Exile, four other annual fasts were observed (Zc. viii. 19), all of them, according to the Talmud, marking disasters in

Jewish history. Est. ix. 31 can be interpreted as implying the establishment of yet another regular fast.

In addition to these there were occasional fasts. These were sometimes individual (*e.g.* 2 Sa. xii. 22) and sometimes corporate (*e.g.* Jdg. xx. 26; Joel i. 14). Fasting gave expression to grief (1 Sa. xxxi. 13; 2 Sa. i. 12, iii. 35; Ne. i. 4; Est. iv. 3; Ps. xxxv. 13, 14) and penitence (1 Sa. vii. 6; 1 Ki. xxi. 27; Ne. ix. 1, 2; Dn. ix. 3, 4; Jon. iii. 5–8). It was a way by which men might humble themselves (Ezr. viii. 21; Ps. lxix. 10). Sometimes it may have been thought of as a self-inflicted punishment (*cf.* the phrase 'to afflict the soul'). Fasting was often directed towards securing the guidance and help of God (Ex. xxxiv. 28; Dt. ix. 9; 2 Sa. xii. 16–23; 2 Ch. xx. 3, 4; Ezr. viii. 21–23). Fasting could be vicarious (Ezr. x. 6; Est. iv. 15–17). Some came to think that fasting would automatically gain man a hearing from God (Is. lviii. 3, 4, RSV). Against this the prophets declared that without right conduct fasting was in vain (Is. lviii. 5–12; Je. xiv. 11, 12; Zc. vii).

II. IN THE NEW TESTAMENT

The usual Gk. words are *nēsteuō* (verb), and *nēsteia* and *nēstis* (nouns). In Acts xxvii. 21, 33 the words *asitia* and *asitos* ('without food') are also used.

As far as general Jewish practice is concerned, the Day of Atonement is the only annual fast referred to in the New Testament (see Acts xxvii. 9). Some strict Pharisees fasted every Monday and Thursday (see Lk. xviii. 12). Other devout Jews, like Anna, might fast often (Lk. ii. 37).

The only occasion when Jesus is recorded as fasting is at the time of His temptations in the wilderness. Then, however, He was not necessarily fasting from choice. The first temptation implies that there was no food available in the place He had selected for His weeks of preparation for His ministry (Mt. iv. 1–4). *Cf.* the forty days' fasts of Moses (Ex. xxxiv. 28) and Elijah (1 Ki. xix. 8).

Jesus assumed that His hearers would fast, but taught them when they did so to face Godward, not manward (Mt. vi. 16–18). When asked why His disciples did not fast as did those of John the Baptist and of the Pharisees, Jesus did not repudiate fasting, but declared it to be inappropriate for His disciples 'as long as the bridegroom is with them' (Mt. ix. 14–17; Mk. ii. 18–22; Lk. v. 33–39). Later, they would fast, like others.

In Acts leaders of the church fast when choosing missionaries (xiii. 2, 3) and elders (xiv. 23). Paul twice refers to his fasting (2 Cor. vi. 5, xi. 27), but it is not clear whether these fasts were voluntary.

The weight of textual evidence is against the inclusion of references to fasting in Mt. xvii. 21; Mk. ix. 29; Acts x. 30; 1 Cor. vii. 5, though the presence of these references in many MSS in itself indicates that there was a growing belief in the value of fasting in the early Church.

H.A.G.B.

FAT. 1. See FOOD, SACRIFICE AND OFFERING. **2.** A wine vat (Is. lxiii. 2; Joel ii. 24). See WINE AND STRONG DRINK.

FATHER. See FAMILY.

FATHERHOOD OF GOD. See GOD.

FATHOM. See WEIGHTS AND MEASURES.

FAVOUR. See GRACE.

FEAR. The Bible uses numerous words to denote fear. The most common of these (giving the noun forms) are Heb. *yir'â*, 'reverence'; Heb. *paḥaḏ*, 'dread', 'fear'; Gk. *phobos*, 'fear', 'terror'. Theologically, four main categories can conveniently be suggested.

a. Holy fear

This comes from the believer's apprehension of the living God. According to Luther, the natural man cannot fear God perfectly; according to Rudolf Otto, he is 'quite unable even to shudder (*grauen*) or feel horror in the real sense of the word'. Holy fear, on the other hand, is God-given, enabling men to reverence God's authority, obey His commandments, and hate and shun all form of evil (Je. xxxii. 40; *cf.* Gn. xxii. 12; Heb. v. 7). It is, moreover, the beginning of wisdom (Ps. cxi. 10); the secret of uprightness (Pr. viii. 13); a feature of the people in whom God delights (Ps. cxlvii. 11); and the whole duty of man (Ec. xii. 13). It is also one of the divine qualifications of the Messiah (Is. xi. 2, 3).

In the Old Testament, largely because of the law's legal sanctions, true religion is often regarded as synonymous with the fear of God (*cf.* Je. ii. 19; Ps. xxxiv. 11, Moffatt), and even in New Testament times the term 'walking in the fear of the Lord' was used in connection with the early Christians. Gentile adherents of the synagogue were called 'God-fearers' (Acts x. 2, *etc.*; *cf.* Phil. ii. 12).

In the New Testament generally, however, emphasis is laid on God as loving and forgiving, the One who through Christ gives to men the spirit of sonship (Rom. viii. 15), and enables them boldly to face up to life (2 Tim. i. 6, 7) and death (Heb. ii. 15) without fear. Nevertheless, a reverent fear remains; for the awesomeness of God has not changed, and there is a day of judgment to be met (2 Cor. v. 10 f.). Godly fear stimulates the believer to seek holiness (2 Cor. vii. 1), and is reflected in his attitude towards his fellow-Christians (Eph. v. 21).

b. Slavish fear

This is strictly a natural consequence of sin (Gn. iii. 10; Pr. xxviii. 1), and can come as a punishment (Dt. xxviii. 28). It was felt by Felix when he heard Paul preach (Acts xxiv. 25); it is felt by Christ-rejecters, for whom remains only 'a fearful expectation of judgment' (Heb. x. 27, RV, 31; *cf.* Rev. xxi. 8). Though not of itself good, this fear is often used by the Holy Spirit for the conversion of men (Acts xvi. 29 ff., *etc.*).

c. Fear of men

This can be expressed as: (i) a reverential awe and regard of men, as of masters and magistrates (1 Pet. ii. 18; Rom. xiii. 7); (ii) a blind dread of them and what they can do (Nu. xiv. 9; Is. viii. 12; Pr. xxix. 25); and (iii) in a peculiar sense a Christian concern for them lest they be ruined by sin (1 Cor. ii. 3; 2 Cor. xi. 3; Col. ii. 1). This kind of fear, and also the slavish fear mentioned in (*b*) above, can be cast out by true love to God (1 Jn. iv. 18).

d. 'Fear' as the object of fear

Fear is used in another sense, as in Gn. xxxi. 42, 53, where God is called the 'fear' of Isaac—*i.e.* the God whom Isaac feared and worshipped. Their 'fear', the thing that terrifies them, comes upon the wicked (Pr. i. 26, 27, x. 24; *cf.* Is. lxvi. 4). When the Hebrews entered the promised land God sent His fear before them, destroying and scattering the Canaanites, or so impressing them with His fear as to render them spiritless and unable to withstand the invaders (Ex. xxiii. 27, 28). Fear in this sense is found also in Jb. iv. 6 (*cf.* ix. 34, xiii. 21): 'Is not this thy fear, thy confidence, thy hope, and the uprightness of thy ways?'

BIBLIOGRAPHY. R. Otto, *The Idea of the Holy*, 1929; J. Murray, *Principles of Conduct*, 1957, pp. 229 ff.; J.-J. von Allmen, *Vocabulary of the Bible*, 1958, pp. 113–119; R. H. Pfeiffer, 'The Fear of God', *IEJ*, V, 1955, pp. 43–48 (a valuable survey of the idea of fear in the non-biblical literatures of the Ancient Near East). J.D.D.

FEASTS. Heb. *ḥag̱*, 'feast' (Lv. xxiii. 6; Dt. xvi. 16), *mô'ᵃḏê Yahweh*, 'feasts of the Lord' (Lv. xxiii. 2, 4; Nu. xv. 3). The terms are expressive of a day or season of religious joy. While some of these feasts coincide with the seasons, it does not follow that they have their origin in the seasonal ritual of the religions of the Ancient Near East. These are associated with the gods of the pantheon who banquet together or feast with men. (See C. H. Gordon, *Ugaritic Literature*, 1949, pp. 57–103; T. Gaster, *Thespis*, 1950, pp. 6–108.) Biblical feasts differ in origin, purpose, and content. To the Israelite the seasons were the work of the Creator for the benefit of man. They manifested the beneficence of God towards His creatures. By these feasts man not only acknowledged God as his Provider but recorded the Lord's unbounded and free favour to a chosen people whom He delivered, by personal intervention, in this world (Ex. x. 2, xii. 8, 9, 11, 14; Lv. xxiii. 5; Dt. xvi. 6, 12). The joy expressed was heartfelt. Religious commitment was not incompatible with pleasure in temporal things conceived as gifts of God (Lv. xxiii. 40; Dt. xvi. 14). The response of the participant was religiously ethical. Acknowledgment of sin and devotion to the law of God was involved (Ex. xiii. 9; Zc. viii. 9). The sacrifices offered bespoke forgiveness of sin and reconciliation with God (Lv. xvii. 11; Nu. xxviii. 22, xxix. 7–11; 2 Ch. xxx. 22; Ezk. xlv. 17, 20). To be withheld from the feast was considered a loss and a bar from privilege (Nu. ix. 7). Not only did the Israelite appear at the feast as a beneficiary of the divine favour, but he made return to the Lord as he had been blessed (Dt. xvi. 10). Only in unauthorized feasts did unbelieving Israelites eat, drink, and play (Ex. xxxii. 6; 1 Ki. xii. 32, 33).

The feasts of the Old Testament do not follow the Ancient Near Eastern pattern of a period of joy preceded by rites of mortification and purgation (T. Gaster, *op. cit.*, pp. 6, 12). The Bible festival itself contained the element of mourning, for this is involved in sacrifice for sin (Lv. xxiii. 27; Nu. xxix. 7). There is no sharp line of demarcation between sorrow for sin and the joy of the Lord.

Prophetical displeasure with the feasts as observed by the Jews (Is. i. 13–20) was not because they were in themselves on a lower plane of piety, but because many Israelites had departed from their spiritual purpose. They made the sum of religion consist in external observance, which was never the divine intent for the feasts from the time of their promulgation (Na. i. 15). In the New Testament this was well understood by our Lord and devout believers who diligently and spiritually observed the prescribed feasts of the old economy (Lk. ii. 41, xxii. 8; Jn. iv. 45, v. 1, vii. 2, 11, xii. 20).

The feasts to which reference is made in the Old Testament are as follows:

1. The Feast of Unleavened Bread, Heb. *ḥag̱ hammaṣṣôṯ* (Ex. xxiii. 15), or Passover (*q.v.*), Heb. *pesaḥ*, Lv. xxiii. 5, was established to commemorate the historical deliverance from Egypt (Ex. x. 2, xii. 8, 14). It was one of the three annual festivals, and was observed on the fourteenth day of the first month. For seven days unleavened bread was eaten and no servile work done. The first and the last day being 'holy convocations', sacrifices were offered (Nu. xxviii. 16–25; Dt. xvi. 1–8).

2. The Feast of Weeks, Heb. *ḥag̱ šāḇû'ôṯ*. It is also called the 'feast of harvest' and 'the day of firstfruits' (Ex. xxiii. 16, xxxiv. 22; Nu. xxviii. 26). Later it was known as Pentecost (*q.v.*) because it was celebrated on the fiftieth day from the sabbath beginning the Passover. It was marked by a holy convocation and the offering of sacrifices.

3. The Feast of Tabernacles (see TABERNACLES, FEAST OF), Heb. *ḥag̱ hassukkôṯ*, or 'the feast of booths', is also called the 'feast of ingathering', Heb. *ḥag̱ hā'āsîp̄* (Ex. xxiii. 16, xxxiv. 22; Lv. xxiii. 34; Dt. xvi. 13). It lasted seven days, the first and last days being holy convocations. Fruit was gathered in and people dwelt in booths made of branches and boughs of trees (Lv. xxiii. 39–43; Nu. xxix. 12–38).

4. The Sabbath (*q.v.*). This is regarded as a feast in Lv. xxiii. 2, 3, and called a 'sabbath of rest'. It was marked by a solemn assembly (Is. i. 13), and cessation from all labour. It was also a day of joy (Is. lviii. 13).

5. The Day of Blowing of Trumpets (Nu. xxix. 1). In Lv. xxiii. 24 it is called 'a memorial of blowing of trumpets' and 'a sabbath'. Sacrifices were offered and hard labour ceased.

6. The Day of Atonement (see ATONEMENT, DAY OF) (Lv. xxiii. 26–31). It was observed on the tenth day of the seventh month, and was a day of a 'holy convocation' in which souls were afflicted and an atonement made for sin. It was observed but once in the year (Ex. xxx. 10).

7. The Feast of Purim, described in Esther ix. Established by Mordecai in the time of Ahasuerus to commemorate the remarkable deliverance from the intrigues of Haman, this was a day of feasting and gladness.

The extra-biblical feast of *ḥ^a^nukkâ* is the celebration of the recovery and cleansing of the Jerusalem Temple by Judas Maccabaeus in 164 BC, after its desecration by Antiochus Epiphanes. It is also called the 'festival of lights'. See Jn. x. 22, where it is called by its Gk. name *enkainia* ('dedication'). D.F.

FELIX, MARCUS ANTONIUS, was the brother of Claudius' favourite and freedman Pallas, through whose influence he was appointed to the procuratorship of Judaea. Tacitus (*Ann.* xii. 54) and Josephus (*BJ* ii. 12; *Ant.* x. 6 ff.) disagree as to the time and circumstances of his arrival in Palestine; he may have been sent to Samaria with the rank of procurator during the trial of Ventidius Cumanus (is the 'many years' of Acts xxiv. 10 some corroboration of this?), but in any case he seems to have held the procuratorship of Judaea from *c.* AD 52. Unrest increased under his rule, for 'with savagery and lust he exercised the powers of a king with the disposition of a slave' (Tac., *Hist.* v. 9), and he was utterly merciless in crushing opposition. In AD 55 he put down the followers of a messianic pretender of Egyptian origin, but the man himself escaped. When the riot recorded in Acts xxi. 27 ff. broke out the tribune Claudius Lysias initially mistook Paul for this Egyptian (Acts xxi. 38).

After his arrest Paul was conveyed to Caesarea, the Roman capital of Palestine, and was tried before Felix. Two well-attested characteristics of the governor stand out in the subsequent narrative: his disregard for justice and his avarice. He kept Paul in prison for two years, hoping he would be paid a fat bribe (Acts xxiv. 26). Disappointed of this hope, he deferred judgment in a case where there was ample evidence of the prisoner's innocence (xxiii. 29, xxiv. 22), and upon his recall he left Paul in prison in order to please the Jews (xxiv. 27) or, according to the Western Text, to please Drusilla (*q.v.*), his wife.

He was recalled by Nero, probably in AD 59 (see FESTUS), and was saved from proceedings instigated by the Jews only through the influence of Pallas. Of Felix' later history nothing is known. E.M.B.G.

FELLOWSHIP. See COMMUNION.

FENCED CITIES. See FORTIFICATION AND SIEGECRAFT.

FERRET. See LIZARD.

FESTUS. Porcius Festus succeeded Felix as procurator of Judaea. Nothing is known of his life prior to his appointment, and he died in office after about two years. According to Josephus (*Ant.* x. 8, 9 f., ix. 1; *BJ* ii. 24. 1), he was a wise and just official, an agreeable contrast to Felix his predecessor and Albinus his successor. In Acts (xxiv. 27–xxvi. 32) he appears in a less favourable light. Though he tried Paul's case with commendable alacrity (xxv. 6), and was convinced of his innocence (xxvi. 31), he was prepared to sacrifice Paul to do the Jews a pleasure (xxv. 9). Hence the scandalous suggestion of re-trial at Jerusalem. Later he deliberately exploited his prisoner for the entertainment of Agrippa and Bernice. As G. P. Gould says, 'Paul's appeal to Nero is the lasting condemnation of Festus.' He was again concerned in an appeal case when the Jewish leaders brought before Nero a successful charge against the younger Agrippa's violation of the privacy of the temple area (Jos. *Ant.* xx. 8. 11). W. M. Ramsay in *Pauline Studies*, p. 348, has shown that Eusebius' evidence, when rightly understood, points to the year AD 59 for the arrival of Festus in Palestine, and some support for this date may be afforded by the sudden change of procuratorial coinage in that year, an event most plausibly attributed to the arrival of a new governor. (See H. J. Cadbury, *The Book of Acts in History*, 1955, pp. 9 f.)

E.M.B.G.

FEVER (Heb. *qaddaḥat*, 'burning heat', Dt. xxviii. 22; Gk. *pyretos*, 'fiery heat', Lk. iv. 38; Acts xxviii. 8, *etc.*). A generic term which in EVV covers various ailments, all of them suggesting the presence of a high temperature. See also DISEASE AND HEALING.

FIELD. A word used in the EVV for several biblical terms. 1. *śāḏeh* (and its poetical form *śāḏay*) is the most common term (*e.g.* Gn. ii. 5) with the simple meaning of 'field', 'plain', 'open space'. 2. *š^e^ḏēmâ* is used six times only (*e.g.* Dt. xxxii. 32) with much the same meaning. 3. *bar* (Aram.) is used only in Dn. ii and iv with the same meaning. 4. *ḥûṣ*, 'the outside', is frequently translated 'abroad' (*e.g.* Dt. xxiii. 13), but twice rendered 'field' (Jb. v. 10; Pr. viii. 26). 5. *ḥelqâ*, in fact, means 'portion of ground' but is translated 'field' in 2 Sa. xiv. 30. 6. *'ereṣ*, the common word for 'earth, land', is translated 'field' in Ezk. xxix. 5 (AV). 7. *y^e^ḡēḇîm*, a word which occurs once only in the Old Testament, is there translated 'field' (Je. xxxix. 10).

8. *agros*, 'field' (*e.g.* Mt. vi. 28), in LXX is used mainly to render *śāḏeh*. 9. *chōra* is usually used of a large region (Acts xvi. 6), but twice rendered 'field' (Jn. iv. 35; Jas. v. 4), and its diminutive *chōrion* is translated 'field' in Acts i. 18, 19.

T.C.M.

FIERY SERPENT. See SERPENT.

FIG, FIG-TREE (Heb. *t*e*'ēnâ*, 'fig', 'fig-tree'; Heb. *paḡ*, 'green fig', Ct. ii. 13 only = Gk. *o'ynthoi*, 'untimely figs', Rev. vi. 13 only; Gk. *sykon*, 'fig', Gk. *sykē*, 'fig-tree').

Indigenous to Asia Minor and Syria, the fig-tree (*Ficus carica*) can grow to about 35 feet and can flourish even in stony soil. Its fruit often appears before the leaves, but the flowers are never conspicuous. Fertilization is effected by small hymenopterous insects.

The fig seems to have been an early inhabitant of Palestine, like the vine and the olive (*e.g.* Jdg. ix. 7 ff.), with which it is associated in God's promises of prosperity and in prophetic warnings (Je. v. 17; Ho. ii. 12; Joel i. 7, 12; Hab. iii. 17). The fig is often planted with the vine (Lk. xiii. 6), so that its branches and the vine's foliage led to the well-known expression 'to sit down under one's own vine and fig-tree' as a symbol of long-continued well-being and prosperity (1 Ki. iv. 25; Mi. iv. 4; Zc. iii. 10; *cf.* 2 Ki. xviii. 31; Is. xxxvi. 16—though some references may refer merely to a rural preference for the cultivation of fig-trees overlooking houses).

The failure or destruction of these slow-growing trees, which demand years of patient labour (Pr. xxvii. 18; Lk. xiii. 7), was a national calamity (Je. v. 17; Hab. iii. 17; *cf.* Ps. cv. 33), and productiveness was a token of peace and of divine favour. Figs are frequently mentioned in conjunction with the vine, palm, and pomegranate (*e.g.* Dt. viii. 8), and their absence formed part of the Israelites' complaint in Nu. xx. 5.

Adam and Eve are said to have been clothed with girdles made from the fig-tree's broad leaves (Gn. iii. 7), and fig leaves are still sewn together in the East and used as wrappings for fresh fruit sent to the markets, where they are a valuable item of commerce. Lumps or cakes of dried figs (from Heb. *d*e*ḇēlâ*, 'pressed together') made an excellent food, were easy to carry, and constituted an acceptable gift (1 Sa. xxv. 18; 1 Ch. xii. 40). Such a mass of figs was prescribed by Isaiah as a poultice for Hezekiah's boil (2 Ki. xx. 7; Is. xxxviii. 21).

There is some difference in terminology about the number of fig crops in the year. W. Corswant (*A Dictionary of Life in Bible Times*, E.T. 1960, pp. 117–118) suggests that for the understanding of certain biblical passages we should regard the fig-tree as bearing successively three kinds of figs: (*a*) the *late or autumn figs* (Je. viii. 13, xxix. 17) which furnish the main crop from August till winter; (*b*) *green or winter figs* (Ct. ii. 13; Rev. vi. 13), which, having had no time to ripen, spend the winter on the branches and grow ruddy at the first touch of spring, yet remain small and are easily blown off by the wind. The remainder stay on the tree and ripen in summer from June onwards. These latter are (*c*) the *first-ripe figs* (Is. xxviii. 4, RV; Je. xxiv. 2; Ho. ix. 10; Mi. vii. 1; Na. iii. 12), much sought after for their freshness and delicious flavour. This would mean that a healthy tree bore fruit for about ten months, and Jesus apparently expected to find green figs on the tree He cursed (Mt. xxi. 18–22; Mk. xi. 12–14, 20–24; but see complete discussions of this intriguing incident in *HDCG*, pp. 593 f.; R. C. Trench, *Notes on the Miracles*, 1886, pp. 468–479; F. F. Bruce, *The New Testament Documents*, 1960, pp. 73, 74).

The fig has inspired numerous similes, metaphors, and proverbs (*e.g.* Je. xxiv. 1 ff.; Mi. vii. 1; Mt. vii. 16; Jas. iii. 12). In Hellenistic times figs were considered so important to the national economy that the Greeks made special laws to regulate their export.

The sycomore tree (Gk. *sykomōraia*; Lat. *Ficus sycomorus*) associated with Zacchaeus in Lk. xix. 4 is often known as the mulberry-fig because it combines the characteristics of both these trees (see 'Sycomore' under TREES).

J.D.D.

FIRE. A word usually represented in the Old Testament by *'ēš* and in the New Testament by *pyr*, the term generally used in the LXX for *'ēš*. These signify the state of combustion, and the visible aspects of it, such as the flame. The production of fire by artificial means was a skill known to man from Stone Age times, but then and in later times great care was taken to preserve a burning fire to avoid the necessity for rekindling. Abraham apparently carried a piece of burning fire with him when he went to offer Isaac (Gn. xxii. 6), and Is. xxx. 14 indicates that this was a common domestic practice. Probably the commonest methods of kindling a flame in biblical times were by means of the fire-drill, attested in the Egyptian hieroglyphic *d'* (XVIIIth Dynasty), and the striking of flint on iron pyrites, a practice attested from Neolithic times and therefore assumed to be in use later. It may be that this latter method is referred to in 2 Macc. x. 3.

Fire was used in the normal course for such purposes as cooking (Ex. xii. 8; Jn. xxi. 9), providing warmth (Is. xliv. 16; Lk. xxii. 55), and refining metals (Ex. xxxii. 24; Je. vi. 29), but also for destroying such things as idols (Ex. xxxii. 20; Dt. vii. 5, 25), Asherim (Dt. xii. 3), chariots (Jos. xi. 6, 9), and cities (Jos. vi. 24; Jdg. xviii. 27), and the culprits in two cases of sexual breach (Lv. xx. 14, xxi. 9). It also played an important part in the worship of the Tabernacle and Temple, where the altars of incense and of burnt offering constantly required it. The fire on the latter having been started by God (Lv. ix. 24; 2 Ch. vii. 1–3), it was kept burning continuously (Lv. vi. 13). This fire was special, and offerings by means of 'strange fire' were not acceptable

(Lv. x. 1; Nu. iii. 4, xxvi. 61). The heathen practice of offering children for burnt offerings (2 Ki. iii. 27, xvii. 31), which is probably what is referred to as 'passing through the fire' and was occasionally practised by the Israelites (2 Ki. xvi. 3, xvii. 17, xxi. 6, xxiii. 10; 2 Ch. xxviii. 3, xxxiii. 6), was included in the condemnations of the prophets (Mi. vi. 7).

Theophanies of God were sometimes accompanied by fire (Ex. iii. 2, xiii. 21, 22, xix. 18; Dt. iv. 11) and the image of fire is used to symbolize God's glory (Ezk. i. 4, 13), protective presence (2 Ki. vi. 17), holiness (Dt. iv. 24), righteous judgment (Zc. xiii. 9), and wrath against sin (Is. lxvi. 15, 16). It is also used of the Holy Spirit (Mt. iii. 11; *cf.* Acts ii. 3), of prophetic inspiration (Je. v. 14, xx. 9, xxiii. 29), and religious feeling (Ps. xxxix. 3). In other contexts fire is used as a literary symbol of sin (Is. ix. 18), lust (Ho. vii. 6), and affliction (Ps. lxvi. 12).

BIBLIOGRAPHY. R. J. Forbes, *Studies in Ancient Technology*, VI, 1958, pp. 4 ff. T.C.M.

FIREPAN (*maḥtâ*, from *ḥaṭâ*, 'to snatch up'). A bowl-shaped utensil with a handle used in connection with the Tabernacle and Temple services for three different purposes. **1.** In some passages it refers to the *snuffdish*, made of gold, which held the pieces of burnt lamp-wick removed by the tongs or snuffers (Ex. xxv. 38, xxxvii. 23; Nu. iv. 9; 1 Ki. vii. 50; 2 Ki. xxv. 15; 2 Ch. iv. 22; Je. lii. 19, the last four of these references being wrongly translated 'censer' and 'firepan' in AV). See also SNUFFERS, SNUFFDISHES. **2.** Elsewhere it refers to the bronze *firepan* which was used to carry coals away from the altar of burnt offering (Ex. xxvii. 3; Nu. iv. 14, the second of these references being wrongly translated 'censer' in AV). **3.** In other passages it is used of the *censer*, also made of bronze, in which incense was burnt (Lv. x. 1, xvi. 12; Nu. xvi. 6, 17, 18, 37–39, 46). See also CENSER. J.C.W.

FIRKIN. See WEIGHTS AND MEASURES.

FIRMAMENT. See CREATION.

FIRSTBORN.

I. IN THE OLD TESTAMENT

The Heb. root *bkr*, represented in many cognate languages, has the general meaning of '(to be) early'; its derivates are used also when speaking of firstfruits. *bᵉḵōr*, however, is used of persons and animals only. In Israel's polygamic society distinction should be made between the firstborn of the father and the firstborn of the mother. The father's firstborn was considered 'the beginning of his strength' (Gn. xlix. 3; Dt. xxi. 17, *cf.* xxxiii. 17), the acme of his (sexual and general) power. (A sore disease is called 'the firstborn of death'; see Jb. xviii. 13.)

In the absence of the father the firstborn son had authority over his brothers (*e.g.* Reuben among the sons of Jacob) and sisters (Gn. xxiv. 55, 60). He ranked highest after the father. The right of the firstborn was greatly appreciated (Gn. xxv. 29–34, xxvii). In cases of misconduct it could be shifted to another son (Gn. xlix. 3, 4; 1 Ch. v. 1, 2). The firstborn inherited twice as much as every other son (*cf.* 2 Ki. ii. 9), and Dt. xxi. 15–17 forbids the arbitrary removal of this right from the actual firstborn son to the son of the most highly-favoured wife. This law does not apply to sons of concubines or handmaids (Gn. xxi. 9–13; Jdg. xi. 1, 2).

Among kings the right of the firstborn implied the succession to his father's rule (2 Ch. xxi. 1–3), but favouritism often played a dangerous rôle, both among kings and commoners (1 Ki. i, ii; 2 Ch. xi. 22, 23; 1 Ch. xxvi. 10). In Harran, firstborn daughters were given in marriage before their younger sisters (Gn. xxix. 26), and this was perhaps the case in Israel too (1 Sa. xviii. 17–27). Ugaritic literature mentions the shifting of the birthright of the eldest daughter to the youngest one. Holy Scripture shows a certain predilection for the youngest son as being the least privileged (Jacob, Ephraim, David). The high rank of the firstborn led to the metaphorical use of the term in Ex. iv. 22; Ps. lxxxix. 27.

On account of the sparing of Israel's firstborn in the night of Passover, the male firstborn of the mother was considered holy to the Lord (Ex. xiii. 2, 12; Nu. iii. 13). The firstborn of the generation of the Exodus were redeemed by the consecration of the Levites (Nu. iii. 40, 41); afterwards every firstborn son, when a month old, was redeemed by paying five shekels to the priests (Nu. xviii. 16, *cf.* iii. 42–51). From excavations we know that young children were often sacrificed among the Canaanites; sometimes the Israelites followed their example (Ezk. xx. 25, 26; Mi. vi. 7), but this was a misinterpretation of Ex. xxii. 29. Male firstlings of clean animals should be sacrificed (Nu. xviii. 17, 18; Dt. xii. 6, 17); if they had any blemish, they should be slaughtered and eaten (Dt. xv. 19–23). Male firstlings of unclean animals should be redeemed (Nu. xviii. 15); in the case of an ass it should be redeemed by a lamb or have its neck broken (Ex. xiii. 13, xxxiv. 20).

II. IN THE NEW TESTAMENT

Jesus was the firstborn (*prōtotokos*) of his mother (Mt. i. 25; Lk. ii. 7); and it is recorded that his parents did 'for him after the custom of the law' (Lk. ii. 27). At the same time Christ is the Firstborn of His heavenly Father and has first rank among His brethren on earth, and complete authority over them (Rom. viii. 29; Heb. i. 6). By His resurrection He is 'the firstborn from the dead' (Col. i. 18; Rev. i. 5). The title 'firstborn of every creature' (Col. i. 15) points to His authority over all creation, but does not imply that He Himself was created. The believers are called 'the firstborn' (Heb. xii. 23), because they are privileged above all other men.

BIBLIOGRAPHY. O. Eissfeldt, *Erstlinge und Zehnten im Alten Testament*, 1917; W. Michaelis, *TWNT*, VII, pp. 872–883. A. VAN S.

FIRSTFRUITS. See SACRIFICE AND OFFERING.

FIR-TREE. See TREES.

FISH, FISHING.

I. KINDS OF FISH AND SOURCES OF SUPPLY

The general Heb. words for water-creatures are *dāḡ* and *dāḡâ*. According to the Mosaic law (Lv. xi. 9–12; Dt. xiv. 9, 10) water-creatures having fins and scales were 'clean', but those without fins and scales (*e.g.* shellfish) were 'unclean'. The creature which swallowed Jonah is called 'a great fish' in Jon. i. 17. Mt. xii. 40 carefully adopts the same designation (Gk. *kētos*, 'a large sea-monster', translated and interpreted by AV and RV as 'whale'). According to Tobit vi. 2 a large fish in the Tigris river threatened to swallow Tobias. The fisherman of the parable of the drag-net (Mt. xiii. 48) discarded some fish because they were too small, inedible, or 'unclean'. The fish in whose mouth Peter found the stater (Mt. xvii. 27) must have had a large mouth, like the fish of the Sea of Galilee called *Chromis simonis* after the apostle. In addition to the common word for fish, *ichthys* (*e.g.* Mt. vii. 10), the New Testament uses the diminutive *ichthydion*, 'little fish' (Mt. xv. 34; Mk. viii. 7, both passages which describe the feeding of the four thousand), and *opsarion*, small fish eaten with bread (Jn. vi. 11, xxi. 9). In the Sea of Galilee today at least twenty-four species of fish are found, sometimes in large shoals.

Fig. 83. An Egyptian dignitary spearing fish with a two-pronged lance from a papyrus skiff in the marshes. From a painting in the tomb of Simut, Thebes, 15th century BC.

The Bible mentions Egypt as a place where fish are plentiful (Nu. xi. 5), and the Sea of Galilee (Lk. v. 6) and Tyre (Ne. xiii. 16) are also noted as ample sources of supply. Fish do not live in the salty waters of the Dead Sea, but Ezk. xlvii. 10 foresees that this lake will be stocked with fish as a sign of the blessings of the kingdom of glory.

II. FISHERMEN AND THEIR METHODS

The strenuous life of fishermen required a strong physique (Lk. v. 2), and their speech was sometimes rough (Mk. xiv. 70 f.). At least seven of Jesus' disciples were fishermen: Peter, Andrew, probably Philip, who also came from Bethsaida (Aram. for 'house of fishing') on the Sea of Galilee, James, John, Thomas, and Nathanael (Mt. iv. 18, 21; Jn. i. 44, xxi. 2). Some of these were partners in fishing and were used to working together (Lk. v. 7, 10).

The Bible mentions fishing by spear or harpoon (Jb. xli. 7, for a crocodile), by hook (Jb. xli. 1, 2; Is. xix. 8; Mt. xvii. 27), and by net. The kinds of nets specified in the Bible are the casting-net (Mt. iv. 18) and the large drag-net (Mt. xiii. 47). See NETS.

On the Sea of Galilee the fishermen used small boats, which were propelled by oars (Jn. vi. 19). The statement that the wind was contrary (Mt. xiv. 24) may indicate the use of a sail as in the present-day fishing-boats on this lake. See SHIPS AND BOATS. Often in the Sea of Galilee fishing was done at night (Lk. v. 5; Jn. xxi. 3). During the day the fisherman on the shore or wading in the water could throw the casting-net (Mt. iv. 18). Larger nets were let down by several men from boats (Lk. v. 4). The fish were either emptied into the boat (Lk. v. 7) or the nets were dragged to the shore (Mt. xiii. 48; Jn. xxi. 8). Then the fish were sorted, the saleable ones were put in baskets, and the useless ones were thrown away (Mt. xiii. 48). The Bible does not refer to fishing as a recreation.

III. MARKETING AND PREPARATION

In Jerusalem there was a Fish Gate (perhaps on the north side of the city), through which traders brought their fish to sell to the populace (Zp. i. 10). From Ne. xiii. 16 we know that Tyrian fish merchants lived in the city after the Exile. In Bible times common methods of preparing fish for eating were roasting (Jn. xxi. 9; Tobit vi. 5), and salting and drying (Tobit vi. 5, Sinaitic Text). The fish which Tyrians sold in Jerusalem and the small fish which were used in the miraculous feeding of the five thousand and of the four thousand (Mt. xiv. 17, xv. 36) were probably prepared in the latter way. See also FOOD.

IV. FISH WORSHIP

Dt. iv. 18 forbids making images of fish for worship. The pagan fish-goddess Atargatis was worshipped at Ascalon and among the Nabataeans. The Oxyrhynchus was worshipped in a nome in Egypt called after that fish.

V. FIGURATIVE AND SYMBOLIC USES

Fishing is used in the Old Testament as a figure of God's judgment on nations or individuals (*e.g.* Je. xvi. 16; Ezk. xxxii. 3). Jesus called disciples to become fishers of men (Mt. iv. 19). The kingdom of heaven is likened to a drag-net (Mt. xiii. 47).

The fish was one of the earliest symbols of Christian art, because the letters of Gk. *ichthys* were taken as an acrostic for *Iēsous Christos Theou Hyios Sōtēr*, 'Jesus Christ, of God the Son, Saviour' (see F. J. Dölger, ΙΧΘΥΣ, 1910–43).

BIBLIOGRAPHY. G. Dalman, *Arbeit und Sitte*, VI, 1939, pp. 343–370. J.T.

Fig. 84. An Assyrian catching fish by hook and line in a pond in the park at Nineveh. Assyrian palace relief, *c.* 700 BC.

FITCHES. 1. Heb. *qeṣaḥ* (Is. xxviii. 25, 27) is taken by some to denote a common herb cultivated as a forage plant, and beaten with a light staff to separate the seeds. RVmg, however, renders 'black cummin' (*Nigella sativa*), whose tiny aromatic seeds, a favourite condiment of ancient Greeks and Romans, are still used in the East for seasoning and carminative purposes.

2. Heb. *kussemeṯ* is rendered 'fitches' in Ezk. iv. 9, 'rye' elsewhere in AV, and (more accurately) 'spelt' in RV. Spelt (*Triticum spelta*) is an inferior kind of wheat which Ezekiel lists as an ingredient of the symbolic bread he was commanded to bake. J.D.D.

FLAG. 1. Heb. *'āḥû*, 'reed'. Rendered 'flag' in Jb. viii. 11, and 'meadow' in Gn. xli. 2, 18, where RV has 'reed-grass', this is a generic word for fen-like plants found in swamps and by river-banks—hence Bildad's rhetorical question ('can the flag grow without water?').

2. Heb. *sûp̄*, 'reed' (Ex. ii. 3, 5; Is. xix. 6). A general term for several sedgy plants still common around the Nile and its canals. The Red Sea (*yam sûp̄*) is literally the 'sea of Reeds' (*cf.* Egyp. *p'-ṯwf*). J.D.D.

FLAGON. Heb. *nēḇel*, Is. xxii. 24, a large, two-handled jar for storing wine (see BOTTLE). AV translates Heb. *'ašîšâ* as 'flagon', following the interpretation of Qimchi. However, Ho. iii. 1 (Heb. *'ašîšê 'anāḇîm* . . . of grapes) and Ct. ii. 5 (parallel to 'refresh me with apples', RSV) suggest a derivation from the root *'šš*, 'be firm', 'compress'. LXX preserves the meaning by translating 'cake from a pan' (*laganon apo tēganou*, 2 Sa. vi. 19); 'raisin cake' (*pemmata meta staphidōn*, Ho. iii. 1); 'sweet cake' (*amoritēn*, 1 Ch. xvi. 3; *amorais*, Ct. ii. 5). Heb. *'ašîšâ* denotes, therefore, a cake of compressed, dried grapes, possibly used as an offering in pagan worship (Ho. iii. 1). See RAISINS. A.R.M.

FLAX (Heb. *pištâ* in Ex. ix. 31 and Is. xlii. 3; *pišteh* elsewhere in the Old Testament; Gk. *linon* in Mt. xii. 20). Used chiefly in making linen (*q.v.*), flax (*Linum usitatissimum*) is the oldest of the textile fibres. The plant grows often to a height of 3 feet, and produces beautiful blue flowers. From the pods comes linseed oil.

Flax was cultivated by the Egyptians before the Exodus (Ex. ix. 31) and, before the conquest, by the Canaanites, who dried the stalks on the housetops (Jos. ii. 6). Among God's judgments in Hosea's day was the taking away of the flax (Ho. ii. 9).

In the single New Testament reference (Mt. xii. 20), an allusion to flax as being slow-burning, Matthew is quoting from Is. xlii. 3. J.D.D.

FLEA. Fleas (*Ctenocephalides* spp.) have always been parasitic on man and his domestic stock, and they are particularly numerous among nomadic peoples. Heb. *par'ōš* occurs only in 1 Sa. xxiv. 14, xxvi. 20. The metaphor is clear, and the jumping habit of the flea confirms the probability of the translation. G.C.

FLESH.

I. IN THE OLD TESTAMENT

In the Old Testament the principal word is *bāśār* (found 269 times), though *še'ēr* (sixteen times, seven times translated 'flesh' in AV) and *ṭibḥâ* (thrice, once translated 'flesh' in AV) also occur. *Bāśār* denotes the principal constituent of the body, human (Gn. xl. 19) or animal (Lv. vi. 27). The latter use leads on to the thought of meat as used for food and to that of the flesh of the animal sacrifices, whether eaten or not. From the former usage 'flesh' comes to mean the whole body (Pr. xiv. 30), and by a natural extension of meaning the whole man, as when the Psalmist says, 'my flesh also shall rest in hope' (Ps. xvi. 9). This leads to the thought of the union of one person with another. Man and wife are 'one flesh' (Gn. ii. 24), and a man can say of his relatives, 'I am your bone and your flesh' (Jdg. ix. 2). Again, the thought of flesh as the whole man leads to the expression 'all flesh', which denotes the totality of human existence, sometimes also including the animal creation. There is sometimes the thought that flesh is weak: 'in God I have put my trust; I will not fear what flesh can do unto me' (Ps. lvi. 4). This is not the thought of moral weakness (perhaps the nearest we get to this is Ps. lxxviii. 39). It is the physical frailty of man that is meant.

II. IN THE NEW TESTAMENT

In the New Testament (apart from two occurrences of *kreas* for 'flesh' or 'meat') the word for 'flesh' is *sarx*. This term reproduces most of the Old Testament meaning of *bāśār*. It denotes the fleshy part of the body, as in references to eating flesh (Rev. xix. 18, *etc.*), or the whole body (Gal. iv. 13 f.). It may mean the whole man, 'our flesh had no rest . . . without were fightings, within were fears' (2 Cor. vii. 5), or 'in me (that is, in my flesh)' (Rom. vii. 18). As in the Old Testament, man and wife are 'one flesh' (Mt. xix. 5 f.), and there are passages referring to 'all flesh' (Jn. xvii. 2). The weakness of the flesh is spoken of in connection with the apostles' failure to watch in Gethsemane (Mk. xiv. 38).

But the New Testament has also some distinctive meanings. Akin to the 'my bone and my flesh' passages of the Old Testament (though not quite the same) are those which refer to physical descent and the like. Thus Christ 'was made of the seed of David according to the flesh' (Rom. i. 3). Paul can speak of 'Israel after the flesh' (1 Cor. x. 18), and the Israelites as his 'kinsmen according to the flesh' (Rom. ix. 3).

'The flesh' may stand for the whole of this physical existence, and there are references to being 'in the flesh' (Col. ii. 1). There is no blame attached to this, and, indeed, Christ is said more than once to have been 'in the flesh' (Eph. ii. 15; 1 Pet. iii. 18; 1 Jn. iv. 2, 3, *etc.*). To be 'in the flesh' is not incompatible with being 'in the Lord' (Phm. 16). The flesh may be defiled (Jude 8) or purified (Heb. ix. 13). The life that Paul the Christian now lived was 'in the flesh' (Gal. ii. 20).

But, by definition, the flesh is the earthly part of man. It has its 'lusts' and its 'desires' (Eph. ii. 3). If a man concentrates on these he may be said to 'mind the things of the flesh' (Rom. viii. 5). And the mind of the flesh 'is death' (Rom. viii. 6). This is explained as 'enmity against God' (Rom. viii. 7). The man whose horizon is limited by the flesh is by that very fact opposed to God. He lives 'after the flesh' (Rom. viii. 13), that flesh that 'lusteth against the Spirit' (Gal. v. 17). For a dreadful list of 'the works of the flesh', see Gal. v. 19–21. The flesh in this sense denotes the whole personality of man as organized in the wrong direction, as directed to earthly pursuits rather than the service of God.

BIBLIOGRAPHY. K. Grayston in *RTWB*; A. R. Johnson, *Vitality of the Individual in the Thought of Ancient Israel*, 1949; J. A. T. Robinson, *The Body*, 1952; E. Schweizer, F. Baumgärtel, and R. Meyer in *TWNT*, VII, 1960, *s.v. sarx*. L.M.

FLESH-HOOK. A bronze implement associated like others with the altar of burnt offering at the tabernacle (Ex. xxvii. 3, xxxviii. 3; Nu. iv. 14) and Solomon's Temple (1 Ch. xxviii. 17; 2 Ch. iv. 16). Seen in use at Shiloh (1 Sa. ii. 13, 14) as a three-pronged fork. K.A.K.

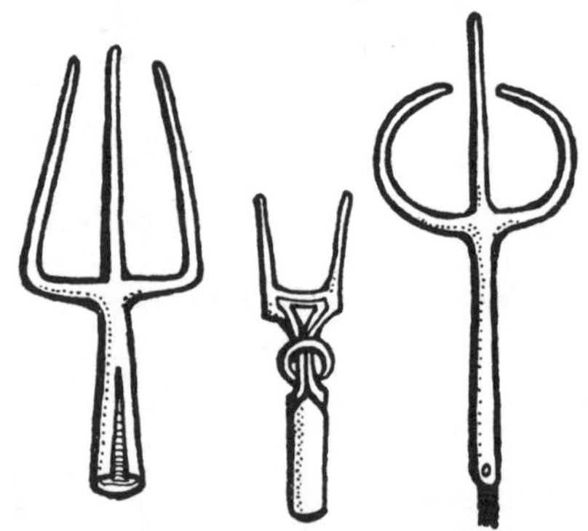

Fig. 85. Bronze forks of the Late Bronze Age, left from Byblos, centre and right from Gezer. Perhaps 'fleshhooks' used in ritual handling of meat for sacrifice (e.g. I Sa. ii. 13).

FLESHPOTS (*sîr*, probably a foreign loanword; *cf.* Arab. *sîr*, 'a large waterjar', and later Gk. *siras*). A large household utensil usually made of metal for placing over a fire (Ec. vii. 6; 2 Ki. iv. 38, AV 'great pot'). It is used symbolically of Jerusalem (Ezk. xi. 3, *etc.*) and in similes for avarice (Mi. iii. 3), and figuratively for speedy vengeance (Ps. lviii. 9). Such pots were in use in the sanctuary (Ex. xxvii. 3; 2 Ki. xxv. 14, *etc.*) and were probably deep bronze cauldrons (so Je. i. 13, RV). They were also used for washing (Ps. cviii. 9). Their shape was that adopted for the excavation of cisterns (2 Sa. iii. 26, RVmg 'cistern of Sirah'). See also POTTER, VESSELS. J.D.D.

FLINT. See MINING AND METALS.

FLOOD. A deluge of water sent by God in the time of Noah to destroy all but a selected few from the earth. The event is described in Gn. vi–

viii. The word used in the Old Testament to describe this phenomenon is *mabbûl*, a word of unknown derivation, and since its only other occurrence outside the narrative of Gn. vi–xi is Ps. xxix. 10, its meaning must be taken to be a cataclysmic deluge such as is described in Genesis. In the LXX, *mabbûl* is translated by *kataklysmos*, and this is the word used in the New Testament (Mt. xxiv. 38, 39; Lk. xvii. 27; 2 Pet. ii. 5) to describe the same event.

In the EVV various other terms are translated by the word 'flood', most of them referring to rivers, either in normal flow or in spate, which was one of the meanings of 'flood' in AV English. Thus in the Old Testament *nāhār* (*e.g.* Jos. xxiv. 2), *y*^e^*'ôr* (*e.g.* Je. xlvi. 7; the form *'ōr* occurs in Am. viii. 8), *naḥal* (*e.g.* 2 Sa. xxii. 5), and *šibbōleṯ* (Ps. lxix. 2, 15; Jdg. xii. 6), and in the New Testament *potamos* (*e.g.* Mt. vii. 25), all bear roughly this meaning. Other words translated 'flood' are *šeṭeṗ*, 'an overflowing' (*e.g.* Ps. xxxii. 6), and the verb *nāzal*, 'to flow', in its participial form 'flower' (*e.g.* Ex. xv. 8) in the Old Testament, and *plēmmyra*, 'high water' (Lk. vi. 48), in the New.

a. The reason for the Flood

'God saw that the wickedness of man was great in the earth, and that every imagination of the thoughts of his heart was only evil continually' (Gn. vi. 5), so He resolved to bring a just destruction upon him (vi. 1–7). But Noah (*q.v.*) was a righteous man, so he and his immediate family were to be spared to make a new start.

b. The preparation

Gn. vi. 3 and 1 Pet. iii. 20 indicate that through the longsuffering of God there would be 120 years' respite before the coming of the Flood. In this period God commanded Noah to build an ark (*q.v.*) and gave him careful instructions for it. He also announced that He would make a covenant with Noah (vi. 18; see (*g*) below).

c. The occupants of the ark

Eight people, Noah and his three sons, Shem, Ham, and Japheth, and their four wives were preserved in the ark (Gn. vi. 18, vii. 7, 13; 2 Pet. ii. 5). There were also two members, a male and a female, of each division (after their kind, *mîn*, not necessarily 'species'; see CREATION, II*d*) of the animal kingdom, including the birds, on board (vi. 19, 20, vii. 8, 9, 14, 15) and in addition to these there were twelve extra creatures, six male and six female, of each clean species, presumably for food and sacrifice (vii. 2, 3; some commentators interpret the numbers as seven, rather than fourteen altogether of each). Vegetable food for all these occupants was also stowed aboard. No mention is made of sea creatures, but these may have been included in 'every living thing of all flesh' (vi. 19), and could have been accommodated outside the ark.

d. The Flood

When Noah and his companions had entered the ark God secured it behind him (vii. 16) and loosed the waters. These came in the form of rain (vii. 4, 12), and of such force that the Bible says 'the windows of heaven were opened' (vii. 11), a very telling metaphor. The level of the waters was also raised from below, as is described in the phrase 'all the fountains of the great deep (*t*^e^*hôm*) were broken up' (vii. 11), but this may be a metaphorical statement, as is suggested by the use of the word *t*^e^*hôm*, which is usually found in poetic passages, so it is not profitable to seek references to geological phenomena in it.

e. The chronology of the Flood

Noah entered the ark on the 17th day of the second month of his 600th year (vii. 11), and the earth was dry on the 27th day of the second month of his 601st year, so, counting 30 days to a month, the Flood lasted 371 days. The rain fell for 40 days (vii. 12) and the waters continued to rise for another 110 (vii. 24) = 150; the waters then fell for 74 days (viii. 5) = 224; 40 days later the raven was sent out (viii. 6, 7) = 264; 7 days later Noah sent out the dove (viii. 8, with implication of 'other 7 days' in viii. 10) = 271; he sent it out again 7 days later (viii. 10) = 278; and for the third time 7 days later (viii. 12) = 285; Noah removed the covering of the ark 29 days later (viii. 13 with vii. 11) = 314; and the earth was finally dry 57 days later (viii. 14) = 371 days altogether. See E. F. Kevan, *NBC*, pp. 84, 85.

f. The extent of the Flood

That everything (vi. 17), including man (vi. 7, vii. 21) and beast (vi. 7, 13, 17, vii. 21, 22), was to be blotted out by the Flood is clearly stated, but it can be argued that these categories are qualified by the statements of locality: upon the earth (*'ereṣ*; vi. 17, vii. 17, 23); under heaven (*šāmayim*; vi. 17, vii. 19); and upon the ground (*'*^a^*ḏāmâ*; vii. 4, 23). *'Ereṣ* can mean 'land' (*e.g.* Gn. x. 10), *šāmayim* can mean 'sky', or the visible part of heaven within the horizon (*e.g.* 1 Ki. xviii. 45), and the extent of *'*^a^*ḏāmâ* would be determined by these other two words; thus it is possible that a flood of unexampled severity might meet these conditions without covering the entire surface of the globe. The argument that such a flood would make the preservation of animals unnecessary might be countered with the suggestion that if a whole environmental zone with its own individual fauna were involved, such a measure would be necessary. The statement that all the high mountains (*har*) under the whole heaven were covered (vii. 19, 20) and that near the end of the Flood they began to be seen (viii. 5) is interpreted in this scheme as a phenomenon due to the cloud and mist that must have accompanied the cataclysm. This interpretation favours a limited Flood, but the text is also capable of bearing the interpretation of a universal Flood, and dogmatism is not reasonable, either way. The theological teaching of the Bible has traditionally been interpreted in the sense that all men except Noah and his family were destroyed.

g. The end of the Flood

God remembered Noah in the ark, and caused the waters steadily to decrease until the ark came to rest on the mountains of Urarṭu (see ARARAT). To find out whether it was safe to disembark Noah sent out a raven first, which was perhaps able to feed on carrion, and perch on the roof of the ark (viii. 7), and then a dove, which on the second attempt brought back an olive leaf, indicating perhaps that the waters had fallen enough for the foothills, where the olive trees grow, to be dry, and therefore sufficient food to be now available for the animals (viii. 8–11). The third time he sent out the dove it did not return (viii. 12), so he deemed it time to leave the ark, and this he was commanded by God to do. Noah then made burnt offerings of every clean beast and bird (see (*c*) above), and God swore not to bring another flood (viii. 21, 22; Is. liv. 9), blessed Noah and his sons (ix. 1), and confirmed it in a covenant (ix. 11), whose sign was a bow in the clouds (ix. 13–17).

h. Cuneiform parallels

A number of versions of a flood account have been found among the cuneiform documents excavated in the Near East. A Sumerian tablet from Nippur in southern Babylonia relates how a king, Ziusuddu, being warned of an approaching deluge which the assembly of the gods has decreed to destroy mankind, builds a great boat and escapes the waters. This tablet dates from about 2000 BC, but the story had probably been known in Mesopotamia for many centuries before this. It is found in Akkadian versions from both Babylonia and Assyria, in more than one composition. One of these, the Atraḫasis Epic, describes a flood, sent among other destructive phenomena to purge mankind; but the best known account of the flood in Akkadian, and one which shows affinities with the Sumerian account, forms part of Tablet XI of a longer composition, the Epic of Gilgamesh. It was an Assyrian recension of this, which had been excavated from Nineveh some twenty years before, that was discovered in the British Museum in 1872 by George Smith. In this version the survivor, Uta-napishtim, describes to Gilgamesh how the god Ea warned him of the impending flood, and he built a boat in which he sheltered all his family as well as craftsmen, animals both domestic and wild, and treasure of gold and silver. The flood lasted seven days, and the boat came to rest on Mount Niṣir (in NW Persia) and Uta-napishtim sent out in succession a dove, a swallow, and a raven, and when the raven did not return the occupants disembarked. Uta-napishtim made a sacrifice, and the gods gathered like flies about it. These cuneiform accounts show similarities with the biblical account, a fact which is possibly to be explained by common reference to an actual original event. The many crude elements in the cuneiform accounts suggest that these are the less reliable of the two.

i. Sources

Many scholars consider that the narrative of the Flood in Gn. vi–ix is composed of two sources, J (Yahwist) and P (Priestly), woven together by a late editor, working after the return from the Exile. According to this theory, oral traditions from early times were brought together, and were committed to writing in the 'document' called J over a period of centuries, beginning in the time of the early Monarchy. The other source (P) was the result of centuries of the traditions of the priests from the time of David, which were written down in the period from perhaps 500 BC to the time of Ezra, drawing, in the case of such sections as that dealing with the Flood, upon the Babylonian traditions as learnt during the Exile. Evidence for the two sources is found in such criteria as the use of the two divine names, *YHWH* in J and *'ᵉlōhîm* in P, and in such observations as that Noah is bidden to take seven (or fourteen) of every clean creature and two of every unclean creature into the ark (Gn. vii. 2, 3 = J), and that he is bidden to take one pair of every species (Gn. vi. 19 = P; see (*c*) above). These matters are susceptible of other explanations, however (see Bibliography), and the unity of the Flood account is suggested by the consistent statements as to the cause of the Flood (Gn. vi. 5–7 (J), 11–13 (P)), the purpose of it (Gn. vi. 7 (J), 13, 17 (P), vii. 4 (J), 21 (P), 22, 23 (J), viii. 21 (J)), and the saving of a representative remnant (Gn. vi. 8 (J), 18–20 (P), vii. 1–3, 7–9 (J), 13–16a (P), 16b (J), viii. 16–19 (P)).

j. Archaeology and the Flood

Excavations at Ur, Kish, Warka, and Farah in southern Mesopotamia have uncovered evidence of serious floods. The excavators of the first two sites, Sir Leonard Woolley and S. H. Langdon, believed that these remains were to be connected with the biblical Flood. There is little likelihood in this, however, since the flood levels at the four sites do not all date from the same period, and in each case they are most readily explained as due to a river inundation of unusual severity. Moreover, the earliest of these, that at Ur, is unlikely to have taken place much before 4000 BC, a date which comes well on in the continuous sequence of prehistoric cultures in the Near East, and one at which there is no sign of a break in other areas. If a serious local flood in the Mesopotamian plan is considered to be all that is implied by the biblical account, one or other of the flood deposits at these sites may be thought to be evidence of it, but if, as seems inescapable, a far more serious event is recorded in Genesis, the evidence from Mesopotamia must be considered irrelevant.

k. Geology and the Flood

No certain geological evidence of the biblical Flood is known. Many phenomena have been noted, however, which in the past, and particularly the nineteenth century, were cited as evidence of a serious flood. The majority of these are today most satisfactorily explained as vestiges of the glacial action of the Quaternary Ice Age. Associated with the ice age, however, were certain changes, such as varying sea-levels through locking up and release of water in the glaciers, and depression and rising of land masses in concord with the increase and decrease in the weight of ice on them, which might well have produced effects in keeping with the biblical account. The effective end of the last glaciation may be dated at about 10,000 BC, so that it may be that Noah and his contemporaries are to be given an antiquity of this magnitude (see GENEALOGY).

No certain evidence is, however, available, and any scheme to place the events described in Genesis in their actual historical setting can be no more than tentative.

BIBLIOGRAPHY. *General:* J. C. Whitcomb and H. M. Morris (eds.), *The Genesis Flood*, 1961; A. Parrot, *The Flood and Noah's Ark*, 1955; A. Heidel, *The Gilgamesh Epic and Old Testament Parallels*², 1949, chapter IV. *Section h:* S. N. Kramer, *History Begins at Sumer*, 1958, pp. 200–205; *ANET*, pp. 72–99, 104–106; *DOTT*, pp. 17–26. *Section i:* O. T. Allis, *The Five Books of Moses*, 1943, pp. 95–99; G. Ch. Aalders, *A Short Introduction to the Pentateuch*, 1949, pp. 45–47. *Section k:* J. K. Charlesworth, *The Quaternary Era*, II, 1957, pp. 614–619. T.C.M.

FLOOR. 1. Heb. *qarqa'*, 'bottom' (thus rendered in Am. ix. 3). See HOUSE. **2.** Heb. *gōren*, 'threshing-floor', Gk. *halōn*. See AGRICULTURE.

FLOWERS. See PLANTS.

FLUTE. See MUSIC AND MUSICAL INSTRUMENTS.

FLY. Although the word fly is widely and loosely used, it is strictly applied only to *Diptera*, a large insect order having only one pair of wings. The word fly occurs only twice in the AV, each time translating Heb. *zᵉḇûḇ*, but nothing in the context of either allows any more precise identification. In Is. vii. 18 it is used figuratively, and Ec. x. 1 is a quotation of the familiar proverb, 'dead flies cause the ointment of the apothecary to stink'. A wide variety of insects, not only true flies, might be attracted to embalmers' spices and unguents.

In addition to this term there is Heb. *'ārōḇ*, translated 'swarms of flies' (Ex. viii. 21 ff.) and 'divers sorts of flies' (Pss. lxxviii. 45, cv. 31). Each passage refers to the plague of flies which God sent upon Egypt. Many species have mass hatchings which cause profuse swarms that are dangerous or gravely inconvenient from sheer weight of numbers. The swarms could well have consisted of 'divers sorts of flies'. G.C.

FOOD. Within this general term are included all the vegetable and animal products used by man to maintain the physical life of his body.

I. IN THE OLD TESTAMENT

a. Earliest periods

From the beginning (Gn. i. 29, 30, ii. 16) all seed-bearing plants (mainly grains and vegetables, presumably) and fruit-bearing trees served as food for man, and natural greenstuffs as food for animals. The fall brought with it the necessity for hard toil in food gathering and production (Gn. iii. 18, 23, iv. 2, 3). Food in the ark was evidently representative of that in common use at the time, but no details of it are given (Gn. vi. 21). After the flood, God promised that seedtime and harvest should not cease while the earth endured, and all living things (besides vegetation) might be used for food, but not their blood (Gn. viii. 22–ix. 4). At the time of Noah's resettlement of the earth after the flood, grape-growing (and, in consequence, drunkenness) first makes its appearance (Gn. ix. 20, 21).

b. The Patriarchal Age

In Egypt, Palestine, and Mesopotamia in the early second millennium BC grain and various breads were a staple diet along with milk, butter, cheeses, water, wine, and beer. Doubtless the semi-nomadic Patriarchs lived mainly on the milk-products of their cattle and flocks, but also had bread (see the supply given to Hagar, Gn. xxi. 14) and sometimes cultivated grain seasonally as did Isaac (Gn. xxvi. 12) and presumably Jacob (*cf.* Gn. xxxvii. 7), since he needed to buy Egyptian grain in time of famine (Gn. xlii. 2, 25 f., xliii. 2, xliv. 1, 2). Lentil soup (a red soup) was probably a common dish in the days when Esau traded his birthright for a meal of it (Gn. xxv. 29–34), as it certainly was later on (*e.g.* 2 Sa. xvii. 28). Honoured guests were treated to the fatted calf accompanied by curds and milk (Gn. xviii. 6–8). With Abraham's action we may compare the references in the N Canaanite texts from Ugarit which mention slaughter and preparation of 'a lamb from the flock' or 'the sleekest of . . . fatlings' (*ANET*, pp. 146, 149, 151). Although meat was not an everyday dish, desert-game was popular in patriarchal Syria–Palestine. Isaac liked his tasty meat from the hunt (Gn. xxvii. 3, 4), just as did the Egyp. Sinuhe in Palestine a little earlier (*ANET*, p. 20). Presents to dignitaries might include nuts and honey as delicacies (Gn. xliii. 11). The tablets from the 18th-century BC palace at Mari indicate that large amounts of honey were provided at banquets for visiting royalty, and during the same period king Ishme-Dagan of Assyria sent pistachio-nuts to his brother ruling at Mari. In Egypt, too, honey was first and foremost the prerogative of royalty and high society, but was also occasionally enjoyed by their inferiors. Finally, the common meal was a recognized token of amity between the two contracting parties of an agreement, *e.g.* Isaac and the Philistines in Gn. xxvi. 30, and Jacob and Laban in Gn. xxxi. 54. No details are given of the meal to which Joseph treated his brothers in Egypt (Gn. xliii. 31–34).

c. Israel in Egypt

In Egypt, despite their hard life, the captive Israelites had had a variety of food that they remembered with nostalgia in the wilderness journeyings: fish in plenty, cucumbers, melons, leeks, onions, garlic (Nu. xi. 5). This list corresponds quite closely with known ancient Egyp. foods, not least in the E Delta (Goshen area) in the 13th century BC. Thus, in praising the region of Ra'amses, a scribe extols its wealth of foods: onions and leeks, seven kinds of fish in its waters, and various fruits and vegetables (*ANET*, p. 471; better, Caminos, *Late-Egyptian Miscellanies*, 1954, p. 74).

d. Food in Israel

(i) *Vegetable foods*. Grain, wine, and olive-oil were the three staple commodities (Dt. vii. 13; Ne. v. 11; Ho. ii. 8). The grain was mainly barley, wheat, and sometimes spelt, an inferior wheat; see Ex. ix. 32 (Egypt); Dt. viii. 8; and Is. xxviii. 25 (note order of grains). For preparation and baking of bread, see BREAD; this basic food was the most appropriate word-picture for Christ Himself, the Bread of Life (*cf.* Jn. vi. 33, 35).

The vine was the second great provider; not only of fresh grapes as a fruit (Nu. vi. 3; Dt. xxiii. 24) but also of dried grapes as raisins (1 Sa. xxv. 18, xxx. 12); of the sweet grape-juice, *'asîs* (Is. xlix. 26; Am. ix. 13; Joel i. 5, iii. 18, AV, 'sweet wine', 'new wine'); of the half-fermented must or new wine (Jdg. ix. 13; Ho. iv. 11; Pr. iii. 10; *etc.*); and of the fully fermented wine (*yayin*). These red juices of the grape were often called 'the blood of the grape' (Gn. xlix. 11; Dt. xxxii. 14). Wine in its various forms was the general drink in ancient Palestine; see VINE, WINE AND STRONG DRINK. Various wines in ancient Egypt, Palestine (*cf.* that of Helbon, in Ezk. xxvii. 18 and Assyr. texts), and Asia Minor were celebrated in antiquity. Vinegar (wine gone acid), diluted with water, helped to refresh field-workers (Ru. ii. 14).

Besides being a general word for fermented drinks, *šēḵār*, 'strong drink', appears to have been applied specifically to beverages brewed from grain (*i.e.* beer; Herodotus, ii. 77) or dates (*ibid.* i. 193) or perhaps even honey. Beer was the more popular drink in Mesopotamia, but wine in Palestine; both were common in Egypt, where date-wine and other drinks are mentioned. For spiced wine, see Seasoning, below.

The third basic commodity, olive-oil, was used both as food and for cooking-fat. With flour, oil went into breads and cakes, or these could be cooked in oil (Ex. xxix. 2); its use was universal, *cf.* the widow of Zarephath (1 Ki. xvii. 12). See OIL.

For vegetables, see sections (*b*) and (*c*) above, Patriarchal Age (lentils) and Israel in Egypt (Nu. xi. 5); beans, *pôl*, were also used (2 Sa. xvii. 28; Ezk. iv. 9). The word occurs also in Egypt from the 13th century BC. Besides the grapes and olives already mentioned, fruits included figs proper, sometimes pressed into fig-cakes (see FIG, FIG-TREE) (*cf.* Is. xxxviii. 21 for a medicinal use; also used medically at Ugarit, for horses), and also sycomore-figs, as in Egypt, that had to be notched to swell to edible size (which was Amos's occupation; Am. vii. 14). Pomegranates were eaten and their juice drunk (Ct. viii. 2). The various nuts available included almonds (Je. i. 11) and pistachio-nuts (see under Patriarchal Age above). In Pr. xxv. 11; Ct. ii. 3, 5, vii. 8, viii. 5; Joel i. 12, the term *tappûaḥ* probably means 'apple', although this interpretation is often questioned (see APPLE). Outside of Egypt and Palestine, Bab. texts indicate a long knowledge of the apple (*ḫašḫûru*) in Mesopotamia, as well as in SE Asia Minor (Purušḫanda, near modern Topada).

(ii) *Animal products*. These include honey, fats, and meat. The honey of wild bees found in rocks, trees, *etc.*, was widely used (Dt. xxxii. 13; Jdg. xiv. 8; 1 Sa. xiv. 25; 2 Sa. xvii. 29). The Old Testament writers do not say whether the Hebrews (like the Egyptians) practised bee-keeping. Honey (*q.v.*) was a delicacy much enjoyed (Ps. xix. 10; Pr. xxiv. 13). Palestine was indeed a land of 'milk and honey' (Ex. iii. 8)—in the 15th century BC the Egyptian pharaoh Tuthmosis III brought back hundreds of jars of honey from Syria–Palestine as tribute (seventh and fourteenth campaigns). See the ecstatic description of Palestine's wealth of grain, wine, oil, honey, fruits, and cattle by Sinuhe, *ANET*, pp. 19, 20.

Milk was another staple item of diet, along with its products butter and cheese. For milk, *cf.* Pr. xxvii. 27; Is. vii. 22; Ezk. xxv. 4; for butter, Pr. xxx. 33; and for cheese, see Jb. x. 10; 1 Sa. xvii. 18; 2 Sa. xvii. 29 (as a gift). Milk was often offered to the unexpected visitor or guest, as it was to Sisera in Jdg. iv. 19, v. 25, and as it had been centuries earlier to the Egyptian fugitive Sinuhe (*ANET*, p. 19).

Meat was eaten only occasionally, except perhaps for the rich, who may have had it regularly. As with Abraham, guests were entertained to calf, kid, or lamb (*cf.* Jdg. vi. 19 ff.; 2 Sa. xii. 4), and these were acceptable gifts alive or already dressed (1 Sa. xvi. 20, xxv. 18). The fatted ox in the stall sometimes provided a princely repast (Pr. xv. 17), just as in Egypt (picture in N. M. Davies, *Egyptian Paintings*, 1955, plate 4) or in Mesopotamia—witness the official, charged with banqueting arrangements for visiting royalty, who reports on a fatted ox so heavy with flesh that 'when he stands up, the blood rushes to his feet and he cannot stand . . .' Eli's renegade sons preferred roast to boiled meat (1 Sa. ii. 13–15), and meat boiled in a pot of water provided Ezekiel with a text (xxiv. 3–5). But a kid was not to be boiled in its mother's milk (Ex. xxiii. 19), perhaps because this appears to have been associated with Canaanite sacrificial practice, and hence would carry similar implications to the 'food offered to idols' of New Testament times. Lv. xi. 1–23, 29 ff. (*cf.* 41 ff.) and Dt. xiv. 3–21 record the law on animals allowed or forbidden as food. In addition to the ox, sheep, and goat, it was permissible to eat seven kinds of venison (Dt. xiv. 5), and all other cloven-hoofed animals that chewed the cud. Those animals which failed to fulfil both demands were forbidden as food and listed as 'unclean', together with more than a score of different kinds of birds. With regard to fish, *etc.*, only those with both fins and scales might be eaten. A very few specified insects might be consumed (the locust-family). Some of the creatures forbidden were simply unfit for human consumption; others (*e.g.* swine) were unsafe in a hot climate; still others may have been too closely identified with surrounding idolatry. For fish, see section (*c*) above on Israel in Egypt, and FISH, FISHING.

Fig. 86. Assyrian slaves bearing sticks of locusts for the table of Sennacherib (705–681 BC). From Nineveh palace relief, *c.* 700 BC.

(iii) *Solomon's palace food-supplies.* In 1 Ki. iv. 7, 22, 23, 27, 28, it is recorded that the governors of the twelve administrative provinces in Israel had each to supply a month's food in the year for Solomon's court: one day's provision being 30 *kōr* of fine flour, 60 *kōr* of meal, 30 cattle, 100 sheep, venison, and fowls, and provender for the royal stables. Similarly, Solomon paid Hiram I of Tyre for his timber and woodcutters with 20,000 *kōr* of wheat per annum, and a corresponding quantity of oil (RSV). This palatial catering was typical of ancient Oriental courts, as is shown by Egyptian and Mesopotamian court-accounts. The courts of Nebuchadrezzar II of Babylon and Cyrus of Persia were apparently supplied by district-officials on a monthly basis, similar to the system in operation in Solomon's court; see R. P. Dougherty, *AASOR*, V, 1925, pp. 23–31, 40–46. Presumably Solomon's monthly supplies were levied either from, or in addition to, the local taxes in kind (grain for flour, livestock) paid by the twelve districts.

Not only the system but also the amount and the probable distribution of Solomon's court-provisions will bear some comparison with the consumption at other royal courts. The court-personnel of the Ancient Orient may be divided conveniently into three classes: first, the king, the royal family, and all the chief ministers of the realm; second, the main body of courtiers and subordinate officials attached to the 'departments' of the chief ministers; and third, the (probably) still greater number of domestic employees of every conceivable kind. The Ancient Near Eastern palace was not just a royal residence but also the practical focus of the entire central government of the state. Partial statistics are available for comparison from Egypt and Mesopotamia. In the 18th century BC royal archives from Mari and Chagar Bazar in NW Mesopotamia record the daily food-supply for the king and his chief officials (*i.e.* the first class); the amounts ran into hundreds of litres (*qa*) of grain, bread, pastries, honey, and syrups each day, averaging 945 litres *per diem* at Chagar Bazar for the 'royal repast' (J. Bottéro, *Archives Royales de Mari*, VII, 1957, pp. 270–273). *Cf.* the great quantities of barley alone which were consumed in the Mari palace itself (see Birot, *ibid.*, IX, 1960, pp. 264, 265). Similar accounts from the Egyptian court of the XIIIth Dynasty (same period) have also survived. Directly comparable is the 726½ litres (10 *ḫar*—sacks) of flour per day used to make bread for the Egyp. court under Sethos I (*c.* 1300 BC) on circuit in Lower Egypt (Spiegelberg, *Rechnungen, Zeit Setis' I*, 1896). Preparations for a pharaoh's arrival in the late 13th century BC included the furnishing of 9,200 loaves (eight varieties), 20,000 biscuits (two kinds), and vast quantities of other victuals (Caminos, *Late-Egyptian Miscellanies*, 1954, pp. 198–201). All these figures also apply principally to 'class 1' consumers (and possibly 'class 2' in the last example), but take no account of the numerous domestics ('class 3')—*e.g.* the 400 palace-women at Mari. Ration-tablets from Babylon in the 10th to 35th years (595–570 BC) of Nebuchadrezzar II give detailed accounts of grain and oil for royal captives, including king Jehoiachin of Judah and his sons, as well as numerous artisans from Egypt, Philistia, Phoenicia, Ionia, Lydia, Cilicia, Elam, Media, and Persia. (For details, see *ANET*, p. 308; W. J. Martin in D. W. Thomas (ed.), *DOTT*, 1958, pp. 84–86; basic source is Weidner, *Mélanges R. Dussaud*, II, 1939, pp. 923–935; for useful background, see Albright, *BA*, V, 1942, pp. 49–55.)

In Solomon's case, if the *kōr* ('measure') be taken as 220 litres (Scott, *BA*, XXII, 1959, p. 31; but *cf.* WEIGHTS AND MEASURES), then his 30 plus

60 *kōr* of flour and meal per day would be some 6,600 plus 13,200 litres respectively, totalling 19,800 litres or 594,000 litres per monthly quota. Bearing in mind the comparative figures given above, 600 litres a day would go to Solomon, his family, and chief ministers (*cf.* 726½ and 945 litres, Egypt and Chagar Bazar, above), *i.e.* 'class 1'; the other 6,000 litres of fine flour would perhaps go to the main body of courtiers and officials ('class 2'), and the 13,200 litres of ordinary meal to the crowd of domestic employees ('class 3'). Evidence from Mari indicates that 1 *iku* of land (3,600 square metres) produced 1 *ugar* of grain (1,200 litres). If Israelite crop-yields were at all similar, and if a litre of grain made about a litre of wholemeal flour, then it is possible to suggest that each month's flour-supply to Solomon's court (594,000 litres) would be roughly equivalent to the grain grown on 495 *iku* or about 424 acres. This represents an area of land about ⅘ mile square (or, ⅗ square mile)—surely no impossible annual burden on each of Israel's twelve administrative districts. As for Hiram's 20,000 *kōr* of wheat per annum, this amount by the same reckoning would take up the crop-yield of about 305 *iku* or 262 acres for each month, *i.e.* from land about ¾ mile square (or, ½–⅔ square mile), again a reasonable kind of figure.

(iv) *Seasoning and cooking.* Cooking included the baking of bread and cakes (with or without leaven), making of soups and stews, and the roasting or boiling of meat (see above). Salt was a prime necessity with a meal (Jb. vi. 6). As already mentioned, sharing a meal marked agreement (Gn. xxvi. 30, xxxi. 54), and the phrases a 'covenant of salt' (Nu. xviii. 19), or 'eating someone's salt' (Ezr. iv. 14, RV), were idioms of the same kind (*i.e.* indicating agreement or loyalty). Other seasonings included dill and cummin (Is. xxviii. 25, 27) and coriander (Ex. xvi. 31; Nu. xi. 7). Common use of these in antiquity is exemplified by actual finds of plants and seeds in Egyptian tombs from the XVIIIth Dynasty onwards, and the mention of them in Egyp. and Bab. texts (*cf.* L. Keimer, *Die Gartenpflanzen im Alten Ägypten*, I, 1924, Nos. 24, 29, 30, pp. 37–38, 40–42 and refs., 147–149).

In Mycenaean Greek tablets from Crete and Greece, written in the 'Linear B' script, and dated to the 15th–13th centuries BC, occur the spices cummin (*ku-mi-no*), coriander (*ko-ri-a-da-na/do-no*), and sesame (*sa-sa-ma*) among others. These names (and probably some of the spices too) were imports from the Near East, *via* Syria-Palestine and Cyprus, and so witness to the antiquity of the use of both spices and names in the Bible lands. Details are given in M. Ventris and J. Chadwick, *Documents in Mycenaean Greek*, 1956, pp. 131, 135–136, 221–231; and Chadwick, *The Decipherment of Linear B*, 1958, pp. 64, 120, contains a brief treatment. Sesame is attested at this same period in Syria itself, at Ugarit (Gordon, *Ugaritic Manual*, III, 1955, p. 331, No. 1898, as *š̌smn*).

Honey could be used in baking (*cf.* Ex. xvi. 31), but not in sacrifice to God (Lv. ii. 11), although the Egyptians offered it to their gods. Sweetened and spiced wines (Ct. viii. 2) and beers are also known from Egyptian and Mesopotamian texts, honey or herbs being used for this purpose. With the rather doubtful 'spice the spicery' in a cooking context in Ezk. xxiv. 10 (meaning spiced meat?), one might compare 'spiced (lit. "sweetened") meat' in Egypt (*ỉwf snḏm*), Gardiner, *Ancient Egyptian Onomastica*, II, 1947, pp. 255*–256*, A. 610.

BIBLIOGRAPHY. See AGRICULTURE, BREAD, FISH, FISHING, MEAT, MILK, WINE AND STRONG DRINK, *etc.* On ancient food generally, see R. J. Forbes, *Studies in Ancient Technology*, III, 1955, pp. 50–105, and on honey and sugars, Forbes, *op. cit.*, V, 1957, pp. 78–88, 97 f. K.A.K.

II. IN THE NEW TESTAMENT

As the food of a typical Heb. family was mainly vegetarian, it is not surprising that the New Testament references to food are almost exclusively to such foodstuffs.

a. Vegetable foods

(i) *Cereals.* The staple diet of man in the Bible is bread, which is made either from wheat flour (Mt. xiii. 33; Lk. xiii. 21) or barley flour (Jn. vi. 9, 13; *cf.* Jdg. vii. 13; 2 Ki. iv. 42). The latter was the usual ingredient of bread for the poorer people (*cf.* Jos., *BJ* v. 10. 2 (Penguin edn., p. 290); and, for the relative value of wheat and barley, Rev. vi. 6). The New Testament witnesses to the primitive method of using corn by plucking the fresh ears (Lv. xxiii. 14, RV) and removing the husk by rubbing them in the hands (Dt. xxiii. 25; Mt. xii. 1; Mk. ii. 23; Lk. vi. 1). When this was done in another man's field it was accounted by the Rabbis as equivalent to reaping, and therefore forbidden on the sabbath (Mishnah, *Shabbath*, vii. 2). Other methods of dealing with the corn are referred to in Mt. iii. 12 = Lk. iii. 17; Lk. xxii. 31. Special mention should be made of the *maṣṣôṯ* or cakes of unleavened pastry, which alone were permitted in Jewish households during the days of the Passover festival (Ex. xii. 19, xiii. 7, *etc.*; 1 Cor. v. 7 f.).

(ii) *Fruits and oil.* From the garden came grapes (Mt. vii. 16) and thereby 'the fruit of the vine' (Mt. xxvi. 29, *etc.*); and olives, although the latter (*cf.* Rom. xi. 17 ff.; Jas. iii. 12) are never expressly recorded as an article of food. The olive, however, provided a most useful oil which was used in the preparation of food, and the olive berry itself was preserved by a process of pickling it in brine. Pickled olives were eaten with bread as a relish. And, in this connection, mention may be made of the sauce compounded of dates, figs, raisins, and vinegar and called *ḥ^a^rōseṯ* which was a feature of the Paschal feast (Mk. xiv. 20; Jn. xiii. 26; in the Mishnah, *Pesaḥim*, ii. 8, x. 3).

The fruit of the fig-tree is spoken of in Mt. vii. 16 in the same context as the grape. These two fruits were much prized in Palestine, whereas at the extreme end of the social scale the fruit or pods of the carob-tree provided the frugal 'husks' which the prodigal would have been glad to eat in his plight (Lk. xv. 16), though they were properly swine-food.

b. Animal products

(i) *Animals* (strictly speaking). The Jewish world of New Testament times was one in which dietary laws were strictly enforced, especially in regard to the distinction between clean and unclean animals and birds (Lv. xi. 1–23; Dt. xiv. 4–20; Acts x. 9 ff.; the Mishnaic tractate *'Abodah Zarah*). The eventual breakdown of these dietary regulations is a notable theme of the New Testament (Mk. vii. 18–20, RV; Acts xv. 20, 29; Rom. xiv; 1 Cor. viii, x: see IDOLS, MEAT OFFERED TO). Among the clean animals which were eaten as food (provided that they had been slaughtered in legitimate fashion and the blood drained away, thereby making them *kosher*) we may note the kid (Lk. xv. 29), and the calf (Lk. xv. 23) which had been specially fattened for a festive occasion.

(ii) *Fish*. Fish were similarly classified as clean and unclean according to the rubric of Dt. xiv. 9 f. (*cf.* Lv. xi. 9–12); and the reader of the gospel story will be familiar with the names of the Galilaean towns which were the centre of the fishing industry on the shores of the lake. The earliest disciples are called 'fishermen' (Mk. i. 16 ff. and parallels). Apart from the reference in Lk. xi. 11 there is the well-known mention of fish in the miraculous feedings of the multitude (Mk. vi. 41 ff. and parallels and Mk. viii. 7 ff. and parallels) as well as in the meals which the risen Lord shared with His own followers (Lk. xxiv. 42, 43; Jn. xxi. 9 ff.). The popularity of the fish-symbol in early Christianity (*cf.* the definitive study of F. J. Dölger, ΙΧΘΥΣ, 1928) and the use of fish at some observances of the Eucharist in early Christian circles are probably derived from these gospel incidents.

(iii) *Birds*. Birds as items of food are not mentioned in the New Testament, apart from the general mention in Acts x. 12 and the implication of the sale of sparrows in Mt. x. 29 and Lk. xii. 6; but their eggs are alluded to in the Lord's teaching in Lk. xi. 12.

(iv) *Insects*. Edible insects include the locust, which, along with wild honey, formed the diet of the Baptist in the Judaean wilderness (Mt. iii. 4; Mk. i. 6).

c. Seasoning

To increase the pleasure of eating, various condiments were employed. The chief of these was salt, which has the property of adding savour to a dish of food (Jb. vi. 6). This fact is made the central feature of some ethical instruction in the Gospels (Mt. v. 13; Mk. ix. 50; Lk. xiv. 34) and Epistles (Col. iv. 6). Compare, for the Jewish background here, T. W. Manson, *The Sayings of Jesus*, 1949, p. 132. Mint, dill, cummin, and rue (conflating Mt. xxiii. 23 and Lk. xi. 42 which adds 'every herb': *cf. ExpT*, XV, August 1904, p. 528) continue the list of spices and herbs used for flavouring; and in Mt. xiii. 31 f. there is a reference to the mustard plant, the leaves of which were cut up and used to give extra flavour. The tiny mustard seed must be sown in the field, according to Jewish practice, and not in the garden; and in Palestine the plant reached a height of 8–10 feet (*EBi*, 1914, col. 3244).

R.P.M.

FOOL. Whereas the wise man (see WISDOM) fears the Lord (Pr. i. 7), the fool disdains moral and pious principles. Is. xxxii. 6 virtually defines 'fool' (*nāḇāl*), stressing moral depravity, spiritual irresponsibility, and social insensitivity. Nabal, the fool *par excellence* (1 Sa. xxv. 25), is labelled 'son of Belial' (*q.v.*), *i.e.* practical atheist (Pss. xiv. 1, liii. 1). Three other words are noteworthy: *'ᵉwîl* (Pr. i. 7, x. 14, xii. 15, xv. 5, xxiv. 9, *etc.*) describes lack of perception stemming from weakness of character (S. R. Driver, *Literature of the Old Testament*[9], p. 398); *kᵉsîl* (Pr. i. 22, x. 23, xiv. 16; Ec. ii. 14, v. 1, *etc.*) implies stubborn obstinacy (*ibid.*); *sāḵāl* probably connotes an almost irrational stubbornness (Je. iv. 22, v. 21; *cf.* 1 Sa. xxvi. 21; 2 Sa. xxiv. 10; Ec. ii. 12, vii. 25, *etc.*).

Christ's warning against branding anybody 'fool' (*mōros*, Mt. v. 22) presupposes these spiritual and moral connotations (see *Arndt* for other explanations). In 1 Cor. i. 25, 27 Paul takes up the term (*mōros*, 'foolishness') used by unbelievers in their faulty evaluation of God's purposes. A man's folly may sometimes lie in his being unable to perceive the issues (*e.g.* Lk. xi. 40; 1 Cor. xv. 36, *aphrōn*), but more likely in the fact that he has made an unworthy choice (*e.g.* Lk. xii. 20, *aphrōn*; Rom. i. 21, *asynetos*; Gal. iii. 1, 3, *anoētos*; Mt. vii. 26, *mōros*).

D.A.H.

FOOT. 1. Heb. *kēn* from a root meaning to be firm, refers to a base, pedestal, or foot, principally of the laver in the tabernacle (Ex. xxx. 18), and in Is. xxxiii. 23, RV, of a ship's mast.

2. Heb. *reḡel*, with parallels in other Near Eastern languages, is used occasionally of objects (Ex. xxv. 26), but mainly of animal or human feet, or, anthropomorphically, of God's feet. Derivatively it is used of the pace (Gn. xxxiii. 14, RV). 3. Heb. *pa'am*, from a root meaning to strike, is used of the step and then of the foot (Is. xxvi. 6). 4. Gk. *pous* is used of the feet of man or beast.

Both in Hebrew and Greek the foot frequently indicates the position, destination, or inclination of the person (Pr. vi. 18, vii. 11; Acts v. 9), and then further in reference to guidance of, and watchful care over, a person, principally by God (1 Sa. ii. 9; Ps. lxvi. 9; Lk. i. 79).

Figuratively the word is often used to symbolize defeat of an enemy, with the picture of putting one's foot on his neck (Jos. x. 24; 1 Cor. xv. 25).

Falling at a person's feet indicates homage or

supplication (1 Sa. xxv. 24; 2 Ki. iv. 27), sitting there implies discipleship or learning (Acts xxii. 3), and casting something at a person's feet indicates an offering (Acts iv. 35). The figure of the foot taken in a snare, or slipping, is used of calamity (Ps. lxxiii. 2; Je. xviii. 22).

The necessity to wash the feet, for comfort and cleanliness, resulted from the dusty roads, and foot-washing was a sign of hospitality, generally performed by the meanest slave (1 Sa. xxv. 41; Lk. vii. 44; Jn. xiii. 5 ff.; Acts xiii. 25). Removing one's dusty sandals was a sign of respect (Ex. iii. 5) and of mourning (Ezk. xxiv. 17). Shaking off the dust from one's feet was a sign of scorn, probably based on the idea that to take so much as dust from a place implied a bond (Mk. vi. 11; *cf.* 2 Ki. v. 17). B.O.B.

FOOTMAN. Heb. *raḡlî* from *reḡel*, 'foot'. The word is used of masculine persons only. Footmen are distinguished from children (Ex. xii. 37; *cf.* Nu. xi. 21). The word is a military term (Jdg. xx. 2), and often denotes soldiers in general (1 Sa. iv. 10, xv. 4; 2 Sa. x. 6; 1 Ki. xx. 29). It is also used to distinguish infantry from chariot-fighters (2 Sa. viii. 4; 2 Ki. xiii. 7; Je. xii. 5; 1 Ch. xviii. 4, xix. 18). AV uses 'footmen' in 1 Sa. xxii. 17 as a translation for *rāṣîm*, 'runners', *i.e.* the fifty men who ran before the king's chariot (1 Sa. viii. 11; 2 Sa. xv. 1; 1 Ki. i. 5). They also acted as a guard (1 Ki. xiv. 27, 28; 2 Ki. x. 25, xi. 4, *etc.*; 2 Ch. xii. 10, 11) and as royal messengers (2 Ch. xxx. 6, 10). Elijah once acted as a runner before Ahab (1 Ki. xviii. 46). The royal posts of the Persian Empire are called 'runners' (AV 'posts') in Est. iii. 13, 15, and retain the name even when mounted (Est. viii. 10, 14). The word is used as a simile in Jb. ix. 25. A. VAN S.

FOOTSTOOL. The word occurs seven times in the Old Testament, but on only one occasion is it used in a literal sense (2 Ch. ix. 18), and there a different word (*keḇeš*) is used; on the other six occasions *hᵃdôm raḡlayim*, 'stool of the feet', is used. The equivalent word in the New Testament (*hypopodion tōn podōn*, 'footstool of the feet') occurs eight times, where again it is only once used literally (and here the word is simply *hypopodion*, Jas. ii. 3), and apart from this reference all the others are quotations from the Old Testament. In its metaphorical sense it has reference to God and applies to the ark of the covenant (1 Ch. xxviii. 2); the Temple (which contains the ark) (Pss. xcix. 5, cxxxii. 7; La. ii. 1); the earth (Is. lxvi. 1; Mt. v. 35; Acts vii. 49); and the enemies of His Messiah King (Ps. cx. 1, referred to six times in the New Testament). See fig. 64. M.A.M.

FOOTWASHING. See FOOT.

FORBEARANCE. See LONGSUFFERING.

FOREHEAD (Heb. *mēṣaḥ*; Gk. *metōpon*, which means literally 'above the eye'). The set of the forehead can indicate opposition, defiance, or rebellion (Je. iii. 3), and hardness of the forehead indicates the determination or power to persevere in that attitude (Ezk. iii. 8 f.; also Is. xlviii. 4, RSV).

The forehead, being open and fully visible, was the most obvious place for a badge or mark (Ezk. ix. 4; Ex. xxviii. 38; Rev. vii. 3, xiii. 16, *etc.*). In Ezekiel this mark was made with ink, but in the Book of Revelation it is a seal, and in Exodus a plaque.

Note also the phylactery worn on the forehead (see EYE). B.O.B.

FOREIGNER. See STRANGER.

FOREKNOWLEDGE. See PREDESTINATION.

FORERUNNER. This word is often used by Christians to describe John the Baptist, because in him the words of Mal. iii. 1 found their fulfilment (Mk. i. 2 and Mt. xi. 10), and also because his father Zacharias prophesied that he would 'go before the face of the Lord to prepare his ways' (Lk. i. 76). The actual word, however, is found only once in the New Testament, with reference to the ascended Christ (Heb. vi. 20). It translates *prodromos*, a military term used of scouts sent on ahead to prepare the way for an advancing army.

Usually a 'forerunner' is of less importance than the person or persons for whose coming he is paving the way. This was true of the runners who preceded the chariots of kings (1 Sa. viii. 11; see FOOTMAN); it was also true of John the Baptist, and of the messengers sent by Jesus to make ready His entrance into the villages of Samaria (Lk. ix. 52). But in the case of Jesus, who entered for us within the veil into the holy of holies, having become our High Priest, the reverse is true. As the supreme Head of the Church He has gone on ahead that His brethren may follow Him in due course. Jesus made it clear to His followers that this was one of the main purposes of His departure to the Father, when He told them in the upper room that He was going to prepare a place for them in the many dwelling-places of His Father's house (Jn. xiv. 2, 3). It is true that *already* Christians have boldness to enter heaven through the blood of Jesus (Heb. x. 19), and that God has already raised them up with Christ and made them to sit with Him in the heavenly places (Eph. ii. 6). They can through prayer and sacrament ascend in heart and mind to their Lord, and with Him continually dwell. But, because Jesus is their Forerunner, they have the assurance that one day they will themselves enter heaven as He has done and enjoy the glory which is now His. Christ will receive them unto Himself that where He is there they may be also (Jn. xiv. 3). 'The Forerunner is also the Way by which, after long following, the whole Church will reach at last the Father's House.' (See H. B. Swete, *The Ascended Christ*, 1911.) R.V.G.T.

FOREST. 1. Heb. *ḥōreš*, 'thicket', 'wood, wooded height', occurs in a number of passages (*e.g.* Ezk. xxxi. 3), though in one of them (2 Ch. xxvii. 4) the text is possibly corrupt and a proper name intended.

2. Heb. *pardēs*, 'park', a loan-word from Persian *pairi-daeza*, 'enclosure', used of a preserve or park containing trees (Ne. ii. 8), fruit-trees (Ct. iv. 13), and laid-out gardens (Ec. ii. 5). See GARDEN.

3. Heb. *ya'ar*, 'outspread place', the most common word, is found thirty-five times in the Old Testament. According to W. F. Albright (*Archaeology of Palestine and the Bible*, 1960, pp. 130–133), much of the hill-country of Canaan was during the Middle Bronze Age (2000–1500 BC) covered with forests. Apart altogether from general uses of the word, the Bible mentions several woods and forests by name, *e.g.* 'forest of Lebanon' (1 Ki. vii. 2 f.). See articles under such place-names. J.D.D.

FORGIVENESS.

I. IN THE OLD TESTAMENT

In the Old Testament the idea of forgiveness is conveyed principally by words from three roots. *Kpr* more usually carries the idea of atonement, and its use in connection with the sacrifices is frequent. Its use for 'forgive' implies that atonement is made. The verb *nś'* means basically 'lift', 'carry', and presents us with a vivid picture of sin being lifted from the sinner and carried right away. The third root is *slḥ*, of unknown derivation, but which corresponds in use pretty closely to our 'forgive'. The first and the last are used always of God's forgiveness, but *nś'* is applied to human forgiveness as well.

Forgiveness is not regarded as a truism, as something in the nature of things. Passages which speak of the Lord as not pardoning certain offences abound (Dt. xxix. 20; 2 Ki. xxiv. 4; Je. v. 7; La. iii. 42). Where forgiveness is obtained it is something to be received with gratitude and regarded with awe and wonder. Sin merits punishment. Pardon is astounding grace. 'There is forgiveness with thee,' says the Psalmist, and then (perhaps surprisingly to us) he adds, 'that thou mayest be feared' (Ps. cxxx. 4).

Forgiveness is sometimes connected with atonement. *Slḥ* is connected with the sacrifices repeatedly. And, as we have seen, the verb from the root *kpr* has the essential meaning 'to make atonement'. Again, it may not be coincidence that *nś'*, besides being used of the forgiveness of sin, is also used of bearing the penalty of sin (Nu. xiv. 33 f.; Ezk. xiv. 10). The two seem to be connected. This does not mean that God is a stern Being who will not forgive without a *quid pro quo*. He is a God of grace, and the very means of bearing sin are instituted by Him. The sacrifices avail only because He has given the blood as the means of making atonement (Lv. xvii. 11). The Old Testament knows nothing of a forgiveness wrung from an unwilling God or purchased by a bribe.

Forgiveness, then, is possible only because God is a God of grace, or in the beautiful expression in Ne. ix. 17 'a God of pardons'. 'To the Lord our God belong mercies and forgivenesses' (Dn. ix. 9). A very instructive passage for the whole Old Testament understanding of forgiveness is Ex. xxxiv. 6 f., 'The Lord, the Lord God, merciful and gracious, longsuffering, and abundant in goodness and truth, keeping mercy for thousands, forgiving iniquity and transgression and sin, and that will by no means clear the guilty.' Forgiveness is rooted in the nature of God as gracious. But His forgiveness is not indiscriminate. He will 'by no means clear the guilty'. On man's side there is the need for penitence if he is to be forgiven. While this is not put into a formal demand, it is everywhere implied. Penitent sinners are forgiven. Impenitent men, who go on still in their wicked way, are not.

It remains to be noticed that the thought of pardon is conveyed in a most graphic way by other imagery than the use of our three basic forgiveness words. Thus the Psalmist tells us that, 'As far as the east is from the west, so far hath he removed our transgressions from us' (Ps. ciii. 12). Isaiah speaks of God as casting all the prophet's sins behind His back (Is. xxxviii. 17), and as 'blotting out' the people's transgressions (Is. xliii. 25; *cf.* Ps. li. 1, 9). In Je. xxxi. 34 the Lord says, 'I will remember their sin no more,' and Micah speaks of Him as casting sins 'into the depths of the sea' (Mi. vii. 19). Such vivid language emphasizes the completeness of God's forgiveness. When He forgives, men's sins are dealt with thoroughly. They see them no more.

II. IN THE NEW TESTAMENT

In the New Testament there are two main verbs to consider, *charizomai* (which means 'to deal graciously with') and *aphiēmi* ('to send away', 'to loose'). The noun *aphesis*, 'remission', is also found with some frequency. There are also two other words, *apolyō*, 'to release', which is used in Lk. vi. 37, 'forgive, and ye shall be forgiven', and *paresis*, 'a passing by', used in Rom. iii. 25 of God's passing over of sins done in earlier days.

In the New Testament there are several points made clear. One is that the forgiven sinner must forgive others. This is manifest in Lk. vi. 37, cited above, in the Lord's Prayer, and in other places. A readiness to forgive others is part of the indication that we have truly repented. Moreover, it is to be wholehearted. It springs from Christ's forgiveness of us, and it is to be like Christ's forgiveness: 'even as Christ forgave you, so also do ye' (Col. iii. 13). Several times Christ insists on the same thing, as in His parable of the unmerciful servant (Mt. xviii. 23–35).

Forgiveness is not often linked directly with the cross, though sometimes this is done, as in Eph. i. 7, 'In whom we have redemption through his blood, the forgiveness of sins.' Similarly, from Mt. xxvi. 28 we find that Christ's blood was shed 'for many for the remission of sins'. More usual is it to find it linked directly with Christ Himse

God 'for Christ's sake hath forgiven you' (Eph. iv. 32). 'Him hath God exalted . . . for to give repentance to Israel, and forgiveness of sins' (Acts v. 31). 'Through this man is preached unto you the forgiveness of sins' (Acts xiii. 38). With these we should place passages wherein Jesus, during the days of His flesh, declared that men were forgiven. Indeed, in the incident of the healing of the paralysed man lowered through the roof, He worked the miracle expressly 'that ye may know that the Son of man hath power on earth to forgive sins' (Mk. ii. 10). But the Person of Christ is not to be separated from His work. Forgiveness by or through Jesus Christ means forgiveness arising from all that He is and all that He does. In particular, it is not to be understood apart from the cross, all the more so since His death is often said to be a death 'for sin' (see on ATONEMENT). In addition to the specific passages which link forgiveness and the death of Christ, there is the whole thrust of the New Testament passages dealing with the atoning death of the Saviour.

Forgiveness rests basically, then, on the atoning work of Christ. That is to say, it is an act of sheer grace. 'He is faithful and just to forgive us our sins' (1 Jn. i. 9). On man's side repentance is insisted upon again and again. John the Baptist preached 'the baptism of repentance for the remission of sins' (Mk. i. 4), a theme which is taken up by Peter with reference to Christian baptism (Acts ii. 38). Christ Himself directed that 'repentance and remission of sins should be preached in his name' (Lk. xxiv. 47). Forgiveness is similarly linked with faith (Acts x. 43; Jas. v. 15). Faith and repentance are not to be thought of as merits whereby we deserve forgiveness. Rather they are the means whereby we appropriate the grace of God.

Two difficulties must be mentioned. One is that of the sin against the Holy Spirit which can never be forgiven (Mt. xii. 31 f.; Mk. iii. 28 f.; Lk. xii. 10; *cf.* 1 Jn. v. 16). This sin is never defined. But in the light of New Testament teaching generally it is impossible to think of it as any specific act of sin. The reference is rather to the continuing blasphemy against the Spirit of God of him who consistently rejects God's gracious call. This is blasphemy indeed.

The other is Jn. xx. 23, 'Whose soever sins ye remit, they are remitted unto them.' It is more than difficult to think of Christ as leaving in men's hands the determination of whether the sins of other men are to be forgiven or not. The important points are the plural 'whose soever' (pointing to categories, not individuals), and the perfect tense rendered 'are remitted' (it means 'have been remitted', not 'will be remitted'). The meaning of the passage then seems to be that as they are inspired by the Holy Spirit (verse 22) the followers of Jesus will be able to say with accuracy which categories of men have sins forgiven, and which not.

BIBLIOGRAPHY. W. C. Morro in *ISBE*; V. Taylor, *Forgiveness and Reconciliation*, 1941; H. R. Mackintosh, *The Christian Experience of Forgiveness*, 1947. L.M.

FORTIFICATION AND SIEGECRAFT.

I. DEFENCE IN THE ANCIENT WORLD

a. Site and size of the fortress

Throughout most of the Bible period the words 'city' and 'fortress' were normally synonyms in Palestine. The detailed story of the rebuilding of Jerusalem under Nehemiah is an excellent demonstration of the fact that walls make a city. Whenever possible a natural defensible site was chosen for the city's location. A steep, isolated peak or the impregnable spur of a hill was an excellent spot, especially if a spring was at hand. Samaria was an ideal example of the former and David's Jerusalem of the latter. Some sites, however, were so valuable that they were occupied although they had no natural defences and the cost of fortifications was therefore much greater. Such a site was Bethel. The large amount of water here, high on the central ridge, was too valuable to go unused.

The very word 'fortress', as well as the related terms 'stronghold' and 'fenced cities', implies a small area, for in Palestine city walls averaged something like 10 feet in width, but at strategic points were over twice as thick. City walls would run as high as 30 feet, the lower two-thirds being built of stone and the upper third of sun-dried brick. In sections of the country where stone was scarce, sun-dried brick was used in greater quantity, and to compensate for this the wall was normally thicker and a secondary wall was sometimes used inside the larger wall. The average town of the Old Testament covered 5–7½ acres in size, although some were only half as large. A city such as the Jerusalem of David's day, or Megiddo, would occupy about 11–13 acres. Hazor was a great metropolis of 100 acres. The capitals of Egypt, Assyria, Babylonia, Persia, and Rome were exceptional in size and differed in many other features from the normal city.

b. The development of city walls

Even as early as Neolithic times, Jericho was a fortified site with a varied history of walls. Some were only stone facings against debris, others free standing and perpendicular, others with battered faces. A fosse or ditch in front of the walls was cut out of solid rock, and a major defence feature was an excellent stone tower 9 metres in diameter with a central stairway. But this was more than four millennia before Abraham, who lived about 1900 BC. Shortly before his time came the transition from Early Bronze to Middle Bronze when Palestine was using the vertical stone wall without a protective revetment at its base. Most of these sites had only a single city wall, although Jericho and Ai had multiple walls. Towers strengthened the walls and offered vantage points of defence.

The Hyksos revolutionized defensive technique by substituting massive *terre pisée* or beaten-earth ramparts, whose outer faces were approximately the angle of rest for the fill. Hazor (*q.v.*) was the most spectacular example, and even today the earth walls still stand out prominently. These camps were rectangular in plan, and were primarily for the protection of chariot warriors. The building of these ramparts, however, was doubtless the work of the conquered people. This new type of wall was also introduced by these conquerors into a number of older Palestinian cities which they re-fortified. Some new stone city walls, however, were also built during the Hyksos period in Palestine.

Fig. 87. The double-walled fortress of Ascalon on its mound ('*tell*'). Egyptian soldiers put scaling-ladders against the outer wall and attack a door with a battleaxe. Pharaoh's arrows smite defenders on the walls who lift their arms in token of surrender. One man holds aloft an incense-burner; in the panic, a woman and child are lowered from turrets on the inner wall. Relief, temple of Karnak (Thebes). Rameses II, *c.* 1280 BC.

After the *terre pisée* defences came a return to the stone wall, either the earlier perpendicular one or the same with a glacis added. The bottom of the latter type of wall reproduced something of the angle of the beaten earth wall but this time it was done in stone and these stones were often of Cyclopean size. Above the revetment rose the perpendicular stone wall and the final superstructure of mud-brick. A cheaper method was to place a dirt fill against a perpendicular wall and then face this fill with heavy stones so placed that, as the fill settled, the stones were interlocked. All revetments were doubtless covered with clay so that the enemy could not determine the quality of the filling underneath. This type of wall seems to have come originally from Asia Minor. Late Bronze, the period between Genesis and Exodus, continued the same patterns of defence.

Joshua was a conqueror of cities rather than a builder, and the archaeologist has found the time of the Judges to have been even more chaotic than a casual reading of that book might imply. With David, however, Israel for a short time became a world power, and city building took a new step forward under him and his son Solomon. The latter called in Phoenician builders with their advanced techniques and dressed masonry. Slightly earlier, however, the casemate wall appeared in Saul's tiny capital of Gibeah. See fig. 95. This was another Anatolian importation which the Hittites had taken into Syria. This new defensive technique consisted of two thin parallel walls joined at various points by transverse walls. This produced long, narrow cells which could either be filled in with earth or used as rooms. The outer wall here was only about 5 feet thick, and the inner one even less. Counting the walls and the earth filled between them, the rampart was 15 feet. Such a wall might look to the enemy like a solid stone wall, but it was decidedly vulnerable. A casemate wall could also be finished off with a glacis. Saul's capital, however, was more like an oversized tower than a city. Samaria was the largest Palestinian city using the casemate wall. But the axes of some of its casemate chambers were at right angles to the walls instead of parallel to them as in the earlier type. Up to the close of the Old Testament, however, the solid stone wall continued in use along with the casemate wall.

In Inter-Testament and New Testament times the solid stone wall was normal. A deep moat in front of any wall was an additional defence and especially helpful in making an enemy's attempt to tunnel into the city more difficult. Herod the Great was the most prolific builder in all of Palestine's history. His best work was at Jerusalem, and it may still be seen in the massive 150-foot high retaining wall at the south-east corner of the temple area, where stones 22 feet in length are still visible above the debris that hides half the height of this wall. The Castle Antonia, where Christ was tried before Pilate, defended the north-west corner of the temple area. Some of its courtyards and cisterns can be seen by the tourist today, although they lie some distance below the modern street level. The lower portion of the so-called tower of David is probably a part of the great tower of Phasael just north of Herod's palace. The last major defence work in biblical Palestine was the third wall of Jerusalem, far to the north of the one used in Christ's time. See JERUSALEM.

c. The city gate

The gate with its adjacent towers was the most important defence feature in a city wall, but nevertheless many a city was captured by the enemy breaking through at this point. In the days of the Patriarchs the city gate was a series of entrances one inside the other. Massive piers held the outer gates, but inside was a second and sometimes a third set of similar piers. Like most of Palestine's military architecture, this gateway came in from Syria. Towers normally flanked the gateway, enabling a larger number of defenders to fight the enemy. In towns the gateway was wide enough for a single chariot; in cities two might pass. A larger city would have more than one gate, as described in the rebuilding of

Nehemiah's Jerusalem. Some of the secondary gates were sortie gates, and might be only wide enough for a single loaded donkey. The gates turned on pivots sunk into holes in the pavement and into the lintel above. Solomonic gateways have been found at Gezer, Megiddo, and Hazor. Here are three sets of long, narrow piers with guard rooms between them. About the 8th century BC a new gate design appeared. This is best represented at Tell en-Nasbeh. In this new gateway the city wall to the right was not only on a line slightly farther out than the city wall to the left of the gate, but it also passed beyond it, making a hollow square between the walls. At the inside end of this passage-way the gate was located—two piers with a guard room on either side between them. The outer wall was finished off with a massive tower which could handle attackers on three sides. Also the inner wall could furnish its quota of defenders against the attackers in the hollow square before the gate. In front of the gate and on either side of this hollow square stone benches were located where the city fathers could hold court. Round towers appeared as part of the Herodian gateway in Samaria, and round towers had appeared earlier in the same city's Hellenistic fortifications. A city's gateway was usually closed by massive double doors of wood bolted into place. Since the enemy would try to burn these doors, they were often covered with metal. In multiple-piered gateways emergency gates were used at the various piers.

d. The problem of water-supply

Second only in importance to the walls and gates of a fortress was its water supply. Until the invention of waterproof plaster and its application to cisterns, every city needed a spring within its walled area or closely adjacent thereto so that it could be reached by a tunnel from inside the city. The most famous of all these is Hezekiah's tunnel in Jerusalem. (See SILOAM.) But other major engineering examples have been found at Gezer, Megiddo, and Gibeon. Cisterns added greatly to a city's ability to withstand a prolonged siege, such as that which the Assyrians made before the surrender of Samaria. Not only did the defenders build up their own water reserve but they sought to lessen the amount available to the invaders. Cisterns were filled with earth, pools were drained, and springs were stopped up wherever possible. Sufficient food was also vital for a siege, and the excavators have uncovered buildings serving as granaries for the defending troops.

e. Citadel and blockhouse

The towers which straddle a city wall or abut on it have already been described, but the term 'tower' was used in two other senses. One is that of a citadel, usually the highest area within the fortifications, where excellent secondary defences would protect the best troops and the royal family. Another use of the word 'tower' is applied to what we would call a blockhouse. These were usually units in a chain of very small fortresses in sparsely settled areas such as the Negeb. They served as police stations for the local area and as alarm posts along a debated frontier. These were still being built in Maccabean times.

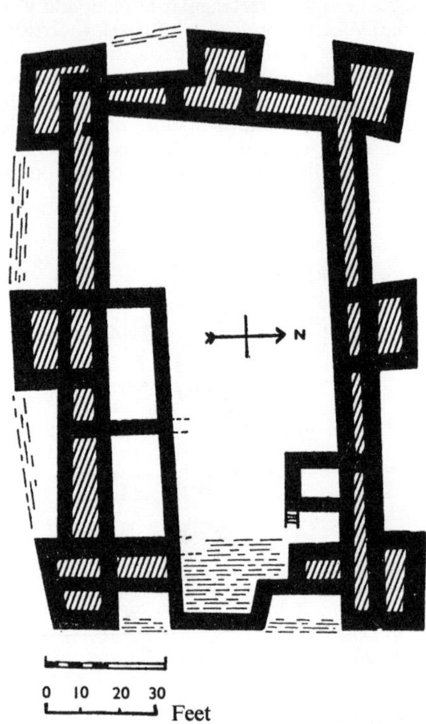

Fig. 88. Plan of a Judaean fort in the desert north of Kadesh-barnea. See also fig. 95.

II. METHODS OF ATTACK

The least costly method of taking a city was, of course, to persuade it to surrender without fighting. The Assyr. Sennacherib used this technique in vain against Jerusalem. Another method was to capture a city by surprise, as David secured Jerusalem. Usually, however, large cities had to be captured by assault or by long siege.

a. The assault

In more difficult assaults the agger or bank was used. The moat in front of the wall was filled in with debris, and then a great bank of earth was erected against the city wall so that the attacking troops could get their machines above the glacis and closer to the top of the wall, where there was usually lighter construction. Towers as high as the city wall might also be pushed up the banks so that the attackers could be on a level with the defenders. Ezk. xxi. 22 summarizes such an assault.

Battering-rams were brought up this ramp and close to the wall so that they could make a breach in the defences. This was more difficult to do quickly if the wall had been built with integrated straddling towers to reduce the effect of the vibration of the rams. The soldiers working these machines were defended by archers and slingers, who were assigned to pick off the defenders on the wall in front of the rams. Catapults were also used to throw large stones against the upper sections of the wall and its defenders. After the breach was made, assault troops swarmed through it into the city. At the same time, at other points along the wall, scaling-ladders were used to put troops on the walls. Other soldiers were probably simultaneously attacking one or more of the city gates, and miners might be at work tunnelling under the walls. In Sennacherib's palace one of the great bas-reliefs pictures vividly the various phases of the assault and capture of Lachish, as well as the exit of prisoners and the impaling of officials.

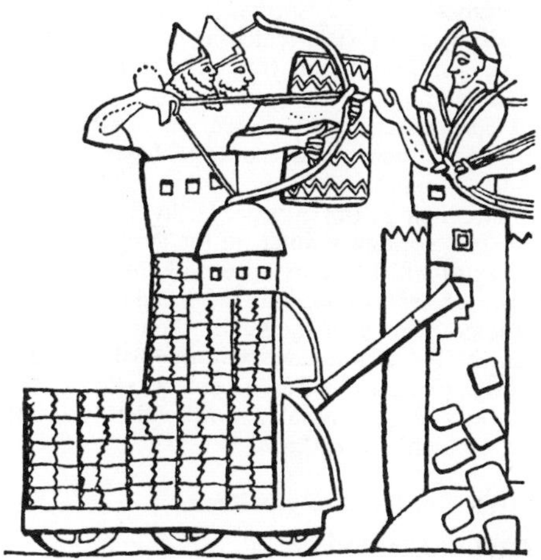

Fig. 89. An Assyrian siege engine. From the tower bowmen shoot into the city, while from the wheeled and armoured cart a metal-tipped battering-ram makes a breach in the walls. Relief of Ashurnasirpal II, 879 BC. See also fig. 94.

Some defenders in the meantime were seeking to burn the battering-rams by dropping firebrands on them, and others were trying to kill the attacking troops adjacent to the machines. The defenders' weapons were arrows, javelins, sling stones, boiling water, *etc.* (See ARMOUR AND WEAPONS.) Other defenders would be tearing down houses opposite the breach and using that stone in erecting an emergency inner wall. As a last resort, the best defending troops would retire to the acropolis for a final stand. At various points during the attack special assault troops would also make sorties out of the city, seeking to destroy the battering-rams and catapults and their protecting troops.

b. The siege

If a city was considered too costly to assault it would be starved out by siege. This was the method tried by Ben-hadad against Samaria, but at the last minute he failed. Samaria later held out against the Assyrians for over two years before surrendering.

c. The capture

After a city was captured it was normally plundered and burned. Most of these captured cities, however, were usually repaired and used again, as it was far too costly to build a completely new city. The most famous destruction of Old Testament times was Nebuchadrezzar's complete obliteration of all the Judaean cities, including Jerusalem itself. The destruction of Jerusalem by Titus in AD 70 was a parallel to that of Nebuchadrezzar, but the lesser cities fared far better under the Romans.

BIBLIOGRAPHY. W. F. Albright, *The Archaeology of Palestine*, 1960. J.L.K.

FORTUNATUS. A member of the Corinthian party which was a blessing to Paul at Ephesus (1 Cor. xvi. 17 f.; see STEPHANAS). Nothing else is certainly known of him. The name is Latin and a common one, and here the man is probably a slave. It has been needlessly assumed that he and Achaicus (*q.v.*) belonged to the household of Stephanas (*cf.* 1 Cor. xvi. 15) or even of Chloe (1 Cor. i. 11). It is attractive to find Fortunatus 'forty years on' in *1 Clement* lxv, but, *pace* Lightfoot (*St. Clement of Rome*, I, p. 62, II, p. 187, *q.v.*), it is not certain that Clement's Fortunatus was a Corinthian. A.F.W.

FOUNDATION.

I. IN THE OLD TESTAMENT

A building was sometimes set upon the surface of the soil or rock which had been levelled either by excavation or by filling up with small stones. But a true foundation was 'laid down' (see Is. xxviii. 16), for much attention was paid to foundations, on the strength of which depended the durability of the upper walls (Je. l. 15). Thus the better buildings had basic layers of stone set out either as a complete foundation course or to support the corners (see CORNERSTONE). Upon this were laid the upper courses of wood or sun-dried brick. The foundation of the Solomonic Temple consisted of large (8 × 10 cubits) and expensively trimmed blocks of stone (1 Ki. v. 17, vi. 37; *cf.* 1 Ch. xxii. 2).

The foundations of the second Temple were laid in two stages; first, under Cyrus, a retaining wall was built to retain a level platform (Aram. *'uššâ*; Akkad. *uššu*, Ezr. v. 16). Darius subsequently gave permission for this to be filled in with earth as a foundation terrace (Ezr. vi. 3) and the normal foundation walls were laid within and upon it (Ezr. iii. 10; Zc. iv. 9). Foundations of this kind were earlier used for the palace and storehouse built by David at Lachish (*q.v.*).

The Heb. *yāsaḏ* and compounds means 'to fix firmly, found' and is thus used generally of all types of foundations, *e.g.* the altar (Ex. xxix. 12). Metaphorically it denotes anything immovably established, as the earth (Ps. xxiv. 2; Is. xxiv. 18);

the inhabited world (Ps. xviii. 15) and the vault of heaven (Am. ix. 6). In this way the future Israel (Is. liv. 11), Zion (Is. xiv. 32), and the righteous (Pr. x. 25) are described.

The rare practice of the heathen people of Jericho who laid a foundation with a human sacrifice, or so-called 'threshold covenant', is not confirmed by archaeology at any Israelite site (1 Ki. xvi. 34; *cf.* Jos. vi. 26). The 'gate of the foundation' in Jerusalem (2 Ch. xxiii. 5, AV) may be the Horse-gate or 'Gate of Sur', while the 'rod of foundation' (Is. xxx. 32, AV 'grounded staff') is probably for 'the rod of discipline' (*mūsār*). D.J.W.

II. IN THE NEW TESTAMENT

Two Greek words are thus translated.

1. *katabolē*, 'a casting or laying down'. All ten occurrences of this word are bound up with the phrase 'the foundation of the world' (*e.g.* Mt. xiii. 35; Lk. xi. 50).

2. *themelios*, 'anything laid', appears sixteen times. Generally this word is found in a figurative sense, but it is used literally in speaking of the wise man who builds his foundation upon a rock (Lk. vi. 48). Christ is spoken of as the foundation of the Church, *i.e.* the true and only basis of our salvation (1 Cor. iii. 11). He is the chief Cornerstone; and the apostles, who are the trustees and publishers of His gospel, are referred to as the foundation on which Christians are built (Eph. ii. 20; *cf.* Rev. xxi. 14, 19). 'Foundation' is used also of one's ministry (Rom. xv. 20; 1 Cor. iii. 10), and in referring to the security of God's seal (2 Tim. ii. 19). The first principles of divine truth are a foundation on which the rest depend (Heb. vi. 1, 2).

In a slightly different use of the word Timothy is instructed to urge those who are 'rich in this world' to lay up a good foundation (1 Tim. vi. 19; *cf.* Heb. xi. 10; Mt. vi. 19, 20) by trusting all to God—perhaps in contrast to the Ephesian merchants who deposited their earthly treasures in the temple of 'the great goddess Diana'.

See also CORNERSTONE.

BIBLIOGRAPHY. J. S. Howson, *The Metaphors of Paul*, 1868. J.D.D.

FOUNTAIN. Palestine, owing to its geological structure, is a land of many springs, as was forecast to the Israelites before they settled there (Dt. viii. 7). As a result of this, several Heb. words were in use which are commonly rendered 'fountain' or 'spring' in the EVV.

1. *'ayin*, 'spring, fountain', the commonest word (*e.g.* Gn. xvi. 7), is well known from the fact that in its construct form, *'ên-* (EVV 'En-'), it is a common element in place-names. Its Arabic cognate is familiar today, as in 'Ain es-Sulṭân, the spring by which the city of Jericho (*q.v.*) stood. The word occurs in a modified form as the place-name Ainōn or Aenōn, where John baptized (Jn. iii. 23). Sometimes translated 'well' (*q.v.*) in AV (*e.g.* Gn. xxiv. 13).

2. *ma'yān*, 'place of springs', is a variant of (1), and rendered in the AV by both 'fountain' (*e.g.* Gn. vii. 11) and 'spring' (*e.g.* Ps. lxxxvii. 7). 3. *mabbûa'*, 'spring', from *nāḇa'*, 'to flow, bubble up', is rendered in the EVV by both 'fountain' (*e.g.* Ec. xii. 6) and 'spring' (*e.g.* Is. xxxv. 7).

4. *māqôr*. This is sometimes used in a figurative sense of, *e.g.*, 'life' (Ps. xxxvi. 9) or in a physiological sense (*e.g.* Lv. xx. 18) and rendered in the EVV by both 'fountain' (*e.g.* Ps. xxxvi. 9) and 'spring' (*e.g.* Pr. xxv. 26). 5. *môṣā'*, 'place of going forth', comes from *yāṣā'*, 'to go out', and is sometimes rendered 'spring' (*e.g.* 2 Ki. ii. 21). 6. *gal* is usually 'heap' (*e.g.* Gn. xxxi. 46), but in Ct. iv. 12 it is translated 'spring' (RSV, however, reads *gan*, 'garden'). 7. *gullâ*, 'basin, bowl', is rendered 'spring' in EVV of Jos. xv. 19 and Jdg. i. 15.

8. *'ašēḏâ*, 'foundation', '(mountain-)slope', which occurs only in the plural, is in the AV sometimes rendered 'spring' (Dt. iv. 49; Jos. x. 40, xii. 8) and thrice treated as part of a place-name, Ashdoth-Pisgah (Dt. iii. 17; Jos. xii. 3, xiii. 20). The other EVV give 'slopes of Pisgah'.

9. *bôr*, 'cistern, well'. In Je. vi. 7, where the *Keṯîḇ* gives *bawir* and the *Qerē bayir*, the AV renders 'fountain' but RV and RSV give 'well'. 10. *ḥay*, 'living'. In Gn. xxvi. 19 'living waters' is rendered 'springing water' in the EVV. 11. *nēḇeḵ* is a word which occurs once only, in the plural construct *niḇeḵê-yām*, in Jb. xxxviii. 16, and rendered 'springs of the sea' in the EVV.

In the New Testament the principal word for 'spring', 'fountain' is *pēgē* (*e.g.* Rev. vii. 17, *etc.*; *cf.* Mk. v. 29; Jn. iv. 6), a word which is, in the LXX, used chiefly for *'ayin*. T.C.M.

FOWL. See BIRDS OF THE BIBLE.

FOWLER. See SNARES.

FOX. Both foxes and jackals are found throughout the Middle East. They are members of the Canidae, the dog family, and closely related, but the fox is usually solitary, whereas jackals often go in packs. It is likely that Heb. *šû'āl* and Gk. *alōpēx* include both fox and jackal (*q.v.*). Both species eat fruit and other vegetable matter, including grapes (Ct. ii. 15). In Jdg. xv. 4 it is likely that the 300 animals caught by Samson were jackals. See fig. 40. G.C.

FRANKINCENSE. This substance consisted of the resinous exudate of certain trees related to the terebinth, the most important being *Boswellia carterii*, *B. papyrifera*, and *B. thurifera*. These species grew abundantly in SW Arabia, Abyssinia, and India. They furnished much of the wealth acquired by those traders who followed the ancient spice-routes from S Arabia to Gaza and Damascus (Is. lx. 6).

The whitish-yellow aromatic resin was obtained by incising the bark, and, although acrid to the taste, frankincense was extremely odoriferous. It comprised one ingredient of the holy anointing oil (Ex. xxx. 34), and was also burned with other substances during the meat-offering (Lv. vi. 15). Frankincense was placed in purified form on the shewbread in the tabernacle (Lv. xxiv. 7). While it gratified the senses (Ct. iii. 6, iv. 6, 14), it was also symbolic of religious fervour (*cf.* Mal. i. 11). The gift of frankincense presented to Christ by the wise men (Mt. ii. 11) has been interpreted as symbolizing His priestly office. See also COSMETICS AND PERFUMERY. R.K.H.

FREEDOM. See LIBERTY.

FREEMAN, FREEWOMAN. Two Gk. words are used. 1. *apeleutheros*, 'one fully freed', applies to a man who, born a slave, has been freed. In 1 Cor. vii. 22 the reference is to one freed by the Lord from the bondage of sin (*cf.* 1 Cor. xii. 13; Col. iii. 11; Rev. xiii. 16, *etc.*). 2. *eleuthera*, 'free woman'. Gal. iv. 22, 23, 30 thus describes Sarah, Abraham's wife, the freewoman, contrasted with Hagar, his concubine, the Egyp. slave-girl. A metaphorical application of this is made in Gal. iv. 31. The masculine form, *eleutheros*, is found in Rev. vi. 15. J.D.D.

FREEWILL. See LIBERTY, PROVIDENCE.

FRIEND OF THE BRIDEGROOM. The Heb. words *rēa'*, *rē'eh*, and *mērēa'*, though often meaning 'friend' in general, sometimes have the special meaning of 'friend of the bridegroom', 'best man'. The ancient versions sometimes show this special meaning. In the case of an abortive marriage Mesopotamian law forbade any marriage between the 'friend' and the forsaken bride. This explains the reaction of the Philistines and of Samson on the marriage of his former fiancée with his best man (Jdg. xiv, xv. 1–6). Jdg. xiv. 20 should be rendered 'to his best man, who had performed for him the offices of a best man'. A metaphorical use of the position of the best man is to be found in Jn. iii. 29 (*cf.* 2 Cor. xi. 2). The position of best man, 'friend' of the king, developed into the office of adviser in family matters and foreign relations.

BIBLIOGRAPHY. A. van Selms, 'The best man and bride—from Sumer to St. John', *JNES*, IX, 1950, pp. 65–75; *id.*, 'The origin of the title "the king's friend"', *ibid.*, XVI, 1957, pp. 118–123. A. VAN S.

FRIEND OF THE KING. A phrase which was applied to various individuals. Ahuzzath was the 'friend' (*mērēa'*) of Abimelech the king of Gerar (Gn. xxvi. 26); Saul had a 'friend' (*mērēa'*) (unnamed, 2 Sa. iii. 8); Hushai the Archite was David's 'friend' (*rē'eh*, 2 Sa. xv. 37); Solomon's 'friend' (*rē'eh*) was Zabud the priest (1 Ki. iv. 5); and Baasha of Israel had a 'friend' (*rēa'*) (unnamed, 1 Ki. xvi. 11). *Rēa'* is the common Old Testament word for 'friend', and *mērēa'* and *rē'eh* are generally taken as variant forms of it. It has been suggested, however, that *rē'eh* is to be connected with Egyp. *rḫ nsw.t*, which came in the Middle Kingdom to mean 'acquaintance of the king', or with *ruḫi šarri* in the Amarna Letters, which has much the same meaning. The title does not seem to have implied any specific function, though marriage arrangements were a special concern, but the importance of the 'friend' is shown by the fact that there was never more than one at a time. A similar title was found later in Persian times, Themistocles, for example, being named a 'King's Friend' by Xerxes.

BIBLIOGRAPHY. R. de Vaux, *Les Institutions de l'Ancien Testament*, I, 1958, pp. 188–189, 332. T.C.M.

FRINGES. A border of tassels along the edges of a garment (Dt. xxii. 12). This was bound by a blue cord, and served to remind the wearer of God's commands and of the need to obey them (Nu. xv. 38, 39). Various monuments show Hebrews and others wearing fringed garments. In New Testament times those who delighted in an outward show of piety put noticeably wide fringed borders on their garments (Mt. xxiii. 5). K.A.K.

FROG. Apart from one figurative use in Rev. xvi. 13 (Gk. *batrachos*), the word 'frog' occurs only in connection with the second of God's plagues upon Egypt (Ex. viii. 2 ff.). Several frogs, especially of the genus *Rana*, are common in the Nile valley, and more than one species could have been the *ṣ*[e]*p̄ardēa'* which caused this plague. G.C.

FRONTLETS. See ORNAMENTS.

FRUIT, FRUITS. The AV translation of the following Heb. and Gk. words, some of which are used interchangeably: Heb. *'ēḇ*, 'budding' (Ct. vi. 11; Dn. iv. 12, 14, 21); *y*[e]*ḇûl*, 'increase' (Dt. xi. 17; Hab. iii. 17; Hg. i. 10); *t*[e]*nûḇâ*, 'increase' (Jdg. ix. 11; Is. xxvii. 6; La. iv. 9); *yeleḏ*, 'child' (Ex. xxi. 22); *leḥem*, 'bread, food' (Je. xi. 19); *nîḇ*, 'utterance' (Is. lvii. 19; Mal. i. 12); *ma'*[a]*ḵāl*, 'eating' (Ne. ix. 25); *m*[e]*lē'â*, 'fulness' (Dt. xxii. 9; also 'ripe fruits' in Ex. xxii. 29); *p*[e]*rî*, 'fruit' (107 times); *t*[e]*ḇû'â*, 'incoming' (thirteen times); *kōaḥ*, 'strength' (Jb. xxxi. 39). Gk. *gennēma*, 'produce' (Mt. xxvi. 29; Mk. xiv. 25; Lk. xii. 18, xxii. 18; 2 Cor. ix. 10); *karpos*, 'fruit' (sixty-four times; *akarpos*, 'without fruit', in Jude 12); *opōra*, 'ripe or full fruits' (Rev. xviii. 14).

a. Literal use

Mosaic law decreed that fruit-bearing trees be regarded as unclean for three years after planting, as the Lord's in the fourth year, and to be eaten by the people only in the fifth year. This preserved the health of the trees against premature plucking, gave God His due place, perhaps commemorated the entrance of sin by forbidden fruit, and certainly inculcated self-discipline. Fruit-trees were so highly valued that for many centuries thereafter, even during the bitterest wars, special efforts were made to protect them (*cf.* Dt. xx. 19, 20). See FOOD, VINE, TREES, APPLE, FIG, and other articles under individual fruits.

Children are sometimes spoken of as the fruit of the body or womb (Dt. xxviii. 4; Ps. cxxvii. 3).

b. Metaphorical use

The term has inspired a large number of metaphorical uses, involving such phrases as the fruit of the Spirit (Gal. v. 22); fruit unto God (Rom. vii. 4) and unto death (Rom. vii. 5; *cf.* Jas. i. 15); fruit of the lips (*i.e.* speaking, Is. lvii. 19; Heb. xiii. 15); fruit unto holiness and life (Rom. vi. 22); fruit of the wicked (Mt. vii. 16) and of self-centredness (Ho. x. 1; *cf.* Zc. vii. 5, 6); fruit in season (*i.e.* true prosperity, Ps. i. 3; Je. xvii. 8); fruits of the gospel (Rom. i. 13; Col. i. 6); of righteousness (Phil. i. 11; Jas. iii. 18); fruits meet for repentance (Mt. iii. 8; *cf.* Am. vi. 12). The unfruitful works of darkness are contrasted with the fruit of light (Eph. v. 9–11).

'The tree of life which bare twelve manner of fruits' (Rev. xxii. 2) some regard as 'a sacrament of the covenant of works, and analogous to the bread and wine used by Melchizedek (Gn. xiv. 18) and to the Christian Eucharist (Mt. xxvi. 29) in the covenant of grace' (*Baker's Dictionary of Theology*, 1960, p. 231). More probably it is a symbol of the gospel and its blessings. J.D.D.

FUEL. Coal (*q.v.*) was unknown to the Hebrews. Charcoal was used by the wealthy (Je. xxxvi. 22; Jn. xviii. 18) and by smiths, while the poor gathered their own sticks (1 Ki. xvii. 10). Ezekiel refers to the use of dried dung (*q.v.*) as a fuel (iv. 12 ff.), which practice obtains today among the poor. Is. xliv. 14–16 lists some of the trees used as fuel, while shrubs (especially 'broom', Ps. cxx. 4, RVmg), briars and thorns (Ec. vii. 6), chaff (Mt. iii. 12) and hay (Mt. vi. 30) were used to obtain a quick, fierce, but evanescent heat. Fuel appears to have been common property among the Hebrews, and to be charged for it was a great hardship (La. v. 4). R.J.W.

FULLER. See ARTS AND CRAFTS.

FULLER'S FIELD. See ARTS AND CRAFTS.

FULNESS. The Gk. word *plērōma*, translated 'fulness', carries three possible connotations: 'that which is filled'; 'that which fills or fills up', *i.e.* 'completes'; 'that which is brought to fulness or completion'.

The first does not seem to be relevant in the Scriptures, but the other two possibilities are important for the interpretation of certain crucial biblical texts. For the second we may cite Ps. xxiv. 1, LXX (= 1 Cor. x. 26); Mt. ix. 16; Mk. vi. 43, viii. 20. The Matthew reference may have the meaning 'that which makes something full or complete', as it refers to a patch which fills up the hole in a torn garment.

Under the third meaning should be placed Rom. xi. 25, 'the full number, the totality of the Gentiles', and Rom. xv. 29 'the full measure of Christ's blessing'. Rom. xiii. 10 describes love as the *plērōma* of the law. This has been construed as 'the sum total of the law's prescriptions and demands'; but it is possible that the correct meaning here is 'fulfilment'. Love, like the Lord Jesus, is the end of the law (Rom. x. 4; *cf.* Gal. v. 14, vi. 2) in that it brings the law to its full realization and perfect completion in the sense of Mt. v. 17, xxvi. 56; Mk. i. 15. This nuance leads on to those verses where the precise meaning of the word is disputed. It is convenient to divide them into two groups.

1. Col. i. 19 and Col. ii. 9 are best taken together. The exegesis of the use of *plērōma* in the latter is undoubtedly 'the fulness of deity, the totality of the Godhead' which dwells in Christ; and this meaning may be decisive in settling the correct interpretation of Col. i. 19. In this text the choice is between taking it as a quasi-technical term of early Gnostic speculation, which used the word *plērōma* to denote the region inhabited by the 'full number' of intermediary beings which were thought to exist between the Creator God and the created world; and taking it in the sense 'God in His fulness', 'the entirety of God's attributes, His full divinity' which was pleased to dwell in Christ (so RSV). On the former view, Paul is combating speculative teachers at Colossae, who reduced Christ to a member of the celestial hierarchy. The apostle asserts in reply to this teaching that He is the fulness of these intermediary beings. They are subsumed in Him, for He is the *plērōma* of them all.

This view, however, which assumes that Paul and the Colossian heretics are using a common term, although supported by many scholars, among whom are Lightfoot, E. F. Scott, and R. Bultmann (*Theology of the New Testament*, II, E.T. 1955, pp. 149 ff.), is open to serious objection. Apart from the lack of convincing evidence for an early Gnostic creed in the 1st century, the most obvious consideration which tells against this proposal is that stated by E. Percy, that there is no trace in i. 19 and ii. 9 of a polemic against the use which the supposed heretical teachers were making of the term *plērōma*, and in any case it is very unlikely that Paul would have borrowed so important a term from such a source. J. A. T. Robinson's suggestion (*The Body*, 1952, p. 67), that the apostle deliberately took over for apologetic use this word which he found in Hellenistic circles, lacks plausibility.

With C. F. D. Moule and C. Masson we may accept the second view and interpret *plērōma* in its Old Testament light, where the Heb. equivalent is *m*ᵉ*lō'*; this reading sees the word as conveying the thought somewhat parallel to the Logos Christology of John, *i.e.* in Christ the sum-total of the divine attributes dwells and is revealed and communicated to men (Jn. i. 14, 16).

2. In Ephesians the term is taken by some commentators as applying to the Church as well as to Christ; and this would confirm the view expressed above that *plērōma* is not being used in any technical 'Gnostic' sense. In Eph. i. 10 there is a meaning similar to that in Mt. v. 17; Mk. i. 15; Gal. iv. 4 with the thought that God's

pre-ordained plan is now about to be consummated.

Eph. i. 22, 23 may be taken in a number of ways, listed with admirable clarity by Moule. The real crux is whether, on the one hand, *plērōma* refers to the Church (so AV, RV, RSV), which is then to be taken actively as that which completes Christ who is filling all things (corresponding to Eph. iv. 10: so J. Dupont, *Gnosis: la connaissance religieuse dans les épîtres de Saint Paul*, 1949, p. 424, n. 1), or, in a passive sense, as that which is filled by Christ: or whether, on the other hand, *plērōma* should be treated as in apposition to 'him' in verse 22 and so taken to apply to the Lord Himself as the One who has been designated by God the Father as the fulness of the Godhead who fills all in all (as in 1 Cor. xv. 28). This latter interpretation has the advantage of harmonizing with the rest of the Epistle (iv. 10) and with the teaching of *plērōma* in Colossians noted above. See Moule for a defence of this view, and F. C. Synge, who also takes *plērōma* as a reference to Christ.

Eph. iii. 19 requires no comment, except that it confirms the understanding of *plērōma* as a Christological title. This verse is another way of expressing the hope that 'Christ may dwell in your hearts by faith' (iii. 17); Eph. iv. 12, 13 holds out the prospect of the whole body of believers coming into such an experience.

Another interpretation takes more seriously the voice of the verb (passive or middle) in the earlier texts. Christ is being fulfilled or is filling Himself: but by or with whom? The answer to this question is that He is fulfilled either by the Christians who, as members of His Body, 'complement' the Head, and together form the 'whole Christ' (so A. Robinson, F. W. Beare); or with W. L. Knox, L. S. Thornton, and J. A. T. Robinson, who propose the translation 'that which is filled by him who is always being filled (by God)' by God, so that the meaning of the whole phrase is that the Church is constantly receiving from Christ its Head the complete fulness which Christ receives from the Father.

BIBLIOGRAPHY. C. F. D. Moule, *The Epistles to the Colossians and to Philemon, Cambridge Greek Testament*, 1957, Appendix IV: 'A Note on PLEROMA'; J. A. T. Robinson, *The Body*, 1952, p. 65, n. 3. See also J. B. Lightfoot, *St. Paul's Epistles to the Colossians and to Philemon*, 1897, pp. 255, 271; C. Masson, *L'Épître de S. Paul aux Colossiens*, 1950; E. Percy, *Die Probleme der Kolosser- und Epheser-briefe*, 1946; E. F. Scott, *The Epistles to the Colossians, to Philemon, and to the Ephesians*, 1930; F. C. Synge, *The Epistle to the Ephesians*, 1941.

R.P.M.

FURLONG. See WEIGHTS AND MEASURES.

FURNACE. A word used in AV to translate five Hebrew terms and one Greek.

1. *'attûn*. An Aramaic word which is used in Dn. iii of the furnace into which Shadrach, Meshach, and Abednego were cast by Nebuchadrezzar. It was probably a loan-word from Akkad. *utūnu*, 'oven', as used for baking bricks or smelting metals.

2. *kiḇšān*. A word occurring four times in the Bible, as a simile to describe the smoke of Sodom and Gomorrah (Gn. xix. 28) and of Mt. Sinai (Ex. ix. 8, 10). In post-biblical Hebrew it was understood to mean a kiln as used for firing pottery or burning lime.

3. *kûr*. A pot or crucible for smelting metals. The word always occurs in the Bible as a metaphor or simile of God's punishment or tempering of man. Egypt was a crucible of iron (Dt. iv. 20; Je. xi. 4; 1 Ki. viii. 51); God will put Israel in the crucible and melt it with His fury (Ezk. xxii. 18, 20, 22); and Israel is passed through the crucible of affliction (Is. xlviii. 10).

4. *'ᵃlîl*. Used only in Ps. xii. 6 in a simile of the words of God which are as silver tried in a furnace. The usage suggests a crucible.

5. *tannûr*. 'Portable stove' or 'oven' (see BREAD), the latter probably being a preferable translation in Ne. iii. 11, xii. 38; Is. xxxi. 9; and perhaps Gn. xv. 17, where AV gives 'furnace'.

6. *kaminos*. 'Oven, furnace', a word used in LXX to translate *'attûn, kiḇšān*, and *kûr*, and in Mt. xiii. 42, 50 and Rev. ix. 2 as a figure of the fires of hell (*cf.* also Rev. i. 15).

Copper-refining furnaces have been excavated in Palestine at Beth-shemesh, Ai, and Ezion-geber, the latter lying at the southern end of the Wadi Arabah, which forms a funnel down which powerful winds blow. Well-preserved furnaces for iron refining built below the level of the ground were found at Tell Jemmeh (see GERAR). See also ARTS AND CRAFTS.

BIBLIOGRAPHY. A. G. Barrois, *Manuel d'Archéologie biblique*, I, 1939, pp. 372, 373; R. J. Forbes, *Studies in Ancient Technology*, VI, 1958, pp. 66 ff.

T.C.M.

FURNITURE. See HOUSE.

Fig. 90. Birds and animals of the Palestinian foothills. Much of the cultivated land is on the lower hills and in the villages among the hills. The black rat (4) never lives far from farms and human dwellings, and it is one of the animals preyed on by the huge eagle owl (1), which is also able to catch hares (6). The wolf (2) hunts many smaller animals and attacks sheep but rarely. Both tortoise (9) and rock partridges (11) can be seen in the farms, the latter more often heard than seen. The hyena (5) is mostly a scavenger. Of many kinds of ant, the harvester ant (8) is one of the most obvious. Typical plants of this region are white mustard (3; *Sinapis alba*), the polyanthus narcissus (7; *Narcissus tazetta*), saffron (10; *Carthamus tinctorius*) and the so-called 'rose of Sharon' (12; *Tulipa sharonensis*). See PLANTS. See also figs. 38, 39, 40.

G

GAAL. Son of Ebed (LXX (B) *Iobel*, possibly Heb. *'Obed*, *cf.* Moore, *ICC*, *Judges*, p. 256, and Jdg. ix. 28); leader of a roving band, who came to Shechem in the reign of Abimelech and tried to take advantage of disaffection in the city. His activity forced Abimelech to attack Shechem; Gaal and his men were expelled by Abimelech's governor, Zebul, before the city was taken (Jdg. ix. 22–45). J.P.U.L.

GABBATHA (Jn. xix. 13). Generally regarded as the Hebrew or Aramaic equivalent of Gk. *lithostrōton*, 'stone-strewn' (*cf.* mosaic pavement of Est. i. 6), but the derivation is obscure. Two languages are cited, possibly to underline the tremendous significance of what was happening (*cf.* Jn. xix. 17, 20). Suetonius (*Vit. Div. Jul.* 46) tells how Julius Caesar carried with him on military business a tesselated pavement which was laid down to mark the spot where his judicial decisions were given, but 'Gabbatha' in this context suggests rather a fixed spot. Many scholars locate it at or near the Tower of Antonia (see JERUSALEM), north-west of the Temple Area, and Père L. H. Vincent claims to have identified part of the paving beneath the present Church of the Dames de Sion (see *Harper's Bible Dictionary*, 1952, p. 210). J.D.D.

GABRIEL (Heb. *Gabrî'ēl*, 'man of God' or 'God has shown Himself strong'). One of the two angels in the Bible who are named; the other is Michael the archangel (Jude 9). In Dn. viii. 16 Gabriel is sent to interpret to Daniel the vision of the Ram and He-goat, and he comes again to give the prophecy of the seventy weeks (Dn. ix. 21 ff.).

Gabriel plays an important rôle in later Jewish apocalyptic. In 1 Enoch, Gabriel is one of the four highest angels (with Michael, Raphael, and Phanuel or Uriel, ix. 1, x. 1, 9, xl. 9) or one of the seven highest (xx. 1–8). He has various functions: he is an angel of punishment (x. 9); is set over Paradise and the serpents and the cherubim (xx. 7); he is set over all powers and intercedes for men (xl. 6, 9); he will execute judgment on the fallen angels (xliv. 6).

In the New Testament Gabriel is the angel who 'stands in the presence of God' (Lk. i. 19), *i.e.* who holds a specially high position in the angelic ranks. He is sent to Zacharias to announce the birth of John the Baptist (Lk. i. 11–22) and to Mary to announce the birth of Jesus (Lk. i. 26–38). In the Bible Gabriel appears to be the messenger angel, while Michael is the warrior angel. G.E.L.

GAD ('good fortune'). **1.** The seventh son of Jacob, his first by Leah's maid Zilpah (Gn. xxx. 10, 11, RV). Gad himself already had seven sons when Jacob and his family entered Egypt (Gn. xlvi. 16); Jacob promised Gad's descendants a troubled life, but foretold that they would hit back (Gn. xlix. 19). They recur later in Moses' blessing (Dt. xxxiii. 20, 21).

2. An Israelite tribe descended from Gad, and the territory they occupied. The tribe in Moses' time had seven clans (Nu. xxvi. 15–18), was commanded and represented by one Eliasaph (Nu. i. 14, ii. 14, vii. 42, x. 20), and supplied a spy for exploration of Canaan (Nu. xiii. 15). When Israel reached the plains of Moab, Reuben, Gad, and half-Manasseh sought permission to settle in Transjordan, which they desired as their share of the promised land, because Gilead (*q.v.*) was so suitable for their considerable livestock. To this Moses agreed, on condition that they first help their fellow-Israelites to establish themselves in W Palestine (Nu. xxxii). The Gadites and Reubenites then promiscuously and hastily repaired cities (including Ataroth) and sheepfolds to safeguard their families and livestock (Nu. xxxii. 34–38, *cf.* 26, 27) while preparing to help their brethren, a promise of help duly kept (Jos. xxii. 1–8). Then came the incident of the altar of witness (Jos. xxii. 9–34). As tribal territory, Reuben and Gad received the Amorite kingdom of Sihon: Reuben had the land from Aroer (*q.v.*) on the Arnon river, northward to a line running from the Jordan's mouth eastward to the region of Heshbon (Jos. xiii. 15–23). North of this line, Gad had all S Gilead, from the Jordan valley eastward as far as the south-to-north course of the upper Jabbok (the border with Ammon), and north generally as far as the east-to-west course of the lower Jabbok, but with two extensions beyond this: first, all the Jordan valley on the east side of Jordan river (formerly Sihon's) between the Dead Sea and the Sea of Galilee (or Chinneroth), and second, across the north-east angle of the river Jabbok to include the district of Mahanaim (*q.v.*) and a fertile tract flanking the east side of N Gilead northward over Gebel Kafkafka to strategic Ramoth-Gilead at modern Tell Ramith, 15 miles north of Jerash (*cf.* Jos. xiii. 24–28). Heshbon was assigned as a levitical city out of the territory of Gad (Jos. xxi. 38, 39); hence perhaps read Jos. xiii. 16, 17 as (Reuben's) 'border was from Aroer . . . and all the plain by Medeba, <unto> Heshbon . . .' (emending only by the addition of one letter, locative-*h*). Dibon, *etc.*, are then cities between these limits, and Heshbon would be the southernmost territory of Gad.

The Gadites doubtless shared the troubles of Transjordanian Israel generally in the judges' period (*e.g.* Jdg. x–xii). In Saul's day the wooded Gileadite hills of Gad offered a place of refuge (1 Sa. xiii. 7), and Gadites among others joined the fugitive David and supported his becoming king (1 Ch. xii. 1, 8–15, 37, 38). Gadites likewise shared in, and were subject to, David's administration (2 Sa. xxiii. 36, xxiv. 5, RSV; 1 Ch. xxvi. 32). On his Moabite Stone, roughly 840/830 BC, King Mesha mentions that the Gadites had long dwelt in the land of Ataroth. Just after this, within Jehu of Israel's reign, Hazael of Damascus smote all Gilead, Gad included (2 Ki. x. 32, 33). In the 8th century BC Gadite settlement apparently extended north-east into Bashan (1 Ch. v. 11–17), until Tiglath-pileser III carried the Transjordanians into exile (2 Ki. xv. 29; 1 Ch. v. 25, 26). Then the Ammonites again invaded Gad (Je. xlix. 1–6). Gad is assigned the southernmost zone in Ezekiel's vision of the tribal portions (xlviii. 27, 28).

3. A prophet or seer, the contemporary of Saul and David; he advised David to leave Moab for Judah (1 Sa. xxii. 5). Later, God through Gad offered a choice of three possible punishments to David after his census, and then commanded that David build an altar on Araunah's threshing-floor (2 Sa. xxiv. 10 ff.; 1 Ch. xxi). Gad helped David and Nathan in organizing music for eventual use in the Temple (2 Ch. xxix. 25), and wrote a history of David's reign (1 Ch. xxix. 29).

4. A pagan deity worshipped by the Canaanites as the god of Fortune for whom they 'prepare a table' (Is. lxv. 11, RV, AVmg).

See also GAD, VALLEY OF. K.A.K.

GAD, VALLEY OF. The place where the census ordered by David was begun is given as 'Aroer, on the right side of the city that is in the middle of the valley (Heb. *naḥal*) of Gad' (2 Sa. xxiv. 5, RV). In Dt. ii. 36, RV, Aroer is described as 'on the edge of the valley (*naḥal*) of Arnon'. Since the census would naturally begin at the southern border of the Transjordan territory, this is probably the place intended. Various MSS of the LXX indicate corruptions in the text of 2 Sa. xxiv. 5, which should read 'towards Gad and Jazer'. G.T.M.

GADARA, GADARENES. The only biblical references to the Gadarene area concern the story of the miracle of Legion and the swine. The word 'Gadarenes' is found in some texts or versions of Mt. viii. 28; Mk. v. 1; and Lk. viii. 26. The probability is, however, that it is the original reading only in Matthew. (Compare these verses in AV and RV.) The actual site of the miracle is in little doubt, at the edge of the Sea of Galilee. It would have been in a sub-district of Gadara, which lay 6 miles south-east of the Sea, near the gorge of the Yarmuk (or Hieromax). The Mishnah claims that Gadara dates from the Old Testament period. It was held variously by Ptolemies, Seleucids, Jews, and Romans between the 3rd century BC and the Jewish War. It was one of the Decapolis cities. The ruins at Umm Qays today mark the site. D.F.P.

GAIUS. A Latin praenomen, used without addition several times in the New Testament.

1. A Macedonian involved in the Ephesian riot (Acts xix. 29; see ARISTARCHUS).

2. A companion of Paul's to Jerusalem, a member of the party which awaited the apostle at Troas (Acts xx. 4 f.), perhaps an official delegate of his church, which on the usual reading was Derbe. It is attractive, however, to follow the Western reading, 'of Doubērus' (a Macedonian town), and also possible to attach 'of Derbe' to Timothy (in which case Gaius would be a Thessalonian). Either way he would be a Macedonian, and thus conceivably the same as (1). Proof is impossible: Luke may rather be interposing two Galatians (Timothy representing Lystra) between two Thessalonians and two Asians.

3. A Corinthian, baptized by Paul (1 Cor. i. 14). The church met in his house, and Paul stayed with him on his third Corinthian visit (Rom. xvi. 23). A suggestion of Ramsay's has been revived that Gaius was the praenomen of Titius Justus (Acts xviii. 7; see JUSTUS). Origen (in Rom. xvi) refers to a tradition that he became first bishop of Thessalonica.

4. The addressee of 3 John: the Elder commends his rectitude and hospitality (of which he asks a renewal), and expects to see him shortly. J. Chapman (*JTS*, V, 1904, pp. 366 ff.) would identify him with any of the preceding, especially (1) and (3), but his reconstruction is highly conjectural.

The name was very common; the four references may well represent four different people. A.F.W.

GALATIA. 1. The ancient ethnic kingdom of Galatia located in the northern part of the great inner plateau of Asia Minor, including a large portion of the valley of the Halys River. A great population explosion in central Europe brought Gauls into this area during the 3rd century BC. Although never in the majority, the Gauls gained the upper hand and ruled over the more numerous tribes of Phrygians and Cappadocians. Ultimately the Gauls separated into three tribes, each inhabiting a separate area: the Trokmi settled in the eastern part which bordered on Cappadocia and Pontus, with Tavium as their capital; the Tolistobogii inhabited the western section bordering on Phrygia and Bithynia, with Pessinus as their chief town; and the Tektosages settled in the central area with Ancyra as their principal city.

2. The Roman province of Galatia. In 64 BC Galatia became a client of the Romans and, after the death of Amyntas, its last king, was given full status as a Roman province (25 BC). The new province of Galatia included not only the old ethnic territory but also parts of Pontus,

Phrygia, Lycaonia, Pisidia, Paphlagonia, and Isauria. Within the provincial Galatia were the towns which the apostle Paul evangelized on his first missionary journey, *viz.* Antioch, Iconium, Lystra, and Derbe (Acts xiii, xiv). The latter two cities were Roman colonies, and the former two had been Romanized by the Emperor Claudius. Large numbers of Romans, Greeks, and Jews were attracted to these population centres because of their strategic geographical location.

A particularly difficult question arises out of Paul's use of the word 'Galatia' in the Epistle to the Galatians (i. 2). Does Paul use the term in its geographical sense, *i.e.* to denote the ancient ethnic kingdom of Galatia, or in its political sense to denote the Roman province by that name? In the past, New Testament scholars have been almost evenly divided on this question. Today, however, the South Galatian theory holds the field, and this is largely due to the historical investigations of Sir William Ramsay. (But see CHRONOLOGY OF THE NEW TESTAMENT for a defence of the North Galatian theory.)

It is clear from the account in Acts xiii and xiv that Paul visited S Galatia and established churches there. Did he ever conduct a mission in N Galatia? Two texts especially have been used to support such a ministry. The first (Acts xvi. 6) reads: 'Now when they had gone throughout Phrygia and the region of Galatia . . .' North Galatian proponents understand 'Phrygia' here to be the territory in which Antioch and Iconium were located, whereas 'Galatia' refers to the geographical or ethnic kingdom by that name. Ramsay, however, takes the phrase *tēn Phrygian kai Galatikēn chōran* to be a composite term describing a single area—the Phrygian-Galatic region. The word *chōra*, 'territory', was the official word used to describe one of the *regiones* into which Roman provinces were divided. Part of the old kingdom of Phrygia belonged to the Roman province of Galatia and another part belonged to the province of Asia. Thus Acts xvi. 6 refers to the parts of Phrygia which had been incorporated into the Roman province of Galatia. This interpretation is supported by the following statement in the Acts account, 'and were forbidden of the Holy Ghost to preach the word in Asia'. The plan of the missionary party apparently was to strike out directly in a westward direction from Antioch of Pisidia, which would have taken them into the province of Asia. Instead they went north towards Bithynia, crossing only a part of Asia.

The other passage is Acts xviii. 23. Here the order of the words is reversed: '. . . and went from place to place through the region of Galatia and Phrygia, strengthening all the disciples', RSV. The 'region of Galatia' here is probably 'Galatic Lycaonia, so called to distinguish it from eastern Lycaonia, which lay, not in the province of Galatia, but in the territory of King Antiochus' (F. F. Bruce, *The Book of the Acts*, 1954, p. 380). 'Phrygia' then would probably include both Galatic and Asiatic Phrygia, since on this occasion there was no prohibition to prevent Paul preaching the word in Asia. In neither of these passages in Acts does there seem to be any good reason to suppose that Galatia means N Galatia. It is doubtful that Paul ever visited the ancient kingdom to the north, much less that he conducted an extensive mission there. See GALATIANS (section IV).

There are three other occurrences of 'Galatia' in the New Testament. 2 Tim. iv. 10 (which has the variant 'Gaul') and 1 Pet. i. 1 are almost certain references to the Roman province, while a decision on 1 Cor. xvi. 1, 'the churches of Galatia', will depend on one's view of the passages discussed above.

BIBLIOGRAPHY. W. M. Ramsay, *An Historical Commentary on St. Paul's Epistle to the Galatians*, 1899, *passim*; *St. Paul the Traveller and Roman Citizen*[3], 1897, pp. 89–151, 178–193; *The Church in the Roman Empire*[3], 1894, pp. 74–111; *HDB*; *HDAC*; K. Lake, *Beginnings*, V, 1933, pp. 231 ff.; G. H. C. Macgregor, *IB*, IX, 1954, pp. 213 f., 247, 252; R. T. Stamm, *IB*, X, 1953, pp. 435 ff.

W.W.W.

GALATIANS, EPISTLE TO THE.

I. OUTLINE OF CONTENTS

Thanks, no doubt, to the sense of urgency with which the Epistle was written, it is difficult to trace a clear progression or sequence in its structure. It may be subdivided as follows.

a. Greetings (i. 1–5).
b. This new 'gospel' is no gospel (i. 6–10).
c. Paul received his commission directly from Christ (i. 11–17).
d. Paul's first visit to Jerusalem after his conversion (i. 18–24).
e. Paul's second visit to Jerusalem (ii. 1–10).
f. Why Paul opposed Peter at Antioch (ii. 11–21).
g. An appeal to their own experience (iii. 1–14).
h. Law and promise (iii. 15–22).
i. Christians are full-grown sons of God (iii. 23–29).
j. Going back to infancy (iv. 1–7).
k. Going back to slavery (iv. 8–11).
l. A further personal appeal (iv. 12–20).
m. Freedom, not bondage (iv. 21–v. 1).
n. Grace, not law (v. 2–12).
o. Liberty, not licence (v. 13–26).
p. A call to mutual aid (vi. 1–5).
q. Sowing and reaping (vi. 6–10).
r. Paul takes up the pen (vi. 11).
s. False and true boasting (vi. 12–16).
t. The true marks of a servant of Christ (vi. 17).
u. Benediction (vi. 18).

II. AUTHORSHIP AND DATE

Except in such extreme and unrepresentative circles as the Van Manen school (whose views received publicity in *EBi*), the Pauline authorship of Galatians has been an axiom of New

Testament criticism. Galatians has traditionally been recognized as one of the four 'capital epistles' of Paul (the other three being Romans and 1 and 2 Corinthians); indeed, it has been regarded as a standard by which other documents' claims to Pauline authorship could safely be measured.

On the 'North Galatian' view of its destination (see section IV below) the Epistle could not have been written before AD 49/50, when Paul's second missionary journey began (Acts xvi. 6), and was more probably written after AD 52, when the third journey began and Paul visited 'Galatia' a second time (Acts xviii. 23), since his reference to having preached to them 'at the first' (Gal. iv. 13)—literally 'the former time' (Gk. *to proteron*)—implies two visits to them. On the 'South Galatian' view the Epistle could have been written earlier; the words 'so soon' (Gal. i. 6) indeed would imply a time not long after the first missionary journey (AD 47–8), and 'at the first' (Gal. iv. 13) could be understood in the light of the fact that in the course of the first journey Paul and Barnabas visited the S Galatian cities twice, going from Pisidian Antioch to Derbe and from there back to Pisidian Antioch (Acts xiv. 21).

A more precise determining of the date depends on the interpretation of Paul's Jerusalem visits listed in Galatians. In arguing that at no time since his conversion had he an opportunity of being commissioned for his missionary service by the Jerusalem apostles, he mentions the occasions on which he had met them since, and tells what happened then. Two Jerusalem visits are mentioned: one three years (or in the third year) after his conversion (Gal. i. 18) and another fourteen years after (Gal. ii. 1). The first of these is certainly that mentioned in Acts ix. 26 ff. The second has generally been identified with that of Acts xv. 2 ff., the visit during which the Council of Jerusalem took place (See COUNCIL, JERUSALEM.) But (i) if Gal. ii. 1–10 and Acts xv. 2–29 purport to relate one and the same set of events, one at least of the two accounts can scarcely be acquitted of misrepresenting the facts; (ii) it is unsatisfactory to suppose that Gal. ii. 1–10 narrates a private interview which Paul and Barnabas had with James, Peter, and John in advance of the public Council; in that case Paul's suppression of the findings of the Council is inexplicable, for they were directly relevant to the Galatian controversy; (iii) the fact that the findings of the Council are not mentioned in Galatians can best be explained if in fact the Council had not yet been held when the Epistle was written; (iv) if the Jerusalem visit of Gal. ii. 1 is that of Acts xv, Paul's critics would have pointed out immediately that he had failed to mention the earlier visit mentioned in Acts xi. 30, xii. 25. (The view that the visit of Acts xi. 30, xii. 25 is a duplicate of that recorded in Acts xv is unacceptable; and the high estimate of the accuracy of the narrative of Acts, which underlies the present discussion, can be defended by strong arguments.) There are weighty reasons for identifying the visit of Gal. ii. 1 with that of Acts xi. 30, and for dating the Epistle shortly before the Council of Jerusalem, *c.* AD 48/49. The incident of Gal. ii. 12 is probably to be correlated with Acts xv. 1. (For a fuller discussion, *cf.* F. F. Bruce, *The Acts of the Apostles*, 1951, pp. 38 f., 287 ff.; *The Book of the Acts*, 1956, pp. 244, 298 ff.)

III. OCCASION OF WRITING

Galatians was plainly written to converts of Paul's who were in imminent danger of adulterating the gospel of Christian freedom which he had taught them with elements of Jewish legalism. Among these elements circumcision took a chief place; they also included the observance of the Jewish calendar (Gal. iv. 10) and possibly Jewish food-laws. The 'churches of Galatia' had evidently been visited by Judaizers who cast doubt on Paul's apostolic status and insisted that, in addition to the faith in Christ which he inculcated, it was necessary to be circumcised and conform in other respects to the Jewish law in order to attain salvation. When news of this reached Paul he wrote this letter in white-hot urgency, denouncing this teaching which mingled grace and law as a different gospel from that which he had preached to them in Christ's name —in fact, no gospel at all—and entreating his readers to stand fast in their new-found liberty and not place their necks again under a yoke of bondage.

IV. DESTINATION

The letter is addressed to 'the churches of Galatia' (i. 2). To us this is a not unambiguous designation, for 'Galatia' was used in two distinct senses in the 1st century AD: it might denote ethnic Galatia in central Asia Minor, or the much larger Roman province of Galatia (see GALATIA). If the letter was sent to people in ethnic Galatia (the view of J. B. Lightfoot and most of the older commentators), we must suppose that that is the region visited by Paul in Acts xvi. 6 and xviii. 23 (or at least in one of these passages). But these two passages should probably be interpreted otherwise (see GALATIA). There is, in fact, little evidence that Paul ever visited ethnic Galatia, whereas there is ample evidence that he visited the southern area of the province of Galatia and planted churches there. The view that this Epistle is addressed to ethnic Galatia is commonly called the 'North Galatian' theory; the 'South Galatian' theory, on the other hand, supposes that the Epistle was sent to the churches of Pisidian Antioch, Iconium, Lystra, and Derbe, all in the south of the Roman province, and all planted by Paul and Barnabas in the course of their first missionary journey (Acts xiii. 14–xiv. 23).

Against the 'South Galatian' theory it has been argued that it would be psychologically inept for Paul to address his readers as 'Galatians' (Gal. iii. 1) if in fact they were not ethnically Galatian. But if they belonged to different ethnic groups (Phrygian and Lycaonian) what common appellation could he have chosen to cover them all except their common political denominator, 'Galatians'? (So a modern writer, addressing a mixed group of English, Welsh, and Scots, would probably address them as 'Britons' or 'British' in the political sense, although in its ethnic sense it would be applicable only to the Welsh members of the group.)

V. PRINCIPAL ARGUMENTS

If a logical analysis of the Epistle as a whole defies us, we can at least recognize the leading arguments which Paul uses in defence of true gospel liberty. Eight of them may be stated briefly as follows.

1. The gospel which Paul preached was the gospel which he received by direct commission from Christ; it came to his hearers with Christ's authority, not with Paul's (i. 11 ff.).

2. If acceptance with God could have been obtained through circumcision and the other observances of the Jewish law, Christ's death was pointless and vain (ii. 21).

3. Christian life, as the Galatian converts knew from their own experience, is a gift of the Spirit of God; when they received it they received at the same time unmistakable proofs of the Spirit's presence and power in their midst. But if they began their Christian life on that high plane it was preposterous to imagine that they should continue it on the lower plane of legal works (iii. 2 ff.).

4. The Judaizers justified their insistence on circumcision by appealing to the example of Abraham: since circumcision was the seal of God's covenant with him, they argued, no uncircumcised person could have a share in that covenant with all the blessings which went with it. But the true children of Abraham are those who are justified by faith in God, as Abraham was; it is they who enjoy the blessings promised to Abraham. God's promise to Abraham was fulfilled in Christ, not in the law; therefore the blessings bestowed by that promise are to be enjoyed not through keeping the law (which came long after the promise and could not affect its terms) but through faith in Christ (iii. 6–9, 15–22).

5. The law pronounces a curse on those who fail to keep it in every detail; those who place their trust in the law therefore put themselves in danger of that curse. But Christ, by His death on the cross, bore the divine curse in His people's place and delivered them from the curse which the law pronounces; His people therefore ought not to go back and put themselves under the law with its attendant curse (iii. 10–14).

6. The principle of law-keeping belongs to the age of spiritual immaturity; now that Christ has come, those who believe in Him have attained their spiritual majority as responsible sons of God. To accept the arguments of the Judaizers would be to revert to infancy (iii. 23–iv. 7).

7. The law imposed a yoke of slavery; faith in Christ brings liberation. Those whom Christ has emancipated are foolish indeed if they give up their freedom and submit afresh to the dictation of those elemental powers through whom the law was mediated (iv. 8–11, v. 1, iii. 19).

8. This freedom which the gospel of grace proclaims has nothing to do with anarchy or licence; faith in Christ is a faith which works by love and thus fulfils the law of Christ (v. 6, v. 13–vi. 10).

These arguments are presented in a more systematic form in the Epistle to the Romans, written eight or nine years later. The basic understanding of the gospel which underlies all these arguments took shape in Paul's mind very probably quite soon after his conversion, although the way in which it finds expression in Galatians is due to the special situation to which Paul addresses himself here. But perhaps for that very reason Galatians has to this day been cherished by Christians as a great charter of gospel liberty.

BIBLIOGRAPHY. J. B. Lightfoot, *St. Paul's Epistle to the Galatians*, 1892; W. M. Ramsay, *An Historical Commentary on St. Paul's Epistle to the Galatians*, 1899; E. D. Burton, *The Epistle to the Galatians, ICC*, 1920; G. S. Duncan, *The Epistle to the Galatians, MNT*, 1934; H. N. Ridderbos, *The Epistle of Paul to the Churches of Galatia, NICNT*, 1953; K. Lake, *The Earlier Epistles of St. Paul*, 1914, pp. 253–323; J. H. Ropes, *The Singular Problem of the Epistle to the Galatians*, 1929. F.F.B.

GALBANUM (Heb. *ḥelbᵉnâ*; etymology uncertain). A fragrant spice, one of the four ingredients of the sacred incense (Ex. xxx. 34), usually regarded as the gum of two umbelliferous plants—*Ferula galbaniflua* and *Ferula rubricaulis*—native to Persia.

GALEED (Heb. *gal'ēḏ*, 'witness pile'). Name given to the cairn erected by Jacob and Laban as a memorial to their covenant made in northern Transjordan (Gn. xxxi. 47, 48, *cf.* PILLAR). By Laban it was given the equivalent Aramaic name *Jegar-sahadutha*. Documents of the earlier second millennium BC reveal a great mixture of ethnic groups in N Mesopotamia. It is quite possible that some Aramaeans were included among them and that their dialect had been adopted by other Semitic groups. Specific evidence of Aramaeans in this area at this date is not yet available (see ARAM). A.R.M.

GALILEE (Heb. *gālîl*, 'ring, circle', hence a 'district, region'). The regional name of part of N Palestine, which was the scene of Christ's boyhood and early ministry. The origin of the name as applied here is uncertain. It occurs occasionally in the Old Testament (*e.g.* Jos. xx. 7; 1 Ki. ix. 11), and notably in Is. ix. 1. The latter reference probably recalls the region's history: it originally formed part of the lands allocated to the twelve tribes, but, owing to the pressure from peoples farther north, its Jewish population found themselves in a kind of northern salient, surrounded on three sides by non-Jewish populations—'the nations'. Under the Maccabees, the Gentile influence upon the Jews became so strong that the latter were actually withdrawn southwards for half a century. Thus Galilee had to be re-colonized, and this fact, together with its diversity of population, contributed to the contempt felt for the Galilaeans by the southern Jews (Jn. vii. 52).

Exact demarcation of the Galilee region is difficult, except in terms of the provincial boundaries of the Roman Empire. The name was evidently applied to the northern marchlands of Israel, the location of which varied from time to time. In the time of Christ, however, the province of Galilee formed a rectangular territory some 40 miles from north to south, and 25 miles from east to west, bordered on the east by the Jordan and the Sea of Galilee (*q.v.*), and cut off from the Mediterranean by the southward extension of Syro-Phoenicia down the coastal plain.

Thus defined, Galilee consists essentially of an upland area, bordered on all sides save the north by plains—the coastlands, the plain of Esdraelon, and the Jordan Rift. It is, in fact, the southern end of the mountains of Lebanon, and the land surface falls, in two steps, from north to south across the area. The higher 'step' forms Upper Galilee, much of which is at 3,000 feet above sea-level; in New Testament times it was a forested and thinly inhabited hill-country. The lower 'step' forms Lower Galilee, 1,500-2,000 feet above sea-level, but falling steeply to more than 600 feet below sea-level at the Sea of Galilee.

It is to this area of Lower Galilee that most of the gospel narrative refers. Well watered by streams flowing from the northern mountains, and possessing considerable stretches of fertile land in the limestone basins among its hills, it was an area of dense and prosperous settlement. It exported olive oil and cereals, and fish from the lake.

'Outside the main stream of Israelite life in Old Testament times, Galilee came into its own in the New Testament' (D. Baly, *The Geography of the Bible*, 1957, p. 190). The Roman region was governed successively by Herod the Great (died 4 BC), Herod Antipas, and Herod Agrippa. Cut off from Judaea—at least in Jewish eyes—by the territory of Samaria, Galilee nevertheless formed an integral part of 'the land', and the Galilaeans had, in fact, resisted the Romans even more doggedly than the southern Jews. In the time of Christ the relationship between the two groups is well described as having been that of 'England and Scotland soon after the Union' (G. A. Smith, *Historical Geography of the Holy Land*[25], 1931, p. 425).

This, then, was the region in which Christ grew up—at Nazareth, in the limestone hills of Lower Galilee. Thanks to its position, it was traversed by several major routeways of the Empire, and was therefore far from being a rural backwater. Its agriculture, fisheries, and commerce provided Him with His cultural background, and are reflected in His parables and teaching. Its people provided Him with His first disciples, and its dense scattering of settlements formed their first mission field.

Today, Galilee and the plain of Esdraelon form the core area of northern Israel, but its modern inhabitants have the task of rehabilitating an area which has lost much of the prosperity it enjoyed in New Testament days. Its forests have been largely replaced by *maquis*, the characteristic scrub of the Mediterranean, and many of its towns and villages, places which Christ knew and visited, have disappeared from the map, leaving hardly a trace behind them.

BIBLIOGRAPHY. G. A. Smith, *The Historical Geography of the Holy Land*[25], 1931, pp. 413–436; D. Baly, *The Geography of the Bible*, 1957.

J.H.P.

GALILEE, SEA OF. A lake in the region of Galilee, also referred to, in the Old Testament, as the 'sea of Chinnereth' (Nu. xxxiv. 11) or Chinneroth (Jos. xii. 3), and in the New Testament as the 'lake of Gennesaret' (Lk. v. 1) and the 'sea of Tiberias' (Jn. xxi. 1). Its modern Heb. name is Yam Kinneret.

The lake is some 13 miles long and up to 7 miles broad, and it lies at 695 feet below sea-level. The river Jordan flows through it from north to south; its waters are therefore sweet—unlike those of the Dead Sea—and its fisheries (see FISH, FISHING), so prominent in the New Testament narrative, were famous throughout the Roman Empire, and produced a flourishing export trade. On the other hand, the position of the lake, in the depths of the Jordan Rift and surrounded by hills, renders it liable to atmospheric downdraughts and sudden storms.

The lake is bordered by a plain of varying width; in general, the slopes on the eastern side are abrupt (Mk. v. 13), and are somewhat gentler on the west. To the north and south are the river plains of the Jordan as it enters and leaves the lake.

The shores of the lake were the site of towns—Capernaum, Bethsaida, *etc.*—where much of Christ's ministry was carried out. In His time they formed a flourishing, and almost continuous, belt of settlement around the lake, and communicated and traded across it with each other. Today, only Tiberias (*q.v.*) remains as a town—even the sites of several other former towns are uncertain—and changed patterns of commerce have robbed the lake of its focal importance in the life of the region.

BIBLIOGRAPHY. G. A. Smith, *The Historical Geography of the Holy Land*[25], 1931, pp. 437–463.

J.H.P.

GALL. The Hebrews used *rôš* and *m^e^rôrâ* to describe a plant and its fruit which were extremely bitter. Variously translated as 'hemlock' (Ho. x. 4), 'poison' (Jb. xx. 16; Je. viii. 14,

RSV), and 'venom' (*cf.* Dt. xxxii. 33), it is frequently associated with the bitter herb wormwood (Dt. xxix. 18; Je. ix. 15; La. iii. 19; Am. vi. 12). Gall is referred to literally as the yellowish-brown secretion of the liver in Jb. xvi. 13, xx. 14, 25. As a plant its identification is obscure.

Metaphorically it denoted travail (La. iii. 5) or any bitter experience (Acts viii. 23). The anodyne offered to Christ during His crucifixion (Mt. xxvii. 34; *cf.* Mk. xv. 23) was a diluted wine containing stupefying drugs. R.K.H.

GALLEY. See SHIPS AND BOATS.

GALLIO. Lucius Junius Annaeus (or Annaeanus) Gallio was the son of Seneca the rhetorician and brother of Seneca the philosopher. An inscription at Delphi (*SIG*, II³, 801; *cf.* text and discussion by K. Lake, *BC*, V, pp. 460 ff.) makes it virtually certain that he was proconsul of Achaia in AD 52–3, in which office we meet him in Acts xviii. 12 ff. A fixed point for Pauline chronology is thus afforded, even though the precise dates of office are unknown. His brother Seneca writes of him (*Ep. Mor.* civ. 1: *Quaest.* iva, pref. 11), as do several other ancient writers (*e.g.* Pliny, *NH* xxi. 33; Tacitus, *Ann.* xv. 73; Dio Cassius, lxi. 35, lxii. 25), with little to his discredit. Luke depicts his vigorous refusal to hear a Jewish-sponsored prosecution of Paul, on the ground that no criminal charge was brought. The now proverbial 'Gallio cared for none of those things' (Acts xviii. 17) denotes less his religious indifference than his connivance at the subsequent outburst of anti-Semitism. Gallio was executed by Nero's order in AD 65. J.H.H.

GALLOWS (Heb. *'ēṣ*, 'tree'). Found only in the book of Esther (eight times). Haman had a gallows (AVmg 'tree') made on which to execute Mordecai, but the mode of the intended execution has been much debated. Hanging was not usual in Persia, where the events took place; it is suggested that the Heb. word means 'pole' or 'stake' (which seems likely), and that, following Persian custom, the victim was to be impaled. See CROSS. J.D.D.

GAMALIEL (Heb. *gamlî'ēl*, 'reward of God'; Gk. *Gamaliēl*). **1.** Son of Pedahzur, and a 'prince of the children of Manasseh' chosen to help Moses in taking the census in the wilderness (Nu. i. 10, ii. 20, vii. 54, 59, x. 23).

2. Son of Simon and grandson of Hillel, Gamaliel was a doctor of the law and a member of the Sanhedrin. Representing the liberal wing of the Pharisees, the school of Hillel, as opposed to that of Shammai, he intervened with a reasoned and persuasive speech at the trial of the apostles (Acts v. 33–40). Paul acknowledged him as his teacher (Acts xxii. 3), and he was held in such high honour that he was designated 'Rabban' ('our teacher'), a higher title than 'Rabbi' ('my teacher'). See F. F. Bruce, *The Book of the Acts*, 1956, pp. 122–126.

The Mishnah (*Soṭa* ix. 15) says, 'Since Rabban Gamaliel the Elder died there has been no more reverence for the Law, and purity and abstinence died out at the same time.' As we might expect from this reputation among the Jews, there is no evidence, despite early suggestions (*e.g. The Clementine Recognitions*, I. 65) that he ever became a Christian. See also PHARISEES. J.D.D.

GAMES.

I. IN THE OLD TESTAMENT

a. Physical sport

In common with their Near Eastern neighbours, the life of the majority of Hebrews left little time or inclination for physical sport. When introduced by Hellenizing Jews in the time of Antiochus Epiphanes (1 Macc. i. 10–14; Jos., *Ant.* xv. 8. 1) and patronized by Jason, the high priest (2 Macc. iv. 7–17), the Greek love of sport was considered irreligious. Nevertheless, there can be little doubt that, despite the absence of explicit references, running, throwing, and hunting were undertaken on occasions when they were not a necessity. Like the Egyptians and Babylonians,

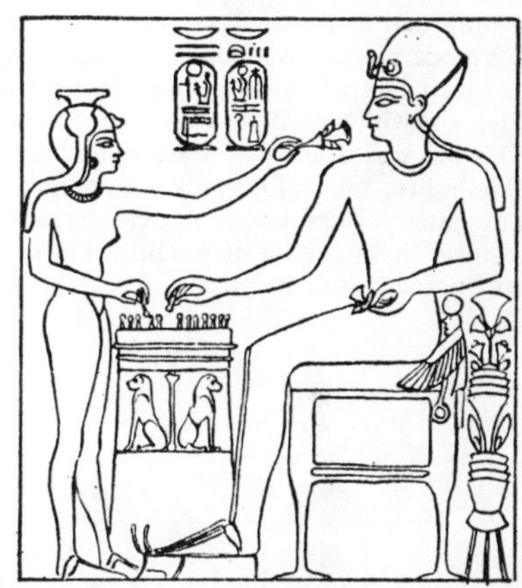

Fig. 91. Rameses III plays draughts with one of the women of his *harim*. Relief in the Gate Tower, temple of Medinet Habu (Thebes), c. 1180 BC.

the people of Palestine would have enjoyed contests at weight-lifting and wrestling. Jacob's long wrestling-match may reflect both practised ability at the sport and the recognition of rules precluding holds below the belt (Gn. xxxii. 24–26). The expression 'hip and thigh' (Jdg. xv. 8) may be a technical wrestling term, like English 'cross-buttock'. It has been suggested that the group combat at Gibeon was initiated as a wrestling-match (2 Sa. ii. 14), wrestling by grasping an opponent's belt being an ancient form of this sport (see fig. 234). Archery could be a game of skill aiming at fixed marks (1 Sa. xx. 20; Jb. xvi. 12; La. iii. 12), as is shown on Assyrian reliefs, as well as a warlike art.

b. Games of chance

Gaming-boards have been discovered at a number of sites. Some made of ivory (Megiddo—*c.* 1350–1150 BC), stone (Gezer *c.* 1200 BC), or wood were in 'human' or 'violin' shape pierced with peg-holes for a game of '55 Holes' commonly found in Egypt and Mesopotamia. Draughts was

Fig. 92. Ivory game pieces from Megiddo. *Left:* A circular disc with the face incised with an ibex and a palm. *Right:* A conical piece, knobbed at the apex similar to modern 'halma' men. 12th century BC. See also fig. 224.

played on boards of twenty or thirty squares made of stone, clay, ebony, or ivory and sometimes hollowed at the back to contain the men. Unlike modern western methods of play in these games, moves were made as a result of the throw of a dice (of which an ivory example of the 17th century BC was found at Tell Beit Mirsim), knuckle-bones, or casting-sticks. Pyramidal or conical game places and counters have been found, also 'halma' men at Lachish. Chess was known in Elam and Babylonia from the third millennium BC and may well have been played in Palestine. Unusual board-games like those discovered at Ur (see fig. 224), Nineveh, and Tell Halaf, Syria (8th century), were played, though the method of play is at present obscure. The Hebrews, with their neighbours, considered that the lot (*pûr*; see DIVINATION) was a means of determining the divine will, and in this way some board-games also had religious significance.

c. Children's games

The young played in the streets (Zc. viii. 5), imitating their elders in daily life or at marriages and funerals. The boys may have imitated the Egyptian team-games shown in paintings and a form of tug-of-war, while the girls practised juggling or ball-games, including catch played by teams with one mounted on another's back. Leather-covered balls have been found. Whistles, rattles, model pots, chariots, and animals (some with wheels) have been recovered and betray an unchanging taste for toys by the youngest. It is unlikely that all the slings found were used only in the serious business of driving birds from the crops or guarding the flocks from straying. There is no evidence that the figurines or small statues with movable joints found at a number of sites were dolls. It is more likely that they were cult objects.

d. Diversion

For the Hebrews of all ages feasting, songs, and music, and especially dancing, were the commonest form of relaxation. Opportunity was taken for this at every domestic rejoicing (Je. xxxi. 4), including merry-making at harvest (Jdg. ix. 27, xxi. 21) as well as at such public and state functions as the royal accession (1 Ki. i. 40) or celebration of victory (Ex. xv. 20; Jdg. xi. 34; 1 Sa. xviii. 6). Story-telling and the art of propounding riddles was also a highly-esteemed practice (Jdg. xiv. 12; Ezk. xvii. 2; 1 Ki. x. 1). See also DANCE and figs. 62, 63.

Fig. 93. Egyptian girls playing ball, keeping several balls in the air at once. Tomb painting, Beni Hasan, *c.* 2000 BC.

BIBLIOGRAPHY. H. J. C. Murray, *A History of Board Games other than Chess*, 1952; P. Montet, *Everyday Life in Egypt*, 1958; *Iraq*, 1, 1935, pp. 45–50, IV, 1938, pp. 11 ff., VIII, 1946, pp. 166 ff.

D.J.W.

II. IN THE NEW TESTAMENT

Apart from one obscure reference to a children's game (Mt. xi. 16, 17), and a possible allusion to a chariot race (Phil. iii. 13 f.), the games mentioned in the New Testament are the Greek athletic contests. Reference to 1 Macc. i. 10–14; 2 Macc. iv. 13, 14 will emphasize the Hellenic outlook of the writers who found metaphor in this worthy subject. The festivals were religious in origin and flavour, encouraged discipline, art, health, and fair play, and were not without diplomatic usefulness (see Lysias, xxxiii). Surviving odes of Pindar reveal the honour paid the victor in the Pythian, Nemean, Isthmian, and above all the Olympic Games.

In the Epistles metaphors are drawn from the Games generally, and from the foot-race and from the chariot race in particular.

In 1 Cor. ix. 24–27 Paul calls attention to the vigorous training of the athlete (a metaphor also used by Epictetus). The athlete is preoccupied not with the immediate token prize of the wreath of wild olive, parsley, pine, or laurel, but with the later reward. The Christian is likewise exhorted to strive 'for the mastery', for his reward is, by contrast, an 'incorruptible' crown (*cf.* 2 Tim. ii. 5, iv. 8; 1 Pet. i. 4, v. 4). Verse 26 depicts a boxing contest. Here the arms and hands were bound with studded leather, which inflicted grave injury, and the combatant therefore sought to evade rather than to parry—hence the phrase 'beating the air'. Having begun with the scene of victory, Paul concludes with a picture of failure. He sees himself as the herald calling others to the contest, but himself disqualified from competing. 'Preached' and 'castaway' (1 Cor. ix. 27) are unhappy renderings (see RV, RSV). Metaphors drawn from the Games would carry particular weight with the readers of this Epistle, since the Isthmian Games were a Corinthian festival.

In Gal. ii. 2, v. 7; Phil. ii. 16; Heb. xii. 1, 2 the reference is to the foot-race, for which a minimum of clothing was worn. 'Every weight' refers probably to weight shed in preparatory training in order to bring the runner to peak condition for the race. 'The sin which envelops' is more clearly a reference to clothing. The 'cloud' is a common metaphor for multitudes. It suggests the runner's blurred vision of the spectators as his eyes are focused on the goal.

The reference in Phil. iii. 13, 14 is probably to a chariot race. Horse-racing with light chariots was well known to the Greeks, and references go back to Homer and Sophocles. They were also a spectacular feature of the festivals. At the time Paul wrote, they were especially in fashion with the Romans, and Philippi was a Roman colony. We may translate these verses: 'I do not count myself to have done this, but this one thing I do, forgetting those things which are behind, and stretching out to those which lie before, I make for the mark, towards the prize of the upward calling of God in Jesus His Anointed.' Paul pictures himself in the chariot, bent over the curved rail against which the charioteer's knees were pressed, and, with the reins round his body, stretching out over the horses' backs and leaning his weight on the reins. In such intense preoccupation a glance at 'the things behind' would have been fatal. E.M.B.

GAMMADIM(S) (RSV 'men of Gammad'). A name occurring only in Ezk. xxvii. 11 and not yet identified, although Kumidi, mentioned in the Tell el-Amarna tablets, has been proposed. The context seems to require a proper name for these people who manned the towers of Tyre. The LXX and the Syr. versions read *šōmᵉrîm*, 'guards', and Lagarde's edition of the Targum, 'Cappadocians', from *gōmᵉrîm*, while the RVmg translates 'valorous men'. R.A.H.G.

GARDEN. It was promised that the lives of God's redeemed people would be like a watered garden, ordered and fruitful (Is. lviii. 11; Je. xxxi. 12; *cf.* Nu. xxiv. 6).

In Egypt the Hebrews had known richly productive vegetable-gardens (Dt. xi. 10; *cf.* Nu. xi. 5; see FOOD). Fed from an irrigation-ditch, or from vessels by hand, a network of little earth channels criss-crossed the vegetable-beds like a chessboard. By merely breaching and resealing the wall of such a channel with the foot, water could be released on to the beds as needed.

In Palestine people cultivated gardens for vegetables ('garden of herbs', 1 Ki. xxi. 2; 'things sown', Is. lxi. 11), and fruit (Am. ix. 14; Je. xxix. 5, 28; Ct. iv. 16). Gardens might be associated with, or even part of, vineyards, olive-groves, or orchards (*q.v.*; Ec. ii. 5; Am. iv. 9; *cf.* 1 Ki. xxi. 2). Spices and choice plants featured in the gardens of royalty and of the nobility (Ct. v. 1, vi. 2, 11 (walnuts); *cf.* iv. 12–16 generally; Ec. ii. 5). These and other gardens were walled round (*cf.* Ct. iv. 12) and had to be kept watered, *e.g.* from a spring or pool (Ct. iv. 15; *cf.* Ec. ii. 5–6; contrast Is. i. 30). They may also have sometimes contained a summerhouse (2 Ki. ix. 27). The 'king's garden' at Jerusalem was a well-known landmark (2 Ki. xxv. 4; Je. xxxix. 4, lii. 7; Ne. iii. 15); and the Persian royal palace is mentioned as having a pleasure-garden (Est. i. 5, vii. 7, 8). Similarly, Egyptian and Mesopotamian kings kept fine gardens; and a garden once occupied a large court inside the sumptuous palace of the kings of Canaanite Ugarit (14th–13th century BC). For full references to gardens in Assyria and Babylonia and the many trees and plants they contained, see in Ebeling, Meissner, and Weidner, *Reallexikon der Assyriologie*, III, 1959, pp. 147–150.

Tombs were sometimes situated in gardens (2 Ki. xxi. 18, 26; Jn. xix. 41); for the garden of Gethsemane (Jn. xviii. 1, 26), see GETHSEMANE. A less happy use of gardens was for pagan rites, perhaps linked with the fertility cults of Canaan (Is. i. 29, lxv. 3, lxvi. 17).

For the Garden of Eden, symbol of God-created fertility (Gn. xiii. 10; Is. li. 3, *etc.*), see EDEN, GARDEN OF. K.A.K.

GARLIC. See PLANTS.

GARMENT. See DRESS.

GARRISON. See FORTIFICATION AND SIEGECRAFT.

GASHMU. See GESHEM.

GATE. See CITY.

GATH. One of the five principal Philistine cities, and formerly occupied by the Anakim (*q.v.*; Jos. xi. 22). The gentilic from the name *gaṯ* was *gittî* or *gittîm* (Jos. xiii. 3), and this accounts for the 'Gittite' of the EVV. When the Philistines captured the ark and it brought ill fortune to Ashdod it was moved to Gath, where the people were struck with bubonic plague, so it was moved on to Ekron (1 Sa. v. 6–10, vi. 17). Gath was famous as the home of Goliath (*q.v.*; 1 Sa. xvii), whom David killed. David later feigned madness to avoid retribution at the hands of Achish, king of Gath, when fleeing from Saul (1 Sa. xxi. 10–15), but subsequently took service under Achish, and lived for more than a year in his territory (1 Sa. xxvii). When David's fortunes revived, and later during Absalom's rebellion, after he had added Gath to his dominions (1 Ch. xviii. 1), he had Gittite friends in his retinue (2 Sa. vi. 10–11, xv. 19–21, xviii. 2) and a Gittite contingent among his mercenaries (2 Sa. xv. 18). Another interesting Gittite is mentioned in 2 Sa. xxi. 20 (= 1 Ch. xx. 6). He was very tall and had six digits on each extremity. Though Achish is still spoken of as king of Gath (1 Ki. ii. 39–41), the city was probably subservient to David, and evidently continued subject to Judah in the time of Rehoboam, who fortified it (2 Ch. xi. 8). It was captured by Hazael of Damascus in the late 9th century (2 Ki. xii. 17), and may have regained its independence by the time Uzziah broke down its wall when he campaigned in Philistia (2 Ch. xxvi. 6); soon afterwards Amos describes it as belonging to the Philistines (vi. 2), so it may have been a Philistine enclave, in loose vassalage, in the territory of Judah. Gath was besieged and conquered by Sargon of Assyria in the late 8th century.

The site has not been identified with certainty. An Israeli expedition under S. Yeivin has excavated since 1956 at Tell el-'Areini some 20 miles north-east of Gaza, supposing it to be ancient Gath, but the finds so far discovered there do not confirm the identification. Another possible location is the adjacent 'Araq el-Menshîyeh, but certainty must await further investigation.

BIBLIOGRAPHY. S. Yeivin, *IEJ*, VI, 1956, pp. 258, 259, VII, 1957, pp. 264, 265, VIII, 1958, pp. 274–276, IX, 1959, pp. 269–271, X, 1960, pp. 122, 123; J. A. Montgomery, *The Books of Kings, ICC*, 1951, pp. 96, 97, 430, 431. T.C.M.

GATH-HEPHER (*gaṯ-haḥēper*, 'winepress of digging'). The rendering Gittah-hepher of Jos. xix. 13 in the AV arose through a misunderstanding of the *he locale*. A town on the border of Zebulon and Naphtali (Jos. xix. 13), the birthplace of the prophet Jonah (2 Ki. xiv. 25). Identified with the present town of el-Meshhed, 3 miles north-east of Nazareth. Ancient and continuous tradition indicated this as the home of the prophet. Jerome in the 4th century AD said that his tomb was about 2 miles from Sepphoris, which would coincide with Gath-hepher.

M.A.M.

GAZA (*'azzâ*, LXX *Gaza*). One of the five principal Philistine cities. Originally inhabited by the Avvim, who were driven out by the Caphtorim (*q.v.*; Dt. ii. 23), it was considered to mark the southern limit of Canaan at the point on the coast where it was situated (Gn. x. 19). Joshua conquered it (Jos. x. 41) and found that some Anakim remained there (Jos. xi. 21, 22); the city was lost to Israel during his lifetime (Jos. xiii. 3). Judah, to whom it was allotted (Jos. xv. 47), recaptured the town (Jdg. i. 18; though some hold that this refers to the same campaign as Jos. x. 41). In the period of the Judges Samson consorted with a harlot of Gaza in connection with which a description of the city gate is given (Jdg. xvi. 1–3). Israel's hold over Gaza must have been lost again at this period, for when the Philistines finally captured Samson they imprisoned him there, and it was there that he 'made sport' for them, and dislodged the pillars of the house, killing many of them (Jdg. xvi. 21–31). It has been pointed out that the description of Samson 'making sport' in front of a pillared building with spectators on the roof is reminiscent of some of the features of Cretan civilization, and this is to be expected in view of the origins of the Philistines (*q.v.*). At the time of the Philistine capture of the ark, Gaza with the other cities suffered from bubonic plague (see EMERODS) and made an offering of an emerod and a mouse of gold to avert it (1 Sa. vi. 17).

The city occupied an important position on the trade routes from Egypt to western Asia, and from the 8th century it is frequently mentioned among Assyr. conquests. Tiglath-pileser III captured it (*Ḫa-az-zu-tu*) in 734 BC, perhaps at the request of Jehoahaz of Judah, the ruler, Hanno, fleeing to Egypt, and Tiglath-pileser set up an image of himself in the palace. Sargon had to repeat the action in 722 BC, for Hanno had returned to Gaza in support of a rebellion led by Hamath. Hanno was taken prisoner to Assyria. The city remained faithful to Assyria, for Sennacherib, when he proceeded against Hezekiah in Jerusalem, gave some of the territory taken from Judah to Ṣillibel, king of Gaza, and Esarhaddon put a strain on this loyalty when he laid heavy tribute on him and twenty other kings of the Hittite country. In the time of Jeremiah the city was captured by Egypt (Je. xlvii. 1). Gaza was taken by Alexander the Great in 332 BC after a five-month siege, and finally desolated—as prophesied by Amos (i. 6, 7), Zephaniah (ii. 4), and Zechariah (ix. 5)—by Alexander Jannaeus in 93 BC.

It is probable, though not certain, that the site

of ancient Gaza is represented by the modern mound of Tell el-'Ajjul about 2½ miles from the coast. On this assumed identification, Flinders Petrie excavated the site from 1930 to 1934, uncovering five occupation levels. The first four dated from the Middle Bronze Age, and the fifth from the Late Bronze Age, but nothing to confirm the identification was found. In 57 BC Gabinius rebuilt the city on a new site to the south of the old, nearer the sea, and it was presumably to distinguish the old abandoned site from this that the angel, who wanted Philip to go to the old site, qualified the name Gaza with the phrase 'the same is desert' (*hautē estin erēmos*, Acts viii. 26). The new site is still occupied today; so that although W. J. Phythian-Adams attempted trial excavations in 1923, little could be uncovered.

BIBLIOGRAPHY. W. M. Flinders Petrie, *Ancient Gaza*, I–IV, 1931–4; J. Garstang, *The Foundations of Bible History: Joshua, Judges*, 1931, pp. 375, 376. T.C.M.

GAZELLE. The word does not appear in AV, but RSV (Dt. xii. 15, *etc.*) translates *ṣᵉḇî* and *ṣᵉḇiyyâ*, 'gazelle', and this is almost certainly correct. Confirmation is found in Acts ix. 36: Tabitha is *ṭaḇyᵉṯâ*, the Aram. equivalent of Heb. *ṣᵉḇiyyâ*, and its Gk. form is *dorcas*. The Dorcas gazelle is one of the two species concerned; the other is the rather smaller Palestine gazelle (*Gazella gazella*). This identification is confirmed by many points in the contexts. See fig. 38. G.C.

GEBA (*geḇa'*, 'a hill'). A town belonging to Benjamin, about 7 miles to the north of Jerusalem and about 3 miles from Gibeah, from which it is to be distinguished; *cf.* Jos. xviii. 24 and 28; Is. x. 29. The *MT* appears to have confused the two names in 1 Sa. xiii. 16; AV makes the necessary emendation. It was assigned to the Levites under Joshua (Jos. xxi. 17; 1 Ch. vi. 60). It was in the descent from here that Jonathan and his armour-bearer revealed themselves to the Philistines during their daring attack (1 Sa. xiv. 1 ff.). In the days of Asa, king of Judah, it was fortified, and it would appear that from these days it was regarded as the northern limit of Judah; it replaced the name of Dan in the saying 'from Dan to Beersheba' (2 Ki. xxiii. 8). It remained prominent after the Exile (Ne. xi. 31, xii. 29). The modern town of Jeba stands on the same site. M.A.M.

GEBAL. 1. A Phoenician seaport (*gᵉḇal*, = *gbl*, the Phoenician and Ugaritic spelling of this city, meaning 'hill', 'bluff'; *Gubla* in Akkadian texts; *Kpn* in Egyptian). Ruins of this ancient port, situated on a bluff overlooking the Mediterranean, adjoin the Lebanese village of Jebeil, 25 miles north of Beirut. The Greeks named the city Byblos, meaning 'papyrus', for here they saw scrolls made from imported Egyptian papyrus reeds. On this ancient writing-material religious texts, expense accounts, and official correspondence were inscribed with ink.

The territory of the Gebalites is mentioned in Jos. xiii. 5; its expert stonemasons, hired by Solomon, in 1 Ki. v. 18, RV; and its shipbuilders, skilful in caulking, in Ezk. xxvii. 9, at a time when Phoenician mariners were colonizing the Mediterranean coastlands. Their cargo ships, successors to the Phoenician 'ships of Tarshish', were dubbed 'Byblos travellers' and sailed between Phoenicia and Egypt exporting masts, flagpoles, hardwoods for furniture, cedar for mummy cases, and resins for mummification. Imports were gold and silver vessels, perfumes, papyrus, linen, rope, and cowhides, as we learn from the tale of the Egyptian priest Wen-amon concerning his trading mission to Byblos around 1100 BC.

Excavations at Gebal directed by Maurice Dunand, begun in 1919, have revealed settlements from Neolithic times to the Crusaders. The lowest level reveals single-room rectangular houses with burials beneath plastered floors, and pottery vessels decorated with bands of herring-bone incisions, as at Jericho before 4000 BC. Jar burials containing human bones, food, copper knives, and jewellery, dated between 4000 and 3000 BC, were found scattered over the hill. By 3100 BC Egyptians were trading at Byblos. During the next millennium this centre of Egyptian influence was fortified by buttressed ramparts. A series of temples, one to the goddess Baalat Gebal, the other to the god Reshef, began around 2800 BC. Gebal was burned about 2150 BC, probably by Amorite invaders. To this period seem to belong the syllabic inscriptions on copper and stone, modelled after Egyptian hieroglyphics. Byblos is the first city to appear in the list of Asiatic rulers execrated by Egyptians at Thebes about 1900 BC. Later in their XIIth Dynasty the Egyptians colonized Byblos. In the Amarna period Ribaddi of Byblos sent over fifty cuneiform letters pleading for help to Pharaoh Ikhnaton. The sarcophagus of King Ahiram (*c.* 1000 BC), inscribed in early Phoenician alphabetic characters, was discovered at Gebal in 1923.

2. A mountainous region east of the Dead Sea (Ps. lxxxiii. 7), whose inhabitants allied with Moab and Arabian nomads against Israel.

BIBLIOGRAPHY. R. Dussaud, 'Byblos et la mention des Giblites dans l'Ancien Testament', *Syria*, IV, 1923, pp. 300 ff. J.R.

GEBER. An Israelite prince, the son of Uri, who was placed by Solomon over his twelfth administrative district, the land of Gilead to the east of Jordan (1 Ki. iv. 19). Over the sixth district, to the north of the twelfth in Transjordan, was Ben-geber (1 Ki. iv. 13, RV). T.C.M.

GECKO. See LIZARD, and fig. 38.

GEDALIAH (Heb. *gᵉḏalyâ* or *gᵉḏalyāhû*, 'Yahweh is great'). **1.** Son of Ahikam, grandson of Shaphan, he was appointed chief minister and ruler of Judah by Nebuchadrezzar II in 587 BC

(2 Ki. xxv. 22). With Jeremiah the prophet he was entrusted with the care of some royal princesses and those persons remaining after the Babylonian war (Je. xli. 16, xliii. 6). He made Mizpah his residence, and there he was joined by Jeremiah (xl. 6) and by many officers and men who had escaped from the enemy. These were granted asylum on condition that they maintained the peace (Je. xl. 7–12). However, Baalis, king of Ammon, plotted against him and provoked a refugee officer, Ishmael, to assassinate Gedaliah (2 Ki. xxv. 25; Je. xli. 1–3). Fear of possible Babylonian reprisals led to further Jewish emigration to Egypt, despite Jeremiah's warning (Je. xlii). The Jewish fast on the third of Tishri commemorates the death of Gedaliah (Zc. vii. 5, viii. 19). A seal impression inscribed 'Belonging to Gedaliah who is over the House' found at Lachish almost certainly refers to this person.

2. Son of Jeduthun, instrumentalist leader of the levitical choir (1 Ch. xxv. 3, 9). **3.** A priest married to a foreign woman in the time of Ezra (Ezr. x. 18). **4.** Son of Pashur, a leading citizen of Jerusalem and opponent of Jeremiah (Je. xxxviii. 1, 4–6). **5.** Grandfather of the prophet Zephaniah and grandson of Hezekiah (Zp. i. 1).

D.J.W.

GEDER. A southern Canaanite town, Jos. xii. 13. LXX (B) reads *asei*, and other minuscules suggest 's' as second letter; *Goshen* may be the correct reading.

GEDERAH. 1. A place in the Shephelah, Jos. xv. 36; the name survives at Kh. Jedireh, a mile west of Latrun (Grollenberg, Kh. Sheikh Ali Jadir); and at Kh. Judraya (Noth, *Josua*, p. 94), north-east of Socoh, more suitable to the context. **2.** The potteries of the monarchy, 1 Ch. iv. 23 (AV 'hedges'). Albright suggests Tell ej-Judeideh, 5 miles south-west of Socoh (*JPOS*, V, 1925, pp. 50 ff.), where a large quantity of stamped jar-handles has been found. **3.** In Benjamin, 1 Ch. xii. 4; possibly Jedireh, a mile north-east of Gibeon, or Kh. Gudeira, east of Beit Liqya.

J.P.U.L.

GEDEROTH. A town in Judah near Aijalon, Jos. xv. 41; 2 Ch. xxviii. 18. Abel (*Géographie*, II, p. 330) discusses the derivation of modern Qatra, but this is too far west (*GTT*, p. 147, Noth, *Joshua*, p. 95). Kh. Jedireh is possible; see GEDERAH (1).

GEDEROTHAIM. 'The two penfolds', Jos. xv. 36 (LXX 'its penfolds', reading *h* for *m*); not a town, the count being correct without it.

GEDOR. 1. A town in the Judaean hills (Jos. xv. 58 and perhaps 1 Ch. iv. 4); Kh. Gedur, 2 km. west of Beit Ummar, just west of the central ridge. Simons (*GTT*, p. 155) identifies it with Beth Gader (1 Ch. ii. 51). **2.** A place south of Hebron, near Socoh and Zanoah (1 Ch. iv. 18), probably GEDERAH (2), *q.v.* **3.** A place in Amalekite territory, at the east end of 'the valley', 1 Ch. iv. 39; probably overlooking the Dead Sea. **4.** A Benjamite, 1 Ch. viii. 31, ix. 37. **5.** A place in Benjamin, 1 Ch. xii. 7; perhaps Kh. el-Gudeira (Abel, *Géographie*, II, p. 330).

J.P.U.L.

GEHAZI. The servant of Elisha. He may be the unnamed 'servitor' of 2 Ki. iv. 43 and the 'servant' of 2 Ki. vi. 15, but he is specifically named on only three occasions.

In 2 Ki. iv he suggests to Elisha that the Shunammite should be rewarded with the promise of a son, and later takes Elisha's staff and lays it upon the dead child in the vain hope of restoring his life.

In 2 Ki. v, after Elisha has refused to take a present from Naaman when his leprosy had been cured, Gehazi obtains presents for himself under false pretences. As a punishment he himself is struck down with leprosy. 2 Ki. v. 27 should be compared with the leprosy regulations of Lv. xiii. 12, 13. When this particular form of skin disease, whatever it may have been, turned the whole skin white, the victim was 'clean', and was not segregated. Hence Gehazi was able to continue as Elisha's servant.

In 2 Ki. viii. 1–6 Gehazi relates to king Jehoram the story of how the Shunammite's son was restored to life. While he is talking the woman herself comes in to appeal to the king for the restoration of her property.

J.S.W.

GEHENNA. See ESCHATOLOGY (x).

GELILOTH. Perhaps means 'circuit, circle' (of stones), compare Gilgal. Only named in Jos. xviii. 17, as on the border of Judah and Benjamin, in terms almost identical with those used of Gilgal (Jos. xv. 7). As Geliloth and Gilgal have more or less the same meaning, both derived from Heb. *gālal*, 'to roll', they are probably variant-names for one and the same place. Simons, *GTT*, p. 173, § 326, thinks of Geliloth as a small region near Jericho. But see also under GILGAL.

K.A.K.

GENEALOGY.

I. IN THE OLD TESTAMENT

a. General

A genealogy in the Old Testament sense is a list of names indicating the ancestors or descendants of an individual or individuals, or simply a registration of the names of people concerned in some situation. The word 'genealogy' in EVV is a translation of Hebrew *yaḥaś*, which occurs only once as a noun, in the phrase *sēp̄er hayyaḥaś*, 'book of the genealogy', in Ne. vii. 5, where it refers to a register of those who returned to Jerusalem with Sheshbazzar. It is thus clear that the term 'genealogy' as used in the EVV is not confined to the sense of the term in modern English usage, of an account of descent from an ancestor by the enumeration of intermediate persons, though this is frequently what is intended.

The genealogies of the Old Testament are found chiefly in the Pentateuch, and in Ezra–Nehemiah and Chronicles, and it is in the latter three books exclusively that the verbal form of *yaḥaś* occurs, always in the intensive reflexive stem (*hiṯyaḥēś*), 'enrol oneself by genealogy' (Ezr. ii. 62, viii. 1, 3; Ne. vii. 5, 64; 1 Ch. iv. 33, v. 1, 7, 17, vii. 5, 7, 9, 40, ix. 1, 22; 2 Ch. xii. 15, xxxi. 16–19). The term *tôlēḏôṯ*, 'generations', is used in Genesis more or less in the sense of 'genealogical history' (see GENERATION).

(i) *Types of genealogies.* The genealogies given in the scriptural record range from a bare list of names as in 1 Ch. i. 1, through the most common type which links the names by means of a standard formula and inserts additional information under some but not all (*e.g.* Gn. v and *cf.* verse 24), to the fully expanded historical account which is based on a framework of names, as in the books of Kings.

Both possible forms of genealogy, ascending and descending, are found in the Old Testament. The former is commonly provided with a linking formula of the type, '*x* the son (*bēn*) of *y*' (*e.g.* 1 Ch. vi. 33–43; Ezr. vii. 1–5), and the latter with one of the type '*x* begat (*yālaḏ*) *y*' (*e.g.* Gn. v; Ru. iv. 18–23; RSV translates 'became the father of'). The descending type of genealogy may include much information as to the age and actions of the individual links, whereas the ascending type is more commonly used to trace the ancestry of an individual back to some important figure of the past, when the doings of the intermediate figures do not affect the issue.

(ii) *Genealogies as sources for chronology.* That some of the genealogies recorded in the Old Testament, as in the New Testament (compare Mt. i. 1 with i. 2–17), omit some generations is demonstrable. For instance, the list of Aaron's descendants in Ezr. vii. 1–5 omits six names which are given in 1 Ch. vi. 3–14. (See also CHRONOLOGY OF THE OLD TESTAMENT, III*a*.) This is readily understandable from the formulae, for the word *bēn* could mean not only son but also 'grandson' and 'descendant', and in like manner it is probable that the verb *yālaḏ* could mean not only 'bear' in the immediate physical sense but also 'become the ancestor of' (the noun *yeleḏ* from this verb has the meaning of descendant in Is. xxix. 23). Various complicating factors, such as the inclusion in Gn. v and xi of the age of each member at the birth of his descendant and the number of years he lived after this, need not militate against an interpretation of these genealogies as being abridgments. It may be that, as Green and Warfield have suggested, the purpose of the mention of the years of age may have been to emphasize the mortality in spite of vigorous longevity of these Patriarchs, thus bearing out one result of the fall.

(iii) *Ancient Near Eastern usage.* Some of the particular characteristics of biblical genealogies may also be observed in the texts, chiefly the lists of kings and rulers, of the surrounding nations. The Sumerian king list, which traces the early rulers of Mesopotamia from the beginning of kingship, mentions one Mes-kiag-Nanna, son of Mes-anni-padda, but from contemporary records it seems probable that he was in fact the grandson of Mes-anni-padda, his father being one A-anni-padda (this may, however, be due to a scribal error). In Babylon, from Kassite times, it was a common practice for the word 'son of' (*mâr*) to be used in the sense of 'descendant of', an interesting case of this being found in the Black Obelisk of Shalmaneser, which refers to Jehu as the son of (*mâr*) Omri, when in fact he was not even a descendant. A remarkable Egyptian example is a brief text in which King Tirhakah (*c.* 670 BC) honours his 'father' Sesostris III (*c.* 1870 BC), who lived some 1,200 years before him. Though care must be exercised in drawing upon modern parallels, the genealogical reckonings of the Arabs exhibit similar characteristics, as estimations on the basis of genealogies obtained in recent times clearly show that only the outstanding links are mentioned. For instance, the late king of Arabia, Abdul 'Aziz, was called Ibn Sa'ud, though he was really the son of Abdur-Rahman, and the Sa'ud whose name he bore died in 1724, though here the question of dynastic names is involved.

There is thus no reason to suppose that all the genealogies in the Bible purport to be complete, since their purpose was more for the establishment of descent from some particular ancestor or ancestors, a purpose unaffected by the omission of names, than the reckoning of exact chronologies (see CHRONOLOGY).

b. Old Testament genealogies

The principal genealogical lists of the Old Testament may be set out as follows.

(i) Adam to Noah (Gn. v; 1 Ch. i. 1–4). Ten names. Each is given in the formula 'A lived *x* years and begat (*yālaḏ*) B, and A lived after he begat B *y* years and begat sons and daughters, and all the days of A were *z* years, and he died'. The figures for *x* and *y* vary to some extent between the *MT*, the Samaritan Pentateuch, and the LXX, though there is a considerable measure of agreement in the totals (*z*), as follows: Adam, 930; Seth, 912; Enos, 905; Cainan, 910; Mahalaleel, 895; Jared, 962 (*MT*, LXX), 847 (Sa.); Enoch, 365; Methuselah, 969 (*MT*, LXX), 720 (Sa.); Lamech, 777 (*MT*), 635 (Sa.), 753 (LXX); Noah's age at the Flood, 600. It is probable that this list is abridged, so that it cannot safely be used as a basis for chronology (*q.v.*). Reminiscent of this genealogy is the first part of the Sumerian king list, which names ten 'great men' who ruled before the Flood. The years of reign for these range in one recension as high as 43,200.

(ii) The descendants of Cain (Gn. iv. 17–22).

(iii) The descendants of Noah (Gn. x; 1 Ch. i. 1–23). The list of the nations who were descended from Shem, Ham, and Japheth (see NATIONS, TABLE OF).

(iv) Shem to Abraham (Gn. xi. 10–26; 1 Ch. i. 24–27). Ten names. A genealogy couched in the same terms as (i) above, except that, while the Samaritan Pentateuch gives the total years (*z*), *MT* and LXX give only the two figures *x* and *y*. The totals given by the Samaritan Pentateuch and worked out for *MT* and LXX are as follows, the *MT* and Samaritan Pentateuch agreeing in most cases against the figures for the LXX. Shem, 600; Arpachshad, 438 (*MT*, Sa.), 565 (LXX); LXX here inserts Kainan, 460, omitted in *MT* and Sa.; Shelah, 433 (*MT*, Sa.), 460 (LXX); Eber, 464 (*MT*), 404 (Sa.), 504 (LXX); Peleg, 239 (*MT*, Sa.), 339 (LXX); Reu, 239 (*MT*, Sa.), 339 (LXX); Serug, 230 (*MT*, Sa.), 330 (LXX); Nahor, 148 (*MT*, Sa.), 208 (LXX); Terah, 205 (*MT*, LXX), 145 (Sa.); Abraham.

(v) The descendants of Abraham by Keturah (Gn. xxv. 1–4; 1 Ch. i. 32, 33). See ARABIA.

(vi) The descendants of Nahor (Gn. xxii. 20–24).

(vii) The descendants of Lot (Gn. xix. 37, 38).

(viii) The descendants of Ishmael (Gn. xxv. 12–18; 1 Ch. i. 29–31).

(ix) The descendants of Esau (Gn. xxxvi; 1 Ch. i. 35–54).

(x) The descendants of Israel (Jacob; Gn. xlvi), 1–6 by Leah; 7, 8 by Bilhah; 9, 10 by Zilpah; and 11, 12 by Rachel.

1. Reuben (Gn. xlvi. 9; Ex. vi. 14; Nu. xxvi. 5–11; 1 Ch. v. 1–10).

2. Simeon (Gn. xlvi. 10; Ex. vi. 15; Nu. xxvi. 12–14; 1 Ch. iv. 24–43).

3. Levi (Gn. xlvi. 11; Ex. vi. 16–26; 1 Ch. vi. 1–53). This was an important genealogy, since the hereditary priesthood resided in this lineage and the high priests were descended from Aaron, whose own genealogy is given in condensed form in Ex. vi. 16–22. The descent of Samuel from Levi is given in 1 Ch. vi and that of Ezra from Aaron in Ezr. vii. 1–5. See also (xi) below.

4. Judah (Gn. xlvi. 12; Nu. xxvi. 19–22; 1 Ch. ii. 3–iv. 22, ix. 4). This was the lineage of David (1 Ch. ii–iii), from whom the line of kings from Solomon to Josiah was descended (1 Ch. iii. 10–15).

5. Issachar (Gn. xlvi. 13; Nu. xxvi. 23–25; 1 Ch. vii. 1–5).

6. Zebulun (Gn. xlvi. 14; Nu. xxvi. 26, 27).

7. Dan (Gn. xlvi. 23; Nu. xxvi. 42, 43).

8. Naphtali (Gn. xlvi. 24; Nu. xxvi. 48–50; 1 Ch. vii. 13).

9. Gad (Gn. xlvi. 16; Nu. xxvi. 15–18; 1 Ch. v. 11–17).

10. Asher (Gn. xlvi. 17; Nu. xxvi. 44–47; 1 Ch. vii. 30–40).

11. Joseph (Gn. xlvi. 20; Nu. xxvi. 28–37; 1 Ch. vii. 14–27), through his two sons, Ephraim and Manasseh, who were accepted by Jacob as equivalent to his own sons (Gn. xlviii. 5, 12; see ADOPTION).

12. Benjamin (Gn. xlvi. 21; Nu. xxvi. 38–41; 1 Ch. vii. 6–12, viii. 1–40, ix. 7, 35–44). This was the lineage of Saul (1 Ch. viii, ix).

In addition to these lists, which establish genealogical relationships, there are a number of other registers of individuals in one context or another, mentioned in connection with certain periods of Old Testament history.

(xi) Registers of Levites (see also (x) 3 above). Of the time of David (1 Ch. xv. 5–24), Jehoshaphat (2 Ch. xvii. 8), Hezekiah (2 Ch. xxix. 12–14, xxxi. 12–17), Josiah (2 Ch. xxxiv. 8–13, xxxv. 8, 9), Zerubbabel and Joiakim (Ne. xii. 1–24), Nehemiah (Ne. x. 2–13).

(xii) Registers of the reign of David. His recruits at Ziklag (1 Ch. xii. 3–13, 20), his mighty men (2 Sa. xxiii. 8–39; 1 Ch. xi. 11–47), his officers over the tribes (1 Ch. xxvii. 16–22), and his other administrative officers (1 Ch. xxvii. 25–31).

(xiii) Registers of families and individuals of the time of the return and the labours of Ezra and Nehemiah. Those who returned with Zerubbabel (Ne. vii. 7–63; Ezr. ii. 2–61), those who returned with Ezra (Ezr. viii. 2–14), the builders of the wall of Jerusalem (Ne. iii. 1–32), those who had foreign wives (Ezr. x. 18–43), those who signed the covenant (Ne. x. 1–27), those resident in Jerusalem (Ne. xi. 4–19; 1 Ch. ix. 3–17).

II. IN THE NEW TESTAMENT

There are two genealogies in the New Testament (Mt. i. 1–17; Lk. iii. 23–38), both of which give the human ancestry of Jesus the Messiah (see GENEALOGY OF JESUS CHRIST).

Apart from the word *genesis* in Mt. i. 1, which is rendered 'genealogy' by RSV, the EVV translate the term *genealogia* thus in 1 Tim. i. 4 and Tit. iii. 9. The corresponding verb, *genealogeō*, 'to trace ancestry', occurs in Heb. vii. 6 in reference to Melchizedek, who did not count his ancestry from Levi. In the passages in Timothy and Titus the word 'genealogies' is used in a depreciatory sense, in Timothy in conjunction with the word *mythos*, 'fable', and in Titus together with 'foolish questions'. It is possible that in speaking of these Paul had in mind either the sort of mythical histories based on the Old Testament which are found in Jewish apocryphal books such as the Book of Jubilees, or else the family-trees of aeons found in Gnostic literature. They obviously do not refer to the genealogies of the Old Testament.

BIBLIOGRAPHY. E. L. Curtis, *HDB*, II, pp. 121–137; P. W. Crannel, *ISBE*, II, pp. 1183–1196; W. H. Green, 'Primeval Chronology', *Bibliotheca Sacra*, 1890, pp. 285–303; B. B. Warfield, 'On the Antiquity . . . of the Human Race', *PTR*, IX, 1911, pp. 1–17; E. J. Young, *WTJ*, XII, XIII, 1949–51, pp. 189–193; W. G. Lambert, *JCS*, XI, 1957, pp. 1–14, 112. For New Testament, see D. Guthrie, *The Pastoral Epistles*, 1957, pp. 58, 208.

T.C.M.

GENEALOGY OF JESUS CHRIST. Twice in the New Testament we are presented with the detailed genealogy of Christ. The first Evangelist introduces his record, in language which echoes Genesis, as 'the book of the generation of Jesus Christ, the son of David, the son of Abraham', and then traces the line of descent through forty-two generations from Abraham to Christ (Mt. i. 1–17). The third Evangelist, immediately after his account of the baptism of Christ, says that 'Jesus himself, when he began, was about thirty years of age, being the son (as was supposed) of Joseph', and then goes back from Joseph through more than seventy generations to 'Adam, the son of God' (Lk. iii. 23–38).

We need not examine the genealogy from Adam to Abraham, which is not given in Matthew, and which Luke patently derived—perhaps *via* 1 Ch. i. 1–4, 24–27—from Gn. v. 3–32, xi. 10–26 (following LXX, since in verse 36 he inserts Cainan between Arphaxad and Shelah). From Abraham to David the two lists are practically identical; the line from Judah to David is based on 1 Ch. ii. 4–15 (*cf.* Ru. iv. 18–22). Mt. i. 5 adds the information that the mother of Boaz was Rahab (presumably Rahab of Jericho). From David to Joseph the lists diverge, for Matthew traces the line through David's son Solomon and the successive kings of Judah as far as Jehoiachin (Jeconiah), whereas Luke traces it through Nathan, another son of David by Bathsheba (1 Ch. iii. 5, where she is called Bathshua), and not through the royal line. In Matthew Jehoiachin is followed by Shealtiel and his son Zerubbabel, and these two names appear also in Luke (iii. 27), but after this momentary convergence there is no further agreement between the lists until we reach Joseph.

It is most improbable that the names in either list which have no Old Testament attestation were simply invented by the Evangelists or their sources. But if we take the lists seriously, the relation between them constitutes a problem. Both make Jesus a descendant of David; His Davidic descent was a matter of common repute during His ministry (Mk. x. 47 f.) and is attested by the apostolic witness (Rom. i. 3; so Heb. vii. 14 assumes that everyone knows that Jesus belonged to the tribe of Judah). But both lists trace His Davidic descent through Joseph, although they appear in the two Gospels which make it plain that Joseph, while Jesus' father *de iure*, was not His father *de facto*. The Lucan genealogy acknowledges this by the parenthetic clause 'as was supposed' in Lk. iii. 23; similarly, the best attested text of Mt. i. 16 says that Joseph was 'the husband of Mary, of whom was born Jesus, who is called Christ'. Even with the Sinaitic Syr. reading of Mt. i. 16 ('Joseph . . . begat Jesus . . .') the biological sense of 'begat' is excluded by the following narrative (verses 18–25), and it is in any case probable that in other parts of this genealogy too 'begat' implies legal succession rather than actual parentage. Matthew's line is probably intended to trace the succession to David's throne, even where it did not run through the direct line from father to son.

In that case it might be expected that Luke, on the contrary, would endeavour to present the line of biological descent. It has accordingly been held by several commentators that the Lucan genealogy traces Jesus' lineage actually, though not explicitly, through Mary, His mother. It is possible to infer from Gabriel's words in Lk. i. 32 that Mary was a descendant of David; although these words may be explained by the reference to 'Joseph, of the house of David' in verse 27, while Mary in verse 36 is a kinswoman of Elizabeth, said to be 'of the daughters of Aaron' (verse 5). No help should be looked for in the Talmudic reference (TJ *Ḥ*[a]*gîgâ* 77d) to one Miriam, a daughter of Eli (*cf.* Heli, Lk. iii. 23), for this Miriam has no connection with the mother of Jesus. In any case, it is strange that, if the Lucan list intended to trace the genealogy through Mary, this was not stated expressly. More probably both lists intend to trace the genealogy through Joseph. If Matthan, Joseph's grandfather in Mt. i. 15, is the same as Matthat, his grandfather in Lk. iii. 24, then 'we should need only to suppose that Jacob [Joseph's father in Mt.] died without issue, so that his nephew, the son of his brother Heli [Joseph's father in Lk.] would become his heir' (J. G. Machen, *The Virgin Birth of Christ*, 1932, p. 208). As for the propriety of tracing Jesus' lineage through Joseph, 'Joseph was the heir of David, and the child, though born without his agency, was born in a real sense "to him"' (*ibid.*, p. 187). A more complicated account, involving levirate marriage, was given by Julius Africanus (*c.* AD 230), on the basis of a tradition allegedly preserved in the holy family (Eus., *EH* i. 7).

If Nathan in Zc. xii. 12 is David's son of that name, his house evidently had some special standing in Israel, and there might then be more significance than meets the eye in the fact that Jesus is made a descendant of his in Lk. iii. 31.

The Lucan list enumerates twenty or twenty-one generations between David and the Babylonian Exile, and as many between the Exile and Jesus, whereas the Matthaean list enumerates only fourteen generations for each of these periods. But several generations are demonstrably omitted from the Matthaean list in the period from David to the Exile, and others may be omitted in the later period. 'Rhesa' in Lk. iii. 27 may originally have been not an individual name, but Aram. *rêšâ* ('prince'), the title of Zerubbabel (in which case the Lucan list may be derived from an Aramaic document).

The main purpose of the two lists is to establish Jesus' claim to be the Son of David, and more generally to emphasize His solidarity with mankind and His close relation with all that had gone before. Christ and the new covenant are securely linked to the age of the old covenant. Marcion, who wished to sever all the links binding Christianity to the Old Testament, knew what he was about when he cut the genealogy out of his edition of Luke.

BIBLIOGRAPHY. J. G. Machen, *The Virgin Birth of Christ*², 1932, pp. 173 ff., 203 ff. F.F.B.

GENERATION. A word used in the EVV to translate various biblical terms.

1. *tôl^eḏôṯ*. A word occurring ten times in Genesis (ii. 4, v. 1, vi. 9, x. 1, xi. 10, 27, xxv. 12, 19, xxxvi. 1, xxxvii. 2) in such a way as to divide it into eleven sections, each being styled 'the generations of . . .' It also occurs in Gn. x. 32, xxv. 13, xxxvi. 9; Ex. vi. 16, 19; Nu. i many times, iii. 1; Ru. iv. 18; 1 Ch. i. 29, v. 7, vii. 2, 4, 9, viii. 28, ix. 9, 34, xxvi. 31. In Ex. xxviii. 10 the EVV translate it 'birth'. The word is formed from *yālaḏ*, 'to bear, beget', and this probably accounts for the English translation 'generation'. From its Old Testament usage, however, it is apparent that the word means 'history' or 'genealogical history', of a family or the like. In the LXX the word is often rendered by *genesis* (see (3) below), and the expression *biblos geneseōs Iēsou Christou*, 'book of the genealogy of Jesus Christ' (RSV), in Mt. i. 1, closely reflects *sēp̄er tôl^eḏôṯ 'āḏām*, 'book of the genealogy of Adam', in Gn. v. 1.

2. *dôr*. A word occurring frequently, which corresponds in general to the word 'generation' as commonly understood in English. It can refer to a generation, as a period in the past (Is. li. 9) or future (Ex. iii. 15), or to the men of a generation (Ex. i. 6). It is the word used in Gn. xvii. 7, 9, where God's covenant with Abraham and his descendants is announced. The word is also used to refer to a class of men, as in 'crooked generation' (Dt. xxxii. 5) or 'generation of the righteous' (Ps. xiv. 5). The Aramaic cognate, *dār*, occurs in Dn. iv. 3, 34.

3. *genesis*. Used chiefly in the LXX for *tôl^eḏôṯ*, and employed in the same sense in Mt. i. 1 (see (1) above). In the other New Testament occurrences, however, it is used in the sense of 'birth' (Mt. i. 18; Lk. i. 14; Jas. i. 23, 'his natural face', lit. 'face of his birth'; Jas. iii. 6, 'course of nature', lit. 'course of birth').

4. *genea*. Used chiefly in the LXX to translate *dôr*, and like it including among its meanings much the same range as English 'generation'. It is used of the people living at a given time (Mt. xi. 16), and, by extension, of the time itself (Lk. i. 50). It is also evidently used to designate the components of a genealogy (Mt. i. 17).

5. *gennēma*, 'child' and 'offspring', occurring in Mt. iii. 7, xii. 34, xxiii. 33; Lk. iii. 7, in each case in the phrase 'generation of vipers', and meaning 'offspring of vipers'.

6. *genos*, 'race'. AV translates the phrase *genos eklekton* in 1 Pet. ii. 9 'chosen generation', but RV 'elect race' or RSV 'chosen race' is to be preferred.

It is sometimes held that a period of forty years, the duration, for instance, of the wilderness wanderings, is to be taken as a round number indicating a generation.

BIBLIOGRAPHY. On (1): P. J. Wiseman, *New Discoveries in Babylonia about Genesis*[6], 1953, pp. 45–57.

T.C.M.

GENESIS, BOOK OF.

I. OUTLINE OF CONTENTS

a. Pre-history: The creation record (i. 1–ii. 3)

b. The story of man (ii. 4–xi. 26)

His creation and fall (ii. 4–iii. 24); his increasing numbers (iv. 1–vi. 8); the judgment of the flood (vi. 9–ix. 29); the rise of nations (x. 1–xi. 26).

c. The choice of Abraham (xi. 27–xxiii. 20)

His entry into the promised land (xi. 27–xiv. 24); the covenant and the promise (xv. 1–xviii. 15); Sodom and Gomorrah (xviii. 16–xix. 38); Sarah, Isaac, and Ishmael (xx. 1–xxiii. 20).

d. The choice of Isaac (xxiv. 1–xxvi. 35)

His marriage with Rebekah (xxiv. 1–67); death of his father and birth of his children (xxv. 1–34); the promise renewed at Gerar (xxvi. 1–35).

e. The choice of Jacob (xxvii. 1–xxxvi. 43)

His obtaining of the blessing by deceit (xxvii. 1–46); his flight to Harran, and renewal of the promise at Bethel (xxviii. 1–22); his life and marriages in Harran (xxix. 1–xxxi. 16); his return to the promised land, and renewal of the promise at Bethel (xxxi. 17–xxxv. 29); Esau's line (xxxvi. 1–43).

f. The choice of Judah, and the story of Joseph (xxxvii. 1–l. 26)

Joseph sold into Egypt (xxxvii. 1–36); Judah and his daughter-in-law (xxxviii. 1–30); Joseph in Egypt (xxxix. 1–xlv. 28); Joseph's father and brothers in Egypt (xlvi. 1–xlvii. 31); Jacob's blessing gives priority to Ephraim and to Judah (xlviii. 1–xlix. 28); deaths of Jacob and Joseph (xlix. 29–l. 26).

The above analysis is intended to show the narrowing of the record and the special promise of God. The general story of man becomes the special story of the line of Judah.

A technical analysis may also be based on the ten occurrences of the phrase (or its equivalent), 'These are the generations of . . .'. 'Generations' (*q.v.*), Heb. *tôl^eḏôṯ*, means 'begettings' or 'genealogical records'. This phrase is used with reference to the heavens and the earth (ii. 4); Adam (v. 1); Noah (vi. 9); the sons of Noah (x. 1); Shem (xi. 10); Terah (xi. 27); Ishmael (xxv. 12); Isaac (xxv. 19); Esau (xxxvi. 1); Jacob (xxxvii. 2).

II. AUTHORSHIP

For a discussion of the authorship of the Pentateuch, see PENTATEUCH. Concerning the authorship of Genesis in particular, there is nothing in the book to indicate its author. There are two widely accepted opinions, though there are variants of each: (*a*) Mosaic authorship, (*b*) non-Mosaic authorship.

a. Mosaic authorship

The education that Moses received at pharaoh's court would have enabled him to read and write (Ex. xxiv. 4; Dt. xxxi. 9, *etc.*), and he would obviously be anxious to preserve the records that had come down. This means that Moses was not so much the author as the editor and compiler of

Genesis. Family records had been handed down either orally or in written form, and Moses brought these together, editing and translating where necessary. The creation story in Gn. i may have been received as a direct revelation from God, since Moses certainly had the experience of immediate contact with God (*e.g.* Ex. xxxiii. 11; Dt. xxxiv. 10). Accordingly, we may legitimately look for documents or for orally transmitted stories in Genesis, and, if we use some recent terminology, we may speak of Moses as the final tradent who faithfully set down what had come to him from past generations.

If we allow for a few later 'footnotes' added by copyists up to the time of the Monarchy to explain points for contemporary readers (*e.g.* xii. 6, xiii. 7, xiv. 17, and parts of xxxvi. 9–43), there is nothing that need be dated after the time of Moses. While the proper interpretation of Ex. vi. 3 does not exclude some use of the name Yahweh in Genesis, it would be perfectly understandable if Moses sometimes substituted the covenant name of his own day for the covenant name 'El Shaddai (God Almighty) of patriarchal times, in order to remind his readers that this was the same God as the God of Sinai.

For this section, see E. J. Young, *Introduction to the Old Testament*, 1949, pp. 51 ff.

b. Non-Mosaic authorship

There is no one theory here that commands general acceptance. Since the days of Jean Astruc, in the 18th century, scholars have looked for various 'documents' in the Pentateuch (and naturally in Genesis also). These for Genesis are, J (which uses Yahweh for the divine name), E (which uses Elohim for the divine name), and P (which is concerned chiefly with religious matters). Early forms of this theory were extremely radical and denied historicity to a great deal in Genesis. More recently it has been argued that the 'documents' grew by the collection of ancient material until they reached their final shape; J in about the 10th or 9th century BC, E a little later, and P in post-exilic times. Historicity is not necessarily denied in the more moderate forms of this theory.

More recently the 'documentary' theory has been abandoned by some who deny that formal documents ever existed. Scholars of this school speak of 'cycles of tradition' which grew up in various areas, chiefly with a religious interest, *e.g.* Ex. i–xii is quoted as a 'cycle of tradition' that has the Passover event as its focal point. Some time later editors collected these materials and cast them into their present shape. For the most part the material was in oral form before collection. Again there is no necessary denial of historicity in this view, although some writers do deny exact historicity, but admit a 'general historicity'. This 'tradition history' school thinks in terms of the development of the traditions around central events which had significance for the religious life of Israel and found expression in their religious rituals and liturgies.

It is not possible to say in general conclusion that any one school today has wide acceptance by all scholars. The exact origin of Genesis remains something of a mystery.

III. THE PLACE OF GENESIS IN THE BIBLE

Genesis is the Book of Beginnings, the great introduction to the drama of redemption. Genesis i–xi may be regarded as the prologue to the drama, whose first act begins at chapter xii with the introduction of Abraham. At the other end of the drama the book of Revelation is the epilogue.

The prologue is cast in universal terms. God made all things (chapter i). In particular, He made man, who became a rebel and a sinner (chapters ii, iii). Sin became universal (chapter iv), and being rebellion against God is always under divine judgment, exemplified in the story of the Flood (chapters vi–ix). Even after God had demonstrated His displeasure by an act of judgment in the Flood, man returned to his rebellion (chapter xi). Yet always God gave evidences of grace and mercy. Adam and Eve were cast out, but not destroyed (chapter iii); Cain was driven out but 'marked' by God (chapter iv); mankind was overwhelmed by the Flood but not obliterated, for a remnant was saved (chapters vi–ix); man was scattered but allowed to live on (chapter xi).

That is the prologue which paints the background for the drama which is about to develop. What was God's answer to the universal, persistent sin of man? As the drama proper opens in Gn. xii we meet Abraham, the first stage in God's answer. He would call out an elect people, from whom in due course would come the Redeemer. That people would proclaim the message of redemption to men everywhere. Genesis tells only the beginning of the story up to the time of Joseph, giving the setting for God's mighty act of deliverance from Egypt, pattern of the greater deliverance yet to be achieved.

IV. GENESIS AND HISTORICITY

It is not always possible to obtain independent evidence as to the historicity of Genesis. This is especially difficult for Gn. i–xi, though easier for Gn. xii–l. It should always be remembered that much in the Bible is beyond scientific investigation, but notably those areas which touch on faith and personal relations. The areas on which one might ask for evidence in Genesis may be summarized as follows:

a. The creation. See CREATION.

b. The origin of man

The Bible asserts that God made man. It does not allow that there was any other source for man's origin. It is not possible, however, to discover from Genesis precisely how God did this. Scientifically, the origin of man is still obscure, and neither archaeology nor anthropology can give a final answer as to the time, place, or means of man's origin. It is safest for the Christian to be cautious about the subject, to be content to assert with Genesis that, however it happened, God lay behind the process, and to be content to await further evidence before rushing to hasty conclusions. See also MAN.

c. The Flood

There is no final evidence here either as to the time, the extent, or the cause. There were certainly extensive floods in the area from which the Patriarchs came, and the ancient Sumerians had a detailed account of a great flood in the ancient world. There are no serious reasons, however, for accepting the suggestion of Sir Leonard Woolley that the flood at Ur, which left a deep deposit of silt revealed by his excavation, was in fact the result of the Bible Flood. See FLOOD.

d. Patriarchal narratives

It is possible today to read the patriarchal narratives against the background of the social, political, and cultural state of the Ancient Near East in the period 2000–1500 BC. While it is not possible to date the events in Genesis, it is true to say that the Bible reflects very closely the life of certain areas of Mesopotamia during these centuries. See PATRIARCHAL AGE; H. H. Rowley, 'Recent Discoveries in the Patriarchal Age', *BJRL*, XXXII, 1949–50, pp. 76 ff. (reprinted in *The Servant of the Lord and Other Essays on the Old Testament*, 1952); J. Bright, *A History of Israel*, 1960, pp. 60–93.

V. GENESIS AND THEOLOGY

It cannot be emphasized too strongly that the primary value of Genesis, as indeed of all Scripture, is theological. It is possible to devote a great deal of time and energy to all kinds of incidental details and to miss the great theological issues. For example, the story of the Flood speaks of sin, judgment, redemption, new life. To be occupied with details about the size of the ark, and with problems of feeding or of the disposal of refuse, is to be concerned with side-issues. While God's revelation was largely in historical events, and while history is of tremendous significance for the biblical revelation, it is the theological significance of events that is finally important. Where corroborative evidence of the Genesis narratives is lacking, the theological significance may still be discerned.

BIBLIOGRAPHY. H. C. Leupold, *Exposition of Genesis*, 1942; E. J. Young, *Introduction to the Old Testament*, 1949; P. J. Wiseman, *New Discoveries in Babylonia about Genesis*, 1948; S. R. Driver, *The Book of Genesis*, *WC*, 1948; C. A. Simpson, *Genesis*, *IB*, I, 1952.

J.S.W.
J.A.T.

GENNESARET, LAKE OF. See GALILEE, SEA OF.

GENNESARET, LAND OF. See CHINNERETH.

GENTILES (Heb. *gôyîm*; Gk. *ethnē* (or *Hellēnes*) *via* Vulg. *gentiles*). This was originally a general term for 'nations', but acquired a restricted sense by usage. In the Old Testament the affinity of all nations is stressed in the tradition of Noah's descendants (Gn. x). In God's covenant with Abraham his descendants are distinguished from other nations, but not in any narrowly exclusive sense (Gn. xii. 2, xviii. 18, xxii. 18, xxvi. 4). Israel became conscious of being a nation uniquely distinct from others by being separated to God after the Exodus (Dt. xxvi. 5), and the covenant of Sinai (Ex. xix. 6). From then on this dedication dominated all her relations with other nations (Ex. xxxiv. 10; Lv. xviii. 24, 25; Dt. xv. 6).

The Israelites were constantly tempted to compromise with the idolatry and immorality practised by other nations (1 Ki. xiv. 24), so bringing God's judgment on themselves (2 Ki. xvii. 7 ff.; Ezk. v. 5 ff.). On their return from the Exile the danger was still more insidious because of the corruptness of the Jews who had remained in Canaan (*cf.* Ezr. vi. 21). This continual struggle against contamination from their neighbours led to so hard and exclusive an attitude to other nations that by the time of Christ for a Jew to stigmatize his fellow as 'Gentile' was a term of scorn equal in opprobrium to 'tax-collector' (*ethnikos*, Mt. xviii. 17), and they earned for themselves from Tacitus the censure that 'they regard the rest of mankind with all the hatred of enemies' (*Histories* v. 5).

Yet the Gentiles were assigned a place in prophecies of the kingdom, merely as the vanquished who would enhance the glory of Israel (Is. lx. 5, 6), or as themselves seeking the Lord (Is. xi. 10), and offering worship (Mal. i. 11) when the Messiah should come to be their Light (Is. xlii. 6), and to bring salvation to the ends of the earth (Is. xlix. 6). In this tradition Simeon hailed Jesus (Lk. ii. 32), and Jesus began His ministry (Mt. xii. 18, 21), and the Jews themselves could question whether He would go to the Gentiles (Jn. vii. 35). Though hesitant and astonished when Cornelius was converted (Acts x. 45, xi. 18), the Church quickly accepted the equality of Jew and Gentile before God (Rom. i. 16; Col. iii. 11), thus revealing the full scope of the gospel and its glorious hope for all (Gal. ii. 14 ff.; Rev. xxi. 24, xxii. 2). P.A.B.

GENTLENESS. The single instance of this word in the New Testament presents the gentleness of Christ (coupled with meekness) in 2 Cor. x. 1. *Epieikeia* suggests the yielding of a judge, who, instead of demanding the exact penalty required by strict justice, gives way to circumstances which call for mercy. Thus the concession of a legal right may avoid the perpetration of a moral wrong (see R. C. Trench, *Synonyms of the New Testament*, pp. 153–157). Similarly in the Old Testament the Heb. '*ānâ*, 'to be humble', and its cognate noun are used of God: 'Thy gentleness hath made me great' (2 Sa. xxii. 36 and Ps. xviii. 35). Although the word itself is rarely used, it expresses the typical condescension of the divine

Judge, whose refusal to exact the full demands of the law lifts up those who would otherwise be crushed under its condemnation. The adjective *epieikēs* describes one of the qualities of the Christlike believer. Note the other qualities with which it is associated in 1 Tim. iii. 3, RV; Tit. iii. 2; Jas. iii. 17; 1 Pet. ii. 18. *Epieikeia* is used in a formal rhetorical sense in Acts xxiv. 4. J.C.C.

GEOGRAPHY OF PALESTINE. See PALESTINE.

GEOLOGY OF PALESTINE. See PALESTINE.

GERAH. See WEIGHTS AND MEASURES.

GERAR (*g^erār*, 'circle'). An ancient city south of Gaza (Gn. x. 19) in the foothills of the Judaean mountains. Both Abraham (Gn. xx–xxi) and Isaac (Gn. xxvi) sojourned there, digging wells, and had cordial relations with Abimelech its king, though Isaac quarrelled with him at one stage. The city lay in the 'land of the Philistines' (*'ereṣ p^elištîm*, Gn. xxi. 32, 34; see also xxvi. 1, 8), not necessarily an anachronistic designation (see PHILISTINES). In the early 9th century BC it was the scene of a great victory by Asa of Judah over the invading Ethiopian army of Zerah (2 Ch. xiv. 13, 14).

The site of Gerar was identified with modern Tell Jemmeh about 8 miles south of Gaza, and the site was excavated by W. J. Phythian-Adams (1922) and by W. M. Flinders Petrie (1927). Though Phythian-Adams recognized a Middle Bronze Age level, Petrie's excavations penetrated only to the time of the XVIIIth Egyptian Dynasty (*c.* 16th–14th centuries BC). After a recent survey by D. Alon, however, a different identification has been suggested which has much to recommend it. This is with Tell Abu Hureira, a mound about 11 miles south-east of Gaza, in the Wadi Eš-Šari'ah. As no pre-Iron-Age remains had been found near it, this site had hitherto been believed to be a natural hill, but Alon's survey has shown that it was first inhabited in Chalcolithic times, and continued in occupation through every period of the Bronze and Iron Ages. The evidence of surface potsherds indicated that the city had a prosperous period in Middle Bronze Age, the age of the Patriarchs.

BIBLIOGRAPHY. Y. Aharoni, 'The Land of Gerar', *IEJ*, VI, 1956, pp. 26–32; *cf.* F. M. Cross Jr. and G. E. Wright, *JBL*, LXXV, 1956, pp. 212, 213. T.C.M.

GERASA. An important city of the classical period, ranking in importance with Palmyra and Petra. Lying in Transjordan, mid-way between the Dead Sea and the Sea of Galilee, and some 20 miles to the east of the Jordan, the site today, still preserving the name in the form *Jaraš*, is one of the best preserved examples of a Roman provincial town in the Middle East. It is only indirectly mentioned in the Bible in the passages describing our Lord's visit to the east side of the Sea of Galilee, where the territory is described as the country of the Gerasenes (RV, Mk. v. 1; Lk. viii. 26, 37, AV 'Gadarenes'; in Mt. viii. 28, AV gives Gergesenes, RV Gadarenes. In all three passages variant MSS give *Gerasēnos*, *Gergesēnos*, and *Gadarēnos* (see GADARA)). The town lies in a well-watered valley with a perennial stream running through the middle of it, and its wealth was probably derived from the cultivation of the fertile corn lands to the east of it. First noted in 1806 by the German traveller Seetzen, it was subsequently visited by many Europeans. In 1867 Charles Warren made many plans and photographs of the ruins. In 1878 a modern village was founded at the site, and the resulting destruction of the buildings led to considerable conservation, reconstruction, and excavation under the auspices of the Department of Antiquities between the wars, a work that still goes on. The extent of the Roman remains makes research into the earlier periods difficult, but Gerasa probably emerged from a village to a Hellenistic town under the name of Antioch, some time after the 4th century BC, when increasing security made prosperity possible. It is first mentioned historically in the writings of Josephus, who states that Theodorus of Gadara took refuge there at the end of the 2nd century BC, but it was soon afterward taken by Alexander Jannaeus, and remained in Jewish hands until Pompey's conquest of 63 BC, when it became part of the province of Syria. The Hellenistic practice of allowing a measure of self-government was continued by Rome, and Gerasa, now one of the cities of the Decapolis (*q.v.*), flourished, carrying on a lively trade with the Nabataeans to the south. This prosperity was such that in the 1st century AD the city was largely rebuilt on a typical Roman plan with a straight main street flanked by columns leading to a forum. There were temples to Artemis and Zeus and two theatres and an enclosing wall round the whole. The 2nd century AD was, however, a period of greater prosperity, and the surviving remains, including a triumphal arch commemorating a personal visit by the Emperor Hadrian in AD 129–130, date largely from that time. In the early 3rd century the city became a colony, but soon thereafter declined, and by the time of the Crusades it had been long deserted.

BIBLIOGRAPHY. C. C. McCown, *The Ladder of Progress in Palestine*, 1943, pp. 309–325; G. Lankester Harding, *The Antiquities of Jordan*, 1959, pp. 78–104; E. G. Kraeling, *Gerasa, City of the Decapolis*, 1938. T.C.M.

GERASENES, GERGESENES. See GADARA, GERASA.

GERIZIM. The more southerly of the two mountains which overshadow the modern town of Nablus, 2 miles north-west of ancient Shechem. It has been called the mount of blessing, because here the blessings for obedience were pronounced at the solemn assembly of Israel described in Jos. viii. 30–35 (see EBAL, MOUNT).

A ledge halfway to the top is popularly called

'Jotham's pulpit', from which he once addressed the men of Shechem (Jdg. ix. 7). On the summit are the bare ruins of a Christian church of the 5th century. Still earlier there stood there a temple of Jupiter, to which a staircase of 300 steps led up, as shown on ancient coins found in Nablus.

Now called Jebel eṭ-Ṭôr, Gerizim remains the sacred mount of the Samaritans; for they have worshipped on this mountain (Jn. iv. 20) for countless generations, ascending it to keep the feasts of Passover, Pentecost, and Tabernacles. According to Samaritan tradition, Gerizim is Mt. Moriah (Gn. xxii. 2) and the place where God chose to place His name (Dt. xii. 5). See further E. Robertson, *The Old Testament Problem*, 1950, pp. 157–171. G.T.M.

GERSHOM, GERSHON, -ITE. The form Gershom is used of the following people.

1. The elder son of Moses, born in Midian (Ex. ii. 22, xviii. 3). The name (construed as 'banishment' or 'a stranger there') commemorated Moses' exile. Gershom's sons counted as Levites (1 Ch. xxiii. 14, 15).

2. A descendant of Phineas the priest (Ezr. viii. 2).

3. Levi's son (elsewhere the allied form, 'Gershon', is used). In the wilderness the Gershonites carried the tabernacle, tent, coverings, hangings, and cords for the door, court, and gate; they received two wagons and four oxen to help in the task. They encamped westward of the tabernacle. Their males, over a month old, numbered 7,500; those who served (age-group 30–50) 2,630 (Nu. iii. 17–26, iv. 38–41, vii. 7). In the land they obtained thirteen cities (Jos. xxi. 6). Under David the Asaphites and Laadanites, both Gershonite families, had special singing and treasury duties (1 Ch. vi. 39, xxiii. 1–11, xxvi. 21–22). Gershonites are mentioned at the bringing up of the ark (1 Ch. xv. 7), at the cleansings of the Temple under Hezekiah and Josiah (2 Ch. xxix. 12, xxxv. 15), and as serving under Ezra (Ezr. iii. 10) and Nehemiah (Ne. xi. 17). D.W.G.

GESHEM. Mentioned in Ne. ii. 19, vi. 1, 2 as one of the chief opponents of Nehemiah, and almost certainly the Gashmu of Ne. vi. 6. In these passages he is called simply 'the Arabian', but is evidently an influential person. Two inscriptions throw a vivid light on this man. One is a memorial in ancient Dedan (modern el-'Ula) dated 'in the days of Jasm (dialect-form of Geshem) son of Shahru', testifying to Geshem's fame in N Arabia. The other is an Aramaic dedication on a silver bowl from an Arabian shrine in the Egyptian E Delta. It reads, 'What Qaynu son of Geshem, king of Kedar, brought (as offering) to (the goddess) Han-'Ilat.' This text of his successor shows that Geshem was none other than king (paramount chief) of the tribesfolk and desert traders of biblically attested Kēdar (*q.v.*) in N Arabia. The Persian kings maintained good relations with the Arabs from the time they invaded Egypt in 525 BC (*cf.* Herodotus, iii. 4 ff., 88), which lends point to Ne. vi. 6, for a complaint by Gashmu to the Persian king would not go unheard. For the silver bowl and full background on Geshem, see I. Rabinowitz, *JNES*, XV, 1956, pp. 2, 5–9, and plates 6, 7. *Cf.* also W. F. Albright, 'Dedan' (also in English) in the Alt anniversary volume, *Geschichte und Altes Testament*, 1953, pp. 4, 6 (Dedan inscription). K.A.K.

GESHUR, GESHURITES. In the list of David's sons in 2 Sa. iii. 3 the third is 'Absalom the son of Maacah the daughter of Talmai king of Geshur', a city in Syria (2 Sa. xv. 8; 1 Ch. iii. 2), to the north-east of Bashan (Jos. xii. 5, xiii. 2, 11, 13).

It was this city to which Absalom fled after the murder of his brother Amnon (2 Sa. xiii. 37) and to which David sent Joab to bring him back (xiv. 23). The young man returned to Jerusalem, but only to plot rebellion against his father (2 Sa. xiv. 32, xv. 8). G.T.M.

GESTURES. The Oriental is much more given to physical gestures than is the Westerner. As might be expected, then, the Bible records numerous gestures. These may be roughly divided into three categories: first, natural physical reactions to certain circumstances; second, conventional or customary gestures; third, deliberate symbolic actions. Gestures of the first type are involuntary, and those of the second often tend to become so, through long habit.

Not many gestures of the first category are recorded; the Bible does not mention, for instance, those shrugs and movements of the head which could be taken for granted by the storyteller. Signs with the hands, for different purposes, are recorded in Mt. xii. 49 and Acts xii. 17. The circumstances of the people around Him also caused Jesus to sigh (Mk. vii. 34) and to weep (Jn. xi. 35).

A great number of conventional actions are to be found in Scripture. When greeting a superior one would bow low, and perhaps kiss his hand. Friends greeting each other would grasp the other's chin or beard, and kiss. Lk. vii. 44–46 records the customary gestures of hospitality. Scorn was expressed by wagging the head and grimacing with the mouth (Ps. xxii. 7). In commerce, a bargain was sealed by 'striking' hands (Pr. vi. 1—the gesture is lost in the RSV paraphrase). Extreme grief was expressed by tearing the garments and placing dust upon the head. This category also includes the physical attitudes adopted for prayer and benediction. Notice also Ex. vi. 6 and Is. lxv. 2.

Symbolic action was a method of prophetic instruction; Ezekiel in particular made great use of it, and many of Jesus' actions were of a symbolic nature. He frequently touched those He meant to heal; He breathed on the disciples, as He imparted the Holy Spirit (Jn. xx.

22). Notice, too, Pilate's eloquent gesture in Mt. xxvii. 24.

See also FOOT, HAND, HEAD, *etc.* D.F.P.

GETHSEMANE (from Aram. *gaṯ šemen*, 'an oil press'). A garden (*kēpos*, Jn. xviii. 1), east of Jerusalem beyond the Kidron valley and near the Mount of Olives (Mt. xxvi. 30). It was a favourite retreat frequented by Christ and His disciples, which became the scene of the agony, Judas's betrayal, and the arrest (Mk. xiv. 32–52). It should probably be contrasted with Eden, as the garden where the second Adam prevailed over temptation. Christ's action in Gethsemane (Lk. xxii. 41) gave rise to the Christian custom of kneeling for prayer. The traditional Latin site lies east of the Jericho road-bridge over the Kidron, and contains olive trees said to date back to the 7th century AD. It measures 150 feet by 140 feet, and was enclosed with a wall by the Franciscans in 1848. It corresponds to the position located by Eusebius and Jerome, but is regarded by Thompson, Robinson, and Barclay as too small and too near the road. The Greeks enclosed an adjacent site to the north. There is a broad area of land north-east of the Church of St. Mary where larger, more secluded gardens were put at the disposal of pilgrims, and Thompson locates the genuine site here. The original trees were cut down by Titus (Jos., *BJ* v. 12. 4).

BIBLIOGRAPHY. W. E. Thompson, *The Land and the Book*, 1888, p. 634; G. Dalman, *Sacred Sites and Ways*, 1935, pp. 321 ff. D.H.T.

GEZER. From the earliest times Gezer was a city of some importance, lying on the road from Joppa to Jerusalem. Originally a Canaanite royal city and stronghold, it was conquered by the Egyptians during the XVIIIth Dynasty and placed under a governor. It regained some measure of independence and had its own king, Horam, at the time the Israelites entered Canaan. In a confederacy with Lachish against Israel, Horam was killed (Jos. x. 33), but the Israelites failed to occupy Gezer. It was nevertheless included in the territory of Ephraim, to whom it paid tribute, and was assigned by them to the Levites. According to the stele of the Pharaoh Merenptah (*c.* 1224 BC), the Egyptians recaptured Gezer shortly after the Conquest. It did not become an Israelite possession until the time of Solomon, when it was given by the pharaoh of Egypt as a gift to his daughter, Solomon's wife (1 Ki. ix. 16). It was rebuilt by Solomon. It figured frequently in the Maccabean struggles. Extensive excavations have been carried out here and important discoveries made, including the famous Gezer Calendar, a schoolboy's mnemonic ditty in verse describing the agricultural seasons, in a script similar to that of the Moabite Stone (see CALENDAR).

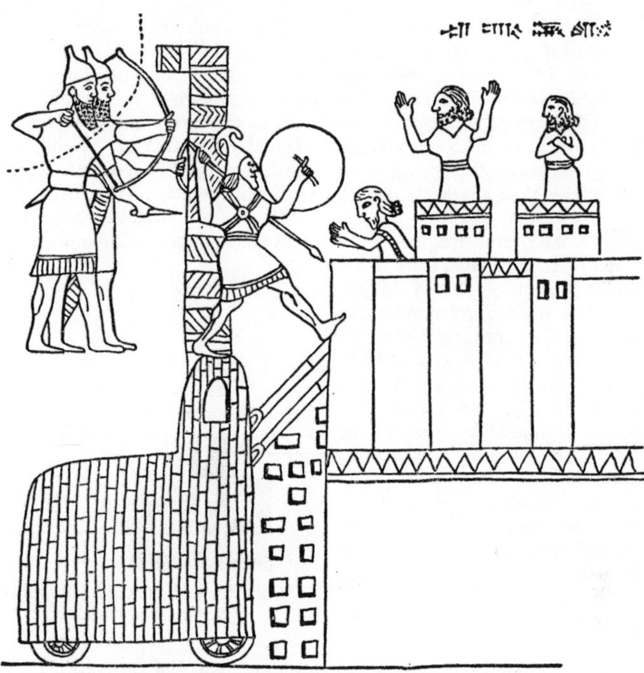

Fig. 94. The assault of the city of Gezer by the army of Tiglath-pileser III. A relief from the south-west palace at Nimrud.

BIBLIOGRAPHY. R. A. S. Macalister, *The Excavations of Gezer*, 1912. M.A.M.

GIANT. A man of great stature. The word is used in EVV, sometimes following LXX, to render various Heb. words.

1. *n^epîlîm* (Gn. vi. 4; Nu. xiii. 33, AV) following LXX *gigas*. RV gives Nephilim (*q.v.*) in these verses.

2. *rāpā'*, *rāpâ*, perhaps variant forms derived from the proper name *r^epā'îm* (see REPHAIM), and so rendered by RV in Dt. ii. 11, 20, iii. 11, 13; Jos. xii. 4, xiii. 12, xv. 8, xvii. 15, xviii. 16 where AV gives 'giant'. In 2 Sa. xxi. 16, 18, 20, 22 and 1 Ch. xx. 4, 6, 8, which speak of certain Philistines as 'sons of the giant', a man of great stature may be meant (*cf.* 2 Sa. xxi. 19, 20); it may be noted here that Goliath is never described as a 'giant' in the Bible (but see GOLIATH), but some scholars hold that these verses indicate descent from the Rephaim. The LXX translates these terms with *gigas* in such other passages as Gn. xiv. 5; Jos. xii. 4, xiii. 12; 1 Ch. xi. 15, xiv. 9, xx. 4, 6.

3. *gibbôr*, 'mighty man', and frequently so translated in EVV (*e.g.* Gn. vi. 4; Jos. i. 14; 1 Sa. ix. 1, *etc.*) but rendered 'giant' in Jb. xvi. 14 (AV, RV; RSV 'warrior'). The word corresponds very much with English 'hero' in meaning. The LXX gives *gigas* for this term in Gn. vi. 4, x. 8, 9; 1 Ch. i. 10; Ps. xix. 5, xxxiii. 16; Is. iii. 2, xiii. 3, xlix. 24, 25; Ezk. xxxii. 12, 21, 27, xxxix. 18, 20.

One other word is translated by *gigas* in the LXX, *'anāq* (see ANAK) in Dt. i. 28, though the EVV do not so take it.

No archaeological remains have been recovered which throw any light on this question, unless the presence of Neanderthal skeletons of Palaeolithic date in the caves of Mount Carmel are considered to do so.

See also EMIM and ZUZIM. T.C.M.

GIBBETHON (*gibb^eṯôn*, 'mound'). A city in Dan (Jos. xix. 44), given to the Kohathite Levites (Jos. xxi. 23). For some time it was in Philistine hands and was the scene of battles between them and northern Israel. Here Baasha slew Nadab (1 Ki. xv. 27) and, about twenty-six years later, Omri was acclaimed king (1 Ki. xvi. 17). Probably modern Tell el-Melât, west of Gezer. G.W.G.

GIBEAH (*giḇ^e'â*, *giḇ^e'aṯ*). A noun meaning 'hill', and often so used in the Bible (*e.g.* 2 Sa. ii. 25 and probably in 2 Sa. vi. 3 with RV and RSV), but also used as a place-name. Owing to its similarity in form with the place-name *geḇa'* (see GEBA), these two are sometimes confused (*e.g.* Jdg. xx. 10).

1. A city in the hill country of Judah (Jos. xv. 57), possibly to be identified with modern el-Jeba' near Bethlehem.

2. A city in Benjamin (Jos. xviii. 28), evidently to the north of Jerusalem (Is. x. 29). As a result of a crime committed by the inhabitants, the city was destroyed in the period of the Judges (Jdg. xix, xx; *cf.* Ho. ix. 9, x. 9). It was famous as the birthplace of Saul (1 Sa. x. 26), *giḇ^e'aṯ šā'ûl*, 'Gibeah of Saul' (1 Sa. xi. 4), and it served as his residence while he was king (1 Sa. xiii–xv), and after David was anointed in his place (1 Sa. xxii. 6, xxiii. 19, xxvi. 1). When David was king it was necessary to allow the Gibeonites to hang up the bodies of seven of Saul's descendants on the walls of Gibeah to make amends for his slaughter of them (2 Sa. xxi. 6; LXX 'Gibeon').

Biblical Gibeah of Saul is almost certainly to be identified with the mound of Tell el-Fûl, which stands about 3 miles north of Jerusalem. Apart from preliminary investigations, the site was excavated by W. F. Albright in 1922–3 with results which agreed with this identification. The situation of the city away from running water meant that it was not occupied until the Israelite Iron Age, when rain-water cisterns came into use in the hill country, so that the first level at Tell el-Fûl is that of the end of the Bronze Age and beginning of the Iron Age, when a fortress was built which was burned near the end of the 12th century. There is good reason to connect this destruction with the crime described in Jdg.

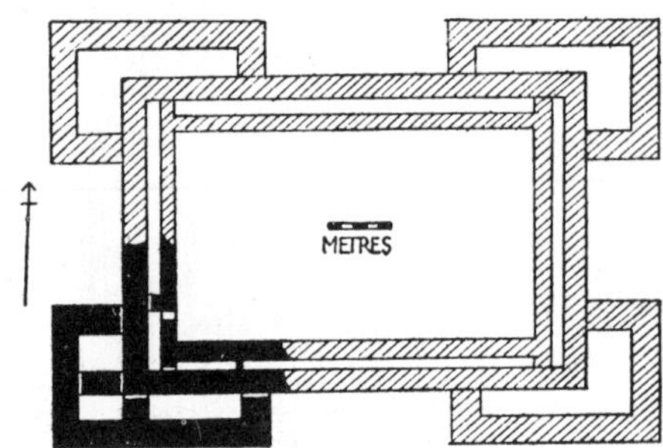

Fig. 95. Plan of a fortified building at Gibeah with casemate walls. 11th century BC.

xix, xx, and the excavations show that the site remained uninhabited for about a century afterwards. The second level represents the time of Saul, and a fortress which must have had a second storey was excavated, in the ground floor store-room of which pottery vessels in keeping with 'a certain measure of rustic luxury' were found. An iron plough-tip from this period was also found, indicating the introduction of iron, monopolized up to now by the Philistines. There are signs that the fortress was pillaged and then abandoned for a few years, presumably at the death of Saul, but the site was soon reoccupied as an outpost in David's war with Ishbosheth. It must have lost its importance with David's conquest of the whole kingdom, however, and the excavations indicate that it now lay deserted for about a century. When the fortress was rebuilt (level III) it was on a smaller scale and was probably in use in the 9th to 7th centuries. Some scholars accordingly hold that 'Geba' in 1 Ki. xv. 22 is to be corrected to 'Gibeah'. The third fortress was destroyed and rebuilt once more, only to be destroyed again, but the authors of neither of these destructions can be named with certainty. After a further period of abandonment lasting some centuries the fort was rebuilt in the Maccabean age, the associated village was resettled, and there was sporadic occupation until the expulsion of all Jews from Jerusalem, when Gibeah presumably fell under the same ban on account of its proximity to the city. It has been abandoned ever since.

BIBLIOGRAPHY. W. F. Albright, 'Excavations and Results at Tell el-Fûl (Gibeah of Saul)', *AASOR*, IV, 1924; L. A. Sinclair, 'An Archaeological Study of Gibeah (Tell el-Fûl)', *AASOR*, XXXIV, 1960. T.C.M.

GIBEON. At the time of the Israelite invasion of Canaan this was an important city inhabited by Hivites (Jos. ix. 7, LXX 'Horites' [*q.v.*] is perhaps preferable) and apparently governed by a council of elders (Jos. ix. 11, *cf.* x. 2). Following the fall of Jericho and Ai, the Gibeonites tricked Joshua into making a treaty with them as vassals. They were reduced to menial service and cursed when their deceit was discovered. The Amorite kings of the southern hill-country attacked Gibeon for its defection to the Israelites, but Joshua led a force to aid his allies and, by means of a hailstorm and a miraculous extension of the daylight, routed the Amorites (Jos. ix–x, xi. 19). The city was allotted to Benjamin and set apart for the Levites (Jos. xviii. 25, xxi. 17). During the struggle between David and the adherents of Ishbosheth the two sides met at Gibeon. Twelve warriors from either side were chosen for a contest, but each killed his opposite number and only after a general mêlée were David's men victorious (2 Sa. ii. 12–17). At 'the great stone which is in Gibeon' Joab killed the dilatory Amasa (2 Sa. xx. 8). This may have been merely a notable landmark, or it may have had some religious significance connected with the high place where the tabernacle and the altar of burnt-offering were, and where Solomon worshipped after his accession (1 Ch. xvi. 39, xxi. 29; 2 Ch. i. 3, 13; 1 Ki. iii. 4, 5). The 'Geba' of 2 Sa. v. 25 should probably be altered to 'Gibeon' in view of 1 Ch. xiv. 16; Is. xxviii. 21 and LXX. The Gibeonites still retained their treaty rights in David's time, so that the only way of removing the guilt incurred by Saul's slaughter of Gibeonites was to hand over seven of his descendants for execution (2 Sa. xxi. 1–11). The close connection of Saul's family with Gibeon (1 Ch. viii. 29–30, ix. 35–39) may well have made his deed appear all the worse. Shishak of Egypt numbers Gibeon among the cities he captured (*ANET*, p. 242; *cf.* 1 Ki. xiv. 25). The assassins of Gedaliah, the governor of Judah appointed by Nebuchadrezzar, were overtaken by the 'great waters' of Gibeon and the prisoners they had taken set free (Je. xli. 11–14). Gibeonites helped Nehemiah to rebuild the walls of Jerusalem (Ne. iii. 7).

Excavations at el-Jib, some 6 miles north of Jerusalem, during 1956, 1957, and 1959 have revealed remains of cities of the Early and Middle II Bronze Age, and of the Iron Age from its beginning to the Persian period. There was also a large town during Roman times. No remains of a Late Bronze Age settlement, which might be considered contemporary with Joshua, have been discovered. Some time in the Early Iron Age a large pit with a stairway descending around it was dug to a depth of 35 feet in the rock. Steps led down a tunnel a further 40 feet to a water-chamber. The purpose of this great pit is in doubt. It seems that it was often almost full of water. At a later date another tunnel was cut leading from the city to a spring outside the walls. The filling of the great pit contained the handles of many storage jars, stamped with a royal seal (*q.v.*) or inscribed with the owners' names and the name Gibeon. Examination of the area around the pit has shown that it was the site of an extensive wine-making industry in the 7th century BC. Sealed jars of wine were stored in cool rock-cut cellars. The evidence suggests that the inscriptions relate to this site and that the city may be identified with Gibeon. Whether the great pit is the pool of the biblical references remains uncertain.

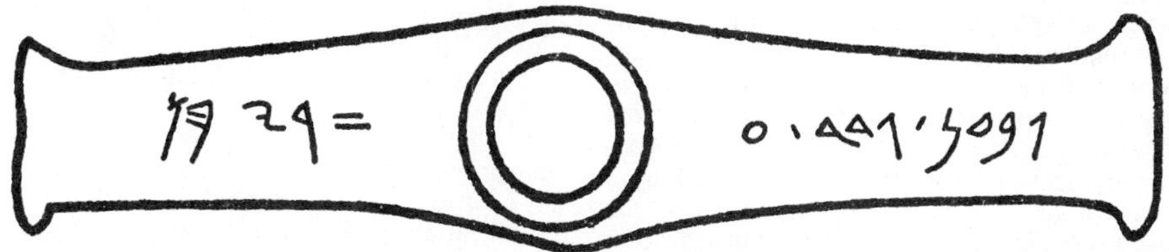

Fig. 96. Handles and mouth of a storage jar from el-Jib, inscribed in old Hebrew *gb'n gdr 'zryhw*, 'Gibeon-Gedor, Azariah'.

BIBLIOGRAPHY. J. B. Pritchard, 'The Water System at Gibeon', *BA*, XIX, 1956, pp. 66–75; *id.*, 'Industry and Trade at Biblical Gibeon', *BA*, XXIII, 1960, pp. 23–29; *id.*, 'Gibeon's History in the Light of Excavation', *VT*, Supplement, VII, 1959, pp. 1–12; *id.*, *Hebrew Inscriptions and Stamps from Gibeon*, University Museum, Philadelphia, 1959. A.R.M.

GIDEON (*giḏe'ôn*, 'hewer, smiter'). Son of Joash, of the clan of Abiezer, of the tribe of Manasseh (Jdg. vi. 11, 15). The judge who delivered Israel from the Midianites, a Bedouin people who were dominating the central area of Palestine (Jdg. vi–viii).

While Gideon was threshing wheat secretly for fear of the Midianites, the angel of Yahweh appeared to call him to deliver his people, confirming it miraculously (Jdg. vi. 11–24). Gideon's first act of defiance was to destroy the Baal-altar and the Asherah, from the consequences of which he was saved by the quick wit of his father (Jdg. vi. 25–32). The gesture of defiance seems to signify a protest against the assimilation of the worship of Yahweh with the Baal-cult. This act is associated with the giving to Gideon of the name Jerubbaal (*yᵉrubba'al*), which is variously interpreted as 'Baal strives', 'Baal founds', or 'may Baal give increase'. Some suggest that this may have been Gideon's earliest name, reflecting the prevailing syncretism, receiving, however, a new significance in view of this act of iconoclasm (*cf.* F. F. Bruce, *The New Bible Commentary*, 1954, p. 245; R. Kittel, *Great Men and Movements in Israel*, 1929, p. 65). In 2 Sa. xi. 21 it appears as Jerubbesheth (*yᵉrubbešeṯ*), replacing the abhorred name Baal with the word for 'shame'.

A further attack by the Midianites led to Gideon's call to action to the tribes of Manasseh, Asher, Zebulun, and Naphtali, followed by the confirmation of his call to leadership by the miracle of the fleece. At God's command he reduced his army from 32,000 to 300, and received personal reassurance during a secret reconnaissance when he heard a Midianite soldier's dream of defeat. He made a sudden night attack which demoralized the enemy and led to a thorough rout (Jdg. vi. 33–vii. 25).

Called in to complete the victory (Jdg. vii. 24), the Ephraimites took offence at the delay in seeking their help, but were mollified by Gideon's tactful words (Jdg. viii. 1–3).

Gideon relentlessly pursued Zebah and Zalmunna, spurred on by the memory of the death of his brothers at their hands. He was refused assistance by the towns of Succoth and Penuel, for which he later punished them. When he eventually captured the kings he put them to death himself (Jdg. viii. 4–21).

After the deliverance Gideon was asked to set up an hereditary monarchy, but he refused. He did, however, accept the golden earrings taken as spoil in battle, with which he made an 'ephod' (probably an image of Yahweh). This he set up in his own city, where it later became a source of apostasy (Jdg. viii. 22–27).

The defeat of Midian was decisive, and Israel had peace throughout the remainder of Gideon's life. The final picture of Gideon is of a peaceful old age, with many wives and sons, among the latter being the notorious Abimelech (Jdg. viii. 28–32).

Heb. xi. 32 gives Gideon a place among the heroes of faith. He trusted in God rather than in a large army, gaining a victory with a handful of men which made it clear it was wholly of God. 'The day of Midian' seems to have become proverbial for deliverance by God without the aid of man (Is. ix. 4). His humility is also apparent, and his refusal of the kingship establishes the fact that Israel's ideal government was a theocracy (Jdg. viii. 23).

BIBLIOGRAPHY. G. Moore, *Judges*, *ICC*, 1895; F. James, *Personalities in the Old Testament*, 1947.

J.G.G.N.

GIER EAGLE. See BIRDS OF THE BIBLE.

GIFT. In the Old Testament a dozen words are used of gifts of one kind or another. The sacrifices and other offerings were gifts to God (Ex. xxviii. 38; Nu. xviii. 11, *etc.*). The Levites were also, in a way, a gift to the Lord (Nu. xviii. 6). Occasionally there is the thought of God's gifts to men, as health and food and wealth and enjoyment (Ec. iii. 13, v. 19). Men gave gifts on festive occasions (Ps. xlv. 12; Est. ix. 22), or in association with a dowry (Gn. xxxiv. 12). Gifts might be tokens of royal bounty (Dn. ii. 6). But there was little goodwill in the 'gifts' the Moabites brought David (2 Sa. viii. 2). Gifts might be the expression of shrewd policy, as when 'a man's gift maketh room for him' (Pr. xviii. 16). Indeed, a gift might be offered with altogether improper motives, so that the word comes to mean much the same as 'bribe'. The Israelites were commanded, 'thou shalt take no gift: for the gift blindeth the wise' (Ex. xxiii. 8).

In the New Testament there is a marked change of emphasis. Some of the nine words for gift refer to men's gifts to God, as *anathēma* (Lk. xxi. 5), and especially *dōron* (Mt. v. 23 f., xxiii. 18 f., *etc.*). Some refer also to men's gifts to one another, *e.g.* *dōron* (Rev. xi. 10), *doma* (Mt. vii. 11; Phil. iv. 17). But the characteristic thing is the use of several words to denote entirely or primarily the gifts that God gives to men. *Dōrea* (the word expresses freeness, bounty) is found eleven times, always of a divine gift. Sometimes this is salvation (Rom. v. 15, 17), or it may be undefined ('his unspeakable gift', 2 Cor. ix. 15), or it is the Holy Spirit (Acts ii. 38). James reminds us that 'Every good gift (*dosis*) and every perfect gift (*dōrēma*) is from above' (Jas. i. 17). A most important word is *charisma*. This may be used of God's good gift of eternal life (Rom. vi. 23), but its characteristic use is for the 'spiritual gifts', *i.e.* the gifts which the Holy Spirit imparts to certain people. Everyone has such a gift (1 Pet. iv. 10), but specific gifts are reserved for individuals (1 Cor. xii. 30), and individuals endowed with these gifts are themselves 'gifts' from the ascended Christ to the Church (Eph. iv. 7 ff.). The important passages are Rom. xii. 6 ff.; 1 Cor. xii. 4–11, 28–30, xiv; Eph. iv. 11 ff. Salvation is God's good gift to men, and all the rest arises from this basic truth.

L.M.

GIHON (*gîḥôn*, 'stream'). **1.** One of the four rivers of the Garden of Eden (see EDEN, GARDEN OF), which has been identified variously with the Oxus, Araxes, Ganges, Nile, and many other rivers. The Nile identification arises from the statement that it wound through (*sāḇaḇ*) the land of Cush (Gn. ii. 13), which is identified with Ethiopia, but it is more probable that the Cush here referred to is the area to the east of Mesopotamia from which the Kassites later descended (see CUSH). If this is so, some river descending to Mesopotamia from the eastern mountains, perhaps the Diyala or the Kerkha, is possible, though the possibility of changed geographical features makes any identification uncertain.

2. The name of a spring to the east of Jerusalem, where Solomon was anointed king (1 Ki. i. 33, 38, 45). It was from this spring that Hezekiah cut a conduit to take the water to the pool of Siloam (2 Ch. xxxii. 30) inside the city walls, and it was still outside the outer wall built by Manasseh (2 Ch. xxxiii. 14). It is probably to be identified with modern 'Ain Sitti Maryām. See fig. 193.

BIBLIOGRAPHY. On (1) see E. A. Speiser, 'The Rivers of Paradise', *Festschrift Johannes Friedrich*, 1959, pp. 473–485; on (2) see J. Simons, *Jerusalem in the Old Testament*, 1952, pp. 162–188. T.C.M.

GILBOA (*gilbōa'*, probably 'bubbling fountain', although there is some doubt about this). Sometimes the name is anarthrous and at others it has the article, while 'Mount Gilboa' also occurs. It was a range of mountains in the territory of Issachar, and so, in 2 Sa. i. 21, David apostrophizes 'ye mountains of Gilboa'. It was the scene of Saul's final clash with the Philistines and of his death (1 Sa. xxviii. 4, xxxi). It may seem surprising to find the Philistines so far north, but the route from Philistia to Esdraelon was an easy one for armies on the march. The hills are now called Jebel Fuḳû'a, but the ancient name is perpetuated in the village of Jelbôn on the hillside. G.W.G.

GILEAD. 1. The son of Machir, son of Manasseh, and progenitor of the Gileadite clan which was a major part of the tribe of Manasseh (Nu. xxvi. 29, 30, xxvii. 1, xxxvi. 1; Jos. xvii. 1, 3; 1 Ch. ii. 21, 23, vii. 14–17). **2.** A descendant of Gad and ancestor of some later Gadites (1 Ch. v. 14). **3.** The father of Jephthah (Jdg. xi. 1, 2).

4. The name applied to the whole or part of the Transjordanian lands occupied by the tribes of Reuben, Gad, and half-Manasseh. Geographically, Gilead proper was the hilly, wooded country north of a line from Heshbon westward to the northern end of the Dead Sea, and extending northward towards the present-day river and Wadi Yarmuk but flattening out into plains from about 18 miles south of Yarmuk. The northern extension of these plains forms the territory of Bashan. Gilead thus defined is divided into northern and southern halves by the east–west course of the lower Jabbok river. South of Gilead proper (*i.e.* south of the Heshbon–Dead Sea line) and reaching to the Arnon river, there is a rolling plateau suitable for grain-growing, cattle, and flocks. This tract, too, was sometimes included under 'Gilead'. But the term Gilead could in its widest application be extended to cover all (Israelite) Transjordan (*cf.* Dt. ii. 36 and especially xxxiv. 1; Jdg. x–xii, xx. 1; 2 Ki. xv. 29). 1 Sa. xiii. 7 is interesting in that it uses 'Gad' in reference to a particular section, and 'Gilead' of the territory in general. It is also used as a general term in 2 Ki. x. 33, where 'all the land of Gilead', *i.e.* (Israelite) Transjordan, includes 'Gilead (*i.e.* Gilead proper, plus the land to the Arnon) and Bashan'. For Gilead in the narrower sense, as the wooded hill-country stretching to the north and south of the Jabbok, see Dt. iii. 10, where it is described as lying between the cities of the plain or tableland south of Heshbon and Bashan in the north, and Jos. xiii. 11 (in context). Either half of Gilead proper could be called simply 'Gilead' (referring to the north, see Dt. iii. 15; Jos. xvii. 1, 5, 6). Where fuller designations were used, Gilead south of the Jabbok (which fell to Gad) was sometimes called 'half the hill-country of Gilead' (RV, Dt. iii. 12, *cf.* 16; Jos. xii. 2, 5, *cf.* xiii. 25), a name also used of Gilead north of the Jabbok (Jos. xiii. 31). The northern half was also known as 'the rest of Gilead' (Dt. iii. 13). In Dt. iii. 12 with 16, and 13 with 15, the sequence of full and abbreviated terms is particularly noteworthy. The simultaneous use of a term or title in both wide and restricted senses, or in both full and abbreviated forms, is a common phenomenon in antiquity and modern times alike. In most Old Testament references to Gilead study of context usually shows the nuance intended.

The balm (*q.v.*) of Gilead was proverbial (Je. viii. 22, xlvi. 11; *cf.* Gn. xxxvii. 25). The rich woodland covering its hills is cited with Lebanon and Carmel as a symbol of luxury (Je. xxii. 6, l. 19; Zc. x. 10). It was the grazing-ground of goats (Ct. iv. 1, vi. 5), and also provided refuge for fugitives. Among those who sought refuge in Gilead were Jacob when he fled before Laban (Gn. xxxi. 21–55), the Israelites who feared the Philistines in Saul's time (1 Sa. xiii. 7), Ishbosheth (2 Sa. ii. 8–9), and David during Absalom's revolt (2 Sa. xvii. 22 ff.).

BIBLIOGRAPHY. On natural geography, *cf.* D. Baly, *The Geography of the Bible*, 1957, pp. 226–236. On the archaeology of the area, *cf.* N. Glueck, *Explorations in Eastern Palestine*, III, *AASOR*, XVIII/XIX, 1939, pp. 151–153, 242–251 (extent and history), and pp. 153–242, 251 ff. (archaeology). See also REUBEN, GAD, MANASSEH, RAMOTH-GILEAD, and MAHANAIM.

K.A.K.

GILGAL. The name can mean 'circle (of stones)', or 'rolling', from Heb. *gālal*, 'to roll'. In its latter meaning the name Gilgal was used by God through Joshua to serve as a reminder to Israel of their deliverance from Egypt when they were circumcised there: 'This day have I rolled away (*gallôṯî*) the reproach of Egypt from off you', Jos. v. 9.

1. Gilgal to the east of Jericho, between it and the Jordan. The exact site of Gilgal within this area is still uncertain. J. Muilenburg (*BASOR*, 140, 1955, pp. 11–27) very tentatively suggests a site just north of Khirbet el-Mefjir, about 1¼ miles north-east of Old Testament Jericho (Tell es-Sulṭan). In support of this approximate location, Muilenburg adduces the combined testimony of the Old Testament references and of later writers (Josephus, Eusebius, *etc.*), and a trial excavation revealed Early Iron Age remains there. J. Simons (*GTT*, pp. 269–270, § 464) criticized Muilenburg's view on the ground that Khirbet el-Mefjir is more fairly north than east of Jericho; but this is not a very strong objection because Khirbet el-Mefjir is as much east as it is north (see Muilenburg's map, *op. cit.*, fig. I, p. 17).

Gilgal became Israel's base of operations after the crossing of Jordan (Jos. iv. 19), and was the focus of a series of events during the conquest: twelve commemorative stones were set up when Israel pitched camp there (Jos. iv. 20); the new generation grown up in the wilderness were circumcised there; the first Passover in Canaan was held there (Jos. v. 9, 10) and the manna ceased (Jos. v. 11, 12). From Gilgal, Joshua led forth Israel against Jericho (Jos. vi. 11, 14 ff.), and conducted his southern campaign (Jos. x) after receiving the artful Gibeonite envoys (Jos. ix. 6), and there began to allot tribal territories (Jos. xiv. 6). Gilgal thus became at once a reminder of God's past deliverance from Egypt, a token of present victory under His guidance, and saw the promise of inheritance yet to be gained. On the camp at Gilgal in Joshua's strategy, compare Y. Kaufmann, *The Biblical Account of the Conquest of Palestine*, 1953, pp. 91–97, especially 92, 95 f. Kaufmann also incisively refutes Alt's and Noth's erroneous views about Gilgal as an early shrine of Benjamite tradition (pp. 67–69).

In later days God's angel went up from Gilgal to Bochim in judgment against forgetful Israel (Jdg. ii. 1); thence Ehud returned to slay a Moabite king for Israel's deliverance (Jdg. iii. 19). Samuel used to visit Gilgal on circuit (1 Sa. vii. 16); there Saul's kingship was confirmed after the Ammonite emergency with joyful sacrifices (1 Sa. xi. 14, 15, *cf.* x. 8). But thereafter, Saul offered precipitate sacrifice (1 Sa. xiii. 8–14), and it was at Gilgal that Samuel and Saul parted for ever after Saul's disobedience in the Amalekite war (1 Sa. xv. 12–35). After Absalom's abortive revolt, the Judaeans welcomed David back at Gilgal (2 Sa. xix. 15, 40). In the days of Ahab and Joram, Elijah and Elisha passed that way just before Elijah's translation to heaven (2 Ki. ii. 1) (although some, quite unnecessarily it would seem, consider this place to be distinct from the historic Gilgal), and there Elisha sweetened the wild gourds in the cooking-pot of a group of prophets who feared poison (2 Ki. iv. 38).

But during the 8th century BC, at least under the kings Uzziah to Hezekiah, Gilgal became a centre of formal and unspiritual worship which like Bethel drew condemnation from Amos (iv. 4, v. 5) and Hosea (iv. 15, ix. 15, xii. 11). The association of Bethel and Gilgal (reflected also in 2 Ki. ii. 1, 2) was strengthened by an important road that connected them (Muilenburg, *op. cit.*, p. 13). Finally, Micah (vi. 5) reminds his people of Gilgal's first rôle in their spiritual pilgrimage, witnessing to God's righteousness and saving power, 'from Shittim to Gilgal', *i.e.* across Jordan into the promised land.

2. In Jos. xv. 7, the northern boundary of Judah at least came in view of a Gilgal that was 'opposite the ascent of Adummim'; in the parallel description of this line, as also the southern boundary of Benjamin (Jos. xviii. 17), Geliloth is so described. But whether *this* Gilgal/Geliloth is the same as the famous Gilgal east of Jericho remains quite uncertain though just possible. Otherwise, it must be some other local 'circle' farther west. Suggestions about this boundary will be found in Simons (*GTT*, pp. 139–140, § 314, 173, § 326), who, however, makes too free a use of emendation.

3. In Dt. xi. 30, the phrase 'opposite Gilgal' may refer to the Canaanites dwelling in the Arabah (Jordan rift valley), rather than to the mountains Ebal and Gerizim. If so, then this is simply the historic Gilgal, see (1) above. Compare *GTT*, p. 35, §§ 87, 88.

4. Among Joshua's defeated enemies occurs the king of Goyyim belonging to Gilgal (Jos. xii. 23) between the kings of Dor and Tirzah. This Gilgal might be the capital of a king ruling over a mixed population on the edge of the maritime plain of Sharon, if—as is sometimes suggested—it is to be placed at Jiljūliyeh, about 5 miles NNE of Aphek or about 11 miles north-east of the coast at Joppa.

5. The Beth-Gilgal from which singers came to the dedication of the walls of Jerusalem by Nehemiah and Ezra is either the famous Gilgal ((1) above) or else remains unidentified (Ne. xii. 29). K.A.K.

GIN. The AV rendering in Pss. cxl. 5, cxli. 9; Am. iii. 5 for Heb. *môqēš*, and in Jb. xviii. 9; Is. viii. 14 for Heb. *paḥ*, both of which words are elsewhere translated 'snare'. See SNARES.

GIRDLE. In AV this word covers several Hebrew terms and body-garments. The word *'aḇnēṭ* is used of the ceremonial sash, especially as worn by the high priest and his associates, made of embroidered linen in blue, purple, and scarlet (Ex. xxviii. 4, 39, 40, xxix. 9, xxxix. 29; Lv. viii. 7, 13, xvi. 4), but worn also by other high dignitaries (Is. xxii. 21). In Ex. xxviii. 8, 27, 28, *etc.*, the 'curious girdle' of AV is *ḥēšeḇ*, 'device', of gold, blue, purple, scarlet, and fine linen, apparently an elaborately worked belt for the ephod (see DRESS, *d*). The term *'ēzôr* usually means 'waistcloth', 'loincloth'. A rough leather one characterized the prophet Elijah (2 Ki. i. 8) and his New Testament counterpart John the Baptist (Mt. iii. 4; Mk. i. 6, RV).

Jeremiah (xiii. 1–11) was bidden to use a spoilt linen loincloth as a symbol that spoilt Judah was good-for-nothing. Centuries later, Agabus bound himself with Paul's girdle in token of Paul's coming captivity (Acts xxi. 11). Besides picturing the onset of Assyrian troops with well-girt loincloths (Is. v. 27; *cf. ANEP*, fig. 236), Isaiah envisaged (xi. 5) righteousness and faithfulness as clothing the son of David like a loincloth. Ezekiel (xxiii. 15) alludes to Babylonians arrayed in vermilion, waistbands, and turbans(?); *cf. ANEP*, fig. 454.

Ḥᵃḡôr, ḥᵃḡôrâ means belt, waistband, or girdle proper. Such belts were often ornate and valuable, including, doubtless, those for sale in Pr. xxxi. 24 and belonging to fashionable women in Is. iii. 24; *cf.* Dn. x. 5; Rev. i. 13, xv. 6. They were used by warriors to support a sword in its sheath (2 Sa. xx. 8; *cf.* 1 Ki. ii. 5 and Hebrew of 2 Ki. iii. 21; *cf. ANEP*, figs. 173, 174), and could be part of presents and rewards (1 Sa. xviii. 4; 2 Sa. xviii. 11). People at work commonly tucked up their clothes into their girdle, as is done in the East today.

The word *mēzaḥ*, 'girdle', occurs in Ps. cix. 19; it and *'aḇnēṭ* may perhaps be connected with the Egyptian words *mḏḥ* and *bnd* respectively (T. O. Lambdin, *JAOS*, LXXIII, 1953, pp. 146, 152).

K.A.K.

GIRGASHITES. A tribe listed among the descendants of Canaan in Gn. x. 16; 1 Ch. i. 14, and part of the very mixed population of Canaan as described in the original promise to Abraham (Gn. xv. 21; *cf.* Ne. ix. 8). In due course they were overcome by Israel (Dt. vii. 1; Jos. iii. 10, xxiv. 11). In N Canaanite Ugarit (14th/13th centuries BC), the Girgashites are indirectly attested by two personal names: *grgš* and *bn-grgš*, *i.e.* Girgash and Ben-Girgash (references in Gordon, *Ugaritic Manual*, 1955, III, p. 252, No. 439). The biblical and Ugaritic Girgash(ites) are probably different from a people in Asia Minor called Karkisa in Hittite annals and *ḳrḳš* in corresponding Egyptian records.

K.A.K.

GIRZITES. In AV 'Gezrites'; either form is possible. Little-known semi-nomadic clans, associated with Geshurites (*q.v.*) and Amalekites (*q.v.*) in the north-west of the Negeb (*q.v.*), and extirpated by David (1 Sa. xxvii. 8) while he governed Ziklag under the Philistine Achish.

K.A.K.

GITTITH. See PSALMS.

GLASS. Seldom mentioned in the Bible, glass was a rare luxury until Roman times. It was considered something precious like gold (Jb. xxviii. 17, AV 'crystal'; Heb. *zᵉḵûḵîṯ*). Several passages translated 'glass' (AV) refer to reflecting metal surfaces used as mirrors (*q.v.*). Glazing was early known and used on beads and brickwork from *c.* 4000 BC, but glass itself is first attested in the Early Bronze Age (*c.* 2600 BC).

By the XVIIIth Egyptian Dynasty (*c.* 1546–1316 BC) a glass factory at El-Amarna in Egypt imitated stone and pottery types and made small unguent vessels by casting, or by winding drawn glass rods round a sand core and re-heating. These products have been found at Gezer, Lachish, Megiddo, and Hazor. Local products also appear at this time, and glazes are mentioned in contemporary Hittite and Assyr. texts. A reference in a Ras Shamra text to *spsg*, 'glaze', makes it probable that this word is found in Pr. xxvi. 23—'like glaze crusted over pottery are smooth lips and an evil heart' (*BASOR*, 98, 1945, pp. 21, 24). Cobalt and manganese were used as colouring agents, but early glass was not very transparent because of impurities in the basic materials. When found it is usually iridescent, due to decomposition and weathering.

In the late Iron and Israelite periods Egyp. glass vessels, now imitating alabaster vessels (hence Gk. *alabastron*), were imported into Syria and Palestine. Local Phoenician products found at Samaria and elsewhere show that glass amphorae, juglets, and aryballoi were in use.

The Hellenistic period brought the additional technique which resulted in gold glass, millefiore, and coloured glasses found at many Palestinian sites. The *alabastron* broken open as a gift for our Lord was probably a long-necked glass ointment bottle, the so-called tear-bottle (Mt. xxvi. 7; Mk. xiv. 3; Lk. vii. 37; AV 'alabaster box').

By the Roman period the invention of glass-blowing methods (at Sidon?) resulted in mass-produced table services which rivalled pottery and metal for ease and cheapness of manufacture. Much of this was translucent, and much like a highly-polished glaze. The latter may be the allusion in the 'glassy sea' (Rev. iv. 6, xv. 2; see SEA OF GLASS) and in the city and street of the New Jerusalem made of pure gold likened to glass (Rev. xxi. 18, 21).

BIBLIOGRAPHY. P. P. Kahane, *Antiquity and Survival*, II, 1957, pp. 208–224; D. B. Harden, 'Ancient Glass', *Antiquity*, 1933.

D.J.W.

GLEANING (*lāqaṭ*, 'to gather, glean'; *'ālal*, 'to roll, glean, suck', usually of grapes). Amid the rejoicing of harvest-time a kindly Israelitish law upheld the custom whereby the poor, orphans, and strangers were allowed to glean grain, grapes, and olives (Lv. xix. 9, 10, xxiii. 22; Dt. xxiv. 19). Ruth (*q.v.*) took full advantage of the practice (Ru. ii. 2 ff.); Gideon used it in striking illustration of the superiority of Ephraim (Jdg. viii. 2); and Jeremiah made of it a metaphor to express the complete annihilation of backsliding Israel (Je. vi. 9, xlix. 9, 10). The custom of gleaning still persists in certain eastern countries. See also AGRICULTURE.

J.D.D.

GLEDE. See BIRDS OF THE BIBLE.

GLORIA IN EXCELSIS. This term refers primarily to a liturgical hymn originating in the patristic church (*cf. SHERK*, VI, 501; F. L. Cross (ed.), *The Oxford Dictionary of the Christian Church*, 1957, *in loc.*) and inspired by the angelic hymn in Lk. ii. 14. As in the visions to Zacharias and Mary (Lk. i. 13, 30), the reassurance of the angel in Lk. ii. 10 is an intimation of the good news which he brings. The previous angelic proclamations were directed particularly to the persons to whom the visions came. The joy of this message is for all the people of God; the shepherds are only representative of the larger group who anticipate and long for the deliverance Messiah brings. The benediction of praise expresses not merely the hope for the future but the reality that has become actual in Messiah's birth:

> To God in the highest, glory!
> To His people on earth, peace!

'Men of God's good will' is the better-attested reading and is parallel to 'the people' in verse 10. It refers to those upon whom God's redemptive mercy has been bestowed and with whom He is well pleased (*cf.* Lk. iii. 22). The peace which the angels announce is not the external and transient *pax Romana*; it is the peace which heals the estrangement between sinful men and a holy God (*cf.* Is. ix. 6 f.; Rom. x. 15). See BENEDICTUS.

E.E.E.

GLORY.

I. IN THE OLD TESTAMENT

'Glory' generally represents Heb. *kāḇôḏ*, with the root idea of 'heaviness' and so of 'weight' or 'worthiness'. It is used of men to describe their wealth, splendour, or reputation (though in the last sense *kāḇôḏ* is often rendered 'honour'). The glory of Israel was not her armies but Yahweh (Je. ii. 11). The word could also mean the self or soul (Gn. xlix. 6).

The most important concept is that of the glory of Yahweh. This denotes the revelation of God's being, nature, and presence to mankind, sometimes with physical phenomena.

In the Pentateuch the glory of Yahweh went with His people out of Egypt and was shown in the cloud which led them through the wilderness (Ex. xvi. 7, 10). The cloud rested on Mount Sinai, where Moses saw His glory (Ex. xxiv. 15–18). No man could see God's face and live (Ex. xxxiii. 20), but some vision of His glory was granted (Ex. xxxiv. 5–8).

The glory of Yahweh filled the tabernacle (Ex. xl. 34, 35) and appeared especially at the hour of sacrifice (Lv. ix. 6, 23). These passages seem all to be connected with a 'thunderstorm-theophany', but there are also passages which suggest more the character of Yahweh which is to be made known throughout the earth (Nu. xiv. 21, 22).

The historical books tell of the Temple's becoming the place where the glory of Yahweh was especially to be located (1 Ki. viii. 11; 2 Ch. vii. 1–3).

In the prophets there is contained both the quasi-physical conception of Yahweh's glory as seen in the visions of Ezekiel (Ezk. i. 28, *etc.*) and also a more spiritualized doctrine (Is. xl. 4, 5, lx. 1–3, *etc.*). The vision of Isaiah in the Temple seems to combine both ideas (Is. vi. 1–4).

There can be found, likewise, in the psalms all the imagery of the storm (Pss. xviii, xxix) and also the idea of the future display of God's character to the world (Ps. lvii. 11, xcvi. 3).

II. IN THE NEW TESTAMENT

Here the LXX is followed in translating *kāḇôḏ* by *doxa*. In secular Greek this means 'opinion' or 'reputation'. The former idea disappears entirely in the LXX and New Testament, and words akin to *kāḇôḏ* are also rendered by *doxa*.

In certain places in the New Testament *doxa* refers to human honour (Mt. iv. 8, vi. 29), but its chief use is to describe the revelation of the character and the presence of God in the Person and work of Jesus Christ. He is the outshining of the divine glory (Heb. i. 3).

The glory of God was seen by the shepherds at the birth of Christ (Lk. ii. 9, 14) and by His disciples throughout His incarnate life (Jn. i. 14). Particularly was it revealed in His *sēmeia* (Jn. ii. 11) and at His transfiguration (Mt. xvii. 1–8; Mk. ix. 2–8; Lk. ix. 28–36). This recalls the ascent of Moses to Sinai (Ex. xxiv. 15) and of Elijah to Horeb (1 Ki. xix. 8) and their visions of the glory of God. Now Christ both sees and reflects the divine glory, but no tabernacle needs to be built because the Word of God has pitched His tent in the human flesh of Jesus (Jn. i. 14) and His glory is to be more fully revealed at the coming exodus at Jerusalem (Lk. ix. 31) and finally at His parousia.

In the Fourth Gospel it is the hour of dedication to death which is essentially the hour of glory (Jn. vii. 39, xii. 23–28, xiii. 31, xvii. 5; *cf.* Heb. ii. 9).

The resurrection and ascension are also seen as manifestations of the glory of God in Christ (Lk. xxiv. 26; Acts iii. 13, vii. 55; Rom. vi. 4; 1 Tim. iii. 16; 1 Pet. i. 21). But above all it is to be revealed in its fulness at the parousia (Mk. viii. 38, xiii. 26, *etc.*).

Man, who was made as the image and glory of God (1 Cor. xi. 7) for relationship with Him, has fallen short of his destiny (Rom. iii. 23), which has been fulfilled only by Christ, the second Adam (Heb. ii. 6–9).

The glory of God in the face of Jesus Christ is still to be seen and reflected by the Church (2 Cor. iv. 3–6). It is the glory of the new covenant (2 Cor. iii. 7–11), and it is especially shared both now (1 Pet. iv. 14) and hereafter (Rom. viii. 18) by those who suffer with Christ. The object of the Church is to see that the world acknowledges the glory which is God's (Rom. xv. 9) and is shown in His deeds (Acts iv. 21), in His disciples (1 Cor. vi. 20), and above all in His Son, the Lord of glory (Rom. xvi. 27).

BIBLIOGRAPHY. A. M. Ramsey, *The Glory of God and the Transfiguration of Christ*, 1949; G. Kittel, '*Doxa*' in *TWNT*. R.E.N.

GNAT. Gnat is an imprecise word applied to several groups of small two-winged insects, similar to and sometimes including midges and mosquitoes. The only New Testament occurrence of *kōnōps* is in Mt. xxiii. 24, which should be read as in RSV, 'straining out a gnat' (AV 'strain at a gnat' is a misprint). This comment was based on the Pharisaic practice of drinking water through a straining cloth to avoid swallowing an insect regarded as unclean. Many small insects breed in or near water, and their larval forms are common in stagnant water. Gk. *kōnōps* probably had as wide an application as the English 'gnat'.

RSV prefers 'gnat' to 'louse' (Heb. *kinnâ*, *kinnâm*) in Ex. viii. 16–18, but the most probable translation is 'tick'. G.C.

GNOSTICISM. A term derived from Gk. *gnōsis*, 'knowledge', and traditionally applied to a body of heretical teaching met by the Church in the first two centuries. It is, however, now widely applied also to those forms of hellenistic religion, both pre-Christian and post-Christian, which display features similar to these heresies (see HERMETIC LITERATURE) and sometimes to any form of religion in which dualism and the possession of knowledge are important: hence to parts of the New Testament, and indeed to Christianity as a whole.

I. CHARACTERISTICS

The classification is in danger of becoming too broad and variable to be serviceable. Since, however, the term Gnostic is by common consent applied to certain Christian heresies, these may serve as an index to its characteristic features. Despite huge differences in intellectual and moral content, and in proximity to central Christianity, it is possible to trace in them a common fund of ideas. Their enemies the Church Fathers provide the main evidence, but they freely quote Gnostic writings, and the recent discoveries at Chenoboskion (*q.v.*) suggest that the Fathers, while trenchant, were not ill-informed.

The Gnostic keynote was knowledge: the possession of secrets which would ultimately serve the soul's union with God. The end of knowledge was thus salvation, comprehending purification and immortality, and it was set in a conceptual framework of contemporary philosophy, mythology, or astrology, different elements prevailing in different systems. In this God's entire separation from matter (conceived, according to Greek dogma, as inherently evil) was assumed, and the drama of redemption enacted within a complex of intermediary beings. The soul of salvable man is a spark of divinity imprisoned in the body: redemption, the soul's escape from corporeal defilement, and its absorption into its Source.

Almost every cardinal Christian doctrine was revised by such thinking. The mythological setting of redemption had no point of contact with the Old Testament (which was rejected or ignored), and diminished the significance of the historic facts of the ministry, death, and resurrection of Jesus. Indeed, the view of God and man which it implied often led to the denial of the reality of Christ's sufferings and sometimes of the incarnation. Creation was an accident, a mistake, even the malevolent act of an antigod. Resurrection and judgment were reinterpreted to refine their 'crudities'. Sin became a defilement which could be sloughed off: the Church was replaced by a club of illuminati possessing secrets hidden from the unsalvable multitude, and even from those uninitiated who claimed the same Redeemer. Ethics centred on maintaining purity: involving in many cases the denial of sex and other bodily appetites, in others (from the same premises) the practice of unrestrained indulgence.

II. DEVELOPMENT

Syncretism and accommodation are of the essence of Gnosticism. The debt—often very indirect—to Greek philosophy is obvious; yet Gnosticism is more than (in Harnack's famous phrase) 'the acute hellenization of Christianity'. Before the coming of Christ, Oriental mysticism, asceticism, and astrology entered a Graeco-Roman world hag-ridden by the fear of death, and there came about what Gilbert Murray called 'The Failure of Nerve' (*Five Stages of Greek Religion*, 1925, chapter iv). Confident rationalism gave way to the quest for salvation. The thought-forms which characterize many of the Christian heresies are observable in some pre-Christian hellenistic religion.

It is urged that Gnostic religious thought emerged from Greek and Oriental elements under the influence, as stimulant or transmitter, of Dispersion Judaism. Support for this view (rejected by Jonas and others) has been drawn from the Chenoboskion documents (see R. M. Grant, *Gnosticism and Early Christianity*, 1959). It is too early to dogmatize; but it is worth noticing that most of the Gnostic-type teachings mentioned in the New Testament (see below) have Judaic elements, that the early Christian congregations were often the heirs of Dispersion synagogues, and that the Fathers see the heresies almost as a succession from Simon Magus (*q.v.*). There are scholars who view Christianity as appropriating and re-interpreting a basic Gnostic Redeemer-Myth (*cf.*, *e.g.*, R. Bultmann, *Primitive Christianity in its Contemporary Setting*, 1956, pp. 162 f.), but it has not yet been shown that such a myth was an integral part of pre-Christian Gnostic thought: nor are the Mandaean documents or their modern descendants (see NAZARENE) highly relevant for primitive Palestinian 'baptist' sects, since they have had such strong later influences.

III. GNOSTICISM AND THE NEW TESTAMENT

The 'Colossian heresy' combined philosophical speculations, astral powers, reverence to angelic intermediaries, food taboos, and ascetic practices with Judaistic borrowings (Col. ii. 8–23; see COLOSSIANS). The Pastoral Epistles denounce preaching compounded of mythology and genealogies (1 Tim. i. 4 ff.) and marked by stringent asceticism (1 Tim. iv. 3 ff.), 'Jewish fables' (Tit. i. 14 ff.), spiritualization of the resurrection (2 Tim. ii. 18), and pernicious moral accompaniments (2 Tim. iii. 5–7)—the whole falsely called *Gnōsis* (1 Tim. vi. 20). The cancerous heresy refuted in the Johannine Epistles denied Christ's humanity (1 Jn. iv. 3; 2 Jn. 7). Of false teachers in Asia the Gnostic-sounding phrase 'the deep things of Satan' is used (Rev. ii. 24, RV).

Some of the less satisfactory features of Corinthian church life reflect terms and concepts developed in Gnosticism; the delight in *Gnōsis* (1 Cor. viii. 1, xiii. 8) and wisdom (i. 17 ff.); the dangerous liberalism of some in sexual matters, whereas others questioned even marriage (1 Cor. vi. 13 ff., vii) and denied the fact of the resurrection (1 Cor. xv. 12). These are only symptoms: certainly they do not constitute a system; but they show the soil in which the Gnostic systems grew so luxuriantly. And Paul in reply can adopt Gnostic vocabulary and disinfect it (1 Cor. ii. 6 ff.; *cf.* Bultmann in *TWNT, s.v. Gnōsis*; E.T. *Gnosis*, 1952): just as he can revolutionize the Gnostic idea of a *plērōma* (*q.v.*) of intermediary beings by declaring that the whole *plērōma* is in Christ (Col. i. 19).

Such depredations, characteristic of the New Testament, upon contemporary religious terminology achieve mental contact with those reared in it without surrendering anything to non-biblical thought. The framework of New Testament thought—whether of election, or knowledge of God, or the Word, or the Redeemer—is provided by the Old Testament revelation, wherever the terminology may come from. Gnosticism with its Greek, Oriental, and Jewish elements, whether viewed as a world-religion (*cf.* G. Quispel, *Gnosis als Weltreligion*, 1951) or simply as a tendency, remained pagan. It attached itself parasitically to Christianity, and took definite shapes from feeding on it. At best it was a desire for Christian ends in a pagan way. *The Gospel of Truth* shows a man holding, through Christian tradition, to a Cross for which his system had small place; but eventually the Christian Gnostic would have to choose between the Gospel and Manichaeism.

BIBLIOGRAPHY. Older texts in W. Völker, *Quellen zur Geschichte der Christlichen Gnosis*, 1932; many translated in R. M. Grant, *Gnosticism: An Anthology*, 1961. For Chenoboskion texts, see NEW TESTAMENT APOCRYPHA. H. Jonas, *The Gnostic Religion*, 1958; R. McL. Wilson, *The Gnostic Problem*, 1958; R. M. Grant, *Gnosticism and Early Christianity*, 1959.

A.F.W.

GOAD. A long-handled, pointed instrument used to urge on the oxen when ploughing. Shamgar used one as a weapon and slew six hundred Philistines (Jdg. iii. 31). The term is employed metaphorically in Ec. xii. 11 to describe the words of the wise, and in Acts ix. 5, xxvi. 14 where Paul's behaviour before his conversion is likened to that of a stubborn ox resisting the goad.

GOAT. As a provider of materials for daily use the goat was second in importance only to the sheep: it had the advantage of being able to live in harder country. Domesticated in antiquity, probably from the wild goat (Heb. *yā'ēl*, 1 Sa. xxiv. 2, *etc.*), the goat was presumably kept by the Patriarchs, and its first mention is Gn. xv. 9. The reference to it in the story of Jacob and Esau (Gn. xxvii. 9) emphasizes its value as meat, but normally only the kids were killed and eaten.

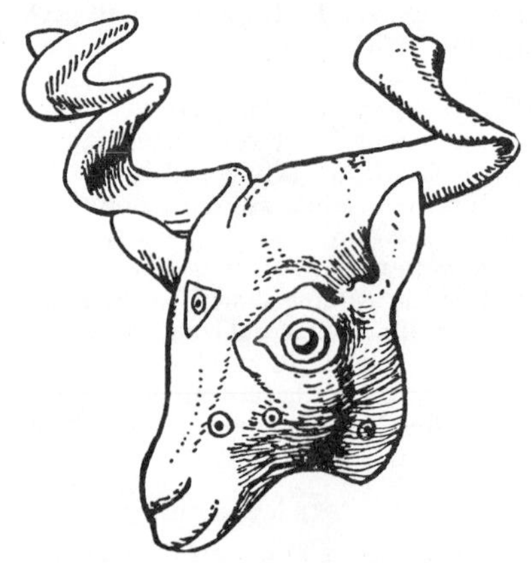

Fig. 97. Copper head of a Markhur goat from Shuruppak, Babylonia. *c.* 2600 BC.

The she-goats provided milk, and the skins were used for leather and as bottles, while the hair of some varieties was woven into cloth. As would be expected in an animal of such importance, it has six or seven different Hebrew names for male (*'attûḏ*, *ṣāpîr*, *śā'îr*, *tayiš*), female (*'ez*, *śᵉ'îrâ*), young (*gᵉḏî*, *gᵉḏî 'izzîm*, pl. *bᵉnê 'izzîm*), *etc.* Of the very numerous Old Testament occurrences, many more than half are concerned with its sacrificial use. Greek words used in the New Testament are *eriphos* (Mt. xxv. 32), *eriphion* (Mt. xxv. 33), and *tragos* (Heb. ix. 12, 13, 19, x. 4).

G.C.

GOD. The derivation of the English word is uncertain. For the Christian conception of God the Bible is our only textbook. In its pages we have the self-revelation of God.

I. HEBREW WORDS FOR GOD

a. 'ēl, 'ĕlōah, 'ĕlōhîm

El derives from a root indicating strength or might, and with this connotation it is applied in the Old Testament to men, and even abstractly to things, as well as to God. When applied to deity it is frequently coupled with some such epithet as 'almighty', *e.g.* El-Shaddai, God Almighty, or All-sufficient. Eloah (rarely used except in poetry) and Elohim are also used, the plural form being the one in common use. Some see in the use of the plural a remnant of polytheism, others an adumbration of the Trinity. It is more likely to be an instance of a usage common in Hebrew by which the plural serves to intensify or enlarge the idea expressed in the singular. It would thus draw attention to the inexhaustible fulness of the Godhead, to the plenitude of life in God.

b. Yahweh

This name, frequently transliterated 'Jehovah', but rendered in AV commonly by 'LORD', is the personal name of the God of Israel, as 'Elohim' is the generic name for deity. It is, therefore, distinctively the name of the living God of biblical revelation. Its derivation is uncertain, though it probably comes from the root *hwh* or *hyh*, conveying the idea of independent and underived existence. When first conveyed to Moses from the burning bush (Ex. iii. 11–15), the flame that derived its sustenance from itself and not from its environment, was an impressive symbol of independent existence. The divine disclosure of the meaning of the name 'I am that I am', or perhaps more accurately 'I will be that I will be', announces the faithfulness and unchangeableness of God, the same yesterday, today, and for ever. While Ex. vi. 3 would suggest that the name Yahweh had not been known before, in view of Gn. xv. 7, xxviii. 13 it can mean no more than that the name had not been formerly revealed in its real meaning and import. It is noteworthy that in this revelation Yahweh declared Himself to be no new or strange God, none other, indeed, than 'Yahweh, the God of your fathers' (Ex. iii. 15).

c. 'ªḏōnāy

This also is a plural form designating God as a Being full of life and power. It signifies 'Lord', or, in its strengthened form, 'Lord of lords', and 'Lord of all the earth', indicating God as the Ruler to whom everything is subject and to whom man is related as servant (Gn. xviii. 27). It was the favourite form of the divine name in later Jewish writers, by whom it was superimposed on the sacred name *YHWH*.

The assumption that the uses of these names point to a distinction in the earlier Old Testament writers between a higher and a lower deity does violence to the facts, and when it is made a criterion for the determination of sources it tends to hopeless confusion. It is not to be denied that the several Old Testament writers emphasize different aspects of the divine character, but this gives no support to the evolutionary view of the religion of Israel from polydaemonism to monotheism. The general tendency in Israel was in the opposite direction, that of the corruption of a pure monotheism into an accommodation to the polytheism of the surrounding nations. While there is historical development in the self-revelation of God to Israel, His nature and character remain consistent throughout.

The God whom Scripture reveals is a Personal Being, self-existent and self-conscious, the Creator of the universe, and the Fountain of life and blessedness. His Being, Character, and Will are the themes that engage the thoughts of all the biblical writers.

See GOD, NAMES OF.

II. THE BEING OF GOD

It is true that Scripture never discusses the Being of God apart from His attributes, inasmuch as God is what He reveals Himself to be. It is possible, however, to conceive of the Being of God in relation to our own beings in the way either of similarity or of contrast, even if His essence must remain incomprehensible. We can say that God is Spirit, Pure, Personal, and Infinite Spirit.

According to Christ's disclosure to the woman of Samaria, God is Spirit (Jn. iv. 24), and we must conceive of Him as Pure Spirit in the sense that He is not complex or made up of parts, but without body or bodily presence, and therefore not visible to the bodily senses (Jn. i. 18).

It is clear also from Scripture that God is a Personal Spirit, rational, self-conscious, and self-determining, an intelligent moral agent. God is supreme Mind and the source of all rationality in His creatures.

God is Infinite Spirit, without bounds or limits to His being or to any of His attributes, and every aspect and element of His nature is infinite. His infinitude in relation to time is spoken of as eternity, in relation to space it is omnipresence. In relation to the universe it implies both transcendence and immanence. By the transcendence of God we mean His detachment from all His creatures as an independent, self-existing Being. He is not shut in by nature, but infinitely exalted above it. Even those passages of Scripture which stress His temporal and local manifestation lay emphasis on His exaltation and omnipotence as a Being external to the world, its sovereign Creator and Judge (*cf.* Is. xl. 12–17).

By the immanence of God we mean His all-pervading presence and power within His creation. He does not stand apart from the world, a mere spectator of the works of His hands; He pervades everything organic and inorganic, acting from within outwards, from the centre of every atom and from the innermost springs of thought and life and feeling, a continuous sequence of cause and effect. In Is. lvii. 15 we have an expression of the transcendence of God as 'the high and lofty one that inhabiteth eternity, whose name is holy', and of His immanence as the One who dwells 'with him also that is of a contrite and humble spirit'.

III. THE CHARACTER OF GOD

If God is a Person, then as a moral agent He possesses character. Thus we may speak of the 'attributes' of God, of qualities we can attribute to the divine character. Though there is no attribute which adequately expresses God's Being, yet the many attributes given in Scripture serve the purpose of giving us a worthy impression of both His transcendence and His immanence. We must, however, bear in mind that the attributes of God belong to the very essence of His Being and that they are therefore co-extensive with His nature. That is to say, in God attributes and being are one. This is not so in the case of men. The attributes of a man's character, because he is finite, are subject to limitation. In him there is a difference between being, living, knowing, and willing, and the most we can expect is that they should be adequately balanced. In God His attributes are all-pervasive, and each of them is infinite and without limitation. For example, we cannot say that God is partly love and partly justice: He is all love and all justice. Each attribute is itself God, and God is fully expressed in each attribute. Then again, man remains man even if he does not possess certain human attributes: God is not God without all His attributes.

It has been found convenient to classify the attributes of God as of two kinds, communicable and incommunicable (sometimes referred to as related and unrelated respectively). Communicable attributes are qualities that can, in measure, be communicated to His rational and moral creatures, such as wisdom, goodness, righteousness, justice, love, that is, attributes that express the immanence of God. Incommunicable attributes are divine perfections which can have no analogy in human character, such as self-existence, immutability, omniscience, eternity, that is, the attributes that emphasize His transcendence. These are capable of definition in part at least. By His self-existence we mean that God has an independent existence by very necessity of His Being; He does not, like His creatures, depend for His existence on anyone outside Himself. By His immutability we mean that He is devoid of all change in His Being, perfections, purposes, and promises. All suggestions of change attributed to Him in Scripture are figures of speech, an accommodation to our human viewpoint. By His eternity we mean that God is above the limitations of time, without beginning and without end, and without succession of moments. This is more readily understood if we remember that time has no existence in and by itself and is but an inseparable accompaniment of created existence. In God there is no time, no becoming; He is the eternal 'I am', and His present is eternity. By the omniscience and omnipresence of God we mean that He is above the limitations of space. God's knowledge is part of His nature and is not acquired like ours. His knowledge is, therefore, complete and absolute, and extends to past and future. Omniscience carries with it omnipresence, inasmuch as God's knowledge involves God's presence in all places and at all times. It is not so much that God is everywhere; He is Himself the Everywhere. Moreover, He is wholly, and not partly, present everywhere. By the omnipotence of God we mean something quite different from power in man. In man power is an effort of will that harnesses or employs pre-existing power; in God power is a creative attribute, it is energy that brings creation out of mere nothing. In God all power is creative.

Holiness may be said to be the distinctive overall attribute of God, the outshining of all that God is. It is His holiness that particularly sets Him apart from all His creation—for He only is holy—and that renders Him unapproachable in all His perfections. It is His intellectual and moral splendour, the ethical purity in virtue of which He delights in good and hates evil (see HOLINESS).

IV. THE WILL OF GOD

The will of God expresses primarily His attribute of self-determination by which He acts in accordance with His eternal power and Godhead. Though God's will cannot be said to be limited in any sense, His perfections ensure that He will never do anything that is incompatible with His nature. Theologians distinguish between the decretive will of God, by which He decrees whatsoever comes to pass, and His preceptive will, by which He enjoins upon His creatures the duties that belong to them. In the light of this definition it can be understood that the decretive will is always accomplished, while the preceptive will is often disobeyed. When we conceive of the sovereign sway of the divine will we recognize that it presents God as the final ground of all existence and of all that ever happens, either actively in bringing it to pass or passively in permitting it to come to pass. Thus, the entrance of sin into the world is attributed to the permissive will of God. The characteristics of the will of God are that there is infinite wisdom and holiness behind it, that it is gracious and kind in its operation, and that it is unconditional in its actions because it is not dependent on anything outside God Himself. Its end is said to be His own glory, or, put otherwise, that manifestation of His glory in which lies the fullest blessedness of His creatures.

The aspect of the will of God that is most frequently alluded to in Scripture is His sovereign purpose. The purpose of God is all-embracing and all-comprehending. This follows from the very nature of God, inasmuch as His knowledge is immediate and complete and He does not need to wait for the unfolding of events as we do. He is thus able to embrace all in one comprehensive plan. His purpose is said to be free, sovereign, and immutable—free in the sense that He cannot be under the influence of anything or anyone outside Himself; sovereign inasmuch as God has the power to carry out His purposes; immutable since there can be no change with God, for change would imply lack of wisdom in planning, or lack of power in executing. It therefore follows that since there can be no unforeseen emergency and no inadequacy of means, the causes of change have no existence for Him.

If we are not able to reconcile God's sovereignty and man's responsibility, it is because we do not understand the nature of divine knowledge and His comprehension of all the laws that govern human conduct. The Bible throughout teaches that all life is lived in the sustaining and upholding power of God 'in whom we live, and move, and have our being', and as a bird is free in the air and a fish in the sea, each in its native element, so man has his true freedom in the will of the God who created him for Himself.

V. THE FATHERHOOD OF GOD

The Christian revelation of God is supremely that of Father. That was Christ's most common designation for God. In Christian theology the designation is reserved specially for the First Person of the Trinity. But inasmuch as the First Person is regarded as the fount of Deity, the one who represents the dignity, honour, and glory of the Trinity, the designation Father is sometimes used when referring to Deity or the Supreme God (*cf.* 1 Pet. i. 17; Jas. i. 27; also Is. ix. 6, where Messiah is called 'Everlasting Father' as the designation of supreme Deity).

The conception of God as Father did not originate with the teaching of Jesus, though He gave it new depth and meaning. The thought is present in the Old Testament, where it expresses both a creative and a theocratic relationship. The fundamental relation of God to men whom He made in His image finds its most full and fitting illustration in the natural relationship which involves the gift of life. Malachi asks the question, 'Have we not one Father, hath not one God made us?' (ii. 10). Isaiah also exclaims 'But now, O Lord, thou art our father; we are the clay, and thou our potter; and we all are the work of thy hand' (lxiv. 8). But it is more particularly for man's spiritual nature that this relationship is claimed. In Heb. xii. 9 God is called 'the Father of spirits', and in Nu. xvi. 22 'the God of the spirits of all flesh'. Paul, when he spoke from Mars' Hill, used this argument to drive home the irrationality of rational man worshipping idols of wood and stone, quoting the poet Aratus ('For we are also his offspring') to indicate that man is a creature of God. Thus the creaturehood of man is the counterpart of the general Fatherhood of God. Without the Creator-Father there would be no race of man, no family of mankind.

The designation of Father is used in the Old Testament also in expression of the covenant relationship of God to His people Israel. In this sense it is a collective relationship that is indicated rather than a personal one. Israel as a covenant nation was the child of God, and she was challenged to recognize and respond to this filial relationship: 'If I then be a Father, where is mine honour?' (Mal. i. 6). But since the covenant relationship was redemptive in its spiritual significance, this may be regarded as a foreshadowing of the New Testament revelation of the divine Fatherhood.

In the New Testament the appellation Father is used in a specific and personal sense. Christ applies it, first of all, to the relationship in which He Himself stood to God. There is every evidence that this relationship is unique and not to be shared by any mere creature. God was His Father by eternal generation, expressive of an essential and timeless relationship. It is significant that Jesus in His teaching of the Twelve never used the term 'our Father' as inclusive of Himself and them. In His resurrection message He indicated two distinct relationships: 'My Father, and your Father' (Jn. xx. 17); but the two are so linked together that the one becomes the ground of the other. His Sonship, though on a level altogether unique, was the basis of their sonship. Now this is the redeeming relationship that belongs to all believers, and in the context of redemption it is viewed from two aspects, that of their standing in Christ and that of the regenerating work of the Holy Spirit in them. From the one aspect they, in living union with Christ, are adopted into the family of God and so granted all the privileges that belong to their filial relationship; 'if children, then heirs' is the sequence (Rom. viii. 17). Under the other aspect they are regarded as born into the family of God by regeneration. The one is the objective aspect, the other the subjective. Because of their new standing (justification) and relationship (adoption) to God the Father in Christ, they become partakers of the divine nature and are born into the family of God.

It is clear that Christ's teaching on the Fatherhood of God restricts the relationship to His believing people. In no instance is He reported as assuming this relationship to exist between God and unbelievers. Not only does He not give a hint of a redeeming Fatherhood of God towards all men, but He said pointedly to the cavilling Jews: 'Ye are of your father the devil' (Jn. viii. 44).

It is under this relationship of Father that the New Testament brings out the tenderer aspects of God's character, His love, His watchful care, His bounty, and His faithfulness. In His training of the Twelve Christ used the figure of an earthly father's relationship to his children and from there proceeded to the higher level: 'How much more shall your heavenly Father . . .'

BIBLIOGRAPHY. T. J. Crawford, *The Fatherhood of God*, 1868; J. Orr, *The Christian View of God and the World*, 1908; A. S. Pringle-Pattison, *The Idea of God*, 1917; G. Vos, *Biblical Theology*, 1948; H. Bavinck, *The Doctrine of God*, 1951.

R.A.F.

GOD, NAMES OF. In considering the various names, titles, or descriptions of God in the Old Testament there are three words of basic importance—*'ēl*, *'ᵉlōhîm*, and *Yahweh* (Jehovah). It is necessary at the outset to realize the meaning of these severally, and their relationship one to another.

I. BASIC NAMES

a. El

El (*'ēl*), EVV 'God' or 'god', has cognate forms in other Semitic tongues, and means a god in the widest sense, true or false, or even an image treated as a god (Gn. xxxv. 2). Because of this general character it is frequently associated with a defining adjective or predicate. For example, in Dt. v. 9 we read, 'I the LORD (*Yahweh*) thy God (*'ᵉlōhîm*) am a jealous God (*'ēl*)', or in Gn. xxxi. 13, 'the God (*'ēl*) of Bethel'. In the Ras Shamra tablets, however, El is a proper noun, the name of the Canaanite 'high God' whose son was Ba'al. The plural of *'ēl* is *'ᵉlōhîm*, and when used as a plural is translated 'gods' (but see below). These may be mere images, 'wood and stone' (Dt. iv. 28), or the imaginary beings which they represent (Dt. xii. 2).

b. Elyon, El Elyon

'Ēl 'elyôn, 'the most high God', was the title of God as worshipped by Melchizedek (see below). *'Elyôn* is found in Nu. xxiv. 16 and elsewhere. In Ps. vii. 17 it is found in combination with *Yahweh*, and in Ps. xviii. 13 in parallel. See also Dn. vii. 22, 25 for the Aram. plural *'elyônîn*; elsewhere in the Aram. of Daniel the equivalent of Heb. *'elyôn* is *'illāyâ* (*e.g.* iv. 17, vii. 25).

c. Elohim

Though a plural form (*'ᵉlōhîm*), Elohim can be treated as a singular, in which case it means the one supreme deity, and in EVV is rendered 'God'. Like its English equivalent, it is, grammatically considered, a common noun, and conveys the notion of all that belongs to the concept of deity, in contrast with man (Nu. xxiii. 19) and other created beings. It is appropriate to cosmic and world-wide relationships (Gn. i. 1), because there is only one supreme and true God, and He is a Person; it approaches the character of a proper noun, while not losing its abstract and conceptual quality.

d. Eloah

This word (*'ᵉlōah*) is a singular form of *'ᵉlōhîm*, and has the same meaning as *'ēl*. In the Old Testament it is chiefly found in poetry (*e.g.* Dt. xxxii. 15, 17; it is most frequent in Job). The corresponding Aramaic form is *'ᵉlāh*.

e. Jehovah

The Heb. word *Yahweh* is in EVV usually translated 'the LORD' (note the capitals) and sometimes 'Jehovah'. The latter name originated as follows. The original Heb. text was not vocalized; in time the 'tetragrammaton' YHWH was considered too sacred to pronounce; so *'ᵃdōnāy* ('my Lord') was substituted in reading, and the vowels of this word were combined with the consonants YHWH to give 'Jehovah', a form first attested at the beginning of the 12th century AD.

The pronunciation Yahweh is indicated by transliterations of the name into Greek in early Christian literature, in the form *iaoue* (Clement of Alexandria) or *iabe* (Theodoret; by this time Gk. *b* had the pronunciation of *v*). The name is certainly connected with Heb. *hāyâ*, 'to be', or rather with a variant and earlier form of the root, *hāwâ*. It is not, however, to be regarded as an imperfective aspect of the verb; the Hiph'îl conjugation, to which alone such a form could be assigned, is not forthcoming for this verb; and the imperfective of the Qal conjugation could not have the vowel *a* in the first syllable. Yahweh should be regarded as a straightforward substantive, in which the root *hwh* is preceded by the preformative *y*. See L. Koehler and W. Baumgartner, *Lexicon in Veteris Testamenti Libros*, 1953, pp. 368 f.; also L. Koehler, *Vom Hebräischen Lexikon*, 1950, pp. 17 f.

Strictly speaking, Yahweh is the only 'name' of God. In Genesis wherever the word *šēm* ('name') is associated with the divine being that name is Yahweh. When Abraham or Isaac built an altar 'he called on the name of Yahweh' (Gn. xii. 8, xiii. 4, xxvi. 25).

In particular, Yahweh was the God of the Patriarchs, and we read of 'Yahweh the God (Elohim) of Abraham' and then of Isaac and finally 'Yahweh, the God of Abraham, and the God of Isaac, and the God of Jacob', concerning which Elohim says, 'this is my name for ever' (Ex. iii. 15). Yahweh, therefore, in contrast with Elohim, is a proper noun, the name of a Person, though that Person is divine. As such, it has its own ideological setting; it presents God as a Person, and so brings Him into relationship with other, human, personalities. It brings God near to man, and He speaks to the Patriarchs as one friend to another.

A study of the word 'name' in the Old Testament reveals how much this word means in Hebrew. The name is no mere label, but is significant of the real personality of him to whom it belongs. It may derive from the circumstances of his birth (Gn. v. 29), or reflect his character (Gn. xxvii. 36), and when a person puts his 'name' upon a thing or another person the latter comes under his influence and protection.

f. Yahweh Elohim

These two words are combined in the narrative of Gn. ii. 4–iii, though 'Elohim' alone is used in the colloquy between Eve and the serpent. If the narrative concerning Eden was related to a Sumerian original it could have been brought by Abraham from Ur, and it would thus be possible to account for the different use in these two chapters from those which precede and follow it.

g. How El, Elohim, and Yahweh are related

We are now in a position to consider how these three words agree or differ in their use. While there are occasions on which any one of them could be used of God, they are by no means identical or interchangeable. In the account of

Gn. xiv, now regarded by many as giving a true picture of the situation in the early second millennium BC, we read how Abraham met with Melchizedek, the priest of *'ēl 'elyôn*, 'the most high God'. Here we have Melchizedek's 'name' or title for the deity he worshipped. It would be clearly wrong to substitute either 'Elohim' or 'Yahweh' for *'ēl 'elyôn* (Gn. xiv. 18). Melchizedek blesses Abraham in the name of *'ēl 'elyôn*, 'possessor of heaven and earth', so identifying *'ēl 'elyôn* as the supreme God (19, 20).

The king of Sodom offers Abraham a gift, which he refuses, lifting up his hand to *Yahweh*, *'ēl 'elyôn*, 'the possessor of heaven and earth' (xiv. 22). He means that he also worships the supreme God, the same God (for there is only one), but knows Him by the name of 'Yahweh'.

To cite a second example, in Gn. xxvii. 20 Jacob deceives his father with the words, 'Because Yahweh thy God (Elohim) brought it to me.' To interchange 'Yahweh' and 'Elohim' would not make sense. Yahweh is the name by which his father worships the supreme God (Elohim).

II. THE REVELATION TO MOSES

The revelation made to Moses at the burning bush is one of the most striking and convincing incidents in the Bible story. After the opening words God introduces Himself thus, 'I am the God (Elohim) of thy father' (Ex. iii. 6). This at once assumes that Moses would know the name of his father's God. When God announces His purpose of delivering Israel by the hand of Moses the latter shows reluctance and begins to make excuse.

He inquires, 'When . . . the children of Israel . . . shall say, What (*mah*) is his name? what shall I say unto them?' (Ex. iii. 13). The normal way to ask a name is to use the pronoun *mî*; to use *mah* invites an answer which goes further, and gives the meaning ('*what?*') or substance of the name.

This helps to explain the reply, namely, 'I AM THAT I AM' (*'ehyeh 'ᵃšer 'ehyeh*), and He said, 'Thus shalt thou say unto the children of Israel, I AM hath sent me unto you' (Ex. iii. 14). By this Moses would not think that God was announcing a *new name*, nor is it called a 'name'; it is just the inner meaning of the name Moses knew. We have here a play upon words; 'Yahweh' is interpreted by *'ehyeh*. M. Buber translates 'I will be as I will be', and expounds it as a promise of God's power and enduring presence with them in the process of deliverance (*Moses*, pp. 39–55). That something like this is the purport of these words, which in English sound enigmatical, is shown by what follows, 'Yahweh, the God of your fathers, the God of Abraham, the God of Isaac, and the God of Jacob, hath sent me unto you: this is my name for ever' (15). The full content of the name comes first, the name itself follows.

III. THE INTERPRETATION OF EXODUS vi. 2, 3

There is a sequel in Ex. vi to the previous revelation; Yahweh further instructs Moses how to deal with Pharaoh and with his own people (Ex. vi. 1–6). This passage has been misconstrued by many adherents of the common documentary hypothesis. According to that hypothesis, this is a 'duplicate' by the Priestly writer (P) of the account in chapter iii. But it is no 'duplicate'; there is no burning bush and no desert scene, no farewell to Jethro; we are already in Egypt. There is no reluctance on Moses' part, Aaron is already his partner; it is a sequel, not a 'doublet'. Thus treated, it makes sense, and presents no contradiction, but a continuation of what precedes it.

The disputed verse is: 'I am JEHOVAH; and I appeared unto Abraham, unto Isaac, and unto Jacob, as God Almighty; but as to my name JEHOVAH I was not made known to them' (Ex. vi. 3, RVmg). The former revelation, to the Patriarchs, concerned promises belonging to a distant future; it supposed that they should be assured that He, Yahweh, was such a God (*'ēl*) as was competent (*šadday*) to fulfil them. The revelation at the bush was greater and more intimate, God's power and immediate and continuing presence with them being all wrapped up in the familiar name of Yahweh. Henceforth, 'I am Yahweh, your God' (Ex. vi. 7) gives them all the assurance they need of His purpose, His presence, and His power.

The hypothesis, based mainly upon the wrong interpretation of Ex. vi. 3, that *'ēl šadday* was the name by which the Patriarchs called upon their God, breaks down therefore at several points. First, *'ēl šadday* is not a 'name', and the writer in Ex. vi. 3 refrains from calling it such. Secondly, Ex. vi. 1–6 is not a doublet, but makes good sense when read as a sequel. Thirdly, it is improbable that this 'P' section would be inserted in JE if it contradicted Ex. iii; and fourthly, in any case the early 'document' JE would be more likely to preserve the true tradition than the post-exilic P.

IV. PARTICULAR NAMES CONTAINING EL OR JEHOVAH

a. 'El 'Ôlām

At Beersheba Abraham planted a tamarisk, and 'called on the name of *Yahweh*', *'ēl 'ôlām* (Gn. xxi. 33). Here 'Yahweh' is the name, and the description follows, 'the everlasting God'. F. M. Cross has drawn attention to the original form of this name—*'El dhū-'Ôlami*, 'God of Eternity'—in a recent communication (*cf.* W. F. Albright in *Bibliotheca Orientalis*, XVII, 1960, p. 242).

b. 'Ēl-'Ĕlōhê-Israel

Jacob, reaching Shechem, bought a piece of land, reared an altar, and called it *'ēl-'ᵉlōhê-Yiśrā'ēl* (Gn. xxxiii. 20), 'God (*'ēl*) is the God (*'ᵉlōhîm*) of Israel'. In this manner he commemorates the recent encounter with the angel at the place he had called Peniel (*pᵉnî-'ēl*, 'the face of God', Gn. xxxii. 30). He thus accepts Israel as his name and so renders worship to God.

c. Jehovah-jireh

In Gn. xxii when the angel of the Lord had pointed to a ram as a substitute for Isaac, Abraham named the place *Yahweh yir'eh*, 'the LORD provides' (verses 8, 14).

d. Jehovah-nissi

In somewhat similar fashion, after the defeat of the Amalekites, Moses erected an altar and called it *Yahweh nissî*, 'the LORD is my banner'. These, however, are not the names of God, but are commemorative of events.

e. Jehovah-shalom

This is the name given by Gideon to the altar he erected in Ophrah, *Yahweh šālôm*, 'the LORD is peace' (Jdg. vi. 24).

f. Jehovah-tsidkenu

This is the name by which Messiah shall be known, *Yahweh ṣiḏqēnû*, 'the LORD (is) our righteousness' (Je. xxiii. 6, AVmg, xxxiii. 16, AVmg), in contrast to the last king of Judah, who was an unworthy bearer of the name Zedekiah (*ṣiḏqiyāhû*, 'Yahweh is righteousness').

g. Jehovah-shammah

This is the name given to the city of Ezekiel's vision, *Yahweh šāmmâ*, 'the LORD is there' (Ezk. xlviii. 35 and mg).

h. The LORD of Hosts

Differing from the preceding names, *Yahweh ṣᵉḇā'ôṯ*, 'the LORD of hosts', is a divine title. It does not occur in the Pentateuch; it appears first in 1 Sa. i. 3 as the title by which God was worshipped at Shiloh. It was used by David in defying the Philistine (1 Sa. xvii. 45); and David again makes use of it as the climax to a glorious song of victory (Ps. xxiv. 10). It is common in the prophets (88 times in Jeremiah), and is used to exhibit Yahweh as at all times the Saviour and Protector of His people (Ps. xlvi. 7, 11). The 'hosts' are all the heavenly powers, ready to do the LORD's command.

i. LORD God of Israel

This title (*Yahweh 'ᵉlōhê Yiśrā'ēl*) is found as early as Deborah's song (Jdg. v. 3), and is frequently used by the prophets (*e.g.* Is. xvii. 6; Zp. ii. 9). It follows in the series 'the God of Abraham, of Isaac, and of Jacob'. In Ps. lix. 5 it is combined with the preceding title.

j. The Holy One of Israel

This title (*qᵉḏôš Yiśrā'ēl*) was a favourite with Isaiah (twenty-nine times—i. 4, *etc.*) in both his earlier and his later prophecies, and also in Jeremiah and the Psalms. Somewhat similar to this is 'the Mighty One of Israel' (*'ᵃḇîr Yiśrā'ēl*, Is. i. 24, *etc.*); also 'the Strength (victory) of Israel' (*nēṣaḥ Yiśrā'ēl*, 1 Sa. xv. 29) used by Samuel.

k. Ancient of days

This is the description (Aram. *'attîq yômîn*) given by Daniel, who pictures God on His throne of judgment, judging the great world-empires (Dn. vii. 9, 13, 22). It alternates with the title 'most High' (Aram. *'illāyâ*, *'elyônîn*, verses 18, 22, 25, 27).

BIBLIOGRAPHY. G. T. Manley, *The Book of the Law*, 1957, pp. 37–47; J. A. Motyer, *The Revelation of the Divine Name*, 1959. G.T.M.

GODLINESS. Gk. *eusebeia* in pagan literature basically means the right respect due to men or gods, but in the Scriptures this word-group (like *theosebeia*, found only in 1 Tim. ii. 10) refers exclusively to reverence towards God (except 1 Tim. v. 4, where 'piety' is proper regard for one's own household). In Peter's denial that the apostles' own *eusebeia* was the source of healing (Acts iii. 12) Alford claims that the term 'bears in it the idea of operative, cultive piety, rather than of inherent character', and translates it, 'meritorious efficacy with God'. Eusebius defines it, 'looking up to the one and only . . . God, and life in accord with Him'. Cornelius is described as *eusebēs* ('devout' in EVV) in Acts x. 2 (*cf.* verse 7) and God-fearing; his godliness being illustrated by his care for his household, almsgiving, and prayers, and his readiness to follow the divine instructions. The word is found most frequently in the Pastoral Epistles (1 Tim. ii. 2, iii. 16, iv. 7, 8, vi. 3, 5, 6, 11; 2 Tim. iii. 5; Tit. i. 1). E. F. Scott regards *eusebeia* as the characteristic word of the Pastoral Epistles and sees in the term 'two things; on the one hand a right belief, on the other hand a right mode of action'. But *eusebeia* is a personal attitude to God rather than a right belief, and the action is not parallel to that attitude but springs directly from it, *e.g.* 2 Tim. iii. 5, where formal godliness is contrasted with that which has power; as also in 2 Pet. i. 3, godliness is derived from divine power. 'The mystery of godliness' (1 Tim. iii. 16) is the fundamental doctrine centred in the Person of Christ, which is the source and criterion of all Christian devotion and behaviour. In 2 Pet. iii. 11 the plural is used to denote godly actions. The noun, 'godliness', does not occur in the Old Testament, but frequently in the Apocrypha, *e.g.* 2 Macc. xii. 45. J.C.C.

GOEL. See AVENGER OF BLOOD, CITIES OF REFUGE, RUTH, BOOK OF.

GOG AND MAGOG. In Ezk. xxxviii. 2 we are introduced to 'Gog of the land of Magog, the chief prince (AV, RVmg, RSV; RV 'prince of Rosh', *q.v.*), of Meshech (*q.v.*) and Tubal'. LXX, probably correctly, understood Magog as a people, not a country. The only reasonable identification of Gog is with Gyges, king of Lydia (*c.* 660 BC)—Assyr. Gugu. The linkage with peoples at the extremities of the then known world (Ezk. xxxviii. 5, 6; *cf.* Rev. xx. 8) suggests that we are to regard them as eschatological figures rather than as a historically identifiable king, *etc.* This is the interpretation in Rev. xx. 8 and rabbinic literature.

Since we need not interpret Ezk. xxxviii, xxxix as earlier in time than Ex. xl–xlviii, and rabbinic tradition places Gog after the days of the Messiah, we need see no contradiction between Ezekiel and Revelation, provided we understand the millennium in the sense the Rabbis gave 'the days of the Messiah'. H.L.E.

GOLAN. A city of refuge in Bashan (Dt. iv. 43) and also a levitical city (Jos. xxi. 27), in the Transjordanian portion of Manasseh. It is probably to be identified with the modern *saḥem el-ğōlān*, about 14 miles west of Aphek (Hippos), though the homonymous district, Gaulanitis, is nearer the Jordan and the sea of Chinnereth. R.F.H.

GOLD. See MINING AND METALS.

GOLGOTHA. See CALVARY.

GOLIATH. A giant (*q.v.*) of Gath serving in the Philistine army (1 Sa. xvii. 4), Goliath may have descended from that remnant of the Rephaim which, after having been scattered by the Ammonites (Dt. ii. 20, 21; 2 Sa. xxi. 22), took refuge with the Philistines. For discussion of his origin, see G. A. Wainwright, 'Early Philistine History', *VT*, IX, 1959, pp. 79 f. His height is given as 'six cubits and a span', *i.e.* 10½ feet, if the cubit is understood as 21 inches (see WEIGHTS AND MEASURES). That this, though an unusual, is not an impossible phenomenon, is confirmed by the discovery in Palestine of human skeletons of similar stature and of roughly the same period.

Goliath was slain by David (*q.v.*) at Ephes-dammim in a duel whose religious character is attested by 1 Sa. xvii. 43, 45; and perhaps also by the Philistines' flight, if this is directly attributed to their conviction that the God of Israel had overcome their god (*cf.* 2 Sa. xxiii. 9–12; 1 Ch. xi. 12 ff.). Goliath's sword, which had been kept in the sanctuary at Nob, was given by the priest Ahimelech to David when the latter was fleeing from Saul to the king of Gath, for whom the weapon was likely to be an acceptable present.

Two later appearances of the name have puzzled scholars. Elhanan is recorded as having slain '(the brother of) Goliath the Gittite'—so AV of 2 Sa. xxi. 19, and again (without parentheses) in 1 Ch. xx. 5, where the victim's name is given as Lahmi. It may be that Elhanan (*q.v.*) was David's original name. On the other hand, some have suggested that this second Goliath could have been the son of David's adversary. For full discussion of the problem and possible emendation, see S. R. Driver, *Notes on the Hebrew Text of the Books of Samuel*, 1913; and E. J. Young, *Introduction to the Old Testament*, 1949, pp. 181 f. J.D.D.

GOMER (*gōmer*, 'completion'). **1.** The eldest son of Japheth and the father of Ashkenaz, Riphath, and Togarmah (Gn. x. 2, 3). In Ezekiel's prophecy (Ezk. xxxviii) the people of Gomer are closely associated with the house of Togarmah in the army of Gog, and are probably to be identified with the ancient Gimirrai (Cimmerians), an Aryan group who conquered Urarṭu (Armenia) from their Ukrainian homeland some time before the 8th century BC, when they appear as enemies of Assyria.

2. The daughter of Diblaim and wife of Hosea (Ho. i. 3). She bore Jezreel, Lo-ruhamah, and Lo-ammi (Ho. i). See HOSEA. G.W.G.

GOMORRAH. See PLAIN, CITIES OF THE.

GOOD. The Hebrew word is *ṭôḇ* ('pleasant', 'joyful', 'agreeable'), signifying primarily that which gratifies the senses and derivatively that which gives aesthetic or moral satisfaction. The LXX renders *ṭôḇ* by *agathos*, the regular Greek word for good as a physical or moral quality, and sometimes by *kalos* (lit. 'beautiful'; hence, in classical as well as biblical Greek, 'noble', 'honourable', 'admirable', 'worthy'). The New Testament reproduces this usage, employing the two adjectives interchangeably (*cf.*, *e.g.*, Rom. vii. 12–21). Paul, following the LXX, uses the noun *agathosynē* for the Christian's goodness, with the accent especially on his beneficence (Rom. xv. 14; Gal. v. 22; Eph. v. 9; 2 Thes. i. 11, RV: for the translation, see the commentaries). He also uses *chrēstotēs* ('goodness', AV, RV; 'kindness', RSV) for the merciful beneficence of God (Rom. ii. 4, xi. 22). 'Goodness' predicated of God in the Old Testament (seven times, AV) is *ḥeseḏ* (RV 'mercy' or 'loving-kindness').

The common element of meaning in the many applications which the word 'good' has in every language is that of approbation, either for inherent value, or for beneficent effect, or both. There is nothing distinctive about the various non-moral senses in which the Bible speaks of things as 'good' (*e.g.* 'useful', as salt, Mt. v. 13; Lk. xiv. 34; 'of high quality', as gold, Gn. ii. 12, cattle, Gn. xli. 26; 'productive', as trees, Mt. vii. 17, ground, Lk. viii. 8; *etc.*). But the biblical concept of moral and spiritual good is thoroughly theological, and stands in sharp contrast with the anthropocentric view of goodness developed by the Greeks and later thinkers in the Greek tradition. This biblical view may be analysed as follows.

a. God is good: for He is morally perfect, and gloriously generous.

The acknowledgment of God as good is the foundation of all biblical thinking about moral goodness. 'Good' in Scripture is not an abstract quality, nor is it a secular human ideal; 'good' means first and foremost what God is ('he is *good*', Ps. c. 5, *et al.*), then what He does, creates, commands, and gives, and finally what He approves in the lives of His creatures. It is not that the biblical writers assess God in terms of a prior concept of goodness, but rather that, contemplating the supreme glory of God's perfections, they apply to Him the ordinary word for acknowledging worth. By so doing, however, they give that word a new depth of meaning. They define good in terms of God; not *vice versa*. Accordingly, the biblical position is that God, and God alone, is good without qualification (Mk. x. 18 and parallels: on which see B. B. Warfield, *The Person and Work of Christ*, 1950, pp. 149 ff.); and He is the arbiter and judge, as He is the norm and standard, of creaturely goodness. Man is good, and things are good, just so far as they conform to the will of God. Woe, then, to those who invert the divine scale of values, giving the name of good to what God calls evil, and *vice versa* (Is. v. 20).

In the Old Testament the goodness of God is frequently invoked as a theme of praise and an argument in prayer (*cf.* 2 Ch. xxx. 18; Ps. lxxxvi. 5). His goodness appears in the good that He does (Ps. cxix. 68), the beneficent activity of His good spirit (Ne. ix. 20; Ps. cxliii. 10), the many-sidedness of His cosmic generosity (Ps. cxlv. 9); most notably, in His kindness to the needy and faithfulness to His covenant (Pss. xxv. 8, lxxiii. 1; La. iii. 25; Na. i. 7). The Psalmists' reiterated exhortation to praise and give thanks to God, 'for he is good: for his mercy endureth for ever' (Pss. cvi. 1, cvii. 1, cxviii. 1, cxxxvi. 1, *cf.* c. 4 f.; also, 1 Ch. xvi. 34; 2 Ch. v. 13, vii. 3), is quoted by Jeremiah as the characteristic motto theme of Israel's worship (Je. xxxiii. 11).

b. The works of God are good: for they reveal His attributes of wisdom and power (see Ps. civ. 24–31), and are the objects of His own approval.

When creation was done, 'God saw every thing that he had made, and, behold, it was very good' (Gn. i. 31, *cf.* verses 4, 10, 12, 18, 21, 25). The whole material order, as such, being God's handiwork, is good (1 Tim. iv. 4; *cf.* Rom. xiv. 14). There is no room for Manichaean dualism in the Bible.

c. The gifts of God are good: for they express His generosity, and make for the welfare of their recipients.

'Beneficial', 'advantageous', is one of the standard secular meanings of 'good' as an adjective; as 'prosperity', 'well-being', is of 'good' as a noun. The Bible integrates this usage into its theology by teaching, not merely that all God's gifts are good, both in intention and in effect, but also that all good is in fact God's gift (Jas. i. 17; *cf.* Ps. iv. 6). It is characteristic of God to do good to the needy, as it was of Jesus, God's anointed (Acts x. 38; Mk. iii. 4). God does good to all men in His ordinary providence, showering on them the blessings of nature (Acts xiv. 17; Ps. cxlv. 9; Lk. vi. 35); and, as a perfect Father, He knows how to give good gifts to those who are His children through Christ (Mt. vii. 11). God's promise to 'do good' to His people is a comprehensive promise of blessing (Je. xxxii. 40, *cf.* xxiv. 6 f.), as the plea that God will 'do good' to them is a comprehensive prayer for it (Pss. li. 18, cxxv. 4). In such passages the 'good' in question is the pledged blessing of the covenant; it is virtually 'salvation' (*cf.* Is. lii. 7). 'Good' on the material level was the promised blessing of the old covenant (with 'evil', the state of blessing withdrawn, as its alternative: Dt. xxx. 15), and 'good' in the realm of spiritual privilege, 'good' not enjoyed under the old covenant, is the gift of the new (Heb. ix. 11, x. 1). Both testaments, however, authorize God's faithful people to rest assured that in God's good time everything that is truly good for them will be made theirs (Pss. lxxxiv. 11, xxxiv. 10, *cf.* lxxxv. 12; Rom. viii. 32; Eph. i. 3).

'Good', as an adjective, is used in various instrumental senses in connection with God's gracious activity of doing good to men. It is used of the word of God that announces blessing, of the hand and work of God that conveys it, of the course of action that leads to enjoyment of it, and of the days in which that enjoyment is experienced (see 1 Ki. viii. 56; Is. xxxix. 8; Je. xxix. 10; Heb. vi. 5; Ezr. vii. 9, viii. 18; Phil. i. 6; 1 Ki. viii. 36; Je. vi. 16; Ps. lxxiii. 28; 1 Pet. iii. 10; *cf.* Ps. xxxiv. 12).

Even when God withdraws the 'good' of outward prosperity from His people and brings upon them 'evil' (hardship) in its place (*cf.* Jb. ii. 10), there is still a sense in which He is doing them good. 'It is good' for a man to be thus afflicted; hereby he receives correction, for his own subsequent benefit (*cf.* Heb. xii. 10), and is exercised and strengthened in faith, patience, and obedience (Ps. cxix. 67, 71; *cf.* La. iii. 26 f.). Anything that drives a man closer to God is for his good, and the Christian's temporary distresses, under God, work for him an eternal weight of glory (2 Cor. iv. 17). Paul is therefore fully entitled to insist that '*all* things (afflictions included) work together for good to them that love God' (Rom. viii. 28). The Christian should regard every circumstance, however ungratifying, as among God's good gifts to him, the expression of a beneficent purpose and, if rightly used, a sure means to his lasting profit.

d. The commands of God are good: for they express the moral perfection of His character and, by showing us how to please Him, mark out for us the path of blessing (Ps. cxix. 39; Rom. vii. 12, xii. 2).

The moral ideal in the Bible is to do the will of God, as revealed in His law. When the rich ruler asked Christ what good thing he should do to gain life, Christ immediately directed him to the Decalogue (Mt. xix. 17 ff.). In a lawless and unloving world, Christians must resist the temptation to do as they are done by, and in face of evil must seek out and hold fast in their conduct that 'good' which the law prescribes (Rom. xii. 9, 21; 1 Thes. v. 15, 21).

e. Obedience to God's commands is good: for God approves and accepts it (1 Tim. ii. 3), and those who yield it profit by it (Tit. iii. 8).

Unredeemed men do not and cannot obey God's law, for they are in bondage 'under sin' (Rom. iii. 9 ff., viii. 7 f.). The evil tree (man as he is in Adam) must be made good before its fruit can be good (*cf.* Mt. xii. 33–35). But those who are in Christ have been freed from sin's bondage precisely in order that they may practise the righteousness which the law prescribes (Rom. vi. 12–22). The characteristic New Testament phrase for this obligatory Christian obedience is 'good works'. The performance of good works is to be the Christian's life's work; it was for this that God saved him (Eph. ii. 10; Col. i. 10; 2 Cor. ix. 8; Tit. ii. 14; Mt. v. 14–16). The Christian is called to be ready for every good work that his circumstances admit of (2 Tim. ii. 21; Tit. iii. 1), so that it is a damning indictment of a man's Christian profession when he is 'unfit for any good work' (Tit. i. 16; *cf.* Jas. ii. 14–26). Good works are the Christian's adornment (1 Tim. ii. 10); God takes pleasure in them, and will reward them (Eph. vi. 8).

Good works are good from three standpoints: they are done (i) in accordance with a right standard (the biblical law: 2 Tim. iii. 16 f.); (ii) from a right motive (love and gratitude for redemption: 1 Thes. i. 3; Heb. vi. 10; *cf.* Rom. xii. 1 ff.); (iii) with a right aim (God's glory: 1 Cor. x. 31; *cf.* 1 Cor. vi. 20; Mt. v. 16; 1 Pet. ii. 12). They take the form of works of love towards God and men, since 'love is the fulfilling of the law' (Rom. xiii. 8–10; *cf.* Mt. xxii. 36–40). This does not, of course, mean that no more is required of a Christian than a right motive; the point is, rather, that the particular acts which the commandments prescribe are to be understood as so many expressions of love, so that without a loving heart the commandments cannot be fulfilled. It is not that a right spirit excuses lapses from the letter of the law, but that rectitude in the letter is no fulfilling of the law where an attitude of love is lacking. The truly good man is no less than the truly righteous man; for, as the truly righteous man observes the spirit as well as the letter of the law (*cf.* Mt. v. 18–20), so the truly good man observes its letter as well as its spirit. Nor is the truly good man any more than the truly righteous man. In Rom. v. 7, where Paul for a moment sets the good man above the righteous man in value, he is speaking popularly, not theologically. The world thinks of righteousness as a merely negative rectitude, and of the kindness and generosity that mark the good man as something more than righteousness; but biblical theology effectively identifies righteousness with goodness, and goodness with righteousness, by insisting that what the law requires is, in fact, love.

Good works, then, are works of love, and the nature of love is to give to the beloved. Love to God is expressed in the gift of personal devotion, however costly (*cf.* Mary's 'good work', Mk. xiv. 3–6). Love to men is expressed by doing them 'good', laying out one's own resources to relieve their need, and seeking their welfare in every possible way (Gal. vi. 9 f.; Eph. iv. 29; *cf.* Pss. xxxiv. 14, xxxvii. 3, 27). The Jerusalem church's poor-relief system (Acts ii. 44 f., iv. 34 ff.), and Paul's collection for the saints (*cf.* 2 Cor. vii–ix) illustrate this. 'Kind', 'generous', are among the ordinary secular meanings of 'good' as a description of persons (*cf.* 1 Sa. xxv. 15; 1 Pet. ii. 18); the Bible comprehends them in the Christian ethic, making the love of God and Christ the model and standard for the kindness and generosity required of Christians (*cf.* Eph. v. 1 f.; Jn. xiii. 14, 34).

The believer who seeks thus to fulfil the law has a 'good conscience' (Acts xxiii. 1; 1 Tim. i. 5, 19; Heb. xiii. 18; 1 Pet. iii. 16, 21)—not because he thinks himself sinlessly perfect, but because he knows that his relationship with God is right, being founded on true faith and repentance. Such a Christian will appear to his fellows as a 'good man' (so Barnabas, Acts xi. 24).

BIBLIOGRAPHY. *Arndt, s.v. agathos, kalos*; G. Vos in *DAC*, II, 470 f.; C. F. H. Henry, *Christian Personal Ethics*, 1957, pp. 209–218.

J.I.P.

GOPHER WOOD (*'aṣê-gōper*), the wood of which Noah's ark was constructed (Gn. vi. 14). Many commentators favour an identification with cypress wood, on the ground of the similarity in name (Gk. *kyparissos*). Others, noting the similarity with Heb. *kōper* (see BITUMEN), suggest a resinous tree. It may be that the word is connected in some way with Akkadian *gubru/gudru*, '(shepherd's) reed hut', and such a cuneiform parallel is further suggested by the construct *'aṣê* which might correspond to the determinative *giš*, which precedes the names of trees and objects of wood, and which is read *iṣu* or *iṣ* in Akkadian. See *The Assyrian Dictionary*, V, 1956, p. 118.

T.C.M.

GOSHEN. 1. The territory assigned to Israel and his descendants during their Egyp. sojourn. Its exact location and extent remain uncertain, but it was certainly in Egypt (Gn. xlvii. 6, 27), and in the E Nile Delta: Gn. xlvii. 6 with 11 clearly equate Goshen with 'the land of Rameses', so named from the residence-city Pi-Ramessē, biblical Ra'amses (*q.v.*), in the NE Delta. The LXX's topographical interpretations are of uncertain authenticity. The E Delta would be suitably 'near' the court (Gn. xlv. 10) for Joseph serving his (probably Hyksos) pharaoh at Memphis (*q.v.*, near Cairo) or Avaris (NE Delta), *cf.* also Gn. xlvi. 28, 29; likewise for Moses interviewing his pharaoh at Pi-Ramessē (Ex. vii–xii). Goshen was a well-favoured region suited to flocks and herds (Gn. xlvi. 34, xlvii. 1, 4, 6, 27, l. 8). It remained the habitat of the Hebrews until the Exodus, being therefore largely shielded from the plagues (Ex. viii. 22, ix. 26); nevertheless, contact was close with Egyptians living in the same general region (*e.g. cf.* Ex. xi. 2, 3, xii. 35, 36). The name *Gsmt* occurring in certain Egyptian texts, once equated with Heb. Goshen through LXX Gesem, should be read *Šsmt* and is therefore irrelevant.

2. A district in the south of Palestine (Jos. x.

41, xi. 16), probably named after **3**, a town in the hills of S Palestine (Jos. xv. 51), possibly near Ẓāhiriyeh, *c.* 12 miles south-west of Hebron (so Abel), or else somewhat farther east (*GTT*, 1959, §§ 285–287, 497). See also GEDER. K.A.K.

GOSPEL (Gk. *euangelion*, 'good news'). In classical literature the word designated the reward given for good tidings, and its later transference to the good news itself belongs to the New Testament and early Christian literature. Even in the LXX its only definite occurrence (2 Sa. iv. 10) carries the classical meaning. That it is found more than seventy-five times in the New Testament suggests a distinctly Christian connotation. The gospel is the good news that God in Jesus Christ has fulfilled His promises to Israel, and that a way of salvation has been opened to all. The gospel is not to be set over against the Old Testament as if God had changed His way of dealing with man, but is the fulfilment of Old Testament promise (Mt. xi. 2–5). Jesus Himself saw in the prophecies of Isaiah a description of His own ministry (Lk. iv. 16–21).

Mark defines the 'gospel of God' in i. 14 (AV, following the Byzantine text, adds 'of the kingdom') as 'The time is fulfilled, and the kingdom of God is at hand.' To believe means salvation: to reject is damnation (Mk. xvi. 15, 16). This same gospel is proclaimed by the first heralds of Christianity, but now the essential message is made more explicit by the death and resurrection of Jesus the Christ. While the gospel came with Jesus (or, rather, the Christ-event *is* the gospel), it was anticipated in God's promise of blessing to Abraham (Gal. iii. 8) and promised in prophetic Scripture (Rom. i. 2).

The gospel not only comes in power (1 Thes. i. 5) but *is* the power of God (Rom. i. 16). It reveals the righteousness of God and leads to salvation all who believe (Rom. i. 16, 17). Paul regards the gospel as a sacred trust (1 Tim. i. 11). Thus he is under divine compulsion to proclaim it (1 Cor. ix. 16), and requests prayer that he may carry out his task with boldness (Eph. vi. 19), even though this involves opposition (1 Thes. ii. 2) and affliction (2 Tim. i. 8). The gospel is 'the word of truth' (Eph. i. 13), but it is hidden to unbelieving men (2 Cor. iv. 3, 4) who demand supernatural verification or rational proof (1 Cor. i. 21–23). Even as it was by revelation that the full theological impact of the gospel came to Paul (Gal. i. 11, 12), so also is it by the response of faith that the gospel breaks in with saving power (Heb. iv. 2).

The use of 'Gospels' as a designation of the first four books of the New Testament is post-biblical (2nd century AD).

BIBLIOGRAPHY. C. H. Dodd, *The Apostolic Preaching and its Developments*, 1936; R. H. Mounce, *The Essential Nature of New Testament Preaching*, 1960; C. Friedrich in *TWNT*, II, pp. 705–735; R. H. Strachan, 'The Gospel in the New Testament', *IB*, VII, pp. 3 ff.

R.H.M.

GOSPELS. The plural form 'Gospels' (Gk. *euangelia*) would not have been understood in the apostolic age, nor yet for two generations following; it is of the essence of the apostolic message that there is only one true *euangelion*; whoever proclaims another, says Paul, is anathema (Gal. i. 8 f.). The four records which traditionally stand in the forefront of the New Testament are, properly speaking, four records of the one gospel—'the gospel of God . . . concerning his Son' (Rom. i. 1–3). It was not until the middle of the 2nd century AD that the plural form came to be used; thus Justin Martyr says that the 'memoirs composed by the apostles' are called 'Gospels' (*First Apology* 66). Earlier writers use the singular, whether they are referring to a single gospel-writing or to a set of such writings (*cf. Didache* viii. 2; Ignatius, *Philadelphians* viii. 2). The traditional titles of the four records imply that in them we have the gospel or good news about Christ according to each of the four Evangelists. And the usage of the singular form to denote the fourfold record continued for long after the earliest attested instance of the plural.

I. THE ORAL STAGE

Most of the material in our Gospels existed for a considerable time in an oral stage before it was given the written form with which we are familiar.

a. The words of Jesus

Jesus began His Galilaean ministry by 'preaching the gospel of God'; the content of this gospel was that the time appointed had arrived and the kingdom of God had drawn near; He urged His hearers to repent and believe the good news (Mk. i. 14 f.; *cf.* Lk. iv. 18–21). His preaching was no bolt from the blue; it was the fulfilment of the promise of God communicated in earlier days through the prophets. Now, at length, God had visited His people; this was the burden not only of Jesus' preaching but of His mighty works (Lk. vii. 16), which were signs that the domain of evil was crumbling before the onset of the kingdom of God (Mt. xii. 22–29; Lk. xi. 14–22). The same theme runs through the parables of Jesus, which call His hearers to decision and watchfulness in view of the advent of the kingdom.

In addition to His public ministry, Jesus took care to give His disciples systematic instruction in a form that they could easily commit to memory. His debates with the Pharisees and other opponents, too, led to pronouncements which, once heard, would not be readily forgotten, and which in fact stood His disciples in good stead later on when they were confronted with controversial issues in which it was helpful to recall their Master's ruling.

b. The apostolic tradition

There are several references in the New Testament Epistles to the 'tradition' (Gk. *paradosis*) received by the apostles from their Lord and delivered by them in turn to their converts. This tradition, in the fullest sense, comprises the apostles' witness to 'all that Jesus began both to do and teach, until the day in which he was taken up' (Acts i. 1 f., *cf.* i. 21 f.). This witness was borne and perpetuated in various ways—principally in missionary preaching, in the teaching of converts, and in Christian worship. An outline of the basic facts of the missionary preaching is given by Paul in 1 Cor. xv. 3 ff.—'that Christ died for our sins according to the scriptures; and that he was buried, and that he rose again the third day according to the scriptures: and that he was seen' by a large number of eye-witnesses, some of whom are named, and most of whom were still alive when Paul was writing. Paul adds that whether the gospel was preached by himself or by the original apostles, the basic facts of the message were the same (1 Cor. xv. 11). This is confirmed by the evidence of the non-Pauline Epistles, and by the extracts from early Christian preaching summarized in Acts. In the preaching the saving events were announced; Jesus was proclaimed as Lord and Christ; men were summoned to repent and receive forgiveness through Him.

Some occasional samples of the teaching of converts appear in the Epistles, from which it is plain that the basis of this teaching was what Jesus Himself had taught. Thus, in giving instruction about marriage Paul quotes Jesus' commandment forbidding divorce (1 Cor. vii. 10); he similarly quotes His ruling about the maintenance of gospel preachers (1 Cor. ix. 14). But there is evidence of more systematic instruction by the catechetical method; and as the number of converts increased, especially in the course of the Gentile mission, 'schools' for the training of instructors would have become almost a necessity, and digests of the teaching of Jesus would inevitably have been drawn up, orally if not in writing. We may envisage such a life-setting for the 'sayings collection' on which Matthew and Luke drew, and at a later date the Matthaean Gospel itself has been viewed as taking shape in such a school.

In worship too the works and words of Jesus were bound to be recalled. In the earliest days of the faith those who had known Jesus could scarcely avoid saying to one another, when they met informally or at the stated occasions of fellowship and worship, 'Do you remember how our Master . . .?' In particular, the Lord's Supper provided a regular opportunity for retelling the story of His death, with the events immediately preceding and following it (1 Cor. xi. 26).

The passion narrative, indeed, being told and retold both in Christian worship and in missionary preaching (*cf.* 1 Cor. ii. 2; Gal. iii. 1), took shape as a connected whole at an early date—a conclusion which is otherwise established by the form criticism of our existing Gospels. By the form-critical method an attempt is made to isolate and classify the various self-contained units which have been brought together in the written Gospels and to envisage the living situations in which they originated and were preserved in the oral stage of transmission. (See BIBLICAL CRITICISM, § III.)

II. THE WRITTEN GOSPELS

The beginning of gospel writing, as we might expect, coincides with the end of the first Christian generation. As those who 'from the beginning were eyewitnesses and ministers of the word' (Lk. i. 2) were removed by death, the necessity of a permanent written record of their witness would be more acutely felt than before. It is just at this point that 2nd-century tradition places the beginnings of gospel writing, and rightly so: all four of our canonical Gospels are probably to be dated within the four decades AD 60–100. We need not suppose that the transmission of the apostolic witness had been exclusively oral before AD 60—some at least of the 'many' who, according to Lk. i. 1, had undertaken to draw up an orderly account of the evangelic events may have done so in writing before AD 60—but no document of an earlier date has survived except in so far as it has been incorporated in our written Gospels.

Several strands of tradition can be distinguished in the four Gospels. In this respect, as in some others, John stands apart from the other Gospels and is best considered independently. The other three Gospels are inter-related to the point where they lend themselves excellently to 'synoptic' study—*e.g.* as when their text is arranged in three parallel columns, so that their coincidences and divergences can be conveniently examined. For this reason they are commonly known as the 'Synoptic Gospels'—a designation first apparently given to them by J. J. Griesbach in 1774.

a. The Synoptic Gospels

A comparative study of Matthew, Mark, and Luke leads to the recognition that there is a considerable body of material common to all three, or to two of the three. The substance of 606 out of the 661 verses of Mark (leaving Mk. xvi. 9–20 out of the reckoning) reappears in abridged form in Matthew; some 380 of the 661 verses of Mark reappear in Luke. This may be stated otherwise by saying that, out of the 1,068 verses of Matthew, about 500 contain the substance of 606 verses of Mark, while out of the 1,149 verses of Luke some 380 are paralleled in Mark. Only thirty-one verses of Mark have no parallel in either Matthew or Luke. Matthew and Luke have each up to 250 verses containing common material not paralleled in Mark; sometimes this common material appears in Matthew and Luke in practically identical language, while sometimes the verbal divergence is considerable. About 300 verses of Matthew have no parallel in any of the other Gospels; the same is true of about 520 verses in Luke.

There is no short cut to a satisfactory account of this distribution of common and special material in the Synoptic Gospels. There is no *a priori* reason for holding one Gospel to be earlier and another later, for holding one to be a source of another and the latter to be dependent on the former. Nor will the objectivity of statistical analysis guarantee a solution. A solution can be attained only by the exercise of critical judgment after all the relevant data have been marshalled and the alternative possibilities assessed. If unanimity has not been reached after a century and a half of intensive Synoptic study, it may be because the data are insufficient for the purpose, or because the field of inquiry has been unduly restricted. Yet certain findings command a much greater area of agreement than others.

One of these is the priority of Mark and its use as a principal source by the other two Synoptic Evangelists. This finding, which may be said to have been placed on a stable basis by C. Lachmann in 1835, depends not merely on the formal evidence that Matthew and Mark sometimes agree in order against Luke; Mark and Luke more frequently against Matthew; but Matthew and Luke never against Mark (which could be explained otherwise), but rather on the detailed comparative examination of the way in which common material is reproduced in the three Gospels, section by section. In the overwhelming majority of sections the situation can best be understood if Mark's account was used as a source by one or both of the others. Few have ever considered Luke as a possible source of the other two, but the view that Mark is an abridgment of Matthew was held for a long time, largely through the influence of Augustine. But where Matthew and Mark have material in common Mark is fuller than Matthew, and by no means an abridgment; and time after time the two parallel accounts can be much better explained by supposing that Matthew condenses Mark than by supposing that Mark amplifies Matthew. While Matthew and Luke never agree in order against Mark, they do occasionally exhibit verbal agreement against him, but such instances mainly represent grammatical or stylistic improvements of Mark, and are neither numerous nor significant enough to be offset against the general weight of the evidence.

The common Markan element in the Synoptic tradition is the more important because of the close relation between the framework of Mark and the apostolic preaching. This relation does not depend so much on the tradition which sees in Peter the authority behind the Markan narrative (a tradition borne out by internal evidence in certain sections of the narrative) as on the fact (demonstrated by C. H. Dodd) that an outline of the primitive preaching, comparable to those outlines which can be discerned in a few passages in the New Testament Epistles and in the reports of speeches in Acts, supplies the thread on which Mark has strung his several units of gospel material.

The material common to Mark and one or both of the other Synoptic Gospels consists mainly of narrative. (The principal exceptions to this are the parables of Mk. iv and the eschatological discourse of Mk. xiii.) On the other hand, the non-Markan material common to Matthew and Luke consists mainly of sayings of Jesus. One might almost say that the Markan material relates what Jesus did; the non-Markan material, what Jesus taught. We have here a distinction comparable to that commonly made (albeit to an exaggerated degree) between apostolic 'preaching' (*kērygma*) and 'teaching' (*didachē*). The non-Markan material common to Matthew and Luke may conveniently, and without prejudice, be labelled 'Q', in accordance with a sixty-year-old custom.

This body of material, extending to between 200 and 250 verses, might have been derived by the one Evangelist from the other, or by both from a common source. Few, if any, can be found to suggest that Matthew derived it from Luke, although some would find it easier to suppose this than to suppose that Luke derived it from Matthew. This latter supposition continues to receive widespread support, but it is specially vulnerable because it implies that Luke reduced to relative disorder the orderly arrangement in which the 'Q' material appears in Matthew, without giving any plausible reason why this should have been done.

The supposition that the 'Q' material was derived from a common source by Matthew and Luke involves fewer difficulties than any alternative supposition.

When we attempt to reconstruct this postulated common source we must beware of thinking that we can do so in anything like a complete form. Yet what we can reconstruct of it reminds us forcibly of the general pattern of the prophetical books of the Old Testament. These books commonly contain an account of the prophet's call, with a record of his oracles set in a narrative framework, but with no mention of his death. So the 'Q' material appears to have come from a compilation which began with an account of Jesus' baptism by John and His wilderness temptations; this forms the prelude to His ministry, and is followed by groups of His sayings set in a minimum of narrative framework; but there is no trace of a passion narrative. There are four main groups of teaching, which may be entitled: (i) Jesus and John the Baptist; (ii) Jesus and His disciples; (iii) Jesus and His opponents; (iv) Jesus and the future.

Since our only means of reconstructing this source is provided by the non-Markan material common to Matthew and Luke, the question whether Mark also made some use of it cannot be satisfactorily answered. That it is earlier than Mark is probable; it may well have been used for catechetical purposes in the Gentile mission based on Antioch. The fact that some of the 'Q' material in Matthew and Luke is almost verbally identical, while elsewhere there are divergences of language, has sometimes been explained in terms of there being two distinct strands of tradition in 'Q,' but a much more probable account is that 'Q' was translated into Greek from Aramaic and that Matthew and Luke sometimes use the same translation and sometimes different ones. In this regard it is apposite to recall the statement of Papias (*apud* Eus., *EH* iii. 39) that 'Matthew compiled the *logia* in the Hebrew [Aramaic] speech, and everyone translated them as best he could'. *Logia* ('oracles') would be a specially appropriate term for the contents of such a compilation as we have tried to recognize behind the 'Q' material.

What other sources were utilized by Matthew and Luke is an even more uncertain question than the reconstruction of the 'Q' source. Matthew appears to have incorporated material from another sayings-collection, parallel to 'Q' but preserved in Judaea rather than in Antioch—the collection conveniently labelled 'M'. Luke has embodied a block of quite distinctive material (found largely between chapters ix and xviii) which may have been derived from Caesarea—the material labelled 'L'. Whether these 'sources' had a written form before they were taken over by the Evangelists is doubtful. Luke has been pictured as amplifying his copy of the 'Q' source by means of the information acquired in Caesarea and elsewhere, thus producing the preliminary draft of his Gospel sometimes called 'Proto-Luke', into which at a later date blocks of Markan material were inserted; but the evaluation of the 'Proto-Luke' hypothesis belongs rather to the special article on LUKE, GOSPEL OF. In general, it may be agreed that Matthew conflates his sources while Luke combines his. The nativity narratives which introduce Matthew and Luke lie outside the general scheme of Synoptic criticism; with regard to them some dependence on Semitic documents cannot be excluded. But it must be emphasized that, fascinating and instructive as Gospel source criticism is, the Gospels themselves are much more important than their putative sources. It is good to consider what sources the Evangelists may have used; it is better to consider what use they made of their sources. Each of the Synoptic Gospels is an independent whole, no mere scissors-and-paste compilation; each has its own view of Jesus and His ministry, and each has its special contribution to make to the full-orbed picture of Jesus with which the New Testament presents us.

b. The Fourth Gospel

John represents a good primitive tradition which was preserved independently of the Synoptic lines of tradition, not only in the memory of the beloved disciple but in a living Christian community, quite probably in the milieu from which at a rather later date came the *Odes of Solomon*. The large area of common background which John shares with the Qumran texts, and the links binding its structure to the Palestinian synagogue lectionary, have in recent times helped to impress upon us that the Johannine tradition has its roots in Jewish Palestine, however much the requirements of a wider Hellenistic audience were borne in mind when this Gospel was given its literary form at the end of the first Christian century. And the fixed outline of the apostolic preaching can be discerned in the Fourth Gospel 'no less clearly than in Mark' (C. H. Dodd, *The Apostolic Preaching and its Developments*, 1950, p. 69). See JOHN, GOSPEL OF.

III. THE FOURFOLD GOSPEL

At an early date after the publication of the Fourth Gospel the four canonical Gospels began to circulate as a collection, and have continued to do so ever since. Who first gathered them together to form a fourfold corpus we do not know, and it is quite uncertain where the fourfold corpus first became known—claims have been made for both Ephesus and Rome. Catholic and Gnostic writers alike show not only acquaintance with the fourfold Gospel but recognition of its authority. The Valentinian *Gospel of Truth* (*c.* AD 140–150), recently brought to light among the Gnostic writings from Chenoboskion (*q.v.*), was not intended to supplement or supersede the canonical four, whose authority it presupposes; it is rather a series of meditations on the 'true gospel' which is enshrined in the four (and in other New Testament books). Marcion stands out as an exception in his repudiation of Matthew, Mark, and John, and his promulgation of Luke (edited by himself) as the only authentic *euangelion*. The documents of the anti-Marcionite reaction (*e.g.* the anti-Marcionite prologues to the Gospels and, later, the Muratorian Canon) do not introduce the fourfold Gospel as something new, but reaffirm its authority in reply to Marcion's criticisms.

In the half-century following AD 95 Theodor Zahn could find only four gospel citations in surviving Christian literature which demonstrably do not come from the canonical four. That the 'memoirs of the apostles' which Justin says were read in church along with the writings of the prophets were the four Gospels is rendered the more probable by the fact that such traces of gospel material in his works as may come from the pseudonymous Gospels of Peter or Thomas are slight indeed compared with traces of the canonical four.

The situation is clearer when we come to Justin's disciple Tatian, whose Gospel harmony or *Diatessaron* (compiled *c.* AD 170) remained for long the favourite (if not the 'authorized') edition of the Gospels in the Assyr. Church. Apart from a small fragment of a Gk. edition of the *Diatessaron* discovered at Dura-Europos on the Euphrates and published in 1935, our knowledge of the work has until recently been indirect, being based on translations (some of them secondary or tertiary) from the Syr. text. But in 1957 a considerable portion of the Syr. original of Ephraem's commentary on the *Diatessaron* (written about the middle of the 4th century) was identified in a parchment manuscript in A.

Chester Beatty's collection; when this text is published by L. Leloir it will no doubt throw valuable light on the early history of the *Diatessaron*.

Tatian began his compilation with Jn. i. 1–5, and perhaps ended it with Jn. xxi. 25. It was the fourfold Gospel that supplied him with the material for his harmony; such occasional intrusions of extra-canonical material as can be detected (possibly from the 'Gospel according to the Hebrews') do not affect this basic fact any more than do the occasional modifications of the Gospel wording which reflect Tatian's Encratite outlook. (See CANON OF THE NEW TESTAMENT.)

The supremacy of the fourfold Gospel which Tatian's work attests is confirmed a decade or so later by Irenaeus. To him the fourfold character of the Gospel is one of the accepted facts of Christianity, as axiomatic as the four quarters of the world or the four winds of heaven (*Adv. Haer.* iii. 11. 8). His contemporary Clement of Alexandria is careful to distinguish 'the four Gospels that have been handed down to us' from uncanonical writings on which he draws from time to time, such as the 'Gospel according to the Egyptians' (*Miscellanies* iii. 13). Tertullian does not even draw upon such uncanonical writings, restricting himself to the canonical four, to which he accords unique authority because their authors were either apostles or men in close association with apostles. (Like other western Christian writers, he arranges the four so as to make the two 'apostolic' Gospels, Matthew and John, precede Luke and Mark.) Origen (*c.* AD 230) sums up the long-established catholic attitude when he speaks of 'the four Gospels, which alone are undisputed in the Church of God beneath the whole heaven' (*Commentary on Matthew* in Eus., *EH* vi. 25. 4). (Like Irenaeus, Origen arranges them in the order with which we are familiar.)

All four of the Gospels are anonymous in the sense that none of them includes its author's name. The first reference to Matthew and Mark as Evangelists is found in Papias, bishop of Hierapolis in Phrygia in the first half of the 2nd century AD. His statement, made on the authority of 'the elder', that 'Mark, the interpreter of Peter, wrote down accurately all the words or deeds of the Lord of which he [Peter] made mention, but not in order . . .', is certainly a reference to our second Gospel. His statement about Matthew's compilation of *logia* (quoted above, under II) is more problematic, and it is still disputed whether it refers to our first Gospel, or to a collection of the sayings of Jesus (as has been suggested in this article), or to a catena of messianic prophecies, or to something else. The earliest explicit references to Luke and John as Evangelists come in the anti-Marcionite Gospel prologues (which to some extent at least draw upon Papias's lost work) and Irenaeus. The latter sums up the account which he had received as follows: 'Matthew put forth a Gospel writing among the Hebrews in their own speech while Peter and Paul were preaching the gospel in Rome and founding the church there. After their departure, Mark, Peter's disciple and interpreter, has likewise delivered to us in writing the substance of Peter's preaching. Luke, the companion of Paul, set down in a book the gospel proclaimed by that apostle. Then John, the disciple of the Lord, who reclined on His bosom, in turn published his Gospel while he was staying in Ephesus in Asia' (*Adv. Haer.* iii. 1. 1).

Without endorsing all that Irenaeus says, we may heartily agree with him that in the canonical Gospels we have the apostolic witness to the redemptive revelation of God in Christ preserved in a fourfold form. (See articles on the four Gospels.)

BIBLIOGRAPHY. K. Aland and others, *Studia Evangelica*, 1959; C. H. Dodd, *The Apostolic Preaching and its Developments*, 1936; *id.*, *History and the Gospel*, 1938; T. W. Manson, *The Sayings of Jesus*, 1949; *id.*, *Studies in the Gospels and Epistles*, 1961; D. E. Nineham (ed.), *Studies in the Gospels*, 1955; J. H. Ropes, *The Synoptic Gospels*, 1934; W. Sanday, *The Gospels in the Second Century*, 1876; B. de Solages, *A Greek Synopsis of the Gospels*, 1959; V. H. Stanton, *The Gospels as Historical Documents*, 3 vols., 1903–20; B. H. Streeter, *The Four Gospels*, 1924; R. V. G. Tasker, *The Nature and Purpose of the Gospels*, 1944; V. Taylor, *The Gospels*[9], 1960; *id.*, *The Formation of the Gospel Tradition*, 1933.

F.F.B.

GOSPELS, APOCRYPHAL. See NEW TESTAMENT APOCRYPHA.

GOURD. 1. AV rendering of Heb. *qîqāyôn*, a plant which the Lord prepared for Jonah, 'that it might be a shadow over his head' (Jon. iv. 6). Its identification has been much disputed. Many scholars, following RVmg ('Palma Christi'), RSVmg, Pliny, and Herodotus, assume it to be the castor-oil plant (*Ricinus communis*; the *krotōn* of the Greeks) which will wither, as Jonah's did, even after only slight handling. Others, starting from LXX (Gk. *kolokyntha*), suggest the bottle-gourd (*Cucurbita lagenaria*; Arab. *ḳar'ah*), which is more adequate botanically, since the biblical context requires a vine rather than a small tree like the castor-oil plant. The reference may therefore be to such a 'lodge' as sheltered watchmen over the cucumbers (see CUCUMBER), and which would also be subject to rapid withering.

2. The 'wild gourds' (Heb. *paqqu'ōṯ*, 'bursters') mentioned in 2 Ki. iv. 39 were from a poisonous plant not exactly defined, but consensus of opinion favours the colocynth (*Citrullus colocynthis*). Resembling the cucumber in smell and appearance, the colocynth is a cathartic, an irritant poison, but a useful medicine when carefully administered. J.D.D.

GOVERNMENT.

1. In the Old Testament.

During the Old Testament period the people of God lived under various types of government.

The Patriarchs might be called semi-nomads. The father was the head of the family and its priest. His jurisdiction extended not only over the members of the immediate family but also over all who were in his employ or subject to him. This type of government was similar to that of the Bedouin nomads of Arabia. In the head of the family (*i.e.* of the clan) there resided even the power of life and death as well as that of making various decisions (*cf.* Jdg. xi. 11 ff.).

In Egypt the descendants of Jacob were in bondage until they were brought forth from the land by Moses. Moses acted as the representative of God, and the people listened to him. At this time also there were officers of the people, although it is difficult to say just how the Israelites were organized in relationship to Egypt. The organization of Sinai was unique in that it consisted in the formation of the tribes into a theocracy (*i.e.* 'the rule of God'—*theos*, 'god'; *kratos*, 'power', 'rule'). This type of government is without parallel, for it is a divinely revealed arrangement. Its essence is set forth in Ex. xix. 5, 6. Primarily it was a rule of God over a nation that was to be holy and a kingdom of priests.

In the wilderness there were elders of the people who assisted Moses in his tasks. The plan of the theocracy was presented to them and they accepted it. God was to rule and He would rule through the agency of a human king. This king should 'reign in righteousness', in that he should give decisions in accordance with strict justice and manifest in his rule the righteousness of God. The people were to be separate from the rest of the world, for they were holy, belonging unto God Himself.

For a time the nation was not ready to accept the full implications of the theocracy. Under Joshua it was necessary that they should obtain possession of the land that had been promised to them. For a time there were rulers or judges over them, but there was no central organization. This condition led them to realize that they must have a king. Their request for a king, however, was made in an untheocratic spirit, for they merely wanted to be like the nations round about them. For this reason Samuel reproached them with having rejected the Lord Himself (1 Sa. viii. 7).

The nation therefore needed not merely to learn that it must have a king but also that it must have the right kind of king. The first king chosen was a man who did not follow the Lord, and for that reason was rejected. In David there was found the man after God's own heart. David rendered the decisions of a more important kind, but minor decisions were left to under-officers. Some of these offices are mentioned in the Scriptures, namely the priests, officers of the household, the cup-bearer, one over the vestry (2 Ki. x. 22), master of the household (1 Ki. iv. 6), scribes, recorders, counsellors, chief of the army, and chief of the king's guard (2 Sa. viii. 18). The ministers of the king served in the administration of the affairs of the state (1 Ki. iv. 2 ff.).

Solomon divided the kingdom into twelve districts, over each of which he placed a prefect to provide victuals for the king and his house (1 Ki. iv. 7 ff.). The Exile brought about a termination of the theocracy, which had long before ceased to be a theocracy in actual fact. After the Exile the Jews were subject to Persia, and were represented by elders and princes, and these were subject to the priests. This same arrangement continued under the Greek period, although at this time a council of elders is introduced. Indeed, the high priest now became a prince of the nation. Thus the nation continued until the time of Herod the Great.

The central point of the theocracy was the Temple, which symbolized the dwelling-place of God in the midst of His people. Thus, Jerusalem, the city in which the Temple was located, became known as the holy city. The formal destruction of the theocracy occurred when the Temple was burned. E.J.Y.

2. In the New Testament.

I. THE SITUATION IN PALESTINE

The land was largely partitioned among a number of republican states (*e.g.* Caesarea and the cities of the Decapolis). This was a device used by the successive supervisory powers, and especially the Romans, to hellenize the population and thus contain Jewish nationalism. The less tractable areas (*e.g.* Galilee) were entrusted to Herodian princes, while Jerusalem itself and its neighbourhood were under the Sanhedrin, a council drawn from the religious aristocracy. The whole complex of governments was supervised in the interests of Roman frontier security by the Caesars, acting at different stages either through a Herodian client king or through a personal deputy, the procurator. Jewish nationalism found institutional expression in a series of religious sects, whose attitudes to the government ranged from terrorism (the Zealots) to detachment (the Essenes), on the one hand, and collaboration (the Sadducees), on the other. All were dedicated in their own way to the restoration of the kingdom.

a. The career of Jesus

Jesus was inextricably involved in this confusion of government. He was attacked at birth (Mt. ii. 16) as a threat to Herod's throne, and denounced in death as a pretender to royal power (Jn. xix. 21). He was dogged on all sides by pressures to avow this goal. The devil's advances (Mt. iv. 9) were mirrored in popular enthusiasm (Jn. vi. 15), the obtuse arrogance of the disciples (Mt. xvi. 22 f.), and the fears of those who precipitated the arrest (Jn. xi. 50). Faced with such a consensus of misconstruction, Jesus generally avoided the claim to kingship, but did not conceal it from the disciples (Lk. xxii. 29, 30) and in the end owned it publicly (Jn. xviii. 36, 37).

b. The teaching of Jesus

Three main assertions about the relation of the kingdom of heaven to temporal government may be singled out. (i) The kingdom of Jesus is not of the same order as the temporal powers. It is not established by political action (Jn. xviii. 36). (ii) Temporal power is not autonomous: it is enjoyed only by permission of God (Jn. xix. 11). (iii) The temporal power therefore has its rights, as does God (Lk. xx. 25): both must be conceded.

c. The church in Jerusalem

After the resurrection the disciples were again instructed in the nature of the kingdom (Acts i. 3). Their view of it was still narrowly political, however (Acts i. 6), and even after the ascension the preaching of Jesus' exaltation at God's right hand (*e.g.* Acts ii. 32–36) was capable of political overtones (Acts v. 31), and certainly taken as politically provocative by the Sanhedrin (Acts v. 33 ff.). The apostles defied a cour order restraining their preaching on the grounds of their prior duty to God (Acts v. 29). The prosecution of Peter and James (Acts xii. 2, 3) may have been political, but in the cases of Stephen (Acts vi. 11) and Paul (Acts xxi. 28) the offences were religious, and reflect the transformation of the Nazarenes into a regular sect of the Jewish religion, differentiated perhaps chiefly by the added sanction that the kingship of Jesus had lent to the law (Jas. ii. 5, 8).

II. THE HELLENISTIC STATES

All the places outside Palestine where churches were established were, along with Rome itself, republican states, either satellites of the Romans or actual Roman colonies. Christians might thus become involved either with the local administration (*e.g.* Acts xvi. 19–21, xvii. 6, 22) or with the superintendent Roman governors (*e.g.* Acts xiii. 7, xviii. 12). The tendency to refer difficult cases to the Roman authority, however, meant that the attitude of that government became the major concern.

a. Support for the government

The only case where Christians were accused of direct opposition to the Caesars (Acts xvii. 7) was fobbed off by the authorities responsible. In all other known cases the charges were not political, and the various governments showed a reluctance to pursue them. Christian writers reciprocated this respectful *laissez-faire* (Rom. xiii. 1–7; 1 Tim. ii. 2; Tit. iii. 1): the teaching of Jesus was elaborated to show that the 'powers that be' (*exousiai*) not only had their authority allowed by God but that they were positively 'God's ministers' for the punishment of evil; to oppose them was to oppose God. This attitude was sustained even (as happened under Nero) when the courts were being used for fabricated charges; the legitimacy of government was studiously defended, while its victims were solaced with the innocent sufferings of Christ (1 Pet. ii. 11–25). Some have held that the restrainer of antichrist (2 Thes. ii. 6–8) is meant to be the Roman government.

b. Criticism of the government

Even Paul had some reservations, however. The responsibility for the crucifixion rests on 'the princes of this world' (1 Cor. ii. 8). Saints must not settle their disputes in civil courts, because their destiny is to 'judge the world' (1 Cor. vi. 2). Attention is repeatedly drawn to the rule of the 'only Potentate, the King of kings' (1 Tim. vi. 15), and the citizenship of the republic that transcends all the barriers of earthly states (*e.g.* Eph. ii. 19). The demonic powers (*archai* or *exousiai*) over whom Christ has triumphed (Col. ii. 15) and with whom we now struggle (Eph. vi. 12) may well be conceived of as the forces behind human government. This is certainly the theme taken up in detail in the Revelation, which envisages a struggle for world government between God and satanic powers. The allusions to the ruler cult (Rev. xiii. 15) seem sufficiently plain to identify the enemy as the Roman Caesars. We know from Pliny (*Ep.* x. 96) that attempts to induce Christians to escape condemnation by making the formal offering to the ruler met with incorrigible obstinacy. They had presumably decided that they were being asked to render to Caesar the things that were God's.

BIBLIOGRAPHY. A. H. M. Jones, *The Herods of Judaea*, 1938, *id.*, *The Greek City from Alexander to Justinian*, 1940; E. Barker, *From Alexander to Constantine, Passages illustrating the History of Social and Political Ideas*, 1956; O. Cullmann, *The State in the New Testament*, 1957; E. A. Judge, *The Social Pattern of the Christian Groups in the First Century*, 1960. E.A.J.

GOVERNOR.

I. IN THE OLD TESTAMENT

Since Israel through her history was involved directly or indirectly with various civilizations, each of which had its own distinctive constitutional system and titles for those in authority, it is not surprising to find a variety of Hebrew terms, and of English translations in AV, *e.g.* 'governor', 'ruler', 'captain'. They may be classed as follows.

a. Technical words

Of these Heb. *peḥâ* (*cf.* Assyr. *paḫatu*) is the most frequent, meaning the ruler of a district under a king, *e.g.* an Assyrian provincial governor (Is. xxxvi. 9), Chaldean and Persian governors (Ezk. xxiii. 6, 23; Est. iii. 12, viii. 9), the Persian Tatnai (Ezr. v. 3, vi. 6), whose satrapy included Palestine, Phoenicia, and Egypt; and Nehemiah and Zerubbabel as governors of Judah (Ne. v. 14; Ezr. vi. 7). The latter are also called 'Tirshatha' (Ezr. ii. 63; Ne. vii. 65, 70) the Heb. form of a Persian title (from Avestan *tarshta*, 'reverenced').

b. General words

Nine other Hebrew terms indicate authority in various spheres. *'allûp̄* (*e.g.* Zc. ix. 7, of governors of Judah), *mōšēl* (Gn. xlv. 26, of Joseph in

Egypt), and *šallîṭ* (Gn. xlii. 6, also of Joseph) are wider terms; the others have more particular references: *pāqîḏ* ('overseer', Je. xx. 1, of a priest; *cf.* Gn. xli. 34, of Egyptian officers), *ḥôqēq* ('lawgiver', Jdg. v. 9, 14), *sāḡān* ('deputy', 'lieutenant', *e.g.* Dn. iii. 2, usually translated 'ruler'), *nāśî'* (indicating social rank, 2 Ch. i. 2), *śar* ('governor of a house', 1 Ki. xxii. 26), and *nāḡîḏ* ('governor of a house', 2 Ch. xxviii. 7).

II. IN THE NEW TESTAMENT

Fewer Greek words are used, and these sometimes imprecisely, sometimes with technical accuracy.

a. Hēgoumai ('lead') and its derivatives occurs most frequently. The term is used for governors in the general sense (Mk. xiii. 9; 1 Pet. ii. 14) but more often describes Roman subordinate rulers, such as Pilate (Mt. xxvii. 2, xxviii. 14), Felix (Acts xxiii. 26), and Festus (Acts xxvi. 30), all of whom were 'procurators' under the legate of the province Syria (the official Gk. equivalent was *epitropoi*).

b. Other terms translated 'governor' appear at Jn. ii. 8 (*architriklinos*, 'controller of a feast'), 2 Cor. xi. 32 (*ethnarchēs*, 'ethnarch', *q.v.*), Gal. iv. 2 (*oikonomos*, 'steward', *cf.* Lk. xii. 42; 1 Cor. iv. 2), and Jas. iii. 4 (*euthynōn*, 'steersman').

B.F.H.

GOZAN, also called Gozar (2 Ki. xvii. 6) or Chôzār (1 Ch. v. 26), is identified with ancient Guzana, modern Tell Halaf, on the Upper Habur river. Israelites from Samaria were deported here in 722 BC (2 Ki. xvii. 6, xviii. 11). Sennacherib, in his letter to Hezekiah (2 Ki. xix. 12; Is. xxxvii. 12), refers to the heavy punishment inflicted on this Assyr. provincial capital when it rebelled in 759 BC. Excavations in 1899, 1911–13, and 1927 (M. von Oppenheim, *Tell Halaf*) produced tablets of the 8th–7th centuries BC, in which W Semitic names may attest, or explain, the presence of the Israelite exiles (*AFO* Beiheft 6). D.J.W.

GRACE, FAVOUR.

I. IN THE OLD TESTAMENT

a. Vocabulary

Grace involves such other subjects as forgiveness, salvation, regeneration, repentance, and the love of God. 'There are "grace-words" which do not contain the word "grace"' (Moffatt); see Dt. vii. 7, ix. 4–6. The two 'grace-words' are: (i) *ḥeseḏ*. This is translated in AV as 'mercy' (149 times), 'kindness' (38), 'lovingkindness' (30), and 'goodness' (12). Luther translates it by *Gnade*, the German word for 'grace'. Despite that, it is not quite the equivalent of grace. It is a two-way word, and can be used of God and man. Of God, it certainly implies grace. Of man, it implies steadfast love to another human being or to God. It is often found in association with the word 'covenant', and denotes the attitude of faithfulness which both parties to a covenant should observe. For God's *ḥeseḏ*, see La. iii. 22; for man's, Ho. vi. 6. Snaith suggests 'covenant love' as the nearest English equivalent. (ii) *ḥēn*. This is not a covenant word and not two-way. It is used of the action of a superior, human or divine, to an inferior. It speaks of undeserved favour, and it is translated 'grace' (38) and 'favour' (26). Examples of man's *ḥēn* are found in Gn. xxxiii. 8, 10, 15, xxxix. 4; Ru. ii. 2, 10. God's *ḥēn* is found in Je. xxxi. 2. No-one can show *ḥēn* to God (as one can show *ḥeseḏ*), for no-one can do Him a favour.

b. The law

(i) Jn. i. 17 puts the law into sharp antithesis with grace. See Tit. ii. 11, which also states that grace came into the world with Christ. That does not mean that grace was non-existent in the Old Testament, but merely that it is not in the foreground, and that it is concerned chiefly with Israel. The Bible often uses antithesis where we would use comparison. (ii) The idea of promise is developed in the New Testament in Galatians (iii. 16–22) and in Hebrews. It shows that grace is prior to law. God dealt with the Patriarchs as individuals by way of promise, and with the nation as a whole by way of law. The law was not primary, but it clarified and emphasized the kind of *ḥeseḏ* that God expected of His covenant people. (iii) Grace is found, however, in the law itself. The election of Israel to be God's people is attributed in the law to God's free choice, and not to Israel's righteousness (Dt. vii. 7, 8; *cf.* viii. 18). The initiative in the Sinai covenant comes from God, just as much as did the covenant of grace with Abraham. Then there is the statement of the converting or restoring power of the law in Ps. xix.

c. The prophets

Repentance is the chief point of interest in the prophetic writings. Typical passages are Am. v. 14; Ho. ii. 7, vi. 1, xiv. 1; Is. i. 16–18; Je. iii. 1, 7, 12–14. The prophets are often accused of a doctrine of repentance which lays stress on human will-power, as did the Pelagian heresy. But the prophets regarded repentance as inward (Joel ii. 13). Ezekiel, who demanded that the individual should make himself a new heart (xviii. 31), also recognized that a new heart can only be a gift of God's grace (xxxvi. 26). With this agrees the 'new covenant' passage in Je. xxxi. 31–34.

d. The Psalms

The word *ḥēn* is almost absent from the Psalms, though its cognates appear. *Ḥeseḏ* is very often found, *e.g.* Pss. v. 7, xxiii. 6, lvii. 3 (all translated 'mercy'), lii. 1 ('goodness', but translated 'mercy' in verse 8), lxxxix. 33 ('lovingkindness'). In the Psalms also is found the increasing use of the cognate word *ḥāsîḏ*, which is found in, *e.g.*, Ps. xii. 1 ('godly man'), lxxix. 2 ('saints'), lxxxvi. 2 ('holy'). The plural of this word (*ḥᵃsîḏîm*) appears as 'Hasidaeans' in 1 Macc. ii. 42, vii. 13; 2 Macc. xiv. 6; it really meant those who were loyal to the covenant, the rigorous, devout, law-keeping party in Judaism, from whose ranks came the Pharisees.

II. IN THE NEW TESTAMENT

a. Vocabulary

Gk. *charis* was the normal word used to translate Heb. *ḥēn*. The nearest corresponding verb, *charizesthai*, was used to denote forgiveness, human as well as divine (Col. ii. 13, iii. 13; Eph. iv. 32). *Eleos* represents the Heb. *ḥeseḏ* and has the meaning of 'mercy'. It is not used very often, and occurs largely in passages based on the Old Testament, such as Rom. ix. 15–18, 23, xi. 30–32. 'Grace' is preferred to 'mercy', because it includes the idea of the divine power which equips a man to live a moral life.

b. The Synoptic Gospels

Quite apart from the word *charis*, which is never placed on the lips of Jesus, the idea of grace is very prominent. Jesus says that He came to seek and save the lost. Many of His parables teach the doctrine of grace. The parable of the labourers in the vineyard (Mt. xx. 1–16) teaches that God is answerable to no-one for His gifts of grace. The parable of the great supper (Lk. xiv. 16–24) shows that spiritual privilege does not ensure final bliss, and that the gospel invitation is to all. The prodigal son was welcomed by his father in a way he did not deserve (Lk. xv. 20–24). Repentance is stressed as a condition of salvation (Mk. i. 15, vi. 12; Lk. xxiv. 47). Faith also has its place (*e.g.* Mk. i. 15; Lk. vii. 50), although there is no theological statement on Pauline lines.

c. The writings of Luke

Both the Gospel and the Acts need special attention. Luke shows flexibility in dealing with the subject. Even the non-religious sense of the noun, of a favour done by one man to another, appears (Acts xxiv. 27, xxv. 3, 9). The Old Testament sense of 'favour' is seen in Lk. i. 30, ii. 52; Acts ii. 47, vii. 10, 46. The dynamic sense of grace resulting in fearless courage and effective witness is seen in Acts iv. 33, xi. 23, xiii. 43 and is used in the context of the universal appeal of the gospel. Luke also brings together, in a way that even Paul does not, the terms 'gospel' ('word') and 'grace' (Lk. iv. 22; Acts xiv. 3, xx. 24).

d. The Pauline Epistles

The word 'grace' has a prominent place in the opening greetings and the closing benedictions of the Epistles, being added to the conventional greeting of 'peace'. The basis of Paul's doctrine is found in Rom. i. 16–iii. 20. Man is shown as a sinner, but by grace he is justified (Rom. iii. 21–iv. 25), *i.e.* God in His grace treats him, though guilty, as if he had never sinned.

Faith (*q.v.*) is the human response to divine grace (Rom. v. 2, x. 9; Eph. ii. 8). This faith is the gift of God (Eph. ii. 8); the words 'not of yourselves' may refer to *sesōsmenoi* ('saved'), but Paul is seeking to point out that the word 'faith' must not be thought to imply some independent action on the part of the believer. See also 2 Cor. iv. 13; Phil. i. 29. This faith, although it implies that there is no salvation through the law, is not unethical. Faith is morally vital by itself. It 'works by love' (Gal. v. 6). C. Anderson Scott (*Christianity according to St. Paul*, 1927, p. 111) says that from the moment that faith was active a transformation of ethical outlook was ideally there.

The believer's position in grace is explained, not by anything in himself, but by the will of God. The doctrine of election (*q.v.*) has two functions: it checks human independence and self-righteousness, and shows that in bestowing favour God is perfectly free (Eph. i. 1–6; 2 Tim. i. 9; Tit. iii. 5). Every step in the process of the Christian life is due to grace—Gal. i. 15 (call); 2 Tim. ii. 25 (repentance); Eph. ii. 8, 9 (faith). In Rom. viii. 28–30 Paul surveys the divine agency from the call to the final glory of the redeemed. He does not, however, overlook man's responsibility. Obedience (Rom. i. 5, vi. 17) is a moral attitude, and cannot be made anything else. A man of himself turns to the Lord (2 Cor. iii. 16). A. Stewart in *HDB* suggests that 1 Thes. iii. 5 teaches that even perseverance is doubted. The two sides are brought together in Rom. ix–x. Chapter ix contains the strongest possible statements of double predestination, while chapter x states that rejection by God is due to unbelief and disobedience, and quotes two 'whosoever' passages. It must be remembered, however, that the primary subject of these chapters is not personal salvation, but the collective functions of those chosen by God to carry out His purpose.

Romans vi uses the figure of baptism to teach the conquest of sin by grace. See also 1 Cor. vi. 11, xii. 13; Eph. v. 26; Col. ii. 12; Tit. iii. 5. H. Wheeler Robinson (*The Christian Doctrine of Man*, 1926, pp. 124–125) holds that believers' baptism is not merely illustrative symbolism but the objective aspect of what is subjectively faith. Others would argue that infant baptism is a means of grace, because the child is a symbol of human inability and helplessness. These views seem to contradict the unvarying Pauline emphasis on faith.

e. The other New Testament writings

It is sufficient briefly to mention the following:

(i) 1 Peter. The apostle emphasizes grace in chapters i, ii by means of the usual variants of covenant election and inheritance; iii. 7 has the unusual phrase 'the grace of life'. Grace is also used in v. 10 in relation to the future glory of the believer.

(ii) Hebrews. The writer uses most of the 'grace-words'. In ii. 9 the grace of God is related to the sufferings of Christ. The word *charis* is used in xii. 28 of human thankfulness to God. Grace is viewed as a calling to consecration in xii. 14, 15. The striking phrase 'the throne of grace' in iv. 16 unites the divine majesty and grace. Another fresh phrase, in x. 29, is 'the Spirit of grace'.

(iii) The Johannine writings. There is surprisingly little directly about grace, but God's love is emphasized throughout. The idea of grace must be related to that of 'eternal life'. Faith is prominent, and John uses a Gk. phrase *pisteuein eis* (believe *into*) of real faith in Christ's person (see FAITH). The 'grace and truth' which characterize the glory of the incarnate Word in Jn. i. 14 (*cf.* verse 17) echo the 'mercy and truth' (*ḥeseḏ we'ᵉmeṯ*) of Ex. xxxiv. 6. (John i. 17 has already been mentioned.)

We conclude with Moffatt that the religion of the Bible 'is a religion of grace or it is nothing . . . no grace, no gospel' (*Grace in the New Testament*, p. xv).

BIBLIOGRAPHY. H. Wheeler Robinson, *The Christian Doctrine of Man*, 1926; N. H. Snaith, *The Distinctive Ideas of the Old Testament*, 1944; J. Moffatt, *Grace in the New Testament*, 1931; N. P. Williams, *The Grace of God*, 1930.

J.H.Sr.

GRAFTING. See OLIVE.

GRAIN (Heb. *ṣᵉrôr*, 'pebble', Am. ix. 9; Gk. *kokkos*, 'kernel', Mt. xiii. 31, *etc.*). The AV rendering nearly always denotes the singular form—*e.g.* 'a grain of mustard seed'. See AGRICULTURE and articles on individual cereals.

GRAPES. See WINE AND STRONG DRINK.

GRASS (Heb. *ḥāṣîr, deše', yereq, 'ēśeḇ*; Gk. *chortos*).

Gn. i. 11 records that the earth brought forth grass on the 'third day' of the creation narrative. In the promised land it provided food for cattle; it would be given to the land by God in response to the people's obedience (Dt. xi. 15). It was the portion of Nebuchadrezzar during his madness (Dn. iv. 15, 25).

Green pastures are not of permanent occurrence in Palestine, but last only for a while after the rains, withering in the dry season. As a result, grass is a fitting symbol of the transitoriness of human life (*e.g.* Ps. ciii. 15; Is. xl. 6, 7), of the brief sway of the rich man (Jas. i. 10, 11), and is a figure of weakness, of perishing enemies (Is. xxxvii. 27 = 2 Ki. xix. 26), of the wicked soon to be cut down (Ps. xxxvii. 2), and of haters of Zion (Ps. cxxix. 6).

The multitude of blades is likened to a multitude of people (Jb. v. 25; Is. xliv. 4) and to a flourishing people (Ps. lxxii. 16), and the luxuriance of green pastures is likened to serenity in the spiritual life (Ps. xxiii. 2). In tender grass can be seen a quality of the just ruler (2 Sa. xxiii. 4), and a benevolent ruler is as refreshing and productive of good as rain upon mown meadows (Ps. lxxii. 6).

In contrast, a barren locality without grass can indicate God's wrath (Dt. xxix. 23). R.A.H.G.

GRASSHOPPER. See LOCUST.

GRAVE. See BURIAL AND MOURNING.

GRAVEN IMAGE. See IMAGE.

GREAVES. See ARMOUR AND WEAPONS.

GREECE. Who the Greeks were is a famous crux. Their language is Indo-European and its earliest known location is in the Mycenaean states of the Peloponnesus (as established by the recent decipherment of the Linear B script) in the second millennium BC. When they emerge into history well into the first millennium they belong indifferently to either side of the Aegean.

The first flowering of the two institutions that became the hallmarks of hellenism, speculative philosophy and republican government, apparently occurred on the Ionian coast of Asia Minor. Ionia is perhaps the Old Testament Javan (Is. lxvi. 19). The area of Greek settlement was never static. The republics were early established throughout the Black Sea, Sicily, and S Italy, and as far west as Marseilles and Spain. After Alexander there were Greek states as far east as India. Under Seleucid and more especially Roman control the wealthy and ancient nations of Asia Minor and the Levant were systematically broken up into many hundreds of Greek republics, leaving only the most backward regions under the indigenous royal or priestly governments. This political fragmentation was always characteristic of the Greeks, as was the consequent subordination to foreign powers. Greece was never a political entity. 'The king of Grecia' (*yāwān*, Dn. viii. 21) must be one of the Macedonian rulers, Alexander or a Seleucid, who controlled the affairs of many but by no means all Greek states. 'Greece' (*Hellas*) in Acts xx. 2 must refer to the Roman province of Achaia, which, while it contained many ancient Greek states, was now almost a backwater of hellenism.

On the other hand, the ever-increasing diffusion of Greek institutions brought unification at a different level. The whole of the eastern Mediterranean and much beyond was raised to the common norm of civilization that hellenism supplied. Both the opulence of the states and the degree of standardization are attested by the splendid ruins that indiscriminately litter these parts today. The ideal of a free and cultivated life in a small autonomous community, once the boast of a few Aegean states, was now almost universally accepted. Athens was still a home of learning, but Pergamum, Antioch, and Alexandria, and many others in the new world, rivalled or eclipsed her.

The states provided not only education but brilliant entertainment and a wider range of health and welfare services than most modern communities. It was membership in such a republic and use of the Greek language that marked a man as civilized (Acts xxi. 37–39). Such a person might be called a Greek, whatever his race (Mk. vii. 26); all others were 'barbarians' (Rom. i. 14). The term 'Grecian' (*hellēnistēs*) in Acts vi. 1, ix. 29 presumably shows that this distinction applied even within the Jewish ethnic community. In Acts xi. 20, however, it refers more probably to non-Jews, for whom the term 'Greek' (*hellēn*) in Acts xviii. 17; Rom. i. 16, *etc.* is the regular New Testament usage, being virtually equivalent to 'Gentile'. Greeks were frequently associated with the synagogues as observers (Jn. xii. 20; Acts xiv. 1, xvii. 4, xviii. 4), but the exclusiveness of Israel as a nation was jealously preserved. It was the agonizing delivery of the gospel from this constricting matrix that marked the birth of the Christian religion in its universal form. The translation from Hebrew into Greek opened the gospel to all civilized men. It also produced the New Testament. See also MACEDONIA, ACHAIA, ATHENS.

BIBLIOGRAPHY. A. H. M. Jones, *The Greek City from Alexander to Justinian*, 1940; H. D. F. Kitto, *The Greeks*, 1951; G. Dix, *Jew and Greek*, 1953. E.A.J.

GREEK. The language of the New Testament, Hellenistic or *koinē* Greek, is to be distinguished from its ancient classical counterpart. The spread of the Athenian Gk. dialect (Attic), which from the 6th to the 4th centuries BC had supplanted other Gk. forms, brought about in time its modification and the emergence of a cosmopolitan dialect, *hē koinē dialektos*. The origin of Hellenistic Greek discloses, says Hastings (*HDB*, iii, p. 36), 'its fitness for its providential office'.

New Testament Greek employs popular idiom, and favours directness more than balance, and simplicity more than conciseness. It is marked by new words (*sēmeioō, hyiothesia, al.*), new forms, grammatical differences and modified meanings. It is also considerably influenced by Hebrew and Aramaic (note especially the transliteration of Semitic words, such as *abba*, Greek words and phrases which have assumed a new meaning under Hebrew influence, and grammatical Hebraisms, many of which appear in LXX), and by Latin. See LANGUAGE OF THE NEW TESTAMENT.

BIBLIOGRAPHY. See N. Turner, 'Philology in New Testament Studies' in *ExpT*, LXXI, 1959–60, pp. 104 ff. for further discussion of the influences on New Testament Greek. S.S.S.

GREEKS. Two words are used with reference to 'Greeks' in the New Testament: *Hellēnes* and *Hellēnistai*. The term *Hellēnes* refers to the inhabitants of Greece or their descendants (*cf.* Acts xvi. 1; Rom. i. 14); but it is also used as a virtual equivalent of 'Gentile', to describe those who are not of Jewish origin (*cf.* Rom. x. 12; Gal. iii. 28).

The term *Hellēnistai* is a crux. It is confined to Acts vi. 1, ix. 29 (where A reads *Hellēnas*) and xi. 20 (as a variant reading, though *Hellēnas*, Aleph[c] A D* 1518, is probably to be preferred). C. F. D. Moule points out (*ExpT*, LXX, 1958–9, p. 100) that the objection to the traditional interpretation of *Hellēnistai* as 'Greek-speaking Jews' is that Paul, who spoke Greek, called himself *Hebraios* (Phil. iii. 5), which in Acts vi. 1 forms the contrast to *Hellēnistai*. He therefore proposes 'Jews who spoke *only* Greek' as the meaning for *Hellēnistai*, and 'Jews who, while able to speak Greek, knew a Semitic language *also*' as the meaning for *Hebraioi*.

BIBLIOGRAPHY. See also J. A. T. Robinson, 'The Destination and Purpose of the Fourth Gospel', in *NTS*, VI, 1960, pp. 117 ff. *Hellēnistai* is here interpreted as 'Greek-speaking Jews of the Diaspora, living *in* Palestine', as opposed to the *Hellēnes*, Greek-speaking Jews who lived beyond Palestine. S.S.S.

GREEK VERSIONS. See TEXT AND VERSIONS.

GREETING. See SALUTATION.

GRINDER (from Heb. *ṭāḥan*, 'to grind'). Grinding in the East is usually done by women (*cf.* Mt. xxiv. 41), but in Ec. xii. 3 the word is used also in a metaphorical sense to denote the teeth (the plain meaning of the word as translated in Jb. xxix. 17; see AVmg). For a full discussion of the Jewish poetic imagery employed here, see *ICC*, *Ecclesiastes*, pp. 186 ff. J.D.D.

GRISLED, GRIZZLED (*bārōḏ*, 'spotted'). A word meaning 'streaked with grey', used to describe goats (Gn. xxxi. 10, 12) and horses (Zc. vi. 3, 6).

GROVE. A word used in the AV forty times to translate Heb. *'ᵃšērâ* (see ASHERAH) and once (Gn. xxi. 33) to translate *'ēšel* (see TREES). This rendering follows LXX (*alsos*) and Vulg. (*lūcus*), but these versions had evidently based their translation only on a tradition or a guess, and reflect an ignorance of the real significance. T.C.M.

GRUDGE. Frequently found in the earliest translations, this word was altered to 'murmur' in most of the AV occurrences, then similarly changed in all but two of the RV passages. Where it is retained in AV several words are thus rendered, *viz.*: Heb. *nāṭar*, 'to keep anger' (Lv. xix. 18); Heb. *lûn, lîn*, 'to murmur' (Ps. lix. 15); Gk. *stenazō*, 'to groan, sigh' (Jas. v. 9); Gk. *gongysmos*, 'grudging', 'murmuring' (1 Pet. iv. 9); Gk. *ek lypēs*, 'grudgingly', 'out of grief' (2 Cor. ix. 7). J.D.D.

GUARD. In the Old Testament the word translates four Heb. terms. 1. *ṭabbāḥ*. The word originally denoted the royal 'slaughterers' (*BDB*), but later came to mean guardsmen or bodyguard and was used of the pharaoh's bodyguard (Gn. xxxvii. 36, xxxix. 1) and of Nebuchadrezzar's bodyguard (2 Ki. xxv. 8–10). The Carites (AV wrongly 'captains') were the royal bodyguard, consisting of Cherethites or Philistines (2 Ki. xi. 4, 19). 2. *Mišma'aṯ*, from *šāma'*, 'hear', 'respond', the attitude of an obedient body of subjects, was sometimes the name given to the bodyguard (2 Sa. xxiii. 23; *cf.* 1 Sa. xxii. 14; RV 'council', RSV 'bodyguard'). 3. *Mišmār* denotes 'guard', 'watch', or 'guardhouse' in a camp (Lv. xxiv. 12; Nu. xv. 34), or 'guard-post' (Ne. vii. 3). 4. *Rāṣîm*, lit. 'runners', were the runners of the king who acted also as the royal bodyguard (1 Sa. xxii. 17; *cf.* 1 Ki. i. 5, xiv. 27). See FOOTMAN.

'Guard' occurs once in the AV New Testament (Acts xxviii. 16), but the text is disputed (see CAPTAIN). The Temple (*q.v.*) had its own police department known as the Temple Guard, who were mostly Levites and whose task, among other things, was to keep out the forbidden Gentile (*cf.* Mt. xxvii. 65, RSV). The Mishnah lists twenty-four guard-points. The *spekoulatōr*, a Latinism found in Mk. vi. 27, was one of ten such officers attached to a legion who acted mostly as couriers but sometimes as executioners. In Mk. vi. 27 the word means 'executioner' in a non-legionary sense. J.A.B.

GUDGODAH. One of four places grouped together as having been visited by the Israelites during their wanderings, in the neighbourhood of Kadesh-barnea (Dt. x. 7); see DEUTERONOMY. In Nu. xxxiii. 33 it is written Hor-ha-gidgad ('the cave (?) of Gidgad'; LXX 'the mountain of Gadgad', reading *har* for *ḥōr*). Perhaps near modern Wadi Ḫadaḫid. G.T.M.

GUEST, -CHAMBER. See HOSPITALITY.

GUILT. See SIN, SACRIFICE AND OFFERING.

GULF (Gk. *chasma*, 'chasm', from *chainō*, 'to gape' or 'yawn'). Found only in the parable of Lazarus and Dives (Lk. xvi. 19–31), this word is sometimes connected with an ill-defined rabbinical belief that the souls of righteous and wicked exist after death in different compartments of Hades (see J. M. Creed, *The Gospel according to St. Luke*, 1942, pp. 212–213), with no road between them, but so situated as to allow the inhabitants of each to see those of the other. There is, however, insufficient evidence for this application of the word. Any interpretation, moreover, must take into account the Oriental love of imagery, for which full scope is provided by a subject such as this (which in various forms was a common feature of the writings of classical antiquity).

The passage seems to imply also that the gulf is seen in this earthly life, in which the respective conditions of Lazarus and Dives are reversed. Abraham, after outlining this aspect, is made to say, 'In all these things' (verse 26 RVmg) '. . . there is a great gulf fixed.' It seems clear that the gulf is in character as well as in condition, otherwise the false impression would be given that some stigma attaches to riches in themselves. The story reminds us that it is of the very essence of the gospel that there is between believers and unbelievers a fundamental difference in this world and in the next. See also LAZARUS AND DIVES, ABRAHAM'S BOSOM. J.D.D.

H

HABAKKUK. See Habakkuk, Book of.

HABAKKUK, BOOK OF.

I. OUTLINE OF CONTENTS

The prophecy attributed to Habakkuk consists of six sections.

a. i. 1–4. The prophet cries to God because of the lawlessness he sees around him and asks how long it will go unpunished.

b. i. 5–11. As if in reply, God announces that He is raising up the Chaldeans and describes the fierceness of their armies and their contempt for all who stand in their way.

c. i. 12–17. But if God is holy, how can He allow the brutal inhumanity and idolatry of the Chaldeans, whose atrocities are worse than the evils that they are sent to punish?

d. ii. 1–5. The prophet waits in imagination upon his watchtower to see if God will resolve his dilemma. The answer comes in the asseveration of the principle that the pride of the Chaldean will be his downfall and the faithfulness of the righteous will be his salvation.

e. ii. 6–20. A taunt-song (*māšāl*) addressed to the Chaldeans, consisting of a series of five woes predicting dire consequences upon them for the acts of inhumanity for which they are responsible.

f. iii. 1–19. If this psalm of Habakkuk has any connection with the theme of the earlier chapters it describes the revelation of God coming in His awful majesty to bring judgment upon the nations and salvation to His people.

II. AUTHORSHIP

So little is known of the prophet Habakkuk that anything that is written about him must be conjectural and based on internal evidence. His name may be connected with a Heb. root meaning 'embrace' (*ḥ-b-q*) or with an Assyr. plant name, *ḫambaḳuḳu*. The Gk. form of his name is *Hambakoum*. The suggestions that he was the son of the Shunammite woman of 2 Ki. iv. 16, or the watchman of Is. xxi. 6, have as little evidence to support them as the tradition associating him with Daniel in the lions' den (so Bel and the Dragon, verses 33 ff.).

III. DATE AND BACKGROUND

There has been considerable discussion among scholars about which if any of these sections are original to Habakkuk, and there is no agreement with regard to unity, authorship, and date. The only clear historical reference is to the Chaldeans in i. 6 and so the prophecy is usually dated at the close of the 7th century BC shortly after the battle of Carchemish (605 BC) when the Chaldeans routed the Egyptians under Pharaoh Necho on the fords of the Euphrates and marched westwards to subjugate Jehoiakim of Judah. The theory of Duhm and C. C. Torrey that 'Chaldeans' (Heb. *kaśdîm*) should read 'Kittim' in the sense of 'Greeks' was based on the problematical i. 9 (Heb. literally 'the eagerness of their faces is *eastwards*'). This would fit in better with Alexander's invasion from the west (and a 4th-century date) than with Nebuchadrezzar's from the north or east. But the text of i. 9 is extremely difficult; there is no textual evidence for the reading 'Kittim' in i. 6; and the traditional dating is to be preferred.

IV. THE PROPHET'S MESSAGE

A unity of theme may be observed throughout the book, though whether this is due to 'the molding influence of liturgical use' (Irwin) or to unity of authorship cannot be known. Habakkuk deals with the moral problem of God's raising up of the Chaldeans to inflict His judgment upon Judah, when their cruelty and barbarity are a denial of His righteousness. The answer given in ii. 4 is that a man's arrogance carries within it the seed of his ruin, whereas the faithful man is assured of living in the light of God's favour. Clearly the full Pauline meaning of faith is not to be found in this oft-quoted scripture (*cf.* Rom. i. 17; Gal. iii. 11; Heb. x. 38); indeed, it is doubtful whether Pauline faith could have been expressed by any Heb. word. But the New Testament gives a legitimate development of the prophet's thought through the medium of the LXX translation, *pistis*.

The Commentary on Habakkuk of the Dead Sea Scrolls interprets i. 4–ii. 20 only in the light of the history of the Qumran sect and throws no light on the meaning of the prophecy. Although on i. 6 and elsewhere it reads 'This means the Kittim', there is no suggestion that the original 'Kasdim' was in need of emendation.

Bibliography. S. R. Driver, *The Minor Prophets*, *Century Bible*, 1906; C. C. Torrey, 'The Prophecy of Habakkuk', in *Jewish Studies in Memory of George A. Kohut*, 1935; W. A. Irwin, 'The Psalm of Habakkuk', *JNES*, I, 1942, pp. 10–40; P. Humbert, *Problèmes du Livre d'Habacuc*, 1944.

J.B.Tr.

HABOR. A river (the modern Ḫâbûr) which carries the waters of several streams draining the Mardin area to the middle Euphrates. It ran through the Assyr. province of Gozan (*q.v.*) (*n*ᵉ*har gôzān*, 'river of Gozan') and was one of the locations to which the Israelites were deported by the Assyrians (2 Ki. xvii. 6, xviii. 11; 1 Ch. v. 26). T.C.M.

HACHILAH (Heb. *ḥᵃḵîlâ*, 'drought'). A hill in the wilderness of Judah where David was hidden when the Ziphites plotted to betray him to Saul (1 Sa. xxiii. 19, xxvi. 1, 3). The site is uncertain, but generally regarded as being near Dahret el-Kôlâ, between Ziph and En-gedi. J.D.D.

HADAD. The name of a Syrian deity meaning 'the Thunderer' (Heb. *hᵃḏaḏ*; Assyr. *Ḫaddu*) who was the Amorite equivalent of the god of storms Baal (so Ras Shamra texts) also written Adad,

Fig. 98. The storm-god Hadad, or Adad, on the back of a bull with forked-lightning in his hands. From Arslan Tash, Syria, 8th century BC.

Adda, Addu. A Hadad temple at Aleppo is known. The personal names Hadad, and their dialectal variant Hadar, are probably abbreviations of names compounded with this divine element (see HADADEZER, BEN-HADAD, HADAD-RIMMON). There is as yet no evidence to support the view that Hadad was a specifically Edomite name, although it was borne by four rulers of that country.

1. The grandson of Abraham, being the son of Ishmael (Gn. xxv. 15 = 1 Ch. i. 30). The *MT* Hadad is supported by LXX readings, while the AV 'Hadar' follows the Syr. and other MSS.

2. A son of Bedad who came from Avith and defeated the Midianites in the plain of Moab. He was succeeded as king of Edom by Samlah (Gn. xxxvi. 35, 36; 1 Ch. i. 46).

3. A later king of Edom, named Hadar in 1 Ch. i. 50, whose native village was Pau.

4. An Edomite of the ruling family who lived in the time of Solomon. He was a young child and fled to Paran when Joab murdered his family after Judah's conquest of Edom. He took refuge in Egypt, where he married the pharaoh's daughter, his son Genubath being brought up at the Egyptian court. When Hadad heard of the death of David and Joab he returned to Edom and plotted against Solomon (1 Ki. xi. 14–22, 25).

BIBLIOGRAPHY. S. Moscati (ed.), *Le Antiche Divinità Semitiche*, 1958, pp. 30 ff. (under Adad). D.J.W.

HADADEZER. This Aramaean personal name, meaning '(the god) Hadad is my helper', was borne by at least two kings of the Damascus region. It is sometimes written 'Hadarezer', perhaps reflecting an Aramaic dialectal variant, in 2 Sa. x. 16–19; 1 Ch. xviii. 3–8 (see HADAD).

Hadadezer, son of Rehob, was king of Zobah, east of Hamath, whose territory at one time included part of the bank of the river Euphrates (2 Sa. viii. 3). He was defeated by David and the gilded shields of his bodyguard taken as trophies to Jerusalem together with booty from the towns of Betah and Berothai in his territory, despite the advance of reinforcements from Damascus. Following this reversal his old enemy, Toi of Hamath, sent gifts to David (verse 10). However, Hadadezer continued to rule his territory and later supported the Ammonites in force in their war with David (2 Sa. x. 16–19; 1 Ch. xviii. 3–8). When the Israelites again defeated the Syrian forces Rezon, a refugee from the court of Hadadezer, became king in Damascus and plotted against Solomon (1 Ki. xi. 23; see REZON).

A Hadadezer (Assyr. *Adad-'idri*), king of Damascus, is named as one of the allies who, with Ahab of Israel, opposed Shalmaneser III at Qarqar in 853 BC (*DOTT*, pp. 47, 48). See BEN-HADAD. D.J.W.

HADAD-RIMMON. The mourning in Jerusalem on the death of Josiah in battle with Necho II of Egypt in 609 BC is compared with that 'of Hadad-Rimmon in the valley of Megiddon' (Zc. xii. 11). It is commonly supposed to be the name of a place near Megiddo and thus to be identified with the modern Rummaneh, south of that city. However, the form of the name meaning '(the god) Hadad is (the god) Rimmon', and the context, may show that it is a composite name. Both elements mean 'the thunderer' and are local names or epithets for Baal, and such a name can be compared with the deity Rashap-Shalmon. The allusion would then be to the great mourning normally associated with this deity personifying the elements in ceremonies at Megiddo, and perhaps a counterpart to that described in Jdg. xi. 37–40 (*DOTT*, p. 133). D.J.W.

HADES. See ESCHATOLOGY, HELL.

HADRACH. A city on the northern boundaries of Syria mentioned in Zc. ix. 1. Usually equated with the Hatarikka of the Assyr. inscriptions, once the seat of a district governor, it is located near Qinneṣrin, some 16 miles south of Aleppo (*HUCA*, XVIII, 1944, p. 449, n. 108). J.D.D.

HAGAR. A Semitic, not an Egyptian, name and thus perhaps given to the woman by Abraham when he left Egypt. It may mean 'flight' or something similar, *cf.* Arab. *hegira.* Hagar was an Egyptian bondservant in Abraham's household, handmaid to Sarah; Abraham probably acquired her during his visit to Egypt. With the passing years Abraham felt keenly the lack of a son and heir, and, after the war of the kings (Gn. xiv), with magnificent faith believed God's promise that he would indeed have a son (Gn. xv. 2–6). But as time still passed, Abraham and Sarah had doubts, and sought to gain an heir by their own unsanctioned efforts: in accordance with the customary law of the period (attested in tablets from Ur and Nuzi), the childless Sarah urged Abraham to have a son by her servant Hagar—so Ishmael was born, the son of a slave-woman (Gn. xvi). In conception, Hagar despised the barren Sarah, and fled into the desert from Sarah's wrath. At a well, God commanded her to return to her mistress and promised her numerous descendants. Awed by this experience of God, Hagar called the well 'the well of him who lives and sees me' (Beer-lahai-roi). In due course (Gn. xxi. 1–7) the promised son, Isaac, was born, the gift of God's initiative and supernatural grace. At Isaac's weaning the half-slave Ishmael mocked; God then commanded Abraham (against the custom of the day) to expel Hagar and her son (Gordon, *BA*, III, 1940, p. 3), for the line of promise was in Isaac, and God had another destiny for Ishmael (Gn. xxi. 9–14). In the wilderness the fugitive pair soon ran out of water, and Hagar sat apart from Ishmael to avoid witnessing his death. God then showed her a well of water. Ishmael grew up in Paran (in NE Sinai) as a hunter with the bow, and Hagar procured him a wife from her Egyp. homeland (Gn. xxi. 15–21).

Two millennia later, Paul had to rebuke his Galatian converts for hankering after a deceptive 'righteousness' gained by self-exertion in obeying the stipulations of the law, instead of continuing in Christ by faith (Gal. iii–v). He used the story of Hagar and Ishmael, Sarah and Isaac, as an allegory. Ishmael was the son, by earthly effort, of Hagar the slave. Similarly, the Jews (*i.e.* 'the present Jerusalem') were 'sons' of the Sinai covenant (pictured as Hagar); their failure to keep it faultlessly demonstrated the power of sin and the futility of seeking justification by self-effort. Isaac was the son of a promise received by faith, the gift of God's grace: Sarah typified the covenant of promise and grace (*cf.* Gn. xv) and all reborn spiritually in saving faith are numbered with Isaac. As Isaac was the true heir and Hagar and Ishmael were expelled, so the law as a limited phase in God's plan of redemption was in due time supplanted by the covenant of faith established finally and eternally in Christ (Gal. iv. 21–v. 1). K.A.K.

HAGGADAH. See TALMUD AND MIDRASH.

HAGGAI. See HAGGAI, BOOK OF.

HAGGAI, BOOK OF.

I. OUTLINE OF CONTENTS

The book contains four prophecies: i. 1–11, ii. 1–9, ii. 10–19, ii. 20–23. There is a brief narrative interlude in i. 12–15. The prophecies are all dated in the 2nd year of Darius I, *i.e.* 520 BC. This corresponds to the date in Ezr. iv. 24, v. 1, 2.

II. AUTHORSHIP AND DATE

Haggai and Zechariah are the first two named prophets after the return from exile in 537 BC. Since they are not mentioned until 520 BC (Ezr. v. 1, 2), it is often supposed that they returned with a fresh group of exiles at about this date. Neither prophet gives any indication of this, and it is equally probable that they were still children when their parents came in 537 BC. Thus Haggai would have witnessed the growing apathy during the period, and when he came of age the Spirit of God came upon him with the gift of prophecy. Apart from Ezr. v. 1, 2, there is no other reference to Haggai outside the book that bears his name.

III. THE FOUR PROPHECIES

a. i. 1–11. 6th month, 1st day. Haggai addresses Zerubbabel and Joshua as leaders. The implication of what follows is that the message was delivered publicly so that all heard. The prophet refers to the neglect of the past sixteen years, during which the people should have been rebuilding the Temple (Ezr. iii, iv). Instead they had turned to elaborating their own houses (Hg. i. 4). Meanwhile they had experienced frustrating natural disasters, which spoiled the crops and kept the people poor. These are God's reminder that they are to put first things first. The interlude (i. 12–15) shows the response of the people within twenty-four days.

b. ii. 1–9. 7th month, 21st day. Words of encouragement to those who felt that the new Temple was a poor thing beside the old one that Solomon built. The Temple in the future is destined for greater glory than it had in the past. While it is tempting to follow the AV in a direct messianic reference in verse 7, the plural verb makes the RV rendering, 'the desirable things', necessary. Haggai is speaking of gifts from Gentile peoples which would help to adorn the Temple. There was a partial fulfilment of this promise within a short time (Ezr. vi. 8, 9). Later Herod the Idumaean reconstructed the Temple and made it even more glorious. Gentiles were attracted to Judaism, and were allowed into the outer courts of the Temple when they came to worship and bring their offerings. But, as with Zc. ii. 11, 12, *etc.*, these words of Haggai come to fruition in the New Temple of Jew and Gentile alike in Christ (Eph. ii. 17–22).

c. ii. 10–19. 9th month, 24th day. Haggai draws a lesson from a point of ritual law. If a man is carrying part of the sacrificial flesh, and his clothes touch something, this thing is not thereby rendered holy. But the clothes of a man who is ritually unclean do contaminate whatever they touch. Thus uncleanness contaminates to the second degree. The Temple ruins are unclean, and they defile the nation and the things that they touch. But the laying of the fresh foundation will make all the difference, and from this time onwards the work of the people will be blessed. It is obvious that the revival had been marked by a fresh foundation ceremony (verse 18; *cf.* Ezr. iii. 10 in 536 BC), and it was customary to have more than one foundation ritual for houses and temples (see J. Stafford Wright, *The Building of the Second Temple*, 1958, p. 17). The date in ii. 18 appears to be a copyist's error, which has confused the 24th of the 6th month (i. 15) with the 24th of the 9th month when this prophecy was spoken (ii. 10).

d. ii. 20–23. 9th month, 24th day. A special promise to Zerubbabel that he will be kept safe in spite of disturbances in the Persian Empire. The reference to the signet in verse 23 is likely to be a reminiscence of the words with which Jeremiah pronounced the fate of Zerubbabel's grandfather, Jehoiachin, in Je. xxii. 24.

BIBLIOGRAPHY. G. A. Smith, *The Book of the Twelve Prophets*², II, 1928, pp. 221 ff.; H. G. Mitchell, *Haggai and Zechariah*, *ICC*, 1912.

J.S.W.

HAGIOGRAPHA. See CANON OF THE OLD TESTAMENT.

HAGRITES, HAGARITES. A wealthy tribe or confederation inhabiting an area east of Palestine which was attacked by Reuben in the days of Saul (1 Ch. v. 10, 18–22). The enmity of the Hagarites towards Israel is mentioned in Ps. lxxxiii. 6–8, but *cf.* 1 Ch. xxvii. 31. The Hagrites have been considered as descendants of Hagar by many Jewish writers; they are mentioned as an Aramaean confederation in Assyrian records (Tiglath-pileser III), and reference is also made to them in Gk. literature (Strabo, xvi. 4. 2).

R.J.W.

HAIL. See PLAGUES OF EGYPT.

HAIR. The normal Israelite custom, for both sexes, seems to have been to let the hair grow to considerable length. Absalom's luxuriant growth is recorded with apparent admiration (2 Sa. xiv. 26). It was only the weight of it that forced him to have it cut annually. Barbers are mentioned (Ezk. v. 1), but their function was to trim rather than to crop the hair. But by the New Testament period long hair was a 'shame' to a man (1 Cor. xi. 14), although Paul made that statement to a church in Greece. Women, on the other hand, wore the hair long and practically uncut in both periods. The Talmud does mention women's hairdressers, but the root of the word (*meḡadde-lā*) is 'to plait' rather than 'to cut'. Baldness was disliked, perhaps because of its possible connection with leprosy (*cf.* Lv. xiii), and evidently the youths' reference to Elisha's baldness was a studied insult. In Egypt the head and face were shaved, however, and Joseph had to comply with the local customs (Gn. xli. 14). Dark hair was admired in both sexes; but grey hair was very

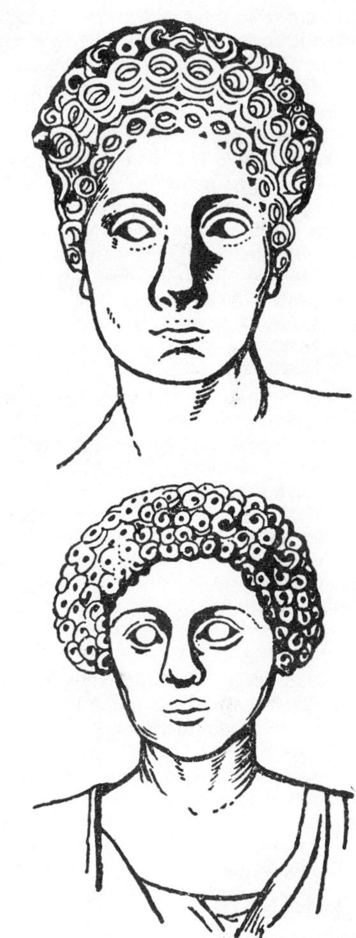

Fig. 99. Heads of Roman ladies of imperial times, illustrating methods of 'plaiting the hair' (I Pet. iii. 3). The coiffure was frequently kept in place by nets of gold thread.

honourable, and revered accordingly (see AGE, OLD AGE). Indeed, we find God Himself portrayed as having grey (or white) hair (Dn. vii. 9; *cf.* Rev. i. 14). But Herod the Great apparently preferred a youthful appearance, for he dyed his hair when it began to go grey.

The hair was treated in various ways. Samson had seven plaits, and women frequently braided or plaited their hair. Soldiers proceeding to battle let it hang loose, but to leave it unkempt was a sign of mourning; tearing it betokened fear and distress. The trimming of it had to be done in special ways; the forelock must never be cut (Lv. xix. 27), since this was a feature of some idolatrous cults (*cf.* Dt. xiv. 1). To this day orthodox Jews observe this custom; small boys can be seen with the whole head cropped close, except for the ringlets hanging at the ears. The priests were given instructions about their hair by Ezekiel (xliv. 20). The Nazirite had to leave his hair untrimmed so long as his vow lasted, and then shave it completely. This shaving signified purification (Lv. xiv. 8). Another special case was that of Samson, the secret of whose strength was his untrimmed hair.

It was a sign of hospitality to anoint a guest's head (Lk. vii. 46). The hair was frequently anointed on festive occasions (*cf.* Ps. xlv. 7). Swearing by the hair (or head) was a custom which Jesus could not commend (Mt. v. 36).

In metaphor and simile the hair was used to denote multitude, insignificance, and fineness (Ps. xl. 12; Mt. x. 29 f.; Jdg. xx. 16).

BIBLIOGRAPHY. L. Köhler, *Hebrew Man*, E.T. 1956, pp. 26 ff. D.F.P.

HALAH. A place in Assyria to which Israelites were deported from Samaria in 722 BC (2 Ki. xvii. 6, xviii. 11; 1 Ch. v. 26). Various locations have been proposed, including Ḫilakku (Cilicia), Ḫalakku (near Kirkuk), an unidentified Ḫalḫu (Strabo's Calachene, Ptolemy's Chalkitis near Gozan), the Baliḫ river or Calah. The last of these is perhaps the most probable, though philologically difficult (see Gn. x. 11), since Heb. names of this period have been found in inscriptions there. D.J.W.

HALAK (Heb. *ḥālāq*, 'smooth, bald'). A mountain (literally 'the bald mountain') in Judaea which marked the southern limit of Joshua's conquests (Jos. xi. 17, xii. 7). Its locality is described as 'going up to Seir'. Probably the modern Jebel Ḫalâq, west of the Ascent of Akrabbim. J.G.G.N.

HALL. See PRAETORIUM.

HALLEL. See HALLELUJAH.

HALLELUJAH. This is a transliteration of the Heb. liturgical call *hallᵉlû-yâh* = 'praise ye Yah', the shortened form of Yahweh (see GOD, NAMES OF), which occurs twenty-four times in the Psalter. Though it is merely one variant of several calls to praise, the fact that with one exception (Ps. cxxxv. 3) it is always found at the beginning or end of psalms, and these all anonymous and so presumably among the later ones, suggests that it had become a standardized call to praise in the temple worship.

The psalms where it is found fall into groups: (1) Pss. civ, cv (at the end), cvi (at the beginning and end, the latter being part of the doxology to the Fourth Book of Psalter). (2) Pss. cxi–cxiii (at the beginning), cxv–cxvii (at the end), LXX is almost certainly correct in placing the repetition at the end of Ps. cxiii at the beginning of Ps. cxiv, thus completing the series. (3) Ps. cxxxv, at the beginning and end, but LXX correctly places the latter at the beginning of Ps. cxxxvi. (4) Pss. cxlvi–cl, at the beginning and end of each.

From the New Testament ('Alleluia', Rev. xix. 1, 3, 4, 6) the call has been taken over into Christian worship. Most of the Hallelujah psalms play a special rôle in synagogue worship. Pss. cxiii–cxviii, the Egyp. Hallel, are sung at the feasts of Passover, Pentecost, Tabernacles, and Dedication (*qq.v.*), at the first Pss. cxiii, cxiv being sung before the meal, Pss. cxv–cxviii after the third cup (*cf.* Mk. xiv. 26). Pss. cxxxv, cxxxvi are sung on the sabbath, and the Great Hallel (Pss. cxlvi–cl), with Ps. cxlv, at all morning services. H.L.E.

HAM. 1. (*ḥām*, LXX *cham*; etym. uncertain) one of the sons of Noah, probably the second (Gn. v. 32, vi. 10, vii. 13, ix. 18; 1 Ch. i. 4, 8; though *cf.* Gn. ix. 20–24), and ancestor of many descendants (see NATIONS, TABLE OF). In 1 Ch. iv. 40 and Pss. lxxviii. 51, cv. 23, 27, cvi. 22 the name is used to indicate one section of his descent: Egypt (see MIZRAIM). From its biblical usage the term 'Hamitic' is applied by modern authors to a group of languages of which Egyptian is one, and for precision it is limited to this linguistic sense, a Hamitic 'race' not being recognized by modern anthropological classifications. In the biblical sense, however, genetic descent is all that is implied, and with the movement and intermarriage of peoples and the changes of language which took place in ancient times common descent from Ham would not necessarily imply common habitat, language, or even race in a recognizable form (see NATIONS, TABLE OF). At the end of the flood when Noah was drunk Ham saw him naked and informed his two brothers, who covered up their father. In consequence of this, Noah put a curse upon Canaan (Gn. ix. 20–27). Many explanations of this apparent cursing of Canaan for what Ham had done have been put forward, perhaps the most plausible being that Canaan did something not recorded which was worthy of cursing and that the phrase 'his younger son' (*bᵉnô haqqāṭān*, literally 'his son/grandson, the little (one)') in verse 24 might refer to Canaan (*NBC*, pp. 85, 86). This would be consistent with the twice-repeated statement (verses 18, 22) that Ham was the father of Canaan.

2. *Hām.* The name of a city whose inhabitants, the Zuzim, were smitten by Chedorlaomer in the time of Abraham (Gn. xiv. 5). The site, though probably somewhere in Transjordan, is unknown. LXX (*hama autois*) interprets the Heb. *bᵉhām* 'in Ham' as *bāhem*, 'with them'. T.C.M.

HAMAN. The villain of the Book of Esther, who plots to massacre the Jews when his vanity is hurt by Mordecai's refusal to bow to him. He is eventually hanged on the gallows that he has prepared for Mordecai. He is called an Agagite (*q.v.*). His name may be derived from the Elamite god, Hum(b)an. See also ESTHER, BOOK OF. J.S.W.

HAMATH (Heb. *ḥ*ª*maṯ*, 'fortress, citadel'). The capital of the kingdom on the banks of the Orontes, lying on one of the main trade-routes to the south from Asia Minor. Gn. x. 18 describes it as a Hamite colony. In David's time, under King Toi (or Tou), it was friendly towards Israel (2 Sa. viii. 9, 10; 1 Ch. xviii. 9, 10). Possibly the worship of Yahweh was introduced then, as Toi's son in 2 Sa. viii. 10 is called Joram ('Yahweh is exalted'), and one of Sargon's inscriptions gives the name of the king of Hamath whom he conquered as *Ia'u-bidi* (*cf. ANET*, p. 285; *DOTT*, p. 59). Solomon controlled it (2 Ch. viii. 4), and it was conquered by Jeroboam II (*c.* 780 BC, 2 Ki. xiv. 28) and Sargon (*c.* 721 BC, *cf.* 2 Ki. xviii. 33 f.; Is. xxxvi. 18 f., xxxvii. 13, 18 f.), some of its inhabitants being settled by the Assyrians in Samaria (2 Ki. xvii. 24). According to the Babylonian Chronicle, it was at Hamath that Nebuchadrezzar overtook the Egyptians fleeing from Carchemish in 605 BC (*cf.* D. J. Wiseman, *Chronicles of Chaldaean Kings*, 1956, p. 69). The city was known in Greek and Roman times as Epiphaneia; today it is *Ḥamāh*. 'The entering-in of Hamath', *i.e.* the opening from the south into the great Syrian valley between the two Lebanon ranges (but perhaps to be translated 'Labo of Hamath', *i.e.* modern Lebweh, 14 miles NNE of Baalbek), was the ideal northern boundary of Israel, *e.g.* Nu. xxxiv. 8; Jos. xiii. 5; Am. vi. 14. J.G.G.N.

HAMMEAH, TOWER OF. In Ne. iii. 1, a Jerusalem tower which stood between the Sheep and Fish Gates, probably near the north-east corner of the city. It should perhaps be equated with Hananel (*q.v.*). The Hebrew is *ham-mē'â*, meaning 'the hundred'; AV reads 'Meah', omitting the definite article, while RSV translates it literally. The name may refer to its height—perhaps 100 cubits; or to the number of its steps; or to the number of the garrison it housed. See JERUSALEM. D.F.P.

HAMMER. See ARTS AND CRAFTS.

HAMMURABI. 1. Hammurabi, king of Babylon (*c.* 1792–1750 BC), the sixth and greatest ruler of the Ist Dynasty of Babylonian kings. His name may mean 'Ammu is great'. (Ammu was the name of an Amorite or East Canaanite god.)

After the fall of the last Sumerian dynasties a number of Amorite kingdoms arose, which were often at war with one another. This unsettled situation gave a number of smaller states the opportunity of achieving independence, among them Babylon. The date of Hammurabi has presented a problem. From a tablet in the British Museum recording observations of the planet Venus for the twenty-one years of Ammiṣaduqa, the tenth king of the Dynasty, J. K. Fotheringham calculated 1921–1900 BC for his reign. When the letters from Mari revealed a synchronism between the last years of Shamshi-Adad I of Assyria and Hammurabi, it was apparent that these dates were much too high. J. W. S. Sewell made a reduction of 275 years, the cycle required for exact repetition, giving 1642–1626 BC for Ammiṣaduqa and 1792–1750 BC for Hammurabi, a reign of over forty-two years; W. F. Albright's dating is 1728–1686 BC.

The death of Shamshi-Adad, or possibly the last year of his reign, marked a turning-point in Hammurabi's career. Until his thirtieth year he maintained peaceful relations with Rim-Sin, the powerful king of Larsa, and Zimrilim of Mari. In this year he attacked and defeated Rim-Sin.

Fig. 100. Diorite head (restored) of a statue, believed to be that of Hammurabi, king of Babylon, c. 1750 BC, because of its similarity to the figure represented on that king's stele.

Some two years later he conquered and destroyed Mari, and then threatened Assyria. With the fall of Mari, the richest source of our historical information, the Mari letters, comes to an end. The reference to the help given by Hammurabi in times of calamity to subjugated lands would seem to confirm that the representation of him as a benefactor was not empty boasting. His territory stretched from the Persian Gulf (at that time much farther inland) to Mari.

The fame of Hammurabi rests, however, not on his military conquests but on his work as a law-giver and administrator. The extant copy of his famous law code is on an 8-foot-high stele of black diorite, discovered in 1902 at Susa, whence it had been carried off as booty. Three earlier collections of laws are known to us: that of Ur-Nammu in Sumerian, near the end of the third millennium; that of Bilalama of Eshnunna in Akkadian about 100 years later; and again after some 150 years that of Lipit-Ishtar, who reverted to Sumerian. Hammurabi's Code, in language and in scope, far surpasses any of its predecessors on which it draws. In its final form it is probably from his closing years, although a part of the Code was, according to the chronological lists, already in existence in his first regnal year, if the statement 'He established justice in the land' refers to the Code. If it does, then the reference would not be to the form of the Code as we know it, for here certain events mentioned in the prologue belong to the latter part of his reign. The language, Akkadian, is already grammatically fully organized and could well be termed classical. By providing a model for later generations, as did the style of Deuteronomy, it may well have proved a greater contribution to literature than to legislation. The upper part of the stele is occupied by a relief depicting Hammurabi, with his right hand raised in supplication, standing before Shamash, the sun-god, whose chief rôle was that of judge. The god, whose feet are resting on conventionalized mountains, is in the act of presenting the king with sceptre and ring. See also fig. 100.

In the lengthy prologue to the Code and the even longer epilogue, titles and high-sounding epithets abound. Hammurabi is the shepherd of the people, and a father to them. He is the protector of the weak and the defender of the oppressed. The state, he affirms, was intended to provide a public declaration of justice for all citizens.

The 282 paragraphs of the Code deal not only with criminal law but contain much that refers to civil and commercial law. The list of crimes differs but little from those found in any code, ancient or modern. One unexpected omission is a reference to homicide in general. The forms of punishments, too, are those common to all periods; capital punishment (in some case by burning, or impaling, or drowning), flogging, maiming, money and property fines. Deprivation of freedom, either by imprisonment or by exile, had not yet become a mode of punishment. Although by no means the equals of men, women nevertheless had considerable rights.

Although there are some resemblances to the Mosaic laws, there is no question of borrowing on the part of the Hebrew codes. The explanation lies in the universal similarity of crimes and their limited variety, together with the limitations in the forms of punishment. The spirit of the Hebrew laws is almost invariably more humane than that of the Babylonian (see COVENANT, BOOK OF LAWS).

Despite the great prestige of Hammurabi and his outstanding achievement in formulating this great Code, the numerous contemporary legal documents fail to provide any evidence of its practical application, or even a reference to it. The imprecations in the epilogue had apparently no effect. It is not easy to offer an explanation of this extraordinary silence. Did it prove to be only an impracticable ideal? This would tally badly with all we know of Hammurabi's executive efficiency. More probably the Code in its definitive form appeared only shortly before his death, so that he himself did not live to insist on its implementation. A late appearance of the Code would explain, too, the absence of any specific reference to it in its final form in the chronological lists. This state of affairs (see Schmökel, *op. cit.*, pp. 74 ff.), so contrary to what one would theoretically expect, shows how fallacious are the deductions concerning the late date of Deuteronomy drawn from its silence on certain matters in the levitical system.

We know practically nothing of the private life of Hammurabi, as is usually the case with rulers of the Ancient East except for the Israelite kings. We may infer from the Code that he had a strong sense of justice. From his activities in the building of temples and his provision of rich offerings, he appears to have been of a religious turn of mind. He did not, however, go through the rite of the 'sacred marriage' leading to deification. Apart from his importance as a great figure of history, his literary remains, the Code, his personal letters, and his building and dedicatory inscriptions constitute one of our most precious legacies from the ancient world. These writings prove beyond a shadow of doubt the advanced state not only of literacy but of literature many centuries before the beginnings of Hebrew literature. The former identification of Amraphel (Gn. xiv. 1) with Hammurabi of Babylon is now seriously questioned.

BIBLIOGRAPHY. S. Smith, *Alalakh and Chronology*, 1940; D. J. Wiseman, *The Alalakh Tablets*, 1953; F. M. Böhl, *King Hammurabi of Babylon in the Setting of his Time*, 1946; W. von Soden, *Herrscher im Alten Orient*, 1954; H. Schmökel, *Hammurabi von Babylon*, 1958; W. J. Martin, 'The Law Code of Hammurabi', in *DOTT*, 1958.

2. Hammurabi was the name borne, according to the Mari letters, by one or more powerful kings of Iamḫad (Aleppo) and a king of Qurda during the early second millennium BC, as well as by one of Zimrilim's officials (J. Bottéro and A. Finet, *Archives Royales de Mari*, XV, 1954, p. 145). W.J.M.

HAMOR. '(He-)ass', see below. The ruler of Shechem in the time of Jacob (Gn. xxxiii. 19–xxxiv), from whose citizens (literally 'sons', a common Sem. usage, *cf.* below) Jacob bought a plot of land (Gn. as cited; Jos. xxiv. 32). Both Hamor and his son Shechem fell in Simeon and Levi's slaughter of the Shechemite men-folk and despoliation of the city in revenge for the humiliation of their sister Dinah (*q.v.*). In the period of the judges Hamor's name was still attached to Shechem (Jdg. ix. 28). In the New Testament, in his dramatic speech to the council, Stephen telescopes Abraham's purchase of the Machpelah cave with Jacob's acquisition of the plot at Shechem—a realistic mark of the rapid flow of Stephen's impromptu, lightning exposition of Israel's history, not an error by Luke (Acts vii. 16).

Animal personal names such as Hamor, 'ass', were common in biblical lands and times. *Cf.*

Merānum ('pup'), the name of a doctor in the Mari tablets of patriarchal date (Bottéro and Finet, *Archives Royales de Mari*, XV, 1954, p. 152, refs.; compare Mendenhall, *BASOR*, 133, 1954, p. 26, n. 3). Egypt also affords many examples.

Killing an ass was sometimes part of covenant-making (Mendenhall, *op. cit.*), but to interpret the phrase 'sons of Hamor' as 'members of a confederacy'—as suggested by Albright, *Archaeology and the Religion of Israel*, 1953, p. 113—is unnecessary. 'Son' of a place or person often means simply a citizen of that place or member of that person's tribal group. *Cf.* the common phrase 'children (sons) of Israel', 'daughter of Jerusalem', as well as Assyr. usage. K.A.K.

HANANEL. In Ne. iii. 1, a Jerusalem tower, lying between the Sheep and Fish Gates, at the north-east corner of the city. It is closely connected with the Tower of Hammeah (*q.v.*), and some scholars would equate the two, or else make them two parts of the same fortress. AV spells the name 'Hananeel'; the Heb. is *ḥananʾēl*, 'God is gracious'. See JERUSALEM. D.F.P.

HANANIAH (Heb. 'Yahweh has been gracious'). A Heb. name occurring frequently in the Old Testament and, under its Gk. form Ananias (*q.v.*), in later times also.

1. A cult-prophet, son of Azur, whom Jeremiah denounced (Je. xxviii) for publicly declaring in the Temple that in two years' time, in opposition to Jeremiah's prophecy of seventy years (xxv. 12), the booty taken from Jerusalem by Nebuchadrezzar would be restored, the captives returned, and the power of Babylon broken. He confirmed his words by the symbolic action of removing from Jeremiah's neck the yoke worn as a symbol of Jeremiah's policy of submission to Babylon (xxvii. 2, 3, 12), and breaking it. Jeremiah's denunciation, 'Yahweh has not sent you' (xxviii. 15), was shown to be true by the death of Hananiah two months later.

2. Father of a prince under Jehoiakim, king of Judah, Je. xxxvi. 12. **3.** Grandfather of Irijah, the officer of the guard who arrested Jeremiah as a traitor (Je. xxxvii. 13). **4.** One of Daniel's companions in captivity, renamed Shadrach (Dn. i. 6, 7, 11, 19). **5.** Son of Zerubbabel (1 Ch. iii. 19, 21). **6.** A Benjamite (1 Ch. viii. 24). **7.** Leader of one of the groups of musicians set up by David for the service of the Temple (1 Ch. xxv. 4, 23). **8.** A captain in Uzziah's army (2 Ch. xxvi. 11). **9.** Commandant of the citadel whom Nehemiah put in charge of Jerusalem (Ne. vii. 2). **10.** Various persons figuring in the lists of Ezra-Nehemiah (Ezr. x. 28; Ne. iii. 8, iii. 30, x. 23, xii. 12, 41). J.B.Tr.

HAND. In comparison with the Gk. word *cheir* (which is translated only by 'hand', with some composite words such as *cheiropoiētos*, 'made with hands'), the two main Heb. words translated 'hand' in AV have very wide meanings. *Yāḏ* has over eighty variant translations in AV, and *kap̄* several, all of which are related to the primary meaning, 'hollow' or 'palm', from a root meaning 'curved' or 'bent'. The latter is also the name of one of the letters of the Heb. alphabet, probably descriptive of its shape, which is like a reversed C.

In common with other parts of the body in Heb. thought, the hand is described as having apparently almost autonomous functions (1 Sa. xxiv. 11; see BODY). But the balancing of the phrases 'my power' and 'the might of mine hand' in Dt. viii. 17, and other examples of parallelism, indicate that this is far from absolute autonomy, the primary reference being to the action of the whole individual, although, at the same time, attention is specifically focused on the relevant functioning part (*cf.* Mt. v. 30).

Like the arm (*q.v.*), the hand (especially the right hand) is used as a symbol of might and power. In the case of 'hand', however, the figurative meaning has gone a step further than with 'arm'. See, *e.g.*, Jos. viii. 20, where *yāḏ* is translated 'power'. There are several very common phrases in which the hand is used as a symbol of power, *e.g.* in or out of 'the hand of one's enemies' (Ps. xxxi. 15; Mk. xiv. 41). Conversely, the dropping of the hands symbolizes weakness or lack of resolution, and to strengthen them is to remedy that (Is. xxxv. 3; Jdg. ix. 24, AVmg). Left-handed persons are specially noted (Jdg. iii. 15).

Lifting the hand is symbolic of violence (1 Ki. xi. 26) as well as of supplication (Ex. ix. 33, xvii. 11; Ps. xxviii. 2), the gesture being indicative of the attitude or action. The word *kap̄*, indicating the open palm, is more frequently used in the latter sense.

Clasping hands (Jb. xvii. 3) ratified an agreement, as did also the placing of one's hand under another's thigh (Gn. xxiv. 9; see THIGH) or raising one's hand, as in a law court today (Gn. xiv. 22; Ex. xvii. 16, where 'the LORD hath sworn' is lit. 'a hand upon the throne of Yah').

The touch of a person's hands was held to communicate authority, power, or blessing, the right hand being more significant in this respect than the left, but both hands were often used (Gn. xlviii. 13, 14; Dt. xxxiv. 9). Notice especially the laying of the hands of the worshipper on the head of his sacrificial beast, where the communication of authority probably signified identity with the offering (Lv. i. 4); and the New Testament communication of the Holy Spirit or performance of miracles by the laying on of hands (Mk. vi. 5; Acts viii. 17–19, xix. 11). This is but another indication that in Hebrew thought, and to a certain extent in the New Testament as well, there was a close relation between what much Gk. and modern thought would designate separately as 'body' and 'spirit'.

'Absalom's monument' (2 Sa. xviii. 18, RV) is literally 'Absalom's hand'.

BIBLIOGRAPHY. A. R. Johnson, *The Vitality of the Individual in the Thought of Ancient Israel*, 1949; C. Ryder Smith, *The Bible Doctrine of Man*, 1951. B.O.B.

HANDBREADTH. See WEIGHTS AND MEASURES.

HANDKERCHIEF (Gk. *soudarion*, in Acts xix. 12, AV; rendered as 'napkin' in Lk. xix. 20; Jn. xi. 44, xx. 7). It transliterates Lat. *sudarium* defined etymologically (*sudor*, 'sweat') as a cloth for wiping perspiration. Catullus, however, uses the word for 'table-napkin' (xii. 14), and Nero (Suet., *Nero* xxv) undoubtedly used *sudarium* with the meaning of 'handkerchief'. E.M.B.

HANES. Is often identified with Egyp. *Ḥ(wt-nnl-)nsw*, Gk.-Lat. Heracleopolis magna, modern Ihnâsyeh el-Medîneh or Ahnâs, about 50 miles upstream (*i.e.* south) of Cairo, and an important city in Middle Egypt. However, this does not really suit Is. xxx. 4, in the two parallel clauses: 'For his princes were (RV, RSV, 'are') at Zoan, and his ambassadors came to (RV, RSV, 'are come to', 'reach') Hanes.' Zoan (*q.v.*) is Tanis in the NE Delta, the seat of the XXIInd–XXIIIrd Dynasty pharaohs, and Lower Egypt advanced-headquarters of the Ethiopian XXVth Dynasty, for Asiatic affairs. Hence the parallelism of the verse seems to demand that Hanes be closely linked with E Delta Tanis, not Upper Egypt Heracleopolis, far distant and irrelevant.

Two solutions are possible. W. Spiegelberg, *Aegyptologische Randglossen zum Alten Testament*, 1904, pp. 36–38, would postulate a 'Heracleopolis parva' in the E Delta, arguing from Herodotus' mention of a province and city of Anysis there (ii. 166, 137); this would then be Egyp. **Ḥ(wt-nnl-)nsw* of Lower Egypt, Heb. *Ḥanes*, and Assyr. *Ḫininsi*. Another explanation (Kitchen) would find even stricter parallelism in Is. xxx. 4: Hanes may merely be a Heb. transcription of an Egyp. **ḥ(wt)-nsw*, 'mansion of the king', as the name of the pharaoh's palace in Zoan/Tanis itself. Either interpretation is plausible, neither is proven. Some refer the 'his' (princes, envoys) of Is. xxx. 4 to the Judaean king; but the natural antecedent is pharaoh in verse 3. Hence, with É. Naville, *Ahnas el Medineh*, 1894, p. 3, these are pharaoh's officials at Zoan and his envoys who come to treat with the Jewish emissaries, either at Hanes as an advance-post for Zoan (Naville, Spiegelberg), or summoned to the 'Ha-nesu', the king's palace, in Zoan itself (Kitchen). K.A.K.

HANGING (EXECUTION). See GALLOWS.

HANGING, HANGINGS. See TABERNACLE.

HANNAH (Heb. *ḥannâ*, 'grace'). The favourite of the two wives of Elkanah, an Ephraimite who lived at Ramathaim-zophim (1 Sa. i). The other wife, Peninnah, tormented her because she had no family. She vowed that if she bore a son she would devote him to God as a Nazarite (*q.v.*). This she did, and named him Samuel (*q.v.*). Her song of thanksgiving (1 Sa. ii. 1–10) suggests that she was a prophetess. It contains the first mention of the king as Yahweh's Messiah ('his anointed'). There are many echoes of it in Mary's song when Christ's birth was announced (Lk. i. 46–55; see MAGNIFICAT). She was in the habit of bringing Samuel a robe every year when she came to Shiloh to worship. She later became the mother of three sons and two daughters (1 Sa. ii. 19, 21). J.W.M.

HARA. With Halah, Habor, and Gozan (*q.v.*) a place to which Tiglath-pileser III removed rebellious Israelites in 734–732 BC (1 Ch. v. 26). An Assyr. site of this name is not known. 2 Ki. xvii. 6, xviii. 11, however, interpret *hārā'* as '*cities* of the Medes' and LXX 'mountains' may represent a Heb. *hārê*, 'hill-country'. D.J.W.

HARAN (Heb. *ḥārān*; Gk. *Charrhan*). The city where Terah settled after leaving Ur (Gn. xi. 31) and from which Abram journeyed to Canaan (Gn. xii. 1). Jacob fled there to escape Esau (Gn. xxvii. 43) and met his bride (xxix. 4). The Mari texts (see ARCHAEOLOGY) tell of Amorite tribes active in the area in the early second millennium BC, which may coincide with Abraham's migration.

Harran (Assyr. *ḫarrānu*, 'main road') is situated *c.* 20 miles south-east of Urfa (Edessa) on the river Baliḫ. Excavations since 1951 show that it was occupied from at least the third millennium BC. It lay on the main route from Nineveh to the river Euphrates and Aleppo, and was a commercial centre in touch with such trading-ports as Tyre (Ezk. xxvii. 23). Its strategic position early resulted in its domination by Assyria. Adad-nirari I (*c.* 1310 BC) fortified the citadel in which Tiglath-pileser I (*c.* 1115 BC) embellished the ancient temple (É.ḫul.ḫul) of Sin, the moon-god. It was for long an Assyrian provincial capital (see TARTAN). Harran rebelled and was sacked in 763 BC, an event used by Rabshakeh (*q.v.*) to intimidate Jerusalem (2 Ki. xix. 12 = Is. xxxvii. 12). The city was restored by Sargon II, and the temple repaired and refurnished by Esarhaddon (675 BC) and by Ashurbanipal. After the fall of Nineveh (612 BC) Harran became the last capital of Assyria until its capture by the Babylonians in 609 BC. The Chaldean Dynasty's interest in the Babylonian temples led to the restoration of the Sin temples at Harran and at Ur. At the former the mother of Nabonidus (who died aged 104), and at the latter his daughter, were made the high-priestesses.

The existing ruins are mainly from the Roman city near which the Parthians slew Crassus (53 BC) and from the later occupation by Sabaean and Islamic rulers in Harran, then called Carrhae. In Acts (vii. 4) the city is named Charran. See also *AS*, I, 1951, pp. 77–111, VIII, 1958, pp. 35–92. D.J.W.

HARARITE. A designation applied to some of David's heroes: Shammah (*šammā'*) son of Agee, who was possibly the same as Shammah (*šammâ*) (2 Sa. xxiii. 11, 33); Jonathan son of Shage (1 Ch. xi. 34); and Ahiam son of Sacar (1 Ch. xi. 35). The name is unknown outside the

Bible, and may be that of a tribe or city, or may simply mean 'mountain dweller' from *har*, 'mountain, hill'. T.C.M.

HARE. The hare (*'arnebet*) is mentioned only as prohibited meat (Lv. xi. 6; Dt. xiv. 7): 'the hare cheweth the cud but divideth not the hoof'. The hare is clearly not a ruminant, but the frequent movement of the mouth and nose might give the appearance of chewing the cud. An Arab. name for it is *'arneb*, and this suggests that the translation 'hare' may be correct. G.C.

HARLOT. See PROSTITUTION.

HAR-MAGEDON (*WH Har Magedon*; TR *Armageddon*; Lat. *Hermagedon*; Syr. Gwy. *Magedon*). The assembly-point in the apocalyptic scene of the great Day of God Almighty (Rev. xvi. 16; unknown elsewhere). If it is symbolic, geographical exactness is unimportant. The earliest known interpretation, extant only in Arabic, is 'the trodden, *level* place (Arab. *'lmwḍ' 'lwṭy* = the Plain ?)' (Hippolytus, ed. Bonwetsch). Of four modern interpretations, namely, 'mountain of Megiddo', 'city of Megiddo', 'mount of assembly' (C. C. Torrey), and 'his fruitful hill', most scholars prefer the first. The fact that the tell of Megiddo was about 70 feet high in John's day, and was in the vicinity of Carmel Range, justifies the use of Heb. *har*, used loosely in the Old Testament for 'hill' and 'hill country' (*BDB*, p. 249; *cf.* Jos. x. 40, xi. 16, RSV). The 'waters of Megiddo' (Jdg. v. 19) and the 'valley-plain of Megiddo' (2 Ch. xxxv. 22, RSV) have witnessed important battles, from one fought by Tuthmosis III in 1468 BC to that of Lord Allenby of Megiddo in 1917. The 'mountains of Israel' witness Gog's defeat in Ezk. xxxix. 1, 4. This may be in the writer's mind. R.J.A.S.

HAROD (*ḥ^arōḏ*, 'trembling'). The spring where Gideon selected, by their manner of drinking its water, those who would go to attack the Midianites (Jdg. vii. 1–7); probably modern 'Ain Jalud. The terrain around the spring emphasized the suitability of the test which Gideon imposed; see G. A. Smith, *The Historical Geography of the Holy Land*, 1931, pp. 397 ff. This may have been the spring where Israel camped prior to the battle on Gilboa (1 Sa. xxix. 1). A tradition says that it was here David slew Goliath. M.A.M.

HAROSHETH. A Canaanite stronghold in the north-west, the headquarters of Sisera (Jdg. iv. 2, 13, 16). It is explicitly called 'Harosheth of the nations' at each reference, and apparently marked the limit of Israelite penetration at the time. Jos. xii. 23b may refer to it (LXX B reads 'in Galilee' for the inexplicable *MT* 'in Gilgal'; see *GTT*, pp. 279 f.). Tell el-Harbaj, a commanding site overlooking the right bank of the Kishon, 2 miles below the ford on the main coastal road skirting Carmel, is most probable; it covered 6 acres, the latest important remains being Late Bronze. Albright prefers Tell el-'Amr, farther upstream, near El-Haritiyeh, which preserves the name.

BIBLIOGRAPHY. J. Garstang, *Joshua–Judges*, 1931, pp. 296 ff., 380 f.; *BSAJ* Bulletins, II, 1922, p. 12, and IV, 1924, p. 46; *GTT*, p. 288. J.P.U.L.

HARP. See MUSIC AND MUSICAL INSTRUMENTS.

HARROW. A toothed implement dragged along the ground to break clods of earth after ploughing. The verb (Heb. *śāḏaḏ*) always occurs parallel to verbs of ploughing or breaking the soil (Jb. xxxix. 10; Is. xxviii. 24; Hos. x. 11, AV 'break'). The actual form of the implement used is uncertain; it was drawn by a led ox (Jb. xxxix. 10, RV), but there is no known representation of anything corresponding to a modern harrow in form.

'Harrows of iron', 2 Sa. xii. 31, AV, are more probably picks or hoes; Heb. *ḥārîṣ* denotes a sharp or pointed instrument. A.R.M.

HART (HIND). These words occur in AV some twenty times, and are the male and female forms of some animal. It is obviously a fairly large ruminant of handsome appearance, and there has been general agreement that the correct translation is 'deer'. No species of deer is at present found in the area concerned, but deer have lived there, and one would expect Heb. *'ayyāl* and *'ayyālâ* to include forms of the red and fallow deer. See fig. 40. G.C.

HARVEST. See AGRICULTURE.

HASIDAEANS. This is a transliteration of *Hasidaioi* in 1 Macc. ii. 42, vii. 13; 2 Macc. xiv. 6, though 'Hasmonaeans' may be the correct reading in the last case. RVmg and modern literature prefer the underlying Heb. *chasidim* (*ḥ^asîḏîm*). This term, meaning fundamentally 'loyal ones', is used frequently in the Psalms (the usual English rendering being 'saints'). It seems to have been adopted by the zealots for the law, when Hellenistic ideas came flooding in early in the 2nd century BC.

Their leader seems to have been the high priest Onias III, deposed by Antiochus Epiphanes. They would have avoided armed struggle against the Syrians by withdrawing into the wilderness, but the implacable hostility of the Hellenizers drove them to support the Maccabees. As soon as they were granted a legitimate high priest they were prepared to return to normal life, but their leaders were murdered by Bacchides (1 Macc. vii. 12–18). They had little sympathy with the nationalistic aims of the Hasmonaeans. Probably already under Simon, their party split in two. The majority, now known as Pharisees (*q.v.*), tried to win the people to their views. The minority, represented by the Essenes and Qumran Covenanters, despaired of all but divine eschatological intervention and withdrew to a greater or lesser degree from public life.

BIBLIOGRAPHY. K. Schubert, *The Dead Sea Community*, 1959. H.L.E.

HASMONAEANS. See MACCABEES.

HAT (Aram. *karbᵉlā'*, Dn. iii. 21 only). A rare Aramaic word which RV and RSV render 'mantle', but whose meaning has not been definitely established. See also DRESS.

HATRED, HATE.

I. IN THE OLD TESTAMENT

Hatred between brothers (Gn. xxvii. 41, xxxvii. 4 f., 8; 2 Sa. xiii. 22) or fellow-Israelites (Ps. lv. 12 f.; Pr. xiv. 20) is condemned (Lv. xix. 17). Dt. iv. 42, xix. 4, 6, 11, and Jos. xx. 5 distinguish between accidental and malicious manslaughter. Sexual love (2 Sa. xiii. 15; Dt. xxii. 13–16, xxiv. 3; *cf.* Jdg. xiv. 16, see III below) may turn to hatred. Personal enmity is sometimes tempered with mercy (Ex. xxiii. 5; Jb. xxxi. 29), but the enemies of Israel (2 Sa. xxii. 41; Ps. cxxix. 5; Ezk. xxiii. 28) or of the godly (Ps. xxxiv. 21; Pr. xxix. 10) are God's enemies too (Nu. x. 35; *cf.* Ex. xx. 5; Dt. v. 9, vii. 10). God hates both evil (Pr. vi. 16; Am. vi. 8) and evil-doers (Dt. xxxii. 41): so therefore do the righteous (Pss. ci. 3, cxxxix. 21 f., cxix. 104, 113). God hates idolatry (Dt. xii. 31, xvi. 22), injustice (Is. lxi. 8), worship that is inconsistent with conduct (Is. i. 14), and even sinful Israel herself (Ho. ix. 15; *cf.* Je. xii. 8).

II. IN THE NEW TESTAMENT

The Father (Jn. xv. 24), Jesus (Jn. vii. 7, xv. 18, 24 f.), and all Christians (Mk. xiii. 13; Lk. vi. 22; Jn. xv. 18–20, xvii. 14; 1 Jn. iii. 13) are hated by the world; but believers must not hate either fellow-Christians (1 Jn. iv. 20) or enemies (Mt. v. 43 f.). Hatred of evil (Heb. i. 9 = Ps. xlv. 7; Rev. ii. 6; *cf.* Mk. iii. 5), though not of persons, is attributed to Christ (see WRATH).

III. CONTRASTED WITH LOVE

'Hate' as opposed to 'love' in Gn. xxix. 31, 33 (*cf.* 30, 'loved . . . more'); Dt. xxi. 15–17; Mt. vi. 24 = Lk. xvi. 13, implies the choice or preference of another rather than active hatred of what is not chosen or preferred. *Cf.* Mal. i. 2 f. = Rom. ix. 13 of God's election of Israel; Lk. xiv. 26 (*cf.* Mt. x. 37, 'loves . . . more'); Jn. xii. 25 of the over-riding claims of discipleship.

BIBLIOGRAPHY. J. Denney, *ExpT*, XXI, 1909–10, pp. 41 f.

P.E.

HAVILAH (*ḥᵃwîlâ*, 'circle', 'district'). **1.** A land (*'ereṣ*) in the neighbourhood of Eden, through which meandered (*sābab*) the river Pishon, and in which was found gold, bdellium (*q.v.*), and *shoham*-stone (Gn. ii. 11, 12). See EDEN, GARDEN OF. The location of the place is unknown.

2. An area mentioned in the phrase 'from Havilah to Shur'; inhabited by the Ishmaelites (Gn. xxv. 18) and Amalekites (1 Sa. xv. 7). It probably lay therefore in the area of Sinai and NW Arabia.

3. A name that occurs twice in Gn. x; as a descendant of Ham through Cush (Gn. x. 7; 1 Ch. i. 9) and as a descendant of Shem through Joktan, Eber, Shelah, and Arpachshad (Gn. x. 29; 1 Ch. i. 23). These may be entirely distinct, but as the names associated with them indicate a possible area of settlement in S Arabia and across the Bab el-Mandeb in Africa, it may be that the name indicates one strong tribe which had absorbed a weaker group.

BIBLIOGRAPHY. J. A. Montgomery, *Arabia and the Bible*, 1934, p. 39.

T.C.M.

HAVVOTH-JAIR (Heb. *ḥawwôṯ yā'îr*, 'the camps (tent-villages) of Jair'). These were probably in the hill-country between Mt. Gilead proper and the Yarmuk; sometimes taken with the Argob region north of the river as part of Bashan, formerly the territory of Og (Dt. iii. 14; Jos. xiii. 30). The area was dotted with tent-villages called *'ᵃyārîm*, Jdg. x. 4; a unique plural of *'îr*, 'town', or a diminutive form (so Rashi, *Commentary*), homonymous with 'ass colts'. Jair was credited with the conquest of the whole region, Dt. iii. 14; 1 Ch. ii. 23 f.; the '60 cities' of Jos. xiii. 30; 1 Ch. ii. 23 refer to the Argob (*cf.* 1 Ki. iv. 13). In Nu. xxxii. 41, where a plural antecedent is not explicit, Bergman (*JPOS*, XVI, 1936, pp. 235 ff.) reads, without altering the consonants, 'the camps of Ham' in northern Gilead (226213), *cf.* Gn. xiv. 5.

J.P.U.L.

HAWK. See BIRDS OF THE BIBLE.

HAZAEL (*ḥᵃzā'ēl*, *ḥᵃzâh'ēl*, 'El sees' or 'whom God beholds'). A powerful king of Syria (Aram), who was God's scourge to Israel during the reigns of Jehoram, Jehu, and Jehoahaz. Elijah was commissioned to anoint him as one of the three ordained to complete the extirpation of Baal-worship that he had begun (1 Ki. xix. 15–17). Later, Hazael, as the emissary of Ben-hadad II to Elisha, learned that he was to be king and would become an oppressor of Israel, a prophecy speedily put into effect by his murder of Ben-hadad and assumption of the throne (2 Ki. viii.

Fig. 101. Ivory plaque inscribed '. . . son of 'Amma, for our lord Hazael, in the year of . . .'. Perhaps part of a tribute brought to Hazael, king of Damascus. From Arslan Tash. 9th century BC.

7–15). He fought against Jehoram at Ramoth-gilead (2 Ki. viii. 28, 29, ix. 14, 15), and frequently defeated Jehu, devastating the country east of Jordan as far south as the Arnon valley (2 Ki. x. 32, 33). He continued his attacks in the reign of Jehoahaz, and Israel was preserved from complete destruction only by God's mercy (2 Ki. xiii. 3, 22 f.). 2 Ki. xii. 17, 18 reveals a Syrian incursion into SW Palestine, probably with the aim of securing the trade-routes. Gath was taken, and Jerusalem threatened, and Hazael was bought off only with a tribute from the temple treasures. Syria's ascendancy was checked only after Hazael's death, and his son, Ben-hadad III, was thrice defeated by Jehoash of Israel (2 Ki. xiii. 24, 25). As one of the chief Syrian oppressors of Israel, the memory of Hazael's might lingered, so that about a century later Amos recalled his name as symbolizing the height of Syria's power which would yet feel the fire of God's judgment (Am. i. 4).

Hazael's name also occurs in Assyrian cuneiform inscriptions as an opponent of Shalmaneser III. The wording of one such text shows that the Assyrians not only knew Hazael to be a usurper ('son of a nobody', *ANET*, p. 280, text (c), 14–ii. 1) but that they also knew that his predecessor was the victim of foul play (Weidner, *Archiv für Orientforschung*, XIII, 1940, pp. 233 f.).

Hazael must have attained his throne before 841 BC (when Shalmaneser III first clashed with him), as his and the Israelite Joram's forces fought in 842 at Ramoth-gilead; 843 BC, as suggested by Unger (*Israel and the Arameans of Damascus*, 1957, p. 75), is an early enough date. Shalmaneser III and Hazael fought again in 837 BC. Thereafter for thirty years no further collision of the two kingdoms is known, until Adad-nirari III in *c.* 805–802 BC cowed the now ageing Hazael into submission (*ANET*, pp. 281, 282; *DOTT*, pp. 51, 52), referring to him as *Marī*', Aramaic for 'lord'. In Syria the earlier redoubtable Hazael had evidently become known as 'the lord' *par excellence*, and this current epithet was simply taken over by the Assyrian annalists. Hazael 'oppressed Israel all the days of Jehoahaz' (2 Ki. xiii. 22), who reigned *c.* 814/3–798 BC, and hence, at least briefly, outlived him, surviving to perhaps *c.* 797 or 796 BC. Assyrian spoils from Hazael's Damascus included ivory-work, one piece inscribed *l-mr'n Ḥz'l*, 'belonging to our lord Hazael', and another the figure of a prince, just possibly a representation of Hazael himself (Parrot, *Samaria*, 1958, pp. 41, 42, figs. VII, VIII).

BIBLIOGRAPHY. On Hazael and Israel generally, see R. de Vaux, *RB*, XLIII, 1934, pp. 512–518, and A. Jepsen, *Archiv fur Orientforschung*, XIV, 1941/4, pp. 153–172. See also ARAM and BEN-HADAD for further background and bibliography.

J.G.G.N.
K.A.K.

HAZARMAVETH (*ḥ^aṣarmāweṯ*). The third son of Joktan (*q.v.*; Gn. x. 26; 1 Ch. i. 20), probably to be identified with the kingdom of Ḥadramaut in S Arabia, written *ḥḍrmt* and later *ḥḍrmwt* in the native inscriptions. The latter form corresponds closely to the unvocalized Heb. *ḥṣrmwt*, Heb. *ṣ* often corresponding to S Semitic *ḍ*. (See ARABIA.)

BIBLIOGRAPHY. G. Ryckmans, *Les Noms propres sud-sémitiques*, I, 1934, p. 338; C. Brockelmann, *Grundriss der vergleichenden Grammatik der semitischen Sprachen*, I, 1908, § 46.

T.C.M.

HAZEL. See ALMOND.

HAZEROTH. A stopping-place on the desert journey of the Israelites (Nu. xi. 35, xxxiii. 17, 18), where Miriam became a leper (Nu. xii. 1–16; *cf.* Dt. i. 1). Generally identified with 'Ayin Khodara, an oasis with a well on the way from Sinai to Aqabah. (See ENCAMPMENT BY THE SEA.)

C.D.W.

HAZOR (*ḥāṣôr*). A place-name, probably meaning 'settlement' or 'village', and therefore used of several places in the Old Testament, of which the most important was a fortified city in the territory of Naphtali (Jos. xix. 36).

I. IN THE OLD TESTAMENT

This city lay in northern Palestine, and at the conquest it was the royal seat of Jabin (called 'king of Hazor', *meleḵ-ḥāṣôr*, Jos. xi. 1), who organized a coalition against Joshua. The Israelites defeated this, however, Jabin was killed, and Hazor was destroyed and burnt (Jos. xi. 1–13, xii. 19). Hazor was the only city thus burnt, perhaps because of its former importance (Jos. xi. 10), but in spite of this destruction a later king of the same name, who this time was styled 'king of Canaan' (*meleḵ-k^ena'an*, Jdg. iv. 2, 24) threatened Israel in the time of Deborah. Though his general, Sisera, had 900 chariots (*q.v.*) at his disposal, the Israelites under Barak were able to defeat him, and crush Jabin (Jdg. iv; 1 Sa. xii. 9). Some two centuries later Hazor was fortified, together with Jerusalem, Megiddo, and Gezer, by Solomon when he was organizing his kingdom (1 Ki. ix. 15), but in the 8th century, in the time of Pekah of Israel, Tiglath-pileser III of Assyria came and destroyed the city and carried off its remaining inhabitants to Assyria (2 Ki. xv. 29).

II. EXCAVATION

The site of Hazor was identified in 1926 by Professor J. Garstang with the abandoned mound of Tell el-Qedah some 5 miles south-west of Lake Huleh in Galilee. He made some trial soundings in 1928, but the first major excavations were carried out from 1955 to 1958 by an Israeli expedition under Dr. Yigael Yadin. The site lies on a north-east facing slope, and consists of the city tell of some 25 acres extent at the southern end, and adjoining this to the north a much larger area of about 150 acres with an earthen rampart on the western or uphill side. The main tell was founded in the third millennium, and the lower city added to it in the early part of the second millennium, probably by the Hyksos. Though Garstang assumed this lower city to be a camping enclosure for horses and chariots, excavation revealed that the whole of this area had been occupied by a built city, which at its height must, with the tell proper, have accommodated up to 40,000 souls. (*Cf.* the size of other cities, in Fortification and Siegecraft.) A further indication of the importance of the city at this time is given by the discovery of a pottery jug with an Akkadian inscription (the earliest known in Palestine) scratched on it. Though crudely done, the inscription has been read as *Iš-me-ilam*, an Akkadian personal name, perhaps that of a Mesopotamian merchant. This lower city was only occupied for about five centuries, having been destroyed in the 13th century and never thereafter inhabited. This destruction is attributed by the excavators to Joshua. Among the remains in this destroyed city were found a Canaanite temple and a small shrine. While the

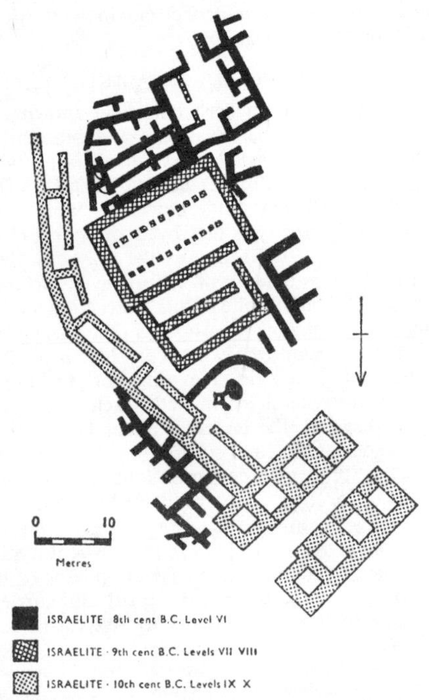

Fig. 102. Plan of Solomonic acropolis. Area 'A'.

lower city lay barren, the tell was reoccupied by the Canaanites, and then by the Israelites. A city gate and casemate wall from the time of Solomon, almost exactly matching those found at Megiddo and Gezer (*qq.v.*; *cf.* 1 Ki. ix. 15), were uncovered. Evidence from the later Israelite period included a pillared public building of the time of Ahab, and a fortress containing a thick layer of ash, in which was a fragment of a wine jar bearing the name Pekah (*pqḥ*), and other signs of violent destruction, probably due to Tiglath-pileser III, who took the city in 732 BC (2 Ki. xv. 29). See fig. 163 and pl. VIII*b*.

III. IN EXTRA-BIBLICAL TEXTS

Hazor is first mentioned in the Egyp. execration texts of the 19th century BC, as a Canaanite city likely to be a danger to the empire. It figures (*ḫa-ṣu-ra*) in the Mari archives of the first quarter of the second millennium, and in a slightly later Bab. text, as an important political centre on the route from Mesopotamia, perhaps to Egypt. In one tablet the ruler is spoken of as a 'king' (*šarrum*), a title not usually applied to city rulers (*cf.* Jos. xi. 1), and his importance is further indicated by the mention of ambassadors from Babylon travelling to see him. One king's name is given as Ibni-Adad, an Akkadian form suggesting Bab. influence, but there was also contact with the north and west, as is manifested in gifts from the king to Ugarit and Crete (*Kaptara*). Hazor is mentioned in the lists of their dominions made by the Egyp. kings Tuthmosis III, Amenhotep II, and Seti I in the 15th and 14th centuries BC. The city is later mentioned in the Amarna letters, of the 14th century, the ruler still being spoken of as a king (*šar ḫa-zu-ra*). Finally, from the next century, the city is mentioned in an Egyp. papyrus (Anastasi I) in a military context. Thus the texts and excavations amply bear out the biblical testimony to the importance of the site.

IV. OTHER PLACES OF THE SAME NAME

1. A place in the south of Judah (Jos. xv. 23) whose site is unknown. **2.** (*ḥāṣôr ḥ^a^dattâ*) 'New Hazor' (Jos. xv. 25), a place in S Judah whose site is unknown. **3.** Another name for Kerioth-Hezron (Jos. xv. 25) in S Judah, site unknown, perhaps the same as (2). **4.** A place in Benjamin (Ne. xi. 33) probably modern Khirbet Hazzur. **5.** An area occupied by semi-nomadic Arabs, mentioned by Jeremiah (xlix. 28, 30, 33).

Bibliography. Preliminary reports of the excavations in *IEJ*, VI, 1956, pp. 120–125, VII, 1957, pp. 118–123, VIII, 1958, pp. 1–14, IX, 1959, pp. 74–88; and *BA*, XXI, 1958, pp. 30–47, XXII, 1959, pp. 2–20; and definitive reports in progress, Y. Yadin *et al.*, *Hazor I*, 1958, *Hazor II*, 1960. See also A. Malamat, *JBL*, LXXIX, 1960, pp. 12–19. T.C.M.

HEAD. The head (Heb. *rō'š*; Gk. *kephalē*) is not regarded as the seat of the intellect, but as the source of life (1 Sa. xxviii. 2; Mt. xiv. 8, 11; Jn. xix. 30). Thus to lift up the head is to grant life in the sense of success (Jdg. viii. 28; Ps. xxvii. 6; Gn. xl. 13, but *cf.* the pun in verse 19), or to expect it in God Himself (Ps. xxiv. 7, 9; Lk. xxi. 28). To cover the head by the hand or with dust and ashes is to mourn the loss of life (2 Sa. xiii. 19; La. ii. 10). Figuratively, headship denotes superiority of rank and authority over another (Jdg. xi. 11; 2 Sa. xxii. 44); though when Christ is spoken of as Head of His body the Church (Eph. v. 23; Col. ii. 19), of every man (1 Cor. xi. 3), of the entire universe (*hyper panta*, Eph. i. 22), and of every cosmic power (Col. ii. 10), and when man is spoken of as the head of the woman (1 Cor. xi. 3; Eph. v. 23; *cf.* Gn. ii. 21 f.), the basic meaning of head as the source of all life and energy is predominant. Hence to interpose allegiance to any other spiritual mediator, as was being done at Colossae, severs the vital connection between the limbs and Christ the Head, the mainspring of all spiritual energy (Col. ii. 18 f.).

The head stone of the corner (Ps. cxviii. 22, quoted messianically five times in the New Testament, Gk. *kephalē gōnias*), like the chief corner-stone (Eph. ii. 20; 1 Pet. ii. 6; Gk. *akrogōniaios*), is generally regarded as the corner foundation-stone from which the rest of the building is measured (G. H. Whitaker, *Expositor*, 8th Series, XXII, 1921, pp. 470 ff.), though J. Jeremias (*ZNW*, XXIX, 1930, pp. 264 ff.) thinks it is the keystone above the door. See S. H. Hooke, 'The Corner-Stone of Scripture', in *The Siege Perilous*, 1956, pp. 235 ff. F.H.P.

HEALTH. The AV renders several Heb. and Gk. words by the single English word 'health'.

1. Heb. *'ᵃrûḵâ*, *'ᵃruḵâ*, meaning literally the new flesh which grows at the wounded spot, hence 'healing of a wound'. Figuratively it is used of the healing and restoration of Israel (Is. lviii. 8; Je. viii. 22, xxx. 17, xxxiii. 6).

2. Heb. *marpē'*, *rip̄'ûṯ* (from *rāp̄ā'*, 'to sew together', 'to mend'), 'health'. Used figuratively in Pr. xii. 18 (of the tongue of the wise), xiii. 17 (of a faithful ambassador), and xvi. 24 (of pleasant words as health to the bones). In Je. viii. 15 it refers to the cure of the nation's sickness because of sin.

3. Heb. *yᵉšû'â* (Pss. xlii. 6, 11, xliii. 5). Literally 'health of my face', a periphrasis for 'my help', 'my deliverer'.

4. Heb. *šālôm*, 'peace', 'completeness' (2 Sa. xx. 9, RSV 'Is it well with you?').

5. Gk. *sōtēria* (Acts xxvii. 34). Common in the papyri in the general sense of 'bodily health', 'well-being', or 'safety', the word is usually translated 'salvation' in the New Testament.

6. Gk. *hygiainō*, 'to be healthy' (3 Jn. 2). Paul uses the word metaphorically of sound doctrine (*i.e.* healthy doctrine) in 2 Tim. i. 13, iv. 3; Tit. i. 9, ii. 1. Luke uses it literally of sound health (Lk. v. 31, vii. 10, xv. 27).

See also DISEASE AND HEALING. D.O.S.

HEART (Heb. *lēḇ* or *lēḇāḇ*, with some other words also translated 'heart', principally *nep̄eš*, which is usually rendered by 'soul' in AV; and Gk. *kardia*).

The term is used of the centre of things (Dt. iv. 11; Jon. ii. 3; Mt. xii. 40), and it is just possible, though unlikely, that the root of the Heb. word, which is obscure, means centre.

The references to the physical organ as such are few and by no means specific. The clearest is 1 Sa. xxv. 37. In 2 Sa. xviii. 14 and 2 Ki. ix. 24 the meaning seems to be wider, indicating the internal organs generally, especially since, in the former passage, Absalom remained alive after three darts had pierced his 'heart'. But this lack of accurate physiological definition is typical of Hebrew thought, particularly in respect of the internal organs (see BOWELS, *etc.*).

In Ps. civ. 15, for instance, the 'heart' is affected by food and drink, and though this may not be true in a direct way physiologically, it certainly is true in experience, if one takes the 'heart' to mean, as outlined below, the inner man, in a wide sense.

The Hebrews thought in terms of subjective experience rather than objective, scientific observation, and thereby avoided the modern error of over-departmentalization. It was essentially the whole man, with all his attributes, physical, intellectual, and psychological, of which the Hebrew thought and spoke, and the heart was conceived of as the governing centre for all of these. It is the heart which makes a man, or a beast, what he is (Pr. xvi. 23, xxiii. 7; Dn. iv. 16), and governs all his actions (Pr. iv. 23). Character, personality, will, mind are modern terms which all reflect something of the meaning of 'heart' in its biblical usage. (But *cf.* BODY where mention is made of synecdoche.)

H. Wheeler Robinson gives the following good classification of the various senses in which the words *lēḇ* and *lēḇāḇ* are used.

a. Physical or figurative ('midst'; 29 times).

b. Personality, inner life, or character in general (257 times, *e.g.* Ex. ix. 14; 1 Sa. xvi. 7; Gn. xx. 5).

c. Emotional states of consciousness, found in widest range (166 times); intoxication (1 Sa. xxv. 36); joy or sorrow (Jdg. xviii. 20; 1 Sa. i. 8); anxiety (1 Sa. iv. 13); courage and fear (Gn. xlii. 28); love (2 Sa. xiv. 1).

d. Intellectual activities (204 times); attention (Ex. vii. 23); reflection (Dt. vii. 17); memory (Dt. iv. 9); understanding (1 Ki. iii. 9); technical skill (Ex. xxviii. 3).

e. Volition or purpose (195 times; 1 Sa. ii. 35), this being one of the most characteristic usages of the term in the Old Testament.

The New Testament usage is very similar, and C. Ryder Smith writes of it as follows: 'It (the heart) does not altogether lose its physical reference, for it is made of "flesh" (2 Cor. iii. 3), but it is the seat of the will (*e.g.* Mk. iii. 5), of the intellect (*e.g.* Mk. ii. 6, 8), and of feeling (*e.g.* Lk. xxiv. 32). This means that "heart" comes the nearest of the New Testament terms to mean "person".'

There is no suggestion in the Bible that the brain is the centre of consciousness, thought, or will. It is the heart which is so regarded, and, though it is used of emotions also, it is more frequently the lower organs (see BOWELS, *etc.*), in so far as they are distinguished, that are connected with the emotions. As a broad general statement, it is true that the Bible places the psychological focus one step lower in the anatomy than most popular modern speech, which uses 'mind' for consciousness, thought, and will, and 'heart' for emotions.

'Mind' is perhaps the closest modern term to

the biblical usage of 'heart', and many passages could well be so translated (*e.g.* Ec. i. 17; Mt. v. 28). The 'heart' is, however, a wider term, and the Bible does not distinguish the rational or mental processes in the way that Gk. philosophy does.

C. Ryder Smith suggests that: 'The First great Commandment probably means "Thou shalt love (*agapān*) the Lord thy God with all thy heart—that is with all thy soul and with all thy mind and with all thy strength" (*e.g.* Mk. xii. 30, 33).'

The heart of man does not always do that, however. It is not what it should be (Gn. vi. 5; Je. xvii. 9), and the Old Testament reaches its highest point in the realization that a change of heart is needed (Je. xxiv. 7; Ezk. xi. 19), and that, of course, is fulfilled in the New Testament (Eph. iii. 17).

There are the exceptional people whose hearts are right with God (1 Ki. xv. 14; Ps. xxxvii. 30, 31; Acts xiii. 22), though it is obvious from what we know of David, the example referred to in the last passage, that this is not true in an absolute sense, but that repentance and conversion are still necessary (2 Ki. xxiii. 25, of Josiah).

The right attitude of heart begins with its being broken or crushed (Ps. li. 17), symbolic of humility and penitence, and synonymous with 'a broken spirit' (*rûaḥ*). This brokenness is necessary because it is the hard or stony heart which does not submit to the will of God (Ezk. xi. 19). Alternatively, it is the 'fat' or 'uncircumcised' heart which fails to respond to Yahweh's will (Is. vi. 10; Ezk. xliv. 7).

Yahweh knows the heart of each one and is not deceived by outward appearance (1 Sa. xvi. 7), but a worthy prayer is, nevertheless, that He should search and know the heart (Ps. cxxxix. 23), and make it clean (Ps. li. 10). A 'new heart' must be the aim of the wicked (Ezk. xviii. 31), and that will mean that God's law has to become no longer merely external but 'written on the heart' (Je. xxxi. 33).

Thus it is that the heart, the spring of all desires, must be guarded (Pr. iv. 23), and the teacher aims to win his pupil's heart to the right way (Pr. xxiii. 26).

It is the pure in heart who shall see God (Mt. v. 8), and it is through Christ's dwelling in the heart by faith that the saints can comprehend the love of God (Eph. iii. 17).

BIBLIOGRAPHY. A. R. Johnson, *The Vitality of the Individual in the Thought of Ancient Israel*, 1949, pp. 77 ff.; C. Ryder Smith, *The Bible Doctrine of Man*, 1951; H. Wheeler Robinson, *The Christian Doctrine of Man*, 1911. B.O.B.

HEATH. See TREES.

HEAVEN. Several words are translated 'heaven', but the only important ones are the Heb. *shāmayim* and the Gk. *ouranos*. The former is plural, and the latter often occurs in the plural. But, just as in English, there does not seem to be any great difference between 'heaven' and 'the heavens'. The term is used of the physical heaven, especially in the expression 'heaven and earth' (Gn. i. 1; Mt. v. 18). Some suggest that the Bible writers thought of heaven in this aspect as solid, and rather like an inverted bowl (the 'firmament', Gn. i. 8). The sun makes his daily pilgrimage across it (Ps. xix. 4–6), and there are windows through which the rain might descend (Gn. vii. 11). Some Hebrews may well have held this idea, but it must not be forgotten that the men of the Old Testament were capable of vivid imagery. It will never do to treat them as wooden literalists. The theological meaning of their language about heaven can be understood without recourse to such hypotheses.

Heaven is the abode of God, and of those closely associated with Him. The Israelite is to pray, 'Look down from thy holy habitation, from heaven' (Dt. xxvi. 15). God is 'the God of heaven' (Jon. i. 9), or 'the Lord God of heaven' (Ezr. i. 2), or the 'Father which is in heaven' (Mt. v. 45, vii. 21, *etc.*). God is not alone there, for we read of 'the host of heaven' which worships Him (Ne. ix. 6), and of 'the angels which are in heaven' (Mk. xiii. 32). Believers also may look forward to 'an inheritance . . . reserved in heaven' for them (1 Pet. i. 4). Heaven is thus the present abode of God and His angels, and the ultimate destination of His saints on earth.

Among many ancient peoples there was the thought of a multiplicity of heavens. It has been suggested that the New Testament bears witness to the rabbinic idea of seven heavens, for there are references to Paradise (Lk. xxiii. 43), and to 'the third heaven' (2 Cor. xii. 2; this was called Paradise on the rabbinic reckoning, *cf.* 2 Cor. xii. 4). Jesus also is said to have passed 'through the heavens' (Heb. iv. 14, RV). These, however, are slender bases on which to erect such a structure. All the New Testament language is perfectly capable of being understood along the lines of heaven as the place of perfection.

Heaven comes to be used as a reverent periphrasis for God. Thus when the prodigal says 'I have sinned against heaven' (Lk. xv. 18, 21), he means 'I have sinned against God'. So with Jn. iii. 27, 'it be given him from heaven'. The most important example of this is Matthew's use of the expression 'the kingdom of heaven', which seems to be identical with 'the kingdom of God'.

Finally, we must notice an eschatological use of the term. In both Old and New Testaments it is recognized that the present physical universe is not eternal, but will vanish away and be replaced by 'a new heaven and a new earth' (Is. lxv. 17, lxvi. 22; 2 Pet. iii. 10–13; Rev. xxi. 1). We should understand such passages as indicating that the final condition of things will be such as fully expresses the will of God. L.M.

HEAVE-OFFERING. See SACRIFICE AND OFFERING (Old Testament), IV*d* (iii).

HEBER. 1. An Asherite, the son of Beriah (Gn. xlvi. 17; Nu. xxvi. 45; 1 Ch. vii. 31, 32; Lk. iii.

35). **2.** The husband of Jael (*q.v.*), known as Heber the Kenite (Jdg. iv. 11, 17, v. 24), though he lived apart from the rest of the Kenites or nomad smiths. The context suggests him to be a man of some importance. **3.** A Judahite, the father of Socho (1 Ch. iv. 18). **4.** A son of Elpaal, a Benjamite (1 Ch. viii. 17). J.D.D.

HEBREW. See LANGUAGE OF THE OLD TESTAMENT.

HEBREWS. From the eponym Eber (Gn. x. 21 ff., xi. 14 ff.) comes the gentilic *'ibrî*, 'Hebrew', used in the Bible as a patronymic for Abraham and his descendants. In the Old Testament *'ibrî* is confined to the narrative of the sons of Israel in Egypt (Gn. xxxix–Ex. x), the legislation concerning the manumission of Heb. servants (Ex. xxi; Dt. xv; *cf.* Je. xxxiv), the record of Israelite-Philistine encounter during the days of Samuel and Saul (1 Sa. iv, xiii, xiv, xxix), plus Gn. xiv. 13 and Jon. i. 9.

'ibrî first appears as an ethnicon for Abraham (Gn. xiv. 13), being prepared for by the notice that Shem was father of all the descendants of Eber (Gn. x. 21). Accordingly, this designation serves to tie the Abrahamic revelation to the covenant promise to Shem. The Noahic doxology in praise of the covenantal union of Yahweh with the family of Shem (Gn. ix. 26) is echoed in Gn. xiv in the doxology of Melchizedek (19, 20) celebrating God's covenantal blessing on Abraham the Hebrew, *i.e.* of the lineage of Shem. That the divine favour is shown to Abraham the Hebrew in a conflict which finds him in military alliance with the 'sons of Canaan' against the forces of an Elamite 'son of Shem' (*cf.* Gn. x. 15 ff., 22) is indicative that the covenantal election of Shem announced by Noah was being more particularly realized through the Eberite (Hebrew) Semites (*cf.* Gn. xi. 10–26).

The broad significance of *'ibrî* in Gn. xiv. 13 might also be plausibly assumed in the Gn. xxxix–Ex. x context (*cf.* especially Gn. xl. 15, xliii. 32; Ex. ii. 11). However, the usage there is perhaps not uniform, since there seems to be a simple equation of Hebrews and Israelites in Ex. v. 1–3 (*cf.* iii. 18), for example, though in speaking of 'the God of the Hebrews' Moses possibly designates his brethren 'Hebrews' as being the Hebrews *par excellence.*

In view of this broader application of *'ibrî*, the appearance of non-Israelite or even non-Abrahamite *'ibrîm* need not come unexpectedly in non-biblical texts of the patriarchal and Mosaic ages. According to a popular theory, the *ḫa-BI-ru*, who figure in numerous texts of the second millennium BC, are such *'ibrîm*. The term *ḫa-BI-ru* is usually regarded as an appellative denoting nomads, dependants, or foreigners. However, the phonetic equation of *'ibrî* and *ḫa-BI-ru* is highly improbable. Moreover, the extant evidence suggests that the *ḫa-BI-ru* were professional militarists with a non-Semitic nucleus drawn from the northern ethnic intrusion which brought the Hurrians and Indo-Aryans into the fertile crescent in the third millennium BC.

On the basis of the interpretation of the term *ḫa-BI-ru* in Nuzi servant contracts as an appellative meaning 'foreign-servant', it has been contended that *'ibrî* in the legislation of Ex. xxi. 2 and Dt. xv. 12, whose terms correspond closely to the stipulations of the *ḫa-BI-ru* contracts, denotes not a specific ethnic identity but the status of an alien and, therefore, that the *'ebed 'ibrî* is like the Nuzi *ḫa-BI-ru* a foreign servant. But that interpretation of *ḫa-BI-ru* in the Nuzi texts seems to be inaccurate, and certainly the biblical legislation is concerned with Israelite servants. Dt. xv. 12 identifies the Heb. servant as 'thy brother' (*cf.* 3; Je. xxxiv. 9, 14). It is objected that what Ex. xxi allows for an *'ebed 'ibrî*, Lv. xxv forbids for an Israelite; but what Ex. xxi. 2 ff. allows is a voluntary perpetuation of an agreeable type of service, while Lv. xxv. 43, 44 forbids compulsorily permanent, rigorous slavery. The Jubilee stipulation of Lv. xxv is a supplementary privilege granted the Heb. servant, which apparently yielded precedence to the servant's further right of voluntary lifelong service (Ex. xxi. 5, 6).

It has been maintained that the *'ibrîm* in 1 Sa. xiii and xiv are non-Israelite mercenaries (a rôle characteristic of the *ḫa-BI-ru*). But in xiii. 3, 4 'the Hebrews' are obviously the same as 'all Israel'. Moreover, it is apparently the 'men of Israel' described in xiii. 6 to whom the Philistines refer in xiv. 11, designating them 'Hebrews'. There is similar identification of the *'ibrîm* in xiii. 19, 20 (*cf.* also iv. 5–9). In xiii. 6, 7 the *'ibrîm* are not, as alleged, distinguished from the 'men of Israel'; rather, two groups of Israelites are described. Verse 6 refers to those who had been excused from military service (2b) and later hid in the hills west of Jordan. Verse 7 refers to certain Israelites, here called 'Hebrews', who had been selected by Saul (2a) but afterwards, deserting, sought refuge east of the Jordan (note the reduction in Saul's army—xiii. 2, 11, 15, xiv. 2). As for xiv. 21, even if, following EVV, the *'ibrîm* are regarded as having fought for the enemy, they might have been Israelite traitors. The original text of verse 21, however, supports the exegesis that certain Hebrews after a lapse of courage resumed their former active hostility against the Philistines by rejoining Saul. These *'ibrîm* are those mentioned in xiii. 7a. Along with the men of Israel who had hidden in the hill-country of Ephraim (xiv. 22, *cf.* xiii. 6) they returned to swell the ranks of Saul's unexpectedly triumphant army.

The Old Testament usage of *'ibrî* is thus consistently ethnic. Most occurrences being in discourse spoken by or addressed to non-Israelites, many would see a derogatory nuance in *'ibrî*. The suggestion that *'ibrî* is an alternative for 'Israelite' in situations where the person is not a free citizen on free soil is perhaps not unsuitable to any of the Old Testament passages. But even if such a connotation were intended it would be neither primary nor permanent. Indeed, by New Testament times, 'Hebrew' had become an exclusivist epithet claimed with pride by those Jews whose basic cultural-religious heritage had not been decisively influenced by the process of Hellenization (*cf.* Acts vi. 1; 2 Cor. xi. 22; Phil. iii. 5). A progressive restricting of the denotation of *'iḇrî* is evident from Abraham to Paul.

BIBLIOGRAPHY. M. G. Kline, 'The Ḫa-BI-ru—Kin or Foe of Israel?', *WTJ*, XX, 1957, pp. 46 ff.; J. Lewy, 'Origin and Signification of the Biblical Term "Hebrew"', *HUCA*, XXVIII, 1957, pp. 1–13. M.G.K.

HEBREWS, EPISTLE TO THE.

I. OUTLINE OF CONTENTS

The doctrinal theme: the superiority of Christ. i. 1–x. 18

a. The Person of Christ, i. 1–iv. 13

(i) *Christ is superior to the Prophets* (i. 1–4). The Prophets are here representative of Old Testament revelation generally.

(ii) *Christ is superior to angels* (i. 5–ii. 18). This is demonstrated by an appeal to various Scriptures, and Christ's apparent inferiority through suffering is then explained.

(iii) *Parenthesis* (ii. 1–4). Solemn warnings are given to those who neglect God's revelation.

(iv) *Christ is superior to Moses* (iii. 1–19). Since Moses was no more than a servant, Christ's sonship establishes His superiority over the great lawgiver. This superiority is also seen by the fact that Moses, unlike Christ, could not lead his people into rest.

(v) *Christ is superior to Joshua* (iv. 1–13). Although Joshua led the Israelites into their inheritance, a better rest, still future, remains for God's people.

b. The work of Christ, iv. 14–x. 18

This is particularly exemplified in His office as Priest.

(i) *His priesthood is divinely appointed* (iv. 14–v. 10). In this section the sympathy of Christ as an essential qualification for the high-priestly office is emphasized.

(ii) *His priesthood is after the order of Melchizedek* (v. 11–vii. 28). This section begins with a long digression consisting of rebuke, solemn warning, and exhortation (v. 11–vi. 8). Then the order of Melchizedek is explained. His priesthood is perpetual (vii. 1–3); it is anterior to, and therefore greater than, the levitical (vii. 4–10); it shows the imperfections of the levitical priesthood (vii. 11–19). Christ's priesthood is seen to be the perfect fulfilment of the order of Melchizedek because it was established by oath, is unaffected by death, and unmarred by sin (vii. 20–28).

(iii) *His work is within the new covenant* (viii. 1–ix. 10). Every aspect of the old order has its counterpart in the new. There is a new sanctuary in which the Mediator of a new covenant has entered to minister.

(iv) *His work is centred in a perfect atonement* (ix. 11–x. 18). Our High Priest offered a unique sacrifice (Himself), and because this offering was made 'through the eternal Spirit' it is superior to the levitical offerings (ix. 11–15). The necessity of Christ's death is demonstrated by an illustration from a legal testament (ix. 16–22). His perfect sacrifice shows up the blemishes of the levitical system (x. 1–10). His ministry, unlike the Aaronic, is complete and effective (x. 11–18).

The practical application of the doctrinal theme. x. 19–xiii. 25

a. Exhortations to hold fast, x. 19–25

b. Parenthesis, x. 26–37

(i) A serious warning against apostasy (x. 26–31).

(ii) Encouragement based on the readers' former experiences (x. 32–37).

c. Examples from the past, xi. 1–40

The writer appeals to the heroes of faith in order to inspire his readers into heroic action.

d. Advice concerning present sufferings, xii. 1–29

(i) Present trials to be regarded as chastisements (xii. 1–13).

(ii) Warnings based on the story of Esau (xii. 14–17).

(iii) A final contrast between the old and the greater glory of the new (xii. 18–29).

e. Christian responsibilities, xiii. 1–25

(i) Various exhortations affecting the social and personal life of the believer (xiii. 1–8).

(ii) A concluding warning to the readers to go forth from the camp (of Judaism) and some final personal references (xiii. 9–25).

II. AUTHORSHIP AND DATE

The question of authorship was of greater importance in the early Church than it is today, for upon it depended the canonicity of the Epistle. Ancient tradition regarding authorship consisted of two divergent opinions, one attributing it to Barnabas (so Tertullian, *De Pudicitia* xx), and the other more dominating tradition attributing it to Paul. This latter view was held by Clement and Origen at Alexandria. Clement seems to have regarded it as written in the Heb. dialect but translated by Luke, and he appears to have received the tradition from his predecessor Pantaenus (the blessed presbyter), while Origen makes clear that it was regarded, not without reason, as Paul's by men of old. The latter mentions that some in his day ascribed it to Clement of Rome and others to Luke, but he himself regarded the thoughts as the apostle's but not the words. His own conclusion regarding authorship was that God alone knows for certain who wrote the Epistle, but this reserve was not followed by the later Alexandrians, who adhered so strongly to Pauline authorship that it became accepted as canonical not only in the east but also in the west, where earlier doubts concerning it were strong. It was not, however, until the time of Jerome and Augustine that canonicity was settled in the west. The tradition of Pauline authorship was not again seriously challenged until the time of the Reformation, when Erasmus, Luther, and Calvin all disputed it. Luther's idea that Apollos was the author has commended itself to many modern scholars, although none would regard it as any more than speculative. Grotius revived the early idea that Luke was the author, and many other suggestions have been offered by modern criticism. But it is significant that few modern scholars have attempted to support the theory of Pauline authorship. It falls down on difference of style, as Origen noted when he recognized the language as 'more Greek'; on different modes of composition, such as the absence of greetings, the manner of introducing exhortations, the method of argument, and the lack of Pauline signature; on the different historical situation in which the author places himself, for whereas Paul never tired of stating that he had received the gospel by revelation, this author makes clear his personal indebtedness to second-hand information (ii. 3, 4); and on the difference of background clearly evident in the absence from this Epistle of any past spiritual crisis dominating the author's thought and in the absence of the familiar Pauline antitheses.

Two interesting alternative suggestions are those of Ramsay, who suggested that Philip wrote the Epistle from Caesarea after contact with Paul and sent it to the Jerusalem church, and of Harnack, who made out a case for Priscilla and Aquila as joint-authors. But at best these are only ingenious guesses, and modern criticism would do well to abide by Origen's caution and allow the author to remain incognito.

Although the information available for dating purposes is scanty, there is enough to enable the most probable period to be ascertained. Since it was cited by Clement of Rome (*c.* AD 95) it must have been produced some while before his time. In all probability it was written before AD 70, as no mention is made of the fall of Jerusalem and as the ecclesiastical situation suits an earlier date (*cf.* xiii. 7, 17, where those in charge are vaguely called 'leaders'). Yet some interval is required after the foundation of the church addressed to allow for the 'former days' of persecution to be regarded in retrospect. If the persecution was that under Nero a date about AD 67–8 would be required, but probably general opposition only is meant, in which case a date before AD 64 would be possible. Some scholars date the Epistle *c.* AD 80–90 on the strength of the author's use of the Pauline Epistles, but since the date of the collection of these Epistles is shrouded in mystery, and since the author does not show the influence of them all, little importance can be attached to this line of evidence.

III. DESTINATION AND PURPOSE

The opening sentences of the Epistle give no indication of the location or identity of the readers, but the traditional title ascribes it simply 'To the Hebrews'. Although this was not part of the original text, it cannot be entirely ignored, since it may preserve genuine tradition. If that is so it must be Jewish Christians and not simply Jews who are intended. Yet a theory which has gained some support in modern times is that the title is no more than an inference from the substance of the Epistle and that it was really sent to Gentiles. Support for this notion is claimed from the consistent citations from LXX rather than the Heb. text of the Old Testament and from the supposed Hellenistic background to which the writer appeals. The Epistle would then set forth the absolute character of Christianity to the Gentile world, showing it to supersede all other faiths, especially the mystery cults. But there is nothing in the Epistle which corresponds to mystery religions or to unbelief in religion as a whole.

Akin to this latter theory is the suggestion that the Epistle was an answer to a pre-Gnostic heresy of a type similar to that combated in Colossians. The passage showing Christ's superiority to angels (Heb. i. 4–14) would certainly give an effective answer to the tendency to angel-worship (*cf.* Col. ii. 18). T. W. Manson went so far as to suggest that Apollos wrote this Epistle to the Colossian church to answer the two main tendencies of reliance on intermediaries (answered in chapters i–iv) and on ritual practices (chapters v–x). Yet there are no evidences of pre-Gnostic tendencies in the situation underlying Hebrews such as clearly existed at Colossae.

The more widely held view is that the Epistle was addressed to Jewish Christians to warn them against apostasy to Judaism. This is based on the serious exhortations in chapters vi and x, which presuppose that there is danger of a definite falling away which would amount to nothing short of crucifying the Son of God afresh (vi. 6) and of profanation of the blood of the covenant (x. 29). Since the author is addressing those who have once tasted the goodness of God (vi. 4, 5) and who are therefore in danger of forsaking Christianity for their old faith, and since the Epistle sets forth the superiority of Christianity to Old Testament ritual, it is natural to suppose that Jewish Christians are in mind. The question then arises as to whether these Jewish Christians can be any more specifically defined, and various answers have been given to this inquiry: (*a*) that the Epistle was designed generally for all Jewish Christians; (*b*) that it was designed for a small house-community of Christians who had the capacity to be teachers (*cf.* v. 12) but who were not exercising it; and (*c*) that the readers were converted Jewish priests. The first view is difficult because of the personal notes in the conclusion (xiii. 22–25) and the direct personal approach in many places in the body of the

Epistle. The second view is for this reason preferable, since a particular historic situation seems to be in mind, and the readers were evidently a group apart from the main body of the church, since v. 12 could not well apply to the whole community. Moreover, the language and concepts of the Epistle presuppose an educated group, and this lends support to the idea of an intellectual clique within the local church. As to the location of these Jewish Christians, various suggestions have been made, depending partially on theories of authorship. Palestine and Alexandria have both found supporters, the former particularly by those regarding Barnabas as the author, but Rome is more favoured, supported by the somewhat ambiguous allusion in xiii. 24 ('They of Italy salute you'). It is not without significance in this connection that the earliest evidence for the use of the Epistle is the writing of Clement of Rome. The third alternative mentioned above, *i.e.* that the readers were converted priests, has gained support from those who claim that the argument of the Epistle would be of great relevance to those who had just recently turned from Jewish ritual practices, and especially to those who had been connected with the Jerusalem Temple (Acts records that a great many of these people were converted through Stephen's ministry). It has been objected that no evidence of separate priestly communities exists from the primitive period, but nevertheless this Epistle may provide such evidence. There seems to be no conclusive reason against this theory, and it must remain an interesting conjecture.

Yet another view, a modification of the last, sees in the Epistle a challenge to restricted Jewish Christians to embrace the world mission. This is based on certain similarities between this Epistle and Stephen's speech, such as the conception of Christianity as superseding Judaism, and the definite call to the people addressed to leave their present position. But the resemblances must not be pressed too far, since Stephen's audience did not consist of Jewish Christians. But nevertheless it is possible that the apostasy danger was the forsaking of the divine world mission purpose. A group of Jewish Christians who regarded Christianity as little more than a sect of official Judaism would certainly have benefited from the arguments of this Epistle, and it seems possible that this view will gain more support.

IV. CANONICITY

The Epistle had an interesting early history, with the west generally more reluctant to accept it than the east. Through the influence of Origen the eastern churches came to accept it, mostly on the strength of Pauline authorship. But although certain of the early western Fathers used it (Clement of Rome and Tertullian), it suffered a period of eclipse, until the time of Jerome and Augustine by whom it was fully accepted, and their opinion settled the matter for the western churches.

V. BACKGROUND

An understanding of the author's milieu is essential for a right appreciation of his thought, and there has been a great deal of discussion on this subject. It may be dealt with under five headings.

a. Old Testament

Since the whole argument of the Epistle revolves around Old Testament history and ritual, it goes without saying that the author was deeply influenced by biblical teaching. In fact, it is to be noted that the basis of his approach is biblical and not Judaistic. His reverence for the sacred text is seen in the care with which he cites it, though always from LXX, in the manner in which he introduces his citations (*e.g.* the repetitive 'he says' in chapter i) and in the strictly historical approach to Old Testament history as contrasted with the contemporary allegorical tendencies. The author, well versed as he is in Old Testament concepts, has clearly thought through the problem of the Christian approach to the Old Testament, and his major emphasis is on the fulfilment in Christ of all that was adumbrated in the old order. This subject is further elaborated in the section on the theology of the Epistle, but for the present it should be noted that the author not only himself accepts the full authority of the Scriptures but clearly expects his readers to do the same.

b. Philonism

At the end of the 19th century a strong movement existed which assumed that the author's mind was so steeped in Philonic thought that it was only possible to understand his Epistle against the background of Philo's philosophical and allegorical expositions. The leading exponent of this view was E. Ménégoz, and one of his presuppositions was that a gap existed between this author's theology and that of Paul, and any similarities were clutched at to prove his indebtedness to Philo rather than to Paul. Yet some similarities cannot be denied. The notion of heaven as real and earth as only a place of shadows and the corresponding antitheses between the old covenant and the new show a similar tendency to Philo. Moreover, many words and phrases may be paralleled in the two authors, some of which occur nowhere else in the New Testament. C. Spicq finds the similarities reaching even to matters of style, schemes of thought, and psychology, and concludes that the author was a converted Philonist. Yet this opinion must be received with reserve, for the author differs from Philo on a number of important issues. His biblical exegesis is more akin to rabbinic methods than Philonic, his understanding of history is not, as Philo's, allegorical, and his idea of Christ as High Priest is far removed from Philo's abstract ideas of the Logos. A Christian Philonist would certainly transform his master's conceptions, but it is questionable whether the Christology of Hebrews stands in direct line of succession from Philo. The author may echo Philonic language and ideas, but his roots are without doubt elsewhere.

c. Primitive tradition

The question arises whether or not this Epistle is to be regarded as being a natural development from primitive Christian theology and whether it has any close connections with Pauline and Johannine theology, or even whether it stands as an unrelated attempt of an author to deal with the Old Testament outside the main stream of development. Increasing interest is being shown in the early roots of the Epistle. The attempt to connect it with the catechesis of Stephen focuses attention on this, but further features from the primitive tradition may also be mentioned by way of illustration. The idea of the continuity between the old and new covenants, the interest in the earthly life of Jesus, the realization that His death must be interpreted, and the mixture of present and eschatological appeals, are all basic to the primitive Christian tradition. The main theme of this Epistle, with its predominant interest in man's approach to God, could not fail to find roots in the earliest preaching and teaching. The author introduces many new features, such as Christ's enthronement and heavenly high priesthood, but he brings in nothing alien to that primitive tradition.

d. Paulinism

It was inevitable under the hypothesis of Pauline authorship which held the field for so long that the Epistle should be regarded as an aspect of Pauline theology, yet with the rejection of Pauline authorship an unfortunate reaction set in against any Pauline influence. Support for this extreme position has declined; but it is undeniable that there are some differences from Paul which would support the theory of the author's belonging to an independent stream of tradition, as, for instance, the different treatment of Christ's relation to the law, for there is an absence of that wrestling with the law which is so evident in Paul's experience. Yet the differences must not be stretched into contrasts, and it remains possible to conceive of the author as having been under Pauline influence while at the same time acknowledging his debt to other influences. In this way he becomes an independent witness, in the truest sense, of the early Christian reflection upon the great themes of the gospel.

e. Johannine thought

Whether there are any close connections between the Johannine literature and this Epistle will clearly depend on the dating of each. It has been argued that Hebrews stands midway between Paul and John in the line of theological development (as, for instance, by R. H. Strachan, *The Historic Jesus in the New Testament*, 1931), but in view of the increasing emphasis which is being placed on the primitive character of the Johannine catechesis, to which the evidence of the Dead Sea Scrolls has lent some support, this notion of theological development must be modified. The main points of contact between Hebrews and the Johannine theology are the common use of antithetic parallelism, the similar conception of Christ's high-priestly work, the description of Christ as Shepherd, the allusion to the propitiatory work of Christ, and the attention given to the perfect character of that work.

To sum up, the author is no antiquary whose researches into the biblical revelation possess no relevance for Christians generally, whether ancient or modern, but a writer who presents a vital aspect of Christian thought, complementary to other streams of primitive tradition.

VI. THEOLOGY

All that precedes has prepared the way for the most important consideration, the theological contribution of the Epistle. The standpoint of the author is to regard Christianity as the perfect revelation of God. This meant that Christianity not only superseded all other faiths, including Judaism, but that it could not itself be superseded. Its salvation is eternal (v. 9), so is its redemption, inheritance, and covenant (ix. 12, 15, xiii. 20), while Christ's offering is described as being 'through the eternal Spirit' (ix. 14). This idea of the perfection and abiding character of Christianity pervades the whole Epistle and furnishes the key for the understanding of all its major themes.

a. Christology

The first part of the Epistle is devoted to demonstrating Christ's superiority to all other intermediaries, to prophets, angels, Moses, Joshua, and Aaron, but the opening chapter strikes the positive and exalted note of His divine sonship. This sonship is conceived of as unique, for Christ is heir of all and agent of creation (i. 2). He is even more closely related to God in i. 3, where He is described as the bursting forth of His glory and the express stamp of His nature, and these two statements taken together exclude the twin errors of difference of nature and lack of distinct personality. The pre-existence of Christ seems to be clearly in the author's mind. The further statement in i. 3 that after effecting purification the Son sat down on the right hand of the majesty on high links this opening Christological statement with the later theme of the Epistle, *i.e.* the processes of redemption. Although some have sought, mistakenly, to trace influences of the currently held enthronement ritual of a king who becomes a god, the idea of Christ's exaltation is firmly rooted in the primitive Christian tradition and is a close corollary to the ascension of Christ. When he comes to his later high priest theme the writer clearly intends to introduce his readers to an exalted Christ who no longer needs liturgical means for the purgation of sins.

The incarnation of the Son is many times mentioned. He was made lower than the angels (ii. 9) in order to taste death for everyone, He partook of the same nature as man (ii. 14), He was made like His brethren in every respect (ii. 17) and is capable of sympathizing with our weaknesses because He was in all points tempted as we are (iv. 15). These statements are a necessary prelude to the high priest theme, since He must be shown to be truly representative (*cf.* v. 1). The earthly life of Jesus comes into focus not only in His temptations (ii. 18, iv. 15) but also in His agony of prayer (v. 7), in His perfect obedience (v. 8), in His teaching ministry (ii. 3), and in His endurance of hostility (xii. 3).

But it is the priestly office of Christ which dominates the author's thought. The Aaronic order was good as far as it went, but its inadequacy is brought out strikingly in contrast to the perfect priesthood of Christ. This leads the author to introduce the mysterious Melchizedek theme before his expositions of the weakness of the levitical economy (v. 6, 10, vi. 20–vii. 19). There is no means of ascertaining whether the writer himself innovated this theme or received it from primitive tradition, as it is nowhere else elaborated in the New Testament. But Ps. cx in which the theme occurs exerted a powerful influence on primitive Christian thought, mainly through our Lord's own use of it, and it is reasonable to suppose that this Psalm provided the author with his conception of a superior order of priesthood. Philo, it is true, had already identified Melchizedek with the Logos, but there is no need to appeal to Philo to account for the usage of this Epistle. Nor is it just to maintain that the Melchizedek exposition is entirely speculative and without any modern relevance, for although the method of argument in vii. 1 ff. borders on the allegorical, the author is clear on the fundamental Christian position that Christ must belong to a higher order than that of Aaron, and in introducing the Melchizedek motive he justifies his contention that, although Christ is not a Priest according to the Aaronic order, He nevertheless is a Priest, and not only a Priest but a King. (See MELCHIZEDEK.)

b. The work of Christ

Against the background of the weaknesses of the Aaronic order the author brings out the positive superiority of Christ's atoning work, and the major factors involved are: (i) the finality of Christ's offering (vii. 27, ix. 12, 28, x. 10); (ii) the personal character of His offering in that He offered Himself (ix. 14); (iii) the spiritual character of the offering (ix. 14); and (iv) the abiding results of His priestly work achieving as it did *eternal* redemption (ix. 12). The Aaronic order, with its constantly repeated ritual, could offer no comparison with this. Even the arrangement of furniture in the holy place and the holiest place is brought into the argument (ix. 1 ff.) in order to contrast this with the greater and more perfect sanctuary into which Christ entered once for all by virtue of His own blood. The climax of the soteriological argument is essentially reached at ix. 14, where Christ is said to have offered Himself 'through the eternal Spirit', which brings into striking contrast the helpless and hapless victims of the Aaronic ritual and the deliberate self-offering of our High Priest. The practical application of all this is found in x. 19, where confidence of approach on the basis of Christ's high-priestly work is urged upon the readers, and this leads on to the mainly practical conclusion of the Epistle.

c. Other theological concepts

One of the great words of the Epistle is 'faith', but it has a different meaning from the Pauline concept. For this writer there is little of the dynamic concept of faith which accepts God's provision of salvation (though x. 22 approximates to this and requires to be so understood). In the use of the concept in the great gallery of heroes in chapter xi, the writer does not give a formal definition but rather gives a description of some of its active qualities. It is essentially practical, comprising rather an approach to life than a mystical appropriation. In various ways the author makes clear the meaning of Christian *salvation*, which has deeply impressed him with its greatness (ii. 3). He makes use of Ps. viii to introduce the fact that it is through humiliation that Christ gained the right to bring 'many sons to glory' (ii. 5–10); he conceives of salvation as deliverance from the power of the devil (ii. 14, 15) and also depicts it as a rest into which believers enter as an inheritance (iii–iv. 13). The processes of salvation are described as sanctification (*hagiasmos*, xii. 14, *cf.* ii. 11, x. 10, 29, xiii. 12) and perfection (*teleiōsis*, vii. 11, *cf.* xi. 40, xii. 23).

BIBLIOGRAPHY. F. J. Badcock, *The Pauline Epistles and the Epistle to the Hebrews*, 1937; W. Manson, *The Epistle to the Hebrews*, 1951; E. Ménégoz, *La Théologie de l'Épître aux Hébreux*, 1894; O. Michel, *Der Brief an die Hebräer, Kritisch-Exegetische Kommentar*, 1949; J. Moffatt, 'The Epistle to the Hebrews', *ICC*, 1924; A. Nairne, 'The Epistle to the Hebrews', *CGT*, 1922; F. D. V. Narborough, 'The Epistle to the Hebrews', *Clarendon Bible*, 1930; T. H. Robinson, 'The Epistle to the Hebrews', *MNT*, 1933; C. Spicq, 'L'Épître aux Hébreux', *Études Bibliques*, 1952; B. F. Westcott, *The Epistle to the Hebrews*, 1892; E. C. Wickham, 'The Epistle to the Hebrews', *WC*, 1910; H. Windisch, *Der Hebräerbrief*, 1931.

D.G.

HEBRON (*ḥeḇrôn*, 'confederacy'; *cf.* its alternative and older name Kiriath-arba, 'tetrapolis'), the highest town in Palestine, 3,040 feet above the level of the Mediterranean, 19 miles SSW of Jerusalem. The statement that it 'was built seven years before Zoan in Egypt' (Nu. xiii. 22) probably relates its foundation to the 'Era of Tanis' (*c.* 1720 BC). Abraham lived in its vicinity for considerable periods (see MAMRE); in his days the resident population ('the people of the land') were 'sons of Heth' (see HITTITES), from whom Abraham bought the field of Machpelah with its cave to be a family burying-ground (Gn. xxiii). There he and Sarah, Isaac and Rebekah, Jacob and Leah were buried (Gn. xlix. 31, l. 13). According to Josephus (*Ant.* ii. 8. 2), the sons of Jacob, with the exception of Joseph, were buried there too. The traditional site of the Patriarchs' sepulchre lies within the great *Ḥaram el-Ḫalîl*, the 'Enclosure of the Friend' (*i.e.* Abraham; *cf.* Is. xli. 8), with its Herodian masonry. During the Israelites' wilderness wandering the twelve spies sent out to report on the land of Canaan explored the region of Hebron; at that time it was populated by the 'children of Anak' (Nu. xiii. 22, 28, 33). After Israel's entry into Canaan Hoham, king of Hebron, joined the anti-Gibeonite coalition led by Adonizedek, king of Jerusalem, and was killed by Joshua (Jos. x. 1–27). Hebron itself and the surrounding territory were conquered from the Anakim by Caleb and given to him as a family possession (Jos. xiv. 12 ff., xv. 13 f.; Jdg. i. 10, 20). In Hebron David was anointed king of Judah (2 Sa. ii. 4) and two years later king of Israel also (2 Sa. v. 3); it remained his capital for seven and a half years. It was here too, later in his reign, that Absalom raised the standard of rebellion against him (2 Sa. xv. 7 ff.). It was fortified by Rehoboam (2 Ch. xi. 10). After the Babylonian captivity it was one of the places where returning exiles settled (Ne. xi. 25; Kiriath-arba = Hebron). Later it was occupied by the Idumaeans, from whom Judas Maccabaeus captured it (1 Macc. v. 65). During the war of AD 66–70 it was occupied by Simon bar-Giora, but was stormed and burnt by the Romans (Jos., *BJ* iv. 9. 7, 9). Under the name of el-Ḫalîl it is one of the four sacred cities of the Muslims.

BIBLIOGRAPHY. L. H. Vincent and E. J. H. Mackay, *Hébron, le Ḥaram el-Khalil, sépulture des patriarches*, 2 vols., 1923. F.F.B.

HEIFER (Heb. *'eḡlâ*, twelve times; Heb. *pārâ*, 'young cow', six times; Gk. *damalis*, 'tamed heifer', Heb. ix. 13 only). Mixed with water, the ashes of an unblemished red heifer, burnt in its entirety 'without the camp', imparted levitical purification (Nu. xix; Heb. ix. 13). A decapitated heifer cleansed the nearest city from the blood-guiltiness of a corpse slain by unknown hands (Dt. xxi. 1–9). Jdg. xiv. 18; Je. xlvi. 20; Ho. iv. 16, *etc.*, are interesting examples of the metaphorical use of the word. R.A.S.

HEIR. See INHERITANCE.

HELAM. A city in Transjordan, probably the modern 'Alma, to which the Syrians from beyond the Euphrates were brought by Hadadezer following the defeat of Syrian forces by David, who subsequently also defeated this reinforced Syrian army (2 Sa. x. 16 f.). As the Gk. form, Eliam, constitutes part of the list of place-names in the LXX of Ezk. xlvii. 16, some have proposed a site on the border between Damascus and Hamath. R.A.H.G.

HELBON (*ḥelbôn*, 'fat', 'fruitful'). A town mentioned in Ezk. xxvii. 18 as trading wine to Tyre. It may be the modern Halbûn, about 13 miles north of Damascus, though *GTT* (p. 456) qualifies this identification with the statement that this place has 'no sufficiently ancient remains of occupation' visible. J.D.D.

HELDAI. *Cf.* Heled. (Heb. *ḥeleḏ* means 'duration of life'; *cf.* Arab. *ḫalada* and *ḫuldun.*)

1. In 1 Ch. xxvii. 15, one of David's famous soldiers who was appointed over 24,000 in the twelfth month. He was a Netophathite, and thus from Judah, from the stock of Othniel (*cf.* Jdg. i. 12–15). The 'Heled' of 1 Ch. xi. 30 is doubtless the same person. He is called a free man (Heb. *gibbôr ḥayil*, verse 26), one of the commanders of the army. We must probably read 'Heled' and not 'Heleb' in 2 Sa. xxiii. 29, and he may have been the same person as the above mentioned.

2. A Heldai is mentioned in Zc. vi. 10 with Tobijah and Jedaiah. After they returned from the Exile, silver and gold was taken from them to make a crown for Joshua, the high priest. Heldai is called Helem in verse 14; this may have been a nickname or may be due to a scribal error. F.C.F.

HELEZ. The Heb. *ḥeleṣ* may mean 'loins' or perhaps 'strength'.

1. One of David's heroes. The Helez of 2 Sa. xxiii. 26 is probably the same as the one of 1 Ch. xi. 27 and xxvii. 10. The problem is that in 2 Samuel he is described as the Paltite (Heb. *palṭî*, a man of *bêṯ peleṭ*, a place in Judah) and in 1 Chronicles as the Pelonite (Heb. *pᵉlōnî* means 'any one'). We have to change 'Pelonite' to 'Paltite' or to accept that Helez of 2 Samuel is not to be identified with the one of 1 Ch. xi and xxvii. In 1 Ch. xxvii. 10 he is called one 'of the sons of Ephraim'. It may be that as a descendant of Ephraim he was regarded as a Pelonite, 'one without any connection to Judah', but lived in Beth Pelet.

2. The son of Azariah, a descendant of Judah (1 Ch. ii. 39). F.C.F.

HELKATH. In the border-territory of Asher (Jos. xix. 25) and a levitical city (Jos. xxi. 31). 1 Ch. vi. 75 gives Hukok as a variant for Helkath. The exact location in the Kishon valley is disputed: a likely site for it is Tell el-Harbaj about 6 miles south-east of Haifa (A. Alt, *Palästinajahrbuch*, XXV, 1929, pp. 38 ff.), or perhaps even better, Tell el-Qasis (or Kussis) about 5 miles SSE of Tell el-Harbaj (Y. Aharoni, *IEJ*, IX, 1959, pp. 119–120). Helkath is probably the *ḥrḳt* in topographical lists of the pharaoh Tuthmosis III, *c.* 1460 BC. K.A.K.

HELKATH-HAZZURIM (*ḥelqaṯ haṣṣurîm*, 'field of flints' or 'field of (sword)-edges'). This is the name given to the place in Gibeon where there was a tournament between the champions of Joab and Abner, which led on to a battle (2 Sa. ii. 16). Other meanings conjectured include 'field of plotters', based on the LXX *meris tōn epiboulōn*, 'field of sides', and 'field of adversaries'. (*Cf.* S. R. Driver, *The Hebrew Text of Samuel*, 1913, *ad loc.*)

J.G.G.N.

HELL. 'Hell' in the AV normally renders one of the three words, Sheol, Hades, and Gehenna.

I. SHEOL

The derivation of the Hebrew word *š^e'ôl* is uncertain. Two main theories have been proposed.

a. It has been held to be derived from the root *š-'-l*, meaning 'ask', or 'enquire'. In this case it may have been originally the place of inquiry, where oracles could be obtained. The root *š-'-l* is frequently used in the Old Testament of consulting oracles, but the idea is certainly not a leading one in the conception of Sheol. There is a connection of *thought* with this root in the personification of Sheol as a gaping, craving monster (Is. v. 14; *cf.* Hab. ii. 5, *etc.*). Delitzsch (Commentary on Is. v. 14) thought that an equivalent Assyrian word had been found in *šualu*, but Jensen and others dispute the existence of this word (*cf. Transactions of the Society of Biblical Archaeology*, VIII, 1885, 269).

b. The second main theory is that *š^e'ôl* is derived from the root *š-'-l*, from which come the words for a hollow hand (Is. xl. 12) and a hollow way (between vineyards, Nu. xxii. 24). In post-biblical Hebrew *ša'al* means the 'deep' of the sea. If this derivation is correct, the original sense will be the hollow, or more probably deep, place.

This word is used in the Old Testament for the place of the dead. In general, we may say that it is the state of death pictured in visible terms (see also ESCHATOLOGY). It has many points of similarity to the Bab. *aralu*. But whereas the latter was ruled over by its own gods, Yahweh was the ruler of Sheol (E. F. Sutcliffe, *The Old Testament and the Future Life*, 1946, pp. 8 ff.). R. H. Charles (*A Critical History of the Doctrine of a Future Life*, 1913, pp. 33 ff.) stated that two contradictory views were current in Israel from the 8th century BC onward: the primitive idea of Sheol as a power independent of Yahweh, and the later realization that His power extended to it (Ps. cxxxix. 8; Am. ix. 2; *cf.* Ps. lxxxviii. 5; Is. xxxviii. 18). Rather, while Sheol is within Yahweh's dominion, its inhabitants do not experience God's workings on earth, and are cut off from the covenant institutions (see also ESCHATOLOGY). Sometimes to descend to Sheol seems to be the penalty for wickedness (Ps. lv. 15; Pr. ix. 18). But this can be accounted for by the biblical doctrine that death is the issue of sin. It would seem also that *premature* committal to Sheol is a special form of judgment. Some have seen in words such as *'^abaddôn*, 'destruction' (Jb. xxxi. 12, xxvi. 6, xxviii. 22; Ps. lxxxviii. 11; Pr. xv. 11, xxvii. 20), *šaḥat*, 'pit', and perhaps sometimes also 'corruption' (E. F. Sutcliffe, *op. cit.*, pp. 39 f.; Jb. xxxiii. 24; Ps. xvi. 10; Ezk. xxviii. 8, *etc.*) and *bôr*, 'pit' (Ps. xxx. 3; Ezk. xxxi. 14), a place of punishment within Sheol. But no passage where they occur necessitates this interpretation, and the idea is not explicitly formulated in the Old Testament. These words are better regarded as synonyms of Sheol, with which they all sometimes occur in parallelism.

In the later Jewish literature we meet with the idea of divisions within Sheol for the wicked and the righteous, in which each experiences a foretaste of his final destiny (Enoch xxii. 1–14). This idea appears to underlie the imagery of the parable of Dives and Lazarus in the New Testament.

II. HADES

The Gk. *haidēs* represents the underworld, or realm of the dead, in the classics. In the LXX it almost always renders *š^e'ôl*, and in the New Testament the Pesh. renders it by *š^eyûl*. It is used in connection with the death of Christ in Acts ii. 27, 31, which quotes Ps. xvi. 10. In Mt. xvi. 18 Christ says that the gates of Hades (*cf.* Is. xxxviii. 10; Pss. ix. 13, cvii. 18) shall not prevail against His Church. As the gates of a city are essential to its power, the meaning here is probably the power of death. The phrase 'brought down to Hades' in Mt. xi. 23 is best understood metaphorically of the depths of shame. For other occurrences in the New Testament, see ESCHATOLOGY.

III. GEHENNA

This name is derived from the Heb. *gê' hinnōm* (see ESCHATOLOGY). Its original derivation is obscure. Some have regarded it as coming from an obsolete Aramaic root meaning 'wailing', but most authorities now regard this as improbable. Hinnom is almost certainly the name of a person. In later Jewish writings Gehenna came to have the sense of the place of punishment for sinners (*Assumption of Moses* x. 10; 2 Esdras vii. 36). The rabbinic literature contains various opinions as to who would suffer eternal punishment. The ideas were widespread that the sufferings of some would be terminated by annihilation, or that the fires of Gehenna were in some cases purgatorial. But those who held these doctrines also taught the reality of eternal punishment for certain classes of sinners (A. Edersheim, *The Life and Times of Jesus the Messiah*, 1894, ii. 440, 791 ff.). Both this literature and the Apocryphal books affirm belief in an eternal retribution (*cf.* Judith xvi. 17, *Psalms of Solomon* iii. 13). The teaching of the New Testament endorses this belief (see ESCHATOLOGY). The passages on which a negation of it has been based do not stand close examination. Thus Lk. xii. 47 f. refers to the intensity, not the duration, of the punishment. Mt. v. 26 is metaphorical, and certainly cannot be pressed into service here; while only by a violent exercise of the imagination can Mt. xii. 32 be made to teach that there is forgiveness of some sins in the world to come, although not in this world.

In 2 Pet. ii. 4 only, we find the verb *tartaroō*, translated in the AV 'cast down to hell', and rendered by the Pesh. 'cast down to the lower regions'. *Tartaros* is the classical word for the place of eternal punishment (*HDB*, *s.v.* 'hell'), but is here applied to the intermediate sphere of punishment for fallen angels.

The fact that, on the one hand, God is omnipotent and God is love, and, on the other, eternal retribution is plainly taught in Scripture, raises problems for our minds that in all probability we cannot fully solve. It is easy in such cases to produce a logical answer at the cost of one side of biblical truth, and this has often been done. E. Brunner, on the other hand, invokes the conception of necessary paradox in God's revelation, saying that the Word of God is not intended to teach us objective facts about the hereafter, but merely to challenge us to action (*Eternal Hope*, 1954, 177 ff.). While not holding this doctrine, we must admit that the counsels of God are past the understanding of our finite minds. The reality and eternity of suffering in Gehenna is an element of biblical truth that an honest exegesis cannot evade. D.K.I.

HELMET. See ARMOUR AND WEAPONS.

Fig. 103. A Roman helmet as worn by the Praetorian Guard in the 1st century AD.

HEM. See FRINGES.

HEMAM. The name of a son of Seir the Horite mentioned in Gn. xxxvi. 22. 1 Ch. i. 39 has 'Hômām', and the LXX in both places has 'Haiman'.

HEMAN (*hêmān*, 'faithful'). **1.** One of the sages whom Solomon excelled in wisdom (1 Ki. iv. 31). Said to be a son of Mahol, but 1 Ch. ii. 6 calls him a son of Zerah, a Judahite. (See MAHOL.)

2. A Kohathite Levite, son of Joel, one of David's leading singers (1 Ch. vi. 33, xv. 17, 19, xvi. 41, 42, xxv. 1, 4–6; 2 Ch. v. 12, xxxv. 15). Probably the 'sons of Heman' in 1 Ch. xxv. 4 are really the titles of parts of a prayer or anthem, the singers receiving names from their parts (*cf.* H. L. Ellison in *The New Bible Commentary*², 1954, p. 351; W. R. Smith, *The Old Testament in the Jewish Church*², p. 143 n.).

3. The Ezrahite named in the title of Ps. lxxxviii. Probably the same as (1) above. J.G.G.N.

HEMLOCK. See WORMWOOD, GALL.

HEN. See BIRDS OF THE BIBLE.

HEN (*ḥēn*, 'favour'). One of the men who were to receive a symbolical crown (Zc. vi. 14), this may be a figurative name for Josiah who had earlier (vi. 10) been similarly described as 'the son of Zephaniah'.

HENA. A city whose god, the Assyrians boasted, could not save it (2 Ki. xviii. 34). It is identified by LXX with Ana on the Euphrates. Hena and Ivvah have been identified as Arab. star names, and consequently taken as the names of deities. This is, however, unlikely, as the latter is almost certainly a place-name identical with Avva (2 Ki. xvii. 24, 31). M.A.M.

HENNA. See PLANTS.

HERALD (Aramaic *kārôz*, 'crier', derived, probably not, as has often been thought, from Gk. *kēryx*, but from Old Persian *khraus*, 'crier'; *cf.* J. T. Nelis *ad loc.*). Found only in Dn. iii. 4, 'an herald cried aloud', the reference being to the royal servant who relayed Nebuchadrezzar's commands. (The causative form of the verbal root *krz* is found in Dn. v. 29, 'made a proclamation'.) RVmg renders Gk. *kēryx* as 'herald' (AV 'preacher') in 1 Tim. ii. 7; 2 Tim. i. 11; 2 Pet. ii. 5. J.D.D.

HERB. A non-woody plant with seasonal foliage and varying life expectation in the root, but biblical usage lacks modern botanical exactitude. The common *deše'* normally denotes grass, the common *ḥāṣîr*, *'ēśeḇ* and less common *yārāq* (Dt. xi. 10; 1 Ki. xxi. 2; Pr. xv. 17) may mean grass, and also herbs or vegetables. The *'ōrōṯ* (Mishnaic *'ôrôṯ*) of 2 Ki. iv. 39 is talmudically rendered 'garden-rocket' or 'colewort' (*eruca*), precision perhaps exceeding the evidence (*Yoma* 18b). Is. xxvi. 19 may speak of the dew of light rather than the dew of herbs. The New Testament uses *chortos* for pasturage, *lachanon* for herbs. R.A.S.

HERD. See CATTLE.

HERESY. The Gk. word *hairesis* properly denotes 'choice', and this is the meaning which it always bears in the LXX; in classical authors, however, it can refer to a philosophical school which the individual chooses to follow. Similarly, the New Testament uses the word to denote a 'party', with the suggestion of self-will or sectarian spirit; but it must be noted that none of the parties thus described is in a state of schism from its parent body. The Sadducees (Acts v. 17) and the Pharisees (Acts xv. 5, xxvi. 5) form sects within the fold of Judaism; and the same word is used to describe Christianity as seen from outside (Acts xxiv. 5, 14, xxviii. 22). When parties appear within the Church they are called 'heresies' (1 Cor. xi. 19, where Paul, either with a touch of irony, or else in acknowledgment of the ways of providence, remarks that they are at least a means of bringing leaders to the top). Such divisions are regarded as a work of the flesh (Gal. v. 20), and primarily as a breach of mutual charity, so that the heretic, *i.e.* the man who stubbornly chooses to follow his own group, is to be rejected after two admonitions (Tit. iii. 10).

The first use of 'heresy' in the modern sense of doctrinal error occurs in 2 Pet. ii. 1, where it includes a denial of the Redeemer. Among incipient heresies mentioned in the New Testament, the most prominent are two: Gnosticism of a Jewish type (Col. ii. 8–23) and Docetism (1 Jn. iv. 2, 3; 2 Jn. 7). G.S.M.W.

HERMAS. One of a group of Christians greeted, some by name, in Rom. xvi. 14. They apparently belonged to a single community, perhaps a house-church. The name is a fairly common diminutive for a number of compound names. Origen's suggestion that the author of *The Shepherd* of Hermas (see PATRISTIC LITERATURE) is indicated here has nothing to commend it. A.F.W.

HERMES. Originally the spirit inhabiting the *herma* or cairn, set up as a guide-mark or boundary. Hence the doorside *herms*, roughly carved phallic stones of Athens, and the god's function as guide of living and dead, as patron of road-users (including footpads), and as Zeus' attendant (Acts xiv. 12). Anthropomorphic myth made him the son of Zeus and Maia, heaven's swift messenger, patron of commerce, eloquence, literature, and youth. Latinized as Mercurius (Mercury). E.M.B.

HERMETIC LITERATURE. A collection of writings associated with the name of 'Hermes Trismegistos' ('Thrice-great Hermes').

I. ORIGIN AND CHARACTER

The writings represent a coalescence of Egyptian and Greek modes of thought, often transfused with mystical personal religion. Hellenistic syncretism identified Thoth, the Egyptian scribe of the gods, with the Greek Hermes, whose functions were not dissimilar. In this way the name of the ancient and wise 'Hermes Trismegistos' became attached to much of the magical and astrological lore of the Egyptian temples, which was now seasoned with Greek science and presented in a revelatory form. The surviving literature of this type may go back to the early 2nd century BC.

More permanent interest attaches, however, to the more recognizably philosophical and religious treatises in Greek, of diverse but unknown authorship, in which Hermes, Tat (really a by-form of Thoth, but regarded as distinct), Asclepius, and others appear as teacher and disciples. The treatises are usually dated in the 2nd and 3rd centuries AD: some may be slightly earlier. The main extant items are a body of eighteen treatises (of which one has been artificially constructed from fragments) preserved in Christian manuscript tradition, and a long tractate dedicated to Asclepius, surviving in a Latin translation, and in a so-far unpublished Coptic version at Chenoboskion (*q.v.*). In addition there are some thirty Hermetic fragments in the *Anthology* of Stobaeus, others in other early writers, and some unpublished Hermetica in the Chenoboskion library.

Some of the tractates are in the form of epistolary discourses: others are Socratic dialogues. The most famous, the *Poimandres*, is a vision reminiscent of that of Hermas (see PATRISTIC LITERATURE).

II. CONTENTS

In some ways the *Poimandres* may be taken as a typical Hermetic work. In it Poimandres (perhaps from the Coptic *p-emi-n-re*, 'knowledge of the (sun) god'), described as 'the Mind (*Nous*) of the Sovereignty', offers to reveal to Hermes what he longs to know: 'the things that are, and to understand their nature, and to know God'. There follows the story of the creation of the universe and the fall of man. The former has elements drawn from Gn. i; the latter describes how archetypal man, God's image, entered into a fatal embrace with Nature, and accordingly became a mixed being, both mortal and immortal. Escape from the dead hand of Nature is, however, possible for those who repent and abandon corruption, till the ascent of the soul is completed at death, when body, passion, feeling are utterly surrendered, and man enters into God.

Not all the Hermetica are as coherent, but the aim expressed and the outlook reflected in the *Poimandres* are generally dominant. Knowledge is the goal; the mortal body the curse; regeneration (enthusiastically described in Treatise XIII), the purification of the soul from the taint of matter, the *summum bonum* the soul's final liberation and absorption into God. There is a warm strain of devotion: the appeal to heedless humanity in the *Poimandres* and the still more impassioned cry of Treatise VII are moving; and the occasional hymns are fervent and rapturous.

To this mystical piety is added rather shop-soiled philosophy, partly Platonic, partly Stoic in origin, with a free use of cosmogonic myth. Judaic sources are under tribute, and there are echoes of the language of the LXX. Indeed, it is arguable that Jewish influences originally stimulated religion of this type. The various elements do not always cohere: there are inconsistencies and contradictions of thought within the corpus. The whole tendency is monotheistic, though not polemically so. Of ceremony or sacrament little is said; and there is no evidence of a Hermetic 'church'.

III. THE HERMETICA AND THE BIBLE

The Hermetic use of the Old Testament, as already noted, is undoubted. The relationship between Hermetic religion and the New Testament is more variously assessed. The Christian Father Lactantius, who thought of 'Hermes' as writing in remote antiquity, delightedly notes his monotheism and his address of God as 'Father' (*Divine Institutes* i. 6). More recent writers point to subtler parallels of thought and language with the New Testament, though not all of equal significance. The Logos in Hermetic thought, for instance, is both cosmic and an activity of the soul: but not personal. A statement like 'Thou who by a word hast constituted all things that are' (*Poimandres* 21) need have no other background than Gn. i: there is no definite article in the original. More striking are phrases like 'No one can be saved before rebirth' (*Treat.* xiii. 1), 'He that loveth the body, the same abideth in darkness' (*Poimandres* 19), and the 'Johannine' vocabulary of light and darkness, life and death, belief and witness. Direct influence by the New Testament on later Hermetica is not impossible, but unproven: direct influence of the Hermetic literature on the New Testament would be even harder to substantiate. However, while our extant religious Hermetica are almost certainly later than most of the New Testament, they clearly derive from a well-established tradition; and those may be right who suggest that John has partly in view a public with this *kind* of education and devotion. We must remember, however, that the Hermetica are but one example of contemporary piety; and the language of the Johannine writings can be paralleled also in the Judaic, and essentially biblical, dualism of Qumran.

As to content, it will be seen that the Hermetic parallels are closest with what might be called the accidentals of the New Testament: with the process of redemption rather than with its essential nature and the means by which it is effected. Concerned with sin as ignorance or passion to be sloughed off, rather than as rebellion requiring reconciliation, and with desire set on a salvation which involved deification through union with God, the motive forces of the Hermetists maintained a pagan, not a biblical, direction. And, while the ethical teaching of the Hermetica is insistent and lofty, its other-worldly nature does not allow for the concreteness of biblical ethics. As C. H. Dodd says, the Hermetists share the second, but not the first half of the description of 'pure religion' in Jas. i. 27. (See also GNOSTICISM.)

BIBLIOGRAPHY. Best edn. by A. D. Nock and A. J. Festugière, *Corpus Hermeticum*², 4 vols., 1960 (with French translation); *cf.* also W. Scott, *Hermetica*, 4 vols., 1924–36; A. J. Festugière, *La Révélation d'Hermès Trismégiste*, I, 1944 (for astral lore); C. H. Dodd, *The Bible and the Greeks*, 1935; *The Interpretation of the Fourth Gospel*, 1953, pp. 10 ff. For the new Hermetica see, provisionally, J. Doresse, *The Secret Books of the Egyptian Gnostics*, E.T., 1960, pp. 275 ff.

A.F.W.

HERMOGENES. Mentioned with Phygellus (RV 'Phygelus') as representative of Asian Christians who once repudiated Paul (2 Tim. i. 15). The language indicates Roman Asia (not, as some suggest, an Asian community in Rome), and a specific action (*cf.* RV)—perhaps breaking off relations (through fear of involvement?) when Paul had a right to expect their support. For the meaning of 'turned away', *cf.* Mt. v. 42: total apostasy is not in question. The occasion, which is unlikely to have been very remote, was known to Timothy, but it is not to us (see also ONESIPHORUS).

A.F.W.

HERMON (*ḥermôn*, 'sanctuary'). A 9,100-foot mountain in the Anti-Lebanon Range, and easily the highest in the neighbourhood of Palestine. It is called also Mt. Sion (Dt. iv. 48), and known to the Sidonians—*i.e.* Phoenicians—as Sirion, and to the Amorites as S(h)enir (Dt. iii. 9). Note, however, that Ct. iv. 8 and 1 Ch. v. 23 explicitly distinguish between Hermon and Senir (*q.v.*; *cf. GTT*, p. 41; *DOTT*, p. 49).

Regarded as a sacred place by the original inhabitants of Canaan (*cf.* 'Baal-hermon', Jdg. iii. 3; 'Baal-gad', Jos. xiii. 5, *etc.*), it formed the northern boundary of Israel's conquests from the Amorites (Dt. iii. 8; Jos. xi. 17, *etc.*). Snow usually lies on the top all year round, causing plentiful dews in stark contrast to the parched land of that region (hence probably the Psalmist's allusion in Ps. cxxxiii. 3), and the melting ice forms a major source of the Jordan. Hermon is identified with the modern Jebel es-Sheik, 'the Sheik's mountain', 30 miles south-west of Damascus (but on this point see *GTT*, p. 83). Its proximity to Caesarea Philippi has made some suggest Hermon as the 'high mountain' (Mk. ix. 2, *etc.*) of the transfiguration (*q.v.*).

A misleading reference to 'the Hermonites' (Ps. xlii. 6, AV) should probably be amended to RV 'the Hermons', signifying the three summits of Mt. Hermon.

J.D.D.

HEROD. 1. Herod the Great, king of the Jews 40–4 BC, born *c.* 73 BC. His father Antipater, a Jew of Idumaean descent, attained a position of great influence in Judaea after the Roman conquest and was appointed procurator of Judaea by Julius Caesar in 47 BC. He in turn appointed his son Herod military prefect of Galilee, and Herod showed his qualities by the vigour with which he suppressed brigandage in that region; the Roman governor of Syria was so impressed by his energy that he made him military prefect of Coele-Syria. After the assassination of Caesar and subsequent civil war Herod enjoyed the goodwill of Antony. When the Parthians invaded Syria and Palestine and set the Hasmonaean Antigonus on the throne of Judaea (40–37 BC) the Roman senate, advised by Antony and Octavian, gave Herod the title 'king of the Jews'. It took him three years of fighting to make his title effective, but when he had done so he governed Judaea for thirty-three years as a loyal 'friend and ally' of Rome.

Until 31 BC, despite Antony's goodwill, Herod's position was rendered precarious by the machinations of Cleopatra, who hoped to see Judaea and Coele-Syria reunited to the Ptolemaic kingdom. This peril was removed by the battle of Actium, after which Herod was confirmed in his kingdom by Octavian (Augustus), the new master of the Roman world. Another source of anxiety for Herod was the Hasmonaean family, who resented being displaced on the throne by one whom they regarded as an upstart. Although he married into this family by taking to wife Mariamne, granddaughter of the former high priest Hyrcanus II, Herod's suspicions led him to get rid of the leading Hasmonaean survivors one by one, including eventually Mariamne herself (29 BC).

Fig. 104. Coin of Herod the Great. *Obverse* shows a helmet with cheek-pieces, surrounded by the inscription *Herodou Basileos*, 'Of King Herod', and in the left field the abbreviation for 'Year 3' (*i.e.* from his accession). *Reverse* shows a Macedonian shield with a radiate disc or sphere upon it.

Herod pacified the territories on his north-eastern frontier in the interests of Rome, and Augustus added them to his kingdom. He furthered the emperor's cultural policy by lavish building projects, not only in his own realm but in foreign cities (*e.g.* Athens). In his own realm he rebuilt Samaria and renamed it Sebaste after the emperor (Gk. *Sebastos* = Lat. *Augustus*); he rebuilt Strato's Tower on the Mediterranean coast, equipped it with a splendid artificial harbour, and called it Caesarea, also in honour of the emperor. Other settlements and strongholds were founded throughout the land. In Jerusalem he built a palace for himself on the western wall; he had already rebuilt the Antonia fortress (called after Antony) north-west of the temple area. The greatest of all his building enterprises was the reconstruction of the Jerusalem Temple, begun early in 19 BC.

Nothing that Herod could do, not even the expenditure lavished on the Temple, endeared him to his Jewish subjects. His Edomite descent was never forgotten; if he was a Jew by religion and rebuilt the Temple of the God of Israel in Jerusalem, that did not deter him from erecting temples to pagan deities elsewhere. Above all, his wiping out of the Hasmonaean family could not be forgiven.

This drastic action did not in fact put an end to his domestic troubles. There was friction between his own female relatives and his wives, and between the children of his respective wives. His two sons by Mariamne, Alexander and Aristobulus, were brought up at Rome and were his designated heirs. Their Hasmonaean descent (through their mother) made them acceptable to the Jewish people. But their privileged position stirred the envy of their half-brothers, and especially of Herod's eldest son Antipater, who set himself to poison his father's mind against them. At last (7 BC) they were found guilty of plotting against their father, and executed. Antipater derived no advantage from their death, for three years later he too fell victim to Herod's suspicions, and was executed only a few days before Herod's own death (4 BC).

Herod's suspicious nature is well illustrated by the story of the visit of the Magi and the slaughter of the infants of Bethlehem (Mt. ii); although this story does not appear elsewhere, any rumour of a rival king of the Jews was bound to rouse his worst fears. This suspicion latterly grew to insane proportions, and in consequence Herod has been remembered more for his murderous outbursts than for his administrative ability.

In his will he bequeathed his kingdom to three of his sons—Judaea and Samaria to Archelaus (Mt. ii. 22), Galilee and Peraea to Antipas, and his north-eastern territories to Philip (Lk. iii. 1). These bequests were ratified by Augustus.

2. Archelaus ('Herod the Ethnarch' on his coins). He reigned in Judaea 'in the room of his father Herod' (Mt. ii. 22) from 4 BC to AD 6, but without the title of king. He was Herod's elder son by his Samaritan wife Malthace, and has the worst reputation of all the sons of Herod. He offended Jewish religious susceptibilities by marrying Glaphyra, the widow of his half-brother Alexander. He continued his father's building policy, but his repressive rule became intolerable; a deputation of the Judaean and Samaritan aristocracy at last went to Rome to warn Augustus that, unless Archelaus were removed, there would be a full-scale revolt. Archelaus was accordingly deposed and banished, and Judaea became a Roman province, administered by procurators appointed by the emperor.

3. 'Herod the tetrarch' (Lk. iii. 19, *etc.*), who bore the distinctive name of Antipas. He was Herod's younger son by Malthace, and inherited the Galilaean and Peraean portions of his father's kingdom. In the Gospels he is conspicuous chiefly for his part in the imprisonment and execution of John the Baptist (Mk. vi. 14–28) and for his brief encounter with Jesus when the latter was sent to him by Pilate for judgment (Lk. xxiii. 7 ff.). Jesus is recorded as having once described him as 'that fox' (Lk. xiii. 31 f.). He was the ablest of Herod's sons, and like his father was a great builder; the city of Tiberias on the Lake of Galilee was built by him (AD 22) and named in honour of the Emperor Tiberius. He married the daughter of the Nabataean king Aretas IV (*q.v.*), but divorced her in order to marry Herodias (*q.v.*), the wife of his half-brother Herod Philip. According to the Synoptic Evangelists, John the Baptist incurred the wrath of Antipas for denouncing his second marriage as unlawful;

Josephus (*Ant.* xviii. 5. 2) says that Antipas was afraid that John's great public following might develop into a revolt. Aretas naturally resented the insult offered to his daughter, and seized the opportunity a few years later to wage war against Antipas (AD 36). The forces of Antipas were heavily defeated, and Josephus says that many people regarded the defeat as divine retribution for Antipas's killing of John the Baptist. In AD 39 Antipas was denounced to the Emperor Gaius by his nephew Agrippa (see (4) below) as a plotter; he was deposed from his tetrarchy and ended his days in exile.

4. 'Herod the king' (Acts xii. 1), otherwise known as Agrippa. He was a son of Aristobulus and grandson of Herod the Great. After his father's execution in 7 BC he was brought up in Rome, in close association with the imperial family. In AD 23 he became so heavily involved in debt that he had to leave Rome. For a time he received shelter and maintenance at Tiberias from his uncle Antipas, thanks to his sister Herodias, whom Antipas had recently married. But he quarrelled with Antipas and in AD 36 returned to Rome. There he offended the Emperor Tiberius and was imprisoned, but on Tiberius's death the following year he was released by the new emperor, Gaius (Caligula), from whom he received the title of king, with territories north-east of Palestine as his kingdom. On Antipas's banishment in AD 39, Galilee and Peraea were added to Agrippa's kingdom. When Claudius became emperor in AD 41 he further augmented Agrippa's kingdom by giving him Judaea and Samaria, so that Agrippa ruled over a kingdom roughly equal in extent to his grandfather's. He courted the goodwill of his Jewish subjects, who looked on him as a descendant of the Hasmonaeans (through his grandmother Mariamne) and approved of him accordingly. His attack on the apostles (Acts xii. 2 f.) was perhaps more popular than it would have been previously, because of their recent fraternization with Gentiles (Acts x. 1–xi. 18). His sudden death, at the age of fifty-four (AD 44), is recorded by Luke (Acts xii. 20 ff.) and Josephus (*Ant.* xix. 8. 2) in such a way that the two narratives supplement each other illuminatingly. He left one son, Agrippa (see (5) below), and two daughters—Bernice (born AD 28), mentioned in Acts xxv. 13 ff., and Drusilla (born AD 38), who became the third wife of the procurator Felix (*cf.* Acts xxiv. 24).

5. Agrippa, son of Herod Agrippa (see (4) above), born in AD 27. He was adjudged too young to be made successor to his father's kingdom. Later, however, he received the title of king from Claudius, with territories north and north-east of Palestine which were increased by Nero in AD 56. He changed the name of his capital from Caesarea Philippi (*q.v.*) to Neronias as a compliment to the latter emperor. From AD 48 to 66 he had the prerogative of appointing the Jewish high priests. He did his best to prevent the outbreak of the Jewish war against Rome in AD 66; when his efforts failed he remained loyal to Rome and was rewarded with a further increase of his kingdom. He died childless about AD 100. He is best known to New Testament readers for his encounter with Paul (Acts xxv. 13–xxvi. 32), whom he charged, in bantering vein, with trying to make a Christian of him (Acts xxvi. 28).

BIBLIOGRAPHY. Josephus, *Ant.* xiv–xx *passim*, *BJ* i–ii *passim*; A. H. M. Jones, *The Herods of Judaea*, 1938; S. Perowne, *Life and Times of Herod the Great*, 1956; *id.*, *The Later Herods*, 1958; F. O. Busch, *The Five Herods*, 1958.

F.F.B.

HERODIANS. They are mentioned as enemies of Jesus once in Galilee, and again at Jerusalem (Mk. iii. 6, xii. 13; Mt. xxii. 16). Their association with the Pharisees in the question regarding the paying of tribute to Caesar suggests agreement with them in the issue at stake, that is, nationalism versus submission to a foreign yoke. This fact and the formation of the word (*cf. Caesariani*) seems to prove that they were a Jewish party who favoured the Herodian dynasty. The view that they were a religious party known in rabbinical literature as 'Boethusians', *i.e.* adherents of the family of Boethus, whose daughter Mariamne was one of the wives of Herod the Great and whose sons were raised by him to the high priesthood, is not now generally held.

J.W.M.

HERODIAS (Mk. vi. 17; Lk. iii. 19), daughter to Aristobulus (son of Herod the Great by Mariamne). She married, first, her uncle Herod Philip (son of Herod the Great by a second Mariamne, and not to be confused with Philip the tetrarch), and secondly, her uncle Herod Antipas (see HEROD (3)). By her first husband she had a daughter Salome, who married her grand-uncle Philip the tetrarch. The identity of Herodias's daughter in Mk. vi. 22 ff. is uncertain. When Antipas was exiled in AD 39 Herodias chose to accompany him rather than accept the favour which Gaius was willing to show to the sister of his friend Agrippa (see HEROD (4)). F.F.B.

HERON. See BIRDS OF THE BIBLE.

HESHBON (*ḥešbôn*, 'device'). Originally a city of Moab, but taken by Sihon king of the Amorites and made his royal city (Nu. xxi. 26). After his defeat by the Israelites (xxi. 21–24) it was given to Reuben (xxxii. 37), but later passed over to Gad, whose land bordered on Reuben, and was assigned by them to the Levites (Jos. xxi. 39). By the time of Isaiah and Jeremiah, at the height of its prosperity, Moab had retaken it (Is. xv. 4; Je. xlviii. 2, *etc.*), but by the time of Alexander Jannaeus it is once more in the hands of Israel (Jos., *Ant.* xiii. 15. 4). Remains of old pools and conduits may be seen in a branch of the present Wadi Hesbān which flows by the city (*cf.* Ct. vii. 4). M.A.M.

HETH. See HITTITES.

HETHLON (*ḥeṯlôn*). A city on the ideal northern boundary of Palestine as seen by Ezekiel, near Hamath and Zedad and referred to only by him (Ezk. xlvii. 15, xlviii. 1). Identified with the modern Heitela, north-east of Tripoli, Syria.

HEXATEUCH. See PENTATEUCH.

HEZEKIAH (*ḥizqîyâ* or *ḥizqîyāhû*, 'Yahweh is (my) strength'). One of the most outstanding kings of Judah, Hezekiah achieved fame both for exceptional piety and for his vigorous political activities. Three full accounts of his momentous reign have been preserved in the Old Testament. Those in Kings (2 Ki. xviii–xx) and Isaiah (Is. xxxvi–xxxix) are virtually identical, except for the addition in Isaiah of Hezekiah's song of thanksgiving on his recovery from his illness (Is. xxxviii. 9–20). In Chronicles (2 Ch. xxix–xxxii) the main emphasis is upon Hezekiah's measures for religious reform. Much detail is provided which is peculiar to this account.

The chronology of Hezekiah's reign presents considerable difficulty. The fall of Samaria occurred in the sixth year of his reign (2 Ki. xviii. 10), *i.e.* 722 BC. Yet the invasion of Judah by Sennacherib in 701 BC is placed in the fourteenth year of his reign (2 Ki. xviii. 13). It seems best to assume that Hezekiah was co-regent with Ahaz from *c.* 729 BC, becoming sole king *c.* 716 BC. The two events will then date respectively from the commencement of the co-regency and from the beginning of his reign as sole king (see CHRONOLOGY OF THE OLD TESTAMENT). Problems also arise over the length of Hezekiah's reign. The last recorded event of his reign was the deliverance of Jerusalem from Sennacherib's army (2 Ki. xix. 35, 36). According to Assyr. records, the invasion of Judah took place in 701 BC. However, the reference to Tirhakah, the king of Ethiopia, in 2 Ki. xix. 9 has occasioned the view that Sennacherib invaded Judah a second time *c.* 688 BC.

As a result of Ahaz's abject submission to Assyria, the religious life of the nation had been contaminated by heathen influences. Isaiah's early prophecies reveal the superstition, idolatry, and spiritual blindness of the people (Is. ii. 6 ff., viii. 16 ff., *etc.*). Hezekiah sought to put matters right at the outset of his reign (2 Ch. xxix. 2 ff.). The Temple was reopened and cleansed from all that made it unfit for use, true worship was re-established, and the ancient covenant between Yahweh and Israel was reaffirmed. The celebration of the Passover on a scale unprecedented since the disruption (2 Ch. xxx. 26) was attended by numerous north Israelites in response to Hezekiah's invitation (2 Ch. xxx. 5 ff.). The reformation was carried beyond Jerusalem, and the high places (*bāmôṯ*) throughout Judah and in Benjamin, and Ephraim and Manasseh, were destroyed (2 Ki. xviii. 4; 2 Ch. xxxi. 1). Hezekiah showed particular courage in doing away with the Mosaic bronze serpent which had become an object of idolatrous veneration (see SERPENT, BRAZEN).

How far the reformation was motivated by political considerations is not easy to determine. The Rabshakeh's speech (2 Ki. xviii. 19 ff.) is evidence that the Assyrians were aware of Hezekiah's reforms, but no political significance was apparently attached to them. Hezekiah was restive under the Assyrian yoke. He appears to have been implicated in the anti-Assyrian revolt of *c.* 711 BC, led by Ashdod at Egyptian instigation. Sargon II claims himself to be the 'subduer of the country of Judah' (*ANET*, p. 287), though the Old Testament contains no evidence that Judah was invaded at this time. Evidently,

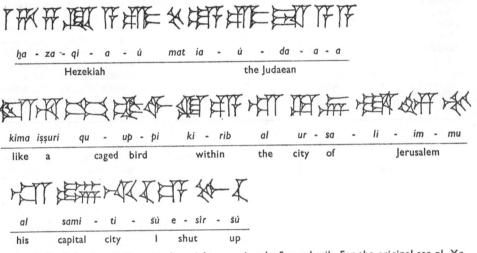

ḫa - za - qi - a - ú mat ia - ú - da - a - a

Hezekiah the Judaean

kima iṣṣuri qu - up - pi ki - rib al ur - sa - li - im - mu

like a caged bird within the city of Jerusalem

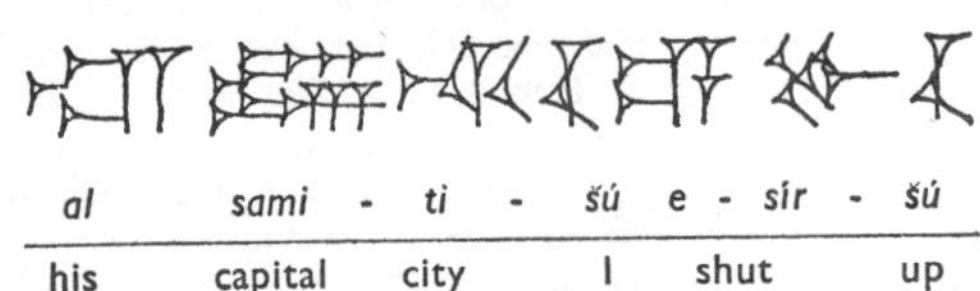
al sami - ti - šú e - sir - šú
his capital city I shut up

Fig. 105. Part of an inscription recording eight campaigns by Sennacherib. For the original see pl. Xa.

Isaiah's warning did not go unheeded (Is. xx). After the death of Sargon, Hezekiah took the lead in the anti-Assyrian revolt in the West. His courteous reception of Merodach-baladan's envoys (2 Ki. xx. 12 ff.) was directly related to his bid for political emancipation. In preparation for the Assyrian invasion, Hezekiah built up the defences of Jerusalem and safeguarded the city's water-supply by constructing the Siloam tunnel (2 Ki. xx. 20; Is. xxii. 9 ff.; see also SILOAM and fig. 193).

Sennacherib's account of his third campaign on the Taylor prism represents Hezekiah as the ring-leader of the western revolt. He there claims to have captured forty-six fortified towns and to have shut up Hezekiah 'like a caged bird within Jerusalem his royal city' (*cf. ANET*, pp. 287 f.). Though Yahweh intervened to save Jerusalem by the destruction of the Assyrian army (2 Ki. xix. 32 ff.), Judah had suffered a crippling blow.

While Hezekiah was doubtless at times too much dominated by his political advisers, his sincerity and devotion to Yahweh cannot be questioned (2 Ki. xviii. 5, 6).

BIBLIOGRAPHY. D. Winton Thomas, *DOTT*, pp. 64–73; article on 'Hezekiah' in *ISBE*.

J.C.J.W.

HEZION. See REZON.

HIDDEKEL. The ancient name of the river Tigris (*q.v.*) used in the account of the Garden of Eden (Gn. ii. 14) and in Daniel's description of his visions (Dn. x. 4) in the third year of Cyrus. The name comes from Akkadian *idiqlat*, which is equivalent to Sumerian *idigna*.

BIBLIOGRAPHY. A. Deimel, *Šumerisches Lexikon*, II, No. 74 (238), p. 163.

T.C.M.

HIEL (*ḥî'ēl*, 'El lives' (*BDB*) or 'brother of God' (C. F. Burney in *HDB*; *cf.* LXX), according to whether it is regarded as a contraction of *y^{e}ḥî'ēl* or *'^{a}ḥî'ēl*). The Bethelite who rebuilt Jericho during Ahab's reign, at the cost of the lives of two of his sons, thus fulfilling Joshua's curse (1 Ki. xvi. 34; *cf.* Jos. vi. 26).

J.G.G.N.

HIERAPOLIS. A city in the Roman province of Asia, in the west of what is now Asiatic Turkey. It was situated about 6 miles north of Laodicea (*q.v.*), on the opposite side of the broad valley of the Lycus. The city was built around copious hot springs, which were famed for their medicinal powers. There was also a subterranean vent of poisonous gases (the Plutonium), which was later filled in by the Christians in about the 4th century AD. These natural features made Hierapolis (the name means 'city of the sanctuary' or 'sacred city') a centre of pagan cults from the earliest times. Its importance and prosperity were almost entirely derived from the fame and popularity of these cults and of the healing powers of the springs. Commercially, it was probably dependent on its near neighbour, the much larger city of Laodicea. There is now only a small village (Ecirliköy) near by; it lies at the foot of spectacular cliffs of lime (pamukkale), which have been deposited over the centuries from the hot-spring water as it flows off the terrace on which the ancient city was built.

The church in Hierapolis was probably founded while Paul was living at Ephesus (Acts xix. 10), perhaps by Epaphras (Col. iv. 12, 13). According to a tradition quoted by Polycrates, bishop of Ephesus about AD 190, the apostle Philip lived and preached, and was buried, at Hierapolis.

M.J.S.R.

HIGGAION. See PSALMS.

HIGH PLACE. The Heb. word *bāmâ* which AV renders 'high place' (but see BAMAH) varies greatly in meaning and application.

1. Used in the plural, it may mean literally 'high places', *i.e.* mountain-tops. This is probably its primitive meaning, as Akkadian and Ugaritic suggest.

2. Since shrines were frequently erected upon hilltops, 'on every high hill' (1 Ki. xiv. 23), it may refer to these, the shrine itself and its elevated position both entering into the meaning.

3. During the monarchy shrines were 'built' in the cities and their 'gates' (2 Ki. xxiii. 8) which are described as 'high places'. The references can be best considered under these three heads.

In the first class are various poetical allusions to battles and victory over enemies (Dt. xxxii. 13; Jdg. v. 18; 2 Sa. i. 19, 25). In these the mountains are viewed as strongholds; in Dt. xxxii. 13, LXX renders *tēn ischyn tēs gēs*. In Is. xiv. 14 *bāmôṯ* is rightly rendered in AV as 'heights', which could equally have been used elsewhere (*e.g.* Mi. iii. 12).

In the second group we have the 'high place' to which Samuel was accustomed to 'go up' to offer sacrifice (1 Sa. ix. 12). Here the 'high place' clearly includes the eminence itself, but associated with it is the altar (though this is not directly mentioned), the 'great chamber' (ix. 18), and possibly other buildings. The word is used again when Saul's company approach the 'hill of God', where they meet a company of prophets 'coming down from the *bāmâ*' (1 Sa. x. 5, 13). Like that of Samuel, the *bāmâ* appears to be an eminence associated with worship.

A third instance of this kind is the high place at Gibeon, 'the great high place' referred to in 1 Ki. iii. 1–4; 2 Ch. i. 2–6, where Solomon sacrificed a thousand rams. Gibeon is the highest point in the immediate area, and LXX renders *hypsēlotatē*, not *megalē*.

There is no suggestion here of idolatry, but a slight shade of disapproval; the people (see 1 Ki. iii. 2) being excused 'because there was no house built for the Lord before those days'.

With the building of the Temple, the rebellion of Jeroboam, and the increase of idolatry, the word *bāmâ* acquires a new and evil meaning. In opposition to the temple worship, Jeroboam set up the golden calves in Bethel and Dan, apparently in conscious imitation of Aaron (1 Ki. xii. 28; *cf.* Ex. xxxii. 4, 8), and so 'made Israel to sin'. He also made a house of high places (*bêṯ bāmôṯ*), and established it with priests of low status (1 Ki. xii. 32). He may have done this in the name of Yahweh to deceive the people, but God was not deceived, and he was rebuked (1 Ki. xiii. 1–6).

Meantime, under Rehoboam, the people of Judah fell headlong into Canaanite idolatry, which is thus described: they 'built them high places, and pillars, and Asherim' on 'every high hill and under every green tree' (1 Ki. xiv. 23), with all their accompanying 'abominations'. Such Canaanite worship is always condemned in the strongest terms. Moses himself had foreseen this danger, and condemned the use of pillars and Asherim, symbols of Baal and Asherah (Ex. xxxiv. 12 f.; Dt. xii. 2 f., xvi. 21 f.).

But there are other high places towards which a different tone is adopted. Thus in the record of King Asa, we are told that he did 'right in the eyes of the Lord', and his zeal to remove all traces of idolatry is recorded; then come the words 'the high places were not removed' (1 Ki. xv. 11–14); and these are repeated in the case of other good kings, zealous for Yahweh. The tone here is the same as that in 1 Ki. iii. 2, and we are led to think of these high places as being like Gibeon, and perhaps like that of Samuel at Ramah. Worship in these and similar places was offered still to Yahweh; it had become irregular now that the Temple had become the true centre. Finally, they were 'removed' by Hezekiah (2 Ki. xviii. 4, 22).

The theory set up by Wellhausen, and adopted with some hesitation by many modern scholars, is different. According to this the 'Book of the Covenant' (Ex. xx–xxiv) was a document of the early monarchy which expressly allowed (Ex. xx. 24) the local sanctuaries, or 'high places'. These were suppressed, in part, by Hezekiah, but only completely by the 'Deuteronomic' reform under Josiah (2 Ki. xxiii). (See DEUTERONOMY; and G. T. Manley, *The Book of the Law*, 1957, chapter ix.) This evidently is not the belief of the author of the two books of Kings, who, after all, was in a better position to judge.

It has been suggested also that the Israelites took over indiscriminately the Canaanite 'high places'. Archaeological research has laid bare, at Gezer and elsewhere, rock eminences used for primitive forms of worship. Some of these have great standing stones, similar to those at Stonehenge. Artificial 'high places' have also been found in temples of the Middle Bronze Age, *e.g.* at Megiddo (*q.v.*) and at Nahariyah (on the coast south of Tyre) where the stones were covered with an oily deposit, apparently the remains of libations. An upright stone pillar stood at the edge of this cairn. This type of shrine continued and was adopted by apostate Israelites. We read that Manasseh 'built up again' those which Hezekiah had removed (2 Ki. xxi. 3); they were found by the men of Josiah in the 'cities of Judah' and one at least in one of the gates of Jerusalem (2 Ki. xxiii. 5, 8). From this we deduce that they were structures of moderate size, suited for the burning of incense or the offering of sacrifices, and of no great strength, since they could without great difficulty be broken down and burned (2 Ki. xxiii. 15). Those erected by Solomon outside Jerusalem may have been larger, for they were only defiled (verse 13).

Several large stone cairns to the west of Jerusalem may be Judaean *bāmôṯ*. Excavation has revealed steps leading up to the top, and pottery of 7th-century date was found in them. No definite traces of the nature of their use have been found; but it is clear that they were not burial mounds.

Recent studies suggest that the religious *bāmâ* was originally a piece of high ground, often, perhaps, the burial-place of some important person, marked by a tumulus or a stone, forming a convenient focal point for assemblies of worshippers. In towns this could take the form of a small artificial mound on which the rites could be performed in the sight of the devotees.

BIBLIOGRAPHY. W. F. Albright, *The High Place in Ancient Palestine*, Supplement to *VT*, IV, 1957, pp. 242–258; L. H. Vincent, 'La Notion Biblique du Haut-Lieu', *RB*, LV, 1948, pp. 245–278, 438–445; M. Dothan, 'Nahariyah', *IEJ*, VI, 1956, pp. 14–25; R. B. K. Amiran, 'Cairns near Jerusalem', *IEJ*, III, 1953. G.T.M.

HIGH PRIEST. See PRIESTS AND LEVITES, I *a*, *e*.

HILKIAH (*ḥilqîyâhû*, *ḥilqîyâ*, 'my portion is Yahweh' or 'he whose portion is Yahweh').

1. The father of Eliakim, Hezekiah's chamberlain (2 Ki. xviii. 18, 26, 37; Is. xxii. 20, xxxvi. 3, 22).

2. The high priest in Josiah's reign. During the repairs on the Temple, he found the book of the law, and brought it to the notice of Shaphan the scribe. Subsequently he was a member of the king's deputation to Huldah the prophetess to learn God's will in the matter, and later he helped to put Josiah's reformation into effect (2 Ki. xxii, xxiii; 2 Ch. xxxiv, xxxv. 8).

3, 4. Levites of the family of Merari (1 Ch. vi. 45, xxvi. 11). **5.** One of those who stood with Ezra the scribe when he read the law of God from a wooden pulpit (Ne. viii. 4). **6.** One of the chiefs of the priests who went up to Judaea with Zerubbabel (Ne. xii. 7, 21). Possibly identical with (5).

7. The father of Jeremiah the prophet, and member of the priestly family of Anathoth (Je. i. 1). Probably a descendant of Abiathar, David's high priest who was rusticated by Solomon for supporting Adonijah (1 Ki. ii. 26). Hilkiah was possibly the officiating priest to the rural community at Anathoth.

8. The father of Gemariah, one of Zedekiah's ambassadors to Nebuchadrezzar (Je. xxix. 3).

J.G.G.N.

HILL, HILL-COUNTRY. These words in AV and RV translate the Heb. words *giḇʻâ* and *har*. The root meaning of the former is convexity; bare hills, like an inverted basin, are a common feature of Palestine, notably the area of Judah. But *giḇʻâ* is often a proper name (Gibeah) to indicate towns built on such eminences, coupled with a distinguishing 'surname' (*e.g.* 'of Saul', 1 Sa. xi. 4).

The second word, *har*, may indicate a single eminence or a range of hills; this leads to some confusion in AV, but RV usually translates by 'hill-country' where a range is meant. The mountainous backbone of Palestine is so styled, sometimes divided into the northern and southern parts of it, respectively called the hill-country 'of Ephraim' and 'of Judah'. It should, however, be noted that it is not always possible to decide whether a single hill or a hilly region is meant.

D.F.P.

HIN. See WEIGHTS AND MEASURES.

HIND. See HART.

HINNOM, VALLEY OF. A valley to the south of Jerusalem, also styled 'the valley of the son (or sons) of Hinnom'. It was associated in Jeremiah's time with the worship of Molech. Josiah defiled this shrine, and put an end to the sacrifices offered there. Later the valley seems to have been used for burning the corpses of criminals and animals, and indeed refuse of any sort. Hence the name came to be used as a synonym for hell, the Heb. phrase *gê* ('valley of') *hinnōm* becoming *geenna* in Greek, whence Gehenna in Latin and English. Jewish tradition at one time held that the mouth of hell was in the valley.

The identification of the valley presents problems. It formed part of the boundary between the territories of Judah and Benjamin, and lay between the 'south side of the Jebusite; the same is Jerusalem' and Enrogel (Jos. xv. 7 f.). So clearly the identification of these two localities will affect our identification of the Valley of Hinnom. If En-rogel was the Virgin's Fountain the Valley of Hinnom can be equated with the Kidron Valley, which runs from the east to the south-east of Jerusalem. But if it was what is now called Bir Eyyub, two possibilities remain: the valley was either the Tyropoeon Valley, running from the centre of Jerusalem to the south-east, or the valley encircling the city on the west and south, now called the Wadi al-Rababi. Each of these three valleys, at its south-eastern extremity, terminates near Siloam. Muslim tradition supports the Kidron Valley identification, but that is the least likely; the great majority of scholars accept the Wadi al-Rababi as the correct identification. See EN-ROGEL. D.F.P.

HIPPOPOTAMUS. See BEHEMOTH.

HIRAM. The king of Tyre, contemporary with David and Solomon; reigned 979/8–945/4 BC (according to Albright, 969–936 BC; see CHRONOLOGY OF THE OLD TESTAMENT).

a. Name

Heb. *Ḥîrām* (Samuel and Kings); *Ḥîrōm* (1 Ki. v. 10, 18); *Ḥûrām* (Chronicles) is a Phoenician name possibly equivalent to, or an abbreviation for, Aḥiram (Nu. xxvi. 38), meaning 'my brother is the exalted (god)', as Ḥiel stands for Aḥiel (1 Ki. xvi. 34).

b. Relations with Judah

Hiram was a great admirer of David (1 Ki. v. 1) and sent materials and craftsmen to aid the building of his palace at Jerusalem (2 Sa. v. 11; 1 Ch. xiv. 1). On Solomon's accession Hiram sent ambassadors to make fresh contacts which led to a trade-treaty whereby he supplied wood from Lebanon and skilled craftsmen for the construction of the new Temple at Jerusalem, in return for an annual payment by Solomon of wheat and fine oil (1 Ki. v. 2–11). Additional payments of barley and wine seem to have been required for the maintenance of the Tyrian workmen, who included technicians acquainted with fabric design and dyes, sent to instruct the Israelites (2 Ch. ii. 3–7).

Twenty years later, on the completion of the Temple, Solomon gave Hiram twenty villages in Galilee, presumably near Tyre, and received in exchange 120 talents of gold (1 Ki. ix. 10–14). Such treaties to adjust the borders between states are known from early Syrian agreements (*e.g.* Alalaḫ). These treaties, which were planned for the economic advantage of both parties, were supplemented by trading operations in which Solomon's ocean-going vessels (see TARSHISH) joined the fleet of Hiram to import gold, silver, and various kinds of rarities, including monkeys (1 Ki. x. 22; 2 Ch. ix. 21; see SHIPS AND BOATS). The vessels sailing from Ezion-geber for Ophir were accompanied by experienced pilots provided by Hiram (1 Ki. ix. 26–28; 2 Ch. viii. 17, 18).

c. The reign of Hiram

Apart from the Old Testament, Hiram's rule is chronicled by Josephus (*Ant.* viii. 2. 6, 7; *Contra Apionem* i. 17 f.), based on the historians Menander and Dius. According to this source, Hiram (LXX *Chiram*, Gk. *Heiramos*, *Heirōmos*) was the son of Abi-baal and reigned thirty-four years before dying at the age of fifty-three. The building of the Temple at Jerusalem began in his eleventh year, *i.e.* the fourth year of Solomon (1 Ki. vi. 1). Hiram warred against Cyprus to enforce the payment of tribute and fortified the island of Tyre, where he built temples to Astarte-Melqart (later Hercules) and enriched the older temples.

Josephus, like Eupolemon and Alexander Polyhistor, recounts the letters, said to have been preserved in the state archives at Tyre, which passed between Hiram and Solomon concerning the building of the Temple. Josephus states also that the two kings engaged in an exchange of riddles until Solomon was defeated by a young Tyrian named Abdemon. Clement of Alexandria and Tatian say that a daughter of Hiram was married to Solomon; with this should be compared the statement that Sidonians were among his wives (1 Ki. xi. 1, 2).

See also TYRE, SIDON, PHOENICIA.

D.J.W.

HIRE, HIRELING. The two main classes of wage-earner in Israel were the foreign mercenary and the agricultural labourer typifying respectively dereliction of duty (Je. xlvi. 21) and stinting service (Jb. vii. 1 f.) under exploitation (Mal. iii. 5). Hence the pejoratives in Jn. x. 12, 13 and Lk. xv. 19. David introduced foreign mercenaries to buttress the newly adopted monarchy (2 Sa. viii. 18). The agricultural labourer was debased by an enclosure movement in the 8th century (Is. v. 8) which dispossessed many freehold farmers of their patrimony and left them in debt. By custom the ultimate discharge of debt was perpetual slavery (2 Ki. iv. 1). The law provided that an Israelite who, through poverty, had to sell himself to a fellow-Israelite should be allowed the status of an employee and be manumitted in the year of Jubilee (Lv. xxv. 39–55). Other laws also protected him (*e.g.* Lv. xix. 13; *cf.* Dt. xxiv. 14, 15). Jacob's two contracts (Gn. xxix) disclose a background of nomadic kinship and recall the great national codes of the second millennium BC. See also SLAVE, SLAVERY.

A.E.W.

HITTITES (Heb. *ḥittim, bene ḥēt*). In the Old Testament the Hittites are, firstly, a great nation which gave its name to the whole region of Syria, 'from the wilderness and this Lebanon even unto the great river, the river Euphrates, all the land of the Hittites, and unto the great sea toward the going down of the sun' (Jos. i. 4); and secondly, an ethnic group living in Canaan from patriarchal times until after the Israelite settlement (Gn. xv. 20; Dt. vii. 1; Jdg. iii. 5), called 'the children of Heth' (Gn. xxiii. 3, *etc.*) after their eponymous ancestor Heth, a son of Canaan (Gn. x. 15).

I. THE HITTITE EMPIRE

The Hittite Empire was founded *c.* 1800 BC by an Indo-European nation which had settled in Asia Minor in city-states some two centuries before. They derived the name 'Hittite' from the Hatti, the earlier inhabitants of the area where they settled (sometimes distinguished as the 'Proto-Hittites'). With the spread of the Hittite Empire the designation 'Hittites' was extended to the peoples and lands which it incorporated.

An early Hittite king, Tudhalia I (*c.* 1720 BC), has been identified with 'Tidal king of nations' of Gn. xiv. 1. About 1600 BC Hattusilis I extended his rule over parts of N Syria. His successor Mursilis I established a new capital at Hattusas (modern Boghaz-Koi), east of the Halys; it is largely to the archives uncovered there since 1906 that we owe our knowledge of Hittite history and literature. Mursilis I captured Aleppo and subsequently (*c.* 1560 BC) raided Babylon—an event which precipitated the fall of the first Babylonian Dynasty.

King Telepinus (*c.* 1480 BC) was the great Hittite legislator. There are some striking affinities between the Hittite law-codes and those of the Pentateuch, although affinities are found in matters of detail and arrangement rather than in general conception. Whereas the Pentateuchal codes resemble the great Semitic law-codes of the Ancient Near East in employing the *lex talionis* as a basic principle, the Hittite laws are dominated by the distinctively Indo-European principle of compensation (*Wergeld*).

The Hittite Empire reached the peak of its power under Suppiluliumas I (*c.* 1380–1350 BC). It was in his province of Kizzuwatna, in SE Asia Minor, that iron was first smelted in the Near East on a scale which justifies one in speaking of the beginning of the Iron Age. He extended his empire over Upper Mesopotamia and over Syria as far south as the Lebanon. The Hittites thus collided with the northern thrust of the Egyptian Empire in Asia, and hostilities continued between the two powers until 1280 BC, when a non-aggression pact between Hattusilis III and Rameses II recognized the Orontes as their common frontier.

The Hittite Empire collapsed around 1200 BC as the result of blows from western enemies.

II. THE HITTITE KINGDOMS

With the fall of the Hittite Empire, twenty-four city-states of the Tabali ('Tubal' in the Old Testament) became heirs to the Hittite home territory north of the Taurus range. In Syria seven city-states which had belonged to the Hittite Empire perpetuated the name 'Hittite' for several centuries; their rulers were called 'the

Fig. 106. Carved relief showing a Hittite king (*right*) pouring a libation before a storm-god who carries a weapon in his right hand and a thunderbolt in his left. From Malataya; c. 9th century BC.

kings of the Hittites'. Hamath on the Orontes and Carchemish on the Euphrates were among the most important of the seven. Hamath was allied with David (2 Sa. viii. 9 ff.), whose kingdom bordered on 'Kadesh in the land of the Hittites' (2 Sa. xxiv. 6, RSV; see TAHTIM-HODSHI). Solomon traded and intermarried with these 'kings of the Hittites' (1 Ki. x. 28 f., xi. 1). In the 9th century BC their military reputation could throw the army of Damascus into panic (2 Ki. vii. 6). But in the following century they were reduced one by one by the Assyrians; Hamath fell in 720 BC and Carchemish in 717 (*cf.* 2 Ki. xviii. 34, xix. 13; Is. x. 9).

The Assyrian and Babylonian records of the period (as late as the Chaldean dynasty) regularly refer to the whole of Syria (including Palestine) as the 'Hatti-land'; Sargon II in 711 BC can speak of the people of Ashdod as 'the faithless Hatti'.

The language of the seven Hittite kingdoms is known from hieroglyphic texts which have been deciphered in recent years; bilingual inscriptions in hieroglyphic Hittite and Phoenician, discovered at Karatepe in Cilicia (1946–7), have helped considerably in their decipherment. The language of these texts shows dialect variations from the official language of the earlier Hittite Empire, which was written in cuneiform script and identified as an Indo-European language in 1917.

III. THE HITTITES OF CANAAN

The Hittites of Canaan in patriarchal times appear as inhabiting the central ridge of Judah, especially the Hebron district. They were probably early migrants from some part of the Hittite Empire; the Hittite Empire itself never extended so far south. In Gn. xxiii the Hittites are the resident population of Hebron ('the people of the land') among whom Abraham lives as 'a stranger and a sojourner' and from whom he buys the field of Machpelah, with its cave, as a family burying-ground. The record of the purchase is said to be 'permeated with intricate subtleties of Hittite laws and customs, correctly corresponding to the time of Abraham' (M. R. Lehmann, *BASOR*, 129, Feb. 1953, p. 18). Esau grieved his parents by marrying two 'daughters of Heth . . . daughters of the land' (Gn. xxvii. 46, *cf.* xxvi. 34 f.)—apparently in the Beersheba region. Jerusalem, according to Ezk. xvi. 3, 45, had a mixed Hittite and Amorite foundation. The name of Araunah the Jebusite (2 Sa. xxiv. 16 ff.) has been thought to be Hittite (see ARAUNAH), and Uriah the Hittite, evidently a Jerusalemite, was one of David's mighty men (2 Sa. xxiii. 39). Ahimelech, one of David's companions in the days of his outlawry, is called a Hittite (1 Sa. xxvi. 6).

The last reference to the Hittites of Canaan is in Solomon's reign (2 Ch. viii. 7); thereafter they were merged in the general population of the land.

BIBLIOGRAPHY. O. R. Gurney, *The Hittites*, 1952; O. R. Gurney and J. Garstang, *The Geography of the Hittite Empire*, 1959; S. Lloyd, *Early Anatolia*, 1956; L. Woolley, *A Forgotten Kingdom*, 1953; C. W. Ceram, *Narrow Pass, Black Mountain*, 1956; E. Neufeld, *The Hittite Laws*, 1951; M. Vieyra, *Hittite Art*, 1955; F. F. Bruce, *The Hittites and the Old Testament*, 1947.

F.F.B.

HIVITE. One of the sons of Canaan (Gn. x. 17; 1 Ch. i. 15); an early inhabitant of Syria and Palestine named as distinct from the Canaanites, Jebusites, Perizzites, Gergashites, and Amorites (Ex. iii. 8; Nu. xiii. 29; Dt. vii. 1), and in association with the Arkites (*q.v.*) known to have dwelt in Lebanon (Gn. x. 17). This accords with their principal location in the Lebanon hills (Jdg. iii. 3) and the Hermon range as far as the valley leading to Hamath (Jos. xi. 3), where they still lived in the time of David, who lists them after Sidon and Tyre (2 Sa. xxiv. 7). Hivites were conscripted as labourers for Solomon's building projects (1 Ki. ix. 20; 2 Ch. viii. 7). Others were settled in Shechem, whose founder is described as son of Hamor, a Hivite, in the time of Jacob (Gn. xxxiv. 2) and near Gibeon (Jos. ix. 7, xi. 19).

Many equate the Hivites (Heb. *Ḥiwwî*; Gk. *Heuaios*) with the Horites (*Ḥorri(m)*), assuming a scribal confusion between the *w*(*āw*) and *r*(*eš*). In Gn. xxxvi. 20–30 Zibeon is called a Horite as opposed to a Hivite in verse 2. Similarly, the LXX of Gn. xxxiv. 2 and Jos. ix. 7 renders 'Horite' for 'Hivite', and some read 'Hittite' (*ḥittî*) for 'Hivite' in Jos. xi. 3; Jdg. iii. 3. The derivation from *ḥawwâ*, 'tent-village', is uncertain, and the identification of the Hivites, otherwise unattested, remains unsolved.

D.J.W.

HOBAB (*ḥōḇāḇ*, 'beloved'). Nu. x. 29 speaks of 'Hobab, the son of Raguel the Midianite, Moses' father in law'—ambiguous wording which leaves unclear whether Moses' father-in-law was Hobab or Raguel (Reuel). Jdg. iv. 11 (*cf.* Jdg. i. 16) says Hobab; Ex. ii. 18 says Reuel; but evidence is too slight to choose between the two accounts. Islamic tradition identifies Hobab with Jethro (*q.v.*), but others suggest an identification between Reuel and Jethro (Ex. ii. 18, iii. 1). The latter would make Hobab the brother-in-law of Moses; but such an interpretation of the Heb. word (*ḥōṯēn*) is questionable. J.D.D.

HOBAH. The name of the place to which Abraham pursued the four kings who had pillaged Sodom and Gomorrah and carried off Lot (Gn. xiv. 15). It lay 'on the left hand of', that is (to one facing east) to the north of Damascus. Though modern sites have been suggested, the place is unknown. T.C.M.

HOLINESS, HOLY, SAINTS. There is probably no religion without a distinction between holy and profane, and in most, if not indeed in all, the religious man is the one to whom something is holy.

The principal biblical words are *qāḏôš* and

qōḏeš in the Old Testament and *hagios* in the New Testament, all words of uncertain derivation. If the Semitic origin of *qāḏôš* be accepted, it may come from a root expressing 'separation' or 'cutting off', applied to the separation of a person or thing to divine use, and so eventually to the state of the object or person so reserved. *Hagios* in the New Testament is the nearest equivalent to the Hebrew *qāḏôš* (probably from the same source as *hagnos* signifying 'pure') and has the same fundamental thought of separation and so of consecration to God. *Hosios* is also used as the equivalent of the Heb. *ḥāsîḏ*; and, like it, implies the right relation to God as holy or pious, with the further connotation, perhaps, of 'beloved' of God. In this latter sense the Messiah is termed the *Holy One* (Acts ii. 27). It may not have, in the first instance, the same ethical implications as *hagios*, though in Tit. i. 8 it certainly connotes holy character.

In the Old Testament holiness is designated of places, things, seasons, and official persons, in virtue of their connection with the worship of God. The first application of the term is to the seventh-day sabbath which God is said to have made holy (Gn. ii. 3). It is likewise applied to the place of worship or sanctuary, and also to things within the sanctuary used in the worship of God. Similarly, it is used in connection with persons, priests, Levites, *etc*., officially connected with the worship of God. In these instances holiness signifies a relation that involved separation from common use and dedication to a sacred one.

a. The holiness of God's character

Holiness in the Old Testament as in the New Testament is applied in the highest sense to God. It denotes, first, His separateness from the creation and elevation above it. It thus sets forth the transcendence of God. Yahweh as the Holy One stands in contrast to false gods (Ex. xv. 11) and to the whole of creation (Is. xl. 25). See also GOD, Section III.

The word also denotes relationship, and signifies God's determination to preserve His own position relative to all other free beings. It is God's self-affirmation, 'the attribute in virtue of which Jehovah makes Himself the absolute standard of Himself' (Godet). Not only does it bring out the contrast between the divine and the human (Ho. xi. 9), but it becomes almost synonymous with supreme deity, and emphasizes, in particular, the awe-inspiring side of the divine character (Ps. xcix. 3).

The ethical quality in holiness is, however, the aspect under which the term is applied most commonly to God. Holiness is a term for the moral excellence of God and His freedom from all limitation in His moral perfection (Hab. i. 13). In this exalted sense God only is holy and so the standard of ethical purity in His creatures.

Since holiness embraces every distinctive attribute of Godhead, it may be defined as the outshining of all that God is. As the sun's rays, combining all the colours of the spectrum, come together in the sun's shining and blend into light, so in His self-manifestation all the attributes of God come together and blend into holiness. Holiness has, for that reason, been called 'an attribute of attributes', that which lends unity to all the attributes of God. To conceive of God's being and character as merely a synthesis of abstract perfections is to deprive God of all reality. In the God of the Bible these perfections live and function in holiness.

For these reasons we can understand why holiness is expressly attributed in Scripture to each Person in the Godhead, to the Father (Jn. xvii. 11), to the Son (Acts iv. 30), and especially to the Spirit as the one who manifests and communicates the holiness of God to His creatures.

b. The holiness of God in relation to His people

The Old Testament applies the word 'holy' to human beings in virtue of their consecration to religious purposes, *e.g.* priests who were consecrated by special ceremonies, and even to the whole nation of Israel as a people separated from the nations and consecrated to God. Thus it was relationship to God that constituted Israel a holy people, and in this sense it was the highest expression of the covenant relationship. This idea is not altogether absent from the New Testament, as in the passage in 1 Cor. vii. 14, where the unbelieving husband is sanctified in virtue of his relationship to the believing wife and *vice versa*.

But as the conception of holiness advanced, alongside the progressive revelation of God, from the outside to the inside, from ceremonial to reality, so it took on a strong ethical significance, and this is its main, and practically its exclusive, connotation in the New Testament. The Old Testament prophets proclaimed it as preeminently God's self-disclosure, the testimony He bears to Himself, and the aspect under which He wills His creatures to know Him. Moreover, the prophets declared that God willed to communicate His holiness to His creatures, and that, in turn, He claims holiness from them. If 'I am holy' is the divine self-assertion, lifting God immeasurably above His creatures, so 'Be ye holy' is the divine call to His creatures to become 'partakers of his holiness' (Heb. xii. 10). It is this imparting of the divine holiness which takes place in the soul of man in regeneration and becomes the spring and foundation of holy character.

Christ in His life and character is the supreme example of the divine holiness. In Him it consisted in more than mere sinlessness: it was His entire consecration to the will and purpose of God, and to this end Jesus sanctified Himself (Jn. xvii. 19). The holiness of Christ is both the standard of the Christian character and its guarantee: 'Both he that sanctifieth and they who are sanctified are all of one' (Heb. ii. 11).

In the New Testament the apostolic designation for Christians is *saints*, and it continued to be used as a general designation at least up to the days of Irenaeus and Tertullian, though after that it degenerated in ecclesiastical usage into an honorific title. Though its primary significance was relationship, it was also descriptive of character, and more especially of Christlike character. The New Testament everywhere emphasizes the ethical nature of holiness in contrast to all uncleanness. It is represented as the supreme vocation of Christians and the goal of their living. In the final assessment of human destiny the two categories known to Scripture are the righteous and the wicked.

c. The eschatological significance of holiness

Scripture emphasizes the permanence of moral character (Rev. xxii. 11). It also emphasizes the retributive aspect of the divine holiness. It involves the world in judgment. From a moral necessity in God life is so ordered that in holiness is welfare, in sin is doom. Since the divine holiness could not make a universe in which sin would ultimately prosper, the retributive quality in the divine government becomes perfectly plain. But retribution is not the end; the holiness of God ensures that there will be a final restoration, a *palingenesia*, bringing to pass a regeneration of the moral universe. The eschatology of the Bible holds out the promise that the holiness of God will sweep the universe clean, and create new heavens and a new earth in which righteousness will dwell (2 Pet. iii. 13).

BIBLIOGRAPHY. A. Murray, *Holy in Christ*, 1888; R. Otto (tr. J. W. Harvey), *The Idea of the Holy*, 1946; *ERE*, VI, pp. 731–759; W. E. Sangster, *The Path to Perfection*, 1943. R.A.F.

HOLY OF HOLIES, HOLY PLACE. See TABERNACLE, TEMPLE.

HOLY ONE OF ISRAEL. See GOD, NAMES OF.

HOLY SPIRIT. In AV the Holy Spirit is referred to, with and without the article, as 'Holy Ghost', 'Spirit', 'Spirit of God', 'Spirit of the Lord', 'Spirit of Christ', and 'the Comforter' (Gk. *Paraklētos*; NEB 'Advocate' (*q.v.*), RSV 'Counsellor': the same word is used to describe our Lord in 1 Jn. ii. 1). The symbols 'breath', 'wind', 'dove', 'finger of God', and 'fire' are also employed. This variety in the terms which Scripture uses gives us an insight into the Spirit's identity and work.

There is no irreconcilable antithesis, as some would suggest, between the teaching of the Old Testament and the teaching of the New on this subject. Just as no dichotomy exists between the Old Testament emphasis on the providential nature of God's dealings with men and the New Testament teaching concerning His grace, or between the activity in creation of the pre-incarnate Logos, on the one hand, and the work of redemption of the incarnate Son, on the other, so it is with the teaching of Scripture concerning the Holy Spirit. It is the same Father and the same Son who are active in both Testaments, and it is the same Holy Spirit who is at work throughout the ages. True, we have to wait for the New Testament revelation before we are given a detailed picture of His activity. But this fuller teaching given by our Lord and His apostles conflicts in no way with what we learn from the Old Testament writers.

Since God is said to be Spirit (Jn. iv. 24), the whole Trinity has been thought of by some in terms of Spirit. This has tended to cloud the distinction between the Spirit, the Father, and the Son. Moreover, to speak, as some do, of the Spirit as the relation of love between the Father and the Son, or further, to define the Spirit as the 'living action of God in the world', while emphasizing a valuable, yet partial, truth, nevertheless tends to depersonalize the Spirit and to reduce Him to an influence or force, albeit a benign one.

Admittedly it is easier in the Old Testament to interpret the activity of the Spirit in an impersonal way than it is in the New Testament; but in both God is personally and powerfully present in His Spirit. In each Testament there is a movement from the more external to the more internal work of the Spirit and from what might be called 'outward application' to inward appropriation. The physical and amoral manifestations lead on to the moral and spiritual.

I. IN THE OLD TESTAMENT

Five differing aspects of the work of the Spirit are discernible in the Old Testament.

a. The work of the Spirit in creation

The Spirit brooding over the primeval waters (Gn. i. 2) and creating man (Gn. ii. 7), the Spirit who garnishes the heavens (Jb. xxvi. 13), sustains animal life, and renews the face of the earth (Ps. civ. 30), is the *rûaḥ* ('breath', 'wind') of God, the outgoing divine energy and power. He is the principle of man's physical and psychological life. Man in every part of his nature—spirit, soul, and body—is meant to be open to the resources of the Spirit of God, learning to reflect God. His spirit is 'the candle of the Lord' (Pr. xx. 27) when in the hand of the Spirit of the Lord. When his spirit is rightly related to the Spirit of God he fulfils God's purpose for his being. (In the Old Testament the fact that a man has a 'spirit' or is a 'spirit' seems to be synonymous with his having a 'heart' or being a 'person'.) Because of sin, man is self-centred; in this state he mars his own personality, dishonours God, and does despite to His Spirit. But when his personality is orientated to the Spirit of God he glorifies God.

b. The work of the Spirit in equipping for service

The Spirit comes upon those whom God selects to do special tasks and (without necessarily transforming them morally) confers upon them skill for their duty, *e.g.* craftsmanship (Ex. xxxi. 3), leadership (Jdg. iii. 10), or physical prowess (Jdg. xiv. 6).

c. The work of the Spirit in inspiring the prophets

on occasions, those who claimed to act by the power of the Spirit of God indulged in extravagances which offended the more spiritually sensitive and circumspect. Some of the prophets, therefore, tended to dissociate themselves from the extremist enthusiasts and laid little claim to the Spirit (see, *e.g.*, Am. vii. 14; Je. xxxi. 33; Ho. ix. 7). Others, however, are very conscious of the Spirit's influence. His work is seen to be of a high moral order, and the possibility of spiritual spontaneity and independent nonconformity is recognized (*cf.* Moses' exclamation in Nu. xi. 29). This is reiterated in principle by Isaiah and Ezekiel, who seem to identify the Spirit unambiguously with God (Is. lxiii. 10, 11), and provide two of the three Old Testament instances of the use of the term 'Holy Spirit'.

d. The work of the Holy Spirit in producing moral living

One of the high marks of Old Testament reference to the Spirit, however, is in the Psalms (*e.g.* li, cxxxix). For the psalmist the Spirit's presence means a broken, contrite spirit in man, a clean heart, constancy, and joy. In Ps. cxxxix. 7 God's Spirit is equated with His presence and both are inescapable. God's proximity and power result in a plea by the psalmist for inward searching and outward leading in the eternal way (verses 23, 24).

e. The work of the Spirit in foretelling the Messiah

While the psalmists record a present experience of the Spirit and by that token, according to some interpretations, represent the high-water mark of Old Testament reference to the Spirit, nevertheless, in the light of the preparatory character of the Old Testament, the highest references may well be those which describe prophetically the future work of the Spirit. The anticipatory references are of two kinds. First, those which prophesy a direct indwelling of the Spirit in one messianic figure (Is. xi. 2–9, xlii. 1–4, lxi. 1, 2; *cf.* Lk. iv. 18); secondly, those indicating the more general experience of the activity of the Spirit by the new covenant people of God (see Ezk. xxxvi. 26, 27, and *cf.* the comprehensive promise in Joel ii. 28 f.).

The inter-testamental period has been traditionally known as an age of decadence in regard to teaching on the Spirit. It supposedly indulged only in wistful, backward glances or in longing for future experience of the Spirit, but had no present, joyous realization of the Spirit's work. The Dead Sea Scrolls, however, are interpreted by some as bearing testimony to experience of the Spirit among the Essenes and probably among other sects prior to the advent of Christ.

II. IN THE NEW TESTAMENT

The New Testament is full of references to the Spirit (Gk. *pneuma*). He is mentioned in every book except 2 and 3 John. Undue attention has been drawn to the contrast between the abundance of references to the Spirit in connection with the main events in the life of Jesus and the striking paucity of His own verbal references to the Spirit's work in the Synoptic record. The latter are only five in number, and by some scholars only one of these is accepted as genuine (Mk. iii. 29 = Mt. xii. 31 = Lk. xii. 10). The other four references are suspected by them on various grounds. This is not the place to consider these objections in detail. Suffice it to say that, even if it were possible to excise Christ's spoken references to the Spirit (as some would wish to do), such procedure is quite impracticable regarding the details of His life as recorded by the Synoptists. The Spirit is associated with the events immediately prior to His birth and related to it (see Lk. i. 15, 35, 41), with the conception, the birth itself and the immediately following events (Lk. ii. 25–27), with the baptism (Mt. iii. 13–17), the temptation (Mt. iv. 1–11), the entry upon His ministry (Lk. iv. 14), and the inaugural address (Lk. iv. 18 ff.), with His exorcizing of evil spirits and His commissioning of His apostles to baptize in the triune name inclusive of the Holy Spirit (Mt. xxviii. 19). These, together with other considerations, sufficiently refute the claim by some scholars that in the 'religion of Jesus' the Spirit occupied a much smaller place than in the 'faith of the early Church', and that our Lord feared the extravagant conceptions of the Spirit which existed at the time and preferred the less spectacular, but intimate, sense of fellowship with His Father.

The fuller references in John xiv–xvi provide an explanation for the paucity of our Lord's verbal references to the Spirit during the earlier part of His ministry. The Spirit was not to function in fulness within believers and towards the world until the Son returned to the Father *via* the cross, the resurrection, and the ascension. While His possession of (and His availability to) the Son was complete (Jn. iii. 34), He was as yet able to be only *with* the disciples (Jn. xiv. 17). But since the Spirit was to be, in a sense, Christ's 'Alter Ego', He was not so necessary to the small number of believers who enjoyed the Son's incarnate presence. Christ Himself was an ever-present Counsellor, Advocate, Comforter, and Strengthener, and not until His departure would the other Comforter (*Paraklētos*) be needed. So long as Christ could be His own interpreter and witness and could repeat His teaching to His disciples there was no need of Another to enlighten, to witness, and to bring His words to remembrance. But His leaving them would necessitate the sending of the Spirit by the Father to undertake these duties among the believers, and to accomplish the further tasks of convincing the world of its sin in terms of its unbelief in Christ; of righteousness because Christ, the objective reference and embodiment of righteousness, was ascended to the Father; of judgment because of the verdict passed upon the prince of this world in the death of Christ (Jn. xvi. 7–11). Christ indicated clearly that the Spirit would not supersede and dispense with His work and Person, but rather dispense and supervise respectively the riches and activity of Christ (*cf.* Acts i.

1, where 'began' implies that Jesus would continue to do and teach by His Holy Spirit).

Scripture, then, in no way warrants the implication that Jesus deliberately neglected, or did not recognize the necessity of, the Spirit, or that where He is recorded as making such recognition the contexts are the influence of the early Church's reading back its Pentecostal and post-Pentecostal experiences into the record.

A further supposed inconsistency in the Fourth Gospel is pointed out, namely, that in the earlier chapters Jesus draws attention to the Spirit as a present reality (Jn. iii. 5–8), but in the latter part of the Gospel He speaks of the Spirit as yet to come. But the considerations already cited show that we must accept a 'both/and' rather than an 'either/or' in this matter. For while John the Baptist's prediction that Christ would baptize with the Spirit and fire was partially fulfilled during our Lord's lifetime, it had to wait for Pentecost for its fuller realization.

The book of Acts recounts the 'outpouring' of the Spirit and His manifold operations. On some occasions the stress is laid chiefly on the energy of the Spirit as if He were acting in an impersonal manner ('falling upon', 'filling'; *cf.* Acts ii. 1 ff.). On other occasions He is manifestly personal, as in Acts v. 1 ff., where He can be lied against, and in other passages which speak of His guiding, appointing, and comforting. In Acts also Christ and the Spirit are clearly distinguished. Notice especially viii. 16 and xix. 1–6, where the gifts of the Spirit are given subsequent to the gift of regeneration and are seemingly more visible and audible. There is no ground, however, for inferring that the experience of the power-gift of the Spirit can be had apart from Christ. It is to those who believe the promise made prior to and by Christ (*cf.* the Old Testament cross-references to Acts ii. 39—Is. liv. 13, lvii. 19; Joel ii. 28–32), and await its fulfilment, that the Spirit comes. The express purpose of the gift of the Spirit is to equip for witness to the mighty works of God in Christ when He wrought salvation in Zion. The Spirit is not to be exulted in for His own sake but rather for Christ's sake. It is in the strong name of Jesus of Nazareth that the Spirit-filled apostles preach and do their miraculous works of love (Acts iii. 6); the Spirit jealously guards the honour of the Son and refuses glory to Himself and to men (*cf.* Jn. xvi. 14).

The most elaborate teaching about the Spirit occurs in the Epistles which deal with the experience of the Spirit-dependent Church. Some scholars discern a chronological development in Paul's teaching on the Spirit. They argue that in his earlier Epistles (1 and 2 Thessalonians) he is in line with the accepted teaching of the early Church, particularly in his uncritical acknowledgment of the overt (and sometimes amoral) gifts of the Spirit (tongues, prophecy, 1 Thes. v. 19, 20) alongside the more inward, moral attributes produced by Him (1 Thes. i. 5, 6). In his next stage (Romans, Corinthians, Galatians) he is concerned, they say, to offset the vagaries of those who make extravagant claims regarding the Spirit and misuse His gifts to the detriment of the harmony of the Church. He places the more spectacular gifts (while still claiming and recognizing his own experience of them as well as that of his fellow-believers) in a secondary position to Christian *agapē*, the love of Christ shed abroad in the heart by the Spirit and indeed called the love of the Spirit (Rom. xv. 30). Stress is placed upon the moral fruit spontaneously produced in the believer by the Spirit rather than on the 'gifts' of the Spirit. The value of the latter is judged in terms of the former (Gal. v. 22, 23).

At this stage also is found the most significant feature of Paul's teaching on the Spirit, *viz.* the integral relation between the Spirit and Christ which is so close and almost indissoluble that he speaks of 'the Spirit of Christ', 'the Spirit of God', 'the Holy Spirit', and 'the Spirit' with seemingly no distinction, and in 2 Cor. iii. 17, 18, he uses the enigmatic phrase 'the Lord the Spirit' ('the Lord is that [or 'who is the'] Spirit').

The last group of letters, traditionally attributed to Paul's imprisonment period (Philippians, Ephesians, Colossians, and the Pastorals), emphasize, according to these interpreters, the communal reference of the Spirit's work in creating and maintaining the unity of the Church (Eph. iv. 3, 4).

In both his earlier and later writings (1 Cor. ii and 2 Tim. iii—if *theopneustos* is regarded as referring to the Spirit-breath of God) Paul shows the relation of the Spirit to revelation and spiritual knowledge, understanding and wisdom. It is the Spirit who knows the mind of God and is alone able to teach the things of God and impart them to the mind (spirit) of man in turn enlightened by Him (1 Cor. ii. 4; Rom. viii. 26, 27). His revelatory work, however, is redemptive. He does not merely impart interesting information about God, but is conjoined in His activity with the demonstration of power (1 Cor. ii. 4). Paul does not write directly about the work of the Spirit in the conviction of the unregenerate, nor indeed does he advert explicitly to His work of regeneration. The activity of the Spirit accompanying, or subsequent to, regeneration, however, is often mentioned. He is the Spirit of adoption who witnesses with man's spirit to his having been brought into the household of faith (Rom. viii. 15, 16; Gal. iv. 6). He sets the seal as the Spirit of promise upon the believer (Eph. i. 13). He is the one Spirit by whom access in Christ is had to the Father—the access in reconciliation and communion, especially in prayer, where, parallel to the Son's intercession at the Father's right hand, He, the Spirit, intercedes for the saint (*cf.* Eph. ii. 18; Rom. viii. 26).

By His self-imparting He is the spiritual life of the believer, causing him to know the indwelling of the risen Christ. He is the Author, Source, and Director of power for the lifelong process of spiritual growth, and it is only as He is the sphere of the believer's walk that victory over sin is possible. Setting the saint free from a stringent, legalistic clinging to the letter of the law, the Spirit is the Spirit of Christ the Liberator, and the Transformer of the sinner, bringing him into conformity with the image of Christ (2 Cor. iii. 17, 18). He is the Spirit of the kingdom, relegating meat and drink to their proper place and giving priority to righteousness, peace, and joy (Rom. xiv. 17). Above all, He is the source of true, holy love which transcends even faith and hope, and heads the list of the fruit of the Spirit which is the spontaneous outcrop of His working (Gal. v. 22, 23). It is in terms of His fruit that His gifts to the Church are to be appraised and used (1 Cor. xii, xiii). He is the one, unifying Spirit and, as He distributes His varied gifts, His concern is to maintain His unity in the bond of peace (Eph. iv. 3). While He is not to be quenched by lack of usage, He is not to be grieved by misuse (1 Thes. v. 19; Eph. iv. 30).

The references to the Spirit elsewhere in the New Testament are relatively few and do not add substantially to the description of His character or conduct. Scripture is His speaking and product (Heb. iii. 7; 2 Pet. i. 21). His relation to Christ is indicated (Heb. ix. 14; 1 Pet. i. 2; 1 Jn. iv. 3). In Revelation the exalted Christ addresses His Church through the transcendent Spirit; the seer in the Spirit is given eschatological perspective and sees enacted on an expansive stage the drama which reaches its climax with the Spirit joining the Bride in hailing the advent of Jesus the Lord.

The biblical data on the Holy Spirit constrain recognition of Him as the uncreated, creative power of the holy, loving God, transcendently other than, but personally present to, the human spirit. The Spirit is sometimes, apparently, an immanent energy, or principle of life, fashioning and sustaining the created cosmos and its inhabitants. Acknowledgment of the Spirit's power even on this level is salutary to man, who at all times, and increasingly with the centuries, manipulates, and is in danger of prostituting the energies of the cosmos to produce chaos and catastrophe. The Old Testament intimations, through Spirit-equipped artisans, inspired prophetic leaders of the people, and penitent saints aspiring to piety, were elaborated and fulfilled in the New Testament supremely in Him who, through the unimpeded breath of God, spoke and was the eloquent saving Word of God. The impediment in man's spirit is atoningly dealt with by Him who through the eternal Spirit offered Himself faultlessly to God, and who through the Spirit of holiness was raised from the dead (Heb. ix. 14; Rom. i. 4). Henceforth the incarnate God with us is experienced as the Lord the Spirit within us. The Son's life, light, liberty, and love are taken over and applied by the Spirit to the spirit of man, so that, convicted of his death, darkness, bondage, and hate of the good and of God, he is remade by a power working unto righteousness, even the Spirit of glory.

Man is alert to the personal operations of the Spirit striving with him, convincing, transforming, constraining, guarding, with gentle warning against quenching or grieving Him and with dread injunction against blaspheming Him. Man is therefore to know that the personal, moral-spiritual results in him cannot be produced by One less than personal and that true enhancement of personality can be realized only by confrontment with the Spirit in whom the I AM encounters man. In this reconciling *rapport* man knows that it is none other than Deity who addresses him. In being united to God in the fellowship of this sanctifying Spirit man knows himself in new relationship with his fellows in Christ and enters into and enjoys the resources and responsibilities of the commonwealth of the Spirit. Only through the Spirit uniting pneumatosomatic humanity to the supreme New Being can a new humanity be formed. Surrounded by sin, distortion of truth, pollution of life, and omens of death, man must cry to the Spirit, who alone can vivify and give reality to his worship, work, and witness. It is only as he now becomes a partaker of the Holy Ghost and reverences the Spirit of grace that he will ever and for ever in the ultimate new creation be in the communion of the Holy Spirit. See ADVOCATE, BAPTISM, SPIRITUAL GIFTS, INSPIRATION, SALVATION, SANCTIFICATION.

BIBLIOGRAPHY. G. S. Hendry, *The Holy Spirit in Christian Theology*, 1957; R. B. Hoyle, *The Holy Spirit in St Paul*, 1928; A. Kuyper, *The Work of the Holy Spirit*, 1900; L. Morris, *Spirit of the Living God*, 1960; G. F. Nuttall, *The Holy Spirit in Puritan Faith and Experience*, 1946; F. W. Dillistone, *The Holy Spirit in the Life of Today*, 1947; H. W. Robinson, *The Christian Experience of the Holy Spirit*, 1928; G. Smeaton, *The Doctrine of the Holy Spirit*, 1889; W. H. G. Thomas, *The Holy Spirit of God*, 1931; H. B. Swete, *The Holy Spirit in the New Testament*, 1909; *id.*, *The Holy Spirit in the Ancient Church*, 1912.

G.W.

HOMER. See WEIGHTS AND MEASURES.

HOMICIDE. See CRIME AND PUNISHMENT.

HONEY, HONEYCOMB (Heb. *d^{e}ḇaš*, 'honey', the usual word; *nōp̄eṯ*, 'juice', 'dropping'; *ya'ar*, 'comb'; *ya'raṯ had-d^{e}ḇaš*, 'comb of honey'; *ṣûp̄ d^{e}ḇaš*, 'a flowing of honey'; Gk. *meli*, 'honey'; *melission kērion*, 'honeycomb'). A favourite food in biblical times (Pr. xxiv. 13; *cf.* Ecclus. xi. 3), honey was found in hollows of the rocks (Dt. xxxii. 13; Ps. lxxxi. 16); in trees (1 Sa. xiv. 25, 26, though the Heb. text here is obscure); in the desert of Judaea (Mt. iii. 4; Mk. i. 6); and in animal carcasses (Jdg. xiv. 8).

Honey was used in cake-making (Ex. xvi. 31), and was regarded as having medicinal properties (Pr. xvi. 24). See FOOD. It was an acceptable gift (2 Sa. xvii. 29; 1 Ki. xiv. 3); a valuable resource (Je. xli. 8); and was evidently plentiful enough to be exported (Ezk. xxvii. 17, but some suggest that in this verse and in Gn. xliii. 11 grape syrup (Arab. *dibs*) may be intended; *cf.* Jos., *BJ* iv. 8. 3). It was forbidden as an ingredient of any meal-offering to Yahweh (Lv. ii. 11) because of its liability to fermentation (so Pliny, *NH* xi. 15), but included in tithes and firstfruits (2 Ch. xxxi. 5), which incidentally suggests domesticated bees. In later times bee-keeping may have been practised by the Jews. See BEE.

Canaan is spoken of as a land 'flowing with milk and honey' (Ex. iii. 8, *etc.*; *cf. ANET*, pp. 19–20), for a discussion of which see T. K. Cheyne's note in *EBi*, 2104. Goshen is similarly described (Nu. xvi. 13).

Honey as the 'chief of sweet things' has inspired many figurative allusions—*e.g.* Ps. xix. 9, 10; Pr. v. 3 (*cf.* Ct. iv. 11); Pr. xxiv. 13, 14 (*cf.* Ecclus. xxxix. 26); Ezk. iii. 2, 3; Rev. x. 9.

J.D.D.

HOOK. AV rendering of several Heb. and one Gk. word. 1. *ḥāḥ* (2 Ki. xix. 28; Ezk. xxix. 4; *etc.*), elsewhere translated 'chain'. This was placed in the nose of a tamed beast to lead it about, or of a wild one to bring it under control. 2. *'agmôn* (Jb. xli. 2). RVmg has 'rope of rushes', and we should probably understand a rush or reed on which small fish are strung. 3. *ṣinnâ* and *sîrôṯ dûgâ* (Am. iv. 2), and Gk. *ankistron* (Mt. xvii. 27) all appear to mean 'fish hook', which is also the RV translation of *ḥakkâ*, rendered by AV as 'hook' in Jb. xli, but elsewhere as 'angle' (Is. xix. 8; Hab. i. 15). 4. *wāw*, 'peg' (Ex. xxvi. 32, *etc.*), is used only in connection with the hangings of the tabernacle (*q.v.*). 5. *shᵉpattayim*, 'double hooks' (Ezk. xl. 43). Perhaps used in the flaying of carcasses, but the meaning is doubtful. RVmg renders as 'ledges'. 6. *mazmērôṯ*, 'pruning hooks' (Is. ii. 4). Small sickle-shaped knives used by vine-dressers, easily convertible to, and probably used as, a weapon of war. 7. *ṣinnōr* (2 Sa. v. 8) is taken to mean 'scaling-hook' by W. F. Albright (*Old Testament Commentary*, ed. H. C. Alleman and E. E. Flack, 1948, p. 149); but is more commonly understood in the sense of 'water shaft' (so RSV). See also FLESH-HOOK, FISH. J.D.D.

HOPE. Hope, it would seem, is a psychological necessity, if man is to envisage the future at all. Even if there are no rational grounds for it, man still continues to hope. Very naturally such hope, even when it appears to be justified, is transient and illusory; and it is remarkable how often it is qualified by poets and other writers by such epithets as 'faint', 'trembling', 'feeble', 'desperate', 'phantom'. The Bible sometimes uses hope in the conventional sense. The ploughman, for example, should plough in hope (1 Cor. ix. 10), for it is the hope of reward that sweetens labour. But for the most part the hope with which the Bible is concerned is something very different; and in comparison with it other hope is scarcely recognized as hope. The majority of secular thinkers in the ancient world did not regard hope as a virtue, but merely as a temporary illusion; and Paul was giving an accurate description of pagans when he said they had no hope (Eph. ii. 12; *cf.* 1 Thes. iv. 13), the fundamental reason for this being that they were 'without God'.

Where there is a belief in the living God, who acts and intervenes in human life, and who can be trusted to implement His promises, hope in the specifically biblical sense becomes possible. Such hope is not a matter of temperament, nor is it conditioned by prevailing circumstances or any human possibilities. It does not depend upon what a man possesses, upon what he may be able to do for himself, nor upon what any other human being may do for him. There was, for example, nothing in the situation in which Abraham found himself to justify his hope that Sarah would give birth to a son, but because he believed in God, he could 'against hope believe in hope' (Rom. iv. 18). Biblical hope is inseparable therefore from faith in God. Because of what God has done in the past, particularly in preparing for the coming of Christ, and because of what God has done and is now doing through Christ, the Christian dares to expect future blessings at present invisible (2 Cor. i. 10). The goodness of God is for him never exhausted. The best is still to be. His hope is increased as he reflects on the activities of God in the Scriptures (Rom. xii. 12, xv. 4). Christ in him is the hope of future glory (Col. i. 27). His final salvation rests on such hope (Rom. viii. 24); and this hope of salvation is a 'helmet', an essential part of his defensive armour in the struggle against evil (1 Thes. v. 8). Hope, to be sure, is not a kite at the mercy of the changing winds, but 'an anchor of the soul, both sure and stedfast', penetrating deep into the invisible eternal world (Heb. vi. 19). Because of his faith the Christian has an assurance that the things he hopes for are real (Heb. xi. 1); and his hope never disappoints him (Rom. v. 5).

There are no explicit references to hope in the teaching of Jesus. He teaches His disciples, however, not to be anxious about the future, because that future is in the hands of a loving Father. He also leads them to expect that after His resurrection renewed spiritual power will be available for them, enabling them to do even greater works than He did, to overcome sin and death, and to look forward to sharing His own eternal glory. The resurrection of Jesus revitalized their hope. It was the mightiest act of God wrought in history. Before it 'panic, despair flee away'. Christian faith is essentially faith in God who raised Jesus from the dead (1 Pet. i. 21). This God towards whom the Christian directs his faith is called 'the God of hope', who can fill the believer with joy and peace, and enable him to abound in hope (Rom. xv. 13). Because of the resurrection, the Christian is saved from the miserable condition of having his hope in Christ limited to this world only (1 Cor. xv. 19). Christ Jesus is his Hope for time and eternity (1 Tim. i. 1). His call to be Christ's disciple carries with it the hope of finally sharing His glory (Eph. i. 18). His hope is laid up for him in heaven (Col. i. 5), and will be realized when his Lord is revealed (1 Pet. i. 13).

The existence of this hope makes it impossible for the Christian to be satisfied with transient joys (Heb. xiii. 14); it also acts as a stimulus to purity of life (1 Jn. iii. 2, 3), and enables him to suffer cheerfully. It is noticeable how often hope is associated in the New Testament with 'patience' or 'steadfastness'. This virtue is vastly different from Stoic endurance, precisely because it is bound up with a hope unknown to the Stoic (see 1 Thes. i. 3; Rom. v. 3–5).

In the light of what has been said it is not surprising that hope should so often be mentioned as a concomitant of faith. The heroes of faith in Heb. xi are also beacons of hope. What is perhaps more remarkable is the frequent association of hope with love as well as with faith. This threefold combination of faith, hope, and love is found in 1 Thes. i. 3, v. 8; Gal. v. 5, 6; 1 Cor. xiii. 13; Heb. vi. 10–12; 1 Pet. i. 21, 22. By its connection with love, Christian hope is freed from all selfishness. The Christian does not hope for blessings for himself which he does not desire others to share. When he loves his fellow-men he hopes that they will be the recipients of the good things that he knows God longs to give them. Paul gave evidence of his hope just as much as his love and his faith when he returned the runaway slave Onesimus to his master Philemon. Faith, hope, and love are thus inseparable. Hope cannot exist apart from faith, and love cannot be exercised without hope. These three are the things that abide (1 Cor. xiii. 13), and together they comprise the Christian way of life.

BIBLIOGRAPHY. E. J. Bicknell, *The First and Second Epistles to the Thessalonians*, *WC*, 1932; J-J. von Allmen, *Vocabulary of the Bible*, 1958.

R.V.G.T.

HOPHNI AND PHINEHAS. The two sons of Eli (*q.v.*), 'priests unto the Lord' at Shiloh (1 Sa. i. 3). They are described as 'men of Belial (*i.e.* unprincipled men) who knew not the Lord nor the due of the priests from the people' (1 Sa. ii. 12, RVmg). They abused their privileges as priests, claiming more than their proper share of the sacrifices and insisting on having it when and as they pleased on threat of force, so that men treated the offerings of the Lord with contempt. Because of this and their licentiousness, a curse was pronounced against the house of Eli, first by an unknown prophet (1 Sa. ii. 27–36) and later by Samuel (1 Sa. iii. 11–14). They died in the battle against the Philistines at Aphek (1 Sa. iv. 11).

J.W.M.

HOPHRA. The pharaoh Ḥa'a'ibrē' Waḥibrē'; Gk. Apries, fourth king of the XXVIth Dynasty, who reigned for nineteen years, from 589 to 570 BC. He was an impetuous king, over-ambitious to meddle in Palestinian affairs. The Hebrew form *Ḥŏpra'* is best derived from his personal name, (Wa)ḥibrē', precisely as with Shishak, Tirhakah, and Necho. 'Pharaoh-hophra' is explicitly mentioned only in Je. xliv. 30, but several other references to 'Pharaoh' in the prophets concern him. Shortly after Hophra's accession, Zedekiah requested forces from him, presumably against Nebuchadrezzar (Ezk. xvii. 11–21). Hophra duly invaded Palestine during Nebuchadrezzar's siege of Jerusalem (Je. xxxvii. 5; perhaps also Je. xlvii. 1 ?), accompanied by his fleet (Herodotus, ii. 161).

Fig. 107. Pharaoh Hophra offering bowls of wine to a god. From a stele dated c. 580 BC.

In 588 Ezekiel prophesied against the Egyptians (Ezk. xxix. 1–16), and Jeremiah prophesied Hophra's retreat (Je. xxxvii. 7). The Babylonians raised the siege of Jerusalem (Je. xxxvii. 11) just long enough to repulse Hophra; whether a battle actually occurred is uncertain. After a disastrous Libyan campaign and a revolt which resulted in Ahmose becoming co-regent, Hophra was slain in conflict with Ahmose (*cf.* Je. xliv. 30).

K.A.K.

HOR. 1. A mountain on the border of Edom where Aaron was buried (Nu. xx. 22–29, xxxiii. 37–39; Dt. xxxii. 50), possibly Moserah (Dt. x. 6), although Nu. xxxiii. 30, 39 distinguishes them. The place was in the region of Kadesh (Nu. xx. 22, xxxiii. 37). More accurately it is 'Hor, the mountain', suggesting that it was a prominent feature.

Josephus (*Ant.* iv. 4. 7) thought it was near Petra, and tradition has identified it with Jebel Nebi Harun, a lofty peak 4,800 feet high, to the west of Edom. This, however, is far from Kadesh.

Jebel Madeira, north-east of Kadesh, on the north-west border of Edom, is more likely, for Israel began the detour round Edom at Mount Hor (Nu. xxi. 4), and Aaron could well have been buried here 'in the sight of all the congregation' (Nu. xx. 22–29).

2. A mountain in northern Palestine between the Mediterranean Sea and the approach to Hamath (Nu. xxxiv. 7, 8), as yet unidentified.

J.A.T.

HOREB. See SINAI.

HORESH. A place in the wilderness of Judaea (1 Sa. xxiii. 15–19, RVmg, RSV, *cf.* LXX). AV and RV translate 'in the wood', which is very doubtful, because it implies an unusual grammatical form and also because a wood adequate for concealment here is unlikely.

G.W.G.

HORITES, HORIM. The ancient inhabitants of Edom, defeated by Chedorlaomer (Gn. xiv. 6), said to be the descendants of Seir the Horite (Gn. xxxvi. 20) and an ethnic group distinct from Rephaim. They were driven out by the sons of Esau (Dt. ii. 12, 22). Esau himself seems to have married the daughter of a Horite chief, Anah (Gn. xxxvi. 25). The Horites (Heb. *ḥōrî*, Gk. *chorraios*) also occupied some places in central Palestine, including Shechem (Gn. xxxiv. 2) and Gilgal (Jos. ix. 6, 7), the LXX reading 'Horite' in both passages (AV 'Hivite').

The Horites were formerly considered to be cave-dwellers (*ḥōrîm*, *cf.* Is. xlii. 22), a view recently revived by Dossin, who considers them to be miners. Others, however, equate them with the Egypt. *Ḫurru*, a designation of Syro-Palestine, named with Israel in the Merenptah stele *c.* 1220 BC. These were the non-Semitic Hurrians who already formed part of the indigenous population of Syria (Alalaḫ) in the 18th century and occupied the area called Subaru (Euphrates–Habur–Tigris region). Under Mitanni leadership they rose to a dominant position in Syria (Alalaḫ–Ras Shamra), S Turkey (Boghaz-Koi) and E Assyria (Nuzi) from *c.* 1550 BC until their subjugation by Assyria *c.* 1150 BC. Since Hurrian names are found in cuneiform tablets from Tell Taanach and Shechem and in the Amarna letters (*e.g.* Arad-ḫepa of Jerusalem and the Hurrian letter of Tushratta to Amenhotep IV), this identification is probable. Albright (*JAOS*, LXXIV, 1954, pp. 226–227) considers the names Abino 'am (Abina 'ami), Job (Aiabi), and Samson (Šapš) to be of Hurrian origin.

Hori was also the personal name both of an Edomite (Gn. xxxvi. 22; 1 Ch. i. 39) and of a Simeonite (Nu. xiii. 5).

BIBLIOGRAPHY. I. J. Gelb, *Hurrians and Subarians*, 1944; E. A. Speiser, *Introduction to Hurrian*, 1941; *Journal of World History*, I, 1953, pp. 311–327.

D.J.W.

HORMAH. An important town in the south, formerly the Canaanite Zephath, which was destroyed by Judahites and Simeonites (Jdg. i. 17) and became Simeonite territory (Jos. xv. 30, xix. 4); its king appears in the list of those defeated under Joshua (Jos. xii. 14). The Israelite name 'sacred' was said to commemorate the sacrifice of the captured town under a national vow made after a previous defeat (Nu. xxi. 1–3; AV 'way of the spies' follows Symmachus, Vulg., *etc.*, emending the *MT* and LXX 'way of Atharim', and there is probably no connection with the events related in Nu. xiv; see *BDB*, *s.v.* *'Atharim*). Zephath was certainly linked with Arad, but is not identical with it; it should be taken as one of 'the cities', in the light of Jdg. i. 17 and other texts.

The references in Jos. xv. 30; 1 Sa. xxx. 30 indicate that Hormah was fairly near Ziklag. Albright (*BASOR*, 15, Oct. 1924; *JPOS*, IV, 1924, p. 155) suggests Tell es-Seri'ah, where an extensive Late Bronze settlement preceded the Early Iron; other sites in northern Simeon are too small.

In Nu. xiv. 45; Dt. i. 44 Hormah is the limit of Canaanite pursuit through Seir towards Kadesh. A position north of Beersheba–Tell el-Milh is hardly compatible with this; Robinson's suggestion, the es-Sufa pass to the south-east, still merits consideration. A compromise position in the valley would really satisfy neither this context nor the Ziklag evidence (stressed by Alt, *JPOS*, XV, 1935, pp. 322 ff.).

BIBLIOGRAPHY. E. Robinson, *Biblical Researches in Palestine*[2], 1856, II, p. 181; Abel, *Géographie*, II, p. 350; *GTT*, pp. 145, 254.

J.P.U.L.

HORN (Heb. *qeren*; Gk. *keras*). **1.** Used literally of the horns of the ram (Gn. xxii. 13; Dn. viii. 3), the goat (Dn. viii. 5), and the wild-ox (Heb. *re'ēm*, Dt. xxxiii. 17; Pss. xxii. 21, xcii. 10; AV 'unicorn', *q.v.*). It was used as a receptacle for oil for ceremonial anointing (1 Sa. xvi. 1, 13; 1 Ki. i. 39). The ram's horn (*qeren hayyôḇēl*) was also used as a musical instrument (Jos. vi. 5; see MUSIC AND MUSICAL INSTRUMENTS; *cf.* 1 Ch. xxv. 5).

2. The horn-shaped protuberances on the four corners of the altars in the Tabernacle and Temple, an example of which has been found at Megiddo. The sacrificial blood was smeared on these (Ex. xxix. 12; Lv. iv. 7, 18, *etc.*) and they were regarded as places of refuge (*cf.* the respective fates of Adonijah and Joab, 1 Ki. i. 50 ff., ii. 28 ff.). See ALTAR and figs. 6, 176.

3. Horns symbolized power, in Zedekiah's prophetic action (1 Ki. xxii. 11) and in Zechariah's vision (Zc. i. 18 ff.), and often the word is metaphorically used in poetic writings. God exalts the horn of the righteous and cuts off the horn of the wicked (Ps. lxxv. 10, *etc.*); He causes the horn of David to sprout (Ps. cxxxii. 17; *cf.* Ezk. xxix. 21). He is spoken of as 'the horn of my salvation' (2 Sa. xxii. 3; Ps. xviii. 2; *cf.* Lk. i. 69), but this may be a metaphor based on the horns of the altar as the place of atonement. Am. vi. 13 'horns' should be read as a place-name, Karnaim.

4. In the peculiar apocalyptic usage of Dn. vii, viii and Rev. xiii, xvii the horns on the creatures in the visions represent individual rulers of each world-empire.

5. For 'ink-horn', see WRITING.

J.B.Tr.

HORNET (Heb. *ṣir'â*). Mention is made of hornets in Ex. xxiii. 28 ('I will send hornets before you'), and in similar contexts in Dt. vii. 20 and Jos. xxiv. 12. Whether or not the use is metaphorical, *ṣir'â* is one of the large colonial wasps whose sting is very painful or even dangerous. Hornets were common in Syria, and still occur frequently in Iraq. J. Garstang's suggestion (*Joshua–Judges*, 1931, pp. 112 ff., 258 ff.) that the 'hornet' of Dt. vii. 20; Jos. xxiv. 12 represents the Egyptian Empire in Canaan has not found much acceptance. G.C.

HORONAIM. A town of Moab (Is. xv. 5; Je. xlviii. 3, 5, 34) which lay at the foot of a plateau close to Zoar. The Moabite Stone refers to it in line 32. (See MOABITE STONE.) Some identify it with el-'Araq, 1,640 feet below the plateau, where there are springs, gardens, and caves. It may be Oronae, taken by Alexander Jannaeus from the Arabs and restored to the Nabataean king by Alexander Jannaeus (Jos., *Ant.* xiii. 15. 4, xiv. 1. 4). J.A.T.

HORONITE. See SANBALLAT.

HORSE. The Old Testament contains numerous references to the horse (*sûs*), but virtually every use of it from Job onwards, as well as in many previous passages, is figurative. Throughout the Old and New Testaments the horse is regularly associated with war and power, whereas the ass usually suggests peace and humility. A further word *pārāš* is rendered 'horseman' in most versions, but this could mean a mounted horse of the cavalry or perhaps a horse with its rider, while *sûs* is a more general word, used in particular for horses drawing chariots.

Of all the animals that have become beasts of burden, the horse is the most important, though it was not the first to be domesticated. In contrast to the wild ass, which lived in the near desert, the ancestors of the horse were native to the grasslands of Europe and Asia. It is likely that domestication took place independently in several different areas—western Europe, southwestern Asia, and Mongolia. The horses in the biblical record presumably come from the second of these sources.

A Babylonian tablet of the period of Hammurabi, *c.* 1750 BC, gives the first record of the horse, referred to as 'the ass from the east'. Horses were already in Egypt when Joseph was in power, and they were used in pursuit at the Exodus. It is perhaps unlikely that the children of Israel owned horses, but in any case they would have been unsuited to a desert journey.

The nations living in Canaan had horses and rode them in battle (Jos. xi. 4, *etc.*); David frequently fought against them, sometimes killing great numbers (2 Sa. x. 18, *etc.*), but he apparently observed the prohibition in Dt. xvii. 16, 'he shall not multiply horses to himself', and the first mention of horses being owned in Israel is 2 Sa. xv. 1: 'Absalom prepared him chariots and horses'. Solomon later had very great numbers of horses, kept in special establishments at Hazor, Megiddo, and Gezer. These were imported from Egypt and Que (Cilicia [AV 'linen yarn', RV 'droves']) and exported to neighbouring states, the price of a horse being 150 shekels of silver (1 Ki. x. 28, 29). G.C.

Fig. 108. Restive horses held by attendants. Relief from Nineveh, *c.* 650 BC. Note the ornamented harness. See also fig. 25.

HORSE-LEACH (Heb. *'ᵃlûqâ*, 'sucking'; Arab. *'alaqeh*). Used in Pr. xxx. 15 to denote insatiability, the word is evidently capable of two interpretations. 1. Most scholars, following EVV, assume a reference to the leech, probably of the same aquatic type (*Limnatis nilotica*) as is still found in stagnant water in Egypt and the Near East, and which constitutes a serious menace to men and animals when swallowed with drinking-water. 2. Others, noting the similarity between the Heb. and Arab. words, identify it with a female demon, perhaps a blood-sucking vampire (*cf.* RVmg), which the Arabs call 'Alūq. On this point, see W. O. E. Oesterley, *The Book of Proverbs*, *WC*, 1929, p. 275. J.D.D.

HOSANNA. The Gk. form of a Heb. term, used at the triumphal entry of Jesus into Jerusalem (Mt. xxi. 9, 15; Mk. xi. 9; Jn. xii. 13). The Heb. consists of the hiphil imperative *hôša'*, 'save', followed by the enclitic particle of entreaty *nā'*, usually translated 'pray', 'we beseech thee'. It does not occur in the Old Testament except in the longer imperative form *hôšî'â nā'* in Ps. cxviii. 25, where it is followed by the words, also quoted at the triumphal entry, 'Blessed is he that cometh in the name of the Lord.' Ps. cxviii was used in connection with the Feast of Tabernacles, and verse 25 had special significance as a cue for the waving of the branches (*lûlāḇ*); see Mishnah, *Sukkah*, 3. 9; 4. 5. But similar expressions of religious enthusiasm were not restricted to the Feast of Tabernacles: 2 Macc. x. 6, 7 implies that psalm-singing and branch-waving were part of the festivities at the Feast of Dedication also. We may reasonably assume that the waving of palm-branches and the cries of Hosanna which welcomed Jesus were a contemporary gesture of religious exuberance, without any reference to a particular festival and without the supplicatory meaning of the original phrase in Ps. cxviii.

J.B.Tr.

HOSEA, BOOK OF.

I. OUTLINE OF CONTENTS

a. The prophet's marriage portrays Israel's relations with her God (i. 1–iii. 5).

b. Hosea denounces Israel's corruption, pride, and idolatry (iv. 1–viii. 14).

c. The certainty of judgment (ix. 1–x. 15).

d. Parenthesis. The triumph of God's love and mercy (xi. 1–11).

e. Israel's unfaithfulness and rebellion will result in judgment and destruction (xi. 12–xiii. 16).

f. God's mercy to a repentant people (xiv. 1–9).

II. AUTHORSHIP AND DATE

Our knowledge of Hosea is flimsy. He was a northerner, the only northern prophet whose writings have survived. Snaith makes the guess (based on the reference in chapter vii to baking) that he was a baker. Agricultural references perhaps suggest that he had some connection with the soil.

His love of humanity shines through his book. He loved his nation. Unlike Amos, he never refers to other nations, except in their relationship to Israel. References to events of which we know nothing (v. 1, vi. 9) indicate his love for the history of his own people.

His love for his wife is more evident. One could say that the book of Hosea is a 'love story that went wrong'. But in that domestic tragedy he found God. Goethe once said, 'I never had a great suffering but I made it into a poem.' Hosea's great suffering has given us this wonderful poem of God's love for Israel. The suffering of Hosea has become a mirror of the suffering of God, expressed in the cry, 'How shall I give thee up, Ephraim?' (xi. 8).

Hosea is the most evangelical and the tenderest of all the prophets. It has been suggested that Hosea suffered, at least in his youth, from 'sex obsession'. According to this theory, Hosea married a harlot. This is an illustration of the 'struggle between the subconscious obsession and the purity of conscious thought, resulting in his involving himself in the thing he most hated' (Oesterley and Robinson). This may well be an illustration of reading the categories of modern psychological study back into the Bible. It is exegetically unnecessary to maintain that Gomer was impure at the time of marriage. There is no evidence of 'sex obsession' in the book. Hosea's disgust at the sexual extravagances of Israel is typically prophetic.

Jewish tradition held that Hosea was the first of the canonical prophets. Most modern scholars would maintain the temporal priority of Amos, but Snaith argues that this is not certain. Both Amos and Hosea foretell immediate trouble for Israel. Estimates of the length of Hosea's ministry vary. i. 4 must have been spoken before the fall of Jehu's house, *i.e.* before the death of Jeroboam II. Therefore Hosea was preaching in 743 BC. His marriage and the birth of Jezreel must have been before that.

III. CIRCUMSTANCES OF WRITING

His preaching must be set against a background of coarseness within Israel and without. In 745 BC Tiglath-pileser III usurped the throne of Assyria, and that usurpation was to send the Assyrian shadow across Israel. Prosperous times under Jeroboam were followed by times of confusion. Jeroboam's son Zechariah was assassinated by Shallum, Shallum by Menahem. Political vacillation towards Assyria ensued. Menahem attempted to court Assyria; Pekah and Hoshea tried resistance. But political vacillation was not limited to Assyria. Hosea was to complain that Israel was like a silly dove, fluttering between Assyria and Egypt, fluttering everywhere but to God (v. 13, vii. 11, xii. 1). But vacillation could not save the kingdom of Israel. It ended with the fall of Samaria in 721 BC.

IV. HOSEA'S DISTINCTIVE MESSAGE

The word *ḥeseḏ* (vi. 6) brings us to the heart of Hosea's message. For him religion was primarily a matter of relationship with God. The personal character of religion penetrates the whole gamut of religion.

a. His view of grace

Ḥeseḏ runs on to grace. (i) Grace in the past. God has taken the initiative in the call of Israel (xi. 1). (ii) Grace in the present is the only hope of Israel. Israel has not the moral and spiritual sinews to turn to God (v. 4, xi. 7). Israel cannot be the bride of God without a betrothal gift (ii. 19). So Israel will be bought back by Yahweh. (iii) Grace in the end. There is the hope that God will be more successful with Israel than the prophet had been with Gomer.

Amos had similarly taught that God had taken the initiative towards Israel (Am. ii. 9–10, iii. 2); but God's initiative in Hosea has tenderer undertones. See the human, kindly picture of God in xi. 3, 4. God is like a father, teaching Israel to walk, healing them when they fall and hurt themselves. He is like a driver going to the animals' heads as they toil up a steep hill, speaking kindly words of encouragement, easing the yoke when it chafes them.

b. His view of sin

Hosea was in thorough agreement with Amos. For both, exile because of sin awaits Israel in the future. The names of Hosea's children point clearly to the judgment of God—Jezreel (standing for the doom of Israel along with the royal house); Lo-ruhamah ('God will not have mercy'); and Lo-ammi (involving denial that Israel is God's people). See also chapters iv, v. 1–14, vi. 4–11, vii–x, xi. 1–7. iv. 17 is especially striking. The verse does not mean that Israel is so thoroughly wedded to idols that she is beyond redemption, but it does reflect a most serious view of sin. Sin befuddles, it deludes, it taints everything it touches (iv. 11). Hosea had saved Gomer from being a thing to be bought and sold for money; but even he could not save her for the old relationship of love that had been ruptured by her faithlessness. He had to let her alone until it was clear that she was no longer joined to her idols of lust and lightness. Discipline did not prove that he no longer cared: it was because he cared that he practised discipline. God only leaves alone those who will not tolerate intervention on His terms. It is His way of bringing them to their senses.

c. His view of repentance

vi. 1–4 is interesting. (i) The passage has been taken as an expression of genuine repentance. (ii) It has been treated as the expression of a cheap and shallow repentance, on the lips of people who cannot shake off the jaunty confidence that they are the sons of God. What can God do with a people whose repentance is spasmodic, as fleeting as a morning cloud that disappears long before noon, or as unsubstantial as dew that evaporates in the sun?

Whatever the exegesis of the passage, there is no doubt that for Hosea there was no easy way to repentance. Idolatry, immorality, formal and easy-going worship were road-blocks on the way. See xiv. 2, where the contrast is not between words and deeds, but between words and idol-worship with its futile kissing of calves and its meaningless mumbo-jumbo. Repentance must be rational and articulate.

d. His view of knowledge of God

We find his diagnosis of the roots of Israel's malady in iv. 6. The verse does not refer merely to intellectual knowledge. Knowledge leads a man to do something. Hosea felt that Israel did not understand God. That lack of knowledge of God resulted in all forms of wickedness 'perjury, lying, and murder, stealing, debauchery, burglary —bloodshed on bloodshed' (iv. 2, Moffatt). If he had been asked about the cure for Israel's malady, he would probably have replied: 'Remember the instructions of your God, handed down by tradition and in sacred writing: remember the great events of your history and the great God to whom they point, a God of great character, great power and great tenderness.' Gomer never understood Hosea. That was why she hurt him as she did. If Israel could be brought to the place of real knowledge of God her behaviour would be transformed.

V. PROBLEMS OF THE BOOK

a. Textual difficulties

'There is no book in the Old Testament which has suffered more from textual corruption than Hosea' (Oesterley and Robinson). This may be a partial explanation of the diversity of approach to a passage such as xi. 1–11. Some translators maintain that there is no hope for the future in the passage, while others claim there is a large hope.

b. Exegetical difficulties

Chapters i–iii have been a battleground of rival interpretations. Hosea's marriage has been looked upon as a vision, as an allegory, and as a historical fact. The last interpretation must surely commend itself. The name Gomer-bath-Diblaim has no allegorical relevance. Again the depth of feeling in the book is best explained by a real rather than a symbolical experience. There are, however, wide differences among those who accept this conclusion, depending on the interpretation of 'a wife of whoredoms and children of whoredoms' (i. 2).

1. Gomer was a harlot when Hosea married her. The words do not necessarily involve this interpretation. Compare Is. vi. 9–12, where it looks as if Isaiah preached in order to blind people. This was the result, rather than the purpose, of preaching. Compare Jesus' use of parable (Mk. iv. 11, 12), and references to the hardening of Pharaoh's heart (Ex. x. 1, xi. 10, xiv. 4), for other passages where result looks like purpose. i. 2 may be a prophetic way of referring to the outcome, which, after all, was known to God from the beginning. 'On that uncertain voyage he

had sailed with sealed orders' (George Adam Smith).

2. Hosea took Gomer, not as a wife but as a concubine. This has nothing to commend it, although it has the support of the great name of Thomas Aquinas.

3. Gomer was pure at the time of marriage. This is psychologically adequate, explaining Hosea's enduring love for Gomer. It is also in accordance with prophetic practice. The prophets always speak of Israel as pure at the time of her union with Yahweh. If Hosea had married a harlot it is unlikely that he would have felt that his marriage could illustrate the divine Bridegroom's marriage to Israel. The prophets speak nostalgically of the 'pure espousals' in the wilderness. If Hosea did not marry a pure girl there was no period of pure espousals to correspond to the 'good old days' in the wilderness.

Snaith accepts this third interpretation in a more complex form. Following Marti, he holds that the woman of chapter iii cannot be Gomer, for she was an adulteress from the beginning. He finds the proof of this in the segregation to which she was committed before there could be any prospect of cohabitation with the prophet. Perhaps she was intended as a secondary wife. Dt. xxi. 15–17 demonstrates the legality of this in Israel. If the woman of chapter iii was not a secondary wife the only alternative, according to Snaith, is to hold that Hosea divorced Gomer and then bought her back from her owner, but not as a wife in any full sense.

Dogmatism in the reconstruction of the story is out of place, but there seem no good reasons against a simpler reconstruction of the tragedy. Gomer left Hosea or was asked to leave. Divorce was not necessarily involved. Subsequently he heard the divine voice calling him to reclaim Gomer from her sordid shame. But there could be no return to marriage in a full sense without discipline.

c. Hope in Hosea

Harper in the *ICC* claims that there is no hope in Hosea. 'The future is altogether dark.' Passages like xiv. 1–8 are not authentic.

Snaith finds Harper's view too sweeping, but holds that there is less hope than appears on the surface. A northerner like Hosea could not, for example, have nourished the hope of a unified Israel and Judah. The oppression of the North under Solomon would have made this impossible.

It would, no doubt, have been impossible for the popular mind, but it is surely permissible to maintain that a man like Hosea, who was ahead of his time in so many ways, might have been ahead of his time in this respect too.

Passages in which Snaith sees clear hope for the future are ii. 14–23, xi. 10, 11, xiv, and vi. 1–3 (this is the supreme example in the book of 'hope of a new beginning and better times').

BIBLIOGRAPHY. G. A. Smith, *The Book of the Twelve Prophets*[2], I, 1928; W. R. Harper, *Hosea*, *ICC*, 1905; H. W. Robinson, *Two Hebrew Prophets*, 1948; W. O. E. Oesterley and T. H. Robinson, *An Introduction to the Books of the Old Testament*, 1935; N. H. Snaith, *Mercy and Sacrifice*, 1953; G. A. F. Knight, *Hosea*, 1960.

E.S.P.H.

HOSHEA (*hôšēa'*). **1.** A variant form of the name of Joshua (Nu. xiii. 8, 16 [where AV inaccurately renders 'Oshea']; Dt. xxxii. 44).

2. The nineteenth and last king of the northern kingdom of Israel. During the reign of Pekah, whom Hoshea assassinated and succeeded (2 Ki. xv. 30), Tiglath-pileser III had overrun Galilee and Transjordan, leaving Hoshea a sadly truncated kingdom. There appear to have been rival political factions in Israel at this time. Pekah had pursued a strong anti-Assyr. policy. Hoshea's conspiracy was doubtless at the instigation of Assyria, and this explains Tiglath-pileser's claim to have set Hoshea over Israel (*ANET*, p. 284). Hoshea was thus an Assyr. vassal from the outset of his reign. In the delusive expectation of support from Egypt, Hoshea ceased paying tribute to Assyria after a time. Shalmaneser V advanced against him. Though Hoshea sought to placate his overlord by a belated act of submission, his endeavour was in vain. His intrigue with Egypt cast grave doubt upon the sincerity of his action (2 Ki. xvii. 3, 4). Accordingly, he was imprisoned and his capital was besieged by the Assyrians. Samaria held out three years before surrendering (2 Ki. xvii. 6). The fate of Hoshea is not recorded. The qualified censure of his reign implies that he sought in measure to reverse the religious policy of his predecessors (2 Ki. xvii. 2). J.C.J.W.

HOSPITALITY. Throughout Scripture the responsibility of caring for the traveller and those in need is largely taken for granted. Thus in the Old Testament we get little in the way of positive injunction to practise hospitality; and in the New the same applies to the duty towards men in general; for the specific commands in the New Testament deal more particularly with the Christian's responsibility to his fellow-believer.

I. IN THE OLD TESTAMENT

We see this normal attitude of readiness to welcome the stranger in the reception given by Abraham to the strangers (Gn. xviii. 1, 2, *cf.* xix. 1). There is a marked courtesy. The strangers are received as honoured guests and the best possible provision is made for them. It can be seen too in the surprise of Reuel that his daughters could meet a stranger and not invite him to a meal (Ex. ii. 20). He orders them rather peremptorily, 'Call him, that he may eat bread.' The word used here for call (*qārā'*) is used elsewhere for a guest, one who is summoned by another to partake of his food (see 1 Ki. i. 41, 49; Pr. ix. 18; Zp. i. 7). An even stronger word of condemnation is the indictment of the Ammonites and Moabites, who failed to meet the children of Israel with bread and water (Dt. xxiii. 4). Even in the rude days of the Judges the same spirit continues. Manoah shows an alacrity in providing for his guest which recalls the generous courtesy of Abraham (Jdg. xiii. 15). Indeed, it is significant that in the licentious atmosphere of Gibeah the lack of any spiritual or moral consciousness in the people is accompanied by a complete lack of hospitality (Jdg. xix. 15). There was, of course, one notable exception, even in Gibeah, the old man who retains something of the spirit of the earlier days and not only receives the stranger but refuses to accept any provision from his guest. In Gibeah we see also another element in the practice of hospitality. Once the guest is welcomed the host becomes responsible for him. If his welfare is endangered the host must protect him. This also appeared earlier in the attitude of Lot in Sodom, when his responsibility as a host was considered even more binding upon him than his duty as a father. Of course the guest too had a duty to behave rightly towards the one who had provided for him. Hence the bitterness of the cry in Ps. xli. 9, that the one who had eaten his bread had risen up against him. There seems to be an awareness of a special duty towards God's servants. We see this in the provision made for Elijah at great cost by the widow of Zarephath (1 Ki. xvii. 10 ff.) or in the permanent provision made for Elisha by the Shunammite woman (2 Ki. iv. 8 ff.). It is significant that in his indictment of the formal religion of his day, with its spiritual barrenness, Isaiah gives as one of the marks of true religion a willingness to care for the hungry and the naked (Is. lviii. 7).

II. IN THE NEW TESTAMENT

When we turn to the New Testament we find the same general pattern of ready hospitality. Indeed, in the parable of the final assize in Mt. xxv the offering or withholding of hospitality when another is in need is considered to be a decisive indication of the presence or absence of spiritual life, and is judged accordingly. We find again the special sense of responsibility towards God's servants. Thus Jesus finds a ready welcome in the home at Bethany. Lydia at Philippi, having heard and received the gospel, urges Paul and his companions to lodge with her. So too when Jesus sends out the Twelve and the Seventy He expects them to be provided for by those to whom they preach (Mt. x. 9; Lk. x. 4), and indeed a refusal to receive them in a hospitable fashion is tantamount to a rejection of their message.

When the guest is received there are certain courtesies to be performed by the host (Lk. vii. 44 ff.). There is the kiss of welcome. Water is provided to wash the dust from his feet, and oil to anoint his head. The guests recline at the meal, and, judging by the easy way in which the woman who anointed Christ came in, there was free access for the passer-by. It was literally an *open house*.

In the Epistles we get definite commands. We might query the reason for this in view of the general pattern. But there were certain reasons for ensuring that the duty of hospitality, especially to fellow-Christians, was not ignored. The persecutions which were already a factor in the New Testament period could lead to the scattering of Christians from their homes, and doubtless led in many cases to a very real material need (Acts viii. 1). Food and lodging became therefore for many an urgent necessity. In addition, there were the brethren who wandered from place to place preaching the gospel. They received nothing from the heathen, and were therefore a charge upon the Christians whose homes they visited. Some of these Christians would, of course, be their own converts (3 Jn. 5, 6, 7). This duty of supporting the peripatetic evangelist is emphasized by the contrasting treatment which is to be accorded to the false teacher. It is a token of the final rejection of his error that he is not to be received into the house (2 Jn. 10). When the further consideration is taken into account that many inns were of rather ill repute—Rahab the harlot doubtless had successors—it will be understood that Christians, whose reputation was so readily assailed, would want to avoid them.

In Rom. xii. 13 the duty of hospitality is closely linked with the particular responsibility of caring for fellow-Christians. It is a task to be carried out with determination. Christians, literally, are to pursue hospitality, not allowing it to elude them because of selfishness or slackness on their part. This special regard to the needs of fellow-Christians is brought out in Gal. vi. 10, where Paul puts it in the context of our duty to do good unto *all men*. Writing to the Colossians, he bids them receive Mark if he comes to them (Col. iv. 10); and in the companion Epistle, to Philemon, he takes the provision of hospitality for granted as he speaks of his hoped-for release, and asks for a room to be prepared for him (Phm. 22). In his directions in the Pastorals concerning the qualification of a bishop, the duty of hospitality stands high on the list (1 Tim. iii. 2; Tit. i. 8).

Peter emphasizes the spirit in which hospitality is to be practised (1 Pet. iv. 9). It springs from love, and so it is to be offered ungrudgingly. There is a similar note in Heb. xiii. 1, where the basis for the call to be hospitable is the exhortation 'Let brotherly love continue'. The love of which Peter speaks (*agapē*) is essentially outward-looking and leads to a readiness in giving to the needs of others. So Christian hospitality is not the grudging performance of a duty but the glad act of a cheerful giver. Furthermore, Peter points out that giving is possible only because we have already received gifts from God. The believer should be constantly aware of the fact that he is in debt to God for all he has; and so the care of others is the discharge of a debt of gratitude.

III. THE BIBLICAL INN

At an early stage we meet with a simple type of inn (*mālôn*) which was probably little more than a place of shelter for the traveller (Gn. xlii. 27, xliii. 21; Ex. iv. 24). The *mālôn* is translated in

LXX by *katalyō* or its cognate *katalyma*, which conveys the idea of unharnessing the beasts. Such an inn was therefore probably rather like a caravanserai. The word *katalyō* acquires the general sense of lodging, for the LXX uses it (Jos. ii. 1) to describe the spies who lodged with Rahab, and presumably they were on foot. The inn at Bethlehem (*katalyma*) may have been the same kind of simple lodging-place. It is hardly likely to have been the guest room of an individual, for no name is given; but it may have been the common responsibility of the village. In other places where the word, or its cognates, is used a guest-chamber in a private residence is indicated (Lk. xix. 7, xxii. 11; *cf.* Mk. xiv. 14). In Lk. x. 34 we get a much more developed type of inn (*pandocheion*). It is open to all and sundry, and it provides not merely shelter for the night, but food and attention, for which there seems to have been a recognized charge. H.M.C.

HOST. See ARMY.

HOST, HOST OF HEAVEN. In AV three words translated 'host' are used in a general sense meaning 'army' (*q.v.*). These are: *ḥayil* (emphasis on 'force'—about thirty times), *maḥ^{a}neh* (emphasis on 'camp'—about fifty times), and the most common word, *ṣāḇā'*, used nearly 400 times. Each of these words, with due regard to its special emphasis, may be used quite neutrally, for example of Pharaoh's 'host' but equally of the 'host' of Israel. However, when used of the host of Israel, there are usually religious overtones, and there are two exclusively religious uses of *ṣāḇā* which must be noted.

a. Host of Heaven

This phrase (*ṣ^{e}ḇā' haššāmayim*) occurs about fifteen times. The two meanings 'celestial bodies' and 'angelic beings' are inextricably intertwined. The LXX translation, using *kosmos*, *stratia*, or *dynamis*, does not help to resolve this. No doubt to the Heb. mind the distinction was superficial, and the celestial bodies were thought to be closely associated with heavenly beings. In fact, the implied angelology of C. S. Lewis's novels (*Out of the Silent Planet*, *etc.*) would probably have commended itself with some force to the biblical writers. The Bible certainly suggests that angels of different ranks have charge of individuals and of nations; no doubt in the light of modern cosmology this concept, if retained at all (as biblically it must be), ought properly to be extended, as the dual sense of the phrase 'Host of Heaven' suggests, to the oversight of the elements of the physical universe—planets, stars, and nebulae.

b. Lord of Hosts (*Yahweh ṣ^{e}ḇā'ôṯ*)

This expression is used nearly 300 times in the Old Testament and is especially common in Isaiah, Jeremiah, Zechariah, and Malachi. It is a title of might and power, used frequently in a military or apocalyptic context. It is significant that the first occurrence is 1 Sa. i. 3 in association with the sanctuary at Shiloh. 'Of Hosts' is rendered in LXX either by transliteration as *sabaōth* (*cf.* Rom. ix. 29; Jas. v. 4) or by use of *pantokratōr* ('almighty'). It is thought by some to have arisen as a title of God associated with His lordship over the 'host' of Israel; but its usage, especially in the prophets, clearly implies also a relationship to the 'host of heaven' in its angelic sense; and this could well be the original connotation. See GOD, NAMES OF. M.T.F.

HOUGH (*'āqar*, 'to root out'). The hough of a horse is the joint between knee and fetlock in the hind leg. In its biblical context the verb (found in Jos. xi. 6, 9; 2 Sa. viii. 4; 1 Ch. xviii. 4) means to cut the tendon of the hough ('tendon of Achilles'), and so render useless the horses of the enemy. J.D.D.

HOUR (Heb., Aram. *šā'â*; Gk. *hōra*) is used in Scripture in a precise sense and in a more general sense.

1. In its more precise sense (which is probably later than the more general sense), an hour is one-twelfth of the period of daylight: 'Are there not twelve hours in the day?' (Jn. xi. 9). They were reckoned from sunrise to sunset, just as the three (Jewish) or four (Roman) watches into which the period of darkness was divided were reckoned from sunset to sunrise. As sunrise and sunset varied according to the time of the year, biblical hours cannot be translated exactly into modern clock-hours; and in any case the absence of accurate chronometers meant that the time of day was indicated in more general terms than with us. It is not surprising that the hours most frequently mentioned are the third, sixth, and ninth hours. All three are mentioned in the parable of the labourers in the vineyard (Mt. xx. 3, 5), as is also the eleventh hour (verses 6, 9), which has become proverbial for the last opportunity. The two disciples of Jn. i. 35 ff. stayed with Jesus for the remainder of the day after going home with Him, 'for it was about the tenth hour' (verse 39), *i.e.* about 4 p.m., and darkness would have fallen before they concluded their conversation with Him. The third, sixth, and ninth hours are mentioned in the Synoptic record of the crucifixion (Mk. xv. 25, 33 f.). The difficulty of reconciling the 'sixth hour' of Jn. xix. 14 with the 'third hour' of Mk. xv. 25 has led some to suppose that in John the hours are counted from midnight, not from sunrise. The one concrete piece of evidence in this connection —the statement in the *Martyrdom of Polycarp* (xxi) that Polycarp was martyred 'at the eighth hour', where 8 a.m. is regarded by some as more probable than 2 p.m.—is insufficient to set against the well-attested fact that Romans and Jews alike counted their hours from sunrise. (The fact that the Romans reckoned their civil day as starting at midnight, while the Jews reckoned theirs as starting at sunset, has nothing to do with the numbering of the hours.) The 'seventh hour'

of Jn. iv. 52 is 1 p.m.; such difficulty as is felt about the reference to 'yesterday' in that verse is not removed by interpreting the hour differently. In Rev. viii. 1 'half an hour' represents Gk. *hēmiōrion.*

2. More generally, 'hour' indicates a fairly well-defined point of time. 'In the same hour' (Dn. v. 5) means 'while the king and his guests were at the height of their sacrilegious revelry'. 'In the selfsame hour' (Mt. viii. 13) means 'at the very moment when Jesus assured the centurion that his plea to have his servant healed was granted'. Frequently some specially critical occasion is referred to as an 'hour': *e.g.* the hour of Jesus' betrayal (Mk. xiv. 41; *cf.* Lk. xxii. 53, 'your hour', *i.e.* 'your brief season of power'); the hour of His parousia, with the attendant resurrection and judgment (Mt. xxv. 13; Jn. v. 28 f.). In John the appointed time for Jesus' passion and glorification is repeatedly spoken of as His 'hour' (*cf.* Jn. ii. 4, vii. 30, viii. 20, also xii. 23, xvii. 1). The present situation between the times is 'the last hour' (1 Jn. ii. 18, RV); the rise of many antichrists indicates that Christ is soon to appear.

BIBLIOGRAPHY. K. Bornhäuser, *Zeiten und Stunden in der Leidens- und Auferstehungsgeschichte,* 1921, summarized by C. Sandegren in *EQ,* XXIV, 1952, pp. 241 ff. F.F.B.

HOUSE.

I. LOCATION

In the Palestine of Bible times the house was part of a great fortress complex. Unfortified housing areas existed only briefly, at prosperous periods, *e.g.* the 8th century BC, when some houses were built outside the walls. But this was a calculated risk, and the owner had to make his wealth quickly before a war jeopardized his investment. Even the farmer lived in the city, although at the harvest season he might camp out, perhaps in a cave, to be nearer to his fields. The threshing-floors were always near the city.

There were some semi-nomads in Palestine, especially in Transjordan. Abraham was the most famous of those who dwelt in a 'house of hair', *i.e.* a goat-hair tent. Lot lived in a cave after his flight from Sodom (Gn. xix. 30), and throughout the biblical period the cave was a not uncommon home for refugees and the poor, but most people in Palestine were city-dwellers.

The words *city* and *fortress* were synonyms, and the size of cities was strictly limited by the labour required to build their massive defences. Most towns probably did not average more than 6 acres in extent (see also FORTIFICATION AND SIEGECRAFT). There was no standard plan for houses, which were therefore of irregular area and crowded together so that every inch of space was utilized. City planning did not come in until Hellenistic times.

II. GENERAL FEATURES

Houses were normally two storeys in height, although a few might be taller, and slave-quarters were often only ground-floor hovels. The walls of the lower storey were built of rough field stones, and were therefore rather thick. The walls of the upper storeys were also thick, although they were usually made of sun-dried bricks. In areas where stone was scarce, the entire house was built of this mud-brick: good foundations of stone were needed in this case, high enough to protect the brickwork from rain-water collecting in the streets. The mud bricks themselves had to be plastered with waterproof marly clay.

Another reason why good foundations and massive corner stones were so important is that Palestine is an earthquake area. Cloudbursts in certain areas are also destructive, as is seen in the parable of the house built upon the sand (Mt. vii. 24–27). The Canaanites occasionally used infant sacrifices as foundation deposits, but these are found only rarely. Some scholars think this use of human sacrifice is referred to in Hiel's rebuilding of Jericho (1 Ki. xvi. 34).

Mortar was seldom used in erecting these stone walls, but the inner faces of the walls were plastered. Rooms were very small by our standards, except in wealthy homes. They were usually about 6 feet high. The floor was made of a marly clay which stands considerable hard usage from bare feet. Some Egyptian village schools still use this kind of floor. More expensive homes had their floors and courtyards paved with flagstones. The roof was commonly made of a thick layer of marly clay, spread over reed mats supported on branches, which in turn were carried on beams. Between rains the clay would crack, and cylindrical stone rollers about 2 feet long were used to roll the roof and keep it waterproof. The tiled roof which came into use before New Testament times could have a steeper pitch. The stone vaulted roof, common in Palestinian houses today, was not used in Bible times.

The roof of the house provided extra accommodation which was often utilized in the summer. The family would sleep there, and use it as a living-room during the day, as well as a storeroom, where raisins, figs, flax, *etc.*, were spread out in the sun. Dt. xxii. 8 required a parapet to be built round it as a safety precaution.

In Jeremiah's day apostate Israelites worshipped Baal and the host of heaven from rooftop altars (Je. xix. 13, xxxii. 29). Pure devotions, however, could also be held on the rooftop (Acts x. 9). The stone or brick stairs used to reach the roof were usually on the outside of the house. Note the phraseology of Mk. xiii. 15. The poor probably used ladders.

The door of the house was small and swung on pivots set in the door-sill and the lintel. A high threshold was useful in keeping the flood water of winter storms from rushing into the house. A doorkeeper who served not only as guard but also as judge of those who should be admitted to the house was often employed in richer homes. Windows were rare on the ground floor, as the open door furnished plenty of light during most of the year. There was another reason for keeping window-space to a minimum: the house was thus kept cooler in summer and warmer in winter. First-floor windows would more likely face the interior courtyard than the street. Those facing the street would be latticed. Glass was not yet available for windows. As little wood as possible was used in houses to reduce the fire hazard. In rich homes, however, it was used for decoration of both walls and ceilings.

The courtyards around which the houses were built served as kitchens except in the most inclement weather. The ovens for baking bread were usually located in the courtyards, and the women did most of their household work there.

After the invention of waterproof plaster the better houses had their own cisterns. The rain-water from the roofs came down a drain and through a settling-basin into the cistern. In earlier days every family fetched its water from a nearby spring.

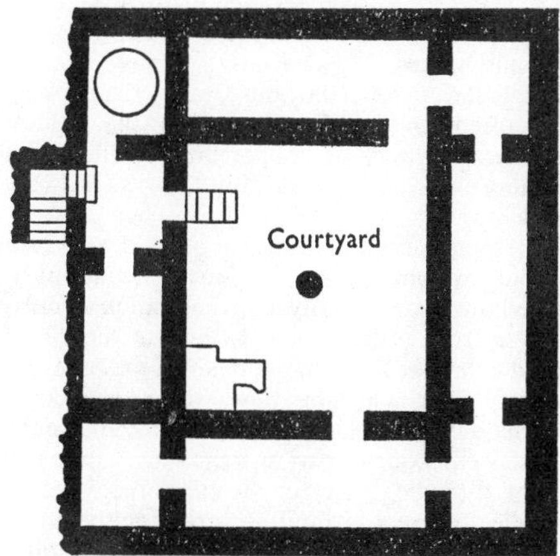

Fig. 109. Plan of a typical villa of the early second millennium. The main rooms are grouped round a central courtyard from which stairs lead to the upper floor. *Cf.* fig. 110.

III. DEVELOPMENTS IN ARCHITECTURE

a. In the days of the Patriarchs

During this period the population of Palestine was divided into patricians and serfs, the former living in mansions, the latter in adjacent single-room hovels. The largest of these patrician houses found to date is about $\frac{1}{2}$ acre in size. The central courtyard of these mansions was normally surrounded on all sides by one or more series of rooms. The family lived on the first floor, and the guard room was there too. The lower floor served for work rooms, storage area, and stable. (The horse was new in Palestine and very valuable.) This type of housing continued in Palestine until Joshua's conquest, but in the period between Genesis and Exodus the country's prosperity declined and its housing became poorer. In a few instances, however, as at Bethel, patrician housing of the Late Bronze period was superior. There was even an excellent system of individual household drains under the floors, sometimes with one drain passing over the other.

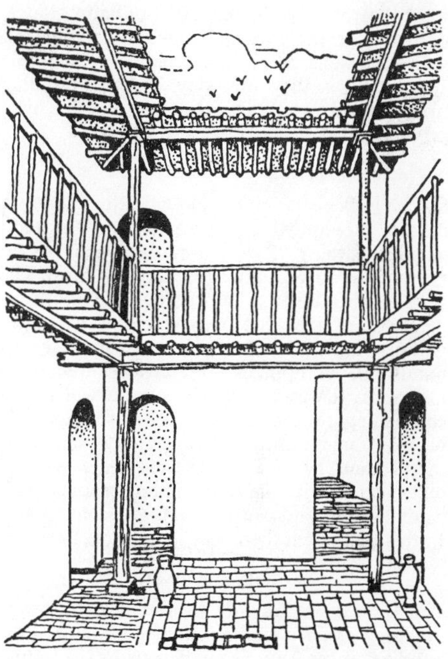

Fig. 110. Reconstruction of a house of the early second millennium BC excavated at Ur. The brick stair leads up to the living-quarters, the ground floor being used for servants and storage.

b. Joshua's conquest

The conquest of the promised land revolutionized the areas where the Israelites settled, but the old order largely continued in the unconquered cities. The Israelites were a democratic people, and the division between lord and serf disappeared—all became commoners. Since the invaders were poor and unskilled after their desert experience, the early Israelite house was almost as poor as the old slave-quarters. There was one new architectural pattern, however, common to all the cities which they occupied. Pillars were used in the building of walls, with the spaces between them filled in with rocks of any kind. The doorway was very low. The poverty of the people is shown by the fact that very few articles are found in their houses and by the cheapness of even these. The most striking difference of all is the absence of Canaanite cult objects in the new Israelite level. Housing was poorest in the period of the Judges, but improved rapidly in the days of David and Solomon, especially through Phoenician influence.

c. During the divided kingdom

As prosperity increased under the divided monarchy, a new type of house for the rich man appeared. The large courtyard was now faced on at least one side of its long axis by a pillared building. The pillars were usually semi-dressed single stones, high enough to hold up the first storey. They reflect the art of quarrying large stone, learned in the days of Solomon. Later, when city property became much more valuable, such mansions were converted into multiple apartments, as they are today. The best building from Persian times is a great house at Lachish, probably used by the governor.

d. Hellenistic period

Some Hellenistic cities of Palestine show a definite attempt at city planning, on the rectangular pattern. The houses also approached much closer to a square or rectangular form. The wealthy now added a bathroom. By New Testament times the rich were making a winter paradise out of Jericho. This excavated city reminds one of Pompeii, but Jericho was more luxurious. It was also spread over a wider area and had spacious gardens. The wealthy house of New Testament times in Palestine was similar to the Roman house everywhere. There was an outer court with its surrounding rooms, and behind it a second court with its adjacent rooms. In this latter area there was the utmost privacy.

IV. ROYAL PALACES

The Bible gives us only a brief description of Solomon's palace, but the detailed account of the building of the Temple enables us to conjecture what the palace looked like, for it was designed by the same architects and constructed by the same craftsmen. The masonry was of dressed stone laid in headers and stretchers. Fine woods, finished to show off their textures, were used for interior decoration. The excavation of the governor's palace at Megiddo has thrown light on Solomon's building programme. The palace of the Omri dynasty at Samaria was also built by Phoenician workmen. The beautiful ivory inlays found here give an excellent clue to the expensive furniture used in the palace (*cf.* pl. V*a*). Herod's palace in Jerusalem, with its extensive gardens, was the last word in luxury, as was also his winter palace at Jericho.

V. LIFE IN THE HOUSE

The house, during most of the Bible period, was usually both a dwelling-place and a store-room. Not only did the farmer live here, but everything he owned was stored here. The plough and other farm tools, grain and other foods sufficient for the family for the winter, and fodder for the animals, were all kept in the house. Archaeologists have been surprised by the amount of carbonaceous matter found in these houses, especially in those destroyed by Joshua's troops. In very cold, wet weather and in times of war, the family would also have to share the house, or at least the courtyard, with the most valuable of the animals.

The furniture for the house varied with the wealth of the inhabitants. The poor could afford only kitchen equipment and bedding. The furniture in the guest room given to Elisha would be typical of that used in the average family (2 Ki. iv. 10). It contained a bed, a table, a chair, and a lamp. The rich used a high bed, others a cot. The poorest used a reed mat on the floor. Plenty of bedding was necessary, for Palestine's winters are cold and damp, and in fact seem much colder than the reading on the thermometer indicates. The table might be high or low, and the same was true of the chair and its cheaper partner the stool. There would be chests to hold clothes and bedding. The furniture of the wealthy was inlaid with ivory, and the middle class sometimes imitated this in common bone inlay. The ivory inlays, in turn, were sometimes also inlaid with gold and precious stones. The hand loom would be found in many homes.

In winter, to keep the house warm, the cooking was often done indoors, and in the coldest weather a pottery or copper brazier filled with burning charcoal was used. But this was not very efficient.

The preparation and serving of food called for special equipment. As we have already mentioned, there was usually an oven built in a courtyard in front of the house. Hollow at the top, it could be about 2 feet in diameter at the base and about 1 foot in height. It was often shaped of alternate layers of clay and potsherds. Inside the house were stone or clay storage bins. Large jars might also be used for keeping the winter's supplies. There was a mill for grinding the grain. Flour was kept in a wide-mouthed jar, and olive oil was stored in a specially designed vessel. Often there was a large stone mortar set in the floor, where various foods could be prepared by grinding with a pestle. If there was no cistern in the house, a large jar for storing water was at hand. Near by were smaller jars with which to carry water from the spring. There were wide-mouthed cooking-pots in which food could be stirred and other narrow-mouthed ones used for heating liquids. There was a wide variety of bowls used in serving foods. The rich used gold and silver tableware, and copper kitchen kettles. Am. vi. 4–6 describes the luxurious life of Israel at its worst.

The Last Supper is a combination of customs both old and new. The diners reclined on couches in the Graeco-Roman style, but the room itself was on an upper floor, the situation of the guest-room from time immemorial.

BIBLIOGRAPHY. W. F. Albright, *The Archaeology of Palestine*, 1954; G. E. Wright, *Biblical Archaeology*, 1957; E. W. Heaton, *Everyday Life in Old Testament Times*, 1956; A. C. Bouquet, *Everyday Life in New Testament Times*, 1955.

J.L.K.

HOZAI. The name of a history, quoted in 2 Ch. xxxiii. 19, RV, which recorded certain of the deeds of King Manasseh, and his prayer. AVmg has 'Hosai'. The AV text translates 'the seers', RSV 'the

Seers', readings which follow LXX and are a translation of the Heb. word (*ḥôzay*, pointed in *MT* as though it meant 'my seers'). R.A.H.G.

HUKKOK. A town on the southern border of Naphtali, listed with Aznoth-tabor (Jos. xix. 34). Generally identified with Yakuk, 5 miles west of the suggested site of Capernaum.

HUKOK. See HELKATH.

HULDAH. This prophetess, wife of Shallum, keeper of the wardrobe (either of priestly vestments or royal robes), lived in the second (western?) quarter of Jerusalem. She was consulted (*c.* 621 BC), on behalf of King Josiah, by Hilkiah the chief priest, Shaphan the scribe, and others, following the discovery of 'the book of the law' in 'the house of the Lord' (2 Ki. xxii. 14; 2 Ch. xxxiv. 22). She accepted the book as the word of Yahweh, and with His authority prophesied judgment against Jerusalem and Judah after Josiah's death. It is noteworthy that, although both Jeremiah and Zephaniah were prophesying at this time, it is she who was approached on this matter of the cultus. M.G.

HUMILITY. The importance of this virtue springs from the fact that it is found as part of the character of God. In Ps. cxiii. 5, 6 God is represented as being incomparably high and great, and yet He humbles Himself to take note of the things which are created, while in Ps. xviii. 35 (*cf.* 2 Sa. xxii. 36) the greatness of God's servant is attributed to the humility (gentleness) which God has displayed towards him.

Wherever the quality is found in the Old Testament it is praised (*e.g.* Pr. xv. 33, xviii. 12) and God's blessing is frequently poured upon those who possess it. Moses is vindicated because of it (Nu. xii. 3), while Belshazzar is reproved by Daniel (v. 22) because he has not profited by the experience of Nebuchadrezzar before him, which might have brought him into an attitude of humility. 2 Chronicles in particular makes it the criterion by which the rule of successive kings is to be judged.

The term is closely connected in derivation with affliction, which is sometimes brought upon men by their fellows, and sometimes attributed directly to the purpose of God, but is always calculated to produce humility of spirit.

Similarly, in the New Testament, at Mt. xxiii. 12 and parallels, the same word is used to express the penalty for arrogance (abasement) and the prerequisite of preferment (humility). In the first case it is a condition of low estate which will be brought about through the judgment of God. In the second it is a spirit of lowliness which enables God to bring the blessing of advancement. Paul too, in Phil. iv. 12, uses it to describe his affliction, but goes on to make clear that the virtue lies in the acceptance of the experience, so that a condition imposed from without becomes the occasion for the development of the corresponding attitude within. In the same Epistle (ii. 8) he cites as an example to be emulated the humility of Christ, who deliberately set aside His divine prerogative and progressively humbled Himself, receiving in due time the exaltation which must inevitably follow.

Like all virtues, humility is capable of being simulated, and the danger of this is particularly plain in Paul's letter to the Colossians. Whatever may be the true rendering of the difficult passage in Col. ii. 18, it is clear that here and in ii. 23 the reference is to a sham. In spite of all the appearances of humility, these false teachers are really puffed up with a sense of their own importance. Setting their own speculative system over against the revelation of God, they deny the very thing which by their asceticism they seem to proclaim. Paul warns his readers against this pseudo-humility and goes on in iii. 12 to exhort them to the genuine thing. F.S.F.

HUNTING, HUNTER. The narratives of the patriarchal period depict the Hebrews as occupied chiefly with the raising of flocks and other semi-sedentary agricultural activities. Hunting was seldom engaged in as a pastime, and was generally resorted to only either at the promptings of hunger or when the wild animals with which Palestine abounded in antiquity (Ex. xxiii. 29) threatened the security of the Hebrews and their flocks (Jdg. xiv. 5; 1 Sa. xvii. 34). Certain individuals, however, were renowned for their hunting prowess, including Ishmael (Gn. xxi. 20) and Esau (Gn. xxv. 27).

By contrast the ancient Mesopotamians and Egyptians spent considerably more time in the pursuit of game. Many Assyrian monuments and bas-reliefs depict hunting-scenes, indicating a long tradition of sporting activity which may well go back as far as Nimrod, the mighty hunter of antiquity (Gn. x. 8) who colonized Assyria (Gn. x. 11). Whereas the Mesopotamians hunted lions and other ferocious beasts, the Egyptians preferred to catch game and predatory birds. In this pursuit dogs and cats frequently participated.

The austerity of the Hebrew diet in ancient times was occasionally relieved by such delicacies as partridge (*cf.* 1 Sa. xxvi. 20), gazelle, and hart meat (Dt. xii. 15). The provision for Solomon's table also included roebucks (1 Ki. iv. 23). Such is the general nature of Old Testament references to hunting that few of the animals are named, and virtually nothing is said of the methods employed or of the accoutrements of the hunter. At Hassuna in Iraq the camp of a hunter was unearthed and found to contain weapons, storage jars, and tools dating back to *c.* 5000 BC. Biblical references allude to bows and arrows (Gn. xxvii. 3), clubs (Jb. xli. 29, RV), slingstones (1 Sa. xvii. 40), nets (Jb. xix. 6), fowlers' snares (Ps. xci. 3), and pits for larger animals such as bears (Ezk. xix. 8). See ARMOUR AND WEAPONS, SNARES.

While hunting was not a common occupation in ancient Palestine, its procedures were sufficiently familiar to be enshrined in figurative speech (Jb. xviii. 10; Je. v. 26). The New Testament employs few hunting metaphors (Lk. xi. 54; Rom. xi. 9; Mt. xxii. 15).

BIBLIOGRAPHY. E. W. Heaton, *Everyday Life in Old Testament Times*, 1956, pp. 112 ff. R.K.H.

3. *'îš 'ᵃdāmâ* means literally 'man of soil', but a comparison of Gn. ix. 20 and Zc. xiii. 5 shows that it refers indifferently to an arable or cattle farmer.

LXX and the New Testament employ *geōrgos*, 'farmer, tenant farmer', throughout. God is pictured as the husbandman of the true vine (Jn. xv. 1) and of the Church (1 Cor. iii. 9).

R.J.W.

Fig. 111. Stags and deer caught in nets. Relief from Nineveh, *c.* 650 BC. See also fig. 25.

HUR (*ḥûr*, 'free', 'noble'). **1.** A prominent Israelite who with Aaron held up the arms of Moses at Rephidim in the battle against Amalek (Ex. xvii. 10, 12), and who also helped Aaron to judge the people while Moses went up into Mt. Sinai (Ex. xxiv. 14).

2. A descendant through Caleb and Hezron of Perez (1 Ch. ii. 19, 20) and grandfather of Bezaleel (*q.v.*; Ex. xxxi. 2, xxxv. 30, xxxviii. 22; 1 Ch. iv. 1; 2 Ch. i. 5). **3.** A son of Ephratah and father of Caleb (1 Ch. ii. 50, iv. 4). **4.** One of the five kings of Midian who were killed with Balaam by the Israelites (Nu. xxxi. 8; Jos. xiii. 21). **5.** The father of one of Solomon's twelve commissariat officers (1 Ki. iv. 8). The son, who was over the district of Mount Ephraim, is not named, so RV transliterates the Heb. 'son of' and names him Ben-hur. **6.** The father of Rephaiah, who helped to rebuild the walls and was ruler over half of Jerusalem in Nehemiah's time (Ne. iii. 9).

T.C.M.

HUSBAND. See MARRIAGE.

HUSBANDMAN. In the Old Testament there are three expressions which are rendered 'husbandman'.

1. *'ikkār*. The cognate Akkadian ideogram describes the *'ikkār* as 'man of the plough'. The exact social position and function of the *'ikkār* is uncertain, but the code of Hammurabi suggests him to have been a hired agricultural foreman. The Old Testament contrasts the shepherd with the *'ikkār* (Is. lxi. 5).

2. *yōḡēḇ* (2 Ki. xxv. 12; Je. lii. 16). Consideration of the related Heb. *gûḇ* and Arab. *ǧāba*, 'to bore', 'hollow out', may suggest that the *yōḡēḇ* was a spade labourer.

HUSHAI. The story of Hushai the Archite (*cf.* Jos. xvi. 2, RV), his devotion to his king, and his readiness to undertake a dangerous errand for him, affords a model for the Christian to study and to follow (2 Sa. xv. 32 ff.). Hushai's arrival at the heights east of Jerusalem where David halted, and his successful mission, defeated the advice of Ahithophel, and came as an answer to David's prayer (verse 31). In a list of David's officers the Chronicler includes Hushai as 'the king's friend' (1 Ch. xxvii. 33; *cf.* 2 Sa. xv. 37). Baanah, Hushai's son, appears in the list of Solomon's local officers (1 Ki. iv. 7, 16).

G.T.M.

HUSHIM. 'Those who hasten'. **1.** A son of Dan (Gn. xlvi. 23), called Shuham in Nu. xxvi. 42. **2.** A son of Aher the Benjamite (1 Ch. vii. 12). **3.** One of the two wives of Shaharaim and the mother of Abitub and Elpaal (1 Ch. viii. 8, 11).

G.W.G.

HUSKS (Gk. *keratia*). A vegetable food eaten by animals and sometimes by the poor. The prodigal son in his hunger would gladly have done so (Lk. xv. 16). It is the pod of the carob tree and is also called the locust bean and St. John's bread from a tradition that they were the 'locusts' which John the Baptist ate. The pods have a leathery shell, and the seeds are embedded in a sweet pulp. They are black when dried and are not unpleasant to the taste. J.W.M.

HUZZAB (*huṣṣaḇ*, uncertain meaning; possibly 'it is fixed, determined'). An obscure word occurring only in Na. ii. 7. AV, RV, and many commentators read as a proper name, referring to the Assyr. queen, but no such name is known in cuneiform texts. RSV renders 'its mistress', but notes that the meaning is uncertain. RVmg and others take it as a verb, 'it is decreed, settled'. LXX gives *hē hypostasis* = Heb. *maṣṣāḇ* = 'standing-place'. The text may be corrupt (*cf.* G. A. Smith, *The Twelve Prophets*, II, 1928, *ad loc.*). J.G.G.N.

HYACINTH. See JEWELS AND PRECIOUS STONES.

HYENA. The striped hyena (*H. hyaena*) is still a well-known scavenging member of the Palestine fauna. It finds no mention in AV, but some authorities are satisfied that *ṣāḇûa'*, translated 'speckled bird' in Je. xii. 9, is the hyena. The context would confirm this; this is the rendering in LXX, and *ṣāḇûa'* is one of four names used of the hyena by talmudic writers. It has also been suggested that 'the valley of Zeboim' (1 Sa. xiii. 18) is from the same root and should be 'the valley of hyenas'. See fig. 90. G.C.

HYMENAEUS. A pernicious teacher associated with Alexander (*q.v.*; 1 Tim. i. 19, 20) and Philetus (2 Tim. ii. 17). Paul's delivery of Hymenaeus and Alexander to Satan recalls 1 Cor. v. 5; both passages have been interpreted of excommunication (*i.e.* surrender to Satan's sphere) and of the infliction of bodily punishment. These are not, of course, incompatible, but the verbal similarity with Jb. ii. 6, LXX, and various other disciplinary transactions in the apostolic Church (*cf.* Acts v. 3–11, viii. 20–24, xiii. 9–11; 1 Cor. xi. 30) suggest that the latter was at least included—even without the parallels in execration texts (*cf. LAE*, p. 302). At all events, the discipline, though drastic, was merciful and remedial in intention.

It had not, however, evoked repentance when 2 Tim. ii. 17 was written. The error of Hymenaeus and others, described in clinical terms as 'feeding like gangrene', was still much in Paul's mind. It involved a 'spiritualization' of the resurrection (including, doubtless, the judgment), doctrine always repugnant to the Greek mind: there were similar misunderstandings at Corinth earlier (1 Cor. xv. 12). Such ideas took various forms in Gnostic religion: *cf.* the claim of the false teachers in the *Acts of Paul and Thecla* xiv (combining two ideas): 'We will teach thee of that resurrection which he asserteth, that it is already come to pass in the children which we have, and we rise again when we have come to the knowledge of the true God' (tr. M. R. James, *Apocryphal New Testament*, p. 275).

The name (that of the marriage-god) is not noticeably frequent. A.F.W.

HYMN. The Gk. *hymnos* was used by the classical writers to signify any ode or song written in praise of gods or heroes, and occasionally by LXX translators of praise to God, *e.g.* Pss. xl. 3, lxv. 1; Is. xlii. 10. In the New Testament the word occurs only in Eph. v. 19 and Col. iii. 16, with the verbal form (*hymneō*) in Mt. xxvi. 30 and the parallel Mk. xiv. 26 (which refer to the singing of the second part of the Hallel, Ps. cxv–cxviii); Acts xvi. 25 (of Paul and Silas singing in prison); and Heb. ii. 12 (a quotation from Ps. xxii. 22, LXX). It is clear, however, that the singing of spiritual songs was a feature of the life of the apostolic church, as is witnessed by 1 Cor. xiv. 15, 26; Jas. v. 13, the Christian canticles recorded by Luke, and the many doxologies found elsewhere in the New Testament. They were used as a spontaneous expression of Christian joy, as a means of instruction in the faith (Col. iii. 16), and, on the basis of synagogue practice, as an integral part of the worship of the Church.

The threefold division of psalms, hymns, and spiritual songs (*ōdai*) must not be pressed too closely, as the terms overlap, but two distinct styles of composition can be observed. The first followed the form and style of the Old Testament psalm and was a Christian counterpart of the psalmodic writing exemplified by the 1st-century BC Psalms of Solomon or the Hymns of Thanksgiving (*Hôḏāyôṯ*) of the Qumran sect. In this category may be included the canticles: Lk. i. 46–55 (Magnificat), i. 68–79 (Benedictus), ii. 29–32 (Nunc Dimittis). The second group consists of doxologies (as Lk. ii. 14; 1 Tim. i. 17, vi. 15, 16; Rev. iv. 8, 11, v. 9, 12, 13, vii. 12, *etc.*), many of which were doubtless used in corporate worship. Some other passages have been loosely described by commentators as hymns, where the majesty of the subject-matter has driven the writer to poetical language, *e.g.* 1 Cor. xiii; Rom. viii. 31–39; Eph. i. 3–14; Phil. ii. 5–11; but there is no certainty that they were ever set to music or recited liturgically. Fragments of liturgical or credal formulae have been detected in Eph. v. 14; 1 Tim. iii. 16; 2 Tim. ii. 11–13; Tit. iii. 4–7. On Phil. ii. 5–11, see R. P. Martin, *An Early Christian Confession*, 1960. J.B.Tr.

HYPOCRITE. In English a hypocrite is one who deliberately and as a habit professes to be good when he is aware that he is not. But the word itself is a transliteration of Gk. *hypokritēs*, which mostly meant play-actor (*cf. Arndt, ad loc.*). Though it was soon in Ecclesiastical Greek to take on its modern meaning, it seems impossible to prove that it bore this meaning in the 1st century AD. In LXX it is twice used to translate *ḥānēp̄*, 'godless'.

In the New Testament, hypocrite is used only in the Synoptic accounts of Christ's judgments on the scribes and Pharisees. Though 'Pharisaic' sources (*Soṭah* 22b) acknowledge and condemn hypocrisy in their ranks, the general tenor of the New Testament, the 1st-century evidences for the teaching of the Pharisees in Talmud and Midrash and their support by the mass of the people (Jos., *Ant.* xiii. 10. 6), all make it hard to accept a general charge of hypocrisy against them. A study of the actual charges against them will show that only in the rarest cases can we possibly interpret them as hypocrisy. We find blindness to their faults (Mt. vii. 5), to God's workings (Lk. xii. 56), to a true sense of values (Lk. xiii. 15), an over-valuation of human tradition (Mt. xv. 7; Mk. vii. 6), sheer ignorance of God's demands (Mt. xxiii. 14, 15, 25, 29), and love of display (Mt. vi. 2, 5, 16). It was only Christ, the sole perfect reader of inward realities (Mt. xxiii. 27, 28), who dared pass this judgment.

BIBLIOGRAPHY. J. Jocz, *The Jewish People and Jesus Christ*, 1949; H. L. Ellison, 'Jesus and the Pharisees' in *JTVI*, LXXXV, 1953; *Arndt* under *hypokritēs*. H.L.E.

HYSSOP. See PLANTS.

I

IBLEAM. A Canaanite town in the northern borderland of Manasseh, whose territory extended to (not 'in') Issachar (Jos. xvii. 11; Y. Kaufmann, *The Biblical Account of the Conquest of Palestine*, 1953, p. 38). During the Israelite settlement, its Canaanite inhabitants were subdued, not expelled (Jdg. i. 27). The site of Ibleam is now Khirbet Bil'ameh, some 10 miles southeast of Megiddo on the road from Beth-shean (2 Ki. ix. 27). It is probably the Bileam of 1 Ch. vi. 70, a levitical city. Ibleam occurs in Egyp. lists as *Ybr'm*. K.A.K.

IBZAN. Known only from Jdg. xii. 8–10; a national judge for seven years, following Jephthah; apparently a person of consequence who raised a large family and arranged marriages for thirty sons. His home and burial-place was Bethlehem, probably of Zebulun (Jos. xix. 15), 7 miles WNW of Nazareth; Jewish commentators assumed Bethlehem-judah, identifying him with Boaz (*q.v.*). J.P.U.L.

ICHABOD (Heb. *'îkābôd*, 'where is the glory?'). The name given by the wife of Phinehas to her child, on hearing that the Philistines had captured the ark (1 Sa. iv. 19–22, *cf.* xiv. 3).

ICONIUM. A city of Asia Minor mentioned in Acts xiii, xiv and 2 Tim. iii. 11 as the scene of Paul's trials, and in Acts xvi. 2 as a place where Timothy was commended. Standing on the edge of the plateau, it was well watered, a productive and wealthy region. It was originally Phrygian, its name Kawania: its religion remained Phrygian into Roman times, the worship of a mother goddess with eunuch priests. After being for a time the chief city of Lycaonia, and passing through various political fortunes, it was at length included in the kingdom of Galatia and a little later in the Roman province of Galatia. Its fame and prestige grew greatly under Roman rule: Claudius honoured it with the title of Claudiconium, and under Hadrian it became a colony in an honorary sense (since no Italians were settled there). In New Testament times, then, it maintained the polity of a Hellenistic city, the juridical powers of the assembly being vested in the two magistrates annually appointed.

The passage in Acts xiv, though brief, gives occasion for differing interpretations. The so-called Western Text implies two attacks on Paul, one open, the second more subtle, after which the apostles flee. Two classes of Jewish leaders are mentioned, 'chief men of the synagogue' and 'rulers', a distinction epigraphically defensible. The text of Codex Vaticanus and its allies has a more difficult text with only one attack of fairly long duration implied. Here the rulers of verse 5 may plausibly be identified with the magistrates of the city, as Ramsay suggests, but whether the Old Uncial text is a bad abbreviation, or the Western Text an attempt at correction of a text perhaps corrupt, has not yet been finally decided.

Iconium is the scene of the well-known apocryphal story of Paul and Thecla, contained in the longer *Acts of Paul*. Apart from the scarcely doubtful existence of an early martyr of the name, there is no ascertainable historical content to be found in the story.

BIBLIOGRAPHY. Commentaries on Acts *in loc.*, especially *BC*, III, pp. 129–132; IV, pp. 160–162; W. M. Ramsay, *Cities of St. Paul*, 1907, part iv. J.N.B.

IDDO. 1. The father of Ahinadab, one of Solomon's commissariat officers, 1 Ki. iv. 14 (*'iddō*', 'timely'). **2.** A Gershonite Levite, 1 Ch. vi. 21 (*'iddô*, 'timely'), who is called Adaiah in 1 Ch. vi. 41 (*cf.* some LXX MSS of 1 Ch. vi. 21). **3.** A tribal prince of the half-tribe of Manasseh in Gilead, 1 Ch. xxvii. 21 (*yiddô*, 'beloved'). **4.** A seer or prophet whose writings were one of the sources of the Chronicler, for the reigns of Solomon (2 Ch. ix. 29, *ye'dî* or *ye'dô*, 'timely'), Rehoboam (2 Ch. xii. 15, *'iddô*), and Abijah (2 Ch. xiii. 22, *'iddô*). **5.** The head of a levitical group at Casiphia (probably near Babylon), Ezr. viii. 17 (*'iddô*, ?'strength'). **6.** One of those guilty of a mixed marriage, Ezr. x. 43, RV (*yiddô* or *yadday*, 'beloved'). **7.** One of the priestly families which returned to Jerusalem with Zerubbabel, Ne. xii. 4, 16 (*'iddô*' or *'aḏāyā*', 'timely'). **8.** The grandfather ('father' in Ezra) of Zechariah the prophet, Zc. i. 1, 7; Ezr. v. 1, vi. 14 (*'iddô* or *'iddô*'). J.G.G.N.

IDOLATRY. The story of Old Testament religion could be told for the most part in terms of a tension between a spiritual conception of God and worship, the hallmark of the genuine faith of Israel, and various pressures, such as idolatry, which attempted to debase and materialize the national religious consciousness and practice. We do not find, in the Old Testament, an ascending from idolatry to the pure worship of God, but rather a people possessing a pure worship, and a spiritual theology, constantly fighting, through the medium of divinely raised spiritual leaders, religious seductions which, nevertheless, often claimed the mass of the people. Idolatry is a declension from the norm, not an earlier stage gradually and with difficulty superseded.

If we consider the broad sweep of evidence for patriarchal religion we find it to be a religion of the altar and of prayer, but not of idols. There are certain events, all associated with Jacob, which might appear to show patriarchal idolatry. For example, Rachel stole her father's teraphim (Gn. xxxi. 19). By itself, this, of course, need prove nothing more than that Jacob's wife had failed to free herself from her Mesopotamian religious environment (*cf.* Jos. xxiv. 15). However, a more likely explanation suggested by archaeology is that these objects were of legal as well as religious significance: the possessor of them held the right of succession to the family

Fig. 112. A small bronze figurine of the intercessory goddess Lama found in a wayside shrine at Ur (*c.* 2000 BC). The arms are missing. It is assumed that they were made of ivory or wood and were raised in the typical attitude of supplication. Cf. fig. 209. The statuette was fixed to a plinth by means of a copper pin, part of which remains in the socket in the foot.

property. See TERAPHIM. This accords well with the anxiety of Laban, who does not appear otherwise as a religious man, to recover them, and his care, when he fails to find them, to exclude Jacob from Mesopotamia by a carefully-worded treaty (Gn. xxxi. 45 ff.). Again, it is urged that Jacob's pillars (Gn. xxviii. 18, xxxi. 13, 45, xxxv. 14, 20) are the same as the idolatrous stones with which Canaan was familiar. The interpretation is not inescapable. The pillar at Bethel is associated with Jacob's vow (see Gn. xxxi. 13), and could more easily belong to the category of memorial pillars (*e.g.* Gn. xxxv. 20; Jos. xxiv. 27; 1 Sa. vii. 12; 2 Sa. xviii. 18). Finally, the evidence of Gn. xxxv. 4, often used to show patriarchal idolatry, actually points to the recognized incompatibility of idols with the God of Bethel. Jacob must dispose of the unacceptable objects before he stands before this God. That Jacob 'hid' them is surely not to be construed as indicating that he feared to destroy them for reasons of superstitious reverence. They were metal objects, and possibly best disposed of in this way.

The weight of evidence for the Mosaic period is the same. The whole narrative of the golden calf (Ex. xxxii) reveals the extent of the contrast between the religion which stemmed from Mt. Sinai and the form of religion congenial to the unregenerate heart. These religions, we learn, are incompatible. The religion of Sinai is emphatically aniconic. Moses warned the people (Dt. iv. 12) that the revelation of God vouchsafed to them there contained no 'form', lest they corrupt themselves with images. This is the essential Mosaic position, as recorded in the Decalogue (Ex. xx. 4) and the so-called ritual Decalogue (Ex. xxxiv. 17), both of which are widely recognized as Mosaic by those who would dispute the Mosaic date of Deuteronomy. The second commandment was unique in the world of its day, and the failure of archaeology to unearth a figure of Yahweh (while idols abounded in every other religion) shows its fundamental place in Israel's religion from Mosaic days.

The historical record of Judges, Samuel, and Kings tells the same story of the lapse of the nation from the spiritual forms proper to their religion. The book of Judges, at least from chapter xvii onwards, deliberately sets out to picture for us a time of general lawlessness (*cf.* xvii. 6, xviii. 1, xix. 1, xxi. 25). We would not dream of seeing in the events of chapter xix the norm of Israelite morality. It is candidly a story of a degraded society. We have as little reason for seeing the story of Micah (Jdg. xvii–xviii) as displaying a lawful but primitive stage in Israel's religion. Significantly, the historian comments on the lawlessness of the days as he records Micah's idolatrous worship (xvii. 5, 6) and his superstitious 'consecration' of the Levite (xvii. 13 = xviii. 1).

We are not told in what form the images of Micah were made. It has been suggested that since they subsequently found a home in the northern Danite sanctuary, they were in the calf or bull form. This is likely enough, for it is a most significant thing that when Israel turned to idolatry it was always necessary to borrow the outward trappings from the pagan environment, thus suggesting that there was something in the very nature of Yahwism which prevented the growth of indigenous idolatrous forms. The golden calves made by Jeroboam (1 Ki. xii. 28) were well-known Canaanite symbols, and in the same way, whenever the kings of Israel and Judah lapsed into idolatry, it was by means of borrowing and syncretism. H. H. Rowley (*Faith of Israel*, pp. 77 f.) urges that such evidences of idolatry as exist after Moses are to be explained either by the impulse to syncretism or by the tendency for customs eradicated in one generation to reappear in the next (*cf.* Je. xliv). We might add to these the tendency to corrupt the use of something which in itself was lawful: the superstitious use of the ephod (Jdg. viii. 27) and the cult of the serpent (2 Ki. xviii. 4).

The main forms of idolatry into which Israel fell were the use of graven and molten images (see IMAGE), pillars, the asherah (AV 'groves', *q.v.*), and teraphim (*q.v.*). The *massēkâ*, or molten image, was made by casting metal in a mould and shaping it with a tool (Ex. xxxii. 4, 24). There is some doubt if this figure, and the later calves made by Jeroboam, were intended to represent Yahweh, or were thought of as a pedestal over which He was enthroned. The analogy of the cherubim (*cf.* 2 Sa. vi. 2, RV) suggests the latter, which also receives the support of archaeology (*cf.* G. E. Wright, *Biblical Archaeology*, p. 148, for an illustration of the god Hadad riding upon a bull). However, while the cherubim were concealed within the Temple, it is likely that the calves were fully visible and were popularly identified with Yahweh.

The pillars and the asherah were both forbidden to Israel (*cf.* Dt. xii. 3, xvi. 21, 22). In Baal sanctuaries the pillar of Baal (*cf.* 2 Ki. x. 27) and the pole of the Asherah stood beside the altar. The pillar was thought of as a stylized representation of the presence of the god at the shrine. It was the object of great veneration: sometimes it was hollowed in part so as to receive the blood of sacrifice, and sometimes, as appears from its polished surface, it was kissed by its devotees. The asherah was wooden, as we learn from its usual destruction by burning (Dt. xii. 3; 2 Ki. xxiii. 6), and probably originated from the sacred evergreen, the symbol of life. The association of these with Canaanite fertility practice sufficed to make them abominable to Yahweh.

The Old Testament polemic against idolatry, carried on chiefly by prophets and psalmists, recognizes the same two truths which Paul was later to affirm: that the idol was nothing, but that nevertheless there was a demonic spiritual force to be reckoned with, and that the idol therefore constituted a positive spiritual menace (1 Cor. viii. 4, x. 19, 20). Thus, the idol is nothing at all: man made it (Is. ii. 8); its very composition and construction proclaims its futility (Is. xl. 18–20, xli. 6, 7, xliv. 9–20); its helpless bulk invites derision (Is. xlvi. 1, 2); it has nothing but the bare appearance of life (Ps. cxv. 4–7). The prophets derisively named them *gillûlîm* (Ezk. vi. 4, and at least thirty-eight other times in Ezekiel. Koehler's *Lexicon* gives the meaning as 'originally "dung pellets"'), and *'ĕlîlîm*, 'godlets'.

But, though entirely subject to Yahweh (*e.g.* Ps. xcv. 3), there are spiritual forces of evil, and the practice of idolatry brings men into deadly contact with these 'gods'. Isaiah, who is usually said to bring the ironic scorning of idols to its peak, is well aware of this spiritual evil. He knows that there is only one God (xliv. 8), but even so no-one can touch an idol, though it be 'nothing', and come away unscathed. Man's contact with the false god infects him with a deadly spiritual blindness of heart and mind (xliv. 18). Though what he worships is mere 'ashes', yet it is full of the poison of spiritual delusion (xliv. 20). Those who worship idols become like them (Ps. cxv. 8; Je. ii. 5; Ho. ix. 10). Because of the reality of evil power behind the idol, it is an abomination (*tô'ēḇâ*) to Yahweh (Dt. vii. 25), a detested thing (*šiqqûṣ*) (Dt. xxix. 17), and it is the gravest sin, spiritual adultery, to follow idols (Dt. xxxi. 16; Jdg. ii. 17; Ho. i. 2). Nevertheless,

Fig. 113. Yehawmilk, king of Byblos, offers a bowl to his goddess Baalath, 'the lady of Byblos'. Stele in the Louvre, c. 450 BC.

there is only one God, and the contrast between Yahweh and idols is to be drawn in terms of life, activity, and government. The idol cannot predict and bring to pass, but Yahweh can (Is. xli. 26, 27, xliv. 7); the idol is a helpless piece of flotsam on the river of history, only wise after the event and helpless in the face of it (Is. xli. 5–7, xlvi. 1, 2), but Yahweh is Lord and controller of history (Is. xl. 22–25, xli. 1, 2, 25, xliii. 14, 15, *etc.*).

The New Testament reinforces and amplifies the Old Testament teaching. Its recognition that idols are both nonentities and dangerous spiritual potencies has been noted above. In addition, Rom. i expresses the Old Testament view that idolatry is a decline from true spirituality, and not a stage on the way to a pure knowledge of God. The New Testament recognizes, however, that the peril of idolatry exists even where material idols are not fashioned: the association of idolatry with sexual sins in Gal. v. 19, 20 ought to be linked with the equating of covetousness with idolatry (1 Cor. v. 11; Eph. v. 5; Col. iii. 5), for by covetousness Paul certainly means sexual covetousness (*cf.* Eph. iv. 19, v. 3; 1 Thes. iv. 6, Gk.; 1 Cor. x. 7, 14). John, having urged the finality and fulness of revelation in Christ, warns that any deviation is idolatry (1 Jn. v. 19–21). The idol is whatever claims that loyalty which belongs to God alone (Is. xlii. 8).

BIBLIOGRAPHY. H. H. Rowley, *Faith of Israel*, 1956, pp. 74 ff.; A. Lods, 'Images and Idols, Hebrew and Canaanite', *ERE*; 'Idol' in J-J. von Allmen, *Vocabulary of the Bible*, 1958; J. Pedersen, *Israel III–IV*, 1926, pp. 220 ff., *passim*; G. E. Wright, *Biblical Archaeology*, 1957, pp. 44,

115 ff., 147 ff.; Y. Kaufmann, *The Religion of Israel*, 1961, *passim*. J.A.M.

IDOLS, MEATS OFFERED TO. Among the questions submitted by the Corinthians for the apostle's ruling was the matter of 'food offered to idols', a phrase which represents one Gk. term, *eidōlothyta*. Paul handles this subject in 1 Cor. viii. 1–13 and x. 14–33. The background of the Corinthians' query may first be sketched.

I. THE BACKGROUND

In the ancient system of sacrifice, which was the centre not only of the religious life of the Graeco-Roman world in the 1st century but also of the domestic and social life, only part of the sacrifice was presented to the god in the temple. The sacrifice was followed by a cultic meal, when the remainder of the consecrated food was eaten either in the precincts of the temple or at home. Sometimes the remaining food was sent to the market to be sold (1 Cor. x. 25).

Evidence for the practice of a meal in the temple is found in the following well-known Oxyrhynchus papyrus which Lietzmann regards as 'a striking parallel' to the reference in 1 Cor. x. 27: 'Chaeremon invites you to dinner at the table of the lord Serapis (the name of the deity) in the Serapeum tomorrow the 15th at 9 o'clock' (quoted in Deissmann, *Light from the Ancient East*[4], 1927, p. 351). Such an invitation to a meal of this character, whether in the temple or in a private house, would be commonplace in the social life of the city of Corinth, and would pose a thorny question for the believer who was so invited. Other aspects of life in such a cosmopolitan centre would be affected by the Christian's attitude to idol-meats. Attendance at the public festivals, which opened with pagan adoration and sacrifice, would have to be considered. Membership of a trade guild, and therefore one's commercial standing, and public-spiritedness were also involved, as such membership would entail 'sitting at meat in an idol's temple' (1 Cor. viii. 10). Even daily shopping in the market would present a problem to the thoughtful Christian in Corinth. As much of the meat would be passed on from the temple-officials to the meat-dealers and by them exposed for sale, the question arose, was the Christian housewife at liberty to purchase this meat which, coming from sacrificial animals which had to be free from blemish, might well be the best meat in the market? Moreover, there were gratuitous banquets in the temple precincts which were a real boon to the poor. If 1 Cor. i. 26 means that some of the Corinthian church members belonged to the poorer classes, the question of whether they were free or not to avail themselves of such meals would have been a practical issue.

II. DIFFERENT REACTIONS

Conviction in the church was sharply divided. One group, in the name of Christian liberty (vi. 12, x. 23, *cf.* viii. 9) and on the basis of a supposed superior knowledge (*gnōsis*, viii. 1, 2), could see no harm in accepting an invitation to a cultic meal and no possible reason why food, formerly dedicated in the temple, should not be bought and eaten. The justification for this attitude of religious syncretism was, first, that the meal in the temple precincts was just a social occasion. They claimed that it had no religious significance at all. And, secondly, they appear to have stated that in any case the pagan gods are nonentities. 'No idol is *anything* in the world, and there is no God but one' was their plea of defence (viii. 4; cited probably from the Corinthians' own letter to Paul).

On the other hand, the 'weak' group (viii. 9; *cf.* Rom. xv. 1) viewed the situation differently. With abhorrence of the least suspicion of idolatry, they believed that the demons behind the idols still exerted malign influence on the food and 'contaminated' it, thus rendering it unfit for consumption by believers (viii. 7; *cf.* Acts x. 14).

III. PAUL'S ANSWER

Paul begins his answer to the Church's inquiry by expressing agreement with the proposition, 'There is no God but one' (viii. 4). But he immediately qualifies this explicit confession of his monotheism by reminding his readers that there are so-called gods and lords which exert demonic influence in the world. He concedes the point, however, that 'for us' who acknowledge one God and one Lord, the power of these demons has been overcome by the cross, so that the Corinthians ought no longer to be in bondage to them (*cf.* Col. ii. 15, 16; Gal. iv. 3, 8, 9). Not all the Corinthian believers have found that freedom in Christ, and their case must be remembered and their weak conscience not outraged by indiscreet action (viii. 7–13). The apostle has a more serious word to say on this matter, which he takes up after a digression in chapter ix.

He comes to grips with the menace of idolatry in x. 14 ff. These verses are an exposition of the inner meaning of the Lord's Table in the light of communion in the body and blood of Christ (x. 16); the unity of the Church as the body of Christ (x. 17, RVmg); the spell cast by demons over their worshippers at idol-feasts which led actually to a compact with the demons (x. 20); and the impossibility of a double allegiance represented by trying to share both the table of the Lord and the table of demons (x. 21, 22). See LORD'S SUPPER.

The apostle in this section, therefore, takes a serious attitude to the implications of attendance at idolatrous banquets (*cf.* x. 14). In line with rabbinical teaching which was later codified in the Mishnah tractate *'Abodah Zarah* ('Strange Worship'), he forbids absolutely the use of food and drink in an idol-temple (x. 19, 20; *cf.* Rev. ii. 14) on the ground no doubt that, as the Rabbis said, 'as a dead body defiles by overshadowing, so also an idolatrous sacrifice causes defilement by overshadowing', *i.e.* by having been brought under a pagan roof, and by this contact becomes ritually unclean. See the Mishnah in Danby's edition, p. 649, n. 3.

But, in regard to food which has formerly been offered in the temple and is afterwards made available for consumption, Paul says that it is permitted on the basis of Ps. xxiv. 1 (1 Cor. x. 25 ff.). Although such food has been dedicated in the temple and is exposed for sale in the meat-market, it may be eaten by virtue of being God's creation (1 Tim. iv. 4, 5). This is a distinct departure from the rabbinical ceremonial rules (and, indeed, from the apostolic decree of Acts xv. 28, 29), and is the practical application of the Lord's word in Mark vii. 19, RV, '*This he said*, making all meats clean' (*cf.* Acts x. 15). The only qualification is that the 'duty of love' (*Liebespflicht*, in Büchsel's word, *TWNT*, II, p. 376) must be observed, and a Christian's own freedom to eat such food must be waived if the conscience of the 'weaker' believer is likely to be damaged and he is thereby caused to stumble (x. 28–32), or if a Gentile is scandalized by this practice (x. 32). The situation envisaged by these verses is a Christian's acceptance of an invitation to a meal in a private house (x. 27). In such a circumstance the believer is free to eat the food set before him, making no inquiries as to its 'past history', *i.e.* where it comes from or whether it has been dedicated in an idol shrine. If, however, a pagan, at the meal, draws attention to the food and says, 'This has been offered in sacrifice'—using the pagan term *hierothyton*—then the food must be refused, not because it is 'infected' or unfit for consumption, but because it 'places the eater in a false position, and confuses the conscience of others' (Robertson–Plummer, *I Corinthians*, p. 219), notably his heathen neighbour (x. 29). This reading differs from the suggestion of Robertson–Plummer in the *ICC*, where they take the speaker in verse 28 to be a Gentile Christian using the terminology of his pre-Christian days; it is better, however, to regard this speaker as 'one of them that believe not' in verse 27; and then the apostle's word links up with the altruism of the Rabbis, who taught that a devout Jew will not countenance idolatry lest he should encourage his Gentile neighbour in his error, for which he would then be responsible (*Aboth* v. 18; *Sanhedrin* vii. 4, 10).

R.P.M.

IDUMAEA, the Gk. form (*idoumaia*) of the Heb. *'ᵉḏôm*, refers to an area in W Palestine, rather than to Edom proper. At the time of the Exodus, Edom extended to both sides of the Arabah, and the western portion reached close to Kadesh (Nu. xx. 16). David subdued Edom, but there was continual conflict between Edom and Judah. (See EDOM.) After the fall of Jerusalem in 587 BC the Edomites took advantage of the calamity to migrate into the heart of S Judah, south of Hebron. Several prophets inveighed against Edom for this (Je. xlix. 7–22; La. iv. 21, 22; Ezk. xxv. 12–14, xxxv. 3; Ob. 10 ff.).

Later, as various Arab groups, notably the Nabataeans, pressed into old Edom, more migrants settled in Judah, and the area they occupied became known as Idumaea (1 Macc. iv. 29, v. 65). Judas Maccabaeus had successful campaigns against these people, and John Hyrcanus subdued them *c.* 126 BC, placed them under Antipater as governor, and compelled them to be circumcised (Jos., *Ant.* xiii. 9. 1). Antipater was the grandfather of Herod the Great (*q.v.*). The word Idumaea occurs in the New Testament only in Mk. iii. 8.

J.A.T.

IGNORANCE. As is the case with knowledge (*q.v.*), ignorance has in Scripture a moral rather than a purely intellectual connotation, except in such casual uses as the Pauline 'I would not have you ignorant, brethren . . .' (Rom. i. 13), which simply means 'I want you to know . . .'

In the books of the Law ignorance is regarded as a palliating feature of sinful acts. For sins done in ignorance (*šᵉgāgâ*) expiation could be made by sacrifice (*cf.* particularly Lv. iv, v; Nu. xv. 22–29). This idea of ignorance as an excuse is reflected in the New Testament uses of the verb *agnoeō*, 'to be ignorant', and its derivatives. Paul declares that he received mercy for his persecution of the Church because he acted ignorantly in unbelief (1 Tim. i. 13); and at Athens he tells his Gentile audience that God overlooked the times of ignorance (Acts xvii. 30, *cf.* iii. 17). Yet although ignorance partly excuses the sins which result from it, ignorance itself is often culpable. It may be linked with hardness of heart (Eph. iv. 18; *cf.* 2 Cor. iv. 4) or even be deliberate (2 Pet. iii. 5; *cf.* Rom. i. 18 ff., x. 3).

Ignorance is used absolutely to refer to the condition of the Gentile world which had not received the revelation of God (Acts xvii. 23, 30; Eph. iv. 18; 1 Pet. i. 14, ii. 15). This usage is found in LXX; *e.g.* Wisdom xiv. 22.

The word *idiōtēs*, translated 'ignorant' in AV of Acts iv. 13, implies the want of special training rather than of knowledge in general; *cf.* the modern somewhat derogatory use of 'layman'.

BIBLIOGRAPHY. R. Bultmann, *Gnosis*, 1952.

M.H.C.

IJON. A town in the hill-country of N Naphtali, taken with Dan and Abel-beth-maachah in Ben-hadad's invasion (1 Ki. xv. 20 = 2 Ch. xvi. 4), and later captured by Tiglath-pileser (2 Ki. xv. 29). Perhaps identical with Tell Dibbîn, near Merjayûn ('the meadow of springs'), which still retains its ancient name.

J.D.D.

ILLYRICUM. The name of the large mountainous region on the east of the Adriatic, extending to the central Balkans in the east and reaching from NE Italy and the Celtic tribes in the north to Macedonia in the south. Its name was derived from that of one of the first tribes within its boundaries that the Greeks came across. Its inhabitants spoke dialects which were probably the linguistic ancestors of modern Albanian. The

Romans had first come into conflict with some of its tribes in the 3rd century BC, but it was not finally conquered till the 1st century AD, when it was divided into the provinces of Pannonia and Dalmatia. The apostle Paul says at the time of writing the Epistle to the Romans (xv. 19) that it was the limit of his evangelistic activity. His reference to it appears to be inclusive, but it is not known when, or from what direction, he had entered it (possibly from Macedonia when he revisited that province after his Ephesian ministry, Acts xx. 1). B.F.C.A.

IMAGE. This word is used throughout the Bible in a literal sense to denote a material representation in animal, human, or mixed form, used for cultic purposes, and in a theological or metaphorical sense to denote a relationship between man and God. Museums are stocked with examples of cult objects which show some aspect of a deity's nature, *e.g.* oxen (power), winged creatures (presence). Israel would not admit any such limitation in the power of God, and viewed with horror the sexual excesses which often accompanied the cultic use of images. See IDOLATRY. Several words are translated 'image', and each has its own particular shade of meaning.

I. IN THE OLD TESTAMENT

a. Material representations

1. *Pesel* was used of the graven image carved out of wood or stone, sometimes with great power and beauty as in the massive Assyrian and Egyptian statuary, but sometimes with obscene crudity. The practice was expressly forbidden to the Israelites by the commands of Ex. xx. 4; Lv. xxvi. 1; Dt. v. 8. Graven images were the subject of Isaiah's bitter mockery, xl. 20 and xliv. 15, and of prophetic condemnation, Je. viii. 19; Ho. xi. 2; Mi. v. 13.

2. *Massēḵâ* indicated the molten image, cast in a mould from copper, silver, or gold. This is the term used of the golden calves made by Aaron (Ex. xxxii. 4) and Jeroboam (1 Ki. xiv. 9). All such objects were forbidden by the Torah (Ex. xxxiv. 17; Lv. xix. 4) and condemned by the Psalmist (Ps. cvi. 19) and the prophets (Is. xxx. 22; Ho. xiii. 2; Hab. ii. 18).

3. *Ḥammānîm* was formerly rendered 'sun images' (Lv. xxvi. 30; Is. xvii. 8; Ezk. vi. 4), but the word actually denotes incense-altars. The *tᵉrāpîm* were household gods (Gn. xxxi. 19; 1 Sa. xix. 13; Ezk. xxi. 21). These were used in personal devotions, and may be connected with divination (*q.v.*).

4. *Ṣelem.* As a general term this word is used in Dn. ii of the great metal figure of which Nebuchadrezzar dreamed, and in Dn. iii of the golden idol which he set up; it is also used of human portrayals (Ps. lxxiii. 20; Ezk. xvi. 17).

b. Theological use

The Genesis account of the creation uses this word in a theological sense. 'God created man in his own image' (Gn. i. 27, ix. 6). In these few words the writer defines both the nature of man and the relation between man and God; on the one hand, there is the fundamental distinction between man and the animals, but on the other hand it is demonstrated that man has not the same status as God, but is dependent on him, and exists only because of the will of God. Because of the sin of Adam this image is blurred, and is therefore not clearly seen in his sons (Gn. v. 3).

II. IN THE NEW TESTAMENT

The word used throughout the New Testament is *eikōn*, which means 'a derived likeness, and implies an archetype' (Abbott-Smith, *Lexicon*, p. 131).

It is used in Rev. xiii. 14, *etc.*, of an idol worshipped by the wicked and depraved. In Mt. xxii. 20 it is used by Jesus of Caesar's portrait stamped on a coin. Elsewhere it is used theologically, of the revelation granted through Jesus Christ, the image of the invisible God (2 Cor. iv. 4; Col. i. 15); of renovation into the image of Christ (Rom. viii. 29) through regeneration (Eph. iv. 24) and lifelong transformation (2 Cor. iii. 18; Col. iii. 10); and of glorification through the resurrection, which crowns this renewing process (1 Cor. xv. 49; *cf.* Phil. iii. 21).

BIBLIOGRAPHY. G. von Rad, G. Kittel, H. Kleinknecht in *TWNT*, *s.v. eikōn*; see also bibliography under IDOLATRY. A.A.J.

IMMANUEL (Heb. *'immānû'ēl*, 'with us is God'). The word is found three times in the Bible, twice in the Old Testament (Is. vii. 14, viii. 8) and once in the New Testament (Mt. i. 23). It may be employed also in Is. viii. 10.

To understand the significance of the word, which in itself means 'God with us', we must note the context in which it appears. Syria and Israel had desired to form a coalition with Judah in order to oppose the increasing power of Assyria. Judah had vacillated, and Syria and Israel determined to punish her. Upon hearing this news, Ahaz trembled. Isaiah was sent to him to inform him that he had nothing to fear. The power of his enemies was about played out, and they could do him no harm. Isaiah even commanded him to ask for a sign in confirmation of the divine message. This Ahaz refused to do. Hence, in reply to the hypocritical king, Isaiah announces that the Lord will give to the people of Judah a sign. In vision the prophet beholds a virgin (*'almâ, i.e.* an unmarried woman), who is with child and about to bear a son and she will call his name Immanuel.

In any interpretation of this prophecy there are three factors which must be kept in mind.

a. The birth of the child is to be a sign. It is true that in itself a sign need not be a miracle, but in this particular context, after the command issued to Ahaz to ask for a sign deep or high one would be justified in expecting a sign such as the recession of the shadow on the sundial. There should be something unusual in the birth; a birth in the ordinary course of nature would not seem to meet the requirements of the sign. In this connection it must be noted that the question is made more difficult by the fact that there cannot be a local reference of the prophecy to Hezekiah, because Hezekiah had already been born.

b. The mother of the child is an unmarried woman. Why did Isaiah designate her by this particular word *'almâ*? It is sometimes said that had he wished to teach a virgin birth there was a good word at his disposal, namely, *b^e^ṯûlâ*. But an examination of the usage of the latter word in the Old Testament reveals that it was very unsatisfactory, in that it would have been ambiguous. The word *b^e^ṯûlâ* may designate a virgin, but when it does the explanatory phrase 'and a man had not known her' is often added (*cf.* Gn. xxiv. 16). The word may also designate a betrothed virgin (*cf.* Dt. xxii. 23 ff.). In this latter case the virgin is known as the wife (*'iššâ*) of the man, and he as her husband (*'îš*). But the word *b^e^ṯûlâ* may also indicate a married woman (Joel i. 8). On the basis of this latter passage a tradition arose among the Jews in which the word could clearly refer to a married woman. Had Isaiah employed this word, therefore, it would not have been clear what type of woman he had in mind, whether virgin or married. Other Heb. words which were at his disposal would not be satisfactory. Had he wished to designate the mother as a young woman he would most likely have employed the common term *na'^a^râ* ('girl'). In using the word *'almâ*, however, Isaiah employs the one word which is never applied (either in the Bible or in the other Near Eastern sources) to anyone but an unmarried woman. This unmarried woman might have been immoral, in which case the birth could hardly have been a sign. We are left then with the conclusion that the mother was a good woman and yet unmarried; in other words, the birth was supernatural. It is the presence of this word *'almâ* which makes an application of the passage to some local birth difficult, if not impossible.

c. We must note the force of the term Immanuel. A natural reading of the passage would lead us to expect that the presence of God is to be seen in the birth of the child himself. This interpretation, however, is seriously disputed, and vigorously rejected by most modern writers on the passage. The presence of God is found, rather, so we are told, in the deliverance of Judah from her two northern enemies. The infancy of the child is made the measure of time that would elapse until the two enemies are removed. Such a period of time would be short—a child learns the difference between good and evil at a tender age. Hence, within, say, two years, or possibly even less, Judah would have nothing to fear from Syria and Israel. In this deliverance the presence of God would be manifested, and as a token or pledge of this deliverance some mother would call her child Immanuel.

This interpretation poses tremendous problems which it does not answer. What warrant would a mother have for naming her particular child Immanuel? How could she know that her own child and no other would be a sign that in two years or so the presence of God would be manifested in the deliverance of Judah from Syria and Israel? Furthermore, how would Israel itself know that a particular child had been born in answer to the prophecy and that the birth of this particular child would be the promised sign? It would seem that, if the prophecy refers to a local birth, the child to be born must be someone prominent. The most prominent person, namely Hezekiah, is ruled out, and therefore we must assume that it is a child of Isaiah or some other child of Ahaz. But this is also ruled out by the word *'almâ*. Neither the wife of Ahaz nor the wife of Isaiah could properly be designated an *'almâ*, for the obvious reason that both were married women.

It seems best, then, to apply the name Immanuel to the Child Himself. In His birth the presence of God is to be found. God has come to His people in a little Child, that very Child whom Isaiah later names 'Mighty God' (*'ēl gibbôr*). This interpretation is strengthened by the fact that Isaiah is seeking to dissuade men from trusting the Assyrian king. The nation's help rests not in Assyria but in God. In this dark moment God is with His people. He is found in the birth of a Child.

The fifteenth and sixteenth verses then use the infancy of the divine Child as a measure of the time that will elapse until Ahaz is freed from the fear of his two northern enemies. Ahaz rejects the sign of Immanuel, and turns to the king of Assyria. That king and his successors caused Judah's downfall, but for the remnant there was given the promise of Immanuel, and in Immanuel they would find their hope and salvation.

BIBLIOGRAPHY. E. J. Young, *Studies in Isaiah*, 1954, pp. 143–198; E. W. Hengstenberg, *Christology of the Old Testament*, 1856, II, pp. 26–66; J. G. Machen, *The Virgin Birth of Christ*, 1930.

E.J.Y.

IMMORTALITY. See ESCHATOLOGY.

IMPRISONMENT. See PRISON.

INCARNATION.

I. MEANING OF THE WORD

Neither the noun 'incarnation' nor the adjective 'incarnate' is biblical, but the Greek equivalent of Lat. *in carne* (*en sarki*, 'in flesh') is found in some important New Testament statements about the person and work of Jesus Christ. Thus the hymn quoted in 1 Tim. iii. 16 speaks of 'he who was manifested in the flesh' (so RV, following the true text; 'God' in AV represents a false reading). John ascribes to the spirit of antichrist any denial that Jesus Christ is 'come in the flesh' (1 Jn. iv. 2; 2 Jn. 7). Paul says that Christ did His reconciling work 'in the body of his flesh' (Col. i. 22, *cf.* Eph. ii. 15), and that by sending His Son 'in the likeness of sinful flesh' God 'condemned sin in the flesh' (Rom. viii. 3). Peter speaks of

Christ dying for us 'in the flesh' (*sarki*, dative of reference: 1 Pet. iii. 18, iv. 1). All these texts are enforcing from different angles the same truth: that it was precisely by coming and dying 'in the flesh' that Christ secured our salvation. Theology calls His coming the incarnation, and His dying the atonement.

What does 'flesh' mean in these texts? In the Bible this word (Heb. *bāśār*, *še'ēr*; Gk. *sarx*) has fundamentally a physiological meaning: 'flesh' is the solid stuff which, together with blood and bones, makes up the physical organism of a man or animal (*cf.* Gn. ii. 21; Lk. xxiv. 39; 1 Cor. xv. 50). Since Hebrew thought associates bodily organs with psychical functions, we find that in the Old Testament 'flesh' can cover the psychological as well as the physical aspects of man's personal life (*cf.* the parallelism between 'flesh' and 'heart', Ps. lxxiii. 26, and between 'flesh' and 'soul', Ps. lxiii. 1). The word, however, bears more than a merely anthropological significance. The Bible sees physical flesh as a theologically significant symbol—a symbol, namely, of the created and dependent sort of life which men and animals share, a sort of life which is derived from God and which, unlike God's own life, requires a physical organism to sustain it in its characteristic activity. Hence 'flesh' becomes a generic term for men, or animals, or men and animals together (*cf.* Gn. vi. 12, vii. 15, 21 f.), viewed as creatures of God, whose life on earth lasts only for the comparatively short period during which God supplies the breath of life in their nostrils. 'Flesh' in this theologically developed sense is thus not something that a man *has*, but something that he *is*. Its mark is creaturely weakness and frailty (Is. xl. 6), and in this respect it stands in contrast with 'spirit', the eternal and unflagging energy that is of God, and is God (Is. xxxi. 3, *cf.* xl. 6–31). (See FLESH.)

To say, therefore, that Jesus Christ came and died 'in the flesh' is to say that He came and died in the state and under the conditions of created physical and psychical life: in other words, that He who died was man. But the New Testament also affirms that He who died eternally was, and continues to be, God. The formula which enshrines the incarnation therefore is that in some sense God, without ceasing to be God, was made man. This is what John asserts in the prologue of his Gospel: 'the Word' (God's agent in creation, who 'in the beginning', before the creation, not only 'was with God', but Himself 'was God', Jn. i. 1–3) 'became flesh' (Jn. i. 14, RV).

II. ORIGIN OF THE BELIEF

Such an assertion, considered abstractly against the background of Old Testament monotheism, might seem blasphemous or nonsensical—as, indeed, orthodox Judaism has always held it to be. It appears to mean that the divine Maker became one of His own creatures, which is a *prima facie* contradiction in theological terms. Whence came the conviction that inspired John's strange statement? How did the early Church's belief that Jesus of Nazareth was God incarnate arise? On the assumption that it was not occasioned by what Jesus Himself said and did, but grew up later, attempts have been made to trace its origin to Jewish speculations about a pre-existent superhuman Messiah, or to the polytheistic myths about redeemer-gods which were characteristic of Hellenistic mystery-religions and Gnostic cults. But it is now generally recognized that these attempts have failed: partly because the differences between these Jewish and Gentile fancies and New Testament Christology have invariably proved to be more substantial and deep-rooted than their surface similarities are; partly because it has been shown that a virtual claim to deity is embedded in the most undoubted sayings of the historical Jesus, as reported in the Synoptic Gospels, and that a virtual acceptance of this claim was fundamental to the faith and worship of the primitive Palestinian Church, as pictured in the first chapters of Acts (the substantial historicity of which is now rarely disputed). The only explanation that covers the facts is that the impact of Jesus' own life, ministry, death, and resurrection convinced His disciples of His personal deity even before He ascended. This, of course, is precisely the account of the matter which the Fourth Gospel itself gives (see especially Jn. xx. 28 ff.). In line with this, Acts tells us that the first Christians prayed to Jesus as Lord (vii. 59), even before Pentecost (i. 21: the 'Lord' who chooses apostles is surely 'the Lord Jesus' of verse 21, *cf.* verse 3); that, beginning on the day of Pentecost, they baptized in His name (ii. 38, viii. 16, xix. 5); that they invoked and put faith in His name (*i.e.* in Himself: iii. 16, ix. 14, xxii. 16, *cf.* xvi. 31); and that they proclaimed Him as the One who gives repentance and remission of sins (v. 31). All this shows that, even if the deity of Jesus was not at first clearly stated in words (and Acts gives no hint that it was), it was nevertheless part of the faith by which the first Christians lived and prayed. *Lex orandi lex credendi.* The theological formulation of belief in the incarnation came later, but the belief itself, however incoherently expressed, was there in the Church from the beginning.

III. STANDPOINT OF THE NEW TESTAMENT WRITERS

It is important to note the nature and limits of the interest which motivates New Testament thinking about the incarnation, particularly that of Paul, John, and the author of Hebrews, who deal with the subject comparatively fully. The New Testament writers nowhere notice, much less handle, the metaphysical questions about the mode of the incarnation, and the psychological questions about the incarnate state, which have been so prominent in Christological discussion since the 4th century. Their interest in Christ's person is not philosophical and speculative, but religious and evangelical. They speak of Christ, not as a metaphysical problem, but as a divine Saviour; and all that they say about His person is prompted by their desire to glorify Him through exhibiting His work and vindicating His centrality in the redemptive purpose of God. They never attempt to dissect the mystery of His person; it is enough for them to proclaim the incarnation as a fact, one of the sequence of mighty works whereby God has wrought salvation for sinners. The only sense in which the New Testament writers ever attempt to explain the incarnation is by showing how it fits into God's over-all plan for redeeming mankind (see, *e.g.*, Rom. viii. 3; Phil. ii. 6–11; Col. i. 13–22; Jn. i. 18; 1 Jn. i. 1–ii. 2; and the main argument of Hebrews, i–ii, iv. 14–v. 10, vii. 1–x. 18).

The exclusiveness of this evangelical interest throws light on the otherwise puzzling fact that the New Testament nowhere reflects on the virgin birth of Jesus as witnessing to the conjunction of deity and manhood in His person—a line of thought much canvassed by later theology. This silence need not mean that any of the New Testament writers were ignorant of the virgin birth, as some have supposed. It is sufficiently explained by the fact that New Testament interest in Jesus centres elsewhere, upon His relation to the saving purposes of God. Proof of this is given by the way in which the virgin birth story is itself told by Matthew and Luke, the two Evangelists who recount it. Each lays all his stress, not on the unique constitution of the Person thus miraculously born, but on the fact that by this miraculous birth God began to fulfil His long-foretold intention of visiting and redeeming His people (*cf.* Mt. i. 21 ff.; Lk. i. 31 ff., 68–75, ii. 10 f., 29–32). The only significance which they, or any New Testament writers, see in the incarnation is directly soteriological. The Scotist speculation, popularized by Westcott, that the incarnation was primarily for the perfecting of creation, and only secondarily and incidentally for the redeeming of sinners, finds not the least support in the New Testament.

The apostolic writers clearly see that both the deity and the manhood of Jesus are fundamental to His saving work. They see that it is just because Jesus is God the Son that they are to regard His disclosure of the Father's mind and heart as perfect and final (*cf.* Jn. i. 18, xiv. 7–10; Heb. i. 1 f.), and His death as the supreme evidence of God's love for sinners and His will to bless believers (*cf.* Jn. iii. 16; Rom. v. 5–10, viii. 32; 1 Jn. iv. 8–10). They realize that it is Jesus' divine Sonship that guarantees the endless duration, sinless perfection, and limitless efficacy, of His High-Priestly service (Heb. vii. 3, 16, 24–28). They are aware that it was in virtue of His deity that He was able to defeat and dispossess the devil, the 'strong man armed' who kept sinners in a state of helpless thraldom (Heb. ii. 14 f.; Rev. xx. 1 f.; *cf.* Mk. iii. 27; Lk. x. 17 f.; Jn. xii. 31 f., xvi. 11). Equally, they see that it was necessary for the Son of God to 'become flesh', for only so could He take His place as the 'second man' through whom God deals with the race (1 Cor. xv. 21 f., 47 ff.; Rom. v. 15–19); only so could He mediate between God and men (1 Tim. ii. 5); and only so could He die for sins, for only flesh can die. (Indeed, the thought of 'flesh' is so bound up with death that the New Testament will not apply the term to Christ's manhood in its glorified and incorruptible state: 'the days of his flesh' (Heb. v. 7) means Christ's time on earth up to the cross.)

We should, therefore, expect the New Testament to treat any denial that Jesus Christ was both truly divine and truly human as a damning heresy, destructive of the gospel; and so it does. The only such denial that it knows is the docetic Christology (traditionally, that of Cerinthus) which denied the reality of Christ's 'flesh' (1 Jn. iv. 2 f.), and hence of His physical death ('blood', 1 Jn. v. 6). John denounces this in his first two Epistles as a deadly error inspired by the spirit of antichrist, a lying denial of both the Father and the Son (1 Jn. ii. 22–25, iv. 1–6, v. 5–12; 2 Jn. 7, 9 ff.). It is usually thought that the emphasis in John's Gospel on the reality of Jesus' experience of human frailty (His weariness, iv. 6; thirst, iv. 7, xix. 28; tears, xi. 33 ff.) is intended to cut at the root of the same docetic error.

IV. ELEMENTS OF THE NEW TESTAMENT DOCTRINE

The meaning of the New Testament claim that 'Jesus Christ is come in the flesh' may be drawn out under three heads.

a. The Person incarnate

The New Testament uniformly defines the identity of Jesus in terms of His relation to the one God of Old Testament monotheism (*cf.* 1 Cor. viii. 4, 6; 1 Tim. ii. 5; with Is. xliii. 10 f., xliv. 6). The basic definition is that Jesus is God's *Son.* This identification is rooted in Jesus' own thought and teaching. His sense of being 'the Son' in a unique sense that set Him apart from the rest of men went back at least to His thirteenth year (Lk. ii. 49), and was confirmed to Him by His Father's voice from heaven at His baptism: 'Thou art my beloved Son' (Mk. i. 11; *cf.* Mt. iii. 17; Lk. iii. 22; *agapētos*, which appears in all three reports of the heavenly utterance, carries the implication of '*only* beloved': so again in the parable, Mk. xii. 6; *cf.* the similar words from heaven at the transfiguration, Mk. ix. 7; Mt. xvii. 5). At His trial, when asked under oath whether He was 'the Son of God' (a phrase which on the high priest's lips probably signified no more than 'Davidic Messiah'), Mark and Luke report Jesus as making an affirmative reply which was in effect a claim to personal deity: *egō eimi* (so Mk. xiv. 62; Lk. xxii. 70 has: 'ye say [*sc.* rightly] that *egō eimi*'). *Egō eimi*, the emphatic 'I am', were words that no Jew would take on his lips, for they expressed the self-identification of God (Ex. iii. 14). Jesus, who according to Mark had used these words before in a similar suggestive way (Mk. vi. 50, *cf.* xiii. 6; and *cf.* the long series of *egō eimi* sayings in John's Gospel: Jn. iv. 26, vi. 35, viii. 12, x. 7, 11,

xi. 25, xiv. 6, xv. 1, xviii. 5 ff.), evidently wished to make it perfectly clear that the divine Sonship to which He laid claim was nothing less than personal deity. It was for this 'blasphemy' that He was condemned.

Jesus' references to Himself as 'the Son' are always in contexts which mark Him out as uniquely close to God and uniquely favoured by God. There are comparatively few in the Synoptic Gospels (Mt. xi. 27 = Lk. x. 22; Mk. xiii. 32 = Mt. xxiv. 36; *cf.* Mk. xii. 1–11), but many in John, both in Jesus' own words and in the Evangelist's commentary. According to John, Jesus is God's 'only' Son (*monogenēs*: i. 14, 18, iii. 16, 18). He exists eternally (viii. 58, *cf.* i. 1 f.). He stands in an unchanging relation of perfect love, union, and communion, with the Father (i. 18, viii. 16, 29, x. 30, xvi. 32). As Son, He has no independent initiative (v. 19); He lives to glorify His Father (xvii. 1, 4), by doing His Father's will (iv. 34, v. 30, viii. 28 f.). He came into the world because the Father 'sent' Him (forty-two references), and gave Him a task to fulfil there (iv. 34, xvii. 4, *cf.* xix. 30). He came in His Father's name, *i.e.* as His Father's representative (v. 43), and, because all that He said and did was according to the Father's command (vii. 16 ff., viii. 26 ff., xii. 49 f., xiv. 10), His life on earth revealed His Father perfectly (xiv. 7 ff.). When He speaks of the Father as greater than Himself (xiv. 28, *cf.* x. 29) He is evidently referring, not to any essential or circumstantial inferiority, but to the fact that subordination to the Father's will and initiative is natural and necessary to Him. The Father is greater than He because in relation to the Father it is always His nature freely and joyfully to act as a Son. But this does not mean that He is to be subordinated to the Father in men's esteem and worship. Just the reverse; for the Father seeks the Son's glory no less than the Son seeks the Father's glory. The Father has committed to the Son His two great works of giving life and executing judgment, 'that all may honour the Son, even as they honour the Father' (v. 21 ff., RV). This amounts to saying that the Father directs all men to do as Thomas did (xx. 28), and acknowledge the Son in the same terms in which they ought to acknowledge the Father Himself—namely, as 'my Lord and my God'.

The New Testament contains other lines of thought, subsidiary to that of divine Sonship, which also proclaim the deity of Jesus of Nazareth. We may mention the more important of these. (i) John identifies the eternal divine *Word* with God's personal Son, Jesus Christ (Jn. i. 1–18, *cf.* 1 Jn. i. 1–3; Rev. xix. 13; see LOGOS). (ii) Paul speaks of the Son as 'the *image* of God', both as incarnate (2 Cor. iv. 4) and in His pre-incarnate state (Col. i. 15), and in Phil. ii. 6 says that prior to the incarnation Jesus Christ was in the 'form' (*morphē*) of God: a phrase the exact exegesis of which is disputed, but which Phillips is almost certainly right to render: 'always . . . God by nature'. Heb. i. 3 (RV) calls the Son 'the effulgence of his (God's) glory, and the *very image of his substance*'. These statements, made as they are within a monotheistic frame of reference which excludes any thought of two Gods, are clearly meant to imply: (1) that the Son is personally divine, and ontologically one with the Father; (2) that the Son perfectly embodies all that is in the Father, or, putting it negatively, that there is no aspect or constituent of deity or character which the Father has and the Son lacks. (iii) Paul can apply an Old Testament prophecy concerning the invocation of 'the Lord' (Yahweh) to the Lord Jesus, thus indicating that it finds its true fulfilment in Him (Rom. x. 13, quoting Joel ii. 32; *cf.* Phil. ii. 10 f., echoing Is. xlv. 23). Similarly, the writer to the Hebrews quotes Moses' exhortation to the angels to worship God (Dt. xxxii. 43, LXX), and the psalmist's declaration: 'Thy throne, O God, is for ever and ever' (Ps. xlv. 6), as words spoken by the Father with reference to His Son (Heb. i. 6, 8). This shows that both writers regard Jesus as divine. (iv) The regular New Testament habit of referring to Jesus as 'Lord'—the title given to the gods of Hellenistic religion (*cf.* 1 Cor. viii. 5), and invariably used in LXX to render the divine name—would seem to be an implicit ascription of deity.

b. The nature of the incarnation

When the Word 'became flesh' His deity was not abandoned, or reduced, or contracted, nor did He cease to exercise the divine functions which had been His before. It is He, we are told, who sustains the creation in ordered existence, and who gives and upholds all life (Col. i. 17; Heb. i. 3; Jn. i. 4), and these functions were certainly not in abeyance during His time on earth. When He came into the world He 'emptied himself' of outward glory (Phil. ii. 7; Jn. xvii. 5), and in that sense He 'became poor' (2 Cor. viii. 9), but this does not at all imply a curtailing of His divine powers, such as the so-called kenosis theories would suggest. The New Testament stresses rather that the Son's deity was not reduced through the incarnation. In the man Christ Jesus, says Paul, 'dwelleth *all the fullness of the Godhead* bodily' (Col. ii. 9, *cf.* i. 19).

The incarnation of the Son of God, then, was not a diminishing of deity, but an acquiring of manhood. It was not that God the Son came to indwell a human being, as the Spirit was later to do. (To assimilate incarnation to indwelling is the essence of the Nestorian heresy.) It was rather that the Son in person began to live a fully human life. He did not simply clothe Himself in a human body, taking the place of its soul, as Apollinaris maintained; He took to Himself a human soul as well as a human body, *i.e.* He entered into the experience of human psychical life as well as of human physical life. His manhood was complete; He became 'the *man* Christ Jesus' (1 Tim. ii. 5; *cf.* Gal. iv. 4; Heb. ii. 14, 17). And His manhood is permanent. Though now exalted, He 'continueth to be, God and man in two distinct natures, and one person, for ever'

(*Westminster Shorter Catechism*, Q. 21; *cf.* Heb. vii. 24).

c. The incarnate state

(i) It was a state of *dependence* and *obedience*, because the incarnation did not change the relationship between the Son and the Father. They continued in unbroken fellowship, the Son saying and doing what the Father gave Him to say and do, and not going beyond the Father's known will at any single moment (*cf.* the first temptation, Mt. iv. 2 ff.). His confessed ignorance of the time of His return (Mk. xiii. 32) should no doubt be explained, not as edifying pretence (Aquinas), nor as evidence of His having laid aside His divine knowledge for the purpose of the incarnation (the kenosis theories), but simply as showing that it was not the Father's will for Him to have this knowledge in His mind at that time. As the Son, He did not wish or seek to know more than the Father wished Him to know.

(ii) It was a state of *sinlessness* and *impeccability*, because the incarnation did not change the nature and character of the Son. That His whole life was sinless is several times asserted (2 Cor. v. 21; 1 Pet. ii. 22; Heb. iv. 15; *cf.* Mt. iii. 14–17; Jn. viii. 46; 1 Jn. ii. 1 f.). That He was exempt from the entail of original sin in Adam is evident from the fact that He was not bound to die for sins of His own (*cf.* Heb. vii. 26), and hence could die vicariously and representatively, the righteous taking the place of the unrighteous (*cf.* 2 Cor. v. 21; Rom. v. 16 ff.; Gal. iii. 13; 1 Pet. iii. 18). That He was impeccable, and could not sin, follows from the fact that He remained God the Son (*cf.* Jn. v. 19, 30). Deviation from the Father's will was no more possible for Him in the incarnate state than before. His deity was the guarantee that He would achieve in the flesh that sinlessness which was prerequisite if He were to die as 'a lamb without blemish and without spot' (1 Pet. i. 19).

(iii) It was a state of *temptation* and *moral conflict*, because the incarnation was a true entry into the conditions of man's moral life. Though, being God, it was not in Him to yield to temptation, yet, being man, it was necessary for Him to fight temptation in order to overcome it. What His deity ensured was not that He would not be tempted to stray from His Father's will, nor that He would be exempt from the strain and distress that repeated insidious temptations create in the soul, but that, when tempted, He would fight and win; as He did in the initial temptations of His messianic ministry (Mt. iv. 1 ff.). The writer to the Hebrews stresses that in virtue of His first-hand experience of temptation and the costliness of obedience He is able to extend effective sympathy and help to tempted and distraught Christians (Heb. ii. 18, iv. 14 ff., v. 2, 7 ff.). See also JESUS CHRIST, LIFE OF; JESUS CHRIST, TEACHING OF.

BIBLIOGRAPHY. J. Denney, *Jesus and the Gospel*, 1908; P. T. Forsyth, *The Person and Place of Jesus Christ*, 1909; H. R. Mackintosh, *The Doctrine of the Person of Jesus Christ*, 1912; A. E. J. Rawlinson, *The New Testament Doctrine of the Christ*, 1926; L. Hodgson, *And was made Man*, 1928; E. Brunner, *The Mediator*, E.T., 1934; D. M. Baillie, *God was in Christ*, 1948; L. Berkhof, *Systematic Theology*[4], 1949, pp. 305–330; G. C. Berkouwer, *The Person of Christ*, 1954; K. Barth, *Church Dogmatics*, I, 2, 1956, pp. 122–202; V. Taylor, *The Person of Christ in New Testament Teaching*, 1958; O. Cullmann, *The Christology of the New Testament*, E.T., 1960.

J.I.P.

INCENSE. A common feature of Old Testament ritual, incense was a costly offering and a sign essentially of the acknowledgment of deity (*cf.* Mal. i. 11). The word has a double application: it refers both to the substance used for burning and to the aromatic odour which is produced. Two Hebrew words are thus rendered: (1) *l^{e}ḇônâ*, 'frankincense'; and (2) *q^{e}ṭōreṯ*, the 'sweet smoke' (EVV 'incense') of Is. i. 13. Among the Israelites only priests were allowed to offer incense. When the Lord gave Moses instructions for Aaron, these included strict regulations concerning the use of incense in the holy place (Lv. xvi. 12 f.). Incense is also used in Scripture as a symbol for prayer (*e.g.* Ps. cxli. 2; Rev. viii. 3 f., Gk. *thymiama*). See also FRANKINCENSE, SACRIFICE AND OFFERING (Old Testament), IV*a*, COSMETICS AND PERFUMERY, V*b* (which includes bibliographical details).

J.D.D.

INCENSE, ALTAR OF. See TABERNACLE, TEMPLE.

INCREASE. A noun or verb meaning multiplication or growth, translating sundry Heb. and Gk. words. Primarily the term involved the natural reproduction and germination of cattle and harvest, but always under God's direction and control (Lv. xxvi. 4; Dt. vii. 13; Ps. lxvii. 6), as acknowledged by the tithe (Dt. xiv. 22; *cf.* Pr. iii. 9). Hence prosperity is a sign of God's favour (Dt. vi. 3), adversity of His displeasure (Je. xv. 8), and man exacting gain from possessions is condemned in the same manner as usury (Lv. xxv. 37; Ezk. xviii. 8 ff.; *cf.* Ps. lxii. 10). The term is used symbolically of Israel's relationship with God (Je. ii. 3) and of the spiritual blessings God imparts (Is. xxix. 19, xl. 29), especially by the coming of the Messiah (Is. ix. 3, 7).

In the New Testament the term is applied to the growth of the Church in numbers (Acts vi. 7, xvi. 5; 1 Cor. iii. 6) and in depth (Eph. iv. 16; Col. ii. 19). It is also applied to individuals generally (Lk. ii. 52; Jn. iii. 30; Acts ix. 22), and specifically with regard to faith (Lk. xvii. 5; 2 Cor. x. 15), love (1 Thes. iii. 12, iv. 10), knowledge (Col. i. 10), or ungodliness (2 Tim. ii. 16).

P.A.B.

INDIA.

I. EARLY PERIOD

Heb. *hōddû*, from Old Persian *hindu* (*cf.* Sanskrit *sindhu*), in inscriptions of Darius I and Xerxes I of Persia. The area so designated was that part of the Indus valley and plains east of the Afghan mountains incorporated into the Persian Empire by Darius I, who made it his eastern boundary (Herodotus, iii. 94, iv. 40, 44). In Est. i. 1, viii. 9 the limits of the dominion of Ahasuerus (Xerxes I) are 'from India unto Ethiopia', *hōddû* and *kûš*; this corresponds with Xerxes I's own Old Persian inscriptions, *cf.* the list of countries including 'Sind' or India (*Hiduš*) and Ethiopia (*Kušiya*) in R. G. Kent, *Old Persian: Grammar, Texts, Lexicon*, 1953 edn., p. 151, ll. 25, 29 and § 3. But long before this, trade between India and Mesopotamia is known as early as *c.* 2100 BC (Ur III period), both in texts and by the presence of Indus Valley seals in Mesopotamia. Some think that Ophir might be Indian (S)upāra (see OPHIR). India was the source of the war-elephants used by Alexander and his Seleucid successors in Syria, and in the Graeco-Roman period many exotic products came from India, usually through S Arabia, either up the Red Sea or overland up the western side of Arabia. On routes and navigation, *cf.* van Beek and Hourani, *JAOS*, LXXVIII, 1958, pp. 146, 147; and LXXX, 1960, pp. 135–139. Greek principalities maintained themselves for some time in parts of NW India; *cf.* W. W. Tarn, *The Greeks in Bactria and India*, 1938. For Indians in Egypt in the Graeco-Roman period, *cf.* Sir H. I. Bell, *Cults and Creeds in Graeco-Roman Egypt*, 1953, p. 48; E. Bevan, *History of Egypt under the Ptolemaic Dynasty*, 1927, p. 155; models from Memphis; Petrie, *Memphis I*, 1909, pp. 16, 17, plate 39.

II. LATER PERIOD

Between the 1st century BC and *c.* AD 200, India and the Mediterranean lands entered into closer commercial and cultural relations, stimulated by the Roman market for Eastern luxuries and facilitated by the discovery of the nature of the monsoons, with the subsequent opening of a regular sea-route to the Tamil towns (mod. Cranganore and Kottayam) and even to Madras (*Sopatma*) and beyond. Against this background we must view the stories of the first introduction of Christianity to India. The unanimous tradition of the old South India Church traces its foundation to Thomas the apostle. The narrative of the gnosticizing *Acts of* (Judas) *Thomas* (see NEW TESTAMENT APOCRYPHA) also sets Thomas's activities in India. In itself it is the wildest legend, but J. N. Farquhar argued that it reflects accurate knowledge of 1st-century India, and postulated that Thomas worked first in the Punjab and later in the south (*BJRL*, XI, 1926, XII, 1927). There seems, however, no other early account of Thomas in India clearly independent of these *Acts* (A. Mingana, *BJRL*, XI, 1926, XII, 1927). The peripatetic Pantaenus is said to have been a missionary in India some time before AD 180, and to have found Christians there with Matthew's Gospel in Hebrew left by Bartholomew (Eusebius, *EH* v. 10); but a loose designation of Aden or some other part of Arabia may be involved. That the Syriac S India Church is very ancient is undeniable: the question of apostolic or sub-apostolic foundation remains open.

BIBLIOGRAPHY. E. H. Warmington, *Indian Commerce*, 1928; L. W. Browne, *The Indian Christians of St. Thomas*, 1956.

K.A.K.
A.F.W.

INGATHERING. See TABERNACLES, FEAST OF.

INHERITANCE.

I. IN THE OLD TESTAMENT

In the Old Testament there are two basic roots for inheritance, *nāḥal* and *yāraš*. In each case the emphasis was much more upon possession generally than upon the process of succession, though this idea is not altogether absent. The words occur only rarely in Genesis and Exodus and are most frequent in Numbers and Deuteronomy, which look forward to the allotment of land in Canaan, and in Joshua, which records how it was put into effect. The law of inheritance was as follows. Land belonged to the family rather than to the individual. There was therefore a strict entail. The eldest son received a double portion and the others equal shares. If a man died leaving no sons the inheritance went to his daughters; if no daughters, to his brothers; if no brothers, to his father's brothers; if no father's brothers, to the next of kin (Nu. xxvii. 8–11). If daughters inherited they had to marry in their own tribe (Nu. xxxvi. 6). The emphasis of the word *yāraš* is on possession, for the heir succeeded by right and not by disposition. Wills were unknown in Israel before the time of Herod. Before the giving of the law the Patriarchs were free to pass over the firstborn in favour of a younger son. Abraham, Isaac, and Jacob were all younger sons. Joseph was preferred to Reuben (1 Ch. v. 1, 2) and Ephraim to Manasseh (Gn. xlviii. 8–20). The giving of the rights of the firstborn to the firstborn of a second and favourite wife was forbidden in Dt. xxi. 15–17. However, in the case of the royal succession David was preferred to his older brothers (1 Sa. xvi. 11) and Solomon to Adonijah (1 Ki. ii. 15), though the normal custom was for the firstborn to succeed (2 Ch. xxi. 3). See also FIRSTBORN.

If a man died childless his brother had to marry his widow (Gn. xxxviii. 8, 9; Dt. xxv. 5–10; Mt. xxii. 23–25). The first son of that union was regarded as the firstborn of the deceased brother, and therefore if there were only one son the surviving brother would have no heir. It was accordingly possible for the brother not to marry his brother's wife, and then the right went to the nearest kinsman (Ru. ii. 20, iii. 9–13, iv. 1–12). In the book of Ruth, Ruth plays the part of Naomi, who was past the age of marriage (Ru. iv. 17). Land could not be sold in perpetuity (Lv. xxv. 23, 24). If it was sold it could be redeemed by the next of kin (Lv. xxv. 25). Naboth knew Ahab's offer was against the law (1 Ki. xxi. 3).

The land of Canaan was regarded as the inheritance of Yahweh in a particular way (Ex. xv.

17; *cf.* Jos. xxii. 19; Ps. lxxix. 1), though He was God of all the earth (Ps. xlvii. 2, *etc.*). It was for that reason that Israel was able to enjoy it as their inheritance.

The promises made to Abraham concerned a land as well as descendants (Gn. xii. 7, xv. 18–21, *etc.*). Abraham's faith was shown in believing that he would have descendants when he was childless and his wife was past childbearing age, and in believing that he would have a land, though during his lifetime he was a nomad with no settled possession (Acts vii. 5). The children of Israel were brought out of Egypt not only to escape from bondage but also to inherit a land (Ex. vi. 6–8). This land was conquered by them, but it was the gift of Yahweh (Jos. xxi. 43–45). He allotted them in it an inheritance which was to last for ever (Gn. xiii. 15, *etc.*).

Lots were cast to discover Yahweh's disposal of portions to individual tribes (Jos. xviii. 2–10). Eventually it was to be a remnant who returned from exile to inherit the land (Is. x. 20, 21, *etc.*). Those who formed that faithful remnant were to inherit the nations as well (Ps. ii. 8).

The Levites were to have no territory because Yahweh was their inheritance (Dt. xviii. 1, 2). Materially this meant that their portion consisted of the dues and firstfruits given by the people to Yahweh (Dt. xviii. 3–5). Spiritually the idea was extended to the whole of Israel (Ps. xvi. 5, 6, *etc.*). Also Israel was to be His inheritance as the people which belonged specially to Him (Dt. vii. 6, xxxii. 9).

II. IN THE NEW TESTAMENT

In the New Testament 'inheritance' renders *klēronomos* and its cognates, derived from *klēros*, meaning a 'lot'. The inheritance is narrowed down to the true Israel, Christ Himself, who is 'the heir' (Mk. xii. 7). As heir of God He enters into a possession given to Him because of His relationship. He has been made heir of everything (Heb. i. 2). Believers in a sense share the divine sonship by adoption and therefore also the divine heirship (Rom. viii. 17). They follow in the footsteps of faithful Abraham as heirs of the promise (Rom. iv. 13, 14) and like Isaac they are his children, heirs according to promise (Gal. iii. 29). Their inheritance is something which is given by God's grace because of their status in His sight, and it is in no sense earned.

The object of the Christian inheritance is all that was symbolized by the land of Canaan, and more. Believers inherit the kingdom of God (Mt. xxv. 34; 1 Cor. vi. 9, 10, xv. 50; Gal. v. 21; Eph. v. 5; Jas. ii. 5). They inherit the earth or 'the land' (Mt. v. 5; *cf.* Ps. xxxvii. 29). They inherit salvation (Heb. i. 14), a blessing (1 Pet. iii. 9), glory (Rom. viii. 17, 18), and incorruption (1 Cor. xv. 50). These are all 'the promises' (Heb. vi. 12), not received in their fulfilment by the believers of the Old Testament (Heb. xi. 39, 40). In Hebrews stress is laid upon the new 'covenant' or 'testament'. It is on this that the promised inheritance is based, especially as it required the death of the testator (Heb. ix. 15–17). Two men asked Jesus what they should do in order to inherit eternal life (Lk. x. 25, xviii. 18), and Christ spoke of that as being part of the blessing of the new world (Mt. xix. 29). A Christian man and wife are joint heirs of the grace of life (1 Pet. iii. 7).

The consummation of the blessings promised will not take place until the parousia. The inheritance is reserved in heaven (1 Pet. i. 4). He who overcomes is to have the inheritance of God (Rev. xxi. 7). However, that does not alter the fact that many of the blessings of heirship may be enjoyed in advance. The Holy Spirit is the agent who makes our position as heirs real (Rom. viii. 16, 17), and He is given to us 'as the guarantee of our inheritance until we acquire possession of it' (Eph. i. 14, RSV). He was sent to the Church after Christ's own entry into His inheritance at His ascension.

In the New Testament we still see God's people as His inheritance (Eph. i. 18), and all the blessings mentioned above show that He Himself is still their inheritance.

But that inheritance is not of right, it is by the free disposition of God, who is able in His sovereign pleasure to dispossess those who seem to have most title to it and give it to others of His choice.

BIBLIOGRAPHY. C. E. B. Cranfield, 'Inherit' in A. Richardson (ed.), *A Theological Word Book of the Bible*, 1950, pp. 112–114; W. Foerster and J. Herrmann in *TWNT*, III, pp. 757–786.

R.E.N.

INK. See WRITING.

INKHORN. See WRITING.

INN. See HOSPITALITY (III).

INNER MAN. Paul uses this phrase (*ho esō anthrōpos*, in Rom. vii. 22; 2 Cor. iv. 16; Eph. iii. 16) to denote the Christian's true self, as seen by God and known (partially) in consciousness. (For a vindication of the view that Rom. vii. 14–26 pictures Paul the Christian, see A. Nygren, *Romans*, 1952, pp. 284 ff.) The contrast, implicit if not explicit, is with *ho exō anthrōpos*, 'the outward man' (2 Cor. iv. 16), the same individual as seen by his fellow-men, a being physically alive and active, known (so far as he is known) through his public behaviour.

This contrast differs both from that which Paul drew between the new and old man (*i.e.* between man's status, condition, and affinities in Christ and apart from Christ), from that which Platonists drew between the immaterial, immortal soul (the real man) and his material, mortal body (his lodging), or, again, between the soul's rational (higher) and sensual (lower) impulses. The contrast in view is rather that between the 'outward appearance' and the 'heart' drawn in 1 Sa. xvi. 7: 'inner man' and 'heart' (*q.v.*) are, indeed, almost synonymous. This contrast reflects two facts. First, God, the searcher of hearts, sees things in a man that are hidden from his fellows, who see only his exterior (*cf.* 1 Sa. xvi. 7; Mt. xxiii. 27 f., and Peter's assertion that meekness and quietness adorn 'the *hidden* man of the heart', which God notices, if men do not, 1 Pet. iii. 3 f.). Secondly, God's renewal of sinners in Christ is a hidden work (Col. iii. 3 f.), of which human observers see only certain of the effects (*cf.* Jn. iii. 8). The sphere of character, and of the Spirit's transforming work, is not the outward, but the inner man. The exact point of the contrast differs in each of the three texts.

1. In 2 Cor. iv. 16 it is between the outward Paul, the Paul whom men saw, worn down by constant work, ill health, anxiety, strain, and persecution, and the Paul whom God knew and who knew God, the Paul who had been re-created, and was now indwelt, by the Spirit (2 Cor. v. 5, 17), and who after physical dissolution would be 'clothed upon' with a resurrection body (2 Cor. v. 1 ff.). The outward Paul was going to pieces; the real Paul was daily renewed.

2. In Rom. vii. 22 f. the contrast is between the 'law (active principle) of sin' in Paul's 'members', influencing his outward actions, and the 'law of my mind', Paul's heart's delight in God's law and heart's desire to keep it, which desire sin constantly frustrated.

3. In Eph. iii. 16–19 the contrast is only implicit. The inward man, the heart, the temple in which Christ dwells and the sphere of His strengthening operation, is the real, abiding self, the self that knows Christ's love and will be filled into God's fulness; but this self is hidden from men. Hence Paul has need to exhort his readers to show the world what God has wrought in them by the quality of their outward conduct (Eph. iv–vi).

BIBLIOGRAPHY. *Arndt, s.v. anthrōpos*; R. Bultmann, *Theology of the New Testament*, I, p. 203; standard commentaries on the texts quoted.

J.I.P.

INSPIRATION. In AV this word occurs twice, in RV not at all.

1. In Jb. xxxii. 8, Elihu says: 'there is a spirit in man: and the inspiration of the Almighty giveth them understanding'. RV corrects to 'breath'.

2. In 2 Tim. iii. 16, Paul says: 'All Scripture is given by inspiration of God, and is profitable for doctrine, for reproof, for correction, for instruction in righteousness'. RV reverts to Tyndale's view of the construction: 'Every scripture inspired of God is also profitable . . .' 'Inspired of God' is, however, no improvement on AV, for the adjective so translated (*theopneustos*) means *out*-breathed rather than *in*-breathed by God—divinely *ex*-spired, rather than *in*-spired. In the last century Ewald and Cremer argued that the adjective bore an active sense, 'breathing the Spirit', and Barth appears to agree (he glosses it as meaning not only 'given and filled and ruled by the Spirit of God', but also 'actively outbreathing and spreading abroad and making known the Spirit of God' (*Church Dogmatics*, I. 2, E.T., 1956, p. 504)); but B. B. Warfield showed decisively in 1900 that the sense of the word can only be passive. The thought is not of God as breathing through Scripture, or of Scripture as breathing out God, but of God as having breathed out Scripture. Paul's words mean, not that Scripture is inspiring (true though this is), but that Scripture is a divine product, and must be approached and estimated as such.

The 'breath' or 'spirit' of God in the Old Testament (Heb. *rûaḥ*, *n*^{e}*šāmâ*) denotes the active outgoing of divine power, whether in creation (Ps. xxxiii. 6; Jb. xxxiii. 4; *cf.* Gn. i. 2, ii. 7), preservation (Jb. xxxiv. 14), revelation to and through prophets (Is. xlviii. 16, lxi. 1; Mi. iii. 8; Joel ii. 28 f.), regeneration (Ezk. xxxvi. 27), or judgment (Is. xxx. 28, 33). The New Testament reveals this divine 'breath' (Gk. *pneuma*) to be a Person of the Godhead (see HOLY SPIRIT). In the texts quoted, Elihu says that God's 'breath' gives spiritual understanding, and Paul says that God's 'breath' (*i.e.* the Holy Spirit) produced Scripture, as a means to the conveyance of spiritual understanding. Whether we render *pasa graphē* as 'the whole Scripture' or 'every text', and whether we follow AV or RV in construing the sentence (either seems possible in each case), Paul's meaning is clear beyond all doubt. He is affirming that all that comes in the category of Scripture, all that has a place among the 'sacred writings' (*hiera grammata*, verse 15, RV), just because it is God-breathed, is profitable for the guiding of both faith and life.

On the basis of this Pauline text, English theology regularly uses the word 'inspiration' to express the thought of the divine origin and quality of Holy Scripture. Actively, the noun denotes God's out-breathing operation which produced Scripture: passively, the inspiredness of the Scriptures so produced. The word is also used more generally of the divine influence which enabled the human organs of revelation—prophets, psalmists, wise men, and apostles—to speak, as well as to write, the words of God.

I. THE IDEA OF BIBLICAL INSPIRATION

According to 2 Tim. iii. 16 what is inspired is precisely the biblical writings. Inspiration is a work of God terminating, not in the men who were to write Scripture (as if, having given them an idea of what to say, God left them to themselves to find a way of saying it), but in the actual written product. It is Scripture—*graphē*, the written text—that is God-breathed. The essential idea here is that all Scripture has the same character as the prophets' sermons had, both when preached and when written (*cf.* 2 Pet. i. 19–21, on the divine origin of every 'prophecy of the scripture'; see also Je. xxxvi; Is. viii. 16–20). That is to say, Scripture is not only man's word, the fruit of human thought, premeditation, and art, but also, and equally, God's word, spoken through man's lips or written with man's pen. In other words, Scripture has a double authorship, and man is only the secondary author; the primary author, through whose initiative, and prompting, and enlightenment, and under whose superintendence, each human writer did his work, is God the Holy Ghost.

Revelation to the prophets was essentially verbal; often it had a visionary aspect, but even 'revelation in visions is also verbal revelation' (L. Koehler, *Old Testament Theology*, E.T., 1957, p. 103). Brunner has observed that in 'the words of God which the Prophets proclaim as those which they have received directly from God, and have been commissioned to repeat, as they have received them . . . perhaps we may find the closest analogy to the meaning of the theory of verbal inspiration' (*Revelation and Reason*, 1946, p. 122, n. 9). Indeed we do; we find not merely an analogy to it, but the paradigm of it; and 'theory' is the wrong word to use, for this is just the biblical doctrine itself. Biblical inspiration should be defined in the same theological terms as prophetic inspiration: namely, as the whole process (manifold, no doubt, in its psychological forms, as prophetic inspiration was) whereby God moved those men whom He had chosen and prepared (*cf.* Je. i. 5; Gal. i. 15) to write exactly what He wanted written for the communication of saving knowledge to His people, and through them to the world. Biblical inspiration is thus verbal by its very nature; for it is of God-given words that the God-breathed Scriptures consist.

Thus, inspired Scripture is written revelation, just as the prophets' sermons were spoken revelation. The biblical record of God's self-disclosure in redemptive history is not merely human testimony to revelation, but is itself revelation. The inspiring of Scripture was an integral part in the revelatory process, for in Scripture God gave the Church His own description of, and commentary on, His saving work in history, and His own authoritative interpretation of its place in His eternal plan. 'Thus saith the Lord' could be prefixed to each book of Scripture with no less propriety than it is (359 times, according to Koehler, *op. cit.*, p. 245) to individual prophetic utterances which Scripture contains. Inspiration, therefore, guarantees the truth of all that the Bible asserts, just as the inspiration of the prophets guaranteed the truth of their representation of the mind of God. ('Truth' here denotes correspondence between the words of man and the thoughts of God, whether in the realm of fact or of meaning.) As truth from God, man's Creator and rightful King, biblical instruction, like prophetic oracles, carries divine authority.

II. BIBLICAL PRESENTATION

The idea of canonical Scripture, *i.e.* of a document or corpus of documents containing a permanent authoritative record of divine revelation, goes back to Moses' writing of God's law in the wilderness (Ex. xxxiv. 27 f.; Dt. xxxi. 9 ff., 24 ff.). The truth of all statements, historical or theological, which Scripture makes, and their authority as words of God, is assumed without question or discussion in both Testaments. The canon grew, but the concept of inspiration, which the idea of canonicity presupposes, was fully developed from the first, and is unchanged throughout the Bible. As there presented, it comprises two convictions.

1. *The words of Scripture are God's own words.* Old Testament passages identify the Mosaic law and the words of the prophets, both spoken and written, with God's own speech (*cf.* 1 Ki. xxii. 8–16; Ne. viii; Ps. cxix; Je. xxv. 1–13, xxxvi, *etc.*). New Testament writers view the Old Testament as a whole as 'the oracles of God' (Rom. iii. 2), prophetic in character (Rom. xvi. 26, *cf.* i. 2, iii. 21), written by men who were moved and taught by the Holy Ghost (2 Pet. i. 20 f.; *cf.* 1 Pet. i. 10–12). Christ and His apostles quote Old Testament texts, not merely as what, *e.g.*, Moses, David, or Isaiah said (see Mk. vii. 10, xii. 36, vii. 6; Rom. x. 5, xi. 9, x. 20, *etc.*), but also as what God said through these men (see Acts iv. 25, xxviii. 25, *etc.*), or sometimes simply as what 'he' (God) says (*e.g.* 1 Cor. vi. 16; Heb. viii. 5, 8), or what the Holy Ghost says (Heb. iii. 7, x. 15). Furthermore, Old Testament statements, not made by God in their contexts, are quoted as utterances of God (Mt. xix. 4 f.; Heb. iii. 7; Acts xiii. 34 f., citing Gn. ii. 24; Ps. xcv. 7; Is. lv. 2 respectively). Also, Paul refers to God's promise to Abraham and His threat to Pharaoh, both spoken long before the biblical record of them was written, as words which *Scripture* spoke to these two men (Gal. iii. 8; Rom. ix. 17); which shows how completely he equated the statements of Scripture with the utterance of God.

2. *Man's part in the producing of Scripture was merely to transmit what he had received.* Psychologically, from the standpoint of form, it is clear that the human writers contributed much to the making of Scripture—historical research, theological meditation, linguistic style, *etc.* Each biblical book is in one sense the literary creation of its author. But theologically, from the standpoint of content, the Bible regards the human writers as having contributed nothing, and Scripture as being entirely the creation of God. This conviction is rooted in the self-consciousness of the founders of biblical religion, all of whom claimed to utter—and, in the case of the prophets and apostles, to write—what were, in the most literal sense, the words of another: God Himself. The prophets (among whom Moses must be numbered: Dt. xviii. 15, xxxiv. 10) professed that they spoke the words of Yahweh, setting before Israel what Yahweh had shown them (Je. i. 7; Ezk. ii. 7; Am. iii. 7 f.; *cf.* 1 Ki. xxii). Jesus of Nazareth professed that He spoke words given Him by His Father (Jn. vii. 16, xii. 49 f.). The apostles taught and issued commands in Christ's name (2 Thes. iii. 6), so claiming His authority and sanction (1 Cor. xiv. 37), and they maintained that both their matter and their words had been taught them by God's Spirit (1 Cor. ii. 9–13; *cf.* Christ's promises, Jn. xiv. 26, xv. 26 f., xvi. 13 ff.). These are claims to

inspiration. In the light of these claims, the evaluation of prophetic and apostolic writings as wholly God's word, in just the same way in which the two tables of the law, 'written with the finger of God' (Ex. xxiv. 12, xxxi. 18, xxxii. 16), were wholly God's word, naturally became part of the biblical faith.

Christ and the apostles bore striking witness to the fact of inspiration by their appeal to the authority of the Old Testament. In effect, they claimed the Jewish Scriptures as the Christian Bible: a body of literature bearing prophetic witness to Christ (Jn. v. 39 f.; Lk. xxiv. 25 ff., 44 f.; 2 Cor. iii. 14 ff.) and designed by God specifically for the instruction of Christian believers (Rom. xv. 4; 1 Cor. x. 11; 2 Tim. iii. 14 ff.; *cf.* the exposition of Ps. xcv. 7–11 in Heb. iii–iv, and indeed the whole of Hebrews, in which every major point is made by appeal to Old Testament texts). Christ insisted that what was written in the Old Testament 'cannot be broken' (Jn. x. 35). He had not come, He told the Jews, to annul the law or the prophets (Mt. v. 17); if they thought He was doing that, they were mistaken; He had come to do the opposite —to bear witness to the divine authority of both by fulfilling them. The law stands for ever, because it is God's word (Mt. v. 18; Lk. xvi. 17); the prophecies, particularly those concerning Himself, must be fulfilled, for the same reason (Mt. xxvi. 54; Lk. xxii. 37; *cf.* Mk. viii. 31; Lk. xviii. 31). To Christ and His apostles, the appeal to Scripture was always decisive (*cf.* Mt. iv. 4, 7, 10; Rom. xii. 19; 1 Pet. i. 16, *etc.*).

The freedom with which New Testament writers quote the Old Testament (following LXX, Targums, or an *ad hoc* rendering of the Hebrew, as best suits them) has been held to show that they did not believe in the inspiredness of the original words. But their interest was not in the words, as such, but in their meaning; and recent study has made it appear that these quotations are interpretative and expository—a mode of quotation well known among the Jews. The writers seek to indicate the true (*i.e.* Christian) meaning and application of their text by the form in which they cite it. In most cases this meaning has evidently been reached by a strict application of clear-cut theological principles about the relation of Christ and the Church to the Old Testament. (See C. H. Dodd, *According to the Scriptures*, 1952; K. Stendahl, *The School of St. Matthew*, 1954; R. V. G. Tasker, *The Old Testament in the New Testament*[2], 1954; E. Earle Ellis, *Paul's Use of the Old Testament*, 1957.)

III. THEOLOGICAL STATEMENT

In formulating the biblical idea of inspiration, it is desirable that four negative points be made.

1. The idea is not of mechanical dictation, or automatic writing, or any process which involved the suspending of the action of the human writer's mind. Such concepts of inspiration are found in the Talmud, Philo, and the Fathers, but not in the Bible. The divine direction and control under which the biblical authors wrote was not a physical or psychological force, and it did not detract from, but rather heightened, the freedom, spontaneity, and creativeness of their writing.

2. The fact that in inspiration God did not obliterate the personality, style, outlook, and cultural conditioning of His penmen does not mean that His control of them was imperfect, or that they inevitably distorted the truth they had been given to convey in the process of writing it down. Warfield gently mocks the notion that when God wanted Paul's letters written 'He was reduced to the necessity of going down to earth and painfully scrutinizing the men He found there, seeking anxiously for the one who, on the whole, promised best for His purpose; and then violently forcing the material He wished expressed through him, against his natural bent, and with as little loss from his recalcitrant characteristics as possible. Of course, nothing of the sort took place. If God wished to give His people a series of letters like Paul's, He prepared a Paul to write them, and the Paul He brought to the task was a Paul who spontaneously would write just such letters' (*The Inspiration and Authority of the Bible*, 1951, p. 155).

3. Inspiredness is not a quality attaching to corruptions which intrude in the course of the transmission of the text, but only to the text as originally produced by the inspired writers. The acknowledgment of biblical inspiration thus makes more urgent the task of meticulous textual criticism, in order to eliminate such corruptions and ascertain what that original text was.

4. The inspiredness of biblical writing is not to be equated with the inspiredness of great literature, not even when (as often) the biblical writing is in fact great literature. The biblical idea of inspiration relates, not to the literary quality of what is written, but to its character as divine revelation in writing.

See HOLY SPIRIT; PROPHECY; SCRIPTURE; AUTHORITY; CANON OF THE OLD TESTAMENT; CANON OF THE NEW TESTAMENT; INTERPRETATION.

BIBLIOGRAPHY. B. B. Warfield, *op. cit.* (much of the relevant material is also in his *Biblical Foundations*, 1958, chapters 1 and 2); A. Kuyper, *Encyclopaedia of Sacred Theology*, E.T., 1899; J. Orr, *Revelation and Inspiration*, 1910; A. H. Strong, *Systematic Theology*, iii, 1907; C. F. H. Henry (ed.), *Revelation and the Bible*, 1958; K. Barth, *Church Dogmatics*, I. 1, 2 (*The Doctrine of the Word of God*), E.T., 1936, 1956; W. Sanday, *Inspiration*, 1893; R. Abba, *The Nature and Authority of the Bible*, 1958; *TWNT*, I, pp. 742–773 (*s.v. graphō*), and IV, pp. 1016–1084 (*s.v. nomos*).

J.I.P.

INTERCESSION. See PRAYER.

INTEREST. See DEBT.

INTERPRETATION, BIBLICAL. The purpose of biblical interpretation is to make the meaning and message of the biblical writings plain to their readers. Some principles of interpretation are common to the Bible and other literature, especially other ancient literature; other principles of interpretation are bound up with the unique place of the Bible in the revelation of God and in the life of His people.

I. GENERAL INTERPRETATION

Each part of the Bible must be interpreted in its context, and that means not only its immediate verbal context but the wider context of time, place, and human situation to which it belongs. Thus there are a number of considerations to be kept in mind if the meaning of the text is to be grasped as fully as is desirable.

a. Language and style

The idioms and constructions of the biblical languages can differ quite widely from those with which we are familiar today, and some acquaintance with these is necessary for a proper interpretation (see LANGUAGE OF APOCRYPHA, OF OLD TESTAMENT, and OF NEW TESTAMENT). The literary categories represented in the Bible should also be noted; this will save us, for example, from interpreting poetry according to the canons of prose narration, or *vice versa*. Most of the literary categories in the Bible are well known from other literature, but biblical prophecy, and still more biblical apocalyptic, have features peculiar to themselves which call for special interpretative procedures.

b. Historical background

The biblical narrative covers the whole span of Near Eastern civilization until AD 100, a period of several millennia within which a succession of sweeping changes took place. It is therefore important to relate the various phases of the biblical revelation to their proper historical context if we are to understand them aright; otherwise we may find ourselves, for example, assessing people's conduct in the Middle Bronze Age by the ethical standards of the Gospels. And we can discern the permanent principles in a biblical document only when we first of all relate that document to the conditions of its own times; we shall then be better able to reapply to our times those features of its teaching which are valid for all time.

c. Geographical setting

We should not underestimate the influence exercised by climate and terrain on a people's outlook and way of life, including its religion. The religious conflicts of the Old Testament are interwoven with the conditions of Palestinian geography. Baal-worship, for example, arose in a land where life depended on rain. To the Canaanites Baal was the storm-god who fertilized the earth, and Baal-worship was a magical ritual calculated to ensure regular rainfall and plentiful harvests. Indeed, to such an extent have geographical conditions entered into the biblical language, literal and figurative, that some acquaintance with these conditions is necessary for an understanding of the language. This is especially true of the Old Testament, but even in the New it has long been recognized, for instance, that the historical geography of Asia Minor makes an important contribution to the interpretation of Acts and the Epistles.

d. The human situation

Even more important than questions of time, place, and language are questions about the everyday life of the people whom we meet in the Bible, their loves and hates, their hopes and fears, their social relations, and so forth. To read the Bible without regard to this living environment is to read it in a vacuum and to put constructions upon it which it was never intended to bear. Thanks largely to archaeological discovery, we are able to reconstruct in fair measure the private and public conditions in which the people of the Bible lived, in age after age; while a sympathetic reading of the text itself enables us in some degree to get under their skins and look at the world through their eyes. It is not unimportant to try to envisage what it must have felt like to be a servant in Abraham's household, an Israelite slave in Egypt, a citizen of Jericho when Joshua's men were marching round the city, or a citizen of Jerusalem in face of Sennacherib's threats, a soldier in David's army, a captive maid waiting on Naaman's wife, or a builder of the wall under Nehemiah. We may then realize that part of the Bible's perennial appeal is due to its concentration on those features of human life that remain basically the same in all times and places.

II. SPECIAL INTERPRETATION

Biblical interpretation involves not only the interpretation of the several documents but their interpretation as part of the Bible, having regard to the way in which each part contributes to the purpose of the Bible as a whole. Since the Bible records God's word to man and man's response to God, since it contains 'all things necessary to salvation' and constitutes the Church's 'rule of faith and life', we may look for such a unity throughout the volume that each part can be interpreted in the light of the whole. We may look, indeed, for some unifying principle of interpretation.

In traditional Jewish interpretation of the Hebrew Scriptures this unifying principle was found in the Law, understood in accordance with the teaching of the great rabbinical schools. The Prophets and the Writings were treated largely as commentaries on the Law. In addition to the surface meaning of the text, the *p*ᵉ*šaṭ*, there was the more extended application, the *d*ᵉ*raš*, derived by the use of various well-defined principles of exegesis, but sometimes appearing far-fetched by the exegetical standards of today.

In the New Testament and early Christian literature the Old Testament oracles are viewed as a unity, making the reader 'wise unto salvation' and equipping him with all that he needs for the service of God (2 Tim. iii. 15 ff.). The prophets, speaking in the power of the Holy Spirit, bear witness to Christ as the One in whom the promises of God find their fulfilment. The New Testament writers—whose diversity of personality, style, and thought must be taken into account in the interpretation of their works—are agreed on this. In Heb. i. 1 f. the 'divers manners' in which God spoke in earlier days are contrasted with the perfect and final word which He has spoken in His Son; in the Pauline writings God's dealings with the world are traced through successive stages associated with Adam, Abraham, Moses, and Christ. Biblical interpretation in the New Testament has Christ as its unifying principle, but this principle is not applied mechanically but in such a way as to bring out the historical and progressive nature of the biblical revelation. This creative principle of interpretation was certainly derived by the apostolic church from Christ Himself.

In post-apostolic times biblical interpretation was influenced by a Gk. concept of inspiration which called for large-scale allegorization of the text. This influence was most apparent in Alexandria, where in the pre-Christian period it is found in the biblical interpretation of Philo. By allegorization, it was believed, the mind of the inspiring Spirit could be ascertained; by allegorization much in the Bible that was intellectually or ethically unacceptable in its literal sense could be made acceptable. This method, developed by the Alexandrian Fathers and taken over from them by many of the Western Fathers, in fact obscured the mind of the Spirit and obliterated the historical character of biblical revelation. In contrast to the Alexandrians the school of Antioch, while not rejecting allegorization entirely, did much more justice to the historical sense of the text.

The distinction between the literal sense of Scripture and the higher or spiritual sense was elaborated in mediæval times, and three varieties of spiritual sense were distinguished—the allegorical, which deduced doctrine from the narrative; the moral, which drew lessons for life and behaviour; and the anagogical, which derived heavenly meanings from earthly things. Yet the early Middle Ages also saw good work done in the field of literal interpretation, notably by the 12th-century school of St. Victor in France.

The Reformers laid fresh emphasis on the literal sense of Scripture, and on the grammatico-historical method of exegesis as the way to establish its literal sense. Grammatico-historical exegesis is fundamental, but when the foundation has been laid by its means theological exegesis and practical application are also called for. Moreover, the use of the Bible in the life of the people of God throughout the centuries continually brings fresh aspects of its meaning to light, although these fresh aspects have general validity only as they are rooted in the true and original sense. Thus, we may understand the Epistle to the Romans better because of the part it played in the lives of Augustine, Luther, and Wesley; but the part it played in their lives owes its significance to the fact that these men had a rare grasp of what Paul really meant when he wrote the Epistle.

Typological interpretation, revived in our own day, must be used (if at all) with caution and restraint. Its most acceptable form is that which discerns in the biblical recital of God's acts of mercy and judgment a recurring rhythm, by virtue of which earlier stages in the recital can be viewed as foreshadowings and illustrations of later stages (*cf.* Paul's use of the wilderness experiences of Israel in 1 Cor. x. 1 ff.).

Christians have an abiding standard and pattern in their Lord's use of the Old Testament, and part of the Holy Spirit's present work for them is to open the Scriptures as the risen Christ opened them for two disciples on the Emmaus road (Lk. xxiv. 25 ff.).

BIBLIOGRAPHY. F. W. Farrar, *History of Interpretation*, 1886; C. W. Dugmore (ed.), *The Interpretation of the Bible*, 1944; N. H. Snaith, *The Distinctive Ideas of the Old Testament*, 1944; B. Ramm, *Protestant Biblical Interpretation*, 1950; B. Smalley, *The Study of the Bible in the Middle Ages*[2], 1952; C. H. Dodd, *According to the Scriptures*, 1952; H. H. Rowley, *The Unity of the Bible*, 1953; E. C. Blackman, *Biblical Interpretation*, 1957; R. M. Grant, *The Letter and the Spirit*, 1957; J. D. Wood, *The Interpretation of the Bible*, 1958. F.F.B.

IRA (Heb. *'îrā'*). **1.** A Jairite, described as a 'priest unto David' (2 Sa. xx. 26, RV), a difficult description to understand, as he was not of the tribe of Levi. However, Pesh. reads 'of Jattir', which was a city of Levi. Alternatively, 'priest' here may mean a chief official (*cf.* 2 Sa. viii. 18, AV; 1 Ch. xviii. 17, AV).

2. An Ithrite, one of David's mighty men (2 Sa. xxiii. 38). May be same as (1) if Pesh. reading is correct.

3. Another of David's heroes, son of Ikkesh the Tekoite (2 Sa. xxiii. 26). M.A.M.

IRON. See MINING AND METALS.

ISAAC (Heb. *yiṣḥāq*, probably 'one laughs'). At the announcement of Isaac's birth Abraham laughed (Gn. xvii. 17), and later Sarah herself laughed at the thought that she who was so old should bear a son (Gn. xviii. 12–15). At Isaac's birth, when Abraham was a hundred years old, Sarah declares that God has made her to laugh (Gn. xxi. 6). On the day of Isaac's weaning Ishmael mocked (Gn. xxi. 9). It is difficult to discover a precise subject for the verb, and possibly it is best to take the form impersonally. Some scholars render 'God laughs', but there is little warrant for this translation.

The two great features of Isaac's life centre about his birth and marriage, and the reason for this is that he was the seed through whom the line of promise was to be continued. Abraham had been sorely tested with respect to the promise of a seed, and now, at an advanced age, when he was as good as dead, that seed came. Thus, it is seen that God is carrying out His purposes in fulfilment of the promises made to Abraham (Gn. xii. 1–3), even though those promises seem to man to be incapable of fulfilment.

At the feast of Isaac's weaning Isaac was made the object of unholy laughter and mocking on the part of his brother Ishmael. Two worlds or seeds were together, and these had to be separated. Hagar and her son Ishmael were therefore driven from the household (Gn. xxi). God then put Abraham to the test, commanding him to slay his son Isaac. Abraham obeyed God, and the Lord intervened, providing a ram for the sacrifice. The promise is then renewed, that Abraham shall have a large seed (Gn. xxii).

The second feature of Isaac's life which is of significance is his marriage. That Isaac should be born was a miracle, and soon afterwards it seemed that he must die. How, then, could he be the promised seed? He lives, however, and attention is centred upon his marriage, for it is to be through him that the line of promise is to be continued. Abraham is concerned that the promised seed be continued and sends his eldest servant to take a wife for Isaac from his own country, Harran. Rebekah, the daughter of Bethuel, Abraham's nephew, is indicated as the intended bride and willingly leaves her home to accompany the servant. Isaac receives her and brings her into his mother's tent. Isaac and Rebekah are married, with love developing as a result of Isaac's considerate and courteous actions (Gn. xxiv).

For twenty years Rebekah was barren, and so it is again seen that the promised seed is not to come merely through the natural means of ordinary fatherhood but through God's supernatural creative power. Rebekah's barrenness causes Isaac to entreat the Lord, and the announcement is made to Rebekah that two children are struggling in her womb (Gn. xxv. 22–26). These two children, representing two nations, will follow mutually hostile courses. Isaac himself is to remain a sojourner in the land, and, instead of going to Egypt in time of famine, remains at Gerar. At the sign of crisis he, like Abraham, seeks to protect his wife by a wrong means. After quarrels with the herdsmen at Gerar he goes to Beersheba, and finally makes an agreement with Abimelech. Mutual antagonism appears between Isaac and Rebekah, occasioned by Jacob's actions. Being deceived, Isaac pronounces the paternal blessing upon Jacob and utters a devout prophetical wish upon Esau. Before his death he acknowledges that the blessing will come through Jacob (Gn. xxviii. 4). Jacob lived to see Isaac again, and, at the age of 180 years, the latter died and was buried by his sons, Esau and Jacob.

E.J.Y.

ISAIAH (Heb. *yᵉšaʿyāhû*, 'Yahweh is salvation'), son of Amoz (Heb. *'āmôṣ*, to be distinguished from the prophet Amos, Heb. *'āmôs*), lived in Jerusalem (Is. vii. 1–3, xxxvii. 2). According to Jewish tradition, he was of royal blood; it has sometimes been inferred from the narratives and oracles of his book that he was, at any rate, of noble descent; but there is no certainty about this. As appears from the superscription to the book (i. 1), he prophesied under Uzziah (791/790–740/739 BC), Jotham (*c.* 740/739–732/731 BC), Ahaz (735–716/715 BC), and Hezekiah (716/715–687/686 BC). (The regnal dates are those assigned by E. R. Thiele.) He was called to be a prophet 'in the year that king Uzziah died' (vi. 1), *i.e.* in 740/739 BC; his last appearance which can be dated with certainty was at the time of Sennacherib's campaign of 701 BC (or *c.* 688 BC, if we assume a second campaign of Sennacherib against Jerusalem). Tradition has it that he was sawn asunder in Manasseh's reign (see the late *Martyrdom of Isaiah*, chapter v); some see a reference to this in Heb. xi. 37, but the reference is dubious, and the tradition appears to have no sound historical basis. It is quite possible that Isaiah survived into Manasseh's reign; the absence of Manasseh's name from i. 1 could be due to the fact that Isaiah played no public part after Manasseh became king.

Isaiah was married; his wife is called 'the prophetess' (viii. 3), perhaps because she too prophesied. Two sons are mentioned, both of whom bear symbolic names (viii. 18)—Shear-jashub, 'Remnant will return' (vii. 3) and Maher-shalal-hash-baz, 'Hasten booty, speed spoil' (viii. 1–4).

Isaiah and Micah were contemporaries (*cf.* i. 1 with Mi. i. 1). Isaiah's activity was preceded by that of Amos and Hosea (Am. i. 1; Ho. i. 1). Amos and Hosea prophesied mainly against the northern tribes; Isaiah and Micah concentrated their prophecies mainly on Judah and Jerusalem (Is. i. 1).

In the first half of the 8th century both Israel, under Jeroboam II (*c.* 782–753 BC), and Judah, under Uzziah, enjoyed a time of great prosperity. This was due in large measure to the weakness of the kingdom of Aram and to Assyria's non-intervention in the west for considerable periods. Uzziah's reign may be described as the most prosperous time that Judah had known since the disruption of the monarchy after Solomon's death. Under Uzziah and Jotham prosperity and luxury abounded in Judah; we have this state of affairs reflected in Is. ii–iv. But with the accession to power of Tiglath-pileser III (745–727 BC), Assyria began once more to impose her yoke on the western lands. Pekah of Israel and Rezin of Damascus formed an anti-Assyrian coalition, and tried to compel Ahaz of Judah to join them. When Ahaz refused, they threatened to depose him and place a puppet of their own on his throne (734 BC). Isaiah's action at this time is recorded in chapter vii. Ahaz committed the sinful folly of asking the Assyrian king for aid; the result was that Judah became a satellite state of Assyria. In 732 BC the Assyrians captured Damascus and annexed the territory of Israel north of the Plain of Jezreel, leaving Hoshea to rule the remainder of the northern kingdom as their vassal. When he revolted, Shalmaneser V (727–722 BC) besieged Samaria, and his successor Sargon II (722–705 BC) captured it in his accession year. Even after that there were various independence movements directed against Assyrian domination. On these occasions Isaiah, who had withdrawn for a time into a smaller circle after his fruitless protest against Ahaz's foreign policy in 734 BC (viii. 16 ff.), raised his voice again to warn Judah against participating in such movements, and particularly against relying on Egyptian aid. According to xiv. 29 the Philistines in the year of the death of Ahaz sent a delegation to Jerusalem to arrange an anti-Assyrian alliance; on this occasion again Isaiah uttered a warning note (xiv. 29–32).

Under Hezekiah there were other movements of this kind, notably the revolt of Ashdod, which was crushed in 711 BC, when the Assyrians besieged and captured Ashdod (*cf.* Is. xx. 1). Judah and Egypt were implicated in this revolt. It is quite possible that Is. xviii should be dated about this time; an Ethiopian dynasty was ruling in Egypt then. After Sargon's death there were widespread risings against his successor Sennacherib (705–681 BC). Judah was one of the states which revolted, and this resulted in Sennacherib's expedition of 701 BC, during which he overran Judah and besieged Jerusalem. Various oracles in chapters xxviii–xxxi may date from the years 705–701 BC, including the warnings against leaning on Egypt in xxx. 1–7, xxxi. 1–3. Chapters xxxvi and xxxvii record Sennacherib's threat to Jerusalem, Jerusalem's liberation, and Isaiah's activity throughout this time of danger. Chapters xxxviii and xxxix, which probably relate to the same period, tell of Hezekiah's sickness and recovery, and the mission of Merodach-baladan (*q.v.*). N.H.R.

ISAIAH, BOOK OF.

I. OUTLINE OF CONTENTS

a. Prophecies relating to Isaiah's own time, i. 1–xxxv. 10

(i) *Introduction* (i. 1–31). Condemnation of a merely external form of worship, *etc.* Date uncertain.

(ii) *Prophecies from Isaiah's earliest period* (for the greater part) (ii. 1–v. 30). Prophecy of the coming kingdom of peace (ii. 2–5; *cf.* Mi. iv. 1 ff.). The day of the Lord which is to bring down everyone who is proud and exalted (ii. 6–22). The haughty women of Jerusalem ('Isaiah's fashion-journal') (iii. 16–iv. 1). The song of the vineyard (v. 1–7).

(iii) *Isaiah's inaugural vision* (vi. 1–13).

(iv) *The present world-empire and the coming kingdom of God* (vii. 1–xii. 6). Chapters vii. 1–ix. 7 originate chiefly from the time of the Syro-Ephraimite war. Rebuke of Ahaz and prophecy of Immanuel (vii. 1–25). Isaiah's temporary withdrawal from the public eye (viii. 11–22). The birth of the Messiah (ix. 1–7). The hand stretched out to smite Ephraim (probably one of Isaiah's earliest oracles) (ix. 8–x. 4). Assyria brought low by the Holy One of Israel (x. 5–34). The Messiah and the kingdom of God (xi. 1–xii. 6); especially here a sharp contrast is drawn between the violent world-empire and the peacefulness of the coming kingdom. Chapter xii contains a song of thanksgiving; it forms a conclusion to this section.

(v) *Mainly prophecies regarding foreign nations* (xiii. 1–xxiii. 18). Babylon (xiii. 1–xiv. 23) (incorporating the impressive taunt-song in xiv. 4–23). Assyria (xiv. 24–27). The Philistines (xiv. 28–32; see under ISAIAH above). Moab (xv. 1–xvi. 14). Aram and Ephraim (xvii. 1–14; probably not long before chapter vii). Ethiopia and Egypt (xviii. 1–xx. 6; xx, and probably xviii, are to be dated *c.* 715 BC, see under ISAIAH above; the date of xix is uncertain). Babylon (xxi. 1–10). Edom ('Watchman, what of the night?') (xxi. 11 f.). Arabia (xxi. 13–17). Jerusalem (xxii. 1–14). Shebna and Eliakim (xxii. 15–25). Phoenicia (xxiii. 1–18).

(vi) *The consummation: the 'Isaianic apocalypse'* (xxiv. 1–xxvii. 13). See below under IIIa (iv).

(vii) *Zion's sin, oppression, and deliverance; Assyria's downfall; Egypt's vain help* (xxviii. 1–xxxiii. 24). Several of the prophecies in these chapters are to be dated between 705 and 701 BC (see under ISAIAH above). The parable of the ploughman (xxviii. 23–29). The messianic kingdom (xxxii. 1–8).

(viii) *A twofold future* (xxxiv. 1–xxxv. 10). The judgment of Edom and the world (xxxiv. 1–17). Salvation for 'the ransomed of the Lord' (xxxv. 1–10).

b. Historical chapters, xxxvi. 1–xxxix. 8

Sennacherib's invasion (xxxvi. 1–xxxvii. 38). Hezekiah's sickness and recovery (xxxviii. 1–22). Mission of Merodach-baladan (xxxix. 1–8).

c. Prophecies which presuppose the Babylonian Exile, xl. 1–lv. 13

These chapters foretell Israel's liberation from exile and the restoration of Zion, and in doing so they proclaim the majesty of Yahweh. They may be divided as follows:

(i) *Introduction* (xl. 1–31). The substance of the following chapters is presented; it consists of four parts; verses 1, 2, verses 3–5, verses 6–11, verses 12–31.

(ii) *Prophecies in which those concerning Cyrus are conspicuous* (xli. 1–xlviii. 22). He is mentioned by name in xliv. 28, xlv. 1. *Cf.* xli. 1–16 (Cyrus's activity will make the nations tremble, but there is no need for Israel to fear), xli. 21–29 (Cyrus's activity will cause Zion to rejoice), xliii. 9–15 (Cyrus overthrows Babylon), xliv. 24–xlv. 13 (Cyrus's victory leads to the rebuilding of Zion), xlvi. 8–13 (amidst prophecies of Babylon's downfall), xlviii. 12–16. *Cf.* also the prophecies of Babylon's downfall, especially xlvi. 1–xlvii. 15. There is a marked contrast drawn between the 'daughter of Babylon' (chapter xlvii) and the 'daughter of Zion' (xlix. 14 ff., *etc.*). Throughout these chapters Israel is comforted in her distress, her deliverance from Babylon is promised (*cf.* xli. 8–20, xlii. 8–xliii. 8, xliii. 16–xliv. 5, xlviii *passim*), Yahweh's majesty is proclaimed, and the contrast between Him and the idols is emphasized (*cf.* xlii. 8–17, xliv. 6–20, xlv. 9–25 *passim*). In xlii. 1–7, the first of the 'Servant Songs', the Servant of the Lord is introduced.

(iii) *Chapters in which the restoration of Zion is prominent* (xlix. 1–liv. 17). *Cf.* xlix. 14–l. 3, li. 17–lii. 12, liv. We hear no more of the conquests of Cyrus or the ruin of Babylon; there is consequently less emphasis on the contrast between Yahweh and the idols. In xlix. 1–9a, l. 4–11, and lii. 13–liii. 12, the second, third, and fourth 'Servant Songs', there are further prophecies concerning the Servant of the Lord, his mission to Israel and the nations, his obedience and suffering, his death and vindication.

(iv) *Exhortation to accept these promises in faith* (lv. 1–13).

d. Various prophecies, lvi. 1–lxvi. 24

It is not easy to summarize the contents of these chapters. The prophecies which they contain are diverse in nature and may even refer to different times. In some places Israel appears to be in exile (lvii. 14, lviii. 12, lx. 10 ff., lxiii. 18, lxiv. 10 f.), in others the nation seems settled in Canaan (*e.g.* lvii. 3–7). Many of the ideas which are expressed in these chapters have already been expressed in the preceding sections of the book.

(i) *Law-abiding proselytes and even eunuchs have a share in God's salvation* (lvi. 1–8; see especially verse 7).

(ii) *Leaders and people alike are rebuked for their sins, particularly for idolatry* (lvi. 9–lvii. 13a). This section may refer to the reign of Manasseh.

(iii) *Comfort for the contrite* (lvii. 13b–21; see especially verse 15); an affinity can be traced here with chapters xl–lv.

(iv) *False and true religion* (lviii. 1–14). Special mention is made of fasting and sabbath-observance.

(v) *Deliverance is conditional upon repentance* (lix. 1–21). Rebuke of sins (verses 1–8); complaint and confession of sin (verses 9–15a); judgment and deliverance (verses 15b–20); Yahweh's covenant (verse 21).

(vi) *Zion's deliverance* (lx. 1–lxii. 12; note again the close affinity with chapters xl–lv). The glorious prospect of salvation for Zion involves blessing for the nations as well (lx. 1–3). The appearance of the messenger of joyful news in lxi. 1 ff. (*cf.* xl. 9, xli. 27, lii. 7) becomes the programme of Jesus' ministry in Lk. iv. 17 ff.

(vii) *Yahweh's vengeance against Edom* (lxiii. 1–6).

(viii) *Penitence and supplication.* God who wrought such wonderful deliverances for His people in the past is entreated to intervene on their behalf again (lxiii. 7–lxiv. 12).

(ix) *Rebels against God and obedient servants* (lxv. 1–25). Idolatry rebuked (verses 3 ff., 11); new heavens and a new earth promised (verse 17).

(x) *Chapter lxvi. 1–24.* Yahweh's repudiation of forbidden forms of sacrificial worship (verses 1–4), Zion glorified and sinners punished (verses 5–24).

II. ORIGIN, CONSTRUCTION, AUTHORSHIP

a. Isaiah's literary activity

We are given but little information about Isaiah's own literary activity. In viii. 1 only a short inscription is involved ('Maher-shalal-hashbaz'); viii. 16 should be understood in a figurative sense; xxx. 8 may relate to the writing down of the brief utterance of verse 7, 'Rahab that sitteth still' (RV), although it is possible that a more extensive passage was to be recorded. The reference to 'the book of the Lord' in xxxiv. 16 implies that the preceding prophecy of chapter xxxiv was written down. The 'I' style in chapters vi and viii tells in favour of the assumption that these chapters were written by Isaiah himself; it is noteworthy, however, that chapter vii speaks of him in the third person (*cf.* chapter xx).

It is very likely, indeed, that more prophecies were written by Isaiah himself than the above-mentioned passages indicate. In favour of this conclusion the high standard and unity of language and style may be taken into consideration. But if Isaiah himself had had a substantial part in the composition of his book, its structure would presumably have been more straightforward than is now the case.

Chapters xxxvi–xxxix are essentially parallel to 2 Ki. xviii. 13–xx. 19. In this connection it should be borne in mind that, according to 2 Ch. xxvi. 22, xxxii. 32, Isaiah also figured as an historical writer. The question whether Isaiah was the author of chapters xxxvi–xxxix cannot be answered with certainty.

b. Construction

The book of Isaiah is decidedly not an arbitrary string of disconnected prophecies. There is a certain chronological arrangement. Chapters ii–v consist to a large extent of prophecies from Isaiah's earliest activity. vii. 1–ix. 7 originate mostly from the period of the Syro-Ephraimite war (734 BC). Chapters xviii–xx take us to the period 715–711 BC, and various prophecies of chapters xxviii–xxxvii belong to the years between 705 and 701 BC. (See under ISAIAH above.) The greater part of chapters xl–lxvi consists of prophecies uttered from an exilic, or perhaps even post-exilic, standpoint.

There is also a certain arrangement according to subject-matter (see the outline of contents). In this regard an outstanding feature is the group of oracles concerning foreign nations in chapters xiii–xxiii; it should also be noted here that most of the prophecies in these chapters are introduced by the words 'The oracle (AV 'burden') concerning . . .' Chapters xl–lv also, to a considerable degree, form a unity. One further point: in xxxix.

6 ff. there is clearly a transition from chapters i–xxxix to chapters xl–lxvi.

On the other hand, chronological order has certainly not been followed throughout. For example, ix. 8–x. 4 contains what is perhaps one of Isaiah's oldest prophecies; chapter xvii may date from the period shortly before 734 BC, *i.e.* close in time to chapter vii; xxviii. 1–6 contains an early prophecy. It should also be noted that, while prophecies from an exilic standpoint occur chiefly in chapters xl ff., chapter xxxv also presupposes the period of the Exile; and we may even be forced to the conclusion that chapters lvi–lxvi set alongside one another prophecies whose respective standpoints are pre-exilic (*e.g.* lvi. 9–lvii. 13), exilic (*e.g.* lx–lxii), and post-exilic (*e.g.* chapter lviii).

Again, it is equally plain that arrangement according to subject-matter has not been carried through with entire consistency. As we have seen, chapters xiii–xxiii consist mainly of prophecies about foreign nations, but chapter xxii forms an exception, and elsewhere there are other prophecies against foreign nations (for example, the oracle against Assyria in x. 5–34 is similar to that in xiv. 24–27).

It should be noted, too, that there are superscriptions in i. 1, ii. 1, and xiii. 1; and further, the account of the vision in which Isaiah received his call to be a prophet does not come until chapter vi.

The situation is involved—more involved, indeed, than might be gathered from the considerations which have been briefly outlined above. It may be taken as certain that our book of Isaiah has been constructed on the basis of shorter collections. But in the end we can only say that the history of its composition can no longer be reconstructed. Scholars have made various attempts to reconstruct the stages of its composition, but have not reached convincing conclusions. Thus, some have supposed that chapters i–xii, xiii–xxiii, xxiv–xxvii, xxviii–xxxv originally formed separate collections. Admittedly these divisions, lying before us in their present arrangement, do form more or less self-contained units. The song of chapter xii or the promise of salvation in chapter xxxv would form an appropriate conclusion to a collection. But we should reckon with the possibility that this is due to the work of the latest redactor.

As for chapters xl–lv, they probably contain a collection of originally independent prophecies: it is hardly to be assumed that they formed a unity from the beginning. On the other hand, in these chapters the same subjects recur time and again. Their arrangement is by no means completely arbitrary; *i.e.* a certain chronological order can be observed (see outline of contents). Many critics are of the opinion that these chapters, in essence at least, come from one author.

c. Authorship

Many scholars nowadays deny great portions of the book to Isaiah—not only in the sense that he did not write them down, but in the sense that their subject-matter does not come from him at all. Even chapters i–xxxv are believed by some to contain much non-Isaianic material. Some scholars go farther than others, but there is a wide measure of agreement that Isaiah cannot be credited with chapters xiii. 1–xiv. 23, xxi, xxiv–xxvii, xxxiv, xxxv. In addition, critical scholars are practically unanimous in the view that chapters xl–lxvi do not come from Isaiah.

Chapters xl–lv are believed to be mainly the work of a prophet to whom the name Deutero-Isaiah ('Second Isaiah') has been given. It is held that his prophecies must be dated between the first victories of the Persian king, Cyrus (*c.* 550 BC), and Cyrus's conquest of Babylon, which was followed by his decree permitting the Jewish exiles to return to their own country (538 BC). Some defend the view that part of Deutero-Isaiah's prophecies should be assigned to the period after 538 BC. Babylon is mostly envisaged as this prophet's field of activity; others think of Palestine, Egypt, and other lands.

As for chapters lvi–lxvi, some scholars, with E. König, credit Deutero-Isaiah with them too, while others ascribe them to a separate author, called Trito-Isaiah ('Third Isaiah'), who is dated either *c.* 450 BC, in the time of Malachi (*e.g.* by B. Duhm), or *c.* 520 BC, in the time of Haggai and Zechariah (*e.g.* by E. Sellin and K. Elliger). Others, again, take the view that the prophecies of chapters lvi–lxvi do not all come from the same time; it has even been held that some come from the 8th century BC, some from the 2nd.

The following considerations are relevant to the Deutero-Isaiah question:

1. The unanimous testimony of tradition credits Isaiah with the authorship of the whole book. Chapters i–xxxix and xl–lxvi have come down to us as a unity; chapter xxxix. 6–8 may certainly be regarded as a planned transition from the first to the second part of the book. From Ecclus. xlviii. 24 f. it is plain that Jesus ben Sira in his time (*c.* 200 BC) considered Isaiah to be the author of chapters xl–lxvi as well as of chapters i–xxxix. The Qumran MSS of Isaiah indicate that, at the time when they were copied (2nd or 1st century BC) the book was regarded as a unity. It is true that the testimony of extra-biblical tradition is not decisive; and in the judgment of the present author it cannot be said that the Old Testament itself points unequivocally to Isaiah as author of the entire book. Even so, two things should be borne in mind.

First, Deutero-Isaiah is taken to be one of the greatest prophets, if not the greatest prophet, of Israel; it would be surprising indeed if every trace of this great prophet had been so thoroughly effaced from tradition that his very name is unknown to us. Secondly, the evidence of the New Testament naturally takes a special place in the testimony of tradition. The following passages from chapters xl–lxvi are introduced in the New Testament by some such words as 'that which was spoken by the prophet Isaiah': xl. 3

(in Mt. iii. 3), xlii. 1–4 (in Mt. xii. 17–21), liii. 1 (in Jn. xii. 38 and Rom. x. 16), liii. 4 (in Mt. viii. 17), lxv. 1 f. (in Rom. x. 20 f.). To this it may be added that those who deny chapters xl ff. to Isaiah usually deny him chapter xiii on similar grounds; but the superscription of this chapter ascribes it to 'Isaiah the son of Amoz'.

2. The weightiest argument for ascribing chapters xl ff. to Deutero-Isaiah is no doubt the fact that these chapters have as their background the period of the Babylonian Exile—more precisely, the closing years of the Exile, from 550 BC onwards. At the very outset it is stated that Israel 'hath received double for all her sins' (xl. 2). Babylon is the oppressing power (xlvi, xlvii), not Assyria, as we should expect in Isaiah's time. The Persian king, Cyrus (559–529 BC), is mentioned by name. While his conquest of Babylon is predicted in xliii. 14, xlviii. 14, *etc.*, it is suggested by xli. 1–7, 25, *etc.*, that he has already achieved his first successes.

It may be said in reply that the Spirit of prophecy can reveal the future to the prophets; and it is true that this fact has not always been taken sufficiently into account by adherents of the Deutero-Isaiah theory. But even those who are prepared to make full allowance for it find themselves faced with difficulties here. It is certainly inconceivable that Isaiah stood in the temple court, comforting his people in view of a calamity which was not to come upon them until more than a century had elapsed. We may indeed suppose that Isaiah communicated these prophecies to the circle of his disciples (*cf.* viii. 16) —or rather that he did not speak them but only committed them to writing. Even so, the question arises: if we credit Isaiah with these chapters, must we not assume that his inspiration took a very 'mechanical' form, bearing no relation to the concepts existing in the prophet's conscious mind? The following suggestion may help in some degree to meet these objections.

Isaiah wrote down these prophecies in Manasseh's reign (see ISAIAH above). He found it impossible to appear in public in those years (*cf.* 2 Ki. xxi. 16). Iniquity had reached such a pitch that Isaiah recognized that the divine judgment was bound to come (*cf.* 2 Ki. xxi. 10–15); indeed, before his mind's eye it had already come. Then the Spirit of prophecy showed him that this judgment in its turn would come to an end (see under III*a* (ii), 'Judgment and Salvation'). It can be said further that the judgment which Isaiah saw as already fulfilled before his mind's eye was 'delayed' by Manasseh's repentance (2 Ch. xxxiii. 12 ff.) and Josiah's reformation (2 Ki. xxii, xxiii). It is, besides, important to observe that, according to Is. xxxix. 5–7, Isaiah knew that a deportation to Babylon would take place.

And while it is true that these prophecies presuppose as their background the closing phase of the Babylonian Exile, and Cyrus is represented as having already entered upon the stage of history, yet in other respects the author expresses himself much less concretely on conditions during the Exile than might have been expected from someone who lived in the midst of it.

3. Attention has been drawn to the differences between chapters i–xxxix and xl–lxvi in matters of language, style, and conceptions. It may indeed be said that in i–xxxix the language is suggestive and full of illustrations, while in xl–lxvi it is often more verbose; that in xl–lxvi the cosmological aspect of the kingship of God is more prominent than in i–xxxix; that while i–xxxix speak of the Messiah-King, this figure is displaced in xl–lxvi by the suffering Servant of Yahweh. Yet these divergences do not make it necessary to abandon belief in the unity of the book. For over against these divergences there are striking points of similarity. As examples of these it may be pointed out, first, that as chapters i–xxxix do not describe only Messiah's glory (*cf.* xi. 1 with liii. 2), so chapters xl–lxvi do not describe only the Servant's suffering (*cf.* xlii. 1–7, liii. 11 f.); and secondly, that the divine appellation 'the Holy One of Israel' occurs twelve times in chapters i–xxxix, thirteen times in chapters xl–lxvi, and only five times in the rest of the Old Testament.

The preceding paragraphs are intended to give some idea of the lines along which the discussion of these problems proceeds and of the arguments which are adduced on either side. The conclusion is that we need not, and indeed should not, deny to Isaiah any share in the composition of chapters xl–lxvi. On the other hand, even those who desire to submit unconditionally to the testimony of Scripture may come to the conclusion that the book of Isaiah contains some parts which are not of Isaianic origin. This is perhaps the situation already in chapters i–xxxix. And especially with regard to chapters xl–lxvi there are reasons for accepting this suggestion; *cf.*, *e.g.*, xlviii. 6, lviii. In the opinion of the present writer it is acceptable to hold that chapters xl–lxvi contain an Isaianic core, upon which the prophet's disciples (men who felt themselves closely bound to him) later worked in the spirit of the original author. It is, however, impossible for us to assess how much belongs to the Isaianic core and how much to the later elaborations.

Two final remarks will close this section.

1. There is a prevalent trend of thought nowadays which lays great emphasis on the significance of oral tradition. According to this trend of thought, a prophet's utterances were handed down orally by the circle of his disciples; in this process they were repeatedly adapted to the changing circumstances of the time. If there is an element of truth in this view it should certainly be taken into account in any attempt to explain the origin of Is. xl–lxvi. It might lead to the conclusion that chapters xl–lxvi contain an Isaianic core but that the subsequent elaboration can no longer be ascertained.

2. It should be remembered that those who deny to Isaiah the whole of chapters xl–lxvi frequently assume that the author or authors of

these chapters belonged to the school of Isaiah. It is admitted that, alongside all the arguments for diversity of authorship, there is a close affinity between chapters i–xxxix and xl–lxvi. See, *e.g.*, what was said above about the divine appellation 'the Holy One of Israel'.

III. THE MESSAGE OF THE BOOK

From ancient times Isaiah has been considered the greatest of Old Testament prophets. He has been called 'the eagle among the prophets', 'the Evangelist of the Old Covenant', and the like. His book is not only lofty in style and conception, but rich in spiritual meaning.

a. Chapters i–xxxix

In endeavouring to outline the message of these chapters we may start with the divine appellation 'the Holy One of Israel' (which, as we have seen, is characteristic of Isaiah), and with the name of one of his sons, Shear-jashub, 'Remnant will return'.

That God was the Holy One was inscribed indelibly on Isaiah's heart as a result of his inaugural vision (vi. 3). As Amos has been called the prophet of righteousness and Hosea the prophet of lovingkindness, so Isaiah has been called the prophet of holiness (*cf.* i. 4, v. 16, 24, viii. 14, x. 17, 20, xii. 6, xvii. 7, xxix. 23, xxx. 11 f., xxxi. 1, xxxvii. 23, *etc.*). God is the Holy One; that means He is so highly exalted above His creatures as to be totally different from them, not only in His moral perfection (*cf.* vi. 5) but also in His power, His wrath, His love, His faithfulness, and all His virtues (*cf.* also xxix. 16, xxxi. 3). Yahweh's holiness is the very essence of His divine being, which causes men to tremble before Him as they worship Him.

This holy God has associated Himself in a special way with Israel (i. 2, v. 1 ff., *etc.*), and in a pre-eminent degree with the house of David (viii. 13, xi. 1, *etc.*). He dwells in the midst of Israel, on Mount Zion (viii. 18, xi. 9, *etc.*).

The fact that God is 'the Holy One of Israel' involves an abiding tension in His relation to His people. On the one hand, He fulminates in a violent way against Israel's sin; on the other hand, He does not break His covenant with Israel. Hence the assurance: 'Remnant will return'. This means first: judgment will come, only a remnant will be left. But it also means: at least a remnant will be left, a remnant will indeed return (*i.e.* to its homeland). In His wrath God remembers mercy. It is also possible to translate: 'Remnant returns to God, changes its mind'; its return and deliverance come along the path of conversion. This remnant-doctrine figures prominently in Isaiah's preaching, from the very first (vi. 13). And he may have seen the beginnings of the remnant in the circle of his disciples, among whom he withdrew himself from public life for a considerable time at an early stage in his ministry (viii. 16–18).

Some of the implications of the outlined teaching of Isaiah may now be elaborated.

(i) *God's requirements and Israel's sin.* The Holy One of Israel requires His people to sanctify Him (viii. 13) by putting their trust in Him alone, by keeping His commandments, by paying heed to the words of His prophets. Because Yahweh has entered into a covenant with Israel, Israel's sin is essentially apostasy (i. 2–4, xxx. 1–9, *etc.*). Instead of preserving due humility in the presence of the Holy One of Israel, they are haughty and frivolous (ii. 6 ff., iii. 8, v. 15 f., 19 ff., xxii. 1 ff., xxviii. 15, xxix. 14 ff., xxxii. 9 ff., *etc.*). Isaiah repeatedly insists that sin, in whatever sphere it may be committed, is first and foremost sin against God.

Isaiah denounces sinful worship (although this is not so prominent a feature of his preaching as of Hosea's); he inveighs against a ritual which confines itself to external matters (i. 10 ff., xxix. 13), against the offering of sacrifices on the high places (i. 29), against heathen worship (ii. 6–8, xvii. 7 f., xxx. 22, xxxi. 7, *etc.*; see also viii. 19).

Especially during the early years of his ministry he also spoke out sternly against sins in the social realm—oppression of the defenceless, immoderate luxury, drunkenness, *etc.* (*cf.*, *e.g.*, i. 15–17, 21–23, iii. 14 f., 16 ff., v. 7, 8, 11 ff., 14, 22 f., x. 1 f., xxviii. 7 ff., xxxii. 9 ff.). In this connection we may think of a possible influence of Amos.

In the political domain, Isaiah's governing demand is trust in the Holy One of Israel (vii. 9 ff., viii. 12 f., x. 20, xvii. 7, xxviii. 16, xxx. 15, *etc.*). What did this involve in practical politics? Isaiah never advocated defencelessness, but he uttered repeated warnings against joining in coalitions, especially with Egypt (xiv. 28–32, xviii, xx, xxx. 1–7, xxxi. 1–3; see ISAIAH above). This abstention from active participation in world-politics would, in the circumstances, also have been a requirement of statecraft (*cf.*, *e.g.*, xxxvi. 5 f.), but Isaiah's warnings should not be attributed to keen political vision, but to divine revelation (see also xxx. 1). Isaiah's warnings may sometimes have been heeded; we do not hear of any open conflict between Assyria and Judah during the years 714–711 BC (see ISAIAH above). But often people would not listen to him. Ahaz's attitude, for example, is made quite clear in chapter vii (*cf.* 2 Ki. xvi. 7 ff.); and as for the time of Hezekiah, see xxix. 15, xxx. 1 ff., xxxi. 1 ff., xxxvi. 4 ff. (*cf.* 2 Ki. xviii. 7).

(ii) *Judgment and salvation.* It is often objected that the preaching of judgment and salvation in Is. i–xxxix contains inherent contradictions. From this it is concluded that various parts of these chapters do not come from Isaiah, or else that Isaiah's views underwent a change; for example, a distinction is drawn between a pro- and an anti-Assyrian period in his ministry. But it has already been said that an inevitable tension is involved in the title 'the Holy One of Israel'. As the situation requires, this may mean that He protects Israel and Jerusalem, the temple city, the royal city; it may mean that He enters into judgment expressly against Israel and

Jerusalem. Therefore there is no need for surprise if Isaiah, in his preaching of judgment and salvation, does not always lay the emphasis in the same place (*cf.* xxviii. 23–29). The persistent emphasis in his preaching is what was revealed to him at the outset, in his inaugural vision (vi. 11–13). A thorough-going judgment is to come upon Judah and upon Jerusalem as well (iii. 1–iv. 1, v. 1–7, 8–24, xxxii. 9–14, *etc.*); in this connection the Assyrians are mentioned (v. 26–30, vii. 17 ff., viii. 5–8, *etc.*); but through and beyond this judgment, which is consequently sometimes portrayed as a purifying judgment (i. 24 ff., iv. 2 ff.), a remnant is saved, and for this remnant a triumphant future breaks (iv. 2 ff., x. 20 ff., *etc.*). But this is not all that should be mentioned here. This thorough-going judgment on Jerusalem does not fall immediately. Isaiah is allowed to prophesy that Pekah and Rezin's attack on Jerusalem will fail (vii. 1–viii. 4), that the Assyrians will overflow Judah and cause great distress to Jerusalem, but will in their turn be struck by divine judgment and not be permitted to capture Jerusalem (viii. 9 f., x. 5–34, xiv. 24–32, xviii, xxix. 1–8, xxxi. 4 ff., xxxvii. 6 f., 21–35). One statement does not contradict another. (It is to be noted too that before the reassuring prophecies of xxxvii. 6 f., 21–35, Sennacherib has dealt treacherously, xxx. 1 ff., *cf.* 2 Ki. xviii. 14 ff., and blasphemed the Holy One of Israel.) That Isaiah's prophecies on this subject are not inherently contradictory is also shown by their fulfilment. The Assyrians did cause much distress to Jerusalem in 701 BC, but were not able to capture it; later on a thorough-going judgment did fall on Jerusalem, at the hand of the Babylonians. Isaiah nowhere mentions *expressis verbis* the Assyrians as the executors of the thorough-going judgment on Jerusalem; in a later time he foretold that the Babylonians would come (xxxix. 5 ff.). Finally, some prophecies, like those of v. 14 ff., have their complete fulfilment only in the eschatological judgment (see below under sub-section (iv)).

The prophet's summons to repentance should also be mentioned in this connection. In a sense his announcement of judgment and salvation is conditional; if they harden their hearts, judgment will follow; if they repent, forgiveness and salvation will be theirs (i. 16 ff., xxx. 15 ff., *etc.*). But this announcement is conditional only in a sense; for as early as Isaiah's inaugural vision it was revealed to him that Yahweh was determined to execute judgment on Judah; the broad masses of the people were sunk so deep in their sins that Isaiah's preaching would have no effect save to harden their hearts still more (vi. 9 ff.). Equally, there is no uncertainty about the coming salvation. And, just as Isaiah's preaching, by hardening his hearers' hearts, contributed to Israel's ripening for judgment, so too it contributed to the postponement of the judgment, the rescue of Jerusalem, and the formation of the remnant on which Yahweh purposed to bestow His salvation.

The salvation proclaimed by Isaiah includes the deliverance of Jerusalem from great distress, but this deliverance is not the full salvation. The promised salvation in its fullest sense is based on the remission of sins (*cf.* i. 18, vi. 5 f., *etc.*), and it consists further in a renewal of the heart (*cf.*, *e.g.*, xxxii. 15 ff.), a life lived in accordance with God's commandments, a life crowned with prosperity and glory. In this salvation Zion would take a central place, but the other nations would participate in it too (*cf.* i. 19, 26 f., ii. 2–5, iv. 2–6, xxxiii. 13 ff.). Special mention should also be made here of the messianic prophecies, which are of paramount importance (*cf.* ix. 1–7, xi. 1–10, where there is a marked contrast with the Assyrian Empire described in x. 5 ff., *cf.* also xvi. 5, xxviii. 16 f., xxxii. 1 ff., xxxiii. 17; the Immanuel prophecy of vii. 14 is also messianic, as its quotation in Mt. i. 22 f. shows, but indirectly so, as verse 16 indicates). In these prophecies Isaiah naturally employs Old Testament terms—the Messiah is portrayed as King of Israel, and the idea is raised that he will liberate his people from the Assyrians (ix. 3, *cf.* xi. 1 ff., with the preceding oracle)—but by means of these terms he gives a glorious portrayal of the coming salvation, which Christians recognize as having been inaugurated with the first advent of Christ, and as coming to its complete fulfilment with His second advent (*cf.* xi. 9, *etc.*).

(iii) *The Holy One of Israel and the nations.* That Yahweh is the only true God is stated even more emphatically in chapters xl ff. than in i–xxxix, but it is stressed plainly enough in the first part of the book (*cf.* ii. 8, xxx. 22, xxxvii. 16, *etc.*). Yahweh is Lord of the whole earth (vi. 3). All that happens is His doing, the execution of His decree (v. 12, 19, xiv. 24, 26, xxxvii. 26, *etc.*). He directs the history of Israel and of the other nations too. Assyria is the rod of His anger (x. 5 ff., *cf.* v. 26, vii. 17 ff., viii. 7 f., *etc.*); but because of the Assyrians' pursuit of their own ambitions (x. 7 ff.), their haughtiness, their violence, their cruelty, their faithlessness, and their blasphemy of Yahweh, they too will have to undergo His judgment (viii. 9 f., x. 5 ff., xiv. 24–27, xviii. 4–6, xxix. 1–8, xxx. 27–33, xxxi. 8 f., xxxiii. 1 ff., xxxvi, xxxvii, *etc.*). See further the prophecies concerning Babylon (xiii, xiv, xxi. 1–10), Moab (xv, xvi, *cf.* also xxv. 10 ff.), Ethiopia and Egypt (xviii–xx), Edom (xxi. 11 f., xxxiv), and other nations. We should observe, too, that Isaiah predicts not only disaster but also blessing for the nations—*e.g.* in the great prophecy of xix. 18–25, with its promise that Egypt, Assyria, and Israel will be joint witnesses for Yahweh (*cf.* xvi. 1 ff., xviii. 7, xxiii. 15–18, and also ii. 2–5, xi. 10, *etc.*).

(iv) *Chapters xxiv–xxvii.* These chapters, which form an epilogue to chapters xiii–xxiii, call for a special mention, because of their eloquent portrayal of world judgment (xxiv) and the great salvation which God will accomplish (all nations will have a share in this salvation: 'He will swallow up death in victory'; *cf.* xxv. 6 ff.) and because of their reference to the resurrection of the just (xxvi. 19).

b. Chapters xl–lv

Jerusalem lies in ruins, Israel is in exile in Babylonia, and the Exile has lasted a long time. The people of Israel are in great distress (xlii. 22, li. 18 ff.), Yahweh's anger lies heavily upon them because of their sins (xl. 2, xlii. 24 f., li. 17, *etc.*); they think that He has forgotten them (xl. 27, xlix. 14). Some of them have come to regard the place of their exile as their homeland (lv. 2). But the prophet promises that Yahweh is about to liberate His people, and he urges his people to believe this promise.

(i) *The Holy One of Israel* (xli. 14, 16, 20, xliii. 3, 14 f., xlv. 11, xlvii. 4, xlviii. 17, xlix. 7, lv. 5) *is able to help.* In view of what is said above, it is not surprising that nowhere in the Old Testament is it asserted so emphatically as in these chapters that Yahweh is the one true God, that He alone can help (*cf.* xli. 1 ff., 21 ff., xliii. 10 f., xliv. 6, 8, xlv. 5, 14, 18, 21 f., xlvi. 9, *etc.*). Trust in other gods is vain, image-worship is sinful folly (xl. 18 ff., xli. 7, 29, xlii. 8, 17, xliv. 6–20, 25, xlv. 20, xlvi. 1 ff., xlvii. 9 ff.). He far transcends all His creatures; He has created all things (this has more stress in chapters xl–lv than in chapters i–xxxix) and directs the course of all things (*cf.* xl. 12–26, which forms the introduction to verses 27–31; xli. 4, xliii. 13, xliv. 7, xlviii. 13, *etc.*). He is the eternal God (xl. 28, xli. 4, xliii. 10, xliv. 6, xlviii. 12); He acts in accordance with His own good pleasure (xlv. 9 ff.), and His decree is certain of accomplishment (xliv. 28, xlvi. 10, *etc.*). His word, spoken by the mouth of His prophets, will not return to Him 'void'—without fulfilling its mission (xl. 6–8, lv. 10 f.). Even a world-conqueror such as Cyrus is but a tool in His hand for the performance of His purpose (xli. 1 ff., 21–29, xliii. 9–15, xliv. 24–xlv. 13, xlvi. 8–13, xlviii. 12–16).

(ii) *The Holy One of Israel is willing to help.* Israel has not deserved His help; she has shown herself unworthy of it (xliii. 22 ff., *etc.*). But Israel is His people (xl. 1, *etc.*; *cf.*, *e.g.*, xliii. 15, xliv. 2), and His name, His reputation, is involved in Israel's deliverance (xlviii. 1–11, *etc.*). His relation to Israel, to Zion, is compared to the marriage bond (l. 1, liv. 5 ff.). He has chosen Israel out of all the nations (xli. 8 f., xlviii. 10, *etc.*) and Israel is His servant—a title which implies both a privilege (xli. 8 f., *etc.*) and a mission (xliii. 10, *etc.*). His love is unchangeably set upon Israel, upon Zion (xl. 11, xliii. 3 f., xlvi. 3 f., xlix. 15 ff., *etc.*), and His righteousness is the guarantee of her liberation (*e.g.* xli. 10, xlv. 24).

(iii) *The Holy One of Israel will certainly help.* The coming salvation is painted in bright colours. The basis of this salvation, and at the same time its very essence, consists in His turning away His anger, His remission of Israel's sin (xl. 2, xliii. 25, xliv. 22, li. 21 ff., *etc.*). He uses Cyrus as His instrument to inaugurate His salvation; Cyrus is described in quite remarkable terms as Yahweh's 'anointed' (xlv. 1), and the man whom He 'loves' (xlviii. 14, *etc.*). Babylon is overthrown by him (xlvi, xlvii, *cf.* xliii. 14, xlviii. 14); Israel is set free, her exiled children are gathered from all the lands of their dispersion, and return to Canaan (xliii. 1–8, 18–21, xlviii. 20 f., xlix. 24–26, lii. 11 f., *etc.*). Yahweh returns to Zion (xl. 9–11, lii. 7 f.), Zion is once again inhabited (xlix. 17–23, liv. 1 ff.), rebuilt (xliv. 28, xlv. 13, liv. 11 f.), and protected (liv. 14–17).

This work of deliverance is described as a new creation (*i.e.* xli. 20, xlv. 8, *cf.* xlv. 18); the miracles which marked the Exodus from Egypt are now to be repeated on a grander scale (xliii. 16 ff., xlviii. 21, li. 9 f., *etc.*). The prophet sees the whole future as a unity. Israel's liberation from exile is viewed as the beginning of the great era of salvation, in which all things will be made new. Here it can be mentioned that Israel's homeward progress is attended by a series of nature-miracles (xli. 17 ff., xliii. 18–21, xlviii. 21, xlix. 9b f., lv. 12 f., *cf.* liv. 13). And it is repeatedly emphasized that the grand aim of all this is the praise and glory of God (xli. 20, xliii. 21, xliv. 23, xlviii. 9–11, *etc.*).

The prophet bends all his energies to persuade the people to accept and believe this assurance of blessing; see especially the closing chapter, lv. He tries to convince them by pointing to Yahweh's majesty in nature and history. He propounds pointed questions, and challenges them to enter into debate (*cf.*, *e.g.*, xl. 12–31, xlix. 14 ff.). He also challenges the Gentile nations and their gods: can *these* gods do what the God of Israel does? It is the God of Israel who has called Cyrus into being and raised him up, in order that he may be the instrument to set Israel free. The God of Israel is therefore the only One who can foretell the result of Cyrus's actions. As certainly as Yahweh made the 'former things' come to pass—that is to say, as certainly as He fulfilled what He foretold in earlier days—so certainly will He bring the 'new things' to pass by the fulfilment of the promises which He now makes through His prophet (xli. 1 ff., 21–29, xliii. 9–15, xliv. 6–xlv. 25, xlvi. 8–13, xlviii. 12–16, *cf.* xlii. 9, xlviii. 1–11). With all this the prophet does not furnish proofs in the strict sense of the word, but he makes a strong appeal to mind, heart, and conscience.

All this underlines the outspoken universalism of these chapters. Yahweh, the Creator of the universe, directs world-events, including the victorious career of Cyrus. He rebukes the nations, particularly Babylon, because of their hostility to Israel and also because of their idolatry (xli. 11–16, xlii. 13, 17, xlvi, xlvii). The goal to which He is directing the course of the world is summed up in the words, 'unto me every knee shall bow, every tongue shall swear' (xlv. 23); in this serving of Yahweh lies also the salvation of the nations of the earth; *cf.*, *e.g.*, xlii. 10–12, xlv. 6, 22–24, li. 4 f.

(iv) On the 'Servant Songs' (xlii. 1–7, xlix. 1–9a, l. 4–11, lii. 13–liii. 12), see SERVANT OF THE LORD.

c. Chapters lvi–lxvi

The following features are specially noteworthy in these concluding chapters:

1. Yahweh is presented as the living God. He is fearful in His anger (lix. 16 ff., lxiii. 1–6), but He bends down in kindness to His people, He shows them mercy and restores their comfort, He delights in Zion (lvii. 15 ff., lx. 10, lxi. 1 ff., lxii. 4 f., lxiii. 7, 15, lxv. 1 f., 8, 19, lxvi. 2, 13). That He is no inflexible or inexorable power is movingly shown in the review of His dealings with Israel in earlier days (lxiii. 8 ff.).

2. A sharp contrast is drawn between those in Israel who love God and those who disobey Him (*e.g.* lvii. 1, lxv. 13 ff., lxvi. 5, *cf.* lxv. 8).

3. It is frequently said, but without justification, that in some parts at least of this section of the book a legalist and nationalist spirit is manifested. True, it is clearly laid down that it is necessary to practise righteousness if one is to share in the coming salvation, and occasionally the importance of keeping the sabbath is stressed (*cf.*, *e.g.*, lvi. 1–8). But this is not intended to inculcate a spirit of ceremonialism and legalism; on the contrary, this very spirit is roundly condemned (*cf.* lviii, lxvi. 1, 5), and an attitude of humility is repeatedly commended (*cf.*, *e.g.*, lvii. 15, lxi. 2 f., lxvi. 2). As to the glorifying of Zion (*cf.*, *e.g.*, lx. 4 ff., lxi. 5 ff., lxvi. 20), this is no mere outburst of nationalist feeling. Zion is not only the capital of Judah but the dwelling-place of God; and the Gentiles who turn to Him participate in His salvation (*e.g.* lvi. 1–8, lx. 3).

BIBLIOGRAPHY. J. Skinner, *Isaiah*, 2 vols., *Cambridge Bible*, 1896; G. B. Gray, *Isaiah i–xxvii*, *ICC*, 1912; G. A. Smith, *The Book of Isaiah*[2], 2 vols., 1927; C. Boutflower, *The Book of Isaiah*, chapters i–xxxix, 1930; E. J. Kissane, *The Book of Isaiah*, 2 vols., 1941, 1943; S. Smith, *Isaiah xl–lv*, Schweich Lectures, 1944; I. W. Slotki, *Isaiah*, *Soncino Bible*, 1949; O. T. Allis, *The Unity of Isaiah*, 1950; U. E. Simon, *A Theology of Salvation*, 1953; E. J. Young, *Studies in Isaiah*, 1955; R. B. Y. Scott, G. D. Kilpatrick, J. Muilenburg, H. S. Coffin, 'Isaiah', *IB*, V, 1956.

N.H.R.

ISCARIOT. See JUDAS.

ISHBOSHETH. The name was originally Eshbaal, *cf.* 1 Ch. viii. 33, ix. 39, so Aq., Symm., Theod., *Eisbaal*; Old Latin *Isbalem*; LXX *Asabal* (elsewhere LXX has *Iebosthe*, but in 2 Sa. iii, iv, *Memphibosthe* by confusion with Mephibosheth), altered by later scribes to avoid an apparently pagan name (see BAAL). A son of Saul, the Ishui of 1 Sa. xiv. 49 (a corruption of Ishiah, *i.e.* Ishbaal). He was made king of Israel at Mahanaim (*q.v.*), out of reach of the Philistines, by Abner, his father's commander. As David's power grew, Abner began an intrigue with him but was murdered. Ishbosheth's supporters lost heart, and two of his cavalry officers, Rechab and Baanah, assassinated him during his midday rest (2 Sa. ii–iv). The LXX account of this crime is more explicit than the *MT* (2 Sa. iv. 6, *cf.* AV with RVmg or RSV), which may be emended to agree with the Greek. The death of Ishbosheth enabled David to gain control of all Israel from the house of Saul.

A.R.M.

ISHI (*'îšî*, 'my husband'). In Ho. ii. 16 the name which the Israelites were to use for God, to supersede 'Baali' with its pagan associations.

ISHMAEL (*yišmā'ē'l*, 'God heareth'). **1.** The son of Abraham by Hagar the Egyptian handmaid of Sarah. When Sarah realized that she was barren, she gave her handmaid to Abraham to conceive seed for her (Gn. xvi. 2). An example of this ancient custom has been discovered in the Nuzi tablets (*ANET*, p. 220). After conceiving by Abraham, Hagar began to despise Sarah, who then drove her out of the home with Abraham's reluctant consent. On her way to Egypt she was met by the angel of Yahweh, who told her to return and submit to Sarah. He also gave her the promise of a multiplied seed through her son Ishmael, who would be 'as a wild ass among men' (xvi. 12, RV; *cf.* Jb. xxxix. 5–8). Ishmael was born when Abraham was eighty-six, eleven years after his arrival in Canaan (xvi. 15, 16, *cf.* xii. 4). Thirteen years later, both Ishmael and his father were circumcised in obedience to God's command (xvii. 25, 26). But on that same day, God had also promised Abraham a son by Sarah. The fact that he had long since centred his hopes on Ishmael caused him to cry out, 'Oh that Ishmael might live before thee!' (xvii. 18). God then assured him that Ishmael would beget twelve princes and ultimately a great nation (xvii. 20, *cf.* xvi. 10, xxv. 13–16). When Ishmael was about sixteen, a great celebration was held at the weaning of the child Isaac (xxi. 8). Ishmael gave vent to his jealousy of 'the child of promise' (Rom. ix. 7–9) by 'mocking' him. The apostle Paul employs the verb 'persecuted' (*ediōke*) to describe this act (Gal. iv. 29) and builds upon it an extended allegory of the opposition of legalistic religionists to those 'born after the Spirit' (Gal. iv. 21–31). Sarah insisted that both Ishmael and Hagar be expelled from the home, and Abraham consented only after the Lord revealed to him that 'in Isaac shall thy seed be called' (Gn. xxi. 12). Hagar and her son nearly perished from thirst in the desert of Beersheba, until the angel of Yahweh pointed her to a well of water in response to Ishmael's cry. He grew to be an archer, married an Egyptian, and begat twelve princes (xxv. 12–16). Esau married one of his daughters (xxviii. 9, xxxvi. 3, 10). He joined Isaac in the burial of their father and died at the age of 137 (xxv. 9, 17).

2. A descendant of Saul and Jonathan, and the son of Azel (1 Ch. viii. 38, *cf.* ix. 44). **3.** A man of Judah, father of the Zebadiah who was a high official under King Jehoshaphat (2 Ch. xix. 11). **4.** The son of Jehohanan, and a captain of hundreds who took part in the conspiracy against Athaliah (2 Ch. xxiii. 1). **5.** A son of Pashur the priest. He was one of those whom Ezra compelled to put away their foreign wives (Ezr. x. 22).

6. The son of Nethaniah, of the seed royal of Judah, who murdered Gedaliah two months after the destruction of Jerusalem in 587 BC. When Gedaliah was appointed by Nebuchadrezzar to be the governor of Judah, many Jews gathered themselves to him at Mizpah for security. Among these, however, was Ishmael, who was jealous of Gedaliah and permitted himself to be hired by Baalis the king of Ammon to plot the governor's death. In spite of Johanan's warnings, Gedaliah trusted Ishmael and invited him and ten of his men to a banquet. They used the occasion to murder Gedaliah and all the others in Mizpah. Two days later they killed a group of Jewish pilgrims and departed for Ammon with many hostages, including Jeremiah and the king's daughters. They were pursued by Johanan and other captains and were overtaken at Gibeon. The hostages were rescued, but Ishmael and eight of his men escaped to Ammon (2 Ki. xxv. 25; Je. xl. 7–xli. 18).

BIBLIOGRAPHY. H. C. Leupold, *Exposition of Genesis*, 1942; C. F. Keil, *Biblical Commentary on the Old Testament*, I, *The Pentateuch*, 1949.

J.C.W.

ISLAND, ISLE (Heb. *'î*, pl. *'iyyîm*; Gk. *nēsos, nēsion*). Etymologically, the Heb. term is frequently supposed to mean 'habitable land', through a cognate Arab. word, but 'coastlands' is a better translation. The general Old Testament usage is to denote the islands and coastlands of the Mediterranean. The idea of distance is also included, *e.g.* Is. lxvi. 19; Je. xxxi. 10. Occasionally it appears to have the strict meaning, *e.g.* 'Kittim' in Je. ii. 10 (probably Cyprus), 'Caphtor' in Je. xlvii. 4 (see RV: probably Crete). Isaiah's usage is interesting. In xlii. 15 it denotes 'dry land' as opposed to water. In xl. 15 it is parallel to 'nations', in xli. 1, xlix. 1 to 'peoples', and in xli. 5 to 'the ends of the earth'.

New Testament usage is unambiguous. Several islands are named, *e.g.* Cyprus (Acts iv. 36, xiii. 4), Crete and Cauda (Acts xxvii), Melita (Acts xxviii. 1), and Patmos (Rev. i. 9). J.G.G.N.

ISRAEL (Heb. *yiśrā'ēl*, 'God strives'). **1.** The new name given to Jacob after his night of wrestling at Penuel: 'Your name,' said his supernatural antagonist, 'shall no more be called Jacob, but Israel, for you have striven [*śārîṯā*, from *śārâ*, 'strive'] with God and with men, and have prevailed' (Gn. xxxii. 28, RSV). With this account, assigned to J in the four-document hypothesis, *cf.* Ho. xii. 3 f., 'in his manhood he [Jacob] strove [*śārâ*] with God. He strove [*wayyāśar*, from the same verb] with the angel and prevailed' (RSV). The re-naming is confirmed at Bethel in Gn. xxxv. 10 (assigned to P), where God Almighty appears to Jacob and says: 'Your name is Jacob; no longer shall your name be called Jacob, but Israel shall be your name.' 'So,' adds the narrator, 'his name was called Israel' (RSV). Thenceforward Israel appears throughout the Old Testament as an occasional synonym for Jacob; it is used most frequently when the Patriarch's descendants are called 'the sons (or "children") of Israel' (Heb. *b^e^nê yiśrā'ēl*).

2. The nation which traced its ancestry back to the twelve sons of Jacob, referred to variously as 'Israel' (Gn. xxxiv. 7, *etc.*), 'the children of Israel' (Gn. xxxii. 32, *etc.*), 'the (twelve) tribes of Israel' (Gn. xlix. 16, 28, *etc.*).

The earliest reference to the nation of Israel in a non-Israelite record appears in an inscription of Merenptah, king of Egypt, *c.* 1230 BC, 'Israel is desolate; it has no seed left' (*DOTT*, p. 139). The next non-Israelite references come in inscriptions of Shalmaneser III of Assyria, *c.* 853 BC, mentioning 'Ahab the Israelite' (*DOTT*, p. 47), and of Mesha of Moab, whose victory-inscription (*c.* 830 BC) makes repeated mention of Israel, including the boast, 'Israel perished utterly for ever' (*DOTT*, pp. 196 f.; see MOABITE STONE. For illustrations see *IBA*, figs. 40, 48, 50, 51.).

I. ISRAEL'S BEGINNINGS

Merenptah's reference practically coincides with the beginning of Israel's national history, for it is the Exodus from Egypt, which took place in his reign or his father's, that marks Israel's birth as a nation. Some generations previously their ancestors, members of a pastoral clan, went down from Canaan to Egypt in time of famine and settled in the Wadi Tumilat. The early kings of Dynasty XIX drafted them in large numbers into forced labour gangs for the building of fortified cities on Egypt's NE frontier. In these circumstances they might have been completely assimilated to their fellow-serfs had not their ancestral faith been reawakened by Moses (*q.v.*), who came to them in the name of the God of their fathers and led them out of Egypt amid a series of phenomena in which he taught them to recognize the power of that God, put forth for their deliverance.

Under Moses' leadership they trekked eastward by 'the way of the wilderness of the Yam Suph' until they reached the place where the God of their fathers had previously revealed Himself to Moses by His covenant-name Yahweh and commissioned him to bring them out of Egypt. There, at the foot of Mt. Sinai, they were brought into special covenant-relationship with Yahweh. He had already shown Himself to be their God by rescuing them from bondage in Egypt; they now undertook to be His people. This undertaking involved their obedience to the 'Ten Words' in which Yahweh made His will known to them. They were to worship Him alone; they were not to represent Him by means of any image; they were to treat His name with due reverence; they were to reserve every seventh day for Him; and in thought, word, and deed they were to behave one towards another in a manner befitting the covenant which bound them together. They were to be a people set apart for

Yahweh, and were therefore to have something of His righteousness, mercy, and truth reproduced in their lives.

This attitude we may call practical monotheism. Whether the gods of neighbouring peoples had any sort of existence or not was a question about which neither Moses nor his followers were likely to trouble their minds; their business was to acknowledge Yahweh as supreme and sole God.

Moses was not only Israel's first and greatest legislator; in his own person he combined the functions of prophet, priest, and king. He judged their lawsuits and taught them the principles of religious duty; he led them from Egypt to the Jordan, and when he died, a generation after the Exodus, he left behind him no undisciplined body of slave-labourers, such as had followed him out of Egypt, but a formidable host ready to invade Canaan as conquerors and settlers.

This host, even before its settlement in Canaan, was organized as an amphictyony of twelve tribes, united in part by a common ancestry but even more so by common participation in the covenant with Yahweh. The visible token of their covenant unity was the sacred ark, housed in a tent-shrine which was located in the centre of their encampment when they were stationary but which preceded them on the march or in battle. They formed close alliances with other nomad groups such as the Kenites (to whom Moses was related by marriage), the Kenizzites and the Jerahmeelites, who in due course appear to have been incorporated into the tribe of Judah. It was probably a breach of alliance on the part of another nomad group, the Amalekites, that was responsible for the bitter feud which Israel pursued against them from generation to generation. Alliance with such pastoral communities was very different from alliance with the settled agricultural population of Canaan, with its fertility cults so inimical to pure Yahweh-worship. Their covenant with Yahweh strictly prohibited the Israelites from making common cause with the Canaanites.

The principal centre of the tribes of Israel in their wilderness period was Kadesh-barnea, evidently (from its name) a sanctuary and also (from its alternative name En-mishpat) a place where causes were heard and judgment pronounced. When they left Kadesh-barnea some of them infiltrated northwards into the central Negeb, but the main body advanced south and east of the Dead Sea, skirting the territories of their Edomite, Ammonite, and Moabite kinsfolk, who had very recently organized themselves as settled kingdoms. Farther north in Transjordan lay the Amorite kingdoms of Sihon and Og, which they entered as hostile invaders. The resisting forces of Sihon and Og were crushed, and their territories were occupied—these are the territories later known as Reuben, Gad, and eastern Manasseh. Part at least of the Israelite community thus settled down to an agricultural way of life even before the crossing of the Jordan.

II. THE SETTLEMENT IN CANAAN

The crossing of the Jordan was followed quickly by the capture and destruction of the fortress of Jericho (*q.v.*). From Jericho they pressed into the heart of the land, taking one fortress after another. Egypt was no longer in a position to send help to her former Canaanite vassals; only along the western coastal road did she now exercise some control, as far north as the pass of Megiddo, and even in that region the Philistine settlement (*c.* 1190 BC) was soon to present a barrier to the extension of Egyptian power.

A coalition of five military governors of Canaanite fortresses attempted to prevent the Israelites from turning south from the central hill-country, where Gibeon and the associated cities of the Hivite tetrapolis had submitted to them as subject-allies. The coalition was completely defeated in the pass of Beth-horon and the road to the south lay open to the invaders. Although the chariot-forces of Canaanite citadels prevented them from operating in more level country, they soon dominated and occupied the central and southern highlands, and also the Galilaean uplands, north of the Plain of Jezreel.

The tribes which settled in the north were cut off from their fellows in central Canaan by a chain of Canaanite fortifications in the Plain of Jezreel, stretching from the Mediterranean to the Jordan. Judah, in the south, was even more effectively cut off from the central tribes by the stronghold of Jerusalem, which remained a Canaanite enclave for two hundred years.

On one notable occasion the northern and central tribes joined forces in an uprising against the military governors of the Plain of Jezreel, who were steadily reducing them to serfdom. Their united rising was crowned with success at the battle of Kishon (*c.* 1125 BC), when a sudden storm flooded the watercourse and put the Canaanite chariotry out of action, so that the light-armed Israelites easily routed them. But even on this occasion, while the call to action went out to all the northern and central tribes, and to those in Transjordan, Judah appears to have received no summons, being too completely cut off from the other tribes.

On an occasion like this, when the tribes of Israel remembered their covenant-bond, their united strength enabled them to resist their enemies. But such united action was rare. The recession of danger was regularly followed by a period of assimilation to Canaanite ways. This assimilation involved intermarriage and the imitation of Canaanite fertility rites, so that Yahweh was thought of rather in terms of Baal, the fructifying rain-god, than as the God of their fathers who had redeemed them from Egypt to be His peculiar people. The covenant-bond was thus weakened, and they became an easy prey to their enemies. Not only did Canaanite city-states try to reduce them to servitude; from time to time they suffered incursions from beyond Jordan, by their own kinsmen the

Moabites and Ammonites, and much more disastrously at the hands of raiding bedouin. The leaders who rallied them in such periods of distress were the charismatic 'judges' after whom this whole settlement period is commonly named; these men not only led them forward to victory against their enemies but back to loyalty to Yahweh.

The greatest and most recalcitrant menace to Israelite independence, however, came from the west. Not long after the Israelites crossed the Jordan, bands of sea-rovers from the Aegean islands and coastlands settled on the western seaboard of Canaan and organized themselves in the five city-states of Ashdod, Ashkelon, Ekron, Gaza, and Gath, each of which was governed by a *seren*—one of the 'five lords of the Philistines'. These Philistines (*q.v.*) intermarried with the Canaanites and soon became Canaanite in language and religion, but they retained the political and military traditions of their homelands. Once they had established themselves in their pentapolis they began to extend control over other parts of Canaan, including those parts occupied by the Israelites. Militarily the Israelites were no match for them. The Philistines had mastered the art of iron-working, and kept it as a monopoly in their own hands. When the Israelites began to use iron implements in their agriculture the Philistines insisted that they must come to Philistine smiths to have them sharpened. This was a means of ensuring that the Israelites would not be able to forge iron implements of war with which they might rise against their overlords.

At last the Philistines extended their domination over the Plain of Jezreel as far as the Jordan. While their suzerainty did not menace Israelite existence, it did menace Israelite national identity. The amphictyonic shrine in those days was established at Shiloh (*q.v.*), in the territory of Ephraim, where the sacred ark was tended by a priesthood tracing its lineage back to Aaron, the brother of Moses. This priesthood took a leading part in an inter-tribal revolt against the Philistines which was an utter failure. The ark was captured, Shiloh and the sanctuary were destroyed, and the central priesthood was practically wiped out (*c.* 1050 BC). All the visible bonds which united the tribes of Israel had disappeared, and Israel's national identity seemed likely to disappear with them.

That it did not disappear, but rather became more vigorous, was due to the character and enterprise of Samuel (*q.v.*), the greatest of Israel's charismatic leaders between Moses and David. Samuel, like Moses, combined the functions of prophet, priest, and judge; and in his own person he provided a rallying-centre for the national life. Under his guidance Israel returned to its covenant loyalty, and with the return of religious devotion came a resurgence of national spirit; after some years the Israelites were able to defeat the Philistines on the very battlefield where they had been so shamefully routed.

As Samuel grew old, the question of the succession became acute. There arose a widespread demand for a king, and at last Samuel consented to this demand and anointed the Benjamite Saul (*q.v.*) to reign over them. Saul's reign began auspiciously with a prompt retort to a hostile show of force by the Ammonites, and this was followed by successful action against the Philistines in the central highlands. So long as Saul accepted Samuel's direction in the religious sphere all went well, but Saul's fortunes began to decline when a breach came about between them. He met his death in battle against the Philistines at Mt. Gilboa, in a bold but vain attempt to bring the northern tribes, beyond the Plain of Jezreel, into the unity of Israel. The Philistine grip on Israel was now firmer than ever (*c.* 1010 BC).

III. DAVID AND SOLOMON

The man who enabled Israel to throw off the Philistine yoke was David (*q.v.*), a member of the tribe of Judah, at one time a military commander under Saul and later a mercenary warrior with the Philistines. On Saul's death he was immediately acclaimed as king of Judah, and two years later the tribes of Israel as a whole also invited him to be their king. In a series of brilliant military actions he inflicted decisive defeats on the Philistines, who thereafter had to live as David's vassals. The capture of Jerusalem by David in the seventh year of his reign provided his kingdom with a strong and strategically situated capital and also with a new religious centre. The ark was brought back from exile and solemnly installed in a tent-shrine on Mt. Zion, later superseded by Solomon's Temple.

After establishing Israelite independence and supremacy in Canaan, David went on by conquest and diplomacy to build up an empire stretching from the Egyptian border and the Gulf of Aqabah to the Upper Euphrates. This empire he bequeathed to his son Solomon, who overtaxed its resources by a grandiose building programme and the maintenance of a splendid court. For the more efficient exploitation of his kingdom's revenue, he divided it into twelve new administrative districts, which took the place of the old tribal divisions, and exacted not only heavy taxes but compulsory labour on public works, ultimately even from his Israelite subjects. The burden at last became intolerable. Towards the end of his reign most of the subject nations had regained their independence, and after his death (*c.* 930 BC) the tribes of Israel themselves split into two kingdoms—the northern kingdom of Israel, which renounced its allegiance to the throne of David, and the southern kingdom of Judah, consisting of the tribal territories of Judah and Benjamin, over which the descendants of David and Solomon continued to reign in their capital at Jerusalem (see JUDAH, IV).

IV. THE KINGDOM OF ISRAEL

Jeroboam, founder of the separate monarchy in the north, elevated the two ancient sanctuaries of

Dan (in the far north) and Bethel (near the frontier with Judah) to the status of national shrines. In both of these golden bull-calves provided the visible pedestals for Yahweh's invisible throne (the function fulfilled by golden cherubs in the Jerusalem Temple). Early in his reign both Hebrew kingdoms were invaded by the Egyptians under Shishak, but the southern kingdom appears to have suffered the more, so that afterwards the northern kingdom had no need to fear an attempt by the Davidic dynasty to regain control of its lost territories.

A more serious threat, however, presented itself from the north. The Aramaean kingdom of Damascus, founded in Solomon's reign, began to encroach on Israelite territory about 900 BC, and this was the beginning of a hundred years of intermittent war which at times reduced Israel to desperate straits.

The security of the kingdom of Israel was also impaired by frequent palace-revolts and dynastic changes. Only two dynasties—those founded by Omri (*c.* 880 BC) and Jehu (*c.* 841 BC)—lasted for more than two generations. Jeroboam's son was assassinated by Baasha, one of his army commanders, in the year after he succeeded to the kingdom; when Baasha had reigned for twenty years his son too fell victim to a similar fate. A few years of civil war followed, from which Omri emerged as the victor.

Omri founded a new capital for his kingdom at Samaria (*q.v.*). Externally he strengthened his position by subduing Moab, east of the Dead Sea, and entering into an economic alliance with Phoenicia. His son Ahab married a Phoenician princess, Jezebel, and also brought the hostility between his kingdom and Judah to an end by means of an alliance which lasted until the dynasty of Omri was overthrown.

The commercial benefits of the Phoenician alliance were great, but in the religious realm it led to a revival of Baal-worship, in which Jezebel played a leading part. The principal champion of pure Yahweh-worship was the prophet Elijah (*q.v.*), who also denounced the royal departure from the old covenant loyalty in the social sphere (notably in the case of Naboth the Jezreelite) and proclaimed the impending doom of the dynasty of Omri.

The war with Damascus continued throughout the reigns of Omri and his descendants, apart from three years during the reign of Ahab, when the kings of Israel and Damascus and neighbouring states formed a military coalition to resist the invading king of Assyria, Shalmaneser III. They gave him battle at Qarqar on the Orontes (853 BC), and he did not invade the western lands again for twelve years. His withdrawal was the signal for the break-up of the coalition and the resumption of hostilities between Israel and Damascus.

The extermination of the house of Omri in Jehu's revolt (841 BC) was followed by the suppression of official Baal-worship. The revolt was supported by the prophetic guilds, who had no reason to love the house of Omri. But it gravely weakened the kingdom of Israel in face of the Aramaean assaults, and the first forty years of the dynasty of Jehu were years of continual tribulation for Israel. Not only were Israel's Transjordanian territories overrun by the enemy but her northern provinces too; the Aramaeans invaded the Plain of Jezreel and made their way along the Mediterranean seaboard as far south as Gath. Israel had been reduced to desperate straits when in 803 BC the Assyrian king Adad-nirari III invaded Syria, raided Damascus and imposed tribute on it. Damascene pressure on Israel was relaxed; and the Israelites were able to take advantage of this turn of fortune and regain many of the cities which the Aramaeans had taken from them.

Throughout the years of tribulation there was one man in Israel whose morale and confidence in Yahweh never wavered—the prophet Elisha (*q.v.*). Well might the king of Israel address him on his deathbed as 'the chariots of Israel and its horsemen' (2 Ki. xiii. 14, RSV). Elisha died with a prediction of victory over the Aramaeans on his lips.

The first half of the 8th century BC witnessed a return of prosperity to Israel, especially under Jeroboam II, the fourth king of Jehu's dynasty. Both Hebrew kingdoms were free from external molestation; Damascus was too weak after her rough handling by Assyria to renew her aggression. Jeroboam extended his kingdom's frontiers and the national wealth increased greatly.

But this increase of national wealth was concentrated in the hands of a relatively small section of the population—the well-to-do merchants and landowners, who enriched themselves at the expense of the peasantry. The smallholders who had formerly tilled their own fields were now obliged in large numbers to become serfs on the growing estates of their wealthy neighbours, cultivating the land which they had once cultivated as independent owners. This increasing disparity between two sections of Israel's freeborn citizens called forth the denunciation of such prophets as Amos and Hosea, the more so as the rich expropriators of their poorer neighbours were punctilious in the performance of what they considered their religious duties. The prophets insisted tirelessly that what Yahweh required from His people was not sacrifices of fatted beasts but righteousness and covenant loyalty, for lack of which the nation faced disaster greater than anything it had hitherto known.

About 745 BC the dynasty of Jehu ended as it had begun, by assassination and revolt. In that year Tiglath-pileser III became king of Assyria and inaugurated a campaign of imperial conquest which in less than a quarter of a century brought an end to the existence of the kingdom of Israel and to the independence of the kingdom of Judah. Menahem of Israel (*c.* 745–737 BC) paid tribute to Tiglath-pileser, but an anti-Assyrian policy was pursued by Pekah (*c.* 736–732 BC), who allied himself for this purpose with Damascus. Tiglath-pileser took Damascus, abolished the monarchy, and transformed the territory into an Assyrian province; the northern and Transjordanian regions of Israel were detached and made into Assyrian provinces. The upper strata of the populations of these areas were deported and replaced by immigrants from other parts of the Assyrian Empire. When Hoshea, the last king of Israel, withheld payment of tribute from Assyria at the instance of Egypt, he was imprisoned. Samaria, his capital, was stormed in 721 BC after a three years' siege, and became the seat of government of the Assyrian province of Samaria. A further deportation took place—according to Assyrian records 27,290 people were taken captive—and foreign settlers were sent to take their place.

V. THE PROVINCE OF SAMARIA

The deportation of Israelites from the northern and Transjordanian territories was so thorough that these territories quite lost their Israelite character. In the province of Samaria it was different; the immigrants in due course adopted Israelite religion—'the law of the god of the land' (2 Ki. xvii. 26 ff., RSV)—and were completely assimilated to the Israelites who had not been carried away; but the Samaritans, as the population of the province of Samaria were later called, came to be despised as racial and religious half-breeds by the people of Judah farther south, especially from the end of the 6th century BC onward.

King Hezekiah of Judah attempted (*c.* 705 BC) to revive the religious unity of Israel by inviting the people of Samaria to come to Jerusalem to worship, but his attempt was rendered ineffective by Sennacherib's invasion of Judah (701 BC). Greater success attended the action of Hezekiah's great-grandson Josiah, who took advantage of the recession of Assyrian power to extend his political sovereignty and religious reformation into the regions formerly belonging to the kingdom of Israel (621 BC). The fact that he tried to bar Pharaoh Necho's advance at Megiddo is evidence enough of the expansion of his kingdom, but his death there (609 BC) brought an end to such hopes as might have been cherished of the reunion of all Israel under a prince of the house of David. The land of Israel passed under the hegemony of Egypt, and a few years later under that of Babylonia.

The Babylonians appear to have perpetuated the Assyrian provincial organization in the west. After the assassination of Gedaliah, governor of Judah under the Babylonians, the land of Judah with the exception of the Negeb (now being occupied by the Edomites) was added to the province of Samaria (*c.* 582 BC). No great change in this respect resulted from the Persian conquest (539 BC), except that the men of Judah exiled under Nebuchadrezzar were allowed to return and settle in Jerusalem and the surrounding area, which now became the separate, if tiny, province of Judaea under a governor appointed by the Persian king (see JUDAH, V).

The Samaritans made friendly overtures to the restored exiles and offered to co-operate in rebuilding the Jerusalem Temple, but these overtures were not welcomed by the Judaeans, who no doubt feared that they would be swamped by the much greater numbers of the Samaritans, and also had serious doubts of the Samaritans' racial and religious purity. In consequence, a long-standing breach which might have been healed at this time became more bitter than ever, and the Samaritans seized every opportunity to represent the Judaeans to the Persian authorities in an unfavourable light. They were unable to prevent the rebuilding of the Jerusalem Temple, which had been authorized by Cyrus in 538 BC, but they had better success for a time in obstructing the Judaeans' attempts to fortify Jerusalem. When, however, Artaxerxes I sent Nehemiah (*q.v.*) to Judah as governor in 445 BC, with express directions to rebuild the walls of Jerusalem, the Samaritans and other neighbours of Judah might betray their chagrin in various ways but could take no effective action in face of the royal edict.

The governor of Samaria at this time was Sanballat (*q.v.*), who continued in office for many years. In 408 BC he is mentioned in a letter from the Jewish community of Elephantine in Egypt, who seek the good offices of Sanballat's sons in procuring permission from the Persian court for the rebuilding of their temple, which had been destroyed in an anti-Jewish riot two or three years previously. This temple had been built more than a century before to serve the religious needs of a Jewish community which the Egyptian kings of Dynasty XXVI had settled on their southern frontier as an insurance against Ethiopian inroads. Before writing to Sanballat's sons, the Elephantine Jews had tried to enlist the aid of the high priest in Jerusalem, but he had paid no attention to their plea; no doubt he disapproved of the existence of a rival temple to that in Jerusalem. Sanballat's sons—not unnaturally, in view of the relations between Samaria and Jerusalem—showed greater alacrity, and procured the necessary permission for the rebuilding of the Elephantine temple.

The fact that it was Sanballat's sons and not their father whom the Elephantine Jews approached suggests that, while Sanballat was still nominally governor, his sons were discharging many of his duties on his behalf, probably because of his age.

The Elephantine papyri which supply us with our information about this Jewish community in Egypt are particularly interesting because they portray a group of Jews who show no signs of having been influenced by the reformation of Josiah's days. In this they form a strong contrast to the Jews who returned from exile to Jerusalem and the surrounding territory. The latter, together with their brethren in Babylonia, had learned the lesson of exile, and were increasingly marked by strict adherence to the Torah, including especially those features of it which were calculated to mark off the people of the law from all other communities. The emergence of the Jews as the people of the law in the most particularist sense is associated above all with the work of Ezra (*q.v.*), under whom the Pentateuchal law became the recognized constitution of the Judaean temple-state, subject to the overriding authority of the Persian court.

The work of Ezra (which had the whole-hearted backing of Nehemiah as governor) meant that the cleavage between the Samaritans and Judaeans was less likely than ever to be mended. Some time before 400 BC a scion of the Jerusalem high-priestly family, Manasseh by name, who had married a daughter of Sanballat, was installed by his father-in-law as high priest of the ancient holy place on Mt. Gerizim, near Shechem, where a temple was built by royal permission. The rival cult thus established to that of Jerusalem has survived to the present day—based, remarkably enough, on the same law-book as that recognized by the Jews (see SAMARITANS).

VI. UNDER THE MACEDONIANS

The conquest of the Persian Empire by Alexander the Great brought no constitutional changes either to Samaria or to Judah. These provinces were now administered by Graeco-Macedonian governors in place of the former Persian governors, and tribute had to be paid to the new overlord in place of the old one. The Jewish *diaspora*, which had been widespread under the Persian Empire—Haman did not exaggerate when he described them to Xerxes as 'dispersed among the peoples in all the provinces of thy kingdom' (Est. iii. 8, RV)—now found new centres to settle in, especially Alexandria and Cyrene. Hellenistic influences inevitably began to give evidence of their presence among them. These influences in some directions were good; we may think in particular of the situation among the Greek-speaking Jews of Alexandria which necessitated the translation of the Pentateuch and other Old Testament writings into Greek in the 3rd and 2nd centuries BC, and thus made the knowledge of Israel's God accessible to the Gentile world (see TEXT AND VERSIONS, Old Testament). On the other hand, there was a tendency to imitate features of Hellenistic culture which were inextricably interwoven with paganism and which otherwise blurred the distinction between Yahweh's 'peculiar people' and their neighbours. How far a prominent Jewish family could go in unscrupulous assimilation to the unworthier aspects of life under the Hellenistic monarchies is illustrated by Josephus's account of the fortunes of the Tobiads, who enriched themselves as tax-collectors on behalf first of the Ptolemies and then of the Seleucids.

Among the dynasties which inherited Alexander's empire, the two which chiefly affect the history of Israel are those of the Ptolemies in Egypt and of the Seleucids who dominated Syria and the lands beyond the Euphrates. From 320 to 198 BC the Ptolemies' rule extended from Egypt into Asia as far as the Lebanon range and the Phoenician coast, including Judaea and Samaria. In 198 BC the Seleucid victory at Panion, near the sources of Jordan, meant that Judaea and Samaria were now tributary to Antioch instead of Alexandria. The defeat which the Seleucid king Antiochus III suffered at the hands of the Romans at Magnesia in 190 BC, and the heavy indemnity which they imposed on him, involved an enormous increase of taxation for his subjects, including the Jews. When his son, Antiochus IV, attempted to redress the situation by imposing his sovereignty over Egypt (in the two campaigns of 169 and 168 BC), the Romans forced him to relinquish these ambitions. Judaea, on the south-western frontier of his kingdom, now became a region of strategic importance, and he felt that there was grave reason for suspecting the loyalty of his Jewish subjects. On the advice of unwise counsellors, he decided to abolish their distinctive nationhood and religion, and the climax of this policy was the installation of a pagan cult—the worship of Zeus Olympios (a name metamorphosed by the Jews into 'the abomination of desolation')—in the Temple at Jerusalem in December 167 BC. The Samaritan temple on Gerizim was similarly diverted to the worship of Zeus Xenios.

Many pious Jews endured martyrdom at this time sooner than forswear their religion. Others took up arms against their overlord. Among the latter were members of the priestly family of the Hasmonaeans, headed by Mattathias of Modin and his five sons. The outstanding son of the five, Judas Maccabaeus, was a born leader of men, who excelled in guerrilla warfare. His initial successes against the royal forces brought many of his fellow-countrymen under his leadership, including a large number of the pious people in Israel, the *ḥ*ᵃ*sîḏîm*, who realized that passive resistance was not enough in face of the present threat to their national and religious existence. Larger armies were sent against them by the king, but they too were routed by the unexpected tactics of Judas and his men.

It became clear to the king that his policy had misfired, and Judas was invited to send ambassadors to Antioch to discuss conditions of peace. Antiochus had military plans for the reconquest of seceding territories in the eastern part of his kingdom, and it was important to reach a settlement on his Egyptian frontier. The basic Jewish condition was, naturally, the complete rescission of the ban on Jewish religious practice. This was conceded; the Jews became free to practise their ancestral religion. The concession was followed at once by the purification of the Temple from the idolatrous cult which had been installed in it, and its rededication to the age-long worship of the God of Israel. The dedication of the Temple at the end of 164 BC (ever afterwards commemorated in the festival of Hanukkah; *cf.* Jn. x. 22) was probably not envisaged in the terms of peace, but in itself it might have been accepted as a *fait accompli*.

It speedily became clear, however, that Judas, with his brothers and followers, was not content with the regaining of religious liberty. Having won that success by force of arms, they continued their struggle in order to win political independence. The dedication of the Temple was followed by the fortification of the Temple hill, over against the citadel or Akra (see JERUSALEM, IV) which was manned by a royal garrison. Judas sent armed bands to Galilee, Transjordan, and other regions where there were isolated Jewish communities and brought them back to the safety of those parts of Judaea which were controlled by his forces.

Such a succession of hostile acts could not be overlooked by the Seleucid government, and further armies were sent against Judas. Judas fell in battle in the spring of 160 BC, and for a time the cause which he had led seemed lost. But events played into the hands of his successors. In particular, the death of Antiochus IV in 163 BC was followed by a lengthy period of intermittent civil war in the Seleucid Empire, between rival claimants to the throne and their respective partisans. Jonathan, the brother of Judas who took his place as leader of the insurgent party, lay low until times were propitious, and then by diplomatic dealing won rapid and astounding advancement. In 152 BC Alexander Balas, who claimed the Seleucid throne on the ground that he was the son of Antiochus IV (the validity of this claim is difficult to assess), authorized Jonathan to maintain his own military force in Judaea and recognized him as high priest of the Jews, in return for Jonathan's promise to support him.

Antiochus IV had begun his intervention in Jewish religious affairs, which ultimately brought about the Hasmonaean rising, by deposing and appointing Jewish high priests at his own discretion, in defiance of ancient custom. Now a Hasmonaean accepted the high priesthood from a man whose title to bestow it was based on his claim to be son and successor to Antiochus IV. So much for the high ideals with which the struggle had begun!

The pious groups who had lent their aid to the Hasmonaeans at a time when it seemed that only by Hasmonaean might could religious freedom be regained, were disposed to be content when that goal was attained, and grew increasingly critical of the Hasmonaeans' dynastic ambitions. But no feature of these ambitions displeased them more than the Hasmonaean assumption of the high-priesthood. Some of them refused to recognize any high-priesthood other than the Zadokite one as legitimate, and looked forward to a day when the sons of Zadok would once more officiate in a purified Temple (see DEAD SEA SCROLLS). One branch of the Zadokite family was permitted to found a Jewish temple at Leontopolis in Egypt and function in the high-priestly office there; but a temple outside the land of Israel could not be countenanced by those *ḥᵃsîḏîm* who had any regard for the law.

In 143 BC Jonathan was trapped and put to death by one of the rival claimants for mastery of the Seleucid kingdom, but he was succeeded by his brother Simon, under whom the Jews achieved complete independence from the Gentile yoke. This independence was granted in a rescript from the Seleucid king Demetrius II in May 142 BC, by which the Jews were released from the obligation to pay tribute. Simon followed up this diplomatic success by reducing the last vestiges of Seleucid ascendancy in Judaea—the fortress of Gazara (Gezer) and the citadel in Jerusalem. Demetrius had embarked on an expedition against the Parthians, and could take no action against Simon, even had he so wished. Simon received signal honours from his grateful fellow-Jews for the freedom and peace which he had secured for them. At a meeting of the popular assembly of the Jews in September 140 BC, it was decreed, in consideration of the patriotic achievements of himself and his brothers before him, that he should be appointed ethnarch or governor of the nation, commander-in-chief of the army, and hereditary high priest. This triple authority he bequeathed to his descendants and successors.

Simon was assassinated at Jericho in 134 BC by his son-in-law Ptolemy, son of Abubus, who hoped to seize supreme power in Judaea. But Simon's son, John Hyrcanus, thwarted the assassin's plans and secured his position as successor to his father.

The Seleucid king Antiochus VII, who had tried to reassert his authority over Judaea during Simon's later years, succeeded in imposing tribute on John Hyrcanus for the first few years of his rule. But the death of Antiochus VII in battle with the Parthians in 128 BC brought Seleucid overlordship over Judaea to a decisive end.

VII. THE HASMONAEAN DYNASTY

In the seventh year of John Hyrcanus, then, the independent state of Judaea was firmly established, forty years after Antiochus IV had abolished its old constitution as an autonomous temple-state within the empire. The devotion of the *ḥᵃsîḏîm*, the military genius of Judas and the statesmanship of Simon, together with increasing division and weakness in the Seleucid government, had won for the Jews more (to all outward appearance) than they had lost at the hands of Antiochus IV. No wonder, then, that the early years of independence under John Hyrcanus were looked back to by later generations as a kind of golden age.

It was in the time of John Hyrcanus that the final breach between the majority of the *ḥᵃsîḏîm* and the Hasmonaean family came about. John was offended by their objections to his tenure of the high-priesthood, and broke with them. From this time onward they appear in history as the party of the Pharisees (*q.v.*), although it is not certain that they owed that name (Heb. *pᵉrûšîm*, 'separated ones') to the fact of their withdrawal from their former alliance with the Hasmonaeans, as has frequently been supposed. They remained in opposition to the régime for fifty years. Those religious leaders who supported the régime and manned the national council appear about the same time with the name Sadducees (*q.v.*).

John Hyrcanus profited by the growing weakness of the Seleucid kingdom to extend his own power. One of his earliest actions after the establishment of Jewish independence was to invade Samaritan territory and besiege Samaria, which held out for a year but was then stormed and destroyed. Shechem was also captured and the Samaritan shrine on Mt. Gerizim was demolished. The Samaritans appealed to the Seleucid king for help, but the Romans warned him not to interfere. The Hasmonaeans, at an early stage in their struggle, had secured a treaty of alliance with the Romans, and this treaty was renewed by John.

To the south of his kingdom John warred against the Idumaeans, conquered them, and forced them to accept circumcision and adopt the Jewish religion. He reduced Greek cities in Transjordan and invaded Galilee.

His work in Galilee was continued by his son and successor Aristobulus I (104–103 BC), who forced the subjected Galilaeans to accept Judaism, as his father had done with the Idumaeans.

According to Josephus, Aristobulus assumed the title 'king' instead of that of 'ethnarch' with which his grandfather and (so far as we know) his father had been content, and wore a diadem in token of his royal estate. No doubt he hoped in this way to enjoy greater prestige among his Gentile neighbours, although his coins designate him, in language more congenial to his Jewish subjects, as 'Judah the high priest'.

Aristobulus died (perhaps of phthisis) after a year's reign and was succeeded by his brother Alexander Jannaeus (103–76 BC), who married his widow Salome Alexandra. A more inappropriate high priest than Jannaeus could hardly be imagined. He did go through the motions of his sacred office on occasions of high ceremony—and did so in a way that deliberately offended the sentiments of many of his most religiously minded subjects (especially the Pharisees). But the master-ambition of his reign was military conquest. His pursuit of this policy brought him many reverses, but by the end of his reign he had brought under his control practically all the territory that had been Israelite in the great days of the nation's history—at a ruinous cost to all that was of value in his people's spiritual heritage.

Greek cities on the Mediterranean seaboard and in Transjordan were his special targets for attack; one after another he besieged and conquered them, showing by his ruthless vandalism how little he cared for the true values of Hellenistic civilization. He modelled his way of life on that of the cruder Hellenistic princelings of W Asia. Feeling against him on the part of many of his Jewish subjects reached such a pitch that, when he suffered a disastrous defeat at the hands of a Nabataean force in Transjordan in 94 BC, they revolted against him and even enlisted the aid of the Seleucid king Demetrius III. But other Jewish subjects of Jannaeus, however much they disliked him, found the spectacle of a Seleucid king being called in to help a revolt against a member of the Hasmonaean family too much for their patriotism; they volunteered to support the cause of their hard-pressed king and enabled him to put down the revolt and send the Seleucid contingents packing. The barbarity of the revenge which Jannaeus took against the leaders of the revolt (who evidently included some outstanding Pharisees) was long remembered with horror.

Jannaeus bequeathed his kingdom to his widow, Salome Alexandra, who ruled it as queen regnant for nine years. She bestowed the high-priesthood on her elder son, Hyrcanus II. In one important respect she reversed the policy of her predecessors; she befriended the Pharisees and paid attention to their counsel throughout her reign.

Her death in 67 BC was followed by civil war between the supporters of the claims of her two sons, Hyrcanus II and Aristobulus II, to succeed to supreme power in Judaea. Aristobulus was a typical Hasmonaean prince, ambitious and aggressive; Hyrcanus was a nonentity, but was easily manipulated by those who supported his claims in their own interests, among whom the dominating personality was the Idumaean Antipater, whose father had been governor of Idumaea under Jannaeus.

The civil strife between the two brothers and their respective partisans was halted by the Romans in 63 BC, in circumstances which brought Judaea's short-lived independence under the Hasmonaeans to an end.

VIII. THE ROMAN SUPREMACY

In 66 BC the Roman senate and people sent their most brilliant general at that time, Pompey, to bring to a successful conclusion the war which they had been waging intermittently for over twenty years with Mithridates, king of Pontus, who had carved out an empire for himself in W Asia from the lands of the decadent Seleucid kingdom and neighbouring states. Pompey was not long in defeating Mithridates (who fled to Crimea and committed suicide there); but having done that, he found himself faced with the necessity of reorganizing the political life of W Asia. In 64 BC he annexed Syria as a province of Rome, and was invited by various parties in the Jewish state to intervene in its affairs too and put an end to the civil war between the sons of Jannaeus.

Thanks to Antipater's shrewd appraisal of the situation, the party favouring Hyrcanus showed itself willing to co-operate with Rome, and

Jerusalem opened its gates to Pompey in the spring of 63 BC. The Temple, however, which was separately fortified and was held by the partisans of Aristobulus, sustained a siege of three months before it was taken by Pompey's forces.

Judaea now became tributary to Rome. She was deprived of the Greek cities which the Hasmonaean kings had conquered and annexed, and the Samaritans were liberated from Jewish control. Hyrcanus was confirmed in the high-priesthood and leadership of the nation; but he had to be content with the title of 'ethnarch', for the Romans refused to recognize him as king. Antipater continued to support him, determined to exploit this new turn of events to his own advantage, which (it must be conceded) coincided largely with the advantage of Judaea.

Aristobulus and his family endeavoured time after time to foment rebellion against Rome so as to secure power in Judaea for themselves. For many years, however, these attempts proved abortive. Successive Roman governors kept a firm grip on Judaea and Syria, because these provinces now lay on the eastern frontier of the Roman Empire, beyond which was the rival empire of Parthia. The strategic importance of this area may be gauged by the number of dominant figures in Roman history who play a part in the history of Judaea in these years—Pompey, who annexed it to the Empire; Crassus, who as governor of Syria in 54–53 BC plundered the Jerusalem Temple and many other temples in Syria while collecting resources for a war against the Parthians, but was defeated and killed by them at Carrhae in 53 BC; Julius Caesar, who became master of the Roman world after defeating Pompey at Pharsalus in 48 BC; Antony, who dominated the eastern provinces of the Empire after he and Octavian had defeated Caesar's assassins and their followers at Philippi in 42 BC; and then Octavian himself, who defeated Antony and Cleopatra at Actium in 31 BC and thereafter ruled the Roman world alone as the Emperor Augustus. Throughout the vicissitudes of Roman civil and external war Antipater and his family made it their settled policy to support the chief representative of Roman power in the east at any one time, whoever he might be and whichever party in the Roman state he might belong to. Julius Caesar in particular had reason to be grateful for Antipater's support when he was besieged in Alexandria during the winter of 48–47 BC, and he conferred special privileges not only on Antipater himself but on the Jews as well.

This confidence which the Romans learned to place in Antipater's family was manifested outstandingly in 40 BC, when the Parthians invaded Syria and Palestine and enabled Antigonus, the last surviving son of Aristobulus II, to regain the Hasmonaean throne and reign as king and high priest of the Jews. Hyrcanus II was mutilated so as to be disqualified from ever becoming high priest again. Antipater was now dead, but an attempt was made to seize and liquidate his family. One son, Phasael, was captured and killed, but Herod, the ablest of Antipater's sons, escaped to Rome, where the senate nominated him king of the Jews, at the instance of Antony and Octavian. It was his task now to recover Judaea from Antigonus (who was left in peace by the Roman commander in Syria when the Parthian invaders were driven out) and to rule his kingdom in the interests of the Romans, as their 'friend and ally'. The task was not easy, and its successful completion in 37 BC, with the storming of Jerusalem after a siege of three months, secured for Herod a bitter ill-will on the part of his new subjects which no effort of his could remove. Antigonus was sent in chains to Antony, who ordered him to be executed. Herod tried to legitimate his position in Jewish eyes by marrying Mariamne, a Hasmonaean princess, but this marriage brought him more trouble, not less.

Herod's position was precarious for the first six years of his reign. Although Antony was his friend and patron, Cleopatra longed to incorporate Judaea in her kingdom, as her earlier Ptolemaic ancestors had done, and tried to exploit her ascendancy over Antony to this end. The overthrow of Antony and Cleopatra in 31 BC, and Herod's confirmation in his kingdom by the conqueror, Augustus, brought him some relief externally, but domestic peace was denied him both in his family circle and in his relations with the Jewish people. Yet he governed Judaea with a firm hand, serving the interests of Rome even better than a Roman governor could have done. (For further details of his reign, see HEROD, 1.)

When Herod died in 4 BC his kingdom was divided among three of his surviving sons. Archelaus governed Judaea and Samaria as ethnarch until AD 6; Antipas governed Galilee and Peraea as tetrarch until AD 39; Philip received as a tetrarchy the territory east and north-east of the Sea of Galilee which his father had pacified in the emperor's interests, and ruled it until his death in AD 34. (See HEROD, 2, 3; PHILIP, 2.)

Antipas inherited a full share of his father's political acumen, and continued the thankless task of promoting the Roman cause in his tetrarchy and the surrounding regions. Archelaus, however, had all his father's brutality without his genius, and soon drove his subjects to the point where they petitioned the Roman emperor to remove him so as to prevent a revolt from breaking out. Archelaus was accordingly deposed and banished, and his ethnarchy was reconstituted as a Roman province of the third grade. In order that its annual yield of tribute to the imperial exchequer might be assessed, the governor of Syria, Quirinius (*q.v.*) held a census in Judaea and Samaria. This census provoked the rising of Judas the Galilaean (*q.v.*), and, while the rising was crushed, its ideals lived on in the party of the Zealots (*q.v.*), who maintained that the payment of tribute to Caesar, or to any other pagan ruler, was an act of treason to Israel's God.

After the census, Judaea (as the province of Judaea and Samaria was called) received a procurator (*q.v.*) as governor. These procurators were appointed by the emperor, and were subject to the general supervision of the governors of Syria. The early Roman procurators exercised the privilege of appointing the high priest of Israel—a privilege which, since the end of the Hasmonaean dynasty, had been exercised by Herod and Archelaus after him. The procurators sold the sacred office to the highest bidder, and its religious prestige was naturally very low. By virtue of his office the high priest presided over the Sanhedrin (*q.v.*), which administered the internal affairs of the nation.

Of the earlier procurators the only one whose name is well known is Pontius Pilate (*q.v.*), whose harsh and stubborn character is recorded in the pages of Josephus and Philo—not to mention the part he plays in the New Testament narrative. His construction of a new aqueduct to provide Jerusalem and the Temple with a better water-supply illustrates the material benefits of Roman rule; his flouting the religious scruples of the Jews by insisting on defraying the expense of it from the sacred Temple-fund illustrates an aspect of Roman rule which was largely responsible for the revolt of AD 66—the insensitivity of many of the governors and their agents to local feeling.

For a short time, between the years 41 and 44, Judaea enjoyed a welcome relief from procuratorial administration. Herod Agrippa I, a grandson of Herod the Great and Mariamne, to whom the Emperor Gaius had given Philip's former tetrarchy as a kingdom in AD 37 (augmenting it by the addition of Galilee and Peraea in AD 39, after the deposition and banishment of Antipas), received Judaea and Samaria as further extensions of his kingdom from the Emperor Claudius in AD 41 (see HEROD, 4). Because of his descent from the Hasmonaeans (through Mariamne) he was popular with his Jewish subjects. But his sudden death in AD 44, at the age of fifty-four, meant that the province of Judaea (now including Galilee as well as Samaria) reverted to government by procurators, since Agrippa's son, Agrippa the Younger (see HEROD, 5), was too young to be entrusted with his father's royal responsibility. One concession was made to Jewish sentiment, however: the privilege of appointing the high priest, which Agrippa had inherited from the procurators who preceded him, did not go back to the procurators who followed him, but was given first to his brother Herod of Chalcis, and then (after the death of that Herod in AD 48) to Agrippa the Younger.

IX. END OF THE SECOND COMMONWEALTH

During the twenty years or so that followed the death of Herod Agrippa I, troubles multiplied in Judaea. The people in general found the re-imposition of procurators all the more irksome after their brief spell of government by a Jewish king; and the procurators themselves did little to conciliate the sentiments of their Jewish subjects. There was a succession of risings stirred up by pseudo-Messiahs such as Theudas (*q.v.*), who was killed by a cavalry detachment sent against him by the procurator Fadus (AD 44–46), or by Zealot leaders such as James and Simon (two sons of Judas the Galilaean), crucified by the next procurator Tiberius Julius Alexander (AD 46–48). The fact that Alexander was a renegade Jew, scion of an illustrious Jewish family of Alexandria, did nothing to ingratiate him with the Jews of Judaea.

It was during the procuratorships of Fadus and Alexander that Judaea was hard hit by the famine of Acts xi. 28. Josephus records how Helena, the queen-mother of Adiabene, east of the Tigris, bought grain in Egypt and figs in Cyprus at this time for the relief of the famine-stricken people of Judaea. The royal family of Adiabene were the most distinguished Jewish proselytes of the period; some of them actually fought on the Jewish side in the war against Rome which broke out in AD 66.

Under the procuratorship of Felix (*q.v.*) disaffection increased in Judaea. Felix set himself energetically to rid the province of insurgent bands, and his severe measures against them were attended by temporary success, but they alienated large numbers of the population, in whose eyes the insurgents were not criminals but patriots.

The closing years of Felix' procuratorship were attended by fierce riots between the Gentile and Jewish inhabitants of Caesarea, arising out of a dispute about civic privileges. Felix sent the leaders of both parties to Rome to have the matter decided by the emperor, but was himself recalled and replaced in the procuratorship by Festus (AD 59). The Caesarean dispute was decided in favour of the Gentiles, and Jewish resentment at the decision, coupled with the Gentiles' malicious exploitation of their victory, was one of the factors in the explosion of AD 66.

Festus (*q.v.*) was a relatively just and mild governor, but he died in office in AD 62, and his two successors, Albinus and Florus, by their persistent offending of Jewish national and religious sentiment, played into the hands of the anti-Roman extremists. The last straw was Florus's sacrilegious seizure of seventeen talents from the Temple treasury. This provoked a riot which was put down with much bloodshed. The moderate elements in the nation, aided by the younger Agrippa, counselled restraint, but the people were in no mood to listen to them. They cut the communications between the fortress of Antonia and the Temple courts, and the captain of the Temple, who was leader of the war-party in Jerusalem, formally renounced the imperial authority by putting an end to the daily sacrifice for the emperor's welfare.

Matters had now escaped Florus's control, and even the intervention of Cestius Gallus, governor of Syria, with stronger military forces than Florus had at his disposal, proved ineffective. Gallus had to withdraw, and his army suffered heavy losses on its retreat through the pass of Beth-horon (November AD 66).

This success, as it seemed to the insurgent Jews, filled them with false optimism. The extremists' policy appeared to have been vindicated: Rome could not stand before them. The whole of Palestine was placed on a war footing.

But Vespasian, who was entrusted with the putting down of the revolt, set about his task methodically. In 67 he crushed the rebellion in Galilee. Some of the leaders of the Galilaean revolt, however, escaped to Jerusalem, and their arrival there added to the internal strife which racked the city during its last years and months. In the summer of 68 Vespasian was approaching Jerusalem itself when news came of Nero's deposition and death at Rome. The ensuing civil war at the heart of the Empire nerved the defenders of Jerusalem with fresh hope; it looked from their standpoint as though Rome and the Empire were on the verge of dissolution and Daniel's fifth monarchy was about to be established on their ruins.

From Caesarea, Vespasian watched the progress of events at Rome. On 1 July, AD 69, he himself was proclaimed emperor at Alexandria by the governor of Egypt (the same apostate Jew, Alexander, who had earlier been procurator of Judaea); the example of Alexandria was swiftly followed in Caesarea and Antioch and by the armies in most of the eastern provinces. Vespasian returned to Rome to occupy the imperial throne, leaving his son Titus to complete the suppression of the revolt in Judaea. By the end of AD 69 all Judaea had been subdued except Jerusalem and three strongholds overlooking the Dead Sea.

Jerusalem was invested in the spring of AD 70. By May half the city was in the hands of the Romans, but the defenders refused to accept terms of submission. On 24 July the fortress of Antonia was stormed; twelve days later the daily sacrifices ceased in the Temple, and on 29 August the sanctuary itself was set on fire and destroyed. Four weeks later the whole city was in Titus's hands. It was razed to the ground, except for part of the western wall, with three towers of Herod's palace on that wall, which provided headquarters for a Roman garrison. The last centre of revolt to be crushed was the almost impregnable fortress of Masada, south-west of the Dead Sea, where a Zealot force held out until the spring of AD 73 and then committed mass-suicide sooner than be captured.

Judaea was reconstituted as a province under its own imperial legate, directly responsible to the emperor and in no way subordinate to the imperial legate of Syria; unlike the procurators, the imperial legates of Judaea had legionary forces under their command. The former Temple tax, which Jews throughout the world had paid for the maintenance of the house of God at Jerusalem, was still exacted, but it was now diverted to the maintenance of the temple of Jupiter on the Capitoline hill in Rome.

With the disappearance of the Temple hierarchy and the Sanhedrin as formerly organized, the chief internal authority in the Jewish nation passed to a new Sanhedrin of Rabbis, led at first by Yohanan ben Zakkai, a teacher of the school of Hillel. This religious court exercised its control through the synagogues, and began the work of codifying the traditional body of oral law which was in due course committed to writing in the Mishnah towards the end of the 2nd century AD. It was in large measure due to the action of Yohanan ben Zakkai and his colleagues and their successors that Israel's national and religious identity survived the downfall of the Temple and the Second Jewish Commonwealth in AD 70. See TALMUD AND MIDRASH.

See also JUDAH. For religion, see SACRIFICE AND OFFERING, LAW, *etc.* For archaeological discoveries, see ARCHAEOLOGY. For individual kings and places, see separate entries.

BIBLIOGRAPHY. W. O. E. Oesterley and T. H. Robinson, *A History of Israel* (2 vols.), 1932; H. M. Orlinsky, *Ancient Israel*, 1954; G. Ricciotti, *The History of Israel* (2 vols.), 1955; M. Noth, *The History of Israel*², 1960; J. Bright, *A History of Israel*, 1960. F.F.B.

ISRAEL OF GOD. Paul's statement that 'not all who are descended from Israel belong to Israel' (Rom. ix. 6, RSV) is in line with the prophetic insistence that the true people of God, those who are worthy of the name of Israel, may be but a relatively small 'remnant' of faithful souls within the nation of Israel. In the New Testament the concept of such a remnant appears in the preaching of John the Baptist, who insists that descent from Abraham is valueless in itself (Mt. iii. 9 = Lk. iii. 8). Jesus' calling of disciples around Himself to form the 'little flock' who were to receive the kingdom (Lk. xii. 32; *cf.* Dn. vii. 22, 27) marks Him out as the founder of the new Israel; He explicitly designated the twelve apostles as judges of 'the twelve tribes of Israel' in the new age (Mt. xix. 28; Lk. xxii. 30). The 'little flock' was to be augmented by the accession of 'other sheep' who had never belonged to the Jewish fold (Jn. x. 16).

Whether the expression 'the Israel of God' in its one appearance in the New Testament (Gal. vi. 16) denotes believing Jews only, or believing Jews and Gentiles without distinction, is disputed; the latter is more probable, especially if the expression is to be construed in apposition to 'all who walk by this rule' (*cf.* RSV). But that the community of believers in Jesus, irrespective of their natural origin, is looked upon as the new Israel throughout the New Testament is clear. They are 'the twelve tribes in the dispersion' (Jas. i. 1, RSV), 'the exiles of the dispersion' (1 Pet. i. 1, RSV), who are further designated, in language borrowed from Old Testament descriptions of Israel, as 'a chosen race, a royal priesthood, a holy nation, God's own people' (1 Pet. ii. 9, RSV).

But the nucleus of this new Israel is Jewish

(Rom. xi. 18). And while the greater proportion of 'Israel according to the flesh' is at present prevented, by a partial and temporary blindness, from recognizing their ancestral hope in Jesus, the time is coming when the veil will be removed from their eyes (2 Cor. iii. 16) and they will be re-established by faith as members of the beloved community: their present estrangement will last only 'until the full number of the Gentiles come in, and so all Israel will be saved' (Rom. xi. 25 ff., RSV).

BIBLIOGRAPHY. L. Gillet, *Communion in the Messiah*, 1942; M. Simon, *Verus Israel*, 1948; A. Oepke, *Das Neue Gottesvolk*, 1950; R. Campbell, *Israel and the New Covenant*, 1954; J. Munck, *Paul and the Salvation of Mankind*, E.T., 1960; *id.*, *Christus und Israel*, 1956. F.F.B.

ISSACHAR. Son of Jacob and Leah, ancestor of one of the twelve tribes of Israel. The name is explained as a compound of Heb. *'îš*, 'man', and *śāḵār*, 'wages', hence 'a hired worker' (Gn. xxx. 18, xxxv. 23).

Issachar's lot fell on the central part of the plain of Jezreel; the boundaries cannot be drawn exactly (Jos. xvii. 10, xix. 17–23). The territory lies between the mountains of Gilboa and Tabor. On the south and west lay Manasseh, on the north Zebulun and Naphtali, on the east the river Jordan. The principal towns included Jezreel (mod. Zer'in), Shunem (mod. Sulem), and En-gannim, a levitical town (probably mod. Jenin).

Issachar was the tribe chiefly involved in the fighting under Deborah, who was herself a member of this tribe (Jdg. v. 15). The battle took place on the plain of Issachar, and the victory secured free passage between the Israelites in the hill country of Ephraim and those in Galilee.

The enjoyment of their rich soil may have produced in the men of Issachar the mood which is reproached in Gn. xlix. 14 f. The reference to 'the mountain' in the blessing of Zebulun and Issachar in Dt. xxxiii. 18 f. does not necessarily imply that Issachar's territory reached the Mediterranean Sea, but simply that there was a market associated with the sacred mountain of Tabor, the frontier-point of the tribes of Zebulun, Issachar, and Naphtali. 'There shall they suck of the abundance of the seas' refers to a commercial route from the coast passing by Mt. Tabor (as against the view that 'the mountain' here is Carmel).

Issachar was one of the twelve administrative districts established under Solomon (1 Ki. iv. 17). A short time before the fall of Nineveh (612 BC) Josiah, king of Judah, was able to extend his authority over Samaria and to penetrate Issachar, which belonged to the Assyrian province of Megiddo after the fall of the northern kingdom (2 Ki. xxiii. 19, 29 f.).

BIBLIOGRAPHY. A. Saarisalo, *The Boundary between Issachar and Naphtali*, 1927; A. Alt, *Palästinajahrbuch*, XXIV, 1928, pp. 47 ff. A.S.

ISSUE, ISSUE OF BLOOD. Apart from the more usual meanings of 'issue', the word is also used biblically in connection with disease. In Lv. xv. 2 ff. Heb. *zôḇ* denotes a discharge which rendered its victims ritually unclean. In Lv. xii. 7; Mk. v. 25; Lk. viii. 43 f.; Mt. ix. 20; Heb. *māqôr*, and Gk. *rhysis* and *haimorrhoeō* (the latter of which is used in Lv. xv. 33, LXX) refer to an issue of blood, translated by NEB New Testament as 'haemorrhages'. See also DISEASE AND HEALING. J.D.D.

ITALIAN BAND. See ARMY.

ITALY (Gk. *Italia*). By the middle of the 1st century this name had come to have substantially its modern geographical meaning. 'All roads led to Rome', and even before the time of Christ many Jews had resorted to Italy, especially to the metropolis. It was because the Emperor Claudius had carried out a purge against the Jews that Paul met Aquila and Priscilla (*q.v.*) (Acts xviii. 2). Italy was the apostle's destination when after his appeal to Caesar he and other prisoners embarked at Caesarea on what was to be his most famous journey (Acts xxvii. 1, 6). In Heb. xiii. 24 we learn that 'they of Italy' (RSV 'those who come from Italy') greet the addressees. See ROME. J.D.D.

ITCH (*ḥeres*, 'heat, sun, itch'). A skin condition, probably akin to eczema, included among the scourges ('which cannot be healed') which would overtake the disobedient (Dt. xxviii. 27). No data are available for precise identification. See also SCAB.

ITHAMAR (Heb. *'îṯāmār*). The meaning of the name is uncertain, but may possibly be 'land of palms'. The youngest of Aaron and Elisheba's four sons (Ex. vi. 23), Ithamar was ordained to the priesthood (Ex. xxviii. 1) and directed the building of the tabernacle (Ex. xxxviii. 21). In the apostasy of Nadab and Abihu he remained faithful in all but the matter of the sin-offering (Lv. x). He was placed over the Gershonites and Merarites (Nu. iv. 28, 33). For evidence that Eli was a descendant of Ithamar, see 1 Sa. xiv. 3, xxii. 9; 1 Ch. xxiv. 3. A man called Daniel, one of his descendants, is named among the returning exiles (Ezr. viii. 2). G.W.G.

ITHIEL. Probably 'God is with me' (correcting Heb. pointing to *'ittî'ēl*). **1.** A Benjamite ancestor of Sallu who resided in Jerusalem in Nehemiah's time (Ne. xi. 7). **2.** A man mentioned with Ucal in Pr. xxx. 1. An altering of the word-divisions results in the more satisfactory rendering: 'I have wearied myself, O God (*lā'îṯî 'ēl*), and am consumed' (ASVmg; *BDB*). D.A.H.

ITHRA (*yiṯrā'*, 'abundance'). Husband of Abigail, David's sister, and father of Amasa, one of David's generals. Called an Israelite in 2 Sa. xvii. 25, the marginal reading and 1 Ch. ii. 17

describe him as an Ishmaelite and give his name as 'Jether' (*cf.* 1 Ki. ii. 5).

ITHRITE, THE. 'Ithrites' was the name given to one of the families descended from Kiriath-jearim (1 Ch. ii. 53). Two members of David's bodyguard, Ira and Gareb, came from this family (2 Sa. xxiii. 38; 1 Ch. xi. 40) and may have originated from the town of Jattir (1 Sa. xxx. 27). See JATTIR. R.A.H.G.

ITTAI (Heb. *'ittay*, ? '(God) is with me'. **1.** The leader of six hundred men from Gath, who joined David shortly before Absalom's rebellion. His fidelity was such that he refused to leave the king when he advised him to return (2 Sa. xv. 19–22). 'Gittite' indicates that he was a Philistine; he was probably a soldier of fortune who found in David a leader worthy of his loyalty. With Joab and Abishai, he was subsequently one of David's three generals (2 Sa. xviii. 2).

2. A Benjamite. One of the 'thirty' of David's mighty men (2 Sa. xxiii. 29; 'Ithai' in 1 Ch. xi. 31). J.G.G.N.

ITURAEA (Gk. *Itouraia*, Lk. iii. 1). The name, mentioned in conjunction with Trachonitis (*q.v.*), almost certainly comes from Heb. *y^{e}ṭûr* (AV 'Jetur'), a son of Ishmael (Gn. xxv. 15, 16; 1 Ch. i. 31), mentioned also as a tribe at war with the Israelites east of the Jordan (1 Ch. v. 19). Little or nothing is known of them thereafter until the time of the Jewish king Aristobulus I (105–104 BC), who is recorded as having fought against the Ituraeans and taken from them a portion of their land (Jos., *Ant.* xiii. 11. 3). Thereafter frequent allusion is made to them by classical writers (Josephus, Strabo, Pliny, Dio Cassius, *etc.*). Sometimes they are called Syrians, sometimes Arabians.

At the time of the Roman conquest they were known as a wild robber tribe especially proficient in the use of the bow (Schürer, *The Jewish People in the Time of Christ*, pp. 326, 327), but not associated with any precisely defined geographical location. It was part of the territory ruled by Herod the Great, after whose death in 4 BC the kingdom was partitioned, and certain lands including Trachonitis and what was called 'the house of Zeno (or Zenodorus) about Paneas' formed the tetrarchy of Philip; see TETRARCH. If, as seems likely, this latter section was inhabited by Ituraeans, it may have been known as Ituraea, for migratory tribes frequently gave their name to their new home. Josephus, in defining the limits of Philip's sovereignty, does not specifically mention Ituraea—some would say because it was indistinguishable from Trachonitis.

Is Luke's reference, then, to be understood as a noun or as an adjectival form? Does he intend the place or the people? 'A very obscure subject', said W. M. Ramsay in 1894, 'in which many statements are glibly made . . . which are quite unproven.' No certainty is possible. Place-names of this region and time are notoriously elastic and liable to corruption, and overlapping is frequently found. The most we can safely say is that it was, in T. W. Manson's words (*Luke* in *MNTC*), 'a hilly country in the Anti-Lebanon range, inhabited by roving Arabs'.

Caligula gave it to Herod Agrippa I. When the latter died it was incorporated into the province of Syria under procurators.

BIBLIOGRAPHY. Discussions by W. M. Ramsay and G. A. Smith in *The Expositor*, IV, IX, 1894, pp. 51–55, 143–149, 231–238; E. Schürer, *The Jewish People in the Time of Christ*, 1905 ed., I, ii, pp. 325–344; A. H. M. Jones, *The Herods of Judaea*, 1938, pp. 9–11, *passim*. J.D.D.

IVAH. A city of Samaria conquered by the Assyrians in the time of Isaiah (2 Ki. xviii. 34, xix. 13). Probably identical with Ava (2 Ki. xvii. 24). The site is unknown, and attempts by older commentators to identify it with Gaza (Cheyne), Ahava of Ezra viii. 15 (Young), or to understand the name as that of one of the gods of Sepharvaim, have not found wide acceptance. R.J.W.

IVORY (Heb. *šēn*, 'tooth', or *šenhabbîm* (1 Ki. x. 22; 2 Ch. ix. 21) thought by some to be 'tooth of elephant' (so LXX), but possibly meaning 'ivory (and) ebony' as in Ezk. xxvii. 15; *cf.* Akkad. *šin piri*).

Ivory was a form of wealth and a mark of luxurious and fine goods (1 Ki. x. 18–22; Rev. xviii. 12, Gk. *elephantinos*). It was used for thrones and sometimes overlaid with gold (1 Ki. x. 18), for couches (Am. vi. 4), and for furnishing and panelling rooms or palaces, hence Ahab's 'house of ivory' (1 Ki. xxii. 39; *cf.* Ps. xlv. 8; see SAMARIA) condemned by Amos (iii. 15). Its commonest use was in the manufacture of small objects and in composite models, where it simulated human flesh and thus was employed figuratively in poetry (Ct. v. 14, vii. 4; in the latter 'tower of ivory' may, however, be a reference to a specific locality).

Most ivory in use in Syria and Palestine came from Syrian (so-called 'Asiatic') elephants (*Elephas maximus*) which inhabited the upper Euphrates until hunted to extinction in the late first millennium BC. Other sources were India, from which tusks (*qarnôṯ šēn*) were imported by ocean-going ships (2 Ch. ix. 17, 21) to Babylonia (Ur) by Phoenicians who decorated their vessels with plaques of ivory (Ezk. xxvii. 6), or overland from the Nilotic Sudan *via* Dedan in central Arabia (verse 15). A tusk was found in the excavations at Alalaḫ (Syria).

In the early third millennium ivory was used for carving small figurines (Beersheba area), animal heads (Jericho), or for silhouettes for inlay, in the early Mesopotamian fashion, in wooden objects (El-Jisr). By the following millennium the trade flourished. Tusks are shown on Egyp. paintings and Assyr. sculpture as valued trophies of war. The Syro-Phoenician trade and guilds of ivory-workers sought to meet a growing export market to Egypt and Assyria, making use of inlay, appliqué, ajouré, veneer, and fretwork techniques. Furniture, especially chairs, beds, caskets, and round boxes (pyxides), are found. some showing foreign influences in design. Remarkable caches of ivories have been recovered from Ras Shamra and Megiddo (see royal scene on the 12th-century panel above). In the Israelite period ivories from Samaria and Hazor attest its use for ladies' hair combs, unguent vases, flasks, and elaborate spoons supported by figures of maidens. See also PHOENICIA, ARTS AND CRAFTS, figs. 24, 58, 146(9) and plates IV*b*, V*a*.

BIBLIOGRAPHY. R. D. Barnett, *The Nimrud Ivories*, 1958; 'Phoenicia and the Ivory Trade', *Archaeology*, IX, 1956, pp. 87–97; J. V. and G. M. Crowfoot, *Early Ivories from Samaria*, 1938. D.J.W.

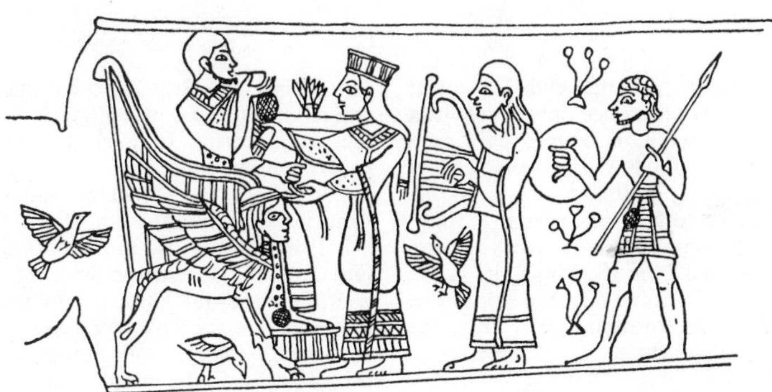

Fig. 114. Part of an ivory panel from Megiddo (12th century BC) showing a king seated on a throne similar to that used by Solomon (I Ki. x. 18–20). A maidservant, lyre-player, and Semitic soldier usher prisoners (not shown here) into the royal presence.

IYE-ABARIM, a stopping-place on the Exodus journey on the borders of Moab (Nu. xxi. 11, xxxiii. 44, 45). Iye-abarim (*'iyyê hā'aḇārîm*, ruins of Abarim, or of the regions beyond) is abbreviated in Nu. xxxiii. 45 AV to Iim. Abel identifies it with the ancient site of Maḥaiy to the south-east of Moab, Glueck places it farther west, and du Buit chooses a site near the river Arnon. Its position is still debatable. J.A.T.

J

JAAR (*ya'ar*, 'forest') in the Old Testament usually means 'forest', but once only it may be a proper name (Ps. cxxxii. 6, RVmg, RSV) as a poetical abbreviation for Kiriath-jearim (city of forests). The allusion in this psalm is to the bringing of the ark to Jerusalem from Kiriath-jearim, where it had lain for twenty years or more after it was recovered from the Philistines (1 Sa. vii. 1, 2; 1 Ch. xiii. 5). Some take the word here, as elsewhere, to mean forest and refer 'it' to the oath in the preceding verses. M.A.M.

JAAZANIAH (Heb. *ya'ᵃzanyāh(ū)*, 'Yahweh hears'). **1.** The Judaean army-commander, son of Hoshaiah, who supported Gedaliah at Mizpah (2 Ki. xxv. 23; Je. xl. 8, xlii. 1). The brother of (or, according to LXX, the same as) Azariah (Je. xliii. 2). A seal found at Mizpah (Tell en-Nasbeh) inscribed 'Ja'azaniah, servant of the king' may be ascribed to this man (*DOTT*, p. 222; pl. 13).

Fig. 115. An onyx scaraboid seal inscribed with the name of 'Jaazaniah, servant of the king'. The owner may have been the commanding officer at Mizpah (2 Ki. xxv. 23). This cock is the earliest representation of this bird yet found on a Palestinian monument. From Tell en-Nasbeh, *c*. 600 BC.

2. Son of Jeremiah, a Rechabite leader (Je. xxxv. 3). **3.** Son of Shaphan, an Israelite elder, seen in a vision by Ezekiel (viii. 11) offering incense to idols in Jerusalem. **4.** Son of Azur, seen by Ezekiel at the east gate of the Temple (Ezk. xi. 1). D.J.W.

JABAL. A son of Adah, wife of Lamech, and ancestor of those 'who dwell in tents and *have* cattle (*ûmiqneh*)', or perhaps better 'who dwell in tents and places of reeds' (*m* (local) + *qāneh*, 'reed'). See Gn. iv. 20.

JABBOK. A river flowing westwards into the river Jordan, some 20 miles north of the Dead Sea. It rises near Amman (see RABBATH-AMMON) and in all is over 60 miles long. It is today called the Wadi Zerqa. It marked a boundary line between Ammonite and Gadite territory (Dt. iii. 16), once the Israelites had defeated the Amorite king Sihon south of the Jabbok (Nu. xxi. 21 ff.). It was also the river forded by Jacob (Gn. xxxii. 22) on the occasion of his wrestling with the angel and subsequent change of name. There may well be a play on words here: 'Jabbok' is in Heb. *yabbōq*, while '[and] . . . wrestled' is [*way*]*yē'āḇēq*. In the unvowelled text there is just an extra letter, an aleph, in the latter word. D.F.P.

JABESH-GILEAD. An Israelite town east of Jordan which took no part in the war against Benjamin (Jdg. xxi), and suffered severe reprisals. Here Saul later proved his kingship by routing the Ammonites who were besieging it (1 Sa. xi). The citizens rescued Saul's body from the Philistines after the battle of Gilboa (1 Sa. xxxi; 1 Ch. x).

Tell Abu-Kharaz, on the north side of the Wadi Yabis where it reaches the plains, is probably the site (Glueck, *BASOR*, 89, 91, 1943). This isolated hill dominates the surrounding country and was heavily fortified in Israelite times; it is 2 miles from the Jordan and 9 from Bethshan. Earlier writers located Jabesh at smaller sites farther upstream, of which only Tell el-Maqlub (on the north bank) is pre-Roman. Noth (*ZDPV*, LXIX, 1953, p. 28) disputes some of Glueck's arguments, but the very existence of Tell Abu-Kharaz makes Maqlub an unlikely location for the biblical narratives. J.P.U.L.

JABEZ (*ya'bēṣ*, 'he makes sorrowful'). **1.** A city, evidently in Judah, inhabited by 'the families of the scribes' (1 Ch. ii. 55). **2.** The head of a family of the tribe of Judah (1 Ch. iv. 9, 10), an 'honourable' man whose prayer God answered. For discussion of a play on the Heb. words here, see C. F. Keil, *Chronicles*, p. 88.

JABIN (*yāḇîn*, possibly '[God] perceives'). **1.** A king of Hazor (*q.v.*), leader of an alliance of northern princes defeated in battle by Joshua, who afterwards slew Jabin (Jos. xi. 1–14). **2.** Another king of Hazor (called 'king of Canaan' in Jdg. iv. 2) who for twenty years 'mightily oppressed' the Israelites, who had been reduced thus to vassalage because of idolatry. Liberation came when Barak and Deborah defeated Jabin's general Sisera (*q.v.*) (Jdg. iv. 3–16), a notable victory immortalized in the Song of Deborah

(Jdg. v) and leading to the destruction of Jabin (Jdg. iv. 23, 24), which is briefly referred to also in Ps. lxxxiii. 9. J.D.D.

JABNEEL (*yaḇne'ēl*, 'God (El) causes to build'), a name, of which a comparable form *Jabni-ilu* occurs in the Amarna letters, which is used of two places in the Bible.

1. A city on the south-western boundary of Judah (Jos. xv. 11) and probably to be identified with Jabneh, a Philistine city which was captured by Uzziah (2 Ch. xxvi. 6). Jabneh was called Jamnia in Greek and Roman periods, and it was at this city that the Sanhedrin re-formed on the destruction of Jerusalem in AD 70, and that the canon of the Jewish Scriptures was confirmed in the last decade of the 1st century AD.

2. A town of Naphtali (Jos. xix. 33), possibly to be identified with modern Khirbet Yamma. T.C.M.

JACHIN and BOAZ. The names of two decorated pillars of bronze which stood to the right and left of the entrance to the Temple of Solomon (1 Ki. vii. 21; 2 Ch. iii. 15–17). At the destruction of Jerusalem in 587 BC they were broken up and the metal was carried off to Babylon (2 Ki. xxv. 13). In Ezekiel's ideal Temple these columns were replaced by wooden pillars (xl. 49). See fig. 116.

I. CONSTRUCTION

The hollow columns were cast by Hiram of Tyre in moulds dug in the ground (Je. lii. 21) using the *cire perdue* method developed by the Assyrians in the time of Sennacherib (*ARAB*, II, 1927, p. 169). They were 18 cubits high and the bronze was 4 fingers thick (1 Ki. vii. 13–15). Reckoning by the royal cubit of 52 cm. (see WEIGHTS AND MEASURES), the columns were 9·56 m. high × 0·988 m. diameter. The capitals were 5 cubits high (2·58 m.), giving a total height of 12·14 m. The Chronicler says there were 'two pillars of 35 cubits high'. This apparent discrepancy has been explained by assuming that Chronicles gives the combined height of both columns, allowing 1 cubit for that part inserted in the base and capitals not shown in 1 Kings. In 2 Ki. xxv. 17 the capitals are said to have been cast solid and 3 cubits high, a reduction in height which some have attributed to possible renovations in the Temple by Joash or Josiah, and others to a faulty reading of the earlier figure.

The pillars were surmounted by 'double' capitals. This refers either to the 'Ionic' form or to the two separately cast parts; these were the 'lotus' work (*šûšān*) or four opened and everted petals 4 cubits 'in width' (*bā'ûlām*, 1 Ki. vii. 19, AV 'in the porch') and the large spherical knob or pommel (verse 41, *gullâ*, RV 'bowl'). A network, *śeḇāḵâ*, of seven strands or chains of interlocking links enveloped the pommel. From this hung a fringe of superimposed golden pomegranates, one hundred to the row, which thus covered the upper part of the lotus flower.

II. PURPOSE

The twin columns were free-standing and did not support the porch roof, but were 'near' (1 Ki. vii. 21) and 'before' it (2 Ch. iii. 17). They are listed with the furnishings but not with the Temple fabric. Similar decorated pillars are shown on models of shrines from Palestine and Cyprus (10th–9th century BC) and on ivories from Arslan Tash and Nimrud, and remains of free-standing pillars from before a temple of Nabu were found at Khorsabad (*c.* 710 BC). Bases for such pillars were found by the 13th-century temple at Hazor. Since Herodotus (ii. 44) describes two large columns near the temple of Hercules at Tyre which 'shone in the night', this confirms that such pillars were common throughout the ancient Near East. There is no evidence that they were bases for divine symbols or lampstands (see ASHERAH). Yeivin suggests that they symbolized the divine presence, as had the pillars of fire and smoke in the desert wanderings (Ex. xxxiii. 9; Dt. xxxi. 15). Staves or pillars of similar import are found from Sumerian to modern times.

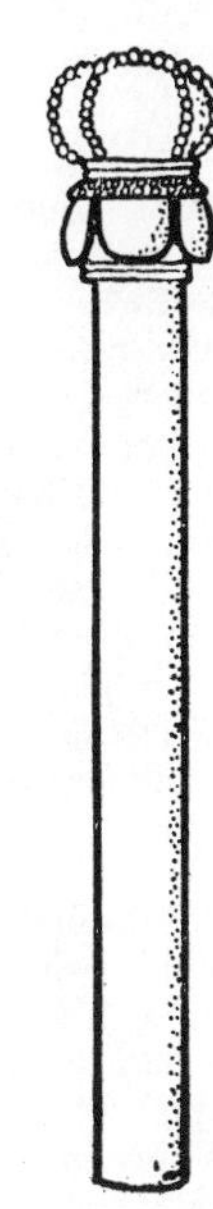

Fig. 116. A reconstruction of one of the two pillars named Jachin and Boaz which stood at the entrance of Solomon's Temple. *Cf.* fig. 204.

III. NAMES

The names of the columns may enshrine the memory of David's ancestry through his mother (Jachin occurs as a Simeonite name [Nu. xxvi. 12] and in a priestly family [1 Ch. xxiv. 17]) and through the paternal line (see BOAZ). However, a more likely theory is that the names may be the first words of oracles giving power to the Davidic dynasty: perhaps 'Yahweh will establish (*yaḵîn*) thy throne for ever' and 'In the strength (*be'ōz*) of Yahweh shall the king rejoice' or something similar.

BIBLIOGRAPHY. R. B. Y. Scott, *JBL*, LVII, 1939, pp. 143 ff.; H. G. May, *BASOR*, 88, 1942, pp. 19–27; S. Yeivin, *PEQ*, XCI, 1959, pp. 6–22.
D.J.W.

JACINTH. See JEWELS AND PRECIOUS STONES.

JACKAL. See FOX.

JACOB. It is fitting that almost a quarter of the book of Genesis should be devoted to the biography of Jacob, the father of the chosen people. Written documents of the second millennium BC have provided extensive material corroborating the background to the stories of Gn. xxvi–l. While this does not prove the existence of the

Patriarch or the historicity of the narrative, it does show that they are not late compositions from the time of the Exile with imaginative and anachronistic details. Rather it suggests that the stories were recorded in writing at an early date (see PATRIARCHAL AGE, TRADITION). Such a frank collection of stories is unlikely to be centred on a mythical figure.

I. DATE

The exact limits of the lifetime of Jacob cannot be fixed because of a lack of explicit correlations between the biblical accounts and the surviving secular records (see CHRONOLOGY OF THE OLD TESTAMENT). Evidence at present available suggests approximately the 18th century BC. Such a date would place his settlement in Goshen, not far from the Egyptian court, early in the period of the Hyksos domination, centred on Tanis (see EGYPT, ZOAN). This date also allows Abraham's life to be placed in the 20th and 19th centuries BC as suggested by biblical and archaeological evidence (see ABRAHAM).

II. BIOGRAPHY

Jacob was born clutching the heel (Heb. *'āqēḇ*) of his elder twin Esau (Gn. xxv. 26), so the name given to him was 'he clutches' or, on another plausible interpretation, 'he clutched' (Heb. *ya'ᵃqōḇ*). This may have been intentional punning on a current name *ya'ᵃqōḇ-il*, 'may God protect' or 'God has protected'. Cuneiform and Egyptian documents of the period contain personal names from the same root (*'qb*), including some of parallel form, in use among people of the West Semitic group (see AMORITES).

Jacob, 'the supplanter' (this is a nuance developed from 'to take by the heel, to overtake', Heb. root *'qb*), obtained the birthright of the elder son by taking advantage of his brother's hunger and then beguiled Isaac into giving to him the blessing which was by custom that of the firstborn. The firstborn son normally inherited twice as much of the paternal estate as each of the other children (*cf.* Dt. xxi. 16). As well as the special legacy, it seems that the heir was marked out for a social and religious position as head of the family. The bestowal of a blessing by the father, and the possession of the household gods, probably symbolized this. These customs may be deduced from contemporary deeds of adoption and legal records as well as from the biblical accounts. The brief narrative of the sale of Esau's birthright for a meal does not tell how the exchange was confirmed or whether it was recorded officially. A document of the 15th century BC records a similar sale of the patrimony of a man in Assyria. A document from the same milieu shows that the oral promise of a man to his son could be upheld in a court of law (see *ANET*, p. 220). So Isaac's blessing was irrevocable, as the text emphasizes (Gn. xxvii. 33 f.). Thus Jacob became the bearer of God's promise and the inheritor of Canaan (*cf.* Rom. ix. 10–13). Esau received the less fertile region, which became known as Edom (*q.v.*). Rebekah, the mother, obtained Isaac's permission for Jacob to flee from Esau's anger to her home in Padan-aram (*q.v.*) (Gn. xxviii. 1 ff.). She used as excuse the need for Jacob to marry a member of the same clan and so avoid mixed marriages such as Esau had contracted with the local people.

The central event of Jacob's life took place during his flight northward. At the end of a day's journey, perhaps the first, he had arrived in the hill-country near Bethel (*q.v.*), some 60 miles from Beersheba. This is a reasonable distance for a fast camel to cover in one day. The first stage of the flight would obviously finish as far from home as possible. There is no indication that Jacob had any knowledge of a particular sanctity attaching to the area, although he may have known of the site of his grandfather's altar (Gn. xii. 8). As he slept he was granted the vision of a ladder between heaven and earth and of the God of his family standing above it. The promise given to Abraham was confirmed to him and he was given a promise of divine protection. Jacob commemorated his dream by setting up the stone on which he had rested his head and pouring a libation of oil over it (Gn. xxviii. 11 ff.). Such simple monuments were often erected in sacred places (see PILLAR). This one marked the place where, for Jacob, God was known to be present.

The narrative leaps from Bethel to the district of Harran at the time of Jacob's arrival. As had Eliezer (Gn. xxiv. 11), so Jacob came first to the well outside the city. Here he was met by his cousin Rachel and taken to Laban, his uncle, who accepted him as his kinsman. When a month had elapsed, Jacob agreed to work for his uncle and, after seven years, to take Rachel as his wife (Gn. xxix. 1 ff.). Another ancient document is a record of a similar transaction, except that the man married immediately. The wedding was duly celebrated in the presence of witnesses who may have signed a marriage contract, legally required in Babylonia to give a woman the status of wife. Laban claimed a local custom as his excuse for actually giving his elder daughter Leah to Jacob. That the elder daughter should be married first is a custom not otherwise known. Jacob acquiesced in Laban's action and a new agreement was made allowing Jacob to marry Rachel after the week (presumably of celebrations) was completed. Seven more years' service were required in place of the money given by a man to his father-in-law (see MARRIAGE).

Eleven sons and one daughter were born to Jacob in Laban's house during the twenty years he stayed there. Leah bore four sons while Rachel remained barren. Her chagrin was partly overcome by giving her maid Bilhah to Jacob and adopting her two sons. Leah did likewise with her maid Zilpah, who also bore two sons. The knowledge that adoption might lead to conception by the adoptive mother may have prompted this (*cf.* Sarah and Hagar, Gn. xvi. 2). Two more sons and a daughter were borne by Leah before Rachel bore Joseph. Several of the names given to Jacob's children also occur in contemporary texts, although there is no mention of the biblical characters known.

Harran was an important trading centre as well as a fertile agricultural and pastoral district. Laban, it may be assumed, had a town house where he lived during the summer harvest season, taking his flocks to pasture on the hills during the winter. As head of what was evidently a fairly wealthy family, he would have had authority over his own household and in the city council. Jacob's request to be allowed to return to his home was, perhaps, made at the end of the fourteen years' service for his two wives. His management of Laban's flocks had been so successful that Laban was unwilling to let him go (Gn. xxx. 25 ff.). An agreement was made whereby Jacob should continue to work for Laban in return for all the beasts of Laban's flocks and herds which were of impure colour. In this way Jacob would build up a capital from which to support his family. Laban, again breaking his agreement, removed all the animals to which Jacob might lay claim, but Jacob, following advice received in a dream, ingeniously turned his father-in-law's trickery to his own advantage without infringing the agreement. His prosperity aroused the envy of Laban's sons, who felt that he was robbing them of their lawful inheritance (Gn. xxxi. 1). A divine command overcame any reluctance Jacob may have had at leaving Harran without Laban's approval. Rachel and Leah supported his plan, since, they claimed, their father had spent the dowry they should have received (see MARRIAGE). The flight was accomplished while Laban was away from home for sheepshearing. A two-day start enabled Jacob and his flocks to travel as far as Gilead in north Transjordan before he was overtaken by Laban (Gn. xxxi. 22 ff.). Seven days for Laban's pursuit, covering about 400 miles, is well within the reach of a riding camel (see CAMEL). Laban complained of Jacob's furtive departure but in particular of the theft of his gods (see TERAPHIM). If possession of these images did indeed mark the head of the family, then Rachel's deed was intended to exalt Jacob. She managed to retain them by a ruse. Jacob in turn reminded Laban of how well he had served him, complying with all the current requirements of a good herdsman, and how ill he had been rewarded. A pact was made, Laban using his authoritative position to dictate the terms: his daughters were not to be maltreated, nor should Jacob take another wife. A pillar was erected to commemorate the covenant and a cairn was built. These also served as points of demarcation beyond which neither party should go; possibly a recognition of the extent of Jacob's territorial rights under the promise. Each party called upon God to be witness and punish whoever might break the covenant. A sacrifice was made and the two parties shared a meal as a sign of their goodwill.

Jacob proceeded to Mahanaim, where an angelic host met him, and then he sent scouts to discover Esau's attitude (Gn. xxxii. 1 ff.). At his approach, Jacob took care to safeguard half of his possessions and also sent a large gift to his brother. After he had asked for divine protection, and as he was about to ford the river Jabbok, he was engaged in a struggle with a stranger who prevailed only by dislocating Jacob's thigh. This incident was regarded as Jacob's redemption 'from all evil' (Gn. xlviii. 16), the new name Israel showing that he was able to contend with God (*cf.* Ho. xii. 4). Esau's friendly greeting did not overcome Jacob's qualms. He turned down to Succoth (*q.v.*) instead of following Esau. From Succoth he moved up to a town in the territory of Shechem and purchased a piece of land. The rape of Dinah and the vengeance taken by her brothers made the area hostile to him (Gn. xxxiv. 1 ff.). God instructed him to go to Bethel, presumably outside the jurisdiction of Shechem, to worship. The various pagan symbols brought from Padan-aram were buried before the family could proceed. As before, Jacob erected a pillar to commemorate his communion with God and poured a libation. He did the same to mark Rachel's tomb at Ephrath (*q.v.*) but without a libation (Gn. xxxv. 1–20). After Isaac's death (Gn. xxxv. 28, 29) he settled in the region of Hebron and there lived as he had in Harran, by herding and by cultivation. When the famine struck and he was invited to Egypt, he first sought assurance that it was right for him to go south of Beersheba (Gn. xlvi. 1 ff.).

Before his death he adopted the two sons of Joseph and gave them a special blessing, preferring the younger over the elder. Joseph was singled out for a double portion (Gn. xlviii). The blessings of the twelve sons are recorded in a poetic composition of unknown date (Gn. xlix. 1–27). It is possible that it is contemporary, but there is no comparative work. Jacob died, over 130 years old, and was buried in the family tomb at Machpelah (*q.v.*) near Hebron (Gn. l. 13).

His descendants called themselves by his name Israel (paralleled by Jacob in poetry). As the chosen people they had the privilege of striving with God. See also ISRAEL, and A. R. Millard, *Archaeology and the Life of Jacob*, 1962.

A.R.M.

III. NEW TESTAMENT REFERENCES

Jacob the son of Isaac is listed in the genealogies (Mt. i. 2; Lk. iii. 34). More significant is the recurring conjunction, Abraham, Isaac, and Jacob, where Jacob stands with the other two as a type of the eternally blessed (Mt. viii. 11; Lk. xiii. 28). All three Synoptists record Jesus' quotation of Ex. iii. 6, 'I am the God of Abraham, and the God of Isaac, and the God of Jacob' (Mt. xxii. 32; Mk. xii. 26; Lk. xx. 37; also Acts vii. 32). This sonorous formula (taken up in the Jewish liturgy, *cf.* the Eighteen Benedictions) gives emphasis and solemnity to the character of God as the One who entered into covenant relation with the Patriarchs of old, and who honours His promises. Peter uses nearly the same formula to heighten his declaration of what God has done in Christ (Acts iii. 13). Stephen mentions Jacob several times (Acts vii. 12, 14, 15, 46). The last time he speaks of 'the God of Jacob', thus giving this Patriarch central importance in the history of religion. Paul refers to Jacob twice, the first time to bring out God's purposes in election (He chose Jacob before the two children were even born, Rom. ix. 11–13), and the second time as a way of symbolizing the nation (Rom. xi. 26). Finally, this Patriarch figures in Hebrews as one of the heroes of faith (Heb. xi. 9, 20 f.).

A Jacob also occurs as the name of the father of Joseph in the Matthean genealogy of our Lord (Mt. i. 15, 16). L.M.

JACOB'S WELL. See SYCHAR.

JAEL (*yā'ēl*, 'wild goat'). The wife of Heber the Kenite, and slayer of Sisera (Jdg. iv. 17–21). The Kenites were a nomadic tribe friendly towards both protagonists (Jdg. i. 16, iv. 17) when the Israelites under Barak defeated the Canaanites (iv. 15). Sisera, the Canaanite general, fled, and Jael invited him into her tent, assured him of protection, and gave him food and a mantle for covering—little more than Oriental hospitality decreed. He specifically enlisted her aid in evading his pursuers, and lay down to sleep. What happened then was as much an outrage against the ethics of her own time as against ours today. The terrible deed done, Jael stood guilty of violating the laws of hospitality, of falsehood, treachery, and murder. That she had fully grasped the course of preceding events (and perhaps felt that prudence counselled favouring the Israelites) can be seen from her opening words when Barak appeared (verse 22).

The victory proved a turning-point in the Israelites' deliverance from oppression, and Jael's action (in a slightly different form) was immortalized in the Song of Deborah (Jdg. v. 24–27) which at the same time involuntarily underlines her baseness (*cf.* verse 28). Even regarded solely as a triumph in a righteous war, it seems strange that such an unnatural act should prove the subject of holy rejoicing.

Jdg. v. 6 ('in the days of Jael') has puzzled commentators who question that the wife of a stranger should be recorded as marking an epoch in the Israelites' history, and suggest that since the Heb. word is masculine the reference may be to a different person, a man. There seems, however, little real evidence for rejecting the verse as an allusion to the wife of Heber. See also SISERA, DEBORAH. J.D.D.

JAHAZ (Heb. *yahaṣ*). A site in the plains of Moab where Israel defeated Sihon, the Amorite king (Nu. xxi. 23; Dt. ii. 32; Jdg. xi. 20). The name occurs in several forms—Jahzah, Jahaza (Jos. xiii. 18), and Jahazah (Jos. xxi. 36; Je. xlviii. 21). It fell in the portion of Reuben, and was assigned to the Merarite Levites (Jos. xiii. 18, xxi. 34, 36). The area was later lost to Israel, but Omri reconquered the land as far as Jahaz. The Moabite Stone (lines 18–20) states that the Israelites dwelt there while they fought Mesha. Finally, Mesha drove them out and added Jahaz to his domains. See MOABITE STONE.

M. du Buit would place the site just off the central highlands road on the right of the Wadi Wali. The city was still in Moabite hands in the days of Isaiah and Jeremiah (Is. xv. 4; Je. xlviii. 21, 34). J.A.T.

JAHZEIAH (*yaḥzᵉyâ*, 'Yahweh sees, reveals'; AV 'Jahaziah', Ezr. x. 15). One of four men mentioned in connection with the controversy over foreign wives. AV regards the four as supporting Ezra, 'being employed about this matter'; but the same Heb. phrase can be translated also as 'stood up against this matter' (so RV, *BDB*, *etc.*). The context would seem to support the AV rendering. J.D.D.

JAIR (*yā'ir*, 'he enlightens'). **1.** Descendant of Manasseh who, during the conquest east of the Jordan under Moses, took several villages on the border of Bashan and Gilead (Nu. xxxii. 41) and named them Havvoth-Jair (*q.v.*). **2.** A judge who judged Israel for twenty-two years (Jdg. x. 3, 5). His thirty sons had thirty cities in Gilead, the name Havvoth-Jair being associated with them. **3.** Father of Mordecai (Est. ii. 5).

4. (*yā'îr*, 'he arouses'.) Father of Elhanan (1 Ch. xx. 5), one of David's heroes; he is called Jaare-oregim (2 Sa. xxi. 19) by a scribal error. See ELHANAN. M.A.M.

JAIRUS. A ruler of the synagogue whose daughter was healed by Christ (Mk. v. 21–43; Lk. viii. 41–56; *cf.* Mt. ix. 18–26). The name may be derived from Heb. *yā'îr*, 'Yahweh enlightens' (*cf.* Jair, Jdg. x. 3). He is named by Mark and Luke but not by Matthew. His duties included the conducting of the synagogue worship and the selection of those who were to lead the prayer, read the Scriptures, and preach in it. There was generally only one *archisynagōgos* to each synagogue (Matthew describes him simply as *archōn*, which here has the same significance).

Jairus came to Jesus after He had crossed the sea of Galilee from the Decapolis and landed near Capernaum. His daughter, aged twelve, was at the point of death, and he asked Him to come and heal her. On the way to his home Jesus healed the woman with a haemorrhage. Then the news came that the girl was dead. Most of those present felt it unnecessary to trouble Christ any further, and they were scornful of His statement that the girl was not dead but asleep. When all but Peter, James, John, Jairus, and his wife had been dismissed, Jesus took her by the hand and she came back to life. He ordered her to be fed and enjoined secrecy upon them.

From a literary point of view it is interesting to see how Matthew compresses the story, so much so as to give the impression that the child was dead when Jairus first approached Jesus. It is also noteworthy that the Aramaic phrase *ṭᵉlîṯâ qûm(î)* is retained by Mark. R.E.N.

JAMBRES. See JANNES.

JAMES (Gk. *Iakōbos,* Heb. *ya'ᵃqōḇ*, 'heel-catcher', 'supplanter').

1. The son of Zebedee, a Galilaean fisherman called with his brother John to be one of the twelve apostles (Mt. iv. 21). He is mentioned in company with John and Peter, to the exclusion of the other apostles, at the raising of Jairus' daughter (Mk. v. 37), and at the transfiguration (Mk. ix. 2). He and John, who were 'nicknamed' by Jesus 'Boanerges, sons of thunder' (Mk. iii. 17), were rebuked by Jesus for their impetuosity and lack of understanding of the purpose of His coming, when they suggested that they should pray for the destruction of the Samaritan village which had repulsed His messengers (Lk. ix. 54). After requesting with his brother a place of honour in Christ's kingdom, he was told that he would drink the cup his Master was to drink (Mk. x. 39), a prophecy which was fulfilled when he was 'slain with the sword' by Herod Agrippa I, *c.* AD 44 (Acts xii. 2).

2. The son of Alphaeus, another of the twelve apostles (Mt. x. 3; Acts i. 13). He is usually identified with James 'the less', the son of Mary (Mk. xv. 40). By the description 'the less' (Gk. *ho mikros*, 'the little') he is distinguished from the son of Zebedee, being either smaller in stature or younger than his namesake.

3. The brother of Jesus mentioned with his brothers Joses, Simon, and Judas (Mt. xiii. 55). He did not apparently accept the authority of Jesus during His earthly life (see Mk. iii. 21, where 'his friends', Gk. *hoi par' autou*, probably includes His brothers). After the risen Jesus had appeared to him (1 Cor. xv. 7) he became a leading member of the Jewish Christian church at Jerusalem (Gal. i. 19, ii. 9; Acts xii. 17). Tradition stated that he was appointed first bishop of Jerusalem by the Lord Himself and the apostles (Eus., *EH* vii. 19). He presided at the first Council of Jerusalem called to consider the terms of admission of Gentiles into the Christian Church, and formulated the decree which was promulgated to the churches of Antioch, Syria, and Cilicia (Acts xv. 19–23). That he continued to have strong *Jewish* Christian sympathies is evident from his request to Paul when the latter visited Jerusalem for the last time (Acts xxi. 18 ff.). Later, according to Hegesippus, he became known as 'the Just' because of his faithful adherence to the Jewish law and his austere manner of life (Eus., *EH* ii. 23). He suffered martyrdom by stoning at the hands of the high priest Ananus during the interregnum after the death of the procurator Festus in AD 61 (Jos., *Ant.* xx. 9). Jerome (*De viris illustribus* ii) records a fragment from the lost apocryphal *Gospel according to the Hebrews* containing a brief and probably unhistorical account of the appearance of the risen Jesus to James. He is the traditional author of the canonical Epistle of James, where he describes himself as 'a servant of God and of the Lord Jesus Christ' (Jas. i. 1).

4. An otherwise unknown James, who is described in Luke vi. 16 and Acts i. 13 as 'the brother' of the apostle Judas (not Iscariot). The Gk. expression 'Judas of James' is, however, more naturally rendered 'Judas the son of James' (so RSV) (see also BRETHREN OF THE LORD). R.V.G.T.

JAMES, EPISTLE OF.

I. THE IDENTITY OF THE AUTHOR

This document did not receive general recognition till the 4th century. Hesitation about accepting it was due to uncertainty as to the identification of the author, who describes himself as 'a servant of God and of the Lord Jesus Christ' (i. 1). It was recognized for the most part that James the son of Zebedee was martyred too early for him to have been the author. A tradition, however, that he wrote the book lingered on in Spain in the Middle Ages, and the book is assigned to him in a 10th-century MS, *Codex Corbeiensis,* which contains a 4th-century Latin version of the Epistle. When it became generally understood that James the brother of the Lord was the probable author, and that he was called an 'apostle' by Paul (Gal. i. 19), the document satisfied the test of apostolicity and was accepted into the canon. There is no evidence that the Epistle was attributed in the early Church to James 'the less' (Mk. iii. 18). Luther's refusal to regard it as on a par with the other canonical books because, in his view, it contradicted Paul on the matter of justification, and was in consequence by comparison with them 'a right strawy Epistle', was his own personal judgment, unsupported by any patristic evidence.

The address 'to the twelve tribes which are scattered abroad' (i. 1), probably a symbolic expression for the congregations of Christian people dispersed throughout the world, naturally caused the Epistle to be grouped with other Epistles that were not addressed to a single community. (See CATHOLIC EPISTLES.) The homiletic character of the work, its Jewish–Christian flavour, its echoes of the later Wisdom literature of Judaism ('wisdom' may be said to be one of its key-words, see i. 5, iii. 17), and of the sayings of Jesus which became embodied in the Sermon on the Mount (*cf.* ii. 13 and Mt. v. 7; iii. 12 and Mt. vii. 16; iii. 18 and Mt. vii. 20; v. 2 and Mt. vi. 19; v. 12 and Mt. v. 34–37), and the note of authority with which the author speaks, are all consonant with the tradition that he was the first 'bishop' of the Jerusalem Church who presided at the conference described in Acts xv. Moreover, although the Epistle contains some curious non-biblical literary phrases (see i. 17, 23, iii. 6), its Hebraic features, coupled with the frequent use of rhetorical questions, vivid similes, imaginary dialogues, telling aphorisms, and picturesque illustrations, make it not unreasonable to suppose that we are listening to the bilingual Palestinian Jewish Christian, who resided at Jerusalem continuously, so far as we know, from the resurrection of Jesus till his martyrdom some thirty years later, and who by virtue of his commanding position was brought into contact with Jews and Christians from all parts of the world. The resemblances in the Greek between the Epistle and the speech of James at the Council of Jerusalem (*cf.* i. 1 and Acts xv. 23; i. 27 and Acts xv. 14; ii. 5 and Acts xv. 13; ii. 7 and Acts xv. 17) afford significant, though not in themselves conclusive, supporting evidence.

II. AUTHORSHIP: OTHER THEORIES

On the other hand, the almost complete lack of references to distinctively Christian doctrines, the disjointed nature of the moral axioms in which the Epistle abounds, and the fact that Jesus Christ is mentioned only twice in it, have led many modern scholars to abandon the view that it was written by James the Lord's brother sometime between AD 40 and 60. Two alternative hypotheses have been favoured. The first supposes that an originally Jewish homily was later adapted for use by the Jewish Christians by the insertion of 'Jesus Christ' at i. 1 and ii. 1. The second regards the Epistle as a late Christian homily written to meet the needs of the more settled Christian communities after early evangelistic fervour had subsided. On either hypothesis, it is possible to assume that the author was either an unknown James or a writer who sought to give authority to his work by using the name either of the son of Zebedee or of the first bishop of Jerusalem.

The first alternative might account for such expressions as 'Abraham our father' (ii. 21) and 'the Lord of Sabaoth' (v. 4), and the emphasis laid upon justification by works (ii. 14–26). It could also explain the phenomena that the writer speaks like a second Amos when he is denouncing the rich (v. 1–6), and that it is to Abraham (ii. 21), Rahab (ii. 25), Job (v. 11), and Elijah (v. 17), and 'the prophets, who have spoken in the name of the Lord' (v. 10) that he turns for example of the virtues he is advocating, and not to Jesus. But these features of the Epistle do not *demand* such an explanation, for the Old Testament was the Bible of the early Christians; and as has been pointed out, 'there is no sentence in the Epistle, which a Jew could have written and a Christian could not'. Moreover, it is difficult to suppose that the imaginary Christian interpolator would have been capable of exercising such excessive restraint!

The second alternative gains credence if it is assumed that ii. 24–26 was written to counteract the antinomian perversion of Paul's doctrine of justification by faith, but it fails to account for the primitive features of the Epistle, such as the use of 'synagogue' for a Christian assembly in ii. 2. Further, if we are to suppose that the author was an unknown James, it is difficult to see why the Epistle received recognition. But if, on the other hand, we assume that it is pseudepigraphic, we are bound to ask why the writer did not describe himself as 'James the apostle' or 'James the brother of the Lord'. Moreover, although it is clear from the evidence of Eusebius and Jerome that many refused to accept the Epistle as genuine on the ground that it might have been written by another using the apostle's name, the fact that it *did* eventually receive recognition at a time when the criterion of apostolicity was so strict at least suggests that the final judgment was not made irresponsibly.

III. TEACHING OF THE EPISTLE

The Epistle has always been highly valued by Roman Catholics because they have regarded it, erroneously, as affording evidence for the doctrine of merit and justification by works, auricular confession (v. 16) and extreme unction (v. 14). Protestants, on the other hand, have tended to be unduly influenced by Luther's devaluation of it, and to regard it as somewhat sub-Christian. There are signs, however, that modern Evangelicals see the folly of under-emphasizing the ethical implications of the doctrine of justification by faith, and the place which good works should occupy in the Christian life. This Epistle, it is clear, supplements but in no way contradicts the teaching of the Epistles to the Galatians and Romans. James, it would seem, is not using the word 'justified' in ii. 21 with reference to the occasion in the story of Abraham alluded to by Paul, *viz.* Gn. xv. 6, but with reference to the incident recorded in Gn. xxii. On the former occasion Abraham was 'justified' by his faith; on the second, he was in effect shown to have been justified by his willingness to offer Isaac in sacrifice, if it should be the Lord's will. As Calvin pointed out, writers of Scripture are not all required to handle the same arguments. He also added that this Epistle contains nothing unworthy of an apostle of Christ, but on the contrary gives instruction on numerous subjects, all of which are important for Christian living, such as 'patience, prayer to God, the excellency and fruit of heavenly truth, humility, holy duties, the restraining of the tongue, the cultivation of peace, the repression of lusts, the contempt of the world and the like'. It is surely remarkable that the only attempted definition of true religion contained in the New Testament should be found in the essentially practical Epistle of James (i. 27). As the present writer has said in *TNTC*, 'Whenever faith does not issue in love, and dogma, however orthodox, is unrelated to life; whenever Christians are tempted to settle down to a self-centred religion, and become oblivious of the social and material needs of others; or whenever they deny by their manner of living the creed they profess, and seem more anxious to be friends of the world than friends of God, then the Epistle of James has something to say to them which they reject at their peril.'

There have not been lacking signs that v. 13–15 has been misinterpreted in recent years to support erroneous teaching about 'spiritual healing', and that the injunction of v. 16 has been appealed to as a justification for the dangerous practice of unrestricted public confession of sins. For these additional reasons the Epistle calls for special study by Christians today. In an age when the severity of the divine nature and the transcendence of God tend to be forgotten, the balance needs to be redressed by the emphasis laid in this Epistle upon the unchangeable God (i. 17), the Creator (i. 18), the Father (i. 27, iii. 9), the Sovereign (iv. 15), the Righteous One (i. 20) untempted with evil (i. 13), to whom man must submit in humility (iv. 7, 10), the Lawgiver, the Judge, the Saviour and Destroyer (iv. 11, 12) who will brook no rivals (see iv. 4, 5, RSV), the Giver of wisdom (i. 5) and grace (iv. 6), who promises the crown of life to those who love Him (i. 12).

BIBLIOGRAPHY. Commentaries by F. J. A. Hort, 1909; J. B. Mayor, 1913; J. H. Ropes, *ICC*, 1916; R. V. G. Tasker, *TNTC*, 1956. See also JAMES and BRETHREN OF THE LORD. R.V.G.T.

JANNES AND JAMBRES. Paul speaks of certain false and morally dangerous teachers as resisting the truth as 'Jannes and Jambres' resisted Moses (2 Tim. iii. 6–8). These names do not occur in the Old Testament, but extra-biblical allusions show that the Egyptian magicians of Ex. vii–viii are intended. Like them, the teachers played on superstitious susceptibilities with a plausibly presented parody of the truth.

The names, of unknown age, occur in various forms. The so-called 'Zadokite Work', now known to belong with the Qumran literature, has Belial raising up 'Yoḥaneh and his brother' against Moses and Aaron (vii. 19 in R. H. Charles, *Pseudepigrapha*, 1913; v. 19 in C. Rabin, *The Zadokite Documents*², 1958, p. 21); the Babylonian Talmud 'Yoḥanē and Mamre' (*Menaḥoth* 85a; *cf.* the spelling 'Mambres' in most Latin and some Greek MSS of 2 Tim. iii. 8). Jewish legend made much of them, even attributing their paternity to Balaam! Pagan sources refer, not always perspicuously, to one or both (*cf.* Pliny, *NH* xxx. 1. 11; Apuleius, *Apology* xc; Numenius of Apamea in Eus., *Praep. Ev.* ix. 8. 1), reflecting the story's celebrity. Origen knew a book on the subject (in Mt. xxiii. 37, xxvii. 9), and the Gelasian Decree a *Penitence of Jannes and Jambres* of which M. R. James identified a fragment in a Saxon MS (*JTS*, II, 1901, pp. 572 ff.). It is improbable, however, that Paul is alluding to the book: he would employ the names simply as being then in common use, with Ex. vii–viii alone in mind.

BIBLIOGRAPHY. E. Schürer, *HJP*, ii, 3, pp. 149 ff.; *SB*, iii, pp. 660 ff. A.F.W.

JANOAH (*yānôaḥ, yānôḥâ*, 'rest'). **1.** A town of Naphtali seized by Tiglath-pileser during Pekah's reign (2 Ki. xv. 29). Possibly modern Yanūḥ, north of Tyre, or Hunîn, west of upper Jordan. **2.** A town of Ephraim, south-east from Shechem, used in defining Ephraim's border with Manasseh (Jos. xvi. 6, 7; AV 'Janohah'). Modern Khirbet Yānun. J.G.G.N.

JAPHETH (*yep̄eṯ*). One of the sons of Noah, usually mentioned last of the three (Gn. v. 32, vi. 10, vii. 13, ix. 18, 23, 27; 1 Ch. i. 4), but his descendants are recorded first in Gn. x (and 1 Ch. i. 5–7). He was the ancestor of a number of tribes and peoples, most of whom had names which in historical times are associated with the regions to the north and west of the Middle East, especially Anatolia, and the Aegean (see NATIONS, TABLE OF; *cf.* map I). Japheth and his wife were among the eight humans who escaped the Flood, and after it was over he and Shem covered the nakedness of their father, Noah. In Noah's prophetic declaration after this episode he prayed that God might enlarge Japheth, and that *he* might dwell in the tents of Shem, and have Canaan as a servant (Gn. ix. 27). Many commentators take this to refer to God rather than Japheth, though either interpretation is possible. If the latter alternative is followed the reference may be to the benefits of the gospel which, coming first to the descendants of Shem, were later extended to the northern peoples. In the above verse the word used for 'may he enlarge' is *yap̄t*, but this is probably only a play on words and does not have anything else to do with the name Japheth (*yep̄eṯ*), which does not occur elsewhere in the Bible or in the ancient inscriptions. Some have connected Japheth, however, with the Gk. mythological figure *Iapetos*, a son of earth and heaven, who had many descendants. The name is not Greek, so may be a form of the biblical name.

BIBLIOGRAPHY. P. Dhorme, 'Les Peuples issus de Japhet, d'après le Chapître X de la Genèse', *Syria*, XIII, 1932, pp. 28–49; D. J. Wiseman, 'Genesis 10: Some Archaeological Considerations', *JTVI*, LXXXVII, 1955, pp. 14 ff.

T.C.M.

JAREB. The name or epithet of a king of Assyria who received tribute from Israel (Ho. v. 13, x. 6). If taken as a personal name it is assumed that the reference is to Tiglath-pileser III and Menahem's attempt to buy off the Assyrians in 738 BC (2 Ki. xv. 19) or to the plea by Ahaz for his help against Rezin of Syria and Pekah of Israel (2 Ki. xvi. 7–10). Sayce's suggestion that it is Sargon II, conqueror of Samaria in 722 BC, is unlikely because of the date and circumstances.

It is more probable, since the customary definite article is here omitted, that *meleḵ yārēḇ* is a title to be translated 'warlike (or contending) king' or, taking *malki raḇ* as an old form for *meleḵ raḇ*, the usual Assyr. royal title of 'great king'. *Cf.* RVmg, 'a king that contends'; AVmg, 'the king that should plead'. On either interpretation the historical reference would be that quoted above. D.J.W.

JARMUTH. 1. Khirbet Yarmuk, a fortified town of the Shephelah in a commanding position on the south side of the Wadi Surar, about 18 road miles from Jerusalem. Late Bronze walls and pottery indicate an occupied area of 6–8 acres and a population of 1,500–2,000 before the Israelite invasion, when Jarmuth was a leading Amorite city. See Jos. x. 3, xv. 35.

BIBLIOGRAPHY. Garstang, *Joshua–Judges*, 1931, p. 171; *PEF Mem.* iii, 1883, 128; *RB*, XXXVIII, 1929, p. 426.

2. A town in Issachar assigned to the Levites (Jos. xxi. 29); LXX(B) *Remmath* corresponds to 'Ramoth' (1 Ch. vi. 73) and probably to 'Remeth' (Jos. xix. 21). The site is unknown. J.P.U.L.

JASHAR, BOOK OF (AV 'Jasher'). In Jos. x. 13 and 2 Sa. i. 18 the book of *yāšār* ('the upright one') is mentioned. Solomon's words in 1 Ki. viii. 12, 13, according to LXX, who put them after viii. 53, are to be found in 'the book of the song'. As 'song', *šyr*, closely resembles *yšr*, probably the same book is meant here. All three quotations are in poetic style. It is possible that more quotations from ancient poetry came from this lost book. Some scholars identify it with 'the book of the wars of the Lord' (Nu. xxi. 14). As the quotations differ in metre, style, and general contents, and date from different times, it is not probable that the book was a 'national epic'; it was rather a collection of songs with short historical introductions, *cf.* Arab. anthologies as, *e.g.*, Ḥamāsa. It must have been composed under Solomon's reign or later. The name *yāšār* is probably related to *yešurûn*, Israel (Dt. xxxii. 15, *etc.*). Printed books of Jashar are modern fabrications.

BIBLIOGRAPHY. S. Mowinckel, 'Hat es ein israelitisches Nationalepos gegeben?', *ZAW*, NF XII, 1935, pp. 130–152. A. VAN S.

JASHOBEAM. 1. 'An Hachmonite, chief of the captains', 1 Ch. xi. 11; 'son of Zabdiel', 1 Ch. xxvii. 2. He is to be identified with 'the Tachmonite that sat in the seat' (2 Sa. xxiii. 8), which might be read 'Josheb-bashebeth the Hachmonite' (*haḥaḵmōnî* for *taḥkemōnî*). LXX *Iebosthe*, *Iesebada*, Lucian *Iesbaal* imply a form 'Ishbaal'. He was David's leading warrior, who slew 'three hundred' (1 Ch.) or 'eight hundred' (2 Sa.), which is more likely, as it gives him superiority over Abishai (2 Sa. xxiii. 18). See CAPTAIN.

2. Another warrior, who joined David at Ziklag (1 Ch. xii. 6). A.R.M.

JASON. 1. Paul's host at Thessalonica (Acts xvii. 5–9). A rabble instigated by Jews raided his house, and, not finding Paul and Silas, seized Jason with some converts, and accused him before the politarchs (local magistrates) of harbouring seditious agitators. The prisoners were released on giving security for good behaviour. Luke does not say whether this involved a promise not to shelter the missionaries (*cf.* T. W. Manson, *BJRL*, XXXV, 1952–3, p. 432), or simply to keep the peace. In either case the effect was the hasty departure of Paul (Acts xvii. 10) in circumstances which precluded an early return (*cf.* 1 Thes. ii. 18). Jason was no doubt a Jew (*cf.* Acts xvii. 2 with xviii. 2–4) and probably a Christian (*cf.* Acts xvii. 7).

2. A Christian at Corinth, sending greetings in Rom. xvi. 21. 'Kinsman' here probably means 'fellow Jew' (*cf.* verses 7, 11 and Rom. ix. 3). Jason may be identical with (1); if Sosipatros is the Sopater (*q.v.*) of Acts xx. 4, Paul may be linking two fellow-Macedonians.

The name—that of the leader of the Argonauts —was very widespread, and Greek-speaking Jews seem to have sometimes used it instead of the similar-sounding, but conspicuously Jewish, name Jesus (Deissmann, *BS*, p. 315 n.). A.F.W.

JASPER. See JEWELS AND PRECIOUS STONES.

JATTIR. Khirbet 'Attir in the SW Judaean hills (Jos. xv. 48), 13 miles from Hebron; assigned to the priests, Jos. xxi. 14. David shared the spoils of the Amalekites with its inhabitants, 1 Sa. xxx. 27. See Alt, *Palästinajahrbuch*, 1932, pp. 15 f.

JAVAN. One of the sons of Japheth (Gn. x. 2; 1 Ch. i. 5) and father of a group of peoples, Elishah, Tarshish, Kittim, and Dodanim (*qq.v.*; Gn. x. 4; 1 Ch. i. 7), whose associations are with the regions to the north and west of the Middle East. It is generally accepted that this name (Heb. *yāwān*) is to be identified with Gk. *Iōnes*, which occurs as *Iaones*, probably for *Iawones*, in Homer (*Iliad*, xiii. 685), and refers to the people who later gave their name to Ionia. The name also occurs in Assyrian and Achaemenian inscriptions (*Iâmanu* and *Yauna* respectively). Isaiah mentions the descendants of Javan (LXX *Hellas*) beside Tubal as one of the nations (*gôyîm*) inhabiting distant islands and coastlands (*'iyyîm*, Is. lxvi. 19). In the time of Ezekiel the descendants of Javan (LXX *Hellas*) were known as traders in men, bronze vessels, and yarn, with Tyre (Ezk. xxvii. 13, 19; in verse 19 RSV prefers to read *mē'ûzāl*, 'from Uzal', for *meûzzāl*, 'that which is spun, yarn'). The name Javan (EVV Greece) is used in the prophecies of Daniel to refer to the kingdom of Alexander of Macedon, and in Zc. ix. 13 the term (EVV Greece, LXX Hellēnes) is probably used of the Seleucid Greeks.

BIBLIOGRAPHY. P. Dhorme, *Syria*, XIII, 1932, pp. 35–36. T.C.M.

JAVELIN. See ARMOUR AND WEAPONS.

JAZER. A town of the Amorite kingdom of Sihon captured by Israel (Nu. xxi. 32) and part of the pasture-lands allotted to the tribe of Gad. It was later given to the Merarite families of the tribe of Levi. During David's reign, Jazer furnished 'mighty men of valour' (1 Ch. xxvi. 31) and was one of the towns on the route of the census-takers (2 Sa. xxiv. 5). The Moabites gained control of it, probably a little before the fall of Samaria (Is. xvi. 8, 9; Je. xlviii. 32, where 'sea of' has been considered a scribal error). Judas

Maccabaeus captured and sacked the town *c.* 164 BC (1 Macc. v. 7, 8). The site may be Khirbet Ġazzir on the Wadi Ša'īb near es-Salt. A.R.M.

JEALOUSY. It is an axiom of the Old Testament that God is a jealous God (Ex. xxxiv. 14), who demands to be worshipped exclusively, and to whom idolatry is the cardinal sin (Ex. xx. 5). His jealousy is a lover's jealousy. As a faithful lover of Israel He demands the faithfulness of His people. It may be to this aspect of the divine nature that the difficult words of Jas. iv. 5 refer (see *TNTC*). Paul insists that for a Christian to run any risk of idolatry would be to 'provoke the Lord to jealousy' (1 Cor. x. 22). As a minister of God's people he has the same jealousy for the purity of their faith and conduct as God Himself (2 Cor. xi. 2). And it is to such godly jealousy that he predicts the unbelieving Israelites will be provoked, in accordance with the prophecy of Dt. xxxii. 21, as they see the Gentiles enjoying the privileges of Israel. Paul is also confident that such jealousy will lead them in the end to claim their own rightful place among God's people (Rom. x. 19, xi. 11). R.V.G.T.

JEBUSITE. The ethnic name of a Canaanite people dwelling in the hills (Nu. xiii. 29; Jos. xi. 3) round about Jerusalem (Jos. xv. 8, xviii. 16). Descended from the third son of Canaan (Gn. x. 16; 1 Ch. i. 14), they are, however, listed as a distinct, but minority, group of people living alongside such peoples as Amorites and Heth. Jebus was a name given to Jerusalem, the principal city in their territory (Jdg. xix. 10, 11; 1 Ch. xi. 4, 5; called Jebusi in Jos. xviii. 16, 28), and 'Jebusite' described the inhabitants of the city (Gn. xv. 21; Ex. iii. 8). Later the term is used of the former inhabitants (Ezk. xvi. 3, 45; Zc. ix. 7).

Unless Melchizedek was ruler of Jerusalem (see SALEM), its earliest king named in the Old Testament is Adoni-zedek (Jos. x. 1), who raised his local Amorite allies (verse 5) to protect the city from the Israelites entering the area. He met his death at Beth-horon (verses 10–11). According to the Amarna tablets (*c.* 1400 BC), *Urusalimmu* was under Abdiḫepa, whose name, like that of a later Jebusite ruler Araunah (2 Sa. xxiv. 24) or Ornan (1 Ch. xxi. 15), is non-Semite, probably Hurrian (see HORITES). Jebus was burnt after its capture by the men of Judah (Jdg. i. 8),

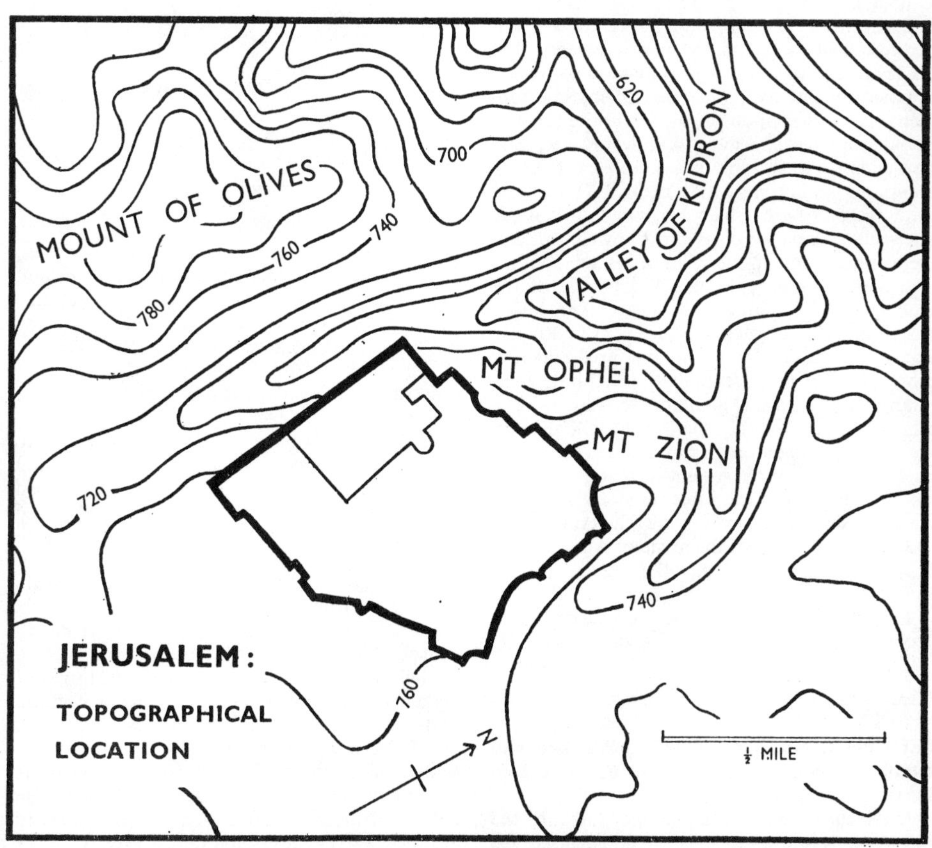

Fig. 117. Plan showing the topographical location of Jerusalem. Contour figures are given in metres. See also pl. XVI.

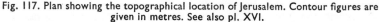

but its original inhabitants regained control at least until the attack by David (2 Sa. v. 6). The Jebusites were allowed to remain on the temple hill until their ground was bought over or the Jebusite minority absorbed by the Judaeans who built a new quarter on Zion (Jdg. i. 21, xix. 11). See JERUSALEM and fig. 119. D.J.W.

JEDIDIAH. See SOLOMON.

JEDUTHUN (*yᵉḏûṯûn*). A Levite appointed by David to conduct the music of the Temple along with Heman and Asaph (1 Ch. xxv. 1, 3, 6, *etc.*). He is also known as Ethan (*q.v.*) (1 Ch. vi. 44, *etc.*), which was possibly his name before his appointment. A variation of the name, Jedithun (*yᵉḏîṯûn*), appears several times in the *Kᵉṯîḇ* (Pss. xxxix, *etc.*). The name appears in the titles of three psalms: xxxix, lxii, lxxvii. In the first of these the title is simply 'to (*lᵉ*) Jeduthun', but in the other two it is ''*al* Jeduthun', which may mean 'according to' or 'over'; if the latter, Jeduthun three means the family or guild of singers called after him. The family continued to officiate after the Exile (Ne. xi. 17). M.A.M.

JEHOAHAZ (*yᵉhô'āḥāz*, 'Yahweh has grasped'). **1.** King of Israel *c.* 815–800 BC. He was the son and successor of Jehu, and his reign was undistinguished except in the negative sense that his religious policy brought almost unparalleled impoverishment to his people. Divine chastisement was visited upon the nation in the form of Syrian military expeditions under Hazael and Ben-hadad which took heavy toll of Israelite manpower and property (2 Ki. xiii. 2–7). So great were the straits to which his kingdom was reduced that Jehoahaz prayed to Yahweh for help. Deliverance came in the reign of his son Joash.

2. King of Judah 608 BC. The people of the land anointed him king on the death of his father Josiah in battle at Megiddo (2 Ki. xxiii. 30). He was not Josiah's eldest son, but was evidently more popular than Jehoiakim (Eliakim). Jeremiah refers to him as Shallum (Je. xxii. 11, 12). His name was probably changed to Jehoahaz on his accession. Pharaoh Necho deposed him when he had reigned three months. He was brought first to Riblah and was later removed to Egypt, where he died (2 Ki. xxiii. 33; 2 Ch. xxxvi. 4).

3. A variant form of the name of Ahaziah, son of Jehoram, king of Judah, 842 BC (2 Ch. xxi. 17, xxv. 23).

4. The full name of Ahaz (*q.v.*), king of Judah, according to an inscription of Tiglath-pileser III (*DOTT*, pp. 56 f.). J.C.J.W.

JEHOASH. See JOASH.

JEHOIACHIN (Heb. *yᵉhôyāḵîn*, 'Yahweh will establish'; 'Jeconiah' in 1 Ch. iii. 16; 'Coniah' in Je. xxii. 24, 28).

Jehoiachin was appointed king of Judah by the Babylonians following the revolt and death of his father Jehoiakim (*c.* 6 December 598 BC). He ruled for three months and ten days (2 Ch. xxxvi. 9; Jos., *Ant.* x. 6. 9). His brief reign is described in 2 Ki. xxiv. 8–16 and 2 Ch. xxxvi. 9, 10. It was marked by evil, and the prophet Jeremiah foretold the end of both his rule and dynasty (Je. xxii. 24–30). According to Josephus, Nebuchadrezzar changed his mind about the appointment and returned to besiege Jerusalem and carried off the eighteen-year-old king, with his mother Nehushta, his family, and fellow Jews, to exile in Babylon. This famous historical event is also described in the Old Testament and in the Bab. Chronicle. The city fell on 16 March 597, and Jehoiachin's young uncle Mattaniah, renamed Zedekiah, was appointed to succeed him (2 Ki. xxiv. 17; Je. xxxvii. 1).

In Babylon Jehoiachin was treated as a royal hostage and received rations from the Babylonian court. He is named (*Ya'u-kîn*) in Bab. tablets, dated between 595 and 570 BC, as receiving such rations in company with his five sons (E. F. Weidner, *Mélanges Syriens offerts à M. René Dussaud*, II, 1939, pp. 923 ff.; *DOTT*, pp. 84–86). While in exile his estates in Judah continued to be managed by a steward Eliakim (*DOTT*, pp. 224). The Jews in Babylonia reckoned the years by those of Jehoiachin's captivity (Ezk. i. 2). After Nebuchadrezzar's death his successor in 561 BC showed Jehoiachin special favour and removed him from prison to the royal palace (2 Ki. xxv. 27–30; Je. lii. 31–34; see EVIL-MERODACH). Jehoiachin's eldest son Shealtiel, the father of Zerubbabel, was born in 598 BC. Another son Shenazar is named in 1 Ch. iii. 18.

BIBLIOGRAPHY. D. J. Wiseman, *Chronicles of Chaldaean Kings*, 1956, pp. 33–35. D.J.W.

JEHOIADA (Heb. *yᵉhôyāḏā'*, 'Yahweh knows') was a popular name in Old Testament times. **1.** The father of Benaiah (2 Sa. viii. 18), a valiant man from Kabzeel in the Negeb (1 Ch. xi. 22); the son was one of David's officers. **2.** The leader of the Aaronites, who supported David at Ziklag (1 Ch. xii. 27). **3.** The son of Benaiah, and grandson of Jehoiada, one of David's counsellors (1 Ch. xxvii. 34).

4. The chief priest of the Temple in Jerusalem during the reigns of Ahaziah, Athaliah, and Joash was also named Jehoiada. He married Jehoshabeath, sister of King Ahaziah, and played a prominent part in political affairs. On the death of Ahaziah he frustrated the queen-mother Athaliah's attempt to destroy all 'the seed royal'. He and his wife hid their nephew, Joash, for six years in the Temple precincts, while Athaliah usurped the throne. Then in a *coup d'état* he brought him out of hiding as the rightful ruler of Judah. A covenant was made for his protection, and another on his proclamation as king (2 Ki. xi. 17). During Joash's minority, Jehoiada virtually ruled on his behalf. He destroyed the shrines of Baal and organized the Levites. He helped in the selection of Joash's two wives to ensure the royal succession (2 Ch. xxiv. 3). After a rebuke from Joash himself he repaired the Temple (2 Ki. xii. 7). When he died at the age of one hundred and thirty, he was buried in the royal tomb, in recognition of his service to the community.

5. A priest in Jerusalem before the Exile, during the lifetime of Jeremiah, who was replaced by Shemaiah (Je. xxix. 26). **6.** The son of Paseah who returned from the Exile with Nehemiah and played his part in the rebuilding programme (Ne. iii. 6). M.G.

JEHOIAKIM (*yᵉhôyāqîm*, 'Yahweh has established'; *cf.* Joakim, 1 Esdras i. 37–39). King of Judah (609–598 BC), a son of Josiah and elder brother of Jehoahaz, whose place he took at the command of Necho II of Egypt. His name was changed from Eliakim as a mark of vassalage. The reign is recorded in 2 Ki. xxiii. 34–xxiv. 6; 2 Ch. xxxvi. 4–8, and as the last-named entry in the 'book of the Chronicle of the Kings of Judah' (2 Ki. xxiv. 5). To pay the Egyp. dues Jehoiakim imposed heavy land taxes (2 Ki. xxiii. 35). He built costly royal buildings, using forced labour (Je. xxii. 13–17), and is described as an oppressive and covetous ruler. The religious decay during his reign is noticed by the contemporary prophets Jeremiah and Habakkuk. Josiah's reforms were forgotten in the reversion to idolatry and introduction of Egyp. rites (Ezk. viii. 5–17). Jehoiakim shed much innocent blood (2 Ki. xxiv. 4) and had the prophet Uriah murdered for opposing him (Je. xxvi. 20). He opposed Jeremiah (xxxvi. 26) and personally burnt the scroll from which Jehudi read the words of the prophet to him (verse 22). He was 'unjust and malignant, neither holy towards God, nor forbearing towards man' (Jos., *Ant.* x. 5. 2), that is, he followed in the tradition of Manasseh's sin (2 Ki. xxiv. 3).

In Jehoiakim's fourth year (605 BC) Nebuchadrezzar defeated the Egyptians and won control of Palestine as far as the Egyp. border (Je. xxv. 1, xlvi. 2; see CARCHEMISH), but it was not until the following year that Jehoiakim, with other rulers, went before Nebuchadrezzar to submit to him as vassal (Je. xxxvi. 9–29; Bab. Chronicle). Three years later, doubtless encouraged by the Egyptian defeat of the Babylonians in 601 BC, but against the advice of Jeremiah, Jehoiakim rebelled (2 Ki. xxiv. 1). Nebuchadrezzar did not at first intervene but sent local Babylonian garrison troops with Syrians, Moabites, and Ammonites to raid Judah (verse 2). At length, three months and ten days before Jerusalem fell to the Bab. besiegers Jehoiakim died, aged thirty-six (*i.e.* 6 December 598 BC). His death occurred on the way to captivity (2 Ch. xxxvi. 6), apparently at the instigation of Nebuchadrezzar, who, according to Josephus (*Ant.* x. 6. 7), had his body thrown outside the city wall as prophesied by Jeremiah (xxii. 18 f.). 2 Ki. xxiv. 6 is silent as to his burial. Jehoiakim was succeeded by his son Jehoiachin. D.J.W.

JEHONADAB (*yᵉhônāḏāḇ*, 'Yahweh is liberal'). **1.** Son of Shimeah, David's brother. His cunning enabled his friend Amnon, David's son, to obtain his foul desire on Tamar, Amnon's half-sister (2 Sa. xiii. 3–5). His knowledge of the death of Amnon would seem to indicate complicity in it, although he was his professed friend (2 Sa. xiii. 30–33). **2.** A son of Rechab, a Kenite (1 Ch. ii. 55; Je. xxxv. 6). He prohibited his clan from engaging in agriculture, possessing vineyards and using their produce, and dwelling in settled communities (Je. xxxv. 6–10). But this may have been codifying what was already general practice. He was a zealous worshipper of Yahweh and assisted Jehu in suppressing the worship of Baal Melqart (2 Ki. x. 15, 23). M.A.M.

JEHORAM (*yᵉhôrām*, 'Yahweh is exalted'). Sometimes the abbreviated form 'Joram' is found.

1. The second eldest son of Ahab who succeeded his brother Ahaziah as king of Israel when the latter died childless (*c.* 851–842 BC). His abandonment of the worship of Baal Melqart of Tyre probably reflects the salutary effect upon him of his brother's fate (2 Ki. iii. 2). Elisha's retort (2 Ki. iii. 13) may perhaps indicate that the break with the foreign cult was not complete. The account of his reign is interwoven with the stories of Elisha (2 Ki. i. 17–ix. 28). As the author of Kings has deliberately suppressed the name of the king of Israel in these narratives (see KINGS, BOOKS OF), it is not certain how many of them belong to the reign of Jehoram. Elisha certainly survived him many years. At the outset of his reign he made an unsuccessful attempt to regain control of Moab with the help of Jehoshaphat of Judah, and Edom (see MOABITE STONE). Jehoram was the first of Jehu's victims, dying from an arrow wound in Jezreel (2 Ki. ix. 24–26).

2. The son of Jehoshaphat and brother-in-law of Jehoram of Israel through his marriage with Athaliah, Ahab's daughter (*c.* 850–843 BC). His reign over Judah (2 Ki. viii. 16–24; 2 Ch. xxi) contrasted sadly with that of his godly father. Early in his reign he had his six brothers put to death, as if to remove in advance all opposition to his intended religious policy, which betrayed the dominating influence of Athaliah and ultimately of Jezebel (2 Ki. viii. 18). His apostasy did not pass unrebuked. A letter from Elijah pronounced the sentence of judgment upon him and foretold his premature death through a fearful disease of the bowels (2 Ch. xxi. 12–15). The successful revolt of Edom and the invasion of Judah by the Philistines and Arabians were other evidences of God's wrath against a worthless and wicked monarch. J.C.J.W.

JEHOSHABEATH, JEHOSHEBA. Daughter of Jehoram, sister or half-sister of Ahaziah. She saved the life of Joash (2 Ki. xi. 2) when Athaliah sought to kill all the royal seed. Her marriage to Jehoiada (2 Ch. xxii. 11) is the only recorded instance of a union between a princess of the royal house and a high priest. M.A.M.

JEHOSHAPHAT (*y^e^hôšāpāṭ*, 'Yahweh has judged'). **1.** The fourth king of Judah and the son and successor of Asa (*c.* 870–845 BC). His reign is recorded at length in Chronicles (2 Ch. xvii. 1–xxi. 1), but the official account of his reign in Kings is brief (1 Ki. xxii. 41–50). Where he appears in other narratives the main interest centres in the northern kingdom (1 Ki. xxii. 1–40; 2 Ki. iii. 4–27).

In the early years of his reign Jehoshaphat took steps to ensure the security of his kingdom from external aggression. He strengthened the defences along his northern frontier, placing permanent garrisons in the towns that lay on or near the boundary between Israel and Judah. Later he reversed the policy of his predecessors and terminated the long-standing feud with Israel by concluding a marriage alliance with the house of Omri (1 Ki. xxii. 44). While it was clearly to Ahab's advantage to have an ally instead of an enemy on his southern border in view of the ever-present threat from Syria, Jehoshaphat had little to gain and, as events were to prove, much to lose by such an alliance. The marriage of his son Jehoram to Athaliah the daughter of Ahab and Jezebel bore evil fruit in later years and brought the Davidic line to the verge of extinction (2 Ki. xi. 1–3).

The widely held view that Judah became virtually a dependency of Israel is based upon the subservient attitude which Jehoshaphat appears to have adopted both towards Ahab in the battle against Ramoth-gilead (1 Ki. xxii. 4, 30) and towards Jehoram in the campaign to subjugate Moab (2 Ki. iii. 7). There is, in fact, no clear evidence that Judah was at this time in any sense subordinate to Israel.

At home Jehoshaphat showed himself to be an able administrator and a man of eminent piety who earnestly sought in all things to honour Yahweh. He was not content simply to purge his kingdom of pagan forms of worship (2 Ch. xvii. 6; *cf.* 1 Ki. xxii. 43 and see HIGH PLACE). He took positive steps to ensure that the Mosaic law was known and understood (2 Ch. xvii. 7–9). He reorganized the judiciary, assigning judges to all the more important cities of his kingdom. The establishment of a special mixed court of appeal in Jerusalem composed of Levites, priests, and elders was a landmark in the legal history of the nation (2 Ch. xix. 5–11).

2. The recorder under David and Solomon (2 Sa. viii. 16, xx. 24; 1 Ki. iv. 3). **3.** One of Solomon's twelve officers (1 Ki. iv. 17). **4.** Father of Jehu, king of Israel (2 Ki. ix. 2, 14). J.C.J.W.

JEHOSHAPHAT, VALLEY OF. The name which Joel gives to the place of the final judgment in Joel iii. 2, 12. In both of these verses 'Jehoshaphat' (meaning 'Yahweh has judged') is associated with statements that God will judge (Heb. *šāpaṭ*). Therefore it is probable that 'the valley of Jehoshaphat', like 'the valley of decision' in verse 14, is a name symbolic of the judgment, not a current geographical name.

The valley of Jehoshaphat has been variously identified. Some have thought that Joel had no definite place in mind; *e.g.* Targum Jonathan translates this name 'the plain of the decision of judgment', and Theodotion renders 'the place of judgment'. Since Joel uses the geographical term 'valley', most students have thought that some location was intended. Ibn Ezra suggests the valley of Berachah south of Bethlehem, where Jehoshaphat's forces gathered after the destruction of enemies (2 Ch. xx. 26), but Zc. xiv locates the judgment near Jerusalem, and according to 1 Enoch liii. 1 all people gather for judgment in a deep valley near the valley of Hinnom. Jewish, Christian, and Muslim traditions identify the place of final judgment as the Kidron valley, between Jerusalem and the mount of Olives. Therefore many have been buried there, Muslims especially on the western slope and Jews especially on the eastern slope of the valley. A Graeco-Roman tomb on the eastern slope has been called mistakenly the tomb of King Jehoshaphat. As early as the Bordeaux pilgrim (AD 333) and Eusebius's *Onomasticon* (*s.v. Koilas*), the name Jehoshaphat was associated with this valley. Some object that Joel uses the word '*ēmeq*, 'broad valley', while the Kidron valley is called *naḥal*, 'ravine' (2 Sa. xv. 23). Other identifications are 'the king's dale' (2 Sa. xviii. 18), which runs into the Kidron valley from the north-west (so C. F. Keil, E. G. Kraeling) and the valley of Hinnom, west and south of Jerusalem (so G. W. Wade). See figs. 117, 119.

BIBLIOGRAPHY. E. Robinson, *Biblical Researches in Palestine*, I, 1856, pp. 268–273; J. A. Bewer in *ICC*, 1912, on Joel iii. (*MT* iv.) 2; E. G. Kraeling, *Rand McNally Bible Atlas*, 1956, p. 342. J.T.

JEHOVAH. See GOD, NAMES OF.

JEHOVAH-JIREH. See GOD, NAMES OF.

JEHOVAH-NISSI. See GOD, NAMES OF.

JEHOVAH-SHALOM. See GOD, NAMES OF.

JEHOVAH-SHAMMAH. See GOD, NAMES OF.

JEHOVAH-TSIDKENU. See GOD, NAMES OF.

JEHU (*yēhû'*—meaning uncertain. Possibly an abbreviation of *y^e^hôhû'*, 'Yahweh is he'). The founder of the fourth and longest-lived dynasty in Israel, Jehu ben-Nimshi (*c.* 842–815 BC)—Nimshi was actually his grandfather; his father was Jehoshaphat—rose to power not solely through personal ambition. Already during Ahab's lifetime Jehu had been designated by God as the instrument of judgment upon the nation (1 Ki. xix. 15–17). God's command to Elijah was entrusted to his successor Elisha and was implemented during the reign of Ahab's son Jehoram. Jehu was the commanding officer of Jehoram's army which had regained control of Ramoth-gilead and continued to defend it against further Syrian assaults. Jehoram had been forced to retire to Jezreel to recover from wounds received in the fighting and had left the army under Jehu's control. It was then that Elisha sent one of the sons of the prophets to anoint Jehu king over Israel with a mandate to exterminate the house of Ahab. His brother officers immediately acquiesced in acclaiming him as king (2 Ki. ix. 1–16).

Jehu wasted no time in carrying out his commission. On his arrival in Jezreel, Jehoram and Ahaziah of Judah who rode out to meet him were both put to death. Jezebel, at his command, was thrown down into the courtyard of the palace, the circumstances of her death exactly corresponding to Elijah's prophecy (2 Ki. ix. 36, 37). The massacre of all seventy of Ahab's male descendants living in Samaria was actually carried out by the leading citizens of the kingdom as evidence of their loyalty to Jehu and in an endeavour to escape a similar fate (2 Ki. x. 1–10). The slaughter of the forty-two relatives of Ahaziah whom Jehu met on their visit to Samaria and his wholesale destruction of the worshippers in the temple of Baal went beyond the terms of his commission and are difficult to justify (2 Ki. x. 12–28; *cf.* Ho. i. 4).

When the 'blood-bath' was over and the foreign cult of Baal had been extirpated, Jehu's true character showed itself in his toleration of the corrupt worship of Yahweh linked with the bull images of Dan and Bethel (2 Ki. x. 29–31). It is scarcely surprising that Israel failed to prosper under him. The renewed threat from Syria found Israel incapable of effective resistance and Hazael overran all her territory east of Jordan (2 Ki. x. 32, 33). Jehu's submission to Shalmaneser III depicted and described on the Black Obelisk is not recorded in the Old Testament, but was doubtless aimed at securing Assyr. support against Hazael (*ANET*, p. 281; see SHALMANESER).

BIBLIOGRAPHY. D. Winton Thomas, *DOTT*, pp. 46–50, and articles in *HDB, ISBE.*

J.C.J.W.

JEHUDI (*y^ehûḏî*). Normally means 'a Jew', as in Zc. viii. 23, but in Je. xxxvi. 14, 21, 23 it is the name of an officer of Jehoiakim's court, who commanded Baruch to read the roll of Jeremiah's prophecies to the princes, and later himself read it to the king, until Jehoiakim personally destroyed it. J.G.G.N.

JEPHTHAH. One of the later (about 1100 BC) Hebrew judges (Jdg. xi. 1–xii. 7), whose name *yip̄tāḥ* is 'probably shortened from *yip̄taḥ-'ēl,* "God opens (*sc.* the womb)", which is cited as a proper name in Sabean' (*NBC*, p. 249). The son of a common heathen prostitute (*zônâ*) and the then childless Gilead, Jephthah felt he had been illegally disinherited by the younger legitimate sons of Gilead. He fled to the land of Tob (*q.v.*). From there he and the renegades he gathered raided settlements and caravans and, like David's gang (1 Sa. xxii. 2, xxvii. 8, 9, xxx), may have protected Israelite villages from marauding tribes, perhaps including the Ammonites.

Thus when the Israelites in Transjordan were threatened by a full-scale invasion of the Ammonites, the elders of Gilead invited Jephthah to be their commander. He consented only when they promised he would continue as their head (*i.e.* judge) after fighting ceased. This pact was confirmed with oaths taken at Mizpeh (Gn. xxxi. 48, 49). Jephthah's attempted diplomacy to dissuade the Ammonites failed (Jdg. xi. 12–28).

Given courage and ingenuity for his task by the Spirit of God, Jephthah passed through Gilead and Manasseh to raise additional troops. He then passed over the Jabbok to Israelite headquarters at Mizpeh. There, before moving against the Ammonites, he vowed a vow (*neḏer*) unto his God, a common practice before battle among ancient peoples. Jephthah intentionally promised Yahweh a human sacrifice, probably intending a slave, because a single animal would have been as nothing from a people's leader. The LXX translation of *hayyôṣē'*, *ho emporeuomenos,* 'whosoever comes by the way', long ago indicated that this is the proper interpretation. Verse 31 should read: 'Then whoever comes forth . . . shall be the Lord's, and I will offer him up for a burnt offering' (RSV). Jephthah was living among heathen who offered human sacrifices to pagan deities (*cf.* 2 Ki. iii. 27) and in a day when the law of Moses was little known or practised. Jephthah might sincerely (although wrongly—Lv. xviii. 21; Dt. xii. 31) suppose 'that Jehovah would need to be propitiated by some offering as costly as those which bled on the altars of Chemosh and Moloch' (F. W. Farrar).

After subduing the Ammonites by faith (Heb. xi. 32) Jephthah returned triumphantly to his headquarters house, only to meet his daughter, his only child, leading a victory procession (*cf.* 1 Sa. xviii. 6; Ex. xv. 20). With utter grief, Jephthah felt he must fulfil his vow by offering her as a burnt-offering (*'ôlâ*, which always was burned). He did not devote her to a life of celibacy (a view not introduced until Rabbi Kimchi), for there is no record that female attendants in Tabernacle or Temple had to be virgins (Anna had been married, Lk. ii. 36).

Jephthah showed himself as stern with his brethren the Ephraimites as he was with his enemies the Ammonites and with himself concerning his daughter. Offended because they had no share in his victory, the Ephraimites threatened his life. Jephthah answered harshly and slaughtered them relentlessly at the Jordan (Jdg. xii. 1–6). J.R.

JERAH. One of the sons of Joktan (*q.v.*; Gn. x. 26; 1 Ch. i. 20), some of whom can be connected with tribes of S Arabia. The name (*yeraḥ*) is identical in form with the Heb. for 'month' (see MOON), and the word occurs in the S Arabian inscriptions (*yrḥ*) with this meaning, so it may be concluded that the descendants of Jerah had likewise settled in S Arabia. The site of Beth-Yerah (Khirbet Kerak) on the Sea of Galilee is probably unrelated.

BIBLIOGRAPHY. J. A. Montgomery, *Arabia and the Bible*, 1934, p. 40. T.C.M.

JERAHMEEL (*yeraḥme'ēl*, 'may God have compassion'). **1.** The ancestor of the Jerahmeelites, a clan on the southern frontier of Judah, 'the Negeb of the Jerahmeelites' (1 Sa. xxvii. 10, RSV; *cf.* xxx. 29), related to the Calebites (*cf.* 1 Sa. xxv. 3) and bordering on the Kenites. Like the Calebites, they were absorbed into the tribe of Judah; their adoptive relationship to other branches of that tribe is given in 1 Ch. ii. 9 ff., together with the sub-divisions of the Jerahmeelite clan itself. They play a very minor part in the Old Testament record, but by dint of large-scale textual emendation T. K. Cheyne concluded that they occupy a position of major importance in the narrative—a theory which retains interest only as a notable aberration in biblical criticism (*cf. EBi*, *s.v.* 'Jerahmeel', *etc.*).

2. In 1 Ch. xxiv. 29 the son of one Kish, a member of the Merarite clan of the tribe of Levi. **3.** In Je. xxxvi. 26 a member of the royal family of Judah (AVmg, RV, RSV, 'Jerahmeel the king's son') who occupied an official position at the court of Jehoiakim. F.F.B.

JEREMIAH.

I. HIS BACKGROUND

Jeremiah's history covered a span of forty years—from his call in the thirteenth year of King Josiah (626 BC) until the fall of Jerusalem in 587 BC. In those four decades he prophesied under the last five kings of Judah—Josiah, Jehoahaz, Jehoiakim, Jehoiachin, and Zedekiah. While he was preaching, important personalities and events were shaping history beyond his native Judah. It was one of the most fateful periods in the history of the ancient Near East and it affected Judah's history too.

The Assyrian Empire disintegrated and Babylon and Egypt were left to struggle against each other for the leadership of the East. The chronology of the last quarter of the 7th century BC has been greatly clarified by the publication of some tablets which were excavated years ago but which had lain in obscurity in the vaults of the British Museum in London. In 1956 Mr. D. J. Wiseman made these Chaldean documents available to students of the ancient Near East, thus making possible a reappraisal of the chronology of the last quarter of the 7th century BC.

Jeremiah's life and times which fall within this all-important period are remarkably well documented, and the intimacies of his personality are more vividly portrayed than those of the more spectral Minor Prophets or even of Isaiah and Ezekiel.

When Jeremiah was called to the prophetic office he was still 'a child' (*na'ar*, i. 6), an ambiguous term descriptive of infancy (Ex. ii. 6) and advanced adolescence (1 Sa. xxx. 17). If the demure Jeremiah simply meant he was spiritually and socially immature the word might indicate that he was not the average age of a prophet, say between twenty and thirty, if we may argue from the rules laid down for Levites (Nu. viii. 24; 1 Ch. xxiii. 24). Assuming, then, that at his call Jeremiah was in his early twenties his boyhood was spent in the reigns of Manasseh and Amon. When the call came to Jeremiah nearly a century had passed since the northern kingdom of Israel (Samaria) had fallen to the Assyrians. Judah in the south, however, contrived to survive. By a miracle it weathered the storm of Sennacherib's invasion as Isaiah had predicted. King Hezekiah initiated reforms in Judah's religion and morals (2 Ki. xviii. 1 ff.), but these had been nullified by the long apostasy of his son Manasseh (2 Ki. xxi. 1 ff.) and the short idolatrous reign of Amon (2 Ki. xxi. 19 ff.). While Judah was wallowing in the slough of idolatry the Assyrians under Esarhaddon and Ashurbanipal conquered Egypt. Under Psammetichus (664–610 BC) Egypt reasserted herself and began afresh to intimidate Judah, who found herself vacillating between now the blandishments, now the menaces of the two world powers, Egypt and Babylon. In this atmosphere of international political tension and national religious declension Jeremiah grew up into boyhood.

Doubtless many in Judah yearned for the dawn that would end the night of sixty years' moral degeneracy. Jeremiah grew up in a pious priestly home (i. 1). His name, 'Yahweh exalts' or 'Yahweh throws down', might well symbolize both his parents' prayers for the disconsolate nation and their aspirations for young Jeremiah. They would communicate to him their anxiety over the religious persecutions and apostasies of Manasseh and Amon, educate him in Israel's laws, and fill his fertile mind with the teachings of Isaiah and other prophets of the previous century.

II. THE FIVE REIGNS

a. Josiah

When God called Jeremiah, Josiah (638–608 BC), who had been on the throne of Judah for twelve years, had already introduced religious reforms (2 Ch. xxiv. 4–7). But it was not until 621 BC, the eighteenth year of his reign, that he initiated a systematic reformation in Judah's religion and morals (2 Ki. xxiii). The impulse to reform was generated by the momentous discovery in the Temple of 'the book of the law' by Hilkiah. Jeremiah had already been a prophet for five years. Probably chapters i–vi describe conditions in Judah before Josiah's main reforms in 622–621 BC. The nation is incorrigibly corrupt, insensible to God's offer of pardon, and oblivious to the menace of an invincible enemy. Apart from xi. 1–8, which may contain hints of Jeremiah's enthusiasm for Josiah's reforms, the prophet has left no reference to the last twelve years of Josiah's reign. In 608 BC the king was killed at Megiddo (2 Ki. xxiii. 29) in an abortive attempt to resist Pharaoh Necho (610–594 BC), successor to Psammetichus. Naturally Jeremiah mourned the premature death of Josiah (xxii. 10a) of whom he thought kindly (xxii. 15 f.).

b. Jehoahaz

Necho continued to meddle in the affairs of Judah. Jehoahaz (or Shallum, Je. xxii. 11) succeeded Josiah, but three months later was deposed by Necho, who imposed on Judah a heavy tribute (2 Ki. xxiii. 31–33) and appointed Jehoiakim (or Eliakim), brother of Jehoahaz, to the throne (2 Ki. xxiii. 34; 2 Ch. xxxvi. 2, 5). Jeremiah lamented Jehoahaz's deposition and exile to Egypt (xxii. 10–12).

c. Jehoiakim

In this reign (607–597 BC) an event of great political significance occurred—the battle of Carchemish (Je. xlvi) in 605 BC. The Egyptians under Necho were crushed by the Chaldeans under Nebuchadrezzar at the battle of Carchemish, on the right-hand bank of the Euphrates north-west of Aleppo and at Hamath. Politically this event was pivotal because it marked the transference of the hegemony of the Middle East to Babylon. Therefore Carchemish also had considerable significance for Judah. Since all routes to the Egyptian border were now under Nebuchadrezzar's control, it was inevitable that the whole Middle East should come under his rule (Je. xxv. 15 ff.). From that moment, therefore, the prophet advocated Judah's submission to Babylonian suzerainty. In 604 BC Nebuchadrezzar sacked the city of Ashkelon, against which Jeremiah (xlvii. 5–7) and Zephaniah (ii. 4–7) prophesy judgment. In Je. xxxvi. 9 ff. a fast in Judah is proclaimed. This undoubtedly points to an approaching national calamity; and indeed the date of Nebuchadrezzar's campaign against Ashkelon coincides with the date of this fast in Judah. Jeremiah anticipates that from Ashkelon Nebuchadrezzar will come against Judah; hence the fast and the proclamation of Jeremiah's message in Jerusalem. But Jeremiah's policy opposed Jehoiakim's domestic and foreign strategy. The king favoured idolatrous usages (2 Ki. xxiii. 37), and his selfishness and vanity aggravated Judah's misfortunes (Je. xxii. 13–19). Jehoiakim had scant respect for the prophet's person (xxvi. 20–23) or message (ix. 26). His vacillating policy of alliance with Egypt, then with Babylon, was probably due to the fact that the outcome of the fighting between Babylon and Egypt in the year 601/600 BC was inconclusive. Three years later he rebelled against Babylon, but failure only brought him under the Babylonian yoke more completely, and this exacerbated Judah's anguish (2 Ki. xxiv. 1 f.). Jeremiah reprimanded the king, the prophets, and the priests, and the hostility which this rebuke engendered is mirrored in his oracles. He was persecuted (xii. 6, xv. 15–18), plotted against (xi. 18–23, xviii. 18), imprisoned (xx. 2), declared worthy of death (xxvi. 10 f., 24, *cf.* verses 20–23, xxxvi. 26). His prophecies in written form were destroyed (xxxvi. 27). But in these depressing circumstances Jeremiah persisted in his ministry—interceding for Judah (xi. 14, xiv. 11, xvii. 16), expostulating with God (xvii. 14–18, xviii. 18–23, xx. 7–18), unmasking the time-serving prophets (xxiii. 9–40), predicting the destruction of the Temple (vii. 1–15) and nation (xviii f.), and lamenting the doom of his people (ix. 1, xiii. 17, xiv. 17). Eventually Jehoiakim's life ended violently in Jerusalem at the close of 598 BC, the eleventh year of his reign, as Jeremiah had foretold (xxii. 18; *cf.* 2 Ki. xxiv. 1 ff.). On the other hand, 2 Ch. xxxvi. 6 f. speaks of Nebuchadrezzar's binding Jehoiakim in fetters to take him to Babylon. Dn. i. 1 f. also speaks of Jehoiakim's exile in the third year of his reign.

d. Jehoiachin

Jehoiachin (or Coniah, xxii. 24, 28, or Jeconiah, xxiv. 1) succeeded Jehoiakim in 597 BC and reaped what his father had sown. This immature youth of eighteen reigned only three months (2 Ki. xxiv. 8). The rebellion of Jehoiachin's father compelled Nebuchadrezzar in the seventh year of his reign to besiege Jerusalem, and the youthful king of Judah 'went out' (2 Ki. xxiv. 12), *i.e.* gave himself up. He, along with the majority of Judah's aristocracy, artisans, and soldiers, was exiled to Babylon (as Je. xxii. 18 f. implies) and the Temple was plundered (2 Ki. xxiv. 10–16). In the Babylonian Chronicle we now find for the first time confirmation of this information from an extra-biblical contemporary source. Jeremiah had already predicted Jehoiachin's fate (xxii. 24–30). Thirty-six years later, however, he was released by the son and successor of Nebuchadrezzar (2 Ki. xxv. 27–30). See JEHOIACHIN.

e. Zedekiah

Zedekiah, the new appointee of Nebuchadrezzar to the throne of Judah, was Josiah's youngest son (Je. i. 3) and uncle of Jehoiachin (2 Ki. xxiv. 17; 2 Ch. xxxvi. 10). This Old Testament account of Zedekiah's appointment by Nebuchadrezzar to succeed Jehoiachin is fully verified by the Babylonian Chronicle. His reign (597–587 BC) sealed Judah's doom (2 Ki. xxiv. 19 f.). He was weak and vacillating, and his officers of state were men of humble station. Having superseded the exiled aristocracy, they now looked upon them with contempt, but Jeremiah had his own convictions concerning the 'bad' and the 'good' figs (xxiv. 1 ff.). It was to the latter that the prophet sent his famous letter (xxix. 1 ff.). But both in Babylon and Judah false prophets sought to have Jeremiah executed (xxviii. 1 ff., xxix. 24 ff.). The main point at issue between them was the length of the captivity. Jeremiah foretold an exile of seventy years, while the false prophets argued that it would last only two years. Jeremiah's main conflict with Zedekiah was over the question of rebellion against Nebuchadrezzar. A revolt was planned in the fourth year of the reign in conspiracy with neighbouring states which the prophet violently opposed (xxvii f.). However, Zedekiah seems to have succeeded in allaying

Nebuchadrezzar's suspicions by visiting Babylon the same year (li. 59).

Finally, however, in the seventh or eighth year of his reign Zedekiah compromised himself irrevocably in the eyes of Nebuchadrezzar by entering into treasonable negotiations with Pharaoh Hophra. The die was cast, and in Zedekiah's ninth year (589) the Babylonians besieged Jerusalem for the second time. But before (xxi. 1–10) and during the siege (xxxiv. 1 ff., 8 ff., xxxvii. 3 ff., 17 ff., xxxviii. 14 ff.) Jeremiah had only one message for Zedekiah—surrender to the Babylonians, for Jerusalem must fall into their hands. Jeremiah's interpretation of the battle of Carchemish seventeen years earlier (605) was being fully vindicated. At one point during the siege, when the Egyptian army's advance compelled the Babylonians to withdraw, hopes that Jeremiah was mistaken were quickly disillusioned. His warning that the Babylonians would annihilate the Egyptians was soon fulfilled and the siege was immediately resumed (xxxvii. 1–10). The perfidy of some Jews towards their slaves at this juncture roused Jeremiah's withering scorn and severest condemnation (xxxiv. 8–22). Thanks to the cowardly vacillations of Zedekiah, the prophet was so rigorously maltreated by his enemies during the siege that he despaired of his life. Arrested on the charge of deserting to the enemy, he was thrown into a dungeon (xxxvii. 11–16), but was later removed to a prison in the guard-court close to the palace (xxxvii. 17–21). He was then accused of treason and thrown into a disused cistern, where he would have died but for the timely intervention of Ebed-melech. He was later transferred to the prison court (xxxviii. 1–13), where the king secretly conferred with him (14–28).

During the last stages of the siege Jeremiah, in a great act of faith, bought the land belonging to his cousin in Anathoth (xxxii. 1–15). At this moment too he proclaimed promises of restoration (xxxii. 36–44, xxxiii. 1–26). To this period too may be assigned his great prophecy of a new covenant (xxxi. 31 ff.), ultimately fulfilled in Christ the Mediator of that covenant. But Judah's cup of iniquity was now full and in 587 judgment engulfed the doomed city of Jerusalem (xxxix). Here too it is instructive to notice that the account of the captivity of Jerusalem in the Babylonian Chronicle agrees in general with the Old Testament account in 2 Ki. xxiv. 10–17; 2 Ch. xxxvi. 17; Je. lii. 28. And it becomes clear that the date of this event is 587 BC, the seventh year of Nebuchadrezzar's reign, and not 586 BC as has for so long been accepted.

Nebuchadrezzar treated Jeremiah kindly, and when he appointed Gedaliah governor of Judah Jeremiah joined him at Mizpah (xl. 1–6). The murder of Gedaliah soon followed (xli. 1 ff.), and the remnant in Mizpah resolved to flee into Egypt in spite of the earnest protestations of Jeremiah, who, along with Baruch his secretary, was compelled to accompany them (xlii. 1–xliii. 7). The last scene in the aged Jeremiah's stormy ministry shows him at Tahpanhes in Egypt still unbowed. He prophesies the conquest of Egypt by Nebuchadrezzar (xliii. 8–13) and rebukes the idolatrous worship of the Jews then residing in Egypt (xliv. 1 ff.). Of subsequent events in his life or the circumstances of his death nothing is known.

III. JEREMIAH'S PERSONALITY

Jeremiah's personality is the most sharply etched of any of the Old Testament prophets. Indeed, it is no exaggeration to say that in order to understand what the Old Testament means by the term prophet it is necessary to study the Book of Jeremiah. Jeremiah's call, his vocation as a bearer of the word of God, the authority which this communicated to him, the manner in which the word was revealed to him, his clear-cut distinctions between the true prophet and the false, his message and the agonizing dilemmas in which his fidelity to it entangled him—all are delineated in Jeremiah's oracles with an authority that is irresistible. This is because of the correlation between the prophet's spiritual and emotional experience and his prophetic ministry.

His emotions are vividly exhibited even in his discourses. From the content of his preaching it is plain that Jeremiah was a man of marked contrasts. He was at once gentle and tenacious, affectionate and inflexible. In him the frailties of the flesh contended with the energies of the spirit. The natural aspirations of youth were to the youthful prophet denied. He insisted on repentance from a people who were incapable of contrition. He unmasked the nation's sins and broadcast its judgment knowing that it would end in futility. Those whom he loved hated him. A loyal patriot, he was branded a traitor. This prophet of undying hope had to exhibit the fallacy of his people's hope. This priestly intercessor was commanded to intercede no more. This lover of Judah was by Judah maligned.

It is impossible to plumb the depths of grief into which Jeremiah was plunged. Despairing of comfort (viii. 18, 21), he desired to dissolve in tears for doomed Judah (ix. 1, xiii. 17) and abandon her to her self-inflicted fate (ix. 2). Convinced of ultimate failure, he cursed the day he was born (xv. 10, xx. 14–18), accused God of having wronged him (xx. 7a), complained of the ignominy that had befallen him (xx. 7b–10), invoked imprecations upon his tormentors (xviii. 18, 21–23). It is in this sense that the emotional, highly-strung Jeremiah was a tragic figure. The tragedy of his life springs from the conflicts which raged within and around him—his higher self wrestling with the lower, courage conflicting with cowardice, certain triumph struggling with apparent defeat, a determination to abandon his calling defeated by an inability to evade it (*cf.* v. 14, xv. 16, 19–21 with vi. 11, xx. 9, 11, xxiii. 29). But these fierce internal conflicts and the ignominy in which his calling involved him (xv. 17 f., xvi. 2, 5, 8) compelled him to find in God a refuge. Thus the Old Testament ideal of communion with God comes to its finest expression in Jeremiah. And it was in this fellowship with God that Jeremiah was able finally to withstand the erosive effects of timidity, anguish, helplessness, hostility, loneliness, despair, misunderstanding, and failure.

IV. HIS MESSAGE

a. Jeremiah's concept of God

God is Creator and sovereign Lord who governs all things in heaven and earth (xxvii. 5, xxiii. 23 f., v. 22, 24, x. 12 f.). While the gods of the nations are nonentities (x. 14 f., xiv. 22), Israel's God disposes all things according to His will (xviii. 5–10, xxv. 15–38, xxvii. 6–8). He knows the hearts of men (xvii. 5–10) and is the fountain of life to all who trust in Him (ii. 13, xvii. 13). He loves His people tenderly (ii. 2, xxxi. 1–3), but demands their obedience and allegiance (vii. 1–15). Sacrifices to pagan gods (vii. 30 f., xix. 5) and oblations offered to Him by a disobedient people (vi. 20, vii. 21 f., xiv. 12) are alike abominations to Him.

b. Jeremiah and idolatry

From the outset the prophet was a proclaimer of judgment. The sinfulness of Judah made this inevitable. The particular evil against which Jeremiah inveighed was idolatry. His many references to the worship of heathen deities confirm that the practice was widespread and diverse. Baal, Moloch, and the queen of heaven are mentioned. Idols were found in the Temple (xxxii. 34), and in the vicinity of Jerusalem children were sacrificed to Baal and Moloch (*cf.* vii. 31, xix. 5, xxxii. 35). Josiah had suppressed the idolatrous practices which his grandfather Manasseh had promoted, but the nation had apostatized after Josiah's death.

c. Jeremiah and immorality

Throughout the Old Testament immorality was a concomitant of idolatry. This principle is powerfully exemplified in Jeremiah's idolatrous generation (v. 1–9, vii. 3–11, xxiii. 10–14). Inescapably moral corruption followed the elimination of the fear of God and reverence for His law. Profligacy and improbity were common even among the priests and prophets (v. 30 f., vi. 13–15, xiv. 14). Instead of arresting immorality, they contributed to its spread. Ironically, idolatrous and immoral Judah was still zealously religious! This explains Jeremiah's oft-reiterated contention that before God the moral law takes precedence over the ceremonial. This principle Jeremiah applies to Judah's reverence for the ark (iii. 16), the tables of the Torah (xxxi. 31 f.), the covenant sign of circumcision (iv. 4, vi. 10, ix. 26), the Temple (vii. 4, 10 f., xi. 15, xvii. 3, xxvi. 6, 9, 12, xxvii. 16), and the sacrificial system (vi. 20, vii. 21 f., xi. 15, xiv. 12).

d. Jeremiah and judgment

Naturally, then, the inevitability of judgment was prominent in Jeremiah's message. Judah's punishment at the hands of God took many forms, such as drought and famine (v. 24, xiv. 1–6) and invasion by a foreign power (i. 13–16, iv. 11–22, v. 15–19, vi. 1–15, *etc.*). And inexorably the great day of doom dawned when God's instrument for punishing apostate Judah appeared (xxv. 9, lii. 1–30). The history of the background against which these oracles of judgment should be set has become much clearer with the publication of *Chronicles of Chaldaean Kings* (*626–556 BC*), to which reference has already been made. It describes a number of international events which took place in Jeremiah's lifetime, and hints of these are found in his oracles against the foreign nations. Doubtless his oracles against the nations in chapter xxv were written under the influence of Nebuchadrezzar's first advance westward (Je. xxv. 1, *cf.* verse 9). Chapter xlvi opens with a reference to the battle of Carchemish in 605. Then comes an oracle relating to Nebuchadrezzar's campaign against Egypt (xlvi. 13–26). The Babylonian Chronicle also provides a factual basis for Jeremiah's oracles against Kedar and Hazor (xlix. 28–33) and Elam (xlix. 34–39). It also relates how Nebuchadrezzar in 599 made raids against the Arab tribes (*cf.* Je. xlix. 29, 32), while in 596 he campaigned against Elam. Hitherto this oracle has had no historical basis. See further for the light shed by the Babylonian Chronicle on the dating and authenticity of the oracles in Jeremiah xlvi–li in *JBL*, LXXV, 1956, pp. 282 f.

e. Jeremiah and the false prophets

Jeremiah's elevated conception of, and total committal to, his call evoked within him an uncompromising antagonism towards the professional prophets and priests, and they in turn were his sworn enemies. Jeremiah's major polemic with the priests was over their policy of making gain of their office and their contention that the Jerusalem Temple would never fall to the Babylonians (vi. 13, xviii. 18, xxix. 25–32, *etc.*). The false prophets confirmed the duped people of Judah in this facile optimism (viii. 10–17, xiv. 14–18, xxiii. 9–40, *etc.*).

f. Jeremiah's hope

By contrast Jeremiah was an uncompromising preacher of judgment. However, his announcement of judgment was shot through and through with hope. Judah's exile in Babylon would not last for ever (xxv. 11, xxix. 10). Indeed, Babylon herself would be overthrown (l f.). This word of hope concerning Judah's survival of judgment was present in Jeremiah's message from the start (iii. 14–25, xii. 14–17), but as the situation became more ominous Jeremiah's confidence shone brighter (xxiii. 1–8, xxx–xxxiii). And it was this hope that gave birth to his great act of faith in the darkest days (xxxii. 1–15).

g. Jeremiah and Judah's religion

Jeremiah could therefore anticipate the destruction of the Temple, the fall of the Davidic dynasty, the cessation of the sacrificial system, and the ministry of the priesthood with perfect equanimity. He even proclaimed that the covenant sign of circumcision was largely meaningless without the circumcision of the heart (iv. 4, ix. 26, *cf.* vi. 10). Confidence in Temple, sacrifice, priesthood, was vain unless accompanied by a change of heart (vii. 4–15, 21–26). Even the ark of the covenant would be dispensed with (iii. 16). Knowledge of the law without obedience to the law was valueless (ii. 8, v. 13, 30 f., viii. 8). Jeremiah therefore sees the necessity of having the law written not on stone but on the heart, thus prompting all to spontaneous and perfect obedience (xxxi. 31–34, xxxii. 40). The passing away of the outward symbols of the covenant signified not the end of the covenant but its renewal in a more glorious form (xxxiii. 14–26).

h. Jeremiah and the ideal future

Thus Jeremiah looks far beyond Judah's return from exile and the resumption of life in Palestine (xxx. 17–22, xxxii. 15, 44, xxxiii. 9–13). In the ideal future Samaria will have a part (iii. 18, xxxi. 4–9), abundance will prevail (xxxi. 12–14), Jerusalem will be holy unto the Lord (xxxi. 23, 38–40), and be named 'the Lord is our righteousness' (xxxiii. 16). Its inhabitants will return to the Lord penitently (iii. 22–25, xxxi. 18–20) and with their whole heart (xxiv. 7). God will forgive them (xxxi. 34b), put His fear within them (xxxii. 37–40), establish the rule of the messianic Prince over them (xxiii. 5 f.), and admit the Gentile nations to a share of the blessing (xvi. 19, iii. 17, xxx. 9).

V. HIS ORACLES

The oracles in Jeremiah's book are not presented to the reader in chronological sequence. His ministry was spread over five reigns, and following Professor C. Lattey, the chapters may be arranged in this order: (i) Josiah: chapters i–xx, except xii. 7–13, 27. (ii) Jehoahaz: nothing. (iii) Jehoiakim: chapters xxvi, xxii, xxiii, xxv, xxxv, xxxvi, xlv, xxxiii, xii. 7–13, 27. (iv) Jehoiachin: chapters xiii. 18 f., xx. 24–30, lii. 31–34, and see discussions on Jehoiachin's reign of three months in *JBL*, LXXV, 1956, pp. 277–282; and *IEJ*, VI, 4, 1956. (v) Zedekiah: warnings: chapters xxiv, xxix, xxvii, xxviii, li. 59, 60; promises of restoration: chapters xxx–xxxiii; the siege: chapters xxi, xxxiv, xxxvii–xxxix. (vi) Following the fall of Jerusalem: chapters xl–xliv. (vii) Prophecies against the nations: chapters xlvi–li. (viii) An historical appendix: chapter lii.

Since, then, the chapters are not arranged chronologically probably their subject-matter has determined their present order. Chapter xxxvi would seem to confirm this suggestion. When Jeremiah's oracles were first committed to writing in the fourth year of Jehoiakim (604 BC) they covered a period of twenty-three years—from the thirteenth year of Josiah (626 BC) until 604 BC. These oracles Jehoiakim destroyed in the fifth year of his reign, but Baruch rewrote them at Jeremiah's dictation, and 'there were added besides unto them many like words' (xxxvi. 32). What these additions were is uncertain, as is also the contents of the original roll which Jehoiakim destroyed. But clearly the original oracles and the additions formed the nucleus of the Book of Jeremiah as it has come down to us; although how the whole was given its final form can only be conjectured. But the disorderly arrangement of the oracles strengthens the conviction that they are the words Jeremiah's inspired lips uttered and were then put together during days of danger and turmoil.

The question of the order of Jeremiah's oracles is also bound up with the relation between the *MT* and LXX text of his book. The Greek translation deviates from the Hebrew text in two respects. (i) It is shorter than the Hebrew text by approximately one-eighth (*i.e.* about 2,700 words). This is the more remarkable when it is recalled that on the whole the text of the LXX corresponds fairly closely to the *MT*. The main exceptions are Jeremiah, Job, and Daniel. (ii) In the LXX the oracles against the foreign nations (xlvi–li) are placed after xxv. 13, and their sequence is also altered. These divergences go back to Origen's time, but it is difficult to believe that the Hebrew and Greek texts represent two different recensions of the Book of Jeremiah. Because of Jeremiah's prophetic stature and spiritual calibre, these two texts of his book must have existed from a very early date, since no text which differed so radically from the received text as the Greek differs from the Hebrew would have been able to gain a foothold if it had been produced centuries after Jeremiah's death.

In the debate on the superiority of one text to the other those who favour the LXX version argue that it gives the oracles against the foreign nations a more natural context, and that some of the omissions (*e.g.* xxix. 16–20, xxxiii. 14–26, xxxix. 4–13, lii, xxviii–xxxiii, *etc.*) could not have been accidental. But the foregoing references to the Babylonian Chronicle have shown how it now enables us to re-create the historical background against which some of these oracles have to be set, especially those against Kedar, Hazor, Elam, and the Arabs. Those who support the claims of the Hebrew text emphasize 'the arbitrary character of the renderings' (Streane), which according to Graf makes it 'altogether impossible to give to this new edition—for one can scarcely call it a translation—any critical authority'. The impression too is that the omissions are not motivated by scholarly interests. And the fact remains that the men of the 'great synagogue' who did so much in determining the Canon of the Old Testament preferred the Hebrew text to the Greek version.

VI. CONCLUSION

In summarizing the greatness of Jeremiah, several things should be stressed. He recognized that Josiah's reforms were in reality a retrograde movement because they threatened to undo the work of the prophets. Reformation in worship without reformation of heart was useless. He also perceived that religion in Judah would continue even though the Temple and Jerusalem were destroyed. In his famous letter to the exiles in Babylon (xxix) he affirmed that in a pagan land Jews could still worship God although denied the ministry of priesthood and the service of sacrifice. Indeed, they could be closer to God in Babylon than were their brethren in Jerusalem, who made the outward trappings of religion a substitute for inward faith.

He saw too that since religion was essentially a moral and spiritual relation with God (xxxi. 31–34) its demands must also be moral and spiritual. With this insight goes also that of the importance of the individual. Individual responsibility was to be the foundation of character and spiritual life. And individuals were to be punished for their own sins, not for those of their fathers. Jeremiah's insight into the importance of the individual was important also because it proved to be a decisive step forward in men's search for a basis for the hope of immortality.

It was no exaggeration on Adam Welch's part, then, when he made Jeremiah the connecting link between Hosea and our Lord. It is significant that Jeremiah borrowed from Hosea and that Christ quotes most frequently from both. It was pre-eminently in the prophecy of the new covenant that Jeremiah spiritualized and individualized religion and insisted upon the primacy of the individual's relation with God. The new law was to be a spiritual bond between God and the individual, a law written on each heart and obeyed in love and loyalty. All this was finally fulfilled in the incarnation of Christ and the gospel He came to proclaim. He was the righteous Branch. He it was who spelled out the name, 'The Lord is our righteousness'.

BIBLIOGRAPHY. A. Bentzen, *Introduction to the Old Testament*, 1948; A. B. Davidson, 'Jeremiah' in *HDB*; A. F. Kirkpatrick, *The Doctrine of the Prophets*, 1906; J. Skinner, *Prophecy and Religion*, 1922; J. G. S. S. Thomson, *The Old Testament View of Revelation*, 1960, chapter 4; A. Condamin, *Le Livre de Jérémie*, 1920; C. Von Orelli, *The Prophecies of Jeremiah*[3], 1905; A. C. Welch, *Jeremiah*, 1928; J. P. Hyatt, *IB*, V, 1956; D. J. Wiseman, *Chronicles of Chaldaean Kings (626–556 BC)*, 1956. J.G.S.S.T.

JEREMIAH, BOOK OF. See previous article, especially Sections IV and V.

JEREMY, EPISTLE OF. See APOCRYPHA.

JERICHO.

I. NAME

The original meaning of the name Jericho is open to doubt. It is simplest to take *yᵉrîḥô* as from the same root as *yārēaḥ*, 'moon', and to connect it with the early W Semitic moon-god *Yariḥ* or *Yeraḥ*. *Cf.* remarks by Albright in *Archaeology and the Religion of Israel*, 1953 edn., pp. 83, 91, 92, 197 note 36, and in *AASOR*, VI, 1926, pp. 73, 74. Some suggest *rwḥ*, 'fragrant place' (*BDB*, p. 437b, after Gesenius), or as 'founded by (deity) Ḥô' (*PEQ*, LXXVII, 1945, p. 13), but this is improbable.

II. SITES

Old Testament Jericho is generally identified with the present mound of Tell es-Sultan *c.* 10 miles north-west of the present mouth of the Jordan at the Dead Sea, 1 mile north-west of er-Riḥa village (modern Jericho), and about 17 miles ENE of Jerusalem. The imposing, pear-shaped mound is about 400 yards long from north to south and roughly 200 yards wide at the broad northern end, and some 70 feet thick. Herodian and New Testament Jericho is represented by the mounds of Tulul Abu el-'Alayiq, 1 mile west of modern er-Riḥa, and so is south of Old Testament Jericho. The mountains of Judaea rise abruptly from the plains of Jericho a little distance to the west.

III. HISTORY

a. Before Joshua

(i) *Beginnings*. The story of Jericho is virtually a précis of the whole archaeological history of Palestine between *c.* 8000 and *c.* 1200 BC. For the special abbreviations used here, see bibliography at the end of this article. Every settlement at Jericho has owed its existence to the fine perennial spring there and the 'oasis' which it waters (*DUJ*, pl. 1); in the Old Testament Jericho is sometimes called 'the city of palm trees' (Dt. xxxiv. 3). Already in the eighth (?) millennium BC, food-gathering hunters may have had a shrine there, and Palestine's earliest-known agriculturists built huts by the spring (*AHL*, pp. 41–43; plate 5A). Early in the seventh millennium BC (Carbon-14 date), the oldest *town* of Jericho was built with a stone revetment-wall that included at least one tower (with built-in stairway) and round houses. Subsequently, spacious rectangular houses became fashionable and skulls of venerated ancestors(?) were embodied in clay-moulded portrait heads of remarkable realism (*DUJ*, pp. 67–73 and pls. 25, 29, 30, or *AHL*, pp. 43–47 and pl. 7, for 'prepottery Neolithic, phase A'; *DUJ*, pp. 51–67 and pls. 20–22, or *AHL*, pp. 47–57, 60 and pls. 13 ff., for 'phase B'). In the fifth and fourth millennia BC later Jericho citizens learned to make pottery, but eventually abandoned the place ('Pottery Neolithic A and B' 'Jericho IX and VIII' of older books, *DUJ*, pp. 79–94, *AHL*, pp. 60–70). Ancient Jericho is currently the primary source of information on the earliest settled life of Palestine; *cf.* also *W*, chapters 2–4 and *GSJ*, pp. 55–72.

(ii) *Early Historical Period.* From *c.* 3200 BC Jericho was again inhabited as a walled and towered town of the Early Bronze Age, when towns famous later (*e.g.* Megiddo) were first founded, contemporary with Egypt's Pyramid

Age and the Sumerian civilization in Mesopotamia (*DUJ*, pp. 167–185; *AHL*, pp. 101–134; *W*, ch. 5; *GSJ*, pp. 75–88, cities I and II). But *c.* 2300 BC Jericho perished violently at the hands of uncultured newcomers who eventually resettled the site (Albright's Middle Bronze Age I; K. M. Kenyon's Amorites of Intermediate Early/Middle Bronze Age, *cf. DUJ*, pp. 186–209; *AHL*, pp. 135–161). These coalesced with the Canaanites of the Middle Bronze Age proper (*c.* 1900–1600/1550 BC). Biblically this was the period of Abraham, Isaac, and Jacob; the remains from contemporary Jericho throw a vivid light on the daily life of Abraham's Canaanite/Amorite town-dwelling neighbours. The tombs have preserved more than the badly-denuded town buildings. Splendid pottery, wooden three- and four-legged tables, stools and beds, trinket-boxes of bone inlay, basketry, platters of fruit and joints of meat, metal daggers and circlets—all have been preserved by peculiar atmospheric conditions (*DUJ*, pp. 210–232 (city), 233–255 (tombs); *AHL*, pp. 162–194; *GSJ*, pp. 91–108). For restoration of a Jericho house-interior, see *DUJ*, endpapers, and fig. 118 above. For reconstructions of the walled city on its mound, see *Illustrated London News*, 19 May 1956, pp. 554, 555; *cf. AHL*, p. 188, fig. 45.

b. Jericho and the Old Testament

(i) *Joshua's invasion.* After *c.* 1600 BC Jericho was violently destroyed, probably by Egypt's XVIIIth Dynasty imperial pharaohs. After this the only (Late Bronze) occupation found at Jericho dates mainly between *c.* 1400 and 1325 BC; from the 13th century BC, the date of the Israelite conquest (see CHRONOLOGY OF OLD TESTAMENT), virtually nothing is known (*DUJ*, pp. 259–263; *AHL*, pp. 197–198, 209–211). Garstang's 'Late Bronze Age' walls (*GSJ*, chapter VII) actually date from the Early Bronze Age, over 1,000 years before Joshua, because of the associated Early Bronze remains, and they are overlaid by Middle Bronze material, only subsequently identified in Miss Kenyon's excavations (*e.g. DUJ*, pp. 170–171, 176–177, and especially 181). It is possible that in Joshua's day (13th century BC) there was a small town on the east part of the mound, later wholly eroded away. Such a possibility is not just a 'harmonistic' or heuristic view, but one suggested by the evidence of considerable erosion of the older settlements at Jericho. The tombs conclusively prove the importance of Middle Bronze Age Jericho (patriarchal period), although on the city mound most of the Middle Bronze town—and even much of the Early Bronze one before it—was eroded away between *c.* 1600 and *c.* 1400 BC (*cf. DUJ*, pp. 170, 171, and also 45, 93, 259–260, 262–263). When so much damage was done by the elements in barely 200 years it is easy to see how much havoc natural erosion must have wrought on the deserted mound in the 400 years that separated Joshua from Jericho's refounding by Hiel the Bethelite (1 Ki. xvi. 34) in Ahab's reign. It seems highly likely that the washed-out remains of the last Late Bronze Age city are now lost under the modern road and cultivated land along the eastern side of the town mound, as the main slope of the mound is from west down to east. It remains highly doubtful whether excavation here (even if allowed) would yield much now. The narrative of Jos. iii–viii within which

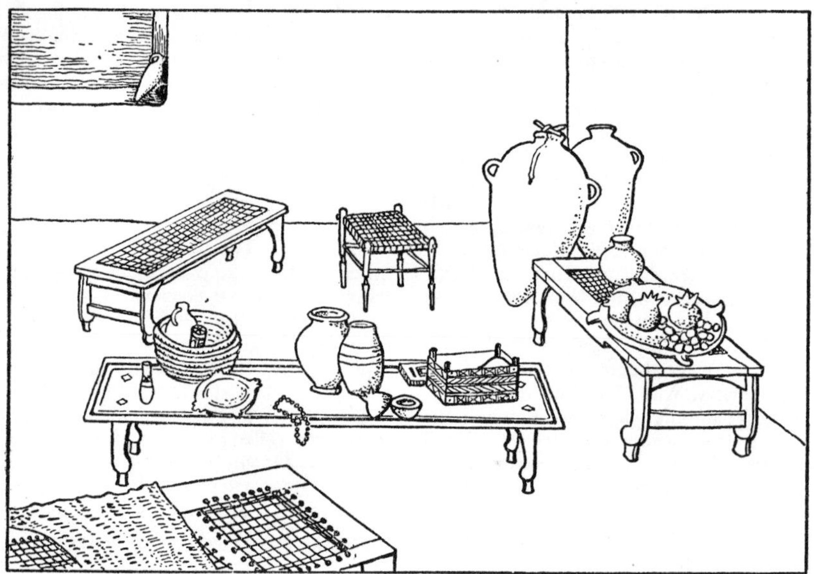

Fig. 118. Reconstruction of a room in Middle Bronze Age Jericho on the basis of the wooden furniture and objects found in the tombs, *c.* 1600 BC.

the fall of Jericho is recounted is known to reflect faithfully conditions in, and topography of, the area, while Joshua's generalship is recounted in a realistic manner. On terrain, *cf.* Garstang, *Joshua-Judges*, 1931, pp. 135–148 (his earth-tremors, providentially sent, remain a valid suggestion, even though his 'Late Bronze' (actually Early Bronze) walls do not now count as direct evidence for Joshua's day). On Joshua's generalship, *cf.* Garstang, *op. cit.*, pp. 149–161, and Y. Kaufmann, *The Biblical Account of the Conquest of Palestine*, 1953, pp. 91–97.

(ii) *From Joshua to Nehemiah.* For centuries no attempt was made to rebuild the town-mound of Jericho in awe of Joshua's curse (Jos. vi. 26), but the spring and oasis were still frequented, perhaps supporting a hamlet there. In the time of the judges, Eglon king of Moab temporarily occupied the oasis (Jdg. iii. 13) and David's envoys tarried there after being outraged by Hanun of Ammon (2 Sa. x. 5; 1 Ch. xix. 5); the 'blockhouse' may have been a guard-post in this latter period (so Albright and Wright (10th century BC), cited by Tushingham, *BA*, XVI, 1953, p. 67). Then in Ahab's reign (*c.* 874/3–853 BC) Hiel the Bethelite refounded Jericho proper and finally fulfilled the ancient curse in the loss of his eldest and youngest sons (1 Ki. xvi. 34). This humble Iron Age Jericho was that of Elijah and Elisha (2 Ki. ii. 4–5, 18–22), and it was in the plains of Jericho that the Babylonians captured Zedekiah, last king of Judah (2 Ki. xxv. 5; 2 Ch. xxviii. 15; Je. xxxix. 5, lii. 8). The remains of this Jericho (9th–6th centuries BC) are very fragmentary (erosion again to blame), but quite definite—buildings, pottery, and tombs; probably the Babylonians destroyed the place in 587 BC (see *BA*, XVI, 1953, pp. 66–67; *PEQ*, LXXXV, 1953, pp. 91, 95; *DUJ*, pp. 263–264). After the Exile, a modest Jericho still existed in Persian times. Some 345 Jerichoans returned to Judaea with Zerubbabel (Ezr. ii. 34; Ne. vii. 36), and their descendants in Jericho helped with repairing Jerusalem's walls in 445 BC under Nehemiah (Ne. iii. 2); a pottery jar-stamp (about 4th century BC) 'belonging to Hagar (daughter of) Uriah' is the last memento of Old Testament Jericho (Hammond, *PEQ*, LXXXIX, 1957, pp. 68–69, with pl. 16, corrected in *BASOR*, 147, 1957, pp. 37–39; *cf.* also Albright, *BASOR*, 148, 1957, pp. 28–30).

c. New Testament Jericho

In New Testament times, the town of Jericho was sited south of the old mound. In that region, Herod the Great (40/37–4 BC) and his successors built a winter palace with ornamental gardens, near the famous palm and balsam groves that yielded lucrative revenues. Fragmentary ruins that may be connected with these great buildings were recently excavated. See Kelso and Baramki, 'Excavations at New Testament Jericho' in *AASOR*, XXIX/XXX, 1955, and *BA*, XIV, 1951, pp. 33–43; Pritchard, *etc.*, *The Excavation at Herodian Jericho* in the *AASOR*, XXXII/XXXIII, 1958, and *BASOR*, 123, 1951, pp. 8–17. Herod brought water by aqueduct from the Wadi Qilt (Perowne, *Life and Times of Herod the Great*, 1956, plates opposite pp. 96–97).

The environs of New Testament Jericho witnessed Christ's healing of blind men, including Bartimaeus (Mt. xx. 29; Mk. x. 46; Lk. xviii. 35). Zacchaeus (Lk. xix. 1) was not the only wealthy Jew who had his home in this fashionable district. The immortal story of the good Samaritan is set on the narrow, bandit-infested road from Jerusalem down to Jericho (Lk. x. 30–37).

IV. BIBLIOGRAPHY

Sir Charles Warren sank shafts at Jericho in about 1868 with little result. The first scientific excavation there (1907–9) was by the Germans Sellin and Watzinger (*Jericho*, 1913), but they could not date their finds properly. Apart from his errors over 'Joshua's Jericho' (see above), Garstang in 1930–6 put the archaeology of the site on a sound basis. The handiest account of his work is J. and J. B. E. Garstang, *The Story of Jericho*, 1948 (*GSJ*). Detailed preliminary reports are in *Liverpool Annals of Archaeology and Anthropology*, XIX, 1932, to XXIII, 1936, and in *PEQ* for the same years. Miss Kenyon reviewed Garstang's results in *PEQ*, LXXXIII, 1951, pp. 101–138. Further older bibliography is in Barrois, *Manuel d'Archéologie Biblique*, I, 1939, pp. 61, 63.

Detailed preliminary reports of Miss Kenyon's excavations from 1952 to 1958 are in *PEQ*, LXXXIV, 1952, to XCII, 1960; *BASOR*, 127, 1952, pp. 5–16; *BA*, XVI, 1953, pp. 45–67, and XVII, 1954, pp. 98–104. For an instructive (and humorous) general account of these excavations, see *W* = M. Wheeler, *The Walls of Jericho*, 1956 (paper-back, 1960). Best detailed over-all account is *DUJ* = K. M. Kenyon, *Digging Up Jericho*, 1957 (fully illustrated), supplemented for the earliest periods by *AHL* = K. M. Kenyon, *Archaeology in the Holy Land*, 1960. The first volume of the definitive publication is K. M. Kenyon and others, *Jericho I*, 1960 (on tombs). General background and a summary in G. L. Harding, *The Antiquities of Jordan*, 1960, pp. 164–174. For New Testament Jericho, see above (section IIIc) and good background by L. Mowry, *BA*, XV, 1952, pp. 25–42. K.A.K.

JEROBOAM (probably 'the people increases'). **1.** An Ephraimite, the son of Nebat, who revolted against Rehoboam and became Israel's first king (*c.* 931–910 BC; 1 Ki. xi. 26–xiv. 20; 2 Ch. x. 2–xiii. 20). Jeroboam was an efficient youth whom Solomon, while building the Millo, put in charge of the work-force of the northern tribes (1 Ki. xi. 28). Apparently his humble origin (his mother was a widow, 1 Ki. xi. 26) and Solomon's oppressive practices led him to foment a revolt resulting in his exile to Egypt until Solomon's death. The LXX contains an unreliable midrash (based partly on Hadad's experiences, 1 Ki. xi. 14–22) which attempts to complete the sketchy biblical picture of Jeroboam's flight. His friendship with Shishak (*q.v.*) was apparently short-lived, for the pharaoh's subsequent invasion proved costly to both Judah and Israel. Rehoboam's rash refusal to initiate a more clement policy than his father's (see SOLOMON) brought the fulfilment of Ahijah's prophecy (1 Ki. xi. 29 ff.): the kingdom was rent asunder. Benjamin alone remained loyal to Judah and became the battle-ground for a series of border skirmishes between the two kings (1 Ki. xiv. 30).

Jeroboam incurred divine wrath by building, in Dan and Bethel, shrines to rival the Jerusalem Temple. The infamous calves were probably not representations of deity but pedestals on which the invisible Yahweh was supposed to stand (*cf.* W. F. Albright, *From the Stone Age to Christianity*², 1957, pp. 299–301). They threatened true religion by encouraging a syncretism of Yahweh worship with the fertility cult of Baal and thus drew prophetic rebuke (*e.g.* the man of God, 1 Ki. xiii. 1 ff.; Ahijah, 1 Ki. xiv. 14–16). Jeroboam's ascent to the throne by popular choice rather than hereditary right contributed to the dynastic instability of the northern kingdom. His royal cult set the pattern for his successors, who are customarily evaluated as perpetuating his sin (*e.g.* 1 Ki. xvi. 26).

BIBLIOGRAPHY. See J. Bright, *A History of Israel*, 1960, pp. 208–214; M. Noth, *The History of Israel*, 1958, pp. 224 ff.

2. Jeroboam II (*c.* 793–753 BC) was the fourth king of Jehu's dynasty and one of Israel's most illustrious rulers (2 Ki. xiv. 23–29). Co-regent for a decade, Jeroboam II carried on Jehoash's policies of aggressive expansion. Aided by Adad-nirari's campaigns (805–802 BC) which broke the back of the Aramaean kingdom and by the Assyr. preoccupation with Armenia, he was able to restore Israel's boundaries virtually to their Solomonic scope and thus fulfil Jonah's prophecy (2 Ki. xiv. 25).

Comparative freedom from foreign attack brought unparalleled economic prosperity. Recent excavations in Samaria (*q.v.*) have demonstrated both the grandeur of Jeroboam's fortress city and the luxury which vexed Amos' righteous soul (*e.g.* vi. 1–7). Extreme wealth and poverty (Am. ii. 6–7), empty religious ritual (Am. v. 21–24, vii. 10–17), and false security (Am. vi. 1–8) are among the characteristics of Jeroboam's lengthy reign. Amos' gloomy prophecy (vii. 9) was verified when Shallum's successful *coup* against Zechariah (2 Ki. xv. 8–12) wrote *finis* to Jehu's house. See J. Bright, *op. cit.*, pp. 238–248; M. F. Unger, *Israel and the Arameans of Damascus*, 1957, pp. 89–95. D.A.H.

JERUBBAAL. See GIDEON.

JERUEL (*yᵉrû'ēl*, 'founded by El'; LXX 'Jeriel'). Mentioned by the prophet Jahaziel as the wilderness where Jehoshaphat would meet and conquer the Moabites and Ammonites (2 Ch. xx. 16). Possibly identical with, or a part of, the wilderness of Tekoa (*q.v.*), the country extending from the west shores of the Dead Sea north of En-gedi.

J.D.D.

JERUSALEM.

I. INTRODUCTION AND GENERAL DESCRIPTION

Jerusalem is one of the world's famous cities. It dates from the second millennium BC, at least; and today is considered sacred by the adherents of the three great monotheistic faiths, Judaism, Christianity, and Islam. The city is set high in the hills of Judah, over 30 miles from the Mediterranean, and over 20 east of the north end of the Dead Sea. It rests on a none-too-level plateau, which slopes noticeably towards the south-east. To the east lies the ridge of Olivet. Access to the city on all sides except the north is hampered by three deep ravines, which join in the Siloam Valley, near the well Bir Eyyub, south-east of the city. The eastern valley is Kidron; the western is now called the Wadi al-Rababi, and is probably to be equated with the Valley of Hinnom; and the third cuts the city in half before it runs south, and slightly east, to meet the other two. This latter ravine is not mentioned or named in Scripture (although Maktesh, Zp. i. 11, may well have been the name of part of it), so it is usually referred to as the Tyropoeon Valley, *i.e.* the Valley of the Cheesemakers, after Josephus. See fig. 119. *Cf.* fig. 117 and see pl. XVI.

Eminences rise each side of the Tyropoeon Valley, and the city can at once be divided into western and eastern halves. Ignoring lesser heights, we may subdivide each of these two sections into northern and southern hills. When considering the growth and development of the city (see IV) it will be important to visualize these details. In discussing the respective heights and depths of these hills and valleys, it must be realized that they have changed considerably over the centuries. This is inevitable in any city continuously inhabited for centuries, and particularly when periodic destructions have taken place. Layer after layer of rubble and débris piles up, amounting here and there to more than 100 feet in parts of Jerusalem. In the case of Jerusalem there is also the factor that deliberate attempts have been made at various periods to fill in valleys and diminish hills.

The water supply is a problem to this day. Apart from Bir Eyyub, the well mentioned above, there is only the Virgin's Spring, which is connected by an aqueduct with the Pool of Siloam. There are, and have been, other reservoirs, of course, such as Bethesda in New Testament times and Mamilla Pool today, but they all depend on the rains or else on aqueducts to fill them. Bir Eyyub and the Virgin's Spring are in all probability the biblical En-rogel and Gihon respectively. Bir Eyyub lies south-east of the city, at the junction of the three ravines mentioned above. The Virgin's Spring is due north of Bir Eyyub, and a little south of the Temple area. Thus it is evident that only the south-east part of Jerusalem has a reliable water supply.

II. NAME

The meaning of the name is not certain. The Hebrew word is usually written *yᵉrûšālaim* in the Old Testament, but this is an anomalous form, since Hebrew cannot have two consecutive vowels. The anomaly was resolved in later Hebrew by inserting the letter 'y', thus giving *yᵉrûšālayim*; this form does in fact occur a few times in the Old Testament, *e.g.* Je. xxvi. 18. This may well have been understood to be a dual (for the ending *-ayim* is dual), viewing the city as two-fold. (Similarly, the Heb. name for 'Egypt', *miṣrayim*, is dual.) But there can be little doubt that the original form of the word in Heb. was *yᵉrûšālēm*; this is evidenced by the abbreviation *šālēm*, English 'Salem', in Ps. lxxvi. 2, and by the Aramaic form of the name, *yᵉrûšlēm*, found in Ezr. v. 14, *etc.*

Most authorities agree that the final part of the word means 'peace' (*cf.* Heb. vii. 2). The first part may mean 'possession' or 'foundation'. But in view of the early mention of the city in the Tell el-Amarna letters (14th century BC) and Assyr. inscriptions, long before it became an Israelite city, bearing the name Urusalim (or Ur-sa-li-im-mu), it is highly probable that the name is not of Heb. origin. The cognate Assyr. language would give a meaning 'city of peace'. This, then, is the most likely derivation of the name. Certainly the initial 'u' of the Assyrian is also found in the Syr. and Arab. forms of the name, *'ûrišlem* and *'ûrušalîm* respectively.

In New Testament Greek the name is transliterated in two different ways, *Hierosolyma* (as in Mt. ii. 1) and *Hierousalēm* (as in Mt. xxiii. 37). The latter is evidently a close approximation to the Heb. pronunciation, and incidentally an additional evidence for an 'e' as the original final vowel in Hebrew. The former is deliberately Hellenized, to make a Gk.-sounding word; the first part of the word at once recalls the Gk. word *hieros*, 'holy', and probably the whole was understood to mean something like 'sacred Salem'. LXX has only the form *Hierousalēm*, whereas Gk. classical writers use *Hierosolyma* (*e.g.* Polybius; so too in Latin, *e.g.* Pliny).

Jerusalem is described in Is. lii. 1 as the holy city, and to this day it often receives this title. The Heb. phrase is *'îr haq-qōḏeš*, literally 'the city of holiness'. Probably the reason for this title was that Jerusalem contained the Temple, the shrine where God deigned to meet His people. Hence the word *qōḏeš* came to mean 'sanctuary' as well as 'holiness'. To Judaism, then, Jerusalem was the holy city without a rival. It was natural for Paul and John, seeing that the earthly city was far from perfect, to designate the place where God dwells in true holiness as 'Jerusalem which is above' (Gal. iv. 26) and 'new Jerusalem' (Rev. xxi. 2).

For other names the city has had, see III, in historical sequence.

III. HISTORY

Jerusalem was in existence in the middle of the second millennium BC, as is shown by the Tell el-Amarna letters. At that time it was under the suzerainty of Egypt, and was probably little more than a mountain fortress. Possible Pentateuchal references to it are as Salem (Gn. xiv. 18) and the mountain in the 'land of Moriah' of Gn. xxii. 2. According to very ancient tradition, the latter was the place where later the Temple was built, but there is no possible proof of this. As for Salem, it is perhaps to be identified with Jerusalem, but this is not certain; the Salem of Ps. lxxvi. 2 is certainly Jerusalem. If the Genesis Salem is the same place, then at this period Jerusalem was ruled by a king, Melchizedek, who was also priest of the most high God (*'ēl 'elyôn*).

When the Israelites entered Canaan they found Jerusalem in the hands of an indigenous Sem. tribe, the Jebusites, ruled over by a king named Adoni-zedek. This ruler formed an alliance of kings against Joshua, who soundly defeated them; but Joshua did not take the city, owing, doubtless, to its natural strength of position. It remained in Jebusite hands, bearing the name Jebus. Comparing Jdg. i. 8 with Jdg. i. 21, it appears that Judah overcame the part of the city outside the fortress walls, and that Benjamin occupied this part, living peaceably alongside the Jebusites in the fortress.

This was the situation when David became king. His first capital was Hebron, but he soon saw the value of Jerusalem, and set about its capture. This was not only a tactical move but also a diplomatic one, for his use of a city on the Benjamin–Judah border would help to diminish the jealousy between the two tribes. The Jebusites felt confident of their safety behind the fortress walls, but David's men used an unexpected mode of entry, and took the citadel by surprise (2 Sa. v. 6–8). In this passage we meet a third name, 'Zion'. This was probably the name of the hill on which the citadel stood; Vincent, however, thinks the name originally applied rather to the fortress building than to the ground it occupied.

Having taken the city, David improved the fortifications and built himself a palace; he also installed the ark in his new capital. Solomon carried the work of fortification further, but his great achievement was the construction of the Temple. After his death and the subsequent division of the kingdom, Jerusalem naturally declined somewhat, being now capital only of Judah. As early as the fifth year of Solomon's successor, Rehoboam, the Temple and royal palace were plundered by Egyptian troops (1 Ki. xiv. 25 f.). Philistine and Arab marauders again plundered the palace in Jehoram's reign. In Amaziah's reign a quarrel with the king of the northern kingdom, Jehoash, resulted in part of the city walls being broken down, and fresh looting of Temple and palace. Uzziah repaired this damage to the fortifications, so that in the reign of Ahaz the city was able to withstand the attacks of the combined armies of Syria and Israel. Soon after this the northern kingdom fell to the Assyrians. Hezekiah of Judah had good reason to fear Assyria too, but Jerusalem providentially escaped. In case of siege, he made a conduit to improve the city's water supply.

Nebuchadrezzar of Babylon destroyed the city and Temple in 587 BC. At the end of that century the Jews, now under Persian rule, were allowed to return to their land and city, and they rebuilt the Temple, but the city walls remained in ruins until Nehemiah restored them in the middle of the 5th century BC. Alexander the Great ended the power of Persia at the end of the 4th century, and after his death his general Ptolemy, founder of the Ptolemaic dynasty in Egypt, entered Jerusalem and included it in his realm. In 198 BC Palestine fell to Antiochus III, the Seleucid king of Syria. About thirty years later, Antiochus IV entered Jerusalem, destroying its walls and plundering and desecrating the Temple; and he installed a Syrian garrison in the city, on the Akra. Judas the Maccabee led a Jewish revolt, and in 165 the Temple was rededicated. He and his successors gradually won independence for Judaea, and the Hasmonaean dynasty ruled a free Jerusalem until the middle of the 1st century BC, when Rome intervened. Roman generals forced their way into the city in 63 and 54; a Parthian army plundered it in 40; and three years after that Herod the Great had to fight his way into it, to take control. He first had to repair the damage created by these various incursions; then he launched a big building programme, erecting some notable towers. His most renowned work was the rebuilding of the Temple on a much grander scale, although this was not finished within his lifetime. One of his towers was Antonia, commanding the Temple area (it housed the Roman garrison which came to Paul's aid, Acts xxi. 34).

The Jewish revolt against the Romans in AD 66 could have but one conclusion; in AD 70 the Roman general Titus systematically forced his way into Jerusalem, and destroyed the fortifications and the Temple. He left three towers standing; one of them, Phasael, still stands, incorporated in the so-called 'Tower of David'. But further disaster awaited the Jews; another revolt in AD 132 led to the rebuilding of Jerusalem (on a much smaller scale) as a pagan city, dedicated to Jupiter Capitolinus, from which all Jews were excluded. This was the work of the Emperor Hadrian; he called the newly constructed city Aelia Capitolina (the name even found its way into Arabic, as Iliya). It was not until the reign of Constantine (early 4th century) that the Jews were again permitted to enter the city. From his reign on, the city became Christian instead of pagan, and many churches and monasteries were built, notably the Church of the Holy Sepulchre.

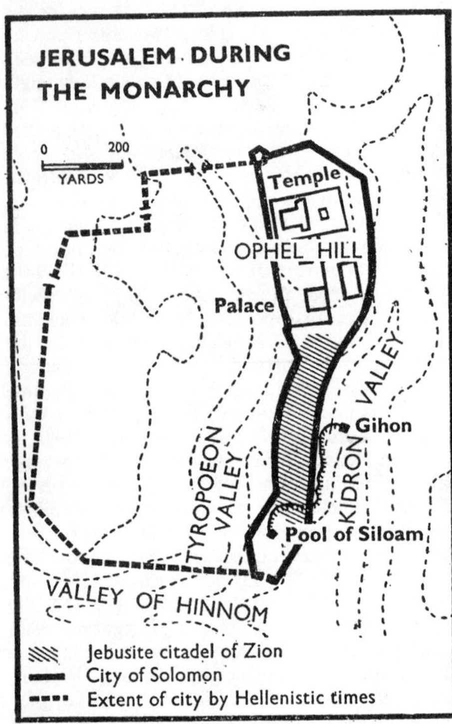

Fig. 119.

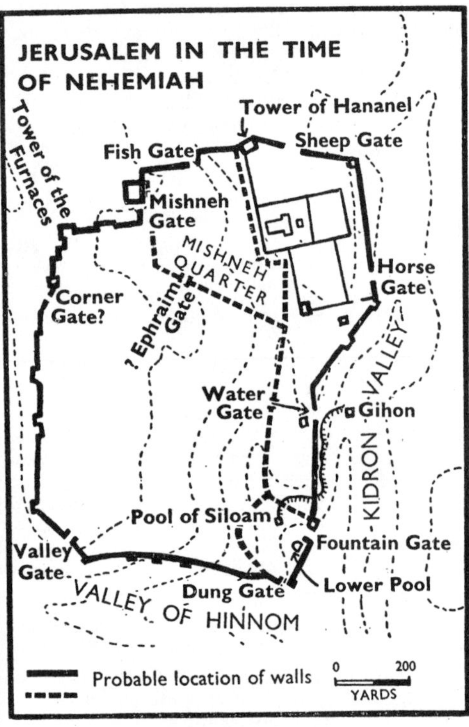

Fig. 120.

After three centuries of Byzantine Christian rule, Jerusalem again suffered a disaster, when the Persians stormed it in 614, destroying buildings and killing and taking prisoners. The Byzantine emperor recovered it, but in 637 the Muslims arrived, led by the Caliph Omar, and Jerusalem has remained in Muslim hands practically ever since. In 691 the Caliph Abd al-Malik erected a magnificent building on the Temple area site, known properly as the Dome of the Rock, but frequently by the incorrect title 'Mosque of Omar'. The Christians and Jews were treated tolerantly by the Muslims until the 11th century, when semi-barbarian Turks displaced the Arabs. The Crusades resulted, and in 1099 Jerusalem was captured by the Crusaders, and a Christian kingdom was established there. Saladin re-conquered it in 1187, and the city was in Egyptian hands, in the main, until 1517, when the Ottoman Turks took control, under Selim I. In 1542 the Sultan Suleiman the Magnificent rebuilt the city walls as they can be seen today. The Ottoman Turks held Palestine until the First World War, when British troops under General Allenby conquered it; Allenby entered Jerusalem in 1917. After that Palestine was under British mandate until 1948, when it was divided between Arabs and Jews. Jerusalem lies on the frontier between Israel and the Hashemite kingdom of Jordan, and so the city is divided. The whole of the walled city (the 'Old City') is in Jordan, and Israel holds little but the fast-growing western suburb. However, Israel does hold the so-called Mount Zion, the hill just south of the south-west corner of the city wall, on which are the traditional sites of the Last Supper room (*coenaculum*) and of the tomb of David. Western Jerusalem bears today its old Heb. name, *Yᵉrûšālayim*; the Arab. form of the name is not unknown, but to Arabs generally the city is known as *Al-Quds al-Sharîf*, 'the noble sanctuary', or more briefly as *Al-Quds*.

IV. GROWTH AND EXTENT

It must be stated at the outset that there is a good deal of uncertainty about the physical history of Jerusalem. This is, of course, partly due to the periodic disasters and destructions, and to the layers upon layers of rubble that have piled up over the centuries. These factors have caused difficulty elsewhere, of course, but archaeologists have often been able to surmount them to a large extent. The particular difficulty with Jerusalem is that it has been continuously inhabited and still is, so that excavations can be made only with difficulty. Archaeologists here have to dig where they can, not where they think it might be profitable. On the other hand, there is an abundance of traditions, Christian, Jewish, and Muslim; but in many cases it is not easy to evaluate them. So uncertainty and controversy remain; however, much valuable archaeological work has been done during the last century, and it has solved some problems.

Scripture nowhere gives a systematic description of the city. The nearest approach to such a description is the account of the rebuilding of the walls by Nehemiah. But there are a great number of references giving some information. These have to be pieced together, and fitted in with the picture we get from archaeology. Our earliest description of the city is that of Josephus (*BJ* v. 136–141); Josephus is here laying a background for his account of the gradual capture of the city by Titus and the Roman armies. This too has to be fitted into the picture.

It is now clear that the original city, the 'Jebus' captured by David, afterwards called the City of David, was the south-east hill (see fig. 119). This has been established by excavations south of the Temple area (which covers the northern part of this south-east hill), and indeed this fits in well with biblical details and the description given by Josephus. There are two facts which must be clearly realized: in the first place, the original city extended considerably south of the present south-east wall of Jerusalem; secondly, this original Zion must not be confused (as it was for centuries) with what is today called Mount Zion, which is the south-west hill. Ancient Jewish tradition erroneously considered the latter to be the original city, a view supported by numbers of scholars last century. Apart from archaeological evidence, it is clear that in the Old Testament Zion could be equated with the Temple, and was the name used for the religious centre of the Jews; had Zion been other than the temple hill, this figurative use of the name could scarcely have occurred.

In times of peace it was common practice for houses to be built outside the walls. This had happened even before David's time, with the Benjamites living alongside the Jebusites, as has already been observed. From time to time further fortifications would be made, to enclose such areas. David and Solomon both repaired the existing fortifications, and Solomon built 'Millo', whatever exactly that may have been. Many suggestions have been made about it, but the paucity of biblical detail precludes dogmatism. It was probably a special feature of the defensive circumvallation of the 'City of David'. The name derives from a Heb. root meaning 'full', so it may be presumed that Millo 'filled up' a breach or deficiency of some kind in the previous fortifications. But the exact limits of David's city are a matter for debate; suffice it to say that traces of early walls have been found in the vicinity of the Pool of Siloam. On the north it must obviously have included the Temple area.

Before Nebuchadrezzar's destruction of the city the populated area had spread on the north, but it is not certain whether the south-west hill was incorporated in the city in pre-exilic days. The first certain references to buildings on this hill date from the Hasmonaean period. Some scholars, then, consider that this hill was never part of the city until after the Exile—a remarkable reversal of the outdated theory that the south-west hill was the original Zion. Simons, on the other hand, takes 'Gareb' (Je. xxxi. 39) as the name of the western hill, and considers it not only pre-exilic but Solomonic. He suggests that Jerusalem and 'the city of David' cannot have been exactly the same place in 1 Ki. iii. 1, and that the former was either the south-west hill alone or else a wider term including both hills. It is convenient here to mention the name Ophel, which apparently referred to the south-east hill. The word means 'swelling', and is used for the citadel hill of other towns too, Samaria for instance. See fig. 119.

Another problem is posed by the 'Second Wall'. When Titus took the city from the north in AD 70 he had three successive walls to overcome. (There was merely a single wall on the other sides of the city, which were more impregnable by the nature of the terrain.) The outer wall had been erected very recently, but Josephus tells us nothing of the date of the origin of the second wall. It may well be that it was pre-exilic, however, for a Second Quarter (RSV) is mentioned in 2 Ki. xxii. 14 and Zp. i. 10. So the Second Wall probably enclosed this quarter.

Nehemiah's work was doubtless a restoration of the walls which Nebuchadrezzar had knocked down. His description of the rebuilding unfortunately presents not a few problems. For one thing, it is not clear which gates were in the city wall and which led into the Temple. For another, there are numerous textual difficulties in the relevant passages of Nehemiah. Again, Nehemiah gives no indication of direction or changes of direction. Add to that the fact that names of gates changed from time to time. At any rate, identification of the starting-point, the Sheep Gate, is fairly safe, in view of the discovery of the Pool of Bethesda, which Jn. v. 2 tells us was near the Sheep Gate. Similarly, the Fountain Gate can safely be placed near the Pool of Siloam, and the Water Gate beside the Virgin's Spring. The Valley Gate led to the Valley of Hinnom, without any doubt. On these foundations a picture can be built up roughly like this: taking the Sheep Gate as approximately marking the north-east corner, the line of the wall ran westwards, *via* the towers of Hammeah and Hananel, the Fish Gate, the 'Mishneh' Gate (*i.e.* the gate that led into the 'Second' Quarter; the name is by textual emendation of the 'Old' Gate of Ne. iii. 6) and the Ephraim Gate to the Corner Gate, where was the tower of the furnaces (Ne. iii. 11); thence south, without gates, as far as the Valley Gate; turning east, it proceeded to the Dung Gate and the Fountain Gate; thence northwards it included the Water Gate, the Horse Gate, and so returned to the Sheep Gate. See fig. 120. Note that the pattern of these walls was by no means an exact square; the line of the north wall in particular undulated considerably. Incidentally a notable omission of Ne. iii is the Ephraim Gate; probably the erection of the Second Wall had robbed it of much of its importance (if indeed it was still in the *external* wall). Nor is the Corner Gate mentioned, but the tower of the furnaces will have been in the same locality. The Second Wall, mentioned above, is one of the problems Josephus sets us. Not only does he omit to mention its date, and builder, but he also neglects to describe the course it took; he gives only its *termini*. Thus it cannot be determined whether or not the site of the Church of Holy Sepulchre was inside the wall of Jerusalem in our Lord's day. (See CALVARY.)

1 Maccabees and Josephus relate that Antiochus IV in 169 BC established a Syrian garrison in Jerusalem, called Akra. Unhappily Josephus, in particular, is loose in his use of the term, and it is difficult to decide where exactly the Akra hill was. 1 Maccabees clearly equates it with the City of David, and relates that Antiochus fortified it strongly (1 Macc. i. 33). At any rate, this fortress clearly dominated the Temple, and must have been near it. Elsewhere Josephus plainly considered the south-west hill, *i.e.* the Lower City, to be the Akra. Vincent accordingly has placed the fortress on an eastern promontory of this hill, that is, due west of the Temple, with the Tyropoeon Valley intervening. Perhaps, however, a distinction is to be drawn between 'the Akra' and 'Akra'; the latter can then be placed (as by Simons) north of the Temple, on the site where later Herod's fortress Antonia stood. In any case, when Simon, brother of Judas the Maccabee, had starved out the Syrian garrison he proceeded to lower the level of the hill, in order that it should not stand higher than the Temple. While the Syrians were in occupation, the Jews made the Temple itself a fortress in opposition.

Not long after the crucifixion, Agrippa I commenced building a third north wall, never thoroughly completed before the Roman destruction in AD 70. Josephus is our only written source of information about these three walls. The first ran from Hippicus to the western portico of the Temple; Hippicus was the north-west corner tower of the city, and the line of this early wall ran roughly due east. The Second Wall (see above) started at the Gennath ('garden') Gate and enclosed the Second Quarter (by New Testament times called Bezetha), ending its course at Antonia, north of the Temple area. The Gennath Gate is nowhere else mentioned, so its position must remain something of a mystery; but it cannot have been far from Hippicus. The Third Wall ran from Hippicus northwards to the tower Psephinus, and then turned, finally linking up with the early circumvallation, and terminating at the Kidron Valley. The *termini* cause no problem whatever; but unfortunately Psephinus cannot be definitely located. Its ruins may be hidden by the present Turkish wall, in which case the line of the Third Wall may well be identical with the present north wall. However, the site of Psephinus may be a large ruined edifice considerably farther north. This building is styled the 'Castle of Goliath' (in Arab. *qaṣr jâlûd*). Excavations west and south-west of it have revealed portions of a wall, which was immediately hailed as the Third Wall of Josephus. The main objection to this identification is the fact that this structure seems to have been too weak to have earned the obvious enthusiasm of Josephus. On the other hand, it does not fit in well with the details of later walls either! So perhaps the matter is best left as an unsolved problem.

Hadrian's rebuilt city was considerably smaller. It was now that the southern extremity of the city was retracted, as it has remained ever since. The southern Turkish wall in effect cuts the ancient Mount Zion in two. The eastern wall still overlooks the Kidron Valley, while the western wall must follow approximately the line it took in New Testament times. As for the north wall, its relation to ancient walls has been shown to be uncertain. Today's city wall has eight gates: the Damascus Gate is at the north-west corner, approximately; on the north wall is Herod's Gate; on the east wall are St. Stephen's Gate and the blocked-up Golden Gate; on the south are the Gate of the Moors (frequently known, erroneously, as the Dung Gate) and Zion Gate; and on the west lie the Jaffa Gate and north of that the New Gate. Jaffa Gate is hard by the 'Tower of David', Herod's Phasael. A large proportion of the 'Old City'—its whole south-eastern corner—is occupied by what is known as the Haram, which is the Dome of the Rock and its courts, where stands the Al-Aqsa mosque as well. Part of the west wall of the Haram enclosure is known as the Wailing Wall; it embodies all that survives (visibly) of Herod's temple, and while they could (till 1948, that is), Jews used to come to this wall to lament the Temple's fate.

The Arab city overflows north of the Old City. Israel holds the vast western suburb, which continues to expand rapidly. Between the two States, just west of the western Turkish wall, lies a stretch of 'no-man's-land', varying in breadth. The only road connecting Israeli and Jordanian Jerusalem officially passes through the Mandelbaum Gate, which is not strictly a gate at all, but merely two check-points.

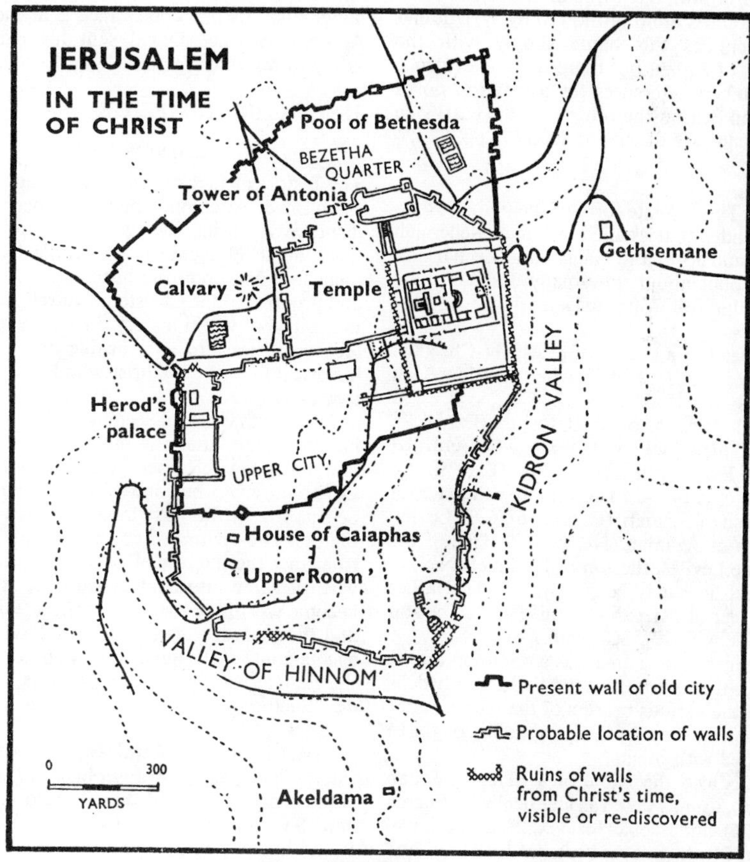

Fig. 121.

BIBLIOGRAPHY. See especially J. Simons, *Jerusalem in the Old Testament*, 1952, and L. H. Vincent, *Jérusalem de l'Ancien Testament*, 1954–6. Then, less recent, W. Besant, *Jerusalem*, 1888; G. A. Smith, *Jerusalem*, 1907. On more detailed points, the following might be recommended: Sukenik and Mayer, *The Third Wall of Jerusalem*,

1930; Macalister and Duncan, *Excavations on the Hill of Ophel*, 1923–5; M. Burrows, *Nehemiah 3: 1–32 as a Source for the Topography of Ancient Jerusalem* (in *AASOR*, XIV, 1934, pp. 115–140).

Simon's and Vincent's works are the fullest and most recent of these. They both give excellent bibliographies, including older works not mentioned here. D.F.P.

JESHIMON (*yᵉšîmōn*, 'a waste', 'a desert'). Mentioned in Nu. xxi. 20, xxiii. 28; 1 Sa. xxiii. 24, xxvi. 1. G. A. Smith, followed by Wright and Filson, identifies this name simply with the Wilderness of Judah, but there is some evidence in the Numbers references for a location north of the Dead Sea on the other (*i.e.* the east) side of the Jordan. See discussion in *GTT*, pp. 22 f. J.D.D.

JESHUA. This is a late form of the name Joshua (the same individual is called Jeshua in Nehemiah and Ezra, and Joshua in Haggai and Zechariah). There is doubt about how many Jeshuas there are, but the following may perhaps be distinguished.

1. The head of a course of priests (1 Ch. xxiv. 11, AV 'Jeshuah'). **2.** A Levite mentioned in Hezekiah's reorganization (2 Ch. xxxi. 15). **3.** The high priest also called Joshua (Ezr. ii. 2, *etc.*). **4.** A man of Pahath-moab who returned from the Exile with Jerubbabel (Ezr. ii. 6). **5.** A head of a house of priests associated with 'the children of Jedaiah' (Ezr. ii. 36). **6.** A Levite, Jeshua son of Azaniah (Ne. x. 9). **7.** One of the chief of the Levites, the son of Kadmiel (Ne. xii. 24; the text here may be corrupt). **8.** The father of Ezer, ruler of Mizpah (Ne. iii. 19). **9.** The son of Nun (Ne. viii. 17). See JOSHUA.

It is clear that the name was a common one at the time of the return from the Exile. But little is told us of the various bearers of the name, and it is possible that some of those in the list ought to be identified with others.

Jeshua is also the name of a place in Judah (Ne. xi. 26), usually taken as identical with Shema (Jos. xv. 26), and Sheba (Jos. xix. 2). The original form would be Shema, *m* becomes *b*, then *w*, and finally *j* is prefixed. L.M.

JESHURUN (*yᵉšurûn*, 'the upright one'; LXX 'the beloved one'). A poetic name for the people of Israel, occurring four times in the Old Testament (Dt. xxxii. 15, xxxiii. 5, 26; Is. xliv. 2, AV 'Jesurun'). Cheyne and others see in this term a synonym for Israel (if the *MT* pointing is correct). If understood as 'righteous nation' it may be both a reminder and a reproach to Israel. See discussion in *EBi*, 2434. J.D.D.

JESSE (*yišay*). Grandson of Boaz and father of David. He lived in Bethlehem and is commonly termed 'the Bethlehemite', but once the 'Ephrathite of Bethlehem-Judah'. He was the father of eight sons (1 Sa. xvi. 10, 11), but only the names of seven are known (1 Ch. ii. 13–15). The eighth is omitted, probably as he had no issue, unless the Elihu of 1 Ch. xxvii. 18 is other than Eliab.

Ancient Jewish tradition (Targ. Ruth iv. 22) followed by later interpreters (*cf.* AVmg) identifies Nahash (2 Sa. xvii. 25) with Jesse. Two other solutions are more probable. Either Abigail and Zeruiah were daughters of Jesse's wife by a former marriage to a Nahash (*cf.* A. P. Stanley, *Jewish Church*, Lect. 22) or Nahash may be a feminine name and taken as the mother of the daughters. His last appearance is at the cave of Adullam, whence David sent his parents for safety to Moab (1 Sa. xxii. 3–4). M.A.M.

JESUS CHRIST, LIFE OF.

I. HISTORICITY

The historical fact of Christ is incontrovertibly established. Attempts which have been made to disprove it during the past two hundred years have failed. Not only is the whole New Testament founded upon the historic Christ; the rise and progress of the Christian Church, and indeed the course of world history during the past nineteen centuries, are inexplicable apart from the historical fact of the Christ who lived, died, and rose again.

The fact that extant secular records of the first hundred years after the ministry of Christ contain only a few references to Him is only natural. Christianity was but one of many religious cults originating in the East in the Roman world of the first two centuries, and there was little in it to attract the interest of pagan historians. Only when it came into conflict with the state did it become worthy of mention in those earlier days, and the earliest pagan writers who refer to it in such a context all significantly mention Christ as the founder of Christianity (Tacitus, *Annals* xv. 44; Suetonius, *Claudius* 25, *Nero* 16; Pliny, *Epistles* x. 96).

Apart from a doubtful and, at best, heavily interpolated passage in Josephus (*Ant.* xviii. 3. 3), Jesus is not mentioned directly in non-Christian Jewish writings of this period. The reason for this is the hostility and resentment with which His memory was regarded by Jewish leaders of the time. There are, however, indirect references to Him in the earlier rabbinical writings which make reasonably recognizable mention of Him as a transgressor in Israel who practised magic, scorned the words of the wise, led the people astray, and said He had come to add to the law, who was hanged on Passover Eve, and whose disciples healed the sick in His name.

In the early centuries AD not even the bitterest enemies of Christianity had any idea of denying that Jesus lived and died in Palestine, and that He performed wonderful works, whatever account they might give of the power by which He performed them. Nor at the present day does any objective historian deny the historical fact of Christ. It is not historians who toy with the fantasy of a Christ-myth. Not only His death but

His resurrection must be reckoned among the best established facts of history.

II. SOURCES

For the essential details of the life of Christ we are entirely dependent on the New Testament. As has been said, not much can be gained from a study of pagan or Jewish literature of the early decades AD, and when we turn to extra-biblical Christian literature of the same period we find very little that is not already in the New Testament. Most of the apocryphal Gospels are so obviously the product of imagination that they only help, by way of contrast, to prove the historical character of the canonical Gospels, but do not add anything to our knowledge of the life of our Lord.

The Gospels are not biographies in the ordinary sense of the word. Each of the four Evangelists had a specific purpose in writing and made an appropriate selection from the information at his disposal regarding our Lord's life. (See GOSPELS.) Although there are many differences in emphasis on certain aspects of His life, all four proclaim one and the same Christ as Lord and Saviour, the perfect Son of man and the only-begotten Son of God.

Because the Gospels are not ordinary biographies but proclamations of the good tidings regarding Jesus as Saviour and Lord, we must not seek in them a strictly chronological arrangement. On the other hand, the Evangelists' religious purpose did not lead them to neglect the historical character of the life of Jesus. As is stated so clearly in the preface to our third Gospel (see LUKE THE EVANGELIST), the authors were keenly aware of the urgent need to make known the truth about Christ. To them and to their fellow-believers faith in Christ was a matter of life and death. Thus they could not afford to base their faith on fantasies, myths, or legends. A faith like that of those first Christian generations demanded absolute loyalty to Christ—even unto death. Such a faith could be built only on assured facts. Moreover, the Gospel-writers were in such close and living contact with many who had heard and seen our Lord that they had unique opportunities of ascertaining those facts. Besides, since the historical facts were known at first hand to so many people, they could not venture to give fictitious accounts.

Although Luke incorporated large sections of Mark in his Gospel and John may well have known the first three Gospels, our four Gospels are essentially four independent sources of information regarding the life of our Lord. Each of them stresses certain aspects of His life and ministry more than the others, but it is essentially the same Christ that we find in all four. This is as true of John as of the Synoptists. John's Gospel supplements the others and, as a result of many years of reflection and more mature insight into the deeper philosophical and theological significance of the Gospel history, concentrates more on the teaching of our Lord regarding His divine Sonship; but even John proclaims no other Christ than the Christ proclaimed by the first three Evangelists (see JOHN, GOSPEL OF).

In short, we have in the four canonical Gospels the best and most reliable sources of information regarding the life of Jesus Christ. Although the rest of the New Testament does not add much to the historical details of the Gospel, it is important to note that the Acts, the Epistles, and the Revelation are all built on the fact that Jesus lived, taught, suffered, and triumphed as the Gospels affirm. Since some of the New Testament Epistles were written as early as AD 50 (or even a little earlier)—1 and 2 Thessalonians and Galatians, and possibly James—we are brought to not more than twenty years from the date of Jesus' crucifixion. Taking further into account the fact that one of the early New Testament writers, Paul, was a bitter persecutor of the followers of Jesus but was converted as early as AD 32 or 33, and that the Epistle of James was written by the brother of Jesus (see JAMES, EPISTLE OF), we realize how close the contact was between the time of our Lord's life on earth (*c.* 6/4 BC–AD 30) and that generation of Christians in whose lifetime the first New Testament documents were written. Paul's summary of the apostolic preaching in 1 Cor. xv. 1–8 (RV) is of great significance: 'Now I make known unto you, brethren, the gospel which I preached unto you, which also ye received, wherein also ye stand, by which also ye are saved. . . . For I delivered unto you first of all that which also I received, how that Christ died for our sins according to the scriptures; and that he was buried; and that he hath been raised on the third day . . .; and that he appeared to Cephas; then to the twelve; *then he appeared to about five hundred brethren at once, of whom the greater part remain until now* [italics mine], but some are fallen asleep; then he appeared to James; then to all the apostles; and last of all, as unto one born out of due time, he appeared to me also.'

In this passage Paul not only proclaims essentially the same gospel as the four Evangelists, but he reveals how intimate the relation was between the early Christian Church and the apostles and other eyewitnesses of our Lord's life. It is thus not surprising to find that our four Gospels, for all their different emphases and varying choice of details, proclaim the same Christ who came to seek and save those who are lost, the divine Lord to whom all power has been given in heaven and on earth (Mt. xi. 27, xxviii. 18; Mk. i. 11, viii. 29; Lk. i. 32, 35, ii. 11, ix. 35, x. 22; Jn. i. 1, xx. 28, *etc.*).

No wonder, then, that after more than a century of acute and ruthless criticism the trustworthiness of the four canonical Gospels has been more securely established than ever. One theory after another, and successive schools of thought which have thrown doubt on the reliability of the Gospels, have crumbled to pieces before the irrefutable historicity of the life of Jesus which they record. Although the Gospels are silent regarding many details which we should naturally like to know, the four Gospels, confirming and supplementing one another, give us all the facts about Jesus which we need to know in order that we may believe in Him as 'the Christ, the Son of God; and that believing ye may have life in his name' (Jn. xx. 31, RV).

III. UNIQUENESS

The life of our Lord is unique in many ways. One aspect of its uniqueness lies in its fulfilment of specific prophecies made hundreds of years before His birth. Jesus Himself, for instance, repeatedly taught His disciples that He would *in accordance with the Scriptures* suffer and die and rise from the dead (*cf.* Lk. xviii. 31–34). After His resurrection, too, He plainly declared that in His life, death, and resurrection the Scriptures had been fulfilled (Lk. xxiv. 25–27, 44–48).

In the speeches of Peter, Stephen, and Paul recorded in the Acts, and in practically all the books of the New Testament the life, suffering, and exaltation of Jesus are repeatedly proclaimed as the fulfilment of the promises of God in the Old Testament (see MESSIAH). There is nothing in the history of the world comparable to the fact that hundreds of years before the birth of Jesus many things regarding Him—even the place of His birth (Mi. v. 2)—had been foretold and recorded in the Old Testament Scriptures. And in many other aspects—from His supernatural conception to His ascension to heaven—the life stands alone. Only in *His* life do we see God become flesh. While the lives of all other founders of religions reveal to us men who sought after truth and strove to attain religious insight, the life of Jesus Christ alone reveals the God of love and righteousness seeking to save fallen humanity.

All the claims made by Jesus regarding His eternal and divine Sonship are confirmed by His life, death, resurrection and triumphant ascension. He is unique among men.

IV. MAIN EPOCHS

Although we cannot construct a detailed or strictly chronological biography of Jesus Christ, the Gospels give us sufficient material to enable us to point to the most important epochs in His life.

a. His supernatural birth

The authors of the Gospels had ample opportunities to discover the truth regarding the birth of Jesus. Apart from the fact that Mary the mother of Jesus was placed in the charge of the beloved disciple (*cf.* Jn. xix. 26, 27), we must remember that James, the brother of Jesus, was for many years one of the leaders of the Christian Church in Jerusalem. After the resurrection and ascension of Jesus, Mary and her sons were freed from all doubt regarding His Lordship and lived in close fellowship with their fellow-believers in the church of Jerusalem (*cf.* Acts i. 14). When the Evangelist Luke accompanied Paul to Jerusalem in AD 56 or 57 one of the people whom he visited was James the brother of Jesus (Acts xxi. 17, 18). At that time, if we may judge from the preface to his Gospel, Luke was already intensely interested in the facts regarding the life of Jesus. Whether Luke met Mary personally we do not know, but it is certain that he had access to information regarding our Lord's birth which ultimately could come from Mary alone. It is basically from her point of view that he relates the story of Jesus' supernatural conception and birth (Lk. i. 26–56, ii. 1–51). Matthew, on the other hand, tells the story more from the point of view of Joseph. But both Gospels agree that Jesus was not the son of a human father but was conceived by the power of the Holy Ghost and born as the Son of God (*cf.* Lk. i. 35; Mt. i. 18–24). In perfect keeping with this fact John opens his Gospel with the words: 'In the beginning was the Word, and the Word was with God, and the Word was God . . . and the Word became flesh, and dwelt among us (and we beheld his glory, glory as of the only begotten from the Father), full of grace and truth' (Jn. i. 1–14, RV). (See INCARNATION.)

b. Infancy, childhood, and growth to maturity

From Lk. ii. 40, 52 it is clear that Jesus' life from childhood to young manhood was normal but also perfect. In His life God's ideal for a perfect human life was realized at every stage. Although He lived in a humble home with Mary, Joseph, and several younger brothers and sisters, His life was at all times in complete agreement with the will of God (Lk. ii. 52), and from an early age (Lk. ii. 49) He appears to have been conscious that He was the Son of God in a special sense. From Lk. ii. 46, 47, it is clear that from His childhood He had made an intensive study of the Old Testament Scriptures; and although Joseph probably died early and Jesus had to work hard as a carpenter in order to provide for Mary and her younger children (Mt. xiii. 55, 56), He gave ample time to meditation on the Scriptures and to prayer.

Apart from the few details given regarding Jesus' childhood and the inferences to be made from the Gospels regarding His life while growing physically, mentally, and spiritually to full maturity, the New Testament passes by in silence those years of preparation.

c. Baptism and temptation

When Jesus (probably in AD 27) had reached the prime of life (about thirty years old, Lk. iii. 23) He left Nazareth and was baptized by John the Baptist. By doing this He publicly accepted His messianic task as the Son of God and Saviour who, sinless Himself, took upon Him the guilt of His people.

God the Father showed His approval of His Son's action in deliberately identifying Himself with His sinful people by the descent of the Spirit 'in bodily form like a dove' and by the heavenly voice which proclaimed: 'Thou art my beloved

Son; in thee I am well pleased' (Lk. iii. 22). These words, combining Ps. ii. 7 and Is. xlii. 1, acknowledged Him as the Messiah but indicated that He was to fulfil His messianic calling in terms of the obedient and suffering Servant of the Lord.

With this assurance in His heart, Jesus was driven by the Spirit into the wilderness of Judaea to be tempted by the devil (Mt. iv. 1). In order to vindicate His competence to be the Saviour of men, He first had to prove His utter and unconditional obedience to His heavenly Father and His power to overcome the great deceiver. The temptation narrative is evidently set in contrast with the story of the fall in Gn. iii; thus, whereas Adam and Eve succumb to temptation in spite of their living under the most favourable conditions, Jesus overcomes although tempted under the most difficult circumstances. After forty days of physical and spiritual strain and privation in the wilderness, He was urged by all the concentrated cunning and power of the tempter to put His Father to the test or reject the path which the heavenly voice had marked out as His Father's will for Him. But Jesus resisted the most subtle temptations and remained unswervingly obedient to His Father's will. He emerged from His spiritual conflict as God's loyal Son and faithful Servant (Mt. iv. 1–11; Mk. i. 12, 13; Lk. iv. 1–13).

d. The beginning of His public ministry

Having triumphed over the titanic onslaughts of the devil, Jesus actively embarked on the first stage of His public ministry, called His first disciples (Jn. i. 35–51), revealed His divine power by changing water into wine (Jn. ii. 1–11), by performing miracles (Jn. ii. 23 ff.), by teaching Nicodemus spiritually revolutionary truths, and by bringing salvation even to the despised Samaritans (Jn. iv. 1–42). This stage of His ministry had been prepared for by John the Baptist (*q.v.*), and reached its climax when some of the Samaritans confessed, 'we . . . know that this is indeed . . . the Saviour of the world' (Jn. iv. 42).

e. Concentrated teaching and ministry in Galilee

John the Baptist's imprisonment was the signal for Jesus to begin His ministry in Galilee, with the proclamation that the appointed time had come and the kingdom of God was at hand (Mk. i. 14 f.). When His claim in the synagogue of Nazareth to be the One through whom the messianic promises were to be fulfilled was rejected by His home town (Lk. iv. 16 ff.) He made Capernaum His new headquarters. Probably for more than a year (see CHRONOLOGY OF THE NEW TESTAMENT) He now worked and taught in Capernaum and in other parts of Galilee (Mt. iv. 12–xiv. 13; Mk. i. 14–vi. 34; Lk. iv. 14–ix. 11; Jn. iv. 46–54, *etc.*), revealing His divine power over nature (Mk. iv. 35–41, vi. 34–51, *etc.*), over the world of spirits and demons (Lk. viii. 26–39, ix. 37–45, *etc.*), over the human body and over physical and spiritual diseases (Mt. viii. 1–17, ix. 1–8, *etc.*), and even over life and death (Lk. vii. 11–17; Mt. viii. 18–26). He furthermore claimed to possess final authority over the eternal destiny of mankind, and in the Sermon on the Mount and other teachings He revealed His unique authority to proclaim the laws of the kingdom of God (Mt. v. 1–vii. 29, *etc.*).

While revealing His supreme authority as the promised Christ, Jesus during this period also revealed His love and sympathy for those in physical or spiritual distress (Mt. ix. 1–8, 18–22; Lk. viii. 43–48, *etc.*). He repeatedly declared that He had come to seek and to save those who were lost, and He exercised the divine prerogative of forgiving sins (Lk. v. 20–26, vii. 48–50).

Out of His much wider group of followers He chose twelve special disciples (Mt. x. 1–4; Lk. vi. 12–16) whom He systematically taught and trained to be His apostles.

The authority with which He taught His hearers and His refusal to be frightened by enemies among the Jewish rulers and Pharisees, added to His many miracles of healing and other manifestations of His power over the created order (Lk. iv. 33–41; Mk. v. 1–42, *etc.*), caused Jesus to become tremendously popular among the masses of Galilee (Lk. iv. 40–42, v. 15, 26, vi. 17–19). This popularity reached its peak in the miracle of the feeding of the 5,000 (Mt. xiv. 13–21; Mk. vi. 30–44; Lk. ix. 10–17; Jn. vi. 5–13), and this clear proof of His messiahship made the masses decide to crown Him King (Jn. vi. 15).

f. The training of the Twelve

After Jesus had refused to be crowned as an earthly Messiah (Jn. vi. 26, 27) the crowds and even many of His wider circle of disciples left Him (Jn. vi. 66, 67). He withdrew to the territory belonging to Tyre, Sidon, and Caesarea Philippi (Mt. xv. 21, xvi. 13; Mk. vii. 31, *etc.*), but could never really escape the public eye. When He again came near the Sea of Galilee, He once more healed and helped many in distress and for a second time miraculously fed the crowds because He had compassion on the multitude (Mt. xv. 29–39). Then, withdrawing from the crowds again, He sought solitude with His disciples and asked them the crucial question: 'But whom say ye that I am?' (Mt. xvi. 15). After Peter, speaking for all the apostles, had openly confessed, 'Thou art the Christ, the Son of the living God', Jesus determinedly began to prepare His disciples for the terrible shock awaiting them in Jerusalem (Mt. xvi. 21–26). But at the same time He clearly and repeatedly taught that the victory would ultimately be His (Mt. xvi. 27, 28) and that His followers thus need not fear (Lk. xii. 4–12, 32–34).

His self-revelation to His disciples culminated in His transfiguration on the mountain when His three closest followers saw Him in divine glory (Mt. xvii. 1–13; Mk. ix. 2–10; Lk. ix. 28–36). Because He came to fulfil both the Law and the Prophets, Moses (typifying the Law) and Elijah (representative of the Prophets) appeared with Him in glory before He finally started on the way to Jerusalem to suffer death for men's salvation. Once again the voice of God from heaven declared Jesus to be His beloved Son to whom all should pay heed (Lk. ix. 35).

g. Mounting antagonism

Having been revealed to His disciples and acknowledged by them as truly the Son of God (Mt. xvii. 1–13; Mk. ix. 2–10; Lk. ix. 18–20), Jesus now prepared them more deliberately than ever for their future task as foundation members of His Church. He taught them many truths, both directly and in the form of parables, and continued to reveal His divine power and authority by healing the sick (Lk. xiv. 1–6, xvii. 11–19) and the blind (Mk. x. 46–52), and relieving others in distress.

The opposition towards Him among the Jewish rulers and religious leaders grew steadily worse (Lk. xiv. 1). Every possible method and scheme was tried to ensnare Him, to break His continuing influence on the masses, and to find a reason to have Him handed over to the Roman authorities for execution (Mt. xix. 1–3; Lk. xi. 53, 54). All His solemn warnings addressed to His enemies, all His penetrating teaching which aimed at bringing them to a change of heart, all His works of benevolence in healing the sick and even raising the dead to life (Jn. xi. 41–45), only inflamed the majority of Pharisees, scribes, and other Jewish leaders with greater hatred against Him (Jn. xi. 46–53).

h. The last week in Jerusalem

Having openly entered Jerusalem as the Messiah amid cheering crowds (Mk. xi. 1–10; Jn. xii. 12–19, *etc.*), Jesus drove the moneychangers and traffickers in sacrificial animals from the outer court of the Temple and so revealed His claim to messianic authority (Lk. xix. 45, 46; Mt. xxi. 12–16). The end was now drawing near. Jesus relentlessly exposed the hypocrisy of His persecutors (Mt. xxiii. 1–39; Lk. xx. 45–47), as He taught in the Temple court during those fateful days (Mt. xxi. 33–44, xxii. 1–14; Mk. xii. 1–12; Lk. xx. 9–47), and prophesied what would happen to the people of Judaea, to Jerusalem, and to the Temple (Lk. xxi. 20–24, *etc.*) in the impending times of distress. He warned His followers regarding the dangers awaiting them (Lk. xxi. 9–19, *etc.*), foretold what was in store for the world and the Church (Lk. xxi. 25–27), and predicted that world history would culminate in His return in majesty to reveal His divine might over all the powers of darkness and usher in His eternal kingdom (Mt. xxiv. 29–31, xxv. 31–46).

On the eve of His passion, as a final preparation of His apostles for the great task awaiting them, Jesus washed their feet (Jn. xiii. 1–11), teaching them an urgently needed lesson in humility (Jn. xiii. 12–17; Lk. xxii. 24–30), announced that Judas was going to betray Him (Mk. xiv. 18–21; Jn. xiii. 21–30), instituted the Lord's Supper (Mt. xxvi. 26–29, *etc.*), and prayed for all His followers (Jn. xvii. 1–26).

Then followed His final and utter self-surrender to the will of His Father in Gethsemane (Mt. xxvi. 39–46, *etc.*). Having taken upon Him the guilt of fallen mankind, He willingly allowed Himself to be arrested, maltreated, falsely condemned, and crucified. His sacrificial and vicarious suffering reached its climax on the cross, when, at the end of the three hours of darkness, He cried with a loud voice: 'My God, my God, why hast thou forsaken me?' (Mt. xxvii. 46). He had told His disciples that He had not come to judge the world but to give His life as a ransom for many (Mt. xxvi. 28; Mk. x. 45, *etc.*). Having voluntarily offered Himself up as the Lamb of God (Jn. i. 29, x. 11–18), His task was now completed. Before commending His spirit into the hands of His Father, He announced triumphantly: 'It is finished' (Jn. xix. 30).

i. Burial, resurrection, and ascension

After His death, He was no longer in the power of His enemies. His body was taken down from the cross (Lk. xxiii. 50–53) and buried in a new tomb in a garden. His promise to rise from the dead was soon fulfilled, and as the risen Christ and living Lord He personally dispelled His followers' fears and doubts (Lk. xxiv. 13–49; Jn. xx. 11–xxi. 22). For forty days He repeatedly appeared to them, opened their minds to understand the Old Testament Scriptures, and promised to send the Holy Spirit to comfort, guide, and empower them to act as His witnesses—starting at Jerusalem and travelling all over the world (Acts i. 8). Having assured them once more that all power had been given to Him in heaven and on earth (Mt. xxviii. 18), He commissioned them to make disciples of all the nations (Mt. xxviii. 19). After He had promised to be with them always, even to the end of the world (Mt. xxviii. 20) He ascended into heaven—with hands lifted up, blessing them (Lk. xxiv. 50).

So the life of Jesus Christ as Man among men on this planet ended triumphantly. The apostolic claim provides a fitting conclusion to His earthly ministry: 'God hath made him both Lord and Christ, this Jesus whom ye crucified' (Acts ii. 36, RV).

See also Chronology of the New Testament, Incarnation, Messiah, Transfiguration, Miracles, Crucifixion, Resurrection, Jesus Christ, Teaching of, *etc.*

Bibliography. O. Borchert, *The Original Jesus*, 1933; G. Bornkamm, *Jesus of Nazareth*, 1960; F. C. Burkitt, *Jesus Christ—an historical outline*, 1932; C. J. Cadoux, *Life of Jesus*, 1948; F. C. Conybeare, *The Historic Jesus*, 1914; H. Daniel-Rops, *Jesus in His Time*, 1955; A. Edersheim, *The Life and Times of Jesus the Messiah*, 1907; F. W. Farrar, *The Life of Christ*, 1874; J. N. Geldenhuys, *Commentary on the Gospel of Luke*, 1950 (especially pp. 36–41, the special notes listed on p. 14, and the Excursus on pp. 649–670); Giovanni Papini, *Life of Christ*, 1925; T. R.

Glover, *The Jesus of History*[13], 1920; M. Goguel, *Life of Jesus*, 1933; F. W. Grosheide (and others), *Christus de Heiland*, 1948; A. C. Headlam, *The Life and Teaching of Jesus*[3], 1936; A. M. Hunter, *The Work and Words of Jesus*, 1950; J. W. Jack, *The Historic Christ*, 1933; S. E. Johnson, *Jesus in His own Times*, 1959; J. Klausner, *Jesus of Nazareth*, 1929; K. S. Latourette, *The First Five Centuries*, 1937 (ch. ii); J. MacKinnon, *The Historic Jesus*, 1931; H. D. A. Major, T. W. Manson, and C. J. Wright, *The Mission and Message of Jesus*, 1940; T. W. Manson, *The Servant-Messiah*, 1953; E. Meyer, *Ursprung und Anfänge des Christentums*, 3 vols., 1921–3; G. Ogg, *Chronology of the Public Ministry of Jesus*, 1940; A. T. Olmstead, *Jesus in the Light of History*, 1942; J. M. Robinson, *A New Quest of the Historical Jesus*, 1959; W. Sanday, *Outlines of the Life of Christ*, 1931; A. Schweitzer, *The Quest of the Historical Jesus*[2], 1936; J. W. Shepard, *The Christ of the Gospels*, 1946; P. C. Simpson, *The Fact of Christ*, 1901; David Smith, *The Days of His Flesh*, 1905; J. Stalker, *The Life of Jesus Christ*, 1891; E. Stauffer, *Jesus and His Story*, 1960; N. B. Stonehouse, *The Witness of Matthew and Mark to Christ*, 1944; *id.*, *The Witness of Luke to Christ*, 1951; R. H. Strachan, *The Historic Jesus in the New Testament*, 1931; V. Taylor, *Life and Ministry of Jesus*, 1954; M. C. Tenney, *New Testament Survey*, 1961; H. E. W. Turner, *Jesus, Master and Lord*, 1953; B. B. Warfield, *The Person and Work of Christ*, 1950; H. G. Wood, *Did Christ Really Live?*, 1938.

J.N.G.

JESUS CHRIST, MUSLIM TRADITIONS ABOUT. There are three general preoccupations of Muslim tradition about our Lord: His miraculous birth and powers, His exemplary asceticism, and His eschatological rôle. Wide but inconclusive issues attach to their origin and currency, which belong with the problems of historical scholarship over the genesis and expansion of Islam.

Jesus is invariably denoted in Islam by the name 'Īsā ibn Maryam, with the title *Al-Masīḥ* (the Christ) frequently added. How the substitution occurred has been variously conjectured—transposition of consonants for rhyming purposes, deliberate misinformation, slow corruption of sources, and usage. Christian thought has sometimes seen in the variant name a symbol of the disparity of beliefs about the person and work of Jesus. Muslim traditions belong within the framework of the Quranic account of Jesus as a wholly human prophet (albeit 'a spirit from God' and 'his word') who was the spokesman of the *Injīl* (or 'gospel' considered as a corpus of teaching) in a succession of prophets and penultimate to Muḥammad, and who was 'raised' to heaven out of a crisis of rejection without having suffered physical crucifixion. The traditions are numerous and full in contrast to the severely brief notices (save of the Nativity) which the Qur'an gives, but they follow the same general pattern of interest in His virgin birth and His works of compassion. The latter are widely embellished from narratives in the Apocryphal Gospels, which doubtless had currency in the early Islamic centuries among Muslims, by virtue of Islam's expansion into mainly Christian areas, its ready absorption of large parts of its converts' heritage (always excluding the Islamically irreconcilable, such as faith in the incarnation and in the redemptive action of God in Christ), and from its conditioned tolerance of continuing Christian communities.

Some of the sayings and stories hold close to the spirit and sense of the Canonical Gospels. 'They saw Jesus coming out of a prostitute's house and someone said to Him: "O Spirit of God, what are you doing with this woman?" And He replied: "The doctor comes only to the sick." ' Or the almost verbatim passage about alms in secret and washing and grooming to prevent fasting becoming ostentatious. By an intriguing adaptation the saying about the 'beautiful' temple which men admired not being left standing 'one stone upon another' is applied (both admiration and ruin) to a mosque. On the other hand, there is frequently around His person, whether in saying or narrative, an aura subtly different from the Gospels. There are miracles of magic such as that of the ten garments all dyed by Jesus in one vat according to the contrasted colours Mary had directed (the tradition of Jesus having been trained as a dyer is frequent). Al-Tha'labī has a story of children changed by Jesus into swine, with whom He also used to liken the 'world' saying: 'Away from me, ye swine.'

The traditional emphasis on the ascetic quality of Jesus' life finds repeated expression in aphorism and story. 'Verily, I have two friends: he who loves them loves me and he who hates them hates me—poverty and distress.' It is a familiar concept, widespread even among illiterate Muslims, that Jesus was *Imām al-Sā'iḥin*, 'the Prince of the wanderers', echoing the status of one who had 'not where to lay his head'. A robe of wool, denoting simplicity, is the characteristic garb with which tradition clothes Him, adding, on His personal appearance, that He was 'a ruddy man, inclined to white, had short hair and never anointed His head: He used to walk barefoot, and He took no house, or adornment, or goods, or clothes, or provision, except His day's food'. In His habitual form of invocation of God, as affirmed by Al-Ghazālī, Jesus says: 'I have become worn out by my labours and there is no poor person poorer than I am.'

The impression of poverty of spirit, as well as of person, is consonant with Jesus' firm Quranic disavowal of what are Quranically seen as the pretensions of Sonship alleged among Christians. Yet the eschatological Jesus in Muslim tradition is a figure of power and authority who will vindicate Islam and finalize its supremacy, breaking all crosses and slaying *Al-Dajjāl*, the antichrist, of whose demise it has much to say, with realistic detail. Within the last century the Aḥmadiyyah movements in Islam have drastically revised these beliefs, holding Jesus to have been buried in Kashmir, at a ripe old age, and denying to Him any rôle in the end time.

BIBLIOGRAPHY. D. S. Margoliouth, 'Christ in Mohammedan Literature', *DCG*, ii. 882; M. Asin y Palacios, 'Logia et Agrapha Domini Jesu apud Moslemicos Scriptores', *Patrologia Orientalis*, XIII, XIX; J. Robson, *Christ in Islam*, 1930; M. Hayek, *Le Christ de l'Islam*, 1959. A.K.C.

JESUS CHRIST, TEACHING OF.

I. SOURCES

The teaching of our Lord is preserved in the main in the four Gospels (see GOSPELS). Although the rest of the New Testament contains comparatively few direct references to His teaching, yet the Acts, the Epistles, and Revelation corroborate its essential content as preserved in the Gospel records. The message of these New Testament documents and of other early Christian writings of the 1st and 2nd centuries is based on the teaching of Jesus. These writings thus serve as important, although indirect, sources. All attempts to prove that the apostles and especially Paul proclaimed a gospel contrary to the teaching of Jesus have completely failed (see PAUL). There is an essential unity between the teaching of our Lord and that of Paul and the early Church.

The supposed clash between the teaching of Jesus as preserved in the Synoptic Gospels and His teaching as presented in the Gospel of John is also only apparent. It is undoubtedly true that the Gospel of John gives more attention to the 'metaphysical' teaching of Jesus and preserves many discourses in which our Lord spoke very directly and intimately regarding His own Person and His relationship to God. There is a difference of accent and emphasis; but the teaching of Jesus in the Synoptic Gospels and in John is basically the same (*cf.* Mt. xi. 25–30, xii. 50, xiv. 33, xvi. 16, xvii. 5, xxv. 34, xxvi. 39, 63–65, xxvii. 43, xxviii. 18–20; Mk. i. 1, 11, ii. 5, 10, viii. 29, 38, ix. 7, 37, x. 29, 30, xii. 6, 35–37, xiii. 26, 31, 32, xiv. 36, 61–64, xv. 39; Lk. i. 30–35, ii. 49, iii. 23, 38, ix. 23–26, 35, x. 21–24, xxii. 69–71, xxiii. 46, xxiv. 36–53, *etc.*, with the contents of the Fourth Gospel).

Each of the Evangelists had his special purpose in view and made his own selection from the teachings of Jesus to suit that purpose. In this way the Gospels supplement but do not contradict one another. Together they give a wonderfully complete report regarding the essential teaching of Jesus Christ. When we study the rest of the New Testament and the life and teaching of the early Church, we see how firmly early Church doctrine and practice are based on Christ's teaching as preserved in the four canonical Gospels.

II. CHRIST'S TEACHING UNIQUE

That our Lord spoke in the language of His times (literally and metaphorically) and that there is much in the outward form of His teaching common to Jewish Rabbis and other religious teachers of His time, may be freely granted. The basic teaching of Jesus Christ is, however, totally new and revolutionary. The words of the Jewish officers who were sent to arrest Him remain true in an even higher sense than they intended: 'Never man so spake' (Jn. vii. 46, RV; *cf.* Mt. vii. 28, 29; Mk. i. 22). It is futile to suppose that the teaching of Jesus is only a natural development of the best Jewish teaching of His age or that it is to a greater or lesser extent the product of the Qumran community or some other Jewish sect. The similarities between His teaching and the teachings of the rabbinical schools and Palestinian religious sects of those times arise from the fact that He lived and taught in the same historical setting. Basically, however, His teaching is not merely new but unique.

III. CHRIST'S TEACHING METHODS

Our Lord used a wide variety of methods of teaching to suit differing circumstances. He read from the Old Testament Scriptures in the synagogue and expounded them to the congregation (Lk. iv. 16–32); He preached in the open air, as may be seen from the incomparable Sermon on the Mount, addressed primarily to His disciples but heard also by many other listeners (Mt. v. 1–vii. 29; Lk. vi. 17–49); He spoke directly and personally to individuals (Mk. x. 21; Lk. x. 39); He asked questions in order to force people to think (Lk. x. 26, xii. 56, 57; Mt. xxiv. 45; Mk. iv. 21). He argued with His enemies in an attempt to rid them of their misconceptions. He engaged in debates in which He proved His points or revealed the folly of His opponents by irresistible logic (Mk. xii. 18–27; Lk. xx. 41–44). He uttered striking paradoxes and terse epigrams to impress certain great truths on the minds of His disciples (Mt. v. 3, 4; Lk. ix. 24, xx. 25). He often quoted Old Testament Scriptures (Mk. xii. 24–27, 35–37; Lk. iv. 4, 8, 12). He made use of object lessons (Jn. xiii. 1–15; Mt. xviii. 2–4, xxi. 18–22). He spoke more intimately and directly to His inner group of disciples (Mt. xvii. 9–13; Mk. xii. 43, 44; Jn. xiii. 1–xvii. 26). He gave impressive prophetical discourses (Mt. xxiv. 5–44; Mk. xiii. 1–37; Lk. xxi. 5–36). He taught His apostles much regarding Himself and God by means of definitely 'metaphysical' declarations (Mt. xi. 25–27; Lk. x. 21, 22; Jn. v. 16–47, vi. 32–71) and very often He taught by means of parables (see PARABLE). Pervading all His teaching is His unique authority. Unlike the prophets of the Old Testament, who spoke with a delegated authority, He spoke with direct, divine and supreme authority (see J. N. Geldenhuys, *Supreme Authority*, 1953, chapter I).

IV. TYPES OF TEACHING

As it is impossible to write an ordinary 'Life of Jesus' so it is impossible to reduce His teaching to an ordinary philosophic, theological, or ethical system; His teaching is so different from that of anyone before or after Him. We may, however, attempt a classification of Christ's teaching under the following heads: ethical (Mt. v–vii; Lk. vi. 17–49, xi. 37–54, *etc.*), metaphysical and theological (Mt. xi. 25–27; Lk. x. 21, 22; Jn. vi. 33–48, viii. 58, *etc.*), social (Lk. xiv. 7–14, xx. 19–25; Mt. xix. 3–12, *etc.*), soteriological (Mt. ix. 12, 13, xi. 28–30, xvi. 24–26, xx. 28; Lk. ix. 23, 24, xiv. 15–24, xv. 1–32, xviii. 9–14, xix. 9, 10; Jn. x. 1–18, *etc.*), and eschatological (Mt. xxiv, xxv; Mk. xiii; Lk. xxi; Jn. xiv. 1–3, *etc.*).

Underlying all His teaching is His direct and indirect teaching regarding Himself. All His teaching is united in His own person.

V. THE BASIC THEME

Unlike all other religious teachers, Jesus did not primarily teach truths regarding God and religion. His teaching is essentially the proclamation of Himself as the Son of God and the Saviour of the world. It is not a mere system of theology but a self-revelation. It is true that He did not proclaim Himself openly and at all times as the Messiah and Son of God. Because of the misconceptions rife among the Jews regarding the character and task of the Messiah (*q.v.*), He was very careful not to say too much to the crowds that He addressed. But a close study of all four Gospels reveals that from the very beginning Jesus taught that He was the Son of God. It is significant to note that in the very first words of Jesus recorded in the Gospels He gently but firmly reminds Mary that His true Father is God (Lk. ii. 48–50); and in the last words which He uttered from the cross He commits Himself to God with the words, 'Father, into thy hands I commend my spirit' (Lk. xxiii. 46). And after His resurrection He told Mary Magdalene to convey His message to His disciples: 'I ascend unto my Father' (Jn. xx. 17).

The most characteristic feature of the teaching of Jesus is His proclamation of the Fatherhood of God. It is true that in a few cases God had already been proclaimed as Father in the Old Testament, but in these cases He is looked upon as Father of His people rather than of the individual believer. Jesus proclaimed God as Father in a new and more personal way. In the Gospels there are about 150 instances in which He refers to God as Father. He taught that God was His own Father in a unique sense (Lk. ii. 49, x. 21, 22, xx. 41–44, xxii. 29; Mt. xi. 25–27, xv. 13, xvi. 13–17, 27, xxi. 37, xxii. 2, xxvi. 29, 63, 64, xxvii. 43, xxviii. 18–20; Mk. viii. 38, xii. 6, 35–37, xiii. 24–27, xiv. 61, 62; Jn. iii. 35, v. 18, 22, 23, *etc.*). He never equated the Fatherhood of God in relation to Himself with the Fatherhood of God in relation to His disciples or to people in general. He never prayed to God as 'our Father' but always directly as 'Father' or 'My Father' (Mk. xiv. 36; Mt. xi. 25; Lk. x. 21; Jn. xi. 41, xvii. 1–26, *etc.*). When speaking to His disciples He never referred to God as 'our Father' but always as 'My Father' (Lk. x. 22; Mt. xi. 27, xii. 50; Jn. xx. 17) or 'your Father' (Mk. xi. 25, 26; Mt. v. 45, 48, *etc.*). This clear demarcation between His own relationship to God and other people's relationship to God pervades all His teaching, in the Synoptic Gospels as well as in the Fourth Gospel. In this Jesus Christ is unique. No religious teacher before or after Him ever claimed that exclusive relationship to God which is expressed in the words, 'All things have been delivered unto me of my Father: and no one knoweth the Son, save the Father, neither doth any know the Father, save the Son, and he to whomsoever the Son willeth to reveal him' (Mt. xi. 27; *cf.* Lk. x. 22; Mk. viii. 38; Jn. xvii. 1–5; *etc.*).

The teaching of Jesus regarding the Fatherhood of God is, however, not limited to the proclamation of this unique relationship between Himself and God the Father. He also taught His disciples to believe in God as Father of all who believe. In the Sermon on the Mount He refers to God as the Father of His disciples no less than fourteen times (see especially Mt. vi. 1–34; *cf.* Lk. vi. 36). Because this relationship between God and man was to be the basis of His followers' spiritual life Jesus taught them to pray to God as 'our Father' (Mt. vi. 9). Because God is their Father they need not fear (Mt. x. 28–30, vi. 26–32); they can and should pray with real faith in Him (Mt. vii. 7–11; Lk. xi. 9–13). Because God is perfect in love and grace they also must be like Him (Mt. v. 43–48; Lk. vi. 36).

The teaching of Jesus regarding the Fatherhood of God struck a death-blow against the prevailing scribal religion, which was overburdened with formalities, ceremonies, and regulations. This is why Jesus said that His teaching was so new that, just as for new wine old wineskins had to be discarded and replaced by new wineskins, so the old ceremonial forms had to be discarded and replaced by the new approach to God through Him (Mk. ii. 22; Mt. ix. 14–17; Lk. v. 33–39).

By teaching that the relationship between God and believers is that of a loving and holy Father to His children, Jesus revolutionized the whole concept of religion. Because God is the Father of grace and love there is hope even for the worst of sinners (*cf.* the parable of the prodigal son who is welcomed and restored to a new life by the forgiving father, Lk. xv. 11–32). As Father, God is interested in even the least of His creatures and cares for them all (Mt. vi. 26, x. 29, 30; Lk. xii. 24–27). As Father, He knows His children's real needs and thus believers should not be worried or afraid (Lk. xii. 4–7, 22–32). As Father, He will remain faithful to them even amid the most trying and dangerous circumstances (Lk. xii. 11, 12; Mk. xiii. 11).

At the same time, however, Jesus clearly taught that God is not only the immanent and omnipresent Father of men, but that He is also the transcendent and almighty Lord of heaven and earth (Mt. xi. 25). Therefore when we pray to God, we must say 'Our Father *which art in heaven*' (Mt. vi. 9). And because God is the almighty Father who created and upholds all things (Lk. x. 21; Mt. xix. 26), the great task and highest privilege of believers is to glorify the name of God (Mt. v. 16, vi. 9; Mk. xii. 17, 30; Lk. viii. 39; Jn. xv. 8). To do the will of the Father then becomes not a wearisome burden but a joyful privilege (*cf.* the words 'Thy will be done, as in heaven, so on earth', Mt. vi. 10, RV, and Jn. xv. 10–15). The incentive for believers to serve their fellow men and to love even their enemies is the desire to be worthy children of their perfect heavenly Father (Mt. v. 44–48).

The teaching of Jesus regarding the Fatherhood of God proclaimed the wonderful truth that God's loving care for believers and for all creation is so all-embracing that He even numbers the hair of His people's heads (Mt. x. 30), He clothes every lily of the field and cares for the most insignificant bird (Mt. vi. 26–30, x. 29). For this reason believers ought not to be anxious about personal requirements or material possessions or about the future (Mt. vi. 25, 34). If they give Him the first place in their hearts and lives He will take care of them in every situation, even the most desperate (Mk. xiii. 11; Lk. xii. 4–12, xxi. 18).

On the other hand, Jesus as clearly taught that those who rejected Him and disobeyed the Father, those who refused His saving mercy, were heading straight for inevitable judgment (Mt. viii. 12, xxi. 43–45, xxii. 13, xxv. 30, 41–46; Mk. viii. 38, xii. 9–12, xiii. 26 f.; Lk. xiii. 27 f., 34 f., xix. 27, xxi. 20–24). He left His hearers in no doubt but that men's eternal destiny depended on their attitude to Him and His words (Mk. viii. 38, x. 29 f., xii. 6–11; Lk. ix. 26; Jn. xii. 48, xiv. 6, 21–24, xv. 22 f.). He came to give His life a ransom for many (Mk. x. 45; Mt. xx. 28, xxvi. 28; Jn. x. 11), and because the Father had delivered all things into His hand He invited all to come to Him and receive eternal life (Mt. xi. 28, xxii. 1–10, xxv. 1–12; Jn. vi. 35–37). The seeking and saving of the lost is the earnest desire and great delight of His Father and Himself (Mt. xxii. 4, 9; Mk. x. 45; Lk. xii. 32, xv. 1–32, xix. 10; Jn. iii. 16 f.); but those who refuse this salvation will bring eternal ruin on themselves (Mk. xii. 9; Mt. xxii. 7, 13, xxv. 30, 41, 46; Jn. viii. 24).

As the Son of man to whom universal sovereignty has been given (Jn. v. 25; *cf.* Dn. vii. 13 f.), Jesus taught that He would execute judgment at the consummation of all things. It is He who will say to the righteous, 'Come, ye blessed of my Father, inherit the kingdom prepared for you . . .' (Mt. xxv. 34), and to the unrighteous, 'Depart from me, ye cursed . . .' (Mt. xxv. 41). The attitude towards Him and His 'brethren', revealed in men's practical lives, is the decisive criterion in the great judgment (Mt. xxv. 31–46; Mk. ix. 37, 41; Lk. x. 10–16; Jn. viii. 51, xii. 26, xv. 23 f.). This is so because Jesus is not merely a wonder-working teacher, or even the Jewish Messiah, but the Son to whom all authority has been given in heaven and on earth (Mt. xi. 27, xxviii. 18–20; Lk. x. 22; Mk. xii. 6; Jn. iii. 34–36, v. 17–27, viii. 58, x. 30).

VI. OTHER IMPORTANT THEMES

Having noted the pre-eminent place given in our Lord's teaching to the Fatherhood of God, we turn to a number of other important themes.

a. The kingdom of God

In Mk. i. 15 Jesus starts His public ministry by preaching the glad tidings of God in these words: 'The time is fulfilled, and the kingdom of God is at hand: repent ye, and believe the gospel.' Not long before this, after Jesus had been baptized, a voice from heaven had proclaimed to Him: 'Thou art my beloved Son, in whom I am well pleased' (Mk. i. 11). To understand Jesus' teaching about the kingdom of God it is essential to note the close relation between His awareness of His unique Sonship and His preaching the good news of the kingdom of God.

The expression 'the kingdom of God' or 'the kingdom of the heavens' (the latter form is peculiar to Matthew) is used by Jesus with a wide variety of meanings (see KINGDOM OF GOD, KINGDOM OF HEAVEN). Basically it denotes the sovereign rule, the royal power of God, more especially as manifested in the ministry of Jesus and destined to be established in its fulness when the Son of man is revealed in glory. Because of the kingly rule of God in the life of mankind, salvation is offered to all who repent of their sins and believe in Jesus Christ; our Lord accordingly started His public ministry by preaching this as God's good tidings (Mk. i. 14, 15; Mt. iv. 17, 23).

In Jesus' day the prevalent Jewish idea of the kingdom of God was in the main the materialistic idea that God would rule over all the heathen through a Messiah and an emancipated Jewish nation. The spiritual aspects of the rule of God as already pictured, dimly in some parts of the Old Testament and more clearly in others, were largely neglected. Jesus, however, not only proclaimed the spiritual character of the divine rule but gave the term 'the kingdom of God' a revolutionary new content. The divine sovereignty which He proclaimed was His Father's, and was inextricably bound to the person and work of Jesus Himself as God's beloved Son (Mk. i. 11, 15, 17, xiii. 26; Mt. vii. 21–27, x. 40, xi. 27, xii. 28–30; Lk. x. 16–24, xi. 20–23, xxi. 27, 31, xxii. 29, 30; Jn. v. 36, x. 30, 37, 38).

Jesus taught that the kingly rule of God was already a present fact in Himself and His ministry (Mk. i. 15; Mt. xi. 27, xii. 28, xiii. 17; Lk. iv. 21, x. 17–24, xi. 20), and that if people would repent and believe they would be partakers of the glorious blessings which it brought (Mk. i. 15, ii. 9–12, x. 45; Mt. xi. 28, xxii. 10; Lk. v. 32, vii. 48–50, xv. 1–32, xviii. 13, 14; Jn. x. 9, 10, 27–29). He also taught very emphatically that the final consummation of the Father's kingly rule was still to come (Mk. xiii. 24–27; Mt. xiii. 40–43, 49, 50, xxiv. 29–31, xxv. 31–46; Lk. xi. 29–32, xxi. 25–31, xxii. 18, 29, 30; Jn. v. 27–29, xiv. 2, 3).

The kingdom of God, viewed as the sum of all possible divine blessings, is proclaimed by Jesus as that supreme good to gain which no price is too high (Mt. xiii. 44–46; Lk. xii. 31). He accordingly called His followers to be prepared to suffer for His sake and to sacrifice life itself in order to be true members of the kingdom (Mk. viii. 34–38; Lk. ix. 23–26, xii. 4–9, 32, xvii. 33; Mt. xvi. 24–27; Jn. xv. 18–21, xvi. 33, xxi. 18, 19).

Basic to all His teaching about the kingdom of God is His unambiguous claim to be the Son to whom all things have been committed by the Father (*cf.* Mt. v. 10, 11, vii. 21, 22, x. 32–40, xi. 27, xxviii. 18; Mk. xii. 6, xiii. 26; Lk. x. 22; Jn. x. 27–30, xvii. 1, 2).

b. The Son of man

Jesus very often referred to Himself as the Son of man. In passages like Mk. viii. 38, xiii. 26, xiv. 62; Lk. xvii. 24, xxi. 27, *etc*., He obviously used this term to describe His character and mission in terms of the vision described in Dn. vii. 13 f., RV: 'there came with the clouds of heaven one like unto a son of man . . . his dominion is an everlasting dominion . . .'. By identifying Himself with the 'Son of man' to whom eternal dominion over all nations is given, Jesus proclaimed His divine Messiahship and the certainty that, in spite of the seeming victory of His enemies and the seeming helplessness of His followers, He would ultimately triumph. The Son of man who humbled Himself to be truly man is at the same time the eternal Victor (Mt. xxiv. 30).

Yet our Lord also clothed the Old Testament term 'Son of man' with new and enriched meaning. This appears from the fact that He often uses this particular self-designation in close association with the necessity of His suffering and sacrificial death (Mk. viii. 31, ix. 31, x. 33, xiv. 21, 41; Lk. xviii. 31, xix. 10; Mt. xx. 18, 28, xxvi. 45). By identifying Himself with guilty humanity 'the Son of man came not to be ministered unto, but to minister, and to give his life a ransom for many' (Mk. x. 45; *cf.* Jn. x. 11, 15). But He never failed to teach also that this suffering would be followed by His resurrection (Mt. xx. 18, 19; Mk. viii. 31, x. 33, 34; Lk. xviii. 31–33), and that the consummation would see ultimate victory for Himself and His followers (Lk. xxi. 25–28, xxii. 29, 30; Mk. xiii. 26, 27, xiv. 24, 25, 62; see also Jn. xiii. 31, 32).

c. The Messiahship of Jesus

That Jesus taught His disciples to believe in Him as the Messiah, the Christ (the anointed King) of God, is evident. But because of the many misconceptions regarding the Messiah among the Jews (*cf.* Jn. vi. 15) He expressly forbade public proclamation regarding His Messiahship (Mk. ix. 7–9; Mt. xvi. 20, xvii. 9). Only after He had completed His public ministry and the time drew near for Him to suffer on the cross did He publicly assume the rôle of the messianic King at His triumphal entry into Jerusalem (Mt. xxi. 1–11; Mk. xi. 1–18; Lk. xix. 1–48; Jn. xii. 12–50). Before His judges He unequivocally claimed that He was indeed the Christ (Mt. xxvi. 63, 64; Mk. xiv. 61, 62; Lk. xxii. 69–71, xxiii. 2, 3) but He was not an earthly Jewish Messiah (Jn. xviii. 36).

It is essential to note that He did not teach that, because He was the Messiah, therefore He was the Son of God. On the contrary, His basic teaching is that He is the Son of God in an absolute sense (*cf.* Mt. xxvii. 43, xi. 27, xxiv. 36; Mk. xiii. 32, *etc*.), and because He is the Son of God He is the real Messiah, the Lord's Anointed. Primarily and essentially He is the eternal and only-begotten Son of the Father (see MESSIAH).

d. The death of Jesus

According to all four Gospels Jesus taught that He would suffer and die. He devoted much attention to His coming death, especially during the last part of His ministry (Mt. xvi. 21; Mk. viii. 31, ix. 31, x. 33, 34; Lk. ix. 22, 44, xxii. 37; Jn. vi. 51, x. 11–18). But as early as Mk. ii. 20 He began to warn His disciples that suffering and death awaited Him. He emphasized that His suffering was in accordance with the will of the Father and at the same time that He Himself freely chose to suffer and die on His people's behalf (Mk. x. 45, xiv. 24; Jn. x. 11–18).

The words spoken by Jesus at the institution of the Lord's Supper plainly teach the sacrificial character of His death. He gave His body to be broken for men and His blood to be poured out for their eternal salvation (Lk. xxii. 19, 20; Mt. xxvi. 27, 28; Mk. xiv. 22–24; *cf.* Jn. xiv. 2, x. 15, xix. 30). Through His death remission of sins would be made possible (Mt. xxvi. 27, 28) and a new covenant between God and man would be established (Lk. xxii. 20). Jesus thus taught that through His death eternal blessing would be procured for many and a new relation established between God and man—through the forgiveness of sins obtained by Him who gave His life as a ransom-sacrifice. The language in which He expressed this is profoundly influenced by the description of the suffering Servant who bore the sin of many and bestowed righteousness upon them (Is. lii. 13–liii. 12).

e. Future events

Not only did Jesus teach that He was going to suffer and die; He taught much more regarding the immediate as well as the distant future.

In the first place He taught that although He was going to give His life as a ransom for many He would rise from the dead (Mk. ix. 9 f., *etc*.).

In the second place He repeatedly taught that, notwithstanding all the hate and power of His enemies and His seeming defeat at their hands He would ultimately triumph over them. A close study of His apocalyptic teaching in the eschatological discourse of Mt. xxiv; Mk. xiii; Lk. xxi. 5–36, and of His other utterances, reveals that He presented His victory over all the forces of evil and the revelation of His divine power as something which would become a practical reality in different stages, as it were. In principle, His triumph was already a glorious reality (Lk. x. 17–22; Mt. xi. 27, xxviii. 18–20; Jn. vi. 35–39). But His disciples still had to pass through many trials before His final coming in glory (Mt. x. 16–23; Mk. xiii. 5–13; Jn. xvi. 33; Lk. xxi. 12, 25, 26). Jesus predicted that in one sense both His enemies and His disciples would soon experience the fact of His victory as the One through whom God the Father revealed His sovereign power (Mt. x. 23, xvi. 28; Mk. ix. 1; Lk. xxii. 69, *etc.*). This was actually fulfilled in the events accompanying His death (Mt. xxvii. 45, 51 ff.; Mk. xv. 33, 38 f.; Lk. xxiii. 44 ff.), in His resurrection and ascension (Mt. xxviii. 1–10; Lk. xxiv; Acts i. 9), in the Pentecostal fulfilment of His promise regarding the Holy Spirit (Acts ii. 1–36; *cf.* Jn. xvi. 7–22; Lk. xxiv. 49), in the establishment and invincible growth of His Church (Acts ii. 37–47 and the rest of Acts), and in the judgment incurred by His enemies, in the destruction of Jerusalem and the Temple and in the tragic fate of the Jewish nation. In all these historical events the kingdom of God was manifested in accordance with the prophetic teaching of Jesus (Mk. xii. 9, xiii. 2, 14–23; Mt. xxi. 43, 44, xxiii. 27–39, xxiv. 1–25; Lk. xix. 41–44, xxi. 5, 6, 20–24).

When speaking of the coming of the kingdom of God and the revelation of His divine might, our Lord every now and then pointed far beyond those initial revelations of His power. He taught that ultimately the kingdom of God would come in consummating glory and that then the Father's sovereign rule would be revealed in the Son on a universal and all-embracing scale (Mt. xxiv. 29–31, xxv. 31–34; Mk. xiii. 24–27; Lk. xxi. 25–27; Jn. v. 28, 29, vi. 44, xiv. 2, 3). That He did not teach that this *final* coming of the kingdom of God would take place within the lifetime of the generation then living is clear from His words in such passages as Mk. xiii. 7, 10, xiv. 9; Mt. xxiv. 14, 36–51, xxv. 1–46 (note especially Mt. xxiv. 14 and xxv. 19; Lk. xix. 11, xxi. 9, 24).

In studying our Lord's teaching regarding the future it is important to remember the different aspects in which He spoke of the coming of the kingdom. In some cases Jesus is viewed as here and now revealing the divine rule—in its saving operation, on the one hand, and in its judicial action, on the other hand. In other cases the emphasis falls rather on the tragic fate awaiting the Jewish nation, with its city and Temple, as a result of its continued rejection of Jesus as its Messiah. But as a mighty mountain-range looms high above the smaller mountains in the foreground, so in prophetic perspective our Lord's teaching reaches up high above the local and national happenings of the nearer future to the universal consummation in the last days. Then the Father will vindicate and acknowledge Jesus as His Son once for all by manifesting His glory as the One to whom He has given eternal and universal dominion (*cf.* especially Lk. xxi. 5–27, and see Geldenhuys, *ad loc.*, pp. 522–545).

VII. THE VINDICATION OF CHRIST'S TEACHING

We have already shown that the teaching of Jesus regarding the future has been vindicated by the facts of history. Much more can be said to show the truth of His prophetic teaching. The fulfilment of what He foretold in Lk. xxi. 24 (*cf.* Mk. xiii. 2, *etc.*) is a striking example of a concrete prophecy which has been and is to this day literally fulfilled. Since its destruction by the Romans in AD 70 the old, original Jerusalem has been 'trodden down of the Gentiles' (Lk. xxi. 24) through all the years during the past nineteen centuries. Nor does the state of Israel yet control the original Jerusalem, the city of David and the Temple area.

In other ways, too, the truth of our Lord's teaching as a whole has been vindicated. Above all, God the Father Himself confirmed His Son's teaching in the following ways.

1. By proclaiming from heaven both at the baptism and on the Mount of Transfiguration that Jesus was indeed His beloved Son in whom He was well pleased (Mk. i. 11, ix. 7, *etc.*).

2. By enabling Him to perform incomparable miracles which revealed His divine power over mental and physical diseases or defects (healing incurable diseases and restoring sight to the blind), over nature (by changing water into wine, by stilling storms, *etc.*), over physical and spiritual death (by raising the dead and by forgiving sinners and changing their lives).

3. By raising Him from the dead and exalting Him to the place of supremacy at His right hand.

4. By the miracle of that first Pentecost, which transformed the small and insignificant group of disciples into the men who laid the foundation of Christ's invincible Church.

5. By directing the history of men and of nations in such a way that all the prophecies of Jesus regarding the future have been or are in the process of being fulfilled. For instance, our Lord taught that, although His followers would suffer many things, His Church would never be destroyed, but on the contrary would continue to proclaim the gospel in ever-wider circles until it had been 'preached in the whole world for a testimony unto all the nations; and then shall the end come' (Mt. xxiv. 14, RV). Humanly speaking, when Jesus spoke these remarkable words, all the odds were against this happening. But God has, in spite of everything, guided and guarded the Church of His Son through nearly 2,000 years and is today enabling the Church to proclaim the gospel to more nations than ever before.

6. By the formation and preservation of the New Testament, which, together with the Old Testament, forms the all-sufficient Word of God and proclaims Jesus as the centre of all things—one with the Father and with the Holy Spirit (Mt. xxviii. 18–20; 2 Cor. xiii. 14).

7. The truth of our Lord's teaching is, finally, attested and established in the life of believers and of the Church by the indwelling Holy Spirit. Thus His promises recorded in Jn. xv. 26 and

xvi. 13–15 continue to be fulfilled, together with His words in Jn. xiv. 25 f.: 'These things have I spoken unto you, while yet abiding with you. But the Comforter, even the Holy Spirit, whom the Father will send in my name, he shall teach you all things, and bring to your remembrance all that I said unto you' (*cf.* Acts i. 4, 5, 8). See also JESUS CHRIST, LIFE OF, CHRONOLOGY OF THE NEW TESTAMENT, LAMB OF GOD, REDEEMER, TRANSFIGURATION, INCARNATION, CRUCIFIXION, SERMON ON THE MOUNT, MIRACLES, SEVEN WORDS, THE, RESURRECTION, LORD'S PRAYER, THE.

BIBLIOGRAPHY. W. F. Adeney, *The Theology of the New Testament*, 1895; G. R. Beasley-Murray, *Jesus and the Future*, 1954; B. H. Branscomb, *Jesus and the Law of Moses*, 1930; A. B. Bruce, *The Parabolic Teaching of Jesus*, 1892; *id.*, *The Training of the Twelve*, 1894; F. F. Bruce, *Second Thoughts on the Dead Sea Scrolls*[2], 1961 (see chapter XII); F. Büchsel, *Theologie des Neuen Testaments*, 1937; R. Bultmann, *Theology of the New Testament*, 1951; G. A. Buttrick, *Jesus Came Preaching*, 1931; *id.*, *The Parables of Jesus*, 1929; C. J. Cadoux, *The Historic Mission of Jesus*, 1941; W. A. Curtis, *Jesus Christ the Teacher*, 1943; G. Dalman, *The Words of Jesus*, 1902; *id.*, *Jesus-Jeshua*, 1929; J. Denney, *Jesus and the Gospel*, 1909; C. H. Dodd, *The Parables of the Kingdom*, 1936; M. S. Enslin, *Christian Beginnings*, 1938; P. Feine, *Theologie des Neuen Testaments*, 1931; F. C. Grant, *The Gospel of the Kingdom*, 1940; M. D. Hooker, *Jesus and the Servant*, 1959; W. F. Howard, *Christianity according to St. John*, 1943; J. Knox, *Christ the Lord*, 1945; J. G. Machen, *The Origin of Paul's Religion*, 1936; C. E. Macartney, *What Jesus really Taught*, 1958; G. C. Morgan, *The Teaching of Christ*, 1946; T. W. Manson, *The Teaching of Jesus*[2], 1943; *id.*, *The Sayings of Jesus*, 1949; J. Moffatt, *The Theology of the Gospels*, 1912; R. Otto, *The Kingdom of God and the Son of Man*[2], 1943; F. C. Porter, *The Mind of Christ in Paul*, 1930; A. E. J. Rawlinson, *The New Testament Doctrine of the Christ*, 1929; T. G. Selby, *The Ministry of the Lord Jesus*, 1903; E. Stauffer, *New Testament Theology*, 1955; J. S. Stewart, *The Life and Teaching of Jesus Christ*[2], 1958; G. B. Stevens, *The Theology of the New Testament*[2], 1918; R. C. Trench, *The Parables of Jesus*, 1902; V. Taylor, *Jesus and his Sacrifice*, 1943; A. N. Wilder, *Eschatology and Ethics in the Teaching of Jesus*, 1939. See also Bibliography to JESUS CHRIST, LIFE OF. J.N.G.

JETHRO. Moses' father-in-law Reuel, called Jethro in Ex. iii. 1, iv. 18. He brought Zipporah and her sons to meet Moses at Mt. Horeb, and held a sacrifice to Yahweh in thanksgiving for the deliverance of Israel. Here he also advised Moses to delegate the administration of justice (Ex. xviii). Moses persuaded Jethro's son Hobab to join the Israelites. In Jdg. iv. 11 'Hobab the Kenite' is called Moses' *ḥōṯēn*, perhaps a broad term for 'in-law'; this, with Jdg. i. 16, is the only evidence for Jethro's Kenite descent. The name may mean 'pre-eminence'. J.P.U.L.

JEW (Heb. *y^ehûḏî*). A term which originally described an inhabitant of Judah (2 Ki. xvi. 6), and as such was employed in contemporary Assyr. texts (*Iaudaia*) from at least the 8th century BC. It was commonly used by non-Jews to refer to the Hebrews, or descendants of Abraham in general (*e.g.* Jeremiah, Ezra, Nehemiah, Esther, Daniel). Thus in Je. xxxiv. 9 'Jew' is used to explain 'Hebrew'. It is also used to describe the local Sem. dialect spoken in Judah ('Jews' language', in 2 Ki. xviii. 26, 28; Is. xxxvi. 11, 13; Ne. xiii. 24). So also 'Jewry' stands in AV for Judah (Dn. v. 13; Lk. xxiii. 5; Jn. vii. 1).

By New Testament times the plural 'Jews' had become a familiar term for all Israelites. The feminine 'Jewess' is used in 1 Ch. iv. 18; Acts xvi. 1, xxiv. 24, and the adjective 'Jewish' in Gal. ii. 14 (Gk.); Tit. i. 14. See JUDAH, JUDAISM. D.J.W.

JEWELS AND PRECIOUS STONES. In biblical times as nowadays various forms of jewellery were worn and highly esteemed by both men and women (Ex. xi. 2; Is. iii. 18–21). They were given as presents (Gn. xxiv. 22, 53), and were an important item of spoil in war (2 Ch. xx. 25). They were a form of wealth, especially before the use of coins (2 Ch. xxi. 3), and were used as a standard of value (Jb. xxviii. 16; Pr. iii. 15; Rev. xxi. 11). Among the various types of jewellery used we find mention of bracelets for the arm (Gn. xxiv. 22, 30, 47; Ezk. xvi. 11), ornaments for the ankles (Is. iii. 18, 20), necklaces (Gn. xli. 42; *cf.* Lk. xv. 8, where the ten pieces of silver are generally regarded as coins strung together to form a necklace), crowns (Zc. ix. 16, RSV; here the Lord's people are likened to shining jewels in a crown), ear-rings (Gn. xxiv. 22), nose-rings (Is. iii. 21), and rings for the fingers (Gn. xli. 42; Est. iii. 10; Lk. xv. 22). These might be made of gold, silver, or other metals (Ex. iii. 22).

A considerable number of precious and semi-precious stones were known and used in jewellery. Inscribed seals have been found in cornelian, chalcedony, jasper, agate, onyx, rock crystal, haematite, jade, opal, and amethyst (D. Diringer, 'Seals', in D. W. Thomas (ed.), *DOTT*, 1958, pp. 218–226). The stones were valued for their rarity, beauty, and durability. The modern method of faceting was not employed; instead, the stones were rounded and polished, and often engraved and sculptured.

In general, the ancients were more familiar with semi-precious than with precious stones. Since many species of stone occur in a variety of colours and since a scientific terminology had not been developed, the identification of the various stones mentioned in the Bible is not always easy, and in some cases we can only guess at the meaning of the terms used.

The **agate** (*š^eḇô*, Ex. xxviii. 19, xxxix. 12) was

probably the modern agate, a type of translucent quartz with layers of different colours. In Is. liv. 12; Ezk. xxvii. 16 (*kadkōd*), a red stone, possibly carbuncle or ruby (RV), may be meant (*cf.* Ezk. xxvii. 16, where Symmachus has *karchēdonion*, *i.e.* carbuncle). For Rev. xxi. 19, RSV, see Chalcedony, below.

The word **alabaster** (*alabastron*, Mk. xiv. 3 = Mt. xxvi. 7; Lk. vii. 37), originally the neuter form of the adjective *alabastros*, was used to mean an alabaster flask with a long neck for storing perfume, the neck being broken off when the contents were used; the word was also used for flasks of this shape of any material. Ancient alabaster was a banded variety of calcium carbonate produced by gradual deposition from solution in water, as in stalactites; modern alabaster is a softer stone, a variety of gypsum.

The **amethyst** (*'aḥlāmâ*, Ex. xxviii. 19, xxxix. 12) was the well-known stone of that name, a purple variety of transparent, crystalline quartz. So also in Rev. xxi. 20 (*amethystos*, so called because it was supposed to prevent intoxication).

The **beryl** (*taršîš*, Ex. xxviii. 20, xxxix. 13; Ct. v. 14; Ezk. i. 16, x. 9, xxviii. 13; Dn. x. 6) was associated with Spain (Tarshish), and was probably a green stone, although some of the LXX translators seem to have thought that it was red. Green chrysoberyl (beryllium aluminate), green peridot (magnesium iron silicate), or ordinary beryl (beryllium alumino-silicate) may be meant. In Rev. xxi. 20 (*bēryllos*) ordinary green beryl is meant.

The **carbuncle** (*bāreqet*, Ex. xxviii. 17, xxxix. 10; *bārᵉqat*, Ezk. xxviii. 13) was probably a green stone in view of the LXX translation as 'emerald' (*smaragdos*) in the Exodus references; possibly green beryl is meant. (But the modern carbuncle is a red stone.) In Is. liv. 12 (*'eqdaḥ*) a red stone is meant in view of the derivation from *qādaḥ*, 'to kindle'.

For **carnelian** (better spelt 'cornelian', the common form being due to confusion with Latin *caro*), see Sardius, below.

The **chalcedony** (*chalkēdōn*, Rev. xxi. 19, RSV 'agate') is usually taken to have been a green stone, since Pliny refers to a kind of emerald and jasper as Chalcedonian (from Chalcedon in Asia Minor). (The word is used in modern writers for various types of translucent quartz, including agate, onyx, carnelian, and chrysoprase.)

The **chrysolite** (*chrysolithos*, Rev. xxi. 20) is the ancient term for the yellow topaz (aluminium fluo-silicate) or yellow quartz. (Note that the ancient chrysolite is the modern topaz, and *vice versa*.) For Ezk. i. 16, x. 9, xxviii. 13, RSV, see Beryl, above.

The **chrysoprasus** (*chrysoprasos*, Rev. xxi. 20, RV and RSV 'chrysoprase') is in modern usage an apple-green form of chalcedony, but the identification here is uncertain.

Coral (*rā'môṯ*, Jb. xxviii. 18; Ezk. xxvii. 16) may be either black or red coral. It is, of course, not strictly a precious stone, being the skeleton of innumerable small marine polyps. *Rā'môṯ* also occurs in Pr. xxiv. 7, *MT*, but this is probably to be read as *rāmôṯ*, 'high'. The RSV translates *pᵉnînîm* as coral in La. iv. 7, where some red stone is meant (see Pearl, below).

Crystal (*zᵉḵôḵîṯ*, Jb. xxviii. 17) is a word applied in the ancient world not simply to rock crystal (pure transparent crystalline quartz) but to any hard, transparent, colourless substance. Glass is probably meant (RV, RSV). *Qeraḥ* (Ezk. i. 22) is elsewhere translated 'frost' or 'ice'. In Rev. iv. 6, xxi. 11, xxii. 1 (*krystallon*, *krystallizō*), either ice or rock crystal may be the rendering.

The **diamond** (*yāhᵃlôm*, Ex. xxviii. 18, xxxix. 11; Ezk. xxviii. 13) is of uncertain identification. The modern diamond was probably unknown in Old Testament times, the first certain reference to it apparently being in Manilius (1st century AD). Probably a white, opaque stone is meant. In Je. xvii. 1 (*šāmîr*) adamant or emery, a form of corundum (the hardest substance known except for diamond), is meant (*cf.* Ezk. iii. 9; Zc. vii. 12).

The **emerald** (*nōpeḵ*, Ex. xxviii. 18, xxxix. 11; also Ezk. xxvii. 16, where various scholars consider the text uncertain) may have been a green stone like the modern emerald, but in view of the LXX translation (*anthrax*, 'a burning coal'), some authorities prefer a red stone. In Rev. iv. 3 (*smaragdinos*) and xxi. 19 (*smaragdos*), the green emerald is meant.

For **hyacinth**, see Jacinth, below.

The **jacinth** (*hyakinthos*, Rev. xxi. 20) was a blue stone, aquamarine (the blue variety of beryl) or sapphire. The name was used to indicate a blue colour (in Classical Greek as a noun it means the hyacinth or bluebell), as in Rev. ix. 17 (*hyakinthinos*), where RV and RSVmg have 'hyacinth' and RSV has 'sapphire'. For Ex. xxviii. 19, xxxix. 12, RSV, see Ligure, below.

The **jasper** (*yāšᵉpeh*, Ex. xxviii. 20, xxxix. 13; Ezk. xxviii. 13) was either modern jasper or possibly nephrite (green jade). In Rev. iv. 3, xxi. 11, 18, 19 (*iaspis*), green quartz may be meant. The ancients used jasper as a name for several colours of stone, whereas in modern usage an opaque, dark-red form of quartz is meant. In xxi. 11 the reference to crystal suggests that a transparent stone may be meant.

For **lapis lazuli**, see Sapphire, below.

The **ligure** (*lešem*, Ex. xxviii. 19, xxxix. 12, RV, RSV 'jacinth'; RVmg 'amber') was probably yellow, but has not been identified.

The **onyx** (*šōham*, Gn. ii. 12; Ex. xxv. 7, xxviii. 9, 20, xxxv. 9, 27, xxxix. 6, 13; 1 Ch. xxix. 2; Jb. xxviii. 16; Ezk. xxviii. 13) may have been a green stone (*cf.* LXX 'beryl' in some of these verses), but was more probably onyx (translucent agate with layers of black and white). The word means 'finger-nail', the stone being so called because it resembles a finger-nail. For Rev. xxi. 20, RSV, see Sardonyx, below.

The **pearl** is found only in the Old Testament (AV) in Jb. xxviii. 18a (*gāḇîš*), where RV and RSV have 'crystal', probably correctly (*cf.* *'elgāḇîš*, 'hail'). In the RSV 'pearl' is found as the translation of *pᵉnînîm* in Jb. xxviii. 18b (AV, RV, 'rubies';

RVmg, 'red coral' or 'pearls'). The same Heb. word occurs in Pr. iii. 15, viii. 11, xx. 15, xxxi. 10, and La. iv. 7 (it is also accepted by some scholars as an emendation in Ps. xlv. 14). In all these references AV has 'rubies'; RV has 'rubies' in the text, but in some editions adds a reference to Jb. xxviii. 18mg.; RSV has 'jewels' or 'costly stones', except in La. iv. 7, where it has 'coral'. *BDB* prefer 'corals', but E. Burrows (*JTS*, XLII, 1941, pp. 53–64) argues that the word properly means 'pearls' but also has the generic sense of 'jewels'. *Unger's Bible Dictionary* (1957, p. 742) suggests that the pink pearls found in the Red Sea are meant, and this would solve the difficulty of La. iv. 7, where a reddish stone is indicated.

There is no doubt that in the New Testament *margaritēs* means 'pearl'. Pearls are noted as articles of feminine ornament (1 Tim. ii. 9, where they are frowned upon; Rev. xvii. 4) and of merchandise (Mt. xiii. 45 f.; Rev. xviii. 12, 16). The gates of the New Jerusalem are each made of a single large pearl or possibly of mother-of-pearl (Rev. xxi. 21). The kingdom of heaven is like a fine pearl which a man will seek to obtain at the cost of all that he has (Mt. xiii. 45 f. In view of the context it is unlikely that this parable refers primarily to Christ giving His life for men, although in fact Christ Himself is the supreme example of giving up all for the sake of the kingdom). On the other hand, it is as foolish to put the Christian message before men who refuse to appreciate it as to cast pearls before swine (Mt. vii. 6; *cf. Didache* ix. 5, where Christ's saying is used to justify exclusion of the unbaptized from the Lord's Supper).

The **ruby** is found in the AV and RV as a translation of *p*ᵉ*nînîm* in six places cited above (see Pearl, above). The RV also has 'ruby' in Is. liv. 12 and Ezk. xxvii. 16 for *kaḏkōḏ* (see Agate, above).

The **sapphire** (*sappîr*, Ex. xxiv. 10, xxviii. 18, xxxix. 11; Jb. xxviii. 6, 16; Ct. v. 14; Is. liv. 11; La. iv. 7; Ezk. i. 26, x. 1, xxviii. 13) was the ancient name for lapis lazuli (*cf.* RSVmg), a deep blue stone with golden flecks of iron pyrites (*cf.* 'dust of gold', Jb. xxviii. 6). Lapis lazuli is also meant in Rev. xxi. 19 (*sappheiros*). The modern sapphire (blue corundum) was scarcely known to the ancients. For Rev. ix. 17, RSV, see Jacinth, above.

The **sardius** (*'ōḏem*, Ex. xxviii. 17, xxxix. 10; Ezk. xxviii. 13) was certainly a red stone (from *'āḏam*, 'to be red'), probably modern sard (a form of cornelian; *cf.* Ezk. xxviii. 13, RSV), *i.e.* a deep brown or red form of quartz. It is also mentioned in Rev. xxi. 20 (*sardios*) and is the **sardine** stone of Rev. iv. 3 (*sardinos*): the RSV has carnelian in both places.

The **sardonyx** (*sardonyx*, Rev. xxi. 20, RSV 'onyx') is in modern usage a form of agate with layers of brown and white; but, according to *LSJ*, in ancient usage a stone was called 'onyx' when the dark ground was simply streaked or spotted with white, and 'sardonyx' when the different colours were arranged in layers.

The **topaz** (*piṭ*ᵉ*ḏâ*, Ex. xxviii. 17, xxxix. 10; Jb. xxviii. 19; Ezk. xxviii. 13) was a yellow stone, probably yellow rock crystal or chrysolite (a pale yellow variety of peridot). So also in Rev. xxi. 20 (*topazion*).

The fullest list of stones in the Old Testament is given in the description of the high priest's breastplate (Ex. xxviii. 17–20, repeated in xxxix. 10–13). This contained four rows of three stones, each stone engraved with the name of one of the twelve tribes of Israel. Later authors commenting on the Old Testament regarded these twelve stones as symbolic of the months of the year or the signs of the zodiac (Philo, *Vit. Mos.* ii. 124 ff.; Jos., *Ant.* iii. 7. 7). Some scholars have rearranged the order of the stones in the *MT* on the basis of the LXX translation, but this is a dubious procedure.

An abbreviated version of the same list of stones is found in Ezk. xxviii. 13 as a description of the covering of the king of Tyre when, according to the poetic imagery used here, he was in Eden, the garden of God. Nine of the stones are mentioned, the ligure, agate, and amethyst being omitted. In the LXX version of this verse, however, the full list of twelve stones is substituted.

A list of twelve stones is given in Rev. xxi. 19 f. as decorations of the foundations of the New Jerusalem. The basis of this description is clearly Is. liv. 11 f. (*cf.* also Tobit xiii. 16–18). The number twelve is clearly significant for John, and various attempts have been made to ascertain whether the twelve stones have any special meaning. It is likely that the form of the vision has been influenced by the description of the twelve stones of the high priest's breastplate; scholars have attempted to relate the two lists of stones more closely to each other, but in view of the difficulties of translation from Hebrew to Greek and the fact that John was probably not quoting verbatim from Exodus, it is very doubtful whether we can say more than that he was generally influenced by the description in Exodus. R. H. Charles (*ICC*, *ad loc.*) has taken up the symbolism of the signs of the zodiac mentioned above, and holds that the stones represent these signs arranged in precisely the opposite order to that in which the sun travels through the zodiac, thus portraying the truth that the New Jerusalem and Christianity bear no relation to those religions in which men worship the sun. It is further possible that the stones, like the twelve gates of the city, are symbolical of the tribes of Israel, but again it seems impossible to work out identifications of individual stones with individual tribes (for an ingenious, but probably unsuccessful, attempt to do so, see A. M. Farrer, *A Rebirth of Images*, 1949, pp. 216 ff.). In the light of xxi. 14 there is perhaps more to be said for the suggestion that the stones represent the twelve apostles, in which case individual identifications are clearly not to be attempted. What is beyond dispute in the symbolism is that in the New Jerusalem we see the fulfilment of the Old Testament prophecy of the perfect city of God in which the saints of the old and new covenants find a place. See also MINING AND METALS. I.H.M.

JEWRY. See JUDAEA.

JEZANIAH (*y^{e}zanyāhû*). One of the Judaean military commanders who joined Gedaliah at Mizpah (Je. xl. 8). He was among those who sought counsel from Jeremiah concerning going down to Egypt (Je. xlii. 1—LXX here has 'Azariah', *cf.* xliii. 2). In 2 Ki. xxv. 23 his name appears as 'Jaazaniah' (*q.v.*). J.C.J.W.

JEZEBEL. 1. The daughter of Ethbaal, priest-king of Tyre and Sidon. She was married to Ahab, to ratify an alliance between Tyre and Israel, by which Omri, Ahab's father, sought to offset the hostility of Damascus towards Israel (*c.* 880 BC). Provision was made for her to continue to worship her native god Baal in Samaria, her new home (1 Ki. xvi. 31–33).

She had a strong, domineering character, and was self-willed and forceful. A fanatical devotee of Melqart, the Tyrian Baal, her staff numbered four hundred and fifty of his prophets, and four hundred prophets of the goddess Asherah, by the time Ahab was king (1 Ki. xviii. 19). She clamoured for her god to have at least equal rights with Yahweh, God of Israel. This brought her into conflict with the prophet Elijah. A battle between Yahweh and Baal was fought on Mount Carmel, when Yahweh triumphed gloriously (1 Ki. xviii. 17–40). Even so, this and the massacre of her prophets, instead of diminishing her zeal, augmented it.

Her conception of an absolute monarchy was at variance with the Heb. covenant-relationship between Yahweh, the king, and the people. She took the lead in the incident of Naboth's vineyard with high-handed, unscrupulous action, affecting the whole community as well as undermining the throne of Ahab. It resulted in the prophetic revolution and the extermination of the house of Ahab.

After Ahab's death, Jezebel continued as a power in Israel for ten years, in her rôle as queen-mother, throughout the reign of Ahaziah, then during Jehoram's lifetime. When Jehoram was killed by Jehu she attired herself regally (2 Ki. ix. 30), and awaited him. She mocked Jehu, and went to her fate with courage and dignity (842 BC).

It is remarkable that Yahweh was honoured in the naming of her three children, Ahaziah, Jehoram, and Athaliah (if indeed she was Athaliah's mother), but they may have been born before her ascendancy over Ahab became so absolute.

The Chronicler makes no reference to her.

2. In the letter to the church at Thyatira (Rev. ii. 20), 'that Jezebel of a woman' is the designation given to a seductive prophetess who encouraged immorality and idolatry under the cloak of religion (see NICOLAS). This could refer to an individual, or to a group within the Church. It indicates that the name had become a byword for apostasy. M.G.

JEZREEL (*yizr^{e}'e'l*, 'God sows'). **1.** The town in the mountains of Judah (Jos. xv. 56); the native place of Ahinoam, one of David's wives (1 Sa. xxv. 43).

2. A city in Issachar and the plain (see ESDRAELON for location) on which it stood (Jos. xix. 18; Ho. i. 5). The city and general neighbourhood are associated with several notable events. By its fountain the Israelites assembled before engaging the Philistines at Gilboa (1 Sa. xxix. 1). It was a part of Ishbosheth's short-lived kingdom (2 Sa. ii. 8 ff.); an administrative district of Solomon (1 Ki. iv. 12); and the scene of the tragedy of Naboth and his vineyard (1 Ki. xxi. 1). Here Joram, who had earlier come to convalesce from war wounds (2 Ki. viii. 29), was slain by Jehu, and his body significantly cast into the vineyard so cruelly appropriated by Ahab and Jezebel (2 Ki. ix. 24–26). Thereafter at Jehu's instigation Jezebel herself (2 Ki. ix. 30–37) and the remnant of Ahab's household (2 Ki. x. 1–11) were slain. Jezreel is identified with the modern Zer'in, about 55 miles north of Jerusalem.

3. The name symbolically given to Hosea's eldest son (Ho. i. 4) and to Israel (Ho. ii. 22). **4.** A Judahite (1 Ch. iv. 3). J.D.D.

JOAB (*yô'āḇ*, 'Yahweh is father'). **1.** Son of Zeruiah, half-sister of David (2 Sa. ii. 18). His father's name is not recorded here, but Josephus (*Ant.* vii. 1. 3) gives it as Suri, whose sepulchre was in Bethlehem (2 Sa. ii. 32).

Joab is first heard of when, with his brothers Asahel and Abishai, he led David's army to victory at Helkath-hazzurim against Ishbosheth's rebel forces under Abner (2 Sa. ii. 12–17). In fleeing, Abner reluctantly killed Asahel in self-defence (see ABNER, ASAHEL), and was himself later treacherously slain by Joab, ostensibly in blood-revenge (2 Sa. ii. 23, iii. 27, 30), but probably also because Abner's new-found loyalty to David confronted Joab with a potential rival for the king's favour.

David was angry with his nephew for this murder, greatly mourned Abner as 'a prince and a great man', and prophesied that God would punish the killer (2 Sa. iii. 31–39). Nevertheless, after taking the Jebusite stronghold, Joab was made commander-in-chief of all Israel (2 Sa. v. 8; 1 Ch. xi. 6, 8), of which David was by this time king.

Joab proved himself a skilful general who greatly helped the establishment of the monarchy, but his character was a strange mixture. Apart from his personal deeds of violence and his opportunism, his cruelty can be seen in the way he swiftly comprehended and carried out David's plan to kill Uriah (2 Sa. xi. 6–26). Yet he could be magnanimous also, as when he gave David the credit after the capture of Rabboth-ammon (2 Sa. xii. 26–31). Perhaps most notably and surprisingly, he tried to dissuade David from numbering the people (2 Sa. xxiv. 2–4).

Joab is found in the rôle of peacemaker, reconciling David and Absalom on one occasion (2 Sa. xiv. 23, 31–33), but later when Absalom's guilt was clearly seen he had a hand in his death (2 Sa. xviii. 14–33), despite David's injunction that the young man's life should be spared. After this David superseded Joab by Amasa as commander (2 Sa. xix. 13), but the resourceful Joab subdued Sheba's revolt and seized the first opportunity to slay the new commander, who had proved inefficient (2 Sa. xx. 3–23). Thereafter for a time Joab seems to have been restored to favour (2 Sa. xxiv. 2).

In David's last days Joab's loyalty to the king faltered, and with Abiathar and others he supported Adonijah as claimant to the throne (1 Ki. i. 5–53), in defiance of David, who had resolved that Solomon should succeed him (1 Ki. ii. 28). For once Joab had supported the wrong side, and it eventually cost him his life (1 Ki. ii. 34), when with the connivance of Solomon he was slain by Benaiah before the altar at Gibeon, where he had fled for sanctuary.

2. Son of Seraiah (1 Ch. iv. 14; *cf.* Ne. xi. 35), a Judahite. **3.** A family which returned with Zerubbabel (Ezr. ii. 6; Ne. vii. 11). Probably the 'Joab' of Ezr. viii. 9 is the same person.

J.D.D.

JOANNA. One of several women, healed by Jesus, who assisted in maintaining the Lord's itinerant company. Her husband, Chuza, was a responsible official of Herod Antipas: whether in the household ('a steward of Herod's', NEB) or in government ('the chancellor', Moffatt) is uncertain (Lk. viii. 1–3). She sought also to share in the last offices to the Lord's body, and became instead one of those who announced the resurrection to the Twelve (Lk. xxiv. 1–10). Luke's notes may indicate personal acquaintance with, and possibly indebtedness for information to, these women.

A.F.W.

JOASH, JEHOASH (*yô'āš*, *y^ehô'āš*, 'Yahweh has given'). A name held, in its shorter or longer form, by a number of Old Testament characters. Omitting those who receive only passing mention, the following are notable.

1. Father of Gideon (Jdg. vi. 11 ff.). Of the Abiezrite clan of Manasseh, he was evidently a man of some status (*cf.* verses 27, 31) and of vigorous independent mind (verses 29–31), the owner of a holy tree (verse 11) and of the altar of Baal in Ophrah (verse 25). He seems to have given Gideon the name of Jerubbaal (verse 32). See GIDEON.

2. Apparently a son of King Ahab (*q.v.*), and perhaps the latter's representative during the king's absence on military business. To Joash was sent Micaiah the prophet for unfavourable prophesying, with instructions that he was to be imprisoned and fed on bread and water (1 Ki. xxii. 26 f.; 2 Ch. xviii. 25). Some suggest that 'king's son' is a title.

3. Son of Ahaziah, and ninth king of Judah (2 Ki. xi f.). As an infant he was rescued by Jehosheba his aunt, wife of Jehoiada (*q.v.*), chief priest of the Temple, when annihilation of the royal family was carried out by Athaliah (*q.v.*). At the age of seven (*c.* 835 BC; see CHRONOLOGY OF THE OLD TESTAMENT) Joash was proclaimed king by Jehoiada, and Athaliah was put to death. Joash is recorded as having reigned forty years, but this may include the six years of the usurping Athaliah. Under Joash the Temple was repaired, and for a time true religion was to a large extent restored in the land. The death of Jehoiada, however, removed a restraining influence, and idolatry crept back again into the national life. Heedless of prophetic warnings, and having slain Jehoiada's son and successor Zechariah, Joash compassed his own destruction. Threatened with a Syrian invasion under Hazael (*q.v.*), he stripped the Temple of its gold and sent it to the Syrian king as a bribe. Soon after, Joash was assassinated by some of his officers. He is one of three kings omitted from the genealogy of Jesus Christ (Mt. i. 8).

4. Son of Jehoahaz, and twelfth king of Israel (2 Ki. xiii. 10–25, xiv. 8–16; 2 Ch. xxv. 17–24). There are indications that he had a successful reign (798–782/1 BC; see CHRONOLOGY OF THE OLD TESTAMENT), and that we may take the condemnatory statement in 2 Ki. xiii. 11 as referring only to his early years as king (*cf.* Jos., *Ant.* ix. 8. 6). The long conflict with Syria which had earlier brought Israel to the verge of destruction (*cf.* 2 Ki. xiii. 7) now turned in Israel's favour, largely because of Assyrian pressure on Syria. In this struggle Joash was encouraged by Elisha, prophet, friend of the king, and foe of Syria. Joash was reluctantly compelled also to accept the rash challenge of Amaziah of Judah, whom he successfully defeated. He captured and despoiled Jerusalem, and took hostages to ensure the future good behaviour of Amaziah (*q.v.*). Joash died soon afterwards, and was buried in Samaria.

J.D.D.

JOB (Heb. *'iyyôḇ*). Apart from the book bearing his name and the passing references to him in Ezk. xiv. 14, 20; Jas. v. 11 we have no reliable information about Job. It is impossible to show that the Jewish, Christian, and Muslim legends about Job (the latter summarized in Stevenson. *The Poem of Job*, chapter VI) have any firm roots in a pre-biblical form of the story. Apart from the tradition of the location of Job's home (see below), which may be no more than intelligent deduction from the Bible, we have the impression of popular or pious fancy.

If we identify the Daniel (*dānī'ēl*) of Ezk. xiv. 14 not with the Daniel (*dāniyyē'l*) of the Exile but with the person mentioned in Ugaritic inscriptions, we can with some confidence date all three names in Ezk. xiv. 14 at a very early date. If we do not accept this clue we have no indication of his date. The location of the land of Uz, where he lived, is uncertain. The modern tendency is to regard it as on the borders of Edom, certain indications in the book being regarded as Edomite; but the traditions placing it in the Hauran (Bashan) are far more probable. Job was a man of great wealth and high social position, but the book is so concerned with stressing his position among the Wise that it avoids precise details; we can, however, unhesitatingly reject the legends that make him a king.

As a result of divine permission Satan robbed him of his wealth, his ten children, and finally his health. There is no agreement on what disease he was smitten with, the main suggestions being elephantiasis, erythema, and smallpox. This wide disagreement is due to the symptoms being given in highly poetic language. His relations and fellow-townsmen interpreted his misfortunes as a divine punishment for gross sin and threw him out of the town, the rabble taking a particular pleasure in this. His wife accepted the common opinion and urged him to expedite the inevitable end by cursing God.

Job was visited by three friends, Eliphaz, Bildad, and Zophar, also members of the Wise, and rich and affluent, as he had been. When they saw his plight they shared popular opinion and could only sit in silence with Job on the dunghill outside the city gate for the seven days of mourning for a man as good as dead. Job's outburst of agony led to a long, vehement discussion, ending with a wordy intrusion by a younger man, Elihu. All this only revealed the bankruptcy of traditional wisdom and theology when faced with an exceptional case like Job's. Though his friends' lack of comprehension drove Job almost to distraction, it also turned him to God and prepared him for the revelation of divine sovereignty, which brought him peace. The mob was confounded by his healing, the doubling of his wealth, and the gift of ten children. H.L.E.

JOB, BOOK OF.

I. OUTLINE OF CONTENTS

Chapters i and ii (in prose) introduce us to the encounter in heaven between God and Satan and its effects on earth. Chapter iii is Job's great 'Why?'; Eliphaz gives his views in chapters iv, v and Job replies in chapters vi, vii. Bildad continues in chapter viii, Job replying in chapters ix, x. The first round of the discussion is completed by Zophar's contribution in chapter xi and Job's reply in chapters xii–xiv. In the second round we hear Eliphaz (xv), Bildad (xviii), and Zophar (xx), with Job's replies in chapters xvi, xvii, xix, xxi. As the text stands (see 'Text', below), the third round is incomplete, only Eliphaz (xxii) and Bildad (xxv) speaking, with Job's replies in chapters xxiii, xxiv, xxvi, xxvii. After an interlude in praise of wisdom (xxviii), Job sums up the debate (xxix–xxxi). Elihu's intervention follows in chapters xxxii–xxxvii, and then God replies to Job in chapters xxxviii–xlii. 6. The book ends with a prose epilogue telling of Job's restored prosperity (xlii. 7–17).

II. AUTHORSHIP AND DATE

The book is anonymous. The 'official' Talmudic tradition, followed by many earlier Christian writers, is that the book was written by Moses (*Baba Bathra* 14b, *seq.*), but the continuation of the passage and other statements show that this is merely a pious pronouncement, based presumably on a feeling of fitness, and not to be taken seriously. The simple fact is that we have no purely objective evidence to guide us either in the question of authorship or of date. The evidence for a very early date lies mostly in the non-mention of any of the details of Israelite history, but this is sufficiently explained by the author's wish to discuss the central problem outside the framework of the covenant. Other evidence, such as the mention of the Chaldeans as nomadic raiders (i. 17) and of the archaic *qᵉśîṭâ* (xlii. 11), point merely to the antiquity of the story and not to that of its present written form. Moderns have varied in their dating from the time of Solomon to about 250 BC, dates between 600 and 400 BC being most popular, though there is a growing tendency to favour later dates. A Solomonic date, accepted by Franz Delitzsch and E. J. Young, is the earliest we can reasonably adopt. The arguments from subject, language, and theology probably favour a somewhat later date, but since the book is *sui generis* in Heb. literature, and the language is so distinctive (some even regard it as a translation from Aramaic, or consider the author lived outside Israel), while the theology is timeless, any dogmatism derives from subjectivism or preconceptions.

III. TEXT

The fact that we are dealing with some of the most difficult poetry in the Old Testament, and that in the vocabulary we have some 110 words (W. B. Stevenson, *The Poem of Job*, p. 71) not found elsewhere, has made the scribe's task very difficult. Unfortunately the versions are no great help in checking the Hebrew text. The LXX must be used with great caution. In its earlier form about 17–25% of the Hebrew is missing, probably because the translators were daunted by their task; the rendering is often free and periphrastic, and not seldom incorrect.

The main textual problem concerns chapters xxvi, xxvii. As they stand they are Job's answer to Bildad's third speech. No objection can be raised to Zophar's failure to speak a third time; it is in keeping with his character, and would be the most obvious proof of Job's verbal triumph over his friends. Indubitably we hear Job speaking in xxvii. 2–6, but in its context it is virtually impossible to ascribe xxvii. 7–23 to him. It is probably part of Zophar's third speech or possibly of Bildad's. If that is so, no entirely satisfactory reconstruction of the text has been suggested, and it may be that part of the original MS has been lost, something that could easily happen with a brittle papyrus roll.

IV. INTEGRITY

Most scholars separate the prose prologue and epilogue from the poetry of chapters iii–xlii. 6. Where this is interpreted as meaning that they are older than the poem, and that the author transformed the heart of the old story into magnificent verse, the theory is unobjectionable and quite possibly correct. There are no objective proofs for the suggestion that the prose was added later to the verse by another hand, whether it is earlier or later in composition. In the hands of W. B. Stevenson (*op. cit.*) this theory has been used to impose a non-natural interpretation on the book.

Very many scholars regard certain portions as later insertions. In descending order of importance the chief are: Elihu's speeches (xxxii–xxxvii), the praise of divine wisdom (xxviii), and certain parts of God's answer (xxxix. 13–18, xl. 15–24, xli. 1–34). In every case the linguistic arguments are very tenuous. The argument from their contents is liable to take the passages in isolation. A very reasonable defence of them in their actual setting can be made.

V. AS WISDOM LITERATURE

R. H. Pfeiffer, *Introduction to the Old Testament*, 1948, pp. 683 f., says very well: 'If our poet ranks with the greatest writers of mankind, as can hardly be doubted, his creative genius did not of necessity rely on earlier models for the general structure of his work. . . . We may regard it as one of the most original works in the poetry of mankind. So original in fact that it does not fit into any of the standard categories devised by literary criticism . . . it is not exclusively lyric . . . nor epic . . . nor dramatic . . . nor didactic nor reflective . . . unless the poem is cut down to fit a particular category.' The convention that calls Job part of Heb. Wisdom literature and aligns it with Proverbs and Ecclesiastes and compares it with certain Egyp. and Bab. 'Wisdom' writings is justified only if we are careful to keep Pfeiffer's warning in mind. For all that, it is clear that Job and his friends are depicted as, and speak primarily as, members of the Wise, and they are so addressed by Elihu (xxxiv. 2).

The Wise in Israel sought to understand God and His ways by studying the great uniformities of human experience by reason illuminated by 'the fear of the Lord'. Proverbs is a typical example of their understanding of life. Job is a flaming protest, less against the basic concept of Proverbs that a God-fearing life brings prosperity, godlessness suffering and destruction, than against the idea that thereby the ways of God are fully grasped. Job is not a type; he is the exception that makes folly of the assumption that through normal experience the depths of God's wisdom and working can be fully grasped.

VI. THE PROBLEM OF JOB

The poem is so rich in its thought, so wide in its sweep, that much in human experience and its mysteries has been found mirrored there. Mostly, however, it has been regarded as concerned with the problem of human suffering. Though he has overstated his case, W. B. Stevenson (*op. cit.*, pp. 34 ff.) makes it clear that in the poem there is far less allusion to Job's physical sufferings than has often been assumed. Job is concerned less with his physical pain than with his treatment by his relations, his fellow-townsmen, the mob, and finally his friends. But these are merely evidence that God has forsaken him. In other words, Job's problem is not that of pain, nor even suffering in a wider sense, but the theological one, why God had not acted as all theory and his earlier experience demanded He should. Being a child of his age, he had naturally built up his life on the theory that God's justice implied the equation of goodness and prosperity.

Taken out of their context, the words of his friends and Elihu are more acceptable than many of the rasher utterances of Job. They are rejected by God (xlii. 7), not because they are untrue, but because they are too narrow. This is made especially clear by the discussion on the fate of the wicked. With all Job's exaggeration we recognize at once that his friends are in fact producing an *a priori* picture of what the fate of the wicked should be. They create their picture of God only by a careful selection of evidence. Job's agony is caused by the breakdown of his theological world-picture.

This explains the apparently unsatisfactory climax in which God does not answer Job's questions or charges, but though He proclaims the greatness of His all-might, not of His ethical rule, Job is satisfied. He realizes that his concept of God collapsed because it was too small; his problems evaporate when he realizes the greatness of God. The book does not set out to answer the problem of suffering but to proclaim a God so great that no answer is needed, for it would transcend the finite mind if given; the same applies to the problems incidentally raised.

BIBLIOGRAPHY. S. R. Driver and G. B. Gray, *The Book of Job*, *ICC*, 1921; G. Hölscher, *Hiob*, 1937; J. C. Rylaarsdam, *Revelation in Jewish Wisdom Literature*, 1946; W. B. Stevenson, *The Poem of Job*, 1947; H. L. Ellison, *From Tragedy to Triumph*, 1958. H.L.E.

JOBAB. 1. A man listed in the genealogies of Gn. x. 29 and 1 Ch. i. 23 as a son of Joktan and a descendant of Shem and Noah. **2.** A king of Edom mentioned in Gn. xxxvi. 33, 34 and 1 Ch. i. 44, 45. **3.** A king of Madon who was allied with Jabin of Hazor and defeated by Joshua (Jos. xi. 1). **4, 5.** The name of two Benjamites (1 Ch. viii. 9, 18). R.A.H.G.

JOCHEBED (*yôḵeḇeḏ*, 'Yahweh is glory'). The mother of Moses, Aaron, and Miriam (Ex. vi. 20; Nu. xxvi. 59), though her name is not recorded in the actual narrative of Moses' birth (Ex. ii). She was a daughter of Levi, and married her nephew Amram, although according to the LXX of Ex. vi. 20 they were cousins. J.G.G.N.

JOEL, BOOK OF.

I. OUTLINE OF CONTENTS

The chief topics of the book of Joel are four: (*a*) the appalling devastation of successive plagues of locusts, which seem literal enough, though they have a meaning beyond themselves; (*b*) the renewed fruitfulness of the land on the repentance of Israel; (*c*) the gifts of the Spirit; (*d*) the final judgment on the nations which have wronged Israel, and the blessedness-to-be of the land of Judah. A primary and a deeper eschatological meaning may be perceived in all these things.

a. The locust plague, i. 1–12

For locusts (*q.v.*) in the Old Testament, *cf.* also Ex. x. 12–15 *et passim*, with Ps. lxxviii. 46, cv. 34; also Pr. xxx. 27; Na. iii. 15, 17, *etc.* See also figs. 86, 136.

(i) Joel claims in customary prophetic manner that he has received the word of the Lord, giving his own name and that of his father, both otherwise unknown (i. 1).

(ii) The burden of his message is prodigious—a locust plague in successive swarms, of frightening dimensions (i. 2–4; *cf.* Ex. x. 14). Full etymological, entomological, and figurative discussion of verse 4 will be found in commentaries.

(iii) The effects of the plague are vividly described (i. 5–12). The first to be mentioned, perhaps in derision, is the loss to the drunkard of his solace. The teeth of the locust host are fearsome (*cf.* Pr. xxx. 14, *etc.*)—the very fig-bark is devoured, and the white, sappy interior uncovered to the world. Temple priests should mourn with the bitterness of an aged virgin whose betrothed died in her youth before marriage, for the very materials of sacrifice are cut off (*cf.* Dn. viii. 11, xi. 31, xii. 11; contrast Is. i. 11–15; Mi. vi. 6; *etc.*). The devastation in cornfield, vineyard, and orchard is vividly described.

b. The fruits of repentance, i. 13–ii. 27

(i) The priests in sackcloth are to lament, with fasting and prayer, the day of God's wrath, the 'conquest from the Conqueror', to reflect palely the striking Heb. assonance (i. 13–15; see Ne. ix. 1; Est. iv. 3, 16; Dn. ix. 3, *etc.*, contrasted with Is. lviii. 4 ff.; Je. xiv. 12; Zc. vii. 5; *etc.*). The Old Testament views on sacrifice and fasting are not contradictory, much depended on circumstance and particular usage. Joel need not stand condemned because he is more ritualistic than Amos or Isaiah.

(ii) It seems reasonable to regard the next section (i. 16–20) as a prayer, despite the vivid initial delineation of locust ravage. Verse 18 should read 'What shall we put in them?'—*i.e.* the flimsy barns not rebuilt through lack of need. The fire and flame of verse 19 may be heat and drought, or even the vivid red colouring in the locust bodies.

(iii) The prophet now reverts from the devastation of the locusts to their initial onslaught, likening it to the Day of the Lord (ii. 1–11). Verse 2b is typical oriental idiom (*cf.* Ex. x. 14). Vividly accurate is the likening of the swarm to an advancing fire. The fruitful earth before them becomes a black desolation as they pass over it (verse 3). First-hand experience is reflected also in the likening of the separate locusts to horsemen, and the parallel drawn between the noise of their advance and the sound of a rapidly spreading bush fire (verses 4, 5). People are horror-stricken before the unswerving, unjostling, accurate advance of myriads of myriads of these insects, invincible through sheer numbers (verses 6–9). The real locusts could be symbols of the Gentiles in the valley of decision, before their judgment.

(iv) In the hour of horror it is not too late to repent, with mortification of the flesh (ii. 12–14). Official rending of the garments may be hypocritical—real repentance is in the heart. This may even make God 'repent' of His recently appropriate judgment, and provide sacrificial materials again. This is oriental symbolism, implying no 'sinful' deity.

(v) A fresh call to special temple worship is given (ii. 15–17). This embraces priests and people, with specific mention of suckling babes, tottering greybeards, and newly-weds, who normally enjoyed far-reaching exemptions from public duties. Bewer (*ICC*) ingeniously points the imperatives as perfects, without consonantal change, making verse 15, not verse 18, the turning-point of the book, and the beginning of continuous narrative.

(vi) The devastation of the locust will be surpassed by the plenty that the Lord will grant on repentance (ii. 18–25). Verse 20 means that physical bodies of locusts in Judaea will be wind-driven into the Dead Sea and the Mediterranean Sea, and this will be followed by the stench of decay (18–25).

c. The gifts of the Spirit, ii. 28–32

The outpouring of the Spirit described in this passage is the apex of prophetic utterance. Verses 28, 29, and 32 were clearly fulfilled at Pentecost; aspects of verses 30 and 31 were fulfilled in the passion of our Lord. Ecstatic prophesying might include the gift of tongues. The pillars of smoke might be sand columns raised by desert whirlwinds, or the conflagration of doomed cities. A solar eclipse can make a blood-red moon. What more saving name could be foreshadowed in verse 32 than that of Jesus? Everything has a meaning—yet there is a deeper meaning belonging to the days when the last sands of human time will sink for evermore.

d. God's enemies judged, iii. 1–21

The surface meaning of this section is the prediction of divine vengeance on the nations which have scattered and persecuted the Jews. The references of verses 3–8 are clearly historical. The locusts might foreshadow these armies of Gentiles in their brief hour of victory. Verses 9–11 are biting in their sarcasm as the prophet urges the heathen to make war on God. God alone will judge the assembled nations in the valley of decision (verses 12, 14; see JEHOSHAPHAT, VALLEY OF). The full horror of verses 15 ff., 19a, and the full benediction of verse 18, are both alike as yet unrealized. Earthly prophecy and eschatology are wedded in a chapter of rich prefiguring. The Christian Church is the heir of the Old Testament, and the sure word of prophecy, be it about Egypt or anything else, will come to pass in God's good time.

II. AUTHORSHIP AND DATE

This is superb extrovert literature, betraying a Judaean flavour, but intrinsically concerned with bigger issues than contemporary politics. This makes dating very difficult. The German scholars Nowack and Marti both regard the book as a literary unity, but of post-exilic origin—the latter particularizes around 400 BC. Bewer (*ICC*) assigns only part of the book to Joel, analysing the deduced additions and interpolations of two subsequent editors, and dating the latest portions about 350 BC. On the unavoidably subjective criterion of Hebrew style, this is a bold assertion. Ancient traditions, borne out by canonical position and frequently reaffirmed by contemporary conservative scholarship, would not only claim the book as one integrated, indivisible whole, but would also claim the man as perhaps the oldest of the writing prophets, a senior contemporary of Amos and Hosea, ministering during the minority of King Jehoash, in the 9th century BC. The intervening centuries have been excluded for historical reasons.

Of the two extremes, the earlier date has much to recommend it. If it be the correct one, certain familiar prophetic battle-cries then find their first known utterance in Joel. Ploughshares might well have been considered the fathers of swords before the hope of the reverse transformation was born (Joel iii. 10; Is. ii. 4).

III. SPECIAL CHARACTERISTICS

Joel was the vehicle of a divine revelation which has a significance perhaps beyond his full understanding. In his book the impinging of the eternal on the temporal, which is the hallmark of genuine inspiration, is undeniably much in evidence. Especially is this true of his arresting description of the destruction caused by the plague of locusts which he uses as a picture of God's wrath and His punishment of sin. There are also his vivid portrayal of God's gracious restoration of His people following upon repentance, and his prophecies concerning events linked with our Lord's death, with the coming of the Holy Spirit, and with both the horror and the hope of the end times. This is one of the briefest and yet one of the most disturbing and heart-searching books of the Old Testament.

BIBLIOGRAPHY. S. R. Driver, *Joel and Amos*, *CBSC*, 1915; A. S. Kapelrud, *Joel Studies*, 1948; J. A. Thompson, 'Joel's Locusts in the Light of Near Eastern Parables', *JNES*, XIV, 1955, pp. 52 ff., *IB*, VI, pp. 727–760. R.A.S.

JOGBEHAH (*yoḡbᵉhâ*, 'height'). A town in Gilead assigned to Gad (Nu. xxxii. 35), named also in Gideon's pursuit of the Midianites (Jdg. viii. 11). It is the modern Jubeihât, about 6 miles north-west of Amman and 3,468 feet above sea-level.

JOHANAN (*yôḥānān*, 'Yahweh is gracious'). A number of men are so called in the Old Testament, the most notable being the son of Kareah. A Jewish leader who supported Gedaliah on the latter's appointment as governor of Judah (2 Ki. xxv. 23; Je. xl. 8) after the fall of Jerusalem, Johanan offered to kill Ishmael, who was plotting Gedaliah's assassination (Je. xl. 13–16). The offer rejected and the warning ignored, Ishmael succeeded in his purpose. Johanan pursued him, rescued the people captured by him (Je. xli. 11–16), and took them and the protesting Jeremiah to Tahpanhes in Egypt (Je. xliii. 1–7).

Others possessing the same name include the eldest son of Josiah, king of Judah (1 Ch. iii. 15); a son of Elioenai (1 Ch. iii. 24); a grandson of Ahimaaz (1 Ch. vi. 9, 10); a Benjamite recruit of David at Ziklag (1 Ch. xii. 4); a Gadite who likewise joined David (1 Ch. xii. 12); an Ephraimite chief (2 Ch. xxviii. 12, where Hebrew has 'Jehohanan'); a returned exile in Artaxerxes' time (Ezr. viii. 12); and a priest in the days of Joiakim (Ne. xii. 22, 23). J.D.D.

JOHN, THE APOSTLE. Our information about John comes from two sources: New Testament and Patristic.

I. NEW TESTAMENT EVIDENCE

a. In the Gospels

John was the son of Zebedee, probably the younger son, for except in Luke–Acts he is mentioned after his brother James. Luke gives the order Peter, John, and James, probably because in the early days of the Church John was closely associated with Peter (Lk. viii. 51, ix. 28; Acts i. 13). That John's mother's name was Salome is an inference from Mk. xvi. 1 and Mt. xxvii. 56; for the third woman who is said to have accompanied the two Marys to the tomb is designated Salome by Mark, and 'the mother of Zebedee's children' by Matthew. Salome is usually regarded as the sister of Mary the mother of Jesus, because in Jn. xix. 25 four women are said to have stood near the cross, the two Marys mentioned in Mark and Matthew, the mother of Jesus, and His mother's sister. If this identification is correct, John was a cousin of Jesus on his mother's side. His parents would appear to have been well-to-do, for his father, a fisherman, had 'hired servants' (Mk. i. 20); and Salome was one of the women who 'provided for Jesus out of their means' (Lk. viii. 3, RSV; Mk. xv. 40). John has often been identified with the unnamed disciple of John the Baptist, who with Andrew was directed by the Baptist to Jesus as the Lamb of God (Jn. i. 35–37); and if *prōtos* is read in Jn. i. 41, it is possible that Andrew was the first of these two disciples to bring his brother Simon to Jesus, and that the unnamed disciple (John) subsequently brought his own brother James. This is not certain, however, as there are textual variants (see *TNTC*). After their subsequent call by Jesus to leave their father and their fishing (Mk. i. 19, 20), James and John were nicknamed by Him *Boanērges*, 'sons of thunder' (Mk. iii. 17), probably because they were high-spirited, impetuous Galilaeans, whose zeal was undisciplined and sometimes misdirected (Lk. ix. 49). This aspect of their character is shown by their outburst after a Samaritan village had refused their Master entrance (Lk. ix. 54). Moreover, their personal ambition was, it would seem, untempered by a true insight into the nature of His kingship; and this lingering trait of selfishness, together with their readiness to suffer for Jesus regardless of self, is illustrated in the request they made to Him (a request encouraged by their mother (Mt. xx. 20)) that they should be allowed to sit in places of special privilege when Jesus entered into His kingdom (Mk. x. 37).

On three important occasions in the earthly ministry of Jesus, John is mentioned in company with his brother James and Simon Peter, to the exclusion of the other apostles—at the raising of Jairus' daughter (Mk. v. 37), at the transfiguration (Mk. ix. 2); and in the garden of Gethsemane (Mk. xiv. 33); and, according to Luke, Peter and John were the two disciples sent by Jesus to make preparations for the final Passover meal (Lk. xxii. 8).

John is not mentioned by name in the Fourth Gospel (though the sons of Zebedee are referred to in xxi. 2), but he is almost certainly the disciple called 'the disciple whom Jesus loved', who lay close to the breast of Jesus at the Last Supper (xiii. 23); who was entrusted with the care of His mother at the time of His death (xix. 26, 27); who ran with Peter to the tomb on the first Easter morning and was the first to see the full significance of the undisturbed grave-clothes with no body inside them (xx. 2, 8); and who was present when the risen Christ revealed Himself to seven of His disciples by the sea of Tiberias. In the account of that last incident in chapter xxi, support is given to the later tradition that John lived on to a great age (xxi. 23). The evidence of Jn. xxi. 24 for the Johannine authorship of this Gospel is capable of different interpretations (see *TNTC*).

b. In the Acts

According to the early narratives of Acts, John, together with Peter, with whom he remained closely associated, had to bear the main brunt of Jewish hostility to the early Christian Church (Acts iv. 13, v. 33, 40). Both men showed a boldness of speech and action which astounded the Jewish authorities, who regarded them as 'uneducated, common men' (Acts iv. 13, RSV). John, it would seem, continued for some years to play a leading part in the church at Jerusalem. On behalf of the other apostles he and Peter laid hands on the Samaritans who had been converted through the ministry of Philip (Acts viii. 14); and he could be described as a reputed 'pillar' of the Jerusalem church at the time when Paul visited the city some fourteen years after his conversion (Gal. ii. 9). We do not know when John left Jerusalem, nor where he went after his departure. Assuming that he is the seer of the book of Revelation, he was presumably at Ephesus when he was banished to Patmos 'for the word of Jesus, and for the testimony of Jesus Christ' (Rev. i. 9), though the date of this exile is uncertain. There is no other mention of John in the New Testament, though some scholars think that he refers to himself under the title 'the elder' in 2 Jn. 1; 3 Jn. 1.

II. PATRISTIC EVIDENCE

There is a certain amount of late but probably unreliable evidence, that John the apostle died as a martyr early in his career, perhaps at the time his brother James was slain by Herod (Acts xii. 2). A 9th-century chronicler, George Hamartolos, reproduces, as we can now see, a statement contained in the history of Philip of Side (*c.* 450), a relevant fragment of which was discovered by de Boor in 1889, to the effect that Papias, Bishop of Hierapolis in the middle of the 2nd century, in the second book of his *Expositions* asserted that *both* the sons of Zebedee met a violent death in fulfilment of the Lord's prediction (Mk. x. 39). Though some scholars accept this testimony as genuine, most regard Philip of Side as an unreliable witness to Papias, and are impressed by the absence from Eusebius of any reference to the early martyrdom of John, and also by the failure of Acts to mention it, if both the sons of Zebedee in fact suffered in the same way at approximately the same time. It is true that some support for Philip of Side's statement seems to be obtainable from a Syr. martyrology written about AD 400, in which the entry for 27 December is 'John and James the apostles at Jerusalem'; and also from a calendar of the church at Carthage, dated AD 505, in which the entry for the same date reads 'John the Baptist and James the apostle whom Herod killed', for it is pointed out by those who accept this evidence that, as the Baptist is commemorated in this calendar on 24 June, the probability is that the entry for 27 December is a mistake for 'John the Apostle'. It is, however, very doubtful whether the Syr. martyrology preserves an ancient tradition independent of the Gk.-speaking church; nor does it follow that, because the two brothers were commemorated on the same day, they were commemorated as being both martyrs in *death* who had been slain at the same time. Nor again does the reference to the sons of Zebedee as 'drinking the cup' and 'being baptized with the baptism of Christ' necessarily imply that both were destined to come to a violent end.

Against this partial and weakly attested tradition must be set the much stronger tradition reflected in the statement of Polycrates, bishop of Ephesus (AD 190), that John 'who reclined on the Lord's breast', after being 'a witness and a teacher' (note the order of the words), 'fell asleep at Ephesus'. According to Irenaeus, it was at Ephesus that John 'gave out' the Gospel, and confuted the heretics, refusing to remain under the same roof as Cerinthus, 'the enemy of truth'; and at Ephesus that he lingered on 'till the days of Trajan', who reigned AD 98–117. Jerome also repeats the tradition that John tarried at Ephesus to extreme old age, and records that, when John had to be carried to the Christian meetings, he used to repeat again and again 'Little children, love one another'. The only evidence that might seemingly conflict with this tradition of John the apostle's residence at Ephesus is negative in character. It is alleged that if, as the writers at the end of the 2nd century assert, John resided long at Ephesus and exercised such influence, it is remarkable that there should be an entire absence of any reference to John in the extant Christian literature which emanated from Asia during the first half of the century, particularly in the letters of Ignatius and the Epistle of Polycarp. But, even if the absence of allusions to John in these documents is significant, it may merely be an indication that 'there was a difference between his reputation and influence at the beginning and at the close of the century' (so V. H. Stanton, *The Gospels as Historical Documents*, I, p. 236). On any score the objection, it would seem, is insufficient to overthrow the tradition which later became so firmly established. Westcott concluded that 'nothing is better attested in early church history than the residence and work of St. John at Ephesus'. It is true that Westcott wrote before the evidence for John's early martyrdom had accumulated, but as we have seen, that evidence is not adequate enough or reliable enough to confute the definite statements of the man who occupied the see of Ephesus at the close of the century, and of the man who at the same period made it his primary aim to investigate the traditions of the apostolic sees.

See also JOHN, EPISTLES OF; JOHN, GOSPEL OF; and REVELATION, BOOK OF.

BIBLIOGRAPHY. See the Commentaries listed under JOHN, GOSPEL OF. R.V.G.T.

JOHN THE BAPTIST. Born (*c*. 7 BC) to an elderly couple, Zacharias a priest and his wife Elisabeth, he grew to manhood in the wilderness of Judaea (Lk. i. 80), where he received his prophetic call, *c*. AD 27 (Lk. iii. 2). The view that his wilderness period was spent in association with the Qumran community or a similar Essene group must be treated with caution; even if it could be substantiated, it was a new impulse which sent him forth 'to make ready a people prepared for the Lord' (Lk. i. 17), and his prophetic ministry must have involved a break with any Essene or similar group with which he may previously have been connected. After the Spirit of prophecy came upon him, he quickly gained widespread fame as a preacher calling for national repentance. Crowds flocked to hear him, and many of his hearers were baptized by him in the Jordan, confessing their sins.

His attitude to the established order in Israel was one of radical condemnation; 'the axe,' he said, 'is laid unto the root of the trees' (Mt. iii. 10; Lk. iii. 9). He denounced the religious leaders of the people as a brood of vipers, and denied that there was any value in the bare fact of descent from Abraham. A new beginning was necessary; the time had come to call out from the nation as a whole a loyal remnant who would be ready for the imminent arrival of the Coming One and the judgment which He would execute. John thought and spoke of himself as a mere preparer of the way for this Coming One, for whom he was unworthy, he said, to perform the lowliest service. Whereas John's own ministry was characterized by baptism with water, the Coming One's ministry would be a baptism with the Holy Spirit and fire.

That John aimed at giving the loyal remnant a distinct and recognizable existence is suggested by the statement in Josephus (*Ant.* xviii. 5. 2) that John was 'a good man who bade the Jews practise virtue, be just one to another, and pious toward God, and come together by means of baptism'; these last words seem to envisage the formation of a religious community which was entered by baptism. This is probably an accurate assessment of the situation. But when Josephus goes on to say that John 'taught that baptism was acceptable to God provided that they underwent it not to procure remission of sins but for the purification of the body, if the soul had first been purified by righteousness', he differs from the New Testament account. The Evangelists say quite plainly that John preached a 'baptism of repentance for the remission of sins'. Josephus is probably transferring to John's baptism what he knew to be the significance of Essene washings; the Qumran *Rule of the Community* gives an account of the significance of such washings almost identical with that which Josephus gives of John's baptism. But John's baptism, like his preaching, may well represent a deliberate turning away from Essene beliefs and practices.

Among those who came to John for baptism was Jesus, whom John apparently hailed as the Coming One of whom he had spoken—although later, in prison, he had doubts about this identification and had to be reassured by being told that Jesus' ministry was marked by precisely those features which the prophets had foretold as characteristic of the age of restoration.

John's ministry was not confined to the Jordan valley. The statement in John iii. 23 that he left the Jordan valley for a time and conducted a baptismal campaign (presumably of brief duration) 'in Aenon near to Salim', where there was abundance of water, has implications which are easily overlooked. For W. F. Albright (*The*

Archaeology of Palestine, 1956, p. 247) is probably right in locating this place south-east of Nablus, near the sources of the Wadi Far'ah—that is to say, in territory which was then Samaritan. This could explain certain features of Samaritan religion attested for the early Christian centuries, but it also illuminates the words of Jesus to His disciples in John iv. 35–38, spoken with regard to the people in this very area, and ending with the statement: 'others have laboured, and ye have entered into their labours'. The harvest which they reaped (Jn. iv. 39, 41) had been sown by John.

After this period of ministry in Samaria John must have returned to the territory of Herod Antipas (see HEROD, 3), probably Peraea. He aroused Antipas's suspicion as the leader of a mass movement which might have unforeseen results; he also incurred his hostility, and still more that of Herod's second wife Herodias (*q.v.*), by denouncing their marriage as illicit. He was accordingly imprisoned in the Peraean fortress of Machaerus (*q.v.*) and there, some months later, put to death.

In the New Testament John is presented chiefly as the forerunner of Christ. His imprisonment was the signal for the start of Jesus' Galilaean ministry (Mk. i. 14 f.); his baptismal activity provided a starting-point for the apostolic preaching (Acts x. 37, xiii. 24 f., *cf.* i. 22 and Mk. i. 1–4). In Jesus' estimation, John was the promised Elijah of Mal. iv. 5 f., who was to come and complete his ministry of restoration on the eve of 'the great and dreadful day of the Lord' (Mk. ix. 13; Mt. xi. 14; *cf.* Lk. i. 17). Jesus also regarded him as the last and greatest member of the prophetic succession: 'the law and the prophets were until John: since that time the kingdom of God is preached' (Lk. xvi. 16). Therefore, while unsurpassed in personal stature, he was (in respect of privilege) less than the least in the kingdom of God; he stood on the threshold of the new order as its herald (as Moses viewed the promised land from Pisgah) without entering in. His disciples preserved their corporate existence for a considerable time after his death.

BIBLIOGRAPHY. C. H. Kraeling, *John the Baptist*, 1951; J. Steinmann, *Saint John the Baptist and the Desert Tradition*, 1958; A. S. Geyser, 'The Youth of John the Baptist', *NovT*, I, 1956, pp. 70 ff.; J. A. T. Robinson, 'The Baptism of John and the Qumran Community', *HTR*, L, 1957, pp. 175 ff.; W. H. Brownlee, 'John the Baptist in the New Light of Ancient Scrolls', in *The Scrolls and the New Testament*, ed. K. Stendahl, 1958, pp. 33 ff.

F.F.B.

JOHN, EPISTLES OF.

I. BACKGROUND AND CIRCUMSTANCES OF 1 JOHN

1 John is headed as an Epistle, but there is nothing 'epistolary' in the strict sense about it (contrast 2 and 3 John), and it is more like a tract addressed to a particular situation.

It was called forth by the activities of false teachers who had seceded from the church (or churches) to which John is writing, and who were attempting to seduce the faithful (ii. 18 f., 26). They formed an esoteric group, believing that they had superior knowledge to ordinary Christians (*cf.* ii. 20, 27; 2 Jn. 9) and showing little love to them (*cf.* iv. 20).

They were forerunners of the later heretics generally known as 'Gnostics' (from Gk. *gnōsis*, meaning 'knowledge') and claimed a special knowledge of God and of theology. See GNOSTICISM. On the basis of their new doctrine they appear to have denied that Jesus was the Christ (ii. 22), the pre-existent (i. 1) Son of God (iv. 15, v. 5, 10) come in the flesh (iv. 2; 2 Jn. 7) to provide salvation for men (iv. 9 f., 14). But the precise form which this heresy took is uncertain. It is generally regarded as having had some affinity with the views held by Cerinthus in Asia Minor at the end of the 1st century, although it was not fully identical with what we know of his teaching. According to Cerinthus, Jesus was a good man who was indwelt by the heavenly Christ from the time of his baptism until just before his crucifixion (Irenaeus, *Adversus Haereses*, i. 26. 1, in J. Stevenson, *A New Eusebius*, 1957, No. 70)—a view which is apparently contradicted in v. 6 and in various verses where belief that Jesus *is* (not simply *was*) the Christ, the Son of God, is emphasized (ii. 22, v. 1, 5). Such teaching was probably bound up with the common gnostic distinction between spirit and matter, according to which a real incarnation of God in man was impossible and was only apparent (as in Docetism) or temporary (as in Cerinthianism).

The false teachers further claimed that they were 'sinless' (i. 8, 10) and possibly also that they did not need redemption through the death of Jesus Christ, while they were in fact morally indifferent, following the ways of the world (*cf.* ii. 15), ignoring the commandments of Christ (ii. 4), and freely doing what they pleased (without, however, indulging in gross sin). They did not realize that sin is a moral category, *i.e.* lawlessness (iii. 4, 7 f.), and consequently they felt quite consistent in claiming sinlessness while indulging in selfishness and lack of love. Probably we are to see here also the influence of the gnostic distinction between spirit and matter: since the body (matter) was evil anyhow and only the (divinely implanted) spirit or soul mattered, their bodily behaviour was irrelevant to their Christian belief.

John writes to provide an antidote to this teaching, and the progress of the argument in his tract is best understood when this is kept in mind. (For attempts to explain its difficult structure in terms of source criticism, see W. Nauck, *Die Tradition und Charakter des ersten Johannesbriefes*, 1957; he suggests that John incorporates a set of antitheses composed earlier by himself.)

II. OUTLINE OF CONTENTS OF 1 JOHN

John begins by stating that his purpose is to explain to his readers what he has heard and seen as regards the word of life manifested in Jesus Christ, so that there may be joyful fellowship between himself, his readers, and God (i. 1–4).

He then states the fundamental proposition, *God is light*, and on the basis of this universally acceptable truth proceeds to take up certain erroneous slogans of his opponents (i. 6a, 8a, 10a, ii. 4a). In opposition to them he asserts that only those who walk in the light can have fellowship with God and cleansing through the blood of Jesus. To deny that one is a sinner in need of cleansing is to commit self-deceit, but sinners can be sure of forgiveness from a faithful God through the righteous Advocate, Jesus Christ. To claim a true knowledge of God without obeying His commandments is to be a liar (i. 5–ii. 6).

Christians, then, are called to obey God's new commandment. Although it is really an old one, yet it is now presented anew as the law of the new era of light which has already begun to shine in the darkness of the old, sinful world. John feels able to address his readers in this way because they have already entered into this new era and enjoy the privileges of forgiveness, knowledge, and power, and he further exhorts them not to cling to the sinful world which is doomed to pass away (ii. 7–17).

One of the marks of the arrival of the new era is the rise of these false teachers who have now left their temporary home in the Church. Their teaching is a denial that Jesus is the Christ, the Son of God, and this really means that they are denying God the Father Himself. They claim special knowledge, to be sure, but John assures his readers that in view of their anointing by God (*i.e.* with the Spirit or perhaps with the Word of God) all Christians have true knowledge (ii. 18–27).

He now counsels them to abide in Christ, the holy and righteous One, and to test themselves and their teachers by their likeness to Him. This leads to the thought of the great privilege of Christians as children of God, and the even greater privilege that at the advent of Christ they will become altogether like Him—all of which constitutes a powerful incentive to holy living (ii. 28–iii. 3).

What, then, is the character of children of God in contrast with those who are the children of the devil? Since Christ came to take away sin, it follows that God's children do not, and in fact cannot, sin, while the children of the devil neither do what is right nor show love. By this uncompromising statement, which must be considered in the light of i. 8, John means that the Christian *as a Christian* cannot sin: he is speaking of the ideal character of the Christian, in contrast with the false teachers who made no attempt to emulate this ideal (iii. 4–10).

In fact, Christians can expect to be hated by children of the devil, just as Abel was murdered by Cain; by contrast, the mark of the true Christian is love, seen not in murder but in self-sacrifice and practical charity (iii. 11–18).

Through such deeds of love a man knows that he is a Christian, so that, even if his conscience at times condemns him, he can still have perfect confidence before his Judge, the God who knows his desire to love and serve Him (*cf.* Jn. xxi. 17); indeed, armed with this confidence, he can be bold in prayer, since he knows that he is pleasing God by keeping His commandment of love, and, further, he will receive inward assurance from the Spirit of God (iii. 19–24).

But how can a Christian be sure that he has the Spirit of *God*? For the false teachers also claim to have the Spirit. John replies that correct belief about Jesus Christ come in the flesh is the sure sign of true inspiration. The false teachers, however, are motivated by the spirit of antichrist (iv. 1–6).

After this digression, John returns to the theme of love. Love, he repeats, is the token that a man is born of God, for, as was shown in the sacrifice of Christ, *God is love*. (This is John's second great declaration about the nature of God.) Even if men cannot see God, they can know that He dwells in them if they show love (iv. 7–12).

John now summarizes the grounds of Christian assurance—possession of the Spirit, confession of Jesus Christ, and the practice of love. These are signs that God dwells in us and give us confidence for the day of judgment, since there can be no fear where there is love. Yet, to avoid any antinomian or 'spiritualistic' misunderstanding, John emphasizes that such love for God is inevitably accompanied by love for the brethren. All who truly confess Jesus Christ love God and their fellow-men. Nor is it difficult to keep this commandment, for by faith those who are born of God can overcome the forces arrayed against them (iv. 13–v. 4).

This leads John back to the theme of faith. True Christian faith is centred on Jesus Christ, who not only submitted to the water of baptism but also shed His blood on the cross, and to whom the Spirit bears witness (Jn. xv. 26). These three—the Spirit, water, and blood—are God's sure testimony to confirm faith in Christ. John possibly also means that the saving activity of the Spirit in the Church (or the individual believer) and the sacraments of baptism and the Lord's supper continue this testimony. To disbelieve this testimony is to make God a liar and to reject the eternal life which He has given to men in His Son (v. 5–12; for the correct text of v. 7 f., see RV, RSV or NEB).

In conclusion, John states that his purpose has been to assure his readers of their salvation. Since they can be sure of divine response to their prayers, they are to win back erring brethren through prayer (although prayer is of no avail in the case of mortal sin, whatever that may be). Finally come three great declarations—that Christians have power not to sin, that they belong to God, and that they are in Jesus Christ who is their great instructor—and a final admonition to avoid idolatry (*i.e.* worship of pagan gods, but the meaning is not certain) (v. 13–21).

III. BACKGROUND AND CONTENTS OF 2 AND 3 JOHN

2 and 3 John are real letters, each long enough to be accommodated on a standard size sheet of papyrus (10 inches by 8 inches) and conforming to the pattern of letter writing of the time. (For a remarkably close parallel to the structure of 3 John, see C. K. Barrett, *The New Testament Background*: *Selected Documents*, 1956, No. 22.)

2 John is addressed from 'the elder' to 'the elect lady and her children'. This is in all likelihood a symbolic manner of addressing a church (*cf.* 1 Pet. v. 13), perhaps intended to baffle any hostile people into whose hands the letter might fall (1–3). The occasion of the letter is similar to that of 1 John (*cf.* 2 Jn. 7 with 1 Jn. iv. 3); false teachers were travelling from church to church and denying that the Son of God had really been incarnate. The elder issues a warning against such teaching; those who 'go on' to accept this new or higher teaching are abandoning their faith in God, the Father of Jesus Christ. He cautions his friends not to extend hospitality to the false teachers, and he encourages them to follow after the truth which already abides in them and to fulfil the command of love (4–11). Finally, he expresses the hope of seeing them soon and adds greetings from his own church (12 f.).

3 John is a private letter (like Philemon) addressed to the elder's friend Gaius, who was a leading member in another church. He is commended for his attachment to the truth and for showing practical love to travelling preachers who depended on the churches for their keep (1–8). His attitude is the reverse of that of Diotrephes, who was seeking to be the leader in his church (probably a neighbouring church to that of Gaius), resisting the advice of John and perhaps withholding a previous letter of his from the church, refusing to welcome the travelling preachers and excommunicating those who did welcome them. It is likely that we see here the difficulties caused by the development of a settled local church leadership alongside the existence of apostolic overseers and travelling teachers, and that Diotrephes was aspiring to the position of 'bishop' in his own church and resented any interference from outside. Such difficulties were no doubt bound to arise as the apostles passed on, but it is clear that Diotrephes was not handling matters in a Christian manner. The elder warns that he will come and deal personally with Diotrephes if necessary (9–11). Finally, a word of commendation is added for Demetrius (the bearer of the letter, or a travelling teacher?), and the letter concludes with warm greetings (12–14).

IV. EXTERNAL ATTESTATION OF THE EPISTLES

1 John was used by Papias (*c.* 140) according to Eusebius, and is quoted by Polycarp (*c.* 110–120) and very probably by Justin (*c.* 150–160). It was accepted as the work of the fourth evangelist, John the apostle, by Irenaeus (*c.* 180), the Muratorian Canon (*c.* 180–200), and Clement of Alexandria (*c.* 200). According to Eusebius, there was never any questioning of its authenticity. 2 and 3 John are probably listed in the Muratorian Canon (J. Stevenson, *op. cit.*, No. 124 and note); 2 John is quoted by Irenaeus, and both Epistles were probably commented on by Clement of Alexandria. Lack of mention and doubts about their canonicity, reflected in Eusebius, who quotes Origen (J. Stevenson, *op. cit.*, No. 289), were due to their slight nature.

V. PROVENANCE, AUTHORSHIP, AND DATE

The Asian provenance of all five Johannine writings is still the most likely. For the epistles this is supported by the Cerinthian teaching which is opposed and by the traditions which connect their author with Ephesus.

The authorship of the Epistles and of the other Johannine writings presents problems which are not yet fully solved.

First, it is certain that one author is responsible for the three Epistles, although this was denied by Jerome and more recently by J. Moffatt (*An Introduction to the Literature of the NT*³, 1918, p. 481). 1 John is anonymous, but we may now assert that its author was also 'the elder'.

Second, it is reasonably certain that John's Gospel and 1 John are by the same author. This is disputed by C. H. Dodd ('The First Epistle of John and the Fourth Gospel', *BJRL*, XXI, 1937, pp. 129–156, summarized in *The Johannine Epistles*, *MNTC*, 1946, pp. xlvii–lvi) and C. K. Barrett (*The Gospel according to St. John*, 1955, pp. 49–52), but convincing proof is given by A. E. Brooke (*The Johannine Epistles*, *ICC*, 1912, pp. i–xix), W. F. Howard (*The Fourth Gospel in Recent Criticism and Interpretation*⁴, 1955, pp. 281–296), and W. G. Wilson (*JTS*, XLIX, 1948, pp. 147–156). There can really be no doubt that John and 1 John represent the same mind at work in two different situations. John is a profound study of the incarnation of Christ addressed primarily as an apologetic to the outside world; 1 John is a tract called forth by a particular situation in the Church. The differences between the two can largely be explained by this difference of audience and purpose. Logically John precedes 1 John, but whether this was the order of composition is hardly possible to determine; John is obviously the work of many years of meditation, and 1 John may have been written in that period.

Third, the relation of Revelation (which is ascribed to John the apostle by strong external evidence) to John and 1–3 John must be considered. The theory of common authorship of all five books is very difficult to maintain, as was seen quite early by Dionysius of Alexandria (J. Stevenson, *op. cit.*, No. 237). There are considerable theological differences between Revelation and the other Johannine writings, although there are also such close similarities that J. Behm (*Die Offenbarung des Johannes*⁴, *Das Neue Testament Deutsch*, 1949, p. 8) could say that John's Gospel and Revelation are inextricably bound up together. Further, the Greek of Revelation is unlike that of any other book in the New Testament; despite suggestions that it was originally written in *Aramaic*, and so possibly by the same person who wrote John and 1–3 John in *Greek*, the theory of common authorship must remain doubtful.

In view of these facts, various theories of authorship have been put forward, of which three deserve attention.

First, the traditional theory, which is supported with reserve by P. Feine and J. Behm (*Einleitung in das Neue Testament*[10], 1954) and W. Michaelis (*Einleitung in das Neue Testament*[2], 1954), attributes all five books to John the apostle. He was known as 'the elder' *par excellence* in Asia Minor on account of his age and authority (*cf.* 1 Pet. v. 1 for a similar title). Against this theory must be reckoned the problems raised by Revelation and the uncertainty which some scholars find in the external evidence for the apostolic authorship of John.

A second solution, which avoids the first of these difficulties, is that John's Gospel and 1–3 John are by John the apostle and Revelation by another John who is otherwise unknown to us. This was essentially the theory of Dionysius of Alexandria, and is supported today by A. Wikenhauser (*New Testament Introduction*, E.T., 1958, pp. 547–553). On this view, some connection between the two Johns must be presupposed to account for the theological similarities between the writings.

A third solution, which avoids the second of the difficulties in the traditional theory, sees a close disciple of John the apostle as the author of John and 1–3 John and John himself as possibly the author of Revelation. (There is no room here to list the varied forms of this theory.) On this view, it was John's disciple who was known as 'the elder'.

Support for this solution has often been sought in a well-known passage in Papias (J. Stevenson, *op. cit.*, No. 31); Papias refers to certain of the apostles, including John, who are apparently dead, as 'elders' and then to two living disciples of the Lord, Aristion and the elder John. Some scholars think that this elder John was a disciple of John the apostle and was the author of John's Gospel and 1–3 John. But this is extremely conjectural. It is not certain whether Papias is here referring to one John (the apostle) twice or to two separate Johns, and weighty names can be quoted for both interpretations. Further, Papias clearly applied the title of 'elder' to more than one person (including John the apostle in any case), and it is not certain that he used the title in the same sense as the author of 2 and 3 John. Finally, Papias does not state that the hypothetical 'elder John' was a disciple of John the apostle. We cannot, therefore, be certain on this theory that the elder of 2 and 3 John was called John or that he was the 'elder John' of Papias.

On the whole, it still remains most plausible that the Gospel and the three letters are the work of John the apostle.

The date of 1–3 John cannot be rigidly determined. The evidence from Qumran *allows* the possibility of an earlier development of the kind of theology found in the Johannine literature than was formerly believed possible. The chief clue, however, is the nature of the heresy attacked and the church situation reflected, both of which suggest a date between the sixties and nineties of the 1st century; our knowledge of the church in this period is so meagre that a closer dating is impossible.

BIBLIOGRAPHY. B. F. Westcott, 1883; A. E. Brooke (*ICC*); C. H. Dodd (*MNTC*); R. Schnackenburg (*Herders Theologischer Kommentar zum Neuen Testament*), 1953. I.H.M.

JOHN, GOSPEL OF.

I. OUTLINE OF CONTENTS

a. The revelation of Jesus to the world, i. 1–xii. 50

(i) Prologue (i. 1–18).
(ii) The manifestation of Jesus (i. 19–ii. 11).
(iii) The new message (ii. 12–iv. 54).
(iv) Jesus, the Son of God (v. 1–47).
(v) The bread of life (vi. 1–71).
(vi) Conflict with the Jews (vii. 1–viii. 59).
(vii) The light of the world (ix. 1–41).
(viii) The good shepherd (x. 1–42).
(ix) The resurrection and the life (xi. 1–57).
(x) The shadow of the cross (xii. 1–36a).
(xi) Epilogue (xii. 36b–50).

b. The revelation of Jesus to His disciples, xiii. 1–xvii. 26

(i) The Last Supper (xiii. 1–30).
(ii) The farewell discourses (xiii. 31–xvi. 33).
(iii) Jesus' prayer for His disciples (xvii. 1–26).

c. The glorification of Jesus, xviii. 1–xxi. 25

(i) The passion of Jesus (xviii. 1–xix. 42).
(ii) The resurrection of Jesus (xx. 1–31).
(iii) The commission to the disciples (xxi. 1–25).

II. PURPOSE

A clear statement of the purpose of John is given in Jn. xx. 30 f. (*Cf.* W. C. van Unnik, *The Purpose of St. John's Gospel*, in *Studia Evangelica* (TU 73), 1959, pp. 382–411.) John has made a selection out of a large number of available 'signs', and his purpose in narrating them is to bring his readers to the belief that Jesus is the Christ (*i.e.* the Messiah) and the Son of God, and thus to bring them into an experience of eternal life.

From this statement we can draw certain conclusions which are amply attested by the substance of the Gospel. First, it is primarily an evangelistic document. Second, its explicit method is to present the work and words of Jesus in such a way as to show the nature of His person. Third, the description of this person as Messiah indicates that a Jewish audience is probably in mind. Since, however, John appears to be writing for an audience outside Palestine and in part ignorant of Jewish customs, it is an attractive hypothesis that he wrote especially for Jews of the Diaspora and proselytes in Hellenistic synagogues. (*Cf.* J. A. T. Robinson, 'The Destination and Purpose of St. John's Gospel', *NTS*, VI, 1960, pp. 117–131.) This naturally does not exclude a Gentile audience from his purview, although the view that the Gospel was written primarily to convert the thoughtful Gentile (*cf.* C. H. Dodd, *The Interpretation of the Fourth Gospel*, 1953) is unlikely.

This main purpose does not exclude other, subordinate aims. Thus, first, it is possible that John consciously stresses points which would refute the false or antagonistic views about Jesus held by Jews in his time. There may also be an attempt to correct an over-zealous veneration for John the Baptist. Second, particularly in xiii–xvii, John addresses Christians and gives teaching about life in the Church. But the view that a principal aim of John was to correct the Church's eschatology (so C. K. Barrett) is not tenable, although this is not to deny that the Gospel contains eschatological teaching. Third, it is often alleged that John was written as a polemic against gnosticism. This view gains some plausibility from the purpose of 1 John, but is not so self-evident as is sometimes supposed; nevertheless, John was no doubt aware of the danger of gnosticism while he wrote, and his Gospel is in fact an excellent weapon against gnosticism.

III. STRUCTURE AND THEOLOGICAL CONTENT

a. The historical structure

As a historical work, John is selective. It begins with the incarnation of the pre-existent Word of God in Jesus (i. 1–18), and then passes straight to the early days of Jesus' ministry—His baptism by John and the call of His first disciples (i. 19–51), and His return from the Jordan to Galilee (i. 43). But the scene of His work is not confined in the main to Galilee, as in the synoptic narrative. Only a few of the incidents related take place there (i. 43–ii. 12, iv. 43–54, vi. 1–vii. 9). Once the scene is Samaria (iv. 1–42), but most frequently it is Jerusalem, usually at the time of a Jewish feast (ii. 13, v. 1, vi. 4, vii. 2, x. 22, xi. 55; *cf.* A. Guilding, *The Fourth Gospel and Jewish Worship*, 1960). The last of these incidents is the raising of Lazarus, which provoked the Jewish leaders to do away with Jesus (xi. 45 ff.), although, as in the synoptic Gospels, their enmity had been mounting for some time (*e.g.* vii. 1). From this point the narrative follows lines familiar to us from the synoptic Gospels—the anointing at Bethany (xii. 1–11), the triumphal entry (xii. 12–19), the Last Supper (xiii), recorded with no reference to its sacramental features, the arrest (xviii. 1–12), trials and Peter's denial (xviii. 13–xix. 16), the crucifixion and resurrection (xx–xxi). Yet in this section also there is much material not found in the synoptic Gospels, especially the last discourses and prayer (xiv–xvi, xvii), the details of the trial before Pilate (xviii. 28–xix. 16), and the resurrection appearances.

There is no need to doubt that this historical outline corresponds broadly to the actual order of events, although it must be remembered that John has recorded only a few incidents and arranged them from the standpoint of his presentation of Jesus as the Messiah.

b. The theological content

(i) *John as revelation.* This historical outline is the vehicle of a theological presentation of Jesus. John's purpose is to reveal the *glory* of Jesus as the Son of God. As the pre-existent Son He shared the glory of the Father (xvii. 5, 24), and in His earthly life His glory was demonstrated to the world—or rather to those who had eyes to see (i. 14)—in the series of signs which He wrought (ii. 11). Yet in these signs Jesus was seeking not His own glory but that of the Father (v. 41, vii. 18). This revelation of Jesus before the world is the theme of i–xii, which concludes with a summarizing passage and a clear break in thought (xii. 36b–50). Since the world had largely not believed in Him (xii. 37), Jesus turned to His disciples, and in xiii–xvii we have a revelation of His glory, seen in humble service, to the disciples, who were themselves also called to a life in which God is glorified (xv. 8, xxi. 19). But a theme which had been hinted at earlier also finds expression here, namely that Jesus is supremely glorified in His passion and death. Thus the third section of the Gospel (xviii–xxi) shows us that the hour has come in which Jesus is glorified as the Son of God and glorifies God.

At the same time the Gospel may be regarded as a revelation of *truth* (i. 14, 17). In the Gospel the world is characterized by error, imperfection, and sin, because it has lost contact with God who is the true One (vii. 28); to it Jesus brings the truth of God (xviii. 37). He Himself is the incarnation of truth (xiv. 6) and will be succeeded by the Spirit of truth (xiv. 17). He leads men to a true worship of God (iv. 23 f.) and frees them from the errors of the devil (viii. 44) through knowledge of the truth (viii. 32). In contrast to the empty satisfactions of the world He brings true, real bread for the souls of men (vi. 32, 55).

(ii) *Signs and witnesses.* The way in which this revelation is brought to men is twofold. First, there are the *signs* or *works* performed by Jesus, seven of which (excluding the resurrection) are related at length. They are signs not simply because they are evidence of a miraculous, supernatural power (iv. 48) but rather because by their character they show that their author is sent by God (ix. 16) as the Messiah and Son of God (iii. 2, vi. 14, vii. 31); they thus authenticate His person to those who have eyes to see (ii. 23, xii. 37).

Usually these signs are the basis of a discourse or dialogue in which their spiritual significance is brought out. There is, however, what may be regarded as a further series of signs in words. Seven times (vi. 35, viii. 12, x. 7, 11, xi. 25, xiv. 6, xv. 1, to which viii. 24 is perhaps to be added)

Jesus says, 'I am . . .' A number of concepts, all of them already current in religious language, are here taken over by Jesus and used to explain who He is and what He has come to do. What is especially significant is that this use of 'I am' contains a veiled claim to deity.

Second, the glory of Jesus is attested by *witnesses*. Jesus Himself came to bear witness to the truth (xviii. 37), and witness is borne to Him by John the Baptist, the woman of Samaria, the crowd who saw His signs (xii. 17), the disciples (xv. 27), the witness at the cross (xix. 35), and the evangelist himself (xxi. 24). Witness is also given by the Scriptures (v. 39), by the Father (v. 37), and by Jesus' signs (x. 25). Such witness was meant to lead men to faith (iv. 39, v. 34).

(iii) *The Person of Jesus.* These signs and witnesses are thus meant to show that Jesus is the Son of God who offers life to men. Right at the beginning of the Gospel He is affirmed to be the *Word* (*Logos*) of God (i. 14, 17). Although this technical term does not recur in John, it is plain that the rest of the Gospel is an exposition and justification of the doctrine that the Word became flesh. The use of 'Word' is singularly happy, for by it John was able to speak to Jews who had already taken some steps towards regarding God's creative Word (Ps. xxxiii. 6) as in some sense a separate being from God (*cf.* the figurative description of Wisdom in Pr. viii. 22 ff.), to Christians who preached the Word of God and virtually identified it with Jesus (*cf.* Col. iv. 3 with Eph. vi. 19), and to educated pagans who saw the Word as the principle of order and rationality in the universe (popular Stoicism). But what John says goes far beyond anything that had previously been said. (See also LOGOS.)

Second, Jesus is the *Messiah* from the house of David awaited by the Jews (vii. 42). In fact, the great question for the Jews is whether Jesus is the Messiah (vii. 26 ff., x. 24), and the confession of the disciples is that this is precisely who He is (i. 41, iv. 29, xi. 27, xx. 31).

Third, He is the *Son of Man.* This term is the key to Jesus' understanding of Himself in the synoptic Gospels, where it is connected with three ideas, the 'hiddenness' of His Messiahship, the necessity of His suffering, and His function as judge at the parousia. These ideas are latent in John (*cf.* xii. 34, iii. 14, v. 27), but the emphasis falls on the two ideas that the Son of Man has been sent from heaven as the revealer of God and the Saviour of men (iii. 13, ix. 35) and that He is glorified by being 'lifted up' to die (xii. 23, 34).

Fourth, He is *Son of God.* This is probably the most important title of Jesus in John. Since the heart of the gospel is that God sent His Son as Saviour (iii. 16), John's purpose is to lead the reader to recognize the claim of Jesus (xix. 7) and make the confession of the disciples (i. 34, 49, xi. 27) that He is the Son of God. As Son, He reveals the Father (i. 18), whose activities of life-giving and judgment He shares (v. 19–29). Through belief in Him men receive salvation (iii. 36) and freedom (viii. 36).

But to say that Jesus is the Son of God is, fifth, to ascribe full deity to Him. Thus He who as the Word of God is Himself *God* (i. 1), is also confessed by men on earth as Lord and God (xx. 28, which is the climax of the Gospel; *cf.* also i. 18, RSVmg).

(iv) *The work of Jesus.* A further set of titles expresses what Jesus came to do for men and what He offers them. These are summed up in xiv. 6, where Jesus claims to be the way, the truth, and the life. The last of these words, *life*, is the favourite word in John for salvation. The world of men is in a state of death (v. 24 f.) and is destined for judgment (iii. 18, 36). What Jesus offers to men is life, defined by John as knowledge of God and Jesus Christ (xvii. 3). Jesus Himself can thus be called the life (i. 4, xi. 25, xiv. 6), the giver of *living water* (*i.e.* life-bestowing water, iv. 14), and *living bread* (vi. 33 f.). To receive Jesus by believing in Him (iii. 36, vi. 29) is to receive the bread of life, and to eat the flesh and drink the blood of Jesus (an expression in which many scholars see an allusion to the Lord's Supper) is to partake of eternal life (vi. 54).

This same truth is presented in the picture of Jesus as the *light* of the world (viii. 12), developed especially in ix. The state of men is now regarded as blindness (ix. 39–41) or darkness (iii. 19, xii. 46), and Jesus is the one who cures blindness and gives the light of life to those who walk in darkness. He is also depicted as the *way* to God (xiv. 1–7). This idea is hinted at in x. 9, where He is the *door* of the sheepfold, but here another idea becomes prominent—that Jesus is the *good shepherd* who gives His life for the sheep and gathers them into His sheepfold. Three vital ideas are contained in this description. First, Jesus is the true fulfilment of the Old Testament promise of a shepherd for the people of God. (Note that life and light are Jewish descriptions of the Law which finds its fulfilment in Jesus.) Second, His death is not simply due to the opposition of His enemies, but is a saving death on behalf of men (x. 11) by which they are drawn to God (xii. 32). Only through a sacrificial death can sin be removed (i. 29) and life be given to the world (vi. 51b). Third, the picture of a flock introduces the idea of the Church.

(v) *The new life.* Jesus is thus portrayed as the *Saviour* of the world (iv. 42). In His presence men face the decisive moment in which they either accept Him and pass from death to life (v. 24) or remain in darkness until the day of judgment (xii. 46–48).

Such acceptance of Jesus occurs when the Father draws men to His Son (vi. 44). Through the work of the Spirit of God, whose movement is beyond human comprehension, there then takes place the radical change known as the *new birth* (iii. 1–21) by which a man becomes a son of God (i. 12).

From the human side this change is the product of *faith*, which is centred on the Son of God who was lifted up on the cross to save the world (iii. 14–18). A distinction is drawn between two kinds of faith—intellectual acceptance of the claims of Jesus (xi. 42, viii. 24, xi. 27, xx. 31), which by itself is not sufficient, and full self-committal to Him (iii. 16, iv. 42, ix. 35–38, xiv. 1).

Such faith is closely related to *knowledge*. Whereas ordinary men have no real knowledge of God (i. 10, xvi. 3), through knowledge of Jesus men can know the Father (viii. 19, xiv. 7). The content of this knowledge is not stated in John; there is no place here for the esoteric revelations characteristic of the mystery religions. Our only clue is that the way in which men know God and are known by Him is analogous to the way in which Jesus knows God and is known by Him (x. 14 f.).

One thing, however, can be said. This new relationship is characterized by *love*. Disciples share in a relationship of mutual love with God like that which exists between the Father and the Son (iii. 35, xiv. 31), though it is to be noted that their love is directed towards the Son rather than towards the Father (xiv. 23, xv. 9, xvii. 26, xxi. 15–17, *cf.* v. 42; 1 Jn. iv. 20 f.).

Other expressions are also used to express this communion of disciples with Jesus. They are said to *abide* in Him (vi. 56, xv. 4–10), and He abides in them (vi. 56, *cf.* xiv. 17). The preposition *in* is also important in describing the close relationship of mutual indwelling between God and Jesus and between Jesus and His disciples (xiv. 20, 23, xvii. 21, 23, 26).

(vi) *The people of God.* Although the word 'church' is not found in John, the idea is most certainly present. To be a disciple is automatically to be a member of the *flock* whose shepherd is Jesus. Jesus also uses the concept of the *vine* (xv. 1–8). A new vine is to replace the old vine (*i.e.* the earthly people of Israel); Jesus Himself is the stem, and from Him life flows to the branches and enables them to bear fruit.

The life of disciples is characterized by a *love* which follows the example of Jesus, who humbly washed His disciples' feet (xiii. 1–20, 34 f.). Such love is in contrast with the attitude of the world which *hates* and *persecutes* the disciples (xv. 18–xvi. 4, 32 f.), and its result is that the Church shows that *unity* for which Jesus prays in xvii.

But the Church is no closed fellowship; others are to come to belief through the word of the disciples (xvii. 20). This is confirmed in xxi, where the idea of *mission* or sending (xx. 21) is developed. The 153 fish are symbolic of the spread of the gospel to all men, and the task of the good shepherd is handed on from the Master to the disciples.

(vii) *Eschatology.* Jesus thus looks forward to the continuing life of the Church after His glorification (xiv. 12). In anticipation of His second advent He promises to come to the Church (xiv. 18) in the person of the *Spirit*. The Spirit comes to the individual disciple (vii. 37–39) and to the Church (xiv. 16 f., 26, xv. 26, xvi. 7–11, 13–15), and His function is to take the place of Jesus (as '*another* comforter') and glorify Him.

It may thus be said that in John the future is 'realized' in the present; Jesus comes again through the Spirit to His disciples, they already partake of eternal life, and already the process of judgment is at work. Yet it would be wrong to conclude that the future activity of God is replaced by His present activity in John. No less than in the rest of the New Testament is the future coming of Jesus (xiv. 3, xxi. 23) and the future judgment of all men (v. 25–29) taught.

IV. TEXTUAL PROBLEMS AND SOURCE CRITICISM

Two passages in the AV of John do not belong to the original text and are removed to the margin in RV and RSV. These are the *Pericope de Adulteria* (vii. 53–viii. 11), a genuine story about Jesus which has been preserved outside the canonical Gospels and found its way into certain late MSS of John, and the explanation of the moving of the water (v. 3b–4), which is omitted in the best MSS.

A special problem is raised by xxi. While E. C. Hoskyns held that it was an integral part of the original Gospel, the majority of scholars think that it was either a later addition of the author or (less probably) that it was added by another hand. The main argument is that xx. 31 reads like the conclusion of a book; some scholars also find stylistic differences between xxi and i–xx, but in the opinion of C. K. Barrett these are not in themselves decisive.

Until recently it was fashionable to believe that the present order of the material in John was not that of the author but had been seriously altered, perhaps by loose sheets of papyrus being combined in the wrong order. There is, however, no objective textual evidence for this, although the phenomenon is not unknown in ancient literature. The displacements found in xviii in certain MSS are clearly secondary, and Tatian (*c.* 170), who made some alterations in order when he was combining the Gospels in a single narrative, does not support modern reconstructions. It is significant that three of the most outstanding recent English writers on John (E. C. Hoskyns, C. H. Dodd, C. K. Barrett) find no need for such theories.

Attempts have also been made, most comprehensively by R. Bultmann, to trace the use of written sources and editorial activity in John. But the literary analysis practised is of doubtful reliability and Bultmann's conclusions have not commended themselves to other scholars.

(For further details, see W. F. Howard, *The Fourth Gospel in Recent Criticism and Interpretation*[4], 1955.)

V. THE BACKGROUND OF THOUGHT

After a period in which John was regarded as a Hellenistic book, to which the closest parallels were to be found in a strongly Hellenized Judaism, mystery religions and even Greek philosophy, there is at present a rediscovery of the essentially Jewish background of the Gospel.

Much evidence has been found of Aramaic

traditions behind the synoptic Gospels and John (M. Black, *An Aramaic Approach to the Gospels and Acts*[2], 1954). There are signs that an Aramaic sayings source lies behind John—Aramaic being, of course, the mother tongue of Jesus. The thought in John is often expressed with the parataxis and parallelism which are well-known features of Semitic writing. All the indications are that the linguistic background of John is Aramaic, although the theory that it was originally written in Aramaic is unconvincing.

This naturally means that the thought of John is likely to be Jewish, which is in fact the case. Although there are comparatively few quotations, most of the key ideas in John are taken from the Old Testament (*e.g.* word, life, light, shepherd, Spirit, bread, vine, love, witness), and Jesus is portrayed as the fulfilment of the Old Testament.

Parallels with contemporary Jewish thought, especially with orthodox rabbinic Judaism, may also be found, it being only natural that Jesus and His followers should often have agreed with the Old Testament scholars of their time and been influenced—both positively and negatively—by them (*cf.* v. 39, vii. 42). Since Palestinian Judaism had been subject to Hellenistic influences for about two centuries, there is no need to look wider for Hellenistic influence upon John. The degree of resemblance between ideas found in John and in Philo of Alexandria is variously estimated.

The Jewish sectarian texts from Qumran also help to fill in the background of John, although their importance for the understanding of the New Testament tends to be exaggerated. Attention is usually drawn to the dualism of light and darkness and to the messianic hopes found in the texts, but the roots of these ideas lie in the Old Testament, and it is doubtful whether a direct influence from Qumran upon John requires to be postulated. (See F. M. Braun, 'L'Arrière-Fond Judaïque de Quatrième Évangile et la Communauté de l'Alliance', *RB*, LXII, 1955, pp. 5–44.)

Other possible formative influences are discussed in detail by C. H. Dodd. He rightly rejects Mandaism, a pagan-Christian syncretism whose earliest literature is considerably later than John. But he devotes considerable attention to Hellenistic mystery religion, especially as depicted in the *Corpus Hermeticum*, a series of tracts probably emanating from Egypt in the 3rd century in their present form. But, while there are interesting parallels of thought which demonstrate that John would be intelligible to pagans and not merely to Jews, a close affiliation of thought is unlikely. (*Cf.* G. D. Kilpatrick in *Studies in the Fourth Gospel*, ed. F. L. Cross, 1957.)

In the 2nd century there was a developed Christian gnosticism, and we must certainly think of some kind of 'pre-gnosticism' in the 1st century, reflected in the polemic in Colossians and 1 John. The theory that John was influenced by the gnostic heretics whom he opposes (*cf.* II above) was propounded by E. F. Scott (*The Fourth Gospel*[2], 1908, pp. 86–103); more recently than this R. Bultmann has argued that in John Jesus is presented in terms of gnostic myths. The view of C. H. Dodd that Johannine Christianity is entirely different from gnosticism in spite of a common background (*op. cit.*, p. 114) does much greater justice to the facts.

Within the early Christian world the Johannine literature occupies a unique place and represents an independently developed strand of thought. Nevertheless, its teaching is that of the Christian Church generally, and the differences from, say, Paul are more of form than of content. (*Cf.* A. M. Hunter, *The Unity of the New Testament*, 1943.)

VI. EXTERNAL ATTESTATION

The existence of John is attested in Egypt before AD 150 by the Rylands Papyrus 457, the earliest known fragment of a New Testament MS.

The use of John as an authoritative Gospel alongside the other three is attested by the Egerton Papyrus 2, also dated before 150 (C. H. Dodd, *New Testament Studies*, 1953, pp. 12–52). It was also used by Tatian in his *Diatessaron*, and Irenaeus (*c.* 180) speaks of a four-Gospel canon. John was certainly also known and used in heretical gnostic circles—*e.g.* by Ptolemaeus, a disciple of Valentinus, by the *Gospel of Peter* (*c.* 150), and (fairly certainly) by the author of the Valentinian *Gospel of Truth*. Knowledge of John by other writers in this period is difficult to attest. There are traces of Johannine language in Ignatius (*c.* 115) and Justin (*c.* 150–160), but it is questionable whether literary dependence is indicated.

Traditions about the authorship of John are given by Irenaeus, who states that John, the disciple of the Lord, gave out the Gospel at Ephesus. This tradition is repeated by Clement of Alexandria (*c.* 200) and the anti-Marcionite prologue to John; the 2nd-century date of the latter is, however, suspect. The Muratorian Canon (*c.* 180–200) gives a legend in which John the apostle is the author, and the apostolic authorship was accepted by Ptolemaeus. But Papias, who had close access to apostolic traditions, is silent on the matter, and Polycarp, who was an associate of John according to Irenaeus, quotes the Epistles but not the Gospel. Nor do the apocryphal *Acts of John* say anything about the Gospel. At the beginning of the 3rd century there was some opposition to the apostolic authorship of John, possibly because of the use made of it by the gnostics.

VII. AUTHORSHIP

At the end of the 19th century the view that John the apostle wrote the Fourth Gospel was widely accepted on the basis of the external evidence set out above and the internal evidence. The latter received its classical formulation from B. F. Westcott and from J. B. Lightfoot (*Biblical Essays*, 1893, pp. 1–198), who demonstrated that the Gospel was written by a Jew, by a Palestinian Jew, by an eye-witness of the events recorded, by an apostle, and, in particular, by the apostle John, who is referred to as the 'beloved disciple'.

A number of arguments have been raised against this chain of reasoning. First, there is the theory that John died as a martyr at an early age, but this is rightly rejected by the majority of scholars. (See JOHN, THE APOSTLE.)

Second, the alleged geographical and historical inaccuracy of John is held to militate against authorship by an eye-witness. The most recent archaeology has, however, confirmed the geographical accuracy of John in a striking way (*cf.* R. D. Potter, 'Topography and Archaeology in the Fourth Gospel', in *Studia Evangelica*, pp. 329–337). For the historical problem, see below.

Third, it is alleged that the apostle John was incapable of writing such a Gospel. He was an unlearned man—a view which finds its only and inadequate basis in a questionable exegesis of Acts iv. 13 and ignores such analogies as Bunyan, the Bedford tinker. As an apostle he could not have written a Gospel so different from the other three—a view which does not take into account the special purpose of John and the fact that we have no other Gospel directly written by an apostle for comparison. As a Jew he could not have the mastery of Hellenistic thought seen in the Gospel—see, however, v above. Finally, nobody would presume to call himself the 'beloved disciple'—which is, however, no more than a subjective argument (those who find it weighty can attribute the use of the title to John's scribe).

Fourth, the weightiest argument is the slowness of the Church to accept John's Gospel. The reliability of Irenaeus has been called in question (but with uncertain justification), and it has been observed that the people who might be expected to know John and quote from it fail to do so. Against this must be pointed out the general weakness of arguments from silence (*cf.* W. F. Howard, *op. cit.*, p. 273) and the fact that the evidence for the acceptance and use of the other three Gospels is almost equally scanty before the period in which we find all four Gospels accepted together. Further, we are completely ignorant of the circumstances of publication of John except for the brief note in xxi. 24.

It may be taken as quite certain that we can safely disregard any theory which denies a connection between John the apostle and the Gospel. Three possibilities then arise. First, John may have composed it himself with the aid of an amanuensis. Second, a disciple of John may have used the memoirs of John or a Johannine tradition as the basis for the Gospel. A third possibility, which is a variant of the second, is that there was a Johannine 'school', possibly to be linked with southern Palestine, in which the characteristic Johannine theology was developed and whose members produced the Johannine literature. It is, however, difficult to bring forward decisive evidence for or against such a theory. (One may compare K. Stendahl's hypothesis of a Matthaean school, the evidence for which is still flimsy.)

It is difficult to decide between the first two theories. But the tradition that John dictated the Gospel is widespread (*cf.* R. V. G. Tasker, *op. cit.* below, pp. 17–20) and bears the marks of genuineness. With all due caution, therefore, it may be suggested that there are still good grounds for maintaining a close association of John the apostle with the actual writing of the Gospel so that he may justly be regarded as its real author.

(For 'John the elder' and the authorship of the other Johannine literature, see JOHN, EPISTLES OF, V.)

VIII. PROVENANCE AND DATE

Early tradition connects John the apostle with Asia Minor and in particular with Ephesus. A connection with Asia Minor is most suitable for 1–3 John and is demanded by Revelation; whether the author of the latter be the evangelist or an associate of his, this strengthens the case for Asia.

The claims of other places cannot, however, be ignored. The apparent lack of knowledge of John in Asia gives weight to the claims of Alexandria: here John was certainly known very early by the gnostics (*cf.* also the papyri), the climate of thought (Hellenistic Judaism) could be regarded as suitable, and the general remoteness of Alexandria would explain the Gospel's slow circulation. There is, however, no tradition connecting John with Alexandria. The claims of Antioch have also been pressed, but they are hardly strong. There is now a tendency to connect John with southern Palestine in view of its background of thought, but this only confirms that for some part of his life the author was resident in Palestine.

John is usually dated in the nineties. This view is based on the assumed dependence of John on the synoptic Gospels (but see IX below) and the alleged post-Pauline character of its theology. While there is no need to regard John as dependent on Paulinism, it is difficult to avoid the impression that it is not an early writing. If it is connected with Ephesus it must be placed after the activity of Paul there; this is confirmed by the date of 1–3 John, which is hardly earlier than the sixties. If John is connected with some other place of composition, *e.g.* Palestine, an earlier date is possible but remains unlikely. The real point of the 'Palestinian background' argument is that the date no longer needs to be put extremely late in order to account for the development of thought. (*Cf.* J. A. T. Robinson, 'The New Look on the Fourth Gospel', in *Studia Evangelica*, pp. 338–350.)

IX. RELATION TO THE SYNOPTIC GOSPELS

a. Knowledge of the synoptic tradition

The accepted opinion until about twenty years ago was that John knew the synoptic Gospels, or at least Mark and Luke, and that he wrote in order to correct, supplement, or replace them. This view has been subjected to sharp criticism by such authors as P. Gardner-Smith (*St. John and the Synoptic Gospels*, 1938) and B. Noack (*Zur Johanneischen Tradition*, 1954), who argue that John was simply dependent on the oral tradition which lies behind the synoptic Gospels, and that he wrote quite independently of them. The closest contacts are between John and Luke, especially in the passion narrative, but it is doubtful whether these prove literary dependence; Luke may well have had access to the traditions recorded in John or even had personal acquaintance with its author (*cf.* G. W. Broomfield, *John, Peter and the Fourth Gospel*, 1934).

The external evidence must also be taken into account. Papias' information about Mark and the Logia came from [John] 'the elder', who *may* be connected with the composition of John. Clement of Alexandria wrote, 'Last of all, John, perceiving that the external facts had been made plain in the Gospel, being urged by his friends, and inspired by the Spirit, composed a spiritual Gospel.' We can, of course, accept this description of John as the spiritual Gospel without believing that John wrote out of a knowledge of the other Gospels, but it is difficult to believe that he did not have some idea of their contents, even if he did not have copies of them before him as he wrote. The question, then, must be regarded as still open.

b. Comparison of the narratives

Two problems arise here. The first is whether the synoptic and Johannine narratives are compatible with each other and can be worked into a single account. It is a fact that attempts can be made to fit the two together in a reasonably convincing manner and thus to shed new light on both. (For a recent attempt, see E. Stauffer, *Jesus and His Story*, 1960.) This is possible because the two accounts describe the activity of Jesus at different periods and in different localities; the old-fashioned idea that the synoptic Gospels leave no room for a ministry in Jerusalem (other than in the passion narrative) is now quite discredited. It must be remembered, of course, that none of the Gospels pretends to give an exact chronological narrative, so that a detailed reconstruction of the order of events is impossible.

The second problem concerns the cases where historical contradictions appear to arise between the Gospels, including cases where it is held that John is consciously correcting data given in the synoptic Gospels. Examples of this are the reason for Jesus' arrest (in particular, the question why the raising of Lazarus is omitted in the synoptic narrative; see a possible answer in J. N. Sanders, 'Those whom Jesus Loved', *NTS*, I, 1954–5, p. 34); the date of the cleansing of the Temple; and the date of the last supper and crucifixion (see N. Geldenhuys, *Commentary on the Gospel of Luke*, 1950, pp. 649–670). The extent of such difficulties can be exaggerated, but it must be admitted that some real problems exist to which answers have yet to be found. In any case the substance of the Gospel records is not affected by these differences.

c. The discourses in John

The teaching ascribed to Jesus in John differs markedly in content and style from that in the synoptic Gospels. Such familiar ideas as the kingdom of God, demons, repentance, and prayer are missing, and new topics appear, such as truth, life, the world, abiding, and witness. At the same time there are close and intricate connections between the two traditions, and common themes appear, *e.g.* Father, Son of Man, faith, love, and sending. The style and vocabulary also differ. There are no parables in John, and Jesus often speaks in long discourses or dialogues which are unparalleled in the synoptic Gospels.

Many scholars, therefore, believe that John gives us his own thoughts or his own meditations upon the words of Jesus rather than His *ipsissima verba*. This conclusion is strongly supported by the fact that a very similar style and content is found in 1 John. Nevertheless, it must be carefully qualified. First, John contains many sayings which are similar in form and content to synoptic sayings (*cf.* B. Noack, *op. cit.*, pp. 89–109; C. H. Dodd, 'Some Johannine "Herrnworte" with Parallels in the Synoptic Gospels', *NTS*, II, 1955–6, pp. 75–86) and which have equal right to be regarded as authentic. Second, there is, on the other hand, at least one famous 'bolt from the Johannine blue' in the synoptic Gospels (Mt. xi. 25–27) which is a standing warning against the facile assumption that the synoptic Jesus did not speak the language of the Johannine Jesus. Third, the same traces of Aramaic speech and the same conformity to Jewish methods of discussion are to be found in John as in the synoptic Gospels.

Thus we can say with considerable confidence that the sayings recorded in John have a firm historical basis in the actual words of Jesus. They have, however, been preserved in a Johannine commentary from which they can be separated only with great difficulty. (*Cf.* the problem of Gal. ii. 14 ff.; where does Paul's speech to Peter end and his meditation upon it begin?) This is no radical conclusion. So conservative a scholar as Westcott saw, for example, the words of John rather than of Jesus in iii. 16–21.

X. HISTORY AND INTERPRETATION IN JOHN

The purpose of John (see II above) demands that, in broad outline at least, the contents of John be regarded as history; it completely fails of attainment if John gives us a legendary construction devised to substantiate the Church's preaching of Jesus as the Messiah instead of the historical facts which lie behind and authenticate that preaching. (See C. F. D. Moule, 'The Intention of the Evangelists', in *New Testament Essays*, ed. A. J. B. Higgins, 1959, pp. 165–179.)

It has already been suggested that many of the

difficulties commonly raised against the historicity of John are by no means so serious as they are often made out to be. There is in fact a growing tendency to recognize that John contains important historical traditions about Jesus and that an adequate understanding of His earthly life cannot be obtained from the synoptic Gospels alone (*cf.* T. W. Manson, 'The Life of Jesus: A Survey of the Available Material (5)', *BJRL*, XXX, 1947, pp. 312–329).

On the other hand, the total impression given by John after a reading of the synoptic Gospels is that here we have an interpretation of Jesus rather than a strictly literal account of His life. The teaching which He gives is different and the picture of His person is also different, particularly as regards His messianic and filial self-consciousness. Yet it would be unwise to over-emphasize these differences. Jesus is no less human in John than in the other Gospels, and even the 'messianic secrecy' of the synoptic Gospels is not altogether absent from John. F. F. Bruce can go so far as to say that there is no fundamental discrepancy between the Jesus of the synoptic Gospels and of John (*The New Testament Documents*: *Are They Reliable?*[5], 1960, pp. 60 f.).

What this amounts to is that John does not contradict the other Gospels but interprets the Person who is depicted in them. While the other evangelists have given us a photograph of Jesus, John has given us a portrait (W. Temple, *op. cit.* below, p. xvi). Consequently, in the light of what has been said, John can be used as a source for the life of Jesus and for John's interpretation of that life, even if it is impossible to separate these two rigidly from each other. The earthly life of Jesus cannot be completely understood in isolation from His revelation of Himself as the risen Lord to His Church. Under the inspiration of the Spirit (*cf.* xiv. 26, xvi. 14) John has brought out the meaning of the earthly life of Jesus; he interprets the story of Jesus, and in doing so he gives us, in the words of A. M. Hunter, 'the true meaning of the earthly story' (*Introducing New Testament Theology*, 1957, p. 129).

Bibliography. Commentaries on the English text: B. F. Westcott, 1882 and later (also on the Gk. text, 1908); E. C. Hoskyns and F. N. Davey[2], 1947; R. H. Lightfoot, 1956; R. V. G. Tasker (*TNTC*), 1960. Commentaries on the Gk. text: C. K. Barrett, 1955. Expository: G. C. Morgan, 1933; W. Temple, 1945. In German: A. Schlatter, 1930 and later; R. Bultmann (*KEK*)[4], 1959.

I.H.M.

JOKNEAM, JOKMEAM. 1. A Canaanite town (Jos. xii. 22), possibly no. 113 of the Tuthmosis III list. It may be identified with modern Tell Keimun on the coastal road, 7 miles north-west of Megiddo, east of the Wadi el-Milh. The river near by marked the western limit of Zebulun (Jos. xix. 11) and, apparently, of a Solomonic district (1 Ki. iv. 12; *MT* *'aḏ mē'ēḇer lᵉyoqmᵉ'ām*; Simons, *GTT*, p. 350, suggests *ma'ᵃḇār*, 'ford' or 'pass'). In Jos. xxi. 34 Jokneam is named as a levitical city in Zebulun. **2.** In 1 Ch. vi. 68 the name Jokmeam is used for the city in south-west Ephraim which is called Kibzaim in Jos. xxi. 22.

Bibliography. Garstang, *Joshua*, p. 91; *GTT*, p. 206; E. Robinson, *Biblical Researches*, 1841, III, pp. 114 f. J.P.U.L.

JOKSHAN. A son of Abraham and Keturah, and father of Sheba and Dedan (Gn. xxv. 2, 3; 1 Ch. i. 32). The name is sometimes assumed to be another form of Joktan (Gn. x. 25–29; 1 Ch. i. 19–23), but the bearers of these names are kept distinct in the genealogical lists. R.J.W.

JOKTAN. A son of Eber of the family of Shem, and father of Almodad, Sheleph, Hazarmaveth, Jerah, Hadoram, Uzal, Diklah, Obal, Abimael, Sheba, Ophir, Havilah, and Jobab (Gn. x. 25, 26, 29; 1 Ch. i. 19, 20, 23), many of whom have been connected with tribes in S Arabia. The name is unknown outside the Bible, but on the basis of the descendants a region of occupation in S or SW Arabia may be postulated. The modern tribes of S Arabia claim that the pure Arabs are descended from Joktan.

Bibliography. J. A. Montgomery, *Arabia and the Bible*, 1934, pp. 37–42; W. Thesiger, *Arabian Sands*, 1960, p. 77. T.C.M.

JONADAB. See Jehonadab.

JONAH. Hebrew personal name, meaning 'dove'. The New Testament form of the name in AV is normally Jonas, twice Jona. **1.** A Hebrew prophet of the reign of Jeroboam II of Israel, in the 8th century BC. He came from Gath-hepher, a Zebulunite town, located in the vicinity of Nazareth. His father's name was Amittai. He predicted the territorial expansion achieved by Jeroboam at the expense of Syria (2 Ki. xiv. 25). This Jonah is also the hero of the book that bears his name, the fifth of the twelve Minor Prophets. The book differs considerably from the other Old Testament Prophets in that it is almost entirely narrative and contains no long prophetic oracles. (See the following article.)

2. The father of Simon Peter, according to Mt. xvi. 17. Some MSS of Jn. i. 42, xxi. 15 ff. also call him Jonah (*cf.* AV rendering), but the best attested reading here is 'John' (*cf.* RV). D.F.P.

JONAH, BOOK OF.

I. OUTLINE OF CONTENTS

The book is divided into four chapters, which neatly divide the subject-matter. The first chapter relates that Jonah, bidden by God to go to Nineveh and protest against its wickedness, rebelled and took ship in the opposite direction. A storm arose, and the sailors eventually threw Jonah overboard, at his own suggestion. A great fish then swallowed the prophet. Chapter ii gives the text of his prayer, or rather psalm of thanksgiving, from the fish's belly. The fish presently disgorged Jonah on to the shore. Chapter iii shows Jonah going to Nineveh, after all. His preaching of doom led the citizens to repent of their evil ways. In chapter iv we find Jonah angry at their repentance and subsequent escape from destruction; whereupon God, by inducing Jonah's pity on a plant, taught him that he must have compassion for all men.

II. AUTHORSHIP AND DATE

The book gives no indication who its author was. Jonah himself may have written it, but the book nowhere uses the first person (contrast, for example, Ho. iii. 1); and the probability of a date later than the 8th century is indicated by the implication of Jon. iii. 3 that Nineveh was no more (it was destroyed in 612 BC). If Jonah was not the author, nobody can say who did write it. The date of writing, then, may have been in the 8th century, but was more probably not earlier than the 6th century. The twelve Minor Prophets were known and venerated by the end of the 3rd century (*cf.* Ecclus. xlix. 10), so a 3rd-century date for the book is the latest it can possibly be allowed. The universalistic emphasis of the book is frequently considered to be a protest against the ultra-nationalistic spirit of the Jews after the time of Ezra. However, universalistic passages occur as early as the 8th century (*cf.* Is. ii. 2 ff.). Thus the universalistic approach does not definitely indicate a post-exilic date; indeed, the book would presumably have received less welcome and ready recognition after the time of Ezra. Nor are the arguments for a late date given above conclusive.

III. MESSAGE AND NATURE

The primary message of the book is clearly that God's interest and mercy extend far beyond the Jews to the whole human race. The readiness of the people of Nineveh to repent was also a salutary lesson to the Jews, who were renowned for their stubbornness and lack of faith. Christ Himself drew this lesson from the book (Mt. xii. 41); He also drew attention to the three days and nights spent by Jonah inside the fish: this 'sign' to the Ninevites He would reproduce for His own generation by spending a similar period in the tomb (Mt. xii. 40; Lk. xi. 30).

The nature of the book is a much more controversial topic. It has been explained as mythology, commentary, allegory, parable, and history. The mythological parallels from the folklore of other nations are, however, few and precarious; the only point of contact is the feature of a man surviving being swallowed by a large sea-creature. Nor is it likely that the book is a commentary on 2 Ki. xiv. 25, relating stories which had gathered round the prophet's name; the book seems too neatly arranged and to have too obvious a didactic purpose for that. The suggestion that it is a Jewish commentary on certain universalistic passages in Isaiah and Jeremiah is somewhat more credible. The allegorical interpretation is less improbable still: Jonah represents the nation of Israel, the fish is Babylon, the swallowing the Exile, *etc.* Such complex allegories are frequent in rabbinic literature, certainly, but at a much later date. The parabolic interpretation is simpler and more likely. Those who hold this view claim that the book is merely a moral tale with a didactic end in view, comparable with Nathan's story to David (2 Sa. xii. 1 ff.) or with our Lord's parable of the Good Samaritan (Lk. x. 30 ff.), which, of course, sought to teach the same lesson as the book of Jonah. The parabolic viewpoint is not merely an expedient to avoid believing in the miracle of Jonah's emerging alive from the fish's belly, as has sometimes been claimed. Such parables are frequent in Scripture; the chief arguments against this interpretation are the unparalleled length of the story, and the fact that the moral is not pointed (contrast the 'Thou art the man' of Nathan, the 'Go and do thou likewise' of our Lord).

IV. HISTORICAL INTERPRETATION

The historical interpretation is based on the obvious sense of the text, and the fact that the story is applied to a definite and historical figure, Jonah the son of Amittai (whereas the characters in the above-mentioned parables are anonymous). Certainly Jewish tradition accepted the book as history, and our Lord's references to it, quoted above, probably, though not necessarily, imply that He did so too. The historical interpretation is, however, challenged on several points, notably the miracle of the fish, the vast size attributed to Nineveh, the statement that its king and citizens not only listened to a Heb. prophet but without hesitation or exception repented, and lastly, the unnaturally fast rate of growth of the gourd. However, it may be that the first was a genuine miracle; in any case the story may have modern parallels. The growth of the gourd might again be miraculous; or, more simply, one can claim that Jon. iv. 10 is not intended to be strictly literal. As for the size of Nineveh (Jon. iii. 3), it is possible that the author intended a much bigger area than the city itself; confirmation of this may be seen in the fact that he refers to a 'king of Nineveh' (iii. 6), whereas other Old Testament writers speak of kings of Assyria, of which country Nineveh was the capital. But see NINEVEH. It can also be asserted that in the low fortunes of Assyria prior to the accession of Tiglath-pileser III (745 BC) the Ninevites would readily have listened to a prophet who forecast disaster unless they repented. Theirs was a polytheistic religion, so they might well have sought to avoid offending even a foreign unknown deity.

It is fair to say that none of the objections to the historical interpretation is insuperable. The same might be said about the parabolic interpretation. The choice seems to rest, therefore, between these two.

V. COMPOSITION

As regards the composition of the book, it appears to be an entity, with the possible exception of the psalm (ii. 2–9). It has been pointed out that ii. 10 follows ii. 1 naturally, without any break in sense; and that this psalm has many parallels with phrases in the book of Psalms. These facts by no means prove that the passage is interpolated, however. The psalm is not inapposite to the situation (*i.e.* Jonah's having been rescued from drowning), even if a plea for deliverance from the fish's belly might have been expected. The fact that the parallels in the Psalms use language of the sea metaphorically is no proof that that is what was intended here. The author (whether Jonah or not) may well have realized how very apt these well-known phrases were to the situation depicted here. Nor is it to be expected that a passage of direct speech would add much to, or alter radically, the narrative of events in which it appears. Perhaps, then, if the author did not compose the psalm himself, he found it, and recognizing it to be suitable for his purpose, utilized it accordingly.

BIBLIOGRAPHY. G. Ch. Aalders, *The Problem of the Book of Jonah*, 1948; A. R. Johnson, 'Jonah ii. 3–10' in *Studies in Old Testament Prophecy*, ed. H. H. Rowley, 1950; and relevant sections in G. A. F. Knight, *Ruth and Jonah*, 1950; E. J. Young, *An Introduction to the Old Testament*, 1949; and A. Bentzen, *Introduction to the Old Testament*, 1948–9. Aalders and Young uphold the historical character of the book. D.F.P.

JONATHAN (*y^e^hônāṯān* or *yônāṯān*, 'Yahweh has given'). There are several occurrences of the name in the Old Testament: **1.** Son of Gershom, descendant of Moses (AV 'Manasseh'). He was hired by Micah to officiate as priest before an idol in Ephraim, then became priest and progenitor of a line of priests to the Danites 'until the day of the captivity of the land' (Jdg. xvii, xviii. 30–31).

2. Eldest son of King Saul by his only wife (1 Sa. xiv. 49, 50), he was his father's heir, which makes his loyalty and affection for David, who succeeded Saul, the more wonderful (1 Sa. xx. 31). Jonathan first appears in the biblical record as the victor at Geba, a Philistine stronghold, though his father's strategy at that time suggests by analogy that he may have taken part in the relief of Jabesh-gilead (1 Sa. xi. 11, xiii. 2). His prowess and courage as a warrior, recalled in David's elegy (2 Sa. i. 22), are clearly seen in his lone attack on another Philistine garrison, an incident which also shows his ability to inspire loyalty as well as to offer it (1 Sa. xiv. 7). It is for his own loyalty to David, however, that he is chiefly remembered; a loyalty made more difficult because it conflicted with his filial duty and affection to Saul, his father and sovereign. As the king, deserted by the Spirit of God and a victim to increasing fears and passions, showed ever greater hatred to 'the man after God's own heart' who was to succeed him, so Jonathan, in fealty to the brotherhood pact sworn with David after the death of Goliath (1 Sa. xviii. 1–4), was driven into defiance and deception of his father, even to the jeopardizing of his own life (1 Sa. xix. 1–7, xx). The parting scene between the two friends is most moving. It does not appear that Jonathan accompanied his father on the two expeditions against David, to En-gedi and Hachilah, and he disappears finally in the tragic Philistine victory at mount Gilboa, along with his father and brothers (1 Sa. xxxi. 2). Gifted physically and morally, he is a model to those of a more favoured dispensation of loyalty to truth and friendship, as well as of that peacemaking which is the rôle of the sons of God.

Others who bore this name are an uncle of David, a counsellor and scribe, perhaps to be identified with the nephew of David who slew a giant (1 Ch. xxvii. 32; 2 Sa. xxi. 21, 22); a son of the high priest Abiathar, who was involved in the attempts on David's throne by Absalom and Adonijah, though not as a rebel (2 Sa. xv. 36, xvii. 15–22; 1 Ki. i. 41–49); one of David's 'mighty men' (2 Sa. xxiii. 32; 1 Ch. xi. 34); a son of Kareah associated with Gedaliah during the domination of Jerusalem by Nebuchadrezzar (Je. xl. 8); and a scribe in whose house Jeremiah was imprisoned (Je. xxxvii. 20). The same name occurs at the time of the restoration (see Ezr. viii. 6, x. 15; Ne. xii. 11, 14, 35).

T.H.J.

JOPPA. Called Japho (Jos. xix. 46). The Heb. word is *yāpô*, the Gk. *Ioppē*, the Arab. *Yâfâ* (whence our 'Jaffa'). It was not in Israelite hands in the early centuries of the history of Israel, but it certainly served as the seaport for Jerusalem, 35 miles away. It is the only natural harbour between the Bay of Acco (*i.e.* the Bay of Haifa) and the Egyp. frontier, so it has a long history. It was a walled town even in the days of Tuthmosis III (and is mentioned in his town lists); and it figures in the Amarna letters. In the days of the Maccabees it was garrisoned by the Syrians, until captured by Simon. Pompey restored it to Syria (63 BC), but within twenty years it was again given to the Jews. It became a centre of piracy in the 1st century AD, and during the Jewish War Vespasian attacked and captured it. Since Roman times it has been in and out of numerous hands, including Napoleon's. Today it is overshadowed by its big neighbour Tel Aviv, and really forms but the southern suburb of it. The two form one municipality.

It also holds a place in Gk. mythology; a rock near the harbour mouth is supposedly the place where Andromeda was chained when Perseus slew the monster. The tourist can see a mosque purporting to mark the site of the house of Simon the tanner; a minaret embellishes a corner of the flat rooftop, which otherwise recalls the story of Acts x. D.F.P.

JORAM. See JEHORAM.

JORDAN. The Jordan depression is unique among the features of physical geography. Formed as a result of a rift valley, it is the lowest depression on earth. The headwaters of the river Jordan, fed by springs, collect into Lake Huleh, 230 feet above sea-level. Ten miles south at Lake Tiberias it is already nearly 700 feet below the Mediterranean, while at the north end of the Dead Sea the floor of the trench has dropped a further 580 feet and the river has plunged to 1,290 feet below sea-level. Thus the name 'Jordan' (Heb. *yardēn*) aptly means 'the descender'. The river is the largest perennial course in Palestine, and its distance of some 75 miles from Lake Huleh to the Dead Sea is more than doubled by its meanders. No other river has more biblical allusions and significance.

a. The Huleh Basin

Although the map might suggest the Jordan rift is continued to the north by the Syrian depression, the latter is mostly traversed by highlands at over 3,000 feet in parts, whereas the Jordan trough plunges steeply to 2,598 feet below sea-level at the northern end of the Dead Sea. Moreover, the Anti-Lebanon highlands form a barrier between Syria and Palestine. The landscape is dominated by the massive shoulder of Mt. Hermon which, at 9,100 feet, is the highest vantage point looking along the Levantine coast. Variously named Senir and Sirion (Dt. iii. 9, iv. 48; Ct. iv. 8), a great temple to Baal-hermon (Jdg. iii. 3) once occupied its summit, the symbol of blessing to the psalmist (Ps. cxxxiii. 3, *cf.* xlii. 6). Abundant springs issue from the limestone to feed the headstreams of the Jordan. The river Liddani receives its flow from springs at Banias (Caesarea Philippi) and at Tell el-Qadi (Dan). Others feed the river Hasbany. Was Banias the seat of the 'Baal-gad in the valley of the Lebanon' (Jos. xii. 7)? Certainly the caverns were the shrines of fertility cults. 'They were wont to say in old times, "let them ask counsel at Abel"' (2 Sa. xx. 18). The inhabitants lived prosperously in lush surroundings (Jdg. xviii. 7) and when the Danites settled they were tempted to follow the local idolatry (Jdg. xviii. 30). Dan was one of the towns where Jeroboam put a golden calf (1 Ki. xii. 29; 2 Ki. x. 29; *cf.* Am. viii. 14). Four miles away, Banias was in Roman times the centre of the worship of Pan, its name being changed to Caesarea Philippi. It was in the haunts of these pagan deities that Jesus chose to ask His disciples the crucial question, 'Whom say ye that I am?' (Mk. viii. 29), and it was probably on some part of Hermon near by that the transfiguration took place (Mk. ix. 2). The district of Dan was the northern limit of Israel, whose inhabitants controlled the vital route into Syria and were likened to a nest of vipers (Gn. xlix. 17).

Overlooking the Huleh basin to the north-west (1 Ki. xv. 20; 2 Ki. xv. 29) is the mound of Tell Abib, a strategic centre once besieged by Joab (see 2 Sa. xx. 14–22). Beyond the shallow swamps of Lake Huleh, a focus of malaria and noted for its high papyrus reeds from which paper may first have been made in Palestine, the Jordan plunges 926 feet in 9 miles of basaltic gorges to reach the small deltaic plain at the head of Lake Tiberias.

b. The Tiberias district

In ancient times this was called Chinnereth, probably because it is harp-shaped, 13 miles long, and about 8 miles across. Fed by numerous thermal springs, its fresh waters are well stocked with fish, the maximum depth of 165 feet permitting vertical migrations of the fish with the seasonal temperatures. It was therefore probably in the hot summer season when the normal winter temperature of 55° F. lies 120 feet below the surface of the lake that Jesus advised the fishermen to 'cast into the deep' (Lk. v. 4). The methods of fishing referred to in the Gospels are still practised: the single-hook line (Mt. xvii. 27); the circular fishing net (Mt. iv. 18; Mk. i. 16); the draw-net cast out by a boat (Mt. xiii. 47 f.); deep-sea nets (Mt. iv. 18 f.; Mk. i. 19 f.); and deep-sea fishing undertaken with two boats (Lk. v. 10). See also FISH, FISHING.

A dense population clustered round the lake in our Lord's day, and it was to the sophisticated city folk of Chorazin, Bethsaida, and Capernaum that His condemnation was given (Mt. xi. 20–24). 'There is no spot in the whole of Palestine where memories heap themselves up to such an extent as in Capernaum' (Dalman). Jewish life throbbed in its synagogues (Mt. xii. 9; Mk. i. 21, iii. 1, v. 22; Lk. iv. 31, vi. 6, viii. 41). There lived Jairus, the chief of the synagogue (Mk. v. 22), the centurion who built a synagogue (Lk. vii. 5), Levi the customs official (Mt. ix. 9; Mk. ii. 14; Lk. v. 27). East of Capernaum was Bethsaida from which Philip, Andrew, and Peter came (Jn. i. 44), and beyond that the less populous district of the Gadarenes, where the heathen reared their pigs (Lk. viii. 32). The interspersed lake plains and steep rocky slopes with boulders and thistle fields provide the setting for the parable of the sower (Mk. iv. 2–8), while in spring the flowered carpets of asphodels, anemones, and irises are also telling sermons (Mt. vi. 28; Lk. xii. 27). The reeded banks of the lake deltas provide other object lessons (Mt. xi. 7; Lk. vii. 24), and the reed given to our Lord in mockery could only have come from the Jordan valley (Mt. xxvii. 29, *cf.* 48).

Hot medicinal springs occur on both sides of the lake, especially at Amatha, and it may have been in the vicinity of el-Hammeh to the south that Naaman dipped himself seven times in Jordan (2 Ki. v. 14). The numerous cases of miracles of healing in the Gospels may reflect the number of patients seeking local medicinal remedies at these spas. Malaria appears to be the cause of some maladies (Mt. viii. 14; Mk. i. 30; Lk. iv. 38; Jn. iv. 52).

Dominating this lake environment are the surrounding mountains, especially those of the north-west, which played so vital a part in the prayer-life of our Lord, where He taught His disciples (Mt. v. 1) and from which He appeared as the risen Lord (Mt. xxviii. 16). The north-east corner of the lake is supposedly the scene of the miracle of the feeding of the five thousand (Lk. ix. 10–17).

c. The 'Ghor' or Jordan valley

This runs for over 65 miles between Lake Tiberias and the Dead Sea. The Yarmuk entering the left bank of the Jordan 5 miles downstream from the lake doubles the volume of flow and the valley is progressively deepened to as much as 150 feet below the floor of the trough. In this sector three physical zones are distinguishable: the broad upper terrace of the Pliocene trough, the *Ghor* proper; the lower Quaternary terrace and flood plain of the river, the *Zor*; and between them the deeply dissected slopes and badlands of the *Qattara*. It is the Qattara and the Zor together, rather than the river Jordan, which have created the frontier character of this obstacle (Jos. xxii. 25). The northern half of the Ghor is a broad, well-cultivated tract, but the Judaean–Gilead dome, crossing the trough, narrows the valley south of Gilead. Beyond it, the trough becomes increasingly more arid until at the head of the Dead Sea there is scarcely more than 2 inches mean annual rainfall. The Qattara badlands, carved grotesquely in soft marls and clays, create a steep, desolate descent to the valley floor. The Zor, making its way in vivid green vegetation cover, stands out in sharp contrast below, hence its name *gā'ôn* ('luxuriant growth') of Jordan (Je. xii. 5, xlix. 19, l. 44; Zc. xi. 3; *cf.* Pss. xlvii. 4, lix. 12; Pr. xvi. 18). The haunt of wild animals (Je. xlix. 19), it is partly flooded in spring (Jos. iii. 15). Thus the question can be understood, 'And though in a land of peace thou art secure, yet how wilt thou do in the Jungle of the Jordan?' (Je. xii. 5).

Between the Yarmuk in the north and the Jabbok are nine other perennial streams entering the left bank of the Jordan, and their water supply explains why all the important settlements were located on the east side of the Ghor, towns such as Succoth, Zaphon, Zaretan, Jabesh-Gilead, and Pella. With the aid of irrigation this was probably the view Lot saw 'as the garden of the Lord' (Gn. xiii. 10). It was on the Jabbok at Penuel that later Jacob wrestled with the Stranger and near by at Succoth where he grazed his flocks (Gn. xxxiii. 16–17). The brook Cherith may well have been a seasonal tributary of the Jabesh farther north, where Elijah, a native of Jabesh-Gilead, hid himself from Ahab (1 Ki. xvii. 1–7). It was from the banks of Jordan that he 'went by a whirlwind into heaven' (2 Ki. ii. 7–11). Between Succoth and Zarthan (identified by Glueck as Tell es-Saidiyeh) Solomon had his copper cast in earthen moulds, using local clay and fuel (1 Ki. vii. 46; 2 Ch. iv. 17). In this section of the valley there are a number of fords, though the river was not bridged until Roman times. Near the mouth of the Jabbok, both Abraham and Jacob crossed it (Gn. xxxii. 10). Somewhere here, the Midianites crossed, pursued by Gideon (Jdg. vii. 24, viii. 4, 5). Twice David crossed it in the rebellion of Absalom (2 Sa. xvii. 22–24, xix. 15–18). But between the Jabbok confluence and the Dead Sea crossings are more difficult owing to the swift current. The miraculous crossing of the Israelites appears to have taken place at Adam (modern Tell Dâmiyeh), 16 miles north of Jericho (Jos. iii. 1–17, iv. 1–24; Ps. cxiv. 3, 5). Near this site the river banks are undercut by the river and earthquakes have caused landslides to block the river. In the night preceding 8 December 1267, a blockage dammed the river for 16 hours. Similar cases occurred in 1906 and 1927—in the latter incident holding back the waters for 21½ hours.

Between the Jabbok and Beth-nimrah for 16 miles (Is. xv. 6) there are no streams entering the Jordan, and little settlement. Oasis towns occur near springs, such as the districts of Beth-shan and Jericho west of the Jordan, and in the plains of Moab (Nu. xx. 1) to the east was Shittim, where the spies were sent (Jos. ii. 1–7). Gilgal and Bethany beyond Jordan are unidentified on the lower course of the Jordan. Of these settlements, Jericho (*q.v.*) is suggested by some to be the most ancient yet known to have been continuously occupied since the dawn of Man.

Despite its oases, the valley is here a desert, the scene of John the Baptist's ministry. The use of the salty waters of the Jordan, unsuitable for the Jewish rites of purification (*cf.* Nu. xix. 17), suggests that his baptism had no connection with Jewish rites. Rather John the Baptist is considered a successor of the prophet Elijah, who also ministered in the same valley (Mt. xi. 14; Mk. ix. 11 ff.). Jesus, too, stayed in the desert. Stones have often been found enclosed in soft lime and appear to take the form of loaves, a reminder today of His temptation to turn those stones into real bread (Mt. iv. 3; Lk. iv. 3). Along the western borders of the Ghor the rift mountains give such extensive views as Jesus saw in His further temptation (Mt. iv. 8; Lk. iv. 5).

BIBLIOGRAPHY. D. Baly, *The Geography of the Bible*, 1957; G. Dalman, *Sacred Sites and Ways*, trans. by P. P. Levertoff, 1935; J. and J. B. E. Garstang, *The Story of Jericho*, 1948; N. Glueck, *The River Jordan*, 1946; K. M. Kenyon, *Jericho I*, 1960.

J.M.H.

JOSEPH.

1. In the Old Testament

I. NAME

Joseph is a jussive form of the verb *yāsap̄*, 'to add'; the name *yôsēp̄* means 'may He (God) add (sons)'; *cf.* Gn. xxx. 24. A Palestinian place-name *yšp-ỉr* (*i.e. y-š-p-'El*) in Egyptian topographical lists of the 15th and 14th centuries BC has been compared with Heb. *yôsēp̄*. But the 's'-sounds are different and the two names are almost certainly not related (so W. F. Albright, *JPOS*, VIII, 1928, p. 249). For the Egyp. *y-š-p-'El*, compare biblical place-names such as Jiphthah-el (Jos. xix. 14, 27).

II. HISTORY

a. Background

Joseph was the eleventh son of Jacob, his first by Rachel (Gn. xxx. 24, xxxv. 24), and his favourite son (Gn. xxxvii. 3, *cf.* xxxiii. 2, 7). The story of Joseph is one of the most graphic and attractive in the Old Testament: a spoilt boy sold into Egyptian slavery by jealous brothers, who makes good in adversity, and from an unjust imprisonment rises to the highest offices of state. By wise planning he averts the scourge of famine, thereby saving Egypt, Canaan, and his own family from starvation. Reconciliation with his brothers follows and the family settles in the pastures of Goshen in the north-east Delta. After burying Jacob in Canaan, Joseph commands that his bones too should be carried there when Israel's descendants eventually leave Egypt for the land of promise. The story as told in Genesis cannot be bettered; the following paragraphs will therefore merely present some Egyptian and related background material and deal with some textual points.

b. Date

The most likely date for Joseph is the period of the Hyksos pharaohs, *c.* 1720–1570 BC (see CHRONOLOGY OF THE OLD TESTAMENT). These were Semitic rulers who had infiltrated from Canaan, but scrupulously observed Egyptian conventions. At first they took over the existing Egyptian bureaucratic administration, but later appointed naturalized Semites to high office. For the historical background, see EGYPT: History.

c. The 'coat of many colours'

Jacob's partiality for Joseph was marked by the 'coat of many colours' (AV, RV) or 'long, sleeved robe' (*cf.* RVmg, RSV). Archaeologically either rendering of the Heb. *keṯōneṯ passîm* is possible. For Semites in multicoloured garb, see *IBA*, p. 29, fig. 25, right, or in colour, E. W. Heaton, *Everyday Life in Old Testament Times*, 1956, dust-jacket; later examples in *IBA*, p. 35, fig. 29 or *ANEP*, p. 17, fig. 52. These same garments, especially the last-cited examples, are also often long and sleeved. In favour of the meaning 'varicoloured', *passîm* has been compared with Assyrian *paspasu*, 'brightly coloured bird' and Arabic *fasafisa*, 'mosaic' (Eisler, *Orientalistische Literaturzeitung*, XI, 1908, 368–371 and *cf. ibid.*, XIV, 1911, 509). The rendering 'long sleeved robe' is attained by taking *pas* as flat of hand or foot, hence *keṯōneṯ passîm* is a 'tunic of (= reaching to) palms and soles' (*BDB*, p. 821a). On dreams, see below.

d. Joseph sold into Egypt

The text records that when Joseph was sent to visit his brothers pasturing the flocks they at first planned to kill him, but instead put him in a cistern at the suggestion of the more scrupulous Reuben, who secretly hoped to rescue him. After the brothers had sat down to a meal, a caravan of Ishmaelite merchants from Gilead appeared in the distance; so they quickly decided to rid themselves of Joseph by selling him off. When the caravan came near, 'they'—Joseph's brothers—sold him to the first of the travellers that they met: '(some) men, Midianites, traders' (Gn. xxxvii. 28). When the caravan had passed on, Reuben returned to the pit and was distraught at finding Joseph gone. This directly suggests that Reuben had been absent from the first appearance of the caravan until it (and Joseph) had passed on.

Certain points require comment. Why should Reuben be absent? Of many possible reasons, the simplest is that when the foreign caravan was sighted, Reuben, the most conscientious of the brothers (and true to character), went off to mount guard among the sheep: passing foreigners could not be trusted not to filch a few choice animals. Reuben would have to wait till they had passed. By the time Reuben could safely return, Joseph was sold and gone; they then sent his blood-stained robe to Jacob.

Who sold Joseph into Egypt? In Egypt the Midianites (actually Medanites, see below) sold Joseph to Potiphar (Gn. xxxvii. 36), who bought him from the Ishmaelites (Gn. xxxix. 1). The caravan was Ishmaelite, including under this designation Midianites or Medanites; the terms overlap. This interchange of terms is most plainly exhibited by Jdg. viii. 24, which explicitly states that the Midianites beaten by Gideon 'had golden earrings, because they were Ishmaelites'. The spelling Medanites in the Hebrew of Gn. xxxvii. 36 may indicate an overlap of a third term; compare Gn. xxv. 2 (= 1 Ch. i. 32), where both Medan and Midian are sons of Abraham by Keturah. The use of multiple terms in a narrative is indicative not of disparate documents but of typical Near Eastern stylistic usage. For similar use of three terms within a few lines compare the Egyptian stele of Sebekkhu (*c.* 1850 BC), who refers to the one general foe of his pharaoh's Palestinian campaign as *Mntyw-Stt*, 'Asiatic bedouin'; as *Rntw ḫst*, 'vile Syrians'; and as *''mw*, 'Asiatics'. There can be no question of separate documents behind this little stone stele, executed as a unit at one man's volition; such examples could be multiplied.

Who sold Joseph to the caravan? 'They drew' (Gn. xxxvii. 28) is at first sight ambiguous, able to refer either to the brothers or to the Midianites. In Gn. xlv. 4, 5 Joseph plainly charges his brothers in private with having sold him into slavery (simple form of the verb), which would refer the 'they' of Gn. xxxvii. 28 to his brothers, not the Midianites. This accords with the syntax of Hebrew and parallel literatures. In Egypt, a text records that when King Tuthmosis II 'flew to heaven', *i.e.* died, his son Tuthmosis III ascended the throne and 'his sister' Hatshepsut governed the land. This latter 'his' refers back, not to Tuthmosis III, but to Tuthmosis II (Schott, *Krönungstag d. Königin Hatschepsut*, 1955, p. 197). Note that 'Midianites' in Gn. xxxvii. 28 has no article, and can mean either just 'Midianites' (undefined) or else '(some) Midianites', *i.e.* part of the main body, there being no indefinite article in Hebrew. Finally, there is Gn. xl. 14, 15, where Joseph tells the butler that he 'was stolen away out of the land of the Hebrews'. Why did he not openly admit that he had been sold into slavery? The reason is perfectly plain. Joseph here desperately pleads his innocence of any offence, seeking to persuade the butler to get him out of prison; it would have wrecked his plea to have revealed the humiliating fact that he had been sold into slavery by his own blood brothers. With his brothers in private (Gn. xlv) Joseph could be frank; but the butler would be bound to think they had had some good reason to rid themselves of him, and Joseph's appeal would be in vain. Joseph therefore said vaguely that he was 'stolen', which was true in so far as his brothers had no right to sell him for gain. This is not a question of harmonization at any price, but of common sense and practical psychology. The truth is that Gn. xxxvii, xxxix, xl, xlv read plainly when put in their proper setting of exact exegesis, Hebrew and other Near Eastern syntax and literary usage, and the motivated actions of individuals.

e. Joseph in Egypt

Joseph was but one of many young Semites who became servants in Egyptian households between 1900 and 1600 BC. The recently published Papyrus Brooklyn 35.1446, part of a prison-register (see below), bears on its reverse a list of seventy-nine servants in an Egyptian household *c.* 1740 BC, of whom at least forty-five were not Egyptians but 'Asiatics', *i.e.* Semites like Joseph. Many of these have good NW Semitic names linguistically related to those of Jacob, Issachar, Asher, Job (Ayyabum), and Menahem. Some were 'domestics' (*ḥry-pr*) just like Joseph in Gn. xxxix. 2 ('in the house'). See Hayes, *A Papyrus of the Late Middle Kingdom*, 1955, and Albright, *JAOS*, LXXIV, 1954, pp. 222–233.

There are ample scattered indications of numbers of Asiatics in Egypt at this period, some of whom reached high and trusted positions under their masters (Posener, *Syria*, XXXIV, 1957, pp. 145–163), rather like Joseph, who became Potiphar's steward (*îmy-r pr*, a common Egyptian title). Potiphar's title (*śar-haṭṭabbāḥîm*) 'captain of the guard', *i.e.* of Pharaoh's bodyguard, would render the Egyptian *sḥḏ-šmsw*, 'Instructor of Retainers'. However, Vergote (*Joseph en Égypte*, 1959, pp. 31–35) has put up a plausible case for interpreting his title as actually 'butler'. For the Egyptian original of Potiphar's name, see POTIPHAR, POTIPHERA. Both Potiphar and the 'butler' and 'baker' of Gn. xl are termed *sārîs*, usually rendered 'officer', but in Semitic it often means 'eunuch'. However, eunuchs are not prominent in Egypt, and *sārîs* in early times meant generally 'courtier, dignitary' as much as 'eunuch' (though this was the main meaning later). See *JFA*, XLVII, 1961, for details.

The incident of Potiphar's covetous wife, who turned the tables on Joseph by asserting the opposite of the truth, is often compared with a very similar incident in the Egyptian *Tale of Two Brothers*. However, there is no other point of contact at all between these two narratives: Joseph's is pure biography, while everything else in the *Two Brothers* is pure fantasy. For a full translation see, *e.g.*, Erman-Blackman, *Literature of the Ancient Egyptians*, 1927, pp. 150–161, as the extracts in *ANET*, pp. 23–25, are abbreviated. More prosaic Egyptian documents reveal that Potiphar's wife was not unique in her sin.

Egyptian prisons served a threefold purpose: as local lock-ups like modern prisons, as forced-labour reserves for state corvée, and as centres for remanded prisoners awaiting trial (*cf.* Joseph). Trials were sometimes conducted in the prisons, whose administration was highly organized, as the Papyrus Brooklyn (Hayes, *op. cit.*) vividly shows; each prisoner's record was filed under seven separate headings, from initial arrest to completion of the sentence. The 'keeper of the prison' (Gn. xxxix. 21–23, *etc.*) probably represents the Egyptian title *s'wty n ḫnrt* which has the same meaning.

The 'butler' of Gn. xl should be rendered 'cupbearer' (*q.v.*), Heb. *mašqeh* being the exact equivalent of Egyptian *wdpw*, later *wb'*, 'cupbearer' (*cf.* Gn. xl. 11, 13). Bakers, too, are well known in Egypt, but chief bakers apparently were not explicitly so called. Perhaps the Egyptian title *sš wdḥw nsw*, 'Royal Table-scribe', is the nearest equivalent. For bread-baskets carried on the head, see *IBA*, p. 33, fig. 28. Dreams (Gn. xxxvii, xl, xli) were considered important also in the non-biblical East (see DREAM). The 'magicians of Egypt' (*ḥarṭummîm*, an Egyptian word) were familiar figures, and special manuals were used for interpreting dreams. For details, see under MAGIC AND SORCERY: Egyptian Magic.

Joseph had to be properly shaved and robed in linen to appear at court (Gn. xli. 14). His practical approach to the threat of famine impressed the pharaoh, who invested him with high office in traditional Egyptian manner, bestowing signet, fine linen, and gold necklace (see fig. 122). Joseph's exact rank is disputed; it seems most probable that he was actually vizier, second only to the pharaoh (so Vergote); but some would make him a minister for agriculture directly responsible to the king in person (Ward, *JSS*, V, 1960, pp. 144–150). The mention of chariots (Gn. xli. 43) and horses (Gn. xlvii. 17) fits the Hyksos period and decades immediately preceding, but not earlier. Remains of horses from the period just before the Hyksos have recently been excavated near Wadi Halfa (Faulkner, *JEA*, XLV, 1959, pp. 1, 2). For the Egyptian names of Joseph and his wife, see ZAPHENATH-PAANEAH and ASENATH.

Egypt was famed for her great agricultural wealth; *cf.* reckoning of grain, *IBA*, p. 32, fig. 27. But Egypt also suffered periodic famines; one oft-quoted biographical text reads: 'When famine came for many years, I gave grain to my town in each famine' (Vandier, *La Famine dans l'Égypte ancienne*, 1936, p. 115). For a graphic scene of famine-starved bedouin, see fig. 82. The Egyptians would not eat with the Hebrews (Gn. xliii. 32) for fear of transgressing various ritual taboos on food (Montet, *L'Égypte et la Bible*, 1959, pp. 99–101). It is possible that Gn. xliv. 5 on divination should be rendered 'is it not from this (= the silver cup) that my lord drinks and *concerning* which he will assuredly divine?' (*cf.* Gn. xliv. 15); for possible cup-divination, see MAGIC AND SORCERY: Egyptian Magic; see also fig. 69.

When pharaoh invited Joseph's family to settle in Egypt (Gn. xlv. 17–21, xlvi. 5), he sent wagons and told them to leave all, for they would have sufficiency in Egypt. Judging from Egyptian scenes 200 years later, such wagons were probably large, two-wheeled ox-carts. (For an excellent picture and discussion of these, see Aldred, *JNES*, XV, 1956, pp. 150–153, pl. 17.) Sinuhe, a fugitive Egyptian in Syria *c.* 1900 BC, was also told to leave all by the pharaoh who recalled him to Egypt. Different customs again explain an allusion in Gn. xlvi. 34b; by this means Joseph's family could be settled in secluded security in Goshen. Joseph's economic policy in Gn. xlvii. 16–19 simply made Egypt in fact what it always was in theory: the land became pharaoh's property and its inhabitants his tenants. The priests were exempt not from taxation but only from Joseph's one-fifth levy, and the temple estates were separately managed (Gn. xlvii. 22, 26). Gn. xlvii. 21 merely indicates that throughout Egypt Joseph brought the people of each district into their nearest cities where the granaries were, the better to feed them; the unsavoury emendation in RSV ('he made slaves of them') is unnecessary. Gn. xlviii, xlix reflect purely Asiatic usage within the patriarchal family; such oral blessings as Jacob's were legally binding in W Asia in the first half of the second millennium BC (*cf.* Gordon, *BA*, III, 1940, p. 8).

f. Death of Joseph

Both Joseph and his father were embalmed in the Egyptian manner (Gn. l. 2, 3, 26), and Joseph was 'put in a coffin in Egypt'. Coffins at this period were anthropoid, wooden ones with a conventional portrait-face at the head-end. The period of embalming varied in length; forty days is one possibility among many. But seventy days' mourning was characteristic. Joseph's age at death, 110 years, is also significant: this was the ideal life-span in Egyptian eyes, and to them would signify divine blessing upon him.

Fig. 122. Investiture of Paser as vizier with a collar (or 'chain') of gold before Pharaoh Sethos I. Painting, tomb of Paser, Thebes, *c.* 1300 BC. *Cf.* Gn. xli. 42.

For background, detailed discussion, and full source references, see J. Vergote, *Joseph en Égypte*, 1959, and K. A. Kitchen, *The Joseph Narrative and its Egyptian Background* (forthcoming).

III. JOSEPH'S DESCENDANTS

The tribes of Ephraim and Manasseh, descended from Joseph's two sons, were sometimes termed '(the tribe of) Joseph', or house of Joseph; 'sons of Joseph' is common (Nu.; Jos.). So, Joseph is blessed as progenitor of the two future tribes by Jacob (Gn. xlix. 22–26, *cf.* xlviii), and Moses also blesses 'Joseph', meaning Ephraim and Manasseh (Dt. xxxiii. 13, 16). Compare also Nu. xiii. 11; Dt. xxvii. 12; Jdg. i. 22, 23, 35; Ps. lxxx. 1 (poetic); and Ezk. xlvii. 13. K.A.K.

2. In the New Testament

The husband of Mary. He is not mentioned in Mark and the references in Jn. i. 45 and vi. 42 are indirect. According to Matthew, he was a descendant of David (Mt. i. 20). It seems that the genealogy in Lk. iii is not that of Joseph but of Mary (but see GENEALOGY OF JESUS CHRIST). Luke had already shown that Jesus was not the son of Joseph. Matthew is tracing the legal relationship back to David and Abraham.

Matthew and Luke both record that Jesus was conceived by the Holy Spirit at a time when Joseph was betrothed to Mary, but before he had intercourse with her (Mt. i. 18; Lk. i. 27, 35). Luke records the revelation by an angel to Mary, Matthew that to Joseph. It seems that Matthew drew his information from Joseph (possibly *via* James, the Lord's brother) and that Luke obtained his from Mary.

Joseph acted as a father towards Jesus, taking Him to Jerusalem for the purification (Lk. ii. 22) and fleeing with Him to Egypt to escape Herod. He returned to Nazareth and settled there (Mt. ii). He took the boy Jesus to Jerusalem each year for the Passover (Lk. ii. 41). Perhaps His words in Lk. ii. 49 indicate that Jesus knew when He was twelve years old that He was not Joseph's son.

It is almost certain that Joseph was not alive during the ministry of Jesus. There is no direct mention of him, and it is hard to explain otherwise the word to John from the cross (Jn. xix. 26, 27) and the reference to Mary and His brothers seeking Jesus (Mt. xii. 46; Mk. iii. 31; Lk. viii. 19). It is natural to assume that the brothers of Jesus were subsequent children of Joseph and Mary.

Others mentioned in the New Testament who bear this name are three ancestors of Joseph the husband of Mary (or ancestors of Mary?) (Lk. iii. 24, 26, 30); Joseph called Barsabas, surnamed Justus, the unsuccessful candidate for the apostleship of Judas (Acts i. 23); and one of the brothers of the Lord (Mt. xiii. 55, RV). It was also the natal name of Barnabas (*q.v.*) (Acts iv. 36, RV; AV has Joses).

For JOSEPH OF ARIMATHAEA, see next article. R.E.N.

JOSEPH OF ARIMATHAEA. A Jew of Arimathaea (*q.v.*), 'a good man, and a just: who waited for the kingdom of God' (Lk. xxiii. 50, 51), 'a disciple of Jesus, but secretly for fear of the Jews' (Jn. xix. 38), and a member of the Sanhedrin who had not voted for Jesus' death. He was rich and, having asked Pilate for Jesus' body, provided fine linen for the burial, laying it in his own, unused, rock tomb (Mt. xxvii. 57–60). (In this Matthew perhaps sees the fulfilment of Is. liii. 9.) In a legend which first appears in William of Malmesbury he is sent by Philip from Gaul to Britain in AD 63 and founded the first Christian settlement in this country, afterwards the site of Glastonbury. There is no reference to this story in Gildas and Bede. J. A. Robinson, in his *Two Glastonbury Legends*, says that the passages are interpolations. A still later legend, probably composed by Walter Map in 1200, tells how Joseph brought the Holy Grail to England. J.W.M.

JOSEPHUS, FLAVIUS. A Jewish historian, who was born AD 37/38, and died early in the 2nd century. He was the son of a priest named Matthias, of the order of Jehoiarib (1 Ch. xxiv. 7), and claimed kinship with the Hasmonaeans, who belonged to that order. After a brief period of association with the Essenes, and with an ascetic wilderness-dweller named Banus, he joined the party of the Pharisees at the age of nineteen. On a visit to Rome in AD 63 he was impressed by the power of the empire. He was strongly opposed to the Jewish revolt against Rome in AD 66, and although he was given a command in Galilee in which he manifested considerable energy and ability, he had no confidence in the insurgent cause. After the Roman seizure of the stronghold of Jotapata, which he had defended until further resistance was useless, he escaped with forty others to a cave. When this refuge in turn was about to be stormed the defenders entered into a suicide pact, and Josephus found himself one of the last two survivors. He persuaded his fellow-survivor that they might as well surrender to the Romans, and then he contrived to win the favour of Vespasian, the Roman commander, by predicting his elevation to the imperial purple. This prediction came true in AD 69. Next year Josephus was attached to the Roman general headquarters during the siege of Jerusalem, acting as interpreter for Titus (Vespasian's son and successor in the Palestinian command), when he wished to offer terms to the defenders of the city. After the fall of Jerusalem Josephus went to Rome, where he settled down as a client and pensioner of the emperor, whose family name, Flavius, he adopted.

Not unnaturally, Josephus' behaviour during the war won for him the indelible stigma of treason in the eyes of his nation. Yet he employed the years of his leisure in Rome in such a way as to establish some claim on their gratitude. These years were devoted to literary activity in which he shows himself to be a true patriot according to his lights, jealous for the good name of his people. His first work was a *History of the Jewish War*, written first in Aramaic for the benefit of Jews in Mesopotamia and then published in a Gk. edition. The account of the outbreak of the war is here preceded by a summary of Jewish history from 168 BC to AD 66. His two books *Against Apion* constitute a defence of his people against the anti-Jewish calumnies of an Alexandrian schoolmaster named Apion; in them, too, he endeavours to show that the Jews can boast a greater antiquity than the Greeks, and in the course of this argument he has preserved for us a number of valuable extracts from ancient writers not otherwise extant. His longest work is his *Jewish Antiquities*, in twenty books, relating the history of his people from earliest times (in fact, he begins his narrative with the creation of the world) down to his own day. This work was completed in AD 93. Finally, he wrote his *Autobiography* largely as a defence of his war record, which had been represented in unflattering terms by another Jewish writer, Justus of Tiberias. It is impossible to reconcile the account of his war activities given in his *Autobiography* with that given earlier in his *History of the Jewish War*.

For the history of the Jews between the reign of Antiochus Epiphanes (175–163 BC) and the war of AD 66–73, and especially for the period beginning with the Roman occupation of 63 BC, the works of Josephus are of incomparable value. He had access to first-rate sources, both published and unpublished: the work of Nicolas of Damascus, historiographer to Herod the Great, supplied a detailed record of that monarch's career; official Roman records were placed at his disposal; he consulted the younger Agrippa (see HEROD, 5) on various details concerning the origin of the Jewish war, and of course could rely on his own immediate knowledge of many phases of it. He can indeed be thoroughly tendentious in his portrayal of personalities and presentation of events, but his 'tendency' is so obvious that the reader can easily detect it and make necessary allowances for it.

The works of Josephus provide indispensable background material for the student of late inter-testamental and New Testament history. In them we meet many figures, both Jewish and Gentile, who are well known to us from the New Testament—members of the Herod family, Roman emperors and procurators, Jewish high priests, and so forth. Sometimes his writings supply a direct commentary on New Testament references, *e.g.* on the mention of Judas of Galilee in Acts v. 37 and of the 'Egyptian' (*q.v.*) in Acts xxi. 38. It is unlikely, however, that his works were known to any New Testament writer. Of special interest are his references to John the Baptist (*Ant.* xviii. 5. 2), to James the Lord's brother (*Ant.* xx. 9. 1), and to our Lord (*Ant.* xviii. 3. 3)—a passage which, while it has been subjected to some Christian editing, is basically authentic.

BIBLIOGRAPHY. The standard edition of Josephus' works in Greek is that by B. Niese (1887–95). The Loeb edition (1926–), in Greek and English, begun by H. St. J. Thackeray and continued by R. Marcus, is not yet complete. The best-known English translation is that by W. Whiston (1736); this has been revised by A. R. Shilleto (1889–90) and (less thoroughly) by D. S. Margoliouth (1906). A most readable new translation of the *Jewish War*, by G. A. Williamson, has appeared in the Penguin Classics (1959). See also H. St. J. Thackeray, *Josephus, the Man and the Historian*, 1929; F. J. Foakes-Jackson, *Josephus and the Jews*, 1930; J. M. Creed, 'The Slavonic Version of Josephus' History of the Jewish War', *HTR*, XXV, 1932, pp. 277 ff.; R. J. H. Shutt, *Studies in Josephus*, 1961.

F.F.B.

JOSHUA. 1. Joshua ben Nun, grandson of Elishama chief of Ephraim (1 Ch. vii. 27; Nu. i. 10), was called by his family *Hoshea'*, 'salvation' (Dt. xxxii. 44; transliterated *Oshea*, Nu. xiii. 8, AV); this name recurs in the tribe of Ephraim (see 1 Ch. xxvii. 20; *cf.* 2 Ki. xvii. 1; Ho. i. 1). Moses added the divine name, calling him *y^ehôšua'*, normally rendered in English *Joshua.* The Gk. *Iēsous* reflects the Aramaic contraction *Yešû'* (*cf.* Ne. iii. 19, *etc.*).

At the Exodus Joshua was a young man (Ex. xxxiii. 11). Moses chose him as personal assistant, and gave him command of a detachment from the as yet unorganized tribes to repel the raiding Amalekites (Ex. xvii). As the Ephraimite representative on the reconnaissance from Kadesh (Nu. xiii, xiv), he supported Caleb's recommendation to go ahead with the invasion. (Caleb (*q.v.*), the senior and leading figure, is sometimes mentioned alone in this connection; but it is unlikely that there was a tradition of the reconnaissance excluding Joshua, or that any later historian denied, or did not know, that he too escaped the curse on the unbelieving people.)

While Moses was alone before God at Sinai, Joshua kept watch; in the Tent of Meeting he also learnt to wait on the Lord; and in the years following something of Moses' patience and meekness was doubtless added to his valour (Ex. xxiv. 13, xxxii. 17, xxxiii. 11; Nu. xi. 28). In the plains by Jordan he was formally consecrated as Moses' successor to the military leadership, co-ordinate with Eleazar's priesthood (Nu. xxvii. 18 ff., xxxiv. 17; *cf.* Dt. iii and xxxi, where Joshua's leadership is naturally emphasized). He was then probably about seventy years old; his senior, Caleb, was a remarkably vigorous eighty-five when he began to occupy the Judaean Hills (Jos. xv. 13–15).

Joshua occupied and consolidated the area of Gilgal, fought successful campaigns against Canaanite confederacies, and directed further operations as long as the united efforts of Israel were required. Settlement of the land depended on tribal initiative, which Joshua sought to encourage by a formal allocation at Shiloh, where the national sanctuary was established. The time had come for him to dissolve his command and set an example by retiring to his own lands at Timnath-serah in Mt. Ephraim. It was perhaps at this time that he called Israel to the national covenant at Shechem (Jos. xxiv). Chapter xxiii may refer to the same occasion; but the substance is different, and seems to imply a different and possibly later period.

Joshua died aged 110, and was buried near Timnath-serah. For JOSHUA, BOOK OF, see the following article.

2. Joshua ben Josedech was high priest of the restoration in 537 BC. Under him the altar was rebuilt and the Temple dedicated. Progress was hindered by opposition, however, until in 520 BC he was strengthened by the prophecies of Haggai and Zechariah, including a remarkable pattern of justification by the grace of God (Zc. iii). He was named prophetically 'the Branch' (or, 'shoot'; *ṣemaḥ*, Zc. vi. 12). See J. Stafford Wright, *The Building of the Second Temple*, 1958, for a review of the problems in Ezra and Haggai.

3. Joshua of Beth-shemesh is mentioned in 1 Sa. vi. 14 as the one into whose field the ark was brought when the Philistines sent it back to Israel. J.P.U.L.

JOSHUA, BOOK OF. The book of Joshua records the invasion of Canaan by Israel and its partition among the tribes. It tells in detail how they crossed the Jordan and secured a bridgehead, describes more briefly two campaigns which broke the power of the Canaanites, and summarizes Israel's further military progress. The account of the partition includes a full description of Judahite territory, together with anecdotes concerning the Kenite settlement of Hebron and the difficulties experienced in N Manasseh. Emphasis is laid on events of religious significance connected with the invasion, the relations of the Transjordanian tribes with the rest of the nation, and Joshua's spiritual testament, the covenant of Shechem.

I. OUTLINE OF CONTENTS

a. The invasion of Canaan (i. 1–xi. 23)

(i) *Change of command* (i. 1–iv. 24). Commission—reconnaissance—the river crossing.

(ii) *The bridgehead* (v. 1–viii. 35). Gilgal—Jericho—Ai.

(iii) *Campaign in the south* (ix. 1–x. 43). The Hivite cities—defeat of the Jerusalem confederacy—cities captured.

(iv) *Campaign in the north, and further progress* (xi. 1–23).

b. The Settlement in Canaan (xii. 1–xxiv. 33)

(i) *List of defeated enemies* (xii. 1–24).

(ii) *The early settlements* (xiii. 1–xvii. 18). Unfinished tasks—Transjordan—Caleb—the land of Judah—allotments for Ephraim and Manasseh.

(iii) *Later settlements* (xviii. 1–xxi. 45). The allotment of Shiloh—cities of refuge—levitical towns.

(iv) *The way ahead* (xxii. 1–xxiv. 33). The witness altar—Joshua's charge—the covenant of Shechem.

II. AUTHORSHIP, SOURCES, AND DATE

The 'Deuteronomist' (D/D_2) may be considered the author, inasmuch as one cannot extract the 'deuteronomic passages' from the narrative and leave complete or intelligible 'source documents'. About D (a cipher for some person or persons unknown) there is no independent evidence. The term 'school' has been used, but is a mere possibility at any period. (For the 7th-century hypothesis, see DEUTERONOMY.) Despite his literary stature and theological leadership, D remains unidentified by history and known only through his work.

Certain written sources are implied (xviii. 6, 9, xxiv. 26), or are probable in the nature of the material (*e.g.* the town lists). The discernment of others is speculative. The Book of Jashar is cited on the battle of Gibeon (x. 12 f.).

The clearest indication of early date is in xiii. 6, designating the Sidonians for expulsion and not mentioning Tyre. The descriptions of Danite and Simeonite territory, and the levitical allocation (never implemented—Kaufmann), appear to be early, probably originating from the Shiloh convention. On the other hand, the language of certain remarks (*e.g.* xv. 63, xvi. 10) would be inappropriate before the monarchy; and the town list of Judah is similarly dated, since it includes the strongholds in the Plain (see SECACAH). The references to memorials supply no latest date. The odd 1st person in Jos. v. 1 (*MT*), and the personal reference to Rahab (vi. 25), are very slight evidence for contemporary writing.

III. COMPOSITION

Chapters i–xi form a continuous, relatively straightforward narrative, though the treatment becomes progressively more summary, ending with a general evaluation of Joshua's achievement (xi. 15–23). In whatever form the author received his material, he has made of it a story of the highest dramatic quality, alike in treatment of the subject and in narrative technique. The terms 'editing' and 'redaction' are quite out of place; but much is omitted or generalized to get the broad picture, in due proportions, in the limited space.

A climax is reached at the end of chapter xi, but the story is not finished, and the 'deuteronomic style' is evident in the setting of the remaining material. This comprises: (i) a summary of victories (*i.e.* the kings defeated; possession is understood to follow, in principle); (ii) an account of the partition convention at Shiloh, interrupted by (iii) details of settlements in Transjordan, Judaea, and Mt. Ephraim; (iv) records of the partition and of the towns allocated as levitical and as sanctuaries; (v) narrative of the dismissal of the Transjordanian contingent and the dispute over the altar Ed; (vi) speeches by Joshua; (vii) epilogue.

Traditional criticism assigned a post-exilic date to matter which was 'systematic' or 'detailed' (*LOT*[9], pp. 12, 126 ff.), or which concerned the priests; such 'P' items in chapters i–xi were ascribed to a priestly redactor, but the criteria were vague and variously applied. Such verses as iv. 13, vii. 1, being designated P, implied a

P-narrative antedating the P-redaction; this has been contested (see C. R. North, *Old Testament and Modern Study*, 1951), and the antiquity of much P-material is being increasingly recognized.

IV. POSITION IN THE BIBLE

In the Hebrew Bible, Joshua heads the 'Former Prophets', which cover Israelite history from the invasion to the Exile. In immediate and natural sequence to Deuteronomy, it extends from Joshua's assumption of command to his passing and the death of Eleazar. Its unity and completeness in this sense are well marked. Because of its continuity with Deuteronomy in content and narrative style, some scholars have considered Genesis–Joshua as a 'Hexateuch', extending their principles of source-analysis through Joshua. Others reject this extension, for example Noth (*Josua*, Introduction, p. 8), who propounds the idea of a 'deut ronomic history' with Joshua as the second book. There are serious difficulties for this theory. We may note in particular: (i) the absence of deuteronomic frameworks for Judges–Kings; (ii) the fact that the 'deuteronomic style' characterizes Joshua specially (S. R. Driver, *LOT*[9], pp. 104, 164, found 'the spirit' of Deuteronomy in the framework of Joshua and Judges, but 'the style' in Joshua only; Burney, *Judges*, 1920, pp. xli ff., defining 'D' stylistically, disallowed it in Judges); and (iii) the clear distinction in Jewish tradition between Law and Former Prophets (*cf.* Josephus, *Contra Apionem*, i. 7 ff.). This last consideration also weighs heavily against the projection into Joshua of Pentateuch 'sources', at any rate as individual continuous narratives (G. A. Smith, *HDB*, II, p. 784; E. J. Young, *Introduction to the Old Testament*, 1949, p. 158).

Passages in Numbers and Deuteronomy recalled in Joshua

Jos.	*Nu.*	*Dt.*	*Subject*	*Notes*
i. 1–9		xxxi	Joshua commissioned	
i. 3–4		xi. 24	Extent of promises	Slight differences of phrasing.
i. 12–15	xxxii	iii. 18 ff.	Eastern tribes	Direct reference to Deuteronomy, phrasing varies.
viii. 30–5		xxvii	Ebal	*Cf.* Dt. xi. 29–32. Jos. abbreviates but also mentions ark and foreigners.
xii. 1–6	xxi. 21–35	ii–iii iv. 45–49	Conquests in Transjordan	Numbers mostly narrative; Deuteronomy has more geographical data, differently arranged.
xiii. 6, 7	xxxiv. 17	i. 38	'divide this land'	
xiii. 8–14 xiii. 15 ff.	xxxii. 33–42	ii. 32 ff.	Settlement in Transjordan	Distinctive description of Aroer in Joshua and Deuteronomy.
xiv. 1	xxxiv. 17		Joshua and Eleazar	*Cf.* Jos. xix. 51.
xiv. 6 ff.	xiv. 24	i. 28–36	Caleb's inheritance	
xv. 1–4	xxxiv. 3–5		South frontier	
xvii. 3–6	xxvii. 1–11		Zelophehad's daughters	
xviii. 4–10	xxxiv. 17 ff.		Partition Commission	Supervisors nominated in Numbers, scribes detailed in Joshua.
xx	xxxv. 9 ff.	xix. 1–13	Sanctuary towns	Joshua assumes procedure detailed in Nu. xxxv. 24 ff.; omits division of land (Dt. xix. 3) and fate of guilty applicant (Dt. xix. 12). Deuteronomy omits Transjordan towns (Jos. xx. 8; Nu. xxxv. 14) and acceptance procedure (Jos. xx. 4).
xxi	xxxv. 2–8		Levitical towns	

V. SPIRITUAL CONTENT

The importance of Joshua for Christians lies chiefly in the evidence it provides of God's faithfulness to His covenant (*cf.* Dt. vii. 7, ix. 5, 6), the development it records of God's purpose for the nation of Israel, the reasons it gives for the failure to carry out God's plan, a failure already becoming evident (see, *e.g.*, xvii. 13, xviii. 3), and the analogies which can be drawn for Christian discipleship because of the spiritual issues of faith, obedience, and purity which the book shows quite clearly were at stake in the invasion.

Israel under Joshua showed better morale than under Moses, but was no less susceptible to polytheism and nature-religion (Nu. xxv; Dt. iv. 3, 23). Determination to extirpate the Canaanites and their religion was therefore of prime importance (*cf.* Gn. xv. 16; Ex. xx. 2–6, xxiii. 23–33, xxxiv. 10–17; Nu. xxxi. 15 ff.; Dt. vii). The Israelites could not yet understand a redemptive approach, while daily contact with Canaanite culture would jeopardize their own faith in a unique, all-powerful God, as well as their moral standards, as the sequel showed. Moreover, spiritual salvation could not be generally offered (as under the New Testament) before its necessary judicial ground had been publicly set out in Christ's death; but we see a pattern of it in God's dealing with Rahab (*cf.* Heb. xi. 31). In general, we may say that God's purpose at the time was not to teach Christian principles, but to prepare the way for Christ through Israel.

As Christians we should note that the experiences of Israel in Canaan, as in the deserts, were 'written for our admonition' (1 Cor. x. 11). In particular, the chief theme of the book is that God gave Israel rest, which their unbelieving fathers had failed to obtain (*cf.* Ps. xcv. 11). In Heb. iv. 1–11 it is shown that this is a 'type'; *i.e.* the principle which the Psalmist applied in his own generation is equally valid for the Christian, and the promise is finally and completely fulfilled (verse 8) only in the rest which God has provided for us in Christ (*cf.* J. N. Darby, *Synopsis*, I, p. 328).

VI. TEXT AND TRANSLATIONS

The Heb. text contains few obscurities. No material corrections are suggested by the Septuagint, which maintains an average standard, not meticulously accurate; its rendering of geographical names is unreliable. The AV requires a few corrections, and a carefully paragraphed format; these the RSV supplies.

BIBLIOGRAPHY. *Text:* Benjamin, *Variations between the Hebrew and Greek Texts of Joshua*, 1921. *Critical:* M. Noth, *Josua*², 1953; H. W. Hertzberg, *Josua, Richter, Ruth, ATD*, 1953; F. M. Abel, *Le Livre de Josué*, École Biblique, 1950. *Expository: Speaker's Bible* (*Deuteronomy–Ruth*), 1924; Calvin, *Joshua*. *Historical evaluation:* Garstang, *Joshua–Judges*, 1931; H. H. Rowley, *From Joseph to Joshua*, Schweich Lectures, 1948; Y. Kaufmann, *Biblical Account of the Conquest of Palestine*, 1953; and relevant portions of general works. J.P.U.L.

JOSIAH (*yō'šiyyāhû*, or rarely, *yō'šiyyâ*, 'Yahweh supports').

1. King of Judah *c.* 639–609 BC. The son of Amon and grandson of Manasseh, Josiah owed his promotion to the throne at the age of eight to 'the people of the land' who also put to death his father's assassins (2 Ki. xxi. 24; 2 Ch. xxxiii. 25). There is no evidence that this popular movement had religious significance. The two accounts of his reign (2 Ki. xxii–xxiii. 30; 2 Ch. xxxiv–xxxv) are focused almost exclusively on the great religious reformation which he inaugurated. Both accounts are agreed that the climax of this reformation was reached in the eighteenth year of his reign when 'the book of the law' was discovered by Hilkiah, the high priest, in the Temple (2 Ki. xxii. 8; 2 Ch. xxxiv. 14, 15). The Chronicler, however, makes it clear that Josiah had actually begun the reformation ten years earlier (2 Ch. xxxiv. 3).

There were in fact three stages in Josiah's programme of reform. In the eighth year of his reign he personally renounced the corrupt, polytheistic religion of the two previous reigns. The effect of this was at first probably confined to court circles. It is not without significance that the last great Assyrian king, Ashurbanipal, died about this time (*c.* 632 BC). This helps to explain how a young man of sixteen could successfully defy his Assyrian overlord by ceasing to honour Assyrian gods and apparently carry the court with him. Four years later, the reform gathered momentum and was extended to Jerusalem and beyond. The call of Jeremiah to be a prophet in the following year may well have some connection with this extension of the reformation (Je. i. 2). The discovery of the law-book in Josiah's eighteenth year (621 BC) gave fresh impetus and urgency to his religious policy, which now entered upon its third and most far-reaching stage.

Even though the author of Kings is chiefly concerned with what took place after the book of the law had been found, his account implies also that the reformation antedated this discovery. That the Temple was undergoing repairs at the time and that money for these repairs had been accumulating over a considerable period (2 Ki. xxii. 3–7) are clear evidence of this. Most assume from the character of Josiah's reforms and from the fact that he renewed the covenant between Yahweh and the people on the basis of it, that the law-book was some form of Deuteronomy. There is in fact no evidence that this was so (but see DEUTERONOMY, BOOK OF).

The reformation itself was more thoroughgoing than Hezekiah's (*cf.* 2 Ki. xxiii. 13) and more extensive. Not only did Josiah destroy all the high places (*bāmôṯ*) in Judah and Benjamin, but his reforming zeal took him through Ephraim and Benjamin and even as far north as Naphtali in Galilee. Everywhere he extirpated every vestige of heathen worship (2 Ki. xxiii. 19, 20; 2 Ch. xxxiv. 6, 7). In particular, he fulfilled the prophecy concerning the high place at Bethel where Jeroboam ben Nebat had first introduced his religious innovations (2 Ki. xxiii. 15–18, *cf.*

1 Ki. xiii. 2). The celebration of the Passover which followed out-rivalled that of Hezekiah's reign, being without parallel since the days of Samuel (2 Ch. xxxv. 18).

Thorough though the reformation was, it was almost entirely external and never effected any real change in the hearts of the people. This is clear both from those prophecies of Jeremiah which belong to this period (Je. ii–vi) and the almost immediate reversion to idolatry after Josiah's death (see JEREMIAH).

Jeremiah speaks with warm appreciation of the justice of Josiah's administration (Je. xxii. 15 f.).

The death of Josiah in battle at Megiddo (609 BC) was as tragic as it was unnecessary. Necho II, king of Egypt, was advancing through Palestine to bring help to the Assyrians making a last desperate stand at Harran. Despite the strongest assurances to the contrary, Josiah regarded Necho's activities as a threat to his kingdom, which by this time probably extended to the Esdraelon Plain, and opposed him (2 Ki. xxiii. 29, 30; 2 Ch. xxxv. 20–24). By this act of folly Judah's godliest king met his end (2 Ki. xxiii. 25).

2. A contemporary of Zechariah (Zc. vi. 10).

BIBLIOGRAPHY. Articles on 'Josiah' in *HDB* and *ISBE* and *DOTT*, pp. 75–78; D. W. B. Robinson, *Josiah's Reform and the Book of the Law*, 1951; M. B. Rowton, 'Jeremiah and the Death of Josiah', *JNES*, X, 1951, pp. 128 ff.

J.C.J.W.

JOT AND TITTLE. In Mt. v. 18 'jot' is a transliteration of *iōta*, the name of the Gk. *i*; here, however, it stands for the corresponding Heb.

Fig. 123. *Left:* A letter *y* (Heb. *yôḏ*, AV 'jot'), the smallest letter in the Hebrew alphabet. *Centre* and *right:* A letter *r* (Heb. *reš*) and a letter *d* (Heb. *dāleṯ*). They are distinguished from each other by the addition of a 'tittle' to the latter.

yôḏ, the smallest letter of the alphabet, the use of which is frequently optional. 'Tittle' is a variant spelling for 'title,' which in older English meant a stroke above an abridged word, and then any minor stroke. Here and in Lk. xvi. 17 it represents *keraia*, meaning a little horn, and refers to the minor strokes which distinguish certain Heb. letters from one another, *e.g.* *bêṯ* and *kap̄*, *dāleṯ* and *rēš*. See fig. 123. H.L.E.

JOTBAH. Birthplace of Manasseh's wife, 2 Ki. xxi. 19. The Talmud names Jotbath (Jotapata in Josephus), 9 miles north of Nazareth, but this is improbable. H. L. Ginsberg (*Alex. Marx Jubilee Volume*, 1950, p. 350) emends to Juttah.

JOTBATH(AH). Probably the modern 'Ain Ṭābah about 22 miles north of Ezion-geber. It was a stopping-place on the route of the Exodus (Nu. xxxiii. 33, 34) and in Dt. x. 7 is described as 'a land of brooks of water', which would refer to its situation in a swampy depression that sometimes becomes a lake in winter. R.F.H.

JOTHAM (*yôṯām*, 'Yahweh is perfect'). **1.** The youngest of the seventy legitimate sons of Jerubbaal (Gideon), and sole survivor of Abimelech's massacre of the other brothers. Through the parable of the trees selecting the bramble to be their king (an honour previously declined by the cedar, the olive, and the vine), Jotham warned the Shechemites against Abimelech (Jdg. ix. 5 ff.). The warning was ignored, and the curse that he uttered was fulfilled three years later (verse 57).

2. Son of Uzziah ('Joatham' in Mt. i. 9), and twelfth king of Judah. He began his reign as co-regent *c.* 750 BC when his father was found to be a leper (2 Ki. xv. 5), and was sole monarch *c.* 740–*c.* 732 BC (see CHRONOLOGY OF THE OLD TESTAMENT). A man who feared God, Jotham built the high gate of the Temple, fortified and extended the land of Judah, and subdued the Ammonites (2 Ch. xxvii. 3–6). **3.** A son of Jahdai and descendant from Caleb (1 Ch. ii. 47).

J.D.D.

JOY. The biblical words are: Heb. *śimḥâ*, verb *śāmēaḥ*, which imply also its outward expression (*cf.* the Arab. cognate, meaning 'to be excited'), and less usually *gîl* (verb and noun); Gk. *chara* (verb *chairō*), and *agalliasis* (frequently used in the LXX, and corresponding to *śimḥâ*), meaning intense joy.

Both in the Old and New Testaments joy is consistently the mark both individually of the believer and corporately of the Church. It is a quality, and not simply an emotion, grounded upon God Himself and indeed derived from Him (Ps. xvi. 11; Phil. iv. 4; Rom. xv. 13), which characterizes the Christian's life on earth (1 Pet. i. 8), and also anticipates eschatologically the joy of being with Christ for ever in the kingdom of heaven (*cf.* Rev. xix. 7).

I. IN THE OLD TESTAMENT

Joy is related to the total national and religious life of Israel, and is particularly expressed in terms of noisy, tumultuous excitement at festivals, sacrifices, and enthronements (Dt. xii. 6 f.; 1 Sa. xviii. 6; 1 Ki. i. 39 f.). Spontaneous joy is a prevailing feature of the Psalter, where it is a mark both of corporate worship (centred largely on the Temple, Ps. xlii. 4, lxxxi. 1) and of personal adoration (Ps. xvi. 8 f., xliii. 4). Isaiah conceives of joy in other than simply ritual terms (though *cf.* Ps. cxxvi), and he associates it with the fulness of God's salvation, and therefore (in terms of a cosmic rejoicing) with the anticipation of a future state (Is. xlix. 13, lxi. 10 f.). In later Judaism, as a result, joy is a characteristic of the last days.

II. IN THE NEW TESTAMENT

The Synoptic Gospels record the note of joy in connection with the proclamation, in its varied forms, of the good news of the kingdom: for example, at the Saviour's birth (Lk. ii. 10), at the triumphal entry (Mk. xi. 9 f.; Lk. xix. 37), and after the resurrection (Mt. xxviii. 8). In the Fourth Gospel it is Jesus Himself who communicates this joy (Jn. xv. 11, xvi. 24), and it now becomes the result of a deep fellowship between the Church and Himself (*cf.* xvi. 22).

In Acts joy marks the life of the early Church. It accompanies the gift of the Holy Spirit to the disciples (Acts xiii. 52), the miracles performed in the name of Christ (viii. 8), and the fact and report of the conversion of the Gentiles (xv. 3); and it also characterizes the eucharistic meal (ii. 46).

Paul uses the term *chara* in three ways. First, progress in the faith on the part of the members of the body of Christ, and particularly those he has led to Christ, is a cause for joy—he describes them, indeed, as *hē chara hēmōn*, 'our joy' (1 Thes. ii. 19 f.; *cf.* Phil. ii. 2). Secondly, Christian joy may paradoxically be the outcome of suffering and even sorrow for Christ's sake (Col. i. 24; 2 Cor. vi. 10; *cf.* 1 Pet. iv. 13; Heb. x. 34, *etc.*), since it is produced by the Lord and not by ourselves. Joy is in fact, finally, a gift of the Holy Spirit (Gal. v. 22), and is therefore something dynamic and not static. Moreover, it derives from love—both God's love and ours—and is therefore closely associated with it in the Pauline list of the fruit of the Spirit. But since it is a gift which may be interrupted by sin, every believer is called upon to share in the joy of Christ by a daily walk with Him and a daily practice of rejoicing in the knowledge of Him and His salvation (1 Thes. v. 16; Phil. iii. 1, iv. 4; 1 Pet. i. 8).

BIBLIOGRAPHY. The standard work on the subject is E. G. Gulin, *Die Freude im Neuen Testament*, 1932; see also J. Moffatt, *Grace in the New Testament*, 1931, p. 168, for the relation between *chara* and *charis*. S.S.S.

JOZACHAR (Heb. *yôzāḵār*). He is named as one of the two assassins of Joash (2 Ki. xii. 21) who was in turn executed by Amaziah when the latter became king (2 Ki. xiv. 5). His name is given as 'Zabad' in 2 Ch. xxiv. 26. This is an abbreviated form of 'Jozabad', which appears in some MSS of the *MT* of 2 Ki. xii. 21. J.C.J.W.

JUBAL. A son of Adah, wife of Lamech, and ancestor of those who 'handle the harp (*kinnôr*) and pipe (*'ûgāḇ*)' (Gn. iv. 21). See MUSIC AND MUSICAL INSTRUMENTS. T.C.M.

JUBILEE. See SABBATICAL YEAR.

JUBILEES, BOOK OF. See APOCALYPTIC.

JUDAEA. The Gk. and Rom. designation of the land of Judah (*q.v.*). The word is actually an adjective ('Jewish') with *gē* ('land') or *chōra* ('country') understood. After the Roman conquest (63 BC) it appears both in a wider sense, denoting all Palestine, including Galilee and Samaria, and in the narrower sense, which excludes these two regions. Herod's kingdom of Judaea (37–4 BC) included all Palestine and some districts east of the Jordan. Archelaus's ethnarchy of Judaea (4 BC–AD 6) embraced Judaea in the narrower sense and Samaria, and the same is true of the Rom. province of Judaea from AD 6 to 41. After the death of Herod Agrippa I in AD 44 the Rom. province of Judaea included Galilee also. See ISRAEL.

The 'wilderness of Judaea' (Mt. iii. 1), associated with John the Baptist, is probably identical with the 'wilderness of Judah' (Jdg. i. 16, *etc.*), *i.e.* the desert to the west of the Dead Sea.

J.D.D.

JUDAH.

I. THE SON OF JACOB

The fourth son of Jacob by Leah (Gn. xxix. 35) was called Judah (*yᵉhûḏâ*); the name is there explained as meaning 'praised', as derived from the root *ydh*, 'to praise'. Gn. xlix. 8 contains a play on this meaning. The derivation is widely rejected, but no other suggested etymology has been generally accepted (for literature, see Köhler and Baumgartner, *Lexicon in Veteris Testamenti Libros*). Judah early took a leading rôle among his brothers, as is shown by the story of Joseph (Gn. xxxvii. 26, 27, xliii. 3–10, xliv. 16–34, xlvi. 28). Gn. xxxviii, though throwing light on the beginnings of the tribe of Judah, clearly stands in its present position to contrast Judah's character with that of Joseph. Though Gn. xlix. 8–12 is not strictly a promise to Judah of kingship, but rather of leadership, victory, and tribal stability, the promise of Shiloh (*q.v.*) involves kingship ultimately. The genealogies of Judah's descendants are found in 1 Ch. ii–iv.

II. OTHER INDIVIDUALS OF THE SAME NAME

After the Babylonian Exile Judah became increasingly one of the favourite names among the Jews. Five men of this name are mentioned in the Old Testament, *viz.* a Levite, ancestor of Kadmiel (Ezr. iii. 9), possibly the father or son of Hodaviah (Ezr. ii. 40); a Levite of the return under Zerubbabel (Ne. xii. 8); a levitical contemporary of Ezra (Ezr. x. 23); a leading Benjamite under Nehemiah (Ne. xi. 9); a priest under Nehemiah (Ne. xii. 36). In Ne. xii. 34 probably members of the tribe in general are meant by 'Judah'. In the New Testament the name is represented by its Hellenized form Judas (shortened to Jude in Jude 1).

III. THE TRIBE OF JUDAH

a. From the Exodus till Saul

Judah plays no special rôle in the story of the Exodus and of the wilderness wanderings, though it is to be noted that he was the leader of the vanguard (Nu. ii. 9). There is no significant change in the two census figures from this period (Nu. i. 27, xxvi. 22).

Achan, a member of the tribe, was the cause of the defeat of Israel before Ai (Jos. vii). This may be the reason for the special task laid on Judah to lead an independent attack on the Canaanites (Jdg. i. 1, 2). No explanation is given, but it is clear that Judah's portion was not allocated by lot in Shiloh (Jos. xviii. 1–10) before its conquest (Jdg. i. 3). It was bounded on the north by the portions of Dan and Benjamin, and ran approximately east and west from the north end of the Dead Sea, south of Jerusalem and the Gibeonite tetrapolis to the Mediterranean. Its west and east frontiers were the Mediterranean and the Dead Sea, and it extended south as far as cultivation permitted (*cf.* Jos. xv).

Judah first overran most of the coastal plain, soon to be occupied by the Philistines (Jdg. i. 18), but evidently quickly withdrew from the struggle (Jdg. i. 19, iii. 3; Jos. xi. 22, xiii. 2, 3). Since it was the best of the land apportioned to him that Judah voluntarily abandoned to Simeon (Jos. xix. 1, 9), it is reasonable to suppose that he hoped to have Simeon as a buffer between him and the unconquered coastal plain.

The story of the conquest of the south in Jdg. i. 1–17 has been very widely interpreted to mean that Judah (and other tribes) entered the land from the south *before* the invasion under Joshua (*cf.* H. H. Rowley, *From Joseph to Joshua*, 1950, pp. 4 f., 101 f., 110 ff., with literature), but the whole trend of modern archaeological discovery seems to be unfavourable to the theory, which is unacceptable on other, general grounds.

The failure to maintain a hold on Jerusalem (Jdg. i. 8, 21), combined with the existence of the semi-independent Gibeonite tetrapolis (Jos. ix; 2 Sa. xxi. 1, 2), created a psychological frontier between Judah and the central tribes. Though there was no barrier to communications (*cf.* Jdg. xix. 10–13), Judah will increasingly have looked south to Hebron rather than to the sanctuary at Shiloh. While Judah provided the first of the judges, Othniel (Jdg. iii. 9–11), and shared in the early action against Benjamin (Jdg. xx. 18), he does not even seem to have been expected to join against Jabin and Sisera (Jdg. v). As a result, when Judah became tributary to the Philistines (Jdg. xv. 11), he seems not to have appealed to the other tribes, nor do they seem to have been concerned.

The fact of this division seems to have been generally recognized, for by Saul's time we find the contingent from Judah separately enumerated (1 Sa. xi. 8, xv. 4, xvii. 52, xviii. 16).

b. Under David and Solomon

After Saul's death this growing split was perpetuated by David's being crowned as king in Hebron over Judah (2 Sa. ii. 4). A. Alt is probably correct in maintaining (*Das Grossreich Davids–Kleine Schriften zur Geschichte des Volkes Israel*, II, pp. 66 ff.) that the crowning of David as king over 'all Israel' (2 Sa. v. 1–5) made him king of a dual kingdom in which Judah kept its separate identity. Certainly during Absalom's rebellion Judah seems to have maintained its neutrality, while the north followed the rebel.

There is no evidence that Solomon showed any favouritism to Judah compared with the other tribes, for 'and one officer, which was in the land' (1 Ki. iv. 19, RVmg) will refer to Judah.

IV. THE KINGDOM OF JUDAH

a. Its relations with Israel

If A. Alt's view is correct, Judah and Israel in accepting different kings were acting in accordance with their rights as separate political entities. Apart from Jeroboam himself, the kings of Israel do not seem to have sought the destruction of Judah (*cf.* 2 Ki. xiv. 13, 14), and the prophets never questioned the right of Israel to exist, though they foresaw the time when it would return to its allegiance to 'David'.

The heritage of Solomon's riches seemed to give Judah the advantage at the disruption, despite its less fertile land and smaller population compared with the north. In spite of claims to the contrary, there is no evidence that Rehoboam later disregarded the command of Shemaiah (1 Ki. xii. 22–24) and attacked Jeroboam. The suggestion that Shishak's attack on Judah (1 Ki. xiv. 25, 26) was in support of his ally Jeroboam has never been able to produce positive evidence in its support. The resultant loss of the wealth Solomon had amassed, even though Israel seems to have suffered from Shishak's attack as well, meant that Judah now stood permanently in a position of material inferiority compared with Israel. The evidence suggests that Judah needed a prosperous Israel for its own prosperity.

One effective test of the absolute, rather than relative, prosperity of Judah was its ability to control Edom, or as much of it as was necessary for the safeguarding of the trade-route to the Gulf of Aqabah. Rehoboam made no effort to maintain his father's precarious hold on the area. Jehoshaphat evidently completely subdued the country (1 Ki. xxii. 47), but later he had to instal a vassal king (2 Ki. iii. 9). Edom regained its independence under his son Jehoram (2 Ki. viii. 20–22). Amaziah, about half a century later, reconquered Edom (2 Ki. xiv. 7). This time the conquest was more effective, and not until the troubles of Ahaz' reign sixty years later was Edom finally able to free itself (2 Ki. xvi. 6, RSV). After this Judah does not seem even to have attempted conquest.

It was only a decisive victory by Abijah (or Abijam) that restored a measure of parity between the kingdoms (2 Ch. xiii). Asa, faced with the capable Baasha, could maintain it only by allying himself with Ben-hadad, king of Damascus (1 Ki. xv. 18–20). The dynasty of Omri, disturbed both by the increasing power of Damascus, and even more by the threat from Assyria (*q.v.*), made peace with Judah, which was later sealed by the marriage of Athaliah, Ahab's daughter, or perhaps sister (2 Ki. viii. 26), with Jehoram. It is widely held that at this time Judah was Israel's vassal. So far from this being true, the evidence suggests that Jehoshaphat used Israel as a buffer between him and Assyria. This is the most likely explanation why Judah does not figure on Shalmaneser's list of his enemies at the battle of Qarqar, nor for that matter on the 'Black Obelisk'. He seems to have looked on, with the sole exception of the battle of Ramoth-gilead (1 Ki. xxii. 1–38), while Israel and Damascus tore at one another's vitals. Hence, by the end of his long reign, he felt himself strong enough to refuse Ahaziah's request for a joint venture to Ophir after the first had failed (1 Ki. xxii. 48, 49 compared with 2 Ch. xx. 35–37). The relative equality between the kingdoms at this time is seen in the fact that Jehu, though he had killed Ahaziah of Judah (2 Ki. ix. 27), did not venture to carry his anti-Baal campaign into Judah, nor, on the other hand, did Athaliah try to avenge her son's death.

In the century between the accession of Jehu and the deaths of Jeroboam II and Uzziah the fortunes of Judah seem to have kept pace with those of Israel both in affliction and prosperity. Probably the latter came more slowly to the south, even as the hollowness of its prosperity was revealed somewhat later than in Israel.

b. Earlier foreign enemies

Until the collapse of Israel the history of Judah is singularly uninfluenced by foreign threats. Shishak's invasion was a last stirring of Egypt's ancient power until the Assyr. advance forced it to measures of self-defence. The Philistines had been so weakened that we find them as aggressors only when Judah was weakest, *viz.* under Jehoram (2 Ch. xxi. 16) and Ahaz (2 Ch. xxviii. 18). At the height of Hazael's power, when he had almost destroyed Israel, Jehoash was forced to become tributary to Damascus, but this cannot have lasted long. In fact, the only two major threats of this period were from those sudden movements that the nomads and semi-nomads of the desert have periodically thrown up. Zerah 'the Cushite' (2 Ch. xiv. 9) is more likely to have been an Arabian (*cf.* Gn. x. 7) than an Ethiopian, *i.e.* a Sudanese. The second was from a sudden movement of the inhabitants of the Transjordan steppe-land (2 Ch. xx. 1, 10).

c. Judah and Assyria

As stated above, the earlier advances of Assyria do not seem to have affected Judah. When Damascus and Israel attacked Ahaz (2 Ki. xvi. 5), it was a last desperate attempt to unite the remnants of the West against the advance of Tiglath-pileser III. There are no grounds for thinking that Judah was threatened by the Assyrians, for until they wanted to challenge Egypt they would hardly alarm it by advancing prematurely to its desert frontier. By accepting the suzerainty of Assyria Ahaz virtually sealed the fate of Judah. On the one hand, it remained a vassal until the approaching doom of Assyria (612 BC) could be foreseen; on the other, it was caught up in the intrigues stirred up by Egypt, for which it duly suffered. Hezekiah's revolt in 705 BC, crushed by Sennacherib four years later, reduced Judah to a shadow of its former self, at least two-thirds of the population perishing or being carried away captive, and a large portion of its territory being lost. For details, see J. Bright, *A History of Israel*, 1960, pp. 267–271, 282–287.

d. Revival and downfall

A revival of religious and nationalistic feeling under the young Josiah began just after Ashurbanipal's death (631 BC), when the weakness of Assyria was already becoming manifest. The steps in reform indicated in 2 Ch. xxxiv. 3, 8 suggest how closely interwoven religion and politics had become, for each step was in itself also a rejection of Assyr. religious and therefore political control. By the height of the reform in 621 BC Josiah, though probably still nominally tributary to Assyria, was in fact independent. With or without the approval of his nominal overlord he took over the Assyr. provinces of Samaria and Eastern Galilee (2 Ch. xxxiv. 6) and doubtless recovered the territory that Hezekiah had lost as a punishment for his rebellion. There is no reliable evidence that the Scythian inroad, which did so much to give Assyria its mortal wound, affected or even reached Judah.

There is no indication that Josiah offered any opposition to Pharaoh Psamatik's expedition in aid of Assyria in 616 BC, but when Pharaoh Necho repeated the expedition in 609 BC Josiah evidently felt that in the new international position his only chance of maintaining Judah's independence was to fight, but in the ensuing battle at Megiddo he met his death. There is no evidence for the suggestion that he was acting in alliance with the rising star of Babylon (*q.v.*).

Egypt marked its victory by deposing Josiah's son Jehoahaz and replacing him by his brother Jehoiakim, who had, however, to accept Babylonian overlordship soon after Nebuchadrezzar's victory at Carchemish (605 BC)—Dn. i. 1; 2 Ki. xxiv. 1. In 601 BC Nebuchadrezzar was checked by Necho in a battle near the Egyp. frontier, and on his withdrawal to Babylon Jehoiakim rebelled. Judah was ravaged by Bab. troops and auxiliary levies (2 Ki. xxiv. 2). Jehoiakim died an obscure death in December 598 BC, before he could suffer the full penalty of rebellion, and Jehoiachin, his eighteen-year-old son, surrendered Jerusalem to Nebuchadrezzar on 16 March 597 BC.

His uncle Zedekiah became the last king of Judah, but revolted in 589 BC. By January 588 BC the Bab. armies were before the walls of Jerusalem. In July 587 BC the walls were breached and Zedekiah was captured to meet a traitor's fate (2 Ki. xxv. 6, 7); a month later the city was burned down and the walls razed.

e. Religion under the Monarchy

This is not the place to describe the religion of Israel, but certain features in Judah need underlining. Popular religion in Judah was probably as degraded by concepts of nature-religion as in Israel, but its relative isolation and openness to the desert will have made it less influenced by its Canaanite forms. Its lack of major sanctuaries —only Hebron and Beersheba are known to us with Gibeon in Benjamin—increased the influence of Jerusalem and its Solomonic Temple. It is questionable whether any king of Israel could even have attempted the centralizing reforms of Hezekiah and Josiah. The Davidic covenant (2 Sa. vii. 8–16), far more than the general atmosphere of the 'Fertile Crescent', made the king the undisputed leader of the national religion, even though cultic functions were denied him (2 Ch. xxvi. 16–21).

The power of the king might be used for good, as in the reformations, but where national policy seemed to demand an acceptance of Baal worship, as under Jehoram, Ahaziah, and Athaliah, or a recognition of the Assyr. astral deities, as under Ahaz and Manasseh, there was no effective power that could resist the royal will. The royal authority in matters of religion will also have helped to make the official cult for many merely an external and official matter.

f. Exile (597–538 BC)

Apart from an unspecified number of ordinary captives destined to slavery, Nebuchadrezzar deported the cream of the population in 597 BC (2 Ki. xxiv. 14; Je. lii. 28—the difference in figures is doubtless due to different categories of captives being envisaged). A few, including the royal family, became 'guests' of Nebuchadrezzar in Babylon; others, *e.g.* Ezekiel, were settled in communities in Babylonia, where they had apparently full freedom apart from the right to change their domicile; the skilled artisans became part of a mobile labour force used by Nebuchadrezzar in his building operations. The destruction of Jerusalem added to the general total of captives (2 Ki. xxv. 11), and Je. lii. 29 shows there was another group of designated deportees. The murder of Gedaliah, whom Nebuchadrezzar had made governor of Judah, led to a large-scale flight to Egypt (2 Ki. xxv. 25, 26; Je. xli–xliii. 7). This, in turn, was followed in 582 BC by another, obviously punitive, deportation to Babylonia (Je. lii. 30).

As the result of deportation and flight Judah was left, and remained, virtually empty (see W. F. Albright, *The Archaeology of Palestine*[2], 1954, pp. 140–142). The land south of a line between Beth-zur and Hebron seems to have been detached from Judah in 597 BC; into it the Edomites gradually moved. As a result, this area was lost to Judah until its capture by John Hyrcanus after 129 BC and the forcible Judaizing of its population. The remainder was placed under the governor of Samaria and deliberately kept virtually empty; there is no evidence for the infiltration of other peoples.

V. POST-EXILIC JUDAH

a. Restoration

Babylon fell to Cyrus in 539 BC, and the next year he ordered the rebuilding of the Jerusalem Temple (Ezr. vi. 3–5); he accompanied this with permission for the deportees and their descendants to return (Ezr. i. 2–4). The list of names, involving a total of some 43,000 persons, in Ezr. ii may well cover the period 538–522 BC, but there are no solid grounds for doubting that there was an immediate and considerable response to Cyrus' decree.

Sheshbazzar, a member of the Davidic royal family, seems to have been Cyrus' commissioner to oversee the rebuilding of the Temple; he will have returned (or died?) after the laying of the foundations (Ezr. v. 14, 16). There is no evidence that Judah was detached politically from the district of Samaria until the time of Nehemiah; the title 'governor' given Sheshbazzar is too narrow a rendering for *pēḥâ*. Zerubbabel, probably heir-apparent of the royal house, does not seem to have held any official position, the title of *pēḥâ* in Hg. i. 1, ii. 21 being probably honorific—note his non-appearance in Ezr. v. 3–17.

By the time of Ezra in the second half of the 4th century it had become apparent to most that political independence and the restoration of the Davidic monarchy were no more than a hope for the more distant future. Ezra transformed the Jews from a national state to a 'church', making the keeping of the Torah the purpose of their existence. The political insignificance of Judaea under the Persians and the relatively peaceful conditions of the country favoured the steady instruction of the mass of the people in the Torah. The only political upheaval of the period may have been a deportation to Babylonia and Hyrcania, though many doubt it (*cf.* Jos., *Contra Ap.* i. 194).

b. The end of Judah

The campaigns of Alexander the Great will hardly have affected Judaea, but his founding of Alexandria provided a centre for a western, and for the most part voluntary, dispersion, which soon rivalled that of Babylonia and Persia in numbers and surpassed it in wealth and influence. The division of Alexander's empire among his generals meant that Palestine became a debatable land between Syria and Egypt. Till 198 BC it was normally in the hands of the Egyp. Ptolemies, but then it became part of the Syrian Seleucid Empire.

The extravagances of the rich Hellenized upper classes of Jerusalem, in large proportion priests, and the unbalanced efforts of Antiochus Epiphanes (175–163 BC) to Hellenize his empire, which led him to forbid circumcision and

Sabbath-keeping and to demand the worship of Greek deities, created an alliance between religious zeal and dormant nationalism. The Jews achieved first religious autonomy and then political freedom (140 BC) for the first time since Josiah. By 76 BC their boundaries extended virtually from the traditional Dan to Beersheba. For the history of this meteoric rise and sudden collapse, see ISRAEL.

When the Romans destroyed the last vestiges of political independence in AD 70, and especially after the crushing of Bar Kochba's revolt in AD 135, Judaea ceased to be a Jewish land, but the name of Judah in its form of Jew became the title of all dispersed through the world who clung to the Mosaic law, irrespective of tribal or national origin.

BIBLIOGRAPHY. Archaeological discovery has put all earlier treatments of the subject to a greater or less degree out of date. John Bright, *A History of Israel*, 1960, gives an up-to-date and balanced presentation with a mention of the most important literature. For the text of *Kings*, see J. A. Montgomery and H. S. Gehman, *The Books of Kings*, *ICC*, 1951. For the archaeological texts, see J. B. Pritchard, *ANET*², 1955, and D. Winton Thomas, *DOTT*, 1958.

H.L.E.

JUDAISM.

I. DEFINITION

Judaism is the religion of the Jews in contrast to that of the Old Testament. While in any full study of it, it would be natural to start with the call of Abraham, this would be solely as an indispensable introduction. Judaism should be regarded as beginning with the Babylonian Exile, but for the period up to AD 70 the term is best used only for those elements which are either modifications or extensions of Old Testament concepts. In German works we frequently find the misleading expression 'late Judaism' used for Jewish religion in the time of Christ. It is derived from the theory that the Priestly Code and history in the Hexateuch are exilic or post-exilic and the true beginning of Judaism.

But it is better to regard Judaism as coming into full existence only after the destruction of the Temple in AD 70 and, except when dealing with those phenomena that continued after this catastrophe, to use the term 'Inter-Testamental Religion' for the period between Ezra and Christ. One important reason for this is that, while primitive Christianity did not reject or ignore all the historical developments in the four centuries after Ezra, it turned its back on precisely that element in Judaism, *viz.* its attitude to and interpretation of the Law, that separates it both from Christianity and the Old Testament.

Judaism reached full development by AD 500, *i.e.* about the same time as Catholic Christianity, and like its sister religion has grown and modified ever since. This article, however, rarely goes beyond AD 200, when with the completion of the Mishnah the main concepts of Judaism had become clear. For later periods the reader is referred to articles on Judaism in *ERE*, *JewE*, *etc.*

II. THE RISE OF JUDAISM

Judaism was made inevitable by Josiah's reformation, which reached its climax in 621 BC. The restriction of legitimate sacrifice to the Temple in Jerusalem inevitably meant that the religion of many became increasingly detached from the sanctuary and sacrifice. The tendency was powerfully reinforced by the Babylonian Exile, even though modern research suggests that the blow of divine judgment was too stunning for any formal non-sacrificial worship to have been developed in exile.

The Exile was a time of waiting for restoration; the refusal of the majority to return in 538 BC made a modification in their religion vital, if they were to survive as Jews. It was not enough to develop non-sacrificial worship (this in its official, formulated expression seems to come later); a new outlook on life completely divorceable from sanctuaries was needed. This was found in the Torah or Law of Moses. It was interpreted less as a law code and more as a set of principles which could and should be applied to every area of life and which were binding on all who wished to be known as Jews (Torah in any case means 'instruction' rather than 'law'). Ezra was the true 'Father of Judaism', for he returned from Babylonia to introduce not a new law but a new way of keeping the old one.

The centuries that followed saw determined opposition to Ezra's policy from the richer priests and others, who by the reign of Antiochus Epiphanes (175–163 BC) were the leaders of the Hellenizers. The majority of the common people (*'am hā-'āreṣ*) tried to evade anything but the clear meaning of the Torah. In the western *diaspora* there was a growing assimilation to Greek modes of thought, helped by the prevalent allegorical interpretation of Scripture.

The next milestone in the development of Judaism was the Hellenization of the leading priests of Jerusalem and the subsequent degeneration of the victorious Hasmonean priest-kings (especially Alexander Jannaeus). Temple-worship for the pious became a duty rather than a joy. While the Qumran Covenanters seem to have turned their backs on the Temple, until God should purge it of its evil priests, the Pharisees (*q.v.* for additional material) exalted the synagogue as the chief means whereby God could be worshipped and His will discovered through the study of the Torah. As a result, by the time of Christ, there were some hundreds of synagogues in Jerusalem itself.

Though the destruction of the Temple in AD 70 came as a shock to the Pharisees and their admirers, they had been prepared for it by its frequent desecration in varying ways from the time of Antiochus Epiphanes onwards, and their synagogue-centred religion was able to adapt itself to the new conditions with great rapidity, the more so as the other religious groups had been destroyed or reduced to impotence. By *c.* AD 90 the Pharisaic leaders, the Rabbis, felt strong enough to exclude those they considered heretics (the *mînîm*), including Hebrew Christians, from the synagogue. By AD 200, after a bitter struggle, they had forced the *'am hā-'āreṣ* to conform, if they wished to be regarded as Jews. From then onwards, until Judaism began to be influenced by modern thought, the terms Jew and normative, rabbinic, orthodox, or traditional Judaism were essentially coterminous.

It should be noted that, though the Pharisees were always a minority group, there is nothing surprising in the triumph of their views. Even though they were often unpopular, their views seemed the most logical adaptation of the Old Testament to the post-exilic scene, and they became common property by their skilful use of the synagogue.

III. THE DOCTRINES OF JUDAISM

It should be clear to the reader of the New Testament that, however bitter the clash between Christ and Paul and their chief opponents, the area of the battle-field was strictly circumscribed. Both sides accepted the same Scriptures—unlike the Sadducees—and, superficially at least, interpreted them in very much the same way. A deep similarity between the teaching of Christ and of the early Rabbis has long been recognized, and the discovery of the Qumran MSS has speeded the recognition that the influence of Hellenism on the New Testament is marginal. Therefore it is sufficient to say here that much of the doctrine of Judaism does not vary significantly either from that of the Old Testament or from that of conservative Christianity. It may therefore be assumed that in matters not mentioned here there was no essential difference down to AD 500. It must be remembered, however, that Judaism's long fight for existence in the face of victorious Christianity has often led to a significant shift of emphasis, which diminishes the apparent area of agreement.

a. Israel

Basic to Judaism is the existence and call of Israel, membership of which is primarily by birth, though the proselyte was very welcome. The latter was conceived of as born into God's people by circumcision, baptism, and sacrifice. There is no evidence of any real understanding of the Old Testament doctrine of the 'remnant'. The aphorism 'All Israel has a share in the world to come' was generally accepted, apostasy (an elastic term) being normally regarded as the only bar to its enjoyment.

Within Israel all were regarded as brothers. Though the natural distinctions of society were never denied, before God rank depended on knowledge of the Torah and its fulfilment. Hence in the synagogue services the only qualifications for leadership were piety, knowledge, and ability. The Rabbis were neither priests nor ministers, nor did they have any form of ordination. They were simply those who knew the Torah well enough to teach it, and recognition by several recognized Rabbis, or even in exceptional cases by the community, was sufficient to make a man a Rabbi.

The woman was looked on as man's inferior because she was under her husband's authority and not able to carry out certain prescriptions of the Torah. But fundamentally Judaism has always maintained the truth of Gn. ii. 18 and woman's essential dignity.

b. Resurrection

Though later, under the influence of Christianity and Greek philosophy, Judaism was to give a somewhat reluctant assent to the doctrine of the immortality of the soul, it has always remained sufficiently true to the spirit of the Old Testament to consider bodily resurrection necessary for true life after death. 2 Tim. i. 10 is no denial of Judaism's hope of resurrection, for it, unlike the Christian faith based on the resurrection of Christ, was deduced from the few indications of the Old Testament and forged in the spiritual anguish that was the lot of the pious from the time of Antiochus Epiphanes.

A clear distinction was made between the *'ôlām ha-zeh* ('this world') and the *'ôlām ha-bā'* ('the world to come'), the latter being always regarded (apart from the more Hellenized members of the western Dispersion) as belonging to this earth. They were linked by the 'Days of the Messiah', always looked on as a limited period.

c. The Torah

The Pharisees seem to have occupied a middle position between the Sadducees, who rejected the authority (though not necessarily the value) of the prophetic books, and the Qumran Covenanters, who gave them high authority when in the hands of a competent expositor. The Pharisees looked on them as divinely inspired commentaries on the Torah, the Pentateuch, which was for them the perfect and final revelation of God's will. The main reason for their rejection of Christ, and why they demanded a sign from Him, was because He appealed to the authority entrusted to Him and not to that of Moses.

The Rabbis so exalted the rôle and value of the Torah that the keeping of it became the explanation and justification of Israel's existence. It was only later, as Judaism faced a politically triumphant Church, that the Torah was given a cosmic position and an existence before the creation of the world, so that it might play the part in Judaism that Christ plays in Christianity. It is easy to understand why Paul, with his doctrine of the addition of the law to bring out the sinfulness of sin, has always been obnoxious to the orthodox Jew.

In Judaism, however, the Pentateuch is only the *tôrâ še-bikeṯāḇ* (the written Torah). If the keeping of the Torah was to become the personal concern of every pious Jew, and if its enactments were to be extended to cover the whole of life, so as to create an essential unity within Israel, then there would have to be agreement on the principles of approach and exegesis. These had probably already been fixed in main outline by the time of Ezra. Together with some customs of immemorial antiquity, *e.g.* the washing of hands, they were attributed to tradition reaching right back to Moses on Mt. Sinai. These principles and their application to everyday life form the *tôrâ še-bᵉʿal-peh* (the oral Torah or law). It has equal authority with the written Torah, for the latter cannot be understood correctly without it.

The development of the oral Torah was approximately as follows. The written Torah was studied to find out the actual commandments in it; they were calculated at 613 in all—248 positive and 365 negative. These were then protected by the making of new laws, the keeping of which would guarantee the keeping of the basic commandments—this is known as 'making a hedge about the Torah'. Finally, the enlarged laws were applied by analogy to all conceivable spheres and possibilities of life.

While in one sense the oral Torah can never be regarded as completed, for with the changes in civilization there are always new situations to which it has to be applied, it is generally considered to have received its definitive form in the Talmud, and to a lesser extent in the Midrashim (sing. Midrash), the official, mainly devotional expositions (*'aggāḏâ*) of the Old Testament books.

The Talmud falls into two parts. The Mishnah is a codification of the oral Torah for which Rabbi Yehuda ha-Nasi (*c.* AD 200) was mainly responsible. In contrast to most Midrashim it is *hᵃlāḵâ*, *i.e.* the laws governing life, and is virtually a commentary on the legal side of the Pentateuch. The Gemara is a prolix commentary on the Mishnah. It not only gives precision to points left unclear but also throws a flood of light on all aspects of early Judaism. The longer Babylonian version was virtually completed by AD 500, the unfinished Palestinian form was broken off about a century earlier. It is much fairer to compare the Talmud with the Church Fathers than with the New Testament.

See further, TALMUD AND MIDRASH.

d. Man and the keeping of the Torah

It would be most unfair to write off Judaism as mere legalism, though this was bound to be prevalent. The favourite passages quoted from the Talmud to prove legalism are typical of any manual seeking to make a casuistic application of law to life. The tendency to legalism was tempered by the Rabbis' insistence that the keeping of the Torah must have the right intention (*kawwānâ*), and that it must be done for its own sake (*lišmâ*) and not for the reward it might bring. They regarded the giving of the Torah as a supreme act of grace, and our keeping of it should be the response of love.

Such a system is bound to stress our measure of success and not failure in the keeping of the Torah. Hence the heinousness of 'respectable' sin and man's inability perfectly to do the will of God were minimized, and this tendency was reinforced by the disappearance of sacrifice in AD 70. Judaism knows nothing really comparable to the Christian doctrine of original sin. It is true that man was conceived of as born with an evil inclination (*yēṣer hā-rāʿ*), but this was balanced by an equally innate good inclination (*yēṣer ha-ṭôḇ*), which if reinforced by the study of Torah would gain the ascendancy. This over-optimistic view of sin and human nature is found throughout Judaism.

More serious is the implicit claim for the autonomy of the man versed in the Torah. Though this claims complete authority over him, God leaves it to the learned to discover what its claims may be. This went so far that in the Talmud (*Menaḥoṯ* 29b) Moses is depicted as unable to grasp Rabbi Akiba's exposition by which he discovered things Moses had never thought were in his laws. On the other hand, direct commands were occasionally deliberately circumvented, for it was felt to be to the common good. The best known example is Dt. xv. 1–3—the example in Mk. vii. 9–13 was not taken up into the Mishnah, possibly because Christ's rebuke was recognized as just. There was an invariable tendency to decrease the burden of any enactment that seemed to press too hardly on the masses (this is no contradiction of Mt. xxiii. 4; it is the learned man's privilege to use his knowledge to lighten his burdens!). It is probably this attitude of self-confident assurance as controllers and moulders of the revelation of God's will that above all lies behind Christ's charge against the Pharisees of hypocrisy (see HYPOCRITE and H. L. Ellison, 'Jesus and the Pharisees', *JTVI*, LXXXV, 1953). In spite of constant rabbinic admonitions to humility the note of Jn. vii. 49 is all too often heard in the literature of Judaism.

Since Judaism lays all its stress on serving God by keeping the Torah, and all its intellectual subtlety was used to find the full scope of God's commands, it has been very little troubled with the type of theological dispute that has been the bane of Christendom. Provided a man accepted the perfect unity and uniqueness of God, the absolute authority and finality of the Torah and the election of Israel, he could, if he kept the demands of the law, hold what philosophical and mystic theories he chose. So much is this true that it has been rightly claimed that orthopraxy rather than orthodoxy is the correct word to apply to Judaism. The only serious schism in Jewry between the triumph of the Pharisaic viewpoint and modern times was that of the Karaites (8th century), and this was concerned with the principles of interpreting the Torah.

Judaism's historic development largely shielded it from Greek influence at its most critical stage. As a result it has preserved a much more even balance between the individual and society than is evident in much Christian practice; it has never been led to depreciate the material and has seldom advocated ascetic practices.

e. The Messiah

Though there was considerable variety of outlook, there are no traces in Judaism down to AD 200 that there would be any supernatural element in the Messiah. He is first the great deliverer from foreign oppression and then the enforcer of true Torah observance. The Days of the Messiah are the link with the world to come, but they are limited in length. For a summary, see J. Klausner, *The Messianic Idea in Israel*, Part III. See MESSIAH.

f. The doctrine of God

Any anthology of rabbinic sayings about God will quickly show that in the vast majority of cases they are true to the Old Testament revelation. They will be found to differ from the Christian concept mainly in the following points. Since a world to come on earth does not imply as close a contact with the Eternal as the concept of a hereafter in heaven, there is less concern with the implications of the absolute holiness of God. Since there is more stress on service than on communion, except among the frequent mystics, the problem of 'at-one-ment' is seldom met. In any case there is no understanding that Israel needs to be reconciled to God. The concept of incarnation is ruled out *a priori*; the gulf between Creator and creation is too great.

The conflict between Judaism and the triumphant Church made it so stress the transcendence of God as to make a real immanence almost impossible. The immanence constantly stressed in Jewish devotion has always something semi-pantheistic about it. God's unity was defined in terms that made Trinitarian doctrine an abomination. Increasingly He was described by negations which made Him unknowable except through His works. In spite of this the Old Testament basis of Judaism has been too strong for the pious Jew to be happy with such a position for long, and he has repeatedly sought to circumvent it by mysticism.

BIBLIOGRAPHY. H. Danby (tr.), *The Mishnah*, 1933; I. Epstein (ed.), *The Talmud*, English translation in 35 vols., 1935–1952; A. Cohen, *Everyman's Talmud*, 1932; H. L. Strack, *Introduction to the Talmud and Midrash*, E.T., 1931; G. F. Moore, *Judaism in the First Centuries of the Christian Era*, 3 vols., 1927, 1930; I. Epstein, *Judaism*, 1959; E. Schürer, *HJP*, E.T., 1898–1900, 3rd and 4th German edn., 1909; H. L. Strack and P. Billerbeck, *Kommentar zum Neuen Testament aus Talmud und Midrasch*, 4 vols., 1922–8; C. G. Montefiore and H. Loewe, *A Rabbinic Anthology*, 1938; J. Jocz, *The Jewish People and Jesus Christ*, 1949. H.L.E.

JUDAS. A number of men are thus designated in the New Testament. **1.** One of the sons of Jacob (Mt. i. 2, 3). See JUDAH. **2.** An ancestor of Jesus (AV 'Juda', Lk. iii. 30). **3.** The Lord's brother (Mt. xiii. 55 = Mk. vi. 3). Perhaps the author of the Epistle of Jude (*q.v.*), who styles himself 'brother of James'. See also BRETHREN OF THE LORD. **4.** The son of James, and one of the Twelve (Lk. vi. 16), called also Lebbaeus (Mt. x. 3) and Thaddaeus (Mk. iii. 18), who asked Jesus a question in the upper room (Jn. xiv. 22). Some regard him as the author of the Epistle of Jude.

5. For Judas Iscariot, see next article.

6. The Galilaean who stirred up a rebellion against the Romans (Acts v. 37). Josephus says he was born in Gamala, and places the rebellion in AD 6. Quirinius (*q.v.*) defeated the rebels and Judas was slain. **7.** A Jew at whose house in Damascus Paul lodged (Acts ix. 11). **8.** A prophet surnamed Barsabas, who with Silas was chosen by the Jerusalem Christian leaders to accompany Paul and Barnabas to Antioch to convey the apostles' decision regarding circumcision (Acts xv. 22–33). J.D.D.

JUDAS ISCARIOT.

I. NAME AND ORIGIN

In the Synoptic lists of the Twelve whom Jesus called that 'they might be with him' (Mk. iii. 14) the name of Judas always appears last, and usually with some description which brands him with an infamous stigma (*e.g.* 'which also betrayed him', Mk. iii. 19; Mt. x. 4; 'which was the traitor', Lk. vi. 16; *cf.* Jn. xviii. 2, 5). We may compare the case of Jeroboam I, in the Old Testament, who is mentioned with horror as the one 'who made Israel to sin'.

The term 'Iscariot' is applied to his name, in the Synoptic texts and in Jn. xii. 4; while in the other Johannine references the textual tradition shows considerable variation, with the name of Simon being given as Judas' father (Jn. vi. 71, xiii. 2, 26), and Iscariot being further explained by the addition *apo Karyōtou* (in certain readings of vi. 71, xii. 4, xiii. 2, 26, xiv. 22). These additional facts supplied by John would confirm the derivation of 'Iscarioth' from Heb. *'îš qerîyôt*, 'a man of Kerioth'. Kerioth is located in Moab, according to Je. xlviii. 24, 41; Am. ii. 2; but there is another possible identification, Kerioth-Hezron (Jos. xv. 25), which is 12 miles south of Hebron. This geographical explanation of 'Iscarioth' is preferable to the view which traces the word to *sikarios*, by way of an Aramaicized *'isqaryā'ā*, 'an assassin' (*cf.* Acts xxi. 38), as suggested by Schulthess and Wellhausen. See G. Dalman, *Jesus–Jeshua*, E.T., 1929, pp. 28, 29.

II. CAREER

In the apostolic band Judas was treasurer (Jn. xiii. 29), while another Johannine text speaks of him as a thief (xii. 6), mainly, we may suppose, on the ground that he 'pilfered' the money which was entrusted to him. For this sense of the verb translated 'took away' in xii. 6, RV, as attested in the papyri, see Deissmann, *Bible Studies*, E.T., 1901, p. 257.

The closing scenes of the Gospel story are

shadowed by the treachery of this 'one of the twelve', as he is repeatedly called (Mk. xiv. 10, *cf.* xiv. 20; Jn. vi. 71, xii. 4). He raises the voice of criticism against the action of Mary, who anointed the Master's feet with the precious ointment (Jn. xii. 3–5). The comment of the Evangelist is intended to stress the avarice of Judas, who saw in the price of the ointment nothing of the beautiful deed which Jesus praised (Mk. xiv. 6) but only a means by which the apostolic fund would be increased, and thereby his own pocket lined. And even this motive was cloaked under a specious plea that the money could be given away to relieve the poor. Thus to covetousness there is added the trait of deceit. Immediately following this incident at Bethany he goes to the chief priests to betray the Lord (Mt. xxvi. 14–16; Mk. xiv. 10, 11; Lk. xxii. 3–6). Mark records simply the fact of the treachery, adding that money was promised by the priests. Matthew supplies the detail of the amount, which may have been a part-payment of the agreed sum (with an implicit allusion to Zc. xi. 12, and possibly Ex. xxi. 32; *cf.* Mt. xxvii. 9). Luke gives the deep significance of the act when he records that Satan entered into the traitor and inspired his nefarious sin (*cf.* Jn. xiii. 2, 27). All Synoptists agree that Judas determined to await a favourable opportunity when he might deliver Jesus up to His enemies 'privately', *i.e.* secretly, by craft (for this rendering in Lk. xxii. 6; Mk. xiv. 1–2, see J. Jeremias, *The Eucharistic Words of Jesus*, E.T., 1955, p. 48).

That opportunity came on the evening when Jesus gathered in the upper room for the last meal with the Twelve (Mk. xiv. 17 ff. and parallels); and this fact is perpetuated in the Church's eucharistic tradition which dates from the time of St. Paul (1 Cor. xi. 23: 'in the night in which he was betrayed'). The Lord, with prophetic insight, foresees the action of the traitor whose presence is known at the table. In the Markan account Judas is not mentioned by name, and there seems to be a general air of bewilderment as to his identity. The conversation of Mt. xxvi. 25 with the question-and-answer dialogue is best understood as spoken in whispered undertones, while the Johannine account preserves the first-hand tradition of the beloved disciple's question and Jesus' action with the Paschal sop, both of which may have been said and done in a secretive fashion. At all events, this is the Lord's final appeal to Judas—and the traitor's final refusal. Thereafter Satan takes control of one who has become his captive; and he goes out into the night (Jn. xiii. 27–30).

The prearranged plan for Jesus' arrest was carried through. The secret which Judas betrayed was evidently the meeting-place in Gethsemane later that night; and to our Lord at prayer there came the band of soldiery, led by Judas (Mk. xiv. 43). The sign of identification was the last touch of irony. 'Whomsoever I shall kiss, that is he'; and with that the traitor's work was completed.

The last chapters of Judas' life are beset with much difficulty. Of his pathetic remorse the Scripture bears witness, yet the only Evangelist to record this is Matthew (xxvii. 3–10). To this account of his agony of remorse and suicide, the account of Acts i. 18, 19 must be added; and also, to complete the evidence, the grotesque testimony of Papias, *Frag.* 3, preserved by Apollinarius of Laodicea. This last-named text may be conveniently consulted in the series *Ancient Christian Writers*, VI, translated and annotated by J. A. Kleist, 1957 edn., p. 119. Papias relates how Judas' body swelled (this may be a possible meaning of Acts i. 18 for the EVV 'falling headlong'; see Arndt-Gingrich, *Lexicon*, *s.v. prēnēs*), and died on his own land. There have been various attempts at harmonization (*e.g.* Augustine's suggestion that the rope broke and Judas was killed by the fall, in the manner of Acts i. 18, thus conflating the Matthean and Acts accounts). But even more terrifying than the gruesome details of these accounts is the plain, stark verdict of Acts i. 25: 'this ministry and apostleship, from which Judas fell away, that he might go to his own place'. The apostle had become an apostate; and had gone to the destiny reserved for such a man.

III. CHARACTER

This reference invites the question of the true character of Judas. If 'his own place' is the place he chose for himself, what motives led him to his awful destiny and fate?, and how can we reconcile this statement with those Scriptures which give the impression that he was predetermined to fulfil the rôle of traitor, that Jesus chose him, knowing that he would betray Him, that he had stamped on him from the beginning the inexorable character of 'the son of perdition' (Jn. xvii. 12)? Psychological studies are indecisive and not very profitable. Love of money; jealousy of the other disciples; fear of the inevitable outcome of the Master's ministry which made him turn king's evidence in order to save his own skin; an enthusiastic intention to force Christ's hand and make Him declare Himself as Messiah—de Quincey's famous reconstruction; a bitter, revengeful spirit which arose when his worldly hopes were crushed and this disappointment turned to spite and spite became hate—all these motives have been suggested. Three guiding principles ought perhaps to be stated as a preliminary to all such considerations. 1. We ought not to doubt the sincerity of the Lord's call. Jesus, at the beginning, viewed him as a potential follower and disciple. No other presupposition does justice to the Lord's character, and His repeated appeals to Judas. 2. The Lord's foreknowledge of him does not imply fore-ordination that Judas must inexorably become the traitor. 3. Judas was never really Christ's man. He fell from apostleship, but never (so far as we can tell) from genuine relationship to the Lord Jesus. So he remained 'the son of perdition' who was lost because he was never 'saved'. His highest title for

Christ was 'Rabbi' (Mt. xxvi. 25). He lives on the stage of Scripture as an awful warning to the uncommitted follower of Jesus who is in His company but does not share His spirit (*cf.* Rom. viii. 9b); he leaves the Gospel story 'a doomed and damned man' because he chose it so, and God confirmed him in that dreadful choice.

BIBLIOGRAPHY. The difficulties associated with the variant details of the death of Judas are discussed by K. Lake in *The Beginnings of Christianity*, I, V, 1933, pp. 22–30; *cf.*, too, Arndt-Gingrich, *loc. cit.* and *s.v.* 'Ioudas', 6; K. Lüthi, *Judas Iskarioth*, 1955; D. Haugg, *Judas Iskarioth in den neutestamentlichen Berichten*, 1930; J. S. Stewart, *The Life and Teaching of Jesus Christ*, 1933, pp. 166–170; P. Benoit, art. 'La mort de Judas' in collected works, *Exégèse et Théologie*, 1961. R.P.M.

JUDE, EPISTLE OF. One of the 'Catholic Epistles' (*q.v.*).

I. OUTLINE OF CONTENTS

The Epistle falls into five parts:

a. Salutation (verses 1, 2).
b. Jude's purpose in writing (verses 3, 4).
c. False teachers denounced and their doom foretold (verses 5–16).
d. Exhortation to Christians (verses 17–23).
e. Doxology (verses 24, 25).

II. AUTHORSHIP, DATE, AND CANONICITY

The author of this little tract identifies himself as 'Jude (RV Judas), the servant of Jesus Christ, and brother of James'. In the early Church there was only one James who could be referred to in this way without further specification—'James the Lord's brother' (as he is called in Gal. i. 19). This points to an identification of the author with the Judas who is numbered among the brothers of Jesus in Mt. xiii. 55 and Mk. vi. 3, the Judas whose two grandsons, according to Hegesippus, were examined and dismissed by Domitian when he was informed that they belonged to the house of David (Eus., *EH* iii. 19, 20). Its date cannot be fixed with certainty; it may be tentatively assigned to the second half of the 1st century AD, after the fall of Jerusalem (verse 17 refers to the apostles in the past). We have express references to it towards the end of the 2nd century, in the Muratorian list and elsewhere; but there are probable allusions to it earlier in that century, in the *Didache* and the *Shepherd* of Hermas. Although its canonicity was long disputed, we may be glad that it was finally established, for (as Origen says) 'while it consists of but a few verses, yet it is full of mighty words of heavenly grace'.

III. OCCASION AND PURPOSE

Jude had projected another treatise, concerning 'our common salvation' (RV), when he found himself obliged to take up a more controversial line, in vigorous defence of the apostolic faith. This defence was made necessary by the alarming advances made by an incipient gnosticism in the circle of Christians to which Jude addresses himself—not in this case an ascetic form of teaching like that attacked by Paul in Colossians, but an antinomian form which may have appealed to Paul's teaching about Christian liberty, misinterpreting that liberty as licence and using it 'for an occasion to the flesh' (*cf.* Gal. v. 13). This is suggested by Jude's description of the false teachers in question as 'turning the grace of our God into lasciviousness' as well as 'denying our only Master and Lord, Jesus Christ' (verse 4, RV).

IV. ARGUMENT OF THE EPISTLE

False teaching requires to be exposed; it is not enough to set the truth alongside it in the expectation that everyone will recognize which is which. The refutation of error is an essential correlative to the defence of the faith 'once for all delivered to the saints' (verse 3, RV).

The doom of these false teachers has been pronounced of old. God's judgment, if slow, is sure, and once executed it abides for ever. This appears from the examples of the disobedient Israelites who died in the wilderness (*cf.* 1 Cor. x. 5; Heb. iii. 17; this was evidently a commonplace of primitive Christian 'typology'), of the rebellious angels of Gn. vi. 1–4, and of the cities of the plain (*cf.* Gn. xix). Like those prototypes, the false teachers defy divinely constituted authority, unlike the archangel Michael, who would not use insulting language even to the devil (verses 8–10). (Clement and Origen tell us that the incident of Michael's dispute with the devil was related in the *Assumption of Moses*, but the part of this work containing the incident is no longer extant.) The examples of Cain, Balaam, and Korah also point the lesson of doom for these latter-day followers of theirs (verse 11).

These false teachers introduce trouble and disgrace into the Church's fellowship, into its very love-feasts; they are shepherds who feed themselves and not the flock ('blind mouths', in Milton's phrase), clouds which blot out the sun but send down no refreshing rain, trees which produce only Dead Sea fruit (verse 12). They are ineffectual as roaring waves whose rage expends itself in froth and foam; they are stars wandering out of their orbits into eternal night (verse 13). The judgment which awaits them at the parousia was foretold by Enoch (verses 14 f.; *cf.* 1 Enoch i. 9).

True believers, however, need not be alarmed at the activity of such people, of whose rise and fall the apostles had given them warning in advance. Let them safeguard themselves by being built up in the faith, praying in the power of the Spirit, continuing steadfastly in the circle of divine love, and looking forward to the consummation of mercy and life at the appearing of Christ (verses 17–21). While they must abhor and avoid all false teachers, they should pity and rescue those who are led astray by them (verses 22, 23).

The Epistle ends with an ascription of praise to God as the One who is able to guard His people from stumbling until they stand without blemish 'before the presence of his glory with exceeding joy'.

BIBLIOGRAPHY. J. B. Mayor, *The Epistle of Jude and the Second Epistle of Peter*, 1907; M. R. James, *2 Peter and Jude*, *CGT*, 1912; J. Moffatt, *The General Epistles*, *MNT*, 1928. F.F.B.

JUDGES. The Heb. word (*šōpēṭ*) means one who dispenses justice, punishing the evil-doer, and vindicating the righteous. The corresponding word for 'judgment' is used to describe a rule by which he must be guided (Ex. xxi. 1).

I. THE MOSAIC INSTITUTION

In the wilderness period Moses wore himself out by sitting to judge the cases brought to him (Ex. xviii. 13–27, and *cf.* Ex. ii. 14). On Jethro's advice he appointed deputies to judge ordinary cases, bringing to him only the most important (see also Dt. i. 9–18).

The Deuteronomic law provides for the appointment of judges, and officers to assist them (Dt. xvi. 18; see OFFICER), 'in all thy gates'. So the more primitive rule of the nomadic period is adapted to the future settlement.

There is insistence upon the need for scrupulous fairness, and impartial justice (Dt. i. 16 f., xvi. 19 f., xxiv. 17 f., xxv. 13–16); and the justice of the courts of which Britons are proud today has its origin in the Word of God. Since the book of the law was in the charge of the priests, the more important cases were to be tried by a judge with priests as assessors (Dt. xvii. 8–13). During the period of the conquest we find judges taking part in assemblies of the nation (Jos. viii. 33, xxiv. 1).

II. THE PERIOD OF THE JUDGES

After the death of Joshua there followed the period of disorganization, tribal discord, and defeat, which is described in the book of Judges. But when the people cried unto the Lord, the author tells us, He 'raised up judges who saved them' (Jdg. ii. 16). These national heroes are sometimes called 'saviours' (iii. 9, 15), and of most of them it is said that they 'judged Israel' for a stated period of years, Othniel being the first (iii. 9) and Samson the last (xvi. 31).

It is clear that this imparts a new meaning into the word 'judge', namely, that of a leader in battle and a ruler in peace. We may see in them a type of Christ, who came to be our Saviour, is with us as our Leader, and will come to be our Judge.

In 1 Samuel there is a transition to the time of the monarchy. Eli 'had judged Israel forty years' (1 Sa. iv. 18), and 'Samuel judged Israel all the days of his life', going in circuit to Bethel and Gilgal and Mizpeh; and appointed his sons also as judges (vii. 15–viii. 1).

III. UNDER THE MONARCHY

Under the kings we find judges engaged in both judiciary and other administration. Among David's officers 'Chenaniah and his sons were for the outward [*i.e.* local] business over Israel, for officers and judges' (1 Ch. xxvi. 29).

After the disruption, Jehoshaphat displayed zeal for 'the book of the law of the Lord' (2 Ch. xvii. 9), appointed judges and officers city by city (xix. 5), and charged them to deal faithfully (2 Ch. xix. 9 f.; *cf.* Dt. xvi. 19 f.).

Finally, on the return from exile, the decree of Artaxerxes bade Ezra set magistrates and judges to administer justice and to teach the people (Ezr. vii. 25).

Later rulers of Phoenician cities took the title *šōpēṭ*; *cf.* the Carthaginian *suffetes*, mentioned by Roman writers (see PHOENICIA). G.T.M.

JUDGES, BOOK OF. As the seventh book of the Old Testament, Judges follows chronologically upon the Pentateuch and Joshua and describes the history of Israel from Joshua's death to the rise of Samuel. It takes its name from its leading characters, the *šôpᵉṭîm* (Jdg. ii. 16). These 'judges', however, were more than judicial arbiters; they were 'saviours' (iii. 9), charismatically empowered by God's Holy Spirit for the deliverance and preservation of Israel (vi. 34) up to the establishment of the kingdom (*cf.* the use of this same word for the chief magistrates of Carthage, and as a synonym for 'king' in ancient Canaanitish Ugarit, *Anat.* v. 40; see JUDGES). Yahweh Himself is the chief *šôpēṭ* (Jdg. xi. 27).

I. OUTLINE OF CONTENTS

a. Events following the death of Joshua (i. 1–ii. 5)

For a few years the tribes of Judah and Simeon advanced devotedly southward to the conquest of Bezek, Jerusalem (not held, i. 21), Hebron and Debir (reoccupied since their devastation in Jos. x. 36, 39), Hormah, and three of the Philistine cities (not held, Jdg. i. 19). The Joseph tribes likewise captured Bethel (i. 22–26), which had revolted (*cf.* Jos. viii. 17, xii. 9). But then came failure: Israel ceased to eradicate the Canaanites, no more cities were taken (Jdg. i. 27–36), and the tribe of Dan actually suffered eviction from its allotted territory (i. 34). Such tolerance of evil necessitated the extended period of chastening that followed (ii. 1–5).

b. Israel's history under the judges (ii. 6–xvi. 31)

(i) *The writer's prophetic understanding of history* (ii. 6–iii. 6). His basic principle is one of divine retribution: that God in His providence recompenses the nation in direct correspondence to the faithfulness of its people. For the people of Israel suffered under constant temptation to adopt the fertility rites of their Canaanitish neighbours, along with their confessedly superior methods of farming and standards of culture. Yahweh had indeed guided Israel in the wilderness, but Baal seemed better able to make the crops come out of the ground! Judges thus exhibits a repeated cycle of sin (Baal worship), servitude (to foreign aggressors), supplication (to the merciful God, for relief), and salvation (through divinely raised up judges).

(ii) *Six successive periods of oppression and the activities of twelve saviour-judges* (iii. 7–xvi. 31).

1. *Invasions of Cushan-rishathaim* (iii. 7–11). Commencing about 1382 BC, Israel suffered for eight years under the depredations of Cushan-rishathaim, an invader who came from Hittite-controlled Mesopotamia (Jdg. iii. 8). The underlying cause, however, lay in Israel's sin (iii. 7) against the moral requirements of God's redemptive covenant (see below, part *c*, appendix). But when they 'cried unto Yahweh, Yahweh raised up a saviour to the children of Israel, even Othniel, Caleb's younger brother' (iii. 9). The forty years of subsequent peace correspond to the parallel period of Hittite overlordship, until some years after the death of Shubbiluliuma in 1345 BC.

2. *Oppression under Eglon* (iii. 12–31). Just prior to the days of international confusion coincident with the rise of Egypt's aggressive XIXth Dynasty, 'Israel again did that which was evil, and Yahweh strengthened Eglon king of Moab against Israel' (iii. 12). 'But when they cried unto Yahweh, he raised them up a saviour, Ehud the Benjamite' (iii. 15), and granted them eighty years of peace, dating from the time of the treaty of 1315, between Seti and Mursil, *cf.* its renewal in 1279 by Rameses II. Neither Egypt nor the Hittites seem to have comprehended their providential function, but the fact remains that the years in which either succeeded in bringing peace to Palestine correspond to the very periods that God had ordained for granting 'rest' to His people (*cf.* John Garstang, *Joshua–Judges*, 1931, pp. 51–66). Shamgar next achieved a limited success against early Philistines, who were better equipped than he (iii. 31).

3. *Deliverance by Deborah* (iv. 1–v. 31). With the decay of the empires and the rise of local Canaanitish oppression under Jabin II of Hazor (iv. 2–3), God raised up the fourth of the judges, the woman Deborah. Her military commander, Barak, proceeded to muster the north-central tribes to the Valley of Esdraelon for war with Jabin's troops led by Sisera. But 'the stars in their courses fought against Sisera' (v. 20, 21): a divinely sent cloudburst immobilized the powerful Canaanitish chariotry, and Sisera was slain in flight by a Kenite woman. The forty years of peace that followed upon Deborah's victory (*c.* 1216–1176 BC) parallel the strong rule of Rameses III, the last great pharaoh.

4. *Deliverance by Gideon* (vi. 1–viii. 32). Next there appeared out of the eastern desert, Midianites and Amalekites to plunder sinful Israel (Jdg. vi. 2–6; *cf.* Ru. i. 1). In about 1169, however, 'the sword of the Lord and of Gideon' cleared Israel of the nomadic raiders (vii. 19–25, viii. 10–12; *cf.* the peaceful background of Ru. ii–iv, some twenty years later).

5. *The rise and fall of Abimelech* (viii. 33–x. 5). The turmoil that resulted from the attempt of Gideon's son Abimelech to make himself king over Israel (Jdg. ix) was rectified by the sixth and seventh judges, Tola and Jair (x. 1–5).

6. *Oppression under Ammon and the Philistines* (x. 6–xvi. 31). But with their deaths in 1103 BC, and the apostasy that subsequently arose, God delivered over His land to simultaneous oppressions by the Ammonites in the east and the Philistines in the west (x. 7). After eighteen years E Israel was freed by Jephthah, the eighth judge (xi), who was succeeded by the three minor judges. W Israel, however, remained subject to the rising power of the Philistines, despite the spectacular exploits of Samson, the twelfth and last judge of the book of Judges (xiii–xvi, to about 1065 BC).

c. An appendix (xvii. 1–xxi. 25)

This provides details on two events from Israel's very first period of apostasy (before 1374 BC; *cf.* the appearance of Phinehas in xx. 28 and the mention of the events of xviii in Jos. xix. 47, the author of which was contemporary with the conquest, Jos. v. 1, vi. 25; but see JOSHUA, II). The purpose of the appendix is to illustrate the depth of Israel's sin, whereby almost every standard of the Decalogue was transgressed. The section on Micah and the Danites (xvii–xviii) relates, for example, how Micah stole from his mother and then converted the proceeds into an idol for his house of gods (xvii. 5). God's Levite, meanwhile, wandered unsupported, until hired by Micah. But he in turn proved false to his employer when offered a position of leadership by the covetous, idolatrous, and murderous Danites (xviii. 25). Yet this Levite was Jonathan, a direct descendant of Moses (xviii. 30, RV). Nothing, admittedly, is said respecting the seventh commandment (on purity); but the following chapters (xix–xxi, the Benjamite outrage) describe not simply civil war and the harbouring of criminals but also harlotry and marital desertion by a Levite's concubine (xix. 2), homosexuality, rape, and adultery (xix. 22–24), and finally mass abduction (xxi. 23). Such were the results when 'every man did that which was right in his own eyes'.

II. AUTHORSHIP AND DATE

The book of Judges makes no direct statement about the date of its writing. The song of Deborah (v. 2–31) does claim contemporary composition (v. 1; *c.* 1215 BC), and its authenticity is generally accepted. But the book as a whole could not have been compiled for another two centuries. It refers to the destruction and captivity of Shiloh (xviii. 30–31) during the youth of Samuel (1 Sa. iv; *c.* 1080 BC); and the last event that it records is the death of Samson (Jdg. xvi. 30–31), which occurred a few years before

Samuel's inauguration as judge (*c.* 1063). Furthermore, the repeated explanation that 'in those days there was no king in Israel' (xvii. 6, xviii. 1, xxi. 25) suggests the book to have been written *after* the accession of Saul as king in 1043 BC. Yet the popular appreciation for the kingship is still fresh; and the book seems to have been composed before the sack of Gezer in 970 BC (1 Ki. ix. 16; *cf.* Jdg. i. 29) or David's capture of Jerusalem in 1003 (2 Sa. v. 6–7; *cf.* Jdg. i. 21).

The writer of Judges must therefore have been a man who was active during the early reign of Saul (before 1020 BC). He must also have been a prophet; for in the Heb. Bible, Judges takes its place in the prophetic division of the canon (the 'former' prophets: Jos., Jdg., Sa., and Ki.), *cf.* the sermonic tone of ii. 10–14, iii. 7–8, *etc.* The most likely possibility is Samuel the prophet, who is indeed identified as the author of Judges according to the Jewish Talmud (*Baba Bathra* 14b). But since this traditional account goes on to make the improbable assertion that Samuel wrote Ruth also, and 'the book which bears his name', we seem justified in concluding only that the author must, at least, have been one of Samuel's prophetic associates.

III. SOURCES OF THE BOOK

The writer of Judges may have relied upon written sources that are now lost, *e.g.* hero-anthologies, such as 'the book of the *yāšār* [upright]' (Jos. x. 13). Modern critics are accustomed to assert that the writer's sources consisted of largely independent materials dating down into the 9th century ('J' document) and 8th century ('E' document) and edited by a Deuteronomist ('D') as late as 550 BC; but this analysis runs counter to the evidence of the book itself and unnecessarily discredits the unity and authenticity of its contents. It seeks, for example, to equate God's call to Gideon at the winepress and his resulting sacrifice (Jdg. vi. 11–24, said to be 'J') with His subsequent command to Gideon to destroy the Baal altar and to replace it with one to Yahweh (vi. 25–32, said to be 'E'), as if these were two conflicting versions of one call. Or again, it confuses Gideon's taking of the Midianite princes Oreb and Zeeb at the fords of the Jordan (vii. 24–25, 'E') with his final capture of the *kings*, Zeba and Zalmunna, farther east (viii. 10–11, 'J'), though it must then eliminate the words in viii. 10, 'all *that were left* of the host', as being an attempt by some later editor to harmonize the supposedly conflicting stories. See also PENTATEUCH.

The Hebrew text of the book of Judges is better preserved than that of any of the other Former Prophets and is generally free from errors of scribal transmission. Its ancient LXX translation, however, exhibits inner-Greek variations to the extent that Rahlfs' edition of the LXX now presents on each page two divergent forms of Greek text, according to codices A and B.

IV. HISTORICAL BACKGROUND

The historical background to the period of Judges concerns, locally, the presence of the Canaanites. Prior to the Heb. conquest, Moses had ordered their 'devotion' (extermination, Dt. vii. 2; *cf.* Jos. vi. 17), both because of long-standing immorality (Dt. ix. 5; *cf.* Gn. ix. 22, 25, xv. 16) and because of their debasing religious influence upon God's people (Dt. vii. 4); for on countless 'high places' the Canaanites worshipped local gods of fertility, the Baalim, with rites that included sacred prostitution and even child sacrifice (xi. 31). Joshua had thus subdued the whole of Canaan (Jos. xi. 16, *cf.* xxi. 43). But its native inhabitants had not yet lost their potential for resistance. Indeed, Moses himself had anticipated a gradual occupation of the land (Ex. xxiii. 28–30; Dt. vii. 22); and much still remained to be possessed (Jos. xiii. 1). On the international scene, the relevant facts may be outlined as follows: (1) At the time of Joshua's death, soon after 1400 BC, XVIIIth Dynasty Egyptian imperial control over Palestine had become ephemeral: Amenhotep III was content to rule in decadent luxury; and his successor, Amenhotep IV (Akhenaten, *c.* 1376–1362 BC), devoted his exclusive attention to monotheistic religious reforms. The contemporary Amarna letters from the Canaanitish city-states contain futile pleas for help against the plundering Habiru. This designation embraces the biblical Hebrews, though it was also used for various Hurrian (?) aggressors from the north (descendants of Eber, Gn. x. 21, 25; *cf.* M. G. Kline, *WTJ*, XIX, May 1957, 184; XX, November 1957, 68). For this era was marked, at the same time, by revived Hittite activity from beyond Syria. King Shubbiluliuma (*c.* 1385–1345 BC), the greatest of the Hittites, at the first encouraged anarchy among the states farther south and later achieved their practical domination for himself and his son Mursil II. (2) But Egypt, under the new XIXth Dynasty (1321–1205 BC), in turn experienced revival. Seti I retook Galilee and Phoenicia in 1318, defeated the Hittites, and three years later concluded a treaty with Mursil, by which Syria was assigned to Hittite control and Palestine and Phoenicia to Egyptian. Young Rameses II (1300–1234) indeed broke the treaty and invaded the Hittite territory. But after years of costly fighting the former division of power was re-established by the treaty of 1279; and peace was kept until the decline of the Hittite Empire, due to the barbarian invasions in the latter part of the century. (3) With the fall of Crete to the barbarians in 1200 BC the ousted Philistines, 'the remnant of the isle of Caphtor' (Je. xlvii. 4) fled eastward to reinforce their older settlements on the coast of Palestine (*cf.* Gn. xxi. 32; Dt. ii. 23). Driven back from Egypt in about 1196 by Rameses III of the XXth Dynasty, they proceeded to consolidate their position in Canaan. Before the end of the century they were thus able to mount the first of their great offensives against Israel, with which event the history of the book of Judges comes to a close.

V. CHRONOLOGY

The over-all chronology of Judges is indicated by the statement of Jephthah, near the conclusion of the period, that Israel had by his time been occupying Palestinian territory for some 300 years (Jdg. xi. 26; *cf.* the similar figure drawn from 1 Ki. vi. 1). The calculation of a more precise chronology, however, depends upon two other facts that appear from the biblical record. First, since the lapse of time from the termination of the conquest in 1400 BC to the commencement of the first (Mesopotamian) oppression is not stated, one must count backward from the accession of Samuel, *c.* 1063 BC (reckoning, from the known date of 930 for the division of the kingdom, 113 years for Solomon, David (over all Israel), and Saul and his successors [1 Ki. xi. 42, ii. 11; Acts xiii. 21], plus twenty years for Samuel [1 Sa. vii. 2; *cf. HDB*, I, p. 399]). Second, since some of the judges overlapped each other (*cf.* Ehud and Shamgar, Jdg. iii. 30–iv. 1), the chronology must be gathered from the dated oppressions and subsequent savings. Of particular significance is the fact that the forty-year Philistine oppression (xiii. 1) in W Palestine continued uninterruptedly from the deaths of Tola and Jair (x. 7), through the judgeships of Jephthah, the three minor judges, Eli, and Samson, down to the victorious advent of Samuel. The following picture results:

	Oppressions		
xiii. 1	Philistine	40	1103–1063
ix. 22	Abimelech	3	1129–1126
vi. 1	Midianite	7	1176–1169
iv. 3	Canaanite	20	1236–1216
iii. 14	Eglon, Moab	18	1334–1316
iii. 8	Mesopotamian	8	1382–1374

	Savings		
x. 3	Tola-Jair	23	1126–1103
	(no separate saving under Jair)		
viii. 28	Gideon	40	1169–1129
v. 31	Deborah	40	1216–1176
iii. 30	Ehud	80	1316–1236
iii. 11	Othniel	40	1374–1334

From the first oppression to Samuel's inauguration, 319 years thus elapse.

(See also CHRONOLOGY OF THE OLD TESTAMENT.)

VI. TEACHING

From the principles stated in Jdg. ii. 6–iii. 6 and the concrete historical examples furnished by the remainder of the book, its teaching may be summarized as follows.

a. God's wrath at sin (ii. 11, 14). Even from a pragmatic viewpoint it appears that Israel's hope for survival was dependent upon their intertribal unity, yet such co-operative effort arose only from a common dedication to their God (*cf.* v. 8–9, 16–18). Loss of faith meant extinction.

b. God's mercy upon repentance (ii. 16). Even foreign oppression served as a medium of divine grace, for Israel's edification (iii. 1–4).

c. Man's total depravity. For after each deliverance, 'when the judge was dead, they turned back and dealt more corruptly than their fathers' (ii. 19). Individualistic society had demonstrated its inherent inadequacy, for man on his own inevitably goes wrong (xvii. 6). Israel needed a king, though indeed only such a king as should accomplish the ultimate will of God (*cf.* viii. 23, ix. 6, 56). The author of Judges was thus one of civilization's first true historians, not simply recording events, but then interpreting the facts on the basis of an explicit philosophy of history. As to the permanent validity of his deuteronomic philosophy of retribution, one must grant that in those early days, when revelation was more limited, providence operated more obviously than at present. But his basic principles remain eternally sound: the sinning nation shall be punished, the repentant shall be saved, and all man-centred systems must ultimately fail. The only valid hope of history lies in the coming of Christ, the King.

BIBLIOGRAPHY. W. F. Albright, 'The Song of Deborah in the Light of Archaeology', *BASOR*, 62, 1936, pp. 26–31; C. F. Burney, *The Book of Judges*, 2nd ed., 1930; John Garstang, *Joshua–Judges*, 1931; J. Myers, *Judges*, *IB*, II, 1953; J. Barton Payne, *An Outline of Hebrew History*, 1954, pp. 78–91; Robert H. Pfeiffer, *Introduction to the Old Testament*, 1941, pp. 314–337; John H. Raven, *The History of the Religion of Israel*, 1933, pp. 156–202; Edward J. Young, *An Introduction to the Old Testament*, 1949, pp. 165–172.

J.B.P.

JUDGING. It is a Christian duty to exercise discrimination. 'Why even of yourselves judge ye not what is right?' (Lk. xii. 57) asked Jesus. Again, He said, 'Judge not according to the appearance, but judge righteous judgment' (Jn. vii. 24). He complained of certain Jews that 'Ye judge after the flesh', and in that situation added, 'I judge no man' (Jn. viii. 15). The Christian is expected not to be credulous. He has an ability to discriminate. He should use it and 'judge righteous judgment'.

The New Testament is clear, however, that the Christian must not pass judgment on his fellow-man. There are many condemnations and prohibitions of this practice. Let us notice four points. First, it is not safe. 'Judge not, that ye be not judged' (Mt. vii. 1). 'Wherein thou judgest another, thou condemnest thyself' (Rom. ii. 1). To pass judgment on others is to invite a similar process with respect to oneself. Secondly, we are not qualified. When the woman taken in adultery was brought before Jesus He said, 'He that is without sin among you, let him first cast a stone at her' (Jn. viii. 7). He counselled the man with a 'beam' in his eye not to concern himself with casting the mote from his brother's eye until he had first dealt with his own condition (Lk. vi. 41 f.). Our own consciences are not so easy that we can indulge in judging others. Such judging is actually harmful, since it distracts us from that self-examination which is a primary duty of the Christian. Thirdly, judging others does not come within our province. 'Who art thou that judgest another man's servant? to his own master he standeth or falleth' (Rom. xiv. 4). Judging is God's business, not ours. 'He that . . . judgeth his brother . . . judgeth the law: but if thou judge the law, thou art not a doer of the law, but a judge' (Jas. iv. 11). To pass judgment on others is to usurp a divine function. Fourthly, such judging is irrelevant. Neither Paul's view of himself nor others' views of him matter in the slightest: 'he that judgeth me is the Lord'. Thus Paul commands 'judge nothing before the time, until the Lord come' (1 Cor. iv. 3–5). L.M.

JUDGMENT. See ESCHATOLOGY, VII.

JUDGMENT-HALL. See PRAETORIUM.

JUDGMENT-SEAT. In Greek states the assembly met in front of a dais (*bēma*) from which all official business was conducted. Thus Herod Agrippa I sits on the dais (AV 'throne') to address the republics of Tyre and Sidon (Acts xii. 21). The term is otherwise used in the New Testament for the *tribunal*, the platform on which a Roman magistrate sat, flanked by his counsellors, to administer justice. It was traditionally erected in some public place, as apparently in the case of Pilate (Jn. xix. 13), or alternatively in an auditorium (Acts xxv. 23). That it was the solemn integrity of Roman justice that prompted the image of 'the judgment seat of Christ' (Rom. xiv. 10; 2 Cor. v. 10) seems likely from the fact that Paul is in either case addressing an audience familiar with direct Roman government.

The English term is also used to render the Gk. *kritērion*, 'a court' (Jas. ii. 6).

BIBLIOGRAPHY. E. Weiss, *RE*, VI.A.2. 2428–30, *s.v. tribunal*. E.A.J.

JUDITH, BOOK OF. See APOCRYPHA.

JULIUS. The family name of the Caesars, which must have become widespread since their rise to power due to the custom of conferring on new citizens the name of the magistrate under whose auspices they were enfranchised. The centurion who escorted Paul to Rome (Acts xxvii. 1) presumably belongs to this class of Julii, since no aristocratic member of the house would serve in that rank. His unit ('Augustus' band', see ARMY) has been thought (by Mommsen and Ramsay) to be the Caesar's regular staff of couriers. The term corresponds exactly, however, to the *cohors Augusta* known from epigraphic evidence. That this was an auxiliary (*i.e.* non-citizen) force, and therefore not likely to supply the escort for a Roman, is not a serious objection, since the centurion himself is manifestly a citizen. Whether enfranchised on promotion, or seconded to the *auxilia* from the legions, he belongs with Paul to the proud and growing body of new citizen families that Roman statesmanship created in the East.

BIBLIOGRAPHY. T. R. S. Broughton, in Jackson, Lake, and Cadbury, *The Beginnings of Christianity*, Part I, V, pp. 427–445. E.A.J.

JUNIA, JUNIAS. See ANDRONICUS AND JUNIA.

JUNIPER. See PLANTS.

JUPITER. The Greek deities, *Zeus* and *Hermēs* (Acts xiv. 12), rendered in AV by their Roman equivalents, Jupiter and Mercurius, presumably in turn represent unknown local gods, whom the Lycaonian-speaking people of Lystra recognized in Barnabas and Paul. Why a miraculous healing should have prompted this particular identification is not clear. Mercurius, the divine wayfarer and messenger of Jupiter, suggested himself for Paul 'because he was the chief speaker'. The fact that there was a local cult of Jupiter (verse 13) may have clinched the identity of Barnabas. The two gods were associated as wanderers on earth in the tale of Philemon and Baucis (Ovid, *Met.* viii. 618–724), who secured their favour by being the only ones to give them hospitality. This possibly explains the anxiety of the Lycaonians not to miss their opportunity.

Paul and Barnabas were naturally greatly distressed and managed only with difficulty to divert the people from their plan to offer sacrifice to them. But Paul also improved the occasion with remarkable dexterity: rising to his rôle of Mercurius, he takes up the familiar picture of Jupiter as the god of the sky who displays himself in the phenomena of the weather, and with delicacy and restraint re-interprets it to display the principles of the gospel.

See also HERMES.

BIBLIOGRAPHY. A. B. Cook, *Zeus*, 1914–40; W. K. C. Guthrie, *The Greeks and their Gods*, 1950. E.A.J.

JUSTICE. The word 'justice' occurs twenty-six times in the AV Old Testament, once translating the Heb. *mišpāṭ*, 'judgment' (Jb. xxxvi. 17), but elsewhere, *ṣeḏeq* or *ṣ*ᵉ*ḏāqâ*. The more frequent rendering of these latter nouns is 'righteousness'; but when *mišpāṭ* and *ṣ*ᵉ*ḏāqâ* appear together the AV translates the whole phrase as 'judgment and justice' (*e.g.* 2 Sa. viii. 15; *cf.* Gn. xviii. 19), though the RV renders the same combination as 'justice and righteousness'. In the AV of Scripture, therefore, 'justice' must be understood as being the same word as 'righteousness', and seldom as denoting the specialized concept of 'fair play', or legal equity, with which the term justice is presently associated (see RIGHTEOUSNESS). The expression. 'to do (someone) justice', occurs twice, being taken from the corresponding

Heb. verbal root, *ṣādaq*, causative, which means 'to declare one right' (2 Sa. xv. 4; Ps. lxxxii. 3). Similarly, the adjective *ṣaddîq*, 'righteous', is over forty times rendered by the word 'just'. In the AV New Testament, the noun 'justice' does not appear; but at over thirty points the adjective *dikaios*, 'righteous', is likewise translated by the English term 'just'.

The biblical concept of justice exhibits development through nine, generally chronological stages.

1. Etymologically, it appears that the root of *ṣᵉḏāqâ*, like that of its kindred noun *yōšer*, 'uprightness' (Dt. ix. 5), signifies 'straightness', in a physical sense (*BDB*, p. 841).

2. But already in the patriarchal age *ṣᵉḏāqâ* has the abstract meaning of conformity, by a given object or action, to an accepted standard of values, *e.g.* Jacob's 'honest' living up to the terms of his sheep-contract with Laban (Gn. xxx. 33). Moses thus speaks of just balances, weights, and measures (Lv. xix. 36; Dt. xxv. 15) and insists that Israel's judges pronounce 'just judgment' (Dt. xvi. 18, 20; see JUDGES). Arguments that are actually questionable may seem, at first glance, to be 'just' (Pr. xviii. 17); and Christian masters are cautioned to provide their servants with what is 'just and equal' (Col. iv. 1). Even inanimate objects may be described as *ṣeḏeq*, if they measure up to the appropriate standards. The phrase, 'paths of *ṣeḏeq*' (Ps. xxiii. 3), for example, designates walkable paths.

3. Since life's highest standard is derived from the character of deity, 'justice', from the time of Moses and onwards (*cf.* Dt. xxxii. 4), comes to distinguish that which is God's will and those activities which result from it. Heavenly choirs proclaim, 'Just and true are thy ways' (Rev. xv. 3). Recognizing the ultimacy of the will of the Lord, Job therefore asks, 'How should man be just with God?' (Jb. ix. 2, *cf.* iv. 17, xxxiii. 12). But even though God stands answerable to no man, still 'to justice . . . he doeth no violence' (xxxvii. 23, RVmg); for the actions of the God who acts in harmony with His own standard are always perfect and right (Zp. iii. 5; Ps. lxxxix. 14). *Ṣᵉḏāqâ* may thus describe Yahweh's preservation of both human and animal life (Ps. xxxvi. 6) or His dissociation from vain enterprise (Is. xlv. 19). In both of the latter verses the EVV translate *ṣᵉḏāqâ* as 'righteousness'; but it might with greater accuracy be rendered 'regularity' or 'reliability'.

4. By a natural transition, 'justice' then comes to identify that moral standard by which God measures human conduct (Is. xxvi. 7). Men too must 'do justice' (Gn. xviii. 19) as they walk with deity (Gn. vi. 9; Mt. v. 48); for not the hearers, but the doers of the law, are 'just before God' (Rom. ii. 13). The attribute of justice is to be anticipated only in the hearts of those who fear God (Lk. xviii. 2), because justice in the biblical sense begins with holiness (Mi. vi. 8; Mk. vi. 20; 1 Thes. ii. 10) and with sincere devotion (Lk. ii. 25; Acts x. 22). Positively, however, the wholehearted participation of the Gadites in the divinely ordered conquest of Canaan is described as 'executing the justice of the Lord' (Dt. xxxiii. 21; *cf.* S. R. Driver, *ICC*). The need for earnest conformity to the moral will of God lies especially incumbent upon kings (2 Sa. viii. 15; Je. xxii. 15), princes (Pr. viii. 15), and judges (Ec. v. 8); but every true believer is expected to 'do justice' (Ps. cxix. 121; Pr. i. 3; *cf.* its personification in Is. lix. 14). Justice constitutes the opposite of sin (Ec. vii. 20) and serves as a marked characteristic of Jesus the Messiah (Is. ix. 7; Zc. ix. 9; Mt. xxvii. 19; Acts iii. 14). In the poetry of the Old Testament there do arise affirmations of self-righteousness by men like David ('Judge me according to my righteousness, and establish the just', Ps. vii. 8–9, *cf.* xviii. 20–24) or Job ('I am . . . the just upright man,' Jb. xii. 4, *cf.* i. 1), that might appear incongruous when considered in the light of their acknowledged iniquity (*cf.* Jb. vii. 21, xiii. 26). The poets' aims, however, are either to exonerate themselves from particular crimes that enemies have laid to their charge (*cf.* Ps. vii. 4) or to profess a genuine purity of purpose and single-hearted devotion to God (Ps. xvii. 1). 'They breathe the spirit of simple faith and childlike trust, which throws itself unreservedly on God . . . and they disclaim all fellowship with the wicked, from whom they may expect to be distinguished in the course of His Providence' (A. F. Kirkpatrick, *The Book of Psalms*, 1906, I, p. lxxxvii). As Ezekiel described such a man, 'He hath walked in my statutes, to deal truly; he is just, he shall surely live, saith the Lord God' (Ezk. xviii. 9).

5. In reference to divine government, justice becomes descriptive in a particular way of punishment for moral infraction. Under the lash of heaven-sent plagues, Pharaoh confessed, 'The Lord is *ṣaddîq*, and I and my people are wicked' (Ex. ix. 27; *cf.* Ne. ix. 33); and the one thief cried to the other as they were crucified, 'We indeed justly . . .' (Lk. xxiii. 41). For God cannot remain indifferent to evil (Hab. i. 13; *cf.* Zp. i. 12), nor will the Almighty pervert justice (Jb. viii. 3; *cf.* viii. 4, xxxvi. 17). Even the pagans of Melita believed in a divine nemesis, so that when they saw Paul bitten by a viper they concluded, 'This man is a murderer, whom . . . Justice hath not suffered to live' (Acts xxviii. 4, RV). God's punitive righteousness is as a consuming fire (Dt. xxxii. 22; Heb. xii. 29; see WRATH), and condemnation is just (Rom. iii. 8, RV).

6. From the time of the judges and onward, however, *ṣᵉḏāqâ* comes also to describe His deeds of vindication for the deserving, 'the righteous acts of the Lord' (Jdg. v. 11). Absalom thus promised to 'do justice' on behalf of his petitioners (2 Sa. xv. 4; *cf.* Ps. lxxxii. 3), and Solomon proclaimed that God 'blesseth the habitation of the just' (Pr. iii. 33; *cf.* Ps. xciv. 15). Divine vindication became also the plea of Isaiah's contemporaries, 'They ask of me the ordinances of justice' (Is. lviii. 2, 3); for though God's

intervention may be delayed (Ec. vii. 15, viii. 14; *cf.* Is. xl. 27), He will yet 'be jealous for his land, and pity his people' (Joel ii. 18).

7. Such words, however, introduce another aspect, in which divine justice ceases to constitute an expression of precise moral desert and partakes rather of divine pity, love, and grace. This connotation appears first in David's prayer for the forgiveness of his crimes over Bathsheba, when he implored, 'Deliver me from bloodguiltiness, O God, thou God of my salvation: and my tongue shall sing aloud of thy *ṣ*ᵉ*ḏāqâ*' (EVV 'righteousness', Ps. li. 14). But what David sought was not vindication; for he had just acknowledged his heinous sin and, indeed, his depravity from birth (Ps. li. 5). His petition sought rather for undeserved pardon; and *ṣ*ᵉ*ḏāqâ* is therefore best translated by simple repetition—O God of my salvation: my tongue shall sing of thy 'salvation'. *Ṣ*ᵉ*ḏāqâ*, in other words, has become redemptive; it is God's fulfilling of His own graciously promised salvation, irrespective of the merits of men (*cf.* David's same usage in Pss. xxxi. 1, ciii. 17, cxliii. 1). David's counsellor Ethan thus moves, in the space of two verses, from a reference to God's 'justice [*ṣeḏeq*, according to sense (4) above] and judgment' (Ps. lxxxix. 14) to the joyful testimony, 'In thy *ṣ*ᵉ*ḏāqâ* [promised grace] shall Israel be exalted' (Ps. lxxxix. 16; *cf.* a similar contrast within Is. lvi. 1). When Isaiah, therefore, speaks of 'a just [*ṣaddîq*] God and a Saviour' (Is. xlv. 21), his thought is not, 'A just God, and yet at the same time a Saviour', but rather, 'A *ṣaddîq* God, and therefore a Saviour' (*cf.* the parallelism of 'righteousness' with salvation in Is. xlv. 8, xlvi. 13; and see RIGHTEOUSNESS). Correspondingly, we read in the New Testament that 'if we confess our sins, he is faithful and just [*dikaios* = "faithful to His gracious promise", not, "demanding justice"] to forgive us our sins' (1 Jn. i. 9). Such concepts of non-judicial 'justice', however, must be limited to those passages in which this usage is specifically intended. In Rom. iii, on the contrary, with its contextual emphasis upon the wrath of God against sin and upon the propitiatory sacrifice of Christ for the satisfaction of the Father's justice, we must continue to understand *dikaios* (Rom. iii. 26) in its traditional sense: 'That he [God] might be just [exacting punishment, according to sense (5) above], and [yet at the same time] the justifier of him which believeth in Jesus' (see Sanday and Headlam, *ICC*; see JUSTIFICATION).

8. As a condition that arises out of God's forgiving 'justice', there next appears in Scripture a humanly possessed *ṣ*ᵉ*ḏāqâ*, which is simultaneously declared to have been God's own moral attribute (*ṣ*ᵉ*ḏāqâ* in sense (4) above), but which has now been imparted to those who believe on His grace. Moses thus describes how Abraham's faith served as a medium for imputed righteousness (Gn. xv. 6), though one must, of course, observe that his faith did not constitute in itself the meritorious righteousness but was merely 'reckoned' so. He was justified *through* faith, not *because of* it (*cf.* John Murray, *Redemption, Accomplished and Applied*, 1955, p. 155). Habakkuk likewise declared, 'The just shall live by his faith' (Hab. ii. 4), though here too the justification derives, not from man's own, rugged 'faithfulness' (RVmg), but from his humble dependence upon God's mercy (contrast the self-reliance of the Babylonians, which the same context condemns; and *cf.* Rom. i. 17; Gal. iii. 11). It was God's prophet Isaiah, however, who first spoke directly of 'the heritage of the servants of the Lord . . . their *ṣ*ᵉ*ḏāqâ* which is of me' (Is. liv. 17, RV). Of this 'righteousness', A. B. Davidson accurately observed, 'It is not a Divine attribute. It is a Divine effect . . . produced in the world by God' (*The Theology of the Old Testament*, 1925, p. 143). That is to say, there exists within Yahweh a righteousness which, by His grace, becomes the possession of the believer (Is. xlv. 24). Our own righteousness is totally inadequate (Is. lxiv. 6); but 'in Yahweh' we 'are righteous' (*ṣāḏaq*) (Is. xlv. 25), having been made just by the imputed merit of Christ (Phil. iii. 9). A century later, Jeremiah thus speaks both of Judah and of God Himself as a 'habitation of justice' (Je. xxxi. 23, l. 7), *i.e.* a source of justification for the faithful (*cf.* Je. xxiii. 6, xxxiii. 16, 'Yahweh our righteousness', Theo. Laetsch, *Biblical Commentary, Jeremiah*, 1952, pp. 254, 191–192).

9. But even as God in His grace bestows righteousness upon the unworthy, so the people of God are called upon to 'seek justice' (Is. i. 17, RV) in the sense of pleading for the widow and 'judging the cause of the poor and the needy' (Je. xxii. 16). 'Justice' has thus come to connote goodness (Lk. xxiii. 50) and loving consideration (Mt. i. 19). Further, from the days of the Exile onward, Aram. *ṣiḏqâ*, 'righteousness', becomes specialized into a designation for alms or charity (Dn. iv. 27), an equivalent expression for 'giving to the poor' (Ps. cxii. 9; *cf.* Mt. vi. 1). One might therefore be led to conceive of biblical 'justice', particularly in these last three, supra-judicial senses, as involving a certain tension or even contradiction: *e.g.* *ṣ*ᵉ*ḏāqâ* in its seventh, gracious sense seems to forgive the very crimes that it condemns in its fifth, punitive sense. The ultimate solution, however, appears in the person and work of the Lord Jesus Christ. The ethical example furnished by His sinless life (Heb. iv. 15) constitutes the climax of biblical revelation on the moral will of God and far exceeds the perverted though seemingly lofty justice of the scribes and Pharisees (Mt. v. 20). Yet He who commanded men to be perfect, even as their heavenly Father is perfect (Mt. v. 48), exhibited at the same time that love which has no equal, as He laid down His life for His undeserving friends (Jn. xv. 13). Here was revealed *ṣ*ᵉ*ḏāqâ*, 'justice', in its ethical stage (5), in its redemptive stage (7), and in its imputed stage (8), all united in one. He came that God might be just and yet the justifier of him that believeth in Jesus (Rom. iii. 26) and

that we might be found in Him, who is made unto us righteousness and sanctification and redemption (1 Cor. i. 30).

BIBLIOGRAPHY. J. A. Bollier, 'The Righteousness of God', *Interpretation*, VIII, 1954, pp. 404–413; A. B. Davidson, *The Theology of the Old Testament*, 1925, pp. 129–144; Gottfried Quell and G. Schrenk, *Righteousness*, trans. by J. R. Coates, 1951 (= *TWNT*); Norman H. Snaith, *Mercy and Sacrifice*, 1953, pp. 70–79; and *The Distinctive Ideas of the Old Testament*, 1946; Geerhardus Vos, *Biblical Theology*, 1948, pp. 270–275.

J.B.P.

JUSTIFICATION.

I. MEANING OF THE WORD

'Justify' (Heb. *ṣāḏaq*; Gk. [LXX and NT], *dikaioō*) is a forensic term meaning 'acquit', 'declare righteous', the opposite of 'condemn' (*cf.* Dt. xxv. 1; Pr. xvii. 15; Rom. viii. 33). Justifying is the judge's act. From the litigant's standpoint, therefore, 'be justified' means 'get the verdict' (Is. xliii. 9, 26).

In Scripture, God is 'the Judge of all the earth' (Gn. xviii. 25), and His dealings with men are constantly described in forensic terms. Righteousness, *i.e.* conformity with His law, is what He requires of men, and He shows His own righteousness as Judge in taking vengeance on those who fall short of it (*cf.* Ps. vii. 11, RV; Is. v. 16, x. 22; Acts xvii. 31; Rom. ii. 5, iii. 5 f.). There is no hope for anyone if God's verdict goes against him.

Because God is King, the thought of Him as justifying may have an executive as well as a judicial aspect. Like the ideal royal judge in Israel, He will not only pass a verdict in favour of the accused, but actively implement it by showing favour towards him and publicly reinstating him. The verb 'justify' may focus on either aspect of God's action. For instance, the justifying of Israel and the Servant, envisaged in Is. xlv. 25, l. 8, is a public vindication through a change in their fortunes. The justification of sinners that Paul expounds, however, is simply the passing of a favourable verdict. Paul certainly believes that God shows favour to those whom He has acquitted, but he uses other terms to describe this (adoption, *etc.*).

'Justify' is also used for ascriptions of righteousness in non-forensic contexts. Men are said to justify God by confessing Him just (Lk. vii. 29; *cf.* Rom. iii. 4, quoting Ps. li. 4), and themselves by claiming to be just (Jb. xxxii. 2; Lk. x. 29, xvi. 15). Jerusalem is ironically said to have 'justified' Sodom and Samaria by outdoing them in sin! (Ezk. xvi. 51). The passive can denote being vindicated by events against suspicion, criticism, and mistrust (Mt. xi. 19; Lk. vii. 35; 1 Tim. iii. 16; *cf.* Jas. ii. 21, 24 f., for which see below).

Lexical support is wanting for the view of Chrysostom, Augustine, and the Council of Trent that when Paul and James speak of present justification they refer to God's work of *making* righteous by inner renewal, as well as of *counting* righteous through remission of sins. James seems to mean neither, Paul only the latter. His synonyms for 'justify' are 'reckon righteousness', 'remit sins', 'not reckon sin' (see Rom. iv. 5–8, RV)—phrases expressing the idea, not of inner transformation, but of conferring a legal status and cancelling a legal liability. Justification, to Paul, is a judgment passed on man, not a work wrought within man. The two things go together, no doubt, but they are distinct.

II. JUSTIFICATION IN PAUL

Out of the thirty-nine occurrences of the verb 'justify' in the New Testament, twenty-nine come in the Epistles or recorded words of Paul; so do the two occurrences of the corresponding noun, *dikaiōsis* (Rom. iv. 25, v. 18). This reflects the fact that Paul alone of New Testament writers makes the concept of justification basic to his soteriology.

Justification means to Paul *God's act of remitting the sins of guilty men, and accounting them righteous, freely, by His grace, through faith in Christ, on the ground, not of their own works, but of the representative law-keeping and redemptive blood-shedding of the Lord Jesus Christ on their behalf.* (For the parts of this definition, see Rom. iii. 23–26, iv. 5–8, v. 18 f.) Paul's doctrine of justification is his characteristic way of formulating the central gospel truth, that God forgives believing sinners. Theologically, it is the most highly developed expression of this truth in the New Testament.

In Romans, Paul introduces the gospel as disclosing 'the righteousness of God' (i. 17). This phrase proves to have a double reference: (1) to the righteous man's status, which God through Christ freely confers upon believing sinners ('the *gift* of righteousness', Rom. v. 17, *cf.* iii. 21 f., ix. 30, x. 3–10; 2 Cor. v. 21; Phil. iii. 9); (2) to the way in which the gospel reveals God as doing what is right—not only judging transgressors as they deserve (ii. 5, iii. 5 f.) but also keeping His promise to send salvation to Israel (iii. 4 f.), and justifying sinners in such a way that His own judicial claims upon them are met (iii. 25 f.). 'The righteousness of God' is thus a predominantly forensic concept, denoting God's gracious work of bestowing upon guilty sinners a justified justification, acquitting them in the court of heaven without prejudice to His justice as their Judge.

Many scholars today find the background of this phrase in a few passages from Is. xl ff. and the psalms in which God's 'righteousness' and 'salvation' appear as equivalents (Is. xlv. 8, *cf.* verses 19–25, xlvi. 13, li. 3–6; Ps. xcviii. 2; *etc.*). This may be right, but since Paul nowhere quotes these verses, it cannot be proved. It must also be remembered that the reason why these texts call God's vindication of His oppressed people His 'righteousness' is that it is an act of faithfulness to His covenant promise to them; whereas Romans deals principally with God's justifying of Gentiles, who previously were not His people and to whom He had promised nothing (*cf.* ix. 24 ff., x. 19 f.)—quite a different situation.

It has been questioned whether Paul's doctrine of justification by faith without works is any more than a controversial device, developed simply as a weapon against the Judaizers. But the following facts indicate that it was more than this.

1. The Epistle to the Romans is evidently to be read as a full-dress statement of Paul's gospel, and the doctrine of justification is its backbone. (See ROMANS.)

2. In three places Paul writes in personal terms of the convictions that had made him the man and the missionary that he was, and all three are couched in terms of justification (Gal. ii. 15–21; 2 Cor. v. 16–21; Phil. iii. 4–14). In Rom. vii. 7 ff. Paul describes his personal need of Christ in terms of the law's condemnation—a need which only God's justifying sentence in Christ could relieve (*cf.* Rom. viii. 1 f.; Gal. iii. 19–iv. 7). Paul's personal religion was evidently rooted in the knowledge of his justification.

3. Justification is to Paul God's fundamental act of blessing, for it both saves from the past and secures for the future. On the one hand, it means pardon, and the end of hostility between God and ourselves (Acts xiii. 39; Rom. iv. 6 f., v. 9 f.). On the other hand, it means acceptance and a title to all blessings promised to the just, a thought which Paul develops by linking justification with adoption and heirship (Gal. iv. 4 ff.; Rom. viii. 14 ff.). Both aspects appear in Rom. v. 1, 2, where Paul says that justification brings both peace with God (because sins are remitted) and hope of God's glory (because the sinner is accepted as righteous). This hope is a certainty; for justification has an eschatological significance. It is the judgment of the last day brought into the present, a final, irreversible verdict. The justified man can accordingly be sure that nothing will ever separate him from the love of his God (Rom. viii. 33–39, *cf.* v. 9). His glorification is certain (Rom. viii. 30). The coming inquisition before Christ's judgment-seat (Rom. xiv. 10 ff.; 2 Cor. v. 10) may deprive him of particular rewards (1 Cor. iii. 15), but not of his justified status.

4. Paul's doctrine of salvation has justification as its basic reference-point. His belief about justification is the source from which flows his view of Christianity as a world-religion of grace and faith, in which Gentiles and Jews stand on an equal footing (Rom. i. 16, iii. 29 ff.; Gal. iii. 8–14, 28 f., *etc.*). It is in terms of justification that he explains grace (Rom. iii. 24, iv. 4 f., 16), the saving significance of Christ's obedience and death (Rom. iii. 24 f., v. 16 ff.), the revelation of God's love at the cross (Rom. v. 5–9), the meaning of redemption (Rom. iii. 24; Gal. iii. 13; Eph. i. 7) and reconciliation (2 Cor. v. 18 f.), the covenant relationship (Gal. iii. 15 ff.), faith (Rom. iv. 23 ff., x. 8 ff.), union with Christ (Rom. viii. 1; Gal. ii. 17, RV), adoption and the gift of the Spirit (Gal. iv. 6–8; Rom. viii. 10, *cf.* verse 15), and Christian assurance (Rom. v. 1–11, viii. 33 ff.). It is in terms of justification that Paul explains all hints, prophecies, and instances of salvation in the Old Testament (Rom. i. 17; Gal. iii. 11, quoting Hab. ii. 4; Rom. iii. 21, iv. 3–8, quoting Gn. xv. 6; Ps. xxxii. 1 f.; Rom. ix. 22–x. 21, quoting Ho. ii. 23, i. 10; Is. viii. 14; Joel ii. 32; Is. lxv. 1, *etc.*; Rom. xi. 26 f., quoting Is. lix. 20 f.; Gal. iii. 8, quoting Gn. xii. 3; Gal. iv. 21 ff., quoting Gn. xxi. 10; *etc.*).

5. Justification is the key to Paul's philosophy of history. He holds that God's central overarching purpose in His ordering of world-history since the fall has been to lead sinners to justifying faith.

God deals with mankind, Paul tells us, through two representative men: 'the first man Adam', and 'the second man', who is 'the last Adam', Jesus Christ (1 Cor. xv. 45 ff.; Rom. v. 12 ff.). The first man, by disobeying, brought condemnation and death upon the whole race; the second man, by His obedience, has become the author of justification and life for all who have faith (Rom. v. 16 ff.).

From the time of Adam's fall, death reigned universally, though sin was not yet clearly known (Rom. v. 12 ff.). But God took Abraham and his family into covenant, justifying Abraham through his faith, and promising that in Abraham's seed (*i.e.* through one of his descendants) all nations should be blessed (*i.e.* justified) (Gal. iii. 6–9, 16; Rom. iv. 3, 9–22). Then through Moses God revealed His law to Abraham's family. The law was meant to give, not salvation, but knowledge of sin. By detecting and provoking transgressions, it was to teach Israelites their need of justification, thus acting as a *paidagōgos* (the household slave who took children to school) to lead them to Christ (Gal. iii. 19–24; Rom. iii. 20, v. 20, vii. 5, 7–13). This epoch of divine preparatory education lasted till the coming of Christ (Gal. iii. 23–25, iv. 1–5).

The effect of Christ's work was to abolish the barrier of exclusivism which Israel's possession of the law and promise had erected between Jew and Gentile (Eph. ii. 14 ff.). Through Christ, justification by faith could now be preached to Jew and Gentile without distinction, for in Christ all believers were made Abraham's seed, and became sons of God and heirs of the covenant (Gal. iii. 26–29). Unhappily, in this situation most Jews proved to be legalists; they sought to establish a righteousness of their own by works of law, and would not believe that faith in Christ was the God-given way to righteousness (Rom. ix. 30–x. 21). So many 'natural branches' had been cut off from the olive-tree of the historic covenant community (Rom. xi. 16 ff.), and the Church was for the present predominantly Gentile; but there was hope that an elect remnant from fallen Israel, provoked by the mercy shown to undeserving Gentiles, would itself come to faith and find remission of sins in the end (Rom.

xi. 23–32). Thus both Jew and Gentile would be saved, not through their own works and effort, but through the free grace of God justifying the disobedient and ungodly; and all the glory of salvation will be God's alone (Rom. xi. 30–36).

These considerations point to the centrality of justification in Paul's theological and religious outlook.

III. THE GROUND OF JUSTIFICATION

As stated by Paul in Romans, the doctrine of justification seems to raise a problem of theodicy. Its background, set out in i. 18–iii. 20, is the solidarity of mankind in sin, and the inevitability of judgment. In ii. 5–16 Paul states his doctrine of the judgment day. The principle of judgment, he says, will be 'to every man according to his works' (verse 6, RV). The standard of judgment will be God's law, in the highest form in which men know it (if not the Mosaic law, then the law of conscience, verses 12–15). The evidence will be 'the secrets of men' (verse 16). Only law-keepers can hope to be justified (verses 7, 10, 12 f.). And there are no law-keepers. None is righteous; all have sinned (iii. 9 ff.). So the prospect is of universal condemnation, for Jew as well as Gentile, for a law-breaking Jew is no more acceptable to God than anyone else (ii. 17–27). All, it seems, are doomed. 'By the works of the law shall no flesh be justified in his sight' (iii. 20, RV, echoing Ps. cxliii. 2).

But now Paul proclaims the present justification of believing sinners (iii. 21 ff.). God reckons righteousness to the unrighteous and justifies the ungodly (iii. 23 f., iv. 5 f.). The (deliberately?) paradoxical quality of the last phrase is heightened by the fact that these very Greek words are used in the LXX of Ex. xxiii. 7 ('I will not justify the wicked') and Is. v. 22 f. ('Woe unto them . . . which justify the wicked . . .'). The question arises: on what grounds can God justify the ungodly without compromising His own justice as the Judge?

Paul maintains that God justifies sinners on a just ground: namely, that Jesus Christ, acting on their behalf, has satisfied the claims of God's law upon them. He was 'made under the law' (Gal. iv. 4) in order to fulfil the precept and bear the penalty of the law in their stead. By His 'blood' (*i.e.* His death: see BLOOD) He put away their sins (Rom. iii. 25, v. 9). By His obedience to God He won for all His people the status of law-keepers (Rom. v. 19). He became 'obedient unto death' (Phil. ii. 8); His life of righteousness culminated in His dying the death of the unrighteous, bearing the law's penal curse (Gal. iii. 13; *cf.* Is. liii. 4–12). In His person on the cross, the sins of His people were judged and expiated. Through this 'one act of righteousness'—His sinless life and death—'the free gift came unto all men to justification of life' (Rom. v. 18, RV). Thus believers become 'the righteousness of God' in and through Him who 'knew no sin' personally, but was representatively 'made sin' (treated as a sinner, and punished) in their place (2 Cor. v. 21). Thus 'Christ . . . is made unto us . . . righteousness' (1 Cor. i. 30). This was the thought expressed in older Protestant theology by the phrase 'the imputation of Christ's righteousness'. The phrase is not in Paul, but its meaning is. The point that it makes is that believers are made righteous before God (Rom. v. 19) through His admitting them to share Christ's status of acceptance. In other words, God treats them according to Christ's desert. There is nothing arbitrary or artificial in this, for God recognizes the existence of a real union of covenantal solidarity between them and Christ. For Paul, union with Christ is not fiction, but fact—the basic fact, indeed, of Christianity; and his doctrine of justification is simply his first step in analysing its meaning. So it is 'in Christ' (Gal. ii. 17, RV; 2 Cor. v. 21) that sinners are justified. God accounts them righteous, not because He accounts them to have kept His law personally (which would be a false judgment), but because He accounts them to be 'in' the One who kept God's law representatively (which is a true judgment).

So, when God justifies sinners on the ground of Christ's obedience and death, He acts justly. So far from compromising His judicial righteousness, this method of justification actually exhibits it. It is designed 'to shew his righteousness, because of the passing over of the sins done aforetime, in the forbearance of God [*i.e.* the sins remitted in Old Testament times]; for the showing, I say, of his righteousness at this present season: that he might himself be just, and the justifier of him that hath faith in Jesus' (Rom. iii. 25 f., RV). The key words are repeated for emphasis, for the point is crucial. The gospel which proclaims God's apparent violation of His justice really reveals His justice. By His method of justifying sinners, God (in another sense) justified Himself; for by setting forth Christ as a propitiation for sins, in whom human sin was actually judged and punished as it deserved, He revealed the just ground on which He was able to pardon and accept believing sinners in Old Testament times (as in fact He did: *cf.* Ps. cxxx. 3 f.), no less than in the Christian era.

IV. THE MEANS OF JUSTIFICATION

Faith in Christ, says Paul, is the means whereby righteousness is received and justification bestowed. Sinners are justified 'by' or 'through' faith (Gk. *pistei*, *dia* or *ek pisteōs*). Paul does not regard faith as the ground of justification. If it were, it would be a meritorious work, and Paul would not be able to term the believer, as such, 'him that worketh not' (Rom. iv. 5); nor could he go on to say that salvation by faith is 'according to grace' (verse 16, RV), for grace absolutely excludes works (Rom. xi. 6). Paul quotes the case of Abraham, who 'believed God, and it was reckoned unto him for righteousness', to prove that a man is justified through faith without works (Rom. iv. 3 ff., RV; Gal. iii. 6; quoting Gn. xv. 6). In Rom. iv. 5, 9 (*cf.* verses 22, 24)

Paul refers to the Genesis text as teaching that Abraham's faith was 'reckoned . . . for righteousness'. All he means, however, as the context shows, is that Abraham's faith—whole-hearted reliance on God's promise (verses 18 ff.)—was the occasion and means of his being justified. 'For' (*eis*) in the phrase 'reckoned for righteousness' could either mean 'as' (by real equivalence, or some arbitrary method of calculation), or else 'with a view to', 'leading to', 'issuing in'. The latter alternative is clearly right. Paul is not suggesting that faith, viewed either as righteousness, actual or inchoate, or as a substitute for righteousness, is the *ground* of justification; Rom. iv does not deal with the ground of justification at all, only with the means of securing it.

V. PAUL AND JAMES

On the assumption that Jas. ii. 14–26 teaches that God accepts men on the double ground of faith and works, some have thought that James deliberately contradicts Paul's teaching of justification by faith without works, supposing it to be antinomian (*cf.* Rom. iii. 8). But this seems to misconceive James' point. It must be remembered that Paul is the only New Testament writer to use 'justify' as a technical term for God's act of accepting men when they believe. When James speaks of 'being justified', he appears to be using the word in its more general sense of being vindicated, or proved genuine and right before God and men, in face of possible doubt as to whether one was all that one professed, or was said, to be (*cf.* the usage in Mt. xi. 19). For a man to be justified in this sense is for him to be shown a genuine believer, one who will demonstrate his faith by action. This justification is, in effect, a manifesting of the justification that concerns Paul. James quotes Gn. xv. 6 for the same purpose as Paul does—to show that it was faith that secured Abraham's acceptance. But now, he argues, this statement was 'fulfilled' (confirmed, shown to be true, and brought to its appointed completion by events) thirty years later, when 'Abraham (was) justified by works, in that he offered up Isaac' (verse 21). By this his faith was 'made perfect', *i.e.* brought to due expression in appropriate actions; thus he was shown to be a true believer. The case of Rahab is parallel (verse 25). James' point in this paragraph is simply that 'faith', *i.e.* a bare orthodoxy, such as the devils have (verse 19), unaccompanied by good works, provides no sufficient grounds for inferring that a man is saved. Paul would have agreed heartily (*cf.* 1 Cor. vi. 9; Eph. v. 5 f.; Tit. i. 16).

See RIGHTEOUSNESS, FAITH.

BIBLIOGRAPHY. *Arndt*; G. Quell and G. Schrenk, *Righteousness*, E.T., 1951 (from *TWNT*); commentaries on Romans: especially C. Hodge, 2nd ed., 1864; W. Sanday and A. C. Headlam, *ICC*[5], 1902; A. Nygren, E.T., 1952; F. J. Leenhardt, E.T., 1961; and on Galatians: especially J. B. Lightfoot, 10th ed., 1890; E. D. Burton, *ICC*, 1921; J. Buchanan, *The Doctrine of Justification*, 1867; C. Hodge, *Systematic Theology*, 1874, III, pp. 114–212; H. R. Mackintosh, *The Christian Experience of Forgiveness*, 1928; V. Taylor, *Forgiveness and Reconciliation*, 1946; L. Morris, *The Apostolic Preaching of the Cross*, 1955; K. Barth, *Church Dogmatics*, IV. 1, E.T., 1956, pp. 514–642; A. Richardson, *Introduction to the Theology of the New Testament*, 1958, pp. 232 ff.; J. Murray, *Romans 1–8*, 1959, pp. 336–362.

J.I.P.

JUSTUS. A Latin name. Lightfoot (on Col. iv. 11) notes its frequency among Jews and proselytes, often combined with a Jewish name (*cf.* 1 and 3 below, and see Deissmann, *BS*, pp. 315 f.), and suggests that it was meant to denote obedience and devotion to the Law.

1. A name of Joseph Barsabas, one of the two conceived as the possible apostolic successor to Judas Iscariot (Acts i. 23). By the context he was thus a consistent disciple from John the Baptist's time. Papias had a story of his survival of a heathen ordeal by poison (Eus., *EH* iii. 39. 9; *cf.* Lightfoot, *Apostolic Fathers*, 1891, p. 531, for another authority). On the name 'Barsabas' ('son of—*i.e.* born on—a Sabbath'?), see H. J. Cadbury in *Amicitiae Corolla*, ed. H. G. Wood, 1933, pp. 48 ff. If it is a true patronymic, Judas Barsabas (Acts xv. 22) could be a brother.

2. Gentile adherent and neighbour of the synagogue in Corinth. When Christian preaching split the synagogue, the house of Justus became Paul's centre (Acts xviii. 7). The MSS variously render his other name as Titus or Titius, or omit it altogether (accepted as the original reading by Ropes, *BC*, III, p. 173). Following the hint of Rom. xvi. 23, Ramsay, and, more fully, Goodspeed (*JBL*, LXIX, 1950, pp. 382 ff.) identify him with Gaius of Corinth (*q.v.*), rendering his name 'Gaius Titius Justus'. The guess that he was the Titus of Paul's letters has nothing but its antiquity to commend it.

3. Alias Jesus, a valued Jewish co-worker of Paul (Col. iv. 11). Nothing more is known of him. It has been conjectured that his name has accidentally dropped out from Phm. 24 (*cf.* E. Amling, *ZNW*, X, p. 261). A.F.W.

JUTTAH. A walled town on a hill 5 miles due south of Hebron, 3 miles south-west of Ziph, assigned to the priests (Jos. xv. 55, xxi. 16); *cf.* 1 Ch. vi. 59, where Juttah appears in LXX as *Atta*, and is required to make the count; modern Yatta; Robinson, *BR*, i. 492. In Luke i. 39 some commentators would read Juttah for Judah, in apposition to *polin*; Abel disagrees emphatically (*Géographie*, II, p. 367). J.P.U.L.

K

KABZEEL. A town in S Judah; birthplace of Benaiah ben-Jehoiada (2 Sa. xxiii. 20); resettled in Nehemiah's time. Khirbet Hora has been suggested; the nearby Wadi el-Ghurra may reflect Jagur (Jos. xv. 21). See further, Abel, *Géographie*, II, pp. 89, 353.

KADESH. 1. Kadesh-barnea. A location apparently in the north-east of the Sinai peninsula: a well, a settlement, and a wilderness region (Ps. xxix. 8). When Chedorlaomer and his allies marched south through Transjordan they penetrated Mt. Seir as far as El Paran, turned back to the north-west, came to En-mishpat (*i.e.* Kadesh) and subdued the Amalekites, before returning north-eastwards to defeat the kings of the Cities of the (Dead Sea) Plain (Gn. xiv. 5–9). In the narrative of the fugitive Hagar's experience of God, the well Beer-lahai-roi is 'between Kadesh and Bered', on the way to Shur (Gn. xvi. 7, 14); Kadesh is also associated with the way to Shur in Gn. xx. 1. Journeying through the Sinai wilderness, the Israelites stayed in the region of Kadesh on the edges of the wildernesses of Paran and Zin more than once (Nu. xiii. 26, xx. 1; Dt. i. 19, 46); from here Moses sent his spies into Canaan. From Horeb or Sinai to Kadesh was eleven days' journey *via* Mt. Seir (Dt. i. 2). From the traditional Mt. Sinai to Dahab on the east coast of Sinai and up the coast and across to Kadesh (Qudeirat) is indeed eleven days' travel, as recently observed by Aharoni (*The Holy Land: Antiquity and Survival*, II, 2/3, pp. 289, 290, and 293, fig. 7; Dahab). See fig. 80.

At Kadesh, after doubting God's ability to give them the promised land, Israel was condemned to wander for forty years until a new generation should arise (Nu. xiv. 32–35; *cf.* Dt. ii. 14). After some time, Israel returned to Kadesh (Nu. xxxiii. 36, 37), Miriam being buried there (Nu. xx. 1). At this time, too, for failing to glorify God when striking water from the rock (Nu. xx. 10–13, xxvii. 14; Dt. xxxii. 51) Moses was denied entry to the promised land; thence, also, he sent messengers in vain to the king of Edom, to grant Israel permission to pass through his territory (Nu. xx. 14–21; Jdg. xi. 16, 17). Kadesh-barnea was to be the southern corner of the south-western boundary of Judah, turning west then north-west to reach the Mediterranean along the 'River of Egypt' (Nu. xxxiv. 4; Jos. xv. 3); it was also included as a boundary-point by Ezekiel (xlvii. 19, xlviii. 28). The south-east to south-west limits of Joshua's South Canaanite campaign were marked by Kadesh-barnea and Gaza respectively (Jos. x. 41).

Kadesh-barnea is often identified with the spring of 'Ain Qudeis, some 66 miles south-west from the south end of the Dead Sea, or about 49 miles south-west of Beersheba. However, the water-supply at 'Ain Qudeis is insignificant; see the unflattering but realistic comments by Woolley and Lawrence ('The Wilderness of Zin', in *Palestine Exploration Fund Annual*, III, 1914/15, pp. 53–57, and plates 10–12, also Baly, *Geography of the Bible*, 1957, p. 266). The name Qudeis may, indeed, have no connection with 'Kadesh' (*cf.* Woolley and Lawrence, *op. cit.*, p. 53 and note*). 'Ain Qudeirat, roughly 5 miles north-west of 'Ain Qudeis, has much more water and vegetation and is a more suitable location for Kadesh-barnea (for this see Aharoni, *op. cit.*, pp. 295, 296, and figs. 1–3 opposite p. 290; and Woolley and Lawrence, *op. cit.*, pp. 59–62, 69–71, and plates 13–15). Probably the whole group of springs was used by the Israelites, Qudeirat being the main one. The general location of Qudeirat/Qudeis sufficiently suits the topographical requirements of the biblical narratives. See further, WILDERNESS OF THE WANDERING.

2. Kedesh in Jos. xv. 23, in the southernmost territory of Judah, is either another otherwise unknown Kadesh, or else is probably identical with Kadesh-barnea (*cf.* xv. 3).

Finally, the emendation of Tahtim-Hodshi (*q.v.*) in 2 Sa. xxiv. 6 to 'the land of the Hittites towards Kadesh' is not very convincing, particularly as the Kadesh on Orontes thus referred to had long passed from history by David's day.

K.A.K.

KADMIEL (*qaḏmî'ēl*, 'The ancient time of El' or 'El is the ancient One, God the Primeval'). A Levite who returned with Zerubbabel, accompanied by his family (Ezr. ii. 40; Ne. vii. 43, xii. 8, 24). He was concerned with the commencement of the Temple rebuilding (Ezr. iii. 9), with the day of national repentance (Ne. ix. 4, 5), and with the sealing of the covenant with Nehemiah (Ne. x. 9).

J.G.G.N.

KADMONITES. A people whose name, *qaḏmōnî*, is identical in form with the adjective *qaḏmōnî*, 'eastern' (*e.g.* Ezk. xlvii. 18) (see EAST), and for this reason may simply mean 'Easterners' and be another designation for the *b*^e^*nê-qedem* (see EAST, CHILDREN OF). The word occurs but once as a name however (Gn. xv. 19, with the article), in the list of peoples to be given to Abraham's seed. It may therefore well be the name of a tribe.

T.C.M.

KAIN. A town to the south of Hebron, Jos. xv. 57. Khirbet Yaqin has been suggested, but its antiquity is uncertain. LXX takes as one name with Zanoah, altering the count; see ZANOAH (2).

KANAH. 1. A wadi running west from the watershed at the head of the Michmethath valley, 4 miles south of Shechem; the natural boundary between Ephraim and Manasseh (Jos. xvi. 8). **2.** A town in the Lebanon foothills, assigned to Asher, Jos. xix. 28. The name survives in a village 7 miles south-east of Tyre. J.P.U.L.

KEDAR (*qēḏār*, probably 'black', 'swarthy'). **1.** One of the sons of Ishmael, and father of the tribe which bears his name (Gn. xxv. 13; 1 Ch. i. 29). See below.

2. Kedar, in its restricted sense, denotes a nomadic tribe which inhabited the Syro-Arabian desert, but the name is often used in Scripture and in rabbinical literature as a collective term for the Bedouin generally. The reference to 'Kedar' in Je. xlix. 28, 29 relates to the actual attack by Nebuchadrezzar on Arabs south-east of Damascus in 599 BC (see D. J. Wiseman, *Chronicles of Chaldean Kings*, 1956, p. 32). They were evidently sheep-breeders on a large scale (Is. lx. 7), and traders with prosperous Tyre (Ezk. xxvii. 21), the nearest seaport. A powerful tribe with skilful archers (Is. xxi. 16, 17), they are coupled with Mesech in Ps. cxx. 5, probably as a type of barbarous people, and their tents are mentioned (Ct. i. 5) to signify dark beauty (*cf. qāḏar*, 'to be black').

Is. xlii. 11 suggests that they dwelt in villages, but these may have been merely temporary encampments (see H. M. Orlinsky, *JAOS*, LIX, 1939, pp. 22 ff.). The tribe is mentioned with the Arabs and Nebaioth in Assyr. inscriptions, and there is an account of the conflicts between Kedar and Ashurbanipal. J.D.D.

KEDEMOTH. Probably the modern qaṣr ez-za'ferān, a twin site about 7½ miles north-east of Dibon. It was a levitical city (1 Ch. vi. 79) from the inheritance of Reuben (Jos. xiii. 18). At the time of the Exodus it must have been a desert area, whence 'the wilderness of Kedemoth' (Dt. ii. 26). R.F.H.

KEDESH, KEDESH-NAPHTALI. 1. A former Canaanite royal city (Jos. xii. 22) which became a principal town in Naphtali (Jos. xix. 37). It was sometimes designated 'of Naphtali' (Jdg. iv. 6) to distinguish it from (2). It was assigned to the Levites (Jos. xxi. 32) and made a city of refuge (xx. 7). Kedesh was also marked by its location in Galilee (Jos. xx. 7; 1 Ch. vi. 76).

This Kedesh may well be the home of Barak where he collected his forces from Naphtali and Zebulun for war against Sisera (Jdg. iv. 9–11). When Tiglath-pileser III of Assyria invaded N Israel in 734–732 BC Kedesh, being on the route south from Hazor, was one of the first cities to fall to him (2 Ki. xv. 29). It was the scene of the great battle fought between the Maccabees and Demetrius (1 Macc. xi. 63). Kedesh is the modern Tell Qades, north-west of Lake Huleh, where soundings and surface finds show it to have been occupied during the early and late Bronze Ages. See further, *Antiquity and Survival*, II, 1957, p. 146.

2. A town of Issachar given to Gershonite Levites (1 Ch. vi. 72). Its place is taken by Kishion in the list of Jos. xxi. 28. It is identified with the modern Tell Abu Qedes, SSW of Megiddo.

3. A city of Judah near the Edomite border (Jos. xv. 23), probably to be identified with Kadesh-barnea (*q.v.*). D.J.W.

KEILAH. A walled town of the Shephelah, attacked by the Philistines in Saul's time; David relieved it, but found Saul's influence too strong for him (1 Sa. xxiii). In the restoration its territory formed two districts (Ne. iii. 17 f.).

Kh. Qila, 6 miles east of Beit Guvrin, crowns a hill commanding the ascent to Hebron which climbs southwards from Socoh, parallel to the Shephelah, behind an outlying ridge of the hills. J.P.U.L.

KENATH (*qenāṯ*, 'possession'). A city in N Transjordan taken from the Canaanites by Nobah, who gave it his name (Nu. xxxii. 42), and reconquered by Geshur and Aram (1 Ch. ii. 23). It is usually identified with the extensive ruins at Qanawât, some 16 miles north-east of Bozrah; but see Abel, *Géographie*, II, p. 417. J.D.D.

KENITES. The Kenites were a Midianite tribe (Nu. x. 29; Jdg. i. 16, iv. 11). The name means 'smith', and the presence of copper south-east of the gulf of Aqabah, the Kenite–Midianite region, confirms this interpretation. The Kenites first appear as inhabitants of patriarchal Canaan (Gn. xv. 19). Subsequently Moses becomes son-in-law of Reuel (Ex. ii. 18), and invites Hobab his son to accompany the Israelites, coveting his nomadic skill (Nu. x. 29). Kenites accompanied Judah into their inheritance (Jdg. i. 16; 1 Sa. xxvii. 10). They were spared by Saul in his Amalekite war (1 Sa. xv. 6), and David cultivated their friendship (1 Sa. xxx. 29). The Rechabites were of Kenite stock (1 Ch. ii. 55), and were prominent in post-exilic times (Ne. iii. 14).

The 'Kenite hypothesis' gives this Midianite clan importance in the religion of Israel. It purports to answer the question: Where did Moses learn the name Yahweh? Rejecting pre-Mosaic knowledge of the name in Israel, some reply that he learned the name from Jethro, the Kenite–Midianite. The later Yahwistic zeal of the Rechabite–Kenites cannot support this theory: it is not unknown for converts to be more zealous than traditional believers! Nor does Jethro's sacrifice (Ex. xviii. 12) bear the weight placed upon it, that Jethro was instructing Moses how Yahweh should be worshipped, for the chapter shows him as the learner, led to faith by

Moses' testimony (verse 11). Apart, therefore, from the unconvincing observation that 'the Kenites were the smiths of the ancient nomad tribes, . . . and undoubtedly Yahweh is a fire-god' (Oesterley and Robinson, *History of Israel*, I, p. 92), the sole support of the Kenite hypothesis is that their ancestor Cain bore the mark of Yahweh (Gn. iv. 15). This hypothesis is advocated, *e.g.*, by L. Koehler, *Old Testament Theology*, p. 45; contested by M. Buber, *Moses*, p. 94. The testimony of Genesis is that the name Yahweh was known to the Patriarchs, and indeed from the earliest times (Gn. iv. 1, 26). The hypothesis is a fruit of the application of documentary analysis, and well merits being called 'the acme of liberal inventiveness' (U. E. Simon, *A Theology of Salvation*, 1953, p. 88).

BIBLIOGRAPHY. H. H. Rowley, *The Faith of Israel*, 1956, pp. 54 ff.; *Joseph to Joshua*, 1950, pp. 149 ff.; Y. Kaufmann, *The Religion of Israel*, 1961, pp. 242 ff. J.A.M.

KENIZZITES. A leading Edomite family, tracing descent from Eliphaz, Esau's eldest son (Gn. xxxvi. 11, 15, 42; 1 Ch. i. 36, 53). Part of them joined the Judahites; their contribution to Israel's history is indicated in 1 Ch. iv. 13–15. (Verse 15 is difficult; perhaps it originally read '. . . (names lost); these were the sons of Kenaz'.) Caleb's Kenizzite descent is always expressed through Jephunneh (Nu. xxxii. 12; Jos. xiv. 6, 14). 'Othniel, son of Kenaz' may simply mean 'Othniel the Kenizzite'; otherwise, this Kenaz would be Caleb's younger brother, and Othniel his nephew, which is less likely. Caleb's history implies that his family was well established in Judah before the Exodus; it may therefore have been Jephunneh's ancestors who first joined the tribe.

The Kenizzites are mentioned, Gn. xv. 19, with nine other nations as occupying the land promised to Abraham; this, apparently defined in terms of settlements made after his time, included the extreme south, but no part of Edom proper (*cf.* Dt. ii. 5). J.P.U.L.

KENOSIS. This Gk. term is formed from the verb *heauton ekenōsen*, 'he emptied himself', which the AV of Phil. ii. 7 renders 'he made himself of no reputation'. As a substantive it is used, in the technical sense, of the Christological theory which sets out 'to show how the Second Person of the Trinity could so enter into human life as that there resulted the genuinely human experience which is described by the evangelists' (H. R. Mackintosh). In its classic form this Christology goes back no farther than the middle of the last century, to Thomasius of Erlangen in Germany. The essence of the original kenotic view is stated clearly by J. M. Creed. 'The Divine Logos by His Incarnation divested Himself of His divine attributes of omniscience and omnipotence, so that in His incarnate life the Divine Person is revealed and solely revealed through a human consciousness' (art. 'Recent Tendencies in English Christology' in *Mysterium Christi*, ed. Bell and Deissmann, 1930, p. 133). This Christological statement is open to damaging theological objections; and, on exegetical grounds too, there is little support for it.

The verb *kenoun* means simply 'to empty'. In the literal sense it is used, for example, of Rebekah's emptying the water from her pitcher into the trough (Gn. xxiv. 20, LXX: the verb is *exekenōsen*). In Je. xiv. 2, xv. 9 the LXX uses the verb *kenoun* to render the *puʿal* of *'āmal*, which the RV translates as 'languish'; and this translation points to a metaphorical usage which prepares the way for the interpretation of the Philippians text. The use of *kenoun* there in the active voice is unique in the New Testament, and the whole phrase with the reflexive is not only un-Pauline but un-Greek too. This fact supports the suggestion that the phrase is a rendering into Greek of a Semitic original, the linguistic solecism being explained by the literal translation from one language into another. Recent scholars (H. W. Robinson, J. Jeremias) have found this original in Is. liii. 12: 'He poured out his soul unto death'. On this reading of Phil. ii. 7, the 'kenosis' is not that of His incarnation but the final surrender of His life, in utter self-giving and sacrifice, on the cross. Even if this novel interpretation is regarded as somewhat forced, it puts us on the right track. The words 'he emptied himself' in the Pauline context say nothing about the abandonment of the divine attributes, and to that extent the kenotic theory is an entire misunderstanding of the Scriptural words. Linguistically the self-emptying is to be interpreted in the light of the words which immediately follow. It refers to the 'pre-incarnate renunciation coincident with the act of "taking the form of a servant" ' (V. Taylor, *The Person of Christ in New Testament Teaching*, 1958, p. 77). His taking of the servant's form involved the necessary limitation of the glory which He laid aside that He might be born 'in the likeness of men'. That glory of His pre-existent oneness with the Father (see Jn. xvii. 5, 24) was His because from all eternity He existed 'in the form of God' (Phil. ii. 6). It was concealed in the 'form of a servant' which He took when He assumed our nature and appeared in our likeness; and with the acceptance of our humanity He took also His destiny as the Servant of the Lord who humbled Himself to the sacrifice of Himself at Calvary. The 'kenosis' then began in His Father's presence with His pre-incarnate choice to assume our nature; it led inevitably to the final obedience of the cross when He did, to the fullest extent, pour out His soul unto death (see Rom. viii. 3; 2 Cor. viii. 9; Gal. iv. 4, 5; Heb. ii. 14–16, x. 5 ff.).

BIBLIOGRAPHY. The fullest modern treatment of the kenosis doctrine, both historically and theologically, is that by P. Henry, art. 'Kénose' in *Supplément au Dictionnaire de la Bible*, Fasc. xxiv, 1950, cols. 7–161: see also R. P. Martin, *An Early Christian Confession: Philippians ii. 5–11 in Recent Interpretation*, 1960. R.P.M.

KERCHIEFS (*mispāḥôṯ*, RSV 'veils', Ezk. xiii. 18, 21). A word associated with the practice of divination (*q.v.*), and found in an obscure passage difficult to interpret. Some understand 'kerchiefs' as denoting long veils or coverings put over the heads of those who consulted false prophetesses. These coverings for 'persons of every stature' reached down to the feet, and were connected with the introduction of the wearer into the magical circle. Others suggest that the word means a close-fitting cap (*cf.* Heb. *sāp̄aḥ*, 'to join'), which also fulfils the condition of certain forms of divination or sorcery that the head should be covered. See also AMULETS and, for full discussion of the context and possible interpretations, G. A. Cooke, *ICC*, *Ezekiel*, 1936, pp. 144 ff. J.D.D.

KEREN-HAPPUCH (*qeren happûḵ*, 'paint-horn', *i.e.* 'beautifier'; LXX *Amaltheias keras*). The name given to the third and youngest daughter of Job after his prosperity had been restored (Jb. xlii. 14). For discussion of the name, see COSMETICS AND PERFUMERY, III (*a*).

KERIOTH. 1. A town in the extreme south of Judah, known also as Kerioth Hezron or Hazor, possibly the modern Khirbet el-Qaryatein (Jos. xv. 25). **2.** A city of Moab (Je. xlviii. 24), formerly fortified (Je. xlviii. 41), and possessing palaces (Am. ii. 2). Some writers identify it with Ar, the ancient capital of Moab, because when Ar is listed among Moabite towns Kerioth is omitted (Is. xv, xvi), and *vice versa* (Je. xlviii). There was a sanctuary there for Chemosh, to which Mesha dragged Arel the chief of Ataroth. See MOABITE STONE. J.A.T.

KESITAH (*qeśîṭâ*, probably 'that which is weighed', 'a fixed weight', from an Arabic word 'to divide, fix'). A unit of unknown value, evidently uncoined money used by the Patriarchs. LXX and other ancient vss render 'lambs', early weights often being modelled in animal-forms (see WEIGHTS AND MEASURES). It occurs only in Gn. xxxiii. 19 and Jos. xxiv. 32 of Jacob's purchase of land at Shechem, and in Jb. xlii. 11 of a congratulatory present. J.G.G.N.

KETURAH (*qeṭûrâ*, 'perfumed one'). Abraham's second wife after the death of Sarah who bore him Zimran, Jokshan, Medan, Midian, Ishbak, and Shuah, who in their turn became the ancestors of a number of N Arabian peoples (Gn. xxv. 1–4; 1 Ch. i. 32, 33). See ARABIA.

BIBLIOGRAPHY. J. A. Montgomery, *Arabia and the Bible*, 1934, pp. 42–45. T.C.M.

KEY (Heb. *map̄tēaḥ*, 'opener'; Gk. *kleis*, 'key'). In its literal sense the word is found only in Jdg. iii. 25; the key was 'a flat piece of wood furnished with pins corresponding to holes in a hollow bolt. The bolt was on the inside, shot into a socket in the doorpost and fastened by pins which fell into the holes in the bolt from an upright piece of wood (the lock) attached to the inside of the door. To unlock the door one put one's hand in by a hole in the door (*cf.* Ct. v. 4) and raised the pins in the bolt by means of the corresponding pins in the key' (F. F. Bruce in *NBC*, p. 242). For a later Roman key see illustration below. The more usual biblical sense

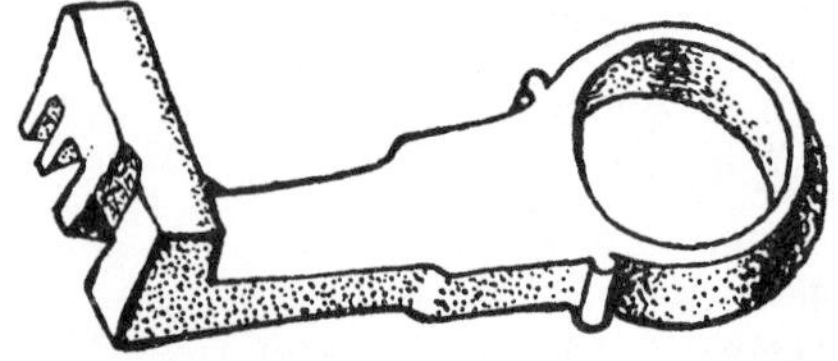

Fig. 124. Roman ring-key. Metal keys which have been found at Pompeii and elsewhere show that the Romans used warded locks made entirely or partly of metal. Some of their keys were made for turning in locks, instead of pushing and sliding, which was the earlier custom.

of the word is as a symbol of power and authority (*e.g.* Mt. xvi. 19; Rev. i. 18; Is. xxii. 22). See especially POWER, III, 'Power of the Keys'. J.D.D.

KIBROTH-HATTAAVAH (*qiḇrôṯ hatta'ᵃwâ*, 'graves of craving'). A camp of the Israelites a day's journey from the wilderness of Sinai. There the people, having craved flesh to eat and been sent quails by the Lord, were overtaken by plague, which caused many fatalities (Nu. xi. 31–34, xxxiii. 16; Dt. ix. 22; *cf.* Ps. lxxviii. 27–31). Some have suggested that the incident at Taberah (Nu. xi. 1–3) had the same location as that at Kibroth-hattaavah, but Dt. ix. 22 seems to argue against this. Grollenberg makes an identification with Ruweis el-Ebeirig, north-east of Mt. Sinai. J.D.D.

KIDNEYS, REINS. In the AV the Heb. word *kᵉlāyôṯ* is translated by 'kidneys' when it refers to the physical organ of sacrificial beasts, principally in Leviticus (iii. 4, iv. 9, vii. 4, *etc.*). The practice was that the two kidneys, together with the fat and part of the liver, were burned on the altar as Yahweh's portion, while the worshippers no doubt consumed the rest. The kidneys along with the blood and other internal organs were held to contain the life, and the kidneys were regarded as a choice portion, perhaps because of their coating of fat. *Cf.* Dt. xxxii. 14, where the meaning is 'rich grains of wheat'.

The same Heb. word is translated 'reins' where it refers, generally figuratively, to the human organs, which were held to possess psychical functions. They are 'troubled' (Jb. xix. 27; Ps. lxxiii. 21), 'rejoice' (Pr. xxiii. 16), and are 'tried' by God (Je. xi. 20).

In the last passage the parallelism reveals how they, along with the heart and indeed the other internal organs (see BOWELS, HEART) were held to be the centre of the personality and will. The only New Testament reference (Rev. ii. 23) is a quotation from, or close parallel to, the Old Testament in this sense.

The reference to the reins instructing one (Ps. xvi. 7) (with a parallel in the Ras Shamra texts, 'his inwards instruct him') is a further similar usage, with which compare the late Jewish concept that one kidney prompts a man to do good and the other to do evil (TJ, *Berakhoth* 61a).

B.O.B.

KIDRON. The brook Kidron, the modern Wadi en-Nar, is a torrent-bed, which begins to the north of Jerusalem, passes the Temple mount and the Mount of Olives *en route* to the Dead Sea, which it reaches by way of the wilderness of Judaea. Its modern name means 'the Fire wadi', and this bears witness to the fact that it is dry and sun-baked for most of the year. Only for short periods during the rainy seasons is it filled with water. It was also called 'the Valley of Jehoshaphat' (*q.v.*). See plate XVI.

On the west side of the Kidron there is a spring known as the Gihon ('Gusher') or 'Virgin's Fountain', the flow of which was artificially diverted by the Jews to serve the needs of Jerusalem. As its name suggests, the water does not come through in a steady flow, but accumulates underground in a reservoir and breaks out from time to time. In 1880 a Heb. inscription was discovered in which information was recorded concerning the making of the tunnel (see SILOAM). This may have reference to the incident recorded in 2 Ch. xxxii. 3, 4. (See fig. 193.)

David passed over the brook Kidron on his way out of Jerusalem during Absalom's revolt (2 Sa. xv. 23). The reforming kings, such as Asa, Hezekiah, and Josiah, used the valley as a place of destruction where heathen idols, altars, *etc.*, were burned or ground to powder (1 Ki. xv. 13, *etc.*). It seems to be taken as one of the boundaries of Jerusalem in 1 Ki. ii. 37 and Je. xxxi. 40.

Some suggest a reference to the Kidron in Ezk. xlvii, where the prophet sees a stream of water issuing from the threshold of the Temple and pursuing its way towards the Dead Sea, making the land fertile in the process. See especially G. Adam Smith, *The Historical Geography of the Holy Land*, 1931, pp. 510 ff.; W. R. Farmer, 'The Geography of Ezekiel's River of Life', *Biblical Archaeologist*, XIX, 1956, pp. 17 ff. That Ezekiel was thinking of the filling-up of the dry bed of the Kidron by the healing stream of water seems probable, but cannot be maintained with certainty.

G.W.G.

KIN, KINSMAN. Israel was originally tribal in nature, and the idea was never entirely lost. Many of her family relationships are to be understood in terms of tribal customs known all over the world. Kinship consisted basically in the possession of a common blood and was strongest nearest to its origin in the father's house, but it was not lost in the further reaches of family relationship. At the head of the family (*mišpāḥâ*) stood the father (*'āḇ*), a word which expressed kinship and authority. The father founded a father's house (*bêṯ 'āḇ*), which was the smallest unit of a tribe. But the strong cohesion of the family extended upwards from the father to the fathers, and downwards from the father to the sons and daughters. Hence the term family could mean the father's house (*bêṯ 'āḇ*), and also the house of the fathers (*bêṯ 'āḇôṯ*). Indeed, at times the whole of Israel was called a family.

The word brother (*'āḥ*) also connoted various things. In its simplest meaning it referred to those who had common parents. In polygamous Israel there were many brothers who had only a common father. These too were brothers, though the brotherhood was not the same as that of men who had a common mother. Thus in Gn. xlii. 4 there are two kinds of brothers, full and half. The full brother was defined by the phrase 'his brother, Benjamin, his mother's son' (Gn. xliii. 29). However, the term extended as far as the feeling of consanguinity extended. Wherever there was a family there were brothers, for all were bearers of kinship (Gn. xxiv. 4, 27, 38; Jdg. xiv. 3). At times all Israelites were called brothers (Ex. ii. 11; Lv. x. 6; 2 Sa. xix. 41, 42).

There were limits to the closeness of relationship permitted when a man came to seek a wife. Abraham would seek a wife for his son Isaac from his kindred (*mišpāḥâ*) and from his father's house (*bêṯ 'āḇ*), not from the daughters of Canaan (Gn. xxiv. 38, 40). She had to be someone of the same flesh and blood. But she could not be of such close relationship as a sister, mother, child's daughter, *etc.* The forbidden areas are defined in Lv. xviii.

There were significant obligations laid on kinsmen. Among the more important we may mention the following.

Since a woman, married to a man, would normally have the privilege of bearing his son and heir, in the case of the untimely death of the husband without a son, the law of levirate (Lat. *levir*, 'husband's brother') marriage came into force, and progeny was raised up to the dead man who had died 'without a name in Israel' by his next of kin (Dt. xxv. 5–10). There is a good illustration of this in the book of Ruth. See also MARRIAGE.

Then in the matter of inheritance, a man's property was normally passed on to his son or sons. Failing these, it went to his daughters, and then in order to his brethren, to his father's brethren, and finally to his kinsman who was nearest to him (Nu. xxvii. 1–11).

Again it was obligatory on a kinsman to redeem the property of a fellow-kinsman who had fallen into the hands of creditors (Lv. xxv. 25 ff.).

In the special circumstance where a man's life was taken by another, since this was part of the life of the family, an obligation rested on the son, or the brother, or the next of kin in order, to take vengeance (*cf.* Gn. ix. 5, 6). Where kinship ends, there is no longer any avenger (*gō'ēl*). See AVENGER OF BLOOD, FAMILY.

BIBLIOGRAPHY. J. Pedersen, *Israel*, I–II, 1926, pp. 49, 52, 58 ff., 284 ff., *etc.* J.A.T.

KING, KINGSHIP. Heb. *meleḵ*; Gk. *basileus*. Both words are of obscure origin; the former, common to all Semitic languages, is possibly connected either with an Arab. root meaning 'possess' or an Assyr. and Aramaic word meaning 'counsel'. The latter is probably taken over from an early Aegean language.

Fig. 125. 'The investiture of the king.' Part of a large wall-painting from the palace at Mari, Syria. The king receives the rod and ring, symbols of authority, from the goddess Ishtar, whose foot rests on a lion. A goddess and other figures are in attendance. 19th century BC.

The office was common in the Middle East from the earliest times, the general pattern apparently being of a ruler who held sway over a settled region, often centred on a city (Gn. xiv. 10, *cf.* v. 13, xx. 1 ff.). His authority seems to have been hereditary (but *cf.* Gn. xxxvi. 31 ff.), and to have derived from the divine-king or god of the land, often spoken of as the ancestor or father of the ruling king (*e.g.* Ras Shamra—Legend of King Keret). In Egypt the tendency was for the king or pharaoh to be regarded as identical with the god; in Assyria, rather as representing the god.

In classical Greek *basileus* denotes the legal hereditary ruler, guiding the life of the people by his justice or injustice, but contrasted with the tyrant or usurper. The king's power is traced back to Zeus. Later, under Plato, we find a movement towards the idea of the king as 'benefactor', whose will is law, leading up to the idea of 'divine-king' in Alexander and the Caesars.

I. EARLY IDEAS IN ISRAEL

In the history of Israel the early nomadic tribes were ruled by the clan Patriarch. During the Exodus from Egypt rule was exercised by Moses, succeeded by Joshua, in what was a virtual theocracy, with the non-hereditary leader elected by divine call and acknowledged by the people, though not without some protest (Ex. iv. 29 ff.; Nu. xvi. 1 ff.). When Israel first settled in Palestine the tribes were ruled largely by village fathers (Jdg. xi. 5), who would call on a certain man to lead the militia against an enemy. Jephthah (Jdg. xi. 9) demanded that he be made 'head' if he took the lead in this way, but his son did not succeed him. Gideon was asked to rule (*mālaḵ*) over Israel (viii. 22) and refused, but his son Abimelech seized a temporary and local kingship after him (ix. 6 ff.). The book of Judges ends on a note of social chaos (chs. xix, xx, xxi), and this is attributed to the lack of a king (xix. 1, xxi. 25).

II. FROM ELI AND SAMUEL

The following period was one of improvement under the religio-judicial lead of Eli and Samuel. Eli was chief priest at the central sanctuary in Shiloh (1 Sa. i. 3, iv. 13); Samuel was a non-hereditary leader (after the style of Moses and Joshua) who, after the destruction of Shiloh, judged Israel from several places which he visited in circuit (vii. 15 f.). Finally, Samuel became the king-maker of Israel, though at the insistence of the people (1 Sa. viii. 4 ff.). This seems to have been regarded as a measure of apostasy from the theocracy (1 Sa. viii. 7). The request was probably made largely in view of the continual Philistine threat, necessitating a sustained army (viii. 20), and Saul's success as a warrior was his main qualification for the rôle as the first king of Israel. Under his reign, however, Samuel, while he lived, preserved the religious leadership (1 Sa. xiii. 9 ff.), and Saul never quite established his position, nor his dynasty.

III. DEVELOPMENT UNDER DAVID

David, however, was eminently successful, and was ever afterwards regarded as the ideal king. He established a dynasty that lasted for over 400 years, until the break-up of the state in 587 BC. The security of David's dynasty seems to have been based largely on what has been called the Davidic covenant (Ps. cxxxii. 11 ff.). The capital city, centrally situated between what became later the northern and southern states, was Jerusalem (2 Sa. v. 5 ff.). It may be that David assumed something of the rôle of priest-king after the style of the Jebusite kings, whose priesthood apparently dated back to the time of Abraham (Gn. xiv. 17 ff.; Ps. cx), since he seems to have taken a lead in the cult (2 Sa. vi. 13 ff.; *cf.* also 1 Ki. viii. 5).

The Davidic covenant may have been an extension of the Mosaic covenant, particularly if G. E. Mendenhall is right in suggesting that the form of the Mosaic covenant was analogous to Hittite treaty patterns. Under these a Hittite overlord granted an enduring dynasty to his vassal, if the vassal king was a relation, but otherwise he was always personally responsible for the appointment of a successor. The reference to the king as the son of God (Ps. ii. 6, 7) and the promise to maintain the dynasty in terms of the covenant (1 Ki. ix. 4, 5) make the suggestion easily credible.

The main responsibility of the king was the maintenance of righteousness (Is. xi. 1–4; Je. xxxiii. 15), possibly signified by the possession of the testimonies or law or *tôrâ* (Dt. xvii. 18 ff.;

1 Sa. x. 25; 1 Ki. ix. 4 ff.; 2 Ki. xi. 12), with the duty not only to act as judge (1 Ki. iii. 28) but to preserve justice and proclaim the law (2 Ki. xxiii. 2; *cf.* 2 Ch. xvii. 7 ff.; *cf.* also Jdg. xvii. 6).

But many of the kings were wicked themselves and encouraged injustice and wickedness to flourish, not only in the schismatic northern kingdom but in the south too (1 Ki. xiv. 16; 2 Ki. xxi. 16). The reform under Josiah (2 Ki. xxii, xxiii) may have been an attempt to revive the Mosaic precepts in connection with the Davidic covenant, but it was above all the prophetic movement which provided a check upon the waywardness of the kings (2 Sa. xii. 1 ff.; 1 Ki. xviii. 17, 18; Je. xxvi. 1 ff.) (see PROPHET; see also the note on 'King's Ministers' below).

It will be noticed that several so-called messianic passages have been applied above to the Davidic dynasty (Ps. ii, cx, cxxxii; Is. xi. 1–4; Je. xxxiii. 15), and it is the considered view of many modern scholars that this is their primary reference, the psalms referred to, being among others, probably coronation psalms used in the Jerusalem Temple. The failure of the kings to live up to the ideal, however, tended to cast the hope for a righteous ruler more and more into the future. With the fall of the southern kingdom, and later the failure of the Davidic prince, Zerubbabel (1 Ch. iii. 19; Hg. ii. 23; Mt. i. 12) to restore the dynasty on the throne of the post-exilic state, the expectation crystallized into what is technically known as the messianic hope, though many scholars believe it began earlier. See MESSIAH.

IV. THE KING'S MINISTERS

But it should be noted that the prophets were not apparently appointed by the king, though the priests were (1 Ki. ii. 27). Both officiated in the installation of a king (i. 34), but the prophet sometimes took the greater initiative, especially with a change of dynasty, as in the northern kingdom (1 Ki. xix. 16). Other servants of the king were the captain of the host (2 Sa. xix. 13); the scribe (2 Sa. viii. 17; 2 Ki. xii. 10), and the recorder, plus sundry others (1 Ki. iv. 5 ff.). The recorder (*mazkîr*, literally one who causes to remember) was perhaps connected with the chronicling of state events (*cf.* 2 Ki. xxi. 25), or the term may signify the advisory and executive position of a prime minister or grand vizier. Another possibility is that it was a vocal office, parallel to the Egyp. *whm.w*, 'court announcer' or 'king's herald'.

V. LATER DEVELOPMENTS

During the period 104–37 BC certain of the Maccabean high priests assumed the title of king, and some were proclaimed as the fulfilment of the messianic hope, but it is essentially the message of the New Testament that this hope was fulfilled only in Jesus Christ (Mt. i. 1–17, xxi. 5, with which compare Zc. ix. 9 and the coronation procedure in the case of Solomon, 1 Ki. i. 33; also Jn. i. 49). Jesus' message began with the proclamation, 'The kingdom of God is at hand' (Mk. i. 15), and announced to the Pharisees that the kingdom was 'among them' (Lk. xvii. 21, see mg or RSV). He pointed out that it was not a kingdom of this world (Jn. xviii. 36), and so offered no direct threat to the position of the Roman governor, Pilate, any more than it would have done to Herod, the Idumaean king of Judah and vassal of Rome (*cf.* Mt. ii. 16).

Though the word translated 'kingdom' (*basileia*) is used in the sense of realm or domain (Mt. xii. 25), the dominant sense is 'sovereignty' or 'kingly rule'. The sovereignty of God is absolute, but not recognized by sinful man, who thus merits destruction. The 'gospel of the kingdom of God' means that men are given an opportunity to receive the kingdom by repentance and faith (Mk. i. 15). This is achieved through Christ the Messiah-King, to whom every knee must bow, whether in willing loyalty or under judgment (Rom. xiv. 10, 11; Phil. ii. 9–11).

The rule of earthly kings is limited, and Christ claims the first allegiance (Mt. vi. 33). His subjects are delivered from the power of darkness (Col. i. 13), and thus are set free to live righteously (Rom. xiv. 17). Christ's kingdom is an everlasting kingdom (2 Pet. i. 11), but yet to be consummated (Lk. xxii. 16; 1 Cor. xv. 24–28).

BIBLIOGRAPHY. S. Mowinckel, *He that Cometh*, 1956; A. R. Johnson, *Sacral Kingship in Ancient Israel*, 1955; G. Widengren, 'King and Covenant', *JSS*, January 1957; G. E. Mendenhall, 'Ancient Oriental and Biblical Law', *BA*, May 1954; and 'Covenant Forms in Israelite Tradition', *BA*, September 1954; H. Frankfort, *Kingship and the Gods*, 1948; K. L. Schmidt *et al.*, *Basileia* (Bible Key Words), 1957.

B.O.B.

KINGDOM OF GOD, KINGDOM OF HEAVEN. The kingdom of heaven or kingdom of God is the central theme of Jesus' preaching, according to the Synoptic Gospels. While Matthew, who addresses himself to the Jews, speaks for the most part of the 'kingdom of heaven', Mark and Luke speak of the 'kingdom of God', which has the same meaning as the 'kingdom of heaven', but was more intelligible to non-Jews. The use of 'kingdom of heaven' in Matthew is certainly due to the tendency in Judaism to avoid the direct use of the name of God. In any case no distinction in sense is to be assumed between the two expressions (*cf.*, *e.g.*, Mt. v. 3 with Lk. vi. 20).

I. IN JOHN THE BAPTIST

John the Baptist first comes forward with the announcement that the kingdom of heaven is at hand (Mt. iii. 2) and Jesus takes this message over from him (Mt. iv. 17). The expression 'kingdom of heaven' (Heb. *malᵉkûṯ šāmayim*) originates with the late-Jewish expectation of the future in which it denoted the decisive intervention of God, ardently expected by Israel, to restore His people's fortunes and liberate them from the power of their enemies. The coming of the kingdom is the great perspective of the future, prepared by the coming of the Messiah (*q.v.*), which paves the way for the kingdom of God.

By the time of Jesus the development of this eschatological hope in Judaism had taken a great variety of forms, in which now the national element and now the cosmic and apocalyptic element is prominent. This hope goes back to the proclamation in Old Testament prophecy concerning both the restoration of David's throne and the coming of God to renew the world. Although the Old Testament has nothing to say of the eschatological kingdom of heaven in so many words, yet in the Psalms and prophets the future manifestation of God's royal sovereignty belongs to the most central concepts of Old Testament faith and hope. Here too various elements achieve prominence, as may be clearly seen from a comparison of the earlier prophets with the prophecies regarding universal world-sovereignty and the emergence of the Son of man in the book of Daniel (*q.v.*).

When John the Baptist and, after him, Jesus Himself proclaimed that the kingdom was at hand, this proclamation involved an awakening cry of sensational and universal significance. The long-expected divine turning-point in history, the great restoration, however it was conceived at the time, is proclaimed as being at hand. It is therefore of all the greater importance to survey the content of the New Testament preaching with regard to the coming of the kingdom.

In the preaching of John the Baptist prominence is given to the announcement of divine judgment as a reality which is immediately at hand. The axe is already laid to the root of the trees. God's coming as King is above all else a coming to purify, to sift, to judge. No-one can evade it. No privilege can buy exemption from it, not even the ability to claim Abraham as one's father. At the same time John the Baptist points to the coming One who is to follow him, whose forerunner he himself is. The coming One comes with the winnowing-fan in His hand. In view of His coming the people must repent and submit to baptism for the washing away of sins, so as to escape the coming wrath and participate in the salvation of the kingdom and the baptism with the Holy Spirit which will be poured out when it comes (Mt. iii. 1–12).

II. IN THE TEACHING OF JESUS

a. Present aspect

Jesus' proclamation of the kingdom follows word for word on John's, yet it bears a much more comprehensive character. After John the Baptist had watched Jesus' appearance for a considerable time, he began to be in doubt whether Jesus was, after all, the coming One whom he had announced (Mt. xi. 2 f.). Jesus' proclamation of the kingdom differs in two respects from that of the Baptist. In the first place, while it retains without qualification the announcement of judgment and the call to repentance, it is the saving significance of the kingdom that stands in the foreground. In the second place—and here is the pith and core of the matter—He announced the kingdom not just as a reality which was at hand, something which would appear in the immediate future, but as a reality which was already present, manifested in His own person and ministry. Although the places where Jesus speaks explicitly of the kingdom as being present are not numerous (see especially Mt. xii. 28 and parallels), His whole preaching and ministry are marked by this dominant reality. In Him the great future has already become 'present time'.

This present aspect of the kingdom manifests itself in all sorts of ways in the person and deeds of Christ. It appears palpably and visibly in the casting out of demons (*cf.* Lk. xi. 20) and generally in Jesus' miraculous power. In the healing of those who are demon-possessed it becomes evident that Jesus has invaded the house of 'the strong man', has bound him fast and so is in a position to plunder his goods (Mt. xii. 29). The kingdom of heaven breaks into the domain of the evil one. The power of Satan is broken. Jesus sees him fall like lightning from heaven. He possesses and bestows power to trample on the dominion of the enemy. Nothing can be impossible for those who go forth into the world, invested with Jesus' power, as witnesses of the kingdom (Lk. x. 18 f.). The whole of Jesus' miraculous activity is the proof of the coming of the kingdom. What many prophets and righteous men desired in vain to see—the breaking in of the great epoch of salvation—the disciples can now see and hear (Mt. xiii. 16; Lk. x. 23). When John the Baptist sent his disciples to ask, 'Art thou he that should come, or look we for another?' they were shown the wonderful works done by Jesus, in which, according to the promise of prophecy, the kingdom was already being manifested; the blind were enabled to see, the lame to walk, the deaf to hear; lepers were being cleansed and dead people raised to life, and the gospel was being proclaimed to the poor (Mt. xi. 2 ff.; Lk. vii. 18 ff.). Also in the last of these—the proclamation of the gospel—the breaking through of the kingdom is seen. Since salvation is announced and offered as a gift already available to the poor in spirit, the hungry, and the mourners, the kingdom is theirs. So too the forgiveness of sins is proclaimed, not merely as a future reality to be accomplished in heaven, nor merely as a present possibility, but as a dispensation offered today, on earth, through Jesus Himself; 'Son, daughter, your sins are forgiven; for the Son of man has power on earth to forgive sins' (see Mk. ii. 1–12, *et passim*).

As appears clearly from this last-quoted word of power, all this is founded on the fact that Jesus is the Christ, the Son of God. The kingdom has come in Him and with Him; He is the *autobasileia*. Jesus' self-revelation as the Messiah, the Son of man and Servant of the Lord, constitutes both the mystery and the unfolding of the whole gospel. It is impossible to explain these sayings of

Jesus about Himself in a future sense, as some have wished to do, as though He referred to Himself only as the future Messiah (*q.v.*), the Son of man who was to be expected on a coming day on the clouds of heaven. For however much this future revelation of the kingdom remains an essential element in the content of the gospel, we cannot mistake the fact that in the Gospels Jesus' Messiahship is present here and now. Not only is He proclaimed as such at His baptism and on the Mount of Transfiguration—as the beloved and elect One of God (plain messianic designations)—but He is also endowed with the Holy Spirit (Mt. iii. 16) and invested with full divine authority (Mt. xxi. 27); the Gospel is full of His declarations of absolute authority, He is presented as the One sent by the Father, the One who has come to fulfil what the prophets foretold. In His coming and teaching the Scripture is fulfilled in the ears of those who listen to Him (Lk. iv. 21). He came not to destroy but to fulfil (Mt. v. 17 ff.), to announce the kingdom (Mk. i. 38), to seek and to save the lost (Lk. xix. 10), to serve others, and to give His life a ransom for many (Mk. x. 45). The secret of belonging to the kingdom lies in belonging to Him (Mt. vii. 23, xxv. 41). In brief, the person of Jesus as the Messiah is the centre of all that is announced in the gospel concerning the kingdom. The kingdom is concentrated in Him in its present and future aspects alike.

b. Future aspect

There is a future aspect as well. For although it is clearly stated that the kingdom is manifested here and now in the gospel, so also is it shown that as yet it is manifested in this world only in a provisional manner. That is why the proclamation of its present activity in the words, 'The blind receive their sight; the dead are raised; the poor have the gospel preached to them', is followed by the warning: 'Blessed is he, whosoever shall not be offended in me' (Mt. xi. 6; Lk. vii. 23). The 'offence' lies in the hidden character of the kingdom in this epoch. The miracles are still tokens of another order of reality than the present one; it is not yet the time when the demons will be delivered to eternal darkness (Mt. viii. 29). The gospel of the kingdom is still revealed only as a seed which is being sown. In the parables of the sower, the seed growing secretly, the tares among the wheat, the mustard seed, the leaven, it is about this hidden aspect of the kingdom that Jesus instructs His disciples. The Son of man Himself, invested with all power by God, the One who is to come on the clouds of heaven, is the Sower who sows the Word of God. He is depicted as a man dependent upon others: the birds, the thorns, human beings, can partially frustrate His work. He has to wait and see what will come of His seed. Indeed, the hiddenness of the kingdom is deeper still: the King Himself comes in the form of a slave. The birds of the air have nests, but the Son of man (Dn. vii. 13) has no place to lay His head. In order to receive everything, He must first of all give up everything. He must give His life as a ransom; as the suffering Servant of the Lord of Is. liii, He must be numbered with the transgressors. The kingdom has come; the kingdom will come. But it comes by the way of the cross, and before the Son of man exercises His authority over all the kingdoms of the earth (Mt. iv. 8, xxviii. 18) He must tread the path of obedience to His Father in order thus to fulfil all righteousness (Mt. iii. 15). The manifestation of the kingdom has therefore a history in this world. It must be proclaimed to every creature. Like the wonderful seed, it must sprout and grow, no man knows how (Mk. iv. 27). It has an inward power by which it makes its way through all sorts of obstacles and advances over all; for the field in which the seed is sown is the world (Mt. xiii. 38). The gospel of the kingdom goes forth to all nations (Mt. xxviii. 19), for the King of the kingdom is also Lord of the Spirit. His resurrection brings in a new aeon; the preaching of the kingdom *and* the King reaches out to the ends of the earth. The decision has already come to pass; but the fulfilment still recedes into the future. What at first appears to be one and the same coming of the kingdom, what is announced as one indivisible reality, at hand and at close quarters, extends itself to cover new periods of time and far distances. For the frontiers of this kingdom are not coterminous with Israel's boundaries or history: the kingdom embraces all nations and fills all ages until the end of the world comes.

III. KINGDOM AND CHURCH

The kingdom is thus related to the history of the Church and of the world alike. A connection exists between kingdom and Church, but they are not identical, even in the present age. The kingdom is the whole of God's redeeming activity in Christ in this world; the Church is the assembly of those who belong to Jesus Christ. Perhaps one could speak in terms of two concentric circles, of which the Church is the smaller and the kingdom the larger, while Christ is the centre of both. This relation of the Church to the kingdom can be formulated in all kinds of ways. The Church is the assembly of those who have accepted the gospel of the kingdom in faith, who participate in the salvation of the kingdom, which includes the forgiveness of sins, adoption by God, the indwelling of the Holy Spirit, the possession of eternal life. They are also those in whose life the kingdom takes visible form, the light of the world, the salt of the earth; those who have taken on themselves the yoke of the kingdom, who live by their King's commandments and learn from Him (Mt. xi. 28–30). The Church, as the organ of the kingdom, is called to confess Jesus as the Christ, to the missionary task of preaching the gospel in the world; she is also the community of those who wait for the coming of the kingdom in glory, the servants who have received their Lord's talents in prospect of His return. The Church receives her whole constitution from the kingdom, on all sides she is beset and directed by the revelation, the progress, the future coming of the kingdom of God, without at any time being the kingdom herself or ever being identified with it.

Therefore the kingdom is not confined within the frontiers of the Church. Christ's Kingship is supreme above all. Where it prevails and is acknowledged, not only is the individual human being set free, but the whole pattern of life is changed: the curse of the demons and fear of hostile powers disappears. The change which Christianity brings about among peoples dominated by nature-religions is a proof of the comprehensive, all-embracing significance of the kingdom. It works not only outwardly like a mustard seed but inwardly like leaven. It makes its way into the world with its redeeming power. The last book of the Bible, which portrays Christ's Kingship in the history of the world and its advancing momentum right to the end, especially illuminates the antithesis between the triumphant Christ-King (*cf.*, *e.g.*, Rev. v. 1 ff.) and the power of Satan and antichrist, which still survives on earth and contends against Christ and His Church. However much the kingdom invades world-history with its blessing and deliverance, however much it presents itself as a saving power against the tyranny of gods and forces inimical to mankind, it is only through a final and universal crisis that the kingdom, as a visible and all-conquering reign of peace and salvation, will bring to fruition the new heaven and new earth.

IV. IN THE REST OF THE NEW TESTAMENT

The expression 'kingdom of heaven' or 'kingdom of God' does not appear so frequently in the New Testament outside the Synoptic Gospels. This is, however, simply a matter of terminology. As the indication of the great revolution in the history of salvation which has already been inaugurated by Christ's coming, and as the expected consummation of all the acts of God, it is the central theme of the whole New Testament revelation of God.

V. IN THEOLOGICAL THOUGHT

As regards the conception of the kingdom of heaven in theology, this has been powerfully subjected to all kinds of influences and viewpoints during the various periods and trends of theological thought. In Roman Catholic theology a distinctive feature is the identification of the kingdom of God and the Church in the earthly dispensation, an identification which is principally due to Augustine's influence. Through the ecclesiastical hierarchy Christ is actualized as King of the kingdom of God. The area of the kingdom is coterminous with the frontiers of the Church's power and authority. The kingdom of heaven is extended by the mission and advance of the Church in the world.

In their resistance to the Roman Catholic hierarchy, the Reformers laid chief emphasis on the spiritual and invisible significance of the kingdom and readily (and wrongly) invoked Lk. xvii. 20 f. in support of this. The kingdom of heaven, that is to say, is a spiritual sovereignty which Christ exercises through the preaching of His word and the operation of the Holy Spirit. While the Reformation in its earliest days did not lose sight of the kingdom's great dimensions of saving history, the kingdom of God, under the influence of the Enlightenment and pietism, came to be increasingly conceived in an individualistic sense; it is the sovereignty of grace and peace in the hearts of men. In later liberal theology this conception developed in a moralistic direction (especially under the influence of Kant): the kingdom of God is the kingdom of peace, love, and righteousness. At first, even in pietism and sectarian circles, the expectation of the coming kingdom of God was maintained, without, however, making allowance for a positive significance of the kingdom for life in this world. Over against this more or less dualistic understanding of the kingdom we must distinguish the social conception of the kingdom which lays all the stress on its visible and communal significance. This conception is distinguished in some writers by a social radicalism (the 'Sermon on the Mount' Christianity of Tolstoy and others, or the 'religious-social' interpretation of, *e.g.*, Kutter and Ragaz in Switzerland), in others by the evolutionary belief in progress (the 'social gospel' in America). The coming of the kingdom consists in the forward march of social righteousness and communal development.

In contrast to these spiritualizing, moralistic, and evolutionary interpretations of the kingdom, New Testament scholarship is rightly laying stress again on the original significance of the kingdom in Jesus' preaching—a significance bound up with the history of salvation and eschatology. While the founders of this newer eschatological direction gave an extreme interpretation to the idea of the kingdom of heaven, so that there was no room left for the kingdom's penetration of the present world-order (Johannes Weiss, Albert Schweitzer, the so-called 'thoroughgoing' eschatology), more attention has been paid latterly to the unmistakable present significance of the kingdom, while this significance has been brought within the perspective of the history of salvation, the perspective of the progress of God's dynamic activity in history, which has the final consummation as its goal.

BIBLIOGRAPHY. The literature on the kingdom of God is immense. For the use of the term in the Gospels, see G. Dalman, *The Words of Jesus*, 1902; *SB*, pp. 172–184; for the interpretation of the kingdom in the history of earlier theology see A. Robertson, *Regnum Dei* (Bampton Lectures), 1901; for the older liberal approach, see E. von Dobschütz, 'The Eschatology of the Gospels', *The Expositor*, Series 7, IX, 1910; for the 'social' interpretation, see N. J. van Merwe, *Die sosiale prediking van Jezus Christus*, 1921; L. Ragaz, *Die Botschaft vom Reiche Gottes*, 1941; for the newer eschatological interpretation (since J. Weiss, *Die Predigt Jesu vom Reiche Gottes*, 1892; Albert Schweitzer, *The Quest of the Historical Jesus*, 1910), see H. M. Matter, *Nieuwere opvattingen omtrent het koninkrijk Gods in Jezus' prediking naar de synoptici*, 1942. More general works: *TWNT*, *s.v. basileia*; F. Holmström, *Das eschatologische Denken der Gegenwart*, 1936; H. D. Wendland, *Die Eschatologie des Reiches Gottes bei Jesus*, 1931; G. Gloege, *Reich Gottes und Kirche im Neuen Testament*, 1929; J. Jeremias, *Jesus der Weltvollender im Neuen Testament*, 1929; H. J. Westerink, *Het Koninkrijk Gods bij Paulus*, 1937; W. G. Kümmel, *Die Eschatologie der Evangelien*, 1936; *id.*, *Promise and Fulfilment*, 1957; R. Otto, *The Kingdom of God and the Son of Man*, 1943; O. Cullmann, *Christ and Time*, 1951; W. A. Visser 't Hooft, *The Kingship of Christ*, 1947; C. H. Dodd, *The Parables of the Kingdom*, 1935; H. Ridderbos, *De Komst van het koninkrijk*, 1950; S. H. Hooke, *The Kingdom of God in the Experience of Jesus*, 1949; G. Vos, *The Teaching of Jesus concerning the Kingdom and the Church*, 1951; G. E. Ladd, *Crucial Questions about the Kingdom of God*, 1952; J. Bright, *The Kingdom of God in Bible and Church*, 1955. H.R.

KINGS, BOOKS OF. The Hebrew title is simply *mᵉlāḵîm*, 'Kings'. Originally there was only one book. The division into two books was first introduced in the LXX, and this for a very practical reason. The Greek translation in which the vowels were written required almost twice as much space as the Hebrew, in which no vowels were used until after AD 600. One large scroll could contain the whole book in Hebrew, but two were required for the Greek translation. The division was introduced into the Hebrew text for the first time in the first edition of Daniel Bomberg's printed Hebrew Bible (Venice, 1516–17). In both the Greek and Latin Bibles the books of Samuel and Kings are treated as one continuous history in four volumes. Some Greek texts vary the point at which Samuel divides from Kings. There is evidence for a division at 1 Ki. ii. 11—the actual termination of David's reign—and at 1 Ki. ii. 46a. Although there is no clear evidence to determine the precise relationship of Kings to Samuel, it is patently obvious that the division between 1 and 2 Kings is quite arbitrary. The artificial nature of the division is borne out by the unnatural interruption of the narrative at the point of division. 1 Kings ends with the commencement of the account of the reign of Ahaziah, king of Israel; the account is concluded in the first chapter of 2 Kings. Still more significant, the major part of Elijah's ministry and his anointing of Elisha to be his successor are contained in 1 Kings, but the magnificent finale of his prophetic career and the whole of Elisha's ministry are recorded in 2 Kings.

I. OUTLINE OF CONTENTS

The history recorded in Kings spans a period of over 400 years, commencing with the last days of David's reign and concluding with the release of Jehoiachin from prison in Babylon in the year 562 BC. There are three main sections:

a. The united kingdom (1 Ki. i. 1–xi. 43)

(i) Solomon's co-regency with David (i. 1–ii. 46).
(ii) The reign of Solomon (iii. 1–vii. 51).
(iii) The Temple dedication (viii. 1–ix. 9).
(iv) The end of Solomon's reign (ix. 10–xi. 43).

b. Israel and Judah (1 Ki. xii. 1–2 Ki. xvii. 41)

(i) The disruption of the kingdom (xii. 1–24).
(ii) Kings of Israel and Judah (xii. 25–xvi. 28).
(iii) Elijah and Ahab (xvi. 29–xxii. 40).
(iv) Further kings of Israel and Judah (xxii. 41–2 Ki. i. 18).
(v) Elisha succeeds Elijah (ii. 1–25).
(vi) Further kings of Israel and Judah (iii. 1–xvi. 20).
(vii) The end of the northern kingdom (xvii. 1–41).

c. The kingdom of Judah (2 Ki. xviii. 1–xxv. 30)

(i) Kings of Judah (xviii. 1–xxiii. 30).
(ii) The destruction of Jerusalem and the Exile (xxiii. 31–xxv. 30).

II. AUTHORSHIP, PURPOSE, AND METHOD

a. Authorship

In the Mishnah (*Baba Bathra* 15a) Jeremiah is credited with the authorship of Kings. The suggestion is most attractive but improbable. The unknown author was doubtless a contemporary of Jeremiah, who lived under the same influences and like him was a prophet. The place of Kings in the second division of the Hebrew Canon—the Prophets (*nᵉḇî'îm*)—along with Joshua, Judges, and Samuel implies that Israel's historians were, for the most part, men who occupied the prophetic office. This anonymous historian was the direct author, however, of only the later period of the history, which belonged to his own times. For the earlier history he was dependent upon written records, three of which he cites by name (see IV below).

b. The author's aim

The author makes it clear that his purpose is not to provide an exhaustive history. He refers his readers repeatedly to his sources for details that he has not seen fit to include (1 Ki. xi. 41, *etc.*). His aim is didactic. Yet his concern is not merely to inculcate the great lessons to be learned from the past, but supremely to present God's view of the history of His people. For Israel was ideally a theocracy. Everything is subordinated to this principal aim. That which does not throw light on the developing purpose of God and that which does not serve to set forth the principles upon which God deals with His people is passed over in silence or accorded the barest notice. From the standpoint of the secular historian, Omri was one of the most important kings of the northern kingdom, yet his reign is dismissed in six verses (1 Ki. xvi. 23–28). Were it not for the fact that he established a new capital at Samaria, he might have been virtually ignored. On the other hand, it is noteworthy that the relatively brief period during which Elijah and Elisha exercised their ministries is given in great detail. Almost a third of the entire book is taken up with this spiritually crucial epoch which saw an outburst of miraculous power such as had not occurred since the time of the Exodus and the conquest. The record of the history is thus inevitably and intentionally uneven.

c. The author's method of writing

Modern historians, having consulted their sources, write their histories as free and original compositions. By contrast, the author of Kings constructed his history by a careful selection of extracts from his written sources. It is a mistake, however, to regard the Hebrew historian as a mere compiler. He himself doubtless wrote the history of his own times. Although he quotes freely from his sources, the final work is not just a collection of extracts, but a carefully planned unity that presents the great religious aim of the prophetic author. He shows particular skill in his treatment of the period of the divided monarchy. He keeps the history of the two kingdoms running parallel. Commencing with an account of Jeroboam's reign over Israel, he traces events down to his death before turning to contemporary events in the kingdom of Judah. The focus of the narrative is then kept on Judah until the death of Asa, who ascended the throne before Jeroboam's reign came to an end. This alternation between Israel and Judah follows this pattern throughout.

Of unusual interest is the way in which the author has dealt with the extensive group of stories about Elisha (2 Ki. iii. 1–viii. 15). These are fitted into the framework of the history and form the basic content of the reign of Jehoram of Israel. The interest shifts from the nation as such. The name of the king of Israel is apparently deliberately suppressed. This fact has been taken to imply that the author recognizes that the nation itself has already been rejected because of her failure to turn back to God after the great demonstration on Mt. Carmel (1 Ki. xviii). Elisha is concerned with building up the righteous remnant that God promised Elijah He would leave in Israel (1 Ki. xix. 18). These Elisha stories have not been kept in precise chronological order. For the author, spiritual considerations override those of chronology.

III. RELIGIOUS STANDPOINT OF THE AUTHOR

The most prominent feature of Kings is the way in which the author assesses the significance of the reigns of the individual kings according to their religious policies, not according to their political achievements. The kings of the northern kingdom alike fall under condemnation (with the possible exception of Hoshea—2 Ki. xvii. 2) because each follows the lead of Jeroboam ben Nebat, who set up bull-images at Bethel and Dan and appointed these sanctuaries the official shrines of his kingdom, thus repudiating the Temple at Jerusalem (1 Ki. xii. 25–33). For this reason he is invariably referred to as having 'made Israel to sin'. When the author has concluded the account of the northern kingdom he breaks off the historical record to reflect upon the moral causes of its downfall (2 Ki. xvii. 7–23). However many factors may have influenced the fortunes of Israel, fundamentally it was the people's attitude to Yahweh, their neglect of His laws, and their adherence to heathen forms of worship which determined the outcome of events. Israel's final overthrow and captivity were nothing less than the judgment of God.

The kings of Judah are broadly classified into two groups according to their religious policy. Some receive unqualified condemnation because they 'walked in the way of the kings of Israel' and 'did evil in the sight of Yahweh' (Jehoram and Ahaziah, 2 Ki. viii. 16–27; Ahaz, 2 Ki. xvi. 1–20; Manasseh and Amon, 2 Ki. xxi. 1–26). The rest are commended for doing what 'was right in the eyes of Yahweh'. For the majority, however, this is a qualified commendation which is frequently followed by expressions indicating that they have fallen short of the Davidic ideal (1 Ki. xi. 4, 6, xv. 3; 2 Ki. xiv. 3) and that they failed to put an end to the worship at the high places (1 Ki. xxii. 43; 2 Ki. xv. 3, 4). Two kings only receive unqualified commendation from the author, Hezekiah and Josiah. These alone abolished the worship at the high places and restricted worship to the Temple at Jerusalem (2 Ki. xviii. 3, 4, xxii. 2, xxiii. 5–8).

It is clear that, for the author of Kings, the building of Solomon's Temple was of immense religious significance. Before the Temple was built, worship at the high places was excusable (1 Ki. iii. 2). But once the Temple was standing, the author finds the continued existence of high places in Judah intolerable. Solomon's Temple was henceforth the one legitimate sanctuary within the kingdom. In this he was doubtless guided by the law of the central sanctuary enunciated in Deuteronomy (Dt. xii. 5–14). In this and in other respects Kings gives evidence of the unmistakable influence of the teaching of Deuteronomy on the author. With Moses in Dt. xxviii he recognizes that obedience to Yahweh is the way to blessing and prosperity for Israel, while disobedience yields the bitter fruit of calamity and disaster. No exception can be taken, therefore, to the application of the epithet 'deuteronomic' to the religious outlook of the author of Kings. But this does not involve an artificial approach to the history, unless one assumes with many modern critics that the book of Deuteronomy was first composed by a reforming group within the nation in the 7th century (see DEUTERONOMY, BOOK OF).

IV. ORIGINAL SOURCES

For the detailed account of the reign of Solomon, the author acknowledges his indebtedness to 'the book of the acts of Solomon' (*diḇerê šelōmô*) (1 Ki. xi. 41). The scope and nature of this work cannot be determined. It may be assumed that it was not merely the official annalistic records of Solomon's reign, but a history based upon them. There is no need to postulate, with some modern critics, that there was an independent temple source which provided the basis of the account of the building of the Temple and the service of dedication (1 Ki. vi–viii), as well as furnishing material for some of the narratives in 2 Kings in which the Temple figures prominently.

Two other works were available for the subsequent history of the divided kingdoms. These were 'the book of the chronicles (*diḇerê hayyāmîm*) of the kings of Israel' (1 Ki. xiv. 19, *etc.*) and 'the book of the chronicles of the kings of Judah' (1 Ki. xiv. 29, *etc.*). The expression 'the book of the chronicles' (lit. 'the book of the affairs of the days') is a technical term for official records of important political events which were kept in the state archives. Such records do not themselves constitute histories as such, but are the raw materials out of which history is fashioned. It is generally agreed that the two works so constantly referred to by the author of Kings were not the official annals, but popular histories based upon them. These books may have contained a number of extended narratives, such as those describing the revolution under Jehu (2 Ki. ix–x) and the overthrow of Queen Athaliah of Judah (2 Ki. xi).

There may well have been other sources in addition to these three main works. The cycles of stories about Elijah and Elisha may have been preserved independently. Such suggestions, however, belong entirely to the realm of conjecture.

V. DATE

The earliest possible date for Kings in its present form is clearly subsequent to the last historical event recorded, the release of Jehoiachin from prison in Babylon (2 Ki. xxv. 27–30). This is carefully dated as occurring in the thirty-seventh year of his captivity, *i.e.* 562 BC, about twenty-five years after the fall of Jerusalem. It is equally plain that the account of his release must have been written considerably after 562, because it is stated that the favours conferred upon him were enjoyed by him to the end of his life. The phrase 'all the days of his life' is used twice over in this passage. The book of Kings, therefore, was not completed until after Jehoiachin's death. Although we have no information as to the date of his death, it is generally assumed that Kings was completed by *c.* 550 BC.

It could be argued, along with many critics, that the account of Jehoiachin's release from prison was appended as a kind of postscript, and that Kings was actually completed considerably earlier. In fact, the majority of critical scholars hold that there were two editions of the book. In accordance with the common theory regarding the date of Deuteronomy, it is natural to assume that the historian so imbued with 'deuteronomic' notions would wish to write a history of his people illustrating how these notions receive corroboration from past history. At the time when Josiah's reform seemed to have achieved its aim and temporal prosperity had returned to the state, the history of Kings would read most convincingly. Subsequent events required the introduction of some modifications. Even granting the basic assumptions, this view is not without great difficulties.

All things considered, it is most likely that Kings, as we now have it, was written during the Exile, when the author would have had leisure for such an undertaking and sufficient time for deep reflection on the causes of his people's misfortunes. The account of Jehoiachin's release is not to be considered a mere appendix, but an intentional conclusion of the history on a note of hope. Here was evidence that God had not abandoned His exiled people and a pledge of their ultimate release also. The Davidic line had not been finally rejected.

VI. THE CHRONOLOGY

This is built up on the basis of the regnal years of the kings. For the period of the divided monarchy the author maintains a careful system of cross-reference between the kings of Judah and Israel. Despite this, the chronology poses a number of problems. The sum of the regnal years of the kings of Israel for a given period fails to yield the same total as the sum of the regnal years of the Judaean kings for the same period. Thus the period from the accession of Rehoboam to the death of Ahaziah is ninety-five years, but the corresponding period in Israel (from the accession of Jeroboam to the death of Joram) spans ninety-eight years. A still greater discrepancy appears in the period that follows. The total of the regnal years from Athaliah to the sixth year of Hezekiah's reign is 165 years, whereas for the same period in Israel (from Jehu to the fall of Samaria) the total yields only 143 years and seven months.

There is no simple solution to these problems. It is, however, clear that discrepancies arise partly through counting parts of years as complete years. The author invariably gives the length of a reign in full years. There is also the matter of co-regencies, when a king associated his son with him on the throne. It appears that this was a more frequent occurrence than the two examples that are explicitly mentioned (David and Solomon, 1 Ki. i. 34, 35, and Azariah and Jotham, 2 Ki. xv. 5). Further difficulties arise when attempts are made to relate the chronology of Kings to the dating of contemporary events in Assyrian inscriptions (see CHRONOLOGY OF THE OLD TESTAMENT).

BIBLIOGRAPHY. C. F. Keil, *Die Bücher der*

Könige, 1865; C. F. Burney, *Notes on the Hebrew Text of the Books of Kings*, 1903; J. Skinner, *Kings, The New Century Bible*; J. A. Montgomery, *The Books of Kings, ICC*, 1951; S. R. Driver, *Introduction to the Literature of the Old Testament*, 1910; R. H. Pfeiffer, *Introduction to the Old Testament*, 1948 (revised edition); E. J. Young, *An Introduction to the Old Testament*, 1949; E. R. Thiele, *The Mysterious Numbers of the Hebrew Kings*, 1951. J.C.J.W.

KING'S GARDEN. An open space in Jerusalem near 'the gate between the two walls' (2 Ki. xxv. 4; Je. xxxix. 4, lii. 7) and close to the Pool of Siloam (*q.v.*) (Ne. iii. 15). The 'two walls' (*cf.* Is. xxii. 11) were probably those below the 'Fountain Gate' (see fig. 120), south-east of Ophel, running along the west side of the eastern hill of Jerusalem, and along the east side of the western hill (S. R. Driver, *Jeremiah*, 1918, p. 239; N. Grollenberg, *Atlas*, Maps 24B & C). J.D.D.

KING'S HIGHWAY. The name given to the direct road running from the Gulf of Aqabah to Syria, east of the Dead Sea and Jordan valley. The route was in use between the 23rd and 20th centuries BC, being marked along its length by Early Bronze Age settlements. It was, therefore, likely that Chedorlaomer and his allies approached Sodom and Gomorrah by this way and were pursued up it by Abraham (Gn. xiv). Its further use in the 13th–6th centuries BC is also marked by datable ruins showing that the road was occupied at the time that the Edomites and the Ammonites prevented Moses and the Israelites from using it (Nu. xx. 17, xxi. 22). In Solomon's reign the highway played an important part as a trade-link between Ezion-geber, Judah, and Syria. Roman milestones show that it was incorporated into Trajan's road built in the 2nd century AD and was used by the Nabataeans. The modern motor-way follows part of the old track, which is still called Tarīq es-Sulṭan.

BIBLIOGRAPHY. N. Glueck, *The Other Side of the Jordan*, 1945. D.J.W.

KIR. In the Heb. text the name of the place of exile of the Syrians (2 Ki. xvi. 9; Am. i. 5), and a country from which Yahweh brought them (Am. ix. 7). This is perhaps not their original home, but a land occupied at some earlier stage in their history, parallel to Israel in Egypt and the Philistines in Caphtor (see SYRIA, PHILISTINES, CAPHTOR). In Is. xxii. 6 Kir is parallel to Elam. No ancient place of this name is known; however, as it simply means 'city', it need not be specific. The LXX does not use a proper name in any of these passages, but translates 'from a pit' (Am. ix. 7, Gk. *ek bothrou*), 'called as an ally' (Am. i. 5, Gk. *epiklētos*) and 'congregation' (Is. xxii. 6, Gk. *synagōgē*), feasible translations of an unpointed Heb. text. The Vulgate follows the mistaken identification with Cyrene made by Symmachus. Kir has been altered to read Koa' (by Cheyne), and said to be Gutium in the Kurdish hills (*cf.* Ezk. xxiii. 23; Is. xxii. 5, 6). The problem is not yet solved. A.R.M.

KIR OF MOAB, KIR-HARESETH. A fortified city of S Moab, attacked but not taken by the kings of Israel, Judah, and Edom (2 Ki. iii). During the siege, Mesha, king of Moab, offered up his eldest son 'for a burnt offering upon the wall'.

The Hebrew name (*qîr ḥ^a^reśet*) means 'the wall of potsherds'. The LXX rendering of Is. xvi. 11 presupposes the Hebrew *qîr ḥ^a^ḏešet*, 'the new city'. Normally the town is called Kir of Moab (Is. xv. 1). Some writers see in Je. xlviii. 36, 37 a play on words in which Kir Heres is parallel to 'bald' (Heb. *qorḥâ*). It is suggested that the original Moabite name was QRḤH, probably the town referred to in the Moabite Stone (lines 22 ff.), where Mesha established a sanctuary for Chemosh and carried out a building project. (See MOABITE STONE.) This would place it near Dibon.

Most writers, however, identify it with Kerak, following the Targum rendering, Kerak of Moab. If that is so, the place was built on a strategic rocky hill 3,370 feet above sea-level, surrounded by steep valleys, some 11 miles east of the Dead Sea and 15 miles south of the Arnon River. Today a medieval castle crowns the hill.

BIBLIOGRAPHY. F. M. Abel, *Géographie de la Palestine*, II, 1933, pp. 418, 419; Nelson Glueck, *AASOR*, XIV, 1934, p. 65. J.A.T.

KIRIATHAIM. The dual form of *qiryâ*, 'city, town', and meaning therefore 'double city', a name applied to two cities in the Bible.

1. A place in the territory allotted to Reuben (Jos. xiii. 19) which had already been conquered and rebuilt by the Reubenites (Nu. xxxii. 37). It is possible that Shaveh Kiriathaim, which is mentioned in the account of the invasion of Chedorlaomer in the time of Abraham (Gn. xiv. 5), refers to this locality, as the 'plain' of Kiriathaim (RVmg), though *šāwēh* is a rare word of uncertain meaning. The city was later in the hands of the Moabites (Je. xlviii. 1, 23; Ezk. xxv. 9), and is mentioned in the 9th-century inscription of King Mesha of Moab (*qrytn*, l. 10) as having been rebuilt by him, so it cannot have remained under Israelite control for more than about three centuries. The site is perhaps to be identified with modern El Quraiyāt about 6 miles north-west of Dibon in Jordan.

2. A levitical city in Naphtali (1 Ch. vi. 76), possibly to be identified with Kartan (*qartān*) of Jos. xxi. 32. The site is unknown, though various suggestions have been made (see *GTT*, §§ 298, 337, 357). T.C.M.

KIRIATH-ARBA (AV Kirjath-arba, Heb. *qiryaṯ 'arba'*, 'city of four', *i.e.* 'tetrapolis'), an earlier name of Hebron (*q.v.*). According to Jos. xiv. 15, it was 'the metropolis of the Anakim' (so LXX; AV makes the numeral *'arba'*, 'four', into a personal name). The name Kiriath-arba occurs once in the story of Abraham (Gn. xxiii. 2) and a few times in the narrative of the conquest (Jos. xiv. 15, xv. 54, xx. 7; Jdg. i. 10); thereafter it evidently fell into disuse. Some attempt may have been made to revive it in the post-exilic age (Ne. xi. 25), but with the Idumaean occupation of the place soon afterwards the old name was completely discontinued. F.F.B.

KIRIATH-JEARIM (*qiryaṯ-y^e'ārîm*, 'city of forests'). A chief city of the Gibeonites (Jos. ix. 17), on the Judah–Benjamin border (Jos. xviii. 14, 15; *cf.* Jdg. xviii. 12), assigned first to Judah (Jos. xv. 60), then, assuming an identification with 'Kiriath', to Benjamin (Jos. xviii. 28). It is called also Kiriath-baal (Jos. xv. 60, suggesting that it was an old Canaanite high place), Baalah (Jos. xv. 9, 10), Baale of Judah (2 Sa. vi. 2), and Kiriath-arim (Ezr. ii. 25).

Here the ark was brought from Beth-shemesh and entrusted to the keeping of Eleazar (1 Sa. vii. 1), whence after twenty years David took it to Jerusalem (2 Sa. vi. 2; 1 Ch. xiii. 5; 2 Ch. i. 4). The home of Uriah the prophet was in Kiriath-jearim (Je. xxvi. 20).

Its precise location has not been determined, but the consensus of opinion favours Kuriet el-'Enab (commonly known as Abu Ghosh), a flourishing little village 9 miles west of Jerusalem on the Jaffa road. It is a well-wooded district (or has been in the past) and it meets other geographical requirements. J.D.D.

KIRIATH-SEPHER. An important Canaanite town in the Judaean Hills; see DEBIR (1).

KISH (*qîš*, 'bow', 'power'). The name of five men in the Old Testament. **1.** A Benjamite, the son of Abiel and father of King Saul (1 Sa. ix. 1, xiv. 51; *cf.* Acts xiii. 21). **2.** The son of Jehiel and Maacah (1 Ch. viii. 29, 30), perhaps the uncle of (1) above. **3.** A Levite, grandson of Merari (1 Ch. xxiii. 21). **4.** Another Levite and Merarite who assisted in the cleansing of the Temple in Hezekiah's time (2 Ch. xxix. 12, 15). **5.** A Benjamite, great-grandfather of Mordecai (Est. ii. 5).

KISHON. The river, modern Nahr el-Muqaṭṭa', which, rising in the hills of N Samaria, drains the plain of Esdraelon and debouches in the bay of Acre to the east of Mount Carmel. Though it winds about, in a general sense it flows in a north-westerly direction parallel with, and to the north-east of, the mountain range which runs from Samaria to Carmel and in the north-eastern passes of which lay Taanach, Megiddo, and Jokneam. The name Kishon is not often used, the river sometimes being indicated by reference to one of the towns overlooking it. Thus it is probably first mentioned in Jos. xix. 11, where the 'river that is before Jokneam' is given as part of the boundary of Zebulun, though in this case only a small section of the river in the vicinity of Jokneam is referred to.

The best-known reference to the river is that connected with the victory of the Israelites under Barak over the Syrians under Sisera (Jdg. iv, v; Ps. lxxxiii. 9). The forces of Sisera, fully armed with chariots, were deployed in the plain, and the Israelites made their attack from the mountains south-west of the river. The success of the Israelites was in large measure due to the river, which was running high, and must have made the surrounding plain too soft for Sisera's chariots, which became bogged down and useless.

The river is referred to in the Song of Deborah as 'the waters of Megiddo' (Jdg. v. 19), and the fact that Megiddo is not otherwise referred to in this account has been taken by Albright to indicate that it was at this time lying in ruins, while Taanach was flourishing. The excavations at Megiddo (*q.v.*) have shown a gap in occupation about 1125 BC between Levels VII and VI, and it may be that the Israelite victory occurred during that period of abandonment, or about 1125 BC.

The river is next mentioned as the scene of the slaughter by Elijah of the prophets of Baal, after the contest on Mt. Carmel (1 Ki. xviii. 40). It is referred to here as a brook (*naḥal*), suggesting that the long drought preceding these events had reduced the river to a low level. The rains which followed must have washed away the traces of the execution.

BIBLIOGRAPHY. G. A. Smith, *The Historical Geography of the Holy Land*[25], 1931, pp. 394–397; W. F. Albright, *The Archaeology of Palestine*, 1960, pp. 117–118. T.C.M.

KISS. A common salutation in the East, this word occurs in the Old Testament as a sign of affection between relatives (*e.g.* Gn. xxix. 11, xxxiii. 4), an expression of love (Ct. i. 2), or lust (Pr. vii. 13), and perhaps as a token of homage (1 Sa. x. 1). The last, kissing 'God's anointed', possibly may be, as Ps. ii. 10, a religious or cultic rite analogous to that found among idol cults: to kiss the hand (Jb. xxxi. 27), or an image (1 Ki. xix. 18; Ho. xiii. 2), is an act of religious worship. In the New Testament *phileō* is used as a sign of friendship or affection (*e.g.* Judas, Mt. xxvi. 48), as is the stronger form *kataphileō* (*e.g.* Lk. vii. 38, xv. 20; Acts xx. 37). The 'holy kiss' (Rom. xvi. 16; 1 Pet. v. 14), which later entered into the Church's liturgy, was an expression of Christian love and presumably was restricted to one's own sex (*cf. Apostolic Constitutions* ii. 57, 12).

E.E.E.

KITE. See BIRDS OF THE BIBLE.

KITTIM (Chittim). One of the sons of Javan (Gn. x. 4 = 1 Ch. i. 7; *kittîm*) whose descendants settled on the island of Cyprus where their name was given to the town of Kition, modern Larnaka, which is referred to in the Phoenician inscriptions as *kt* or *kty*. They engaged in sea trade (Nu. xxiv. 24), and the name seems to have come to apply to the whole island of Cyprus (Is. xxiii. 1, 12), and then in a more general way to the coastlands of the E Mediterranean (*'iyyê* *kittiyyîm:* Je. ii. 10; Ezk. xxvii. 6). In Daniel's fourth vision, which probably deals with the period from Cyrus to Antiochus Epiphanes, the latter's failure to conquer Egypt, due to the intervention of Rome, is probably referred to in xi. 30, where 'the ships of Chittim' must be Rome. The name occurs in the Dead Sea Scrolls, also probably with reference to Rome, being used, for instance, in the Commentary on Habakkuk as an interpretation of the 'Chaldeans' of that prophet.

BIBLIOGRAPHY. H. H. Rowley, 'The Kittim and the Dead Sea Scrolls', *PEQ*, LXXXVIII, 1956, pp. 92 ff.; F. F. Bruce, *The Teacher of Righteousness in the Qumran Texts*, 1957, pp. 10, 11. T.C.M.

KNEADING-TROUGH. A large shallow bowl in which dough was prepared, made of pottery or wood. Modern Arab nomads often use wooden bowls for this purpose. See Ex. xii. 34; *cf.* Dt. xxviii. 5, 17 (AV 'store'). For a model, *c.* 700 BC, see *ANEP*, no. 152. See also BREAD. A.R.M.

KNEE, KNEEL. The concrete imagery of the Old Testament expresses weakness or fear as 'feeble knees' (Jb. iv. 4; Is. xxxv. 3) or as 'the knees smite together' (Na. ii. 10; Dn. v. 6). The fifteen references in the New Testament are, with the exception of Heb. xii. 12, always used in connection with bowing. The action may indicate a sign of respect (Mk. i. 40; *cf.* 2 Ki. i. 13; Mk. xv. 19), or subjection (Rom. xi. 4, xiv. 11; *cf. 1 Clement* lvii. 1, 'bending the knees of your heart'), or of religious adoration or worship (Lk. v. 8). In the latter sense kneeling is sometimes the posture of prayer (Lk. xxii. 41; 1 Ki. viii. 54, *cf.* xviii. 42). The universal recognition of Christ's Lordship is thus signified: 'every knee should bow' (Phil. ii. 10; *cf.* Rom. xiv. 10 f.; 1 Cor. xv. 25). *Cf. TWNT.* E.E.E.

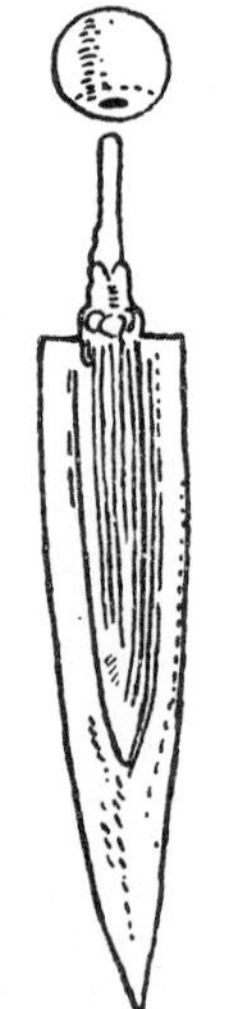

Fig. 126. Bronze dagger with a limestone pommel. Of the Middle Bronze Age (early second millennium BC) from Megiddo.

KNIFE. The primitive flint-knife survived well into the Bronze Age for ordinary use, alongside various metal forms. In the Old Testament, however, it is connected with ritual acts; *e.g.* the circumcision of Moses' son and of Israel (Ex. iv. 25; Jos. v. 2, 3). The Heb. *ḥereḇ* used in these passages, and for the self-mutilation of the frenzied priests of Baal (1 Ki. xviii. 28), usually denotes a short sword. In Pr. xxx. 14 this is parallel to Heb. *ma'ᵃḵelet*, a knife used in eating. It was such a short sword that Abraham took to kill Isaac and the Levite used to dismember his concubine (Gn. xxii. 6, 10; Jdg. xix. 29). Heb. *śakkîn* (Pr. xxiii. 2) is possibly to be connected with Assyr. *šikkatu*, 'plug', rather than with Aramaic *sakkînâ*, Arab. *sikkîn*, 'knife'.

AV and RV follow Vulg. *cultri* in rendering the unique Heb. *maḥᵃlāpîm*, 'knives' (Ezr. i. 9, *cf.* Syr. *ḥlāpâ*). RSV 'censers' is taken from 1 Esdras ii. 9 (Gk. *thyiskai*). The LXX 'of a different sort' (Gk. *parēllagmena*) translates the Hebrew but does not throw light on the meaning. A.R.M.

KNOP (= knob). In AV this translates two Heb. words. 1. *kap̄tôr*, which denotes either an ornamental round protrusion (LXX *sphairōtēr*) in the lampstand (Ex. xxv. xxxvii; see LAMP), or the capitals (so RV, AVmg) of pillars (Am. ix. 1; Zp. ii. 14). 2. *pᵉqā'îm*, which has reference to the knob-like ornaments carved on the Temple walls and cast on the 'sea' (1 Ki. vi. 18, vii. 24). The precise meaning is uncertain; but from the etymological connection with *paqqu'ōṯ* (*Citrullus colycynthis*) most scholars render it 'gourds'. The Targum has 'eggs'. D.W.G.

KNOWLEDGE. The Greek ideal of knowledge was a contemplation of reality in its static and abiding being; the Heb. was primarily concerned with life in its dynamic process, and therefore conceived knowledge as an entry into relationship with the experienced world which makes demands not only on understanding but also on will.

I. IN THE OLD TESTAMENT

Thus it is that the Old Testament speaks of knowing (*yāḏa'*) the loss of children (Is. xlvii. 8), grief (Is. liii. 3), sin (Je. iii. 13), God's hand and His might (Je. xvi. 21), His vengeance (Ezk. xxv. 14). The intimate sexual relationship is spoken of as knowing a man or a woman (*e.g.* Gn. iv. 1; Jdg. xi. 39). Above all, to know God is not simply to be aware of His existence; for the most part this is taken for granted in Heb. writings. To know Him is to recognize Him for what He is, the sovereign Lord who makes a demand on man's obedience and especially upon the obedience of His people Israel, with whom He has made a covenant. He is the God whose holiness and loving-kindness are 'known' in the experience of nation and individual. The criterion of this knowledge is obedience, and its opposite is not simply ignorance but rebellious, wilful turning away from God (*cf.* 1 Sa. ii. 12, iii. 7; 2 Ch. xxxiii. 13; Is. i. 3; Je. viii. 7, xxiv. 7, xxxi. 34). Furthermore, the acknowledgment of the Lord's claims involves a rejection of the heathen gods, knowing that they are not gods (*cf.* Is. xli. 23).

On God's side of the relationship between Himself and man there is also knowledge. Here especially there can be no question of theoretical observation; for man and all things are God's creation. It is from this fact that God's omniscience springs: He knows the world and man within it because it is at His command that they come to be (Jb. xxviii. 20 ff.; Ps. cxxxix). In particular, God knows those whom He has chosen to be His agents: His knowledge is spoken of in terms of election (Je. i. 5; Ho. xiii. 5; Am. iii. 2).

II. IN THE NEW TESTAMENT

To speak of knowledge in these ways is natural in addressing a people who all formally believe that God exists but fail to acknowledge His claims. In Hellenistic Judaism and in the New Testament use of *ginōskein*, *eidenai*, and their derivatives we find Heb. thought modified by the fact that the Gentiles were ignorant even of God's existence (see IGNORANCE). In general, however, the Heb. conception is retained. All men ought to respond to the revelation in Christ which has made possible a full knowledge of God, no mere intellectual apprehension but an obedience to His revealed purpose, an acceptance of His revealed love, and a fellowship with Himself (*cf.* Jn. xvii. 3; Acts ii. 36; 1 Cor. ii. 8; Phil. iii. 10). This knowledge of God is possible only because God in His love has called men to it (Gal. iv. 9; 1 Cor. xiii. 12; 2 Tim. ii. 19). The whole process of enlightenment and acceptance may be called coming to the knowledge of the truth (1 Tim. ii. 4; 2 Tim. ii. 25, iii. 7; Tit. i. 1; *cf.* Jn. viii. 32).

Both Paul and John write at times in conscious contrast with and opposition to the systems of alleged esoteric knowledge purveyed by the mystery cults and syncretistic 'philosophy' of their day (*cf.* 1 Tim. vi. 20; Col. ii. 8). To these knowledge was the result of an initiation or illumination which put the initiate in possession of spiritual discernment beyond mere reason or faith. Against them Paul (particularly in 1 Corinthians and Colossians) and all the Johannine writings stress that knowledge of God springs from committal to the historic Christ; it is not opposed to faith but forms its completion. We need no revelation other than that in Christ. See GNOSTICISM.

BIBLIOGRAPHY. R. Bultmann, *Gnosis*, 1952.

M.H.C.

KOA. Ezekiel (xxiii. 23) prophesies that this people, together with other dwellers in Mesopotamia, will attack Jerusalem. Koa has been identified with the people called in Assyr. texts *Kutu*, who lived east of the Tigris in the region of the upper 'Adhaim and Diyala rivers. Assyr. records often couple this people with the *Sutu*, called Shoa in Ezk. xxiii. 23, as warring against Assyria. Some (*e.g.* O. Procksch) find Koa in Is. xxii. 5, but only by a doubtful emendation of the word usually translated 'walls'.

BIBLIOGRAPHY. Friedrich Delitzsch, *Wo lag das Paradies?*, 1881, pp. 233–237; G. A. Cooke in *ICC*, 1936, on Ezk. xxiii. 23.

J.T.

KOHATH, KOHATHITES. Kohath, second son of Levi, was founder of one of the three great Levite families. His family was subdivided into the houses of Amram, Izhar, Hebron, and Uzziel, and Moses and Aaron were Amramites (Ex. vi. 20). In the wilderness the Kohathites carried the tabernacle furniture and vessels. They camped on the south side of the tabernacle. Their males over a month old numbered 8,600; those who actually served (age-group 30–50), 2,750 (Nu. iii. 27–32, iv. 36). In the land the Kohathites, who, being sons of Aaron, were priests, were allotted thirteen cities, the rest ten cities (Jos. xxi. 4, 5). Under David's reorganization the Kohathites held a wide variety of offices, including a share in the Temple singing (1 Ch. vi. 31–38, *cf.* ix. 31–32, xxvi. 23–31). Kohathites are mentioned again under Jehoshaphat, Hezekiah, and Josiah (2 Ch. xx. 19, xxix. 12, xxxiv. 12), and at the return from the Exile (*cf.* Ezr. ii. 42 with 1 Ch. ix. 19; Korahites were Kohathites). See also KORAH.

D.W.G.

KORAH (*qōraḥ* = baldness?). **1.** Duke of Edom, son of Esau (Gn. xxxvi. 5, 14, 18; 1 Ch. i. 35). **2.** Duke of Edom, son of Eliphaz (Gn. xxxvi. 16). As the name is omitted from Gn. xxxvi. 11 and 1 Ch. i. 36, some think this to be a gloss. **3.** A son of Hebron (1 Ch. ii. 43). **4.** A grandson of Kohath and ancestor of a group of sacred musicians ('sons of Korah') to whom Ps. xlii and eleven other Psalms are addressed (1 Ch. vi. 22).

5. A Levite ('Core' in Jude 11, AV), a Kohathite of the house of Izhar, perhaps identical with (4). With Dathan, his brother Abiram, and another Reubenite, On, Korah rebelled against Moses and Aaron. Three grounds of revolt are stated, and although these have led some commentators to assume composite authorship according to the documentary hypothesis, the narrative reads naturally as a harmonious unity. Numbers xvi records discontent on the grounds: first, that Moses and Aaron have set themselves above the rest of Israel (verses 3, 13); secondly, that Moses has failed to bring Israel to the promised land (verse 14); and thirdly, that he and Aaron have arrogated the priesthood to themselves (verses 7–11). That different grievances should be used unitedly is not unfamiliar in both ancient history and modern. As the rebels prepare to offer incense, the wrath of God is kindled, and after Moses has interceded for the congregation of Israel the rebels and their followers are destroyed by the earth opening to swallow them, and by fire. *Cf.* Nu. xxvi. 9; Dt. xi. 6; Ps. cvi. 17.

T.H.J.

L

LABAN (Heb. *lāḇān*, 'white'). **1.** Son of Bethuel and brother of Rebekah (Gn. xxiv. 29, xxv. 20, xxviii. 5), and thus uncle of Jacob and Esau (Gn. xxvii. 43, xxviii. 2), and later Jacob's father-in-law. This branch of the family had remained in Harran after Abraham and Lot had migrated, and it was there that both Isaac and Jacob found their wives. Laban first appears giving permission for the marriage of Rebekah to Isaac, apparently playing a more prominent rôle in the negotiations than his father (Gn. xxiv). When Jacob fled to him from Esau, Laban, realizing his value as a servant, made use of Jacob's passion for Rachel to trick him into serving him for fourteen years. But Jacob was more than his match in guile, and Laban found himself defrauded (Gn. xxix, xxx). Subsequently, Jacob fled with his family and possessions, and Laban pursued them, but, being warned in a dream not to be violent, he eventually made a covenant with Jacob (Gn. xxxi). Laban's duplicity, seemingly a family characteristic, was ultimately thwarted, not merely by Jacob's superior cunning, but by the covenant-grace of God; see JACOB.

2. An unknown place mentioned in describing the location of Moses' charge to Israel (Dt. i. 1). Possibly in the plains of Moab, or it may be identical with Libnah, a halting-place on the Israelites' journey (Nu. xxxiii. 20). J.G.G.N.

LACHISH. An important fortified city in the lowland of Judah, guarding the main road leading up to Jerusalem (*c.* 30 miles to the north-east). The modern site at Tell ed-Duweir, 15 miles west of Hebron, covers 18 acres, and thus Lachish (Heb. *Lāḵîš*; LXX *Lachis*) was, at its greatest period, larger than Jerusalem and Megiddo. It was excavated by the Wellcome–Marston Archaeological Expedition in 1932–8.

I. HISTORY

Finds in caves outside the city walls show that Lachish was occupied from at least the Early Bronze Age. By the Hyksos period (*c.* 1720–1550 BC) it was a military site defended by a deep-ditched enclosure protected by a ramp built over older foundations. According to the Amarna letters, the city, under its own ruler, helped the incoming semi-nomadic Habiru and was strong enough to require its opponents to appeal for help to Egypt. In this Canaanite period Lachish was one of the four most important strongholds ruled by Japhia, who was defeated by Joshua in a battle at Gibeon and then put to death at Makkedah (Jos. x. 3–6). Joshua captured Lachish in an attack lasting two days (x. 32), and in accordance with his general policy (*cf.* Jos. xi. 10–13) burned the city. There are extensive traces of burning *c.* 1220–1200 BC which may well be ascribed to this attack. This interpretation agrees well with an inscribed Egyptian tax-collector's memorandum dated in 'the fourth year' (probably of Merenptah). A small Fosse Temple shows the ritual of the Late Bronze Age (*c.* 1600–1200 BC) with its altars for incense and sacrifice. Of the victims the animal bones were all identifiable as the upper part of the right foreleg, the priests' portion of the Israelite sacrifice. There is little to indicate whether the site was rebuilt during the succeeding two centuries.

A stone platform 105 feet square built upon a retaining wall filled with earth (see FOUNDATION) may be the type of construction described as Millo ('Filling') at Jerusalem (2 Sa. v. 9). It is not known whether this was built in David's reign or, like the large storehouse in the citadel, as part of Solomon's administrative reforms. The city was chosen as a place of refuge by Amaziah in his flight from the rebels in Jerusalem, but he was pursued and slain there (2 Ki. xiv. 19; 2 Ch. xxv. 27).

Rehoboam rebuilt Lachish as one of fifteen defence centres to protect Judah from attack by Philistines or Egyptians (2 Ch. xi. 5–12). This reliance upon the military strength of Lachish was one of the sins condemned by Micah (i. 13), in a play on the word *reḵeš* (AV 'swift beast'). The double defences consisted of a ring wall (19 feet thick) round the summit and a further wall 50 feet down the slope. The masonry was found to be of crudely squared boulders with more carefully prepared corner-stones erected by Rehoboam or his grandson Asa (2 Ch. xiv. 6). These walls, with their bastions, towers, battlements, and towered gateway, remained in use until the Assyr. siege. Inside the city a street lined with shops led to the palace and store-rooms sited on a platform 256 feet long. The water supply was assured by a deep well or cistern cut 144 feet down at the north-west corner, requiring the excavation of more than half a million cubic yards of limestone. The town of the later monarchy has not yet been explored.

When Sennacherib attacked Judah in 701 BC he first moved to besiege Lachish (2 Ki. xviii. 13–17; 2 Ch. xxxii. 2) and thus to cut Jerusalem off from any possible support from Egypt. From here he sent messengers to Hezekiah demanding his surrender. The siege of Lachish is depicted on the reliefs on the walls of Sennacherib's palace at Nineveh (now preserved in the British Museum). The inscription above this scene shows that it represents 'Sennacherib, King of Assyria, sitting on his throne while the spoil from the city of Lachish passed before him'. Archaeological confirmation of this attack is provided by the discovery of a heavy destruction level (III) marked by scattered arrowheads, scale-armour sling stones, and an Assyr. helmet crest found near the ramp leading to the gateway as shown in the sculpture. The intensity of the siege is also perhaps shown by the communal grave on the north-west slope holding 1,500 bodies, subsequently desecrated by pig bones scattered over it.

After the victory Sennacherib moved to Libnah to meet the Egyptians moving up towards Jerusalem (2 Ki. xix. 8; Is. xxxvii. 8). Lachish was administered after its fall by an Assyr. governor and was the rallying-point for levies from Philistia. Part of the ruined citadel was cleared and the gateway reconstructed on a narrower scale. There are archaeological traces of the presence of Scythian warriors in the city in the late 7th century BC and this may account for the lack of rebuilding.

By the time of Jehoiakim Lachish had been rebuilt on a large enough scale to warrant an attack by the Babylonian army under Nebuchadrezzar II in 597 BC. The city gate and citadel were partially destroyed at the same time as Jerusalem was attacked. However, it was during the final siege of Judah in 589–587 BC that the full force of the Bab. army was turned on Lachish, which, with Azekah, alone remained a heavily fortified position outside the capital (Je. xxxiv. 7). The heavy destruction by fire can be seen throughout the site (level II) where the walls were demolished. Above the débris the seal impression of 'Gedaliah who is over the House', the governor of Judaea appointed by Nebuchadrezzar (2 Ki. xxv. 22–25; Je. xxxix. 14) may show that the town was quickly reoccupied once the war was over in 581 BC.

There is scant archaeological evidence for the period to *c.* 400 BC when a large Persian villa was built on the summit of the ruin-mound. The plan (level I) is similar to Parthian buildings in Babylonia, and the house may have been the residence of Geshem (Gashmu), the Arab governor of Idumaea (Ne. vi. 1). Although Lachish was reoccupied by Jews returning from exile (Ne. xi. 30), there is little to suggest that it ever again became an important place.

For details of other objects found at Lachish, see WEIGHTS AND MEASURES, JEWELS AND PRECIOUS STONES, ARCHAEOLOGY.

II. INSCRIPTIONS

Among the smaller finds at Lachish was a bronze dagger inscribed with four pictographic signs (*c.* 1700 BC) and an ewer inscribed with a dedication in eleven archaic letters, the earliest 'Hebrew' inscription known. The most important epigraphic find from Palestine itself was made in 1935, when eighteen ostraca inscribed in a cursive Hebrew of the time of Jeremiah were found in a small guard-room under the gate-tower of Lachish, and three years later three further fragments of similar sherds were found (see fig. 161). As well as being of value as the only known copies of documents in classical Hebrew yet discovered, the texts throw light on the conditions prevailing during the Bab. attack. The only addressee named in the letters is Yaosh, military governor of the city, to whom, on at least one occasion (see below, letter III), Hoshayahu, a subordinate officer in charge of an outpost (perhaps located 4 miles to the north-east [Mareshah] and within visual range of Azekah), was to send fire or smoke signals (*cf.* Je. vi. 1, xxxiv. 7). Letter IV reads: 'May YHWH cause my lord to hear now at this time good tidings! And now, according to all that my lord has written, so has thy servant done. I have written on the door (scroll?) according to all that my lord hath sent me. With regard to what my lord has written about the matter of Bethharaphid, there is no-one

Fig. 127. Judaean prisoners going into captivity after the fall of Lachish to the Assyrians. From a bas-relief in the palace of Sennacherib at Nineveh, *c.* 690 BC.

there. And as for Semakiah, Shemaiah has taken and brought him up to the capital (Jerusalem).... And let my lord know that we are watching for the fire-signals of Lachish according to the signs my lord has given, for we cannot see Azekah.'

The longest letter (III) refers to 'a letter of Tobiah, servant of the king, which came to Shallum, son of Jadduah, through the prophet, saying, "Beware! thy servant hath sent it to my lord." ' It is by no means certain who was the prophet who was bearer of the letter. An ostracon (XVI) also refers to 'the prophet', but the name being broken (. . *iah*) opinions are divided over an identification with Uriah who fled to Egypt (Je. xxvi. 20) with Jeremiah, or an otherwise unnamed prophet of this period. See also WRITING.

BIBLIOGRAPHY. The excavations have been fully reported in a series *Lachish*—I, H. Torczyner, *The Lachish Letters*, 1935; II, O. Tufnell, *The Fosse Temple*, 1940; III, *The Iron Age*; IV, *The Bronze Age*. See also O. Tufnell, *PEQ*, XCI, 1959, pp. 90–105 for chronological problems; R. D. Barnett, 'The Siege of Lachish', *IEJ*, VIII, 1958, pp. 161–164; D. Winton Thomas, 'Letters from Lachish', *DOTT*, pp. 212–217. D.J.W.

LADDER. See FORTIFICATION AND SIEGECRAFT (II*a*).

LAHMI. A personal name found only in 1 Ch. xx. 5 and applied to the brother of Goliath the Gittite, who is there stated to have been slain by Elhanan. There is no valid reason why this should not be accepted, but it is possible that the reading may be a copyist's error for 'Beth-lehemite' (*cf.* 2 Sa. xxi. 19), the last part of which is identical to 'Lahmi' in Hebrew. There is, however, no MS authority for this conjecture. See GOLIATH. G.W.G.

LAMB. See SHEEP.

LAMB OF GOD. This expression occurs twice only in the New Testament (Jn. i. 29, 36). The word *amnos* is also found in Acts viii. 32 and 1 Pet. i. 19, *arnos* occurs in Lk. x. 3, and *arnion* is found once in Jn. xxi. 15 and twenty-eight times in Revelation. The words 'Behold the Lamb of God, which taketh away the sin of the world' (Jn. i. 29) are attributed to John the Baptist when acclaiming Jesus. Many possible interpretations of the word 'lamb' have been canvassed.

Some suggest that it refers to the lamb of the sin-offering, and the phrase 'which taketh away the sin of the world' lends support to this. The fact that propitiatory ideas do not seem to be found elsewhere in the Fourth Gospel is not a sufficient reason for rejecting this.

Others believe there is a reference to the paschal lamb. The Jewish festivals have great significance in John, and Jn. xix. 36 may well be alluding to the lamb of the Passover. But this would not explain the whole phrase, as the paschal lamb did not take away sins.

Some maintain that we have here a reference to the suffering servant of Is. liii. The word *amnos* occurs in the LXX of Is. liii. 7. The Baptist quoted from Is. xl the day before and he may have been meditating on those chapters. The sin-bearing function is clear in Is. liii. The suggestion that *amnos* is a mistranslation of the Aramaic *ṭalyā'* meaning 'servant' is ingenious, but it has not been proved.

Another possible reference is to the horned ram who led the flock. The 'lamb of God' would thus be the same as the 'king of Israel'. This view is acceptable only if it is claimed that *ho airōn tēn hamartian* has no propitiatory meaning.

It seems likely that, whatever the Baptist intended, the evangelist intended his readers to think of the lamb offered in the Temple, the paschal lamb, and the suffering servant. The 'Lamb of God' also reminds us of God's provision of a lamb for Abraham (Gn. xxii. 8).

BIBLIOGRAPHY. *Arndt*; *TWNT*; standard commentaries on John's Gospel; C. H. Dodd, *The Interpretation of the Fourth Gospel*, 1953, pp. 230–238. R.E.N.

LAMECH (Heb. *lemeḵ*, possibly from an Arabic word meaning 'a strong young man'; so Dillmann, Holzinger). **1.** A descendant of Cain (Gn. iv. 18 f.), and the first polygamist. He had two wives, Adah and Zillah. One of his sons was Tubal-cain, the first worker of metals, and Lamech's song in Gn. iv. 23 f. is frequently thought to be a 'sword-lay' glorifying the weapons of war invented by his son. He boasts to his wives that he has killed men, and, because of his superior strength due to his weapons, he has no need of God's protection, but is well able to defend himself. He appears as 'a cruel man, destitute of all humanity' (Calvin).

2. A descendant of Seth and father of Noah (Gn. v. 25–31; 1 Ch. i. 3). From the fact that 'Lamech' and 'Enoch' occur in both Cainite and Sethite genealogies, and from other likenesses, it has been conjectured that they are variants of one original list (*cf.* S. R. Driver, *WC*, p. 80). But there are also differences, one of which appears in the character of this Lamech, when he voices the pious hope that with the birth of Noah the curse of Adam would be removed (Gn. v. 29; *cf.* iii. 17 ff.). J.G.G.N.

LAMENESS. See DISEASE AND HEALING.

LAMENTATIONS, BOOK OF. In the Heb. Bible Lamentations (called *'êḵâ*, the characteristic lament 'how!'; *cf.* i. 1, ii. 1, iv. 1) is included among the five scrolls, since it is read on the ninth of Ab, the day of mourning over the destruction of the Temple (*q.v.*). The EVV follow the LXX (*thrēnoi*, 'wailings' or 'dirges') and the Vulg. (whose sub-title *Lamentationes* supplied the English name) in placing Lamentations after the book of Jeremiah.

I. OUTLINE OF CONTENTS AND LITERARY STRUCTURE

The first four chapters are acrostic poems, each containing sixty-six lines, except chapter iv, which has forty-four. Chapter iii is noteworthy because each of the twenty-two Heb. letters is used for three successive one-line verses. One purpose of an acrostic is to aid memorization. But in a collection of acrostics the alphabetic pattern would not help one remember which verse beginning with a given letter belongs in which chapter. This carefully wrought, highly artificial style seems to have a further purpose: 'to encourage completeness in the expression of grief, the confession of sin and the instilling of hope' (N. K. Gottwald, *Studies in the Book of Lamentations*, 1954, p. 28). The acrostic speaks to the eye, not the ear, and conveys an idea not merely a feeling. Gottwald stresses the cathartic rôle of the acrostic: 'to bring about a complete cleansing of the conscience through a total confession of sin' (*op. cit.*, p. 30). Though curbing spontaneity, the acrostic lends a restraint, a gentle dignity, to what could have become an unfettered display of grief.

The dirge-like rhythm of chapters i–iv helps to convey the feeling of grief. Characteristic of Heb. elegies (*e.g.* 2 Sa. i. 19 ff.; Am. v. 2), this *qînâ* rhythm drives home its message with short, sobbing lines. An important device in *qînâ* poetry is *dramatic contrast* in which the former state of the deceased or bereaved is described in glowing terms to sharpen the sense of tragedy (*e.g.* i. 1, iv. 1, 2; *cf.* 2 Sa. i. 19, 23).

Chapter iii, though written in *qînâ* rhythm, is an *individual lament* rather than a funeral dirge (*cf.* Pss. vii, xxii, *etc.*), containing elements typical of this category: a figurative description of suffering (iii. 1–18) and an affirmation that God will answer the suppliant's plea (iii. 19–66), the climax of the book. Though the form is *individual* the intent is *national*; the author speaks for the nation. Chapter v, neither acrostic nor *qînâ*, resembles closely in form the psalms of *communal lament* (*e.g.* xliv, lxxx).

II. AUTHORSHIP AND DATE

Though anonymous, Lamentations has been attributed to Jeremiah by the LXX, Vulg., and Jewish tradition (Targum at Je. i. 1; Talmud, *Baba Bathra* 15a), probably on the basis of 2 Ch. xxxv. 25 which mentions Jeremiah's lamenting over Josiah's death.

The evidences for and against a Jeremianic authorship approach a stalemate. S. R. Driver and E. J. Young cite similar lines of evidence and reach differing conclusions, Young voting *pro* and Driver *contra*. The chief arguments for the traditional view are the similarity in temperament between Lamentations and Jeremiah, their unanimity in attributing Jerusalem's destruction to God's judgment, and certain stylistic parallels. Against these one must consider the variation in alphabetic order of the acrostic poems (ch. i, *s*, ', *p*; ch. ii–iv, *s*, *p*, '), which may hint at multiple authorship, alleged conflicts in viewpoint, such as the author's apparent dependence on Egypt (*cf.* iv. 17 with Je. xxxvii. 5–10) or his support of King Zedekiah (*cf.* iv. 20 with Je. xxiv. 8–10), and the contrast between Jeremiah's spontaneity and the stylized acrostics of Lamentations (see S. R. Driver, *Literature of the Old Testament*, pp. 462–464, for details of the various arguments).

Attempts to attribute the first four poems to different times and authors have generally proved too subjective to gain wide acceptance. These chapters seem to be the work of an eye-witness of Jerusalem's calamity (*c.* 587 BC), who recorded his impressions while they were still fresh. Chapter v may date from a slightly later period when the intense anguish of the catastrophe had given way to the prolonged ache of captivity. No part of the book need be dated later than the return in 538 BC.

III. MESSAGE AND SIGNIFICANCE

Lamentations is by no means barren theologically. Gottwald's analysis is convincing in its main thrusts if not in all details (*op. cit.*, pp. 47–110). Finding the central theme in the *tragic reversal*, the contrast between past glory and present degradation, he discusses the theology in terms of *doom* and *hope*.

The prophets had heralded Judah's doom, convinced that a righteous God would act in history to punish His people's sin. Lamentations continues this prophetic emphasis by seeing in the ashes of Jerusalem the vindication of God's righteousness (i. 18). The city's destruction is no capricious coincidence; it is the logical and inevitable result of defying God's law. Even where God is chided (*e.g.* ch. ii) for His severity, the deep-seated sense of guilt which permeates the book is evident (ii. 14, *cf.* i. 5, 8, 9, 18, 22, iii. 40–42, iv. 13, 22, v. 7). The sense of tragedy is heightened by the recognition that it was avoidable. The manifold picture of the wrath of God (*e.g.* i. 12 ff., ii. 1–9, 20–22, iii. 1–18, iv. 6, 11) makes Lamentations a key source for any study of this aspect of God's nature.

Judah's plight is desperate but not hopeless. Though the aspects of her hope are not delineated, her reason for hope is cogently stated: the faithfulness of a covenant-keeping God (iii. 19–39). It was one thing for the prophets to forecast a better day before the disaster struck; it is another thing for our prophet to appropriate this hope in the midst of appalling circumstances. His recognition of the disciplinary rôle of suffering and its relationship to God's goodness (iii. 25–30) is cogent testimony to his prophetic insight.

Lamentations is a meeting-place of three great strands of Heb. thought: prophecy, ritual, and wisdom. The priestly influence is evident in the liturgical forms of the poems. The wisdom emphasis is stressed in the willingness to contemplate the mysteries of God's ways with men, especially in regard to the timeless problem of suffering.

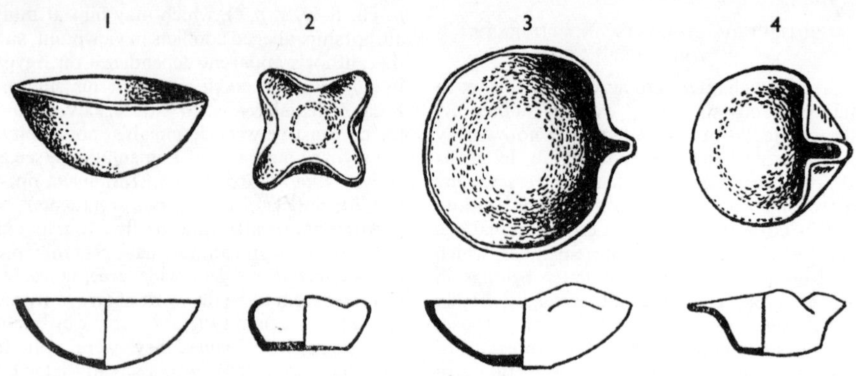

BIBLIOGRAPHY. I. Bettan, *The Five Scrolls*, 1950; H. L. Ellison, *Men Spake from God*, 2nd edn., 1958, pp. 149–154; Max Haller, *Die fünf Megilloth*, J. C. B. Mohr, 1940; T. J. Meek, *Lamentations* in *IB*; T. H. Robinson, *The Poetry of the Old Testament*, 1947, pp. 205–216; N. K. Gottwald, *Studies in the Book of Lamentations*, 1954. D.A.H.

LAMP, LAMPSTAND.

I. DESIGN AND DEVELOPMENT

Small open bowls with a slight lip, which can be certainly identified as lamps (Heb. *nēr*; Gk. *lychnos, lampas*) first appear in the Middle Bronze Age. This simple form continued in use throughout the Iron Age, the lip becoming more pronounced. The final development, the spouted lamp, took place in the Hellenistic period. The rim was pinched in so far that the opposite sides met. Mass-production, typical of this period, was facilitated by the use of moulds, one making the bowl and another the lid. This lid had a central hole through which the oil was poured (*cf.* Mt. xxv. 4). A very long spout for the wick characterizes Hellenistic lamps. Roman lamps are normally rounder, often with moulded designs on the lid. In the 4th century Christian symbols (alpha and omega, fishes, crosses, *etc.*) form decorative motifs, continued on the oval lamps of the Byzantine period. Other lamps are distinctively Jewish, stamped with the *menorah*. Some Israelite pottery lamps are provided with pedestal bases, particularly larger ones with up to seven lips (see *BASOR*, 79, 19, fig. 10; *cf.* Zc. iv. 2; see *IBA*, fig. 117). Bronze lamps found at Megiddo had separate tripod stands, but a simple wooden one would serve most households (Heb. *mᵉnôrâ*, 2 Ki. iv. 10; Aramaic *neḇraštâ*, Dn. v. 5; Gk. *lychnia*, Mt. v. 15; *cf. ANEP*, no. 657, left edge).

In the Tabernacle stood an elaborate golden lampstand (Ex. xxv. 31 ff.). See plate XIV*a*. Three branches ending in flower-shaped lamp-holders protruded from either side of the main stem, which also supported a lamp-holder. Representations on certain Maccabean coins and a relief on the Arch of Titus in Rome supplement Hebrew descriptions. Ten similar lampstands were made for Solomon's Temple.

Hanging lamps have not been found before the Rom. period. Out-of-doors torches were used (Heb. *lappîḏ*, Jdg. vii. 16, xv. 4; see also below). The lamp is often made a simile, *e.g.* 2 Sa. xxi. 17; Ps. cxix. 105; see also below. A.R.M.

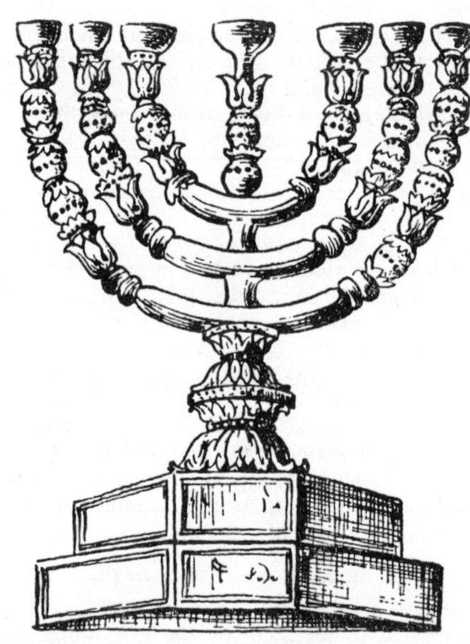

Fig. 129. The seven-branched lampstand from Herod's Temple, as depicted in a relief on the Arch of Titus, Rome.

II. SYMBOLIC AND OTHER USES IN THE NEW TESTAMENT

In the New Testament 'lamp' occurs seven times in AV, on each occasion rendering *lampas.* RV renders *lampas* as 'torch' in Jn. xviii. 3 (following AV) and in Rev. viii. 10, as 'light' in Acts xx. 8 (following AV), and as 'lamp' in Mt. xxv. 1, 3, 4, 7, 8; Rev. iv. 5 (following AV). RV renders *lychnos* (AV 'light' six times, 'candle' eight times) as 'lamp' on every occasion.

The RV rendering must be accepted apart from

5

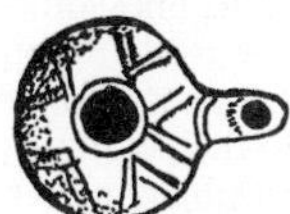

6

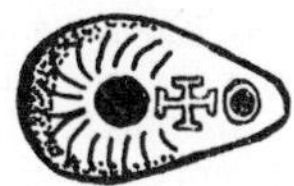

Fig. 128. The development of the lamp: 1. End of Early Bronze Age (Jericho). 2. Middle Bronze Age (Jericho). 3. Late Middle Bronze Age (Jericho). 4. Late Israelite (Samaria). 5. Hellenistic (*c.* 1st century BC–AD). 6. Christian (4th century AD).

All drawings are reduced approximately 1 : 5.

the translating of *lampas* by 'lamp' in Mt. xxv and Rev. iv. 5. In the latter RSV has 'torch'. In the parable of the virgins (Mt. xxv. 1–13) RVmg should be followed, where 'torch' is read. The conventional lamp was for indoor use, and what was needed (and what is still sometimes used) at a wedding was a torch (*q.v.*). The rags which formed its wick needed to be soaked in oil. It seems that the foolish virgins had no oil at all (verse 3), and therefore when they lit their torches they went out straightaway (verse 8). The wise had taken oil in separate containers ready for use at the appropriate moment. The difference between them seems to have been not in the quantity of oil that they possessed but in the fact of their possessing or not possessing any at all. The foolish could have gone and bought some had they acted in time.

Lychnos is used frequently in a symbolic sense. It is the lamp which must be put on a stand to give light to all in the house (Mt. v. 15). John the Baptist was 'the lamp that burneth and shineth' (Jn. v. 35, RV), who came 'that he might bear witness of the light' (Jn. i. 7, RV). It is Christ who is the light (*phōs*). In Mt. vi. 22 the eye is called 'the lamp of the body' because it receives the light from outside.

Lychnia is rendered 'candlestick' by AV *passim* and 'stand' by RV in the Gospels. RV translates this 'candlestick' in Heb. ix. 2 and in Revelation seven times, but in Revelation gives 'lampstand' in mg. RSV has 'lampstand' throughout. The seven churches (Rev. i. 12, 13, 20, ii. 1, 5) and the two witnesses (Rev. xi. 4) are symbolized by lampstands, similar to those used in the Tabernacle (Heb. ix. 2). R.E.N.

LANDMARK. Canaan was divided among the Israelite tribes, and to each family was given a plot of land to provide its livelihood. This was passed from father to son, or at least kept within the tribe (Nu. xxvii. 1–11, xxxvi), from which it was, theoretically, inalienable (see the story of Naboth, 1 Ki. xxi). Inevitably many lost their land through debt, so that the situation in which every man owned his own plot was looked upon as an ideal (Zc. iii. 10). The landmark was an inscribed stone on which the boundaries of the property were defined. (*Cf.* the Bab. *kudurru*, *ANEP*, nos. 519–522, contemporary with the Israelite settlement of Canaan.) To remove this was tantamount to removing a man's claim, and was a lawless act (Dt. xix. 14, xxvii. 17; Pr. xxii. 28, xxiii. 10). (For an Egyp. parallel, *cf. ANET*, p. 422, Sixth Chapter.) It was a sign of evil times when men dared to do so (Jb. xxiv. 2; Ho. v. 10). A.R.M.

LANGUAGE OF THE APOCRYPHA. The so-called 'Apocrypha' (*q.v.*) comprises a heterogeneous group of books, so that to talk of its language is in fact to talk of the individual books and the problems of language which they pose. They have been preserved for us in MSS of the LXX and so lie before us like that translation in Greek. Their Greek varies widely: *e.g.* an evident 'translation Greek' in Tobit, Judith, Ben-Sira, 1 Maccabees; a relatively idiomatic Greek in 1 Esdras and Wisdom of Solomon i–ix, in which nonetheless may be perceived traces of its original; the rest of Wisdom and 2 Maccabees in a Greek uninfluenced by any other tongue, although these two works differ widely in their literary merit. In this Greek dress, then, the Apocrypha presents instances of a variety of popular Greek works current among Jewish people in the three centuries immediately before Christ. The writings pose textual problems which fall within the general pattern of the textual criticism of the LXX.

It has often been assumed that Hebrew is the original tongue of those works in this group which are evidently based on a Semitic original. C. C. Torrey, however, in this as in the New Testament field, opened the pertinent question whether Aramaic is not the original language, at least in certain cases. His knowledge of Aramaic was vast and his contributions to biblical learning always challenging and stimulating, sometimes providing solutions to problems old and new, but not always convincing or even necessary (see the review by G. R. Driver of his posthumously published work on the Apocalypse: *JTS*, XI, 1960, pp. 383–389). This must be borne in mind in evaluating his views on the language of the Apocrypha.

The Hebrew origin of a number of books is not controverted even by Torrey. 1 Maccabees has been translated from Hebrew by one better acquainted with Greek than Hebrew: signs of its origin are to be seen in, for instance, i. 28, ix. 24, xiv. 28. Judith is plainly from Hebrew, as phrases such as *apo prosōpou*, *eis prosōpon*, and instrumentally used *en* show. The prologue to the Wisdom of Ben-Sira, or Ecclesiasticus, as it is often called, expressly states Hebrew to be the original, and a large part of this was discovered in the Cairo Geniza in 1896. The additions to Daniel are shown to be Hebrew in origin by passages such as the Prayer of Azariah 17 (iii. 40 in continuous Greek text) and Susanna 15. The Greek of the Prayer of Manasses is fluent, but the obscurities of verses 4 and 7, for example, appear to derive from imperfectly expressed Hebrew locutions. Baruch displays in iv. 5 evidence of a scribal error in the Hebrew (*zikrôn* read instead of *zikrû*) translated into Greek. 1 Esdras is a rendering of a known original, part Hebrew, part Aramaic: it is idiomatically rendered. Finally, within this group, the first nine chapters of the Wisdom of Solomon are now widely acknowledged to be based on a Hebrew original; they are translated by the author of the rest of the book, to whose original additions we should perhaps also attribute vi. 22–viii. 1.

Tobit is generally conceded to be translated from some Semitic language. Pfeiffer admits that both Hebrew and Aramaic can be proposed but that the case for Aramaic is the stronger. Torrey proposed to find evidence for this latter hypothesis in the meaningless Manasses of xiv. 10 (MSS B and A), an original participle with objective suffix *m*ᵉ*nassēh*, 'the one who exalted him', 'his benefactor'. (Fragments of Tobit in both Hebrew and Aramaic have been identified among the Qumran texts.) The Epistle of Jeremy admits of debate: some still maintain a Greek original. A crucial point is 'the harlots on the roof' (verse 11). Torrey sees here evidence of a misrendering of *'al 'agrā*, 'for their hire', as *'al 'iggārā*. However, both readings in the Greek (*stegous/tegous*) may be understood as 'brothel', so that the mistranslation seems to be an unnecessary hypothesis in this case. In the case of 2 Esdras (not extant in Greek) variant hypotheses have been advanced for both Hebrew and Aramaic originals. The question of the additions to Esther is larger than merely discussion of language: if the argument of Torrey that this represents the original form of the book be correct, then Aramaic may well have been its original. But this argument has not been accepted by the majority of scholars.

Lastly, 2 Maccabees is a composition in Greek, a highly artificial attempt at the attainment of rhetorical heights. The letters which are found in chapters i and ii may be original, and appear to be from a Semitic source, perhaps in Aramaic.

In these linguistic debates it may be well to bear in mind the remarks of G. R. Driver (*op. cit.*) to the effect that in the case of one author at least both Hebrew and Aramaic must be considered. As the one was spoken increasingly during the time of the composition of the Apocrypha and the other was still a literary medium and sometimes spoken, it may be that both have left their imprint upon the eventual Greek form of these books: and that this fact has led to the possibility of such different arguments upon a single matter.

BIBLIOGRAPHY. R. H. Charles, *The Apocrypha and Pseudepigrapha of the Old Testament*, 2 vols., 1913; C. C. Torrey, *The Apocryphal Literature*, 1945; R. H. Pfeiffer, *History of New Testament Times with an Introduction to the Apocrypha*, 1949; E. A. Speiser, 'The Hebrew Origin of the First Part of the Book of Wisdom', *JQR* (NS), XIV, 1924, pp. 455–482; C. E. Purinton, 'Translation Greek in the Wisdom of Solomon', *JBL*, XLVII, 1928, pp. 276–304; C. C. Torrey, 'The Older Book of Esther', *HTR*, XXXVII, 1944, pp. 1–40. J.N.B.

LANGUAGE OF THE OLD TESTAMENT.

I. HEBREW

Hebrew belongs to the western group of the Semitic languages (the word Semitic is formed from the name of Shem, Noah's eldest son). It is most closely related to the language of ancient Ugarit, the capital of a petty kingdom on the north Syrian coast (now Ras Shamra), and to Phoenician and Moabite. In the Old Testament it is called the 'language (lit. "lip") of Canaan' (Is. xix. 18), or Judaic (2 Ki. xviii. 26 f.; *cf.* Is. xxxvi. 11 ff. and Ne. xiii. 24). The designation 'Hebrew' first occurs in Ben-Sira (*c.* 130 BC).

Characteristic of the Semitic languages is the triconsonantal root acting as a sort of a frame for a series of vowel-patterns. The insertion of the vowel-pattern into the frame gives it its specific meaning. In *kōhēn*, for instance, *k-h-n* would be the consonantal frame and *o-e* would be the vowel-pattern. The force of the *o-e* is roughly equivalent to that of the present participle in English, thus *kōhēn*, 'ministering (one)'. Hebrew began early to discard case-endings, but a few remnants still remain. The verbal system has been schematized.

Hebrew script is a descendant of the North Semitic or Phoenician script (see WRITING). It consists of twenty-two consonants (later *š* and *ś* were distinguished, making twenty-three). It is written from right to left. The letters are also used to denote numbers. It contains various sounds not found in Indo-European languages; *e.g.* emphatic consonants (*ṭ*, *ḳ* (*q*), and *ṣ*) and the laryngal *'ayin* ('). The latter was often transliterated into Greek by *gamma*, as for instance in 'Gomorrah'. The form of the script known as *Assyrian* (probably for *Syriac*), or *Square* script, was introduced before 200 BC, but the Jewish tradition that Ezra brought it back from the Exile is without support. Vowel-signs were not used, but as a consequence of certain phonetic changes, etymological spellings with *w* and *y* arose, and these letters then came to be used in other places to represent long vowels. A complete system of vocalization, on the model of the Nestorian system, was introduced by the Jewish scribes, probably in the 6th century AD. Three different systems were developed: in the Babylonian and Palestinian the signs were placed above the consonants (supralinear), and in the Tiberian, the one commonly found in our Hebrew Bibles, the signs (with the exception of that for *ō*) were placed beneath the consonants (infralinear). This vocalization represents an important synchronic stage in Hebrew, and it is the product of a highly enlightened and reliable tradition, as is shown, for instance, by the care with which it observes the distinction that originally obtained between certain vowels of 'substantival' and 'adjectival' verbs, where modifications of the consonantal frame reveal their primitive forms. There are also a number of extra-alphabetical and punctuation or intonation signs. For biblical Hebrew the pronunciation most commonly adopted is the Sephardic (Judaeo-Spanish).

The scribes scrupulously avoided making any change in the consonantal text. Where they presumed that there had been a transcriptional error, or where a word was no longer in polite use, they placed what they considered was the right or preferable word in the margin and the vowels of this word were added to the word in the text (over which a small circle was often placed). The consonants in the text are referred to as *Keṯîḇ* ('the written'), those in the margin as the *Qerē'* ('that which is to be read').

Hebrew possesses no indefinite article. The definite article (*ha-*) is prefixed to the noun. Its use differs in many details from that of the definite article in English. For example, demonstrative pronouns and adjectives take it when used attributively with a noun determinate in its reference. It is also used with a member of a class or with something previously mentioned.

Nouns in Hebrew distinguish gender and number. Gender is grammatical: inanimate as well as animate things are assigned gender. The feminine has usually a specific termination (*-â*). A number of feminine nouns, however, have no termination, but their gender is indicated by the agreement of adjectives and verbs. Hebrew also possesses a specific termination for the dual, largely confined to members of the body occurring in pairs.

There are two main classes of verbs: those with *substantival* cognates and those with *adjectival* cognates. Broadly speaking, the 'substantival' verb is dynamic, whereas the 'adjectival' (often called 'stative') is static. The verb indicates primarily the kind of the action, and distinguishes two main aspects: completed action (perfective) and incompleted (imperfective). For the perfective, the pronominal element is suffixed: for the imperfective it is prefixed. In the perfective, gender is distinguished in the 3rd person singular and in the 2nd person singular and plural, and in the imperfective also in the 3rd person plural. Hebrew has a number of verb-forms for particular categories of action, such as iterative, causative, tolerative, *etc.* There are several classes of irregular verbs, in which the deviations are due to the phonetic character of a small number of consonants or of semi-vowels.

Nouns are formed in many ways: by a variety of vowel-patterns, and with or without the addition of certain consonants. When consonants are used they are usually prefixed. The most commonly used are *m* and *t*. Wide use is made of the singular as a collective, with the result that the feminine termination is sometimes used as a kind of singulative ending, *e.g.* *śē'ār*, 'hair', *śa'arâ* (fem.), 'single hair'. Zero forms, that is forms in which a morphological element common to a class is missing, are not uncommon; *ṣō'n* (fem.), 'flocks', *cf.* *ṣō'n 'ōḇeḏôṯ*, 'lost sheep', where *ôṯ* indicates the element missing. The noun preceding a genitive has its vowels reduced to the minimum and omits the definite article. The group is treated virtually as an inseparable compound. Possessive pronouns appear as suffixes to the noun.

Generally adjectives have one particular form of stress-pattern which limits the number of vowel-patterns in use. They may be used either predicatively, when they do not take the definite article and usually precede the noun, or attributively, when they follow the noun and take the definite article if the noun has it. The adjective may also take the definite article and be used independently, having the value of a substantive. Comparison is rendered by the use of the preposition *min*, 'from', equivalent to the English 'more . . . than'. The highest degree of a quantity is often left unexpressed, *e.g.* 'the good', namely 'the best', or the superlative is expressed by a phrase consisting of a singular form followed by a plural, *e.g.* 'song of the songs', *i.e.* the greatest or best song.

The use of the numerals shows several peculiarities. One and two agree in gender with their noun, but three to ten disagree. This may indicate a late introduction of grammatical gender.

The 'verbless' or nominal sentence in which the predicate consists of a noun, a pronoun, or adjective, is widely used. Usually we supply in translation some part of the verb 'to be', *e.g.* 'the servant of Abraham (am) I'. In sentences with a finite verb the word-order usually follows the pattern—verb, subject, object. Often with the accusative the particle *'eṯ* is used. If the object consists of a pronoun it can be appended to the accusative particle, or it can be added as an enclitic form to the verb. An indirect object consisting of a preposition and a pronominal suffix normally comes before the subject. If there is an adverbial extension it usually follows the object. Where English might use the impersonal 'one', *e.g.* in 'one says', Hebrew uses either the 3rd singular masculine or the 3rd plural, or the 2nd singular masculine.

The most distinctive feature of Hebrew style is its syndetic or co-ordinative character, that is, the prevalence of the simple conjunction 'and', and the infrequent use of subordinating conjunctions. Compared with English, it might seem to be less abstract, but this is partly because many of our terms for abstract ideas are not native, and where they had originally a concrete association this easily escapes us. Hebrew, for instance, makes extensive use of terms for physical attitudes to describe psychological states, or organs of the body are associated with mental attitudes. It is most difficult for anyone inured to Indo-European procedure to dissociate his mind from the original meanings; this is particularly so when a work is replete with them, as for instance, in the 'Song of Songs'.

The imagery of Hebrew is largely drawn from the things and activities of everyday life. It has, therefore, a universal quality and lends itself without difficulty to translation. Hebrew makes use of all the common figures of speech, parables (*e.g.* 2 Sa. xii), similes, metaphors, *e.g.* 'star' or 'lion' for hero, 'rock' for refuge, 'light' for life and for the divine revelation, 'darkness' for sorrow and ignorance.

Hebrew, in common with linguistic usage in general, makes wide use of anthropomorphic expressions; that is, the transference or adaptation of terms for parts of the human body and for human activities to the inanimate world and other conditions to which they are not strictly attributable. These expressions have their origin in metaphor and come under the heading of 'extension of meaning', a device essential apparently to mechanism of languages in general. They occur as frequently in other Semitic languages as in Hebrew. Akkadian, for instance, refers to the keel of a ship as the 'backbone', to which the 'ribs' are attached. Hebrew speaks about the 'head' of a mountain, the 'face' of the earth, the 'lip' (shore) of the sea, the 'mouth' of a cave, the 'going' of water (a verb often used elsewhere with the meaning of 'walking'). These and many other expressions had obviously become 'fossilized' metaphors. When such expressions are applied to the activities or attributes of God it would be indefensible on linguistic grounds to interpret them in a literal sense, or to base theories of beliefs on what are intrinsic modes of expression dictated by the very nature of linguistic communication.

Elliptical expressions, by which the semantic content of a full phrase is vested in a single member of the group, are not uncommon. The omission may be a verbal form, as in the common ellipsis of the finite verb after the so-called 'infinitive absolute', or of the object of a verb, as the omission of 'voice' after 'to lift up' (Is. xlii. 2). Although one of the earliest references to semantic change occurs in the Old Testament (1 Sa. ix. 9), there is little evidence of change in Hebrew in the course of the centuries. In the nature of the case, it would not be easy to detect loan-words from cognate languages. Examples are *hêkāl*, 'temple', from Akkad. *ekallu*, 'palace', which in turn was borrowed from Sumerian *e-gal*, 'great house'; *'argāmān*, 'purple', comes from Hittite. The great divergences between Hebrew and the other cognate languages, largely due to the action of semantic change, make it extremely hazardous to attempt on etymological grounds to assign meanings to Hebrew words of infrequent occurrence.

The high literary style of much of the Old Testament would seem to indicate the early existence of literary models or of a 'grand style'. Much that has been written about divergences in Hebrew style is, in the absence of proper criteria, valueless.

While it is now clear that the influence of Hebrew on New Testament Greek is not as extensive as was formerly held by many scholars, nevertheless it has left its mark both on vocabulary and syntax. There are a number of loan-words and many loan-translations, *e.g. hilastērion* for the covering of the ark which, on the Day of Atonement, was sprinkled with blood, and an expression like 'Blessed art thou among (lit. "in") women', where the Greek follows the Hebrew in the use of the preposition.

The influence of Hebrew on European literature is incalculable, even though much of it may have come indirectly through the Vulgate. Among the many Hebrew loan-words in English are: sabbath, sack, Satan, shekel, jubilee, hallelujah, aloes (fragrant resin), and myrrh. The use of 'heart' as the seat of the emotions and will and of 'soul' for person are probably loan-translations.

II. ARAMAIC

Aramaic, a close cognate, not a derivative, of Hebrew, is the language of Dn. ii. 4–vii. 28; Ezr. iv. 8–vi. 18, vii. 12–26; Je. x. 11; two words in Gn. xxxi. 47; and of the Targums (Aramaic translations of parts of the Old Testament). The oldest extra-biblical specimen may be the Melqart stele, possibly 9th century BC (*DOTT*, pp. 239 ff.). The inscriptions from Zenjirli, one of which mentions Tiglath-pileser (745–728 BC), are from the 8th century BC. A relief from his reign depicts two scribes (see fig. 182), one of whom holds a roll of papyrus or leather, probably to record in Aramaic. There are also Aramaic notes on some Assyrian and Babylonian tablets. From the 5th century we have the papyri from a colony of Jewish mercenaries stationed on Elephantine, an island in the Nile near Aswan. See plate XIII*a*.

The reference in 2 Ki. xviii. 26 shows that already in the time of Sennacherib (705–681 BC) Aramaic was a diplomatic language. In the Persian Empire (550–450 BC) it was the official language.

S. R. Driver (*LOT*, pp. 502 ff.) affirmed that the Aramaic of Daniel was a *Western* Aramaic dialect and hence late. When he wrote, the only material available was too late to be relevant. Subsequently R. D. Wilson, making use of earlier material that had come to light, was able to show that the distinction between Eastern and Western Aramaic did not exist in pre-Christian times. This has since been amply confirmed by H. H. Schaeder. Schaeder also drew attention to the fact that the static nature of 'Imperial Aramaic', as it has come to be called, precludes the possibility of dating documents in it, including Daniel and Ezra. He showed that the criteria adduced to assign to Daniel and Ezra a late date are merely the result of a process of orthographical modernization going on in the 5th century BC (see F. Rosenthal, *Aramaistische Forschung*, p. 676). From what we know from contemporary documents of the extent of trade and diplomatic contacts, we are not surprised to find loan-words in the most unexpected places. The cosmopolitan character of Babylon in the time of Nebuchadrezzar II, as revealed by the Jehoiachin tablets, must have left its mark on the various languages (*DOTT*, p. 86). As Rosenthal says, the linguistic argument used by Driver and others 'has been shelved'.

The script is the same as Hebrew, and Aramaic has approximately the same phonological characteristics, including the position of the stress. The vowel-patterns are on the whole more attenuated and on occasions preserve more primitive forms. The consonantal shift between the two languages lacks the consistency of a law. Heb. *z* = Aram. *d*(*ḏ*), Heb. *š* = Aram. *t*, Heb. *ṣ* = Aram. *ṭ*, *etc*., but the change of Heb. *ṣ* to Aram. ' and *q* is phonetically hard to explain.

The definite article is *-â* and is suffixed to its noun. The genitive relation can be expressed as in Hebrew, the noun preceding the genitive is shortened if possible and the group is treated as inseparable. The relationship is more often expressed by *dî*, originally a demonstrative pronoun, thus *ḥezwâ dî lēlyâ*, 'vision of the night'.

As in Hebrew, the noun has singular, dual, and plural. There are two genders: masculine and feminine. The feminine termination is *-â*, but many feminine nouns are without any indication. Possessive pronouns are suffixed to the noun.

The verb possesses two tense-aspects: perfective (completed action) with pronominal elements suffixed, and imperfective (incompleted action) with the pronominal elements prefixed. The active participle is widely used to express present or future. There are some eight 'verb-forms' or conjugations: Primary Form, with modifications for active, passive, and reflexive; Intensive; and the Causative, designated by either a prefixed *h*, ', or *š*. The verb 'to be', *h^{a}wâ*, comes to be used very much like an auxiliary verb.

The verbless sentence is common. In verbal sentences either the verb or the subject may come first, but the latter order seems more common. Word-order is less rigid than in Hebrew.

BIBLIOGRAPHY. *Hebrew:* A. B. Davidson, *An Introductory Hebrew Grammar*[24], 1932; G. Beer and D. R. Meyer, *Hebräische Gram*., I, 1952, II, 1955; J. Weingreen, *Practical Grammar for Classical Hebrew*, 1959; H. Bauer and P. Leander, *Historische Gram. der Hebräischen Sprache*, 1918–19; C. Bergsträsser, *Hebräische Grammatik*[29] (Gesenius-Kautzsch); W. Gesenius, *Hebrew Grammar* (tr. A. E. Cowley), 1910; F. Böttcher, *Lehrbuch der Hebräischen Sprache*, 1861; P. Joüon, *Grammaire de l'Hébreu Biblique*, 1923; E. König, *Lehrgebäude der Hebräischen Sprache*, 1881–1897; S. R. Driver, *Tenses in Hebrew*, 1892; E. König, *Stilistik*, 1900; *id*., *Rythmik*, 1914; C. Brockelmann, *Hebräische Syntax*, 1956; Gesenius–Buhl, *Handwörterbuch*, 1921; L. Koehler, *Lexicon in Veteris Testamenti libros*, 1948 ff.; *BDB*.

Aramaic: Reallexikon der Assyriologie (*s.v*. 'Aramu'); R. D. Wilson, *Aramaic of Daniel*, 1912; *id*., *Studies in the Book of Daniel*, 1917; H. H. Rowley, *The Aramaic of the Old Testament*, 1929; F. Rosenthal, *Aramaistische Forschung*, 1939; H. H. Schaeder, *Iranische Beiträge*, I, 1930; *Grammars*—by H. Bauer and P. Leander, 1927; H. Strack, 1921; W. B. Stevenson, 1924; *Lexicons*—those listed under *Hebrew* contain Aramaic supplements. W.J.M.

LANGUAGE OF THE NEW TESTAMENT.

I. GENERAL CHARACTERISTICS

a. The nature of 'common Greek'

The language in which the New Testament documents have been preserved is the 'common Greek' (*koinē*), which was the *lingua franca* of the Near Eastern and Mediterranean lands in Rom. times. It had been established over this wide territory by the conquests and express cultural purpose of Alexander the Great, whose colonies provided *foci* for the continued use of the language. It exercised influence in vocabulary upon Coptic, Jewish Aramaic, rabbinical Hebrew, and Syriac, and was spoken as far west as the Rhone valley, colonized from the province of Asia. It represents, as its morphology and accidence show, a mingling of the Attic, Ionic, and NW Greek dialects, which in the course of Gk. political history before and after Alexander's conquests became fused together into a fully unified language with little trace of dialectal differentiation, so far as our records go. It is the direct ancestor of Byzantine and Modern Greek which have recently been much utilized to cast light on its development and normative forms.

A number of the writers of the Rom. period strove to attain the Attic ideal, and thus the living dialect is largely obscured in their works (Dionysius of Halicarnassus, Dio Chrysostom, Lucian); and even those who wrote in the *koinē* were inevitably influenced at times by their literary background (Polybius, Diodorus Siculus, Plutarch, Josephus). For the language of the common man we may turn rather to inscriptions and papyri, the latter mainly derived from Egypt, the former from a wider area. The New Testament, together with the *Discourses* of Epictetus, form the chief literary monument of the language of the common man as typified in the sources named above, but here utilized for lengthy exposition of high and serious matters. It was not until the discovery of the masses of papyri at Oxyrhynchus and other sites that this close link between the New Testament and the Greek of everyday life was fully understood; since these have been examined, we may no longer speak of biblical Greek as a separate dialect but simply as the *koinē*, exemplified in a conveniently gathered and well-known collection homogeneous in theological interest, but representing a fairly wide linguistic range from the Apocalyptist's work to the highly wrought periods of parts of Hebrews.

The *koinē* is characterized by the loss or attenuation of many subtleties of the classical period, and by a general weakening in force of particles, conjunctions, and the *Aktionsart* of verbal conjugations. The extent and particular instances of this tendency to simplification naturally vary even within the New Testament, and much more within the whole range of the linguistic monuments of the dialect. The dual number has totally disappeared. The optative mood is little used and scarcely ever strictly according to the canons of classical Attic. The distinction of perfect and aorist is sometimes not observed, a feature often reflected in variant readings. Certain particles, *e.g. te, hōs*, and even *ge*, are used as mere otiose supplements to others. Distinctions between different prepositions, *e.g. eis* and *en*, *hypo* and *apo*, are blurred; and similarly, the use of the same preposition (*e.g. epi*) with differing cases of the noun.

In vocabulary, compound verbs take the place of simple, thematic of non-thematic, back-formations appear; while in the noun there is a marked inclination to use diminutives without due implication of smallness. Similarly, the usage of such conjunctions as *hina* and *mē* has been greatly extended; and the pattern of conditional sentences (whether with *ei* or with a relative) has lost its clearly defined nuances. This is not to imply that the language was in this form totally weakened and bereft of all its powers and subtleties—it remained a keen and precise instrument of expression—but without cognizance of the attenuating processes which were at work the expositor stands in danger of oversubtlety in exegesis.

During the period of our New Testament writings, under Roman domination, the *koinē* was exposed to the influence of Latin, and this has left its mark upon the language. However, this impression is mainly upon vocabulary and is to be seen in two forms, transliterated words (*e.g. kentyriōn*) and literally transposed phrases (*e.g. to hikanon poiein* = *satisfacere*). An attempt has been made to argue that the original tongue of Mark's Gospel was Latin, as some Syr. colophons say, and a plausible case erected; but the thesis has not met with acceptance, since much of its evidence may be paralleled either in the papyri or in modern Greek. It is in fact an unchallenged axiom of present-day scholarship in this field that that which is at home in modern Greek is the development of a natural Hellenistic locution, and in its appearance in the New Testament cannot be the result of a foreign influence upon New Testament Greek. As regards the language of Mark, it should also be noted that Latinisms of both kinds are to be found in Matthew and John and even in Luke, while the African Lat. text, claimed as the original text, is in fact extant for all four Gospels, and not only for Mark.

b. Hebraisms in the New Testament

No local dialects are observable within the *koinē*, and in extant records there seems to be little local variation. A few 'Phrygianisms' and 'Egyptianisms' have been isolated. But in the New Testament writings we meet the particular problem of Semitisms, *i.e.* abnormal locutions which reveal an underlying or otherwise influencing Hebrew or Aramaic. We find that here we are dealing with an extremely subtle problem, in solving which a number of different types of influence and reflection may be discerned. Much that seemed curious to earlier scholars and was put down to Hebraism has, since the discoveries of the papyri, proved to be but the common Greek of the period. Yet certain features remain about which debate continues.

Hebraisms are mainly of Septuagintal origin. The Septuagint was the Bible text chiefly known and used in the period of the formation of the New Testament. Its influence upon the New Testament writers varies. To trace this is again somewhat difficult, except in the case of explicit citation or phraseology, because of different strata in the Septuagint itself, some parts of which are written in idiomatic *koinē*, others in good literary *koinē*, while the Pentateuch and some other portions, largely for reverential reasons, closely adhere to the Heb. text, even when this entails a certain wresting of the grammatical usage of Greek. Heb. phrases are rendered word for word into Greek, *e.g. pasa sarx*, 'all flesh'; *akrobystia*, 'uncircumcision', *enōpion tou kyriou*, 'before the Lord'; pronouns are much used, following Heb. usage; various verbal features of Hebrew, especially the infinitive absolute, are rendered as literally as possible into Greek, *e.g.* in this case by pleonastic participle or cognate noun in the dative case; various periphrastic prepositional forms are used in imitation of Hebrew, *e.g. en mesō, dia cheiros*. In some cases, for instance the last named, this represents simply an over-use of a development already observable in popular Greek of the period.

Except perhaps in one instance, however, the Greek of the New Testament is not translated from Hebrew; and where (citations, *etc.*, apart) Hebraism is observable, it is in works otherwise high in the scale of stylistic and literary elegance in the New Testament. These are Luke, whose Septuagintalism is probably the result of deliberate pastiche, and Hebrews, whose author is steeped in the LXX while himself being capable of a highly complex and subtle Gk. style. In Revelation, parts of which at least were translated from Hebrew (probably; though perhaps from Aramaic), the Greek is curious and unusual; having thrown away much of normal Gk. grammar and syntax, the author (or his circle) has created his own almost rigidly observed rules.

The resultant style is not, however, noticeably Septuagintal, though it is thoroughly Hebraized.

c. The so-called 'Aramaic Approach'

This approach is a method even more difficult to pursue than the tracing of Hebraism. This is due to many factors. First, there has been considerable debate over the appropriate dialect of the widespread Aramaic language, in which the sayings of Jesus may be presumed to have been uttered and preserved. In the upshot it would appear that the Palestinian Targum, the Aramaic portions of the Talmud Yerushalmi, and Samaritan Aramaic sources are probably the safest guide, with Biblical Aramaic and Christian Palestinian Syriac as useful auxiliary aids. Secondly, whereas for Hebraisms we have a known translation from Hebrew to guide us, in the case of Aramaic there is no translated literature apart from the versions of biblical books known to have been translated from Aramaic, and various pseudepigrapha presumably translated; and only in the first of these cases have we the originals by which to control our understanding. Josephus's *Jewish War*, originally composed in Aramaic, has been skilfully rendered into Greek in a version which shows little or no trace of its original language. Thirdly, a number of alleged signs of Aramaic origin (*e.g.* asyndeton, parataxis, an extended use of *hina* said to be based on the Aramaic d^e) are also to be found in the *koinē*, where simplicity of construction is often found and finer shades of meaning are sometimes lost.

In view of these difficulties, one needs to proceed with care. The more ambitious hypotheses which find all the Gospels and parts of Acts to be translations from Aramaic have failed to meet with general acceptance. More sober positions need to be taken up. We have to assess the probabilities largely by an 'un-Greek' preponderance of, or predilection for, certain locutions, or by means of patent ambiguities directly attributable to errors of translation. We find, then, that, broadly speaking, sayings and discourse material prove to be that which displays the most unambiguous signs of translation out of Aramaic: *viz.* sayings, complexes of sayings, parables, in the Synoptics; peculiarly Johannine discourse material; speeches in Acts. In these sections a number of ambiguities have been resolved by recourse to the syntax and style of Aramaic: this is the most securely established conclusion of this method. The majority of attempts to find flagrant mistranslations, however, in the *cruces interpretum* of the Greek, have not met with general agreement; each scholar tends to put forward his own suggestions, to the detriment of others and in criticism of theirs. In the case of John not all would be willing to find Aramaic sources even behind the discourses: rather, the work of a bilingual author has been postulated, in which the more natural Aramaic has left its indelible imprint on the more mannered Greek. This is certainly so in the case of Paul, whose rugged and vigorous *koinē* is marked throughout by his close acquaintance with the LXX and by his native Aramaic.

II. INDIVIDUAL STYLISTIC FEATURES

Having thus summarized the general characteristics of New Testament Greek, we may give a brief characterization of each individual author. Mark is written in the Greek of the common man; our increased knowledge of the papyri has done much to illuminate his usage, though Aramaisms still remain, notably his impersonal use of the third person plural of the active verb to express a general action or thought. Matthew and Luke each utilize the Markan text, but each corrects his solecisms, and prunes his style, in accordance with principles which we may find illustrated in their extreme form in Phrynichus. Matthew's own style is less distinguished than that of Luke—he writes a grammatical Greek, sober but cultivated, yet with some marked Septuagintalisms; Luke is capable of achieving momentarily great heights of style in the Attic tradition, but lacks the power to sustain these; he lapses at length back to the style of his sources or to a very humble *koinē*. In both evangelists, of course, the Aramaic background of the material reveals itself again and again, especially in sayings. The first two chapters of Luke have led to some debate: it is common to describe them as a pastiche of the LXX, but it may be plausibly argued that they are translated directly from a Heb. source. John's Greek can be closely paralleled from Epictetus, but in the opinion of most scholars appears to be a *koinē* written by one whose native thought and speech were Aramaic; there may even be passages translated from that language. Certain qualities of his style, notably the 'I AM' type of theophanic declaration, are most closely to be paralleled from the Mandaean writings which have their roots in W Syria; this too underlines the description of the Gospel as markedly Semitic. Acts is clearly the work of Luke, whose style fluctuates here as in the Gospel, and in spite of his spasmodic achievements remains at the mercy of his sources.

Paul writes a forceful Greek, with noticeable developments in style between his earliest and his latest Epistles. The development in Ephesians and in the Pastorals is so striking as to have led to hypotheses of pseudonymous composition; it is naturally patient of other explanations in the view of conservative scholars (see PSEUDONYMITY). Hebrews is written in a very polished Greek of one acquainted with the philosophers, and with the type of thought and exegesis exemplified in Philo, yet the LXX has affected the language and style as it has not in Philo's case. James and 1 Peter both show close acquaintance with classical style, although in the former some very 'Jewish' Greek may also be seen. The Johannine Epistles are closely similar to the Gospel in language, but are more uniform and, even, duller in style, though the wide differences of literary type and subject may well be the operative factor in this. Jude and 2 Peter both display a highly tortuous and involved Greek; the latter has in fact with some justification been accused of Atticizing, and has been described as the one New Testament writing which gains by translation. The Apocalypse, as we have indicated, is *sui generis* in language and style; its vigour, power, and success, though a *tour de force,* cannot be denied.

III. CONCLUSION

So New Testament Greek, while showing a markedly Semitic cast in places, remains in grammar, syntax, and even style essentially Greek. Semantically, however, it has come to be increasingly acknowledged that its terminology is as strongly moulded by the usage of the Septuagint as by its origins, etymology, and usage in Greek. This realization has led to the *TWNT* founded by Kittel, and has made a major contribution towards the current investigations of Biblical Theology; readily accessible to the English reader, there is also the work of C. H. Dodd in this field, especially in *The Bible and the Greeks* and *The Interpretation of the Fourth Gospel.* Behind 'righteousness' and 'justification', behind 'faith' and 'to believe', behind 'knowledge' and 'grace', stand Heb. concepts which quite transform the Gk. significance and which must be comprehended if the gospel is not to be misunderstood. Much of the legalism and sacramentalism of the Fathers and the mediaeval theologians stems from lack of this knowledge—and even later theologians have suffered from lack of it. The realization of it is one of our greatest gains from modern biblical research.

In summary, we may state that the Greek of the New Testament is known to us today as a language 'understanded of the people', and that it was used with varying degrees of stylistic attainment, but with one impetus and vigour, to express in these documents a message which at any rate for its preachers was continuous with that of the Old Testament scriptures—a message of a living God, concerned for man's right relation with Himself, providing of Himself the means of reconciliation. This gospel has moulded the language and its meaning so that even the linguistic disciplines of its analysis become ultimately parts of theology.

BIBLIOGRAPHY. F. Blass and A. Debrunner, *Grammatik der neutestamentlichen Griechisch*[8], 1949; Ludwig Radermacher, *Neutestamentliche Grammatik*[2], 1925; J. H. Moulton, *Grammar of New Testament Greek*, I[3], 1908, II (ed. W. F. Howard), 1929, III in progress; A. T. Robertson, *A Grammar of the Greek New Testament*[3], 1919; F. M. Abel, *Grammaire du Grec Biblique*, 1927; Matthew Black, *An Aramaic Approach to the Four Gospels and Acts*[2], 1953; Walter Bauer, *Griechisch-Deutsches Wörterbuch zu den Schriften des Neuen Testament und der übrigen urchristlichen Literatur*[5], 1957–8; W. F. Arndt and F. W. Gingrich, *A Greek–English Lexicon of the New Testament*, 1957 (translated with some supplementation from the work of Bauer); *Theologisches Wörterbuch zum Neuen Testament*, founded by G. Kittel, 1933– ; C. H. Dodd, *The Bible and the Greeks*, 1934, and *The Interpretation of the Fourth Gospel*, 1953. J.N.B.

LANTERN (Gk. *phanos*). Found only in Jn. xviii. 3 in connection with the party who came to arrest Jesus. It may refer to some kind of torch, or perhaps simply to a covered lamp (*q.v.*).

Fig. 130. A Roman bronze lantern. 1st century AD.

LAODICEA. A city in the Roman province of Asia, in the west of what is now Asiatic Turkey. It was founded by the Seleucid Antiochus II in the 3rd century BC, and called after his wife Laodice. Owing to its position, it was an extremely prosperous commercial centre, especially under Roman rule. For example, when it was destroyed by a disastrous earthquake in AD 60 it could afford to reject the proffered imperial subsidy. It lay on a very important cross-road; the main road across Asia Minor ran west to the ports of Miletus and Ephesus about 100 miles away, and east by an easy incline on to the central plateau and thence towards Syria; and another road ran north to the provincial capital at Pergamum and south to the coast at Attaleia. It was therefore an important centre of banking and exchange. In addition, lying in the broad valley of the Lycus (a tributary of the Meander), the city was surrounded by fertile land. Its distinctive products included garments of glossy black wool, and medicinal tabloids or powders. Its site had one disadvantage: being entirely determined by the road-system, there was no permanent water supply near at hand. Water had to be piped to the city from hot springs some way off, and probably arrived lukewarm. See fig. 131. The site was eventually abandoned, and the modern town (Denizli) grew up around the springs.

Lying on the natural route of innumerable travellers and traders, Laodicea was reached by the gospel at an early date, probably while Paul was living in Ephesus (Acts xix. 10), and perhaps through Epaphras (Col. iv. 12, 13). Although Paul mentions the church there (Col. ii. 1, iv. 13–16), there is no record that he visited it. It is evident that the church maintained close connections with the communities in the neighbouring cities of Hierapolis and Colossae (*q.v.*). The

Fig. 131. Ancient water pipes at the site of Laodicea. The pipes were constructed of cubical blocks of stone, approximately 3 feet across, bored through the centre and cemented end to end. The relatively large original bore has been partially blocked by precipitated mineral matter.

'letter from Laodicea' (Col. iv. 16) is thought by many to refer to a copy of 'Ephesians' which had been received by the Laodicean church. The last of the Letters to 'the seven churches of Asia' was addressed to the 'angel of the church of the Laodiceans' (Rev. iii. 14–22). It appears to contain many allusions to the character and circumstances of the city. For all its wealth, the city could produce neither the healing power of hot water, like its neighbour Hierapolis (*q.v.*), nor the refreshing power of cold water to be found at Colossae; but merely lukewarm water, useful only as an emetic. The church was charged with a similar uselessness (see M. J. S. Rudwick and E. M. B. Green, 'The Laodicean Lukewarmness', *ExpT*, LXIX, 1957–8, pp. 176–178). Like the city, the church thought it had 'need of nothing', whereas in fact it needed 'gold', 'white raiment', and 'eyesalve' more effective than its bankers, clothiers, and doctors could supply. Like citizens inhospitable to a traveller who offers them priceless goods, its members had closed their doors and left their real Provider outside (verse 20).

BIBLIOGRAPHY. W. M. Ramsay, *The Letters to the Seven Churches of Asia*, 1904. M.J.S.R.

LAPPIDOTH (*lappîḏôt*, 'torches', AV 'Lapidoth'). The husband of Deborah (Jdg. iv. 4). Some Jewish commentators, taking it as a description of Deborah, would render the Hebrew as 'a woman of lightning flashes', but there is little evidence to support this view; other Jewish commentators (with equal lack of evidence) identified him with Barak (Jdg. iv. 6), whose name means 'lightning'.

LAPWING. See BIRDS OF THE BIBLE.

LASEA, presumably the same town as the Lasos mentioned by Pliny (*NH*, iv. 59), has been identified with ruins some 5 miles east of Fair Havens (*q.v.*). If this identification is correct, one of the disadvantages of Fair Havens as a winter harbour would be the distance of the town from it. K.L.McK.

LASHA. Probably *leša'*, but written *lāša'* in the interests of prosody in its sole occurrence, which is at the end of a verse (Gn. x. 19). It figures in the designation of the limits of the territory of Canaan in a context which suggests that one travelling from the Mediterranean coast would encounter it as the farthest inland of a group consisting of Sodom, Gomorrah, Admah, and Zeboim. This points to a locality somewhere near the south-east shore of the Dead Sea, but no site of this name is known there. Ancient tradition equated it with the hot springs of *Kallirrhoē*, modern Zarqa Ma'in south-west of Madaba near the east coast of the Dead Sea, and some modern scholars prefer to identify it with *layiš* (see DAN), but neither of these can be substantiated.

T.C.M.

LASHARON (RV 'Lassharon', AVmg 'Sharon') A Canaanite royal city mentioned with Aphek as taken by Joshua (xii. 18). LXX (B) reads 'the king of Aphek in Sharon'. However, Eusebius (*Onomasticon*, *s.v.* 'Saron') mentions a district called Sarona, between Mt. Tabor and the Sea of Tiberias, and this ancient site, 6½ miles south-west of Tiberias, may be the biblical Lasharon.

J.D.D.

LAST SUPPER. See LORD'S SUPPER.

LATCHET. A leather thong for tying on sandals (Gn. xiv. 23; Mk. i. 7). To servants was assigned the menial task of untying it. See sandals under DRESS.

LATIN. The word is mentioned only twice in the New Testament (Lk. xxiii. 38; Jn. xix. 20). An Indo-European language, it was spoken first in Rome and the contiguous Latian plain by racial elements which entered Italy, probably from the north, before 900 BC. Latin was confined to the Latian enclave by the alien Etruscan language to the north, and to the east and south by the allied languages, Oscan and Umbrian, which came with a later wave of immigrants, possibly across the Adriatic. Latin expanded with Rome, became the second speech of the Western Mediterranean, fathered the Romance languages, and contributed major elements to the vocabularies of the Teutonic and Slavonic languages. Latin words appearing in the New Testament are: *as, charta, census, centurio, colonia, custodia, denarius, forum, flagellum, grabbatus, legio, lenteum, libertini, lolium, praetorium, quadrans, macellum, membrana, modius, raeda, semicinctium, sicarius, speculator, sudarium, taberna, titulus, zizanium.* E.M.B.

LATIN VERSIONS. See TEXT AND VERSIONS.

LATTICE. See CASEMENT.

LAVER. See TABERNACLE, TEMPLE.

Fig. 132. A basalt laver supported by two bulls. Early first millennium BC from Carchemish.

LAW.

I. IN THE OLD TESTAMENT

a. The etymology of tôrâ

Following the ancient versions, most modern translations use the word 'law' to render Heb. *tôrâ*, a word which occurs about 220 times in the Old Testament. There are widely divergent opinions about its etymology. We know that this noun is undoubtedly related to the Heb. verb *hôrâ*, 'to direct, to teach, to instruct in'. But whether its root *yrh* (of which the qal does not occur) is related to the verb *yārâ*, 'to throw, to cast', hiph'îl 'to shoot' (arrows), is very uncertain. The theory that the relation is based on the Arabian usage of obtaining oracles by shooting arrows is now abandoned. As the verb is never used with *gôrāl*, 'lot', as an object, the idea that *tôrâ* was originally the casting of lots in order to obtain an oracle is improbable. In the highdays of Pan-babylonianism *tôrâ* was considered a loan-word from Accadian *tērtu*, 'oracle', a theory which nowadays will find few advocates. The verb *hôrâ* may be related to an Accadian root *(w)arū*, 'to guide', or to colloquial Arab. *warrā*, 'to show'. In any case *hôrâ*, 'to instruct', is well attested in Hebrew, *cf.* Pr. iv. 4; Jb. vi. 24, viii. 10, *etc.*, and the noun *môreh*, 'teacher', *e.g.* Pr. v. 13; *tôrâ* therefore may be rendered by 'instruction'.

b. The origin of tôrâ

Such instruction is given by fathers, or the wise men who address the pupil as 'son' (Pr. iii. 1, vi. 23, vii. 2, xiii. 14), or by mothers (Pr. i. 8, vi. 20, xxxi. 26). Its parallels are *mûsār*, 'direction', *ḥoḵmâ*, 'wisdom', and especially *miṣwâ*, 'commandment'. In most instances, however, the instruction stems not from human beings, but from God. *Tôrâ* is never used when describing direct communication between God and men; therefore it is lacking in the stories of Genesis (with the exception of Gn. xxvi. 5 only). *Tôrâ* is given by God, but through human intermediaries, such as Moses, priests, prophets, or the Servant of the Lord (Is. xlii. 4).

From the beginning the term *tôrâ* was used to describe single instructions, decisions taken in concrete dilemmas. A good example is to be found in Hg. ii. 11–13, where the priests' decision is asked in a matter of ritual cleanness. The priests' decision, their directive for the behaviour of the community, is called *tôrâ*, 'instruction'. The task of delivering such directives has been entrusted to the priests by God (Mal. ii. 6, 7), and their decisions therefore have divine authority. Important decisions have a longer life than the situation which called them forth; they are retained by the people whose life they govern. Oral tradition eventually brings these single decisions together into small lists of 'instructions' which are made known by the priests who are not only the revealers of the divine decisions, but also transmit these decisions to the next generation.

In due time collections of *tôrôṯ* are put into writing. Such collections of directives for ritual or other purposes are then also called a *tôrâ*, often in the singular, though the plural also occurs. Such a written *tôrâ* is guarded by the priests at the sanctuary (Dt. xxxi. 24–26). At the end of this development the whole of the Pentateuch or even the whole of the Old Testament is quoted as 'the *tôrâ*'. Divine instruction therefore was part of the task of priests, but while giving divine instruction the priests performed a prophetic function, as the authority of their *tôrâ* depended on revelation. So the prophets as well often gave *tôrâ* (Is. i. 10, viii. 16, 20, xxx. 9, 10). This does not mean, however, that there was not any *tôrâ* before the prophets of the 8th century raised their voice; Ho. viii. 12 expressly mentions a written collection of *tôrôṯ*, and in general we may say that the prophetic admonitions would have had little sense for their first hearers without the existence of a well-known and generally accepted authoritative *tôrâ*. Just as the early prophets brought their messages in rhythmical, poetical form, divine instruction often seems to have had a fixed poetical scheme, which certainly recommended itself for mnemonic purposes. In Ex. xxi. 12 ff., *e.g.*, a series of verses, each consisting of 3–2 metrical stresses, and all ending on 'shall be surely put to death', has been detected. In the same way we find in Dt. xxvii. 15 ff. twelve lines, each of four stresses, and all beginning with 'cursed be he that . . .'. The decalogue and its counterparts (Ex. xx. 1–17; Dt. v. 6–21; Ex. xxxiv. 10–26) show a somewhat more advanced form, in which metrical interest does not play an important rôle any more.

c. The Book of the Covenant

Alongside these smallest collections (*cf.* also Pss. xv. 2–5, xxiv. 4–6), which describe the religious and moral attitude the Lord demands from those who belong to the people of His covenant, larger collections of a more technical nature are to be found. There is no reason to suppose that the small collections as such must be older than the larger ones; the difference is accounted for by the difference in aim: the small collections for popular usage and instruction, the larger as handbooks for priests and judges.

A very old larger collection is the so-called Book of the Covenant (Ex. xxi–xxiii). Most scholars nowadays admit that this book must date from pre-royal times (see COVENANT, BOOK OF). Whereas the 'categoric' commandments in this collection ('Ye shall not afflict any widow or fatherless child') are supposed by Alt to derive from Israelite priestly revelation of divine instruction, the same scholar maintains that the 'casuistic' commandments ('If a thief be found breaking up, and be smitten that he die, there shall no blood be shed for him') find their origin in Canaanite customary law, taken over by the Israelites after the invasion of Canaan. In that case the Book of the Covenant, as it stands now, must be post-Mosaic. Another argument for post-Mosaic dating has often been brought forward, the fact that it presupposes a society in which agriculture plays an important rôle (Ex. xxii. 1–4, 5, 6, 29, xxiii. 10, 11, 14–16). But during their sojourn in Goshen the Israelites certainly were not a nomadic society; one may suppose that they brought along, when migrating into Egypt, elements from Canaanite customary law, and the Book of the Covenant therefore could be described as a codification of the rules prevailing among the Hebrews in Egypt, enriched by the 'categoric' commandments obtained by priestly-prophetic revelation. If that be true there is nothing against the assumption of Mosaic authorship.

d. The Deuteronomic Code

Another easily recognizable collection of laws is the Deuteronomic code, the legal prescriptions of which are found in Dt. xii–xxv. Though it is still very probable that it was this code whose recovery by Josiah is described in 2 Ki. xxii, it cannot be maintained that the prescriptions of this code date from the reign of Josiah or shortly before that period. Many of its regulations betray an archaic character, and if we are not prepared to deny the historical value of the books of Chronicles the influence of certain passages from Deuteronomy is traceable in the centuries preceding Josiah (*cf.* Dt. xvii. 8–13 with 2 Ch. xix. 5–11; Dt. xxiv. 16 with 2 Ch. xxv. 4). Moreover, the analogy with other ancient Oriental codes induces us to assume that the Deuteronomic compilation must have had a prologue and an epilogue, to be found in the chapters preceding xii and following xxv. An early date for the main corpus of Deuteronomy therefore seems indicated; this assumption does not exclude, however, that a new edition in Josiah's time offered the opportunity, as well in the prologue and epilogue as in the legislative kernel, to expand upon the ancient original. That would account for the fact that the institution of kingship plays such an unimportant rôle in Deuteronomy, though it is mentioned in Dt. xvii. 14–20 (with mental references to 1 Sa. viii and 1 Ki. x. 26–xi. 8). See DEUTERONOMY.

e. The law of holiness

A third compilation of laws is the so-called 'law of holiness' found in Lv. xvii–xxvi, a compilation of ritual and moral prescriptions which centre around the tabernacle, the priests officiating there, and the nation which supports this cult. Ritual as well as moral holiness are described as the essential characteristics of the nation which by the delivery from Egypt and the conclusion of the covenant has become the Lord's property. Many prescriptions have a sharp edge against Canaanite ritual and social practice. Based on Mosaic principles, the laws reflect the struggle against Canaanite culture. The keyword of this compilation is Lv. xxi. 8: 'for I the Lord, which sanctify you, am holy', often shortened into 'I am the Lord'. This 'law of holiness' has influenced the book of Ezekiel, and therefore is certainly pre-exilic; its separate ordinances often go back to the time of Israel's wanderings (see LEVITICUS).

f. Later developments

The same holds true for many other regulations which in general reflect the rules governing the cult in the Jerusalem sanctuary. It is evident that after the foundation of this Temple the officiating priesthood in general did not create new customs, but continued the ritual as formerly performed around the tabernacle and in sanctuaries like those in Shiloh and Gibeon. Even if prescriptions for sacrifice as laid down in Lv. i–vii in their written form could be proved to exist since the Exile only, there is no doubt that, though unwritten, their contents were observed from time immemorial at Israel's sanctuaries. Gradually the different compilations were brought together, their historical introductions were imbedded in the great historical relation of Israel's origins, and the result was the Pentateuch in its final form as proclaimed by Ezra (Ne. viii, *c.* 450 BC).

This does not mean, however, that Ezra was the author of substantial parts of the Pentateuch. The mere fact that the Samaritans, mortal foes of the work of Ezra and Nehemiah, have the same Pentateuch which differs from the Jewish copy in very immaterial details only, is sufficient proof that the Pentateuch already existed in Ezra's day. But it was Ezra who made the Pentateuch into the base of the whole of Jewish life. By his work *tôrâ* became the constitution of the state, the base of Jewish society, and the law, in the legal meaning of the word, enforced by state authority, regulating every detail in the religious, ritual, and moral life of every individual.

g. Biblical law compared with other ancient codes

Archaeological researches of this century have yielded many ancient Oriental codes. We have, apart from smaller and older Sumerian fragments, the Accadian laws of Eshnunna (1850 BC, *ANET*, pp. 161–163); the Sumerian code of Lipit-Ishtar (a few decades younger, *ANET*, pp. 159–161); the code of Hammurabi, the longest and best preserved of all (1700 BC, *ANET*, pp. 163–180); the Hittite laws (15th century?, *ANET*, pp. 188–196); the Middle Assyrian laws (12th century, *ANET*, pp. 180–188). All these compilations contain chiefly regulations of the 'casuistic' type, starting with 'if . . .'. There is, therefore, a certain resemblance between the ancient Oriental codes in general and some of the biblical injunctions. The material resemblances have been greatly exaggerated; even the most quoted example, the laws concerning the 'goring ox', is not at all convincing; there are seven points of difference between the biblical and the Mesopotamian regulations.

More important than certain accidental resemblances between separate paragraphs is a comparison between biblical and Oriental law in general. In biblical law the divine origin is stressed nearly everywhere, giving to the injunctions their authority. Indeed, the whole of the *tôrâ* is considered as the most striking instance of the Lord's favour to His chosen people (Ps. cxlvii. 19, 20). In the Oriental codes religion plays only a subordinate part; it is the king, not the divinity, who gives his authority to the code. In popular literature it is often mentioned that the bas-relief at the top of the stele of Hammurabi depicts the sun-god giving his laws to the king; in reality this scene shows us the god investing the king with the symbols of rulership (ring and staff; see *IBA*, fig. 24). In general, the Oriental codes deal with legal matters only, leaving morals and religious exhortations to other branches of literature. In the biblical *tôrâ* legal, moral, and religious prescriptions form one inseparable unit.

To the modern mind this unity of ethical values, religious ritual, and judicial prescriptions makes a baffling impression; in this respect the Oriental codes are more 'modern' than the biblical ones. For the biblical mind, however, the separation of religion from morals and of morals from law which we see today would be proof of a most unhealthy condition of society. One of the effects of the blending of religion, morals, and law is the admonitory character biblical law often assumes. In contrast to all ancient Oriental codes biblical prescriptions often contain some motivation which appeals to the religious and ethical sense of the hearer—the so-called motive clauses which, though superfluous from a legalistic standpoint, are essential parts of biblical *tôrâ*.

A striking feature in Israel's legislation are the numerous paragraphs which protect the rights of the weak, *e.g.* the blind (Lv. xix. 14; Dt. xxvii. 18), the deaf (Lv. xix. 14), the widows and fatherless children (Ex. xxii. 21–22; Dt. xxiv. 17, *etc.*), the 'strangers' (*gērîm*, Ex. xxiii. 9; Lv. xix. 10, *etc.*), the poor (Ex. xxiii. 6; Dt. xv. 7–11), the debtors who sold themselves into slavery (Ex. xxi. 1–11; Dt. xv. 12–18), and even the born slaves (Ex. xxiii. 12). The laws concerning the sabbath, the sabbatical year, and the jubilee, and those regulating religious festivals (*e.g.* Dt. xiv. 29, xvi. 11, 14) point to the same social attitude, in sharp contrast, for example, to the Hammurabi code, in which the tendency to secure the interests of the ruling classes is prevailing. Again, Dt. xxiii. 15 stands in sharp contrast to the Bab. laws concerning fugitive slaves. In this respect biblical law is certainly more 'modern' than any ancient code.

As a final difference between the *tôrâ* of the Bible and the ancient codes may be mentioned the historical setting of the Pentateuchal laws; very often the special circumstances which led to the revelation of new stipulations are mentioned (*e.g.* Lv. x, xxiv. 10–16; Nu. xv. 32–36). Though the prologues of Oriental codes often contain historical allusions, the laws themselves are free from all historical indications; they are timeless abstractions. The historical setting of biblical law is the more remarkable because at the same time there is a prophetic and even eschatological tendency in the laws of the Pentateuch; these are the laws given with an eye to a future event, the invasion of Canaan where the theocracy is still to be founded. The laws regulate everything which is of importance for this theocracy; civil laws, as, *e.g.*, the law of contracts, are not written down in the sacred documents, though doubtless they must have existed, albeit in oral form.

h. Tôrâ in the life of Israel

The influence of the *tôrâ* on the life of Israel must have been considerable, even in times when contemporary authors deplore its neglect. We have remarked above that prophecy in Israel presupposes the existence of oral or written *tôrâ* (*cf.* also Mi. vi. 8; Ho. iv. 2; Je. vii. 9). Books such as Judges, Samuel, and Kings present Israel's history from the viewpoint of the *tôrâ*, indicating that periods of obedience to the divine injunctions were times of material and spiritual prosperity, whereas neglect of the *tôrâ* always brought calamities over Israel. Psalms i, xix, and cxix glorify the *tôrâ* as God's greatest gift, and even in the book of Proverbs, where *tôrâ*, as we have seen, often has the meaning of human instruction, divine law is praised as the principle of all wisdom and happiness (see Pr. xxviii. 4, 7, 9, xxix. 18). The final proclamation of the Pentateuch as the textbook of all *tôrâ*, coinciding as it did with the extinguishing of the prophetical spirit, led to the rise of a new kind of spiritual leader, the 'scribes', with Ezra as their prototype (Ezr. vii. 6; Ne. viii. 1–8). Hand in hand with their work went the shifting of Israel's spiritual centre from the Temple to the synagogue. In the *diaspora* the *tôrâ* proved more important than the sacrificial cult of Jerusalem. It was translated into the languages of the countries Jews were living in. The translation of the word *tôrâ* into Gk. *nomos* has often been criticized, and not without foundation, as *tôrâ*, as we have seen, has a wider and deeper meaning, and above all implicates, more than *nomos*, a living and merciful God as the giver of this 'instruction'. One should not forget, however, that the LXX in this respect had a predecessor in the Aramaic parts of Ezra, where *tôrâ* is rendered by the Aramaic (originally Persian) word *dāṯ*, which in Ezr. vii. 26 is used both of Persian state-law and of divine *tôrâ*. Nevertheless, it is true that in such a way the first steps have been made along a path which ultimately led to a purely legalistic conception of the *tôrâ* as found among leading circles in Jewry in New Testament times. In this conception the living and merciful Lord disappears behind legal paragraphs and the commentaries thereupon.

BIBLIOGRAPHY. G. Oestborn, *Tōrā in the Old Testament*, 1945; J. Begrich, 'Die priesterliche Tora', in P. Volz, F. Stummer, and J. Hempel, *Werden und Wesen des Alten Testaments*, 1936, pp. 63–88; A. Alt, *Die Ursprünge des israelitischen Rechts*, 1934; L. Köhler, *Die hebräische Rechtsgemeinde*, 1931; B. Gemser, 'The importance of the motive clause in Old Testament law', *Supplements to VT*, I, 1953, pp. 50–66; J. A. Wilson, E. A. Speiser, *etc.*, *Authority and Law in the Ancient Orient* (Supplement to the *Journal of the American Oriental Society*, 17), 1954.

A. VAN S.

II. IN THE NEW TESTAMENT

a. The meaning of the term

There is much flexibility in the use of the term 'law' (*nomos*) in the New Testament.

1. Frequently it is used in the canonical sense to denote the whole or part of the Old Testament writings. In Rom. iii. 19a it clearly refers to the Old Testament in its entirety; Paul has quoted from various parts of the Old Testament in the preceding context, and he must be understood as culling these quotations from what he calls 'the law'. But the flexibility of his use of the term is apparent. For, when he speaks of those 'under the law' in the next clause, 'law' in this instance has a different meaning. It is likely that this broader denotation comprising the Old Testament as a whole is the sense in Rom. ii. 17–27. It is likewise apparent in the usage of our Lord on several occasions (*cf.* Mt. v. 18; Lk. xvi. 17; Jn. viii. 17, x. 34, xv. 25).

But the term is also used in a more restricted canonical sense to designate a part of the Old Testament. In the expression 'the law and the prophets' it will have to be understood as comprising the whole of the Old Testament not included in 'the prophets' (*cf.* Mt. v. 17, vii. 12, xi. 13, xxii. 40; Lk. xvi. 16; Acts xiii. 15; Rom. iii. 21b). In a still more restricted sense it is used to denote the Pentateuch as distinct from the other two main divisions of the Old Testament (*cf.* Lk. xxiv. 44). There are some instances in which it is uncertain whether 'the law of Moses' refers merely to the Pentateuch or is used in the more inclusive sense to denote the rest of the Old Testament not included in 'the prophets' (*cf.* Jn. i. 45; Acts xxviii. 23). It is possible that, since the simple term 'the law' can be used in a more inclusive sense, so 'the law of Moses' could even be understood as embracing more than was strictly Mosaic. This again is symptomatic of the flexibility of terms in the usage of the New Testament, arising, in this connection, from the fact that the expression 'the law and the prophets' is a convenient designation of the Old Testament in its entirety.

2. There are instances in which the term designates the Mosaic administration dispensed at Sinai. This use is particularly apparent in Paul (*cf.* Rom. v. 13, 20; Gal. iii. 17, 19, 21a). Closely related to this denotation is the use by Paul of the expression 'under the law' (1 Cor. ix. 20; Gal. iii. 23, iv. 4, 5, 21; *cf.* Eph. ii. 15; 'of the law' in Rom. iv. 16). This characterization, in these precise connections, means to be under the Mosaic economy or, in the case of 1 Cor. ix. 20, to consider oneself as still bound by the Mosaic institutions. The Mosaic economy as an administration had divine sanction and authority during the period of its operation. This use of the term 'under law' must not be confused with another application of the same expression which will be dealt with later.

3. Frequently the term is used to designate the law of God as the expression of God's will. The instances are so numerous that only a fraction can be cited (Rom. iii. 20, iv. 15, vii. 2, 5, 7, 8, 9, 12, 16, 22, viii. 3, 4, 7, xiii. 8, 10; 1 Cor. xv. 56; Gal. iii. 13; 1 Tim. i. 8; Jas. i. 25, iv. 11). The abiding obligation and sanctity of the law as the expression of God's character as holy, just, and good lie on the face of such references. The obligation for men involved is expressed in terms of being 'under law' (1 Cor. ix. 21, *ennomos*).

4. On occasion 'law' is used as the virtual synonym of law specially revealed in contrast with the work of the law natively inscribed on the heart of man (Rom. ii. 12–14). It is to be understood that law in the other senses is law specially revealed. But in the instance cited attention is focused on this consideration because of the

contrast respecting mode of revelation. There is no indication that a different law is in view. The emphasis falls upon the greater fulness and clearness of special revelation and the correlative increase of responsibility for the recipients.

5. In varying forms of expression 'law' is used in a depreciatory sense to denote the status of the person who looks to the law, and therefore to works of law, as the way of justification and acceptance with God. The formula 'under law' has this signification (Rom. vi. 14, 15; Gal. v. 18). As indicated above, this use of the formula is not to be confused with the same when applied to the Mosaic dispensation (*cf.* Gal. iii. 23 and others cited). Interpretation of the New Testament, particularly of the Pauline Epistles, has been complicated by failure to recognize the distinction. The person who is 'under law' in the sense of Rom. vi. 14 is in bondage to sin in its guilt, defilement, and power. But this was not the consequence of being under the Mosaic economy during the period from Moses to Christ. Nor is 'under law', in this sense, to be confused with a similar term as it applies to a believer in Christ (1 Cor. ix. 21). Of the same force as 'under law' in this depreciatory sense is the expression 'of law' (Rom. iv. 14; Gal. iii. 18; Phil. iii. 9); and the phrase 'of works of law' (Rom. iii. 20; Gal. ii. 16, iii. 2, 5, 10) refers to the same notion. 'Apart from works of law' (Rom. iii. 28) expresses the opposite. Several expressions are to be interpreted in terms of this concept and of the status it denotes. When Paul says, 'a righteousness without law has been manifested' (Rom. iii. 21), he means a righteousness apart from works of law, and therefore antithetical to a works-righteousness. When he says that we have been put to death to the law and discharged from the law (Rom. vii. 4, 6), he refers to the breaking of that bond that binds us to the law as the way of acceptance with God (*cf.* also Gal. ii. 19). Law as law, as commandment requiring obedience and pronouncing its curse upon all transgression, does not have any potency or provision for the justification of the ungodly. The contrast between law-righteousness, which is our own righteousness, and the righteousness of God provided in Christ is the contrast between human merit and the gospel of grace (*cf.* Rom. x. 3; Gal. ii. 21, v. 4; Phil. iii. 9). Paul's polemic in the Epistles to the Romans and Galatians is concerned with that antithesis.

6. Law is sometimes used in the sense of an operating and governing principle. In this sense Paul speaks of 'the law of faith' (Rom. iii. 27), which is contrasted with the law of works. The contrast is that between the principle of faith and that of works. It is the same idea that offers the best interpretation of the word 'law' in Rom. vii. 21, 23, 25b, viii. 2.

There is thus great diversity in the denotation of the word 'law', and sometimes there is deep-seated difference in connotation. The result is that a meaning totally diverse from that intended by the New Testament speaker or writer would be imposed upon his words if we did not appreciate the differentiation which appears in the usage. There are instances, especially in Paul, where transition from one meaning to another appears in adjacent clauses. In Rom. iii. 21, if we did not appreciate the two distinct senses of the word, there would be patent contradiction. In Rom. iv. 14 the expression 'of law' is exclusive of faith. However, in verse 16 'of the law' is not exclusive of faith, for those of the law are represented as having the promise made sure to them. Different senses are thus demanded. There are other classifications beyond those given above that other nuances of meaning and application would suggest. And on numerous occasions it is difficult to ascertain what the precise denotation is. In the main, however, when the distinctions given above are recognized, interpretation will be relieved of frequent distortions and needless difficulties will be resolved.

b. Law and gospel

The foregoing analysis makes it apparent how important is the question of the relation which a believer sustains to the law of God. To be 'under law' in one sense (Rom. vi. 14) excludes a person from the enjoyment of the grace which the gospel imparts; to be 'under law' is the opposite of being 'under grace' and means that the person is the bondslave of the condemnation and power of sin. In this sense, therefore, it is by the gospel that we are delivered from the law (Rom. vii. 6) and put to death to the law (Rom. vii. 4)—'we died to that wherein we were held' (*cf.* Gal. ii. 19). The gospel is annulled if the decisiveness of this discharge is not appreciated. In that event we have fallen away from grace and Christ becomes of no effect (*cf.* Gal. v. 4).

But this is not the whole account of the relation of law and gospel. Paul said also in the heart of his exposition and defence of the gospel of grace, 'Do we then make void the law through faith? God forbid: yea, we establish the law' (Rom. iii. 31). As a believer he protests that he consents unto the law that it is good, that he delights in the law of God after the inward man, that with the mind he serves the law of God (Rom. vii. 16, 22, 25), and that the aim of Christ's accomplishment was that the righteousness of the law might be fulfilled in those who walk not after the flesh but after the Spirit (Rom. viii. 4). When we look for an example of the law he had in mind we find it in Rom. vii. 7. And no doubt can remain that in Rom. xiii. 9 he provides us with concrete examples of the law which love fulfils, showing thereby that there is no incompatibility between love as the controlling motive of the believer's life and conformity to the commandments which the law of God enunciates. The conclusion is inescapable that the precepts of the Decalogue have relevance to the believer as the criteria of that manner of life which love to God and to our neighbour dictates. The same apostle uses terms which are to the same effect as that of being 'under law' when he says, 'being not without law to God, but under law to Christ' (1 Cor. ix. 21). In respect of obligation he is not divorced from the law of God, he is not lawless in reference to God. And this is validated and exemplified in his being bound to the law of Christ.

When Paul says that 'love is the fulfilling of the law' (Rom. xiii. 10) it is obvious that the commandments appealed to in the preceding verse are examples of the law in view. But by the words 'if there be any other commandment' he intimates that he has not enumerated all the commandments. The distinction is, therefore, that 'the law' is the generic term and the commandments are the specific expressions. Hence, although the apostle John does not speak in terms of fulfilling the law, the emphasis placed upon the necessity of keeping and doing the commandments (1 Jn. ii. 3, 4, iii. 22, 24, v. 2, 3) is to the same effect. And when he writes that 'whoso keepeth his word, in him verily is the love of God perfected' (1 Jn. ii. 5), he is pointing to what he elsewhere defines as that of which the love of God consists, namely, that 'we keep his commandments' (1 Jn. v. 3). The sum is that the keeping of God's commandments is the practical expression of that love apart from which we know not God and our Christian profession is a lie (*cf.* 1 Jn. ii. 4, iv. 8). John's teaching is the reproduction of our Lord's, and it is John who records for us Jesus' corresponding injunctions (Jn. xiv. 15, 21, xv. 10). It is also significant that our Lord Himself should enforce the necessity of keeping commandments by appealing to His own example of keeping the Father's commandments and thus abiding in and constraining the Father's love (*cf.* Jn. xv. 10, x. 17, 18).

No New Testament writer is more jealous for the fruits that accompany and vindicate faith than James, the author of the Epistle bearing his superscription. This jealousy is the distinctive feature of his Epistle. The criterion by which these fruits are to be assessed is 'the perfect law of liberty' (Jas. i. 25). James, like other New Testament writers, is well aware that love is the motive power. The 'royal law' is 'Thou shalt love thy neighbour as thyself' (Jas. ii. 8). But for James also neither love nor law is conceived of apart from the concrete examples of law and expressions of love in commandments, instances of which he provides (Jas. ii. 11). It is by this law that we shall be judged (Jas. ii. 12); it is in this law we are to continue (Jas. i. 25); it is this law we are to keep in each of its demands (Jas. ii. 10); it is this law we are to perform (Jas. iv. 11).

The reason for this sustained appeal to the law of God as the norm by which the conduct of the believer is to be judged and by which his life is to be governed resides in the relation of the law to the character of God. God is holy, just, and good. Likewise 'the law is holy, and the commandment holy, and just, and good' (Rom. vii. 12). The law is, therefore, the reflection of God's own perfections. In a word, it is the transcript of God's holiness as the same comes to expression for the regulation of thought and behaviour consonant with His glory. We are to be holy in all manner of life because He who has called us is holy (1 Pet. i. 15, 16). To be relieved of the demands which the law prescribes would contradict the relation to God which grace establishes. Salvation is salvation from sin, and 'sin is the transgression of the law' (1 Jn. iii. 4). Salvation is, therefore, to be saved from transgression of the law and thus saved to conformity unto it. Antinomian bias strikes at the nature of the gospel. It says, in effect, let us continue in sin.

A believer is re-created after the image of God. He therefore loves God and his brother also (1 Jn. iv. 20, 21). And because he loves God he loves what mirrors God's perfection. He delights in the law of God after the inward man (Rom. vii. 22). Obedience is his joy, disobedience the plague of his heart. The saint is destined for conformity to the image of God's Son (Rom. viii. 29) and he is re-made after the pattern of Him who had no sin and could say, 'yea, thy law is within my heart' (Ps. xl. 8).

BIBLIOGRAPHY. J. Durham, *The Law Unsealed*, 1802; S. H. Tyng, *Lectures on the Law and the Gospel*, 1849; W. S. Plumer, *The Law of God as Contained in the Ten Commandments*, 1864; P. H. Eldersveld, *Of Law and Love*, 1954; C. H. Dodd, 'Ennomos Christou' in *Studia Paulina*, 1953, pp. 96–110; C. H. Dodd, *Gospel and Law*, 1953; E. F. Kevan, *The Evangelical Doctrine of Law*, 1955; H. N. Ridderbos, *When the Time Had Fully Come*, 1957. See also ETHICS, BIBLICAL.

J.M.

LAWGIVER (Heb. *meḥōqēq*; Gk. *nomothetēs*). The word occurs only seven times; all of the six Old Testament occurrences are in poetry. In Gn. xlix. 10; Nu. xxi. 18; Ps. lx. 7 (= Ps. cviii. 8) the rendering 'staff' or 'sceptre' makes better sense in context and with parallels. Dt. xxxiii. 21; Jdg. v. 14; Is. xxxiii. 22 ascribe judicial leadership to Gad, Manasseh, and the Lord. James (iv. 12) rebukes censoriousness among his readers by reminding them that God alone is judge.

The idea is much more widespread. In particular, Christ is characterized as Lawgiver by His respect for the Mosaic Law (Mt. v. 17, 18), and by comparison with Moses (Mt. xvii. 3; Jn. i. 17). The superiority of Christ is emphasized in His own pronouncements (Mt. v. 22, *etc.*, xxii. 36–40) and elsewhere by stressing His status (Gal. iii. 19; Heb. vii. 11), the scope of His law (Rom. x. 4, xiii. 8 ff.), and its spiritual nature (Rom. vii, viii; Jas. i. 25, *etc.*).

P.A.B.

LAWYER. The New Testament title *nomikos* was used of the scribes synonymously with *grammateus* and *nomodidaskalos*. All scribes were originally students of Scripture, but by the 2nd century BC lay scribes had begun to expound the minutiae of the law without direct reference to Scripture. Lawyers had seats in the Sanhedrin (Mt. xvi. 21; Lk. xxii. 66; Acts iv. 5).

R.K.H.

LAYING ON OF HANDS. Actions with the hands were an important part of ancient religious ritual, as, for example, in prayer (1 Ki. viii. 54; 1 Tim. ii. 8) and invocation of divine blessing (Lv. ix. 22; Ecclus. l. 20; Lk. xxiv. 50). Jacob blessed the sons of Joseph by laying (*šîṯ*) his hands upon their heads (Gn. xlviii. 8–20), and Jesus similarly blessed children brought to Him (Mk. x. 16; Mt. xix. 13–15). Jesus also touched (*e.g.* Mk. i. 41, vii. 33), or laid His hands on, the sick (Mk. v. 23, vi. 5, vii. 32, viii. 23, 25; Mt. ix. 18; Lk. iv. 40, v. 13, xiii. 13), as did the apostles (Acts ix. 12, 17, xxviii. 8; *cf.* longer ending of Mk. xvi. 18). The action was symbolic of spiritual blessing flowing from one person to another (*cf.* Mk. v. 30).

I. IN THE OLD TESTAMENT

On the day of atonement Aaron placed (*sāmaḵ*) his hands on the head of the goat which was to be sent into the wilderness and confessed the people's sins over it, thus putting them upon the goat (Lv. xvi. 21). A similar rite accompanied the burnt, peace, sin, and ordination offerings (*e.g.* Lv. i. 4, iii. 2, iv. 4; Nu. viii. 12), indicating the 'identification' of the people with their offering. (In Lv. xxiv. 14 (*cf.* Susanna 34) the people who put their hands upon a blasphemer were probably 'thrusting' his guilt upon him.)

The Levites, who as priests represented the people before God, were ordained by the people placing their hands upon them (Nu. viii. 10). Moses ordained his successor Joshua by placing his hands upon him and thus investing him with some of his authority (Nu. xxvii. 18–23). This passage describes Joshua as 'a man in whom is the spirit' before his ordination, but Dt. xxxiv. 9 states that he was full of the spirit of wisdom because Moses had laid his hands upon him. The implication would appear to be that a worthy person, possessed of the divine Spirit, received additional spiritual gifts when commissioned for service by this rite. At the same time the rite indicated a transfer of authority.

II. IN THE NEW TESTAMENT

In the New Testament baptism and the reception of the Spirit were on occasion accompanied by the laying on of hands. In Acts viii. 14–19 the gift of the Spirit was conferred only when baptism had been followed by apostolic laying on of hands. It is unlikely that the laying on of hands by Ananias in Acts ix. 12, 17 (where it precedes baptism) is to be understood similarly. Acts xix. 6 links laying on of hands with baptism and the gift of the Spirit expressed in tongues and prophecy, and Heb. vi. 2 refers to teaching about baptisms and laying on of hands, probably as instruction given to new converts. Elsewhere, however, the gift of the Spirit was given without mention of laying on of hands, and once even before baptism (Acts x. 44–48), and it is unlikely that in the New Testament period baptism was always accompanied by laying on of hands.

Following the Old Testament analogies and what was almost certainly contemporary rabbinic practice, laying on of hands was also the rite of ordination for Christian service. After the congregation had chosen the seven 'deacons' they (or possibly the apostles) prayed and laid hands on them (Acts vi. 5 f.); similarly, the church at Antioch prayed and laid hands on Barnabas and Saul for mission work (Acts xiii. 3). In 1 Tim. v. 22 Timothy is urged not to be hasty in laying on of hands; this may refer to the ordination of elders or to the restoration of backsliders to fellowship with an act of blessing. 2 Tim. i. 6 refers to Timothy's own reception of the gift of God for the work of the ministry by the laying on of Paul's hands. *Cf.* 1 Tim. iv. 14, where, however, it is the 'presbytery' which laid hands on him. The simplest and best solution is that Paul and the local elders were associated in the act, but D. Daube thinks that the phrase in question means 'ordination to the rank of presbyter'. Such ordination, carried out under divine guidance (Acts xiii. 3; *cf.* 1 Tim. i. 18), was an outward sign that God gave to the person His gifts for some task of ministry in the Church, and by it the Church acknowledged the divine commission and enabling and associated itself with the Spirit in commissioning and authorizing the minister for his task.

BIBLIOGRAPHY. J. Behm, *Die Handauflegung im Urchristentum*, 1911; G. W. H. Lampe, *The Seal of the Spirit*, 1951, ch. 5; E. Lohse, *Die Ordination im Spätjudentum und im Neuen Testament*, 1951; D. Daube, *The New Testament and Rabbinic Judaism*, 1956, pp. 224 ff.

I.H.M.

LAZARUS AND DIVES. In the story, which occurs in Lk. xvi. 19–31, Dives, the rich man, is nowhere named. He failed to take notice of the plight of Lazarus, the beggar at his gate. After death Lazarus went to Abraham's bosom (*q.v.*) and Dives to Hades. It was impossible for any contact to be made between them. Nor was there any point in Abraham's sending Lazarus to the brothers of Dives, as they had sufficient in Moses and the prophets to bring them to repentance.

The story teaches the dangers of wealth in blinding men to the need of their fellows and the irrevocable decision of our eternal destiny in our life on earth. It does not suggest that poverty is a virtue and wealth a vice, for Abraham was a rich man. Dives failed to learn the unjust steward's lesson (Lk. xvi. 9). The reference to resurrection in xvi. 31 applies more naturally to that of Christ than to that of Lazarus of Bethany. See also GULF.

R.E.N.

LAZARUS OF BETHANY. Students of the New Testament know well the two sisters of the Bethany home, but they know nothing whatever about the character and the temperament of Lazarus. The theory that he may be identified with the rich young ruler is nothing more than a flight of fancy. He appears in the gospel story, not because of any shining qualities in his personality nor because of any resounding achievement, but solely because of the amazing miracle that was wrought upon him. He was perhaps quite an undistinguished sort of man, 'scarcely heard of half a mile from home', and yet it was to him that the very wonderful thing happened.

The laborious attempts made by rationalists to explain, or to explain away, the miracle are condemned by their patent absurdity. To believe, as Renan did, that the disciples arranged with Lazarus to pretend to be dead in order that Jesus might gain renown by pretending to raise him from the dead, and that Jesus agreed to take part in such an imposture, is an astounding *tour de force* of ingenious scepticism. All such absurdities must be abandoned, and the story must be taken, as it deserves to be, as a sober and a really convincing account of an actual happening.

The early part of John xi reads like the writing of an eye-witness and ear-witness of what is recorded, one who was with Jesus on the east of Jordan and who wondered why He remained two days there after He had heard of the sickness of Lazarus (verse 6); one who can record striking sayings of Jesus, such as the one about the number of the hours (verse 9) or the tremendous claim reported in verse 25; one who knows the exact distance between Bethany and Jerusalem, no doubt because he had often walked that road (verse 18); one who can report words spoken by Thomas and the other disciples (verses 8, 12–16). The facts mentioned form a small part of the many indications that the Fourth Gospel comes from an eye-witness of the deeds of Jesus and an ear-witness of His words, who was familiar with the thoughts, the fears, and the difficulties of the disciples, because he was, almost certainly, one of them, who brings to us first-hand information.

If he narrates the events in the early part of the chapter faithfully and soberly, why should he be accused of romancing when he comes to the grave of Lazarus? The *Gospel of Peter*, in its fantastic account of the resurrection of Jesus, shows us what the inventive mind of man can accomplish when it attempts to describe an event which no human eye saw; on the other hand, the quiet sobriety of the story of what happened at the grave of Lazarus seems to prove that it comes from a man who is describing something that he saw, exactly as he saw it.

Would a romancer who, according to sceptical theories, was intent on multiplying miraculous details, have been likely to represent Jesus as weeping, not long before He called Lazarus out of the grave? The tears of Jesus there may in some ways be a mystery to us, but we are not concerned with that mystery at present. The point we make is that a man who is fabricating a story about a stupendous miracle would scarcely have added a touch like that. The mention of the tears of Jesus may be regarded as an indirect confirmation of the authenticity of the narrative, since 'a cold or stony-hearted raiser of the dead would belong to the region of fiction' (E. W. Hengstenberg).

It can fairly be said that the silence of the narrative is as impressive as its contents. Not a single word of Lazarus is recorded. Nothing is told us about his experiences during 'those four days', and no revelation is made concerning the conditions of life in the other world.

'Behold a man raised up by Christ!
The rest remaineth unrevealed;
He told it not; or something sealed
The lips of that Evangelist.'

A.R.

LEAD. See MINING AND METALS.

LEAH (Heb. *lē'â*, 'wild cow' (?)). The elder daughter of the Aramaean, Laban. Through his deception she became the wife of Jacob, because of the local custom prohibiting the younger daughter from marrying before the elder (Gn. xxix. 21–30). She was, not unnaturally, jealous of her more attractive sister Rachel.

As the mother of Reuben, Simeon, Levi, Judah, Issachar, Zebulun, and Dinah she was acclaimed with Rachel as one of the builders of the house of Israel (Ru. iv. 11). Together they allied with Jacob against Laban, and when they went to meet Esau she was given a place in the middle of the procession.

Her burial took place at Machpelah, in Hebron, presumably before Jacob's descent to Egypt (Gn. xlix. 31).

M.G.

LEATHER. See ARTS AND CRAFTS.

LEAVEN (*śe'ōr*, 'leaven', 'leavened bread' in Dt. xvi. 4; *hāmēṣ*, 'anything leavened or fermented'; *cf. maṣṣâ*, 'without leaven', Lv. x. 12; Gk. *zymē*, 'leaven'; Lat. *levare*, 'to raise').

In Heb. life leaven came to play an important part, not only in bread-making, but also in law, ritual, and religious teaching. It was made originally from fine white bran kneaded with must; from the meal of certain plants such as fitch or vetch; or from barley mixed with water and then allowed to stand till it turned sour. As baking developed, leaven was produced from bread flour kneaded without salt and kept till it passed into a state of fermentation.

a. In bread-making

In bread-making the leaven was probably a piece of dough, retained from a former baking, which had fermented and turned acid. This was then either dissolved in water in the kneading-trough before the flour was added, or was 'hid' in the flour (AV 'meal') and kneaded along with it. The bread thus made was known as 'leavened', as distinct from 'unleavened' bread (Ex. xii. 15, *etc.*). See BREAD. There is no clear trace of the use of other sorts of leaven, although it has often been suggested that the Jews used also the lees of wine as yeast.

b. In law and ritual

The earliest Mosaic legislation (Ex. xxiii. 18, xxxiv. 25) prohibited the use of leaven during the

Passover (*q.v.*) and the 'feast of unleavened bread' (*azymos*) (Ex. xxiii. 15; Mt. xxvi. 17, *etc.*). This was to remind the Israelites of their hurried departure from Egypt, when without waiting to bake leavened bread they carried dough and kneading-troughs with them, baking as they wandered (Ex. xii. 24 ff.; Dt. xvi. 3, *etc.*), much as the Bedouin still do.

The prohibition on leaven, as that on honey (Lv. ii. 11), was possibly made because fermentation implied disintegration and corruption, and to the Hebrew anything in a decayed state suggested uncleanness. Rabbinical writers often used leaven as a symbol of evil and of man's hereditary corruption (*cf.* also Ex. xii. 8, 15–20). Plutarch echoes this ancient view when he describes leaven as 'itself the offspring of corruption, and corrupting the mass of dough with which it is mixed'. *Fermentatum* is used in Persius (*Sat.* i. 24) for 'corruption'.

Doubtless for this reason it was excluded also from the offerings placed upon the altar of Yahweh, only cakes made from flour without leaven (*maṣṣôṯ*, Lv. x. 12) being allowed. See also SHOWBREAD.

Two exceptions to this rule should, however, be noted (Lv. vii. 13; *cf.* Am. iv. 5). 'Leavened bread' was an accompaniment of the thank-offering, and leavened loaves were used also in the wave-offering—*i.e.* at the Feast of Pentecost.

c. In religious teaching

The figurative uses of leaven in the New Testament to a large extent reflect the former view of it as 'corrupt and corrupting'. Jesus utters warnings against the leaven of the Pharisees, Sadducees, and Herodians (Mt. xvi. 6; Mk. viii. 15): the Pharisees' hypocrisy and preoccupation with outward show (Mt. xxiii. 14, 16; Lk. xii. 1); the Sadducees' scepticism and culpable ignorance (Mt. xxii. 23, 29); the Herodians' malice and political guile (Mt. xxii. 16–21; Mk. iii. 6).

The two Pauline passages in which the word occurs support this view (1 Cor. v. 6 ff.; Gal. v. 9), with the former going on to contrast 'the leaven of malice and wickedness' with 'the unleavened bread of sincerity and truth', remembering the new significance of the old feast: that 'Christ our passover is sacrificed for us'.

No such meaning attaches, however, to Jesus' brief but profoundly significant parable which (following that of the slow-growing mustard seed) compares the kingdom of God with 'leaven which a woman took, and hid in three measures of meal, till the whole was leavened' (Mt. xiii. 33; Lk. xiii. 21), clearly an allusion to 'the hidden, silent, mysterious, but all-pervading and transforming action of the leaven in the . . . flour' (*ISBE*, III, p. 1862).

BIBLIOGRAPHY. *ISBE*; J. Lightfoot, *Horae Hebraicae*, 1859, II, pp. 232, 233; O. T. Allis, 'The Parable of the Leaven', *EQ*, XIX, 1947, pp. 254–273; R. S. Wallace, *Many Things in Parables*, 1955, pp. 22–25. J.D.D.

LEBANON. A mountain range in Syria. The name is also more loosely applied to the adjoining regions (Jos. xiii. 5), and is also that of a modern republic.

I. NAME

Heb. *Lᵉḇānôn* is derived from the root *lbn*, 'white'. The range owes this name to two factors: the white limestone of the high ridge of Lebanon and especially to the glittering snows that cap its peaks for six months of the year; *cf.* Je. xviii. 14. Lebanon is attested in ancient records from at least the 18th century BC onwards; see on history, below. The Assyrians called it *Lab'an*, then *Labnanu*; the Hittites, *Niblani*; the Egyptians, *rmnn* or *rbrn*; and the Canaanites themselves, *e.g.* at Ugarit, *Lbnn* just as in Hebrew.

II. TOPOGRAPHY

The southernmost end of the Lebanon range is a direct continuation of the hills of N Galilee, and is divided from them only by the deep east–west gorge of the lower reaches of the Litani river, which enters the sea a few miles north of Tyre. The Lebanon range is a ridge almost 100 miles long, following the south-west to north-east trend of the Phoenician coast from behind Sidon northward to the east–west valley of the Nahr el-Kebir river (the river Eleutherus of antiquity), which divides Lebanon from the next north–south mountain range extending still farther north (Nuseiri or Ansariya Mts.).

This ridge is marked by a series of peaks. From south to north, the principal ones are Gebel Rihan, Tomat, and Gebel Niha (from over 5,300 feet high to nearly 6,200 feet) behind Sidon; Gebel Baruk, Gebel Kuneiyiseh, and Gebel Sunnin (roughly 7,200 feet, 6,800 feet, and 8,500 feet high respectively) behind Beirut; Qurnet es-Sauda, the highest at about 10,000 feet, east-south-east of Tripoli; northernmost is Qurnet Aruba, about 7,300 feet high. These high mountains and the coastal strip have a good rainfall, but in the 'rain-shadow' area Damascus and the northern half of the Biqā' plain have less than 10 inches a year and must depend on stream water.

The west flanks of this range sweep right down to the Mediterranean, leaving only a narrow coastal plain for the Canaanite/Phoenician cities, and sometimes reach the sea, roads having had to be cut by man round such headlands. Typical of these is the headland of the Nahr el-Kelb just north of Beirut. The east flanks of Lebanon descend into the Biqā'. This plain, or broad vale, is highest in the vicinity of Baalbek, and it is the 'valley (*biq'aṯ*) of Lebanon' of Jos. xi. 17. It descends northwards with the Orontes and southwards with the Litani and headwater streams of the Jordan. It is the classical Coelesyria (*q.v.*; 'Hollow Syria') and is bounded along its east side by the corresponding mountain range of Antilebanon. This latter range also runs from south-west to north-east and is broken in two by the plateau from which the Barada river descends eastward to water the incredibly rich oasis of Damascus. The highest peak is Mt. Hermon (over 9,000 feet) in the southern half of the range. The structure of the whole region is clearly expressed in the diagram of D. Baly, *Geography of the Bible*, 1957, p. 11, fig. 3. For routes connecting the Biqā', Antilebanon, and Damascus, see *ibid.*, pp. 110, 111.

Mt. Hermon in Antilebanon was called Sirion by the Sidonians (*i.e.* Phoenicians), and Senir by the Amorites (Dt. iii. 9). Both names are independently attested in antiquity. Senir is mentioned as Saniru by Shalmaneser III of Assyria in 841 BC (*ANET*, p. 280b; *DOTT*, p. 48). Besides a Hittite mention of Sirion as Sariyana about 1320 BC (*ANET*, p. 205a), the use of the name Sirion for Hermon by the Canaanites/Phoenicians is confirmed by the Ugaritic texts of the 14th/13th centuries BC that picture Lebanon and Sirion as yielding timber for Baal's temple (*ANET*, p. 134a, § vi). Hermon is often thought to be the 'many-peaked mountain, mountain of Bashan' in Ps. lxviii. 15; but Baly (*op. cit.*, pp. 194, 220, 222) suggests that it could equally well be the impressive peaks of the Gebel Druze. See also BASHAN, HERMON, SENIR, SIRION.

The biblical writers sometimes define the promised land in general terms as extending 'from the wilderness to Lebanon and from the river . . . Euphrates to the western sea' (Dt. xi. 24; Jos. i. 4, RSV), *i.e.* within these south–north and east–west limits. For the Phoenician coastal cities, the Lebanon mountain ridge formed a natural barrier to invaders from inland. The Assyrian king Shamshi-Adad I reached Lab'an in the 18th century BC (*ANET*, p. 274b) and the Hittite emperor Suppiluliuma made it his south-west boundary in the 14th century BC (Mt. Niblani, *ANET*, p. 318b), without their disturbing the coastal cities to any extent.

III. RESOURCES

Lebanon was above all famous for its former dense forest cover (see fig. 158). The ample November and March rainfall and limestone ridges gave rise to many springs and streams flowing down to east and west (Ct. iv. 15; Je. xviii. 14). The coastland, Biqā', and lower mountain-slopes support garden-cultivation, olive-groves, vineyards, fruit-orchards (mulberries, figs, apples, apricots, walnuts), and small cornfields (Rawlinson, *Phoenicia*, p. 17). Higher still rises the forest-cover of myrtles and conifers, culminating in the groves of mighty cedars, of which, alas, only one or two isolated groves survive (because of excessive deforestation), the main one being at Bsharreh south-east of Tripoli (picture in L. H. Grollenberg, *Shorter Atlas of the Bible*, 1959, p. 13). The fertility and fruitfulness of the Lebanon region is reflected in scriptures such as Ps. lxxii. 16; Ct. iv. 11; Ho. xiv. 5–7, as well as in early inscriptions (Tuthmosis III, 5th and 7th campaigns, 15th century BC, *ANET*, p. 239a and b). Wild beasts also lurked there (*e.g.* 2 Ki. xiv. 9; Ct. iv. 8).

The mighty cedars were apt symbols of majesty and strength in biblical imagery; *cf.* Jdg. ix. 15; 1 Ki. iv. 33; 2 Ki. xiv. 9 (= 2 Ch. xxv. 18); Pss. xcii. 12, civ. 16; Ct. v. 15; Is. xxxv. 2, lx. 13. They were also symbols of earthly pride subject to divine wrath; *cf.* Ps. xxix. 5, 6; Is. ii. 13, x. 34; Je. xxii. 6; Ezk. xxxi. 3–14; Zc. xi. 1, 2. These forests afforded a refuge (Je. xxii. 23). But above all, Lebanon's cedars and conifers (firs, cypresses, *etc.*) furnished the finest building timber in the Ancient East, sought by the rulers of Egypt, Mesopotamia, and Syria-Palestine alike. The most celebrated of such deliveries of timber were those sent to Solomon by Hiram I of Tyre for the Temple at Jerusalem (1 Ki. v. 6, 9, 14 (= 2 Ch. ii. 8, 16), vii. 2, x. 17, 21 (= 2 Ch. ix. 20)). For the price in foodstuffs paid by Solomon for his timber, *etc.*, see FOOD (Solomon's palace food-supplies). The firs of Lebanon and Antilebanon (Sirion) provided ships for Tyre (Ezk. xxvii. 5) and sacred barges for Egypt (*ANET*, pp. 25b, 27a; *c.* 1090 BC), as well as furniture (Ct. iii. 9). Wood for the second Jerusalem Temple was also cut in Lebanon (Ezra iii. 7).

IV. HISTORY

The history of Lebanon is essentially that of the Phoenician cities on its littoral and the story of the exploitation of its splendid timber. From south to north, the Canaanite/Phoenician cities of Tyre, Ahlab, Zarephath, Sidon, Beirut, Byblos (Gebal, modern Jebail), and Simyra (north of Tripoli) all had the wealth of the Lebanon as their hinterland besides their maritime trade. For their detailed histories, see separate articles on each of these cities; see also CANAAN and PHOENICIA.

The Lebanon timber-trade goes back to the earliest times. The IVth Dynasty pharaoh Snofru fetched forty shiploads of cedars as early as *c.* 2600 BC (*ANET*, p. 227a), and various of his successors followed suit in later centuries. Byblos in particular became virtually an Egyptian dependency and its princes thoroughly assimilated to Egyptian culture, even writing their Semitic names in hieroglyphs (*cf. ANET*, p. 229a). In exchange for timber, they received handsome gold jewellery from the XIIth Dynasty pharaohs (*c.* 1900–1800 BC).

When the New Kingdom pharaohs conquered Syria they exacted a regular annual tribute of 'genuine cedar of Lebanon' (*ANET*, p. 240b: Tuthmosis III, *c.* 1460 BC), and a relief of Sethos I (*c.* 1300 BC) actually depicts the Syrian princes hewing down the timbers of Lebanon for the pharaoh (*ANEP*, p. 110, fig. 331, or Grollenberg, *Shorter Atlas of the Bible*, p. 14; *cf. ANET*, p. 254, § c, end). In later days (XXth Dynasty) the pharaohs had to pay handsomely for such timber (*cf.* Solomon), as Wenamun, envoy of Rameses XI, found to his cost (*ANET*, p. 27a).

From Canaan itself in the second millennium BC, the Ugaritic epics about Baal and Anath and Aqhat allude to 'Lebanon and its trees; Sirion, its choice cedars' providing timber for the house (*i.e.* temple) of Baal (*ANET*, p. 134a, § vi; C. H. Gordon, *Ugaritic Literature*, 1949, p. 34), and furnishing material for a bow (*ANET*, p. 151b, § vi; Gordon, *op. cit.*, p. 90).

The Assyrians, too, exacted a tribute of timber from Lebanon for temple-building—so Tiglath-pileser I, *c.* 1100 BC (*ANET*, p. 275a) and Esarhaddon about 675 BC (*ANET*, p. 291b)—but also often drew upon the Amanus forests farther north (*ANET*, pp. 276b, 278a); *cf.* here, 2 Ki. xix. 23; Is. xxxvii. 24. Nebuchadrezzar followed their example (*ANET*, p. 307; *DOTT*, p. 87). Habakkuk (ii. 17) refers to Babylonian despoliation of Lebanon, also foreseen by Isaiah (xiv. 8).

BIBLIOGRAPHY. In addition to works already cited above for particular points, see also P. K. Hitti, *Lebanon in History*, 1957, and his *History of Syria with Lebanon and Palestine*, 1951.

K.A.K.
A.K.C.

LEB-KAMAI. An artificial word (Je. li. 1), formed by the device known as Athbash (explained under SHESHACH, *q.v.*). The Heb. consonants *l-b-q-m-y* really represent *k-ś-d-y-m, i.e. kaśdîm*, 'Chaldeans'. The vowels added by the Massoretes give the word a quasi-meaning, 'the heart of those that rise up against me' (*cf.* RVmg). The verse mentions Babylon openly, so the device is here word-play rather than cipher. D.F.P.

LECTIONARY. See TEXT AND VERSIONS.

LEEKS (Heb. *ḥāṣîr*, 'herb'). Only in Nu. xi. 5; the Heb. word is elsewhere translated 'grass' or 'herb'. The leek (*Allium porrum*) has always been a great favourite in Palestine and Egypt, and is mentioned among the delicacies which the querulous Israelites hankered after during their wanderings. J.D.D.

LEES (*šᵉmārîm*, 'preserves', Is. xxv. 6; Je. xlviii. 11; Zp. i. 12). The dregs at the bottom of wine-jars. See WINE AND STRONG DRINK, and an excellent comprehensive article under 'Shemarim' in Kitto, *A Cyclopaedia of Biblical Literature*. The expression is used only figuratively in the Old Testament. J.D.D.

LEG. A number of Heb. words and one Gk. word are translated thus in the AV.

1. *kᵉrā'ayim.* This occurs chiefly in ritual passages, *e.g.* Ex. xii. 9, xxix. 17; Lv. i. 9, 13, iv. 11, *etc.* In Lv. xi. 21 it describes the bending hind-legs of locusts permitted for food, and provides an illustration of judgment in Am. iii. 12.

2. *reḡel.* This normally means 'foot', but it is used of Goliath's legs in 1 Sa. xvii. 6.

3. *šôq* means the upper leg, and is synonymous with 'thigh'. It is used of men in Dt. xxviii. 35; Ps. cxlvii. 10; Pr. xxvi. 7; Ct. v. 15; Is. xlvii. 2; Dn. ii. 33. In Jdg. xv. 8 it is translated 'hip'. It is also used with reference to animals. It is translated 'shoulder' in AV of several ritual passages, *e.g.* Ex. xxix. 22, 27; Lv. vii. 32–34, viii. 25, 26; Nu. vi. 20, *etc.*, and in 1 Sa. ix. 24 (RV 'thigh'). This was one of the choicest pieces, reserved for priests.

4. *šōḇel.* This is incorrectly translated 'leg' in AV of Is. xlvii. 2 (RV 'train').

5. Gk. *skelos.* The word occurs only in Jn. xix. 31 ff., when the legs of those crucified with Jesus were broken to hasten death. J.G.G.N.

LEGION. Legion, *legeōn* (from Lat. *legio*), used four times in the New Testament, was a division of the Roman army numbering (on paper) 6,000 men and divided into ten cohorts. Sometimes a small cavalry division or *ala* (about 120) was attached. (For the auxiliary cohorts, which had a paper strength of 1,000 each, see ARMY.) These forces have their spiritual counterpart, for Christ is able to summon twelve legions of angels to His aid (Mt. xxvi. 53).

'Legion' is also the name of the Gerasene demoniac (Mk. v. 9, 15; Lk. viii. 30), so called because of the large but indefinite number of demons which possessed him; *cf.* verse 13, '2,000 swine'. As a demon is unwilling to identify itself, it perhaps gave its number instead. Also demons prefer to be in groups or troops (Lk. viii. 2; Mt. xii. 45). J.A.B.

LEHABIM. The third son of Mizraim (Gn. x. 13; 1 Ch. i. 11). The name (*lᵉhāḇîm*) is unknown apart from these references, but many scholars would equate it with *lûḇîm* of 2 Ch. xii. 3, *etc.* (see LUBIM), which is generally identified as referring to the Libyans. In support of this is the LXX reading *Labieim* and the fact that these people, who figure in the ancient Egyp. inscriptions as *rbw*, are not elsewhere mentioned in Gn. x, unless *lûḏîm* (verse 13) is to be read for *lûḇîm*, as some scholars hold (see LUD, LUDIM). The matter therefore remains uncertain. T.C.M.

LEHI (*lᵉḥî, leḥî*, 'jawbone', Jdg. xv. 9, 14, 19; 'Ramath-lehi' in Jdg. xv. 17). The place in Judah where Samson slew a thousand men with the jawbone of an ass. The site is unknown, but see F. F. Bruce, in *NBC*, p. 253.

LEMUEL. King of Massa (*q.v.*) whose mother's instructions concerning good government and the dangers of sensuality and over-indulgence in wine are recorded in Pr. xxxi. 1–9. Modern scholars have not generally accepted the rabbinic tradition, which says that Lemuel and the names in xxx. 1 are attributes of Solomon, an attempt to credit Proverbs entirely to Solomon (*cf.* L. Ginzberg, *The Legends of the Jews*, 1946, VI, p. 277).
D.A.H.

LENDING. See DEBT, DEBTOR (*a*).

LENTILS (*'ᵃḏāšîm*, AV 'lentiles'). A small pea-like plant (*Lens esculenta*, sometimes called *Ervum lens*) of the vetch family, lentils are easily grown and are still a favourite food throughout the Near East. The parched seeds are regarded as the best food to carry on a long journey or in an emergency (*cf.* Ezk. iv. 9). Lentils formed the 'red pottage' associated with Esau in the famous story (Gn. xxv. 29–34), and were among the foods offered to David at Mahanaim (2 Sa. xvii. 28). A field of lentils is mentioned in 2 Sa. xxiii. 11, 12 as the scene of an Israelite warrior's doughty deeds against the Philistines. J.D.D.

LEOPARD. In popular English usage the word leopard, usually with a qualifying word, stands for a number of different spotted cats. It is similarly likely that Heb. *nāmēr* refers to both the true leopard and the cheetah (hunting leopard), and also to one or two other spotted wild cats of Palestine. All references are proverbial and figurative, and the precise species is therefore immaterial. Perhaps the most familiar use of this word is the proverb in Je. xiii. 23, 'Can the Ethiopian change his skin, or the leopard his spots?'

The jungle cat (*Felis chaus*) is still found in more wooded parts, especially in Galilee, but the leopard (*Felis pardus*) has probably disappeared from Israel, though still found rarely in adjacent countries. G.C.

LEPROSY. See DISEASE AND HEALING, CLEAN AND UNCLEAN.

LETHEK. See WEIGHTS AND MEASURES.

LETTER. See WRITING.

LEVI. The third son of Jacob and Leah (Gn. xxix. 34). The name (*lēwî*) is here linked with the root *lāwâ* (to join), and a play upon this meaning is found in Nu. xviii. 2, 4.

The only detail of his life known to us, apart from those events common to all Jacob's sons, is his treacherous attack on Shechem in company with Simeon (Gn. xxxiv. 25, 26). It should in fairness be noted that the natural meaning of Gn. xxxiv. 13, 27 is that the two brothers were acting with the connivance of all. The two were specially concerned because Dinah was their full sister. The two lads could carry out the massacre with the help of their father's slaves.

It has almost universally been taken for granted that Gn. xlix. 5–7 refers to this incident, but this is most doubtful. There is no validity in the versional variation in the last clause of verse 6 represented by AV, 'they digged down a wall'; the Heb. 'they houghed an ox' (RV) is seemingly contradicted by Gn. xxxiv. 28. It is better to take the tenses in verse 6 as 'perfects of experience' and render, 'For in their anger they slay men and in their wantonness they ham-string oxen' (RSV). They were cursed for a life of violence and cruelty in which Shechem was merely an early and outstanding example. Later history was to show that the loyalty of Levi's descendants to Yahweh could turn the curse to a blessing, and their division and scattering in Israel was as His representatives. None the less, the curse seems to have hit Levi very heavily. The total census figure in Nu. iii. 22, 28, 34 of males from a month upward is strikingly below all the tribal figures in Nu. i of males from twenty years upwards. No indication is given how this happened. Levi seems to have had only three sons, Gershon, Kohath, and Merari, all born before he went down with Jacob to Egypt.

Modern critical scholarship has questioned the biblical account of the origin of the tribe of Levi in various ways, but most of them have by now fallen into disfavour. We need mention only the conjecture of Lagarde that the Levites were those Egyptians that 'joined themselves' to the Israelites at the Exodus, and that of Baudissin that they were those 'joined to', *i.e.* escorting, the ark—in other words priestly servants. Much more important is Hommel's linking of *lēwî* with *lawi'a*, meaning 'priest', in Minaean N Arabian inscriptions. The facts and a valuable discussion will be found in G. B. Gray, *Sacrifice in the Old Testament*, pp. 242–245. He points out that the Minaeans *might* have borrowed the term from Israel. In fact, an overwhelming majority of scholars agree that Gn. xlix. 5–7 is proof positive that Levi must have originated as a secular tribe.

For Levi the son of Alphaeus, one of the Twelve (Mk. ii. 13), see MATTHEW. The name also occurs twice in the genealogy of our Lord (Lk. iii. 24, 29). H.L.E.

LEVIATHAN is a transliteration of a Heb. word which occurs in only five passages in the Old Testament. It is generally thought to be from a root *lāwâ*, *cf.* Arab. *lawā*, 'bend', 'twist'. Its literal meaning would then be 'wreathed', *i.e.* 'gathering itself in folds'. Some scholars have suggested that it may be a foreign loan-word, possibly of Bab. origin. The context of its use in the Old Testament indicates some form of aquatic monster. In Ps. civ. 26 it is clearly of the sea and is generally thought to be the whale, although the dolphin has been suggested. It is used twice symbolically in Is. xxvii. 1, referring to the Empires of Assyria (the 'piercing' (RV 'swift') serpent is the swift-flowing Tigris) and Babylonia (the 'crooked' (RV 'winding') serpent is the Euphrates). In Ps. lxxiv. 14 it occurs in reference to Pharaoh and the Exodus in parallel with the Heb. *tannîn*, 'sea or river monster'. This word occurs again in Ezk. xxix. 3–5 symbolically of Pharaoh and the Egyptians, where the description of its scales and jaws makes it clear that the crocodile is intended.

Leviathan is referred to twice in Job. In iii. 8 (see mg) it is generally held to be the dragon which according to popular ancient mythology was supposed to cause eclipses by wrapping its coils around the sun. The longest description of Leviathan occupies Jb. xli. 1–34, and most scholars agree that here the creature is the crocodile. Some have objected that the crocodile would not have been described as unapproachable and that there is no reference in the Old Testament to crocodiles in Palestine. However, the author probably had in mind the crocodile of the Nile, and the description of the creature's invincibility is rhetorical. The only alternative interpretation of any significance regards Leviathan as a mythical monster, perhaps to be identified with the Bab. chaos-dragon Tiamat. The word is cognate with Ugaritic *lotan*, the seven-headed monster whose description as 'the fleeing serpent, . . . the tortuous serpent' smitten by Baal is so reminiscent of the language of Is. xxvii. 1.

BIBLIOGRAPHY. C. F. Pfeiffer, 'Lotan and Leviathan', *EQ*, XXXII, 1960, pp. 208 ff.

D.G.S.

LEVIRATE LAW. See MARRIAGE (IV).

LEVITES. See PRIESTS AND LEVITES.

LEVITICAL CITIES. See PRIESTS AND LEVITES, I*a*.

LEVITICUS, BOOK OF. The third book of the Pentateuch is referred to in Jewish usage as *wayyiqrā'* ('and he called'), this being the word with which it begins in Hebrew. In the Mishnah the book is variously named *tôraṯ kôhᵃnîm*, 'priests' law', *sēp̄er kôhᵃnîm*, 'priests' book', *tôraṯ haqqorbānîm*, 'law of the offerings'; these names refer to the contents of the book. In the LXX it is called *Leueitikon* or *Leuitikon* (*sc. biblion*), 'the Levitical (book)'. The Latin Vulg. entitles it *Leviticus* (*sc. liber*), which similarly means 'the Levitical (book)'; in some Latin manuscripts the name appears as *Leviticum*. The Peshitta calls it 'the book of the priests'.

It can be objected to the name Leviticus that the book has much less to do with Levites than with priests. But the priests in question are levitical priests (*cf.* Heb. vii. 11, 'the Levitical priesthood'). The name Leviticus indicates clearly enough that the book has to do with the cult; this name may indeed have been chosen because 'Levitical' was understood in the sense of 'cultic' or 'ritual'.

I. OUTLINE OF CONTENTS

Leviticus consists mainly of laws. The historical framework in which these laws are set is Israel's residence at Sinai. The book may be divided as follows:

a. Laws concerning offerings (i. 1–vii. 38).

b. The tabernacle service put into operation (viii. 1–x. 20).

c. Laws concerning purity and impurity (xi. 1–xv. 33).

d. The great Day of Atonement (xvi. 1–34).

e. Various laws (xvii. 1–xxv. 55).

f. Promises and warnings (xxvi. 1–46).

g. Appendix: valuation and redemption (xxvii. 1–34).

As may be seen from this outline, the contents consist largely of ritual law. At the same time it must be noted that the intention is to continue the narrative of Israel's experiences at Sinai. This is evident from the first words of the book, and from the repeated formula 'And the Lord spake unto Moses' (i. 1, iv. 1, v. 14, *et passim*), with which we should compare 'And the Lord spake unto Aaron' (x. 8) and 'And the Lord spake unto Moses and to Aaron' (xi. 1, *cf.* xiii. 1, *etc.*). The historical setting must not be lost sight of. The book must be seen as part of the complete Pentateuch. It occupies its own place in the Pentateuchal narrative.

At Mt. Sinai the nation of Israel is equipped for its task, a task stated in the words 'And ye shall be unto me a kingdom of priests, and a holy nation' (Ex. xix. 6). Israel had already had committed to it the Decalogue, the Book of the Covenant, and the regulations with regard to the tabernacle. This dwelling-place for the Lord had already been set up in the midst of the camp (Ex. xl). It is possible that the laws concerning the offerings (Lv. i–vii) once existed as a separate unit (*cf.* vii. 35–38). But they fit very well into the Pentateuchal context in which they now appear. The history of sacrificial offerings, about which the book of Leviticus provides such important information, and in which Christians ought to take a special interest because we know how perfectly their inmost significance was fulfilled by the obedience of Jesus Christ, begins as early in the Pentateuch as Gn. iv. 3–5. There are also other passages in the Pentateuch before the book of Leviticus in which sacrifices and offerings are mentioned. But in Leviticus the Lord regulates the whole sacrificial service and institutes a special form of it as a means of atonement for Israel. Lv. xvii. 11 states the reason for the ban upon eating blood ('the life of the flesh is in the blood'); the ban has already been imposed in iii. 17 and vii. 26 f., but in neither of these places is the reason for it explicitly stated. It is in the light of xvii. 11 that the shedding of blood and sprinkling with blood prescribed in chapters i–vii must be viewed. This is an indication of the unity of the book.

Another indication of its unity is the fact that vii. 21 prepares us for the transition to the regulations regarding impurity, which come up for detailed treatment in chapters xi–xv. Similarly, x. 10 looks forward to the transition to the detailed distinctions between clean and unclean which we have in chapter xi. Kuenen himself had to admit that chapters xi–xv are inserted in a very appropriate position; that is certainly true. Viewed in the light of the whole book of Leviticus, the laws concerning purity and impurity point to the necessity laid upon Israel to keep sin at a distance. It is sin which brings about separation between the Lord and His people, so that they have to approach Him through the mediation of sacrifice (chapters i–vii) and priesthood (chapters viii–x). Lv. xvi. 1 follows close on xv. 31 and refers back to x. 1 f. In xx. 25 we have a clear allusion to the law concerning clean and unclean animals in chapter xi; and this verse provides a closer link between the commandments of chapters xviii–xx and those of chapters xi–xv. This does not support the view of those who accept the existence at one time of a separate Holiness Code, preserved for us in chapters xvii–xxvi. In xxi. 1–xxii. 16 expressions like those of xi. 44 f., xix. 2, xx. 7 are repeated with reference to the priests (*e.g.* xxi. 8, 'I the Lord, which sanctify you, am holy'). Lv. xxv. 1 states that the words which follow were revealed to Moses on Mt. Sinai, just as is stated of the laws summarized in vii. 37 f.

In the form in which we now possess Leviticus, it forms a well-knit and coherent whole, provided that we do not apply western standards of today to a book which arose in the East centuries ago.

The historical portion is larger than one might think at first sight (*cf.* x. 1–7, xxiv. 10–23, viii–x, and the formula 'And the Lord spake unto Moses').

Attention is also paid to marriage and chastity, the sanctification of daily life, and Israel's attitude to the commandments of her God (*cf.* xviii. 3–5, 30, xix. 1–3, 18, 37, xx. 26, xxii. 31–33, xxvi, *etc.*).

In view of the character of its contents throughout, we can call Leviticus 'the book of the holiness of Yahweh', whose fundamental requirement is 'And ye shall be holy unto me: for I the Lord am holy' (xx. 26). His holiness appears in His punishing the sin of Nadab and Abihu (x. 1–7) and that of the blasphemer (xxiv. 10–23). It is His holiness that necessitates the laws concerning offerings and food, purification and chastity, festivals and other ceremonies. The priests are indispensable as intermediaries between Yahweh and Israel. Life under the covenant is a life that must be continually regulated by all kinds of provisions. The ideal is such a lofty one that nothing but sacrifice can provide a covering for Israel before the eye of Yahweh, since Israel remains far short of His holy requirements. The blood on the altar is indispensable. This atoning blood points forward to Him who comes to fulfil, to bring to completion, all Leviticus, all the Pentateuch, all the Old Testament. So Leviticus proclaims to us 'It is finished'. It points us to our liberation; it points us also to our obligation to be holy in the sight of Him who gave His own Son as priest and sacrifice for our sins.

II. AUTHORSHIP AND COMPOSITION

The author of Leviticus is not named in the book. Yahweh does indeed speak repeatedly to Moses, to Moses and Aaron, or to Aaron; but no command is given to make a written record of what He says. We owe the contents of the book to divine revelation given at Sinai in the time of Moses (*cf.* vii. 37 f., xxvi. 46, xxvii. 34); but that does not settle the question of the authorship of Leviticus. Moses is not named as the author of any single part of the book, as he is named with regard to certain sections of Exodus (*cf.* Ex. xvii. 14, xxiv. 4, xxxiv. 27). It may be that a later writer set in order the Mosaic material of which Leviticus consists. It may equally well be that Moses himself set it in order in the form which has been handed down to us.

The question of authorship is bound up with the whole question of the composition of the Pentateuch. Leviticus is commonly assigned to P (the Priestly Code). But in P itself two separate elements are distinguished, called, for example, by Kuenen P^1 and P^2. P^1 is exilic, while P^2 is post-exilic. Other adherents of the documentary hypothesis make other distinctions, but they are all agreed that Leviticus belongs to P.

The objections to this documentary hypothesis in general are equally valid as regards their application to Leviticus. The name 'Holiness Code', given to Lv. xvii–xxvi, is due to August Klostermann, who in 1877 wrote for the *Zeitschrift für lutherische Theologie* an article entitled 'Ezechiel und das Heiligkeitsgesetz' ('Ezekiel and the Law of Holiness'), which was reprinted in his book *Der Pentateuch*: *Beiträge zu seinem Verstandnis und seiner Entstehungsgeschichte* (*The Pentateuch*: *Contributions to its understanding and the history of its composition*), 1893, pp. 368–418. The name 'Holiness Code' came into wide vogue; many found it especially apt because of the explicit and repeated emphasis on holiness and sanctification in xix. 2, xx. 7, 8, 26, xxi. 6–8, 15, 23, xxii. 9, 16, 32. It is not possible to debate the whole question here; reference should be made to the case for the separate existence of H, based upon distinctive features of style and language, as presented, *e.g.*, in S. R. Driver, *Literature of the Old Testament* (9th edn., 1913), pp. 47 ff. A close relationship is pointed out between H and Ezekiel; indeed, some have seen in Ezekiel himself the author or redactor of H, while others take the view that Ezekiel was acquainted with H. But the majority opinion is that H is earlier than Ezekiel. According to Baentsch, H is the law-code of the Exile. Elliott-Binns dates H in the closing period of the monarchy, but before Josiah (*cf.* *ZAW*, LXVII, 1955, pp. 26–40). The hypothesis of an H-document is opposed by, among others, Hoffmann, Eerdmans, Noordtzij, Clamer, and Küchler; their arguments are strong and from every point of view worthy of consideration.

None of the arguments for the view that Lv. xvii–xxvi should be regarded as a separate law-code seems to be conclusive. We must not forget that here as elsewhere the investigator of the Old Testament is greatly influenced by the attitude which he adopts to Holy Scripture as the Word of God. For example, the argument that Lv. xxvi must be dated in the time of the Exile, because this exile is foretold in that chapter, is far from doing justice to divine revelation. The absence of a special superscription at the head of Lv. xvii is best explained by the view that here the book of Leviticus continues quite ordinarily.

III. SIGNIFICANCE

Leviticus is a book of great significance from many points of view.

First of all, it provides us with a background

to all the other books of the Bible. If we wish to understand references to sacrificial offerings and ceremonies of purification, or institutions such as the sabbatical year or the year of jubilee, it is this book that we must consult.

In the second place, it is of interest from a general religious viewpoint. Thanks especially to archaeological excavation, we can compare the institutions dealt with in Leviticus with those of other peoples, *e.g.* the Phoenicians, Canaanites, Egyptians, Assyrians, Babylonians, and Hittites.

In the third place, orthodox Jews have to this day found their binding regulations—*e.g.* with regard to food—in this book. Hoffmann, a Jewish exegete of Leviticus, points out that other confessions which draw upon the Old Testament chiefly select Genesis as the subject of their study, while Jews pay special attention to Leviticus.

Fourthly, Leviticus proclaims to us who are Christians the way in which the God of Israel combats sin in Israel. He combats it by means of His institutions of sacrifice and purification—social sin by means of the sabbatical year and year of jubilee, sexual sins by means of the laws of chastity—and also by means of His promises and warnings. And in this combating of sin the book of Leviticus presents to us Christ as the means of atonement, the means of purification, the great Priest, Prophet and Teacher, the King who rules us through His ordinances. That is the abiding significance of Leviticus. It is the book of sanctification, of the consecration of life (the burnt-offering stands in the forefront of the book), the book of the avoidance and atonement of sin, the combating and removal of sin among the people of the Lord. The Day of Atonement occupies a central place in it (Lv. xvi); the ceremony of the two goats prescribed for that day reminds us that 'as far as the east is from the west, so far hath he removed our transgressions from us' (Ps. ciii. 12). See LAW; PENTATEUCH.

BIBLIOGRAPHY. A. A. Bonar, *Commentary on Leviticus*[4], 1861; S. H. Kellogg, *The Book of Leviticus, Expositor's Bible*, 1891; S. R. Driver and H. A. White, *The Book of Leviticus*, 1898; A. T. Chapman and A. W. Streane, *The Book of Leviticus, CBSC*, 1914; W. H. Gispen, *Het Boek Leviticus*, 1950; N. Micklem, *Leviticus, IB*, II, 1955; H. Cazelles, *Le Lévitique, Bible de Jérusalem*[2], 1958. W.H.G.

LIBERTINES. The Greek of Acts vi. 9 makes it difficult to determine whether the *Libertinoi*, the members of a Jewish synagogue at Jerusalem, worshipped by themselves, or with the Cyrenians, the Alexandrians, the Cilicians, and the Asiatics. The meaning of the name is equally uncertain, and this has given rise to a number of variants for this verse (notably the reading 'Libyans' for 'Libertines', which appears in the Armenian vss and the Syriac). Schürer suggests that the Libertines were Rom. freedmen descended from Jews who had been prisoners of war under Pompey (63 BC) and subsequently released. Possibly only one synagogue is referred to here (then *kai Kyrēnaiōn . . . Asias* is epexegetic of *Libertinōn*), which was attended by Jewish freedmen or their descendants from the places mentioned (so F. F. Bruce, *The Acts of the Apostles*[2], 1952, p. 156).

S.S.S.

LIBERTY. The biblical idea of liberty (freedom) has as its background the thought of imprisonment or slavery. Rulers would imprison those whom they regarded as wrongdoers (Gn. xxxix. 20); a conquered nation might be enslaved by its conqueror, or a prisoner of war by his captor, or an individual might, like Joseph, be sold into slavery. When the Bible speaks of liberty, a prior bondage or incarceration is always implied. Liberty means the happy state of having been released from servitude for a life of enjoyment and satisfaction that was not possible before. The idea of liberty appears in Scripture in its ordinary secular application (*e.g.* Ps. cv. 20; Acts xxvi. 32); but it also receives a significant theological development. This sprang from Israel's realization that such freedom from subjugation by foreigners as she enjoyed was God's gift to her. In the New Testament liberty becomes an important theological concept for describing salvation.

I. ISRAEL'S LIBERTY

At the Exodus God set Israel free from bondage in Egypt, in order that henceforth the nation might serve Him as His covenant people (Ex. xix. 3 ff., xx. 1 ff.; Lv. xxv. 55; *cf.* Is. xliii. 21). He brought them into the 'land flowing with milk and honey' (Ex. iii. 8; *cf.* Nu. xiv. 7 ff.; Dt. viii. 7 ff.), settled them there, and undertook to maintain them in political independence and economic prosperity as long as they eschewed idolatry and kept His laws (Dt. xxviii. 1–14). This meant that Israel's freedom would not depend upon her own efforts in either the military or the political realm, but on the quality of her obedience to God. Her freedom was a supernatural blessing, Yahweh's gracious gift to His own covenant people; unmerited and, apart from Him, unattainable in the first instance, and now maintained only through His continued favour. Disobedience, whether in the form of religious impiety or social injustice, would result in the loss of freedom. God would judge His people by national disaster and enslavement (Dt. xxviii. 25, 47 ff.; *cf.* Jdg. ii. 14 ff., iii. 7 ff., 12 ff., iv. 1 ff., vi. 1 ff.); He would raise up hostile powers against them, and would ultimately cause them to be deported into a land where no tokens of His favour could be expected (Dt. xxviii. 64 ff.; Am. v; 2 Ki. xvii. 6–23; *cf.* Ps. cxxxvii. 1–4).

The structure of the theological idea of liberty is here fully evident. Liberty, as the Old Testament conceives it, means, on the one hand, deliverance from created forces that would keep men from serving and enjoying their Creator, and, on the other hand, the positive happiness of living in fellowship with God under His covenant in the place where He is pleased to manifest Himself and to bless. Liberty is *from* slavery to powers that oppose God *for* the fulfilment of His claims upon one's life. Liberty is not man's own achievement, but a free gift of grace, something which apart from God's action man does not possess at all. In its continuance, liberty is a covenant blessing, something which God has promised to maintain as long as His people are faithful. Liberty does not mean independence of God; it is precisely in God's service that man finds his perfect freedom. Man can enjoy release from bondage to the created only through bondage to his Creator. Thus, the way that God sets men free from their captors and enemies is to make them His own slaves. He liberates them by bringing them to Himself (Ex. xix. 4).

The Isaianic prophecies of the release from captivity and the restoration of Jerusalem gave added religious content to the idea of liberty by stressing that these events would herald a new and unprecedented experience of joyful and satisfying fellowship with Israel's gracious God (Is. xxxv. 3–10, xliii. 14–xliv. 5, xlv. 14–17, xlix. 8–l. 3, li. 17–lii. 12, liv, lxi. 1 ff., *etc.*; *cf.* Ezk. xxxvi. 16–36, xxxvii. 15–28).

Since all members of the liberated nation were, as such, God's servants (Lv. xxv. 42, 55), Israelites who through pressure of poverty sold themselves into household service were not to be treated like foreign slaves, as mere property, in their master's hereditary possession (Lv. xxv. 44 ff.). Every seventh year they were to be released (unless they had voluntarily chosen to make their service permanent) in memory of God's release of Israel from Egyptian bondage (Dt. xv. 12 ff.). Every fiftieth year, in addition to a release of Israelite servants, alienated land was also to revert to its hereditary owner (Lv. xxv. 10). Jeremiah denounced the people because, having thus 'proclaimed liberty' for Hebrew servants, they went back on it (Je. xxxiv. 8–17).

II. THE CHRISTIAN'S LIBERTY

The full development of the idea of liberty appears in the Gospels and Pauline Epistles, where the enemies from whom God through Christ liberates His people are revealed to be sin, Satan, the law, and death.

Christ's public ministry was one of liberation. He opened it by announcing himself as the fulfilment of Is. lxi. 1: '. . . he hath anointed me . . . to preach deliverance to the captives' (Lk. iv. 16 ff.). Ignoring Zealot hankerings after a national liberation from Rome, Christ declared that He had come to set Israelites free from the state of slavery to sin and Satan in which he found them (Jn. viii. 34–36, 41–44). He had come, He said, to overthrow 'the prince of this world', the 'strong man', and to release his prisoners (Jn. xii. 31 f.; Mk. iii. 27; Lk. x. 17 f.). Exorcisms (Mk. iii. 22 ff.) and healings (Lk. xiii. 16) were part of this work of dispossession. Christ appealed to these (Lk. xi. 20; *cf.* Mt. xii. 28) as proof positive of the coming among men of the kingdom of God (*i.e.* the promised eschatological state in which men effectively receive God's forgiveness and salvation and are effectively made subject to His will). (See KINGDOM OF GOD.)

Paul makes much of the thought that Christ liberates believers, here and now, from destructive influences to which they were previously in bondage: from sin, the tyrannical overlord whose wages for services rendered is death (Rom. vi. 18–23); from the law as a system of salvation, which stirred sin up and gave it its strength (Gal. iv. 21 ff., v. 1; Rom. vi. 14, vii. 5–13, viii. 2; 1 Cor. xv. 56); from the demonic 'power of darkness' (Col. i. 13); from polytheistic superstition (1 Cor. x. 29; Gal. iv. 8); and from the burden of Jewish ceremonialism (Gal. ii. 4). To all this, Paul affirms, freedom from the remaining partial bondage to indwelling sin (Rom. vii. 14, 23), and from physical corruption and death, will in due course be added (Rom. viii. 18–21).

This freedom, in all its aspects, is the gift of Christ, who by death bought His people out of bondage (1 Cor. vi. 20, vii. 22 f.). (There may be an allusion here to the legal fiction by which Greek deities 'bought' slaves for their manumission.) Present freedom from the law, sin, and death is conveyed to believers by the Spirit, who unites them to Christ through faith (Rom. viii. 2; 2 Cor. iii. 17). Liberation brings with it adoption (Gal. iv. 5); those set free from guilt become sons of God, and receive the Spirit of Christ as a Spirit of adoption, assuring them that they are in truth God's sons and heirs (Gal. iv. 6 f.; Rom. viii. 15 f.).

Man's response to the divine gift of liberty (*eleutheria*), and indeed the very means of his receiving it, is a free acceptance of bondservice (*douleia*) to God (Rom. vi. 17–22), to Christ (1 Cor. vii. 22), to righteousness (Rom. vi. 18), and to all men for the sake of the gospel (1 Cor. ix. 19–23) and of the Saviour (2 Cor. iv. 5). Christian liberty is neither an abolishing of responsibility, nor a sanctioning of licence. The Christian is no longer 'under law' (Rom. vi. 14, RV) for salvation, but he is not therefore 'without law to God' (1 Cor. ix. 21). The divine law, as interpreted and exemplified by Christ Himself, remains a standard expressing Christ's will for His own freed bondservants (1 Cor. vii. 22). Christians are thus 'under law to Christ' (1 Cor. ix. 21, RV). The 'law of Christ' (Gal. vi. 2)—James' 'law of liberty' (Jas. i. 25, ii. 12)—is the law of love (Gal. v. 13 f.; *cf.* Mk. xii. 28 ff.; Jn. xiii. 34), the principle of voluntary and unstinting self-sacrifice for the good of men (1 Cor. ix. 1–23, x. 23–33) and the glory of God (1 Cor. x. 31). This life of love is the response of gratitude which the liberating gospel both requires and evokes. Christian liberty is precisely freedom for love and service to God and men, and it is therefore abused when it is made an excuse for unloving licence (Gal. v. 13; *cf.* 1 Pet. ii. 16; 2 Pet. ii. 19), or irresponsible inconsiderateness (1 Cor. viii. 9–12).

Paul wrote the Epistle to the Galatians (*q.v.*) to counter the threat to Christian liberty which Judaizing theology presented. The basic issue, as he saw it, was the sufficiency of Christ for salvation apart from works of law. The Judaizers held that Gentiles who had put faith in Christ still needed circumcision for salvation. Paul argued that if this were so, then by parity of reasoning they would need to keep the whole Mosaic law for salvation; but this would be seeking justification by the law, and such a quest would mean a falling away from grace and from Christ (Gal. v. 2–4). The Christian, Jew or Gentile, Paul maintained, is free from all need to perform works of law for acceptance, for as a believer in Christ he is fully accepted already (Gal. iii. 28 f.), as the gift of the Spirit to him proves (Gal. iii. 2 f., 14, iv. 6, v. 18). There is no reason why a Gentile convert should burden himself with Mosaic ceremonies (circumcision, the festal calendar (Gal. iv. 10), *etc.*), which in any case belonged to the pre-Christian era. The redeeming work of Christ has freed him completely from the need to seek salvation through law (Gal. iii. 13, iv. 5, v. 1). His task now is, first, to guard his God-given liberty against any who would tell him that faith in Christ alone is not enough to save him (Gal. v. 1) and, second, to put his liberty to the best use by letting the Spirit lead him into responsible fulfilment of the law of love (Gal. v. 13 ff.).

Paul makes a similar point elsewhere. The Christian is free from the need to work for his salvation, and he is bound neither by Jewish ceremonialism nor by pagan superstition and taboos. There is a large realm of things indifferent in which 'all things are lawful unto me' (1 Cor. vi. 12, x. 23). In this realm the Christian must use his liberty responsibly, with an eye to what is expedient and edifying and with a tender regard for the weaker brother's conscience (*cf.* 1 Cor. viii–x; Rom. xiv. 1–xv. 7).

III. 'FREE WILL'

The historic debate as to whether fallen men have 'free will' has only an indirect connection with the biblical concept of freedom. Distinctions must be made to indicate the issues involved.

1. If the phrase 'free will' be taken morally and psychologically, as meaning the power of unconstrained, spontaneous, voluntary, and therefore responsible, choice, the Bible everywhere assumes that all men, as such, possess it, unregenerate and regenerate alike.

2. If the phrase be taken metaphysically, as implying that men's future actions are indeterminate and therefore in principle unpredictable, the Bible seems neither to assert nor to deny an indeterminacy of future action relative to the agent's own moral or physical constitution, but it does seem to imply that no future event is indeterminate relative to God, for He foreknows and in some sense foreordains all things; see PROVIDENCE, PREDESTINATION.

3. If the phrase be taken theologically, as denoting a natural ability on the part of unregenerate man to perform acts that are good without qualification in God's sight, or to respond to the gospel invitation, such passages as Rom. viii. 5–8; Eph. ii. 1–10; Jn. vi. 44 seem to indicate that no man is free for obedience and faith till he is freed from sin's dominion by prevenient grace. All his voluntary choices are in one way or another acts of serving sin till grace breaks sin's power and moves him to obey the gospel. (*Cf.* Rom. vi. 17–22; and see SIN, REGENERATION.)

BIBLIOGRAPHY. *Arndt*; *MM*; H. Schlier in *TWNT*; *LAE*, pp. 326 ff.; Calvin, *Institutio*, III. xix.

J.I.P.

LIBNAH. 1. A fortified town in the Shephelah, between Aijalon and Lachish, taken by Joshua and assigned to the priests; revolted from Jehoram (2 Ki. viii. 22); withstood siege by Sennacherib, where his army was decimated by pestilence (2 Ki. xix. 8); birthplace of Josiah's wife Hamutal. Bliss and Macalister (*Excavations 28*, pp. 63 ff.) recognized Libnah ('white') in Tell es-Safi, the Crusaders' Blanchegarde with its limestone cliffs. This crescent-shaped hill, 4 miles west of Azekah and just south of the wadi, commands the entrance to the Vale of Elah (Abel, *Géographie*, II, pp. 369 f., *RB*, XXXVIII, pp. 427 f.; Garstang, *Joshua*, p. 392). More recently Tell Bornat, 6 miles farther south, has been preferred (Albright, *BASOR*, 15, p. 19; Elliger, *PJB*, 1934, pp. 58 ff.), and Gath (G. A. Smith, pp. 193, 222) or Makkedah (Albright) suggested for Safiyeh.

2. A camping place in the wilderness (Nu. xxxiii. 20; *cf.* Dt. i. 1), the site of which is unknown.

J.P.U.L.

LIBNI. A son of Gershon mentioned in Ex. vi. 17; Nu. iii. 18; 1 Ch. vi. 17, 20. In 1 Ch. vi. 29 Libni is listed as a son of Merari. The patronymic 'Libnites' is mentioned in Nu. iii. 21, xxvi. 58.

R.A.H.G.

LIBRARY. See WRITING.

LIBYA, LIBYANS. See LUBIM.

LICE. See PLAGUES OF EGYPT.

LIE, LYING (Heb. *šeqer*, 'falsehood', 'deception'; *kāzāḇ*, 'lie' or 'deceptive thing'; Gk. *pseudos* and cognates). Essentially, a lie is a statement of what is known to be false with intent to deceive (Jdg. xvi. 10, 13). Biblical writers severely condemn aggravated forms of lying, *e.g.* that which perpetrates a fraud (Lv. vi. 2, 3), that which secures wrongful condemnation (Dt. xix. 15), and the testimony of false prophets (Je. xiv. 14). Lies may be expressed in words (Pr. vi. 19), a way of life (Ps. lxii. 9), error (2 Thes. ii. 11), or a false form of religion (Rom. i. 25). The prophets regarded lying as a specific expression of the principle of evil (Ho. xii. 1). Lying is prohibited as repugnant to the moral conscience of Israel (Pr. xix. 22), because of its anti-social effects (Pr. xxvi. 28), and, above all, as incompatible with the divine nature (Nu. xxiii. 19). Jesus declares that Satan is the father of lies (Jn. viii. 44). All falsehood is forbidden in the Christian community (Col. iii. 9).

Lying is characterized in various ways, *e.g.* Cain's evasive answer (Gn. iv. 9), Jacob's deliberate falsehood (Gn. xxvii. 19), Gehazi's misrepresentation of his master (2 Ki. v. 21–27), and the deception practised by Ananias and Sapphira (Acts v. 1–10). Lying is the sin of antichrist (1 Jn. ii. 22), and all habitual liars forfeit eternal salvation (Rev. xxi. 27).

1 Sa. xvi. 2 does not justify the expedient lie. God merely suggested an ostensible reason for Samuel's visit to Bethlehem, and the prophet was under no obligation to divulge his real purpose. Again, 1 Ki. xxii. 20–23 implies that God permitted a subterfuge that His righteous judgment should be enacted upon Ahab. In such passages as Gn. xii. 10–20 it is clear that deception is not condoned nor recorded as an example to follow. See TRUTH.

BIBLIOGRAPHY. John Murray, *Principles of Conduct*, 1957, chapter VI; *HDB*, III. A.F.

LIEUTENANT. See SATRAP.

LIFE.

I. IN THE OLD TESTAMENT

a. Terms and concepts

1. Inherent in 'life' (*ḥayyîm*) is the idea of activity. Life is 'that which moves' (Gn. vii. 21 f.; Ps. lxix. 34; *cf.* Acts xvii. 28) in contrast to the relaxed, dormant, or inert state of non-life (*cf.* Rom. vii. 8; Jas. ii. 17, 20). Running water is 'living' (Gn. xxvi. 19), and rapid labour in childbirth indicates the mother's 'aliveness' (Ex. i. 19). The word's frequently plural form emphasizes the intensity of the concept. Life is associated with light, gladness, fullness, order, and active being (Ps. xxvii. 1; Jb. xxxiii. 25 ff.; Pr. iii. 16; Gn. i) and contrasted with the darkness, sorrow, emptiness, chaos, and silence which are characteristic of death and inanimate being (Ec. xi. 8; Ps. cxv. 17).

2. Soul (*nep̄eš*), as 'being' or 'self', is common to man and beast, living and dead (Lv. xxi. 11; Jb. xii. 10; Rev. viii. 9, xvi. 3). But its meaningful state is 'living soul' (*nep̄eš ḥayyâ*, Gn. ii. 7) and, therefore, may simply mean 'life'. To die is to breathe out one's soul, and to revive is to have it return (Je. xv. 9; 1 Ki. xvii. 21; *cf.* Acts xx. 10); or, seated in the blood, it is 'poured out' at death (Lv. xvii. 11; La. ii. 12; Is. liii. 12). While the soul may continue in spilt blood (Rev. vi. 9; Gn. iv. 10) or, corporately, in one's name or descendants, 'life' and 'self' are so closely parallel that to lose one's life means virtually to lose one's self (Pedersen, *Israel*, I, 1926, 151 ff.; Jb. ii. 4; Ezk. xviii).

3. Similarly, spirit (*rûaḥ*) or breath (*nešāmâ*), as the principle which distinguishes the living from the dead, often may be rendered life (1 Sa. xxx. 12; Jb. xxvii. 3 f.). To die is to lose one's breath or spirit (Jb. xxvii. 3; Ps. civ. 29 f.; *cf.* Mt. xxvii. 50); to revive is to 'have it come again' (*cf.* Lk. viii. 55; Rev. xi. 11, xiii. 15).

4. Life is given to man as a psycho-somatic unity in which 'our own distinctions between physical, intellectual, and spiritual life do not exist' (von Allmen, pp. 231 f.); and the Old Testament view of man may be described as 'animated body' (Robinson, p. 27). Thus soul may be paralleled with flesh (Ps. lxiii. 1; *cf.* Mt. vi. 25; Acts ii. 31), life (Jb. xxxiii. 28), or spirit (Ps. lxxvii. 2 f.; *cf.* Lk. i. 46 f.), and all terms viewed as the self or 'I'. It is the 'I' which lives—and which dies (*cf.* Gn. vii. 21; Ezk. xviii. 4).

b. Life unto death

1. What will man give for his life (Jb. ii. 4; *cf.* Mk. viii. 37)? Man is not only a unified being, he is a being threatened by death—mortal (Jb. iv. 17), barred from the tree of life (Gn. iii. 24), existing like cut grass or a morning's dew (Jb. vii. 9; Pss. xxxix. 4 f., xc. 5 f.; *cf.* 1 Pet. i. 24; Jas. iv. 14). Death is at work in the midst of life, and life, therefore, is a battle against the dissolution of death, an ebb and flow, possessed in greater or less degree. The tired slave rests and is 'ensouled' (Ex. xxiii. 12). Deliverance from sickness or an enemy or sorrow is deliverance from death, and to be sick or troubled is to be in Sheol (Nu. xxi. 8 f.; Jos. v. 8; Ps. xxx. 2 f.; *cf.* Ps. lxxxvi. 13, lxxi. 20). It is not that these are equated with death but that anything threatening life is viewed as an invasion of death upon the soul. Thus, Adam and Eve 'died' when they disobeyed (Gn. ii. 17); Abimelech, incurring God's displeasure, is a 'dead man' (Gn. xx. 3); and Jonah (ii. 2) in the fish is in Sheol. Standing under threat of death, one may be viewed from that perspective (*cf.* Lk. ix. 60).

2. Likewise long life as the gift of Wisdom or God (Pr. iii. 16; Dt. v. 16) has implicit in it the idea of the good life. 'I have set before thee . . . life and good, and death and evil' (Dt. xxx. 15). 'Long live the King' (1 Sa. x. 24, RSV) does not mean merely length of life but a reign of peace, prosperity, and victory. The death of the righteous at an old age (see AGE) and full of years is a blessing in that life has been lived to the full and a progeny blessed by God carries on the name (Gn. xxv. 8; Nu. xxiii. 10).

3. Nevertheless, the present life is life unto death. 'What man is he that liveth and shall . . . deliver his soul from the hand of the grave?' (Ps. lxxxix. 48). Man is a thing moulded of clay; his breath goes back to God, man dies and returns to dust (Gn. iii. 19; Jb. x. 9; Ps. cxliv. 4; Ec. xii. 7). One may continue to 'live' in his name or progeny (Ps. lxxii. 17; Is. lxvi. 22), and in a very real way these are viewed as a corporate extension of one's own soul (Pedersen, I, 254 ff.). But personal life ends and personal being belongs no more to the 'land of the living' (*cf.* Ps. lii. 5; Je. xi. 19). To live is to speak of *my* life; in death

a man's plans perish and he returns to the common earth, gathered to and sleeping with the fathers (Gn. xxv. 8, xxxvii. 35; Dt. xxxi. 16). Man's end is 'like water spilt on the ground, which cannot be gathered up again' (2 Sa. xiv. 14, RSV).

4. Death is not merely the momentary event of dying; it is the death state, *i.e.* Sheol. Sheol is 'in the dust' (Jb. xvii. 13 ff.) and is probably best understood generically as 'the grave'. As a synonym for death it is the common goal and final leveller of all life: man and beast, righteous and wicked, wise and foolish (Jb. iii. 13 ff.; Ps. xlix; Ec. ii. 14, iii. 19). It is a state of sleep, rest, darkness, silence, without thought or memory (Jb. iii. 16 f., xvii. 13 ff.; Ps. vi. 5; Ec. ix. 5, 10) in which one does not praise God and from which one does not return (2 Sa. xii. 23; Jb. vii. 9; Ps. xxx. 9; Is. xxxviii. 18). It is like an insatiable monster and its prospect, except in the most desperate straits, is one of foreboding (Hab. ii. 5; *cf.* 2 Sa. xxii. 5 f.).

A few times Sheol is pictured as a massive grave in which, amidst the maggots, an enfeebled ghost-life continues (Ezk. xxxi, xxxii; Is. xiv. 4 ff.) and from which one's 'shade' may be called up (1 Sa. xxviii. 8 ff.). While the first two passages are obviously poetic symbolism, the Witch of Endor séance reflects a common—though forbidden—practice. It is not representative of the general Old Testament view, which sees life and death in utter opposition (*contra* Johnson, p. 89).

Although not strictly non-being, Sheol is the end of meaningful existence and is 'virtual annihilation' (Johnson, p. 93). 'The paths of glory lead but to the grave', and this conclusion to human life gives rise to the Preacher's refrain: 'Vanity of vanities, all is vanity' (Ec. xii. 8; Ps. lxxxix. 47). To this victory of death the Old Testament does offer a hopeful answer; it lies not in the nature of man but in the power of the living God.

c. The Living God

1. The common formula for an oath, 'as the Lord liveth' (*cf.* Nu. xiv. 21, 28; 1 Sa. xiv. 39), stresses that God is the God who speaks and acts because he is 'the living God'. This quality distinguishes Yahweh from all idols and attests not only His own vitality but His creative power and providential activity (Jos. iii. 10; Je. x. 10; Is. xlvi. 5 ff.). He is the source and upholder of all life, the spring of living water (Je. xvii. 13; Ps. xxxvi. 9 f.), who gives man breath and who, delivering from Sheol, leads one in the path of life (Gn. ii. 7; Ps. xvi. 11; Pr. v. 6). God is the God who makes alive and who kills (Gn. vi. 17; Dt. xxxii. 39; Jdg. xiii. 3, 23; 1 Sa. ii. 6; 2 Ki. v. 7).

2. Such is man's dependence upon God for life that man's breath or spirit may be called God's breath and God's spirit (Jb. xxvii. 3 f., xxxiii. 4; Gn. vi. 3; Is. xlii. 5). God gave manna in the wilderness that Israel might learn that even physical life is maintained by 'every word that proceedeth out of the mouth of God' (Dt. viii. 3; *cf.* Mt. iv. 4; Lk. xii. 15, 20). God imparts breath and man lives (Gn. ii. 7; *cf.* Rev. xi. 11); if God 'gather unto himself his spirit and his breath all flesh shall perish together and man shall turn again unto dust' (Jb. xxxiv. 14 f.; *cf.* Ec. xii. 7; Ps. xc. 3, civ. 29 f.). Man's life then is loaned to him at God's good pleasure, and true life consists not in the transient, even though prosperous, life of the wicked, but in having God as 'my portion for ever' (Ps. lxxiii. 17, 26). One's life is assured if he is 'bound up in the bundle of life with the Lord' (1 Sa. xxv. 29).

3. Because life is 'life in relatedness to God', life and death are moral alternatives. The fate of the individual and nation, whether blessing and life or misfortune and death, hangs upon one's righteousness or sinfulness, obedience or disobedience to Yahweh (Dt. xxx. 15 ff.; Jdg. ii. 18 ff.; Ezk. xviii). Universal death is viewed (when viewed at all) as a judgment upon sin: because of disobedience man is barred from the 'tree of life' (Gn. iii. 17 ff.; *cf.* Jb. xiv. 1 ff., 16 f.; contrast Ps. lxxxix. 47). Although not always apparent, righteousness tends to life and evil to death (*cf.* Ps. lxxiii. 17; Pr. xi. 19); righteousness is a 'way of life', and by it one is delivered from the threats of Sheol (Am. v. 4, 14; Pr. vi. 23; Hab. ii. 4).

4. God has no relationship to Sheol or to those in it. But this must not be confused with the mistaken notion that God has no power in Sheol. It is basic to the Old Testament faith—as expressed in all strata of the literature—that Yahweh, the Living God, reigns over death and/or Sheol. To heal (2 Ki. v. 7, 14), to raise the dead (1 Ki. xvii. 20 ff.; 2 Ki. iv. 16, 33 ff.), to deliver Israel from national death (Jdg. vii. 2 ff.; Ho. xiii. 14; Ezk. xxxvii), to cause life to bud in a barren woman (Gn. xvii. 15 ff.; Jdg. xiii. 2 f.; 1 Sa. i. 19 f., ii. 6)—all these reveal God's power over Sheol, for the maladies are themselves invasions of death into which God interjects resurrection power.

While God's power to deliver individuals from Sheol is implicit throughout the Old Testament, His purpose to do so comes to explicit expression in comparatively few passages (*cf.* Is. xxv. 8, xxvi. 19; Jb. xix. 26; Ps. xvi. 8–11, xlix. 14 f.; Dn. xii. 2). When it does appear, however, the conviction is full-grown and seemingly is not an innovation (W. O. E. Oesterley, *The Jews and Judaism during the Greek Period*, 1941, p. 183). The concept is related to and perhaps an inference from: (1) God's expressed relationship to the righteous dead, and (2) God's redemption of Israel understood within the framework of a 'corporate personality' in which the reality of the individual is preserved in the reality of the whole. In a later day Jesus Christ, as well as other Rabbis, urged the former as a key to the proper understanding of the Old Testament at this point (Mt. xxii. 31 f.; Lk. xx. 37 f.; *cf.* Strack-Billerbeck, I, 893 ff.): (1) God says to Moses, 'I am the God of Abraham.' (2) Abraham is in Sheol. (3) God is the God of the living and has no relationship with Sheol. (4) Therefore, it is to be inferred that God will resurrect Abraham from Sheol.

5. Resurrection-life is pictured (as in inter-testament Judaism) in materialistic terms. It is restored life in which 'life', *i.e.* prosperity, peace, and fulness, is multiplied and Sheol threats are removed (Is. xxvii; *cf.* Rev. xxi, xxii). Its realization (in Is. xxvi. 19; Dn. xii. 2) belongs to the coming messianic deliverance and, as creation life, it is solely the result of God's sovereign and gracious act. God, who by His creative word called man into being, again calls dust into life through resurrection.

II. IN THE NEW TESTAMENT

a. Terms and concepts

1. Life (*bios*), means 'course of life' or 'necessities of life maintenance' (Mk. xii. 44; 1 Tim. ii. 2; 1 Jn. iii. 17). While *zōē* characteristically (and always in the Johannine literature) describes resurrection-life, it also denotes 'course of life' (Lk. xvi. 25; Phil. i. 20; *cf.* Lk. xv. 13; Rom. vi. 2), soul-life or natural vitality (Acts viii. 33, xvii. 25; Phil. i. 20; 1 Tim. iv. 8; *cf.* Jn. iv. 50), and life duration (Jas. iv. 14). Soul (*psychē*) and spirit (*pneuma*) continue their ambiguous rôle of 'self' and 'life'. As life, soul is simply 'being', 'natural-life' (Lk. ix. 25; Mk. viii. 36). It may be preserved to resurrection-life (Jn. xii. 25), but at present it exists as natural vitality, lost at death (Mt. ii. 20; Jn. xv. 13; Acts xx. 10; 1 Jn. iii. 16) or, more importantly, as Adamic life, life of the old age, life under divine judgment (Lk. xii. 20; *cf.* 1 Cor. ii. 14, xv. 44 ff.; Jas. iii. 15). While spirit can mean, as in ancient Israel, the vitalizing principle of Adamic life (Jn. xix. 30; Acts vii. 59), it tends to be associated with resurrection-life and, as such, to stand in contrast to soul-life, *i.e.* life under judgment (*cf.* Jude 19; Jn. vi. 63; 1 Cor. xv. 45).

2. As in the Old Testament, man's life and being, although viewed from different aspects, is a psycho-somatic unity (*cf.* Bultmann). The Gk. soul-body dualism is incidentally reflected in the parable of Lk. xvi. 19 ff., but is not in accord with the general New Testament outlook or teaching.

b. Life under death

1. The Old Testament view continues. (1) Life is borrowed, transitory, dependent upon and at the disposal of God (*cf.* Mt. iv. 4). Man can neither prolong his soul-life nor destroy it (Mt. vi. 25 ff.; Lk. xii. 25; Jas. iv. 15); God can either forfeit it or redeem it to resurrection-life (Mt. x. 28; Lk. xii. 20; 1 Cor. xv. 44; 1 Jn. v. 16; *cf.* Jas. v. 20). (2) Life is ebb and flow: to live is to live in health (Jn. iv. 50).

2. In radical development of Old Testament thought the moral quality of life as relationship to God comes into sharp focus. One related to God, although dead, may be viewed as 'living' (Lk. xx. 38). On the other hand, soul-life alienated from the life of God (Eph. iv. 18) is no life at all. Anyone in it—not only those under immediate threat of Sheol (Mk. v. 23; *cf.* Mt. ix. 18)—may be regarded as 'dead' (Lk. ix. 60; Rom. viii. 10; 1 Jn. iii. 14; Rev. iii. 1; *cf.* Lk. xv. 24). Even when called life, 'this life' is contrasted to real life (1 Cor. xv. 19; 1 Tim. vi. 19) and has meaning only in conjunction with the life of the new age (Gal. ii. 20; Phil. i. 22; 1 Tim. iv. 8).

3. The cry of John the Baptist, 'Repent ye', sets the mood of the New Testament (Mt. iii. 2; *cf.* Acts xi. 18, xvii. 30 f.). All life stands under imminent judgment, and decision is demanded of all who would share the life of the new age. Criminals suffering ignominious execution are not special sinners: 'except ye repent ye shall all likewise perish' (Lk. xiii. 3). Nor can prosperity be relied upon as a token of God's favour: in the midst of man's ease God speaks, 'Fool, this night your soul is demanded from you' (Lk. xii. 20). While this (OT) view of the judgment of the soul-life by physical death is present, more often the *locus* of judgment shifts to the eschatological consummation—the parousia (Mt. xxiv. 36 ff., xxv. 31 ff.), the resurrection of judgment (Jn. v. 28 f.), the second death (Rev. xxi. 8)—in which God destroys 'soul and body' in hell (Mt. x. 28). Soul-life (*psychē*), in contrast to resurrection-life (*zōē*), is Adamic life, life under judgment, which without *zōē* must perish (Jn. iii. 16). Indeed the 'soulish' man is one directing his life toward the perishing old age, the 'soulish' body one controlled by the Sheol-power dominating the old age (1 Cor. ii. 14, xv. 44; Jas. iii. 15; Jude 19).

4. The judgment of death is executed corporately and representatively in Jesus Christ, the eschatological Adam (1 Cor. xv. 45), who 'becomes sin' and voluntarily delivers His soul to Sheol as 'a ransom' (Mk. x. 45; Jn. x. 15; 2 Cor. v. 21; *cf.* Mk. xiv. 34; Is. liii. 6, 10; Acts viii. 32 ff.; 1 Pet. ii. 24) to give resurrection-life to the world (Jn. vi. 51). However, Christ's soul is not left in Sheol; in resurrection victory He takes His soul again (Acts ii. 31; Jn. x. 17). And by the power of an 'indestructible life' He becomes a 'life-giving spirit' who shares His victory and imparts resurrection-life to whom He will (Heb. vii. 3; 1 Cor. xv. 45; Eph. iv. 8; Jn. v. 21, xvii. 2). Thereby, Christ removes for ever the Sheol threat to man's soul.

5. Man's soul-life, then, need not be forfeited. If he loves it or seeks to preserve it, he will lose it, but if he loses it or gives it up for Christ, the gospel, or the brethren, it will be preserved, caught up in resurrection-life (Mk. viii. 35 f.; Jn. xii. 25; 1 Jn. iii. 16; 2 Cor. xii. 15; Phil. ii. 30; Rev. xii. 11). To believe or to convert a sinner is to save a soul from death (Heb. x. 39; Jas. i. 21, v. 20; 1 Pet. i. 9). One who believes shall never taste real death (Jn. viii. 51 f., xi. 26; *cf.* Jn. x. 28; Mk. ix. 1), for in Christ death is transformed into a temporary 'sleep in Jesus' (1 Thes. iv. 14; *cf.* Mk. v. 39; Jn. xi. 11). Both soul-life and resurrection-life are the life of the self, the whole man. The latter does not displace the former, but preserves it and transforms it.

c. Resurrection-life

1. The Old Testament ideal of the good life has in the New Testament an eschatological fulfilment as resurrection-life (*zōē*). Since it is the only true life, it may be called simply 'life' (Acts v. 20, xi. 18; Rom. v. 17; 2 Pet. i. 3; 1 Jn. v. 16). It is associated with light (Jn. viii. 12), glory (1 Pet. v. 1, 4; *cf.* Jas. i. 12), honour (Rom. ii. 7), abundance (Jn. x. 10), immortality (2 Tim. i. 10), resurrection (Jn. vi. 40, xi. 25), eternal life, the kingdom of God (Col. i. 13; Mt. xxv), holiness (Rom. vi. 22 f.), joy (1 Thes. ii. 19), spirit (Jn. vi. 63; *cf.* 1 Cor. xv. 45), the imperishable (Heb. vii. 16; 1 Pet. i. 23); and is contrasted with darkness (Col. i. 13), dishonour (Rom. ii. 7), death (1 Jn. iii. 14), mortality (2 Cor. v. 4), destruction (Mt. vii. 13 f.), judgment (Jn. v. 28 f.), corruption (Gal. vi. 8), wrath (Rom. ii. 7 f.; Jn. iii. 36), eternal punishment (Mt. xxv. 46). To have life is to 'abide' (Jn. vi. 27). To lack it is to wither and be burned as a severed branch (Mt. vii. 13, 19; Lk. iii. 9; *cf.* Jn. xv. 6) and to be destroyed in hell (Mt. x. 28; Mk. ix. 43 ff.; Rev. xx. 14 f.).

2. As in the Old Testament, life is properly the life of God, the Ever-Living One (Rom. v. 21; Rev. iv. 9), who has life in Himself and alone has immortality (Jn. v. 26; 1 Tim. vi. 16). He can make alive and He can kill (Rom. iv. 17; 2 Cor. i. 9; 1 Tim. vi. 13; Mt. x. 28 f.; Jas. iv. 14 f.; Lk. xii. 20).

3. This life of God is manifest in Jesus Christ. In the Synoptic Gospels Jesus simply assures His followers of resurrection-life (Mk. viii. 34 ff., ix. 41 ff., x. 29 f.; Mt. xxv. 46) and evidences His power to bestow it: to heal is to 'save souls' (Lk. vi. 9) and cause to 'live' (Mk. v. 23). Sheol itself is robbed by Christ's creative word (Mk. v. 39 ff.; Lk. vii. 14 f.; *cf.* Jn. xi. 43). The Fourth Gospel and the Epistles, written with Christ's resurrection in more deliberate perspective, are more explicit and elaborate: Christ is 'the true God, and eternal life' (1 Jn. v. 20; Jn. i. 4, xiv. 6), the 'Prince of life' (Acts iii. 15), to whom the Father has granted 'to have life in himself' (Jn. v. 26). He is 'the resurrection and the life' (Jn. xi. 25), 'the bread of life' (Jn. vi. 35), and His words are 'spirit and life' (Jn. vi. 63). By His resurrection He manifests Himself Lord and Judge over the living and the dead (Mt. xxv. 31 ff.; Mk. xiv. 62; Jn. v. 27 ff.; Acts x. 42, xvii. 31; Rom. x. 9 f., xiv. 9; 2 Tim. iv. 1; *cf.* 1 Pet. iv. 5; Rev. xi. 18).

In Jesus Christ's resurrection immortal life has been actualized on the plane of history. His resurrection becomes the basis for all resurrection, and all resurrection is to be understood in terms of His (*cf.* 1 Cor. xv; Col. iii. 4; 1 Jn. iii. 2). No longer does the hope of resurrection rest, as in the Old Testament, merely upon prophetic vision or upon inferences from God's covenant relationships. No longer is resurrection to be defined simply as renewed life out of Sheol. Resurrection-life now finds its meaning in the image of Jesus Christ (Rom. viii. 29).

4. For man, then, true life is grounded in Jesus Christ who 'became a life-giving spirit' (1 Cor. xv. 45; *cf.* Jn. vi. 63; 2 Cor. iii. 17). The core of the Gospel proclamation is that He who was dead is 'alive for evermore' (Acts ii. 31 ff.; 1 Cor. xv. 3 ff.; Rev. i. 5, 18) and by the power of an indestructible life gives life to the world (Heb. vii. 16; Jn. vi. 33). If Christ has not been raised from death one must write over the Christian dead, *finis* (1 Cor. xv. 18, 32). But Christ is risen and has the 'keys to Sheol'; because Sheol could not conquer Him, neither can it prevail against His Church (Mt. xvi. 18; Rev. i. 18). His Life is mediated to the believer through repentance, faith, and baptism (Acts xi. 18; Jn. iii. 16, xi. 25 f.; Rom. vi. 4); by it one is 'saved' (Rom. v. 10). In Christ's death and resurrection God pierces radically into the world of man to make him see the fatality of sin and the utter grace of the new life from God—an unfathomable, unexpected, and freely bestowed act of salvation.

5. Resurrection-life, like Adamic soul-life, is imparted and sustained by God's creative word. Man has no control over it. He may inherit, receive, or enter it (Mk. ix. 43 ff., x. 17, 30; Tit. iii. 7; 1 Pet. iii. 7). By evil deeds or rejection of the Gospel he may judge himself unworthy of it (Acts xiii. 46; *cf.* Rom. i. 32) or, conversely, by the Spirit he may perform deeds yielding eternal life (Mk. x. 17 ff.; Jn. v. 28 f.; Rom. ii. 7; 2 Cor. v. 10; Gal. v. 22, vi. 8). Such deeds are possible only by a relationship to Christ through faith (Rom. i. 17; Jn. xx. 31) which itself imparts life (Jn. vi. 53 f.; Rom. vi. 23; Col. iii. 3; 1 Jn. iii. 14, v. 13). God gives life to those whom He wills (Jn. i. 13, v. 21), who are ordained for it, and who from the foundation of the world are written in the book of life (Acts xiii. 48; Rom. ix. 11; Phil. iv. 3; Rev. xvii. 8, xx. 12 ff.). The new life is a resurrection, a new birth, a sovereign and gracious act of the creator God (Jn. v. 24 f.; Rom. vi. 4; Col. iii. 1 ff.; Eph. ii. 1 ff.; Jn. i. 13).

6. In the Synoptic Gospels life is always viewed as future and associated with the coming kingdom of God (Mk. x. 17, 23, ix. 43, 47; Mt. xxv. 46). The way to it is blocked by sin and found by few; yet to attain life is the highest possible goal and worthy of any sacrifice (Mk. ix. 42 ff.; Mt. vii. 14, xiii. 44 ff.), for only in this way can one's soul be preserved (Mk. viii. 34 ff.; *cf.* Jn. xii. 25).

7. In the Johannine and Pauline literature this parousia perspective continues (Jn. v. 24, 28 f., vi. 40, xi. 24, xiv. 3, 6, 19; Rom. v. 10, vi. 22; 2 Cor. v. 4, xiii. 4; Phil. iii. 10 f., *cf.* 1 Cor. xv. 52 ff.), but resurrection-life is also viewed as a present possession of the believer. One passes 'from death to life' at conversion (1 Jn. iii. 14; *cf.* Jn. v. 24; Eph. ii. 1 ff.), and one may even speak in the past tense of having been crucified, raised to life, brought into Christ's kingdom, glorified, and made to sit in heaven (Gal. ii. 20; Eph. ii. 5 f.; Col. i. 13; Rom. viii. 30). However, in Paul (and probably in John) this is always viewed as a corporate participation in Christ's

death and resurrection (Rom. vi. 4, viii. 2; 2 Tim. i. 1; *cf.* Jn. vi. 33, 51 ff.) vouchsafed by the Spirit, the 'down-payment' of the new-age life (*cf.* 2 Cor. iv. 12, v. 5). Our life is hid with Christ (Col. iii. 3), and to have life means simply to have Christ (1 Jn. v. 11 f.). Individually, resurrection-life is now being realized in ethical renewal and psychological transformation (Rom. viii. 10, xii. 1; Gal. v. 22 f.; Col. iii. 1 ff., 9 f.; Eph. iv. 18 ff.); but the self in its mortality remains under death. Only in the parousia is mortality 'swallowed by life' and Sheol's power vanquished (1 Cor. xv. 26, 52 ff.; 2 Cor. v. 4; *cf.* Rev. xx. 13). At present the victory is actualized personally only in Jesus Christ, 'the firstfruits of those who have fallen asleep', 'the firstborn among many brethren' (1 Cor. xv. 20; Rom. viii. 29).

8. As in ancient Israel, the problem of death finds its answer neither in philosophical speculation about immortality nor in the sub-life of Sheol but in deliverance from Sheol; to be a son of God is to be a son of the resurrection (Lk. xx. 36). And it is the resurrected Son of God who imparts this victory to His Church; in Adam all die, so in Christ all shall be made alive (1 Cor. xv. 22). Not Bach's 'come, sweet death' but John's 'come, Lord Jesus' expresses the New Testament attitude towards death.

Resurrection-life is bodily life—the life of the whole man (Lk. xxiv. 39 ff.; Jn. v. 28 f.; 1 Cor. xv; Phil. iii. 21; Rev. xx. 13). It is to be with Christ (Jn. xiv. 3; Col. iii. 4; 1 Thes. iv. 17), to have a full vision of God (1 Cor. xiii. 12; 2 Cor. v. 7; 1 Jn. iii. 2; Rev. xxii. 4), to enter the kingdom (Mt. xxv. 34, 46), to enjoy the fulfilment of 'righteousness and peace and joy in the Holy Spirit' (Rom. xiv. 17; *cf.* Rev. xxi, xxii) in which all Sheol-threats are removed.

Resurrection-life will be 'my life'. One's personal continuity does not rest, however, in the residual monad of Leibnitz nor in the escaping soul of Plato. It rests in God in whose mind 'all live' (Lk. xx. 38) and 'who can bring the dead to life and can call to himself the things that do not exist as though they did' (Rom. iv. 17, Williams).

BIBLIOGRAPHY. J.-J. von Allmen, ed., *Vocabulary of the Bible*, 1958, pp. 231–237; R. Bultmann, *The Theology of the New Testament*, 1955, I, pp. 191–227, 324–329; E. de W. Burton, *Spirit, Soul, and Flesh*, 1918; O. Cullmann, *Immortality of the Soul or Resurrection of the Dead?*, 1958; and 'The Proleptic Deliverance of the Body according to the New Testament', *The Early Church*, 1956, pp. 165–173; C. H. Dodd, *The Interpretation of the Fourth Gospel*, 1954, pp. 144–150, 201 ff.; E. E. Ellis, *Paul and his Recent Interpreters*, 1961, pp. 35–48; A. R. Johnson, *The Vitality of the Individual in the Thought of Ancient Israel*, 1949; F. Muszner, *ΖΩΗ: Die Anschauung vom 'Leben' im vierten Evangelium*, 1952; J. Pedersen, *Israel: Its Life and Culture*, 1926, I, pp. 99–181, 453–496; H. W. Robinson, *The Christian Doctrine of Man*, 1926; *TWNT*, II, pp. 833–874.

E.E.E.

LIGHT. The word is used in connection with joy, blessing, and life in contrast to sorrow, adversity, and death (*cf.* Gn. i. 3 f.; Jb. x. 22, xviii. 5 f.). At an early time it came to signify God's presence and favour (*cf.* Ps. xxvii. 1; Is. ix. 2; 2 Cor. iv. 6) in contrast to God's judgment (Am. v. 18). From this and other sources arises an ethical dualism between light and darkness, *i.e.* good and evil, which is quite marked in the New Testament (*cf.* Lk. xvi. 8; Jn. iii. 19 ff., xii. 36; 2 Cor. vi. 14; Col. i. 12 f.; 1 Thes. v. 5; 1 Pet. ii. 9). Some, *e.g.* C. H. Dodd, have regarded Hellenistic parallels to be significant in this regard, but the presence of this usage in Judaism, *e.g. The War of the Sons of Light and the Sons of Darkness* in DSS, makes such an inference unnecessary and provides a more pertinent commentary on the New Testament concepts. See LIFE.

God's holiness is expressed in terms of light, *e.g.* in 1 Tim. vi. 16, where He is said to dwell 'in the light which no man can approach unto'; see HOLINESS (*a*). *Cf.* 1 Jn. i. 5 where it is said that 'God is light' and other passages in that Epistle where the implications of this for the believer are worked out. The same thought is seen in the typically Hebrew expression 'children of light' which is twice used by Paul (Eph. v. 8; 1 Thes. v. 5; *cf.* Jn. xii. 36).

In John's Gospel the term light refers not so much to God's holiness as to the *revelation* of His love in Christ and the penetration of that love into lives darkened by sin. So Christ refers to Himself as 'the light of the world' (Jn. viii. 12, ix. 5, xii. 46), and in the Sermon on the Mount applies this term to His disciples (Mt. v. 14–16). Similarly Paul can refer to 'the light of the glorious gospel of Christ' and to God Himself who 'hath shined in our hearts' (2 Cor. iv. 4–6).

BIBLIOGRAPHY. *Arndt*; *ISBE*; C. H. Dodd, *The Interpretation of the Fourth Gospel*, 1954, pp. 201–212; D. Flusser, 'The Dead Sea Sect and Pre-Pauline Christianity', *Aspects of the DSS*, ed. C. Rabin and Y. Yadin, 1958, pp. 215–266.

E.E.E.

LIGHTNING. 1. Lightning which accompanies a thunderstorm is a well-known phenomenon in Palestine, especially in the cool season, with a maximum in November or December. In AV the word is sometimes rendered 'glitter' or 'glittering' (Dt. xxxii. 41; Jb. xx. 25; Ezk. xxi. 10, 28; Na. iii. 3; Hab. iii. 11) and 'bright' (Ezk. xxi. 15), and lightning is a figure used for brightness of countenance (Dn. x. 6; Mt. xxviii. 3) and of raiment (Lk. xxiv. 4). In some passages the usage of 'fire' refers to lightning (*e.g.* Ex. ix. 23; 1 Ki. xviii. 38; 2 Ki. i. 10, 12, 14; 1 Ch. xxi. 26; Jb. i. 16; Pss. cv. 32, cxlviii. 8). Lightning is poetically described in association with thunderstorms (2 Sa. xxii. 15; Pss. xviii. 14, xcvii. 4, cxxxv. 7; Je. x. 13, li. 16).

2. Lightning is associated with theophanies as at Sinai (Ex. xix. 16, xx. 18), in Ezekiel's vision (Ezk. i. 13–14) and several times in the

Apocalypse (Rev. iv. 5, viii. 5, xi. 19, xvi. 18). It is regarded as an instrument of God's judgment (Ps. cxliv. 6; Zc. ix. 14; Hab. iii. 11; Lk. x. 18). See also THUNDER. J.M.H.

LIGN ALOES. See ALOES.

LIGURE. See JEWELS AND PRECIOUS STONES.

LILITH (*lîlîṯ*, Is. xxxiv. 14, RVmg; LXX *onokentauros*; Symm., Vulg. *lamia* (Jerome, 'avenging fury'); AV 'screech owl'; AVmg, RV 'night-monster').

This name appears in a description of the terrible desolation of Edom, and presents great difficulties of interpretation. At a time when Bab. and Persian influence was developing, Lilith appears evidently as a loan-word derived from the Assyr. female demon of the night, *Lilitu*.

It may, however, be misleading to regard the creature as necessarily associated with the night: the darkness which some demons were said to love was that caused by desert storms (*cf.* Sumerian *LIL.LÁ*, 'storm-wind'; and also a possible conclusion from Jerome's translation cited above). Some scholars regard it as the equivalent of the English vampire (see HORSE-LEACH).

Later Jewish literature speaks variously of Lilith as the first wife of Adam, but she flew away and became a demon; as a fabulous monster which stole and destroyed newly born infants; and as a demon against which charms were used to keep it from the haunts of men, lest it enter and bring disease.

There is, however, no real evidence for insisting on a mythological interpretation of the word, and it is perhaps significant that most of the other creatures listed in Is. xxxiv are real animals or birds. If the LXX rendering is understood as something akin to a tail-less monkey (*cf.* G. R. Driver, *loc. cit.*, p. 55), it seems an unlikely habitué of a desolate place. A similar objection applies also to both the tawny and the night owl, neither of which is a desert bird. Driver suggests a goat-sucker or night-jar, several species of which are found in waste land.

BIBLIOGRAPHY. *JewE*; G. R. Driver, 'Lilith', *PEQ*, XCI, 1959, pp. 55–58. J.D.D.

LILY. See PLANTS.

LIME, LIMESTONE. Chemically, lime is calcium oxide, made by heating limestone in a kiln, of which there must have been many in ancient Palestine. The Heb. Bible uses three words, *śîḏ*, 'plaster', 'lime', or 'whitewash' (Dt. xxvii. 2, 4; Is. xxxiii. 12; Am. ii. 1), *gîr*, 'chalk' or 'lime' (Dn. v. 5), and *'aḇnê gîr*, 'stones of lime' (Is. xxvii. 9).

Limestone is abundant in Palestine. Geologically it was formed from the compacting together of shells, *etc.*, on the sea bed, which was then thrust up by earth movement. Palestine was under the sea more than once, at least in part. The bulk of the limestone visible today on both sides of the Jordan is from the Cretaceous period.

BIBLIOGRAPHY. Denis Baly, *The Geography of Palestine*, 1958, p. 16. J.A.T.

LINE. Six Heb. words and one Gk. word are translated 'line' in the Bible.

The commonest word is *qaw*, *qāw*, or *qeweh*, denoting a measuring line such as was used to measure the circumference of the Temple laver (1 Ki. vii. 23) or to mark out a city, or land for building (Is. xxxiv. 17; Je. xxxi. 39; Zc. i. 16). It is used for measuring distances of 1,000 cubits from Ezekiel's Temple to test the water depth (Ezk. xlvii. 3), and by an extension of meaning it is the plumbline used to check the integrity of a city or land (2 Ki. xxi. 13; Is. xxviii. 17, xxxiv. 11; La. ii. 8), or the lines of instruction of a teacher (Is. xxviii. 10, 13, where the picture is one of children reciting the alphabet, *qāw* being an alternative way of naming the letter *qōp̄*).

The word *ḥeḇel*, 'cord' or 'rope', also refers to an instrument for dividing up land or an inheritance (Ps. xvi. 6, lxxviii. 55; Am. vii. 17; Zc. ii. 1). In 2 Sa. viii. 2 it is used of the lines of Moabites drawn up by David, some destined for life and some for death.

The words *ḥûṭ* (1 Ki. vii. 15), *pāṯîl* (Ezk. xl. 3), and *śereḏ* (Is. xliv. 13) have special uses. Rahab's red cord is *tiqwâ* (Jos. ii. 18, 21). In the New Testament the word is *kanōn* (2 Cor. x. 16).

See WEIGHTS AND MEASURES, ARTS AND CRAFTS. J.A.T.

LINEN. AV thus translates different Heb. and Gk. words. The Heb. word *šēš* (Egyp. *sś*) is rendered 'fine linen'. The following Heb. words are rendered by 'linen' in AV, *baḏ*, *pištâ*, *bûṣ*, *'ēṭûn* (*cf.* Egyp. *'idmy*, 'yarn' in RV) and *miqweh* (*cf.* Accadian *qû* 'cord', 'a drove' in RV). The word *pištâ* means actually the flax of which linen was made. As early as the 14th century BC the word *pšt*, or plural *pštm*, was used in Ugarit for linen (*cf.* Virolleaud, *PRU*, Mission Ras Shamra VII, II). *Bûṣ* is present only in later books (*cf.* Gk. *byssos*). AV renders the following Gk. words by linen, *sindōn*, *othonion*, and *linon*.

Linen is made of flax (*Linum usitatissimum*). After treatment the thread of the rind gives linen and the seed linseed-oil. After the flax was treated it was spun by women and made into material (Pr. xxxi. 13, 24). Flax was never extensively grown in Palestine in Old and New Testament times. According to Ex. ix. 31, Ho. ii. 5, and probably Jos. ii. 6, it was, however, cultivated from early times. An extra-biblical witness is the Gezer calendar (*c.* 1000 BC), where we read in the fourth line: 'His month is hoeing up of flax' (Albright's translation in Pritchard, *ANET*[2]). The great cultivator and exporter of flax was Egypt. In Pr. vii. 16 we read of Egyptian linen (*cf.* Heb. *ḥᵃṭuḇôṯ*, 'many coloured'). Red linen was especially precious in ancient Egypt and was called 'royal linen'. It is quite probable that linen (*cf.* Egyp. words *sś* and *'idmy* as possible loan-words in Hebrew and Canaanite) was imported from Egypt by the inhabitants of Palestine from the earliest times. We know from Egyp. documents that linen was exported from Egypt to Phoenicia (*cf.* also Ezk. xxvii. 7) and especially Byblos through many centuries (*cf.* H. Kees, *Aegypten*, 1933, *KAO*, 118).

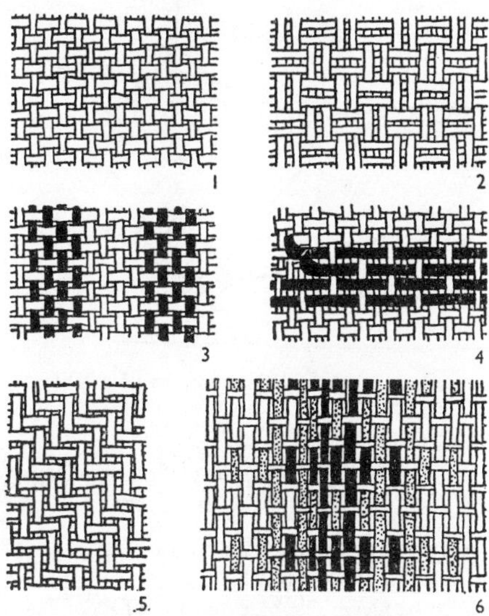

Fig. 133. Some examples of ancient weaving patterns, probably Egyptian. Items 3, 4, and 6 show the introduction of additional colours.

The use of linen in Old Testament times was prescribed for priests (Ex. xxviii. 39). The coat, turban, and girdle must be of fine linen. This is, according to Ezk. xliv. 17, prescribed for the coolness of the material. The high priest used a woollen overcoat, but was draped in linen on the great Day of Atonement (Lv. xvi. 4, 23). Linen the Israelites brought along from Egypt was used for the ten curtains of the tabernacle (Ex. xxvi. 1), the veil (xxvi. 31), and the screen of the door of the tent (xxvi. 36). Samuel wore an *'ēpôḏ* of linen (1 Sa. ii. 18); David danced in front of the ark draped in a linen *'ēpôḏ* (2 Sa. vi. 14). It seems as if the use of linen was associated with special, holy persons, *e.g.* the man with the writing-case in Ezk. ix. 2 and the man Daniel saw in Dn. x. 5 and xii. 6, 7. Linen and fine linen were regarded as precious gifts to the woman a man loved. In Ezk. xvi. 10, 13 the Lord speaks to Jerusalem as a husband to his wife and reminds her how He has decked her with linen and fine linen. It is obvious from Pr. xxxi. 22 that the use of linen by women was highly esteemed. The word *bûṣ*, 'linen', is used in the later books as the material for the rich and important people, *e.g.* Mordecai went to the Persian king draped with a mantle of fine linen (Est. viii. 15). See fig. 133.

The word linen is sparingly used in the New Testament. In the parable of the rich man and the beggar Lazarus the former is described as decked out in fine linen (Gk. *byssos*) and purple (Lk. xvi. 19). The young man who followed Christ to Gethsemane lost his linen cloth (or sheet?) in his flight from the scene (Mk. xiv. 51). The body of Christ was wrapped in linen according to Mt. xxvii. 59 and parallel texts. According to Rev. xix. 8, the Bride of the Lamb is clothed in fine linen, which is the righteous deeds of the saints. In Rev. xix. 14 the eschatological armies are described as arrayed in fine white linen.

BIBLIOGRAPHY. K. Galling, *BRL*, 1937; F. J. Bruijel in *Bijbelsche Encyclopaedie*, 1950; W. Corswant, *Dictionnaire d'archéologie biblique*, 1956; F. Nötscher, *Biblische Altertumskunde*, 1940. F.C.F.

LINTEL. See HOUSE.

LINUS. A Rom. Christian who greeted Timothy, 2 Tim. iv. 21; for his relation to others *in loc.*, see CLAUDIA. The name (a son of Apollo) is not common. Succession lists show a Linus, identified by Irenaeus (*Adv. Haer.* iii. 3. 2) and subsequent writers with Timothy's friend, as first bishop of Rome after the apostles. On the problems of such lists, *cf.* Lightfoot, *Clement I*, pp. 201–345; A. Ehrhardt, *The Apostolic Succession*, 1953. Writers dominated by later practice (*e.g.* Rufinus, Preface to *Clem. Recog.*) labour to reconcile the apostolic appointment of both Linus and Clement (*q.v.*). Linus made little further mark on tradition or legend. (*Cf. Liber Pontificalis*, ed. Duchesne, I, pp. 53, 121, for meagre notices; Tischendorf, *Acta Apocrypha*, pp. xix f., for martyrdoms of Peter and Paul.) A.F.W.

LION. At one time the Asiatic lion was found from Asia Minor through the Middle East and Persia to India, and a lion found in Greece up to nearly AD 100 was probably very similar. This European/Asiatic lion resembles the African lion fairly closely, but too few specimens have been collected to know how distinct it is. It is thought that lions were exterminated from Palestine about the time of the Crusades, but in 1900 lions were still known in Persia; these had been killed out by 1930, or perhaps earlier still. Lions were reported in Syria up to 1851 by Burton (*Travels in Syria*) and in parts of Iraq up till the early 1920s. The few Asiatic lions surviving today are in a small patch of forest in the Kathiawar peninsula of India.

The word 'lion' occurs some 130 times in AV, with one general Heb. word *'aryeh* and eight other words applied to various ages of the two sexes. This rich vocabulary suggests that the lion was common and well known in Old Testament times, and many contexts confirm this, even though the usage is largely metaphorical for strength. The lion was also a symbol of royalty in the Ancient Near East (see next article). Lions were frequently kept in captivity (*cf.* Dn. vi. 7 ff.). They were being bred by Ashurnasirpal II (883–859 BC) at Nimrud (see CALAH) and kept in large numbers (E. W. Budge and L. W. King, *Annals of the Kings of Assyria*, 1901). G.C.

LION OF JUDAH. An abbreviated form of one of Christ's messianic titles found in Rev. v. 5: 'the Lion of the tribe of Judah'. An obvious allusion to Gn. xlix. 9, 'Judah is a lion's whelp', this title depicts Christ as the culmination of the courage, might, and ferocity of the tribe of Judah. Like a lion Satan stalks the saints (1 Pet. v. 8), but Christ is the conquering lion, worthy to open the seven seals of judgment. The use of the term 'lion' (*q.v.*) in connection with judgment may reflect passages like Is. xxxviii. 13; La. iii. 10; Ho. v. 14, xiii. 8, where God's judgment is likened to a lion's attack. Emperors of Ethiopia, convinced that they stem from Judah as descendants of Solomon and the Queen of Sheba, have proudly appropriated this title. D.A.H.

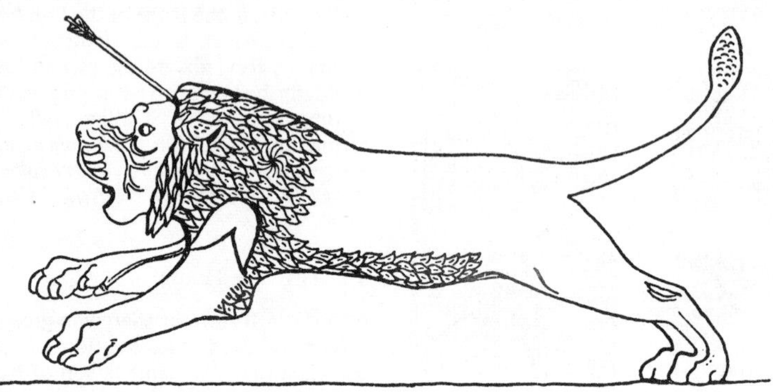

Fig. 134. One of the lions depicted in the lion-hunt scene on the reliefs from the palace of Ashurbanipal. Nineveh, *c.* 650 BC. See also fig. 25.

LIP. Both the Heb. word *śāpâ*, and (less frequently) the Gk. word *cheilos*, mean not only the human lips but also the brink or shore of the sea, or the bank of a river (Gn. xxii. 17, xli. 3; Heb. xi. 12) and, in the case of the Heb. word, border of a garment (Ex. xxviii. 26), though the primary application is to lips. Another Heb. word *śāpām* refers to the upper lip or moustache, always in respect of covering it, with the hand or garment, as a sign of grief or shame (Lv. xiii. 45). *Cf.* the reference to covering the face in 2 Sa. xix. 4.

In the case of the lips we find clear examples of the Hebrew way of speaking whereby the organs seem to feel and act themselves, which is partly synecdoche, and partly due to the lack of physiological understanding of the nervous system (see BODY).

However, the connection of the lips with the heart is brought out in Pr. xvi. 23. For an explanation of this connotation, see HEART.

The lips not only speak (Jb. xxvii. 4) but rejoice (Ps. lxxi. 23), quiver (with fear) (Hab. iii. 16), preserve knowledge (Pr. v. 2), offer praise (Ps. lxiii. 3), plead (Jb. xiii. 6), and possess ethical qualities of truthfulness, or righteousness, or, conversely, sinning or speaking lies (Jb. ii. 10; Pr. xii. 19, xvi. 13).

The parallelism with tongue or mouth is natural, and these are used in much the same senses (Pss. xxxiv. 13, li. 15). Just as with these words, lip can be extended to mean speech, words (Jb. xii. 20), or language (Gn. xi. 1; Is. xix. 18). (See MOUTH, TONGUE.) B.O.B.

LIVER. Only in the Old Testament does this word occur. The Heb. *kāḇēḏ* is from a root meaning 'to be heavy', or by extension of meaning 'to be honoured'. So, it is the heavy organ. Of the fourteen occurrences, eleven are in Exodus and Leviticus, referring to the liver of a sacrificial beast.

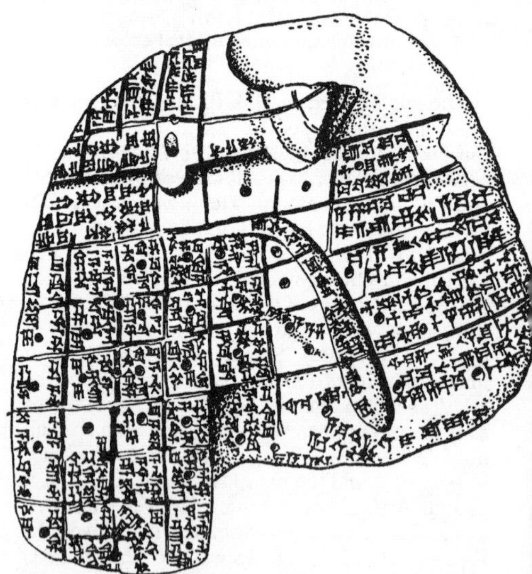

Fig. 135. Clay model of liver, inscribed in fifty-five sections. Used as a text-book for divination by the priests of Babylon (*c.* 1830–1530 BC).

The 'caul above or from the liver' (see CAUL),

always associated with the kidneys, was burned on the altar. Josephus lists the parts burned on the altar (*Ant.* iii. 9. 2) 'the kidneys, and the caul, and all the fat, and the lobe of the liver'.

It is, however, unlikely that the 'caul', *yōṯereṯ*, refers to a lobe of the liver, but probably to fat upon it, or possibly the pancreas. The word literally means 'remainder' or 'appendage', so it is not stated specifically that the liver itself was burned on the altar, but the internal fat and the kidneys.

From Ezekiel (xxi. 21) it appears that the liver was the material for a form of divination, based on the internal markings of the liver. Many artificial livers of clay have been unearthed in the Middle East, and were made for this purpose. A similar practice was known among the Etruscans, from whom it passed to the Romans (Lat. *haruspices* = 'liver diviners').

A wound in the liver was apparently regarded as fatal (Pr. vii. 23), though a wound in the 'heart' (2 Sa. xviii. 14) was not, but Heb. physiology of the internal organs is vague (see HEART; BOWELS).

The reference in La. ii. 11 is better rendered with the Gk., Lat., and Syr. versions, by 'my glory', *keḇōḏî* for *keḇēḏî*, but, on the other hand, in Ps. xvi. 9 it makes better sense to read it *vice versa*.

B.O.B.

LIZARD. Six words, each denoting some kind of lizard, appear in a list of unclean animals in Lv. xi. 29, 30. They are (with the AV translations): (1) *ṣāḇ*, 'tortoise' (RV 'great lizard'); (2) *'anāqâ*, 'ferret' (LXX 'shrew-mouse'; RV 'gecko'); (3) *kōaḥ*, 'chameleon' (Vulg. *stellio*; RV 'land crocodile'); (4) *leṭā'â*, 'lizard' (RV 'lizard') (a general Talmudic name for the *Lacertilia*); (5) *ḥōmeṭ*, 'snail' (RV 'sand-lizard'); (6) *tinšemeṯ* (= 'breathing', 'blowing'), 'mole' (RV 'chameleon'). In addition, another probable reference to a lizard is (7) *śemāmîṯ* (Pr. xxx. 28), 'spider' (RV 'lizard').

Each of the seven names occurs only once, the philological evidence is obscure, and it is difficult to make accurate identification. RVmg, indeed, has against numbers (2), (3), (4), (5) above, the marginal note: 'Words of uncertain meaning, but probably denoting four kinds of lizards.'

Although the Israelites were not allowed to eat the unclean animals named, the Bedouin have been known to consume them in times of need.

More than forty species of lizard are known to Palestine, the most common of which are the green lizard (*Lacerta viridis*) and its varieties, and the wall-lizard of the genus *Zootoca*. They are generally to be found lurking in uninhabited areas, in warm crannies of rocks, on trees, and on walls and ceilings of houses. The gecko (*Ptyodactylus Hasselquistii*) was called also *abu-brais*, 'father of leprosy', perhaps because of its colour, perhaps because of supposed poisonous qualities. For discussion of others named above, see TORTOISE, CHAMELEON, SNAIL, MOLE, SPIDER, and figs. 38, 39, 40, 90.

J.D.D.

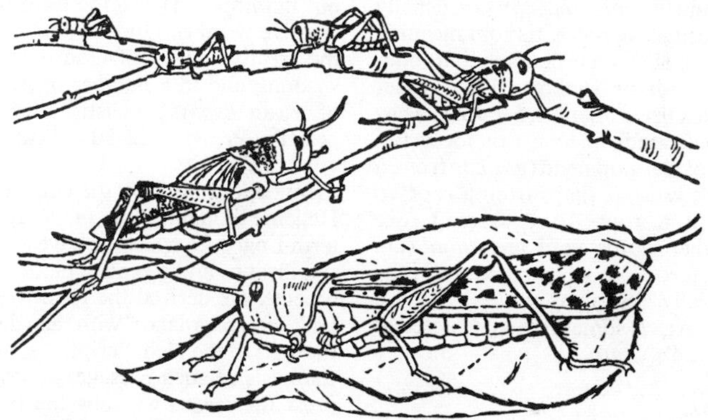

Fig. 136. Six stages in the life-cycle of the migratory or desert locust with the winged adult in the foreground. Two-thirds average natural size. See also fig. 86.

LOAF. See BREAD.

LOAN. See DEBT, DEBTOR (*a*).

LOCK. See KEY.

LOCUST. The locust is frequently mentioned in the Old Testament on account of its devastating habits. It is alluded to in AV under the names 'beetle', 'cankerworm', 'caterpillar', 'grasshopper', 'locust', and 'palmer-worm' (*q.v.*). It belongs to the family *Orthoptera* which consists of two groups, 'runners' (*Cursoria*), unclean under the levitical law, and 'leapers' (*Saltatoria*), 'which have legs above their feet, to leap withal upon the earth' regarded as clean (Lv. xi. 20–23).

There are numerous species of locusts. The Rabbis say there were 800. They are migratory, but their migrations do not take place at fixed seasons of the year nor at definite intervals of time. Their swarms are driven along by the wind, as they have little power of guiding their own flight. They usually invade Palestine from the Arabian desert on the south or south-east.

The female locust lays her eggs in holes in the

earth, which she digs by means of a special apparatus. They hatch out as wingless larvae, which hop about devouring all vegetation on which they alight. After a series of moults they develop wings and rise in clouds into the air. In each stage they are equally voracious, and there are numerous accounts by different observers of their ravages. They are, however, edible and form a palatable food (Lv. xi. 22; Mt. iii. 4). See fig. 86.

Nine different Heb. words are used in the Old Testament where the locust is intended. The commonest (*'arbeh*), the general term, occurs twenty-four times. It is usually connected with a root (*rāḇâ*), 'to multiply'. It is used of the Egyp. plague (Ex. x. 4–6) and is listed as one of four insects mentioned in Lv. xi. 22. The other three are also members of the locust family. Two occur only in this verse: *sol'ām* (AV 'bald-locust', from a rabbinical statement that its head was bald in front) and *ḥargōl* (AV incorrectly 'beetle', RV 'cricket'). The fourth word (*ḥāgāḇ*) (AV usually 'grasshopper') occurs five times. Its root meaning is 'to hide', and the allusion is perhaps to its concealing the sun with its swarms. Three other words are used in a list in Joel i. 4. See JOEL. They are either different kinds of locust or locusts in different stages of development (*gāzām*, from a root 'to cut off'; *yeleq*, perhaps from a root 'to lick'; *ḥāsîl*, from a root 'to consume'). See fig. 136. The other words used are *ṣᵉlāṣal* (Dt. xxviii. 42), from a root 'to whirr', and *gôḇ* (Na. iii. 17, *etc.*), literally 'a swarm'.

A plague of locusts is sometimes interpreted as a visitation of God's wrath. D.G.S.

LOD. See LYDDA.

LO-DEBAR. Where Mephibosheth lived before David recalled him (2 Sa. ix. 4); east of the Jordan (*cf.* 2 Sa. ii. 29, xvii. 27); probably DEBIR (3).

LODGE. See CUCUMBER.

LOG. See WEIGHTS AND MEASURES.

LOGIA. See ORACLE.

LOGOS. A common Gk. word used in a quasi-technical sense as a title of Christ in the Johannine writings. It carries a large number of different meanings: its basic translation is 'word', *i.e.* meaningful utterance, whence develop its many senses 'statement, declaration, discourse, subject-matter, doctrine, affair' and, by another development, 'reason, cause, sake, respect'. As a grammatical term it means a finite sentence, in logic a factual statement, definition, or judgment, in rhetoric a correctly constructed piece of oratory. As a term of psychology and metaphysics it was used by the Stoa, following Herakleitos, to signify the divine power or function by which the universe is given unity, coherence, and meaning (*Logos Spermatikos*, 'seminal Word', which, like seed, gives form to unformed matter): man is made in accordance with the same principle, and is himself said to possess Logos, both inwardly (*Logos Endiathetos*, reason) and expressed in speech (*Logos Prophorikos*). The term is also used as the pattern or norm of man whereby he may live 'according to Nature'.

In the LXX Logos is used to translate Heb. *dāḇār*. The root of this signifies 'that which lies behind', and so when translated as 'word' it, too, means meaningful sound; it may also mean 'thing'. In accordance with a common feature of Heb. psychology a man's *dāḇār* is regarded as in some sense an extension of his personality and further as possessing a substantive existence of its own. The Word of God, then, is His self-revelation through Moses and the prophets; it may be used to designate *both* single visions and oracles *and* the whole content of the total revelation, and thus especially the Pentateuch. The Word possesses a like power to the God who speaks it (*cf.* Is. lv. 11) and effects His will without hindrance. Hence the term may refer to the creative word of God. In the Wisdom literature the creative power of God is referred to as His wisdom, and in a number of passages is spoken of as an *hypostasis* distinct from Him (see especially Pr. viii. 22–30: Wisdom of Solomon vii. 21 ff.).

Influenced both by the Old Testament and by Hellenic thought, Philo made frequent use of the term Logos, to which he gave a highly developed significance and a central place in his theological scheme. He derived the term from Stoic sources and, in accordance with his discovery of Gk. thought in the Heb. Scriptures, made use of it on the basis of such passages as Ps. xxxiii. 6 to express the means whereby the transcendent God may be the Creator of the universe and the Revealer of Himself to Moses and the Patriarchs. On the Gk. side he equates the Logos with the Platonic concept of the World of Ideas so that it becomes both God's plan and God's power of creation. On the side of biblical exegesis the Logos is identified with the Angel of the Lord and the Name of God, and is described by a variety of terms as High Priest, Captain and Steersman, Advocate (Paraclete), and Son of God. It is termed a second God and, on the other hand, described as the Ideal Man, the Pattern of God's earthly creation of man. In spite of all this terminology of personification, however, the term remains—inevitably, in view of Philo's staunch Judaism (at least, in intention) —a philosophical and theological term and tool.

A further possible determining factor in the use of Logos in the passages which we need to review is the use of the term to signify the gospel message. The term is used absolutely (*e.g.* to preach the Word) and with a number of genitives (the Word of God, of Christ, of the Cross, of reconciliation, of life, *etc.*). These show that the gospel story is seen in the New Testament as essentially a presentation of Jesus Himself; He is the Word which is preached. But this is by no means always implicit in the phrase.

Three places are found at which the use of Logos in a technical sense has been concerned, *viz.* Jn. i. 1 and 14; 1 Jn. i. 1–3; Rev. xix. 13.

Jn. i. 1 is the only unambiguous case. Here we have a highly metaphysical prologue to the Gospel in which the significance of the Christ is interpreted theologically. Divergence is found among scholars only in the identification of the primary source of these verses and the chief meaning of Logos here. Attempts have been made to link the prologue primarily with the Old Testament use of *dāḇār* alone, or with the rabbinical teaching concerning the Torah. These fail because these concepts are not sufficiently differentiated from the supreme Godhead to stand without alteration in verse 14. The figure of Wisdom provides more parallels but lacks identification in our sources with the Word: the teaching about the Primal or Heavenly Man which others have invoked is too conjectural to command much confidence. Only the Philonic Logos-teaching provides a clear theological scheme in which the Word possesses a like unity with God and a like distinction from Him, and in which both creative and sustaining activity in the universe and revelatory activity towards man is ascribed to it. Further, the necessarily unique concept of incarnation is nevertheless a proper development of the identification of Philo's Logos with the Ideal Man. Either a direct use of Philo or a similar background in intellectual circles of Hellenistic Jewry may lie behind this.

In 1 Jn. i. 1 the phrase 'Word of life' is unlikely to bear the meaning of Logos in its technical theological sense; both context and construction are against this. Even if this be from the same pen as the Gospel (which some scholars regard as doubtful) the letter may date from a time prior to the adoption of a full-grown Logos-doctrine. The sense of 'Christian gospel' fits this context best.

In Rev. xix. 13 the sense of 'gospel' may lie behind the ascription of the title Logos of God to the triumphant figure; compare vi. 2, where in the view of some exegetes the mounted figure is the triumphant advancing gospel.

We may compare also the imagery of Wisdom of Solomon xviii. 15, 16. But since in Revelation the figure is explicitly declared to be King of kings and Lord of lords, some more metaphysical meaning must be latent here. The literary genre of the book amply explains why this meaning is not developed here in the same fashion as in the Fourth Gospel.

All three places illustrate how the fulness of Christ consistently exhausts all preparatory imagery and thought; and how many places need an exegesis which draws on many sources for full exposition. Jesus gives fresh meaning to terminology which prior to Him was expressive of lesser mysteries.

BIBLIOGRAPHY. *TWNT* (*s.v. legō*); Pauly-Wissowa, art. 'Logos'; C. H. Dodd, *The Interpretation of the Fourth Gospel*, 1954. J.N.B.

LOIS. Timothy's grandmother, presumably Eunice's mother (2 Tim. i. 5). Paul doubtless alludes to her Christian faith: had she been simply a godly Jewess, her devotion is less likely to have been known to him. (See also EUNICE.) The name is hard to parallel in the period.

A.F.W.

LONGSUFFERING. In the Old Testament the quality of longsuffering is frequently attributed to God, and represents the restraint of His anger in the face of provocation. Whenever He is described as longsuffering, or as being slow to anger (Heb. *'ereḵ 'appayim*; *cf.* Ex. xxxiv. 6; Nu. xiv. 18; Ps. lxxxvi. 15, *etc.*), it is almost invariably in association with His gracious and merciful character towards sinful and rebellious men. In the book of Proverbs this quality is commended among men as having practical value in the avoidance of strife and the wise ordering of human affairs, particularly where provocation is involved. The use of the term in Je. xv. 15 is doubtful: 'Take me not away in thy longsuffering'. If the text is correct the natural meaning of the sentence would seem to demand a bad sense for longsuffering, unless it be referred to God's longsuffering in respect of the prophet's enemies.

In the New Testament longsuffering (and patience) is again attributed to God. In Romans Paul twice speaks of His longsuffering, Gk. *makrothymia*, towards sinful men (i. 4, ix. 22), and Peter uses the verb in a similar context (2 Pet. iii. 9). There is throughout the Epistles also a strong emphasis upon its necessity in human relationships within the Christian fellowship. As one of the fruits of the Spirit (Gal. v. 22) it is to characterize the ministry. In several instances the idea of human provocation is absent, such as in Jas. v. 7, where the believer is exhorted to emulate the husbandman who waits for the fruit of the earth, and in the same Epistle (v. 10), where it is related to affliction. F.S.F.

LOOM. See SPINNING AND WEAVING.

LOOPS. See TABERNACLE.

LORD. See GOD, NAMES OF.

LORD OF HOSTS. See GOD, NAMES OF.

LORD'S DAY. The expression is found only once in Scripture. In Rev. i. 10 John discloses that the vision of the Apocalypse came to him while he was rapt 'in the Spirit on the Lord's day'. This is the first extant occurrence in Christian literature of *hē kyriakē hēmera*. The adjectival construction suggests that it was a formal designation of the Church's worship day. As such it certainly appears early in the 2nd century (Ignatius, *Epistle to the Magnesians*, i. 67).

Little support can be adduced for the theory that the term referred to Easter day, except, of course, in the sense that each Lord's day is a paschal recapitulation. But it must be noted that such reputable scholars as Wettstein, Deissmann, and Hort, among others, prefer to interpret the verse as indicating that John was transported in his spiritual ecstasy to the great day of judgment itself (*cf.* Rev. vi. 17, xvi. 14). Lightfoot believes that there are 'very good, if not conclusive reasons' for such a view (*The Apostolic Fathers*, II, Section I, Part II, p. 129). The majority opinion, however, inclines to feel with Swete that such an interpretation is foreign to the immediate context and contrary to linguistic usage (LXX always has *hē hēmera tou kyriou* for the prophetic 'day of the Lord': *kyriakos* does not appear). It would seem reasonably safe, therefore, to conclude that as the actual location of John's vision is recorded in verse 9, so the actual occasion is recorded in verse 10.

Even if a late date for Revelation be accepted (*c.* AD 96), it is not necessary to assume with Harnack that *hē kyriakē hēmera* was not in use before the close of the 1st century. It may even have emerged as soon as AD 57 when Paul wrote 1 Corinthians. In xi. 20 he speaks of *kyriakon deipnon* (AV 'the Lord's supper'). It is interesting that Pesh. reads 'Lord's day' here. But it would hardly appear that the term was in current use, for later in the Epistle Paul has *kata mian sabbatou* (xvi. 2).

Deissmann has thrown further light upon the title by showing that in Asia Minor and Egypt even before the Christian era the first day of each month was called Emperor's day or *Sebastē*. This may eventually have been transferred to a day of the week, probably Thursday (*dies Iovis*). 'If these conclusions are valid,' comments R. H. Charles, 'we can understand how naturally the term "Lord's Day" arose; for just as the first day of each month, or a certain day of each week, was called "Emperor's Day", so it would be natural for Christians to name the *first day* of each week, associated as it was with the Lord's resurrection and the custom of Christians to meet together for worship, as "Lord's Day". It may have first arisen in apocalyptic circles when a hostile attitude to the Empire was adopted by Christianity' (R. H. Charles, *The Revelation of St. John*, 1920, I, p. 23; *cf. BS*, pp. 218 ff.).

'Lord' here clearly signifies Christ and not God the Father. It is Christ's own day. It belongs to Him because of His resurrection, when He was 'declared to be the Son of God with power' (Rom. i. 4). McArthur is surely right in claiming that the title ultimately derives from the Lordship of Jesus Christ which was made manifest in the resurrection on 'the first day of the week' (Mk. xvi. 2; see A. A. McArthur, *The Evolution of the Christian Year*, 1953, p. 21). Christian worship is essentially an *anamnēsis* (remembrance) of the Easter event which revealed the triumph of God's redemptive purpose. Hence the prevailing note of joy and praise. The first day was also appropriate, as it recalled the initial day of creation, when God made light, and the fact that the Christian Pentecost fell on Sunday. Furthermore, it may well have been the expectation of the primitive Christians that our Lord's return would take place on His own day.

The earliest piece of evidence relating to the Christian observance of the first day of the week lies in 1 Cor. xvi. 1, 2, but there is no explicit reference to an actual assembly. Acts xx. 7 is more specific and probably reflects the continued Christian use of the Jewish calendar under which the Lord's day would begin at sunset on Saturday. Alford sees in the readiness of Gentiles to accept this Jewish reckoning 'the greatest proof of all that this day was thus observed' (Henry Alford, *The New Testament for English Readers*, n.d., p. 788). On the other hand, there is no trace in the New Testament of any sabbatarian controversy. The Lord's day, while fulfilling all the beneficent purposes of God in the institution of the Sabbath for mankind, was kept 'in newness of the spirit, and not in oldness of the letter' (Rom. vii. 6, RV). A.S.W.

LORDS OF THE PHILISTINES. An expression in which the word translated 'Lords' is *s^e^rānîm*, probably having a singular form *seren*, though this does not occur. The word is applied only to the Philistine rulers of the five cities Ashdod, Ashkelon, Ekron, Gath, and Gaza (*qq.v.*; Jos. xiii. 3; Jdg. iii. 3, xvi. 5, 8, 18, 27, 30; 1 Sa. v. 8, 11, vi. 4, 12, 16, 18, vii. 7, xxix. 2, 6, 7; 1 Ch. xii. 19) and is used nowhere else in the Bible. It is generally believed that the word *seren* is to be derived from the same pre-Hellenic (perhaps Indo-European) word as that from which the Gk. *tyrannos* (*c.* 700 BC), was taken. Since the exact connotation of the word *seren* is as yet unknown, the translations 'lord' (AV, RV) or 'ruler' (RSV) are both a satisfactory generalization. T.C.M.

LORD'S PRAYER, THE. The prayer which our Lord taught His disciples as the model prayer for believers and for His Church of all ages. In Mt. vi. 9–13 it is given as an integral part of the Sermon on the Mount. But in Lk. xi. 2–4 it is given by our Lord in totally different circumstances. It is obvious that since He meant this prayer to serve as a model and pattern for all His disciples and for all times, He would have repeated it on different occasions. The fact that the Gospels mention only the two occasions does not preclude the probability that our Lord taught His disciples at other times too to pray this perfect prayer.

In Mt. vi. 9–13 our Lord gives it as an example of prayer which complies with all the requisites which He Himself had laid down as essential for true prayer. He declares in Mt. vi. 9: 'After this manner therefore pray ye.' He was thus continuing to teach His disciples *how* to pray. After having warned them not to pray as hypocrites (vi. 5) nor to use 'vain repetitions' as the heathen do (vi. 7) our Lord taught them what sort of prayer is acceptable before God. But in Lk. xi. 1–4 we see that in response to the request of a disciple, who had just seen Jesus pray, our Lord gives the prayer this time, not only as an example of a prayer which complies with His teaching, but as a definite prayer which must be prayed by His followers. For in xi. 2 He declares: 'When ye pray, say . . .'

Although in Lk. xi. 2–4 the prayer is given in a shorter form than in Mt. vi. 9–13, its contents are essentially the same. We may perhaps surmise that our Lord in Lk. xi. 2–4 gave the absolute minimum wording of the prayer which we should pray, not mechanically or purely formally, but in spirit and in truth. In Mt. vi. 9–13, where He gave the prayer as an example of how His followers should pray, He gave a more detailed prayer. We shall thus consider the contents of this longer form of our Lord's prayer. It is obvious that our Lord gave the prayer originally in Aramaic. By the time Matthew and Luke wrote their Gospels, however, the prayer would naturally have been used by Christians in Greek also. This probably explains why Mt. vi and Lk. xi have general agreement in language and both use the unique term *epiousion* (rendered 'daily') in the prayer.

By the opening words of the prayer—'Our Father which art in heaven'—we are taught the correct attitude and spirit in which we should pray to God. Addressing Him as 'Our Father', we look up to Him in love and faith, as to the One who is near us in perfect love and grace. By the words 'which art in heaven' we give expression to our holy reverence for Him who is the Almighty Ruler over heaven and earth. The introductory words of the prayer also remind us of the fact that all Christian believers are one in Him, for we are to pray to God as '*Our* Father'.

The believer's heart being rightly attuned by the invocation, the first petitions are those concerning the glory and divine purpose of our heavenly Father. 'Hallowed be thy name' (*hagiasthētō*) is a prayer asking God to enable us and all men to recognize and honour Him—to work inwardly upon us and upon all humanity so that we and everyone shall worship and serve Him as the holy, almighty, heavenly Father. His name, *i.e.* Himself in His self-revelation, is to be acknowledged as holy; and He is to receive all the honour and glory due to Him who has revealed Himself both as the One who perfectly loves us and as the holy and omnipotent Creator. (See GOD, NAMES OF.) The petition 'thy kingdom come' asks God to let His divine rule and sovereignty (*basileia*) continually and ever more gloriously attain its rightful place; so that instead of living in sin and rebellion against God, we should all, through the might of His Spirit, be brought more and more to accept His sovereign rule and thus be freed from the powers of darkness. (See KINGDOM OF GOD.) It is a supplication that the divine dominion of God will be extended 'here and now' (in this present age) in the heart of individuals as well as in the world as a whole. In the last instance, however, this petition has an eschatological connotation also. It is ultimately a supplication that the kingly rule of God, which has come with power into the life of individuals and of mankind through the first coming of Jesus, and which is continually coming, shall come in full glory and divine perfection through the second coming of Christ as the Lord of lords.

The third petition, 'Thy will be done, as in heaven, so on earth' (RV), which is absent in the authentic text of Lk. xi. 2, is practically an elaboration of the previous petition. In heaven, where the rule of God is gladly and unconditionally accepted by all, the will of God is spontaneously and joyfully obeyed by all and at all times. Believers should thus pray that God's will shall in the same way be obeyed by all on earth. This petition is primarily meant for the present age, but it opens up vistas to the time after the consummation of all things, when every knee shall bow before Him who is the King of kings and the powers of darkness will be finally and totally destroyed. God will then be all in all and His will will reign supreme in heaven and on the new earth (1 Cor. xv. 25–28).

The first three petitions having centred upon the glorification of God, the next three petitions are concerned with the physical and spiritual well-being of believers. Because, as a result of sin and rebellion against the Lord, the dominion of God is not universally recognized and His will is not completely obeyed in the present age on earth, there are always material and spiritual needs experienced in the life of individual believers and unbelievers alike.

Believers should thus pray expressly for the aid and blessing of God regarding all aspects of life in this world. The petition 'Give us this day our daily bread' asks God as our heavenly Father to grant us the physical necessities of life. The word 'bread' here symbolizes all that we really need for our earthly existence. In view of the foregoing petitions, this is a supplication asking God continually to supply us with the material necessities of life in such a way that we shall in the highest degree be able to sanctify His Name, to labour for the coming of His kingdom, and to do His will, as in heaven so on earth. Our prayer for daily sustenance is thus not meant to be a selfish prayer, or a prayer for material luxury, but a prayer in which we confess our utter dependence on God, and look to Him in faith and love to supply us with all things which we really need to enable us to live according to His will.

The Gk. word *epiousion*, translated in the AV and RV by 'daily', occurs only in Mt. vi. 11 and Lk. xi. 3. Although finality has not yet been reached regarding its correct etymological derivation, and some prefer to translate it by 'for the coming day' or 'that is needful or sufficient', the translation 'daily' seems to be quite in order. According to the context, what is meant is the constant provision of what is really needed and adequate for us day by day in the realm of our physical, material existence.

The next petition, 'And forgive us our debts, as we also have forgiven our debtors' (RV), is both a prayer and a confession. For he who prays for forgiveness at the same time admits that he has sinned and is guilty. In Lk. xi. 4 this petition reads: 'And forgive us our sins; for we ourselves also forgive every one that is indebted to us.' The Gk. word *hamartias*, here rendered 'sins', has the primary meaning of 'missing the mark' and thus 'acting wrongly' and 'breaking the law of God'. In Mt. vi. 12 *opheilēmata* ('debts') is used, and designates our sins as those things which make us guilty and load us with debts before God—the true, filial relation to God has been broken and we have incurred a moral and spiritual debt to our Father and our Creator, who has full authority over our lives. In this petition we therefore humbly ask our heavenly Father for a remission of our debts, seeing that we ourselves can never earn our forgiveness. Because Jesus came to give His life as a ransom for our sins, He could teach believers to pray thus.

The words 'as we also [*hōs kai hēmeis*, 'in the same way also as we'] have forgiven [aorist] our debtors' (Mt. vi. 12) and 'for we ourselves also forgive [present indicative] every one that is indebted to us' do not mean that we are to ask forgiveness on the ground that we have forgiven and are forgiving those who sin against us. We can receive forgiveness through grace alone. But in order to pray to God for forgiveness in sincerity and without hypocrisy, we must be free from every spirit of hatred and revenge. Only when God has given us the grace truly to forgive our debtors can we utter a true prayer for forgiveness. This demand that we should be free of insincerity and hypocrisy, when we pray to our heavenly Father for forgiveness, was looked upon by our Lord as of such importance that He reiterated it in Mt. vi. 14, 15.

The final petition in Lk. xi. 4 reads: 'And bring us not into temptation'. In Mt. vi. 13, RV, the words 'but deliver us from the evil one' follow. But as these additional words are only an elaboration of the foregoing, the petition is essentially the same in Luke and Matthew. They who sincerely pray for forgiveness of sins long to be enabled not to sin again. Thus it is fitting that this petition follows the previous one. The Gk. *peirasmos*, rendered 'temptation', cannot in the context of Mt. vi. 13 mean 'trial' or 'affliction', but only 'temptation'. The meaning of this petition is, 'And do not allow us to be brought into situations where we shall be exposed to evil temptation'. God never tempts anyone to do evil (Jas. i. 13), but He controls the circumstances of our lives. In this prayer we humbly confess that we are prone to sin and thus plead with Him not to allow us to be brought into situations or conditions which involve grave temptation to sin. As a further elaboration of this there follows 'but deliver us from the evil one', *i.e.* shield, protect, guard (*rhyesthai*) us against the onslaughts of the devil (*tou ponērou*). This final petition, although applicable to every day in our lives, points very strongly to the consummation when our Lord at His second coming shall bring a decisive end to all that is evil, and establish His eternal kingdom on the new earth where righteousness and holiness will reign for ever.

In some ancient and many later MSS of Mt. vi a doxology follows. In the AV it reads, 'For thine is the kingdom, and the power, and the glory, for ever. Amen'. Although the most authoritative MSS do not have the doxology, it has been used in the Christian Church from the very earliest times (*cf.* the *Didache* and the Western Text), and it is certainly a most suitable and worthy ending for the Lord's Prayer. That it does not, however, belong to the original text of Matthew is apparent from the fact that verses 14 and 15 follow naturally after verses 12 and 13a as we have them in the RV.

Someone has rightly said that the Lord's Prayer is the Sermon on the Mount summarized in prayer form. It is the prayer which all Christians should regularly offer to God in order to be enabled to obey the laws of His kingdom ever more completely until the day when His divine sovereignty will be finally and perfectly established.

It should be noted that our Lord (when teaching His disciples this prayer) did not say, '*We* must pray' but '*ye* pray'. The Lord's Prayer is not a prayer which He Himself ever prayed or could pray. In the first place He never prayed to God as 'Our Father' but only as 'My Father'. For His Sonship is a unique Sonship; He is the only begotten of the Father. In the second place He never prayed to God to forgive Him because He is the divine Son who always did the will of the Father perfectly, and who, although He bore our sins on the cross, never Himself sinned.

While the individual petitions in the Lord's Prayer are paralleled in various contexts in Jewish religious literature, nothing comparable to the prayer as a whole is found. The Lord's Prayer is unique, and unsurpassed even to this day—gathering in a few words all the essentials of true prayer.

BIBLIOGRAPHY. R. V. G. Tasker, *Matthew*, *TNTC*, 1961; J. N. Geldenhuys, *Luke*, *New London Commentary*, 1951, and other commentaries on Matthew and Luke. J.N.G.

LORD'S SUPPER, THE. It will be most convenient to set out the New Testament evidence for the Christian ordinance under the headings of 'The Last Supper'; 'The Breaking of Bread'; 'The Pauline Eucharist'; and 'Other New Testament Material'.

I. THE LAST SUPPER

a. Was it the Passover?

The precise nature of the meal which the Lord shared with His disciples on the night in which He was betrayed is one of the most warmly debated topics of New Testament history and interpretation. Various suggestions have been made.

1. The traditional explanation is that the meal was the customary Passover feast, and this can claim the support of the Gospel records, both Synoptic (*e.g.* Mk. xiv. 1, 2, 12–16) and Johannine (*e.g.* xiii. 21–30). There are features of the meal which Jewish scholars (notably Billerbeck and Dalman) have noted as distinguishing features of the Paschal feast, *e.g.* reclining at the table (see ABRAHAM'S BOSOM), the distribution of alms (*cf.* Jn. xiii. 29), and the use of the 'sop' which is dipped in the special *ḥaroseth* sauce as a memorial of the bitterness of the Egyp. bondage. See the full details in Dalman, *Jesus–Jeshua*, E.T., 1929, pp. 106 ff., and J. Jeremias, *The Eucharistic Words of Jesus*, E.T., 1955, pp. 14 ff. But the evidence is not so compelling as to exclude all other interpretations, although there is a tendency today, especially since the publication of Jeremias' book in 1949, to give more respectful consideration to the Passover view than was formerly done. The earlier judgment was similar to that expressed by Hans Lietzmann, who dismissed the Paschal theory of the Supper as containing scarcely 'a glimmer of probability' (*Messe und Herrenmahl*, 1926, p. 212). There has been a reaction from this extreme negativism.

2. The data which caused some questioning of the traditional view are mainly derived from the Fourth Gospel, which apparently dates the events of the Supper evening and the passion a day earlier than the Synoptics. According to Jn. xiii. 1, xviii. 28, xix. 14, 31, 42, the crucifixion happened a day before Nisan 15, which is the Synoptic reckoning, and the Last Supper was, of course, eaten on the evening before that. Thus it cannot have been the regular paschal meal, for the Lord died at the same time as the lambs for that meal were being immolated in the Temple ritual. Thus there is an apparent *impasse*, which is further complicated by the allegation that the Synoptic account is not consistent with itself; for instance, Lk. xxii. 15 may be read as an unfulfilled wish. For those scholars who prefer to support the Johannine dating (*e.g.* Bernard in the *ICC* on *John*) and believe that the last meal could therefore not have been the Passover, the question arises, what type of meal, then, was it? They answer this question by postulating a sabbath *Qiddūsh*, *i.e.* according to this view, Jesus and His followers constituted a religious group which met on the eve of the sabbath and the Passover, and held a simple service in which a prayer of sanctification (*Qiddūsh*) over a cup of wine was said.

3. As a modification of this suggestion Lietzmann put forward the idea that the meal was an ordinary one, and the Lord and His disciples, who shared it, formed a religious association called a *ḥabūrāh*, similar to the groups in which the Pharisees met. All these ideas have met with severe criticism, and there is apparent deadlock in the debate; though it is now being reopened through the investigation of the new evidence of the Qumran scrolls.

4. In the light of recent researches into the influence of separate calendars which were used for calculating feast-days, it is now possible to consider again the older submissions of Billerbeck and Pickl that the two strata of Gospel evidence may be harmonized on the assumption that both are right, each reflecting a different tradition. Billerbeck and Pickl distinguished between the Pharisaic date of the Passover which Jesus used and the Sadducean dating a day earlier which lies behind the Fourth Gospel. This was dismissed by critics as lacking in supporting evidence, but the Dead Sea Scrolls show that there were divergent calendars in use in heterodox Jewry, and it is possible that separate traditions were, in fact, in vogue at the time of the passion. Mlle A. Jaubert has recently reconstructed the events on this basis so as to harmonize the data of the Gospels and early liturgical witnesses (in her book *La date de la Cène, Calendrier biblique et liturgie chrétienne*, 1957, with a summary in English of her thesis in *Scripture*, October 1957, IX (8), pp. 108–115: 'The date of the Last Supper', by L. Johnston; and critical review by Jeremias in *JTS*, NS, X, 1959, pp. 131–133).

Whether the date of the Supper will ever be conclusively determined is uncertain; but we may certainly believe that, whatever the exact nature of the meal, there were Passover ideas in the Lord's mind when He sat down with the disciples. The Jewish Passover, based on Ex. xii and interpreted in the *Haggādāh* for Passover and the Mishnaic tractate *Pesaḥim*, provides the indispensable key to an understanding of the meal and also the meaning of the Lord's Supper in the early Church. This conclusion is reinforced by recent studies in typology which have shown the importance of the Old Testament events in their 'typological' significance for the New Testament writers; and no complex of saving events comes more decisively to the foreground in the thinking of early Christianity than the Exodus and redemption from Egypt (*cf.* H. Sahlin, 'The New Exodus of Salvation according to St. Paul', in *The Root of the Vine*, ed. A. Fridrichsen, 1953, pp. 81–95; J. Daniélou, *Sacramentum Futuri*, 1950, Book IV, pp. 131 ff.). Reference may also be made to the important contribution of T. Preiss, *Life in Christ*, E.T., 1954, p. 90, who shows the place of 'the totality of the events of the Exodus centring on the Passover' in both Jewish and Christian traditions.

b. The words of institution

We turn now to examine more closely the last meal in the upper room. Two questions immediately arise. What was the *form* of the words of institution, spoken over the bread and wine? And what was their *meaning*?

1. The original form of the words is not easily discoverable because there are two sets of variants, represented in the Markan and the Pauline traditions respectively. Lk. xxii. 15–20 has peculiarities of its own, both textual and hermeneutic. There is a recent tendency to accept the longer recension of the Lucan text against the

shorter readings of the Western manuscript D and certain Old Lat. MSS which omit verses 19b and 20. The value of the Lucan *pericope* lies in its place as independent evidence of the same tradition as that used by Paul with the unusual order 'cup—bread' in Lk. xxii. 17–19 and 1 Cor. x. 16, 21 (*cf. Didache* ix); and the preservation in both accounts of the command to repeat the rite (Lk. xxii. 19b; 1 Cor. xi. 25).

On the issue of Markan versus Pauline form the arguments on both sides are inconclusive. Some scholars feel that Jesus could never have suggested that the disciples were to drink His blood, even symbolically, and the Pauline version, 'This cup is the new covenant in my blood' (1 Cor. xi. 25), is more likely to be original, especially as the Markan formula is liturgically symmetrical with that about the bread, and is aligned to Ex. xxiv. 8 (LXX). Against this it has been contended by A. J. B. Higgins that the Markan form is more primitive because of its harsh Semitisms in the Greek and the obvious dependence on the Servant passages in Isaiah, although Higgins would wish to excise some of the Markan phrases. At all events, we may consider the following to be somewhere near the original: 'Jesus took a loaf, pronounced a blessing, broke it and said, This is my body. And he took a cup, blessed it and said, This cup is the new covenant in my blood (Paul), or, This is my blood of the covenant (Mark).' Then followed the eschatological pronouncement, *cf.* Mk. xiv. 25; 1 Cor. xi. 26.

2. If we begin with the eschatological utterance this will be explained as the hope of the early believers, instructed by the Lord, that their fellowship with Him will be fulfilled in the perfected kingdom of God; and this sets a *terminus ad quem* for the Pauline eucharist, for when the Lord returns in glory to unite His people in fellowship the memorial table-fellowship will cease (*cf.* Dibelius, *From Tradition to Gospel*, E.T., 1934, p. 208).

The interpretative words over the elements have been variously estimated. There is no ground for a literal equivalence as in the doctrine of transubstantiation. The copula 'is' is the exegetical *significat* as in Gn. xli. 26; Dn. vii. 17; Lk. viii. 11; Gal. iv. 24; Rev. i. 20; and in the spoken Aramaic the copulative would be lacking, as in Gn. xl. 12; Dn. ii. 36, iv. 22. The figurative, non-literal connotation 'ought never to have been disputed' (Lietzmann).

The words, 'body, blood', are sometimes taken in the sense that Jesus is referring to His impending death on the cross when His body was broken (but *cf.* Jn. xix. 31–37) and His blood shed in violent death. The principal objection to this symbolic view is that the word over the bread was not spoken when it was broken but when it was distributed, and the wine had been poured out at an earlier part of the paschal meal. Also there is nothing unusual or unique in the fact that bread was broken. 'To break bread' was a common Jewish expression for the sharing of a meal.

Another view takes the Gk. term *sōma* (body) to denote the Aramaic *gûp̄*, which means not only 'body' but 'person', as though Jesus said, 'This is my person, my real self'; and points to His continuing fellowship as risen Lord with His people as they repeat the table-fellowship. Jeremias, however, has objected to this suggestion of Dalman (*op. cit.*, p. 143) by remarking that the true counterpart to 'blood' is not 'body', *sōma*, but 'flesh', *sarx*, for which the Aramaic is *bisrī*, 'my flesh'.

The most valuable clue to the meaning of the Lord's instituting words is to be found in the part which food and drink play in the Passover ritual. Following Higgins' interpretation, we may take the words of the institution to be the Lord's own addition to the order of the paschal liturgy at two vital points, before and after the main meal. He tells His disciples, by His words and prophetic symbolism, that the original meaning of the paschal rite has now been transcended, inasmuch as He is the paschal Lamb fulfilling the Old Testament prefigurement (1 Cor. v. 7). His words and action in taking the bread and the cup are parables which announce a new significance. The bread becomes under His sovereign word the parable of His body yielded up in the service of God's redeeming purpose (*cf.* Heb. x. 5–10); and His blood outpoured in death, recalling the sacrificial rites of the Old Testament, is represented in the cup of blessing on the table. That cup is invested henceforward with a fresh significance as the memorial of the new Exodus, accomplished at Jerusalem (Lk. ix. 31).

The function of the elements is parallel, then, to that of the Passover dishes. At the annual feast the Israelite is linked, in a realistic and dynamic way, with his forebears whom the Lord redeemed from Egypt. The bread on the table is to be regarded as though it were 'the bread of affliction' which the Jews of old ate (Dt. xvi. 3 as interpreted in the Passover *Haggādāh*); he is to account himself as though he personally was set free from Egyp. tyranny in that first generation of his nation long ago (Mishnah, *Pesaḥim* x. 5). At the Lord's Table which is genetically related to the upper room the Church of the new Israel is gathered as the people of the new covenant (Je. xxxi. 31 ff.); is confronted afresh with the tokens of that once-offered sacrifice; and relives that experience by which it came out of the Egypt of sin and was ransomed to God by the precious death of God's paschal Victim.

II. THE BREAKING OF BREAD

In the early Church of the Acts there are scattered references to table-fellowship, *e.g.* Acts ii. 42, 46 where the phrase is 'breaking of bread'. In Acts xx. 7 (but not xxvii. 35, which describes an ordinary, non-cultic meal) there is a reference to a fellowship meal, using the identical phrase. The fact that no mention of the cup is ever made in Acts leads H. Lietzmann (see *ExpT*, LXV, pp. 333 ff. for a clear, yet critical, statement of his theory) to the elaborate thesis that this

Jerusalem communion in one kind is the earliest and most original form of the sacrament, though hardly deserving the name. It was, *ex hypothesi*, a fellowship meal beginning with the familiar Jewish custom of breaking of bread—a continuation, in fact, of the common meals of the Galilaean ministry when the Lord fed the crowds and in which the Lord and His disciples formed a *ḥabūrāh*. The motif of the Jerusalem rite was not the death of Jesus, but the invisible presence of the exalted Lord in their midst. The Lord's Supper of 1 Cor. xi with its emphasis on the atoning significance of the death of Christ was Paul's own new contribution, received by special revelation from the Lord in glory. So Lietzmann suggests.

But this elaboration is unnecessary. There is little suggestion that Paul was such an innovator. As A. M. Hunter remarks, 'It staggers belief that he could have successfully foisted his innovation . . . on the church at large' (*Paul and His Predecessors*, 1940, p. 91). The non-mention of the cup may not be significant; the name 'breaking of bread' may be a quasi-technical expression for the whole meal. What is significant about the early form of the Eucharist is the note of *joy* which stems directly, not so much from the Galilaean meals as from the post-resurrection appearances, many of which are associated with a meal between the victorious Lord and His own (Lk. xxiv. 30–35, 36–48; Jn. xxi. 9 ff.; Acts i. 4 (RVmg), x. 41; Rev. iii. 20).

III. THE PAULINE EUCHARIST

The common meals of the Galilaean ministry are more likely to find their fulfilment in the *agapē* or love feast of the Corinthian church (1 Cor. xi. 20–34). At Corinth there were two parts of the cultic observance: a common meal, taken for the purpose of nourishment (*cf. Didache* x. 1: 'after you are filled'), followed by a solemn rite of the Eucharist. (See LOVE FEAST.) There were serious excesses within the Corinthian assembly, such as greediness, selfishness, drunkenness, and gluttony. Paul issued a grave warning, and the impression we gather is that it was his desire to have the two parts kept separate, as happened in the later Church. Let the hungry eat at home, and come with reverence and self-examination to the Table, is his caution (xi. 22, 30–34).

Paul's distinctive eucharistic teaching serves to enhance the significance of the Supper by anchoring it firmly in God's redeeming purpose; so that it proclaims the Lord's death (1 Cor. xi. 26) as the Passover ritual set forth (hence the title, *Haggādāh*, *i.e.* declaration, for which the Gk. equivalent would be the Pauline *katangellein* of 1 Cor. xi. 26) the redeeming mercy of God under the old covenant. He also expounds the inner meaning of the Table as a communion (*koinōnia*) with the Lord in His death and risen life, signified in the bread and the wine (1 Cor. x. 16). Therein he discovers the unity of the Church, for as the members share together the one loaf they sit down as the one body of Christ (*cf.* A. E. J. Rawlinson's essay in *Mysterium Christi*, ed. Bell and Deissmann, 1930, pp. 225 ff.). There are eschatological overtones likewise, as in the evangelic tradition, with the forward look to the advent in glory. *Marānā-thā* in 1 Cor. xvi. 22 may very well be placed in a eucharistic setting so that the conclusion of the letter ends with the invocation 'Our Lord, come!' and prepares the scene for the celebration of the meal after the letter has been read to the congregation (*cf.* Lietzmann, *op. cit.*, p. 229; J. A. T. Robinson, 'Traces of a Liturgical Sequence in 1 Cor. xvi. 20/24', *JTS*, NS, IV, 1953, pp. 38–41; but see C. F. D. Moule, *NTS*, VI, 1959–60, pp. 307 ff.).

IV. OTHER NEW TESTAMENT MATERIAL

It is surely significant that there is little other *direct* New Testament witness to the sacrament apart from the references we have already given. This fact is especially important when it comes to an assessment of Paul's so-called 'sacramentalism'. The writer of 1 Cor. i. 16, 17 could never have been one who regarded the sacraments as the last word about the Christian faith and practice; yet we must equally admit that, in C. T. Craig's words, 'Paul would not have understood an expression of Christian faith apart from a community in which the Lord's Supper was celebrated' (quoted by A. M. Hunter, *Interpreting Paul's Gospel*, 1954, p. 105). Adolf Schlatter, we believe, gives the truest estimate in his observation on the apostle's sacramental theology: Paul 'can express the word of Jesus, not in half measure but completely, without mentioning the sacraments at all. But if they come into view he connects with them the entire riches of the grace of Christ, because he sees in them the will of Jesus, not partially but fully expressed and effective' (*Die Briefe an die Thessalonicher, Philipper, Timotheus und Titus*, 1950, p. 262).

What is true of Paul is true of the other New Testament writers. There may be allusions to the Lord's Supper in such places as Heb. vi. 4, xiii. 10; and John's Gospel contains the notable synagogue discourse which many scholars relate to the eucharistic tradition of the later Church (Jn. vi. 22–59); but we should not overpress these references, as O. Cullmann seems to have done in finding numerous subtle references to sacramental worship in the Fourth Gospel (see his *Early Christian Worship*, 1953, pp. 37 ff., especially p. 106).

There is the witness of 2 Pet. ii. 13 and Jude 12 to the *agapē* meal. Apart from these somewhat exiguous data and meagre details, the New Testament is silent about the ordering and observance of eucharistic worship in the primitive communities, owing mainly to the fact that what is generally received and practised is not usually the subject of extended comment. For the development of the rite, and, it must be confessed, a fruitful source of heresy and confused doctrine, we must await the correspondence, epistles, and liturgies of the 2nd and subsequent centuries, from *1 Clem.* xl. 2–4; Ignatius, *Smyr.* viii. 1; *Didache* ix–x, xiv onwards.

BIBLIOGRAPHY. This article has mentioned some of the main works of importance. Of special value is A. J. B. Higgins, *The Lord's Supper in the New Testament*, 1952; and for the later development, J. H. Srawley, *The Early History of the Liturgy*, 1947. See also A. M. Stibbs, *Sacrifice, Sacrament and Eucharist*, 1961. A useful survey of recent discussion of the New Testament evidence is that by E. Schweizer, 'Das Herrenmahl im Neuen Testament', in *Theol. Literaturzeitung*, X, October 1954, cols. 577–592.

R.P.M.

LOT (Heb. *lôṭ*, 'covering' (?)). The son of Haran, Abraham's youngest brother, and so Abraham's nephew. Apart from the account of his life in Genesis, his name is absent from the Old Testament (except for references to his descendants in Dt. ii. 9, 19; Ps. lxxxiii. 8), but he is mentioned by our Lord in Lk. xvii. 28–32 and also by Peter in 2 Pet. ii. 7 f.

He accompanied Terah, Abram, and Sarai as they journeyed from Ur to Harran, and went on with Abram and Sarai into Canaan, down into Egypt, and then out again into Canaan (Gn. xi. 31, xii. 4, 5, xiii. 1). Flaws in his character first appear when he selfishly chose the well-watered Jordan valley (Gn. xiii. 8–13). This brought him into the midst of the wicked men of Sodom, and he had to be rescued from the results of his folly, first by Abraham (Gn. xiv. 11–16), and then by the two angels (Gn. xix). In the latter incident he revealed both his weakness and his inclination to compromise. His salvation from Sodom is expressly linked with God's remembrance of Abraham in Gn. xix. 29.

Through his drunkenness his two daughters obtained children by him, and these became the ancestors of the Moabites and the Ammonites (Gn. xix. 30–38; *cf.* Dt. ii. 9, 19; Ps. lxxxiii. 8).

Our Lord illustrated His teaching on the subject of His return from the story of Lot and his wife (Lk. xvii. 28–32), thus setting His seal upon its historicity, and 2 Pet. ii. 7 f. emphatically asserts his righteousness. It is probable that Peter is here deliberately alluding to Abraham's prayer for the 'righteous' in Sodom. G.W.G.

LOTS. See DIVINATION (*g*).

LOVE, BELOVED.

I. IN THE OLD TESTAMENT

a. Etymology

Love is the translation in the EVV primarily of the Heb. *'āhēḇ*, which is in every way as broad in its usage as the English word, and easily the most common word for every range of its meaning. Other Heb. words are *dôḏ* and *ra'yâ* (respectively of passionate love and its female object, especially in Ct.), *yāḏaḏ* (*e.g.* Ps. cxxvii. 2), *ḥāšaq* (*e.g.* Ps. xci. 14), *ḥāḇaḇ* (only Dt. xxxiii. 3), *'āgaḇ* (*e.g.* Je. iv. 30, of paramours), and *rāḥam* (Ps. xviii. 1).

In the Old Testament love, whether human or divine, is the deepest possible expression of the personality and of the closeness of personal relations. In the non-religious sense *'āhēḇ* is most commonly employed of the mutual urge of the sexes, in which there is no restraint or sense of uncleanness (see The Song of Solomon for its most sublime expression). It is also used of a multitude of personal (Gn. xxii. 2, xxxvii. 3) and sub-personal (Pr. xviii. 21) relations which have no connection with the sexual impulse. Fundamentally it is an inner force (Dt. vi. 5, 'might') which impels to performing the action which gives pleasure (Pr. xx. 13), obtaining the object which awakens desire (Gn. xxvii. 4), or in the case of persons to self-sacrifice for the good of the loved one (Lv. xix. 18, 34), and unswerving loyalty (1 Sa. xx. 17–42).

b. God's love for men

(i) *Its object.* This is primarily a collective group (Dt. iv. 37, 'thy fathers'; Pr. viii. 17, 'them that love me'; Is. xliii. 4, 'Israel'), though the implication is clear that the individual shares in the divine regard for the group. Only in three places is God said in so many words to love an individual, and in each case a king (2 Sa. xii. 24 and Ne. xiii. 26, Solomon; Is. xlviii. 14, ?Cyrus). Here the special relationship may be because Israel's king is in some sense regarded as a son of God (*cf.* 2 Sa. vii. 14; Pss. ii. 7, lxxxix. 26 f.), while Cyrus in the Isaianic passage may be a representative figure.

(ii) *Its personal nature.* Being rooted firmly in the personal character of God Himself, it is deeper than that of a mother for her children (Is. xlix. 15, lxvi. 13). This is most clear in Ho. i–iii, where (in whatever order the chapters are to be read) the relation between the prophet and his unfaithful wife Gomer is illustrative of the ultimate basis of the divine covenant in a deeper than legal relationship, in a love that is willing to suffer. God's love is part of His personality, and cannot be swayed by passion or diverted by disobedience (Ho. xi. 1–4, 7–9, RSV; this passage is the nearest the Old Testament approaches to a declaration that God is love). Israel's unfaithfulness can have no effect upon it, for 'I have loved thee with an everlasting love' (Je. xxxi. 3). The threat to 'love them no more' (Ho. ix. 15) is best interpreted as one to be their God no more.

(iii) *Its selectiveness.* Dt. in particular bases the covenant relationship between Israel and God on God's prior love. Unlike the gods of other nations, who belong to them for natural and geographic reasons, Yahweh took the initiative and chose Israel because He loved her (Dt. iv. 37, vii. 6 ff., x. 15; Is. xliii. 4). This love is spontaneous, not evoked by any intrinsic worth in its object, but rather creating that worth (Dt. vii. 7). The corollary is also true, that God hates those whom He does not love (Mal. i. 2 f.). Although in various passages, notably Jonah and the Servant

Songs of Isaiah, a doctrine of universal love is foreshadowed, it nowhere finds concrete expression.

c. Love as a religious duty

(i) *Towards God.* Love for God with the whole personality (Dt. vi. 5) is God's demand; though this is not to be understood as meaning merely a punctilious observance of an impersonal divine law but rather as summoning to a relationship of personal devotion created and sustained by the work of God in the human heart (Dt. xxx. 6).

It consists in the simple joyful experience of communion with God (Je. ii. 2, RSV; Ps. xviii. 1, cxvi. 1), worked out in daily obedience to His commandments (Dt. x. 12, 'to love him and to serve'; Jos. xxii. 5, 'to love and to walk in all his ways'). This obedience is more fundamental to the nature of love for God than any feeling. God alone will be the judge of its sincerity (Dt. xiii. 3).

(ii) *Towards fellow-men.* Love is ordained by God to be the normal, ideal human relationship, and as such is given the sanction of the divine law (Lv. xix. 18), though the parallel prohibition of hatred with its reference to the heart (Lv. xix. 17) shows clearly that this too is deeper than a merely legal relationship. An enemy is never commanded to be loved, though he is to be helped (Ex. xxiii. 4 f.), even if for somewhat selfish motives (Pr. xxv. 21 f.).

II. IN THE NEW TESTAMENT

a. Etymology

The most common word for all forms of love in the New Testament is *agapē, agapaō.* This is one of the least common words in classical Greek, where it expresses, on the few occasions it occurs, that highest and noblest form of love which sees something infinitely precious in its object. Its use in the New Testament derives not directly from classical Greek so much as from the LXX, where it occurs in 95% of all cases where EVV translate the Hebrew by 'love', and in every case of love from God to man, man to God, and man to his neighbour. The dignity which the word possesses in the New Testament has been contributed by its use as a vehicle of the Old Testament revelation. It is pregnant with Old Testament associations.

Phileō is the alternative word to *agapaō.* It is more naturally used of intimate affection (Jn. xi. 3, 36; Rev. iii. 19), and of liking to do things which are pleasant (Mt. vi. 5), though there is considerable overlapping of usage between the two words. Much exegesis of Jn. xxi. 15–17 has turned on Peter's willingness to say *philō se* ('I am your friend', J. B. Phillips), and apparent reluctance to say *agapō se.* It is difficult to see why a writer of such simple Greek as John should have used the two words in this context unless he intended a distinction to be drawn between their meanings. The existence of any clear distinction, here or elsewhere, is, however, seriously disputed by scholars, and is not noticed by ancient commentators, except perhaps by Ambrose (*On Luke* x. 176) and in the Vulg., which in this passage employs *diligo* and *amo* to translate *agapaō* and *phileō* respectively. (B. B. Warfield, 'The Terminology of Love in the New Testament', *PTR*, XVI, 1918; J. H. Bernard, *St. John, ICC*, II, 1928, pp. 701 ff.)

b. God's love

(i) *For Christ.* The relationship between the Father and the Son is one of love (Jn. iii. 35, xv. 9; Col. i. 13, RSV). The word 'beloved' (*agapētos*), carrying with it a strong sense of 'only-beloved', is employed in the Synoptics only of the Christ, either directly (Mt. xvii. 5; Mk. i. 11) or by inference (Mt. xii. 18; Mk. xii. 6) (B. W. Bacon, 'Jesus' Voice from Heaven', *American Journal of Theology*, IX, 1905, pp. 451 ff.). This love is returned and mutual (Jn. xiv. 31; *cf.* Mt. xi. 27). Since this love is historically prior to creation (Jn. xvii. 24), it follows that, though known by men only as revealed in Jesus Christ and in redemption (Rom. v. 8), it is of the very nature of the Godhead (1 Jn. iv. 8, 16), and that Jesus Christ, who is love incarnate and personified (1 Jn. iii. 16, RSV 'that he') is God's self-revelation.

(ii) *For men.* Jesus is not recorded in the Synoptic Gospels as using *agapaō* or *phileō* to express God's love for men. Rather He revealed it by His countless acts of compassionate healing (Mk. i. 41; Lk. vii. 13), His teaching about God's acceptance of the sinner (Lk. xv. 11 ff., xviii. 10 ff.), His grief-stricken attitude to human disobedience (Mt. xxiii. 37; Lk. xix. 41 f.), and by being Himself a friend (*philos*) of tax-collectors and outcasts (Lk. vii. 34). This saving activity is declared in John to be a demonstration of the love of God, imparting an eternal reality of life to men (Jn. iii. 16; 1 Jn. iv. 9 f.). The whole drama of redemption, centring as it does around the death of Christ, is divine love in action (Gal. ii. 20; Rom. v. 8; 2 Cor. v. 14).

As in the Old Testament, God's love is selective. Its object is no longer the old Israel, but the new, the Church (Gal. vi. 16; Eph. v. 25). God's love and His choosing are closely connected, not only in Paul but clearly too by inference in certain sayings of Jesus Himself (Mt. x. 5 f., xv. 24). Those whom God's life-giving love does not reach are 'children of wrath' (Jn. iii. 35 f.; Eph. ii. 3 ff.) and of 'the devil' (Jn. viii. 44). God's intention, however, is clearly the salvation of the whole world (Mt. viii. 5, xxviii. 19; Rom. xi. 25 f.), which is ultimately the object of His love (Jn. iii. 16, vi. 51), through the preaching of the gospel (Acts i. 8; 2 Cor. v. 19). Individuals are loved by God under the new covenant (Gal. ii. 20), though response to His love involves fellowship in the people of God (1 Pet. ii. 9 f., a passage generally regarded as having a baptismal context).

c. Love as a religious duty

(i) *Towards God.* Man's natural state is to be God's enemy (Rom. v. 10; Col. i. 21), and to hate Him (Lk. xix. 14; Jn. xv. 18 ff.), this enmity being seen for what it is in the crucifixion. This attitude is transformed into one of love by the prior action of God in loving man (1 Jn. iv. 11, 19). So closely related is God's love for man and man's for God that it is often difficult to decide whether the phrase 'the love of God' denotes a subjective or objective genitive (*e.g.* Jn. v. 42).

Jesus Himself, though He accepted and underlined the Shema with His own authority (Mk. xii. 28 ff.), and expected men to love God and Himself when there was ample opportunity for them not to (Mt. vi. 24, x. 37 f.; Lk. xi. 42; Jn. iii. 19), preferred to speak of the ideal man–God relationship as one of faith (Mt. ix. 22; Mk. iv. 40). The word love appears not to have sufficiently emphasized for Him the humble trust which He regarded as vital in man's relationship to God. Accordingly, though love to God, worked out in service to one's fellows, is enjoined in the rest of the New Testament (1 Cor. ii. 9; Eph. vi. 24; 1 Jn. iv. 20, v. 2 f.), the writers more commonly follow Jesus' example and enjoin faith.

(ii) *Towards fellow-men.* As in the Old Testament, mutual love is to be the ideal human relationship. Jesus corrected contemporary Jewish thought in two directions. (1) He insisted that the commandment to love one's neighbour is not a limiting ordinance (Lk. x. 29), as in much rabbinic exegesis of Lv. xix. 18, but rather means that the neighbour is to be the first object, because the nearest, of the love which is the characteristic of the Christian heart (Lk. x. 25–37). (2) He extended this demand for love to include enemies and persecutors (Mt. v. 44; Lk. vi. 27), though none but the new people of God can be expected to have this attitude, for the demand belongs to a new time (Mt. v. 38 f.), involves supernatural grace ('reward', Mt. v. 46; 'thank', Lk. vi. 32 ff.; 'more', Mt. v. 47), and is addressed to a group of 'hearers' (Lk. vi. 27), who are sharply differentiated from sinners (Lk. vi. 32 ff.) and publicans (Mt. v. 46 f.).

This new attitude is far from a sentimental utopianism, for it must issue in practical help to those who need it (Lk. x. 33 ff.), nor is it a superficial virtue, for it involves a fundamental response of the heart (1 Cor. xiii *passim*) to the prior love of God (1 Jn. iv. 19, RSV), and an acceptance of the work of the Spirit in the depths of a man's being (Gal. v. 22).

The characteristic form of this love in the New Testament is love for the fellow-Christian (Jn. xv. 12, 17; Gal. vi. 10; 1 Pet. iii. 8, iv. 8; 1 Jn. ii. 10, iii. 14), love for the outsider being expressed in the evangelistic outreach (Acts i. 8, x. 45; Rom. i. 15 f.) and in the patient endurance of persecution (1 Pet. ii. 20). The Christian loves his brother: (1) to imitate God's love (Mt. v. 43, 45; Eph. v. 2; 1 Jn. iv. 11); (2) because he sees in him one for whom Christ died (Rom. xiv. 15; 1 Cor. viii. 11); (3) because he sees in him Christ Himself (Mt. xxv. 40). The very existence of this mutual love, issuing as it does in the unity of Christian people (Eph. iv. 2 f.; Phil. ii. 1 ff.), is the sign *par excellence* to the outside world of the reality of Christian discipleship (Jn. xiii. 35).

BIBLIOGRAPHY. G. Quell and E. Stauffer, *TWNT*, art. 'Love', tr. by J. R. Coates, 1949; J. Moffatt, *Love in the New Testament*, 1929; A. Nygren, *Agape and Eros*, Pt. I, tr. P. S. Watson, 1953. F.H.P.

LOVE FEAST. The Christian duty to love one another has always been expressed in gatherings for fellowship. Such fellowship was realized from early times by participation in a common meal, and love feasts, *agapai*, are mentioned by Jude (verse 12; *cf.* 2 Pet. ii. 13, RV). Among the Jews meals for fellowship and brotherhood were common, and similar convivial gatherings took place among the Gentiles. It was natural, therefore, that both Jewish and Gentile Christians should adopt such practices. The name *agapē* was later given to the fellowship meal. It is an anachronism, however, to apply it in its later sense to the conditions described in Acts and 1 Corinthians. 'The breaking of bread' referred to in Acts ii. 42, 46 may describe a common meal which included both Agapē and Eucharist (see F. F. Bruce, *Acts of the Apostles*, 1951). St. Paul's account (in 1 Cor. xi. 17–34) of the administration of the Eucharist shows it set in the context of a fellowship supper. His farewell discourse at Troas which continued till midnight was delivered at a fellowship meal on the first day of the week which included the Eucharist (Acts xx. 7 ff.).

Although the common custom of fellowship meals among the Jews may have been sufficient ground for the primitive Agapē, some would trace the practice to the actual circumstances of the Last Supper. The sacrament was instituted at a Passover meal. Some scholars contend for another type of fellowship meal customary in the *qiddush* and *ḥaburah* gatherings. The early disciples probably reproduced the setting of the first Eucharist, preceding it with such a fellowship meal. The separation of the meal or Agapē from the Eucharist lies outside the times of the New Testament. The theory of Lietzmann that Eucharist and Agapē can be traced to two different types of sacramental observance in the New Testament is generally rejected. See also LORD'S SUPPER.

For later development of Agapē and Eucharist, see Pliny's letter to Trajan, *Didache*, Justin Martyr, *Apol.* i. 67, Tertullian, *de Corona* 3.

BIBLIOGRAPHY. J. H. Kelly, *Love Feasts: A History of the Christian Agape*, 1916; J. H. Srawley, *Early History of the Liturgy*, 1947; G. Dix, *Shape of the Liturgy*, 1944. R.J.C.

LOVING-KINDNESS. One rendering given in all EVV from the time of Coverdale (except RSV) of the Heb. word *ḥeseḏ*. Most of its occurrences are in the Psalms, but it occurs seven times elsewhere in AV, which has ten other renderings of it, the most frequent of which are 'mercy', 'kindness', and 'goodness'. There have been many suggestions as to how it should best be translated, among these being 'leal-love' (G. Adam Smith), 'piety' (C. H. Dodd), 'solidarity' (Koehler-Baumgartner), and 'covenant-love' (N. Snaith). RSV frequently, although not consistently, renders it 'steadfast love'. Its etymological origin is uncertain. An examination of the passages where it is found (*e.g.* Ps. lxxxix, where it is rendered 'mercy' as well as 'lovingkindness' in AV) reveals that it is closely connected with the two ideas of covenant and faithfulness. Its meaning may be summed up as 'steadfast love on the basis of a covenant'. It is employed both of God's attitude towards His people and of theirs to Him, the latter especially in Hosea.

BIBLIOGRAPHY. N. Snaith, *The Distinctive Ideas of the Old Testament*, 1944, chapter 5.

G.W.G.

LOWLAND. See SHEPHELAH.

LUBIM. First occurs as *Rbw* (= Libu) in Egyp. texts of 13th–12th centuries BC, as a hostile Libyan tribe (Sir A. H. Gardiner, *Ancient Egyptian Onomastica*, I, 1947, pp. 121*–122*). Libu as *lûḇîm* became a Heb. term for Libya, Libyans (*q.v.*), and as *libys* became the general Gk. term 'Libyan' for the land and people west of Egypt. Thus the Heb. and Gk. terms cover other Libyans besides the tribe *Rbw*. During the 12th–10th centuries BC, Libyans entered Egypt as raiders, settlers, or soldiers in Egypt's armies. Hence the prominence of Lubim in the forces of Shishak (*q.v.*), 2 Ch. xii. 3; of Zerah (*q.v.*), 2 Ch. xiv. 9 with xvi. 8; and among the troops of the Ethiopian pharaohs that failed to protect No-Amon (Thebes) from Assyr. devastation (Na. iii. 9). *Lubbîm*, Dn. xi. 43, may be the same word. See also LEHABIM; PUT, PHUT.

K.A.K.

LUCIFER (Lat. 'light-bearer'). This was the Lat. name for the planet Venus, the brightest object in the sky apart from the sun and moon, appearing sometimes as the evening, sometimes as the morning, star. In Is. xiv. 12 it is the translation of *hêlēl* ('shining one': LXX *heōsphoros*, 'light-bearer'; *cf.* the Arabic for Venus, *zuhratun*, 'the bright shining one'), and is applied tauntingly as a title for the king of Babylon, who in his glory and pomp had set himself among the gods. This name is appropriate, as the civilization of Babylon began in the grey dawn of history, and had strong astrological connections. Babylonians and Assyrians personified the morning star as Belit and Ištar. Some have considered that the phrase 'son of the morning' might refer to the crescent moon; *cf.* Gray in *ICC ad loc.*; others (*e.g.* S. H. Langdon, *ExpT*, XIII, 1930–1, pp. 172 ff.) argue for an identification with the planet Jupiter. The similarity of the description here with that of such passages as Lk. x. 18 and Rev. ix. 1 (*cf.* xii. 9) has led to the application of the title to Satan. The true claimant to this title is shown in Rev. xxii. 16 to be the Lord Jesus Christ in His ascended glory.

D.H.W.

LUCIUS. Gk. *Loukios*, transcribing or imitating the Roman praenomen. *Loukas* (Luke) was a diminutive. (*Cf.* Ramsay, *BRD*, pp. 370–384, for inscriptions.)

1. A Cyrenian prophet and teacher of Antioch (Acts xiii. 1), probably one of its first missionaries (*cf.* Acts xi. 19–21). A strange African quotation of Acts xiii. 1 noted by Zahn (*cf. INT*, III, pp. 28 f.) adds 'who remains to this day'. Probably this writer, like Ephraem Syrus *in loc.*, identifies Lucius with the traditionally Antiochene Luke.

2. A companion of Paul in Corinth, sending greetings in Rom. xvi. 21. He is Paul's 'kinsman', *i.e.* a Jew (*cf.* Rom. ix. 3). Origen *in loc.* mentions an identification with Luke.

That either is Luke is improbable. They were undoubtedly Jews; Luke was almost certainly a Gentile (see Col. iv. 11, 14).

BIBLIOGRAPHY. H. J. Cadbury, *BC*, V, pp. 489–495.

A.F.W.

LUD, LUDIM. In Gn. x. 22 and 1 Ch. i. 17 Lud is one of the descendants of Shem, and Josephus (*Ant.* I. 6. 4) refers to the Lydians (see LYDIA) as his descendants. Herodotus' account of the Lydians (I. 7) does not preclude a Semitic origin. In Is. lxvi. 19 Lud is a Gentile nation characterized by the use of the bow (probably not true of Lydia); in Ezk. xxvii. 10 and xxx. 5 they are allies of Tyre and of Egypt respectively, and as such Lydia (*Lūdu*) is mentioned in Neo-Babylonian annals.

Ludim appears in Gn. x. 13 and 1 Ch. i. 11 as a descendant of Ham, and in Je. xlvi. 9 as a bow-bearing auxiliary of Egypt. This may be an unknown African nation, but some scholars emend to *Lubim* (Libya), and even the singular *Lud* to *Lub* in some passages.

K.L.McK.

LUHITH, ASCENT OF. A place in Moab where the people fled from the Babylonians (Is. xv. 5; Je. xlviii. 5). Eusebius places it between Areopolis and Zoar, but it has not yet been certainly identified.

LUKE THE EVANGELIST. It is the unanimous teaching of early Christian tradition that our third Gospel and the Acts of the Apostles were written by a Greek-speaking Gentile (probably from Antioch) who was an educated physician and fellow-traveller of the apostle Paul with the name Luke (Gk. *Loukas*).

From the contents of the third Gospel and Acts we learn to know the author in a very intimate way. He is a humble and disciplined writer, who keeps himself in the background, and lets all the light fall on the great theme of his two-fold book, namely the glad tidings that Jesus Christ is both Lord and Saviour, and that the victorious Redeemer chose, equipped, and used His apostles, and especially Paul, to proclaim the gospel throughout the then known world. Although Luke in self-effacing loyalty to his Lord refrained from pushing himself into the limelight, he does not hesitate, however, to claim in the prologue to his Gospel that he had done a thorough and intensive work in investigating all the relevant facts before he wrote his book. In the so-called 'we-sections' in Acts (xvi. 10–17, xx. 5, xxi. 18, xxvii. 1–xxviii. 16) Luke unequivocally claims to be an intimate companion of Paul and an eye-witness of the happenings related in those sections.

From the literary style of Luke and Acts, and from the character of the contents of the books, it is clear that Luke was a well-educated Greek. His fine qualities as one of the very best and most reliable historians of antiquity are today being admitted by most impartial scholars. That he was an educated physician is borne out by the character of the contents of Luke and Acts, as well as by the specific terminology used in describing cases of illness in these writings.

Paul writes of Luke in Col. iv. 14 as 'the beloved physician', who is with him, and in Phm. 24 he names him as one of his fellow-labourers. These two letters were written by Paul when he was a prisoner in Rome. This agrees with the last two chapters of Acts, according to which Luke was with Paul on his eventful voyage to Rome and was one of his intimate followers when he arrived there.

In 2 Tim. iv. 11 Paul (during his second imprisonment in Rome, shortly before his martyrdom; probably in AD 64) wrote these moving words: 'Only Luke is with me.' This agrees with the earliest Christian tradition that Luke the beloved physician remained a faithful co-worker of Paul until the end. What happened to him after the martyrdom of his great friend and leader we do not know for certain. According to the anti-Marcionite prologue to his Gospel, he continued to serve the Lord without the distraction of family responsibilities until he died in Boeotia in Greece at the age of 84. Through intimate contact over many years with Paul and many other Christian leaders (*e.g.* Philip, Timothy, Silas, Mark, Barnabas, James the brother of Jesus, *etc.*), and as a consequence of the fact that he was in Jerusalem (*cf.* Acts xxi. 17 ff.), Caesarea and other places intimately associated with Jesus and with His first apostles, Luke had the very best opportunity to obtain first-hand knowledge regarding our Lord and the history of the earliest Christian Church. That he definitely and purposefully made full use of these opportunities is claimed by him in Lk. i. 1–4, and is corroborated by the sterling quality and historical accuracy of both Luke and Acts.

BIBLIOGRAPHY. For a more detailed discussion and for an extensive bibliography, *cf.* Norval Geldenhuys, *Commentary on the Gospel of Luke*, 1950, pp. 15–50. See also D. J. Theron, *Evidence of Tradition*, 1957, and the introductory chapters to F. F. Bruce, *The Acts of the Apostles*, 1951.

J.N.G.

LUKE, GOSPEL OF.

I. OUTLINE OF CONTENTS

See also section IX below.

a. Prologue (i. 1–4).

b. The birth and childhood of Jesus (i. 5–ii. 52).

c. The baptism, genealogy, and temptation of Jesus (iii. 1–iv. 13).

d. The ministry in Galilee (iv. 14–ix. 50).

e. Teaching and healing during the journey to Jerusalem (ix. 51–xix. 28).

f. The entry into Jerusalem and ministry there (xix. 29–xxi. 38).

g. The trial, crucifixion, and resurrection appearances (xxii. 1–xxiv. 53).

II. AUTHORSHIP AND DATE

For details regarding the author of this Gospel and of Acts, see under LUKE THE EVANGELIST.

In view of the fact that Acts was written (probably shortly) after the Gospel (*cf.* Acts i. 1–3), the date of composition of Luke depends on what date we accept as probable for Acts. See, therefore, ACTS OF THE APOSTLES. Here we need only point out that there is nothing in the Gospel which demands a date later than AD 70. The fact that the Christians of Jerusalem and its surroundings understood the words of Jesus in His prophetical discourse as meaning that they should flee in time from the doomed city and that they actually fled to Pella (the modern Khirbet el-Fahil) in obedience to Him, does not prove that Lk. xix. 42–44 and xxi. 20–24 must have been written after AD 70. All available evidence seems to prove that Luke was written in about the year AD 60 (*cf.* the writer's *Commentary on the Gospel of Luke*, pp. 30–35, and F. F. Bruce, *The Acts of the Apostles*, pp. 10–14). Since Luke used Mark as one of his sources of information, the Gospel was written after the composition of Mark. See MARK, GOSPEL OF. There is, however, no reason to assume that Luke wrote his Gospel a long time after Mark. Luke was in very close contact with Mark (*cf.* Col. iv. 10, 14; Phm. 24, and see also Luke's intimate knowledge regarding Mark in Acts xii. 12, 25, xiii. 13, xv. 37–41, and note especially Paul's words in 2 Tim. iv. 11–13). It is thus quite probable that he was able to read the Gospel of Mark immediately or soon after Mark had written it. Mark could even have allowed him to consult his manuscript while he was still busy writing the Gospel.

III. SOURCES

Luke declares in his prologue (i. 1–4) that he made an intensive study of the gospel history in order to be able to write a reliable account. The excellent opportunities he had to become acquainted with the true facts we have noticed in the previous paragraph. His prologue teaches clearly that he not only consulted those who knew at first hand the truth regarding the gospel, but that he also had access to quite a number of written documents containing authoritative information from reliable eye-witnesses (*cf.* Lk. i. 2). It can be accepted as a firmly established fact that one of these written documents is the Gospel of Mark. The attempts to prove that Luke and Matthew used the document 'Q' seem, however, to have failed (but see GOSPELS; MATTHEW, GOSPEL OF). Nobody at present knows which written documents other than Mark were used by Luke as sources. Neither does anyone know for certain what the relationship is between Luke and Matthew. From his prologue (i. 1–4) we know, however, that Luke made the best and most careful use of the many written and oral sources of information regarding the gospel history which were at his disposal.

Judging from the contents of his Gospel, Luke had access to the most intimate and direct sources of information. These covered not only the parents of John the Baptist, but also the events accompanying the supernatural birth of the Saviour known only to those most closely concerned. From Acts xxi. 18 it is clear that Luke met James the brother of Jesus personally; and it is certain that during his long stay in Palestine (*cf.* Acts xxi. 17–xxvii. 1) he had direct personal contact with many eye-witnesses of the facts which he describes in his Gospel. When Luke was accompanying Paul there were still many people alive who had seen and heard Jesus, some of whom were His most intimate disciples (*cf.* 1 Cor. xv. 6). He was therefore able to trace the course of all things regarding Jesus accurately, so that he could write a Gospel which would enable Christians to know with certainty the facts on which their faith was based (*cf.* i. 3–4).

IV. PLACE AND CIRCUMSTANCES OF COMPOSITION

Luke may have begun to gather and to write down the facts regarding our Lord and His teaching soon after he started to accompany Paul on his missionary journeys; later, when Paul was a prisoner in Palestine, and Luke had contact with many ear- and eye-witnesses of the ministry of Jesus (*cf.* Acts xxi. 33–xxvii. 1), he may have done much preparatory work (*cf.* Lk. i. 1–4) for the writing of Luke and Acts, and when he was with Paul in Rome he would have had ample opportunity to continue his task. Paul would naturally have encouraged Luke and given him help and advice (*cf.* 2 Tim. iv. 11–13). The contact between Luke and Paul was so intimate that early Christian writers mistakenly spoke of the Gospel of Luke as Paul's Gospel (*cf.* Tertullian, *Contra Marcion.* iv. 5, and especially Irenaeus, *Adv. Haer.* iii. 1. 1–2).

Exactly where Luke completed his Gospel we do not know. But as the Gospel was soon widely used, and from the very beginning Christian tradition was unanimous in honouring Luke as author, it would seem probable that (through the help of men like Theophilus, *cf.* Lk. i. 3 and Acts i. 1) copies of the Gospel were soon distributed in different countries. This last consideration is possibly the reason why the early tradition is not so unanimous regarding the locality where the Gospel was originally 'published'.

V. HISTORICAL ACCURACY

Since he was well educated (*cf.* the classical style of his prologue) and scientifically minded (*cf.* i. 3, 4), and because of the special opportunities he had to obtain first-hand information, we can expect Luke's writings to be historically accurate and reliable. From Lk. i. 3, 4, it is clear that he was deeply conscious of the urgent necessity for Christian believers to have their faith built on a firm foundation. He realized that religious faith cannot be established on myths, legends, or half-truths. Therefore he took much trouble (*cf.* i. 3) to discover the facts and to write a comprehensive, accurate, and orderly account. During the last century the historical trustworthiness of the Gospel was questioned by many, but it is generally admitted by scholars today that the author's historical accuracy has been remarkably vindicated (*cf.* the writer's *Commentary on the Gospel of Luke*, pp. 39 f., and F. F. Bruce, *The Acts of the Apostles*, pp. 15–18).

VI. MAIN THEME

Luke did not intend to write an ordinary historical treatise or a biography. As a faithful companion of the great missionary apostle Paul, his religious faith was to him a matter of life or death. His Gospel was accordingly not intended as a formal, historical treatise, and it was in no way the result of philosophical speculations or the impersonal product of the study. He believed in Jesus Christ as the Saviour of the world and as the Son of God. With piety, sincerity, and accuracy he made sure regarding all the essential facts concerning the gospel history; and from the large amount of reliable information which he had gathered he selected what would most help him to present the good news regarding his Redeemer in such a way that every believer might know the certainty concerning the things wherein he had been instructed (*cf.* Lk. i. 4). From beginning to end Luke focuses attention upon Him who came to 'seek and to save that which was lost' (xix. 10). His Gospel is a proclamation of Jesus Christ as the Son of God who has power and authority to save sinners. The self-revelation of Jesus as Saviour and as the almighty Son of God forms the main theme of the Gospel. Already in the first chapter Luke recalls the fact that the angel, who announced the coming birth of the Saviour, commanded Mary to call his name Jesus (*i.e.* Saviour), and added, 'He shall be great, and shall be called the Son of the Highest' (i. 31, 32). And in the next chapter he records that when the birth of Jesus was announced to the shepherds the angel referred to him as the 'Saviour . . . which is Christ the Lord' (ii. 11). Even where Luke narrates the history of John the Baptist, he is actually engaged in proclaiming Jesus as Redeemer and

Lord. John's work is preparatory (*cf.* i. 17 and iii. 16) for the coming of Him who, by the voice of God from heaven, is announced as the beloved Son of God in whom He is well pleased (iii. 22). From chapter iv onwards, Luke shows how Jesus revealed Himself more and more as the Son of God in a unique and absolute sense and as the One who came to call and save the lost (*cf.* iv. 18–21, 43, v. 8–10, 31, 32, vii. 47–50, viii. 28, ix. 1, 18–20, xxi. 27, 33, xxii. 69, 70, xxiii. 43, 46, xxiv. 5, 6, 15, 36–38, 45–53).

VII. SPECIAL CHARACTERISTICS

In the following features Luke may further be distinguished from the other Gospels to a greater or lesser degree.

a. He lays special stress on the fact that Jesus is the divine Saviour in a *universal* sense. Jesus offers forgiveness and redemption freely to all—irrespective of race, sex, or merit. Salvation is offered to Samaritans (ix. 52–56, x. 30–37, xvii. 11–19) and pagans (ii. 32, iii. 6, 8, iv. 25–27, vii. 9, x. 1, xxiv. 47) as well as to Jews (i. 33, ii. 10, *etc.*); to women as well as to men (many examples in the Gospel); to outcasts, publicans, and sinners (iii. 12, v. 27–32, vii. 37–50, xix. 2–10, xxiii. 43) but also to respectable people (vii. 36, xi. 37, xiv. 1); to the poor (i. 53, ii. 7, vi. 20, vii. 22) as well as to the rich (xix. 2, xxiii. 50).

b. Luke stresses the fact that Jesus is the Saviour who has divine power to heal both soul and body. His salvation is an all-embracing salvation—for time and eternity.

c. Luke describes more than any other evangelist how often Jesus went aside to pray.

d. Luke shows more clearly, and gives more particulars regarding, the redeeming and uplifting work which Jesus accomplished among women. He emphasizes the sympathy with which Jesus acted towards women (in contrast with the unsympathetic and even harsh attitude revealed towards them by many Jews and Gentiles of those times).

e. Luke gives a prominent place to parables of Jesus in which the redeeming love of God is depicted (*cf.* xv. 1–32).

f. No other Gospel gives such a comprehensive history of Jesus. He tells us in his prologue that, 'having traced the course of all things accurately from the first', he has decided to write the Gospel in an orderly manner. A close study reveals the extent to which the gospel history is written in a well-ordered and comprehensive form. Starting with the history of the parents of John the Baptist, the forerunner of the Saviour, Luke depicts the close link between the Old and the New Testament periods. He then gives details regarding the birth of John and of Jesus and essential details of the childhood and growth to maturity of Him who is both perfect Man and perfect God (*cf.* ii. 40, 42, 52). Having described the preparatory work of John in iii. 1–20, he describes the baptism of Jesus, and then gives our Lord's genealogy (tracing it right back through Adam to God, iii. 38). This is followed in iv. 1–13 by a description of how Jesus, in the most difficult circumstances, warded off all the onslaughts of Satan. From iv. 14 onwards he shows how Jesus through word and deed revealed Himself more and more as the Son of God and the almighty Saviour. Having narrated the history of His sufferings, death, and resurrection, Luke ends His Gospel by describing how Jesus first opened the minds of His disciples to understand the Scriptures (xxiv. 44–47), and then, having assured them that He would send forth the promise of His Father upon them, commanded them to wait until they were clothed with power from on high (xxiv. 49). Finally, he narrates how the victorious Redeemer returned to the Father while blessing His disciples (xxiv. 50, 51), who now know Him as their almighty Saviour and worship Him as their Lord. So the Gospel ends on a note of wonderful joy and victory and in an atmosphere of genuine and unreserved devotion to God, who in Christ wrought such a perfect redemption.

VIII. LITERARY STYLE AND LANGUAGE

It is generally admitted that Luke is the most literary author of the New Testament. His prologue proves that he was able to write in irreproachable, pure, literary Greek. His style was, however, so versatile that he switched over to a Hebraistic style whenever he was narrating history with a predominantly Hebraistic atmosphere (*cf.* i. 5, ii. 39). His familiarity with the Gk. version of the Old Testament (the Septuagint) undoubtedly helped him to adapt his style to the character of the contents of the Gospel.

Luke was a real 'painter in words', and his pictures of people and situations have captured the minds and imagination of many artists through almost two thousand years. There is much idyllic charm, simplicity, and purity in his style, and his whole Gospel is characterized by an earnest, devotional spirit.

IX. CONTENTS PECULIAR TO LUKE

As a result of his thorough investigations (*cf.* i. 1–4) and the splendid opportunities he had to obtain the information he needed, Luke preserved many of the words, and especially some important parables, of Jesus which would otherwise have been irrevocably lost. Some of the most beautiful and significant narratives regarding Jesus are found only in Luke. The following are the most important of these:

The promise of John the Baptist's birth (i. 5–25); the annunciation (i. 26–38); the visitation (i. 39–56); the birth of John the Baptist (i. 57–80); the birth of Jesus and the history of the shepherds (ii. 1–20); the circumcision of Jesus, His presentation in the Temple, and the joy of Simeon and Anna (ii. 21–40); Jesus' visit to Jerusalem and the Temple when He was twelve years of age (ii. 41–52); the replies of John the Baptist to those coming for baptism (iii. 10–14); John's imprisonment (iii. 19–20); an extensive description of the preaching of Jesus in Nazareth and His subsequent rejection (iv. 16–30); the miraculous draught of fishes (v. 1–11); the woes (vi. 24–26); the son of the widow of Nain (vii. 11–17); the woman who was saved by Jesus (vii. 36–50); the women who followed and served Jesus (viii. 1–3); the Samaritan villages which refused to accept Jesus (ix. 51–56); the parable of the good Samaritan (x. 30–37); Martha and Mary (x. 38–42); the friend at midnight (xi. 5–8); the blessedness of those who obey the Word of God (xi. 27–28); parable of the rich fool (xii. 13–21); many or few stripes (xii. 47–48); the call to repentance (xiii. 1–9); the healing of another woman (xiii. 10–17); the departure from Galilee (xiii. 31–33); the healing of a man with dropsy (xiv. 1–6); teaching on humility (xiv. 7–14); the parable of the prodigal son (xv. 11–32); the parable of the unjust steward (xvi. 1–13); the hypocrisy of the Pharisees (xvi. 14–15); the parable of the rich man and Lazarus (xvi. 19–31); the servant's duty (xvii. 7–10); the healing of the ten lepers (xvii. 11–19); on the kingdom of God (xvii. 20–21); the parable of the unjust judge (xviii. 1–8); the parable of the Pharisee and the publican (xviii. 9–14); Zacchaeus (xix. 1–10); the two swords (xxii. 35–38); Jesus before Herod (xxiii. 6–16); Jesus and the weeping women (xxiii. 27–31); the repenting thief and the crucified Saviour (xxiii. 40–43); the women from Galilee and the burial of Jesus (xxiii. 55–56); the men of Emmaus and the risen Lord (xxiv. 13–35); appearance of the risen Saviour in Jerusalem (xxiv. 36–49); the ascension (xxiv. 50–53).

X. THE GOSPEL AND ACTS

From the prologue to Luke and the introductory words to Acts, and from the contents of the two works, it is clear that Luke wrote his two treatises in closest relationship to each other. We may even look upon the Gospel and Acts as one book written in two volumes. The way in which Luke gives a very short summary of the history of the ascension of Jesus in the last chapter of his Gospel and then in Acts gives a more detailed, supplementary account may indicate that when he wrote his Gospel he had already planned his second treatise. He may even then have had most of his material ready for Acts. By saying in Acts i. 1, 2 that he wrote 'the former treatise [his Gospel] concerning all that Jesus began both to do and to teach until the day in which he was received up' Luke made it clear that there is the most intimate relation between the history recorded in his Gospel and the history of how the risen Lord continued His redemptive work through His chosen apostles, whom He equipped with the power of the Holy Spirit. Luke–Acts thus forms one great proclamation of Jesus as the divine Lord and almighty Saviour—Son of man and Son of God. This central theme indissolubly unites his two-fold work. See ACTS.

BIBLIOGRAPHY. An extensive bibliography is given in *Commentary on the Gospel of Luke*, by J. Norval Geldenhuys, 1950, pp. 47–50. See also the following works: F. Godet, *Commentary on the Gospel of Luke*, 1879; A. Plummer, *Gospel according to St. Luke*[5], *ICC*, 1922; A. Schlatter, *Das Evangelium des Lukas*, 1931; Strack and Billerbeck, *Das Evangelium nach Lukas*, vol. II in *Kommentar zum Neuen Testament aus Talmud und Midrasch*, 1924; Theodor Zahn, *Das Evangelium des Lukas*, 1913; S. Greijdanus, *Het Heilig Evangelie naar het Beschrijving van Lukas*, 2 vols., 1950; J. M. Creed, *The Gospel according to St. Luke*, 1926; A. R. C. Leaney, *The Gospel according to Luke*, 1958; N. B. Stonehouse, *The Witness of Luke to Christ*, 1951. J.N.G.

LUNATIC. See POSSESSION.

LUST. The English word was originally a neutral term describing any strong desire; hence its use in early translations of Gn. iii. 16; Jn. i. 13; Nu. xiv. 8; Heb. x. 6. In its modern restricted sense of sexual passion it cannot adequately render many familiar contexts in AV.

The Heb. *nep̄eš* expresses craving or desire in Ex. xv. 9 and Ps. lxxviii. 18, and carries the promise of satisfaction in Pr. x. 24. Gk. *epithymia* expresses any strong desire, the context or a qualifying adjective determining its nature, whether good or evil. Hence it is used of the intensely pure desire of Christ, Lk. xxii. 15, and of Paul's desire to be with Christ, Phil. i. 23, and of his longing to see his converts, 1 Thes. ii. 17. Yet in 1 Pet. iv. 3 it stands among a list of Gentile vices, and the adjectives 'worldly', 'evil', 'youthful', and 'deceitful' are attached to it in Tit. ii. 12; Col. iii. 5; 2 Tim. ii. 22; and Eph. iv. 22 respectively. The restricted reference to sexual passion is found in Eph. ii. 3; 1 Jn. ii. 16; 1 Pet. ii. 11 (*cf.* LXX and Jos., *Ant.*). The strong desire of the Spirit is set over against that of the flesh in Gal. v. 17. Other cognate words are *pathos*, 'passion' (1 Thes. iv. 5); *orexis*, 'strong desire' (Rom. i. 27), and *hēdonē*, 'pleasure' (Jas. iv. 3). The word 'lusty' when used in Jdg. iii. 29 (AV); Is. lix. 10 (RV); Ps. lxxiii. 4 (Prayer Book) carries no derogatory tone, and simply means able-bodied or vigorous.

BIBLIOGRAPHY. *Arndt*; *HDB*; B. S. Easton, *Pastoral Epistles*, 1947, 186 ff.; *MM*. D.H.T.

LUTE. See MUSIC AND MUSICAL INSTRUMENTS.

LUZ. The ancient name of Bethel (*q.v.*), which was so named by Jacob after he had dreamed of the ladder from heaven to earth after spending the night near to the city (Gn. xxviii. 19, xxxv. 6, xlviii. 3). It was the site of Jacob's sojourn near to the city, rather than the city itself, that received the name Bethel (Jos. xvi. 2), but this site later became so important that the name was applied to the city as well (Jos. xviii. 13; Jdg. i. 23). The city was, however, still known to the Canaanite inhabitants as Luz, because when the Israelites took the city at the time of the conquest a Canaanite whom they pressed to show them the entrance to it in return for his life escaped to the 'land of the Hittites' and founded another city of that name (Jdg. i. 24–26). At that time the 'land of the Hittites' was probably the region of N Syria, and the place-name *Lazi* in the Alalaḫ tablets is possibly to be connected with it, though the site is unknown.

BIBLIOGRAPHY. F. M. Abel, *Géographie de la Palestine*, II, 1938, p. 371; D. J. Wiseman, *The Alalakh Tablets*, 1953, pp. 155, *etc.* T.C.M.

LYCAONIA, a territory in south-central Asia Minor, so called from the *Lykaones* who inhabited it, mentioned by ancient writers from Xenophon (early 4th century BC) onwards. In Pompey's settlement of Western Asia Minor (64 BC) the western part of Lycaonia was added to Cilicia, the eastern part to Cappadocia, and the northern part to Galatia (*q.v.*), which became a Roman province in 25 BC. Eastern Lycaonia later became independent of Cappadocia and from AD 37 onwards formed part of the client kingdom of Antiochus, king of Commagene, and was known as Lycaonia Antiochiana. In the New Testament 'Lycaonia' denotes that part of the territory which constituted a region of the province of Galatia, Lycaonia Galatica. Lystra and Derbe are designated 'cities of Lycaonia' in Acts xiv. 6, in a context which implies that Iconium lay on the Phrygian side of the frontier separating Lycaonia Galatica from Phrygia Galatica. W. M. Ramsay has put it on record that it was this geographical note that led to his 'first change of judgment' with regard to the historical value of Acts. Paul and Barnabas on their first 'missionary journey' (AD 47–8) doubtless recognized that they had crossed a linguistic frontier between Iconium and Lystra, for in the latter place (near modern Hatunsaray) they heard the indigenous population use 'the speech of Lycaonia' (Acts xiv. 11, Gk. *lykaonisti*). Lycaonian personal names have been identified in inscriptions hereabout, *e.g.* in one at Sedasa which records the dedication to Zeus of a statue of Hermes (*cf.* Acts xiv. 12). When, after leaving Lystra, Paul and Barnabas came to Derbe (modern Kerti Hüyük) and planted a church there, they turned back; had they gone farther they would have crossed into the kingdom of Antiochus, but it was no part of their plan to evangelize non-Roman territory. See fig. 26 and map 17.

BIBLIOGRAPHY. W. M. Ramsay, *Historical Commentary on Galatians*, 1899, pp. 185 f., 215 ff.; M. Ballance, *AS*, VII, 1957, pp. 147 ff.

F.F.B.

LYCIA. A small district on the south coast of Asia Minor which contains the broad valley of the river Xanthus, and mountains rising to over 10,000 feet. Although some sculptures and inscriptions have been preserved, the origin of the Lycian people is obscure. They alone of the peoples of W Asia Minor successfully resisted the Lydian kings, but after fierce fighting they succumbed in 546 BC to the Persians.

Freed by Greeks in the following century, they were greatly influenced by Gk. civilization and eventually submitted voluntarily to Alexander. They adopted the Gk. language and script, and were thoroughly Hellenized by the time they came under Roman protection in the 2nd century BC. Claudius in AD 43 annexed Lycia to the province of Pamphylia, but apparently Nero restored their freedom, for Vespasian again reduced them to provincial status. Through these vicissitudes the federation of Lycian cities maintained its general political framework. See MYRA, PATARA. K.L.McK.

LYDDA. A town some 11 miles south-east of the coast at Jaffa, in the Shephelah plain. It is almost certainly to be identified with the Old Testament Lod, which is mentioned in the Karnak list of Thothmes III. In Israelite times it was a Benjamite town; reoccupied after the Bab. Exile, it later fell to the authority of the governor of Samaria, and was not reclaimed by the Jews till 145 BC (1 Macc. xi. 34). It was burnt down in Nero's reign. After the fall of Jerusalem (AD 70) it became a rabbinical centre for a period. It had a bishop in the early Christian centuries. Since then it has borne the names Diospolis, Ludd, and Lod again (today). D.F.P.

LYDIA. A woman of Thyatira in Lydia, who at Philippi became Paul's first European convert, and gave him hospitality, with Silas and Luke (Acts xvi. 14, 15, 40). Lydia may be an adjectival form, 'the Lydian woman' (such ethnic names were common), but it was also a personal name (*e.g.* Hor., *Od.* i. 8, iii. 9, vi. 20). Evidently a woman of rank (*cf.* Acts xvii. 4, 12), she was head of a household, and thus either widowed or unmarried. Lydian purple dye, in which she traded, was renowned (*cf.* Hom. ii. 4. 141). She was a Jewish proselyte, engaging in prayers and ablutions at the riverside on the sabbath; her connection with the Jewish faith probably went back to the colony in Thyatira. For the Christian church established there, *cf.* Rev. i. 11, ii. 18–29. Lydia may be included in Paul's reference in Phil. iv. 3, but since she is unmentioned by name she may have died or left the city. Her hospitality became traditional in the church there (*cf.* Phil. i. 5, iv. 10). B.F.H.

LYDIA, a district in the centre of the western slope of Asia Minor, included the Caÿster and Hermus valleys, the most fertile and highly cultivated areas of the peninsula, and between them the mountains of Tmolus, rising to 6,000 feet. Besides its natural wealth its position on the main routes from the coast to the interior of Asia Minor gave its cities (including Sardis, Thyatira, and Philadelphia) great commercial importance. Lydia was bordered by Mysia, Phrygia, and Caria. Some of the coastal cities (including Smyrna and Ephesus) were sometimes reckoned as Lydian, sometimes as Greek.

The origins of the Lydian race are obscure, but there may have been Semitic elements (see LUD). Building on the foundations laid by his predecessors, King Croesus dominated the whole of Asia Minor before being conquered by Cyrus the Persian in 546 BC. The region was subsequently ruled by Alexander and his successors, and became part of the Attalid kingdom of Pergamum before passing to the Romans in 133 BC, when it was incorporated in the province of Asia. Some Lydian inscriptions of the 4th century BC have been discovered, but by the beginning of the Christian era Greek had become the common language and, according to Strabo, Lydian was little used.

Lydia was the first state to use coined money and was the home of some innovations in music.

For Je. xlvi. 9 and Ezk. xxx. 5, see RV.

K.L.McK.

LYRE. See MUSIC AND MUSICAL INSTRUMENTS.

LYSANIAS, listed in Lk. iii. 1 as 'tetrarch of Abilene' *c.* AD 27–8. So Josephus (*Ant.* xx. 7. 1) speaks of 'Abila, which had been the tetrarchy of Lysanias'. His name appears on an inscription of Abila, dated between AD 14 and 29, recording a temple dedication by a freedman of 'Lysanias the tetrarch' (*CIG*, 4521). It is uncertain whether coins superscribed 'Lysanias tetrarch and high priest' refer to him or to an earlier Lysanias, 'king of the Ituraeans' (so Dio Cassius), executed by Antony *c.* 36 BC (Jos., *Ant.* xv. 4. 1). Two members of this family called Lysanias, of different generations, are named in *CIG*, 4523. See ABILENE.

F.F.B.

LYSIAS, CLAUDIUS. See CLAUDIUS LYSIAS.

LYSTRA. An obscure town on the high plains of Lycaonia (near modern Hatun Sarai), singled out by Augustus as the site of one of a number of Roman colonies that were intended to consolidate the new province of Galatia. Its advantages are not known. Its remote position and proximity to the unsettled southern mountains suggest defensive motives, as also does the considerable Latin-speaking settlement implied by surviving inscriptions. If it was the security of such a place that attracted Paul and Barnabas in their hasty retreat from Iconium (Acts xiv. 6) they were badly let down. Superstitious veneration, disabused by the apostles themselves, was converted by agitators into drastic hostility, which apparently secured official support for the stoning that was inflicted upon Paul (verse 19). There is no suggestion of Roman order or justice. Nor does the New Testament even disclose that it was a colony. There was plainly a substantial non-hellenic population (verse 11), as well as the usual Greeks and Jews (Acts xvi. 1). Nevertheless, a church was established (Acts xiv. 20–23) which provided in Timothy (unless, as is just possible, he came from the nearby Derbe, Acts xvi. 1, 2) Paul's most devoted retainer. See fig. 26.

BIBLIOGRAPHY. D. Magie, *Roman Rule in Asia Minor*, 1950, pp. 463, 1324; Ruge, *RE*, XIII. 2. 2258–65.

E.A.J.

M

MAACAH, MAACHAH. 1. Maachah is used as a man's name for the following: the father of Shephatiah, one of David's henchmen (1 Ch. xxvii. 16); the father of Hanun, one of David's warriors (1 Ch. xi. 43); the father of Achish, king of Gath at the time of Solomon (1 Ki. ii. 39).

2. It is also used as a woman's name for the following: the concubine of Caleb, mother of Sheber and Tirhanah (1 Ch. ii. 48); the wife of Machir, mother of Peresh (1 Ch. vii. 16); the wife of Gibeon, or Jehiel, one of the ancestors of Saul (1 Ch. viii. 29, ix. 35); the daughter of Talmai, king of Geshur, who married David and was the mother of Absalom and Tamar (2 Sa. iii. 3); the favourite wife of Rehoboam and the mother of Abijah and the daughter of Absalom (2 Ch. xi. 20–22); the mother of Asa, the queen-mother of Judah until she was removed because of her idolatry (2 Ch. xv. 16). See QUEEN.

3. The child of Nahor, the brother of Abraham, and his concubine Reumah, was called Maachah, but there is no indication as to sex (Gn. xxii. 24).

4. It is also the name for a small state to the south-east of Mt. Hermon, on the edge of the territory of the half-tribe of Manasseh (Dt. iii. 14; Jos. xiii. 8–13) and possibly extending across the Jordan to Abel-beth-Maacah. At the time of David, its Aramaean king provided one thousand soldiers for the Ammonite and Aramaean attempt to crush Israel. Following the defeat at Helam, Maacah probably became tributary to David (2 Sa. x). Maacah was later absorbed into the kingdom of Damascus, which had been re-established during Solomon's reign (1 Ki. xi. 23–25).

BIBLIOGRAPHY. B. Mazar, 'Geshur and Maacah', *JBL*, LXXX, 1961, pp. 16 ff M.G.
A.R.M.

MAALEH-ACRABBIM. See AKRABBIM.

MAAREH-GEBA (Jdg. xx. 33, RV; AV 'meadows of Gibeah'). Heb. *ma'ᵃrēh* means 'open, bare place', but LXX(A) *dysmōn* and Vulg. *occidentali urbis parte* suggest Heb. *ma'ᵃrāḇ*, 'west', which yields a better sense in the context. See GEBA.
A.R.M.

MACCABEES. *Makkabaios* was the Greek form of the surname of the Jewish hero Judas ben Mattathias (1 Macc. ii. 4): its application has been extended to his family and his party. The derivation is quite obscure: 'the hammerer' or 'the eradicator' are perhaps the commonest modern interpretations. According to Josephus the family name seems to have been Ḥašmōn: hence the title 'Hasmonaeans' reflected in rabbinic literature.

I. THE MACCABEAN REVOLT

Palestine was perennially a theatre for the power politics of the Seleucid and Ptolemaic heirs of Alexander the Great's empire. One result was the growth of a pro-Syrian and a pro-Egyptian party in Judaea, and tension between these groups was inextricably bound up with Jewish internal politics and family jealousies, and with a movement among 'liberal' Jews to adopt the customs and standards of the Greek world. Resulting conflict brought about the decisive intervention of Syria. The Seleucid king, Antiochus IV (Epiphanes), who was mad, bad, and dangerous, sold the high-priesthood to the highest bidder, one Menelaus, who was quite unentitled to it, and when, in 168 BC, his nominee was ejected, Antiochus sent his officer to sack Jerusalem and butcher its inhabitants.

Soon afterwards, Antiochus instituted a religious persecution of unprecedented bitterness. sabbath-keeping and the practice of circumcision were forbidden under pain of death: pagan sacrifices and prostitution were established in the Temple; and law-loving Jews were subjected to every degradation and brutality (*cf.* Dn. xi. 31–33). Doubtless many succumbed, but many endured heroic suffering (1 Macc. i. 60 ff., ii. 29 ff.; 2 Macc. vi. 18 ff.), and Antiochus could not have estimated the sober resilience of the Ḥasidim (or men of the covenant), who 'offered (themselves) willingly for the law' (1 Macc. ii. 42). More drastic action began in Modein, some twenty miles from Jerusalem, where the aged Mattathias angrily killed a Jew who had come to sacrifice on the royal altar, and the Syrian officer who had come to supervise, and then called on everyone zealous for the Law to follow him and his five sons, John, Simon, Judas, Eleazar, and Jonathan, to the mountains. The Maccabean revolt had begun.

II. JUDAS MACCABAEUS

The Judaean hills were suited to guerrilla warfare. Mattathias and his sons were joined by many Ḥasidim, and at first were content with terrorizing apostates, destroying altars, and enforcing the Law. Mattathias died, and his third son, Judas, proved a leader of Gideon's type and stature. Perhaps no army has ever had higher morale than the force with which he won his brilliant victories against numerically superior Syrian forces. Antiochus was occupied in larger wars with the Parthians, and his regent Lysias had no option but to conclude peace with Judas and withdraw the abominable decrees in 165 BC. Amid great rejoicing, Judas marched to Jerusalem, the Temple was solemnly cleansed, and the worship of God restored (1 Macc. iv)—an event commemorated by the Feast of Hanukkah, or the Dedication (Jn. x. 22).

Maccabean success had led to furious persecution of Jewish minorities in cities of mixed population. Judas raised the cry 'Fight this day for your brethren' (1 Macc. v. 32) and, with his brother Jonathan, carried out effective punitive expeditions in Transjordan, while Simon dealt similarly with Galilee. On the death of Antiochus Epiphanes in 164/3 BC Judas tried to seize the *Akra*, the Syrian fortress in Jerusalem, the symbol of Seleucid suzerainty: he was trapped, and was on the brink of disaster when political upheaval in Syria caused a diversion, and the Syrians had to be content with a treaty virtually securing the *status quo*.

Eventually Demetrius I (Soter) made good his claim to the throne, and he appointed a pro-Syrian high priest, Alcimus. Many Ḥasidim were prepared to support this man, since he was an Aaronite, but his outrageous actions played into Judas's hands. Judas took revenge on deserters, and a large Syrian force had to be called in. The Syrians were defeated at Adasa, but, after an interval, scattered the Jewish army at Elasa, where Judas was killed in battle in 161 BC.

III. JONATHAN

Jonathan, youngest of the brothers, now headed the Maccabean party. For a long time he was reduced to guerrilla fighting in the hills, but internal faction had become endemic in the Seleucid Empire, and he was more and more left to himself by the Syrians. In time he was the effective ruler of Judaea, and rival claimants to the Seleucid throne competed for his support. One such, Alexander Balas, appointed him high priest in 153 BC, and military and civil governor in 150. He continued to exploit Seleucid weakness until treacherously murdered by a pretended ally in 143 BC.

IV. SIMON

The last survivor of the sons of Mattathias showed a resolution not inferior to that of his brothers. He drove a hard bargain with Demetrius II whereby the latter virtually resigned the suzerainty of Judaea and 'the yoke of the heathen was taken away' (1 Macc. xiii. 41). The Syrians were ejected from the *Akra*, Judaea was aggrandized at the expense of her neighbours at several points, and a period of relative peace and prosperity began, with Simon as high priest and unchallenged ruler.

V. THE LATER HASMONAEANS

Simon died at the hand of his son-in-law in 135 BC. His son John Hyrcanus was forced into temporary submission to the disintegrating Seleucid Empire, but at his death in 104 BC the Jewish realm was at its greatest extent since Solomon's time. His son Aristobulus (104–103 BC) formally claimed the title of king, and with him begins the sorry story of murder and intrigue and family jealousy which left the Jewish state a prey to the rising power of Rome. Antigonus, the last of the Hasmonaean high-priestly kings, was executed in 37 BC, and the pro-Roman Herod the Great began a new era (see HEROD). Several later members of the house of Herod had Hasmonaean blood by the maternal side.

VI. THE SIGNIFICANCE OF THE MACCABEES

According to Dn. xi. 34, the Maccabean revolt was to be only 'a little help' to God's people, for Daniel depicts events on the huge canvas of God's ultimate gracious purpose. Many Ḥasidim, looking for God to accomplish this, probably thought military action had gone far enough when the proscription of Judaism was abrogated and the Temple cleansed in 165 BC. At all events there are after that date increasing signs of Ḥasidim and Maccabees parting company. The assumption of the high-priesthood by Jonathan, and then Simon and his family, who were all of priestly but not Aaronic stock must have been bitter to the Ḥasidim, and the latter's heirs, the Pharisees, were wholly alienated from the worldly and tyrannical Hasmonaean high-priest kings, who reached a grotesque climax in the drunken and unhinged Alexander Jannaeus (103–76 BC).

It would, nevertheless, be a mistake to divide Maccabean aims into the achievement first of religious liberty, and then of political liberty. Judas and his brethren were fighting for *Israel*, and desired, in the name of the God of Israel, to take away the 'yoke of the heathen'. The easy and natural process whereby the hereditary high-priesthood, which comprehended unquestioned civil leadership, assumed into itself the revived monarchy, is eloquent. John Hyrcanus and the Hasmonaean kings in their campaigns clearly have the ideal of the Davidic kingdom in mind, and there are records of some territories they conquered being forcibly Judaized.

In some respects, the Maccabees set the pattern of Jewish nationalism and messianic thought for the New Testament period. Judas and his successors were invariably on good terms with the Romans, but in their day Rome was not yet ready to control Palestine. By New Testament times the Jews were firmly under 'the yoke of the heathen' once more, this time that of Rome. But the memory lingered of how Israel had once in the name of God defied another heathen empire, engaged her in single combat, and won; of how her borders had approached those of her Davidic glory. 'The ministry of Jesus falls . . . when the Jews of Palestine had still the memory of the Maccabean triumphs and no foreknowledge of the horrors of the siege under Titus' (T. W. Manson, *The Servant-Messiah*, 1953, p. 4).

W. R. Farmer has pointed to the preponderance of Maccabean names among anti-Roman agitators of New Testament times, and has associated the Zealot party (*q.v.*) with Maccabean ideals, and the crowd's reaction to our Lord's triumphal entry with the deliberate recall of the triumphs of Judas and Simon.

The once fashionable habit of dating many Psalms in the Maccabean period has almost passed. For other literary questions, see APOCRYPHA, DANIEL, BOOK OF, PSEUDEPIGRAPHA, ZECHARIAH.

BIBLIOGRAPHY. 1 and 2 Maccabees (see APOCRYPHA); Jos., *Ant.* xii–xiv; E. Schürer, *HJP*, I, i; W. O. E. Oesterley, *History of Israel*, II, 1932, chs. xvi–xxii; E. Bickerman, *The Maccabees*, 1947; W. R. Farmer, *Maccabees, Zealots and Josephus*, 1956 (*cf. JTS* (NS), III, 1952, pp. 62 ff.). A.F.W.

MACCABEES, BOOKS OF. See APOCRYPHA.

MACEDONIA. A splendid tract of land, centred on the plains of the gulf of Thessalonica, and running up the great river valleys into the Balkan mountains. It was famous for timber and precious metal. Anciently ruled by cavalry barons under a hellenized royal house, its kings dominated Gk. affairs from the 4th century BC, and after Alexander Macedonian dynasties ruled throughout the Eastern Mediterranean until superseded by the Romans. The home monarchy was the first to go when in 167 BC Macedonia was constituted a series of four federations of republics (to which structure Acts xvi. 12 may refer), thus completing its hellenization. They were subsequently grouped under Roman provincial control, and, until the consolidation of Moesia and Thrace as provinces in New Testament times, were heavily garrisoned against the intractable northern frontier. The province embraced the northern part of modern Greece from the Adriatic to the Hebrus river, and was crossed by the Via Egnatia, the main land route from Italy to the east. After 44 BC the proconsul sat at Thessalonica, while the assembly of the Greek states met at Beroea, the seat of the imperial cult. The province included six Roman colonies, of which Philippi was one. There were also tribally organized communities. In spite of this diversity, the area is normally treated in the New Testament as a unit, following Roman usage.

Paul's vision of 'a man of Macedonia' (Acts xvi. 9) marks a distinct development in his methods of evangelism. At Philippi (Acts xvi. 37) for the first time he took advantage of his high civil station. He now enjoyed support in the cultivated circles to which he naturally belonged (Acts xvi. 15, xvii. 4, 12) in contrast to their hostility at earlier points on his route (Acts xiii. 50, xiv. 5). He looked back upon Macedonia with profound affection (1 Thes. i. 3; Phil. iv. 1), and was always eager to return (Acts xx. 1; 2 Cor. i. 16). The Macedonians were willing donors to his Jerusalem fund (2 Cor. viii. 1–4), and several of their number were added to his regular retinue of assistants (Acts xix. 29, xx. 4). It was in Macedonia then, it seems, that Paul finally proved himself as an independent missionary leader.

BIBLIOGRAPHY. J. Keil, *CAH*, XI, pp. 566–570; J. A. O. Larsen, *Representative Government in Greek and Roman History*, 1955, pp. 103, 104, 113–115; *id.* in T. Frank, *An Economic Survey of Ancient Rome*, V, 1940, pp. 436–496. E.A.J.

MACHAERUS. A fortress east of the Dead Sea (modern el-Mekawar), near the southern frontier of the region of Peraea, built by Alexander Jannaeus (103–76 BC), destroyed by the Roman commander Gabinius (57 BC), rebuilt by Herod (37–4 BC), who appreciated the hot springs at Calirrhoe not far away (Wadi Zerka Ma'in). Here, according to Josephus (*Ant.* xviii. 5. 2), Herod Antipas imprisoned John the Baptist and later had him put to death; here too Antipas's first wife, the daughter of the Nabataean king Aretas IV, broke her journey on her way home to her father's capital at Petra when Antipas divorced her for Herodias. When Peraea was added to the province of Judaea (AD 44), Machaerus was occupied by a Roman garrison, which evacuated the place on the outbreak of war in AD 66. It was then occupied by a force of Jewish insurgents, but surrendered to the governor Lucilius Bassus in AD 71.

BIBLIOGRAPHY. Jos., *BJ* vii. 6. 1–4. F.F.B.

MACHIR (Heb. *māḵîr*). Two men in the Old Testament bear this name. **1.** A grandson of Joseph and son of Manasseh was named Machir (Gn. l. 23). We later learn that he begat Gilead, ancestor of the Gileadites (Nu. xxvi. 29). His children later took Gilead, dispossessing the Amorites who dwelt in it (Nu. xxxii. 39, 40). Gilead is later attributed to Machir (Jos. xvii. 1–3). For other references, *cf.* Dt. iii. 15; Jos. xiii. 31; Jdg. v. 14; 1 Ch. ii. 21–23, vii. 14–17.

2. The son of Ammiel who protected Mephibosheth in Lo-debar (2 Sa. ix. 4, 5). Later Machir was one of those who brought provisions to David (2 Sa. xvii. 27–29). E.J.Y.

MACHPELAH. The name applied to the field, cave, and surrounding land purchased by Abraham as a burial-place for his wife Sarah (Gn. xxiii). It was purchased from Ephron, a Hittite, for 400 shekels of silver (verses 8–16). It lay east of Mamre (verse 17) in the district of Hebron. Here were later buried Abraham (Gn. xxv. 9), Isaac and Rebekah (Gn. xlix. 31), and Jacob (Gn. l. 13).

The Heb. (*hammaḵpēlâ*) implies that the name is in some way descriptive and the Gk. (*to diploun*, 'the double') is taken to describe the form of the cave in Gn. xxiii. 17 (LXX). The reading of Shechem for Hebron in Acts vii. 16 may be due to the summary nature of the record of this speech, which originally referred also to Joseph's burial at Shechem.

The modern site of the burial-cave (197 feet × 111 feet), now incorporated in the southern end of the Ḥaram al-Ḥalîl at Hebron, is much venerated by Jews, Christians, and Muslims. It is jealously guarded by massive stone walls, probably of Herodian work, though the antiquity of the cave itself and its furnishings has not been verified by archaeological research. The 'cenotaph of Sarah' is still to be seen among others in the mosque above the cave (Vincent, Mackay, and Abel, *Hébron, le Haram al Khalîl*, 1923).

Recent comparisons of the details of Abraham's purchase of Machpelah with Middle Assyr. and Hittite laws support the antiquity of Gn. xxiii. Thus M. R. Lehmann draws attention to the inclusion of the number of the trees, the weighing of silver at the current merchant valuation, and the use of witnesses at the city-gate where the transaction was proclaimed (verses 16–18). These accord with Hittite laws which fell into oblivion by *c.* 1200 BC. The desire of Ephron to sell all the property rather than 'the cave at the edge of the field' (verse 9) may be linked with legal and feudal requirements of the time (*BASOR*, 129, 1953, pp. 15–23). D.J.W.

MADAI. See MEDES.

MADMANNAH. In SW Judah (Jos. xv. 31), probably Khirbet umm Deimneh, 12 miles northeast of Beersheba. At one time Calibbite (1 Ch. ii. 49), it may have passed to Simeon and become known as Beth-marcaboth. This theory is based on the close parallelism of Jos. xv. 31 and xix. 5. See Albright, *JPOS*, IV, 1924, pp. 159 f.
J.P.U.L.

MADMEN. A town of Moab against which Jeremiah prophesied (xlviii. 2). Since it is otherwise unknown, it has been suggested, either that the Heb. text read *gm-dmm tdmm*, 'also thou (Moab) shalt be utterly silenced' (LXX, Syr., Vulg.), or that it stands for Dimon, a possible (but unlikely) rendering of the name of the capital *Dîḇôn*. This place cannot be the same as Madmannah, which lay in the Negeb (Jos. xv. 31; 1 Ch. ii. 49). D.J.W.

MADMENAH. A city mentioned only once in the Bible. Isaiah includes it in his description of the route taken by an invading army approaching Jerusalem from the north (Is. x. 31). The site is unknown though, from the context, the vicinity of Jerusalem seems likely.

See *JPOS*, XIII, 1933, pp. 90–93. T.C.M.

MADON. A city of the northern Canaanites, it appears in the list of Tuthmosis III (*Mdn*, no. 20). It is possibly the Bronze Age site Qeren Hattin, on a hill overlooking Lake Tiberias; nearby Khirbet Madjan preserves the name. Garstang (*Joshua–Judges*, 1931, pp. 102, 109) thinks it was farther north. Mentioned in Jos. xi. 1, xii. 19.
J.P.U.L.

MAGADAN. See MAGDALA.

MAGBISH (*maḡbîš*, probably 'strong'). A town in Central Palestine to which returned 156 of its 'children' (Ezr. ii. 30) with Zerubbabel, but which is not mentioned in the parallel passage in Ne. vii. The location is unknown, but see note in *GTT*, p. 380.

MAGDALA, MAGDALENE. The name 'Magdala' occurs only once in the New Testament (Mt. xv. 39, AV), where the best MSS (followed by RV and RSV) read 'Magadan'. Some MSS, however, also read 'Magdala' or 'Magadan' for 'Dalmanutha' (otherwise unknown, *q.v.*) in Mk. viii. 10. The town of Magdala (or Tarichaea) stood on the western shore of the Sea of Galilee, north of Tiberias and Hammath, and south of Capernaum. The name derives from the Heb. *miḡdāl*, 'tower'. It is probable that the modern Khirbet Mejdel stands on the site today. Magadan was the *locality* on the western shore of the lake to which Jesus crossed after feeding the crowds, and it probably included the town of Magdala. Evidently Mary called Magdalene came from this town or area. (For 'Mary Magdalene', see MARY.) S.S.S.

MAGI. The term is used in Herodotus (i. 101, 132) of a tribe of the Medes who had a priestly function in the Persian Empire; in other classical writers it is synonymous with priest. Complementing this, Daniel (i. 20, ii. 27, v. 15) applies the word to a class of 'wise men' or astrologers who interpret dreams and messages of the gods. In the New Testament the usage broadens to include all who practise magic arts (*cf.* Acts viii. 9, xiii. 6, 8).

Both Daniel and Herodotus may contribute to the understanding of the Magi of Mt. ii. 1–12. Apparently they were non-Jewish religious astrologers who, from astronomical observations, inferred the birth of a great Jewish king. After inquiring of Jewish authorities, they came to Bethlehem to do homage. Whether 'the East' from which they came is Arabia, Babylon, or elsewhere is uncertain.

The historicity of the visit of the Magi has been questioned on account of the silence of other sources concerning both the event and Herod's subsequent slaughter of the infants, and also because of what is regarded as the legendary character of parts of the narrative. While full weight must be given to the poetic descriptions in the story (*e.g.* the star standing over Bethlehem), descriptive symbolism neither affirms nor negates the historicity of the event involved. A literalist approach, either to de-historicize the story or to exaggerate the miraculous, is out of keeping with the evangelist's meaning. For Matthew the Magi's visit represents the Messiah's relationship to the Gentile world and is also a fitting introduction to other prophetically significant events of Christ's infancy. The story is in keeping with the 'royal' messianic expectations of the Jews and with the character of Herod. Perhaps there is some astronomical confirmation of the star (*q.v.*) in the conjunction of Jupiter and Saturn in 7 BC and in the report of a later (4 BC) evanescent star in

Chinese records. But such parallels must be applied with caution.

Later Christian traditions regard the Magi as kings (because of Ps. lxxii. 10; Is. xlix. 7, lx. 3?) and number them at three (because of the gifts) or twelve. In the Christian calendar Epiphany, originally associated with Christ's baptism, reflects the importance of the Magi's visit for later Christendom. E.E.E.

MAGIC AND SORCERY.

1. The biblical view

Magic and sorcery attempt to influence people and events by supernatural or occult means. They may be associated with some form of divination (*q.v.*), though divination by itself is the attempt to use supernatural means to discover events without influencing them.

Magic is universal, and may be 'black' or 'white'. Black magic attempts to produce evil results through such methods as curses, spells, destruction of models of one's enemy, and alliance with evil spirits. It often takes the form of witchcraft. White magic tries to undo curses and spells, and to use occult forces for the good of oneself and others. The magician tries to compel a god, demon, or spirit to work for him; or he follows a pattern of occult practices to bend psychic forces to his will. There is no doubt that magic and sorcery are not always mere superstitions, but have a reality behind them. They must be resisted and overcome through the power of God in the name of Jesus Christ.

I. BIBLICAL TERMS

The following root words are used in Scripture to denote magical practices and practitioners. The Scripture references in each case are not exhaustive.

a. In the Old Testament

1. *kšp̄*. Translated 'sorcerer', 'sorcery', 'witch-(craft)'. The root probably means 'to cut', and could refer to herbs cut for charms and spells (*e.g.* Ex. xxii. 18; Dt. xviii. 10; Is. xlvii. 9, 12; Je. xxvii. 9).

2. *ḥrṭm*. Translated 'magician'. This term derives from Egyp. *ḥry-tp*, 'chief (lector-priest)', the title borne by Egypt's most renowned magicians; see below in paragraph (*d*) of Egyptian magic.

3. *lḥš*. Translated 'charm(er)', 'whisper', 'enchantment', 'ear-ring' (see AMULETS) (*e.g.* Is. iii. 20; used of serpent charmers in Ps. lviii. 5; Ec. x. 11).

4. *ḥb̄r*. Translated 'enchantment', 'charmer' (*e.g.* Dt. xviii. 11; Is. xlvii. 9, 12). The root has the idea of binding, probably with amulets and charms.

5. *kaśdîm*. Translated 'Chaldeans'. In Daniel the term is used both racially and of a special class who are linked with magicians. It is difficult to see how the exclusive technical sense could occur as early as the conquest of Babylon (Chaldaea) by Cyrus, but, since most of the technical references occur in the Aramaic section of Daniel, which may be a later translation from Hebrew, it is likely that the translator used it as the equivalent in his day of another word which stood in the original; possibly *galdu*, which on Bab. inscriptions seems to mean 'astrologers'. The only two references in the Heb. sections (ii. 2, 4) were then assimilated.

b. In the New Testament

1. *magos* (and cognates). Translated 'sorcerer', 'sorcery'; in Mt. ii, 'wise men'. Originally a magian, a racial group in Media, it came, like 'Chaldean', to have a technical use (*e.g.* Acts viii. 9, 11, xiii. 6, 8; found only in Matthew and Acts; see MAGI).

2. *pharmakos* (and cognates). Translated 'sorcerer', 'sorcery', 'witchcraft'. The root idea is that of drugs, potions, poisons (Rev. ix. 21, xviii. 23, xxi. 8, xxii. 15; elsewhere only in Gal. v. 20).

3. *goēs*. Translated 'seducer' (2 Tim. iii. 13; RV 'impostor'), it may signify rather a spell-binding magician. Although it means literally 'a wailer', it has the magical sense in classical and hellenistic Greek.

II. THE BIBLICAL JUDGMENT ON MAGIC

The references given in the first part of this article show that magic and sorcery are always condemned in Scripture. Magic is a rival to true religion, though it can be practised in conjunction with false religious ideas. True religion centres in the personal experience of the one God, with an attempt to live a life that is conformable to His will. The believer walks humbly with his God, prays to Him, and is prepared to accept the circumstances of life as the sphere in which to glorify Him. Magic, on the other hand, deals with lower supernatural beings, or attempts to force issues by using psychic forces, irrespective of whether the issues are for the glory of God. The following practices come under the specific condemnation of the Bible.

a. The wearing of charms

Among the list of women's ornaments in Is. iii. 18–23 it is usually thought that the word translated 'ear-rings' (see I*a* (iii) above) in verse 20 is a charm. The word is associated with whispering and snake-charming. Some think that the charm had good spells whispered into it; others consider that the word may originally have been *nḥš*, 'serpent', in which case the charm would have been a serpent figure. In this same passage there is a reference in verse 18 to 'round tires like the moon' (RV 'crescents'). These are clearly moon-images, and the only other occurrence of the word (*śahᵃrōnîm*) is in Jdg. viii. 21, 26, where they are worn both by camels and by the kings of Midian (in both places they are translated 'ornaments'). The previous word in Is. iii. 18 (*šᵉb̄îsîm*), translated 'cauls', occurs only here in Scripture, but a similar word in the Ras Shamra tablets apparently denotes sun-pendants, and this would make good sense in the context.

It is probable that there is a reference to

charms in Gn. xxxv. 2–4, where Jacob's household put away their 'strange gods' and their 'ear-rings'. This is the normal word for ear-ring, but the association with idols here suggests that they were charms of some kind.

b. Workers of magic; sorcerers; witches

Genesis and Exodus speak of the magicians of Egypt, and 2 Tim. iii. 8 names two of them as Jannes and Jambres. The Exodus record says that the Egyp. magicians copied Moses in turning their rods into serpents (vii. 11), in turning water into blood (vii. 22), and in producing frogs (viii. 7), but failed to produce the lice (viii. 18, 19), and were themselves incapacitated by the boils (ix. 11). The account leaves us free to decide whether they were clever conjurors or whether they used occult methods.

There is little direct allusion to sorcerers and witches in Israel. It is incorrect to speak of the 'witch' of Endor, since the Bible describes her as a medium, and not as a worker of magic. It is significant that Jezebel was known to practise witchcraft (2 Ki. ix. 22), and the allusion in Mi. v. 12 suggests that it was by no means rare. Manasseh personally encouraged it among other evils (2 Ki. xxi. 6).

In Is. iii. 3 the final word is *laḥaš*, which we have already noted (I*a* (iii) above) as connected with magic. Hence it is better to follow RV here, and translate as 'skilful enchanter'. There is another indication of magical practices in Is. xxviii. 15, where presumably people were initiated into some magical pact which they believed would give immunity from death.

The most striking reference to Heb. witchcraft is Ezk. xiii. 17–23. Here Heb. prophetesses were also practising magic arts for the preservation and destruction of individuals. In this they were going farther than the false prophets of Mi. iii. 5, who gave messages of good or ill to individuals according to whether they were prepared to pay. The details of the magical practices here are not easy to follow. The RSV 'magic bands upon all wrists' is more likely than the AV and RV 'pillows to all arm-holes (elbows)'. The purpose of the bands on the wrists and the veils (kerchiefs) on the head is said to be for hunting souls to death or for preserving them alive. One would assume from Ezk. xiii. 18 that the bands and veils were put on their clients, but verse 20 says that the bands will be torn from the arms of the witches, and verse 21 most naturally says the same of the veils. There are two main interpretations. G. A. Cooke (*ICC*) thinks that bands were placed on the wrists of the client and a covering on the head of the witch. In verse 20 he emends the text to read 'their arms'. He thinks that the binding was a piece of sympathetic magic, and represented the binding of the client's enemy for destruction. The veil was for loosing someone from death. The other interpretation is that of J. G. Frazer in his *Folk-Lore in the Old Testament*. This is that the women professed to catch souls and bind them up on cloth bands. The imprisonment would cause the owner of the soul to waste away. In return for money a wandering soul would be restored to a sick person. This view is commonly rejected on the ground that the Hebrews had no conception of a soul (*nep̄eš*) existing apart from the body. The present writer is inclined to doubt this, and thinks that Frazer may basically be correct, but, if the *ICC* view is the true one, then *nep̄eš* here, as frequently, must be translated 'person'.

III. DOES THE BIBLE COUNTENANCE MAGIC?

We now deal with some of the passages where the Bible might seem to countenance magic and superstition.

a. The use of mandrakes

Down through the centuries eastern women have made use of mandrakes to ensure conception (*cf.* Gn. xxx. 14–18). Since modern investigations have shown that primitive medicines often contain some element that is really effective, it would be foolish to dismiss this example as magic.

b. Jacob and the peeled rods

In the passage concerned (Gn. xxx. 37–41) Jacob was probably influenced by primitive ideas of the effect of seen objects upon the unborn young. But verse 40 indicates that the results really came about through selective breeding (see D. M. Blair, *A Doctor Looks at the Bible*, 1959, p. 5).

c. Samuel and the water

This incident (1 Sa. vii. 6) is often thought to denote sympathetic magic, the solemn pouring out of water to induce a storm. There is, however, not the slightest indication of this in the context. Water poured on the ground, according to 2 Sa. xiv. 14, is a symbol of human frailty and impermanence, and Samuel's action may best be interpreted as a sign of abasement and humiliation before God.

d. Samson's hair

Frazer and others have produced stories from all parts of the world in which the soul or the strength of someone resided in his hair, or even in some external object. The biblical story, however (Jdg. xvi), shows that Samson's uncut hair denoted his faithfulness to the Nazirite vow, and that the Spirit of God empowered him so long as he was faithful to this vow (*e.g.* Jdg. xiii. 25, xiv. 19). Those who wish to argue from a natural level may note that the loss of strength could be accounted for on psychological grounds when Samson realized his guilt. There are well-recognized cases of hysterical blindness, paralysis, *etc.*

e. Rousing up leviathan

Job asks that the day of his birth should be cursed by those who curse the day, who are ready to rouse up leviathan (Jb. iii. 8, RV). Some find here a reference to magicians who were thought to rouse up a dragon to swallow the sun at an eclipse. If this is correct, it is part of the extravagant language of Job, who calls upon everyone, bogus or true, who might claim to bring ill-luck on his birthday.

f. The power of blessing and cursing

The Old Testament lays great stress on this. The Patriarchs bless their children, and Isaac cannot reverse what he has promised to Jacob (Gn. xxvii. 33, 37). Balaam is called upon to curse Israel (Nu. xxii f.). Throughout the rest of the Old Testament there are other incidental references. It should be noted that the Bible does not visualize anyone's pronouncing an effective blessing or curse contrary to God's will. The Patriarchs believe that God is showing them the future of their descendants, and their blessing is declaratory of this. Balaam cannot effectively curse those whom God has blessed (Nu. xxiii. 8, 20). The psalmist knows that God can turn the undeserved curse into a blessing (Ps. cix. 28), while David's reluctance to interfere with Shimei is based on the fear that God may have inspired the curse for something that David had done (2 Sa. xvi. 10).

J.S.W.

2. Egyptian and Assyro-Babylonian.

I. EGYPTIAN MAGIC

a. Its rôle

Where the ordinary relationships and processes of life could readily be regulated through observation of obvious cause and effect, and by acting on an acquired modicum of knowledge and/or skill, this sufficed. But where mystery shrouded the causes of effects, and when ordinary means did not suffice to obtain desired results, then magic was appealed to. In Egypt magic was the exploitation of miraculous or occult powers by carefully specified methods to achieve ends otherwise unattainable.

Magic and religion were closely linked in Egypt, in that whereas 'society' principally covers relationships between man and man, and 'religion' the relationships between deity and mankind, the powers of magic found application in both spheres. The nearest term in Egyptian for 'magic' is *hīke*' (*ḥk*'); the concept *Hike*', 'Magic', was even personified as a deity from the third millennium BC onward. Patrons of magic were Thoth, god of learning and letters, and the wily goddess Isis.

b. Its uses

The Egyptians drew upon magic for the welfare of the living and for security in the life after death, only rarely using it for harmful ends. Its main uses may conveniently be labelled Defensive, Productive, Prognostic, Malevolent (these, after Gardiner), Funerary, and Wonder-working.

(i) *Defensive magic* was early deemed a gift of the sun-god who 'made for them (*i.e.* mankind) magical spells for defence against things that might happen' (*c.* 2200 BC), in the *Instruction for King Merikarē*, *e.g.* onset of death, scorpions, snakes, lions, *etc.* This shades into curative magic, overlapping with medicine: 'medical' writings ranged from the almost wholly observational and inductive (like the surgical Edwin Smith Papyrus) to collections of mixed medicinal remedies and magical spells, and mere collections of spells.

(ii) *Productive magic* was used to ease childbirth, aid love-making, and avert storms and bad weather.

(iii) *Prognostic magic* sought to know future events—*e.g.* would a newborn child survive? Divination as understood in Babylonia was not typical and mainly confined to late epochs, except for the interpretation of dreams (see II*a* below).

(iv) *Malevolent magic* is black magic, used to harm others; this was punishable at law just like any other misdemeanour.

(v) *Funerary magic*, intimately bound up with the cult of the dead, conveniently covers the numerous spells that were put at the disposal of deceased persons in the world beyond, to enable them to overcome hostile beings, gain sustenance, enjoy their faculties, change into various bodily forms at will, *etc.* For the Pyramid Texts, Coffin Texts, and Book of the Dead, see EGYPT, Religion.

(vi) *Wonder-working magic* exhibited the prowess of Egypt's renowned sages, usually in tales and short stories (see EGYPT, Literature). In the *Tales of the Early Magicians* in Papyrus Westcar of the Hyksos period (*c.* 1650 BC), four great sages of the Pyramid Age (*c.* 2700 BC) are able to produce a wax crocodile which becomes real or reverts to wax at the utterance of a spell, or they can double back the waters of a pleasure-lake to recover a girl's trinket, or restore to wholeness and life animals and birds whose heads had been severed (see translation in A. Erman and A. M. Blackman, *Literature of the Ancient Egyptians*, 1927, pp. 36–47). Such stories of great magicians remained popular in Egypt down to the 1st century AD, as is evidenced by the tales told of Neneferkaptah, Khamwēsē, and others, including a contest between an Egyptian and an Ethiopian magician (see F. Ll. Griffith, *Stories of the High Priests of Memphis*, 1900, pp. 54–65). Hence the Bible's association of magic with Egypt reflects authentic Egyptian background.

c. Its methods

Egyptian magical procedure was largely based on the 'sympathetic' principle, *i.e.* the enacted ritual often mimed the desired result (such as burning wax figures to destroy enemies). Accurate pronunciation of the potent words of the spell and proper performance of the rites laid down, using correct images, *etc.*, made from prescribed materials, were considered essential for success. Hence in Egypt, exploitation of occult powers depended on technical learning and strict rule, not on the magician's personality. Considerable collections of magical spells and rites occur therefore in papyri and other inscriptions. For a typical text, see A. Massart, *The Leiden Magical Papyrus I 343 + I 345*, 1954. Magicians' spells usually invoke help from the gods and often personify the evil forces to be exorcised, while they command, persuade, threaten, or curse the personalized hostile force that it leave the afflicted person.

d. Its practitioners

Learned in sacred writings, rituals, and spells, trained in the 'House of Life' (temple 'schools' where this and other literature was composed, copied, and taught), Egypt's greatest magicians were the chief lector-priests, in Egyp. *ḫry-ḥbt ḥry-tp*, later abbreviated by Moses' time (13th century BC) to *ḥry-tp*. This very title gave the Heb. *ḥarṭōm*, 'magician'. This essentially Egyp. term recurs in an Assyr. document (7th century BC), as *ḫar-ṭibi*, and as *ḥrtb* in the 1st-century AD tales of magicians mentioned in (*b*) above. (See A. H. Gardiner, *JEA*, XXIV, 1938, pp. 164, 165; and, more fully, J. Vergote, *Joseph en Égypte*, 1959, pp. 66–94, 206, with full references.) Thus the association of 'magicians' with 'wise men' generally in Gn. xli. 8 and Ex. vii. 11 reflects authentic Egyp. tradition; see paragraphs II*a* and II*c* below.

BIBLIOGRAPHY. For a good formal analysis of Egyptian magic, see A. H. Gardiner in *ERE*, VIII, pp. 262–269. Much material is collected (texts and pictures) in F. Lexa, *La Magie dans l'Égypte Antique*, 3 vols., 1925.

II. EGYPTIAN MAGIC IN THE BIBLE

a. Magicians and dreams of Joseph's pharaoh

In Gn. xli. 8, Joseph's pharaoh calls upon his magicians and wise men to interpret his dreams. This reflects the importance of dreams in ancient Egypt and the East; dreams and their interpretations were gathered into manuals, veritable handbooks of dream-interpretation. The original of one such MS, Papyrus Chester Beatty III (XIXth Dynasty, 13th century BC) may date back to the Middle Kingdom age, while the Papyri Carlsberg XIII and XIV of the 2nd century AD contain further collections from early sources. The common pattern is, that if a man sees himself in a dream doing or experiencing such-and-such, it is good or bad, and means that so-and-so will befall him. For this whole topic, see A. L. Oppenheim, *The Interpretation of Dreams in the Ancient Near East*, 1956; *Sources Orientales, II: Les Songes et leurs Interprétations*, 1959.

b. Joseph and divination

In Gn. xliv. 4, 5, 15, Joseph play-acts the learned Egyptian, master of the divinatory art, before his brothers. Two interpretations of this incident are possible.

(i) Joseph had it said by his steward, according to the usual translations of verse 5, that he divined by means of his silver cup; this would imply knowledge of cup-divination (lecanomancy) in Hyksos-period Egypt, *c.* 1700 BC. By this technique, omens for interpretation were obtained by observing the movement or configuration of drops of oil upon water in a cup. This technique is of Mesopotamian origin, apparently already used by the Sumerians (*cf.* B. Meissner, *Babylonien und Assyrien*, II, 1925, p. 284). A handbook to this technique is preserved on two cuneiform tablets dating from the 19th–17th centuries BC, *i.e.* within Joseph's general period.

In Egypt, however, cup-divination is attested only twice, once doubtfully. Two small statuettes of apparently Middle Kingdom date (*c.* 1900–1700 BC) each show a figure kneeling with chin on a cup held in the hands (see fig. 69), and it is just possible that these depict cup-divination (J. Capart, *Chronique d'Égypte*, XIX, 1944, p. 263). Egypt offers no further example until the technique recurs in papyri of the 2nd century AD. But Bab. influence, including divination, was already felt in Palestine in the second millennium BC. The Mari letters show regular, even intensive, relations between Hammurabi's Babylon and Hazor in the west in the 18th century BC; the contemporary king of Hazor even bore a Bab. name, Ibni-Adad. Moreover, Bab. divinatory practice is archaeologically attested at Hazor: in Temple II of the 15th century BC was found a clay model liver inscribed in cuneiform (see Y. Yadin, *BA*, XXII, 1959, p. 7 with fig. 5). Hence on this evidence there is no difficulty whatever in presupposing some knowledge of other forms of Mesopotamian divination such as lecanomancy in the Palestine of Joseph's day or in the immediately adjacent Egyp. East Delta, then under Hyksos (Semitic) control.

(ii) One may, on the other hand, render Joseph's steward's speech as 'Is it not from this cup that my lord drinks, and *concerning* which he will assuredly divine?', *i.e.* to unmask the theft. On this rendering Joseph's cup is solely a drinking-vessel, cup-divination would not be alluded to, and the form of his pretended divination remains wholly unspecified. This fits well with verse 15 when Joseph says to his brothers, 'Know you not that such a one as I can certainly divine?', *i.e.* he pretends to have apprehended them in their theft by divination, to recover his cup. For this view, see J. Vergote, *Joseph en Égypte*, 1959, pp. 172, 173.

c. Moses and the magicians

In Ex. vii. 8–13, when Aaron at Moses' command casts down his rod as a serpent before Pharaoh, his magicians and sorcerers 'did in like manner with their enchantments' (verse 11). For this kind of conjuring, it would appear that the Egyp. cobra (Arab. *naja haje*) can be rendered immobile (catalepsy) if pressure be applied to the muscles at the nape of the neck; *cf.* L. Keimer, *Histoires de Serpents dans l'Égypte ancienne et moderne* (*Mémoires, Institut d'Égypte*, L), 1947, pp. 16–17. The serpent must first be charmed, then seized at the neck as shown on several ancient Egyptian scarab-amulets (Keimer, *op. cit.*, figs. 14–21) and thus be temporarily immobilized. This feat was performed in Egypt as recently as 1954 and there photographed (*cf.* H. S. Noerdlinger, *Moses and Egypt*, 1956, p. 26; *EBr*[11], VI, p. 613). Aaron's serpent restored to a rod manifested the wholly-other omnipotence of God, however. On the plagues, see PLAGUES OF EGYPT.

III. ASSYRO-BABYLONIAN MAGIC

a. Its rôle

As in Egypt, Assyro-Babylonian magic supplemented the ordinary usages of society and religion by exploitation of occult or supernatural powers; in its origins, it goes back largely to the Sumerians of the third millennium BC.

b. Its uses and methods

Here again magic was primarily for mankind's advantage, though noxious spells cast by sorcerers were much feared. Its main spheres were Defensive (especially curative), Prognostic (divination), and Malevolent (sorcerers' black magic). Again, as in Egypt, magical practice consisted of exact manual rites and properly enunciated spells, and drew largely on the sympathetic principle.

(i) *Defensive and curative magic* was mainly resorted to to obtain deliverance from affliction —illness, demon possession, *etc.*—which may originate with the sufferer. Has he offended some deity through a ritual or moral fault? The exorcist might then often employ rites and spells from the 'handbook' *Šurpu*, 'Burning' (*i.e.* in purificatory rite), listing every conceivable fault the sufferer might have committed. Or affliction may have entered from without—some sorcerer's evil spell. To counter such, there was the companion 'handbook' of tablets, *Maqlu*, also 'Burning' (of wax or wooden effigies of sorcerers this time). 'As this image quivers, dissolves and melts away, even so may the sorcerer and sorceress quiver, dissolve and melt away!' (E. A. W. Budge, *British Museum: A Guide to the Babylonian and Assyrian Antiquities*, 1922, p. 201). Collections of prayers for release or absolution also exist. There is a full modern translation of *Šurpu* in E. Reiner, *Šurpu, A Collection of Sumerian and Akkadian Incantations*, 1958; of *Maqlu* in G. Meier, *Die Assyrische Beschwörungssammlung Maqlû*, 1937.

(ii) *Prognostic magic, i.e.* divination, was based on the conviction that any event, good or ill, may be announced or accompanied by some portent observable by men. By knowledge of such portents, men might then foresee impending events or experiences and welcome or avert them according to their nature. Learned priests systematically compiled long series of omens with interpretations in veritable reference-manuals. One such eventually occupied over 170 cuneiform tablets! Omens were either observed from signs in nature or sought by specific techniques.

1. Natural portents were taken from the whole gamut of man's observation: haloes and eclipses of sun and moon, conjunctions of heavenly bodies, positions of planets and stars, atmospheric phenomena, *etc.* (astrology); the flight of birds, actions and states of animals (snakes, dogs, mice, *etc.*) and insects (scorpions, beetles, *etc.*); births of animals and humans, especially if abnormal—all in long series of omen-tablets. For a sick person, omens good or bad would determine their survival or decease (see R. Labat, *Traité Akkadien de Diagnostics et Prognostics Médicaux*, 2 vols., 1951).

2. Specific techniques of divination included observation of configurations of and on a sheep's liver (hepatoscopy, extispicy), and observation of patterns of oil on water (or *vice versa*) in a cup (lecanomancy). Vast technical detail occupies the tablet-handbooks of hepatoscopy, for instruction in which suitably inscribed clay model livers were used. For English translations of reports recording observed formations of the liver, see A. Goetze, *JCS*, XI, 1957, pp. 89–105. This most famous form of Bab. divinatory magic penetrated among the Hittites of Asia Minor and the Canaanites in N Syria and Palestine alike (see Egyptian Magic, II*b* above). For a cup-divination handbook of the 18th century BC, see the same paragraph.

3. Dream-interpretation was as important as in Egypt, and Bab. and Assyr. dream-manuals are likewise known. Besides dreams that just happen, priests sometimes deliberately sought dreams by incubation to receive revelation from a deity.

(iii) *Malevolent magic* was the work of unofficial sorcerers; for the handbook *Maqlu* employed to counter their black magic, see on Defensive magic above.

c. Its practitioners

As in Egypt, magic was practised by priestly scholars attached to the temples. Exorcisms were performed by the *ašipu*-priest (*cf.* Heb. *'aššāpîm*, 'enchanters', Dn. i. 20) by virtue of the gods Ea and Marduk, the master-magicians. The elaborate apparatus of divination was the province of the *bârû*-priest; he had to be physically perfect, undertake long studies, and be initiated. Those attached to the royal court were called upon at any time to interpret all manner of things. See G. Contenau, *Everyday Life in Babylon and Assyria*, 1954, pp. 281–283, 286–295.

BIBLIOGRAPHY. On Mesopotamian magic, see also briefly L. W. King, *ERE*, IV, 1911, pp. 783–786, VIII, 1915, pp. 253–255. Useful notes can be found in É. Dhorme and R. Dussaud, *Les Religions de Babylonie et d'Assyrie . . . des Hittites, etc.*, 1949, pp. 258–298. Fully detailed surveys of magic and divination respectively, with copious translations from texts, can be found in M. Jastrow, *Die Religion Babyloniens und Assyriens*, I and II, 1912. Specific studies are by G. Contenau, *La Magie chez les Assyriens et les Babyloniens*, 1940; B. Meissner, *Babylonien und Assyrien*, II, 1925, pp. 198–282.

IV. ASSYRO-BABYLONIAN MAGIC IN THE BIBLE

a. Balaam

Balaam of Nu. xxii–xxiv is apparently a diviner turned prophet under divine constraint. Thus Balak sent emissaries to hire Balaam 'with the fees for divination in their hand' (Nu. xxii. 7, RSV, *cf.* verse 18), and at first Balaam went 'to meet with omens', their nature unspecified (Nu. xxiv. 1, RSV). Balak evidently required of Balaam evil omens wherewith to curse Israel. For Bab.-type divination at Hazor, see Egyptian Magic II*b* above; also an astrological text was found at Qatna (*Revue d'Assyriologie*, XLIV, 1950, pp. 105–112) and *bârû*-diviners in 18th- and 14th-century BC texts from Alalaḫ (D. J. Wiseman, *The Alalakh Tablets*, 1953, p. 158 *sub* '*bârû*'), both in N Syria. Further, an early second millennium seal of one 'Manum the *bârû*(-diviner)' turned up at Beth-shan in Jezreel in levels of the 13th century BC, Balaam's own period, to which his oracles can be dated linguistically (W. F. Albright, *JBL*, LXIII, 1944, pp. 207–233). It is therefore wholly in keeping with known facts that a Moabite ruler should hire a diviner from N Syria (Pethor by the River (Euphrates)), in the land of the sons of Amaw (Nu. xxii. 5, RSV; *cf.* Albright, *BASOR*, 118, 1950, pp. 15, 16, note 13).

b. The law and magic in Canaan

The prohibitions in the Mosaic law against the magic and sorcery practised by other nations (*e.g.* Lv. xix. 26, xx. 27; Dt. xviii. 10–14) were very relevant to conditions in contemporary Canaan. For Bab. influence there, see above Egyp. Magic II*b*, and on Balaam see section (*a*) above. The N Canaanite epics from Ugarit/Ras Shamra (tablets of the 14th/13th century BC, but epics are even older) indicate that womenfolk practised magical arts—witness Puǵat, who possibly divines from the flight of birds (*1 Aqht*: 32–36, see C. H. Gordon, *Ugaritic Literature*, 1949, p. 94, or G. R. Driver, *Canaanite Myths and Legends*, 1956, p. 59) and who certainly practised astrology 'knowing the courses of the stars' (*1 Aqht*: 50, 194, 201; Gordon, *op. cit.*, pp. 95, 100, or Driver, *op. cit.*, pp. 61, 65). That Ex. xxii. 18 expressly condemns sorceresses is thus noteworthy.

c. Isaiah

Is. xlvii. 9–13, directed against Babylon's hoary magical lore and priestly interpreters of heavens, stars, and moon, accurately reflects the facts set forth in III*b* above.

d. Ezekiel

Just before the final siege of Jerusalem in 589/587 BC, Ezekiel (xxi. 21, 22) envisages Nebuchadrezzar of Babylon using divination for military purposes, as often in the cuneiform records. His shaking (RV, RSV) of arrows, belomancy, is not yet attested from Bab. sources (although in general keeping with them) and *teraphim* are still rather obscure, but 'looking in the liver' is the famed Mesopotamian practice of hepatoscopy, so well known from first-hand documents; see Prognostic magic III*b*(ii) above.

e. Daniel

In Dn. i. 4 the procedure for educating the well-favoured Heb. youths in Bab. learning as laid down by Nebuchadrezzar accurately reflects that which was usual for the *bârû* scholar-magicians. Like their Bab. colleagues, Daniel and his friends could be called upon without notice by the king for counsel or interpretations (Dn. i. 20). In Dn. ii, because they were not told the content of Nebuchadrezzar's dream, the Bab. magicians could not resolve it by consulting their dream-manuals; Daniel drew on a Source infinitely higher than his Bab. training. In Dn. iv the narrative wording of verse 7 ('*did not* make known') hints that this time the diviners had some idea of the second dream's ominous nature, but for their own sakes professed inability to interpret it (verse 18, leading Nebuchadrezzar to say they 'are *not able* to make known . . .'), leaving this unpleasant duty to Daniel. In Dn. v Belshazzar's magicians apparently found the writing on the wall too cryptic for their lore.

To 'dissolve doubts' (Dn. v. 12, 16), *i.e.* to dissipate anxiety caused by a (yet unexplained) dream or omen (*cf.* Dn. iv. 5), was the purpose of interpreting or 'resolving' dreams. Then a good dream's benefits could be accepted and the threat from a bad one averted magically. On this, see Oppenheim, *The Interpretation of Dreams in the Ancient Near East*, pp. 218–220, 300–307. This emphasis on dreams is characteristic of the neo-Bab. kings, particularly Nabonidus, father of Belshazzar. For his dreams, see Oppenheim, *op. cit.*, pp. 202–206, 250, and, in part, T. Fish in *DOTT*, pp. 89 f. New texts of, and new dreams by, Nabonidus and his venerable mother come from recently discovered stelae of this king at Harran; see C. J. Gadd, *AS*, VIII, 1958, pp. 35–92 and plates 1–16, especially pp. 49, 57, 63. Closely parallel to Dn. iv is the 'Prayer of Nabonidus' in the Dead Sea Scrolls in which an exiled Jewish sage (name not preserved) is granted to that king to explain the cause of the latter's affliction. English translation in M. Burrows, *More Light on the Dead Sea Scrolls*, 1958, p. 400; text published by J.-T. Milik, *RB*, LXIII, 1956, pp. 407–415; brief comments, D. N. Freedman, *BASOR*, 145, 1957, pp. 31, 32.

BIBLIOGRAPHY. 'Magic (Jewish)' in *ERE*; E. Langton, *Good and Evil Spirits*, 1942; *id.*, 'The Reality of Evil Powers Further Considered', *HJ*, CXXXII, July 1935, pp. 605–615; M. F. Unger, *Biblical Demonology*, 1952, pp. 107–164.

See also DANIEL, BOOK OF. K.A.K.

MAGISTRATE. In the Old Testament the word occurs twice. In Ezr. vii. 25 it translates the Heb. *šōpēṭ*, 'judge' (see JUDGES), and in Jdg. xviii. 7 'there was no magistrate in the land' is a paraphrase of the Heb. idiom *yāraš ʿeṣer*, 'to possess restraint'.

In the New Testament Luke uses in his Gospel (xii. 11, 58) the words *archē* and *archōn* ('rule' and 'ruler') to refer to civil authorities in general. Paul was beaten, imprisoned, and subsequently released by the magistrates at Philippi (Acts xvi. 20, 22, 35, 36, 38). Here the Gk. word is *stratēgoi*, which literally means generals, or leaders of the host, and is used as an equivalent for Lat. *praetores*. This latter was the title found in some inscriptions as a popular designation for the leading men of the colony, though their correct title was *duoviri*. Evidence for the titles of the Philippian magistrates is to be found in *CIL* iii. 633, 654, 7339, 14206^{15}.

See also SANHEDRIN, SERJEANTS. D.H.W.

MAGNIFICAT. Like other hymns in Lk. i–ii, the prophecy of Mary (Lk. i. 46–55) takes its name from the Lat. Vulg. Believing 'Mary' (Lk. i. 46) to be the secondary reading, some commentators accept the less well-attested reading 'Elizabeth' (*cf.* Creed). It may be that Luke originally wrote simply 'she said', and that both 'Mary' and 'Elizabeth' were attempts of copyists to assign the song to a particular person. The reading 'Mary' became universally accepted. Scholars are divided on the question of whether the contents of the hymn are more suitable to Mary or Elizabeth. The episode which forms the setting is, however, transitional from the annunciation to the birth stories; it stands in close conjunction with the former and continues its messianic theme. Most probably, therefore, Luke viewed it as *Mary's* song regarding Christ.

This lyrical poem is modelled upon Old Testament psalms and has also a special affinity to the Song of Hannah (1 Sa. ii. 1–10). The sequence of the narrative is moulded by Luke's theme; and the hymn need not be regarded as Mary's spontaneous or exact reply. But neither should it be considered merely as an editorial reconstruction. Its significance for Luke lies in the fact that it is Mary's prophecy, *i.e.* that its contents sprang from her lips and express her mind and her heart.

As this lyric forms a climax to the section, so also within the Magnificat itself the mood rises to a crescendo. It is divided into four strophes, describing (1) Mary's joyous exaltation, gratitude, and praise for her personal blessing; (2) the character and gracious disposition of God to all who reverence Him; (3) His sovereignty and His special love for the lowly in the world of men; and (4) His peculiar mercy to Israel. The cause of Mary's song is that God has deigned to choose her, a peasant maid of low estate, to fulfil the hope of every Jewish maiden. For it is probable that, in Judaism, that which gave deepest meaning and joy to motherhood was the possibility that this child might be the Deliverer.

The last part of the poem is a description of God's messianic deliverance and is a virtual paraphrase of Old Testament passages. This redemption is prophesied in terms of a national deliverance from human oppressors. This is a typical mode of expression of pre-Christian messianism. The New Testament does not contradict it, but does transfer it to Messiah's parousia in the eschatological 'age to come' (*cf.* Acts i. 6 ff.). As is often the case in Old Testament oracles, these messianic acts of God are viewed as though they were already accomplished: the promise of God has the efficacy of the act itself (*cf.* Gn. i. 3); His word is the word of power. The specific object of God's mercy is 'Israel his servant' (Lk. i. 54 f.; *cf.* Acts iii. 13, 26, iv. 27, 30). Whether there is reflected here the Old Testament distinction between the whole nation and the righteous remnant is uncertain; the concept is often left in an undifferentiated whole, and the contrast in verses 51–53 may be only between the Jewish nation and the Gentile overlord. But in the mind of Luke—and in the mind of his first readers—certainly the distinctly Christian interpretation in such concepts as 'Israel' (*cf.* Lk. xxiv. 21–26; Jn. xii. 13; Acts i. 6; Rom. ix. 6), 'servant', and 'the seed' (Jn. viii. 39; Gal. iii. 16, 29) is not absent, and it probably enters into his understanding and interpretation of Mary's prophecy. See BENEDICTUS.

BIBLIOGRAPHY. J. M. Creed, *The Gospel according to St. Luke*, 1942, pp. 21–24; C. Neil and J. M. Willoughby, *The Tutorial Prayer-Book*, 1959, pp. 117, 118. E.E.E.

MAGOG. See GOG AND MAGOG.

MAGOR-MISSABIB (Heb. *māḡôr missāḇîḇ*, 'terror on every side'). A symbolic name which Jeremiah gave to Pashur son of Immer (Je. xx. 3; see PASHUR, 1).

MAGUS. See SIMON.

MAHALATH. See PSALMS.

MAHANAIM (*maḥanayim*, 'two camps'). A place in Gilead where Jacob saw the angels of God before he reached Penuel and met Esau (Gn. xxxii. 2). Appointed to be a levitical (Merarite) city from the territory of Gad (Jos. xxi. 38; 1 Ch. vi. 80), Mahanaim was on the border of Gad with Gileadite Manasseh (Jos. xiii. 26, 30). It was briefly capital of Ishbosheth, Saul's son (2 Sa. ii. 8, 12, 29), and later David's refuge from Absalom (2 Sa. xvii. 24, 27, xix. 32; 1 Ki. ii. 8), and then became the seat of a district-officer of Solomon's (1 Ki. iv. 14). The location of Mahanaim is still uncertain; it is usually placed in the middle of N Gilead at Khirbet Mahneh, 12½ miles north of the Jabbok river, but as the boundary of Gad is linked with the course of the Jabbok, Mahanaim is probably better located somewhere on (or overlooking) the north bank of the Jabbok. Mahanaim was at some distance from the Jordan, on the evidence of 2 Sa. ii. 29, however 'Bithron' be interpreted. If (as is commonly taken) Bithron means 'cleft, ravine', Abner went from Jordan up the vale of the Jabbok eastward and through its narrow part before reaching Mahanaim. If the RSV reading be adopted, then 'the whole forenoon' was needed in any case for Abner's eastward flight from the Jordan to Mahanaim. Hence perhaps Mahanaim is located somewhere in the Jerash area, or up to 5–10 miles south-south-west to south-west of Jerash, overlooking the north bank of the river Jabbok. *Cf.* also GAD, GILEAD. K.A.K.

MAHANEH-DAN (*maḥᵃnēh-ḏān*, 'camp of Dan'). The place where 'the Spirit of the Lord began to move (Samson)' (Jdg. xiii. 25), and where 600 Danites camped before the capture of Laish (Jdg. xviii. 11, 12, 27). It is described respectively as 'behind Kiriath-jearim' and as 'between Zorah and Eshtaol', but scholars have found it difficult to reconcile these two locations, and the site is unknown. See discussion in *GTT*, p. 301. J.D.D.

MAHER-SHALAL-HASH-BAZ. A symbolical name ('speed the spoil, hasten the prey') given to one of Isaiah's sons to signify the speedy removal of Syria and Israel as enemies of Judah by the Assyrians. This removal was to take place before the child could lisp 'my father and my mother' (Is. viii. 3, 4). See ISAIAH. E.J.Y.

MAHLI (*maḥlî*, 'weak', 'sickly'). **1.** Eldest son of Merari and grandson of Levi (Ex. vi. 19, AV 'Mahali'; Nu. iii. 20; 1 Ch. vi. 19, 29, xxiii. 21, xxiv. 26, 28; Ezr. viii. 18). His descendants are mentioned in Nu. iii. 33, xxvi. 58. **2.** The son of Mushi, another son of Merari (1 Ch. vi. 47, xxiii. 23, xxiv. 30); therefore nephew of (1) above.

MAHOL (*māḥôl*, 'dance'). The father of certain sages whom Solomon excelled in wisdom (1 Ki. iv. 31). But in 1 Ch. ii. 6 these sages are said to be the sons of Zerah. 'Sons' may simply mean 'descendants' in either case. 'Sons of Mahol' may, however, be an appellative expression meaning 'sons of the dance' (*cf.* 'daughters of music' in Ec. xii. 4). Such dancing would be part of the ritual of worship, as in Pss. cxlix. 3, cl. 4. (*Cf.* also the titles of Pss. lxxxviii, lxxxix.) J.G.G.N.

MAIL, COAT OF. See ARMOUR AND WEAPONS.

MAKKEDAH. A town in the Shephelah captured by Joshua (Jos. x. 28, xii. 16); grouped with Lachish and Eglon (Jos. xv. 41); named in Shishak's list (no. 27) and possibly in that of Tuthmosis III (no. 30). Adonizedek and his allies hid after their defeat in a cave near by (Jos. x. 16 ff.). El Mughar ('the cave'), 7 miles from the coast opposite Aijalon, has been proposed as its site; but there are many caves in this country, and Israelite occupation seems unlikely so far west. Eusebius (*Onom.*, p. 126) put Makkedah 8 Roman road miles from Beit Guvrin; this may indicate Khirbet el-Kheishum, north-east of Azekah, a considerable ruin near a prominent hilltop with caves (Abel, *Géographie*, II, p. 378).

BIBLIOGRAPHY. *GTT*, p. 273; Garstang, *Joshua–Judges*, p. 181. J.P.U.L.

MAKTESH. A site in Jerusalem or near by (Zp. i. 11). The name means 'mortar' or 'trough'. The oldest suggestion is that it was the Kidron Valley; so says the Targum. But most scholars today believe it to have been some part of the Tyropoeon Valley, within the walls of the city, where foreign merchants gathered. D.F.P.

MALACHI, BOOK OF.

I. AUTHORSHIP, DATE, AND BACKGROUND

The LXX takes the word not as a proper name but as a common noun, and renders 'my messenger', which is the meaning of the Heb. word. Many scholars follow LXX, and believe that the name of the author is not given. But the analogy of the other prophetical books which give the author's name would support the view that the name is here intended to indicate the author. This is supported by the Targum, which adds the phrase 'whose name is called Ezra the scribe'.

From internal evidence the approximate date of the prophecy may be determined. Sacrifices were being offered in the Temple (i. 7–10, iii. 8). This implies that the Temple was standing; indeed, that it had been standing for some time, a fact which would point to the post-exilic period. This is substantiated by the reference in i. 8 to the *peḥâ* or Persian governor. Mixed marriages seem to have been practised (ii. 10–12). The phrase 'the daughter of a strange god' means 'a woman of foreign or strange religion'. Apparently this practice was so widespread that the earlier prohibitions had long since been forgotten. Nor was great care exhibited in the offering of the sacrifices (i. 7). The priests had despised the Lord in offering polluted bread. When blemished offerings are brought it is a sign of a lax condition, and such a condition would not well comport with the early zeal displayed by the returned exiles. This appears to have been accompanied by a neglect in paying the requisite tithes (iii. 8–10). When one reads the book one finds that the abuses which Malachi condemns are those which Nehemiah sought to correct. It is impossible to date the book precisely, but it may be that it was composed during the time of Nehemiah's visit to Susa. At least it would seem to come from approximately this time.

II. OUTLINE OF CONTENTS

The book falls into two main parts, and its purpose may best be ascertained through a study of its contents. The first part (chapters i and ii) deals with the sin of Israel, and the second part (chapters iii and iv) with the judgment that will befall the wicked and the blessedness that will come upon those who repent.

We may analyse the prophecy as follows:

a. The superscription (i. 1)

There is a connection between this heading and that found at the beginning of chapter iii. If Malachi be a proper name, it at least exemplifies the fact that he is a messenger of God.

b. The Lord's love for Israel (i. 2–5)

God declares His love for the people in that He chose Jacob and hated Esau. This fact is seen in that Edom is devastated because of her wickedness and the wrath of the Lord, whereas Israel is to learn that the Lord will be magnified from her border.

c. A delineation of Israel's sin (i. 6–ii. 9)

In bold fashion the prophet now begins to delineate the chief and characteristic sins of the nation, those sins which were bringing the wrath of God upon the nation's head. God is the Father of the people, for He has nourished and brought them up. A father is deserving of honour and love, but such have not been shown to God by Israel. This complaint is directed particularly to the priests who are the representatives of the people before God. These priests who should have set the example of godly fear in worship have, in fact, despised the name of the Lord. Isaiah had earlier uttered the same type of condemnation. In punishment for their former sins, the Exile had been brought upon Judah. Now, however, the Exile is past, and its lessons have not yet been learned. Restored to her land, able to worship in the Temple, Judah yet sins against the Lord in the same manner as before.

The accusation against Israel is carried on in the form of a dialogue. Against each charge of the Lord a question of challenge is raised. For example, God charges that the priests have offered polluted bread. They reply, 'Wherein have we polluted thee?' (i. 7). It is thus brought out in clear-cut fashion that the priests have been bringing blemished sacrifices. This was in direct contravention of the law, which required that the offerings should be whole. Instead, however, they had brought what was blind and lame, and in so doing had exhibited contempt for the Lord.

When such sacrifices come from their hands, how can they expect Him to accept them as individuals and to find favour with Him? (i. 9). It would be better that the gates of the Temple be closed entirely than for such offerings to be brought (i. 10). Both the offerer and his offering are decidedly displeasing to the Lord, who is of purer eyes than to behold iniquity.

Such sacrifices are not desired of God, for even among the Gentiles His name proves itself to be great so that pure sacrifices are offered to Him (i. 11). This does not refer to the offerings which the heathen nations bring to their gods, nor does it refer to the sacrifice of the Mass, but to the time when the true gospel will be spread throughout the world and the true God worshipped by all peoples. Israel, however, had profaned the Lord's table, and found His service boring, which resulted in a people who practised deception and were selfish.

If there is no repentance, then a curse will come upon the priests. In ii. 5–7 the Lord makes clear what the true duty of the priest is to be, and thus there appears a great contrast between what the priest should be and what he actually was. Indeed, through his own poor example, he, instead of instructing others, has led them astray. He has been partial in the law (ii. 9b).

d. Condemnation of mixed marriages and divorce (ii. 10–17)

Israel had a common Father. God had created her. Therefore, she should have manifested unity. Instead of that, however, she had dealt treacherously. She had profaned the holiness of the Lord in the practice of mixed marriages. Those who have thus acted, however, are to be cut off. Divorce was also common, and the Lord hates divorce. These sins had been glossed over, and rationalized. The Lord declares that the people have wearied Him with their words. They have ignored Him and acted as though He did not exist.

e. The coming Day of the Lord (iii. 1–6)

Malachi now breaks forth into the exalted language of prophecy in declaring that the messenger of the Lord will truly come and prepare the day for the Lord whom the people seek. He will appear as a refiner, to purify and purge the nation, and who may abide the day of His coming? As a result of His work, the offering of Judah and Jerusalem will be pleasant (iii. 4). Yet the coming will bring judgment, and this will fall upon those in the nation who do wickedly. Nevertheless, Jacob will not be consumed, for the Lord changes not; He remains faithful to His promises (iii. 6).

f. Repentance and tithing (iii. 7–12)

The nation's apostasy is not new, but has continued from of old. For one thing, it has shown itself in withholding from God the tithes which had been commanded. This was a robbing of God. If the nation would bring the tithes as it should, God would respond to its worship and pour upon it a blessing such as it could not contain, and in addition other peoples also would then look upon Israel as truly blessed.

g. A promise of deliverance for the godly (iii. 13–iv. 3)

The nation's sinful speech has been hard and insistent against God. It would seem that the people concluded that the service of God was vain and of no profit. But among the people there were also those who feared the Lord, and they spoke with one another. These the Lord takes note of, and them He will spare in the day when He makes up His jewels. The day of judgment will surely come, and it will consume the wicked, but to those who fear the Lord's name righteousness, the sum and substance of salvation, will rise like a sun, and in its wings there will be healing.

h. Conclusion (iv. 4–6)

The prophecy closes with an exhortation to remember the law of Moses, and with the announcement that Elijah will come before there appears the great and terrible Day of the Lord.

BIBLIOGRAPHY. Marcus Dods, *The Post-Exilian Prophets*, 1881; G. C. Morgan, *Wherein Have We Robbed God?*, 1898; E. J. Young, *Introduction to the Old Testament*, 1958, pp. 301–303. E.J.Y.

MALCAM. 1. A Benjamite, son of Shaharaim by Hodesh (1 Ch. viii. 9).

2. God of the Ammonites, possibly their chief deity (Am. i. 15, AV 'their king'), almost certainly to be identified with Milcom (1 Ki. xi. 5, 33; 2 Ki. xxiii. 13), and Molech or Moloch (Lv. xviii. 21; 1 Ki. xi. 7; Je. xxxii. 35, *etc.*). All these terms have the basic root *mlk* which conveys the idea of king, kingship. Both AV and RV translate *malkām* as 'their king' in Je. xlix. 1, 3. *Cf.* Zp. i. 5. (See MOLOCH, MILCOM.) J.A.T.

MALCHIJAH ('Yah is King'). This is a common Old Testament name, sometimes translated as Malchiah. It was the name of the following: **1.** A descendant of Gershom and ancestor of Asaph (1 Ch. vi. 40); **2.** a priest, the father of Pashur (1 Ch. ix. 12; Je. xxi. 1); **3.** the head of a priestly course (1 Ch. xxiv. 9), perhaps the same as (2); **4, 5, 6.** three Israelites who had taken strange wives in post-exilic times (Ezr. x. 25, 31). In 1 Esdras ix. 26, 32 they are called Melchias, Asibias, and Melchias respectively; **7.** 'the son of Rechab', who repaired the dung gate (Ne. iii. 14); **8.** 'the goldsmith's son', possibly the same as (4), (5), (6), or (7), who helped to repair the wall (Ne. iii. 31).

9. One who stood beside Ezra at the reading of the Law (Ne. viii. 4); **10.** one who sealed the covenant, perhaps the same as (9) (Ne. x. 3); **11.** a priest who took part in the purification of the wall (Ne. xii. 42), perhaps the same as (9) and/or (10).

12. The owner of the pit in which Jeremiah was imprisoned and probably a member of the royal family (Je. xxxviii. 6, AVmg, RV, RSV).

J.D.D.

MALCHUS (Gk. *Malchos* from Heb. *meleḵ*, 'king'). The high priest's servant whose ear Peter cut off when Jesus was arrested in the Garden of Gethsemane (Mt. xxvi. 51; Mk. xiv. 47; Lk. xxii. 50; Jn. xviii. 10). Only John mentions the man's name, thus confirming his close acquaintance with the high priest Caiaphas and his household (*cf.* Jn. xviii. 15); and only Luke (xxii. 51) mentions the healing of the ear. J.D.D.

MALICE. In the New Testament this translates Gk. *kakia*, which has the following meanings: 1. 'Wickedness', 'evil' (so RSV in 1 Cor. xiv. 20; Jas. i. 21; 1 Pet. ii. 1, 16; and also in Acts viii. 22, of an individual sinful act). 'Malice' in 17th-century English had primarily this meaning. 2. 'Ill-will', 'spitefulness'; *i.e.* 'malice' in the modern sense of the word. 3. 'Trouble', 'harm' (Mt. vi. 34). In lists of sins (*e.g.* Rom. i. 29; Col. iii. 8; Tit. iii. 3), sense (2) is probably to be preferred, except, perhaps, in 1 Pet. ii. 1 and Eph. iv. 31, where 'all *kakia*' implies 'all kinds of wickedness'.

Malice characterizes the life of men under the wrath of God (Rom. i. 29). It is not only a moral deficiency but a 'fellowship-destroying power' (W. Grundmann in *TWNT*). For believers it belongs to the old life (Tit. iii. 3); but there is still need for exhortation to 'clean it out' (1 Cor. v. 7 f.) or 'strip it off' (Jas. i. 21; Col. iii. 8). Christians are to be 'babes in evil' (1 Cor. xiv. 20), for Christian liberty is not lawlessness (1 Pet. ii. 16).

P.E.

MALLOWS. See PLANTS.

MALTA. See MELITA.

MAMMON. This word occurs in the Bible only in Mt. vi. 24 and Lk. xvi. 9, 11, 13, and is a transliteration of Aramaic *māmônâ*. It means simply wealth or profit, but Christ sees in it an egocentric covetousness which claims man's heart and thereby estranges him from God (Mt. vi. 19 ff.): when a man 'owns' anything, in reality it owns him. (*Cf.* the view that Mammon derives from Bab. *mimma*, 'anything at all'.) 'Mammon of unrighteousness' (Lk. xvi. 9) is dishonest gain (*TWNT*) or simply gain from self-centred motives (*cf.* Lk. xii. 15 ff.). The probable meaning is that such money, used for others, may be transformed thereby into true riches in the coming age (Lk. xvi. 12). E.E.E.

MAMRE (*mamrē'*). **1.** A place in the Hebron district, westward from Machpelah (Gn. xxiii. 17, 19, xlix. 30, l. 13), associated with Abraham (Gn. xiii. 18, xiv. 13, xviii. 1) and Isaac (Gn. xxxv. 27). Abraham resided for considerable periods under the terebinth of Mamre; there he built an altar, there he learned of the capture of Lot, there he received Yahweh's promise of a son and pleaded for Sodom, and from there he saw the smoke of Sodom and its neighbour-cities ascend. The site has been identified at Râmet el-Khalîl, 2 miles north of Hebron. Here Constantine built a basilica beside an ancient terebinth which was pointed out in his day (as by Josephus 250 years earlier) as the tree beneath which Abraham 'entertained angels unawares' (Gn. xviii. 4, 8). There was a shrine there under the Monarchy, but it was a sacred place before Abraham's time, in the Early Bronze Age.

2. An Amorite chief at Mamre who with his brothers Eshcol and Aner joined Abraham's expedition against Chedorlaomer (Gn. xiv. 13, 24).

BIBLIOGRAPHY. E. Mader, *Mambre*, 2 vols., 1957. F.F.B.

MAN. The Genesis account of creation accords to man a supreme place in the cosmos. Not only is his creation the final work of God, but in it the work of the other five days finds its fulfilment and its meaning. Man is to possess the earth, make it serve him, and to rule the other creatures (Gn. i. 27–ii. 3). The same witness to man's dominion and centrality in creation is given elsewhere (Am. iv. 13; Is. xlii. 5 f.; Pss. viii. 5 f., civ. 14 f.), and is supremely given in the incarnation (*cf.* Heb. ii).

a. Man in nature

It is emphasized throughout the Bible that man is part of nature. Being dust, and made from dust (Gn. ii. 7), his biological and physical similarity to the animal creation is obvious in many aspects of his life (Gn. xviii. 27; Jb. x. 8, 9; Ps. ciii. 14; Ec. iii. 19, 20, xii. 5–7). Being 'flesh' he shares in the helpless dependence of the dumb creation on God's mercy (Is. ii. 22, xl. 6; Ps. ciii. 15, civ. 27–30). Even in making nature serve him he has to serve nature, tend it, and bring it to fruition (Gn. ii. 15). He is subject to the same laws as the natural world, and can find himself overwhelmed in the midst of the grandeur of the world in which he lives (Jb. xxxviii–xlii).

Nature is not simply a neutral framework or background for man's life. Between nature and man there are deep and mysterious bonds. The natural world falls under the curse of corruption through the fall of man (Gn. iii. 17, 18), and now suffers pain and death, waiting for the final redemption of mankind before it can expect its own (Rom. viii. 19–23). Nature is regarded in the Bible as rejoicing in the events that lead to man's redemption (Ps. xcvi. 10–13; Is. xxxv, iv. 12, 13) when it, too, shall enjoy deliverance (Is. xi. 6–9, lxv. 25). Man, on his side, has an instinctive sympathy with nature (Gn. ii. 19) and must respect its ordinances (Lv. xix. 19; Dt. xxii. 9, 10; Jb. xxxi. 38–40), realize his dependence on it, and toil to gain from his natural environment sustenance for his life and enrichment for his culture (Gn. iii. 17, ix. 1–7).

b. Man's destiny

Yet man cannot find the true meaning of his life within this context. The animals can provide no help meet for him. He has a history and a destiny to fulfil, unique among the rest of creation. He is made 'in the image of God' (Gn. i. 27). While some have suggested that this image is expressed in man's dominion over the earth, or in his power of reasoning, or even in his physical characteristics, it seems better to find it neither in man's relationship with the world nor in any static impress on man's being, but in his responsibility towards his Creator. In the Genesis account of creation God, when He creates man, is regarded as taking up an attitude of deeper personal concern for him (Gn. i. 26, *cf.* i. 3, 6, *etc.*), and an approach that involves Himself in a closer relationship with man His creature (Gn. ii. 7) than with the rest of creation. God approaches man and addresses him as a 'thou' (Gn. iii. 9), and man is made to respond to God's gracious word in personal love and trust. Only in this response can man be what he truly is. God's word by which he lives (*cf.* Mt. iv. 4) offers him a relationship that lifts him above the rest of creation around him, and confers on him his dignity as a child of God, made in His image and reflecting His glory. This dignity, moreover, is not something he possesses as an isolated individual before God, but only as he also stands in responsible and loving relationship to his fellow-men. It is as man within his family and social relationships that he truly reflects the image of God (Gn. i. 27, 28, ii. 18).

c. Man's structure

Various words are used to describe man in his relationship to God and to his environment, and in the structure of his own being. These are: spirit (Heb. *rûaḥ*, Gk. *pneuma*), soul (Heb. *nep̄eš*, Gk. *psyche*), body (only in New Testament Gk., *sōma*), flesh (Heb. *bāśār*, Gk. *sarx*). These words are used according to the different aspects of man's activity or being which it is intended to emphasize, but they must not be regarded as describing separate or separable parts which go to make up what man is. The use of the word 'soul' may emphasize his individuality and vitality with emphasis on his inner life and feeling and personal consciousness. The use of the word 'body' may emphasize the historical and outward associations that affect his life. But the soul is, and must be, the soul of his body, and *vice versa.* Man is also in such a relation to the Spirit of God that he has spirit, and yet not in such a way that he can be described as spirit, or that spirit can be regarded as a third aspect of his identity. Man as 'flesh' is man in his connection with the realm of nature and with humanity as a whole, not only in its weakness but also in its sinfulness and opposition to God.

Other words are used to define the seat of certain particular aspects or functions of man. In the Old Testament emotional impulses and feelings are attributed, really and metaphorically, to organs of the body such as the heart (*lēḇ*), liver (*kāḇēḏ*), kidneys (*kelāyôṯ*), and bowels (*mēʿîm*). The blood is also regarded as being closely identified with the life or *nep̄eš*. It is especially the heart (*lēḇ*) that is the seat of a wide range of volitional and intellectual as well as emotional activities, and tends to denote the soul, or man viewed from his inward and hidden side. In the New Testament the same use is made of the Gk. word *kardia* (= heart or *lēḇ*). Two more words, *nous*, 'mind', and *syneidēsis*, 'conscience', are brought into use, and a clearer distinction is made between the 'inward' and 'outward' man, but these two aspects of the one man cannot be separated, and the future holds not the mere 'immortality of the soul' but the 'resurrection of the body', which means the salvation and renewal of the whole man in the fullness of his being.

d. Man's sin

The fall of man (Gn. iii) involves his refusal to respond to God's word, and to enter the relationship in which he can fulfil the purpose for which he was created. Man seeks to find within himself the justification for his existence (Rom. x. 3). Instead of seeking to enter a true relationship with God and his fellow-men in which he can reflect God's image and glory, he seeks to find the meaning of his destiny merely in his relationship with the created world in the context of his immediate environment (Rom. i. 25). The result is that his life has become characterized by bondage (Heb. ii. 14, 15), conflict with evil powers (Eph. vi. 12), frailty and frustration (Is. xl. 6; Jb. xiv. 1), and he is so perverted and evil in his mind and heart (Gn. viii. 21; Jb. xiv. 4; Ps. li. 5; Mt. xv. 19, 20, xii. 39) that he turns the truth of God into a lie (Rom. i. 25).

e. Man in God's image

Yet in spite of the fall, man under the promise of Christ must still be regarded as in the image of God (Gn. v. 1 ff., ix. 1 ff.; Ps. viii; 1 Cor. xi. 7; Jas. iii. 9), not because of what he is in himself, but because of what Christ is for him, and because of what he is in Christ. In Christ is now to be seen the true meaning of the covenant which God sought to make with man in the Word, and the destiny which man was made to fulfil (*cf.* Gn. i. 27–30, ix. 8–17; Ps. viii; Eph. i. 22; Heb. ii. 6 ff.), for the unfaithfulness of man does not nullify the faithfulness of God (Rom. iii. 3). Therefore in the sight of God, man, seen both in the individual (Mt. xviii. 12) and corporate (Mt. ix. 36, xxiii. 37) aspects of his life, is of more value than the whole realm of nature (Mt. x. 31, xii. 12; Mk. viii. 36, 37), and the finding of the lost man is worth the most painful search and complete sacrifice on His part (Lk. xv).

Jesus Christ is the true image of God (Col. i. 15; 2 Cor. iv. 4) and thus the true man (Jn. xix. 5). He is both the unique individual and the inclusive representative of the whole race, and His achievement and victory mean freedom and life for all mankind (Rom. v. 12–21). He fulfils the covenant in which God bestows on man his true destiny. In Christ, by faith, man finds himself being changed into the likeness of God (2 Cor. iii. 18) and can hope confidently for full conformity to His image (Rom. viii. 29) at the final manifestation of His glory (1 Jn. iii. 2). In 'putting on' this image by faith he must now 'put off the old nature' (Eph. iv. 24; Col. iii. 10), which seems to imply a further renunciation of the idea that the image of God can be thought of as something inherent in the natural man, though even the natural man must be regarded as being created in the image of God (*cf.* 2 Cor. v. 16, 17).

In the development of the doctrine of man, the Church came under the influence of Gk. thought with its dualistic contrast between matter and spirit. Emphasis was placed on the soul with its 'divine spark', and there was a tendency to regard man as a self-contained individual entity whose true nature could be understood by the examination of the separate elements constituting his being. Emphasis was placed by some of the Fathers on the rationality, freedom, and immortality of the soul as being the main element in man's likeness to God, though others found the image of God also in his physical being. Irenaeus regarded the image of God as a destiny which man was created to grow into. Augustine dwelt on the similarity between the Trinity and the threefold structure in man's memory, intellect and will.

An exaggerated distinction was also suggested between the meanings of the two words 'image' and 'likeness' (*ṣelem* and *d*[e]*mûṯ*) of God, in which man was said to be created (Gn. i. 26), and this gave rise to the scholastic doctrine that the 'likeness' (Lat. *similitudo*) of God was a supernatural gift given by God to man in his creation, *i.e.* an original righteousness (*justitia originalis*) and perfect self-determination before God, which could be, and indeed was, lost in the fall. The 'image' (*imago*), on the other hand, consisted of what belonged to man by nature, *i.e.* his freewill, rational nature, and dominion over the animal world, which could not be lost even in the fall. This means that the fall destroyed what was originally supernatural in man, but left his nature and the image of God in him wounded, and his will free.

At the Reformation Luther denied the distinction between *imago* and *similitudo*. The fall radically affected the *imago*, destroyed man's freewill (in the sense of *arbitrium*, though not of *voluntas*), and corrupted man's being in its most important aspects, only a tiny relic of his original image and relationship to God being left. Calvin, however, also stressed the fact that the true meaning of man's creation is to be found in what is given to him in Christ, and that man comes to be in God's image as he reflects back to Him His glory, in gratitude and faith.

In later Reformed dogmatics the concepts of *imago* and *similitudo* were again differentiated when theologians spoke of the essential image of God which could not be lost, and the accidental but natural endowments (including original righteousness) which might be lost without the loss of humanity itself. In more modern times Brunner has attempted to use the concept of the 'formal' *imago* consisting of the present structure of man's being, based on law. This has not been lost in the fall, and is a point of contact for the gospel. It is one aspect of a unified theological nature of man which even in its perversion reveals traces of the image of God. 'Materially', however, for Brunner, the *imago* has been completely lost. R. Niebuhr has returned to the scholastic distinction between, on the one hand. the essential nature of man which cannot be destroyed, and, on the other hand, an original righteousness, the virtue and perfection of which would represent the normal expression of that nature.

Karl Barth, in formulating his doctrine of man, has chosen a path different from that followed by Church tradition. We cannot know real man till we know him in and through Christ, therefore we must discover what man is only through what we find Jesus Christ to be in the gospel. We must not take sin more seriously than grace, therefore we must refuse to regard man as being no longer the one God made him. Sin creates the conditions under which God acts, but does not so change the structure of man's being that when we look at Jesus Christ in relation to men and mankind, we cannot see within human life analogical relationships which show a basic form of humanity corresponding to and similar to the divine determination of man. Though man is not by nature God's 'covenant-partner', nevertheless in the strength of the hope we have in Christ human existence is an existence which corresponds to God Himself, and in this sense is in the image of God. Barth finds special significance in the fact that man and woman together are created in the image of God, and stresses the mutual communication and helpfulness of man to man as being of the essence of human nature. But only in the incarnate Son, Jesus Christ, and through his election in Christ, can man know God and be related to God in this divine image.

BIBLIOGRAPHY. H. Wheeler Robinson, *The Christian Doctrine of Man*, 1926; O. Weber, *Dogmatik*, I, 1955, pp. 582–640; E. Brunner, *Man in Revolt*, E.T., 1939; K. Barth, *Church Dogmatics*, E.T., III/1, pp. 176–211, 235–249, and III/2, *Christ and Adam*, E.T., 1956; David Cairns, *The Image of God in Man*, 1953; R. Niebuhr, *The Nature and Destiny of Man*, 1941; T. F. Torrance, *Calvin's Doctrine of Man*, 1947; Gustaf Wingren, *Man and the Incarnation*, 1959; Günther Dehn, *Man and Revelation*, 1936, pp. 9–37; H. Heppe, *Reformed Dogmatics*, E.T., 1950, pp. 220–250; C. Hodge, *Systematic Theology*, II, 1883, pp. 3–116; W. Eichrodt, *Man in the Old Testament*, E.T., 1951; George A. F. Knight, *A Christian Theology of the Old Testament*, 1959, pp. 25–39, 119–130; Charles West, *Communism and the Theologians*, 1957; W. A. Whitehouse, 'The Christian View of Man', *SJT*, II, 1949, pp. 57–82.

R.S.W.

MAN OF SIN. See ANTICHRIST.

MANAEN. The Gk. form of the Heb. name Menahem ('comforter'). Brought up with ('foster-brother of') Herod Antipas, Manaen's life took a very different turn from that of the tetrarch, and he is found as one of the Christian leaders at Antioch along with Paul and Barnabas (Acts xiii. 1). He may have been related to an earlier Manaen, an Essene who, according to Josephus (*Ant*. xv. 10. 5), was a friend of Herod the Great.

J.D.D.

MANAHATH, MANAHETHITES. 1. Son of Shobal, son of Seir the Horite (Gn. xxxvi. 23; 1 Ch. i. 40), who was the eponymous ancestor of a clan of Mt. Seir later absorbed by Edom.

2. The name of a city to which certain Benjamites were carried captive (1 Ch. viii. 6), and which seems to have been somewhere in the vicinity of Bethlehem (so *GTT*, p. 155). *ISBE* and Grollenberg suggest an identification with Manocho, a town in the hill-country of Judah listed in Jos. xv. 59, LXX, and probably to be identified with the modern Malîha, south-west of Jerusalem. Mahanath may also be the 'Menuhah' of Jdg. xx. 43, RVmg, where AV renders 'with ease' (*cf.* 'Manahath' = 'resting-place').

Inhabitants of Manahath (called Manahethites in AV) are mentioned in 1 Ch. ii. 52, 54. They were the descendants of Caleb. One-half of them were the progeny of Shobal, and the other of Salma (*qq.v.*).

J.D.D.

MANASSEH ('making to forget'). **1.** Elder son of Joseph, born in Egypt of an Egyptian mother, Asenath (*q.v.*), daughter of Potiphera (*q.v.*), the priest of On (Gn. xli. 51). Israel accepted Manasseh and Ephraim as co-equals with Reuben and Simeon, but Manasseh lost the right of *firstborn* (*b*ᵉ*ḵôr*) in favour of his younger brother Ephraim (Gn. xlviii. 5, 14). An interesting and early parallel is found in Ugaritic literature, *Keret Legend* (Tab. 128, III. 15), 'The youngest of them I will make *firstborn* (*abrkn*).'

2. The tribe of Manasseh derived from seven families: one from Machir, and the remaining six from Gilead. They occupied land on both sides of Jordan; the eastern portion being granted by Moses, the western by Joshua (Jos. xxii. 7). After the crossing of Jordan and the settlement in the land, Joshua permitted the half-tribe of Manasseh, together with Reuben and Gad, to return to the conquered territory of Sihon, king of Heshbon, and Og, king of Bashan (Nu. xxxii. 33). The eastern lot of the half-tribe of Manasseh covered part of Gilead and all of Bashan (Dt. iii. 13). The western half of the tribe was granted good land north of Ephraim, and south of Zebulun and Issachar (Jos. xvii. 1–12). This western part was divided into ten portions: five to those families having male descendants, and five to Manasseh's sixth family, namely, the posterity of Hepher, all females and daughters of Zelophehad (Jos. xvii. 3). Western Manasseh included a chain of Canaanite fortresses and strong cities, among which were Megiddo, Taanach, Ibleam, and Bethshan (*qq.v.*). These they failed to conquer but compelled their inhabitants eventually to pay tribute. Though the lot of Manasseh and Ephraim, the tribe of Joseph, was large, they lodged a complaint with Joshua for more land. In reply he advised them to show their worth by clearing the unclaimed forest areas (Jos. xvii. 14–18). Golan, a city of Bashan, in eastern Manasseh, was one of the six 'cities of refuge' (Jos. xx. 8, xxi. 27).

The tribe was renowned for its valour; among its heroes was Gideon in the west (Jdg. vi. 15), and Jephthah in the east (Jdg. xi. 1). Some of the tribe of Manasseh deserted to David at Ziklag (1 Ch. xii. 19, 20), and also rallied to his support at Hebron (verse 31). Manassites were among those deported to Assyria by Tiglath-pileser (1 Ch. v. 18–26).

Difficulties have been found in the genealogies of the tribe of Manasseh, given in Nu. xxvi. 28–34; Jos. xvii. 1–3; 1 Ch. ii. 21–23, vii. 14–19 (see *HDB* on 'Manasseh'). But if allowance is made for a corrupt text in 1 Ch. vii. 14, 15, then harmony can be restored. It is probable that the words 'Huppim and Shuppim' are glossed into verse 15 from verse 12, and possible that the word 'Asriel' is a dittograph.

A comparison of the Heb. text of these verses with LXX, Syr. Peshitta, and Vulg. indicates that the original text may have had the following words: 'The son of Manasseh (Asriel) . . . whom his Syrian concubine . . . bore Machir the father of Gilead and Machir took a wife . . . and his sister's name Maacha and the name of the . . . Zelophehad and Zelophehad had daughters . . .' Apart from these verses, the genealogies are consistent, as may be seen below:

Assyria and a fascination for her cults. This resulted in a syncretism of Baalism, a cult of Astarte at the 'high places', astral worship, with spiritism and divination. His long reign was bloody and reactionary, and notorious for the introduction of illegal altars into the Temple courts, and 'the passing of his sons through the fire' in the valley of the son of Hinnom.

The name 'Manasseh, king of Judah' appears on the Prism of Esarhaddon (*Me-na-si-i šar Ia-ú-di*), and on the Prism of Ashurbanipal (*Mi-in-si-e šar Ia-ú-di*), among twenty-two tributaries of Assyria (*ANET*, pp. 291, 294). The Chronicler narrates Manasseh's deportation to Babylon, his repentance and release (2 Ch. xxxiii. 10–13). A parallel to this is the capture and the subsequent release of Necho I, king of Egypt, by Ashurbanipal (*Rassam Cylinder*, *ANET*, p. 295). Since a revolt against Assyria occurred in Manasseh's reign, in support of Shamash-shum-ukin, viceroy of Babylon, he may well have been involved in it (*ANET*, p. 298). His reformation appears to have been superficial and was swept away in the reign of his son. R.J.A.S.

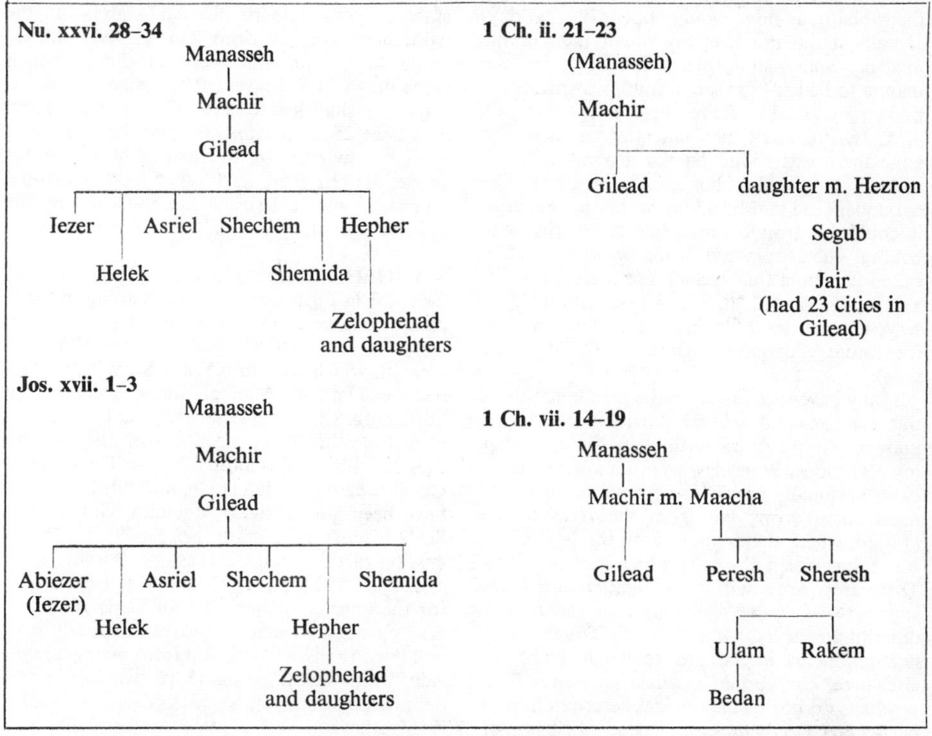

3. Son of Hezekiah and Hephzibah, he began his reign in Jerusalem at the age of twelve and reigned fifty-five years (2 Ki. xxi. 1; 2 Ch. xxxiii. 1); probably as co-regent with his father 696–686 BC, and as sole ruler 686–642 BC (E. R. Thiele, *The Mysterious Numbers of the Hebrew Kings*, 1951, pp. 154 ff.). His reign was a time of religious retrogression, caused by terror of

MANDRAKE. See PLANTS, MAGIC AND SORCERY, 1, III*a*.

MANEH. See WEIGHTS AND MEASURES.

MANGER. The feeding-trough for animals in a stall or stable. In AV and RV it is translated 'crib' (Jb. xxxix. 9; Pr. xiv. 4; Is. i. 3). Gk. *phatnē* has an extended meaning of 'stall' (Lk. xiii. 15), and is used in LXX to translate various Heb. words, *'urwâ*, 'stall' (2 Ch. xxxii. 28), *rep̄eṯ* (Hab. iii. 17), *'ēḇûs* (Jb. xxxix. 9; Pr. xiv. 4; Is. i. 3). In the New Testament it occurs in Lk. ii. 7, 12, 16, xiii. 15.

Mangers are known in other lands besides Palestine. In Palestine the stable or stall was attached to the owner's house and was furnished with a manger. The royal stables at Megiddo had hollowed-out limestone blocks for feed boxes. Christian tradition holds that Jesus was born in a cave in the neighbourhood of Bethlehem. In that case the manger may have been cut out of the rock walls. J.A.T.

MANNA. A substance which was the Israelites' chief food during their forty years' sojourn in the wilderness (Ex. xvi. 35). When Israel grumbled at the lack of food in the wilderness of Sin, God gave them 'bread from heaven' (Ex. xvi. 4; Ps. lxxviii. 23, 24), and this provision did not cease until they crossed into Canaan and ate the food of that land (Jos. v. 12), despite their grumbling (Nu. xi. 6; *cf.* Ne. ix. 20). The Israelites were to collect an omer each for five days and double that amount on the sixth day to last them over the sabbath, as none would appear on that day. Usually it did not keep overnight but became maggoty and malodorous if left over, but the manna to be kept for sabbath use was preserved by being cooked or baked beforehand (Ex. xvi. 4, 5, 16–30). Each morning after the dew had gone there was found on the ground a 'small, round thing' like hoar-frost, whitish, like coriander-seed and bdellium, with a honey taste; it could be ground and used in cooking and baking. The people said, 'what (*man*) is it?', and called it manna (*man*). Such are the data in Ex. xvi. 14, 15, 31; Nu. xi. 7–9. An omerful was preserved by Aaron at God's command as a witness for future generations (Ex. xvi. 33, 34; Heb. ix. 4).

Many have speculated on the precise nature of this manna, and several partial parallels are known. To the present time in Sinai, certain insects produce honeydew excretions on tamarisk-twigs seasonally every June for some weeks. At night these drops fall from the trees to the ground, where they remain until the heat of the sun brings forth the ants which remove them. These drops are small, sticky, light-coloured, and sugary-sweet, quite strikingly like the biblical descriptions in Ex. xvi and Nu. xi. Other honeydew-producing insects are known in Sinai and elsewhere, *e.g.* certain cicadas. However, these products do not fit the biblical description in all particulars. On them, see F. S. Bodenheimer, *BA*, X, 1947, pp. 1–6; for a photo of tamarisk-twigs with drops, see W. Keller, *The Bible as History*, 1956, plate between pp. 112, 113. In S Algeria in 1932 and also about seventy years before, after unusual weather 'there were falls of a whitish, odourless, tasteless matter of a farinaceous kind which covered tents and vegetation each morning' (A. Rendle Short, *Modern Discovery and the Bible*[3], 1952, p. 152). Also in 1932, a white substance like manna one morning covered an area of ground 2,100 by 60 feet on a farm in Natal and was eaten by the natives (H. S. Gehman in *Westminster Bible Dictionary*, 1944, p. 375a). None of these phenomena satisfy the biblical data, and the provision of the manna remains ultimately in the realm of the miraculous, especially in its continuity, quantity, and six-day periodicity. The partial parallels cited above may indicate, however, the kind of physical bases used by God in this provision.

The manna was used by God to teach lessons for spiritual instruction as well as physical sustenance. Israel was told that with the failure of other food ('suffered thee to hunger'), His provision of manna was to 'make thee know that man doth not live by bread only, but by every word that proceedeth out of the mouth of the Lord doth man live' (Dt. viii. 3, *cf.* 16). God used the provision of manna on six days and not the seventh to teach Israel obedience, and convicted them of disobedience (Ex. xvi. 19, *cf.* 20, 25–30). Jesus Christ uses the manna, God-given 'bread from heaven', as a type of Himself, the true bread of life, and contrasts the shadow with the substance: 'your fathers did eat manna in the wilderness, and are dead' (Jn. vi. 49), but He could say, 'I am the bread of life . . . which came down from heaven; if any man eat of this bread, he shall live for ever' (Jn. vi. 35, 51, and *cf.* verses 26–59 *passim*). Eternal life was made available to man by the merits of His death (verse 51). In Rev. ii. 17 the 'hidden manna' represents spiritual sustenance imparted by the Spirit of Christ. K.A.K.

MANOAH. Samson's father. The name is identical in form with a word meaning 'resting-place, state or condition of rest' from the root *nwḥ*, 'to rest' (*BDB*), and with the Wâdi el-Munâḥ, which runs into Wâdi Ṣarâr from Tibneh (= Timnah). Manoah was a Danite from Ṣor'â (Jdg. xiii. 2), and one name may be derived from the other. A connection with the Manaḥtites of 1 Ch. ii. 54 is more dubious. These were a Calebite clan of Judah (1 Ch. ii. 50 ff.), and may have been among those Judahites who lived in Ṣor'â in post-exilic times (Ne. xi. 29). For a discussion of these coincidences, see Burney, *Book of Judges*, 1920, p. 341. Manoah is best known for the angelic annunciation of Samson's birth. He appears as a man of prayer and godly fear, and tried to dissuade his son from marrying outside the covenant people (Jdg. xiv. 3). He predeceased his son (Jdg. xvi. 31). A.G.

MANSIONS (Gk. *monai*, Vulg. *mansiones*, RVmg 'abiding-places'). Various speculations have been made about this figure of speech used by our Lord in Jn. xiv. 2 (*e.g.* B. F. Westcott, *The Gospel according to St. John*, II, 1908, p. 167). Most scholars agree that what is intended is that the Father will provide room and to spare in the eternal abode. The Gk. word elsewhere occurs only in verse 23 of this chapter. J.D.D.

MANSLAYER. See KIN, KINSMAN.

MANTLE. See DRESS.

MANUSCRIPTS. See TEXT AND VERSIONS, WRITING.

MAON, MAONITES. 1. Descendants of the Calebite branch of the tribe of Judah. Maon was the son of Shammai and the father of the inhabitants of Beth-zur (1 Ch. ii. 45). The town Maon features in Judah in the list in Jos. xv. 55. In this area David and his men sheltered from Saul (1 Sa. xxiii. 24, 25), and the churlish Nabal lived there (1 Sa. xxv. 2). The Maonites are mentioned in the official list of those who returned from Exile (Ezr. ii. 50, AV 'Mehunim', RV 'Meunim'; Ne. vii. 52, 'Meunim'). Khirbet Ma'în, 8½ miles south of Hebron, marks the ancient site. It is surrounded by pasture lands, probably the 'wilderness of Maon' where David sought refuge from Saul (1 Sa. xxiii. 24, 25) and was saved by a Philistine raid (1 Sa. xxiii. 27 f.).

2. A hostile people in Transjordan, linked with Amalek and the Zidonians as oppressors of Israel (Jdg. x. 12); a pastoral people attacked by Hezekiah (RV 'Meunim', 1 Ch. iv. 41), and Uzziah (2 Ch. xxvi. 7). Their association with Arabs and Ammonites (RVmg, 2 Ch. xx. 1) suggests *Ma'ān*, south-east of Petra, as their home.

J.A.T.

MARA (*mārā'*, 'bitter'). The name by which Naomi wished to be called (Ruth i. 20) on her return from Moab, where her husband and two sons had died. Her own name (which meant 'pleasant') seemed no longer appropriate.

MARAH (*mārâ*, 'bitter'). This was the first camp of the Israelites after the Red Sea crossing, called Marah because only bitter water was found there (Ex. xv. 23; Nu. xxxiii. 8, 9), and perhaps also by comparison with the sweet water of the Nile Valley to which they had been accustomed. It is often identified with the modern 'Ain Hawârah, several miles inland from the Gulf of Suez. In recent years, however, H. H. Rowley (*From Joseph to Joshua*, 1950, p. 104) and J. Gray (*VT*, IV, 1954, pp. 149 f.) have espoused the theory which identifies Marah with Kadesh (*q.v.*), a location refuted by *GTT*, p. 252, n. 218; *cf.* B. Rothenberg, *God's Wilderness*, 1961, pp. 11, 93 f., 142 ff. See also WILDERNESS OF THE WANDERING.

J.D.D.

MARANATHA. An Aramaic formula used in transliteration without explanation at 1 Cor. xvi. 22. In the *Didache* (x. 6) it figures as part of the eucharistic liturgy. The phrase is probably to be resolved as *māranâ ṯâ*, 'our Lord, come!' (see Dalman, *Grammatik des jüdisch-palästinisch Aramäisch*, pp. 120, n. 2; 297, n. 2: also *Jesus-Jeshua*, 1929, p. 13, for the resolution *māran 'eṯâ* of identical meaning). The anticipation and longing expressed in this early Christian prayer may be seen reflected in 1 Cor. xi. 26 (*cf.* the context in the *Didache*) and in Rev. xxii. 20. The occurrence of the phrase at 1 Cor. xvi. 22 derives from the idea of judgment implicit in verse 21, which is closely linked with the idea of the second coming (*cf.* the Old Latin MS g and the Ethiopic version, which render *maranatha* as 'at the coming of the Lord').

In Gk. MSS with accents and punctuation the phrase is often written as if it represented *māran 'aṯâ*, 'our Lord has come'. This seems less likely in view of the ideas of the Eucharist and the judgment with which it is linked in the context, unless it be a reference to the Lord's manifestation of Himself through the Eucharist.

BIBLIOGRAPHY. Zahn, *Introduction to the New Testament*, 1909, I, pp. 303–305; *TWNT*, IV, pp. 470 ff. (K. G. Kuhn); *Arndt, s.v.* J.N.B.

MARBLE. See MINING AND METALS.

MARCUS. See MARK (JOHN).

MARESHAH. A town on the edge of the Shephelah, now Tell Sandahannah, near Keilah and Achzib (Jos. xv. 44; Mi. i. 15); fortified by Rehoboam; birthplace of the prophet Eliezer, 2 Ch. xx. 37; subsequently a Sidonian colony and an important Idumaean stronghold, mentioned by Zeno (Cairo Museum, pap. 59006); destroyed by the Parthians, 40 BC (1 Macc. v. 66; 2 Macc. xii. 35; Jos., *Ant.* xii. 8. 6, xiv. 12. 9, 13. 9). In this area Zerah of Ethiopia was defeated by Asa. The inhabitants claimed descent from Shelah (1 Ch. iv. 21). With the rise of Eleutheropolis, now Beit Guvrin, 1½ miles farther north, the old site remained unoccupied; there was a village to the east, now Khirbet Mar'ash. The name was probably derived from *rō'š* (head), and may not have been unique (see W. Rudolph on 1 Ch. ii. 42).

J.P.U.L.

MARI. See ARCHAEOLOGY, VIIIc.

MARK, GOSPEL OF.

I. OUTLINE OF CONTENTS

a. Prologue (i. 1–13)

The ministry of John (i. 1–8); baptism and temptation of Jesus (i. 9–13).

b. The earlier Galilaean ministry (i. 14–vi. 44)

The kingdom of God in Galilee (i. 14–45); the beginning of conflict (ii. 1–iii. 6); conflict increases (iii. 7–35); division fixed (parables of the Kingdom) (iv. 1–34); Jesus, by-passing the synagogue, communicates Himself to Israel (iv. 35–vi. 44).

c. The later Galilaean ministry (vi. 45–ix. 50)

Jesus, removing the barriers, communicates Himself to Gentiles (vi. 45–viii. 10); the Pharisees are refused a sign and the disciples cannot see one when it is given (viii. 11–26); confession and transfiguration (viii. 27–ix. 10); the passion foretold (ix. 11–50).

d. The road to Jerusalem (x. 1–52)

Debates in Peraea (x. 1–34); the test of greatness (x. 35–45); the healing of Bartimaeus (x. 46–52).

e. The Jerusalem ministry (xi. 1–xiii. 37)

Entry into Jerusalem (xi. 1–14); cleansing of the Temple (xi. 15–19); exhortation and debate (xi. 20–xii. 44); the Olivet discourse (*q.v.;* xiii. 1–37).

f. Passion and resurrection (xiv. 1–xvi. 8)

The Last Supper (xiv. 1–25); agony in Gethsemane (xiv. 26–42); the arrest (xiv. 43–52); Jesus before the Sanhedrin (xiv. 53–72); Jesus before Pilate (xv. 1–15); the crucifixion (xv. 16–41); burial and resurrection (xv. 42–xvi. 8).

(xvi. 9–20 form a later addition to the Gospel.)

The scope of Mark's Gospel is thus identical with that of the primitive apostolic preaching, beginning with John the Baptist and ending with the resurrection (*cf.* Acts x. 36–43, xiii. 24–37).

II. AUTHORSHIP

This record of our Lord's ministry, the shortest and simplest of all the Gospels, was traditionally compiled by John Mark of Jerusalem, who at different times was a younger companion of Paul, Barnabas, and Peter (see MARK (JOHN)).

a. Evidence of Papias

The earliest statement about the origin of this Gospel is that given by Papias (preserved in Eus., *EH* iii. 39): 'Mark, who was the interpreter of Peter, wrote down accurately all that he remembered, whether of sayings or doings of Christ, but not in order. For he was neither a hearer nor a companion of the Lord; but afterwards, as I have said, he accompanied Peter, who adapted his instruction as necessity required, not as though he were making a compilation of the Lord's oracles. So then Mark made no mistake when he wrote down thus some things as he remembered them; for he concentrated on this alone—not to omit anything that he had heard, nor to include any false statement among them.'

Papias's information (*c.* AD 140) is amplified a generation or so later in the anti-Marcionite prologue to Mark and in Irenaeus. The anti-Marcionite prologue, only part of which has survived, says that Mark 'was called "stumpy-fingered" (*kolobodaktylos*) because his fingers were short in relation to the rest of his body; he was Peter's interpreter, and after Peter's departure he committed his Gospel to writing in the parts of Italy'. Irenaeus (*Against Heresies*, iii. 1. 1), after referring to Mark as having been written 'when Peter and Paul were preaching the gospel in Rome and founding the church there', adds that 'after their departure (*exodos*) Mark, Peter's disciple, has himself delivered to us in writing the substance of Peter's preaching'.

b. Influence of Peter

Mark's Gospel has sometimes been popularly called Peter's Gospel (to be distinguished from later heretical works with this or similar titles), not only because of the evidence of these 2nd-century writers but also since, even if the hand be Mark's, the voice is Peter's voice, to judge from the nature of the incidents, choice of matter, and manner of treatment. It may thus be no empty tradition that this is the written record of the preaching of Peter, originally delivered to Christian catechumens, whether at Rome, or in the Gk. east, and reduced to writing either on the death of its oral source or when the death became imminent. This would put the date of the Gospel somewhere in the second half of the 1st century, but the question is more complicated, as will be seen below.

Others have chosen to describe it as the Gospel for the Romans, or the Gospel for the Gentiles; but in the first of these identifications they may have been influenced more by the Lat. name borne by Mark, in addition to his Heb. name of John, and by the traditional place of origin of the Gospel, rather than by a strictly empirical examination of the contents of the book. Luke has more claim, in every way, to be regarded as the Gentile Gospel; and, while Peter was initially used by God for the conversion of the Gentile Cornelius (Acts xv. 7), yet he was universally recognized in the early Church as apostle to the circumcision (Gal. ii. 8), not apostle to the Gentiles, as was Paul. Thus it is *a priori* unlikely that Peter's teaching forms would be specifically aimed at, and adapted to, Gentile audiences. In any case, modern scholarship shows increasingly the thoroughly Jewish nature of *all* the Gospels, so that the question is not of prime importance.

III. RELATIONSHIP TO MATTHEW AND LUKE

For over a century, since Lachmann's day, the question of the assumed literary relationship of Mark to the other Gospels has attracted the attention of western scholars. Apart from the Gospel of John, which in many ways stands by itself, it is obvious that some close link exists between the other three, usually called the Synoptic Gospels because, taken together, they present a very similar picture of the ministry and teaching of Christ. Source criticism is the science of investigation of the assumed direct literary dependence of one Gospel upon another, or of both alike upon some third document, either present or hypothetical.

a. Primacy of Mark's Gospel

Most subsequent Protestant scholars have held firmly, with Lachmann, to the primacy of Mark, considering it to be one of the earliest of these formulations, if not in its present form, at least in what might be called an early edition. If this were true, Mark would underlie both Matthew and Luke as a principal source. A second presumed early written source was a mass of non-

Markan matter common to Matthew and Luke; this, when isolated, was denoted by the symbol 'Q', for German *Quelle*, 'source'. Mark and Q were thus two of the earliest strands in the Gospel tradition, although Matthew and Luke were acknowledged each to have their own peculiar material as well, for which suitable alphabetical symbols were adopted. Mark, under this system, was considered as a product of the years immediately preceding the fall of Jerusalem in AD 70, and the first Gospel to be written; some of its peculiarities were thus explained, as arising from its 'primitive' nature. The danger was that, if Matthew and Luke seemed to deviate from Mark, they would be considered as less reliable, as having manipulated their source for some end of their own. Thus at times the exponents of this method used very cavalier methods in dealing with the text of Scripture.

b. Primacy of Matthew's Gospel

Roman Catholic scholars for a long time would have none of this; for them it was an article of faith to believe in the primacy of Matthew, and they argued their case with great ingenuity, although without producing much conviction outside their own ranks. They could at least argue that the early Church believed in the primacy of Matthew—else why put Mark as the second Gospel? But the principle of arrangement of books within the various sections of the New Testament is still too little understood to make such a psychological argument valid. Their view, if true, would make Mark only a secondary authority, and his words would tend to be treated as less weighty than those of Matthew. The battle raged; mathematical symbols multiplied, and ultimately the multiplication of assumed literary sources led to fragmentation. Instead of Gospels, there were bundles of documents, and scholars were left in a morass of literary agnosticism. Was there a way out? As men said of contemporary Old Testament scholarship, the literary hypothesis had broken down under its own weight.

c. Form Criticism

Meanwhile, on the flank, a new enemy had arisen, which would in itself nullify and make meaningless the whole battle. This was Form Criticism, originated about 1920 by M. Dibelius, followed closely by R. Bultmann. This might be described as the abandonment of the study of the whole in favour of the study of the part, and, in origin, was purely a descriptive and classificatory science, although it rapidly became far more formidable. The various incidents and sayings recorded in Mark were now examined, and classified by nature and content. So far, so good. This classification was studied from a new angle, had the merit of freshness, and produced some positive and valuable results. But the next step was to examine the hypothetical circumstances that led to the preservation and repetition of each saying; and to make exegesis dependent upon hypothetical reconstruction is very dangerous. In the case of extreme critics, this meant the view that the story was either created or moulded by the needs of the infant Church, and was no true record of the sayings or doings of Christ. Thus, what had begun as a purely neutral movement ended by passing judgments on the historicity of the text of Scripture. In a sense, such a statement as the last phrase is meaningless to an adherent of this school, for documentary hypotheses have been abandoned in favour of oral tradition, exactly as in contemporary Old Testament scholarship. It is doubtful, however, whether there is any ultimate difference between considering a particular mass of material as a written document or as a complex of oral tradition, especially in view of the known fixity of oral tradition in the Ancient Near East.

Nevertheless, this stress on Form Criticism and oral tradition has hopelessly outdated rather than solved much of the old discussion. Further, it has made the question of the date of Mark's Gospel unanswerable, if not meaningless. The scholar may tentatively date the compilation of the oral tradition in its present literary form, but the origins of Mark lie much farther back, in the oral traditions of the generation of the crucifixion and resurrection. This, of course, has its good side, in that the reader is confronted directly with the recollections of those who had themselves been eye-witnesses of the events (Lk. i. 2). Much work along these lines has been constructive and cautious; and valuable results have emerged. Nevertheless, in this whole field of study many will feel that there has been an incommensurate pile of chaff for a few grains of wheat.

d. Recent discoveries

As against this swing towards oral tradition, a reaction in favour of early written documents as sources has been helped by the discovery in Egypt, during the last generation, of several early Gk. papyri containing portions of both canonical and uncanonical gospels. By their early date, these have pushed back the emergence of written gospels, in the modern sense of the word, to at least the end of the 1st Christian century. These finds, important as they are, have been overshadowed by the discovery in 1947 and the following years, in caves near Qumran, in the territory of Jordan, of caches of manuscripts in Hebrew, Aramaic, and Greek. These Dead Sea Scrolls (*q.v.*) are largely of pre-Christian date, apparently the property of a semi-monastic community of Jewish sectaries. The very existence of these manuscripts proves that there is no *a priori* evidence against the existence of 1st-century Christian documents, Greek or Aramaic, as sources of the Gospels.

e. Aramaic influences

Further, the discovery of such Semitic documents has raised again the issue, already live for half a century, as to whether Greek or Aramaic was the original language of the sources of the Gospels, oral or written. This leads to the further question, as to how far the Greek of Mark is not only *koinē* Greek, the *lingua franca* of the 1st-century Roman Mediterranean (see LANGUAGE OF THE NEW TESTAMENT), but actually 'translation Greek'. The many Semitisms in Mark would thus be due, not to Old Testament reminiscences, nor to influence by the 'translation Greek' of the Septuagint, the Gk. Old Testament, but directly to the Aramaic originals lying before the Evangelist. Indeed, to scholars pursuing this line, many difficult verses in Mark have appeared either as misunderstandings or mistranslations of a lost Aramaic original, whether written or spoken. It appears certain that Aramaic was the mother-tongue of the Lord and His apostles, to judge from the fossilized Aramaic words and phrases that appear even in Gk. dress (*cf.* Mk. v. 41, vii. 34, xv. 34). While C. C. Torrey's theory of entirely translated Gospels has not generally commended itself to scholars as it is too extreme and involves too many forced arguments, yet few would deny the importance of the underlying Aramaic substratum in every Gospel, and the value of considering Aramaic vocabulary or idiom when the Gk. text presents difficulties. Recent and more cautious approaches in English have been made, especially by Matthew Black. There is traditional support for some such translation process in the evidence of Papias of Hierapolis, preserved in Eusebius; but as it relates directly only to Matthew, it may be left with this mention.

IV. SPECIAL CHARACTERISTICS

Basically, Mark is the most blunt and clipped of the Gospels; Matthew contains much of specifically Jewish interest nowhere to be found in Mark, and Luke has much of a 'medical' or of a 'human' interest omitted in Mark, as for example the three famous parables of Luke xv. The abrupt ending of Mark is a problem in itself, although it is probably to be seen as a textual rather than a literary problem, since the various alternatives put forward by the manuscripts suggest that the original was lost at a very early date. It will be objected that the above is a purely negative definition of Mark's nature and contents. Indeed, this was precisely why, in the hey-day of Source Criticism, Mark was seen as the earliest and most primitive of the Gospels, and as a source for both the other Synoptists. But if all documentary sources alike disappear in a welter of oral tradition, possibly only first formulated and codified as the four Gospels known today, what then? The basic observation as to the nature and style of Mark still holds good. Nor is this a purely subjective impression on the part of the 20th century; Papias of Hierapolis shows that the problem was felt equally keenly in the 2nd century. If Mark knew more facts about the Lord, why did he not recount them? Why does he omit so much that the other Evangelists record? (On the other hand, his narratives are commonly more detailed and more vivid than parallel accounts in the other Gospels, especially Matthew's, when such parallels are available for comparison.) In addition, Mark appears on first sight to be constructed on a chronological framework of the Lord's life. But is Mark so constructed? and, if not, is there any discernible principle of arrangement? In the days when Mark was taken as the prime literary source of both Matthew and Luke, attempts were made to fit the other Gospels willy-nilly into Mark's assumed chronological framework. But this proved impossible, for Matthew and Luke had to be distorted or mutilated to fit it even awkwardly.

Perhaps the answer is to be found in the cautious use of the new understanding of the nature and importance of oral tradition as underlying the present Gospel of Mark. For it is a plain fact that constant oral repetition leads not to diversity but to uniformity, especially when such repetition is by unimaginative and elderly teachers, whose aim is not to entertain but to instruct. Stories are not ramified but simplified, if told with a purely didactic end in view; events are boiled down to their bare bones. Variant stories do not grow from one original in such a tradition; if anything, the tendency is to assimilate original variants, all unconsciously. Scholars have not always recognized this, because they have too often considered the earliest custodians of Christian tradition in the light of professional story-tellers, Arabic, Celtic, or Scandinavian, according to the culture-pattern the scholars already knew. The aged Sunday-school teacher in a country church might be a closer parallel, for with his continual tendency of 'extempore prayer' he tends to become in such circumstances quasi-liturgical, and fixed in form. Seen in this light, Mark is not the most primitive and least developed of the Gospels. The second Gospel is not the bare recital of facts, to which other writers have added flowery details, as imagination prompted them. Rather, Mark is the most developed of the Gospels; it is threadbare with use, pared of all but significant fact, the record of teaching forms that have stood the test of time.

This, of course, does not say anything about the actual date of the writing of Mark in its present form, but merely the empirical observation that it bears, more clearly than any other Gospel, the marks of being a virtual 1st-century Teachers' Handbook, a summary of facts, with all save what was deemed significant ruthlessly pruned. By contrast, Luke was specifically composed *de novo* as a written document, and in the face of other existing written documents (Lk. i. 1–4), and in deliberate and pointed contrast to such oral instruction as Mark records. Luke, in fact, had claims to be regarded as a work of literature, as had Acts (Acts i. 1); Mark had none. Even Matthew and John bear marks of careful arrangement, although on varying principles; but, for such matters as Mark contains, the principle of arrangement seems to be broadly mnemonic. Stories and sayings are linked by keywords or similarity of subject rather than by strict chronological sequence; and where the order of incident varies, as against that given in Matthew and Luke, it is sometimes demonstrably because a different keyword or link is used.

All this would fit perfectly with the above sketch of the origin and nature of Mark, and when it is found to accord exactly with the earliest traditions about the Gospel the case becomes even stronger. For Papias, our oldest witness, in the extract quoted above, appears to be defending Mark against exactly the charges which a modern scholar might bring against him —omission of significant detail and lack of chronological arrangement. The defence is seen to lie in the very nature of the Gospel, which, says Papias, is but a permanent record of the teaching of Peter, thus preserved for posterity at a time when its primary source was passing away. Careful chronological order and full cataloguing of fact, says Papias, are not to be found in Peter because they were not his aim, which was purely practical and instructional; it is unfair to blame any man for failure to achieve something not attempted because he considered it foreign to his purpose. If all this be so, Mark is absolved, with Peter his source, and the reasons for many other aspects of his Gospel become apparent at once. (See GOSPELS.)

BIBLIOGRAPHY. Commentaries by A. Menzies, *The Earliest Gospel*, 1901; H. B. Swete, 1913; C. H. Turner, 1928; A. E. J. Rawlinson, 1936; V. Taylor, 1952; C. E. B. Cranfield, 1960; M. Black, *An Aramaic Approach to the Gospels and Acts*, 1946; G. R. Beasley-Murray, *A Commentary on Mark Thirteen*, 1957; N. B. Stonehouse. *The Witness of Matthew and Mark to Christ*, 1958.

A.C.

MARK (JOHN). The author of the second Gospel (see MARK, GOSPEL OF), apparently a Jew, and a native of Jerusalem. His Heb. name was the Old Testament *Yoḥānān*, 'Yahweh has shown grace' (*cf.* 2 Ki. xxv. 23, *etc.*), shortened in English to the familiar 'John'. The reason for his adopted Lat. name of 'Marcus' is uncertain; sometimes Jewish families that had been captured as slaves in war, and later freed, took, as 'freedmen', the name of the Roman family to which they had been enslaved; but this is unlikely in his case, the more so as Marcus is a praenomen, not a family name. It was not uncommon for 1st-century Jews to bear a Gk. or Rom. name in addition to their Heb. name, 'in religion'; see Acts i. 23 for another such 'surname', again Latin and not Greek in origin. The same phenomenon is common among Western Jews today. If his early nickname of *kolobodaktylos*, 'stumpy-fingered', is a genuine tradition (see the anti-Marcionite prologue to Mark, dating from the later 2nd century, which is the earliest evidence for it), then it may refer either to a physical peculiarity on the part of the author or to some strange stylistic features of the Gospel which have puzzled critics of all ages. It may, however, be only a late conjecture, due to the confusion of his name Marcus with the Lat. adjective *mancus*, 'maimed'.

Scripture gives some very clear evidence about his family, and there are also several conjectures of varying degrees of probability. His mother, named Mary, was related to Barnabas (Col. iv. 10), the wealthy Levite from Cyprus, who was a landowner (Acts iv. 36) and, whatever his country of origin, was a resident of Jerusalem in the days of the opening chapters of Acts. Mary herself appears to have been a woman of wealth and position, as well as a Christian; certainly her house was large enough to house a number of people, boasted at least one maidservant, and was used as a meeting-place by the apostolic Church even in time of persecution (Acts xii. 12). It is significant that Peter, released from prison, has no doubt as to where he will find the Christians gathered. John Mark's father is nowhere mentioned in Scripture, and, from the fact that the house of Acts xii. 12 is called Mary's, it has been inferred, probably correctly, that he was dead by that date, and Mary a widow. To John Mark himself there is no certain early reference, although the young man of Mk. xiv. 51, who saved himself by ignominious flight, is usually taken to be Mark. It would be neither safe nor customary for an author to mention his own name in such circumstances (*cf.* Jn. xxi. 24 for similar deliberate anonymity). Less likely, as partly dependent on the above tentative identification, is the theory that the Last Supper of Mk. xiv actually took place in John Mark's house; the shadowy 'goodman of the house' of verse 14 would thus be John Mark's father, still alive then, although dead before the date of Acts xii. 12.

John Mark apparently remained at home until brought to Antioch by Barnabas and Paul, who were returning from a relief mission to Jerusalem (Acts xii. 25). When the two departed to Cyprus on the first missionary journey some time later he accompanied them, as travelling companion and attendant on the two older men (Acts xiii. 5). When, however, the party reached Perga, on the mainland of Asia Minor, John Mark left them, and returned to Jerusalem (Acts xiii. 13), while Barnabas and Paul continued alone. Paul apparently regarded this as desertion, and thus, when Barnabas suggested Mark as a travelling companion for the second journey, he refused point-blank (Acts xv. 38). With both men, the attitude towards John Mark was no whim, but a point of principle (*cf.* Acts ix. 27 and xi. 25 for the character of Barnabas), so a separation was inevitable, Barnabas taking Mark back to Cyprus with him, and Paul taking Silas instead.

After that, Mark is lost to view in Acts, but appears spasmodically in the Epistles. By the date of Col. iv. 10 he is in the company of Paul the prisoner, presumably at Rome; Paul is apparently intending to send him on a mission to Colossae, so that he must have forgiven and forgotten the past. Phm. 24 also mentions him among the same apostolic group, which includes Luke. By the time of writing 2 Tim. iv. 11 Mark is now away with Timothy, but there has been no rift; presumably this means that Paul had sent Mark on the mission to Asia Minor envisaged above, if Timothy was indeed in Ephesus.

In the Petrine correspondence there is one significant mention, in 1 Pet. v. 13, where the wording shows the 'paternal' relationship existing between the older and younger disciples. If, as is probable, 'Babylon' in this verse stands for 'Rome', then the early tradition of the origins of Mark's Gospel may well be true. The tradition that Mark later founded the church of Alexandria (Eusebius, *EH* ii. 16) lacks support. For Bibliography, see under MARK, GOSPEL OF. A.C.

MARKET, MARKET-PLACE. In the Old Testament this translates Heb. *ma'arāḇ*, 'merchandise', in Ezk. xxvii. 13, 17, 19, 25. In Is. xxiii. 3 (AV 'mart') the word is *sāḥār*, 'emporium'. Both describe the trading centre of an eastern town.

In the New Testament the word used is *agora*, 'place of assembly', the chief place not only of trade but of public resort, often ornamented with statues and colonnades. Here the sick were brought (Mk. vi. 56, AV 'streets'), children played games (Mt. xi. 16; Lk. vii. 32) and idlers waited to hire out their services (Mt. xx. 3; *cf.* Acts xvii. 5, *agoraioi*, 'of the baser sort'). In the market-places greetings were exchanged, according to social rank, and this the Pharisees particularly loved (Mt. xxiii. 7; Mk. xii. 38; Lk. xi. 43, xx. 46), but they were careful to remove any defilement (Mk. vii. 4). Here also in Gentile towns preliminary trial hearings were held (Acts xvi. 19; *cf.* xix. 38 ff.) and philosophical or religious discussions took place (*e.g.* Paul in Athens, Acts xvii. 17, 18). B.F.H.

MARKS. Various 'marks' are referred to in the Old and New Testaments. Their variety is reflected in the number of different Heb. and Gk. words used to describe them.

1. The various verbal forms which occur both in the Old and New Testaments correspond to our English verb 'to mark' in the sense of 'to consider' (Ps. xlviii. 13), 'pay attention to' (Ps. xxxvii. 37), 'scrutinize with fixed gaze' (1 Sa. i. 12), 'observe closely' (Lk. xiv. 7), *etc.* In very few instances does the AV use the phrase 'to make a mark'. Isaiah refers to the carpenter who draws a line with pencil and compasses (xliv. 13), while Jeremiah speaks of Judah's sins being indelibly marked like a stain on cloth which neither lye nor soap can eradicate (ii. 22).

2. The first arresting use of 'mark' as a noun is found in Gn. iv. 15. Here it is a translation of Heb. *'ôṯ*, which describes the mark on Cain's forehead. In the Old Testament *'ôṯ* usually means 'sign', but it signifies also 'omens' (1 Sa. x. 7, 9), 'symbols' (Is. viii. 18), 'miracles' (Ex. vii. 3). However, underlying many of these different uses is the common idea of 'pledge', as, *e.g.*, of good (Ps. lxxxvi. 17), of God's presence (Ex. iv. 8 f.), and of covenant (Gn. ix. 12, 13, 17). Hence *'ôṯ*, when used with reference to the mark on Cain's brow, should be understood in terms of a sign, a pledge, or token, of the Lord's protection which would shield him from retribution. If this is correct, then *'ôṯ* might signify a token of some kind of covenant by which God promises to protect Cain (Gn. iv. 15).

3. 'Mark' in the sense of 'target' is a rendering of the Heb. *maṭṭārā'* (1 Sa. xx. 20). Job complains that God has made him a target at which He shoots His arrows (xvi. 12; *cf.* La. iii. 12).

4. In Ezk. ix. 4, 6, the Heb. word *tāw* is rendered 'mark' in the sense of 'sign'. This is the mark which is placed on the forehead of the righteous, and was an attestation that those who bore the sign were the Lord's people (*cf.* Jb. xxxi. 35, RV, where *tāw* is rendered 'signature'), were distinguished from idolaters, and were therefore exempt from judgment because of the Lord's protection (*cf.* Ex. xii. 22 f.). Here 'mark' might mean 'seal' (*cf.* Rev. vii. 3, xiv. 1, xxii. 4).

5. Another word which is rendered 'mark' occurs only once in the Bible: *qa'ᵃqa'*. Its etymology is obscure, but in Lv. xix. 28 it probably refers to tattoo marks which, along with 'cuttings in your flesh' (*i.e.* 'incisions' or 'lacerations'), the Israelites were forbidden to make. The prohibition probably points to their having pagan and magical associations.

6. In the well-known Pauline metaphor of 'pressing towards the mark' (*skopos*) in order to win the prize (Phil. iii. 14) 'mark' signifies the 'goal'. The apostle here uses the language of the chariot races to describe the intensity with which he concentrates on winning the crown—the honour of being called by God in Christ.

7. The next Gk. word rendered 'mark' is one that has entered the English language without undergoing any alteration, *stigma*. Like *skopos*, it occurs only once (Gal. vi. 17). The root means 'to prick', but probably Paul uses it in the sense of tattoo- or brand-marks with which slave-owners stamped their slaves for identification purposes. Paul was proud of being Christ's bondslave (*cf.* Rom. i. 1, RVmg); for him no stigma attached to Christ's brand-marks with which he had been branded (Gal. vi. 17) in the course of his ministry (2 Cor. xi. 23–27).

8. The last word, *charagma* (Rev. xiii. 16), is reminiscent of Heb. *tāw* in Ezk. ix. 4, 6, but the circumstances are reversed. In Rev. xiii. 16 it is 'the mark of the beast', and is borne by the followers of anti-christ, who is the embodiment of apostasy. Whether a literal or a moral designation, this 'mark' may have stood for a travesty of God's 'seal' upon the Christians. J.G.S.S.T.

MARRIAGE. Marriage is the state in which men and women can live together in sexual relationship with the approval of their social group. Adultery and fornication are sexual relationships that society does not recognize as constituting marriage. This definition is necessary to show that in the Old Testament polygamy is not sexually immoral, since it constitutes a recognized married state; though it is generally shown to be inexpedient.

I. THE STATUS OF MARRIAGE

Marriage is regarded as normal, and there is no word for 'bachelor' in the Old Testament. The record of the creation of Eve (Gn. ii. 18–24) indicates the unique relationship of husband and wife, and serves as a picture of the relationship between God and His people (Je. iii; Ezk. xvi; Ho. i–iii) and between Christ and His Church (Eph. v. 22–33). Jeremiah's call to remain unmarried (Je. xvi. 2) is a unique prophetic sign, but in the New Testament it is recognized that for specific purposes celibacy can be God's call to Christians (Mt. xix. 10–12; 1 Cor. vii. 7–9), although marriage and family life are the normal calling (Jn. ii. 1–11; Eph. v. 22–vi. 4; 1 Tim. iii. 2, iv. 3, v. 14).

Monogamy is implicit in the story of Adam and Eve, since God created only one wife for Adam. Yet polygamy is adopted from the time of Lamech (Gn. iv. 19), and is not forbidden in Scripture. It would seem that God left it to man to discover by experience that His original institution of monogamy was the proper relationship. It is shown that polygamy brings trouble, and often results in sin, *e.g.* Abraham (Gn. xxi); Gideon (Jdg. viii. 29–ix. 57); David (2 Sa. xi, xiii); Solomon (1 Ki. xi. 1–8). In view of Oriental customs Heb. kings are warned against it (Dt. xvii. 17). Family jealousies arise from it, as with Elkanah's two wives, one of whom is an adversary to the other (1 Sa. i. 6; *cf.* Lv. xviii. 18). It is difficult to know how far polygamy was practised, but on economic grounds it is probable that it was found more among the well-to-do than among the ordinary people. Herod the Great had nine wives at one time (Jos., *Ant.* xvii. 1. 3). Polygamy continues to the present day among Jews in Muslim countries.

When polygamy was practised the status and relationship of the wives can be gathered both from the narratives and the law. It was natural that the husband would be drawn to one rather than another. Thus Jacob, who was tricked into polygamy, loved Rachel more than Leah (Gn. xxix). Elkanah preferred Hannah in spite of her childlessness (1 Sa. i. 1–8). In Dt. xxi. 15–17 it is admitted that the husband may love one wife and hate the other.

Since children were important to carry on the family name, a childless wife might allow her husband to have children by her slave. This was legal in civilized Mesopotamia (*e.g.* The Code of Hammurabi, §§ 144–147), and was practised by Sarah and Abraham (Gn. xvi) and Rachel and Jacob (Gn. xxx. 1–8), though Jacob went farther and accepted Leah's maid also, even though Leah had already borne him children (Gn. xxx. 9). In these cases the rights of the wife are safeguarded; it is she who gives her maid to her husband for a specific occasion. It is difficult to give a name to the status of the maid in such a relationship; she is a secondary, rather than a second, wife, though, if the husband continued to have relations with her, she would have the position of concubine. This is perhaps why Bilhah is called Jacob's concubine in Gn. xxxv. 22, while Hagar is not classed with Abraham's concubines in xxv. 6.

Wives would normally be chosen from among the Hebrews (*e.g.* Ne. xiii. 23–28). Betrothal and marriage would then follow a normal pattern (see below). Sometimes they were bought as Heb. slaves (Ex. xxi. 7–11; Ne. v. 5). It is commonly asserted that the master of a household had sexual rights over all his female slaves. No doubt there were flagrant examples of such promiscuity, but the Bible says nothing about them. It is noteworthy that Ex. xxi. 7–11 and Dt. xv. 12 distinguish between an ordinary female slave, who is to be released after seven years, and one who has been deliberately taken as a wife, or concubine, and who cannot claim her release automatically. Since her rights are here established by law, the head of the house or his son must have gone through some ceremony, however simple, of which the law can take cognizance. In speaking of her rights this passage does not make them depend upon her word against the word of the head of the house, nor even upon her having borne him or his son a child. It is difficult to say what her status was. No doubt it varied according to whether she was the first, second, or only 'wife' of the householder. Where she was given to the son of the house, she might well have full status as his wife. The fact is that this law, as the context shows, deals with her rights as a slave and not primarily as a wife.

Wives might also be taken from among captives after a war, provided that they were not Palestinians (Dt. xx. 14–18). Some writers regard these captives as concubines, but the regulations of Dt. xxi. 10–14 regard them as normal wives.

There is no law dealing with concubines, and we do not know what rights they had. Obviously they had an inferior position to the wives, but their children could inherit at their father's discretion (Gn. xxv. 6). Judges records the rise to power of Abimelech, the son of Gideon's concubine (Jdg. viii. 31–ix. 57), and also tells the tragic story of the Levite and his concubine (Jdg. xix). The impression given by xix. 2–4 is that this concubine was free to leave her 'husband', and that the man relied on persuasion to bring her home. David and Solomon copied Oriental monarchs in taking many wives and concubines (2 Sa. v. 13; 1 Ki. xi. 3; Ct. vi. 8, 9). In the last two passages it seems that the concubines were drawn from a lower class of the population.

In normal marriages the wife came to the husband's home. There is, however, another form of marriage in Jdg. xiv, xv. This is practised among the Philistines, and there is no record of it among the Israelites. Here Samson's wife remains at her father's home, and Samson visits her. It might be argued that Samson had intended to take her home after the wedding, but went off alone in a rage after the trick that she had played on him. Yet she is still at her father's house in xv. 1, even though in the meantime she has been married to a Philistine.

II. MARRIAGE CUSTOMS

The marriage customs of the Bible centre in the two events of betrothal and wedding.

a. Betrothal

In the Near East betrothal (Talmudic *'ērûsîn* and *qiddûšîn*) is almost as binding as marriage itself. In the Bible the betrothed woman was sometimes called 'wife' and was under the same obligation of faithfulness (Gn. xxix. 21; Dt. xxii. 23, 24; Mt. i. 18, 20), and the betrothed man was called 'husband' (Joel i. 8; Mt. i. 19). The Bible does not legislate for broken betrothals, but the Code of Hammurabi (§§ 159, 160) stipulated that if the future husband broke the engagement the bride's father retained the bride-gift; while if the father changed his mind he repaid double the amount of the gift (see also the Law codes of Lipit-Ishtar, 29, and Eshnunna, 25). Presumably there was some formal declaration, but the amount of publicity would depend on the bridegroom. Thus Joseph wished to dissolve the betrothal to Mary as quietly as possible (Mt. i. 19).

God's love and faithfulness towards His people is pictured in terms of a betrothal in Ho. ii. 19, 20. The betrothal included the following steps:

(i) *Choice of a spouse.* Usually the parents of a young man chose his wife and arranged for the marriage, as Hagar did for Ishmael (Gn. xxi. 21) and Judah for Er (Gn. xxxviii. 6). Sometimes the young man did the choosing, and his parents the negotiating, as in the case of Shechem (Gn. xxxiv. 4, 8) and Samson (Jdg. xiv. 2). Rarely did a man marry against the wish of his parents, as did Esau (Gn. xxvi. 34, 35). The girl was sometimes asked whether she consented, as in the case of Rebekah (Gn. xxiv. 58). Occasionally the girl's parents chose a likely man to be her husband, as did Naomi (Ru. iii. 1, 2) and Saul (1 Sa. xviii. 21).

(ii) *Exchange of gifts.* Three types of gifts are associated with betrothal in the Bible: 1. The *mōhar*, translated 'marriage present' in RSV and 'dowry' in AV (Gn. xxxiv. 12, for Dinah; Ex. xxii. 17, for a seduced maiden; 1 Sa. xviii. 25, for Michal). The *mōhar* is implied but not so named in such passages as Gn. xxiv. 53, for Rebekah; xxix. 18, the seven years' service performed by Jacob for Rachel. Moses' keeping of the sheep for his father-in-law may be interpreted in the same way (Ex. iii. 1). This was a compensation gift from the bridegroom to the family of the bride, and it sealed the covenant and bound the two families together. Some scholars have considered the *mōhar* to be the price of the bride, but a wife was not bought like a slave. 2. The dowry. This was a gift to the bride or the groom from her father, sometimes consisting of servants (Gn. xxiv. 59, 61, to Rebekah; xxix. 24, to Leah) or land (Jdg. i. 15, to Achsah; 1 Ki. ix. 16, to Pharaoh's daughter, the wife of Solomon), or other property (Tobit viii. 21, to Tobias). 3. The bridegroom's gift to the bride was sometimes jewellery and clothes, as those brought to Rebekah (Gn. xxiv. 53). Biblical examples of oral contracts are Jacob's offer of seven years' service to Laban (Gn. xxix. 18) and Shechem's promise of gifts to the family of Dinah (Gn. xxxiv. 12). In TB a contract of betrothal is called *šᵉṭar qiddûšîn* (*M.K.* 18b) or *šᵉṭar 'ērûsîn* (*ḳid.* 9a). In the Near East today the contributions of each family are fixed in a written engagement contract.

b. Wedding ceremonies

An important feature of many of these ceremonies was the public acknowledgment of the marital relationship. It is to be understood that not all of the following steps were taken at all weddings.

(i) *Garments of bride and groom.* The bride sometimes wore embroidered garments (Ps. xlv. 13, 14), jewels (Is. lxi. 10), a special girdle or 'attire' (Je. ii. 32), and a veil (Gn. xxiv. 65). Among the adornments of the groom might be a garland (Is. lxi. 10). Eph. v. 27; Rev. xix. 8, xxi. 2 refer figuratively to the white garments of the Church as the Bride of Christ.

(ii) *Bridesmaids and friends.* Ps. xlv. 14 speaks of bridesmaids for a royal bride, and we assume that lesser brides had their bridesmaids also. Certainly the bridegroom had his group of companions (Jdg. xiv. 11), spoken of in the New Testament as 'sons of the bridechamber' (Mt. ix. 15, RV). One of these corresponded to the best man at our weddings, and is called 'companion' in Jdg. xiv. 20, xv. 2, and 'the friend of the bridegroom' in Jn. iii. 29. He may be the same as 'the governor of the feast' in Jn. ii. 8, 9.

(iii) *The procession.* In the evening of the day fixed for the marriage the bridegroom and his friends went in procession to the bride's house. The wedding supper could be held there: sometimes circumstances compelled this (Gn. xxix. 22; Jdg. xiv), but it may have been fairly common, since the parable of the Ten Virgins in Mt. xxv. 1–13 is most easily interpreted of the bridegroom going to the bride's house for the supper. One would, however, expect that more usually the bridegroom escorted the bride back to his own or his parents' home for the supper, though the only references to this in Scripture are in Ps. xlv. 14 f.; Mt. xxii. 1–14 (royal weddings), and probably in Jn. ii. 9 f.

The procession might be accompanied by singing, music, and dancing (Je. vii. 34; 1 Macc. ix. 39) and by lamps if at night (Mt. xxv. 7).

(iv) *The marriage feast.* This was usually held at the house of the groom (Mt. xxii. 1–10; Jn. ii. 9) and often at night (Mt. xxii. 13, xxv. 6). Many relatives and friends attended; so the wine might well run out (Jn. ii. 3). A steward or friend supervised the feast (Jn. ii. 9, 10). To refuse an invitation to the wedding feast was an insult (Mt. xxii. 7). The guests were expected to wear festive clothes (Mt. xxii. 11, 12). In special circumstances the feast could be held in the bride's home (Gn. xxix. 22; Tobit viii. 19). The glorious gathering of Christ and His saints in heaven is figuratively called 'the marriage supper of the Lamb' (Rev. xix. 9).

(v) *Covering the bride.* In two cases in the Old Testament (Ru. iii. 9; Ezk. xvi. 8) the man covers the woman with his skirt, perhaps a sign that he takes her under his protection. D. Mace follows J. L. Burckhardt (*Notes on the Bedouin*, 1830, p. 264) in saying that in Arab weddings this is done by one of the bridegroom's relations. J. Eisler, in *Weltenmantel und Himmelszelt*, 1910, says that among the Bedouin the bridegroom covers the bride with a special cloak, using the words, 'From now on, nobody but myself shall cover thee.' The Bible references suggest that the second custom was followed.

(vi) *Blessing.* Parents and friends blessed the couple and wished them well (Gn. xxiv. 60; Ru. iv. 11; Tobit vii. 13).

(vii) *Covenant.* Another religious element was the covenant of faithfulness which is implied in Pr. ii. 17; Ezk. xvi. 8; Mal. ii. 14. According to Tobit vii. 14, the father of the bride drew up a written marriage contract, which in the Mishnah is called *k^e^ṯûḇâ*.

(viii) *Bridechamber.* A nuptial chamber was specially prepared (Tobit vii. 16). The Heb. name for this room is *ḥuppâ* (Ps. xix. 5; Joel ii. 16), originally a canopy or tent, and the Gk. word is *nymphōn* (Mk. ii. 19). The word *ḥuppâ* is still used among Jews today of the canopy under which the bride and bridegroom sit or stand during the ceremony.

(ix) *Consummation.* The bride and groom were escorted to this room, often by the parents (Gn. xxix. 23; Tobit vii. 16, 17, viii. 1) or by the 'sons of the bridechamber' (Mt. ix. 15). Before coming together, for which the Hebrew uses the idiom 'to know', prayer was offered by husband and wife (Tobit viii. 4).

(x) *Proof of virginity.* A blood-stained cloth or chemise was exhibited as a proof of the bride's virginity (Dt. xxii. 13–21). This custom continues in some places in the Near East.

(xi) *Festivities.* The wedding festivities continued for a week (Gn. xxix. 27, Jacob and Leah) or sometimes two weeks (Tobit viii. 20, Tobias and Sarah). These celebrations were marked by music (Ps. xlv, lxxviii. 63, RSV) and by joking like Samson's riddles (Jdg. xiv. 12–18). Some interpret Canticles in the light of a custom among Syrian peasants of calling the groom and bride 'king' and 'queen' during the festivities after the wedding and of praising them with songs.

III. FORBIDDEN DEGREES OF MARRIAGE

These are listed in Lv. xviii in detail, and less fully in Lv. xx. 17–21; Dt. xxvii. 20–23. They are analysed in detail by David Mace, *Hebrew Marriage*, pp. 152 f. We presume that the ban held good both for a second wife during the first wife's lifetime and for any subsequent marriage after the wife's death, except for marriage with the wife's sister: for Lv. xviii. 18, in saying that the wife's sister may not be married during the wife's lifetime, implies that she may be married after the wife is dead.

Abraham (Gn. xx. 12) and Jacob (Gn. xxix. 21–30) married within degrees of relationship that were later forbidden. The scandal in the Church at Corinth (1 Cor. v. 1) may have been marriage of a stepmother after the father's death, but, since the woman is called 'his father's wife' (not *widow*), and the act is called *fornication*, it is more likely to be a case of immoral relationship with the father's young second wife.

IV. THE LEVIRATE LAW

The name is derived from Lat. *levir*, meaning 'husband's brother'. When a married man died without a child his brother was expected to take his wife. Children of the marriage counted as children of the first husband. This custom is found among other people besides the Hebrews.

The custom is assumed in the story of Onan in Gn. xxxviii. 8–10. Onan took his brother's wife, but refused to have a child by her, because 'the seed should not be his' (verse 9), and his own children would not have the primary inheritance. This verse does not pass any judgment on birth control as such.

Dt. xxv. 5–10 states the law as applying to brethren who dwell together, but allows the brother the option of refusing.

The Book of Ruth shows that the custom extended farther than the husband's brother. Here an unnamed kinsman has the primary duty, and only when he refuses does Boaz marry Ruth. A further extension of the custom here is that it is Ruth, and not Naomi, who marries Boaz, presumably because Naomi was too old to bear a child. The child is called 'a son to Naomi' (iv. 17).

The levirate law did not apply if daughters had been born, and regulations for the inheritance of daughters are given to the daughters of Zelophehad in Nu. xxvii. 1–11. It might seem strange that verses 9–11 seem to ignore, or even contradict, the levirate law. It could be argued that Dt. xxv. 5–10 had not yet been promulgated. On the other hand, when a law arises out of a specific occasion one must know the exact circumstances in order to judge what the law professes to cover. There would be no contradiction of the levirate law if Zelophehad's wife had died before he did, and the law here confines itself to similar cases. Thus the levirate law and its extension would be valid, though not compulsory, when there were no children. Nu. xxvii. 8–11 would operate when there were daughters only, or when a childless wife had predeceased her husband, or when the late husband's brother refused to take the childless widow, or when the wife remained childless after the brother had married her.

In Lv. xviii. 16, xx. 21 a man is forbidden to marry his brother's wife. In the light of the levirate law this clearly means that he may not take her as his own wife, whether she has been divorced during her husband's lifetime or has been left with or without children at her husband's death. John the Baptist rebuked Herod Antipas for marrying the wife of his brother Herod Philip (Mt. xiv. 3, 4); Herod Philip was still alive.

In the New Testament the levirate law is used by the Sadducees to pose a problem about the resurrection (Mt. xxii. 23 ff.).

V. DIVORCE

a. In the Old Testament

In Mt. xix. 8 Jesus Christ says that Moses 'suffered', *i.e.* 'allowed', divorce because of the hardness of the people's hearts. This means that Moses did not command divorce, but regulated an existing practice, and the form of the law in Dt. xxiv. 1–4 is best understood in this sense. AV and RV imply a command in the second half of verse 1, but the RSV follows Keil, Delitzsch, S. R. Driver, and LXX, in making the 'if' of the protasis extend to the end of verse 3, so that verse 4 contains the actual regulation. On any translation we gather from this section that divorce was practised, that a form of contract was given to the wife, and that she was then free to remarry.

The grounds of divorce here are referred to in such general terms that no precise interpretation can be given. The husband finds 'some uncleanness' in his wife. The Heb. words, *'erwaṯ dāḇār* (literally, 'nakedness of a thing'), occur elsewhere only as a phrase in Dt. xxiii. 14. Shortly before the time of Christ the school of Shammai interpreted it of unfaithfulness only, while the school of Hillel extended it to anything unpleasing to the husband. We must remember that Moses is not here professing to state the grounds of divorce, but accepting it as an existing fact.

There are two situations in which divorce is forbidden: when a man has falsely accused his wife of pre-marital unfaithfulness (Dt. xxii. 13–19); and when a man has had relations with a girl, and her father has compelled him to marry her (Dt. xxii. 28, 29; Ex. xxii. 16, 17).

On two exceptional occasions divorce was insisted on. These were when the returned exiles had married pagan wives (Ezr. ix, x; Ne. xiii. 23 ff.). In Mal. ii. 10–16 some had put away their Jewish wives so as to marry pagans.

b. In the New Testament

In comparing the words of Jesus Christ in Mt. v. 32, xix. 3–12; Mk. x. 2–12; Lk. xvi. 18, we find that He brands divorce and remarriage as adultery, but does not say that man *cannot* put asunder what God has joined together. In both passages in Matthew fornication is given as the sole ground on which a man may put away his wife, whereas there is no such qualification in Mark and Luke. *Fornication* is commonly taken as here being equivalent to *adultery*; similarly, the conduct of the nation as Yahweh's wife is branded both as adultery (Je. iii. 8; Ezk. xxiii. 45) and as fornication (Je. iii. 2, 3; Ezk. xxiii. 43); in Ecclus. xxiii. 23 an unfaithful wife is said to have committed adultery in fornication (*cf.* also 1 Cor. vii. 2).

The reason for the omission of the exceptive clause in Mark and Luke could be that no Jew, Roman, or Greek ever doubted that adultery constituted grounds for divorce, and the evangelists took it for granted. Similarly, Paul in Rom. vii. 1–3, referring to Jewish and Roman law, ignores the possibility of divorce for adultery which both these laws provided.

Other theories have been held about the meaning of Christ's words. Some refer *fornication* to pre-marital unfaithfulness, which the husband discovers after marriage. Others have suggested that the parties discover that they have married within the prohibited degrees of relationship, a thing which must have happened too rarely for it to be the subject of a special exception in Christ's words. Roman Catholics hold that the words sanction separation, but not remarriage. It is difficult to exclude permission to remarry from Mt. xix. 9; and among the Jews there was no such custom as separation without permission to remarry.

Some have doubted the authenticity of Mk. x. 12, since a Jewish wife could not normally divorce her husband. But a wife could appeal to the court against her husband's treatment of her, and the court could compel the husband to divorce her. Moreover, Christ may have had Gk. and Rom. law in mind, and here the wife could divorce her husband, as Herodias had divorced her first husband.

There is a strong body of opinion both among Protestants and Roman Catholics that 1 Cor. vii. 10–16 gives another ground for divorce. Here Paul repeats the teaching that the Lord had given when on earth, and then, under the guidance of the Spirit, gives teaching beyond what the Lord had given, since a new situation had arisen. When one party in a pagan marriage is converted to Christ he or she must not desert the other. But if the other insists on leaving the Christian 'a brother or sister is not under bondage in such cases'. This latter clause cannot simply mean that they are free to be deserted, but must mean that they are free to be remarried. This further ground, which on the face of it is of limited application, is known as the 'Pauline Privilege'.

In the present modern tangle of marriage, divorce, and remarriage the Christian Church, in dealing with converts and repentant members, is often compelled to accept the situation as it is. A convert who previously has been divorced, on sufficient or insufficient grounds, and who has remarried cannot return to the original partner, and the present marriage cannot be branded as adulterous (1 Cor. vi. 9, 11).

BIBLIOGRAPHY. W. R. Smith, *Kinship and Marriage in Early Arabia*, 1903; E. A. Westermarck, *The History of Human Marriage*, 3 vols., 1922; H. Granquist, *Marriage Conditions in a Palestinian Village*, 2 vols., 1931, 1935; M.

Burrows, *The Basis of Israelite Marriage*, 1938; E. Neufeld, *Ancient Hebrew Marriage Laws*, 1944; D. R. Mace, *Hebrew Marriage*, 1953; John Murray, *Divorce*, 1953; D. S. Bailey, *The Man–Woman Relation in Christian Thought*, 1959.

J.S.W.

J.T.

MARSHAL. There are two words rendered 'marshal' in RV and RSV. 1. *sōpēr* (Jdg. v. 14, 'they who wield the marshal's baton'). The word *sōpēr* usually means 'writer' (so AV and Syr., Targ.; *cf.* LXX *grammateus*, 'scribe'). 2. *ṭipsār* (Je. li. 27) or *ṭapsēr* (Na. iii. 17). Probably from Akkadian *dupšarru*, 'tablet writer'; hence 'official', 'marshal'. For both these instances, *cf.* 1 Macc. v. 42, where Gk. *grammateus* means 'marshal'.

The seeming proper name *Tartan* (Is. xx. 1; 2 Ki. xviii. 17) is from the Akkadian *turtanu*, a title of high military rank which may be rendered 'marshal'. See TARTAN. R.J.W.

MARS' HILL. See AREOPAGUS.

MARTHA. The name derives from an Aramaic form not found in Hebrew, meaning 'lady' or 'mistress'. It occurs only in the New Testament, and is used of only one person (Lk. x. 38–41; Jn. xi. 1, 5, 19–39, xii. 2). Martha was the sister of the Mary who anointed our Lord shortly before His death (Mt. xxvi. 6 ff., and parallels); and Lazarus, whom Jesus raised from the dead (Jn. xi), was their brother. According to Jn. xi. 1 the family came from Bethany, a village probably about 2 miles from Jerusalem on the road to Jericho. Luke seems to suggest by his placing of events that Martha's house was in Galilee (Lk. x. 38). This difficulty is removed, however, if we allow either the possibility that the Lucan incident is chronologically misplaced (so *HDB*, III, p. 277) or, more reasonably, take it that this was one of the several journeys undertaken by Jesus to Jerusalem during the last six months of His earthly life (*cf.* Jn. x. 22).

Matthew, Mark, and John all agree that our Lord was anointed in Bethany, and Matthew and Mark specify (presuming the same occasion is referred to) that it took place in the house of Simon the leper. Since Jesus was received into Martha's house in the Lucan record, and Martha served at the supper in Simon's house at Bethany during which Mary anointed our Lord, it has been supposed that Martha was the wife (or even the widow) of Simon. The lead she takes on both occasions suggests that she was the elder sister.

In Luke's narrative (x. 38 ff.) Martha is gently rebuked by Christ for her impatience with her sister, and her excessive concern for the practical details of the meal (verse 40). She was no less devoted to Jesus than Mary but she failed to see the way of receiving Him which would please Him most—'one thing is needful'. Some of the oldest MSS (including Aleph, B, L) read at this point, 'few things are needful, or only one' (so RSVmg). 'Few' refers presumably to material provision, 'one' to spiritual apprehension.

See the comment on Lk. x. 38–42 in N. Geldenhuys, *Commentary on the Gospel of Luke*, 1950, pp. 315–317. (See also MARY (2).) S.S.S.

MARTYR. See WITNESS.

MARY. The name appears as *Maria* or *Mariam* in the New Testament. Both are Graecized forms of the Hebrew name Miriam, which appears in LXX as Mariam (used of the sister of Moses), and may just possibly be derived from Egyptian *Maryē*, 'beloved', though this is extremely doubtful; see Gardiner, *JAOS*, LVI, 1936, pp. 194–197. In the New Testament the name is used to refer to the following:

1. Mary the mother of the Lord. Our information about the mother of Jesus is largely confined to the infancy narratives of Matthew and Luke. There we learn that when the angelic announcement of the birth of Jesus occurred, Mary was living at Nazareth, in Galilee, and was engaged to a carpenter named Joseph (Lk. i. 26 f.). Luke tells us that Joseph was of Davidic descent (*ibid.*), and, although no mention of Mary's lineage is made, it is possible that she came of the same line, particularly if, as seems likely, the genealogy of Christ in Lk. iii is to be traced through His mother (see GENEALOGY OF JESUS CHRIST). The conception of Jesus is described as 'of the Holy Ghost' (Mt. i. 18; *cf.* Lk. i. 35), and His birth as taking place at Bethlehem towards the end of the reign of Herod the Great (Mt. ii. 1; Lk. i. 5, ii. 4).

It is recorded in both Mt. ii. 23 and Lk. ii. 39 that after the birth the Holy Family lived at Nazareth. Matthew alone mentions the flight into Egypt, where Joseph and Mary and the child Jesus took refuge from the jealous anger of Herod. Luke records Mary's visit to her cousin Elizabeth, who greeted her with the words 'Blessed art thou among women', as 'the mother of my Lord' (i. 42 f.), and also Mary's song of praise (i. 46–55, where a few ancient witnesses read 'Elizabeth' for 'Mary' as the name of the speaker; see MAGNIFICAT). The single appealing glimpse of Christ's childhood is given to us by Luke (ii. 41–51), who records the typically anxious words of His mother at the discovery of the lost boy (verse 48), and the famous reply, 'Did you not know that I must be in my Father's house?' (verse 49, RSV).

The remaining references to Mary in the Gospels are few and relatively uninformative. Apparently she did not accompany our Lord on His missionary journeys, though she was present with Him at the marriage in Cana (Jn. ii. 1 ff.). The rebuke uttered by Jesus on this occasion, 'O woman, what have you to do with me?' (verse 4, RSV), reveals amazement rather than harshness (*cf.* Lk. ii. 49, and the tender use of the same word *gynai*, 'woman', in Jn. xix. 26; see also Mk. iii. 31 ff., where the Lord places spiritual fidelity above family relationship; with verse 35 *cf.* Lk.

xi. 27 f.). Finally, we meet Mary at the foot of the Saviour's cross (Jn. xix. 25), when she and the beloved disciple are entrusted by Him to each other's care (verses 26, 27). The only other explicit New Testament reference to Mary is in Acts i. 14, where she and the disciples are described as 'devoting themselves to prayer'.

The brief New Testament sketch of Mary and her relationship to our Lord leaves many gaps in the record which pious legend has not been slow to fill. But we are not able to press the Gospel records beyond their historical limit, and this means that we must be content at least to notice Mary's humility, obedience, and obvious devotion to Jesus. And as she was the mother of the Son of God, we cannot say less about her than did her cousin Elizabeth, that she is 'blessed *among* women'. (For the Virgin Birth, see under INCARNATION.)

2. Mary the sister of Martha. She appears by name only in Luke and John. In Lk. x. 38–42 it is recorded that after the return of the Seventy Jesus came into 'a certain village' (identified subsequently in Jn. xi. 1 as Bethany, about 1 mile east of the summit of the Mount of Olives), where Martha (*q.v.*), who had a sister called Mary, received Him into her house. In the account which follows Martha is rebuked by the Lord for complaining about her sister Mary, who listened to His 'word' rather than helping with the work.

John xi gives us the description of the meeting at Bethany between Jesus and the sisters Martha and Mary, on the occasion of the death of Lazarus their brother. Mary is now described (verse 2) as the one who 'anointed the Lord with ointment, and wiped his feet with her hair'; and after the raising of Lazarus by Jesus (xi. 43, 44) we are told almost immediately of this anointing (xii. 1 ff.).

All four Gospels contain an account of the anointing of Jesus by a woman (Mt. xxvi. 6–13; Mk. xiv. 3–9; Lk. vii. 37–50; Jn. xii. 1–8). The difficulty is to decide whether these four accounts report an identical occasion, and if not whether more than one woman is involved. Matthew and Mark more or less agree in their versions, the Lucan account differs widely (particularly in placing the event in Galilee while John the Baptist was in prison, rather than in Bethany shortly before the death of Christ), while the Johannine account is independent of all three. Only in John is the woman named, and there, as we have seen, she is clearly identified as Mary the sister of Martha. Luke alone adds that the woman was 'a sinner' (vii. 37), Matthew and Mark set the scene specifically 'in the house of Simon the leper', and Matthew and Mark agree against Luke and John that it was the head and not the feet of Jesus that the woman anointed.

There have been various attempts to resolve these differences. One is to suggest that Luke describes a different occasion, but that it is the same woman who performs the anointing. The difficulty in this view (mostly held in the Latin Church) is the earlier description *hamartōlos* for the saintly Mary of Bethany. It was this ascription indeed, together with the absence of further information, which led mediaeval scholars to identify the sinful woman of Luke's account with Mary Magdalene (for a discussion of which see below under 'Mary Magdalene'), and the Magdalene herself, by the further confusion just noted, with Mary of Bethany. Yet John, for one, could not have been unaware of the real identity of the two Marys, or been content to confuse his readers. There is really no justification for identifying Mary of Bethany with Mary Magdalene, and certainly none for associating either with the sinful woman of Lk. vii.

The second main view is that two anointings of our Lord occurred during His earthly ministry, one administered by a penitent sinner of Galilee, and the other by Mary of Bethany. In this case the description of Mary in Jn. xi. 2, as the one who 'anointed the Lord', has a prospective reference. The only difficulty in this view is the repetition of what is evidently regarded by Jesus as an otherwise unique action, the singular character of which He clearly intends to underline by His commendation (Mt. xxvi. 13; Mk. xiv. 9). This interpretation seems the most satisfactory one, however, and it solves more problems than it raises. Origen suggested that at least three anointings took place, involving either two or three different people.

The action of Mary is recognized as a spontaneous expression of devotion to the Saviour, which in its character as well as its timing anticipates His death and is therefore associated with it.

3. Mary Magdalene. The name probably derives from the Galilaean town of Magdala (*q.v.*). Her appearance prior to the passion narratives is confined to Lk. viii. 2, where we read that among the women cured of possession by evil spirits who accompanied the Lord and His disciples during their evangelistic ministry was 'Mary called Magdalene, out of whom went seven devils' (*cf.* Mk. xvi. 9, in the longer ending).

It is not possible, at least from the biblical evidence, to limit the illness from which Mary was healed to one sphere alone, the physical, the mental, or the moral. This is a further reason for resisting any identification between Mary Magdalene and the 'sinful woman' of Lk. vii (see above, under 2). If Luke had known that the Mary of chapter viii was the same person as the sinner of chapter vii is it not probable that he would have made the connection explicit?

Mary reappears at the crucifixion, in company with the other women who had journeyed with our Lord from Galilee (see below, under 4). In the Johannine account of the resurrection we have the description of the Lord's appearance to Mary alone. Mark's report, in the longer ending, is brief and not placed chronologically. Slight differences occur in the reports of the arrival of the women at the tomb. Mary sets out with the others (Mt. xxviii. 1; Mk. xvi. 1), but apparently runs ahead of them and arrives first at the tomb (Jn. xx. 1). She then tells Peter and the beloved disciple what has happened (Jn. xx. 2), and is joined there by the other women (Lk. xxiv. 10). She returns with Peter and the beloved disciple to the tomb, and lingers behind weeping after they have gone (Jn. xx. 11). It is then that she sees two angels (verse 12), and finally the risen Christ Himself (verse 14), who addresses to her the famous *noli tangere* injunction (verse 17). Clearly Mary's relationship to her Lord, following His resurrection, is to be of a different kind and to continue in another dimension.

4. Mary the mother of James; 'the other Mary'; Mary of Clopas. It is very probable that these three names all refer to the same person. Mary the mother of James and Joses is listed with Mary Magdalene among the women who accompanied our Lord to Jerusalem and were present at the crucifixion (Mt. xxvii. 55 f.). When Mary Magdalene and 'the other Mary' are described immediately afterwards (verse 61) as 'sitting over against the sepulchre' after the burial it seems likely that the same Mary, the mother of James, is intended. 'The other Mary' again appears with Mary Magdalene on the resurrection morning (Mt. xxviii. 1).

From the other Synoptists we learn further details. Mark refers to her (xv. 40) as 'Mary the mother of James the less and of Joses', who was present at the crucifixion in the company of Mary Magdalene and Salome. In Mk. xv. 47 she is called *Maria hē Iōsētos*, and in xvi. 1 she reappears (as 'Mary the mother of James') with Salome and Mary Magdalene as one who brought spices to the tomb on the morning of the resurrection to anoint the dead body of Jesus. Luke adds (xxiv. 10) that Joanna, as well as Mary Magdalene and Mary the mother of James, was among the women who had been onlookers at the passion of Christ, and who reported the events of the resurrection to the apostles.

It is John who uses the descriptive term *Klōpa* ('of Clopas') for this Mary, when he records (xix. 25) that standing by the cross of Jesus were His mother and His mother's sister, Mary 'the wife of Clopas' (RV, RSV) and Mary Magdalene. It appears correct to translate the genitive *Klōpa* as '(wife) of Clopas', rather than as '(daughter) of Clopas'. Judging, then, by the list given in Mk. xv. 40, and noted above, it seems fairly clear that Mary of Clopas (*pace* Jerome) is the same person as Mary of James. Hegesippus tells us (see Eus., *EH* iii. 11) that Clopas (AV Cleophas) was the brother of Joseph, the husband of the Virgin Mary.

5. Mary the mother of Mark. The sole New Testament reference to this Mary occurs in Acts xii. 12. After Peter's escape from prison (xii. 6 ff.) it is to her house in Jerusalem, evidently a meeting-place for Christians, that he goes first. Since Mark is described as the cousin of Barnabas (Col. iv. 10), Barnabas was evidently Mary's nephew (see MARK (JOHN)).

6. Mary greeted by St. Paul. Her name appears among the twenty-four people listed in Rom. xvi to whom Paul sent greetings (verse 6). There she is described as one who 'worked hard' (RSV) in (or for) the church. Otherwise nothing is known of her. S.S.S.

MASCHIL. See PSALMS.

MASON. See ARTS AND CRAFTS, III*d*.

MASSA. The seventh of the twelve princes of Ishmael according to Gn. xxv. 14 and 1 Ch. i. 30, who apparently settled in N Arabia. Probably this tribe is to be identified with the Mas'a who paid tribute with Tema to Tiglath-pileser III (*ANET*, p. 283) and with the *Masanoi*, located by Ptolemy (v. 19, 2) north-east of Duma. Perhaps Meshech in Ps. cxx. 5 should be emended to Massa, which more closely parallels Kedar. In Pr. xxx. 1 and xxxi. 1 *hammaśśā'* ('the prophecy' in AV) should possibly be read as a proper name (ASVmg, RSV). If Agur and Lemuel (*q.v.*) are Massaites, their collections of proverbs are examples of the international character of Heb. wisdom literature (*q.v.*), which on occasion was adopted and shaped by the Israelites to conform to their historic faith. D.A.H.

MASSAH. Massah and Meribah describe an event at the Israelite camp-ground at Rephidim (see REPHIDIM). Massah (*massâ*, from *nāsâ*, 'to test', 'prove') means 'testing'; Meribah (*m^e^rîḇâ*, from *rîḇ*, 'to strive', 'contend', 'find fault', 'quarrel') means 'quarrelling' or 'dissension'. These names occur together as applied to the same event or place only in Ex. xvii. 7 and Ps. xcv. 8. In all other passages the names are kept distinct, as referring to two separate events or places. If, as is evident from the record, Israel strove repeatedly against God, so may the descriptive name, Meribah, be repeated. 'Massah' seems to refer only to the above-mentioned event at Rephidim, before Israel reached Mt. Sinai. When they did not find the water which Moses evidently had promised them at the springs in Wadi Feiran they 'chided' (*wayyāreḇ*, from *rîḇ*) or found fault with Moses as to the divine validity of his leadership. They grumbled against Moses, Yahweh's agent, and thus put God Himself to the test (*cf.* Dt. vi. 16, ix. 22).

'Meribah' more often refers to an event near Kadesh-barnea (Nu. xx. 13, 24, xxvii. 14; Dt. xxxii. 51; Ps. cvi. 32). Towards the close of their wanderings the oases of Kadesh dried up, and the Israelites again contended with Moses. Instead of only speaking to the rock at hand as God directed, Moses angrily accused the congregation of rebelling against himself and Aaron and struck the rock twice. Thus not only did the people test God but in return He was proving them (Ps. lxxxi. 7) and striving with the tribe of Levi in the person of Moses their leader (Dt. xxxiii. 8). J.R.

MASSORAH, MASSORETES. See TEXT AND VERSIONS.

MASTER. The AV translation of five Hebrew and seven Greek words. In the Old Testament the most common term is *'āḏôn*, 'lord', 'sir', found ninety-six times, particularly when the reference is to persons other than God—*e.g.* a master of servants (Gn. xxiv. 14, *etc.*). *Ba'al*, 'owner', 'master', appears five times, generally denoting the master of a house (Jdg. xix. 22; *cf.* Gk. *oikodespotēs*, Mt. x. 25). (For the Phoenician god, see BAAL.) *Raḇ*, 'great', 'elder', occurs four times, notably in combination with another word —*e.g.* 'master of the magicians' (Dn. iv. 9, v. 11), 'master of his eunuchs' (Dn. i. 3). On two occasions the Hebrew word is *śar*, 'prince', 'chief', 'commander' (Ex. i. 11; 1 Ch. xv. 27), and once it is *'ēr*, 'to awake', 'to stir up' (Mal. ii. 12), where RV and AVmg render 'him that waketh' and RSV has 'any to witness' (reading *'ēḏ* for *'ēr*).

In the New Testament the most frequent term is *didaskalos*, 'teacher', 'instructor', found forty-seven times, all in the Gospels except for Jas. iii. 1. *Despotēs* generally denotes a master over slaves, and is used five times (*e.g.* 1 Tim. vi. 1, 2). A word peculiar in this connection to Luke's Gospel and found there six times, always when the disciples are addressing Jesus, is *epistatēs*, 'superintendent', 'overseer' (*e.g.* Lk. v. 5). *Kyrios*, 'lord', 'sir', is translated 'master' fourteen times, often signifying God or Christ (*e.g.* Mk. xiii. 35; Eph. vi. 9). Another word translated as master is *kathēgētēs*, 'a leader', 'a guide' (in the scholastic sense) (Mt. xxiii. 8, 10). Gk. *rhabbi*, 'Rabbi', from Heb. *rabbî*, 'my master', is found eight times in the Gospels (*e.g.* Jn. iv. 31), and used of Jesus only. (See RABBI.) Finally, *kybernētēs*, 'ship-master', 'pilot', is found twice (Acts xxvii. 11; Rev. xviii. 17). J.D.D.

MATTANIAH. See ZEDEKIAH.

MATTHEW. Matthew appears in all the lists of the twelve apostles (Mt. x. 3; Mk. iii. 18; Lk. vi. 15; Acts i. 13). In Mt. x. 3 he is further described as 'the tax-collector' (RSV). In Mt. ix. 9 Jesus finds him 'sitting at the tax-office' (RSV) and bids him follow Him. In the parallel passages in Mark and Luke the tax-collector called from the tax-office is designated Levi, Mark adding that he was 'the son of Alphaeus'. The *Gospel of Peter* also speaks of Levi the son of Alphaeus as a disciple of Jesus. Subsequently, Jesus is a fellow-guest with many tax-collectors and sinners. Neither Mt. ix. 10 nor Mk. ii. 15 makes it clear at whose house the meal was held, but Lk. v. 29 states that 'Levi made him a great feast in his own house'. From this evidence it is usually supposed that Matthew and Levi were the same person.

The statement of Papias that Matthew 'compiled the oracles' (*synegrapsato ta logia*) in Hebrew was taken by the early Church as evidence that Matthew was the author of the Gospel which had been handed down as 'according to Matthew'. Most modern scholars believe that Papias was referring to a compilation by Matthew either of the sayings of Jesus or of messianic proof-texts from the Old Testament. It may be that the subsequent embodiment of some of these sayings or proof-texts in the Gospel was the reason why that document came to be styled 'according to Matthew' from the middle of the 2nd century. For Bibliography, see under MATTHEW, GOSPEL OF. R.V.G.T.

MATTHEW, GOSPEL OF.

I. OUTLINE OF CONTENTS

a. Events associated with the birth of Jesus the Messiah (i. 1–ii. 23).

b. Jesus is baptized and tempted and begins His Galilaean ministry (iii. 1–iv. 25).

c. The ethics of the kingdom of God are taught by Jesus by injunctions and illustrations (v. 1–vii. 29).

d. Jesus demonstrates His power over disease, the devil, and nature (viii. 1–ix. 34).

e. Jesus commissions the Twelve and sends them out as preachers (ix. 35–x. 42).

f. Jesus commends John the Baptist, issues a gracious invitation to the heavy laden, claims to be Lord of the sabbath day, argues that He cannot be Beelzebub, and explains the qualifications for membership in His new family (xi. 1–xii. 50).

g. Jesus gives seven parables about the kingdom of heaven (xiii. 1–52).

h. Jesus is rejected by His fellow-townsmen of Nazareth, and John the Baptist is martyred (xiii. 53–xiv. 12).

i. Further miracles are performed by Jesus, who is acknowledged to be the Christ by Peter. Later Jesus is transfigured before three disciples and predicts His coming death and resurrection (xiv. 13–xvii. 27).

j. Jesus teaches His disciples to be humble, careful in conduct, and very forgiving in practice (xviii. 1–35).

k. Jesus travels to Jerusalem. On the way He gives teaching on divorce, the position of children, the snare of riches, and the wickedness of God's people the Jews; He heals two blind men at Jericho (xix. 1–xx. 34).

l. After making a triumphal but humble entry into Jerusalem, Jesus shows His authority by cleansing the Temple, by cursing a fruitless fig-tree, and by attacking and counter-attacking the chief priests and Pharisees (xxi. 1–xxiii. 35).

m. Jesus predicts the fall of Jerusalem and His own glorious second coming (xxiv. 1–51).

n. Jesus gives three parables on judgment (xxv. 1–46).

o. Jesus is betrayed, tried, denied, mocked, crucified, and buried (xxvi. 1–xxvii. 66).

p. Jesus is raised from the dead and is seen by His friends (xxviii. 1–10).

q. Jesus gives His final orders before returning to God in heaven (xxviii. 11–20).

II. CHARACTERISTICS AND AUTHORSHIP

In this Gospel the incidents in the life of Jesus which constituted 'the gospel' preached by the apostles are combined to a greater extent with the ethical teaching of Jesus than elsewhere in the New Testament; and it is this feature of the book, together with the orderly manner in which the material is presented, which made it from the earliest days the most widely read and in some respects the most influential of the four Gospels. Modern scholars hesitate to accept the tradition that its author was the apostle Matthew, for he seems to have been dependent upon a document composed by a non-apostolic writer, the Gospel of Mark, to a degree improbable in an original apostle. The book was styled 'according to Matthew', probably because it embodies a translation of a collection of the sayings of Jesus made by him (see MATTHEW); but the Gospel itself is an original Greek work.

III. THE INFLUENCE OF MARK

It is clear that Matthew has included almost the whole of Mark, though he has greatly abbreviated the Markan stories of the miracles to make space for the large amount of non-Markan material he desires to insert (see GOSPELS and MARK, GOSPEL OF). Along with the stories from Mark, the evangelist inserts numerous sayings of Jesus, taken, it would seem, from a source common to himself and Luke; and he conflates these sayings with others found only in his Gospel, the resultant groupings constituting five blocks of teaching, *viz.* v–vii, x, xiii, xviii, and xxiv–xxv, each block ending with the formula: 'It came to pass when Jesus had finished these sayings'. The subject-matter of the Gospel is rendered complete by the addition of several narratives found nowhere else. These would appear for the most part to be elaborations of traditions used by Christians for apologetic purposes in defence against Jewish slanders. Evidence of style suggests that these particular narratives were first put in writing by the evangelist himself (see G. D. Kilpatrick, *The Origins of the Gospel according to St. Matthew*, 1946).

IV. DIFFERENCES FROM MARK'S GOSPEL

The fact that this Gospel originated in a Gk.-speaking Jewish–Christian community accounts largely for the particular emphasis which it places upon the different elements that composed the primitive Christian preaching, and also for the manner in which the teaching of Jesus is presented. The note of *fulfilment* finds stronger emphasis here than in the Gospel of Mark. The author is most concerned to establish the truth that the earthly history of Jesus, in its origin and its purpose, and in the actual manner of its unfolding, was the activity of God Himself, who was therein fulfilling His own words spoken by the prophets. No Gospel links together so closely the Old and New Testaments; and no document in the New Testament sets forth the person of Jesus, and His life and teaching, so clearly as the fulfilment of 'the law and the prophets'. Not only does the evangelist add Old Testament references to passages taken over from Mark, as, *e.g.*, at xxvii. 34 and 43; but at various points in the narrative he introduces with the impressive formula 'that it might be fulfilled which was spoken by the prophet, saying' some eleven special quotations from the Old Testament, the cumulative effect of which is remarkable (see i. 23, ii. 18, ii. 23, iv. 15 f., viii. 17, xii. 18 ff., xiii. 35, xxi. 5, and xxvii. 9 f.). Events are recorded as happening in the way they did because God had willed that it should be so. They were not freak events isolated and unexplained. They happened 'according to the Scriptures', in which God's will had been expressed.

V. THE STORY OF JESUS

The record of the events in the life and death of Jesus which were of special importance and significance for the Christian gospel that we find presented in Matthew is for the most part Mark's story. Our evangelist collects in chapters viii and ix, in three groups of three, many of the Markan narratives of the miracles; and in chapters xi and xii he combines from Mark and other sources stories about the relations of Jesus with prominent people of His day such as John the Baptist and the Pharisees. He makes no attempt to relate these incidents in chronological sequence. Such sequence is to be found only in the story of the passion, which, because it lay at the centre of the Christian gospel, was probably told in chronological form from very early days. Matthew, however, renders Mark's story of the life of Jesus more complete by prefacing it with a genealogy and traditions about the infancy of Jesus and by following it with accounts of two of the appearances of the risen Jesus. The infancy narratives of Matthew do not contain an account of the birth of Jesus, which is mentioned only in passing in ii. 1. The purpose of the evangelist seems to be, by the genealogy, to show that Jesus, though born of a virgin-mother, was nevertheless legally of Abraham's seed and a son of the royal house of David; and, by the material contained in i. 18–25 to answer the calumny that Jesus was an illegitimate child of Mary, and to defend the action of Joseph. The subsequent story of the flight into Egypt is partly an answer to the Jewish cavil why, if Jesus, known as Jesus of Nazareth, was really born in Bethlehem, so much of His life was spent at Nazareth.

The two resurrection appearances peculiar to Matthew (xxviii. 9, 10, 16–20) may be an attempt to round off the Markan story. Certainly, the abruptness of Mark's ending is avoided by the statement that the women, instead of saying nothing to anybody of what they had heard and seen, at once obeyed the angel's command to report to the Lord's brethren that they were to go to Galilee where they would see Him, and that, as the women were setting out on their errand, they met the risen Jesus. The momentous disclosure by the risen Jesus in Galilee that by His victory over death universal sovereignty had been given Him, and His commission to the eleven disciples to embark upon a world-wide evangelistic mission with the assurance that He would be with them to the end of time, provides the climax of the Gospel of Matthew.

In these infancy and post-resurrection narratives Matthew is making definite additions to the story of Jesus as it had been set forth in Mark. Where he expands such Markan stories as he embodies, it is usually by adding material which reflects interests that were of concern to the Christian Church at the time he was writing. For example, the story of Peter walking over the waves to Jesus (xiv. 28–31) and the famous Petrine passage in xvi. 18, 19 were important at a time when that apostle was playing a leading part in the Church; and the problem presented by taxation, especially after AD 70, when, on the destruction of the Temple, the tax for its upkeep was transferred to the temple of Jupiter Capitolinus, would receive some elucidation from the narrative recorded in xvii. 24–27. Moreover, as time went on, and biographical curiosity tended to increase, greater attention seems to have been paid to the secondary characters in the story of Jesus. Thus the Matthaean account of the fate of Judas Iscariot (xxvii. 3–10) and the incident of Pilate's wife (xxvii. 19) would help to answer the puzzling questions 'Why did Judas betray his Master?' and 'Why did Pilate condemn Jesus?'

In his account of the crucifixion and resurrection Matthew makes four main additions to the Markan narrative which at this point he is following closely. He relates that at the moment of Jesus' death an earthquake occurred accompanied by a resurrection of the saints, who had foretold the coming of the Messiah and who now rose to salute His death on Calvary (xxvii. 51–53). The three further additions of Matthew to Mark's resurrection narrative, *viz.* the special guarding and sealing of the tomb (xxvii. 62–66); the failure of these precautions due partly to the semi-mortification of the guards after another earthquake and partly to the presence of an angelic visitor who rolled the stone from the tomb (xxviii. 2–4); and the bribing of the guards to circulate the story, still current in the evangelist's day, that the disciples of Jesus had come during the night and stolen the body (xxviii. 11–15)—are all of an apologetic nature. Their purpose is to dismiss the possibility that the body of Jesus could have been removed from the grave except in a supernatural manner. In many respects the Gospel of Matthew might be called an early Christian apology.

VI. THE NEW ISRAEL

The chief consequence of the life and death of Jesus emphasized in the Gospel of Matthew is the coming into being of the universal Church of God, the new Israel, in which Gentiles as well as Jews find a place. The Gospel opens with the prophecy that Jesus is Emmanuel, God with us (i. 23); and it closes with the promise that this same Jesus, now the risen Christ, will be with His disciples, drawn from all the nations, till the end of time. The note of universality, sounded at the beginning in the story of the manifestation of Jesus to the Magi, is re-echoed in the command with which the Gospel closes to go into all the world and make disciples of all nations. The evangelist finds significance in the fact that the ministry of Jesus was exercised partly in 'Galilee of the Gentiles' (iv. 15); and describes Him as God's servant who would 'declare judgment to the Gentiles . . . and in whom the Gentiles would hope' (xii. 18, 21). The Christian Church, universal in its membership, is, however, no new Church. It is the old Israel transformed and widened because of Jesus' rejection by the majority of the Jews. It was to 'the lost sheep of the house of Israel' that Jesus confessed Himself primarily to have been sent (xv. 24); and it was to the same lost sheep that He despatched His apostles to proclaim the arrival of the kingdom (x. 6). But greater faith was found in a Roman centurion than in any in Israel (viii. 10); and in consequence the places at the messianic banquet, unfilled by the Jew, would be thrown open to believers from east and west, while 'the sons of the kingdom' would remain outside (viii. 11, 12). Because the messiahship of Jesus had become to the Jews 'a stone of stumbling', the kingdom would be taken away from them and given to a nation 'bringing forth the fruits thereof' (xxi. 42, 43). The patriarchs of the new Israel, the apostles, would share in the Messiah's final victory, acting as His co-assessors in judgment, as Jesus makes clear in the words recorded by Matthew in xix. 28, and as the evangelist emphasizes by inserting the words 'with you' in the Markan saying inserted at xxvi. 29.

VII. JESUS AS JUDGE

The fourth element in the primitive preaching was the call to repentance in view of the return of Jesus as Judge of living and dead. This call is sounded loudly in Matthew. John the Baptist in this Gospel calls Israel to repent in the same words as Jesus because they stand on the threshold of the Messiah's ministry (iii. 2); and at the close of the teaching of Jesus we read the parable of the great assize, found only in this Gospel (xxv. 31–46). This parable concludes a group of sayings and parables concerned exclusively with the coming of the Messiah in judgment. By the time the Gospel was written, perhaps in the early eighties of the 1st century, part of the divine judgment had already descended upon Israel in the fall of Jerusalem; and the words of xxi. 41 and xxii. 7 had indeed been fulfilled.

Many of the parables peculiar to Matthew, such as the tares of the field, the unforgiving debtor, the guest without a wedding garment, and the ten virgins, stress the inevitability and the serious nature of the divine judgment; and it is in them that we find constantly repeated the solemn phrases peculiar to this Gospel, 'the outer darkness', 'the consummation of the age', and 'the weeping and gnashing of teeth'. In the perspective of this Gospel this final coming of the Christ, though absolutely certain, is not pictured as immediate, because, as we have seen, the closing pronouncement of the risen Christ implies a period of indefinite duration, during which He is present and exercises His reign in His Church, before His final appearance as Judge. It is probable, therefore, that in the light of the teaching of the Gospel as a whole we ought to interpret the two very difficult sayings in x. 23 and xvi. 28 as referring to the exaltation of Jesus to the right hand of God after the triumph of His resurrection, when He entered upon a more extended reign in the hearts of His followers. Otherwise we are forced to the unsatisfactory conclusion that either they remained unfulfilled, and were therefore false prophecies, or that they are not genuine sayings of Jesus.

VIII. ETHICAL TEACHING

The Gospel of Matthew is also remarkable for the extent to which and the manner in which the ethical teaching of Jesus is presented. To this evangelist, as to Jewish Christians generally, and also to Paul (for the very phrase is his), there is such a thing as 'the law of Christ'. Some scholars have thought that the five groups of teaching in this Gospel were regarded by the author as comparable to the five books of the law. Be this as it may, it would seem clear that he presents Jesus as the great Teacher who proclaims a revised law for the new Israel from the mountain (v. 1), even as Moses had spoken the divine law given to him on Mt. Sinai. The Messiah calls Israel not only to repentance but to good works; and the desire to do them, and the willingness to suffer for doing them, render the doers blessed (v. 6, 10). The righteousness of Christ's disciples must exceed that of the Pharisees (v. 20). It is true that by their traditions, by their slavery to isolated texts, and their failure to grasp the wider implications of the law, the Pharisees had rendered much of it void; but the law remained an integral part of divine revelation. It is this law which finds its fulfilment in Christ, who came not to destroy it but to supply what it lacked and to correct scribal misinterpretations of it (v. 17). Accordingly, a large part of the Sermon on the Mount is taken up with an explanation of the Decalogue in which Jesus lays down the moral standards by which the conduct of His disciples is to be judged.

One of the major difficulties of this Gospel is that it presents Jesus as upholding the validity of the Mosaic law and also claiming authority so to 'fulfil' it that sometimes He has been thought to be contradicting it. That He regarded the Old Testament as possessing permanent validity as the Word of God is explicit in the uncompromising saying of v. 17–19. At the same time, so strongly is the binding authority of Christ's own utterances stressed, that in certain instances the abiding nature of the old law *seems* to be denied. In view, however, of the categorical statement about the law's validity, the evangelist cannot have meant his readers to infer that there was any real antithesis between the statements contained in it and Jesus' comments upon them. Six times in the Sermon on the Mount He appears to be setting His own pronouncements against what had been previously spoken, and in each instance what had been previously spoken consists of, or at least includes, a quotation from the Mosaic law.

It has, however, been well pointed out that the expressions in chapter v, 'You have heard that it was said' or 'It was said', do not correspond exactly to 'It is written', which Jesus so often uses when He is appealing to the authority of Scripture. By them He is, in fact, drawing attention not only to what the law said but to what the people had been told by their teachers was its meaning. In Judaism the law occupied the supreme position. In Christianity that place is occupied by Christ Himself. In the Jewish-Christian Gospel of Matthew Christ remains the dominant authority. It is significant that it is in this Gospel alone that we read His gracious but imperious invitation, 'Come unto me, all ye that labour and are heavy laden, and I will give you rest. Take my yoke upon you, and learn of me; for I am meek and lowly in heart: and ye shall find rest unto your souls. For my yoke is easy, and my burden is light' (xi. 28–30).

BIBLIOGRAPHY. N. B. Stonehouse, *The Witness of Matthew and Mark to Christ*, 1944. Commentaries: A. H. McNeile, 1915; F. W. Green, *Clarendon Bible*, 1936; B. T. D. Smith, *CGT*, 1927; T. H. Robinson, *MNT*, 1928; P. P. Levertoff, 1940; F. V. Filson, *Black's N.T. Commentaries*, 1960. R.V.G.T.

MATTHIAS. The successor of Judas Iscariot, following the latter's defection from the Twelve (Acts i. 15–26). The fact and manner of his election have sometimes been called in question as hasty and unspiritual, and supervening on the place intended for Paul (*cf.*, *e.g.*, G. Campbell Morgan, *Acts*), but Luke gives no hint of such a view: the basis of the lot-casting, with its Old Testament precedent (*cf.* 1 Sa. xiv. 41, and see URIM AND THUMMIM), was that God had *already chosen* His apostle (verse 24), and it was fitting that the foundational apostolate should be complete at the outpouring of the Spirit on the Church and its first preaching (see APOSTLE). That Matthias fulfilled the qualifications of verses 21, 22 makes the statement of Eusebius (*EH* i. 12) that he was one of the Seventy not unlikely.

Of his later career nothing is known. His name was often confounded with that of Matthew, a process doubtless encouraged by the Gnostic groups who claimed secret traditions from him (Hippolytus, *Philos.* vii. 8). A book of so-called traditions was known to Clement of Alexandria (*Strom.* ii. 9, iii. 4, *cf.* vii. 17). Other apocryphal literature was fathered upon him.

The early identification of Matthias with Zacchaeus (Clement, *Strom.* iv. 6) may also arise from confusion with Matthew the Publican. The substitution of 'Tholomaeus' in the Old Syriac of Acts i is harder to understand.

The name is probably a contraction of the Maccabean Mattathias. A.F.W.

MATTOCK. In AV this word covers three different Hebrew terms. 1. Heb. *maḥ^{a}rēšā* in 1 Sa. xiii. 20 (end), 21, and the similar form *maḥ^{a}rešeṯ* (earlier in verse 20) represent cutting instruments (root *ḥrš*, 'to plough, engrave'), *i.e.* probably mattocks and hoes. Among other terms in these verses, the second one, Heb. *'ēṯ*, is a metal head: of an axe in 2 Ki. vi. 5 and so perhaps of a ploughshare or more strictly a metal cap for a wooden plough (rather than AV's 'coulter'); *cf.* Is. ii. 4 = Mi. iv. 3; Joel iii. 10, feasible adaptations as well as evocative. The third term in verse 20 (*qardōm*) is a pickaxe (AV 'axe'). See ARTS AND CRAFTS.

2. Heb. *ma'dēr* in Is. vii. 25 is a hoe, used in the vineyard terraces, *cf.* also Is. v. 6.

3. Heb. *b^{e}ḥarbōṯêhem* in 2 Ch. xxxiv. 6 should probably be rendered 'in their ruins' with RV, RSV (from *ḥorbâ*), rather than 'with their mattocks' or 'axes' (AV, RVmg).

For an iron mattock of about 10th century BC found at Tell Jemmeh in SW Palestine, see G. E. Wright, *Biblical Archaeology*, 1957, p. 92, fig. 57:3. K.A.K.

MAZZAROTH. See STARS.

MAZZOTH. See SHOWBREAD.

MEADOW. 1. Heb. *'āḥū*: AV 'meadow'; RV, RSV 'reed grass'. This Hebrew word is a loan-word from Egyp. *'ḥ(y)* and, like it, means 'papyrus thicket(s)'. The picture of cattle pasturing in the papyrus thickets and marshes (Gn. xli. 2, 18) is typically Egyptian: cattle are shown thus in tomb-scenes, while texts mention bringing 'best grass from the papyrus marshes' for livestock. In Jb. viii. 11 *gōme'* and *'āḥū* are parallel: 'papyrus' or 'reeds' and 'papyrus thicket', which must have mud and water. In Ho. xiii. 15 it is possible to render *'aḥîm* as 'reed thickets' rather than 'brothers' (*cf.* RSV). See J. Vergote, *Joseph en Égypte*, 1959, pp. 59–66 (especially 62 ff.) for full references; also *cf.* T. O. Lambdin, *JAOS*, LXXIII, 1953, p. 146, for other related Egyptian and Ugaritic terms.

2. In Jdg. xx. 33 AV renders *ma'^{a}rēh-ḡeḇa'* as 'meadows of Geba'. This may be the 'bare place' by Geba, or perhaps a place Maareh-Geba close to Geba, or possibly (with LXX) to be read as *ma'^{a}raḇ-geḇa'*, '(on) west of Geba' (RSV). K.A.K.

MEAL. See BREAD.

MEAL-OFFERING. See SACRIFICE AND OFFERING (OLD TESTAMENT) IV*d*(ii).

MEALS.

I. NON-BIBLICAL SOURCES

What is probably the oldest banquet scene in the world has been preserved on a lapis-lazuli cylinder seal recovered from the mound at Ur in Mesopotamia. Now in the University of Philadelphia Museum, the artefact dates from the time of Queen Shub-ad (*c.* 2600 BC). It depicts a meal at which the royal guests are seated on low stools (*cf.* fig. 198) and are being served with beakers of wine by attendants who wear skirts of fleece. Musical entertainment is provided by a harpist, while other servants employ fans in an attempt to cool the guests in the hot Mesopotamian air.

Similar scenes have been preserved by Babylonian artists from subsequent periods, one of the more interesting of which is a large bas-relief from Assyria (see fig. 137). King Ashurbanipal is seen eating with his wife in the garden of the royal palace at Nineveh. As the king reclines on a pillowed dining-couch he raises a bowl of wine to his lips. His wife is also shown drinking from an elegant bowl, but she is seated upon a small chair which has a low shelf in the form of a foot-rest. As in the case of the Ur artefact, attendants stand ready with fans to cool the diners and dispel annoying insects. The relief shows a few musical instruments placed on the ground beside some vines and palm trees in readiness for the court musicians.

The earliest detailed menu of which we have any record relates to a feast given by Ashurnasirpal II at the dedication of his new palace at Nimrud. It was attended by 69,574 persons and lasted for ten days. The details are given on a monument set up in 879 BC (see *IBA*, fig. 43).

II. BIBLICAL REFERENCES

a. Palace meals

The type of elegance mentioned above, which was characteristic of Mesopotamian antiquity, was far surpassed by the delicacy and expertise which surrounded the royal meals of ancient Egypt. Paintings on the walls of tombs and other buildings have furnished remarkable evidence of the splendour surrounding such a celebration as the palace birthday banquet of pharaoh in the time of Joseph (Gn. xl. 20). On such occasions the guests, elegantly bewigged and perfumed, were seated on couches near to low tables. Their food would include a variety of roast fowl, vegetables, roast beef, a wide range of pastries, and numerous sweetmeats. Popular beverages included beer brewed from barley, and wine. Representations on tomb walls show servants bringing in large containers of wine and handing the guests bent glass tubes which were then dipped into the jar. The guests drank until they were inebriated and fell to the floor near their dining-couches.

Banqueting customs in Persia in the 5th century BC have been preserved by the Book of Esther, which describes no fewer than five such festive occasions at Susa. The first was a marathon feast lasting 180 days, given by the king in honour of the Persian and Median princes (Est. i. 3 ff.). This was followed by a seven-day banquet in the royal gardens, to which all the palace staff were invited. The guests were shielded from the sunlight by awnings of blue, green, and white, the royal Persian colours, while the dining-couches were inlaid with gold and silver. The other feasts mentioned included one for the palace women (Est. i. 9), the wedding feast of Queen Esther (ii. 16–18), the wine-banquet given to Ahasuerus and Haman (v. 4, vii. 1–8), and the festival period known as Purim (ix. 1–32).

By contrast the Heb. palace meals were austere until the days of Solomon. Guests and retainers were numerous even in the time of Saul, and the royal displeasure could be incurred by refusing an invitation to dine with the king (1 Sa. xx. 6). The generosity of David was shown in the provision made at the royal board for Mephibosheth, the crippled son of Jonathan (2 Sa. ix. 7). Solomon imitated the monarchs of surrounding nations in the elaborateness and splendour of his feasts. It has been suggested that Solomon would probably have his summer meals served in some such garden as that mentioned in Canticles. In the royal court at Samaria Queen Jezebel supported a retinue of 400 prophets of the Asherah and 450 Baal prophets (1 Ki. xviii. 19). The poverty of post-exilic Judaea contrasted sharply with the fare provided by Nehemiah the governor. He supported 150 Jews in addition to other guests, and the day's food included six sheep, an ox, numerous fowls, fruit, and wine (Ne. v. 17–19).

b. Working-class meals

For the labouring classes in biblical times, however, the situation was very different. The day began early, and instead of eating a formal breakfast, the workers carried in their girdles or in other containers small loaves, goat's-milk cheese, figs, olives, and the like, of which they partook as they journeyed to work. The Egyptians apparently had their main meal of the day at noon (Gn. xliii. 16), but Heb. workers generally contented themselves with a light repast and a rest period (Ru. ii. 14). Abstinence from this meal constituted fasting (Jdg. xx. 26; 1 Sa. xiv. 24). Supper, the most important meal of the day, took place after the work had been done (Ru. iii. 7). Once the food had been prepared, the entire family dined together along with any guests who might be present. On festive occasions it was customary for entertainment to be provided, and this included riddles (Jdg. xiv. 12), music (Is. v. 12), and dancing (Mt. xiv. 6; Lk. xv. 25). In the patriarchal period the diners sat in a group on the ground (Gn. xviii. 8, xxxvii. 25), but at a later time it became customary for them to sit at a table (1 Ki. xiii. 20; Ps. xxiii. 5; Ezk. xxiii. 41) after the Egyptian fashion, but perhaps in a semi-recumbent position (Est. vii. 8).

c. Seating arrangements

In New Testament times meals were often eaten on a floor above that normally occupied by animals and domestic pets (*cf.* Mk. vii. 28). Guests invariably reclined on couches, which were arranged on three sides of a square around a low table. Normally not more than three persons reclined on each couch, though occasionally this number was increased to four or five. Each couch was provided with cushions on which the left elbow rested and the right arm remained free, following the contemporary Graeco-Roman fashion. The guests so arranged themselves on the couches that each person could rest his head near the breast of the one who was reclining immediately behind him. He was thus reclining 'in the bosom' of his neighbour (Jn. xiii. 23; *cf.* Lk. xvi. 22), the close proximity of whom furnished adequate opportunity for an exchange of confidential communications. The place of greatest honour or 'highest couch' was the one immediately on the right of the servants as they entered the room to serve the meal. Conversely, the 'lowest room' was on the left of the servants, directly opposite to the 'highest couch'. The three guests on each couch were spoken of as highest, middle, and lowest, a designation which was

Fig. 137. Ashurbanipal, king of Assyria 669–*c.* 627 BC, reclines on a couch beneath a vine while he feasts in his garden with his queen. From a relief in his palace at Nineveh, *c.* 660 BC.

suggested by the fact that a guest who reclined on another's bosom always appeared to be below him. The most coveted seat (Mt. xxiii. 6) was therefore the 'highest' place on the 'highest' couch. No questions of physical elevation were involved in such a usage of 'high' and 'low'.

d. The meal itself

The main meal of the day was generally a relaxed, happy occasion. Guests always washed their hands before partaking of food, since it was customary for all of them to eat from a communal dish. This was a large pottery container filled with meat and vegetables, and was placed on a table in the centre of the couches. Only one instance is recorded in the Old Testament of a blessing being pronounced before food was eaten (1 Sa. ix. 13), but the New Testament mentions several occasions on which Christ pronounced grace before a meal commenced (Mt. xv. 36; Lk. ix. 16; Jn. vi. 11).

While the general practice was for each guest to dip his hand into the common bowl (Mt. xxvi. 23), there were occasions when separate portions were served to each guest (Gn. xliii. 34; Ru. ii. 14; 1 Sa. i. 4, 5). In the absence of knives and forks, small pieces of bread were held between the thumb and two fingers of the right hand to absorb the gravy from the dish (Jn. xiii. 26). They were also used after the fashion of spoons to scoop up a piece of meat, which was then conveyed to the mouth in the form of a sandwich. If a guest acquired a particularly delectable morsel by such means it was deemed an act of great politeness for him to hand it over to a companion (Jn. xiii. 26). When the meal was at an end it was customary for grace to be pronounced once again in compliance with the injunction of Dt. viii. 10, after which the guests washed their hands a second time.

It would appear from instances such as those of Ruth among the reapers (Ru. ii. 14), Elkanah and his two wives (1 Sa. i. 4, 5), and the sons and daughters of Job (Jb. i. 4) that the womenfolk commonly partook of their meals in company with the men. But since it is probable that the task of preparing the food and waiting upon the guests normally devolved upon the women of the household (Lk. x. 40), they would doubtless be forced to take a somewhat more irregular and brief repast.

An ordinary family meal would not involve the preparation of more than one dish of food, so that when it had been served the member of the household who had cooked the meal would have no further work to do. This thought probably underlies the rebuke to Martha (Lk. x. 42), when Christ suggested that only one dish was really necessary. In Old Testament times, when the meal had been brought in by the person who had prepared it (1 Sa. ix. 23), the head of the household allotted the various servings (1 Sa. i. 4), the size of which might well vary with the preference which he exercised towards individuals in the assembled group (Gn. xliii. 34; 1 Sa. i. 5).

e. Special meals

Special feasts celebrating birthdays, marriages, or the presence of honoured guests were normally marked by an increased degree of ceremony. Visitors were received by the host with a kiss (Lk. vii. 45) and provided with a refreshing foot-bath (Lk. vii. 44). On certain occasions special clothing was furnished (Mt. xxii. 11) and the guests were decked out with floral wreaths (Is. xxviii. 1). The head, beard, face, and sometimes even the clothes were anointed with perfumes and ointments (Ps. xxiii. 5; Am. vi. 6; Lk. vii. 38; Jn. xii. 3) in celebration of an important festal occasion. The conduct of the banquet itself was under the direction of a special person known in New Testament times as the 'governor' of the feast (Jn. ii. 8), to whom fell the task of sampling the various items of food and drink before they were placed on the table.

Guests were seated according to their respective rank (Gn. xliii. 33; 1 Sa. ix. 22; Mk. xii. 39; Lk. xiv. 8; Jn. xiii. 23), and were often served with individual portions of food (1 Sa. i. 4, 5; 2 Sa. vi. 19; 1 Ch. xvi. 3). Honoured guests were usually singled out by being offered either larger (Gn. xliii. 34) or more delectable (1 Sa. ix. 24) portions than the others who were present at the banquet.

In the days of Paul the banquet was an elaborate meal which was generally followed by a symposium or intellectual discussion. On such occasions the discourse would often last far into the night, and would treat of such subjects as politics and philosophy.

f. Jesus' presence at meals

The New Testament records a number of occasions on which Jesus was a guest at an evening meal. The wedding feast at Cana (Jn. ii. 1–11) was a festal occasion for which formal invitations had been issued, as was also the case in the parable of the king who gave a feast when his son was married (Mt. xxii. 2–14). The occasion on which Matthew was host at a banquet (Mt. ix. 10) followed the more formal pattern of 1st-century AD Graeco-Roman meals. Jesus reclined at the table in company with His disciples, the tax-collectors, and other invited guests. It is probable that the dining-room opened on to the street, with curtains placed near the entrance so that the guests would be shielded to some extent from the curious gaze of passers-by. The customs of the day, however, permitted people to look in through the curtains and gossip about those present at the feast. It was this practice which prompted the Pharisees to question the propriety of Christ's dining with publicans and sinners (Mt. ix. 11).

On another occasion in a similar dining-room (Lk. vii. 36–50) Jesus was noticed by a passing woman who returned with an alabaster cruse from which she poured ointment on the feet of Christ. Her action was interpreted as supplying the traditional unguent of hospitality which the host had neglected to furnish in honour of his guest. It would also appear that he had failed to provide a container of water in which the guest could wash his feet, an omission which constituted a grave breach of courtesy in those days. The meal served to Jesus in Jericho by Zacchaeus (Lk. xix. 6) was probably of lavish proportions. More modest were the family gatherings in Bethany (Lk. x. 40; Jn. xii. 2), and the interrupted meal at Emmaus (Lk. xxiv. 30–33) on the first Easter day. Occasionally Christ omitted the traditional hand-washing as a preliminary to a meal in order to teach an important spiritual principle (Lk. xi. 37–42).

g. Meals on journeys

Persons undertaking journeys to parts of the country where hospitality was uncertain usually carried an earthen bottle of water (Gn. xxi. 14) and items of food, such as cakes of figs or raisins, bread, and parched corn. The plight of those who 'forgot to take bread' (Mk. viii. 1–9, 14) could be very serious under certain circumstances.

III. RELIGIOUS SIGNIFICANCE OF MEALS

a. Among the Semites

The communal aspect of a meal was carried over into the religious sphere by all Semitic peoples. Archaeological discoveries at Ras Shamra (Ugarit) have shown the prevalence of such meals in Canaanite religious life. Baal temples were frequently dedicated amidst prolonged feasting and revelry. At Shechem the remains of a Hyksos temple indicated the presence of rooms for banquets consequent upon the performance of sacrificial rites. The Hebrews sought both divine fellowship and pardon by means of meals (see PASSOVER, SACRIFICE, WORSHIP) at which the blood and fat were the divine perquisite, while the priests and people received their appointed portions (Lv. ii. 10, vii. 6). Such sacrifices were common in the kingdom period (1 Sa. ix. 11–14, 25; 1 Ch. xxix. 21–22; 2 Ch. vii. 8–10), but were devoid of the licentiousness and debauchery which characterized Canaanite religious meals.

b. In Christianity

The principal sacred meal of Christianity was the Lord's Supper, instituted by Christ just prior to His crucifixion (Mk. xiv. 22–25; Mt. xxvi. 26–29; Lk. xxii. 14–20; see LORD'S SUPPER). In the early Church the Agape, a communal meal denoting brotherly love among believers, frequently preceded celebrations of the Lord's Supper (see LOVE FEAST). See also FOOD.

BIBLIOGRAPHY. *EBi*, III, 2989–3002; E. W. Heaton, *Everyday Life in Old Testament Times*, 1956, pp. 81 ff. R.K.H.

MEASURES. See WEIGHTS AND MEASURES.

MEASURING-LINE. See ARTS AND CRAFTS, III*b*.

MEAT-OFFERING. See SACRIFICE AND OFFERING (Old Testament) IV*d*(ii).

MECHONA, MEKONA. A town near Ziklag occupied by the Jews under Nehemiah, Ne. xi. 28. Simons (*GTT*, p. 155) equates it with Madmannah, but Grollenberg with Machbena, named separately from Madmannah as a Calebite settlement, 1 Ch. ii. 49. J.P.U.L.

MEDAD. See ELDAD.

MEDAN. A son of Abraham by Keturah (*q.v.*; Gn. xxv. 2; 1 Ch. i. 32). The names of some of the other sons and descendants of Keturah, such as Midian and Dedan, were later known as those of N Arabian tribes (see ARABIA), so it may be assumed that Medan likewise settled in this area, though the name is unknown outside the Bible. T.C.M.

MEDEBA (*mêḏᵉḇā'*, possibly 'water of quiet'). A plain and city of Reuben (Jos. xiii. 9, 16) on the right side of the Arnon. An old Moabite town taken from Moab by Sihon (Nu. xxi. 21–30), it was used by the Syrian allies of Ammon as a camping-site after their defeat at the hand of Joab (1 Ch. xix. 6–15). Thereafter it seems to have changed hands several times. It is mentioned in the Moabite Stone (*q.v.*) as having been taken by Omri, perhaps from Moab, and as recovered by Mesha and fortified. Recaptured from Moab by Jeroboam II, it is again Moabite in Is. xv. 2.

It figured also in the history of the intertestamental era (1 Macc. ix. 36 ff. as 'Medaba'; Jos., *Ant.* i. 2. 4), before being captured by Hyrcanus after a long siege (Jos., *Ant.* xiii. 9. 1).

The site, today called Mādabā, is 6 miles south of Heshbon. There in 1896, during excavation of the site of a church, was discovered a 6th-century AD mosaic map showing part of Palestine from Beth-shan to the Nile. See M. Avi-Yonah, *The Madaba Mosaic Map*, 1954. In addition, there are considerable ruins, dating mainly from the Christian era, including a large temple and extensive cisterns. J.D.D.

MEDES, MEDIA (Heb. *madai*; Assyr. *(A)mada*; O. Pers. *Mada*; Gk. *Medai*).

Media was the ancient name for NW Iran, west of the Caspian Sea and south of the Zagros Mountains. This territory thus covered the modern province of Azerbaijan and part of Persian Kurdistan. The inhabitants were called Medes or Medians and were Japhethites (Gn. x. 2), whose Aryan lineage is confirmed by Herodotus (vii. 62), Strabo (xv. 2. 8), and by the surviving traces of their language. The Medes were steppe-dwellers whose name is first mentioned by Shalmaneser III in his raid into their plains in 886 BC to obtain the finely bred horses for which they were famous. His action was followed by later Assyr. kings, who also sought to keep the eastern passes open to the traders. Adad-nirari III (810–781 BC) claims to have conquered 'the land of the Medes and Parsua (Persia)', as did Tiglath-pileser III (743 BC) and Sargon II (716 BC). The latter transported Israelites to Media (2 Ki. xvii. 6, xviii. 11) after he had overrun the part of the land ruled by Dayaukku (Deioces), whom he exiled for a time to Hamath.

Esarhaddon bound his Median vassals by treaty (*Iraq*, XX, 1958, pp. 1–91), but they soon rebelled and joined the Scythians (Ashguza) and Cimmerians against the declining power of Assyria after 631 BC. Under Phraortes there began the open attacks which culminated in the fall of Nineveh (612 BC) and Harran (610 BC) to Kyaxares of Media and his Bab. allies. The Medes controlled all lands to the north of Assyria and clashed with Lydia until peace was negotiated in 585 BC.

Fig. 138. Head of a Mede wearing a round hat. He fingers the fringe of his garment. Another person touches the 'hem' of his garment. Period of Darius–Xerxes (521–465 BC). From Persepolis.

In 550 BC Cyrus of Anshan (see ELAM) defeated Astyages and brought Media under control, capturing the capital Ecbatana and adding 'King of the Medes' to his titles. Many Medes were given positions of responsibility and their customs and laws were combined with those of the Persians (Dn. vi. 8, 15). Media was sometimes used to denote Persia but more usually combined with it as a major part of the new confederation (Dn. viii. 20; Est. i. 19). The Medes, as seen by the prophets Isaiah (xiii. 17) and Jeremiah (li. 11, 28), took part in the capture of Babylon (Dn. vi. 28). The new ruler of Babylon, Darius, was called 'the Mede' (Dn. xi. 1), being the son of Ahasuerus of Median origin (Dn. ix. 1). See DARIUS, CYRUS.

The Medes later rebelled under Darius I and II (409 BC). The history of the Jews in Media is recounted in Esther (i. 3, 14, 18, 19) and the Medians under Syrians (Seleucids) and Parthians are referred to in 1 Macc. v. 46, xiv. 1–3; Jos., *Ant.* xx. 2. Media was organized as the 11th and 18th Satrapies. The Medes are mentioned, with the Parthians and Elamites, in Acts ii. 9. After the Sassanids Media was used only as a geographical term.

D.J.W.

MEDIATOR. The term occurs infrequently in the Scriptures (Gal. iii. 19, 20; 1 Tim. ii. 5; Heb. viii. 6, ix. 15, xii. 24; Jb. ix. 33, LXX). But the idea of mediation and therefore of persons acting in the capacity of mediator permeates the Bible. The function of a mediator is to intervene between two parties in order to promote relations between them which the parties themselves are not able to effect. The situation requiring the offices of a mediator is often one of estrangement and alienation, and the mediator effects reconciliation. In the sphere of human relations Joab acted the part of mediator between David and Absalom (2 Sa. xiv. 1–23). Job expresses the need in regard to his relations to God when he said, 'Neither is there any daysman betwixt us, that might lay his hand upon us both' (Jb. ix. 33).

I. IN THE OLD TESTAMENT

In the Old Testament the prophet and the priest fulfilled, most characteristically, the office of mediator in the institution which God established in terms of covenant relations with His people. The prophet was God's spokesman; he acted for God in the presence of men (*cf.* Dt. xviii. 18–22). The priest acted on behalf of men in the presence of God (Ex. xxviii. 1; Lv. ix. 7, xvi. 6; Nu. xvi. 40; 2 Ch. xxvi. 18; Heb. v. 1–4; *cf.* Jb. xlii. 8). In the Old Testament, however, Moses, of all human instruments, was the mediator *par excellence* (*cf.* Ex. xxxii. 30–32; Nu. xii. 6–8; Gal. iii. 19; Heb. iii. 2–5). He was the mediator of the old covenant, because it was through his instrumentality that the covenant at Sinai was dispensed and ratified (*cf.* Ex. xix. 3–8, xxiv. 3–8; Acts vii. 37–39). It is with Moses that Jesus as Mediator of the new covenant is compared and contrasted.

II. CHRIST AS MEDIATOR

The designation 'Mediator' belongs pre-eminently to Christ, and even those men who executed mediatory offices in the Old Testament institution were thus appointed only because the institution in which they performed these functions was the shadow of the archetypal realities fulfilled in Christ (*cf.* Jn. i. 17; Heb. vii. 27, 28, ix. 23, 24, x. 1). Jesus is the Mediator of the new covenant (Heb. ix. 15, xii. 24). And it is a better covenant (Heb. viii. 6) because it brings to consummate fruition the grace which covenant administration embodies (see COVENANT). Christ is the 'one mediator between God and men' (1 Tim. ii. 5). To invest any other with this prerogative is to assail the unique honour that belongs to Him as well as to deny the express assertion of the text.

Though the title 'Mediator' is not often used, the Scripture abounds in references to the mediatory work of Christ.

a. Pre-incarnate mediation

As the eternal and pre-existent Son He was Mediator in the creation of the heavens and the earth (Jn. i. 3, 10; Col. i. 16; Heb. i. 2). This activity in the economy of creation is correlative with His mediatorship in the economy of redemption. The omnipotence evidenced in the former and the prerogatives that belong to Him as Creator are indispensable to the execution of redemption. It is in redemption, however, that the extensiveness of His mediation appears. All along the line of the redemptive process from its inception to the consummation His mediacy enters.

Election as the ultimate fount of salvation did not take place apart from Christ. The elect were chosen in Him before the foundation of the world (Eph. i. 4) and they were predestinated to be conformed to His image (Rom. viii. 29).

b. Mediation in salvation and redemption

It is particularly in the once-for-all accomplishment of salvation and redemption that His mediatory action is patent (*cf.* Jn. iii. 17; Acts xv. 11, xx. 28; Rom. iii. 24, 25, v. 10, 11, vii. 4; 2 Cor. v. 18; Eph. i. 7; Col. i. 20; 1 Jn. iv. 9). The accent falls upon the death, blood, and cross of Christ as the action through which redemption has been wrought. In the Scriptures the death of Christ is always conceived of as an event in which Jesus is intensely active in obedience to the Father's commandment and in fulfilment of His commission (*cf.* Jn. x. 17, 18; Phil. ii. 8). It is Jesus' activity as Mediator in the shedding of His blood that accords to His death its saving efficacy. When salvation wrought is viewed as reconciliation and propitiation, it is here that the mediatory function is most clearly illustrated. Reconciliation presupposes alienation between God and men and consists in the removal of that alienation. The result is peace with God (*cf.* Rom. v. 1; Eph. ii. 12–17). Propitiation is directed to the wrath of God and Jesus, as the propitiation, makes God propitious to us (*cf.* 1 Jn. ii. 2).

c. Continued mediation

Christ's mediation is not confined to His finished work of redemption. His mediatory activity is never suspended. In our participation of the fruits of redemption we are dependent upon His continued intervention as Mediator. Our access to God and our introduction into the grace of God are through Him; He conveys us into the Father's presence (Jn. xiv. 6; Rom. v. 2; Eph. ii. 18). It is through Him that grace reigns through righteousness unto eternal life, and grace and peace are multiplied unto the enjoyment of the fulness of Christ (*cf.* Rom. i. 5, v. 21; 2 Cor. i. 5; Phil. i. 11). The most characteristic exercises of devotion on the part of the believer are offered through Christ. Thanksgiving and prayer are not only exercised in the grace which Christ imparts but are also presented to God through Christ (*cf.* Jn. xiv. 14; Rom. i. 8, vii. 25; Col. iii. 17; Heb. xiii. 15). The acceptableness of the believer's worship and service springs from the virtue and efficacy of Christ's mediation, and nothing is a spiritual sacrifice except as rendered through Him (1 Pet. ii. 5). Even the pleas presented to others for the discharge of their obligations derive their most solemn sanction from the fact that they are urged through Christ and in His name (Rom. xv. 30; 2 Cor. x. 1; *cf.* Rom. xii. 1).

The continued mediation of Christ is specially exemplified in His heavenly ministry at the right hand of God. This ministry concerns particularly His priestly and kingly offices. He is a Priest for ever (Heb. vii. 21, 24). An important aspect of this priestly ministry in the heavens is intercession directed to the Father and drawing within its scope every need of the people of God. Jesus is exalted in His human nature, and it is out of the reservoir of fellow feeling forged in the trials and temptations of His humiliation (Heb. ii. 17, 18, iv. 15) that He meets every exigency of the believer's warfare. Every grace bestowed flows through the channel of Christ's intercession (Rom. viii. 34; Heb. vii. 25; *cf.* 1 Jn. ii. 1) until the salvation which He has secured will reach its fruition in conformity to His image. The priestly ministry of Christ, however, must not be restricted to intercession. He is High Priest over the house of God (Heb. iii. 1–6), and this administration involves many other functions. In His kingly office He is exalted above all principality and power (Eph. i. 20–23), and He will reign to the end of bringing all enemies into subjection (1 Cor. xv. 25). This is Christ's mediatorial dominion, and it embraces all authority in heaven and in earth (Mt. xxviii. 18; Jn. iii. 35, v. 26, 27; Acts ii. 36; Phil. ii. 9–11).

It is eschatology that will finally manifest and vindicate Christ's mediatorship; the resurrection and judgment will be wrought by Him. All the dead, just and unjust, will be raised by His summons (Jn. v. 28, 29). It is in Him that the just will be raised to immortality and incorruption (1 Cor. xv. 22, 52–54; 1 Thes. iv. 16), and with Him they will be glorified (Rom. viii. 17; *cf.* Jn. xi. 25; Rom. xiv. 9). The final judgment will be executed by Him (Mt. xxv. 31–46; Jn. v. 27; Acts xvii. 31).

d. Conclusion

Christ's mediatorship is thus exercised in all the phases of redemption from election in God's eternal counsel to the consummation of salvation. He is Mediator in humiliation and exaltation. There is, therefore, multiformity attaching to His mediatorial activity, and it cannot be defined in terms of one idea or function. His mediatorship has as many facets as His person, office, and work. And as there is diversity in the offices and tasks discharged and in the relations He sustains to men as Mediator, so there is also diversity in the relations He sustains to the Father and the Holy Spirit in the economy of redemption. The faith and worship of Him require that we recognize this diversity. And the unique glory that is His as Mediator demands that we accord to no other even the semblance of that prerogative that belongs to Him as the one Mediator between God and man.

BIBLIOGRAPHY. J. Calvin, *Institutes of the Christian Religion*, II, xii; G. Stevenson, *Treatise on the Offices of Christ*, 1845; R. I. Wilberforce, *The Doctrine of the Incarnation of Our Lord Jesus Christ*, 1875, pp. 166–211; P. G. Medd, *The One Mediator*, 1884; W. Symington, *On the Atonement and Intercession of Christ*, Part II, 1839; W. L. Alexander, *A System of Biblical Theology*, 1888, I, p. 425, II, p. 212; J. S. Candlish, *The Christian Salvation*, 1899, pp. 1–12; E. Brunner, *The Mediator*, 1934; H. B. Swete, *The Ascended Christ*, 1916, pp. 87–100; V. Taylor, *The Names of Jesus*, 1954, pp. 110–113. J.M.

MEDICINE. See DISEASE AND HEALING.

MEEKNESS. The high place accorded to meekness in the list of human virtues is due to the example and teaching of Jesus Christ. Rarely was it commended by pagan writers, who paid greater respect to the self-confident man. However, its roots lie in the Old Testament, where the adjective usually translated 'meek' (*'ānāw*) basically means poor and afflicted, from which the spiritual quality of patient submission, humility, is derived. In this sense it is used in the Psalms, *e.g.* Pss. xxii. 26, xxv. 9, cxlvii. 6. Meekness is a quality of the messianic King (Ps. xlv. 4) and the theme of Ps. xxxvii. 11, 'the meek shall inherit the earth', is repeated by our Lord in the Beatitudes (Mt. v. 5). In meekness Moses, while maintaining strength of leadership, was ready to accept personal injury without resentment or recrimination (Nu. xii. 1–3).

In the New Testament meekness (*praotēs* and adjective *praos*) refers to an inward attitude, whereas gentleness (*q.v.*) is expressed rather in outward action. It is part of the fruit of Christlike character produced only by the Spirit (Gal. v. 23). The meek do not resent adversity because they accept everything as being the effect of God's wise and loving purpose for them, so that they accept injuries from men also (as Moses above), knowing that these are permitted by God for their ultimate good (*cf.* 2 Sa. xvi. 11). The meekness and gentleness of Christ was the source of Paul's own plea to the disloyal Corinthians (2 Cor. x. 1). He enjoined meekness as the spirit in which to rebuke an erring brother (2 Tim. ii. 25) and when bearing with one another (Eph. iv. 2). Similarly, Peter exhorted that the inquiring or arguing heathen should be answered in meekness (1 Pet. iii. 15). Supremely meekness is revealed in the character of Jesus (Mt. xi. 29, xxi. 5), demonstrated in superlative degree when He stood before His unjust accusers without a word of retort or self-justification. J.C.C.

MEGIDDO. An important Old Testament city which lay in the Carmel range some 20 miles SSE of the modern port of Haifa.

I. BIBLICAL EVIDENCE

The city of Megiddo (*m^eḡiddô*) is first mentioned among the cities which Joshua 'smote' during his conquest of Palestine (Jos. xii. 21) and was subsequently allotted to Manasseh in the territory of Issachar (Jos. xvii. 11; 1 Ch. vii. 29). Manasseh, however, did not destroy the Canaanites in the city, but put them to menial labour (Jdg. i. 28). A curiously indirect reference is made to Megiddo in the Song of Deborah, where Taanach (*q.v.*) is described as 'by the waters of Megiddo' (*'al-mê m^eḡiddô*, Jdg. v. 19), but no mention of Megiddo as a city as opposed to the name of a watercourse is made (see KISHON). The next reference to the city comes from the time of Solomon, when it was included in his fifth administrative district under Baana (the son of Ahilud) (1 Ki. iv. 12) and was selected, with Hazor and Gezer, to be one of his main fortified cities outside Jerusalem, in which he had accommodation for chariots and horses (1 Ki. ix. 15–19). Megiddo is briefly mentioned as the place where Ahaziah of Judah died after being wounded in his flight from Jehu (2 Ki. ix. 27), and it was later the scene of the death of Josiah when he tried to prevent Necho (*q.v.*) of Egypt from going to the aid of Assyria (2 Ki. xxiii. 29, 30; 2 Ch. xxxv. 22, 24). The name occurs in the form *m^eḡiddôn* in the prophecy of Zechariah (xii. 11), and it is this form which is used in the New Testament Armageddon (*q.v.*), from *har-m^eḡiddôn*, 'hill of Megiddo'.

II. EXTRA-BIBLICAL SOURCES

The site of ancient Megiddo has been identified with the modern deserted mound of Tell el-Mutesellim, which lies on the north side of the Carmel ridge and commands the most important pass from the coastal plain to the valley of Esdraelon. The tell stands nearly 70 feet high, with an area on the summit of over 10 acres, and the earlier cities lower down in the mound were still larger than this. The first excavations were carried out by a German expedition under G. Schumacher from 1903 to 1905. A trench was cut across the top of the mound, and a number of buildings were found, but owing to the limited knowledge of pottery at the time little was learnt. The site was not excavated again until 1925, when the Oriental Institute of the University of Chicago under the direction of J. H. Breasted selected it as the first major project in an ambitious scheme of excavations all over the Near East. The work was directed successively by C. S. Fisher (1925–7), P. L. O. Guy (1927–35), and G. Loud (1935–9). The original intention was to clear the entire mound, level by level, to the base, and to this end an area at the foot of the slope was excavated at an early stage to release it for the subsequent dumping of earth from the tell. War brought the work to an end, and though the lay-out of the entire city in Iron Age times had been revealed, the earlier levels were known only in a relatively small area. A brief excavation was carried out in 1960 by Y. Yadin to elucidate some problems of the stratigraphy of levels V–III.

Twenty main occupation levels were identified, dating back to Chalcolithic settlements in the early fourth millennium (levels XX, XIX). An interesting feature of level XIX is a small shrine with an altar in it. During the Early Bronze Age (third millennium) there was a considerable city at Megiddo (levels XVIII–XVI), one interesting feature of which was a circular platform of boulders approached by a flight of steps, which was covered with animal bones and broken pottery. It may be that this was a *bāmâ* (see HIGH PLACE). This platform continued in use in the Middle Bronze Age (levels XV–X; first half of the second millennium), a period of Egyp. influence the start of which was marked by widespread rebuilding, in which the circular platform became the nucleus of three megaron-shaped temples with altars (*q.v.*). A fine triple-piered gateway, of a type which originated in Mesopotamia, was also found in these levels, and the necessity of such strong gates was shown by the evidence of a number of major destructions in the latter part of the period, culminating in a great devastation probably to be connected with the Egyp. reconquest of Palestine following the expulsion of the Hyksos from Egypt.

The evidences of periodical violence are less frequent in the Late Bronze Age (levels VIII, VII), and though this was a period of Egyp. domination the culture of Palestine reflected the Canaanite civilization of the north to a considerable extent. It was in this period that perhaps the most fully reported battle of antiquity was fought when Tuthmosis III routed an Asiatic coalition at Megiddo *c.* 1468 BC. Architectural remains of this period include a temple, a palace, and a gate, and the northern cultural influence is clearly seen in a great hoard of over 200 objects of carved ivory which was found in a subterranean treasury under the level VII palace (see fig. 114). This is one of the earliest collections of a type of art which was well known in Iron Age times from as far afield as Assyria (see also SAMARIA), and though practically no examples have yet been discovered in Phoenicia it is

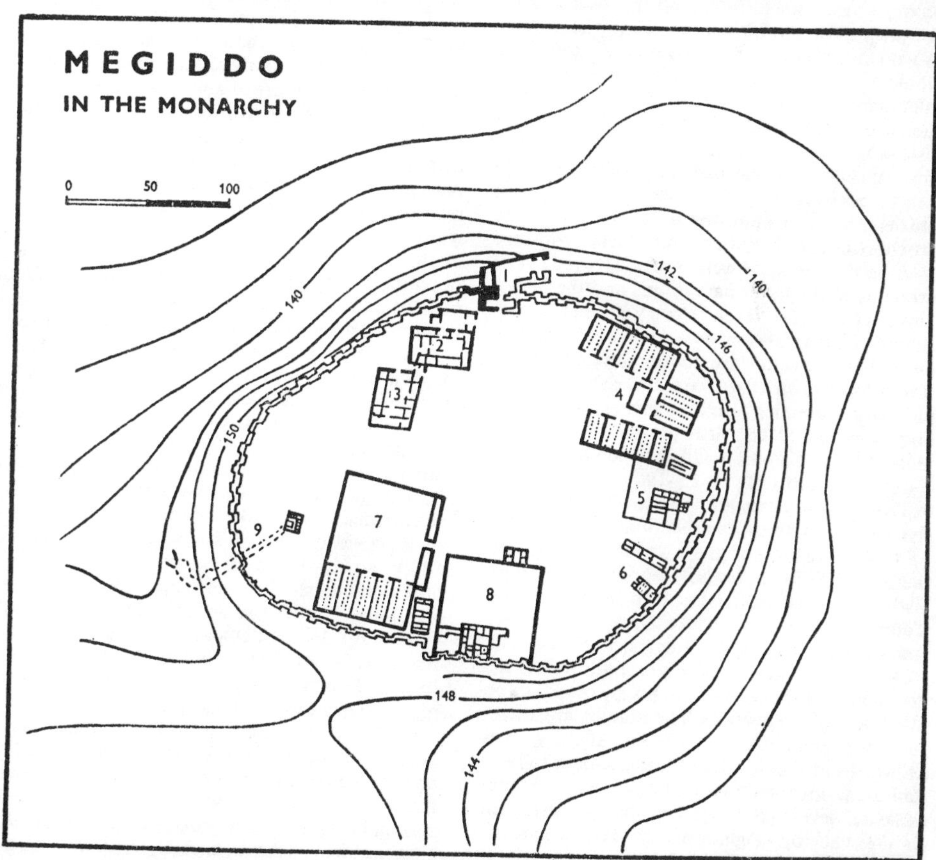

Fig. 139. *Key* (numbers in brackets refer to levels). 1. City Gate (III); 2, 3. Unidentified buildings (III); 4. North stable compound (IV); 5. Unidentified (IV); 6. 'Shrine' (V); 7. South stable compound (IV); 8. Palace compound (IV); 9. Water-supply system, with tunnel to external spring. Scale is in metres.

probable that many of them were made either in Phoenician workshops or by expatriate Phoenician craftsmen. That there were contacts with Mesopotamia at this period is shown by the recent discovery on the edge of the mound of a fragment of the Bab. Epic of Gilgamesh which can be dated by its cuneiform script to the 14th century BC.

Another discovery, probably of this period, was the city water-supply system. An unbuilt zone of the mound was excavated by a pit 120 feet deep, the bottom section of which consisted of a shaft with a staircase round its side, cut into the rock at the base. From the foot of the shaft, the staircase entered a tunnel which, finally levelling off, led, some 165 feet farther on, into a cave with a spring of water at the far end. It appeared that this spring had originally given on to the slope outside the city, but at a later period the tunnel had been cut from inside the city and the cave was blocked and masked from the outside for strategic reasons.

Though there are signs of destruction towards the end of the 12th century, some time after the arrival of the Israelites, and evidence of a temporary abandonment following this destruction, the people responsible for resettling the mound (V) do not seem to have been Israelites. This would accord with the biblical statement that the inhabitants of Megiddo were not driven out at the time of the conquest, and were later put to task work (Jdg. i. 27, 28). A number of cult objects, limestone horned incense altars (see ALTAR and fig. 6), clay incense stands, and braziers, from this and the following levels, are probably due to these Canaanites, who, contrary to God's command, were not destroyed. It is probably to the latter part of this and the beginning of the next level (VA–IVB) that a six-chambered city gate and associated casemate wall (see ARCHITECTURE) are to be assigned, as Y. Yadin has shown. These are almost identical in plan with examples found at Hazor and Gezer, and are probably with little doubt to be assigned to the time of Solomon, a fact which illuminates the statement in 1 Ki. ix. 15–19.

The pre-war excavations uncovered an extensive series of stables, capable of accommodating up to 450 horses, and the excavators connected these with Solomon, who was known to have instituted a chariot (*q.v.*) arm in his forces; but Yadin's investigations have shown that these stables date from the latter part of level IV (IVA), which was probably rebuilt after the destruction of the Solomonic city by the Pharaoh Sheshonq (see SHISHAK). The stables are therefore very probably the work of Ahab, who is known from the Annals of Shalmaneser to have had a chariot force of 2,000 vehicles. The final Israelite level (III) was probably destroyed in 733 BC by Tiglath-pileser III, when the city became the capital of an Assyr. province. With the decline in the fortunes of Assyria, this city (level II) came once more within the territory of Israel, and the defeat and death of Josiah there in 609 BC is probably marked by its destruction.

The excavations at Megiddo have shown what a formidable civilization the Israelites under Joshua had to encounter when they invaded the land.

BIBLIOGRAPHY. G. Schumacher and C. Steuernagel, *Tell el-Mutesellim*, I, *Fundbericht*, 1908; C. Watzinger, II, *Die Funde*, 1929; R. S. Lamon and G. S. Shipton, *Megiddo I: Seasons of 1925–34*, 1939; G. Loud, *Megiddo II: Seasons of 1935–1939*, 1948; H. G. May, *Material Remains of the Megiddo Cult*, 1935; R. S. Lamon, *The Megiddo Water System*, 1935; P. L. O. Guy and R. M. Engberg, *Megiddo Tombs*, 1938; G. Loud, *The Megiddo Ivories*, 1939; W. F. Albright, *AJA*, LIII, 1949, pp. 213–215; G. E. Wright, *JAOS*, LXX, 1950, pp. 56–60; *BA*, XIII, 1950, pp. 28–46; Y. Yadin, *BA*, XXIII, 1960, pp. 62–68; A. Goetze and S. Levy, 'Fragment of the Gilgamesh Epic from Megiddo', *'Atiqot*, II, 1959, pp. 121–128. T.C.M.

MELCHIZEDEK (Heb. *malkî-ṣeḏeq*, 'Ṣedeq is (my) king' or, as in Heb. vii. 2, 'king of righteousness'). He was the king of Salem (probably Jerusalem) and priest of 'God Most High' (*'ēl 'elyôn*) who greeted Abram on his return from the rout of Chedorlaomer (*q.v.*) and his allies, presented him with bread and wine, blessed him in the name of God Most High, and received from him a tenth part of the booty which had been taken from the enemy (see Gn. xiv. 18 ff.). Abram thereupon declined the king of Sodom's offer to let him keep all the booty apart from the recovered prisoners, swearing by God Most High that he would allow no man to have the honour of making him rich (verse 22, where *MT*, but not Samaritan, LXX, or Pesh., adds *Yahweh* before *'ēl 'elyôn*, thus emphasizing that the two names denote one and the same God). The incident is probably to be dated in the Middle Bronze Age (see ABRAHAM). Melchizedek's name may be compared with that of a later king of Jerusalem, Adoni-zedek (Jos. x. 1 ff.).

In Ps. cx. 4 a Davidic king is acclaimed by divine oath as 'a priest for ever after the order of Melchizedek'. The background of this acclamation is provided by David's conquest of Jerusalem *c.* 1000 BC, by virtue of which David and his house became heirs to Melchizedek's dynasty of priest-kings. The king so acclaimed was identified by Jesus and His contemporaries as the Davidic Messiah (Mk. xii. 35 ff.). If Jesus is the Davidic Messiah He must be the 'priest for ever after the order of Melchizedek'. This inevitable conclusion is drawn by the writer to the Hebrews, who develops his theme of our Lord's heavenly priesthood on the basis of Ps. cx. 4, expounded in the light of Gn. xiv. 18 ff., where Melchizedek appears and disappears suddenly, with nothing said about his birth or death, ancestry or descent, in a manner which declares his superiority to Abram and, by implication, to the Aaronic priesthood descended from Abram. The superiority of Christ and His new order to the levitical order of Old Testament times is thus established (Heb. v. 6–11, vi. 20–vii. 28).

BIBLIOGRAPHY. Commentaries on Genesis, Psalms, and Hebrews cited in bibliographies appended to these entries; H. H. Rowley, 'Melchizedek and Zadok', *Festschrift für A. Bertholet* (ed. W. Baumgartner *et alii*), 1950, pp. 461 ff.; A. R. Johnson, *Sacral Kingship in Ancient Israel*, 1955; O. Cullmann, *The Christology of the New Testament*, 1959, pp. 83 ff.

F.F.B.

MELITA. Mentioned in Acts xxviii. 1; the modern Malta, an island in the centre of the Mediterranean, 60 miles south of Sicily and in area about 95 square miles (not to be confused with the island Meleda or Melitene off the Dalmatian coast). Here Paul's ship was driven from Crete by the east-north-east wind Euraquilo (xxvii. 14, AV 'Euroclydon'). After being shipwrecked he spent three months on the island before continuing his journey to Rome *via* Syracuse, Rhegium, and Puteoli (xxviii. 11–13). Paul performed acts of healing, and the party was treated with great respect.

Melita had been occupied in the 10th century BC by Phoenicians. The name itself means 'refuge' in that language (J. R. Harris, *ExpT*, XXI, 1909–10, p. 18). Later, Sicilian Greeks also came; there are bilingual inscriptions of the 1st century AD on the island. In 218 BC the island passed from Carthaginian to Roman control (Livy, xxi. 51), later gaining the 'civitas'. Its inhabitants were 'barbarians' (xxviii. 2, 4) only in the sense of not speaking Greek. Luke may refer to one of their gods in verse 5 as *Dike* (Justice, AV 'vengeance'). Publius, 'the chief man' (verse 7), probably served under the propraetor of Sicily. His title (Gk. *prōtos*) is attested by inscriptions (*CIG*, xiv. 601, *CIL*, x. 7495).

The site of the shipwreck is thought to have been 'St. Paul's Bay', 8 miles north-west of modern Valletta (*cf.* W. M. Ramsay, *St. Paul the Traveller*[4], 1920, pp. 314 ff.).

BIBLIOGRAPHY. J. Smith, *Voyage and Shipwreck of Paul*[4], 1880; W. Burridge, *Seeking the Site of St. Paul's Shipwreck*, 1952.

B.F.H.

MELONS (*'ᵃbaṭṭiḥîm*). Mentioned in Nu. xi. 5 when the desert-wandering Israelites in grumbling mood were lamenting the various delicacies no longer available to them since their departure from Egypt. The reference is to the water-melon (*Citrullus vulgaris*), a member of the family *Cucurbitaceae*, cultivated from the earliest times in Egypt and the Orient, and seeds of which have been frequently found in Egyp. tombs. J.D.D.

MELZAR. The subordinate official in charge of Daniel and his companions, to whom Daniel appealed for a change of diet (Dn. i. 11, 16). AV, with Theodotion, Lucian, Syr., Vulg., and Arab. vss, translates as a proper name, while LXX gives 'Abiesdri', identifying him with the chief of the eunuchs in verse 3. Most scholars now regard it as a title. Some derive it from the Bab. *maṣṣar* ('watch'). Probably we should read 'steward' (RV), 'guardian' (*BDB*), or 'warden' (J. A. Montgomery, *Daniel*, *ICC*, 1926; *q.v.*). J.G.G.N.

MEMPHIS (Egyp. *Mn-nfr*; Heb. *Mōp̄* and *Nōp̄*). Situated on the Nile, at about 15 miles from the apex of the Delta. It was a foundation of Menes (The White Walls), the pharaoh who united Upper and Lower Egypt. The name *Mn-nfr* is short for that of the temenos of the pyramid of Pepi (*c.* 2400 BC). It was the capital of Egypt during the Old Kingdom. It remained an important city up to the conquest by Alexander the Great (331 BC). Principal gods were Ptah, the demiurge, Sekhmet, Nefertem, and Sokaris. The name *Hwt-k'-Ptḥ*, 'mansion of the Ka of Ptah', is the origin of the name Egypt. Very little remains of the city of the living (Mît-Rahîna); the necropolis is better known with the important ruins of Djeser at Saqqara, the pyramid of Djedefrê at Abu Rawash, the pyramids of Kheops, Khephren, and Mykerinos at Gîza, and those of the Vth Dynasty at Abusîr. Rameses II, Merenptah, and Psammetichus pursued extensive building in the region. The temple is described by Herodotus (ii. 153), and writers of old describe the place where the living Apis bull was kept. During the New Kingdom, as a consequence of Asiatic immigration, we find that foreign gods, such as Qadesh, Astarte, and Baal, were worshipped at Memphis.

The city was taken by the Ethiopians (Piankhy 730 BC), the Assyrians (Esarhaddon 671, Ashurbanipal 666), and the Persians (Cambyses 525).

Since the 7th century BC, colonies of foreigners established themselves in the place, and, after the destruction of Jerusalem, also Jews (Je. xliv. 1). The city is mentioned several times by the prophets (Ho. ix. 6; Is. xix. 13; Je. ii. 16, xlvi. 14, 19; Ezk. xxx. 13, 16).

BIBLIOGRAPHY. F. Petrie, *Memphis*, I, II, III, 1909–10; Kees, in *RE s.v.*; Porter and Moss, *Topographical Bibliography*, III, 1931. C.D.W.

MENAHEM (*mᵉnaḥēm*, 'comforter', 2 Ki. xv. 14–22). The son of Gadi, and military governor of Tirzah, the older capital of Israel. When Shallum (*q.v.*) usurped the throne during a time of anarchy, Menahem resisted, attacked Shallum in Samaria, captured the city, put the usurper to death, and was himself proclaimed king (*c.* 752 BC; see CHRONOLOGY OF THE OLD TESTAMENT). Some opposition to him continued, and in the town of Tiphsah Menahem suppressed a serious rebellion, evidently with needless cruelty. To strengthen his position he became a vassal of Pul, king of Assyria (see TIGLATH-PILESER III). This privilege cost Menahem 1,000 talents, which he exacted from wealthy men in his realm. The alliance turned out to be a disastrous one for Israel, for it led eventually to an Assyrian annexation of the nation. Menahem's policy was resisted in Israel by an anti-Assyrian party, but he maintained his position till his death (*c.* 742/1) and was succeeded by his son Pekahiah. Menahem was the last king of Israel whose son followed him on the throne. For a discussion of the chronology of his reign, see H. Tadmor, *Studies in the Bible*, 1961, pp. 248–266. J.D.D.

MENE, MENE, TEKEL, UPHARSIN. The writing on the wall at Belshazzar's feast (Dn. v. 25, RSV 'MENE, MENE, TEKEL, and PARSIN', since the *u* of *u-pharsin* is the conjunction 'and', after which *p* becomes the spirant *ph* [*p̄*]). In Daniel's interpretation (verses 26–28) *m^enē'* is derived from Aramaic *m^enā'*, 'to number', indicating that the days of the Chaldean Empire have been *numbered* and brought to an end; *t^eqēl* is derived from Aramaic *t^eqal*, 'to weigh' (*cf.* Heb. *šāqal*, whence 'shekel'), indicating that Belshazzar has been *weighed* in the divine scales and found wanting; and the plural *parsîn* is replaced by the singular *p^erēs*, which is derived from Aramaic *p^eras*, 'to divide', indicating that his empire is to be *divided* between the Medes and the Persians (*pārās*, with a further play on the root *prs*).

Fig. 140. Aramaic writing of the 6th–5th centuries BC of the type interpreted by Daniel at Babylon. It reads *mn' mn' tql prs*, which AV renders as MENE; TEKEL; PERES (Dn. v. 26–28).

The mystery lay not in the decipherment of the Aramaic words, but in their significance. On the surface they denoted a series of weights or monetary units, 'a mina, a mina, a shekel, and half-shekel' (Bab. *parisu*)—or, if the first word were regarded as imperative of the verb *m^enā'*, 'number a mina, a shekel, and half-shekel'. But there was no context which could make these words seem relevant to the king or his wise men. Various attempts have been made to relate the specified units to successive rulers of Babylon, *e.g.* Nebuchadrezzar (a mina), Belshazzar (a shekel), Medes and Persians (divisions) (C. S. Clermont-Ganneau, A. H. Sayce); Evil-Merodach and Neriglissar (two minas), Labashi-Marduk (a shekel), Nabonidus and Belshazzar (two half-minas) (E. G. Kraeling); Nebuchadrezzar (a mina), Evil-Merodach (a shekel), Belshazzar (one half-mina) (H. L. Ginsberg); Nebuchadrezzar (a mina), Nabonidus (a shekel), Belshazzar (one half-mina) (D. N. Freedman, who concludes from the Qumran *Prayer of Nabonidus* that the Daniel story originally knew these three Chaldean kings). These attempts are fascinating but inconclusive.

BIBLIOGRAPHY. Commentaries on Daniel by S. R. Driver, 1900, J. A. Montgomery, 1927, C. Lattey, 1948, E. J. Young, 1949, E. W. Heaton, 1956, and A. Jeffery (*IB*, VI, 1956), *ad loc.*; C. S. Clermont-Ganneau, *Journal Asiatique*, Series VIII, I, 1886, pp. 36 f.; A. H. Sayce, *The Higher Criticism and the Verdict of the Monuments*, 1895, pp. 530 f.; E. G. Kraeling, *JBL*, LXIII, 1944, pp. 11 ff.; H. L. Ginsberg, *Studies in Daniel*, 1948, pp. 24 ff.; D. N. Freedman, *BASOR*, 145, February 1957, pp. 31 f.

F.F.B.

MEONENIM, OAK OF. The RV rendering of the phrase *'ēlôn m^e'ôn^enîm* in Jdg. ix. 37, which is translated 'plain of Meonenim' in AV and 'Diviners' Oak' in RSV. The word *m^e'ôn^enîm* is the intensive participle of the verb *'ānan*, 'to practise soothsaying', used, for instance, in 2 Ki. xxi. 6 = 2 Ch. xxxiii. 6 (RV 'observed times') and Lv. xix. 26, where the practice is forbidden. The participial form, meaning 'soothsayer' (*q.v.*) or 'diviner' (see DIVINATION), occurs also in Dt. xviii. 10, 14 and in Mi. v. 12 (Heb. 13) but is treated only as a proper name by AV and RV in the passage in Judges. The reference is probably to a tree where Canaanite or apostate Israelite soothsayers carried out their business. The site is unknown. T.C.M.

MEPHIBOSHETH. The original form of the name was either Meribba'al, perhaps 'Baal is advocate' (1 Ch. viii. 34, ix. 40a), or Meriba'al, 'hero of Baal' (1 Ch. ix. 40b). In the Lucianic recension of the LXX (except at 2 Sa. xxi. 8) the form is Memphibaal, perhaps 'one who cleaves Baal in pieces' (*cf.* Dt. xxxii. 26). This transitional form was further modified by the replacement of *ba'al* with *bōšet*, 'shame' (*cf.* Ishbosheth, Jerubbesheth in 2 Sa. xi. 21, and the LXX 'prophets of shame' for 'prophets of Baal' in 1 Ki. xviii. 19, 25; see further BAAL). See *BDB*; Smith, *ICC*, *Samuel*, 1899, pp. 284, 285; S. R. Driver, *Notes on the Hebrew Text of the Books of Samuel*², 1913, pp. 253–255 with references.

There were two men of this name. **1.** The son of Jonathan, Saul's son. When they were killed he was five years old and became lame owing to an injury sustained in flight with his nurse (2 Sa. iv. 4). David spared his life, gave him an honourable place at court for Jonathan's sake, and appointed Ziba, one of Saul's slaves, to serve him (2 Sa. ix, xxi. 7). Ziba's treachery and Mephibosheth's reconciliation with David at the time of Absalom's revolt are related in 2 Sa. xvi. 1–6, xix. 24–30. **2.** Saul's son by his concubine Rizpah. He was among those executed by the Gibeonites to expiate Saul's massacre (2 Sa. xxi. 8). A.G.

MERAB. Saul's elder daughter (1 Sa. xiv. 49). She was promised to David but given instead to Adriel, the Meholathite (1 Sa. xviii. 17–20), an incident the LXX omits. Many scholars substitute Merab for Michal in 2 Sa. xxi. 8, regarding it as an ancient scribal error, saying that after her death her sons were hanged to atone for Saul's slaughter of the Gibeonites, a breaking of Israel's covenant (Jos. ix). M.G.

MERARI, MERARITES. Merari, third son of Levi, was founder of one of three great Levite families. His family was subdivided into the houses of Mahli and Mushi. In the wilderness the Merarites carried the tabernacle frames (boards), bars, and sockets, and the court pillars, sockets, pins, and cords. Four wagons and eight oxen were given them to help in the task. They encamped on the north side of the tabernacle. Their males over a month old numbered 6,200; those who actually served (age-group 30–50), 3,200 (Nu. iii. 33–39, iv. 42–45, vii. 8). In the land they were assigned twelve cities (Jos. xxi. 7).

Under David's reorganization the Merarite family of Ethan (Jeduthun) shared in the temple singing duties, while others were porters (1 Ch. vi. 31–48, xxv. 3, xxvi. 10–19). Merarites are mentioned as being present at the bringing up of the ark (1 Ch. xv. 6), and again at the successive cleansings of the temple under Hezekiah and Josiah (2 Ch. xxix. 12, xxxiv. 12). Some also are recorded as serving under Ezra (Ezr. viii. 18, 19) and Nehemiah (*cf.* Ne. xi. 15 with 1 Ch. ix. 14). D.W.G.

MERATHAIM (*m^{e}rāṯayim*). A term found in Je. l. 21, having the dual meaning of 'double bitterness' or 'double rebellion'. Some hold that the dual expresses merely intensity of rebellion against the Lord (*cf.* verse 24); other scholars now suggest an identification of the word with Bab. *nār marrātu* (Persian Gulf) = Southern Babylonia (so *BDB*; *GTT*), but this is questionable. J.D.D.

MERCHANDISE, MERCHANT. See TRADE AND COMMERCE.

MERCURY. See HERMES.

MERCY, MERCIFUL. The tracing of the concept of mercy in the English Bible is complicated by the fact that 'mercy', 'merciful', and 'have mercy upon' are translations of several different Heb. and Gk. roots, which are also variously rendered in other occurrences by other synonyms, such as 'kindness', 'grace', 'favour' (and cognate verbs). To picture this concept we would require a group of overlapping linguistic circles.

I. IN THE OLD TESTAMENT

1. *ḥeseḏ*: the etymological origin of this root is possibly 'keenness, eagerness' (Snaith). Its semantic core is best expressed by 'devotion'. Used nearly 250 times, it is translated in AV predominantly by 'mercy', but also by 'kindness', 'lovingkindness', 'goodness' (LXX, *eleos*; Luther, *Gnade*). Its range of meaning is: 'solidarity, kindness, grace' (G. Lisowsky, *Konkordanz*, 1958). It denotes devotion to a covenant, and so, of God, His covenant-love (Ps. lxxxix. 28). But God's faithfulness to a graciously established relationship with Israel or an individual, despite human unworthiness and defection, readily passes over into His mercy. 'This steady, persistent refusal of God to wash his hands of wayward Israel is the essential meaning of the Heb. word which is translated loving-kindness' (Snaith). RSV renders it often by 'loyalty', 'deal loyally', but chiefly by 'steadfast love'.

2. *ḥānan* is translated in AV chiefly as 'have mercy upon', be 'gracious', 'merciful'; and *ḥēn* by 'grace' and 'favour' (LXX mostly *charis*). 'It is the gracious favour of the superior to the inferior, all undeserved' (Snaith).

3. *rāḥam* may share common origin with *reḥem*, meaning 'womb', and hence denote 'brotherly' or 'motherly feeling' (*BDB*—*cf.* Is. xiii. 18, xlix. 15). AV: 'have mercy' or 'compassion', and once (Ps. xviii. 1) 'love'. The plural *raḥ^{a}mîm* is rendered 'tender mercies' (LXX *splanchna, oiktirmoi, eleos*). It expresses the affective aspect of love: its compassion and pity. 'The personal God has a heart' (Barth).

II. IN THE NEW TESTAMENT

In the New Testament the meanings of *ḥeseḏ* and *ḥēn* are largely combined in *charis*, 'grace'. The specific notion of mercy—compassion to one in need or helpless distress, or in debt and without claim to favourable treatment—is rendered by *eleos, oiktirmos*, and *splanchnon* (and cognate verbs). Grace is concerned for man, as guilty; mercy, as he is miserable (R. C. Trench, *Synonyms of the New Testament*, pp. 166 ff.). (Lk. xviii. 13: *hilaskomai*, see PROPITIATION.)

God is 'the Father of mercies' (2 Cor. i. 3; Ex. xxxiv. 6; Ne. ix. 17; Pss. lxxxvi. 15, ciii. 8–14; Joel ii. 13; Jon. iv. 2). 'His compassion is over all that he has made' (Ps. cxlv. 9, RSV), and it is because of His mercy that we are saved (Eph. ii. 4; Tit. iii. 5). Jesus was often 'moved with compassion', and He bids us to be 'merciful, as your Father also is merciful' (Lk. vi. 36; Mt. xviii. 21 ff.). Christians are to put on 'heartfelt compassion' (Col. iii. 12). The merciful are blessed, and will receive mercy (Mt. v. 7; also Jas. ii. 13, on which see R. V. G. Tasker, *TNTC, ad loc.*).

BIBLIOGRAPHY. N. H. Snaith, *The Distinctive Ideas of the Old Testament*, 1944; A. Richardson, *A Theological Word book of the Bible*, 1950 ('Lovingkindness', 'Mercy'); Karl Barth, *Church Dogmatics*, II, 1, 1957, section 30, pp. 368 ff. J.H.

MERCY-SEAT. See TABERNACLE.

MERIBAH. See MASSAH.

MERODACH. The deity Marduk, 'king of the gods', who early in the second millennium BC was worshipped as the supreme deity of the Babylonians (Je. l. 2). Earlier, as a Sumerian god *Amar-utu* he was named with such deities as Anu and Bel, whose attributes he was later to take over. The Babylonian Creation Epic was probably composed in his honour. He may be represented on the Stele of Hammurabi (see *IBA*, fig.

24). Merodach occurs as the divine element in personal names (see EVIL-MERODACH, MERODACH-BALADAN, MORDECAI, BABYLONIA). D.J.W.

Fig. 141. The god Marduk, wearing a high Babylonian crown and holding a curved sword and the 'rod and ring' symbols of authority, stands upon water by the crouching horned dragon (*mušruššu*), his symbol (see also fig. 150). Lapis-lazuli. 4 inches high, *c.* 950 BC.

MERODACH-BALADAN. The Hebrew spelling (*cf.* Berodach-Baladan, 2 Ki. xx. 12) of the name of Marduk-apla-iddina II, the king of Babylon who sent an embassy to Hezekiah (Is. xxxix. 1). He was a ruler of the Chaldean district of Bit-Yakin, north of the Persian Gulf, who claimed descent from Eriba-Marduk king of Babylon *c.* 800 BC, when Tiglath-pileser III entered Babylonia in 731 BC. Merodach-baladan brought presents to him at Sapia and supported the Assyrians against a rebellious sheikh Ukīn-zēr (*Iraq*, XVII, 1953, pp. 44–50). On the succession of Sargon in 721 BC Merodach-baladan entered Babylon and claimed the throne. The Assyrians reacted and attacked the Elamite allies of Babylon the following year. The outcome of the battle is obscure except in that Merodach-baladan remained on the throne until 710 BC, when Sargon, having previously neutralized the Elamites, entered Babylon unopposed. When the Assyrians moved south into Bit-Yakin Merodach-baladan was retained as local ruler and did not openly oppose his overlord during the rest of his reign.

On Sargon's death in 705 BC, however, Merodach-baladan began to work for his independence from Assyria. It was probably at this time that he sent an embassy to Hezekiah, and was shown the resources of Judah (2 Ki. xx. 12–19; Is. xxxix), with the aim of encouraging action against Assyria by the west. Not only did Isaiah's opposition to this scheme thwart Merodach-baladan's plan, but the Babylonians themselves forestalled him by setting up their own nominee, Marduk-zakir-šum, in 703 BC. He was therefore forced to act prematurely, to depose the newly appointed king in Babylon and to rule from near-by friendly Borsippa. Despite the aid of Elamite troops under Imbappa sent by Šutur-Naḫundu, Sennacherib defeated the rebels in battles at Kutha and Kish and entered Babylon, where he set Bel-ibni on the throne. Bit-Yakin alone was despoiled and Merodach-baladan fled to SW Elam, where he died before Sennacherib's naval expedition arrived in 694 BC. D.J.W.

MEROM (WATERS OF). Rendezvous of the Hazor confederacy against Joshua, who surprised and routed them there, Jos. xi. 5, 7. It lies between Lakes Huleh and Tiberias, 10 miles west of Jordan, and copious springs flow southwards by the village of Meiron, down a valley opening into Galilee (Noth, *Joshua*, p. 67). This location is preferable to Jebel Marun (Garstang, *Joshua–Judges*, pp. 193 ff., 395) or L. Huleh (see Abel, *RB*, LVI, 1949, pp. 335 ff., who expounds Joshua's tactics on this basis). J.P.U.L.

MERONOTHITE. A designation applied to Jehdeiah (1 Ch. xxvii. 30) and Jadon (Ne. iii. 7). Although the latter verse seems to suggest that Meronoth was close to Gibeon and Mizpah, *GTT* (p. 387) points out that 'Mizpah' is itself a doubtful reading. The exact place has not been identified.

MEROZ (Heb. *mērōz*), in Jdg. v. 23 a community (doubtfully identified with Khirbet Maruṣ, 7½ miles south of Barak's home at Kedesh-naphtali) on which Deborah pronounces a curse for its failure to take part in the campaign against Sisera. The bitterness of the curse suggests that Meroz was under a sacred obligation to obey Barak's summons. F.F.B.

MESHA. 1. A king of Moab who threw off the yoke of Israel on Ahab's death (2 Ki. iii. 4, 5). His country was invaded by the kings of Judah, Israel, and Edom (2 Ki. iii), but the expedition failed. He built many towns and guaranteed a good water supply for Moab. He left a lengthy account of his achievements on the famous Moabite Stone (see MOAB, MOABITE STONE).

2. Caleb's firstborn son (1 Ch. ii. 42). **3.** A Benjamite born in Moab, son of Shaharaim by Hodesh (1 Ch. viii. 9). J.A.T.

MESHA. A place mentioned as the limit of the territory of the descendants of Joktan (Gn. x. 30), the other limit being Sephar (*q.v.*). Some scholars would identify it with *maśśā'* in N Arabia (see MASSA), but the probable location of Sephar in S Arabia suggests a similar locality for

Mesha, though no place of that name has been suggested in that region.

For Mesha king of Moab see MOABITE STONE.

T.C.M.

MESHACH (*mēšaḵ*). The name given to Mishael ('Who is as God?'), one of Daniel's three companions, by the chief eunuch in captivity (Dn. i. 7, ii. 49, *etc.*). No Bab. name of this form is known, and it may be a hybrid Aramaism ('Who is this?') built on the similarity to the Heb. name and thus avoiding giving offence to a pious Jew. (See ABED-NEGO, SHADRACH.)

D.J.W.

MESHECH (*MT mešeḵ*; LXX *Mosoch*). One of the sons of Japheth (Gn. x. 2 = 1 Ch. i. 5) mentioned here and elsewhere in association with Tubal (*q.v.*). He is mentioned in 1 Ch. i. 17 as a descendant of Shem by Aram, while in the parallel passage in Genesis (x. 23) the name given is Mash. It is presumed that one of these is a slip, perhaps the most likely being the dropping of *k* from a supposed *mšk* in Gn. x. 23 (LXX *Mosoch*). The intermarriage implied by the presence of the same name among the children of Japheth and Shem, which such a view would involve, would not be impossible (see NATIONS, TABLE OF).

The descendants of Meshech are later mentioned as exporting slaves and copper (Ezk. xxvii. 13), as a warlike people threatening from the north (Ezk. xxxii. 26, xxxviii. 2, 3, xxxix. 1), and as typical of a barbarous society (Ps. cxx. 5). The close association of the name with Tubal renders likely their identification with the people referred to as *Tabâl* and *Musku* or *Mušku* in the Assyr. inscriptions and *Tibarēnoi* and *Moschoi* in Herodotus, in both of which sources these names are closely associated. The *muš-ka-a-ia* are first mentioned in the annals of Tiglath-pileser I at the end of the 12th century, as mounting an army of 20,000 men in the north, and it may be that they were already in the region south-east of the Black Sea a century earlier when the Hittite texts mention one Mitas in that area, for this name is similar to that of the king of the Muški in the 8th century. They are mentioned in the annals of Tukulti-Ninurta II and Ashurnasirpal II in the 9th century and of Sargon in the 8th. This king mentions the name of *mi-ta-a* their ruler, and some scholars suggest that this name is to be equated with that of Midas of Phrygia, the kingdom which succeeded the Hittites in Asia Minor, and that the Muški are therefore to be equated with the Phrygians. The name Mušku is not mentioned in the Achaemenian inscriptions, but Herodotus names the Moschoi as falling within the 19th Satrapy of Darius (iii. 94) and as forming a contingent in the army of Xerxes (vii. 78). This information leads to the conclusion that Meshech refers to a people perhaps speaking an Indo-European language who entered the Near East from the northern steppe, and imposed themselves as rulers upon the indigenous population of an area in eastern Anatolia.

BIBLIOGRAPHY. E. Dhorme, *Syria*, XIII, 1932, pp. 39, 40.

T.C.M.

MESOPOTAMIA. The Gk. *Mesopotamia*, 'between the two rivers', is AV borrowing from LXX to render the Heb. *'ᵃram nahᵃrayim* (except in the title of Ps. lx). This was the fertile land east of the river Orontes covering the upper and middle Euphrates and the lands watered by the rivers Habur and Tigris, *i.e.* modern E Syria–N Iraq. It includes Harran (to which Abraham moved after leaving Ur in Babylonia) and its surrounding townships, to which Eliezer was sent to find a wife for Isaac (Gn. xxiv. 10). Mesopotamia was the original home of Balaam (Dt. xxiii. 4; see PEOR) and was the country ruled by Cushan-rishathaim when he oppressed Israel (Jdg. iii. 8–10). In David's time Mesopotamia provided charioteers and horsemen to support his Ammonite opponents (1 Ch. xix. 6). This accords with the evidence for the occupation of this whole area by the Indo-Aryan Mitanni and Hurrians (see HORITES) in the second millennium.

The Greek and Roman writers after the 4th century BC extended the use of 'Mesopotamia' to describe the whole Tigris–Euphrates valley, that is, the modern state of Iraq. Thus Stephen referred to Abraham's original home of Ur in Babylonia as in 'Mesopotamia, before he dwelt in Charran' (Acts vii. 2). The inclusion of Mesopotamians with Parthians, Medes, and Elamites may indicate that the Jews of the Diaspora in Babylonia were present in Jerusalem to hear Peter (Acts ii. 9). Thus the New Testament follows the wider use of the geographical name which is still adopted by some modern scholars.

See also ARAM, SYRIA; and for the history of the region, ASSYRIA and BABYLONIA.

BIBLIOGRAPHY. R. T. O'Callaghan, *Aram Naharaim*, 1948.

D.J.W.

MESSIAH.

I. IN THE OLD TESTAMENT

This word, used as the official title of the central figure of Jewish expectation, is a product of later Judaism. Its use is, of course, validated by the New Testament, but the term is found only twice in the Old Testament (Dn. ix. 25, 26).

The idea of anointing, and of the anointed person, is a well-established Old Testament usage (see ANOINTING). One particular example, which has sometimes caused difficulty to Old Testament students, is in fact specially helpful in defining the term. In Is. xlv. 1 the Persian, Cyrus, is addressed as 'his (*i.e.* Yahweh's) anointed (*mᵉšîḥô*)'. There are here five features which, in the light of the rest of Scripture, are clearly definitive of certain main lines of Old Testament messianism. Cyrus is a man of God's choice (Is. xli. 25), appointed to accomplish a redemptive purpose towards God's people (xlv. 11-13), and a judgment on His foes (xlvii). He is given dominion over the nations (xlv. 1-3); and in all his activities the real agent is Yahweh Himself (xlv. 1-7). The anointed status of Cyrus, as such, simply shows that there is a 'secular' (so to speak) usage of the terminology of messiahship (*cf.* the 'anointing' of Hazael, 1 Ki. xix. 15). But, while not desiring to prove an Old Testament point by dogmatic appeal to the New Testament, it is quite clear that these five points are pre-eminently true of the Lord Jesus Christ, who saw Himself as the fulfilment of the Old Testament messianic expectations. In the light of this, the best and simplest plan for our study is to apply the word 'messianic' to all those prophecies that place a person in the limelight as the figure of salvation (so Vriezen).

How old is the messianic expectation? One major line of argument on this question (suggested by Mowinckel) is that the Messiah is an eschatological figure in the strict sense of the term: that is to say, not merely a figure of future hope, but emphatically belonging to the 'last days'. Consequently, since all properly defined eschatological passages look back upon the fall of the Davidic monarchy as a fact of past history, the Messiah must belong to post-exilic times, and is not found as a matter of prediction in pre-exilic documents. Seemingly messianic passages belonging to monarchic times must be interpreted as simple addresses to the reigning king, and of no messianic, that is, eschatological, significance. Later editing, it is urged, may have adapted them messianically, and later messianic writers may have drawn from them some of their imagery, but in themselves, and properly considered, they are not messianic.

Against this it is urged (*e.g.* by Knight), with great weight, that it is hardly credible that the monarchs known to us in the Books of Kings could have been seriously addressed or thought of in the terms used, for example, in the Royal Psalms. We shall demonstrate this contention presently, and for the moment must be content to say that such passages point to a conception of Israelite kingship as such, and to an expectation resident in the kingly office itself. Even if Mowinckel has correctly insisted that Messiah must be an eschatological figure, by no means all Old Testament specialists would agree that eschatology must be post-exilic (*cf.*, *e.g.*, Vriezen), but it may certainly be asked if he has not defined the concept of eschatology too rigidly. If, for example, he denies the description 'eschatological' to any passage which depicts the survival and life of a remnant after the divine intervention, the logical consequence of this is to deny that the Lord Jesus Christ is an eschatological figure, and thereby to contradict the biblical view of the 'last days' (*e.g.* Heb. i. 2; 1 Jn. ii. 18). It is much more satisfactory to define the Messiah as a 'teleological figure'. Unique in Israel was their apprehension of purpose in life. They possessed this awareness from the beginning (*cf.* Gn. xii. 1-3), and this made them alone the true historians of the ancient world.

The specific attachment of this hope to a royal figure of the future is in no way dependent on the historical fall of the monarchy, for the Davidic line was a failure from the start, and the expectation, even longing, for the royal Messiah need not be later than the time of Solomon. Our plan therefore will be to seek in the Old Testament for a 'figure of salvation', and, by associating our search with Israelite teleology, rather than with a narrowly defined eschatology, we will find good reasons to hold that such a hope was early embraced by the chosen people, taking its rise from the famous 'protevangelium' of Gn. iii. 15.

a. Messiah as the antitype of great historical figures

Israel's teleological view of life on earth, already mentioned, was rooted in the knowledge of the unique God who revealed Himself to them. The faithfulness and self-consistency of their God provided them with a key to the future, in so far as it was necessary for faith to discern things to come. God had acted 'typically' and characteristically in certain great persons and events of the past, and, because God does not change, He will so act again. Three such persons of the past were specially woven into the messianic pattern: Adam, Moses, and David.

(i) *The Messiah and Adam.* There are certain features of the messianic future which are very clearly reminiscent of the Edenic state: for convenience we group them under the two headings of prosperity (Am. ix. 13; Is. iv. 2, xxxii. 15, 20, lv. 13; Ps. lxxii. 16) and peace (the harmony of the world of living creatures: Is. xi. 6-9; and of the world of human relations: Is. xxxii. 1-8). Viewing the fall in its effects purely upon this world, these were the things lost as God's curse took effect. When the curse is reversed and God's Man restores all things the Edenic scene reappears. This is not merely wishful thinking, but a logical and proper extension of the doctrine of creation by a holy God. All the passages cited above concern the messianic King and the nature of His rule and kingdom. Here is the real recapitulation of the first man, for he had 'dominion' over the rest of created things (Gn. i. 28, ii. 19, 20), but fell when he allowed his dominion to be usurped (*cf.* Gn. iii. 13). Dominion will be restored in the Messiah. It may frankly be admitted that the notion of the Messiah as a new Adam is neither lengthily nor specifically developed, 'but it is not unlikely that we have evidence that the royal ideology was sometimes influenced by the conception of the king of paradise' (Mowinckel). The New Testament doctrine of the 'Second Adam' has a clear Old Testament root in the passages quoted.

(ii) *The Messiah and Moses.* It is not surprising that the Exodus and its leader should have so impressed the mind of Israel that the future was seen in this mould. As it was recorded and presented to succeeding generations of the nation, the pattern of the first Exodus constituted an eternal revelation of God (Ex. iii. 15). The conception of the second Exodus is not always in a specifically messianic setting. Sometimes the fact is stressed that God will do again what He did at the Exodus, only in a surpassing way, but without mentioning any man by whom God will so work as formerly He wrought by Moses (*e.g.* Ho. ii. 14–23; Je. xxxi. 31–34; Ezk. xx. 33–44—note 'king' (RV, RSV) in verse 33: it may be that Moses is called 'king' in Dt. xxxiii. 5). Sometimes, however, the forecast of the second Exodus is messianic. Such references are Is. li. 9–11, lii. 12; Je. xxiii. 5–8. Once again, it is only fair to notice that the matter is, at best, inferentially expressed. However, in the case of Moses we can take the study a stage farther, for we have his own prophecy recorded in Dt. xviii. 15–19 that the Lord will raise up a prophet 'like unto me'.

In general, the exegesis of this passage has tended to the exclusive advocacy of one or other point of view: either that the Messiah is here foretold or that the reference is simply to the providential provision of a continuing line of prophets. In recent work the latter has the support of the majority, although sometimes it has been allowed that the messianic meaning may also, though secondarily, be admitted. However, the passage itself seems to require both interpretations, for some features in it can be satisfied only by the line of prophets, and others only by the Messiah.

Thus the context is very weighty for the former view. Moses insistently warning his hearers against Canaanite abomination stresses especially divinatory practices for ascertaining the future. The warning is buttressed by this prophecy of the Mosaic Prophet. Here, says Moses, is the Israelite alternative to divination; the living are not to consult the dead, for the God of Israel will speak to His people through a man raised up for that purpose. This seems to be a promise of continuous revelation; a prediction of a far-off Messiah would not meet the need for guidance of which Moses is speaking.

Again, verses 21, 22, supplying a test for prophets, may be seen as anticipating the situation which often arose in the days of the canonical prophets, and which caused such bitterness of soul to Jeremiah (xxiii. 9 ff.). However, this consideration is not of equal weight with the foregoing, for it would not be at all improper that some test for the Messiah should be provided. A false Messiah is as likely as a false prophet and, indeed, to take the matter no farther, Jesus Himself rested His claims on the coincidence of His words and works, and His Jewish opponents were continually pressing for an unequivocal messianic sign.

If we take Moses' words as prophetic of a line of prophets, they were, of course, amply fulfilled. Every true prophet was 'like Moses', for he existed to teach Moses' doctrine. Both Jeremiah (xxiii. 9 ff.) and Ezekiel (xiii. 1–xiv. 11) distinguish the true prophet from the false by the content of his message: the true prophet has a word to speak against sin, the false prophet has not. This is simply to say that the theology of true prophecy derives from Sinai. This truth is taught also in Deuteronomy, for the question of false prophecy is raised in chapter xiii, and it is precisely required that every prophet must be brought into comparison with the Exodus revelation (verses 5, 10) and with the teaching of Moses (verse 18). Moses is the normative prophet; every true prophet, as such, is a prophet 'like Moses'.

But there is another side to the exegesis of this passage. According to Dt. xxxiv. 10, Moses is unique, and his like has not yet appeared. On any view of the date of Deuteronomy, this verse points to an understanding of Dt. xviii. 15 ff. as messianic: for if Deuteronomy is as late as some hold, or if xxxiv. 10 represents later editorial comment, then we are here being informed that no single prophet, nor yet the prophets collectively, was regarded as having fulfilled the prediction of xviii. 15 ff.

Furthermore, when we come to the passage itself, special regard ought to be had to the very precise terms of the comparison with Moses. The passage does not say, in a large and undefined way, that there will arise a prophet 'like Moses', but specifically a prophet who, in his person and work, may be compared with Moses at Horeb (verse 16). Now this comparison was not fulfilled by any of the Old Testament prophets. Moses at Horeb was the mediator of the covenant; the prophets were preachers of the covenant and foretellers of its successor. Moses was an originator; the prophets were propagators. With Moses, Israel's religion entered a new phase; the prophets fought for the establishment and maintenance of that phase, and prepared the way for the next, to which they looked forward. The strict requirement of verses 15, 16, therefore, can be met only by Messiah.

How, then, are these two interpretations to be reconciled? We remarked above, relative to Israel's continuing need of the voice of God, that a far-off Messiah would not meet that need. In so saying, we spoke as if 20th-century information was at the disposal of the ancient Israelite. This passage certainly foretells the prophet-Messiah, but it says nothing about His being 'far off'. Only the actual passage of time could show that. Here, then, is the reconciliation: in respect of prophets, Israel was in exactly the same situation as in respect of kings (see further below). The line of kings proceeded under the shadow of the promise of the coming great King, and each successive king was hailed in deliberately messianic terms, both to remind him of his vocation to a certain type of kingship and to express the national longing that at last Messiah might have come. So too with the prophets. They likewise live under the shadow of the promise; they too have a pattern to fulfil. Each king must be, as best he can, like the king of the past (David) until the coming of the One who is able to reformulate the

Davidic type and be the king of the future; so, too, each prophet must be, as best he can, like the prophet of the past (Moses) until the coming of the One who is able to reformulate the Mosaic type and be the prophet, lawgiver, and mediator of the future, new covenant.

(iii) *The Messiah and David.* The dying Jacob is recorded (and there is no good reason for doubting the ascription) as prophesying about the future of his sons. The prophecy about Judah has deservedly attracted great attention (Gn. xlix. 9, 10). Dispute has necessarily centred on the meaning of *'aḏ kî yāḇô' šîlôh.* Ezk. xxi. 27 seems to suggest the interpretation 'until he come, whose right it is', and this certainly is the most venerable approach to the problem. More recently the view has been taken that we have here an Akkadian loan-word meaning 'his (*i.e.* Judah's) ruler'. We need not pause to debate the point. At all events, tribal rule is vested in Judah, and some pre-eminent Judahite ruler is foreseen as the consummation of the sovereignty. In an initial, and at the same time normative, sense, this came to pass in David of Judah, with whom all succeeding kings, for good or ill, were compared (*e.g.* 1 Ki. xi. 4, 6, xiv. 8, xv. 3, 11–14; 2 Ki. xviii. 3, xxii. 2). However, it is one thing to see that David, as a matter of fact, was the normative king; it is another matter altogether to say just why he should be the type of the king to come. The prophecy of Nathan (2 Sa. vii. 12–16) does not precisely require a single king as its fulfilment, but rather predicts a stable house, kingdom, and throne for David. We must presume that, as one failure after another ascended the Davidic throne, the days of David glowed (deservedly) brighter and brighter in Israel's memory, and hope crystallized into the 'David' of the future (*e.g.* Ezk. xxxiv. 23). At all events, such was the expectation, as is shown particularly by two groups of passages in the Old Testament Scriptures.

1. The Psalms. It would take us far off course to discuss what cultic use was made of the Royal Psalms; our concern is only with their content. There are certain psalms which centre round the king, and, limiting inquiry to those psalms which are indisputably royal, they depict a very precise character and career. Summarizing, this king meets world-opposition (ii. 1–3, cx. 1), but, as a victor (xlv. 3–5, lxxxix. 22, 23), and by the activity of Yahweh (ii. 6, 8, xviii. 46–50, xxi. 1–13, cx. 1, 2), he establishes world-rule (ii. 8–12, xviii. 43–45, xlv. 17, lxxii. 8–11, lxxxix. 25, cx. 5–6), based on Zion (ii. 6), and marked by a primary concern for morality (xlv. 4, 6, 7, lxxii. 2, 3, 7, ci. 1–8). His rule is everlasting (xxi. 4, xlv. 6, lxxii. 5); his kingdom is peaceful (lxxii. 7), prosperous (lxxii. 16), and undeviating in reverence for Yahweh (lxxii. 5). Pre-eminent among men (xlv. 2, 7), he is the friend of the poor and the enemy of the oppressor (lxxii. 2–4, 12–14). Under him the righteous flourish (lxxii. 7). He is remembered for ever (xlv. 17), possesses an everlasting name (lxxii. 17), and is the object of unending thanks (lxxii. 15). In relation to Yahweh, he is the recipient of His everlasting blessing (xlv. 2). He is the heir of David's covenant (lxxxix. 28–37, cxxxii. 11, 12) and of Melchizedek's priesthood (cx. 4). He belongs to Yahweh (lxxxix. 18) and is devoted to Him (xxi. 1, 7, lxiii. 1–8, 11). He is His son (ii. 7, lxxxix. 27), seated at His right hand (cx. 1), and is himself divine (xlv. 6).

The messianic pattern as deduced from Cyrus above is clearly here. It is inconceivable that such notions were entertained in any directly personal way concerning the line of monarchs who followed David in Judah. We have here, therefore, either the most blatant flattery the world has ever heard, or else the expression of a great ideal. Some comment is necessary on the ascription of divinity in Ps. xlv. 6. Unquestionably there are ways in which the address to the king as 'God' may legitimately be avoided (see Johnson), but such interpretations are not necessary in the light of the fact so clearly taught elsewhere in the Old Testament that a divine Messiah was expected. It is no argument against this that verse 7 of the psalm, still addressing the king, speaks of 'God, thy God'. Certainly we are intended to gather that there is some distinction between God and the king, even if the king can be spoken of as 'God', but this need occasion no surprise, because exactly the same thing occurs throughout messianic expectation, as we shall see, and also in the case, for example, of the Angel of the Lord, who is both Himself divine and also distinct from God.

2. Isaiah vii–xii, *etc.* Isaiah faced Ahaz at a critical moment for the Davidic dynasty. In all the intervening years since David, son had succeeded father without intermission or dynastic threat, but now, for the first time, it seemed as if the long reign of David's house had come to an end. The northern powers, Syria and Ephraim, intent upon unifying Palestine, by force if necessary, against Assyria, purposed to invade Judah, take Jerusalem, and set up a puppet king. Isaiah's message was two-fold: in the name of Yahweh he declared that this threat was transient and would not be accomplished (vii. 7, 16), but that nevertheless the moment was decisive for the house of David. It would not be overthrown by a northern force, but it could be overthrown by unbelief (vii. 9). Everything depended on the manner in which Ahaz faced the crisis. Let him face it on the basis of faith in the promises of Yahweh concerning David and Zion, and all would be well; let him turn to political expediency, and appeal to the help of Assyria, and he—and how insistently Isaiah identified Ahaz and the dynasty (verses 2, 13, 17)—would have no future at all. In order to urge faith upon the faithless king, Isaiah offered a sign (verse 11), but this was refused; the way of faith was abandoned, and the pattern of doom established. In judgment upon this faithlessness, 'the Sovereign Himself' (verse 14) declared a sign: Immanuel is to be born, an heir to the devastation caused by

King Ahaz. Before the child can grow to any years, the threat will be gone, but the prosperity of land and people will go with it; for the Assyrian is no friend or deliverer, but a destroyer in whose wake there remains but a small population (verse 21) in a weed-infested waste (verses 23, 24).

However, no sooner has Isaiah declared the seemingly immediate birth of Immanuel than he transfers this immediacy to another, his own child, Maher-shalal-hashbaz (*q.v.*). Now, and for a reason soon to appear, it is he whose birth is both the sign and the time factor in the dispersal of the northern threat (viii. 1–4). The Assyrian appears again as the destroyer, but it is now Immanuel's land (verse 8) which he will overrun; yet, somehow, Immanuel is the guarantee that no alien purpose can triumph (verses 9, 10). None the less, for a people which has rejected God, only banishment can ensue (verses 19–22). But this is not the end, for 'in the latter time' (ix. 1) a great light dawns (verse 2), joy is multiplied (verse 3), slavery is ended (verse 4), victory is won (verse 5), and all this because a prince with four names is born (verse 6). He is a Counsellor of such wisdom that it must be called 'supernatural' (*pele'*, *cf.* xxviii. 29); he is the Hero-God, divine in nature (*cf.* x. 21); he will rule for ever with a father's benevolence, and as Prince he shall bring his people that full well-being of mind and spirit, of body and circumstances which Hebrew expresses by the word 'peace'. His sway, as he occupies David's throne, will know no end in time or space (verse 7). His prime concern is for a righteous, moral rule, and the guarantee of his coming and kingdom is the 'zeal of Yahweh'.

When the passage is thus seen as a unity, the identity of Immanuel with the 'prince of the four names' can hardly be questioned, and the similarity of the messianic content with that already found in the Psalms is remarkable. Isaiah first holds up before Ahaz the hope inherent in the Davidic house, the coming divine King. Using phrases doubtless made familiar by the king-cultus, he allows the hapless king to foresee the long-awaited fulfilment of the promise in the setting of the doom which his faithlessness has brought upon the nation. Then Isaiah switches the time factor to Maher-shalal-hashbaz, whose four-fold name is full of foreboding. Then, having clarified that Immanuel was indeed the expected heir of David, he holds up before the troubled gaze of the doomed community the hope of Immanuel's distant but certain birth. The substance of the section opening at ix. 8 is that the northern kingdom of Israel is to fall, because of its rejection of God's word (ix. 8–x. 4). Isaiah shows that though Judah will not go into captivity before the Assyrian, yet the captivity is ultimately certain; but so, also, is the regathering of a remnant of both Israel and Judah (x. 5–23). Judah is encouraged against the Assyrian (x. 24–34), and beyond the tribulations, again for the encouragement of faith, rises the Davidic king, uniquely endued with the divine Spirit, his kingdom of moral and spiritual righteousness (xi. 1–6), godly peace (verses 6–9), ingathered nations (verse 10), and restored Israel (verses 11–16). The same king, the same personal and public characteristics, and the same kingdom appear again in chapter xxxii. It is not necessary to go into detail about the character of the king: it is the same as is described in the Psalms. It ought, however, to be noticed particularly that here, too, his deity is set forth in precisely the same fashion. He is God (*'ēl*) (ix. 6) and yet is established by the 'zeal of Yahweh'.

b. Other messianic figures

(i) *The Servant.* As with the delineation of the king in Is. vii ff., we shall try to display the unity of the treatment of the Servant in Is. xl ff. In chapter xl God's people are found in some trouble, there unnamed but later (xliii. 14, *etc.*) disclosed as Babylonian captivity. Their deliverance is certain, because there is no God but theirs. In pursuit of His purpose of deliverance, Yahweh has raised up a conqueror (xli). Isaiah's certainty that Israel will be delivered is thus theologically based upon the greatness of Israel's God, as sole God, Creator God, and sole Mover in history. But the more he exalts Yahweh, the more futile by contrast do the gods of the heathen appear to be, and the more awful the plight of those committed to such gods (xl. 18 ff., xli. 6 ff., 21 ff.). Isaiah's awareness of heathen darkness rises to a climax in xli. 28 f., where he poses the problem of the greater part of humanity. But the only God has an answer to this problem: His Servant will bring forth revelation ('judgment') to the Gentiles. Thus it is that the Servant, without introduction or identification, but with the presumption that Israel is intended, appears with a mission to the Gentiles (xlii. 1–4). Hardly, however, has this mission been reaffirmed (xlii. 5–17) than the exact state of Yahweh's servant Israel is disclosed (xlii. 18–25): blind, deaf, imprisoned, and (verse 25) of such spiritual obtuseness that the disciplinary purpose of the calamity has not been seen, nor has the nation been morally reformed by it.

It is this theme of Israel's national and spiritual need which now occupies the prophet until xlviii. 22. Cyrus is foretold as national deliverer, and it is repeatedly asserted that Yahweh will forgive Israel's sin. However, we see Israel leaving Babylon without knowing the peace of God (xlviii. 20–22). But Yahweh has the answer to His people's spiritual need. Cyrus will bring them back from Babylon; the Servant will bring them back to Yahweh (xlix. 1–6). The Servant is called Israel (verse 3), not because the nation, or any part of it, either as it is or viewed in any idealized mode, is the servant, but because the nation has forfeited the name (xlviii. 1), and he alone has the right to use it. Israel has been reduced to One. Having reaffirmed the double task of the Servant (xlix. 7–13), Isaiah proceeds to make clear the distinction between him and the nation: they are despondent (xlix. 14–26) and unresponsive (l. 1–3), but the Servant is full of hope, and obedient at the expense of great suffering (l. 4–9). Now the Servant begins to stand out in his individuality. He is commended to the faithful in the nation for their imitation (l. 10, 11). This shows that he cannot be identified with the 'remnant', the more so in that the latter are now called to watch the great salvation, national (li. 1–3) and universal (li. 4–6) which he will accomplish. It is the national aspect chiefly (though not exclusively, see lii. 10) which occupies the prophet until the moment when he is able to display its great Accomplisher: 'Behold, my Servant' (lii. 13). The Servant's career is summarized in three verses (verses 13–15): exaltation, following on suffering, issuing in world-wide influence. Chapter liii elaborates, showing us the Servant's life among men (verses 1–3), his substitutionary death (verses 4–9), and the inner explanation of it all in the will of Yahweh, who brings His Servant to victory and life after his passion (verses 10–12). Two further chapters complete the story; chapter liv calls Israel into the new covenant, and in chapter lv the call goes out to all the needy to enter a free salvation.

This all too hasty summary has at least displayed the Servant's work, and thereby shown the new feature which the doctrine of the Servant-Messiah introduces into the messianic conception: salvation by means of his vicarious suffering in the place of sinners, for Jew and Gentile alike. We must note also the indications given concerning his person. It is clearest of all that he is a man among men (xlix. 1, l. 4–6, liii. 2, 3, 7–9). Equally, he has remarkable endowments from God: the divine Spirit (xlii. 1) and Word (xlix. 2, l. 4). Two other matters may be noticed. First, it seems likely that in lv. 3, 4 the Servant is identified with the Davidic Messiah. Certainly it is on the basis of the Servant's work that the everlasting covenant is established (*cf.* lv. 3 with liv. 10 and liii. 5b). This covenant is now described as the Davidic mercies, and the leader offered to the peoples is David. Secondly, it may be suggested that by calling the Servant the 'Arm of Yahweh' Isaiah is affirming exactly that identity of and distinction between the Servant and God which has already been noted in the case of the other messianic figures. Certainly, he addresses the Arm of Yahweh in li. 9 as a person and ascribes to it the acts of Yahweh Himself. In liii. 1 he says 'Who could have believed what we heard? Who could have seen here the arm of Yahweh?' (Mowinckel's translation). It is hard to resist the suggestion that the Servant is here set forth in divine terms, at once identified with and distinguished from Yahweh.

(ii) *The Anointed Conqueror.* Isaiah showed a king reigning over Jews and Gentiles (xi), but gave no indication how the Gentiles were to be gathered in. By his teaching on the Servant he completed this picture, depicting a world-wide salvation with all the redeemed brought under David's rule. But in both the kingly and Servant sections (*e.g.* ix. 3–5, xlii. 13, 17, xlv. 16, 24, xlix. 24–26) it was made clear that the work of the king and Servant included the exacting of vengeance on Yahweh's foes. In his third, and complementary, messianic picture the prophet elaborates on this topic. One who, like the king (xi. 2, 4) and the Servant (xlii. 1, xlix. 2), is anointed with the Spirit and the Word appears without warning (just as the others did in their place) in lix. 21. Chapters lvi–lix have been occupied with the moral collapse of God's people and their total inability to keep the law and to save themselves. Yahweh Himself dons the armour of salvation (lix. 16 ff.), whereby He will rout His foes and redeem His people. But the ensuing covenant is made by a mediator, described in terms indubitably reminiscent, as indicated above, of Isaiah's two other messianic figures. The joy of this salvation, which is shared by Jew and Gentile, and which makes Israel supreme over the nations (*cf.* xlv. 14–25), occupies chapter lx.

In chapter lxi the one endowed with Spirit and Word appears again, personally declaring his work of bringing in the acceptable year and the day of vengeance (lxi. 1–3). This task is reaffirmed by Yahweh in verses 4–9, and then again the speaker returns to testify his joy in wearing the garments of salvation. By his being thus apparelled, 'the Lord God will cause righteousness and praise to spring forth before all nations'; *i.e.* he is clothed in the interests of a universal work, of which, none the less, Yahweh is the Doer. Chapter lxii takes up a fuller description of this work in its effects on Zion and the nations (*cf.* the relation of li. 17–lii. 12 to lii. 13 ff.), and in chapter lxiii. 1–6 the Anointed Conqueror, wearing the appointed vesture, accomplishes vengeance and redemption. In his person, this messianic conqueror hardly differs from the king and the Servant. He has the same spiritual endowment; he is a man among men. But two other sidelights are given. First, he is described as the conqueror of Edom, a task accomplished by no other Israelite king but David (*cf.* Nu. xxiv. 17–19). May we not see here the identity of the Anointed Conqueror with the Davidic Messiah? Secondly, in the development of the theme it is he who at the last wears the garments of salvation and vengeance which Yahweh Himself was seen to don (lix. 16 ff.). Once more the prophet introduces the messianic motif: the identity and the distinction of Yahweh and His Anointed.

(iii) *The Branch.* Under this messianic label there is a beautifully unified series of predictions in the Old Testament. Je. xxiii. 5 ff. and xxxiii. 14 ff. are virtually identical. Yahweh will raise a Branch 'unto David'. He is a king in whose days Israel will be saved. His rule is marked by judgment and righteousness. His name is 'Yahweh our Righteousness'.

The second of these passages associates the Branch prophecy with the assertion that the priests shall never want a man to offer sacrifice. This might seem somewhat extraneous were it not for the subsequent use made by Zechariah of the same messianic figure. In Zc. iii. 8 Joshua and his fellow-priests are declared to be a sign of Yahweh's purpose to bring forth 'my servant the Branch', who will accomplish the priestly work of removing the iniquity of the land in one day. Again, in vi. 12 ff., Zechariah returns to the Branch, who shall grow up in his place, build the Temple of Yahweh, be a priest upon his throne, and enjoy perfect, covenanted peace with Yahweh. The Branch is clearly, therefore, the Messiah in his kingly and priestly offices. He is the fulfilment of Ps. cx, with its designation of the king as an eternal Melchizedek-priest.

Having reached this point, it is now fair to refer to Is. iv. 2–6. The messianic reference of verse 2 is a matter of dispute, and is often denied, but, seeing that the following verses agree exactly with the use of the Branch in the passages already cited, the inference can hardly be resisted that the Messiah is found here too. He is the Branch of Yahweh, and he is associated with the priestly work of purging the filth of the daughters of Zion (verse 4) and with the kingly reign of Yahweh in Jerusalem (verses 5, 6). The picture of the Branch summarizes in one figure what Isaiah elsewhere extended and analysed into the work of King, Servant, and Conqueror. The messianic motifs of humanity and divinity, and of identity and distinction in Deity, are present, for the Branch 'belongs to David' and yet is 'Yahweh's'—the very imagery speaking of origin and nature; he is 'my servant', and yet his name is 'Yahweh our righteousness'.

(iv) *The Seed of the Woman.* We have noticed throughout this study that the humanity of the Messiah is stressed. In particular, it is often through the mother that the human origin is described. It is easy to over-emphasize small details, but nevertheless it should be noted that both Immanuel (Is. vii. 14) and the Servant (Is. xlix. 1) are cases in point. Likewise, Mi. v. 3 speaks of 'she that travaileth', and very likely the difficult Je. xxxi. 22 refers to the conception and birth of a remarkable child. The most notable prophecy of the seed of the woman, and the one from which the whole notion may well have arisen, is given in Gn. iii. 15. It has become almost an accepted thing to refuse any messianic reference here, and to regard the verse as 'a quite general statement about mankind and serpents, and the struggle between them' (Mowinckel). But as a direct matter of the exegesis of these chapters in Genesis, and apart altogether from the question of their historicity or otherwise, it is unfair to isolate this verse from its context and to treat it aetiologically. In order to see the force of the promise made in iii. 15, we must pay heed to the part played by the serpent in the tragedy of the fall. Gn. ii. 19 shows man's superiority over the animal creation. The Creator graciously instructs the man as to his difference from the mere animals: he can impose his order upon them, but among them there is not found any 'help meet for him'. His like is not there.

But now, in chapter iii, another phenomenon meets us: a talking animal, an animal which somehow has risen above its station, and presents itself as man's equal, able to engage him in intelligent conversation, and even as his superior, able to instruct him in matters wherein he was formerly misguided, to give him what purports to be a correct understanding of God's law and God's person. The serpent speaks as one well able to weigh God in the balances and find Him wanting, to discern the inner thoughts of the Almighty and to expose His underhand motives! Even more, he displays open hostility to God; a hatred of God's character, a readiness to destroy His creation-plan, a sneering mockery of the most High. It is simply not good enough to see in the serpent the spirit of man's irrepressible curiosity (Williams) or any such thing. The Bible knows only one who displays this ungodly arrogance, this hatred of God, and it is exegetically required that the serpent in Eden is but the tool of 'the old serpent, which is the Devil, and Satan' (Rev. xx. 2). But where sin abounds, grace superabounds, and so it is that at the very moment when Satan seems to have scored a signal triumph it is declared that the seed of the woman will crush and destroy Satan. He will be himself bruised in the process, but will be victorious. The seed of the woman will reverse the whole calamity of the fall.

(v) *The Son of Man.* We end our survey of Old Testament messianism by a brief reference to Daniel's vision of the Son of Man (Dn. vii. 1–28). In a matter which has aroused so much discussion and difference of opinion it is only possible here, as throughout this article, to state one point of view. The essence of the vision is the judgment scene, wherein the Ancient of Days disposes of the worldly and hostile powers—we note in passing the reappearance of the kingly motif of Psalm ii—and there is brought to him 'with the clouds of heaven one like unto a son of man' who receives a universal and everlasting dominion. It is clear that the general reference here must be associated in some way with the universal dominion already generally observed in the messianic passages, but the question whether the 'one like unto a son of man' is the messianic individual or is intended to be a personification of the people of God must not be thus summarily settled. It is urged that verses 18 and 22 speak of judgment and the kingdom being given to the 'saints of the most High', and that therefore reason demands that the same recipients must be intended by the single figure of verses 13, 14.

However, we may also notice that there is a double description of the beasts who are the enemies of the saints. Verse 17 says 'these great beasts . . . are four kings' and verse 23 says 'the fourth beast shall be the fourth kingdom'. The figures are both individual (kings) and corporate (kingdoms). We must adopt the same preliminary reference for the 'one like unto a son of man'. Next, we must view the king–kingdom relationship in its Old Testament context. The king is prior, and the kingdom is derivative. It is not the kingdom which fashions the king, but the reverse. As for the beast-kings, they are the personal enemies of the kingdom of the saints, and they involve their kingdoms with them; equally the 'one like unto a son of man' receives universal dominion, and in this is implicated the dominion of his people (*cf.* the dominion of Israel in the dominion of the conqueror, Is. lx, *etc.*). On this ground it is urged that the 'one like unto a son of man' is the messianic individual. As such, he fits into the general pattern found throughout the whole series of expectations: he is a king, opposed by the world, but achieving universal dominion by the zeal of the Lord, *i.e.* from the Ancient of Days, in Daniel's imagery; he is man, by the terms of his title, and yet he does not originate among men but comes 'with the clouds of heaven', a position characteristic of God (see, *e.g.*, Ps. civ. 3; Na. i. 3; Is. xix. 1). Here is the same polarity of human and divine which is found almost without exception in Old Testament messianism, and which in the fulness of time was fully perfected in our Prophet, Priest, and King, Jesus the Messiah. J.A.M.

II. IN THE NEW TESTAMENT

Heb. *māšîaḥ* or Aramaic *m^ešîḥā'* is twice transliterated into Gk. as *messias* (Jn. i. 41, iv. 25, in both of which places the word is glossed by *christos*). Elsewhere it is represented by Gk. *christos* ('anointed', verbal adjective from *chriō*, 'anoint'), rendered 'Christ' in AV, RV, RSV. Since, however, in modern usage 'Christ' is practically an alternative or additional name of Jesus, and does not immediately suggest its original sense, NEB frequently translates *christos* by 'Messiah' where the original sense is plainly required (*cf.*, *e.g.*, Mt. i. 18, xvi. 16, 20, xxvi. 63, xxvii. 22; Mk. viii. 29, xiv. 61; Lk. ii. 11, 26, ix. 20, xxii. 67; Jn. iv. 29, vii. 26 f., 31, 41 f., ix. 22, x. 24; Acts ii. 36, iii. 20, iv. 26 f., v. 42, ix. 22, xvii. 3, xviii. 28, xxvi. 23).

The Messiah is Jesus of Nazareth, who at His baptism was 'anointed . . . with the Holy Ghost and with power' (Acts x. 38; *cf.* the implication of Jesus' quotation of Is. lxi. 1 in Lk. iv. 18). But He Himself rarely employed the term, no doubt because of the misunderstanding to which its employment would give rise. When Peter confessed Him to be the Christ He accepted the designation, but ordered His disciples not to tell anyone else (Mk. viii. 29 f.). In His conversation with the Samaritan woman (Jn. iv. 25 f.) the term would be understood in the light of the Samaritan expectation of the *Taheb* or 'restorer', the prophet like Moses promised in Dt. xviii. 15 ff. When, however, He was challenged by the high priest at His trial to say whether or not He was 'the Christ, the Son of the Blessed', He agreed that He was, and the language of His reply, with its implied claim to be the peer of the Almighty, led to a unanimous verdict of guilty on the score of blasphemy (Mk. xiv. 61–64). This verdict, with the ensuing death-sentence, was reversed by God, who raised Him from the dead and exalted Him to His 'right hand', thus proclaiming the crucified Jesus as 'Lord and Messiah' (Acts ii. 36, NEB; *cf.* Rom. i. 4).

But Jesus understood and fulfilled His messianic vocation in a different way from that popularly associated with the expected Messiah. The heavenly voice at His baptism (Mk. i. 11) acclaimed Him as the Davidic Messiah, in the words 'Thou art my Son' of Ps. ii. 7, but by adding words in which the Servant of Yahweh is introduced in Is. xlii. 1 indicated that His Messiahship was to be realized in terms of the portrayal of the Servant, humble, obedient, suffering, accomplishing His mission by passing through death, and committing His vindication confidently to God. His ministry, crowned by His passion, was characterized by steadfast adherence to the path thus marked out for Him by His Father; and in consequence Jesus has given to the word 'Messiah' a new meaning, transcending every connotation which it previously bore.

BIBLIOGRAPHY. (The occasional names bracketed above refer to the authors and works now listed.) H. Ringgren, *The Messiah in the Old Testament*, 1956; A. Bentzen, *King and Messiah*, 1955; H. L. Ellison, *The Centrality of the Messianic Idea for the Old Testament*, 1953; F. Delitzsch, *Messianic Prophecies in Historical Succession*, 1891; N. P. Williams, *The Ideas of the Fall and of Original Sin*, 1927, pp. 43 ff.; S. Mowinckel, *He That Cometh*, 1956; J. Klausner, *The Messianic Idea in Israel*, 1956; B. B. Warfield, 'The Divine Messiah in the Old Testament', reprinted in *Biblical and Theological Studies*, 1952; H. H. Rowley, *The Servant of the Lord*, 1952; O. T. Allis, *The Unity of Isaiah*, 1951; E. J. Young, *Daniel's Vision of the Son of Man*, 1958; *id.*, *Studies in Isaiah*, 1954; *id.*, *Old Testament Theology Today*, 1958, pp. 65 ff.; A. R. Johnson, *Sacral Kingship in Ancient Israel*, 1955; *id.*, 'The Psalms', in *The Old Testament and Modern Study* (ed. H. H. Rowley), 1951; Th. C. Vriezen, *An Outline of Old Testament Theology*, 1958, pp. 350 ff.; G. A. F. Knight, *A Christian Theology of the Old Testament*, 1959, pp. 294 ff.; H. Gressmann, *Der Messias*, 1929; W. Manson, *Jesus the Messiah*, 1943; T. W. Manson, *The Servant-Messiah*, 1953; Y. Kaufmann, *The Religion of Israel*, 1961, *s.v.* 'Messiah'. F.F.B.

METALS. See MINING AND METALS.

METHEG-AMMAH. Apparent textual corruption in 2 Sa. viii. 1 makes this name difficult to understand. No certainty seems possible, and at least three alternative interpretations present themselves. 1. That it is a place-name, evidently near Gath in the Philistine plain. 2. That the RV translation, 'the bridle of the mother city', be preferred—*i.e.* regarding it as a figurative name for Gath, a chief city of the Philistines (*cf.* 1 Ch. xviii. 1). 3. That LXX be followed and the verse rendered as 'and David took the tribute out of the hand of the Philistines'. J.D.D.

METHUSELAH (*m*ᵉ*ṯûšelaḥ*). The eighth Patriarch listed in the genealogy of Gn. v. He was the son of Enoch and grandfather of Noah. He lived to the great age of 969 years according to the Hebrew and the LXX (the Samaritan gives 720 years). Though they are both rendered in the LXX by *Mathousala*, there is no reason to assume that *m*ᵉ*ṯûšelaḥ* and *m*ᵉ*ṯûšā'ēl* (Gn. iv. 18) were the same person. T.C.M.

MEUNIM. See MINAEANS, MAON, MAONITES.

ME-ZAHAB. The grandfather of Mehetabel who was the wife of Hadar (see HADAD), king of Edom (Gn. xxxvi. 39 = 1 Ch. i. 50). The form is that of a place- rather than personal-name (*mê-zāhāḇ*, 'waters of gold'), but a man may sometimes be named after a place with which he is associated. T.C.M.

MICAH, MICAIAH ('who is like Yah?'). A common Hebrew name, variously spelt in both AV and *MT*. Of the many men named with one of these forms, three are better known than the rest. **1.** Micah of Moresheth the prophet. (See under MICAH, BOOK OF.) **2.** Micah of Mt. Ephraim, whose strange story is told in Jdg. xvii, xviii, presumably to explain the origin of the sanctuary at Dan and incidentally relating the migration of the Danites to their new territory. **3.** Micaiah the son of Imlah, a prophet in Israel in the days of Ahab (1 Ki. xxii. 4–28; 2 Ch. xviii. 3–27). Nothing is known of him except for this single interview he had with Ahab, but we may deduce that he had prophesied before and that Ahab was aware of his unfavourable messages. Probably he was brought out of prison to appear before Ahab, and there may be some truth in Josephus' tradition that he was the unknown prophet of 1 Ki. xx. 35–43.
J.B.Tr.

MICAH, BOOK OF (*mîḵâ*, abbreviated form of *mîḵāy*ᵉ*hû*, 'who is like Yahweh?').

I. OUTLINE OF CONTENTS

a. The coming judgment upon Israel (i. 1–16).

b. Israel to be punished, then restored (ii. 1–13).

c. Condemnation of the princes and prophets (iii. 1–12).

d. The coming glory and peace of Jerusalem (iv. 1–13).

e. The suffering and restoration of Zion (v. 1–15).

f. Prophetic and popular religion contrasted (vi. 1–16).

g. Corruption of society; concluding statement of trust in God (vii. 1–20).

II. AUTHORSHIP AND DATE

Authorship is usually attributed to Micah of Moresheth (i. 1), whose home, identified with Moresheth-gath (*q.v.*) in the Shephelah or lowlands of Judah, was the general locale of his prophetic activity (i. 14). A younger contemporary of Isaiah, he uttered his sayings during the reigns of Jotham (*c.* 742–735 BC), Ahaz (*c.* 735–715 BC), and Hezekiah of Judah (*c.* 715–687 BC).

Some modern scholars have maintained that only Mi. i. 2–ii. 10 and parts of chapters iv and v are the work of the prophet himself. While the last two chapters of the book have much in them that is akin to the work of Micah, critics have urged that the difference in background and style from earlier portions of the prophecy, and the comparatively subordinate position which they occupy in the book, require them to be assigned to a time later than the 8th century BC. In particular, vii. 7–20 is held to be definitely post-exilic.

Other scholars have claimed that the forceful, descriptive style which is evident in each chapter of the prophecy, and the consistent revelation of divine judgment, compassion, and hope, are powerful arguments for the unity of authorship of the prophecy. Arguments from style are never particularly strong at the best, since style can be altered so easily with a change of subject-matter. Furthermore, it is not easy to see why vii. 7–20 should be assigned to a post-exilic period, since there is nothing in the content which is in the slightest degree at variance with the language or theology of the 8th-century BC prophets. The closing verses of the book are read each year by Jewish worshippers in the afternoon service on the Day of Atonement.

III. BACKGROUND AND MESSAGE

Although he lived in rural surroundings, Micah was familiar with the corruptions of city life in Israel and Judah. His denunciations were directed particularly at Jerusalem (iv. 10), and like Amos and Isaiah he noted how the wealthy landowners took every advantage of the poor (ii. 1 f.). He condemned the corruption rampant among the religious leaders of his day (ii. 11) and the gross miscarriages of justice perpetrated by those dedicated to the upholding of the law (iii. 10). The fact that all this was carried on in an atmosphere of false religiosity (iii. 11) proved for Micah to be the crowning insult.

Like his 8th-century BC contemporaries Amos, Hosea, and Isaiah, Micah stressed the essential righteousness and morality of the divine nature. He was concerned also to point out that these qualities had pressing ethical implications for the life of the individual and the community alike. If the people of Israel and Judah were to take their covenant obligations at all seriously the justice which characterized the nature of God must be reflected in a similar state of affairs among the people of God.

Whereas Amos and Hosea had a good deal to

say about the idolatry and immorality which were rampant in Israel and Judah as a result of the influence of pagan Canaanite religion, Micah confined his utterances to the problems arising from the social injustices perpetrated upon the small landowners, farmers, and peasants. He warned those who wrongfully deprived others of their possessions that God was devising a drastic punishment for them. His denunciation of the rulers of Israel (iii. 1–4) and the false prophets (iii. 5–8) envisaged the ultimate destruction of Jerusalem because the corruption which they represented had permeated to the very core of national life.

Micah was in general accord with Amos, Hosea, and Isaiah in his belief that God would use a pagan nation to punish His own guilty people. As a result he foretold clearly the depredations of Shalmaneser V in the northern kingdom, and the ultimate destruction of Samaria, capital of Israel (i. 6–9). He did not view the collapse of the northern kingdom in quite the same broad terms as did Isaiah, however. To Micah it brought the threat of invasion to the very doors of 'this family' (ii. 3), making the Assyr. invader Sennacherib the herald of a larger doom (v. 5 ff.).

There is a striking resemblance between the prophecies of devastation proclaimed for Samaria (i. 6) and Jerusalem (iii. 12). A century after his death the words of Micah concerning the downfall of Zion were still remembered (Je. xxvi. 18 f.). On that occasion the prophet Jeremiah might well have been put to death for prophesying destruction for the Temple and the Holy City had not certain elders of the land recalled that Micah of Moresheth had said precisely the same thing a hundred years earlier. For Micah there could be no question as to the ultimate fate of the house of Judah. So pervasive and influential was the depraved religion of Canaan, and so widespread was the resultant corruption of society that nothing short of the exercise of divine judgment upon the southern kingdom could avail for the ultimate salvation of the people of God. But before the remnant of Jacob could experience this saving grace it would be necessary for all idolatry and social corruption to be rooted out (v. 10–15).

This experience would be one of tribulation and sorrow, during which the voice of prophecy would cease (iii. 6, 7), and the sin of the nation would become evident (iii. 8). Consequent upon this would come the destruction of Jerusalem and the shame of captivity in the midst of other peoples (v. 7, 8). Restoration would be marked by a new universalistic religion in a restored Jerusalem. Under divine judgment swords would be beaten into ploughshares and spears into pruning-hooks (iv. 3), and the people of God would honour His name only (iv. 5). Prominent in the thought of Micah was the expectation of a Messiah to be born in Bethlehem (v. 2). This personage would come forth from the common people, delivering them from oppression and injustice and restoring the remainder of the Israelite family to fellowship with the remnant in Zion.

Micah was at pains to point out that the saving grace of God could not be earned (vi. 6–8), either by pretentious sacrificial offerings or by indulgence in elaborate ritual forms of worship. Humility, mercy, and justice must be an everyday experience in the life of the person who was to be well-pleasing to God.

BIBLIOGRAPHY. P. Haupt, *Amer. Journ. Sem. Lang. Lit.*, XXVII, 1910, pp. 1–63; W. Nowack in *HDB*, 1900; A. J. Tait, *The Prophecy of Micah*, 1917; J. M. P. Smith, *ICC*, 1911, pp. 5–156; G. A. Smith, *The Book of the Twelve Prophets*, I, 1928, pp. 381 ff.; S. Goldman in *Soncino Commentary*, 1948. R.K.H.

MICE. See MOUSE.

MICHAEL (*mîḵā'ēl*, 'who is like God?'—synonymous with Micaiah and Micah). The name of eleven biblical characters, only one of whom gets more than a passing reference. The exception is the angel Michael, who in pseudepigraphic literature is regarded as the patron of, and intercessor for, Israel (1 Enoch xx. 5, lxxxix. 76). In the Book of Daniel he is more particularly the guardian of the Jews from the menace of the godless power of Greece and Persia (xii. 1), and is styled as 'one of the chief princes' and as 'your prince' (x. 13, 21). In this capacity it is peculiarly fitting that he should be the archangel represented (Jude 9) as 'contending with the devil . . . about the body of Moses', that great leader of God's people to whom an angel (perhaps Michael) spoke in Mount Sinai (Acts vii. 38). Michael further appears in Rev. xii. 7 as waging war in heaven against the dragon. For further discussion, see ANGEL and R. H. Charles, *Studies in the Apocalypse*, 1913, pp. 158–161. J.D.D.

MICHAL (*mîḵal*) was Saul's younger daughter (1 Sa. xiv. 49). Instead of her sister Merab she was married to David, for a dowry of a hundred Philistine foreskins (1 Sa. xviii. 20 ff.). Her prompt action and resourcefulness saved him from Saul (1 Sa. xix. 11–17). During his exile she was given in marriage to Phalti(el), son of Laish, of Gallim (1 Sa. xxv. 44). After Saul's death, when Abner wanted to treat with him, David demanded her restitution—a political move to strengthen his claim to the throne. Having brought the ark to Jerusalem, he danced before it with such abandon that Michal despised him (2 Sa. vi. 12 ff.). For this reason she remained childless for ever (2 Sa. vi. 23). Five sons are mentioned (2 Sa. xxi. 8), but tradition holds that they were Merab's (so LXX and two Heb. MSS), and that Michal 'reared them'.

On one view David married Michal at Hebron 'to unite the tribes of Israel and the clans of Judah' (*EBi*); but the idea that she had one son, Ithream, her name being corrupted to Eglah (2 Sa. iii. 5), is without foundation. M.G.

MICHMASH, MICHMAS. A city of Benjamin east of Bethel and 7 miles north of Jerusalem, 2,000 feet above sea-level, on the pass from Bethel to Jericho. In Geba, just south of this pass, Jonathan made a successful foray against the Philistine garrison (1 Sa. xiii. 3), whereupon the Philistines gathered a large well-equipped army and occupied Michmash, causing the scattered flight of the Hebrews (xiii. 5 ff.). Thereafter Saul's army camped at Geba (or Gibeah) with the Philistines on the other side of the pass (xiii. 23).

Unknown to Saul, Jonathan and his armour-bearer descended from Geba and, ascending the southern slope, surprised the Philistines and caused confusion in the enemy camp (for a description of this feat, see S. R. Driver, *Notes on the Hebrew Text of the Books of Samuel*[2], 1913, p. 106). Aided by Hebrew prisoners who had been in Philistine hands, by refugees from the previous defeat, and by Saul's army, they put the Philistines to rout (1 Sa. xiv. 1 ff.).

In his prophetic description of the coming attack on Jerusalem Isaiah (x. 24, 28) represents the taking of Michmash by the Assyrians. After the Exile members of the Jewish community lived in Michmash (Ezr. ii. 27; Ne. vii. 31, xi. 31), and it was later the residence of Jonathan Maccabeus (1 Macc. ix. 73).

It is the present Mukhmâs, a ruined village on the northern ridge of the Wadi Suweinit.

J.D.D.

MICHTAM. See PSALMS.

MIDIANITES. They consisted of five families, linked to Abraham through Midian, son of the concubine Keturah. Abraham sent them away, with all his other sons by concubines, into the east (Gn. xxv. 1–6). Thus the Midianites are found inhabiting desert borders in Transjordan from Moab down past Edom. They were desert-dwellers associated with Ishmaelites and Medanites (Gn. xxxvii. 28, 36) when Joseph was sold into Egypt; for the partial overlap of these three terms, see JOSEPH and *cf.* Jdg. viii. 24, where the Midianites defeated by Gideon are said to have been Ishmaelites because of their use of gold ear- or nose-rings. Moses had a Midianite wife, Zipporah, father-in-law, Jethro/Reuel (Ex. ii. 21, iii. 1, *etc.*), and brother-in-law, Hobab (Nu. x. 29; Jdg. iv. 11, RV). As a man of the desert, Hobab was asked by Moses to guide Israel in travelling through the steppe (or 'wilderness') (Nu. x. 29–32).

Later, in the plains of Moab, the chiefs of Midian and Moab combined in hiring Balaam to curse Israel (Nu. xxii ff.) and their people led Israel into idolatry and immorality (Nu. xxv), and so had to be vanquished (Nu. xxv. 16–18, xxxi). The five princes of Midian were confederates of the Amorite king Sihon (Jos. xiii. 21). In the time of the judges, through Gideon and his puny band (Jdg. vi–viii, ix. 17), God delivered Israel from the scourge of camel-riding Midianites, Amalekites, and other 'children of the east', an event remembered by psalmist and prophet (Ps. lxxxiii. 9; Is. ix. 4, x. 26). This is at present the earliest-known reference to full-scale use of camels in warfare (W. F. Albright, *Archaeology and the Religion of Israel*, 1953, pp. 132, 133), but by no means the first occurrence of domesticated camels (see CAMEL; and W. G. Lambert, *BASOR*, 160, 1960, pp. 42, 43, for indirect Old Babylonian evidence). The dromedaries of Midian recur in Is. lx. 6. In Hab. iii. 7 Midian is put in parallel with Cushan, an ancient term that probably goes back to *Kushu* mentioned in Egyptian texts of *c.* 1800 BC (see W. F. Albright, *BASOR*, 83, 1941, p. 34, note 8; *cf.* G. Posener, *Princes et Pays d'Asie et de Nubie*, 1940, p. 88, and B. Maisler, *Revue d'Histoire Juive en Égypte*, No. 1, 1947, pp. 37, 38). See also ETHIOPIAN WOMAN.

K.A.K.

MIDRASH. See TALMUD AND MIDRASH.

MIDWIFE (Heb. *m*[e]*yalle̱ḏet*, 'one who helps to bear'). The midwife helped at childbirth by taking the new-born child, cutting its umbilical cord, washing the babe with water, salting, and wrapping it (Ezk. xvi. 4); the birth was then announced to the father (Je. xx. 15). In Hebrew tradition, midwives are first mentioned in the time of Jacob, attending on Rachel (Gn. xxxv. 17) and Tamar (Gn. xxxviii. 28); in the latter case the midwife put a red thread on one twin to mark the first one born, *i.e.* technically the eldest.

In Mesopotamia and Egypt and among the Hebrews women very often crouched down in childbirth upon a pair of bricks or stones—the *'o̱ḇnayim* of Ex. i. 16—or on a birthstool of similar pattern. All this can be well illustrated from ancient sources. The Egyptian Papyrus Westcar, written in the Hyksos period (*c.* 1700/1600 BC), records how three goddesses delivered a priest's wife of three sons: one took each child on her arms, they cut the umbilical cord, washed the children, and put them on a cloth on a little brick bench, then went to announce the births to the waiting husband (Erman-Blackman, *Literature of the Ancient Egyptians*, 1927, pp. 44, 45). This text also illustrates the giving of punning names to children at birth as in Genesis and elsewhere. In Egyptian the two bricks or stones (and also birthstools) were called *ḏb't*, 'the brick(s)', or *msḫnt*, the latter word being followed in writing by the hieroglyph of a brick or of a pair of bricks, or of a birthstool (plan-view), *etc.* The Egyptian word *msỉ*, 'to give birth', was often followed by the hieroglyph of a crouching woman in the act of birth, and in one late text the figure is actually shown crouching on two bricks or stones. See W. Spiegelberg, *Aegyptologische Randglossen zum Alten Testament*, 1904, pp. 19–25.

K.A.K.

MIGDOL. The name is used of a Canaanite fort. Mentioned as a place-name in Ex. xiv. 2; Nu. xxxiii. 7; Je. xliv. 1, xlvi. 14; Ezk. xxix. 10, xxx. 6. Several Migdols were built in the neighbourhood of the Egyptian border, but none of them can be accurately located. The Migdol of the Prophets, in the north of Egypt (possibly at Tell el-Her), is different from that in the south (P. Anastasi V), which is probably the Migdol of Succoth (Old Egyp. *ṯkw*). The Migdol in the north may be the Magdolum of *Itinerarium Antonini*, at 12 Roman miles from Pelusium. See ENCAMPMENT BY THE SEA. C.D.W.

MIGRON. 1. A place mentioned in 1 Sa. xiv. 2 situated on the outskirts of Saul's home at Gibeah, where he remained during the first stage of the Philistine invasion after his election as king. It is possibly identical with **2,** a locality mentioned in the march of the Assyr. army in Is. x. 28, the modern Tell Miryam, north of Michmash.

MILCAH (*milkâ*, 'counsel'). **1.** The daughter of Haran (Abraham's brother) and wife of Nahor (Gn. xi. 29). Her children are named in Gn. xxii. 20 ff. Rebekah was her granddaughter (Gn. xxiv. 15, 24, 47). **2.** One of the five daughters of Zelophehad of the tribe of Manasseh. Because they had no brothers, they were given an inheritance when the land was divided (Nu. xxvi. 33, xxvii. 1, xxxvi. 11; Jos. xvii. 3). See ZELOPHEHAD.

MILCOM. The national deity of the Ammonites (see MALCAM, MOLECH). The basic root *mlk* enables an identification of these three forms of the name of this god (*milkōm*, *malkām*, *mōleḵ*). Solomon married an Ammonite princess and went 'after Milcom the abomination of the Ammonites' (1 Ki. xi. 5). Josiah was later to break down the high place that Solomon erected for this god (2 Ki. xxiii. 13). J.A.T.

MILDEW (*yērāqôn*, 'paleness', 'greenness'; *cf.* LXX *ikteros*, 'jaundice'). A common species of fungus (*Puccinia graminis*) which, produced by moisture, attacks the crops in Palestine. In biblical times it was regarded as God's punishment on the disobedient (Dt. xxviii. 22; Am. iv. 9; Hg. ii. 17), and Solomon prayed for deliverance from it (1 Ki. viii. 37; 2 Ch. vi. 28). The Bible always mentions mildew in conjunction with the opposite condition, 'blasting' (Heb. *šiddāpôn*, lit. 'scorching'), a drying up of plants by the hot *ḥemsīn* wind from the south. J.D.D.

MILE. See WEIGHTS AND MEASURES.

MILETUS. The southernmost of the great Ionian (Gk.) cities on the west coast of Asia Minor. It flourished as a commercial centre, and in the 8th, 7th, and 6th centuries BC established many colonies in the Black Sea area and also had contact with Egypt. Pharaoh Necho dedicated an offering in a Milesian temple after his victory at Megiddo in 608 BC (2 Ki. xxiii. 29; 2 Ch. xxxv. 20 ff.). The Milesians resisted the expansion of Lydia, and in 499 BC initiated the Ionian revolt against Persia, but their city was destroyed in 494. In its period of great prosperity Miletus was the home of the first Gk. philosophers Thales, Anaximander, and Anaximenes, and of Hecataeus the chronicler and map-maker. Milesian woollen goods were world famous.

After its Persian destruction the city had many vicissitudes, and when Paul called there (Acts xx. 15; 2 Tim. iv. 20) it was largely living on its past glories. At this time it was part of the Roman province of Asia, and due to the silting up of its harbour (nowadays an inland lake) by deposits from the river Maeander it was declining commercially. An inscription in the ruins shows the place reserved in the stone theatre for Jews and 'god-fearing' people. K.L.McK.

MILK (Heb. *ḥālāḇ*; Gk. *gala*). Milk was part of the staple diet of the Hebrews from patriarchal times, and where there was abundance of milk (Is. vii. 22) it was possible to enjoy the added delicacy of cream or curdled milk (Heb. *ḥem'â*, 'butter'). Hence the attraction of the land of Canaan as a land flowing with milk and honey (Ex. iii. 8), for the rich supply of milk was an indication of the pasturage available. *ḥālāḇ* might be the milk of cows or sheep (Dt. xxxii. 14; Is. vii. 22), goats (Pr. xxvii. 27), or possibly in patriarchal times of camels also (Gn. xxxii. 15). It was contained in buckets, if RVmg is the correct rendering of the *hapax legomenon* in Jb. xxi. 24, and in skin-bottles (Jdg. iv. 19), from which it could conveniently be poured out for the refreshment of strangers (Gn. xviii. 8) or as a drink with meals (Ezk. xxv. 4). It is coupled with honey frequently, and with wine (Gn. xlix. 12; Is. lv. 1; Joel iii. 18), with which it may sometimes have been mingled as a rich delicacy (Ct. v. 1). The phrase 'honey and milk are under thy tongue' (Ct. iv. 11) refers to the sweet conversation of the loved one.

Its metaphorical use to describe the land of Canaan has been mentioned; Egypt was also so described by the embittered Israelites during the years of wandering (Nu. xvi. 13). Elsewhere it stands alone as a symbol of prosperity and abundance (Is. lx. 16; Joel iii. 18), and it is therefore not surprising that later Judaism compared it with the Torah. Kimchi says of Is. lv. 1, 'As milk feeds and nourishes a child, so the law feeds and nourishes the soul.' This is a similar figure to that used in the New Testament of young converts imbibing the 'sincere milk of the word' (1 Pet. ii. 2; RSV 'pure spiritual milk'), though Paul carries the metaphor further and considers milk unworthy of mature disciples (1 Cor. iii. 2; *cf.* Heb. v. 12 f.).

The strange Mosaic prohibition of seething a kid in its mother's milk (Ex. xxiii. 19, xxxiv. 26; Dt. xiv. 21) probably referred originally to a Canaanite ritual. On this verse, however, has been built the entire Jewish dietary law forbidding milk to be consumed at any meal at which meat is eaten, the cleavage between the two foods being so great that among orthodox Jews separate kitchen equipment has to be provided for the preparation of milk and meat dishes. J.B.Tr.

MILL, MILLSTONE. The oldest and most common method of grinding corn was to spread it on a flat stone slab and rub it with a round stone muller. Such stone querns have been found in the early Neolithic town at Jericho, together with stone mortars (*PEQ*, LXXXV, 1953, pl. XXXVIII. 2; for an Egyptian model, see *ANEP*, no. 149). The rotary quern came into general use in the Iron Age. This consisted of two circular stone slabs, each about 18 inches across, the upper one (Heb. *reḵeḇ*, 'rider') pierced through to revolve on a pivot fixed to the lower (*cf.* the illustration of a potter's wheel, fig. 20). A wooden stick projecting from a hole near the outer edge of the upper stone was the handle. The grain was poured through the pivot-hole in the upper stone and crushed as this turned, so that the flour spilled from between the two stones (Heb. *rēḥayîm*) on to the ground. It was the woman's task to grind the corn (Ex. xi. 5; Mt. xxiv. 41), but it was also imposed upon prisoners as a menial service (Is. xlvii. 2; La. v. 13). Larger types of rotary quern were turned by animals, or by prisoners (Samson, Jdg. xvi. 21) and were kept in a mill-house (Mt. xxiv. 41, Gk. *mylōn*).

Since the Israelite depended on the hand-mill for his daily bread, he was forbidden to give it in pledge (Dt. xxiv. 6). Cessation of the steady, constant sound of grinding was a sign of desolation and death (Je. xxv. 10; Rev. xviii. 22, a simile for the old man's teeth; Ec. xii. 4). The upper stone was used on occasion as a missile in war (Jdg. ix. 53; 2 Sa. xi. 21) and as a weight (Mt. xviii. 6, Gk. *mylos onikos*, the largest sort of mill-stone, turned by an ass; Rev. xviii. 21). See MORTAR AND PESTLE. A.R.M.

MILLENNIUM. See ESCHATOLOGY (IX).

MILLO. A place-name derived from the verb *mālē*', 'to be full', 'to fill'. It is used in Jdg. ix. 6, 20 of a place near Shechem, the 'house of Millo', perhaps a fortress; but its principal use is in connection with Jerusalem (*q.v.*). It was probably part of the fortification of the Jebusite city, perhaps a solid tower ('full') or a bastion 'filling' some weak point in the walls, for it was evidently already in existence in the time of David (2 Sa. v. 9 = 1 Ch. xi. 8). It was rebuilt by Solomon (1 Ki. ix. 15, 24, xi. 27; the 'breach' here referred to was probably a different thing) as part of his programme of strengthening the kingdom, and was again strengthened some two and a half centuries later when Hezekiah was preparing for the Assyrian invasion (2 Ch. xxxii. 5). This verse is taken by some to indicate that Millo was another name for the whole city of David, but it is more probable that it formed part of the defences of this, the south-eastern hill of later Jerusalem. Many theories have been put forward as to what part of the city of David was strengthened by the Millo, but excavation has not yet been sufficiently systematic to make identification possible. Millo is only otherwise mentioned as the place where Joash was murdered (2 Ki. xii. 20). The LXX usually translates Millo by the name Akra, but this was a Maccabean structure. For a suggestion as to the type of construction indicated by the term *millô*', see ARCHITECTURE.

BIBLIOGRAPHY. J. Simons, *Jerusalem in the Old Testament*, 1952, pp. 131–144. T.C.M.

MINAEANS. The people of the kingdom of Ma'īn which flourished in SW Arabia (in the north of modern Yemen) in the first millennium BC. The name is that of a tribe which became dominant in a state known from inscriptions to have been established with Qarnāw as its capital by about 400 BC. It was active in establishing trade links with the north, having colonies along the Red Sea coastal route to Palestine, the best known being Dedan (*q.v.*). Towards the end of the 1st century BC Ma'īn was absorbed by the expansion of its southern neighbour Saba (see SABAEANS) and its northern colonies lost their Minaean identity. The name does not occur with certainty anywhere in the Bible, though some scholars would see it in Jdg. x. 12 (Maonites); 1 Ch. iv. 41 (AV 'habitation'); 2 Ch. xx. 1 (altering Ammonites); 2 Ch. xxvi. 7 (Mehunims); Ezr. ii. 50 = Ne. vii. 52 (Mehunim). See MAONITES and also ARABIA.

BIBLIOGRAPHY. J. A. Montgomery, *Arabia and the Bible*, 1934, pp. 60, 61, 133–138, 182–184; S. Moscati, *Ancient Semitic Civilizations*, 1957, pp. 184–194. T.C.M.

MIND. See HEART.

MINING AND METALS. The theatre of Old Testament history is the so-called 'Fertile Crescent' (*i.e.* Mesopotamia, Syria, Palestine and the Nile Delta). The alluvial plains of the Tigris–Euphrates and Nile valleys provide but little stone. Much of Assyria's gypsum, indeed, comes from stone quarries near Mosul; and there is a worked vein of stone near Ur. But for the most part in those valleys clay bricks were used for building purposes in ancient times (Gn. xi. 3; Ex. i. 11–14, v. 7–19).

The 'Crescent' is bounded on the north and east by high folded mountain chains consisting of rocks of many types and ages. The ranges are well mineralized and provide ores of gold, silver, copper, tin, lead, and iron. On the south a complex of ancient rocks appears in which such types as granite, diorite, and porphyry occur. This group extends along the eastern desert between the river Nile and the Red Sea, across the southern half of the Sinai peninsula and eastwards into the Arabian plateau. In some of these rocks occur gold, silver, iron, turquoise, and other semi-precious stones, together with building stones of many kinds.

North of Sinai and the Arabian plateau lie the desert, Transjordan, and Palestine. These are composed mainly of cretaceous rocks (limestone, chalk, and sandstone), but north and east of the upper Jordan are areas of newer volcanic basalts. See fig. 155.

I. NON-METALLIC MATERIALS

a. Flint

Tools of this material have been found in Palestine dating from the Old to the New Stone Age. This covers a vast period of time measured in thousands of years. The New Stone Age (Neolithic) ended about 6,000 years ago. Flint occurs abundantly in the chalk of the area and in gravels derived from the chalk. Flint is a close-grained hard rock which a knife-blade will not scratch. It breaks with a hollow, shell-like fracture, which makes it ideal for producing a sharp cutting edge. Stone-Age man made arrow-heads, chisels, scrapers, and knives of it. Flints continued to be used well into the Bronze period. Zipporah, wife of Moses, circumcised her son with a flint knife (Ex. iv. 25). Flint is referred to in Scripture to denote hardness, inflexibility, steadfastness (Dt. viii. 15; Ps. cxiv. 8; Is. l. 7; Ezk. iii. 9).

b. Stone

Away from the alluvial plains of Mesopotamia and Lower Egypt supplies were plentiful. In Egypt granite, diorite, and other igneous rocks, together with sandstones and limestones, were at hand, and in Palestine limestone, sandstone, and basalt, which occurred east of the upper Jordan valley. The quarrying and erection of huge standing stones in Neolithic times gave experience for future quarrying and mining. Limestone is easily worked, being fairly soft, and was used for the excavation of cisterns, tombs, and the making of such things as water-pots (Je. ii. 13; Mt. xxvii. 60; Jn. ii. 6).

c. Marble

This is a close-grained crystalline limestone, usually white or cream in colour. It may be pink or veined in red or green. The best statuary marble in the Near East came from Paros (Minoa), but it also occurs on the western coast of the Gulf of Suez, in southern Greece, and in Assyria east of the river Tigris. 'Marble stones in abundance' are mentioned in 1 Ch. xxix. 2, and may have been polished local limestone, but, considering that trade was vigorous and far-flung in David and Solomon's time, it may have been brought by sea or from the north-east.

II. METALS AND MINING

The order in which the principal metals came into use was gold, copper (bronze), and iron. Gold is the first metal mentioned in Scripture (Gn. ii. 11), and is thereafter closely associated with silver, the other *noble* metal of antiquity. All the above can occur in the native state, and as such they were first used. Silver is often found alloyed with gold. After the period when native metals were used, mainly for ornament, copper ores were won from outcrops at the surface, but mining began at a very early date, and an advanced stage of the working of the metal (not mining) had been reached at Ur more than a thousand years before Abraham's time. According to R. J. Forbes (*Metallurgy in Antiquity*, 1950, p. 297), 'it is certain that every form of mining from open-cut mining to the driving of galleries into the mountainside to follow up the copper-bearing strata was practised in Antiquity. But the details given on ancient mines are few.'

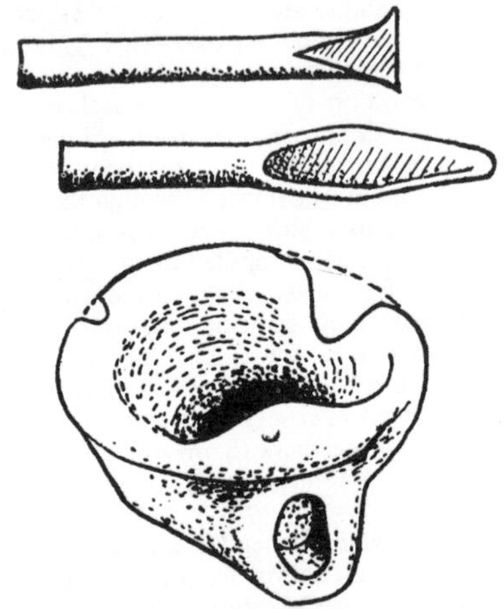

Fig. 142. Two copper chisels and a crucible from Sinai, c. 1500 BC.

Mining for turquoise and for copper began in the time of the Ist Dynasty of Egypt before 3000 BC at Magharah and Serabit el-Khadim in W Sinai, and copper mines at Ezion-Geber at the north of the Gulf of Aqabah were in full production in the time of Solomon, and are much older. Shafts more than 100 feet in depth have been found in mines in Egypt. Tunnels, ventilated by shafts, were driven into hillsides, pillars being left in broad excavations to support the roof. At first stone tools were used, but later bronze and stone continued to be used together. Wedges and fire were used to split the rock, and the ore was separated by crushing, washing, and hand-picking. Smelting was usually done on the spot in clay crucibles using charcoal and primitive bellows. Such crucibles and slag heaps are found at many old sites. Baskets were used for transporting the ore, and drainage tunnels constructed to get rid of surplus water. Moffatt's translation of Jb. xxviii. 1–11 gives a vivid picture of mining in ancient times.

a. Gold

This occurs native, usually alloyed with silver in varying amounts. It is extremely malleable and ductile and does not tarnish. This property made it a very acceptable material for ornaments, such as beads and rings, even to Stone Age man. Gold was prescribed for use in the most important furnishings in the Mosaic tabernacle (Ex. xxv) and in Solomon's Temple (1 Ki. vi). The metal was especially abundant in the alluvium of the eastern desert of Egypt, and the Israelites must have removed large quantities of it at the Exodus. Other sources known to the ancient world were the western coast of Arabia, the mountains of Armenia and Persia, western Asia Minor, and the Aegean islands. Gold early became a valuable article of currency.

b. Silver

This is ranked next to gold as a noble metal, with which it is often linked in Scripture. It does not tarnish in a pure atmosphere and will take a mirror-like polish. It is usually extracted from the sulphide ore of lead (galena), but may occur native. Silver was so plentiful in biblical times that the extraction and refining processes must have been known from an early date. Jeremiah (vi. 29, 30) uses the failure of the refining process of lead and silver as an illustration of the refusal of the people to become obedient to God. Sources of the metal are the same as those for lead, namely, Asia Minor, the islands of the Aegean, Laurion in southern Greece, Armenia, and Persia. Three or four localities occur in the eastern desert of Egypt also.

c. Lead

This occurs in Scripture in a few lists of metals. It was used occasionally as tablets for inscriptions (Jb. xix. 24).

d. Copper (Bronze, Brass)

Heb. *n^eḥōšeṯ* is translated 'copper' in Ezr. viii. 27, AV, but elsewhere in AV is called 'brass'. Bronze is not mentioned in Scripture, but it was in common use from before patriarchal times (Abraham lived in the Middle Bronze Age). The 'brass' of Scripture may therefore be any of the three, except that true brass, an alloy of copper and zinc, came into use only at a late stage. Heb. *ḥašmal* in Ezk. i. 4 (AV, RV 'amber'; RSV 'gleaming bronze') probably denotes true brass. Pure copper was first of all used before the art of alloying tin with copper was known. True brass was first made about 1000 BC, and so bronze or copper must have been used before the monarchy was established. The ores of copper which appear at the surface are brightly coloured green and blue carbonates, and so would attract attention, native copper being associated with them. The coloured ores were used in Egypt and elsewhere as eye-paint as well as the black ore of lead (galena, lead sulphide; see COSMETICS AND PERFUMERY). The ores were widespread around the 'Fertile Crescent' in Sinai, Midian, E Egypt, Armenia, Syria, and Persia. The metal was used for a host of purposes. In addition to its use in the Tabernacle and Temple, household articles, such as basins, ewers, idols, musical instruments, as well as armour, mirrors, *etc.*, were all made of it.

e. Tin

Tin is mentioned in Scripture only in lists of metals. It was often confused with lead in ancient times. A small percentage mixed with copper produces bronze. As tin often occurs in association with copper, the first bronze was probably made by accident. The dark heavy oxide ore, cassiterite, was taken mainly from stream-sands and was not mined, as were the other metals, until about Roman times.

f. Iron

Iron is known to have been used in very ancient times, but only in the native form, which has its origin in fragments of 'shooting stars' or meteors. This is probably the explanation of its early mention in Gn. iv. 22, which belongs to a time long before the true Iron Age begins. Experiments with iron went on for a long time before tools could be made of it, since this depends for success on producing a metal with the properties of steel. The Hittites were probably the first to solve the problem, and when their kingdom came to an end the knowledge spread farther. The Philistines brought the art to Palestine, and indeed, they were a nation of smiths. The Israelites found themselves at a disadvantage in this respect (Jdg. i. 19; 1 Sa. xiii. 19–22). The balance was restored in the reigns of David and Solomon (1 Ch. xxix. 7). Iron was abundant along with copper in the Wadi Arabah between the Dead Sea and the Gulf of Aqabah, and the mines were in production in the reign of Solomon. Iron ores were plentiful around Palestine and were to be found near Mt. Carmel, Mt. Hermon, SW Midian, in Syria, Cyprus, the Pontus coast of Asia Minor, as well as in the Aegean Islands. The fact that both copper and iron could be mined within the confines of Solomon's realm near Ezion-geber was a literal fulfilment of Dt. viii. 9.

Steel is mentioned in the AV of 2 Sa. xxii. 35 (= Ps. xviii. 34); Jb. xx. 24; Je. xv. 12, but the Heb. word is that for copper or bronze (*n^eḥōšeṯ*); accordingly, RV renders 'brass' and RSV, more accurately, 'bronze'.

BIBLIOGRAPHY. R. J. Forbes, *Metallurgy in Antiquity*, 1950; A. Lucas, *Ancient Egyptian Materials and Industries*[3], 1948; L. Woolley, *Ur of the Chaldees*, 1938; W. A. Ruysch (ed.), *The Holy Land, Antiquity and Survival*, II, 2, 3, 1957; T. Löw, *Die Mineralia der Juden*, 1935.

A.St.

MINISTER. The Heb. term *m^ešārēṯ* (LXX *leitourgos*) and its correlates normally refer to temple service, or else to the ministration of angels (Ps. civ. 4); but in a more general sense Joshua is the *m^ešārēṯ* or 'minister' of Moses (Ex. xxiv. 13; Jos. i. 1), and Solomon's ministers (1 Ki. x. 5) are his domestic servants. In the New Testament the characteristic word is *diakonos*, at first in a non-technical sense, and then in Phil. i. 1 and in the Pastorals as the title of a subordinate church-officer. It refers to service in general, temporary or permanent, either by bond or free; but it has the special connotation of waiting at table (the corresponding verb is used in this sense,

Lk. xii. 37, xvii. 8, and Martha's trouble was excess of *diakonia*, Lk. x. 40). Christ appears among the disciples as *ho diakonōn*, 'he that serveth' (Lk. xxii. 27), and He can be described as a *diakonos* of the circumcision (Rom. xv. 8); following the example of this lowly service, the greatest of Christians should be a minister to the rest (Mt. xx. 26; Mk. x. 43).

Thus we find the apostles and their helpers designated as ministers of God (2 Cor. vi. 4; 1 Thes. iii. 2), of Christ (2 Cor. xi. 23; Col. i. 7; 1 Tim. iv. 6), of the gospel (Eph. iii. 7; Col. i. 23), of the new covenant (2 Cor. iii. 6), of the Church (Col. i. 25), or absolutely (1 Cor. iii. 5; Eph. vi. 21; Col. iv. 7). But it is to be noted that Satan can also have his ministers (2 Cor. xi. 15) and that there might be a minister of sin (Gal. ii. 17); further, the secular power can be regarded as a minister of God (Rom. xiii. 4). The Seven were appointed to serve tables (*diakonein trapezais*, Acts vi. 2); it is unlikely that the word is here used to denote a technical office, since it is immediately afterwards (verse 4) contrasted with the apostles' *diakonia* of the word, and in fact Stephen and Philip did the work of evangelists rather than of deacons; however, the Seven may in some sense have provided a prototype for the later administrative assistants mentioned in Phil. i. 1 along with bishops, and characterized in 1 Tim. iii. 8 ff. as men of serious, honest, sober, and faithful disposition. Their primary work seems to have been, not that of teaching, but visiting from house to house and relieving the poor and sick; deacons were thus the chief agents through which the Church expressed its mutual fellowship of service.

It is uncertain whether 1 Tim. iii. 11 refers to deacons' wives or to deaconesses; Phebe is described (Rom. xvi. 1) as a *diakonos* (common gender) of the church at Cenchrea, but this probably means that she was a helper rather than that she held an official position; the two *ministrae* mentioned by Pliny in his letter to Trajan may have been deaconesses, but this office was not really developed until the 3rd century.

The lowliness of Christian service is emphasized even more strongly by the use of the word *doulos* or slave; it was the form of such a bond-servant that Christ assumed (Phil. ii. 7), and, following His example, the apostles and their fellow-labourers are designated as the slaves of God or Christ (Rom. i. 1; Gal. i. 10; Col. iv. 12; Tit. i. 1; Jas. i. 1; 2 Pet. i. 1).

Another term is *hypēretēs*, properly meaning an under-rower in a galley, and then anyone in a subordinate position. This word is used for the *ḥazzān*, a sort of verger in the Jewish synagogue, who had custody of the sacred books (Lk. iv. 20); it also describes John Mark (Acts xiii. 5) when he acted in the capacity of batman to Paul and Barnabas. But Paul himself was proud to claim a similar position in relationship to Christ (Acts xxvi. 16; 1 Cor. iv. 1), and Luke (i. 2) employs it as a generic term for the servants of the word.

Finally, the term *leitourgos* is taken over by the New Testament in a Christian sense. Originally it referred to public service, such as might be offered by wealthy citizens to the State; then it acquired a distinctively religious connotation, as in the LXX usage. Thus Christ appears as a *leitourgos* of the heavenly temple (Heb. viii. 2), and the angels are 'liturgical', *i.e.* ministering spirits (Heb. i. 14). The corresponding verb is used when prophets and teachers minister to the Lord at Antioch (Acts xiii. 2); similarly, Paul describes himself as the *leitourgos* of Jesus Christ, ministering (*hierourgōn*) the gospel of God (Rom. xv. 16). But the New Testament terminology remains sufficiently fluid for the same word to be used of Epaphroditus as a minister to Paul's wants (Phil. ii. 25), of Gentile assistance to Jews in carnal things (Rom. xv. 27), and of the civil power as the servant of God (Rom. xiii. 6). In the Christian understanding of ministry (*q.v.*), whether official or otherwise, the minister renders a lowly but loving service to God or man.

BIBLIOGRAPHY. See under MINISTRY.

G.S.M.W.

MINISTRY. To express the idea of professional or priestly ministration, the Old Testament normally employs the verb *šāraṭ* and its correlates (LXX *leitourgein*), while *'āḇaḏ* (*latreuein*) refers rather to the religious service of the whole congregation or of an individual. In the New Testament the characteristic term is *diakonia*, which appears only in Esther among the Old Testament books, but is not there used of any priestly function; and the change in language implies a change also in doctrine, since ministry in the New Testament sense is not the exclusive privilege of a priestly caste. *Leitourgia* is retained to describe the work of the Jewish priesthood (Lk. i. 23; Heb. ix. 21), and it is applied also to the more excellent ministry of Christ (Heb. viii. 6); further, it can be applied, in a metaphorical sense, to the spiritual service rendered by prophets and preachers of the gospel (Acts xiii. 2; Rom. xv. 16). But it remains true in general that the New Testament uses priestly language only in reference to the body of believers as a whole (Phil. ii. 17; 1 Pet. ii. 9).

I. CHRIST THE PATTERN

The pattern of Christian ministry is provided by the life of Christ, who came not to receive service but to give it (Mt. xx. 28; Mk. x. 45); the verb used in these texts is *diakonein*, which suggests something like waiting at table, and recalls the occasion when He washed the disciples' feet (Jn. xiii. 4 ff.). It is significant that in the first recorded instance of ordination to the Christian ministry, the purpose of the office is stated to be that of 'serving tables' (Acts vi. 2); and the same word is used in the same chapter (verse 4) to describe the service of the word exercised prior to this by the twelve apostles. The minister (*q.v.*) of Christ, following the example of his Master, renders a humble but loving service to the needs of humanity at large, in the same spirit as that in which angels (Mt. iv. 11; Mk. i. 13) and women (Mt. xxvii. 55; Lk. viii. 3) had ministered to the Lord on earth. Such service is reckoned as being done to Christ in the persons of the needy (Mt. xxv. 44); it is most frequently rendered to the saints (Rom. xv. 25; 1 Cor. xvi. 15; 2 Cor. viii. 4, ix. 1; Heb. vi. 10); but it is a mutual service within the fellowship of Christ's body (1 Pet. iv. 10); and, as the ministry of the gospel (1 Pet. i. 12), it is in fact a ministry of reconciliation (2 Cor. v. 18) for the world.

The ability to perform such work is a gift of God (Acts xx. 24; Col. iv. 17; 1 Tim. i. 12; 1 Pet. iv. 11); already in Rom. xii. 7 it is being classified in a list of other spiritual gifts; and in 1 Tim. iii. 8 ff. the diaconate has become a recognized church office. But even so, the term is still being used in a wider sense; Timothy is to fulfil his ministry by doing the work of an evangelist (2 Tim. iv. 5); and this work of service has as its great object the edification of the body of Christ (Eph. iv. 12). In the words of Hort, Christ lifted 'every grade and pattern of service into a higher sphere . . . ministration thus became one of the primary aims of all Christian actions'; and the generic term is applied to all forms of ministry within the Church.

II. PASTORAL MINISTRY

Christ is not only the pattern of the diaconate, but also, as the good Shepherd (Jn. x. 11), He is the great Bishop (*q.v.*) of men's souls (1 Pet. ii. 25). In a sense, both of these offices originate from the example of Christ Himself, while that of the presbyter (*q.v.*) is a reflection of the ministry instituted by Him in the apostolate (*cf.* 1 Pet. v. 1). Thus it may be said that the elder rules in virtue of a commission granted by his King (Lk. xxii. 29, 30), while the work of bishops or pastors and of deacons is modelled on the prophetic and priestly offices of Christ. But it would be wrong to stress these distinctions, since the terms bishop and presbyter are virtually synonymous, and the diaconate embraces many forms of ministry. Pastoral care of the flock is an outstanding part of ministerial duty (Jn. xxi. 15–17; Acts xx. 28; 1 Pet. v. 2), and is closely associated with the preaching of the word (1 Cor. iii. 1, 2) as the bread of life (Jn. vi. 35), or pure nourishing milk (1 Pet. ii. 2). The parable in Lk. xii. 41–48 implies that some ministry of this character is to continue in the Church until Christ's return.

III. SACRAMENTAL DUTIES

The New Testament has comparatively little to say on the subject of sacramental duties; Paul regarded the administration of baptism as a very subordinate activity (1 Cor. i. 17), which he was accustomed to delegate to his assistants; and although it is natural for an apostle, if present, to preside at the breaking of bread (Acts xx. 7), the celebration of the Lord's Supper is normally regarded as an activity of the entire congregation. However, a president must have been needed from the first; and in the absence of an apostle, prophet, or evangelist, this duty would naturally fall to one of the local presbyters or bishops.

IV. SPIRITUAL GIFTS

In its earliest form the Christian ministry is charismatic, *i.e.* it is a spiritual gift or supernatural endowment, whose exercise witnesses to the presence of the Holy Spirit in the Church. Thus prophecy and *glossolalia* occur when Paul lays his hands on some ordinary believers after baptism (Acts xix. 6); and the words there used imply that the occurrence was to some extent a repetition of the Pentecostal experience (Acts ii).

Three lists are provided in the Pauline Epistles of the various forms which such ministry may take, and it is notable that in each list administrative functions are included along with others more obviously spiritual (see CHURCH GOVERNMENT). In Rom. xii. 6–8 we have prophecy, ministry (*diakonia*), teaching, exhortation, almsgiving, ruling, and 'showing mercy' (?visitation of the sick and poor). 1 Cor. xii. 28 lists apostles, prophets, teachers, together with those endowed with power to work miracles, heal the sick, help, govern, or speak with tongues. The more official catalogue in Eph. iv. 11 mentions apostles, prophets, evangelists, pastors, and teachers, who all labour to perfect the saints in their Christian service, so that the whole Church grows up in organic connection with her divine Head. Here, emphasis is laid on the ministration of the word, but the fruit of such ministry is mutual service in love. The various gifts listed in these passages are functions or ways of serving, rather than regular and stereotyped offices; one man might act in several capacities, but his ability to fulfil any depended on the prompting of the Spirit.

Not only the Twelve were included in the apostolate, but also Paul and Barnabas (1 Cor. ix. 5, 6), James the Lord's brother (Gal. i. 19), and Andronicus and Junias (Rom. xvi. 7). The primary qualification of an 'apostle' (*q.v.*) was that he had been an eye-witness of Christ's earthly ministry, particularly of the resurrection (Acts i. 21, 22), and his authority depended on the fact that he had been in some way commissioned by Christ either in the days of His flesh (Mt. x. 5, xxviii. 19) or after He was risen from the dead (Acts i. 24, ix. 15). Apostles and elders might meet in council to decide a common policy for the Church (Acts xv. 6 ff.), and apostles could be sent as delegates from the original congregation to superintend some new development in another locality (Acts viii. 14 ff.). But the picture of an apostolic college in permanent session at Jerusalem is quite unhistorical, and the great work of an apostle was to act as a missionary for the propagation of the gospel, in which capacity his labours should be confirmed by signs of divine approval (2 Cor. xii. 12). Thus the apostolic ministry was not confined by local ties, though a division of labour might be made, as for example between Peter and Paul (Gal. ii. 7, 8).

The 'evangelist' exercised a similar ministry of

unrestricted mission, and his work seems to have been identical with that of the apostle, except in so far as he lacked the special qualifications for the higher function; Philip, one of the original Seven, became an evangelist (Acts xxi. 8), and Timothy is called by the same title (2 Tim. iv. 5), though he is by implication excluded (2 Cor. i. 1) from the rank of apostle.

Prophecy was by its very nature a gift of intermittent occurrence, but some individuals were so regularly endowed with it that they formed a special class of 'prophets'. Such men were found at Jerusalem (Acts xi. 27), Antioch (Acts xiii. 1), and Corinth (1 Cor. xiv. 29); those mentioned by name include Judas and Silas (Acts xv. 32), and Agabus (Acts xxi. 10), together with Anna (Lk. ii. 36) and the pretended prophetess Jezebel (Rev. ii. 20). Prophecy provided edification, exhortation, and comfort (1 Cor. xiv. 3), and might therefore be described as inspired preaching. The prophet could issue a specific direction (Acts xiii. 1, 2) or on occasion foretell the future (Acts xi. 28). Being delivered in a known tongue, his messages were more profitable than mere *glossolalia* (1 Cor. xiv. 23–25). But the gift was particularly liable to the danger of imposture, and although it should be controlled only by those possessing it (1 Cor. xiv. 32), its content must agree with the fundamental teaching of the gospel (1 Jn. iv. 1–3), or else the prophet must be dismissed as one of the false pretenders whose coming had been foretold by Christ (Mt. vii. 15).

'Pastors' are presumably to be identified with the local ministers instituted by the apostles (Acts xiv. 23) or their assistants (Tit. i. 5) to serve the needs of a particular congregation, and described indifferently as presbyters or bishops. 'Teachers', who might be of either sex, gave authoritative instruction in knowledge of the Bible and in the performance of Christian duty (*cf.* Tit. ii. 3–5). 'Governors' seems to be a generic name for those who administered the affairs of local congregations, while 'helpers' were engaged in works of charity, especially in attending to the sick and poor. Miraculous powers of healing and speaking with tongues were a marked feature of the apostolic age, but they appear to have been withdrawn thereafter, although their renewal has been claimed at various periods from the Montanist revival onwards.

V. THE ORIGIN OF THE MINISTRY

There has been much debate over the precise relationship between the original and unrestricted mission of apostles and evangelists, on the one hand, and the permanent and local ministry of pastors, teachers, governors, and helpers, on the other. The latter class appears always to have been appointed by the former; but if Acts vi may be taken as describing a typical ordination, popular election played a part in the choice of candidates. Rom. xii and 1 Cor. xii might seem to imply that the Church, as the Spirit-filled community, produces its own organs of ministration; on the other hand, Eph. iv. 11 asserts that the ministry is given to the Church by Christ. It may be suggested that, while Christ is the source of all authority and the pattern of every type of service, the Church as a whole is the recipient of His divine commission. At all events, the New Testament is not concerned to indicate possible channels of transmission; its main preoccupation in this regard is to provide a doctrinal test for the orthodoxy of ministerial teaching.

BIBLIOGRAPHY. J. B. Lightfoot, 'Dissertation on the Christian Ministry' in *Philippians*, 1868; A. von Harnack, *The Constitution and Law of the Church in the First Two Centuries*, E.T., 1910; H. B. Swete, *Early History of the Church and Ministry*, 1918; B. H. Streeter, *The Primitive Church*, 1929; K. E. Kirk (ed.), *The Apostolic Ministry*, 1946; D. T. Jenkins, *The Gift of Ministry*, 1947; T. W. Manson, *The Church's Ministry*, 1948; K. M. Carey (ed.), *The Historic Episcopate*, 1954; J. K. S. Reid, *The Biblical Doctrine of the Ministry*, 1955; T. F. Torrance, *Royal Priesthood*, 1955. G.S.M.W.

MINNI. A people summoned by Jeremiah, with Ararat (Armenia) and Ashkenaz, to make war on Babylonia (Je. li. 27). The Mannai, whose territory lay south-east of Lake Urmia, are frequently named in texts of the 9th–7th centuries BC. The Assyrians dominated them until 673 BC, when they were controlled by the Medes (verse 28). In the light of Jeremiah, it is interesting to note that the Mannai were allied with the Assyrians, their former enemies, against the Babylonians in 616 BC (Bab. Chronicle). They were probably present with the Guti and other hill-folks at the capture of Babylon in 539 BC. D.J.W.

MINNITH. Mentioned in Jdg. xi. 33 as the limit of Jephthah's invasion of Ammon. According to the indication of Eusebius (*Onom.*, p. 132), it lay at the head of a natural route from the Jordan to the uplands between Rabbath-Ammon and Heshbon. The exact site is unknown.

Ezk. xxvii. 17 may refer to the same; but Cornill and others doubt the reading and emend to 'spices'; see *ICC, ad loc.* J.P.U.L.

MINT. See PLANTS.

MIRACLES. A number of Heb., Aramaic, and Gk. words are used in the Bible to refer to the activity in nature and history of the living God. They are variously translated in the English versions by 'miracles', 'wonders', 'signs', 'mighty acts', 'powers'. Thus, for example, the Heb. word *môpēṯ*, which is of uncertain etymology, is translated in AV by 'miracle' (Ex. vii. 9; Dt. xxix. 3), 'wonder' (*e.g.* Ex. vii. 3; Dt. iv. 34; Ps. lxxviii. 43), and 'sign' (*e.g.* 1 Ki. xiii. 3, 5).

The words used by the English translators preserve in general, though not always in particular instances, the three distinctive emphases of the originals. These characterize God's activity as being:

1. Distinctive, wonderful; expressed by Heb.

derivatives of the root *pl'*, 'be different', particularly the participle *niplā'ōṯ* (*e.g.* Ex. xv. 11; Jos. iii. 5), by Aramaic *ṯᵉmāh* (Dn. iv. 2, 3, vi. 27), and by Gk. *teras* (*e.g.* Acts iv. 30; Rom. xv. 19).

2. Mighty, powerful; expressed by Heb. *geḇûrâ* (Ps. cvi. 2, cxlv. 4) and Gk. *dynamis* (*e.g.* Mt. xi. 20; 1 Cor. xii. 10; Gal. iii. 5).

3. Meaningful, significant; expressed by Heb. *'ôṯ* (*e.g.* Nu. xiv. 11; Ne. ix. 10), by Aramaic *'āṯ* (Dn. iv. 2, 3, vi. 27), and by Gk. *sēmeion* (*e.g.* Jn. ii. 11, iii. 2; Acts viii. 6).

I. MIRACLES AND THE NATURAL ORDER

A great deal of confusion on the subject of miracles has been caused by a failure to observe that Scripture does not sharply distinguish between God's constant sovereign providence and His particular acts. Belief in miracles is set in the context of a world-view which regards the whole of creation as continually dependent upon the sustaining activity of God and subject to His sovereign will (*cf.* Col. i. 16, 17). All three aspects of divine activity—wonder, power, significance—are present not only in special acts but also in the whole created order (Rom. i. 20). When the psalmist celebrates the mighty acts of God he moves readily from the creation to the deliverance from Egypt (Ps. cxxxv. 6–12). In Jb. v. 9, 10, ix. 9, 10 the word *niplā'ōṯ* refers to what we would call 'natural events' (*cf.* Is. viii. 18; Ezk. xii. 6).

Thus when the biblical writers refer to the mighty acts of God they cannot be supposed to distinguish them from 'the course of nature' by their peculiar causation, since they think of all events as caused by God's sovereign power. The particular acts of God highlight the distinctive character of God's activity, different from and superior to that of men and more particularly that of false gods, almighty in power, revealing Him in nature and history.

The discovery of, say, causal connections between the different plagues of Egypt, a repetition of the blocking of the Jordan, or increased knowledge of psychosomatic medicine could not of themselves contradict the biblical assertion that the deliverance from Egypt, the entry to Canaan, and the healing works of Christ were mighty acts of God. 'Natural laws' are descriptions of that universe in which God is ever at work. It is only by an unwarranted philosophical twist that they are construed as the self-sustaining working of a closed system or the rigid decrees of a God who set the universe to work like some piece of machinery.

It has been argued by some philosophers and theologians that the working of miracles is inconsistent with God's nature and purpose. He is the Alpha and Omega, He knows the end from the beginning; He is the Creator who fashioned all things unhampered by any limitation imposed by pre-existent matter; He is the unchanging One. Why, then, should He need to 'interfere' with the working of the natural order?

This objection based on the character of God arises from a failure to grasp the biblical understanding of God as living and personal. His changelessness is not that of an impersonal force but the faithfulness of a person: His creative act brought into being responsible creatures with whom He deals not as puppets but as other persons over against Himself. Miracles are events which dramatically reveal this living, personal nature of God, active in history not as mere Destiny but as a Redeemer who saves and guides His people.

A fuller knowledge of the ways of God's working may show that some supposedly unique events were part of a regular pattern. It can, however, never logically exclude the exceptional and extraordinary. While there is no such radical discontinuity between miracles and the 'natural order' as has been assumed by those who have most keenly felt the modern doubts on the subject, it is clear that Scripture speaks of many events which are extraordinary or even unique so far as our general experience of nature goes.

II. MIRACLES AND REVELATION

If it be granted that *a priori* objections to miracle stories are invalid it still remains to ask what precise function these extraordinary events perform in the total self-revelation of God in history. Orthodox theologians have been accustomed to regard them primarily as the authenticating marks of God's prophets and apostles and supremely of His Son. More recently it has been argued by liberal critics that the miracle stories of the Old and New Testaments are of the same character as the wonder-stories told of pagan deities and their prophets. Both these views fail to do justice to the integral relationship between the miracle stories and the whole self-revelation of God. Miracles are not simply an external authentication of the revelation but an essential part of it, of which the true purpose was and is to nourish faith in the saving intervention of God towards those who believe.

a. False miracles

Jesus consistently refused to give a sign from heaven, to work useless and spectacular wonders, simply to guarantee His teaching (see SIGN). In any case the simple ability to work miracles would have been no such guarantee. There is frequent reference both in Scripture and elsewhere to wonder-working by those who were opposed to the purposes of God (*cf.* Dt. xiii. 2, 3; Mt. vii. 22, xxiv. 24; 2 Thes. ii. 9; Rev. xiii. 13 ff., xvi. 14, xix. 20). The refusal to do wonders for their own sake sharply marks off the biblical miracle stories from the general run of *Wundergeschichten.*

It is noteworthy that the word *teras*, which of all the biblical terms has most nearly the overtones of the English 'portent', is always used in the New Testament in conjunction with *sēmeion* to stress that only significant portents are meant. The only exception is the Old Testament quotation in Acts ii. 19 (but *cf.* Acts ii. 22).

The mere portent or the false miracle is distinguished from the true by the fact that the true miracle is congruous with the rest of the revelation. It harmonizes with the knowledge which believers already possess concerning God, even where it also carries that knowledge farther and deeper. Thus Israel is to reject any miracle-worker who denies the Lord (Dt. xiii. 2, 3) and thus also we may rightly discern between the miracle stories of the canonical Gospels and the romantic tales or ludicrous stupidities of the apocryphal writings and mediaeval hagiography.

b. Miracles and faith

The working of miracles is directed to a deepening of men's understanding of God. It is God's way of speaking dramatically to those who have ears to hear. The miracle stories are intimately concerned with the faith of observers or participants (*cf.* Ex. xiv. 31; 1 Ki. xviii. 39) and with the faith of those who will hear or read them later (Jn. xx. 30, 31). Jesus looked for faith as the right response to His saving presence and deeds; it was faith which 'made whole', which made the difference between the mere creation of an impression and a saving communication of His revelation of God.

It is important to observe that faith on the part of human participants is not a necessary condition of a miracle in the sense that God is of Himself unable to act without human faith. Mk. vi. 5 is often quoted to support such a view, but Jesus could do no mighty work in Nazareth, not because the people's unbelief limited His power—Mark tells us that He healed a few sick people there—but rather because He could not proceed with His preaching or with the deeds which proclaimed His gospel in action where men were unready to accept His good news and His own person. Wonder-working for the crowds or the sceptics was inconsistent with His mission: it is in this sense that He could not do it in Nazareth.

c. Miracles and the Word

It is a notable feature—in some cases the chief feature—of miracles that even where the matter of the event is such that it can be assimilated to the ordinary pattern of natural events (*e.g.* some of the plagues of Egypt), its occurrence is predicted by God to or through His agent (*cf.* Jos. iii. 7–13; 1 Ki. xiii. 1–5) or takes place at an agent's command or prayer (*cf.* Ex. iv. 17; Nu. xx. 8; 1 Ki. xviii. 37, 38); sometimes both prediction and command are recorded (*cf.* Ex. xiv). This feature emphasizes yet again the connection between miracles and revelation, and between miracles and the divine creative Word.

d. The crises of the sacred history

Another connection between miracles and revelation is that they cluster about the crises of sacred history. The pre-eminently mighty acts of God are the deliverance at the Red Sea and the resurrection of Christ, the first the climax of the conflict with Pharaoh and the gods of Egypt (Ex. xii. 12; Nu. xxxiii. 4), the second the climax of God's redeeming work in Christ and the conflict with all the power of evil. Miracles are also frequently noted in the time of Elijah and Elisha, when Israel seemed most likely to sink into complete apostasy (*cf.* 1 Ki. xix. 14); in the time of the siege of Jerusalem under Hezekiah (2 Ki. xx. 11); during the Exile (Dn. *passim*); and in the early days of the Christian mission.

III. MIRACLES IN THE NEW TESTAMENT

Some liberal treatments of the question of miracles draw a marked distinction between the miracles of the New Testament, particularly those of our Lord Himself, and those of the Old Testament. Both more radical and more conservative critics have pointed out that in principle the narratives stand or fall together.

The contention that the New Testament miracles are more credible in the light of modern psychology or psychosomatic medicine leaves out of account the nature miracles, such as that at the wedding-feast in Cana and the calming of the storm, the instantaneous cures of organic disease and malformation, and the raising of the dead. There is no *a priori* reason to suppose that Jesus did not make use of those resources of the human mind and spirit which today are employed by the psychotherapist; but other narratives take us into realms where psychotherapy makes no assertions and where the claims of spiritual healers find least support from qualified medical observers.

There is, however, evidence for regarding the miracles of Christ and those done in His name as different from those of the Old Testament. Where before God had done mighty works in His transcendent power and revealed them to His servants or used His servants as the occasional agents of such deeds, in Jesus there confronts us God Himself incarnate, freely active in sovereign authority in that world which is 'his own'. When the apostles did like works in His name they acted in the power of the risen Lord with whom they were in intimate contact, so that Acts continues the story of the same things which Jesus began to do and teach in His earthly ministry (*cf.* Acts i. 1).

In stressing the direct presence and action of God in Christ we do not deny the continuity of His work with the previous course of God's dealing with the world. Of the list of works given by our Lord in answering the Baptist's inquiry (Mt. xi. 5) it is the most wonderful, the healing of lepers and the raising of the dead, which have Old Testament parallels, notably in the ministry of Elisha. What is remarkable is the integral relationship between the works and words of Jesus. The blind receive their sight, the lame walk, the deaf hear, and at the same time that gospel is preached to the poor by which spiritual sight and hearing and a power to walk in God's way are given to the spiritually needy.

Again, the frequency of healing miracles is far

greater in the time of the New Testament than at any period of the Old. The Old Testament records its miracles one by one and gives no indication that there were others unrecorded. The Gospels and the New Testament in general repeatedly claim that the miracles described in detail were but a fraction of those wrought. Isolated instances of the divine exercise of sovereign power here give way to a wholesale onslaught on the forces of evil and disease.

Jesus' works are clearly marked off from others by their manner or mode. There is in Jesus' dealing with the sick and demon-possessed a note of inherent authority. Where prophets did their works in the name of God or after prayer to Him, Jesus casts out demons and heals with that same air of rightful power as informs His pronouncement of forgiveness to the sinner; indeed, He deliberately linked the two authorities (Mk. ii. 9–11). At the same time Jesus stressed that His works were done in constant dependence on the Father (*e.g.* Jn. v. 19). The balance between inherent authority and humble dependence is the very mark of the perfect unity of deity and humanity.

In general, it may be said of Jesus' works that in their integral relation to His mission, their frequency, and their authoritative manner they are distinctively messianic.

Above all, the virgin birth, the resurrection, and the ascension manifest the newness of what God did in Christ. He is born of a woman in the genealogy of Abraham and David, but of a virgin; others had been raised from death, only to die again; He 'ever liveth' and has ascended to the right hand of power. It is, moreover, true of the resurrection as of no other individual miracle that on it the New Testament rests the whole structure of faith (*cf.* 1 Cor. xv. 17). This event was unique as the decisive triumph over sin and death.

The miracles of the apostles and other leaders of the New Testament Church spring from the solidarity of Christ with His people. They are works done in His name, in continuation of all that Jesus began to do and teach, in the power of the Spirit He sent from the Father. There is a close link between these miracles and the work of the apostles in testifying to the person and work of their Lord; they are part of the proclamation of the kingdom of God, not an end in themselves.

The debate continues over the contention that this function of miracle was of necessity confined to the apostolic age. But we may at least say that the New Testament miracles were distinct from any subsequent ones by virtue of their immediate connection with the full manifestation of the incarnate Son of God, with a revelation then given in its fullness. They do not, therefore, afford grounds in themselves for expecting miracles to accompany the subsequent dissemination of the revelation of which they formed an integral part.

BIBLIOGRAPHY. It is impossible to list here even a representative selection of the very extensive literature on the many aspects of the question of miracles. The following works represent points of view discussed above and will also provide references for further study: J. B. Mozley, *Eight Lectures on Miracles*, 1865; F. R. Tennant, *Miracle and its Philosophical Presuppositions*, 1925; D. S. Cairns, *The Faith that Rebels*, 1927; A. Richardson, *The Miracle Stories of the Gospels*, 1941; C. S. Lewis, *Miracles, A Preliminary Study*, 1947. M.H.C.

MIRIAM. (For derivation, see MARY.) **1.** The daughter of Amram and Jochebed, and the sister of Aaron and Moses (Nu. xxvi. 59). It is generally agreed that it was she who watched the baby Moses in the bulrushes and suggested her mother as his nurse. The term 'the prophetess' was used to describe her as she led the women in music, dancing, and singing a paean of praise to celebrate the crossing of the Red Sea (Ex. xv. 20 f.).

Miriam and Aaron rebelled against Moses, supposedly because of his marriage to the Cushite woman, but in reality because they were jealous of his position. Divine judgment descended upon Miriam and she became leprous, whereupon Moses interceded for her and she was cleansed, but she was excluded from the camp for seven days (Nu. xii).

She died at Kadesh and was buried there (Nu. xx. 1). There is no record of her marriage in the Bible, but rabbinical tradition makes her the wife of Caleb and mother of Hur.

2. In his genealogy the Chronicler lists Miriam as one of the children of Ezra (1 Ch. iv. 17). M.G.

Fig. 143. Egyptian mirror of polished copper or bronze, with handle shaped like a papyrus-column. New Kingdom, *c.* 1570–1085 BC.

MIRROR. During the Old Testament period mirrors were made of metal, cast and highly polished (Jb. xxxvii. 18). Several bronze examples dating from the Middle Bronze Age onwards have been found in Palestine. These are of a form common throughout the Near East (see fig. 143); *cf.* those used by the Israelite women in Ex. xxxviii. 8 (see *ANEP*, No. 71). The meaning of Heb. *gillāyôn* in Isaiah's list of finery (iii. 23) is uncertain; it may mean mirrors (Targ., AV, RV) or garments of gauze (LXX, RSV). Glass mirrors were probably introduced in the 1st century AD. Whether of metal or glass, these mirrors never gave a perfect reflection (1 Cor. xiii. 12). It is probable that in 2 Cor. iii. 18 (Gk. *hēmeis . . . katoptrizomenoi*) Paul's idea is that we see merely a reflection (AV); but it may be that we reflect (RV; see *Arndt*, pp. 425–426; R. V. G. Tasker, *2 Corinthians*, *TNTC*, 1958, pp. 67–68). James gives a simple illustration from the use of a mirror (i. 23). A.R.M.

MISHNAH. See TALMUD AND MIDRASH.

MISREPHOTH-MAIM. At the north end of the Acre plain, below the rocky headland of Rosh Haniqra, the Bronze Age site Khirbet el-Mushreifeh probably marks the limit of pursuit from Merom (Jos. xi. 8), and the southern border of Zidon (Jos. xiii. 6). Zarephath, 27 miles farther north between Tyre and Zidon, is unlikely to have been the border.

BIBLIOGRAPHY. Garstang, *Joshua*, 1931, p. 190; Welch, *HDB*, *s.v.* J.P.U.L.

MITE. See MONEY (II*a*).

MITHREDATH ('given by Mithra', the Persian god of light. *Cf.* Gk.-Lat. 'Mithridates'). **1.** The treasurer of Cyrus king of Persia, who in 536 BC restored to Sheshbazzar the sacred vessels confiscated by Nebuchadrezzar from Jerusalem (Ezr. i. 8). **2.** A Persian officer in Samaria, one of those who wrote to Artaxerxes ('Longimanus') protesting against the rebuilding of the walls of Jerusalem (Ezr. iv. 7) in the Syrian, *i.e.* Aramaic, language. B.F.H.

MITRE (Heb. *miṣnep̄et̲*). One of the high priest's holy garments. From the use of the verb in Is. xxii. 18 it is thought to have been a kind of turban wound round the head. It is described in Ex. xxviii. 4, 36–39. On it was worn 'the plate of the holy crown' engraved 'HOLINESS TO THE LORD' (Ex. xxxix. 28, 30 f.). Aaron wore it for his anointing (Lv. viii. 9) and on the Day of Atonement (Lv. xvi. 4). To be uncovered was a sign of mourning (Ezk. xxiv. 17), and uncleanness (Lv. xiii. 45, *cf.* x. 6), and was specifically forbidden to the high priest (Lv. xxi. 10–12)—*cf.* the 'bonnets' (*mig̱bā'ôt̲*) of inferior priests—so that Ezekiel (xxi. 26) prophesies of the removal of the mitre because of the profanity of Israel, and Zechariah (iii. 5) sees Joshua invested with it (*ṣānîp̄*) as a sign of his cleansing and acceptance by God. Israel's ultimate renewal is symbolized by calling her a royal mitre in the hand of God (Is. lxii. 3). P.A.B.

MITYLENE. An ancient republic of the Aeolian Greeks and the principal state of the island of Lesbos. Its situation at the cross-roads of Europe and Asia frequently placed its political fortunes in jeopardy, until under the pax Romana it settled down as an honoured subordinate, highly favoured by the Romans as a holiday resort. A capacious harbour facing the mainland of Asia Minor across the straits made it a natural overnight stop for Paul's vessel on the southward run to Palestine (Acts xx. 14).

BIBLIOGRAPHY. R. Herbst, *RE*, XVI. 2. 1411. E.A.J.

MIXED MULTITUDE. When Israel left Egypt under Moses there went with them a motley crowd whose motives for leaving Egypt were doubtless as mixed as their origins (Ex. xii. 38, *'ēreb̲rab̲*, 'mixed crowd'; *cf.* English 'riffraff'). In the 13th century BC the evidence of foreign names in Egyptian texts indicates the presence of all manner of foreigners in Egypt; the E Delta would have the highest proportion of such. In the wilderness it was this element that craved meat, despising the God-given manna (Nu. xi. 4, Heb. *'ᵃsap̄sup̄*, 'rabble'). In other scriptures *'ēreb̲* (AV often 'mingled people') indicates foreigners, *e.g.* in Egypt (as at the Exodus), mixed tribal folk in the deserts (Je. xxv. 20, 24, RSV), foreign troops in Babylon (Je. l. 37), and those of foreign descent excluded from the Hebrew commonwealth under Nehemiah (Ne. xiii. 3, *cf.* 23–25). For Ezk. xxx. 5, *cf.* RSV. K.A.K.

MIZAR. A hill mentioned in Ps. xlii. 6, in connection with Mt. Hermon. It may be presumed that Hermon was visible from it; in which case it would have been in the Galilee region—note the reference to the Jordan. The word in Hebrew (*miṣ'ār*) means 'smallness'. Some scholars emend the text of Ps. xlii. 6 slightly, making *miṣ'ār* an adjective, 'small', referring to Mt. Zion. In this case the Psalmist would be stating his preference for Zion rather than Hermon's great bulk. D.F.P.

MIZPAH, MIZPEH. The basic meaning of the word is 'watchtower', 'place for watching'. It is vocalized as *miṣpâ* and *miṣpeh*, and is found usually with the article. It is natural to look for places so named on high vantage points. The following may be distinguished:

1. The place where Jacob and Laban made a covenant (see COVENANT) and set up a cairn of stones as a witness (Galeed, *gal'ēd̲* in Hebrew, or *yᵉg̱ar śāhᵃdûṯā'* in Aramaic). God was the watcher between them (Gn. xxxi. 44–49).

2. Either the same place as above or a town in Gilead, east of the Jordan. The article is used both in Gn. xxxi. 49 (*hammiṣpâ*), and in Jdg. x. 17, xi. 11, 34. The place features in the story of Jephthah. When Ammon encroached on Gilead the Israelites assembled at Mizpah (Jdg. x. 17), the home of Jephthah, from which he commenced his attack and to which he returned to carry out his rash vow (Jdg. xi. 11, 29, 34). Its identification with Ramoth-gilead is urged by some writers (J. D. Davis, *The Westminster Dictionary of the Bible*, 1944, p. 401), but is rejected by F. M. Abel and du Buit, who identify it with Jal'ûd. It is possibly the same as Ramath-mizpeh or height of Mizpeh (Jos. xiii. 26).

3. A place in Moab to which David took his parents for safety (1 Sa. xxii. 3), possibly the modern Rujm el-Meshrefeh, west-south-west of Madaba. **4.** A place at the foot of Mt. Hermon (Jos. xi. 3), referred to as 'the land of Mizpeh' or 'the valley of Mizpeh' (verse 8), the home of the Hivites. Opinions differ as to its identification, but Qal'at eṣ-Ṣubeibeh on a hill 2 miles north-east of Banias has much support. **5.** A town in the Shephelah (lowlands) of Judah named along with Joktheel, Lachish, and Eglon (Jos. xv. 38, 39). The two sites of Khirbet Ṣāfiyeh, 2 miles north-east of Beit Jibrin, and Ṣufiyeh, 6 miles north, are possible choices for this Mizpeh.

6. A town of Benjamin (Jos. xviii. 26), in the neighbourhood of Gibeon and Ramah (1 Ki. xv. 22). In the days of the Judges, when the Benjamites of Gibeah outraged the Levite's concubine, the men of Israel assembled here (Jdg. xx. 1, 3, xxi. 1, 5, 8). Here Samuel assembled Israel for prayer after the ark had been restored to Kiriath-jearim (1 Sa. vii. 5, 6). The Philistines attacked them, but were driven back (verses 7, 11), and Samuel erected a stone of remembrance near by at Ebenezer (verse 12). Here also Saul was presented to the people as their king (1 Sa. x. 17). Mizpeh was one of the places visited by Samuel annually to judge Israel (1 Sa. vii. 16).

King Asa fortified Mizpeh against Baasha of Israel, using materials his men took from Baasha's fort at Ramah, after Asa had asked the Syrian Ben-hadad to attack Israel (1 Ki. xv. 22; 2 Ch. xvi. 6). After the destruction of Jerusalem by Nebuchadrezzar in 587 BC Gedaliah was appointed governor of the remainder of the people, the governor's residence being fixed at Mizpeh (2 Ki. xxv. 23, 25). The prophet Jeremiah, released by Nebuzar-adan, the captain of the guard, joined Gedaliah at Mizpeh (Je. xl. 6), and refugee Jews soon returned (Je. xl. 8, 10, 12, 13, 15). Soon after, Ishmael of the royal seed slew Gedaliah and the garrison at the instigation of Baalis, king of Ammon. Two days later he murdered a company of pilgrims and threw their bodies into the great cistern Asa had built. He imprisoned others and sought to carry them to Ammon, but was frustrated by Johanan (Je. xli. 1, 3, 6, 10, 14, 16).

Two references to a Mizpah in post-exilic times occur in Ne. iii. 15, 19. It is possible that one or both of these refer to Mizpah of Benjamin, though they may represent different places.

Mizpah was the scene of an important assembly in the days when Judas Maccabaeus called the men of Judah together for counsel and prayer (1 Macc. iii. 46), 'a place of prayer aforetime in Israel'.

Two identifications are offered today—Nebi Samwil 4½ miles north-west of Jerusalem, 2,935 feet above sea-level and 500 feet above the surrounding country, and Tell en-Nasbeh on the top of an isolated hill about 8 miles north of Jerusalem. The latter site has been excavated by F. W. Badé, who found a long period of occupation here from the Early Bronze Age to the Maccabean period, with evidence of strong fortification in Asa's time. Stamped jar handles found here bore the letters MṢH and MṢP, the latter suggesting Mizpah. Opinion today is strongly in favour of identifying Mizpah with Tell en-Nasbeh, though some doubt remains.

BIBLIOGRAPHY. F. M. Abel, *Géographie de la Palestine*, 1933, II, pp. 388–390; M. du Buit, *Géographie de la Terre Sainte*, 1958, p. 213; Nelson Glueck, *BASOR*, 92, 1943, pp. 10 ff.

J.A.T.

MIZRAIM. 1. Second son of Ham and progenitor of Ludim, Anamim, Lehabim, Naphtuhim, Casluhim, and Caphtorim (*qq.v.*) (Gn. x. 6, 13; 1 Ch. i. 8, 11).

2. *Miṣrayim* is also the regular Hebrew (and common Semitic) term for Egypt. For all full details on this name, see EGYPT (Name).

3. In 1 Ki. x. 28, 29, it is possible to argue that the first *miṣrayim* is not Egypt but a land Muṣur in SE Asia Minor, and to render (modifying RSV) 'Solomon's import of horses was from Muṣur and from Que' (Cilicia), but this would require the *miṣrayim* of 2 Ch. ix. 28 to be taken also as Muṣur and not Egypt. It is perhaps better to render *miṣrayim* as Egypt in these two passages as in all other Old Testament references. On the various lands Muṣur, besides references given under EGYPT (Name), see also P. Garelli, *Muṣur*, in Vigouroux and Cazelles, *Supplément au Dictionnaire de la Bible*, V, fasc. 29, 1957, cols. 1468–1474. K.A.K.

MNASON. 'An early (original) disciple'—*i.e.* at least from Pentecost—and Paul's host (Acts xxi. 16). Like Barnabas, he was a Jewish Cypriot. The name is Greek, and common.

Vulg., AV, RV, NEB understand the passage 'Caesarean disciples brought Mnason' (but why should they bring the prospective host?); RSV translates 'bringing *us* to the house of Mnason'. Neither is easy; probably *Mnasōni* has been attracted into the case of its relative (*cf.* A. T. Robertson, *Gram.*, p. 719). One would infer Mnason's residence in Jerusalem: a Hellenist host might not embarrass Paul's Gentile friends. The Western reading, valueless in itself, has 'reaching a village, we were with Nason': perhaps a guess, for the journey would require a night-stop; but perhaps correctly interpreting Luke. Mnason's house would then lie between Caesarea and Jerusalem: hence the escort, and the reference to Jerusalem in verse 17.

Luke's allusion may indicate that Mnason provided source-material (*cf.* Ramsay, *BRD*, p. 309 n.).

BIBLIOGRAPHY. H. J. Cadbury in *Amicitiae Corolla*, 1933, pp. 51 ff.; F. F. Bruce, *The Acts of the Apostles*, 1951, *ad loc.* A.F.W.

MOAB, MOABITES. Moab (*mô'āḇ*) was the son of Lot by incestuous union with his eldest daughter (Gn. xix. 37). Both the descendants and the land were known as Moab, and the people also as Moabites (*mô'āḇî*). The core of Moab was the plateau east of the Dead Sea between the

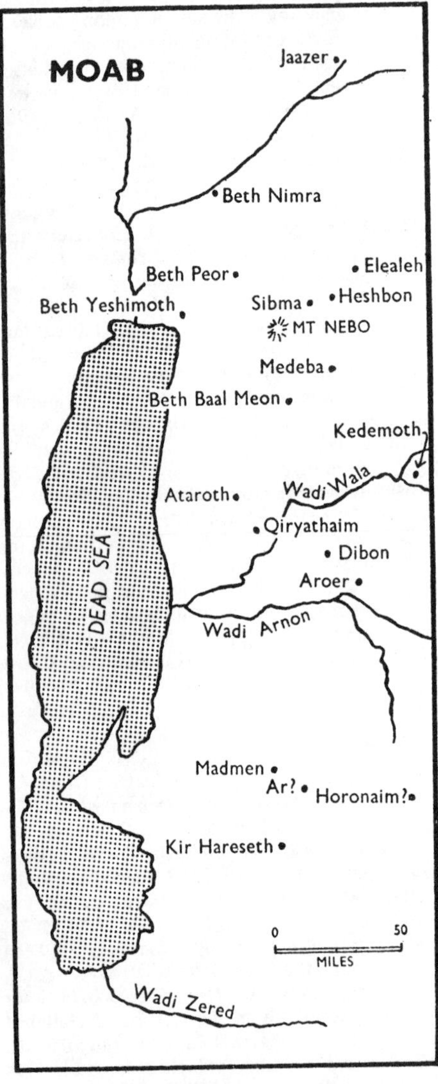

Fig. 144.

wadis Arnon and Zered, though for considerable periods Moab extended well to the north of the Arnon. The average height of the plateau is 3,000 feet, but it is cut by deep gorges. The Arnon itself divides about 13 miles from the Dead Sea and several times more farther east into valleys of diminishing depth, the 'valleys of the Arnon' (Nu. xxi. 14, RSV). The Bible has preserved the names of many Moabite towns (Nu. xxi. 15, 20, xxxii. 3; Jos. xiii. 17–20; Is. xv, xvi; Je. xlviii. 20 ff.).

In pre-Exodus times Moab was occupied and had settled villages until about 1850 BC. Lot's descendants found a population already there, and must have intermarried with them to emerge at length as the dominant group who gave their name to the whole population. The four kings from the East invaded Moab and overthrew the people of Shaveh-Kiriathaim (Gn. xiv. 5). Either as a result of this campaign, or due to some cause unknown, Transjordan entered on a period of non-sedentary occupation till just before 1300 BC, when several of the Iron Age kingdoms appeared simultaneously. Moab, like the others, was a highly organized kingdom with good agricultural and pastoral pursuits, splendid buildings, distinctive pottery, and strong fortifications in the shape of small fortresses strategically placed around her boundaries. The Moabites overflowed their main plateau and occupied areas north of the Arnon, destroying the former inhabitants (Dt. ii. 10, 11, 19–21; *cf.* Gn. xiv. 5). These lands were shared with the closely related Ammonites.

Just prior to the Exodus, these lands north of the Arnon were wrested from Moab by Sihon, king of the Amorites. When Israel sought permission to travel along 'the King's Highway' which crossed the plateau, Moab refused (Jdg. xi. 17). They may have had commercial contact (Dt. ii. 28–29). Moses was forbidden to attack Moab despite their unfriendliness (Dt. ii. 9), although Moabites were henceforth to be excluded from Israel (Dt. xxiii. 3–6; Ne. xiii. 1).

Balak, king of Moab, distressed by the Israelite successes, called for the prophet Balaam to curse Israel now settled across the Arnon (Nu. xxii–xxiv; Jos. xxiv. 9).

As Israel prepared to cross the Jordan, they camped in the 'plains of Moab' (Nu. xxii. 1; Jos. iii. 1) and were seduced by Moabite and Midianite women to participate in idolatrous practices (Nu. xxv; Ho. ix. 10).

In the days of the Judges, Eglon, king of Moab, invaded Israelite lands as far as Jericho and oppressed Israel for eighteen years. Ehud the Benjamite assassinated him (Jdg. iii. 12–30). Elimelech of Bethlehem migrated to Moab and his sons married Moabite women, Orpah and Ruth. Ruth later married Boaz and became the ancestress of David (Ru. iv. 18–22; Mt. i. 5–16). Saul warred with the Moabites (1 Sa. xiv. 47) and David lodged his parents there while he was a fugitive (1 Sa. xxii. 3, 4). Later David subdued Moab and set apart many Moabites for death (2 Sa. viii. 2, 12; 1 Ch. xviii. 2, 11). After Solomon's death, Moab broke free, but was subdued by Omri of Israel. (See MESHA, MOABITE STONE.) Towards the close of Ahab's life Moab began to break free again. Jehoram of Israel sought the help of Jehoshaphat, king of Judah, and the king of Edom to regain Moab, but the campaign was abortive (2 Ki. i. 1, iii. 4–27). Later, Jehoshaphat's own land was invaded by a confederacy of

Moabites, Ammonites, and Edomites, but confusion broke out and the allies attacked one another so that Judah was delivered (2 Ch. xx. 1–30).

In the year of Elisha's death, bands of Moabites raided Israel (2 Ki. xiii. 20). During the latter part of the 8th century BC Moab was subdued by Assyria and compelled to pay tribute (Is. xv, xvi), but after Assyria fell Moab was free again. Moabites entered Judah in the days of Jehoiakim (2 Ki. xxiv. 2). At the fall of Jerusalem in 587 BC some Jews found refuge in Moab, but returned when Gedaliah became governor (Je. xl. 11 ff.). Moab was finally subdued by Nebuchadrezzar (Jos., *Ant.* x. 9. 7) and fell successively under the control of the Persians and various Arab groups. The Moabites ceased to have independent existence as a nation, though in post-exilic times they were known as a race (Ezr. ix. 1; Ne. xiii. 1, 23). Alexander Jannaeus subdued them in the 2nd century BC (Jos., *Ant.* xiii. 13. 5).

In the prophets they are often mentioned and divine judgment pronounced on them (see Is. xv, xvi, xxv. 10; Je. ix. 26, xxv. 21, xxvii. 3; Ezk. xxv. 8–11; Am. ii. 1–3; Zp. ii. 8–11).

BIBLIOGRAPHY. Nelson Glueck, *The Other Side of Jordan*, 1940, pp. 150 ff.; *id.*, *AASOR*, XIV, XV, XVIII, XIX, many references; F. M. Abel, *Géographie de la Palestine*, I, 1933, pp. 278–281; M. du Buit, *Géographie de la Terre Sainte*, 1958, pp. 142, 143; D. Baly, *The Geography of the Bible*, 1958, p. 19.

J.A.T.

MOABITE STONE. A black basalt inscription left by Mesha king of Moab, at Dhiban (biblical Dibon) to commemorate his revolt against Israel and his subsequent rebuilding of many important towns (2 Ki. iii. 4, 5).

The stone was found on 19 August 1868, by the Rev. F. Klein, a German missionary working with the Church Missionary Society. An Arab sheikh named Zattam showed him an inscribed slab some 3 feet 10 inches high, 2 feet broad, and 2½ inches thick, rounded at the top and containing thirty-four lines of writing. Klein copied a few words and reported his find to Dr. Petermann the German consul, who began negotiations to obtain the inscription for the Berlin Museum. Unfortunately, C. S. Clermont-Ganneau of the French Consulate sought to obtain it for the Paris Museum. He sent independent messengers to obtain a squeeze of the inscription, but a dispute arose and the messengers fled with the squeeze in several pieces. The Arabs, sensing the value of the stone, had forced the price up. When the Turkish officials interfered the local Arabs kindled a fire under the stone and poured water over it to break it into fragments, which were carried away as charms to bless their grain. Clermont-Ganneau subsequently recovered several fragments, made fresh squeezes, and finally reconstructed the stone in the Louvre in Paris (see *IBA*, p. 54). Out of an estimated 1,100 letters, 669 were recovered, rather less than two-thirds, but the original squeeze, though somewhat marred, preserved the greater part of the story.

The inscription refers to the triumph of 'Mesha, son of Chemosh, king of Moab', whose father reigned over Moab thirty years. He tells how he threw off the yoke of Israel and honoured his god Chemosh by building a high place at Qarḥoh (QRḤH) in gratitude. The account continues as follows—'As for Omri King of Israel, he humbled Moab many years [lit. days] for Chemosh was angry at his land. And his son followed him and he also said "I will humble Moab". In my time he spoke (thus) but I have triumphed over him and over his house, while Israel hath perished for ever! (Now) Omri had occupied the land of Medeba and (Israel) had dwelt there in his time and half the time of his son (Ahab), forty years; but Chemosh dwelt there in my time.'

This account seems to imply that Mesha broke free from Israel before Ahab's death and thus appears to clash with 2 Ki. i. 1. There need not be any contradiction, however, for during the last years of Ahab's life he was sore pressed by the Syrian wars and probably lost his control over Moab. From Mesha's angle, his freedom dated from then, but from Israel's viewpoint Moab could not be regarded as free till after the abortive campaign conducted by Ahab's son Joram (2 Ki. iii).

The stone continues with an account of the building of Baal-meon, Qaryaten, Qarḥoh, Aroer, Beth-bamoth, Bezer, Medeba, Beth-diblathen, Beth-baal-meon. Ataroth, built by the king of Israel for the men of Gad, was captured, its people slain, and its chieftain Arel (or Oriel) dragged before Chemosh in Kerioth. Nebo was taken and 7,000 devoted to Ashtar-Chemosh. Yahaz, built by the king of Israel, and his centre during the fighting, was taken and attached to Dibon.

Mesha referred to the reservoirs and cisterns, the walls, gates, towers, and the king's palace he constructed in Qarḥoh with Israelite slave labour. He also made a highway in the Arnon valley.

The great importance of this inscription linguistically, religiously, and historically lies in its close relation to the Old Testament. The language is closely akin to Hebrew. Both Chemosh the god of Moab and Yahweh the God of Israel are mentioned, and we have an interesting insight into Moabite beliefs, akin in some ways to those of Israel. Chemosh may be angry with his people, forsake them, deliver them to their enemies, and finally save them. He might command Mesha in words like those that Yahweh used for His servants. The rite of *ḥērem* and the existence of sanctuaries in high places occur here as well as in the Old Testament. Although the authenticity of the stone has been disputed, there are no adequate grounds for this. It must be dated towards the end of Mesha's reign, *c.* 830 BC. It is translated and annotated by E. Ullendorff in *DOTT*, pp. 195 ff., and by W. F.

Albright in *ANET*, pp. 320 f. For a careful study of the text see S. R. Driver, *Notes on the Hebrew Text of the Books of Samuel*², 1913, pp. lxxxiv ff. For reproductions of the Stone see *IBA*, p. 54; *DOTT*, facing p. 198; *ANEP*, No. 274 (and alphabetic table in No. 286). (See MOAB, MESHA, CHEMOSH, DIBON.) J.A.T.

MOLADAH. A town in S Judah, Simeonite before David's reign (1 Ch. iv. 28), and occupied under Nehemiah (Ne. xi. 26). Robinson identified it as Tell el-Milh, 12 miles east of Beersheba, probably the Roman headquarters Moleatha (Abel, *Géographie*, II, p. 391); Simons prefers Quseife, 4 miles up-country towards Arad (Malaatha in Eusebius); so Albright, *JPOS*, IV, 1924, pp. 149 ff. J.P.U.L.

MOLE. Of two Heb. words translated mole in AV, *tinšemeṯ* (Lv. xi. 30) is so vague that its identity remains very uncertain; there is more agreement about *ḥᵃp̄arpereṯ* (Is. ii. 20), which RSV also renders mole. The animal in question is more likely to be the mole-rat (*Spalax sp*.). This is a rodent, but burrows and pushes up heaps after the manner of a mole: these heaps are seen in great numbers in many parts of the Middle East. See also LIZARD. G.C.

MOLECH, MOLOCH. A god worshipped by the Ammonites. Usually the name is Molech (*mōleḵ*), but twice in AV it is Moloch (Am. v. 26; Acts vii. 43), though the Heb. text, RV, and RSV have 'your king'. Some commentators suggest that the Heb. consonants of *meleḵ*, 'king', and the vowels of *bōšeṯ*, 'shame', were combined to form Heb. *mōleḵ*, which expressed contempt for the heathen god. Heb. *mōleḵ* (LXX *moloch*) is probably related to the Carthaginian–Phoenician *molok*, known from inscriptions of the period 400–150 BC, and occurring as *molc* in Lat. inscriptions from Carthage about AD 200 (W. F. Albright, *Archaeology and the Religion of Israel*, 1953, pp. 162 ff.). The god is related to *muluk*, worshipped at Mari about 1800 BC, and *malik*, known in Akkadian texts, and appearing in the compound forms Adrammelech and Anammelech, 2 Ki. xvii. 31. The name is related, through the common root *mlk*, to Milcom and Malcam (*qq.v.*). In the Old Testament Molech generally carries the article (Lv. xviii. 21, xx. 2–5; 2 Ki. xxiii. 10; Je. xxxii. 35), suggesting that the word may have been an appellative for 'the one who rules'. Je. xxxii. 35 points to some connection with Baal, whose name is also an appellative, and to whom, as Baal-Melqart, human sacrifices were offered at Tyre.

The worship of Molech was associated with the sacrifice of children in the fire (Lv. xviii. 21, xx. 2, 3, 4, 5; 2 Ki. xxiii. 10; Je. xxxii. 35; *cf.* 2 Ki. xvii. 31). The practice is attested in documents from Syria (W. F. Albright, *op. cit.*, p. 163).

The law of Moses demanded the death of anyone who offered his child to Molech (Lv. xviii. 21, xx. 2, 3, 4, 5). Later, Solomon built a high place for this god in 'the hill that is before [east of] Jerusalem', *i.e.* the Mount of Olives (1 Ki. xi. 7). Several references in the Old Testament to child-sacrifice, while not referred specifically to Molech, may be included here (Ps. cvi. 38; Je. vii. 31, xix. 4, 5; Ezk. xvi. 21, xxiii. 37, 39). King Ahaz, *c.* 730 BC, burned his children in the fire (2 Ch. xxviii. 3), and Manasseh did the same (2 Ki. xxi. 6). Samaria was judged for this sin (2 Ki. xvii. 17). Josiah, in Judah, destroyed the high places of Molech (2 Ki. xxiii. 10, 13). Ezekiel was still condemning the practice early in the 6th century (Ezk. xvi. 20 ff., xx. 26, 31, xxiii. 37). The Exile seems to have put an end to this worship but it lingered on in N Africa among the Carthaginian Phoenicians into the Christian era.

BIBLIOGRAPHY. W. F. Albright, *Archaeology and the Religion of Israel*, 1953, pp. 162 ff.; O. Eissfeldt, *Molk als Opferbegriff* . . ., 1935. J.A.T.

MOLID. A name found in the genealogy of Jerahmeel (1 Ch. ii. 29). Moladah may be connected, but evidence is lacking (*GTT*, pp. 48, 144).

MOLTEN SEA. See TEMPLE.

MONEY.

I. IN THE OLD TESTAMENT

Before the introduction of coinage in the late 8th century BC (see *c* below) the medium of exchange in commercial transactions was a modified form of barter. Throughout the Ancient Near East staple commodities, both those which were perishable, such as wool, barley, wheat, and dates, and those which were non-perishable, including metals, timber, wine, honey, and livestock, served as 'exchangeable goods'. The texts show that from the earliest times periodic attempts were made to stabilize the values of these commodities with respect to each other. Thus wealth was measured by possession of cattle (Jb. i. 3) and precious metals. Abraham was 'rich in cattle, in silver, and in gold' (Gn. xiii. 2).

a. Metal as an exchange commodity

Since silver (Heb. *kesep̄*) was the commonest metal available in Palestine (as in Assyria and Babylonia), it appears as the most frequently used (AV often translates *kesep̄* as 'money', *e.g.* Gn. xvii. 13). Thus in ordinary transactions the term silver is often omitted, as understood; Solomon purchased chariots at 600 (shekels weight of silver) and horses at 150 (1 Ki. x. 29; *cf.* Lv. v. 15). His revenue was reckoned in silver by talents (1 Ki. x. 14; see WEIGHTS AND MEASURES), for silver was as common in Jerusalem as stones (1 Ki. x. 27). Until post-exilic times the 'shekel' bears its literal meaning of a certain weight rather than denoting a coin.

Silver was used for the purchase of real estate, whether a field, such as that purchased by Jeremiah at Anathoth for 17 shekels of silver

(Je. xxxii. 9), the cave at Machpelah bought by Abraham for 400 shekels of silver (Gn. xxiii. 15, 16), the village and hill of Samaria bought by Omri for 2 talents of silver (1 Ki. xvi. 24), or the threshing-floor of Araunah bought by David for 50 shekels (2 Sa. xxiv. 24). Silver also formed the basis of a dowry (Ex. xxii. 17) or a bride purchase-price (Ho. iii. 2).

Gold, being more rarely obtained, often figures after silver, and is mentioned with it in large quantities in the payment of tribute. Thus Hezekiah paid Sennacherib in 701 BC 300 talents of silver and 30 talents of gold (2 Ki. xviii. 14), while Menahem had bought off the Assyrians for 1,000 talents of silver (2 Ki. xv. 19). Gold played a prominent part in inter-state border transactions, and Hiram paid 120 talents of gold to Solomon for the villages ceded to him (1 Ki. ix. 10–14).

In many inter-state and local transactions payment in goods might be agreed as a supplement or substitute for precious metal. Mesha of Moab offered sheep and wool (2 Ki. iii. 4); Sennacherib was given precious stones, in addition to gold and silver, by Hezekiah according to the Assyr. annals, and Jehu's tribute to Shalmaneser III included blocks of antimony, lead, golden vessels, and rare fruits (see JEHU). Barley (Ho. iii. 2), spices (2 Ki. xx. 13), or clothing might be part of the agreed price or gift (2 Ki. v. 23). Copper (AV 'brass') was another metal in use as currency (Ex. xxxv. 5; 2 Sa. xxi. 16) of less value than gold (Is. lx. 17).

To control the use of metals as currency they had to be weighed out (Heb. *šql*, hence 'shekel') by the purchaser and checked by the vendor in the presence of witnesses (Gn. xxiii. 16; Je. xxxii. 9, 10). The standard of weight agreed was that in force by local standards called the 'silver of city X' or 'the silver (current with) the merchant' (Gn. xxiii. 16; Bab. *kaspum ša damqarim*). This agreed standard is also implied by payment 'in full weight' (Gn. xliii. 21). Thus merchants were 'weighers of silver'. Another check was made on the quality of the metal by stamping it with its place of origin. Gold of Ophir (1 Ki. x. 11) or Parvaim (2 Ch. iii. 6) was highly prized, while gold and silver were sometimes classified as 'refined' (AV 'pure, purified').

b. Forms of currency

To enable metal used as currency to be transportable it was kept either in the form of jewellery, of objects in daily use, or in characteristic shapes. Thus Abraham gave Rebekah a gold ring (weighing) half a shekel and bracelets of 10 shekels (Gn. xxiv. 22). Gold was often carried as thin bars or wedges (Heb. 'tongue'), like that weighing 50 shekels found by Achan at Jericho (Jos. vii. 21) or the 'golden wedge of Ophir' (Is. xiii. 12). The latter was probably engraved with the name, since a pot marked 'For the gold of Ophir' has been discovered at Qasileh in Palestine (see OPHIR). Gold and silver were also held as ingots, vessels, dust (Jb. xxviii. 6), or small fragments, and could be melted and used immediately for many purposes. In these forms Joseph increased the revenue of Egypt (Gn. xlvii. 14).

On a journey the small pieces of metal were carried in a pouch or bag of leather or cloth (AV 'bundles of money', Gn. xlii. 35; Pr. vii. 20) which, if holed, would easily lead to loss (Hg. i. 6). A talent of silver seemed to require two bags (2 Ki. v. 23). To guard against loss the money bags were often placed inside other sacks or receptacles (Gn. xlii. 35). Silver was also moulded into small drops or beads (1 Sa. ii. 36, *'ᵃgōrâ*) or lumps. It is probable that the half-shekel used for payment into the sanctuary was an unminted lump of silver (Ex. xxx. 13; 2 Ki. xii. 9–16), though normally such temple dues as taxes could be paid either in silver or in kind (Dt. xxvi; Ne. v. 10).

Copper, being of less value than gold and silver, was transported as flat circular discs, hence the term *kikkār* ('a round', 'flat round of bread', Assyr. *kakkāru*) was used for the 'talent', the heaviest weight.

c. The introduction of coinage

Coinage, a piece of metal struck with a seal authenticating its title and weight so that it would be accepted on sight, first appears in Asia Minor in the late 8th century BC. Though Sennacherib (*c.* 701 BC) refers to the 'minting of half-shekel pieces', there is no evidence that this refers to anything more than a bronze-casting technique, for no coins of this early period have been found as yet in Assyria, Syria, or Palestine. Early silver coins have been found at Aegina, but the first staters were struck in electrum (an alloy of gold and silver) by Croesus of Lydia (561–546 BC). Herodotus (i. 94) attributes to him the introduction of coinage, his gold coins being designated 'Croesides'. It would seem that after the Persian wars against Lydia, coinage was introduced into Persia by Darius I (521–486 BC), whose name was used to denote the thick gold coin, or *daric*, which portrays the king, half-length or kneeling, with bow and arrow; with the die-punch mark in reverse (see Herodotus iv. 166). This daric weighed 130 gr., the *siglos* or shekel 86½ gr. *Cf.* fig. 145, no. 4.

The daric (AV 'dram') was known to the Jews in exile (Ezr. ii. 69, viii. 27; Ne. vii. 70, 71) and the reference to a daric in the time of David (1 Ch. xxix. 7) shows that the text at this point was giving the equivalent term at the time of compilation of this history. The change to payment of workmen in coin instead of in kind is attested by the Persepolis Treasury texts (*c.* 450 BC), confirming a ratio of 13 :1 gold to silver. The spread of coinage to Judah seems to have been slow, perhaps because of the images they bore. It is therefore uncertain whether the silver shekels of Ne. v. 15, x. 32 were weights, as in the earlier period, or money in coin. Since the Persian satraps were allowed to mint only silver coins, gold Achaemenian coins were rare in Palestine.

The Phoenician traders had early taken up the

Fig. 145. A selection of coins in circulation in biblical times. 1. A silver tetradrachm of Ephesus (4th century BC). The bee and the stag were symbols connected with the worship of Diana (Artemis). 2. A Roman silver denarius (*c.* 180 BC) showing the head of Roma (*obverse*) and the Dioscuri charging with levelled lances (*reverse*). 3. A bronze coin of Aelia Capitolina, the name given to Jerusalem after its re-building by the Emperor Hadrian in AD 136. It shows the head of Hadrian and, on the reverse, a representation of him ploughing the first furrow of the new city. 4. Silver siglos of Darius II of Persia (424–405 BC) showing him kneeling with spear and bow; probably one of the earliest coins to circulate in Palestine. 5, 6, 7. Three bronze coins of Alexander Jannaeus (103–76 BC). The first has a Hebrew inscription (*obverse*) and a poppy between a double cornucopia (*reverse*). The second shows a Greek inscription with an anchor (*obverse*) and a Hebrew inscription within an encircled star (*reverse*).

use of coins, and by the 5th–4th centuries many coins were issued from mints at Aradus, Byblos, Tyre, and Sidon, and the coinage of Asia Minor, Greece, Ptolemaic Egypt, and Syria entered Judah, where these coins, along with those of the ruling Persian, as later Greek, rulers were used. Hoards found in Palestine include coins of Ptolemy Soter I (3rd century BC) and Demetrius I (294–289 BC) at Beth-shan; of Alexander the Great at Bethel; of the Seleucids and Maccabees at Beth-zur and Jerusalem.

With the Hellenization of Syria and Palestine, Greek coinage brought the talents and drachmas, which continued into common use into New Testament times (1 Macc. xi. 28; 2 Macc. iv. 19). However, the discovery of three coins inscribed *yhd* (Aramaic for 'Judah') of the first half of the 4th century BC implies an early attempt at a native coinage; the reverse shows a design of a male deity seated on a chariot holding a hawk, with square frame (see *IBA*, p. 89). Somewhat later comes a coin inscribed 'Hezekiah' (the high priest under Alexander the Great) found at Beth-zur.

In the struggle for independence under the Maccabees John Hyrcanus (134–104 BC) struck small bronze coins of $\frac{1}{2}$, $\frac{1}{4}$, and $\frac{1}{3}$ shekel showing (obverse) an olive wreath with the inscription 'Jehohanan, the high-priest and the community of the Jews'; the reverse imitated Greek coins with its double cornucopia. The coins once attributed to Simon Maccabaeus, who won the right to coin money for his nation with his own stamp (1 Macc. xv. 6), have now been identified as later (see, *e.g.*, the silver shekels of the First Revolt).

BIBLIOGRAPHY. R. de Vaux, *Les Institutions de l'Ancien Testament*, I, 1958, pp. 313–317; E. S. G. Robinson, 'The Beginnings of Achaemenid Coinage' in *Numismatic Chronicle* (6th Series), XVIII, 1958, pp. 187–193. D.J.W.

II. IN THE NEW TESTAMENT

During New Testament times money from three different sources was in circulation in Palestine. There was the official imperial money coined on the Roman standard; provincial coins minted at Antioch and Tyre, which held mainly to the old Gk. standard, and circulated chiefly among the

No. 7 has the obverse similar to No. 6, but the reverse has a Hebrew inscription around a flower. 8. A bronze coin of Herod the Great (37–4 BC). This again bears the anchor motif on the obverse. The reverse shows a herald's wand (caduceus) between a double cornucopia. 9. A bronze coin of Herod Archelaus (4 BC–AD 6), showing a bunch of grapes and a plumed helmet. 10. A bronze coin of Herod Agrippa I (AD 37–44). The obverse shows an umbrella-shaped canopy, the reverse three ears of barley. 11. A silver tetradrachm of Antioch on the Orontes, showing the head of the Emperor Augustus. Coins such as these would have been in circulation in Jerusalem during the time of our Lord, and may have been used by the chief priests for their payment to Judas. 12. The obverse of a denarius showing a portrait of the Emperor Nero (AD 54–68). For other coins see figs. 9, 10, 47, 79.

inhabitants of Asia Minor; and the local Jewish money, coined perhaps at Caesarea. Certain cities and client-kings were also granted the right to strike their own bronze coins. With coins of so many different scales in circulation it is obvious that there was need of money-changers at Jerusalem, especially at feasts when Jews came from all parts to pay their poll-tax to the Temple treasury. On these occasions the money-changers moved their stalls into the Court of the Gentiles, whence Jesus expelled them (Jn. ii. 15; Mt. xxi. 12; Mk. xi. 15; Lk. xix. 45 f.) because of their avaricious practices.

Mt. x. 9 serves as a useful reminder that in those days, as now, money was coined in three principal metals, gold, silver, and copper, bronze, or brass. Bronze (Gk. *chalkos*) is used as a general word for money in Mk. vi. 8 and xii. 41, but as only the coins of smaller value, the Roman *as* (Gk. *assarion*) and Jewish *lepton* were minted in bronze, the more common general term for money in the New Testament is silver (Gk. *argyrion*; see Lk. ix. 3; Acts viii. 20; *etc.*). The most common silver coins mentioned in the New Testament are the Attic tetradrachm and the Roman *denarius*. Gk. *chrysos*, gold, is most frequently used to refer to the metal itself, except in Mt. x. 9; Acts iii. 6, possibly also Acts xx. 33; 1 Pet. i. 18; Jas. v. 3; Mt. xxiii. 16 f., though these instances might equally well refer to gold vessels and ornaments.

Other general terms used for money in the New Testament are the common Gk. word *chrēma*, meaning property or wealth, as well as money (Acts iv. 37, viii. 18, 20, xxiv. 26), *kerma*, or small change (from Gk. *keirō*, 'I cut up'), used in Jn. ii. 15, and nearly always denoting copper coins, and *nomisma*, or money introduced into common use by law (*nomos*). This last is found only in Mt. xxii. 19, where the phrase *nomisma tou kēnsou* means the legal coin for paying the tax.

a. Jewish coins

In 141–140 BC Antiochus VII granted permission to Simon Maccabaeus 'priest and governor of the Jews . . . to coin money for thy country with thine own stamp' (1 Macc. xv. 6), and from that time Jewish coins were minted, mainly in bronze, as neighbouring cities produced an abundance of silver coins. Early Jewish coins heeded the second commandment, and so their devices adhered strictly to horticultural designs and inanimate objects. Coins minted under the Herods show one or two breaches of this rule, as they displayed sometimes the reigning emperor's head, sometimes their own, on the obverse (see Wiseman, *Illustrations from Biblical Archaeology*, p. 86). During the time of the First Revolt (AD 66–70) the Jews proudly coined their own silver for the first time, issuing silver shekels and quarter- and half-shekel pieces as well as their own bronzes. Following this revolt, the Temple treasures were seized, and so the Jews had no further supplies of metal to coin their own silver during the second revolt (AD 132–135). They therefore celebrated their independence by overstriking old foreign coins with Jewish dies containing the inscription 'deliverance of Jerusalem'.

The only Jewish coin mentioned in the New Testament is the bronze *lepton* (from Gk. *leptos*—'small, fine'). This is the widow's 'mite' of Mk. xii. 42; Lk. xxi. 2, also called a 'farthing' in Lk. xii. 59, where it stands for the smallest coin imaginable. It was equivalent to half the Roman *quadrans*, and so one-eighth of the *assarion* (see below).

b. Greek coins

The basic Greek coin was the silver *drachmē*, of which there were 100 to the *mna*, or mina, and 6,000 to the talent. The drachm was roughly equivalent to 1*s*. 2*d*. sterling or 16 cents of American money today, but this is no guide to its purchasing power. About 300 BC it was the price of a sheep: an ox cost 5 *drachmai* (Demetrius Phalereus).

The *drachmē* is mentioned only in Lk. xv. 8 f. in the New Testament, where it is translated 'pieces of silver' (EVV): it is thought that the woman in the parable may have had this as an ornament. It was regarded as approximately equivalent to the Roman *denarius* (see below).

The *didrachmon* or 2-drachm piece was used among the Jews for the half-shekel required for the annual Temple tax (Mt. xvii. 24). This regulation derived from the atonement-money prescribed in Ex. xxx. 11–16, which, according to Maimonides, later developed into a regular annual poll-tax (see Jos., *Ant*. xvi. 6). After the fall of Jerusalem and the destruction of the Temple this tax had to be paid into the Roman treasury (Jos., *BJ* vii. 6. 6). It seems most likely that the coins used for this tax would be those of Tyre, for the Talmudic law forbade the use of Antiochene money for the Temple treasury, not for any religious reasons, but because it did not contain enough silver.

The *statēr*, *tetradrachmon*, or 4-drachm piece, is found only in Mt. xvii. 27, where it is the coin which would pay the Temple tax for Jesus and Peter. As it was a more common coin than the didrachm, it would appear that Jews frequently united to pay the Temple tax in pairs by means of the tetradrachm. It was minted at Antioch, Caesarea in Cappadocia, and in Tyre. Pompey fixed the rate of exchange of tetradrachms from Antioch and Tyre at 4 *denarii* (*c*. 65 BC), and Josephus refers to the same rate for the Tyrian tetradrachm in his day (*BJ* ii. 21. 2). Antiochene tetradrachms were, however, tariffed by the imperial government at 3 *denarii* only. Most numismatists agree that this was the coin in which Judas received his thirty pieces of silver (Mt. xxvi. 15; see fig. 145, no. 11). The use of the term *argyria hikana*, 'large silver-money', in Mt. xxviii. 12, 13 has been thought by some to suggest that the coins with which the Sanhedrin bribed the guards of the tomb were the large silver staters and not the smaller *drachmai* or *denarii*, though it is possible that the adjective here refers to quantity rather than size.

The *mna*, translated 'pound', occurs in the parable of Lk. xix. 11–27.

The 'talent' was not a coin, but a unit of monetary reckoning. Its value was always high, though it varied with the different metals involved and the different monetary standards. The Roman–Attic was equivalent to 240 *aurei* (see below). It was mentioned by Jesus in two parables: in Mt. xviii. 24 ten thousand talents is figurative for a very large sum of money, and in the parable of the talents in Mt. xxv. 15–28 it is referred to in verse 18 as *argyrion*, which may suggest that our Lord had the silver talent in mind.

c. Roman coins

The basic Roman coin, mentioned above, was the silver *denarius*. There were 25 *denarii* to the golden *aureus*, the weight of which was fixed by Julius Caesar in 49 BC at 126·3 grs., though subsequent debasing of the coinage under Augustus and his successors brought the weight down to 115 grs. by Nero's time.

The *quadrans* (Gk. *kodrantēs*) was one-quarter of the copper *as* (see below). It is referred to by both Horace (*Satires*, ii. 3. 93) and Juvenal (vii. 8) as the smallest Roman coin: Mk. xii. 42 states that the widow's two *lepta* (see (*a*) above) were equivalent to a *quadrans*. Mt. v. 26 uses *quadrans* for the smallest coin, which must be paid to clear a debt in full, while the Lucan parallel (xii. 59) has *lepton*, except in the Western Text, which agrees with Matthew.

The copper *as* (Gk. *assarion*) was a quarter of the bronze *sestertius* and one-sixteenth of the silver *denarius*. It occurs in Mt. x. 29 and Lk. xii. 6, where it is translated by the AV as 'farthing' and RV as 'penny', the price at which two sparrows are sold (Lk. has five sparrows for two farthings).

The *denarius* (Gk. *dēnarion*) gained its name (*deni* = ten at a time) from the fact that at first it was the equivalent in silver of 10 copper *asses*. From 217 BC it was worth 16 *asses*, when the weight of the latter coin was fixed at 1 ounce. It is regarded today as equivalent to about 1*s*. 2*d*. or 16 cents (not in purchasing power), but was rendered consistently as 'penny' by the translators of the AV and RV (but see the note on Mt. xviii. 28 in the RVmg), owing to the fact that British currency, modelled on that of Rome, still uses *d.* for *denarius* as the abbreviation for penny.

It would appear from the parable of Mt. xx. 1–16 to have been the daily wage of a labourer, and two *denarii* was the sum paid by the good Samaritan to the innkeeper (Lk. x. 35): that should give some idea of its purchasing power. In Rev. vi. 6 'a measure of wheat for a *denarius*, and three measures of barley for a *denarius*' is an indication of famine prices (see WEIGHTS AND MEASURES).

From Mt. xxii. 19; Mk. xii. 15; Lk. xx. 24 we learn that it was the coin used to trick Jesus in the question concerning the payment of tribute-money. Silver *denarii* of the time have been discovered which carry the laureate head of the Emperor Tiberius on the obverse, with his mother, Livia, in the rôle of Pax, holding a branch and sceptre, on the reverse (see *IBA*, p. 87, fig. 90).

The *aureus*, or *denarius aureus* (golden denarius), was a gold coin introduced by Julius Caesar in his financial reforms of 49 BC. It finds no mention in the Bible, but is referred to in Jos., *Ant.* xiv. 8. 5: it may be the 'gold' of Mt. x. 9.

d. Evaluation of money

In view of fluctuating economic conditions it is extremely difficult to evaluate the money of the New Testament in modern terms, but the table given below may serve as a rough guide.

Jewish	*Greek*	*Roman*	*English*	*American*
1 *lepton*		½ *quadrans*	0.1075*d.*	⅛ cent
		1 *quadrans*	0.215*d.*	¼ cent
		1 *as*	0.86*d.*	1 cent
	1 *drachmē*	1 *denarius*	13.76*d.*	16 cents
	1 *statēr*	4 *denarii*	55.04*d.*	64 cents
	25 *drachmai*	1 *aureus*	£1 8*s.* 8*d.*	4 dollars
	1 *mna*	100 *denarii*	£5 14*s.* 8*d.*	16 dollars
	1 *talent*	240 *aurei*	£344	960 dollars

These figures are based on the current rate of exchange at the time of writing of 7*s.* 2*d.* to the dollar, and it should again be emphasized that they are no guide to the purchasing power of the coins mentioned. Before the devaluation of the pound in 1949 the *aureus* was reckoned as roughly equivalent to the pound, and the *denarius* consequently about 9½*d.*

BIBLIOGRAPHY. H. A. Grueber, *Coins of the Roman Republic in the British Museum*, 3 vols., 1910; Garnet R. Halliday, *Money Talks about the Bible*, 1948; G. F. Hill, *Catalogue of Greek Coins in the British Museum*, vol. on Palestine, 1914; Mattingley and Sydenham, *The Roman Imperial Coinage*, vols. i and ii, 1923, reprinted 1948; E. Rogers, *A Handy Guide to Jewish Coins*, 1914; Paul Romanoff, *Jewish Symbols on Ancient Jewish Coins*, 1944; F. A. Banks, *Coins of Bible Days*, 1955; A. Reifenberg, *Israel's History in Coins from the Maccabees to the Roman Conquest*, 1953.

D.H.W.

MONEY-CHANGERS. The 'exchangers' of Mt. xxv. 27 were regular bankers (*trapezitai*); *cf.* the saying commonly ascribed to our Lord, 'Be expert bankers'—*i.e.* trustworthy and skilled in detecting counterfeits. A specialized class of 'exchanger' officiated in the Temple precincts, probably in the Court of the Gentiles—the *kollybistai* (Mt. xxi. 12; Mk. xi. 15; Jn. ii. 15) or *kermatistai* (Jn. ii. 14). The former title derived from a word of Semitic origin denoting exchange-rate or commission; the latter would, strictly speaking, relate to a dealer in small change. The trade arose from the fact that money for the Temple, including the obligatory half-shekel (Ex. xxx. 13; *cf.* Mt. xvii. 24, and see E. Schürer, *HJP*, II. i, pp. 249 ff.) had to be in Tyrian standard coin, and not in the current Roman standard (which had heathen embellishments). A surcharge was made (Mishnah tractate *Sheqalim, passim*) and the way opened for various malpractices (add passages in J. Lightfoot, *Horae Hebraicae* on Mt. xxi. 12 to those in *SB*). The Lord's cleansing of the Temple included the overthrow of the counters of these dealers at the (doubtless highly lucrative) Passover season.

A.F.W.

MONTH. See CALENDAR.

MOON. The creation of the moon is recorded in Gn. i. 16, where it is referred to as 'the lesser light' in contrast to the sun. It was placed in the heavens to rule the night, and with the other luminaries to be 'for signs, and for seasons, and for days, and years' (i. 14). Its appearance in regular phases in the night sky afforded a basis for early calendars (see CALENDAR), and the word most commonly used for it (*yārēaḥ*) is closely related to *yeraḥ*, 'month'. The same word occurs in Akkadian ((*w*)*arḫu*), Ugaritic (*yrḫ*), Phoenician (*yrḥ*), and other Semitic languages. Another word, used less often for it, is *l*ᵉ*bānâ*, 'white one' (Ct. vi. 10; Is. xxiv. 23, xxx. 26).

The first day of each new month was considered holy. Hence the association in the Old Testament of the monthly 'new moon' with the weekly sabbath (*e.g.* Is. i. 13). This fresh beginning was marked by special sacrifices (Nu. xxviii. 11–15) over which the trumpets were blown (Nu. x. 10; Ps. lxxxi. 3). Amos depicts the merchants of his day anxiously awaiting the end of the new moon and of the sabbath so that they could resume their fraudulent trading. It seems therefore to have been regarded, like the sabbath, as a day on which normal work was not done. The reference may be, however, to the new moon of the seventh month, regarding which the law stated specifically that no servile work was to be done on it (Lv. xxiii. 24, 25; Nu. xxix. 1–6). 2 Ki. iv. 23 suggests that both new moon and sabbath were regarded as providing opportunity for consulting the prophets, and Ezekiel marks out the new moon as a special day for worship (Ezk. xlvi. 1, 3).

The moon is mentioned with the sun as a symbol of permanence (Ps. lxxii. 5). It is quoted as a wonder of creation (Ps. viii. 3), and as marking by its behaviour the coming of the Messiah (Mk. xiii. 24; Lk. xxi. 25). Ps. cxxi. 6 suggests that it was recognized as capable of affecting the mind, and in the New Testament Greek words meaning literally 'moon struck' are used in Mt. iv. 24 and xvii. 15.

The moon is named as an object of idolatrous worship in Jb. xxxi. 26, and archaeology has shown that it was deified in ancient W Asia from early Sumerian to Islamic times. In Mesopotamia the Sumerian god Nanna, named Sin by the Akkadians, was worshipped in particular at Ur, where he was the chief god of the city, and also in the city of Harran in Syria, which had close religious links with Ur. The Ugaritic texts have shown that there a moon deity was worshipped under the name *yrḫ*. On the monuments the god is represented by the symbol of a crescent moon (see also AMULETS). At Hazor in Palestine a small Canaanite shrine of the late Bronze Age was discovered which contained a basalt stele depicting two hands lifted as if in prayer to a crescent moon, perhaps indicating that the shrine was dedicated to the moon god (see *IBA*, fig. 112).

T.C.M.

MORALITY. See ETHICS, BIBLICAL.

MORASHTITE. See MORESHETH-GATH.

MORDECAI (Heb. *mordᵉḵay*; *mordᵒḵay*; Ezr. ii. 2).

1. A leader of the exiles who returned with Zerubbabel (Ezr. ii. 2; Ne. vii. 7; 1 Esdras v. 8).

2. A Jewish exile who had moved to the Persian capital Susa (see SHUSHAN), where he was employed in the palace. He was a Benjamite son of Jair and descendant of Kish, who had been taken prisoner to Babylon by Nebuchadrezzar (Est. ii. 5, 6). He brought up his orphaned cousin Hadassah (see ESTHER) and was rewarded, by being mentioned in the royal chronicles, for revealing a plot against King Xerxes (ii. 7, 21–23).

He opposed the vizier Haman who plotted to kill all Jews (Est. iii). When this evil deed was turned against Haman Mordecai succeeded him in office, being then next in rank to the king (v–vi, x). He used this position to encourage the Jews to defend themselves against the massacre inspired by Haman. In respect for Mordecai the Persian provincial officials to whom he wrote assisted in protecting the Jews. The celebration of this event by an annual feast (see PURIM) was later connected with the 'day of Mordecai' (2 Macc. xv. 36).

Rawlinson suggested that Mordecai is to be identified with Matacas, a minister of Xerxes (so Ctesias); but this is uncertain, since domestic annals of this reign are wanting. For the same reason attempts to demonstrate the unhistorical nature of the story of Mordecai are unjustified. Mordecai may be the Heb. rendering of the common Bab. personal name Mardukaia.

D.J.W.

MOREH (*mōreh*, 'teacher', 'diviner'). **1.** The name of a place near Shechem mentioned in Gn. xii. 6, where *'ēlôn mōreh* may be translated 'the teacher's oak' (or 'terebinth'). Dt. xi. 30 makes reference to the 'oak of Moreh' (RSV) in the district of Gilgal (*i.e.* the Shechemite Gilgal). It is recorded that Abraham pitched his camp there on arriving in Canaan from Harran, and it was there that God revealed Himself to Abraham, promising to give the land of Canaan to his descendants (see MAMRE). This tree may also be the one mentioned in Gn. xxxv. 4 where Jacob hid foreign gods, and a reference to the place also occurs in the story of Abimelech (Jdg. ix. 37).

2. The hill of Moreh at the head of the northern side of the valley of Jezreel, south of Mt. Tabor, 1 mile south of Nain, and *c.* 8 miles north-west of Mt. Gilboa, is the modern Jebel Dahi; it features in Jdg. vii. 1, where, in the encounter between Gideon and the Midianites, the Midianites encamped in the valley, by the hill of Moreh, to the north of Gideon's camp by the spring of Harod. R.A.H.G.

MORESHETH-GATH. Mentioned only in Mi. i. 14, it is almost certainly the modern Tell el-Ǧudeideh, about 20 miles south-west of Jerusalem. Morashtite is the gentilic adjective of a shortened form of the name, Moresheth, and is used to describe the prophet Micah, whose home town it was (Je. xxvi. 18; Mi. i. 1). R.F.H.

MORIAH. A place-name occurring twice in the Old Testament. In Gn. xxii. 2 it is recorded that God commanded Abraham to take Isaac to 'the land of Moriah' (*'ereṣ hammōriyyâ*) and there to offer him as a burnt offering upon one of the mountains (*har*). The mountain chosen was three days' journey (xxii. 4) from the land of the Philistines (xxi. 34; the region of Gerar, *q.v.*), and was visible from a distance (xxii. 4). The other mention of the name occurs in 2 Ch. iii. 1, where the site of Solomon's Temple is said to be 'in mount Moriah' (*bᵉhar hammōriyyâ*), in the threshing-floor of Ornan the Jebusite where God appeared to David (iii. 2). It should be noted that no reference is made here to Abraham in connection with this site. It has been objected that Jerusalem is not sufficiently distant from S Philistia to have required a three days' journey to get there, and that one of the characteristics of Jerusalem is that the Temple hill is not visible until the traveller is quite close, so that the correctness of the biblical identification is called in question. The Samaritan tradition identifies the site with Mt. Gerizim, and this is claimed to fulfil the conditions of Gn. xxii. 4 adequately. However, the distance from S Philistia to Jerusalem is about 50 miles, which might well have required three days to traverse, and in Genesis the place in question is not a 'mount Moriah' but one of several mountains in a land of that name, and the hills on which Jerusalem stands are visible at a distance. There is no need to doubt therefore that Abraham's sacrifice took place in the site of later Jerusalem, if not on the Temple hill.

BIBLIOGRAPHY. Abel, *Géographie de la Palestine*, I, 1933, pp. 374, 375. T.C.M.

MORTAR, MORTER. See HOUSE.

MORTAR AND PESTLE. This formed an alternative to the stone mill (see MILL, MILLSTONE). While in the wilderness the Israelites ground the manna (*q.v.*) either in mills or in a mortar (Nu. xi. 8; Heb. *m^eḏōḵâ*), and olive oil was produced in the same way ('beaten oil', Ex. xxvii. 20). Pr. xxvii. 22 shows that evil cannot be removed from a wicked man even if he were to be crushed small (Heb. *maḵtēš*, 'mortar'; '*elî*, 'pestle'). For Egyptians using mortar and pestle, see *ANEP*, no. 153, upper right, and 154, lower part. The mortar was either a hollowed stone or a deep wooden bowl, the pestle a stout wooden pole. A small hollow in the land could also be called 'mortar' from its form, so Jdg. xv. 19; Zp. i. 11 (see MAKTESH). A.R.M.

MOSERAH, MOSEROTH. The name, meaning 'chastisement(s)', is applied to the place, or rather to the event, of Aaron's death, which took place on Mt. Hor (Nu. xx. 23–29). This was regarded as a chastisement for the trespass at Meribah (Nu. xx. 24; Dt. xxxii. 51). Aaron died on the mountain, the people camped below and mourned, and the incident and the camping-place were called Moseroth (Nu. xxxiii. 31; Dt. x. 6). His brother's death, and his own exclusion from this land, lay heavily on Moses' heart (Dt. i. 37, iii. 23–27). G.T.M.

MOSES. The great leader and lawgiver through whom God brought the Hebrews out of Egypt, constituted them a nation for His service, and brought them within reach of the land promised to their forefathers.

I. NAME

In Ex. ii. 10 it is said that 'she called his name *Mōšeh*: and she said, Because I drew him (*m^ešîṯî-hû*) out of the water'. Most interpreters identify the 'she' as Pharaoh's daughter, and this has led many to assume an Egyptian origin for the name *Mōšeh*, Egyp. *ms*, 'child' or '(one) born' being the best possibility. However, the antecedent of 'she' could as easily be 'the woman', *i.e.* Moses' own mother and nurse, who '*had* called his name . . .' (so W. J. Martin). Ex. ii. 10 clearly links the name of *Mōšeh* with his being taken from the waterside (*māšâ*, 'to draw forth'). This pun would come naturally to a Hebrew speaker but not to an Egyptian; which fact would favour the view just mentioned that it was Moses' own mother who first named him, rather than Pharaoh's daughter.

Mōšeh as it stands is an active participle meaning 'one who draws forth', and may be an ellipsis for some longer phrase. In the 14th/13th centuries BC Egyp. *ms*, 'child' (and the related grammatical form in such names as Ramose, 'Rē, is born') was pronounced approximately *măsĕ*, becoming *Mōšeh*, and there is no philological or other reason why Moses' Egyptian adoptive mother should not have assimilated a Semitic **māši* or *Mōšeh* to the common name-word *Măsĕ*, *Mōšeh*, in her own tongue. Compare assimilations such as German Löwe to English Lowe, or Goldschmidt to Goldsmith, in our own day. Hence Moses' name may simply be Semitic assimilated to Egyptian while in Egypt. The majority view, however, is that the daughter of Pharaoh called him *Mōšeh*, 'child' (or—less suitably—a theophoric name in *-mose*), which passed into Hebrew speech as *Mōšeh*. This view, however, fails to account adequately for the Semitic pun, which there is no objective reason to reject as unhistorical, as it is a common practice in Egypt and elsewhere (including the Old Testament) long before Moses; such a view, moreover, runs into real phonetic difficulties over Egyp. *s* appearing as *š* in *Mōšeh* but as *s* in Ra'amses and Phinehas in Hebrew, as was pointed out long ago by A. H. Gardiner, *JAOS*, LVI, 1936, pp. 192–194—a problem in no way solved by J. G. Griffiths, *JNES*, XII, 1953, pp. 225–231, the best and latest statement of this view.

II. LIFE AND BACKGROUND

a. Ancestry

Moses belonged to the tribe of Levi, to the clan of Kohath, and to the house or family of Amram (Ex. vi. 16 ff.). That he was the distant descendant, not the son, of Amram by Jochebed is hinted at inasmuch as his parents are not named in the detailed account of his infancy (Ex. ii), and is made almost certain by the fact that Amram and his three brothers had numerous descendants within a year of the Exodus (Nu. iii. 27 f.); see also CHRONOLOGY OF THE OLD TESTAMENT: Date of the Exodus, for further indications.

b. Egyptian upbringing

To save her baby son from the pharaonic edict ordering the destruction of Hebrew male infants,

Moses' mother put him into a little basket of pitch-caulked reeds or papyrus among the rushes by the stream bank and bade his sister Miriam keep watch. Soon a daughter of Pharaoh came with her maidservants to bathe in the river, found the child, and took pity on him. Miriam discreetly offered to find a nurse for the child (in fact, his mother), and so Moses' life was saved. When weaned, he was handed over to his adoptive 'mother', the Egyptian princess (Ex. ii. 1–10). Of Moses' growth to adult maturity in Egyptian court society no detail is given, but a boy in his position in New Kingdom period court circles could not avoid undergoing a substantial basic training in that 'wisdom of the Egyptians' with which Stephen credits him (Acts vii. 22).

Modern knowledge of Ancient Egypt yields a rich background for the early life of Moses in Egypt. The pharaohs of the New Kingdom period (*c.* 1570–1085 BC) maintained residences and *harîms* not only in the great capitals of Thebes, Memphis, and Pi-Ramessē (Ra'amses) but also in other parts of Egypt, especially in pleasure-resorts. Typical is the long-established *harîm* in the Fayum, a marshland region then, much favoured by the pharaohs for fishing and bird-shooting expeditions. Papyrus documents indicate that this *harîm* was no prison of enforced idleness for its inmates in pharaoh's absence; the royal ladies supervised a hive of domestic industry, spinning and weaving done by servants (Gardiner, *JNES*, XII, 1953, pp. 145–149, especially p. 149). Distinguished ladies might be found in such a *harîm*, such as Maa-Hor-neferu-Rē', a Hittite princess married to Rameses II, mentioned by the Fayum records (Gardiner, *loc. cit.*). However, the regular inmates would be mainly royal concubines and 'favourites' of lesser rank and origin, and the 'daughter of Pharaoh' who adopted Moses would be the adolescent offspring of a king by one of these and not one of the chief princesses of the full blood royal, heiresses of the kingdom, who are much more prominent in the available records than their more obscure (half-)sisters. But the pleasures of fishing and fowling and the *harîms* associated with them were not restricted to the Fayum. An early precursor of Walton's *Compleat Angler* includes in its list of good sporting-grounds various localities in the E Delta (R. A. Caminos, *Literary Fragments in the Hieratic Script*, 1956, pp. 19, 20; *Sḫt-Ḏ'* (Field of Zoan), Avaris, *etc.*) adjoining Goshen. Suitable *harîms* would not be lacking in the region either (*cf.* the inference of H. Kees, *Ancient Egypt: A Cultural Topography*, 1961, p. 201, in another connection), and one such must have been Moses' first Egyptian home.

Anciently, children of *harîm*-ladies could be educated by the Overseer of the *harîm* ('a teacher of the children of the king', F. Ll. Griffith and P. E. Newberry, *El Bersheh*, II, 1894, p. 40). In due course princes were given a tutor, usually a high official at court or a retired military officer close to the king (H. Brunner, *Altägyptische Erziehung*, 1957, pp. 32, 33); Moses doubtless fared similarly. Egyptian education included reading and writing of the hieroglyphic and hieratic scripts (see WRITING), the copying of texts (especially classical literature), instruction in letter-writing and other administrative accomplishments. Royal princes were trained also in archery and other physical attainments. On Egyptian education, see the work of Brunner mentioned above for full sources. Princes found various employments: in the armies of the pharaoh, superintending great building projects, holding high-priestly office in important provincial temples (H. Kees, *Das Priestertum im Ägyptischen Staat*, 1953, pp. 66, 67, 93–96), or even as administrators of crown or temple estates (Gardiner, *JEA*, V, 1918, p. 133: J).

Moreover, as a Semite in Egypt, Moses would have had no difficulty whatever in learning and using the twenty or so letters of the proto-Canaanite linear alphabet, especially if he had been submitted to the much more exacting discipline of a training in the scores of characters and sign-groups of the Egyptian scripts (though even these require only application, not genius, to learn them). The fact that Egypt, not Palestine, was his home would be no barrier to familiarity with this simple linear script. The 'proto-Sinaitic' inscriptions of the early 15th century BC are certainly just informal dedications, work-notes, and brief epitaphs (for offerings) by Semitic captives from the Egyptian E Delta (or Memphis settlements) employed in the turquoise-mines (*cf.* W. F. Albright, *BASOR*, 110, 1948, pp. 12, 13, 22), and illustrate free use of that script by Semites under Egyptian rule nearly two centuries before Moses. Still more eloquent of the ready use of the linear script by Semites in Egypt is an ostracon from the Valley of the Queens at Thebes, some 350 miles south of Palestine, Sinai, or the Delta (J. Leibovitch, *Annales du Service des Antiquités de l'Égypte*, XL, 1940, p. 119, fig. 26, and plates XVI, XIX:50); the one word fully preserved can be reasonably read *'mht*, 'maid-servants' (Albright, *op. cit.*, p. 12, n. 33).

If mere workmen (or their foremen) at Theban tomb-sites and Sinai mines have no inhibitions about using this script for mundane lists and religious memorials, then it is unwarranted and unrealistic to ascribe just such inhibitions to the eventual leader of an embryo nation, especially one conditioned in Egyptian attitudes to the written word, in favour of a theoretical oral traditionism patently at variance with the usage of the Ancient Near East when properly understood; and it is grotesque to try to limit this script to 'the specialist' (as would E. Nielsen, *Oral Tradition*, 1954, pp. 24 ff. (after H. S. Nyberg), with radical misuse of Near Eastern data, *passim*).

c. Foreigners at the Egyptian court

Semites and other Asiatics could be found at every level of Egyptian society in the New Kingdom. Besides thousands of prisoners brought from Canaan to be slaves (*cf. ANET*, pp. 246b, 247b), foreign artisans, Syrian warriors in Egyptian service (*e.g. ANEP*, fig. 157), Asian youths as attendants, fanbearers, *etc.*, at court (Caminos, *Late-Egyptian Miscellanies*, 1954, pp. 117, 200, 201), Semites in Egypt could rise to the highest levels of the social pyramid. They were couriers between Egypt and Syria (*ANET*, p. 258b), charioteers who themselves owned servants (J. Černý, *JEA*, XXIII, 1937, p. 186), and merchants (Caminos, *op. cit.*, p. 26: 'Aper-Ba'al); the daughter of a Syrian sea-captain Ben-'Anath could marry a royal prince (W. Spiegelberg, *Recueil de Travaux*, XVI, 1894, p. 64).

But above all, some reached positions of high influence and responsibility in the state and its administration. One such was the architect Bunaia (*c.* 1440 BC), son of a Horite Aritenni; he repeatedly entitles himself a *ḫrd-n-k'p*, 'child of the (court-) harîm', *i.e.* brought up at court. Later, the butlers Heqareshu and Heqa-erneheh, apparently foreigners with Egyptian names, were tutors to royal princes (W. Helck, *Zur Verwaltung des Mittleren und Neuen Reichs*, 1958, p. 273). In the period of the Amarna letters (*c.* 1360 BC) the Semite Yanhamu was governor of the Egyptian province of Canaan (Helck, *Mitteilungen der Deutschen Orient-Gesellschaft*, No. 92, 1960, p. 7 and n. 38), and Dudu or Tutu in these letters (virtually Foreign Minister) was probably another Semite. Under the Ramesside kings Asiatics were still more prominent. Thus, one of King Merenptah's trusted cupbearers was the Syrian Ben-'Ozen of Ṣûr-Bashan ('Rock-of-Bashan'), who accompanied the vizier in overseeing work on that pharaoh's tomb in the Valley of the Kings (*JEA*, XXXIV, 1948, p. 74). Further, at the very end of the XIXth Dynasty, a Syrian very briefly took over control of Egypt itself: he was very possibly the immensely powerful Chancellor Bay (Černý in Gardiner, *JEA*, XLIV, 1958, pp. 21, 22). For further examples of, and references for, highly placed Semites in New Kingdom Egypt, see EGYPT: History, under XIXth Dynasty.

In New Kingdom Egypt, Canaanite and other Asiatic deities were accepted (Baal, Resheph, 'Ashtaroth, 'Anath, *etc.*; *cf. ANET*, pp. 249, 250); and as well as innumerable loan-words, Canaanite literary themes were current, either borrowed or assimilated to Egyptian ones (W. F. Albright, *Archaeology and the Religion of Israel*, 1953, pp. 197, 198 (rape of 'Anath); T. H. Gaster, *BO*, IX, 1952, pp. 82–85, 232; and G. Posener, *Mélanges Isidore Lévy*, 1955, pp. 461–478 (the greed of the Sea); and reference to a story of Qazardi, *ANET*, p. 477b). Some Egyptian officials prided themselves on being able to speak the lip of Canaan as well as know its geography (*ANET*, p. 477b), not to mention those who had to learn Babylonian cuneiform for diplomatic purposes (*cf.* Albright, *Vocalization of the Egyptian Syllabic Orthography*, 1934, p. 13, n. 50, and *JEA*, XXIII, 1937, pp. 191, 196–202).

The foregoing sketch (which is far from exhaustive) of the background against which the early career of a Moses must be set does not and cannot mechanically prove that the biblical Moses in particular actually had an Egyptian training and a literary and administrative background. But this kind of material does enforce two points. First, the upbringing and training of foreigners, especially Semites, in *harîms* and at Court, and their employment in posts of confidence (*e.g.* royal tutors) and responsibility (*e.g.* governors of major provinces), show that the royal upbringing of Moses recorded in Ex. ii. 10a, 11 would be nothing exceptional, but is, in fact, characteristic for New Kingdom Egypt. Second, once the veracity of Ex. ii. 10a, 11 is granted, that Moses did have a court upbringing (which the Egyptian background makes natural and typical), then the assumption becomes obligatory that Moses was subjected to the kind of intellectual training referred to above in Egyptian scripts, literature, and administrative methods, and would be free to use his native tongue and simple NW Semitic linear script, living in a social climate where 'Asiatic' modes, words, literature, *etc.*, were fashionable.

d. In Midian and Sinai

Moses felt for his labouring brethren (*cf.* Acts vii. 24) and slew an Egyptian overseer whom he found beating a Hebrew (Ex. ii. 11 f.); but the deed reached Pharaoh's ears, so Moses fled east over the border to Midian for safety (Ex. ii. 15 ff.). Flight over the eastern border was the escape chosen also by Sinuhe 600 years earlier (*ANET*, p. 19) and by runaway slaves later in the 13th century BC (*ANET*, p. 259b). Moses helped the daughters of a Midianite shepherd-priest Reuel/Jethro to water their flocks, and married one of them, Zipporah, who bore him a son, Gershom (Ex. ii. 16–22). While Moses kept Jethro's sheep and doubtless gained a knowledge of Sinai and Midian invaluable in later days, pharaohs came and went; but Israel's hard labour continued without break.

God had prepared His man, however, trained in Egyptian skills and now tempered in spirit with long years in the silent grandeur of the wilderness (Acts vii. 29 f.). Through the wonder of the burning bush that was not consumed came his call from God, the God of ancestral Abraham, Isaac, and Jacob (Ex. iii. 6) and not just of his Midianite/Kenite in-laws, except in so far as they too were descendants of Abraham (*cf.* Gn. xxv. 1–6) and may have retained the worship of Abraham's God. After some procrastination, Moses obeyed the call (Ex. iii, iv). Apparently Moses had omitted to circumcise one of his sons, perhaps under Zipporah's influence. At any rate, under threat of Moses' death by God's agency, she circumcised the boy, calling her husband 'a bridegroom of blood' (Ex. iv. 24–26, RSV) because circumcision was binding on him and his people (but perhaps not on her people?). Moses may have gone on alone from this point, as later on Zipporah returns to Moses from Jethro's care (Ex. xviii. 1–6).

e. On the eve of the Exodus

After meeting his brother and the elders of Israel (Ex. iv. 27–31), Moses with Aaron went before the pharaoh in the name of the God of Israel to request that he release the people to hold a feast to the Lord in the wilderness. But Pharaoh contemptuously dismissed this God as one more obscure Semitic godling—there were already enough religious holidays and festivals on which no work was done, and this was just an excuse to be idle (Ex. v. 8, 17). To discourage such 'idleness', Pharaoh decreed that the Hebrews must henceforth gather their own straw for the brick-making, but still produce the same quota of bricks (Ex. v. 7–14). Failure to complete quotas meant beatings for the Hebrew foremen from the taskmasters, and Israel seemed to be in worse case than ever (Ex. v. 23). Egyptian monuments and texts vividly illumine these events.

That Moses should be able to gain ready access to the pharaoh is not very surprising, especially if the pharaoh of the Exodus was Rameses II. P. Montet (*L'Égypte et la Bible*, 1959, p. 71) appositely refers to Papyrus Anastasi III, which describes how the 'young people of (Pi-Ramessē) Great of Victories . . . stand by their doors . . . on the day of the entry of Wosermaetrē'-Setepenrē' (*i.e.* Rameses II) . . ., every man being like his fellow in voicing his petitions' (*i.e.* to the king), *cf. ANET*, p. 471b. For the brickmaking of the Israelites and use of straw, see BRICK; for a taskmaster with his sticks watching Semitic, Libyan, and other labourers making bricks, see fig. 44. The organization of labour into gangs of workmen under foremen responsible to taskmasters is at once authentic and natural.

As for absence from work, Egyptian ostraca (*q.v.* under PAPYRI AND OSTRACA) include journals of work that give a day-to-day record of absenteeism, names of absentees, and reasons. One ostracon shows that the workmen of the royal tomb were idle at one period for thirty days out of forty-eight. One journal of absences takes note of several workmen, 'offering to his god' (A. Erman, *Life in Ancient Egypt*, 1894, pp. 124, 125), and the laconic entry *wsf*, 'idle', is not infrequent in such journals. That the Hebrews should go three days' journey into the wilderness to celebrate their feast and not arouse Egyptian religious antagonism (Ex. viii. 26 f., x. 9, 25 f.) is, again, thoroughly realistic as is pointed out by Montet (*op. cit.*, pp. 99–101 with references), with reference to sacred animals, especially the bull-cults in the Egyptian Delta provinces (see CALF, GOLDEN).

After the rebuff from Pharaoh, Moses was reassured by God. He had established His covenant with the Patriarchs, and this He would fulfil to their descendants, bringing them from Egypt to Palestine (Ex. vi. 2–9). It should be noted that Ex. vi. 3 does *not* deny knowledge of the name of YHWH to the Patriarchs, though it may possibly deny real knowledge of the significance of the name; see on this, W. J. Martin, *Stylistic Criteria and the Analysis of the Pentateuch*, 1955, pp. 16–19, and J. A. Motyer, *The Revelation of the Divine Name*, 1959, pp. 11–17. God's deliverance of His people was to be wrought by great judgments upon Egypt, its kings, gods, and people. For the successive plagues that demonstrated the God of Israel's power to Pharaoh in judgment, and compelled the king to let Israel leave (Ex. vii. 14–xii. 36), see PLAGUES OF EGYPT. On the eve of the last plague, the smiting of the first-born, the families of Israel had to kill a spotless lamb and mark the jambs and lintels of their house-doors with the blood, so that God should not destroy their first-born: 'the sacrifice of the Lord's passover' (Ex. xii. 27). It has been suggested by B. Couroyer (*RB*, LXII, 1955, pp. 481–496) that the Hebrew *psḥ* is derived from the Egyptian *p(')-sẖ*, 'the stroke, blow' (*i.e.* of God), but this meaning does not fit all the Hebrew evidence, and so remains doubtful.

f. From Succoth to Sinai

On the date of the Exodus, see CHRONOLOGY OF THE OLD TESTAMENT; for its route from Ra'amses and Succoth out of Egypt, see ENCAMPMENT BY THE SEA, PITHOM; for travels in Sinai, see WILDERNESS OF WANDERING. See also fig. 80. When Israel encamped by the *yam sûp̄*, 'sea of reeds', the pharaoh and his people imagined that the Hebrews were trapped by the natural obstacles, and so he led out his élite chariot-corps to the attack (Ex. xiv. 1–9). For the figure of over 600 chariots (Ex. xiv. 7), compare the figures of 730 and 1,092 (*i.e.* 60 + 1032) Syrian chariots captured in Canaan on two campaigns by Amenophis II (*ANET*, pp. 246, 247); on the rôle of chariots in the Egyptian army, *cf.* R. O. Faulkner, *JEA*, XXXIX, 1953, p. 43. But God divided the waters, led His people to safety, and turned the waters upon the Egyptian forces. Then Moses and the Hebrews raised their song of God's triumph (Ex. xv), taken up by Miriam and the womenfolk. In the ensuing three months Israel learned to feed on manna (Ex. xvi), repulsed the Amalekites (Ex. xvii), met Jethro again, who restored Zipporah to Moses, and reached Sinai (Ex. xix. 1). On the journeyings thus far, and after leaving Sinai, and on the numbers of the Israelites, *cf.* WILDERNESS OF WANDERING.

Israel encamped at the foot of the mount, and Moses went up the mountain to commune with God and receive the terms of the covenant (the 'ten commandments' of Ex. xx), which were the foundation of Israel's subsequent rôle as the people of God (He being their Great King), and also the series of statutes carrying the commandments into effect (Ex. xxi–xxiii). Then was held a solemn ceremony and feast to seal the covenant between God and the people (Ex. xxiv). Thereafter Moses returned to the mountain for forty days and nights (Ex. xxiv. 12–18) to receive the stone tablets bearing the Ten Commandments, Israel's 'title deed' of covenant, and God instructed Moses to gather from Israel the materials for making a portable shrine—the tabernacle, its furnishings, and the ark of the covenant, all according to the pattern that God impressed on him (Ex. xxv–xxxi).

After the idolatrous lapse over the golden calf (*q.v.*) and the restoration of the covenant so quickly violated, with further reinforcing of its laws (Ex. xxxii–xxxv. 3), the tabernacle, ark, and furnishings were duly made and inaugurated for the worship of God (Ex. xxxv. 4–xl); details of that worship are set forth in the book Leviticus (*q.v.*). The techniques used for the portable tabernacle (of gold-covered wooden frames of beams and bars easily erected and dismantled, with curtains to cover) reflect Moses' Egyptian training in so far as such techniques had been used in Egypt for portable structures (religious and otherwise) for over a thousand years before his time (*cf.* Kitchen, *Tyndale House Bulletin*, 5/6, 1960, pp. 7–13). However, the representational and didactic nature of the tabernacle sacrifices stands out in marked contrast to Egyptian ritual. The Hebrew sacrifices speak in picture-language of the offensiveness of sin in God's sight, and of the need of atonement for its cancellation, and were not merely a magically efficacious re-enactment of daily life needed to keep the god fed and flourishing as in Egyptian ritual.

At Sinai a census was taken, the manner of Israel's camp and marching order laid down. Levitical care for the tabernacle and its contents was arranged (Nu. i–iv) among other things on the eve of leaving Sinai (Nu. v. 1–x. 10). The arrangement of the tribes by their standards in a 'hollow rectangle' round the tabernacle is also probably a mark of God's use of Moses' Egyptian training (*cf.* Kitchen, *op. cit.*, p. 11). The long, silver trumpets and their use for civil assembly and military and religious purposes (Nu. x. 1–10) is illustrated by contemporary Egyptian use of such trumpets (*cf.* H. Hickmann, *La Trompette dans l'Égypte Ancienne*, 1946, especially pp. 46–50); silver trumpets were found in the tomb of Tutankhamūn (*c.* 1350 BC). The six ox-wagons for the tabernacle structure fit in well also. Ox-wagons were regularly used on campaigns in Syria by the pharaohs from Tuthmosis III (*c.* 1470 BC) onwards (*ANET*, p. 240a, 'chariot'), *e.g.* by Rameses II, *c.* 1270 BC, at Qadesh (C. Kuentz, *La Bataille de Qadech*, 1928/34, plate 39, left centre). With Moses' wagons each drawn by a span of (two) oxen in Sinai, compare the ten wagons (Egyp. *'grt* from Heb. *'glt*, same word, in Nu. vii. 3, 6, 7) each drawn by six spans of oxen that carried supplies for 8,000 quarrymen of Rameses IV (*c.* 1160 BC) from the Nile valley into the deserts of Wadi Hammamat between the Nile and the Red Sea, in very similar conditions to Sinai (*ARE*, IV, § 467).

g. From Sinai to Jordan

In their second year out from Egypt (Nu. x. 11), Israel left Sinai and reached Kadesh-barnea in the region of Paran, not far from the promised land. At that time Miriam and Aaron criticized Moses over his marriage with a Cushite woman (Nu. xii. 1, RSV; see ETHIOPIAN WOMAN). From the region of Kadesh, with Israel doubtless eager to go forward into the promised land, Moses sent the spies into Canaan. The land was a goodly one, but its inhabitants were powerful (Nu. xiii. 17–33). At this report, faithless Israel rebelled against Moses and Aaron, decided to return to Egypt, and would have stoned their leaders had not God intervened. Amidst all this, with splendid magnanimity, Moses still pleaded with God to spare Israel for His own name's sake, rather than strike them down in judgment (Nu. xiv. 5–19). Therefore the Lord decreed instead that Israel's travels in the wilderness should last forty years until the rebellious generation had died and given place to a new one (Nu. xiv. 20–35).

It is very easy to forget that, prior to this tragic episode, Israel was intended to have crossed from Egypt—*via* Sinai—directly to the promised land within a few years; the forty years in the wilderness was purely a commuted sentence (Nu. xiv. 12, 20–30, 33) and *not* part of God's 'first and best' plan for Israel. This should be remembered when reading the laws in Ex. xxii, xxiii, relating to agriculture, vineyards, *etc.*; Israel at Sinai had had four centuries living in Egypt amid a pastoral and agricultural environment (*cf.* Dt. xi. 10), neither they nor their patriarchal forefathers were ever true desert nomads (*cf.* Gn. xxvi. 12 and xxxvii. 6–8), and at Sinai they might well count themselves within striking distance of the land where these laws would find a speedy application. Israel had no need to settle in Canaan before such laws could be given, as is so often asserted (*cf.* Kitchen, *op. cit.*, pp. 13, 14).

The long, dreary period of wanderings was marked by further troubles; on the twin rebellion of Korah against the ecclesiastical rôle (Nu. xvi. 3), and Dathan and Abiram against the civil authority (Nu. xvi. 13), of Moses and Aaron, see further in WILDERNESS OF WANDERING. This double revolt was followed by the threat of general revolt, and again Moses and Aaron pleaded for the people, many being smitten with a plague as God's judgment (Nu. xvi. 41–50). Back at Kadesh-barnea, where Miriam died, Moses himself and Aaron sinned openly before God; He promised water from the rock, but Moses and Aaron blasphemously cast themselves in God's rôle: 'hear now, ye rebels, shall *we* [not God] bring you water out of this rock?' (Nu. xx. 10, RV); their punishment was that neither should enter the promised land, and was one which Moses later felt very keenly (Dt. iii. 24–27). The Edomites (Nu. xx. 14–21; also Moab, *cf.* Jdg. xi. 17) refused Israel passage through their territories so that Israel must go round their borders. At this time Aaron died and was buried in Mt. Hor (Nu. xx. 22–29). Yet again Israel was rebellious, God punished them by sending serpents among them, and once more Moses interceded for them. God commanded him to set up a bronze serpent on a pole (Nu. xxi.

4–9), to which those bitten might look and live, through faith in the Healer. (See SERPENT; SERPENT, BRAZEN.) Once past Edom and Moab, Israel were confronted by the Amorite kingdom of Sihon. Again Israel asked permission to pass through, and Sihon not only refused this, but marched—unprovoked—to attack Israel, into whose hand God then delivered him and his land; Og of Bashan, likewise hostile, met a similar fate (Nu. xxi. 21–35).

At last, Israel encamped in the plains of Moab by Jordan opposite Jericho (Nu. xxii. 1, xxv. 1), where the menace of idolatry and immorality from Moabite and Midianite sources had to be combated. A second census was carried out, and preparations for apportioning the promised land were begun. A punitive war was conducted against Midian, and the tribes of Reuben, Gad, and half-Manasseh were allowed to take Transjordan as their portion on condition that they would help their brethren beyond Jordan after Moses' death.

Deuteronomy (*q.v.*) gives Moses' farewell addresses to his people, and the reaffirmation, revision, and expansion to some of the statutes originally given at Sinai so many years before. Above all, the covenant between God and Israel, from which these laws stem as its stipulations, was renewed and placed under sanctions of blessing and cursing in a manner calculated to be widely understood in the 14th/13th centuries BC (as shown by covenants or treaties from the contemporary Hittite state archives, *cf.* G. E. Mendenhall, *BA*, XVII, 1954, pp. 53–60 and *passim*). Finally, Moses saw to it that Israel had her covenant-law in written form, appropriately placed alongside the ark of the covenant (Dt. xxxi. 24), left them a song to enjoin on them obedience to that law (Dt. xxxii, especially verses 44–47), and laid upon them his dying blessing (Dt. xxxiii) before ascending Mt. Nebo to view the land he was not destined to enter, and being laid to rest by his Lord in the land of Moab (Dt. xxxii. 48–52, xxxiv. 1–8).

III. THE WORK OF MOSES

a. Leader

As a leader of his people, Moses was not only equipped technically through his Egyptian upbringing and training (Acts vii. 22), but was also, on a much more fundamental level, a supreme leader by being a close follower of his God by faith (Heb. xi. 23–29; *cf.* Acts vii. 23–37). Such a man did God raise up to lead His people from bondage to promise. Time and again, beginning with the outcome of Moses' first interview with Pharaoh (Ex. v. 19–21) right down to the war with Midian on the eve of Moses' death (Nu. xxxi. 14–16), Israel failed to have faith in the saving power of their God in all circumstances, broke the commandments, and rejected God's leadership in rebelling against Moses (sometimes Moses and Aaron) through whom that leadership was manifested (*e.g.* Nu. xiv. 4, 10, xvi. 41 f.). Moses' own family let him down: witness Aaron's weak defection over the golden calf (Ex. xxxii. 1 ff., 21), and Miriam and Aaron's jealousy of his position and criticism of his marriage (Nu. xii. 1 f.). Great indeed was Moses' meekness and forbearance through all this (Nu. xii. 3); he was constantly interceding with God for sinning Israel (*e.g.* Nu. xiv. 13 ff., xvi. 46, *etc.*) and pleading with Israel to be faithful to their delivering God (*e.g.* Nu. xiv. 5–9). The wonder is not that Moses sinned openly once (though grievously, Nu. xx. 10 ff.) but that he did not more readily despair of the 'stiff-necked and rebellious' people and his consequently onerous commission, and fail them many more times. That he was a man of enduring faith in the invisible God (Heb. xi. 27b) and so jealous for God's name (*cf.* Nu. xiv. 13 ff.) can alone explain his achievement (*cf.* Phil. iv. 13).

b. Prophet and lawgiver

As one especially prominent in declaring and teaching the will, commandments, and nature of God, Moses was characteristically the model of all later true prophets until the coming of that One of whom he was forerunner (Dt. xviii. 18; Acts iii. 22 f.), to whom all the prophets bear witness (Acts x. 43). He was called by God (Ex. iii. 1–iv. 17) not only to lead the people out of bondage but to make known God's will. So did he in announcing the coming deliverance (Ex. iv. 30 f., vi. 8 f.), in communicating God's periodic commands to Israel on the eve of deliverance, and especially at the Passover (Ex. xi. 1–3, xii. 21, 28, 35 f., xiii. 3 ff., xiv. 1), and in proclaiming in word and act God's deliverance through the sea (Ex. xiv. 13, 21–28). Typical is Ex. xix. 3, 7: God speaks to Moses, and he to the people.

Moses communed with God long (Ex. xxiv. 18) and often (*e.g.* Ex. xxxiii. 7–11, RV, RSV), as did later prophets (*cf.* Samuel's life of prayer, 1 Sa. vii. 5, viii. 6, xii. 23, xv. 11). To Moses was given the high privilege of declaring the covenant by which Israel should serve the Lord their God, the Ten Commandments and their applications (Ex. xx, xxi–xxiii; *cf.* also Dt. v. 2–5). Just as the covenant was declared and renewed (Dt. xxix. 1) through Moses, so the later prophets in turn repeatedly reproved Israel for breaking the covenant and its conditions (*e.g.* 1 Ki. xviii. 18; 2 Ki. xvii. 15, 35–40; 2 Ch. xv. 1 f., 12; Je. vi. 16, 19, viii. 7 f., xi. 1–5, 6–10; Ho. vi. 7; Am. ii. 4; Hg. ii. 5; Mal. ii. 4 ff.), though Jeremiah (xxxi. 31–34) could also look forward to a new covenant.

The term 'code' often given to various parts of the Pentateuch is misleading: Moses was not simply the promulgator of some kind of ideal, civil 'code Napoléon' for Israel. Contemporary Near Eastern treaty-documents of the 13th century BC show that Moses was moved by God to express Israël's relationship to God in the form of a 'suzerainty' treaty or covenant, by which a great king (in this case, God, the King of kings) bound to Himself a vassal-people (here, Israel), the form in question being uniquely transmuted to the religious and spiritual plane. This was a kind of formulation that would be universally understood at the time. Such a covenant was rooted in the 'prevenient grace' of the great King (here, God's saving Israel from bondage, Ex. xx. 1) and laid His subjects under a bond of indebtedness and gratitude, to be expressed in practice by their obedience to explicit stipulations and detailed regulations laid on them and their leader(s) by the great King. For Israel, the basic stipulations of their covenant were the Ten Commandments, in effect moral law as the expression of God's will; and the detailed covenant-obligations took the form of 'civil' statute rooted in the moral law of the Ten Commandments (*e.g.* Ex. xxi–xxiii; Dt. xii–xxvi, *etc.*), and even of prescriptions governing the forms of permissible and authorized religious practice (*e.g.* Ex. xxv. 1 ff., xxxv. 10 ff.; Lv.); Israel's life in every way was to be marked by righteousness and holiness as issuing from obedience to the covenant or, in other words, fulfilling the law. Attainment, however, waited upon further divine provision, *cf.* Gal. iii. 23 ff. (also 15–22, especially 21 f.).

Because Israel's covenant was not merely a treaty of political obligations but regulated their daily life before God, its ordinances served also as a minimum basis of 'civil' law for the people. Because in its ordinary forms of society, sources of economy, geographical conditions, possible range of crime, *etc.*, Israel's everyday life necessarily had much in common with that of other peoples of the ancient biblical world, so both Israel and her neighbours shared to some extent a common ancient heritage of law and custom in such matters. It is thus no surprise to find similarities at various points in the Mosaic stipulations and the laws of Hammurabi (five centuries earlier) and other still earlier Mesopotamian rulers (*cf.* W. J. Martin, *DOTT*, pp. 28, 36, 37), while the existence of long series of laws promoted by individual heads of state from the end of the third millennium BC onwards makes it superfluous to date the giving of the pentateuchal laws any later than Moses (13th century BC). It must constantly be remembered that even earliest Israel came *late* in the long and interwoven, multi-millennial history of the Ancient Near East, allowing Israel *no* opportunity to start from a truly primitive level—a situation too often forgotten or ignored in practice in Old Testament studies.

The number or quantity of 'civil' laws in the Pentateuch is in no way excessive or exceptional when compared with the collections issued elsewhere. In Ex. xxi–xxiii may be discerned about forty 'paragraphs', in Lv. xviii–xx more than twenty 'paragraphs', and in Dt. xii–xxvi nearly ninety 'paragraphs', of very variable length from a chapter or half-chapter of the present-day text-divisions down to one short sentence; say, about 150 'paragraphs' in these sections altogether, leaving aside the more obviously religious prescriptions. This figure compares very reasonably with the 282 paragraphs of Hammurabi's laws, the 115 surviving paragraphs of the Middle Assyrian laws (many more being lost), or the 200 paragraphs of the Hittite laws.

c. Author

In modern times estimates of Moses' rôle as an author have varied over the whole range of conceivable opinion between the two extremes of either attributing to him every syllable of the present Pentateuch, or denying his very existence. It is singularly unfortunate that the words 'Moses', 'Mosaic' have become illegitimately charged with the emotional overtones of chopping-block and rallying-flag for opposed theological camps over the last eighty years; the pentateuchal data should be treated seriously and *ab initio* in the strict context of the contemporary Ancient Near East, and obsolete controversies and subjective critical methods be relegated to long-overdue oblivion. See the articles PENTATEUCH, BIBLICAL CRITICISM, and EGYPT: Literature (Egyptian Literature and the Old Testament), to which the following is supplementary.

That Moses' name was attached to parts of the Pentateuch right from the start is clearly shown by the biblical text itself. Thus, at an utter minimum, Moses as a writer is undeniably credited with the following: a brief document on God's judgment against Amalek (Ex. xvii. 14); the 'book of the covenant' (Ex. xxiv. 4–8; on the external parallels, this must include Ex. xx and xxi–xxiii, the commandments and attendant laws); the restoration of the covenant (Ex. xxxiv. 27, referring to xxxiv. 10–26); an itinerary (Nu. xxxiii. 1 f., referring to the document that furnished xxxiii. 3–40); the major part of Deuteronomy to xxxi (Dt. xxxi. 9–13, 24 ff., referring to renewal of the covenant and re-enforcement of its laws that precede xxxi); and two poems (Dt. xxxii, *cf.* xxxi. 22; and Ps. xc by title, which there is no objective evidence to doubt). Later Old Testament and New Testament references to Moses in this connection are collected by various scholars, *e.g.* by E. J. Young, *An Introduction to the Old Testament*, 1949, pp. 50 f.

The ability to write historical narrative, record laws, and compose poetry in one man is not unique. An Egyptian example of this kind of ability seven centuries before Moses is probably furnished by Khety (or Akhtoy), son of Duauf, a writer under the pharaoh Amenemhat I (*c.* 1991–1962 BC), who was apparently educator, political propagandist, and poet. He wrote the *Satire of the Trades* for use in scribal schools, was probably commissioned to give literary form to the 'Teaching of Amenemhat I', a political pamphlet, and may have been author of a well-known Hymn to the Nile often copied out by scribes along with the other two works (*cf.* Gardiner, *Hieratic Papyri in the British Museum, Third Series*, 1935, I, pp. 40, 43, 44, and Posener, *Littérature et Politique dans l'Égypte de la XIIe Dynastie*, 1956, pp. 4–7, 19, n. 7, 72, 73). However, beyond the 'utter minimum' already mentioned above, there is no objective reason why

Moses should not have written, or have caused to be written (at dictation—hence third person pronouns), considerably more of the contents of the present Pentateuch, though just how much must remain a matter of opinion.

Nearly the whole body of material could have been arranged in practically its present form as early as Joshua, with a minimum of later orthographic and linguistic revision. As explained and illustrated above in sections II*b* and *c* (especially end)—if any veracity at all be accorded to Ex. ii on Moses' early life in Egypt—modern knowledge of conditions in New Kingdom Egypt make the assumption that Moses received literary and other training, if not inevitable, at least the only reasonable one. The onus of proof rests upon those disposed to assert the contrary. Nowadays, the objection to Mosaic authorship is often not that Moses could not write but that he *would* not write, and large appeal is made to 'oral tradition' and writing up and editing of documents at relatively later dates. Against this contention stands the whole evidence of the Ancient Near East. Matters that were considered important or that should go on permanent record for posterity were *written*, inscribed, in the lands of the contemporary Near East, not left to the care of bards and camp-fire romancers (*cf.* WRITING).

d. Later fame

From Joshua (viii. 31; *cf.* 1 Ki. ii. 3; 2 Ki. xiv. 6; Ezr. vi. 18, *etc.*) to New Testament times (Mk. xii. 26; Lk. ii. 22; Jn. vii. 23), the name of Moses was associated with the Old Testament, especially the Pentateuch; note 2 Cor. iii. 15, where 'Moses' stands *pars pro toto* for the Old Testament. And it was Moses and Elijah, the representatives of Old Testament law and prophecy, who stood with Christ on the Mount of Transfiguration (Mt. xvii. 3 f.). Space forbids inclusion of any appreciation of the impact of the figure of Moses upon writers and leaders in more recent history and in our own times.

BIBLIOGRAPHY. H. Gressmann, *Mose und seine Zeit*, 1913; M. Buber, *Moses*, 1947; O. T. Allis, *God Spake by Moses*, 1951; H. H. Rowley, 'Moses and the Decalogue', *BJRL*, XXXIV, 1951–2, pp. 81 ff.; G. von Rad, *Moses*, 1960; and works cited in the article. K.A.K.

MOST HIGH. See GOD, NAMES OF.

MOTE. The word occurs in Mt. vii. 3, 4, 5, and almost identically in the Lucan parallel (Lk. vi. 41, 42 *bis*). The Gk. word is *karphos* (RSV 'speck'), and is cognate with the verb *karphō*, 'to dry up'. The noun means a small, dry stalk or twig, a light piece of straw, or even of wool such as might fly into the eye. Metaphorically it is used by our Lord to denote a minor fault.

S.S.S.

MOTH. Heb. *'āš* and Gk. *sēs* are rendered moth in ten different places (Jb. iv. 19, xiii. 28, xxvii. 18; Ps. xxxix. 11; Is. l. 9, li. 8; Ho. v. 12; Mt. vi. 19, 20; Lk. xii. 33), and the context of all confirm identification with the clothes moth. In countries with fairly high average temperatures for most of the year and with clothes regarded as a form of wealth and therefore stored in quantity, damage by the larvae of clothes moths was likely to be serious. G.C.

MOTHER. See FAMILY.

MOUNT (Heb. *sōlᵉlâ*, Je. vi. 6; Ezk. xvii. 17). The earthworks thrown up around a besieged city (*cf.* FORTIFICATION AND SIEGECRAFT).

MOUNT, MOUNTAIN. The topographical terms *giḇ'â* and *hār* in Hebrew, and *bounos* and *oros* in Greek, are best translated by the English 'hill' and 'mountain' respectively. The term *giḇ'â*, 'hill', is specific, referring to an elevated site, slope, or ascent. Its root meaning, 'bowl' or 'hump-backed', refers accurately to the rounded hills which form the backbone of central Palestine, carved out of the hard and folded arches of Cenomanian limestone. Their eroded form is distinct from the deep dissection of the soft Senonian limestones which flank the Judaean highlands, which are more graphically described as 'slippery places' (Dt. xxxii. 35; Pr. iii. 23; Je. xxiii. 12, xxxi. 9). Specific sites of the hills and mountains are often personified in Scripture with descriptive titles. Such are: head (Gn. viii. 5; Ex. xix. 20; Dt. xxxiv. 1; 1 Ki. xviii. 42), ears (Jos. xix. 34), shoulder (Jos. xv. 8, xviii. 16), side (1 Sa. xxiii. 26; 2 Sa. xiii. 34), loins (Jos. xix. 12), rib (2 Sa. xvi. 13), back—possible derivation of Shechem, backed by Mt. Gerizim—and thigh (Jdg. xix. 1, 18; 2 Ki. xix. 23; Is. xxxvii. 24).

The term *hār*, generally translated mountain in the RV, is more general, used indiscriminately of a single mount, a mountain range, or a tract of mountainous terrain. In English mountain and hill are relative terms associated with altitudinal differences, but AV regards the terms *giḇ'â* and *hār* as almost interchangeable. Jesus, *e.g.*, is described as coming down the 'hill' (Lk. ix. 37) which He ascended the previous day as the 'Mount' of Transfiguration. In the following passages AV would be better rendered 'mountain': Gn. vii. 19; Ex. xxiv. 4; Nu. xiv. 44, 45; Dt. i. 41, 43, viii. 7, xi. 11; Jos. xv. 9, xviii. 13, 14; Jdg. ii. 9, xvi. 3; 1 Sa. xxv. 20, xxvi. 13; 2 Sa. xiii. 34, xvi. 13, xxi. 9; 1 Ki. xi. 7, xvi. 24, xx. 23, xxii. 17; 2 Ki. i. 9, iv. 27; Pss. xviii. 7, lxviii. 15, 16, lxxx. 10, xcv. 4, xcvii. 5, xcviii. 8, civ. 10, 13, 18, 32, cxxi. 1; Lk. ix. 37. On the other hand, the term *hār* is correctly termed 'hill-country' (AV of Jos. xiii. 6, xxi. 11; Lk. i. 39, 65) when applied to a regional tract of land such as Ephraim and Judah. It is also used of the land of the Amorites (Dt. i. 7, 19, 20), of Naphtali (Jos. xx. 7), of the Ammonites (Dt. ii. 37) and of Gilead (Dt. iii. 12).

The identification of specific sites is therefore not always possible, as in the cases of the high mountain of temptation (Lk. iv. 5), the mount of the Beatitudes (Mt. v. 1), and the Mount of

Transfiguration (Mt. xvii. 1; Mk. ix. 2; Lk. ix. 28). Mt. Sinai cannot be identified if, as some have suggested, it was a previously active volcano (Ex. xix. 16; Pss. civ. 32, cxliv. 5). The traditional location in the Sinai Peninsula (Jebel Mūsa) would in that case be impossible geologically, as the ancient rocks of the district show no evidence of recent volcanicity. Two pleistocene volcanic cones, perhaps active in historic times, occur on the east side of the Gulf of Aqabah, but some authorities cannot see how this fits with the route of the Exodus described. See EXODUS and fig. 80.

The Mount of Congregation (see CONGREGATION) in AV of Is. xiv. 13 occurs in the boast of the king of Babylon, and may be an allusion to a probable Bab. legend relating to the dwelling of the gods (*cf.* Jb. xxxvii. 22; Ezk. xxviii. 13 f.).

Armageddon or the Hebraicized Har-magedon (Rev. xvi. 16) may refer to the mountain district of Megiddo (*q.v.*), *i.e.* Mt. Gerizim, which overlooks the plain of Megiddo, the location of other apocalyptic scenes (*cf.* Zc. xii. 11).

Mountains have great significance in the geography and history of Palestine (see PALESTINE). Consequently they are frequently referred to in the Scriptures. They provide vistas—'go up to top of Pisgah and lift up your eyes' (Dt. iii. 27, RSV; *cf.* Lk. iv. 5). Their influence on higher rainfall makes them a symbol of fertility (Dt. xxxiii. 15; Je. l. 19; Mi. vii. 14), grazing-places (Ps. l. 10) and hunting-grounds (1 Sa. xxvi. 20). They are associated with pagan sanctuaries (1 Ki. xviii. 17–46; Is. xiv. 13, lxv. 7; Ezk. vi. 13). Their inaccessibility makes them places of refuge (Jdg. vi. 2; 1 Sa. xiv. 21, 22; Ps. lxviii. 15, 22; Mt. xxiv. 16).

Mountains are a symbol of eternal continuance (Dt. xxxiii. 15; Hab. iii. 6) and stability (Is. liv. 10). They are considered as the earliest created things (Jb. xv. 7; Pr. viii. 25), of ancient origin (Ps. xc. 2) and objects of the Creator's might (Ps. lxv. 6) and majesty (Ps. lxviii. 16). They are the scenes of theophanies, melting at Jehovah's presence (Jdg. v. 5; Ps. xcvii. 5; Is. lxiv. 1; Mi. i. 4) and shuddering at His judgments (Ps. xviii. 7; Mi. vi. 1 f.). They are called to cover the guilty from His face (Ho. x. 8; Lk. xxiii. 30). When God touches them they bring forth smoke (Ps. civ. 32, cxliv. 5). They also rejoice at the advent of Israel's redemption (Ps. xcviii. 8; Is. xliv. 23, xlix. 13, lv. 12), leap at the praise of the Lord (Ps. cxiv. 4, 6) and are called to witness His dealings with His people (Mi. vi. 2).

Mountains are also symbols of difficult paths in life (Je. xiii. 16), obstacles (Mt. xxi. 21), and other difficulties (Zc. iv. 7), the removal of which is possible to those of strong faith (Mt. xvii. 20).

J.M.H.

MOURNING. See BURIAL AND MOURNING.

MOUSE. Mouse (*'akbār*) is found six times in AV (four times in 1 Sa. vi, in the incident of the pestilence that struck the Philistines). The symptoms described fit bubonic plague precisely and it is therefore likely that the 'mice' were black rats (*Rattus rattus*), whose fleas are the carriers of plague. 'Mouse' is always a rather vague term and may be expected to include all small or medium-sized rodents of the rat family.

G.C.

MOUTH. Heb. *peh* with several other words occasionally translated mouth, and Gk. *stoma.* Both are used not only of the mouth of man or beast, or anthropomorphically of God, but are often translated 'edge', in the phrase 'edge of the sword'. *Peh* is used also of the mouth of a well (Gn. xxix. 2), a sack (Gn. xlii. 27), or a cave (Jos. x. 22).

The general usage is very close to and almost interchangeable with lip or tongue (*qq.v.*). The hand laid upon the mouth, like the lip, was a sign of shame (Mi. vii. 16). The mouth can sin (Ps. lix. 12) or utter good. The tendency to speak of the mouth as acting independently, by synecdoche or ignorance of physiology, is not as marked as in the case of lip. This may be because the Hebrew did not distinguish clearly between the supposed functions of the internal organs, and the mouth, being partly internal, was obviously connected with them (see HEART and *cf.* Pr. xvi. 23).

Frequently the mouth is said to be filled with words of one kind or another, or a spirit which causes certain words to be spoken (1 Ki. xxii. 22; Ps. xl. 3). By extension the word *peh* came to mean words or commandments (Ex. xvii. 1).

B.O.B.

MUFFLER (Heb. *re'ālâ*). An elaborate kind of veil mentioned among a list of feminine accoutrements in Is. iii. 19. AVmg reads 'spangled ornaments'. See also DRESS.

MULBERRY-TREE. See TREES.

MULE. Although the English word has a number of other meanings, it is primarily applied to the offspring of a horse by a donkey. It is likely that these hybrids were first bred soon after the horse was introduced into areas where the donkey was kept, but such breeding appears to be specifically forbidden by Lv. xix. 19, 'Thou shalt not let thy cattle gender with a diverse kind.' This may explain why it was not until towards the end of David's reign (2 Sa. xiii. 29) that mules appear in the record. (It is generally agreed that *yēmîm* is incorrectly translated 'mules' in Gn. xxxvi. 24, AV; it should perhaps be translated 'warm springs'.) *Pered* and *pirdâ* are used for the male and female, but this hybrid is always sterile. Mules are valuable in that they combine the strength of the horse with the endurance and sure-footedness of the donkey, as well as having the extra vigour characteristic of hybrids.

In Est. viii. 14 Heb. *rekeš* is perhaps better translated 'swift horses', as in RSV.

G.C.

MUNITION. See FORTIFICATION AND SIEGECRAFT.

MURDER. See Crime and Punishment.

MURRAIN. See Plagues of Egypt.

MUSIC AND MUSICAL INSTRUMENTS.

I. MUSIC

It is evident from the frequent references in the Old Testament that music played an important part in Heb. culture. According to tradition Jubal, the son of Lamech, who 'was the father of all such as handle the harp and organ' (Gn. iv. 21), was the inventor of music. The close relation between the pastoral and the musical arts is shown in that Jubal had an elder brother Jabal who was 'father of such as dwell in tents, and of such as have cattle' (Gn. iv. 20).

At a later stage music was consecrated to the service of the Temple worship, but initially its uses seem to have been secular. The first allusion to music after the flood was made by Laban when he reproached Jacob for stealing away without allowing him to cheer his departure 'with mirth, and with songs, with tabret, and with harp' (Gn. xxxi. 27). It was frequently used on occasions of rejoicing, when it was regularly linked with dancing (see Dance). There were songs of triumph after victory in battle (Ex. xv. 1 ff.; Jdg. v. 1 ff.). Miriam and the women celebrated the downfall of Pharaoh and his horsemen 'with timbrels and with dances' (Ex. xv. 20 ff.), and Jehoshaphat returned victorious to Jerusalem 'with psalteries and harps and trumpets' (2 Ch. xx. 28). Music, singing, and dancing were common at feasts (Is. v. 12; Am. vi. 5). In particular, they were features of the vintage festivals (Is. xvi. 10) and of marriage celebrations (1 Macc. ix. 37, 39). Kings had their singers and instrumentalists (2 Sa. xix. 35; Ec. ii. 8). The shepherd boy also had his lyre (1 Sa. xvi. 18). The young men at the gates enjoyed their music (La. v. 14). Even the harlot increased her seductive powers with song (Is. xxiii. 16).

Music was used at times of mourning as well as at times of gladness. The dirge (*qînâ*) which constitutes the Book of Lamentations and David's lament over Saul and Jonathan (2 Sa. i. 18–27) are notable examples. It became the custom to hire professional mourners to assist at funerals. These regularly included flautists (Mt. ix. 23). According to Maimonides, the poorest husband was expected to provide at least two flautists and one mourning woman for the funeral of his wife (*Mišnāyôṯ*, chapter IV).

As music formed an integral part of Heb. social life, so it had its place in their religious life. 1 Ch. xv. 16–24 contains a detailed account of the organization by David of the levitical choir and orchestra. Apart from this passage there are only scattered and indirect references to the use of music in religious worship, and there is little evidence on which to form any clear impression of the character of the musical service of the Temple.

Of the nature of the music performed by the Heb. musicians we have no knowledge whatever. It is uncertain whether they had any system of notation. No identifiable system has survived. Attempts have been made to interpret the accents of the Heb. text as a form of notation, but without success. These accents were a guide to recitation rather than music and were, in any case, of late origin. Although we have no evidence regarding the instrumental music of the Temple, we can discover from the form of the psalms that they were intended to be sung antiphonally either by two choirs (Pss. xiii, xx, xxxviii), or by a choir and the congregation (Pss. cxxxvi, cxviii. 1–4). It appears that after the captivity the choirs were formed of an equal number of male and female voices (Ezr. ii. 65). But it is not clear whether each choir was of mixed voices or whether one was of male and the other of female voices. They probably chanted rather than sang, although the manner of their chanting is obscure and was certainly very different from modern ecclesiastical chanting.

II. MUSICAL INSTRUMENTS

We have a little more knowledge of the musical instruments of the Bible, although there is no definite information regarding their form or construction. Instruments have, however, been found belonging to other ancient nations of the Middle East, notably the Egyptians (see figs. 146, 147). The etymology of the Hebrew words helps a little, and also the ancient versions, but still our knowledge is very slight. The instruments mentioned in the Bible can be divided into the three main groups: strings, wind, and percussion.

a. Strings

(i) *Harp*. The *kinnôr*, which is regularly rendered 'harp' by AV, is the first musical instrument mentioned in the Bible (Gn. iv. 21) and is the only stringed instrument referred to in the Pentateuch. It is one of the instruments with which Laban the Syrian would have wished to send Jacob on his way, had he not departed so suddenly (Gn. xxxi. 27). This allusion suggests that the instrument may have been of Syrian origin. There has been difference of opinion whether it was truly a harp or a lyre. The balance of opinion is in favour of the lyre, which word is used in RSV. That it was portable and therefore small is evidenced by the fact that it was one of the four musical instruments borne before the young prophets (1 Sa. x. 5). Ancient Egyptian tomb-paintings represent foreigners, thought to be Semitic, bearing lyres played with a plectrum in their hands. However, the identity of these strangers has not been positively established. Nor is it clear whether the *kinnôr* was played with a plectrum or by hand. In 1 Sa. xvi. 23 'David took an harp, and played with his hand'; but the absence of mention of a plectrum is no proof that the strings were plucked by the fingers alone. There is no certainty about the number of strings on the *kinnôr*. Josephus thought it had ten. Another suggestion, based on the association of the instrument with Heb. *šᵉmînîṯ* ('eighth', LXX *hyper tēs ogdoēs*) in

1 Ch. xv. 21, is that it had eight strings; but the allusion in the passage is far from certain.

The *kinnôr* was a wooden instrument, David's being made probably of cypress (2 Sa. vi. 5). Those which Solomon had made for the Temple were constructed of almug (1 Ki. x. 12), and were evidently very valuable. Josephus (*Ant*. viii. 3. 8) records that their framework was fitted with electrum, *i.e.* either a mixed metal or amber.

The word 'harp' is used also by AV in translating Aramaic *qîṯrôs*, which occurs only among the instruments of Nebuchadrezzar's orchestra in Dn. iii. It is the same root from which the European word 'guitar' has sprung.

(ii) *Psaltery*. This word is derived from Gk. *psaltērion*, which denotes an instrument plucked with the fingers instead of with a plectrum. The Gk. verb *psallō* means to touch sharply or pluck. It is the word most often used to translate Heb. *nēḇel*, although occasionally the rendering 'viol' is found, and in the Prayer Book version of the Psalms the word 'lute' is used. In LXX *nēḇel* is variously rendered (*psaltērion, psalmos, kithara, nablion, nabla, nablē, naula*, and *nablas*). It is generally accepted that it was a kind of harp, as it is rendered in RSV, although its exact description is uncertain. It is first mentioned in 1 Sa. x. 5, and this seems to confirm the opinion that it was of Phoenician origin, since there was little close contact between Israel and Phoenicia before this date. Attempts have been made to reconstruct the shape of the *nēḇel* by identifying it with a root meaning a skin-bottle, jar, or pitcher. It has been suggested that it had a bulging resonance body at its lower end. This identification of the root has even led to the supposition that the instrument was a form of bagpipe. But these suggestions are mere conjecture.

Like the *kinnôr*, the *nēḇel* was made of cypress wood, and later of almug. It is clear that David was able to play the *nēḇel* as well as the *kinnôr*. As it is commonly linked in the Bible with other musical instruments, it is generally thought to have supplied the bass.

Heb. *'āśôr* is frequently linked with *nēḇel*. This word is from the root meaning 'ten', and is generally thought to indicate that the instrument had ten strings. This interpretation is found also in LXX and Vulg. (*psaltērion decachordon* and *psalterium decem chordarum*). In all probability the *nēḇel 'āśôr* was simply a variety of *nēḇel*.

The word 'psaltery' appears also in AV as a translation of Aramaic *psantērîn* (Dn. iii. 5 ff.), another of the instruments in Nebuchadrezzar's orchestra. The Aramaic word appears to be a rendering of Gk. *psaltērion*, and is translated in RSV 'harp'. J. Stainer (*The Music of the Bible*, pp. 40–55) argues at some length that the instrument referred to is in fact the dulcimer. It is, however, impossible to say more with confidence than that it was a stringed instrument.

(iii) *Sackbut*. This word occurs in AV only in Dn. iii as a translation of Aramaic *sabbᵉḵâ*. It was one of the instruments of Nebuchadrezzar's orchestra, and was therefore not a Heb. instrument. The AV translation is clearly wrong, as the sackbut was a wind instrument, being in fact a kind of bass trumpet with a slide rather like a modern trombone. The *sabbᵉḵâ* is usually identified with Gk. *sambykē*, by which it is translated in Dn. iii, LXX. This has been described as either a small triangular harp of four or more strings and high pitch, or a large, many-stringed harp. Whichever description is correct, it was a stringed and not a wind instrument. According to Strabo (x. 471) it was of barbaric origin. RSV more correctly renders 'trigon'.

(iv) *Dulcimer*. This is the AV translation of Aramaic *sûmpônyâ*, which is generally regarded as a Gk. loan-word. It occurs in the Bible only in the orchestra of Dn. iii. The AV rendering is incorrect, as it is not a stringed instrument. It is now generally supposed to have been a form of bagpipe (as rendered in RV, RSV). The modern Italian rendering of the word is *sampogna*, a kind of bagpipe in current use in that country.

b. Wind instruments

(i) *Pipe*. This is Heb. *ḥālîl*, rendered 'pipe' in AV, 'flute' in RSV. The word occurs only six times in the Old Testament. In the New Testament the pipe is Gk. *aulos*, used in LXX for the *ḥālîl*. Vulg. uses *tibia*. Both *aulos* and *tibia* are general terms covering both reed instruments, such as the oboe and the clarinet, and instruments played by blowing across or through a hole, such as with the flute.

The word *ḥālîl* derives from a root meaning to bore or pierce. The word *aulos* is from a root meaning to blow. But neither the derivation of *ḥālîl*, nor its rendering in LXX, gives any indication of the nature of the instrument. The balance of opinion seems to be in favour of the oboe rather than the flute, but there is no certainty on the matter. Just as today, it was apparently customary in ancient times for the player of a reed instrument to carry with him a supply of reeds in a box (Gk. *glōssokomon*). It was in fact a reed-box and not a 'bag', as AV renders it, which Judas used as a money-box (Jn. xii. 6, xiii. 29).

The pipe was used in festival processions (Is. xxx. 29), at times of national rejoicing (1 Ki. i. 40), and also in mourning at funerals (Mt. ix. 23). That it could produce a plaintive note is evidenced by the allusion to it in Je. xlviii. 36.

(ii) *Flute*. This is the AV translation of Aramaic *mašrôqîṯâ*. It occurs only in Dn. iii, and is derived from the root *šāraq*, an onomatopoeic word meaning 'to whistle' or 'hiss'. The playing of most types of pipe or flute is usually accompanied by a hissing sound. It is therefore a reasonable supposition that the instrument referred to is of that class.

(iii) *Organ*. This word (Heb. *'ûgāḇ*) occurs only four times in the Old Testament. In Gn. iv. 21 it is evidently a generic term covering all wind instruments, just as the parallel word in the verse, *kinnôr*, is the general term for all stringed instruments. In Jb. xxx. 31 it again occurs in

Fig. 146. Musical instruments in the ancient Near East. Musicians playing a guitar (1), a flute (2), and a harp and flute (3) in a tomb relief of the XVIIIth Dynasty from Saqqara. 4. Musicians playing a lute, double pipes, and clappers in a relief of the 9th–8th centuries BC from Carchemish. 5. A nomad playing a lyre in a tomb painting of the 19th century BC from Beni Hasan. 6. Musicians playing a horn and drum in a 9th–8th-century BC relief from Carchemish. 7. An Assyrian trumpeter. 8. A trumpeter from the temple of Rameses III at Medinet Habu. 9. A scene on an ivory pyxis showing a procession of worshippers playing (*left to right*) psalteries, timbrel and double pipes. 8th century BC from Nimrud.

association with the *kinnôr*, and in Jb. xxi. 12 it represents the wind section in parallel with members of the stringed and percussion families. We find it again in Ps. cl. 4 among numerous other instruments. LXX gives no guide as to the nature of the instrument, for it uses no fewer than three different words. (In Gn. iv. 21 *kithara*, 'guitar'; in the two passages in Job *psalmos*, 'psaltery'; and in Ps. cl. 4 *organon*, 'organ'.) The derivation of the Heb. word is uncertain. Some have linked it with a root meaning 'to lust', 'have inordinate affection', thus alluding to its sensuous or appealing tones; but this is no more than conjecture. The instrument must be some form of pipe or possibly a group of pipes.

(iv) *Horn.* This word (Heb. *qeren*) occurs frequently in the Old Testament. Cognate with it are Gk. *keras* and Lat. *cornu*. It appears to have been used in biblical times for two purposes: as a flask for carrying oil and as a kind of trumpet. In this latter sense it occurs in only three passages. In Jos. vi it is used synonymously with *šôp̄ār* ('trumpet', see (v) below) in the account of the capture of Jericho. In 1 Ch. xxv. 5 are listed those who were appointed by David to play it, and in Dn. iii it is one of the instruments of Nebuchadrezzar's orchestra. The earliest trumpets were evidently made out of the horns of animals. These were later imitated in metal.

(v) *Trumpet.* There is frequent mention of the trumpet in the Bible. In AV it is used chiefly as a translation of two different Heb. words, *šôp̄ār* and *ḥ^{a}ṣōṣ^{e}râ*. It is used once also for Heb. *yôḇēl*, which means literally a ram's horn. LXX renders uniformly *salpinx*, which is used also in the New Testament.

The *šôp̄ār*, a long horn with a turned-up end, was the national trumpet of the Israelites. It was used on military and religious occasions to summon the people. The *šôp̄ār* is still used in Jewish synagogues today.

The *ḥ^{a}ṣōṣ^{e}râ* was a trumpet made of beaten silver. Moses was commanded by God to make two of them for summoning the congregation and for breaking camp. Nu. x. 1–10 contains God's instructions to Moses regarding the occasions for the blowing of the trumpet. It was principally a sacred and not a martial instrument.

(vi) *Cornet.* The word appears in AV as the translation of three different words. In Dn. iii it is used for *qeren*, elsewhere translated 'horn' (see (iv) above). In four passages the Heb. word is *šôp̄ār*, which occurs frequently in the Old Testament and is in all other instances translated 'trumpet' (see (v) above).

In 2 Sa. vi. 5 the Heb. word is *m^{e}na'an'îm*, which occurs only in this passage. It is used in conjunction with the cymbals (see *c* (ii) below) among other instruments on which David and the children of Israel played before the Lord. The root from which it is derived means 'to quiver', 'vibrate', and it is probable that the instrument was a kind of rattle. LXX renders *kymbala*, 'cymbals', and is therefore less accurate than Vulg. *sistra*, 'rattles' (Gk. *seistron* from *seiō*, 'shake', 'move to and fro'). RSV renders 'castanets'. Illustrations have been preserved of ancient Egyptian rattles consisting of an oval hoop on a handle, to which were affixed rods carrying loose rings which jangled together when the instrument was shaken (see fig. 147).

c. Percussion

(i) *Bells.* Two different Heb. words are rendered 'bells' in AV: *pa'^{a}môn*, from a root meaning 'strike', occurs four times in Exodus, referring to the bells of gold on Aaron's high-priestly robes; the other word, *m^{e}ṣillâ*, is found only once, in Zc. xiv. 20. AVmg follows LXX (*chalinoi*), reading 'bridles'. The Heb. word is from the same root as that rendered 'cymbals' in AV, and probably refers to the metal discs or cups fixed to the bridles of horses either as an ornament or in order to produce a jingling sound. See fig. 34.

(ii) *Cymbals.* This word comes from Gk. *kymbalon*, which occurs once in the New Testament (1 Cor. xiii. 1) and also in LXX as a translation of Heb. *m^{e}ṣiltayim* and *ṣelṣ^{e}lîm*. *Kymbalon* is

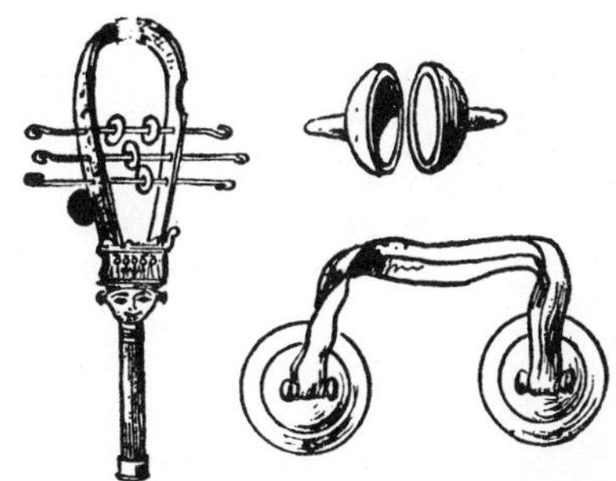

Fig. 147. Bronze sistrum and cymbals of types used in Egypt and Western Asia from the second millennium BC onwards.

derived from *kymbē*, which means a bowl or hollowed plate. The two Heb. words are derived from the same root, an onomatopoeic word meaning to whirr or quiver. *M^{e}ṣiltayim* seems to be a later form of the word occurring about twelve times in the books of Chronicles and once each in Ezra and Nehemiah. The earlier form *ṣelṣ^{e}lîm* is found in the Psalms and once in 2 Samuel. In Ps. cl the word is used twice in one verse with different adjectives. Two kinds of cymbals are known to have existed in ancient times. One kind consisted of two shallow metal plates held one in each hand and struck together. The others were cup-like in shape, one being held stationary while the other was brought down sharply against it. It has been suggested that in Ps. cl these two kinds of cymbals are alluded to, but this is merely conjecture.

In all the passages where cymbals are mentioned they are used in religious ceremonies. Gk. *kymbalon* is used in 1 Sa. xviii. 6 LXX to translate Heb. *šālîš*, which is from the root meaning 'three'. The Vulg. renders *sistrum*, 'rattle'. Suggestions have been made that it was a triangle or a three-stringed instrument, but there is no certainty as to what is denoted.

(iii) *Timbrel* and *tabret*. These are each used eight times in AV, translating Heb. *tōp̄* (LXX *tympanon*). The instrument was a kind of tambourine held and struck with the hand. It was used as an accompaniment to singing and dancing (Ex. xv. 20). It is always associated in the Old Testament with joy and gladness, and is found accompanying the merriment of feasts (Is. v. 12) and the rejoicing of triumphal processions (1 Sa. xviii. 6).

BIBLIOGRAPHY. J. Stainer, *The Music of the Bible*, 1914; C. H. Cornill, *Music in the Old Testament*, 1909; *ISBE*; S. B. Finesinger, 'Musical Instruments in the Old Testament' in *Hebrew Union College Annual*, III, 1926, pp. 21–75; F. W. Galpin, *The Music of the Sumerians and their Immediate Successors*, 1937; K. Sachs, *A History of Musical Instruments*, 1940. D.G.S.

MUSTARD. See PLANTS.

MUTH-LABBEN. See PSALMS.

MYRA. With its port, about 2 miles away, Myra was one of the chief cities of Lycia, a province on the south-west tip of Asia Minor. There Paul and his centurion escort boarded an Alexandrian corn ship bound for Italy (Acts xxvii. 5, 6). Called Dembre by the Turks, Myra displays some impressive ruins, including a well-preserved theatre. J.D.D.

MYRRH (Akkadian *murru*; Heb. *mōr*). The resinous exudate from the stems and branches of a low shrubby tree, either the *Commiphora myrrha* (variously *Balsamodendron myrrha* Nees) or the closely related *Commiphora kataf*. Both species are native to the Arabian deserts and parts of Africa. The gum drips from the shrub on to the ground, where it hardens to form an oily yellowish-brown resin.

Myrrh was an ingredient of the holy anointing oil (Ex. xxx. 23–33). It was prized for its aromatic qualities (Ps. xlv. 8; Pr. vii. 17; Ct. iii. 6, iv. 14, v. 5, 13), and was one of the substances used in female purification rites (Est. ii. 12), as well as in cosmetic preparations (see COSMETICS AND PERFUMERY). Myrrh was presented to the infant Jesus by the magi (Mt. ii. 11); it formed part of an anodyne offered to Him on Calvary (Mk. xv. 23), and was one of the spices employed at His burial (Jn. xix. 39).

The 'myrrh' of Gn. xxxvii. 25, xliii. 11 (Heb. *lōṭ*) carried by Ishmaelite traders to Egypt was probably the resin of the *Cistus villosus* L., or commercial ladanum. R.K.H.

MYRTLE. See PLANTS.

MYSIA. The homeland of one of the pre-hellenic peoples of Asia Minor, never a political unit in classical times, and therefore never precisely defined. It centred on the heavily forested hill country on either side of the main north road from Pergamum to Cyzicus on the Sea of Marmora, a tract which stretched from the border of Phrygia westwards to the promontory of the Troad. Troas itself, together with Assos and a number of other Gk. coastal states, and even Pergamum may be regarded as part of Mysia. It was the northern portion of the Rom. province of Asia. Paul had reached its eastern limits on his way through Phrygia to Bithynia (Acts xvi. 7) when he was diverted through Mysia (verse 8) to Troas, probably following a route through the south of the region. E.A.J.

MYSTERY.

I. IN THE OLD TESTAMENT

The only Old Testament appearance of the word is in the Aramaic section of Daniel (ii. 18, 19, 27–30, 47, iv. 9), where LXX renders Aram. *rāz* by *mystērion* (AV, RV 'secret'; RSV 'mystery'). In this context the word carries a specialized reference, and, as in the phrase 'there is a God in heaven who reveals mysteries' (ii. 28, RSV), it means primarily that which is hidden and still needs to be made known. Yet even here the meaning of the term is not unrelated to its New Testament use and significance, since the mysteries of which Daniel speaks in this chapter are contained within the eternal plan of God, and also made known by Him in advance to His servants ('thoughts of what would be hereafter', ii. 29, RSV).

Daniel's use of *rāz*, 'mystery', with the correlative *p*[e]*šar*, 'solution', 'interpretation', was taken over by the Qumran sect, whose use of this terminology has provided an illuminating background for understanding the New Testament occurrences of the term *mystērion*.

II. IN THE NEW TESTAMENT

a. Meaning

The meaning of the term *mystērion* in classical Greek is 'anything hidden or secret' (*vide HDB*, III, p. 465), and it was used in the plural particularly (*ta mystēria*) to refer to the sacred rites of the Gk. mystery religions in which only the initiated shared. The root verb is *myō*, which means primarily 'to close the lips (or eyes)' (Lat. *mutus*). But whereas 'mystery' may mean, and in contemporary usage often does mean, a secret for which no answer can be found, this is not at all the connotation of the term *mystērion* in classical and biblical Greek. In the New Testament *mystērion* signifies a secret which is being, or even has been, revealed, which is also divine in scope, and needs to be made known by God to men through His Spirit. In this way the term comes very close to the New Testament word *apokalypsis*, 'revelation'. *Mystērion* is a temporary secret, which once revealed is known and understood—a secret no longer; *apokalypsis* is a temporarily hidden eventuality, which simply awaits its revelation to make it actual and apprehended (*cf.* 1 Cor. i. 7, for example, where *apokalypsis* is used, as so often, in reference to

Christ Himself; and Rom. viii. 19, where Paul describes the creation as waiting with eager longing for its *apokatastasis* in the coming age of glory, which is to be revealed (*apokalyphthēnai*) at the *apokalypsis* of the sons of God themselves).

b. Usage

(i) *In the Gospels.* The single occurrence of the word *mystērion* in the Gospels is in Mk. iv. 11 = Mt. xiii. 11 (plural) = Lk. viii. 10 (AV 'mystery', RSV 'secret'). Here the term is used to refer to the kingdom of God, the knowledge of which, just because it is *God's* kingdom, is reserved for those to whom it is 'given'. As a result the unrevealed mystery is, for those 'outside' (*exō*), hidden in 'parables' (*q.v.*).

(ii) *In the Pauline Epistles.* Paul uses the word frequently, and indeed, apart from four occurrences of the word in Revelation and the three just noted in the Synoptic Gospels, the appearance of *mystērion* in the New Testament is confined to the Pauline Epistles (twenty-one times). The character of *to mystērion* in Paul's theology is fourfold.

1. It is eternal in its scope, in so far as it relates to the divine plan of salvation, the *Heilsgeschichte* itself. The 'mystery' is the good news which forms the content of God's revelation (*cf.* Eph. vi. 19); it is the mystery of God Himself, the focus of which is in Christ (Col. ii. 2, reading *tou mystēriou tou theou, Christou*, with P46, B, *et al.*; *cf.* 1 Cor. ii. 1, where B, D, and other MSS read *martyrion* for *mystērion*). As such it is contained within God's everlasting counsels and hidden in Him (Eph. iii. 9), decreed 'before the ages' (1 Cor. ii. 7) and declared as God's *sophia*, and veiled to human understanding, though awaiting its disclosure, throughout the ages (1 Cor. ii. 8; Rom. xvi. 25, where the adjectival participle is *sesigēmenon*).

2. It is historical in its announcement. This mystery is also the 'mystery of Christ', announced historically and definitively by God in Christ Himself (Eph. i. 9, iii. 3 f., where the *mystērion* is described as revealed to Paul *kata apokalypsin*; *cf.* Col. iv. 3) when the 'fulness of the time' had arrived (Gal. iv. 4). It is precisely this mystery, centred and declared in the person of the Lord Jesus Christ, through whose death God reconciles us to Himself (2 Cor. v. 18 f.; *cf.* 1 Cor. ii. 2), that Paul was commissioned to proclaim (Eph. iii. 8 f.; *cf.* 1 Cor. iv. 1). In his letter to the Ephesians Paul considers particularly, against the background of a general and gradual movement towards a Christ-centred inclusiveness (*vide* J. A. Robinson, *Ephesians*, 1903, pp. 238 f.), the dominant and related notions of 'hope' and 'mystery'. Christ is the hope of men (i. 12) and of the universe (i. 10), and we possess as a result a hope which is both glorious (i. 18) and real—already the Christian is saved, and raised with Him (ii. 4–6, where the verbs are in the aorist). Not only so, but also, and this is the particular character of the *mystērion* which Paul has been sent to preach, and which in the Epistle to the Ephesians he is chiefly concerned to outline, the new hope, and thus also the new *life* in Christ, is available for Jew and Gentile alike (iii. 8; *cf.* Col. i. 27, where the content of the mystery is qualified as 'Christ in you, the hope of glory').

3. It is spiritual in its perception. We have seen already from the Synoptic Gospels that the mystery of the kingdom is spiritually perceived. Paul retains this idea when he regards the mystery of Christ (the focus of which is particularly 'the Gentiles as fellow-heirs') as revealed to apostles and prophets by the Spirit (*en Pneumati*, Eph. iii. 5; *cf.* also 1 Cor. xiii. 2, xiv. 2). In line with this must be understood the term as it is used derivatively by Paul in connection with Christian marriage (Eph. v. 32), and the 'man of lawlessness (or sin)' (2 Thes. ii. 7). The divine significance of these 'mysteries' is apprehended by a conjunction of revelation and spiritual understanding (*cf.* also Rev. xvii. 3–7).

4. It is eschatological in its outcome. The mystery which has been revealed in time still awaits its divine consummation and fulfilment in eternity. This is the sense in which the term must be understood in Rev. x. 7: the 'mystery of God' already announced will be corporately fulfilled without delay, 'in the days of the trumpet call to be sounded by the seventh angel' (RSV). And this is equally true in terms of personal salvation—the 'mystery' of 'being changed' when the trumpet sounds, of mortality's being finally replaced by immortality (1 Cor. xv. 51 ff.). Such a mystery, even when it is made known, overwhelms us still with the depth of nothing less than the wisdom and the knowledge of God Himself (Col. ii. 2).

The use of the word 'mystery' with reference to the Sacraments (Vulg. translates *mystērion* as *sacramentum*) is entirely post-biblical.

BIBLIOGRAPHY. E. Hatch, *Essays in Biblical Greek*, 1899, pp. 57–62; C. L. Mitton, *The Epistle to the Ephesians*, 1951, pp. 86–90; G. Bornkamm in *TWNT*. See also the parallel article in *Vocabulary of the Bible*, ed. J.-J. von Allmen, E.T., 1958, pp. 276 ff. S.S.S.

N

NAAMAH ('pleasant'). **1.** A daughter of Zillah and sister of Tubal-cain (Gn. iv. 22). **2.** 'The Ammonitess', the mother of Rehoboam (1 Ki. xiv. 21). **3.** A city in lowland Judah (Jos. xv. 41), probably identical to modern Nā'neh, 6 miles south of Lydda. Zophar, one of Job's 'comforters', was a Naamathite, but it is unlikely that he originated from the same Naamah.

G.W.G.

NAAMAN (*na'amān*, 'pleasant'). The highly-successful commander-in-chief under Ben-hadad (*q.v.*), king of Damascus and sworn enemy of Israel (*cf.* 1 Ki. xx). His story is told in 2 Ki. v. He was 'a great man with his master, and honourable . . . mighty in valour, but . . . a leper'. In Israel this affliction would have cast him out from human society (*cf.* Lv. xiii, xiv), but in Syria it did not even preclude his holding high office. Because of some words spoken by a little Israelite slave-girl in his household, and taken up by the king, Naaman was sent to Samaria and sought a cure at the hand of Elisha. He took with him to Israel such presents as were appropriate to the occasion and to Naaman's rank (*cf.* C. F. Keil, *The Books of the Kings*, n.d., p. 317).

Though displeased and humiliated, both at the manner of his reception and by the counsel which the prophet gave, Naaman is prevailed upon to follow Elisha's instructions, chiefly through the striking common sense of his servants ('if the prophet had bid thee do some great thing, wouldest thou not have done it?').

On being cleansed from his leprosy Naaman confesses that Israel's God is the one true God, and requests two mules' burden of earth from Canaan—perhaps an indication of his conviction that Yahweh could be worshipped only on His own ground (*cf.* Ex. xx. 24). Moreover, he shows the contemporary pagan idea of religious syncretism as permissible (perhaps even desirable) by raising with Elisha the interesting problem of his future ostensible conformity to idol-worship in Syria—a subject on which the prophet declines to commit himself.

His leprosy gone and with a new faith, Naaman willingly presses upon the opportunist Gehazi (*q.v.*) some of the gifts which the prophet of the Lord had declined.

A Jewish legend, preserved by Josephus (*Ant.* viii. 15. 5), identifies Naaman with the man who 'drew a bow at a venture' and mortally wounded King Ahab (1 Ki. xxii. 34), but this has never been substantiated.

Naaman is mentioned also briefly in Lk. iv. 27.

The same name is borne by a grandson of Benjamin (Gn. xlvi. 21) whose descendants are the Naamites (Nu. xxvi. 40), and by a son of Ehud (1 Ch. viii. 7) whom some consider to be the same as the former.

J.D.D.

NABAL ('fool'). A wealthy inhabitant of Maon, south-east of Hebron, of the tribe of Caleb, who pastured sheep and goats on adjacent Carmel. During his exile in the reign of Saul, David heard that Nabal was shearing his sheep, a traditional time of hospitality, and sent ten of his men with the request that Nabal should provide David's force with hospitality on a feast-day in return for the protection from brigands David had given his flocks.

Nabal, referring to David as a nobody (*i.e.* as a usurper), refused his request, whereupon David with 400 men marched up. When Abigail, the beautiful and intelligent wife of Nabal, heard of the messengers' visit she arranged for food and wine to be sent on ahead and went to meet David. This prevented David from committing the crime of blood guilt upon Nabal.

On her return Abigail found her husband drunk. The following day Nabal suffered a paralytic stroke on hearing of his wife's action, and he died about ten days later (1 Sa. xxv).

R.A.H.G.

NABATAEANS. Nebaioth, son of Ishmael and brother-in-law of Edom (Gn. xxv. 13, xxviii. 9), is possibly to be considered the ancestor of the Nabataeans, who may also be the Nabaiate of inscriptions of Ashurbanipal of Assyria (*c.* 650 BC, *ANET*, pp. 298, 299). A difference in spelling between these two names (with *tāw*) and the native *nbṭw* (with *ṭēth*) precludes certain identification. Diodorus Siculus (*c.* 50 BC) brings the Nabataeans into recorded history in his account of the end of the Persian Empire and the career of Alexander. Quoting from an earlier source, he describes them as a nomadic Arab tribe who neither build houses nor till the soil. Their territory, the area south and east of the river Jordan, straddled the trade routes from the Orient to the Mediterranean, and their capital, Petra, 50 miles south of the Dead Sea, formed a base from which caravans could be attacked. Antigonus, who gained power in Syria after Alexander's death, sent two expeditions to Petra to subdue the Nabataeans and gain control of the trade (312 BC). Both were unsuccessful. It is clear that at this time Petra was at least a stronghold, and Gk. potsherds of *c.* 300 BC found there suggest a permanent settlement.

Contact with the settled communities of Palestine during the 2nd and 3rd centuries BC resulted in the development of Nabataean villages and towns and in intensive cultivation of formerly barren desert areas. This was aided by well-organized lines of frontier posts to guard against Arab marauders and by the skill of Nabataean engineers in constructing irrigation systems to conserve the scanty rainfall. Many of their dams and reservoirs are still usable. Petra is surrounded by high cliffs, pierced by narrow ravines, which form an almost impregnable defence.

When a Nabataean ruler arose (the earliest known king is Aretas I, *c.* 170 BC, 2 Macc. v. 8) who was able to safeguard the caravans, Nabataean merchants led trade from S Arabia and from the Persian Gulf to Petra, whence it was forwarded to the coast, particularly Gaza. Increased demands by the Rom. world for spices, silks, and other luxuries from India and China swelled enormously the revenues of a power which could levy tolls on all goods passing through its territory. The re-direction of the trade routes across the Red Sea to Egypt after Augustus' failure to conquer Arabia (25 BC) was an important factor in the decline of Nabataean prosperity.

Native records (coins and dedicatory inscriptions) are written in Aramaic in a curiously heightened form of the 'square' script (see WRITING). Papyri from the Judaean desert and ostraca from Petra exhibit a cursive form of this writing from which the Arab. scripts are derived. Use of Aramaic indicates a wide assimilation of the culture of neighbouring settled peoples. This is evidenced by Nabataean sculptures which contain features found in Syrian work and traceable in early Islamic ornamentation. It may be seen also in the acceptance of Syrian deities, Hadad and Atargatis (Astarte) into the Nabataean pantheon. These two may have been identified with Dushara and his consort Allat, the national deities. Many open-air shrines (*e.g.* the high place at Petra) and temples (*e.g.* Khirbet et-Tannur) have been discovered on isolated hill-tops. The gods worshipped were especially associated with weather and fertility. Nabataean potters developed a distinctive ware of their own unsurpassed in Palestine (see POTTER).

Nabataean history, as reconstructed from incidental references by Jewish and Gk. authors, consists mainly of struggles to gain control of the Negeb in the south and of Damascus in the north. Aretas III (*c.* 70 BC) and Aretas IV (*c.* 9 BC–AD 40) succeeded in holding both these areas for a few years, so obtaining complete control of east–west trade. It was an officer (Gk. *ethnarchēs*) of Aretas IV who attempted to detain Paul in Damascus (2 Cor. xi. 32). Malichus III and Rabbel II, the last Nabataean kings, moved the capital from Petra to Bostra, 70 miles east of Galilee. This became the capital of the Rom. province of Arabia following Trajan's conquests in AD 106. Petra enjoyed considerable prosperity during the 2nd century AD when most of the rock-cut façades were made. The rise of Palmyra diverted the trade which formerly went to Petra from the east, and that city gradually declined. The Nabataean people became absorbed in the surrounding population, although the script continued in use into the 4th century.

BIBLIOGRAPHY. J. Starcky, 'The Nabataeans: A Historical Sketch', *BA*, XVIII, 1955, pp. 84–106; G. L. Harding, *The Antiquities of Jordan*, 1959; *PEQ*, LXXXVIII, 1958, pp. 12–15, on recent work at Petra; N. Glueck, *The Other Side of the Jordan*, 1940, pp. 158–200; S. Moscati, *The Semites in Ancient History*, 1959, pp. 117–119.

A.R.M.

NABOTH. 1 Ki. xxi tells how Ahab and Jezebel obtained the vineyard of Naboth the Jezreelite, after suborning false witnesses to accuse him of blasphemy against God and the king. Unjustly convicted, Naboth was stoned to death, according to law, outside the town (*cf.* Lv. xxiv. 16). If Naboth had heirs, either they shared his fate or the estate of those convicted of blasphemy (which in Israel was treason) was automatically confiscated by the king (see ARCHAEOLOGY, VIII).

God sent Elijah to condemn Ahab (*q.v.*) and his house for this cruel deed. The king, because of a passing repentance, escaped for a time, but later died a violent death (1 Ki. xxii. 34–40). The deaths of Joram and Jezebel (2 Ki. ix. 25, 36) near the spot of Naboth's execution were regarded as divine retribution on the cruel deed.

J.D.D.

NADAB (*nāḏāḇ*, 'generous', 'noble'). **1.** Aaron's eldest son (Nu. iii. 2). Intimately present at Sinai (Ex. xxiv. 1) and later a priest (Ex. xxviii. 1), he transgressed the law (Ex. xxx. 9) with his brother Abihu in offering 'strange fire' to God, for which they both died (Lv. x. 1–7; *cf.* Nu. xxvi. 61). 'Strange fire' may mean either fire or incense kindled elsewhere than at the altar (Lv. xvi. 12) or incense offered at the wrong time ('which he commanded them not'). Lv. x. 8, 9 hints at the possibility that drunkenness was an element in the sin.

2. A son of Shammai, of the house of Jerahmeel, of the tribe of Judah (1 Ch. ii. 28). **3.** A son of Gibeon, of the tribe of Benjamin (1 Ch. viii. 30). **4.** A king of Israel, successor to his father, Jeroboam I. He reigned *c.* 915–914 BC, being assassinated and succeeded by Baasha while besieging Gibbethon (1 Ki. xiv. 20, xv. 25–28).

T.H.J.

NAG HAMMADI. See CHENOBOSKION.

NAHALAL, NAHALOL. A town assigned to Zebulun, but held by Canaanites (Jos. xix. 15, xxi. 35; Jdg. i. 30). Ma'lul, north-east of modern Nahalal and 4 miles west of Nazareth, is identified in the Talmud, but is not sufficiently old. Simons (*GTT*, p. 182) favours Tell el-Beida, south of Nahalal; Albright (*Cont. Hist. Geog. Pal.*, p. 26) suggests Tell en-Nahl near Haifa (*cf.* Gn. xlix. 13). J.P.U.L.

NAHALIEL. A stage on Israel's advance northward from the Arnon; now Wadi Zerka Ma'in; famous in Roman times for its warm springs, which flow into the Dead Sea 11 miles from the Jordan mouth (Jos., *BJ* i. 33. 5, vii. 6. 3). J.P.U.L.

NAHASH. 1. An Ammonite king who attacked Jabesh-Gilead in Saul's reign (1 Sa. xi, xii). His relations with David were friendly (2 Sa. x. 2; 1 Ch. xix. 1). **2.** Father of Abigail and Zeruiah, David's sisters, 2 Sa. xvii. 25. LXX (B) and Origen support this reading against other Gk. MSS which give 'Jesse' (Driver, *Samuel*), possibly by assimilation to 1 Ch. ii. 13–16. The Chronicler may mean that Abigail and Zeruiah were Jesse's step-daughters; their sons appear to have been of about David's age. J.P.U.L.

NAHOR. 1. Son of Serug, and grandfather of Abraham (Gn. xi. 22–25; 1 Ch. i. 26).

2. Son of Terah, and brother of Abraham and Haran. He married his niece Milcah, Haran's daughter (Gn. xi. 26, 27, 29). Nahor probably journeyed to Harran with Terah, Abram, and Lot despite the silence of Gn. xi. 31 to this effect, for Harran became known as 'the city of Nahor' (Gn. xxiv. 10; *cf.* xxvii. 43). He was the progenitor of twelve Aramaean tribes which are listed in Gn. xxii. 20–24. This reflects the close relationship of the Hebrews and the Aramaeans. A place Nahur in the vicinity of Harran is named in the Mari tablets (18th century BC).

The two other passages where Nahor is mentioned need to be compared to reveal that Nahor was a devotee of the false god of his father Terah (Gn. xxxi. 53; *cf.* Jos. xxiv. 2). This implies that the consecration at Mizpah (Gn. xxxi. 43 ff.) took place in the presence of Yahweh and Terah's god. R.J.W.

NAHSHON (Heb. *naḥšôn*, possibly from *nāḥāš*, 'serpent'; Gk. *Naassōn*). Aaron's brother-in-law (Ex. vi. 23; AV gives 'Naashon'), son of Amminadab and prince of Judah (Nu. i. 7, ii. 3, vii. 12, 17, x. 14; 1 Ch. ii. 10). He is mentioned as an ancestor of David in Ru. iv. 20, and of our Lord in Mt. i. 4 and Lk. iii. 32. J.G.G.N.

NAHUM, BOOK OF.

I. AUTHORSHIP AND DATE

Nahum was a prophet from Elkosh, possibly in Judah. It is difficult to date his prophecy precisely, but we may note that the capture of Thebes (*i.e.* No-ammon) is regarded as already having taken place. This event occurred under Ashurbanipal in the years 664–663 BC. At the same time, Nineveh, the object of Nahum's preaching, is still standing. Nineveh fell in 612 BC, and so we may roughly place the prophecy between these two dates. More precise than this, however, it is impossible to be.

II. SUMMARY OF CONTENTS

Each of the three chapters is a unit in itself, and we may best understand the prophecy by considering these chapters one after another.

a. An acrostic poem and declaration of judgment, i. 1–15

Chapter i falls into three principal sections; the superscription (verse 1), the description of God's majesty (verses 2–8), and the declaration of judgment to come (verses 9–15). The superscription describes the message as a *maśśā'*, *i.e.* 'burden', a word which often denotes a message involving threatening. It also declares that the work is a 'book of the vision of Nahum', *i.e.* it is a book in which the vision received by Nahum is written down. The supernatural character of the message is thus early acknowledged.

The prophet immediately plunges into a statement of the jealousy of God. The zeal of the Lord is His determination to carry out His purposes both in the bringing in of His own kingdom and in the punishment of His adversaries. It is this latter aspect of God's jealousy which is here prominent. God is slow to anger, says the prophet (verse 3); nevertheless, He will take vengeance on His enemies. When these terms are applied to God we must understand that they are used anthropomorphically; they do not contain the sinister connotations that adhere to them when they are used of men. That God is able so to carry out His purposes is a matter that admits of no doubt. He can control the forces of nature, the storm, the rivers, the sea, Bashan, *etc.* For those who trust in Him He is a stronghold, but for the wicked He is darkness.

The enemies of the Lord refuse to believe that He will smite them. Hence, God announces that in a time when they expect it not the enemy will be devoured as stubble that is wholly dry. Yet there is also to be an announcement of salvation, and Judah is commanded to keep her solemn feasts and to perform her vows.

b. The siege and sack of Nineveh, ii. 1–13

In ii. 1–6 Nahum describes the enemy who lay siege to Nineveh. These are the Medes who came from the plain of Persia and were turning their attention against the Assyrians of the Mesopotamian plain. They are described as those that dash in pieces (verse 1). In attacking the city they open the sluices so that the waters of the river may overflow and then they enter the city to destroy her palace.

Huzzab, a word which probably designates the queen, is taken away into captivity, and her female attendants follow her. Nineveh, the object of attack, has become like a pool of water. Into her much trade has poured and many goods have been brought, so that she is now filled. Nevertheless, men will flee from her, and those who cry

'Stand!' will not be able to stay those who would take refuge in flight. Plunder then begins in earnest, and the few survivors who remain behind look on in grief and terror as the city is despoiled.

Nineveh had once been a lion, a veritable den of lions. She had engaged in search for prey. Now, however, she is herself the object of such search and herself becomes a prey. What has become of Nineveh? The answer is that the Lord of hosts is against her, and He has determined to act in such a way as to remove her strength and power from her.

c. A description of the city and a comparison with Egypt, iii. 1–19

Chapter iii consists of a description of the wicked character of the city of Nineveh. She was a bloody city and full of cruelty. She was a warring city, and there were many that were slain. Through her whoredoms she sold nations, and dealt in witchcrafts. Hence, the Lord had set Himself against her and would expose her so that she would become a laughing-stock to all who looked upon her.

Nahum then makes a brief comparison with Egypt (iii. 8–15). Egypt had become strong, had revelled in her strength, and acted as had Nineveh, yet her ruin had surely come. So also would it be with Nineveh. There could be no escape. Thus the prophet works up to a mighty climax, and announces that there is no healing for the bruise of Assyria, 'Thy wound is grievous' (iii. 19a).

In this small prophecy of doom we learn that the God of Israel, the nation whom Assyria had despised, is truly the God who controls the destinies and the actions of all nations.

BIBLIOGRAPHY. Walter A. Maier, *Nahum*, 1959; W. J. Deane, *Nahum*, 1913; E. J. Young, *Introduction to the Old Testament*, 1958, pp. 286, 287. E.J.Y.

NAIL. 1. Finger-nail (Heb. *ṣippōren*; Aram. *ṭeᵉpar*). Captive women were commanded to shave the head and pare the nails (Dt. xxi. 12). Nebuchadrezzar had 'nails like birds' claws' (Dn. iv. 33, *cf.* vii. 19).

Fig. 148. Bronze nail from the gates of the temple of Imgut-Bel at Balawat near Nineveh. It was used for fixing to the wooden frame the bronze reliefs depicting the campaigns of Shalmaneser III (859–824 BC).

2. A wooden tent peg (Jdg. iv. 21, Heb. *yāṯēḏ*), used by Jael to slay Sisera. It was sometimes used for suspending objects as in Ezk. xv. 3. Isaiah likened Eliakim to 'a nail in a sure place' on which the 'glory of his father's house' might hang. Such a nail was driven into a wall.

3. A metal nail or pin (*yāṯēḏ*) for driving into wood or other material to hold objects together, or left projecting to suspend objects. In the tabernacle the nails were of brass (Ex. xxvii. 19, xxxv. 18, xxxviii. 20, 31, xxxix. 40; Nu. iii. 37, iv. 32). Delilah used such a nail (pin) to bind Samson (Jdg. xvi. 14). The word *masmēr* refers to nails of iron (1 Ch. xxii. 3) or of gold (2 Ch. iii. 9), driven into a wall (Ec. xii. 11), or used to secure idols in their place (Is. xli. 7; Je. x. 4).

4. In New Testament times victims were affixed to a cross by nails driven through hands and feet (Gk. *hēlos*, Jn. xx. 25).

Numerous specimens of nails, both bronze and iron, have been found in excavations in Palestine covering the time range of the biblical references.

J.A.T.

NAIN. Mentioned only in Lk. vii. 11. There is a small village still bearing this name in the Plain of Jezreel, a few miles south of Nazareth, at the edge of Little Hermon, and it is generally accepted as the scene of the gospel narrative. It is certainly to be distinguished from the Nain of Jos., *BJ* iv. 9. 4, which was east of the Jordan. The name is perhaps a corruption of the Heb. word *nā'îm*, 'pleasant', which adjective well describes the area and the views, if not the village itself. A problem is raised, however, by the reference to the city gate (Lk. vii. 12); for the village today called Nain was never fortified, and so would never have had a gate in the proper sense of the word. But the word 'gate' may be used loosely, to indicate the place where the road entered between the houses of Nain. An ingenious suggestion solves the difficulty by proposing that the site was Shunem (as in the similar story of 2 Ki. iv), an original *synēm* becoming accidentally reduced to *nēm*, and then confused with Nain. Shunem, in any case, is in the same general area.

D.F.P.

NAIOTH. A place or quarter in Ramah where Samuel supervised a community of prophets and to which David fled from Saul (1 Sa. xix. 18, 19, 22, 23). When Saul sent messengers there to seek David, each in turn 'prophesied'. Later, when Saul came in person he too 'prophesied' (verse 24), giving rise to a proverb: 'Is Saul also among the prophets?' The Heb. word *nāyôṯ* is related to *nāweh*, 'pasture ground' or 'abode', and is commonly translated 'habitation'. J.A.T.

NAME. Although certain aspects of the biblical notion of 'name' survive in modern usage, *e.g.* the use of someone's name as a reference, yet to us the name is to a large extent nothing more than a personal label. This was hardly, if at all, the case in the Bible. We have only to consider how particular God was to name chosen individuals (*e.g.* Gn. xvii. 5, 15, 19; Is. xlv. 3, 4; Mt. i. 21), and how solemnly He revealed the meaning of His own name, and used it (Ex. iii. 13–15, xxxiii. 19, xxxiv. 5, 6) to realize that the concept of 'name' is both deep and clearly conceived.

I. THE GIVING OF A NAME

To give a name is the prerogative of a superior, as when Adam exercised his dominion over the animals, by giving them their names (Gn. ii. 18 ff.), or when the victorious pharaoh renamed the conquered Judaean king (2 Ki. xxiii. 34). Likewise, the parent (the mother on twenty-eight occasions, the father on eighteen) names the child.

When a superior thus exercised his authority, the giving of the name signified the appointment of the person named to some specific position, function, or relationship. The dying Rachel would have called her new-born son Ben-oni ('son of my sorrow'), for this was the relation in which he stood to her; his father prized this son of his loved wife more highly and decided his status differently, Benjamin ('son of the right hand', Gn. xxxv. 18). In the same way Solomon's other name, Jedidiah, was given 'because of Yahweh', *i.e.* to signify the love which Yahweh bore to him (2 Sa. xii. 25). The names Isaac (as given by God, Gn. xvii. 19) and John (Lk. i. 13) have no stated significance. The giving of the name signifies in these cases the bare notion of appointment (*cf.* Phil. ii. 10).

Often, however, the giving of the name had a deeper and more personal significance, the positive donation of new character and capacity. This could be only a pious hope in the case of human namings (*e.g.* 2 Ki. xxiv. 17, where the new name 'Yahweh is righteousness' presumably expressed a hope concerning a corresponding fidelity of the vassal to his overlord!), and we shall say more of this presently. But when God renamed an individual it was equivalent to regeneration (as in Gn. xvii. 5, 15, xxxii. 28) or to condemnation (as in Je. xx. 3). The name confirmed that person in the possession of a certain quality of being; God had fixed his nature, capacity, and destiny. For the same reason, God selected the name His Son should bear (Mt. i. 21); the name must match the character and function.

The most frequent source of the name which was selected in any given case was some circumstance at the time of birth. This is the explanation of Peleg (Gn. x. 25), Zoar (Gn. xix. 22), Edom (Gn. xxv. 30), and very many others. In some cases this circumstance was prophetic, as in the naming of Jacob (Gn. xxv. 26). The name given describes the character of the man who was to be.

The relation between the name and the circumstance may be used to illustrate a feature of the whole custom of giving significant names: sometimes the name and the circumstance have an exact philological equivalence, as in the case of Peleg, which means 'division'; sometimes, however, the association is simply one of sound: thus Joseph called his son 'Ephraim', a name somewhat reminiscent of the verbal root *pārâ*, expressing fruitfulness (Gn. xli. 52), and Moses called his son 'Gershom', similar in sound to the word *gēr*, 'a resident alien'.

Another motive for the selection of the name was hope or prophecy. God could use names to act as proofs positive of coming events (*e.g.* Ho. i. 4; Is. viii. 1–4, *cf.* viii. 18), but human parents could only express hopes, as, for example, the pitiable Leah did, seeing in each successive child the indication that now at last Jacob would love her truly (Gn. xxix. 32, 33, 34, 35). Under the same heading of hope we may observe that many names were implied prayers. 'Joseph' is interpreted as 'May the Lord add to me another son!' (Gn. xxx. 24, RSV). Surely we must include the wretched Nabal (1 Sa. xxv. 25) here also, for how else can we explain such a dreadful name except as an implied prayer that the child would be kept from folly? Unfortunately the parents were, apparently unwittingly, skilled in prophecy! Koehler (*op. cit. inf.*, p. 65) speaks of such names as talismans: 'There hovers over the life of the child the fear of what might come upon it, and this is expressed in a name which says what the child should not be.' Many of the names compounded with Yahweh, or *'ēl* ('God') are to be understood as prayers; *e.g.* 'Joshua' = 'Yahweh is salvation', *etc.*

One final feature of the giving of the name may be noted. Where the name-giver places his own name upon the person named, the giving of the name signifies the joining of two hitherto separate persons in the closest unity. The wife receives the name of her husband (Is. iv. 1). In particular, Israel is called by Yahweh's name, and thus becomes the holy people of the holy God (Dt. xxviii. 9, 10; *cf.* Is. xliii. 7, lxiii. 19, lxv. 1). On the basis of the shared name, Jeremiah appealed to Yahweh to save Israel (xiv. 9); it is also the basis of his own personal fellowship with God (xv. 16). Again, Jerusalem (Je. xxv. 29; Dn. ix. 18 f.), the Temple (Je. xxxii. 34), and possibly the ark as well (2 Sa. vi. 2) are called by the Name, signifying the same closeness of association with Yahweh's holy person. This, of course, has doctrinal implications of the greatest importance, for, in the New Testament, one regular idiom used in connection with baptism is 'to baptize into the Name' (*eis* with the accusative, *e.g.* Mt. xxviii. 19; Acts viii. 16; 1 Cor. i. 13, 15), signifying designation for union, the passing into new ownership, and loyalty, and fellowship (*cf.* Jas. ii. 7).

II. THE NAME AND THE PERSON

So far we have studied what was involved in the giving of a name, and what bearing it had on the relationship between giver and receiver. We now ask concerning the relationship between the name and the person who bore it. The biblical teaching can be stated in three propositions: the name is the person; the name is the person revealed; and the name is the person actively present.

a. The name is the person

This proposition hardly needs demonstration beyond what has been given already. The new man, Abraham, is the new name, Abraham. There are, however, other usages of the concept of the name which make the equation between name and bearer exact. Thus, the idea of total personal extinction is expressed as the cutting off (Jos. vii. 9), destroying (Dt. vii. 24), taking away (Nu. xxvii. 4, RSV), blotting out (2 Ki. xiv. 27), rotting (Pr. x. 7) of the name. The man who leaves neither name nor remainder (2 Sa. xiv. 7) is utterly quenched as a person. In the case of God the evidence is even more dramatic, for He can be spoken of as 'the Name' (Lv. xxiv. 11, RSV; Pr. xviii. 10; Is. xxx. 27).

b. The name is the person revealed

These forms of expression are so strange that there must be some further meaning involved in them. Why does Isaiah speak of the 'name of Yahweh' coming, rather than simply of 'Yahweh' coming? The answer is that the 'name' means the person as revealed: the 'name of Yahweh' means Yahweh in all that fulness of divine power, holiness, wrath, and grace which He has revealed as His character. The 'name' is a place of refuge because the God who bears the name has so revealed Himself (Je. x. 6; and especially Ps. lxxvi. 1). The name is what is known of the person. Moses, wishing to express that degree of intimate knowledge which Yahweh has of him, said 'Thou hast said, I know thee by name' (Ex. xxxiii. 12; *cf.* Ps. ix. 10; Jn. x. 3); and, again, foreseeing that the Israelites in Egypt would desire to know what revelation of God he brought, he poses their question, 'What is his name?' (Ex. iii. 13). He went to Egypt equipped to reveal the meaning of the name, just as the Psalmist, having experienced the activity of Yahweh, says 'I will declare thy name . . .' (Ps. xxii. 22; *cf.* Jn. xvii. 6; Acts ix. 15).

The Psalms delight to associate the name of Yahweh with the acts in which He displays Himself: His name is linked with His righteousness (lxxxix. 15, 16), faithfulness (lxxxix. 24), salvation (xcvi. 2), holiness (xcix. 3), goodness (c. 4, 5), mercy (cix. 21), love (cxix. 55), truth (cxxxviii. 2), and glory (cxlviii. 13). The adjective most often associated with the name of God is 'holy', which thus becomes the primary description of the divine nature.

We may adduce two other lines of evidence in support of the proposition that name means revealed character. First, the expression 'for my/thy name's sake', which may mean 'for purely personal reasons, reasons hidden within the heart of the subject' (*e.g.* Ezk. xx. 44; 1 Sa. xii. 22), often means 'out of loyalty to revealed character' (Pss. xxiii. 3, xxv. 11; Je. xiv. 7, 8). Secondly, we read of people acting towards the name of God in a way which involves the notion of the name as expressive of the quality of God Himself as revealed. His name can be blasphemed (Is. lii. 5), polluted (Je. xxxiv. 16), handled violently (Pr. xxx. 9); on the other hand, God's people can love (Ps. v. 11), or can praise (Joel ii. 26), walk in (Mi. iv. 5), think upon (Mal. iii. 16), wait on (Ps. lii. 9), give thanks to (Ps. liv. 6, RSV), fear (Mal. iv. 2), call upon (Ps. xcix. 6), proclaim (Is. xii. 4, RSV), and bless (Ps. cxlv. 1, 2) God's name.

c. The name is the person actively present

However, some of the passages quoted immediately above call for further explanation. For example, what is the difference between calling upon the name and calling upon God? It is here that the third aspect of the relation between name and person comes to the fore. The name signifies the active presence of the person in the fulness of the revealed character. On Mt. Carmel Elijah proposed a contest between 'names' (1 Ki. xviii. 24), *i.e.* reality of deity is to be demonstrated by present personal action (*cf.* Ps. lxxvi. 1). The same truth is expressed when name means personal reputation. Sometimes, when Yahweh is said to act 'for his name's sake', the meaning clearly is 'out of regard for His reputation' (Ps. lxxix. 9, 10; Ezk. xxxvi. 21–23). Where His name is implicated He is personally involved, and will take personal action; this is the truth stated in Ex. xxxiv. 14, where His name is said to be 'jealous'. Similarly, prophets (Dt. xviii. 20), messengers (1 Sa. xxv. 5), and letters (1 Ki. xxi. 8) are sent 'in the name', which means not only that they are consonant with the will of the person named but also that they carry his personal authority: they are as if he were personally present and active (*cf.* 2 Cor. v. 20). Likewise, to impart a blessing from God is to put God's name upon someone (Nu. vi. 27), that is, a prayer that the one blessed may know the active presence of God in the fulness of His revealed character (Jn. xvii. 11, 12). To revert again to the terminology of baptism, we find that sometimes the New Testament speaks of baptizing 'upon the name . . .' (*epi* with the dative, *e.g.* Acts ii. 38, x. 48), signifying that baptism rests upon the authority of the Lord Jesus and is spiritually effective only through His personal presence and activity.

III. 'NAME THEOLOGY'

Many times there is mention of the place where God will cause His name to dwell (Dt. xii. 5, 11, 21, xiv. 23, 24, xvi. 2, 6, 11; 2 Sa. vii. 13; 1 Ki. iii. 2, viii. 16–20, 29, ix. 3; Je. vii. 12). This has been given a good deal of publicity as name-theology, characteristic of the Deuteronomists, as distinct from the *kāḇôḏ* or 'glory'-theology of the Priestly School (see von Rad, *op. cit. inf.*). This notion is suspect on three grounds: first, because the rigid distinction between 'name' and 'glory' cannot be pressed. Yahweh's name is His glory, the manifested perfection of His presence. Moses prayed that he might see the glory, and he found it to be inseparable from the name (Ex. xxxiii. 18–23, xxxiv. 6–8). Secondly, the 'placing' of Yahweh's name is not peculiar to Deuteronomy, but is found also in Exodus (xx. 24). Thirdly, and specially, the name-theology is said to involve a 'theologically sublimated idea': 'It is not Jahweh himself who is present at the shrine, but only his name. . . . Deuteronomy is replacing the old crude idea of Yahweh's presence and dwelling at the shrine' (von Rad). It is difficult to see quite what is 'crude' about the notion of God dwelling among His people; but it is more difficult to understand why Deuteronomy should replace it by an idea which rather enforces and emphasizes it, since the name is the person actively present in revealed character. The 'angel' who accompanied Israel is to be regarded with all the reverence due to Yahweh Himself, 'for my name is in him' (Ex. xxiii. 21); in Ezk. xliii. 8 the picture of Yahweh Himself resident in the sanctuary could not be more baldly painted, and yet He says that it was His 'name' which was profaned; when the Psalmist prays 'the name of the God of Jacob protect thee' he is not dealing with a 'theologically sublimated idea' but with the practical religious truth that the name is the person, actively present in the fulness of his revealed character.

BIBLIOGRAPHY. L. Koehler, *Hebrew Man*, 1956, pp. 63 ff.; J.-J. von Allmen, *Vocabulary of the Bible*, 1958, *s.v.* 'Name'; J. Pedersen, *Israel*, I and II, 1926, pp. 245–259 *et passim*; A. B. Davidson, *The Theology of the Old Testament*, 1904, pp. 36 ff.; G. A. F. Knight, *A Christian Theology of the Old Testament*, 1959, Index, *s.v.* 'Name'; G. von Rad, *Studies in Deuteronomy*, 1953, pp. 37–44; G. T. Manley, *The Book of the Law*, 1957, pp. 33, 122 ff. J.A.M.

NAOMI (*na'ᵒmî*, 'my delight'). During the period of the judges there was a famine in Bethlehem of Judah, which caused Elimelech, a citizen of that place, to take his wife Naomi, and their two sons, Mahlon and Chilion, to Moab. There she was widowed, and her sons married Moabite girls, Orpah and Ruth, who were widowed in their turn. (See RUTH.)

Naomi decided to return to her own people alone, while her daughters-in-law remarried, but Ruth insisted on accompanying her. At Bethlehem she planned a levirate marriage for Ruth with her near kinsman, Boaz. Their first child, Obed, was reckoned as hers, and he was the grandfather of David (Ru. iv. 16 f.). M.G.

NAPHISH. The eleventh son of Ishmael (Gn. xxv. 15; 1 Ch. i. 31). His descendants have not been definitely identified, but may be the 'Nephish' of 1 Ch. v. 19; 'the children of Nephusim' of Ezr. ii. 50; and the 'Nephishesim' (RV 'Nephushesim') of Ne. vii. 52. J.D.D.

NAPHTALI (*napṯālî*, 'wrestler'). Fifth son of Jacob (Gn. xxx. 7 f.); his mother was Rachel's maidservant Bilhah. The description of him as 'a hind let loose' in Gn. xlix. 21 may mark him out as fleet of foot. The Targum of Pseudo-Jonathan gives him a life-span of 132 years.

In Nu. ii. 29–31 his tribe comes last in the survey of the wilderness encampments; it was included under the standard of Dan.

After the settlement the tribal territory of Naphtali lay west of the Sea of Galilee and the upper Jordan. Its frontiers are detailed in Jos. xix. 32–34, *cf.* 22. Here Naphtali lived among the Canaanites. Galilee (Heb. *gālîl*) applied originally to a district around the hill-country of Naphtali (Jos. xx. 7, xxi. 32), but later covered a wider region to the west and south, called *gᵉlîl haggōyîm* (Is. ix. 1); *Galilaia allophylōn* (1 Macc. v. 15; *cf.* Mt. iv. 15).

Barak from Kedesh-Naphtali (north-west of Lake Huleh) gained himself a national name in Israel (Jdg. iv. 6). Exposed to constant marauding attacks, the men of these uplands developed a marked degree of courage and hardihood. Their bravery is commended in the song of Deborah (Jdg. v. 18); they served valiantly under Gideon (Jdg. vii. 23), and made an important contribution to David's strength at Hebron (1 Ch. xii. 34). Lying on the northern border, Naphtali suffered much during the wars of the kings. The territory was ravaged about 885 BC by Ben-hadad I, the Syrian king of Damascus (1 Ki. xv. 20). In 734 BC Naphtali was annexed by Tiglath-pileser III, king of Assyria. Its people were the first west of Jordan to be taken captive (2 Ki. xv. 29).

Nineteen fenced cities in Naphtali are mentioned in Jos. xix. 32–39. In addition to the famous city of refuge, Kedesh-Naphtali, the territory included also the great city of Hazor, and the two Canaanite holy cities Beth-anath and Beth-shemesh. Jos. xix. 35 names three cities which can be located beside the Sea of Galilee: Hammath (south of Tiberias), Rakkath (north of Tiberias), and Chinnereth (west of Capernaum). The district around the springs of the Jordan was included in the lot of Naphtali. From this northernmost part Naphtali could not drive out the Canaanites, who worshipped Anath and Shemesh (Jdg. i. 33). These the Danites found in possession at the time of their raid of Laish, apparently with no opposition on the side of Naphtali (Jdg. xviii).

The territory of Naphtali includes many pastoral mountains and arable valleys. It was one of the districts from which Solomon drew provisions; its governor was the king's son-in-law (1 Ki. iv. 15). To the north-west of the Sea of Galilee there is the fertile plain of Gennesaret on the seashore. Water is plentiful, supplied by copious springs. The plain was dotted with villages in the time of Jesus. The apricot, fig, mulberry, olive, pomegranate, and vine gave splendid harvests. Pine and terebinth grow on the lofty mountains, of which Jebel Jermuk is the highest in Palestine.

In the land of Naphtali Jesus spent the greatest part of His public life. The plain of Gennesaret, Bethsaida, Capernaum, Chorazin, all lay within its boundaries (Mt. iv. 15). In Naphtali were the headquarters of the Jewish Zealots, who fought against the Roman oppressors. Even one of the twelve disciples was a Zealot. Josephus (*BJ* iii. 3) praises the people of Naphtali as robust warriors.

BIBLIOGRAPHY. A. Saarisalo, *The Boundary between Issachar and Naphtali*, 1927; *id.*, 'Topographical Researches in Galilee', *JPOS*, VIII, IX, 1928, 1929; A. Alt, *Palästina-Jahrbuch*, 1928.

A.S.

NAPHTUHIM. Classed with Mizraim (Egypt), Gn. x. 13; 1 Ch. i. 11. Its identity is uncertain, but Lower Egypt, specifically the Nile Delta, would be very appropriate alongside Pathrusim (*q.v.*) for Upper Egypt. Hence Brugsch and Erman emended the Heb. to fit Egyp. *p' t'-mḥw*, 'Lower Egypt'. Another Egyp. equivalent, without emendation, might be a *n'(-n-)/n'(yw-) p' idḥw*, 'they of the Delta (lit. marshland)', Lower Egypt(ians). Alternatively, *nap̄tuḥîm* may be an Egyp. *n'(-n-)/n'(yw-) p' t' wḥ'(t)*, 'they of the Oasis-land', *i.e.* the oases (and inhabitants) west of the Nile valley.

K.A.K.

NAPKIN. See HANDKERCHIEF.

NARCISSUS. Paul salutes 'them that be of Narcissus' (Rom. xvi. 11). The phrase suggests the slaves of a prominent household. The rich freedman Narcissus, who brought about the fall of Messalina (Tacitus, *Annals* xi, *passim*), had committed suicide some little time before Romans was written (*ibid.*, xiii. 1); but his slaves ('Narcissiani' are mentioned in *CIL*, III, 3973, VI, 15640) would pass to Nero and still be a recognizable entity. Though the name is also common outside Rome, it is tempting to see in Rom. xvi. 11 a Christian group within this body.

A.F.W.

NARD. See SPIKENARD.

NASH PAPYRUS. See WRITING, *Vb*(v)2.

NATHAN (*nāṯān*, 'he [*i.e.* God] has given'). Of some eleven men of this name in the Old Testament, the following at least can be identified as separate individuals:

1. A prophet (*nāḇî'*) involved in the story of King David. He appears without introduction when David expresses his wish to build a temple (2 Sa. vii = 1 Ch. xvii). Nathan approves at first, but after speaking with God informs David that this task is for David's descendant, though David apparently arranges, at Nathan's instigation, the music for Temple worship (1 Ch. xxix. 25). When Adonijah plans to seize his father's throne, Nathan advises Bathsheba to remind David of his promise to name Solomon his successor. Supporting this reminder, Nathan is instructed to proclaim Solomon (1 Ki. i. 11–45). Nathan is best known for his fearless denunciation of David's double sin against Uriah the Hittite, and the parable in which it was couched (2 Sa. xii).

2. Relative of two of David's warriors (2 Sa. xxiii. 36; 1 Ch. xi. 38). **3.** Son of David, born in Jerusalem (2 Sa. v. 14). This line of descent is cited in Zc. xii. 12 and in our Lord's genealogy in Lk. iii. 31. Either this Nathan or the prophet is referred to in 1 Ki. iv. 5. **4.** A man of Judah (1 Ch. ii. 36). **5.** One of Ezra's companions to Jerusalem (Ezr. viii. 16). **6.** Son of Bani, who put away his foreign wife at Ezra's instigation (Ezr. x. 39).

T.H.J.

NATHANAEL. The name means 'gift of God', and it occurs only in Jn. i. 45–51, xxi. 2. He seems to be one of the Twelve and he has been variously identified, especially with Bartholomew. The name Bartholomew is a patronymic, and its bearer would have another name too. Bartholomew is next to Philip in the lists of the Twelve in the Synoptics (Mt. x. 3; Mk. iii. 18; Lk. vi. 14). Some, with but little justification, have identified Nathanael with Matthew, Matthias, John, Simon the Cananaean, or Stephen. Others, with even less justification, have denied his real existence.

He was from Cana in Galilee and he was brought by Philip to Jesus, sceptical about the possibility of a Messiah from Nazareth. He was astonished that Jesus knew him already, having seen him under the fig-tree. (This means a display of supernatural power, though the 'fig tree' may be symbolic of the study of the Law or of prosperity.) He confessed that Jesus was Son of God and King of Israel. This was the confession of an 'Israelite indeed in whom was no guile', but it seems to limit the Messiahship to Israel. Christ promised him a greater vision, that of the Son of man as the link between heaven and all mankind (Jn. i. 45–51). He was one of those who saw Christ on His resurrection appearance by the Sea of Tiberias (Jn. xxi. 2).

R.E.N.

NATIONS. TABLE OF. An account, recorded in Gn. x, and with a few minor variations in 1 Ch. i. 5–23, of the descendants of Noah by his three sons, Shem, Ham, and Japheth (*qq.v.*).

I. THE TABLE

The table on p. 866 represents the relationships by placing the names of the descendants of an individual below and to the right of the ancestor's name.

II. POSITION IN GENESIS

If Genesis is divided into sections by means of the recurring formula 'these are the generations (*tôl^e^ḏôṯ*) of . . .' (see GENERATION) the Table of Nations falls within the section Gn. x. 2–xi. 9, the formula occurring in Gn. x. 1 and xi. 10. Different views are held as to whether these formulae constitute headings or colophons, but it does not affect the issue in the present case whether the Table of the Nations, together with the account of the tower of Babel, be regarded as part of the *tôl^e^ḏôṯ* of the sons of Noah (if x. 1 is the heading) or of Shem (if xi. 10 is the colophon).

III. ARRANGEMENT

Verse 32 summarizes the Table, stating that it gives the families (*mišp^e^ḥôṯ*, see FAMILY, Old Testament) of the sons or descendants (*b^e^nê*) of Noah, with reference to their histories (*l^e^ṯôl^e^ḏôṯ*, see GENERATION) in their nations (*b^e^ḡôyim*), and from these (*mē'ēlleh*, *i.e.* either the 'families' or

Japheth	Ham	Shem
Gomer	Cush	Elam
Ashkenaz	Seba	Asshur
Riphath	Havilah	Arpachshad
Togarmah	Sabtah	Shelah
Magog	Raamah	Eber
Madai	Sheba	Peleg
Javan	Dedan	Joktan
Elishah	Sabteca	Almodad
Tarshish	Nimrod	Sheleph
Kittim	Mizraim	Hazarmaveth
Dodanim	Ludim	Jerah
Tubal	Anamim	Hadoram
Meshech	Lehabim	Uzal
Tiras	Naphtuhim	Diklah
	Pathrusim	Obal
	Casluhim	Abimael
	Philistines	Sheba
	Caphtorim	Ophir
	Put (Phut)	Havilah
	Canaan	Jobab
	Zidon	Lud
	Heth	Aram
	Jebusite	Uz
	Amorite	Hul
	Girgashite	Gether
	Hivite	Mash
	Archite	
	Sinite	
	Arvadite	
	Zemorite	
	Hamathite	

the 'nations' making these up) were divided the nations (*gôyīm*) in the earth (*'ereṣ*) after the flood. While this verse forms a colophon to the Table as a whole, verses 5, 20, and 31 form colophons to the subsections verses 2–4, 6–19, and 21–30 which give the descendants of Japheth, Ham, and Shem respectively. Their general tendency is the same as verse 32, but they further state that their lists give the names 'with reference to' their families (*mišpeḥôṯ*) and their tongues (*lešōnôṯ*; Japheth's colophon varies with '(each) man according to his tongue'), and in their lands and their nations (*gôyīm*). In Japheth's colophon these are presented in a different order, and it is further stated that 'from these were the isles of the Gentiles divided'. Many commentators consider that this phrase applies to the descendants of Javan alone, since the designation 'isles' is not appropriate to the other members of the group. It is further suggested on the basis of the analogous statements in verses 20 and 31 that the phrase 'these are the sons of Japheth' originally stood before 'in their lands . . .' in verse 5, and inadvertently dropped out in transmission. This view is adopted in the RSV and may be correct.

Within the three lineages the names are related to each other, either by the formula 'these are the sons of (*benê*) . . .' or '. . . begat (*yālaḏ*) . . .' (see GENEALOGY). The latter is not found in the list of Japheth's descendants, but under Ham is used of Nimrod, and the descendants of Mizraim and of Canaan, and under Shem is used of the section from Shelah to Jobab, that is, all the descendants of Arpachshad. One exception to these two formulae is found in the Philistines who 'went forth' or 'were begotten' (*yāṣā'*) from Casluhim. The regular arrangement into three lists of names is modified by the insertion of other verses which give additional information, either in relating the names to each other, or in giving further information about individuals. The arrangement of the chapter may be summarized as follows:

Heading (or colophon to previous section) (1)
- Japheth's descendants (2–4)
  - Details concerning Javan (5a)
  - Colophon (5b)
- Ham's descendants (6–7, 13–18a)
  - Details concerning Nimrod (8–12) and Canaan (18b–19)
  - Colophon (20)
- Shem's descendants (22–29a)
  - Details concerning Shem (21), and Joktan (29b–30)
  - Colophon (31)

Colophon to whole (32)

The order, in which Shem is given last, is in accordance with the usage of Genesis whereby the chosen line is reserved for treatment after the collateral lines have been discussed. The genealogy in Gn. xi carries on the line through Peleg to Abraham.

IV. CONTENTS

Many of the names in the Table have been connected with names of peoples or regions known in the ancient inscriptions, and there is sufficient agreement on a number of these to make possible a general idea of the scope of the three lists.

a. Preliminary consideration

The names in the Table were probably originally the names of individuals, which came to be applied to the people descended from them, and in some cases to the territory inhabited by these people. It is important to note that such names could have different meanings at different points in history, so that the morphological identification of a name in Gn. x with one in the extra-biblical sources can be completely valid only if the two occurrences are exactly contemporary. The changes in significance of names of this kind are due largely to movements of peoples, in drift, infiltration, conquest, or migration.

There are three principal characteristics of a people which are sufficiently distinctive to form some nuance of their name. These are race or physical type; language, which is one constituent of culture; and the geographical area in which they live or the political unit in which they are organized. Racial features cannot change, but they can become so mixed or dominated through intermarriage as to be indistinguishable. Language can change completely, that of a subordinate group being replaced by that of its rulers, in many cases permanently. Geographical habitat can be completely changed by migration. Since at times one, and at other times another, of these characteristics is uppermost in the significance of a name, the lists in Gn. x are unlikely to have been drawn up on one system alone. Thus, for instance, the descendants of Shem cannot be expected all to have spoken one language, or to have lived all in one area, or even to have belonged to one racial type, since intermarriage may have obscured this. That this could have taken place may be indicated by the presence of apparently duplicate names in more than one list, Asshur (see ASSYRIA), Sheba, Havilah, and Lud(im) under both Shem and Ham, and probably Meshek (Mash in Shem's list; see MESHECH) under Shem and Japheth. Though these may indicate names that are entirely distinct, it is possible that they represent points where a strong people has absorbed a weaker.

It is necessary to observe that names have been adopted from this chapter for certain specific uses in modern times. Thus in language study the terms 'Semitic' and 'Hamitic' are applied, the former to the group of languages including Hebrew, Aramaic, Akkadian, Arabic, *etc.*, and the latter to the group of which (ancient) Egyptian is the chief. This is a usage of convenience, however, and does not mean that all the descendants of Shem spoke Semitic languages or all those of Ham Hamitic. Thus the entry of Elam under Shem, and Canaan under Ham, is not necessarily erroneous, even though Elamite was a non-Semitic and Canaanite was a Semitic tongue. In short, the names in Gn. x probably indicate now geographical, now linguistic, and now political entities, but not consistently any one alone.

b. Japheth

In this list the following identifications receive general, though not universal, agreement: Gomer = Cimmerians; Ashkenaz = Scythians; Madai = Medes; Meshek = Muški, peoples who entered the ancient Near East from the northern steppe. Javan = Ionians, and his descendants, including Elishah = Alašia (in Cyprus) and Dodanim [probably a corruption for Rodanim; *cf.* 1 Ch. i. 7, RV] = Rhodes, were probably a western group of the northern peoples who passed through Ionia to the islands and coastlands (*'iyyê*, verse 5) of the Aegean and Mediterranean. From these indications it appears that the descendants of Japheth were people who in the second millennium were found in the regions to the north and north-west of the Near East.

c. Ham

Here the following identifications are accepted in general: Cush = Ethiopia; Sheba = Saba (in S Arabia); Dedan = Dedan (in N Arabia); Mizraim = Egypt; Ludim = Lydia (?); Philistines = Philistines; Caphtorim = Cretans; Put = Libya; Canaan = Canaan; Zidon = Sidon; Heth = Hittites; Amorite = Amorites; Hivites = Hurrians (see HIVITES); Hamathites = Hamathites.

Under Nimrod (*q.v.*) an additional note is provided to the effect that the beginning of his kingdom was in Shinar = Babylonia (see SHINAR) where he ruled in Babel = Babylon, Erech = Uruk, Accad = Agade, and Calneh (*q.v.*, possibly to be vocalized *kullānâ*, 'all of them'), the first three being important cities in S Mesopotamia, though the site of Agade is as yet unknown. From there he went to Asshur = Assyria (or 'Asshur went forth'; *cf.* AV) and built Nineveh, Rehoboth-Ir, Calah = Kalḫu, and Resen. Nineveh and Kalḫu were Assyrian royal cities, the other two names are unknown.

According to the situation revealed in the extra-biblical inscriptions, the statements that the inhabitants of Mesopotamia (Nimrod) came from Ethiopia, and that the Philistines and Cretans came from Egypt might appear to be erroneous, but the nature and origins of all the elements in the early population of Mesopotamia are still obscure, and Egypt's early connections with Crete and the Aegean area show the possibility of earlier unrecorded contacts. In general, the peoples to the south of the Near East are indicated in this list.

d. Shem

In Shem's list a few identifications are generally accepted: Elam = Elam (the south-eastern part of the Mesopotamian plain); Asshur = Aššur (or Assyria); Hazarmaveth = Ḥaḍramaut (in S Arabia); Sheba = Saba; Lud = Lydia (?); Aram = Aramaeans. These names suggest that the general area settled by the group stretched from Syria in the north, through Mesopotamia to Arabia.

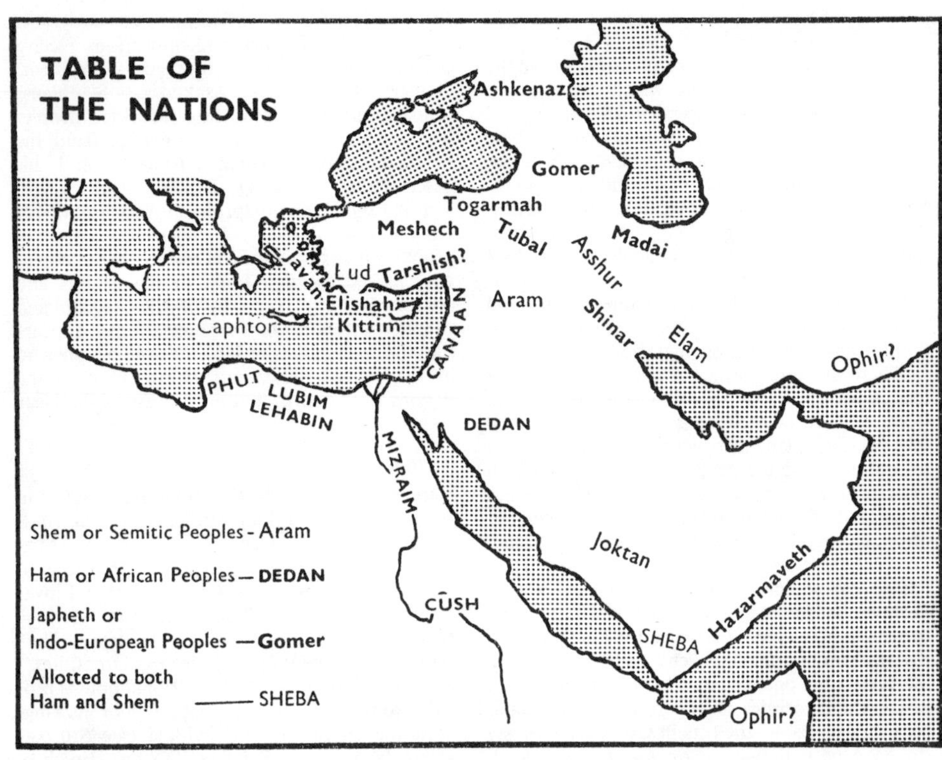

Fig. 149.

the Mediterranean ('Upper Sea'), the Taurus ('Silver Mountain'), and Anatolia (Burušḫatum) in the north, and in the south with Bahrain (Dilmun), where recent excavations have revealed a centre trading with Arabia and India. In the 18th century BC a colony of Assyrian merchants maintained themselves in Cappadocia (Kültepe), and from about this period a merchant's itinerary from southern Mesopotamia to this station is known (*JCS*, VII, 1953, pp. 51–72).

Movements in the third millennium on the northern steppe resulted in the arrival in the Near East during the early second millennium of such peoples as the Kassites and later the rulers of Mitanni, who probably brought with them a knowledge of the northern lands.

V. SOURCES

The study of the Ancient Near East gives some idea of the horizons of geographical knowledge of the second millennium BC and earlier.

a. Mesopotamia

In the fourth millennium BC the evidence of prehistoric archaeology shows that at times a common culture flourished over an area stretching from the Persian Gulf to the Mediterranean. By about 3000 BC contacts through trade are attested with the Arabian peninsula, Anatolia, Iran, and India. The cuneiform records take up the tale in the late third and the second millennia. Early rulers had business relations and other contacts with Iran, the Lebanon ('Cedar Forest'),

b. Egypt

In pre-historic times the inhabitants of the lower Nile had trading contacts with the Red Sea, Nubia, Libya, and perhaps other places in the Sahara, and during the early Dynasties in the third millennium regular expeditions were made to Sinai, and to Byblos on the Syrian coast. In the early second millennium trade contacts with Cyprus, Cilicia, and particularly Crete are attested by finds of objects at both ends. The Egyptians were given to listing names, and the execration texts of the 18th century and the lists of 'subject' cities and peoples of the pharaohs of the 15th show a geographical knowledge of Palestine and Syria. In the 14th century the archive of cuneiform tablets found at el-Amarna shows that one language (Akkadian) was used for diplomacy over the whole Near East and that a good knowledge of other areas was possible.

c. Literary criticism

It is believed by many scholars that the distinction between the *bᵉnê* and *yālad* formulae in the arrangement of the Table betrays composite authorship. According to this, the main framework, making use of the *bᵉnê* formula, is to be ascribed to the Priestly Code (P), and the parts introduced by *yālad*, together with other matter which gives additional information on some names in the lists, is derived from the earlier less scientific Yahwistic document (J) which was woven into their framework by the more methodical Priestly writers. The resulting division is: P = 1a, 2–7, 20, 22, 23, 31, 32; J = 1b, 8–19, 21, 24–30. This variation can be just as well understood, however, as the licence of style, and in the light of the geographical knowledge of the second millennium BC it is no longer necessary to assume a date of composition as late as the early monarchy (J) and the post-exilic period (P). Indeed, the absence of Persia from the list would be difficult to explain if the Table was largely compiled and put into its final form by priests who owed their very return from exile to the tolerant policy of the Persians.

VI. SCOPE

Apart from those theories which would set the Table down as late and unreliable, there are two main views as to its scope. Some maintain that this Table names the peoples of the whole world, others that it mentions only those peoples of the Near East with whom the Israelites were likely to come in contact. This depends largely upon the word *'ereṣ* in verse 32. This is taken in EVV in the sense of 'earth', but it is a term whose significance could vary from 'the whole earth' through 'the known world' to a limited 'country' according to the context (see EARTH). The general view which can be obtained from the commonly accepted identifications of names in the Table supports the opinion that *'ereṣ* here means 'the known world'; but the fact that many of the names in the Table are as yet unidentified shows that the other view cannot be completely ruled out. To accept the former view does not imply that others besides Noah survived the flood, for the Table does not claim to name all the descendants of Noah's three sons, or indeed of himself. The possibility that Noah had other children after the flood cannot be ignored.

VII. AUTHORSHIP AND DATE

The facts mentioned above show that the contents of the Table would not necessarily have been beyond the knowledge of a person educated in the Egyptian schools of the 15th or 14th century. Those who argue for a post-Mosaic date do so largely on the basis of the fact that such peoples as the Cimmerians, Scythians, Medes, and perhaps Muški do not appear in the written documents until the first millennium and on the basis of this a date in the early first millennium is postulated. These peoples must, however, have existed as tribes or larger groups before they are mentioned in the extant records, and it is possible that such earlier invaders as the Kassites and the rulers of Mitanni, who had had contacts with the more northerly tribes, might have preserved a knowledge of them. It is also commonly held that the Philistines (verse 14) did not appear in the biblical world until the 12th century, but various considerations point to the possibility of earlier contacts with these people (see PHILISTINES). Likewise the S Arabian peoples mentioned in the Table, who do not appear in the written records until the first millennium, must have existed as tribes before then.

In brief, therefore, though there are some difficulties in the view, it is not impossible that the Table of Nations could have been compiled in the 13th century BC, perhaps by Moses.

BIBLIOGRAPHY. W. F. Albright, *Recent Discoveries in Bible Lands*, 1955, pp. 70–72; W. Brandenstein, 'Bemerkungen zur Völkertafel der Genesis', *Festschrift . . . Debrunner*, 1954, pp. 57–83; E. Dhorme, 'Les peuples issus de Japhet . . .', *Syria*, XIII, 1932, pp. 28–49; G. Hölscher, *Drei Erdkarten . . .*, 1949, chapter v; J. Simons, 'The Table of Nations (Gen. x): Its General Structure and Meaning', *Oudtestamentische Studiën*, X, 1954, pp. 155–184; D. J. Wiseman, 'Genesis 10: Some Archaeological Considerations', *JTVI*, LXXXVII, 1955, pp. 14–24, 113–118; most of the earlier views are discussed in S. R. Driver, *The Book of Genesis*[12], 1926, pp. xxvi, xxvii, 112–132; G. R. Driver, *ibid.*, pp. 444–447; J. Skinner, *Genesis*[2], 1930, pp. 196–207. T.C.M.

NATURE. There are few words more dangerously ambiguous than 'nature'. It is impossible here to distinguish carefully all its various uses; the following analysis deals only with the words translated 'nature', 'natural', 'naturally' in the AV. It is significant that even these spring from four distinct roots, one Hebrew and three Greek.

1. The Heb. word *lēaḥ*, rendered 'natural force' at Dt. xxxiv. 7, has the root idea of 'freshness', 'moistness', and so of the vigour usually associated with the suppleness of youth.

2. The Gk. adverb *gnēsiōs* and the noun *genesis* stem from a root indicating 'birth', 'coming into being'. The former, although rendered 'naturally' in AV, Phil. ii. 20, had lost its etymological sense in Hellenistic Greek and is better translated 'genuinely', 'sincerely' (*cf. MM s.v.* for the history of this change in meaning). The noun *genesis* occurs in the genitive case in Jas. i. 23, iii. 6. In the first case AV renders the genitive by 'natural', in the second 'of nature'. The idea is that of the successive birth, decay, and new birth characteristic of the world around us. A man sees in a mirror the face which has

come to be what it is through this process (i. 23): iii. 6 further brings out the sense of continuous process with the phrase 'the wheel' or 'course' of the changing world. There is abundant evidence in Philo for the contrast between *genesis*, the changing scene around us, and the eternity of God.

3. The word translated 'natural' in 1 Cor. ii. 14, xv. 44, 46 and 'sensual' in Jas. iii. 15; Jude 19 is the Greek *psychikos*. This adjective is used in the New Testament to refer to that which belongs to *psychē*, not in the most general sense of 'life', 'soul', but as it is distinguished from *pneuma*. *Psychē* in this sense is the life of sensation, emotion, intellect apart from all conscious contact with God. The natural body of 1 Cor. xv is a body which answers to the needs of this lower *psychē*; similarly, the spiritual body, otherwise undefined, will be a body not necessarily 'composed of spirit' but a fit 'vehicle', as it were, for the functioning of the spirit.

4. The words most frequently translated 'nature', 'natural', are *physis* and *physikos*. The basic meaning of *physis* is 'the process of growth' and hence that which comes into being by such a process; *cf.* Rom. xi. 21, 24 for the distinction between *physis*, the normal growth of a plant, and the results of grafting. Every order of beings has its own *physis*, Jas. iii. 7 (*cf.* RVmg); it is even possible to speak of the distinctive *physis* of God (2 Pet. i. 4), though no process of growth is conceivable within the divine Being itself.

The precise meaning of *physis*, *physikos*, is often determined by that with which *physis* is contrasted. Thus it may be regarded as characteristic of brute beasts as opposed to humanity (2 Pet. ii. 12; Jude 10) or be contrasted with that which is commonly but falsely believed (Gal. iv. 8, Moffatt—'gods who are really', *physei*, 'no gods at all'; *cf.* 1 Cor. viii. 5).

Of special importance are the Pauline uses of *physis* in contrast with (i) the perversions of Gentile society, (ii) the free grace of God in Christ and its consequences in man's life.

The former use is found in Rom. i. 26, 27; sexual perversion is there viewed as a departure from the norm recognized by 'natural' man. The same idea is probably present in 1 Cor. xi. 14, though *physis* could have here a reference to its primary sense 'the process of growth' and physiological facts about the length of uncut hair.

Physis as distinguished from grace gives the Jew a place of comparative privilege (Gal. ii. 15); it marks him off from the Gentile outside the covenant (Rom. xi. 21, 24), though it does not of itself save. On the other hand, the Gentile, despite his not having the sign of the covenant and being, *ek physeōs*, uncircumcised, is sometimes able *physei* to do the works demanded by the law (Rom. ii. 14, 27). Over against all privilege or good works, however, stands the fact that all men are *physei* children of wrath (Eph. ii. 3). Thus *physis*, *physikos*, in these passages refer to all that belongs to the state of the world, Jewish and Gentile, apart from God's gracious act in Christ. M.H.C.

NAZARENE. According to Mark, the designation *Nazarēnos* was applied to our Lord by demons (i. 24), the crowd (x. 47), a domestic (xiv. 67), and the messenger of the resurrection (xvi. 6). It is used also in Lk. iv. 34 (= Mk. i. 24) and Lk. xxiv. 19 (the Emmaus disciples). But Matthew, Luke, and John normally employ *Nazōraios* (Mt. xxvi. 71; Lk. xviii. 37; Jn. xviii. 5 ff., xix. 19; Acts ii. 22, iii. 6, iv. 10, vi. 14, xxii. 8, xxvi. 9). Both terms are translated in AV and RV as 'of Nazareth'. *Nazōraios*, 'Nazarene', is applied also to Jesus in Mt. ii. 23, and occurs as a popular designation of the Christian 'sect' in Acts xxiv. 5. This is maintained in Jewish use (*cf.* the oldest Palestinian form of the *Shemoneh 'Esreh*, where at about AD 100 execration is pronounced on the *noṣrîm*) and in Arabic, apparently as a general designation for Christians (*cf.* R. Bell, *The Origin of Islam in its Christian Environment*, 1926, pp. 147 ff.). The Christian Fathers knew of Jewish-Christian groups who called themselves 'Nazarenes' (Jerome, *De vir. ill.* 2, 3, *Epist.* xx. 2) or 'Nazorenes' (Epiphanius, *Haer.* xxix. 7, 9), and Epiphanius—never too reliable on such matters—mentions an aberrant Jewish sect, the Nasarenes (*Haer.* i. 18).

In the New Testament the title is never applied to our Lord without the name 'Jesus', and to identify a man by his place of origin (*e.g.* John of Gischala) was a common Jewish practice. Linguistic objections have been raised, however, against deriving *Nazarēnos*, still more *Nazōraios*, from 'Nazareth', even issuing in a suggestion that Nazareth was created out of a misunderstanding of the title Nazorean (*cf.* E. Nestle, *ExpT*, XIX, 1908, pp. 523 f.). These objections have been faithfully dealt with by G. F. Moore, but are still sometimes raised.

The allusion to *Nazōraios* as a title given to the Messiah in prophecy (Mt. ii. 23) has been frequently taken as a reference to the 'Branch' (*nēṣer*) of Is. xi. 1 and similar passages, or to the Nazirite (*nāzîr*, *cf.* Jdg. xiii. 7) in his character as God's holy one (*Nazir* is used non-technically, and was perhaps interpreted messianically, in Gn. xlix. 26; Dt. xxxiii. 16; see H. Smith, *JTS*, XXVIII, 1926, p. 60). Another ancient suggestion (Jerome, *in loc.*) is that Matthew alludes to the passages which speak of the Messiah as despised (*cf.* Jn. i. 46). At all events the different quotation formula in Mt. ii. 23 from that in, *e.g.*, Mt. i. 22, ii. 15, 17, suggests that a prophetic *theme*, not a specific prediction, is in mind.

The fact that the Mandaean Manichaean–Gnostic sect call themselves *Naṣorayya* has attracted attention. Moore has sufficiently disposed of the 'evidence' for a pre-Christian 'Nazarene' cult adapted to a Jewish *milieu*, but M. Black accepts Lidzbarski's derivation of *Naṣorayya* from *nāṣar*, 'to guard' (*sc.* the tradition), and points to the Mandaean claim to preserve the rites of John the Baptist. Rejecting on linguistic grounds any connection of *Nazōraios* with either *nēṣer* or *nāzîr*, he suggests the suitability of 'Nazarenes' as a title for the followers of John, that it is preserved by the Mandaeans and perhaps Epiphanius, and became applied to the 'Jesus-movement' which arose in the wake of John's. Ingenious as this is, it is perhaps oversubtle. It may be that word-play between *nēṣer* or *nāzîr* or both and the name 'Nazareth' is all that is involved; and it is noteworthy that the Syriac versions, doubtless reflecting Aramaic speech, spell Nazareth with *ṣ* not *z*. A different paronomasia is used in the Qur'an (*Sura* iii. 45, xi. 14), and yet another derivation has appeared in the Chenoboskion *Gospel of Philip*, Log. 47.

BIBLIOGRAPHY. G. F. Moore, *BC*, I, 1920, pp. 426 ff.; W. O. E. Oesterley, *ExpT*, LII, 1941, pp. 410 ff.; W. F. Albright, 'The Names "Nazareth" and "Nazarene"', *JBL*, LXV, 1946, pp. 397 ff.; M. Black, *Aramaic Approach to the Gospels and Acts*[2], 1954, pp. 143 ff. For the modern Mandaeans, see the works of Lady E. S. Drower, and especially *The Secret Adam*, 1960.

A.F.W.

NAZARETH. A town of Galilee where Joseph and Mary lived, and the home of Jesus for about thirty years until He was rejected (Lk. ii. 39, iv. 16, 28–31). He was therefore called Jesus of Nazareth. It is not mentioned in the Old Testament, the Apocrypha, by Josephus, or in the Talmud. The reason for this was first geographical and later theological. Lower Galilee remained outside the main stream of Israelite life until New Testament times, when Rom. rule first brought security. Even then Sepphoris was the chief town of the area, a little to the north of Nazareth. But Nazareth lay close enough to several main trade-routes for easy contact with the outside world, while at the same time her position as a frontier-town on the southern border of Zebulun overlooking the Esdraelon plain produced a certain aloofness. It was this independence of outlook in Lower Galilee which led to the scorn in which Nazareth was held by strict Jews (Jn. i. 46; see NAZARENE).

Nazareth is situated in a high valley among the most southerly limestone hills of the Lebanon range; it runs approximately from SSW to NNE. To the south there is a sharp drop down to the plain of Esdraelon. The base of the valley is 1,200 feet above sea-level. Steep hills rise up on the northern and eastern sides, while on the western side they reach up to 1,600 feet and command an impressive view. Major roads from Jerusalem and Egypt debouched into the Esdraelon plain in the south; caravans from Gilead crossed the Jordan fords and passed below; the main road from Ptolemais to the Decapolis and the north, along which the Rom. legions travelled, passed a few miles above Nazareth. Such a location may have given rise to the name, which is possibly derived from the Aramaic *nāṣ*[e]*raṯ*, 'watch-tower'. Another suggested derivation is from the Heb. *nēṣer*, 'shoot', advocated in Eusebius' *Onomasticon* and by Jerome (*Epist.* xlvi, *Ad Marcellam*). The mild climate in the valley causes wild flowers and fruit to flourish.

To judge by the rock-tombs, the early town was higher up the western hill than the present Nazareth. There are two possible water-supplies. The first, which is the larger, lies in the valley and has been called 'Mary's Well' since AD 1100, but there is no trace of early dwellings near by. The second is a very small fountain, called 'the New Well', in an angle formed by a projection of the western hill; the Byzantine church and town lay closer to this. The steep scarp of Jebel Qafsa, overlooking the plain, is traditionally but erroneously called 'the Mount of Precipitation', since this was not the hill 'whereon their city was built' (Lk. iv. 29).

BIBLIOGRAPHY. G. H. Dalman, *Sacred Sites and Ways*, 1935, pp. 57 ff.

J.W.C.

NAZARITE (RV 'Nazirite'; Heb. *nāzîr*, from *nāzar*, 'to separate, consecrate, abstain'; *cf.* *nēzer*, 'a diadem', the 'crown of God', sometimes identified with the Nazirite's uncut hair). In Israel the Nazirite was one who separated himself from others by consecration to Yahweh with a special vow.

The origin of the practice is pre-Mosaic and obscure. Semites and other primitive peoples often left the hair uncut during some undertaking calling for divine help, and thereafter consecrated the hair (*cf.* modern echoes of this among Arab tribes in A. Lods, *Israel*, 1932, p. 305; see also Jdg. v. 2).

I. LEGISLATION IN NUMBERS VI

Although chronologically not the first biblical reference to the subject, the rules for the Nazirite outlined in Nu. vi provide the fullest and most convenient basis for discussion. The legislation has three sections.

a. Prohibitions

(i) The Nazirite had to abstain from wine and intoxicating drinks, vinegar and raisins. This may have been aimed at safeguarding the integrity and holiness of the Nazirite from possession by a spirit other than that of Yahweh (*cf.* Pr. xx. 1). Like an officiating priest, the Nazirite renounced wine so as the more worthily to approach God. R. Kittel, however, sees in the abstention a protest against Canaanite culture, and a desire to return to nomadic customs (*Geschichte des Volkes Israel*[6], II, 1925, p. 250).

(ii) He must not cut his hair during the time of consecration (*cf.* *nāzîr* = 'unpruned vine', Lv. xxv. 5, 11). The hair was regarded as the seat of life, 'the favourite abode of spirits and magical influences', to be kept in its natural state until its burning ensured its disappearance without fear of profanation.

(iii) He must not go near a dead body, even that of his nearest relation, a prohibition which applied also in the case of the high priest.

b. Violation

If the last-named rule was inadvertently broken, the Nazirite had to undergo closely-detailed purificatory rites, and to begin all over again. It is notable, however, that the terms of the Nazirite vow did not preclude the carrying out of other domestic and social duties.

c. Completion

At the end of his vow the Nazirite had to offer various prescribed sacrifices, and thereafter cut his hair and burn it on the altar. After certain ritual acts by the priest, the Nazirite was released from his vow.

The distinctive features of the original Nazirate were a complete consecration to Yahweh, in which the body, not regarded merely as something to be restrained, was enlisted into holy service; an extension to the layman of a holiness usually associated only with the priest; and an individualistic character in contrast to groups such as Rechabites (*q.v.*).

II. PROBLEMS CONCERNING THE NAZIRATE

It is clear from the provisions in (*c*) above that the Nazirate was for a fixed term only. But against that, and pre-dating the above legislation (for the dating of which, see NUMBERS, BOOK OF), there are instances during the pre-exilic era of parents dedicating children to be Nazirites all their lives. There is, for example, the consecration of Samuel (1 Sa. i. 11), who is not called a Nazirite in *MT* (but in a Qumran text, 4Q Sam[a], 1 Sa. i. 22 ends with the words, 'a Nazirite for ever all the days of his life'). There is also the express Nazirate of Samson (Jdg. xiii), elements of whose story may date from the 10th century BC. That Samuel and Samson were Nazirites has been questioned (see G. B. Gray, *Numbers*, *ICC*, 1903, pp. 59, 60). The Samson narrative conspicuously does not give the impression that he abstained from wine! It may be that the term 'Nazirite' was loosely applied to one devoted to Yahweh.

Absalom, moreover, has often been regarded as a type of perpetual Nazirite (for the cutting of the hair of such, see G. B. Gray, 'The Nazirite', *JTS*, I, 1900, p. 206). Amos, in whose day Nazirites appear to have been numerous, clearly speaks of Nazirites whom the people seek to deflect from their abstinence (ii. 11, 12). During the whole pre-exilic period it is difficult to find direct evidence of temporary Nazirites.

III. LATER DEVELOPMENTS

From the time of the Exile the Nazirate seems to have been for a fixed term only. Extraneous elements crept in, and no longer was the motive for taking the vow exclusively one of penitence and devotion. On occasion it was practised in order to gain certain favours from Yahweh (*cf.* Jos., *BJ* ii. 15. 1, where Bernice undertakes a thirty days' vow), as a meritorious ritual activity, or even for a bet (Mishnah, *Nazir* v. 5 ff.). Wealthy Jews often financed the final sacrifice; Herod Agrippa I is said to have done so (Jos., *Ant.* xix. 6. 1), and Paul was persuaded to perform this service for four members of the church of Jerusalem (Acts xxi. 23 ff., *cf.* xviii. 18 for Paul's personal undertaking of a Nazirite vow). Casuistry was inevitably introduced, and a special tractate of the Mishnah (*Nazir*) fixed the minimum duration of the Nazirate at thirty days.

From the references in Josephus it appears that Nazirites were a common feature of the contemporary scene. For the suggestion that John the Baptist and James the Lord's brother were Nazirites, and for the whole subject, see G. B. Gray in the *JTS* article cited above. J.D.D.

NEAPOLIS (the 'new city'). A town, mod. Kavalla, in Macedonia which served as the port of Philippi, 10 miles inland. Originally thought to have been called Daton, it occupied a position on a neck of land between two bays, which gave it a useful harbour on both. Paul arrived here from Troas on his second missionary journey (Acts xvi. 11), after receiving his call to Macedonia. He may have visited the city on his third journey also. J.H.P.

NEBAIOTH. The eldest son of Ishmael (Gn. xxv. 13, xxviii. 9, xxxvi. 3; 1 Ch. i. 29). His descendants, an Arabian tribe mentioned in conjunction with Kedar in Is. lx. 7, are possibly to be identified with the later Nabataeans (*q.v.*).

NEBAT. A name which occurs only in the phrase 'Jeroboam the son of Nebat' (1 Ki. xi. 26, *etc.*), apparently to distinguish Jeroboam I from the later son of Joash.

NEBO (*n*ᵉ*ḇô*). The Bab. deity Nabu, son of Bel (Marduk), and thus descriptive of the power of Babylon itself (Is. xlvi. 1). The name occurs as part of such appellatives as Nebuchadrezzar and perhaps Abed-nego (*q.v.*). Nabu was considered the god of learning and thus of writing, astronomy, and all science. His symbol was a wedge upon a pole, signifying either the cuneiform script or a sighting instrument used in astronomy. He was the principal deity of Borsippa (7 miles SSW of Babylon), but a temple Ezida ('the House of Knowledge') was dedicated to him in each of the larger cities of Babylonia and Assyria. D.J.W.

NEBO. 1. Mt. Nebo, from which Moses viewed the promised land, sometimes also described as Mt. Abarim, this more general term signifying the range (Nu. xxvii. 12; Dt. xxxii. 49, xxxiv. 1).

Christian tradition has given the name Jebel Neba to a mountain some 12 miles west of the north end of the Dead Sea. Much to be preferred, for several reasons (see G. T. Manley, *The Book of the Law*, 1957, pp. 63 ff.), is Jebel Osha, approved by the local Muslim tradition. This is much higher, overlooks Jericho, and the view agrees minutely with the description in Dt. xxxiv. 1, 2. See ABARIM, PISGAH.

2. A town in Judah (Ezr. ii. 29; Ne. vii. 33).
3. A town in Moab (Nu. xxxii. 3, 38). G.T.M.

NEBUCHADREZZAR, NEBUCHADNEZZAR. The king of Babylon (605–562 BC) frequently named by the prophets Jeremiah, Ezekiel, and Daniel, and in the history of the last days of Judah. His name in Hebrew (*n[e]būkaḏre'ṣṣar*) transliterates the Bab. *Nabū-kudurri-uṣur*, meaning perhaps 'Nabu has protected the succession-rights'. The alternative Heb. rendering (*n[e]būkaḏne'ṣṣar*; *cf.* Gk. *Nabochodonosor*) may be derived from an Aramaic form of the name.

According to the Bab. Chronicle this son of the founder of the Chaldean dynasty, Nabopolassar, first commanded the Bab. army as 'crown-prince' in the fighting in N Assyria in 606 BC. In the following year he defeated Necho II and the Egyptians at Carchemish and Hamath (2 Ki. xxiii. 29 f.; 2 Ch. xxxv. 20 ff.; Je. xlvi. 2). 'At this time he conquered the whole of Hatti' (*i.e.* Syria and Palestine, so Bab. Chronicle; 2 Ki. xxiv. 7; Jos., *Ant.* x. 6). Daniel was among the hostages taken from Judah (Dn. i. 1), where Jehoiakim was in his fourth regnal year (Je. xxxvi. 1). While in the field Nebuchadrezzar heard of his father's death and rode across the desert to claim the Babylonian throne, which he ascended on 6 September 605 BC.

In the following year, the first of his reign, Nebuchadrezzar received tribute in Syria from the kings of Damascus, Tyre and Sidon and others, including Jehoiakim, who was to remain his faithful vassal for only three years (2 Ki. xxiv. 1; Je. xxv. 1). Ashkelon refused and was sacked. In the campaign of 601 BC the Babylonians were defeated by Egypt, whereupon Jehoiakim transferred his loyalty, despite the warnings of Jeremiah (xxvii. 9–11), to the victors. When his army had been re-equipped Nebuchadrezzar raided the Arab tribes of Qedar and E Jordan in 599/8 BC, as predicted by the same prophet (Je. xlix. 28–33), in preparation for subsequent reprisals on Jehoiakim and Judah (2 Ch. xxxvi. 6). Thus in his seventh year Nebuchadrezzar 'marched to Palestine and besieged the city of Judah which he captured on the second day of the month Adar' (= 16 March 597 BC). He then 'seized its king and appointed a king of his own choice, having received heavy tribute which he sent back to Babylon' (Bab. Chronicle B.M. 21946). This capture of Jerusalem and its king Jehoiachin (Jehoiakim's son and successor), the choice of Mattaniah-Zedekiah as his successor, and the taking of booty and prisoners, form the subject of the history recorded in 2 Ki. xxiv. 10–17. Nebuchadrezzar removed the temple vessels to the temple of Bel-Marduk in Babylon (2 Ch. xxxvi. 7; 2 Ki. xxiv. 13; Ezr. vi. 5). The Judaean captives were marched off about April 597, 'in the spring of the year' (2 Ch. xxxvi. 10), which marked the beginning of his eighth regnal year (2 Ki. xxiv. 12). Jehoiachin and other Jewish captives are named in inscriptions from Babylon dated in the years of this Bab. king (*ANET*, p. 308; *DOTT*, pp. 83–86).

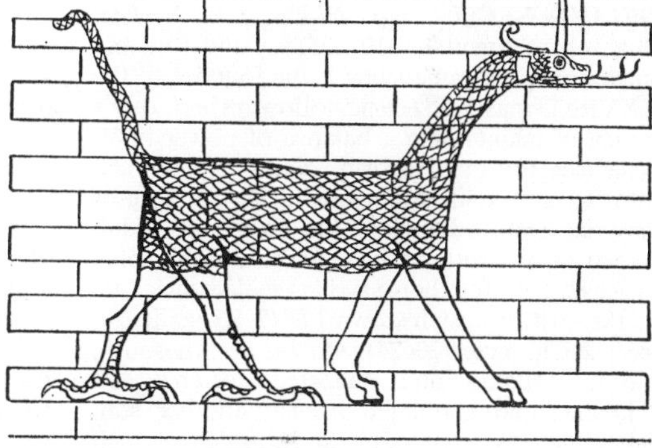

Fig. 150. One of composite creatures (*mušruššu*) with which the Ishtar gate at Babylon was decorated in the time of Nebuchadrezzar II, 605–562 BC. It is made up of the head of a serpent, a lion's body, and the hind claws of an eagle. Glazed and coloured relief on kiln-baked bricks. See also plates VIII*a*, IX*a*.

In 596 BC Nebuchadrezzar fought a battle with Elam (so also Je. xlix. 34), and in the next year mastered a rebellion in his own country. Thereafter the Bab. historical texts are wanting, but in his seventeenth–nineteenth years he campaigned again in the west. From his headquarters at Riblah he directed the operations which led to the sack of Jerusalem in 587 BC and the capture of the rebel Zedekiah (Je. xxxix. 5, 6, lii). For a time the siege was raised when Apries, the successor of Necho II of Egypt, invaded Phoenicia and Gaza (Je. xlvii. 1). In Nebuchadrezzar's twenty-third year (582) a further deportation of Judaeans to Babylon was ordered (Je. lii. 30). About this time also the thirteen-year siege of Tyre was undertaken (Ezk. xxvi. 7; see TYRE).

A fragmentary Bab. text tells of Nebuchadrezzar's invasion of Egypt in 568/7 BC (*cf.* Je. xliii. 8–13). Since little is yet known of the last thirty years of his reign, there is no corroboration from external sources of his madness which occurred for seven months (or 'times') as recorded in Dn. iv. 23–33. With the aid of his wife Amytis, he undertook the rebuilding and embellishment of his capital Babylon. A religious man, he rebuilt the temples of Marduk and Nabu with many shrines in Babylon and provided regular offerings and garments for the divine statues (*cf.* the golden image of Dn. iii. 1). He also restored temples in Sippar, Marad, and Borsippa and boasted of his achievements, especially in the two defence walls, the gateway of Ishtar, the ziggurat, and the sacred processional way through his own city, which he provided with new canals (Dn. iv. 30). See BABYLON. Some of his architectural works were classed among the seven wonders of the world. Herodotus calls both Nebuchadrezzar and Nabonidus (556–539) by the name of Labynetus. Nebuchadrezzar died in August–September 562 BC and was succeeded by his son Amēl-Marduk (see EVIL-MERODACH).

BIBLIOGRAPHY. D. J. Wiseman, *Chronicles of Chaldaean Kings*, 1956; A. Malamat, 'A New Record of Nebuchadrezzar's Palestinian Campaigns', *IEJ*, VI, 1956. D.J.W.

NECHO, NECO. Egyp. *Nỉ-k'w*, Gk. *Nechao.* Pharaoh of Egypt *c.* 610–595 BC, and son and successor of Psammetichus I, the founder of the XXVIth Dynasty. In 609 BC, following his father's policy of maintaining a balance of power in W Asia (see EGYPT: History), Necho II marched into Syria to assist Aššur-uballiṭ II, last king of Assyria, against Babylon. But Josiah of Judah forced a battle with Necho at Megiddo; this delay of Egyp. help for the Assyrians sealed their fate at the cost of Josiah's own life (2 Ki. xxiii. 29, RSV; 2 Ch. xxxv. 20–24). On his return south, Necho deposed and deported Josiah's son Jehoahaz and appointed instead another son, Jehoiakim, as vassal-king in Jerusalem, which was obliged to pay tribute to Egypt (2 Ki. xxiii. 31–35; 2 Ch. xxxvi. 1–4). Egypt claimed Palestine as her share of the former Assyr. empire, but in the battle of Carchemish, in May/June 605 BC, Nebuchadrezzar stormed that Egyp. outpost and pursued the remnants of the Egyp. forces through Syria as they scurried home to Egypt; Judah thus exchanged an Egyp. for a Bab. master (2 Ki. xxiv. 1, 7).

Necho wisely desisted from any further Palestinian adventures. But the Bab. Chronicle shows that in 601 BC Nebuchadrezzar marched against Egypt; Necho met him in open battle, and both sides suffered heavy losses. Nebuchadrezzar therefore had to spend the next year at home in Babylon to refit his army. This Egyp. rebuff for the Babylonians perhaps tempted Jehoiakim to revolt against Babylon as recorded in 2 Ki. xxiv. 1, but no help came from neutral Egypt.

At home, Necho II followed his father's policy of fostering Egypt's internal unity and prosperity, granting trading-concessions to Gk. merchants to this end. He undertook the cutting of a canal from the Nile to the Red Sea, completed by Darius the Persian, and sent out a Phoenician fleet that circumnavigated Africa as recorded by Herodotus (iv. 42), whose scepticism of this achievement is refuted by its cause, namely that the voyagers reported that the sun eventually rose on their right hand.

BIBLIOGRAPHY. For Necho, see Drioton and Vandier, *L'Égypte*, Coll. Clio, 1952; H. De Meulenaere, *Herodotos over de 26ste Dynastie*, 1951. For his conflicts with Babylon, see D. J. Wiseman, *Chronicles of Chaldaean Kings* (626–556 BC), 1956. C.D.W.

NECK. 1. Heb. *'ōrep̄* is used of the neck, or back of the neck; it is also translated 'back' in AV and RV, when used of enemies turning their back in flight (*e.g.* Ex. xxiii. 27). It is used of similar ideas in respect of conflict (Gn. xlix. 8; Jb. xvi. 12), and also in the descriptive metaphor of the hardened or stiffnecked, meaning obstinate or rebellious (Dt. xxxi. 27; 2 Ki. xvii. 14; Is. xlviii. 4).

2. *gārôn* is also used, meaning the front of the neck (Is. iii. 16; Ezk. xvi. 11), or throat (Ps. v. 9; Je. ii. 25), and so voice (Is. lviii. 1, 'cry aloud', lit. 'with thy throat').

3. The commonest Heb. word is *ṣawwā'r*, used of the neck generally; bearing a yoke, symbolizing servitude (Gn. xxvii. 40; Je. xxx. 8); wearing a necklace (Gn. xli. 42); of falling on a person's neck in embrace (Gn. xxxiii. 4), or of the neck placed under the foot of a conqueror (Jos. x. 24) (see FOOT).

4. Gk. *trachēlos* is used of embrace (Lk. xv. 20), of being under a yoke (Acts xv. 10), or of wearing a millstone, a large flat stone with a hole in the centre, to weigh the body down (Mt. xviii. 6). Paul also speaks of laying down the neck in respect of the custom of beheading (Rom. xvi. 4). *Cf.* the modern idiom, 'risked his neck'. From *trachēlos* comes the verb *trachēlizō*, 'to expose the neck or throat', used in the perfect participle passive in Heb. iv. 13 in the sense of 'laid open' (AV 'opened'). B.O.B.

NECROMANCY. See DIVINATION.

NEEDLE'S EYE. In three of the Gospels (Mt. xix. 24; Mk. x. 25; Lk. xviii. 25) we find the statement of Jesus: 'It is easier for a camel to go through the eye of a needle, than for a rich man to enter into the kingdom of God.' This form of words, familiar in rabbinic writings, signifies something both very unusual and very difficult—*e.g.* in the Talmud an elephant passing through the eye of a needle is twice used of what is impossible, and a camel is portrayed as dancing in a very small corn measure (*cf.* also J. Lightfoot, *Horae Hebraicae*, II, 1859, pp. 264, 265). Some scholars interpret 'needle's eye' as a reference to a narrow gateway for pedestrians, but there is no historical evidence to support this. See F. W. Farrar, 'The Camel and the Needle's Eye', *The Expositor*, III, 1876, pp. 369–380. J.D.D.

NEEDLEWORK. See EMBROIDERY.

NEGEB. Heb. *neg̱eḇ*, 'the dry', refers to the southern lands of Palestine. Misconceptions arise from its translation as 'the South' in both

AV and RV, where some forty passages have described it inaccurately in this way. An indefinite region, it covers approximately 4,520 square miles or nearly one-half of the area of the modern state of Israel. The northern boundary may be drawn conveniently south of the Gaza–Beersheba road, along the approximate alignment of the 8-inch-mean annual isohyet (see fig. 156), then due east of Beersheba to the Dead Sea through Ras ez-Zuweira. The southern boundary merged traditionally into the highlands of the Sinai Peninsula is now drawn politically south of the Wadi el-Arish to the head of the Gulf of Aqabah at Eilat. The Wadi Arabah, now the political frontier with Jordan, is overlooked to the east by the Arabah escarpment, the traditional boundary. For the description of the geographical features of the Negeb, see PALESTINE.

Mention of the Negeb is almost entirely confined to pre-exilic times, apart from allusions in Zc. vii. 7 and Ob. 20. Five districts in the N Negeb are referred to: the Negeb of Judah, of the Jerahmeelites, of the Kenites (1 Sa. xxvii. 10), of the Cherethites, and of Caleb (1 Sa. xxx. 14). These occupied the grazing and agricultural lands between Beersheba and Bir Rikhmeh and the western slopes of the central highlands of Khurashe-Krmub. This district was settled by the Amalekites (Nu. xiii. 29), the ruins of whose fortified sites are still seen between Tell Arad (Nu. xxi. 1, xxxiii. 40), 20 miles east of Beersheba and Tell Jemmeh or Gerar (Gn. xx. 1, xxvi. 1). At the Exodus the spies had been awed by their defences (Nu. xiii. 17–20, 27–29), lasting until the early 6th century BC, when they were probably destroyed finally by the Babylonians (Je. xiii. 19, xxxiii. 13). The sites of the twenty-nine cities and their villages in the Negeb (Jos. xv. 21–32) are unknown, only Beersheba ('well of seven', or 'well of oath', Gn. xxi. 30), Arad, Khirbet Ar'areh or Aroer (1 Sa. xxx. 28), Fein or Penon (Nu. xxxiii. 42), and Tell el-Kheleifeh or Ezion-geber, having been identified.

The strategic and economic importance of the Negeb has been significant. The 'Way of Shur' (see fig. 80) crossed it from central Sinai north-eastwards to Judaea (Gn. xvi. 7, xx. 1, xxv. 18; Ex. xv. 22; Nu. xxxiii. 8), a route followed by the Patriarchs (Gn. xxiv. 62, xxvi. 22), by Hadad the Edomite (1 Ki. xi. 14, 17, 21, 22), and probably the escape route used by Jeremiah (xliii. 6–12) and later by Joseph and Mary (Mt. ii. 13–15). The route was dictated by the zone of settled land where well water is significant, hence the frequent references to its wells (*e.g.* Gn. xxiv. 15–20; Jos. xv. 18, 19; Jdg. i. 14, 15). Uzziah reinforced the defence of Jerusalem by establishing cultivation and defensive settlements in his exposed southern flank of the N Negeb (2 Ch. xxvi. 10). It seems clear from the history of the Near East that the Negeb was a convenient vacuum for resettlement whenever population pressure forced out migrants from the Fertile Crescent. Also significant was the location of copper ores in the E Negeb and its trade in the Arabah. Control of this industry explains the Amalekite and Edomite wars of Saul (1 Sa. xiv. 47 f.) and the subsequent victories of David over the Edomites (1 Ki. xi. 15 f.). It also explains the creation by Solomon of the port of Ezion-geber, and, when it got silted up, the creation of a new port at Elath by Uzziah (1 Ki. ix. 26, xxii. 48; 2 Ki. xiv. 22). The abiding hatred of the Edomites is explained by the struggles to control this trade (*cf.* Ezk. xxv. 12 and the Book of Obadiah).

BIBLIOGRAPHY. For the occupation of the Negeb (though not mentioned by name) in the time of Abraham, see N. Glueck in *BA*, XVIII, February 1955, pp. 2–9; *BA*, XXII, 1959, pp. 81–100. See also N. Glueck, *Rivers in the Desert*, 1959; C. L. Woolley and T. E. Lawrence, *The Wilderness of Zin*, 1936.

J.M.H.

NEGINAH, NEGINOTH. See PSALMS.

NEHELAMITE. An epithet applied to Shemaiah, a false prophet who withstood Jeremiah (Je. xxix. 24, 31, 32), and whose place of origin is not known. Verse 24 AVmg renders the word as 'dreamer', thus implying some connection with Heb. *ḥālam*, 'to dream'. M. F. Unger suggests a punning allusion to the dreams of the false prophets.

J.D.D.

NEHEMIAH. Our only knowledge of Nehemiah comes from the book that bears his name. He was cupbearer to the Persian King Artaxerxes I (465–424 BC). This was a privileged position. Since there is no mention of his wife, it is possible that he was a eunuch. On receiving news of the desolate state of Jerusalem (probably the result of the events of Ezr. iv. 7–23), he obtained permission to go to his own country, and was appointed governor. In spite of intense opposition (see SANBALLAT, TOBIAH), he and the Jews rebuilt the walls of Jerusalem in fifty-two days. He and the other Jews then called on Ezra to read the Law, and pledged themselves to observe its commands. During his absence in Persia, some of the abuses that he had put down reappeared, and on his return he had to carry out fresh reforms. His personal memoirs occupy a large part of the Book of Nehemiah, and they reveal him as a man of prayer, action, and devotion to duty.

For dating his movements we have the following references:

ii. 1. His appointment as governor in 445 BC.
v. 14, xiii. 6. His return to Persia in 433 BC.
xiii. 6. His return to Jerusalem 'after certain days'.

The suggestion in ii. 6 is that his first appointment was short, and he may have returned to Persia for a brief time between 445 and 433 BC. Since his absence from Jerusalem in xiii. 6 was long enough for considerable abuses to arise, and for the Levites to be driven out to work in the fields, we must conclude that the 'certain days' were at least eighteen months, and possibly more.

J.S.W.

NEHEMIAH, BOOK OF.

I. OUTLINE OF CONTENTS

a. Nehemiah in Persia hears of Jerusalem's distress, and prays to God (i. 1–11).

b. King Artaxerxes appoints him governor of Jerusalem (ii. 1–11).

c. His plans to rebuild the ruined wall (ii. 12–20).

d. The list of builders and their allotted work (iii. 1–32).

e. Threats to the work: sarcasm (iv. 1–6); sudden attacks (iv. 7–23); disunity within (v. 1–19); false accusations (vi. 1–14).

f. Completion of the wall (vi. 15–vii. 4).

g. The register of the returned exiles (vii. 5–73).

h. Ezra and the Levites read and expound the law (viii. 1–18).

i. A corporate prayer of repentance (ix. 1–38).

j. The sealing of a covenant promise to obey (x. 1–39).

k. Register of dwellers in Jerusalem and neighbourhood (xi. 1–36).

l. List of priests and Levites (xii. 1–26).

m. The dedication of the walls and arrangements for worship (xii. 27–47).

n. Abuses and reforms (xiii. 1–31).

II. COMPOSITION

The book of Nehemiah originally was one book with Ezra, and the two probably were a continuation of Chronicles (see EZRA, BOOK OF, and CHRONICLES, BOOKS OF). In Nehemiah the compiler has used the following:

a. Personal memoirs of Nehemiah, retained in the 1st person: i. 1–ii. 20, iv. 1–vii. 5, x. 28–xi. 2, xii. 27–xiii. 31.

b. Narrative in the 3rd person, which may have come from Nehemiah's memoirs or from Temple records: vii. 73–ix. 38.

c. Lists: 1. Builders: iii. 1–32, almost certainly from Nehemiah's memoirs.

2. Returned exiles: vii. 6–73, from the same source as Ezr. ii.

3. Those who set their seal to the covenant: x. 1–27, either from Nehemiah's memoirs or from Temple records.

4. Dwellers in Jerusalem and neighbourhood: xi. 3–36, probably from Temple records. The section xi. 3–19 is virtually the same as 1 Ch. ix. 2–17.

5. Priests, Levites, and high priests: xii. 1–26, from Temple records.

All these have been brought together to form one historical record.

III. THE PLACE OF EZRA

Nehemiah's personal memoirs in xii. 36 mention Ezra as leading one procession at the dedication of the walls. Those who date Ezra long after Nehemiah are bound to hold that here the compiler has created an artificial set of memoirs, or doctored genuine memoirs. This is a wholly gratuitous assumption. The description here is as natural as in the rest of the memoirs.

The reading of the law by Ezra in chapter viii is in a different category, since this section is not written in the 1st person. Some wish to attach it to the end of the book of Ezra. It is indeed attached to the end of 1 Esdras. The compiler of 1 Esdras alters the order of the Hebrew stories in the first part of his book, and it is fair to assume that he has neatly rounded off the story of Ezra by including the reading of the law at this point, and taking it from its original position in the story of Nehemiah. The position of the story in 1 Esdras does not help the argument that Ezra came after Nehemiah, since there is no mention of Nehemiah and no place for him earlier in 1 Esdras, which covers the period from the time of the first return from exile.

See also JERUSALEM, TEMPLE.

BIBLIOGRAPHY. See under EZRA. J.S.W.

NEHILOTH. See PSALMS.

NEHUSHTA (*n^{e}ḥuštā'*). The wife of Jehoiakim and mother of Jehoiachin, a native of Jerusalem (2 Ki. xxiv. 8) who was taken prisoner with her son when the Babylonians captured the city in 597 BC (verse 12; also Jos., *Ant.* x. 6, 7). Her name may allude to her complexion (*cf.* Jb. vi. 12) or to bronze (*n^{e}ḥūšâ*) or even to the serpent (*q.v.*). Heb. personal names relating to colours, metals (see BARZILLAI), or animals are characteristic of this period. D.J.W.

NEHUSHTAN. See SERPENT (BRAZEN).

NEIGHBOUR. In the Old Testament 'neighbour' translates the Heb. *šāḵēn*, *'āmîṯ*, *qārôḇ*, and *rēa'*. In Lv. xix. 18 LXX has *ho plēsion.* In the New Testament (in which this commandment is quoted eight times) Luke and John alone use the words *geitōn* and *perioikos*; elsewhere (and also Lk. x. 27–36; Acts vii. 27) the LXX expression is used.

The Heb. *rēa'* is of more general application than English 'neighbour'. It is used, even of inanimate objects (Gn. xv. 10), in the expression 'one *another*'; but it is also used in the sense of 'bosom friend' (Pr. xxvii. 10), 'lover' (Ct. v. 16), even 'husband' (Je. iii. 20). Like *'āmîṯ*, *rēa'* is almost exclusively used in contexts where moral principles are in question (*qārôḇ* and *šāḵēn* expressing mere geographical or physical proximity). Of passages where *rēa'* is defined in the context (*i.e.* refers to particular people) there are only three (1 Sa. xv. 28, xxviii. 17; 2 Sa. xii. 11) which do not admit the translation 'friend', and these are all susceptible of ironical interpretation. Thus it is either used definitely, in which case it means one who has acted—or *surprisingly* has not acted (Ps. xxxviii. 11)—in the appropriate manner, hence a 'friend'; or indefinitely of those towards whom appropriate behaviour is due. *Rēa'* is often found in parallel with *'āḥ*, 'brother', and the Bible uses this dichotomy of other people in a developing series of senses. Thus a relative is contrasted with another within the clan, a fellow Hebrew with a Gentile, and finally a fellow Christian with an unbeliever.

It is important to love those to whom one has a natural or covenanted obligation, but it is as important to love those with whom one's only contact is through circumstances: the distinct ideas *ḥesed* and *'ahᵃḇâ* ('covenant' and 'elective' love—*cf.* N. H. Snaith, *Distinctive Ideas of the Old Testament*, 1944, pp. 94, 95) merge in the New Testament into the one *agapē* required of a Christian both to those within and without the Church. The Bible teaches this in the following ways:

1. It praises those who were exemplary neighbours to those whom they might have been expected to hate: particularly *cf.* Rahab's treatment of the spies (Jos. ii. 1); Ruth's refusal to desert her mother-in-law, though in a sense free from obligation after the death of her husband (the whole story is most instructive in this connection, and it is perhaps no accident that 'Ruth' is the abstract noun from the same root as *rēa'*); the widow's entertainment of Elijah (implicitly compared with the unclean birds (1 Ki. xvii. 6) who fed him: Zarephath was in the territory of Sidon from which Jezebel came).

2. It rebukes the proud independence of the Jew (*cf.* Am. ii. 6 ff.; Is. i. 17; Jonah *passim*; Jb. xii. 2).

3. In the parable of the Good Samaritan an explicit epitome of biblical teaching is given which combines (1) and (2). To the question, 'Who is my neighbour?' Jesus replies, 'Who was neighbour unto him that fell among the thieves?' (Lk. x. 36). J.B.J.

NEPHEW. Where this word occurs in the AV (Jdg. xii. 14; Jb. xviii. 19; Is. xiv. 22; 1 Tim. v. 4) it should be understood as 'grandson' or 'descendant'.

NEPHILIM. See GIANT.

NEPHTOAH. Mentioned only in the expression 'the fountain of the water of Nephtoah' (Jos. xv. 9, xviii. 15). The context shows that it was on the borders of Judah and Benjamin. It is usually identified with Lifta, a village 2 miles north-west of Jerusalem. The linguistic equation Nephtoah = Lifta is very doubtful, but no other site seems to have strong claims. L.M.

NEREUS. A Christian greeted with his sister (not named, but conceivably Nereis) in Rom. xvi. 15. He is grouped with three others and 'the saints which are with them', perhaps because they belonged to the same house-church. The name (a Greek sea-god) is found in many areas, usually of freedmen and the lower orders (including slaves of 'Caesar's household'). Strangely, Paul's friend seems not to have been assimilated to the early Roman martyr commemorated in the Acts of SS. Nereus and Achilleus (*Acta Sanctorum*, III, Maii, pp. 4 f.; *cf.* Lightfoot, *Clement*, I, pp. 42 ff., especially p. 51 n.). A.F.W.

NERGAL (*nērᵉḡal*; Sumerian U.GUR; Bab. *ne-uru-gal*, 'Lord of the great city'). This Bab. deity had his cult-centre at Cuthah (modern Tell Ibrahim, north-east of Babylon), where he was worshipped with his consort Ereshkigal, as lord of the underworld. Men from Cutha continued to worship him as exiles in Samaria (2 Ki. xvii. 30), but, though he was the god of hunting, they feared the lions sent by Yahweh (verse 26). Nergal was worshipped throughout Assyria and Babylonia as a deity having the sinister aspects of the sun, bringing plague, war, flood, and havoc. He was also identified with Mars. Temples at Larsa, Isin, and Assur were dedicated to him. His name is commonly found as the divine element in personal names (see NERGAL-SHAREZER). D.J.W.

NERGAL-SHAREZER. Heb. equivalent of Bab. *Nergal-šar-uṣur* (Gk. Neriglissar) meaning 'O Nergal, protect the king'. The name of a senior official with Nebuchadrezzar's army at Jerusalem in 587 BC (Je. xxxix. 3, 13). It is possible that two persons of the same name are listed in verse 3; if so, the first may be the Neriglissar who was one of the Bab. army commanders, son of Bel-šum-iškun and married to Nebuchadrezzar's daughter. He succeeded to the throne at Babylon in 560 BC. The Nergal-sharezer qualified as Rab-mag (*q.v.*) seems to have held a position of lower rank. D.J.W.

NERO. Son of a distinguished family of the old Roman aristocracy, the Domitii, and on his mother's side the great-great-grandson of Augustus, he was adopted by Claudius as his heir and duly took his place in the Caesarian succession in AD 54. His atrocities and feebleness finally destroyed the credit of his house, whose long ascendancy he finally brought to an end with his suicide in the face of the revolts of AD 68. A youth of exquisite taste, he fascinated and scandalized his contemporaries with his artistic pursuits. To the Greeks in particular he endeared himself; they never tired of flattering his longing for prizes in literary festivals; and he reciprocated this whimsy by abolishing Rom. control over the states of Achaia. After his premature death his legend flourished in the east, and his reincarnation was fervently expected, and even announced. On the other hand, within his domestic circle and among his aristocratic peers, his behaviour was monstrously sinister. The belief that his mother had murdered Claudius after marrying him to ensure her son's succession scarcely mitigated the horror when Nero himself had her done to death. Although there seems to have been a period of stable government while he remained under the influence of the senators Burrus and Seneca, he eventually freed himself from their restraints as well and was driven by his bloodthirsty suspicions to the inevitable end.

Nero is indirectly concerned with the New Testament at three points.

1. It was Nero to whose superior justice Paul

appealed against the vacillations of his deputy, Festus (Acts xxv. 10, 11), and Nero whose God-given authority he had studiously supported in writing to the Romans (Rom. xiii. 1–7). There is a horrible and tragic irony in this: 'he beareth not the sword in vain' (verse 4). We do not know the outcome of Paul's appeal, but the Christians of Rome were treated for their loyalty to one of the most barbaric pogroms in history.

Fig. 151. Head of Nero, the Caesar to whom Paul appealed (Acts xxv. 11). He was emperor of Rome AD 54–68.

2. In AD 64 much of the city of Rome was destroyed by fire. To divert the suspicion that he had started it for his own entertainment, Nero accused another party about whom the public were also prepared to believe the worst. Having forced a conviction for arson against certain Christians, he conducted mass arrests, and among other tortures burnt his victims alive in public (Tacitus, *Ann.* xv. 44). The important things about this were that Christians were clearly distinguished from Jews (Nero's wife Poppaea was pro-Jewish), and that it was plausible to accuse them of such crimes. Although Tacitus makes it clear that the charges were a fabrication, and that they even attracted some sympathy to the Christians, he equally reveals that the public was profoundly suspicious of the morals of the Christians. Suetonius (*Nero* xvi. 2), without mentioning the fire, lists the attack on the Christians with a number of other reforms that are put down to Nero's credit. What was disastrous for the Christians was that Nero's action had left a legal precedent for translating this popular odium into official action. The First Epistle of Peter reflects this kind of situation. Christians are in the agonizing position of being committed to honour the authorities, while knowing that any moral lapse may lead to legal proceedings against them, and that they may even be prosecuted on grounds of their membership in the Christian society alone.

3. In the closing years of Nero's régime his commanders in Palestine were drawn into the war that ended with the destruction of Jerusalem in AD 70, an event that finally set the Christian churches free from their Zionist orientation. Nero played no part in the campaigns, and was apparently oblivious of the issues involved: the critical year AD 67 found him engrossed in literary triumphs on the stages of Greece.

BIBLIOGRAPHY. A. Momigliano, *CAH*, X, pp. 702–742. E.A.J.

NEST (Heb. *qēn* from *qinnēn*, 'make a nest'; Gk. *kataskēnōsis*, 'place for roosting in'). The word is employed in its customary sense in Dt. xxii. 6, xxxii. 11 (speaking of 'nestlings'); Jb. xxxix. 27; Ps. civ. 17; Pr. xxvii. 8; Is. xvi. 2. It is found metaphorically (notably of a lofty fortress) in Nu. xxiv. 21; Je. xlix. 16; Ob. 4; with reference to the secure home of Israel in Ps. lxxxiv. 3, 4; and of the Chaldeans' strong abode in Hab. ii. 9. Job (xxix. 18) speaks of his lost home as a 'nest'. In Gn. vi. 14 'nests' (*qinnîm*, AV 'rooms') is used to describe the subdivisions within the ark. In Mt. viii. 20; Lk. ix. 58 Jesus contrasts His homeless situation with that of the birds who have their nests (RVmg 'lodging-places'). See also BIRDS OF THE BIBLE. J.D.D.

NETHANIAH (*n*[e]*ṯanyāhū*, 'Yahweh has given'; LXX *Nathanias*; *cf.* NATHANAEL). **1.** The father of Ishmael, the murderer of Gedaliah (Je. xl. 8, 14, 15; xli. 9). In 2 Ki. xxv. 23 the LXX reads *Maththanias*. **2.** An Asaphite, leader of the fifth group of the temple choir (1 Ch. xxv. 2, 12). **3.** Father of Jehudi (Je. xxxvi. 14). **4.** A Levite accompanying the teaching mission sent by Jehoshaphat to Judah (2 Ch. xvii. 8). D.J.W.

NETHINIM. Apart from 1 Ch. ix. 2 (parallel to Ne. xi. 3) these people are mentioned only in Ezra and Nehemiah. They are listed among the returned exiles in Ezr. ii. 43–58, where they are grouped with 'the children of Solomon's servants'. When Ezra brings back a fresh party he sends to a place named Casiphia to obtain Levites and Nethinim (Ezr. viii. 17, 20). In Jerusalem they had special quarters in the Ophel district near the Temple (Ne. iii. 26, 31, xi. 21). This may have been where they lived when they were on duty, since Ezr. ii. 70; Ne. vii. 73 refer to cities in which they lived; it is possible, however, that the reference here is to the period before the rebuilding of the Temple.

The name means 'those who are given', and Ezr. viii. 20 says that David and the princes had given them for the service of the Levites. It has been held that they and the children of Solomon's servants were the descendants of Canaanite or foreign prisoners, like the Gibeonites of Jos. ix. 27. The foreign names in Ezr. ii. 43–58 would support this. In 1 Esdras v. 29 and Josephus (*Ant.* xi. 5. 1) they are called 'temple slaves', *hierodouloi*. It has been supposed that Ezekiel protests against them in xliv. 6–8, but it is hardly likely that the Nethinim would have remained uncircumcised as Ezekiel here says, and their inclusion in the Ezra list, and the position given to them in Ezra–Nehemiah shows that the rigoristic Chronicler had no objection to them. Similarly, the reference to the Canaanite in the house of the Lord in Zc. xiv. 21 is more likely in the context to refer to Canaanite traders, as in Pr. xxxi. 24 (RVmg).

BIBLIOGRAPHY. E. Schürer, *HJP*, II, i. 273; L. W. Batten, *Ezra–Nehemiah*, *ICC*, 1913, p. 87.

J.S.W.

NETOPHAH ('a dropping'). A city, or group of villages (1 Ch. ix. 16; Ne. xii. 28), near Bethlehem (Ne. vii. 26). The inhabitants are called Netophathites in EVV. 'Netophathi' in Ne. xii. 28, AV, should be 'the Netophathites'. It was the home of some of David's mighty men (2 Sa. xxiii. 28, 29). It is mentioned as a place to which returning exiles came (Ezr. ii. 22). That it was near Bethlehem is clear, but it cannot be identified conclusively with any modern site. G.W.G.

NETS. Nets in the Bible are instruments of meshed strings for fishing or hunting, or reticulate designs or gratings. See fig. 111.

a. Nets for fishing and hunting

Words from four Heb. roots are translated 'net' in the Old Testament. 1. From *yrš*, 'take', *rešeṯ* is a net to catch birds (Pr. i. 17) or water creatures (Ezk. xxxii. 3), and is often used figuratively of the plots of evil men (*e.g.* Ps. ix. 15, laid to catch the feet), or of God's judgments (*e.g.* Ezk. xii. 13, cast over the prey). 2. *ḥerem*, 'something perforated', is a large net which may be spread out on the shore to dry (Ezk. xxvi. 5) and is used figuratively of an evil woman's heart (Ec. vii. 26), of God's judgment of Pharaoh (Ezk. xxxii. 3), of predatory individuals (Mi. vii. 2), and of the Chaldeans' military power (Hab. i. 15). 3. From the root *ṣûḏ*, 'hunt', *m*[e]*ṣôḏâ* is a fish-net (Ec. ix. 12), *māṣûḏ* and *m*[e]*ṣuḏâ* are used of God's judgments (Jb. xix. 6, surrounding the prey; Ps. lxvi. 11), and *māṣôḏ* in Pr. xii. 12 is perhaps a snare for evil men. 4. From the root *kmr*, which in Arabic means 'overcome' or 'cover', Heb. *mikmōreṯ* is the net which Egyptian fishermen spread over the water (Is. xix. 8), *mikmereṯ*, AV 'drag', RSV 'seine', is a symbol of the Chaldeans' army (Hab. i. 15), *mikmôr* is used to catch an antelope (Is. li. 20, RSV), and *mikmār* is figurative of the plots of the wicked (Ps. cxli. 10).

In the New Testament three Gk. words are translated 'net'. 5. From *diktyō*, 'to net', *diktyon*, the most common and general word for net. This type of net was used by Jesus' disciples (Mt. iv. 20, 21); it was let down (Lk. v. 4) or cast (Jn. xxi. 6) in the water, and emptied into a boat (Lk. v. 7) or dragged to shore (Jn. xxi. 8). 6. From *amphiballō*, 'cast around', *amphiblēstron*, 'a casting net', also used by the disciples of Jesus (Mt. iv. 18). 7. From *sassō*, 'fill', *sagēnē* (related to English 'seine'), a drag-net to which our Lord compared the kingdom of heaven (Mt. xiii. 47). It required several men to draw this large net to shore (Mt. xiii. 48).

The care of nets included washing (Lk. v. 2), drying (Ezk. xlvii. 10), and mending (Mt. iv. 21).

BIBLIOGRAPHY. G. Dalman, *Arbeit und Sitte*, VI, 1939, pp. 335–337, 343–363.

b. Nets as designs or gratings

Around the base of the brazen altar of burnt offering of the Tabernacle was grating of net design (*rešeṯ*, Ex. xxvii. 4, 5) or net work (*ma'aśēh rešeṯ*, Ex. xxxviii. 4). See fig. 176. This grating may have had both artistic and practical purposes, since it would be lighter to carry than solid metal.

The capitals of the two pillars before Solomon's Temple were decorated with a net design (Heb. *ś*[e]*ḇāḵâ* from a root meaning 'interweave', 1 Ki. vii. 17; Je. lii. 22). Those who think these pillars were cressets point out that open net work would give air for burning inside the capital, but this feature is not mentioned in the Bible and is uncertain. See fig. 116.

BIBLIOGRAPHY. H. G. May, *The Two Pillars before the Temple of Solomon*, *BASOR*, 88, December 1942, pp. 19–27. J.T.

NETTLES. There is some uncertainty about the precise plants referred to in the above translation of the two Heb. words. 1. *ḥārûl*, perhaps from the obsolete root *ḥāral*, 'to be sharp', 'to sting'. Found in Jb. xxx. 7 (LXX 'wild brushwood'); Pr. xxiv. 31; Zp. ii. 9. RVmg in each case renders 'wild vetches'. 2. *qimmôś* (Is. xxxiv. 13; Ho. ix. 6). Probably the true nettle, of which the most common Palestine variety is the *Urtica pilulifera*, which abounds in desolate places.

For general discussion and botanical details, see THORNS. J.D.D.

NEW BIRTH. See REGENERATION.

NEW MOON. See MOON.

NEW TESTAMENT. See BIBLE, CANON OF THE NEW TESTAMENT.

NEW TESTAMENT APOCRYPHA. The extent of the New Testament Apocrypha is more difficult to determine than that of the Old Testament. The term will here be confined to non-canonical works attributed to, or purporting to give extra-canonical information about, Christ or the apostles. Works written without such pretensions are thus excluded, even where they enjoyed quasi-canonical status in some churches for a time (see PATRISTIC LITERATURE); so are Christian attributions to (or Christianized versions of works attributed to) Old Testament characters (see PSEUDEPIGRAPHA), and the interpolation or rehandling of New Testament texts with alien material (see TEXT AND VERSIONS, New Testament section).

A huge literature remains, preserved partly in Greek and Latin, but still more in Coptic, Ethiopic, Syriac, Arabic, Slavonic, and even in

Anglo-Saxon and contemporary West European languages. Some works that we know to have been very influential have been almost lost, and many of the most important exist only in fragmentary state. New discoveries, however, often of much importance for early Christian history, are constantly being made. Complex literary problems are frequently met, for many of the apocryphal works lent themselves to re-telling, interpolation, and plagiarization.

I. FORMS

A large proportion of the apocryphal literature falls into one of the New Testament literary forms: Gospel, Acts, Epistle, Apocalypse. But this formal similarity is often accompanied by a huge difference in conception. This is particularly noticeable with the Gospels: we have Infancy Gospels, Passion Gospels, sayings documents, and theological meditations; but (if we exclude the early fragmentary Gospels on which we are in any case ill-informed), it is hard to find works which, like the canonical Gospels, have any interest in the words and works of the incarnate Lord. Acts form a numerous and probably the most popular class, doubtless through the wide and non-sectarian appeal of many of the stories. Epistles are not common: despite the fact that nearly all the works in the New Testament sometimes said to be pseudepigraphic are Epistles. For apocalypses, there was Jewish precedent for attributing them to a celebrity of the past.

Another class of literature developed which took over some features of apocryphal literature: the Church Orders of Syria and Egypt. These collections of canons on Church discipline and liturgy, of which the *Apostolic Constitutions* is the most popular, claiming to represent apostolic practice, came by convention to claim apostolic origin: and the most daring, the *Testament of our Lord*, purports to be a post-resurrection discourse of Christ. The custom was perhaps stimulated by its success in the 3rd-century *Didascalia*, and misunderstanding of the claim to apostolicity of the *Apostolic Tradition* of Hippolytus—two works which they plundered heavily—together with, in some cases, the popularity of the Clementine romance. (*Cf. Studia Patristica*, edited by K. Aland and F. L. Cross, II, 1957, pp. 83 ff.)

II. MOTIVES

The creation of apocryphal literature had begun in apostolic times: Paul has apparently to authenticate his signature because of forgeries circulating (*cf.* 2 Thes. iii. 17). In the 2nd century the literature comes into its own, and gathers momentum thenceforth, particularly in Egypt and Syria. It continues into the Middle Ages (where the older legends were still loved), and, occasionally, through sentiment, *parti pris*, or sheer eccentricity, in our own day. The various motives behind it are thus related to the whole trend of Christian and sub-Christian history; but some of the motives operative at the beginning are particularly important.

a. Romance and the literary impulse

This shows itself in various forms. There is the desire to satisfy curiosity on matters of which the New Testament says nothing. A flood of worthless Infancy Gospels covers the silent years from Bethlehem to the baptism. As the Virgin Mary becomes more prominent in theology and devotion, pseudo-apostolic works describe her birth, life, and, eventually, her assumption into heaven. A reader of Col. iv. 16 felt it incumbent upon him to supply the apparently missing letter to the Laodiceans. It appears above all in the novelistic Acts and romances and some of the Gospels—bizarre, fetid, but packed with wonders and anecdotes, and many of them, with all their faults, having a certain animation. We best understand this movement as a branch of popular Christian literature, and, studied in this light, the earliest books reveal some of the issues which occupied congregations in the 2nd and 3rd centuries: relationships with the state, controversies with the Jews, debates on marriage and celibacy: and, by their belligerent insistence on miracles, reveal that the real age of miracles had passed. The productions are crude, even vulgar; but their authors knew their public. For many they must have replaced erotic pagan popular literature, and in many cases, with a real desire to edify. The authors would doubtless be hard put to it to differentiate their motives from those of the author of *The Robe* or *The Big Fisherman*. There is no need to question the sincerity of the Asian presbyter who was unfrocked for publishing the *Acts of Paul* when he said that he did so 'for love of Paul', and Paul for him was almost as distant as Charles Simeon is for us. This helps to explain how stories and whole books originating in heretical circles retained and increased their currency in orthodox quarters. It was heretical teachers who made the earliest effective use of this form of literature; and so successful was it that others transmitted, expurgated, and imitated the forms designed as vehicles for their propaganda.

b. The inculcation of principles not, to the author's mind, sufficiently clearly enunciated in the New Testament books

Naturally, even in a work 'for love of Paul' any doctrinal disproportion or aberration of the author passed into his work; indeed part of his edificatory aim might well be to inculcate the aberration: the Asian presbyter, for instance, had an obsession with virginity which makes his work, otherwise more or less orthodox, remote from evangelic spirit. But there are many works the aim of which is deliberately sectarian: to promulgate a body of doctrine to supplement or supersede that of the undisputed books. These were mainly the fruit of the two great reactionary movements of the 2nd century, Gnosticism (*q.v.*) and Montanism. The Montanist 'Scriptures' arose almost by accident, and were not in our sense strictly apocryphal, for, though they claimed to preserve the living testimony of the Holy Spirit, they were not pseudonymous; they have virtually disappeared (but *cf.* those collected in R. M. Grant, *Second Century Christianity*, pp. 95 ff.). Writings from the multiform expressions of Gnosticism, however, have survived in quantity. Such works as the *Gospel of Truth*, a meditation in Gnostic terms reflecting the language of the undisputed Scriptures, are less common than works which select, modify, and interpret those Scriptures in a sectarian direction (*cf.* the Chenoboskion *Gospel of Thomas*), those which blatantly profess to contain secret doctrine not available elsewhere (*cf.* the *Apocryphon of John*), and those which simply attribute to the Lord or the apostles the commonplaces of Gnostic teaching. And for all these purposes the apocryphal form became conventional.

The reason is not far to seek. In the subapostolic age and after, with the immense expansion of the Church, the intensifying of the danger of persecution and the proliferation of false teaching, apostolicity became the norm of faith and practice: and, as the living memory of the apostles receded, apostolicity was increasingly centred in the Scriptures of our New Testament, over the majority of which there was unanimity in the Church. If, therefore, a new form of teaching was to spread, it had to establish its apostolicity. This was commonly done by claiming a secret tradition from an apostle, or from the Lord through an apostle, either as a supplement to the open tradition of the Gospels or as a corrective. The favoured apostle varies: many sects had Judaic leanings, and James the Just and, curiously, Salome, are frequent sources of tradition; Thomas, Philip, Bartholomew, and Matthias also appear constantly. In the Chenoboskion *Gospel of Thomas*, for instance, it is Thomas who shows fullest understanding of the Lord's person (Matthew and Peter—perhaps as the apostles behind the Church's first two Gospels—appear to their disadvantage). The still more weird *Pistis Sophia* envisages a sort of congress of the apostles and the women with the Lord, but indicates that Philip, Thomas, and Matthias are to write the mysteries (*Pistis Sophia*, chapter 42, Schmidt). Local factors probably contribute something to the choice of apostle—all those named were associated with Syria and the East, some of the most fertile soil for literature of this type; and speculations about Thomas as the Lord's twin exercised an additional fascination. The process brought about a new emphasis on the post-resurrection period, in which discourses of the Lord were usually set; significantly, for little is said of this period in the undisputed Gospels, and it was a constant Gnostic feature to undervalue the humanity of the incarnate Lord. It is worth noticing that, while those syncretistic sects who adopted some Christian elements could get their revelations whence they would, Christian Gnosticism had to show that its knowledge was derived from an apostolic source.

c. The preservation of tradition

Inevitably in early days words of the Lord were handed down outside the canonical Gospels. Some were probably transformed out of recognition in the process, others tendentiously twisted. The celebrated preface of Papias (Eusebius, *EH* iii. 39), showing him collecting oracles of the Lord for his Expositions, reveals how conscious orthodox Christians in the early 2nd century were of this floating material and the problems of collecting it. Papias, whatever his shortcomings, was conscientious in scrutinizing his material: yet the results were not always happy, and perhaps not all his contemporaries had his compunction. Genuine material may thus sometimes have been preserved amid undisputed rubbish.

Similarly, memories of the lives and deaths of apostles would be likely to linger, and the apocryphal Acts, even when dubious theologically, may sometimes preserve genuine traditions, or reflect appropriate situations.

The desire to transmit such memories undoubtedly played its part in the production of the apocryphal literature; but it could not defeat the tendency to invent, elaborate, improve, or redirect. Any winnowing process is thus hazardous: and, as scholars like Origen knew, was already hazardous in patristic times. In consequence, the necessity of building squarely upon what was undisputed was universally recognized.

III. THE APOCRYPHAL LITERATURE IN THE EARLY CHURCH

The presence of such various writings under apostolic names when apostolicity was the norm made it urgent to be assured which the truly apostolic writings were, and the early Christian scholars were not deficient in insight and critical acumen (see CANON OF THE NEW TESTAMENT). But it is striking how little the generally received list of canonical books is affected by discussions over apocryphal literature. Some churches were slow in receiving books now regarded as canonical. Some gave high place to such works as *1 Clement* and Hermas. But hardly any of the books in, say, James' *Apocryphal New Testament* were ever in any sense 'Excluded books of the New Testament'. They were beyond consideration. The Petrine literature caused more heart-searching than any other (*cf.* R. M. Grant and G. Quispel, *VC*, VI, 1952, pp. 31 ff.). By Eusebius' time the discussion, save on 2 Peter, is closed (*EH* iii. 3), but there is positive evidence that at least the *Apocalypse of Peter* was for a time employed in some areas (see below).

In this connection the letter of Serapion, Bishop of Antioch to the congregation at Rhossus about AD 190, is of interest (*cf.* Eusebius, *EH* vi. 12). The Church had begun to use the *Gospel of Peter*. There had evidently been opposition to it, but Serapion, satisfied of the stability of the congregation, had, after a cursory glance, sanctioned its public reading. Trouble followed. Serapion read the Gospel more carefully and found not only that it was accepted by churches whose tendencies were suspect, but that it reflected at some points the Docetic heresy (denyng the reality of Christ's manhood). He sums it up 'most is of the Saviour's true teaching', but some things (of which he appended a list) were added. He says, 'We accept Peter and the other apostles as Christ, but as men of experience we test writings falsely ascribed to them, knowing that such things were not handed down to us.'

In other words, the list of apostolic books was already traditional. Other books might be read, provided they were orthodox. The *Gospel of Peter* was *not* traditional: its use at Rhossus was the result of a specific request, and was not unopposed. At first Serapion had seen nothing to require prolonged controversy: if spurious, it was at least harmless. When closer examination revealed its tendencies its use in any form in church was forbidden.

The course of events seems best understood if, following the hint of Serapion's action, we recognize that the acknowledgment of a book as spurious did not necessarily involve complete refusal to allow its public reading, providing it had some devotional value and no heretical tendency: a sort of intermediate status analogous to that of the Apocrypha in the sixth Anglican Article. But even a heretical book, if it had other appeal, might still be read privately and laid under tribute. By these means the apocryphal literature came to have a permanent effect on mediaeval devotion and Christian art and story.

There is, however, nothing to suggest that it was an accepted part of catholic practice in the 1st or 2nd century to compile works in the name of an apostle, a process implied in some theories of the authorship of certain New Testament books (*cf.* D. Guthrie, *ExpT*, LXVII, 1956, pp. 341 f.), and the case of the author of the *Acts of Paul* is one example of drastic action against such publication.

Passing from any of the New Testament writings to the best of the New Testament apocrypha—the true creation of the early Christian community—one moves into a different world. If 2 Peter—to take the New Testament writing most commonly assigned to the 2nd century—be an apocryphon, it is unique among the apocrypha.

IV. SOME REPRESENTATIVE WORKS

A few representatives of different apocryphal forms may be given. They are, generally speaking, some of the more important older works. Few have a complete text: for some we are dependent on quotations from early writers.

a. Early apocryphal Gospels

A number of fragments from early Gospels are quoted by 3rd- and 4th-century writers. Debate continues on the nature and inter-relationships of these Gospels. The *Gospel according to the Hebrews* was known to Clement of Alexandria, Origen, Hegesippus, Eusebius, and Jerome, who says (though he is not always believed) that he translated it into Greek and Latin (*De Vir. Ill.* 2) from Aramaic in Hebrew characters, and that it was used by the Nazarenes, a Jewish-Christian group. Most people, he says, mistakenly thought it was the Hebrew original of Matthew mentioned by Papias (see MATTHEW, GOSPEL OF), which recalls that Irenaeus knew of sects which used only Matthew (*Adv. Haer.* i. 26. 2, iii. 11. 7). Some of the extracts we possess have certainly points of contact with Matthew; others reappear in other works, most recently the Chenoboskion *Gospel of Thomas*. There is a strong Jewish–Christian tone, and a resurrection appearance to James the Just is recorded. Eusebius refers to a story, found both in Papias and in the *Gospel of the Hebrews*, of a woman accused before Jesus of many sins. This has been often identified with the story of the adulteress found in many MSS of Jn. viii.

The Gospel probably reflects the activity of Syrian Jewish Christians using Matthaean (the 'local' Gospel) and other local tradition, some of it doubtless valid. The Nazarenes called it 'The Gospel according to the Apostles' (Jerome, *Dial. Pelag.* iii. 2)—a suspiciously belligerent title. (See V. Burch, *JTS*, XXI, 1920, pp. 310 ff.; M. J. Lagrange, *RB*, XXXI, 1922, pp. 161 ff., 321 ff.; and for its defence as a primary source, H. J. Schonfield, *According to the Hebrews*, 1937.)

Epiphanius, ever a confused writer, mentions a mutilated version of Matthew used by the Jewish–Christian sect he calls 'Ebionites'. This has been identified with the Hebrews Gospel, but the extracts given show a different view of the nativity and baptism, and the work is clearly sectarian and tendentious. It may be the same as the *Gospel of the Twelve Apostles* mentioned by Origen (*Lk. Hom.* 1; *cf.* J. R. Harris, *The Gospel of the Twelve Apostles*, 1900, pp. 11 f.).

The *Gospel of the Egyptians* is known mainly through a series of quotations in the *Stromateis* of Clement of Alexandria. Some Gnostics used it (Hippolytus, *Philos.* v. 7), and it doubtless arose in an Egyptian sect. Extant portions relate to a dialogue of Christ and Salome on the repudiation of sexual relations.

The papyri have yielded a number of fragments of uncanonical Gospels. The most celebrated, P. Oxy., 1, 654, 655, will be considered later under the Chenoboskion *Gospel of Thomas*. Next in interest comes the so-called *Unknown Gospel* (P. Egerton, 2) published by H. I. Bell and T. C. Skeat in 1935, describing incidents after the Synoptic manner but with a Johannine dialogue and vocabulary. The MS, dated *c.* AD 100, is one of the oldest known Christian Greek MSS. It has been held by some to draw on the Fourth Gospel and perhaps one of the Synoptics also, and by others to be an early example of Christian popular literature independent of these (*cf.* Lk. i. 1). (See H. I. Bell and T. C. Skeat, *The New Gospel Fragments*, 1935; C. H. Dodd, *BJRL*, XX, 1936, pp. 56 ff. = *New Testament Studies*, 1953, pp. 12 ff.; G. Mayeda, *Das Leben-Jesu-Fragment Egerton 2*, 1946; H. I. Bell, *HTR*, XLII, 1949, pp. 53 ff.)

b. Passion Gospels

The most important Gospel of which we have any substantial part is the (mid?) 2nd-century *Gospel of Peter*, of which a large Coptic fragment, covering from the judgment to the resurrection, exists (The Akhmim Fragment). It has been identified with the 'memoirs of Peter', perhaps mentioned by Justin (*Trypho* 106), but this is inappropriate. (*Cf.* V. H. Stanton, *JTS*, II, 1900, pp. 1 ff.)

The miraculous element is heightened. The watch see three men come out from the tomb, two whose heads reach the sky and one who overpasses it. A cross follows them. A voice from heaven cries, 'Hast thou preached to them that sleep?' and a voice from the cross says, 'Yes' (*cf.* 1 Pet. iii. 19). Pilate's share of blame is reduced, and that of Herod and the Jews emphasized: perhaps reflecting both an apologetic towards the state and controversy with the Jews.

Serapion's judgment (see above) did not err; most of it is lurid, but not dangerous. But there are tell-tale phrases: 'He kept silence as one feeling no pain', and the rendering of the cry of dereliction, 'My power, thou hast forsaken me', followed by the pregnant 'he was taken up', show that the author did not properly value the Lord's humanity. (See L. Vaganay, *L'Évangile de Pierre*, 1930.)

The *Gospel of Nicodemus* is the name given to a composite work existing in various recensions in Greek, Latin, and Coptic, of which the principal elements are 'The Acts of Pilate', supposedly an official report of the trial, crucifixion, and burial, an abstract of the subsequent debates and investigations of the Sanhedrin, and a highly coloured account of the 'Descent into Hell'. There are various appendices in the different versions; one, a letter of Pilate to the Emperor Claudius, may give the earliest example of 'Acts of Pilate'. Apologists like Justin (*Apol.* 35, 48) appeal confidently to the trial records, assuming they exist. Tertullian knew stories of Pilate's favourable reports to Tiberius about Jesus (*Apol.* 5, 21). Such 'records' would be constructed in time: especially when a persecuting government, *c.* AD 312, used forged and blasphemous reports of the trial for propaganda purposes (Eusebius, *EH* ix. 5). Our present 'Acts' may be a counter to these. The 'Descent into Hell' may be from rather later in the century, but both parts of the work probably draw on older material. The striking feature is the virtual vindication of Pilate, doubtless for reasons of policy. As the stories passed into Byzantine legend, Pilate became a saint, and his martyrdom is still celebrated in the Coptic Church.

There is no proper critical text. See J. Quasten, *Patrology*, I, pp. 115 ff. for versions.

c. Infancy Gospels

The *Protevangelium of James* had a huge popularity: many MSS exist in many languages (though none in Latin), and it has deeply influenced much subsequent Mariology. It was known to Origen, so must be 2nd century. It gives the birth and presentation of Mary, her espousal to Joseph (an old man with children), and the Lord's miraculous birth (a midwife attesting the virginity *in partu*). It is clearly written in the interests of certain theories about the perpetual virginity. The supposed author is James the Just, though at one point Joseph becomes the narrator. (See E. de Strycker, *Le Protévangile de Jacques*, A newly discovered Greek text is given by M. Testuz, *Papyrus Bodmer V*, 1958.)

The other influential infancy Gospel of antiquity was the *Gospel of Thomas*, which tells some rather repulsive stories of the silent years. Our version seems to have been shorn of its Gnostic speeches. It is distinct from the Chenoboskion work of the same name (see below): it is sometimes difficult to be sure to which work patristic writers refer.

d. The Gospels from Chenoboskion

Chenoboskion (*q.v.*) has produced several Gospels in Coptic which were not previously known, besides new versions of others. It is too early for anything but the briefest mention.

One text opens '*The Gospel of Truth* is a joy' (an *incipit*, not a title), and proceeds to a verbose and often obscure meditation on the scheme of redemption. Gnostic terminology of the type of the Valentinian school is evident, but not in the developed form we meet in Irenaeus. It alludes to most of the New Testament books in a way which suggests recognition of their authority. It has been commonly identified with the 'Gospel of Truth' ascribed to Valentinus by Irenaeus, though this has been denied (*cf.* H. M. Schenke, *Th.Lit.*, LXXXIII, 1958, pp. 497 ff.). Van Unnik has attractively proposed that it was written before Valentinus' break with the Roman church (where he was once a candidate for an episcopal chair), when he was seeking to establish his orthodoxy. It would thus be an important witness to the list of authoritative books (and substantially similar to our own) in Rome *c.* AD 140. (See G. Quispel and W. C. van Unnik in *The Jung Codex*, ed. by F. L. Cross, 1955; text by M. Malinine *et al.*, *Evangelium Veritatis*, 1956; E.T. and commentary by K. Grobel, *The Gospel of Truth*, 1960.)

The now famous *Gospel of Thomas* is a collection of sayings of Jesus, numbered at about 114, with little obvious arrangement. A high proportion resemble sayings in the Synoptic Gospels (with a bias towards Luke) but almost always with significant differences. These often take a Gnostic direction, and among other Gnostic themes the Old Testament is minimized and the necessity for obliterating consciousness of sex is stressed. It has been identified with the Gospel used by the Naassene Gnostics (*cf.* R. M. Grant with D. N. Freedman, *The Secret Sayings of Jesus*, 1959; W. R. Schoedel, *VC*, XIV, 1960, pp. 225 ff.), but its originally Gnostic character has been doubted (R. McL. Wilson, *Studies in the Gospel of Thomas*, 1961), and some are prepared to see independent traditions of some value in it. G. Quispel has found the variants similar in type to those in the Bezan ('Western') Text (*VC*, XIV, 1960, pp. 204 ff.) as well as in Tatian's *Diatessaron* and the Pseudo-Clementines (see below). The Oxyrhynchus Logia P. Oxy., 1, 654, 655, including the celebrated 'Raise the stone and thou shalt find me', recur in a form which suggests that they were part of an earlier Greek version of the book. Thomas (probably thought of as the twin of Jesus) plays the central rôle in the tradition (see above), but James the Just is said to become chief of the disciples—one of several indications that a Jewish–Christian source is under tribute.

Many problems beset this curious and inconsistent book, but so far it seems safe to place its origin in Syria (which may explain the Semitisms of the language), where there was always a freer attitude to the Gospel text and more contamination than elsewhere. (See text and translation by A. Guillaumont *et al.*, 1959; B. Gärtner, *The Theology of the Gospel of Thomas*, 1961; Bibliography to 1960 in J. Leipoldt and H. M. Schenke, *Koptisch-Gnostische Schriften aus den Papyrus-Codices von Nag-Hamadi*, 1960, pp. 79 f.)

The chief interest of the *Gospel of Philip* (Gnostic, though the sect is hard to identify) lies in its unusually developed sacramental doctrine, in which there are greater mysteries in chrism and the 'bridechamber' than in baptism (see E. Segelberg, *Numen*, VII, 1960, pp. 189 ff.). The language is repulsive: interest in sexual repudiation amounts to an obsession. (German translation in Leipoldt and Schenke, as above.)

e. The 'Leucian' Acts

The five major apocryphal acts must serve as representatives of a large number. They were gathered into a corpus by Manicheans, who would inherit them from Gnostic sources. The 9th-century bibliophile Photius found the whole attributed to one 'Leucius Charinus' (*Bibliotheca*, 114), but it is probable that Leucius was simply the fictitious name of the author of the *Acts of John*, the earliest (and most unorthodox) of the corpus.

It belongs to about AD 150–60 and describes miracles and sermons (definitely Gnostic) by John in Asia Minor. It reflects ascetic ideals, but has some pleasant anecdotes amid more disreputable matter. It affects also to relate John's own accounts of some incidents with the Lord, and His farewell and death. Liturgically it is of some interest, and includes the first known eucharist for the dead.

The *Acts of Paul* is also early, for Tertullian knew people who justified female preaching and baptizing therefrom (*De Baptismo* 17). He says it was written ostensibly 'for love of Paul' by an Asian presbyter, who was deposed for the action. This must have happened before AD 190, probably nearer AD 160. The Acts reflect a time of persecution. There are three main sections:

(i) The Acts of Paul and Thecla, an Iconian girl who breaks off her engagement at Paul's preaching, is miraculously protected from martyrdom (winning the interest of 'Queen Tryphaena'—see TRYPHAENA AND TRYPHOSA) and assists Paul's missionary travels. There may have been some historical nucleus even if not a written Thecla source (so Ramsay, *CRE*, pp. 375 ff.).

(ii) Further correspondence with the Corinthian church.

(iii) The martyrdom of Paul (legendary).

The tone is intensely ascetic (*cf.* Paul's Beatitudes for the celibate, chapter 5), but otherwise orthodox. There are many incomplete MSS, including a sizeable section of the original Greek. See L. Vouaux, *Les Actes de Paul*, 1913; E. Peterson, *VC*, III, 1949, pp. 142 ff.

The *Acts of Peter* is somewhat later, but still well within the 2nd century. The main MS, in Latin (often called the Vercelli Acts), opens with Paul's farewell to the Roman Christians (perhaps from another source). Through the machinations of Simon Magus (*q.v.*) the Roman church falls into heresy, but, in response to prayer, Peter arrives, and defeats Simon in a series of public encounters. There follows a plot against Peter initiated by pagans whose wives have left them as a result of his preaching, Peter's flight including the *Quo Vadis?* story, and his return to crucifixion, which was head downwards. A Coptic fragment and allusions to a lost portion suggest that other stories dealt with questions raised in the community about suffering and death. Like other Acts, it sees Peter's work and Paul's as supplementing each other: and the Roman church is a *Pauline* foundation. The ascetic tone is as intense as ever, but otherwise the Gnostic element is not often obtruded; we may, however, have expurgated editions. The place of origin is disputed, but it was almost certainly eastern. See L. Vouaux, *Les Actes de Pierre*, 1922.

The *Acts of* (*Judas*) *Thomas* stand apart from the other Acts. They are a product of Syriac Christianity, and were almost certainly written in Syriac in Edessa in the early 3rd century. They describe how the apostles divided the world by lot, and Judas Thomas the Twin was appointed to India. He went as a slave, but became the means of the conversion of King 'Gundaphar' and many other notable Indians. Everywhere he preaches virginity and is frequently imprisoned in consequence of his success. Finally, he is martyred.

The Acts have certain Gnostic features: the famous 'Hymn of the Soul' which appears in them has the familiar Gnostic theme of the redemption of the soul from the corruption of matter—the king's son is sent to slay the dragon and bring back the pearl from the far country. There is clearly some relation, as yet unascertained, to the Chenoboskion *Gospel of Thomas*: and the title of Thomas, 'Twin of the Messiah', is eloquent. The appeal for virginity is louder, shriller, than in any of the other Acts, but this was a characteristic of Syriac Christianity. Of Gnosticism in the sense of the possession of hidden mysteries there is little trace: the author is too much in earnest in preaching and recommending his Gospel.

There are complete versions in Syriac and Greek. The Acts seem to show some real knowledge of Indian history and topography (see INDIA). (See A. A. Bevan, *The Hymn of the Soul*, 1897; F. C. Burkitt, *Early Christianity outside the Roman Empire*, 1899; J. Doresse, *L'Évangile selon Thomas*, 1959; A. F. J. Klijn, *VC*, XIV, 1960, pp. 154 ff.)

The *Acts of Andrew* is the latest (*c.* AD 260?) and, in our MSS, the most fragmentary of the 'Leucian' Acts. It is closely related to the *Acts of John*, and its Gnostic character is mentioned by Eusebius (*EH* iii. 25). It describes preachings among the cannibals, miracles, exhortations to virginity, and, perhaps added from another source, martyrdom in Greece. An abstract is given by Gregory of Tours. (See P. M. Peterson, *Andrew, Brother of Simon Peter*, 1958; F. Dvornik, *The Idea of Apostolicity in Byzantium and the Legend of the Apostle Andrew*, 1958, pp. 181 ff.; G. Quispel, *VC*, X, 1956, pp. 129 ff.)

f. Apocryphal Epistles

The most important are the *Third Epistle to the Corinthians* (see *Acts of Paul*, above); the *Epistle of the Apostles*, really a series of early 2nd-century apocalyptic visions cast in the form of an address in the name of all the apostles, to convey post-resurrection teaching of Christ (important as one of the earliest examples of this form); the *Correspondence of Christ and Abgar*, in which the King of Edessa invites the Lord to his state, and of which Eusebius affords an early translation from the Syriac (*EH* i. 13); the Latin *Correspondence of Paul and Seneca* (see Jerome, *De Vir. Ill.* 12), a 3rd-century apology for Paul's diction, evidently intended to gain a reading of the genuine Epistles in polite circles; and the *Epistle to the Laodiceans*, in Latin, a cento of Pauline language evoked by Col. iv. 16. The Muratorian Fragment mentions Epistles to the Laodiceans, and to the Alexandrians, of Marcionite origin: of these there is no trace. The commonly quoted Letter of Lentulus describing Jesus and allegedly addressed to the Senate is mediaeval. (See H. Duensing, *Epistula Apostolorum*, 1925; J. de Zwaan in *Amicitiae Corolla* edited by H. G. Wood, 1933, pp. 344 ff.; L. Vouaux, *Les Actes de Paul*, 1913, pp. 315 ff. for all the pseudo-Pauline letters.)

g. Apocalypses

The *Apocalypse of Peter* is the only strictly apocryphal work of which there is positive evidence that it held quasi-canonical status for any length of time. It occurs in the Muratorian Fragment, which does not mention 1 Peter (but *cf.* Zahn, *Geschichte des Neutestamentliche Kanons*, II, i, pp. 105–110, 142), but with the note that some will not have it read in church. Clement of Alexandria seems to have commented on it as if it were canonical in a lost work (Eusebius, *EH* vi. 14), and in the 5th century it was read on Good Friday in some Palestinian churches (Sozomen, *Eccles. Hist.* vii. 19). But it was never universally accepted, and its canonicity was not a live issue in Eusebius' day (*EH* iii. 3). Its substantial orthodoxy seems certain. An old stichometry gives it 300 lines: about half of this appears in the main copy of the *Gospel of Peter* (see above). It contains visions of the transfigured Lord, and lurid accounts of the torments of the damned: with perhaps a confused reference to future probation. (See M. R. James, *JTS*, XII, 1911, pp. 36 ff., 362 ff., 573 ff.; XXXII, 1931, pp. 270 ff.).

There were several Gnostic *Apocalypses of Paul*, one known to Origen, inspired by 2 Cor. xii. 2 ff. A version of one (which influenced Dante) has survived (see R. P. Casey, *JTS*, XXIV, 1933, pp. 1 ff.).

h. Other Apocryphal Works

The *Kerygma Petrou*, or *Preaching of Peter*, is known to us only in fragments, mostly preserved by Clement of Alexandria. Origen had to deal with Gnostic scholars who employed it, and challenges those who do so to prove its genuineness (in Jn. xiii. 17, *De Princ.* Pref. 8). It has been postulated as a source of the original Clementine romance (see below). The fragments we have claim to preserve words of the Lord and of Peter, and at least one accords with the *Gospel of the Hebrews*.

The *Clementine Homilies* and the *Clementine Recognitions* are the two chief forms of a romance in which Clement of Rome, seeking for ultimate truth, travels in the apostle Peter's footsteps and is eventually converted. It is probable that both derive from an immensely popular 2nd-century Christian novel, which may have used the *Preaching of Peter*. The literary and theological problems involved are very complex. The Homilies in particular commend a Judaized sectarian form of Christianity. (See O. Cullmann, *Le Problème Littéraire et Historique du Roman Pseudo-Clémentin*, 1930; H. J. Schoeps, *Theologie und Geschichte des Judenchristentums*, 1949; E.T.s of Homilies and Recognitions in Ante-Nicene Christian Library.)

The *Apocryphon of John* was popular in Gnostic circles, and has reappeared at Chenoboskion. The Saviour appears to John on the Mount of Olives, bids him write secret doctrine, deposit it safely, and impart it only to those whose spirit can understand it and whose way of life is worthy. There is a curse on anyone imparting the doctrine for reward to an unworthy person. It is to be dated before AD 180, probably in Egypt. (See W. C. Till, *Die Gnostischen Schriften des koptischen Papyrus Berol. 8502*, 1955; *cf. JEH*, III, 1952, pp. 14 ff.)

The *Apocryphon of James* has been discovered at Chenoboskion. It is an exhortation to seek the kingdom, cast in the form of a post-resurrection discourse to Peter and James, who ascend with the Lord, but are unable to penetrate the third heaven. Its interest lies in its early date (AD 125–150?), the prominence of James (the Just?), who sends the apostles to their work after the ascension, and, in van Unnik's opinion, its freedom from Gnostic influence. (See W. C. van Unnik, *VC*, X, 1956, pp. 149 ff.)

The *Pistis Sophia* and the *Books of Jeû* are obscure and bizarre Gnostic works of the 2nd or 3rd century. (See C. Schmidt, *Koptisch-gnostische Schriften*[3], edited by W. Till, 1959; G. R. S. Mead, *Pistis Sophia*[3], 1947, E.T.—*cf.* F. C. Burkitt, *JTS*, XXIII, 1922, pp. 271 ff.; C. A. Baynes, *A Coptic Gnostic Treatise*, 1933.)

GENERAL BIBLIOGRAPHY. Critical editions of many of these works are still needed. Greek and Latin texts of the earlier Gospel discoveries are provided by C. Tischendorf, *Evangelia Apocrypha*, 1886, to be supplemented by A. de Santos, *Los Evangelios Apocrifos*, 1956 (with Spanish translations). The best collection of texts of the Acts is R. A. Lipsius and M. Bonnet, *Acta Apostolorum Apocrypha*, 1891–1903. Some newer texts and studies are provided in M. R. James, *Apocrypha Anecdota*, I, 1893, II, 1897. M. R. James, *ANT* (a splendid collection of English translations up to 1924); E. Hennecke–W. Schneemelcher, *Neutestamentliche Apokryphen*[2], I (Gospels), 1959, II in preparation (indispensable for serious study). Non-canonical sayings: A. Resch, *Agrapha*[2], 1906; B. Pick, *Paralipomena*, 1908; J. Jeremias, *Unknown Sayings of Jesus*, 1957. Church orders: J. Cooper and A. J. Maclean, *The Testament of our Lord*, 1902; R. H. Connolly, *The So-Called Egyptian Church Order and its Derivatives*, 1917. A.F.W.

NICODEMUS. The name is Greek and means 'conqueror of the people'. He is mentioned only in the Fourth Gospel, where he is described as a Pharisee and ruler of the Jews (*i.e.* a member of the Sanhedrin) who visited Jesus by night (Jn. iii. 1–21). He seems to have been an earnest man attracted by the character and teaching of Jesus but afraid to allow this interest to be known by his fellow Pharisees. He was unable to understand the spiritual metaphors used by Christ. Nicodemus fades from the scene and we are left with the voice of Christ to a Judaism wrapped in darkness.

Nicodemus is mentioned again in Jn. vii. 50–52, where he showed more courage in protesting against the condemnation of Christ without giving Him a hearing. The final reference is in Jn. xix. 40, where he is said to have brought a lavish gift of spices to anoint the body of Christ. Nothing more is known of him despite a large number of legends (*e.g.* in the apocryphal *Gospel of Nicodemus*). His identification with the wealthy and generous Naqdimon ben Gorion of the Talmud is uncertain. R.E.N.

NICOLAS, NICOLAITANS. Nicolas of Antioch (Acts vi. 5) is supposed to have given his name to a group in the early Church who sought to work out a compromise with paganism, to enable Christians to take part without embarrassment in some of the social and religious activities of the close-knit society in which they found themselves. It is possible that the term Nicolaitan is a Graecized form of Heb. Balaam, and therefore allegorical, the policy of the sect being likened to that of the Old Testament corruptor of Israel (Nu. xxii). In that case the Nicolaitans are to be identified with groups attacked by Peter (2 Pet. ii. 15), Jude (11), and John (Rev. ii. 14 and possibly ii. 20–23), for their advocacy within the Church of pagan sexual laxity. References in Irenaeus, Clement, and Tertullian suggest that the group hardened into a Gnostic sect traceable as far as AD 200. E.M.B.

NICOPOLIS ('city of victory'). A town built as the capital of Epirus by Augustus on a peninsula of the Ambraciot Gulf, where he had camped before his victory at Actium in 31 BC. It was a Rom. colony, and derived some of its importance from the Actian games, also established by Augustus.

Although there were other towns named Nicopolis, this was the only one of sufficient standing to warrant Paul's spending a whole winter in it (Tit. iii. 12), and its geographical position would suit its selection as a rendezvous with Titus. Paul may have planned to use it as a base for evangelizing Epirus. There is no ancient authority for the AV subscription to the Epistle to Titus.

K.L.McK.

NIGER. See SIMEON (5).

NIGHT-HAWK. See BIRDS OF THE BIBLE.

NIGHT-MONSTER. See LILITH.

NILE.

I. TERMINOLOGY

The origin of Gk. *Neilos* and Lat. *Nilus*, our 'Nile', is uncertain. In the Old Testament, with a few rare exceptions, the word *y*e*'ôr*, 'river, stream, channel', is used whenever the Egyptian Nile is meant. This Hebrew word is itself directly derived from Egyp. *ỉtrw* in the form *ỉ'r*(*w*) current from the XVIIIth Dynasty onwards, meaning 'Nile-river, stream, canal', *i.e.* the Nile and its various subsidiary branches and channels (A. Erman and H. Grapow, *Wörterbuch der Aegyptischen Sprache*, I, 1926, p. 146; T. O. Lambdin, *JAOS*, LXXIII, 1953, p. 151). In AV the word *y*e*'ôr* is hidden under various common nouns, 'river, flood', *etc.* Just once the word *nāhār*, 'river', is used of the Nile as the river of Egypt in parallel with the Euphrates, the *nāhār*, 'river', *par* *excellence*, the promised land lying between these two broad limits (Gn. xv. 18). *Naḥal*, 'wadi', is apparently never used of the Nile, but of the Wadi el-'Arish or 'river of Egypt', while the Shihor (*q.v.*) is the seaward end of the easternmost Delta branch of the Nile; see EGYPT, RIVER OF.

II. COURSE OF THE RIVER

The ultimate origin of the Nile is the streams such as the Kagera that flow into Lake Victoria in Tanganyika; from the latter, a river emerges northward, *via* Lake Albert Nyanza and the vast Sudd swamps of the S Sudan, to become the White Nile. At Khartoum this is joined by the Blue Nile flowing down from Lake Tana in the Ethiopian (Abyssinian) highlands, and their united stream is the Nile proper. After being joined by the Atbara river some 200 miles north-east of Khartoum, the Nile flows for 1,700 miles through the Sudan and Egypt northward to the Mediterranean without receiving any other tributary; the total length of the river from Lake Victoria to the Mediterranean is roughly 3,500 miles. Between Khartoum and Aswan, six 'sills' of hard granite rocks across the river's course give rise to the six cataracts that impede navigation on that part of its course.

Within Nubia and Upper Egypt, the Nile stream flows in a narrow valley which in Egypt is never much more than 12 miles wide and often much less, bounded by hills or cliffs, beyond which stretch rocky deserts to east and west; see EGYPT: Natural Features. Some 12 miles north of Cairo, the river divides into two main branches that reach the sea at Rosetta in the west and Damietta in the east respectively; between and beyond these two great channels extend the flat, swampy lands of the Egyptian Delta. In Pharaonic Egypt three main branches of the Delta Nile seem to have been recognized ('Western river', Canopic branch?; 'the Great river', very roughly the present Damietta branch; 'the Waters of Rēʻ', or Eastern, Pelusiac branch, Heb. Shihor), besides various smaller branches, streams, and canals. Greek travellers and geographers reckoned from five to seven branches and mouths of the Nile. See A. H. Gardiner, *Ancient Egyptian Onomastica*, II, 1947, pp. 153*–170*, with map between pp. 131* and 134*, on this tricky question; also J. Ball, *Egypt in the Classical Geographers*, 1942; and the works they cite.

III. THE INUNDATION AND AGRICULTURE

The most remarkable feature of the Nile is its annual rise and flooding over its banks, or inundation. In spring and early summer in Ethiopia and S Sudan the heavy rains and melting highland snows turn the Upper Nile—specifically the Blue Nile—into a vast torrent bringing down in its waters masses of fine, reddish earth in suspension which it used to deposit on the lands flooded on either side of its banks in Egypt and Nubia. Thus, until the perennial irrigation-system of dams at Aswan and elsewhere was instituted last century, those areas of the Egyptian valley and Delta within reach of the floods received every year a thin, new deposit of fresh, fertile mud. The muddy flood-waters used to be held within basins bounded by earthen banks, to be released when the level of the Nile waters sank again. In Egypt the Nile is lowest in May; its rise there begins in June, the main floodwaters reach Egypt in July/August, reach their peak there in September, and slowly decline again thereafter. But for the Nile and its inundation, Egypt would be as desolate as the deserts on either hand; wherever the Nile waters reach, vegetation can grow, life can exist. So sharp is the change from watered land to desert that one can stand with a foot in each. Egypt's agriculture depended wholly on the inundation, whose level was checked off against river-level gauges or Nilometers. A high flood produced the splendid crops that made Egypt's agricultural wealth proverbial. A low Nile, like drought in other lands, spelt famine; too high a Nile that swept away irrigation-works and brought destruction in its wake was no better. The regular rhythm of Egypt's Nile was familiar to the Hebrews (*cf.* Is. xxiii. 10; Am. viii. 8, ix. 5, RSV), and likewise the dependence of Egypt's cultivators, fisherfolk, and marshes on those waters (Is. xix. 5–8, xxiii. 3, RSV). More than one prophet proclaimed judgment on Egypt in terms of drying up the Nile (Ezk. xxx. 12, *cf.* xxix. 10; Zc. x. 11, RSV), as other lands might be chastised by lack of rain (*cf.* FAMINE). Jeremiah (xlvi. 7–9) compares the advance of Egypt's army with the surge of the rising Nile. On the inundation of the Nile, see G. Hort, *ZAW*, LXIX, 1957, pp. 88–95; J. Ball, *Contributions to the Geography of Egypt*, 1939, *passim*; H. R. Hall, *General Introductory Guide to Egyptian Collections, BM*, 1930 ed., pp. 10–12.

IV. OTHER ASPECTS

The Nile in dominating Egypt's agriculture also affected the form of her calendar, divided into three seasons (each of four thirty-day months and excluding five additional days) called *'Akhet*, 'Inundation'; *Peret*, 'Coming Forth' (*i.e.* of the land from the receding waters); and *Shomu*, 'Dry(?)' or Summer season. The waters of the Nile not only supported crops but formed also the marshes for pasture (*cf.* Gn. xli. 1–3, 17, 18) and papyrus (see PAPYRI AND OSTRACA), and contained a wealth of fish caught by both line and net (Is. xix. 8), *cf.* R. A. Caminos, *Late-Egyptian Miscellanies*, 1954, pp. 74, 200 (many sorts), and G. Posener *et al.*, *Dictionnaire de la Civilisation Égyptienne*, 1959, figures on pp. 214, 215. On the plagues of a blood-red Nile, dead fish and frogs, *etc.*, see PLAGUES OF EGYPT. For Na. iii. 8, see No. The Assyrian's boast of drying up Egypt's streams (2 Ki. xix. 24 = Is. xxxvii. 25) may refer to moats and similar river-defence works. For Moses in the rushes by the Nile, see MOSES. The Nile was also Egypt's main arterial highway; boats could sail northward by merely going with the stream, and could as readily sail southward with the aid of the cool north wind from the Mediterranean. In the religious beliefs of the Egyptians the spirit of the Nile-flood was the god Ha'pi, bringer of fertility and abundance.

K.A.K.

NIMRIM, WATERS OF. The waters of Nimrim are mentioned twice (Is. xv. 6; Je. xlviii. 34). In substantially identical terms the prophets tell of the overthrow of Moab; cries of anguish go up from the cities of Moab, and 'the waters also of Nimrim shall be desolate'. Both in Isaiah and (especially) in Jeremiah the sequence of place-names suggests a site in south Moab, the now-customary identification with Wadi en-Numeirah, 10 miles from the southern tip of the Dead Sea. This is to be distinguished from Nimrah (Nu. xxxii. 3) or Beth-nimrah (Nu. xxxii. 36) about 10 miles north of the Dead Sea.

J.A.M.

NIMROD. The name of the son of Cush, an early warrior, or hero (*gibbōr*), who lived in Babylonia, where his kingdom included Babylon, Erech, and Akkad (Gn. x. 8–10; 1 Ch. i. 10). He was father or founder of Nineveh and Calah in Assyria (Gn. x. 11) and was famous as a hunter (verse 9). The land adjacent to Assyria was later referred to as the 'land of Nimrod' (Mi. v. 6).

His name is perpetuated in several place-names, including Birs Nimrud, south-west of Babylon, and Nimrud in Assyria (see CALAH). This, with the legends concerning him preserved in Sumerian, Assyr., and later literature, implies a wider basis in the tradition than is provided in Genesis. Many scholars therefore compare him with Sargon of Agade, *c.* 2300 BC, who was a great warrior and huntsman and ruler of Assyria (see fig. 2). He led expeditions to the Mediterranean coast and into S Anatolia and Persia, and the splendour of his age and achievements led to its being recalled as a 'golden age'. Since only the throne-name of Sargon is known, it is possible that he bore other names. Others see in Nimrod exploits attributed to such early deities as Ninurta (Nimurda), the Bab. and Assyr. god of war, and the hunter, or Amar-utu, the Sumerian name of the god Marduk (see MERODACH). No certain identification is yet possible. D.J.W.

NINEVEH. A principal city, and last capital, of Assyria. The ruins are marked by the mounds called Kuyunjik and Nabi Yunus ('Prophet Jonah') on the river Tigris opposite Mosul, Iraq.

I. NAME

The Heb. *nînᵉwēh* (Gk. *Nineuē*; classical *Ninos*) is a translation of the Assyr. *Ninua* (Old Bab. *Ninuwa*), a rendering of the earlier Sumerian name *Nina*, a name of the goddess Ishtar written with a sign depicting a fish inside a womb. Despite the comparison with the history of Jonah, there is probably no connection with the Heb. *nūn*, 'fish'.

II. HISTORY

According to Gn. x. 11 Nineveh was one of the northern cities founded by Nimrod or Ashur after leaving Babylonia. Excavation 82 feet down to virgin soil shows that the site was occupied from prehistoric times (*c.* 4500 BC). 'Ubaid (and Samarra) type pottery and pisée-buildings may indicate a southern origin. Although first mentioned in the inscriptions of Gudea of Lagash who campaigned in the area *c.* 2200 BC, the texts of Tukulti-Ninurta I *c.* 1250 BC tell how he restored the temple of the goddess Ishtar of Nineveh founded by Manishtisu, son of Sargon, *c.* 2300 BC (see NIMROD).

By the late second millennium the city was in contact with the Assyrian colony of Kanish in Cappadocia, and when Assyria became independent under Shamshi-Adad I (*c.* 1800 BC) the same temple of Ishtar (called E-mash-mash) was again restored. Hammurabi of Babylon (*c.* 1750 BC) adorned the temple, but the expansion of the town followed the revival of Assyrian fortunes under Shalmaneser I (*c.* 1260 BC), and by the reign of Tiglath-pileser I (1114–1076 BC) it was established as an alternative royal residence to Assur and Calah. Both Ashurnasirpal II (883–859 BC) and Sargon II (722–705 BC) had palaces there. It was, therefore, likely that it was to Nineveh itself that the tribute of Menahem in 744 BC (2 Ki. xv. 20) and of Samaria in 722 BC (Is. viii. 4) was brought.

Sennacherib, with the aid of his W Semitic Queen Nakiya-Zakuta, extensively rebuilt the city, its defence, walls, and water supply. For the last-named he built a canal leading 30 miles from a dam on the river Gomel to the north, and controlled the flow of the river Khasr, which flowed through the city, by the erection of another dam at Ajeila to the east. He also provided new administrative buildings and parks. The walls of his new palace were decorated with reliefs depicting his victories, including the successful siege of Lachish (*q.v.*). The tribute received from Hezekiah of Judah (2 Ki. xviii. 14) was sent to Nineveh, to which Sennacherib himself returned after the campaign (2 Ki. xix. 36; Is. xxxvii. 37). It is possible that the temple of Nisroch (*q.v.*), where he was murdered, was in Nineveh (see SENNACHERIB). His account of his siege of Hezekiah in Jerusalem is recorded on a clay prism (Taylor Prism) found in the Nabi Yunus mound at Nineveh in 1830.

Ashurbanipal (669–*c.* 627 BC) again made Nineveh his main residence, having lived there as crown prince. The bas-reliefs, depicting a lion hunt (British Museum) which were made for his palace, are the best examples of this form of Assyr. art. The fall of the great city of Nineveh, as predicted by the prophets Nahum and Zephaniah, occurred in August 612 BC. The Bab. Chronicle tells how a combined force of Medes, Babylonians, and Scythians laid siege to the city, which fell as a result of the breaches made in the defences by the flooding rivers (Na.

ii. 6–8). The city was plundered by the Medes, and the king Sin-shar-ishkun perished in the flames, though his family escaped. The city was left to fall into the heap of desolate ruin which it is today (Na. ii. 10, iii. 7), a pasturing-place for the flocks (Zp. ii. 13–15), which gives the citadel mound its modern name of Tell Kuyunjik ('mound of many sheep'). When Xenophon and the retreating Greek army passed in 401 BC it was already an unrecognizable mass of debris.

At the height of its prosperity Nineveh was enclosed by an inner wall of *c.* 7¾-miles circuit within which, according to Felix Jones' survey of 1834, more than 175,000 persons could have lived. The population of 'this great city' of Jonah's history (i. 2, iii. 2) given as 120,000, who did not know right from wrong, accords well with the evidence from Nimrud, a city of less than half the size, which accommodated 69,574 persons in 879 BC. The 'three days' journey' required to traverse Nineveh (Jon. iii. 3) probably refers to the whole administrative district of Nineveh, which was about 30–60 miles across (Hatra–Khorsabad–Nimrud). The day's journey of Jon. iii. 4 might refer to the distance from the southern suburbs (*e.g.* Balawat) to the north of the city. The Heb. translation by using *nînᵉwēh* in each case did not differentiate between the district (Assyr. *ninua*(*ki*)) and metropolis ((*al*)-*ninua*). There is no external evidence for the repentance of the people of Nineveh (Jon. iii. 4, 5), the Ninevites whose action was commended by Jesus Christ (Lk. xi. 30; Mt. xii. 41).

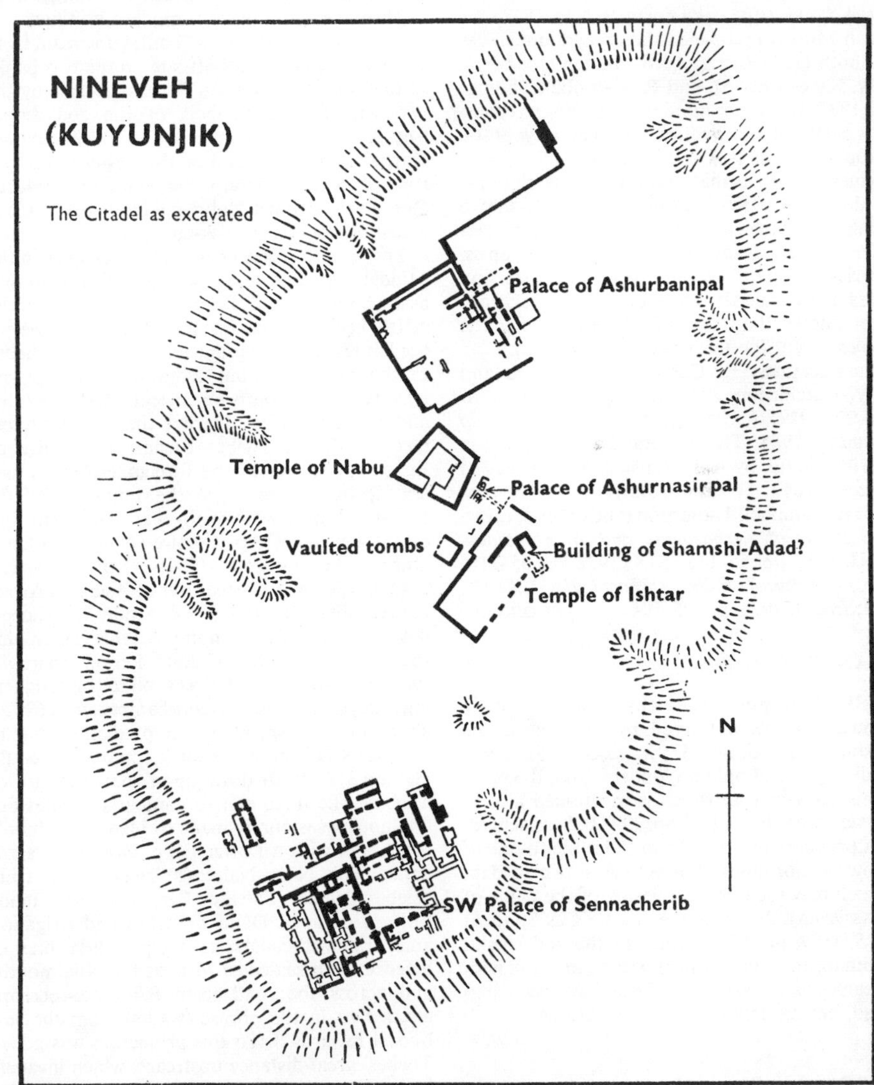

Fig. 152.

III. EXPLORATION

Following reports made by such early travellers as John Cartwright (17th century AD) and plans drawn by C. J. Rich in 1820, interest was reawakened in the discovery of the Old Testament city. Excavation was at first undertaken by P. E. Botta (1842–3), but with little success, and he abandoned the site, believing Khorsabad (10 miles to the north) to be the biblical Nineveh. However, the diggings of Layard and Rassam (1845–54), which resulted in the discovery of the reliefs from the palaces of Sennacherib and Ashurbanipal together with many inscriptions, placed the identification beyond question. Following the identification, among the 25,000 inscribed tablets from the libraries of Ashurbanipal and of the temple of Nabu (see WRITING), of a Bab. account of the flood (Epic of Gilgamesh) in 1872, the British Museum reopened the excavations under G. Smith (1873–6); E. A. W. Budge (1882–91); L. W. King (1903–5), and R. Campbell Thompson (1927–32). The mound of Nabi Yunus covering a palace of Esarhaddon has been as yet little explored because it is still inhabited.

Nineveh, with its many reliefs and inscriptions, has done more than any other Assyrian site to elucidate the ancient history of the country (see ASSYRIA and BABYLONIA), while the epics, histories, grammatical and scientific texts and letters have made the literature of the Assyrians better known than that of any ancient Semitic peoples except the Hebrews (see WRITING).

BIBLIOGRAPHY. R. Campbell Thompson and R. W. Hutchinson, *A Century of Exploration at Nineveh*, 1929; A. Parrot, *Nineveh and the Old Testament*, 1955. The exploration of Nineveh is described in full by A. H. Layard, *Nineveh and its Remains*, 1849; G. Smith, *Assyrian Discoveries*, 1875; R. Campbell Thompson (and others), *Liverpool Annals of Archaeology and Anthropology*, XVIII, 1931, pp. 55–116; XIX, 1932, pp. 55–116; XX, 1933, pp. 71–186; *Archaeologia*, LXXIX, 1929; *Iraq*, I, 1934, pp. 95–104. D.J.W.

NISAN. See CALENDAR.

NISROCH (*nisrōḵ*). The deity in whose temple Sennacherib was murdered by his sons as he worshipped (2 Ki. xix. 37; Is. xxxvii. 38). There is a divergence of opinion in identifying the place of this assassination which is mentioned also in Assyrian records (*DOTT*, pp. 70–73). Sennacherib most probably returned from Palestine to one of his own major cities, Nineveh, Assur, or Calah. Nisroch may then be a rendering of the name of the Assyrian national god, Ashur (*cf.* LXX *Esorach*; *JRAS*, 1899, p. 459). A form of the god Nusku (assuming an original *nswk*) or a connection with the eagle-shaped army standards have been suggested, but are less likely identifications.

D.J.W.

NITRE (*neṯer*). The modern name denotes saltpetre (sodium or potassium nitrate), but the biblical name refers to natron (carbonate of soda), which came chiefly from the 'soda lakes' of Lower Egypt. In Pr. xxv. 20 the effect of songs on a heavy heart is compared to the action of vinegar on nitre (RVmg 'soda')—*i.e.* producing strong effervescence. LXX renders 'it is like pouring vinegar on a wound'. In Je. ii. 22 nitre (RV 'lye') is used in a purificatory sense: mixed with oil it formed a kind of soap (*q.v.*). See ARTS AND CRAFTS, III*h*.

BIBLIOGRAPHY. R. J. Forbes, *Studies in Ancient Technology*, III, 1955. J.D.D.

NO, NO-AMON. Generally identified with Thebes in Upper Egypt, once Egypt's most magnificent capital. Heb. *No* corresponds to the Egyp. *nìw*(*t*), 'the City' *par excellence*, and No-Amon to the Egyp. phrase *nìw*(*t*)-'*Imn*, 'the City of (the god) Amūn'. In Greek it is called both Thebes, the usual term in modern writings, and Diospolis magna. Some 330 miles upstream from Cairo as the crow flies, its site on the two banks of the Nile is marked on the eastern side by the two vast temple-precincts of the god Amūn (see AMON), now known by the Arab. names Karnak and Luxor, and on the western side by a row of royal funerary temples from modern Qurneh to Medinet Habu, behind which extends a vast necropolis of rock-cut tombs.

Thebes first rose to national importance in the Middle Kingdom (early second millennium BC), as the home town of the powerful pharaohs of the XIIth Dynasty (see EGYPT, History); however, the land was then administered not from Thebes in the far south, but from the better-placed Itjet-Tawy just south of ancient Memphis (*q.v.*) and modern Cairo. During the Second Intermediate Period Thebes became the centre of Egyp. opposition to the foreign Hyksos kings, and from Thebes came the famous XVIIIth Dynasty kings, who finally expelled them and established the Egyp. Empire (New Kingdom). During the imperial XVIII–XXth Dynasties, *c.* 1570–1085 BC, the treasures of Asia and Africa poured into the coffers of Amūn of Thebes, now state god of the Empire. All this wealth plus the continuing gifts of Late Period pharaohs such as Shishak (*q.v.*) fell as spoil to the conquering Assyrians under Ashurbanipal in 663 BC amid fire and slaughter. In predicting mighty Nineveh's fall, no more lurid comparison could Nahum (iii. 8–10) draw upon than the fate of Thebes. The force of this comparison rules out attempts occasionally made to identify Nahum's No-Amon with a Lower Egyp. city of the same name. The Nile, Nahum's 'rivers', was truly Thebes' defence. The Late Period pharaohs made full use of its E Delta branches and irrigation and drainage canals as Egypt's first line of defence, with sea-coast forts at the Nile mouths and across the road from Palestine—perhaps alluded to in the phrase 'wall(s) from the sea' (-coast inwards?). To this protection was added Thebes' great distance upstream, which invaders had to traverse to reach her. In the early 6th century BC both Jeremiah (xlvi. 25) and Ezekiel

(xxx. 14–16) proclaimed judgment against No and other cities. K.A.K.

NOAH. The last of the ten antediluvian Patriarchs and hero of the Flood (*q.v.*). He was the son of Lamech, who was 182 (Samaritan Pentateuch, 53; LXX, 188) years old when Noah was born (Gn. v. 28, 29; Lk. iii. 36).

a. Name

The etymology of the name, *nōaḥ*, is uncertain, though many commentators connect it with the root *nwḥ*, 'to rest'. In Genesis (v. 29) it is associated with the verb *nḥm* (translated 'comfort' in AV and RV; 'bring relief in RSV), with which it is perhaps etymologically connected; though this is not necessarily required by the text. Names similar to this are known from the cuneiform sources, one being on a fragment of what is probably a Hurrian version of the Mesopotamian flood story, which was discovered at Boghaz-Koi in Asia Minor. On this a name occurs, written with the divine determinative, which may be read *na-aḫ-ma-ú/al-li-el*. It has been suggested that this name might be a compound of *nḥm* and *'el*, 'God brought relief', agreeing with the use of the word *nḥm* in Genesis. This text is too fragmentary, however, for its purport to be certain. The LXX gives the name as *Nōe*, in which form it appears in the New Testament, and is consequently rendered Noe in the AV New Testament.

b. Life and character

Noah was a righteous man (Gn. vi. 9, *ṣaddîq*), having the righteousness that comes of faith (Heb. xi. 7, *hē kata pistin dikaiosynē*, literally 'the according to faith righteousness'), and had close communion with God, as is indicated by the expression he 'walked with God' (Gn. vi. 9). He is also described as without fault among his contemporaries (Gn. vi. 9; AV 'perfect in his generations') who had all sunk to a very low moral level (Gn. vi. 1–5, 11–13; Mt. xxiv. 37, 38; Lk. xvii. 26, 27), and to them he preached righteousness (2 Pet. ii. 5), though without success, as subsequent events showed. Like the other early Patriarchs, Noah was blessed with great length of years. He was 500 years old when his first son was born (Gn. v. 32), 600 when the Flood came (Gn. vii. 11), and died at the age of 950 (Gn. ix. 28, 29). According to the most likely interpretation of Gn. vi. 3, together with 1 Pet. iii. 20, when Noah was 480 years old God informed him that He was going to destroy man from the earth but would allow a period of grace for 120 years, during which time Noah was to build an ark (*q.v.*), in which he would save his immediate family and a representative selection of animals (Gn. vi. 13–22). It was probably during this period that Noah preached, but there was no repentance, and the Flood (*q.v.*) came and destroyed all but Noah, his three sons, and their four wives (Gn. vii. 7; 1 Pet. iii. 20).

After the Flood Noah, who had probably been a farmer before it, planted a vineyard (Gn. ix. 20; 'And Noah, the husbandman, began and planted a vineyard . . .', which is to be preferred to the EVV) and, becoming drunk, behaved in an unseemly way in his tent. Ham, seeing his father naked, informed his two brothers, who covered him, but it is probable that Canaan, Ham's son, did something disrespectful to his grandfather, for Noah placed a curse on him when he awoke (Gn. ix. 20–27; see HAM).

c. God's covenant with Noah

The covenant implied in Gn. vi. 18 might be interpreted as salvation for Noah conditional upon his building and entering the ark, which obligations he fulfilled (verse 22). On the other hand, it may be that this passage simply makes reference to the covenant which God made with Noah after the Flood, and which He sealed by conferring a new significance on the rainbow (Gn. ix. 9–17; *cf.* Is. liv. 9). The main features of this covenant were that it was entirely instituted by God, that it was universal in scope, applying not only to Noah and his seed after him but to every living creature, that it was unconditional, and that it was everlasting. In it God undertook from His own free lovingkindness never again to destroy all flesh with a flood.

d. Descendants

Noah is stated to have had three sons, Shem, Ham, and Japheth (*qq.v.*; Gn. v. 32, ix. 18, 19, x. 1), who were born before the Flood, and accompanied him in the ark. After the Flood their descendants were dispersed over a wide area, and the Table of the Nations (see NATIONS, TABLE OF) in Gn. x gives an account of where they later travelled. It is probable that Noah had other children and descendants who are not mentioned in the biblical narratives, for Gn. x lays no claim to being exhaustive.

e. Cuneiform parallels

In the flood accounts which have been preserved in Akkadian the name of the hero is Utanapishtim, which corresponds to the name Ziusuddu in a Sumerian account of the early second millennium BC, which probably lies behind the Akkadian versions (see FLOOD). Though in the principal version of the Sumerian king list only eight rulers are named before the Flood, of whom Ziusuddu is not one, other texts list ten rulers, the tenth being Ziusuddu, who is credited with a reign of 36,000 years. The same is found in a late account in Greek by the Babylonian priest Berossos, whose flood hero Xisouthros is the tenth of his pre-flood rulers.

BIBLIOGRAPHY. J. Murray, *The Covenant of Grace*, 1954, pp. 12–16; E. A. Speiser, *Mesopotamian Origins*, 1930, pp. 160, 161; T. Jacobsen, *The Sumerian King List*, 1939, pp. 76, 77 and n. 34. T.C.M.

NOB. A locality mentioned in three passages of the Old Testament, all of which may refer to the same place.

In 1 Sa. xxii. 19 it is referred to as a city of priests; presumably Yahweh's priests had fled there with the ephod after the capture of the ark and the destruction of Shiloh (1 Sa. iv. 11). David visited Nob after he had escaped from Saul when Ahimelech was priest there and ate holy bread (1 Sa. xxi. 6). When Saul heard the news that the priest of Nob had assisted the fugitive David he raided the shrine and had Ahimelech, along with eighty-five other priests, put to death (1 Sa. xxii. 9, 11, 18, 19).

Isaiah prophesied that the Assyrian invaders would reach Nob, between Anathoth, 2½ miles north-east of Jerusalem, and the capital (Is. x. 32), and the city is also mentioned in Ne. xi. 32 as a village which was reinhabited after the return from exile.

The latter two references indicate a locality near Jerusalem, probably the modern Râs Umm et-Tala on the eastern slopes of Mt. Scopus, north-east of Jerusalem (Grollenberg, *Atlas of the Bible*, 1956). S. R. Driver (*Notes on the Hebrew Text of the Books of Samuel*², 1913, p. 172) suggests perhaps a spot on the Rās el-Meshārif, 1 mile north of Jerusalem, a ridge from the brow of which (2,685 feet) the pilgrim along the north road still catches his first view of the holy city (2,593 feet). R.A.H.G.

NOBAH. 1. An Amorite locality settled and named by Nobah and his followers; probably the same which lay on the line of Gideon's pursuit of the Midianites *via* Succoth and Jogbehah (Jdg. viii. 11). If so, its position cannot be exactly determined. The Amorite name Kenath has been linked with Kanawat (Eusebius' *Kanatha*), a city in Hellenistic times, 60 miles east of lake Tiberias; but this is improbably far afield.

2. A Manassite leader (Nu. xxxii. 42). J.P.U.L.

NOD. A land to the east of, or in front of, Eden (*qiḏmaṭ-'ēḏen*, Gn. iv. 16), to which Cain was banished by God after he had murdered Abel. The name (*nôḏ*) is the same in form as the infinitive of the verb *nûḏ* (*nwd*), 'to move to and fro, wander', the participle of which is used in Gn. iv. 14 when Cain bemoans the fact that he will become a 'vagabond' (RV 'wanderer'). The name is unknown outside the Bible, but its form and the context suggest that it was a region where a nomadic existence was necessary, such as is today found in several parts of the Middle East. T.C.M.

NODAB. A tribe which, among others, is mentioned in 1 Ch. v. 19 as having been conquered by Reuben, Gad, and half-Manasseh, and about whom nothing more is definitely known. See HAGRITES.

NOMADS. A human group which changes its area of residence seasonally within a larger domain which is its home territory.

I. IN THE BIBLE

The word 'nomad' does not occur in EVV of the Bible, the nomadic groups appearing in it under other names.

The first nomad was Cain (*q.v.*), who was banished from his kindred to be a wanderer (Gn. iv). A number of nomadic groups are mentioned in the Table of the Nations in Gn. x (see NATIONS, TABLE OF). Among the descendants of Japheth are such names as Gomer (Cimmerians), Madai (Medes), Meshek (perhaps Phrygians), and Ashkenaz (Scythians) (*qq.v.*), all peoples who probably came originally from the northern steppe. Heth, among the children of Ham, may be the Hittites of Asia Minor, though it is perhaps more probable that the reference is to the later Neo-Hittite states of N Syria (see HITTITES). Among the descendants of Shem are listed Aram (Aramaeans) (*q.v.*), and a number of Arabian tribes, some of them still nomadic in historical times, who stemmed from the Arabian peninsula.

The patriarchal period was largely a time of nomadism for God's chosen remnant. It is uncertain whether Abraham was actually living a sedentary life within the city of Ur when he was called by God. He is later called 'the Hebrew' (Gn. xiv. 13), and this may indicate that he was one of the Habiru (see HEBREWS) living outside the city in perhaps a client status. In such a situation he could still be a man of substance, as he undoubtedly was. How long he and his fathers had been at Ur is not stated, but when he left he began a nomadic life which was continued by Isaac and Jacob for two long generations, before the children of Israel settled to the sedentary life of Egypt (*cf.* Heb. xi. 9). This was not the regular seasonal movement of nomads within a set territory, but a wandering from place to place; and, though Abraham had camels (*e.g.* Gn. xxiv; for the view of some scholars that patriarchal camels are anachronistic, see CAMEL), his herds were largely of sheep and goats, and included asses (Gn. xxii. 3), so that some would class him as a semi-nomad or an 'ass-nomad'. Such a life would fit in well with the times as illuminated by the Mari archives (see ARCHAEOLOGY, VIII, *c*). Terah and his sons Nahor and Haran by remaining at Harran established affiliations with another nomadic group, the Aramaeans, as is shown by the reference to a 'wandering Aramaean' as the ancestor of the Israelites (Dt. xxvi. 5, RSV).

After experiencing the luxuries of a sedentary life in Egypt, even though oppressed, the Israelites at the Exodus were reluctant to return to the rigours of wandering. The forty years in the wilderness was a unique episode, for without the miraculous supply of food provided by God the numbers of the people would have been far too great to be supported by the natural resources of the area.

After the settlement in the promised land the true nomadic life ceased for the Israelites, but various reminiscences of it survive in the Old

Testament. For instance, in many cases a man's house is referred to as his 'tent' (*e.g.* Jdg. xix. 9, xx. 8; 1 Sa. iv. 10, xiii. 2; 2 Sa. xviii. 17, xx. 1; 1 Ki. viii. 66, xii. 16, xxii. 17, 36). To express the idea of rising early the verb *šāḵam* (in the Hiph'il stem), which properly means 'to load the backs (of beasts)', is used (*e.g.* Jdg. xix. 9; 1 Sa. xvii. 20). Certain metaphors used in poetry suggest a nomadic background: in Jb. iv. 21 (RV) the plucking up of a tent cord signifies death; in Je. x. 20 the breaking of tent cords indicates desolation, and conversely, a sound tent speaks of security (Is. xxxiii. 20); in Is. liv. 2 a prosperous people is signified by an enlarged tent space.

The Israelites came in contact with various nomadic groups after they had settled in the land. The Aramaeans had by the first millennium largely settled in the city states of Syria, so that the nomadic threat came mostly from the east and south, where the *bᵉnê qeḏem*, 'the Children of the East' (*q.v.*; *cf.* Ezk. xxv. 4) and such associated peoples as the Midianites, Amalekites, Moabites, Edomites, Ammonites, and Kedarites (*qq.v.*) would always take advantage of weakness in the settled territories. Solomon's commercial expansion in the 10th century brought contacts with Arabia (*q.v.*) and the caravan traders of that area. In the 9th century Jehoshaphat was able to exact tribute from the Arabs (2 Ch. xvii. 11), but the family of Jehoram were carried off by this people in a raid (2 Ch. xxi. 16, 17). Throughout the Monarchy, the Arabs are mentioned in various capacities (*e.g.* Is. xiii. 20, xxi. 13; Je. iii. 2, xxv. 23, 24; Ezk. xxvii. 21).

After the return from the Exile the nomadic traders who were settling on the eastern fringes of Syria–Palestine are exemplified by Geshem (*q.v.*) the Arab, who tried to hinder the rebuilding of Jerusalem (Ne. ii. 19, vi. 6). These people were followed in New Testament times by the Nabataeans (*q.v.*).

With the moral corruption which accompanied the settlement in the land, the prophets used the ideal of the nomadic life as a figure of spiritual health. They condemned the luxuries of city life (Am. iii. 15, vi. 8) and spoke of a return to the simplicity of the early days of Israel in the wilderness (Ho. ii. 14, 15, xii. 9). It is probable that this call to the desert was put into practice from time to time, as is evidenced by the Qumran Community (see QUMRAN) in the inter-testamental period, and by John the Baptist, and Jesus Christ and His disciples in New Testament times. Though this was not nomadism in the strict sense, it was a manifestation of that value of nomadism which has always been held forth as an aim for God's people; to be pilgrims in this world, and to avoid the laying up of treasure upon earth. See also RECHABITES; KENITES.

II. WAY OF LIFE

A nomadic group depends for its livelihood upon herds of animals such as the horse, camel, sheep, goat, or ox, and the pasturing needs of the herds determine the movements of the community. This way of life is required by the terrain inhabited, which usually consists mainly of an area of steppe or plain which provides temporary pasture in the wet or cool season, and either oases or uplands to which a retreat is made in the dry season. Under normal conditions a nomadic tribe will have a recognized home territory, different parts of which it visits regularly in a seasonal cycle. Thus each tribe or, in more barren areas, smaller group visits annually its recognized tract of pasture, and returns annually to the same oasis or upland territory. Mobile dwellings are provided by tents of skins, felt, or wool, and all equipment is strictly limited. There are variations from area to area. Some groups, mainly camel herders, abandon the plain for an oasis or upland only when compelled by drought; others, particularly shepherds, have semi-permanent dwellings at the oasis, even planting and raising crops, and go out on the plain only when the animals' needs for pasture compel it. Peoples of this latter type are sometimes called semi-nomads.

Such an economy is finely adjusted, and the natural increase of population disturbs the balance. In consequence, a growing group may encroach on a neighbour's traditional territory, and the weaker group is displaced, perhaps setting up a chain effect which may cause the fringe groups to look abroad. Sedentary farming communities fall an easy prey to the overspilling nomads who may set themselves as a military aristocracy over the less-vigorous population. A few generations, however, usually suffice for the interlopers to be absorbed by the dominant though less-aggressive culture of the settled peoples.

The most advantageous situation for a nomadic group is in a mixed country where city-states and their surrounding tilled territory are interspersed by less-intensively settled areas where the nomad can make his encampments and exploit the vulnerable settlements. This may be done either by mobile raids or by taking service either as mercenary troops or as labourers.

Certain values arise from the demands of the nomadic life. The mutual dependence of the members of a tribe, together with the consciousness of common descent, lead to great solidarity (see FAMILY) and to such concomitant practices as blood revenge (see AVENGER OF BLOOD) for murder or manslaughter. The need for mobility results in the reduction of property to that which is movable, wealth being accumulated in livestock. The rigours of life lead also to hospitality to the traveller and to chivalry, sometimes of a kind strange to the sedentary farmer.

III. THE ANCIENT NEAR EAST

There were two main areas supporting nomadic populations in ancient times, from which the more settled regions of the Near East suffered the influx of marauders. These were the peninsula of Arabia and the steppe of S Russia. Access from Arabia was easier than from the north, since the latter area lay across a mountain barrier, and for the nomads of N Arabia some of the oases visited seasonally lay on the very margins of the settled areas of Palestine and Syria.

a. The southern nomads

It is probable that Arabia was the immediate homeland of the Semites (Semitic speakers), and since from the earliest historical times in Mesopotamia the Semitic Akkadians formed part of the population, a continual influx of nomads from the Arabian peninsula may be inferred. Knowledge of the arrival of nomads from Arabia is very much conditioned by the surviving evidence. Written records are meagre from Palestine, intermittent from Syria, but more extensive from Mesopotamia. In Mesopotamia, however, the fullest records come from periods of political strength, when encroaching nomads could be most effectively resisted, and indeed, according to the records, the best-attested route of overt entry to Mesopotamia was from the north, though a peaceful infiltration into Babylonia from the west may be assumed. The early part of the second millennium BC, following the fall of the IIIrd Dynasty of Ur, was a period of weakness in Babylonia, and of consequent nomadic invasions from the north, the invaders, particularly the 'Amorites' (*q.v.*), finally establishing themselves as ruling dynasties in the cities of Babylonia. During the time of the greatest of these dynasties, the 1st of Babylon, the diplomatic archives discovered at the city of Mari (see ARCHAEOLOGY, VIII, *c*) on the Middle Euphrates give a glimpse of the situation in N Mesopotamia–Syria, where the city states were interspersed by territory occupied by nomadic groups. One group known as the Hanaeans (*Ḫanû*) provided the king of Mari with mercenary troops, and, though they lived in encampments, some of them were beginning to settle in permanent dwellings. A more troublesome group were the Benjaminites (Bini-Iamin, written TUR(pl)-*ia-mi-in*; however, the logogram TUR, 'son', was perhaps more likely to have been read *mâru* than *binu*; see BENJAMIN), who spread through the steppe area between the Ḫabur river and the Euphrates and farther west, particularly in the vicinity of Harran, being frequently mentioned as raiding settlements and even attacking towns. The Sutaeans (*Sutû*) likewise raided farther south, particularly on the trade routes connecting the Euphrates with Syria. Another group of people, the Habiru (see HEBREWS), who are mentioned in the second half of the second millennium in documents from Nuzi, Alalaḫ, Hattusas, Ugarit, El-Amarna, and in native Egyptian documents, are already mentioned earlier (18th century BC) in the Mari letters and in documents of the same general period from Alalaḫ, Cappadocia, and S Mesopotamia. These people seem to have been nomads or semi-nomads who are found now as raiders, now as settlers in the towns, serving sometimes as mercenary troops, and sometimes as labourers or even slaves.

These are the principal nomadic groups mentioned in the Mari archives from this period, but they were no doubt typical of peoples at other periods who menaced the isolated city-states, particularly of N Mesopotamia and Syria–Palestine. Some were probably more in the nature of travelling craftsmen than raiders, and such a group is depicted on a 19th-century BC wall painting at Beni Hasan in Egypt (see fig. 146, No. 5; see also *IBA*, fig. 25).

In the succeeding centuries another nomadic group which spread through Syria–Palestine and into Egypt was the Hyksos (see EGYPT), and again mainly during the second millennium yet another body of nomads, the Aramaeans (*q.v.*), and a related group, the Aḫlamu, began to come into prominence. During the centuries around the turn of the second to the first millennium, these people and their congeners flooded W Asia, putting a halt to the growing dominion of Assyria, and founding many city-states in the area of Syria and N Mesopotamia.

These groups of nomads are the principal ones known from the written documents, who probably came ultimately from the Arabian peninsula. More directly from the peninsula were groups of Arabs (see ARABIA), who are mentioned in the Assyrian inscriptions and depicted in the bas-reliefs as riding camels and living in tents (see fig. 50). Later in the first millennium such posts as Petra and Palmyra on the fringes of the sown were settled by Arab tribes who were able to profit from the caravan traffic.

b. The northern nomads

Access to the Near East was more difficult for the northern nomads who inhabited the S Russian steppe; the principal route of entry was between the Caspian and the Black Seas and into Asia Minor and Iran. Signs of the influx of the northern nomads are found already in the middle of the third millennium at the 'Royal Tombs' of Alaca Hüyük in central Asia Minor, where a warrior aristocracy had imposed itself on the peasant population. These were predecessors of the Indo-European-speaking Hittites who established an empire in Asia Minor in the second millennium. It is clear that, like the Hittites, many of the invaders from the North were Indo-European-speaking. In the second millennium the Kassites in Babylonia and the rulers of Mitanni in N Mesopotamia betray, in their names and certain elements of vocabulary, their Indo-European origins. These people were among the first to introduce the horse and chariot (*qq.v.*) to W Asia, and it is probable that this was a combination developed on the steppe. In the late second millennium the Phrygians in Asia Minor repeated the pattern of a dominating warrior aristocracy, and later the Cimmerians are encountered as warlike raiders. In the first millennium the Medes and Persians came to prominence in Iran, the latter finally founding an empire which dominated the entire Near East. In the Assyrian inscriptions the earlier groups of the raiding warriors are known as Ummanmanda (see ASSYRIA).

BIBLIOGRAPHY. *General:* C. D. Forde, *Habitat, Economy and Society*[4], 1942, pp. 308–351. *Bible:* R. de Vaux, *Les Institutions de l'Ancien Testament*, I, 1958, pp. 15–33, 319–321; D. J. Wiseman, *The Word of God for Abraham and Today*, 1959, pp. 10–12; H. Charles in L. Pirot *et al.* (eds.), *Dictionnaire de la Bible, Supplément*, VI, 1959, coll. 541–550. *Ancient Near East:* F. Gabrieli (ed.), *L'Antica Società Beduina*, 1959; J. R. Kupper, *Les nomades en Mésopotamie au temps des rois de Mari*, 1957; S. Moscati, *The Semites in Ancient History*, 1959; T. T. Rice, *The Scythians*, 1958, esp. pp. 33–55. T.C.M.

NOSE, NOSTRILS (Heb. *'ap̄*, 'nose' or 'nostril'). The organ of breathing, used also of the face, perhaps by synecdoche, especially in the expression 'face to the ground' in worship or homage. The Hebrews apparently thought no further into the respiratory process, and no word for lung occurs in the Bible. The presence of breath in the nostrils was connected with life (see LIFE, SOUL, SPIRIT) (Gn. ii. 7; Jb. xxvii. 3), and the temporary nature thereof (Is. ii. 22). The word also denotes the nose as the organ of smelling (Dt. xxxiii. 10, RVmg; Ps. cxv. 6; Am. iv. 10). When breath was emitted visibly (called 'smoke', Ps. xviii. 8) it was connected with the expression of inner emotion, principally anger. By metonymy the word *'ap̄* often comes to mean 'anger' (Gn. xxvii. 45; Jb. iv. 9), and is used figuratively thus in the Old Testament far more frequently than in the literal sense. It is apparent from cognate languages (*e.g.* Akkadian *appu*, 'face') that the physical designation is the original. The word is not found in the New Testament. B.O.B.

NUMBER.

I. GENERAL USAGE

Israel shared with most of her Mediterranean and Near Eastern neighbours, *e.g.* Assyria, Egypt, Greece, Rome, and Phoenicia, the decimal system of counting. The numbers recorded in the Hebrew text of the Old Testament are written in words, as in the main are the figures in the Greek text of the New Testament. Numbers are also written in word form on the Moabite Stone and the Siloam Inscription.

In Hebrew the number one is an adjective. A series of nouns denote the numbers two to ten. Combinations of these numbers with ten give eleven to nineteen. After twenty the tens are formed in a pattern similar to that used in English, *i.e.* three, thirty. A separate word denotes one hundred; two hundred is the dual form of this, and from three to nine hundred there is again a pattern similar to that found in the English numeral system. The highest number expressed by one word is twenty thousand, the dual form of ten thousand.

Aramaic papyri from Egypt from the 6th to the 4th centuries BC, Aramaic endorsements on cuneiform tablets from Mesopotamia and Aramaic ostraca found at Samaria provide evidence of an early system of numerical notation within the Old Testament period. Vertical strokes, generally grouped in threes, were used for digits and horizontal strokes for tens. These latter generally had a downward hook on the right, and they were written one above the other to form a double hook for twenties. A stylized *mem* represented a hundred, with vertical strokes added to indicate hundreds. An abbreviation of the word 'a thousand' was used to indicate this figure. Hebrew ostraca from the kingdoms also show vertical strokes for units, and it is considered that a sign resembling a Greek lambda represented ten and a sign similar to an early *gimel* stood for five on Hebrew ostraca from Samaria dating from before the 7th century. (See also WEIGHTS AND MEASURES for marking of denominations on weights.)

H. L. Allrick (*BASOR*, 136, December 1954, pp. 21–27) proposes that originally the lists in Ne. vii and Ezr. ii were written in the early Hebrew–Aramaic numeral notation, and he suggests that an explanation of certain differences between the lists may be found in this fact.

The idea of using letters of the alphabet for numerals originated from Greek influence or at least during the period of Greek influence, and, as far as is known, first appeared on Maccabean coins. The first nine letters were used for the figures one to nine, the tens from ten to ninety were represented by the next nine, and the hundreds from one hundred to four hundred by the remaining four letters. The number fifteen, however, was denoted by a combination of *ṭeth* (equals nine) and *waw* (equals six), as the two letters *yod* (equals ten) and *he* (equals five) were the consonants of Yah, a form of the sacred name Yahweh. Further numbers were denoted by a combination of letters. There are ordinal numbers in biblical Hebrew from one to ten, after which the cardinal numbers are used. There are also words for fractions from a half to a fifth. Numbers in biblical Greek follow the pattern used in Hellenistic Greek.

An indication of the mathematical concept of infinity may be found in the statement in Rev. vii. 9 where the redeemed are 'a great multitude, which no man could number'. In a concrete image this concept is expressed in the Old Testament as, *e.g.*, Gn. xiii. 16, RSV: 'I will make your descendants as the dust of the earth: so that if one can count the dust of the earth, your descendants also can be counted.' *Cf.* also Gn. xv. 5, RSV: 'Look toward heaven, and number the stars, if you are able to number them.'

The elementary processes of arithmetic are recorded in the Old Testament, *e.g.* addition, Nu. i. 17 ff. and Nu. i. 45; subtraction, Lv. xxvii. 18; multiplication, Lv. xxv. 8.

In certain passages it is evident that numbers are being used in an approximate sense. The numbers 'two', 'two or three', 'three or four', 'four or five' are sometimes used with the meaning of 'a few', *e.g.* 1 Ki. xvii. 12, where the widow of Zarephath says, 'I am gathering two sticks', and also Lv. xxvi. 8 'five of you shall chase an hundred'. Similar usages are found in 2 Ki. vi. 10; Is. xvii. 6; for 'three or four', see Am. i. 3 ff. and Pr. xxx. 15 ff. From the New Testament we may quote the use of round numbers by Paul in 1 Cor. xiv. 19. 'Yet in the church I had rather speak five words with my understanding, that by my voice I might teach others also, than ten thousand words in an unknown tongue.' *Cf.* also Mt. xviii. 22.

It would seem that 'ten' was used as the equivalent of 'quite a number of times,' and we may instance Jacob's words in Gn. xxxi. 7, where it is recorded that Laban changed his wages 'ten times'; *cf.* also Nu. xiv. 22. That Saul, David, and Solomon are recorded as having reigned for forty years, and the recurring statement in the book of Judges that the land had rest forty years (Jdg. iii. 11, v. 31, viii. 28) seem to indicate that forty was used to stand for a generation, or quite a considerable number, or length of time. A hundred, *e.g.* Ec. vi. 3, would equal a large number, and a thousand, ten thousand (Dt. xxxii. 30; Lv. xxvi. 8), and forty thousand (Jdg. v. 8) provide instances of round numbers which indicate an indefinitely large number. In the case of large numbers for the strength of armies, *e.g.* 2 Ch. xiv. 9, these are in all probability approximate estimates, as also seems to be the case with the number of David's census (2 Sa. xxiv. 9; *cf.* 1 Ch. xxi. 5), and perhaps the 7,000 sheep sacrificed in Jerusalem (2 Ch. xv. 11).

II. LARGE NUMBERS IN THE OLD TESTAMENT

The large numbers recorded in certain parts of the Old Testament have occasioned considerable difficulties. These are concerned chiefly with the chronology of the early periods of Old Testament history, where the problem is further complicated by the presence of differing figures in the various texts and versions, with the numbers of the Israelites at the time of the Exodus, and the numbers of warriors in various armies, and especially of the numbers of the slain of enemy forces. With regard to the first problem one may instance that the Hebrew text gives 1,656 years as the time between the creation and the flood, the LXX 2,262 years, and the Samaritan 1,307. Or for the age of Methuselah the Hebrew text gives 969 years and the Samaritan 720. (See CHRONOLOGY OF THE OLD TESTAMENT.) A similar problem exists in the New Testament regarding the number of persons on board the ship on which Paul travelled to Rome. Some MSS give 276 and others 76 (Acts xxvii. 37). Again the number of the beast (Rev. xiii. 18) is given variously as 666 and 616.

The possibility that error occurred during the transmission of numbers in the text of the Scriptures must therefore be conceded. See, for example, 2 Sa. xv. 7, where 'four' should be read for 'forty', a confusion of tens and units which is the type of error which could creep in during copying of the text when, as in the Old Testament (see above), numbers are written as words.

Some conservative scholars have accepted the large numbers mentioned in Nu. i. 46 for the total of Israelite warriors aged twenty years and above, and from this census we may calculate a total population for the multitude of Israelites in the wilderness of between two and three millions. Such scholars have pointed to the miraculous preservation and sustaining power of God (*cf.*, *e.g.*, *NBC*, p. 165, on Nu. i. 17–46). More critical scholars, however, have regarded the numbers as being unreal, *e.g.* G. B. Gray, *ICC*, *Numbers*, 1903, pp. 11–15, where some of the difficulties which these large numbers entail are mentioned.

Archaeological discoveries have enabled us to re-create a picture of the age and conditions of life in Egypt, the wilderness, and Canaan, and so the problems to which these large numbers give rise are seen more acutely. Some account of these difficulties will be found in J. Garstang, *Joshua–Judges*, 1931, p. 120, and of particular relevance is the fact that the population of Canaan must have been well below three million, whereas it is inferred in Ex. xxiii. 29 and Dt. vii. 7, 17, 22 that the Israelites were less in number than the Canaanites.

Various attempts have been made to retranslate the numbers and so reduce them. In certain instances the Hebrew word *'elep̄*, 'a thousand', can be translated 'family' or 'tent-group'; *e.g.* Jdg. vi. 15, 'my family (*'alpî*) is poor in Manasseh'. Hence Sir Flinders Petrie has suggested (*Egypt and Israel*, 1911, p. 42 ff.) that the word translated 'thousands' in the two censuses should be retranslated as 'families', and this would give totals from five to six thousand warriors. A more up-to-date presentation of what is substantially the same argument, in the light of modern archaeological knowledge, is given by G. E. Mendenhall, 'The Census Lists of Numbers 1 and 26', *JBL*, LXXVII, 1958, pp. 52 ff. C. S. Jarvis, *Yesterday and Today in Sinai*, 1936, calculates from the number of fighting men that a total of at least 27,000 Israelites was involved in the Exodus and wilderness pilgrimage, and this figure would fit the general historical picture.

In a paper on 'The Large Numbers of the Old Testament' (*JTVI*, LXXXVII, 1955, pp. 82 ff.), R. E. D. Clark has endeavoured in a similar manner to reduce these, and some of the other large numbers in the Old Testament, *e.g.* the death of 50,070 male inhabitants of Beth-shemesh who were killed for irreverent treatment of the ark of God (1 Sa. vi. 19), the number of Jehoshaphat's army of 1,160,000 (2 Ch. xvii). 1 Ki. xx. 30 records that a wall fell and killed 27,000 people. He points out that another translation of *'elep̄* (or, otherwise vocalized, *'allup̄*) is 'captain'. Thus in 1 Ch. xii the 50,000 of Zebulun would mean fifty captains, and the total number of men who feasted with David, *i.e.* the captains, would be considerably reduced.

With regard to the enormous numbers who are often stated as having fallen in battle, he points out that in ancient battles the mighty men did most of the fighting, as, for example, in the contest between David and Goliath, and therefore it would be so many 'mighty men', rather than so many 'thousands', who fell in battle.

Hence in the census in Nu. i it could be that at some stage in the transmission of the text *'elep̄* (*'allup̄*), 'captain', has been confused with *'elep̄*, 'a thousand', and he suggests that, *e.g.*, the 62,700 for the tribe of Dan might originally have read sixty captains and 2,700 warriors.

III. SIGNIFICANT NUMBERS

In addition to the above consideration of numbers in the Bible, mention must also be made of the use of numbers with a symbolical or theological significance.

One is used to convey the concept of the unity and uniqueness of God, *e.g.* Dt. vi. 4, 'The Lord our God is one Lord'. The human race stems from one (Acts xvii. 26). The entry of sin into the world is through one man (Rom. v. 12). The gift of grace is by one man, Jesus Christ (Rom. v. 15). His sacrifice in death is a once for all offering (Heb. vii. 27), and He is the firstborn from the dead (Col. i. 18), the firstfruits of the dead (1 Cor. xv. 20). 'One' also expresses the unity between Christ and the Father (Jn. x. 30), the union between believers and the Godhead, and the unity which exists among Christians (Jn. xvii. 21; Gal. iii. 28). 'One' further expresses singleness of purpose (Lk. x. 42). The concept of union is also found in the saying of Jesus concerning marriage, 'and the twain shall become one flesh' (Mt. xix. 6, RV).

Two can be a figure both of unity and of division. Man and woman form the basic family unit (Gn. i. 27, ii. 20, 24). Animals associate in pairs and enter the ark in twos (Gn. vii. 9). Two people often work together in companionship, *e.g.* Joshua's spies (Jos. ii. 1), and the Twelve and Seventy disciples were sent out in pairs (Mk. vi. 7; Lk. x. 1). In addition, at Sinai there were two stone tablets, and animals were often offered for sacrifice in pairs. By contrast two is used with separating force in 1 Ki. xviii. 21, 'How long halt ye between two opinions?', as it is also implied in the two 'ways' of Mt. vii. 13, 14.

Three. It is natural to associate the number three with the Trinity of Persons in the Godhead, and the following references among others may be instanced: Mt. xxviii. 19; Jn. xiv. 26, xv. 26; 2 Cor. xiii. 14; 1 Pet. i. 2, where this teaching is implied. The number three is also associated with certain of God's mighty acts. At Mt. Sinai the Lord was to come down to give His Law on 'the third day' (Ex. xix. 11). In Hosea's prophecy the Lord would raise up His people 'in the third day', probably meaning a short time (Ho. vi. 2). There is a similar usage of 'three' in Lk. xiii. 32, where 'third day' is 'poetical for the moment when something is finished, completed, and perfected' (N. Geldenhuys, *Commentary on the Gospel of Luke*, 1950, p. 384, n. 4). Jonah was delivered (Jon. i. 17; Mt. xii. 40), and God raised Christ from the dead, on the third day (1 Cor. xv. 4). There were three disciples admitted to special terms of intimacy with Christ (Mk. ix. 2; Mt. xxvi. 37), and at Calvary there were three crosses. Paul emphasizes three Christian virtues (1 Cor. xiii. 13). A further instance of three being used in connection with periods of time is the choice offered to David of three days' pestilence, three months' defeat, or three years' famine (1 Ch. xxi. 12). The deployment of Gideon's army furnishes an example of division into three (Jdg. vii. 16), and the fraction, a third, is employed in Rev. viii. 7–12.

Four, the number of the sides of a square, is one of symbols of completion in the Bible. The divine name Yahweh has four letters in Hebrew (YHWH). There were four rivers flowing out of the garden of Eden (Gn. ii. 10) and there are four corners of the earth (Rev. vii. 1, xx. 8), from whence blow the four winds (Je. xlix. 36; Ezk. xxxvii. 9; Dn. vii. 2). In his vision of the glory of God, Ezekiel saw four living creatures (chapter i), and with these we may compare the four living creatures of Rev. iv. 6.

The history of the world from the time of the Babylonian Empire is spanned by four kingdoms (Dn. ii, vii). Four is a prominent number in prophetic symbolism and apocalyptic literature, as the following additional references show: four carpenters (RSV 'smith') and four horns (Zc. i. 18–21), four chariots (Zc. vi. 1–8), four horns of the altar (Rev. ix. 13), four angels of destruction (Rev. ix. 14). In addition, there are four Gospels, and at the time when the gospel was extended to the Gentiles Peter saw in a vision a sheet let down by its four corners.

Five and *ten*, and their multiples, occur frequently on account of the decimal system used in Palestine. In the Old Testament ten Patriarchs are mentioned before the flood. The Egyptians were visited with ten plagues and there were Ten Commandments. The fraction one-tenth formed the tithe (Gn. xiv. 20, xxviii. 22; Lv. xxvii. 30; 2 Ch. xxxi. 5; Mal. iii. 10). In the parable of Lk. xv. 8 the woman possessed ten coins, and in the parable of the pounds mention is made of ten pounds, ten servants, and ten cities (Lk. xix. 11–27). Of the ten virgins, five were wise and five foolish (Mt. xxv. 2). Five sparrows were sold for two farthings (Lk. xii. 6); Dives had five brothers (Lk. xvi. 28); the woman by the well had had five husbands (Jn. iv. 18), and at the feeding of the five thousand the lad had five loaves. There are ten powers which cannot separate the believer from the love of God (Rom. viii. 38 f.) and ten sins which exclude from the kingdom of God (1 Cor. vi. 10). The number ten, therefore, also signifies completeness; ten elders form a company (Ru. iv. 2).

Six. In the creation narrative God created man and woman on the sixth day (Gn. i. 27). Six days were allotted to man for labour (Ex. xx. 9, xxiii. 12, xxxi. 15; *cf.* Lk. xiii. 14). A Hebrew servant had to serve for six years before he was freed.

The number six is therefore closely associated with man.

Seven has an eminent place among sacred numbers in the Scriptures, and is associated with completion, fulfilment, and perfection. In the creation narrative God rested from His work on the seventh day, and sanctified it. This gave a pattern to the Jewish sabbath on which man was to refrain from work (Ex. xx. 10), to the sabbatic year (Lv. xxv. 2–6), and also to the year of jubilee, which followed seven times seven years (Lv. xxv. 8). The Feast of Unleavened Bread and the Feast of Tabernacles lasted seven days (Ex. xii. 15, 19; Nu. xxix. 12). The Day of Atonement was in the seventh month (Lv. xvi. 29), and seven occurs frequently in connection with Old Testament ritual, *e.g.* the sprinkling of bullock's blood seven times (Lv. iv. 6) and the burnt-offering of seven lambs (Nu. xxviii. 11); the cleansed leper was sprinkled seven times (Lv. xiv. 7), and Naaman had to dip seven times in Jordan (2 Ki. v. 10). In the tabernacle the candlestick had seven branches (Ex. xxv. 32).

Other references to be noted are: the mother of seven sons (Je. xv. 9; 2 Macc. vii. 1 ff.); seven women for one man (Is. iv. 1); a loving daughter-in-law preferable to seven sons (Ru. iv. 15). The Sadducees proposed a case of levirate marriage with seven brothers (Mt. xxii. 25). The priests encompassed Jericho seven times (Jos. vi. 4). Elijah's servant looked for rain seven times (1 Ki. xviii. 43). The psalmist praised God seven times a day (Ps. cxix. 164), and Gn. xxix. 18, xli. 29, 54 and Dn. iv. 23 mention seven years (times). The early Church had seven deacons (Acts vi. 3) and John addresses seven churches in the book of Revelation, where there is mention of seven golden candlesticks (i. 12) and seven stars (i. 16). At the miraculous feeding of four thousand from seven loaves and a few fishes (Mk. viii. 1–9), the seven basketsful collected afterwards may indicate that Jesus can satisfy completely. The complete possession of Mary Magdalene is effected by seven demons (Lk. viii. 2), while the dragon of Rev. xii. 3 and the beast of Rev. xiii. 1, xvii. 7 has seven heads.

Eight. 1 Pet. iii. 20 records that eight people were saved in the ark of Noah. Circumcision of a Jewish boy took place on the eighth day (Gn. xvii. 12; Phil. iii. 5). In Ezekiel's vision of the new Temple the priests make their offering on the eighth day (xliii. 27).

Twelve. The Hebrew year was divided into twelve months, the day into twelve hours (Jn. xi. 9). Israel had twelve sons (Gn. xxxv. 22–27, xlii. 13, 32) and there were twelve tribes of Israel, the people of God (Gn. xlix. 28). Christ chose twelve apostles (Mt. x. 1 ff.). Twelve is therefore linked with the elective purposes of God.

Forty is associated with almost each new development in the history of God's mighty acts, especially of salvation, *e.g.* the flood, redemption from Egypt, Elijah and the prophetic era, the advent of Christ, and the birth of the Church. The following periods of forty days may be listed: the downpour of rain during the flood (Gn. vii. 17); the despatch of the raven (Gn. viii. 6); Moses' fasts on the mount (Ex. xxiv. 18, xxxiv. 28; Dt. ix. 9); the spies' exploration of the land of Canaan (Nu. xiii. 25); Moses' prayer for Israel (Dt. ix. 25); Goliath's defiance (1 Sa. xvii. 16); Elijah's journey to Horeb (1 Ki. xix. 8); Ezekiel's lying on his right side (Ezk. iv. 6); Jonah's warning to Nineveh (Jon. iii. 4); Christ's stay in the wilderness prior to His temptation (Mt. iv. 2), His appearances after His resurrection (Acts i. 3).

For forty years, the general designation of a generation, the following may be quoted: the main divisions of Moses' life (Acts vii. 23, 30, 36; Dt. xxxi. 2); Israel's wandering in the wilderness (Ex. xvi. 35; Nu. xiv. 33; Jos. v. 6; Ps. xcv. 10); the recurring pattern of servitude and deliverance in the era of the judges (*e.g.* Jdg. iii. 11, xiii. 1); the reigns of Saul, David, and Solomon (Acts xiii. 21; 2 Sa. v. 4; 1 Ki. xi. 42); the desolation of Egypt (Ezk. xxix. 11).

Seventy is often connected with God's administration of the world. After the flood the world was repopulated through seventy descendants of Noah (Gn. x); seventy persons went down to Egypt (Gn. xlvi. 27); seventy elders were appointed to help Moses administer Israel in the wilderness (Nu. xi. 16); the people of Judah spent seventy years of exile in Babylon (Je. xxv. 11, xxix. 10); seventy weeks, 'sevens', were decreed by God as the period in which messianic redemption was to be accomplished (Dn. ix. 24); Jesus sent forth seventy disciples to prepare His way (Lk. x. 1); He enjoined forgiveness 'until seventy times seven' (Mt. xviii. 22).

666 (*or 616*) is the number of the beast in Rev. xiii. 18. Many interpretations of this number have been proposed, and by *gematria*, in which figures are given the value of corresponding letters, the number 666 has been identified with the numerical values of the names of a variety of personalities from Caligula and Nero Caesar onwards, and with such concepts as the chaos monster.

For a full discussion, see commentaries on the book of Revelation, especially *NBC*, p. 1185b; H. B. Swete, *The Apocalypse of St. John*, 1906, pp. 175–176; J.-J. von Allmen, art. 'Number' in *Vocabulary of the Bible*, 1958.

Rev. vii. 4, xiv. 1 records the number *144,000* 'which were sealed'. It is the number twelve, the number of election, squared, and multiplied by a thousand, an indefinitely large number, and symbolizes the full number of saints of both covenants who are preserved by God. R.A.H.G.

NUMBERS, BOOK OF. The synagogue named this book after its first word or after one of the first words (*wayᵉḏabbēr*, 'and He spoke'; or *bᵉmiḏbar*, 'in the desert'). The Greek translators called it *arithmoi*, 'numbers'. Where the four other parts of the Pentateuch are concerned, the Greek names are commonly used; in this fifth part, in some countries the Greek has been translated into the native language: 'Numbers', *etc.*; in other countries the Latin translation of the Greek name is used: *Numeri*. The title is given because the book's first few chapters (and chapter xxvi) contain many numbers, especially census-numbers.

I. OUTLINE OF CONTENTS

a. The numbering of the Israelites. The marshalling of the tribes (i. 1–iv. 49).

b. The law regarding jealousy, legislation for the Nazirites and other laws (v. 1–vi. 27).

c. The offerings for the consecration of the tabernacle (vii. 1–89).

d. The candlestick. The consecration of the Levites; their time of service (viii. 1–26).

e. The second Passover; the cloud; the two silver trumpets (ix. 1–x. 10).

f. The departure from Sinai (x. 11–36).

g. Taberah. The quails. The seventy elders (xi. 1–35).

h. Miriam and Aaron against Moses (xii. 1–16).

i. The twelve spies (xiii. 1–xiv. 45).

j. Miscellaneous commandments regarding, *inter alia*, meat and drink offerings, offerings where a person has sinned through ignorance, and commandments about sabbath-breaking (xv. 1–41).

k. Korah, Dathan, and Abiram. The blossoming rod of Aaron (xvi. 1–xvii. 13).

l. The position of the priests and Levites (xviii. 1–32).

m. The water of separation for purification of sins (xix. 1–22).

n. The death of Miriam. Meribah (xx. 1–13).

o. Edom refuses to give Israel passage. Death of Aaron (xx. 14–29).

p. The struggle at Hormah. The serpent of brass. To the plains of Moab. The fight against Sihon and Og (xxi. 1–35).

q. Balaam (xxii. 1–xxiv. 25).

r. Baal-peor (xxv. 1–18).

s. The second numbering of the Israelites (xxvi. 1–65).

t. The right of inheritance of daughters. The successor of Moses (xxvii. 1–23).

u. Commandments regarding offerings. Vows of the women (xxviii. 1–xxx. 16).

v. Vengeance taken against the Midianites (xxxi. 1–54).

w. The allotment of the land on the east side of Jordan (xxxii. 1–42).

x. The places where Israel camped during their journeys through the desert (xxxiii. 1–49).

y. Directions concerning the conquest of Canaan. The borders of Canaan. Regulations concerning the division of the land. The cities of the Levites. Cities of refuge (xxxiii. 50–xxxv. 34).

z. The marriage of daughters possessing an inheritance (xxxvi. 1–13).

II. AUTHORSHIP AND DATE

Regarding the book of Numbers there is insufficient ground for, and even objection to, our following the tradition according to which Moses is the author of the whole of the Pentateuch. Only in chapter xxxiii is a literary activity of Moses mentioned (verse 2, *cf.* v. 23, xi. 26); this is not repeated in any other part of Numbers; for the contrary case, see *e.g.* Dt. xxxi. 9. Various data point to a later time than that of Moses, or at least to another author than Moses; *cf.* xii. 3, xv. 22 f. (Moses in the third person), xv. 32, xxi. 14 (perhaps the 'book of the wars of the Lord' originates from the post-Mosaic time), xxxii. 34 ff. Nevertheless, the book repeatedly states that the regulations and the laws have been given through the agency of Moses (and Aaron), i. 1, *etc.*; it is also clear that the laws and regulations give the impression that they were enacted during the wanderings through the desert (v. 17, xv. 32 ff., *etc.*). For that matter it is possible that the laws have gone through a process of growth: afterwards there may have been alterations made in them, *e.g.* for the purpose of adapting them to altered circumstances. Sometimes there are definite marks of these processes; thus there are differences between Nu. xv. 22–31 and Lv. iv. If, in addition, we note the fact that Nu. xv. 22 f. speaks about Moses in the third person, it is not unlikely that Nu. xv. 22–31 is a later version of Lv. iv.

We shall have to assume that the laws substantially originate from the Mosaic time. We can also assume that the noting down of both the laws and the stories was already begun during the Mosaic time. The time when the book received its final form is unknown to us. In the opinion of the present writer, it is a plausible view that the major points were already recorded in writing, *e.g.* in the early days of the monarchy. It is significant that there are no *post-Mosaica* pointing unmistakably to a time much later than that of Moses.

Since the critical activity of Wellhausen and others, many scholars have adopted the view that Numbers belongs for the greater part to the so-called Priestly Code, which is said to have its origin in the post-exilic age. At present, however, scholars are inclined, more than Wellhausen was, to accept the view that Numbers contains material dating from old, even very remote, times, admitting that in Nu. v. 11 ff., xix, ancient rites are described, and that other material points to a similar conclusion. Many scholars are willing to accept that the cult, as it is described in Numbers, was in use, so far as concerns the main points, in pre-exilic Jerusalem. See also the articles on PENTATEUCH, MOSES, WILDERNESS OF THE WANDERING, *etc.*, and articles under particular subjects such as BALAAM, CITIES OF REFUGE, *etc.*

III. FURTHER SUMMARY OF CONTENTS

1. The division of the Pentateuch into five books is not original. Thus, even though it is not without meaning that with Nu. i. 1 a new book begins (in which the first four chapters form the preparation for the departure from Sinai), this book nevertheless forms a unity with the preceding books. In the same way it may be said that

Deuteronomy is the continuation of Numbers, but the separation between Numbers and Deuteronomy is more fundamental than the separation of Leviticus and Numbers.

2. The history narrated in Numbers covers thirty-eight years—the period between the second year and the fortieth year after the Exodus (see the definitions of the time in i. 1, vii. 1, ix. 1, 15, x. 11, xxxiii. 38; *cf.* Ex. xl. 2; Dt. i. 3).

In the first part Israel is still staying near Mt. Sinai (Ex. xix. 1 tells of their arrival at Sinai). Nu. x. 11–xii. 16 deals with the departure from Sinai and the journey to Kadesh (*cf.* xiii. 26); in the second year after the Exodus Israel had already arrived at Kadesh (*cf.* Dt. ii. 14). Because Israel put faith in the defeatist words of the spies, there ensued a prolonged wandering in the desert (xiii, xiv). Little is known to us of the fortunes of Israel during the thirty-eight years of their wanderings (xv. 1–xx. 13). We should reckon with the possibility that Kadesh was for a long time a sort of centre for Israel, while various groups of Israelites were wandering about the Sinai Peninsula. After these thirty-eight years Israel leaves Kadesh for Canaan; marches round Edom, comes into the plains of Moab, and defeats Sihon and Og (xx. 14–xxi. 35). The last part of the book describes the actions of Balaam, Israel's idol-worship of Baal-peor, and the punishment of the Midianites.

3. Besides dealing with history, this book contains all kinds of regulations and laws. The relation between laws and history and between one law and another is often not very clear to us. Nevertheless, the author will, at least in many cases, have intended a connection. The simplest solution is to suppose that there is a chronological connection. Sometimes there is also a material connection; see, *e.g.*, how well v. 1–4, xviii correspond with what precedes, and x. 1–10 with what follows; after a survey of the journey through the desert has been given (xxxiii. 1–49), the narrative continues (xxxiii. 50–xxxv. 34) with regulations concerning the conquest of Canaan and laws for when they are dwelling in it. Finally, we should bear in mind that the construction of many Old Testament books raises similar questions to those we have referred to here (see PSALMS, PROVERBS, ISAIAH, *etc.*).

Many laws (but not all of them) concern ritual matters. The Israelites did not distinguish between cultic, moral, juridical, and social laws in the same way as we usually do. All the laws and regulations have as their object that Israel should be prepared to live in Canaan in the sight of the Lord, as an independent and well-conducted nation.

4. In Numbers Moses is again the dominant figure, depicted in all his greatness and weakness, and guiding the people in every respect. Through his mediation the Lord gives Israel a variety of laws and regulations, speaking to His servant 'mouth to mouth' (xii. 6–8). Over and over again Moses acts as intercessor for the people (xi. 2, xii. 13, xiv. 13 ff., xvi. 22, xxi. 7). He was 'very meek, above all the men which were upon the face of the earth' (xii. 3, *cf.* xiv. 5, xvi. 4 ff.), yet he had his share of human failings. Contrary to the Lord's order he strikes the rock (xx. 10 f.), and on occasion he makes temperamental complaints (xi. 10 ff., *cf.* xvi. 15). Next to Moses in prominence is Aaron (i. 3, 17, 44, ii. 1, *etc.*, especially xii, xvi, xvii).

IV. THE MESSAGE OF THE BOOK

In Numbers, as in the case of the whole Bible, the almighty and faithful God of the covenant reveals Himself; it is this revelation that joins the different parts of Numbers into a unity. In the regulations and laws He imposes, God shows His care of His people. Israel frequently revolts against Him. As a result the anger of the Lord is kindled: He does not allow the sin to go unpunished (xi. 1–3, 33 f., xii. 10 ff., xiv, *etc.*); Moses and Aaron are not allowed to enter Canaan (xx. 12 f.). But the Lord does not repudiate His people; He remains faithful to His covenant. He guides Israel through the desert, so that the land promised to their fathers is reached. This is prevented neither by Israel's unfaithfulness nor by the power of the nations that turn against Israel.

Special attention should be paid to certain aspects of the revelation of God in Numbers.

1. The Lord is, indeed, unchangeable in His faithfulness (*cf.* xxiii. 19), but this does not imply that He is an unmovable being (see especially the touching story in xiv. 11 ff.). In this connection we should note the strong anthropomorphisms (see, *e.g.*, x. 35 f., xv. 3 ('a sweet savour unto the Lord'), xxviii. 2 ('my bread'), *etc.*); expressions which, while we must not take them in a strictly literal sense, show at the same time how deeply the Lord is involved in the doings of Israel.

2. God's holiness is specially emphasized. The stories do this (see, *e.g.*, xx. 12 f.), and so also, in a different way, do the laws and regulations: when a man approaches God he has to fulfil all kinds of prescribed rules, he has to be free from every uncleanness (*cf.* also i. 50 ff., *etc.*).

3. Very detailed prescriptions are given in this book: God exercises His sovereign dominion over everything, even over the smallest details.

4. As soon as the children of Israel have arrived at the borders of the promised country they yield to the temptation to serve the gods of the new land. But the Lord is not only the Lord of the desert: He engages a heathen fortune-teller (xxii–xxiv), and punishes Israel for their idol-worship (xxv), together with those who had seduced His people (xxxi).

In what is said above, the Christological character of this book has already been mainly indicated. In Numbers, as elsewhere, God reveals Himself as the faithful God of the covenant. In other words, He reveals Himself in the countenance of Christ. In addition, there is much in this book which has a typological meaning: in persons (especially Moses and Aaron), in occurrences, and in laws, the coming Christ casts His shadow before Him (*cf.* Jn. iii. 14; 1 Cor. x. 1 ff.; Heb. iii. 7 ff., ix. 13; *etc.*).

BIBLIOGRAPHY. See the various Introductions to the Old Testament—*e.g.* A. Bentzen, *Introduction to the Old Testament*[2], 1952; O. Eissfeldt, *Einleitung in das Alte Testament*[2], 1956; E. J. Young, *An Introduction to the Old Testament*[3], 1957; and the various Commentaries—*e.g.* G. B. Gray, *Numbers, ICC*, 1903; L. E. Binns, *The Book of Numbers, WC*, 1927; S. Fish, *The Book of Numbers*[2], 1950, in *The Soncino Books of the Bible*; J. Marsh, *Numbers, IB*, II, 1953; W. H. Gispen, *Het boek Numeri*, I, 1959, in *Commentaar op het Oude Testament*. N.H.R.

NUNC DIMITTIS. The prophecies accompanying Christ's advent occur not (as with John the Baptist) at circumcision but at the rites of purification a month later. According to an ancient custom babies were brought to an old doctor or Rabbi in the Temple for a blessing. Perhaps in this setting Simeon, taking the Lord Jesus, uttered his *nunc dimittis* (Lk. ii. 29–35). Simeon is characterized as receiving a 'spirit which was holy', which in Jewish tradition is equated with the 'spirit of prophecy'. According to the Rabbis the Spirit departed from Israel after the prophet Malachi, and His return was indicative of the messianic age (*cf.* Strack-Billerbeck, *in loc.*). In the case of Simeon three specific 'acts of the Spirit' occur: (1) he receives by divine revelation assurance that he shall see the Lord's Messiah; (2) under the influence of the Spirit (*cf.* Rev. i. 10) he is led to encounter and recognize Jesus as Messiah (*cf.* 1 Sa. xvi. 6 ff.); (3) he utters a prayer and prediction which, in Luke's context, is clearly to be regarded as prophetic.

Nunc Dimittis is divided into two parts, the first a prayer to God (liturgically, this alone came to be designated the 'Nunc Dimittis') and the second a prophecy spoken to Mary. Their mood and theme stand in stark contrast to each other. The prayer is joyful, expressing the messianic hope of Judaism in its most exalted tone: in Messiah the Gentiles will receive the truth of God and thus, in him, Israel's glory as God's instrument of revelation and redemption will be fully manifest (*cf.* Is. xlix. 6; Acts i. 8; Rom. xv. 8 ff.). But, in the second section, as if to counterbalance the impression of the prayer, praise gives way to warning. The Messiah shall cause division and shall be rejected by many (*cf.* Rom. ix. 33).

In Simeon's prophecy to Mary the concept of a Suffering Messiah appears. Israel's destiny is glorious, but it is one of conflict. As a sign or pointer to the redemption of Israel Jesus shall be attacked and rejected (*cf.* Lk. xi. 30), for the kind of redemption He represents will not be welcomed by all. Although this will bring anguish to Mary, through it men will be brought to decision and thus their real selves, their hidden selves, be uncovered. See BENEDICTUS. E.E.E.

NURSE. 'Nurse' in the English Bible may mean a wet-nurse, translating Heb. *mêneqet*, used of Deborah (Gn. xxiv. 59), of Moses' mother (Ex. ii. 7), and of the nurse of the infant Joash (2 Ki. xi. 2; 2 Ch. xxii. 11). Suckling is usually continued in the Near East for two years, and the nurse often remains with the family as a trusted servant, as in the case of Deborah (Gn. xxxv. 8). The same word is used in a figurative sense of queens who will care for God's people in the glorious future (Is. xlix. 23). Paul compares his care for believers to that of a nurse (Gk. *trophos*) for her own children (1 Thes. ii. 7).

In the more general sense of one who cares for children, 'nurse' translates Heb. *'ōmeneṯ*; for example, Naomi (Ru. iv. 16) and the governess of five-year-old Mephibosheth (2 Sa. iv. 4) are so described. The masculine form of this Heb. word, *'ōmēn*, translated 'nursing father', is used figuratively of Moses' care for the Israelites (Nu. xi. 12) and of kings who will serve the people of God (Is. xlix. 23). *Cf.* Acts xiii. 18, RVmg.

BIBLIOGRAPHY. H. Granquist, *Birth and Childhood among the Arabs*, 1947, pp. 107–117, 246–252. J.T.

NUTS. Two Heb. words are thus translated. 1. *'ᵉgôz* (Arab. *gawz*), in Ct. vi. 11 only—probably referring to the walnut, a delicacy. The walnut is strictly not a nut, but a drupe or stone-fruit, like the plum or olive—only here the kernel, not the integument, is edible. 2. *boṭnîm* (Gn. xliii. 11 only) were pistachio nuts with green, edible kernels. Not grown in Egypt, they were an acceptable gift to Joseph. A rabbinic scholar was likened to a nut—the shell (his personality) might be soiled by sin, but the Torah in him (the kernel) remained unsullied. Ability to distinguish between a nut and a pebble qualified a Jewish child to receive and possess a gift (*Giṭṭîn* 64 b). R.A.S.

NUZI. See ARCHAEOLOGY.

NYMPHA, NYMPHAS. Owner of a house in Laodicea (or possibly somewhere else near Colossae) in which a church met (Col. iv. 15). Though many MSS read 'his house', as AV, most of the best read either 'her house' (*cf.* RSV, NEB) or 'their house' (*cf.* RV). The name is in the accusative and, unaccented, could represent a masculine Nymphas (pet-form for Nymphodorus?) or a feminine Nympha (*cf.* J. H. Moulton, *Grammar*, I, p. 48, for alleviation of the cause of Lightfoot's reserve). On either rendering the reading 'their house' is so hard to explain that it may well be correct. Perhaps it refers back to 'the brethren which are in Laodicea' (Lightfoot proposes a Colossian family there, or, alternatively, that *autōn* stands for 'Nymphas and his friends').

Nympha(s), like Philemon and Archippus (*q.v.*), displays Paul's friendships (made in Ephesus?) in an area he had not visited (*cf.* Col. ii. 1). A.F.W.

O

OAK. See Trees.

OAR. See Ships and Boats.

OATHS. Heb. *šᵉḇûʿâ* and *'ālâ*; Gk. *horkos*. *'ālâ* is the stronger of the two Heb. words: it means an execration or curse invoked upon the person who breaks an oath; *šᵉḇûʿâ* comes from the word for 'seven', the sacred number, and has reference to the ritual of the oath.

Scripture has much to say about oaths taken by men. An oath is the invocation of a curse upon one if he breaks his word (1 Sa. xix. 6), or if he is not speaking the truth (Mk. xiv. 71). See Curse. This idea of invoking a curse upon oneself has led some scholars to suggest that in invoking God's Name in an oath a Hebrew 'released the action of God', or 'committed to God the duty of taking action against the perjured or false man' (A. Lelièvre, in *Vocabulary of the Bible* (ed. J.-J. von Allmen), 1958). See also Covenant.

In taking oaths various means (Gn. xxiv. 2; Dt. xxxii. 40) and formulae (Nu. v. 22; Gn. xxxi. 50; Jdg. viii. 19; 2 Ki. ii. 2; Je. xlii. 5; Mt. v. 34–36, xxiii. 16) were adopted. Frequently the dire effects of non-fulfilment were not expressed (2 Sa. iii. 9, but see Je. xxix. 22).

The seriousness of oaths is emphasized in the laws of Moses (Ex. xx. 7; Lv. xix. 12). Israelites were forbidden to swear their oaths by false gods (Je. xii. 16; Am. viii. 14). Ezekiel speaks as if perjury were punishable by death (xvii. 16 ff.), but in the law the false swearing by a witness, and the denial on oath regarding something found or received (Lv. v. 1–4, vi. 1–3), could be atoned for by a sin-offering (Lv. v. 5 ff., vi. 4 ff.).

Christ taught that oaths were binding (Mt. v. 33). The Christian's daily conversation is to be as sacred as his oaths. He is not to have two standards of truth as certain Jews had when they introduced a sliding scale of values in regard to oaths. In the kingdom of God oaths will finally become unnecessary (Mt. v. 34–37). Christ Himself accepted the imprecatory oath (Mt. xxvi. 63 ff.), and Paul also swore by an oath (2 Cor. i. 23; Gal. i. 20).

Scripture also testifies that God bound Himself by an oath (Heb. vi. 13–18). What the Lord bound Himself to perform was His promises to His covenant people: *e.g.* His promises to the Patriarchs (Gn. l. 24), His promises to the Davidic dynasty (Ps. lxxxix. 19–37, 49), His promises to the messianic Priest-King (Ps. cx. 1–4). The Guarantor of all these promises is Jesus Christ in whom they find the answering 'amen' (2 Cor. i. 19 f.; *cf.* Is. lxv. 16, rvmg). In His advent Jesus Christ fulfilled God's ancient oaths to Patriarchs (Lk. i. 68–73, ii. 6–14), to David (Acts ii. 30), and to the Old Testament priest-king (Heb. vii. 20 f., 28). See R. C. Walls in *A Theological Word Book of the Bible* (ed. A. Richardson), 1950, pp. 159 f. J.G.S.S.T.

OBADIAH (*'ōḇaḏyāhû*, *'ōḇaḏyâ*). A Heb. name meaning 'servant of Yahweh' or 'worshipper of Yahweh'. At least twelve men in the Old Testament bear this name.

1. The steward, or major domo, in charge of the palace of King Ahab of Israel (1 Ki. xviii. 3–16). From his youth he was a devout worshipper of Yahweh. When Jezebel was persecuting the prophets of Yahweh, Obadiah hid 100 of them in two caves. During a drought while Obadiah was seeking grass for the royal horses and mules, Elijah met him and persuaded him to arrange a meeting with Ahab, which led to the contest between Elijah and the prophets of Baal. The TB (*Sanhedrin* 39b) mistakenly identifies him with the prophet Obadiah. An ancient Hebrew seal reading 'To Obadiah servant of the King' may have belonged to this man.

2. A descendant of David (1 Ch. iii. 21). **3.** A chief of Issachar (1 Ch. vii. 3). **4.** A descendant of Saul (1 Ch. viii. 38, ix. 44). **5.** A Levite (1 Ch. ix. 16), identical with Abda (Ne. xi. 17) and probably with Obadiah, a gate-keeper of the Temple (Ne. xii. 25). **6.** A Gadite captain who joined David at Ziklag (1 Ch. xii. 9).

7. A Zebulonite (1 Ch. xxvii. 19). **8.** One of the princes sent out by King Jehoshaphat to teach the law in the cities of Judah (2 Ch. xvii. 7). **9.** A Levite overseer of the repair of the Temple in the time of Josiah (2 Ch. xxxiv. 12). **10.** An Israelite leader who returned from Babylonia to Jerusalem with Ezra (Ezr. viii. 9). **11.** A priest who sealed the covenant with Nehemiah (Ne. x. 5).

12. A prophet, presumably of Judah (Ob. 1). The Bible gives nothing directly about his life. Though some locate him before the Exile, it is more likely that he lived in the 5th century BC (see Obadiah, Book of). If the latter view is correct it is chronologically impossible to identify him with King Ahab's steward, as does the TB (*Sanhedrin* 39b), or with King Ahaziah's captain (2 Ki. i. 13–15) as Pseudo-Epiphanius does in *The Lives of the Prophets*. The talmudic tradition that he was a proselyte of Edomite origin is improbable in view of his strong denunciation of Edom. J.T.

OBADIAH, BOOK OF. The fourth of the Minor Prophets in the Hebrew Bible and the fifth in the order of the LXX. For a note on the author, see the previous article (12).

I. OUTLINE OF CONTENTS

a. The judgment of Edom (verses 1–14).
(i) Title (verse 1a).
(ii) Warning of Edom's doom (verses 1b–4).
(iii) Completeness of Edom's destruction (verses 5–9).
(iv) Reasons for Edom's judgment (verses 10–14).
b. Universal judgment (verses 15, 16).
c. Restoration of Israel (verses 17–21).

II. HISTORICAL BACKGROUND

a. Before the Exile

Jewish tradition in the Talmud (*Sanhedrin* 39b) placed Obadiah in the reign of Ahab in the 9th century BC, and the order of the Minor Prophets in the Heb. Bible includes Obadiah among the pre-exilic prophets. Some scholars have suggested that the background for the whole of Obadiah is the attack of the Arabians and Philistines on Judah in the reign of Jehoram mentioned in 2 Ch. xxi. 16, 17 (so Keil), or the Edomite attack on Judah in the reign of Ahaz described in 2 Ch. xxviii. 17 (so J. D. Davis). Many think that only the older oracle against Edom, which Obadiah embodies in verses 1–6, 8, 9, has a pre-exilic background. Arab raids on Palestine, and presumably on Edom, are recorded in the 9th century BC (2 Ch. xxi. 16, 17) and in the 7th century BC (Assyr. Annals).

b. After 587 BC

Most scholars think that the calamity to Jerusalem described in Ob. 11–14 is its capture by the Chaldeans in 587 BC. This is the only capture of Jerusalem, in which it is recorded that Edomites participated (Ps. cxxxvii. 7; 1 Esdras iv. 45). The references to the sufferings caused by the fall of Jerusalem are so vivid that G. A. Smith would place Obadiah soon afterwards during the exilic period. Many, however, think that the latter part of Obadiah reflects a post-exilic background. Verse 7 states that the Edomites have been driven out of their old land (*cf.* Mal. i. 3, 4). After the fall of Jerusalem Edomites under Arab pressure began moving into the Negeb (1 Esdras iv. 50), which came to be called Idumaea, and by the late 6th century BC Arabs had largely pushed them out of the area of Petra, once the Edomite capital. Verses 8–10 announce the future wiping out of the Edomites as a nation, and this prophecy must have been made before the fulfilment which took place in the Maccabean period (Jos., *Ant.* xiii. 9. 1). The territory occupied by the Jews according to verses 19, 20 is the area around Jerusalem, as in the days of Nehemiah (Ne. xi. 25–36). Thus the latest clear indication of date in the prophecy is in the mid-5th century BC, about the time of Malachi.

III. PARALLELS IN OTHER PROPHECIES

Other prophetic denunciations of Edom include: Is. xxxiv. 5–17, lxiii. 1–6; Je. xlix. 7–22; La. iv. 21–22; Ezk. xxvi. 12–14, xxxv; Joel iii. 19; Am. i. 11–12.

The many identical phrases in Ob. 1–9 and Je. xlix. 7–22 prove some literary relationship between the two passages. The different order of the phrases in the two prophecies makes it probable that they are both quoting some earlier divine oracle against Edom. Since some of the additional material in Jeremiah is characteristic of that prophet, and since the order is more natural in Obadiah, it is likely that the latter is closer in form to the original prophecy. Some scholars, however, hold that either Jeremiah (so Keil) or Obadiah (so Hitzig) made use of the other.

Several phrases are found in both Obadiah and Joel: Ob. 10=Joel iii. 19; Ob. 11=Joel iii. 3; Ob. 15=Joel i. 15, ii. 1, iii. 4, 7, 14; Ob. 18=Joel iii. 8. In ii. 32 Joel indicates by the words 'as the Lord hath said' that he is quoting, probably from Ob. 17. Therefore Obadiah preceded Joel and doubtless influenced him in some of the other phrases common to the two prophets.

IV. STYLE

Obadiah, the shortest book of the Old Testament, is marked by vigorous poetic language. The prevailing poetic metre is the pentameter (3 + 2), but other metres are used for variety (*e.g.* 3 + 3 and 3 + 3 + 3). Much of the prophecy consists of God's own words to personified Edom (verses 2–15), and this feature gives a direct and personal quality to the book. Vividness is enhanced by the use of the prophetic perfect tense (verse 2) to describe a judgment yet to be fulfilled, and by the use of prohibitions (verses 12–14) forbidding atrocities which had actually been perpetrated. Various striking comparisons and metaphors are used: the mountain fastness of Edom is like an eagle's eyrie (verse 4); the plunderers of Edom are compared to night thieves and gleaners of grapes (verse 5); the judgment of the nations is a bitter drink which they must swallow (verse 16); the avenging Israelites are called a fire, and the Edomites are called stubble (verse 18). Edom's crimes are listed in climactic order (verses 10–14). The completeness of Israel's restoration is expressed by the specification of its expansion in the four cardinal directions (verses 19, 20). Sin and doom in verses 1–16 are sharply contrasted with hope and victory in verses 17–21. Obadiah proceeds from the particular to the general, from the judgment of Edom to the universal judgment, from the restoration of Israel to the establishment of the kingdom of God.

V. LITERARY ANALYSES

Some hold that Obadiah was the original author of the whole prophecy (so Keil). Most scholars believe that he adapted an older oracle in verses 1–6, 8, 9. Some have found various other fragments, but the uniform historical background supports the literary unity of the remainder of the prophecy.

VI. LEADING MESSAGES

1. *Divine inspiration.* Four times (verses 1, 4, 8, 18) the prophet claims a divine origin for his words.

2. *Divine judgment.* The main message of this prophecy is God's moral judgment of nations. Edom is judged because of inhumanity to Israel, who also has been punished. Ultimately all nations will be judged in the Day of the Lord.

3. *The divine kingdom.* The final goal, according to Obadiah, is that 'the kingdom shall be the Lord's' (*cf.* Rev. xi. 15). His hope for the restoration of his own people rises above mere nationalism, for in their victory he sees the establishment of the kingdom of God (verse 21). That kingdom will be characterized by 'deliverance' and 'holiness' (verse 17), ideas which are amplified in the New Testament.

BIBLIOGRAPHY. *Commentaries* by E. B. Pusey, 1860; C. F. Keil in *Biblischer Commentar über das Alte Testament*, 1873; J. A. Bewer in *ICC*, 1911; H. C. O. Lanchester in *CBSC*, 1918; G. W. Wade in *WC*, 1925; G. A. Smith in *Expositor's Bible*, 1928; E. Sellin in *Kommentar zum Alten Testament*, 1929; T. H. Robinson in *Handbuch zum Alten Testament*, 1938; D. W. B. Robinson in *The New Bible Commentary*, 1953; J. A. Thompson in *IB*, 1956.

Special studies: G. L. Robinson, *The Sarcophagus of an Ancient Civilization*, 1930; W. Rudolph, 'Obadja', *ZAW*, VIII, 1931, pp. 222–231.

J.T.

OBAL. See EBAL.

OBED ('*ôḇēḏ*, 'servant'). **1.** The son of Ruth and Boaz (Ru. iv. 17), and grandfather of David (Ru. iv. 21 f.; 1 Ch. ii. 12; Mt. i. 5; Lk. iii. 32). Obed's birth brought comfort to Naomi's old age. **2.** A Jerahmeelite (1 Ch. ii. 37 f.). **3.** One of David's mighty men (1 Ch. xi. 47). **4.** A son of Shemaiah and grandson of Obed-edom, of the Korahite family (1 Ch. xxvi. 7). **5.** The father of Azariah, a captain who served under Jehoiada (2 Ch. xxiii. 1).

J.D.D.

OBED-EDOM ('*ōḇēḏ 'ᵉḏôm*, 'servant of [god?] Edom'). **1.** A Philistine of Gath living in the neighbourhood of Jerusalem. Before taking it to Jerusalem David left the ark in his house for three months after the death of Uzzah, during which time its presence brought blessing to the household (2 Sa. vi. 10 ff. = 1 Ch. xiii. 13 f., xv. 25).

2. The ancestor of a family of doorkeepers (1 Ch. xv. 18 ff., xvi. 38, xxvi. 4 ff.; 2 Ch. xxv. 24). **3.** A family of singers in post-exilic times (1 Ch. xv. 21, xvi. 5).

J.D.D.

OBEDIENCE. The Hebrew verb translated 'obey' in EVV is *šāma' bᵉ*, lit. 'hearken to'. The verb used in LXX and the New Testament is *hypakouō* (noun, *hypakoē*; adjective, *hypēkoos*), a compound of *akouō*, which also means 'hear'. *Hypakouō* means literally 'hear *under*'. The New Testament also uses *eisakouō* (1 Cor. xiv. 21), literally 'hear *into*', *peithomai*, and *peitharcheō* (Tit. iii. 1). The two latter words express respectively the ideas of yielding to persuasion and submitting to authority. The idea of obedience which this vocabulary suggests is of a hearing that takes place *under* the authority or influence of the speaker, and that leads *into* compliance with his requests or orders.

For obedience to be due to a person, he must: (*a*) have a right to command, and (*b*) be able to make known his requirements. Man's duty to obey his Maker thus presupposes: (*a*) God's Lordship, and (*b*) His revelation. The Old Testament habitually describes obedience to God as obeying (hearing) either His *voice* (accentuating (*b*)) or His *commandments* (assuming (*b*), and accentuating (*a*)). Disobedience it describes as not hearing God's voice when He speaks (Ps. lxxxi. 11; Je. vii. 24–28).

According to Scripture, God demands that His revelation be taken as a rule for man's whole life. Thus obedience to God is a concept broad enough to include the whole of biblical religion and morality. The Bible is insistent that isolated external acts of homage to God cannot make up for a lack of consistent obedience in heart and conduct (1 Sa. xv. 22; *cf.* Je. vii. 22 f.).

The disobedience of Adam, the first representative man, and the perfect obedience of the second, Jesus Christ, are decisive factors in the destiny of everyone. Adam's lapse from obedience plunged mankind into guilt, condemnation, and death (Rom. v. 19; 1 Cor. xv. 22). Christ's unfailing obedience 'unto death' (Phil. ii. 8; *cf.* Heb. v. 8, x. 5–10) won righteousness (acceptance with God) and life (fellowship with God) for all who believe on Him (Rom. v. 15–19).

In God's promulgation of the old covenant the emphasis was on obedience as His requirement if His people were to enjoy His favour (Ex. xix. 5, *etc.*). In His promise of the new covenant, however, the emphasis was on obedience as His gift to them, in order that they might enjoy His favour (Je. xxxi. 33, xxxii. 40; *cf.* Ezk. xxxvi. 26 f., xxxvii. 23–26).

Faith in the gospel, and in Jesus Christ, is obedience (Acts vi. 7; Rom. vi. 17; Heb. v. 9; 1 Pet. i. 22), for God commands it (*cf.* Jn. vi. 29; 1 Jn. iii. 23). Unbelief is disobedience (Rom. x. 16; 2 Thes. i. 8; 1 Pet. ii. 8, iii. 1, iv. 17). A life of obedience to God is the fruit of faith (*cf.* what is said of Abraham, Gn. xxii. 18; Heb. xi. 8, 17 ff.; Jas. ii. 21 ff.).

Christian obedience means imitating God in holiness (1 Pet. i. 15 f.) and Christ in humility and love (Jn. xiii. 14 f., 34 f.; Phil. ii. 5 ff.; Eph. iv. 32–v. 2). It springs from gratitude for grace received (Rom. xii. 1 f.), not from the desire to gain merit and to justify oneself in God's sight. Indeed, law-keeping from the latter motive is not obedience to God, but its opposite (Rom. ix. 31–x. 3).

Obedience to divinely-established authority in

the family (Eph. v. 22, vi. 1 ff.; *cf.* 2 Tim. iii. 2), in the Church (Phil. ii. 12; Heb. xiii. 7), and in the state (Mt. xxii. 21; Rom. xiii. 1 ff.; 1 Pet. ii. 13 ff.; Tit. iii. 1), is part of the Christian's obedience to God. When claims clash, however, he must be ready to disobey men in order not to disobey God (*cf.* Acts v. 29). J.I.P.

OBELISK. See PILLAR.

OBLATION. See SACRIFICE AND OFFERING (Old Testament), I.

ODED. 1. Father of Azariah the prophet (2 Ch. xv. 1) in the reign of Asa. Verse 8 has either included a marginal gloss or omitted 'Azariah the son of'. **2.** A prophet of Samaria (2 Ch. xxviii. 9–15) who met the victorious army of the northern kingdom returning with a number of enslaved captives from Judah, and remonstrated with them to return the slaves. His pleadings, joined by those of some Samaritan leaders, were successful. M.A.M.

OFFENCE. See STUMBLING-BLOCK.

OFFERING. See SACRIFICE AND OFFERING.

OFFICERS. (Heb. *šōṭēr*, one who 'writes' or 'records'.) Officers appear as overseers over the rank and file (Pr. vi. 7, 'overseers', Heb. *šōṭerîm*) and at the same time as assistants, or recorders assisting the chiefs under whom they serve. This is precisely the function of the 'officers' named in Ex. v. 6–19. Israelite foremen are set over the people to keep count of their tally of bricks. There is abundant evidence of such recording of the work of slaves in the Egyp. records and in remains of the Mosaic period and earlier. It is therefore natural that we should find officers taking a place in the Mosaic law. For the dispensation of justice, 'judges and officers' are to be appointed in all their gates (Dt. xvi. 18), the duty of the officers being to keep the records, *cf. EQ*, XXVII, 1957, pp. 149–157 (see JUDGES).

Dt. xx contains laws for the coming invasion in which 'officers' are to proclaim exemption from service, after which 'captains' are to be appointed to lead. We find officers performing a somewhat similar service at the crossing of the Jordan (Jos. i. 10 f., iii. 1 f.). They are counted in with elders and judges in Jos. viii. 33, xxiii. 2, xxiv. 1. Under David's civil administration 'for the outward business over Israel' (apparently east and west of Jordan), there were 'officers and judges'; and west of Jordan, 1,700 officers for the business of the Lord and the service of the king (1 Ch. xxvi. 29 f.). In addition, there were officers attached to the army (1 Ch. xxvii. 1). The correspondence with the Deuteronomic law is too striking to be missed. Under Jehoshaphat also a distinction is made between 'matters of the Lord' and 'the king's matters', officers being employed in both (2 Ch. xix. 11). Other references show that the officers, though recorders, were distinct from 'the scribes' (2 Ch. xxvi. 11, xxxiv. 13). G.T.M.

OG (*'ôḡ*). An Amorite king of Bashan, of the giant race of Rephaim at the time of the conquest of Palestine (Nu. xxi. 33; Jos. xiii. 12). His kingdom was a powerful one, having sixty cities 'fenced with high walls, gates and bars' (Dt. iii. 4, 5), extending from Mt. Hermon to the Jabbok. These included two royal cities, Ashtaroth and Edrei, at the latter of which the Israelites defeated and slew him. His territory was given to the half tribe of Manasseh (Dt. iii. 13), which remained east of the Jordan. His defeat was one of the signal victories of Israel (*cf.* Jos. ix. 10; Ne. ix. 22; Pss. cxxxv. 11, cxxxvi. 20).

His bed (*'ereś*) was renowned as made of black basalt. Some have conjectured that it was in reality a sarcophagus, although the word nowhere else bears this meaning; but many such sarcophagi have been found in the region. It appears to have fallen into the hands of the Ammonites and was kept in Rabbah (Dt. iii. 11). M.A.M.

OHOLAH AND OHOLIBAH (AV Aholah and Aholibah). These are the allegorical names given to Samaria (the northern kingdom) and Judah in Ezk. xxiii. They mean 'Her tent' and 'My tent is in her' respectively. A criticism of the state cultus of the north is implied in the former name. The two kingdoms are pictured as sisters both married to Yahweh; in an allegory the contradiction with the prohibition in Lv. xviii. 18 should cause no difficulty. They are both charged with adultery against Yahweh, their husband, by their voluntary political entanglements and alliances with other nations—in the concept of the time an alliance between two nations involved an alliance between their gods. Oholibah is warned that her not learning from her sister's fate guarantees her own. H.L.E.

OIL. Unless cosmetic ointments (2 Sa. xiv. 2; Ps. civ. 15; Ru. iii. 3) or oil of myrrh (Est. ii. 12) are indicated, all other biblical references to oil are to the expressed product of the oil-berry. The abundance of olive-trees (*Olea europaea* L.) in ancient Palestine enabled a flourishing trade in oil to be carried on with Tyre and Egypt. See OLIVE. Solomon supplied large quantities of oil to Hiram as part-payment for the construction of the Temple (1 Ki. v. 11; Ezk. xxvii. 17), while Egypt imported substantial quantities of Palestinian oil (*cf.* Ho. xii. 1), probably because Egyp. olives produced an inferior grade of oil.

As an important element of religious observances, oil was prominent among the firstfruit offerings (Ex. xxii. 29) and was also an object of tithing (Dt. xii. 17). The meal-offerings were frequently mixed with oil (Lv. viii. 26; Nu. vii. 19), while the sanctuary lamp (Ex. xxv. 6) was replenished from a supply of freshly processed oil (Lv. xxiv. 2). Oil was employed ceremonially at the consecration of priests (Ex. xxix. 2), at the purification of lepers (Lv. xiv. 10–18), during the daily sacrifice (Ex. xxix. 40), and at the completion of the Nazirite's vow (Nu. vi. 15). But certain ceremonies were devoid of oil, such as the jealousy-offering (Nu. v. 15) and the sin-offering (Lv. v. 11).

Olive oil was widely employed in the preparation of food, replacing butter in cooking (1 Ki. xvii. 12–16). An equally popular usage in the domestic sphere was that of a fuel for the small lamps found in abundance from an early period in Palestine (see fig. 128). Both portable and other types of lamps generally had an indentation in the brim into which the wick of flax (Is. xlii. 3) or hemp was put. When the lamp was filled with olive oil the wick maintained a steady flame until the supply of fuel was depleted. When such lamps were being carried about it was customary in New Testament times for the bearer to attach a small container of olive oil to one finger by means of a string. Then if the lamp needed to be replenished at any time an adequate supply of oil was readily available (*cf.* Mt. xxv. 1–13).

Apart from the use of oil at the consecration of the priests (Ex. xxix. 2), it was an important ritual element in the ceremonial recognition of the kingly office (1 Sa. x. 1; 1 Ki. i. 39). As a medicine olive oil was used both internally and externally. Its soothing protective qualities made it a valuable remedy for gastric disorders, while its properties as a mild laxative were also recognized in antiquity. Externally it formed a popular unguent application for bruises and wounds (Is. i. 6; Mk. vi. 13; Lk. x. 34).

In Old Testament times olive oil was produced either by means of a pestle and mortar (Ex. xxvii. 20) or by grinding the olives in a stone press. Excavations at Taanach, Megiddo, and Jerusalem have uncovered presses hewn out of the solid rock. A large stone roller manipulated by two people crushed the olives to a pulp, which was then either trodden out (Dt. xxxiii. 24) or subjected to further pressing. After impurities had been removed the oil was ready for use. The Garden of Gethsemane (*gaṯ-šemen*, 'oil press') received its name from the stone presses set up to extract oil from the berries gathered on the Mount of Olives.

Oil was commonly used for anointing the body after a bath (Ru. iii. 3; 2 Sa. xii. 20), or as part of some festive occasion (*cf.* Ps. xxiii. 5). In ancient Egypt a servant generally anointed the head of each guest as he took his place at the feast. The anointing of the sick (Jas. v. 14) in New Testament times had become a quasi-sacramental rite. Josephus records as a peculiarity of the Essenes that they did not anoint themselves with oil (*BJ* ii. 8. 3).

The presence of oil symbolized gladness (Is. lxi. 3) while its absence indicated sorrow or humiliation (Joel i. 10). Similarly oil was used as an image of comfort, spiritual nourishment, or prosperity (Dt. xxxiii. 24; Jb. xxix. 6; Ps. xlv. 7).

BIBLIOGRAPHY. H. N. and A. L. Moldenke, *Plants of the Bible*, 1952, pp. 97 f., 158 ff.

R.K.H.

OIL-TREE. See TREES.

OINTMENT (Heb. *mirqaḥaṯ*, *šemen*; Gk. *myron*). Unguent preparations of various kinds were widely used throughout the whole of the ancient Near East. Their primary use was cosmetic in nature, and they probably originated in Egypt. See COSMETICS AND PERFUMERY. Toilet boxes, of which alabaster ointment containers formed a part, have been recovered in considerable numbers from Palestinian sites (see fig. 42). The Egyptians apparently found the application of unguents soothing and refreshing. It was their custom at feasts to place small cones of perfumed ointment upon the foreheads of guests. Bodily heat gradually melted the ointment, which trickled down the face on to the clothing, producing a pleasant perfume. This practice was adopted by the Semites (Ps. cxxxiii. 2), and continued into New Testament times (Mt. vi. 17; Lk. vii. 46).

Other ancient peoples followed the Egyptians in using ointments to reduce chafing and irritation caused by the heat. In localities where water was frequently at a premium, aromatic unguents were employed to mask the odour of perspiration. At other times they were used along with cosmetics in personal toilet procedures. Ointments were compounded either by apothecaries (2 Ch. xvi. 14), perfumers (Ex. xxx. 35), priests, or private individuals, using a wide variety of aromatic substances.

The holy anointing oil (Ex. xxx. 23–25) prescribed for use in Tabernacle rituals was required to be compounded according to the art of the perfumer. It consisted of olive oil, myrrh, cinnamon, calamus, and cassia, the solid ingredients probably being pulverized and boiled in the olive oil (*cf.* Jb. xli. 31). The manufacture of this preparation by unauthorized persons was strictly prohibited (Ex. xxx. 37, 38).

According to Pliny, unguents were preserved most successfully in alabaster containers. Under such conditions they improved with age, and became very valuable after a number of years. Thus the alabaster box of ointment mentioned in the Gospels (Mt. xxvi. 7; Mk. xiv. 3; Lk. vii. 37) was a very costly one containing spikenard (*Nardostachys jatamansi*). This herb, related to valerian, was imported from N India and used widely by Hebrews and Romans alike in the anointing of the dead. The qualifying adjective *pistikē* in Mk. xiv. 3 and Jn. xii. 3 may perhaps mean either 'liquid' or 'genuine'.

Ointments were employed in a quasi-sacramental sense when new kings were consecrated for their office. Thus Samuel anointed Saul (1 Sa. x. 1), Elijah anointed Jehu (2 Ki. ix. 3), and Jehoiada anointed Joash (2 Ki. xi. 12). Palestinian shepherds compounded an ointment of olive oil which they rubbed on to the bruised faces of sheep (*cf.* Ps. xxiii. 5). In New Testament times the sick were often anointed during a religious rite (Jas. v. 14). Unguents perfumed with myrrh were used to anoint the dead (Lk. xxiii. 56; Mk. xiv. 8).

BIBLIOGRAPHY. H. N. and A. L. Moldenke, *Plants of the Bible*, 1952, pp. 148 f. R.K.H.

OLD GATE. See JERUSALEM, IV.

OLD LATIN VERSIONS. See TEXT AND VERSIONS.

OLD TESTAMENT. See BIBLE, CANON OF THE OLD TESTAMENT.

OLIVE (Heb. *zayiṯ*; Gk. *elaia*). One of the most valuable trees of the ancient Hebrews, the olive is first mentioned in Gn. viii. 11, when the dove returned to the ark with an olive branch. When the Israelites took possession of Canaan it was a conspicuous feature of the flora (*cf.* Dt. vi. 11). At a later time the olive was esteemed with the vine as a profitable source of revenue (1 Sa. viii. 14; 2 Ki. v. 26).

Although the botanical name of the olive is *Olea europaea* L., the tree is thought to be a native of W Asia, being reintroduced subsequently into the Mediterranean region. Oriental peoples regarded the olive as a symbol of beauty, strength, divine blessing, and prosperity. In harmony with the Noahic tradition, the olive and the dove have been venerated ever since as symbols of friendship and peace (*cf.* Ps. lii. 8).

In many parts of Palestine the olive, of which there are four varieties in the Near East, is still very often the only tree of any size in the immediate locality. The cultivated olive grows to about 20 feet in height, with a contorted trunk and numerous branches. The tree develops slowly, but often attains an age of several centuries if left undisturbed. If cut down, new shoots spring up from the root, so that as many as five new trunks could thus come into being. Moribund olives usually sprout in this manner also (*cf.* Ps. cxxviii. 3). Olive groves were chiefly valued for their potential oil resources (see OIL), although they were also highly esteemed as a shelter from the burning sun and as a place where one could meditate (Lk. xxii. 39).

In antiquity olive-trees were distributed profusely across Palestine. The groves on the edge of the Phoenician plain were particularly impressive, as were those in the plain of Esdraelon and the valley of Shechem. Bethlehem, Hebron, Gilead, Lachish, and Bashan were all renowned in Bible times for their wealth of olive groves.

The berries borne by the olive ripened in the early autumn, and were harvested towards the end of November. The primitive and rather injurious method of gathering the olive berries described in Dt. xxiv. 20, whereby the trees were either shaken or beaten with poles, is still widely employed. In antiquity a few berries were left on the tree or on the ground beneath it for the benefit of the poor. The olive harvest was normally transported to the presses in baskets on the backs of donkeys. The oil was usually extracted from the berries by placing them in a shallow rock cistern and crushing them with a large upright millstone. Occasionally the berries were pounded by the feet of the harvesters (Dt. xxxiii. 24; Mi. vi. 15), but this was a rather inefficient procedure. After being allowed to stand for a time the oil separated itself from foreign matter, and was then stored in jars or rock cisterns.

The cherubim of the Solomonic Temple were fashioned from olive wood (1 Ki. vi. 23), and since they were some 18 feet high with a wing-spread of about 20 feet, it has been conjectured that they were composed of several pieces of wood joined together. While olive-wood is still used in Palestine for fine cabinet-work, the short gnarled trunks do not provide very lengthy pieces of timber. After it has been seasoned for a number of years the rich amber-grained wood can be polished to a high gloss.

So prolific a tree as the olive was naturally turned to a wide variety of usages. It was deemed worthy of being called the king of the trees (Jdg. ix. 8), and at coronations its oil was employed as an emblem of sovereignty. Olive boughs were used to construct booths during the Feast of Tabernacles (Ne. viii. 15). Fresh or pickled olives eaten with bread formed an important part of ancient Palestinian diet. The oil constituted the base of many unguent preparations, and was also used as a dressing for the hair. In addition it did duty as a fuel (Mt. xxv. 3), a medicine (Lk. x. 34; Jas. v. 14), and a food (2 Ch. ii. 10).

The olive-tree enjoyed wide symbolic usage among the Hebrews. The virility and fruitfulness of the tree suggested the ideal righteous man (Ps. lii. 8; Ho. xiv. 6), whose offspring was described as 'olive branches' (Ps. cxxviii. 3). An allusion to the facility with which the olive sometimes sheds its blossoms is found in Jb. xv. 33, where Eliphaz states that the wicked will 'cast off his flower as the olive'. In Zc. iv. 3 the two olive-trees were emblems of fruitfulness, indicating the abundance with which God had provided for human needs.

The fruit of the olive in its wild state is small and worthless. To become prolific the olive must be grafted, a process by which good stock is made to grow upon the wild shrub. Paul uses this fact as a powerful allegory (Rom. xi. 17) in showing how the Gentiles are under obligation to the true Israel, indicating that it is contrary to nature for a wild olive slip to be grafted on to good stock.

BIBLIOGRAPHY. W. M. Ramsay, *Pauline and Other Studies*, 1906, pp. 219 ff.; H. N. and A. L. Moldenke, *Plants of the Bible*, 1952, pp. 157–160.

R.K.H.

OLIVES, MOUNT OF. Olivet, or the Mount of Olives, is a small range of four summits, the highest being 2,723 feet, which overlooks Jerusalem and the Temple Mount from the east across the Kidron Valley and the Pool of Siloam. Jesus knew the Mount as a thickly wooded locality, rich in the olives which occasioned its name; but it was stripped bare of trees in the days of Titus. All the ground is holy, for He unquestionably walked there, but the exact location of any gospel incident is not necessarily demonstrated by the church now erected on the slopes of the Mount.

If, after the baptism, Jesus raised His eyes from Jordan's bank, far below sea-level, He would see the distant summit nearly 4,000 feet above, for Palestine is a small land of long perspectives.

The Old Testament references to Olivet at 2 Sa. xv. 30; Ne. viii. 15; Ezk. xi. 23 are slight. 1 Ki. xi. 7 and 2 Ki. xxiii. 13 refer to Solomon's idolatry, the erection of high places to Chemosh and Molech, which probably caused one summit to be dubbed the Mount of Offence. In the eschatological future God will part the Mount in two as He stands on it (Zc. xiv. 4).

Jews resident in Jerusalem used to announce the new moon to their compatriots in Babylonia by a chain of beacons starting on Olivet, each signalling the lighting of the next. But the wicked Samaritans lit false flares, and eventually human messengers had to replace the old beacons. Dalman feels the Mishnaic claim that this beacon service stretched as far afield as Mesopotamia is perfectly feasible (*Sacred Sites and Ways*, 1935, p. 263, n. 7). The Mount has close connections with the red heifer (see CLEAN AND UNCLEAN) and its ashes of purification (Nu. xix; *Parah* iii. 6, 7, 11), as with other ceremonies of levitical Judaism. According to one legend, the dove sent forth from the ark by Noah plucked her leaf from Olivet (Gn. viii. 11; Genesis Rabbah, xxxiii. 6). Some authorities considered the Jewish dead as unfit for resurrection save in Israel—the faithful who died abroad would eventually be rolled back through underground cavities (*Ketuboth* 111a), emerging at the sundered Mount of Olives (*Rabbinic Anthology*, 1938, pp. 660 ff.). When the Shekinah, or radiance of God's presence, departed from the Temple through sin, it lingered 3½ years on Olivet, so it is said, vainly awaiting repentance (Lamentations Rabbah, Proem XXV). The name 'Mountain of Three Lights' comes from the glow of the flaming Temple altar reflected on the hillside by night, the first beams of sunrise gilding the summit, and the fact that olives grown there once produced oil for the Temple lamps.

Hard by the Church of All Nations, at the base of Olivet, are some impressively ancient olive-trees, though not demonstrably as old as the time of Jesus. This is the area of the Garden of Gethsemane, and the precise spot of the agony is close, though undetermined. Half-way up the hill is the Church of Dominus Flevit. But why should He weep there? *HDB* cogently argues that Jesus really approached Jerusalem by Bethany, round the southern shoulder of Olivet, and that He wept when the city burst suddenly into view. Why should He scale the higher summit unnecessarily, walk half-way down with the city in full view, and then weep? A succession of Churches of the Ascension have long crowned the reputed summit of our Lord's assumption, and His supposed footprints were carefully preserved there as a tangible fulfilment of Zc. xiv. 4. Luke's Gospel favours the Bethany area as the real scene of the ascension. The visitor to Palestine learns the futility of pondering insolubles. R.A.S.

OLIVET DISCOURSE. According to all three Synoptists, our Lord delivered an eschatological discourse to His disciples on the Mount of Olives during the last week of His life (Mk. xiii. 3–37; Mt. xxiv. 3–xxv. 46; Lk. xxi. 5–36). As He faces rejection and humiliation (probably on the Tuesday, significantly the day after the cleansing of the Temple and two days before His agony and betrayal and arrest on the same mount), He calls on the disciples to watch and to take heed, for they too shall endure sorrows and suffer tribulations and be arrested (*cf.* Col. i. 24). On the eve of inaugurating the kingdom by His imminent death and resurrection, He warns them that although the kingdom will be truly established, 'the end is not yet'. They will *see* the kingdom of God (*q.v.*) in outward glory only after an interim period of suffering and persecution, during which the old Temple, the symbol of so many false messianic nationalistic hopes, will be completely destroyed.

The occasion of the discourse was a remark by an unnamed disciple about the grandeur of the Temple buildings. The massive stones with their apparent stability spoke of God's enduring presence among His people Israel. To the disciples' astonishment, Jesus predicts the complete destruction of the Temple. Consequently, at the end of the day, when Jesus, on His way back to Bethany, had paused to sit on the Mount of Olives in full view of the Temple, four of the disciples question Him about His prediction. They ask Him the time-question, 'When shall these things be?', and what sign will accompany them. Matthew expands 'these things' to include a reference to the *parousia* and the end of the age. By way of reply Jesus delivers the ensuing discourse about both the fall of Jerusalem (AD 70) and the return of the Son of man in outward glory.

The significant thing about the discourse is that Jesus deliberately does not answer the 'time-question', except to refer to the imminence of these eschatological events (Mk. xiii. 30) and to express His ignorance of the precise time of the end (verse 32). Instead, what He does, in effect, is to draw a distinction between *two conditions* of the kingdom.

a. There will be a prior condition when the glory of the kingdom, realized *de facto* by His death and resurrection, will be *hidden* behind a veil of suffering and sorrow and tribulation both in the world and in the Church. During this interim period (between the ascension and the *parousia*, when the Church lives by faith and not by sight (*cf.* 2 Cor. v. 7)), certain signs will be given that the old order is passing away and that the new messianic age has dawned. For example, there will be the destruction of the Temple (Mk. xiii. 14–20), the sign that, with the advent of the kingdom, the Jewish ritual has been fulfilled and abrogated, that the one true Sacrifice has abolished for ever the need for the Temple sacrifices (*cf.* the Epistle to the Hebrews). Deceivers will arise (verse 6), there will be sufferings, common to all men (verses 7, 8), suffering and persecution peculiar to the Church (verses 9–13), and false messiahs will come (verses 21–23). This prior condition of the kingdom, the time between the times, is variously described in the New Testament as 'the beginnings of sorrows' (verse 8), 'those days' (verses 17, 19, 24), 'the days' (verse 20, RV), 'the last days' (Acts ii. 17; 2 Tim. iii. 1; 2 Pet. iii. 3), 'the last hour' (1 Jn. ii. 18, RV), 'the last time' (Jude 18), 'the end of the ages' (Heb. ix. 26, RV). In this interim period God gives time for the gospel of the kingdom to be preached and for men to decide (Mk. xiii. 10).

b. Then comes the ultimate condition of the kingdom, when the glory of the Messiah's kingdom, which is a present reality, will be outwardly revealed to *sight* in the coming of the Son of man in power and glory (verses 24–27). (The phrase 'Son of man' in the New Testament, like the 'clouds', is always in the language of vision.) This is the *parousia* (Mt. xxiv. 3), 'the end' (Mk. xiii. 7), 'that day', 'that hour' (verse 32), 'the *kairos*' (verse 33), 'when the master . . . cometh' (verse 35), the 'day of the Lord' (Acts ii. 20; 2 Thes. ii. 2, RV), 'the end of all things' (1 Pet. iv. 7). This ultimate condition will be immediately heralded by cosmic signs (Mk. xiii. 24, 25) and the reason for the coming of the Son of man 'then' is to gather 'his elect' (verse 27).

If the disciples distinguish these two conditions of the kingdom the time question will look after itself (*cf.* 1 Thes. v. 1). They will not be discouraged when they endure suffering. Suffering is not a sign that the kingdom has not come, but merely that 'the end is not yet' (Mk. xiii. 7, RV). (This is also the burden of Paul's letters to the Thessalonians.) The signs therefore are given, on the one hand, that they might 'know' (verse 28), and, on the other hand, to make them 'take heed' and 'watch' (verses 5, 9, 23, 33, 34, 35, 37). The whole discourse is intensely practical and concludes with the application 'watch ye therefore', the parable of the fig-tree, 'learn' (verse 28), 'verily' (verse 30), 'take heed' (verse 33).

The Olivet discourse is sometimes called the 'Little Apocalypse', because it is thought by many critics to be a piece of Jewish–Christian apocalyptic literature incorporated into the Synoptic Gospels, either by the Evangelists themselves or by the early Church. This theory was originally put forward by Timothy Colani in his *Jésus-Christ et les Croyances Messianiques de son Temps* (1864) and taken up by Wendt, Hölscher, and others, although often in a modified form. Although our Lord is undoubtedly using symbolic apocalyptic imagery as plastic material in His hands (W. Manson) for the practical purpose of exhortation, this is clearly not typical apocalyptic literature with its usual 'orderly succession of events' (V. Taylor) and extravagant predictions (C. H. Dodd, T. F. Glasson). Such literature was rarely hortative or so full of imperatives, but was rather almost entirely predictive. Again, the critics seize on the point that the discourse does not answer the 'time question' put by the disciples, and therefore was probably an insertion. Similarly, they point to certain alleged inconsistencies in the discourse, for example, between the idea of a sudden *parousia* (Mk. xiii. 30) and a *parousia* heralded by signs (verses 5–25); between Jesus' profession of ignorance of the time of the end (verse 32) and this apparent 'orderly succession of events' prior to the end (verses 5–31); between this discourse and Jesus' teaching elsewhere. These criticisms reflect in the main a theological failure to see that there is 'intentional paradox' (Cranfield) in our Lord's distinction between the two conditions of the kingdom, and a deliberate refusal to answer the time-question.

Paradox lies at the heart of all New Testament eschatology. It is the core of the gospel to see that, in this interim period, we live in the tension between faith and sight, between being now in the realized kingdom and waiting until we see it. We know that the end is not yet and yet that it is near, even at the doors. We do not know the time of the *parousia*, we can only observe the signs of the times and watch and pray. Apocalyptic imagery is the language of faith waiting and longing to be turned into sight. It is faith's way of expressing an eschatological understanding of history, not a flight from history. If we rationalize this paradox between the two conditions of the kingdom, we shall inevitably see 'inconsistencies'. See also MARK, GOSPEL OF.

BIBLIOGRAPHY. G. R. Beasley-Murray, *Jesus and the Future*, 1954; *id., A Commentary on Mark XIII*, 1957; C. E. B. Cranfield, 'St. Mark xiii', *SJT*, VI, 1953, pp. 189–196, 287–303, VII, 1954, pp. 284–303; *id., The Gospel according to St. Mark*, 1959; W. G. Kümmel, *Promise and Fulfilment*, E.T., 1957; K. Barth, *Church Dogmatics*, III, 2, 1960, pp. 437–511. J.B.T.

OLYMPAS. An otherwise unknown but influential Christian greeted by Paul in Rom. xvi. 15. As the name, probably an abbreviation of Olympiodorus, was common throughout the Empire, its presence in this verse throws no light on the problem of the destination of Rom. xvi.

R.V.G.T.

OMEGA. See ALPHA AND OMEGA.

OMENS. See DIVINATION.

OMER. See WEIGHTS AND MEASURES.

OMRI (*'omrî*). **1.** 'Captain of the host' to Elah, the last king of the dynasty of Jeroboam the son of Nebat. Omri was with the Israelite army besieging the Philistine city of Gibbethon when news came that Zimri (*q.v.*) had slain the king and assumed the kingship (1 Ki. xvi. 16 ff.). The army elected Omri as successor (*c.* 885 BC; see CHRONOLOGY OF THE OLD TESTAMENT), and, raising the siege, he marched swiftly to Tirzah. Zimri, resigned to his fate, set fire to the palace and perished in the flames. Further opposition came from a rival group led by Tibni (LXX mentions also his brother Joram), and only after four years was Tibni defeated and killed.

Omri's choice of the hill of Samaria (1 Ki. xvi. 24) as the new capital of the northern kingdom was a master-stroke. The beautiful site's strategic position enabled the Israelites to repulse successive Syrian and Assyrian sieges until its capture by Sargon in 722 BC (even then only after a three-year siege). See SAMARIA.

Unsuccessful in his conflict with Damascus, Omri was compelled to cede certain cities to the Syrians (1 Ki. xx. 34). Apparently in an attempt to strengthen his position he married his son Ahab (*q.v.*) to the Tyrian daughter of Ethba'al, a high priest of Tyre. Her rôle in Israel's history was to bring bitter consequences. Omri so completely subdued Moab that not until Mesha's reign was that people strong enough to rebel against Israel (2 Ki. iii. 4 ff.; *cf.* the Moabite Stone (*q.v.*), lines 4 ff.). From the time of Shalmaneser III to that of Sargon, northern Israel appears in some Assyrian inscriptions as 'the land of the house of Omri', a probable indication that under Omri the Israelites first paid tribute to the Assyrians.

Though historically important, little is recorded of Omri's twelve-year reign. The first of a dynasty of four, he is said to have done 'evil in the sight of the Lord', and may have countenanced syncretistic practices in religion (*cf.* Mi. vi. 16). However, his death (*c.* 874 BC) evidently saw a quiet and prosperous kingdom inherited by his son Ahab.

2. A Benjamite, son of Becher (1 Ch. vii. 8). **3.** A Judahite, descendant of Pharez (1 Ch. ix. 4). **4.** Prince of Issachar in the time of David (1 Ch. xxvii. 18). J.D.D.

ON. 1. A venerable city, Egyp. *'Iwnw* ('city of the pillar'), Gk. Heliopolis, now represented by scattered or buried remains at Tell Ḥiṣn and Maṭariyeh, 10 miles north-east of Cairo. From antiquity it was the great centre of Egyp. sun-worship, where the solar deities Rē' and Atum were especially honoured, and the home of one of Egypt's several theological 'systems'. The pharaohs embellished the temple of Rē' with many obelisks—tall, tapering, monolithic shafts of square or rectangular section, each ending at the top in a pyramidally shaped point; such a 'pyramidion' represented the *benben* or sacred stone of Rē', as first to catch the rays of the rising sun. Each pharaoh from the Vth Dynasty onward (25th century BC) was styled 'son of Rē' ', and the priestly corporations of On/Heliopolis were equalled in wealth only by that of the god Ptah of Memphis and exceeded only by that of the god Amūn of Thebes, during *c.* 1600–1100 BC.

The prominence of On is reflected in Gn. xli. 45, 50, xlvi. 20, where Joseph as Pharaoh's new chief minister is married to Asenath, daughter of Potiphera, 'priest of On'. This title might mean that Potiphera was high priest there. His name, very fittingly, is compounded with that of the sun-god Rē' or P'Rē' whom he served (see POTIPHERA).

On next recurs in Heb. history under the appropriate pseudonym Beth-shemesh, 'House of the Sun', when Jeremiah (xliii. 13) threatens that Nebuchadrezzar will smash 'the pillars of Beth-shemesh', *i.e.* the obelisks of On/Heliopolis. Whether Isaiah's 'city of the sun' (xix. 18) is On is less clear. Aven (Heb. *'awen*) of Ezk. xxx. 17 is a variant pointing of *'ôn*, 'On', perhaps as a pun on *'awen*, 'trouble, wickedness', in Ezekiel's judgment on Egypt's cities.

2. On, son of Peleth, a Reubenite chief, rebelled with Korah against Moses in the wilderness, Nu. xvi. 1. K.A.K.

ONAN (*'ōnān*, 'vigorous'). The second son of Judah (Gn. xxxviii. 4, xlvi. 12; Nu. xxvi. 19; 1 Ch. ii. 3). On the death of his elder brother Er, Onan was commanded by Judah to contract a levirate marriage with Tamar, Er's widow. Onan, unwilling to follow this traditional practice, took steps to avoid a full consummation of the union, thus displeasing the Lord, who slew him (Gn. xxxviii. 8–10). Judah evidently attached some blame for his sons' deaths to Tamar herself (verse 11). For levirate marriage see MARRIAGE, IV. J.D.D.

ONESIMUS. A runaway slave belonging to Philemon, an influential Christian at Colossae. He made the acquaintance of Paul, while the latter was a prisoner, either at Rome or Ephesus (according to the view which is taken of the provenance of Colossians). He was converted by the apostle (Phm. 10), and became a trustworthy and dear brother (Col. iv. 9). His name, which means 'useful', was a common name for slaves, though not confined to them; and he lived up to it by making himself so helpful to Paul that the latter would have liked to have kept him to look after him as, Paul feels, Philemon would have wished (Phm. 13). But the apostle felt constrained to do nothing without Philemon's willing consent; so he returned the slave to his former owner, with a covering note—the canonical Philemon (*q.v.*). In this the apostle plays on the slave's name by describing him as 'once so little use to you, but now useful indeed, both to you and me'; and hints, tactfully but clearly, that he expects Philemon to take Onesimus 'back for good, no longer as a slave, but as more than a slave—as a dear brother, very dear indeed to me and how much dearer to you, both as man and as Christian' (Phm. 15, 16, NEB). Nevertheless, Paul admits that sending him back is like being deprived of a part of himself (Phm. 12).

The mention of Onesimus is one of the links which bind together Colossians and Philemon, and shows that they were sent from the same place at the same time. Some scholars believe that the Onesimus known to Ignatius and described by him in his Epistle to the Ephesians as 'a man of inexpressible love and your bishop' was none other than the runaway slave. This hypothesis, though not impossible, would seem improbable on chronological considerations. It is urged in its support that it supplies a reason why Philemon was preserved as a canonical book. On the other hand, its close connection with Colossians, and its importance for the light it throws on the Christian treatment of slaves, would seem to provide adequate reasons for its canonicity. See also PHILEMON. R.V.G.T.

ONESIPHORUS. In the Second Epistle to Timothy, written by Paul to Timothy at Ephesus, the apostle sends greetings to the household of Onesiphorus (iv. 19), and prays that the Lord's mercy may rest upon it, and that Onesiphorus himself may find mercy from the Lord on the great day of judgment. This true Christian friend had often brought relief to the apostle in his troubles, and had taken pains to search out and find him in Rome, where Paul was now in prison. His conduct in this respect, Paul notices, stood out in marked contrast to other Asian Christians who had deserted Paul in his hour of need. Like Onesimus, Onesiphorus had lived up to his name, which means 'profit-bringer'. The apostle reminds Timothy that he knew better than Paul himself about the many services rendered by Onesiphorus to the Christians at Ephesus (i. 16–18). R.V.G.T.

ONIONS (*b^{e}ṣālîm*). One of the vegetables for which the disgruntled Israelites sighed in the wilderness, the onion (*Allium cepa*) is mentioned only once in the Bible (Nu. xi. 5). Nevertheless, it was a common and much appreciated food, as it still is in the Near East. It was regarded, moreover, as possessing medicinal qualities. Cultivated by the Egyptians from the earliest times, the onion is represented on some of their tomb-paintings. J.D.D.

ONO. A town first mentioned in the lists of Thothmes III (1490–1436 BC). The Benjamites rebuilt it after the conquest of Canaan (1 Ch. viii. 12), and they reoccupied it after the Exile (Ne. xi. 31–35). The area was called the Plain of Ono (Ne. vi. 2). It lay near Lydda. Perhaps it is modern Kafr 'Anâ. D.F.P.

ONYCHA. Incorrectly interpreted as nominative in Vulg. and EVV, it is the Gk. accusative of *onyx* as used in LXX—an error conveniently distinguishing it from the precious stone. 'Onyx' means talon or claw, but 'onycha', Heb. *š^{e}ḥēleṯ* (Ex. xxx. 34 only), is a component of the holy incense made by Moses at God's bidding. It is produced by burning the claw-shaped valves closing the shell apertures of certain molluscs. R.A.S.

ONYX. See JEWELS AND PRECIOUS STONES.

OPHEL. See JERUSALEM, IV.

OPHIR (*'ôpir*, Gn. x. 29; *'ôp̄îr*, 1 Ki. x. 11). **1.** The name of the son of Yoqtān in the genealogy of Shem (Gn. x. 29 = 1 Ch. i. 23). This tribe is known from pre-islamic inscriptions (G. Ryckmans, *Les noms propres sud-sémitiques*, 1934, pp. 298, 339 f.). Their area lies between Saba in the Yemen and Ḥawilah (Ḥawlān) as described in Gn. x. 29. Islamic tradition equates Yoqtān with Qaḥtān, a son of Ishmael and 'father of all Arabs'.

2. The country from which fine gold was imported to Judah (2 Ch. viii. 18; Jb. xxii. 24, xxviii. 16; Ps. xlv. 9; Is. xiii. 12), sometimes in large quantities (1 Ch. xxix. 4), and with valuable almug(sandal?)-wood (1 Ki. x. 11), silver, ivories, and two kinds of apes (1 Ki. x. 22), and precious stones (2 Ch. ix. 10). It was reached by Solomon's fleet from Ezion-geber on the Gulf of Aqabah (1 Ki. ix. 28) employing 'ships of Tarshish', which might be ships normally used for carrying ore (1 Ki. xxii. 48; see SHIPS AND BOATS). These voyages took 'three years', that is perhaps one entire year and parts of two others. The trade was sufficiently well known for Ophir to be synonymous with the fine gold which was its principal product (Jb. xxii. 24). In Is. xiii. 12 Ophir is paralleled with *'ôqir*, 'I will make precious' (*Hebrew Union College Annual*, XII–XIII, 1937–8, p. 61). A confirmation of this trade is found in an ostracon, found at Tell Qasile (Afek) north-east of Tel Aviv in 1946, inscribed *zhb 'p̄r lbyt ḥrn š≡*, 'gold from Ophir for Beth Horon 30 shekels' (*JNES*, X, 1951, pp. 265–267).

Various theories have been put forward for the site of Ophir.

a. SW Arabia as in (1) above.

b. SE Arabia: Oman. These are not far from Ezion-geber, and it is necessary to assume both that the three-year voyage included laying up during the hot summer and that some commodities (*e.g.* apes) not commonly found in S Arabia were brought to Ophir as an entrepôt from more distant places.

c. NE African coast: Somaliland, *i.e.* the Egyp. *Punt*, a source of the frankincense and myrrh and those items described as from Ophir (W. F. Albright, *Archaeology and the Religion of Israel*, 1953, pp. 133–135, 212).

d. (S)upāra, 60 miles north of Bombay, India. Jerome and LXX interpreted Ophir as India. In favour of this interpretation are the facts that all the commodities named are familiar in ancient India, and it is known that from the second millennium BC there was a lively sea-trade between the Persian Gulf and India.

e. Other, more doubtful, suggestions include Apir, Baluchistan (Hommel), and Zimbabwe, S Rhodesia. D.J.W.

OPHRAH. 1. A city in Benjamin (Jos. xviii. 23; 1 Sa. xiii. 17). It has been identified with modern et-Tayibeh, a commanding hilltop position some 6 miles north-east of Michmash. Probably identical with the Ephraim of 2 Sa. xiii. 23; 2 Ch. xiii. 19; Jn. xi. 54.

2. Ophrah in Manasseh was Gideon's home and the place where his altar of Jehovah-shalom was shown in later times (Jdg. vi. 24). The following identifications have been suggested: (*a*) Fer'a-ta, west of Gerizim (Conder). This location is certainly near Shechem, but it is inaccessible from the east. Philologically, it suits Pirathon (Jdg. xii. 15) better. (*b*) Tell el-Far'a (Dalman, *PJB*, VIII, 1912, pp. 31 f. *et al.*), a stronghold 7 miles north-east of Shechem; contested by Albright (*JPOS*, XI, 1931, pp. 245 ff.), and now identified as the site of the biblical Tirzah (see ARCHAEOLOGY). (*c*) Et-Tayibeh, 8 miles from Beth-shan towards Tabor (Abel, *JPOS*, XVII, 1937, pp. 39 ff.). If not too exposed to the Midianites, this is perhaps most likely. Arabs often substituted *ṭaiyibeh* ('fortunate') where the place-name *'ōprâ* persisted in the Middle Ages, as it suggested black magic (Abel, *JPOS*, XVII, 1937, p. 38).

J.P.U.L.

ORACLE. The translation 'oracle' occurs seventeen times in the AV of the Old Testament. Sixteen times it is the consistent mistranslation of the Heb. *d*[e]*ḇîr*, used exclusively of the inner shrine of Solomon's Temple (see fig. 204). The faulty derivation from *dibber*, 'speak', rather than from *dāḇar* in the sense of 'to be behind' stems from the translations of Aquila and Symmachus (who used *chrēmatistērion*, 'oracle') and the Vulgate (*oraculum*). That in heathen temples the chambers where the gods delivered their utterances (the oracular shrine of Apollo at Delphi was the most famous of these) were designated 'oracles' undoubtedly influenced the change as well.

In 2 Sa. xvi. 23 'oracle' translates the Heb. *dāḇār* and refers simply to the *word* or *utterance* of God without any specific indication of how this would be elicited; although some have here inferred a reference to the Urim and Thummin (*q.v.*) (1 Sa. xxviii. 6). In the RVmg 'oracle' is sometimes used in place of 'burden' in the title of certain prophecies as a translation of the Heb. *maśśā'*.

In the New Testament 'oracle' occurs four times (each time in the plural) as the exclusive translation of the Gk. *logia.* Here it stands for a divine utterance and refers generally to the entire Old Testament or some specific part of it. In Acts vii. 38 the reference is either to the Decalogue or the entire content of the Mosaic law. These oracles are said to be 'living', *zōnta*, that is, 'enduring' or 'abiding'. In Rom. iii. 2 the reference is to all the written utterances of God through the Old Testament writers, but with special regard to the divine promises made to Israel. The 'oracles of God' in Heb. v. 12 represent the body of Christian doctrine as it relates both to its Old Testament foundation and to God's final utterance through His Son (Heb. i. 1). 1 Pet. iv. 11 teaches that the New Testament preacher must speak as one who speaks the oracles of God; treating his words as carefully as if they were inspired Scripture.

The theological significance of the oracle is emphasized by B. B. Warfield when he concludes that *ta logia*, as employed in the New Testament, are 'divinely authoritative communications before which men stand in awe and to which they bow in humility' (*The Inspiration and Authority of the Bible*, 1948, p. 403).

R.H.M.

ORATOR. The *rhētōr* was a professional teacher of rhetoric, or, as Tertullus (Acts xxiv. 1), a speech writer who might accept a barrister's brief himself. The extreme refinement of the rhetorical art, which formed the hallmark of higher education, and the difficulties of a hearing before a foreign court, made his services indispensable to the Jews. They were rewarded with a fine speech, notable for its ingratiating exordium. Paul, a master of the art himself, was able to reply in his own person. Elsewhere (1 Cor. ii. 4) he disdained professional skill.

BIBLIOGRAPHY. M. L. Clarke, *Rhetoric at Rome*, 1953.

E.A.J.

ORCHARD. Well known in various Bible lands throughout antiquity, these were plantations of fruit trees, specifically including pomegranates (Ec. ii. 5 and Ct. iv. 13 where 'orchard' renders Heb. *pardēs*). The *pardēs* of Ne. ii. 8 furnished timber, and so is there rendered 'forest' (*q.v.*).

K.A.K.

ORDER. See PRIESTS AND LEVITES.

ORDINANCE. See DECREE.

ORDINATION. Considering the rôle played by the ministry throughout the history of the Church, references to ordination are surprisingly few in the New Testament. Indeed, the word 'ordination' does not occur, and the verb 'to ordain' in the technical sense does not occur either. A number of verbs are translated 'ordain' in AV, but these all have meanings like 'appoint'. For example, *cheirotoneō* is used of the institution of elders in certain Galatian churches (Acts xiv. 23), but before we think of this as denoting 'ordination' in our sense of the term we must note its use in passages such as 2 Cor. viii. 19, where it refers to the brother who was 'chosen of the churches to travel with us . . .'

The Twelve were chosen by Christ to be very near to Himself and to be sent forth to minister (Mk. iii. 14). But there is no word of any ceremony of ordination. Mark says that Jesus 'made (*poieō*)' twelve, and Luke that He 'chose (*eklegō*)' them (Mk. iii. 14; Lk. vi. 13). This was a very solemn occasion (Luke tells us that Jesus prayed all night before making His selection). But there is no 'ordination' mentioned. John speaks of the risen Lord as breathing on the ten, saying, 'Receive ye the Holy Ghost' (Jn. xx. 22); but it is difficult to see an ordination in this. It is probably significant that when Matthias took the place of Judas there is again no mention of any ordination. Lots were cast, and when the choice of Matthias was known he was simply 'numbered' with the others (Acts i. 26). Similarly, prophets and others are called directly by God, though some at least are said to be 'for the work of ministry' (Eph. iv. 12; the word 'ministry' here is, of course, used of service in a wide sense).

Luke tells us of the appointment of the Seven (Acts vi), and this is often understood as the institution of the diaconate. This may indeed be the case, but it is far from certain. Some think that the presbyterate is meant, and others deny that there is ordination to any ecclesiastical office. They think that Luke is describing nothing more than a temporary measure to meet a difficult situation. If the traditional view is accepted, then the essential thing about ordination is the laying on of hands with prayer. But in view of the uncertainties, and the wide use in antiquity of the laying on of hands, it is not possible to build much on this passage. Nor are we any better off when we read of elders as being appointed in the Galatian churches (Acts xiv. 23), for, while we may be tolerably sure that they were ordained in some way, nothing at all is told us of how this was done or what was expected of it.

Our most important information comes from the Pastoral Epistles. Paul counsels Timothy, 'Neglect not the gift that is in thee, which was given thee by prophecy, with the laying on of the hands of the presbytery' (1 Tim. iv. 14). This passage yields us three items of information about Timothy's ordination. First, it meant the giving to him of a 'gift' (*charisma*), the spiritual endowment needed for the work of ministering. Secondly, this came to him 'by (*dia*) prophecy'. Thirdly, it came with (*meta*) the laying on of hands by the elders. The essential thing about ordination is the divine gift. Nothing can compensate for its lack. But there is also an outward act, the laying on of hands. It is likely that Paul refers to the same rite when he speaks of his own laying on of hands on Timothy (2 Tim. i. 6), though the possibility should not be overlooked that some other rite is in mind, perhaps something more akin to our confirmation than to our ordination. We might be able to make a better judgment if we knew when this took place, whether at the beginning of Paul's association with Timothy, or not long before the writing of the letter. If with most commentators we take this to refer to ordination, the meaning will be that Paul joined with the elders in the laying on of hands, which in any case would be antecedently likely. It is probable that we have a third reference to the same ordination in the words about 'the prophecies which went before on thee' (1 Tim. i. 18).

Ordination is always a solemn affair, and it may be that the words 'lay hands suddenly on no man' (1 Tim. v. 22) emphasize this. But in view of the context it is perhaps more likely that they refer to the reception of penitents back into fellowship.

All this makes for a somewhat meagre harvest, which is all the more disappointing, since the Pastorals show us how important the ministry was, especially the offices of presbyter and deacon. Titus, for example, is bidden 'ordain (*kathistēmi*) elders in every city' (Tit. i. 5), and much attention is paid to the qualifications for ministers. It is possible to suggest that the Christians took over the ordination of elders from the similar Jewish institution, but this does not get us far. All that we can say for certain is that the important thing for ministering is the divine gift, and that the essential rite in the earliest time appears to have been that of the laying on of hands with prayer. See MINISTRY, SPIRITUAL GIFTS, LAYING ON OF HANDS. L.M.

OREB (Heb. *'ōrēḇ*, 'raven'). **1.** A Midianite prince in the army routed by Gideon. **2.** The rock of Oreb, named after this prince, and remembered for the great defeat of Midian (Jdg. vii. 25; Is. x. 26). The Ephraimites cut off the enemy's retreat at the fords of Jordan, presumably not far from Jezreel (Bethbarah might be a ford named 'Abarah, 12 miles south of the Sea of Galilee). The rock was probably west of Jordan, as it is likely that most of the enemy who crossed made good their escape. J.P.U.L.

ORGAN. See MUSIC AND MUSICAL INSTRUMENTS, II*b*.

ORION. See STARS.

ORNAMENTS. From Palaeolithic times ornament has been used by man to adorn the objects which surround him in his daily life. When the intention is right, the skill of the craftsman is a thing pleasing to God, and indeed for the building of the tabernacle Bezaleel was filled with the spirit (*rûaḥ*) of God (Ex. xxxi. 1–5), as were those who were to make the garments for the high priest (Ex. xxviii. 3).

Archaeological discoveries have shown that in biblical times the carving of wood and ivory was done with great skill; weaving and embroidery reached a high standard; and the techniques involved in fine metalwork were well understood (see ARTS AND CRAFTS). Three main divisions of ornamented objects may be distinguished.

I. PERSONAL

There is no evidence for the practice of ornamental tattooing in the Ancient Near East, but clothing was often elaborately decorated, and jewellery was widely used. Though few examples of textiles have been recovered outside Egypt, the Assyrian and Persian sculptured reliefs, and mural paintings at Mari on the Euphrates give, sometimes in great detail, representations of garments with fine embroidery (see figs. 25, 70, 77). The Egyptian tomb paintings likewise depict clothing in detail, and in one tomb at Beni Hasan a group of Asiatic nomads with brightly-coloured costumes (*cf.* fig. 70, No. 12; see also *IBA*, fig. 25) gives an idea of the sort of ornamental clothing perhaps worn by the Patriarchs (see DRESS).

Many examples of jewellery (see JEWELS AND PRECIOUS STONES) have been found in excavations, perhaps the most outstanding being those from the 'Royal Tombs' at Ur (see plate I*c*).

Various terms referring to objects of personal adornment are translated 'ornament' in AV, but their precise significance is in many cases uncertain. Among these are the following: 1. *ḥ^alî* (Pr. xxv. 12), perhaps from a Semitic root *ḥlh*, 'to adorn'; all EVV translate 'ornament'. The word also occurs in Ct. vii. 1 where EVV translate it 'jewel'. 2. *liwyâ* (Pr. i. 9, iv. 9; lit. 'twisted thing'); RV renders 'chaplet' and RSV 'garland'. 3. *'^aḏî* (Ex. xxxiii. 4–6; 2 Sa. i. 24; Is. xlix. 18; Je. ii. 32, iv. 30; Ezk. vii. 20, xvi. 7, 11, xxiii. 40), derived from *'āḏâ*, 'to ornament', 'to deck oneself'; all EVV translate 'ornament'. 4. *p^e'ēr* (Is. lxi. 10), from *pā'ar* in the Pi'el, meaning 'to beautify'; RV and RSV translate 'garland'. 5. *ṣ^e'āḏâ* (Is. iii. 20), of unknown etymology. It probably signifies an 'armlet' (so RSV); RV gives 'ankle chain'. 6. *'eḵes* (Is. iii. 18), perhaps connected with Arab. *'ikāsu*, 'to hobble (a camel)', from *'akasa*, 'to reverse, tie backwards', whence RV, RSV 'anklet'. The root occurs as a verb in Is. iii. 16, where it is translated 'making a tinkling'.

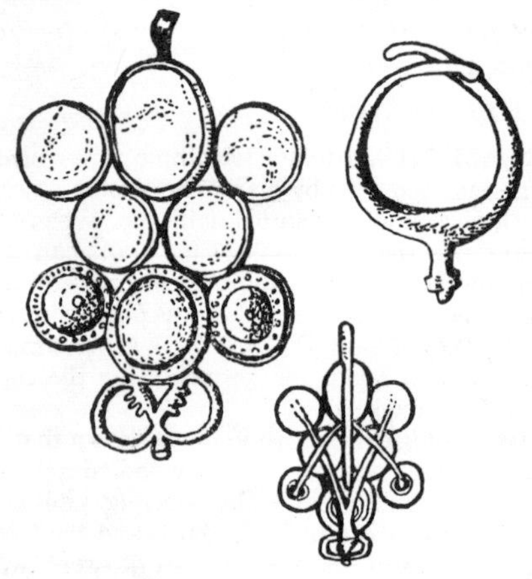

Fig. 153. *Left:* An elaborate ear-ring of gold and faience. *Below:* A reduced drawing of the same ornament as seen from the back, showing detail of the construction. *Right:* A gold nose-ring (not to same scale). Both from Megiddo, 16th–15th centuries BC.

Though on an occasion such as a wedding the putting on of ornaments and jewels by the participants is treated as right and proper (Is. lxi. 10), the immoderate use of personal ornament is roundly condemned (Is. iii. 18–23; 1 Tim. ii. 9). Is. iii provides a catalogue of different kinds of ornaments which are translated variously in EVV. Some of these are *hapax legomena*, and little can be added to the AV interpretation. The 'bracelet' (*šērâ*) of verse 19 is supported by the probable Akkadian cognate *šemêru* (*šewêru*) with this meaning. Likewise in verse 21, 'ring' (*ṭabba'aṯ*, RSV 'signet ring') is supported by Akkad. *ṭimbu'u*, *ṭimbûtu*, 'seal ring' (see SEAL). AV renderings which have been radically altered in the later versions are verse 20 'earring' (*lahaš*; RV, RSV 'amulet', *q.v.*), and verse 22 'wimple' (*miṭpaḥaṯ*; RV 'shawl', RSV 'cloak') and 'crisping pin' (*ḥārîṭ*; RV 'satchel', RSV 'handbag').

Among other articles of personal adornment were: 1. *ḥāḥ*, usually a hook or ring for holding a man (2 Ki. xix. 28) or animal (Ezk. xxix. 4) captive, but in Ex. xxxv. 22 an ornament (AV 'bracelet', RV, RSV 'brooch'); 2. *śah^arôn*, probably a crescent-shaped object which was used on camels (Jdg. viii. 21; AV 'ornament', RV 'crescent') and humans (Jdg. viii. 26; Is. iii. 18, AV 'round tire like the moon', RV 'crescent'); and many different kinds of chain ornaments, including 3. *rāḇîḏ*, probably a twisted circlet for the neck (Gn. xli. 42; Ezk. xvi. 11); 4. *'^anāq*, a more elaborate form made of plaited wire which might have pendants attached (Jdg. viii. 26; Pr. i. 9; Ct. iv. 9); 5. *šarš^erâ*, probably a more flexible chain of the link type (Ex. xxviii. 14, 22, xxxix. 15; 1 Ki. vii. 17; 2 Ch. iii. 5, 16); 6. *ḥārûz*, a necklace of beads strung on a thread (Ct. i. 10; RV 'string of jewels').

Another type of ornament, mentioned in 1 Macc. x. 89, xi. 58, xiv. 44, is the 'buckle' (Gk. *porpē*, 'buckle pin', 'buckle brooch').

A special case of personal ornament is found in the garments of the high priest (see DRESS (*d*)). The linen coat was of an ornamental weave (Ex. xxviii. 39, RV, RSV; see fig. 133), the ephod and the girdle were decorative (Ex. xxviii. 6, 8) and round the hem of the robe of the ephod were alternate bells and pomegranates (Ex. xxviii. 31–35). In addition to these the breastplate (see BREASTPLATE OF THE HIGH PRIEST) contained ornamental elements.

The ancient Hebrews, like their neighbours, probably wore amulets and personal seals for ornamentation (see AMULETS; SEAL, and figs. 7, 187).

In Ex. xiii. 16 and Dt. vi. 8, xi. 18 the word 'frontlets' (*ṭôṭāp̄ôṯ*) may refer to some ornament of the head. A connection with Akkad. *ṭaṭāpu*, 'to encircle', has been suggested, but this remains uncertain.

II. MOVABLE OBJECTS

From very early times painted or incised decoration was used on pottery (*q.v.*), and though in historical times the abundance of other possessions resulted in absence of decoration, certain wares such as Mycenaean and that called 'Philistine' are easily distinguishable and provide useful criteria for dating to the archaeologist (see ARCHAEOLOGY). Archaeology has shown that tools and weapons had, on occasion, appropriate decorations, but the class of small object which often called forth the most elaborate and delicate ornamentation was that of cosmetic equipment. Boxes, jars for unguents (fig. 42), palettes for mixing pigments (fig. 58), and mirror handles (fig. 143) of elaborately carved bone and ivory have been excavated in Syria, Palestine, Mesopotamia, and Egypt. Furniture, especially in royal palaces, was sometimes richly ornamented with carved ivory panels (*cf.* 1 Ki. x. 18; 2 Ch. ix. 17; Am. vi. 4 and IVORY; see figs. 56, 114). That ornamental carpets were used is shown by stone paving slabs carved in replica of carpets from the Assyrian royal palaces. Elaborately ornamented horse harnesses are portrayed on the Assyrian palace reliefs (see figs. 25, 108), and camel harness was also evidently decorated (Jdg. viii. 21, 26).

The tabernacle and its contents were ornamented, under the skill of Bezaleel, with cunning workmanship (see TABERNACLE). This was also a pagan practice, as is shown by discoveries of temple furniture from Megiddo, Beth-shan, and other sites, where incense and offering stands are decorated with birds, animals, serpents (symbol of fertility), and human figures (see fig. 18). These were the common trappings of the pagan cults of the Israelites' neighbours, and often the most elaborate ornament was reserved for the casquet of the deceased. Elaborately carved stone sarcophagi are known from Phoenicia and Egypt, and the discoveries in the 'Royal Tombs' at Ur (see plates I*b*, *c*) and in the tomb of Tutankhamūn show the wealth of ornamental riches that accompanied the dead to the grave.

III. ARCHITECTURAL

Buildings in antiquity, particularly palaces, were decorated both inside and out. The inside walls of important rooms in the palaces of the Assyrian kings at Nineveh and Khorsabad were adorned by carved bas-reliefs (see, *e.g.*, plates VI*a*, VII*b*) and the doorways guarded by great composite beasts (*IBA*, fig. 44). These reliefs were probably partially coloured in antiquity, being in fact glorified murals, examples of which from the Assyrian period were discovered at Til Barsip. In the early second millennium palace at Mari remains of several mural paintings were recovered suggesting that such decoration has not been discovered more often only on account of its perishable nature.

In Egypt, while the best-known mural paintings are found in rock-cut tombs, palaces with murals have been excavated at Malkata (Amenophis III) and el-Amarna (Amenophis IV). The great temples at Karnak and Luxor were decorated with carved (*e.g.* fig. 87) and painted murals (*cf.* fig. 125) and hieroglyphic inscriptions, the hieroglyphs forming ornamental elements. Ivory was probably used not only for the decoration of furniture but also for application to suitable parts of important rooms, as is suggested by caches of carved ivories found at Nimrud, Arslan Tash, Megiddo, and Samaria (*cf.* 1 Ki. xxii. 39; Ps. xlv. 8; Am. iii. 15; see IVORY).

Outside decoration, while in earlier periods it might consist of revetted walls, or in Assyria guardian beasts at gateways, reached a sumptuous level in Nebuchadrezzar's Babylon, where excavation has revealed great façades of coloured glazed bricks with animals and rosettes at intervals (see fig. 150 and plate VIII*a*).

The Persians in the latter part of the first millennium BC recruited craftsmen from all over the Middle East to build and decorate the great ceremonial city of Persepolis, even employing men from as far afield as the Aegean. Aegean influences had already been felt in the second millennium (Alalaḫ, Ugarit), and it is probable that the term *kap̄tôr* in Ex. xxv. 31–36, xxxvii. 17–22 (AV 'knop') and Am. ix. 1; Zp. ii. 14 (AV 'lintel') refers to some decorative architectural feature, perhaps a column capital, derived from Crete or the Aegean (see CAPHTOR).

There is reason to believe that under the Monarchy the kings and the wealthy would have followed the customs of the surrounding peoples in the decoration of their palaces and houses.

BIBLIOGRAPHY. No one work covers the whole subject. Relevant material is to be found incidentally in C. Singer, E. Holmyard, and A. Hall, *A History of Technology*, I, 1954, especially pp. 413–447, 623–703, and *passim* in H. Frankfort, *The Art and Architecture of the Ancient Orient*, 1954; W. S. Smith, *The Art and Architecture of Ancient Egypt*, 1958; and for Palestine, A. G. Barrois, *Manuel d'Archéologie Biblique*, I–II, 1939–53. T.C.M.

ORPAH. A Moabitess, the daughter-in-law of Naomi, and Ruth's sister-in-law (Ru. i. 4). After their husbands died they came from Moab to Judah, but Orpah, following Naomi's advice, remained, to return to her former home and the worship of Chemosh (Ru. i. 15; 1 Ki. xi. 33). Even so, Naomi commended her to Yahweh's protection. M.G.

ORPHAN, FATHERLESS (Heb. *yāṯôm*; Gk. *orphanos*). The care of the fatherless was from earliest times a concern of the Israelites, as of the surrounding nations. The Covenant Code (Ex. xxii. 22), and the Deuteronomic Code particularly, were most solicitous for the welfare of such (Dt. xvi. 11, 14, xxiv. 17), protecting their rights of inheritance and enabling them to share in the great annual feasts and to have a portion of the tithe crops (Dt. xxvi. 12). It is specifically stated, moreover, that God works on their behalf (Dt. x. 18), and that condemnation awaits those who oppress them (Dt. xxvii. 19; *cf.* Mal. iii. 5).

Though many orphans would be aided by kindred and friends (Jb. xxix. 12, xxxi. 17), there was a general failure to fulfil the provisions of the Codes, testified by the accusations and laments found in the prophets, in the Psalms, and in the Book of Job. 'In thee,' says Ezekiel (xxii. 7), speaking of Jerusalem, 'have they vexed the fatherless and the widow'. Justice, it is averred, was withheld from orphans; their plight is pitiable, for they are robbed and killed (Jb. xxiv. 3, 9; Ps. xciv. 6; Is. i. 23, x. 2; Je. v. 28), making even more vivid the Psalmist's words against the wicked: 'Let his children be fatherless . . .' (cix. 9).

God, however, is specially concerned for the fatherless (Pss. x. 14, 18, lxviii. 5, cxlvi. 9; Ho. xiv. 3; *cf.* Jn. xiv. 18), especially when they look in vain to men for help (*cf.* Ps. xxvii. 10).

The only New Testament occurrence of the

word in AV makes an integral part of true religion the visiting of 'the fatherless and widows in their affliction . . .' (Jas. i. 27). J.D.D.

Fig. 154. A captured ostrich with its feathers and eggs. From a tomb of the XVIIIth Dynasty at Thebes.

OSNAPPAR. See ASHURBANIPAL.

OSPREY. See BIRDS OF THE BIBLE.

OSSIFRAGE. See BIRDS OF THE BIBLE.

OSTRACA. See PAPYRI AND OSTRACA.

OSTRICH. See BIRDS OF THE BIBLE.

OTHNIEL (*'oṯnî'ēl*, LXX *Gothoniel*). Brother, or perhaps nephew, of Caleb ben Jephunneh (Jdg. i. 13). In the context, the phrase 'Caleb's younger brother' probably applies to Othniel not Kenaz. Distinguishing himself in the sack of Kiriath-sepher (Debir), he married Achsah, Caleb's daughter. Later he saw the beginnings of apostasy and the domination by Cushan-rishathaim (*q.v.*), against whom he led a successful revolt, becoming the first of the judges. Jdg. iii. 10 indicates that he was a charismatic leader, and he first restored authority and order ('judged' means this as well as deliverance; *cf.* 1 Sa. vii. 15, viii. 20).

His family provided a duty officer under David (1 Ch. xxvii. 15). See JUDGES. J.P.U.L.

OVEN. See BREAD.

OWL. See BIRDS OF THE BIBLE.

OX. See CATTLE.

P

PADAN, PADAN-ARAM. The 'field' or 'plain' of Aram (RSV 'Mesopotamia') is the name given in the area around Harran in Upper Mesopotamia, north of the junction of the rivers Ḫabur and Euphrates in Gn. xxv. 20, xxviii. 2, xxxi. 18, *etc.*, and is identical with Aram-naharaim, 'Aram of the rivers', of Gn. xxiv. 10; Dt. xxiii. 4; Jdg. iii. 8. Abraham dwelt in this area before emigrating to Canaan. He sent his servant there to provide a bride for Isaac, and thither Jacob fled from Esau. For a suggested identification of Padan-aram, near Harran, see *AS*, II, 1952, p. 40. R.A.H.G.

PAHATH-MOAB (lit. 'Governor of Moab'). Perhaps an ancestor had been a governor of Moab when Moab was subject to Israel. The name of a Jewish clan consisting of two families, Jeshua and Joab, 2,812 of whom returned to Judah with Zerubbabel, Ezr. ii. 6 (Ne. vii. 11 gives the figure 2,818) and 201 with Ezra (Ezr. viii. 4). Of this clan certain members are listed in Ezr. x. 30 as having married foreign women. Ne. x. 14 records that Pahath-moab among princes, priests, and Levites set his seal to the covenant made on the return of the exiles to Jerusalem. R.A.H.G.

PAINT, PAINTING. See ART, COSMETICS AND PERFUMERY.

PALACE. Used in AV to describe the following:

1. The royal residence (*bêṯ hammeleḵ*) where dwelt the king, his family, advisers, and servants (2 Ch. ix. 11; 2 Ki. vii. 9). It was sometimes referred to by the king's name ('house of David', 2 Ch. viii. 11).

2. The 'great house' (AV 'palace', 'temple'; Heb. *hêḵāl*; Akkadian *ekallu*) was the principal building in a city. The use of the term did not necessarily imply any religious association. Thus the palace of Ahab at Jezreel (1 Ki. xxi. 1), of the Assyrian king at Nineveh (Na. ii. 6), of the Babylonians at Babylon (2 Ki. xx. 18; Dn. iv. 4), and of the Persian ruler at Susa (Ezr. iv. 14) are so described.

3. The prominent building on the citadel (Heb. *'armôn*; Ugar. *rmm*), with special reference to Jerusalem (Is. xxxii. 14), Samaria (Am. iii. 10, 11), and Israel (Am. vi. 8). This term is used for the palaces of Damascus (Ben-hadad) in Am. i. 4; Je. xlix. 27; Tyre in Is. xxiii. 13; Babylon in Is. xxv. 2; Edom in Is. xxxiv. 13; and by Amos for Gaza, Ammọn, Bozrah, Ashdod, and Egypt (i. 7, 12, iii. 9). The 'palace' of Samaria (Am. iv. 3, AV; *haharmônâ*) is possibly to be translated 'to Rimmon'.

4. The aspect of the palace as a fortress is also emphasized. This was the 'palace' (Aram. *bîrâ*, *bîrāniyâ*) at Jerusalem (1 Ch. xxix. 1, 19; Ne. ii. 8) and at Susa (Ne. i. 1; Est. i. 2, *etc.*). The 'palace garden' (*ginnaṯ habbîṯān*) was an 'inner garden' (Akkad. *bitanu*) found in the courtyard of many large buildings (Est. vii. 7, 8). The 'palace of silver' (Ct. viii. 9, RV 'turret') and the 'palaces' of the Ammonites (Ezk. xxv. 4, *ṭîrâ*) are 'enclosures'. The tents of the palace seen by Daniel (xi. 45) may be the general quarters (tents) or a pillared hall (*'appeḏen*, *cf.* Old Persian *apadāna*, 'palace').

5. The 'palace' of the high priest (Mt. xxvi. 3; Jn. xviii. 15) and of the nobles (Lk. xi. 21) was a court (*aulē*). Adjacent to this in Jerusalem was the residence of the state-governor or 'praetor's' court (*praitōrion*, Mt. xxvii. 27; Mk. xv. 16; Jn. xviii. 28). At Caesarea this was part of Herod's palace (Acts xxiii. 35). The 'palace' in Phil. i. 13, AV (Gk. *praitōrion*) was either the headquarters of the praetorian guard in Rome or the official residence in Ephesus of the Roman governor of the province of Asia.

The palace in a faithful nation is marked by peace (Je. xxx. 18; Ps. cxxii. 7) and Paul uses it (Gk. *oikodomē* as the usual translation of Heb. *hêḵāl*) to describe the great 'building' of the Church of the body of Christ (1 Cor. iii. 9). Alternatively, the palace was condemned as the symbol of luxury (Am. vi. 8) and the object of the divine wrath (Is. xiii. 22).

Archaeological excavation shows that the palaces of Palestine differed little from those of their neighbours (see ARCHITECTURE). The fortress-palace of Saul at Gibeah (see fig. 95) was probably similar in lay-out to the Jebusite palace occupied by David in Jerusalem (2 Sa. v. 7–9). His own plans for a palace built with Tyrian help were completed by Solomon, whose palace is described in 1 Ki. vii. 1–12. This consisted of a hyperstyle entrance hall of 100 by 50 cubits named 'House of the Forest of Lebanon' (after its cedar columns) and a waiting-room outside the throne-room, off which led the royal apartments, harem, and servants' quarters, which were built round a courtyard with an entrance into the southern portico of the Temple.

Parts of the palace of Ahab-Jeroboam at Samaria (*q.v.*), the Persian governor at Lachish (*q.v.*), and the Hellenistic residence of the Tobiads (see fig. 14; ARCHITECTURE) have been uncovered. Herod the Great installed himself in the tower of Hananel, which he rebuilt and called Antonia (see JERUSALEM). Of his later palace the tower of Phasael still stands (*cf.* Jos., *BJ* v. 6. 4).

He built himself other palaces at Machaerus (*q.v.*), Herodium, and Jericho (*q.v.*). See also HOUSE, ARCHAEOLOGY (for references to other palaces excavated at Ai, Tell en-Nasbeh, *etc.*).

D.J.W.

PALESTINE. The term 'Palestine', originally applied to the territory of Israel's foes, the Philistines, was first used by Herodotus as a designation of southern Syria. In the form of *Palaestina*, it was also used by the Romans. The older term 'Canaan' has a similar history. In the Tell el-Amarna letters (14th century BC) Canaan was limited to the coastal plains, then with the Canaanite conquests of the interior it was applied to all the lands west of the Jordan valley. The terms 'land of Israel' (1 Sa. xiii. 19) and 'the land of promise' (Heb. xi. 9) are associated with the Israelites in the same area, the latter usually connected with the area from Dan to Beersheba, north of the Negeb. The Israelite settlement of two-and-a-half tribes east of the Jordan seems to have resulted from unforeseen circumstances and the hold on that side of the valley appears to have been generally precarious. After the division of the kingdom, the name Israel was usually given to the northern realm. In the Middle Ages, the term 'the Holy Land' was often adopted (*cf.* Zc. ii. 12).

I. THE POSITION AND HIGHWAYS OF PALESTINE

The mediaeval perspective of Jerusalem as the centre of the earth is not so absurd as might generally be thought, for on the tiny Syrian corridor that unites the world island of Europe, Asia, and Africa, the five seas of the Mediterranean, Black Sea, Caspian, Red Sea, and the Persian Gulf narrow the greatest land mass of our planet into a single isthmus. All the important continental routes must go across this corridor, and the great sea-routes of antiquity between the Indies and the Mediterranean must in turn be linked by land communications across the Sinai Peninsula. The high mountain chains which run eastwards from Asia Minor to Kurdistan and the deserts to the south and east further help to concentrate the routeways of 'the Fertile Crescent', which, sickle-shaped, runs from Palestine and southern Syria to the alluvial valley basins of the Tigris and Euphrates. It is, of course, 'fertile' only in comparison with the surrounding desert and mountainous terrain, since most of it is either Mediterranean scrub or steppe. At either end of the Fertile Crescent a great locus of civilization developed in the lower basin of Mesopotamia and the lower Nile valley respectively, whose fortunes dominated the history of the Near East for almost two millennia.

Three great trade routes have always traversed Palestine. The great Trunk Road, perhaps described in Is. ix. 1 as 'the way of the sea', runs along the low coast from Egypt to the Vale of Esdraelon. Then it is diverted inland by the Syrian mountains to skirt the west side of the Lake of Galilee, then through the Syrian Gate and central depression to Damascus, where it joins the desert caravan trails across to Mesopotamia. Two other routes are of great antiquity although of lesser importance. The King's Highway (*q.v.*) follows the edge of the Transjordan plateau from the Gulf of Aqabah towards Damascus. It marks a zone of increased rainfall and was followed in part by the Israelites during the Exodus (Nu. xxi, xxii), and all the towns enumerated in Nu. xxi, xxvii–xxx lie along it. The watershed of central Palestine is followed by another route, the shortest between Sinai and Canaan. In the northern Negeb it links an important series of wells, keeping west of the forbidding, barren depressions of the eastern Negeb that are still difficult to traverse. It links all the important historic centres from Kadesh-barnea and Beersheba to Hebron, Jerusalem, Shechem, and Megiddo (see fig. 80). Heavily travelled from the Abramic (Middle Bronze I) period onwards, it was also made famous by the journey of Joshua and his fellow-spies. All these routes emphasized the north–south alignment of Palestine, which benefited from their fertilizing contacts of trade and culture. But Israel was rarely able to control these highways without upsetting the strategic interests of the great powers that dominated their terminals. Even in Solomon's day the coastal highway was too tightly controlled by the sea-powers to warrant interference there (1 Ki. ix. 11, x. 22; Ezk. xxvii. 17), while Edom was for long Israel's deadly enemy because it dominated the routes from the Gulf of Aqabah where Israel obtained its copper (Ob. 3).

A number of minor transverse routes have joined these parallel highways. Of these the most important have been: (1) Gaza–Beersheba–Petra; (2) Ashkelon–Gath–Helvan; (3) Joppa–Bethel–Jericho (*cf.* Jos. x. 6–14) and Joppa–Shechem–Adam–Gilead (Jos. iii. 16); (4) Vale of Esdraelon–Megiddo–Gilead. Exposed to coastal sedimentation from the Nile, the coast of Palestine as far as Carmel has been unfavourable for port development, so the chief towns have been route centres at important road junctions, either in the strategic plain of Esdraelon or along the hilly dorsal of Judaea and Samaria. The sea was an unfamiliar medium of communication to the Hebrews (*cf.* Ps. cvii), while the desert was also feared as 'a land of trouble and anguish' (Dt. viii. 15; Is. xxx. 6). Perched precariously between them, the Hebrew highlanders sought a protracted aloofness from both environments and their peoples. Thus autonomy of spirit became a major characteristic of the Israelites, despite their nodal position at the hub of the ancient world's trade routes.

II. THE GEOLOGICAL STRUCTURE AND RELIEF

For some 420 miles from the borders of Egypt to Asia Minor, the Levant consists of five major zones: (1) the littoral; (2) the western mountain chain (the Judaean–Galilaean Highlands, Lebanon and Ansariya mountains); (3) the rift valleys

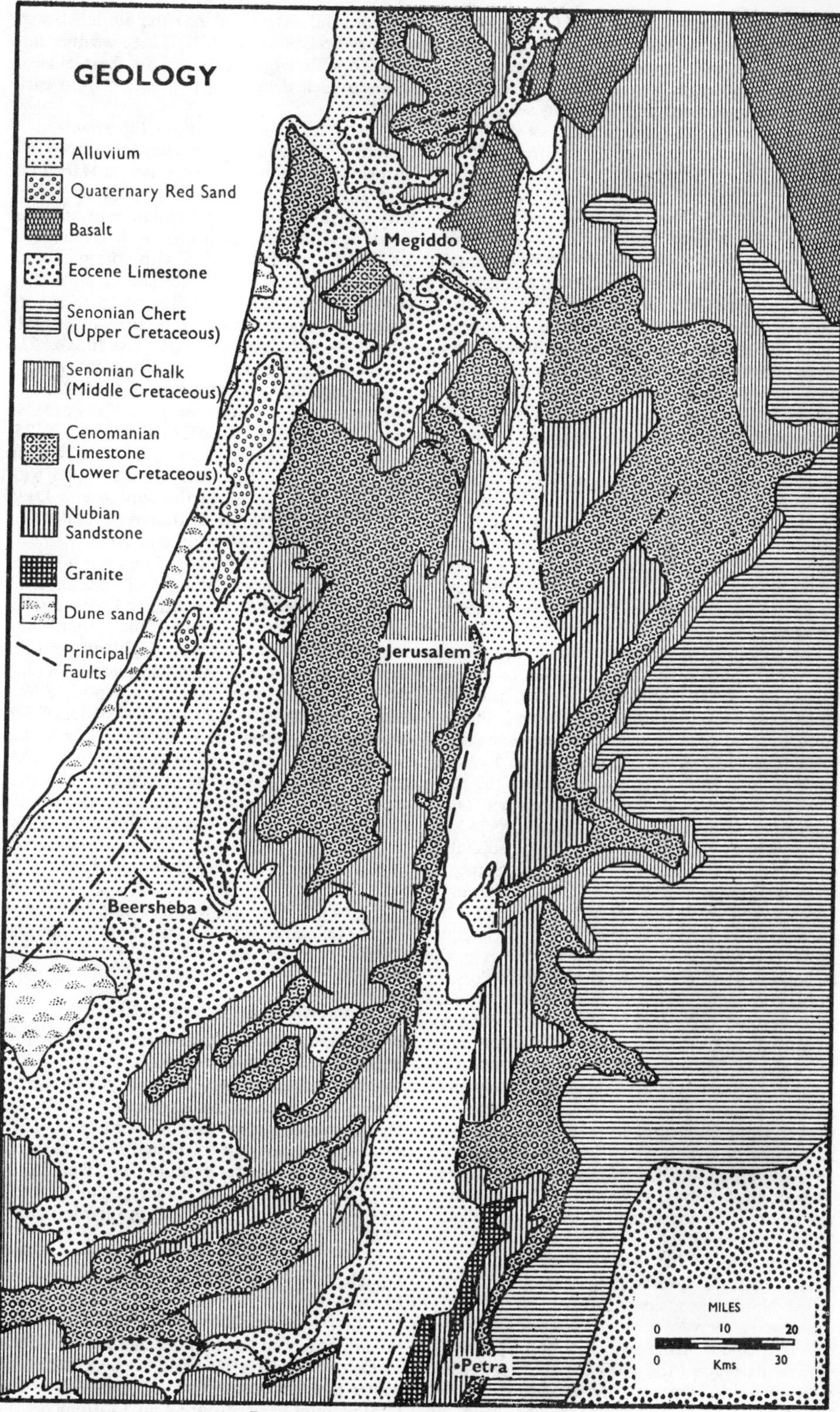

Fig. 155. Palestine: geological structure.

(Arabah, Jordan valley, Biqa', and Ghôr); (4) the eastern mountains (highlands of Transjordan, Hermon, and Anti-lebanon); and (5) the deserts of Negeb, Arabia, and Syria. But the contrasts between the northern and southern sections of these zones explain the individuality of Palestine. North of Acre, the mountains rise abruptly from the sea, limiting the narrow coastal plains to discontinuous stretches but providing the famous harbours of Sidon, Tyre, Beirut, Tripoli, and Ras Shamra. The limited hinterlands of each unit have encouraged independent maritime city-states where 'the families of the Canaanites spread abroad' (Gn. x. 18). South of Mt. Carmel, however, the coast opens into a broad continuous plain, harbourless except for artificial ports erected by the Philistines and later sea-peoples. A second contrast is to be found in the Rift Valley sectors. In Syria the Biqa' depression is a broad, fertile plain between the lofty ranges of Lebanon and Anti-lebanon, with wide access to other rolling plains, and studded with historic centres such as Kadesh, Homs, and Hamath. To the south, the depression blocked by recent basaltic lavas narrows into deep gorges before opening into the swamp of Lake Huleh, making north–south communication difficult. These features have tended to isolate Palestine from the northern territory.

The rocks of Palestine are notably limestone, volcanics, and recent deposits such as marls, gravels, and sands. The Rift Valley represents an ancient planetary lineament that is traceable as far as the East African Lakes. Broadly speaking, it has operated like a hinge, so that the areas to the west of it have been mostly under the sea, whereas the Arabian block has been generally continental. Thus, west of the Rift the rocks are predominantly limestone laid down specially during the Cretaceous and Eocene eras. Some of these are hard and dolomitic (Cenomanian and Eocene), explaining the steep headland of Mt. Carmel, the twin mountains of Ebal and Gerizim above Shechem, and generally all the rugged, higher relief of the Judaean–Galilaean dorsal. But the Senonian is a soft chalk, easily eroded into gaps and valleys that breach the highlands, notably at Megiddo, the valley of Aijalon, and the moat of Beth-shemesh which separates the Eocene foothills of the Shephelah from the Judaean plateau. These limestones have been upworked along the central dorsal and gently folded in a series of arches which become more complicated farther north in Samaria and Galilee. They occur, however, horizontal in Transjordan, resting upon the continental block beneath them. The ancient block is exposed in the south-east in the high cliffs of the Wadi Arabah and in the Sinai Peninsula. Overlapping them are the so-called Nubian sandstones, whose desert origin prolonged over vast geological periods explains the red colour from which Edom probably derives its name ('the red'). In the north-east, recent basaltic lavas cap the limestones in the broad, undulating plateaux in the land of Bashan, and extending into the Jordan trough around the Lake of Galilee. These weather into the rich soils which attracted to the Galilaean shores a high density of population from early times.

Crustal instability has been the *alter ego* of Palestine. Volcanic eruptions have continued into historic times, notably in the cases of Harrat en-Nar, south-east of the Gulf of Aqabah, which were active as late as the 8th and 13th centuries AD. It is tempting to equate the descriptions of Ex. xix. 18 and Ps. lxviii. 8 with volcanic manifestations, but the traditional site of Sinai is in an area of ancient, crystalline rocks where no recent volcanic action has occurred. The fate of Sodom and Gomorrah (Gn. xiv. 10, xix. 23–28) is a memory of some kind of volcanic phenomena, associated probably with the intrusion of sulphurous gas and liquid asphalt. There are also the biblical records of earthquakes (Gn. xix. 25; 1 Sa. xiv. 15; Am. i. 1) and geological faulting (Nu. xvi. 31–35). All these are associated with the Great Rift Valley of the Jordan and Dead Sea, or with the series of transverse faults that form the Vale of Esdraelon and divide Samaria and Galilee into a complicated series of highland blocks and depressions floored with sediments.

Under the semi-arid conditions, badland relief is typical, especially around the eastern and southern rims of the Judaean highlands and the western edge of the Transjordan plateau. Within the deep Jordan valley, soft marls deposited by a lake more extensive than the present Dead Sea have been dissected to form the Ghôr in the middle of the trough, lying at more than 1,200 feet below sea-level. The seasonal wadis that drain into the Arabah trough have also deeply dissected their slopes. Thus the biblical references to the 'slippery places' are a characteristic feature of many parts of the Negeb and the Jordan (Dt. xxxii. 35; Pr. iii. 23; Je. xxiii. 12, xxxi. 9). Much of the Negeb is a rock waste of hammadas, and direct reference to the wind-borne loessial deposits is made (Ex. x. 20–23; Dt. xxviii. 24; Na. i. 3).

III. THE CLIMATE AND VEGETATION

In the Levant three climatic zones may be distinguished: a Mediterranean, a steppe, and a desert zone, each with its distinct type of vegetation. Along the coast as far south as Gaza, the Mediterranean zone has mild winters (53·6° F. mean monthly average for January at Gaza) compared with the severer conditions of the interior hills (Jerusalem 44·6° in January). But summers are everywhere hot (Gaza 78·8° in July, Jerusalem 73·4°). The prolonged snow cover of the high Lebanon mountains (Je. xviii. 14) is exceptional, though snow is not infrequent in the Hauran. Elsewhere it is a rare phenomenon (2 Sa. xxiii. 20). Less than one-fifteenth part of the annual rainfall occurs in the summer months from June to October; nearly all of it is concentrated in winter to reach a maximum in mid-winter. The total amount varies from about 14–16 inches on the coast to about 30 inches on Mt. Carmel and the Judaean, Galilaean, and Transjordan mountains. In the Beersheba area to the south, and in parts of the Jordan valley and of the Transjordan plateau the climate is steppe, with only 8–12 inches of rain, though temperature conditions are comparable to those of the Judaean hills. The deep trough of the Jordan has sub-tropical conditions with stifling summer heat; at Jericho mean daily maxima remain above 100° from June to September, with frequent records of 110–120°. The winter, however, has enjoyable conditions of 65–68° (January mean daily maximum). In the Negeb, the southern part of the Jordan valley, and the country east and south of the Transjordan steppe the climate is desert, with less than 8 inches of rain a year.

There is no archaeological evidence that climate has changed since biblical times. Near the Gulf of Aqabah, a number of recently excavated Roman gutters still fit the springs for which they were constructed, and wherever the Byzantine wells of the Negeb have been kept clean and in constant use, the water still rises to the ancient levels. Thus the biblical narrative gives a convincing picture of the present climate. Distinction is made between the hot and cold seasons (Gn. viii. 22; Am. iii. 15), and the inception of the autumn rains is clearly described (Dt. xi. 14; Ho. vi. 3; Joel ii. 23). Variability in the amount and distribution of rainfall is common (Am. iv. 7), and the incidence of prolonged drought is recorded on a number of occasions (1 Ki. xvii. 7; Je. xvii. 8; Joel i. 10–12, 17–20).

Because of the contrasts of relief, from 3,336 feet above sea-level near Hebron, to 1,290 feet below sea-level at the Dead Sea, the flora of Palestine is very rich (about 3,000 vascular plants) for such a small area. A large proportion of them are annuals. Few districts have ever had dense forests, though remnants have been preserved in Mts. Hermon and Lebanon (*q.v.*) with their cedars, firs, oaks, and pines, and in the biblical Golan (Jaulan), where forests of pine and oak still exist. Lebanon has always been noted for its cedars. The Israelites had their share in deforestation of the Mediterranean woodland

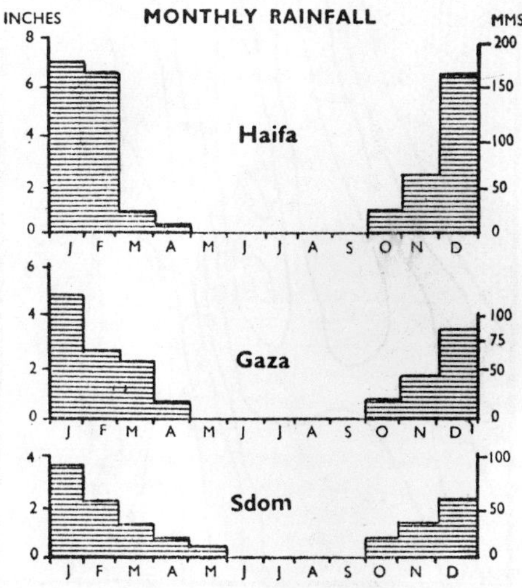

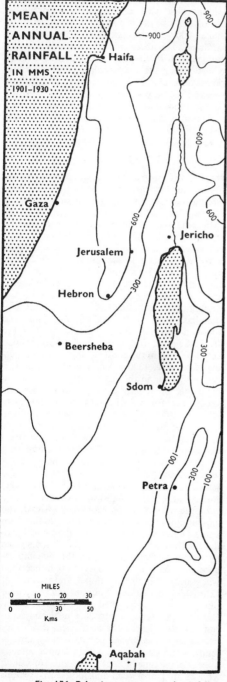

Fig. 156. Palestine: mean annual rainfall and monthly totals at Haifa, Gaza, and Sdom.

that once covered the central dorsal (Jos. xvii. 18), and today there are no traces of the woodlands that once existed at Bethel (2 Ki. ii. 24), Ephraim (Jos. xvii. 15), and Gilead near the Jordan valley.

Oak forests long existed in Sharon, whose name means forest, but biblical prophecy states three forested regions were to be turned into sheep pastures, the coastal Sharon, northern Gilead, and south-eastern Galilee (see Is. lxv. 10). The development of pastoralism must be blamed for much of this forest clearance in Palestine (*cf.* 2 Ki. iii. 4). But under Mediterranean conditions 'the pastures of the wilderness' are seasonally short-lived, so Rabbi Akiba (*c.* AD 100) observed shrewdly that 'those who rear small cattle and cut down good trees . . . will see no sign of blessing'. Deterioration of the woodland scrub had gone so far in Palestine before the establishment of the new state of Israel in AD 1948 that most of the uncultivated land was a dreary expanse of *batha*, low scrub with open, rock outcrops. Towards the steppe and the desert, the colour of the landscape is governed more by the rocks than the plant cover, with only a few shrubby elements, such as wormwood, broom, saltwort, and tufts of xerophytic grasses. Only along the banks of the Jordan is there a dense and wide gallery forest of various willows, poplar, tamarisk, oleander, *etc.*

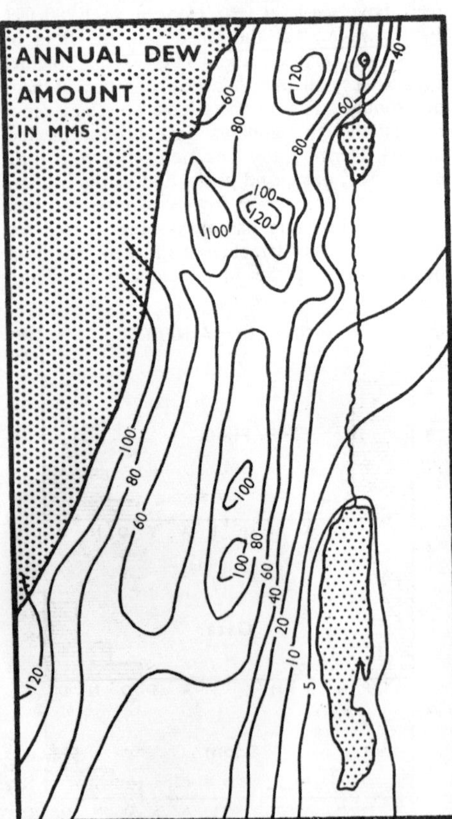

Fig. 157. Palestine: annual dew amount.

But many of the Palestinian hill lands, eroded of their productive *terra vessa* soils, have been the graveyard of former civilizations, especially with the decay of terrace-cultivation. One estimate is that since Roman times 2,000–4,000 million cubic metres of soil have been worked off the eastern side of the Judaean hills, sufficient to make 4,000–8,000 square kilometres of good farmland. This threat of soil erosion is possibly alluded to in Jb. xiv. 18, 19, and the easy spread of fire during the summer drought is described (Ps. lxxxiii. 13, 14). These features of Mediterranean instability are recognized in the need for balance and restraint, in a land which lies so precariously between the desert and the sown (Ex. xxiii. 29, 30; Pr. xxiv. 30–34).

See also DEW, RAIN, and WIND.

IV. WATER SUPPLY AND AGRICULTURE

It is not by chance that the names of over seventy ancient sites in Palestine contain the word *'ain*, 'spring', and another sixty such sites the word *bîr*, 'well'. Apart from the Jordan, a few of its tributaries and four or five small coastal streams that are fed from springs, all the remaining rivers of Palestine are seasonal. Snow-fed streams account for their maximum volume in May–June (Jos. iii. 15), but the majority dry up in the hot summer (1 Ki. xvii. 7; Jb. xxiv. 19; Joel i. 20), notably in the Negeb (Ps. cxxvi. 4). With the autumn rains the sudden spate is graphically described (Jdg. v. 21; Mt. vii. 27). Thus 'the fountain of living waters' was the ideal of the Israelite settler. The invention of a mortar which could be used in the construction of rain-collecting cisterns (*c.* 1300 BC) may well have been a decisive factor in the rapid colonization of the highlands of Judaea by the Israelite settlers. Wells dug for watering the stock are early alluded to (Gn. xxvi, *etc.*) and irrigation was well known (Gn. xiii. 10). Reservoirs too for the needs of the urban population are frequently mentioned (Ct. vii. 4), some fed through imposing rock-cut tunnels (2 Ki. xx. 20). The need for water often pointed a moral lesson to the Israelites (Dt. viii. 7–10, xi. 10–17; 1 Ki. xviii; Je. ii. 13, xiv. 22). See also CISTERN, WELL.

Before the rise of the Monarchy at least, the agricultural population of central Palestine consisted of small landowners, and the typical produce of the land is described in the presents given by Abigail to David (1 Sa. xxv. 18). The importance in Judaea of the barley crop rather than wheat because of its low rainfall, and the fame of Carmel for its vines and Ephraim and Galilee for olives, have been justified since biblical times. But droughts tend to introduce debt and servitude, so that despite the ideological democracy envisaged in the jubilee year (Lv. xxv), crownlands, large estates, and forced labour already appear in the time of Saul (1 Sa. viii. 16, xxii. 7, xxv. 2). In Transjordan and the Negeb it seems that the pastoral life has been traditionally supplemented by settled agricultural practices wherever wells and oases permitted. But the decline of agriculture has been constantly threatened by over-grazing by sheep and goats, apart from the more catastrophic incursions from the desert.

V. THE SETTLEMENTS

A major problem in the historical geography of Palestine has been the identification of place-names. There are approximately 622 place-names west of Jordan recorded in the Bible. The lists of Tuthmosis III, Sethos I, Rameses II, and Sheshonq I at Karnak throw some light on Palestinian topography. The Onomasticon of Eusebius and Jerome is another valuable source. The work of R. Reland (1714) paved the way for the modern topographical work of Dr. Edward Robinson when he visited Palestine in 1838. He identified 177 place-names, few of which have been subsequently changed. In 1865 the Palestine Exploration Fund was established, and by 1927 about 434 place-names had been located; Conder in particular added 147 new names. A number of these are still disputed, and modern scholarship has continued to revise a few of them.

The startling discoveries of Miss K. Kenyon at Jericho since 1952 indicate that there has been a semblance of urban life there since 6000–8000 BC with an 8-acre site occupied by some 3,000 inhabitants (see ARCHAEOLOGY). Indeed, the Jordan valley seems to have been from early times an area of dense settlement. N. Glueck notes some seventy sites there, many founded over 5,000 years ago, and over thirty-five of them still inhabited by Israelite times. It was only later that this valley which Lot found so attractive (Gn. xiii. 10) became more desolate, probably with the advent of malaria. It has been suggested that some of the Tells were artificial mounds built deliberately above the swampy ground, though added to by subsequent settlement. But everywhere water supply has been the decisive factor of settlement. Fortified towns and castles were built at important perennial springs such as Jericho, Beth-shan, and Aphek (famous from the wars of the Israelites with the Philistines). Indeed, it is a corollary that sites with abundant springs have usually had the most continuous settlement from remote times.

Along the coastal plain south of Carmel settlement has been relatively dense since antiquity, favoured by the ease with which wells could be dug through the sandy soils to the lenticular beds of clay that hold suspended water-tables. But farther north in the Vale of Sharon and Upper Galilee, where the water supply is abundant, relatively dense woodland made human occupancy difficult until more recent centuries. In the basins of lower Galilee and Samaria population has for long been dense, scattered in numerous villages, but south of Jerusalem village sites become fewer and more nucleated, until around Beersheba settlement has been limited to strategic fortified well sites. In Transjordan the edge of the plateau is marked by a number of fortresses such as Petra, Bozrah (Buseira) and Tophel (Tafileh). Beyond them to the east is the narrow stretch of agricultural land with its scattered villages along which ran the King's Highway. Within these patterns of settlement dictated largely by water conditions, the strategic and most important towns have grown up at cross-roads where the proximity of some defile enabled the transverse roads to link with the main north-to-south highways. Such were in biblical times Beersheba, Hebron, Jerusalem, Bethel, Shechem, Samaria, Megiddo, Beth-shan, and Hazor. Hence the psalmist could exclaim: 'He led them by a straight way, till they reached a city to dwell in' (Ps. cvii. 7, RSV).

VI. THE REGIONS OF PALESTINE

The geographer can create as many regions as there are problems worth studying, so it is absurd to suggest that the delimitation of areas within Palestine has a permanent validity. But certain regional units have appeared again and again in the history of Palestine, and should be recognized. The broad divisions already noted are distinct: the coastal plains, the central hill lands, the Rift Valley, the plateaux of Transjordan, and the desert.

The coastal plains stretch for a distance of about 120 miles from the borders of Lebanon to Gaza, interrupted by Mt. Carmel in the north. To the north of it, the plain of Asher runs for 25 miles to the ancient Ladder of Tyre, where the Galilaean hills crowd close to the coast. It played no part in the life of Israel, but to the south-east of it the valley of Jezreel and plain of Esdraelon has been of major significance. Stretching for 30 miles into the interior and some 12 miles at its widest, this formed the main road from Egypt to Damascus and the north. Along it were situated the strategic centres of Megiddo, Jezreel, and Beth-shan, famous in many of Israel's wars (Jdg. v, vii. 1; 1 Sa. xxix. 1, xxxi. 12) and the apocalyptic site of the future (Rev. xvi. 16). South of Carmel, which shelters the small plain of Dor, is the plain of Sharon with its five great Philistine strongholds of Ekron, Ashdod, Ashkelon, Gath, and Gaza, merging eastwards into the hill lands of the Shephelah, a buffer between Israel and Philistia. These hills were once heavily wooded with sycamores (1 Ki. x. 27; 2 Ch. i. 15, ix. 27) and crossed transversely by narrow valleys which witnessed the early struggles of Israel from the times of the Judges to David, notably Aijalon (Jos. x. 10–15; 1 Sa. xiv. 31), Sorek (Jdg. xvi), and Elah (1 Sa. xvii. 1, 2).

The Central Hills run some 200 miles from northern Galilee to Sinai, made up of interlocking hills and plateaux. In the south, Judah has gently undulating folds except in the east, where the deeply dissected chalky relief of the Wilderness of Judah, or Jeshimon, descends steeply to the Rift Valley. This Judaean plateau runs north into the hill country of Ephraim with its easy transverse passages, but to the north the hills of

Samaria decrease gently from the Judaean heights of over 3,000 feet to an average of just over 1,000 feet in the central basin, in which are situated the biblical sites of Gibeah, Shalem, Shechem, and Sychar. Above it tower the heights of Ebal (3,100 feet) and Gerizim (2,910 feet). Together with other fertile basins, Samaria was exposed to outside influences, and its faith early corrupted. North of the plain of Esdraelon lies Galilee, divided into southern or lower Galilee, which has a similar landscape to the lands of Samaria, and northern or upper Galilee, where the moun-

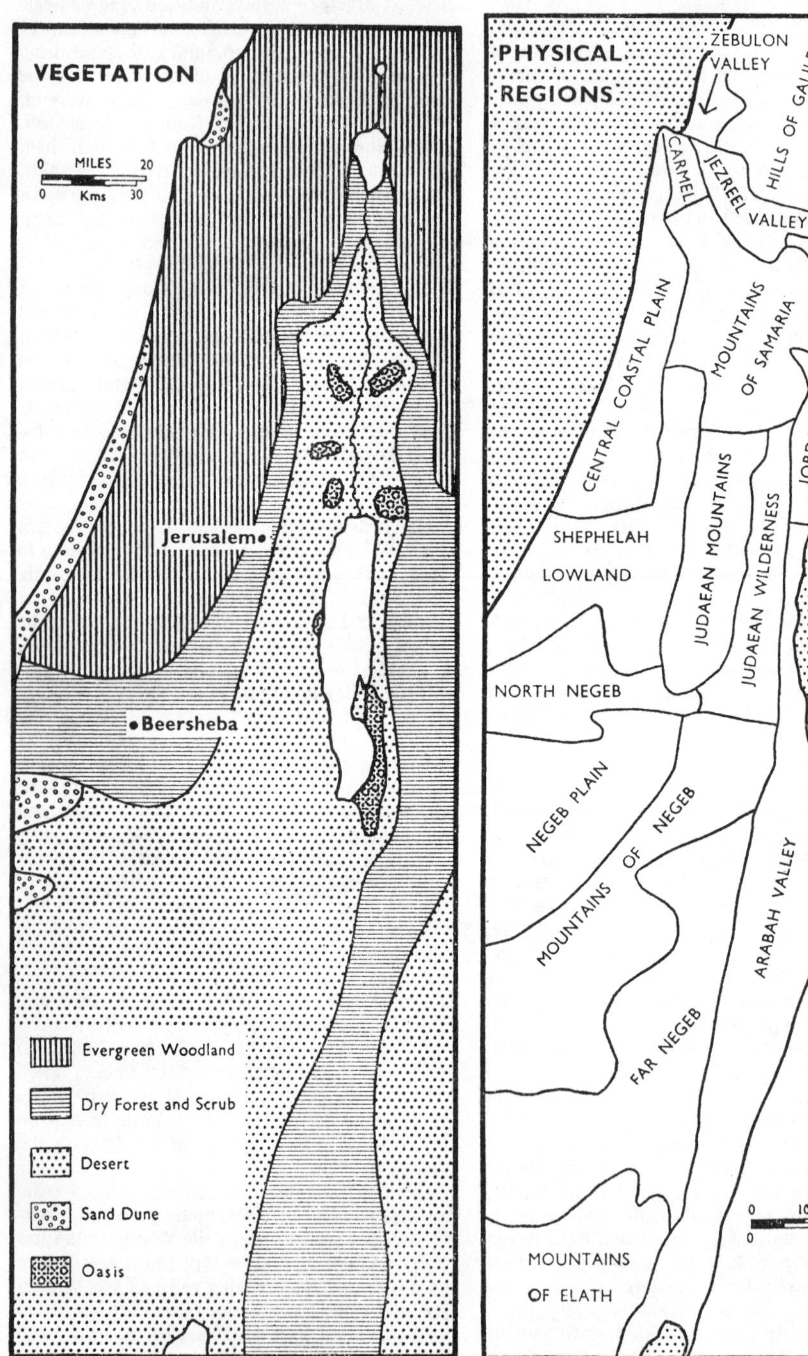

Fig. 158. Palestine: vegetation.

Fig. 159. Palestine: physical regions.

tains reach over 3,000 feet. A number of basins, notably Nazareth, provide easy passage and rich cultivation between the coast and the Lake area, densely settled in our Lord's day.

Slicing across Palestine for over 60 miles, the Jordan follows the great Rift Valley. Its northern sector is occupied also by the lakes Huleh and Galilee, surrounded by high mountains, notably Hermon, the source of the Jordan (Dt. iii. 9, iv. 48). Below the basin of Huleh, the Jordan has cut through the basaltic dam that once blocked the depression in a gorge to enter the lake Tiberias or Sea of Galilee 600 feet below sea-level. Beyond it the river Yarmuk adds its waters to the Jordan and the valley gradually widens southwards towards the Dead Sea trough. South of the cliffs of 'Ain Khaneizer commences the Arabah, stretching 100 miles to the Gulf of Aqabah, a desert dominated by the great wall of the Transjordan tableland. Westwards stretches the desolate hilly relief of the central Negeb and its steppe plains, towards Beersheba. Eastwards over the edge of the Transjordan plateaux extend a series of regions well known in Bible times: the tableland of Bashan dominated eastwards by the great volcanic caves of Jebel Druze; Gilead situated in a huge oval dome 35 miles by 25 miles wide and famed for its forests (Je. xxii. 6; Zc. x. 10); the level steppes of Ammon and Moab; and south of the Zered valley (Dt. ii. 13; Is. xv. 7) the faulted and tilted block of Edom with its impregnable strongholds. Beyond to the east and the south are the deserts, tablelands of rock and sand, blasted by the hot winds. See also JORDAN, NEGEB, SHARON, ZIN. For archaeology of Palestine, see ARCHAEOLOGY; for history of Palestine, see CANAAN, ISRAEL, JUDAH, PHILISTINES, *etc.*

BIBLIOGRAPHY. F.-M. Abel, *Géographie de la Palestine*, 1933 (2 vols.); D. Baly, *The Geography of the Bible*, 1957; G. Dalman, *Sacred Sites and Ways*, 1935; M. du Buit, *Géographie de la Terre Sainte*, 1958; N. Glueck, *The River Jordan*, 1946; *id.*, *Rivers in the Desert*, 1959; W. J. Phythian-Adams, 'The Land and the People' in *A Companion to the Bible* (ed. T. W. Manson), 1944, pp. 133–156; A. Reifenberg, *The Struggle between the Desert and the Sown in the Levant*, 1956; G. A. Smith, *The Historical Geography of the Holy Land*[25], 1931. J.M.H.

PALMER-WORM. See LOCUST.

PALM-TREE. See TREES.

PALSY. See DISEASE AND HEALING.

PALTITE, THE. The name given to the inhabitants of Beth-pelet, situated in the Judaean Negeb (Jos. xv. 27; Ne. xi. 26). Helez, one of David's thirty heroes, was a native of this town (2 Sa. xxiii. 26). In 1 Ch. xi. 27 and xxvii. 10 he is called 'the Pelonite' (*q.v.*). R.A.H.G.

PAMPHYLIA. A coastal region of S Asia Minor on the great bay of the Mare Lycium, lying between Lycia and Cilicia (see fig. 26). It is mentioned in Acts xiii. 13, xiv. 24, and xv. 38 in connection with Paul's first journey, a visit which Ramsay believed was cut short through illness and the enervating climate (*St Paul the Traveller and Roman Citizen*, pp. 89 ff.). According to tradition, the area was colonized by Amphilochus and Calchas (or Mopsus, his rival and successor) after the Trojan War. Linguistic evidence confirms a mixed settlement. The chief towns were Attaleia, Paul's probable landing-place, founded by Attalus II of Pergamum after 189 BC with Athenian colonists; Aspendus, a Persian naval base which claimed Argive foundation; Side, founded by Aeolian colonists; and Perga (*q.v.*). The region was under Persian rule until Alexander, after which, apart from brief occupations by Ptolemy I and Ptolemy III, it passed to the possession of the Seleucids of Syria. After the defeat of Antiochus III, C. Manlius took the region over for Rome and the main cities were associated in alliance. The Attalids at this time (189 BC) received the coastal strip, where they founded Attaleia. Many readjustments followed. From 102 BC Pamphylia was a part of the province of Cilicia, but about 44 BC was included in Asia. In 36 BC Antony made the territory over to his ally Amyntas, king of Galatia. Thanks to his timely desertion to Octavian before Actium Amyntas retained possession until his death in battle against a highland tribe in 25 BC. From this date until AD 43 Pamphylia was part of the province of Galatia. In that year Claudius formed the province of Lycia-Pamphylia. There were later reorganizations under Galba and Vespasian. The church founded at Perga is the only one mentioned in the 1st century, but there were at least twelve foundations at the time of Diocletian's persecution in AD 304.

BIBLIOGRAPHY. A. H. M. Jones, *Eastern Cities*, 1937, pp. 124 ff. E.M.B.

PAN. See VESSELS.

PANNAG. A Hebrew word, found only in Ezk. xxvii. 17, signifying some type of merchandise, presumably edible. AV and RV transliterate, since the meaning is unknown. A few scholars have proposed to read *dônag̱*, 'wax'. A simpler emendation is *paggag̱*, 'unripe figs'; this involves the change of a single letter in Hebrew; and indeed three Hebrew MSS have this reading, which has been accepted by RSV. D.F.P.

PAPER. See WRITING.

PAPHOS. The name of two settlements in SW Cyprus in New Testament times, distinguished by scholars as Old and New Paphos. The former was a Phoenician foundation of great antiquity lying slightly inland from the coast. New Paphos grew up, after the Romans annexed the island in 58 BC, as the centre of Roman rule, and it was here that Paul met the proconsul Sergius (Acts xiii. 6, 7, 12) on his first missionary journey. Here, too, he had his encounter with Elymas the sorcerer (Acts xiii. 6–11). Old Paphos was the site of a famous shrine, probably of Phoenician or Syrian origin, but later devoted to the worship of Aphrodite. J.H.P.

PAPYRI AND OSTRACA.

I. EGYPTIAN

a. Papyrus

(i) *Name.* The term papyrus applies to a large aquatic plant of the sedge family, to the writing material prepared from its pith, and to individual manuscripts made from this material. The origin of Gk. *papyros* (from which come 'papyrus', 'paper') is still uncertain. Some think that it derives from an assumed *papūro* in Coptic (last stage of the ancient Egyptian language), which would mean 'belonging to the King', reflecting the fact that production of papyrus was a royal monopoly in the Graeco-Roman epoch.

Fig. 160. The *Cyperus papyrus* plant.

(ii) *The plant and its uses.* In antiquity, the plant *Cyperus papyrus* L. grew throughout Egypt, especially in the Delta, in marshes and lakes; but the plant is not now found in the wild state north of the Sudan, although it still grows in the marshes of Lake Huleh in Palestine and is found in Sicily. From roots in the mud, the great stems, triangular in section, grew to heights of 10 and even 20 feet, ending in large, open, bell-shaped flowers. (See H. Frankfort, *Birth of Civilization in the Near East*, 1951, pl. 2, and for a representation in antiquity, W. Stevenson Smith, *Art and Architecture of Ancient Egypt*, 1958, plate 129A.) The graceful form of the papyrus was a favourite motif in Egyptian art and architecture. Heb. *gōme'* (AV 'bulrushes', 'rush', 'rushes') appears to signify the papyrus-plant; see also RUSH, RUSHES. The biblical references to it tally well with the known nature and uses of papyrus. It indeed grew in the mire (Jb. viii. 11) and fittingly symbolized luxuriant, swampy growth by contrast with the desert sands (Is. xxxv. 7). The little basket or 'ark' in which the infant Moses was placed was of papyrus (Ex. ii. 3); and in Egypt and Ethiopia papyrus vessels and skiffs were to be seen on the Nile and its marshes (Is. xviii. 2) as ancient pictures show (see fig. 83; and *e.g.* M. Murray, *The Splendour that was Egypt*, 1949, p. 83, pl. 19). Besides the manufacture of reed boats and baskets, papyrus was used for making ropes, sandals, and some clothing, and its roots were even used as food for the poor.

(iii) *Papyrus 'paper'.* To make this, the plant-stems were stripped of their outer rinds, cut up into lengths of about 16–18 inches, and the fresh, pithy inner stem was cut into thin strips. These were laid out side by side, overlapping each other, on a hard wooden surface; more strips were similarly laid across these at right-angles; and the two layers were then welded into a whole simply by hard beating, *e.g.* with mallets. Trimmed and smoothed, the result was a sheet of whitish paper that was durable but yellowed with age. The side showing horizontal fibres was usually written on first (except for letters) and is called the recto; the 'back' with the vertical fibres is termed the verso. These sheets were pasted end to end, with slight overlaps, to form a papyrus roll. The standard length was twenty sheets, but this could be shortened by cutting or lengthened by pasting on more, as need arose. The longest known papyrus is the great *Papyrus Harris I*, *c.* 1160 BC, in the British Museum; it is some 133 feet long. The height of a papyrus varied according to the use to which it was to be put: the larger sizes (maximum, 18½ inches; usually 14 inches and 16½ inches in Dynasties XVIII and XIX–XX) for official and business papers and accounts (with long columns of figures); and the smaller ones (about 7 inches and 8¼ inches, but often less) for literary compositions.

(iv) *The use of papyrus.* This was governed by definite conventions. As Egyptian script usually runs from right to left, the scribes always began at the right-hand end of a papyrus and wrote to the left—at first in vertical lines (usual until *c.* 1800 BC), thereafter in horizontal lines of modest length, grouped in successive 'columns' or 'pages'. For scripts used, punctuation, writing equipment, manuscripts, *etc.*, see WRITING; TEXT AND VERSIONS.

Papyrus was used from the beginning of Egyptian history (*c.* 3000 BC) down into the early Islamic period (7th century AD and later). The oldest (blank) rolls are of Dynasty I, the first written ones are of Dynasty V, *c.* 2500 BC. Large quantities were made and used in Egypt in the second and first millennia BC for every kind of written record; but papyrus was not cheap, and the backs and blank spaces of old rolls were often used up, or an old text washed off to make room for a new one.

Before the end of the second millennium BC, papyrus was being exported extensively to Syria–Palestine and doubtless beyond. About 1090 BC Zakarbaal, the prince of Phoenician Byblos, quoted timber-prices to the Egyptian envoy

Wenamun from the rolls of accounts kept by his predecessors, and in Wenamun's part-payment for timber were included '500 (rolls of) finished papyrus' (*ANET*, pp. 27a, 28a). For the use of papyrus for Hebrew and Aramaic, and in New Testament times, see separate sections below. On all aspects of papyrus as a writing-medium in Egypt, see J. Černý, *Paper and Books in Ancient Egypt*, 1952. For pictures of funerary and administrative papyri respectively, see D. J. Wiseman, *IBA*, pp. 36, 37, figs. 30, 31.

b. Ostraca

The plural of *ostrakon*, a Greek word originally meaning 'oyster-shell', but applied by the Greeks to the potsherds on which they recorded their votes (hence English 'ostracize, -cism'). In Egypt this term is applied to slips of limestone or potsherds bearing ink-written inscriptions and drawings. Although such ostraca are known from most periods in Egyptian history and from various sites, the vast majority are of New Kingdom date (*c.* 1570–1085 BC) and come from Thebes in Upper Egypt, specifically from the Valleys of the Tombs of the Kings and the Queens and the village for the workers at these tombs (modern Deir el-Medineh). Most Egyptian ostraca are written in the cursive hieratic script; those in the more formal, pictorial hieroglyphic script are much rarer. The ostraca with drawings are often delightful, sketched by artists in their spare time. The inscribed ostraca fall into two classes: literary and non-literary. The former contain portions of Egyptian literary works (stories, poems, wisdom, hymns, *etc.*), written out as school exercises, test of memory, or for pleasure; these ostraca often preserve literary works (or parts of them) still unknown from any other source. Much more varied are the non-literary ostraca. These were the Egyptians' equivalent of memo-pads, jotters, and scrap paper, and reflect every conceivable aspect of daily life: rosters of workmen with note of absentees, reports on work done (*cf.* Ex. v. 18, 19), distribution of food-allowances and oil, innumerable accounts of bricks, straw, vegetables, vessels, *etc.*, lawsuits, marriage-contracts, bills of sale and demand-notes for debts, many letters and memoranda, and much else besides. The total of this material gives a vivid insight into Egyptian daily life during and after the time of Israel's sojourn and exodus and can provide useful background for the Exodus narratives. See also LACHISH, SAMARIA.

BIBLIOGRAPHY. On scope and importance of ostraca, see J. Černý, *Chronique d'Égypte*, VI/No. 12, 1931, pp. 212–224, and S. Sauneron, *Catalogue des Ostraca Hiératiques Non Littéraires de Deir el Medineh*, 1959, Introduction, pp. vi–xviii, who gives ample reference to other publications. In English, see W. C. Hayes, *The Scepter of Egypt*, II, 1959, pp. 176–178, 390–394, 432. For pictures of typical ostraca, see Hayes, *op. cit.*, p. 177, fig. 98.

II. HEBREW AND ARAMAIC

a. Hebrew papyri

By far the oldest Hebrew papyrus known is the palimpsest found at the Wadi Murabba'at by the Dead Sea. It contains a list of personal names, written in the palaeo-Hebrew ('Phoenician') script, and dates from the 7th, or even 8th, century BC. At Qumran many papyrus fragments have been found, many of which have yet to be identified. Noteworthy is a copy of the sectarian work *The Rule of the Community*, in a proto-cursive script, found in Cave IV; it dates from the Hasmonaean period. Some letters of the Jewish rebel leader of AD 132–5, usually known as Bar Kokhba, have been found at Murabba'at and Wadi Heber; the fourteen papyri discovered in the latter locality in 1960 also include correspondence in Greek and Aramaic.

Till the Qumran discoveries were made, the earliest extant Hebrew Old Testament MS was the Nash Papyrus, which contains part of Dt. v–vi, and may date from as early as the 2nd century BC The majority of the biblical MSS from Qumran are not papyri; however, papyrus fragments of the books of Kings and Daniel were found in Cave VI.

b. Hebrew ostraca

The most significant discoveries are those of Samaria and Lachish. In 1908–10 sixty-five ostraca were discovered at Samaria, and others have been found there since. Written in the palaeo-Hebrew script, they appear to be invoices concerning vineyard produce. Since they were found in the remains of the royal palace, it may be assumed that they refer to royal property. They probably date from the reign of Jeroboam II. They contain many personal names and some place-names; the former include compounds of Yahweh, El, and Baal.

Excavations at Tell ed-Duweir (the Old Testament Lachish, *q.v.*) in 1935 and 1938 unearthed twenty-one ostraca. Most of them appear to be letters, written in the palaeo-Hebrew script (see fig. 161). Not all of them can be read or dated, but those that have been translated indicate a date *c.* 588 BC, for the recipient (where named) was the military governor of the city during the last few years of the kingdom of Judah, when the Babylonian armies were reducing the fortified cities one by one. The ostraca reflect on this situation, and there are some contacts with the Book of Jeremiah. Indeed, Ostracon III refers to a prophet, whom some have conjecturally (with little warrant) identified with Jeremiah. Perhaps the most interesting feature of the Lachish Letters is the recurrent use of the name YHWH (*i.e.* Yahweh; the ostraca omit all vowels). It is surprising to find the ineffable name used freely in an ordinary military letter.

A few Hebrew (and Aramaic) sherds have also appeared at Qumran and Murabba'at, but they are of little consequence. Excavations at Jerusalem in 1923–5 revealed the 'Ophel' Ostracon, which gives a list of names. It is in the palaeo-Hebrew script, and may date from the 7th century BC.

c. Aramaic papyri

Near Aswan (the ancient Syene) there is an island in the Nile which once bore the Greek name Elephantine. Here a Jewish colony flourished, and left behind a large number of documents, mostly papyri, which have gradually come to light since 1893. The papyri all date from the 5th century BC, when this colony acted as a military garrison for the Persian conquerors of Egypt. The language of the papyri is Aramaic, not unlike the Aramaic of Daniel and Ezra. They include legal documents and letters. It is evident that the colonists were not of the main stream of Jewish religious thought; for instance, they had their own temple to Yahu (*i.e.* Yahweh), despite the Deuteronomic prohibition of sanctuaries outside Jerusalem. When they needed help to rebuild this temple they wrote optimistically to the Jerusalem priesthood. A clear evidence of their syncretism is the mention of Anath-Yahu, *i.e.* a Canaanite goddess linked with Yahweh; it is unlikely that they were polytheistic, but evidently there were pagan elements in their Yahweh worship.

These papyri have contacts with the Book of Nehemiah; *e.g.* they mention Sanballat, governor of Samaria (*cf.* Ne. iv. 1).

From the general area of Murabba'at, Bedouin have brought to light some papyri in the Nabataean dialect of Aramaic. One of them is a property deed, and dates from *c.* AD 100. They add considerably to our knowledge of Nabataean.

d. Greek Old Testament papyri

Of the Old Testament in Greek, there are extant a considerable number of papyri, almost invariably fragmentary and mutilated. The oldest of these is the John Rylands Library Papyrus Greek 458, which consists of fragments of Dt. xxiii–xxviii, and dates from the 2nd century BC. The Papyrus Fouad 266 is of almost equal antiquity; it contains part of Dt. xxxi–xxxii. The Chester Beatty collection has a number of Greek Old Testament papyri, consisting of parts of Genesis, Numbers, Deuteronomy, Esther, Isaiah, Jeremiah, Ezekiel, and Daniel as well as Ecclesiasticus; they range in date from the 2nd to the 4th centuries AD. From the early 3rd century AD there is the Freer Greek MS V, a papyrus codex of the Minor Prophets. Other papyri of somewhat later date give parts of the Psalter. See plates XII*b c.*

In Cave IV at Qumran some papyrus fragments of the book of Leviticus were found, dating from the 1st century BC. Cave VII has revealed fragments of what appears to be the Epistle of Jeremy (Baruch vi).

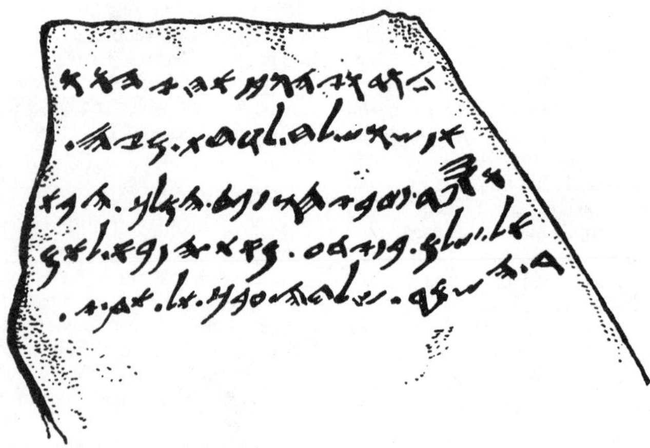

Fig. 161. Drawing of an inscribed ostracon from Lachish. This letter, written in cursive Hebrew of the time of Jeremiah, was found in a small guard-room under the gate-tower of Lachish, *c.* 589–587 BC.

BIBLIOGRAPHY (for Hebrew, Aramaic, and Greek Old Testament material). A. Cowley, *Aramaic Papyri of the Fifth Century BC*, 1923; E. G. Kraeling, *The Brooklyn Museum Aramaic Papyri*, 1953; *DOTT*, pp. 204–208, 212–217, 256–275; J. B. Pritchard (ed.), *ANET*[2], 1955, pp. 321 f., 427–430, 491 f.; F. F. Bruce, *The Books and the Parchments*, 1950, pp. 141–155; F. G. Kenyon, *Our Bible and the Ancient Manuscripts*[5] (revised by A. W. Adams), 1958, pp. 114–119; B. J. Roberts, *The Old Testament Text and Versions*, 1951, pp. 145–149.

See also DEAD SEA SCROLLS for relevant material and bibliography.

III. NEW TESTAMENT

a. Introduction

The discovery of the Greek papyri in Egypt during the last eighty years has had important results for New Testament studies. In the initial finds biblical papyri were rare, but with the commencement of systematic excavations by Grenfell and Hunt in 1896 large quantities of papyri came to light, including either portions of the New Testament books themselves or documents of the early centuries which helped our understanding of them. The most fruitful sites of all were south of Fayum, at Behnesa (Oxyrhynchus), Eshmunen (Hermopolis), Kom Ishgau (Aphroditopolis), and Akhmim (Panopolis).

It had long been assumed by many scholars that New Testament Greek was *sui generis*, 'a language of the Holy Ghost', but there were some, such as Masson, Lightfoot, and Farrar, who anticipated the fact soon to be proved, that the New Testament writers used the common tongue of the Greek world in the 1st century AD, approximating more often to the spoken than to the literary form of *koinē* Greek. Thanks to the papyri, we now have illustrations of the contemporary 'secular' use of the vast majority of New Testament words. It is still true, in a restricted sense, that the language is *sui generis*, because of the frequent substratum of Hebrew and Aramaic. 'The tension between the Jewish heritage and the Greek world vitally affects the language of the New Testament' (Hoskyn and Davey, *The Riddle of the New Testament*, 1931, p. 20). Another tendency corrected by the study of the papyri was the inclination of scholars to judge the New Testament by Attic standards of grammar and syntax, and also of literary taste. It was now made doubly clear that the *koinē* of the first Christian centuries was in a comparatively rapid state of evolution, which culminated in Byzantine and finally in modern Greek, and must therefore be evaluated in the light of this. It would be wrong to claim too much for these advances, but they have provided an indispensable aid to the study of the New Testament text, language, and literature, and thus for its theological interpretation. In his Schweich Lecture of 1946 (published in 1953 as *The Text of the Epistles*) Dr. G. Zuntz makes a plea for the active conjunction of these two fields of study. 'The theologian who studies the New Testament must assume the quality also of the philologist' (p. 3). Perhaps the finest work exemplifying this is the *Theologisches Wörterbuch zum Neuen Testament* (1933–), edited by G. Kittel and G. Friedrich.

The original documents of the New Testament were all written on papyrus rolls (apart from one or two of the shortest Epistles, which may have been written on individual sheets of papyrus), and it may here be mentioned that the transmission of the text played an important part in the development of new techniques. In the rest of the Roman world papyrus codices did not begin to replace rolls until the 3rd century AD, but from Egypt we have evidence that the Christian communities developed the codex form considerably earlier. Ten Bible fragments have been found dated to the 2nd and early 3rd centuries, and of 111 fragments of the 3rd and 4th only twelve were in the form of papyrus rolls. The text of Romans would have required a roll of 11½ feet, Mark 19 feet, Acts about 32 feet (*cf.* 2 Tim. iv. 13 referring to rolls and the parchment wrappings which protected them). But as the need arose for copies of the Gospels and Epistles in larger bulk, the use of codices naturally developed, *i.e.* leaves of papyrus folded and arranged in quires, much as in modern books. A single codex could now contain the four Gospels and Acts, or the whole of Paul's Epistles.

b. List of the most notable papyri

The latest official tabulation, that of K. Aland (1957), contains more than 241 entries, of which sixty-eight are listed in the critical editions of the New Testament text. Many are comparatively small, but the importance of the more substantial texts is great.

P^1 (3rd or 4th century) contains Mt. i. 1–9, 12–20; P^4 (4th century) Lk. i. 74–80, vi. 1–4; P^5 (3rd century) Jn. i. 23–31, 33–41 and xx. 11–17, 19–25; it comprises the two leaves of a single quire, and illustrates the family from which the Codices Sinaiticus and Vaticanus later derived. P^8 (4th century) contains Acts iv. 31–37, v. 2–9, vi. 1–6, 8–15; P^{13} (3rd century, written on the back of an Epitome of Livy) Heb. ii. 14–v. 5, x. 8–22, x. 29–xi. 13, xi. 28–xii. 17; P^{20} (3rd century) Jas. ii. 19–iii. 9; P^{22} (3rd century) Jn. xv. 25–xvi. 2, 21–32; P^{27} (3rd century) Rom. viii. 12–22, 24–27, 33–ix. 3, 5–9; P^{37} (3rd century) contains Mt. xxvi. 19–52; P^{38} (4th century) Acts xviii. 27–xix. 6, xix. 12–16.

Of the Chester Beatty Papyri ($P^{45, 46, 47}$), Nos. 1 and 2 are of particular interest. P^{45} (early 3rd century) contains portions of thirty leaves out of a codex of 220 including the Gospels and Acts; it has parts of Matthew, Mark, Luke, John (seventeen leaves) and Acts (thirteen leaves). P^{46} (also early 3rd century) contains eighty-six leaves, found over a period in three groups, and has Romans, Hebrews, 1, 2 Corinthians, Galatians, Ephesians, Philippians, Colossians, 1, 2 Thessalonians, except for small gaps. It is notable that the concluding doxology of Romans here occurs at the end of chapter xv. P^{47} (3rd century, ten leaves) has Rev. ix. 10–xvii. 2; P^{48} (3rd century, similar to P^{38}) has Acts xxiii. 11–16, 24–29. P^{52} (the famous 'John Rylands' fragment, 3½ inches by 2½ inches) was identified by C. H. Roberts in 1935 as Jn. xviii. 31–33, 37, 38 and belonging to the early 2nd century. P^{64} (2nd century) contains portions of Mt. xxvi; P^{66} (*c.* AD 200), the 'Bodmer papyrus II', has 108 leaves in five quires, each 6½ inches by 5½ inches, and contains Jn. i. 1–xiv. 26. *Cf.* plate XII*b*.

The textual relation of these and many lesser papyri to the most important vellum codices and early versions of the New Testament has been the subject of close study.

c. Effect on the textual study of the New Testament

To describe this, a brief sketch of the history of the Greek text up to the papyrus discoveries is necessary. The AV of 1611 was based on the Greek New Testament edition prepared by Stephanus (Robert Estienne) in 1550, the 'Textus Receptus', which itself drew largely on the edition of Erasmus published in 1516. Stephanus had made use of only fifteen MSS, all of them of late date, and representing the Byzantine or Eastern tradition of the text. The event which stimulated a serious search for all available MSS was the appearance in England in 1627 of the Codex Alexandrinus, a vellum codex of the 5th century AD. But it was not until the discovery of Codex Sinaiticus and the appearance of Tischendorf's edition of Vaticanus, in 1859 and 1867 respectively, that any great advance in textual study was possible. This came just as scholars began to realize the potential wealth of Egypt in papyri. Westcott and Hort published a revised Greek text in 1881, which was used extensively in the English RV of that year. These scholars postulated four main families of texts, Syrian, Neutral, Alexandrian, and Western, and themselves gave most weight to the Neutral family, consisting of the Codices Vaticanus and Sinaiticus, the Coptic Versions and kindred MSS.

New Testament papyri have played a prominent part in the extension and modification of their results. Further study convinced scholars that Westcott and Hort's groups had been distinguished too sharply from each other; and B. H. Streeter, using the minuscule groups of MSS isolated by Ferrar and Abbott, and by K. Lake, together with the Koridethi MS (9th century) demonstrated the close relation these all bore to Origen's text of the New Testament, and postulated at any rate for the Gospel of Mark the 'Caesarean' family (Origen having spent his latter years at Caesarea). The text of the Gospels in the Freer MSS (the 'Washington Gospels') and the Chester Beatty papyri further showed that the 'Caesarean' family of texts probably originated in Egypt, and went from Alexandria to Caesarea with Origen. The Chester Beatty group, especially P^{46}, have been of immense value. They prove that the codex was early in use for collections of the Gospels and Pauline Epistles, the circulation of which greatly assisted towards the formation of the canon of the New Testament. Their firm dating to the 3rd century AD means that we now possess a line of textual evidence going beyond the great vellum codices of the 4th and 5th centuries, upon which scholars had depended so heavily, and earlier than the New Testament collections which Eusebius was ordered to produce for use in the churches, following the Edict of Milan in AD 313. Still earlier fragments, in particular the 'John Rylands' fragment of John's Gospel, take us into the first half of the 2nd century, *i.e.* to within a single generation of the last writings of the New Testament, the Johannine Corpus.

The general picture of the transmission of the text which emerges is that of many groups or families arising, as copies were made for public and private use, sometimes by trained scribes, but more often by untrained Christians. The need for a standard text had not yet arisen, and local attempts at the collation of different texts were never very widely used. We must also assume that in the persecutions, *e.g.* that of Decius in AD 250, many copies of the New Testament perished. The papyri have helped to reveal the complexity of this early stage of transmission; if we are still far from fulfilling Bentley's aim to make the text so undoubtedly true 'ut e manibus apostolorum vix purior et sincerior evaserit', at least the story is one of continuous advance. See TEXT AND VERSIONS (New Testament).

d. Effect on the study of New Testament language and literature

As noted above, the Greek of the New Testament has affinities with both the literary and the non-literary forms of the *koinē*, principally the latter, which is now known so fully from papyrus documents of every type from Graeco-Roman Egypt—Imperial rescripts, judicial proceedings, tax and census papers, marriage contracts, birth, death, and divorce notices, private letters, business accounts, and a host of others. There are without doubt many Semitisms in the New Testament, all the writers except one being Jewish, but their estimated number has been greatly reduced by the discovery of parallel expressions in the papyri. 'Even Mark's Semitisms are hardly ever barbarous Greek, though his extremely vernacular language makes us think so, until we read the less educated papyri' (Howard). An example is the expression *blepein apo* at Mk. viii. 15. Many new word formations of New Testament Greek have been paralleled, *e.g.* substantives ending in *-mos, -ma, -sis, -ia*; adjectives ending in *-ios*, new compound adjectives and adverbs, new words with the privative *a-* prefix; foreign words, technical words used of the Roman army and administration. Problems of orthography have been settled, *e.g. genēma* (Mt. xxvi. 29), *tameion* (Lk. xii. 3), *sphyris* (Mt. xv. 37); and of morphology, *e.g. gegonan* (Rom. xvi. 7), *elthatō* (Mt. x. 13), *ēlthan* (Mk. iii. 8); and of syntax, *e.g.* the consecutive use of *hina* clauses (as in Jn. xvii. 3), the interchangeability of *eis* and *en* (as in Jn. i. 18; Mt. xviii. 19).

New Testament vocabulary was abundantly illustrated. Instead of the numerous *voces biblicae* of the older scholars, it became possible to show, as did Deissmann and Bauer, that only about 1 per cent of the vocabulary, about fifty words, was in fact peculiar to it. A better sense could be given to words like *hēlikia* (*e.g.* Lk. ii. 52 = 'age'), *meris* (Acts xvi. 12 = 'district'), *anastatoō* (lit. 'drive out of hearth and home', used metaphorically in Acts xvii. 6 and Gal. v. 12), *hypostasis* (Heb. xi. 1 = 'title-deeds'), *parousia* (*passim*; = visit of royalty or other notable person), *arrhabōn* (*e.g.* Eph. i. 14 = 'deposit paid'), *leitourgia* (2 Cor. ix. 12; of both private and public service). The common terms *adelphoi* and *presbyteroi* were frequently illustrated, from social and religious fraternities and from village and temple officials.

At the time the New Testament was written a revised Atticism was popular, an essentially artificial movement which affected to recognize only 5th-century Attic Greek as the norm. But there were notable secular writers, such as Plutarch, Strabo, Diodorus Siculus, and Epictetus, who shunned Atticism, and the New Testament itself represents a revolt against it by its use of the vernacular tongue. *Koinē* is not, as it were, pure gold accidentally contaminated, but something more like a new and serviceable 'alloy' (Moule). The LXX had already set a precedent for such a use of popular Greek, and the writers, all of whom might have written in Aramaic, wrote in Greek from deliberate choice. The literary standard of their work of course varies enormously. 2 Peter most nearly approaches a fully literary level, and Luke and the author of Hebrews are also conscious stylists. But Luke and Paul, though obviously capable of speaking and writing Greek in its classical form (*cf.* the prefaces to Luke and Acts, and Acts xvi. 22 ff.) did not hesitate to use highly colloquial forms. The extreme case is the Revelation, written in laboured and sometimes barbarous Greek, which clearly reflects the influence of Semitic terms and modes of thought. But it still remains true that 'the Greek in which the author expresses himself was more like the Greek of the Egyptian papyri' (A. Robinson). See LANGUAGE OF THE NEW TESTAMENT.

e. Ostraca

We have noted already that ostraca or 'potsherds' were used extensively in antiquity as the cheapest possible writing material. Their seeming insignificance (*cf.* Is. xlv. 9) caused them to be neglected as being of any value for the study of *koinē* Greek. As we might expect, among the large numbers found in Egypt, covering a period of nearly a thousand years, the vast majority are documents, or fragments of them, belonging to the life of the lower classes. A few have been found bearing short literary texts, no doubt for use in schools, and we have ostraca with short passages of the New Testament inscribed on them (verses from Mk. ix and Lk. xxii) and one of the 6th century AD with a hymn to Mary influenced by Lk. i. But more comprise brief letters, contracts, and, above all, tax receipts. Many languages are used, including Greek, Latin, Aramaic, Coptic, and Old Egyptian.

Occasionally a New Testament expression is illuminated. Several ostraca give details of receipts dated to the day called *Sebastē*, meaning 'Emperor's Day', and perhaps parallel to the use by Christians of *kyriakē* as 'the Lord's day'. The title *Kyrios*, 'Lord', appears on ostraca referring to the emperors Nero and Vespasian (*cf.* Jude 4). Receipts from Thebes dated to the first century have thrown light on the New Testament use of *logeia* (*e.g.* 1 Cor. xvi. 1–2 = 'collections') and also on the verb *apechō* signifying the receipt of a payment (*cf.* Mt. vi. 2 = 'they have received their reward in full'). The common phrase *eis to onoma* ('in the name') is shown by ostraca to have been a regular legal formula, of the authority under which something is done. Ostraca thus supplement, on a comparatively minor scale, the evidence of the papyri as to New Testament language and idiom.

f. Apocryphal and non-canonical papyri

These deserve mention because of the assistance they have given to the understanding of the form and content of New Testament writings. Most notable are the *Logia* or Sayings of Jesus. The first of those (found at Oxyrhynchus in 1896 and 1897) was the leaf of a codex dated to the 3rd century, containing sayings some of which were familiar, others of a more mystical type; the second, of the late 2nd century, had the sayings written on the back of a roll about land surveys. A third contained fragments of a non-canonical Gospel, and another of this type was discovered in 1934; it comprises fragments of three leaves of a codex, assigned to *c.* AD 150, and narrates four incidents from Christ's life, similar to those in the Gospels. Then, among thirteen papyrus rolls found near Nag Hammadi in 1946 was the *Gospel of Thomas*, an important collection of Sayings in which Gnostic influence mingles with the Synoptic, Johannine, and other traditions, evidently a Coptic version of the work of which the Oxyrhynchus Logia are fragments.

Several apocryphal works have been recovered in whole or in part. The Chester Beatty collection includes fourteen leaves of the Book of Enoch, from a 4th-century codex, and part of a homily by Melito of Sardis on the passion. One papyrus leaf of Gnostic origin has come to light (early 3rd century), out of the *Gospel of Mary*. At Akhmim fragments were found of the *Gospel* and *Apocalypse of Peter* (probably written in the 2nd century). The former has Docetic tendencies, and the latter is much inferior to the Revelation of John. In the Amherst collection is the major portion of the *Ascension of Isaiah*, and in the Hamburg State Library are eleven leaves of the *Acts of Paul*, a late 2nd-century 'religious romance'. Finally, the Oxyrhynchus papyri have provided some of the Greek text of the well-known *Shepherd* of Hermas. This work later appears in full in the Codex Sinaiticus. See CANON OF THE NEW TESTAMENT.

BIBLIOGRAPHY (listed according to the above sections).

a. F. G. Kenyon, *Our Bible and the Ancient Manuscripts*[5], 1958; *id.*, *The Bible and Archaeology*, 1940; E. Hoskyns and F. N. Davey, *The Riddle of the New Testament*, 1931; A. Deissmann, *LAE*[4], 1929; F. F. Bruce, *The New Testament Documents: Are They Reliable?*[5], 1959.

b. G. Maldfeld and B. M. Metzger, 'Detailed list of the Greek Papyri of the New Testament', *JBL*, LXVIII, 1949, pp. 359–370; W. H. P. Hatch, *The Principal Uncial MSS of the New Testament*, 1939; F. G. Kenyon (ed.), *The Chester Beatty Biblical Papyri* (fasc. I–VII), 1933–7.

c. F. G. Kenyon, *The Text of the Greek Bible*, 1937; L. Vaganay, *Introduction to the Textual Criticism of the New Testament* (translated

Miller), 1937; A. H. McNeile, *Introduction to the New Testament*[2], 1953, chapter xi.

d. A. Wikenhauser, *New Testament Introduction*, 1958, Part II; G. A. Deissmann, *Bible Studies*[2], 1909; F. Blass, *Grammatik des Neutestamentlichen Griechisch*[6], 1931; J. H. Moulton and W. F. Howard, *A Grammar of New Testament Greek*, I, 1926, II, 1929; C. F. D. Moule, *An Idiom Book of New Testament Greek*, 1953; J. H. Moulton and W. Milligan, *Vocabulary of the Greek New Testament*, 1930; *Arndt*, 1957; A. T. Robertson, *A Grammar of the Greek New Testament*[3], 1919; L. R. Palmer, *A Grammar of the Post-Ptolemaic Papyri*, 1946.

e. U. Wilcken, *Griechische Ostraka aus Ägypten und Nubien*, 1899; G. Lefebvre, *Fragments grecs des Évangiles sur ostraca*; H. R. Hall, *Coptic and Greek Texts of the Christian Period from Ostraca, Stelae, etc., in the British Museum*, 1905.

f. H. I. Bell and T. C. Skeat, *Fragments of an Unknown Gospel*, 1935; B. P. Grenfell, A. S. Hunt, and others, *The Oxyrhynchus Papyri*, I–XXVII, 1898–1952; R. M. Grant and D. N. Freedman, *The Secret Sayings of Jesus*, 1960; R. McL. Wilson, *Studies in the Gospel of Thomas*, 1960.

K.A.K.
D.F.P.
B.F.H.

PARABLE.

I. PARABLES AND ALLEGORIES

The word 'parable' (Gk. *parabolē*) by derivation means 'putting things side by side', and is similar to the word 'allegory', which by derivation means 'saying things in a different way'. The object of teaching by parables and allegories is the same. It is to enlighten the listener by presenting him with interesting illustrations, from which he can draw out for himself moral and religious truth. The value of such a method of teaching is twofold. First, it makes the assimilation of such truth easier, for 'truth embodied in a tale shall enter in at lowly doors'; and secondly, the truth so learned is more likely to remain fixed in the memory, for by drawing his own deductions from the illustrations the learner is in effect teaching himself. But, while 'parable' and 'allegory' are by derivation and meaning almost indistinguishable, in common usage 'parable' has come to be limited to the somewhat protracted simile or the short descriptive story, designed to inculcate a single truth or answer a single question. 'Allegory', on the other hand, denotes the more elaborate tale, in which a comparison is to be found in all or most of the details.

II. THE INTERPRETATION OF THE PARABLES

In the case of the parables of Jesus some difficulty has arisen, because the same word 'parable' is used both in the Gospels themselves, and by students of the Gospels, to describe the great variety of illustrations to be found in the teaching contained in them. What we would normally call a 'proverb' (*q.v.*) is designated a 'parable' in Lk. iv. 23 (so RV, following the Gk.; AV and RSV translate 'proverb'). The 'parable' referred to in Mt. xv. 15 is almost in the nature of a conundrum. The simple illustration, that leaves on a tree are signs of the approach of summer, is called a 'parable' in Mk. xiii. 28. The more elaborate comparison between children at play and the reaction of Jesus' contemporaries to John the Baptist and Himself is usually spoken of as 'the *parable* of the children's game' (Lk. vii. 31, 32). On the other hand, the parables of the sower and the tares of the field are both given detailed allegorical interpretations (Mt. xiii. 18–23, 36–43); and the parables of the drag-net (Mt. xiii. 47–50), the wicked husbandmen (Mk. xii. 1–12), the marriage feast (Mt. xxii. 1–14), and the great supper (Lk. xiv. 16–24) should more accurately be called 'allegories'.

Christian preachers in all ages have striven, for homiletic purposes, to find more truth embodied in the parables of Jesus than was originally intended. Small details have been allegorized so as to teach truths not in the least obvious in the stories themselves, and irrelevant to the context in which they are found. As a result, the inevitable critical reaction set in. Scholars, such as Jülicher, asserted that the parables were intended to illustrate one truth only (though there might be considerable difference of opinion as to what that one truth was); and they regarded the allegorical interpretations of the parables of the sower, and of the tares, as early examples of the dangerous process of allegorization which had done so much harm in the Christian Church. But, as we have seen, it is in reality impossible to draw such a clear-cut distinction between parable and allegory in the stories told by Jesus; and in some of His parables *several* lessons are to be learned, as, *e.g.*, in that of the prodigal son, where stress is laid upon the joy the Father-God has in forgiving His children, upon the nature of repentance, and upon the sin of jealousy and self-righteousness (Lk. xv. 11–32).

More recent scholars, such as Jeremias, have attempted to distinguish within the Gospels themselves between the comparatively simple lessons that Jesus meant His parables to convey and the more elaborate meaning given to them by early Christian teachers before the stories became finally embodied in the Gospels. But such attempts to disentangle primary and secondary elements must always be more subjective than scientific. What is clear, however, is that the Gospels do not always tell us either the occasion on which a particular parable was first spoken or the person to whom it was originally addressed. In the case of the parables of the good Samaritan (Lk. x. 25), the two debtors (Lk. vii. 41), the children's game (Lk. vii. 31, 32), and the parable of the pounds (Lk. xix. 11), the context is clearly given and provides a clue to the interpretation. Very often, however, it would seem that the stories of Jesus were remembered long after the circumstances that gave rise to them were forgotten; and the evangelists have fitted them in to their narratives, sometimes, but not always, suggesting the motive which prompted their original utterance (see Lk. xviii. 19). A collection of seven parables, detached from their contexts, is to be found in Mt. xiii.

Over-elaboration and over-simplification are both to be avoided in the interpretation of the parables, for in few spheres of Gospel exegesis is it easier to be tendentious. As the present writer has said elsewhere, 'It is, for example, misleading to say that the parable of the prodigal son contains "the gospel within the Gospels" and to deduce from it that no doctrine of atonement is vital to Christianity: or to suppose from the story of the good Samaritan that practical service to our fellow men is the be-all and end-all of Christianity' (R. V. G. Tasker, *The Nature and Purpose of the Gospels*, 1957, pp. 57, 58). Equally mistaken is the attempt to bring ethical or economic considerations to bear upon the interpretation of the parables, when such considerations are in fact irrelevant. For example, the parable of the unjust steward (Lk. xvi. 1–9) teaches that the future matters, and that men must prepare themselves for it; but the question of the morality of the action taken by the fictitious steward has no bearing on the main lesson of the story. Similarly, it is beside the point to ask whether the man who discovered a great treasure in a field was morally justified in obtaining the purchase of the field for much less than he now knew it to be worth (Mt. xiii. 44). The lesson of the parable is that no treasure is comparable in value to the treasure of the kingdom of God, and that the sudden 'discovery' of it is a matter for great joy. Once again, it is futile to suggest that the parable of the labourers in the vineyard (Mt. xx. 1–16) throws any light whatever on the problem of wages. It illustrates the goodness of God, who deals with men graciously and not strictly in accordance with their merits.

III. CHARACTERISTICS OF THE PARABLES

Jesus would seem to have taken the illustrations for His parables sometimes from nature, as in the parables of the sower (Mk. iv. 1–9), the seed growing secretly (Mk. iv. 26–29), the mustard seed (Mk. iv. 30–32), and the tares (Mt. xiii. 24–30); sometimes from familiar customs of everyday life, as in the parables of the leaven (Mt. xiii. 33), the lamp set on a stand (Mk. iv. 21), the lost sheep and the lost coin (Lk. xv. 3–10), the importunate man (Lk. xi. 5–8), and the ten virgins (Mt. xxv. 1–13); sometimes from well-known events in recent history (Lk. xix. 14); and sometimes from what might be conceived as occasional happenings, or not improbable contingencies, as in the parables of the unjust judge (Lk. xviii. 2–8), the children's game (Lk. vii. 31–35), the labourers in the vineyard (Mt. xx. 1–16), the unjust steward (Lk. xvi. 1–9), and the prodigal son (Lk. xv. 11–32). When the truth to be taught is something beyond the experience of His listeners the parable not only becomes more fictitious but more didactic in character, as in the case of the parable of the rich man and Lazarus (Lk. xvi. 19–21), where Jesus concludes the story with the emphatic utterance: 'If they hear not Moses and the prophets, neither will they be persuaded, though one rose from the dead.'

Sometimes the lesson of a parable is sufficiently obvious from the story itself, as in the story of the rich fool, where a *reductio ad absurdum* is reached when the rich man dies at the very moment when the preparations for him to retire in security and comfort have been completed (Lk. xii. 16–21); but even here the story is 'capped' with the dictum: 'So is he that layeth up treasure for himself, and is not rich toward God.' On other occasions, we find Jesus eliciting from a listener the point of a parable by a question, *e.g.* 'Tell me therefore, which of them will love him most?' (Lk. vii. 42). Or He may point the moral Himself, either at the conclusion of a story (as in Mt. xviii. 23, where He concludes the parable of the unforgiving servant with the words 'So likewise shall my heavenly Father do also unto you, if ye from your hearts forgive not every one his brother their trespasses'), or in response to a subsequent request for elucidation (as in Mt. xv. 15, where Peter asks Him to 'declare' the parable, *i.e.* to explain what He meant by saying that what enters a man's mouth cannot defile him, but that what comes out of it can). More often, the story is told without additions, and the hearers are left to draw their own deductions from it. That the right inference was often drawn, even though it proved unacceptable, is seen from the statement in Mk. xii. 12 that the religious leaders knew that Jesus had spoken the parable of the wicked husbandmen against them.

IV. THE KINGDOM OF GOD

Many of the parables of Jesus are concerned with some aspect of *the kingdom of God* (*q.v.*), its nature, its coming, its value, its growth, the sacrifices it calls for, the sphere of its operations, and so forth. Very naturally the interpretation given to these parables has been largely influenced by the view of the kingdom of God held by individual interpreters. Theologians, for example, of the 'thorough-going' eschatological school, such as Schweitzer, who regarded it as axiomatic that Jesus envisaged the coming of the kingdom of God as a supernatural event which would take place suddenly and catastrophically in the near future, found here the clue to the meaning of all the parables of the kingdom. Even parables which appeared to imply growth or progress did not in fact do so. It was, for example, in the suddenness of the rising of the leaven, not in its slow working, that the meaning of that parable was to be found. On the other hand, scholars of the school of 'realized eschatology' assume that the kingdom of God is wholly present in the teaching and deeds of Jesus. Consequently, to them the parables of the kingdom are essentially parables of fulfilment.

The harvest prepared for in past ages has now come; the mustard seed planted long ago has now become a tree in whose branches birds of every kind are roosting. It would seem that neither of these extreme types of exegesis does full justice to the material. Both err by oversimplification.

If we are to give to the parables of the kingdom their *prima facie* meaning, we must suppose that, while Jesus regarded the kingdom or kingship of God as present indeed in His own words and actions, He also anticipated a period, the length of which He did not know (Mk. xiii. 32), during which that kingship would be a reality within the society of His followers who would constitute His world-wide Church, and predicted that the kingdom would not come in its fulness till He Himself returned in glory. The contrast between the apparent lack of response with which His teaching was at first received and the final outcome of it is suggested in the parables of the sower, the seed growing secretly, and the mustard seed, which are recorded by Mark significantly at the point in the ministry of Jesus when He begins to limit the sphere of His activities to those who have responded to Him, and to speak in parables the meaning of which will be clear only to those to whom 'it is given to know the mystery of the kingdom of the God'. The nature of this 'mystery' is suggested in the parable of the sower: 'Know ye not *this* parable? and how then will ye know all parables?' (Mk. iv. 13). It is the mystery of the varied response to the proclamation of the kingdom. The behaviour expected of those who have responded to Christ during the period between His first and second comings, is brought out in numerous parables; some of them are called parables of the kingdom and others remain unspecified. The disciples are to be persistent in prayer, to forgive others, to serve their neighbours, to use the gifts God has given them, to be free from covetousness, to remain alert, to be faithful stewards, and to remember that their final judgment is being determined by their present conduct.

V. THE PURPOSE OF THE PARABLES

Some have found the section Mk. iv. 10–12 very difficult to understand, for it seems to suggest that the specific purpose which led Jesus to teach in parables was not to enlighten the unenlightened, but that the unbeliever might become hardened in his unbelief. It is probable, however, that what seems to be a clause of purpose in Mk. iv. 12 is in fact a clause of consequence (so Mt. xiii. 11). The parables of Jesus may have, and often have had, the effect of hardening the unbeliever. For the truth is that the parables of Jesus are unique. The parables of other teachers and moralists can to some extent be separated from the teachers themselves. But Jesus and His parables are inseparable. To fail to understand *Him* is to fail to understand His parables. Consequently, to those who remain unaware of who He really is, or ignorant of the nature of the gift that He came to bring mankind, the mysteries of the kingdom of God, however many parables they may hear about it, must remain mysteries. 'Unto them that are without, *all* these things are done in parables' (Mk. iv. 11). The *whole* of Jesus' ministry, *everything* He says, not merely that part of His teaching that is spoken in 'parables', and *all* His miracles remain on the level of earthly stories, and portents devoid of any deeper significance. It is 'because they seeing, see not; and hearing they hear not, neither do they understand' (Mt. xiii. 14) that the words of Isaiah's prophecy, quoted in Mt. xiii. 14, 15 and Mk. iv. 12 are fulfilled in them. It is important to notice that this same quotation from Isaiah is found in John xii. 40 to explain the disbelief of the Jews in Jesus 'though he had done so many *miracles* before them'.

VI. JOHN'S GOSPEL

In Jn. x. 6 the allegory of the true and false shepherds is called a *paroimia*, meaning by derivation 'something said by the way'. This is translated, probably rightly, by 'parable' in AV and RV, as the words seem in this passage to be synonyms. On the other hand, in Jn. xvi. 25 the same word *paroimia* is translated 'proverb' in AV and RV; here it seems to be used in its LXX sense, where it translates *māšāl*, meaning a difficult saying which needs further explanation. The RSV translates *paroimiai* 'figures'; and it is true that in this Gospel, which contains no 'parables', Jesus uses many 'figurative' or allegorical descriptions of Himself, *e.g.* 'the Good Shepherd', 'The True Vine', 'The Door', 'The Light of the World', 'The Way, the Truth, and the Life'.

BIBLIOGRAPHY. C. H. Dodd, *The Parables of the Kingdom*, 1935; J. Jeremias, *The Parables of Jesus*, 1954; W. O. E. Oesterley, *The Gospel Parables in the Light of their Jewish Background*, 1936; B. T. D. Smith, *The Parables of the Synoptic Gospels*, 1937. R.V.G.T.

PARACLETE. See ADVOCATE, HOLY SPIRIT.

PARADISE. Paradise is a loan-word from ancient Iranian (*pairidaēza-*) and means a garden with a wall. The Greek word *paradeisos* is used for the first time by Xenophon for the gardens of the Persian kings. LXX translates *gan 'ēḏen* of Gn. ii. 8 by *paradeisos.*

a. In the Old Testament

The word paradise (Heb. *pardēs*) appears in Ne. ii. 8; Ec. ii. 5; Ct. iv. 13. AV renders it by 'king's forest' in Nehemiah and 'orchard' in Ecclesiastes and Canticles. The actual word is thus nowhere used in the Old Testament in an eschatological sense, which meaning developed in the later Jewish world. The following trends can be discerned. The word paradise (Aram. *pardēsā'*) was used to give expression to the meaning of primeval times (German *Urzeit*) and then expanded to include fantastic speculations on the glory and bliss of those times. This was connected with the expectations of a wonderful messianic time in the future. This coming age of glory would be indentical with the garden of Eden of ancient times. The Jews believed also that paradise was present in their own time, but concealed. This concealed paradise was the place to which the souls of the Patriarchs, the chosen and the righteous people, were taken. The ancient, future, and present paradise were regarded as being identical.

b. In the New Testament

The word paradise (Gk. *paradeisos*) occurs in only three instances in the New Testament (Lk. xxiii. 43; 2 Cor. xii. 4; Rev. ii. 7). The context shows that the predominating sense is that of the later development of the word. In Lk. xxiii. 43 the word 'paradise' is used by Jesus for the place where souls go immediately after death, *cf.* the concealed paradise in later Jewish thought. The same idea is also present in the parable of the rich man and Lazarus (Lk. xvi. 19–31).

In 2 Cor. xii. 2–4 Paul wrote in the third person of his experience of being caught up into paradise where he heard unspeakable words (Gk. *arrhēta rhēmata*). In this case paradise is heaven with its glory, the same as in Lk. xxiii. The only place where paradise is used in an eschatological sense is in Rev. ii. 7. The promise is made by Christ that He will give paradise as a gift to the one who overcomes. The present paradise will come in its full glory with the final consummation. The idea of a garden of God in the world to come is strongly emphasized in the last chapters of Revelation. The symbols of the tree of life, of life-giving water, and of the twelve kinds of fruit are all witnesses to the glory of the coming paradise (Rev. xxii). F.C.F.

PARAN. A wilderness situated in the east central region of the Sinai peninsula, north-east from the traditional Sinai and south-south-east of Kadesh, with the Arabah and the Gulf of Aqabah as its eastern border. It was to this wilderness that Hagar and Ishmael went after their expulsion from Abraham's household (Gn. xxi. 21). It was crossed by the Israelites following their Exodus from Egypt (Nu. x. 12, xii. 16), and from here Moses despatched men to spy out the land of Canaan (Nu. xiii. 3, 26). The wilderness was also traversed by Hadad the Edomite on his flight to Egypt (1 Ki. xi. 18).

1 Sa. xxv. 1 records that David went to the wilderness of Paran on the death of the prophet Samuel, but in this instance we may read with the Greek 'wilderness of Maon'.

El-paran, mentioned in Gn. xiv. 6 as on the border of the wilderness, may have been an ancient name for Elath. Mt. Paran of the Song of Moses (Dt. xxxiii. 2) and of Hab. iii. 3 was possibly a prominent peak in the mountain range on the west shore of the Gulf of Aqabah.

R.A.H.G.

PARBAR. 1 Ch. xxvi. 18 describes the place where gatekeepers to the court of the Temple were stationed 'at the western *parbar*, four at the causeway and two inside the *parbar*'. Gesenius suggested that *parbar* is a rare word for 'colonnade' or other opening for light on the basis of the Persian *parwār*, 'possessing light'. This meaning might suit 2 Ki. xxiii. 11 (LXX *pharoureim*), which qualifies the location of the house of Nathan-melekh as 'in *parwārîm*' (RV 'precincts'; AV 'suburbs' follows the Targ. and Mishnah, for the city suburbs consisted of 'summer' or veranda-houses). Schick located these colonnades on his Temple plan (*ZDPV*, 1894, p. 13) but the precise meaning of *parbar* is still unknown, for the (pre-exilic) use of a Persian word is unlikely. The suggested emendation to *p^erāḏîm*, '(who was over) the mules', is unsupported.

D.J.W.

PARCHED CORN (*qālî*, *qālâ*, 'roasted'). Ears or grains of wheat (Lv. xxiii. 14; Ru. ii. 14; 1 Sa. xvii. 17, xxv. 18; 2 Sa. xvii. 28) roasted over a blazing fire, usually on an iron pan or flat stone. See also PULSE.

PARCHMENT. See WRITING.

PARDON. See FORGIVENESS.

PARENTS. See FAMILY.

PAROUSIA. See ESCHATOLOGY.

PARTHIANS. Parthia, a district south-east of the Caspian Sea, was part of the Persian Empire conquered by Alexander the Great. In the middle of the 3rd century BC Arsaces led the Parthians in revolt against their Seleucid (Macedonian) rulers, and his successors eventually extended their empire from the Euphrates to the Indus. Their exclusive use of cavalry-bowmen made them a formidable enemy, as the Romans discovered to their cost. In the 1st century AD the Parthians changed their capital from Ecbatana to Ctesiphon and sought to revive the Iranian elements of their civilization at the expense of the Greek.

The Parthians were governed by a land-owning aristocracy, and controlled the lucrative trade with the Far East. Their own religion was Iranian Mazdaism, but they were generally tolerant of other peoples' religions.

Parthia was one of the districts in which the deported Israelites had been settled, and according to Josephus their descendants continued to speak an Aramaic dialect and to worship the true God, sending tribute to the Temple at Jerusalem. Consequently the Parthians in Jerusalem on the day of Pentecost (Acts ii. 9) may have been only Israelites from that district ('language' in verse 8 could equally well be 'dialect'), but there may have been Parthian proselytes with them.

BIBLIOGRAPHY. N. C. Deberoise, *Parthia*, 1938; F. F. Bruce, *The Acts of the Apostles*, 1951, p. 84; *BC*, IV, p. 19. K.L.McK.

PARTRIDGE. See BIRDS OF THE BIBLE.

PARVAIM. The place which produced the gold used for ornamenting Solomon's Temple (2 Ch.

iii. 6). The location is obscure. Some suggest Farwa in Yemen. Gesenius, identifying it with Sanskrit *parvam*, understands it to be a general term for the eastern regions. See also OPHIR.

PASHUR. This name is probably of Egyptian origin (Heb. *paš-ḥûr* from Egyp. **p(s)š-ḥr*, 'portion of (the god) Horus').

1. Pashur son of Immer. A priest, the chief officer of the house of the Lord, in the reign of Zedekiah or earlier, who put Jeremiah in the stocks and whose fate Jeremiah prophesied as exile in Babylon (Je. xx. 1–6).

2. Pashur son of Malchijah. Sent by King Zedekiah to inquire of Jeremiah (Je. xxi. 1), he was among those who incarcerated the prophet in the slimy pit-dungeon of the king's son Malchijah (the father of this Pashur?); Je. xxxviii. 1–13. He is possibly identical with the head of a priestly family of which some members were exiled to Babylonia. Some later members of this family returned to Jerusalem with Zerubbabel (Ezr. ii. 38 = Ne. vii. 41), six of them having to put away foreign wives there (Ezr. x. 22). Others volunteered for the fuller reoccupation of Jerusalem under Nehemiah (Ne. xi. 12; probably the same Adaiah as in 1 Ch. ix. 12).

3. Pashur father of Gedaliah. His son Gedaliah was among those who imprisoned Jeremiah in Malchijah's dungeon (Je. xxxviii. 1–13); see (2) above. This Pashur might conceivably be identical with (1) or (2) above.

4. Pashur, a priest, was among those who set their seal to the covenant under Nehemiah which followed Ezra's reading of the law (Ne. x. 3).

K.A.K.

PASSION. The word occurs only three times in AV.

1. In Acts i. 3 it translates *pathein* and refers to Christ's suffering and death. This use of the term is still current. Elsewhere the same word is translated 'suffer' (*e.g.* Lk. xvii. 25, xxiv. 26; Acts xvii. 3; Heb. xiii. 12, *etc.*).

2. In Acts xiv. 15 and Jas. v. 17 it translates *homoiopathēs*. RSV 'of like nature' gives the sense of the Greek.

3. The RV and RSV use the term in its bad sense to translate *pathos* in Rom. i. 26; Col. iii. 5; 1 Thes. iv. 5 (in the New Testament this word always has the meaning 'evil desire'), and *pathēmata* in Rom. vii. 5 and Gal. v. 24 (a word which usually has the sense of 'sufferings'). RSV also uses it fifteen times to translate *epithymia*, 'desire' (usually in the plural) in the bad sense of that word. See LUST.

P.E.

PASSOVER. In Christian thought, as in Judaism, the Passover, the Feast of Unleavened Bread, and the dedication of the first-born have been traditionally regarded as closely connected memorials of interdependent events of the historic Exodus, instituted by Moses himself at God's specific command. Passover means, of course, two things—the historic event and its later recurrent institutional commemoration (Mishnah, *Pesaḥim* ix. 5). The conjoined prohibition of leaven (*q.v.*) symbolizes the haste of that unforgettable night in Egypt, and the dedication of the first-born is a later statutory offering of thanksgiving for God's wondrous deliverance.

It has been argued that the Passover is an adaptation of something much older than Moses—whether a circumcision ceremonial (*JewE*), or an anti-demonic threshold rite (*HDB*, *IB*), or a shepherds' festival (*JewE*), or a sacrificial attempt to enhance the vitality both of the flock and of the celebrant (Mowinckel, *op. cit.*, pp. 58, 103), or a sacrifice of the first-born as old as Cain and Abel, defining by its very reference the offence and punishment of Pharaoh (*HDB*), or a common meal of communion or magic (Gaster). This list is by no means exhaustive.

I. IN THE OLD TESTAMENT

It has been suggested also that the authority for the existence and manner of the Passover rests on documents centuries later than Moses. The most important relevant passages of the Old Testament are Ex. xii. 1–13, 21–27, 43–49 and Dt. xvi. 1–8. According to Driver's analysis and dating of the Pentateuch, the earliest (or JE) portion of this material is Ex. xii. 21–27, which he regards as earlier than 750 BC. The other relevant verses in Ex. xii are assigned to the P document, perhaps about 550 BC, while Dt. xvi. 1–8 is dated a little before 621 BC. This is merely a sample chronology—other scholars propose other dates. Whether the period of Moses be dated in the 15th or 13th century BC, the implications of these later documentary datings are obvious.

The position here taken is not that the entire Pentateuch consists of the precise words of Moses, but that the ultimate sanction of his divinely inspired authority, oral or written, substantially underlies the books traditionally ascribed to him, whatever be the precise method of its transmission to the point of a fixed scriptural text. If the writer of Ex. xii is not Moses himself, it is difficult to resist the conclusion that he knew the mind of his master remarkably well, and possessed the details of a strong eyewitness tradition. The Deuteronomy passage is certainly a little later than the Exodus one, but its dubiety as to the precise location of the Temple (verses 2, 6) has a forward look about it, and is difficult to reconcile with a date centuries after the conquest.

Ex. xii, the natural starting-point of study, suggests the following principal considerations.

1. Passover, Heb. *pesaḥ*, comes from a verb meaning 'to pass over', in the sense of 'to spare' (Ex. xii. 13, 27, *etc.*). There seems to be nothing except perspicuity to condemn the view that God simply and literally passed over the blood-sprinkled Israelite houses, while smiting the Egyptians. The term is used both for the ordinance and for the sacrificial victim. (There is a verb with the same radicals meaning 'to limp',

which has suggested alternative theories; *cf.* Gaster, *op. cit.*, pp. 23–25.)

2. Abib, later called Nisan, the month of the ripening ears and of the first Passover, was made in honour the first month of the Jewish year (Ex. xii. 2; Dt. xvi. 1; *cf.* Lv. xxiii. 5; Nu. ix. 1–5, xxviii. 16).

3. Of especial interest is the identity of the Paschal victim, whether or not it be the lamb popularly conceived, of which Christ is the antitype. In Dt. xvi. 2 the choice of animal is unquestionably much wider; in Ex. xii. 3–5 it is a matter of exegesis. The Hebrew word *śeh* (verse 3) means sheep or goat, irrespective of age, but, unlike the more general word in Deuteronomy, it excludes all other kinds. Whether the choice be further limited to a lamb or kid depends on the precise translation of *ben-šānâ* (verse 5), lit. 'son of a year'. If, as some maintain, this really means a yearling animal, between twelve and twenty-four months in age (*cf.* Gesenius–Kautsch–Cowley, *Hebrew Grammar*, section 128, v; Gray, *op. cit.*, pp. 345–351), then a full-grown sheep or goat is meant. But the traditional exegesis, which takes twelve months as the upper, not as the lower, age limit is by no means disproved. The rabbinic evidence on this point is interesting, but not conclusive. The Talmud in general would seem to limit the legitimacy of the Passover victim to the sheep and goat families, following Exodus rather than Deuteronomy (see, *e.g.*, *Menaḥoth* vii. 5 with Gemara). Beyond this lies a realm of controversy, with certain pointers. The choice of lamb or kid, lamb or goat is several times asserted (*Pesaḥim* viii. 2; 55 b; 66 a), yet the over-all evidence does suggest a certain preference for the lamb; it would scarcely be honest to say more than that (*Shabbath* xxiii. 1; *Kelim* xix. 2; *Pesaḥim* 69 b; *etc.*). One ruling, without precisely specifying the age of the paschal victim, excludes a female animal, or a male which has passed the age of two years—which would lend tacit support to the yearling interpretation and the modern critics (*Pesaḥim* ix. 7). Yet a contradictory passage declares categorically that a Passover offering is valid from the eighth day of its life (*Parah* i. 4). If the universal use of a lamb cannot be certainly demonstrated from Scripture or Talmud, it is at least clear that this acquired strong consuetudinary sanction, and that the typologies 'Christ our Passover', 'Lamb of God', rested on widespread precedent.

4. It is laid down in Ex. xii. 46 and Nu. ix. 12 that no bone of the Passover victim is to be broken. This small detail is typologically fulfilled when it is reverently applied to the crucified One (Jn. xix. 36).

5. There is no blood ritual in Dt. xvi. In Ex. xii, however, it is commanded that on the Passover night in Egypt, the lintel and side-posts of each Israelite door should be smeared with the victim's blood. This is applied with hyssop, the foliage of the marjoram plant, a common emblem of ritual purity in the Pentateuch and elsewhere, and the blood is carried in a basin (Heb. *sap̄*; the Hebrew word also means 'threshold', which would alter slightly, though not basically, the meaning of verse 22). This smearing has been interpreted as apotropaic, that is to say, intended to ward off evil spirits. The biblical story has even been rewritten with Yahweh Himself as the demonic spirit to be warded off (Gray, *op. cit.*, pp. 355–364). There is surely greater cogency in accepting the tremendous biblical story, and in fitting it into its place in the long history of the theology of atonement by blood, culminating in the Epistle to the Hebrews.

6. The phrase 'between the two evenings' in Ex. xii. 6 (*cf.* Ex. xvi. 12; Lv. xxiii. 5; Nu. ix. 3, 5, 11) has been accorded two variant renderings according to community practice; either between noon and sunset, or between sunset and dark. The matter is important to Jews, but can scarcely be determined by etymology.

7. Ex. xii. 43–49 certainly excludes Gentiles from participation in the Passover, but it leaves the door noticeably wide for conscientious proselytes willing to meet the conditions required.

The whole drama and inner meaning of Ex. xii is concentrated into seventeen pregnant Greek words in Heb. xi. 28.

The Passover depicted in Dt. xvi differs in several important respects from that of Ex. xii. The blood emphasis has disappeared; the essentially domestic ceremony has become a more formal sacrifice at a central sanctuary with a considerably wider choice of victim. Passover and Unleavened Bread, here called the bread of affliction, are integrated more thoroughly than in Exodus. This is development, event changing to institution, not contradiction. It is not absolutely necessary to assume a vast time gap between the two passages; the necessary changes of circumstance could have taken place in the wilderness period. It is further recorded that a second Passover, a month later, was instituted for the benefit of those who had been levitically unclean at the time of the first (Nu. ix. 1–14).

Passover was celebrated in the plains of Jericho during the conquest (Jos. v. 10 f.). In the observances of Hezekiah (2 Ch. xxx. 1–27) and Josiah (2 Ch. xxxv. 1–19), the proper place is considered to be the Jerusalem Temple. Hezekiah's ceremony takes advantage of the legitimate second Passover mentioned above, because the people are not gathered in Jerusalem, and the priests are not in a state of levitical purity, at the earlier date. The brief reference of Ezekiel (xlv. 21–24) deals with Passover in the ideal Temple of his conceiving. The three points of interest are the fuller participation of the secular leader, the fact of a sin-offering, and the complete change-over from family celebration to public ceremony. The victims specified include bullocks, rams, and kids. The prescriptions of Deuteronomy are considerably extended, though not in any new thought-pattern.

Jewish usage in the last days of the Herodian Temple is reflected in the Mishnah tractate *Pesaḥim*. The common people gathered in the outer Temple court in companies to slaughter the Passover victims. The priests stood in two rows; in one row each man had a golden, in the other each man a silver, basin. The basin which caught the blood of the expiring victim was passed from hand to hand in continuous exchange to the end of the line, where the last priest tossed the blood in ritual manner on the altar. All this was done to the singing of the *Hallel*, or Pss. cxiii–cxviii. These and other details were very different from the simple ceremony in Egypt.

II. IN THE NEW TESTAMENT

In New Testament times the Passover victim was ritually slaughtered in the Temple, but the meal could be eaten in any house within the city bounds. A company bound together by some common tie, such as Jesus and His disciples, could celebrate as though they formed a family unit. Christians must have perceived at a date soon after the close of the New Testament canon that the Lord's Supper replaces Passover completely, and that this was its intended purpose.

After the destruction of the Jerusalem Temple in AD 70, any possibility of slaughtering a victim in ritual manner utterly ceased, and the Jewish Passover reverted to the family festival it had been in the earliest days—the wheel had turned full circle. The minimal obligatory four cups of wine were a later innovation, not exempt from the possibility of abuse. There is still vitality in the institutions which Judaism perpetuates. (*Cf.* Gaster, *op. cit.*, pp. 52–66.)

BIBLIOGRAPHY. Babylonian Talmud, *passim*; T. H. Gaster, *Passover: Its History and Traditions*, 1949; G. B. Gray, *Sacrifice in the Old Testament*, 1925, pp. 337–397; S. Mowinckel, *Religion und Kultus*, 1953; W. R. Smith, *Religion of the Semites*[2], 1894; *TWNT*, *s.v.* '*pascha*'.

R.A.S.

PASTORAL EPISTLES. The three Epistles, 1 and 2 Timothy and Titus, were first called the Pastoral Epistles in the 18th century, and the name has become generally used to denote them as a group. The title is only partially an accurate description of their contents, for they are not strictly pastoral in the sense of giving instruction on the care of souls. (See TIMOTHY AND TITUS, EPISTLES TO.) D.G.

PATARA. A seaport of SW Lycia (*q.v.*), in the Xanthus valley. Besides local trade it was important as being a suitable starting-point for a sea passage direct to Phoenicia (see SHIPS AND BOATS). According to the commonly accepted Alexandrian text of Acts xxi. 1, Paul transshipped at Patara on his way to Jerusalem. The Western Text, possibly influenced by Acts xxvii. 5, 6, adds 'and Myra' (see MYRA), which would imply that he coasted farther east before transshipment. There is reason to believe that the prevailing winds made Patara the most suitable starting-point for the crossing, and Myra the regular terminal for the return journey.

Patara was also celebrated for its oracle of Apollo. K.L.McK.

PATHROS, PATHRUSIM. Classed under Mizraim (Egypt), Gn. x. 14; 1 Ch. i. 12. Pathros is Egyp. *p' t'-rs(y)*, 'the Southland', *i.e.* Upper Egypt, the long Nile valley extending north to south between Cairo and Aswan; the name is attested in Assyrian inscriptions as Paturisi. Thus, the terms Mizraim for Egypt, especially Lower Egypt, Pathros for Upper Egypt, and Cush (*q.v.*) for 'Ethiopia' (N Sudan) occur in this significantly geographical order both in a prophecy of Isaiah (xi. 11) and in a subsequent inscription of Esarhaddon, king of Assyria, who also boasts himself 'king of Muṣur, Paturisi and Cush'. Jeremiah similarly identifies Pathros with Egypt (Je. xliv. 15) and specifically Upper Egypt as distinct from the cities (and land) of Lower Egypt (Je. xliv. 1). Pathros also appears as Upper Egypt and as the homeland of the Egyptian people in Ezk. xxix. 14, xxx. 14. K.A.K.

PATIENCE. Biblical patience is a God-exercised, or God-given, restraint in face of opposition or oppression. It is not passivity. The initiative lies with God's love, or the Christian's, in meeting wrong in this way. In the Old Testament, the concept is denoted by Heb. *'ārēḵ*, meaning 'long'. God is said to be 'long' or 'slow' to anger (see Ex. xxxiv. 6; Nu. xiv. 18; Ne. ix. 17; Pss. lxxxvi. 15, ciii. 8, cxlv. 8; Joel ii. 13; Jon. iv. 2). This idea is exactly represented in the Gk. *makrothymia*, often translated 'longsuffering', and defined by Trench as 'a long holding out of the mind' before it gives room to anger.

Such patience is characteristic of God's dealings with sinful men, who are fully deserving of His wrath (Is. xlviii. 9; Ho. xi. 8). His protecting mark on the murderer Cain (Gn. iv. 15), His providential rainbow sign to a world that had forfeited its existence (Gn. ix. 11–17; *cf.* 1 Pet. iii. 20), His many restorations of disobedient Israel (Ho. xi. 8, 9), His sparing of Nineveh (Jonah), His repeated pleadings with Jerusalem (Mk. xii. 1–11; Lk. xiii. 1–9, 34; Rom. ix. 22), His deferment of His second coming (2 Pet. iii. 9)—these are all expressions of His patience. Christians are to show a like character (Mt. xviii. 26, 29; 1 Cor. xiii. 4; Gal. v. 22; Eph. iv. 2; 1 Thes. v. 14).

The patience of God is a 'purposeful concession of space and time' (Barth). It is opportunity given for repentance (Rom. ii. 4; 2 Pet. iii. 9). God's forbearance has been a 'truce with the sinner' (Trench, on *anochē*, Rom. ii. 4, iii. 25), awaiting the final revelation and redemption in Christ (Acts xvii. 30). Prayer may prolong the opportunity for repentance (Gn. xviii. 22 ff.; Ex. xxxii. 30; 1 Jn. v. 16).

The Christian's patience in respect of persons (*makrothymia*) must be matched by an equal patience in respect of things (*hypomonē*), that is, in face of the afflictions and trials of the present age (Rom. v. 3; 1 Cor. xiii. 7; Jas. i. 3, v. 7–11; Rev. xiii. 10). God is the God who gives such

Christlike patience (Rom. xv. 5; 2 Thes. iii. 5), and Jesus is the great Exemplar of it (Heb. xii. 1–3). He who thus endures to the end, by his patience will gain his soul (Mk. xiii. 13; Lk. xxi. 19; Rev. iii. 10).

BIBLIOGRAPHY. R. C. Trench, *Synonyms of the New Testament*[9], 1880, pp. 195 ff.; Karl Barth, *Church Dogmatics*, II, 1, 1957, sect. 30, pp. 406 ff.: 'The Patience and Wisdom of God'.

J.H.

PATMOS. An island of the Dodecanese, lying some 35 miles off the south-western coast of Asia Minor, at 37° 20′ N, 26° 34′ E. To this island the apostle John was banished, evidently for some months about the year AD 95, from Ephesus, and here he wrote his Revelation (Rev. i. 9). The island is about 8 miles long, with a breadth of up to 4 miles, and it has been suggested that the scenery of its rugged volcanic hills and surrounding seas find their reflection in the imagery of the Apocalypse. The island now belongs to Greece.

J.H.P.

PATRIARCHAL AGE, THE.

I. THE BIBLICAL PICTURE

The patriarchal age, covering the life-spans of Abraham, Isaac, and Jacob (between 1900 and 1600 BC), is presented in the Bible as an age in which urban life is set alongside nomadic or semi-nomadic life. Among the towns which archaeology shows to have been occupied at that time, and which figure in the biblical accounts of the Patriarchs, of special interest are Ur (Gn. xi. 28, 31, xv. 7), Harran (Gn. xi. 31, 32, xii. 4, 5, xxvii. 43, xxviii. 10, xxix. 4), Nahor (Gn. xxiv. 10), and Shechem (Gn. xii. 6, xxxiii. 18); there are others, such as Gerar (Gn. xx. 1, xxvi. 1, 6, *etc.*), Dothan (Gn. xxxvii. 17), Hebron (Gn. xiii. 18, xxiii. 2, 19, xxxv. 27), Sodom and Gomorrah (Gn. xiii. 12, xix. 1 ff.). Some of these may have been villages, but others were walled. In some passages lists of towns are given, *e.g.* Ashteroth-karnaim, Ham, and Shaveh-kiriathaim, towns along the road traversed by the invading kings of the east (Gn. xiv. 5); the 'cities of the plain' (Gn. xiii. 12, xix. 25, 29); the towns which Jacob passed through on his way back to Bethel (Gn. xxxv. 5), and towns in Egypt (Gn. xli. 35, 48, xlvii. 21). It is clear that from Mesopotamia to Egypt there were centres of settlement both small and large. In Palestine proper most of the towns were confined to the lowlands or to the highways.

Outside the settled areas the semi-nomads moved about with their flocks. For much of their lifetime the Patriarchs seem to have belonged to this class, from Abraham's migration from Ur with his father (Gn. xii. 5) until the day of Jacob's migration to Egypt (Gn. xlvi). The valued possessions of the Patriarchs were sheep, asses, oxen, flocks and herds, and even camels (*q.v.*) (Gn. xii. 16, xiii. 5, 7, xx. 14, xxi. 27–30, xxx. 29, xxxi. 1–10, 38, xxxii. 13–16, xxxiv. 28, xlvi. 32, xlvii. 16–18). The term 'cattle' (*b*[e]*hēmâ*) in some of these passages is a comprehensive one for small beasts, although the Patriarchs did have cattle in our sense of the word, called 'oxen', *bāqār* (Gn. xii. 16, xx. 14, xxi. 27, xxxiv. 28).

At times there were clashes between the semi-nomads and the settled town dwellers over water supplies and pasture lands (Gn. xxi. 22–34, xxvi. 17–32).

Travel seems to have been common. Abraham moved from Ur in Mesopotamia to Egypt in the course of his life; Jacob travelled from Palestine to Harran and back (Gn. xxviii, xxxv), and later to Egypt. Probably there were well-trodden trade routes used by merchants, a group of whom took Joseph to Egypt (Gn. xxxvii. 28–36).

Something is told us about the rulers of the day. Inside each family the father was the head of the clan, and a patriarchal system prevailed. In the wider world there were rulers of various kinds. The term *meleḵ*, often translated 'king', covers a wide variety of rulers from real kings to petty chieftains. Thus in Gn. xiv. 1–2 we read of four great kings from lands to the north and east who invaded Transjordan and crossed into Western Palestine where they fought five kings of city-states near the south end of the Dead Sea. The same chapter tells of Melchizedek (*q.v.*), king of Salem. In Edom there were 'dukes' (*'allûp̄*), and later kings (Gn. xxxvi. 19, 31). In the same area the Horites had 'dukes' (Gn. xxxvi. 29). In Egypt the pharaoh was ruler (Gn. xii. 15–20, xxxvii. 36, xxxix. 1, *etc.*), and in places like Gerar there were local governors, *e.g.* Abimelech (*q.v.*) (Gn. xx, xxi, xxvi). The total picture is not easy to reconstruct from Genesis, but it would seem that there were a few powerful rulers, a great number of lesser petty rulers who may have been little more than chieftains, and a number of officials who represented foreign powers that had some control over parts of Palestine. Abimelech was perhaps the representative of a 'Philistine' ruler from the Aegean Sea. The semi-nomads probably paid little attention to these sedentary rulers as they moved to various pastures and wells.

The daily life of the Patriarchs was governed by a variety of customs of long standing and widespread usage. The father, as head of the family, led the worship of the family, and had wide powers. Normally the eldest son succeeded him as heir to his position and his property. In the absence of a natural heir, a slave might inherit the position (Gn. xv. 2 f.), or the son of a handmaiden who became a kind of subsidiary wife (Gn. xvi. 1 ff.). In the latter case the son born was regarded as the son of the true wife, who had indeed presented the slave-woman to her husband (Gn. xvi. 2). Should a son be born to the true wife in due course he became the heir automatically (Gn. xv. 4, xvii. 19).

Marriage was a complex affair. Polygamy seems to have been common (Gn. xvi. 4, xxix. 23, 24, 28, 29). At times the suitor in marriage seems to have worked for his prospective father-in-law for an agreed period before he received the daughter in marriage (Gn. xxix. 18, 27). A handmaiden was given as a gift, and such a woman might bear children who were regarded as part of the family (Gn. xxix. 24, 29). Slave women too were taken at times to raise up an heir (Gn. xvi). Sometimes further marriages were forbidden to a man (Gn. xxxi. 50).

The patriarchal blessing was important, and once given could not be revoked (Gn. xlviii, xlix).

In matters of religion few details are given. It is clear, however, that the Patriarchs knew the need for a personal faith in God who guided them through life and who encouraged them with His promises (Gn. xii. 1–3, xv. 4 ff., xvii, xxviii. 11–22, *etc.*). Once God's will became known the only course was to obey (Gn. xxii). Prayer and the offering of sacrifices (Gn. xii. 8, xiii. 4, 18, xxvi. 25, xxxv. 1, 3, 7) were part of the regular worship of the Patriarchs. Circumcision was a religious rite to mark those who were in the covenant family. An intense awareness of God's activity among them caused the Patriarchs to name places and children according to some evidence of God's dealings with them (Gn. xvi. 11, 14; all the names of Jacob's children in Gn. xxix. 31 ff.; *cf.* Gn. xxxii. 30, xxxv. 15, *etc.*). Each Patriarch seems to have had his own special name for God, which suggests a sense of special personal relationship; the 'Fear' or, as W. F. Albright suggests, the 'Kinsman' (*paḥaḏ*) of Isaac (Gn. xxxi. 42, 53), the Mighty One (*'ᵃḇîr*) of Jacob (Gn. xlix. 24). The sense of personal relationship, the knowledge of God's promises and the awareness that obedience to the will of God is of the essence of true faith, may be said to form the heart of patriarchal religion.

II. MODERN DISCOVERY AND THE PATRIARCHAL AGE

The precise date of the patriarchal age is difficult to determine, but there are strong reasons for placing it in the Middle Bronze Age, *c.* 2000–1550 BC (see ABRAHAM). Modern excavations and historical research have transformed our knowledge of these times. The following outline will give an idea of the more important of the discoveries of recent years (see also ARCHAEOLOGY).

a. Peoples

The first half of the second millennium was a time of considerable folk-migration in many parts of the Near East. Amorites, Hurrians (Horites), Hittites, and numbers of smaller groups of people were all on the move seeking new homes. In addition, conquering kings were conducting expeditions such as that depicted in Gn. xiv. In this very chapter it would seem that Amraphel was an Amorite, Arioch a Hurrian, and Tidal a Hittite, while Chedorlaomer is named as an Elamite. It is precisely these peoples who are known from the texts to have been active in the years under discussion. Unfortunately we are not able to identify any of these kings with sufficient certainty to reach a precise date for this event.

b. Cities

Excavation shows that in Abraham's day the Near East had already an ancient civilization and that several of the towns in the biblical record had been in existence already for some time. The most spectacular of these towns was Ur (*q.v.*). But others, as Harran, Shechem, and Dothan, were in existence in these times. Details of the life lived in these towns may be learned from the house ruins, the pottery and art work, and in some cases from the written records left behind in the ruins. The town of Harran, for example, is known from clay tablets found in Mari, a large town on the banks of the Euphrates with a palace of some 15 acres in size which produced over 20,000 tablets during excavation. These tablets refer to both Nahor and Harran (Gn. xi. 24, xxiv. 10). Abraham may well have passed by Mari on his way north to Harran.

Some important Egyptian records, the execration texts, of the late 20th century BC suggest that at that time nearly all Palestine and southern Syria was organized along tribal lines. However, by 1800 BC most of western Palestine and southern Syria was organized as city-states.

c. Personal names

The patriarchal name system is now known to have been that of the lands to the north-east of Palestine in the Amorite territories. Such names as Jacob and Isaac were probably abbreviations of some such form as *Ya'ᵃqōḇ-'ēl* and *Yiṣḥāq-'ēl*, which were common at the time. Both personal and place-names agree with the types found in the Middle Bronze Age.

d. Travel, trade, and commerce

There was a good deal of trade and travel all over the Near East at this time. Clay tablets from Cappadocia indicate that as early as 2000 BC there was trade in copper and wool between Asia Minor and Assyria. Other records tell of movements of armies and the transport of booty, *etc.*, all over the Near East. Great routes crossed from Mesopotamia to Asia Minor and Palestine, and others down into Egypt. That a great road traversed Transjordan (the King's Highway (*q.v.*), Nu. xx. 17), is clear from the line of ancient towns strung out along the route not far from the modern highway. Pictures from Beni Hasan in Egypt dating to about 1900 BC depict travelling nomads, possibly metal-workers, from the general area of Palestine. From these we gain a good idea of the dress and the possessions of these people in Abraham's time. Their main beasts of burden seem to have been asses and donkeys.

e. The customs of the age

These have come to light from the tens of thousands of clay tablets which represent the documents of everyday life, legal, commercial, religious, and private. There are in addition some important documents which give lists of laws, such as the Code of Hammurabi (about 1700 BC), the Code of the town of Eshnunna (19th or 18th century BC), and the fragmentary Sumerian Codes of Kings Lipit-Ishtar and Ur-Nammu (between the 21st and the 19th centuries BC). Of the more informal documents, those of Nuzi (15th century BC), Mari (17th century BC), and Ras Shamra (various dates from the 20th century onwards, but especially *c.* 1400 BC), should be mentioned. These combine to give a picture of the life in N Mesopotamia in the period 2000–1500 BC and numerous parallels with the patriarchal customs are to be seen. Customs do change in the course of time, and the parallels are not always complete, but there is nothing quite so comparable in the centuries that followed.

The archives from Nuzi offer some of the best parallels.

Adoption practices here were very like those in the patriarchal narratives. A man who had no heir could adopt a slave, a relative, or a free-born man as his heir. Alternatively, he could receive from his wife a slave woman and raise up a son from her. If subsequently a true son were born he became the heir automatically, although the other sons took a share in the inheritance.

Marriage practices at Nuzi were parallel to those in the patriarchal stories. In Nuzi a man often worked for a period for the father of a girl before he could obtain her as his wife. Women without sons presented a slave-woman to their husbands to raise up a son, and then claimed the child as their own. Cases are known where further marriages were forbidden to a man by the father of the girl he had taken in marriage. Quite regularly a handmaiden accompanied the daughter as a marriage gift, and children were raised up from her as well. The practice of levirate marriage (see MARRIAGE) was also known.

Other customs such as the importance of the dying words of the patriarch, the distinction between free women and slave women (*cf.* Gn. xxi. 10), the exchange of garments, shoes, *etc.*, on the occasion of certain transactions (Ru. iv. 7 f.; Am. ii. 6, viii. 6) were current at Nuzi and carried over into Israel, it would seem, with the Patriarchs. (See also ARCHAEOLOGY under Alalaḫ, Mari, Nuzi.)

III. THE HISTORICAL VALUE OF THE PATRIARCHAL RECORDS

A notable change in opinion has come over scholarship since the days of J. Wellhausen at the end of the 19th century. His view was that we can attain no historical knowledge of the Patriarchs from the biblical records, but that these are rather a reflection of the times of those men who wrote the stories in a much later day. The general opinion today (apart from the school of A. Alt and M. Noth) is that the patriarchal narratives record customs which do not recur in the Old Testament in later periods, but which accurately reflect the social conditions in those parts of Mesopotamia from which the Patriarchs came. Many of these customs were obsolete in later centuries, but they were transmitted faithfully through the centuries, either orally or in written form, in the patriarchal narratives. Today when we are able to read once again the life of the period 2000–1500 BC, we discover a remarkable and pervasive faithfulness to the picture which was to be found in the lands to the north-east of Palestine in precisely the period of the Patriarchs.

Many problems remain. Exact dating is still not possible. Explorations of N. Glueck in western Palestine provide some evidence for a date somewhere close to 1900 BC. Material from Mari and Nuzi suggests a somewhat later date. The wisest course to follow at present is to await further evidence from all the sources. More research will enable the scholars to fit together the biblical and the non-biblical material. Meanwhile there is today a disposition among scholars of all shades of opinion to treat the patriarchal records with far more respect than some earlier scholars accorded them.

BIBLIOGRAPHY. H. H. Rowley, 'Recent Discovery and the Patriarchal Age', *BJRL*, XXXII, 1949–50, pp. 44 ff., reprinted in *The Servant of the Lord and Other Essays on the Old Testament*, 1952, pp. 269 ff.; R. de Vaux, 'Les patriarches hébreux et les découvertes modernes', *RB*, LIII, 1946, pp. 321 ff., LV, 1948, pp. 321 ff., LVI, 1949, pp. 5 ff.; N. Glueck, 'The Age of Abraham in the Negeb', *BA*, XVIII, 1955, pp. 2 ff., *BASOR*, 149, February 1958, pp. 8 ff., *ibid.*, 152, December 1958, pp. 18 ff.; *id.*, *The Other Side of Jordan*, 1940; *id.*, *Rivers in the Desert*, 1959; C. H. Gordon, 'Biblical Customs and the Nuzu Tablets', *BA*, III, 1940, pp. 1 ff.; E. A. Speiser, *JBL*, LXXIV, 1955, pp. 252 ff.; J. R. Kupper, *Les Nomades en Mésopotamie au temps des rois de Mari*, 1957; D. J. Wiseman, *The Word of God for Abraham and To-day*, 1959.

J.A.T.

PATRISTIC LITERATURE. The importance for many branches of New Testament study of the extra-canonical early Christian literature, both the fragments from unorthodox writings and the New Testament Apocrypha (*q.v.*), on the one hand, and the patristic writings (*i.e.* the non-apocryphal and non-sectarian ancient Christian writings), on the other, is widely recognized. For the history of the Canon of the New Testament (*q.v.*) and the establishment of its text (see TEXT AND VERSIONS, IV) the patristic allusions and quotations from biblical books are obviously indispensable. In exegesis, also, the Greek Fathers in particular have to be taken into account and what writers such as Irenaeus, Clement of Alexandria, and, above all, Origen say about unwritten traditions demands attention. But, in a wider aspect, the 2nd-century Greek- and Latin-speaking Church, with all its differences in ethos from the apostolic age, is the outcome of the Jerusalem Pentecost assembly, and any illumination of the path between them is likely to cast its light backwards as well as forwards.

Unfortunately, at present a very ill-lit tunnel extends from the later apostolic age to the great apologists of the middle and later 2nd century. It is a period of intensified persecution and pernicious propaganda (as predicted in 2 Tim. iii and elsewhere); the Church is widely spread through and (in the east) beyond the Roman Empire; Israel has been repudiated in AD 70, and with it any effective primacy of the Jerusalem church has ended. The name 'Apostolic Fathers', originally meant to designate men in contact with, or appointed by, the apostles, has long been given to writings associated with this period; but lists of the Apostolic Fathers vary considerably. To three—Clement of Rome, Ignatius, Polycarp—this title is regularly applied, though only for Polycarp is there unmistakable evidence of direct contact with the apostles. All these early writings are practical, not scholarly or speculative. If one senses the immediate drop from the New Testament, the contrast of their directness with the tortuous intellectualism of, say, the *Gospel of Truth*, their contemporary, or with the fetid atmosphere of the apocrypha is also marked.

The works listed below represent some of the earlier patristic writings.

I. CLEMENT OF ROME

A long Greek letter addressed from the church of God sojourning in Rome to that in Corinth has come down under the name of Clement. There is no ground for identifying him with the Clement of Phil. iv. 3, or with Flavius Clemens, Domitian's cousin. He is doubtless the person who appears third in Roman episcopal succession lists, but the term 'Bishop of Rome' in the usual sense would be an anachronism, for in the letter 'bishop' is equivalent to 'presbyter'.

The occasion is a disturbance in the church at Corinth in which legitimately appointed presbyters have been ejected. Clement, on behalf of his church, appeals for peace and order, and asks them to remember the analogy of the ordered worship of old Israel and the apostolic principle of appointing a continuance of reputable men.

The date is almost certainly about the time of Domitian's persecution, AD 95–96, *i.e.* within the New Testament period.

The so-called second Epistle of Clement is a homily of unknown (though 2nd-century) date and authorship.

II. IGNATIUS

Ignatius, bishop of Antioch, was on his way to martyrdom in Rome in Trajan's reign (AD 98–117—probably late in that period) when he wrote seven letters which were gathered into a corpus: to the Asian churches at Ephesus, Magnesia, Tralles, Philadelphia, and Smyrna, to his friend Polycarp, bishop of Smyrna, and to the Roman church, asking them not to intervene to prevent his martyrdom.

Ignatius approaches nearer than any other 2nd-century writer to sublimity as he speaks of the mysteries of incarnation and salvation. But he writes hurriedly and often obscurely: and he is consumed with the desire for martyrdom and obsessed with the necessity for close adhesion to the bishop. Some have taken this to imply that government by a single bishop, as distinct from presbyters, was still fairly new in Asia. Ignatius mentions no bishop when writing to Rome.

The letters were heavily interpolated and others added by forgers, usually dated in the 4th century (but see J. W. Hannah, *JBL*, LXXIX, 1960, pp. 221 ff.). On the setting see V. Corwin, *St. Ignatius and Christianity in Antioch*, 1960.

III. POLYCARP

Polycarp was one of the most revered figures of Christian antiquity. He was bishop of Smyrna when Ignatius wrote: at a great age he was martyred. The date of his martyrdom, of which a moving early account survives, is disputed: AD 155/6 and AD 168 are canvassed (see W. Telfer, *JTS* (NS), III, 1952, pp. 79 ff.). He had known the apostles, and John in particular, and he taught Irenaeus (Irenaeus, *Adv. Haer*. iii. 3. 4; Eusebius, *EH* v. 20). He thus links the apostolic age and the late 2nd-century church. A letter to the Philippians survives, earnest and gracious. Chapter 13 is written without news of Ignatius' fate. P. N. Harrison (*Polycarp's Two Epistles to the Philippians*, 1936) argues that it is a separate early letter, and that chapters 1–12 were written *c.* AD 135–7 and conflated with it.

IV. THE DIDACHE

This is a problematical work, consisting of teaching (which appears in other works) on the ways of life and of death, a brief church order, dealing with baptism, fasting, prayer, eucharist, ministers and prophets, and closing with an apocalypse. It has many peculiar features, according exactly neither with church order in the New Testament nor what we know of the 2nd-century Church. It has been argued that it is a genuine early work (*e.g.* J. P. Audet, *La Didache*, 1958, dates it AD 60), that it is a late-2nd-century reconstruction, or that it represents a church out of the main stream. It seems to be Syrian.

V. PAPIAS

Papias was bishop of Hierapolis in the early 2nd century and devoted much care to a five-volume 'Exposition of the Oracles of the Lord', which survives only in tantalizing fragments in Irenaeus and Eusebius. Its date is uncertain: nothing later than AD 130 is likely. At all events he was in contact with hearers of the apostles (see MARK, GOSPEL OF; MATTHEW, GOSPEL OF).

VI. BARNABAS

An Epistle, probably Alexandrine, from the early 2nd century. It is strongly anti-Jewish in tone, and marked by forced allegorical exegesis. It includes a form of the 'Two Ways'. The work is anonymous; its attribution to Barnabas (if the apostle is meant) is doubtless an early guess. It may, however, have led to its being read for a time in some churches (*cf.* Eusebius, *EH* iii. 25). See further L. W. Barnard, *JEA*, XLIV, 1958, pp. 101 ff.

VII. HERMAS

The *Shepherd of Hermas* is a symbolic work intended to rouse a lax church and call to repentance Christians who had sinned: making clear—obviously a disputed point—that post-baptismal sin was not necessarily unforgivable. It is divided, rather artificially, into Visions, Tractates, and Mandates.

Critical and historical problems abound. The Muratorian Fragment says it was written recently, by the brother of bishop Pius of Rome (*c.* AD 140), but there are some marks of earlier date, and, inferior work as it seems now, it had a period of reception as Scripture in some churches. It appears in Codex Sinaiticus of the New Testament. See H. Chadwick, *JTS* (NS), VIII, 1957, pp. 274 ff.

BIBLIOGRAPHY. J. B. Lightfoot, *The Apostolic Fathers*, 5 vols. (a mine of information and judicious comment, with texts of Clement, Ignatius, and Polycarp); J. B. Lightfoot–J. R. Harmer, *The Apostolic Fathers*, 1891 (handy texts and translations); K. Lake, *The Apostolic Fathers* (texts and translations), 1917–19; T. F. Torrance, *The Doctrine of Grace in the Apostolic Fathers*, 1948. A.F.W.

PAUL.

I. LIFE

a. Background

From Paul's birth until his appearance in Jerusalem as a persecutor of Christians there is little information concerning his life. Although of the tribe of Benjamin and a zealous member of the Pharisee party (Rom. xi. 1; Phil. iii. 5; Acts xxiii. 6), he was born in Tarsus a Roman citizen (Acts xvi. 37, xxi. 39, xxii. 25 ff.). Jerome cites a tradition that Paul's forbears were from Galilee. It is not certain whether they migrated to Tarsus for commercial reasons or were colonized by a Syrian ruler. That they were citizens suggests that they had resided there for some time.

Sir William Ramsay and others have shown us that Tarsus truly was 'no mean city'. It was a centre of learning, and scholars generally have assumed that Paul became acquainted with various Greek philosophies and religious cults during his youth there. In recent years van Unnik has challenged this assumption. He argues that the relevant texts (Acts xxii. 3, xxvi. 4 f.) place Paul in Jerusalem as a very small child; Acts xxii. 3 is to be read in sequence: (i) born in Tarsus; (ii) brought up at my mother's knee (*anatethrammenos*) in this city; (iii) educated at the feet of Rabbi Gamaliel. As a 'young man' (Acts vii. 58; Gal. i. 13 f.; 1 Cor. xv. 9) Paul was given official authority to direct the persecution of Christians and as a member of a synagogue or Sanhedrin council 'cast my vote against them' (Acts xxvi. 10, RSV). In the light of Paul's education and early prominence we may presume that his family was of some means and of prominent status; his nephew's access to the Jerusalem leaders accords with this impression (Acts xxiii. 16, 20).

Of Paul's personal appearance the canonical account suggests only that it was not impressive (1 Cor. ii. 3 f.; 2 Cor. x. 10). A more vivid picture, which Deissmann (p. 58) and Ramsay (*The Church in the Roman Empire*, pp. 31 f.) incline to credit, occurs in the apocryphal *Acts of Paul and Thecla*: 'And he saw Paul coming, a man little of stature, thin haired upon the head, crooked in the legs, of good state of body, with eyebrows joining, and nose somewhat hooked, full of grace: for sometimes he appeared like a man, and sometimes he had the face of an angel.'

b. Conversion and early ministry

While there is no evidence that Paul was acquainted with Jesus during His earthly ministry (2 Cor. v. 16 means only to 'regard from a human point of view'), his Christian kinsmen (*cf.* Rom. xvi. 7) and his experience of the martyrdom of Stephen (Acts viii. 1) must have made an impact upon him. The glorified Jesus' question in Acts xxvi. 14 implies as much. The result of Paul's encounter with the risen Christ gives ample assurance that it was an experience of a healthy mind; and it can be adequately interpreted, as indeed Luke does interpret it, only as a miraculous act, which transformed Christ's enemy into His apostle. The three accounts in Acts (chapters ix, xxii, xxvi) attest not only the significance of Paul's conversion for Luke's theme (*cf. CBQ*, XV, 1953, pp. 315–338), but also, as Munck and others have suggested, its essential importance for Paul's interpretation of his ministry to the Gentiles, and of his union with Christ.

Apart from an interval in the Transjordan desert, Paul spent the three years following his baptism preaching in Damascus (Gal. i. 17; Acts ix. 19 ff.). Under pressure from the Jews he fled to Jerusalem, where Barnabas ventured to introduce him to leaders of the understandably suspicious Christians. His ministry in Jerusalem lasted scarcely two weeks, for again the Jews sought to kill him. To avoid them, Paul returned to the city of his birth, spending there a 'silent period' of some ten years. No doubt it is silent only to us. Barnabas, hearing of his work and remembering their first meeting, requested Paul to come to Antioch to help in a flourishing Gentile mission (Gal. i. 17 ff.; Acts ix. 26 ff., xi. 20 ff.). These newly named 'Christians' soon began their own missionary work. After a year of notable blessing Paul and Barnabas were sent on a 'famine visit' to help stricken Christians in Jerusalem.

c. Mission to Galatia—the Council of Jerusalem—mission to Greece

Upon their return from Jerusalem—about AD 46—Paul and Barnabas, commissioned by the church in Antioch, embarked on an evangelistic tour. It took them across the island of Cyprus and through 'South Galatia' (Acts xiii, xiv; see map 17). Their strategy, which became a pattern for the Pauline missions, was to preach first in the synagogue. Some Jews and Gentile 'God-fearers' accepted the message and became the nucleus for a local assembly. When the mass of Jews rejected the gospel, sometimes with violence, the focus of the preaching shifted to the Gentiles (*cf.* Acts xiii. 46 f.). Despite these perils and the defection at Perga of their helper, John Mark, the mission succeeded in establishing a Christian witness in Pisidian Antioch, Iconium, Lystra, Derbe, and possibly Perga.

Meanwhile the influx of Gentiles into the Church raised serious questions concerning their relation to Jewish laws and customs. A number of Jewish Christians were insisting that Gentiles must be circumcised and observe the Mosaic law if they were to be received 'at par' in the Christian community. Upon his return to Antioch (*c.* AD 49), Paul, seeing in this Judaizing movement a threat to the very nature of the gospel, expressed his opposition in no uncertain terms: First, he rebuked Peter publicly (Gal. ii. 14), after the latter, to avoid a breach with certain Judaizers, had separated himself from Gentile Christians. Secondly, hearing that the Judaizing heresy was infecting his recently established churches, Paul wrote a stinging letter of warning to the Galatians in which the Pauline *credo*, 'Salvation by grace through faith', was forcefully presented.

These events in Antioch gave rise to the first great theological crisis in the Church. To resolve the problems which it raised, the church in Antioch sent Paul and Barnabas to confer with the 'apostles and elders' in Jerusalem (Acts xv). The ensuing council gave the judgment that Gentiles should have 'no greater burden' than to abstain from food offered to idols, blood-meat, meat from strangled animals, and unchastity (or incest marriage). The effect of this decision was to sustain Paul's contention that Gentiles were under no obligation to keep the Mosaic law. The restrictions mentioned seem to have been principally for local application (*cf.* 1 Cor. viii) and as an aid to Jewish–Gentile relations.

Because of differences with Barnabas (over taking John Mark with them again) Paul took a new companion, Silas, on his second missionary tour (Acts xv. 40–xviii. 22; see map 17). From Antioch they travelled overland to the churches of 'South Galatia' and at Lystra added young Timothy to the party. Forbidden by the Holy Spirit to evangelize westward, they journeyed northward through 'North Galatia', where some converts may have been made (*cf.* Acts xvi. 6, xviii. 23). At Troas Paul in a vision saw a 'man of Macedonia' beckoning to him. Thus his evangelization of Greece began. In Macedonia missions were established in Philippi, Thessalonica, and Beroea; in Achaia, or Southern Greece, Athens and Corinth were visited. In the latter city Paul remained almost two years founding a Christian fellowship that was to be the source of both joy and trial in the future. Through his helpers (Luke the physician joined the party in Troas) and by correspondence (the Epistles to the Thessalonians) he kept in touch also with the struggling young churches in Macedonia. The Holy Spirit now moved Paul to turn his eyes once more upon the earlier forbidden province of Asia. Departing from Corinth, he stopped briefly at Ephesus, the commercial metropolis of Asia, and left as an advance party two Corinthian friends, Priscilla and Aquila. In a quick trip back to Antioch—*via* Jerusalem—Paul completed his 'second missionary journey' and, after a final sojourn in Antioch, prepared to move his base of operation westward to Ephesus.

d. The Aegean ministry

In many ways the Aegean period (*c.* AD 53–58; Acts xviii. 23–xx. 38) was the most important of Paul's life. The province of Asia, so important for the later Church, was evangelized; and the Christian outposts in Greece secured. During these years he wrote the Corinthian letters, Romans, and probably the Prison Epistles, which in the providence of God were to constitute a holy and authoritative Scripture for all generations. For the apostle this was a time of triumph and defeat, of gospel proclamation and threatening heresies, of joy and frustration, of activity and prison meditation. The risen Christ used all these things to mould Paul into His image and to speak through Paul His word to the Church.

From Antioch Paul travelled overland through the familiar Galatian region to Ephesus. There he met certain 'disciples', including Apollos, who had known John the Baptist and, presumably, Jesus (Acts xviii. 24 ff.). On this foundation the Church grew and evangelized the whole province of Asia. God performed such extraordinary miracles that certain Jewish exorcists began, without success, to use the name of 'Jesus whom Paul preaches'. Opposition from devotees of the city's patron goddess, Artemis (Diana), was soon aroused; and Demetrius, a prosperous idol-maker, succeeded (from motives other than piety) in inciting the people to riot. Paul doubtless had made a number of short trips from Ephesus; he took this occasion, some three years after his arrival, to make a final visit to the churches in the Aegean area. Through Troas he came to Macedonia, where he wrote 2 Corinthians and, after a time, travelled southward to Corinth. There he spent the winter and wrote a letter to the 'Romans' before retracing his steps to Miletus, a port near Ephesus. After a touching farewell Paul, 'bound in the Spirit' and under threatening clouds, sailed towards Jerusalem and almost certain arrest. These things did not deter him. For Asia had been conquered, and he had visions of Rome.

e. The Caesarean and Roman imprisonment—Paul's death

Paul disembarked at Caesarea and, with a collection for the poor, arrived at Jerusalem at Pentecost (Acts xxi. 23 f.; *cf.* 1 Cor. xvi. 3 f.; 2 Cor. ix; Rom. xv. 25 ff.). Although he was careful to observe the Temple rituals, Jewish pilgrims from Ephesus, remembering 'the apostle to the Gentiles', accused him of violating the Temple and incited the crowds to riot. He was placed under arrest but was permitted to address the crowd and later the Sanhedrin.

To prevent his being lynched, Paul was removed to Caesarea, where Felix (*q.v.*), the Roman governor, imprisoned him for two years (Acts xxiii–xxvi). At that time Festus, Felix's successor, indicated that he might give Paul to the Jews for trial. Knowing the outcome of such a 'trial', Paul, as a Roman citizen, appealed to Caesar. After a moving interview before the governor and his guests, King Agrippa and Bernice, he was sent under guard to Rome. Thus, under circumstances hardly anticipated, the risen Christ fulfilled the apostle's dream and His own word to Paul: 'You must bear witness also at Rome' (Acts xxiii. 11, RSV). Paul had a stormy sea-voyage and, after being wrecked, spent the winter on Malta (*c.* AD 61). He reached Rome in the spring and spent the next two years under house arrest 'teaching about the Lord Jesus Christ quite openly' (Acts xxviii. 31, RSV). Here the story of Acts ends, and the rest of Paul's life must be pieced together from other sources. (The most helpful survey of the apostolic age, and Paul's place in it, is A. Schlatter's *The Church in the New Testament Period*, 1955.)

Most probably Paul was released in AD 63 and visited Spain and the Aegean area before his re-arrest and death at the hands of Nero (*c.* AD 67). The Letter of Clement (v. 5–7; AD 95), and the Muratorian Canon (*c.* AD 170), and the apocryphal (Vercelli) *Acts of Peter* (i. 3; *c.* AD 200) witness to a journey to Spain; and the Pastoral Epistles, or at least 2 Timothy, involve a post-Acts ministry in the East. To the end Paul fought the good fight, finished the course, and kept the faith. His crown awaited him (*cf.* 2 Tim. iv. 7 f.).

II. CHRONOLOGY

a. General reconstruction

The Book of Acts, augmented with data from the Epistles and from Jewish and secular sources, continues to serve as the chronological framework of most scholars. However, its sketchiness and chronological vagueness, even in those periods treated, is increasingly conceded; and there is a growing willingness to interpolate (*e.g.* an Ephesian imprisonment) into the framework from other data or reconstructions. Fixed dates with secular history are not numerous. The most certain is the proconsulship of Gallio (*cf.* Acts xviii. 12), which may be fixed in AD 51–2 (Deissmann) or, more probably AD 52–3 (Jackson and Lake, Feine-Behm). If in Acts xviii. 12 Gallio had only recently assumed office (Deissmann), Paul's sojourn in Corinth may be dated between the end of AD 50 and the autumn AD 52. This accords with the 'recent' expulsion of Priscilla and Aquila from Rome (Acts xviii. 2), which is to be dated AD 50 (Feine-Behm; W. M. Ramsay, *St. Paul the Traveller and Roman Citizen*). The astronomer Gerhardt (*cf.* Feine-Behm, pp. 126 f.), following Zahn's exegesis of Acts xx. 6 ff. (that the Passover mentioned occurred on a Tuesday), dated the passage in AD 58. If so, it would place the accession of Festus (Acts xxiv. 27) in AD 60 and give a second firm date. But there are a number of variables which make the calculation only a probability.

Besides the three dates above, the mention of King Aretas of Nabatea (2 Cor. xi. 32), the famine in Judaea (Acts xi. 28), and Paul's trip to Spain and martyrdom in Rome under Nero (Rom. xv. 28; *1 Clement* 5; Eus., *EH* ii. 25–iii. 1) provide some less specific chronological data as follows. First, Damascus coins showing Roman occupation are present until AD 33, but from AD 34 to 62 they are lacking; this places a *terminus a quo* for Paul's conversion at AD 31 (*i.e.* AD 34 minus 3; *cf.* Gal. i. 18; *ICC* on 2 Cor. xi. 32). Secondly, Josephus notes a severe famine *c.* AD 44–8, probably to be located in AD 46. Thirdly, from tradition Paul's death may be dated with some probability in the latter years of Nero, *c.* AD 67. See CHRONOLOGY OF THE NEW TESTAMENT.

b. The relation of Acts and Galatians

The only fully satisfying chronology is one in which there is a consensus of Acts, the Epistles, and extra-biblical sources. One continuing problem for such a synthesis has been the relation between Acts and Galatians. The identification of Paul's visit to Jerusalem in Gal. i. 18 with Acts ix. 26 ff. is seldom questioned: the second visit in Gal. ii. 1 ff. poses the basic problem. Three views are current: Galatians ii equals Acts xv, Acts xi. 27–30, or Acts xi and xv. In the past the first view has commanded the largest advocacy (*cf.* E. de W. Burton, *The Epistle to the Galatians*, 1921, pp. 115 ff.), and it continues to attract some commentators (*cf.* H. Schlier, *An die Galater*, 1951, pp. 66 ff.; H. Ridderbos, *Galatians*, 1953, pp. 34 f.). The following objections, among others, have combined to undermine it: Gal. ii pictures a second visit and a private meeting without reference to any document; Acts xv is a third visit involving a public council and culminating in an official decree. Many scholars regard it as incredible that Galatians would, in a highly relevant context, omit mention of the Apostolic Council and decree.

The second view, often associated with the S Galatian theory, revives an interpretation of Calvin and removes a number of these objections. Acts xi is a second visit, by revelation, and concerned with the poor (*cf.* Gal. ii. 1, 2, 10); the Apostolic Council in Acts xv occurs after the writing of Galatians and, therefore, is not germane to the problem. Advanced in modern times by Ramsay (*op. cit.*, pp. 54 ff.) and recently advocated by Bruce (*Acts*, Greek Text, pp. 38 f.), it is probably the prevailing view among British scholars (*cf.* C. S. C. Williams, *The Acts of the Apostles*, 1957, pp. 22 ff.).

Dissatisfied with both alternatives, most Continental writers (*e.g.* Goguel, Jeremias), followed by a number in Britain and America (*e.g.* K. Lake, A. D. Nock), regard Acts xi and Acts xv as duplicate accounts of Gal. ii, which Luke, using both sources, failed to merge (*cf.* Haenchen, pp. 57 f., 328). Against Ramsay, Lake urges that if the Judaizing problem is settled in Acts xi (= Gal. ii), Acts xv is superfluous. Gal. ii. 9, however, pictures not a settlement but only a private, tacit approval of Paul's gospel and is incidental to the purpose of the visit which, as Lake admits, is the 'care of the poor' (*The Beginnings of Christianity*, V, pp. 201 f.). Haenchen (p. 328) rejects Ramsay's 'crucial' application of Gal. ii. 10 to the famine visit. He may be correct in identifying the 'poor' with the Gentile mission (Gal. ii. 9), but it scarcely has the vital significance which he attributes to it. Ramsay's reconstruction, even with some exegetical gnats, remains the more probable alternative. Basically the view identifying Acts xi and Acts xv arises from the traditional equation of Gal. ii and Acts xv, and also from an excessively negative estimate of Luke's acquaintance with and interpretation of the primary sources. Since Gal. ii = Acts xi provides 'a perfectly clear historical development' (W. L. Knox, *The Acts of the Apostles*, 1948, p. 49), the other is unnecessarily complex. Other views of the problem are expressed by T. W. Manson (*BJRL*, XXIV, 1940, pp. 58–80), who identifies Gal. ii with a visit prior to Acts xi, and M. Dibelius (p. 100), whose somewhat excessive *tendenz* criticism absolves both Acts xi and Acts xv of any claim to historicity. See GALATIANS, EPISTLE TO.

c. A new reconstruction

Convinced that the Acts framework is unreliable, John Knox (*Chapters in a Life of Paul*, 1950, pp. 74–88) offers an imaginative chronological reconstruction from the evidence of the letters. A fourteen-year 'silent period' (AD 33–47) is impossible; therefore, the apostle's missionary activities and some letters are largely to be placed between his first (AD 38; Gal. i. 18) and second (AD 51; Gal. ii = Acts xv) visits to Jerusalem. The final tour ends with his 'collection visit' and arrest (AD 51–3; Rom. xv. 25; 1 Cor. xvi. 3 f.). Why a silent period (which means simply that it yields no extant letters and did not fit Luke's theme) is so impossible is not readily apparent; and the traditional equation of Acts xv and Gal. ii also is open to question. Knox's fertile mind has found here more admirers than followers, for 'it is difficult to exchange tradition with imagination (as we find it in Acts) for imagination (however reasonable) without tradition' (Davies, 'Paul', p. 854).

III. HISTORY OF CRITICISM

a. Early developments

In a brilliant historical survey Albert Schweitzer (*Paul and his Interpreters*, *cf.* also Feine, *Paulus*, pp. 11–206) traces the development of critical studies in Germany following the Reformation. For the orthodox, Scripture sometimes was little more than a mine of credal proof texts; exegesis became the servant of dogma. The 18th century witnessed a reaction by pietists and rationalists, who, each for his own purpose, sought to distinguish exegesis from credal conclusions. Philological exegesis and the interpretation of Scripture by Scripture became normative for scientific interpretation.

This development perhaps finds its most important expression in J. S. Semler, who, with J. D. Michaelis, pioneered the development of literary–historical criticism. His 'Prolegomena' to theological hermeneutics, 'Paraphrases' of Romans and Corinthians, and other writings emphasize that the New Testament is a temporally conditioned document in which the purely cultural references are to be distinguished and/or eliminated. Philology exists to serve historical criticism. Our copies of Paul's letters have a 'church liturgy' format and we must, then, face the possibility that they originally had a different form. Specifically, Semler suggests that Rom. xv and xvi; 2 Cor. ix, xii. 14–xiii. 14 were separate documents, later incorporated into the larger Epistles. Foreshadowing the conclusions of F. C. Baur, Semler contrasts Paul's non-Jewish ideas with the Jewish-Christian party whom the apostle opposed; the General Epistles reflect an effort to mediate in this conflict.

b. The Tübingen School

In 19th-century Germany exegesis was fully transformed from the 'servant of dogma' to the 'servant of scientific philosophy' (*cf.* G. W. Bromiley, *Biblical Criticism*, 1948). In Pauline studies a trend appeared in J. E. C. Schmidt (1805), who, on literary grounds, doubted the authenticity of 1 Timothy and 2 Thessalonians. Schleiermacher (1807), Eichhorn (1812), and De Wette (1826) brought 2 Timothy, Titus, and Ephesians under question. After F. C. Baur's thorough-going scythe activity, only five of the twenty-seven New Testament documents remained uncontested witnesses from the apostolic period. Apart from Revelation, all were Paul's (Romans, Corinthians, Galatians).

F. C. Baur of Tübingen was not content merely to test the authenticity of ancient documents, a popular practice since the Renaissance. His was a 'positive criticism' which sought to find the documents' true historical setting and meaning. In *Symbolik und Mythologie*, the book which brought about his faculty appointment, he revealed the set of his mind and of his future work with the declaration that 'without philosophy history seems to me dumb and dead' (*cf. SHERK*, II, pp. 7 f.). Baur's philosopher was Hegel, and his history was the apostolic Church. To apply the Hegelian dialectic, which viewed all historical movement as a series of theses (advance), antitheses (reaction), and syntheses (= a new thesis), Baur needed an interpretative key. He found it in

1 Cor. i. 12: conflict between Paul, the apostle to the Greeks (advance), and the narrow Jewish Christianity of the original disciples (reaction) was the clue to the history of the apostolic age. Only under the threat of Gnosticism was Catholic unity (synthesis) achieved in the late 2nd century. In this 'tendency criticism' all New Testament writings which 'tended' towards compromise between Paul and the original apostles were viewed as later attempts at unity through rewriting history. The then current literary analysis of Paul's letters favoured Baur's reconstruction and, in turn, the latter accentuated and confirmed the suspicions of the more extreme literary critics. The Tübingen School rapidly became the dominant factor in New Testament criticism.

Using Baur's logic and sparked by Bruno Bauer's commentary on Acts (1850), an ultra-radical school questioned the genuineness of all Pauline literature. First, Acts knows no Pauline letters, and its simple picture of the apostle may be more primitive than the letters; disagreements even within Romans and Galatians suggest several hands and a later time. Secondly, if Pauline thought (Paulinism) is the Hellenization of Christianity, as Baur thought, is it possible that this was accomplished so quickly and by one man? Could anti-Jewish feeling or Paul's high Christology have developed in a Palestinian-based Church so soon after Jesus' death? No; the conflict itself is the climax of a long development, and Paulinism is to be identified with a 2nd-century Gnostic party who used the apostle's 'letters' as an authoritative vehicle for their own ideas. Why letters? Because apostolic letters already had a position of authority. Why Paul? This is impossible to say.

For all their logic the radicals succeeded only in convincing themselves. The citation of Paul in *1 Clement* (AD 95) and Ignatius (AD 110), and the neglect of Paulinism and lack of any anti-Jewish conflict in the post-apostolic literature were fatal to their argument. The omission in Acts of Pauline literary activity was a (not very strong) argument from silence. The net result of the 'ultra-Tübingen school' was to undermine Tübingen itself. For, within their common assumption that Paul was the Hellenizer of Christianity and that Hegel supplied the key to history, the radicals had the better argument.

Baur's views came under attack from the conservatives (*e.g.* J. C. K. von Hofmann) and the followers of Schleiermacher (*e.g.* Ewald); perhaps the cruellest and most telling blow was from A. Ritschl, a former disciple. Both Ritschl and von Hofmann rejected the alleged hostility between Paul and the original disciples. The latter's emphasis upon the unity of apostolic teaching was in the next century to find renewed expression in the writings of P. Feine and A. Schlatter and in the kerygmatic theology of C. H. Dodd. A moderating literary criticism, even among Baur's disciples (*e.g.* Pfleiderer), revised the estimate of genuine Pauline Epistles sharply upward. Apart from the Pastorals, the majority excluded only 2 Thessalonians and Ephesians, and their acceptance (*e.g.* by Harnack, Jülicher) was no longer a mark of conservatism.

With its literary and philosophical presuppositions undermined, the influence of Tübingen waned. Nevertheless, by tying literary analysis to an imaginative philosophical synthesis Baur, whom Godet called Semler *redivivus*, dominated New Testament criticism (as Semler never did) for half a century. Again, although his own exegesis proved to have a philosophical bias unacceptable to later historians (and to all committed to a theistic interpretation of history), Baur brought into prominence an inductive historical approach to earliest Christianity and freed research from a tradition which came to much of the data with its conclusions already assumed. For this, all students can appreciate his labours. Finally, because Baur's reconstruction placed in bold relief the problems facing historians of the apostolic age, he largely set the course of future studies. What was the relationship between Paul and Jesus? What was the influence of Jewish and Hellenistic thought in the apostolic Church? What are the proper philosophical presuppositions for a study of Christian origins? The Tübingen school died, and there is no apparent sign of an early resurrection. (Its recent airing in S. G. F. Brandon's *The Fall of Jerusalem and the Christian Church*, 1951, does not appear to have imparted life.) But the forces which gave it birth continued fecund and, for a corpse, Tübingen retained a remarkable familiarity with the following generations.

c. British contributions in the nineteenth century

British (and American) scholars interacted with the Tübingen reconstruction; but, with one or two exceptions (*e.g.* S. Davidson), they did not find it persuasive. Likewise, the Pauline Corpus (minus Hebrews) continued to find acceptance. In America some rejected the Pastorals (*e.g.* B. W. Bacon, A. C. McGiffert); Britain, following J. B. Lightfoot (*Biblical Essays*, 1904, pp. 397–410), generally accepted them in a post-Acts setting. Nevertheless, with characteristic *Vorsichtigkeit*, British scholars influenced future criticism more than is generally realized by solid historical exegesis (*e.g.* Lightfoot, Ramsay) and by relating Paul to contemporary Jewish thought (*e.g.* F. W. Farrar, H. St. J. Thackeray). Sir William Ramsay's espousal of the Lucan authorship of Acts after thorough-going archaeological and historical research was particularly influential for the critical reconstruction of Paul's life (*cf. Traveller*, pp. 20 ff.; W. K. Hobart's conclusions regarding *The Medical Language of St. Luke*, 1882, also remain, with qualifications, a valid contribution in this area). With the advocacy of Harnack and Deissmann (*Paul*, p. 26) this conclusion has been strengthened, although some recent students, as Haenchen, have argued anew against the tradition.

d. Trends in the twentieth century

Literary criticism in the present century has focused upon: (i) a continuing effort towards a general historical reconstruction (*cf.* Pauline Thought, *infra*); (ii) the publication of the Pauline Corpus; (iii) the provenance and date of the Prison Epistles; (iv) authorship; and (v) other questions concerning individual Epistles.

(i) *A historical reconstruction.* In spite of the demise of the Tübingen school its historical reconstruction, and some of its literary foibles, have continued to be assumed in much contemporary critical study. Johannes Munck (pp. 70–77) has rightly objected that when the literary conjectures failed, the dependent historical conjectures ought to have been revised ('it was not enough merely to transfer the problem from the two centuries to the three decades'; p. 70). Munck himself proposes such a revision. (1) The Jerusalem church, *i.e.* the original disciples, even as Paul, had no interest in excluding or 'Judaizing' Gentiles. (2) It was Paul's conviction, and his sole difference with the Jerusalem church, that Gentiles must *first* be won. Thus, as *the* apostle to the Gentiles (Gal. ii. 7) he restrains antichrist (2 Thes. ii. 7), by evangelism brings in (representatively) the 'fullness of the Gentiles' (Rom. xi. 25, xv. 19) and, as a decisive eschatological act, initiates Israel's redemption by making her jealous (Rom. xi. 11) in taking the 'Gentile' collection to Jerusalem (Acts xx. 4; 1 Cor. xvi. 3). Israel's 'No' issues in Paul's arrest and death, but Paul dies, as did Jesus, knowing God will yet answer that 'No' in the fullness of time. In interpreting Paul's ministry within the framework of his initial call and of his eschatology, Munck gives due heed to critical emphases; on balance, his work marks a constructive advance.

(ii) *The Pauline Corpus.* E. J. Goodspeed, departing from Harnack and earlier authorities, drew fresh attention to the formation of the Pauline Corpus. He conjectured that about AD 90 an admirer of Paul in Ephesus published the apostle's letters (excepting the Pastorals) and wrote Ephesians himself as an 'Introduction'. J. Knox (*Philemon*, pp. 98 ff.) took the hypothesis a step further and identified that admirer with Onesimus the slave, and later bishop of Ephesus. While receiving considerable acceptance (*cf.* C. L. Mitton, *The Formation of the Pauline Corpus of Letters*, 1955), the theory has been unpersuasive to many. (1) The text demands some addressee, and the primitive omission of such points to a circular letter, hardly suitable for a corpus introduction. (2) Ephesians never introduces or ends the Pauline Corpus in any ancient MS. (3) It is very doubtful that the content of Ephesians can be properly described as a non-Pauline summation of Pauline thought. (4) G. Zuntz (pp. 14 ff., 276–279), while recognizing the possibility of an earlier pre-corpus collection in Ephesus, finds that the textual and other evidence points to *c.* AD 100 and to 'the scholarly Alexandrian methods of editorship'.

(iii) *The provenance and date of the Prison Epistles.* The provenance of Paul's prison letters has been a matter of increasing interest since G. S. Duncan, following Lisco and Deissmann, located them in *St. Paul's Ephesian Ministry* (1929). (A Caesarean provenance has few advocates today.) Although Acts mentions no Ephesian imprisonment, Paul's letters imply it (*e.g.* 1 Cor. xv. 32; 2 Cor. i. 8, vi. 5, xi. 23); also the setting, journeys, and personages of the prison letters fit Ephesus better than distant Rome (*cf.* Phm. 22; Phil. ii. 24 with Rom. xv. 24 ff.; *NTS*, III, 1956–7, pp. 211–218). J. Knox (*Philemon*, p. 33), Michaelis (pp. 205 ff., 220), and as to Philippians, Bruce (*Acts*, English Text, p. 341) and T. W. Manson (*BJRL*, XXII, 1939, pp. 182 ff.) are sympathetic to Duncan. C. H. Dodd (*Studies*, pp. 85–108) and Percy (pp. 473 f.) object. (1) The tradition apart from Marcion's Prologue is unanimous for Rome, and such probably (though not certainly) is the meaning of Phil. iv. 22. (2) Such references as 1 Cor. xv. 32 are to be taken metaphorically. (3) The 'developed theology' of the captivity Epistles suggests the later Roman date. On balance, the Ephesian provenance is inviting and, at least in the case of Philippians, may prove to be a permanent advance.

(iv) *Authorship.* At the beginning of the century some attention was given to interpolation criticism, a kind of New Testament Wellhausenism, which sought to distinguish Pauline and other hands according to style and/or subject-matter. The arbitrary selection of criteria caused Schweitzer (*Interpreters*, p. 147) to remark that one scholar's 'Pauline' core had a suspicious resemblance to the Good Friday meditations of his 'Christian Century'! While such criticism generally has been rejected, fragment hypotheses are still applied to 2 Corinthians and the Pastorals. Using more objective criteria derived from the nature and practice of ancient letter writing, Otto Roller gives a verdict of genuine to all thirteen Pauline letters. Roller's important work illustrates the considerable shift in the climate of scholarship since Deissmann (*Paul*, pp. 15 f.), some fifty years ago, felt it necessary to rebuke the delusion 'that a biblical scholar's scientific reliability is to be assessed according to the number of his critical verdicts of "not genuine" '.

(v) *Individual Epistles.* Critical emphases within the individual letters have shifted, except in the case of Ephesians and the Pastorals, from authorship to other matters. (See separate articles on the various Epistles.) Many British and American scholars favour an early date for *Galatians* (*c.* AD 49 from Antioch) and a S Galatia destination, *i.e.* to the churches founded on Paul's first mission tour. On the Continent, N Galatia, *i.e.* the ethnic region (Acts xvi. 6,

xviii. 23), and a post-Acts xv chronology remain popular. The order of *1* and *2 Thessalonians* is reversed by T. W. Manson; and differences of style and subject-matter caused Harnack to suppose that 2 Thessalonians was written to the Jewish Christians (*cf.* Davies, 'Paul'). Munck (pp. 36 ff.; contrast *NIC*), following Cullmann, identifies the restraining power in 2 Thes. ii. 6 f. with Paul himself.

The *Corinthians correspondence* includes, in addition to the canonical Epistles, a letter prior to 1 Corinthians (v. 9) and a 'painful letter' (*cf.* 2 Cor. ii. 4, vii. 8) which are identified by some scholars with 2 Cor. vi. 14–vii. 1 and 2 Cor. x–xiii respectively. In *TNTC*, R. V. G. Tasker argues for the unity of our second Epistle. A more plausible case for the combination of two letters occurs in *Romans*, where the concluding doxology occurs after xiv. 23 and xv. 33 in a number of MSS, and the addressees in Rom. i. 7, 15 are missing in a few. Of several explanations the one given by T. W. Manson (*BJRL*, XXXI, 1948, pp. 224–240), among others, is most attractive; Rom. i–xv was a circular letter to which chapter xvi, an introduction of Phoebe to the Ephesians, was attached in the Ephesus copy. Nevertheless, the traditional view continues to find wide support (*cf.* Davies, 'Paul').

A 'circular letter' appears to be indicated in the case of *Ephesians* by: (1) the currency of the practice in the first century (*cf.* Zuntz, p. 228), and (2) the necessity for, and yet manuscript omission of, an addressee. Such a view would militate against Goodspeed's corpus introduction theory, but it would leave open Sanders' view (*cf.* F. L. Cross, *supra*) that Ephesians is not an Epistle but Paul's 'spiritual testament'. It might also explain the title 'to the Laodiceans', which, according to Tertullian, Marcion gave the letter (*cf.* Col. iv. 16). E. Percy has given the most recent argument for the Pauline authorship; C. L. Mitton in *Epistle to the Ephesians* (1951) argues against it. A more popular 'pro and con' is found in F. L. Cross's symposium, *Studies in Ephesians* (1956). 'Which is more likely,' asks H. J. Cadbury (*NTS*, V, 1958–9, p. 101), 'that an imitator of Paul in the first century composed a writing ninety or ninety-five per cent in accordance with Paul's style or that Paul himself wrote a letter diverging five or ten per cent from his usual style?' With the increased tendency to allow for variation in Pauline literary and theological expression the arguments against genuineness have become less compelling; they are weakened even further by the Dead Sea Scrolls parallels (*cf.* Flusser, p. 263).

Most students consider the 19th-century 'non-Pauline' verdicts valid only for the Pastorals. (In recent years Pauline authorship of the Epistle to the Hebrews has been seriously argued only by the Roman Catholic scholar, William Leonard.) Anglo-American opinion has followed P. N. Harrison's 'fragment hypothesis', *i.e.* Pauline fragments supplemented and edited; most Continentals who reject the Pastorals favour, with Dibelius, a later Paulinist author. The case for genuineness has found support in Roller's 'secretary hypothesis', *i.e.* that stylistic variations stem from Paul's amanuensis (*cf.* Feine-Behm); the traditional view has been argued anew by Spicq and Michaelis. The growing dissatisfaction with Harrison's hypothesis expressed, *e.g.*, in Guthrie, Michaelis, and Metzger (*ExpT*, LXX, 1958–9, pp. 91 ff.) may forecast a general reappraisal of the prevailing view (*cf.* *EQ*, XXXII, pp. 151–161).

IV. PAULINE THOUGHT

a. Background

The Reformation emphasis upon righteousness or justification by faith (Rom. i. 17) continued in the following centuries to be the controlling factor in the interpretation of Paul's doctrine. With the rise of literary criticism the absence of this motif became sufficient reason to suspect or even reject a 'Pauline' letter; and in the incipient development of Paulinism, *i.e.* the system of Pauline thought, 'righteousness' was regarded as the key to the apostle's mind. (In the following sketch compare especially Schweitzer, *Interpreters.*)

(i) *Paul's doctrine of redemption.* L. Usteri (1824) and A. F. Daehne (1835) sought to explain the whole of Pauline thought in terms of the imputed righteousness of Romans (*e.g.* iii. 21 ff.). In contrast, the rationalist H. E. G. Paulus, starting from texts stressing the 'new creation' and sanctification (*e.g.* 2 Cor. v. 17; Rom. viii. 29) insisted that Pauline righteousness was an ethical, moral concept; faith in Jesus meant ultimately the faith of Jesus. These two ideas and their relationship had a continuing significance throughout the 19th century.

F. C. Baur, within the framework of Hegelian idealism, sought at first (1845) to explain Paul the Hellenizer in terms of the Spirit given through union with Christ by faith. Later, however, Baur reverted to the Reformation pattern, a compartmentalized presentation of the various Pauline doctrines without any attempt to view them from a unified concept. This *loci* approach was followed by succeeding writers who gave minute descriptions of Pauline doctrine, innocently supposing 'that in the description they possessed at the same time an explanation' (Schweitzer, *Interpreters*, p. 36).

Nevertheless, some writers pressed towards the discovery of a unifying concept for Pauline thought. R. A. Lipsius (1853) had recognized two views of redemption in Paul, the juridical (justification) and the ethical ('new creation'). Hermann Luedemann, in his book *The Anthropology of the Apostle Paul* (1872), concluded that the two views of redemption actually rested on two views of the nature of man. In Paul's earlier 'Jewish' view (Galatians; Rom. i–iv) redemption was a juridical verdict of acquittal; for the mature Paul (Rom. v–viii) it was an ethical-physical transformation from 'flesh' to 'spirit' through communion with the Holy Spirit. The source of the first idea was Christ's death; the second, His resurrection. On the other hand, Richard Kabisch concluded that Pauline redemption essentially meant deliverance from coming judgment, and its significance, therefore, was to be found in the eschatology of the apostle. The Christian must walk in newness of life to show that he actually shared Christ's resurrection. 'Spiritual' life and death in the modern religious sense are unknown to Paul; both concepts are, *e.g.* in Rom. vi, always physical; and the new life is a mystical union with Christ. Thus, future deliverance from satanic powers is anticipated by the possession of the Holy Spirit, who manifests the new age in the present and inseminates our corporal being with a super-earthly substance.

For both Luedemann and Kabisch: (1) Paul's doctrine of redemption emanates from one fundamental concept. (2) It is a physical redemption to be understood in terms of Pauline anthropology. (3) To be redeemed means to share Christ's death and resurrection, which involves union with Christ and the abolition of the 'flesh'. (4) Although future, this redemption is mediated in the present by the Holy Spirit.

But questions remained. In what sense can Christ's death and resurrection be repeated in the believer? In what sense can the Christian be 'a new creation' and yet outwardly appear unchanged? Albert Schweitzer, building upon the interpretations of Luedemann and Kabisch, sought an answer in the following synthesis. (1) Paul, as did Jesus, interpreted Jesus' death and resurrection to be eschatological, *i.e.* an end of the world event, bringing the kingdom of God and the resurrection life to all the elect. (2) But the world did not end, and believers did not in fact enter into resurrection life; in time the temporal separation between Christ's resurrection and the (anticipated) resurrection of believers became the chief problem for Paul's teaching. (3) To answer it Paul posits a 'physical mysticism': through the sacraments the Holy Spirit mediates in the present time Christ's resurrection to the 'last generation' believers. (4) This present union with Christ in the Spirit ensures to the believer a share in the 'messianic resurrection' at the parousia.

(ii) *Pauline eschatology*. Thus, Schweitzer set the stage for 20th-century discussions of Pauline eschatology. It was his great merit that he sought to understand Paul's thought in terms of one fundamental concept, that he recognized the central importance of eschatology and (Jewish) anthropology in the apostle's doctrine of redemption, and that he recognized the Holy Spirit and the *en Christō* union as the realization of the new age in the present. But Schweitzer's interpretation of Paul's eschatology as a makeshift expedient (and as a sacramental mysticism) is questionable, to say the least. For, as Hamilton's critique has pointed out (pp. 50 ff.), the exalted Christ, not the 'delay' in the parousia, determines Paul's eschatology. Also, if Paul's thought patterns are Jewish (as Schweitzer rightly recognized), sacramental mysticism is a rather awkward explanation of the realism of the 'new creation' in Christ.

(iii) *Paul's thought patterns*. In addition to eschatology as the key to Paulinism, a closely related question important for the future also had its rise in the 19th century. Are Paul's thought patterns Jewish or Hellenistic? Kabisch and Schweitzer insisted that Pauline thought was Jewish to the core. Others, following F. C. Baur's reconstruction of Paul as the 'Hellenizer of Christianity', interpreted Pauline anthropology and eschatology from the standpoint of a modified Hellenistic dualism. The antithesis between 'flesh' and 'spirit' in Rom. vi–viii was an ethical dualism, and 'dying' and 'rising' a spiritual transformation. This has its roots in an anthropological dualism; thus, in the future, redemption involves the deliverance of the 'soul' from its house of clay. But Paul also speaks of the resurrection of the whole man from death (1 Thes. iv; 1 Cor. xv). Otto Pfleiderer (*Paulinism*, 1891, p. 264) concluded that Paul held Jewish and Greek views simultaneously, 'side by side, without any thought of their essential inconsistency'. In interpreting Pauline eschatology elsewhere (*cf.* Schweitzer, *Interpreters*, p. 70) he posits a development from 1 Thes. iv through 1 Cor. xv to 2 Cor. v. The first is simply Jewish resurrection eschatology; in 2 Cor. v the believer goes to the heavenly realms at death.

b. The origin of Paul's religion: Hellenism

Twentieth-century studies of Pauline thought have devoted themselves primarily to three questions. What is the relation between Paul and Jesus? What are the sources for Pauline thought? What is the rôle of eschatology in the mind of Paul?

(i) *Paul's relation to Jesus*. The distinction raised a half century earlier between 'juridical' (Rom. i–iv) and 'ethical' (Rom. v–viii) righteousness had borne much fruit, and the latter came to be regarded as the more central and decisive Pauline concept. A. Deissmann (*Paul*, pp. 148 ff.) viewed 'in Christ' as an intimate spiritual communion with Christ, a Christ mysticism; more often the 'mysticism' was interpreted as a sacramental reality based upon Jewish eschatology (Schweitzer) or the Hellenistic mysteries (J. Weiss, *Earliest Christianity*, 1959 (1937), II, pp. 463 f.). Somewhat later J. S. Stewart (*A Man in Christ*, 1935, pp. 150 ff.) reflected this trend in British scholarship, regarding union with Christ as the central element in Paul's thought. This emphasis had important consequences for the course of Pauline studies in the 20th century.

The contrast between the 'liberal Jesus' and Paul's indwelling and yet transcendent Christ called forth at the turn of the century a spate of books on the relationship of Jesus and Paul (*cf.* P. Feine, *Paulus*, pp. 158 ff.). W. Wrede's influential *Paulus* (1905) put the matter in the starkest terms: Paul was not truly a disciple of Jesus; he was actually the second founder of Christianity. The individual piety and future salvation of the Rabbi Jesus had been transformed by the theologian Paul into a present redemption through the death and resurrection of a christ-god. Paul's ideas could not, of course, be accepted at face value. To do so would, as Weinel (*St. Paul*, 1906, p. 11) remarked, 'stifle the claims of reason for the sake of Christianity, for reason is ever-repeating . . . that the modern conception of the world is the right one'. Nevertheless, the historian's task remained. If Paul's doctrines did not arise from and build upon the mind of Jesus, what was their origin?

(ii) *Sources of Pauline thought.* F. C. Baur sought to explain the mind of Paul in the context of Church controversy: Paul was the champion of Gentile freedom. For Schweitzer the origin of Paul's thought was his peculiar eschatological problem forged in the mental cauldron of late Judaism. However, the rising 'History of Religion' (*Religionsgeschichte*) school found no evidence to ground Paul's sacramental mysticism in Judaism. While recognizing the eschatological problem, it built upon Baur's 'Gentile' Paul and developed still another elaborate reconstruction of the apostolic age. Represented most notably by R. Reitzenstein and W. Bousset, it interpreted Paulinism in the framework of Oriental–Hellenistic mystery religions. The Mysteries spoke, as did Paul, of a dying-rising god, of 'Lord', of sacramental redemption, of 'mysteries', *gnōsis*, and 'spirit'. As a boy in Tarsus and later as a missionary the apostle came under the influence of these ideas, and they exerted a profound influence on his theology. Schweitzer (*Interpreters*, pp. 179–236), H. A. A. Kennedy (*Mystery Religions*; *cf. Biblica*, XXXIX, 1958, pp. 426–448; XL, 1959, pp. 70–87; *CBQ*, XX, 1958, pp. 417–443), and J. G. Machen (pp. 255–290) subjected this reconstruction to a thorough critique, pointing out that, in ignoring the Old Testament–Judaism background of the parallels (which Kennedy showed to be quite plausible) and the late date of its sources, the theory reflected a weakness in methodology. The principal contribution of the History of Religion school was to raise the important question of Paul's theological relation to the Gentile religious world. The 'mystery religion' reconstruction did not win general approval, but in a more recent gnostic dress its general outlines continue to be strongly advocated.

The mystery religion parallels paled; nevertheless, the conviction remained strong that Paul's thought was substantially Hellenistic. R. Bultmann (1910) had shown the affinity of Paul's literary style with the Stoic diatribe; others regarded Paul's doctrine of the 'corporate body' (*cf.* W. L. Knox, *Gentiles*, pp. 160 ff.), his natural theology in Rom. i (*cf.* Acts xvii), and his concept of conscience (E. Norden, *Agnostos Theos*, 1913) as rooted in Stoicism. The inadequacy of these conclusions was pointed out, respectively, by E. Best (pp. 83 ff.), B. Gaertner (pp. 133–169), and C. A. Pierce (pp. 16 ff.). Gaertner argues that Paul's 'natural theology' is thoroughly Old Testament–Jewish; however, Pierce (pp. 22 ff., 57 ff.) concludes that the New Testament adopts in the case of 'conscience' a general Hellenistic usage.

To determine the relationship of Paul to Hellenistic thought, the area currently receiving most attention is Gnosticism. This religious-philosophical movement stressed a metaphysical dualism, deliverance from 'matter' through a divine gift and power of *gnōsis*, *i.e.* a special knowledge of God, and mediating angels to assist one to salvation. Long ago J. B. Lightfoot (*Colossians and Philemon*, 1886, pp. 71–111) detected elements of Gnosticism in the Colossian heresy. Early in the 20th century Bousset and J. Weiss (*op. cit.*, II, pp. 650 f.) urged that aspects of Paul's own thought lay in this direction. R. Bultmann (with his 'school') is the chief representative and developer of Bousset's reconstruction today. From existentialist considerations Bultmann again makes 'justification' a central Pauline motif, although it is far from a return to Baur or to the Reformers; for the same reasons Paul's anthropology is given a thorough exposition (*Theology*, I, pp. 190–227). But the real clue to Bultmann's understanding of Paulinism is his grounding of Pauline thought in Hellenistic Judaism and Hellenistic Christianity. From this background Paul obtained a number of concepts, *e.g.* sacramental redemption and ethical dualism, which were Gnostic or gnosticized in some degree (*Theology*, I, pp. 63 ff., 124 ff., 151–188). While Paul opposed the Gnostics, *e.g.* at Colossae, in the process he modified not only his terminology but also his concepts, particularly his Christology (Messiah Jesus becomes a heavenly Lord; *cf.* Bousset) and cosmogony (the demon-controlled world is redeemed by a heavenly man; *cf.* W. L. Knox, *Gentiles*, pp. 220 ff. But see G. B. Caird, *Principalities and Powers*, 1956; *TWNT*, II, pp. 568–570).

Schweitzer (*Interpreters*, p. 231) predicted that a Hellenized Paulinism was a half-way house which must carry its conclusions even to the genesis of Christianity. His prediction was more than fulfilled by the discovery of the Dead Sea Scrolls with their ethical dualism and emphasis on 'knowledge'. The Scrolls are an embarrassment for Bultmann's reconstruction, for 'pre-Gnostic' is about the closest identification most scholars care to make for them. Also, there is little reason to believe that Paul reflects, *e.g.*, 'an earlier Gnostic doctrine about the descent of a redeemer, especially since there is no evidence that such a doctrine existed' (R. M. Grant, *Gnosticism*, p. 69; *cf.* pp. 39–69). Almost all else Bultmann chooses to refer to Gnostic influence likewise suffers from the same chronological strictures. Grant, looking back to Schweitzer, interprets Gnosticism as arising from a failure of the apocalyptic hope; unlike Schweitzer, Grant views Paul as a man whose spiritual world lies somewhere between Jewish apocalyptic and the fully developed Gnosticism of the 2nd century (p. 158). Grant sees the latter tendency in Paul's interpretation of Christ's resurrection as a realized (eschatological) victory over the cosmic powers. More cautiously, R. McL. Wilson, in a valuable assessment (*The Gnostic Problem*, pp. 75–80, 108, 261), concludes that Paul adopts a Hellenistic cosmogony and terminology only to oppose Gnosticism and to interpret Jesus' authority over the (Gnostic) 'powers'; the apostle rejects the gnosticizing interpretation. However, J. Dupont (*Gnosis: La Connaissance Religieuse dans les Épîtres de Saint Paul*, 1949) argues that Pauline *gnōsis* is strictly Old Testament–Jewish.

All the 'Greek' reconstructions of Paul have their root in F. C. Baur's interpretation of Paul as the exponent of Gentile Christianity. When W. Wrede and others recognized the redemptive–eschatological character of Pauline thought, the apostle was set in opposition not only to Jewish Christianity but to the 'liberal' Jesus Himself. But, as Schweitzer had shown, the 'liberal' Jesus was not the Jesus of the Gospels. Bultmann (*Theology*, I, pp. 23, 30 ff.) accepted Schweitzer's 'apocalyptic' Jesus but insisted that God's demand for man's decision, not the apocalyptic window-dressing, was the essence of Jesus' eschatology. The suffering, resurrected, and returning Son of man was a 'mythologized' picture of the later Hellenistic Christology. The mind of Paul remained far distant from the mind of the earthly Jesus or of His earliest disciples. One's estimate of Paulinism is closely tied, therefore, to one's estimate of the Gospels' picture of Jesus.

A number of mediating scholars, taking their cue from B. Weiss, see 'development' as the key to Paul's thought. In view of fading parousia hopes Paul's anthropology and eschatology move towards a Greek dualism (Dodd) and his cosmogony towards Gnosticism (R. M. Grant).

In its present *religionsgeschichtliche* format the Hellenistic school is subject to a number of criticisms. There is a tendency to convert parallels into influences and influences into sources. Some of its 'sources' for Pauline thought come from a period considerably later than the apostle's lifetime. (Bultmann's Paul may have more than a casual relation to the Gnostic 'Paul' of the ultra-Tübingen school.) Also, its historical inquiry has sometimes been compromised by an inadequate world-view. For example, Bultmann, like Weinel, views the natural world as a 'self-subsistent unity immune from the interference of supernatural powers' (*Kerygma and Myth*, ed. H. W. Bartsch, 1953, p. 7; *cf.* pp. 5–8, 216, 222; *cf.* Hamilton, pp. 71–82).

Perhaps the most basic questions are these: Is Paulinism best understood as an amalgam, gathered here and there, or as the expansion and application of a central tradition rooted in the mind of Jesus Christ and the earliest Church? Is Paul's mind most adequately explained within a Hellenistic syncretism or within the bosom of Palestinian Judaism and the primitive Church? Does the Hellenization of Christianity begin in Paul and pre-Pauline Christianity (Bultmann) or in Paul's Gentile disciples; and does it arise from a failure of the primitive eschatology in Paul (Grant) or from a misunderstanding of it (and Paul) in his churches?

c. The origin of Paul's religion: Judaism

(i) *Paul's link with the earliest Church.* Both Ritschl and von Hofmann had argued, *contra* Baur, for the unity of Paul's teaching with that of the earliest Church. A. Resch, in the 'Jesus or Paul' debate, upheld this view. His thorough investigation of *Der Paulinismus und die Logia Jesu* (1904) concluded that the words of Jesus were a primary source of Pauline thought. But could not rather Paul be the source of the Synoptic Jesus? The research of several writers has substantiated the priority argued by Resch. C. H. Dodd (*Preaching*, p. 56) established that a *kerygma, i.e.* a gospel-core proclamation, underlay both the Gospels and Paul, 'a tradition coeval with the Church itself'. The same writer (*According to the Scriptures*, 1952, pp. 108 ff.), building upon Rendel Harris's *Testimonies* (1916, 1920), found a 'substructure of New Testament theology' to which Paul was indebted and whose origin pointed to Christ Himself. E. E. Ellis, examining the hermeneutical principles of *Paul's Use of the Old Testament* (pp. 97 f., 107–112), suggested that some common (pre-Pauline) exegetical tradition originated with 'prophets' of the earliest Church. E. Lohmeyer (*Kyrios Jesus*, 1928) interprets Phil. ii. 5 ff. as a primitive Christian hymn probably arising in Aramaic circles (*cf.* L. Cerfaux, pp. 283 ff.; R. P. Martin, *An Early Christian Confession*, 1960, pp. 8–16; E. G. Selwyn, *First Epistle of St. Peter*, 1946, pp. 365–369, 458–466). Similarly, the pre-Pauline character of the *Primitive Christian Catechism* (1940) was demonstrated by P. Carrington.

O. Cullmann ('Tradition', pp. 69–99), K. H. Rengstorf ('Apostleship', *Bible Keywords*, II, ed. J. R. Coates, 1958), and H. Riesenfeld (*The Gospel Tradition and Its Beginnings*, 1957) point to a rationale for this understanding of Christian origins. The New Testament concept of apostle has its origin in the rabbinic *šālîaḥ*, an authorized agent equivalent to the sender himself. The apostles witnessed to a tradition or *paradosis*, given to them by Christ. 'But since everything has not been revealed to each individual apostle, each one must first pass on his testimony to another (Gal. i. 18; 1 Cor. xv. 11), and only the entire *paradosis*, to which all the apostles contribute, constitutes the *paradosis* of Christ' (Cullmann, 'Tradition', p. 73). Thus, as an 'apostle' Paul's message is defined in terms of what he has received: his catechesis, kerygma, and the wider 'tradition' should be, and critical study finds them to be, rooted in the earliest Church and ultimately in the teaching of Jesus. This teaching of Jesus seems to have been not merely moral instruction or apocalyptic warning, but creative, theological synthesis which envisaged a post-resurrection ministry by His disciples (*cf.* J. Jeremias, *Jesus' Promise to the Nations*, 1958). If these writers are correct (to say nothing of J. Munck's recent thesis; *cf. supra*), the dichotomy between Paul and the primitive Jewish Church, which has been urged from Baur to Bultmann, is an assumption which must be abandoned.

(ii) *Paul's milieu.* To understand a writer it would seem to be proper to give priority to that milieu to which he appeals and to which he presumably belongs. In interpreting Pauline concepts it is not the categories of a 2nd-century Hellenistic Gnosticism (however easily they may be 'read back') but the categories of 1st-century rabbinic/apocalyptic Judaism which demand first claim upon the critical historian's mind.

The nature of 1st-century Judaism is complex, and it is easy to overdraw or wrongly define the contrast between the 'Hellenized' and 'Orthodox' (terms not to be equated with '*diaspora*' and 'Palestinian'; *cf.* Acts vi. 1; Davies, pp. 1–8). Nevertheless, considerable research relates the thought of Paul, the Pharisee and 'Hebrew of the Hebrews' (Phil. iii. 5), with Palestinian rabbinism and apocalypticism rather than with a Hellenized *diaspora*. Van Unnik has raised at least the probability that Paul's early youth was passed not in Tarsus but in Jerusalem. Certainly Paul used the Septuagint and preached among the *diaspora*, and he could employ Hellenistic religious terminology. He may have been acquainted with the syncretistic Judaism exemplified by Philo; but with the doubtful exception of the Wisdom of Solomon, his relationship to the *diaspora* literature is not direct and probably reflects only traditions which both had in common (*cf.* Ellis, *Testament*, pp. 76–84). His more direct relationships lie in another direction. W. D. Davies, in a significant work (1948), has demonstrated that the relation of Paul and Rabbinic Judaism forms the background of many Pauline concepts formerly labelled Hellenistic. The Dead Sea Scrolls have also confirmed in remarkable fashion the Jewishness of Pauline and New Testament backgrounds (*cf.* Stendahl, pp. 94–113, 157–182; Bruce, *Qumran Texts*, pp. 66–77; Flusser).

(iii) *Specific Pauline concepts.* Passing to specific Pauline concepts, anthropology and the nature of the 'in Christ' relationship have had a central importance since the days of F. C. Baur. It is widely recognized today that Paul views man in an Old Testament–Jewish framework and not in the Platonic dualism of the Hellenistic world (*cf.* LIFE; Bultmann, *Theology*, I, pp. 209 f.; Cullmann, *Immortality*, pp. 28–39; J. A. T. Robinson, *The Body*, 1952). The corporate 'body of Christ' also is best understood not in terms of a Gnostic mythology (Käsemann) nor a Stoic metaphor (W. L. Knox) but as the Old Testament–Jewish concept of corporate solidarity. Davies (*Judaism*, pp. 53 ff.) has related Paul's thought here to the rabbinic speculations on the body of Adam. R. P. Shedd's *Man in Community* (1958) correctly finds Paul's ultimate rationale in the realism of Semitic thought patterns, as they are applied to Messiah and His people (*cf.* J. A. T. Robinson, *Body*, pp. 56 ff.; Ellis, *Testament*, p. 136). E. Best (pp. 83–95, 112 f.) falls short of this realism in viewing the concept metaphorically (*cf.* further the essays of K. Barth and J. Murray). D. R. G. Owen, in *Body and Soul* (1956), offers an illuminating comparison of biblical anthropology with the modern scientific view of man. The study of D. Cox (*Jung and St. Paul*, 1959) seeks to define in other areas the relevance of Paul for current faith and practice.

Whether Paul's eschatology is rooted in Jewish or Greek concepts is a matter of continuing debate. The importance of this question for Paulinism requires that some detailed attention now be given to it.

d. The eschatological essence of Pauline thought

C. A. A. Scott's well-written *Christianity according to Saint Paul* (1927), over against Albert Schweitzer's eschatological interpretation, identifies salvation as the fundamental concept of Paulinism. But what is the factor determining the character of Paul's 'already but not yet' redemption theology? Not grasping Schweitzer's real question, Scott does not really pose an alternative: he found a motif to describe Paul, not a key to explain him. (*Cf.* also recent Christological approaches, *e.g.* L. Cerfaux, *Christ in the Theology of St. Paul*, 1959.) Schweitzer may not have stated the problem, or the solution, satisfactorily; but his identification of the key concept remains valid.

(i) *The views of Schweitzer and Dodd.* Until recently discussion of New Testament eschatology has revolved about the views of Schweitzer and C. H. Dodd. (For Bultmann, eschatology has nothing to do with the future or with history; it is the realm of existential living. Like F. C. Baur, Bultmann uses New Testament language to clothe an imposing philosophy of religion; exegesis becomes the servant of existentialism. *Cf.* N. Q. Hamilton's *The Holy Spirit and Eschatology in Paul*, pp. 41–90, for a lucid summation and critique of the eschatology of Schweitzer, Dodd, and Bultmann.) Schweitzer argued that Paul's '*en Christō*' concept arose from the failure of the kingdom of God, *i.e.* the end of the world, to arrive at Christ's death and resurrection. Against Schweitzer, Dodd contended that in Christ's death the 'age to come' did arrive; eschatology was 'realized' as much as it ever would be in history. The believer already participates in the kingdom (*e.g.* Col. i. 13), and at death he fully enters the eternal, *i.e.* eschatological, realm. Eschatology, therefore, does not refer to an end-of-the-world event; in Platonic fashion it is to be understood 'spatially' rather than temporally, eternity over against time. How, then, is Paul's anticipation of a future parousia to be accounted for? Believing it to be a hang-over from apocalyptic Judaism (and quite alien to the central message of Jesus), Dodd goes back to Pfleiderer for an answer: in 1 Thes. iv Paul has a strictly Jewish eschatology but in 1 Cor. xv modifies it with the concept of a 'spiritual' body; 2 Cor. v, which then places the believer in heaven at death, expresses the view of the mature (and 'Greek') Paul. J. A. T. Robinson's *Jesus and His Coming* (1958, pp. 160 ff.) is essentially an elaboration of Dodd's thesis.

It is Dodd's great merit that he saw, as Schweitzer did not, the essential meaning for New Testament thought (and for the relevance of the gospel in the present world) of the 'realized' aspect of the kingdom of God. But in adopting an unbiblical 'Greek' view of time Dodd failed to do justice to the futurist and temporal character of eschatological redemption. Also, a development (*i.e.* Hellenization) of Pauline eschatology involves an un-Pauline anthropological dualism and, in part, reflects a misunderstanding of the texts. Both Schweitzer and Dodd make admirable attempts to achieve a comprehensive interpretation of New Testament eschatology. Although 'futurist or realized' has now been recognized as an improper either/or, the contributions of Schweitzer and Dodd remain fundamental landmarks in the progress of the research.

The important monographs of W. G. Kuemmel (*Promise and Fulfilment*, 1957, pp. 141–155; *cf.* 'Futurische und Präsentische Eschatologie im Ältesten Urchristentum', *NTS*, V, 1958–9, pp. 113–126) argue convincingly that both 'present' and 'future' eschatology are equally and permanently rooted in the teaching of Jesus and of Paul. Oscar Cullmann's most significant publication, *Christ and Time* (1951), contrasts the Greek idea of redemption, *i.e.* to escape the time 'circle' at death, with the biblical concept that redemption is tied to resurrection in future 'linear' time, *i.e.* at the parousia. These works, plus a proper appreciation of Paul's Old Testament–Jewish anthropology and of the Semitic concept of corporate solidarity, form a proper foundation for understanding Paul's eschatology—and thus his total doctrine of redemption.

(ii) *The pre-eminence of a theology of redemption.* Historical research since the Reformation has recognized that Pauline theology is above all a theology of redemption. The 19th century witnessed a growing emphasis upon the present 'union with Christ' (rather than imputed righteousness) as the central aspect of this redemption. Since Albert Schweitzer two eschatological *foci*, Christ's death and resurrection and the parousia, have been recognized as the key to the meaning of 'union with Christ'.

Jesus Christ in His death and resurrection defeated for all time the 'powers' of the old aeon—sin, death, and the demonic 'rulers of this darkness' (Eph. vi. 12; Col. ii. 15). Now Christians were crucified, resurrected, glorified, and placed at God's right hand with Christ (Gal. ii. 20; Eph. ii. 5 f.). 'In Christ' Christians have entered the resurrection age; the solidarity with the first Adam in sin and death has been replaced by the solidarity with the eschatological Adam in righteousness and immortal life.

This corporate redemption in and with Jesus Christ, this 'new age' reality, which the believer enters at conversion (*cf.* Rom. vi), finds an individual actualization in the present and the future (*cf.* Ellis, 'Eschatology', pp. 211–216). In the present life it means a transformation through the indwelling Spirit, the firstfruits of the new resurrection life (Rom. viii. 23; 2 Cor. v. 5), of one's ethic (Col. ii. 20, iii. 1, 9 f., 12) and of one's total world view (Rom. xii. 1 ff.). However, in the midst of moral–psychological renewal the Christian remains, in his mortality, under the death claims of the old age. But this too is to be understood no longer in terms of 'in Adam', but as a part of the 'in Christ' reality; for 'the sufferings of Christ abound to us' (2 Cor. i. 5; *cf.* Phil. iii. 10; Col. i. 24), and the Christian dead have fallen asleep 'in Jesus' (1 Thes. iv. 14; *cf.* Phil. ii. 17; 2 Tim. iv. 6). The individual actualization of Christ's sufferings is, of course, in no wise a self-redemption process; rather, it means to be identified with Christ 'in the likeness of his death' (Rom. vi. 5). The 'likeness of his resurrection' awaits its actualization at the parousia, when the individual Christian, raised to immortal life, shall be 'conformed to the image of his Son, that he might be the firstborn among many brethren' (Rom. viii. 29; *cf.* 1 Cor. xv. 53 ff.).

Thus, Pauline redemption is not a 'spiritual' deliverance culminating in the escape of the 'soul' at death (Dodd); it is a physical redemption culminating in the deliverance of the whole man at the parousia (Cullmann). It is to be understood not in terms of a Greek dualism but in the framework of Old Testament–Jewish view of man as a unified being and as one who lives not only as an individual but in 'corporate solidarities'. The future that has become present in the resurrection of Jesus Christ is a future which the Christian realizes now only corporately, as the 'body of Christ'. However, at the parousia faith shall become sight, 'away' shall become 'at home', and the solidarities of the new age shall become individually actualized in all their glory. This is the living hope of Paul's heart; it is also the meaning of his theology.

BIBLIOGRAPHY. W. Barclay, *The Mind of St. Paul*, 1959; K. Barth, *Christ and Adam*, 1956; E. Best, *One Body in Christ*, 1955; G. Bornkamm, *Das Ende des Gesetzes*, 1958; W. Bousset, *Kurios Christos*, 1913; F. F. Bruce, *The Acts of the Apostles*, 1951 (*NLC*, 1954); *id.*, *Biblical Exegesis in the Qumran Texts*, 1959; R. Bultmann, *Theology of the New Testament*, 2 vols., 1952; J. Coppens, *L'état présent des études pauliniennes*, 1956; O. Cullmann, *The State in the New Testament*, 1957; *id.*, *Immortality of the Soul or Resur-*

rection of the Dead?, 1958; *id.*, 'The Tradition', *The Early Church*, 1956, pp. 57–99; W. D. Davies, *Paul and Rabbinic Judaism*, 1955; *id.*, 'Paul', *Twentieth Century Encyclopedia*, 1955; A. Deissmann, *Paul*, 1927; M. Dibelius, *Studies in the Acts of the Apostles*, 1956; M. Dibelius and W. G. Kuemmel, *Paul*, 1953; C. H. Dodd, *New Testament Studies*, 1953; *id.*, *The Apostolic Preaching and Its Development*, 1936; E. E. Ellis, *Paul's Use of the Old Testament*, 1957; *id.*, 'II Corinthians v. 1–10 in Pauline Eschatology', *NTS*, VI, 1959–60, pp. 211–224; P. Feine, *Der Apostel Paulus*, 1927; P. Feine and J. Behm, *Einleitung in das Neue Testament*, 1950; D. Flusser, 'The Dead Sea Scrolls and Pre-Pauline Christianity', *Aspects of the Dead Sea Scrolls*, ed. C. Rabin and Y. Yadin, 1958, pp. 215–266; F. J. Foakes-Jackson and K. Lake, *The Beginnings of Christianity*, 5 vols., 1933; B. Gaertner, *The Areopagus Speech and Natural Revelation*, 1955; A. S. Geyser, 'Paul, The Apostolic Decree and the Liberals in Corinth', *Studia Paulina, Festschrift* for J. de Zwaan, 1953, pp. 124–138; E. J. Goodspeed, *The Meaning of Ephesians*, 1933; R. M. Grant, *Gnosticism and Early Christianity*, 1959; D. Guthrie, *The Pastoral Epistles*, 1959; E. Haenchen, *Die Apostelgeschichte*, 1956; N. Q. Hamilton, *The Holy Spirit and Eschatology in Paul*, 1957; P. N. Harrison, *The Problem of the Pastoral Epistles*, 1921; H. A. A. Kennedy, *The Theology of the Epistles*, 1919; *id.*, *Saint Paul and the Mystery Religions*, 1913; T. S. Kepler, ed., *Contemporary Thinking about Paul: An Anthology*, 1950; J. Knox, *Philemon among the Letters of Paul*, 1959 (1935); W. L. Knox, *Saint Paul and the Church of the Gentiles*, 1939; W. G. Kümmel, *Das Neue Testament: Geschichte der Ersforschung seiner Probleme*, 1958; W. von Loewenich, *Paul: His Life and Work*, 1960; J. G. Machen, *The Origin of Paul's Religion*, 1947 (1925); B. M. Metzger, *Index to Periodical Literature on the Apostle Paul*, 1960; W. Michaelis, *Einleitung in das Neue Testament*, 1954; O. Moe, *The Apostle Paul*, 2 vols., 1954 (1928); J. Munck, *Paul and the Salvation of Mankind*, 1960; J. Murray, *The Imputation of Adam's Sin*, 1960; A. D. Nock, *Saint Paul*, 1938; E. Percy, *Probleme der Kolosser- und Epheserbriefe*, 1946; C. A. Pierce, *Conscience in the New Testament*, 1955; F. Prat, *The Theology of St. Paul*, 2 vols., 1945; W. M. Ramsay, *The Church in the Roman Empire*, 1893; *id.*, *St. Paul the Traveller and Roman Citizen*, 1895; R. Reitzenstein, *Die hellenistischen Mysterienreligionen*, 1927; H. Ridderbos, *Paul and Jesus*, 1958; O. Roller, *Das Formular der Paulinischen Briefe*, 1933; H. J. Schoeps, *Paulus, Die Theologie des Apostels im Lichte der judischen Religionsgeschichte*, 1959, E.T. 1961; A. Schweitzer, *The Mysticism of Paul the Apostle*, 1931; *id.*, *Paul and His Interpreters*, 1912; K. Stendahl (ed.), *The Scrolls and the New Testament*, 1957; W. C. van Unnik, *Tarsus of Jerusalem, De Stadt van Paulus' Jeugd*, 1952; G. Vos, *The Pauline Eschatology*, 1952 (1930); A. Wikenhauser, *Pauline Mysticism*, 1960; R. McL. Wilson, *The Gnostic Problem*, 1958; G. Zuntz, *The Text of the Epistles*, 1953. E.E.E.

PAULUS, SERGIUS, more correctly **PAULLUS,** was the proconsul (Gk. *anthypatos*) of Cyprus (*q.v.*) in AD 47/8 when the apostle Paul visited that island (Acts xiii. 7). His name suggests that he was a member of an old Roman senatorial family: if he was the L. Sergius Paullus mentioned in *CIL*, VI. 31545, he was one of the Curators of the Banks of the Tiber under Claudius. Another inscription (*Inscriptiones Graecae ad res Romanas pertinentes*, iii. 930; *cf. EGT*, II, 1900, p. 286) found in Cyprus refers to the proconsul *Paulos*, while an inscription discovered at Pisidian Antioch in honour of a L. Sergius Paullus, propraetor of Galatia in AD 72–4, is probably a commemoration of his son. W. M. Ramsay (*The Bearing of Recent Discovery on the Trustworthiness of the New Testament*, 1914, chapter xii) discusses the evidence that Paullus's belief (Acts xiii. 12) was a real Christian faith (see also G. L. Cheeseman in *JRS*, III, 1913, pp. 262 f.). D.H.W.

PAVEMENT. See GABBATHA.

PAVILION (Heb. *sōḵ*, *sukkâ*). A covered place, tent, booth, or shelter, where a person or beast may hide or be sheltered. The same word is

Fig. 162. The royal pavilion of Shalmaneser III of Assyria set up in Syria in 858 BC. An attendant stands before a table and a pot-stand. From the Balawat Gates.

translated den (Ps. x. 9), tabernacle (Ps. lxxvi. 2), covert (Je. xxv. 38), booth (Jon. iv. 5), and lodge (Is. i. 8), and thus represents something used by beasts, worshippers, travellers, and soldiers. It is translated only six times in the AV as pavilion. In 1 Ki. xx. 12, 16 it refers to the army tents in which Ben-hadad and his soldiers were resting and drinking when they were campaigning against Ahab. Such tents are illustrated on the sculptured reliefs of the Assyrian kings Shalmaneser III and Sennacherib (British Museum). The other uses of the word are metaphorical. It represents the place of divine protection in the day of trouble (Ps. xxvii. 5, xxxi. 20), or the place where God is hidden with dark waters and thick clouds for His pavilion (Ps. xviii. 11; 2 Sa. xxii. 12). J.A.T.

PEACE. Basically the Old Testament word for peace, *šālôm*, means 'completeness', 'soundness', 'well-being'. (See *BDB*.) It is used when one asks of or prays for the welfare of another (Gn. xliii. 27; Ex. iv. 18; Jdg. xix. 20), when one is in harmony or concord with another (Jos. ix. 15; 1 Ki. v. 12), when one seeks the good of a city or country (Ps. cxxii. 6; Je. xxix. 7). It may mean material prosperity (Ps. lxxiii. 3) or physical safety (Ps. iv. 8). But also it may mean spiritual well-being. Such peace is the associate of righteousness and truth, but not of wickedness (Ps. lxxxv. 10; Is. xlviii. 18, 22, lvii. 19–21).

Because of the world's chaos through man's sin, and because peace comes only as God's gift, the messianic hope was of an age of peace (Is. ii. 2–4, xi. 1–9; Hg. ii. 7–9), or of the advent of the Prince of peace (Is. ix. 6 f.; *cf.* Je. xxxiii. 15 f.; Ezk. xxxiv. 23 ff.; Mi. v. 5; Zc. ix. 9 f.). The New Testament shows the fulfilment of this hope. In Christ peace has come (Lk. i. 79, ii. 14, 29 f.). By Him it is bestowed (Mk. v. 34; Lk. vii. 50; Jn. xx. 19, 21, 26), and His disciples are its messengers (Lk. x. 5 f.; Acts x. 36).

In classical Greek *eirēnē* had a primarily negative force; but by way of the LXX, the word in the New Testament has the full content of the Old Testament *šālôm*, and nearly always carries a spiritual connotation. The breadth of its meaning is especially apparent from its linking with such key-words as grace (Rom. i. 7, *etc.*), life (Rom. viii. 6), righteousness (Rom. xiv. 17), and from its use in benedictions such as 1 Thes. v. 23 and Heb. xiii. 20 f. (*cf.* 2 Pet. iii. 14).

For sinful man there must first be peace with God, the removal of sin's enmity through the sacrifice of Christ (Rom. v. 1; Col. i. 20). Then inward peace can follow (Phil. iv. 7), unhindered by the world's strife (Jn. xiv. 27, xvi. 33). Peace between man and man is part of the purpose for which Christ died (Eph. ii) and of the Spirit's works (Gal. v. 22); but man must also be active to promote it (Eph. iv. 3; Heb. xii. 14), not merely as the elimination of discord, but as the harmony and true functioning of the body of Christ (Rom. xiv. 19; 1 Cor. xiv. 33).

BIBLIOGRAPHY. W. Foerster and G. von Rad on '*eirēnē*' in *TWNT*. F.F.

PEACE-OFFERING. See SACRIFICE AND OFFERING.

PEACOCK. See BIRDS OF THE BIBLE.

PEARL. See JEWELS AND PRECIOUS STONES.

PEDAIAH ('Yahweh has redeemed'). **1.** Father of Joel, ruler (under David) of Manasseh, west of the Jordan (1 Ch. xxvii. 20). **2.** Grandfather of King Jehoiakim (2 Ki. xxiii. 36). **3.** Third son of King Jehoiachin (1 Ch. iii. 18). According to 1 Ch. iii. 19, he was called the father of Zerubbabel, who elsewhere is named as the son of Shealtiel, brother of Pedaiah. **4.** A son of Parosh, who helped to repair the wall of Jerusalem (Ne. iii. 25). **5.** One who stood on Ezra's left when he read the law to the people (Ne. viii. 4); perhaps identical with (4) above. **6.** A Levite appointed by Nehemiah to assist in distributing the tithes (Ne. xiii. 13). **7.** A Benjamite (Ne. xi. 7). J.D.D.

PEKAH (*peqaḥ*, 'opening'). Pekah, the son of Remaliah, was the 'third man' (*šālîšâ*) in Pekahiah's war chariot. With the help of Gileadites he murdered Pekahiah, successor of Menahem, at Samaria (2 Ki. xv. 21 ff.). He then seized the throne and reigned as king of Israel from *c.* 737 to 732 BC. His accession was in the fifty-second year of Uzziah of Judah (verse 27), and in his second year Jotham succeeded Uzziah (verse 32).

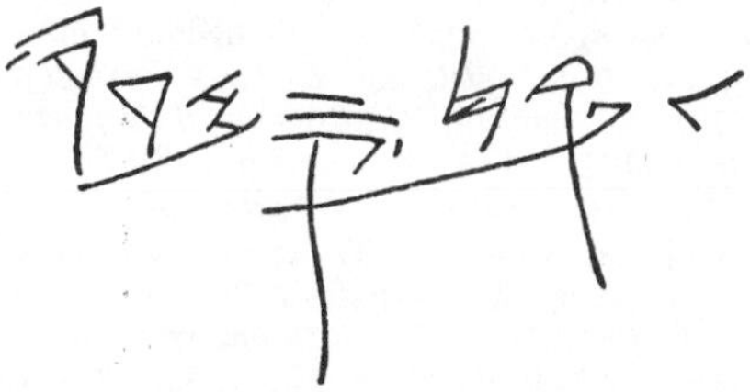

Fig. 163. Hebrew inscription on a fragment of an 8th-century BC wine jar from Hazor. It reads 'For Peqah, Semader', probably a reference to Pekah, king of Israel, and to a kind of wine (Heb. *s^e^māḏēr*).

Pekah adopted an anti-Assyrian policy and allied himself to Rezin of Syria. Together they brought pressure on Jotham of Judah, probably to join them (verse 37). Isaiah, however, advised him and his successor Ahaz to be neutral. Pekah moved in force against Jerusalem, which was unsuccessfully besieged (2 Ki. xvi. 5; Is. vii. 1). His Syrian allies took Elath, while Pekah fought the Judaeans, slaying many and taking many prisoners from the Jericho district back to Samaria (2 Ch. xxviii. 7, 8). These were later released on the intercession of the prophet Oded (verses 8–15).

Faced with this invasion Ahaz appealed for help to Tiglath-pileser III of Assyria, who was campaigning in Syria. In 732 BC the Assyrians captured Damascus and invaded N Israel. A list of the places invaded, as far south as Galilee, is given in 2 Ki. xv. 25–29 and is partly paralleled by Tiglath-pileser's own Annals. Excavation at Hazor confirms the Assyrian destruction there at this time. A wine-jar inscribed *lpqḥ*, 'belonging to Pekah', was found among the objects from the period of Pekah's occupation. See fig. 163 above.

Following the swift Assyrian invasion of more

than half of Israel, Hoshea, son of Elah, conspired against Pekah, whom he slew. Since Tiglath-pileser claims in his Annals to have replaced Pekah (*Paqaḫa*) by Hoshea (*'Ausi*), it is clear that this act was approved, if not instigated, by the Assyrians. Pekah's reign was considered to have followed the evil tradition of Jeroboam (2 Ki. xv. 28). D.J.W.

PEKAHIAH (*p^eqaḥyâ*, 'Yahweh has opened (his eyes)'). Son of Menahem, king of Israel, whom he succeeded *c.* 742/1 BC (2 Ki. xv. 23–26; see also CHRONOLOGY OF THE OLD TESTAMENT). His assassination in the second year of his reign suggests that he continued his father's policy of submission to Assyria. The revolutionaries, led by Pekah son of Remaliah, may have been in league with Rezin, king of Damascus, for they came from Gilead, adjacent to his territory. The king was killed while in the keep (Heb. *'armôn*) of the palace at Samaria. The words 'with Argob and Arieh' (2 Ki. xv. 25) seem to have been transposed from verse 29. See also MENAHEM, PEKAH, SAMARIA, ARGOB. A.R.M.

PEKOD. In his picture of judgment on Babylon, Jeremiah (l. 21) includes an attack on the territory of Pekod, with perhaps a reference to the meaning of this word as a common noun, 'visitation' (RVmg). Ezekiel (xxiii. 23) prophesies that this people, together with other dwellers in Mesopotamia, will attack Jerusalem. According to Akkadian sources, the *Puḳudu* were an Aramaean tribe in the area east of the lower Tigris who fought against Assyria and were subdued by Nebuchadrezzar. They gave their name to a city and a canal in this area which are mentioned in Assyrian records and in TB (*Betzah* 29a, *Ketuboth* 27b, *Hullin* 127a).

BIBLIOGRAPHY. A. Neubauer, *La Géographie du Talmud,* 1868, pp. 363–369; Friedrich Delitzsch, *Wo lag das Paradies?*, 1881, pp. 240, 241; S. Schiffer, *Die Aramaër*, 1911, pp. 126–130; G. A. Cooke in *ICC*, 1936, on Ezk. xxiii. 23. J.T.

PELATIAH (Heb. *p^elaṭyāh(û)*, 'Yahweh delivers'; Gk. *Phaltias, Phalettia*). **1.** A witness to the covenant in Ne. x. 22. This may well be the same man as the grandson of Zerubbabel, a descendant of Solomon (1 Ch. iii. 21). **2.** A Simeonite captain who occupied ex-Amalekite territory (1 Ch. iv. 42). **3.** A leader (*'Pelatiahu'*) whom Ezekiel pictured as devising mischief and giving wicked counsel in Jerusalem. He fell dead while Ezekiel prophesied (Ezk. xi. 1–13).

For the name, *cf.* Palṭi, Pilṭi, Palṭi'el, Yaphleṭ in contemporary inscriptions. D.J.W.

PELEG (*peleḡ*, 'water-course, division'). The son of Eber, brother of Yoqtan (see JOKTAN), and grandson of Shem (Gn. x. 25). In his time the earth was 'divided', the word used (*nip̄l^eḡâ*) being a play on, or explanation of, his name. This is commonly held to refer to the splitting up of the world's population into various geographical and linguistic groups (Gn. xi. 1–9). It may equally well mark the development by the semi-nomad sons of Eber (see HEBREW) of cultivation, using artificial irrigation canals (Assyr. *palgu*); *peleḡ* is used in this sense in Is. xxx. 25, xxxii. 2; Jb. xxix. 6, xxxviii. 25. Peleg was father of Reu (Gn. xi. 19). D.J.W.

PELETHITES. See CHERETHITES.

PELICAN. See BIRDS OF THE BIBLE.

PELONITE. The name given to two of David's mighty men, Helez and Ahijah (1 Ch. xi. 27, 36, xxvii. 10). The former is described as the Paltite (*q.v.*) in the parallel text, 2 Sa. xxiii. 26, and the Syriac has this reading in 1 Ch. xi. 27. In view of 2 Sa. xxiii. 34 some commentators prefer to emend 1 Ch. xi. 36b to 'Eliam the son of Ahithophel the Gilonite'. R.A.H.G.

PEN. See WRITING.

PENDANTS. See AMULETS, ORNAMENTS.

PENIEL. See PENUEL.

PENKNIFE. See WRITING.

PENNY. See MONEY.

PENTATEUCH. The first five books of the Old Testament (Genesis, Exodus, Leviticus, Numbers, Deuteronomy) constitute the first and most important section of the three-fold Jewish Canon (*q.v.*). Usually called by the Jews *sēp̄er hattôrâ*, 'the book of the law', or *hattôrâ*, 'the law' (see *KB*, p. 403, for suggested derivations of the word, which seems to mean basically 'teaching' or 'instruction'), the Pentateuch (Greek *pentateuchos*, 'five-volumed [*sc.* book]') is also known as the 'five-fifths of the law'. For the past century or so, many higher critics, following the lead of Alexander Geddes (*c.* 1800), have tended to disregard the traditional five-book division in favour of a Hexateuch comprising the Pentateuch and Joshua (*cf.* J. Wellhausen, *Die Composition des Hexateuchs*, 1876–7). On the other hand, I. Engnell has suggested the word 'Tetrateuch' to separate Deuteronomy from the first four books (*Gamla Testamentet*, I, 1945). The critical presuppositions which underlie these suggestions are evaluated below.

The antiquity of the five-fold division is attested by the Samaritan Pentateuch and the LXX, which gave the books their traditional names; the Jews identify them by the first word or phrase. The divisions between the books were determined both by topical and practical considerations: papyrus scrolls could contain only about one-fifth of the *tôrâ*. Jewish tradition prescribes that a section of the Law be read weekly in the synagogue. Three years were required for the completion of the Pentateuch in Palestine; the modern lectionary, in which the Pentateuch is read through in one year, is derived from that used in Babylonia. It may well be that a psalm was read along with the traditional reading from the prophetic writings (*hap̄ṭārâ*). The five books of the Psalter are probably patterned after the Pentateuch (*cf.* N. H. Snaith, *Hymns of the Temple*, 1951, pp. 18–20).

References to the Pentateuch in the Old Testament are largely restricted to the writings of the Chronicler, who uses several designations: the law (Ezr. x. 3; Ne. viii. 2, 7, 14, x. 34, 36, xii. 44, xiii. 3; 2 Ch. xiv. 4, xxxi. 21, xxxiii. 8); the book of the law (Ne. viii. 3); the book of the law of Moses (Ne. viii. 1); the book of Moses (Ne. xiii. 1; 2 Ch. xxv. 4, xxxv. 12); the law of the Lord (Ezr. vii. 10; 1 Ch. xvi. 40; 2 Ch. xxxi. 3, xxxv. 26); the law of God (Ne. x. 28, 29); the book of the law of God (Ne. viii. 18); the book of the law of the Lord (2 Ch. xvii. 9, xxxiv. 14); the book of the law of the Lord their God (Ne. ix. 3); the law of Moses the servant of God (Dn. ix. 11; *cf.* Mal. iv. 4). One cannot say for certain whether references to the law in the historical writings refer to the Pentateuch as a whole or to parts of the Mosaic legislation, *e.g.* the law (Jos. viii. 34); the book of the law (Jos. i. 8, viii. 34; 2 Ki. xxii. 8); the book of the law of Moses (Jos. viii. 31, xxiii. 6; 2 Ki. xiv. 6); the book of the law of God (Jos. xxiv. 26).

The New Testament uses similar designations: the book of the law (Gal. iii. 10); the book of Moses (Mk. xii. 26); the law (Mt. xii. 5; Lk. xvi. 16; Jn. vii. 19); the law of Moses (Lk. ii. 22; Jn. vii. 23); the law of the Lord (Lk. ii. 23, 24). The descriptions of the Pentateuch in both Testaments serve to emphasize its divine and human authorship, its binding authority as *the law*, and its inscripturated form in *the book*.

I. CONTENTS

The Pentateuch narrates God's dealings with the world and especially the family of Abraham from creation to the death of Moses. There are six main divisions. First, the origin of the world and of the nations (Gn. i–xi). This section describes the creation (*q.v.*), the fall of man, the beginnings of civilization, the flood, the Table of the Nations, and the tower of Babel. Secondly, the patriarchal period (Gn. xii–l) depicts the call of Abraham, the initiation of the Abrahamic covenant, the lives of Isaac, Jacob, and Joseph, and the settling of the covenant-clan in Egypt. Thirdly, Moses and the Exodus from Egypt (Ex. i–xviii). Fourthly, legislation at Sinai (Ex. xix–Nu. x. 10), which includes the giving of the law, the building of the Tabernacle, the establishment of the levitical system, and the final preparations for the journey from Sinai to Canaan. Fifthly, the wilderness wanderings (Nu. x. 11–xxxvi. 13). This section describes the departure from Sinai, the acceptance of the majority report of the spies, God's consequent judgment, the encounter with Balaam, the appointment of Joshua as Moses' successor, and the apportionment of the land to the twelve tribes. Sixthly, the final speeches of Moses (Dt. i–xxxiv) recapitulate the Exodus events, repeat and expand the Sinaitic commandments, clarify the issues involved in obedience and disobedience, and bless the tribes, who are poised to enter Canaan. This section ends with the cryptic description of Moses' death and burial.

II. AUTHORSHIP AND UNITY

For centuries both Judaism and Christianity accepted without question the biblical tradition that Moses wrote the Pentateuch. Ben-Sira (Ecclus. xxiv. 23), Philo (*Life of Moses*, iii. 39), Josephus (*Ant.* iv. 8. 48), the Mishnah (*Pirqê Abôth* i. 1), and the Talmud (*Baba Bathra* 14b) are unanimous in their acceptance of the Mosaic authorship. The only debate centred in the account of Moses' death in Dt. xxxiv. 5 ff. Philo and Josephus affirm that Moses described his own death, while the Talmud (*loc. cit.*) credits Joshua with eight verses of the *tôrâ*, presumably the last eight.

a. Pentateuchal criticism before AD 1700

The tradition expressed in 2 Esdras xiv. 21, 22 that the scrolls of the Pentateuch, burned in Nebuchadrezzar's siege of Jerusalem, were rewritten by Ezra was apparently accepted by a number of the early Church Fathers, *e.g.* Irenaeus, Tertullian, Clement of Alexandria, Jerome. They did not, however, reject the Mosaic authorship of the original law. The first recorded instance of such a rejection is the statement of John of Damascus concerning the Nasaraeans, a sect of Jewish Christians (*cf.* J. P. Migne, *PG*, XCIV, 688, 689). The *Clementine Homilies* teach that diabolical interpolations were made in the Pentateuch to try to put Adam, Noah, and the Patriarchs in a bad light. Any passage out of harmony with the Ebionite assumptions of the author was suspected in this early attempt at higher criticism. Among the stumbling-blocks to the faith which Anastasius the Sinaite, patriarch of Antioch (7th century AD), attempted to remove were questions dealing with the Mosaic authorship of, and alleged discrepancies in, Genesis (*cf.* J. P. Migne, *PG*, LXXXIX, 284, 285).

During the mediaeval era, Jewish and Muslim scholars began to point out supposed contradictions and anachronisms in the Pentateuch. For instance, Ibn Ezra (d. 1167), following a suggestion of Rabbi Isaac ben Jasos (d. 1057) that Gn. xxxvi was written not earlier than Jehoshaphat's reign because of the mention of Hadad (*cf.* Gn. xxxvi. 35; 1 Ki. xi. 14), maintained that such passages as Gn. xii. 6, xxii. 14; Dt. i. 1, iii. 11 were interpolations.

The Reformer Carlstadt (1480–1541), observing no change in the literary style of Deuteronomy before and after Moses' death, denied that Moses wrote the Pentateuch. A Belgian Roman Catholic, Andreas Masius, produced a commentary on Joshua (1574) in which he credited Ezra with certain pentateuchal interpolations. Similar positions were maintained by two Jesuit scholars, Jacques Bonfrère and Benedict Pereira. Two famous philosophers helped pave the way for modern higher critics by voicing in their widely circulated writings some of the contemporary criticisms of the unity of the law: Thomas Hobbes (*Leviathan*, 1651) credited Moses with everything attributed to him in the Pentateuch, but suggested that other parts were written more about Moses than by him; Benedict Spinoza (*Tractatus Theologico-politicus*, 1670) carried the observations of Ibn Ezra farther by noting doublets and alleged contradictions, and concluding that Ezra, who himself wrote Deuteronomy, compiled the Pentateuch from a number of documents (some Mosaic). Seventeenth-century criticism of the Pentateuch was climaxed in the works of the Roman Catholic Richard Simon and the Arminian Jean LeClerc in 1685. LeClerc replied to Simon's view that the Pentateuch was a compilation based on many documents, both of divine and human origin, by asserting that the author must have lived in Babylonia between 722 BC and Ezra's time.

b. Pentateuchal criticism from AD *1700 to 1900*

(i) *The question of Mosaic authorship.* Despite the questions raised by Catholics, Protestants, and Jews in the period discussed above, the vast multitude of scholars and laymen clung firmly to belief in the Mosaic authorship. A milestone in Pentateuchal criticism was reached in 1753, when the French physician Jean Astruc published his theory that Moses had composed Genesis from two main ancient *mémoires* and a number of shorter documents. The clue to the identification of the two *mémoires* was the use of the divine names: one employed *Elohim*; the other, *Yahweh.* Astruc maintained the Mosaic authorship of Genesis, but posited his theory of multiple sources to account for some of the repetitions and alleged discrepancies which critics had noted. J. G. Eichhorn (*Einleitung*, 1780–83) expanded Astruc's views into what is called 'the early documentary theory'. Abandoning the Mosaic authorship, he credited the final editing of the Elohistic and Yahwistic documents of Genesis and Ex. i, ii to an unknown redactor. K. D. Ilgen (*Die Urkunden des Jerusalemischen Tempelarchivs in ihrer Urgestalt*, 1798) carried the documentary theory a step farther when he discovered in Gn. xvii independent sources traceable to three authors, two of whom use *Elohim* and the other *Yahweh.*

A Scottish Roman Catholic priest, Alexander Geddes, pursued Astruc's identification of several *mémoires* and developed (between 1792 and 1800) the *fragmentary theory* which holds that the Pentateuch was composed by an unknown redactor from a number of fragments which had originated in two different circles—one Elohistic, the other Yahwistic. Two German scholars embraced and expanded the fragmentary theory: J. S. Vater (*Commentar über den Pentateuch*, 3 vols., 1802–5) tried to trace the growth of the Pentateuch from over thirty fragments; W. M. L. De Wette (*Beiträge zur Einleitung in das Alte Testament*, 1807) stressed the comparatively late nature of much of the legal material and, significantly for later research, identified Josiah's book of the law as Deuteronomy (in this identification he had been anticipated by Jerome 1,400 years earlier).

De Wette's emphasis on one basic document augmented by numerous fragments was developed by H. Ewald, who in 1831 suggested that the chief document was the Elohistic source which carried the narrative from the creation into the book of Joshua and was supplemented by the account of the Yahwist, who was also the final redactor. Though Ewald later retreated from this 'supplementary theory', it survived in the writings of F. Bleek (*de libri Geneseos origine*, 1836) and F. Tuch (*Genesis*, 1838).

The 'new documentary theory' was fathered by H. Hupfeld (*Die Quellen der Genesis und die Art ihrer Zusammensetzung*, 1853), who, like Ilgen, found three separate sources in Genesis—the original Elohist (E^1), the later Elohist (E^2), and the Yahwist (J). A year later, when E. Riehm published his *Die Gesetzgebung Mosis im Lande Moab* in 1854, which purported to demonstrate the independent character of Deuteronomy, the four major documents had been isolated and dated in the order E^1, E^2, J, D.

K. H. Graf (in 1866) developed the suggestion of E. G. Reuss, J. F. L. George, and W. Vatke and affirmed that E^1 (called P for Priestly Code by modern scholars), rather than being the earliest of the documents, was the latest. The debate then centred in the question as to whether E^2(E)JDP(E^1) or JEDP was the proper chronological order. A. Kuenen's work, *The Religion of Israel* (1869–70), assured the triumph of the latter order and set the stage for the appearance of the star actor in the drama of Pentateuchal criticism, Julius Wellhausen.

(ii) *Wellhausen's views.* Wellhausen's important publications from 1876 to 1884 gave the documentary theory its most cogent and popular setting. Stated simply, this theory holds that J (*c.* 850 BC) and E (*c.* 750 BC) were combined by a redactor (R^{JE}) about 650 BC. When D (the Deuteronomic laws, *c.* 621) was added by R^D (*c.* 550) and P (*c.* 500–450) by R^P about 400 BC, the Pentateuch was basically complete. In Wellhausen's presentation more was involved than mere documentary analysis. He linked his critical studies to an evolutionary approach to Israel's history which minimized the historicity of the patriarchal period and tended to detract from Moses' prominence. The religion of Israel advanced from the simple sacrifices on family altars in the days of the settlement to the intricately legalistic structure of Leviticus (P), which stemmed from Ezra's era (see PRIESTS AND LEVITES). Similarly, Israel's concept of God evolved from the animism and polytheism of the patriarchal days, through the henotheism of Moses' time and the ethical monotheism of the 8th-century prophets to the exalted sovereign Lord of Is. xl ff.

So fundamental for later scholarship were

Wellhausen's ideas that his influence in biblical studies has frequently been likened to Darwin's in the natural sciences. Largely through the writings of W. Robertson Smith and S. R. Driver, Wellhausen's documentary analysis gained a widespread acceptance throughout the English-speaking world. The following summary (somewhat oversimplified) outlines the basic characteristics of the Pentateuchal documents according to the Wellhausenian school.

The *Yahwist's narrative* (J) is said to date from early in the monarchy (*c.* 950–850 BC). Allusions to territorial expansion (Gn. xv. 18, xxvii. 40) and the ascendancy of Judah (Gn. xlix. 8–12) allegedly point to a Solomonic date. The J document tells the story of God's dealings with man from the creation of the universe to Israel's entry of Canaan. The combination of majesty and simplicity found in J marks it as an outstanding example of epic literature worthy of comparison with Homer's *Iliad.* Originating in Judah, the Yahwist document has some distinctive literary traits in addition to the preference for the name Yahweh: *šip̄ḥâ*, 'maidservant', is preferred to *'āmâ* (E); Sinai is used instead of Horeb (E); popular etymologies occur frequently, *e.g.* Gn. iii. 20, xi. 9, xxv. 30, xxxii. 27.

Intensely nationalistic, the J narrative records in detail the exploits of the patriarchal families, even those that are not particularly praiseworthy. Theologically J is noted for its anthropopathisms and anthropomorphisms. God in quasi-human form walks and talks with men, although His transcendence is never doubted. The transparent biographies of the Patriarchs, deftly and simply narrated, are an outstanding feature of J.

The *Elohist's narrative* (E) is usually dated about a century after J, *i.e.* about 850–750 BC. A northern (Ephraimitic) origin for E has been suggested on the basis of the omission of the stories of Abraham and Lot, which centre in Hebron and the Cities of the Plain, and the special emphasis given to Bethel and Shechem (Gn. xxviii. 17, xxxi. 13, xxxiii. 19, 20). Joseph, the ancestor of the northern tribes Ephraim and Manasseh, plays a prominent rôle. More fragmentary than J, E nevertheless has its own stylistic peculiarities: 'the River' is the Euphrates; repetition is used in direct address (*cf.* Gn. xxii. 11; Ex. iii. 4); 'Here am I' (*hinnēnî*) is used in replies to the Deity.

Though less noteworthy as a literary composition than J, the E document is noted for its moralistic and religious emphases. Sensitive to the sins of the Patriarchs, E attempts to rationalize them, while the anthropomorphisms of J are replaced by divine revelations through dreams and angelic mediation. An outstanding contribution of E is the story of God's testing of Abraham in the command to sacrifice Isaac (Gn. xxii. 1–14). With powerful simplicity the picture of conflict between love of family and obedience to God is painted, and with prophetic force the lesson concerning the inwardness of true sacrifice is conveyed.

The *Deuteronomist document* (D), in Pentateuchal studies, corresponds roughly with the book of Deuteronomy (*q.v.*). Essential to the documentary hypothesis is the view that Josiah's book of the law (2 Ki. xxii. 3–xxiii. 25) was part, at least, of Deuteronomy. The correspondences between D and the terms of Josiah's reformation are noteworthy: the worship is centralized at Jerusalem (2 Ki. xxiii. 4 ff.; Dt. xii. 1–7); acts of false worship are specifically forbidden (2 Ki. xxiii. 4–11, 24; Dt. xvi. 21, 22, xvii. 3, xviii. 10, 11). D lays great stress on God's love for Israel and her obligation to respond, a philosophy of history which spells out the terms of God's blessing and judgment, and the necessity for a vigorous sense of social justice under the terms of the covenant. A collection of sermons rather than narratives, D is a congeries of legal and hortatory materials compiled during the exigencies of Manasseh's reign and combined with JE after the time of Josiah.

The *Priestly document* (P) draws together laws and customs from various periods of Israel's history and codifies them in such a way as to organize the legal structure of post-exilic Judaism. P contains some narratives, but is more concerned with genealogies and the patriarchal origins of ritual or legal practices. Formal divisions such as the ten 'generations' of Genesis (*q.v.*) and the covenants with Adam, Noah, Abraham, and Moses are generally credited to P. The complexity of the legal and ritual structure of P is usually interpreted as a sign of a post-exilic date, especially when P (*e.g.* Ex. xxv–xxxi, xxxv–xl; Leviticus; the laws in Numbers) is compared with the simple ritualism of Judges and 1 Samuel. As a literary document P cannot be compared with the earlier sources, because the penchant for laborious details (*e.g.* the genealogies and detailed descriptions of the tabernacle) tends to discourage literary creativity. The concern of the priestly movement for the holiness and transcendence of God reveals itself in P, where the entire legislation is viewed as a means of grace whereby God bridges the gap between Himself and Israel.

c. Pentateuchal criticism after AD 1900

Documentary analysis did not stop with Wellhausen's researches. Rudolf Smend, expanding a suggestion made in 1883 by Karl Budde, attempted to divide the Yahwistic document into J^1 and J^2 throughout the Hexateuch (*Die Erzählung des Hexateuch auf ihre Quellen untersucht*, 1912). What Smend had called J^1 Otto Eissfeldt identified as a Lay-source (L), because it contrasts directly with the Priestly document and emphasizes the nomadic ideal in opposition to the Canaanite mode of life. Julian Morgenstern's Kenite (*q.v.*) document (K), purportedly dealing with Moses' biography and the relations between Israel and the Kenites (*HUCA*, IV, 1927, pp. 1–138), R. H. Pfeiffer's S (South or Seir) document in Genesis, corresponding somewhat to Eissfeldt's L (*ZAW*, XLVIII, 1930, pp. 66–73), and Gerhard von Rad's division of the priestly document into P[A] and P[B] (*Die Priesterschrift im Hexateuch*, 1934) are further refinements of a documentary criticism which had reached its extreme in the detailed dissections of P in B. Baentsch's work on Leviticus (1900), where seven main sources of P are further modified by the discovery of one or more redactors. This atomizing tendency is given a contemporary form in the works of C. A. Simpson (notably *The Early Traditions of Israel: a Critical Analysis of the Pre-Deuteronomic Narrative of the Hexateuch*, 1948).

d. Reactions to the Graf–Wellhausen theory

Conservatives, convinced that their view of inspiration and the whole structure of theology built on it were at stake, joined battle almost immediately with Pentateuchal critics. In the van of this reaction were E. W. Hengstenberg (*Dissertations on the Genuineness of the Pentateuch*, 1847) and C. F. Keil. After the appearance of Wellhausen's monumental synthesis the battle was continued by W. H. Green (*The Higher Criticism of the Pentateuch*, 1895) and James Orr (*The Problem of the Old Testament*, 1900), whose careful scrutiny of the documentary analyses found them wanting in terms of both literary evidence and theological presuppositions. The pattern set by these scholars has continued in the researches of R. D. Wilson (*A Scientific Investigation of the Old Testament*, 1926, reprinted 1959), G. Ch. Aalders (*A Short Introduction to the Pentateuch*, 1949), O. T. Allis (*The Five Books of Moses*, 1943), and E. J. Young (*Introduction to the Old Testament*, 1949).

(i) *The use of the divine names.* Conservative attacks on the Wellhausenian theory have generally taken shape along the following lines. The use of the divine names as a criterion for separating documents has been questioned at four points: (1) The evidence of textual criticism, especially from the Pentateuch of the LXX, suggests that there was less uniformity and more variety in early manuscripts of the Pentateuch than in the *MT*, which has traditionally been used as the basis of documentary analysis (although J. Skinner's *The Divine Names in Genesis*, 1914, has weakened the force of this argument). (2) R. D. Wilson's study of the divine names in the Qur'an (*PTR*, XVII, 1919, pp. 644–650) brought to light the fact that certain suras of the Qur'an prefer *Allah* (iv, ix, xxiv, xxxiii, xlviii, *etc.*), while others prefer *Rab* (xviii, xxiii, xxv, xxvi, xxxiv, *etc.*), just as certain sections of Genesis use *Elohim* (*e.g.* Gn. i. 1–ii. 3, vi. 9–22, xvii. 2 ff., xx, *etc.*) and others *Yahweh* (*e.g.* Gn. iv, vii. 1–5, xi. 1–9, xv, xviii. 1–xix. 28, *etc.*), although there is no support among scholars for a documentary approach to Qur'anic studies based on the divine names.

(3) The use of *Yahweh Elohim* (Gn. ii. 4–iii. 24; *cf.* also Ex. ix. 30) presents a special problem for the Wellhausen theory, since it involves a combining of the divine names which are supposed to be clues to separate documents; the LXX apparently contains many more instances of this combination (*e.g.* Gn. iv. 6, 9, v. 29, vi. 3, 5), while there is ample evidence of compound names for deities in Ugaritic, Egyptian, and Greek literature (*cf.* C. H. Gordon in *Christianity Today*, 23 November 1959). (4) It is likely that the interchange of Yahweh and Elohim in the Pentateuch reflects an attempt on the part of the author to stress the ideas associated with each name (*cf.* I. Engnell, *Gamla Testamentet*, I, 1945, pp. 194 ff.). These and similar problems pertaining to the divine names have long since caused documentary critics to minimize what was once the starting-point of the whole process of documentary analysis.

(ii) *Diction and Style.* Differences in diction and style, an important link in the chain of evidence for the Wellhausen theory, have been called into question by a number of conservatives. Stress has been laid on the fact that the Pentateuchal stories are too fragmentary to give an adequate sampling of an author's vocabulary and that insufficient attention has sometimes been given to the fact that different types of literature call for differing vocabularies. Words supposedly peculiar to one document are sometimes credited to a redactor when they occur in another source. This use of a redactor when the facts call in question critical theories seems a somewhat too convenient method of dealing with difficulties. As for matters of style, conservatives and others have frequently pointed out the subjectivity in such judgments and the very great difficulty involved in subjecting such opinions to scientific examination. What seems to be a graphic, vibrant narrative to one critic may seem dull or turgid to another. W. J. Martin has highlighted some of the difficulties encountered by literary critics in his *Stylistic Criteria and the Analysis of the Pentateuch*, 1955, although caution is imperative in the use of analogies from western literary criticism for the study of Oriental literature.

(iii) *Double narratives.* The occurrence of double narratives (sometimes called doublets) has been considered key evidence for a diversity of sources. Aalders (*op. cit.*, pp. 43–53) and Allis (*op. cit.*, pp. 94–110, 118–123) have examined a number of these repetitions (*e.g.* Gn. i. 1–ii. 4a, ii. 4b–25, vi. 1–8, 9–13, xii. 10–20, xx, xxvi. 6–11) and have sought to show that their presence in the text need not be interpreted as evidence for multiplicity of sources. On the contrary, repetition within Hebrew prose may be connected with the characteristically Hebrew (and indeed Semitic) use of repetition for emphasis. Ideas are underscored in Hebrew literature not by the logical connection with other ideas but by a creative kind of repetition which seeks to influence the reader's will. (*Cf.* J. Muilenburg, 'A Study in Hebrew Rhetoric: Repetition and Style' in Supplements to *VT*, I, 1953, pp. 97–111; J. Pedersen, *Israel*, I–II, 1926, p. 123.)

So far as Genesis is concerned, a conservative contribution was made by P. J. Wiseman in *New Discoveries in Babylonia about Genesis*, 1936, in which it was suggested that the *tôlēḏôt* passages (those beginning or ending with some such phrase as 'These are the generations . . .') mark the various sources available to Moses for compiling earlier narratives. This approach was popularized by J. Stafford Wright in *How Moses Compiled Genesis: A Suggestion*, 1946. For suggested replies to the Wellhausenian theory of the development of the levitical system, see PRIESTS AND LEVITES.

Conservatives have been quick to draw upon the conclusions of non-conservatives when these conclusions tended to question the validity of the documentary hypothesis. The sustained attack on the theories of Wellhausenians by B. D. Eerdmans is a case in point. Though denying the Mosaic authorship of the Pentateuch, Eerdmans staunchly defended the basic authenticity of the patriarchal narratives and affirmed his confidence in the antiquity of the ritual institutions of P. Further, Oestreicher and Welch endeavoured to tumble the documentary theory by removing the key-stone—the identification of D with Josiah's book of the law. E. Robertson (*The Old Testament Problem*, 1950) regards Deuteronomy as having been compiled under Samuel's influence as a law-book for 'all Israel', as having fallen into disuse when the disruption of the nation made its application impossible, and as having been opportunely rediscovered in Josiah's reign at a time when it was possible to treat 'all Israel' as a religious unit once more. The Decalogue and the Book of the Covenant, with which the Hebrews entered Canaan, were preserved in the early days of the settlement at various local sanctuaries, where they gathered around themselves bodies of divergent though related laws and traditions; the beginnings of national reunion in Samuel's day necessitated the compilation, on the basis of this material, of a law-book for the central administration. R. Brinker, a pupil of E. Robertson, elaborated certain aspects of this theory in *The Influence of Sanctuaries in Early Israel*, 1946. Using linguistic and stylistic criteria, U. Cassuto (*La Questione della Genesi*, 1934) argued for the unity of Genesis, while F. Dornseiff (*ZAW*, LII–LIII, 1934–5) defended the literary unity of the whole Pentateuch; *cf.* his *Antike und Alter Orient*, 1956.

From another angle A. R. Johnson warns us against what 'seems to be a real danger in Old Testament study as a whole of misinterpreting what may be different but contemporary *strata* in terms of corresponding *stages* of thought, which can be arranged chronologically so as to fit into an over-simplified evolutionary scheme or similar theory of progressive revelation' (*The Vitality of the Individual in the Thought of Ancient Israel*, 1949, p. 3).

(iv) *Form criticism.* While not abandoning the documentary hypothesis, the pioneer form critics, H. Gunkel and H. Gressmann, laid stress both on the literary qualities and on the lengthy process of oral tradition which had shaped the various narratives into aesthetic masterpieces. This welcome relief from the coldly analytical approach of the documentary critics, who in their detailed dissection of the Pentateuch tended to neglect the power and beauty of the stories, paved the way for the researches of a group of Scandinavian scholars who have discarded the documentary approach in favour of an emphasis on oral tradition. Following the lead of J. Pedersen who in 1931 formally rejected the documentary theory (*ZAW*, XLIX, 1931, pp. 161–181), I. Engnell (*Gamla Testamentet*, I, 1945) affirmed that, far from being the result of the compilation of written documents, the Pentateuch is a combination of reliable oral traditions collected and shaped in two main traditionist circles: a 'P-circle' responsible for the Tetrateuch and a 'D-circle' which formulated Deuteronomy, Joshua, Judges, Samuel, and Kings. The actual writing of the books is relegated to exilic or post-exilic times. Key factors in the development of this traditio-historical school are the advanced knowledge of Hebrew psychology and the growing understanding of ancient Oriental literature. According to Engnell, the devotees of the Wellhausenian approach tend to interpret the Old Testament in terms of European literary methods and western logic. See Eduard Nielsen, *Oral Tradition*, 1954, for a concise presentation of the views of the Scandinavian School.

As H. Gunkel's preoccupation with the various literary units (identifiable by literary *form* within the Pentateuch) represented a kind of return to the *fragmentary* approach of Geddes, Vater, and De Wette, so P. Volz (and to some extent W. Rudolph) called for a revival of a *supplementary* hypothesis by minimizing the importance of the Elohist, who is at the most, in Volz's view, a later editor of the great author of Genesis, the Yahwist. In somewhat similar fashion G. von Rad (*Das formgeschichtliche Problem des Hexateuchs*, 1938) has stressed the dominant rôle played by the Yahwist as both collector and author of the Pentateuchal materials which took shape over a lengthy period of time and have a rich history of tradition behind them. The generally accepted dates for the documents are highly tentative, according to von Rad, and represent the final stages in the compilation of the materials.

M. Noth (*Überlieferungsgeschichte des Pentateuch*, 1948) has approximated some of the results of the Uppsala school of Engnell *et al.* without abandoning a documentary approach. Rather, he has paid close attention to the history of the oral traditions which lie behind the documents, while maintaining an approach to J, E, and P which is quite conventional. Perhaps his divergence from the Wellhausenian tradition is best seen in his refusal to recognize a 'Hexateuch' and his removal of most of Deuteronomy from the province of Pentateuchal criticism.

(v) *The evidence of archaeology*. The march of modern archaeology has contributed to the re-evaluation of the documentary hypothesis. The basic reliability of the historical narratives has been confirmed time and again, especially in the patriarchal period. (See H. H. Rowley, 'Recent Discovery and the Patriarchal Age' in *The Servant of the Lord*, 1954.) The evolutionary reconstruction of Israel's history and religion has been questioned more than once by outstanding archaeologists such as W. F. Albright (*e.g. From the Stone Age to Christianity*, 1957, pp. 88 ff., 282) and C. H. Gordon (*e.g. Ugaritic Literature*, 1949, pp. 5–7; 'Higher Critics and Forbidden Fruit', *Christianity Today*, 23 November 1959). A drastic re-appraisal of the documentary hypothesis from the standpoint of Israel's religion is found in the researches of Yehezkel Kaufmann, who affirms the antiquity of P and its priority to D. Furthermore, he separates Genesis from the rest of the Pentateuch, maintaining that it is 'a stratum in itself whose material is on the whole most ancient' (*The Religion of Israel*, 1960, p. 208).

e. The position today

The insights gained from these criticisms of the Graf–Wellhausen hypothesis, together with the continuing researches of its exponents, have resulted in considerable modification of the old theory. The simple evolutionary views of Israel's history and religion have been cast aside. The basic authenticity of the patriarchal stories is recognized by many scholars, since the light of archaeology has illuminated the setting of these stories. The Egyptian *milieu* of the Joseph cycle and the Exodus account has been established by archaeological, literary, and linguistic considerations (*cf.* A. S. Yahuda, *The Language of the Pentateuch in its Relation to Egyptian*, 1931; C. H. Gordon, *The World of the Old Testament*, 1958, p. 139). The rôle of Moses (*q.v.*) as the great lawgiver and the dominant figure in Israel's religion has been reaffirmed.

Though not discarded, the documentary theory has been modified by contemporary scholars. The development of each document is exceedingly complex and is generally considered to represent a whole 'school' rather than a single author. The growth of the various documents is not consecutive but parallel, since there are ancient elements found in each, as the use of pentateuchal elements by the prophets indicates (*cf.* Aalders, *op. cit.*, pp. 111–138). Minute dissections of verses and positive assignment of their parts to diverse sources have generally been abandoned. These modifications in the documentary hypothesis should be viewed by conservatives as a medical chart, not as an obituary. The Wellhausenian theory is still very much alive and remains a constant challenge to orthodox scholarship, which has sometimes been content to take comfort in the reactions against the documentary hypothesis without producing a thorough introduction to the Pentateuch, which states positively the evidence for the basic unity of the law while taking into full consideration the indications of diversity on which the documentary theory is based.

Aalders' studies have broken fresh ground and point the way for further advance. Of particular interest are his recognition of post-Mosaic and non-Mosaic elements in the Pentateuch (*e.g.* Gn. xiv. 14, xxxvi. 31; Ex. xi. 3, xvi. 35; Nu. xii. 3, xxi. 14, 15, xxxii. 34 ff.; Dt. ii. 12, xxxiv. 1–12) and his awareness of the fact that neither Testament ascribes the entire work to Moses, although both attribute substantial parts of it to him. The great legal codes, for instance, are credited specifically to Moses (*e.g.* Ex. xx. 2–xxiii. 33, xxxiv. 11–26; Dt. v–xxvi; *cf.* Dt. xxxi. 9, 24), as is the Israelites' itinerary mentioned in Nu. xxxiii. 2. As far as the Genesis stories are concerned, Moses may or may not have been the one who compiled them from their written and oral forms. The evidences of post-Mosaic editing of the Pentateuch are found in the references cited above, and especially in the mention of such ancient documents as 'the book of the wars of the Lord' (Nu. xxi. 14). It is difficult to date the final redaction of the Pentateuch. Aalders' suggestion that it took place some time within the reigns of Saul and David is credible, although some further allowance should probably be made for the modernizing of vocabulary and style.

III. THE RELIGIOUS MESSAGE OF THE PENTATEUCH

'*The Pentateuch must be defined as a document which gives Israel its understanding, its aetiology of life*. Here, through narrative, poetry, prophecy, law, God's will concerning Israel's task in the world is revealed' (A. Bentzen, *Introduction to the Old Testament*[2], 1952, II, p. 77). A record of revelation and response, the Pentateuch testifies to the saving acts of God who is sovereign Lord of history and nature. The central act of God in the Pentateuch (and indeed the Old Testament) is the Exodus from Egypt (*q.v.*). Here God broke in upon the consciousness of the Israelites and revealed Himself as the redeeming God. Insights gained from this revelation enabled them under Moses' leadership to re-evaluate the traditions of their ancestors and see in them the budding of God's dealings which had bloomed so brilliantly in the liberation from Egypt.

Having powerfully and openly proved Himself as Lord in the Exodus, God led the Israelites into the realization that He was the creator and sustainer of the universe as well as the ruler of history. The order is important: a knowledge of the *Redeemer* led to a knowledge of the *Creator*; an understanding of the God of *grace* prompted an understanding of the God of *nature*. The display of control over nature apparent in the plagues, the crossing of the sea, and the sustenance in the wilderness may well have influenced the Israelites to view God as Lord of nature as well as of history.

God's grace is not only revealed in His deliverance and guidance, but in the giving of the law and the initiation of the covenant. Israel's pledge of obedience, her oath of loyalty to God and His will is her response; but even her response is a gift of God's grace, for it is He who, though free from obligation, has fixed the terms of the covenant and provided the sacrificial system as a means of spanning the gap between Himself and His people. God's grace demands a total recognition of His Lordship, a complete obedience to His will in every sphere of life. This demand is gracious because it involves what is good for Israel, what will help her realize her true potential, and what she could not discover without divine revelation.

Whatever the origin of the Pentateuch, it stands now as a document possessing a rich inner unity. It is the record of God's revelation in history and His Lordship over history. It testifies both to Israel's response and to her failure to respond. It witnesses to God's holiness, which separates Him from men, and His gracious love, which binds Him to them on His terms. See GENESIS, EXODUS, LEVITICUS, NUMBERS, DEUTERONOMY.

BIBLIOGRAPHY. A. T. Chapman, *An Introduction to the Pentateuch*, 1911; G. Ch. Aalders, *A Short Introduction to the Pentateuch*, 1949; O. T. Allis, *The Five Books of Moses*[2], 1949; A. Bentzen, *Introduction to the Old Testament*, II, 1952, pp. 9–80; B. D. Eerdmans, *Alttestamentliche Studien*, I–IV, 1908–12; H. F. Hahn, *The Old Testament in Modern Research*, 1956; Y. Kaufmann, *The Religion of Israel*, 1960, pp. 153–211; W. J. Martin, *Stylistic Criteria and the Analysis of the Pentateuch*, 1955; J. A. Motyer, *The Revelation of the Divine Name*, 1959; A. Noordtzy, 'The Old Testament Problem', *BS*, 1940–1; C. R. North, 'Pentateuchal Criticism', *OTMS*, pp. 48–83; N. H. Ridderbos, 'Reversals of Old Testament Criticism', in *Revelation and the Bible*, ed. C. F. H. Henry, 1958; H. H. Rowley, 'Moses and the Decalogue', *BJRL*, XXXIV, 1951, pp. 81–118; *id.*, *The Biblical Doctrine of Election*, 1950; W. Rudolph, *Der 'Elohist' von Exodus bis Josua*, *BZAW*, LXVIII, 1938; P. Volz and W. Rudolph, *Der Elohist als Erzähler: ein Irrweg der Pentateuchkritik?*, *BZAW*, LXIII, 1933; J. Wellhausen, *Prolegomena to the History of Ancient Israel*, E.T. 1885, reprinted 1957; G. E. Wright, *God Who Acts*, 1952; *id.*, *The Old Testament against its Environment*, 1950; P. J. Wiseman, *New Discoveries in Babylonia about Genesis*, 1936; J. S. Wright, *How Moses Compiled Genesis: A Suggestion*, 1946; E. Robertson, *The Old Testament Problem*, 1950; R. Brinker, *The Influence of Sanctuaries in Early Israel*, 1946.

D.A.H.

PENTECOST, FEAST OF. In Lv. xxiii. 16 LXX reads *pentēkonta hēmeras* for the Hebrew *ḥᵃmiššîm yôm*, 'fifty days', referring to the number of days from the offering of the barley sheaf at the beginning of the Passover. On the fiftieth day was the Feast of Pentecost. Since the time elapsed was seven weeks, it was called *ḥaḡ šāḇuʿôṯ*, 'feast of weeks' (Ex. xxxiv. 22; Dt. xvi. 10). It marks the completion of the barley harvest, which began when the sickle was first put to the grain (Dt. xvi. 9), and when the sheaf was waved 'the morrow after the sabbath' (Lv. xxiii. 11). It is also called *ḥaḡ haqqāṣîr*, 'feast of harvest', and *yôm habbikkûrîm*, 'day of the firstfruits' (Ex. xxiii. 16; Nu. xxviii. 26). The feast is not limited to the times of the Pentateuch, but its observance is indicated in the days of Solomon (2 Ch. viii. 13), as the second of the three annual festivals (*cf.* Dt. xvi. 16).

The feast was proclaimed as a 'holy convocation' on which no servile work was to be done, and at which every male Israelite was required to appear at the sanctuary (Lv. xxiii. 21). Two baked loaves of new, fine, leavened flour were brought out of the dwellings and waved by the priest before the Lord, together with the offerings of animal sacrifice for sin- and peace-offerings (Lv. xxiii. 17–20). As a day of joy (Dt. xvi. 16) it is evident that on it the devout Israelite expressed gratitude for the blessings of the grain harvest and experienced heart-felt fear of the Lord (Je. v. 24). But it was the thanksgiving and fear of a redeemed people, for the service was not without sin- and peace-offerings, and was, moreover, a reminder of their deliverance from Egypt (Dt. xvi. 12) as God's covenant people (Lv. xxiii. 22). The ground of acceptance of the offering presupposes the removal of sin and reconciliation with God.

In the inter-testamental period and later, Pentecost was regarded as the anniversary of the law-giving at Sinai (Jubilees i. 1 with vi. 17; TB, *Pesaḥim* 68b; Midrash, *Tanḥuma* 26c). The Sadducees celebrated it on the fiftieth day (inclusive reckoning) from the first Sunday after Passover (taking the 'sabbath' of Lv. xxiii. 15 to be the weekly sabbath); their reckoning regulated the public observance so long as the Temple stood, and the Church is therefore justified in commemorating the first Christian Pentecost on a Sunday (Whit Sunday). The Pharisees, however, interpreted the 'sabbath' of Lv. xxiii. 15 as the Festival of Unleavened Bread (*cf.* Lv. xxiii. 7), and their reckoning became normative in Judaism after AD 70, so that in the Jewish calendar Pentecost now falls on various days of the week.

In the New Testament there are three references to Pentecost: (1) Acts ii. 1 (Gk. *tēn hēmeran tēs pentēkostēs*). On this day, after the resurrection and ascension of Christ (*c.* AD 30), the disciples were gathered in a house in Jerusalem, and were visited with signs from heaven. The Holy Spirit descended upon them, and new life, power, and blessing were evident, which Peter explained was in fulfilment of the prophecy of Joel. (2) Acts xx. 16. Paul was determined not to spend time in Asia and made speed to be in Jerusalem by the day of Pentecost (AD 57). (3) 1 Cor. xvi. 8. Paul purposed to stay at Ephesus until Pentecost (AD

54 or 55), because an effectual door was opened to him for his ministry.

BIBLIOGRAPHY. Mishnah *Menaḥoṯ* x. 3; Tosefta *Menaḥoṯ* x. 23, 528; TB, *Menaḥoṯ* 65a; L. Finkelstein, *The Pharisees*, 1946, pp. 115 ff. D.F.

PENUEL. 'The face of God' was the name that Jacob gave to the place where he crossed the Jabbok on his way back to meet Esau. It is possible that it had been called Penuel before, perhaps after a peculiarly shaped rock, and that Jacob endorsed the name as a result of his experience with the angel (*cf.* 2 Sa. v. 20). The blessing which he sought (Gn. xxxii. 26) materialized in Esau's conciliatory attitude (*cf.* xxxiii. 10: 'Truly to see your face is like seeing the face of God').

That Penuel was the site of an important pass is shown by the fact that a tower was built there, which Gideon destroyed after defeating the Midianites (Jdg. viii. 8 ff.), and Jeroboam rebuilt the city there, presumably to defend the invader's route from the east to his new capital at Shechem. The exact site is unknown, but S. Merrill, *East of Jordan*, 1881, pp. 390–392, makes a good case for the ancient ruins 4 miles east of Succoth on two hills called Tulul ed-Dahab. J.B.J.

PEOPLE. 1. *le'ôm* is occasionally used in the singular, frequently in the plural (*le'ummîm*). It may mean: (i) a race or ethnic aggregate (Gn. xxv. 23, singular and plural); (ii) the sum total of the populace subject to a ruler, the same concept from a different viewpoint (Pr. xiv. 28, singular); (iii) the totality of an ethnic community considered as the vehicle of judgment and feeling (Pr. xi. 26, singular); (iv) exceptionally, the Jewish people (Is. li. 4, singular); (v) frequently, in the plural, the non-Jewish nations (*e.g.* Is. lv. 4).

2. *gôy*, 'nation', 'people', came by association rather than etymology to mean specifically the Gentiles. When the word is applied to Israelites it likens them, in their backsliding and religious unfaithfulness, to Gentiles (Jdg. ii. 20; Is. i. 4; *et frequenter*). The metaphorical usage for the swarm of locusts in Joel i. 6 is vividly descriptive. LXX regularly uses *ethnos* for *gôy*, yet the New Testament occasionally uses *ethnos* for Israel, reminding us that acquired and artificial associations cannot be too rigidly pressed.

3. With trifling exceptions (*cf.* Gn. xxvi. 11, 'Philistines'; Ex. ix. 15, 'Egyptians') *'am*, 'people', came to be applied so exclusively to Israel as the chosen race that the terms became almost synonymous. Once again, this meaning is acquired, not intrinsic. The LXX equivalent is *laos*. Further exceptions are the metaphorical usages for ants and conies in community (Pr. xxx. 25 f.). The unusual negative of Dt. xxxii. 21, directly attached to the noun, denies to a physical people those moral and spiritual characteristics which justify the name (*cf.* 'Lo-ammi', Ho. i. 9). The biblical phrase *'am hā'āreṣ* means in the earlier books the common 'people of the land', as distinct from rulers and aristocracy. In the Ezra–Nehemiah period the phrase sharpened to focus those Palestinians whose Judaism was mixed or suspect, with whom the more scrupulous Jews could not intermarry; *cf.* Ezr. ix. 1, 2, *etc.* In the rabbinic literature the term—now used in the singular of an individual, in the plural (*'ammê hā'āreṣ*) of a class—came to mean specifically all those who failed to observe the whole traditional law in all its details. A clear premonition of the rabbinic contempt for such persons is seen in Jn. vii. 49.

4. The common New Testament equivalent to *'am* is *laos* or *dēmos*, as opposed to *ochlos*, which merely means a crowd. R.A.S.

PEOR. 1. A mountain somewhere to the north of the Dead Sea and opposite Jericho, described as looking towards the desert, but its location is not certainly identified. It was the last place from which Balaam blessed Israel (Nu. xxiii. 28). See Joussen-Savignac, *Mission en Arabie*, pp. 2, 650 f.

2. The name of a deity, more fully Baal-Peor (*q.v.*), to which the Israelites were attracted (Nu. xxv. 3) and for the worship of which they were severely punished. Their punishment left a vivid impression and was recalled as a warning and example (Nu. xxxi. 16; Dt. iv. 3; Jos. xxii. 17). M.A.M.

PERAEA. A district in Transjordan, corresponding roughly to the Gilead (*q.v.*) of the Old Testament. It is never mentioned by name in the New Testament—that is left to Josephus—but is the district referred to several times (*e.g.* Mt. xix. 1) as the land 'beyond Jordan'. The name Peraea came into use after the Exile, to denote an area east of the Jordan about 10 miles wide, stretching from the river Arnon in the south to some point between the Jabbok and the Yarmuk in the north. It comprised essentially the edge of the 3,000-foot scarp overlooking the Jordan, with its towns, and was thus a highland region, with adequate (30 inches per annum) rainfall and tree cover in its higher parts. See figs. 156, 158. At intermediate elevations there were olives and vines, and cultivation tailed off eastwards through the wheatfields and then the steppe pastures of lower lands. It was evidently an attractive region in Old Testament times, for after seeing it and adjacent areas the tribes of Gad and Reuben (Nu. xxxii. 1–5) lost interest in crossing Jordan with their cattle.

In the time of Christ Peraea was occupied by Jews and ruled by Herod Antipas, and by Jews it was regarded as possessing equality of status with Judaea and Galilee. As it adjoined both of these across the Jordan, it was possible by traversing its length to follow an all-Jewish route from Galilee to Judaea, thus by-passing the territory of the Samaritans. J.H.P.

PERDITION (*apōleia*, 'loss', 'destruction'). A word employed by AV eight times in the New

Testament, usually in the sense of 'destruction' and with special reference to the fate of the wicked and their loss of eternal life (Phil. i. 28; 1 Tim. vi. 9; Heb. x. 39; 2 Pet. iii. 7; Rev. xvii. 8, 11). See HELL, ESCHATOLOGY.

In addition, the phrase 'son of perdition' occurs twice, a form of speech in which the Jews often expressed a man's destiny (*e.g.* 'sons of light', 'children of disobedience'; *cf.* Mt. ix. 15, xxiii. 15; Lk. x. 6, RVmg). It is applied to Judas Iscariot (Jn. xvii. 12) in a vivid sense which the English does not fully convey as meaning literally 'not one perished but the son of perishing'. The term is used also by Paul to describe the 'man of sin' (2 Thes. ii. 3), for which see ANTICHRIST. The phrase 'sons of perdition' is found in Jubilees x. 3, with reference to those who perished in the flood.

The Greek word stands in direct antithesis to full and complete blessedness (*sōtēria*). J.D.D.

PEREZ, PEREZITES. Perez (*pereṣ*), one of the sons of Judah by Tamar his daughter-in-law (1 Ch. ii. 4, iv. 1), was so named because though his twin Zarah put out his hand first, Perez was the first delivered, and it was said that he had 'broken forth' (*pāraṣ*; Gn. xxxviii. 29). He was the father of Hezron and Hamul (Gn. xlvi. 12; Nu. xxvi. 21; 1 Ch. ii. 5), whose descendants were called Perezites (*parṣî*; Nu. xxvi. 20; AV 'Pharzites'; see also Ne. xi. 4, 6). Through him and Hezron passed the genealogy of the Messiah (1 Ch. ix. 4; Ru. iv. 18; Mt. i. 3; Lk. iii. 33; *cf.* Ru. iv. 12). The name occurs in LXX and New Testament as *Phares*, and this name is taken over unchanged into the AV New Testament. In the Old Testament the AV gives 'Pharez' in all occurrences except 1 Ch. xxvii. 3, and Ne. xi. 4–6. In the later EVV the form Perez is used throughout. It may be compared with the Assyrian personal name *Parṣi* found in documents of the 8th century BC. See K. Tallqvist, *Assyrian Personal Names*, 1914, p. 180. T.C.M.

PERFECTION. The biblical idea of perfection is of a state of ideal wholeness or completion, in which any disabilities, shortcomings, or defects that may have existed before have been eliminated or left behind.

In the Old Testament, two Hebrew roots express this idea: *šlm* and *tmm*. (For the literal sense of the adjective *šālēm*, see Dt. xxv. 15, xxvii. 6; for that of *tāmîm*, see Lv. iii. 9, xxiii. 15.) In the New Testament the usual adjective (nineteen times) is *teleios* (noun *teleiotēs*, Col. iii. 14; Heb. vi. 1), which expresses the thought of having reached the appropriate or appointed *telos* ('end' in the sense of 'goal', 'purpose'). The corresponding verb, *teleioō* (sixteen times in this sense), means to bring into such a condition. In secular Greek *teleios* means also: (i) adult, full-grown, as opposed to immature and infantile, and (ii), in connection with mystery-cults, fully initiated. The former sense shines through in 1 Cor. xiv. 20; Eph. iv. 13; Heb. v. 14, *cf.* vi. 1; the latter in 1 Cor. ii. 6 and perhaps Phil. iii. 15; Col. i. 28. Two adjectives of similar meaning are: (i) *artios* (2 Tim. iii. 17; AV 'perfect', RV 'complete'), denoting ability and readiness to meet all demands made upon one, and (ii) *holoklēros* (Jas. i. 4, with *teleios*; 1 Thes. v. 23, RV 'entire', RSV 'sound'), for which Arndt gives 'whole, complete, undamaged, intact, blameless'. The New Testament also uses (seven times) the verb *katartizō*, translated 'perfect' in AV, meaning 'put in order', or 'bring to a fit state', by training, or supplying some lack, or correcting some fault.

Perfection is a relative term, meaning simply the attainment of a due end, or the enjoyment of an ideal state. What that end and state is varies in different cases. The Bible speaks of perfection in three distinct connections.

I. THE PERFECTION OF GOD

Scripture speaks of God (Mt. v. 48), His 'work' (Dt. xxxii. 4), His 'way' (2 Sa. xxii. 31 = Ps. xviii. 30), and His 'law' (Ps. xix. 7; Jas. i. 25) as perfect. In each context some feature of His manifested moral glory is in view, and the thought is that what God says and does is wholly free from faults and worthy of all praise. In Mt. v. 48, Christ holds up the ideal conduct of the heavenly Father (particularly, in the context, His kindness to those who oppose Him) as a pattern which His children must imitate.

II. THE PERFECTION OF CHRIST

The writer to the Hebrews speaks of the incarnate Son of God as having been made 'perfect through sufferings' (Heb. ii. 10). The reference here is not to any personal probation of Jesus as man, but to His being fitted by His experience of the power of temptation and the costliness of obedience for the high-priestly ministry to which God had called Him (Heb. v. 7–10, *cf.* vii. 28, RV). As High Priest, having 'offered one sacrifice for sins for ever' (Heb. x. 12), He became 'the author of eternal salvation unto all them that obey him' (Heb. v. 9), securing for them by His intercession constant access to God (Heb. vii. 25, x. 19 ff.) and giving them the constant sympathy and help that they need in their constant temptations (Heb. iv. 14 ff.). It was His own first-hand experience of temptation that fitted Him to fulfil this latter ministry (Heb. ii. 17 f., v. 2, 7 ff.).

III. THE PERFECTION OF MAN

This is spoken of with reference (*a*) to God's covenant relationship with man and (*b*) to His work of grace in man.

a. God's covenant relationship with man

The Bible speaks of *man's perfection in the covenant with God.* This is the perfection which the Old Testament demands of God's people (Gn. xvii. 1; Dt. xviii. 13) and ascribes to individual saints (Noah, Gn. vi. 9; Asa, 1 Ki. xv. 14; Job, Jb. i. 1): loyal, sincere, whole-hearted obedience to the known will of their gracious God. It is faith at work, maintaining a right relationship with God by reverent worship and service. This perfection is essentially a matter of the heart (1 Ki. viii. 61; 2 Ki. xx. 3; 1 Ch. xxix. 9); outward conformity to God's commands is not enough if the heart is not perfect (2 Ch. xxv. 2). Perfection is regularly linked with uprightness, as its natural outward expression (Jb. i. 1, 8, ii. 3; Ps. xxxvii. 37; Pr. ii. 21). In Mt. xix. 21 *teleios*, as well as expressing the negative thought, 'lacking nothing', would seem to carry the positive meaning, 'sincerely and truly in covenant with God'.

The Bible also speaks of *God's perfecting of His covenant relation with man.* This is the perfecting of men through Christ with which the writer to the Hebrews deals. 'The perfecting of men refers to their covenant condition. . . . To perfect . . . is to put the People into the true covenant relation of worshippers of the Lord, to bring them into His full fellowship' (A. B. Davidson, *Hebrews*, p. 208). God did this by replacing the old covenant, priesthood, tabernacle, and sacrifices by something better. The 'old covenant' in Hebrews means the Mosaic system for establishing living fellowship between God and His people; but, says the writer, it could never 'perfect' them in this relationship, for it could not give full assurance of the remission of all sins (Heb. vii. 11, 18, ix. 9, x. 1–4). Under the new covenant, however, on the ground of Christ's single sacrifice of Himself, believers receive God's assurance that He will remember their sins no more (x. 11–18). Thus they are 'perfected for ever' (verse 14). This perfection of fellowship with God is something that Old Testament saints did not know on earth (xi. 40)—though, through Christ, they enjoy it now, in the heavenly Jerusalem (xii. 23 f.).

b. God's work of grace in man

The Bible speaks of *God's perfecting of His people in the image of Christ.* God means those who through faith enjoy fellowship with Him to grow from spiritual infancy to a maturity (perfection) in which they will lack nothing of the full stature of Christ, in whose likeness they are being renewed (Col. iii. 10). They are to grow till they are, in this sense, complete (*cf.* 1 Pet. ii. 2; Heb. v. 14, vi. 1; Gal. iii. 14; Eph. iv. 13; Col. iv. 12). This thought has both a corporate and an individual aspect: the church corporately is to become 'a perfect man' (Eph. iv. 13, *cf.* ii. 15; Gal. iii. 28), and the individual Christian will be 'made perfect' (Phil. iii. 12, RV). In either case the conception is Christological and eschatological. The realm of perfection is 'in Christ' (Col. i. 28), and perfection of fellowship with Christ, and likeness to Christ, is a divine gift that will not be enjoyed till the day of His coming, the Church's completing, and the Christian's resurrection (*cf.* Eph. iv. 12–16; Phil. iii. 10–14; Col. iii. 4; 1 Jn. iii. 2). Meanwhile, however, mature and vigorous Christians may be said to have attained a relative perfection in the realms of spiritual insight (Phil. iii. 15, *cf.* verse 12), tempered Christian character (Jas. i. 4), and confident love towards God and men (1 Jn. iv. 12, 17 f.).

The Bible nowhere relates the idea of perfection directly to law, nor equates it directly with sinlessness. Absolute sinlessness is a goal which Christians must seek (*cf.* Mt. v. 48; 2 Cor. vii. 1; Rom. vi. 19) but which they do not as yet find (Jas. iii. 2; 1 Jn. i. 8–ii. 2). No doubt when the Christian is perfected in glory he will be sinless, but to equate the biblical idea of perfection with sinlessness and then to argue that, because the Bible calls some men perfect, therefore sinlessness on earth must be a practical possibility, would be to darken counsel. The present perfection which, according to Scripture, some Christians attain is a matter, not of sinlessness, but of strong faith, joyful patience, and overflowing love. See SANCTIFICATION.

BIBLIOGRAPHY. *Arndt*; R. C. Trench, *New Testament Synonyms*[10], 1880, pp. 74–77; B. B. Warfield, *Perfectionism*, I, 1931, pp. 113–301; R. N. Flew, *The Idea of Perfection in Christian Theology*, 1934, pp. 1–117; V. Taylor, *Forgiveness and Reconciliation*, 1941, chapter v; commentaries on Hebrews by A. B. Davidson, 1882, pp. 207–209, and Westcott[3], 1903, pp. 64–68; J. Wesley, *A Plain Account of Christian Perfection*, 1777.

J.I.P.

PERFUMER. See COSMETICS AND PERFUMERY.

PERGA. An ancient city of unknown foundation in Pamphylia (*q.v.*), well-sited in an extensive valley, watered by the Cestrus. It was the religious capital of Pamphylia, like Ephesus, a 'cathedral city' of Artemis, whose temple stood on a nearby hill. Like most cities on that pirate-ridden coast, Perga stands a little inland, and was served by a river-harbour. Attaleia, founded in the 2nd century BC, later served as Perga's port, but also absorbed her prosperity. Some ruins remain, giving a pleasant impression of the ancient Perga, but Attaleia survives as an active port, the modern Adalia, one of the beauty-spots of Anatolia, so completely did Attalus' foundation overwhelm the more ancient towns. E.M.B.

PERGAMUM. A city of the Roman province of Asia, in the west of what is now Asiatic Turkey. See fig. 26. It occupied a commanding position near the seaward end of the broad valley of the Caicus, and was probably the site of a settlement from a very early date. When Philetaerus revolted against the Thracian Lysimachus in 282 BC it became the capital of his kingdom, which in 133 BC was bequeathed by Attalus III to the Romans, who formed it into the province of Asia. The first, and for some time the only, temple of the imperial cult was built there (about 29 BC) in honour of Rome and Augustus. This and other later honours, besides its former capital status, indicate that it was the official administrative capital of the province, even though Ephesus or Smyrna may have been the first city from a commercial point of view. As such, it was the centre of the official religion, and the seat of imperial authority and justice in the province. It was also a centre of four of the greatest pagan cults, of Zeus, Athena, Dionysus, and Asclepius. A small town (Bergama) still stands on the plain below the site of the ancient city.

In the letters to the 'seven churches of Asia' Pergamum is listed third (Rev. i. 11). This is appropriate if the order is taken to be geographical: starting at the great port of Ephesus, the list follows the coast road north through Smyrna to Pergamum, and then turns south-east along another important road through Thyatira, Sardis, and Philadelphia to Laodicea, which is on the great main road running back direct to Ephesus. Pergamum is the place 'where Satan's seat is' (Rev. ii. 13). This can hardly refer to the pagan cults—though relations with these may be involved in the 'doctrine of Balaam' (verse 14)—for the cults were equally strong in other cities in the province. Far more probably it alludes to the official position of Pergamum as the centre of the imperial religion. Pergamum was seen as the seat of the power of evil, because in the imperial cult the God-given power of the State had been harnessed to the blasphemous worship of a man. Worship of the emperor had been made the touchstone of civic loyalty, so that a faithful Christian, however loyal to the secular authority of the State, was branded as a traitor. Antipas (verse 13) is probably cited as a representative (perhaps the first) of those who were brought to Pergamum as suspects and executed there after refusal to worship the emperor.

In view of this perversion of the divine authority of the State, the Christ is described as the real and ultimate possessor of this authority, symbolized by the sharp two-edged sword (verse 12). The meaning of the 'white stone' (verse 17) is uncertain; a small cube, *tessara hospitalis*, of the kind which was often used as a ticket, is intended, and perhaps symbolizes the permanent and individual covenant between Christ and the faithful believer. See W. M. Ramsay, *The Letters to the Seven Churches of Asia*, 1904, chapters xxi, xxii.

M.J.S.R.

PERIZZITES. These are mentioned: (1) among the occupants of Canaan generally (Gn. xv. 20; Ex. iii. 8; Dt. vii. 1, xx. 17; Jos. iii. 10, ix. 1; Jdg. iii. 5; 1 Ki. ix. 20; 2 Ch. viii. 7; Ezr. ix. 1; Ne. ix. 8); (2) with the Jebusites, *etc.*, in the hills (Jos. xi. 3); (3) with the Canaanites near Bethel (Gn. xiii. 7), near Shechem (Gn. xxxiv. 30), and in the Judaean hills (Jdg. i. 4 f.); (4) with the Rephaim (Jos. xvii. 15). (Noth thinks 'Rephaim' implies a Transjordanic setting, but this is debatable.) They were apparently hill-dwellers; this suits the interpretation of 'Perizzites', favoured by most commentators, as 'villagers' (from *perāzâ*, 'hamlet'), rather than as the name of an ethnic group. *BDB* is cautious, however, as *perizzî* occurs only in the contexts enumerated, and *perāzî* only in Dt. iii. 5; 1 Sa. vi. 18 (LXX 'Perizzites'); and Est. ix. 19; *cf.*, perhaps, *perāzôn* (Jdg. v. 7, 11). Gn. x. 15 ff. does not mention Perizzites among the branches of the Canaanites.

J.P.U.L.

PERSECUTION. As encountered by Christians, this was nothing new. It was part of their Jewish heritage. The association of witness and suffering, begun as early as the second part of Isaiah, was crystallized in the Seleucid struggle. A theory of martyrdom rewarded by personal immortality grew up till it dominated the outlook of the Jews towards the Roman government (4 Macc. xvii. 8 ff.). The possibility of death for Torah became accepted as a demand of Judaism. Thus the Jews were not averse to martyrdom; despite official Roman toleration of their religion, their cohesiveness, non-co-operation, and uncanny financial success won them widespread hatred and spasmodic persecution, especially outside Palestine: pogroms were common in Alexandria. This legacy was taken over by the Christians. Their willingness to face suffering was intensified by the example of Jesus and by the association of persecution with the longed-for end of the age (Mk. xiii. 7–13). Even so, we must ask what aroused such animosity towards them among both the Jews and the Romans.

a. Opposition from the Jews

This gradually grew in intensity. The preaching of a crucified Messiah whose death was publicly blamed on the Jewish leaders was highly provocative. Even so, the people were favourable (Acts ii. 46 f., v. 14) and the Pharisees moderate (Acts v. 34 ff., xxiii. 6 ff.), while opposition arose, naturally enough, among the Sadducees (Acts iv. 1, 6, v. 17). Stephen's preaching of the transitoriness of the law (Acts vi. 14) turned public opinion and brought about the first persecution in Jerusalem and elsewhere, *e.g.* Damascus. In AD 44 James was executed by Herod Agrippa, and throughout the Acts the Jews appear as Paul's most vehement enemies. This attitude could only have been made worse by the Apostolic Council which repudiated the need for circumcision, and it culminated in the excommunication of Christians at Jamnia, *c.* AD 80.

b. Opposition from the Romans

Rome's attitude underwent a marked change. At first, as we see in Acts, she gave Christians toleration and even encouragement. This soon gave way to fierce opposition. In Rome (Tac., *Ann.* xv. 44) such was their unpopularity by AD 64 that Nero could make them scapegoats for the fire. In Bithynia (Pliny, *Ep.* x. 96, 97) by *c.* AD 112 persistence in Christianity was a capital offence, though Trajan would not allow anonymous delation and he deprecated 'witch hunting'. Three explanations of this changed attitude have been suggested:

(i) That Christians were prosecuted only for specific offences, such as cannibalism, incendiarism, incest, magic, illicit assembly, and *majestas* (in their case, refusal to sacrifice to the *numen* of the emperor). There is, indeed, evidence that they were accused on all these counts, but 1 Pet. ii. 12, iv. 14–17; Pliny, *Ep.* x. 97; and Suet., *Nero* 16, all make clear that at an early date the *nomen ipsum* of Christian, irrespective of the *cohaerentia flagitia* associated with it in the popular mind, was punishable.

(ii) That there was a general law throughout the Empire, the *institutum Neronianum*, which proscribed Christianity. Tertullian makes this claim, and says that this was the only one of Nero's *acta* not rescinded later (*Ad. Nat.* 1. 7, see also *Apol.* 5), and the evidence of Suetonius, 1 Peter, and Revelation is patient of this interpretation. However, Christianity was probably not important enough to evoke such a general law, and if there was one it is hard to explain Pliny's ignorance of it, Trajan's failure to mention it, the property rights enjoyed by the Church prior to the Decian persecution, and the remarkable lack of uniformity in its execution.

(iii) That persecution was at the discretion of the governor, who acted only in response to private accusation: there was no public prosecutor in Roman society. Whatever the formal charge, it is clear that by Pliny's time active membership of an organization believed to be criminal, and therefore, like the Bacchanals and the Druids, banned because in all three cult and *scelera* appeared indistinguishable, constituted an actionable offence, and *contumacia*, persistent refusal to recant, met with death. The competence of proconsuls and city prefects in *crimina extra ordinem* has been shown in recent years to have been very great. If a governor wished to take action against Christians he had the Neronian precedent to guide him and his coercive *imperium* to support him. Alternatively, it lay within his discretion, like Gallio (Acts xviii. 14–16), to refuse jurisdiction. If in doubt he could refer to the emperor, whose rescript would be binding on him as long as he remained in the province, though not necessarily upon his successors.

It is because the governors enjoyed such discretion that Tertullian addressed his Apology not to the emperor but to the governor: for it was in his hands that the remedy lay. This accounts for the spasmodic nature of persecution until the days of Decius. It depended so much on the policy of the governor and whether the extent of the unpopularity of Christians in the province was such as to drive private individuals to prosecute them. There is no satisfactory evidence (despite Orosius, vii. 7) for believing that there was any general action against Christians throughout the Empire under Nero, though the sect seems to have become *illicita* in Rome itself (Suet., *Nero* 16). The actual evidence for a Domitianic persecution of the Church is precarious despite the invective heaped on that emperor by the Fathers. A broad generalization in Dio. (lxvii. 14), the death of Flavius Clemens, who was possibly, and Acilius Glabrio, who was probably, a Christian, and the banishment of Domitilla, is about all that can be summoned. But it is quite possible that Domitian, who minutely inspected and vigorously exacted the Jewish revenue (Suet., *Domit.* 12), discovered uncircumcised Christians sheltering under the religious privileges of the Jews and instituted against them a general persecution of which we have vivid traces in the Apocalypse, if this is to be dated under Domitian rather than Nero.

Persecution was therefore restricted by three factors: (i) that the Roman governors were reluctant to admit charges concerning private religious opinions (*superstitiones*) and tried to confine their attention to real offences; (ii) that accusations had to be made personally and publicly—and to bring a capital charge was both dangerous and difficult; (iii) that in each province only one man, the governor, could pass the death sentence.

These three factors combined to protect the majority of Christians long enough for the Church to become firmly established throughout the empire.

Bibliography. Recent studies include T. W. Manson, 'Martyrs and Martyrdom', *BJRL*, XXXIX, 1956–7, pp. 463 ff.; H. B. Mattingley, *JTS* (NS), IX, 1958, pp. 26 ff.; F. W. Clayton, *CQ*, XLI, 1947, pp. 83 ff.; A. N. Sherwin-White, *JTS* (NS), III, 1952, pp. 199 ff.; H. Last, *JRS*, XXVII, 1937, pp. 80 ff.; E. M. Smallwood, *Classical Philology*, LI, 1956, pp. 5–11.

E.M.B.G.

PERSEVERANCE. The strictly biblical, as distinct from the later theological, significance of this term is indicated by the context of its sole occurrence in AV as a rendering of *proskarterēsis* in Eph. vi. 18. The implication of steadfastness, patience, persistence is confirmed by the use of the verb *proskartereō*, to attend constantly, continue unswervingly, adhere firmly, hold fast to (*MM*, p. 548). It is used in Mk. iii. 9 to describe a skiff quietly waiting to carry Jesus from the surging crowd, and in Acts x. 7 of the soldiers in Cornelius' bodyguard who were in uninterrupted attendance upon him. In its spiritual application it always has to do with continuance in the Christian way, particularly in relation to prayer (*cf.* Acts i. 14, ii. 42, 46, vi. 4, viii. 13; Rom. xii. 12, xiii. 6; Col. iv. 2).

No doctrinal undertones attach to the term in the New Testament. It relates simply to the continual and patient dependence of the Christian upon Christ. Our Lord's parable of the importunate widow is the most relevant commentary (*cf.* Lk. xviii. 1–8). Christian perseverance is only a quality in the believer because initially it is a gift of God. It is by His power that those who trust in Him are 'kept . . . through faith unto salvation ready to be revealed in the last time' (1 Pet. i. 5).

A.S.W.

PERSIA, PERSIANS. The Indo-European Persians, nomadic pastoralists from S Russia, probably entered the Iranian plateau late in the second millennium BC. In 836 BC Shalmaneser III of Assyria received tribute from rulers of a Parsua near Lake Urmia. His successor found the land of Parsuash in the south where several tribes finally settled. This area, east of the Persian Gulf, is still called Farsistan. Persepolis and Parsagarda were the chief towns (see map 9). Heb. *pāras*, 'Persia', refers to this land.

I. PERSIAN AND JEWISH HISTORY

The early traditions of the Persian people are recorded in the sacred book, the Zend-Avesta. The earliest recorded kings ruled from Anshan, north-west of Susa. The Achaemenes who was claimed as founder of the Dynasty by later kings probably reigned *c.* 680 BC. His grandson, Cyrus I, opposed Ashurbanipal of Assyria but later submitted. Cyrus II, grandson of Cyrus I, rebelled against his Median suzerain, Astyages, killing him and taking over his capital, Ecbatana (see ACHMETHA), in 550 BC. This success was followed by the subjugation of Anatolia and the conquest of Croesus of Lydia (547 BC). Cyrus then turned eastward to extend his realm into NW India. By 540 BC he was sufficiently strong to attack Babylonia. After several battles he entered Babylon in triumph on 29 October 539 BC, seventeen days after the city had fallen to his army (Dn. v. 30 f.; see CYRUS). The king soon returned to Susa, but his son Cambyses remained in Babylon to represent him in religious ceremonies. The whole empire was divided into large regions ruled by satraps (see SATRAP), chosen from Persian or Median nobles but with native officers under them (*cf.* Dn. vi). Various statues of gods which had been collected into Babylon by the last native king, Nabonidus (perhaps reflected in Is. xlvi. 1 f.), were returned to their own shrines. As there was no image of Yahweh to return to Jerusalem, Cyrus gave back to the Jews the precious vessels looted from the Temple by Nebuchadrezzar (Ezr. i. 7 ff.; *cf. DOTT*, pp. 92–94). More important, he gave royal authorization for the rebuilding of the Temple to any Jew who wished to return to Judah (Ezr. i. 1–4). One Sheshbazzar was appointed governor (Ezr. v. 14). He was evidently a special officer responsible to the king. The governor of the province of 'Across the River' (the country west of the Euphrates) was clearly unaware of Cyrus' edict when in 520 BC he attempted to delay the work. His letter went to his superior, the satrap who had charge of Babylon and the West. No record was found among the archives kept at Babylon, but a memorandum was found at Ecbatana, where Cyrus had resided during his first regnal year. Darius I (522–486 BC) confirmed the decree and ordered his officials to help the Jews.

Darius and his successor Xerxes I (486–465 BC) expended considerable energy in an attempt to conquer the Greeks of the Peloponnese, almost the only area remaining outside the Persian Empire in the known world, for Cambyses II (530–522 BC) had annexed Egypt in 525 BC. The defeat at Marathon (490 BC) by a small Greek army was the only rebuff suffered by Darius. His reorganization of the satrapies, his system of military commanders, and his introduction of coinage, legal, and postal systems lasted as long as the Empire. These facilities coupled with the considerable degree of autonomy allowed to subject peoples contributed greatly to the stability of the Empire and allowed such a small community as Judah to survive.

Fig. 164. Relief on glazed tiles of an archer-spearman of the Persian royal guard. From Susa, 5th century BC.

Under Artaxerxes I (465–424 BC) Jewish affairs had official representation at court. Ezra, it seems, was 'Secretary of State for Jewish Affairs' (Ezr. vii. 12). He was accredited as special envoy to reorganize the Temple services at Jerusalem (458 BC). The eager Jews were led on by the encouragement they received to exceed the terms of Ezra's commission and rebuild the city wall. This was reported to the king by the governor of Samaria, who evidently had some responsibility for Judah. The royal reply (Ezr. iv. 17–23) ordered the cessation of the work, for search of the records had shown that the city had revolted against earlier kings. Artaxerxes was faced with rebellion in Egypt (*c.* 460–454 BC), so he could not allow the construction of a fortress so near to that country. However, the royal cupbearer was a Jew, Nehemiah, who was able to reverse the effects of this decree by having himself appointed governor of Judah (Heb. *tiršāṯā'*, Ne. viii. 9; see GOVERNOR) with permission to rebuild the walls (445 BC). No record remains of relations between the Persian rulers and the Jews after this period. When the Persian Empire was in the power of Alexander (331 BC) the Jews simply transferred their allegiance from one monarch to another. See also EZRA, NEHEMIAH.

II. PERSIAN CULTURE

The Indo-European Persian language was written in a cuneiform script composed of fifty-one simple syllabic signs (see WRITING). This script was in use by *c.* 650 BC (gold tablet of Ariaramnes, R. Ghirshman, *Iran*, 1954, fig. 48). The imperial chancery used Aramaic language and characters for official communications (*e.g.* the letters in Ezra, *cf. DOTT*, pp. 256–269).

The luxury of the Persian court as described in the book of Esther (*q.v.*) is attested by objects found at several sites. A number of stone bas-reliefs depict the king and his courtiers and the tribute of the vanquished. Portraits of the different racial groups are especially fine examples of Persian stone carving. The Oxus treasure (now mostly in the British Museum) and other chance finds show the skill of goldsmiths and jewellers. Greek influences may be seen in some Persian works and Greek craftsmen appear among lists of palace dependants.

III. PERSIAN RELIGION

The early Persians revered gods of nature, fertility, and the heavens. The tribe of the Magi were nearly exclusively the priests. During the early 6th century BC Zoroaster proclaimed a religion of lofty moral ideals based on the principle 'Do good, hate evil'. For him there was one god, Ahura-mazda, the Good, represented by purifying fire and water. Opposed to the good was a dark power of Evil. This creed was adopted by Darius I, but soon became lost among the more ancient cults. Zoroaster's doctrines survived and were spread abroad. Their influence has been traced in the writings of early Judaism (see DEAD SEA SCROLLS) and, by some scholars, in the New Testament.

BIBLIOGRAPHY. A. T. Olmstead, *History of the Persian Empire*, 1948; R. Ghirshman, *Iran*, 1954; J. Bright, *A History of Israel*, 1960, Part Five.

A.R.M.

PESTILENCE. See PLAGUE.

PESTLE. See MORTAR AND PESTLE.

PETER.

I. EARLY BACKGROUND

Peter's original name was apparently the Hebrew Symeon (Acts xv. 14; 2 Pet. i. 1, RV): perhaps, like many Jews, he adopted also 'Simon', usual in the New Testament, as a Greek name of similar sound. His father's name was Jonah (Mt. xvi. 17); he himself was married (Mk. i. 30), and in his missionary days his wife accompanied him (1 Cor. ix. 5). The Fourth Gospel gives Bethsaida (*q.v.*), just inside Gaulanitis, and a largely Greek city, as his place of origin (Jn. i. 44), but he had also a home in Capernaum in Galilee (Mk. i. 21 ff.). Both places were at the lakeside, where he worked as a fisherman, and in both there would be abundant contact with Gentiles. (His brother's name is Greek.) Simon spoke Aramaic with a strong north-country accent (Mk. xiv. 70), and maintained the piety and outlook of his people (*cf.* Acts x. 14), though not trained in the law (Acts iv. 13; literacy is not in question). It is likely that he was affected by John the Baptist's movement (*cf.* Acts i. 22): his brother Andrew was a disciple of John (Jn. i. 39 f.).

II. CALL

The Fourth Gospel describes a period of Christ's activity before the commencement of the Galilaean ministry, and to this may be referred Peter's first introduction to Him, by Andrew's agency (Jn. i. 41). This makes the response to the subsequent call by the lakeside (Mk. i. 16 f.) more intelligible. The call to the intimate band of the Twelve followed (Mk. iii. 16 ff.).

It was as a disciple that Simon received his new title, the Aramaic *Kepha* (AV 'Cephas'), 'rock' or 'stone' (1 Cor. i. 12, xv. 5; Gal. ii. 9), usually appearing in the New Testament in the Greek form *Petros*. According to Jn. i. 42, Jesus conferred this title (not known as a personal name previously) at their first encounter. John's usual designation is 'Simon Peter'. Mark calls him Simon up to iii. 16, and Peter almost invariably thereafter. There is nothing in any case to suggest that the solemn words of Mt. xvi. 18 represented the first bestowal of the name.

III. PETER IN THE MINISTRY OF JESUS

Peter was one of the first disciples called; he always stands first in the lists of disciples; he was also one of the three who formed an inner circle round the Master (Mk. v. 37, ix. 2, xiv. 33, *cf.* xiii. 3). His impulsive devotion is frequently portrayed (*cf.* Mt. xiv. 28; Mk. xiv. 29; Lk. v. 8; Jn. xxi. 7), and he acts as spokesman of the Twelve (Mt. xv. 15, xviii. 21; Mk. i. 36 f., viii. 29, ix. 5, x. 28, xi. 21, xiv. 29 ff.; Lk. v. 5, xii. 41). At the crisis near Caesarea Philippi he is the representative of the whole band: for the question is directed to them all (Mk. viii. 27, 29), and all are included in the look that accompanies the subsequent reprimand (viii. 33).

On any satisfactory interpretation of Mk. ix. 1 the transfiguration is intimately related to the apostolic confession which precedes it. The experience made a lasting impression on Peter: 1 Pet. v. 1; 2 Pet. i. 16 ff. are most naturally interpreted of the transfiguration, and, for what they are worth, the *Apocalypse* and *Acts of Peter* (see

NEW TESTAMENT APOCRYPHA) show that their authors associated the preaching of this subject with Peter.

In a measure, the disastrous boast of Mk. xiv. 29 ff. is also representative of the disciples; and, as Peter's protestations of loyalty are the loudest, so his rejection of the Lord is the most explicit (Mk. xiv. 66 ff.). He is, however, specially marked out by the message of the resurrection (Mk. xvi. 7), and personally receives a visitation of the risen Lord (Lk. xxiv. 34; 1 Cor. xv. 5).

IV. THE COMMISSION OF PETER

Mt. xvi. 18 ff. is one of the most discussed passages of the New Testament. Rejection of the genuineness of the saying is arbitrary, and generally based on dogmatic assumptions (sometimes the assumption that Jesus never meant to found the Church). Others have argued that the saying is genuine but displaced. Stauffer would see it as a resurrection commission, like Jn. xxi. 15, Cullmann would set it in a passion context, like Lk. xxii. 31 f. Such reconstructions hardly do justice to the distinctiveness of Mt. xvi. 18 ff. It is a benediction and a promise: the other passages are commands. We need not undervalue Mark's vivid account of the Caesarea Philippi incident, which concentrates attention on the disciples' failure to understand the nature of the Messiahship they have just confessed, to acknowledge that the 'rock' saying belongs to the occasion of the confession.

There is still no unanimity in interpreting the passage. The suggestion that 'rock' is simply a misunderstanding of a vocative 'Peter' in the underlying Aramaic (*SB*, I, p. 732) is too facile: the passage has obviously something to do with the significance of Peter's name, which various Gospel sources show as having been solemnly bestowed by Jesus. From early times two main interpretations have been held, with many variants.

1. That the rock is substantially what Peter has said: either Peter's faith or the confession of the Messiahship of Jesus. This is a very early interpretation (*cf.* Origen, *in loc.*, 'Rock means every disciple of Christ'). It has the great merit of taking seriously the Matthaean context, and emphasizing, as Mk. viii does in a different way, the immense significance of the Caesarea Philippi confession. In historical perspective we should probably see the rock as, not simply faith in Christ, but the apostolic confession of Christ, spoken of elsewhere as the foundation of the Church (*cf.* Eph. ii. 20). The 'rock' saying touches the core of the apostolic function (see APOSTLE), and Peter, first among the apostles, has a name which proclaims it. That his own faith and understanding is as yet anything but exemplary is irrelevant: the Church is to be built on their confession.

2. That the rock is Peter himself. This is found almost as early as the other, for Tertullian and the bishop, whether Roman or Carthaginian, against whom he thundered in *De Pudicitia*, assume this, though with different inferences. Its strength lies in the fact that Mt. xvi. 19 is in the singular, and must be addressed directly to Peter even if, like Origen, we go on to say that to have Peter's faith and virtues is to have Peter's keys. Comparison might also be made with the Midrash on Is. li. 1. When God looked on Abraham who was to appear, He said, 'Behold, I have found a rock on which I can build and base the world. Therefore he called Abraham a rock' (*SB*, I, p. 733).

Many Protestant interpreters, including notably Cullmann, take the latter view; but, despite his disclaimer (p. 184), it is perhaps significant that he cuts the saying from the Matthaean setting. To read it where Matthew places it is surer than to treat it as an isolated logion.

It must be stressed, however, that the exegesis of this point has nothing to do with the claims for the primacy of the Roman Church or its bishop with which it has through historical circumstances become involved. Even if it could be shown that Roman bishops are in any meaningful sense the successors of Peter (which it cannot), the passage does not allow for the transfer of its provisions to any successors whatever. It refers to the foundation of the Church, which in the nature of things cannot be repeated.

The words that follow about the keys of the kingdom should be contrasted with Mt. xxiii. 13. The Pharisees, for all their missionary propaganda, shut up the kingdom: Peter, recognizing the Son who is over the house and who holds the keys (*cf.* Rev. i. 18, iii. 7, xxi. 25), finds them delivered to him (*cf.* Is. xxii. 22) to open the kingdom. See also POWER OF THE KEYS. The 'binding and loosing' (*q.v.*), a phrase for which there are illuminating rabbinic parallels, is here addressed to Peter, but elsewhere is assigned to all the apostles (*cf.* Mt. xviii. 18). 'The apostle would, in the coming Kingdom, be like a great scribe or Rabbi, who would deliver decisions on the basis, not of the Jewish law, but of the teaching of Jesus which "fulfilled" it' (A. H. McNeile, *in loc.*).

But that here and elsewhere a primacy among the apostles is ascribed to Peter is not in doubt. Lk. xxii. 31 ff. shows the strategic position of Peter as seen by both the Lord and the devil and, in full knowledge of the approaching desertion, marks out his future pastoral function. The risen Lord reinforces this commission (Jn. xxi. 15 ff.), and it is the Fourth Gospel, which demonstrates the peculiar relationship of the apostle John to Christ, that records it.

V. PETER IN THE APOSTOLIC CHURCH

The Acts shows the commission in exercise. Before Pentecost it is Peter who takes the lead in the community (Acts i. 15 ff.); afterwards, he is the principal preacher (ii. 14 ff., iii. 12 ff.) the spokesman before the Jewish authorities (iv. 8 ff.), the president in the administration of discipline (v. 3 ff.). Though the Church as a whole made a deep impression on the community, it was to Peter in particular that supernatural powers were attributed (v. 15). In Samaria, the Church's first mission field, the same leadership is exercised (viii. 14 ff.).

Significantly also, he is the first apostle to be associated with the Gentile mission, and that by unmistakably providential means (x. 1 ff., *cf.* xv. 7 ff.). This immediately brings criticism upon him (xi. 2 ff.); and not for the last time. Gal. ii. 11 ff. gives us a glimpse of Peter at Antioch, the first church with a significant ex-pagan element, sharing table-fellowship with the Gentile converts, and then meeting a barrage of Jewish-Christian opposition, in the face of which he withdraws. This defection was roundly denounced by Paul; but there is no hint of any theological difference between them, and Paul's complaint is rather the incompatibility of Peter's practice with his theory. The old theory (revived by S. G. F. Brandon, *The Fall of Jerusalem and the Christian Church*, 1951), of persistent rivalry between Paul and Peter, has little basis in the documents.

Despite this lapse, the Gentile mission had no truer friend than Peter. Paul's gospel and his had the same content, though a somewhat different expression: the Petrine speeches in Acts, Mark's Gospel, and 1 Peter have the same theology of the cross, rooted in the concept of Christ as the suffering Servant. He was ready with the right hand of fellowship, recognizing his mission to Jews and Paul's to Gentiles as part of the same ministry (Gal. ii. 7 ff.); and at the Jerusalem Council is recorded as the first to urge the full acceptance of the Gentiles on faith alone (Acts xv. 7 ff.).

Peter's career after the death of Stephen is hard to trace. The references to him in Joppa, Caesarea, and elsewhere suggest that he undertook missionary work in Palestine (James no doubt now assuming leadership in Jerusalem). He was imprisoned in Jerusalem, and on his miraculous escape he left for 'another place' (Acts xii. 17). Attempts to identify this place are fruitless. We know that he went to Antioch (Gal. ii. 11 ff.); he may have gone to Corinth, though probably not for long (1 Cor. i. 12). He is closely associated with Christians in northern Asia Minor (1 Pet. i. 1), and possibly the prohibition on Paul's entry into Bithynia (Acts xvi. 7) was due to the fact that Peter was at work there.

Peter's residence in Rome has been disputed, but on insufficient grounds. 1 Peter was almost certainly written from there (1 Pet. v. 13, and see PETER, FIRST EPISTLE OF). That book shows signs of being written just before or during the Neronian persecution, and *1 Clement* v implies that, like Paul, he died in this outburst. Doubts cast on the interpretation of *1 Clement* (*cf.* M. Smith, *NTS*, IX, 1960, pp. 86 ff.) have little foundation. On the other hand, Cullmann's suggestion, based on the context in *1 Clement* and Paul's hints in Philippians of tensions in the church in Rome, that Peter, perhaps at Paul's request, came specifically to heal the breach, and that bitterness among Christians led to the death of both, is worth serious consideration. The story in the *Acts of Peter* of his martyrdom by crucifixion (*cf.* Jn. xxi. 18 ff.) head downwards cannot be accepted as reliable, but this work (see NEW TESTAMENT APOCRYPHA) may preserve some valid traditions. Certainly these Acts, like other 2nd-century witnesses, emphasize the co-operation of the apostles in Rome.

Excavations in Rome have revealed an early cultus of Peter under St. Peter's (*cf.* Eusebius, *EH* ii. 25): it is not safe to claim more for them.

See also PETER, FIRST and SECOND EPISTLES OF; NEW TESTAMENT APOCRYPHA.

BIBLIOGRAPHY. F. J. Foakes Jackson, *Peter, Prince of Apostles*, 1927; E. Stauffer, *Zeitschrift für Kirchengeschichte*, LXII, 1944, pp. 1 ff. (*cf. New Testament Theology*, 1955, pp. 30 ff.); O. Cullmann, *Peter: Disciple—Apostle—Martyr*, 1953, *JEH*, VII, 1956, pp. 238 f. (on excavations); J. Toynbee and J. Ward Perkins, *The Shrine of St. Peter and the Vatican Excavations*, 1956; H. Chadwick, *JTS* (NS), VIII, 1957, pp. 31 ff.

A.F.W.

PETER, FIRST EPISTLE OF. The letter is sent in the name of the apostle, to whose status and experience there is a modest allusion in v. 1. A certain function is ascribed to Silvanus (v. 12)—almost certainly the Silas (*q.v.*) of Acts. The address is the widest in the New Testament (i. 1); to the Christians of five provinces (of which Bithynia and Pontus were for administrative purposes merged).

I. OUTLINE OF CONTENTS

a. Address and greeting (i. 1, 2)

Trinitarian in form and concerned with the work of salvation.

b. Thanksgiving (i. 3–12)

In form a *Berakhah*, or blessing of God, for the privileges of salvation (contrast Paul's thanksgivings), making reference to present suffering.

c. The implications of salvation (i. 13–ii. 10)

God's purpose for His people: the nature of redemption and the call of the redeemed to fear God and love one another: the privileges of belonging to the people of God. The section includes the call to 'put off' the characteristics of the old life.

d. Christian relationships (ii. 11–iii. 12)

The appeal to good behaviour among the Gentiles: careful subjection to lawfully constituted authority; the duties of slaves, under good and bad masters, with the example of Christ; the duties for wives and husbands; the call to unity, love, gentleness, and humility, swelling into Ps. xxxiv.

e. Suffering and the will of God (iii. 13–22)

Preparedness to suffer injustice: Christ's suffering and its triumphant consequences.

f. Holy living (iv. 1–11)

Includes a call to watch: culminates in a benediction.

g. The fiery trial (iv. 12–19)

A sudden resumption of the theme of imminent suffering: its inherent blessing: the glory of suffering for the Name: the coming judgment.

h. Address to elders (v. 1–4)

i. General address and benediction (v. 5–11)

Including a renewal of the call to vigilance and to resistance to the evil one.

j. Personalia and greetings (v. 12–14)

II. EXTERNAL ATTESTATION

The use of 1 Peter in the primitive Church is at least as well attested as most of the Epistles. Eusebius says that 'the ancient elders' made free use of it (*EH* iii. 3); some have found echoes of it in Clement of Rome (*c.* AD 96), and rather more in Ignatius, Hermas, and Barnabas, belonging to different parts of the world, but all to the early 2nd century. Beyond question is its use by Polycarp (who may have been baptized as early as AD 69) and Papias, also of the sub-apostolic generation (Eusebius, *EH* iii. 39). It is reflected in the *Gospel of Truth*, which seems to use the books regarded as authoritative in Rome *c.* AD 140 (see NEW TESTAMENT APOCRYPHA). From the second half of the century onwards it seems universally known and read, at least in the Greek-speaking Church. There are fewer signs of it in Latin writers. It is not mentioned—possibly by accident (*cf.* T. Zahn, *Geschichte des Neuetestamentlichen Kanons*, II. 1, 1890, pp. 105 ff., 142)—in the Muratorian Fragment. By Eusebius' time, no question was remembered of its authenticity, though other writings bearing Peter's name had long caused discussion (*EH* iii. 3).

Obviously the Epistle had considerable influence on the thought and expression of early Christians, and nothing suggests that it was ever attributed to anyone but Peter. Some who have on other grounds questioned its authenticity have been driven by its evident early attestation to the desperate conclusion that it must have circulated anonymously.

A date about AD 100–111 has often been urged for the passages about persecution. It is worth remembering that Polycarp and Papias, both Asians, were the one certainly, the other almost certainly, mature men at that time.

III. PLACE OF WRITING

The letter conveys greetings from the church in 'Babylon' (v. 13). Mesopotamian Babylon is unlikely: it is too much of a coincidence that Mark and Silvanus, old colleagues of Paul, should be there too. Still less can be said for Babylon on the Nile, a military depot. It is far more likely that, as in Rev. xiv. 8, xvii. 5, *etc.*, Babylon stands for Rome. The Old Testament had compared it as a symbol of godless prosperity (*cf.* Is. xiv); theories that it is a general allegory for 'the world' or a cryptogram for security purposes are needless. There are grounds for believing Peter worked in Rome, and the presence of Mark and Silvanus would be explained.

IV. STYLE AND LANGUAGE

The Greek of the Epistle is good and rhythmic, the style not pretentious but with a certain delicacy. Simple rhetorical devices are effectively used, but there are also some grammatical features best explained by Semitic influence. The quotations from and allusions to the Old Testament almost invariably follow the LXX in a way which suggests thorough familiarity with it.

Some of these facts, reinforced by an exaggeration of the classical character of the Greek, have seemed at once to overthrow any claim to authorship by an Aramaic-speaking Galilaean. A number of assumptions here, however, require testing. Greek was widely understood and spoken, and was a vital cultural force, throughout 1st-century Palestine, and especially Galilee. Peter's own brother has a Greek name, and Peter would doubtless be quite at home in the language. Further, the LXX was the Authorized Version of most early Christians, and everyone connected with the Gentile mission would be familiar with it, and especially with the key passages most frequently in use.

These factors, however, would not themselves justify an easy assumption that Peter could write Greek prose of the type of 1 Peter. But we must here ask, in what sense is the letter 'by' Silvanus (v. 12)? Were he simply the messenger, one would expect the expression 'sent by' (*cf.* Acts xv. 27). Contemporary literature attests that in the ancient world secretaries were often entrusted with considerable powers (*cf.* J. A. Eschlimann, *RB*, LIII, 1946, pp. 185 ff.). Probably, therefore, 1 Pet. v. 12 indicates, and the diction and style evidence, the assistance of Silvanus in drafting the letter.

Silvanus, we learn from Acts, was a Jew, a Roman citizen, acceptable for the delicate task of explaining the resolutions of the Jerusalem Council (Acts xv. 22 ff.), and a devoted worker in the Gentile mission. He had been associated with Paul in the sending of 1 and 2 Thessalonians (1 Thes. i. 1; 2 Thes. i. 1). Selwyn has pointed to verbal parallels and connections of thought between those Epistles and 1 Peter (pp. 369 ff., 439 ff.) which, after due weight has been given to the criticisms of B. Rigaux (*Les Épîtres aux Thessaloniciens*, 1956, pp. 105 ff.) and others, will repay careful study. An interesting light may be cast, for instance, on 1 Pet. iii. 7 and 1 Thes. iv. 3–5 if the one is read in the light of the other.

Those who deny the Petrine authorship usually write off the reference to Silvanus as part of the pseudepigraphic machinery. If, however, the hypothesis of a secretary introduces factors beyond proof it is also true that this method was used in antiquity, and must be allowed for.

V. THE HISTORICAL BACKGROUND

The principal data come from the references to persecution (i. 6 f., iii. 13–17, iv. 12–19, v. 9). In the first two passages trials exist, unjust suffering is a possibility; in the second two a fierce ordeal is imminent: so much so that some have even urged that iv. 12 ff. comes from a later period. The vocabulary, however, is very similar: in each case *peirasmos*, 'trial', is used (i. 6 and iv. 12); persecution is a ground of rejoicing (i. 6, iv. 13); the same beatitude is applied (iii. 14, iv. 14); the glory of suffering for doing good, or as a Christian, is proclaimed (iii. 17, iv. 16); the undeserved suffering of Christians is linked with the will of God (iii. 17, iv. 19); obedience to the civil power in things lawful and honest is enjoined (ii. 13 ff., iv. 15), and the example of Christ's sufferings is set forth (i. 11, iii. 18, iv. 13). The readers are also told that their fiery trial should be no surprise (iv. 12): and suffering they already know (*cf.* i. 6 ff.). All this suggests that if the peril in iv. 12 ff. is new, it is in degree, not kind.

The antithesis in iv. 12 ff. between suffering for wrong committed and suffering for the name of Christ has attracted comparison with a letter from Pliny, appointed Governor of Bithynia–Pontus in AD 110/111 to the usually liberal-minded Emperor Trajan (Pliny, *Ep.* x. 96).

Pliny, faced with vast numbers of Christians in his province, asks whether age, sex, or recantation is to be allowed for in prescribing punishment: and, further, if the name of Christian (*nomen ipsum*) is sufficient reason for punishment, or only the crimes (putatively) congruent therewith (*flagitia cohaerentia*).

His own line of conduct had been to inquire whether people were Christians and to give them free pardon if they sacrificed to the emperor's genius; and, if they refused, to execute them for contumacy (*contumacia*). Some of those who sacrificed said they had ceased to be Christians twenty years back; but neither from them nor from two Christian girls (see DEACONESS), whom he tortured, could he find anything very reprehensible save a rather disgusting superstition. His vigorous action was having effect, and disused heathen rites were recommencing.

Trajan's reply (*Ep.* x. 97) generally approves these actions but lays down that Christians are not to be sought out: if they are regularly accused and fail to recant they must suffer.

Pliny also says that Christians took an oath of abstention from crime (*cf.* 1 Pet. iv. 15). And this all takes place in part of the area to which 1 Peter is addressed.

There is no evidence of widespread state-sponsored persecution in the provinces before this date: the savage pogroms of Nero and Domitian were directed at Roman Christians. Accordingly, many have seen in 1 Peter a tract designed for Pliny's time (*cf., e.g.*, J. Knox, *JBL*, LXXII, 1953, pp. 187 ff.).

To this thesis there are four strong objections.

1. 'The name' is used in 1 Peter in a primitive Christian, not a juristic Roman, sense. The 'name' of Jesus was immensely significant for Christians of the apostolic age, and in particular the accounts which we have of Peter's Jerusalem preaching (*cf.* Mk. ix. 37, 41, xiii. 13; Lk. xxi. 12; Acts ii. 21, 38, iii. 6, 16, iv. 12, 17 f., 30, v. 28). Even in Jerusalem days persecution was for 'the name' (Acts v. 41, ix. 16, *cf.* ix. 4 f.). The background of 'the name' in 1 Peter iv surely lies in these passages.

2. When Pliny talks of *flagitia cohaerentia* he is doubtless thinking of the common slander that Christians were guilty of cannibalism, incest, and other horrors in their rites—he is looking for evidence. But the warnings in 1 Pet. iv. 15 f. have no such undertones: and 'a busybody' does not denote a criminal offence at all.

3. The language of 1 Peter does not necessarily indicate legislative action. It is implied in ii. 14, iii. 15 ff. that, in the ordinary administration of justice, Christians would have nothing to fear: though the same passages make clear that they might on occasions be subjected to flagrant injustice. In iii. 15 ff. the danger seems to be primarily from ill-disposed neighbours; in iv. 14 reproach is specifically mentioned; and the readers' sufferings are the same as other Christians know elsewhere (v. 9). Jewish jealousy, private spite, enraged commercial interests, mob violence, and ill-judged actions by local magistrates could have dire effects (Acts *passim*; 2 Cor. xi. 22 ff.; 1 Thes. ii. 14 f.; 2 Tim. iii. 11 f.; Heb. xii. 4 ff.).

4. Pliny's jurisdiction extended over Bithynia–Pontus only: nothing suggests an enforcement of his policy in the other areas to which 1 Peter is addressed.

Pliny's action must have had its roots well in the past (*cf.* Ramsay, *CRE*, pp. 245 ff.). Though not sure of the technicalities, he takes for granted that Christians must be punished for *something*: and even he does not execute for the *nomen ipsum* but for *contumacia*. Nor does Trajan give him a straight answer: it is still not clear whether Christianity is a crime or not. The law, kept deliberately vague, puts Christians at the mercy of gossips.

There is no need, however, to look to Vespasian's or Domitian's time: nothing in the *language* of 1 Peter requires a date later than the sixties. If a note of particular urgency appears at iv. 12 ff. the outbreak of the Neronian persecution would afford ample justification.

It seems certain that Peter suffered in Rome under Nero (see PETER, above), and 'Babylon' (v. 13) almost certainly indicates that city. The eastern provinces tended to copy imperial actions on their own initiative. Rev. ii, iii suggests that this happened in Domitian's persecution in the nineties. From Rome, in the first rumblings of Nero's anti-Christian movement that became literally a fiery trial, Peter would have reason to predict an intensification of the suffering of his brethren in the East.

A suitable date for 1 Peter would thus be just before the outbreak of Nero's persecution: AD 63 or early 64; perhaps after Paul had died and left his colleagues Silvanus and Mark.

VI. THE AUTHOR'S BACKGROUND

A rewarding study can be made of the connection between 1 Peter and the other parts of the New Testament with which Peter is associated: Mark's Gospel and the early speeches in Acts. It is not simply a matter of verbal links between 1 Pet. ii. 20 ff. and Mark's passion narrative (*cf.* Selwyn, p. 30). Mark, the Petrine speeches, and 1 Peter all set forth Christ in terms of the suffering Servant of Isaiah liii; 1 Peter and Mark both expound the Lord's death as a ransom (*cf.* Mk. x. 45 with 1 Pet. i. 18). Other New Testament writings, of course, are indebted to Is. liii, but it is remarkable that these three have this prophetic passage so deeply impressed that it may be regarded as their central thought about Christ. 1 Pet. ii, like Is. liii, describes both the Servant's conduct and sufferings and the significance of them. Much has been said of the call to the imitation of Christ in 1 Peter; but there is far more than a description of the passion and an appeal to imitation: the thought moves on to what is for ever inimitable, the redemption which only His suffering could effect.

The Petrine speeches in Acts share with 1 Peter the same sense of prophetic fulfilment (Acts ii. 16 ff., iii. 18; 1 Pet. i. 10 ff., 20), the insistence on the cross as the foreordained action of God (Acts ii. 23; 1 Pet. i. 20), the same connection of the resurrection and exaltation (Acts ii. 32 ff.; 1 Pet. i. 21); the call to repentance and faith-baptism (Acts ii. 38, 40; 1 Pet. iii. 20 ff.); the certainty of Christ's judgment of the living and dead (Acts x. 42; 1 Pet. iv. 5); joyous recognition of the Gentile mission and its blessings (Acts x. 9 ff., xi. 17, xv. 7 ff.; 1 Pet. i. 1, 4–12, ii. 3–10), expressed from a Jewish standpoint. It would take a Jew of Peter's views to speak of Gentile Christians as 'elect . . . sojourners of the Dispersion' (i. 1, RV), and to describe them as entering Israel (ii. 9 f.—note the modification of Hosea: the readers had *never been* God's people before). A Jew, too, could describe their background as 'what the Gentiles like to do' (iv. 3, RSV).

Again, in both 1 Peter and the Petrine speeches we are, as we have seen, in an atmosphere where the 'name' of Jesus means much (see v above). Even details may be significant: the use of the oracle about the stone (Acts iv. 10 ff.; 1 Pet. ii. 7) and the use of *xylon*, properly 'wood', for the cross (Acts v. 30, x. 39; 1 Pet. ii. 24).

1 Peter contains an unusual number of apparent reminiscences of the Lord's words: generally not as formal quotations, but woven into the framework of the discourse (*e.g.* 1 Pet. i. 16, Mt. v. 48; i. 17, Mt. xxii. 16; i. 18, Mk. x. 45; i. 22, Jn. xv. 12; ii. 19, Lk. vi. 32 and Mt. v. 39; iii. 9, Mt. v. 39; iii. 14, Mt. v. 10; iv. 11, Mt. v. 16; iv. 13, Mt. v. 10 ff.; iv. 18, Mt. xxiv. 22; v. 3, Mt. xx. 25 f.; v. 7, Mt. vi. 25 ff.), and other passages take on a richer meaning if Peter were in fact the author. These connections are not exclusively from the Markan tradition: but 1 Peter and Mark alike display the theme of the sufferings and the glory.

Some have sought the author's background in the Asian mystery cults (see R. Perdelwitz, *Die Mysterienreligionen und das Problem des 1 Petrusbriefes*, 1911, and *cf.* Beare) and found the letter too colourless in its treatment of the Lord's life for the work of one of the Twelve. The proponents of the mystery religion theory have, however, not made their case in a matter where dating is notoriously uncertain; and the parallels with the Galilaean Gospel tradition are far more impressive. Eloquent is the judgment of Cullmann, who, while not discussing the authorship of 1 Peter, can be assured that it was written with knowledge of Peter's dominant theological themes (*Peter*, p. 68).

VII. I PETER AND THE REST OF THE NEW TESTAMENT

The theology of 1 Peter is essentially Pauline. This is not, as some think, an argument against authenticity: there is reason to hold that Peter stood close to Paul in theology (see PETER, above) and none to think that he was an original theologian. Silvanus, too, had long worked with Paul. Moreover, though the agreement is close, the setting and expression of the theology in terms of the Servant is quite independent of Paul. It is worth remark that K. Lake, drawn to a late date by the persecution passages, could say, 'The simplicity of the theology is marked, and affords an argument for an early date' (*EBr*[11], XXI, p. 296) and that F. L. Cross can point to 'that remarkable co-presence of the end as future and yet as already here from which second century writings depart' (pp. 42 f.).

More remarkable are the literary resemblances between 1 Peter and other New Testament writings, especially Romans, Ephesians, Hebrews, and James. Not all can be fortuitous: for instance, the unusual divergence from the LXX in the quotation in 1 Pet. ii. 4–8 appears also in Rom. ix. 32 f. Problems of priority in literary relationships are always difficult and can rarely command certainty. C. L. Mitton claims to have proved the dependence of 1 Peter on Ephesians (*JTS* (NS), I, 1950, pp. 67 ff.)—the significance of this, if ascertained, will depend on the date given to Ephesians. Beare claims, with less demonstration, that the author of 1 Peter must have had access to the published Pauline Corpus (*The First Epistle of Peter*[2], p. 195).

A fruitful development in recent literary criticism has been the attention given to the common patterns of Christian teaching which appear in diverse New Testament writings (see P. Carrington, *The Primitive Christian Catechism*, 1946). A pattern of instruction for converts has been recovered, associated by many scholars, perhaps too categorically, with baptism. James and 1 Peter, as well as Ephesians and Colossians, reflect this pattern, which had among its components:

1. The call to put away sins and desires of the old pagan life (1 Pet. ii. 1, 11).

2. The call to Christian humility, subjection, and the subordination of self-interest—addressed to particular classes of society (1 Pet. ii. 11–iii. 9—there are parentheses).

3. The call to watch and pray: twice in 1 Peter (1 Pet. iv. 7, v. 8).

4. The call to resist the devil (1 Pet. v. 8 f.). Many of the strongest resemblances between 1 Peter and other Epistles occur in just these sections, and it seems probable that the explanation lies in the common forms of catechetical training, not in direct literary dependence.

Selwyn has gone further and seen other common patterns reflected in 1 Peter, more especially a body of teaching on persecution which declared it to be a ground of rejoicing, a test of character, a necessary visitation, and a sign of the imminence of divine judgment and vindication: and which was anchored in the words of the Lord. Selwyn finds this same pattern in 1 and 2 Thessalonians, also associated with Silvanus. In common with other writers, he sees various hymns and liturgical fragments (*e.g.* 1 Pet. ii. 6–10, iii. 18–22; and use of Ps. xxxiv in iii. 10 f.).

VIII. THE NATURE AND PURPOSE OF I PETER

1 Peter has long been treated as a sermon cast into epistolary form, dealing with baptism. This was given a new form by H. Preisker in 1951, who saw in the section i. 3–iv. 11 indications of a rite in progress and references to baptismal practice, and declared the work to be a baptismal liturgy with the rubrics omitted. Preisker's hypothesis was marred by stylistic hypercriticism, but this feature has been removed by F. L. Cross, who urges, with a wealth of illustration from patristic sources and especially from the *Apostolic Tradition* of Hippolytus, that 1 Peter is the president's part for an Easter baptismal eucharist: i. 3–12 is the president's opening solemn prayer; i. 13–21 his formal charge to the candidates. The baptism takes place at this point, and i. 22–25 gives the welcome to the newly baptized: passing to a discourse on the fundamentals of sacramental life (ii. 1–10), an address on Christian duties (ii. 11–iv. 6), and closing with admonitions and a doxology (iv. 7–11). It is a weakness of the theory that no explanation is given of iv. 12 ff.

This thesis rests on a vast amount of detailed study which cannot be discussed here. Many of the details have been called in question. (See the examination by T. C. G. Thornton, *JTS* (NS), XII, 1961, pp. 14 ff.) A few general points, however, suggest the need for reserve.

First, baptism is less prominent in the Epistle than the discussions of recent years suggest. There is only one explicit reference to it, and that is a parenthesis (iii. 21). Other allusions to baptism which some find are highly dubious: the 'begetting again' (i. 3, *cf.* i. 23) is already realized, and its result enjoyed: it cannot refer to an event to take place after i. 21. Its corresponding member in the catechetical form in Jas. i. 18 makes it clear that the begetting relates to the gospel, not baptism, and this is confirmed by i. 23, where the 'word of God' is defined as the enduring gospel preached to the readers. The repeated 'now' need not relate to a rite in progress; it is due rather to an exultant sense of the last times: and the 'now' in iii. 21 in the context of baptism surely only points to a contrast with the ancient flood.

Second, many of the allusions can be readily understood without the theory. The emphasis on Exodus typology is valuable, but this typology is not restricted to baptism. Van Unnik, for example, points to a rabbinic saying that proselytes entered Israel in the same way as Israel entered the covenant and infers that 1 Peter stresses the transition that the readers have made. They know God's election and covenant sprinkling (i. 2 ff.); they are now Israel (i. 18 f.); those who had never been God's people have become that people (ii. 10); the work of Christ is to bring us (*prosagein*) to God: and *prosagein* represents a technical term for becoming a proselyte.

On a reading like this, while conversion and the radical break with the old life are much to the fore, baptism in itself is not. The question of authorship is not, of course, directly affected by the formal nature of the work. Peter might preach a sermon and send it as a letter (though it is very hard to see a motive for converting a liturgical text into a letter). But 1 Peter as we have it *is* a letter, and on the sound critical principle of making sense of what we have, we must so read it.

See also DESCENT INTO HADES; PERSECUTION.

BIBLIOGRAPHY. Commentaries by R. Leighton (d. 1684), *Practical Commentary upon 1 Peter*; F. J. A. Hort (posthumous, unfinished, Greek text); E. G. Selwyn, 1946 (indispensable for Greek text); H. Windisch–H. Preisker, 1951; F. W. Beare[2], 1959 (denies Petrine authorship; the second edition has an important supplement and bibliography); C. E. B. Cranfield[2], 1961; A. M. Stibbs and A. F. Walls, *TNTC*, 1959. F. L. Cross, *1 Peter: a Paschal Liturgy*, 1955; W. C. van Unnik, *ExpT*, LXVIII, 1956, pp. 79 ff.; C. F. D. Moule, *NTS*, III, 1957, pp. 1 ff.

A.F.W.

PETER, SECOND EPISTLE OF.

I. OUTLINE OF CONTENTS

After the salutation (i. 1, 2) the author speaks of the reliability of the Christian faith, attested as it is by growing personal experience (i. 3–11), the testimony of eye-witnesses (i. 12–18), and inspired ancient prophecy (i. 19–21). Mention of true prophecy leads him on to condemn false prophecy (ii. 1–iii. 10). Current false teachers are the successors of the Old Testament false prophets, and will incur the same judgment (ii. 1–9). Their depravity is shown by throwing off God's restraints in unbridled licence (ii. 10–18), which brings not liberty but bondage (ii. 19–22). Therefore judgment awaits them, despite their scepticism about the parousia. They should recall that a catastrophic end of the world had been foretold (iii. 1–4), and the certainty of this prophecy is substantiated by the flood (iii. 5–7). The second coming is delayed because of the longsuffering of a God who is outside time (iii. 8, 9), but, though delayed, it is none the less certain (iii. 10). It is the duty of the faithful not to be led away by the libertinism and scepticism of the false teachers, but to live an upright life in anticipation of Christ's return (iii. 11–end).

II. OCCASION

The recipients are not defined, though their having 'like precious faith *with us*' (i. 1) and their having 'escaped the corruption of the world' (i. 4) suggests a predominantly Gentile audience. The writer has had a long and intimate acquaintance with them (i. 12, 13, iii. 1) and writes to warn them against a false teaching both antinomian in practice and radical in belief. The immorality (ii. 12 ff.), insubordination to church leaders (ii. 10), scepticism (iii. 3), twisting of Scripture (they exploited in particular, no doubt, the Pauline doctrine of justification, iii. 16), and greed of these false teachers (ii. 3, 15) evoke his most stringent denunciation. He writes to warn the church members of their moral and intellectual danger, to assure them of the basis for their belief, to explain their main problem—the parousia—and to encourage holy living and growth in grace. If the author was Peter the date would be around the mid-sixties (he is anticipating death, i. 14). If not, the letter may have been written in the late 1st or early 2nd century. No mention is made of its provenance or destination: it may well have been written, like 1 Peter, from Rome to Asia Minor.

III. AUTHORSHIP AND DATE

The authorship of this Epistle is hotly contested on both external and internal grounds.

a. The external evidence

This is inconclusive. While no book in the Canon is so poorly attested in the Fathers, no book excluded from the Canon can claim comparable support. Origen, early in the 3rd century, is the first to cite it by name; he records the doubts which surrounded it, but himself accepts it. So does Jerome, while Eusebius is uncertain. After its inclusion in the Festal Letter of Athanasius in AD 367 and its ratification by the Council of Carthage in AD 397, its position in the Canon was unquestioned until the Reformation, when Luther accepted it, Erasmus rejected it, and Calvin was dubious. Though not quoted by name until Origen, it was used much earlier; Clement of Alexandria had it in his Bible; Valentinus in the *Gospel of Truth*, Aristides in his *Apology* (AD 129) and Clement of Rome (*c*. AD 95) appear to allude to it. More probable still is its use by the author of the *Apocalypse of Peter*, whose existence is attested by the end of the 2nd century AD. For this reason many of the scholars who on other grounds reject the Epistle nevertheless regard its external attestation as sufficient.

b. The internal evidence

Many scholars are inclined to adjudge it a pseudepigraph, on the following grounds:

(i) *Its relationship with Jude*. There is an undeniable literary relationship between the two letters; which way it lies has not been fully established, although the majority today think 2 Peter borrowed from Jude. This, it is argued, would in itself rule out the possibility of apostolic authorship. No such conclusion is warranted. If, as is certain, Paul borrowed from a variety of sources, and if, as is possible, 1 Peter borrowed from James, it would not be surprising to find the same thing in 2 Peter. On the other hand, both 2 Peter and Jude may have incorporated a common document denouncing false teaching, just as Matthew and Luke appear to have drawn from 'Q' their common sayings-material. In neither case need the priority of Jude affect the authenticity of 2 Peter, whereas if Jude drew from 2 Peter (as Bigg and Zahn maintain), the apostolic authorship of the Epistle could hardly be denied.

(ii) *Its relationship with 1 Peter*. The marked difference of diction and style between the two letters led to the doubts of the early Church about 2 Peter. Jerome thought that Peter used two different amanuenses (a possibility enhanced by the researches of E. G. Selwyn into the probable influence of Silvanus on 1 Peter), and this suggestion must be taken seriously, for despite the wide differences no book in the New Testament is so like 2 Peter as 1 Peter. They have been shown (by A. E. Simms, *The Expositor*, V, 8, 1898, pp. 460 ff.) to have as close an affinity on a purely linguistic basis as 1 Timothy and Titus, where unity of authorship is universally admitted.

Modern writers concentrate less on the linguistic than on the doctrinal differences between the Epistles, and they are very different in this respect. The subject-matter of 1 Peter is hope, of 2 Peter knowledge. 1 Peter is written to Christians facing persecution, and therefore stresses the great events of the life of Christ for emulation and comfort; 2 Peter is written to Christians facing false doctrine and practice and therefore stresses the great hope of the return of Christ for warning and challenge. The best safeguard against the false teaching is full knowledge (*gnōsis*, *epignōsis*) of Christ, and it is this, accordingly, which is stressed in 2 Peter. The teaching of both letters is conditioned by the pastoral needs which evoked them. The differences can, in fact, easily be exaggerated; both letters draw attention to the warnings of the flood, the small number saved, the longsuffering of God. Both emphasize prophecy, the inspiration of the Old Testament, the solidarity of the Old and the New Israel, and the value of eye-witness testimony. Both emphasize the primitive eschatological tension derived from the Christian's dual membership of this age and the age to come, with its consequences in holy living, in sharp contrast with the 2nd-century neglect of this doctrine. In short, the divergence of doctrinal emphasis in the two letters is great, but not impossible.

(iii) *Its anachronisms.* 1. Such concepts as 'partakers of the divine nature' (i. 4), 'escaping the corruption of the world' (i. 4), and the repeated emphasis on knowledge and eye-witness (*epoptai*, i. 16, is a favourite word of the mystery-religions) suggest to some scholars a 2nd-century origin for the letter. There is no need to postulate so late a date, since the discovery of the Carian Inscription of AD 22 and parallel passages in Philo and Josephus show that this was the common cultural language of the day in the 1st century.

2. The destruction of the world by fire (iii. 7) was a common topic in the 2nd century, and may thus be an indication of a late date for 2 Peter. On the other hand, there is some reason to believe that the distinctly Christian belief in the destruction of the world by fire (as seen in Barnabas and Justin) may ultimately derive from this Epistle (see J. Chaine, *RB*, XLVI, 1937, pp. 207 ff.).

3. The phrase 'since the fathers fell asleep' (iii. 4) is held to favour a late date when the first Christian generation had almost disappeared. Even if these words did apply to the Christian 'fathers', it would not necessitate a late date. As early as 1 Thes. iv. 15–17 or 1 Cor. xv. 6, the state of those who had died before the parousia was a burning topic that had to be faced. However, here the context suggests that 'the fathers' refers to the Old Testament fathers ('from the beginning of the *creation*') as elsewhere in the New Testament (*e.g.* Heb. i. 1; Rom. ix. 5).

4. The inclusion of Paul's letters among the 'other scriptures' favours the hypothesis of a late date, and suggests the formation of the Pauline Corpus of letters. If this is the case, to make Peter call Paul a 'beloved brother' was a stroke of genius in the *falsarius* unparalleled in the 2nd century, when divergencies between Peter and Paul were constantly exacerbated. No mention is made here of a corpus of letters, and the only real difficulty lies in one apostle's regarding the letters of another as Scripture. In view, however, of the apostolic assertion that the same Holy Spirit who inspired the Old Testament writings was active in their own (1 Cor. ii. 13), and the claims of Paul to have the mind of Christ (1 Cor. ii. 16) and to lay down rules for all the churches (1 Cor. vii. 17) which are equated with the commandment of Christ (1 Cor. xiv. 37) and rejection of which will bring rejection by God (1 Cor. xiv. 38, RSV), this possibility cannot be excluded.

IV. CONCLUSION

The evidence does not suffice to justify a dogmatic answer one way or the other to the question of authorship. There is nothing that forbids us to entertain the possibility of Petrine authorship, though many regard it as unlikely in view of the cumulative effect of the difficulties outlined above. However, no alternative solution is free from difficulty. The doctrine of the letter and the character of the false teaching do not readily fit into the 2nd-century scene. 2 Peter as a pseudepigraph has no satisfactory *raison d'être*; it adds nothing to our knowledge of Peter, has no unorthodox tendency, is no romance, makes no reference to burning 2nd-century problems, such as chiliasm, gnosticism, or church leadership; in fact, it bears no resemblances to the undoubted pseudepigrapha of the Petrine circle. At all events, it is certain that the early Church which deposed the author of the *Acts of Paul* for forgery (Tertullian, *de Baptismo* 17) and forbade the use of the *Gospel of Peter* because it was Petrine neither in authorship nor doctrine (Eus., *EH* vi. 12) thoroughly investigated 2 Peter's claims to authenticity. It passed the test before that same Council of Carthage which excluded from the Canon *Barnabas* and *Clement of Rome*, which had long been read in the churches. It cannot be shown that they were right; but it has still to be shown that they were wrong.

BIBLIOGRAPHY. Among those who reject the Petrine authorship are F. H. Chase, *HDB*, III, 1900, pp. 796 ff.; J. B. Mayor, *The Epistle of Jude and the Second Epistle of Peter*, 1907; C. E. B. Cranfield, *I and II Peter and Jude*, 1960; E. Käsemann, *ZTK*, XLIX, 1952, pp. 272 ff.; J. Moffatt, *Introduction to the New Testament*[3], 1918, pp. 358 ff.; E. A. Abbott, *The Expositor*, II, 3, 1882, pp. 49 ff., 139 ff., 204 ff. Those who accept the Epistle as Peter's include B. Weiss, *A Manual of Introduction to the New Testament*, II, 1888, pp. 154 ff.; T. Zahn, *Introduction to the New Testament*, II, 1909, pp. 194 ff.; J. Chaine, *Les Épîtres Catholiques*, 1939; C. Bigg, *St. Peter and St. Jude, ICC*, 1902; E. I. Robson, *Studies in 2 Peter*, 1915; E. M. B. Green, *2 Peter Reconsidered*, 1961. See also R. V. G. Tasker, *The Old Testament in the New Testament*[2], 1954, p. 129.

E.M.B.G.

PETHOR. A city of N Mesopotamia, south of Carchemish, mentioned in Nu. xxii. 5 as by the river (*i.e.* the Euphrates) and in Dt. xxiii. 4 as in Mesopotamia, it was the home of Balaam. Thither Balak sent messengers to call him to curse Israel. Pethor in 'Amaw is the Pitru of Assyrian texts (*cf. ANET*, p. 278), described as on the river Sāgūr (modern Sājūr), near its junction with the Euphrates. On 'Amaw, see Albright, *BASOR*, 118, 1950, pp. 15, 16 note 13, and for 'the eastern mountains (or hills)' note that in a 15th-century BC Egyptian text, chariot-wood from 'Amaw is said to come from 'god's land (= the east) in the hill-country of Naharen'—*i.e.* hills overlooking

'Amaw on the Sājūr river flowing into the Euphrates on its western bank; this western extension of (Aram-) Naharaim is attested both by Hebrew and Egyptian references.

R.A.H.G.

PHARAOH.

I. THE TERM

The common title in Scripture for the kings of Egypt. It derives from Egyp. *pr-*'', 'great house'. This term was by origin simply a name for the royal palace and the Egyptian court, and is so used in the Old and Middle Kingdoms (see EGYPT, History) in the third and first half of the second millennium BC. But in the mid-XVIIIth Dynasty (*c.* 1450 BC) the term came to be applied to the person of the king himself, as a synonym

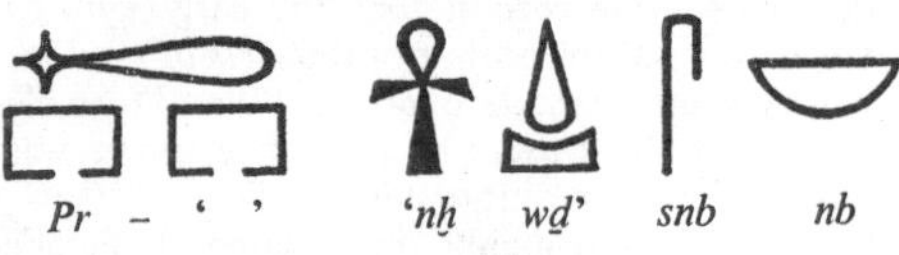

Fig. 165. The address on a 14th-century BC letter. It reads: 'Pharaoh, life, prosperity, health, the Master'.

for 'His Majesty'. The first examples of this usage apparently date from the reigns of Tuthmosis III(?) and IV, then under Amenophis IV/Akhenaten. From the XIXth Dynasty onward, the simple term 'pharaoh' is constantly used in documents, just as it is particularly in Genesis and Exodus. From the XXIInd Dynasty onward (945 BC), the term 'pharaoh' could also be coupled with the king's name: thus, 'Pharaoh Sheshonq' occurs on a stele then, just like the slightly later Old Testament references to Pharaoh-necho and Pharaoh-hophra. See Sir A. H. Gardiner, *Egyptian Grammar*[3], 1957, p. 75; J. Vergote, *Joseph en Égypte*, 1959, pp. 45–48, and the references they cite.

II. SPECIFIC PHARAOHS

1. A contemporary of Abraham (Gn. xii. 15–20). As Abraham lived *c.* 1900 BC (see CHRONOLOGY OF THE OLD TESTAMENT), his pharaoh was most likely one of the several kings Amenemhat and Sesostris of the XIIth Dynasty (*c.* 1991–1778 BC).

2. A contemporary of Joseph (Gn. xxxvii–l). Joseph lived *c.* 1700 BC (see CHRONOLOGY OF THE OLD TESTAMENT); his pharaoh therefore would most likely be one of the Hyksos kings of the XVth Dynasty (see EGYPT, History; JOSEPH).

3. The pharaoh(s) of the oppression. The number of individual rulers covered by the terms 'king of Egypt' and 'pharaoh' in Ex. i, ii is a matter of interpretation—one, or two. In any case, he/they would directly precede the pharaoh of the Exodus.

4. The pharaoh of the Exodus (Ex. v–xii). If the Exodus occurred in the first half of the 13th century BC, as seems likeliest on the evidence available (see CHRONOLOGY OF THE OLD TESTAMENT), the pharaoh of the Exodus and last oppressor would be Rameses II.

5. The father of Bithiah, wife of Mered of the tribe of Judah (1 Ch. iv. 18). The date of Bithiah and so of her royal father is uncertain, and therefore he has not yet been identified.

6. The pharaoh who received the young prince Hadad of Edom as a refugee from David and Joab's devastation of the Edomites (1 Ki. xi. 18–22), and married him off to his sister-in-law. The pharaoh in question would be late in the XXIst Dynasty, *i.e.* Amenemope or Siamūn. The obscurities of XXIst Dynasty chronology forbid any closer dating.

7. The pharaoh who reduced Gezer and bestowed it as dowry on that daughter of his whom he gave in marriage to Solomon (1 Ki. ix. 16, *cf.* also iii. 1, vii. 8, ix. 24, xi. 1). Shishak's raid into Palestine in 925 BC, the fifth year of Rehoboam, was not later than his own twenty-first year, and he acceded *c.* 945 BC. Solomon died in 931/30 BC after a forty-year reign which began *c.* 970 BC; hence Shishak acceded in Solomon's twenty-fifth year. Therefore Solomon's Egyptian contemporaries for his first twenty-five years of reign would be the last two kings of the XXIst Dynasty, Siamūn and Psusennes II. Of these two, Siamūn is perhaps the pharaoh who took Gezer and bestowed it with his daughter upon Solomon; a triumphal scene of his from Tanis (Zoan) may provide evidence for warlike activity of Siamūn in Philistia. On this period of Egypto-Israelite relations, see B. Grdseloff, *Revue de l'Histoire Juive en Égypte*, No. 1, 1947, pp. 90–92.

8. Shishak (*q.v.*), who is Sheshonq I, founder of the XXIInd (Libyan) Dynasty. **9.** So (*q.v.*), contemporary of Hoshea. **10.** Tirhakah (*q.v.*), of the XXVth (Ethiopian) Dynasty. **11.** Necho (*q.v.*), second king of the XXVIth Dynasty, is the pharaoh of Je. xxv. 19. **12.** Hophra (*q.v.*), fourth king of the XXVIth Dynasty, is apparently the pharaoh of Je. xxxvii. 5, 7, 11; Ezk. xvii. 17, xxix. 2, 3; and possibly of Je. xlvii. 1. Zerah (*q.v.*) was almost certainly *not* a pharaoh.

III. OTHER REFERENCES

These are found mainly in the prophets. Is. xix. 11 is part of a passage reflecting disruption in Egypt. Such internal fragmentation first became chronic early in Isaiah's time, in the late XXIInd–XXIVth Dynasties (*c.* 750–715 BC), and continued under the overlordship of the Ethiopian kings of the XXVth Dynasty (*c.* 715–664 BC). Pride in the long and exalted continuity of pharaonic tradition in accordance with verse 11 was reflected in the deliberate archaisms fostered by the XXVth and XXVIth Dynasty kings, who sought thus to recall the glories of earlier epochs. The deceptive outward repute of the Ethiopian kings and their actual inability to help Israel against Assyria's armies are epitomized in Is. xxx. 2, 3. Shebitku ('Shabataka') was on the throne in 701 BC when the Assyrian Rab-shakeh dismissed pharaoh as a 'broken reed' (Is. xxxvi. 6 = 2 Ki. xviii. 21). For 'Pharaoh's house in Tahpanhes' (Je. xliii. 9), see TAHPANHES.

Both Jeremiah (xlvi. 25, 26) and Ezekiel (xxx. 21–25, xxxi. 2, 18, xxxii. 31, 32) from 587 BC onward prophesied that Egypt would be worsted by Nebuchadrezzar II of Babylon (*q.v.*). In 568 BC Nebuchadrezzar did actually war against Egypt, as indicated by a fragmentary Babylonian text, though the extent of his success against Ahmose II (Amasis) is still unknown because of the lack of relevant documents. Lastly, Ct. i. 9 merely reflects the great fame of the chariot-horses of the pharaohs of the New Kingdom (*c.* 1570–1085 BC) and later. See also EGYPT, History. K.A.K.

PHAREZ. See PEREZ, PEREZITES.

PHARISEES.

I. HISTORY

The work of Ezra (*q.v.*) was continued by those who tried to master the text and teaching of the law in every detail—the scribes in the New Testament were their spiritual descendants—and the wider circle of those who meticulously tried to carry out their teaching. Early in the 2nd century BC we find them called *ḥ*^{a}*sîḏîm*, *i.e.* God's loyal ones (see HASIDAEANS).

The name Pharisee first appears in contexts of the early Hasmonaean priest-kings. The Ḥasidim had probably divided. The minority, basing itself on the illegitimacy of the high-priesthood and the abandonment of certain traditions, withdrew from public life awaiting an eschatological intervention from God. The majority aimed at controlling the religion of the State. The traditional interpretation of Pharisees as 'the separated ones' is much more probable than T. W. Manson's suggestion of the nickname 'the Persians'. Their views on tithing (see below) made separation from the majority inescapable.

Under John Hyrcanus (134–104 BC) they had much influence and the support of the people (Jos., *Ant.* xiii. 10. 5–7), but when they broke with him he turned to the Sadducees. Pharisaic opposition under Alexander Jannaeus (103–76 BC) went so far that they even appealed for help to the Seleucid king, Demetrius III. Jannaeus triumphed and crucified some 800 of his leading opponents (Jos., *Ant.* xiii. 14. 2). On his deathbed, however, he advised his wife, Alexandra Salome, who succeeded him (76–67 BC), to put the government in the hand of the Pharisees, who from this time held a dominating position in the Sanhedrin.

They suffered heavily under Antipater and Herod (Jos., *BJ* i. 33. 2, 3) and evidently learnt that spiritual ends could not be attained by political means, for after Herod's death we find them petitioning for direct Roman rule. For the same reason the majority of them opposed the revolt against Rome (AD 66–70). Hence Vespasian favoured Yohanan ben Zakkai, one of their leaders, and permitted him to establish a rabbinic school at Jamnia. By now the controversies between the party of the rigorist Shammai and of the more liberal Hillel had ended in compromise, the Sadducees had disappeared and the Zealots were discredited—after the defeat of Bar Kochba in AD 135 they too disappeared—and so the Pharisees became the unquestioned leaders of the Jews. By AD 200 Judaism and Pharisaic teaching had become synonymous.

II. RELATION TO OTHER PARTIES

The Pharisees were always a minority group. Under Herod they numbered something over 6,000 (Jos., *Ant.* xvii. 2. 4). The later bitterness of their relationship to the common people (*'am ha-'āreṣ*), shown by many Talmudic passages from the 2nd century AD, indicates that the rigour of their interpretation of the law had no intrinsic appeal. The apocalyptists had little influence except through the Zealots, and their appeal seems to have been mainly to a desperate proletariat. The Sadducees were drawn mainly from the richer landowners; Talmudic tradition distinguishes clearly between them and their allies, the house of Boëthus, the high-priestly clan. In their own way they were as rigorist as the Pharisees, only they applied the laws and their traditions irrespective of consequences—they were rich enough to bear them. The Pharisees were always mindful of the public interest. It is no coincidence that Shammai, the rigorist Pharisee, came of a rich, aristocratic family, while Hillel was a man of the people. The main attraction of the Pharisees for the people was that they came mostly from the lower middle and better artisan classes and, understanding the common man, did genuinely try to make the law bearable for him.

The differences stressed by Josephus (*BJ* ii. 8. 14)—the Pharisees' belief in the immortality of the soul, which would be reincarnated (*i.e.* re-animated by the resurrection body), and in the overruling of fate (*i.e.* God), and the Sadducees' disbelief in either (*cf.* Mt. xxii. 23; Acts xxiii. 8)—were obviously secondary. Fundamentally the Sadducees considered that Temple worship was the centre and main purpose of the law. The Pharisees stressed individual fulfilment of all sides of the law, of which the cultus was only a part, as the reason for its existence. The outward differences expressed their inner attitudes.

III. TEACHING

Basic to the Pharisaic conception of religion was the belief that the Babylonian Exile was caused by Israel's failure to keep the Torah (the Mosaic law), and that its keeping was an individual as well as a national duty. But the Torah was not merely 'law' but also 'instruction', *i.e.* it consisted not merely of fixed commandments but was adaptable to changing conditions, and from it could be inferred God's will for situations not expressly mentioned. This adaptation or inference was the task of those who had made a special study of the Torah, and a majority decision was binding on all.

One of the earliest tasks of the scribes was to establish the contents of the written Torah (*tôrâ še-biḵṯāḇ*). They determined that it contained 613 commandments, 248 positive, 365 negative. The next step was to 'make a hedge' about them, *i.e.* so to interpret and supplement them that there would be no possibility of breaking them by accident or ignorance. The best-known example is the frequently cited thirty-nine principal species of prohibited acts on the sabbath. There is, however, nothing unreasonable or illogical about them once we grant the literal prohibition of sabbath work. The commandments were further applied by analogy to situations not directly covered by the Torah. All these developments together with thirty-one customs of 'immemorial usage' formed the 'oral law' (*tôrâ še-b*[e]*-'al peh*), the full development of which is later than the New Testament. Being convinced that they had the right interpretation of the Torah, they claimed that these 'traditions of the elders' (Mk. vii. 3) came from Moses on Sinai.

Beyond an absolute insistence on the unity and holiness of God, the election of Israel and the absolute authority of the Torah for him, all the stress in the Pharisee's religion was ethical, not theological. Our Lord's condemnation of them (see HYPOCRITE) has to be interpreted in the light of the undoubted fact that they stood ethically higher than most of their contemporaries. The special Pharisaic stress on tithing and their refusal to buy food from or to eat in the homes of non-Pharisees, lest the food should not have been tithed, was due to the very heavy burden created by tithes superimposed on Hasmonaean, Herodian, or Roman taxation. For the Pharisee full taxation was a mark of loyalty to God.

BIBLIOGRAPHY. G. F. Moore, *Judaism in the First Centuries of the Christian Era*, 1927; A. T. Robertson, *The Pharisees and Jesus*, 1920; L. I. Finkelstein, *The Pharisees*, 1938; J. Jocz, *The Jewish People and Jesus Christ*, 1949. H.L.E.

PHARPAR ('swift'). One of the two 'rivers of Damascus' of which Naaman boasted (2 Ki. v. 12). Forty miles long, it is one of the tributaries of the Abana (*q.v.*) or Barada, flows eastward from Hermon a little south of Damascus, and is today called the 'Awaj'. J.D.D.

PHEBE. Lady Bountiful of Cenchreae (eastward port of Corinth, where hospitality would be important); 'deaconess' (AV 'servant') of the church and 'patroness' (AV 'succourer') of many, including Paul (Rom. xvi. 1–2; the terms are probably semi-technical; see DEACONESS). She apparently carried Paul's letter, and he asks worthy hospitality for her. E. J. Goodspeed (*HTR*, XLIV, 1951, pp. 55 ff.) holds that Rom. xvi is a separate letter to Ephesus to secure her a reception with those named. But would such oblique personal references be necessary?

The name (meaning 'radiant') is a surname of Artemis. A striking epitaph to 'The second Phoebe', a later deaconess, is cited in *MM* (*s.v. koimaomai*). See further M. D. Gibson, *ExpT*, XXIII, 1911–12, p. 281. A.F.W.

PHENICE. See PHOENIX (2).

PHEREZITE. See PERIZZITES.

PHILADELPHIA. A city in the Roman province of Asia, in the west of what is now Asiatic Turkey (see fig. 26). It was founded by Eumenes, king of Pergamum, in the 2nd century BC, and named after his brother Attalus, whose loyalty had earned him the name Philadelphus. It was situated near the upper end of a broad valley leading down through Sardis to the sea near Smyrna; and it lay at the threshold of a very fertile tract of plateau country, from which much of its commercial prosperity derived. The area was subject to frequent earthquakes. A severe one in AD 17 destroyed the city; and as the shocks continued intermittently the people took to living outside the city in tents. After an imperial bounty had helped it to recover, the city voluntarily assumed the new name of Neokaisareia. Later, under Vespasian, it took another imperial name, Flavia. The city was remarkable for the number of its temples and religious festivals. The site is now occupied by the town of Alaşehir.

The letter to 'the angel of the church in Philadelphia' (Rev. iii. 7–13) probably alludes to some of the circumstances of the city. As Philadelphus was renowned for his loyalty to his brother, so the Church, the true Philadelphia, inherits and fulfils his character by its steadfast loyalty to Christ (verses 8, 10). As the city stands by the 'open door' of a region from which its wealth derives, so the church is given an 'open door' of opportunity to exploit (verse 8; *cf.* 2 Cor. ii. 12). The symbols of the 'crown' and the 'temple' (verses 11, 12) point to a contrast with the religious festivals and rites of the city. In contrast to the impermanence of life in a city prone to earthquakes, those who 'overcome' are promised the ultimate stability of being built into the temple of God; and whereas the city has taken new names from the divine emperors, those who 'overcome' will be given new names which will denote their permanent membership of the city of the true God (verse 12). As at Smyrna, the Church had encountered opposition from the Jews in the city (verse 9). (See W. M. Ramsay, *The Letters to the Seven Churches of Asia*, 1904, ch. xxvii, xxviii.) Ignatius later visited the city on his way from Antioch to martyrdom in Rome, and subsequently sent a letter to the church there. M.J.S.R.

PHILEMON. The owner of Onesimus (*q.v.*) and almost certainly a resident of Colossae (but see PHILEMON, EPISTLE TO, for other views). Though Paul had not himself visited Colossae (Col. ii. 1), Philemon was apparently converted through him (Phm. 19) and had been a colleague (the normal meaning of 'fellow-worker', Phm. 1, RV)—both, perhaps, in Ephesus, the provincial capital (*cf.* Acts xix. 31). The argument of J. Knox (who applies Phm. 19 to Archippus) that Paul would regard the work of any of his associates as his own is hardly borne out by Col. i. 7 f., which he cites, nor is Phm. 5 ('*hearing* of thy love') incompatible with past acquaintance. A.F.W.

PHILEMON, EPISTLE TO.

I. OUTLINE OF CONTENTS

a. Address and greeting (verses 1–3).

b. Thanksgiving: introducing themes, to be developed later, of love, fellowship (*koinōnia*; *cf. koinōnos*, 'partner' in verse 17) and refreshment (*cf.* verse 20) (verses 4–7).

c. The request for Onesimus (verses 8–21).

d. A request for hospitality (verse 22).

e. Greetings from Paul's friends (verses 23, 24).

f. Blessing (verse 25).

II. SIGNIFICANCE

The earliest extant lists of the Pauline Corpus (Marcion's 'canon' and the Muratorian fragment) contain Philemon, even though they omit the Pastoral Epistles. In the 4th century complaints appear not so much against its authenticity as of its alleged triviality (*cf.* Jerome, Preface to Philemon): most generations, however, have better valued the grace, tact, affection, and delicacy of feeling which mark this little letter. Tertullian remarked that it was the only Epistle which Marcion left uncontaminated by 'editing' (*Adv. Marc.* v. 21), and its authenticity has never been responsibly questioned. In recent years it has become a bastion of the theory of the Pauline Corpus associated with E. J. Goodspeed and John Knox (see CANON OF THE NEW TESTAMENT); gratitude for the fresh interest they have stimulated in Philemon, and the adoption of some of their suggestions, does not, however, demand acceptance of this highly dubious reconstruction.

III. FORM

The personal and informal nature of Philemon (*cf.* Deissmann, *LAE*, pp. 234 f., and see EPISTLE) may distract attention from its extremely careful composition and observance of literary forms (*cf.* Knox, pp. 18 f.). It should also be noted that a house-church is in mind as well as the people named in the address (verse 2). Goodspeed and Knox over-emphasize the part the church is expected to play in swaying the slave-owner to 'do the Christian thing' (Goodspeed, p. 118): the second person singular is used throughout, even for the greetings: the only exceptions are in verses 22 (the hoped-for visit) and 25 (the benediction). This affords a contrast with Ignatius's letter to Polycarp, which is addressed to an individual but with frequent passages in the second person plural which show that the church is being harangued. Philemon is addressed to the slave-owner, with his family and church presumably linked with him after the manner of Rom. xvi. 5; Col. iv. 15.

Comparison has often been invited with Pliny's letter (*Ep.* ix. 21) on behalf of an errant but repentant freedman.

IV. PURPOSE AND OCCASION

The core of the Epistle is an appeal by Paul on behalf of one Onesimus, a slave from Colossae (Col. iv. 9) whose conduct had contrasted with his name ('useful'—a pun is involved in Phm. 10, 11). It seems that Onesimus had robbed his master (verse 18) and run away (verse 15—not quite explicit). By some means unstated—perhaps his fellow-townsman Epaphras (Col. iv. 12) was instrumental—he was brought into contact with the imprisoned Paul and radically converted. Not only so, but strong affection developed between Paul and his new 'son', in whom the veteran saw rich potential.

Under contemporary law, almost limitless vengeance could be wreaked on Onesimus by his owner: Graeco-Roman society was never free from the phobia of a servile war, and even an otherwise good master might think it his duty to society to make an example of the runaway. Frightful penalties also awaited those who harboured runaways (*cf.* P. Oxy. 1422). It is at this point that Paul interposes with his brother (verses 7, 20), not commanding, but begging (verses 8, 9) that his owner will receive Onesimus as he would Paul himself (verse 17), and solemnly undertaking all the slave's debts (verses 18, 19).

But probably Paul is asking more than mercy. Knox points out that *parakaleō* followed by *peri* (as in verse 10) usually means in late Greek 'to ask *for*' rather than 'on behalf of'. Paul highly valued Onesimus; his departure caused him great sorrow; and but for the necessity of obtaining his owner's permission would have liked to keep him with him (verses 11–14). The fulness of Paul's request would be that Onesimus might be released to Paul for Christian service. He would thenceforth stand in an unspeakably closer and more permanent relationship than the old domestic one (verses 15, 16). In any case, to Paul's ministry this correspondent owes his own conversion (verse 19).

Paul is in prison (9, 10): the occasion is the same as that indicated in Colossians, for Onesimus is to accompany Tychicus, the bearer of that letter (Col. iv. 9). Paul's party in Phm. 23 f. is the same as that in Col. iv. 10–14, with the exception of Jesus Justus (unless this is a scribal omission; *cf.* E. Amling, *ZNW*, X, p. 261). The place of imprisonment will be decided mainly on grounds external to the letter: the real alternatives are Rome, in the first imprisonment (*c.* AD 62) or Ephesus about AD 55 (see PAUL; CHRONOLOGY OF THE NEW TESTAMENT). Either city might have attracted Onesimus. Ephesus was near home, but large enough to be lost in, Rome was a haven for displaced persons of every kind. In either case there is some expectation of release and a journey to Philemon's area in the foreseeable future.

There are other links with Colossians. Col. iii. 22 ff. (*cf.* Eph. vi. 5–9) could hardly have been written without Onesimus, and the possible effect on his career, in mind. Knox and Goodspeed have, however, little reason to associate the charge to Archippus and the 'Epistle from Laodicea' (Col. iv. 16, 17) with the Onesimus case. Knox himself has disposed of Goodspeed's suggestion that Onesimus' owner lived at Laodicea (pp. 40 ff.), but his own suggestion that Philemon received the letter first as the (Laodicean) superintendent of the Lycus churches and that Archippus in Colossae was the slave-owner and principal addressee, fares no better. It requires an unnatural reading of the address, and a heavy burden on a few words (*e.g.* 'fellowworker' and 'fellowsoldier' in verses 1 and 2). Whether the epistle of Col. iv. 16 was Ephesians (*q.v.*) or some unknown letter is uncertain, but nothing suggests that it was Philemon.

See also APPHIA; ARCHIPPUS; ONESIMUS; PHILEMON.

BIBLIOGRAPHY. Commentaries (with Colossians) on the Greek text by J. B. Lightfoot[3], 1879, and C. F. D. Moule, 1957; on the English text by H. C. G. Moule, *CB*, 1893, J. Knox, *IB*, 1955, and H. M. Carson, *TNTC*, 1960; E. J. Goodspeed, *Introduction to the New Testament*, 1937, pp. 109 ff.; J. Knox, *Philemon among the Epistles of Paul*[2], 1959. A.F.W.

PHILETUS. A teacher representative of those undermining the Christian doctrine of the resurrection (2 Tim. ii. 17). See HYMENAEUS.

PHILIP (Gk. *philippos*, 'horse-lover'). There are four characters of this name known to the writers of the New Testament.

1. A son of Herod the Great and Mariamne, the daughter of Simon the high priest. For a time he was next in succession to Antipater (Jos., *Ant.* xvii. 3. 2), but this arrangement was revoked by later wills, and he lived as a private citizen. A. H. M. Jones (*The Herods of Judaea*, 1938, p. 176 n.) claims that his name was Herod, not Philip. (Jos., *Ant.* xviii. 5. 4, calls him Herod, but so many members of the Herod family bore this name that an additional name was almost obligatory.) His wife Herodias, the mother of Salome, left him in order to live with Herod Antipas, his half-brother (Mt. xiv. 3; Mk. vi. 17; Lk. iii. 19). See HEROD, HERODIAS.

2. A son of Herod the Great by his fifth wife, Cleopatra of Jerusalem; Jos., *Ant.* xvii. 1. 3 states that he was brought up at Rome. By Augustus' settlement of Herod's will Philip was granted the tetrarchy of Gaulanitis, Trachonitis, Auranitis, Batanaea (Jos.), and Ituraea (Lk. iii. 1). He ruled for thirty-seven years until his death in the winter of AD 33/34, and differed from his kinsfolk in the moderation and justice of his rule (Jos., *Ant.* xviii. 4. 6). At his death the territory was incorporated into the province of Syria until AD 37, when the Emperor Gaius Caligula granted it to Agrippa (the Herod of Acts xii. 1, 19–23), son of Aristobulus and grandson of Herod and Mariamne. Philip rebuilt Panias (modern Banyas) as Caesarea Philippi (Mt. xvi. 13; Mk. viii. 27) and Bethsaida Julias (Jos., *Ant.* xviii. 2. 1; *BJ* ii. 9. 1), both names reflecting his pro-Roman sympathies. He was the first Jewish prince to impress the heads of Roman emperors on his coins. He married Salome, the daughter of Herodias (*q.v.*), and had no children (Jos., *Ant.* xviii. 5. 4).

3. Philip the apostle was called to follow Jesus on the day following the call of Andrew and Simon, and was instrumental in bringing Nathanael to follow Him (Jn. i. 43–46). His home was Bethsaida (Jn. i. 44): this was the Bethsaida of Galilee (Jn. xii. 21), the home town of Andrew and Simon, and is thought to have been a fishing-village on the western shore of the lake (see BETHSAIDA). In the lists of the apostles in Mt. x. 3; Mk. iii. 14; Lk. vi. 14 he is placed fifth in order, with Bartholomew sixth: Acts i. 13 places him fifth, but puts Thomas in the sixth place. The only other references to him in the New Testament tell of his inability to suggest to Jesus how to supply the food for the five thousand (Jn. vi. 5), his bringing the Greeks to Jesus (Jn. xii. 21 f.), and his request of Jesus to see the Father (Jn. xiv. 8). Papias ii. 4 refers to him as one of the *presbyteroi* (see further below).

4. Philip was one of the 'Seven' who were chosen as officials (the first 'deacons') of the church at Jerusalem (Acts vi. 5). See DEACON. On the persecution of the Church following the martyrdom of Stephen he took the gospel to Samaria, where his ministry was much blessed (Acts viii. 5–13), and subsequently he was sent south to the Jerusalem–Gaza road to lead the Ethiopian eunuch to Christ (Acts viii. 26–38). After this incident he was 'Spirited' away to Azotus, the Philistine Ashdod, and from there conducted an itinerant ministry until he reached the port of Caesarea (Acts viii. 39, 40), where he appears to have settled (Acts xxi. 8). He was known as 'the evangelist', presumably to distinguish him from the apostle (3, above), and had four daughters who were prophetesses (Acts xxi. 9). Luke is here at great pains to distinguish the evangelist from the apostle. Eusebius twice (*EH* iii. 31, v. 24) quotes Polycrates as referring to Philip, 'one of the twelve apostles', and his two aged virgin daughters as being buried at Hierapolis, while another daughter was buried at Ephesus. Perhaps this last was the one mentioned in iii. 30 (quoting Clement of Alexandria, who uses the plural here perhaps loosely) as having been given in marriage. Papias is also cited (*EH* iii. 39) as stating that 'the apostle Philip' and his daughters lived at Hierapolis and the daughters supplied him with information. A quotation from the *Dialogue of Gaius and Proclus* in Eus., *EH* iii. 31 that the tomb of Philip and his four prophesying daughters may be seen at Hierapolis, followed by a reference to Acts xxi. 8, 9, shows that the historian had confused the apostle and the evangelist. It would seem most likely that both the apostle and the evangelist had daughters, which would lead to their confusion.

Lightfoot (*Colossians*, pp. 45 ff.) is most probably right in maintaining that it was the apostle who died in Hierapolis. D.H.W.

PHILIPPI. In the course of his apostolic travels Paul received in a vision the invitation of the man of Macedonia who implored, 'Come over into Macedonia, and help us' (Acts xvi. 9). Interpreting this plea as a summons from God, Paul and his party sailed for Neapolis, the port of Philippi, 8 miles south of the city and the terminus of the Egnatian Way, a military road which joined Rome and the East as a much valued line of communication.

The arrival at Philippi is marked in Acts xvi. 12 by a description of the city: 'a city of Macedonia, the first of the district, a *Roman* colony' (RV). The stages by which the city attained the rank of this noble description may be traced.

The town derives its name from Philip of Macedon, who took it from the Thasians about 300 BC. He enlarged the settlement, and fortified it to defend his frontiers against the Thasians. At this time the gold-mining industry was developed, and gold coins were struck in the name of Philip and became commonly recognized. After the battle of Pydna in 168 BC it was annexed by the Romans; and when Macedonia was divided into four parts for administrative purposes Philippi was included in the first of the four districts. This fact supports the reading of *prōtēs* in place of the Received Text's *prōtē* in Acts xvi. 12, suggested by Field and accepted by Blass, who explained it by this reference to the division of Macedonia into four districts by Aemilius Paullus in 167 BC (Livy, xlv. 17, 18, 29). On this emended reading the verse runs: 'a city of the first division of Macedonia'. If the text is not changed, Philippi's claim to be 'chief city of the district' can be accepted only in a general sense, as Ramsay observes (*St. Paul the Traveller and Roman Citizen*[15], 1925, pp. 206 f.). The comment possibly reflects Luke's special interest in the city, which may have been his birth-place.

In 42 BC the famous battle of Philippi was fought with Antony and Octavian ranged against Brutus and Cassius. After this date the town was enlarged, probably by the coming of colonists; the title *Colonia Iulia* is attested at this time. This prominence was enhanced further when, after the battle of Actium in 31 BC, in which Octavian defeated the forces of Antony and Cleopatra, the town 'received a settlement of Italian colonists who had favoured Antony and had been obliged to surrender their land to the veterans of Octavian' (Lake and Cadbury, p. 187). Octavian gave the town its notable title, *Col(onia) Iul(ia) Aug(usta) Philip(pensis)*, which has appeared on coins. Of all the privileges which this title conferred, the possession of the 'Italic right' (*ius Italicum*) was the most valuable. It meant that the colonists enjoyed the same rights and privileges as if their land were part of Italian soil.

The civic pride of the Philippians (who are given the equivalent of their Latin name *Philippenses* in Paul's letter, iv. 15) is a feature of the Acts narrative, and reappears in allusions the apostle makes in the Epistle. See Acts xvi. 21, *cf.* xvi. 37. Official names are used (*duoviri* in xvi. 19; 'praetors' in xvi. 20; 'lictors' in xvi. 35). The Greek word translated 'uncondemned' in xvi. 37 probably reflects the Latin *re incognita* or *indicta causa, i.e.* 'without examination'. In the letter to the Philippian Church two passages, i. 27 and iii. 20, speak of 'citizenship', a term which would have special appeal to the readers; and the virtues listed in iv. 8 are those which the Roman mind would particularly appreciate.

After the apostle's first visit with his preaching, imprisonment, and release, his further contact with the city is inferred from references in Acts xx. 1; 6; 1 Tim. i. 3.

BIBLIOGRAPHY. Historical details are supplied in Lake and Cadbury, *The Beginnings of Christianity*, I, IV, 1933, *ad loc.*; F. W. Beare, *The Epistle to the Philippians*, 1959, Introduction, section II, which describes the religious *milieu* of the city at the time of Paul's arrival there; while for archaeological information the work of P. Collart, *Philippes, ville de Macédoine*, two volumes containing plates and text, 1937, may be mentioned. R.P.M.

PHILIPPIANS, EPISTLE TO THE. The church at Philippi was brought into being during the apostle's second missionary journey, recorded in Acts xvi. 12–40. See PAUL, PHILIPPI. Paul's letter to this Christian community has always been looked upon as a most personal and tender communication, although there is a noticeable change at the introduction to chapter iii.

I. OUTLINE OF CONTENTS

a. Address and greeting (i. 1, 2).
b. Paul's thanksgiving and confidence (i. 3–7).
c. An apostolic prayer (i. 8–11).
d. Paul's great ambition and joy (i. 12–26).
e. Exhortation and example (i. 27–ii. 18).
f. Future plans (ii. 19–30).
g. The great digression (iii. 1–21).
h. Encouragements, appreciations, and greetings (iv. 1–23).

II. DATE AND PROVENANCE

From the record of Paul's life in the Acts of the Apostles we know of only three imprisonments (xvi. 23–40, xxi. 32–xxiii. 30, xxviii. 30), during one of which this letter was written (Phil. i. 7, 13, 14, 16, AV). It obviously cannot have been written during the first; and it seems at first sight that the choice is a simple one between his captivity at Caesarea and the two years' detention at Rome.

a. The Caesarean hypothesis

This view goes back to 1731, when it was propounded by Oeder of Leipzig. Rather surprising support came later from E. Lohmeyer in the Meyer commentary, but on the whole scholars have not been attracted to this position. The suggestion of the letter's composition during the imprisonment at Caesarea bristles with difficulties, which may be enumerated as follows:

1. The custody of Acts xxiii. 35 does not suggest the imminent martyrdom which Lohmeyer takes as the controlling theme of the entire letter (*cf.* his analysis of the letter in these terms, pp. 5 f.).

2. The size and type of the Christian community at the place of his captivity do not tally with what we know of the church at Caesarea (i. 14 ff.), as Moffatt indicates (*An Introduction to the Literature of the New Testament*, 1918, p. 169).

3. The apostle's outlook at the time of Acts xxiii, xxiv was bound up with a visit to Rome, but of this desire there is no hint in Philippians; rather he looks forward to a return visit to Philippi (ii. 24 ff.).

b. The Roman hypothesis

The alternative proposal is that the letter was written and despatched during the apostle's Roman captivity; and this remains the traditional view, with many adherents. It has considerable evidence in its favour:

1. The allusions to the *praetorium* (i. 13) and to 'Caesar's household' (iv. 22) correspond to the historical detail of the Roman detention, whatever the precise meaning of the terms may be.

2. The gravity of the charge and of the impending verdict (i. 20 ff., ii. 17, iii. 11) suggests that Paul is on trial for his life in the highest judicial court, from which there can be no appeal. It is submitted that this piece of evidence shows that it cannot have been a provincial court whose judgment Paul awaits, for even if the verdict there were unfavourable, he would still have a 'trump card' (in C. H. Dodd's phrase) to play which would quash this local sentence and transfer his case to Rome. That he does not appear to have recourse to this is presumptive evidence that he has in fact so appealed, and that the appeal has brought him to the imperial city.

3. The church at Rome would correspond, in size and influence, to the references in i. 12 ff., which point to a Christian fellowship of considerable importance.

4. The length of the imprisonment is sufficient, according to the proponents of this view, to allow for the journeys mentioned or implied by the letter. But this is a matter of debate.

5. There is indirect witness to the Roman provenance of the Epistle in the Marcionite prologue to the letter, which says, 'The apostle praises them from Rome in prison by Epaphroditus.'

There are, however, certain difficulties about this time-honoured view which have made scholars hesitate before accepting it. A. Deissmann was apparently the first to formulate these doubts, which we may state thus:

1. Deissmann drew attention to the fact that journeys to and from the place of captivity imply that the place cannot have been far from Philippi. It was argued that on the Roman hypothesis it is difficult to fit 'those enormous journeys', as he called them, into the two years mentioned as the duration of the Roman imprisonment.

2. Moreover, the situation reflected in the letter, with its foreboding of imminent martyrdom, hardly corresponds with the comparative freedom and relaxed atmosphere of Acts xxviii. 30, 31. If the letter came out of that detention it is clearly necessary to postulate an unfavourable development in the apostle's relations with the authorities which led to a change for the worse in his conditions and prospects.

3. A telling criticism of the traditional theory is the witness of ii. 24, which expresses the hope that, if the apostle is set free, he intends to revisit the Philippians, and also to take up his missionary and pastoral work in their midst once again. This is an important *datum* from the internal evidence of the letter itself, for we know from Rom. xv. 23, 24, 28 that at that time he considered his missionary work in the east as completed, and was setting his face to the west, notably to Spain. If the letter emanates from Rome (*i.e.* if it is later than the writing of Rom. xv) it is necessary to believe that a new situation had arisen which led him to revise his plans. This possibility, indeed, is not unthinkable, as we know from his movements at Corinth; but it does show that the Roman view is not entirely free from weaknesses.

c. The Ephesian hypothesis

In place of the Roman dating it is proposed to place the letter in a putative Ephesian captivity. The evidence for this imprisonment is inferential and therefore lacking in complete cogency; but the scholars who support it find that the locating of the letter in this period of Paul's life eases the difficulties which the Roman theory encounters. For example, the intended re-visit to Philippi is then fulfilled in Acts xx. 1–6, with Timothy's movements also tallying with the record of Acts. W. Michaelis, who has consistently championed the Ephesian origin, shows persuasively how, on this view, the movements mentioned both in Acts and in Philippians dovetail like the pieces of a jig-saw puzzle. The shorter distance between Philippi and Ephesus makes the journeys more within the bounds of likelihood, while there is inscriptional evidence that satisfies the requirement of i. 13 and iv. 22. Ephesus was the centre of the imperial administration in Asia, and there would be a *praetorium* there.

The main difficulties which stand in the way of accepting this novel theory are:

1. Its speculative character. The Ephesian imprisonment cannot be proved from a direct source, although there is much indirect attestation of it, especially in 1 and 2 Corinthians.

2. The absence of any mention of a matter which (so it is argued) must have filled the apostle's mind at the time of this suggested dating, *viz.* the collection for the churches in Judaea.

3. Perhaps the strongest counter-objection is the failure to explain why it was that, if Paul were in jeopardy at Ephesus, he did not use his right as a Roman citizen and extricate himself by an appeal to the emperor to be tried in Rome. Of this possibility there is no mention in the letter.

Our conclusion, then, must be a disappointing one to those who expect a firm answer. The evidence, we feel, is finely balanced, and a final decision is not possible. The Roman dating may still be accepted with caution and one or two lingering doubts. The Ephesian hypothesis would have to be sufficiently strong to reverse the judgment of centuries, and this it fails to do completely, although it has many points in its favour; and were it more securely anchored in direct evidence it would command wider support. See PAUL, III*d* (iii).

III. THE UNITY OF THE LETTER

In the textual history the letter is known only as a complete whole; but there are many suggestions which contest its unity, mainly on the ground of an abrupt change in tone, style, and content at the beginning of chapter iii. Explanations of this sudden change are given under the headings of 'Interpolation' and 'Interruption'.

a. Interpolation

On this view the reason for the abrupt change at iii. 1b is that this verse introduces an interpolated fragment from another Pauline letter which has somehow become interwoven into the canonical Epistle. There is little agreement as to where the interpolation ends, whether iv. 3 (so K. Lake), iv. 1 (A. H. McNeile–C. S. C. Williams, F. W. Beare), or iii. 19 (J. H. Michael). Beare, who is one of the most recent commentators, envisages the letter as a composite document made up of three elements: a letter of thanks, acknowledging the Philippians' gift by Epaphroditus (iv. 10–20); an interpolated fragment which denounces the false teaching of the Jewish missionaries and the antinomianism of Gentile Christians (iii. 2–iv. 1), and may be directed to some church other than Philippi, as J. H. Michael earlier proposed; and the framework of the Epistle (i. 1–iii. 1, iv. 2–9, 21–23), regarded as being the last of Paul's extant letters and, in a sense, his farewell message to the Church militant on earth. This analysis is reminiscent of that described by P. Benoit in his commentary in *La Bible de Jérusalem*, 1956, p. 19.

b. Interruption

The sudden change in style and outlook may more plausibly be accounted for by the interruption of the apostle as he dictated his letter, as Lightfoot suggested. See also E. Stange, 'Diktierpausen in den Paulusbriefen', in *ZNW*, XVIII, 1917–18, pp. 115 f.

On this interpretation, iii. 1a is the intended conclusion of the letter. Paul is disturbed by stirring news which has just reached him, and quickly turns aside to dictate a vehement warning. 'The same things' is a prospective term, looking forward to the serious admonitions to watchfulness against the Judaizers which are to follow.

The integrity of the letter is, therefore, to be accepted, with a possible reservation only in the case of ii. 5–11, which some regard as a pre-Pauline or post-Pauline composition, while F. W. Beare breaks new ground with the submission that this section owes its origin to an unknown Gentile writer who came under Pauline influence during the apostle's lifetime. Paul accepts his writing with his *imprimatur* by including it in his Epistle. There is a full discussion of the authorship and provenance of the Christological hymn in ii. 5–11 in the Tyndale Lecture, noted below.

IV. THE OCCASION AND PURPOSE OF THE LETTER

The most obvious reason why the letter came to be written is to be found in Paul's situation as a prisoner, and his desire to commend his colleagues Timothy and Epaphroditus to the church. Paul writes as though he wanted to prepare the way for the coming of these men, and particularly to disarm any criticism which might be raised against Epaphroditus (*cf.* ii. 23 ff.).

There is also the note of appreciation for the Philippians' gift, to which he alludes in several places (i. 5, iv. 10, 14 ff.). This gift had evidently come through Epaphroditus, and Paul gratefully acknowledges both the gift and the presence of their messenger (ii. 25).

Epaphroditus had, it is clear, also brought news of the outbreak of various troubles at Philippi, especially the disturbing news of disunity within the ranks of the church members. This is clear from ii. 2–4, 14, iv. 2, where the disputants are named, and perhaps i. 27. Paul gently reproaches them for this, and recalls them to agreement in the Lord.

Another source of confusion in the fellowship seems to have been the existence and influence of a 'perfectionist' group within the church. It is true that there is no direct mention of such a wing of opinion, but the way in which the apostle writes in chapter iii endorses the verdict of E. F. Scott that 'it can hardly be doubted that Paul here deals with a question which was warmly debated in the Philippian church'.

The Christian cause at Philippi seems to have been the object of persecution and attack from the outside world. There is definite allusion to the church's 'enemies' (i. 28), and a description of the type of society in which the church was called upon to live and bear witness to Christ is given (ii. 15). Hence the oft-repeated call to stand fast (i. 27, iv. 1). We may detect in a ministry of encouragement a further reason for the letter, although Lohmeyer's interpretation of the entire Epistle as a 'tract for martyrs' is somewhat extreme.

V. THE VALUE OF THE LETTER

Two outstanding features of the letter may be mentioned. First, the Philippian letter will always remain as a tribute to the apostle's attitude to his sufferings. By the grace of God he is able to rejoice under the most trying circumstances of his captivity and impending fate. His constant call to rejoicing (the word 'joy' and its cognate forms is found sixteen times) is a distinguishing characteristic, as Bengel noted in his famous phrase: '*summa epistolae*; *gaudeo, gaudete*'. And the secret of that joy is fellowship with the Lord who is the centre of his life, whatever the future may hold (i. 20, 21).

Secondly, no introduction to the letter would be complete without a reference to the great passage in ii. 5–11. Here we find the *locus classicus* of Paul's doctrine of the person of Christ, and for that reason the Philippian Epistle will ever remain in the forefront of Pauline studies so long as the great apostle's writings continue to engage the attention of Christian students.

BIBLIOGRAPHY. In the recent commentary on this Epistle by the present writer (*TNTC*, 1959) and that by F. W. Beare (1959) full bibliographies are given to which the reader is referred. For the hymn in ii. 5–11 the author has essayed a full presentation of the problems and solutions in the Tyndale monograph, *An Early Christian Confession: Philippians ii. 5–11 in Recent Interpretation*, 1960.

R.P.M.

PHILISTINES, PHILISTIA.

I. NAME

In the Old Testament the name Philistine is written *pᵉlištî*, usually with the article, and more commonly in its plural form *pᵉlištîm* (rarely *pᵉlištiyyîm*) generally without the article. The territory which they inhabited was known as 'the land of the Philistines' (*'ereṣ pᵉlištîm*) or Philistia (*pᵉlešet*). It is from these that the modern name 'Palestine' derives. In the LXX the word is variously rendered *Phylistieim* (mainly in the Pentateuch, Joshua, and Judges), *Hellēnas* (Is. ix. 12 (Heb. 11)), and *allophylos, -oi*, 'stranger, foreigner' (but not in the Pentateuch or Joshua). It is probable that this name is to be identified with the name written *prst* in the Egyptian texts (the hieroglyphic script using *r* for the *l* sound, which is not represented, in the writing of foreign names) and *palastu* in the Assyrian cuneiform inscriptions.

II. IN THE BIBLE

a. Origin

The Philistines 'came out from' Casluhim, the son of Mizraim (Egypt) the son of Ham (Gn. x. 14; 1 Ch. i. 12). When they later appeared and confronted the Israelites they came from Caphtor (*q.v.*; Am. ix. 7).

b. In the time of the Patriarchs

Abraham and Isaac had dealings with a Philistine, Abimelech, the king of Gerar, and his general Phichol (Gn. xx, xxi, xxvi). In the time of the Monarchy the Philistines were almost proverbially aggressive, but Abimelech was a reasonable man. He had adopted many of the customs of the country, for he bore a Semitic name, and engaged with Isaac in a covenant (*q.v.*).

c. At the time of the Exodus and the Judges

When the Israelites left Egypt the Philistines were extensively settled along the coastal strip between Egypt and Gaza, and they were obliged to detour inland to avoid 'the way of the land of the Philistines' (Ex. xiii. 17). The adjacent section of the Mediterranean was in fact referred to as the sea of the Philistines (Ex. xxiii. 31). It is presumably the Philistines in this area who are referred to as Caphtorim in Dt. ii. 23.

The Israelites did not encounter the Philistines in Canaan during the conquest, but by the time Joshua was an old man they were established in the five cities, Gaza, Ashkelon, Ashdod, Ekron, and Gath, where they were ruled by five 'lords' (Jos. xiii. 2, 3; see LORDS OF THE PHILISTINES). From this time for many generations these people were used by God to chastise the Israelites (Jdg. iii. 2, 3). Shamgar ben Anath repulsed them temporarily (Jdg. iii. 31), but they constantly pressed inland from the coast plain, and the Israelites even adopted their gods (Jdg. x. 6, 7). The great Israelite hero of the period of the Judges was Samson (Jdg. xiii–xvi). In his time there was intercourse between the Philistines and Israelites, for he married a Philistine wife, and later had relations with Delilah, who, if not a Philistine herself, was in close contact with them. The hill-country was not under Philistine control, and Samson took refuge there after his raids. When he was finally taken by them he was bound with bronze fetters (xvi. 21) and forced to make sport for them while they watched from inside and on the roof of a pillared building (xvi. 25–27).

d. In the reigns of Saul and David

It was probably largely due to the continuing pressure of the Philistines that the need for a strong military leader was felt in Israel. The ark was captured by the Philistines in a disastrous battle at Aphek and the shrine at Shiloh was destroyed (1 Sa. iv), and at this time they probably controlled Esdraelon, the coast plain, the Negeb, and much of the hill-country. They also controlled the distribution of iron, and thus prevented the Israelites from having useful weapons (1 Sa. xiii. 19–22). Saul was anointed king by Samuel, and after a victory over the Philistines at Michmash, drove them from the hill-country (1 Sa. xiv). His erratic rule, however, allowed the Philistines to continue to assert themselves, as when they challenged Israel at Ephes-dammim, and David killed Goliath (1 Sa. xvii, xviii). Saul turned against David, who became an outlaw and finally a feudatory vassal of Achish king of Gath (1 Sa. xxvii). He was not called upon to fight against Israel at the battle of Mt. Gilboa when Saul and his sons were killed, and when he took over the kingship of Israel he must have remained on peaceful terms with Gath at least, and in fact maintained a personal Philistine bodyguard throughout his reign (see CHERETHITES). A final conflict had to come, however. David drove the Philistines out of the hill-country and struck a heavy blow in Philistia itself (2 Sa. v. 25), putting an end to the power of the Philistines as a serious menace.

e. During the divided Monarchy

The Philistines continued to cause trouble throughout the Monarchy. With the weakening of the kingdom at the death of David the Philistine cities (except for Gath, 2 Ch. xi. 8) were independent and there was fighting on the frontier (1 Ki. xv. 27, xvi. 15). Jehoshaphat received tribute from some of the Philistines (2 Ch. xvii. 11), but under Jehoram the border town of Libnah was lost to Israel (2 Ki. viii. 22). They were still aggressive in the time of Ahaz (Is. ix. 8–12), and the last time they are mentioned in the Bible is in the prophecy of Zechariah, after the return from the Exile.

III. PHILISTIA

The area which took its name from the Philistines was that of the nucleus of their settlement. This centred on the five main Philistine cities Gaza, Ashkelon, Ashdod, Ekron, and Gath, and comprised the coastal strip south of Carmel, extending inland to the foothills of Judah. Other cities particularly associated with the Philistines in the Bible are Beth-shan and Gerar (*qq.v.*). The five Philistine cities have not all been identified with certainty owing to continued occupation of many of the sites in the area (see under separate city names).

Fig. 166. Philistinian soldiers as depicted on a relief showing a sea-battle in the mortuary temple of Rameses III at Medinet Habu (1191 BC).

IV. IN THE INSCRIPTIONS

The Philistines are first mentioned by name (*prst*) in the annals of Rameses III for his 5th (1165 BC) and subsequent years, inscribed in his temple to Ammon at Medinet Habu near Thebes. This describes his campaign against an invasion of Libyans and various other peoples generally known as the 'Sea Peoples', of whom the *prst* were one. Other members of the 'Sea Peoples' had already been mentioned in the inscriptions of Merenptah, Rameses II, and in the 14th-century Amarna Letters (Lukku, Šerdanu, Danuna). The carved reliefs in the temple at Medinet Habu show the Sea Peoples arriving with their families and chattels by wagon (see fig. 52) and ship, and the *prst* and another group closely associated with them, the *ṯkr* (Tjekker), are depicted wearing head-dresses of feathers rising vertically from a horizontal band (see fig. 166). A head wearing a similar head-dress is one of the pictographic signs on a clay disk found at Phaistos in Crete, and usually dated to the 17th century BC. A recent attempted decipherment of this document (Schwartz) would reduce its date to the late 15th century and read the place-name *pi-ri-ta*, Philistia, on it.

The Assyrian inscriptions mention Philistia as an area often in revolt. The first occurrence is in an inscription of Adad-nirari III (810–782 BC), where Philistia is mentioned among other states, including Israel, as paying tribute. Later Philistia or cities in it is mentioned in the annals of Tiglath-pileser III, Sargon, and Sennacherib, usually to state that a rebellion has been put down.

In a group of cuneiform documents of the time of the Exile found at Babylon, the issue of rations to expatriates is recorded. Among these are mentioned men from Philistia.

V. ARCHAEOLOGY

a. Pottery

A type of pottery has been found in a number of sites centring on Philistia and from levels of the late second millennium BC. Since this was the area and period of the Philistines, this pottery is usually attributed to them. In its decoration it shows marked affinities with that of the Aegean, and recent excavations at Enkomi and Sinda in Cyprus have brought to light locally made pottery (*c.* 1225–1175 BC) which is classified as Mycenaean III. C. 1. b, deriving from Aegean originals, and most probably representing the forerunner of the Philistine pottery.

b. Clay coffins

Clay coffins, each with a face moulded in relief at the head end, have been discovered at Beth-shan, Tell el-Far'a, and Lachish, which are probably to be connected with similar coffins found in Egypt, notably at Tell el-Yehudiyeh in the Delta. The date and distribution of these suggest that they may be attributed to the Philistines, a view supported by the fact that some of the faces are surmounted by a row of vertical strokes, perhaps indicating the feathered head-dress.

c. Weapons

The Egyptian reliefs show the *prst*, with the Tjekker and Serdanu, as armed with lances, round shields, long broadswords, and triangular daggers (see fig. 166). They arrived in Palestine at the period of transition from the Bronze to Iron Age, so that the biblical statements that they bound Samson with fetters of bronze but, by the time of Saul, controlled the iron industry of the area are quite consistent.

VI. CULTURE

The Philistines, while retaining a few cultural features bespeaking their foreign origin, were largely assimilated to the Canaanite culture that surrounded them.

a. Government

The five Philistine cities were each ruled by a *seren* ('Lord', see LORDS OF THE PHILISTINES). This word has been connected with Gk. *tyrannos*, and it may be that it is similarly to be connected with *tarwana*, 'judge(?)' (rendered by Phoenician *ṣdq* in the Karatepe bilingual) of the Hittite hieroglyphic inscriptions. From its usage, this word has been compared semantically with Heb. *šōpēṭ*, 'judge' (Laroche).

b. Language

No Philistine inscriptions have been recovered, and the language is unknown, though some scholars have surmised that it may have derived from a possibly Indo-European, pre-Greek speech of the Aegean area. Certain words in the Bible may be Philistine loan-words. In addition to *seren*, which is probably one, the word for helmet, whose foreign origin is betrayed in the variant spellings *kôḇa*' and *qôḇa*', is usually attributed to the Philistines. Another word which some scholars would label as Philistine is *'argāz*, 'box' (1 Sa. vi. 8, 11, 15, AV 'coffer'). Other words have been designated as Philistine from time to time, but without general assent. Among the names, Achish (*'āḵîš*) is probably the same as *'kš*, which is listed as a *kftyw* (see CAPHTOR) name in an Egyptian inscription of about the XVIIIth Dynasty. Aside from these few words, it is clear that the Philistines adopted the Semitic tongue of the peoples they dispossessed.

c. Religion

Knowledge of the Philistine religion depends upon the Bible. The three gods mentioned, Dagon, Ashtoreth, and Baalzebub (*qq.v.*), were all Near Eastern, and it is perhaps to be assumed that they identified their own gods with those they found in Palestine, and accommodated their own religion to that already there. The excavator of Beth-shan (*q.v.*) suggested that two temples found there might be those of Dagon and Ashtoreth, where Saul's trophies were hung (see figs. 36, 61), but no excavated temples may be certainly identified as Philistine. They offered sacrifices (Jdg. xvi. 23) and wore charms into battle (2 Sa. v. 21).

VII. ORIGIN AND RÔLE

The cumulative evidence leaves little doubt that the Philistines came immediately, though probably not ultimately, from the Aegean. Some scholars would equate the name with that of the *Pelasgoi*, the pre-Greek inhabitants of the Aegean, a view which is weighted by the occurrence of the name twice in Greek literature, spelt with a *t* rather than a *g*. This view is still debated, and even granting it, the classical references to the *Pelasgoi* are too inconsistent to be helpful.

It seems that the Philistines were one of the Sea Peoples who, in the later second millennium, moved out of the Aegean, probably as a result of the arrival of the Greeks, and migrated by land and sea, some *via* Crete and Cyprus, to the Near East, where they forced a foothold, first as mercenary troops of the pharaohs, the Hittite kings, and the Canaanite rulers, and finally as settlers who were absorbed in the basic population. Though they retained their name for many centuries, the biblical Philistines, the Tjekker who occupied an adjacent coastal region, and doubtless others of the Sea Peoples, became for all practical purposes Canaanites.

VIII. PHILISTINES IN THE PATRIARCHAL NARRATIVES

Since the Philistines are not named in extra-biblical inscriptions until the 12th century BC, and the archaeological remains associated with them do not appear before this time, many commentators condemn their mention in the patriarchal period as anachronistic. Two considerations must be entertained, however. There is evidence of a major expansion of Aegean trade in the Middle Minoan II period (*c.* 1900–1700 BC; see CRETE) and objects of Aegean manufacture or influence have been found from this period at Ras Shamra in Syria, Hazor, and perhaps Megiddo in Palestine, and Ṭôd, Harageh, Lahun, and Abydos in Egypt. It is likely that a large part of this trade consisted in perishable goods such as textiles. A new type of spiral design which appears in Egypt and Asia (Mari) at this time may support this. Further evidence of contacts is afforded by a tablet from Mari (18th century) recording the sending of gifts by the king of Hazor to Kaptara (see CAPHTOR). Secondly, ethnic names in antiquity were not used with particular precision. The members of a mixed group such as the Sea Peoples were unlikely to be carefully distinguished by name, so that the absence of one name from the inscriptions may simply mean that the particular group was not sufficiently prominent to find special mention. The Sea Peoples, and their predecessors who traded with the Near East, arrived in waves, and dominant in a 12th-century wave were the Philistines, who consequently figured in the records. There is no reason why small groups of Philistines could not have been among the early Aegean traders, not prominent enough to be noticed by the larger states.

BIBLIOGRAPHY. R. A. S. Macalister, *The Philistines, Their History and Civilization*, 1914; W. F. Albright, *AASOR*, XII, 1932, pp. 53–58; E. Grant, *JBL*, LV, 1936, pp. 175–194; O. Eissfeldt in G. Wissowa, *RE*, XXXVIII, 1938, cols. 2390–2401; A. Furumark, *The Chronology of Mycenaean Pottery*, 1941, pp. 118–121; A. H. Gardiner, *Ancient Egyptian Onomastica*, Text, I, pp. 200*–205*; V. Georgiev, *Jahrbuch für Kleinasiatische Forschung*, I, 1950, pp. 136–141; J. Bérard, *RAr*, XXXVII, 1951, pp. 129–142; C. H. Gordon, *Antiquity*, XXX, 1956, pp. 22–26; T. Dothan, *Antiquity and Survival*, II, 1957, pp. 151–164; G. E. Wright, *BA*, XXII, 1959, pp. 54–66; K. M. Kenyon, *Archaeology in the Holy Land*, 1960, pp. 221–239. T.C.M.

PHILO. Among the many bearers of the name Philo in antiquity, the most important for the student of the Bible is Philo of Alexandria, a member of a rich and influential Jewish family in that city in the 1st century. His brother Alexander was one of the richest men of his day, while his nephew Tiberius Alexander became in due time Procurator of Judaea and Prefect of Egypt, having apostatized from the Jewish faith.

Little is known of the life of Philo himself; neither his birth nor his death may be dated, the one sure date in his career being his membership in the embassy to Gaius (Caligula) in AD 39. From this it is evident that he was quite old at that time, and conjecturally we may place his dates as approximately 20 BC to AD 45. From his writings it may be deduced that, as a leader of the Jewish community, he spent much of his life in the duties of public service. His natural bent, however, was to the life of contemplation and the pursuit of philosophy, in which, as he asserts, he spent his youth (*Concerning the Special Laws*, iii. 1), perhaps in such a community as the Therapeutae, described by him in *Concerning the Contemplative Life*. Although he was obliged to leave this to take up his duties, he found opportunity to produce a body of writings on philosophical and theological topics.

His early work was on philosophical themes, in which he shows little originality, but provides valuable source material for the study of a little-known period of Hellenistic philosophy. His main work, however, was the production of expositions of the Pentateuch; he was motivated by the desire to demonstrate that the philosophical and religious quests of the Gentile world of the day found their true goal in the God of Abraham. Three large works remain, none of them complete nor in exact order, their several sections having been transmitted often as separate treatises in the MS tradition: *The Allegory of the Laws* (a commentary on Genesis); *Questions and Answers on Genesis and Exodus* (a shorter work of the same kind); and *The Exposition of the Laws* (a review of the history in the Pentateuch). By means of allegorical exegesis he is able to extract moral and mystical teaching from all parts of these books. His method of allegory is derived from that already applied to the Homeric books by philosophers. It may be analysed as: (i) 'cosmological' ('physiological' in his own terminology) in which allegory concerning the nature (*physis*) of things is perceived (*e.g.* the high priest and his vestments seen as the Logos and the universe, *Life of Moses*, II, 117 ff.), and (ii) 'ethical', in which reference to human psychology and moral struggle is seen (*e.g.* etymological interpretations of such figures as Isaac (= joy)). The basis of both the cosmology and psychology is the Stoic system, although it is evident that Pythagorean and Platonist are also laid under contribution in some details, a feature which probably reflects the eclecticism of the period.

Philo's greatest contribution to thought, according to recent students, is his use of philosophy in this way to provide a rationale of religion; he is in fact the 'first theologian', and philosophy is significant to him primarily as the handmaid of theology. The motivation of his work may be seen not simply in his missionary zeal, common to many Jews of that era, but also in the mystical experiences of the reality of his God of which he writes movingly in several places (*e.g. Special Laws, loc. cit.*). Central to his understanding both of the universe and of religious experience is the concept of the Logos, a term of Stoic origin which, in Philo, linked with such a concept as the Platonic World of Ideas, signifies the mode whereby the transcendent God creates and sustains the world, and further, reveals Himself to His creatures. Moses is expounded as a type of the Logos by whom men are led to knowledge of God; the Patriarchs as instances of those who have freed themselves from the bondage of material things and are united with the divine Wisdom.

The definitive edition of the Greek text of Philo is the six volumes by L. Cohn and P. Wendland, published 1896–1914, with a seventh volume of Indices (1926–30) by H. Leisegang. A number of works, extant only in Armenian, were edited by the Mechitarist J. B. Aucherian in 1822 and 1826; the version dates from the 5th century. There is also an Old Latin version of Philo, of some value for the construction of his text. The most recent translation of Philo's extant works, both Greek and Armenian, is that in the Loeb Classical Library by F. H. Colson, G. H. Whittaker, and R. Marcus (9 vols. plus 2 supplementary vols., 1929–).

As the best preserved and most extensive of Hellenistic Jewish writings, Philo's works are of value in illuminating the thought world of the New Testament. Certain of his Old Testament citations bear upon the problem of the origin of the LXX (see P. Katz, *Philo's Bible*). Two writings at least of the New Testament may not be adequately understood without reference to his thought and method. The Epistle to the Hebrews in its treatment of the tabernacle and the figure of Melchizedek shows close affinity to his allegory, while its doctrine of the Son is related in several particulars to his Logos-teaching. The Gospel of John bears no resemblance to Philonic allegory (as has sometimes been asserted), but in the cosmology explicit in the Prologue and elsewhere implicit there is evidently close kinship to the Philonic allegory. This need not imply that these writers were directly dependent on Philo. A plausible explanation might be that they come from a like background of thought. Both possibilities have been pursued and demand still further investigation.

BIBLIOGRAPHY. H. Leisegang, article 'Philo' in Pauly-Wissowa; E. Bréhier, *Les Idées Philosophiques et Religieuses de Philon d'Alexandrie*, 1925; E. R. Goodenough, *An Introduction to Philo Judaeus*, 1939; *id.*, *By Light, Light*, 1935; and appropriate chapters in C. H. Dodd, *The Interpretation of the Fourth Gospel*, 1953, and C. Spicq, *L'Épitre aux Hébreux*, 1952. J.N.B.

PHINEHAS. A name of Egyptian origin, *P'-nḥsy*, 'the Nubian'; popular in Egypt during the New Kingdom (16th to 12th centuries BC). It is borne in the Old Testament by three individuals.

1. Son of Eleazar, and grandson of Aaron (Ex. vi. 25; 1 Ch. vi. 4, 50; Ezr. vii. 5), with priestly descendants (Ezr. viii. 2). He slew an Israelite and the (pagan) Midianite woman he had taken, after Israel became involved in paganism at Shittim (Nu. xxv; Ps. cvi. 30), and shared in the subsequent war against Midian (Nu. xxxi. 6). Under Joshua, Phinehas helped settle the dispute with the Transjordanian tribes over their memorial altar (Jos. xxii. 9 ff.). After burying his father in his own hill (Jos. xxiv. 33) Phinehas was officiating priest early in the Judges' period (Jdg. xx. 28; perhaps 1 Ch. ix. 20).

2. Younger of the high priest Eli's two disreputable sons, late in the Judges' period (1 Sa. i. 3, *cf.* ii. 12–17, 34). He was slain in the battle of Aphek when the Philistines captured the ark (1 Sa. iv). A grandson of this Phinehas was a priest in Saul's reign (1 Sa. xiv. 3). **3.** The father of a priest Eleazar in Ezra's time (Ezr. viii. 33). K.A.K.

PHOENICIA, PHOENICIANS. The territory on the E Mediterranean coast covering about 150 miles between the rivers Litani and Arvad (modern Lebanon–S Latakia) and its inhabitants (see maps 8, 16).

Phoenicia (AV Phenice) as such is named only in the New Testament as the place of refuge for Christians fleeing from persecution following the death of Stephen (Acts xi. 19); through this land Paul and Silas journeyed on their way from Samaria to Antioch (Acts xv. 3). Later Paul landed on the Phoenician coast near Tyre on his way to Jerusalem (Acts xxi. 2, 3). In the time of our Lord Phoenicia was referred to as 'the coast and region about Tyre and Sidon' (Mt. xv. 21; Lk. vi. 17), and the inhabitants, including Greeks, were considered 'Syro-Phoenicians' (Mk. vii. 26).

In Old Testament times the territory occupied by the Phoenicians was called by the Hebrews 'Canaan' (Is. xxiii. 11), 'Canaanite' (*i.e.* 'merchant') being probably the name applied by the inhabitants to themselves (Gn. x. 15). It was, however, the common practice in all periods to refer to Phoenicia by the name of its principal cities (see SIDON, TYRE), since there was little political cohesion between them except for periods such as the reign of Hiram I.

I. HISTORY

The origin of the sea-faring Phoenicians is obscure, though according to Herodotus (i. 1, vii. 89) they arrived overland from the Persian Gulf area, *via* the Red Sea, and first founded Sidon. The earliest archaeological evidence of their presence comes from the proto-Phoenician finds at Byblos (ancient Gubla or Gebal, Ezk. xxvii. 9, modern Gebail) dated *c.* 3000. This important site has been excavated since 1924 by the French under Montet and Dunand. Byblian ships are depicted on Egyptian reliefs of the time of Sahure in the Vth Dynasty (*c.* 2500 BC) and there can be no doubt that by the 18th century there was an extensive trade in timber and artistic commodities between Phoenicia and Egypt (see SHIPS). The Phoenicians by this time had founded their first colonies along the coast at Joppa, Dor (Jdg. i. 27–31), Acre, and Ugarit (Ras Shamra). They chose easily defensible natural harbours and gradually dominated the local population as at Ras Shamra (level IV).

For some centuries Phoenicia was under the economic and quasi-military control of the Egyptian XVIIIth and XIXth Dynasties, and Arvad was among the places claimed to have been captured by Tuthmosis III (*c.* 1485 BC). Nevertheless, the letters written by Rib-Addi of Byblos and Abi-milki of Tyre to Amenophis III at Amarna in Egypt show that, by *c.* 1400 BC, Ṣumuru and Berut had disaffected and with Sidon, which appears to have maintained its independence, were blockading Phoenician cities (see Amarna under ARCHAEOLOGY). When the 'sea-peoples' invaded the coast *c.* 1200 BC Byblos, Arvad, and Ugarit were destroyed and the Sidonians fled to Tyre, which now became the principal port, or, as Isaiah claims, 'the daughter of Sidon' (xxiii. 12).

By the time of David Tyre was ruled by Hiram I son of Abi-Baal and his reign began a golden age. Phoenicia was allied commercially with David (2 Sa. v. 11; 1 Ki. v. 1) and Hiram by treaty supplied Solomon with wood, stone, and craftsmen for the construction of the Temple and palace (1 Ki. v. 1–12; 2 Ch. ii. 3–16), and ships and navigators to assist the Judaean fleet and to develop the port of Ezion-geber as a base for long voyages (1 Ki. ix. 27). This aid resulted in territorial advantages, for Tyre was given twenty villages on her border in part payment (verses 10–14). Phoenicia, herself long influenced by Egyptian art, motifs, and methods, was now in a position to influence Hebrew thought. Hiram was a conqueror and builder of several temples at Tyre, and a successful administrator who settled colonial revolts (W. F. Albright in the *Leland Volume*, 1942, pp. 43 f.). It was probably due to his initiative that by the 9th century Phoenician colonies were founded in Sardinia (Nova, Tharros), Cyprus (Kition), and Karatepe (N Taurus). Utica had been settled in the 12th century and Carthage, Sicily (Motya), and Tunisia by the 8th.

Hiram's successor, a high priest named Ethbaal, furthered the alliance with Israel by the marriage of his daughter Jezebel to Ahab (1 Ki. xvi. 31), with the consequence that the worship of the Phoenician Baals was increased (1 Ki. xviii. 19). Elijah fled for a while to Zarephath, which was part of the coast controlled by Sidon, and therefore at this time independent of Tyre (1 Ki. xvii. 9).

The Assyrian advances brought pressure on the Phoenician cities. Ashurnasirpal II (884–859 BC) counted among the tribute he received from Tyre, Sidon, Gebal, and Arvad garments and cloth, many dyed, precious metals, and carved ivory and wood. This tribute was renewed when Shalmaneser III besieged Damascus and marched to the Mediterranean coast at the Dog river in 841 BC. The act of submission to him and the gifts sent by Tyre and Sidon are pictured on the bronze gates set up in the Assyrian temple at Balawat (see R. D. Barnett, *Assyrian Palace Reliefs*, 1960, pl. 139). Adad-nirari III claimed Tyre and Sidon among his vassals in 803 BC (*DOTT*, p. 51). Hirammu of Tyre, Sibitti-Bi'ili of Gubla (Byblos) sent tribute to Tiglath-pileser III during his siege of Arpad (*c.* 741 BC) about the same time as Menahem of Israel submitted to him. A few years later the Assyrian sent his *rab šaqe*—official (see RAB-SHAKEH)—to collect taxes from Metenna of Tyre. Letters addressed to the Assyrian king show that Tyre and Sidon were under direct supervision of an Assyrian official, who forwarded the taxes, mostly paid in timber and goods, direct to Calah (*Iraq*, XVII, 1955, pp. 126–154). In 734 BC Tiglath-pileser captured the fortress of Kashpuna, which guarded the approaches to Tyre and Sidon, who were now allied in defence.

Sargon continued to raid the Phoenician coastlands, and Sennacherib (*c.* 701 BC) captured Ušše near Tyre and carried Phoenician prisoners off to Nineveh to build his new palace (British Museum reliefs) and to Opis to build the fleet planned to pursue the rebel Merodach-baladan (*q.v.*) across the Persian Gulf. Nevertheless, the larger cities clung to their independence until Esarhaddon sacked Sidon and settled the survivors from it in a new town called 'Walled City of Esarhaddon' and in fifteen adjacent villages. Other towns were placed under Ba'ali of Tyre, who was bound by treaty to Esarhaddon. This named Arvad, Acre, Dor, Gebal and Mt. Lebanon and regulated trade and shipping. However, Ba'ali, incited by Tirhakah of Egypt, revolted. Tyre was besieged and Phoenicia subordinated to a province. The rulers of the cities, including Milki-ašapa of Gebal, and Matan-Ba'al of Arvad, were made to 'bear the corvée basket', that is, to act as labourers at the foundation of Esarhaddon's new palace at Calah as Manasseh did in Babylon (2 Ch. xxxiii. 11).

Ashurbanipal continued the war against Phoenicia containing Ba'ali by an attack in 665 BC prior to his advance on Egypt. He took Ba'ali's daughters as concubines and also received a heavy tribute. On the death of Ba'ali Azi-Ba'al was made king and Yakinlu appointed to rule Arvad.

Fig. 167. Ahiram, king of Tyre, seated on his throne with his Phoenician courtiers and servants before him. From a sarcophagus relief, *c.* 1000 BC.

With the decline of Assyria the cities regained their independence and traded with new ports opened in Egypt. Their Punic kinsfolk founded colonies in Algeria, Spain, and Morocco in the 7th–5th centuries and by a naval victory over the Etruscans in 535 BC finally closed the W Mediterranean to the Phoenician traders.

Nebuchadrezzar II of Babylon in his advance towards Egypt besieged Tyre for thirteen years *c.* 585–573 BC (Ezk. xxvi. 1–xxix. 1 ff.), but, though Ithobaal was carried off prisoner to Babylon, the city retained a measure of autonomy, which it held throughout the Neo-Babylonian and Persian rule, trading with Egypt (Zp. i. 11) and supplying fish and other commodities to Jerusalem (Ne. xiii. 16) and in return probably receiving wood and homespun textiles (Pr. xxxi. 24, RSV; see also ARTS AND CRAFTS).

Alexander the Great captured the island city of Tyre by means of an artificially constructed causeway. The slaughter and destruction was heavy, but the city recovered and, like Sidon, was prosperous in Hellenistic and Roman times (*e.g.* Mt. xv. 21).

II. RELIGION

The idolatrous religion of Phoenicia was condemned by Elijah (1 Ki. xviii–xix) and later Hebrew prophets (Is. lxv. 11). The early period, seen in the Ras Shamra texts (see ARCHAEOLOGY), reveals a polytheistic and natural mythology centred round Baal, also called Melek 'king', the sun-god Saps, and Keshep (Mikkal) an underworld deity. Fertility cults honoured 'Anat (Astarte, Ashtart) and the popular blend of Semitic and Egyptian ideas resulted in the cult of Adonis and Tammuz (*q.v.*), in which the former was identified with Osiris. Other deities included Eshmun, the god of healing (Gk. Asklepios), and Melqart.

III. ART

The syncretistic tendencies of Phoenician religions are to be seen in the art which combines Semitic, Egyptian, and Hurrian elements. This is due to the geographical location and the interchange of materials and influence which followed trade. The Phoenicians were primarily sea-traders and artists. They exported silk, linen, and wool, dyed, woven, and embroidered locally, hence the name Phoenicia may be derived from Gk. *phoinios*, 'red-purple' (see ARTS AND CRAFTS), and from their unbounded supplies in the hinterland of the Lebanon shipped wood and its products. The craftsmen worked stone (*e.g.* Aḥiram sarcophagus *c.* 900 BC; *BASOR*, 134, p. 9; *Syria*, XI, pp. 180 ff.), ivory (*q.v.*), and glass (*q.v.*), and though the Hebrews did not themselves allow images or the portrayal of the human figure (see ART), Phoenician silver and bronze coins are found inland in numbers from the 4th century BC onwards. The requirements of their trade led to the development of writing (the so-called Phoenician, Byblian, and Ugaritic alphabets), the *abacus* for counting, and papyrus books (see PAPYRUS, BOOK). It is much to be regretted that the Phoenician literature, including the mythology of Sanchuniathon of Byblos and the history of Menander of Tyre, has survived only in a few quotations in later authors, for it was probably through their literature that much of the learning of the East reached Greece.

See also WRITING.

BIBLIOGRAPHY. R. D. Barnett, 'Phoenicia and the Ivory Trade' in *Archaeology*, IX, 1956.

D.J.W.

PHOENIX. 1. A mythical bird, anciently thought to be born directly from its parent's corpse. Some early Christians (Tertullian, *De Resurr.* xiii. 6, *cf. 1 Clement* xxv), seeing an analogy of resurrection, warranted it by Ps. xcii. 12 (LXX xci. 13), but *phoinix* there clearly means 'palm-tree'. Phoenix-and-palm became frequent in Christian art.

2. The harbour (AV 'Phenice') the nautical experts, despite Paul's entreaties, made for in winter (Acts xxvii. 12). Data given by Strabo, Ptolemy, and other writers seem to indicate the Cape Mouros area, where modern Loutro is the only safe harbour in southern Crete (James Smith, *Voyage and Shipwreck of St. Paul*[3], 1866, p. 90 n.). But Luke says Phoenix 'lieth toward the south-west and north-west (*sc.* 'winds')', *i.e.* faces west, while Loutro faces east. A narrow peninsula separates it from a west-facing bay, but one offering little shelter. Smith, urging the danger of westerly winter gales, suggested that Luke meant the direction *towards which* the winds blew, *i.e.* looking north-east and south-east (*cf.* RV, RSV); but this is unsubstantiated unless we assume some lost nautical idiom. Ramsay thought that Luke might have excusably misunderstood Paul's account of the discussion, but left open the possibility of a change in coastline (*cf. HDB*). Ogilvie's recent examination strongly suggests this occurred. The western bay was once better protected, and earthquake disturbance has apparently covered an inlet facing north-west in classical times. A south-western-facing inlet remains, and the disused western bay is still called Phinika. Ogilvie also found that locally the winter winds are north and east: in Acts xxvii it was an east-north-east wind (see EUROCLYDON) which caused the disaster.

BIBLIOGRAPHY. J. B. Lightfoot on *1 Clement* xxv; J. Smith, *op. cit.*, pp. 87 ff., 252 ff.; R. M. Ogilvie, *JTS* (NS), IX, 1958, pp. 308 ff.

A.F.W.

PHRYGIA. A tract of land centred on the western watershed of the great Anatolian plateau, and reaching northwards into the valley of the upper Sangarius, south-westwards down the valley of the Maeander, and south-eastwards across the plateau, perhaps as far as Iconium. The Phrygians formed the (legendary?) kingdom of Midas. They fell under direct Hellenic influence during the era of the Attalid kings of Pergamum, and in 116 BC most of Phrygia was incorporated by the Romans into their province of Asia. The eastern extremity (Phrygia Galatica) was included in the new province of Galatia in 25 BC. The Romans were deeply impressed by the ecstatic Phrygian cult of Cybele, and the national fanaticism apparently lies behind the defiant tombstones, presumably Montanist, of the 2nd century AD, which represent the earliest extant public manifesto of Christianity. There is no evidence of any indigenous Christian church in New Testament times, however. Such churches as fall technically within Phrygia (Laodicea, Hierapolis, Colossae, Pisidian Antioch, and probably Iconium; see fig. 26) were established in Greek communities. It was most probably Jewish members of these Greek states who visited Jerusalem (Acts ii. 10). If Col. ii. 1, as is just possible, is not taken to exclude a visit by Paul, it would be natural to assume that it is the first three of these cities, on the upper Maeander, that are referred to in Acts xvi. 6, xviii. 23. Failing that, we may resort to the view that 'Phrygia and the region of Galatia' is a composite technical term for Phrygia Galatica and refers in particular to the churches at Iconium and Pisidian Antioch (see GALATIA). Otherwise we cannot identify the disciples Paul left in 'Phrygia'.

BIBLIOGRAPHY. Strabo, xii; *Monumenta Asiae Minoris Antiqua; Anatolian Studies*; J. Friedrich, *RE*, XX, 1, pp. 781–891; W. M. Ramsay, *Cities and Bishoprics of Phrygia*, 1895–7; A. H. M. Jones, *Cities of the Eastern Roman Provinces*, 1937; D. Magie, *Roman Rule in Asia Minor*, 2 vols., 1950. E.A.J.

PHYLACTERIES. The name is a transliteration of Gk. *phylaktērion*, meaning 'a means of protection' or 'amulet'. Though some Jews have regarded them superstitiously, this attitude has always been marginal, so the Greek name probably derives from heathen misinterpretation (see AMULETS). The Jew speaks of *t^e^pillâ* (lit. 'prayer'), pl. *t^e^pillîn*. They represent the interpretation by the pious of Ex. xiii. 9, 16; Dt. vi. 8, xi. 18. Their present form became standardized by the early years of the 2nd century AD and consists of two hollow cubes made of the skin of clean animals. They vary between ½ inch and 1½ inches a side. That for the head is divided into four equal compartments; that for the hand has no divisions. In them are placed the four passages Ex. xiii. 1–10, xiii. 11–16; Dt. vi. 4–9, xi. 13–21 written by hand on parchment (on four pieces for the head, on one for the hand). The phylacteries are attached to leather straps by which they are fastened to the left hand and the centre of the forehead by the men before morning prayers, whether in the home or the synagogue, except on the sabbath and high festivals. They are put on after the praying shawl (*ṭallîṯ*), that for the hand coming first. Both they and the straps are always coloured black. The phylactery for the head can be recognized by a three- and four-armed *šin* on its right and left sides.

In the Qumran (*q.v.*) discoveries portions of phylacteries have been found, which show they were not absolutely standardized before the destruction of the Temple. The main difference, however, was the inclusion of the Ten Commandments on the parchment in them. Their exclusion later, just like their exclusion from the daily services, was a reaction against the Jewish Christians.

Though Christian exegesis has always understood the above-mentioned passages as metaphorical, our increasing knowledge of the ancient Near East would not rule out their possible literal intent (or for that matter of Dt. vi. 9, xi. 20, which the Jew fulfils by enclosing a parchment containing Dt. vi. 4–9, xi. 13–21 in a box called a *m^e^zûzâ* and affixing it to his door-post). All available evidence suggests, however, that they were a late innovation brought in by the *ḥ^a^sîḏîm* (see HASIDAEANS), being intended as a counterblast to increasing Hellenistic influence. There is no mention of them in the Old Testament, and they seem always to have been unknown to the Samaritans. LXX clearly takes the passages on which the custom is based as metaphorical. The *Letter of Aristeas* mentions apparently only that for the arm and Philo that for the head.

Both the somewhat later Talmudic acknowledgment that they were not worn by the common people (*'am hā-'āreṣ*) and the failure of pagan writers to mention them indicate that in the time of Christ they were still worn only by a minority of the people. We may be sure that all Pharisees wore them, not merely during morning prayer but throughout the hours of daylight. Their later restriction to the time of prayer was due to their providing an all too easy mark of recognition of the Jew in times of persecution. We have no reason for thinking that they were worn either by Christ or His disciples. Even the condemnation in Mt. xxiii. 5 suggests the temptation to the ultra-pious of stressing their adherence to a custom that was only slowly winning its way. Their use will have become universal before the end of the 2nd century AD.

The orthodox Jew interprets their use in a highly spiritual way. This is shown by the meditation to be used while putting them on, which is given early in the morning service in any standard Jewish Prayer Book.

BIBLIOGRAPHY. See the article in *JewE* and *SB*, IV, Excursus 11. H.L.E.

PHYSICIAN. See DISEASE AND HEALING.

PI-BESETH. Bubastis (Egyp. *Pr-B'stt*, 'mansion of the goddess Ubastet'), today Tell Basta, is situated on the Nile (Tanitic branch) south-east of Zagazig. It is mentioned in Ezk. xxx. 17 with the more important city of Heliopolis (On or Aven). Of the main temple described by Herodotus (ii. 138), little remains. Ubastet was a lioness or cat-goddess. Bubastis existed already in the time of Kheops and Khephren (IVth Dynasty, *c.* 2600 BC) and Pepi I (VIth Dynasty, *c.* 2400 BC). There are a few remains of the XVIIIth Dynasty (14th century BC). The town was important under the Ramesside kings (XIXth Dynasty, 13th century BC) and gave its name to the XXIInd Dynasty—that of Shishak, *c.* 945 BC—for whom it served as a residence like Tanis.

BIBLIOGRAPHY. E. Naville, *Bubastis*, 1891, and *The Festival Hall of Osorkon II*, 1892; Labib Habachi, *Tell Basta*, 1957. C.D.W.

PIETY. In AV the word occurs only in 1 Tim. v. 4, of dutiful care for a widowed mother or grandmother (*cf.* the Latin *pietas*, and the English 'filial piety'). The verb is *eusebeō*, the regular Hellenistic word for performing acts of religious worship (so in Acts xvii. 23), which indicates that, to Paul, care for these widowed relatives was part of a Christian's religious duty. This is understandable in the light both of the fifth commandment and of the fact that hereby the Christian relieves the Church of responsibility for supporting the widows concerned.

The corresponding noun, *eusebeia*, usually translated 'godliness' in EVV, appears fourteen times in the Pastorals and 2 Peter (elsewhere only in Acts iii. 12, where RSV renders 'piety') as a comprehensive term for the practice of Christian personal religion, the worship and service of God and the rendering of reverent obedience to His laws. In the plural the word denotes specific acts of piety (2 Pet. iii. 11). Christian *eusebeia* springs from the divine gift of an inner principle of life and power (2 Pet. i. 3; 2 Tim. iii. 5), which in its turn is bestowed with and through the sinner's believing response to the prior gift of saving truth (1 Tim. iii. 16: the 'mystery'—revealed secret—from which 'godliness' springs is the gospel message of the incarnate and reigning Christ). It is characteristic of gospel truth that it is 'according to godliness' (1 Tim. vi. 3; Tit. i. 1), *i.e.* godliness is the natural and necessary outcome of receiving it, so that ungodliness in those who profess it is presumptive evidence that they have not truly and heartily received it at all (*cf.* 2 Tim. iii. 2–8; Tit. i. 16; 2 Pet. ii. 19–22). All allegedly evangelical teaching should be tested by asking whether it makes for godliness—*i.e.* whether it enforces God's demands adequately, and whether it exhibits correctly the gift of renewal in Christ from which alone godliness can spring (2 Tim. iii. 5–8). (See GODLINESS.)

The Bible views the piety that it inculcates from several complementary standpoints. The Old Testament calls it 'the fear of God', or 'the Lord' (over thirty times), thus showing that true piety is rooted in an attitude of reverence, submission, and obedience towards God (see FEAR). The New Testament calls it 'obeying the gospel' or 'the truth' (Rom. x. 16; Gal. v. 7; 2 Thes. i. 8; 1 Pet. i. 22; *cf.* Rom. vi. 16), thus characterizing piety as a response to revelation. From another standpoint, as the maintaining of a state of separation from the world and consecratedness to God, the New Testament calls it simply 'holiness' (*hagiasmos, hagiōsynē*: see 1 Thes. iv. 3; Heb. xii. 14; 2 Cor. vii. 1; 1 Thes. iii. 13; *etc.*). Christ taught that the 'work of God', the single comprehensive divine requirement in which all the individual 'works of God' are embraced, is faith in Himself (Jn. vi. 28 f.); and Christian piety means simply living by this faith, and living it out. Accordingly, John characterizes the piety that God commands and accepts by singling out the two features that are most essential to it, and most distinctive of it—faith in Christ, and love to Christians (1 Jn. iii. 22–24).

A full analysis of New Testament piety would include the practical expression of faith in a life of repentance, resisting temptation, and mortifying sin; in habits of prayer, thanksgiving, and reverent observance of the Lord's Supper; in the cultivation of hope, love, generosity, joy, self-control, patient endurance, and contentment; in the quest for honesty, uprightness, and the good of others in all human relations; in respect for divinely constituted authority in Church, State, family, and household. All these attitudes and practices are commanded by God, and glorify Him.

BIBLIOGRAPHY. *Arndt*; *MM*; Richard Baxter, *A Christian Directory* (*Practical Works*, 1830, I–V; 1838, I). J.I.P.

PIGEON. See BIRDS OF THE BIBLE.

PIHAHIROT(H). An unidentified place on the border of Egypt (Ex. xiv. 2, 9; Nu. xxxiii. 7, 8). Several Old Egyptian equivalents have been proposed: *pr-qrḥt* (Naville), *pr-ḥwt-ḥr* (Clédat), *P'-Ḥwir* (Cazelles), *Pr-Ḥrt* (Albright), none of which is conclusive. See ENCAMPMENT BY THE SEA. C.D.W.

PILATE. Pontius Pilatus was a Roman of the equestrian, or upper middle-class, order: his *praenomen* is not known, but his *nomen*, Pontius, suggests that he was of Samnite extraction and his *cognomen*, Pilatus, may have been handed down by military forbears. Little is known of his career before AD 26, but in that year (see Hedley in *JTS*, XXXV, 1934, pp. 56–58) the Emperor Tiberius appointed him to be the fifth procurator (Gk. *epitropos*) of Judaea, and in accordance with a recent reversal in the policy of the Senate (in AD 21—Tacitus, *Annals* iii. 33, 34) Pilate took his wife with him (Mt. xxvii. 19). As procurator he had full control in the province, being in charge of the army of occupation (1 ala—*c.* 120 men—of cavalry, and 4 or 5 cohorts—*c.* 2,500–5,000 men—of infantry), which was stationed at Caesarea, with a detachment on garrison duty at Jerusalem in the fortress of Antonia. The procurator had full powers of life and death, and could reverse capital sentences passed by the Sanhedrin, which had to be submitted to him for ratification. He also appointed the high priests and controlled the Temple and its funds: the very vestments of the high priest were in his custody and were released only for festivals, when the procurator took up residence in Jerusalem and brought additional troops to patrol the city.

Even pagan historians mention Pilate only in connection with his authorization of the death of Jesus (Tacitus, *Annals* xv. 44): his only appearance on the stage of history is as procurator of Judaea.

Josephus relates (*Ant.* xviii. 3. 1; *BJ* ii. 9. 2, 3) that Pilate's first action on taking up his appointment was to antagonize the Jews by setting up the Roman standards, bearing images of the emperor, at Jerusalem: previous procurators had avoided using such standards in the holy city. Because of the determined resistance of their leaders in spite of threats of death, he yielded to their wishes after six days and removed the images back to Caesarea. Philo (*De Legatione ad Gaium* xxxviii) tells how Pilate dedicated a set of golden shields in his own residence at Jerusalem. These bore no image, only an inscription with the names of the procurator and the emperor, but representations were made to

Tiberius, who sensibly ordered them to be set up in the temple of *Roma et Augustus* at Caesarea.

Josephus (*Ant.* xviii. 3. 2; *BJ* ii. 9. 4) and Eusebius (*EH* ii. 7) allege a further grievance of the Jews against Pilate, in that he used money from the Temple treasury to build an aqueduct to convey water to the city from a spring some 25 miles away. Tens of thousands of Jews demonstrated against this project when Pilate came up to Jerusalem, presumably at the time of a festival, and he in return sent his troops in disguise against them, so that a large number were slain. It is generally considered that this riot was caused by the Galilaeans mentioned in Lk. xiii. 1, 2 (whose blood Pilate had mingled with their sacrifices), and Noldius (*De Vita et Gestis Herodum* ccxlix) claims that Herod's enmity against Pilate (Lk. xxiii. 12) arose from the fact that Pilate had slain some of Herod's subjects. This explains Pilate's subsequent care (Lk. xxiii. 6, 7) to send Jesus to be tried before Herod. It is not known whether the tower at Siloam which collapsed (Lk. xiii. 4) was part of this aqueduct.

Pilate finally over-reached himself by the slaughter of a number of Samaritans who had assembled at Mt. Gerizim in response to the call of a deceiver who had promised to show them that Moses had hidden the sacred vessels there. In spite of the obvious falsehood of this claim (Moses had never crossed Jordan: some consider that there is a textual error, *Mōÿseōs* for *Ōseōs*, and Josephus is referring to the Samaritan tradition that Uzzi the high priest (1 Ch. vi. 6) had hidden the ark and other sacred vessels in Mt. Gerizim), a great multitude came armed to the mountain, and Pilate surrounded and routed them, capturing many and executing their ring-leaders. A Samaritan delegation went with a protest to Vitellius, who was then governor of Syria, and he ordered Pilate to answer this accusation of the Jews before the emperor, ordering Marcellus to Judaea in Pilate's place (Jos., *Ant.* xviii. 4. 1, 2). Pilate was on his journey to Rome when Tiberius died (AD 37). We know nothing of the outcome of the trial, but Eusebius (*EH* ii. 7) preserves a report of Greek historians that Pilate was forced to commit suicide during the reign of Gaius (AD 37–41).

Philo can find no good thing to say of Pilate: in *De Virtutibus et Legatione ad Gaium* (xxxviii) he describes him as 'by nature rigid and stubbornly harsh' and 'of spiteful disposition and an exceeding wrathful man', and speaks of 'the bribes, the acts of pride, the acts of violence, the outrages, the cases of spiteful treatment, the constant murders without trial, the ceaseless and most grievous brutality' of which the Jews might accuse him. The verdict of the New Testament is that he was a weak man, ready to serve expediency rather than principle, whose authorization of the judicial murder of the Saviour was due less to a desire to please the Jewish authorities than to fear of imperial displeasure if Tiberius heard of further unrest in Judaea. This is made abundantly evident by his mockery of the Jews in the wording of the superscription (Jn. xix. 19–22). It is most unfortunate that we do not know anything of his record apart from his government of the Jews, towards whom he would appear to have shown little understanding and even less liking.

In 1961 the first inscription providing archaeological evidence of Pilate's existence came to light when a stone slab was discovered at Caesarea bearing the Latin names *Pontius Pilatus* and *Tiberius*. A third line of the inscription had not been deciphered at the time of writing this article.

For an interesting discussion of the significance of the inclusion of 'suffered under Pontius Pilate' in Christian creeds see S. Liberty, 'The Importance of Pontius Pilate in Creed and Gospel', *JTS*, XLV, 1944, pp. 38–56.

There are a number of *Acta Pilati* in existence: none of which is considered to be genuine.

D.H.W.

PILGRIMAGE. A man may sojourn in a foreign land, and then return home; similarly, he may sojourn in the flesh, with a foreshortened view of heavenly things, and then enter or re-enter the eternal realm. By established metaphor, the earthly life-span came to be called a pilgrimage instead of a sojourn—but English biblical translation has not been entirely consistent, and there have been confusions in a few passages.

The Hebrew noun *m^eḡûrîm*, plural in form, commonly denotes the act of dwelling in a strange country, and sometimes stands in apposition to *'ereṣ*, the word for 'land'. The LXX generally uses the verb *paroikeō* or a cognate (Gn. xvii. 8, xxviii. 4, xxxvi. 7, xxxvii. 1; Ex. vi. 4; *etc.*). 'Sojourning' translates accurately in each case—the Hebrew plural is grammatical, not numerical, and the singular would be preferable in RV and RSV. In the Genesis passages AV has 'land wherein thou art a stranger' or some variant. This is precisely correct. (*Cf.* also Ezk. xx. 38; and Ps. lv. 15; Jb. xviii. 19, where 'dwellings' could express a comparable idea, but would be better singular.) The AV and RV text perceptively render the same word twice as 'pilgrimage' in Gn. xlvii. 9—this may be upheld against RVmg and RSV, because the meaning here is life's total span and experience. The LXX underlines this by using *zōē*, 'life'. There is a close parallel in Ps. cxix. 54, where 'the house of my pilgrimage' means simply 'my mortal body throughout its earthly existence'. The 'land of their pilgrimage' of Ex. vi. 4, AV, looks at first sight inconsistent—yet it could well mean the land where future Israelites are to live out their mortal pilgrimage. The AV is sometimes more sensitive to delicate nuances than the later versions.

There are two technical terms for a resident alien—usually a Gentile dweller in Palestine—*gēr*, from the same Hebrew root as *m^eḡûrîm*, and *tôšāḇ*. The first word usually implies a longer, the second a shorter, association, so that the difference is chiefly one of intensity. The coupling of the two lays tremendous emphasis on transitoriness. The second then follows climactically. The LXX translates the first term by *paroikos*, the second in its happier moments by *parepidēmos*. The four words may be found literally used in Gn. xxiii. 4, *MT* and LXX. The metaphorical usages, stressing the brevity of life, are Ps. xxxix. 12; 1 Ch. xxix. 15. The LXX spoils the sense in the second passage by substituting *katoikountes* for *parepidēmoi*. This verb suggests settled dwelling where the whole emphasis is the reverse. In both cases 'pilgrim' would afford a good translation. (See further *TWNT*, II, pp. 63 f., V, pp. 153–157, 840 ff.; also *MM*.)

The 'weary pilgrimage' of the familiar paraphrase has a similar ring about it, but strictly it is a mistranslation. Jacob in his vow (Gn. xxviii. 20) actually uses the word *dereḵ*, 'road' or 'way'—metaphorically, manner of life, human or animal—even behaviour of inanimate but propelled objects. (Pr. xxx. 19 aptly illustrates all three.) Jacob's reference is personal, practical, specific, and contemporary. This in no way invalidates the familiar hymn—the intensification is in the right direction.

Paroikos and *parepidēmos* or their cognates are used in the New Testament independently (1 Pet. i. 1, 17) and in Old Testament quotation (Heb. xi. 13; 1 Pet. ii. 11). By New Testament times it is probably true to say that the *paroikos* not only resided longer in a place than the *parepidēmos* but also that he was more fully incorporated into the civic life and fiscal obligations of his adopted community. The *eklektoi parepidēmoi* of 1 Pet. i. 1 are more than 'elect sojourners'—their political status is mere metaphor for the fact that they are God's pilgrims—persons now in time and flesh, chosen for eternal life through Christ Jesus, and therefore greatly different from the worldling. The *paroikia* of 1 Pet. i. 17 reverts by stylistic variation to the *gēr* emphasis, but still means essentially 'pilgrimage'. The 'strangers and pilgrims' of Heb. xi. 13 translates the Greek beautifully. There is a verbal echo of Ps. xxxix. 12 and 1 Ch. xxix. 15, with perhaps a sidelong glance at Gn. xlvii. 9. The phrase is more telling in view of the writer's 'idealist epistemology'—the Temple and all earthly things are but copies and shadows of heavenly things, and the real world is the unseen one. The comparable verbal echo in 1 Pet. ii. 11 calls for no special comment.

The concept of pilgrimage as a journey of religious volition or obligation to a sacred spot, such as Abraham's visit to Mt. Moriah, is known from remote antiquity, though the Bible lacks a technical term for it. Any place held in veneration was liable to attract pilgrims, as even the earliest records of the Old Testament show. Journeys to the main feasts at Jerusalem, where the Temple came to enjoy an exclusive prestige, were well established by New Testament times. The one described in Lk. ii. 41 ff. is a particularly famous example. Before the partition of Jerusalem, Jews regularly lamented at the Wailing Wall, which is all that remains of the Herodian Temple. See STRANGER.

BIBLIOGRAPHY. D. J. Wiseman, *The Word of God for Abraham and To-day*, 1959. R.A.S.

PILLAR.

a. Structural

Pillars of wood, stone, or mud-brick were used from the earliest times to support the roofs of large rooms or to provide monumental decoration (as at Erech in S Mesopotamia; H. Frankfort, *Art and Architecture of the Ancient Orient*, 1954, pl. 2). From the latter part of the second millennium onwards rectangular stone pillars or wooden posts on stone bases were used in larger Palestinian houses for carrying upper storeys or balconies on one or all sides of the central courtyard (see HOUSE and fig. 110). The evidence of Philistine sites suggests that the pillars held by Samson were of wood, set on stone bases (Jdg. xvi. 23–30; *cf.* R. A. S. Macalister, *Bible Sidelights from the Mound of Gezer*, 1906, pp. 135–138).

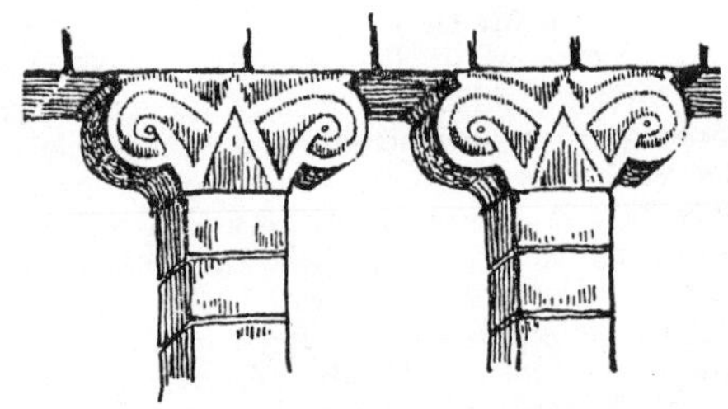

Fig. 168. Reconstructed capitals of pilasters from Samaria of the period of the Monarchy. These probably represent a style of design which was later adapted in Greek architecture.

From the early Monarchy have survived several examples of official buildings with rows of pillars (*cf.* the seven pillars of Wisdom's house, Pr. ix. 1). In the stables at Megiddo pillars also served as hitching-posts (see *ANEP*, nos. 741, 742, and, for official and private buildings at Hazor, *BA*, XIX, 1956, p. 7, fig. 3, XXI, 1958, p. 45, fig. 15). Of finer quality, and showing possible Phoenician influence, are the carved capitals (called proto-Aeolic or Ionic) found at several sites. While the majority were made for rectangular attached pillars (*e.g.* those from the palace at Samaria, *cf.* W. F. Albright, *Archaeology of Palestine*, 1960, p. 127, fig. 35), one has recently been discovered at Hazor which belonged to a free-standing column about 8 feet high (*BA*, XXII, 1959, p. 11, fig. 8). The rows of pillars in Solomon's palace may well have taken this form (1 Ki. vii. 2–6). This simple design was elaborated, producing finally the complicated capitals at the Persian palaces of Persepolis and Susa (Est. i. 6, see R. Ghirshman, *Iran*, 1954, pl. 17b). Simple cylindrical pillars of this period have been found at Lachish (*PEQ*, LXIX, 1937,

p. 239) and possibly Bethel (*BASOR*, 127, 1955, fig. 3).

During the Hellenistic and Roman periods pillars were widely employed as decorative features, *e.g.* lining the main streets of towns, as at Jerash (G. L. Harding, *Antiquities of Jordan*, 1959, pl. 10). The entrance to Solomon's Temple was flanked by two gigantic bronze pillars of uncertain significance (1 Ki. vii. 15–22; see JACHIN AND BOAZ). It was apparently by one of these that the king stood on ceremonial occasions (2 Ki. xi. 14, xxiii. 3; 2 Ch. xxiii. 13; *cf.* the coronation of Abimelech, Jdg. ix. 6, RV).

'Pillar' is also used to describe: Lot's wife smothered by salt (Gn. xix. 26); the smoke and fire which protected the camp of Israel (Ex. xiii. 21); a palm-like column of smoke spreading at the top (Ct. iii. 6; Joel ii. 30, Heb. *tîmārâ*). The supporting function is used figuratively of: (i) the pillars of heaven and earth over which God alone has power (1 Sa. ii. 8; Jb. ix. 6, xxvi. 11; Ps. lxxv. 3); (ii) the legs of the beloved and the feet of an angel (Ct. v. 15; Rev. x. 1); (iii) the Church as upholding the truth (1 Tim. iii. 15); (iv) the position of James, Cephas, and John in the Church of Jerusalem (Gal. ii. 9).

b. Monumental

Stones set up on end are to be found throughout the ancient world, often associated with a shrine or temple (*e.g.* an early Neolithic shrine at Jericho contained a niche in which was a stone cylinder, see *PEQ*, LXXXIV, 1952, p. 72, pl. XIX. 1) or standing alone (the Celtic *menhir*). A consideration of all the Old Testament passages in which such a pillar (Heb. *maṣṣēḇâ*, something erected) is mentioned shows that the basic significance was that of a memorial. Rachel's grave was thus marked (Gn. xxxv. 20), and Absalom, being childless, set up a pillar, to which he gave his own name, as his own memorial (2 Sa. xviii. 18). The name conferred on the stone identified it with the bearer of that name (see WORD, NAME). Important events were likewise commemorated. Jacob set up the stone he had used as a pillow, clearly a small slab, after the first theophany at Bethel and another stone after the second theophany. Libations were poured on both of these, marking them out from other stones. By naming the stones 'House of God' (Heb. *bêṯ'ēl*), Jacob recorded their significance to him (Gn. xxviii. 18–22, xxxv. 13–15). The covenants between Jacob and Laban and between Yahweh and Israel were also visibly indicated in this way (Gn. xxxi. 45–54; Ex. xxiv. 4; Jos. xxiv. 26, 27). So too were the crossing of the Jordan (Jos. iv. 1–9) and the victory over the Philistines at Mizpah (1 Sa. vii. 12, named 'stone of help', Heb. *'eḇen hā'ēzer*). This is the significance of the victorious Christian who will be a pillar in the temple of God, bearing the names of God, the new Jerusalem and the new name of the Son of man (Rev. iii. 12).

In Canaanite religion the pillar had so far become identified with deity (particularly male deity) as to be an object of veneration. It was therefore forbidden to the Israelites, who were told to destroy all they found (Ex. xxiii. 24; Dt. xvi. 22; *cf.* ASHERAH). Of the many standing stones found in and around Palestine (*e.g.* at Gezer, Lejjun, Byblos, Ras Shamra) the best examples are those at Hazor. An upright stone, with the top broken off, was found standing by the entrance to an important building in the Canaanite citadel, an offering before it (*BA*, XXII, 1959, p. 14, fig. 12). In the lower city lay a small shrine containing a row of several slabs about eighteen inches high and many more stacked in a side room (*BA*, XIX, 1956, p. 10, fig. 7). These may well be ancestral monuments destroyed by the Israelites (*cf. ANEP*, nos. 630, 635). The practice continued in neighbouring countries and Isaiah foretold that the Egyptians would set up a pillar to Yahweh on their border when they turned to Him (Is. xix. 19). A.R.M.

PILLOW. 1. Heb. *k^{e}ḇîr* (1 Sa. xix. 13, 16). Read with RVmg 'quilt' or 'network'. 2. Heb. *m^{e}ra'^{a}šôṯ* (Gn. xxviii. 11, 18, *etc.*). Read with RV 'under his head'. 3. Heb. *k^{e}sāṯôṯ* (Ezk. xiii. 18). Meaning uncertain; probably fillets used as charm. 4. Gk. *proskephalaion* (Mk. iv. 38), a cushion or head-rest, *cf.* V. Taylor, *ad loc.* J.B.J.

PIM. See WEIGHTS AND MEASURES.

PINE. See TREES.

PINNACLE (Gk. *pterygion*, 'a little wing'; Vulg. *pinnaculum*; NEB 'highest ledge'). A part of the buildings of the Temple (Mt. iv. 5; Lk. iv. 9) mentioned in connection with the temptation of Jesus. Its precise location is uncertain, but two relevant factors should be noted. (i) Despite the AV's use of the indefinite article, we should follow other EVV in reading '*the* pinnacle of the temple' (*i.e.* suggesting that there was only one). (ii) The context calls for a position from which there was both a fearful drop and an impressive view of the surrounding countryside. These latter conditions are met if we locate the pinnacle in the south-east corner of the Temple area, overlooking the Kidron Valley (*cf.* Jos., *Ant.* xv. 11. 5). Different opinions have, however, been expressed. See, *e.g.*, Lightfoot's *Horae Hebraicae . . .*, 1859, IV, pp. 85, 86. For a plan of the Temple and courts see fig. 207.

J.D.D.

PIPE. See MUSIC AND MUSICAL INSTRUMENTS.

PIRATHON. Fer'ata, 6 miles west-south-west of Shechem, home of the Ephraimite judge Abdon ben Hillel (Jdg. xii. 13, 15) and of David's captain Benaiah (2 Sa. xxiii. 30; 1 Ch. xi. 31, xxvii. 14); probably not the Pharathon fortified by the Maccabees in Benjamin (1 Macc. ix. 50), though the name Abdon is otherwise Benjamite (Moore, *ICC*, Jdg. xii. 13; Burney, *Judges*, *ad loc.*; the *Sellem* of the Greek is a corruption of 'Hillel'). The district was known as the Amalekite hills (*MT* and LXX B; LXX A, 'hill of Anak'); *cf.* Jdg.

v. 14, though here also LXX A ('in the valley') disagrees. J.P.U.L.

PISGAH, ASHDOTH PISGAH. Wherever this word occurs in the Hebrew text it is accompanied by the definite article, showing that it is not a single spot, but a common noun. It is derived from a root, which in later Hebrew meant 'to cleave'; and in the LXX is translated by several words meaning 'cleft'. Various pisgahs are mentioned; they usually involve an ascent, and afford a view. From this we gather that a pisgah is a ridge crowning a hill or mountain, and which from below or from a distance presents a broken outline; and such ridges are common in Transjordan.

The first to be mentioned is the pisgah (AVmg 'hill') which the people ascended as they left the way along the Arabian desert, towards which this pisgah looked (Nu. xxi. 18–20, RV).

A second pisgah was ascended by Balak and Balaam, from the field of Zophim, in order to view the Israelites (Nu. xxiii. 13 f.). But the view was incomplete, and they went on to 'the top of Peor' (verse 28; see Dt. iii. 29).

Special interest attaches to the pisgah which Moses was bidden to ascend in order to view the land from every point of the compass (Dt. iii. 27). This is carefully described in Dt. xxxiv. 1 as being 'the mountain of Nebo, to the top of (the) Pisgah, that is over against Jericho'. (For the identification of this pisgah with Jebel Osha, see NEBO.) From this marvellous viewpoint can be seen snow-capped Hermon on the north, and the Dead Sea, and the *neḡeḇ* or south, as well as other parts named.

The word also occurs in the combination Ashdoth-pisgah, 'slopes of the pisgah' (Dt. iii. 17), which stood above the eastern bank of the Dead Sea, which formed the limit of the Reubenite territory; and again in Dt. iv. 49 (*'ašdôṯ happisgâ*, AV 'the springs of Pisgah') as the limit of the newly-conquered territory (see also Jos. xii. 7, xiii. 20). G.T.M.

PISIDIA. A highland area in Asia Minor bounded by Lycaonia to the east and north, Pamphylia to the south, and the province of Asia to the north and west (see fig. 26). The district lay at the western end of the Taurus range, and was the home of lawless mountain tribes who defied the efforts of the Persians and their Hellenistic successors to subdue them. The Seleucids founded Antioch (called 'the Pisidian' to distinguish it rather from the Phrygian Antioch on the Maeander than from the Seleucid capital of Syria) in order to control the Pisidian highlanders, and Amyntas with like aim founded a colony there about 25 BC, and linked the city with similar strongpoints by a system of military roads. Paul's 'perils of robbers . . . perils in the wilderness' (2 Cor. xi. 26) may have reference to this area, and it is a fair guess that, even in his day, the tradition of predatory independence was not yet dead among the mountaineers. Pisidia was part of the kingdom of Galatia assigned by Antony to Amyntas in 36 BC, and it was in warfare against the Pisidian hill tribes that Amyntas perished in 25 BC. Sulpicius Quirinius finally imposed some sort of order, and incorporated the region in the province of Galatia. The Roman Peace brought prosperity to the district and in the 2nd century several prosperous towns sprang up together with at least six strong churches. E.M.B.

PIT. Basically a deep hole, either natural or artificial, in the ground. In the AV the word is used to translate twelve Hebrew and two Greek words.

1. *bôr*, 'a deep hole', used to describe the place where Joseph was cast by his brethren (Gn. xxxvii. 20, 22, 24, *etc.*), a place to hide (1 Sa. xiii. 6), a place where lions lurked (2 Sa. xxiii. 20; 1 Ch. xi. 22), a place where prisoners were shut up (Is. xxiv. 22; Zc. ix. 11; *cf.* Je. xxxviii. 6), and where the rebel Ishmael cast the bodies of the men of Shechem, Shiloh, and Samaria (Je. xli. 7, 9).

The laws of Ex. xxi. 33, 34 were directed to Israelites who opened up holes and left them uncovered (*cf.* Ec. x. 8, where the word is *gûmmāṣ*).

Metaphorically the word is used to describe the underworld, the place of departed spirits (Ps. xxviii. 1, xxx. 3, lxxxviii. 4, 6, cxliii. 7; Pr. i. 12; Is. xiv. 15, 19, xxxviii. 18; Ezk. xxvi. 20, xxxi. 14, 16, xxxii. 18, 24, *etc.*). A second metaphorical use describes the place from which God brings up His saints (Ps. xl. 2; Is. li. 1).

2. *b*ᵉ*'ēr*, a well. The vale of Siddim was full of slime (bitumen) pits (Gn. xiv. 10). Used metaphorically, it is the pit of destruction (Ps. lv. 23, lxix. 15). A harlot is described in Pr. xxiii. 27 as a narrow pit. 3. *gēḇ* or *geḇe'*, a place where water is collected (Is. xxx. 14; Je. xiv. 3). 4. *paḥaṯ*, 'a hole for trapping animals' (2 Sa. xvii. 9, xviii. 17; Is. xxiv. 17, 18; Je. xlviii. 43, 44). 5. *š*ᵉ*'ôl*, the underworld (Nu. xvi. 30, 33; Jb. xvii. 16). The same Hebrew word is translated elsewhere in other ways. See HELL.

6. Three words from the root *šwḥ*: (i) *šûḥâ*, 'a pit in the desert' (Je. ii. 6), a place where Jeremiah was trapped by wicked men (Je. xviii. 20, 22), and the mouth of a strange woman (Pr. xxii. 14). (ii) *šaḥaṯ*, a trap in the ground for wild animals (Ps. xxxv. 7; Ezk. xix. 4, 8), or, more usually, the underworld (Jb. xxxiii. 18, 24, 28, 30; Pss. ix. 15, xxx. 9, xciv. 13; Is. xxxviii. 17, li. 14; Ezk. xxviii. 8). (iii) *šîḥâ*, a trap (Pss. lvii. 6, cxix. 85; Je. xviii. 22).

7. Two words from the root *šḥh*. *š*ᵉ*ḥuṯ*, the pit which the wicked prepare for the righteous, into which they fall themselves (Pr. xxviii. 10), and *š*ᵉ*ḥîṯ*, the lot of Zedekiah in 587 BC when he was taken in the pits of the enemy (La. iv. 20).

8. In the New Testament the pit into which an ass falls is *bothynos* in Mt. xii. 11 and *phrear* in Lk. xiv. 5. The bottomless pit of Rev. ix. 1, 2 is also *phrear*. See also ABYSS.

Some idea of pits is to be obtained from

archaeological discoveries. Quite regularly the cistern which served as a pit had a neck about the width of a man some 3 or 4 feet in depth, and then opened out into a large bulbous cavity of varying size. Broken pottery and other remains in these pits are useful aids to dating the period when they were in use. See POOL, ARCHAEOLOGY.

J.A.T.

PITCH. See BITUMEN.

PITCHER. See VESSELS.

PITHOM (Old Egyp. *Pr-ìtm*, 'mansion of the god Atum'). The city of Egypt where the Israelites were afflicted with heavy building burdens (Ex. i. 11). Since the excavations of Naville in 1883, it is generally accepted that this city was situated in the eastern part of Wadi Tumilat (Tell el-Maskhouta). Other scholars (*e.g.* Gardiner) place it in the western part of this wadi. Not far away from this place was the migdol of Tjeku, which may be the biblical Succoth (Ex. xii. 37, xiii. 20; Nu. xxxiii. 5, 6). In Papyrus Anastasi, V, 19. 5–20. 6 we read that the chief of the archers went to Tjeku to prevent slaves from running away, but he came too late. Somebody had seen them crossing the north wall of the migdol of Seti-Merenptah. A second report, in Papyr. Anas., V, 18. 6–19. 1, refers to Libyan mercenaries who tried to flee and were taken back to Tjeku. A third mention, in Papyr. Anas., VI, 5. 1, emanates from a civil servant who had finished passing Shasu-nomads from Edom, south of the Dead Sea, into Egypt, at the fort of Tjeku, towards the marshes of Pithom of Merenptah of Tjeku. See ENCAMPMENT BY THE SEA.

BIBLIOGRAPHY. E. Naville, *The Store-City of Pithom*, 1903; Montet, *Géographie de l'Égypte ancienne*, I, 1957, pp. 214–219. C.D.W.

PITY. See COMPASSION.

PLAGUE, PESTILENCE. The AV rendering of five Hebrew and three Greek words connected with disease, death, or destruction. 1. *Deḇer*, 'pestilence, plague'. Originally meaning 'destruction', this word is used comprehensively for all sorts of disasters, and is often linked with the sword and famine (which three evils generally go hand in hand; *cf.* Je. xiv. 12; Ezk. vi. 11, *etc.*), and with divine visitation. It describes also the virulent epidemic which, after David's numbering of the people, cut off 70,000 Israelites (2 Sa. xxiv. 15; *cf.* Jos., *Ant.* vii. 13. 3), and is probably the same affliction as destroyed 185,000 of Sennacherib's men (2 Ki. xix. 35; Is. xxxvii. 36; see SENNACHERIB). The same word is found in Solomon's dedication prayer (1 Ki. viii. 37; 2 Ch. vi. 28); is employed in an unusual sense to describe God's effect on death (Ho. xiii. 14); and, translated 'murrain', is connected with a disease of cattle (Ex. ix. 3; *cf.* Ps. lxxviii. 50, AVmg).

2. *Maggēpâ*, 'plague, smiting' (Ex. ix. 14; Zc. xiv. 12, *etc.*). 3. *Makkâ*, 'a smiting, beating' (Lv. xxvi. 21; Je. xix. 8, *etc.*). 4. *Negaʿ*, 'a touch, smiting'. This word, associated most often with leprosy (Lv. xiii, xiv), also denotes any great distress or calamity (Ps. xci. 10, *etc.*), or inward corruption (1 Ki. viii. 38). 5. *Negep̄*, 'a stumbling, plague' (Ex. xii. 13; Jos. xxii. 17, *etc.*). 6. *Mastix*, 'a scourge, whip, plague' (Mk. iii. 10, v. 29, 34; Lk. vii. 21). This is used as a synonym for disease in general.

7. *Loimos*, 'a plague, pestilence' (Mt. xxiv. 7; Lk. xxi. 11; *cf.* Jos., *BJ* vi. 9. 3). In both biblical references it is coupled with famine, but RV follows some older MSS in omitting 'pestilence' in Mt. xxiv. 7. 8. *Plēgē*, 'a stroke, plague'. This word is thus translated only in Revelation (ix. 20, xi. 6, *etc.*), in connection with the judgment that shall overtake the wicked.

See also PLAGUES OF EGYPT; DISEASE AND HEALING. J.D.D.

PLAGUES OF EGYPT. In commissioning Moses to lead Israel out of Egypt, God had warned him that this would come about only through God's supreme power overcoming all the might of Pharaoh, whereby Egypt would be smitten with wonders or signs from God (*cf.* Ex. iii. 19, 20). After the sign of the rod that became a serpent and swallowed up those of the Egyptian magicians, which left Pharaoh unmoved, God's power was demonstrated to him and his people in a series of ten judgments. They were so applied as to portray clearly the reality and power of Israel's God, and thus by contrast the impotence of Egypt's gods. The first nine of these plagues bear a direct relation to natural phenomena in the Nile valley, but the tenth, the death of the firstborn, belongs wholly to the realm of the supernatural.

These first nine plagues demonstrate the divine use of the created order to achieve His ends, and recent studies tend to confirm both the reality of what is described in Ex. vii–xii and the powers of accurate, first-hand observation of the narrator of this part of Exodus. The element of miracle in these plagues is usually bound up with their intensity, timing, and duration. By far the most painstaking study of the plague phenomena is that by G. Hort in *ZAW*, LXIX, 1957, pp. 84–103, and *ZAW*, LXX, 1958, pp. 48–59. While her treatment of the first nine seems excellent, her attempt to explain the tenth as 'firstfruits' instead of firstborn is decidedly artificial and unlikely.

Hort has pointed out that the first nine plagues form a logical and connected sequence, beginning with an abnormally *high* Nile-inundation occurring in the usual months of July and August and the series of plagues ending about March (Heb. *Abib*). In Egypt too high an inundation of the Nile was just as disastrous as too low a flood.

The first plague (Ex. vii. 14–25)

Moses was commanded to stretch his rod over the Nile waters, that they should be 'turned to blood'; the fish in the river would die, the river stink, and its water be unpalatable; no immediate ending of these conditions is recorded. This would correspond with the conditions brought about by an unusually high Nile. The higher the Nile-flood, the more earth it carries in suspension, especially of the finely-divided 'red earth' from the basins of the Blue Nile and Atbara. And the more earth carried, the redder became the Nile waters. Such an excessive inundation could further bring down with it microcosms known as *flagellates* and associated bacteria: besides heightening the blood-red colour of the water, these would create conditions so unfavourable for the fish that they would die in large numbers as recorded. Their decomposition would foul the water and cause a stench. The rise of the Nile begins in July/August, reaches its maximum about September, and then falls again; this plague would therefore affect Egypt from July/August to October/November.

The second plague (Ex. viii. 1–15)

Seven days later (vii. 25) Egypt was afflicted by swarms of frogs which, in accordance with God's promise, died *en masse* the following day and quickly decayed. That the frogs should swarm out of the river in August was most unusual. The numerous decomposing fish washed along the banks and backwaters of the Nile would pollute and infect the river-shore haunts of the frogs and the frogs themselves, which then came ashore in numbers, heading for the shelter of houses and fields. The sudden death and malodorous and rapid putrefaction of the frogs would indicate internal anthrax (from *Bacillus anthracis*) as the infection and cause.

The third plague (Ex. viii. 16–19)

Hort suggests that this was an abnormal plague of mosquitoes (AV 'lice'), whose already high rate of reproduction would be further encouraged by the specially-favourable breeding-conditions provided by an unusually high Nile.

The fourth plague (Ex. viii. 20–32)

The particular 'fly' in question here was probably *Stomoxys calcitrans*. See below on the sixth plague, for which this insect is the likeliest agent.

The fifth plague (Ex. ix. 1–7)

A 'grievous murrain' upon all the Egyptians' cattle actually in the fields (not all livestock). A cattle pest that affected only the animals out in the fields might indicate that they had contracted anthrax from the infection carried into their fields by the frogs. If the Israelites' cattle were in their stalls they would not have been affected.

The sixth plague (Ex. ix. 8–12)

The boils 'with blains' were probably skin anthrax passed on by the bites of the carrier-fly *Stomoxys calcitrans*, which breeds in decaying vegetation and would have become a carrier of the disease from the infected haunts of the frogs and cattle. The boils 'with blains' may have affected particularly the hands and feet (Ex. ix. 11: the magicians could not stand before Moses; *cf.* Dt. xxviii. 27, 35), which would be a further clue in favour of the proposed identifications of the disease and its carrier, which would strike by about December/January. See also BOILS.

The seventh plague (Ex. ix. 13–35)

Heavy hail with thunder, lightning, and rain. This ruined ('smote') the barley and flax, but not the wheat and spelt, which were not yet grown up. This would fit early February. The concentration at this season of this sudden plague in Upper Egypt, but not in Goshen nearer the Mediterranean seaboard, fits the climatic phenomena of these areas.

The eighth plague (Ex. x. 1–20)

The heavy precipitation in Ethiopia and the Sudan which led to the extraordinarily high Nile would also provide favourable conditions for a dense plague of locusts by about March. These, following the usual route, would in due course be blown into northern Egypt by the east wind; the 'west wind', *rûaḥ-yām*, is literally 'sea-wind': *i.e.* really a north (or north-west) wind, and this would blow the locusts right up the Nile valley. Hort would then emend 'Red Sea' (*yām sûp̄*) to 'South' (*yāmîn*), but this is not strictly necessary.

The ninth plague (Ex. x. 21–29)

The 'thick darkness' which could be felt. This was a *khamsin* dust-storm, but no ordinary one. The heavy inundation had brought down and deposited masses of 'red earth', now dried out as a fine dust over the land. The effect of this when whirled up by a *khamsin* wind would be to make the air extraordinarily thick and dark, blotting out the light of the sun. The 'three days' of Ex. x. 23 is the known length of a *khamsin*. The intensity of the *khamsin* may suggest that it was early in the season, and would thus come in March. If the Israelites were dwelling in the region of Wadi Tumilat as their part of Goshen, they would miss the worst effects of this plague.

The tenth plague (Ex. xi. 1–xii. 36)

So far God had demonstrated His full control over the natural creation. He had caused His servant Moses to announce the successive plagues and brought them to pass in invincible sequence and growing severity when the pharaoh ever more persistently refused to acknowledge Israel's God in face of the clearest credentials of His authority and power. In this final plague came the most explicit sign of God's precise and full control: the death of the firstborn only. Nor did it come without adequate warning (Ex. iv. 23); the pharaoh had had every opportunity to acknowledge God and obey His behest, and so had to take the consequences of refusal.

Other aspects

In later days Joshua reminded Israel in Canaan of their mighty deliverance from Egypt through the plagues (Jos. xxiv. 5). The Philistines also knew of them and feared their Author (1 Sa. iv.

8). Later still, the psalmist sang of these awe-inspiring events (Ps. lxxviii. 43–51).

In Ex. xii. 12 God speaks of executing judgments against all the gods of Egypt. In some measure He had already done so in the plagues, as Egypt's gods were much bound up with the forces of nature. Ha'pi, the Nile-god of inundation, had brought not prosperity but ruin; the frogs, symbol of Heqit, a goddess of fruitfulness, had brought only disease and wasting; the hail, rain, and storm were the heralds of awesome events (as in the Pyramid Texts); and the light of the sun-god Rēʿ was blotted out, to mention but a few of the deities affected.

The account of the plagues is emphatically a literary unity: it is only the *total* details of the whole and unitary narrative that correspond so strikingly with observable physical phenomena. The mere fragments of plagues that would feature in supposed documentary sources (J, E, P, *etc.*) and the schematic uniformity of features postulated for these correspond to no known phenomena. Arbitrary adaptation of such partial and stylized accounts into a new and conflated narrative that somehow then happens to correspond exactly to observable phenomena long past and in a distant land is surely beyond serious belief (so Hort). The plainer explanation and the unity of the narrative is to be preferred to a theory which involves unattested phenomena.

K.A.K.

PLAIN, CITIES OF THE. The cities of the plain were, chiefly, Sodom, Gomorrah, Admah, Zeboiim, and Bela or Zoar (Gn. xiv. 2). It used to be held that these were located north of the Dead Sea, where the Jordan Valley broadens into the 'Circle' or 'plain' of the Jordan (*cf.* Dt. xxxiv. 3), the evidence being 'that Abraham and Lot looked upon the cities from near Bethel (Gn. xiii. 10), that *Circle of Jordan* is not applicable to the south of the Dead Sea, that the presence of five cities there is impossible, and that the expedition of the Four Kings (Gn. xiv. 7), as it swept north from Kadesh Barnea, attacked Hazazon-tamar, probably Engedi, *before* it reached the Vale of Siddim and encountered the king of Sodom and his allies' (G. A. Smith, *Historical Geography of the Holy Land*[25], 1931, pp. 505 f.).

In the light of archaeological assurance that the cities lie buried beneath the shallow waters of the southern tip of the Dead Sea (G. E. Wright, *Westminster Historical Atlas*, 1945, pp. 26, 65, 66; *Biblical Archaeology*, 1957, p. 50), these facts must be re-assessed. Firstly, Gn. xiii. 10 says that Lot saw, not the cities of the plain, but the 'Circle' (AV 'plain') of Jordan. He was attracted not by urban facilities but by good pasturage. Secondly, refusal to give the name 'Circle of Jordan' to, and denial of the possibility of five cities at, the south of the Dead Sea depends on present-day configuration, and disregards any alterations made by the overthrow. Thirdly, there is the identification of Hazezon-tamar with En-gedi. This depends on 2 Ch. xx. 2, where the advancing Moabites and Ammonites are said to be 'in Hazazon-tamar, which is En-gedi'. The qualifying phrase ought not to be taken in this case as identifying the two places (as, *e.g.*, in Gn. xiv. 3), unless we make the absurd assumption that after the time of Jehoshaphat the name En-gedi replaced Hazezon-tamar, thus necessitating an explanation of the archaism. The qualification 'that is, En-gedi' must, therefore, state more precisely where the enemy was in the general district designated by the first place-name. This suits the usage in Gn. xiv. 7 where, in a chapter full of parenthetic explanations of archaic place-names, Hazezon-tamar is left unexplained. We may therefore picture the cities of the plain as sited in the now-flooded area which once formed the southern extension of the Circle of the Jordan.

As Lot saw it, the Circle was supremely attractive from every material viewpoint (Gn. xiii. 10), but, as archaeological investigation shows, about 2000 BC (G. E. Wright, *Westminster Historical Atlas*, p. 26; D. J. Wiseman, *IBA*, p. 30) there was a catastrophe which emptied the area of settled occupation for 600 years. The efficient cause of this evacuation of the cities was probably an earthquake, with an accompanying release and explosion of gaseous deposits. Biblically, and fundamentally, it was God's judgment, remembered again and again throughout the Bible (Dt. xxix. 23; Is. i. 9; Je. xlix. 18; La. iv. 6; Am. iv. 11; Lk. xvii. 29; 2 Pet. ii. 6); and Sodom became synonymous with brazen sin (Is. iii. 9; La. iv. 6; Jude 7). Whereas Ezk. xvi. 49 lists the sins of Sodom as pride, prosperous complacency, and 'abomination', Gn. xix. 4, 5 concentrates on sexual perversion, particularly homosexuality. Lot's vicious offer of his daughters (verse 8) indicates the life and demoralizing influence of Sodom. (Note, however, that 'Sodomite', translating *qāḏēš*, *e.g.* 2 Ki. xxiii. 7, see RSV, is wholly misleading.)

The story of Sodom does not merely warn, but provides a theologically documented account of divine judgment implemented by 'natural' disaster. The history is faith's guarantee that the Judge of all the earth does right (Gn. xviii. 25). Being personally persuaded of its justice and necessity (Gn. xviii. 20, 21), God acts; but in wrath He remembers mercy, and in judgment discrimination (Gn. xix. 16, 29).

J.A.M.

PLANE. See ARTS AND CRAFTS, IIIc.

PLANTS. Any attempt to pronounce upon the nature and identity of the various biblical plants must avoid a number of pitfalls. One of these is the tacit assumption that they are identical with those designated by the same names in different parts of the world today. Another is the assumption that plants found in Palestine today were also native to that area in biblical times. In addition, different versions of Scripture frequently reflect wrong identifications and there is confusion of botanical nomenclature and the like by the translators. This is partly due to the fact that for the original writers present-day standards of accuracy in botanical matters were not pressing considerations, and, in addition, their terminology was by no means as comprehensive as that of the modern botanist. The AV contributed materially to the degree of confusion already existing regarding the identification of plants. Thus the apricot is termed an 'apple', the terebinth becomes an 'elm', eaglewood is designated 'aloes', the acanthus is described as a 'nettle', and so on.

The following represent some of the more important biblical plants:

1. *Anise* (*Pimpinella anisum* L.) is the name used in the AV for 'dill'. The true anise grows in Palestine today, but it is probably not the plant mentioned by Christ (Mt. xxiii. 23) as being scrupulously tithed. Dill (*Anethum graveolens*) is a rather weedy plant resembling fennel and parsley. In antiquity it was used as a condiment and medicinal herb.

2. *Broom*. A more accurate rendering of the Hebrew words translated by 'juniper' in the AV, with which the true juniper (*Juniperus*) has no connection. The scriptural 'juniper' is actually the white broom (*Retama raetam*), a dense bush sometimes growing to 12 feet in height and occurring abundantly in the Palestinian wastelands. The phrase 'coals of juniper' (Ps. cxx. 4) refers to the highly combustible charcoal derived from the wood of the white broom. The 'juniper roots' of Jb. xxx. 4 were edible, and hence not the nauseous roots of the white broom. Probably the parasitic plant *Cynomorium coccineum* L., which often grows on broom, was meant. See fig. 38.

3. *Camphire*. The AV rendering (Ct. i. 14, iv. 13) of *kōp̄er*. However, the true camphire or camphor (*Camphora officinarum* Nees) has no connection with that mentioned in Canticles. Solomon probably envisaged the henna plant, *Lawsonia inermis* L., which was widely used in the Near East as a cosmetic. The ancient custom of dyeing the nails and hair with henna was frowned on in Dt. xxi. 12.

4. *Dill*. The *anēthon* of Mt. xxiii. 23, translated by 'anise' in the AV, is most probably *Anethum graveolens* L., an annual umbellifer whose seeds were widely used for culinary and medicinal purposes in antiquity. Dill is a native of Europe.

5. *Garlic*. Nearly seventy species of garlic (Heb. *šûmîm*) and onion have been reported from Palestine. The reference in Nu. xi. 5 may be to the common garlic, *Allium sativum* L., well known in Egypt before the days of Moses, or perhaps to the shallot, *Allium ascalonicum* L. The former species is probably Asiatic in origin, while the latter is unknown in a wild state. Onions (*q.v.*) were a popular dietary item in antiquity, while garlic was additionally regarded as an anthelmintic.

6. *Henna*. *Lawsonia inermis* L., the 'camphire' of Ct. i. 14, iv. 13, is a shrub originating in N India. The pulverized leaves were made into a paste and used from earliest times as a cosmetic. Egyptian women employed it to dye their hair, finger and toe nails, hands and feet. Men coloured their beards with henna, and often the tails and manes of their horses. See COSMETICS AND PERFUMERY. Any women thus adorned who fell captive to the Hebrews were required to remove all traces of the dye (Dt. xxi. 11, 12). The orange or bright yellow colour probably had pagan associations. The shrub grows wild in Palestine, and may attain a height of twelve feet. It has spiny branches bearing clusters of whitish fragrant flowers at the tips.

7. *Hyssop*. Occurring several times in Scripture, this plant (Heb. *'ēzôḇ*; Gk. *hyssōpos*) is extremely difficult to identify, since the references do not always suggest the same species. It is not the familiar herb *Hyssopus officinalis* L., which is not native to Palestine, being found in southern Europe. Among others the thorny caper (*Capparis spinosa* L.), sorghum (*Sorghum vulgare*), the wall-rue (*Asplenium ruta-muraria* L.), and the common caper (*C. sicula*) have been suggested as the true hyssop. See fig. 39.

Probably most Old Testament references are to the Syrian marjoram (*Origanum maru* L.) or the Egyptian variety (*O. aegyptiacum* L.). The hyssop of 1 Ki. iv. 33 may be a fern such as the wall-rue or the maidenhair spleenwort, and is certainly different from the hyssop used in the Passover rites (Ex. xii. 22). The plant employed at the Crucifixion was probably the *Sorghum vulgare*, var. *durra* (Jn. xix. 29), a maize-like grass attaining at least 6 feet in height. Hyssop, with cedar and scarlet wool, formed part of the purification rite for lepers (Lv. xiv. 4, 6), for plague (Lv. xiv. 49–52), and the red heifer sacrifice (Nu. xix. 2–6; *cf.* Heb. ix. 19). The purifying qualities of hyssop are referred to in Ps. li. 7.

8. *Juniper*. The scriptural juniper is the white broom, *Retama raetam*, which grows in desert areas. An attractive shrub, the broom often reaches a height of 12 feet. The reference in Ps. cxx. 4 alludes to the combustible nature of the charcoal produced from the white broom. Its fierce fire would constitute an adequate punishment for deceitful tongues. See above under 'Broom'. See also fig. 38.

9. *Lily*. A bulbous plant and its flower, of which several varieties abound in Palestine, but which are not specified in translations. Most of the references in Canticles are probably to the hyacinth (*Hyacinthus orientalis* L.), although the lily-like lips of Ct. v. 13 may allude to the red anemone (*Anemone coronaria* L.), while in Ct. vi. 2 the madonna lily (*Lilium candidum* L.) may be meant. This latter has been shown to be a native Palestinian plant. The 'lily' of Ecclus. l. 8 and Ho. xiv. 5 is probably the iris (*Iris pseudacorus* L.).

The references to 'lily-work' on the columns of the Solomonic Temple in 1 Ki. vii. 19, 22, 26 and 2 Ch. iv. 5 are probably to carved representations of the *Nymphaea*. The magnificent Egyptian lotus (*Nymphaea lotus* L.) exercised a wide influence over ancient Near Eastern art, as evidenced by the presence of the lotus motif on

Fig. 169. Some plants of the Bible: 1. Anise (*Pimpinella anisum* L.); 2. Myrtle (*Myrtis communis* L.); 3. Camphire (*Lawsonia nermis* L.); 4. Garlick (*Allium sativum* L.); 5. Rue (*Ruta graveolens* L.); 6. Lily (*Iris pseudacorus* L.); 7. Hyssop (New Testament) (*Sorghum vulgare*); 8. Rose (*Rosa phoenicia*); 9. Mandrake (*Mandragora officinarum* L.); 10. Hyssop (Old Testament) (*Origanum maru var: aegyptiacum*); 11. Saffron (*Crocus sativus* L.). See also figs. 38, 39, 40, 90, 196.

many Egyptian and Palestinian archaeological *objets d'art*. The 'lilies of the field' (Mt. vi. 28; Lk. xii. 27) seem to refer to whole families of flowers, including the lily, anemone, iris, narcissus, hyacinth, and cyclamen. An alternative suggestion envisages a reference to the Palestinian chamomile (*Anthemis palaestina*; see fig. 39), a common plant of daisy-like appearance.

10. *Mallows*. The AV rendering of the Hebrew *mallûaḥ* in Jb. xxx. 4. The term implies 'saltiness', whether referring to the taste of the plant itself or to the place where it is found. The most common identification is with various species of saltwort (*Atriplex*), of which over twenty occur in Palestine at the present day. Some commentators, however, think that 'mallows' may be a general term covering *Atriplex*, *Chenopodium*, and others found in eastern Syria. See fig. 38.

11. *Mandrake* (*Mandragora officinarum* L.). The 'love-apple' is mentioned only in Gn. xxx. 14–16; Ct. vii. 13, and is a stemless perennial of the nightshade family, having emetic, purgative, and narcotic qualities. The forked, torso-like shape of the tap-root gave rise to many superstitions. Aphrodisiac properties were ascribed to it at an early period (Gn. xxx. 14). Ct. vii. 13 alludes to the fragrance of mandrakes. The plant grew widely in Palestine in deserted areas, being native to the Mediterranean region generally. The identification of mandrakes with *Cucumis dudaim* L. is incorrect.

12. *Mint*. Of the several varieties found in Palestine, the horse-mint, *Mentha longifolia*, is probably the one referred to in Mt. xxiii. 23 and Lk. xi. 42. The characteristic essential oils present in mint species made the herb a desirable condiment. Scriptural references, however, merely point out the ostentation and hypocrisy of the Pharisees, who tithed even the commonest garden herbs. See fig. 40.

13. *Mustard*. Much controversy surrounds the identification of the plant whose seed was used by Christ as an illustration of something which develops rapidly from small beginnings, such as the kingdom of heaven (Mt. xiii. 31; Mk. iv. 31; Lk. xiii. 19) or the faith of an individual (Mt. xvii. 20; Lk. xvii. 6). Some scholars think that the black mustard (*Sinapis nigra* L.) is indicated, since in New Testament times its seeds were cultivated for their oil as well as for culinary purposes. Others have identified the mustard of Christ's parables with white mustard (*Sinapis alba* L.), a closely related species. Though both varieties have been reported growing to a height of about 15 feet, they do not normally exceed 4 feet at maturity. See fig. 90.

A different plant, the *Salvadora persica* L., found near the Dead Sea, has been suggested as an alternative. This shrub grows to nearly 10 feet in height, but was not found in Galilee where Christ uttered His parables. Furthermore, the seeds of this plant are fairly large, unlike those of *Sinapis*, and in other respects also it is much more improbable.

14. *Myrtle* (*Myrtis communis* L.). The rendering of *hᵃḏas*, a popular Palestinian evergreen sometimes attaining a height of 30 feet. The fragrant leaves and scented white flowers were used as perfumes. Scriptural references envisage the myrtle as symbolizing divine generosity. Isaiah foresaw the myrtle as replacing the brier in the wilderness (Is. xli. 19, lv. 13). Zechariah, in a vision symbolizing peace, saw a grove of myrtle trees (Zc. i. 8–11), while in Ne. viii. 15 the Jews brought myrtle branches from Olivet to construct booths at the original Feast of Tabernacles in 445 BC. The name Hadassah (Esther) was derived from the Hebrew term.

15. *Rose*. Numerous references to this plant occur in Scripture, but the fact that the AV appears to indicate several different 'roses' makes the matter of their identification by botanists extremely controversial. While there are reasons for believing that true roses existed in Palestine in the biblical period, it is difficult to say precisely how many flourished at that time. At least four wild species now exist in Palestine, while others grow in Lebanon and Syria.

The reference to the rose in Is. xxxv. 1 is more probably to some bulbous plant. This may be gathered from the presence of the Hebrew *hᵃḇaṣeleṯ* ('bulb') in the text, which is rendered by *krinon* ('lily') in the LXX. Probably the polyanthus narcissus, *Narcissus tazetta* L., was envisaged. This fragrant flower occurs in several varieties and grows abundantly on the plain of Sharon. The familiar 'rose of Sharon' (Ct. ii. 1) has been variously identified with *Anemone fulgens*, *Colchicum autumnale*, *Cistus*, and *Narcissus tazetta*. A bulbous plant is again envisaged, the most probable being the *Tulipa sharonensis*, a close relative of the Syrian mountain-tulip. The modern 'rose of Sharon' (*Hibiscus syriacus* L.) is native to China and not Palestine, despite its Latin name. The 'rose' of Ecclus. l. 8 bloomed in spring, and may be either a tulip, narcissus, or crocus. In Ecclus. xxiv. 14 and xxxix. 13 the references are probably to the *Nerium oleander* L. The 'rose' of 2 Esdras ii. 19 and 'rose-buds' of Wisdom ii. 8 have been variously regarded as species of rock-rose (*Cistus*), dog-rose (*Rosa canina* L.), or oleander. More probably these passages referred to the Phoenician species *Rosa phoenicia*, and not to the rhododendron. See figs. 40, 90.

16. *Rue*. The translation of *pēganon* in Lk. xi. 42 is correct, but does not indicate which species of rue is meant. The common variety, *Ruta graveolens* L., grew to about 3 feet in height, emitting a strong odour from its grey-green foliage. The African rue, *Ruta chalepensis*, var. *latifolia*, was also cultivated in Palestine in New Testament times. Rue was highly prized for its medicinal values, having alleged disinfectant and antiseptic properties. Christ criticized the Pharisees for their hypocrisy in tithing so inconsequential a plant. As a kitchen herb it was used for flavouring food.

17. *Saffron*. This substance (Heb. *karkōm*, LXX *krokos*) is produced from several species of *Crocus*, particularly the *C. sativus* L., a native

of Greece and Asia Minor. The styles and stigmas of the plant are collected, dried, and packed into small cakes. In antiquity saffron was used for dyeing and for colouring foodstuffs. It was also popular as a therapeutic agent, being used as an emmenagogue, stimulant, and antispasmodic. The ancient Egyptians reputedly employed a different kind of plant, the *Carthamus tinctorius* L., (fig. 90) which yields a dye similar to saffron, for colouring the grave-clothes of mummies. The reference in Ct. iv. 14 is to the true saffron.

18. *Saltwort.* The 'mallows' of the AV rendering of Jb. xxx. 4. Some botanists have suggested that certain species of the true mallow (genus *Malva*), such as *M. sylvestris* L. (marshmallow) or *M. rotundifolia* L. (dwarf mallow), are referred to here. Most modern authorities, however, identify 'mallows' with saltwort (genus *Atriplex*), of which twenty-one kinds are found in modern Palestine. The species most favoured is *A. halimus* or shrubby orach, a sturdy shrub related to the spinach, found abundantly on the Mediterranean littoral. In the Dead Sea region it is said to attain a maximum height of 10 feet. See above under 'mallows'. See also fig. 38.

BIBLIOGRAPHY. H. N. Moldenke, *Plants of the Bible*, 1952; I. Löw, *Die Flora der Juden*, 1924–34, I–IV; W. Walker, *All the Plants of the Bible*, 1957; R. K. Harrison, 'The Biblical Problem of Hyssop', *EQ*, XXVI, 1954, pp. 218–224; *ib.*, 'The Mandrake and the Ancient World', *EQ*, XXVIII, 1956, pp. 87–92. R.K.H.

PLASTER, PLAISTER. 1. The inner, and sometimes outer, walls of buildings were covered with a plaster commonly made of clay (Lv. xiv. 42, 43; Heb. *ṭûaḥ*, 'to coat, overlay'; Arab. *ṭāḥa*). A better plaster was made by heating crushed limestone or gypsum (Heb. *śîḏ*, 'to boil'). This enabled rough stones or brickwork to be covered with a fine surface which could be painted or inscribed, as was done on the altar at Ebal (Dt. xxvii. 2, 4). A glazed surface on brickwork was obtained by firing in a kiln (Is. xxvii. 9; Heb. *gîr*). Such a 'plaister' (AV) was broken by the handwriting on the palace wall in Babylon (Dn. v. 5; Aram. *gîrâ*). See GLASS.

2. The plaister used to cure Hezekiah (Is. xxxviii. 21, AV; Heb. *māraḥ*) was a poultice made of crushed figs. A similar medical term is used in the Ras Shamra texts and Egyp. Ebers Papyrus.

D.J.W.

PLEDGE. See DEBT.

PLEIADES. See STARS.

PLOUGH. See AGRICULTURE and fig. 4.

PLUMBLINE, PLUMMET. See ARTS AND CRAFTS.

POETRY.

I. IN THE OLD TESTAMENT

Poetry, especially in the form of song or hymn, occupies an important place in Hebrew literature. The Jews were evidently a music-loving people and famous for their songs. Hezekiah in 701 BC included in his tribute to Sennacherib male and female musicians (*i.e.* those who accompanied their songs with instruments) (*DOTT*, p. 67), and the exiles in Babylon were pressed by their captors to sing one of their songs, of whose fame they must have heard (Ps. cxxxvii. 3). Little of their secular poetry has remained, but references to it in the Old Testament seem to indicate that it was of considerable volume. The 'Song of the Well' (Nu. xxi. 17, 18) was probably a work-song or chorus used at the well or by well-diggers. Other occupations probably had special songs: reaping (Is. ix. 3), and vintaging (Is. xvi. 10). Songs were also used on special occasions. Laban would have made use of songs at a farewell for Jacob (Gn. xxxi. 27). No marriage feast would be complete without them (*cf.* Je. vii. 34). Laments for the dead were often in poetic form. The elegies of David for Saul and Jonathan (2 Sa. i. 19–27), and for Abner (2 Sa. iii. 33, 34), are poetic compositions of the highest order. The short lament over Absalom has been called 'a masterpiece of rhythm' (2 Sa. xviii. 33).

Songs were nearly always accompanied by instrumental music (Ex. xv. 20; Is. xxiii. 16; 1 Ch. xxv. 6). In fact, instruments would appear to have existed for the sole purpose of accompanying song (Am. vi. 5). Hebrew poetry has rightly been called lyric poetry, and as such it is in a class by itself.

Among the terms used for poetic compositions are: *šîr*, 'song' (with or without an instrument); *mizmôr*, 'psalm' or 'hymn' (with instruments); *qînâ*, 'elegy' or 'lament'; *tᵉhillâ*, 'hymn of praise'; *māšāl*, in addition to its more usual meaning of 'proverb', is a 'satirical song'.

The largest collection of Hebrew poetry is in the book of Psalms, and it is here that we have the richest material for the study of poetic forms. There is, however, no consensus of opinion among scholars as to the nature of Hebrew poetry. Some hold that in a corpus of writings, such as the Psalms, covering many centuries no uniform system is to be expected. Others hold that without a knowledge of the original pronunciation, it is impossible to recover the original forms. Some, again, think that the late introduction of vowel-signs may have brought with it many innovations in vocalization. Others raise the problem of the possibility of transcriptional errors. It would certainly be hazardous in the absence of any indication of vowel-patterns and stress-patterns to defend dogmatically any theory of the principles of Hebrew prosody.

It is generally accepted that metre, as we understand it, is absent from Hebrew poetry. There is nothing corresponding to the unit of metrical measure (the 'foot'), whether of vowel-quantity or of stress formation. In the absence of 'feet', measured sequence between the 'accents' is hardly to be expected. There is wide agreement that Hebrew poetry is 'accentual' in character and that the 'accent' or 'ictus' coincides with grammatical stress. As the number and disposition of unstressed syllables seem to play no essential part, they would be ignored in scanning. Variable rhythm, therefore, takes the place of definite metre. The absence of mechanical measure might seem to indicate a variety of *vers libre*, but in Hebrew there is no deliberate admixture. It would be misleading, too, to compare it with logaoedic rhythm, a cross between the rhythm of prose and that of poetry, found on occasion in Greek poetry, for it is true poetry. Perhaps as good a description as any would be the term 'Sprung Rhythm', coined by Gerard Manley Hopkins. Describing this rhythm, he said: 'It consists in scanning by accents or stresses alone, without any account of the number of syllables, so that a foot may be one strong syllable or it may be many light and one strong.'

To scan Hebrew poetry, then, one should count merely the number of 'ictus units' or 'stress units', each one, irrespective of the number of syllables, providing only one 'beat'. Resultant groupings, corresponding very roughly to dimeter, trimeter, *etc*., and combinations of these, could be made. In the nature of the case the procedure here is bound to be to a greater or lesser extent subjective. Nevertheless, there seem to be many instances of rhythmic patterns (*e.g.* in Ps. xxix). It would, however, be unreasonable to expect rigid uniformity in poetry as subjective as Hebrew. The Procrustean treatment meted out to Hebrew poetry by some scholars is symptomatic of insensibility and not of insight.

One type of poem, the lament or dirge (*qînâ*), has, according to the view of many scholars, a particular metre. The verse here consists of five anapaests with a caesura after the third. If this is so the choric use to which such a poem was put may well have dictated the form. In the case of other poems used in congregational singing, use may have been made of 'reciting notes'.

A common feature of Hebrew poetry particularly in the Psalms is 'parallelism', as it was called by R. Lowth (*De sacra poesi Hebraeorum*, 1753). In its simplest form it is the restating by the second line of a couplet what has been expressed in the first. The relationship of the second line or 'stichos' of the couplet (distich) to the first may be synonymous, or synthetical, or antithetical, or climactic. Occasionally the stanza is a tristich, and then all three 'stichoi' may be involved in the parallelism.

An example of synonymous parallelism is 'Deliver me from my enemies, O God, protect me from those who rise up against me' (Ps. lix. 1, RSV). Ps. civ is full of parallelisms of this kind. In synthetic parallelism the second line amplifies or complements the first, *e.g.* 'Oh that I had wings like a dove! I would fly away and be at rest' (Ps. lv. 6, RSV). In antithetical, the second line expresses a contrast to the first, *e.g.* 'The Lord knoweth the way of the righteous; but the way of the ungodly shall perish' (Ps. i. 6). In climactic parallelism there is a heightening of the effect in the second line (*cf.* Ps. lv. 12, 13). Less common forms, such as bimorphic parallelism, occur, *i.e.* one line followed by two different parallels (Ps. xlv. 1).

With the exception of rhyme, Hebrew makes full use of literary devices common to all poetry. Assonance is not absent. Simile and metaphor abound. Alliteration, usually as 'concealed', is enlisted. Anadiplosis and anaphora are used with telling effect (Jdg. v. 19, 27). The mnemonic help of the acrostic is invoked. The best-known example is that of Ps. cxix, which is arranged in stanzas of eight verses, and in which a letter of the alphabet is assigned to each stanza, and each verse begins with this letter.

Nowhere is the genius of Hebrew poetry more apparent than in its imagery. It lays heaven and earth under tribute. It steals music from the morning stars, and light from the bridegroom who needs no virginal lamps. Its eternal summer fades not, and its snows are undefiled. It rules the raging of the sea, it drives on the clouds, and goes on the wings of the wind. It makes the royal gold richer, the myrrh more fragrant, and the frankincense sweeter. The offerings it takes from the shepherd suffer no death, and his flock is folded in evergreen pastures. The bread of its harvest will never waste, the oil from its press never fail, and its wine is for ever new. So long as men can breathe, its eternal lines will form the litany of the praying heart. The strings it touches are the strings of the harp of God.

The rhythm of Hebrew poetry is not the measured beat of the earth-locked body. It is the majestic rhythm of the soaring spirit, felt only by him who has the music of heaven in his soul. It rises above the metrical to a loftier plane and to a new dimension—the dimension of the spirit, where they who worship God worship Him in spirit and in truth.

Its proper object is the Highest, the God of heaven and earth; its source and fount, the depths of the God-hungry heart. Its great theme is the personal encounter with the living God.

BIBLIOGRAPHY. R. Lowth, *De sacra poesi Hebraeorum*, 1753; E. Sievers, *Metrische Studien*, 1901–7; G. B. Gray, *The Forms of Hebrew Poetry*, 1915; G. A. Smith, *The Early Poetry of Israel*, 1912; C. F. Burney, *The Poetry of our Lord*, 1925; T. H. Robinson, *The Poetry of the Old Testament*, 1947; W. F. Albright, 'A Catalogue of Early Hebrew Lyric Poems', *HUCA*, XXIII, i, 1950–1, pp. 1 ff.; F. F. Bruce, in *NBC*, 1953, pp. 39 ff.

W.J.M.

II. IN THE NEW TESTAMENT

a. Psalms

Three, perhaps four, typical Hebrew hymns are preserved in Luke's Gospel: the *Magnificat* (Lk. i. 46–55), the *Benedictus* (Lk. i. 68–79), the *Nunc Dimittis* (Lk. ii. 29–32), and the *Gloria* (Lk. ii. 14). All of these passages are in the style and spirit of Old Testament psalms, majestic in language, and constructed on the pattern of verbal parallelism proper to Hebrew poetry. See MAGNIFICAT; BENEDICTUS; NUNC DIMITTIS.

b. Hymns

Early Christian hymns may have been poems of mixed tradition (Eph. v. 19), reflecting both the form of the Hebrew psalm and that of the Greek lyric. It has been suggested that numerous passages in the New Testament are direct and indirect quotations from this corpus of sacred poetry: *e.g.* Eph. v. 14 and 1 Tim. iii. 16, where the Hebraic structure is especially striking. Perhaps Col. i. 13–20 and 2 Cor. v. 14–18 are of the same order.

c. Poetic language

This may be discussed under three heads:

(i) It is impossible decisively to distinguish between what may have been direct quotation of rhythmical and poetic utterance, and exalted prose couched in poetic language. In the warm, emotive style of Hebrew writing it is always difficult to distinguish sharply poetry from prose, and in passages of deep emotion the New Testament often adopts such a style. Consider brief ascriptions of praise such as Jude 24 and 25, and Rev. v. 12–14; rhythmic constructions such as Jn. xiv. 27, Rom. xi. 2, 33, and 1 Cor. xv. 54–57; or parallelisms strong in their antitheses such as Jn. iii. 20 and 21, or Rom. ii. 6–10; and parallelism of chiastic form and pattern such as Phil. iii. 3–10, and Jn. x. 14 and 15. All these passages, and many others, reveal the influence of the poetry of the Old Testament on the language of the New Testament, both in form and colouring. Less in debt to Hebrew speech, but still of the nature of poetry, are such lofty passages as Rom. xii, 1 Cor. xiii, and Phil. ii.

(ii) Tropes and figures are part of the language and tradition of poetry, and have found some mention under *c* (i) above. Paronomasia and alliteration may, however, be separately considered. In several passages the Greek of the New Testament reveals an artificial assonance, accompanied sometimes by alliteration: *e.g.* Lk. xxi. 11 (*loimoi, limoi*); Rom. i. 29 (*phthonou, phonou*); Acts xvii. 25 (*zōēn, pnoēn*); Heb. v. 8 (*emathen, epathen*); Rom. xii. 3 (*hyperphronein, phronein, sōphronein*). Mt. xvi. 18 (*Petros, petra*) and Phm. 10 and 20 (*Onēsimus, onaimēn*) involve puns. Acts viii. 30 (*ginōskeis, anaginōskeis*) is probably accidental.

(iii) Mt. xxiv and the parallel Synoptic passages, together with the whole of the Apocalypse, are couched in the traditional language of Hebrew apocalyptic poetry or prophecy, a type of literature found in Daniel, Ezekiel, and Zechariah. It is based on imagery of an allusive nature, and is sometimes designed for private interpretation. It is not unlike certain forms of modern poetry, first brought into fashion by G. M. Hopkins, and practised with some skill by T. S. Eliot. It follows that the 'poetic' interpretation is one legitimate approach to the Apocalypse, and certainly a rewarding one. It may also be remarked that some of the imagery of the book may lack interpretation because of the loss of the key to the allusion, once doubtless possessed.

d. Quotation

The New Testament is uncommonly full of quotation from the poetic literature of the Old Testament. Parts of the Epistle to the Hebrews are composed almost entirely of such references. So are parts of the Epistle to the Romans. These quotations need not be listed. More elusive and less frequent are some direct quotations from Greek literature. Acts xvii. 28, 'for we are also his offspring', is the former half of an hexameter by Aratus of Soli in Cilicia (315–240 BC). The same phrase occurs in a surviving fragment of Cleanthes, who was the head of the Stoic school from 263 to 232 BC. There is some evidence that the passage contains a more remote quotation from Epimenides, the half-legendary Cretan poet from whom Paul quotes a complete hexameter at Tit. i. 12. Then, in 1 Cor. xv. 33, an iambic trimeter of Menander (342–291 BC), the Athenian comic poet, is quoted ('evil communications corrupt good manners'). Again, the Greek of Jas. i. 17 contains a pure hexameter. So does Heb. xii. 13 (reading the aorist imperative), and there is an iambic measure at Acts xxiii. 5. It is impossible to say whether quotation is involved in these cases. Metrical writing can be accidental, *e.g.* 'Husbands love your wives and be not bitter against them.'

BIBLIOGRAPHY. C. F. Burney, *The Poetry of our Lord*, 1925. E.M.B.

POISON. In Israelite thinking poison came either from plants, water or food, or from adders, vipers, serpents, *etc.* The commonest word for poison, *ḥēmâ*, means, basically, heat, and may derive from the burning sensation which followed the taking of poison or from the sting of a reptile.

There were poisonous plants in Palestine like hemlock (Ho. x. 4), and the poisonous gourd (2 Ki. iv. 39), and, although the word is not used, the waters of Marah (Ex. xv. 23) and Jericho (2 Ki. ii. 19) were clearly regarded as poisonous (2 Ki. ii. 21). See GALL, WORMWOOD.

Several passages refer to the poison of reptiles, serpents (Dt. xxxii. 24; Ps. lviii. 4), dragons (Dt. xxxii. 33), and adders (Ps. cxl. 3). Zophar, in the story of Job, told how the wicked would suck the poison (*rō'š*, lit. 'head') of asps (Jb. xx. 16).

Metaphorically, the Almighty is said to send forth His arrows which give forth poison to distress one's spirit (Jb. vi. 4). Again, the poison of the wicked is as the poison of serpents (Ps. lviii. 4), and the poison of adders is under their lips (Ps. cxl. 3). With this latter verse compare Rom. iii. 13 (Gk. *ios*). Jas. iii. 8 describes the tongue as full of poison (*ios*). J.A.T.

POLLUX. See CASTOR AND POLLUX.

POLYGAMY. See MARRIAGE.

POMEGRANATE (Heb. *rimmôn*). A smallish tree (*Punica granatum*) growing wild in some eastern countries, but much prized and cultivated from earliest times, several places in Palestine bearing its name, *e.g.* Rimmon (Jos. xv. 32), Gath-rimmon (Jos. xix. 45), En-rimmon (Ne. xi. 29). It has numerous spreading branches, dark green leaves, occasional thorns, large tough calyxes, and bright red flowers. When fully ripe the apple-shaped fruit is a mixture of yellow, brown, and maroon in colour, and contains multitudinous seeds covered with thin skin and surrounded by red pulp. There are two varieties, sweet and acid. A refreshing drink is made from the juice, a syrup, called grenadine, from the seeds, and an astringent medicine from the blossoms. Ornamental pomegranates decorated the high priest's robe (Ex. xxviii. 33), the capitals of Solomon's Temple pillars (1 Ki. vii. 20), and the silver shekel of Jerusalem in circulation 143–135 BC. D.W.G.

POND. See POOL.

PONTUS. The coastal strip of N Asia Minor, reaching from Bithynia in the west into the highlands of Armenia to the east. See fig. 26. The region was politically a complex of Greek republics, temple estates, and Iranian baronies in the interior. One of these houses established a kingdom whose greatest ruler, Mithridates, temporarily ejected the Romans from Asia Minor early in the 1st century BC. After his defeat the western part of Pontus was administered with Bithynia as a Roman province, the eastern part being left under a Greek dynasty. The Jews from Pontus (Acts ii. 9, xviii. 2) presumably came from the Greek coastal states. We know nothing of the origin of Christianity there, but it was represented by the time of 1 Pet. i. 1.

BIBLIOGRAPHY. J. Keil, *CAH*, XI, pp. 575 ff.; D. Magie, *Roman Rule in Asia Minor*, 2 vols., 1950. E.A.J.

POOL. During the summer, water which had collected in pools during the winter and spring formed an important source of supply. The ability to collect and keep water in artificial pools enabled the Israelites to settle uninhabited parts of Palestine (see CISTERN). Artificial pools were dug inside walled cities, often fed through a tunnel leading from a spring outside, ensuring a supply in time of siege. Examples have been found at Gezer, Megiddo, Gibeon (*cf.* 2 Sa. ii. 13), and elsewhere (see J. B. Pritchard, 'The Water System at Gibeon', *BA*, XIX, 1956, pp. 65–75). 'Hezekiah's tunnel' and the pool of Siloam, lying at the southern end of Ophel in Jerusalem, are perhaps the best-known examples (Jn. ix. 7, 11; Ne. iii. 15). Lack of evidence precludes the certain location of the other pools named in Jerusalem (the lower and old pools, Is. xxii. 9, 11; the king's pool and the artificial pool, Ne. ii. 14, iii. 16). The pool of Bethesda (*q.v.*) is usually located in the north-eastern corner of the city, near the Sheep Gate. A.R.M.

POOR. See POVERTY.

POPLAR. See TREES.

PORCH. Heb. *'ûlām* (*cf.* Assyr. *ellamu*, 'front') is used of the vestibule of Solomon's Temple (1 Ki. vi. 3) and of the gateways of Ezekiel's Temple (Ezk. xl). Solomon's palace included a porch of pillars with a porch in front and another porch for the judgment throne (1 Ki. vii. 6, 7). These buildings may well be derived from the Syrian *bit hilāni*, a suite of rooms, consisting of a portico entered by a flight of steps and leading to an audience chamber, various other rooms and a stairway to an upper floor or roof. The unique Heb. *misd^erôn* (Jdg. iii. 23, from root *sdr*, 'to set in order, arrange') is perhaps a portico of this nature in an upper storey, the word describing the row of pillars (see H. Frankfort, *Art and the Architecture of the Ancient Orient*, 1954, pp. 167–175, and the reconstruction in Sir Leonard Woolley's *A Forgotten Kingdom*, 1953, p. 113). Five porches (Gk. *stoa*) surrounded the pool of Bethesda to give shelter (Jn. v. 2). Peter denied his Lord in the entrance to the courtyard of the high priest's house (Mt. xxvi. 71, *pylōn*; Mk. xiv. 68, *proaulion*). Solomon's Porch was a covered walk 30 cubits wide with two rows of pillars 25 cubits high along the east side of the Court of the Gentiles in Herod's Temple (Jn. x. 23; Acts iii. 11, v. 12; Jos., *Ant.* xv. 11); see TEMPLE and fig. 207. A.R.M.

PORCUPINE. See BITTERN.

PORPOISE. See BADGERS' SKINS.

PORTER. See HOUSE.

POSSESSION. Apparent possession by spirits is a world-wide phenomenon. It may be sought deliberately, as by the shaman and witch-doctor among primitive peoples, and by the medium among both primitive and civilized men and women. It may come upon individuals suddenly, as with watchers at the Voodoo rites, or in the form of what is generally known as demon-possession. In each case the possessed person behaves in a way that is not normal for him or her, speaks in a voice totally different from normal, and often shows powers of telepathy and clairvoyance.

In the Bible the pagan prophets probably sought possession. The prophets of Baal in 1 Ki. xviii would come in this category. Mediums, who were banned in Israel, must have deliberately cultivated possession, since the law regards them as guilty people, not as sick (*e.g.* Lv. xx. 6, 27). In the Old Testament Saul (*q.v.*) is an outstanding example of unsought possession. The Spirit of the Lord leaves him, and 'an evil spirit from the Lord troubled him' (1 Sa. xvi. 14, xix. 9). We may fairly interpret this by saying that, if a person has been powerfully open to the Holy Spirit in a charismatic way, disobedience is liable to be followed by the entry into his life of an evil spirit allowed by God. On the other hand, we may simply say that evil has no moral connotation here, but signifies depression. The spirit is driven away by David's playing: since playing was normally accompanied by singing, it was probably David's psalm-singing that drove away the spirit, as Robert Browning implies in his poem *Saul*.

The New Testament records many cases of possession. It is as though Satan had concentrated his forces in a special way to challenge Christ and His followers. The Gospel records show that Christ distinguished between ordinary illnesses and those that accompanied demon possession. The former were healed by laying on of hands or anointing, the latter by commanding the demon to depart (*e.g.* Mt. x. 8; Mk. vi. 13; Lk. xiii. 32; also Acts viii. 7, xix. 12). Possession was apparently not always continuous, but when it came it produced effects that were often violent (Mk. ix. 18). Blindness and dumbness, when caused by possession, would presumably have been persistent (*e.g.* Mt. ix. 32, 33, xii. 22).

Most psychologists dismiss the idea of demon possession. A good representative writer is T. K. Oesterreich, whose German work is published in English as *Possession, Demoniacal and Other, among Primitive Races, in Antiquity, the Middle Ages, and Modern Times*, 1930. He maintains that the equivalents of possession today are 'a particularly extensive complex of compulsive phenomena' (p. 124). On the other hand, there is the classic by J. L. Nevius, a missionary doctor in China, *Demon Possession and Allied Themes*, 1892. This book, now hard to obtain, takes demon-possession as a genuine phenomenon, and most missionaries would probably agree.

It is possible to take an intermediate position, and to hold that a demon can seize on a repressed facet of the personality, and from this centre influence a person's actions. The demon may produce hysterical blindness or dumbness, or symptoms of other illnesses, such as epilepsy. We mention epilepsy, since among many peoples an epileptic fit has been regarded as a sign of possession by a spirit or a god, and indeed epileptics are often psychically sensitive. The Bible does not link epilepsy with demon-possession, and even

Fig. 170. Reconstruction of the entrance porch of the royal palace at Alalaḫ, Syria, *c*. 1450 BC.

the description of the fits of the possessed boy in Mt. xvii. 14 f.; Mk. ix. 14 f.; Lk. ix. 37 f., seem to indicate something more than mere epilepsy. The nature of epilepsy is still unknown, but it can be artificially induced in apparently normal people (W. G. Walter, *The Living Brain*, 1953, pp. 60 f.). Students of personality disorders know that it is often impossible to say just how these are triggered off. We are not saying that all, or even the majority, are due to demon-possession, but some may be.

The Bible does not say what conditions predispose to demon-possession, though Christ's words in Mt. xii. 44–45 indicate that an 'empty house' can be reoccupied. The early Church cast out demons in the name of Jesus Christ (Acts xvi. 18), but it would seem that there were also non-Christian exorcists who met with some success (Lk. xi. 19; though note Acts xix. 13–16).

The command to 'try the spirits' in 1 Jn. iv. 1–3 shows that there were false prophets in the Church who spoke under possession. Since the spiritualists make much of this verse, it should be noted that the Bible never speaks of possession by any good departed spirit or by an angel. The alternatives are either the Holy Spirit or an evil spirit. See also 1 Cor. xii. 1–3.

BIBLIOGRAPHY. W. M. Alexander, *Demonic Possession*, 1902; M. F. Unger, *Biblical Demonology*, 1952; L. D. Weatherhead, *Psychology, Religion, and Healing*, 1951, pp. 97 ff.; V. White, *God and the Unconscious*, 1952, chapter x; J. S. Wright, *What is Man?*, 1955, p. 126 ff.

J.S.W.

POST, COURIER. Urgent messages were sent in antiquity by a swift runner (*rāṣ*), often a member of the royal bodyguard or 'out-runners' (2 Sa. xv. 1). So the late term 'runner' or royal messenger (Je. li. 31) was used for those who carried letters between cities (2 Ch. xxx. 6, 10), usually on swift horses (Est. viii. 10, 14). Thus the term 'post' was synonymous with speed (Jb. ix. 25). Throughout the Persian Empire, as in earlier Babylonian times, regular posts were established between provincial capitals (G. R. Driver, *Aramaic Documents of the Fifth Century BC*, 1956, pp. 10–12). D.J.W.

POST, DOOR-POST, GATE-POST. 1. *Meẓûzâ*, the post on which the door turned, usually of wood. Used of private houses (Ex. xii. 7), the Temple (1 Sa. i. 9; 1 Ki. vi. 33; Ezk. xli. 21), and of city gates (Jdg. xvi. 3). These were usually made from tree-trunks. In later times the term was transferred to the cylinder attached to the door-post containing a strip of parchment bearing Dt. vi. 4–9, xi. 13–21.

2. *'ayil* (1 Ki. vi. 31, AV 'post') is thought to be a pilaster, or projection in the wall at the porch (hence perhaps connected with *'ûlām*, 'porch').

3. *sap̄* (RV 'threshold') is probably the cupped stone socket in which the hinge-post turned; such door-sockets and 'thresholds' were often inscribed.

Is. vi. 4 (*'ammôṯ sippîm*) is uncertain but may mean that the supports (*cf.* RV 'foundations') of the door-sockets slipped, and thus the door fell open revealing the holy place to the prophet. D.J.W.

POT. See FLESHPOTS, VESSELS.

POTIPHAR. A high officer of Pharaoh, to whom the Midianites sold Joseph (Gn. xxxvii. 36, xxxix. 1), and in whose household Joseph became chief steward (Gn. xxxix). His name is Egyptian, of the type *P'-dỉ-X*, X being a deity. The simplest, but not wholly satisfactory, explanation of Potiphar is that it is an abbreviated variant of Potiphera (*q.v.*), with loss of final *'ayin*. Two high officials at court with the same or similar names is not without parallel in Egyptian history.

K.A.K.

POTIPHERAH (better, 'Potiphera', RV). The 'priest of On', whose daughter, Asenath, Joseph received in marriage from Pharaoh (Gn. xli. 45, 50, xlvi. 20). He was possibly (but not certainly) high priest of the sun-god Rē' in On (*q.v.*) (Gk. Heliopolis). Potiphera (Heb. *Pôṭîpera'*) is universally admitted to be Egyp. *P'-dỉ-P'R'*, 'he whom P'Rē' (= sun-god) has given', on pattern *P'-dỉ-X*, X being a deity. The exact form *P'-dỉ-P'R'* is inscriptionally attested only late (*c.* 1000–300 BC), but is merely a full Late-Egyptian form of this name-type which is known from the Empire period, especially the XIXth Dynasty (13th century BC), the age of Moses. Potiphera/*P'-dỉ-P'R'* may be simply a modernization in Moses' time of the older form *Dỉdỉ-R'*, with the same meaning, of a name-pattern (*Dỉdỉ-X*) which is particularly common in the Middle Kingdom and Hyksos periods, *i.e.* the patriarchal and Joseph's age (*c.* 2100–1600 BC). See Kitchen, *The Joseph Narrative and its Egyptian Background*, 1962. K.A.K.

POTSHERD. See PAPYRI AND OSTRACA.

POTTAGE. See FOOD, Ib.

POTTER, POTTERY. A reasonable explanation of the introduction of pottery is that a clay-lined basket was accidentally burnt, baking the lining and rendering it usable (see S. Cole, *The Neolithic Revolution*, 1959, p. 41). Pottery first appears in Neolithic times in the Near East. Until the invention of the potter's wheel (see WHEEL) late in the fourth millennium BC, all pots were built up by hand, by the same methods which continue to be used for making large vessels in Palestine (G. M. Crowfoot, 'Pots Ancient and Modern', *PEQ*, LXIV, 1932, pp. 179–187). Examples of the professional potter's workshop discovered in Palestine (*e.g.* at Lachish (*PEQ*, LXX, 1938, p. 249, pl. XXV) and Khirbet Qumrān (*RB*, LXIII, 1956, p. 543, pl. XI)) show that the potter sat on the edge of a small pit in which stood the wheels (Heb. *'oḇnayim*), usually two stones, one pivoted over the other, which he turned with his feet (see fig. 20). Pebbles, shells, bone implements, and broken shards were used in smoothing and burnishing the surface, in shaping and decorating. The power of the potter (Heb. *yôṣēr*; Gk. *kerameus*) over the clay (Heb. *ḥōmer*; Gk. *pēlos*) is used as a simile in Je. xviii. 1–12 and by Paul (Rom. ix. 21).

I. ANCIENT POTTERY

Simply because it is by nature common, but fragile, pottery in large quantities lies strewn on every ancient tell (*cf.* Jb. ii. 8). Careful observation of the stratigraphical relationship of fragments found on one site enables a distinction to be made between the earliest pieces and the latest (usually those found at the bottom and the top of the mound respectively). Comparison with similar shards from other sites shows the contemporaneity or otherwise of the various levels (see ARCHAEOLOGY, fig. 12). Records of pottery finds from several sites in Palestine have enabled a sequence of forms to be drawn up which can be dated by other evidence. As a result, it is now possible to date pottery found on one site—and thus the site—by comparison with recognized dated forms. It is dangerous, however, to give a date more precisely than approximately fifty years either way solely on the evidence of pottery. Population movements and trade routes can be followed by plotting the distribution of types over a large area. The following brief description of some features of pottery found in Palestine should be read in conjunction with the chart (fig. 171). The superior figures refer to the numbers of the various objects included in it.

Neolithic pots are of simple but diverse form, with burnishing and incised or painted decoration, perhaps imitating basket and leatherwork. The ware is mostly coarse, tempered with chopped straw. Some contact with Syria and Mesopotamia is suggested by the painted decoration of the next period (Chalcolithic). Definite rim-forms and ledge-handled jars now occur, and unique to it are long, barrel-like vessels with a loop handle either end and a neck in the middle. These are probably churns, imitating skin originals[2].

The Early Bronze Age may be divided into three phases on the basis of pottery types. Globular jars with parallel lines of reddish paint covering the whole body are typical of the earliest phase in southern Palestine, while broad strokes of thick and thin paint appear in the north[9]. A grey-burnished ware was probably introduced by immigrants[14]. Ledge-handled jars, common at this time, were exported to Egypt. Several pieces of Early Bronze II ware have been found in Egyptian tombs of the Ist Dynasty. Especially noticeable are single-handled pitchers[8] and red-burnished dishes. Migrations from Anatolia *via* Syria brought a distinctive red- or black-burnished pottery with plastic decoration (Khirbet Kerak ware, Early Bronze III[10,15]). This was used alongside local styles which are also found in Egyptian tombs of the Pyramid Age.

The different civilization of the Middle Bronze Age is apparent in the new pottery forms. Jars with short, narrow necks, and broad, flat bases are typical of the first phase, as are spouted pots[9,16]. It may be that these forms were associated with the spread of the Amorites. Certainly the very fine pottery of the second phase can be linked with the movements which culminated in the Hyksos. General use of the wheel and careful burnishing produced wares that rivalled, but did not oust, expensive vessels of metal and stone. Jars and pitchers have small round or pointed bases. The lamp first came into use at this period. Juglets of black ware with incised decoration filled with white paste found widely on sites of this period may be associated with the Hyksos[22].

II. LATER STYLES

Towards the end of the Middle Bronze Age and during the first part of Late Bronze I, jugs and bowls with red and black geometric designs and animals appear[28]. This ware was exported to Cyprus and possibly to Cilicia. Mycenaean pottery[30] (F. H. Stubbings, *Mycenaean Pottery from the Levant*, 1951) was imported in large quantities in the second phase together with Cypriot wares (the metallic 'base-ring' and 'milk-bowl' types)[33,37]. The break in culture between the Bronze and Iron Ages (see ARCHAEOLOGY) is clearly recognizable in the pottery. From the coastal plain, known to have been occupied by the Philistines, come large two-handled bowls and beer-jugs of cream ware, decorated with red and black geometric designs and stylized birds[36,29]. This is a local imitation of the later forms of Mycenaean wares. Pottery from the highlands is, in some cases, a degenerate continuation of Late Bronze Age styles, but new forms of coarse ware and crude shape also appear. Cylindrical jars with rounded bases and wide collared mouths are typical of the Settlement period.

During the Monarchy there is a greater regularity of form and gradual improvement in ware. A tendency to angular shapes may be noticed[41]. Many dishes were burnished while turning on the wheel, but the finest are very thin and decorated with bands of red slip ('Samaria ware')[48]. Large storage jars[39] were often stamped on the handles with a royal seal bearing the name of one of four towns, possibly factories (Hebron, Ziph, Socoh, and one unidentified, *Mmšt*, *cf.* 1 Ch. iv. 23, RSV; *DOTT*, p. 219; *BA*, XII, 1949, pp. 70–86). The mining communities of the Negeb used crude, hand-made pots (*BA*, XXII, 1959, p. 93, figs. 10, 16).

Persian and Hellenistic pottery shows development of some forms (*e.g.* the amphora[52]) under Greek influence. Athenian black- and red-figured wares were imported. Narrow, elongated flasks were often placed in tombs at this time. A ribbed appearance is common on coarse pottery

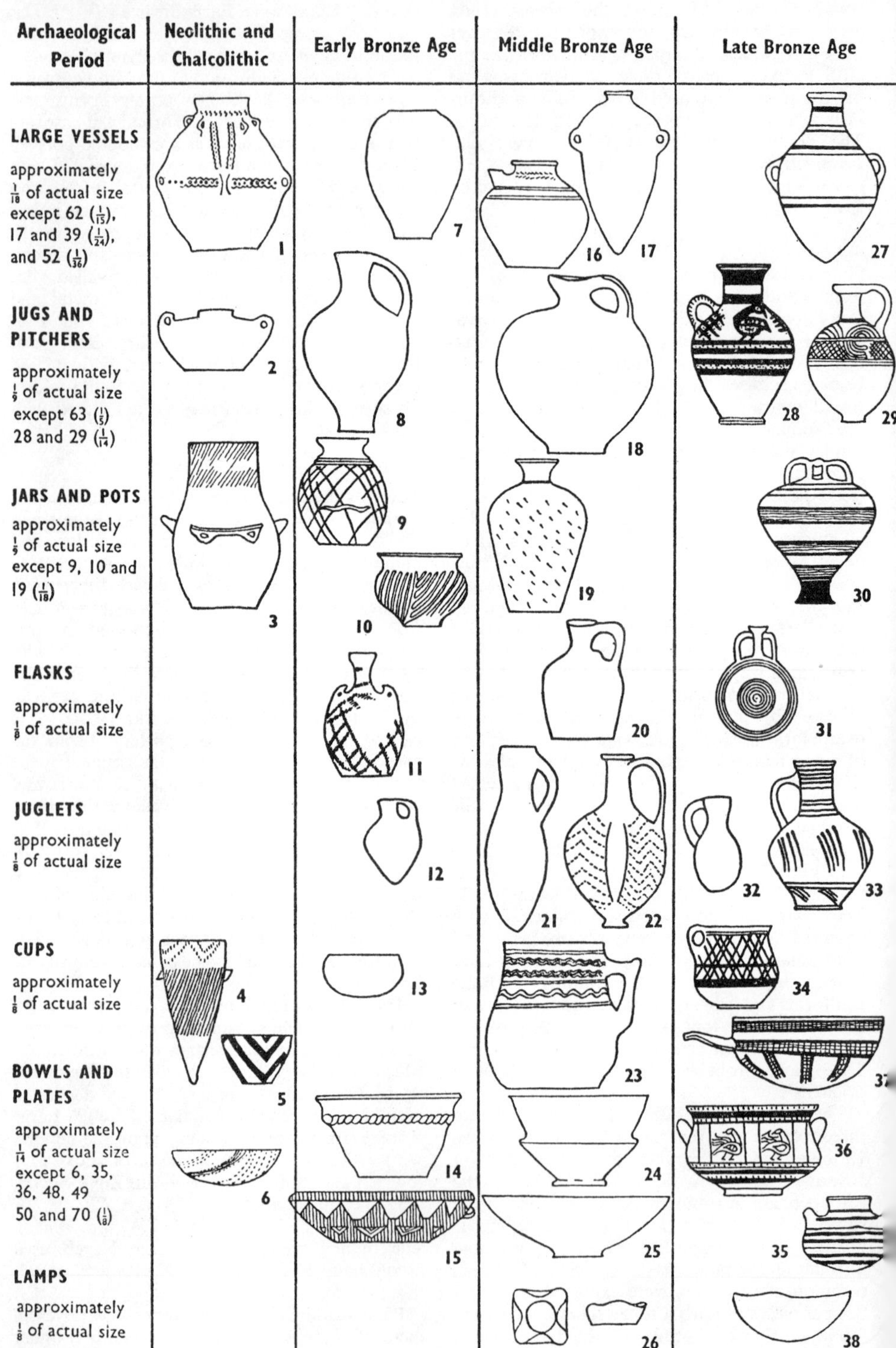

Archaeological Period
Neolithic and Chalcolithic
Early Bronze Age
Middle Bronze Age
Late Bronze Age
LARGE VESSELS
approximately 1/18 of actual size except 62 (1/15), 17 and 39 (1/24), and 52 (1/36)
JUGS AND PITCHERS
approximately 1/9 of actual size except 63 (1/5) 28 and 29 (1/14)
JARS AND POTS
approximately 1/9 of actual size except 9, 10 and 19 (1/18)
FLASKS
approximately 1/8 of actual size
JUGLETS
approximately 1/8 of actual size
CUPS
approximately 1/8 of actual size
BOWLS AND PLATES
approximately 1/14 of actual size except 6, 35, 36, 48, 49 50 and 70 (1/8)
LAMPS
approximately 1/8 of actual size

Fig. 171. Chart showing the development of pottery from Neolithic times
reference is made by means of superior figures to som

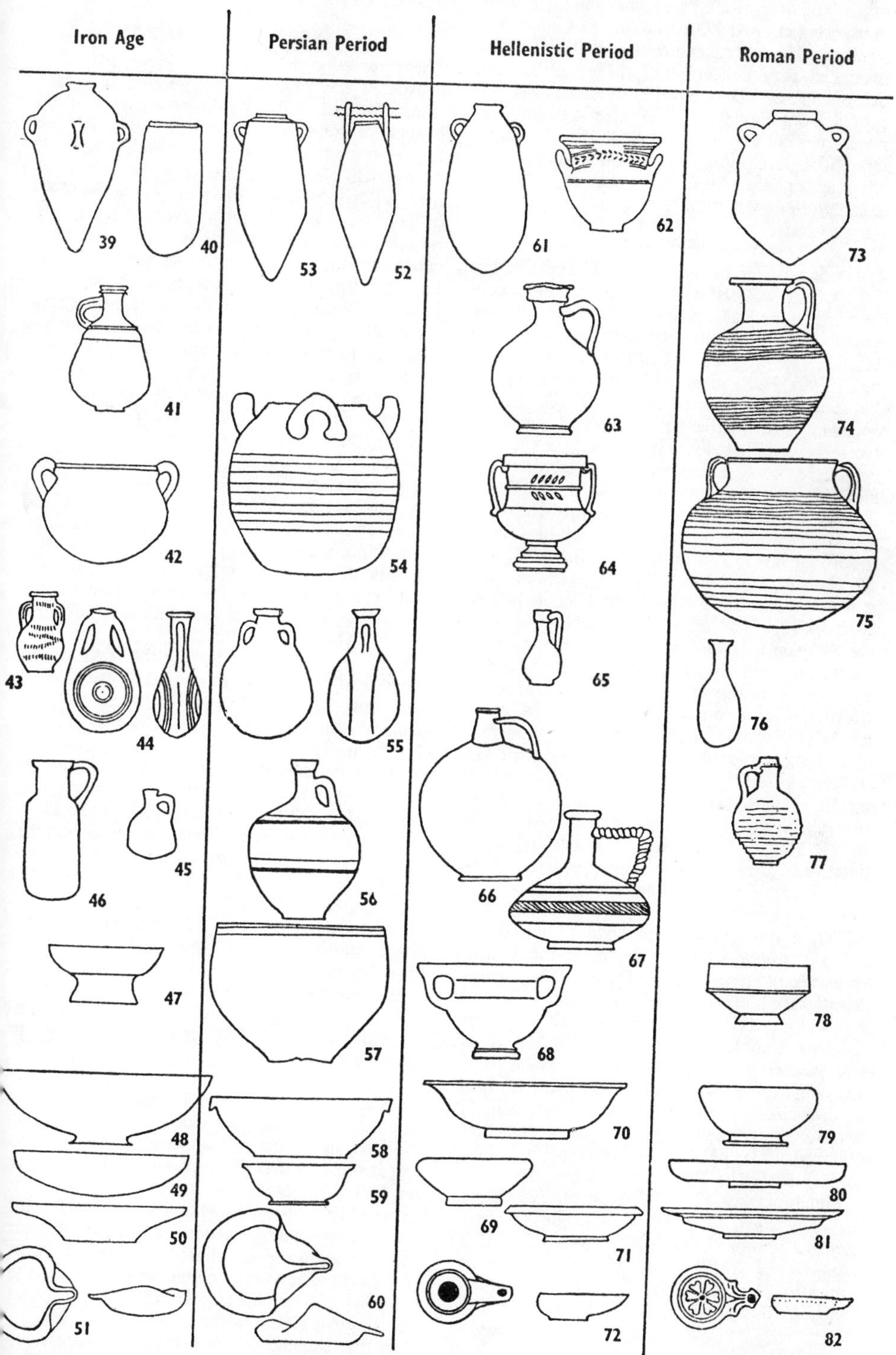

r a discussion of special features see article POTTER, POTTERY, where the objects in this chart. See also figs. 41, 42, 128, 225.

of the Roman period[74,75]; most of the finer wares in use were imported (*e.g.* Italian and Gallic *terra sigillata*). The Nabataean centres in Transjordan produced very delicate buff dishes with floral designs in red. Glazed ware (faience) was imported from Egypt in the Bronze Age but was never very common. (Pr. xxvi. 23 may be translated 'like glaze poured over pottery' taking Heb. *spsyg* as cognate with Hittite *zapzaga(y)a* 'glaze', *BASOR*, 98, 1945, pp. 21, 24.)

III. HEBREW NAMES

It is not possible to identify the Hebrew names for pottery vessels with certainty; these suggestions follow J. L. Kelso, *Ceramic Vocabulary of the Old Testament*, *BASOR* Supplementary Studies, 5, 6, 1948 (*cf. PEQ*, LXXI, 1939, pp. 76–90). Heb. *'aggān*, a large bowl, see CUP; *'āsûḵ*, a large, spouted oil-jar (2 Ki. iv. 2); *baqbûq*, the distinctive narrow-necked jug of the Iron II period (1 Ki. xiv. 3; Je. xix. 1, 10); *gāḇîa'*, Je. xxxv. 5, evidently a ewer, *cf.* CUP; *dûḏ*, a spherical cooking-pot (1 Sa. ii. 14; Jb. xli. 20); see also BASKET; *kaḏ*, pitcher, probably both the large handled jar and the crock-like, hole-mouth jar (Gn. xxiv. 14 ff.; Jdg. vii. 16 ff.); *kôs*, see CUP; *kiyyôr*, a bowl of pottery (Zc. xii. 6) or metal (Ex. xxx. 18; 1 Ki. vii. 20; 1 Sa. ii. 14); on 2 Ch. vi. 13, see W. F. Albright, *Archaeology and the Religion of Israel*, 1956; *kîrayîm*, clay rings on which round-based jars stood (Lv. xi. 35); *maḥᵃḇaṯ*, a pottery or metal disc or griddle on which pancakes were baked (Lv. ii. 5; Ezk. iv. 3); *marḥešeṯ*, a cooking-pot (Lv. ii. 7, vii. 9); *maśrēṯ*, a cooking-pot or handled pan (2 Sa. xiii. 9); *miš'ereṯ*, kneading-trough (*q.v.*); *nēḇel*, large wine jar (Is. xxx. 14; Je. xlviii. 12; La. iv. 2), see BOTTLE; *sîr*, any large cooking-pot (2 Ki. iv. 38; Jb. xli. 31), see FLESHPOTS; *cf.* WASHPOT; *sap̄*, a bowl, see CUP; *sēp̄el*, a large, valuable bowl (Jdg. v. 25, vi. 38); *paḵ*, juglet, see BOX; *pārûr*, a pot with a handle for heating liquids (Jdg. vi. 19); *ṣᵉlōḥîṯ*, a deep handle-less bowl (2 Ki. ii. 20, xxi. 13); *ṣāmîḏ*, a shallow bowl serving as a lid (Nu. xix. 15; see G. R. Driver, *The Hebrew Scrolls*, 1951, frontispiece); *ṣappaḥaṯ*, a flask or juglet (1 Sa. xxvi. 11 ff.; 1 Ki. xvii. 12 ff., xix. 6); *qallaḥaṯ*, a cooking-pot (1 Sa. ii. 14; Mi. iii. 3); Gk. *modios*, a vessel holding one peck (Mt. v. 15); *niptēr*, a wash-basin, defined as foot-wash-basin in papyrus Bodmer II (Jn. xiii. 5); *potērion*, see CUP; *tryblion*, a fairly large bowl (Mt. xxvi. 23); *phialē*, a broad dish for holding unguents (Rev. v. 8).

BIBLIOGRAPHY. K. M. Kenyon, *Archaeology in the Holy Land*, 1960; W. F. Albright, *Archaeology of Palestine*, 1960; M. Burrows, *What Mean These Stones?*, 1941, pp. 159–171; R. B. K. Amiran, *The Story of Pottery in Palestine* (*Antiquity and Survival*, II, 2, 3), 1957, pp. 187–207.

A.R.M.

POTTER'S FIELD. See AKELDAMA.

POUND. See WEIGHTS AND MEASURES, MONEY.

POVERTY.

I. IN THE OLD TESTAMENT

The impression is sometimes given that God prospered the righteous with material possessions (Ps. cxii. 1–3). While it is true that the benefits of industry and thrift to individuals and to the nation are clearly seen, and that God promises to bless those who keep His commandments (Dt. xxviii. 1–14), there were numbers of poor people in Israel at every stage of the nation's history. Their poverty might have been caused through natural disasters leading to bad harvests, through enemy invasion, through oppression by powerful neighbours, or through extortionate usury. There was an obligation on the wealthier members of the community to support their poorer brethren (Dt. xv. 1–11). Those who were most likely to suffer poverty were the fatherless and the widows and the landless aliens (*gērîm*). They were often the victims of oppression (Je. vii. 6; Am. ii. 6, 7a), but Yahweh was their vindicator (Dt. x. 17–19; Ps. lxviii. 5, 6). The law commanded that provision should be made for them (Dt. xxiv. 19–22), and with them were numbered the Levites (Dt. xiv. 28, 29) because they had no holding of land. A man could sell himself into slavery, but if he were a Hebrew he had to be treated differently from a foreigner (Lv. xxv. 39–46).

It was a problem to some of the psalmists to understand how in so many cases wealth had come into the wrong hands. On purely material grounds it might seem vain to serve Yahweh (Ps. lxxiii. 12–14), but in the end the wicked would come to destruction while the righteous enjoyed the richest possession—the knowledge of Yahweh Himself (Ps. lxxiii. 16–28). But so often were the rich oppressors that 'the poor' became almost a synonym for 'the pious' (Ps. xiv. 5, 6).

II. IN THE NEW TESTAMENT

There were heavy taxes of various kinds imposed on the Jews in New Testament times. Probably many were in severe economic straits, while others made considerable profits from collaborating with the Romans. The worldly-minded Sadducees were generally wealthy, as were the tax-collectors.

Jesus was the son of poor parents (Lk. ii. 24), but there is no reason to suppose He lived in abject poverty. As the eldest son, He would probably have inherited something from Joseph, and it appears that He used to pay the Temple tax (Mt. xvii. 24). Some of His disciples were reasonably well-to-do (Mk. i. 20) and He had some fairly wealthy friends (Jn. xii. 3). He and the Twelve, however, shared a common purse (Jn. xii. 6). They were content to go without the comforts of home life (Lk. ix. 58), and yet found occasion for giving to the poor (Jn. xiii. 29).

In the teaching of Jesus material possessions are not regarded as evil, but as dangerous. The poor are often shown to be happier than the rich, because it is easier for them to have an attitude of dependence upon God. It was to them that He came to preach the gospel (Lk. iv. 18, vii. 22). It is they who are the first to be blessed and to be assured of the possession of the kingdom of God (Lk. vi. 20), if their poverty is the acknowledgment of spiritual bankruptcy (Mt. v. 3). A poor person's offering may be of much greater value than a rich man's (Mk. xii. 41–44). The poor must be shown hospitality (Lk. xiv. 12–14), and given alms (Lk. xviii. 22), though charity was to be secondary to worship (Jn. xii. 1–8).

The early Church made an experiment in the communal holding of wealth (Acts ii. 41, 42, iv. 32). This led at first to the elimination of poverty (Acts iv. 34, 35), but it has often been held that it was responsible for the later economic collapse of the Church at Jerusalem. Much of the ministry of Paul was concerned with raising money in the Gentile Churches to assist the poor Christians in Jerusalem (Rom. xv. 25–29; Gal. ii. 10). These churches were also taught to provide for their own poor members (Rom. xii. 13, *etc.*). James is especially vehement against those who allowed distinctions of wealth in the Christian community (Jas. ii. 1–7). The poor were called by God and their salvation brought glory to Him (1 Cor. i. 26–31). The material wealth of the church of Laodicea was in sad contrast with her spiritual poverty (Rev. iii. 17).

The most systematic exposition about poverty and wealth in the Epistles is found in 2 Cor. viii, ix, where Paul sets the idea of Christian charity in the context of the gifts of God and especially that of His Son who, 'though he was rich, yet for your sakes he became poor, that ye through his poverty might become rich' (RV). In the light of that, running the risk of material poverty will lead to spiritual blessing, just as the apostles were poor but made many rich (2 Cor. vi. 10). See also ALMS, ORPHAN. R.E.N.

POWER.

I. IN THE OLD TESTAMENT

Various Hebrew words are rendered 'power', the principal ones being *ḥayil*, *kōaḥ*, and *'ōz*. True power, the ability to exercise authority effectively, belongs to God alone (Ps. lxii. 11). The power of God is shown in the creation (Ps. cxlviii. 5), and the sustaining of the world (Ps. lxv. 5–8). Some of His authority is delegated to mankind (Gn. i. 26–28; Ps. viii. 5–8, cxv. 16), but God actively intervenes on many occasions, showing His power in miraculous deeds of deliverance. It was 'with mighty hand and outstretched arm' that He brought His people out of Egypt (Ex. xv. 6; Dt. v. 15, *etc.*), and He demonstrated His power in giving them the promised land (Ps. cxi. 6).

II. IN THE NEW TESTAMENT

'Power' in EVV represents chiefly Gk. *dynamis* and *exousia*. *Exousia* means derived or conferred 'authority', the warrant or right to do something (Mt. xxi. 23–27); from this it comes to denote concretely the bearer of authority on earth (Rom. xiii. 1–3), or in the spirit world (Col. i. 16). *Dynamis* is ability (2 Cor. viii. 3) or strength (Eph. iii. 16), or it may mean a powerful act (Acts ii. 22) or a powerful spirit (Rom. viii. 38). Christ had all authority given Him by His Father (Mt. xxviii. 18) and He used it to forgive sins (Mt. ix. 6) and to cast out evil spirits (Mt. x. 1). He gave authority to His disciples to become sons of God (Jn. i. 12) and to share in His work (Mk. iii. 15).

Jesus came to His ministry in the power (*dynamis*) of the Spirit (Lk. iv. 14), and His power was operative in healing miracles (Lk. v. 17) and He did many mighty works (Mt. xi. 20). This was evidence of the power of the kingdom of God as a prelude to the new Exodus (Lk. xi. 20; *cf.* Ex. viii. 19). But the kingdom had not yet come in its full power. That would happen at Pentecost (Lk. xxiv. 49; Acts i. 8; ? Mk. ix. 1) and there would be the consummation at the parousia (Mt. xxiv. 30, *etc.*).

In the Acts we see the power of the Spirit operative in the life of the Church (iv. 7, 33, vi. 8; *cf.* x. 38). Paul looks back to the resurrection as the chief evidence of God's power (Rom. i. 4; Eph. i. 19, 20; Phil. iii. 10) and sees the gospel as the means by which that power comes to work in men's lives (Rom. i. 16; 1 Cor. i. 18). See also AUTHORITY.

BIBLIOGRAPHY. *TWNT*, *s.v. dynamia/dynamis, exousia, ischyō/ischys*; D. M. Lloyd-Jones, *Authority*, 1958. R.E.N.

III. 'THE POWER OF THE KEYS'

This phrase is used to describe the authority given by our Lord to His disciples as described in Mt. xvi. 19, xviii. 18; Jn. xx. 22, 23. It is a power which may be said to operate in two ways. First, by preaching the gospel the kingdom of God is opened to believers and shut to the impenitent, and secondly, by discipline, serious offenders are excluded from the Church until they repent, whereupon they are readmitted. In either case, forgiveness is mediated through the Church, acting in the Spirit and through the Word.

Since it is the doctrine of the gospel that opens heaven to us, it is beautifully expressed by the metaphorical appellation of 'keys'. '*Ac ligare & solvere prorsus aliud nihil est quam Evangelium praedicare & applicare*' (Luther). That keys and doctrine are so connected is seen from the fact that the delivery of a key was part of a scribe's ordination (Mt. xiii. 52; Lk. xi. 52). Through the preaching of the gospel some men are reconciled to God by faith, others are more firmly bound by unbelief. The Church, acting as Christ's representative (Lk. x. 16), pronounces absolution to the penitent. This is a real transaction only in so far as the Church is filled with the Spirit of God, so that then it gives the actual judgment of God Himself. Binding and loosing (*q.v.*) mean not merely the authoritative announcement of the conditions of entrance into the kingdom; a stronger sense is necessary—determining which individuals have accepted the conditions.

This power was given in a special sense to Peter, for he, at Pentecost, opened the door of faith to the Jews, and later to the Gentiles and Samaritans. But it was given to all the apostles (Jn. xx. 23) and to men of like faith and spirit ever since.

In the further exercise of the power of the keys, in ecclesiastical discipline, the thought is of administrative authority (Is. xxii. 22) with regard to the requirements of the household of faith. The use of censures, excommunication, and absolution is committed to the Church in every age, to be used under the guidance of the Spirit. 'Whoever, after committing a crime, humbly confesses his fault and entreats the Church to forgive him, is absolved not only by men, but by God Himself; and, on the other hand, whoever treats with ridicule the reproofs and threatenings of the Church, if he is condemned by her, the decision which men have given will be ratified in Heaven' (Calvin on 1 Cor. v).

Since the Reformers it has been accepted that 'the power of the keys' represented this 'duplex ministerium', a real power of spiritual binding and loosing. But this judicial sense has been sharply challenged of late in favour of a legislative sense whereby 'loose' means 'permitted', and 'bind' means 'forbidden'. This is in agreement with rabbinic usage: the school of Shammai was said to *bind* when it declared that there was only one ground for divorce; the school of Hillel *loosed* when it allowed more laxity in this and other questions. For this use, see also Mt. xxiii. 4; Rom. vii. 2; 1 Cor. vii. 27, 39. So Peter, in T. W. Manson's words, is to be 'God's vicegerent . . . The authority of Peter is an authority to declare what is right and wrong for the Christian community. His decisions will be confirmed by God' (*The Sayings of Jesus*, 1954, p. 205). But note that this special rabbinical application of the words was based on the juristic character of the rabbinic literature, and that it was originally used of the full power of the judge (*cf. TWNT, s.v.* 'Keys'). Even granting a late origin for Mt. xviii. 18, we are left with the question as to why a context of Church discipline should early seem suitable for the words 'bind' and 'loose'. A. H. McNeile questions the authenticity of this passage altogether, but J. Jeremias has argued ingeniously for its trustworthiness *TWNT, op. cit.*).

In any case, it is hardly right to make Peter, as this view does, a scribe in the kingdom of God. 'The apostle would, in the coming kingdom, be like a great scribe or Rabbi, who would deliver decisions on the basis . . . of the teaching of Jesus' (A. H. McNeile). But there is a great difference between the pronouncements of the apostles on ethical matters and the encyclopaedic casuistry of the scribes. Mt. xxiii. 8 made it impossible for Peter to aspire to such a function. The principle of Christian ethics is to look after the big things (mercy, love, truth) and the little things will then look after themselves; not detailed prescribed legislation, but the guidance of the Spirit.

BIBLIOGRAPHY. Calvin's Commentaries on the Matthaean passages and on 1 Cor. v present a fair representation of the views of all the Reformers. In addition to the modern writers cited, Dr. R. N. Flew discusses these questions in *Jesus and His Church*, 1938, p. 131 f. See also *DCG* (*s.v.* 'Absolution'); *ERE* (*s.v.* 'Discipline'); Calvin, *Institutes*, iv. 12; *TWNT* (*s.v.* 'Keys'). R.N.C.

PRAETORIUM. Originally the tent of the commander, or praetor, and, in consequence, the army headquarters (Liv., vii. 12; Caes., *BC* i. 76). By extension the word came to mean the residence of a provincial governor (Mt. xxvii. 27; Mk. xv. 16; Jn. xviii. 28, 33, xix. 9; Acts xxiii. 35). If Paul was writing from Rome, Phil. i. 13 may refer to the emperor's residence on the Palatine. The word seems not to have been used for the permanent camp of the praetorian guards by the Porta Viminalis. It does, however, sometimes mean the forces of the praetorian guards (*CIL*, v. 2837, viii. 9391), and, whether the letter was written at Ephesus or Rome, this gives good sense to Paul's phrase. Detachments of *praetoriani* were sent to the provinces, and in Rome they would have charge of prisoners in imperial custody. E.M.B.

PRAISE. In the Old Testament the words for praise mainly used are *hālal*, the root meaning of which is connected with making a noise; *yāḏâ*, which was originally associated with the bodily actions and gestures which accompany praising; and *zāmar*, which is associated with the playing or singing of music. In the New Testament, *eucharistein* (lit. 'to give thanks') is the favourite word, implying on the part of the person who praises the attitude of one more intimate with the person praised than in the more formal *eulogein*, 'to bless'.

The whole of the Bible is punctuated with outbursts of praise. They rise spontaneously from the 'basic mood' of joy which marks the life of the people of God. God takes pleasure and delight in His works of creation (Gn. i; Ps. civ. 31; Pr. viii. 30, 31), and all creation, including the angels, expresses its joy in praise (Jb. xxxviii. 4–7; Rev. iv. 6–11). Man also was created to rejoice in God's works (Ps. xc. 14–16) and fulfils this purpose by accepting God's gifts (Ec. viii. 15, ix. 7, xi. 9; Phil. iv. 4, 8; *cf.* also W. Eichrodt, *Man in the Old Testament*, 1951, p. 35).

The coming of the kingdom of God into the midst of this world is marked by the restoration of joy and praise to the people of God and the whole creation (Is. ix. 2; Ps. xcvi. 11–13; Rev. v. 9–14; Lk. ii. 13, 14), a foretaste of which is already given in the ritual and worship of the Temple where praise arises from sheer joy in the redeeming presence of God (Dt. xxvii. 7; Nu. x. 10; Lv. xxiii. 40). The praise of God is rendered on earth for the works both of creation and redemption (Ps. xxiv, cxxxvi), this being an echo on earth of the praise of heaven (Rev. iv. 11, v. 9, 10). Praise, therefore, is a mark of the people of God (1 Pet. ii. 9; Eph. i. 3–14; Phil. i. 11). It is the mark of the heathen that they refuse to render it (Rom. i. 21; Rev. xvi. 9). The act of praising implies the closest fellowship with the One who is being praised. 'Therefore praise not merely expresses but completes the enjoyment; it is its appointed consummation. . . . In commanding us to glorify Him, God is inviting us to enjoy Him' (C. S. Lewis, *Reflections on the Psalms*, 1958, p. 95).

Yet praise to God is frequently commanded from men as a duty and is obviously not meant to depend on mood or feeling or circumstances (*cf.* Jb. i. 21). To 'rejoice before the Lord' is part of the ordered ritual of the common life of His people (Dt. xii. 7, xvi. 11, 12), in which men encourage and exhort one another to praise. Though there are psalms which express the praise of the individual, it was always felt that praise could best be rendered within the congregation (Pss. xxii. 25, xxxiv. 3, xxxv. 18), where praise not only gives honour and pleasure to God (Ps. l. 23) but also bears testimony to God's people (Ps. li. 12–15).

Elaborate arrangements were made for the conduct of praise in the Temple by the Levites. The Psalms were used in the liturgy and in sacred processions with 'glad shouts and songs' (Ps. xlii. 4). The singing was probably antiphonal, involving two choirs, or soloist and choir. Dancing, from earliest times a means of expressing praise (Ex. xv. 20; 2 Sa. vi. 14), was also used in the Temple to this end (Pss. cxlix. 3, cl. 4). Ps. cl gives a list of musical instruments used in the praise. See MUSIC AND MUSICAL INSTRUMENTS.

The early Christians continued to express their gladness by attending worship in the Temple (Lk. xxiv. 53; Acts iii. 1). But their experience of new life in Christ was bound to express itself in new forms of praise (Mk. ii. 22). Joy was the dominant mood of the Christian life, and though the formal worship and praise which it inspired is not explicitly described or prescribed, this was because it was so much taken for granted. As those who experienced and witnessed the healing and cleansing power of Jesus broke out spontaneously into praise (Lk. xviii. 43; Mk. ii. 12), so also in the apostolic Church there are frequent examples of such spontaneous outbursts, as men began to see and understand the power and goodness of God in Christ (Acts ii. 46, iii. 8, xi. 18, xvi. 25; Eph. i. 1–14).

The Psalms were undoubtedly used to express the praise of the early Church (Col. iii. 16; *cf.* Mt. xxvi. 30). There were also new Christian hymns (*cf.* Rev. v. 8–14), referred to in Col. iii. 16; 1 Cor. xiv. 26. We have examples of such inspiration to new forms of praise in the *Magnificat*, *Benedictus*, and *Nunc Dimittis* (*qq.v.*) (Lk. i. 46–55, 68–79, ii. 29–32). Elsewhere in the text of the New Testament there are examples of the formal praise of the early Church. It seems likely from its literary form and content that Phil. ii. 6–11 was composed and used as a hymn of praise to Christ. Probably there are echoes of, or quotations from, early hymns in such passages as Eph. v. 14 and 1 Tim. iii. 16. The doxologies in the book of Revelation (*cf.* Rev. i. 4–7, v. 9–14, xv. 3, 4) must have been used in public worship to express the praise of the congregation (*cf.* A. B. Macdonald, *Christian Worship in the Primitive Church*, 1934).

The close connection between praise and sacrifice should be noted. In the sacrificial ritual of the Old Testament a place was found for the sacrifice of thanksgiving as well as of expiation (*cf.* Lv. vii. 11–21). Gratitude was to be the fundamental motive behind the bringing of the first-fruits to the altar (Dt. xxvi. 1–11). In the sincere offering of praise itself there is a sacrifice which pleases God (Heb. xiii. 15; Ho. xiv. 2; Ps. cxix. 108). In the priestly self-offering of Jesus this aspect of thanksgiving finds its place (Mk. xiv. 22, 23, 26; Jn. xvii. 1, 2; Mt. xi. 25, 26). The life of the Christian should, correspondingly, be a self-offering of gratitude (Rom. xii. 1) in fulfilment of his royal priesthood (Rev. i. 5, 6; 1 Pet. ii. 9), and the fact that such a sacrificial self-offering can be made in a real way in the midst of suffering, links suffering and praise together in the Christian life (Phil. ii. 17). Thanksgiving sanctifies not only suffering but all aspects of the life of the Christian (1 Tim. iv. 4, 5; 1 Cor. x. 30, 31; 1 Thes. v. 16–18). Whatever else be the burden of prayer, it must include praise (Phil. iv. 6).

R.S.W.

PRAYER.

I. INTRODUCTION

In the Bible prayer is worship that includes all the attitudes of the human spirit in its approach to God. The Christian worships God when he adores, confesses, praises, and supplicates Him in prayer. This highest activity of which the human spirit is capable may also be thought of as communion with God, so long as due emphasis is laid upon divine initiative. A man prays because God has already touched his spirit. Prayer in the Bible is not a 'natural response' (see Jn. iv. 24). 'That which is born of the flesh is flesh.' Consequently, the Lord does not 'hear' every prayer (Is. i. 15, xxix. 13). The biblical doctrine of prayer emphasizes the character of God, the necessity of a man's being in saving or covenant relation with Him, and his entering fully into all the privileges and obligations of that relation with God.

II. IN THE OLD TESTAMENT

Köhler (*loc. cit.*, p. 251, n. 153) finds 'about eight-five original prayers in the Old Testament. In addition there are about sixty whole psalms and fourteen parts of psalms which may be called prayers.'

a. The patriarchal period

In the patriarchal period prayer is calling upon the name of the Lord (Gn. iv. 26, xii. 8, xxi. 33); *i.e.* the sacred name is used in invocation or appeal. There is, consequently, an unmistakable directness and familiarity in prayer (Gn. xv. 2 ff., xviii. 23 ff., xxiv. 12–14, 26 f.). Prayer is also closely connected with sacrifice (Gn. xiii. 4, xxvi. 25, xxviii. 20–22), although this association appears in later periods too. This offering of prayer in a context of sacrifice suggests a union of man's will with God's will, an abandonment and submission of the self to God. This is especially so in Jacob's conjoining prayer with a vow to the Lord. The vow, itself a prayer, promises service and faithfulness if the blessing sought is granted (Gn. xxviii. 20 ff.).

b. The pre-exilic period

1. In this period one of the main emphases in prayer is intercession; although this was also a factor in patriarchal times (Gn. xviii. 22 ff.). Intercession was especially prominent in the prayers of Moses (Ex. xxxii. 11–13, 31 f., xxxiii. 12–16, xxxiv. 9; Nu. xi. 11–15, xiv. 13–19, xxi. 7; Dt. ix. 18–21, x. 10). Dt. xxx is also largely a prayer of intercession, as are also the prayers of Aaron (Nu. vi. 22–27), Samuel (1 Sa. vii. 5–13, xii. 19, 23), Solomon (1 Ki. viii. 22–53), and Hezekiah (2 Ki. xix. 14–19). The inference seems to be that intercession was confined to outstanding personalities who, by virtue of their position assigned to them by God as prophets, priests, and kings, had peculiar power in prayer as mediators between God and men. But the Lord always remained free to execute His will; hence we hear of unsuccessful intercession (Gn. xviii. 17 ff.; Ex. xxxii. 30–35). In Am. vii. 1–6 'the Lord repented' concerning a certain course of action in answer to the prophet's intercession, and in the next verses (vii. 7–viii. 2) Israel is to be led away captive after all. Jeremiah is even forbidden to intercede with God (Je. vii. 16, xi. 14, xiv. 11). On the other hand, success attended the intercession of Lot (Gn. xix. 17–23), Abraham (Gn. xx. 17), Moses (Ex. ix. 27–33; Nu. xii. 9 ff.), and Job (Jb. xlii. 8, 10). It is the strongly personal relation with God in which those mediators stood that underlies these intercessory prayers.

2. It is surprising that among all the legal enactments of the Pentateuch there is nothing about prayer apart from Dt. xxvi. 1–15. Even here it is formulae for worship rather than prayer that are being emphasized. In verses 5–11 there is thanksgiving, and in verses 13, 14 there is a profession of past obedience, but only in verse 15 is there supplication. However, we are probably right in assuming that sacrifice would often be offered with prayer (Ps. lv. 14), and where it was not it might be reproved (Ps. l. 7–15). On the other hand, the almost total absence of prayer in those parts of the Pentateuch where sacrifice is regulated suggests that sacrifice without prayer was fairly common.

3. Prayer must have been indispensable in the ministry of the prophets. The very reception of the revelatory Word from God involved the prophet in a prayerful relation with Yahweh. Indeed, it might well have been that prayer was essential to the prophet's receiving the Word (Is. vi. 5 ff., xxxvii. 1–4; Je. xi. 20–23, xii. 1–6, xlii. 1 ff.). The prophetic vision came to Daniel while he was at prayer (Dn. ix. 20 ff.). On occasion the Lord kept the prophet waiting for a considerable time in prayer (Hab. ii. 1–3). We know from Jeremiah's writings that while prayer was the essential condition of, and reality in, the prophet's experience and ministry, it was often a tempestuous exercise of the spirit (xviii. 19–23, xx. 7–18), as well as a sweet fellowship with God (i. 4 ff., iv. 10, x. 23–25, xii. 1–4, xiv. 7–9, 19–22, xv. 15–18, xvi. 19, xvii. 12 ff.).

4. The Psalms. In the Psalms there is a blending of pattern and spontaneity in prayer. Alongside the more formal 'sanctuary' prayers (*e.g.* xxiv. 7–10, c, cl) there are personal prayers for pardon (li), communion (lxiii), protection (lvii), healing (vi), vindication (cix), and prayers that are full of praise (ciii). Sacrifice and prayer also blend in the psalms (liv. 6, lxvi. 13 ff.).

c. The exilic period

During the Exile the important factor in religion for the Jews was the emergence of the synagogue. The Jerusalem Temple was in ruins, and altar rites and sacrifices could not be performed in unclean Babylon. A Jew was now no longer one who had been born into the community, and was residing in it, but rather one who *chose* to be a Jew. The centre of the religious community was the synagogue, and among the accepted religious obligations such as circumcision, fasting and sabbath observance, prayer was important. This was inevitable because each little community in exile now depended upon the synagogue service where the Word was read and expounded, and prayers were offered. And after the return to Jerusalem, just as the Temple was not allowed to displace the synagogue, nor the priest the scribe, nor sacrifice the living Word, so ritual did not displace prayer. Both in Temple and synagogue, in priestly ritual and scribal exposition, the devout worshipper now sought the face of Yahweh, His personal presence (Pss. c. 2, lxiii. 1 ff.), and received His blessing in terms of the light of His countenance shining upon him (Ps. lxxx. 3, 7, 19).

d. The post-exilic period

After the Exile there was undoubtedly a framework of devotion, but within it freedom was secured for the individual. This is exemplified in Ezra and Nehemiah, who, while insisting upon cult and law, and upon ritual and sacrifice and, therefore, upon the social aspects of worship, yet emphasized also the spiritual factor in devotion (Ezr. vii. 27, viii. 22 f.; Ne. ii. 4, iv. 4, 9). Their prayers are also instructive (Ezr. ix. 6–15; Ne. i. 5–11, ix. 5–38; *cf.* also Dn. ix. 4–19). We may also note here that concerning posture in prayer there were no fixed rules (Ps. xxviii. 2; 1 Sa. i. 26; 1 Ki. viii. 54; Ezr. ix. 5; 1 Ki. xviii. 42; La. iii. 41; Dn. ix. 3 and verse 20 where we should read 'towards' instead of 'for'). So also in the matter of hours for prayer: prayer was effective at any time, as well as at the stated hours (Ps. lv. 17; Dn. vi. 10). In the post-exilic period, then, we find a blending of orderliness of temple ritual, the simplicity of the synagogue meeting, and the spontaneity of personal devotion. Prayer being what it is, it would be manifestly impossible to systematize it completely. Within the Old Testament there are certainly patterns for prayer but no binding regulations governing either its contents or its ritual. Mechanical prayer, prayer hemmed in by coercive prescriptions, did not come until towards the close of the inter-testamental period, as the Gospels make clear. Then, alas, both through Temple sacrifice in Jerusalem, and in the *diaspora* through the praise, prayer, and exposition of the synagogue service, and through circumcision, sabbath observance, tithes, fasting, and supererogatory deeds, worshippers in both Temple and synagogue sought to merit acceptance with God.

III. IN THE NEW TESTAMENT

There are certain clearly-defined areas where the New Testament teaching on prayer is set forth, but the fountain-head from which all its instruction in prayer flows is Christ's own doctrine and practice.

a. The Gospels

1. As to Jesus' doctrine of prayer this is set out principally in certain of His parables. In the parable of the friend who borrowed three loaves at midnight (Lk. xi. 5–8) the Lord inculcates importunity in prayer; and the ground on which the confidence in importunate prayer is built is the Father's generosity (Mt. vii. 7–11). The parable of the unjust judge (Lk. xviii. 1–8) calls for tenacity in prayer, which includes persistence as well as continuity. God's delays in answering prayer are due not to indifference but to love that desires to develop and deepen faith which is finally vindicated. In the parable of the publican and the Pharisee (Lk. xviii. 10–14) Christ insists on humility and penitence in prayer, and warns against a sense of self-superiority. Self-humiliation in prayer means acceptance with God, self-exaltation in prayer hides God's face. Christ calls for charity in prayer in the parable of the unjust servant (Mt. xviii. 21–35). It is prayer offered by a forgiving spirit that God answers. Simplicity in prayer is taught in Mt. vi. 5 f., xxiii. 14; Mk. xii. 38–40; Lk. xx. 47. Prayer must be purged of all pretence. It should spring from simplicity of heart and motive, and express itself in simplicity of speech and petition. The Lord also urged intensity in prayer (*cf.* Mk. xiii. 33, xiv. 38; Mt. xxvi. 41). Here watchfulness and faith combine in sleepless vigilance. Again, in Mt. xviii. 19 f. unity in prayer is emphasized. If a group of Christians who have the mind of Christ pray in the Holy Spirit their prayers will be effectual. But prayer must also be expectant (Mk. xi. 24). Prayer that is an experiment achieves little; prayer which is the sphere where faith operates in surrender to God's will achieves much (Mk. ix. 23).

2. On objectives in prayer Jesus had singularly little to say. Doubtless He was content to let the Holy Spirit prompt His disciples in prayer. What aims He referred to in prayer are to be found in Mk. ix. 28 f.; Mt. v. 44, vi. 11, 13, ix. 36 ff.; Lk. xi. 13.

3. As to method in prayer the Lord had two important things to teach. First, prayer is now to be offered to Him, as it was offered to Him when He was on earth (*e.g.* Mt. viii. 2, ix. 18). As He insisted on faith then (Mk. ix. 23), and tested sincerity (Mt. ix. 27–31), and uncovered ignorance (Mt. xx. 20–22) and sinful presumption (Mt. xiv. 27–31), in those who petitioned Him, so He does today in the experience of those who offer prayer to Him. Secondly, prayer is now also to be offered in the name of Christ (Jn. xiv. 13, xv. 16, xvi. 23 f.), through whom we have access to the Father. To pray in the name of Christ is to pray as Christ Himself prayed, and to pray to the Father as the Son has made Him known to us: and for Jesus the true focus in prayer was the Father's will. Here is the basic characteristic of Christian prayer: a new access to the Father which Christ secures for the Christian, and prayer in harmony with the Father's will because offered in Christ's name.

4. As to the Lord's practice of prayer it is well known that He prayed in secret (Lk. v. 15 f., vi. 12); in times of spiritual conflict (Jn. xii. 20–28; Lk. xxii. 39–46); and on the cross (Mt. xxvii. 46; Lk. xxiii. 46). In His prayers He offered thanksgiving (Lk. x. 21; Jn. vi. 11, xi. 41; Mt. xxvi. 27), sought guidance (Lk. vi. 12 ff.), interceded (Jn. xvii. 6–19, 20–26; Lk. xxii. 31–34; Mk. x. 16; Lk. xxiii. 34), and communed with the Father (Lk. ix. 28 ff.). The burden of His high-priestly prayer in Jn. xvii is the unity of the Church.

5. Since the Lord's Prayer (*q.v.*) is treated more fully elsewhere it will suffice to point out that after the invocation (Mt. vi. 9b) there follow six petitions (9c–13b), of which the first three have reference to God's name, kingdom and will, and the last three to man's need of bread, forgiveness, and victory: the Prayer then closes with a doxology (13c) which contains a threefold declaration concerning God's kingdom, power, and glory. It is 'after this manner' that the Christian is now enjoined to pray.

b. The Acts of the Apostles

The Acts is an excellent link between the Gospels and the Epistles, because in Acts the apostolic Church puts into effect our Lord's teaching on prayer. The Church was born in the atmosphere of prayer (i. 4). In answer to prayer the Spirit was poured out upon her (i. 4, ii. 4). Prayer continued to be the Church's native air (ii. 42, vi. 4, 6). There remained in the Church's thinking a close connection between prayer and the Spirit's presence and power (iv. 31). In times of crisis the Church had recourse to prayer (iv. 23 ff., xii. 5, 12). Throughout the Acts the Church leaders emerge as men of prayer (ix. 40, x. 9, xvi. 25, xxviii. 8) who urge the Christians to pray with them (xx. 28, 36, xxi. 5).

c. The Pauline Epistles

It is significant that immediately after Christ revealed Himself to Paul on the Damascus road it is said of Paul, 'Behold, he prayeth' (Acts ix. 11). Probably for the first time Paul discovered what prayer really was, so profound was the change in his heart which conversion had effected. From that moment he was a man of prayer. In prayer the Lord spoke to him (Acts xxii. 17 f.). Prayer was thanksgiving, intercession, the realization of God's presence (*cf.* 1 Thes. i. 2 f.; Eph. i. 16 ff.). He found that the Holy Spirit assisted him in prayer as he sought to know and do God's will (Rom. viii. 14, 26). In his experience there was a close connection between prayer and the Christian's intelligence (1 Cor. xiv. 14–19). Prayer was absolutely essential for the Christian (Rom. xii. 12). The Christian's armour (Eph. vi. 13–17) included prayer which Paul describes as 'all prayer', to be offered at 'all seasons', with 'all perseverance', for 'all saints' (verse 18). And Paul practised what he preached (Rom. i. 9; Eph. i. 16; 1 Thes. i. 2); hence his insistence upon prayer when writing to his fellow-believers (Phil. iv. 6; Col. iv. 2).

In his Epistles Paul is constantly breaking out into prayer, and it is instructive to glance at some of his prayers because of their content. 1. In Rom. i. 8–12 he pours out his heart to God in thanksgiving (verse 8), insists upon serving Christ with his spirit (verse 9a), intercedes for his friends in Rome (verse 9b), expresses his desire to impart to them a spiritual gift (verses 10 f.), and declares that he too is depending upon them for spiritual uplift (verse 12).

2. In Eph. i. 15–19 Paul again thanks God for his converts (verses 15 f.), and prays that they may receive the Spirit through whom comes knowledge of God and illumination of heart (verses 17, 18a), in order that they may know the hope of God's calling, the wealth of God's inheritance, and the greatness of God's power which had been demonstrated in Christ's resurrection (verses 18b, 19).

3. Again, in Eph. iii. 14–18 the apostle pleads with the Father (verses 14 f.) for his fellow-Christians that they might be increasingly conscious of God's power (verse 16), to the end that Christ might indwell them, and that they might be rooted in love (verse 17), that each together, being perfected, might be filled with the fulness of God (verse 18 f.). Both of these 'Ephesian' prayers are well summed up in Paul's threefold desire that Christians should receive knowledge and power, issuing in the love of Christ, through which as individuals and a group they should achieve perfection.

4. In Col. i. 9 ff. Paul again prays that the believers should know God's will through spiritual wisdom and understanding (verse 9), that practice might agree with profession (verse 10), that they might have power for their practice (verse 11), and be thankful for their immense privilege and position in the Lord Jesus (verses 12 f.).

But perhaps Paul's greatest contribution to our understanding of Christian prayer is in establishing its connection with the Holy Spirit. Prayer is in fact a gift of the Spirit (1 Cor. xiv. 14–16). The believer prays 'in the Spirit' (Eph. vi. 18; Jude 20); hence prayer is a co-operation between God and the believer in that it is presented to the Father, in the name of the Son, through the inspiration of the indwelling Holy Spirit.

d. Hebrews, James, and 1 John

The Epistle to the Hebrews makes a significant contribution to an understanding of Christian prayer. iv. 14–16 shows why prayer is possible: it is possible because we have a great High Priest who is both human and divine, because He is now in the heavenly place, and because of what He is now doing there. When we pray it is to receive mercy and find grace. The reference to the Lord's prayer life in v. 7–10 really teaches what prayer is: Christ's 'prayers' and 'supplications' were 'offered up' to God, and in this spiritual service He 'learned obedience' and therefore 'was heard'. In x. 19–25 the emphasis is upon corporate prayer, and the demands and motives which it involves. The place of prayer is described in vi. 19.

The Epistle of James has three significant passages on prayer. Prayer in perplexity is dealt with in i. 5–8; correct motives in prayer are underlined in iv. 1–3; and the significance of prayer in time of sickness is made clear in v. 13–18.

In his first Epistle, John points the way to boldness and efficacy in prayer (iii. 21 f.), while in v. 14–16 he establishes the relation between prayer and the will of God, and shows that efficacy in prayer is especially relevant to intercession, but that situations do arise where prayer is powerless.

IV. CONCLUSION

The heart of the biblical doctrine of prayer is well expressed by Westcott: 'True prayer—the prayer that must be answered—is the personal recognition and acceptance of the divine will (Jn. xiv. 7; *cf.* Mk. xi. 24). It follows that the hearing of prayer which teaches obedience is not so much the granting of a specific petition, which is assumed by the petitioner to be the way to the end desired, but the assurance that what is granted does most effectively lead to the end. Thus we are taught that Christ learned that every detail of His life and passion contributed to the accomplishment of the work which He came to fulfil, and so He was most perfectly "heard". In this sense He was "heard for his godly fear".'

BIBLIOGRAPHY. H. Trevor Hughes, *Prophetic Prayer*, 1947; F. Heiler, *Prayer*, 1932; J. G. S. S. Thomson, *The Praying Christ*, 1959; Ludwig Köhler, *Old Testament Theology*, 1957; Th. C. Vriezen, *An Outline of Old Testament Theology*, 1958. J.G.S.S.T.

PRAYER OF MANASSES. See APOCRYPHA.

PREACHING. In the New Testament, preaching is 'the public proclamation of Christianity to the non-Christian world' (C. H. Dodd, *The Apostolic Preaching and its Developments*, 1944, p. 7). It is not religious discourse to a closed group of initiates, but open and public proclamation of God's redemptive activity in and through Jesus Christ. The current understanding of preaching as biblical exposition and exhortation, while a valid extension of the term, has tended to obscure its primitive meaning.

I. THE BIBLICAL TERMS

The choice of verbs in the Greek New Testament for the activity of preaching points us back to its original meaning. The most characteristic (occurring more than sixty times) is *kēryssō*, 'to proclaim as a herald'. In the ancient world the herald was a figure of considerable importance (*cf.* the article by Friedrich in *TWNT*). A man of integrity and character, he was employed by the king or State to make all public proclamations. Preaching is heralding; the message proclaimed is the glad tidings of salvation. While *kēryssō* tells us something about the activity of preaching, *euangelizomai*, 'to bring good news' (from the primitive *eus*, 'good', and the verb *angellō*, 'to announce'), a common verb, used over fifty times in the New Testament, emphasizes the quality of the message itself. It is worthy of note that the RV has not followed the AV in those places where it translates the verbs *diangellō*, *laleō*, *katangellō*, and *dialegomai* by 'to preach'. This helps to bring into sharper focus the basic meaning of preaching.

It is not unusual to draw a rather sharp line of distinction between preaching and teaching—between *kērygma* (public proclamation) and *didachē* (ethical instruction). An appeal is made to such verses as Matthew's summary of Jesus' Galilaean ministry, 'Jesus went about all Galilee, *teaching . . . preaching . . .* and *healing*' (Mt. iv. 23), and Paul's words in Rom. xii. 6–8 and 1 Cor. xii. 28 on the gifts of the Spirit. While the two activities, as ideally conceived, are distinct, both are based upon the same basic facts. The *kērygma* proclaims what God has done, while the *didachē* teaches the implications of this for Christian conduct.

While we have defined preaching within narrow limits in order to emphasize its essential New Testament meaning, this is not to suggest that it is without precedent in the Old. Certainly the Hebrew prophets as they proclaimed the message of God under divine impulse were forerunners of the apostolic herald. Jonah was told to 'preach' (LXX *kēryssō*; Heb. *qârâ'*, 'to call out'), and even Noah is designated a 'preacher (*kēryx*) of righteousness' (2 Pet. ii. 5). The LXX uses *kēryssō* more than thirty times, both in the secular 'sense of official proclamation for the king and the more religious sense of prophetic utterance (*cf.* Joel i. 14; Zc. ix. 9; Is. lxi. 1).

II. NEW TESTAMENT FEATURES

Perhaps the most prominent feature in New Testament preaching is the sense of divine compulsion. In Mk. i. 38 it is reported that Jesus did not return to those who sought His healing power but pressed on to other towns *in order that He might preach*—'for therefore came I forth'. Peter and John reply to the restrictions of the Sanhedrin with the declaration, 'We cannot but speak the things which we have seen and heard' (Acts iv. 20). 'Woe is unto me, if I preach not the gospel', cries the apostle Paul (1 Cor. ix. 16). This sense of compulsion is the *sine qua non* of true preaching. Preaching is not the relaxed recital of interesting but morally neutral truths: it is God Himself breaking into the affairs of man and confronting him with a demand for decision. This sort of preaching meets with opposition. In 2 Cor. xi. 23–28 Paul lists his sufferings for the sake of the gospel.

Another feature of apostolic preaching was its transparency of message and motive. Since preaching calls for faith, it is vitally important that its issues be not obscured with eloquent wisdom and lofty words (1 Cor. i. 17, ii. 1–4). Paul refused to practise cunning or to tamper with God's Word, but sought to commend himself to every man's conscience by the open statement of the truth (2 Cor. iv. 2). The radical upheaval within the heart and consciousness of man which is the new birth does not come about by the persuasive influence of rhetoric but by the straightforward presentation of the gospel in all its simplicity and power.

III. THE ESSENTIAL NATURE OF PREACHING

In the Gospels Jesus is most characteristically portrayed as One who came 'heralding the kingdom of God'. In Lk. iv. 16–21 Jesus interprets His ministry as the fulfilment of Isaiah's prophecy of a coming Servant-Messiah through whom the kingdom of God would at last be realized. This kingdom is best understood as God's 'kingly rule' or 'sovereign action'. Only secondarily does it refer to a realm or people within that realm. That God's eternal sovereignty was now invading the realm of evil powers and winning the decisive victory was the basic content of Jesus' *kērygma*.

When we move from the Synoptics into the rest of the New Testament we note a significant change in terminology. Instead of the 'kingdom of God' we find 'Christ' as the content of the preached message. This is variously expressed as 'Christ crucified' (1 Cor. i. 23), 'Christ . . . raised' (1 Cor. xv. 12, RSV), 'the Son of God, Jesus Christ' (2 Cor. i. 19), or 'Christ Jesus the

Lord' (2 Cor. iv. 5). What accounts for this change of emphasis? Simply that Christ *is* the kingdom. The Jews anticipated the universal establishment of the sovereign reign of God, *viz.* His *kingdom*, and the death and resurrection of Jesus Christ was the decisive act of God whereby His eternal sovereignty was realized in human history. With the advance of redemptive history the apostolic Church could proclaim the kingdom in the more clear-cut terms of decision concerning the King. To preach Christ *is* to preach the kingdom.

One of the most important advances of New Testament scholarship in our generation has been C. H. Dodd's crystallization of the primitive *kērygma*. Following his approach (comparing the early speeches in Acts with the pre-Pauline credal fragments in Paul's Epistles) but interpreting the data with a slightly different emphasis, we find that the apostolic message was 'a proclamation of the death, resurrection, and exaltation of Jesus that led to an evaluation of His person as both Lord and Christ, confronted man with the necessity of repentance, and promised the forgiveness of sins' (R. H. Mounce, *The Essential Nature of New Testament Preaching*, 1960, p. 84).

What true preaching really is is best understood in terms of its relation to the wider theme of revelation. Revelation is essentially God's self-disclosure apprehended by the response of faith. Since Calvary is God's supreme self-revelation, the problem is, How can God reveal Himself in the present through an act of the past? The answer is, through preaching—for preaching is the timeless link between God's great redemptive act and man's apprehension of it. It is the medium through which God contemporizes His historic self-disclosure in Christ and offers man the opportunity to respond in faith.

BIBLIOGRAPHY. In addition to the books mentioned above, *cf.* E. P. Clowney, *Preaching and Biblical Theology*, 1961; H. H. Farmer, *The Servant of the Word*, 1950; P. T. Forsyth, *Positive Preaching and the Modern Mind*, 1949; J. Knox, *The Integrity of Preaching*, 1957; J. S. Stewart, *Heralds of God*, 1946; J. R. W. Stott, *The Preacher's Portrait*, 1961; L. J. Tizard, *Preaching: the Art of Communication*, 1958. R.H.M.

PRECIOUS STONES. See JEWELS AND PRECIOUS STONES.

PREDESTINATION.

I. BIBLICAL VOCABULARY

The English 'predestinate' comes from Lat. *praedestino*, which the Vulgate uses to translate the Gk. *proorizō*. AV renders *proorizō* as 'predestinate' in Rom. viii. 29, 30; Eph. i. 5, 11; but not Acts iv. 28; 1 Cor. ii. 7. Presumably the translators demurred at using 'predestinate' without a personal object. RV has 'foreordain' in all six places.

Proorizō, which the New Testament uses only with God as subject, expresses the thought of appointing a situation for a person, or a person for a situation, in advance (*pro-*). The New Testament uses other *pro-* compounds in a similar sense: (1) *protassō*, 'arrange beforehand' (Acts xvii. 26); (2) *protithemai*, 'propose' (Eph. i. 9; of a human proposal, Rom. i. 13; *cf.* use of the cognate noun *prothesis*, 'purpose', 'plan', Rom. viii. 28, ix. 11; Eph. i. 11, iii. 11; 2 Tim. i. 9); (3) *proetoimazō*, 'prepare beforehand' (Rom. ix. 23; Eph. ii. 10); (4) *procheirizō*, 'appoint beforehand' (Acts iii. 20, xxii. 14); (5) *procheirotoneō*, 'choose beforehand' (Acts x. 41). *Problepō*, 'foresee', carries the thought of God's effective preordaining in Gal. iii. 8; Heb. xi. 40; as the context shows. So does *proginōskō*, 'foreknow' (Rom. viii. 29, xi. 2; 1 Pet. i. 20), and its cognate noun *prognōsis* (1 Pet. i. 2; Acts ii. 23). The same sense is sometimes conveyed by the uncompounded verbs *tassō* (Acts xiii. 48, xxii. 10) and *horizō* (Lk. xxii. 22; Acts ii. 23), the former implying a precise setting in order, the latter an exact marking out. This varied vocabulary well suggests the different facets of the idea expressed.

The New Testament formulates the thought of divine foreordination in another way, by telling us that what motivates and determines God's actions in His world, and among them the fortunes and destiny which He brings upon men, is His own will (nouns, *boulē*, Acts ii. 23, iv. 28; Eph. i. 11; Heb. vi. 17; *boulēma*, Rom. ix. 19; *thelēma*, Eph. i. 5, 9, 11; *thelēsis*, Heb. ii. 4; verbs, *boulomai*, Heb. vi. 17; Jas. i. 18; 2 Pet. iii. 9; *thelō*, Rom. ix. 18, 22; Col. i. 27), or His 'good-pleasure' (noun, *eudokia*, Eph. i. 5, 9; Mt. xi. 26; verb, *eudokeō*, Lk. xii. 32; 1 Cor. i. 21; Gal. i. 15; Col. i. 19), *i.e.* His own deliberate, prior resolve. This is not, indeed, the only sense in which the New Testament speaks of the will of God. The Bible conceives of God's purpose for men as expressed both by His revealed commands to them and by His ordering of their circumstances. His 'will' in Scripture thus covers both His law and His plan; hence some of the above terms are also used with reference to particular divine demands (*e.g. boulē*, Lk. vii. 30; *thelēma*, 1 Thes. iv. 3, v. 18). But in the texts referred to above it is God's plan of events that is in view, and it is this that predestination concerns.

The Old Testament lacks words for expressing the idea of predestination in an abstract and generalized form, but it often speaks of God purposing, ordaining, or determining particular things, in contexts which call attention to the absolute priority and independence of His purposing in relation to the existence or occurrence of the thing purposed (*cf.* Ps. cxxxix. 16; Is. xiv. 24–27, xix. 17, xlvi. 10 f.; Je. xlix. 20; Dn. iv. 24 f.).

The usage of the New Testament word-group is in favour of the traditional practice of defining predestination in terms of God's purpose regarding the circumstances and destinies of men. The wider aspects of His cosmic plan and government are most conveniently subsumed under the general head of providence (*q.v.*). To grasp the meaning of predestination as Scripture presents it, however, it must be set in its place in God's plan as a whole.

II. BIBLICAL PRESENTATION

a. In the Old Testament

The Old Testament presents God the Creator as personal, powerful, and purposeful, and assures us that as His power is unlimited, so His purposes are certain of fulfilment (Ps. xxxiii. 10 f.; Is. xiv. 27, xliii. 13; Jb. ix. 12, xxiii. 13; Dn. iv. 35). He is Lord of every situation, ordering and directing everything towards the end for which He made it (Pr. xvi. 4), and determining every event, great or small, from the thoughts of kings (Pr. xxi. 1) and the premeditated words and deeds of all men (Pr. xvi. 1, 9) to the seemingly random fall of a lot (Pr. xvi. 33). Nothing that God sets before Himself is too hard for Him (Gn. xviii. 14; Je. xxxii. 17); the idea that the organized opposition of man could in any way thwart Him is simply absurd (Ps. ii. 1–4). Isaiah's prophecy expands the thought of God's plan as the decisive factor in history more fully than does any other Old Testament book. Isaiah stresses that God's purposes are everlasting, that Yahweh planned present and future happenings 'long ago', 'from the beginning' (*cf.* Is. xxii. 11, RSV, xxxvii. 26, xliv. 6–8, xlvi. 10 f.), and that, just because it is He, and no-one else, who orders all events (Is. xliv. 7), nothing can prevent the occurrence of the events that He has predicted (Is. xiv. 24–27, xliv. 24–xlv. 25; *cf.* 1 Ki. xxii. 17–38; Ps. xxxiii. 10 f.; Pr. xix. 21, xxi. 30). Yahweh's ability to predict the seemingly incredible things that are going to happen proves His control of history, whereas the inability of the idols to foretell these things shows that they do not control it (Is. xliv. 6–8, xlv. 21, xlviii. 12–14).

Sometimes Yahweh is pictured as reacting to developing situations in a way that might seem to imply that He had not anticipated them (*e.g.* when He repents, and reverses His prior action, Gn. vi. 5; Je. xviii. 8, 10, xxvi. 3, 13; Joel ii. 13; Jon. iv. 2). But in their biblical context it is clear that the purpose and point of these anthropomorphisms is simply to emphasize that Israel's God is really personal, and not to throw doubt on whether He really foreordains and controls human affairs.

That Yahweh governs human history teleologically, to bring about His own predestined purpose for human welfare, is made clear in the Bible story as early as the protevangelium (Gn. iii. 15) and the promise to Abraham (Gn. xii. 3). The theme develops through the wilderness promises of prosperity and protection in Canaan (*cf.* Dt. xxviii. 1–14), and the prophetic pictures of the messianic glory which would succeed God's work of judgment (Is. ix. 1 ff., xi. 1 ff.; Je. xxiii. 5 ff.; Ezk. xxxiv. 20 ff., xxxvii. 21 ff.; Ho. iii. 4 f., *etc.*); and it reaches its climax in Daniel's vision of God overruling the rise and fall of pagan world-empires in order to set up the rule of the Son of man (Dn. vii, *cf.* ii. 31–45). A global eschatology of this order could not be seriously put forward save on the presupposition that God is the absolute Lord of history, foreseeing and foreordaining its whole course.

It is in terms of this view of God's relation to human history that the Old Testament describes God's choice of Israel to be His covenant people, the object and instrument of His saving work. This choice was *unmerited* (Dt. vii. 6 f.; Ezk. xvi. 1 ff.) and wholly gracious. It was *purposeful*; Israel was appointed a destiny, to be blessed and so to become a blessing to other nations (*cf.* Ps. lxvii; Is. ii. 2–4, xi. 9 f., lx; Zc. viii. 20 ff., xiv. 16 ff.). It was, however, for the time being *exclusive*; the selection of Israel meant the deliberate passing-by of the rest of the nations (Dt. vii. 6, see RVmg; Ps. cxlvii. 19 f.; Am. iii. 2; *cf.* Rom. ix. 4; Eph. ii. 11 f.). For more than a millennium God left them outside the covenant, objects only of His judgment for their national crimes (Am. i. 3–ii. 3) and for their malice against the chosen people (*cf.* Is. xiii–xix, *etc.*).

b. In the New Testament

The New Testament writers take for granted the Old Testament faith that God is the sovereign Lord of events, and rules history for the fulfilling of His purposes. Their uniform insistence that Christ's ministry and the Christian dispensation represented the fulfilment of biblical prophecies, given centuries before (Mt. i. 22, ii. 15, 23, iv. 14, viii. 17, xii. 17 ff.; Jn. xii. 38 ff., xix. 24, 28, 36; Acts ii. 17 ff., iii. 22 ff., iv. 25 ff., viii. 30 ff., x. 43, xiii. 27 ff., xv. 15 ff.; Gal. iii. 8; Heb. v. 6, viii. 8 ff.; 1 Pet. i. 10 ff.; *etc.*), and that God's ultimate aim in inspiring the Hebrew Scriptures was to instruct Christian believers (Rom. xv. 4; 1 Cor. x. 11; 2 Tim. iii. 15 ff.), is proof enough of this. (Both convictions, be it noted, derive from our Lord Himself: *cf.* Lk. xviii. 31 ff., xxiv. 25 ff., 44 ff.; Jn. v. 39.) A new development, however, is that the idea of election, now applied, not to national Israel, but to Christian believers, is consistently individualized (*cf.* Ps. lxv. 4) and given a pre-temporal reference. The Old Testament assimilates election to God's historical 'calling' (*cf.* Ne. ix. 7), but the New Testament distinguishes the two things sharply, by representing election as God's act of predestinating sinners to salvation in Christ 'before the foundation of the world' (Eph. i. 4; *cf.* Mt. xxv. 34; 2 Tim. i. 9); an act correlative to His foreknowing Christ 'before the foundation of the world' (1 Pet. i. 20). The uniform New Testament conception is that all saving grace given to men in time (knowledge of the gospel, understanding of it and power to respond to it, preservation, and final glory) flows from divine election in eternity.

Luke's language in the narrative of Acts bears striking witness to his belief, not merely that Christ was foreordained to die, rise, and reign (Acts ii. 23, 30 f., iii. 20, iv. 27 f.), but that salvation is the fruit of prevenient grace (ii. 47,

xi. 18, 21–23, xiv. 27, xv. 7 ff., xvi. 14, xviii. 27) given in accordance with divine foreordination (xiii. 48, xviii. 10).

In John's Gospel Christ says that He has been sent to save a number of particular individuals whom His Father has 'given' Him (Jn. vi. 37 ff., xvii. 2, 6, 9, 24, xviii. 9). These are His 'sheep', His 'own' (x. 14 ff., 26 ff., xiii. 1). It was for them specifically that He prayed (xvii. 20). He undertakes to 'draw' them to Himself by His Spirit (xii. 32, *cf.* vi. 44, x. 16, 27, xvi. 8 ff.); to give them eternal life, in fellowship with Himself and the Father (x. 28, *cf.* v. 21, vi. 40, xvii. 2; Mt. xi. 27); to keep them, losing none (vi. 39, x. 28 f., *cf.* xvii. 11, 15, xviii. 9); to bring them to His glory (xiv. 2 f., *cf.* xvii. 24), and to raise their bodies at the last day (vi. 39 f., *cf.* v. 28 f.). The principle that those who enjoy salvation do so by reason of divine predestination is here made explicit.

The fullest elucidation of this principle is found in the writings of Paul. From all eternity, Paul declares, God has had a plan (*prothesis*) to save a Church, though in earlier times it was not fully made known (Eph. iii. 3–11). The aim of the plan is that men should be made God's adopted sons and be renewed in the image of Christ (Rom. viii. 29), and that the Church, the company of those so renewed, should grow to the fulness of Christ (Eph. iv. 13). Believers may rejoice in the certainty that as part of His plan God predestinated them personally to share in this destiny (Rom. viii. 28 ff.; Eph. i. 3 ff.; 2 Thes. ii. 13; 2 Tim. i. 9; *cf.* 1 Pet. i. 1 f.). The choice was wholly of grace (2 Tim. i. 9), having no regard to desert—being made, indeed, in defiance of foreseen ill-desert (*cf.* Jn. xv. 19; Eph. ii. 1 ff.). Because God is sovereign, His predestinating choice guarantees salvation. From it flows an effectual 'calling', which elicits the response of faith which it commands (Rom. viii. 28 ff., *cf.* ix. 23 f.; 1 Cor. i. 26 ff.; Eph. i. 13; 2 Thes. ii. 14); justification (Rom. viii. 30); sanctification (1 Thes. ii. 13); and glorification (Rom. viii. 30, where the past tense implies certainty of accomplishment; 2 Thes. ii. 14). Paul gives this teaching to Christians, persons who were themselves 'called', in order to assure them of their present security and final salvation, and to make them realize the extent of their debt to God's mercy. The 'elect' to whom, and of whom, he speaks in each Epistle are himself and/or the believers to whom he addresses it ('you', 'us').

It has been argued that God's foreknowledge is not foreordination, and that personal election in the New Testament is grounded upon God's foresight that the persons chosen will respond to the gospel of themselves. The difficulties in this view seem to be: (1) this asserts in effect election according to works and desert, whereas Scripture asserts election to be of grace (Rom. ix. 11; 2 Tim. i. 9), and grace excludes all regard to what a man does for himself (Rom. iv. 4, xi. 6; Eph. ii. 8 f.; Tit. iii. 5, RV); (2) if election is *unto* faith (2 Thes. ii. 13) and good works (Eph. ii. 10) it cannot rest upon foresight of these things; (3) on this view, Paul ought to be pointing, not to God's election, but to the Christian's own faith, as the ground of his assurance of final salvation; (4) Scripture does appear to equate foreknowledge with foreordination (*cf.* Acts ii. 23).

III. ELECTION AND REPROBATION

'Reprobate' appears first in Je. vi. 30 (*cf.* Is. i. 22), in a metaphor taken from metal refining. The thought is of something that, by reason of its corrupt condition, does not pass God's test, and which He therefore rejects. The metaphor reappears in the New Testament. It is used of the Gentile world (Rom. i. 28) and of professing Christians (1 Cor. ix. 27; 2 Cor. xiii. 5 f.; *cf.* 2 Tim. iii. 8; Tit. i. 16). Christian theology since Augustine has, however, spoken of reprobation, not as God's rejection of particular sinners in history, but as that which (it is held) lies behind it—God's resolve, from all eternity, to pass them by, and not to give them His saving grace (*cf.* 1 Pet. ii. 8; Jude 4). It has thus become common to define predestination as consisting of election and reprobation together.

It is disputed whether reprobation ought to be thus included in God's eternal *prothesis*. Some justify the inclusion by appeal to Rom. ix. 17 f., 21 f., xi. 7 f. It seems hard to deny, in face of ix. 22, that the hardening and non-salvation of some, which in verses 19–21 Paul proved to be within God's right, is actually part of His predestinating purpose; though it should be noticed that Paul is concerned to stress, not God's implacability towards the reprobate, but His long restraint of His wrath against persons who have become ripe for destruction (*cf.* ii. 4). But to determine the exact scope of these verses in their context is not easy; see the commentaries.

See ELECTION, PROVIDENCE, REPROBATE.

BIBLIOGRAPHY. *Arndt*; B. B. Warfield, 'Predestination', and J. Denney, 'Reprobation', in *HDB*; Calvin, *Institutio*, III. xxi–xxiv; *id.*, *Concerning the Eternal Predestination of God*, E.T. by J. K. S. Reid, 1960; E. Jacob, *Theology of the Old Testament*, E.T., 1958, pp. 183–207; G. C. Berkouwer, *Divine Election*, 1960; commentaries on Rom. ix–xi, esp. Sanday and Headlam, *ICC*, 1902.

J.I.P.

PREPARATION. The Greek word *paraskeuē* is found in the New Testament with a twofold connotation. In its meaning of a definite day of preparation, it is used of the day preceding the weekly sabbath and the day which prepares for the annual Jewish Passover festival (*cf.* Jos., *Ant.* xvi. 6. 2), see Mt. xxvii. 62; Mk. xv. 42; Lk. xxiii. 54; and especially Jn. xix, which mentions both types of preparation day. The reference in Jn. xix. 14 is to *'ereḇ ḥa-pesaḥ*, *i.e.* the eve of the Passover (*cf.* *Pesaḥim* x. 1 in the Mishnah). In Jn. xix. 31, 42 there is no accompanying genitive, so the word must mean *'ereḇ šabbāṯ*, *i.e.* the day before the sabbath (as clearly in Mk. xv. 42). This would be the 24 hours from 6 p.m. Thursday to 6 p.m. Friday. The second meaning is extended, in later Christian literature, to designate the sixth day of the week, *i.e.* Friday (*cf. Martyrdom of Polycarp* vii. 1; *Didache*, viii. 1); and this is the sense of *paraskeuē* in modern Greek.

For the controverted meaning of the phrase in Jn. xix. 14, see J. Jeremias, *The Eucharistic Words of Jesus*, E.T., 1955, pp. 54, 55. R.P.M.

PRESBYTER, PRESBYTERY. In the Old Testament the elders of Israel, of the people, or of the congregation are frequently mentioned; Jewish synagogues were normally governed by a council of elders, under the chairmanship of a 'ruler of the synagogue', whose office was perhaps held in rotation; and the entire Jewish people was subject in religious matters to the Sanhedrin of seventy-one members, in which the high priest, during the New Testament period, was chairman *ex officio*. A similar organization was naturally followed in the Christian Church, and the *zāqēn* (elder) of the Old Testament became the *presbyteros* (Vulg. *senior*) of the New.

But although the name continued, the content of the office changed. Pastoral visitation of the sick (Jas. v. 14) is a strikingly new feature of the Christian elder's duties. Moreover, although Jewish elders were not necessarily preachers, some of their Christian counterparts laboured in the word and doctrine (1 Tim. v. 17). General oversight of the congregation remained their primary task, and the verb *episkopein* is used to describe this function in 1 Pet. v. 2. The elders of the Jerusalem church received gifts on behalf of the community (Acts xi. 30), and took part in council with the apostles (Acts xv. 4, 6, 23, xvi. 4). Paul and Barnabas ordained elders in all the Asian churches (Acts xiv. 23); Paul enjoined Titus to do the same in Crete (Tit. i. 5); and the elders at Ephesus (Acts xx. 17, 28) are also called *episkopoi* or overseers, from which it appears that the names 'presbyter' and 'bishop' are interchangeable in New Testament usage (see BISHOP).

All elders seem to be of equal rank, though the elder of 2 Jn. 1 and 3 Jn. 1 has some personal pre-eminence by virtue of his seniority. If the author of these letters is the apostle John he is merely following the practice of 1 Pet. v. 1 in calling himself an elder. The Christian eldership acted in a corporate capacity, and the word *presbyterion*, 'presbytery', is used (1 Tim. iv. 14) to describe the body of elders that ordained Timothy, in which Paul on this occasion at least must have occupied the chair (*cf.* 2 Tim. i. 6). The same word is employed (Lk. xxii. 66; Acts xxii. 5) to denote the Jewish Sanhedrin (see also CHURCH GOVERNMENT, MINISTRY). G.S.M.W.

PRESS, WINEFAT. A word which is used indiscriminately of the instrument for pressing out the grapes, and the trough for holding the resultant juice. Its fulness was a sign of prosperity, while its emptiness represented famine.

It is used metaphorically in Is. lxiii. 3, and in Joel iii. 13, where the full press and overflowing vats indicate the greatness of the threatened carnage. It is a striking simile in La. i. 15, and in Rev. xiv. 18–20 forms part of the apocalyptic language following on the predicted fall of Babylon. F.S.F.

PRIDE. The emphasis placed on pride, and its converse humility, is a distinctive feature of biblical religion, unparalleled in other religious or ethical systems. Rebellious pride, which refuses to depend on God and be subject to Him, but attributes to self the honour due to Him, figures as the very root and essence of sin.

We may say with Aquinas that pride was first revealed when Lucifer attempted to set his throne on high in proud independence of God (Is. xiv. 12–14). The fallen devil (Lk. x. 18) instilled the craving to be as gods into Adam and Eve (Gn. iii. 5), with the result that man's entire nature was infected with pride through the fall (*cf.* Rom. i. 21–23). Hence we find a sustained condemnation of human arrogance throughout the Old Testament, especially in the Psalms and Wisdom Literature. In Pr. viii. 13 both *gē'â*, 'arrogance', and *ga'ᵃwâ*, 'insolence', are hateful to the divine wisdom: their manifestation in the form of national pride in Moab (Is. xvi. 6), Judah (Je. xiii. 9), and Israel (Ho. v. 5) are especially denounced by the prophets. The notorious 'pride which goes before a fall' is called *gā'ôn*, 'swelling excellence', in Pr. xvi. 18, and is rejected in favour of the lowly spirit. 'Haughtiness', *gōḇah*, appears as a root cause of atheism in Ps. x. 4. It is the downfall of Nebuchadrezzar in Dn. iv. 30, 37. A milder word, *zāḏôn*, 'presumption', is applied to David's youthful enthusiasm in 1 Sa. xvii. 28, but in Ob. 3 even this is regarded as a deceitful evil. Further warnings against pride occur in the later Wisdom Literature, *e.g.* Ben-Sira x. 6–26.

Greek teaching during the four last centuries BC was at variance with Judaism in regarding pride as a virtue and humility as despicable. Aristotle's 'great-souled man' had a profound regard for his own excellence; to underestimate it would have stamped him as mean-spirited. Similarly, the Stoic sage asserted his own moral independence and equality with Zeus. Insolence (*hybris*), however, is a deep source of moral evil in the Greek tragedy (*cf.*, *eg.*, the *Antigone* of Sophocles).

The Christian ethic consciously rejected Greek thought in favour of the Old Testament outlook. Humility was accorded supreme excellence when Christ pronounced Himself 'gentle and lowly in heart' (Mt. xi. 29). Conversely, pride (*hyperēphania*) was placed on a list of defiling vices proceeding from the evil heart of man (Mk. vii. 22). In the Magnificat (Lk. i. 51 f.) God is said to scatter the proud and exalt the meek. In both Jas. iv. 6 and 1 Pet. v. 5, Pr. iii. 34 is quoted to emphasize the contrast between the meek (*tapeinois*), whom God favours, and the proud (*hyperēphanois*), whom God resists. Paul couples the insolent (*hybristas*) and the boastful (*alazonas*) with the proud sinners in his sketch of depraved pagan society in Rom. i. 30; *cf.* 2 Tim. iii. 2. Arrogant display or ostentation (*alazoneia*) are disparaged in Jas. iv. 16 and 1 Jn. ii. 16. Love, in 1 Cor. xiii. 4, is stated to be free from both the arrogance and the self-conceit which mar the heretical teachers of 1 Tim. vi. 4.

Paul saw pride ('boasting' in knowledge of the law and in works/righteousness) as the characteristic spirit of Judaism and a direct cause of Jewish unbelief. He insisted that the gospel is designed to exclude boasting (Rom. iii. 27) by teaching men that they are sinners, that self-righteousness is therefore out of the question, and that they must look to Christ for their righteousness and take it as a free gift by faith in Him. Salvation is 'not of works, lest any man should boast'; it is all of grace. No man, therefore, not even Abraham, may glory in the achievement of his own salvation (see Eph. ii. 9; 1 Cor. i. 26–31; Rom. iv. 1, 2). The gospel message of righteousness through Christ sounds the death-knell of self-righteousness in religion; that is why it was a stumbling-block to the proud Jews (Rom. ix. 30–x. 4).

This New Testament emphasis made a deep impact on early and mediaeval ethics. Augustine, Aquinas, and Dante all characterized pride as the ultimate sin, while Milton and Goethe dramatized it.

BIBLIOGRAPHY. *ERE*; *Arndt*; *MM*; R. Niebuhr, *The Nature and Destiny of Man*, 1944–5, ch. 7. D.H.T.

PRIESTS AND LEVITES. The relationship between the priests, who are the descendants of Aaron, and the Levites, the other members of Levi's tribe, is one of the thorny problems of Old Testament religion. Not only are the biblical data many and varied, but the problems have been compounded by Julius Wellhausen's critical re-interpretation of the evidence which forms one of the cornerstones of the impressive edifice of Wellhausenian criticism. Any treatment, therefore, of the Levites must deal with the biblical evidence, Wellhausen's evaluation of it, and the numerous ways in which contemporary scholars have reacted to his evolutionary approach.

I. THE BIBLICAL DATA

a. The Pentateuch

The Levites come into prominence in the Pentateuch in connection with Moses and Aaron (Ex. ii. 1–10, iv. 14, vi. 16–27). After Aaron led the people into apostasy with the golden calf (Ex. xxxii. 25 ff.), the sons of Levi avenged the Lord's honour by punishing many of the miscreants. This display of fidelity to God may partially account for the signal responsibilities given the tribe in the pentateuchal legislation. J. Pedersen (*Israel*, III–IV, 1940, pp. 172, 173) sees in this story a reflection of the Levites' ruthless fight against Israelites who adopted the Canaanite religion. The intensity of this struggle accounts, according to Pedersen, for Levi's growth as a priestly tribe.

The rôle of the Levites as ministers in the tabernacle, clearly enumerated in Numbers, is anticipated in Ex. xxxviii. 21, where they co-operate (how is not clear) in the construction of the tabernacle under the supervision of Aaron's son, Ithamar. In the laws preparatory to the wilderness march, Levi was separated by God from the other tribes and placed in charge of the dismantling, carrying, and erecting of the tabernacle (Nu. i. 47–54). The sons of Levi camped around the tabernacle and apparently served as buffers to protect their fellow-tribes from God's wrath, which threatened them if they unwittingly came in contact with the holy tent or its furnishings (Nu. i. 51, 53, ii. 17).

Forbidden to serve as priests, a privilege reserved, on penalty of death, for Aaron's sons (Nu. iii. 10), the Levites were dedicated to an auxiliary ministry for the priests, especially in regard to the manual labour of caring for the tabernacle (Nu. iii. 5 ff.). In addition, they performed an important service for the other tribes by substituting for each family's first-born, to whom God was entitled in view of the fact that He spared Israel's first-born at the passover in Egypt (*cf.* Ex. xiii. 2 ff., 13). As representatives of the tribes' first-born, the Levites were part of 'the far-reaching principle of *representation*' by which the concept of a people utterly dependent upon and totally surrendered to God was put across (*cf.* H. W. Robinson, *Inspiration and Revelation in the Old Testament*, 1953, pp. 219–221). The details of this representation are stated in Nu. iii. 40 ff., where a five-shekel redemption tax is exacted for the 273 first-born of Israel over and above the 22,000 Levites.

Each of the three families of Levi had specific duties. The sons of *Kohath* (numbering 2,750 in the age-group from thirty to fifty according to Nu. iv. 36) were in charge of carrying the furniture after it had been carefully covered by the priests, who alone could touch it (Nu. iii. 29–32, iv. 1 ff.). The Kohathites were supervised by Aaron's son, Eleazar. The sons of *Gershon* (2,630; Nu. iv. 40) cared for the coverings, screens, and hangings under the supervision of Aaron's son Ithamar (Nu. iii. 21–26, iv. 21 ff.). *Merari's* sons (3,200; Nu. iv. 44) had the task of carrying and erecting the frame of the tabernacle and its court (Nu. iii. 35–37, iv. 29 ff.). The sons of Gershon were given two wagons and four oxen and the sons of Merari four wagons and eight oxen, while the Kohathites were obliged to carry the furnishings, which were too sacred and precious to be conveyed by ox-cart (Nu. vii. 1 ff.).

The representative function of the Levites is symbolized in the rituals of cleansing and dedication (Nu. viii. 5 ff.). For instance, both the fact that the Israelites (probably through their tribal leaders) laid hands on the Levites (viii. 10), acknowledging them as substitutes (*cf.* Lv. iv. 24, *etc.*), and the fact that the priests offered the

Levites as a wave-offering (probably by leading them to and then from the altar) from the people (viii. 11), suggest that the Levites were given by the Israelites to serve Aaron's sons in their stead. This is made explicit in viii. 16 ff., where Levi's sons are called *nᵉṯûnîm*, 'gifts'.

Their service began at twenty-five years of age and continued until the fiftieth year, when the Levite went into a kind of semi-retirement with limited duties (Nu. viii. 24–26). There may have been a five-year apprenticeship, because apparently the full responsibility of carrying the tabernacle and its furnishings fell on the shoulders of the men from thirty years to fifty (Nu. iv. 3 ff.). When David established a permanent site for the ark, the age was lowered to twenty years because there was no longer a need for mature Levites as porters (1 Ch. xxiii. 24 ff.).

The levitical responsibility of representing the people carried with it certain privileges. Although they had no inheritance in the land (*i.e.* no portion of it was appointed for their exclusive use: Nu. xviii. 23, 24; Dt. xii. 12 ff.), the Levites were supported by the tithes of the people, while the priests received the parts of the offerings not consumed by sacrifice, the firstlings of flock and herd, and a tithe of the levitical tithes (Nu. xviii. 8 ff., 21 ff.; *cf.* Dt. xviii. 1–4). Occasionally both priests and Levites shared in the spoils of battle (*e.g.* Nu. xxxi. 25 ff.). In addition, the Levites had permission to reside in forty-eight cities set aside for their use (Nu. xxxv. 1 ff.; Jos. xxi. 1 ff.). Surrounding each city an area of pasture-land was marked off for them. On the apparent contradiction between the 1,000 cubits (Nu. xxxv. 4) and the 2,000 cubits (verse 5), see Keil and Delitzsch's commentary *in loc.* Six of the cities, three on each side of the Jordan, served as cities of refuge (*q.v.*). The levitical cities do not seem to have been the exclusive possessions of the tribe, but rather the Levites had certain privileges within them, including the right to redeem mortgaged houses after the year for redemption had passed. Their pasture-land could not be sold at all, but remained their perpetual possession (Lv. xxv. 32–34).

The transition from the wilderness marches to settled life in Canaan (anticipated in Nu. xxxv in the establishing of levitical cities) brought with it both an increased concern for the welfare of the Levites and an expansion of their duties in order to cope with the needs of the decentralized pattern of life. In Deuteronomy great stress is laid on the Israelites' responsibilities towards the sons of Levi, who were to share in the rejoicing of the tribes (xii. 12), in their tithes and certain offerings (xii. 18, 19, xiv. 28, 29), and in their chief festivals, especially Weeks and Tabernacles (xvi. 11–14). The Levites dispersed throughout the land were to share equally both the ministry and the offerings with their brethren who resided at the central shrine (xviii. 6–8).

Whereas Numbers characteristically calls the priests the *sons of Aaron*, Deuteronomy frequently uses the expression 'the priests the Levites', *i.e.* 'the *Levitical priests*' (RSV). Though some scholars (see below) have held that no distinction is made between priest and Levite in Deuteronomy, the fact that different portions are ascribed to priests in Dt. xviii. 3 ff. and to Levites in xviii. 6 ff. suggests that the distinction is maintained. The phrase 'the priests the Levites' (*e.g.* Dt. xvii. 9, 18, xviii. 1, xxiv. 8, xxvii. 9; *cf.* Jos. iii. 3, viii. 33) seems to mean 'the priests of the tribe of Levi'. To them the Deuteronomic code assigns numerous duties in addition to the care of the sanctuary: they serve as judges in cases involving difficult decisions (xvii. 8, 9), regulate the control of lepers (xxiv. 8), guard the book of the law (xvii. 18), and assist Moses in the ceremony of covenant renewal (xxvii. 9).

Within the family of Kohath the office of high priest (Heb. *hakkōhēn*, 'the priest' [Ex. xxxi. 10, *etc.*]; *hakkōhēn hammāšîaḥ*, 'the anointed priest' [Lv. iv. 3, *etc.*]; *hakkōhēn haggāḏōl*, 'the high priest' [Lv. xxi. 10, *etc.*]) was exercised by the eldest representative of Eleazar's family, unless the sanctions of Lv. xxi. 16–23 were applicable. He was consecrated in the same manner as the other priests and shared in their routine duties. He alone wore the special vestments (Ex. xxviii; see BREASTPLATE OF THE HIGH PRIEST, MITRE, DRESS) and interpreted the oracles (see URIM AND THUMMIM). On the Day of Atonement he represented the chosen people before Yahweh, sprinkling the blood of the sacrificial goat on the mercy-seat (see ATONEMENT, DAY OF; SACRIFICE AND OFFERING).

b. The Former Prophets

The priests play a more prominent rôle than the Levites in the book of Joshua, especially in the story of the crossing of Jordan and the conquest of Jericho. Sometimes called 'the priests the Levites' (*e.g.* Jos. iii. 3, viii. 33) and more often simply 'the priests' (*e.g.* Jos. iii. 6 ff., iv. 9 ff.), they had the crucial task of bearing the ark of the Lord. The tabernacle, however, carried by the Levites is not mentioned (with the possible exception of vi. 24) until it was pitched at Shiloh (xviii. 1, xix. 51) after the conquest of Canaan. Apparently the carrying of the ark was entrusted to the priests rather than the Kohathites (*cf.* Nu. iv. 15) because of the supreme importance of these journeys: God, whose presence the ark symbolized, was marching forth conquering and to conquer. The Levites came into the forefront only when the time for dividing the land was at hand (*cf.* Jos. xiv. 3 ff.). The distinction between priests and Levites is clearly maintained: the Levites remind Eleazar, the priest, and Joshua of Moses' command concerning levitical cities (Jos. xxi. 1–3); the Kohathites are divided into two groups—those who have descended from Aaron (*i.e.* the priests) and the rest (Jos. xxi. 4, 5).

The list of cities in Jos. xxi is problematic. W. F. Albright, on archaeological grounds, dates it in the early monarchy between Saul and Solomon (*Louis Ginzberg Jubilee Volume*, 1945; *cf.* also B. Mazar in *BIES*, XXIII, 1959), while

Y. Kaufmann (*The Biblical Account of the Conquest of Palestine*, 1953) regards it as a utopian list forecasting the ideal distribution of priests and Levites and dating from the period of conquest. See J. Bright's *Early Israel in Recent History Writing*, 1956, pp. 60 ff., for an evaluation of various approaches to this list, including M. Noth's view that it stems from the Persian period.

The general laxness of worship during the days between the conquest of Canaan and the establishment of the monarchy is illustrated in the two levitical stories in Judges. Micah's Levite (Jdg. xvii, xviii) is said to hail from Bethlehem and to be a member of the family of Judah (xvii. 7). How was he both Levite and Judahite? The answer hangs on whether the Levite is to be identified with Jonathan (*q.v.*), the son of Gershom (xviii. 30). If they are identical (as seems likely), then the Levite's relationship to Judah must be geographical, not genealogical, in spite of the phrase 'family of Judah' (xvii. 7). If the two men are not identical, then the Levite may be an example of the possibility that men of other tribes could, in this period, join themselves to the priestly tribe. This may have been the case with Samuel (*q.v.*), an Ephraimite (*cf.* 1 Sa. i. 1; 1 Ch. vi. 28). There is some evidence that the term *Levite* may have been a functional title meaning 'one pledged by vow' as well as a tribal designation (*cf.* W. F. Albright, *Archaeology and the Religion of Israel*[3], 1953, pp. 109, 204 ff.); however, T. J. Meek (*Hebrew Origins*[3], 1960, pp. 121 ff.) maintains that the Levites were originally a secular tribe who assumed a priestly function not only in Israel but perhaps in Arabia as well. The oracular function of the Levite in this story is noteworthy: he is viewed by the Danites as an augur who can determine the will of God. It is hazardous to draw definite conclusions about the levitical office from this story, since Micah's idolatry, his appointing of his own son as priest (xvii. 5), and the Levite's willingness to accept the more lucrative position with the Danites who stole Micah's images are illustrative of the chaos of the times. 'There was no king in Israel, but every man did that which was right in his own eyes' (xvii. 6, *cf.* xix. 1). The macabre story of the Levite and his concubine (Jdg. xix) is further testimony to the itinerations of the Levites and to the general laxness of the era. Lack of central authority curtailed the control which the central sanctuary at Shiloh should have enjoyed (Jdg. xviii. 31) and allowed numerous shrines to exist which paid little heed to the Mosaic regulations.

Levites appear only rarely in the rest of the Former Prophets, usually in connection with their rôle in carrying the ark (1 Sa. vi. 15; 2 Sa. xv. 24; 1 Ki. viii. 4). When Jeroboam I (*q.v.*) set up rival shrines at Dan and Bethel, he staffed them with non-levitical priests, probably in order to sever relationships with the Jerusalem Temple as completely as possible (1 Ki. xii. 31; *cf.* 2 Ch. xi. 13, 14, xiii. 9, 10). Royal control of the centre of worship in both kingdoms was an important feature of the Monarchy and helps to account for the vast contrast between the *laissez-faire* religious patterns in the period of the Judges and the more highly-regulated worship which David and his heirs maintained.

c. The Chronicles

The priestly perspective from which the Chronicler writes (see CHRONICLES, BOOKS OF) tends to accentuate the rôle of the Levites and fills in numerous details of their ministry which the authors of Kings have omitted. In the genealogies of 1 Ch. vi, which also describe the rôle of Aaron's sons (vi. 49–53) and the distribution of levitical cities (vi. 54–81), special attention is focused on the levitical singers, Heman, Asaph, Ethan, and their sons, who were put in charge of the temple music by David (vi. 31 ff.; *cf.* 1 Ch. xv. 16 ff.). The list of Levites in 1 Ch. ix bristles with problems. The similarities between it and Ne. xi have led some (*e.g.* ASV, RSV) to treat it as the roll of Levites who returned to Jerusalem from the captivity (*cf.* 1 Ch. ix. 1). Others (*e.g.* C. F. Keil) view it as a list of early inhabitants of Jerusalem. Both the carefully organized assignments of duty and the numbers of Levites involved (*cf.* the 212 gatekeepers of 1 Ch. ix. 22 with the ninety-three of 1 Ch. xxvi. 8–11) suggest a period subsequent to that of David. The close co-operation between Levites and sons of priests (*cf.* 1 Ch. ix. 28 ff.) and the fact that Levites cared for some of the holy vessels and helped to prepare the showbread may indicate that the rigid division of duties suggested in Nu. iv and xviii broke down during the Monarchy, perhaps because the sons of Aaron were not numerous enough (the 1,760 in 1 Ch. ix. 13 probably refers to the number of kinsmen, not to the number of heads of houses) to cope with the demands of their office. Therefore, in addition to their regular tasks as singers and musicians, gatekeepers, porters, *etc.*, the Levites had to help in the actual preparation of the sacrifices. In addition, the Levites, including Moses' sons (xxiii. 14), were to assist the sons of Aaron in the care of the courts and chambers, the cleansing of the holy things and the preparation of the showbread, the cereal offering, the unleavened bread, the baked offering, *etc.*

David's orders in 1 Ch. xxiii illustrate the two dominant factors which produced substantial changes in the levitical offices. The first was the permanent location of the ark in Jerusalem. This act of David automatically made obsolete all the regulations concerning the Levites' function as porters. The second factor was the centralization of responsibility for the official religion (as for all other affairs of life) in the king. The Hebrew view of corporate personality saw the king as the great father of the nation whose essential character was derived from him. Though the sons of Aaron had weighty responsibilities, they could not and would not be able to discharge them without the active support of their monarch. As

David brought the central shrine to Jerusalem (1 Ch. xiii. 2 ff.) and established the patterns of its function (1 Ch. xv. 1 ff., xxiii. 1 ff.) in accordance with the principles of the Mosaic legislation, so Solomon built, dedicated, and supervised the Temple and its cult according to his father's plan (1 Ch. xxviii. 11–13, 21; 2 Ch. v–viii; note especially viii. 15: 'And they did not turn aside from what the king had commanded the priests and Levites . . .', RSV). Similarly, Jehoshaphat commissioned princes, Levites, and priests to teach the law throughout Judah (2 Ch. xvii. 7 ff.) and appointed certain Levites, priests, and family heads as judges in Jerusalem (2 Ch. xix. 8 ff.) under the supervision of the chief priest. Joash (2 Ch. xxiv. 5 ff.), Hezekiah (2 Ch. xxix. 3 ff.), and Josiah (2 Ch. xxxv. 2 ff.) supervised the priests and Levites and re-established them in their functions according to the Davidic pattern. Josiah's command in 2 Ch. xxxv. 3 emphasizes the transition that took place when the Levites were no longer needed to carry the tabernacle: they assist the priests by slaying and flaying the passover sacrifices.

The relationship between the levitical office and the prophetic is a moot question. Were some Levites cult-prophets? No firm answer is possible, but there is some evidence that Levites sometimes exercised prophetic activity: Jahaziel, a Levite of the sons of Asaph, prophesied Jehoshaphat's victory over the Moabite–Ammonite coalition (2 Ch. xx. 14 ff.) and Jeduthun, the Levite, is called the king's *seer* (2 Ch. xxxv. 15).

d. The Latter Prophets

Isaiah, Jeremiah, and Ezekiel touch briefly upon the rôle of the Levites after the Exile. Is. lxvi. 21 speaks of God's gathering of dispersed Israelites (or perhaps converted heathen) to serve Him as priests and Levites. Jeremiah (xxxiii. 17 ff.) envisages a covenant with the levitical priests (or perhaps priests and Levites; *cf.* Syr. and Vulg.) which is as binding as God's covenant with David's family (*cf.* 2 Sa. vii). Ezekiel forces a sharp cleavage between the levitical priests, whom he calls the sons of Zadok (*e.g.* xl. 46, xliii. 19), and the Levites. The former are deemed to have remained faithful to God (xliv. 15, xlviii. 11), while the latter went astray after idols and therefore could not approach the altar or handle the most sacred things (xliv. 10–14). Actually Ezekiel's suggestion seems to be a return to the careful distinction between priest and Levite found in Numbers from the somewhat more lax view which prevailed during the Monarchy.

e. The post-exilic writings

Under Joshua and Zerubbabel 341 Levites returned (Ezr. ii. 36 ff.) with the 4,289 members of priestly families, and the 392 temple servants (*n*ᵉ*tînîm, i.e.* 'given', 'appointed', who were apparently descendants of prisoners of war pressed into temple service; *cf.* Jos. ix. 23, 27; Ezr. viii. 20). The difference between the large number of priests and the comparatively small number of Levites may be due to the fact that many Levites took on priestly status during the Exile. The other Levites responsible for menial tasks in the Temple seem to have been reluctant to return (Ezr. viii. 15–20). The Levites played a prominent part at the laying of the foundation (Ezr. iii. 8 ff.) and at the dedication of the Temple (Ezr. vi. 16 ff.). Ezra, after recruiting Levites for his party (Ezr. viii. 15 ff.), instituted a reform to ban foreign marriages in which even priests and Levites had become involved (Ezr. ix. 1 ff., x. 5 ff.).

Similarly in Nehemiah, the Levites and priests engaged in their full range of duties. After repairing a section of the wall (Ne. iii. 17), the Levites were busily occupied with instruction in the law (Ne. viii. 7–9) and participation in the religious life of the nation (Ne. xi. 3 ff., xii. 27 ff.). They were to receive tithes from the people and in turn to give a tithe of the tithes to Aaron's sons (Ne. x. 37 ff., xii. 47). The need for a central authority to enforce the levitical regulations was shown by the deterioration of the cult during Nehemiah's absence from Jerusalem: Tobiah, the Ammonite, was allowed to occupy the room in the Temple which should have served as a storeroom for the levitical tithes (Ne. xiii. 4 ff.); deprived of their support, the Levites had forsaken the Temple and fled to their fields in order to sustain themselves (Ne. xiii. 10 ff.).

If Malachi (see MALACHI, BOOK OF) reflects this period of slackness during Nehemiah's absence, the indictment of the priesthood in Mal. ii. 4 ff. adds to the darkness of the picture: the priests put personal gain above their covenanted responsibility to teach the law and accepted corrupt sacrifices (i. 6 ff.). So concerned was Malachi with these failures that he saw the purification of the sons of Levi as one of God's central eschatological missions (iii. 1–4).

The high priesthood remained in the family of Eleazar until the time of Eli (*q.v.*) who was descended from Ithamar. The conspiracy of Abiathar (*q.v.*) led Solomon to depose him (1 Ki. ii. 26 f.). The office thus returned to the house of Eleazar in Zadok (*q.v.*) and remained in that family until political intrigues resulted in the deposition of Onias III by the Seleucid king Antiochus Epiphanes (*c.* 174 BC). Thereafter it became the patronage of the ruling power.

f. The New Testament

The traditional distinction between priests and Levites is maintained in the New Testament, as both the parable of the good Samaritan (Lk. x. 31, 32) and the Jewish emissaries to John the Baptist (Jn. i. 19) indicate. The missionary Barnabas was a Levite (Acts iv. 36).

II. WELLHAUSEN'S RECONSTRUCTION

The development of the documentary hypothesis with its emphasis on the post-exilic date for the completion of the priestly code (see PENTATEUCH) brought with it a drastic re-evaluation of the development of Israel's religion. The classical form of this re-evaluation was stated by Julius Wellhausen (1844–1918) in his *Prolegomena to the History of Israel* (1878; E.T. 1885), which contains two chapters pertinent to the present topic: 'The Priests and the Levites' and 'The Endowment of the Clergy'.

The crux of the relationship between priest and Levite for Wellhausen was Ezekiel's banning of Levites from priestly duties (xliv. 6–16). From Ezekiel's statement Wellhausen drew two inferences: the separation of the holy from the profane was not part of the temple procedure, as the use of heathen temple servants (see above) indicates; Ezekiel reduced the Levites, who had hitherto performed priestly functions, to the status of temple-slaves. The sons of Zadok were exempt from Ezekiel's indictment because they served at the central sanctuary in Jerusalem and had not defiled themselves by service at the high places throughout the land. The Levites of the high places suffered the same fate as their shrines, in spite of the Deuteronomist's willingness to let them share in the Jerusalem cult. When the sons of Zadok objected to relinquishing their exclusive control, Ezekiel devised 'moral' grounds for maintaining their exclusiveness, although actually the distinction between priests and Levites was accidental not moral (the priests *happened* to be at Jerusalem, the Levites at the high places). Noting that Ezekiel's distinction between priest and Levite appeared to be an innovation, not a return to the pattern of Numbers, Wellhausen concluded that the priestly law of Numbers did not at Ezekiel's time exist.

Since the Aaronic priesthood is stressed only in the priestly code, it was viewed by Wellhausen as a fiction (in the same sense as the tabernacle is a fiction) in order to give the priesthood an anchor in the Mosaic period. The genealogies in Chronicles are artificial attempts to link the sons of Zadok with Aaron and Eleazar.

Central in Wellhausen's reconstruction was the striking contrast between the 'elaborate machinery' of the wilderness cult and the decentralization of the period of the Judges, when worship played apparently only a minor rôle according to Jdg. iii–xvi. The latter period he took to be the authentic time of origin of Israelite worship, which began simply as various family heads offered their own sacrifices, and developed as certain families (*e.g.* Eli's at Shiloh) gained prominence at special sanctuaries. A startling example of the contrast between the complexity of the wilderness religion and the simplicity during the settlement was the fact that Samuel, an Ephraimite, slept nightly beside the ark (1 Sa. iii. 3) in the place where, according to Lv. xvi, only the high priest could enter annually.

The centralization enforced by the monarchy brought with it a corresponding centralization of the priesthood, which greatly strengthened the status of the priests, particularly the family of Zadok (*q.v.*), whom David appointed along with Abiathar to succeed the family of Eli. When Solomon built the permanent shrine for the ark the prominence of the Jerusalem priests was assured. Like Judah, like Israel: Jeroboam's shrines were royal shrines and the priests were directly responsible to him (Am. vii. 10 ff.). In Judah the process of centralization reached its acme when Josiah's reform abolished the high places, reduced their priests to subsidiary status in the central sanctuary, and set the stage for Ezekiel's crucial declaration.

Against this evolutionary schematization, Wellhausen set the various strata of the Pentateuch and found a remarkable degree of correspondence. In the laws of J (Ex. xx–xxiii, xxxiv) the priesthood is not mentioned, while the other parts of J mark Aaron (Ex. iv. 14, xxxii. 1 ff.) and Moses (Ex. xxxiii. 7–11) as founders of the clergy. The mention of other priests (*e.g.* Ex. xix. 22, xxxii. 29) was disregarded by Wellhausen, who considered these passages as interpolations. It was in D (Dt. xvi. 18–xviii. 22) that he saw the beginning of the use of the name *Levites* for the priests. Levite, Wellhausen held, was originally an official name and was applied to the tribe only in a secondary sense after the priests in Israel began to claim kinship with Moses. The hereditary character of the priesthood began not with Aaron (who, according to Wellhausen, 'was not originally present in J, but owed his introduction to the redactor who combined J and E') but during the monarchy with the sons of Zadok. Recognizing the basic authenticity of the inclusion of Levi in the tribal blessings of Gn. xlix, Wellhausen believed that this tribe 'succumbed at an early date' and that the supposed tie between the official use of the term *Levite* and the tribe of Levi was artificial, while admitting the possibility that Moses, a descendant of Levi, was the bridge between the official and tribal uses of the term.

The priestly code (P) not only strengthened the hand of the clergy but introduced the basic division into the ranks of the clergy—the separation of priests (Aaron's sons) from Levites (the rest of the tribe). Therefore, while the Deuteronomist spoke of levitical priests (*i.e.* the priests the Levites) the priestly writers, especially the Chronicler, spoke of priests and Levites.

Another priestly innovation was the figure of the high priest, who loomed larger in Exodus, Leviticus, and Numbers than anywhere else in the pre-exilic writings. Whereas in the historical books the king dominated the cult, in the priestly code it was the high priest. Anointed, crowned, and clad like a king, the high priest assumed a regal status, which, according to Wellhausen, could only reflect a period when the civil government of Judah was in the hands of foreigners and Israel was not so much a people as a Church—the post-exilic period. The priestly code, then, was an attempt to give the *status quo* of post-exilic religious life roots in Mosaic soil.

Though in part modified by the advances in archaeology, fresh approaches to the documentary hypothesis, and a widespread suspicion of the neat evolutionary structure (see PENTA-

TEUCH), Wellhausen's approach to the position of the Levites (which he called 'the Achilles heel of the Priestly Code') remains a central pillar of Old Testament criticism. One need only consult such representative works as Max Loehr's *A History of Religion in the Old Testament*, 1936, *e.g.* pp. 136, 137; W. O. E. Oesterley and T. H. Robinson's *Hebrew Religion*, 1930, *e.g.* p. 255; and R. H. Pfeiffer's *Introduction to the Old Testament*, 1948, *e.g.* pp. 556, 557, to see the stubbornness with which Wellhausen's reconstruction has persisted.

III. SOME REACTIONS TO WELLHAUSEN'S RECONSTRUCTION

Among the conservatives who have set out to tumble Wellhausen's structure, three names are noteworthy: James Orr (*The Problem of the Old Testament*, 1906), O. T. Allis (*The Five Books of Moses*[2], 1949, pp. 185–196), G. Ch. Aalders (*A Short Introduction to the Pentateuch*, 1949, pp. 66–71).

Basic to Wellhausen's reconstruction is the assumption that the Levites who were invited in Dt. xviii. 6, 7 to serve at the central shrine were the priests who had been disfranchised by the abolition of their high places during Josiah's reform. But solid evidence for this assumption is lacking. In fact, 2 Ki. xxiii. 9 affirms the opposite: the priests of the high places did not come up to the altar of the Lord in Jerusalem. The critical view that priests and Levites are not clearly distinguished in Deuteronomy has been discussed above, where it was seen that a clear distinction was made between them in regard to the people's responsibility towards them (Dt. xviii. 3–5, 6–8). Nor can the view that the phrase 'the priests the Levites' (Dt. xvii. 9, 18, xviii. 1, xxiv. 8, xxvii. 9), not found elsewhere in the Pentateuch, argues for the identity of the two offices in Deuteronomy be maintained. The phrase serves merely to link the priests with their tribe. No distinction, therefore, should be made in Deuteronomy between the priests and the priests the Levites (*cf.* also the 'priests, the sons of Levi'; Dt. xxi. 5, xxxi. 9). Confirmation for this seems to be found in 2 Ch. xxiii. 18 and xxx. 27, where the 'priests the Levites' are distinguished from other Levites (xxx. 25), gatekeepers, *etc.* (xxiii. 19). The tendency of Wellhausen and his followers to regard as interpolations passages which call into question their theories is evidenced in their handling of the reference to priests and Levites in connection with the bringing of the ark to Solomon's Temple (1 Ki. viii. 4).

Attention has frequently been directed by Wellhausen and others to the apparent discrepancy between the law of tithes (see TITHE) in Nu. xviii. 21 ff. (*cf.* Lv. xxvii. 30 ff.), which earmarks the tithes for the Levites, and the counterpart in Dt. xiv. 22 ff., which allows Israelites to eat of the tithes in a sacrificial meal while enjoining them to share it with the Levites. Judaism has traditionally reconciled these passages by calling the tithe of Deuteronomy 'a second tithe', *e.g.* in the Talmudic tractate *Ma'aśer Sheni*. This explanation may not be so acceptable as James Orr's (*op. cit.*, pp. 188, 189): the laws of Deuteronomy, he held, apply to a time when the tithe-laws (and those relating to levitical cities) could not be fully enforced, since the conquest was not complete and there was no central agency to enforce them. In other words, Nu. xviii. 21 ff. deals with Israel's ideal while Dt. xiv. 22 ff. is an interim programme for the conquest and settlement. The contradictory reasoning involved in the critical view, which suggests that the Levites were priests deposed in Josiah's day and yet supported after their disestablishment by a complex law of tithes drawn up in the post-exilic period, is apparent.

Pivotal in Wellhausen's reconstruction is his interpretation of Ezekiel's denunciation of the Levites (xliv. 4 ff.), in which he finds the origin of the cleavage between priests (the sons of Zadok) and Levites (priests who had previously engaged in idolatry at the high places). But this is not the only interpretation of the passage. James Orr (*op. cit.*, pp. 315–319, 520) makes a number of apt observations. Calling attention to the deplorable condition of the priesthood just prior to Ezekiel's time, he points out that Ezekiel did not establish the law but rather re-established [illegible] by depriving Levites of privileges not rightly theirs, which they had usurped during the Monarchy and by demoting idolatrous priests to the already well-established lower rank of Levite. Furthermore, the ideal context of Ezekiel's pronouncement suggests that the degradation in view may never have been carried out, at least not literally. The tone of Ezekiel stands in contradiction to that of the priestly code in that the latter knows nothing of priestly degradation but stresses divine appointment. In addition, the priests in P are not Zadok's sons but Aaron's sons. It seems questionable that such drastic changes could have been so readily accepted by a people noted for its historical memory, its sensitivity to its own past. (*Cf.* J. Pedersen, *Israel*, III, IV, 1940, p. 185.)

The office of high priest has been largely relegated to the post-exilic period by the Wellhausenian school. Though the title itself occurs only in 2 Ki. xii. 10, xxii. 4, 8, xxiii. 4 in pre-exilic writings (usually considered by documentary critics to be post-exilic interpolations), the existence of the office seems to be indicated by the title '*the* priest' (*e.g.* Ahimelech, 1 Sa. xxi. 2; Jehoiada, 2 Ki. xi. 9, 10, 15; Urijah, 2 Ki. xvi. 10 ff.) and by the fact that a priesthood of any size at all involves an administrative chief, even if the king is the head of the cult. (*Cf.* J. Pedersen, *Israel*, III, IV, p. 189.)

Yehezkel Kaufmann's criticisms of Wellhausen's reconstruction are trenchant. In *The Religion of Israel*, 1960, this Jewish scholar examines a number of Wellhausen's key conclusions and finds them wanting. The high priest, for instance, far from being a royal figure reflecting the post-exilic religious leaders, faithfully mirrors the conditions of the military camp which is subject to the authority of Moses not Aaron (*op. cit.*, pp. 184–187).

Following an argument that the tithe laws of Nu. xviii are definitely pre-exilic and were not observed in the second Temple (pp. 187–193), Kaufmann turns his attention to 'the one pillar of Wellhausen's structure that has not been shaken by later criticism'—the reconstruction of the relationship between priests and Levites. Noting the absence of evidence for the demotion of the rural priests, he then calls attention to a basic weakness in the documentary view: 'Nothing can make plausible a theory that the very priests who demoted their colleagues saw fit to endow them with the amplest clerical due, a theory the more improbable when the great number of priests and paucity of Levites at the Restoration (4,289 priests, Ezr. ii. 36 ff.; 341 Levites plus 392 temple servants, Ezr. ii. 43 ff.) is borne in mind' (p. 194).

Where, Kaufmann asks, are the priestly laws which provide for the disqualification of priests? Furthermore, why did the priests preserve the story of the Levites' faithfulness during Aaron's defection (Ex. xxxii. 26–29), while glossing over the idolatry, which, for Wellhausen, was responsible for their degradation, and according the Levites the honour of divine appointment rather than punishment? After affirming that the Levites are clearly a distinct class in the Exile, he points out that they could not have developed as a distinct class in the brief period between Josiah's reform (to say nothing of Ezekiel's denunciation) and the return, and that on foreign soil.

Kaufmann's own reconstruction may not prove entirely satisfactory. He denies an hereditary connection between the sons of Aaron and the Levites, since he deems the Aaronides to be 'the ancient, pagan priesthood of Israel' (p. 197), and thus rejects the firm biblical tradition connecting Moses, Aaron, and the Levites (*cf.* Ex. iv. 14). In the golden calf incident the old secular tribe of Levi rallied with Moses against Aaron, but was forced to yield the privilege of altar service to the Aaronides (p. 198), while they themselves had to be content as *hierodules*. This raises the question as to how, apart from a connection with Moses, the Aaronides survived the catastrophe of the golden calf and continued as priests. Kaufmann's opinion that the Deuteronomic legislation was compiled during the latter part of the Monarchy and thus is considerably later than the priestly writings may be more of a return to an old critical position (*i.e.* that of Th. Noeldeke and others) than a fresh thrust at Wellhausen.

W. F. Albright has called into question a number of the basic assumptions of the Wellhausenian school. Rejecting the linear view of institutional evolution which was a main plank in Wellhausen's platform, he notes that Israel would be unique among her neighbours had she not enjoyed during the period of the judges and afterwards a high priest, usually called (in accordance with Semitic practice) *the priest* (*Archaeology and the Religion of Israel*[3], 1953, pp. 107, 108). The lack of emphasis on the high-priestly office during the monarchy represents a decline, while, after the monarchy's collapse, the priesthood again rose to a position of prestige. Albright accepts the historicity of Aaron and finds no reason for not considering Zadok an Aaronid. Concluding that the Levite had first a functional (see above) and then a tribal significance, Albright points out that Levites may sometimes have been promoted to priests and that 'we are not justified either in throwing overboard the standard Israelite tradition regarding priests and Levites, or in considering these classes as hard and fast genealogical groups' (*op. cit.*, p. 110).

The assumption that the tabernacle in the wilderness was the idealization of the Temple and had no historical existence, so basic to Wellhausen's reconstruction, has now largely been abandoned (although *cf.* R. H. Pfeiffer's *Religion in the Old Testament*, 1961, pp. 77, 78). Both arks and portable tent-shrines are attested among Israel's neighbours, as archaeology has revealed. Far from being figments of a later period, these, as John Bright notes, are 'heritages of Israel's primitive desert faith' (*A History of Israel*, 1960, pp. 146, 147).

Obviously the last word has not been said on this puzzling problem of the relationship between priests and Levites. The data from the period of the conquest and settlement are meagre. It is hazardous to assume that the pentateuchal legislation, representing the ideal as it often does, was ever carried out literally. Even such stalwart kings as David, Jehoshaphat, Hezekiah, and Josiah were not able to ensure complete conformity to the Mosaic pattern. But it is even more tenuous to hold that because laws were not enforced they did not exist. The combination of argumentation from silence, straight-line evolutionary reconstruction, and a resort to textual emendations and literary excisions when passages prove troublesome, has resulted more than once in interpretations of biblical history which have proved to be too facile to stand permanently in the face of the complexities of biblical data and Semitic culture. Wellhausen's ingenious reconstruction of the history of the Levites may prove to be a case in point.

BIBLIOGRAPHY. In addition to works cited above, R. Brinker, *The Influence of Sanctuaries in Early Israel*, 1946, pp. 65 ff.; R. de Vaux, *Les Institutions de l'Ancien Testament*, II, 1960, pp. 195 ff., with bibliography on pp. 446–450.

D.A.H.

PRINCE. Fifteen different Hebrew words are translated 'prince' in the AV; but not all are only so represented. 'Ruler', 'leader', 'captain', *etc.*, are also used, because the translators were following (though not entirely consistently) the LXX *archōn*, a word which represents more than twenty Hebrew words, the most important of which is the word for 'head', *rō'š*.

The Hebrew words fall into two categories. First, loan-words from other languages, usually referring to foreign dignitaries. For example, *khshathrapavan*, 'satrap', and *fratama*, 'foremost', are Persian words transliterated in Dn. iii. 2, *etc.* (Aram. *'ahašdarpan*), i. 3 (Heb. pl. *part^emîm*). Secondly, words of indigenous origin representing the following salient ideas: (1) *śar*, 'exercising dominion', whether as supreme or subordinate to an overlord; (2) *nāgîḏ*, 'being in front', especially of military leader; (3) *nāśî'*, 'being exalted'; (4) *nāḏîḇ*, 'a volunteer', perhaps signifying a contrast with those whom a king might compel to fight on his behalf; (5) *qāṣîn*, 'a judge'.

Ezekiel often uses *nāśî'* of the Messiah: it corresponds with his conception of the true David (Ezk. xxxvii. 24, 25). In Daniel, *śar* and *nāgîḏ* are used of Him, corresponding to the military imagery with which the cosmic struggle is depicted. *Śar* is also used of the guardian angels of countries, and particularly of Michael (Dn. x. 13, 21).

In the New Testament *archōn* is used of Satan, 'prince of this world', *etc.*, and, in the plural, of the Roman or Jewish authorities ('rulers'). It is used once of Christ (Rev. i. 5), 'prince of the kings of the earth', but elsewhere, where 'prince' occurs in AV, the LXX *archēgos* (for *nāśî'* and *qāṣîn*) is used of Christ, gathering from its Greek connections the additional idea of 'author', 'pioneer'. J.B.J.

PRISCILLA, PRISCA. See AQUILA.

PRISON.

I. IN THE OLD TESTAMENT

The first mention of the word in Scripture is Joseph's prison in Egypt (Gn. xxxix. 20–23). For this the Hebrew text uses a special term *bêṯ-sōhar*; *sōhar* is usually compared with other Semitic words for 'round' or 'enclosure', and Joseph's prison is therefore commonly considered to be, or be in, a fortress. The comparison of Heb. *sōhar* with Egyp. *Ṯ'rw*, 'Silē' (modern Qantara), is false, as this word is really *Ṯl* (J. Vergote, *Joseph en Égypte*, 1959, pp. 25–28). However, there is an Egyp. word *ṯ'rt*, occurring as early as *c.* 1900 BC as well as later, which means 'enclosed building', 'store', '(ship's) cabin', and this might just conceivably be connected with *sōhar*. Egyptian prisons served as forced-labour compounds, as 'lock-ups', and as places of remand for people like Joseph awaiting trial. The butler and baker were put in *mišmār*, detention, virtually house-arrest, in Joseph's prison (Gn. xl. 2, 3) until their case was decided. Joseph's brothers were likewise detained for three days (Gn. xlii. 17, 19). See also JOSEPH. After capture by the Philistines, Samson was kept in prison, the 'house of the prisoners' (Jdg. xvi. 21, 25; lit. 'those bound'); a very similar term is used in Ec. iv. 14.

In Judah the guardrooms of the palace guards served as a temporary prison for Jeremiah (xxxii. 2, 8, 12, xxxiii. 1, xxxvii. 21, xxxviii. 28; *cf.* also Ne. iii. 25, xii. 39). Both there and in a private residence, a cistern could be used as a dungeon, which would often be very unpleasant (Je. xxxvii. 16, 20, xxxviii. 6, 13) and dark (Is. xlii. 7), a symbol of bondage from which the Lord's servant should deliver His people (Acts xxvi. 15–18; Lk. i. 79). Nor was Jeremiah the only prophet imprisoned for his faithfulness in declaring God's message: Asa of Judah put Hanani the seer into the stocks (2 Ch. xvi. 10), and Ahab had Micaiah put in prison on rations of bread and water (1 Ki. xxii. 27; 2 Ch. xviii. 26). Defeated kings were sometimes imprisoned by their conquerors: so Hoshea of Israel by the Assyrians (2 Ki. xvii. 4), Jehoiachin of Judah by Nebuchadrezzar (*cf.* Je. xxiv. 1, 5; D. J. Wiseman, *Chronicles of Chaldaean Kings*, pp. 33–35, 73), and Zedekiah of Judah likewise (Je. lii. 11). At Babylon Jehoiachin was but one of many noble captives and artisans detained under 'house-arrest' at the royal palace and environs. Ration-tablets for him, his five sons, and many other foreigners were found at Babylon (*ANET*, 308b; *DOTT*, pp. 84–86; E. F. Weidner, *Mélanges R. Dussaud*, II, 1939, pp. 923–935; Albright, *BA*, V, 1942, pp. 49–55). Eventually Evil-merodach granted him a greater measure of freedom (2 Ki. xxv. 27, 29; Je. lii. 31, 33). Ezekiel (xix. 9) pictures Jehoiachin being brought to Babylon in a cage (RV, RSV); for a much earlier Egyptian picture of a Semitic prince as a prisoner in a cage, see Montet, *L'Égypte et la Bible*, 1959, p. 73, fig. 12. K.A.K.

II. IN THE NEW TESTAMENT

Four Greek words are translated by 'prison' in the EVV. John the Baptist was imprisoned in a *desmōtērion*, a 'place of bonds'. This was at Herod's fortress at Machaerus in Peraea, east of the Dead Sea (Jos., *Ant.* xviii. 5. 2), where two dungeons have been discovered, one still showing traces of fetters. *Phylakē*, a 'place of guarding', is the most general and frequently used term. It suggests a place where the prisoners were closely watched. The chief priests imprisoned the apostles (Acts v. 19) in what is also called a *tērēsis dēmosia*, a 'public place of watching' (*cf.* Acts iv. 3).

When Herod put Peter in prison, probably in the fortress of Antonia, where Paul was later lodged (Acts xxi. 34, xxiii. 30) and referred to here as an *oikēma*, 'house', the apostle was guarded continually by four soldiers, two chained to him and two outside the door (Acts xii. 3–6). Beyond this there would appear to have been another guard and then the iron outer gate (Acts xii. 10). At Philippi Paul was in custody in the town jail, under the charge of a keeper, where there was an inner, perhaps underground, chamber containing stocks (Acts xvi. 24). These would have several holes, allowing the legs to be forced wide apart to ensure greater security and greater pain. In Caesarea Paul was imprisoned (Acts xxiii. 35) in Herod's castle, but when a prisoner at Rome he was allowed to stay in his own lodging, with a soldier always chained to him (Acts xxviii. 16, 30). D.H.W.

PRIZE. See GAMES.

PROCONSUL (Gk. *anthypatos*, AV 'deputy'). In the Roman Empire as organized by Augustus this was the title of governors of provinces which were administered by the Senate because they did not require a standing army. Proconsuls mentioned in the New Testament are L. Sergius Paullus (*q.v.*), proconsul of Cyprus when Paul and Barnabas visited that island *c.* AD 47 (Acts xiii. 7), and L. Junius Gallio (*q.v.*), whose proconsulship of Achaia (AD 51–2) overlapped Paul's eighteen-month stay in Corinth (Acts xviii. 12). In Acts xix. 38 'proconsuls' may be a generalizing plural; the proconsul of Asia had recently been assassinated (October AD 54) and his successor had not yet arrived. F.F.B.

PROCURATOR. In Roman imperial administration the word indicated the financial officer of a province, but was also used as the title of the governor of a Roman province of the third class, such as Judaea (Gk. *epitropos*; but in the New Testament the procurator of Judaea is regularly described as the 'governor', Gk. *hēgemōn*). Judaea was governed by imperial procurators from AD 6 to 41 and from 44 to 66. Three procurators are mentioned in the New Testament: Pontius Pilate, AD 26–36 (Mt. xxvii. 2, *etc.*), Antonius Felix, 52–9 (Acts xxiii. 24 ff.), and Porcius Festus, 59–62 (Acts xxiv. 27 ff.). The procurators were generally drawn from the equestrian order (Felix, a freedman, was an exception). They had auxiliary troops at their disposal and were generally responsible for military and financial administration, but were subject to the superior authority of the imperial legate (propraetor) of Syria. Their seat of government was Caesarea. See FELIX, FESTUS, JUDAEA, PILATE. F.F.B.

PROGNOSTICATOR. See MAGIC AND SORCERY.

PROMISE. There is in the Hebrew Old Testament no special term for the concept or act of promising. Where our English translations say that someone promised something, the Hebrew simply states that someone said or spoke (*'āmar*, *dāḇar*) some word with future reference. In the New Testament the technical term, *epangelia*, appears—chiefly in Acts, Galatians, Romans, and Hebrews.

A promise is a word that goes forth into unfilled time. It reaches ahead of its speaker and its recipient, to mark an appointment between them in the future. A promise may be an assurance of continuing or future action on behalf of someone: 'I will be with you', 'They that mourn shall be comforted', 'If we confess our sins, God will forgive us our sins.' It may be a solemn agreement of lasting, mutual (if unequal) relationship: as in the covenants. It may be the announcement of a future event: 'When you have brought the people from Egypt, you will serve God on this mountain'. The study of biblical promises must therefore take in far more than the actual occurrences of the word in the EVV. See also WORD, PROPHECY, COVENANT, and OATHS. An oath often accompanied the word of promise (Ex. vi. 8; Dt. ix. 5; Heb. vi. 13 ff.).

That what He has spoken with His mouth He can and will perform with His hand is the biblical sign manual of God, for His word does not return void. Unlike men and heathen gods, He knows and commands the future: 1 Ki. viii. 15, 24; Is. xli. 4, 26, xliii. 12, 19, *etc.*; Rom. iv. 21; Pascal, *Pensées*, 693. Through the historical books, a pattern of divine promise and historical fulfilment is traced (G. von Rad, *Studies in Deuteronomy*, 1953, pp. 74 ff.), expressive of this truth.

The point of convergence of the Old Testament promises (to Abraham, Moses, David, and the Fathers through the prophets) is Jesus Christ. All the promises of God are confirmed in Him, and through Him affirmed by the Church in the 'Amen' of its worship (2 Cor. i. 20). The Old Testament quotations and allusions in the Gospel narratives indicate this fulfilment. The Magnificat and the Benedictus rejoice that God has kept His word. The promised Word has become flesh. The new covenant has been inaugurated—upon the 'better promises' prophesied by Jeremiah (Je. xxxi; Heb. viii. 6–13). Jesus is its guarantee (Heb. vii. 22), and the Holy Spirit of promise its first instalment (Eph. i. 13, 14).

Awaiting the promise of Christ's coming again and of new heavens and a new earth (2 Pet. iii. 4, 9, 13), the Church sets forth on her missionary task with the assurance of His presence (Mt. xxviii. 20) and with the news that 'the promise of the Father'—the Holy Spirit (after Joel ii. 28)—is given to Jew and pagan in Jesus Christ, fulfilling the promise to Abraham of universal blessing through his posterity. The promise is correlated to faith and open to all who, by imitating Abraham's faith, become 'children of the promise' (Gal. iii; Rom. iv, ix). See ESCHATOLOGY; SCRIPTURE.

BIBLIOGRAPHY. G. K. Chesterton, *A Defence of Rash Vows*, 1901. J.H.

PROPHECY, PROPHETS.

I. THE PROPHETIC OFFICE

a. The normative prophet

The first person whom the Bible calls a prophet (Heb. *nāḇî'*) was Abraham (Gn. xx. 7; *cf.* Ps. cv. 15), but Old Testament prophecy received its normative form in the life and person of Moses, who constituted a standard of comparison for all future prophets (Dt. xviii. 15–19; see MESSIAH; Dt. xxxiv. 10). Every feature which characterized the true prophet of Yahweh in the classical tradition of Old Testament prophecy was first found in Moses.

He received a specific and personal call from

God. The initiative in making a prophet rests with God (Ex. iii. 1–iv. 17; *cf.* Is. vi; Je. i. 4–19; Ezk. i–iii; Ho. i. 2; Am. vii. 14–15; Jon. i. 1), and it is only the false prophet who dares to take the office upon himself (Je. xiv. 14, xxiii. 21). The primary object and effect of the call was an introduction into God's presence, as the passages noted above show. This was the 'secret' or 'counsel' of the Lord (1 Ki. xxii. 19; Je. xxiii. 22; Am. iii. 7). The prophet stood before men, as a man who had been made to stand before God (1 Ki. xvii. 1, xviii. 15).

Again, the prophetic awareness of history stemmed from Moses. When Isaiah makes his tremendous polemic against idolatry, one of his most potent contentions, that Yahweh alone is the Author of prophecy and that the idols are at best wise after the event (*e.g.* xlv. 20–22), stems directly from Moses and the Exodus. Yahweh sent Moses into Egypt possessed of the clues necessary to interpret the great events which were to follow. History became revelation because there was added to the historical situation a man prepared beforehand to say what it meant. Moses was not left to struggle for the meaning of events as or after they happened; he discerned them beforehand and was warned by God of their significance. So it was with all the prophets. Alone of the nations of antiquity, Israel had a true awareness of history. They owed it to the prophets, and, under the Lord of history, the prophets owed it to Moses.

Likewise they owed to him their ethical and social concern. Even before his call Moses concerned himself with the social welfare of his people (Ex. ii. 11 ff., *cf.* verse 17), and afterwards, as the prophetic lawgiver, he outlined the most humane and philanthropic code of the ancient world, concerned for the helpless (Dt. xxiv. 19–22, *etc.*) and the enemy of the oppressor (*e.g.* Lv. xix. 9 ff.).

Many of the prophets were found confronting their kings and playing an active, statesman's part in national affairs. This was a function of the prophet which found its prototype in Moses, who legislated for the nation, and was even called 'king' (Dt. xxxiii. 5). It is interesting that the first two kings of Israel were also prophets, but this union of offices did not continue, and the Mosaic–theocratic rule was prolonged by the association of the anointed king and the anointed prophet.

We also find in Moses that combination of proclamation and prediction which is found in all the prophets. This will concern us in greater detail presently, as a feature of prophecy at large. We will pause only to show that Moses established the norm here also, namely, that in the interests of speaking to the present situation the prophet often undertakes to enlarge upon events yet to come. It is this interlocking of proclamation and prediction which distinguishes the true prophet from the mere prognosticator. Even when Moses uttered his great prophecy of the coming Prophet (Dt. xviii. 15 ff.) he was dealing with the very pressing problems of the relation of the people of God to the practices and allurements of pagan cults.

Two other features characteristic of the prophets who were to succeed him are found in Moses. Many of the prophets used symbols in the delivery of their message (*e.g.* Je. xix. 1 ff.; Ezk. iv. 1 ff.). Moses used the uplifted hand (Ex. xvii. 8 ff.) and the uplifted serpent (Nu. xxi. 8), not to mention the highly symbolic cultus which he mediated to the nation. And finally, the intercessory aspect of the prophetic task was also displayed in him. He was 'for the people to God-ward' (Ex. xviii. 19; Nu. xxvii. 5) and on at least one notable occasion literally stood in the breach as a man of prayer (Ex. xxxii. 30 ff.; Dt. ix. 18 ff.; *cf.* 1 Ki. xiii. 6; 2 Ki. xix. 4; Je. vii. 16, xi. 14, xiv. 11).

b. The titles of the prophets

Two general descriptions appear to have been used for prophets: the first, 'man of God', describes how they appeared to their fellow-men. This title was first used of Moses (Dt. xxxiii. 1) and continued in use till the end of the Monarchy (*e.g.* 1 Sa. ii. 27, ix. 6; 1 Ki. xiii. 1, *etc.*). That it was intended to express the difference of character between the prophet and other men is made perfectly clear by the Shunammite: 'I perceive that this is a holy man of God . . .' (2 Ki. iv. 9). The other general title was 'his, thy, or my servants'. It does not appear that any man ever addressed the prophet as 'servant of God', but God often described the prophets as 'my servants' and consequently the other pronouns, 'his' and 'thy', were also used (*e.g.* 2 Ki. xvii. 13, 23, xxi. 10, xxiv. 2; Ezr. ix. 11; Je. vii. 25). Here the other relationship of the prophet, that towards God, is expressed, and this also was first a title of Moses (*e.g.* Jos. i. 1, 2).

However, passing from the general to the particular, there are three Hebrew words used of the prophet: *nāḇî'*, *rō'eh*, and *ḥōzeh*. The first of these is always translated 'prophet', the second, which is, in form, an active participle of the verb 'to see', is translated 'seer'. The third, also an active participle of another verb 'to see', is unfortunately without English equivalent and is translated either 'prophet' (*e.g.* Is. xxx. 10) or 'seer' (*e.g.* 1 Ch. xxix. 29).

The derivation of *nāḇî'* has been the subject of long debate. The word can be traced to an Akkadian root, and the choice is between the prophet as one who is called, or one who calls, *i.e.* to men in the name of God. Either of these will admirably suit the nature of the prophet as found in the Old Testament, and therefore we need not prolong the discussion. The possibility that the prophet is one who calls to God, in prayer, has not been canvassed, but that too, and apparently from the start (Gn. xx. 7), was a mark of a prophetic man.

Equally extensive discussion has centred on the relation of the three words *nāḇî'*, *rō'eh*, and *ḥōzeh* to each other. Verses such as 1 Ch. xxix. 29, which appear to use the words with great discrimination (Gad is described in the Hebrew as *ḥōzeh*), suggest that we ought to find a precise shade of meaning in each word. This, however, is not borne out by an examination of Old Testament usage as a whole. The use of the words falls into two periods, marked out by 1 Sa. ix. 9: first, there was the period when *nāḇî'* and *rō'eh* meant something different, the early period; then came the period, in which the author of 1 Sa. ix. 9 lived, when *nāḇî'* had taken on the force of a synonym of *rō'eh*, with or without losing its own earlier meaning. The source document for the early period is 1 Sa. ix–x, and it certainly seems that we can decide the force of the two words as far as those chapters are concerned: the *nāḇî'* is a member of a group, given to corporate and infectious ecstasy (1 Sa. x. 5, 6, 10–13, xix. 20–24), whereas the *rō'eh* is solitary, and altogether a more important and impressive person. Out of a total of ten occurrences of the title, it is used six times of Samuel (1 Sa. ix. 11, 18, 19; 1 Ch. ix. 22, xxvi. 28, xxix. 29). He, therefore, demonstrates the *rō'eh par excellence.*

However, when we move to the later period indicated in 1 Sa. ix. 9 it is impossible to be so precise. While it is noticeable that throughout Chronicles the *ḥōzeh* is always (except in 2 Ch. xxix. 30) mentioned in association with the king, the attractive suggestion that he was employed as a resident clairvoyant is not in accordance with the evidence. Even in Chronicles he often acts precisely as a *nāḇî'* would have done (*e.g.* 2 Ch. xix. 2, xxxiii. 18), and the task most frequently attributed to him was that of court historian—a task equally found in the *nāḇî'* and the *rō'eh* (2 Ch. ix. 29, xii. 15; *cf.* 1 Ch. xxix. 29).

In general Old Testament usage every shade of meaning in the verb *ḥāzâ* can be paralleled in the verb *rā'â*: both are used in connection with divination (Zc. x. 2; Ezk. xxi. 21), a connection which they share also with the *nāḇî'* (Mi. iii. 11); both are used for the perception of the meaning of events (Ps. xlvi. 8; Is. v. 12), and of the assessment of character (Ps. xi. 4, 7; 1 Sa. xvi. 1); both are used of the vision of God (Ps. xxvii. 4; Is. vi. 5), and of prophetic activity (Is. i. 1; Ezk. xiii. 3); both are used of seeing vengeance carried out (Ps. lviii. 10, liv. 7). In Is. xxix. 10 *nāḇî'* and *ḥōzeh* are parallel; in Is. xxx. 10, *rō'eh* and *ḥōzeh* are parallel; in Am. vii. 12 ff. Amaziah addresses Amos as *ḥōzeh*, urging him to prophesy (*nibbā'*) in Judah, and Amos replies that he was not a *nāḇî'*; in Ezk. xiii. 9 the reverse procedure is found: the noun *nāḇî'* is the subject of the verb *ḥāzâ*. These references could be prolonged extensively, and we are forced to conclude that the words are synonymous.

c. Foretelling and forthtelling

Too often in studies of the phenomenon of prophecy lip-service has been paid to the uniqueness of this movement in Israel, and at the same time it has been brought under judgment and criticism as though it were not unique, and as though the evidence could be explained on purely rationalistic grounds. We have only one mine of information about the Old Testament prophet, however, and that is the Old Testament itself, which must be treated therefore as a primary source document.

The prophet was primarily a man of the word of God. Even when he seemed to undertake other functions, such as the elaborate 'miming' of Ezekiel, it was subordinated to the interests of bringing the word of God to his fellow-men. This word was not, so to speak, a mere passive opinion, as though God were anxious simply that men should be aware how He saw matters before they decided for themselves. It was rather the prophets' conviction that the proclamation of God's word radically changed the whole situation. For example, Is. xxviii–xxix shows us a picture of a people struggling for a satisfactory solution to a pressing problem of political expediency, and, in the process, rejecting God's word; chapters xxx onwards reveal the situation which then transpires: the problem is no longer one of political balance of power as between Judah, Assyria, and Egypt, but one of spiritual relationship between Judah, Assyria, and Egypt, on the one hand, and the word of God, on the other. The word is an active ingredient added to the situation, which is henceforth impelled forward in terms of the word spoken (Is. xl. 8, lv. 11; see, *e.g.*, CURSE).

Clearly, however, the prophets spoke to their situation primarily by means of warnings and encouragements concerning the future. Almost every prophet first appears as a foreteller, as, for example, Am. i. 2. There are three grounds of this practice of foretelling: in the first place, it is clearly necessary if people are to exercise due moral responsibility in the present that they should be aware of the future. This at once lifts Old Testament prediction out of the realm of mere prognostication and carnal curiosity. Calls to repentance (*e.g.* Is. xxx. 6–9) and calls to practical holiness (*e.g.* Is. ii. 5) are equally based on a word concerning the future; the vision of wrath to come is made the basis of a present seeking of the mercy of God; the vision of bliss to come calls to a walking in the light now.

Secondly, prediction arises from the fact that the prophets speak in the name of the holy Ruler of history. We have already mentioned that the prophet's call was primarily to a knowledge of God. Out of this knowledge sprang the awareness of what He would do, as He guided history according to the unchangeable principles of His holy nature. This is to say, that, as prophets, they possessed all the basic information, for by Moses and the Exodus God had declared His name for ever (Ex. iii. 15). They were 'in the know' (Am. iii. 7).

Thirdly, prediction seems to belong to the very idea of the prophetic office. We may see this in Dt. xviii. 9 ff.: Israel, entering the land of Canaan, is not only warned about the abominations of the Canaanite cults, such as infant sacrifice, but also about Canaanite religious practitioners, such as diviners. Certainly these men were concerned with what we call 'fortune-telling'; they offered to probe the future by one means or another. For Israel, instead of all these, there will be a prophet whom the Lord will raise up from among their brethren. This prophet, speaking in the name of the Lord, is to be judged by the accuracy of his forecasts (verse 22)—a clear proof that Israel expected prophetic prediction, and that it belonged to the notion of prophecy.

We may note here the extraordinarily detailed telepathic and clairvoyant gifts of the prophets. Elisha had the reputation of knowing what was said in secret afar off (2 Ki. vi. 12) and gave evidence that it was not an inaccurate assessment of his powers. Ezekiel is justly famed for his detailed knowledge of Jerusalem at the time of his residence in Babylon (Ezk. viii–xi). It is needless to try to evade this part of the biblical testimony. The prophets were men of remarkable psychic powers. It is equally unnecessary to question foreknowledge of personal names, such as is exemplified in 1 Ki. xiii. 2; Is. xliv. 28 (*cf.* Acts ix. 12). Since there is no textual uncertainty at these points, the question is simply one of whether we accept the Old Testament evidence as to what constitutes Old Testament prophecy or not. The occurrence of such detailed prediction is perfectly 'at home' in the general picture of prophecy as the Bible reveals it. We should remember that it is illegitimate to pose the problem in terms of our knowledge of the lapse of time between prediction and fulfilment: 'How could the prophet know the name of someone not born till hundreds of years after his time?' There is nothing about 'hundreds of years' in the passages mentioned. This is our contribution to the question, because we know of the time lapse. The real question is much simpler in statement: 'From what we know of the Old Testament prophet, is there anything against his foreknowledge of personal names?' In the light of the Old Testament, there is only one possible answer.

II. PROPHETIC INSPIRATION AND METHODS

a. Modes of inspiration

How did the prophet receive the message which he was commissioned to convey to his fellows? The answer given in the vast majority of cases is perfectly clear and yet tantalizingly vague: 'The word of the Lord came . . .', literally, the verb being the verb 'to be', 'the word of the Lord became actively present to . . .' It is a statement of a direct, personal awareness. This is the basic experience of the prophet. It is stated for the first time in Ex. vii. 1, 2 (*cf.* iv. 15, 16). God is the author of the words, which He conveys to the prophet, and through him to the people. It is this same experience which Jeremiah had when the Lord's hand touched his mouth (Je. i. 9), and this passage tells us as much as we are permitted to know: that in the context of personal fellowship which God has brought about the prophet receives a donation of words. Jeremiah later expressed this experience as that of 'standing in the counsel of the Lord' (xxiii. 22), whereby one was then able to make the people hear God's words. This, however, adds nothing in the way of psychological explanation.

Dreams and visions also had their place in the inspiration of the prophet. It is sometimes urged that Je. xxiii. 28 teaches the invalidity of dreams as a method of ascertaining the word of the Lord. However, in the light of Nu. xii. 6, 7 and 1 Sa. xxviii. 6, 15, which teach the validity of the dream, we see that Je. xxiii. 28 is to be understood as 'a mere dream' or 'a dream of his own fancy'. Indeed, Jeremiah himself appears to have enjoyed the word of God through a dream (xxxi. 26). The experience of visions is best exemplified in the prophet Zechariah, but, like dreams, adds nothing to our knowledge—or rather our ignorance—of the mechanics of inspiration. Exactly the same may be said of the cases where the word is perceived through a symbol (Je. xviii; Am. vii. 7 ff., viii. 1–3). Inspiration is a miracle; we do not know in what way God makes the mind of a man aware of His word.

This raises the question of the activity of the Spirit of God in prophetic inspiration. There are eighteen passages which associate prophetic inspiration with the activity of the Spirit: in Nu. xxiv. 2 the reference is to Balaam; Nu. xi. 29; 1 Sa. x. 6, 10, xix. 20, 23 deal with the prophetic ecstasy; the plain assumption that prophecy arises from the Spirit of God is found in 1 Ki. xxii. 24; Joel ii. 28, 29; Ho. ix. 7; Ne. ix. 30; Zc. vii. 12; a direct claim to the inspiration of the Spirit is made in Mi. iii. 8; the Spirit's inspiration of the prophetic word is claimed by 1 Ch. xii. 18; 2 Ch. xv. 1, xx. 14, xxiv. 20; Ne. ix. 20; and Ezk. xi. 5. It is clear that this evidence is not evenly spread through the Old Testament, and in particular that the pre-exilic prophets are sparsely represented. Indeed, Jeremiah does not mention the Spirit of God in any context whatever! This has been taken as showing a distinction between the 'man of the word' and the 'man of the Spirit' (see L. Koehler, *Old Testament Theology*, 1957; E. Jacob, *Theology of the Old Testament*, 1958; T. C. Vriezen, *An Outline of Old Testament Theology*, 1958). The early prophets were anxious to dissociate themselves from the group inspiration and frenzy of the so-called spirit-possessed men. This is not a necessary, nor even a probable, conclusion. For one thing, a straightforward identification of the earlier group-ecstatics with the later false prophets is not possible; and, for another, as Jacob points out, 'the word presupposes the spirit, the creative breath of life, and for the prophets there was such evidence of this that they thought it unnecessary to state it explicitly'.

b. Modes of communication

The prophets came before their contemporaries as men with a word to say. The spoken oracle is the form in which the word of God is expressed.

Each prophet stamped the marks of his own personality and experience on this word: the oracles of Amos and Jeremiah are as unlike as are the personalities of the two prophets. There is, therefore, a double awareness in the books of the prophets: on the one hand, these words are the words which God gave to the prophet. God took this man to be His mouthpiece; they are the words of God. On the other hand, these words are the words of a certain man, spoken at a certain time, under certain circumstances. It is customary among modern writers (*e.g.* Rowley, *The Servant of the Lord*, 1952, p. 126) to draw the conclusion that the word thus became to an extent imperfect and fallible, because it was the word of imperfect and fallible men. We ought to be clear that such a conclusion must rest on grounds other than the testimony of the prophets themselves in so far as we have it in the books. This is not the place to discuss the relation between the words of inspired men and the words of the God who inspired them, but it is the place to say that the books of the prophets may be searched without discovering any trace of suggestion that the prophets thought the word through them was in any way less than the word of God. We shall note presently that most of the prophets seemed totally unaware of the existence of voices other than, or contradictory to, their own. They possessed an overwhelming certainty concerning their words, such as is proper either to lunatics or to men who have stood in the counsel of God and received there what they are to say on earth.

Sometimes the prophets couched their oracles in the form of parable or allegory (*e.g.* Is. v. 1–7; 2 Sa. xii. 1–7; and especially Ezk. xvi and xxiii), but the most dramatic presentation of their message was by means of the 'acted oracle'. If we start by thinking of the acted oracle as a 'visual aid' we will undoubtedly end with the wrong conception of its nature and function. Of course, it was a visual aid, but, in association with the Hebrew notion of the efficacy of the word, it served to make the discharge of the word into the contemporary situation rather more powerful. This is best seen in the interview between King Joash and the dying Elisha (2 Ki. xiii. 14 ff.). In verse 17 the arrow of the Lord's victory is shot against Syria. The prophet has introduced the king into a sphere of symbolic action. He now inquires how far the king has faith to embrace that word of promise: the king smites three times, and that is the extent to which the effective word of God will achieve accomplishment and not return void. Here we see very vividly the exact relation in which the symbol stood to the word, and in which both stood to the course of events. The word embodied in the symbol is exceedingly effective; it cannot fail to come to pass; it will accomplish exactly what the symbol declared. Thus, Isaiah walked naked and barefoot (Is. xx), Jeremiah smashed a potter's vessel in the place of potsherds (Je. xix), Ahijah tore his new coat into twelve pieces and gave Jeroboam ten (1 Ki. xi. 29 ff.), Ezekiel besieged a model city (Ezk. iv. 1–3), dug through the house wall (xii. 1 ff.), did not mourn for his dead wife (xxiv. 15 ff.). We need to distinguish sharply between the acted oracle of the Israelite prophet and the sympathetic magic of the Canaanite cults. Essentially the latter is a movement from man to God: the performance of a certain action by man is an attempt to coerce Baal, or whatever god was in mind, to function correspondingly. The acted oracle was a movement from God to man: the word of God, the activity on which God had already decided, was thus declared and promoted on earth. In this, as in every other aspect of biblical religion, the initiative rests solely with God.

c. The Books of the Prophets

The question of the formation of the Canon does not concern us here, but we cannot evade the question of the compilation of the writings of each prophet. It ought to be taken for granted that each of the prophetic books contains only a selection of the utterances of that prophet, but who did the selecting, editing, and arranging? For example, the Judaean references in the book of Hosea are probably correctly seen as editorial work after the fall of Samaria, when the prophet's oracles were carried south. But who was the editor? Or, again, the series of questions and answers in Malachi are clearly a deliberate arrangement to convey a total message. Who arranged them? Or, on a larger scale, the book of Isaiah is manifestly a well-edited book; we have only to think of the way in which the series of six 'woes' (chapters xxviii–xxxvii) fall into two groups of three within which the first three respectively are exactly matched by the second three, or of the way chapters xxxviii, xxxix have been taken out of chronological order so that they may become an historical preface to chapters xl–lv. But who was the careful editor?

If we consult the books themselves we find three hints as to their written composition. First, that the prophets themselves wrote at least some of their oracles (*e.g.* Is. xxx. 8; Je. xxix. 1 ff.; *cf.* 2 Ch. xxi. 12; Je. xxix. 25; *cf.* the use of the 1st person in Ho. iii. 1–5); secondly, that in the case of Jeremiah, at least, a lengthy statement of his prophecies so far was made out with the help of a secretary (Je. xxxvi), and that the command is both given and received without any sign that it was at all out of the way; and thirdly, that the prophets are sometimes associated with a group which was, presumably, the recipient of the teaching of the master-prophet, and may have been the repository of his oracles. Such a group is mentioned as 'my disciples' in Is. viii. 16. These slender pieces of evidence suggest that the prophet himself was behind the recording of his words, whether by personal act, or by dictation, or by teaching. It could easily have been that the oracles of Isaiah took their present form as a manual of instruction for the prophet's disciples.

The name 'sons of the prophets' is used of these groups of disciples. It is actually found in the times of Elijah and Elisha, though Am. vii. 14 shows that it survived as a technical term long after. We would gather from 2 Ki. ii. 3, 5 that there were known groups of men settled here and there in the land under the general superintendence of the 'authorized' prophet. Elijah, in his effort to spare Elisha the strain of parting, appears to make a customary journey. Elisha in his turn had the management of the prophetic groups (2 Ki. iv. 38, vi. 1 ff.), and availed himself of their services (2 Ki. ix. 1). Clearly the members of these groups were men of prophetic gift (2 Ki. ii. 3, 5), but whether they joined the group by divine call or attached themselves to the prophet, attracted by his teaching, or were called by him, we are not in a position to say.

There is no need to see in Am. vii. 14 a slur on the prophetic groups, as though Amos were indignantly distinguishing himself from them. Amos could hardly be denying prophetic status to himself, seeing he is about to assert that the Lord commanded him to 'prophesy' (Heb. *hinnāḇē'*, to perform the part of a *nāḇî'*, vii. 15). We may therefore take the words either as an indignant rhetorical question: 'Am I not a prophet, and a prophet's son? Indeed, I was a herdman . . . and the Lord took me', or, preferably (*cf.* AV), 'I was no prophet . . . I was a herdman, . . . and the Lord took me.' Amos is making no sinister accusation against the sons of the prophets as necessarily professional time-servers, but is alleging the authority of a spiritual call as against the accusation of lack of official status and authorization.

Very likely, at any rate, it is to such men, grouped round the great prophets, that we owe the safeguarding and transmission of their oracles.

III. TRUE AND FALSE PROPHETS

When Micaiah the son of Imlah and Zedekiah the son of Chenaanah confronted each other before King Ahab, the one warning of defeat and the other promising victory, and both appealing to the authority of the Lord (1 Ki. xxii), how could they have been distinguished, the true from the false? When Jeremiah faced Hananiah, the former bowing under a yoke symbolizing servitude and the latter breaking the yoke symbolizing liberation (Je. xxviii), how could they have been distinguished? Or, a more extreme case, when the 'old prophet in Bethel' brought back the 'man of God' out of Judah with a lying message, and then rounded upon him with the true word of God (1 Ki. xiii. 18–22), was it possible to tell when he spoke with truth and when he spoke with deceit? The question of the discrimination of prophets is by no means academic but thoroughly practical and of the highest spiritual importance.

Certain external characteristics of a general kind have been alleged as distinguishing the true from the false. It has been urged that the prophetic ecstasy was the mark of the false prophet. We have already noted that group-ecstasy was the common mark of the *nāḇî'* in the time of Samuel (1 Sa. ix, x, *etc.*). This ecstasy was apparently spontaneous, or it could be induced, notably by music (1 Sa. x. 5; 2 Ki. iii. 15) and by the ritual dance (1 Ki. xviii. 28). The ecstatic person apparently became very self-forgetful and quite insensible to pain (1 Sa. xix. 24; 1 Ki. xviii. 28). It is easy, and indeed almost inevitable, that we should look with suspicion on a phenomenon such as this: it is so alien to our taste, and it is known as a feature of Baalism, and of Canaan in general. But these are not sufficient grounds for a plain identification between ecstatic and false. For one thing, there is no indication that the ecstasy was in any way frowned upon either by the people at large or by the best of their religious leaders. Samuel foretold with apparent approbation that Saul would join the ecstatic prophets and that this would signify his becoming a new man (1 Sa. x. 6). Also, the emissary of Elisha is called by Jehu's fellow captains 'this mad fellow' (2 Ki. ix. 11), probably indicating that the ecstasy was still a feature of the prophetic group. Furthermore, Isaiah's temple experience was certainly an ecstasy, and Ezekiel was without doubt an ecstatic.

Another suggested identification of false prophecy was professionalism: they were the paid servants of some king or other and it was to their interest to say what would please the king. But, again, this will hardly serve as a criterion. Samuel was clearly a professional prophet but was not a false prophet; Nathan was very likely a court official of David, but yet professionalism was by no means equivalent to sycophancy. Even Amos may have been professional, but Amaziah urges upon him that the living is better in Judah for a prophet like him (Am. vii. 10 ff.). Like the ecstatics, the court prophets are found in groups (1 Ki. xxii), and no doubt their professional status could have been a corrupting influence, but to say that it was so is to run beyond the evidence. Jeremiah made no such accusation against Pashhur (Je. xx), though it would have been greatly to his advantage to have had a ready-made proof of his adversary's error.

There are three notable discussions of the whole question of false prophecy in the Old Testament. The first is in Deuteronomy xiii and xviii. Dealing with the latter chapter first, it states a negative test: what does not come to pass was not spoken by the Lord. The wording here ought to be strictly observed; it is not a simple statement that fulfilment is the hall-mark of genuineness, for, as xiii. 1 ff. indicates, a sign may be given and come to pass and yet the prophet be false. Inevitably, fulfilment was looked for as proof of genuine, godly utterance: Moses complained when what was spoken 'in the name' failed to have the desired effect (Ex. v. 23); Jeremiah saw in the visit of Hanamel a proof that the word was from the Lord (Je. xxxii. 8). But Deuteronomy states only the negative, because that alone is safe and correct. What the

Lord says will always find fulfilment, but sometimes the word of the false is fulfilled also, as a test for God's people.

Thus, we turn to Dt. xiii, and the answer to the problem of discerning the false prophet: the test is a theological one, the revelation of God at the Exodus. The essence of the false prophet is that he calls the people 'after other gods, which thou hast not known' (verse 2), thus speaking 'rebellion against the Lord your God, who brought you out of the land of Egypt' (verses 5, 10, RSV). Here we see the final feature of Moses, the normative prophet: he also fixed the theological norm by which all subsequent teaching could be judged. A prophet might allege that he spoke in the name of Yahweh, but if he did not acknowledge the authority of Moses and subscribe to the doctrines of the Exodus he was a false prophet.

This is substantially the answer, also, of Jeremiah. This sensitive prophet could not carry off the contest with the robust assurance which seemed so natural to Isaiah and Amos. The question of personal certainty was one which he could not evade, and yet he could not answer it except by the tautologous 'certainty is certainty'. We find him in the heat of the struggle in xxiii. 9 ff. It is clear from a reading of these verses that Jeremiah can find no external tests of the prophet: there is here no allegation of ecstasy or professionalism. Nor does he find the essence of the false prophet to consist in the acquisition of his oracles by dreams: that is, there is no test based upon prophetic technique. This is what Jeremiah alleges: the false prophet is a man of immoral life (verses 10–14) and he places no barrier to immorality in others (verse 17); whereas the true prophet seeks to stem the tide of sin and to call people to holiness (verse 22). Again, the message of the false prophet is one of peace, without regard to the moral and spiritual conditions which are basic to peace (verse 17); whereas the true prophet has a message of judgment upon sin (verse 29).

We might interject here that Jeremiah ought not to be understood to say that the true prophet cannot have a message of peace. This is one of the most damaging notions that has ever entered the study of the prophets and has been responsible for more subjective carving up of prophetic texts than any other. There is a time when peace is the message of God; but it will always be in Exodus terms, that peace can come only when holiness is satisfied concerning sin. And this is exactly what Jeremiah is urging: the voice of the true prophet is always the voice of the law of God, once for all declared through Moses. Thus Jeremiah is bold to say that the false prophets are men of borrowed testimony, feigned authority, and self-appointed ministry (verses 30–32), whereas the true prophet has stood in the counsel of Yahweh, and heard His voice, and has been sent by Him (verses 18, 21, 22, 28, 32). Jeremiah's final position is in fact that 'certainty is certainty', but he is rescued from tautology by the positive revelation of God. He knows he is right because his experience is the Mosaic experience of standing before God (*cf.* Nu. xii. 6–8; Dt. xxxiv. 10).

The answer of Ezekiel is substantially that of Jeremiah, and is found in Ezk. xii. 21–xiv. 11. Ezekiel tells us that there are prophets who are guided by their own wisdom and have no word from Yahweh (xiii. 2, 3). Thus they make people trust in lies and leave them without resource in the day of trial (xiii. 4–7). The mark of these prophets is their message: it is one of peace and shallow optimism (xiii. 10–16), and it is devoid of moral content, grieving the righteous, and encouraging the wicked (verse 22). By contrast, there is a prophet who insists on piercing to the core of the matter, answering folk not according to their ostensible queries but according to their sinful hearts (xiv. 4, 5), for the word of Yahweh is always a word against sin (xiv. 7, 8). We see again that the true prophet is the Mosaic prophet. It is not just that in a vague sense he has a direct experience of God, but that he has been commissioned by the God of the Exodus to reiterate once again to Israel the moral requirements of the covenant.

IV. THE PROPHETS IN THE RELIGION OF ISRAEL

a. Cultic prophets

Prophecy in a cultic setting is found in 2 Ch. xx. 14. In a time of national anxiety King Jehoshaphat has led his people in public prayer in the court of the Lord's house. Immediately upon the conclusion of the prayer, a Levite, inspired by the Spirit of God, brings a word from the Lord promising victory. Here, then, is a Levite, that is, a cultic official, with a prophetic capacity. A further indication of the same happening is said to occur in some psalms (*e.g.* lx, lxxv, lxxxii, *etc.*). In all these psalms there is a section in which a first person singular voice speaks: this is the oracular response, the prophet associated with the cult, bringing the contemporary utterance of God to His people. The suggestion made is that the guilds of levitical singers in the post-exilic period are the survival of groups of cultic prophets attached to the various sanctuaries in pre-exilic times. At every sanctuary, working alongside the priests, who had charge of the sacrificial aspect of the worship, there were prophets who declared the word of God publicly for the nation or privately for individual guidance.

The evidence for this practice, known, of course, in Canaanite circles, is largely inferential: we first meet a prophetic guild at the high place at Gibeah (1 Sa. x. 5); Samuel the prophet was an official at Shiloh (1 Sa. iii. 19), and presided at a cultic meal at Ramah (1 Sa. ix. 12 ff.); the prophet Gad commanded David to erect the altar in Araunah's threshing-floor (2 Sa. xxiv. 11, 18), and revealed God's will concerning the guilds of temple singers (2 Ch. xxix. 25); the prophet Nathan was consulted about the building of the Temple (2 Sa. vii. 1 ff.); Elijah staged a cultic scene at an ancient shrine (1 Ki. xviii.

30 ff.); it was customary to visit the prophet on cultic occasions (2 Ki. iv. 23); there are numerous references in which prophet and priest are coupled together in a way suggesting professional association (2 Ki. xxiii. 2; Is. xxviii. 7; Je. ii. 26, viii. 10, xiii. 13, *etc.*); there were prophetic quarters within the Temple (Je. xxxv. 4).

It is difficult to see how any theory could be stable when it rests on such slight foundation. For example, the apparently strong connection established between prophet and Temple by the allocation of quarters, in Je. xxxv. 4, is utterly negatived by the fact that the same verse speaks of chambers allocated to the princes. Again, the fact that prophets and guilds are found at cultic centres need mean nothing more than that they too were religious people! Amos was found at the sanctuary of Bethel (vii. 13), but this does not prove that he was paid to be there. David's consultation of his prophets tells us more about David's good sense than about his prophets' cultic associations. The theory of the cultic prophet remains a theory.

b. The prophets and the cultus

Even if the theory of the cultic prophet could be proved, it would still leave unsettled the relation of the canonical, or writing, prophet to the cultus. Their view of the cultus is somewhat of a crux of interpretation, and centres round six brief passages which are supposed by some to contain an outright condemnation of all cultic worship and a denial that it was ever the will of God. The verses in question are Am. v. 21–25; Ho. vi. 6; Is. i. 11–15, xliii. 22–24; Mi. vi. 6–8; Je. vii. 21–23.

We may remark at once what a small number of verses is involved. If the prophets were so opposed to the cultus as some commentators have urged, it is extraordinary that their opposition was so rarely voiced, and then in such a manner as to leave it open to doubt whether they intended to condemn the cultus as such or the cultus as then abused. Furthermore, in other parts of their writings some of these prophets do not seem to take such a strong line about ceremonial and sacrifice. For example, Ho. viii. 13 mentions the 'sacrifices of mine offerings', a strange utterance for the God in whose name Hosea is supposed to be rejecting all cultic worship. Again, Isaiah, in his inaugural vision, certainly met with God and with peace of heart in a cultic setting. Are we to believe that he thought the cultus was worth nothing? Or again, Jeremiah, in chapter vii, the chapter from which the proof text is drawn, does not condemn people for offering cultic worship (verses 9, 10) because Yahweh has forbidden it but because they couple it with moral indifference and iniquity; in verse 11 the Temple is 'this house, which is called by my name' and in verse 12, Shiloh is 'my place', which, incidentally, was destroyed, not to manifest divine rejection of the cultus but because of the iniquity of the worshippers. This all suggests, what detailed study of the verses will also indicate, that the anger of the prophets is directed against the cultus abused.

The heart of the exegetical problem in Am. v. 21–25 is in the last verse: 'Have ye offered unto me sacrifices and offerings in the wilderness forty years . . .?' In order to support the theory that Amos is a root-and-branch opponent of sacrifice, we must see him confidently expecting the answer 'No' to this question. But this is exactly what he could not have done. On any view of the origin of the Pentateuch, the traditions current in Amos' day would have spoken of sacrifice in the time of Moses, and of the Patriarchs before him. Verses 21–23 tell of God's spurning of their current cultic practice. Verse 24 tells us what is missing: a moral concern, a holy life. Verse 25 is intended to enforce the truth that these things are not an 'either/or' but are the inseparable sides of religion according to the will of God. If we translate verse 25 so as to bring out the emphasis of the prophet, we read: 'Was it sacrifices and offerings ye brought to me in the wilderness forty years . . .?' If they trace their religion back to its root in revelation, what do they find but a divine requirement of sacrifice in the context of a life obedient to the law of God? Because of their failure to follow this pattern (verses 26 f.) they will go into captivity. Mere *opus operatum* ritual is not worship of the God of the Bible.

According to Pr. viii. 10, we are to 'Receive my instruction, and not silver; and knowledge rather than choice gold.' Clearly this is a statement of priorities, not an exclusion of one thing in favour of the other. The importance of this verse is that its Hebrew is exactly parallel in construction to that of Ho. vi. 6. In the light therefore of Hosea's failure to maintain an attitude of rejection towards the cultus throughout the rest of his prophecy we may hold that he intends here a statement of priorities such as was given classical expression by Samuel: 'To obey is better than sacrifice' (1 Sa. xv. 22).

The difficulty with the passage in Isaiah i is that it proves a great deal too much if it is taken simply as outright condemnation. Certainly verses 11, 12 appear to be a very strong attack on sacrifice, but no stronger than the attack upon the sabbath in verse 13, and upon prayer in verse 15. It cannot be that the prophet is utterly repudiating the sabbath and prayer. It must be that the final clause of verse 15, while referring directly to the earlier part of the verse, refers also to all the preceding condemnations. The prophet is simply urging that no religious activity avails in the context of a blatantly sinful life. This interpretation is proved to be correct by the initial verbs of verse 16, the first of which is constantly used throughout the levitical code for ceremonial purification, a very unlikely verb for the prophet to use if he considered all such things contrary to God's will; the second verb applies to moral purgation. The prophet's message is thus the Bible's message: the message of the joint requirement of the moral and ceremonial law.

We notice next Mi. vi. 6–8. We have a somewhat analogous situation in the words of our Lord to the rich young ruler (Mk. x. 17 ff.). By His exclusive reply in terms of the moral law does He intend to deny the divine authority of the ceremonial law of atoning sacrifice? In view of His constant regard for the Mosaic legislation (*e.g.* Mt. viii. 4), not to mention His authentication of the terms of Old Testament sacrifice by His teaching concerning His own death (Mk. xiv. 24), this is an unlikely interpretation of the words. Or again, we might ask if Lv. xviii. 5, presenting the moral law as a way of life, intends to invalidate the ceremonial law. Likewise, in the case of Micah, we must not understand him to reject whatever he does not specifically approve.

We have already noted certain background facts relative to the study of Je. vii. 21–23. If Jeremiah, in the immediate context, seems, at the least, not to condemn sacrifice as *per se* unacceptable, may we so interpret vii. 22? The difficulty is that, on the face of it, the words seem to require us to do so. However, closer examination of the Hebrew suggests that the difficulty belongs more to the English translation than to the original. The preposition which the English gives as 'concerning'—the vital word in the whole verse—is the Hebrew *'al-diḇrê*, which can only mean 'concerning' by a radical weakening of its real significance 'because of' or 'for the sake of' (*cf.* Gn. xx. 11, xliii. 18; Ps. vii, title; Je. xiv. 1; *etc.*). According to this, the verse says that Yahweh did not address Israel either 'because of' sacrifices: that is to say, the performance of sacrifice is not a means whereby pressure may be applied to God; nor did He address them 'for the sake of' sacrifices, for the living God stands in no need of anything man can supply. The nation has missed the divine priority by its concentration on the mere operation of a cult, for the cult is not a thing which exists on its own but rather for the sake of the spiritual needs of a people committed to obedience to the moral law of God.

We may allude finally to Is. xliii. 22 ff., which is, in many ways, the most difficult verse of all. The emphasis in verse 22 requires the translation, 'Not me hast thou called . . .' On the supposition that this sets the tone of address throughout the verses, we are clearly within the same circle of possibilities: either, there is an indignant repudiation of the whole idea of divine authorization of sacrifice: 'whoever you may think you appeal to in your cultus, it is not I, for I did not burden you with offerings'; or the accusation is that they abused the divine intention: 'in all your cultic labour you have not really called upon Me, for it was never My plan that the cultus should turn you into slave-labour of ritual'. These alternatives of interpretation are so clear in the text that we may simply ask whether there are any other evidences whereby we might decide between them. The general consent of Scripture points to the second suggestion. Since there is no need to interpret the other crucial verses as an outright denial of sacrifice, we ought to reject that meaning here also. Moreover, within Isaiah, we have to reckon with xliv. 28, clearly approving the rebuilding of the Temple: for Isaiah to repudiate sacrifice and yet rejoice in the Temple would involve a complete contradiction in terms. There is also the inescapably sacrificial language of Isaiah liii.

c. The unity of Israel's religion

The religion of Israel began, as to its normative form, with the prophet-priest Moses, and it continued as a religion jointly of prophet and priest. This is declared in the covenant ceremony in Ex. xxiv. 4–8. Yahweh has redeemed His people according to promise and they have acquiesced in the law He has imposed upon them as His redeemed people. Moses expressed the relationship symbolically: twelve pillars grouped round an altar (xxiv. 4). Here is the visual expression of the fulfilment of the covenant promise: 'I will take you to me for a people, and I will be to you a God' (Ex. vi. 7). Notably, God is represented as an altar, for the holy God—the primary revelation of God to Moses (Ex. iii. 5)—can dwell among sinners only by virtue of the atoning blood. Hence, the first thing Moses does with the blood is to sprinkle it upon the altar. As at the Passover, the initial movement of the blood is towards God in propitiation (Ex. xii. 13).

The ceremony proceeds with the people's self-dedication to obedience to the law, and then the blood is sprinkled upon them. It is thus declared that while the people are brought to God by means of the blood of propitiation, the people themselves need the blood also in the context of their obligation to keep God's holy law. This, then, is the unity of prophet and priest: the former calls continually to obedience, the latter reminds constantly of the efficacy of the blood. If we drive them asunder the former becomes a moralist and the latter a ritualist; if we keep them together, as the religion of Israel does, and as the Bible does, we see the whole wonder of the God whom prophet and priest—and apostle too—proclaimed: a just God, and a Saviour, who will never relax His demand that His people walk in the light and be holy as He is holy, and who sets alongside that inflexible demand the blood which cleanses from all sin.

V. PROPHETS IN THE NEW TESTAMENT

a. The authentication of the Old Testament prophets

Prophecy and the prophets form the greatest link of continuity between the Old and New Testaments. The prophetic line did not end with Malachi, so to speak, but with John the Baptist. This is the express teaching of our Lord: 'For all the prophets and the law prophesied until John . . .' (Mt. xi. 13). The customary division into two 'Testaments' unfortunately obscures this marvellous unity of God's programme of revelation, but the line is continuous from Mo-to John. We see in John, as indeed in his father, Zacharias (Lk. i. 67–79), the pattern of Old Testament prophecy repeated: the unity of proclamation and prediction. It was the prediction of wrath to come (Lk. iii. 7) and of grace to come (Lk. iii. 16; Jn. i. 29 ff.) that gave John such a potent message for his generation.

Furthermore, the New Testament stands in a relation of fulfilment to the actual message of the Old Testament prophets. Time and again this is the burden of the New Testament: what God said of old He has now brought to pass (Mt. i. 22, xxvi. 56; Lk. xxiv. 25, 27, 44; Acts x. 43, *etc.*). The importance of this feature of the New Testament in authentication of the Old Testament can hardly be over-emphasized. The prophets can never be men of mere antiquarian attraction for us. Though a persecuted minority (Mt. v. 12, xxiii. 29–37; Lk. vi. 23, *etc.*), they are the most important voice coming to us from the ancient past, for they are not mere dreamers or idle speculators. They are raised to the level of proclaimers of eternal truth by the verification of their greatest words in the greatest of all events, the person and work of Christ.

We can state the matter more completely. The Lord Jesus Christ Himself points us back to the prophets and their message as a permanent revelation of God. They stand in the relation of authorized teachers of the Christian Church, men whose words are still to be heeded as the word of God. For God has set His seal to their message, both by the fact of fulfilment and by the positive teaching of His Son (Mt. v. 17, *etc.*).

b. Prophets in the Christian Church

Every Christian is potentially a prophet. The pouring out of the Spirit on all flesh carries with it this result, 'and they shall prophesy' (Acts ii. 18). Paul called upon the Corinthian Christians to 'desire earnestly spiritual gifts, but rather that ye may prophesy' (1 Cor. xiv. 1, RV). We see this actually happening in the case of the Ephesians in Acts xix. 6, in the daughters of Philip (Acts xxi. 9), and in the men and women of the Corinthian Church (1 Cor. xi. 4, 5).

However, there seem to have been, in the New Testament Church, also a special group known as 'prophets' set apart for the ministry of prophecy. They are mentioned next after apostles in the lists of ministries (1 Cor. xii. 28, 29; Eph. iv. 11); they are associated with teachers in the church at Antioch (Acts xiii. 1), the two senior grades of ministry under the apostles. As we meet them in Acts and Epistles, their function was the customary double prophetic ministry of proclamation and prediction. Agabus, one of the few prophets named for us, is noted for prediction (Acts xi. 28, xxi. 10, 11), making use of this power of foresight to issue spiritual guidance to the Church. The whole book of Revelation is the most outstanding example in the Bible of foretelling harnessed to the task of forthtelling. In their capacity as preachers to the Church, their work is described as exhortation (Acts xv. 32), edification, and consolation (1 Cor. xiv. 3). The reaction of the non-Christian to the ministry of the prophets (1 Cor. xiv. 24, 25) shows that they were preachers of the whole message of sin and salvation, wrath and grace.

In the context of the church meeting (1 Cor. xiv. 26 ff.) the ministry of the prophet is spoken of as revelation (verse 30). This could take the form of spontaneous utterance, and is associated with the activity of the Spirit of God (*cf.* 1 Thes. v. 19). This prophetic activity is not the same as speaking with tongues (see 1 Cor. xiv. 22–25, 27–29), nor is it the interpretation of tongues. It is some perception of the truth of God intelligibly made to the assembly. It was an abuse of prophecy to pretend to an ecstatic frenzy so that the prophets became, as it were, out of hand. Paul insists that 'the spirits of the prophets are subject to the prophets', that is to say, each is in full possession of his faculties and is able to restrain the impulse to speak if the interests of order so require (verses 32, 33). Most important of all, the prophets were not to be given undiscerning credence.

Two tests were applied to any prophetic utterance: first, there was the test of the experience of other prophets present. The apostle says, 'let the others discern' (verse 29, RV), that is, let them subject the utterance which is being made to their knowledge of God and His truth. Secondly, there is the over-all test of the apostolic deposit. The test of the true prophet, or any man who lays claim to spirituality, is that he takes 'knowledge of the things which I write unto you, that they are the commandment of the Lord', for apart from this there is nothing but ignorance (verses 37, 38, RV). This teaches us that the prophets were not sources of new truth to the Church, but expounders of truth otherwise revealed. Just as the Old Testament prophet stood in a subordinate relation to Moses, who provided the doctrinal norm of sound teaching, so the New Testament prophet stood towards the apostles, and was bound to submit all to the test of that which they declared as the word of God. It is in this sense that the apostle urged the Church of his day, and would urge us also, to desire earnestly to prophesy: not to desire the notoriety of doctrinal innovators, but to contend earnestly for the truth once for all delivered to the saints.

BIBLIOGRAPHY. H. H. Rowley, *The Servant of the Lord*, 1952, chapter 3; *id., The Unity of the Bible*, 1953, chapters 2, 4; *id.* (ed.), *Studies in Old Testament Prophecy*, 1950; *id.* (ed.), *The Old Testament and Modern Study*, 1951, chapters 5, 6; H. W. Robinson, *Inspiration and Revelation in the Old Testament*, 1946, Parts III and IV; A. R. Johnson, *The Cultic Prophet in Ancient Israel*, 1944; A. B. Davidson, *Old Testament Prophecy*, 1904; C. Kuhl, *The Prophets of Israel*, 1960; S. H. Hooke (ed.), *Myth, Ritual, and Kingship*, 1958, chapter 8; E. J. Young, *My Servants the Prophets*, 1955; A. Lods, *Israel*, 1932; *id., The Prophets and the Rise of Judaism*, 1937; A. F. Kirkpatrick, *The Doctrine of the Prophets*, 1897;

W. R. Smith, *The Prophets of Israel*, 1882; T. H. Robinson, *Prophecy and the Prophets in Ancient Israel*, 1923; J. Skinner, *Prophecy and Religion*, 1926; A. Guillaume, *Prophecy and Divination*, 1938; M. Noth, 'History and the Word of God in the Old Testament', *BJRL*, XXXII, 1949–50, pp. 194 ff.; O. T. Allis, *The Unity of Isaiah*, 1950, chapters 1 and 2; H. L. Ellison, *Men Spake from God*, 1952; S. H. Blank, *Of a Truth the Lord hath sent me*, 1955; J. G. S. S. Thomson, *The Word of the Lord in Jeremiah*, 1959; Y. Kaufmann, *The Religion of Israel*, 1961, Part III. J.A.M.

PROPHETESS (Heb. *nᵉḇî'â*; Gk. *prophētis*). Throughout both Testaments 'prophetess' is used in as wide a sense of women as 'prophet' is of men.

Prophetesses specifically named are Miriam, sister of Moses, who led a choral dance in celebration of Israel's deliverance from Egypt (Ex. xv. 20), Deborah, wife of Lappidoth, 'a mother in Israel' (Jdg. v. 7), who was consulted as an intertribal judge (Jdg. iv. 4), Huldah, wife of the keeper of the royal wardrobe, who declared the divine will to Josiah after the discovery of the law-book (2 Ki. xxii. 14), Noadiah, who joined other prophets in attempting to intimidate Nehemiah (Ne. vi. 14), and Anna, who praised God in the Temple at the appearance of the infant Christ (Lk. ii. 36 ff.).

Isaiah's wife is called 'the prophetess' (Is. viii. 3), perhaps because she was a prophet's wife. Philip's four unnamed daughters prophesied in Caesarea (Acts xxi. 9). In the early Church, as Paul's Corinthian correspondence indicates, the gift of prophecy was exercised by various Christians irrespective of sex (*cf.* 1 Cor. xi. 4 f.). This was in accordance with the prediction of Joel ii. 28 ('your sons and your daughters shall prophesy'), fulfilled on the day of Pentecost (Acts ii. 16 ff.).

There were false prophetesses as well as false prophets in Israel (*cf.* Ezk. xiii. 17). In the New Testament unenviable notoriety is attained by 'that woman Jezebel, which calleth herself a prophetess' (Rev. ii. 20). See PROPHECY, PROPHETS. M.G.

PROPITIATION. Propitiation properly signifies the removal of wrath by the offering of a gift. In the Old Testament it is expressed by the verb *kipper* (see ATONEMENT). In the New Testament the *hilaskomai* word group is the important one. In modern times the whole idea of propitiation has been strongly criticized as savouring of unworthy ideas of God. Many suggest that the term 'propitiation' should be abandoned in favour of expiation (*q.v.*).

The objection to propitiation arises largely from an objection to the whole idea of the wrath of God, which many exponents of this view relegate to the status of an archaism. They feel that modern men cannot hold such an idea. But the men of the Old Testament had no such inhibitions. For them 'God is angry with the wicked every day' (Ps. vii. 11). They had no doubt that sin inevitably arouses the strongest reaction from God. God is not to be accused of moral flabbiness. He is vigorously opposed to evil in every shape and form. While He may be 'slow to anger' (Ne. ix. 17, *etc.*) His anger is yet certain in the face of sin. We may even read 'The Lord is longsuffering, and of great mercy, forgiving iniquity and transgression, and by no means clearing the guilty' (Nu. xiv. 18). Even in a passage dealing with the longsuffering of God His refusal to condone guilt finds mention. The thought that God is slow to anger is to men of the Old Testament far from being a truism. It is something wonderful and surprising. It is awe-inspiring and totally unexpected.

But if they were sure of the wrath of God against all sin, they were equally sure that this wrath might be put away, usually by the offering of the appropriate sacrifice. This was ultimately due, not to any efficacy in the sacrifice, but to God Himself. God says, 'I have given it to you upon the altar to make an atonement for your souls' (Lv. xvii. 11). Pardon is not something wrung from an unwilling deity. It is the gracious gift of a God who is eager to forgive. So the psalmist can say, 'He, being full of compassion, forgave their iniquity, and destroyed them not: yea, many a time turned he his anger away, and did not stir up all his wrath' (Ps. lxxviii. 38). The averting of the wrath of God is not something which men bring about. It is due to none less than God Himself. It is He who 'turned his anger away'.

In the New Testament there are several passages where the expression 'the wrath of God' occurs, but the relevant evidence is not limited to these alone. Everywhere in the New Testament there is the thought that God is vigorously opposed to evil. The sinner is in no good case. He has put himself in the wrong with God. He can look for nothing other than the severity of the divine judgment. Whether we choose to call this 'the wrath of God' or not, it is there. And, while wrath is a term to which some objections may legitimately be raised, it is the biblical term and no satisfactory substitute has been suggested.

We see the force of the New Testament idea of propitiation from the occurrence of the term in Rom. iii. 24 f. We are 'justified freely by his grace through the redemption that is in Christ Jesus: whom God hath set forth to be a propitiation through faith in his blood'. The force of Paul's argument up to this point is that all, Jew and Gentile alike, are under the condemnation of God. 'The wrath of God is revealed from heaven against all ungodliness and unrighteousness of men' (Rom. i. 18). Paul shows first that the Gentile world stands under God's condemnation and then that the Jewish world is in the same plight. It is against this background that he sees the work of Christ. Christ did not save men from nothing at all. He delivered them from a very real peril. The sentence of judgment had been passed against them. The wrath of God hung over them.

Paul has strongly emphasized the wrath of God throughout these opening chapters, and therefore Christ's saving work must include deliverance from this wrath. This deliverance is described by the word 'propitiation'. There is nothing else to express this thought in the critical passage Rom. iii. 21 ff., which sets out the way in which God has dealt with this aspect of man's plight. *Hilastērion* must be held here to signify something very like 'propitiation'. See further *NTS*, II, 1955–6, pp. 33–43.

In 1 Jn. ii. 2 Jesus is described as 'the propitiation for our sins'. In the previous verse He is our 'advocate with the Father'. If we need an advocate with God, then our position is indeed a dangerous one. We are in dire peril. All this helps us to see that 'propitiation' is to be taken here in its usual sense. The writer is describing Jesus' activity for men as one of turning away the divine wrath.

But the Bible view of propitiation does not depend on this or that specific passage. It is a reflection of the general import of its teaching. 'Propitiation' is a reminder that God is implacably opposed to everything that is evil, that His opposition may properly be described as 'wrath', and that this wrath is put away only by the atoning work of Christ.

BIBLIOGRAPHY. C. H. Dodd, *The Bible and the Greeks*, 1935; R. Nicole, *WTJ*, XVII, 1954–5, pp. 117–157; Leon Morris, *NTS*, 1955–6, II, pp. 33–43; *id.*, *The Apostolic Preaching of the Cross*, 1955.

L.M.

PROSELYTE. In assessing the Old Testament view of proselytes, it is necessary to look beyond terminology to the concept. The Hebrew word *gēr* undoubtedly meant at first a resident alien, who might profess no religious affiliation whatever—the same word is used freely for Israelites dwelling outside their own land (*cf.* Gn. xv. 13; Ex. xxiii. 9). Afterwards *gēr* came to mean full proselyte, but whether within the Old Testament canon or at a later date is a matter of dispute. The term *tôšāḇ* has the same civil restriction as the earlier usage of *gēr*, but with a lesser implication of permanence. The LXX renders the common *gēr* about a dozen times by *paroikos*, 'neighbour' —a word which cannot mean religious proselyte —occasionally by some other term, and over seventy times by *prosēlytos*. Here the Greek language reflected sympathetically the conceptual development of the Hebrew one, though transition details are once again in controversy.

Several passages in the Old Testament would suggest something of the warmth of the later meaning. There is a remarkable spirit of charity in Lv. xix. 34 and parallels, a willingness to receive foreigners into religious fellowship on the condition of circumcision (Ex. xii. 48), or even without this (Nu. xv. 14–16)—a recognition of one law for the miscreant Israelite and foreigner (Nu. xv. 30). The alien is also enjoined to observe the sabbath in Jewish company (Ex. xx. 10, *etc.*). The most important teachings do not use the term. Vastly more impressive than anything above are the generous prayers of 1 Ki. viii. 41–43, and the glowing universalism of Is. ii. 2–4, xlix. 6, lvi. 3–8; Je. iii. 17; Zp. iii. 9. The whole book of Ruth is the story of a particular lady proselyte whose memory later Judaism greatly honoured.

Political and geographical circumstances may have kept the number of converts relatively small in Old Testament times. Such persons would normally be aliens resident in Palestine, voluntarily accepting circumcision, and with it the whole burden of the law. Yet Is. xix. 18–25 and Zp. ii. 11 undoubtedly think in terms singularly unfettered by tradition and prejudice. If certain strains of later Judaism were unwilling to receive proselytes, they could find no valid excuse in the Old Testament.

In the period of the Graeco-Roman Dispersion, proselytes became numerous. Despite the Gentile abhorrence of circumcision, sabbaths, and abstention from pork, Jewish morality and monotheism appealed to some. Certain converts underwent instruction, circumcision, and baptism, and then offered sacrifice in the Temple. None could go farther than that. Others admired Judaism, but could not wholly meet its requirements. They worshipped and studied in the synagogue, but remained uncircumcised, rather like Christian adherents who are not communicants. Many scholars have dubbed these 'half-proselytes', and debated as to whether they are the 'God-fearers' of contemporary literature. Lake's epigrammatic remark that 'fractional proselytes are impossible' pinpoints a cardinal truth, but in a slightly arbitrary manner—some name must be found for this class that undoubtedly existed. Why not call them uncircumcised sympathizers? (Philo, Josephus, and many other writers, ancient and modern, might be further consulted.)

In the rabbinic literature, the term *gēr* unquestionably means a full proselyte. A resident alien is a *gēr tôšāḇ* in the Mishnah; later, in mediaeval literature, a 'proselyte of the gate'. A convert through fear is contemptuously called a 'lion proselyte', in reference to 2 Ki. xvii. 25 ff. In the eighth chapter of Midrash Rabbah on Numbers, in the passages cited in the *Rabbinic Anthology*, and in innumerable contexts throughout the literature, it is insisted that the privileges of the proselyte should be equal to, if not greater than, those of the Jew by birth, and that he should be the special object of human and divine love.

Many Rabbis, however, had very different views. The Babylonian Talmud insists in one context that the proselyte has a strong predisposition to sin, because of his evil background (*Bāḇā' Meṣî'ā'* 59b). Surely the potentiality of a real conversion should be admitted in generosity. In deprecating the admission of proselytes to Judaism, the same Talmud elsewhere likens them to a sore on the skin of Israel (*Yeḇāmôṯ* 109b)—an ugly sentiment, whatever its political pretext. It is unlikely that the proselyte ever attained in practice a real, as distinct from his theoretical, equality with his Jewish-born brethren, even though Scripture and the best rabbinic teachings ordained that he should. Exclusiveness has been typical of Judaism throughout its history, though much of this is the fruit of suffering. The Old Testament rebukes this spirit in many places, especially in the book of Jonah.

By New Testament times there must have been a steady stream of proselytes into the Jewish fold, as the book of Acts confirms (ii. 10, vi. 5, xiii. 43). The more precise determination of its extent lies beyond the scope of this article. *Diaspora* Judaism was considerably more hospitable to the proselyte and honest inquirer than was the more narrow, legalistic, and traditional cult of Palestine and Babylonia. There must have been a vastly greater number of those uncircumcised sympathizers from which the infant Church was largely recruited. To some who were deterred by circumcision, the cross proved no stumbling-block. World history was trembling in the balance while Paul and his Judaistic colleagues argued over the circumcision controversy. Had this been made the necessary condition of Christian conversion, candidates might have been few, and world history would have been very different.

There has been much controversy as to why Jesus should have used the words of Mt. xxiii. 15 when the scribes and Pharisees were so notoriously indifferent to proselytization. The 'one' might refer to their meagre returns, or the verse could point to a particular historical incident, when four leading Rabbis attempted to secure a distinguished Roman convert (so Grätz, cited *JewE*).

BIBLIOGRAPHY. F. J. Foakes-Jackson and K. Lake, *The Beginnings of Christianity*, V, 1933, pp. 80–84; E. Schürer, *History of the Jewish People* . . ., 1901, II (ii), pp. 291–337; R. A. Stewart, *Rabbinic Theology*, 1961, see Index.

R.A.S.

PROSTITUTION. This evil was known from Israel's early days (Gn. xxxviii. 15; Jdg. xi. 1); and found in Canaan (Jos. ii. 1); Philistia (Jdg. xvi. 1); and in other lands (Pr. ii. 16, xxix. 3): the last two references relating to foreigners. The law of Moses forbids a father to prostitute his daughter (Lv. xix. 29). A priest must not marry a prostitute (Lv. xxi. 7), especially a high priest (Lv. xxi. 14). The penalty for prostitution, in the case of the daughter of a priest, was death by fire (Lv. xxi. 9); in other cases stoning (Dt. xxii. 21: *cf.* Jn. viii. 5). The pecuniary gains from this illicit practice were banned from the temple revenues (Dt. xxiii. 17, 18); and the destruction of the Canaanites was said to be partly due to their immoral habits (Lv. xx. 23).

The worst form of prostitution was that which was given a religious sanction. This was a prominent feature in Canaanitish worship, both male and female prostitutes being attached to the sanctuaries and shrines. The female class is known in the Old Testament as the *qᵉḏēšâ* and the male as *qāḏēš*. The illicit gains of the latter are called 'the wages of a dog' (Dt. xxiii. 18). Among the Ugaritic Tablets a male class is referred to as *qdšm* along with the priests (*khnm*), as temple personnel (*Ugar. tabs.* 63. 3; 81. 2; 113.73 *et al.*). These may be the Canaanite 'sodomites' of the Old Testament, but this is not certain (see A. van Selms, *Marriage and Family Life in Ugaritic Literature*, 1954, pp. 80 f.).

In the thought of the Old Testament prophets harlotry and national apostasy were closely associated (Is. i. 21; Je. xiii. 27; Ezk. xvi. 16; Ho. i. 2; *et al.*), the one leading to the other. So the Old Testament speaks of 'going a-whoring after other gods'.

In the New Testament our Lord rebukes Pharisaical censoriousness towards sexual immorality (Jn. viii. 7; Mt. xxi. 31 f.; Lk. vii. 37–50). Paul had to combat sexual immorality in the church at Corinth (1 Cor. v. 1 ff., vi. 15, 16). The early Church made a solemn pronouncement against it (Acts xv. 20, 29, where, however, *porneia* may have the semi-technical sense of unions within forbidden degrees, as in Mt. v. 32, xix. 9; 1 Cor. v. 1). In Rev. xvii the term 'the great harlot' denotes the city of Rome as a power inimical to God and His people (*cf.* the description of Nineveh as 'the wellfavoured harlot' in Na. iii. 4).

R.J.A.S.

PROVERB. In AV the word 'proverb' has a wider range of meanings than in normal English usage, due especially to the many meanings of *māšāl* (probably related to *mšl*, 'to be like', 'to be compared with', although some relate it to *mšl*, 'to rule'; hence a word spoken by a ruler). In addition to denoting 'a pithy saying, especially one condensing the wisdom of experience' (*cf.* 1 Sa. x. 12, xxiv. 13; 1 Ki. iv. 32; Pr. i. 1, 6, x. 1, xxv. 1; Ec. xii. 9; Ezk. xii. 22, 23, xvi. 44, xviii. 2, 3), 'proverb' may also serve as a synonym for 'byword' (*e.g.* Dt. xxviii. 37; 1 Ki. ix. 7; 2 Ch. vii. 20; Ps. lxix. 11; Je. xxiv. 9; Ezk. xiv. 8). The point seems to be that the sufferer becomes an object-lesson from which others may learn appropriate lessons. Similarly, 'proverb' may mean 'taunt-song' as in Is. xiv. 4 ff., where the disastrous effects of the king of Babylon's presumptuous pride are paraded. In Hab. ii. 6 'proverb' translates *ḥîḏâ*, 'riddle', 'perplexing question'.

Two words are rendered 'proverb' in the New Testament: *parabolē* (Lk. iv. 23) and *paroimia* (Jn. xvi. 25, 29; 2 Pet. ii. 22). In the Johannine passages *paroimia* apparently denotes a 'dark saying' or 'figure of speech in which . . . lofty ideas are concealed' (*Arndt*). The didactic rôle of proverbs in both Testaments should not be underestimated. Along with parables, proverbs played a major part in the teaching ministry of Christ (*e.g.* Mt. vi. 21; Lk. iv. 23; Jn. xii. 24). See WISDOM LITERATURE, PARABLE.

BIBLIOGRAPHY. A. R. Johnson, 'Mashal' in *Wisdom in Israel and in the Ancient Near East*, ed. M. Noth and D. W. Thomas, 1955.

D.A.H.

PROVERBS, BOOK OF. The Hebrew title *mišlê*, 'proverbs of', is an abbreviation of *mišlê šelōmōh*, 'the proverbs of Solomon', i. 1. The English name is derived from the Vulg. *Liber Proverbiorum*. A collection of collections, Proverbs is a guidebook for successful living. Without overtly stressing the great prophetic themes (*e.g.* the covenant), the proverbs show how Israel's distinctive faith affected her common life.

I. OUTLINE OF CONTENTS

a. The importance of wisdom (i. 1–ix. 18)

Following an introductory statement of purpose (i. 1–6), the writer instructs his son or pupil concerning the worth and nature of wisdom. In contrast to the proverbs of x. 1 ff., each idea is discussed at some length in a didactic poem. These poetic essays are a highly polished development of the *māšāl* (see PROVERB, WISDOM LITERATURE).

The author's aim is to paint the strongest possible contrast between the results of seeking wisdom and living a life of folly. He sets the stage for the several hundred specific proverbs which follow. Certain temptations loom large in the sage's mind: crimes of violence (i. 10–19, iv. 14–19); the binding of oneself by a rash pledge (vi. 1–5); sloth (vi. 6–11); duplicity (vi. 12–15); and especially sexual impurity (ii. 16–19, v. 3–20, vi. 23–35, vii. 4–27, ix. 13–18). To the one who avoids these snares, Wisdom (*q.v.*) offers happiness, long life, wealth, and honour (iii. 13–18). The deeply religious nature of this section (*e.g.* i. 7, iii. 5–12), its sensitive moral tone, and its hortatory, didactic style are reminiscent of Deuteronomy.

Apparently the writer of these chapters is anonymous, since i. 1–6 probably refers to the entire book and x. 1 introduces a collection of proverbs which purport to be Solomonic. This section is customarily dated among the latest in the collection. Though its final editing may be relatively late (*c.* 600 BC), much of the material may be considerably earlier. W. F. Albright has drawn attention to the number of parallels in thought and structure between this section, especially viii, ix, and Ugaritic or Phoenician literature (*Wisdom in Israel*, pp. 7–9). He also suggests that 'it is entirely possible that aphorisms and even longer sections go back into the Bronze Age in substantially their present form' (p. 5). For the personification of Wisdom in viii. 22 ff., see WISDOM.

b. The proverbs of Solomon (x. 1–xxii. 16)

This section is probably the oldest in the book, and there is a growing tendency among scholars to accept the accuracy of the tradition reflected in 1 Ki. iv. 29 ff.; Pr. i. 1, x. i, xxv. 1 honouring Solomon as the sage *par excellence*. His contacts with the court of Egypt, the far-reaching network of his empire (see SOLOMON), and the combination of wealth and respite from war enabled him to devote himself to cultural pursuits on a scale denied his successors.

About 375 proverbs occur in this collection. Their structure is largely *antithetic* in x–xv and *synthetic* or *synonymous* in xvi–xxii. Most of the proverbs are unrelated; no system of grouping is discernible.

Though a religious note is by no means absent (*cf.* xv. 3, 8, 9, 11, xvi. 1–9, *etc.*), the bulk of the proverbs contain no specific reference to Israel's faith but are based on practical observations of everyday life. The extremely practical nature of the instruction which stresses the *profits* of wisdom has drawn the criticism of those who hold that pure religion should be disinterested. But how would a practical sage to whom God had not yet revealed the mystery of life after death make the issues clear without pointing out the blessings of the wise and the pitfalls of the fool?

c. The words of the wise (xxii. 17–xxiv. 22)

The title is obscured in *MT* and EVV, being incorporated in xxii. 17. However, the obvious title 'These also are sayings of the wise' (RSV, xxiv. 23) suggests that xxii. 17–xxiv. 22 should be considered a separate collection. These maxims are more closely related and sustained in theme than those of the previous section. The topics are manifold: regard for the poor (xxii. 22, 27), respect for the king (xxiii. 1–3, xxiv. 21, 22), discipline of children (xxiii. 13, 14), temperance (xxiii. 19–21, 29–35), honour of parents (xxiii. 22–25), chastity (xxiii. 26–28), *etc.* Religious emphasis, though not dominant, is not lacking (*e.g.* xxii. 19, 23, xxiv. 18, 21).

A formal relationship between the Egyptian proverbs of Amenemope and xxii. 17–xxiii. 11 is widely recognized. The debate centres in the question, Which influenced which? W. Baumgartner (*The Old Testament and Modern Study*, ed. H. H. Rowley, 1951, p. 212) notes that 'the . . . theory that Amenemope is the original . . . has now been generally accepted'. This view, however, has now been challenged from within Egyptology itself, by É. Drioton, who has put up weighty reasons for a view that the Egyptian Amenemope is, in fact, merely a translation (sometimes too literal) from a Hebrew original into Egyptian; this Hebrew original would then be the 'words of the wise' from which Proverbs independently drew. See Drioton, *Mélanges André Robert*, 1957, pp. 254–280, and *Sacra Pagina I*, 1959, pp. 229–241. Against this, however, see R. J. Williams, *JEA*, XLVII, 1961, pp. 100–106. The passage has been so refined by Israel's faith that, whatever its origin, it belongs to the Old Testament revelation.

d. Additional sayings of the wise (xxiv. 23–34)

This brief collection exhibits the same irregularity of form as the one above. There are brief proverbs (*e.g.* verse 26) and extended maxims (*e.g.* verses 30–34; *cf.* vi. 6–11). The religious element is not prominent, but there is a keen sense of social responsibility (*e.g.* verses 28, 29). These two collections are apparently not Solomonic but are part of the legacy of Israel's sages, who created or collected and polished a vast body of wisdom sayings (*cf.* Ec. xii. 9–11).

e. Additional proverbs of Solomon (xxv. 1–xxix. 27)

In content this section is not unlike x. 1–xxii. 16 (*e.g.* xxv. 24—xxi. 9; xxvi. 13—xxii. 13; xxvi. 15—xix. 24, *etc.*). However, the proverbs here are less uniform in length; antithetic parallelism, the backbone of the earlier section, is less common, although xxviii and xxix contain numerous examples; comparison, rare in x. 1 ff., occurs frequently (*e.g.* xxv. 3, 11–14, 18–20, *etc.*).

The statement in xxv. 1 has influenced the Talmudic opinion (*Baba Bathra* 15a) that Hezekiah and his company wrote the Proverbs. The rôle of Hezekiah's men in the editing of the book is not clear, but there is no reason to question the accuracy of xxv. 1, which relates to the sayings in xxv–xxix. Hezekiah's interest in Israel's literature is attested in 2 Ch. xxix. 25–30, where he restores the Davidic order of worship, including the singing of the psalms of David and Asaph. A. Bentzen suggests that these proverbs were preserved *orally* until Hezekiah's time, when they were transcribed (*Introduction to the Old Testament*, II, p. 173). S. R. Driver (*An Introduction to the Literature of the Old Testament*, p. 401) lists a number of proverbs which reflect a restiveness concerning the monarchy (xxviii. 2, 12, 15 f., 28, xxix. 2, 4, 16). In the selection of these proverbs, is there a reflection of the turbulence of the 8th century BC?

f. The words of Agur (xxx. 1–33)

Agur, his father Jakeh, Ithiel, and Ucal (xxx. 1) defy identification. See ITHIEL for an adjustment in the word divisions which eliminates the last two names completely. *Oracle* (xxx. 1) should probably be read as a proper name *Massa* (*q.v.*).

The first few verses are difficult to interpret, but seem to be agnostic in tone. This agnosticism is answered (5, 6) with a statement about the unchangeable word of God. Following a brief but moving prayer (7–9), the chapter concludes with a series of extended proverbs describing some commendable or culpable quality. In many of these the number *four* is prominent. Several exhibit the x, x + 1 pattern well attested in the Old Testament (*e.g.* Am. i, ii; Mi. v. 5) and common in Ugaritic (*cf.* C. H. Gordon, *Ugaritic Handbook*, 1947, pp. 34, 201).

g. The words of Lemuel (xxxi. 1–9)

This king of Massa (*q.v.*) is unknown (see LEMUEL). His mother's advice includes warnings against sexual excess and drunkenness and encouragement to judge even the poor with rectitude. The influence of Aramaic on this section is noteworthy (*e.g. bar*, 'son'; *mᵉlāḵîn*, 'kings').

h. In praise of a virtuous wife (xxxi. 10–31)

This well-wrought acrostic poem has no title, but is so different from the preceding section that it must be considered separately. Its stylized form suggests that it should be viewed among the latest sections of the book. The description of an industrious, conscientious, and pious woman is a fitting conclusion to a book which discusses the practical out-workings of a God-directed life.

II. DATE

Proverbs could not have been completed before Hezekiah's time (*c.* 715–686 BC). However, the acrostic poem (xxxi. 10–31) and the sayings of the Massaites (xxx. 1–33, xxxi. 1–9) may well have been added in the exilic or post-exilic period. A reasonable date for the final editing is the 5th century BC. The individual proverbs date in most cases from well before the Exile. W. F. Albright notes (*op. cit.*, p. 6) that the contents of Proverbs must, on literary grounds, be dated before the Aramaic sayings of Ahiqar (7th century BC).

III. PROVERBS AND THE NEW TESTAMENT

Proverbs has left its stamp on the New Testament by several quotations (*e.g.* iii. 7a—Rom. xii. 16; iii. 11, 12—Heb. xii. 5, 6; iii. 34—Jas. iv. 6 and 1 Pet. v. 5b; iv. 26—Heb. xii. 13a; x. 12—Jas. v. 20 and 1 Pet. iv. 8; xxv. 21, 22—Rom. xii. 20; xxvi. 11—2 Pet. ii. 22) and allusions (*e.g.* ii. 4—Col. ii. 3; iii. 1–4—Lk. ii. 52; xii. 7—Mt. vii. 24–27). As Christ fulfilled the Law and the Prophets (Mt. v. 17), so He fulfilled the wisdom writings by revealing the fulness of God's wisdom (Mt. xii. 42; 1 Cor. i. 24, 30; Col. ii. 3). If Proverbs is an extended commentary on the law of love, then it helps to pave the way for the One in whom true love became incarnate. See C. T. Fritsch, 'The Gospel in the Book of Proverbs', *Theology Today*, VII, 1950, pp. 169–183.

BIBLIOGRAPHY. A. Cohen, *Proverbs*, 1945; C. T. Fritsch, *Proverbs* in *IB*; B. Gemser, *Sprüche Salomos*, 1937; W. O. E. Oesterley in *WC*; T. T. Perowne, *The Proverbs*, 1916; C. I. K. Story in *JBL*, LXIV, 1945, pp. 319–337; D. W. Thomas, *Wisdom in Israel and in the Ancient Near East*, 1955, pp. 280–292; C. H. Toy in *ICC*, 1899.

D.A.H.

PROVIDENCE. No single word in biblical Hebrew or Greek expresses the idea of God's providence. *Pronoia* is used for God's purposive foresight by Plato, Stoic writers, Philo, who wrote a book *On providence* (*Peri pronoias*), Josephus, and the authors of Wisdom (*cf.* xiv. 3, xvii. 2) and 3, 4 Macc.; but in the New Testament *pronoia* occurs only twice (Acts xxiv. 2; Rom. xiii. 14), both times denoting, not God's care and forethought, but man's. The cognate verb *pronoeō*, too, is used only of man (Rom. xii. 17; 2 Cor. viii. 21; 1 Tim. v. 8).

Providence is normally defined in Christian theology as the unceasing activity of the Creator whereby, in overflowing bounty and goodwill (Ps.

cxlv. 9; *cf.* Mt. v. 45–48), He upholds His creatures in ordered existence (Acts xvii. 28; Col. i. 17; Heb. i. 3), guides and governs all events, circumstances, and free acts of angels and men (*cf.* Ps. cvii; Jb. i. 12, ii. 6; Gn. xlv. 5–8), and directs everything to its appointed goal, for His own glory (*cf.* Eph. i. 9–12). This view of God's relation to the world must be distinguished from: (*a*) *pantheism*, which absorbs the world into God; (*b*) *deism*, which cuts it off from Him; (*c*) *dualism*, which divides control of it between God and another power; (*d*) *indeterminism*, which holds that it is under no control at all; (*e*) *determinism*, which posits a control of a kind that destroys man's moral responsibility; (*f*) the doctrine of *chance*, which denies the controlling power to be rational; and (*g*) the doctrine of *fate*, which denies it to be benevolent.

Providence is presented in Scripture as a function of divine sovereignty. God is King over all, doing just what He wills (Pss. ciii. 19, cxxxv. 6; Dn. iv. 35; *cf.* Eph. i. 11). This conviction, robustly held, pervades the whole Bible. The main strands in it may be analysed as follows.

a. Providence and the natural order

God rules all natural forces (Ps. cxlvii. 8 f.), all wild animals (Jb. xxxviii–xli), and all happenings in the world, great and small, from thunderstorms (Jb. xxxvii; Ps. xxix) and plagues (Ex. vii. 3–xi. 10, xii. 29 ff.; Joel ii. 25) to the death of a sparrow (Mt. x. 29) or the fall of a lot (Pr. xvi. 33). Physical life, in men and animals, is His to give and to take away (Gn. ii. 17; 1 Sa. i. 27; 2 Sa. xii. 19; Jb. i. 21; Pss. cii. 23, civ. 29 f., cxxvii. 3; Ezk. xxiv. 16 ff.; Dn. v. 23, *etc.*); so are health and sickness (Dt. vii. 15, xxviii. 27, 60), prosperity and adversity ('evil', Am. iii. 6; *cf.* Is. xlv. 7), *etc.*

Since the regularity of the natural order is thought of as depending directly upon the divine will (*cf.* Gn. viii. 22), the Bible finds no difficulty in the idea of an occasional miraculous irregularity; God does what He wills in His world, and nothing is too hard for Him (*cf.* Gn. xviii. 14).

God's providential government of the created order proclaims His wisdom, power, glory, and goodness (Pss. viii. 1, RV, xix. 1–6; Acts xiv. 17; Rom. i. 19 f.). The man who in face of this revelation does not acknowledge God is without excuse (Rom. i. 20).

The Bible presents God's constant fulfilling of His kindly purposes in nature both as matter for praise in itself (*cf.* Pss. civ, cxlvii) and as a guarantee that He is lord of human history, and will fulfil His gracious promises in that realm also (*cf.* Je. xxxi. 35 ff., xxxiii. 19–26).

b. Providence and world history

Since the fall, God has been executing a plan of redemption. This plan pivots upon Christ's first coming and culminates in His return. Its goal is the creation of a world-wide Church in which Jew and non-Jew share God's grace on equal terms (Eph. iii. 3–11), and through this the reintegration of the disordered cosmos (Rom. viii. 19 ff.), under the rule of Christ at His second coming (Eph. i. 9–12; Phil. ii. 9 ff.; Col. i. 20; 1 Cor. xv. 24 ff.). Through Christ's present reign and future triumph, the Old Testament prophecies of God's messianic kingdom (*cf.* Is. xi. 1–9; Dn. ii. 44, vii. 13–27) are fulfilled. The unifying theme of the Bible is God's exercise of His kingship in setting up this kingdom. No foe can thwart Him; He laughs at opposition to His plan (Ps. ii. 4), and uses it to His own ends (*cf.* Acts iv. 25–28, quoting Ps. ii. 1 f.). The climax of history will be the overthrow of those who fight against God and His kingdom, as the book of Revelation shows (Rev. xix, *etc.*).

Paul analyses the steps in God's plan in terms of the Jew–Gentile and law–grace relationships in Gal. iii; Rom. ix–xi; *cf.* Eph. ii. 12–iii. 11.

c. Providence and personal circumstances

God told Israel as a nation that He would prosper them while they were faithful but bring disaster on them if they sinned (Lv. xxvi. 14 ff.; Dt. xxviii. 15 ff.). The attempt to understand the fortunes of individual Israelites in the light of this principle raised problems. Why does God allow the wicked to prosper, even when they are victimizing the just? And why is disaster so often the lot of the godly?

The first question is always answered by affirming that the wicked prosper only for a moment; God will soon visit them and take vengeance (Pss. xxxvii *passim*, l. 16–21, lxxiii. 17 ff.), though for the present He may forbear, in order to give them further opportunity for repentance (Rom. ii. 4 f.; 2 Pet. iii. 9; Rev. ii. 21). The New Testament identifies the day of God's visitation with the final judgment (*cf.* Rom. ii. 3 ff., xii. 19; Jas. v. 1–8).

The second question is tackled in several ways. It is asserted: (i) that the righteous will be vindicated when the day of visitation for the wicked comes (Ps. xxxvii; Mal. iii. 13–iv. 3); (ii) that meanwhile suffering is valuable as a God-given discipline (Pr. iii. 11 ff.; Ps. cxix. 67, 71); (iii) that suffering, faithfully borne, even if not understood, glorifies God and leads to blessing in the end (Jb. i, ii, xlii); (iv) that communion with God is the supreme good, and to those who enjoy it outward impoverishments are of no ultimate importance (Ps. lxxiii. 14, 23 ff.; Hab. iii. 17 f.).

In the New Testament the fact that believers suffer ill-treatment and adverse circumstances is no longer a problem, since it is recognized that fellowship in Christ's sufferings is fundamental to the Christian vocation (*cf.* Mt. x. 24 f.; Jn. xv. 18 ff., xvi. 33; Acts ix. 16, xiv. 22; Phil. iii. 10 ff.; 1 Pet. iv. 12–19). This recognition, in conjunction with the Old Testament principles mentioned above, completely disposed of the 'problem of suffering' for the first Christians. Knowing something of their glorious hope (1 Pet. i. 3 ff.), and of the strengthening and sustaining power of Christ (2 Cor. i. 3 ff., xii. 9 f.), they could contentedly face all situations (Phil. iv. 11) and rejoice in all troubles (Rom. viii. 35 ff.), confident that through adversity their loving Father was disciplining them in sanctity (Heb. xii. 5–11), developing their Christian character (Jas. i. 2 ff.; 1 Pet. v. 10; *cf.* Rom. v. 2 ff.), proving the reality of their faith (1 Pet. i. 7), and so ripening them for glory (1 Pet. iv. 13). In all things God works for the spiritual welfare of His people (Rom. viii. 28); and He supplies them with whatever material things they need throughout their earthly pilgrimage (Mt. vi. 25–33; Phil. iv. 19).

Belief in providence determines many of the basic attitudes of biblical piety. The knowledge that God determines their circumstances teaches the faithful to wait on Him in humility and patience for vindication and deliverance (Pss. xxxvii, xl. 13 ff.; Jas. v. 7 ff.; 1 Pet. v. 6 f.). It forbids them to grow despondent or despairing (Pss. xlii, xliii), and brings them courage and hope when harassed (Pss. lx, lxii). It inspires all prayers for help, and praise for every good thing enjoyed.

d. Providence and human freedom

God rules the hearts and actions of all men (*cf.* Pr. xxi. 1; Ezr. vi. 22), often for purposes of His own which they do not suspect (*cf.* Gn. xlv. 5–8, l. 20; Is. x. 5 ff., xliv. 28–xlv. 4; Jn. xi. 49 ff.; Acts xiii. 27 ff.). God's control is absolute in the sense that men do only that which He has ordained that they should do; yet they are truly free agents, in the sense that their decisions are their own, and they are morally responsible for them (*cf.* Dt. xxx. 15 ff.). A distinction, however, must be drawn between God's allowing (or 'giving up') sinners to practise the evil that they have preferred (Ps. lxxxi. 12 f.; Acts xiv. 16; Rom. i. 24–28), and His gracious work of prompting His people to will and do what He commands (Phil. ii. 13); for in the former case, according to the biblical rule of judgment, the blame for the evil done belongs entirely to the sinner (*cf.* Lk. xxii. 22; Acts ii. 23, iii. 13–19), whereas in the latter case the praise for the good done must be given to God (*cf.* 1 Cor. xv. 10).

See PREDESTINATION, LIBERTY.

BIBLIOGRAPHY. *Arndt*; A. E. Garvie, in *HDB*; A. H. Strong, *Systematic Theology*[12], 1949, pp. 419–443; L. Berkhof, *Systematic Theology*[4], 1949, pp. 165–178; Calvin, *Institutio*, I. xvi–xviii; K. Barth, *Church Dogmatics*, III. iii, E.T., 1960, pp. 3–288; A. S. Peake, *The Problem of Suffering in the Old Testament*, 1904; O. Cullmann, *Christ and Time*, E.T., 1951; G. C. Berkouwer, *The Providence of God*, 1952. J.I.P.

PROVINCE. Originally the word denoted a sphere of duty or administration. The *praetor urbanus*, for example, held an *urbana provincia*, and this was defined as the administration of justice within the city (Livy, vi. 42, xxxi. 6). Tacitus speaks of the suppression of a slave revolt at Brundisium in AD 24 by a quaestor 'whose province was the hill-country pastures', *calles* (Tac., *Ann.* iv. 27). The reading is confirmed by Suetonius (*Iul.* xix), who speaks of 'provinces' covering the supervision of 'woods and pasture-lands'. The reference shows that long after the term developed territorial and geographical significance it retained its ancient meaning. The intermediate use is seen in the employment of the term for a military command. 'To Sicinius,' says Livy, 'the Volsci were assigned as his province, to Aquilius the Hernici' (ii. 40). That is, the task of pacification in these two Italian tribal areas was allotted respectively to these two consuls. It was an easy step from, for example, Spain as a military command to Spain as a conquered territory and defined area of administration. In this later, commoner, and wider sense of the word, there were no provinces until Rome extended her conquests beyond the Italian peninsula. Sicily was the first country to be made thus into 'a Roman province' (Cic., *In Verr.* ii. 2). This was in 241 BC. Sardinia followed in 235 BC. In 121 BC Rome annexed a piece of territory in S Gaul between the Alps and the Cévennes to secure communications with Spain, and this area, Gallia Narbonensis, became known as 'the Province' above all others, and its inhabitants *provinciales*. Hence Provence today. Similarly the rest of the provinces were acquired piecemeal, the list being closed by the annexation of Britain by Claudius and Dacia by Trajan.

The earliest provinces were administered by magistrates elected for the purpose. For example, two additional praetors were elected from 227 BC for Sicily and Sardinia, and two more, twenty years later, to govern the two Spanish provinces. The scheme was then discontinued for over a century, Macedonia (148 BC), Achaea and Africa (146 BC), and Asia (133 BC), for example, being ruled by magistrates already in office, their *imperium* being extended for the purpose. The term *proconsul* signified a consul whose *imperium* was thus 'prorogued' after his year of office, for the purposes of a provincial governorship. A proconsulship could, however, be held without preceding tenure of the consulship. This was the case with Pompey in 77, 66, and 65 BC.

Under the principate the provinces were divided into senatorial and imperial. The former were governed by ex-consuls and ex-praetors with the title of *proconsul* (*q.v.*), normally in yearly tenure, the latter were administered by legates of the emperor (*legati Augusti pro praetore*), men of senatorial rank, or selected equestrian officials. Tenure of office was at the emperor's pleasure. Imperial provinces were usually those involving legionary garrisons. Transference from one list to another was not uncommon. Tacitus mentions the transfer of Achaea and Macedonia from the senate to the emperor in AD 15 (*leuari proconsulari imperio tradique Caesari . . .*) (*Ann.* i. 76). Cyprus is a similar example. Annexed in 57 BC, it was incorporated in Cilicia in 55 BC and made an imperial province in 27 BC. In 22 BC Augustus transferred it and Gallia Narbonensis to the senate in exchange for Dalmatia. Hence there was a proconsul in command, as Luke, with his usual accuracy, indicates (Acts xiii. 7). See also ROMAN EMPIRE.

BIBLIOGRAPHY. T. Mommsen, *The Provinces of the Roman Empire from Caesar to Diocletian*, 1909; G. H. Stevenson, *Roman Provincial Administration*, 1939. E.M.B.

PSALMS, BOOK OF.

I. THE IMPORTANCE OF THE PSALTER

It is impossible to overestimate the significance, for Jew and Gentile, of the Book of Psalms. Here are mirrored the ideals of religious piety and communion with God, of sorrow for sin and the search for perfection, of walking in darkness unafraid by the lamp of faith; of obedience to the law of God, delight in the worship of God, fellowship with the friends of God, reverence for the Word of God; of humility under the chastening rod, trust when evil triumphs and wickedness prospers, serenity in the midst of storm.

The Hebrew poets were inspired to take these timeless spiritual insights and religious experiences and make them the themes of their songs. But it should be remembered that 'the Psalms are poems, and poems intended to be sung, not doctrinal treatises, nor even sermons' (C. S. Lewis, *Reflections on the Psalms*, 1958, p. 2)—hence the Hebrew title of the Psalms, *t*[e]*hillîm*, 'songs of praise'—and also that they were giving expression to the religion of Israel to which the psalmists were heirs, not merely to their personal religious experiences. Indeed, these Hebrew poets have mirrored the spiritual experience of the human soul, of humanity. In other words, the Psalms belong to all 'believers', Jew and Gentile. Therein lies the importance of the Psalter.

II. THE FORMATION OF THE PSALTER

It has been customary to describe the Book of Psalms as 'the hymn-book of the Second Temple', and such it undoubtedly was. The title is misleading, however, if it is interpreted to mean that all the psalms were written in the exilic or post-exilic periods. It is important to notice that this type of literature is not only not confined to the Psalter in the Old Testament but is found in many different periods in Hebrew history. It is found among the Hebrews as early as the Exodus period (Ex. xv), and another example comes from a time subsequent to, but relatively close to, the invasion of Canaan under Joshua (Jdg. v). Hannah's psalm (1 Sa. ii. 1–10) comes at the close of the Judges period.

The pre-exilic prophetic literature also contains examples of psalm composition (*cf.*, *e.g.*, Ho. vi. 1–3; Is. ii. 2–4, xxxviii. 10–20; Je. xiv. 7–9; Hab. iii. 1 ff., *etc.*). And from the post-exilic period come such passages as Ezr. ix. 5–15 and Ne. ix. 6–39, which are strongly reminiscent of many of the psalms. Clearly, then, the Psalter is not an isolated literary phenomenon. Indeed, the same type of poetry is found among the Babylonians and the citizens of Ugarit as the Ras Shamra tablets testify. The Old Testament Psalter is a collection of poems which are typical of a literary form which the Hebrews, in common with other cultures, used from at least the Exodus right up until the post-exilic or second Temple period. And, of course, if one reckons with the non-canonical psalms it is clear that this literary form persisted among the Jews until quite a long way into the Christian era.

a. Authorship

No fewer than seventy-three psalms are attributed to David. Other authors named in the titles are Asaph (l, lxxiii–lxxxiii), the sons of Korah (xlii–xlix, lxxxiv, lxxxv, lxxxvii), Solomon (lxxii, cxxvii), and Heman (lxxxviii), Ethan (lxxxix), both Ezrahites, and Moses (xc), who have one psalm each attributed to them. Davidic authorship of many of the psalms has often been denied, principally on the ground that David the psalmist of popular belief bears no resemblance to David the warrior of the books of Samuel and Kings. We do know, however, that David was a musician (1 Sa. xvi. 14 ff.) and a poet (2 Sa. i. 17 ff., iii. 33 f.). The attempts of some scholars to disprove the Davidic authorship assigned to 2 Sa. xxii. 1 ff., xxiii. 1–7, and to excise the words 'like David' from Am. vi. 5 (where the tradition of David and his music and songs is referred to three hundred years after his death) have been far from successful. Tradition itself points to the strong probability of there being psalms in the Psalter which came from the pen of David.

This hymn-book of the second Temple contains very ancient material. This is not at all surprising when it is recalled that the Ras Shamra tablets show that, when Israel invaded Canaan, the type of poetry represented in the Psalms was already a long-established tradition among the inhabitants of Ugarit. The Song of Moses, then, in Ex. xv, and the Song of Deborah (Jdg. v), were neither isolated nor unprecedented examples of Semitic poetry. The Mosaic and Solomonic authorships referred to in the titles of three psalms suggest that the ancient religion of the tabernacle and the first Temple would require its sacred music. The fact too that certain psalms were connected with sacrificial worship among the Jews (*e.g.* Ps. xxx was used at the festival of the Dedication of the Temple, Ps. xcii was used on the sabbath, others at the thank-offering, *etc.*) also points to the great age of some of the material in the Old Testament Psalter. Religion in the days of Amos (v. 21–23) and Isaiah (xxx. 29), during the Exile (Ps. cxxxvii. 1 ff.) and the period following the return, and the building of the second Temple, would also require its solemn chants. With the gradual undermining of the Graf–Wellhausen theory of Old Testament history, and the acknowledgment that 'P', written, it used to be said with assurance, during or after the Exile, has nothing to say about Hebrew psalmody or cultic hymns, it is being increasingly conceded that the Psalter contains very ancient compositions as well as post-exilic psalms.

b. Organization

The Old Testament Psalter as we now have it consists of five books. This division goes back to the LXX version, which was begun as early as 300 BC. Every section is easily recognizable because a doxology closes each book. These doxologies are short except the one that ends Book V; there an entire psalm is given over to the closing doxology. The five divisions of the Psalter are as follows: Book I, Pss. i–xli; Book II, Pss. xlii–lxxii; Book III, Pss. lxxiii–lxxxix; Book IV, Pss. xc–cvi; Book V, Pss. cvii–cl. Many have seen in this fivefold division an attempt to imitate the division of the Torah into five books, the Pentateuch. See N. H. Snaith, *Hymns of the Temple*, 1951, pp. 18–20, where the significance of this is discussed.

The first book consists for the most part of psalms attributed to David. Then Pss. xlii–lxxxiii include compositions mainly from three sources—the sons of Korah, David, and Asaph. Then Pss. xc–cl contain psalms which are nearly all anonymous. Probably also many were intended for use in the Temple: *cf.*, *e.g.*, xcv–c and cxlv–cl. There is also a short collection of psalms (cxx–cxxxiv) which are often called 'Songs of Degrees', more properly 'Songs of Ascents' (see DEGREES). These were almost certainly separate original collections of psalms, and it may be that these collections provide the key to an understanding of the stages leading to the formation of the Psalter as it has come down to us.

On the basis of Gray's suggestions set out in his *Critical Introduction to the Old Testament*, 1913, it may be supposed that the psalms attributed to David would be the first unit, but probably the seventy-two psalms of Davidic authorship were originally two collections, as is suggested by their now being found divided between the two first main groups of psalms, iii–xli and li–lxxii. It is thought that the next two compilations were the two groups of psalms attributed to Asaph (l, lxxiii–lxxxiii) and the sons of Korah (xlii–xlix). Another two collections have been postulated; the first consists of the second of the Davidic group and the Korahite and Asaphic (xlii–lxxxiii), and the second contains Pss. lxxxiv–lxxxix. These two collections have one thing in common—the use of the Hebrew word *'ᵉlōhîm* for God. 'The Songs of Ascents' probably formed the nucleus of the collection containing xc–cl. When the one hundred and fifty psalms were finally brought together Robertson Smith thinks they may have already been reduced to three compilations: i–xli, xlii–lxxxix, xc–cl, and then were eventually rearranged into their present fivefold division to correspond to the division of the Law.

III. THE TITLES IN THE PSALTER

The title of the book in Hebrew is *tᵉhillîm*, 'Songs of Praise', or 'Praises'. In English the title *Psalter* comes from LXX A *Psaltērion*, while *The Psalms* comes from LXX B *Psalmoi* or the Vulg. *Liber Psalmorum*. In addition to the title given to the book, the majority of individual psalms have separate headings. These tend to puzzle the reader who has no knowledge of Hebrew, and the following remarks may be found useful.

Following Mowinckel, Professor E. A. Leslie, in his Introduction to the Psalms, *The Abingdon Bible Commentary*, 1929, pp. 509 ff., divides the titles of the Psalms into four categories.

1. The titles which are technical designations of the Psalms. *Mizmôr*, a melody, usually rendered 'psalm' (*e.g.* xxiv), suggesting that these psalms were sung to musical accompaniment; *šîr*, a song, hence a religious song sung in worship (*e.g.* xlvi); *šîr hamma'ᵃlôṯ*, a song of ascents, a pilgrim song sung by worshippers as they processed behind the ark in celebration of a religious festival (cxx–cxxxiv); *miḵtām*, a technical term of which the root meaning is unknown. The LXX rendering suggests the idea of engraving on tablets, but the notion of atonement is suggested because all *miḵtām* psalms are lamentations (xvi, lvi–lx); *maskîl*, a didactic poem, hence a composition setting forth divine insights, and which therefore instructs (lxxiv, lxxviii, lxxix); *šiggāyôn* (vii), another obscure technical designation. If the word comes from *šāgâ*, 'to swerve, reel', then the title might mean a wild rhythmic song and may have had connections with some part of the cult which now escapes us; *tᵉpillâ*, 'prayer', hence a poetic or liturgical prayer of petition (cxlii).

2. Some titles throw light on the purpose of the psalm: *tôḏâ*, 'thanksgiving', suggests a psalm to express praise in Temple liturgy (c); *lᵉ'annôṯ* should probably be derived from a root meaning 'to be afflicted', and the psalm so entitled would then be an expression of penitence for those who humble themselves; *hazkîr*, 'to commemorate', hence a psalm in which either the individual worshipper recalls his sins, or in which the priest brings to remembrance the sins of the worshipper (xxxviii, lxx); *yᵉḏûṯûn* is probably to be connected with the idea of confession, the *yᵉḏûṯûn* psalms (xxxix, lxii, lxxvii) would then be expressions of confession and penitence; *lammēḏ*, 'to teach', indicates that such a psalm imparts religious instruction (lx).

3. There are some titles which are clearly cultic (*cf.* Hab. iii) in meaning and intention: the well-known *mᵉnaṣṣēaḥ*, which *BDB* renders 'musical director' or 'choirmaster' and conjectures that the fifty-five psalms so entitled once formed a 'Director's Collection', is by Mowinckel connected with a root meaning 'to shine' and is understood to signify the shining of God's face in terms of His blessing on the worshippers in the Temple; others again think the term should be connected with the idea of God's victory, which was celebrated in the cult; the title *yônaṯ 'ēlem rᵉḥōqîm*, 'to the dove of distant terebinths' (*BDB*), usually understood to be the name of the melody to which the psalm (lvi) was set, may have a connection with the sacrifice of the dove upon which was laid the sins of the worshipper (Lv. v. 6–10); the title *'ayyeleṯ haššaḥar*, 'hind of the

dawn', may also point to another sacrifice which was offered to the accompaniment of the psalm (xxii) so entitled; another title, *šōšannîm*, 'lilies' (xlv, lxix; variant forms are found in Pss. lx, *šûšan 'ēḏûṯ*; lxxx, *šōšannîm 'ēḏûṯ*, 'lily (lilies), remembrance'), may point to the use of flowers in some festal procession; if the title *maḥalaṯ* (liii, lviii) comes from a root meaning 'to be sick', then these two psalms may have been used in the purification ritual after illness. There are several other titles which are thought to connect the psalms where they are found with specific cultic acts, *e.g.* the titles common to Pss. lvii–lix, lxxv, Pss. viii, lxxxi, lxxxiv, and Pss. vi, xii; but a great deal of dispute and doubt concerning their meaning and interpretation still exists. *mûṯ labbēn* (ix), 'die for the son' (?), is one of these.

4. Two titles are thought to be musical references. They are *n^eḡînôṯ* (vi, liv, lv, lxvii), which means 'the music of stringed instruments' or the instruments themselves, and may indicate that these psalms were sung to the accompaniment of the harp; and *selâ*, which occurs seventy-one times in thirty-nine psalms (*BDB*). It signifies 'lift up', and probably marked the points in the psalms at which the worshippers were to lift up their voices, crying out, 'Blessed be Yahweh for ever', or 'Yahweh endureth for ever'. In many of the instances where *selâ* occurs the words 'amen' or 'hallelujah' might easily be substituted, and should perhaps be classed with them. And since *selâ* occurs with *higgāyôn* in ix. 16 the latter is thought to be identical in meaning to the former. The obscure *n^eḥîlôṯ* ('flutes'?) may fall into this category.

IV. THE POETRY OF THE PSALTER

An appreciation of the principles and structure of Hebrew poetry is essential to a proper understanding of the psalms and their interpretation. It is also necessary to realize that what we in the West today mean by poetry bears little resemblance to what the Hebrews meant by the term. In Hebrew poetry rhyme does not exist, and it is more accurate to speak of rhythm rather than metre. There is a rhythmic accentuation in each clause, and a rhythmical balance of clauses, but no metrical system dependent upon the quantity or number of syllables or accents in each line. Attempts to discover a metrical system in the poetry of the Psalter have not met with much success. It is because Hebrew poetry depends upon the rhythmical balance of clauses and not upon rhyme and metre (in the classical sense of these terms) that it loses so little, comparatively speaking, in translation.

It was Robert Lowth (1710–87), Professor of Poetry at Oxford, who first drew attention to the fundamental principle of Hebrew poetry. In his treatise, *De Sacra Poesi Hebraeorum: Praelectiones Academicae Oxonii habitae* (1753), Lowth pointed out that the distinctive feature of Hebrew poetry was parallelism, that is to say the correspondence of one line of poetry with another, or the repetition of the same thought in different words. It is important that in translation Hebrew poetry should be printed as poetry, that is to say, in lines and not as prose. This enables the reader who has no knowledge of Hebrew to recognize the members or lines of which the verses are composed, and to notice the parallelism between the members (usually two); that is to say, to notice how the second line of the verse repeats the thought of the first line, but in different words. It is essential to be able to recognize this law of parallelism in Hebrew poetry because it has great exegetical value. It can often be used by the exegete when he has to decide such important questions as the construction or connection of words, the elucidation of the meaning of a verse, and on occasion the choice between various possible readings.

Various types of parallelism have been distinguished.

1. Synonymous parallelism. This type is found in every verse throughout Ps. cxiv, but is extremely common throughout the Psalter. It is called 'synonymous' because the statement in the first line of the verse is repeated exactly, but with different words, in the second line: *cf.* also l. 11, 13, 19, lxxx. 13.

2. Antithetical or contrasted parallelism. In this type the statement in the first line of the verse is affirmed, not by its repetition in the second line but by its opposite: *e.g.* Pss. i. 6, xxx. 5, xxxvii. 21.

3. Synthetical or constructive parallelism. Here the two members or lines of the verse do not say the same thing but rather the statement in the first serves as the basis upon which the second rests, or the relation is that of cause and effect: *e.g.* Pss. xix. 7–10, ii. 6, xxii. 4, cxix. 121.

4. Climactic or ascending parallelism, where often the first line of the verse is incomplete but the second takes up some words from it and completes it: Pss. xxix. 1, cxxi. 1–4, xxii. 4.

The question, Were the Psalms originally divided into strophes? cannot be answered with complete certainty. That there are strophic arrangements in some psalms is quite clear. It is tolerably certain that the refrains which are found in Pss. xli, xlii, xlvi, lvii, lxxx, xcix, cvii, indicate strophic arrangements. It is possible too that the musical reference *selâ* may also have served to divide a psalm into stanzas or strophes, as in Pss. iii and iv. Other psalms fall into strophes naturally; *e.g.* the general sense of Ps. ii leads to a natural fourfold division: verses 1–3, 4–6, 7–9, 10–12. So also does Ps. xcii: verses 1–3, 4–8, 9–11, 12–15. Occasionally an alphabetical arrangement was used to divide a psalm into stanzas. The best-known example of this device is, of course, Ps. cxix. The probability is that not all Hebrew poetry was originally strophic, and the attempts on the part of Duhm, Briggs, and others to force many psalms into strophic form by means of emendation have been both unsuccessful and infelicitous.

Another feature of Hebrew poetry to which attention should be drawn is the use of acrostic or alphabetic devices. There are nine alphabetic psalms in the Psalter, and these show a great deal of variation in their alphabetic structure; *e.g.* in Pss. cxi and cxii each line begins with a different letter of the Hebrew alphabet, but in Ps. cxi the lines are arranged in eight pairs of verse lines or couplets and in Ps. cxii the lines are arranged in two tristichs. In Pss. xxv, xxxiv, and cxlv each letter of the alphabet begins a couplet. In Ps. cxix, where the verses are arranged in strophes of eight verses each, the same letter begins every verse in the stanza. Pss. ix, x, and xxxvii are also alphabetic in structure. The contents of these psalms show that this acrostic device did not fetter the poet's inspiration any more than the metre or rhyme which has been a general feature of more modern poetry has cramped the style of western poets.

V. THE INTERPRETATION OF THE PSALTER

The question of interpretation is closely dependent upon that of classification, and there is by no means complete unanimity on the second of these questions. Different authorities proceed on different principles when endeavouring to determine the classification of the Psalms. If the use of the Psalms in temple worship be the determining principle then some such classification as the following will emerge: (1) hymns of praise; (2) prayers of thanksgiving; (3) prayers of petition; (4) prayers of lamentations; (5) spiritual and wisdom psalms. Of the first four types there are, of course, both public and individual psalms.

Some authorities classify the Psalms according to their subjects: (1) hymns of adoration; (2) psalms which celebrate God's kingdom; (3) royal psalms; (4) psalms of meditation; (5) psalms of worship and thanksgiving; (6) psalms which recount Israel's history; (7) psalms of imprecation; (8) psalms of penitence; (9) psalms of petition. If one attempts to classify the Psalms on a psycho-religious basis, then they would be grouped according to whether they expressed such sentiments as hatred, penitence, piety, patriotism, sense of wonder, trust in God, self-reliance, *etc.*

Perhaps the most satisfactory classification of the Psalms would follow these lines:

1. Psalms which are prayers in which the psalmists petition God for blessing and protection (*e.g.* lxxxvi, cii).

2. Psalms of praise, in which the thanksgiving may be for specific mercies, or the praise may spring from God's majesty in the world of nature, or praise in worship and adoration (*e.g.* xlvii, lxviii, civ, cxlv–cl).

3. Psalms which plead for divine intervention and deliverance in time of sickness, calamity, and danger (*e.g.* xxxviii, lxxxviii).

4. Psalms which are confessions of faith that God is the Lord, Creator, King of the nations, Judge and moral Ruler of the universe (*e.g.* xxxiii, xciv, xcvii, cxxxvi, cxlv).

5. Psalms of penitence for sin, of which there are seven (vi, xxxii, xxxviii, li, cii, cxxx, cxliii), but in only one (li) of these penitential psalms is confession of sin prominent; indeed, two of them (vi, cii) make no reference to sin at all, the chief concern being forgiveness not confession.

6. Psalms of intercession, in which the psalmists intercede for the king, their own people, other nations, the house of David, and Jerusalem (*e.g.* xxi, lxvii, lxxxix, cxxii).

7. Imprecatory psalms, which are discussed more fully below, but it should be noted here that these imprecations are really the psalmists' reply to those of Israel's enemies (*e.g.* xxxv, lix, cix).

8. Psalms of wisdom in the form of spiritual or religious homilies, which offer instruction on patience when the wicked prosper, on Jerusalem's true glory, on true kingship, on false prosperity, on true service for God, on God's providential care over the nation, on God's power in the world of nature, and His rule in all history (*e.g.* xxxvii, cxxii, xlv, xlix, l, lxxviii, civ, cv–cvii).

9. Psalms which deal with the strange providences that befall God's people, and with such questions as the future life, why the wicked prosper, and with speculations on the possibility of rewards after death (*e.g.* xciv, xlix, xvi, xvii, lxxiii).

10. Psalms which extol the greatness of the Law. The very first psalm is concerned with the joys and blessings that attend the man who studies and practises the Torah. Ps. xix describes the nature of the Law and its effects upon the obedient heart, while Ps. cxix is one sustained paean of praise to God for His greatest of all gifts to Israel, His Law, and the revelation of His will for His covenant people which it mediates.

Modern interpreters of the Psalms, in addition to emphasizing the value of knowing the class to which a psalm belongs, also insist on being guided by other principles. They underline the importance of studying the historical situation out of which the various psalms arose. It is self-evident that this 'historical' method of interpreting the Psalms is of great importance, but when one attempts to apply it the difficulties in the way of determining the date of a psalm and the circumstances in which it was written are almost insurmountable. These difficulties have led to a great deal of conjecture and speculation on the historical background, and hence on the categories to which individual psalms belong. Historical allusions are certainly important *where these are found,* but they are often so vague that it is impossible to identify them with certainty.

A much safer criterion is the character of the religious ideas found in each psalm. That is to say, what the psalmist's concept of God was, what his hopes were, his aspirations after God, his fears, his endeavours to please God. This approach is important because modern studies in the Psalms have resulted in establishing an earlier date for the Psalter than was hitherto thought possible. Many of them are undoubtedly pre-exilic in origin, but the association of the Psalter with the Temple worship suggests that it was the hymn-book and prayer-book of the Second Temple. In other words, the Psalter as a whole grew out of those centuries when Israel was being compelled to re-think her way through her religious convictions and past history, and search for their meaning and relevancy concerning Israel's place in the world and the probable fate of the nation and the individual in the age in which she now found herself.

But how is this conviction that the Psalter belongs to the age of the Second Temple to be interpreted? Does it mean simply that all the psalms were written for use in the Temple ritual, and the majority were for congregational use, but some were to be used in private? Some scholars have gone far beyond such a simple interpretation. The name of Sigmund Mowinckel, the Scandinavian scholar, is justly famous for the original work he has done on the Psalter, although there has been much hesitancy in accepting his theories. In the main these are twofold.

While agreeing that the psalms were written to meet ritual needs, he suggested, as early as 1921 in his *Psalmenstudien*, Part I, that many were in the main powerful spells which, when written and later recited, released a dynamic force against one's enemies who by sorcery sought to injure the psalmist. Where the foes in question were numerous Mowinckel assumed that they were daemonic forces. These were 'workers of mischief' because they practised magic and the black art (*cf.* x. 7, vi. 6–8, xciv. 3–7, lxiv. 2–4). Mowinckel, however, is really not basing his arguments on what he finds in the psalms; he is in fact arguing from analogy. This realm of ideas very clearly forms the background from which Babylonian and Assyrian psalms come, but there is nothing to suggest that the same is true of the Old Testament Psalter. In any case, to say that the 'workers of mischief' in the Psalms were sorcerers who practised the black art is pure assumption.

Another hypothesis with which Mowinckel's name is associated concerns what are called the 'Accession Psalms'. Here too he is largely dependent upon knowledge of the annual accession festival in Babylonian culture. In these Mesopotamian accession festivals the reigning monarch received his kingdom annually from the deity, Marduk, his overlord. In addition to this fundamental significance were subsidiary ideas. For example, in the accession festivals there took place a ritual conflict in which the deity overthrew the monarch's enemies, after which he ascended the throne again for another year. Part of the festival took the form of a procession in which the deity's image was set on a throne. The well-known ritual of the god's dying and rising may also have been part of the Babylonian annual accession festival, as well as a ritual marriage in which the reigning monarch, as the deity's substitute, 'married' someone who represented the goddess. But while there is irrefragable evidence that these annual accession festivals were an integral part of Babylonian civilization, there is no such evidence that such annual accession festivals were in vogue in Israel. That Saul (1 Sa. x. 1, 24, xi. 4–11) and David (2 Sa. ii. 3 f., v. 1–3) were *confirmed* in their kingdoms cannot be taken as evidence of an annual accession festival in Israel. Moreover, while the seven 'Accession Psalms' (xlvii, xciii, xcv–xcix) may plausibly be interpreted in terms of an annual accession day of Yahweh which was held as a religious festival every New Year's Day (Nu. xxix. 1), yet this interpretation is based on an analogy from Babylonian cultic literature, not on Old Testament history or the Psalter.

VI. THE RELIGION OF THE PSALTER

It cannot be said too often that the Psalter is a mirror which reflects not so much the religious experience of individuals as the experience of 'the religious soul of Israel' conceived as a corporate personality. The message of the Psalter is mediated through the varieties of religious experience which find expression in it. Man's highest duty is to love God by worshipping Him, praying to Him, participating in public service, obeying His commandments in which He has revealed His will for man. He must pray to God at all times and in all circumstances. The workers of iniquity he must shun, and he must associate with the pious. He should be faithful, kind, honest, holy. His worship should consist of adoration, thanksgiving, praise, and the sacrifices of a contrite heart. God's house, God's law, God's service, and the liturgy as well, are to be the means of grace indispensable to the man of God.

The Psalter lays great stress on the place of public worship in the religious life of the individual Hebrew. In this connection it is interesting to notice the lack of emphasis on the sacrificial system in the temple cultus. In the Psalter participation in it is enjoined (iv. 5, xx. 3, li. 19, lxvi. 13–15); but on the other hand, a non-ritual type of religion is not to be despised. Indeed, this latter expression of man's religious life is acceptable to God (xl. 6, l. 9), but substitutes for sacrificial offerings are to be offered to the Lord, such as obedience (xl. 6 ff.), gratitude (l. 14, 23), contrition (li. 16 ff.), meditation (xix. 14), prayer (cxli. 2), morality (xv. 1 ff.), and faith (iv. 5). Here spiritual values are being given their proper place in Hebrew religion.

This tendency to deprecate the Pentateuchal system of sacrifice must also have contributed to the discovery of the value of the individual before God. And this religion of the individual before God as reflected in the Psalter was supremely an expression of confident trust in the Lord, of praise to God, of acceptance with God. It was rooted in obedience to the law of God and of fellowship with God. That many in Israel set their hearts to attain such an experience of God cannot be doubted when due regard is given to the bitternesses of life as these are reflected in the Psalter. Gentile often lorded it over Jew, rich over poor, and false friends, false witnesses, and slanderers often made life unbearable; and sickness unto death was a constant reminder of the dark hopelessness of sheol. If the pious in Israel, the 'afflicted', the 'needy', the 'meek', were to cope with life as they knew it and retain their faith and fidelity, and maintain this otherworldliness without compromise, then the religious experience which is mirrored in the Psalter was their only refuge.

VII. THE THEOLOGY OF THE PSALTER

1. The marrow of the religious life of the psalmists was undoubtedly their *conception of God.* They never tire of singing His majesty in creation. In all His works in the heavens, the earth, and the sea He has made Himself known as the all-powerful, the all-knowing, the everywhere-present God. He is also the God of all history who guides everything towards the final goal which He has purposed to fulfil. But this Ruler of the world, this King of kings, is also Lawgiver and Judge, the Vindicator of all who are oppressed and their Saviour. He is therefore merciful and faithful, just and righteous, the Holy One whom men and angels adore. But the God of the psalmists is also, and uniquely, the God of Israel. The God who revealed Himself to Abraham, Isaac, and Jacob, who through Moses delivered Israel from Egypt, entered into covenant with them and gave them the promised land, is the God of Israel still, the Lord and Defender of the chosen people.

With such a high conception of God it is not surprising that the psalmists found their chief delight and privilege in prayer to God. There is a directness, a spontaneity, and an immediacy in the prayers of the psalmists that convince us of the reality of prayer for them. They believe in His providence, trust in His presence, rejoice in His righteousness, rest in His faithfulness, confide in His nearness. In their prayers they praise, petition, and commune with their God, and find refuge from sickness, want, pestilence, and slander, and humble themselves under His mighty hand. In the progressive life of the community their behaviour is marked by fidelity to God, reverent obedience to the law, kindness to the oppressed, and joy in the worship of God's people.

2. Set against such a background of faith and obedience *the imprecatory psalms* (see especially xxxv. 1–8, lix, lxix, cix) may be felt to constitute a 'moral difficulty'. Similar prayers for vengeance are found in Jeremiah xi. 18 ff., xv. 15 ff., xviii. 19 ff., xx. 11 ff. The underlying idea in these passages in the Psalter, where curses and revengeful punishments are invoked upon the enemy, is expressed in cxxxix. 21 f., 'Do not I hate them, O Lord, that hate thee? . . . I count them my enemies.' That is to say, the psalmists are not motivated by desires for personal revenge not by zeal for the Holy One of Israel who must exercise retribution in the present moral order in the world. Behind the imprecations is a recognition of a divine moral governance in the world, a belief that right and wrong are meaningful for God, and that therefore judgment must operate in the moral world order as well as grace. It was natural, then, for men living under the dispensation of the law to pray for the destruction of *God's* enemies through judgment, although Christians now living in the dispensation of grace pray for all men that they may be saved, while still believing in the reality of a here-and-now judgment as well as judgment that is a future event.

It should be remembered too that while the psalmists were aware of the tensions between righteousness and unrighteousness, between the people of God and the enemies of God, they had as yet no conception of judgment in an eschatological sense, nor had they any doctrine of a future state in which the ungodly would be punished and the godly rewarded. Therefore if righteousness is to be vindicated it has to be vindicated now, if wickedness is to be punished it has to be punished now. For when the righteous man prayed for the destruction of wickedness he did not distinguish in his mind between the ungodly and his ungodliness. The destruction of the one without the other was unthinkable to the pious Hebrew. It was even difficult if not impossible for some psalmists to distinguish between the ungodly man and his family. All that belonged to the wicked man was involved with him in his wickedness. The Christian therefore must have these things in mind when he reads these imprecatory psalms. He must not empty them of all significance. They were at least a powerful reminder of the reality of judgment in this moral world, and they testify to a burning zeal for the cause of righteousness which flamed in the hearts of some of the psalmists, and to their refusal to condone sin.

3. Has the Psalter a theology of *a future life*? The answer here is, No. There is a hope but no assured belief concerning the future. No psalmist, of course, ever thinks of death in terms of annihilation, but death is to be feared because it separates from God. Since death is the lot of the godly and the ungodly, it means that the existence of the dead is devoid of all moral as well as religious significance. The most that the pious man could hope for was survival in a happy posterity. There is no *certain* reference to resurrection in the Psalter. Flashes of revelation or insight concerning the future life there may be, but there is no doctrine, no such article of religious faith. The germ of such a hope may be found in Pss. xvi, xvii, xlix, lxxiii, but a hope it remains. Nowhere does a psalmist attain to an assured belief in resurrection.

4. The *messianic psalms*. One of the most important factors in the national survival of Israel has been the messianic hope. This hope centres around the return of the age of David whose reign in the past marked the golden age in Israel's history; and it is against this background that the messianic hope in the Psalter should be viewed. The picture of the Messiah that emerges from the Psalter is a twofold one.

First, since Messiah is to be a scion of the Davidic dynasty, He is to be the *King* of the messianic age. The Psalter envisages a divine messianic King against whom nations will rebel in vain (Ps. ii). The messianic age is depicted in Ps. lxxii, while in Ps. ii the kingdom is described as a universal kingdom which belongs to God but over which Messiah rules in association with the Lord. In Ps. cx Messiah is King, Priest, and Victor who sits in glory at God's right hand. Ps. xlv speaks of eternal dominion, while Ps. lxxii emphasizes the universality of Messiah's rule.

But secondly, the Psalter also prepares men's minds for a suffering Messiah. Is. liii has its counterpart in the Psalter. The anointed Son of Yahweh, the Priest-King whose throne will stand for ever and whose reign of peace and righteousness will cause all nations to be blessed in Him, is to submit Himself to dreadful suffering (Pss. xxii, lxix, *etc.*). However, not until Christ interpreted the Psalter to the apostles were these and similar psalms considered to be messianic (Lk. xxiv. 27–46). Only as the Lord enlightened the disciples' minds did the Church understand the meaning of these passages in the Psalter and make it the hymn-book and the prayer-book of the Church.

VIII. THE CHRISTIAN AND THE PSALTER

Apart from the inherent religious and devotional qualities of the Psalms two factors have compelled the Christian Church to make the Psalter her prayer-book.

1. There is the fact that the Psalter occupied such a large place in the life and teaching of our Lord. It was the prayer-book which He would use in the synagogue service, and His hymn-book in the Temple festival. He used it in His teaching, met temptation with it, sang the Hallel from it after the Last Supper, quoted it from the cross, and died with it on His lips.

2. Moreover, from earliest times the Psalter has been both the hymn-book and the prayer-book of the Christian Church. Some of her great hymns of praise are modelled on the psalms (Lk. i. 46 ff., 68 ff., ii. 29 ff.). The Psalter was the inspiration of the apostles in persecution (Acts iv. 25 f.), it was embedded in their message (Acts ii. 25 ff., xiii. 33), it was used to set forth their profoundest beliefs concerning the Lord (Heb. i. 6, 10–13, ii. 6–8, v. 6, x. 5–7). In all ages the Church has found in the Psalter 'a Bible in miniature' (Luther), or 'the Bible within the Bible'. And while this 'Bible in miniature' originated in the Jewish Church, and is intimately related to the Old Testament, yet, because it is illumined by the light that breaks from the Gospels, the Christian Church claims it and uses it too in all her access to God whom she evermore worships and adores.

BIBLIOGRAPHY. In addition to works already referred to, and from a vast literature, see S. Mowinckel, *He that Cometh*, 1956; H. H. Rowley (ed.), *The Old Testament and Modern Study*, 1951, ch. vi; A. S. Rappoport, *The Psalms*, 1935; D. C. Simpson, *The Psalmists*, 1926; W. E. Barnes, *The Psalms*, Introduction, *WC*, 1931; A. C. Welch, *The Psalter in Life, Worship and History*, 1926; A. F. Kirkpatrick, *The Book of Psalms*, 1921; W. O. E. Oesterley, *The Psalms*, 1939.

J.G.S.S.T.

PSALMS OF SOLOMON. See NEW TESTAMENT APOCRYPHA, PSEUDEPIGRAPHA, I.

PSALTERY. See MUSIC AND MUSICAL INSTRUMENTS.

PSEUDEPIGRAPHA. The term is used to describe those Jewish writings which were excluded from the Old Testament Canon and which find no place in the Apocrypha. For the purpose of this article the term will also exclude the sectarian documents of the Qumran library (for which see DEAD SEA SCROLLS). Unlike the Apocrypha, which were included in the Greek Scriptures, these pseudepigrapha never approached canonical status. They nevertheless played an important rôle during the inter-testamental period and are valuable for the light they shed on the Jewish background of the New Testament. While not all the writings included in this group are pseudepigraphic in the strict sense of writings published under assumed names (see PSEUDONYMITY), the majority of them are and the name is therefore generally appropriate. It will be convenient to divide them roughly between Palestinian and Jewish–Hellenistic groups, as their place of origin strongly affected their form and purpose. Because of a dominant thread which runs through the majority of these writings they have aptly been described as the literature of the apocalyptic movement.

I. THE PALESTINIAN GROUP

The Palestinian group contains three different literary types, poetry, legend, and apocalypse. The **Psalms of Solomon** almost certainly belongs to the period at the end of the Maccabean age and is an example of the anti-Sadducean polemic of the Pharisees at that period. In the majority of these eighteen psalms, which are modelled on the Davidic Psalms, there is no reference to the Messiah (*Ps. Sol.* xvii is the main exception); but much about the messianic kingdom. The overthrow of the Hasmonean dynasty by the Roman Pompey is regarded as a divine act, although Pompey himself is condemned for his profanation of the Temple. There were other psalm collections during the inter-testamental period, an example of which is the **Psalms of Joshua** found in the Qumran library.

There were many books which were legendary expansions of biblical history, based mainly on the law, although including some legends about the prophets. Among the earliest of these is the **Testaments of the Twelve Patriarchs**, based on Gn. xlix. Each of Jacob's sons gives his instructions to his descendants and much of this teaching is of a high moral order. They are represented as reviewing their own failings to serve as a warning to others, but two of the Patriarchs,

Joseph and Issachar, are able to commend their own virtues. The original work was a Pharisaic production written towards the end of the 2nd century BC, but this was later expanded by additions. The library at Qumran contained certain parts of an earlier recension of the *Testaments* of Levi and Naphtali, in Aramaic and Hebrew, but does not appear to have possessed the whole. This new evidence has confirmed Charles' opinion that the *Testaments* contained some late Jewish and Christian additions. There are in these writings some similarities to the teachings of Jesus, as, for example, exhortations to humility, brotherly love, and almsgiving. These parts represent some of the best moral injunctions of pre-Christian Judaism.

Another book based on Genesis is the **Book of Jubilees,** so styled from its system of dating. The author advocated a 364-day year in order to assist the Jews to keep the feasts on the proper day. This is typical of his legalistic approach. The whole book, in fact, purports to be a revelation to Moses on Mt. Sinai and is clearly intended to uphold the eternal validity of the law. The Pharisaic author was intent on combating the encroachments of Hellenism during the latter part of the 2nd century BC. In the course of the revelations there are many legendary accretions to the biblical history, as for example the attribution to Satan and not to God of the suggestion that Abraham should sacrifice Isaac (xvii. 16, xviii. 9, 12). The author insisted on the strict observance of Jewish rites, particularly circumcision and Sabbath observance (xv. 33 f., ii. 25–31, l. 6–13).

In a similar vein to the *Testaments of the Twelve Patriarchs* is the **Testament of Job,** in which Job delivers to the children of his second wife a parting address. He is represented as reviewing his past life, and the book concludes with an account of the special ability granted to his three daughters to sing heavenly songs while his soul is transported by chariot to heaven. The book appears to have been the work of an author belonging to one of the stricter Jewish sects (possibly the *ḥasidim*) and may be dated possibly about 100 BC.

Several legendary works of a similar character, but which at least in their extant texts appear to have been subjected to Christian influence, must be included among this group of writings. The **Life of Adam and Eve,** which was at one time erroneously described as an Apocalypse of Moses, is an imaginative reconstruction of the history subsequent to the fall, and in the course of it Adam has a vision in which he sees a picture of the developments of Jewish history to post-exilic times. It is generally dated between AD 20 and 70, since it supposes that Herod's Temple is still standing (xxix. 6 f.).

The **Martyrdom of Isaiah** is a partly Jewish and partly Christian book, extant only in Ethiopic. It tells how Isaiah came to be 'sawn asunder' (*cf.* Heb. xi. 37) with a wood saw (i–v). A *Vision of Isaiah,* which has been interpolated into the original work, is clearly a Christian addition because it records the devil's indignation over Isaiah's foretelling of redemption through Christ and mentions Christian history up to the time of the Neronian persecutions (iii. 13–iv. 18). The part of the book known as the *Ascension of Isaiah* is also Jewish-Christian, for Isaiah is not only told by God of the coming of Jesus but witnesses the birth, death, and resurrection of the Coming One.

In addition to these there was some pre-Christian pseudo-Jeremianic and pseudo-Danielic literature which has only recently come to light from the Qumran library and which has not been sufficiently investigated at the time of writing for an account of it to be included in this survey. But a previously extant work known as the **Paralipomena of Jeremiah the Prophet,** which shows marked Christian influences, may well look back to some earlier Jeremianic cycle. It is aimed particularly against mixed marriages.

By far the most important group of Jewish pseudepigrapha is the apocalypses, among which the **Book of Enoch** takes pride of place. It is a composite work, of which the various parts were composed at different times during the last two centuries BC. The oldest sections belong to the Maccabean period according to Rowley and Torrey, although Charles had earlier maintained a pre-Maccabean date. There are five main divisions in the book as it now exists. The first describes a vision given to Enoch of future judgment, especially of the fallen angels. The second, known as *The Similitudes of Enoch*, consists of three parables dealing mainly with the theme of judgment upon the world, but with assurances to the righteous through the messianic hope. The third is an astronomical book. The fourth consists of two visions, one about the flood and the other recounting the history of the world down to the messianic age. The fifth is a miscellaneous collection of exhortations and other material, of which the most notable is an *Apocalypse of Weeks* which divides world-history into ten weeks, the last three being apocalyptic. This book is of great importance for studies in the inter-testamental period and furnishes valuable data for pre-Christian Jewish theology. It is also of interest in being cited in the New Testament Epistle of Jude.

There was another book which circulated under the name of Enoch, commonly known as the **Book of the Secrets of Enoch** or **2 Enoch.** It is also sometimes described as the *Slavonic Enoch* because it is extant only in some Slavonic manuscripts. Unlike *1 Enoch* it comes from a Hellenistic background and parts of the work are believed to belong to the Christian period. Since it was cited in the later parts of the *Testaments of the Twelve Patriarchs*, at least a section of *2 Enoch* must have preceded those parts. The whole is generally dated during the 1st century AD. It consists of an account of Enoch's journey through the seven heavens, together with certain revelations given to Enoch about creation and the history of mankind and includes Enoch's admonitions to his children. Much of the ethical instruction is noble in character and is reminiscent of the type of teaching in Ecclesiasticus.

The **Assumption of Moses** may have consisted of two distinct works known as the *Testament*, and *Assumption, of Moses* respectively (according to Charles, but Pfeiffer is reserved about this). In any case no manuscript is extant which gives the dispute over the body of Moses, which formed the basis of the *Assumption* (it is alluded to in the Epistle of Jude), but in the *Testament* Moses gives to Joshua an apocalyptic review of Israel's history from the occupation of Canaan until the end of time. There is a marked absence of any messianic hope in the book, which appears to be of Pharisaic origin (*c.* AD 6–30).

Another work belonging to the Christian period is the **Apocalypse of Ezra** (or **2** (or **4**) **Esdras**). In this book various visions are ascribed to Ezra in Babylon which deal with the problem of Israel's sufferings and bring the issue down to the author's own day (*i.e.* to the period after AD 70 when the problem became acute). The sense of hopelessness pervading the account is finally relieved only by the vague belief in a coming golden age. The book is a sincere but unsuccessful attempt to solve a pressing problem.

About the same time appeared the **Apocalypse of Baruch** (or *Syriac Baruch*), which has many similarities of thought with the last-mentioned book. It is in fact regarded by some scholars as an imitation of the more brilliant *2 Esdras*. Through the pessimism resulting from the overthrow of the city of Jerusalem there is faint hope until the messianic reign of peace begins. The present is unrelieved despair, typified by very dark waters, but the coming of Messiah, represented by lightning, brings consolation.

II. THE JEWISH–HELLENISTIC GROUP

Among the more notable Jewish–Hellenistic pseudepigrapha are propaganda works (the *Letter of Aristeas* and parts of the *Sibylline Oracles*), legendary history (*3 Maccabees*), philosophy (*4 Maccabees*) and apocalyptic (part of the *Slavonic Enoch* already mentioned and part of the *Greek Baruch* (see APOCRYPHA)).

The **Letter of Aristeas** purports to come from the time of the production of the LXX said to have been proposed by Ptolemy II, Philadelphus, of Egypt (285–245 BC). The narrative itself is legendary and was written in fact by a Jew (*c.* 100 BC) who wished to commend the Jewish law and religion to his hellenistic contemporaries. It is an apology for Judaism against its Gentile detractors.

About 140 BC an Alexandrian Jew produced some **Sibylline Oracles** in imitation of the ancient Greek oracles attributed to the Sibyl, a pagan prophetess held in high regard not only by contemporary Greeks but also among many Jews and even Christians at a later period. Numerous additions were subsequently made to these oracles. Of the twelve extant books the majority appear to be Christian in origin, but books III–V are generally regarded as Jewish. These are specifically devoted to propaganda and consist particularly of judgments on Gentile nations. In book III occurs a review of Israelitish history from Solomon's time down to Antiochus Epiphanes and his successors, but the Jews are to benefit by the coming Messiah. There is a special appeal to Greece to cease its pagan worship, and this strong apologetic purpose is further seen in the claim that the Sibyl is in reality a descendant of Noah.

3 Maccabees, like *2 Maccabees*, is a legendary embellishment designed for the glorification of the Jews in Egypt under Ptolemy Physcon. **4 Maccabees** is a philosophical homily in which a Hellenistic Jewish author, of a definitely legalistic persuasion, discourses on the main theme of the control of the passions by reason, and in this he betrays his Stoic leanings. But his real admiration is nevertheless for the Mosaic law, and he seeks unsuccessfully to achieve a synthesis between the two.

As a whole this pseudepigraphic literature throws interesting light on the preparation period for the gospel. It belongs to times when prophetic declarations had ceased and when there was an increasing reverence for the law. They were times of perplexity, and apocalyptic emerged to attempt to reconcile the prophetic promises with the disastrous course of current history and to project the fulfilment of these promises into an age yet to come. These books had wide circulation among the Jews, and many of the New Testament writers may have been acquainted with them.

The literary device used seems strange to modern ideas, but the great preponderance of pseudonymous ascriptions in these books is evidence of its contemporary effectiveness. It may have been adopted by reason both of security and of the need to ensure the maximum authority for the writings (see PSEUDONYMITY).

There are many theological differences and developments in this literature as compared with the earlier prophetical period. The future age differs essentially from the present. It has a supernatural origin and will displace the present age, which is conceived of as under the domination of evil influences. This doctrine of the two ages is characteristic of the inter-testamental period and finds some echoes in New Testament thought. It is significant that owing to this apocalyptic approach to future history the messianic hope was not as dominant during this period as it had been earlier. The clearest picture is in the *Book of Enoch*, where the messianic conception has become more transcendental, parallel with the increasing transcendentalism of the conception of God. The Son of man as a heavenly pre-existent Being is conceived as sharing with God in judgment. Another striking feature of this literature is the receding interest in pure nationalism and in the development of individualism, on the one hand, and universalism, on the other. But perhaps the greatest service rendered by the literature was its antidote to the increasing legalism of Judaism, particularly among the Pharisees, in spite of the fact that this legalism is not entirely lacking from many of these books.

See also APOCALYPTIC, APOCRYPHA.

BIBLIOGRAPHY. R. H. Charles (ed.), *The Apocrypha and Pseudepigrapha in English*, 1913; W. Fairweather, *The Background of the Gospels*, 1926; E. Kautzsch (ed.), *Die Apokryphen und Pseudepigraphen des Alten Testaments*, 1900; R. H. Pfeiffer, *History of New Testament Times with an Introduction to the Apocrypha*, 1949; H. H. Rowley, *The Relevance of Apocalyptic*, 1944; E. Schürer, *Geschichte des Jüdischen Volkes im Zeitalter Jesu Christi*[4], III, 1909 (E.T.: *A History of the Jewish People in the Time of Jesus Christ*, 1886–90); C. C. Torrey, *The Apocryphal Literature*, 1945.

D.G.

PSEUDONYMITY. Pseudonymity is the practice of attributing literary works to assumed names, a device widely used in the ancient world. Numerous examples are known from the Graeco-Roman world, but in studying the Christian attitude towards such a device the Jewish pseudepigrapha are very much more significant (see PSEUDEPIGRAPHA, Section I). The former were not, as the latter were, expressions of a religious approach, and because of the wide differences in content between secular and religious writings the Jewish writings naturally form a closer parallel with the numerous Christian pseudepigrapha circulating during the first three centuries AD.

There is no doubt that these writings enjoyed considerable popularity, and for this reason demand some explanation of their character and method. It is difficult for modern minds accustomed to the literary condemnation of plagiarism (the use of another's material) to appreciate this ancient practice of using another's name. But it is often assumed that the ancient approach was essentially different from the modern and implied nothing reprehensible. Undoubtedly many of the authors who resorted to this practice were men of sincerity, and herein lies the problem. Are there any ascertainable principles which throw any light on the apparent contradiction?

I. THE GREEK APPROACH

There are many causes which are thought to account for the abundance of pseudonymous writings among the Greeks. There was a tendency to ascribe anonymous works to some well-known author of works of the same kind, for instance epics to Homer or Virgil. Many writings by scholars were attributed to their masters, from whom they had learnt their wisdom, as, for example, among the followers of Plato. Moreover, rhetorical exercises were frequently attributed to famous persons (*cf.* the forgery known as the *Epistle of Phalaris*). A more deliberate type of forgery prevalent in the Greek world was the practice of publishing manuscripts under the names of popular authors as a method of selling them. A later motive was the desire to produce documents in support of certain doctrines by attributing them to some ancient and honoured teacher (*e.g.* among the Neopythagoreans, and in a Christian context the Clementine literature and the works attributed to Dionysius the Areopagite).

II. THE JEWISH APPROACH

This seems to have inherited little directly from Greek practices, since the majority of the pseudonymous writings were the products of Palestinian Judaism. The widespread Greek secular usage may have had some small impact, although the *Letter of Aristeas* and the *Slavonic Enoch* are almost the only clear instances of the practice even among the Hellenistic Jews. See PSEUDEPIGRAPHA, Section II. The main causes for pseudonymity must clearly be sought elsewhere. Undoubtedly the most significant factor was the rigidity of the law and the cessation of prophecy. An authoritative message for the contemporary Jews of the two centuries before Christ could be established, it was thought, only by attributing such a message to some hero of the past whose authority was unquestioned. This accounts for the prominence of the patriarchal names among the pseudepigrapha. Indeed, all the assumed authors except Aristeas are mentioned either in the Law or the Prophets. This illustrates clearly the fundamental difference between Greek and Jewish pseudonymous practice. The latter possessed what the former lacked, an authoritative body of writings which formed the basis of their religious beliefs, and their pseudonymous productions were therefore extensions of canonical material (the nearest Greek parallel is the *Sibylline Oracles*). It is this phenomenon which raises problems for Jewish pseudonymity which were almost entirely absent from the Greek world. The Jewish authors were religious men, and it is not easy to see how they could resort to a literary method which to us seems morally questionable. There are a number of possible explanations.

The false ascription may have been occasioned by the use of materials traditionally handed down in association with some famous name. Some scholars, for instance, have virtually maintained this viewpoint when suggesting that Jude cites not the *Book of Enoch* but an earlier oral ascription believed to have been a true saying of Enoch which was later incorporated into the pseudonymous book (*cf.* Jude 14). But unfortunately data for verifying this procedure are practically non-existent. Another suggestion arises from the nature of apocalyptic. This mode of thought frequently made use of symbolic figures of speech, which the readers were clearly not expected to take literally, and the same tacit assumption may have been made over the pseudonym. Sometimes the device may have been used in self-defence when the author was not anxious to parade his identity for fear of arousing the suspicions of the tyrannical occupying power. In this case the readers would readily appreciate the reason for the pseudonym and would absolve the writer from any moral censure. Yet in few cases is this explanation clearly applicable. It is possible that the Jews paid little attention to literary property and were far more concerned with contents than authorship, and if this were generally so it might explain the readiness with which the writings circulated.

III. THE CHRISTIAN APPROACH

There is no doubt that the prevalence of pseudonymous early Christian writings owed more to Jewish than to Greek influences. By the 2nd century AD a canon of Christian writings had come into existence which, although lacking formal codification (except in the case of Marcion), was nevertheless real and authoritative. There were pseudonymous counterparts to all four types of New Testament Literature—Gospels, Acts, Epistles, and Apocalypses. The majority of these sprang from heretical sources, and in these cases the use of the pseudonymous device is transparent. Esoteric doctrines outside the theology of orthodoxy sought support by the theory that secret teachings had been handed down to the initiates of a particular sect but had been hidden from others. The production of pseudonymous apostolic writings was thus made easy. Since the interval separating the assumed author from the real author was not as great as in the majority of Jewish writings of this character, it did not stretch the credulity of the readers too much to be told that some new writing was in fact an apostolic production, assuming, of course, that they were ignorant of its true source.

In spite of the fact that pseudonymity was a widespread practice, it must not be assumed that it would have been regarded as a harmless literary device among the orthodox Christians. What external evidence there is suggests rather that the Church took a firm stand against the practice (*e.g.* the Muratorian Canon, Serapion, Tertullian). Tertullian in fact records the unfrocking of the Asian presbyter who confessed to writing the *Acts of Paul* out of his love for Paul, which does not suggest it was an acknowledged practice to produce such literature. For this reason the assumption by some scholars that certain New Testament books are really pseudonymous raises an acute psychological and moral problem, which many of the supporters of these hypotheses are willing to admit. There is a presumption against New Testament canonical pseudepigrapha which can be nullified only by overwhelming and conclusive evidence to the contrary, and even here each case must be judged entirely on its own merits.

On the question of pseudonymity in Old Testament literature, see DANIEL, BOOK OF, DEUTERONOMY, ECCLESIASTES, PENTATEUCH.

BIBLIOGRAPHY. R. H. Charles, *Religious Development between the Old and the New Testaments*, 1914; W. Fairweather, *The Background of the Gospels*, 1926, pp. 216 ff.; J. Moffatt, *An Introduction to the Literature of the New Testament*[2], 1912, pp. 40 ff.; H. J. Rose, 'Pseudepigraphic Literature', *Oxford Classical Dictionary*, 1949; R. D. Shaw, *The Pauline Epistles*[4], 1913, pp. 477 ff.; and especially F. Torm, *Die Psychologie der Pseudonymität im Hinblick auf die Literatur des Urchristentums*, 1932. D.G.

PTOLEMAIS.

I. IN THE OLD TESTAMENT

The name given in the late 3rd or early 2nd century BC by Ptolemy I or II of Egypt to the seaport of Accho, on the north point of the Bay of Acre (named from Accho), about 8 miles north of Carmel headland which faces it across the bay. Accho was the only natural harbour on the coast south of Phoenicia in Old Testament times, and various routes connected it with Galilee and its lake, the Jordan valley, and beyond. The only reference to Accho in the Old Testament is in Jdg. i. 31, where it is assigned to Asher, but the tribe failed to capture it, and it probably remained Phoenician throughout the Old Testament period. Some would emend Ummah in Jos. xix. 30 to read Accho (*e.g. GTT*, p. 139), though this is but a conjecture.

Accho is more frequently mentioned in non-biblical texts. A prince of Accho (Egyp. *'ky*) is apparently already mentioned in the Egyptian execration texts of the 18th century BC (G. Posener, *Princes et Pays d'Asie et de Nubie*, 1940, p. 87, E49; *ANET*, p. 329, n. 9). Accho later appears in topographical lists of the 15th and 13th centuries BC, in the Amarna tablets of the 14th century BC (*e.g. ANET*, pp. 484–485, 487), and in an Egyptian satirical letter of *c.* 1240 BC (*ANET*, p. 477b). In later days Sennacherib of Assyria mentions Accho as part of the realm of Tyre and Sidon on his Palestinian campaign of 701 BC (*ANET*, p. 287b), and Ashurbanipal attacked it in the 7th century BC (*ANET*, p. 300b). On the relation of Accho to Asher and Galilee inland, see D. Baly, *Geography of the Bible*, 1957, pp. 128–131.

K.A.K.

II. IN THE NEW TESTAMENT

During the inter-testamental period the name Accho was changed to Ptolemais, presumably in honour of Ptolemy Philadelphus (285–246 BC). Under this name it played an important rôle in the Jews' struggle for freedom under the Maccabees (*cf.* 1 Macc. v. 15, xii. 45–48), but is only once noticed in the New Testament (Acts xxi. 7). Paul, sailing from Tyre to Caesarea towards the end of his third missionary journey, put in at Ptolemais, and while his ship lay at anchor in the harbour spent a day with the Christians of the place. This was probably not the only time he passed through the city, since he came along the Phoenician coast a number of times.

In Paul's day Ptolemais was a *colonia*, the Emperor Claudius having settled a group of veterans there. After the Roman period it assumed its original name Akka and has maintained it to the present day. During the Crusades

Ptolemais rose to importance under the Gallicized name Acre or St. Jean d'Acre. Today it is overshadowed by the prominence of the city of Haifa, which lies directly across the bay.

W.W.W.

PTOLEMY. The name borne by the fourteen kings of the purely Macedonian Greek dynasty that ruled Egypt *c.* 323 to 30 BC.

I. THE EARLY PTOLEMIES

After the death of Alexander the Great at Babylon in 323 BC one of his marshals, Ptolemy son of Lagus, had himself appointed as satrap of Egypt, recognizing the nominal reigns of Alexander's half-brother Philip Arrhidaeus and infant son Alexander the younger, as did the great conqueror's other marshals in Babylon, Syria, Asia Minor, and Greece. But in 310 BC the boy Alexander had been murdered, and each marshal tried unsuccessfully to take the whole Empire from his rivals, so that it was carved up between them. Ptolemy therefore took the title king of Egypt in 304 BC, reigning till 285. Under him, his son Ptolemy II Philadelphus (285–246 BC), and his grandson Ptolemy III Euergetes I (246–221 BC), Egypt became once more a power in the Near East, no longer as a pharaonic but as a Hellenistic monarchy. Ptolemy IV Philopator (221–205 BC) was a dissolute ruler, echoes of whose Syrian wars occur in 3 Macc. i. 1–5.

Like the Ptolemaic kings themselves, all their chief ministers, all the upper ranks of the vast, centralized bureaucracy now instituted to govern Egypt, the main armed forces, the official language of administration—all were Greek. Egypt was the king's personal estate and run on strictly business lines to extract the maximum profit for the Crown. Alexandria (*q.v.*) was the capital, famous for its buildings, institutions ('Museum', Library, Serapeum, *etc.*, see fig. 5), and its exports of grain, papyrus, perfumes, glass, *etc.* There was early a large community of Greek-speaking Jews in Alexandria; in the 3rd century BC the law was rendered into Greek for their use, and the rest of the Old Testament followed, and thus was born the Septuagint version (see TEXT AND VERSIONS).

The Ptolemies endeavoured to retain the loyalty of the native population of Egypt by gifts of money, lands, and new temple buildings to the great, traditional Egyptian priesthoods. Large new temples arose (*e.g.* at Edfu, Dendera, Kom Ombo) in the old pharaonic style, but the 'pharaohs' sculptured on their walls bear in hieroglyphs the names of the Ptolemies. The long hieroglyphic texts in these temples were written in a specially intricate way by the nationalistic priests so that no foreigners should penetrate their secret traditions; they contain a vast deposit of information on Egyptian religion and mythology, much of it handed down from, and valuable for the study of, pharaonic Egypt.

At first, Palestine—including the Jewish community—and Coele-Syria (*q.v.*) formed part of the Ptolemaic kingdom along with Cyprus and Cyrenaica. But after a series of battles in 202–198 BC Antiochus III of Syria finally drove the forces of young Ptolemy V Epiphanes (205–180 BC) out of Syria–Palestine; this area, with its Jewish inhabitants, thus passed under Syrian (Seleucid) rule. The Rosetta Stone is a decree of Ptolemy V, *c.* 196 BC, inscribed in both Egyptian (hieroglyphs and demotic) and Greek; its discovery in 1799 provided the key for the decipherment of the Egyptian hieroglyphs and the founding of modern Egyptology (see WRITING).

II. THE LATER PTOLEMIES

The change from an Egyptian to a Syrian overlord was to have drastic consequences for the Jews some thirty years later, under Antiochus IV (see ANTIOCHUS). Down to this period, some of the clashes between the kingdoms of Egypt and Syria (of the 'South' and 'North') are foreshadowed in Dn. xi. 4 ff. (see DANIEL, BOOK OF). Under Ptolemy VI Philometor (180–145 BC) dynastic strife first divided the royal family; his ruthless brother Ptolemy VIII Euergetes II was for a time joint king and eventually succeeded him. Ptolemy VI favoured the Jews in Egypt and permitted the dispossessed high priest, Onias (III) of Jerusalem, to establish a rival temple in Egypt at Leontopolis, about 12 miles north of Heliopolis. Ptolemy VI's activities in Syria are mentioned in 1 Macc. x. 51–57, xi. 1–18; those of Ptolemy VIII (145–116 BC) in 1 Macc. i. 18 and xv. 16 (links with Rome). Other, non-royal, Ptolemies who are named in the Apocrypha are a general of Antiochus IV Epiphanes (1 Macc. iii. 38; 2 Macc. iv. 45, vi. 8, viii. 8, and perhaps x. 12) and a son-in-law of Simon Maccabaeus who murdered Simon and two brothers-in-law at Dok near Jericho in 135 BC (1 Macc. xvi. 11 ff.).

Under the later Ptolemies the Egyptian state steadily declined. Native revolts were more frequent; the kings and their ruthless queens (Cleopatras and Berenices) were dissolute (family murders being common), while the power of Rome grew apace. Last of the line were the brilliant but unscrupulous Cleopatra VII and her son by Julius Caesar, Ptolemy XV Caesarion. She captivated both Caesar and Antony, but made no impression on Octavian (Augustus), and so committed suicide to avoid the humiliation of appearing in a Roman triumphal procession. So Egypt passed under the heel of Rome in 30 BC.

BIBLIOGRAPHY. By far the best account of the Ptolemies is that by E. Bevan, *A History of Egypt under the Ptolemaic Dynasty*, 1927; see also *CAH*, VII, 1928; and for the religious background, Sir H. I. Bell, *Cults and Creeds in Graeco-Roman Egypt*, 1953. For the numbering and reigns of the Ptolemies, *cf.* T. C. Skeat, *The Reigns of the Ptolemies*, 1954.

K.A.K.

PUBLICAN. In the Synoptic Gospels the word 'publican' (Gk. *telōnēs*) means a collector of tax or custom on behalf of the Romans, employed by a tax farmer or contractor. As early as 212 BC there had existed in Rome a class of men (*ordo publicanorum*, Livy, xxv. 3. 8–19) who undertook state contracts of various kinds. They were closely associated with, and supported by, the Equestrian Order; and at a later date were active in a number of provinces (Cicero, *In Verrem*, ii. 3. 11, §§ 27, 28), where their work included the collection of tithes and various indirect taxes. The system was very open to abuse, and the *publicani* seem to have been prone to extortion and malpractice from the very beginning, so that while the grossest excesses were restrained by the government, and cases sometimes brought to justice, a generally bad reputation has come down to us. Cicero considered such occupations as that of customs officer vulgar on account of the hatred they incurred (*de Officiis*, i. 42, § 150) and Livy records the opinion, expressed in 167 BC, that where there is a publican allies have not liberty (xlv. 18. 3–4). The central contractors were often foreign to the provinces whose taxes they farmed, though there was nothing to prevent their being natives, and they might employ native sub-contractors. (The expression *architelōnēs* in Lk. xix. 2 seems to imply that Zacchaeus was the contractor for the whole of the taxes of Jericho and had collectors under him—Strack-Billerbeck, II, 249.) But the collectors were usually from the native population, and their generally extortionate practices (*cf.* what amounts to an admission in the words of Zacchaeus, Lk. xix. 8, and the conditions implied by the counsel of John the Baptist, Lk. iii. 13) made them an especially despised and hated class, so that our Lord could refer to them as typical of a selfish attitude (Mt. v. 46). For the strict Jew, however, this quite natural attitude of hatred was aggravated and altered in character by the religious consideration that the publican was regarded as ceremonially unclean, on account of his continual contact with Gentiles. This uncleanness, and the Rabbis' teaching that their pupils should not eat with such persons, account for the attitude evidenced by the expressions *publicans and sinners* (Mt. ix. 10 f., xi. 19; Mk. ii. 15 f.; Lk. v. 30, vii. 34, xv. 1) and *publicans and harlots* (Mt. xxi. 31), and for the questions of Mt. ix. 10 f., xi. 19; Mk. ii. 15 f.; Lk. v. 29 f. (*cf.* Strack-Billerbeck, I, 498 f.), and indicates the intention of the command of Mt. xviii. 17. This also lends point to both the negative and positive aspects of the denunciation of the chief priests and elders in Mt. xxi. 31b, to the statement of Mt. xi. 19; Lk. vii. 34, and to the story of the Pharisee and the publican, Lk. xviii. 10 ff.

BIBLIOGRAPHY. *Arndt*; *OCD*, *s.v. decumae, portoria, publicani, vectigalia*; E. Schürer, *HJP*[4], I, 116, 474 f., 479; *SB*, I, 377 f., 498 f., 770 f., II, 249. J.H.H.

PUBLIUS. *Poplios* is the Greek version of the Latin name, probably *praenomen*, of the 'chief man of the island' of Malta in Acts xxviii. 7. The title appears to be correct local usage (*IG*, XIV. 601; *CIL*, X. 7495), and may refer either to a native officer or to the chief Roman official. In the latter case the use of *praenomen* alone may perhaps be explained as the familiar usage of the local inhabitants.

BIBLIOGRAPHY. W. M. Ramsay, *SPT*, p. 343; *BC*, IV, *in loc.*; *Arndt*. J.H.H.

PUDENS. A Roman Christian who joined Claudia and others in greeting Timothy (2 Tim. iv. 21). Martial (iv. 13) salutes Aulus Pudens and his bride Claudia, and another Pudens ('modest') and Claudia are linked in an inscription (*CIL*, vi. 15066): but identification with Timothy's friends is improbable (see CLAUDIA). Tradition called Pudens a senator, locating his house-church at the Church of S. Pudentiana (*cf. Liber Pontificalis*, ed. Duchesne, I, pp. 132 f.); for excavations, *cf.* R. Lanciani, *Pagan and Christian Rome*, 1895, pp. 110 ff., and references there.

A.F.W.

PULSE (*zērō'îm*, 'seeds', Dn. i. 12; *zērᵉ'ōnîm*, 'seeds', RVmg 'herbs', Dn. i. 16). A general Hebrew word for something that is sown, but usually denoting edible seeds which can be cooked, such as lentils, beans, *etc.* In the biblical context the word is used of the plain vegetable food sought by Daniel and his friends in preference to the rich diet of the king's table.

J.D.D.

PUNISHMENT. See CRIME AND PUNISHMENT.

PURIFICATION. See CLEAN AND UNCLEAN; PURITY.

PURIM. A Jewish festival celebrated during the 13–15th days of the month Adar. On this occasion the book of Esther is read, and traditionally the congregation in the synagogue shouts and boos whenever the name of Haman is mentioned. The book of Esther gives the origin of the festival. In the reign of Ahasuerus, probably Xerxes (485–465 BC) but possibly Artaxerxes II (404–359 BC), Haman, the vizier, determined to massacre all the Jews. Since he was a superstitious man, he cast lots to find an auspicious day. The word *pûr*, which in Est. iii. 7, ix. 24, 26, is said to mean 'lot', is not a Hebrew word, but is almost certainly the Assyrian *puru*, which means a pebble, or small stone, which would be used for casting lots.

The earliest reference to the festival outside the Old Testament is 2 Macc. xv. 36, where a decree is made in 161 BC to celebrate annually the defeat of Nicanor by Judas Maccabaeus on 'the thirteenth day of the twelfth month, which in the Syrian tongue is called Adar, the day before Mardocheus' (Mordecai's) day.' If 2 Maccabees is dated somewhere in the middle of the 1st century BC, this shows that by 50 BC Purim was celebrated on the 14th of Adar. The parallel passage in 1 Macc. vii. 49 speaks of the institution of what was later called Nicanor's Day on the 13th of Adar, but makes no reference to Purim on the 14th. No conclusions can be drawn from this silence.

Josephus, at the end of the 1st century AD, says that Nicanor's Day was kept on Adar 13 (*Ant.* xii. 10. 5) and Purim on Adar 14 and 15 (*Ant.* xi. 6. 13). Curiously enough, Josephus does not use the term *Purim*, but says that the Jews call the two days *phroureas* (other readings are *phrouraias*, *phroureous*, *phrouraios*). This Gk. word seems to be based on the verb *phroureō*, meaning 'guard', 'protect'.

Nicanor's Day was not observed after the 7th century AD, but Adar 13 was gradually made part of Purim. As opposed to Adar 14 and 15, which were days of lively celebration, Adar 13 was a day of fasting.

Purim is not mentioned in the New Testament, unless it is the feast of Jn. v. 1. J.S.W.

PURITY. The original biblical significance was ceremonial. It was to be obtained by certain ablutions and purifications which were enjoined upon the worshipper in the performance of his religious duties. Purifications were common to many other religions, but there they were merely ceremonial and had no ethical significance. In the case of Israel most of the ceremonial purifications had both sanitary and ethical significance. Though Gn. xxxv. 2 and Ex. xix. 14 indicate that the general idea did not originate with the Mosaic law, it is clear that only with the giving of the ceremonial law under Moses were these regulations codified and detailed. In the teaching of the prophets the significance largely passed from the merely ceremonial to the ethical. In the New Testament the teaching of Christ and the descent of the Spirit lifted the meaning of purity into the moral and spiritual sphere.

In the general sense common to the New Testament, and to the devotional literature of the Old, purity indicates a state of heart where there is complete devotion to God. As unadulterated water is said to be pure, and gold without alloy is pure gold, so the pure heart is the undivided heart where there is no conflict of loyalties, no cleavage of interests, no mixture of motives, no hypocrisy, and no insincerity. It is wholeheartedness God-wards. This is probably the sense in which our Lord used it in the Beatitudes (Mt. v. 8). The reward of the undivided heart is the vision of God. No vision of God can come to the heart that is unclean because it is out of harmony with the nature and character of God. In the further teaching of Christ (see Mk. vii. 14–28) He transfers the state of defilement, and so of purity, entirely from the outer to the inner man. Purity in this sense may be said to be a state of heart reserved completely for God and freed from all worldly distractions.

In the specialized sense purity came to mean freedom from sensual pollution, particularly in the sexual life, though the New Testament does not teach that sexual activity is polluting in itself and, indeed, makes it clear that rightly ordered sexual behaviour is not (*cf.* Heb. xiii. 4). Nevertheless, the New Testament teaches the sanctity of the body as the temple of the Holy Spirit (*cf.* 1 Cor. vi. 19 f.) and inculcates the duty of self-restraint and self-denial even to the extent of personal loss. Purity is thus the spirit of renunciation and of the obedience which brings every thought and feeling and action into subjection to Christ. It begins within and extends outwards to the entire life, cleansing all the centres of living and controlling all the movements of body and spirit. R.A.F.

PURPLE. See COLOURS, LYDIA.

PURSE. See BAG.

PUT, PHUT. 1. Third son of Ham (Gn. x. 6; 1 Ch. i. 8). **2.** Warriors alongside Lubim (*q.v.*), Egyptians, and Ethiopians unable to save No-Amon (Thebes) from Assyria (Na. iii. 9). Elsewhere the word is found only in Je. xlvi. 9; Ezk. xxx. 5 (as Egyptian allies), in Ezk. xxxviii. 5 (in Gog's armies; AV 'Libya(ns)', *q.v.*), and in Ezk. xxvii. 10 (warriors of Tyre). Put is certainly African, but its location is disputed. Claiming that Lubim (Libyans) and Put are distinct in Na. iii. 9, some wish to equate Put with *Pw(n)t* (Somaliland(?)) of Egyptian texts. But Old Persian *putiya* and Bab. *puṭa* (= Heb. *pûṭ*) become *T' Ṯmḥw*, 'Libya', in Egyptian, thus making Put Libya (G. Posener, *La Première Domination Perse en Égypte*, 1936, pp. 186, 187). Lubim and Put in Na. iii. 9 are like Lubim and Sukkiim (*q.v.*) in 2 Ch. xii. 3. Also, Tyre would employ Libyan rather than Somali auxiliaries. *Pûṭ* may derive from Egyp. *pḏty*, 'foreign bowman', or similar; especially as the Libyans were archers (W. Hölscher, *Libyer und Ägypter*, 1937, pp. 38, 39). K.A.K.

PUTEOLI. Modern Pozzuoli, near Naples, a Samian colony from Cumae founded in the 6th century BC. Puteoli probably fell into Roman hands with Capua in 338 BC, and rapidly became an important arsenal and trading port. Livy mentions a garrison of 6,000 during the Hannibalian invasion (xxiv. 13), and the embarkation of large reinforcements for Spain (xxvi. 17). Rome's eastern traffic, notably the Egyptian grain, passed through Puteoli. Seneca describes the arrival of the Alexandrian corn-fleet (Ep. lxxvii), and Paul arrived on an Alexandrian freighter (Acts xxviii. 13). The Via Domitiana linked Puteoli with the Via Appia. Considerable ruins remain. E.M.B.

PYGARG. Referred to solely in the list of allowed meats in Dt. xiv. 5, this pygarg (*dîšôn*) must be one of the ruminants. Pygarg is derived from the LXX translation *pygargos*, meaning 'white-rumped' and is mentioned by Herodotus and Pliny. It could be the addax, a striking black-and-white desert antelope, or the Arabian oryx:

other less likely suggestions are the Arabian ibex and one of the gazelles. G.C.

PYTHON. This is the Greek name given to the mythological serpent or dragon which lived at Pytho beneath Mount Parnassus, and guarded the Delphic oracle. Apollo slew it, but the name was then applied to anyone who prophesied under the inspiration of Apollo. Such persons generally spoke with the mouth closed, uttering words quite beyond their own control, and so were also known as *engastrimythoi* or ventriloquists (Plutarch, *De Defectu Oraculorum*, ix, p. 414E).

Acts xvi. 16 records how Paul met and subsequently exorcized a young woman with such a spirit of divination at Philippi: it is significant that Luke uses a word with pagan connections, *manteuomenē*, not elsewhere employed in the New Testament, to describe her oracular speech, obviously inspired by a demonic power.

D.H.W.

Q

QUAIL. See BIRDS OF THE BIBLE.

QUARRY. 1. Heb. *šᵉḇārîm*, a place from which stone is dug. In Jos. vii. 5, AV and RV Shebarim should follow RVmg, 'quarries', in describing the place to which the Israelites fled after their abortive attack on Ai. Stone was quarried through the centuries in Palestine. Good limestone lies close to the surface in most places and is broken out of its bed by cracking the stone along lines of cleavage. The so-called stables of Solomon in Jerusalem near to the Temple area are almost certainly ancient quarries.

2. The word *pᵉsîlîm* (Jdg. iii. 19, 26) refers to the product of the quarry in the shape of a graven image. This word, translated 'quarries' in Jdg. iii. 19, 26 is translated elsewhere as graven image (Dt. vii. 5; Ps. lxxviii. 58; Is. x. 10; Mi. v. 13). J.A.T.

QUARTUS. The Latin name, meaning 'fourth', of a Christian at Corinth whose greetings Paul conveys (Rom. xvi. 23). He is called 'the brother'. This may mean either 'brother of Erastus', mentioned with him (several Corinthian Christians have Latin names); or 'our brother', *i.e.* our 'fellow-Christian', the title balancing the appellations of the others in verses 21–23; or 'your brother', *i.e.* 'fellow-Roman Christian' (*cf.* 1 Cor. i. 1, and see SOSTHENES). Later, menologies allocated him to the Seventy (*Acta Sanctorum*, Nov. 1, p. 585). A.F.W.

QUEEN (Heb. *malkâ*, Gk. *basilissa*). The word 'queen' is not widely used in the Bible. It is used to describe women from countries outside Palestine who were reigning monarchs in their own right. Examples of this are the queen of Sheba (1 Ki. x. 1; *cf.* Mt. xii. 42; Lk. xi. 31), and Candace, queen of Ethiopia (Acts viii. 27). (See CANDACE, ETHIOPIA, SHEBA.)

In this same sense the word is used once in Israelite history with reference to Athaliah, who usurped the throne of Judah and reigned for six years (2 Ki. xi. 3). In post-biblical Jewish history Salome Alexandra, widow of Alexander Jannaeus, succeeded her husband as queen regnant for nine years (76–67 BC).

As consort the wife of the reigning monarch did not as a rule concern herself with affairs of state. Among the most noteworthy exceptions to this are Bathsheba (1 Ki. i. 15–31) and Jezebel (1 Ki. xxi). The most important woman in the royal household, in Israel and Judah as in neighbouring lands, was the queen-mother. She was pre-eminent among the ladies of the court, and sat at the monarch's right hand (Bathsheba, 1 Ki. ii. 19), crowned (Nehushta, Je. xiii. 18). In the history of Judah the queen-mothers were always named. A king might have many wives, but he had only one mother, and he was under obligation to honour her (Ex. xx. 12). That her position was more than an honorary one is evident from the record of Maacah, who was queen-mother not only during the reign of her son Abijam but also during the reign of her grandson Asa, until the latter deposed her for idolatry (1 Ki. xv. 2, 10, 13; 2 Ch. xv. 16). The Chaldean queen of Dn. v. 10 was probably the queen-mother; the same may be true of the Persian queen of Ne. ii. 6 and (possibly) the Assyrian queen of Na. ii. 7 (see HUZZAB). M.G.

QUEEN OF HEAVEN. Cakes were made for the *mᵉleḵeṯ* of the heavens by the inhabitants of Jerusalem (Je. vii. 18) and incense burnt as to a deity (Je. xliv. 17–19, 25). The unusual word is rendered as 'queen' (*malkaṯ*) in AV, and is thus considered to be the Phoen. Astarte, Assyr.

Fig. 172. Ishtar, the goddess of war and love, among whose titles was 'Queen of heaven', shown upon a lion, receiving a worshipper. From an Assyrian seal, 7th–6th century BC.

Ishtar. See ASHTAROTH. *Cf.* the female personal name (*Ham*)*mōleḵeṯ* (1 Ch. vii. 18). Alternatively, this may be a rare writing of *mᵉle'ḵeṯ*, 'the worship (or creative work)' of the heavens, also denoting an idolatrous practice. D.J.W.

QUICKSANDS (Gk. *syrtis*, 'a sandbank', RV 'Syrtis', Acts xxvii. 17). The ship in which Paul was travelling found it necessary to take precautions against being driven on to the Greater Syrtis, quicksands west of Cyrene on the North African coast. Now called the Gulf of Sidra, its treacherous sands and waters were greatly feared by sailors.

QUIRINIUS (Lk. ii. 2, RV, RSV, NEB; AV 'Cyrenius', corresponds closely to Gk. *Kyrēnios*). Publius Sulpicius Quirinius was consul at Rome in 12 BC, and not long afterwards conducted a campaign against the unruly Homanadensians of central Asia Minor. In 3 BC he became proconsul of Asia; in AD 3–4 he was adviser to the imperial heir-apparent, Gaius Caesar, during the latter's Armenian expedition; from AD 6 to 9 he was imperial legate (*legatus pro praetore*) of Syria-Cilicia. This appears to have concluded his public career; thereafter he lived at Rome, where he died in AD 21. At the beginning of his governorship of Syria–Cilicia he organized the census in Judaea when that territory became a Roman province on the deposition of Archelaus (see HEROD (2)). This census, recorded by Josephus (*Ant*. xviii. 1. 1), is that referred to in Acts v. 37. From the *Lapis Venetus* (*CIL*, III. 6687) we gather that it was not only in Judaea that a census was held under Quirinius's auspices; this inscription records the career of an officer who served under Quirinius during his legateship of Syria–Cilicia and held a census on his behalf in the Syrian city of Apamea. The census of Lk. ii. 1 ff., however, must be at least nine years earlier (see CENSUS).

The statement in Lk. ii. 2 about this earlier census has been understood in two alternative ways: 'This was the first registration of its kind; it took place when Quirinius was governor of Syria' (NEB), or 'This was the first registration carried out while Quirinius was governor of Syria' (NEBmg). The possibility that Quirinius may have been governor of Syria on an earlier occasion (see CHRONOLOGY OF THE NEW TESTAMENT) has found confirmation in the eyes of a number of scholars (especially W. M. Ramsay) from the testimony of the *Lapis Tiburtinus* (*CIL*, XIV. 3613). This inscription, recording the career of a distinguished Roman officer, is unfortunately mutilated, so that the officer's name is missing, but from the details that survive he cannot be other than Quirinius. It contains a statement that when he became imperial legate of Syria he entered upon that office 'for the second time' (Lat. *iterum*). The question is: did he become imperial legate of Syria for the second time, or did he simply receive an imperial legateship for the second time, having governed another province in that capacity on the earlier occasion?

The wording is ambiguous. Ramsay held that he was appointed an additional legate of Syria between 10 and 7 BC, for the purpose of conducting the Homanadensian war, while the civil administration of the province was in the hands of other governors, including Sentius Saturninus (8–6 BC), under whom, according to Tertullian (*Adv. Marc*. iv. 19), the census of Lk. ii. 1 ff. was held. A strong case, however, has been made out (especially by R. Syme) for the view that Quirinius's earlier legateship was not over Syria but over Galatia, where the Homanadensians would have been on his doorstep. In that case we should consider the possibility that 'Saturninus', which Tertullian appears to have read in his copy of Lk. ii. 2, was the original reading rather than 'Quirinius' (so B. S. Easton, *The Gospel according to St. Luke*, 1926, p. 20; J. W. Jack, 'The Census of Quirinius', *ExpT*, XL, 1928–9, pp. 496 ff.).

BIBLIOGRAPHY. W. M. Ramsay, *Was Christ Born in Bethlehem?*, 1905; L. R. Taylor, 'Quirinius and the Census of Judaea', *American Journal of Philology*, LIV, 1933, pp. 120 ff.; R. Syme, 'Galatia and Pamphylia under Augustus', *Klio*, XXVII, 1934, pp. 122 ff.; and other literature listed in *TCERK*, I, 1955, p. 222 (*s.v*. 'Census').

F.F.B.

QUIVER. See ARMOUR AND WEAPONS.

QUMRAN, the name of a wadi and of an ancient ruin in its vicinity, north-west of the Dead Sea (see map 16). The derivation of the name is uncertain; attempts (*e.g*. by F. de Saulcy) to connect it with Gomorrah are unacceptable. The name was recorded by a number of travellers who passed that way, but was practically unknown until the manuscript discoveries in neighbouring caves, in 1947 and the following years, put it on the map (see DEAD SEA SCROLLS). The excavations carried out at Khirbet Qumran ('ruin of Qumran') between 1951 and 1955 are generally regarded as demonstrating that this complex of buildings formed the headquarters of the community to which the Qumran manuscripts belonged. A cemetery lying between Khirbet Qumran and the Dead Sea (investigated by C. S. Clermont-Ganneau in 1873) was probably the burying-ground of the community; over 1,000 burials have been identified here, the bodies lying north and south, with the head to the south.

The site was evidently occupied in the period of the Judaean monarchy, to which period a circular cistern is assigned (*cf*. 2 Ch. xxvi. 10; and see SALT, CITY OF). The most interesting phases of occupation, however, are those generally associated with the 'people of the scrolls'. Phase Ia (*c*. 130–110 BC) was marked by the clearing of the old circular cistern and the construction of two new rectangular cisterns, together with a few rooms and a potter's kiln. This was followed by Phase Ib, marked by a thoroughgoing reconstruction of the headquarters on an elaborate scale, evidently to meet the requirements of a greatly enlarged community. This phase came to an end when the buildings were seriously damaged by the earthquake of 31 BC (mentioned in Josephus, *Ant*. xv. 5. 2). The site lay derelict until *c*. 4 BC, when the damaged buildings were repaired and strengthened. This marks the beginning of Phase II, during which the place evidently served the same purpose as it had done during Phase Ib. Among the installations which can be clearly identified are assembly rooms, scriptorium, kitchen, laundry, pottery factory (the best-preserved one thus far known from ancient Palestine), flour mills, storage bins, ovens, smelting furnaces, metal workshops, and an elaborate system of cisterns, into which water was led by an aqueduct fed from rock-hewn cisterns in the hills to the north-west.

The phases of occupation are fairly clearly indicated by the coin record, several hundreds of contemporary coins having been found in the course of the excavations. This record suggests that Phase II came to an end *c.* AD 68. Evidence of another kind shows that the end of Phase II was violent; the walls were demolished, a layer of black ash covered the site, and a quantity of arrow-heads added their silent testimony to the general picture. It is tempting to connect these events with mopping-up operations in that region at the time of the Roman occupation of Jericho in the summer of AD 68. Whether the Qumran

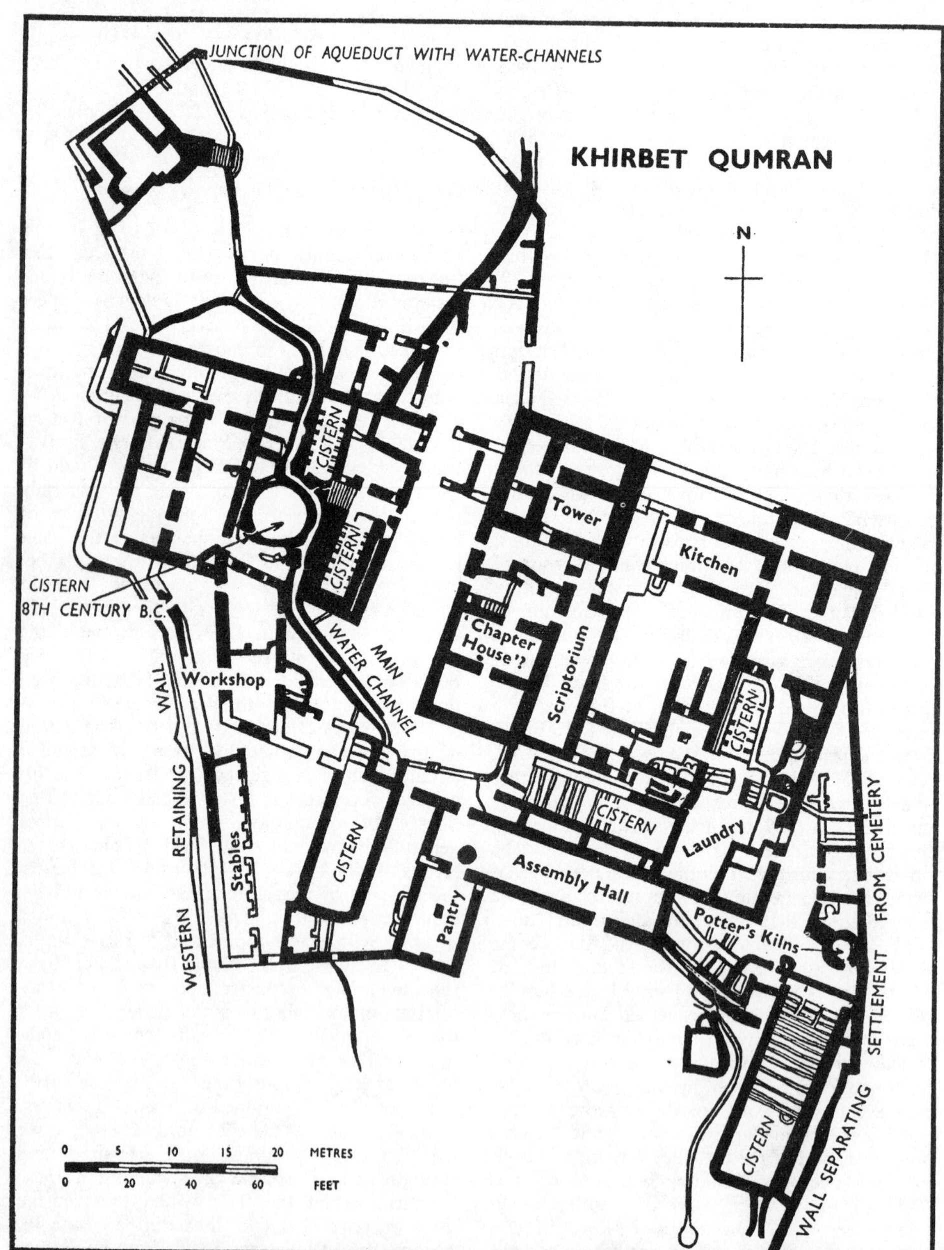

Fig. 173. Plan of the headquarters of the monastic settlement at Qumran, *c.* 31 BC.

community had remained in possession up to that time, or an insurgent garrison had taken over such well-built headquarters, remains uncertain.

A few rooms were built over the ruins and manned for some years by a Roman garrison (Phase III).

Since the excavation of Khirbet Qumran it has been widely identified with the Essene settlement referred to by Pliny the Elder (*NH* v. 17) as lying above Engedi (see ESSENES).

BIBLIOGRAPHY. Literature listed under DEAD SEA SCROLLS and ESSENES; with H. Bardtke, *Die Handschriftenfunde am Toten Meer*, 2 vols., 1953, 1958; J. van der Ploeg, *The Excavations at Qumran*, 1958; C. Roth, 'Did Vespasian capture Qumran?', *PEQ*, XCI, 1959, pp. 122 ff.

F.F.B.

QUOTATIONS (IN THE NEW TESTAMENT). There are some 250 express citations of the Old Testament in the New. If indirect or partial quotations and allusions are added, the total exceeds a thousand. The book of Revelation, for example, has no quotations, but is virtually interlaced with allusions to Old Testament texts. The importance of the Old Testament, which is indicated by this usage, is further defined by the introductory formulas: to say 'the Scripture says' is equivalent to saying 'God says' (*e.g.* Mt. xix. 4); 'that it might be fulfilled' (*e.g.* Mt. ii. 15) points to the essential connection between the message of God in the old covenant and in the new (*cf.* Warfield, pp. 299–350; Ellis, pp. 22–25).

Some citations are taken from an Old Testament Targum (Rom. xii. 19) or from the Hebrew text itself (Rom. xi. 35; 1 Cor. iii. 19). However, as one would expect in a Greek document written for Greek readers, the large majority of quotations are derived from the LXX, but with varying degrees of exactness. (Although textually dated, Turpie's manual is still helpful for classification and comparison of the Greek and Hebrew texts.) The inaccuracies which occur show the lack of concern (more than memory lapse) of the biblical writers for verbal exactness: it is the meaning rather than the words in themselves that are important.

In a considerable number of cases variant renderings are deliberately chosen, *ad hoc* or from other known versions, for the purpose of bringing out the meaning desired by the New Testament writer (*e.g.* 1 Cor. xv. 54 f.). In this process quotation and commentary are sometimes merged in what is known as a *midrash pesher*. Stendahl has shown the affinity of this hermeneutical method in Matthew with the practices of the Qumran community; it is also present in Paul (Ellis, pp. 139–149). Interpretative or *pesher* renderings may not have originated with the New Testament writer himself. Rendel Harris suggested that behind some New Testament quotations lay a pre-canonical 'testimony book', a collection of selected, combined (*e.g.* Mk. i. 2 f.), and interpreted Old Testament passages, worked out in the early Christian community for apologetic purposes (*contra*, see *NovT*, III, 1958, pp. 268–281). While C. H. Dodd has suggested some modifications to this theory, the presence of *testimonia* in the Dead Sea Scrolls shows that the practice was not unknown and substantiates, in some measure, Harris's conjecture. It also appears probable that some of these paraphrases originated in the oracles of primitive Christian prophets (Ellis, pp. 107–112). Thus the problem of textual variation points beyond itself to the larger question of interpretation and application of the Old Testament by the New.

Often Old Testament passages are applied quite at variance with the original historical meaning. Hosea's reference to the Exodus of Israel is 'fulfilled' in the baby Jesus' return from Egypt (Mt. ii. 15). A number of passages having historical reference to Israel are referred by the New Testament to the Church (*e.g.* Rom. viii. 36; Eph. iv. 8). A passage referring to Solomon, king of Israel, is applied both to Jesus Christ (Heb. i. 5) and to the Church (2 Cor. vi. 18). The rationale for this usage seems to lie (1) in a typological (see TYPOLOGY) correspondence between Old Testament *Heilsgeschichte* and the 'new age' fulfilment in Jesus Christ; (2) in the Semitic idea of corporate solidarity in which the king of Israel and Israel, Christ (Israel's true king) and the 'body of Christ', stand in realistic relationship to one another; and (3) in the conviction that the Church is the true Israel and, therefore, the heir to the promises and the object of the prophecies. While the subject-matter of New Testament quotations covers virtually all doctrinal issues, the emphasis throughout is on the Messiah and messianic age fulfilments. Sometimes the application of the quotations is dependent upon the wider context of the Old Testament (*e.g.* Acts viii. 49 f.); such 'pointer' quotations also may have been designed to call the reader's attention to a wider theme or topic (Dodd, p. 126).

Quotations other than from the Old Testament also appear. Eph. v. 14 (*cf.* 1 Cor. xv. 45b; 1 Tim. v. 18b) may be an excerpt from an early Christian hymn or oracle; Jude 14 is taken from the pseudepigraphical Book of Enoch; and Acts xvii. 28 is a quotation from a pagan writer. The first appears to be regarded on a par with 'Scripture'; the last two are used for illustrative purposes. For the nature of the speeches in Acts as quotations, *cf.* F. F. Bruce, *The Speeches in Acts*, 1942.

BIBLIOGRAPHY. B. F. C. Atkinson, *The Christian's Use of the Old Testament*, 1952; 'The Textual Background of the Use of the Old Testament by the New', *JTVI*, LXXIX, 1947, pp. 39–69; C. H. Dodd, *According to the Scriptures*, 1952; E. E. Ellis, *Paul's Use of the Old Testament*, 1957; J. R. Harris, *Testimonies*, 2 vols., 1916, 1920; T. W. Manson, 'The Old Testament in the Teaching of Jesus', *BJRL*, XXXIV, 1952, pp. 312–322; K. Stendahl, *The School of St. Matthew*, 1954; R. V. G. Tasker, *The Old Testament in the New Testament*, 1954; D. M. Turpie, *The Old Testament in the New*, 1868; B. B. Warfield, *The Inspiration and Authority of the Bible*, 1948. E.E.E.

R

RAAMAH (*ra'mâ, ra'mā*, 'trembling'). A 'son' of Cush (Gn. x. 7; 1 Ch. i. 9). The tribe of Raamah has not been identified, but inscriptions found in Sheba suggest a location near Havilah and Sheba, and east of Ophir. Like Sheba (*q.v.*), Raamah traded with Phoenician Tyre (Ezk. xxvii. 22).

RA'AMSES, RAMESES (Egyp. *Pr-R'mssw*, Pi-Ramses, 'Mansion of Rameses'). A city of Egypt mentioned in connection with Pithom, where the Hebrews were afflicted with heavy burdens (Ex. i. 11, xii. 37; Nu. xxxiii. 3). This was the famous residence of Rameses II (*c.* 1290–1224 BC) in the Delta. The kings of the XVIIIth Dynasty did no building here. For a number of years, scholars located Pi-Ramses at Pelusium, but after the excavations of Montet at Tanis (the Zoan of Ps. lxxviii. 12, 43) most scholars now believe that Pi-Ramses was situated at or near Tanis (Ṣân-el-Ḥagar), though several would place it at Qantîr, about 19 miles south of Tanis. Pi-Ramses was the starting-point of the Exodus (see fig. 80). Centuries before, Jacob had established himself in the neighbourhood (Gn. xlvii. 11). See ENCAMPMENT BY THE SEA.

BIBLIOGRAPHY. P. Montet, 'Tanis, Avaris et Pi-Ramsès', *RB*, XXXIX, 1930, pp. 5–28, and 'Avaris, Pi-Ramsès, Tanis', *Syria*, XVII, 1936, pp. 200–202; Labib Habachi, 'Khatâ'na-Qantîr: Importance', *Annales du Service des Antiquités de l'Égypte*, LII, 1954, pp. 443–562. C.D.W.

RABBAH. 1. A town with associated villages in the hill country of Judah (Jos. xv. 60), but not now identifiable. Possibly it is Rubute of the Amarna letters.

2. The capital of Ammon, represented today by Amman, capital of Jordan, 22 miles east of Jordan. Normally in the Old Testament it is *Rabbâ*, but twice in AV it is called Rabbath. Here rested the 'bedstead of iron' (iron sarcophagus) belonging to Og, king of Bashan (Dt. iii. 11).

Little is heard of Rabbah till David's time. Messengers sent to sympathize with Hanun the new king of Ammon, on the death of his father Nahash, were insulted and Hanun, suspecting treachery, obtained the help of Aramaean auxiliaries and declared war. David sent Joab to meet the enemy concentrated round Medeba (1 Ch. xix. 6, 7). Joab was beset before and behind, but, dividing his own forces, he overcame the enemy (2 Sa. x). Later David defeated the Aramaeans at Helam (2 Sa. x. 17) and was able to concentrate on Ammon. While David tarried at home, Joab besieged Rabbah and ravaged the land. Finally, Joab took the 'city of waters' but left David the honour of taking the main citadel. The inhabitants were condemned to forced labour (2 Sa. xii. 26–31; 1 Ch. xx. 1–3).

After Solomon's death Ammon broke free and troubled Israel. The prophets spoke against Rabbah as representing the people of Ammon (Je. xlix. 2, 3; Ezk. xxi. 20, xxv. 5; Am. i. 14).

Rabbah, rebuilt and renamed Philadelphia by Ptolemy Philadelphus (285–246 BC), became one of the cities of the Decapolis and an important trading centre. Considerable archaeological remains exist in the whole vicinity of Amman today, reaching back to the centuries before the Exodus.

BIBLIOGRAPHY. F. M. Abel, *Géographie de la Palestine*, II, 1933, pp. 423–425; G. L. Harding, *Antiquities of Jordan*, 1959, pp. 61–70. J.A.T.

RABBI, RABBONI. Heb. *raḇ* meant 'great', hence 'master', and later 'teacher'. 'Rabbi', 'my teacher', a reverential form of address in the time of Christ, later became a title for the authorized Jewish teachers. In the New Testament the Greek *rabbi* (or *rabbei*) is applied once to John the Baptist and twelve times to our Lord. In Mt. xxiii. 7 f., in contrast to the scribes' delight in being called 'rabbi', the disciples are told not to be so called—for them only one is Teacher. Here the explanatory Greek word in many MSS, *kathēgētēs*, is essentially similar in meaning to *didaskalos*, the interpretation given for 'rabbi' in Jn. i. 38 and xx. 16.

'Rabboni' (or *rabbouni*) is a heightened form of 'rabbi' used to address our Lord in Mk. x. 51 and Jn. xx. 16.

BIBLIOGRAPHY. G. H. Dalman, *The Words of Jesus*, 1902, pp. 331–340. F.F.

RAB-MAG. The official position of the Babylonian Nergal-sharezer (*q.v.*) at the time of the sack of Jerusalem in 587 BC (Je. xxxix. 3, 13). It has been compared with *rabu emga*, 'noble and wise', a royal title claimed by Neriglissar, and with *rab maḫḫu*, 'chief of the *maḫḫu* (administrative rather than religious) officials'. However, it may well be the Hebrew form of *rab mu(n)gu*, the title of a high Babylonian official, the precise meaning of which is unknown. D.J.W.

RAB-SARIS. The title (so RV) of the following officials: **1.** One of the three Assyrian officials sent by Sennacherib to parley with Hezekiah at Jerusalem (2 Ki. xviii. 17; *cf.* Is. xxxvi. 3, where it is omitted). **2.** The Babylonian Nabushazban who removed Jeremiah from prison and handed him over to Gedaliah (Je. xxxix. 13). **3.** Sarsechim, one of three Babylonians who sat as judges in the gate of Jerusalem after its capture in 587 BC (Je. xxxix. 3). See SARSECHIM.

The office of 'chief of the eunuchs' was held by a high-ranking palace dignitary (*cf.* Dn. i. 7). It is, however, attested in extra-biblical texts only in an Aramaic docket from Nineveh (B.M. 81–2–4, 147). For this reason attempts have been made to equate the office with the well-known Assyr. *rab šareši*, 'chief of the nobles'. This is unlikely; see RAB-SHAKEH. D.J.W.

RAB-SHAKEH. The title of the Assyrian official who, with the Tartan and Rab-saris (*q.v.*), was sent by Sennacherib, king of Assyria, from Lachish to demand the surrender of Jerusalem by Hezekiah (2 Ki. xviii. 17, 19, 26–28, 37, xix. 4–8; Is. xxxvi. 2, 4, 11–13, 22, xxxvii. 4, 8). He acted as spokesman for the delegation, addressing the citizens in the Judaean dialect. Hezekiah's representatives asked him to speak in Aramaic to avoid disclosing his mission. He refused and, at the failure of his task, returned to Lachish.

The office (*rab̲šaqēh*) ranked below that of the army commander, after whom it is listed (see TARTAN). The Assyr. *rab* ('chief') *šaqe* was once thought to be 'chief cupbearer' (Heb. *mašqeh*), but is now known to be connected with *šaqū*, 'to be high'; Sum. SAG = Assyr. *rēšu*, lit. 'head'. The Assyr. SAG is used both of officials and nobles. The title in question is probably therefore the Assyr. *rab ša reši*, 'chief of the nobles' (*cf.* RAB-SARIS), who is frequently mentioned as governor of the Assyrian province east of Harran. D.J.W.

RACA. This is probably an Aramaic word *rêqā'* or *rêqâ*, which means 'scoundrel' or 'fool'. Since the discovery in a papyrus of Gk. *rhachas* (of which *rhacha* may be a vocative), used in a bad sense (*Antiochon ton rhachan*), some scholars have suggested that the word is Greek. Raca is, however, to be derived from Aramaic and Hebrew. Heb. *rêqîm* is used in the Old Testament for good-for-nothings. In Jdg. xi. 3 the men who associated themselves with Jephthah are called *rêqîm*; in 2 Sa. vi. 20 Michal despised David because he uncovered himself as one of the *rêqîm* (AV 'vain fellows'). The word is also used in Zadokite Documents (x. 18), where it is combined with *nāb̲āl* (*cf.* Mt. v. 22, Gk. *mōre* for Heb. *nāb̲āl*) as an adjective to 'word'. Raca is abundantly used in rabbinical literature (*cf.* Strack-Billerbeck, I, 278, 279) in the sense of 'fool'.

The word *raca* is present in Mt. v. 22 in the Sermon on the Mount. Jesus gave a new spirit to the well-known law of homicide. It is not actually a question of killing, but also of disposition. People are not allowed to call their brother names in their resentment. In spirit this is as big a transgression as real murder. F.C.F.

RACE. See GAMES.

RACES. See NATIONS.

RACHEL (Heb. *rāḥēl*, 'ewe'; LXX *Rachēl*). The younger daughter of Laban, favourite wife of her first cousin Jacob, and mother of Joseph and Benjamin. She was a woman of great beauty (Gn. xxix. 17), but was capable of unprincipled action (Gn. xxxi. 19, 34, 35). Jacob first met her when he was approaching Harran in Padan-aram whither Isaac had sent him to seek a wife from among his mother's kin (xxviii. 1–2; see FAMILY). She came to water her father's sheep, and Jacob rolled away the stone from the well's mouth for her (xxix. 2–10). He immediately loved her (xxix. 11), to the extent that when he served seven years for her hand in marriage 'they seemed unto him but a few days, for the love he had to her' (xxix. 20). It is possible that at this time Laban had no sons, so that when he learned of the arrival of a near kinsman, and possible future son-in-law who would secure the descent and inheritance (*q.v.*) within the family should he himself die sonless, he made much of him (xxix. 12–14). Laban agreed to Jacob's proposal that he should work seven years for him in return for Rachel as his wife (see MARRIAGE), but, providing a feast and then taking advantage of Jacob, he passed off on him Leah, his elder daughter, saying, 'It must not be so done in our country, to give the younger before the firstborn' (xxix. 15–26). It was necessary therefore for Jacob to work a further seven years for Laban to earn Rachel as his wife (xxix. 27–30). Though there is no indication that Laban adopted Jacob, the relationship between the two is somewhat comparable to that sometimes found in the 14th-century Akkadian documents from Nuzi in N Mesopotamia. In one of these a certain Nashwi, who had no son, adopted a young man named Wullu, who at the same time married his daughter, with the intention that all his property should be inherited by Wullu (see ARCHAEOLOGY, Nuzi). The custom of the elder daughter's having the prior claim to a bridegroom, appealed to by Laban to justify his duplicity, was not widespread in the ancient Near East, and is not attested in the Nuzi documents. It seems strange that Jacob should not have known about such a custom after living for seven years in the locality, so it may be that Laban invented it as an excuse, though this cannot be certain. In the early years of her marriage Rachel was barren, and consequently provided Jacob with her handmaid Bilhah to bear children to him (xxx. 1–8). This was a normal practice of the times which was followed by Sarah with Hagar, and Leah with Zilpah, and is attested in other texts (see ARCHAEOLOGY, Nuzi, Alalaḫ). In one Nuzi text it is laid down that if the wife be childless she shall take a Lullu woman (*i.e.* a slave) and give her to her husband as a wife (*aššatu*; *cf.* xxx. 4, where Bilhah is designated *'iššâ*). If she should subsequently have children herself these would take precedence in inheritance, but the offspring of the concubine could not be turned out. After two sons, Dan and Naphtali, had been born to Bilhah, Rachel bore Joseph (xxx. 22–24). Whether her obtaining of Reuben's mandrakes (xxx. 14, 15) had anything to do with this is not stated. It was after this that Jacob resolved to return to Canaan (xxx. 25, 26), but it was another six years before God commanded him to go (xxxi. 3). By this time Laban had sons of his own (xxxi. 1), and this must have altered the status and prospects of Jacob, so that both Rachel and Leah endorsed his decision to leave (xxxi. 14–16). In the Nuzi document quoted above it is stated that should Nashwi, the father, subsequently have a son of his own the inheritance would be divided evenly between him and Wullu the adopted son, but that the true son would take the gods (*ilāni*). In the light of this Rachel may have felt that Jacob was not being treated fairly, so when Jacob and his family left by stealth (xxxi. 17 ff.) she took her father's gods (*'ᵉlōhîm*, xxxi. 30; see TERAPHIM), perhaps with a view to securing for Jacob and her children rights and privileges which should have fallen to Laban's true sons (xxxi. 19). When Laban pursued Jacob and his family, Rachel deceived him in his understandable search for his gods (xxxi. 34, 35), the theft of which was regarded by Jacob, who was unaware of Rachel's action, as sufficiently serious to require the death of the culprit (xxxi. 32). The result of this action is not related, though the teraphim were later disposed of (xxxv. 2–4), and in spite of it Jacob still held her in high esteem when he met Esau, as is indicated by his care to keep her and Joseph from harm (xxxiii. 1, 2). Rachel died soon after this while giving birth to Benjamin (xxxv. 16–20). This was between Bethel and Bethlehem, and there she was buried and Jacob raised a pillar (*maṣṣēḇâ*) over her tomb. The location of this was still known in the time of Saul, when it is described as on the border of Benjamin at Zelzah (*q.v.*; 1 Sa. x. 2). Its site is now unknown, but the prophetic figure in Je. xxxi. 15 (see Mt. ii. 18) indicates that it was somewhere near Ramah, which lies about 5 miles north of Jerusalem. Through the recognition of Joseph's sons as his own by Jacob, Rachel became the ancestress of the three tribes of Benjamin, Ephraim, and Manasseh, and in Ru. iv. 11 she is held up with Leah as a builder of the house of Israel.

BIBLIOGRAPHY. C. J. Gadd, *Revue d'Assyriologie*, XXIII, 1926, pp. 126, 127; E. A. Speiser, *AASOR*, X, 1930, pp. 31–33; *ANET*, pp. 219, 220; C. H. Gordon, *Adventures in the Nearest East*, 1957, pp. 119, 120. T.C.M.

RAHAB (Heb. *rāḥāḇ*, possibly connected with root *rḥb*, 'broad'). A harlot who lived in a house on the town wall of Late Bronze Age Jericho. Joshua's two spies lodged with her, and she hid them from the city police by covering them with drying stalks of flax on the roof. Having set a false trail for the police, she made terms with the spies. The renown of Yahweh's might convinced her that Jericho must fall to His people, so she requested protection for herself and her family. A scarlet cord in her window was the agreed signal to mark her house. She facilitated the spies' escape by letting them down through a window in the town wall, where it formed one wall of her house, and warned them which way to take (Jos. ii). When Jericho fell, she and her family alone of its citizens had their lives spared; they subsequently became naturalized Israelites (Jos. vi. 17, 22–25).

In the New Testament the writer to the Hebrews includes her among ancient examples of faith in God (Heb. xi. 31), and she is quoted as one who was justified by her works in Jas. ii. 25. She is almost certainly to be identified with Rahab (AV 'Rachab'), the wife of Salmon and mother of Boaz, ancestor of David, who is included in our Lord's genealogy in Mt. i. 5.

M.G.

RAHAB (Heb. *rahaḇ*, lit. 'pride', 'arrogance'), the female monster of chaos (*cf.* Babylonian Tiamat), closely associated with Leviathan (*q.v.*). The curbing of the forces of chaos (pre-eminently the unruly sea) at the creation is poetically described in terms of God's smiting through Rahab (*cf.* Jb. xxvi. 12, and more generally Jb. ix. 13, xxxviii. 8–11). But this imagery in the Old Testament is usually transferred from the creation story to the narrative of the redemption of Israel from Egypt, when God again showed His mastery over the sea and other forces opposed to His will; it is the Exodus that is indicated by references to the smiting of Rahab in Ps. lxxxix. 10; Is. li. 9 (*cf.* Ps. lxxiv. 12 ff., where the sense is the same, although Rahab is not expressly mentioned). From this usage Rahab comes to be employed quite generally as a poetic synonym for Egypt, as in Ps. lxxxvii. 4 ('I will make mention of Rahab and Babylon as among them that know me', RV) and Is. xxx. 7 ('Rahab that sitteth still', RV); and her dragon-associate becomes a figure of Pharaoh (*cf.* Ezk. xxix. 3). F.F.B.

RAHEL. See RACHEL.

RAIMENT. See DRESS.

RAIN. The importance and character of rainfall is emphasized in the Old Testament by the use of several words. The general term is *māṭār*, combined sometimes with *gešem*, a violent downpour (1 Ki. xviii. 41; Ezr. x. 9, 13), to suggest torrential rains (Zc. x. 1; Jb. xxxvii. 6); *zerem*, a rain-storm (Is. xxv. 4, xxviii. 2, xxxii. 2; Hab. iii. 10; Jb. xxiv. 8), is sometimes accompanied by hail (Is. xxviii. 2, xxx. 30). In contrast are the *rᵉbîḇîm*, 'showers' (Dt. xxxii. 2; Ps. lxv. 10; Je. iii. 3, xiv. 22; Mi. v. 7), and *rᵉsîsîm*, a 'rain-mist' (Ct. v. 2). Seasonal rainfall, *yôreh* and *môreh*, 'former rains', and *malqôš*, 'the latter rain', are a reference to the onset and termination of the rainy season (Dt. xi. 14; Jb. xxix. 23; Ho. vi. 3; Joel ii. 23; Zc. x. 1 f.; Jas. v. 7).

Frequently the term *māṭār* indicates that this source of blessing to man comes from God

Himself, from the heavens. The Baalim were early associated with the springs, wells, and streams, but Jehovah was the rain-giver (Je. xiv. 22), for can 'any among the vanities of the Gentiles . . . cause rain?' This challenge was vindicated by Elijah before the priests of Baal (1 Ki. xviii. 17–40). Heaven is thus invoked for rainfall (Ps. lxxii. 6), and its blessings are compared with the mechanical devices of the Egyptian *shaduf* for lifting river water from the Nile (Dt. xi. 11). Heb. *šeṭep̄*, 'torrential rain', 'flood-water' (Ps. xxxii. 6; Pr. xxvii. 4; Dn. ix. 26, xi. 22; Na. i. 3), is used in the plural in Jb. xxxviii. 25 to denote irrigation channels (normally *peleḡ*, as in Pss. i. 3, cxix. 136; Pr. v. 16, xxi. 1; Is. xxx. 25, xxxii. 2; La. iii. 48), as though a heavy downpour were likened to a channel of water poured from the reservoir of heaven (*cf.* 'the *peleḡ* of God', Ps. lxv. 9; also Gn. vii. 11, where the *'ᵃrubbôṯ* or 'sluices' of the sky are opened). Gentle rain or rain-mist (*ṭal*) is associated with beneficent gifts (Dt. xxxiii. 13). It is the first of blessings promised to Jacob's land (Gn. xxvii. 28) and to Israel (Dt. xxviii. 12). The descent of rain is likened to the blessings of the kingdom (Ps. lxxii. 6, 7). In contrast, the presence of clouds and wind without rain is likened to a man who 'boasteth himself of his gifts falsely' (Pr. xxv. 14, RV). See DEW.

The rainfall of Palestine is so closely identified with the cool season that the Arab. *šitā'* refers to both winter and rain. There is the same significance in Ct. ii. 11, 'For, lo, the winter is past, the rain is over and gone.' Equally the summer season is suggestive of the hot, dry period, *e.g.* 'My strength was dried up as by the heat of summer' (Ps. xxxii. 4, RSV). During the preliminary period of mid-September to mid-October the moist sea air encountering the very hot dry air from the land surface causes thunderstorms and the irregular distribution of rainfall. This is vividly described in Am. iv. 7, 'I caused it to rain upon one city, and caused it not to rain upon another city: one piece was rained upon, and the piece whereupon it rained not withered.' The onset of the effective rains usually begins in mid- or late October, but may be delayed until even January. These 'former rains', so earnestly longed for, cause a fall in temperature so that convectional currents are eliminated and the damp atmosphere produces a brilliance in the sky, described by Elihu: 'And now men cannot look on the light when it is bright in the skies, when the wind has passed and cleared them' (Jb. xxxvii. 21, RSV). The cool, rainy season is the pastoral setting to the joys described by the psalmist (Ps. lxv. 12, 13). Between April and early May, the 'latter rains' describe the last showers at the close of the rainy season (Am. iv. 7). See fig. 156.

Modern scholars agree that no climatic change has occurred within historic times. See J. W. Gregory, 'The Habitable Globe: Palestine and the Stability of Climate in Modern Times', *Geog. Journ.*, LXXVI, 1947, pp. 487 ff.; W. C. Lowdermilk, *Palestine, Land of Promise*, 1944, pp. 82 ff.; A. Reifenberg, *The Struggle between the Desert and the Sown*, 1956, pp. 20–24; N. Shalem, 'La Stabilité du Climat en Palestine', *Proc. Desert Research*, UNESCO, 1953, pp. 153–175. This does not mean that there have not been minor fluctuations in climate, but they have not been great enough to influence civilizations materially. Prolonged droughts such as those recorded in 1 Ki. xvii. 7; Je. xvii. 8; Joel i. 10–12, 17–20, indicate their disastrous effects, especially when there is no dew to compensate the lack of rainfall (2 Sa. i. 21; 1 Ki. xvii. 1; Hag. i. 10). See also articles on CLOUD, DEW, PALESTINE, and figs. 156, 157. J.M.H.

RAINBOW. There is no special word for rainbow in Hebrew. The ordinary word for war-bow (Heb. *qešeṯ*) is used. The New Testament word is *iris*. In Gn. ix. 13, 15, God's war-bow, *qešet*, is said to be put in the clouds as the sign of His covenant with Noah, and was His pledge that never again would He destroy all flesh by a flood.

The meaning seems to be that what was ordinarily an instrument of war, and a symbol of vengeance, became a symbol of peace and mercy by virtue of its now being set in the clouds. Against the black storm clouds God's war-bow is transformed into a rainbow by the sunlight of His mercy and grace. God is at peace with His covenant people.

So also in Ezk. i. 28 the rainbow of mercy appears around the throne of divine glory and judgment. In Rev. iv. 3, x. 1, John has a vision similar to Ezekiel's. J.G.S.S.T.

RAISINS (*ṣimmûqîm*, 'dried fruits'). Dried grapes (*cf.* Nu. vi. 3) have from earliest times been a staple food in biblical lands. The grapes were laid out, often on house-tops, to dry in the hot sun (see Pliny, *NH* xiv). A welcome food for the hungry (1 Sa. xxx. 12; 1 Ch. xii. 40), raisins were an easily carried and acceptable gift (1 Sa. xxv. 18; 2 Sa. xvi. 1). See also VINE. J.D.D.

RAM. See SHEEP.

RAMAH. The name *rāmâ* from the root *rûm*, 'to be high', was used of several places, all of them on elevated sites.

1. Ramah of Benjamin, near Bethel, in the area of Gibeon and Beeroth (Jos. xviii. 25), was a resting-place on the road north. Here the Levite and his concubine planned to stay (Jdg. xix. 13). Deborah the prophetess lived close by (Jdg. iv. 5). When Asa of Judah and Baasha of Israel were at war, Baasha built a fort here, but when the Syrians attacked Israel Asa destroyed it and built Geba and Mizpah with the materials (1 Ki. xv. 17, 21, 22; 2 Ch. xvi. 1, 5, 6).

Here Nebuzaradan gathered the exiles after the fall of Jerusalem and released Jeremiah (Je. xl. 1). The town was reoccupied after the return from Babylon (Ezr. ii. 26; Ne. xi. 33).

Ramah features in the messages of some of the prophets (Ho. v. 8; Is. x. 29; Je. xxxi. 15). It is probably to be identified with Er-Ram, 5 miles north of Jerusalem, near the traditional tomb of Rachel (Je. xxxi. 15; 1 Sa. x. 2; Mt. ii. 18; Jos., *Ant.* viii. 12. 3).

2. The birthplace and subsequent home of Samuel, also called Ramathaim-zophim (1 Sa. i. 19, ii. 11), from which he went on circuit annually (1 Sa. vii. 17). Here Saul first met him (1 Sa. ix. 6, 10), and here the elders of Israel came to demand a king (1 Sa. viii. 4 ff.). After his dispute with Saul Samuel came here (1 Sa. xv. 34 ff.). David found refuge in Ramah and later fled to Nob (1 Sa. xix. 18, xx. 1).

Four sites are proposed for Ramah today: Ramallah, 8 miles north of Jerusalem; Beit Rama, 12 miles north-west of Bethel; Er-Ram, the Ramah of Benjamin; and Nebi Samwil. Some uncertainty remains.

The word is also used as the name for **3.** a town on the boundary of Asher (Jos. xix. 29); **4.** a walled town of Naphtali (Jos. xix. 36); **5.** a town of Simeon (Jos. xix. 8; 1 Sa. xxx. 27); and **6.** an abbreviation for Ramoth-gilead (*cf.* 2 Ki. viii. 28, 29 and 2 Ch. xxii. 5, 6).

See F. M. Abel, *Géographie de la Palestine*, II, 1933, p. 427. J.A.T.

RAMESES. See RA'AMSES.

RAMOTH-GILEAD. A walled city in the territory of Gad, east of the Jordan, which featured frequently in Israel's wars with Syria. It was one of the cities of refuge (*q.v.*) (Dt. iv. 43; Jos. xx. 8) and was assigned to the Merarite Levites (Jos. xxi. 38; 1 Ch. vi. 80). It has been identified with Mizpeh, Mizpeh of Gilead (Jdg. xi. 29), and Ramath-mizpeh ('height of Mizpeh', Jos. xiii. 26). Modern equivalents suggested are Huṣn-'Ajlûn and Remtheh, but the suggestion of Nelson Glueck (*BASOR*, 92, December 1943) that it is Tell-Rāmîth has strong claims.

It was probably the home of Jephthah (Jdg. xi. 34). Ben-geber, one of Solomon's twelve administrators, lived here (1 Ki. iv. 13). According to Josephus (*Ant.* viii. 15. 3 ff.), the city was taken by Omri from Benhadad I. The town changed hands between Israel and the Syrians several times. Even after Ahab had defeated the Syrians (1 Ki. xx), it remained in their hands and Ahab enlisted the help of Jehoshaphat of Judah to retake it (1 Ki. xxii. 3, 4). He was wounded and died (1 Ki. xxii. 1–40; 2 Ch. xviii). His son Joram took up the attack but was likewise wounded (2 Ki. viii. 28 ff.). During his absence from the camp at Ramoth-gilead, Jehu the army captain was anointed at Elisha's instigation (2 Ki. ix. 1 f.; 2 Ch. xxii. 7). Jehu later murdered all the seed royal, but Josephus says that the city was taken before Jehu departed (*Ant.* ix. 6. 1).

BIBLIOGRAPHY. N. Glueck, 'Ramoth Gilead', *BASOR*, 92, December 1943, pp. 10 ff.; F. M. Abel, *Géographie de la Palestine*, II, 1933, pp. 430, 431. J.A.T.

RANSOM. See REDEEMER.

RAS SHAMRA. See ARCHAEOLOGY, VIII*e*.

RAVEN. See BIRDS OF THE BIBLE.

REAPING. See AGRICULTURE.

REBEKAH, REBECCA (Heb. *riḇqâ*, 'a looped cord for tying young animals', from Arab. *raboqa*, 'to tie fast'; Gk. *rhebekka*). The daughter of Bethuel, Abraham's nephew (Gn. xxii. 23), and the wife of Isaac. The story of the choice of Rebekah, finely told in Gn. xxiv, strongly emphasizes the guidance and overruling providence of God. Abraham sent his chief steward, probably Eliezer, to his home-country to seek a wife for his son. The steward prayed, and was led directly to Rebekah. Bethuel and her brother, Laban, having heard all the circumstances, agreed to the marriage.

She was barren for the first twenty years of her marriage. Isaac entreated God, and she bore twin sons, Esau and Jacob, receiving from Yahweh before the birth an oracle in which their divergent destinies were foretold (Gn. xxv. 20–26). The beginning of tragedy is foreshadowed in Gn. xxv. 28, where we read that Isaac loved Esau while Rebekah loved Jacob; the result of such favouritism was the destruction of the family unity.

The next incident involving Rebekah was during Isaac's sojourn in Gerar, when he deceived Abimelech and the Philistines by pretending, as did Abraham in similar circumstances, that his wife was his sister (Gn. xxvi. 1–11). Both parents were grieved at Esau's marriages to women of alien race (Gn. xxvi. 34 f.).

In the deed of treachery when Jacob supplanted Esau in obtaining the blessing from his aged father, Rebekah took the initiative and planned the act of deception (Gn. xxvii. 5–17). When this was successful, fearing that Esau would kill Jacob, she sent him away to his uncle Laban in Paddan-aram, justifying the action to Isaac by suggesting that Jacob ought to seek a wife of their own people (Gn. xxvii. 42–xxviii. 5).

The only remaining episodes recorded concerning Rebekah are the death of her nurse Deborah (Gn. xxxv. 8), and her burial with Isaac in the family grave in the cave at Machpelah (Gn. xlix. 31).

In the New Testament, the sole reference to Rebekah is in Rom. ix. 10, where EVV follow the Vulg. spelling 'Rebecca'. Paul refers to the oracle she received before the birth of Esau and Jacob as illustrating God's election of grace.

Rebekah was a woman of strong will and ambition, devoted at first to her husband, but later transferring that devotion to her younger son, with disastrous results for the life of the family, though the sequel shows that in the overruling of God even this was converted to the furtherance of His purpose.

BIBLIOGRAPHY. S. R. Driver, *The Book of Genesis*[7], *WC*, 1909; W. Vischer, *The Witness of the Old Testament to Christ*, tr. A. B. Crabtree, 1949, pp. 147–149. J.G.G.N.

RECHABITES. Jehonadab (or Jonadab), the son of Rechab, and the man who gave to the name 'Rechabite' its special connotation, appears first in 2 Ki. x. 15–31. Jehu son of Nimshi was in the midst of his savage ascent to the throne of Israel (*c.* 840 BC) when he chanced to meet Jehonadab 'coming to meet him' (verse 15). By thus deliberately and wholeheartedly associating himself with the militant Yahwism of Jehu and the atrocious massacre of the worshippers of Baal, Jehonadab shows himself to be an extremist with more zeal for Yahweh than discrimination. This same unrealistic extremism is found in the regulations he imposed on his family; but at the same time it says much for his force of character that his descendants were still obedient to him over 200 years later, as Je. xxxv shows (*c.* 600 BC). In response to Jeremiah's offer of wine (verses 5–10), they describe their distinctive life. They eschew all the marks of a settled, agricultural civilization—a house, the regular sowing of crops, the vine which demanded years of unbroken attention if it was to bear fruit—and follow the nomad life as in the wilderness period when Israel walked faithfully with God (*e.g.* Je. ii. 1–3). To preserve the outward marks of this pure following of God, and not as a 'temperance order', the Rechabites obeyed their ancestor's regulations, and it was their obedience which won divine approval (Je. xxxv. 18, 19). J.A.M.

RECONCILIATION. There are four important New Testament passages which treat of the work of Christ under the figure of reconciliation, namely, Rom. v. 10 f.; 2 Cor. v. 18 ff.; Eph. ii. 11 ff.; Col. i. 19 ff. The important Greek words are the noun *katallagē* and the verbs *katallassō* and *apokatallassō*. Reconciliation properly applies not to good relations in general but to the doing away of an enmity, the bridging over of a quarrel. It implies that the parties being reconciled were formerly hostile to one another. The Bible tells us bluntly that sinners are 'enemies' of God (Rom. v. 10; Col. i. 21; Jas. iv. 4). We should not minimize the seriousness of these and similar passages. An enemy is not someone who comes a little short of being a friend. He is in the other camp. He is altogether opposed. The New Testament pictures God in vigorous opposition to everything that is evil.

Now the way to overcome enmity is to take away the cause of the quarrel. We may apologize for the hasty word, we may pay the money that is due, we may make what reparation or restitution is appropriate. But in every case the way to reconciliation lies through an effective grappling with the root cause of the enmity. Christ died to put away our sin. In this way He dealt with the enmity between man and God. He put it out of the way. He made the way wide open for men to come back to God. It is this which is described by the term 'reconciliation'.

It is interesting to notice that no New Testament passage speaks of Christ as reconciling God to man. Always the stress is on man's being reconciled. This in the nature of the case is very important. It is man's sin which has caused the enmity. It is man's sin that has had to be dealt with. Man may very well be called on in the words of 2 Cor. v. 20 to be 'reconciled to God'. Some students go on from this to suggest that Christ's reconciling activities are concerned only with man. But it is difficult to harmonize this with the general New Testament position. That which set up the barrier was the demand of God's holiness for uprightness in man. Man, left to himself, is content to let bygones be bygones. He is not particularly worried by his sin. Certainly he feels no hostility to God on account of his sin. The barrier arises because God demands holiness in man. Therefore when the process of reconciliation has been effected it is impossible to say it is completely man-ward, and not God-ward in any sense. There must be a change from God's side if all that is involved in such expressions as 'the wrath of God' is no longer exercised towards man.

This does not mean a change in God's love. The Bible is very clear that God's love to man never varies no matter what man may do. Indeed, the whole atoning work of Christ stems from God's great love. It was 'while we were yet sinners' that 'Christ died for us' (Rom. v. 8). This truth must be zealously guarded. But at the same time we must not allow ourselves to slip into the position of maintaining that reconciliation is a purely subjective process. Reconciliation in some sense was effected outside man before anything happened within man. Paul can speak of Christ 'by whom we have now received our reconciliation' (Rom. v. 11, RSV). A reconciliation that can be 'received' must be proffered (and thus in some sense accomplished) before men received it. In other words, we must think of reconciliation as having effects both God-ward and man-ward.

BIBLIOGRAPHY. *Arndt*; *TWNT*; J. Denney, *The Christian Doctrine of Reconciliation*, 1917; L. Morris, *The Apostolic Preaching of the Cross*, 1955. L.M.

RECORDER. See KING, IV.

RED HEIFER. See CLEAN AND UNCLEAN, VI.

RED SEA. In modern geography, the sea that divides NE Africa from Arabia and extends some 1,200 miles from the straits of Bab el-Mandeb near Aden northward to the south tip of the Sinai peninsula. For nearly another 200 miles, the Gulfs of Suez and Aqabah continue the sea northward on the western and eastern sides of the Sinai peninsula respectively. In classical antiquity the name Red Sea (*erythra thalassa*) included also the Arabian and Indian Seas to the north-west coast of India. In the Old Testament the term *yam sûp̄*, 'sea of reeds' (and/or 'weed'), is used to cover: (*a*) the Bitter Lakes region in the Egyptian

Delta north of Suez along the line of the present Suez Canal; and (*b*) the Gulfs of Suez and Aqabah and possibly the Red Sea proper beyond these.

I. THE BITTER LAKES REGION

In general terms, the Israelites were led from Egypt on the way of the wilderness and the *yam sûp̄* (Ex. xiii. 18). Ex. xiv and xv are more specific: on leaving Succoth (Tell el-Maskhuta) and Etham, Israel were to turn back and camp before Pihahiroth, between Migdol and the 'sea', before Baalzephon (Ex. xiv. 1, 2, 9; *cf.* ENCAMPMENT BY THE SEA). It was this 'sea', near all these places, that God drove back and divided by a 'strong east wind' for Israel to cross dryshod, and then brought back upon the pursuing Egyptians (Ex. xiv. 16, 21–31, xv. 1, 4, 19, 21). From the 'sea of reeds', *yam sûp̄*, Israel went into the wilderness of Shur (Ex. xv. 22; Nu. xxxiii. 8) and then on towards Sinai. Various points suggest that this famous crossing, the Exodus in the narrow sense, took place in the Bitter Lakes region, roughly between Qantara (30 miles south of Port Said) and just north of Suez. First, geographically, the wilderness of Shur, which Israel entered directly from crossing the *yam sûp̄* (Ex. xv. 22), is opposite this very area (see SHUR). Secondly, geophysically, the reedy waters of the Bitter Lakes and Lake Menzaleh can be affected by strong east winds precisely in the way described in Ex. xiv. 21 and experienced on a small scale by Aly Shafei Bey in 1945–6 (*Bulletin de la Société Royale de Géographie d'Égypte*, XXI, August 1946, 231 ff.). Thirdly, philologically, the Heb. word *sûp̄* is generally admitted to be a loan-word from Egyp. *ṯwf(y)*, 'papyrus', and *p'-ṯwf*, a location, 'the papyrus-marshes' *par excellence* in the north-east part of the Delta between Tanis (Zoan), Qantir, and the present line of the Suez Canal north of Ismailia, on the former Pelusiac arm of the Nile. For all relevant details and references, see Gardiner, *Ancient Egyptian Onomastica*, II, 1947, pp. 201*–202*; Caminos, *Late-Egyptian Miscellanies*, 1954, p. 79; Erman and Grapow, *Wörterbuch d. Aegypt. Sprache*, V, 1931, p. 359: 6–10. Ps. lxxviii. 12, 43, puts the great events preceding the Exodus in the 'field of Zoan', *i.e.* in the North-East Delta. See fig. 80.

II. THE GULFS OF SUEZ AND AQABAH

Turning south from Shur *via* Etham, Marah, and Elim, the Israelites pitched by the *yam sûp̄* and then went on to Sin and Dophkah (Nu. xxxiii. 10, 11). This would appear to refer to the Gulf of Suez. Whether Ex. x. 19 during the plagues refers to the Lakes region, the Gulf of Suez, or the Red Sea proper is not certain; see PLAGUES OF EGYPT (eighth plague) and G. Hort, *ZAW*, LXX, 1958, pp. 51, 52. The *yam sûp̄* of Ex. xxiii. 31 is ambiguous, but perhaps it is the Gulf of Aqabah.

Various references clearly show the term *yam sûp̄* applied to the Gulf of Aqabah. After their first halt at Kadesh-barnea (see KADESH), the Israelites were ordered into the wilderness by the way to the *yam sûp̄* (Nu. xiv. 25; Dt. i. 40, ii. 1), *i.e.* by the Arabah towards the Gulf of Aqabah as suggested by the physical circumstances in which the earth swallowed Korah and his company (see WILDERNESS OF WANDERING, and Hort, *Australian Biblical Review*, VII, 1959, pp. 19–26). Later still, after a second sojourn at Kadesh, Israel went by the way of the *yam sûp̄* to go round Edom (Nu. xxi. 4; Jdg. xi. 16), again with reference to the Gulf of Aqabah. Solomon's seaport of Ezion-geber or Elath (*q.v.*) on this gulf is placed on the *yam sûp̄* by 1 Ki. ix. 26; the association of the term with Teman (in Edom) in Je. xlix. 21 is another example.

That the term *yam sûp̄* should have a wider use for the two northern arms of the Red Sea as well as the more restricted application to the line of reedy lakes from Suez northwards to Lake Menzaleh and the Mediterranean is not specially remarkable or unparalleled. About 1470 BC, for example, Egyptian texts of a single epoch can use the name *Wadj-wer*, 'Great Green (Sea)', of both the Mediterranean and Red Seas (Erman-Grapow, *op. cit.*, I, p. 269: 13, 14, references), and *Ta-neter*, 'God's Land', of both Punt (Somaliland?) in particular and Eastern lands generally (*ibid.*, V, p. 225: 1–4, references).

K.A.K.

REDEEMER, REDEMPTION. Redemption means deliverance from some evil by payment of a price. It is more than simple deliverance. Thus prisoners of war might be released on payment of a price which was called a 'ransom' (Gk. *lytron*). The word group based on *lytron* was formed specifically to convey this idea of release on payment of ransom. In this circle of ideas Christ's death may be regarded as 'a ransom for many' (Mk. x. 45).

Again, slaves might be released by a process of ransom. In the fictitious purchase by a god the slave would pay the price of his freedom into the temple treasury. Then he would go through the solemn formality of being sold to the god 'for freedom'. Technically he was still the slave of the god, and some pious obligations might accordingly be laid upon him. But as far as men were concerned he was thenceforth free. Alternatively, the slave might simply pay his master the price. The characteristic thing about either form of release is the payment of the ransom price (*lytron*). 'Redemption' is the name given to the process.

Among the Hebrews we may discern a different situation, well illustrated in Ex. xxi. 28–30. If a man had a dangerous ox he must keep it under restraint. If it got out and gored someone so that he died the law was plain, 'the ox shall be stoned, and his owner also shall be put to death'. But this is not a case of wilful murder. There is no malice aforethought. Thus, it is provided that a ransom (Heb. *kōp̄er*) might be 'laid upon him'. He could pay a sum of money and thus redeem his forfeited life.

Other usages of redemption in antiquity provide for the redemption of property, *etc.*, but the three we have noticed are the most important. Common to them all is the idea of freedom secured by payment of a price. Outside the Bible the usage is practically unvarying. A few metaphorical passages occur, but these serve only to make clear the basic meaning of the word. The payment of a price for deliverance is the basic and characteristic thing.

It is this which makes the concept so useful for the early Christians. Jesus had taught them that 'Whosoever committeth sin is the servant (Gk. "slave") of sin' (Jn. viii. 34). In line with this, Paul can think of himself as 'carnal, sold under sin' (Rom. vii. 14), sold as under a cruel slave-master. He reminds the Romans that in earlier days they had been 'the slaves of sin' (Rom. vi. 17). From another point of view men were under sentence of death on account of their sin. 'For the wages of sin is death' (Rom. vi. 23). Sinners are slaves. Sinners are doomed to death. Either way the ancient world would have regarded the situation as crying out for redemption. Failing redemption, the slavery would continue, the sentence of death be carried out. The cross of Christ is seen against this background. It is the price paid to release the slaves, to let the condemned go free.

What gives the metaphor force is the constant presence of the price-paying idea. But it is precisely this that is disputed by some who think that redemption is no more than another way of saying 'deliverance'. The big reason for thinking this is that there are some Old Testament passages where Yahweh is said to have redeemed His people (Ex. vi. 6; Ps. lxxvii. 14 f., *etc.*), and it is unthinkable that He should pay a price to anyone. But too much is being deduced. The metaphor has not been robbed of its point. Sometimes in the Old Testament Yahweh is thought of as being so powerful that all the might of the nations is but a puny thing before Him. But redemption is not used in such passages. Where redemption occurs there is the thought of effort. Yahweh redeems 'with a stretched out arm'. He makes known His strength. Because He loves His people He redeems them at cost to Himself. His effort is regarded as the 'price'. This is the whole point of using the redemption terminology.

The characteristic New Testament word for redemption is *apolytrōsis*, a comparatively rare word elsewhere. It is found ten times in the New Testament and only eight times in all the rest of Greek literature. This may express the conviction of the early Christians that the redemption wrought in Christ was unique. It does not mean, as some have thought, that they understand redemption simply as 'deliverance'. For that they use such a word as *rhyomai*, 'rescue'. *Apolytrōsis* means deliverance on payment of a price, and that price is the atoning death of the Saviour. When we read of 'redemption through his blood' (Eph. i. 7), the blood of Christ is clearly being regarded as the price of redemption. It is not otherwise with Rom. iii. 24 f., 'Being justified freely by his grace through the redemption that is in Christ Jesus: whom God hath set forth to be a propitiation through faith in his blood.' Here Paul is using three metaphors, those of the law court, and of the sacrifices, and of manumission. Our concern is with the last. Paul envisages a process of freeing, but by the payment of a price, the blood of Christ. Redemption is linked with Christ's death also in Heb. ix. 15. Sometimes, again, we have the mention of price, but not redemption, as in references to being 'bought with a price' (1 Cor. vi. 19 f., vii. 22 f.). The basic idea is the same. Christ bought men at the price of His blood. In Gal. iii. 13 the price of redemption is given thus: 'being made a curse for us'. Christ redeemed us by taking our place, by bearing our curse. This points us to the definitely substitutionary idea in redemption, an idea which sometimes receives stress, as in Mk. x. 45 ('a ransom for many').

Redemption does not only look back to Calvary. It looks forward to the freedom in which the redeemed stand. 'Ye are bought with a price,' Paul can say, 'therefore glorify God in your body, and in your spirit, which are God's' (1 Cor. vi. 20). Precisely because they have been redeemed at such a cost believers must be God's men. They must show in their lives that they are no longer caught up in the bondage from which they have been released. They may be exhorted to 'stand fast therefore in the liberty wherewith Christ hath made us free' (Gal. v. 1).

BIBLIOGRAPHY. *LAE*, pp. 318 ff.; Leon Morris, *The Apostolic Preaching of the Cross*, 1955, chapter I; *TWNT*; B. B. Warfield, *The Person and Work of Christ*, ed. S. G. Craig, 1950, chapter IX.

L.M.

REED (Heb. *qāneh*; Gk. *kalamos*). Tall grasses growing in wet places (marshes, river-banks, *etc.*), often the haunts of large aquatic animals (*cf.* Jb. xl. 21; Is. xix. 6, 7, xxxv. 7, RSV). The Hebrew and Greek words are both quite general terms, although some think that the *Arundo donax* of Palestine and Egypt, growing to 10 feet high or more, is the plant usually intended. Israel under God's judgment is like a reed shaken in the water (1 Ki. xiv. 15); and in Christ's words, wind-blown reeds and richly dressed courtiers will not be found in a dry wilderness (Mt. xi. 7, 8; Lk. vii. 24). If undue weight be rested on a reedstalk it will buckle up without snapping right off, and the snags will pierce the hand. Just so did Egypt fail Israel in the days of Isaiah (xxxvi. 6; 2 Ki. xviii. 21) and Jeremiah (Ezk. xxix. 6, 7). The 'bruised reed' could be symbolic of the weak whom the Messiah would not break off (Is. xlii. 3; Mt. xii. 20).

Before the crucifixion, the soldiers gave Christ a reed as a mock sceptre, and then smote Him with it (Mt. xxvii. 29, 30; Mk. xv. 19). On the cross He was offered a spongeful of vinegar on the end of a reed (Mt. xxvii. 48; Mk. xv. 36). A reed could serve as a measuring-rod, and gave its name to a measure of 6 cubits (Ezk. xl. 3–8, xli. 8 (the 6 cubits), xlii. 16–19; Rev. xi. 1, xxi. 15, 16), as did the same term *qanu* in Mesopotamia (see WEIGHTS AND MEASURES).

In Je. li. 32, the word *'ᵃgammîm*, rendered 'reeds' by AV and RV (mg: 'marshes', 'pools'), is closely similar to Bab. *agammu*, 'reed-marsh'; RSV renders 'bulwarks'. Closely related is *'aḡmōn*, 'rush', in Is. ix. 14, xix. 15; see RUSH.

K.A.K.

REFINER, REFINING. The Heb. root *ṣrp* expresses the melting, testing, and refining of metals, especially precious metals such as gold and silver. This same terminology was also used of God testing men and of God's tried and tested word. A less-common term for refining or purifying was *zqq*. In the ancient world crude metal was customarily remelted to remove impurities by various means and to make metal castings (tools, weapons, images, *etc*.). The metal was heated in pottery crucibles ('fining pot', Pr. xvii. 3, xxvii. 21) in ovens or hearths, bellows often being used to provide a draught to create greater heat (see fig. 174).

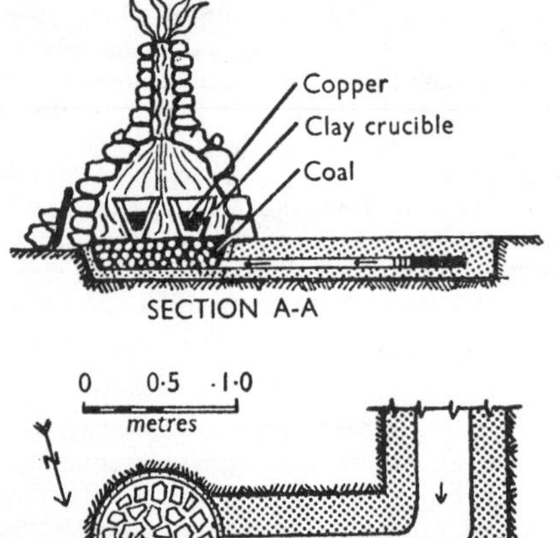

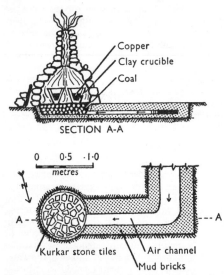

Fig. 174. Section and plan of copper-smelting furnace found at Tell Qasileh, *c*. 1000 BC.

The Heb. term *ṣōrēp̄* for refiner, metal-worker, is often rendered as goldsmith in EVV. In the days of the Judges Micah's mother had a silver image cast (Jdg. xvii. 4), while much later Isaiah (xl. 19, xli. 7, xlvi. 6) and Jeremiah (x. 8, 9, li. 17) graphically describe the futile manufacture of metal and metal-plated idols. David provided refined gold and silver for the future Temple at Jerusalem (1 Ch. xxviii. 18, xxix. 4); various metal-smiths shared in the repair of Jerusalem's walls under Nehemiah (Ne. iii. 8, 31, 32).

God, like a master-refiner seeking the pure metal, is often said to try or test (*ṣrp*) men's hearts. *Cf*. Jdg. vii. 4 (Gideon's men); Pss. xvii. 3b, xxvi. 2b, lxvi. 10, cv. 19; Is. xlviii. 10; Je. ix. 7; Zc. xiii. 9; Mal. iii. 2, 3. See also the graphic pictures in Ps. xii. 6 and Pr. xxx. 5 of God's Word. For the latter concept, *cf*. also 2 Sa. xxii. 31 (= Ps. xviii. 30); Ps. cxix. 140. Pure metal was used for casting (*cf*. Pr. xxv. 4). God sought to purify His people from sin as the removal of dross and alloy (Is. i. 25), but in simile even a fire heated with the bellows was not enough sometimes to do this (Je. vi. 29, 30). Trials are sometimes used to refine men, and the wise refine (purify) themselves (Dn. xi. 35, xii. 10). Wine is once so referred to (Is. xxv. 6). See also ARTS AND CRAFTS.

BIBLIOGRAPHY. For Egyptian scenes of such metal-working, actual moulds and crucibles, see *ANEP*, p. 40, figs. 133–136; Singer, Holmyard, and Hall, *A History of Technology*, I, 1954, p. 578, fig. 383 (use of bellows). In general, see *ibid*., pp. 577–584; R. J. Forbes, *Studies in Ancient Technology*, VI, 1958, pp. 70–73, 81–85; A. Lucas, *Ancient Egyptian Materials and Industries*, 1948, ch. XI; and G. E. Wright, *Biblical Archaeology*, 1957, pp. 194, 195 and fig. 140 (furnace).

K.A.K.

REFUGE, CITIES OF. See CITIES OF REFUGE.

REGENERATION. The noun regeneration (*palingenesia*) occurs only twice in the New Testament (Mt. xix. 28; Tit. iii. 5). In the Matthew passage it is used eschatologically to refer to the restoration of all things, reminding us that the renewal of the individual is part of a wider and cosmic renewal. In Titus the word is used with an individual reference.

Elsewhere various words are used to express the change which the Holy Spirit effects. *Gennaō* (with *anōthen*, Jn. iii. 3, 7), meaning 'to beget' or 'give birth to', is used in Jn. i. 13, iii. 3, 4, 5, 6, 7, 8; 1 Jn. ii. 29, iii. 9, iv. 7, v. 1, 4, 18. In 1 Pet. i. 3, 23 the word *anagennaō*—'to beget again' or 'to bring again to birth'—is found. These words are used to describe the initial act of renewal. The words *anakainōsis* (Rom. xii. 2; Tit. iii. 5) with the verb *anakainoō* (2 Cor. iv. 16; Col. iii. 10) denote a making anew or renewing. The references will indicate that the use of these two words is not limited to the initial renewal but extends to the resultant process. We may note with reference to the result of the new birth such terms as *kainē ktisis*, 'a new creation' (2 Cor. v. 17; Gal. vi. 15), and *kainos anthrōpos*, 'a new man' (Eph. ii. 15, iv. 24). Twice we have the term *synzōopoieō*, 'to make alive with' (Eph. ii. 5; Col. ii. 13), which hints at a change, not only as dramatic as birth, but as dramatic as resurrection. *Apokyeō* (Jas. i. 18) denotes to bear or bring forth.

Surveying the above terms, we notice that they all indicate drastic and dramatic change which may be likened to birth, rebirth, re-creation, or even resurrection. Several of the terms in their context indicate that this change has permanent and far-reaching effects in its subject.

I. OLD TESTAMENT PRESENTATION

The idea of regeneration is more prominent in the New Testament than in the Old. Many Old Testament passages have the concept of national renewal. This thought is present in the statements concerning the new covenant and the law being written in the heart or the giving of a new heart (Je. xxiv. 7, xxxi. 31 f., xxxii. 38 f.; Ezk. xi. 19, xxxvi. 25–27, and the 'valley of dry bones' passage, xxxvii. 1–14).

Although it is the nation that is in view in these scriptures, a nation can be renewed only when the individuals within it are changed. Thus, in the very idea of national renewal we find the concept of 'new hearts' being given to individuals. Other passages deal more directly with the individual (*cf.* Is. lvii. 15). We notice especially Ps. li, where David's prayer is expressed in verse 10. Considering the serious view of sin and its effects expressed in this Psalm, it is hardly surprising to find more than a hint of the need for individual renewal.

II. NEW TESTAMENT PRESENTATION

This doctrine must be considered in the context of man in sin (Jn. iii. 6; Eph. ii. 1–3, 5). The effects of sin on human nature are considered to be so serious that, without the new birth, the sinner cannot see, let alone enter into, the kingdom of God (Jn. iii. 3, 5; *cf.* 1 Cor. ii. 6–16).

The initiative in regeneration is ascribed to God (Jn. i. 13); it is from above (Jn. iii. 3, 7) and of the Spirit (Jn. iii. 5, 8). The same idea occurs in Eph. ii. 4, 5; 1 Jn. ii. 29, iv. 7; *etc.* This divine act is decisive and once for all. Aorists are used in Jn. i. 13, iii. 3, 5, 7. The use of perfects indicates that this single, initial act carries with it far-reaching effects, as in 1 Jn. ii. 29, iii. 9, iv. 7, v. 1, 4, 18. The abiding results given in these passages are doing righteousness, not committing sin, loving one another, believing that Jesus is the Christ, and overcoming the world. These results indicate that in spiritual matters man is not altogether passive. He is passive in the new birth; God acts on him. But the result of such an act is far-reaching activity; he actively repents, believes in Christ, and henceforth walks in newness of life.

Jn. iii. 8 serves to warn us that there is much in this subject that is inscrutable. Yet we must inquire what actually happens to the individual in the new birth. It would be safe to say that there is no change in the personality itself; the person is the same. But now he is differently controlled. Before the new birth sin controlled the man and made him a rebel against God; now the Spirit controls him and directs him towards God. The regenerate man walks after the Spirit, lives in the Spirit, is led by the Spirit, and is commanded to be filled with the Spirit (Rom. viii. 4, 9, 14; Eph. v. 18). He is not perfect; he has to grow and progress (1 Pet. ii. 2), but in every department of his personality he is directed towards God.

We may define regeneration as a drastic act on fallen human nature by the Holy Spirit, leading to a change in the person's whole outlook. He can now be described as a new man who seeks, finds, and follows God in Christ.

III. THE MEANS OF REGENERATION

In 1 Pet. iii. 21 baptism is closely connected with entry into a state of salvation, and in Tit. iii. 5 we have the reference to the washing of regeneration. 1 Pet. i. 23 and Jas. i. 18 mention the Word of God as a means of new birth. Many, from such scriptures, contend that these are the necessary channels by which regeneration comes to us. With 1 Cor. ii. 7–16 in mind, we must question whether the Word of God is a means of regeneration in this way. Here we are clearly taught that the natural man is in such a state that he cannot receive the things of the Spirit of God. A divine intervention which makes the natural man receptive to God's Word must be antecedent to hearing the Word in a saving manner. When this has occurred the Word of God brings the new life into expression. It is clear that the new birth of 1 Pet. i. 23; Jas. i. 18 is conceived more comprehensively than in John. John distinguishes between regeneration and the faith which results from it (*e.g.* Jn. i. 12, 13; 1 Jn. v. 1); Peter and James, by including the reference to the Word as the means, show that they have in mind the whole process whereby God brings men to conscious faith in Christ.

There are further biblical objections to the idea that baptism itself conveys regenerating grace. To look at baptism in this *ex opere operato* manner is contrary to other scriptures, especially the prophetic protest against the abuse of priestly rites, and Paul's strictures on Jewish views concerning circumcision (*cf.* Rom. ii. 28 f., iv. 9–12). We actually have incidents of conversion without baptism (Acts x. 44–48, xvi. 14, 15). The latter case is especially interesting, for the opening of Lydia's heart is specifically mentioned before baptism. If it be argued that things are different concerning Christians of subsequent generations, Paul's attitude to similar views with regard to circumcision ought to settle the issue. Regenerating grace comes direct by the Spirit to lost sinners. The Word of God brings it into expression in faith and repentance. Baptism bears witness to the spiritual union with Christ in death and resurrection through which new life is conveyed, but does not convey it automatically where faith is not present. See also BAPTISM, FAITH, LIFE.

BIBLIOGRAPHY. Articles on Regeneration by J. V. Bartlet (*HDB*, 5 vols.), J. Denney (*DCG*), *TWNT*. Most works on Systematic Theology deal with this subject—especially note Hodge (vol. III, pp. 1–40) and Berkhof (pp. 465–479); T. Boston, *Human Nature in its Fourfold State*, 1720, pp. 131–168; B. Citron, *The New Birth*, 1951.

M.R.G.

REHOB (Heb. *rᵉḥōḇ*, 'open place, market-place (of town or village)', a name occurring in the

Bible as a personal and as a place-name). **1.** The most northerly city observed by Joshua's spies in Canaan (Nu. xiii. 21). It was an Aramaean centre which supplied the Ammonites with troops in the time of David (2 Sa. x. 6–8). The name is written 'Beth-rehob' in 2 Sa. x. 6 and in Jdg. xviii. 28, which latter passage suggests that it was situated near the source of the Jordan, though the precise location is unknown.

2. A city in Canaan which fell to the lot of Asher (Jos. xix. 28, 30) and was declared a levitical city (Jos. xxi. 31; 1 Ch. vi. 75), though it was among the cities not taken at the time of the conquest (Jdg. i. 31). The suggested identification with Tell eṣ-Ṣârem south of Beth-shan is unsubstantiated.

3. The father of Hadadezer, the king of Zobah in the time of David (2 Sa. viii. 3, 12). Compare Ruḫubi, the name of the father of Ba'sa, the Ammonite ally of Ahab at the battle of Qarqar in 854 BC (Shalmaneser III, Kurḫ Stele ii. 95).

4. One of the Levites who sealed the covenant in the time of Nehemiah (Ne. x. 11).

See REHOBOTH and REHOBOTH-IR.

BIBLIOGRAPHY. W. F. Albright, *BASOR*, 83, 1941, p. 33; J. Garstang, *Joshua–Judges*, 1931, pp. 73–74, 241. T.C.M.

REHOBOAM (*reḥaḇ'ām*, 'may the people expand'). The son of Solomon (*q.v.*) by Naamah, an Ammonite princess, Rehoboam was the last king of the united Monarchy and the first of the southern kingdom of Judah.

The events connected with his reign are recorded in 1 Ki. xii, xiv. 21–31; 2 Ch. ix. 31–xii. 16. Scholars differ about the precise dating and duration of Rehoboam's reign. Assuming that it lasted seventeen years (2 Ch. xii. 13), the dates have been put as early as 937 BC for his accession and as late as 907 for his death. W. F. Albright, moreover, using the antedating system, shortens Rehoboam's reign by some eight or nine years, and suggests his dates to have been *c.* 922–915 BC (*BASOR*, 100, December 1945, p. 20). See also CHRONOLOGY OF THE OLD TESTAMENT.

Rehoboam went first to Shechem, where the people had assembled to make him king, but matters did not run smoothly. Incited by Jeroboam, who had previously incurred the wrath of Solomon (1 Ki. xi. 28–40) and who was encouraged by Shishak (*q.v.*) king of Egypt, the people offered Rehoboam the sovereignty on condition that he would alleviate the forced labour and excessive taxation laid upon them by Solomon in pursuing his building projects. After three days' deliberation Rehoboam rejected the advice of his father's counsellors and, spurred on by some hotheaded contemporaries of his own, arrogantly told the people of his intention to load them with even more grievous burdens, and to punish them more severely than his father had done (1 Ki. xii. 14). This rash decision spelt the end of what was ostensibly a united kingdom, but which in fact was little more than a loose confederation of tribes.

The ten tribes, led by Jeroboam (*q.v.*), who was to become the first king of the northern kingdom, indignantly decided to depart, washing their hands of Rehoboam and the house of David. Rehoboam sent his treasurer Adoram to bring them to a better frame of mind, but he was stoned, perhaps because he was associated with the former repressive régime. Rehoboam thereupon fled to Jerusalem, where the tribes of Judah and Benjamin acknowledged him as king. He raised a huge army to subdue the rebels, but Shemaiah the prophet dissuaded him and asserted that what had happened was God's doing (1 Ki. xii. 22–24).

To strengthen his kingdom, probably with an apprehensive eye on Egypt, Rehoboam further fortified the cities of Judah, including Bethlehem, Tekoa, Beth-zur, Gath, Mareshah, Lachish, and Azekah (see W. F. Albright, *The Biblical Period*, 1955, p. 30). Judah was strengthened in another sense by the influx of the priests and Levites who left the northern kingdom because of the God-rejecting practices they had found there (2 Ch. xi. 13–17).

For a time Rehoboam and his subjects followed the Lord and prospered, though evidence is not lacking that he shared his father's expensive tastes (2 Ch. xi. 18–23). Gradually, however, there crept in idolatrous altars, statues, groves, and high places, and men and women were appointed as public prostitutes (1 Ki. xiv. 22–24). To punish this wickedness God allowed Shishak to ravage the land and carry off the Temple and palace treasures (see K. A. Kitchen, 'Egypt and the Bible: Some Recent Advances', *Faith and Thought*, XCI, 1959–60, p. 193).

After Shemaiah the prophet had pointed out that these calamities came because of the national sin, Rehoboam and his princes repented and acknowledged the Lord's hand and His justice in their miseries. When Shishak eventually departed, Rehoboam and his people restored the worship of God, though the high places were not removed. The king caused brazen shields to be made for his Temple guard, instead of the golden ones made by his father, which Shishak had appropriated.

Rehoboam was not one of Judah's outstanding rulers (*cf.* Jos., *Ant.* viii. 10. 2), but his difficulties were many, and his reign marked particularly by sporadic war with the northern kingdom. When he died he was buried in the city of David among the 'good kings'. See also JUDAH.

The name appears as 'Roboam' in the genealogy of Mt. i. 7. J.D.D.

REHOBOTH (*reḥōḇôṯ*, 'broad places, room'; LXX *eurychōria*). **1.** A well dug by Isaac near Gerar (Gn. xxvi. 22), so named because no quarrel ensued with the herdsmen of Gerar. **2.** A city 'by the river' (Gn. xxxvi. 37), probably beside the Wadi el-Hesā, which divides Moab from Edom. 'The River' is normally the Euphrates (see RSV), but the context here forbids it. J.W.C.

REHOBOTH-IR (*reḥōḇōṯ ʻîr*). One of four cities built by As(s)hur (RV 'Nimrod') in Assyria (Gn. x. 11, 12). Of these Nineveh and Calah are well known, but no Assyrian equivalent is known for this place. Since the large and ancient city of Aššur (50 miles south of Nineveh) would be expected in the context, some consider this name an interpretation from the Sum. *AŠ.UR* (*AŠ* = Assyr. *rebātu*; *UR* = Assyr. *ālu*; Heb. *ʻîr*). A suburb of Nineveh (*rebit Ninua*) is mentioned in Assyrian texts (Esarhaddon), and this may have been founded at the same time. The phrase 'city of open-places (piazzas)' may here be a description of Nineveh itself. The LXX read as a proper name (*Rhoōbōth*). See G. Dossin, *Le Muséon*, XLVII, 1934, pp. 108 ff.; W. F. Albright, *Recent Discoveries in Bible Lands*, 1955, p. 71. D.J.W.

REHUM. A name borne by several men in post-exilic times, including Rehum the chancellor who joined in writing the letter of complaint in Ezr. iv. 8. His title *beʻēl ṭeʻēm* means 'lord of judgment' (or 'report'), and may refer either to administration ('commander', RSV) or to communication (A. H. Sayce suggests 'postmaster'). See POST. J.S.W.

REI. Occurs in 1 Ki. i. 8 only. EVV render it as a personal name, thus linking Rei with the group of Solomon's supporters. J. Taylor (*HDB in loc.*) suggests that he was an officer of the royal guard. Josephus (*Ant.* vii. 14. 4) translates 'the friend of David' instead of 'and Rei, and the mighty men which belonged to David', but this indicates that he was probably following a shorter Hebrew text, and the longer form is difficult to account for if it is not original. Suggested conjectural emendations and identification with other persons of the Davidic period are unconvincing. G.W.G.

REINS. See KIDNEYS.

RELIGION. The word 'religion' came into English from the Vulg., where *religio* is used to translate Gk. *thrēskeia*. One of its earliest recorded uses is in a 13th-century paraphrase of Jas. i. 26 f. Apart from its use in this passage, the word occurs in the AV only in Acts xxvi. 5, where it means Judaism (*cf.* Gal. i. 13 f.). Here and in the Apocrypha, *thrēskeia* refers to the outward expression of belief, and does not mean (as does our use of the word 'religion' in such phrases as 'the Christian religion contrasted with Buddhism') the content of belief. Because of the association of *thrēskeia* with Judaism, it is probable that James' use is ironical. The things which he calls the elements of 'pure *thrēskeia* and undefiled' would not, in the view of his opponents who restricted it to ritual, have counted as *thrēskeia* at all.

Hesitance today in using the word 'religion', either of the content of the Christian faith or of its expression in worship and service, is due to a conviction that Christianity differs from all other religions in that its content has been revealed by God and its outward expression by believers is not an attempt to secure salvation but a thank-offering for it. J.B.J.

REMNANT. See ISRAEL OF GOD, ISAIAH, BOOK OF, III.

REMPHAN, REPHAN. The name of a god identified or connected with the planet Saturn, quoted in Acts vii. 43 from the LXX translation of Am. v. 26. There the *MT* has *kiyyûn* (= Akkad. *kaiwanu*). See CHIUN. Just how the LXX obtained its form *Rhaiphan* (BA; *Rhemphan* 239) is a moot point. The two main suggestions are: (1) by mistaken transliteration; (2) by deliberately substituting another name, of obscure origin and sometimes thought to be Egyptian, although there appears to be no adequate evidence to substantiate this latter supposition. D.W.G.

REPENTANCE.

I. IN THE OLD TESTAMENT

In the AV the terms 'repent' and 'repentance' are seldom used in the Old Testament with reference to men (*cf.* Ex. xiii. 17; Jdg. xxi. 6, 15; 1 Ki. viii. 47; Jb. xlii. 6; Je. viii. 6; Ezk. xiv. 6, xviii. 30). As translations of the Hebrew root *nāḥam*, they are applied most frequently to God (*cf.* Gn. vi. 6, 7; Ex. xxxii. 14; Jdg. ii. 18; 1 Sa. xv. 11; 2 Sa. xxiv. 16; 1 Ch. xxi. 15; Je. xviii. 8, 10, xxvi. 3, 13, 19, xlii. 10; Joel ii. 13, 14; Am. vii. 3, 6; Jon. iii. 9, 10, iv. 2). The negative with reference to God also appears with equal emphasis (*cf.* Nu. xxiii. 19; 1 Sa. xv. 29; Ps. cx. 4; Je. iv. 28; Ezk. xxiv. 14; Ho. xiii. 14).

The term used most frequently to denote human repentance is not *nāḥam* but *šûḇ*, which means to turn or return and is applied to turning from sin to God. This is the characteristic Old Testament way of expressing repentance towards God; it is to turn to the Lord with all the heart and soul and might (*cf.* 2 Ki. xvii. 13, xxiii. 25; 2 Ch. vi. 26, vii. 14, xv. 4, xxx. 6; Ne. i. 9; Ps. lxxviii. 34; Is. xix. 22, lv. 7; Je. iii. 12, 14, 22, xviii. 8; Ezk. xviii. 21, xxxiii. 11, 14; Dn. ix. 13; Ho. xiv. 1, 2; Joel ii. 13; Jon. iii. 10; Zc. i. 3, 4; Mal. iii. 7).

When repentance is predicated of God, either in the direction of judgment or of mercy, there is reference to the change that takes place in His relations to men. God is immutable in His being, perfections, and purposes. But He changes His relationship and attitude, in judgment upon sin from complacency to wrath, in mercy from wrath to favour and blessing. The latter is frequently expressed in the Old Testament in terms of turning from the fierceness of His anger (*cf.* Ex. xxxii. 12; Jos. vii. 26; 2 Ch. xii. 12, xxix. 10; Is. xii. 1; Ho. xiv. 4; Joel ii. 14; Jon. iii. 9). This has the same force as repenting Him of the evil.

II. IN THE NEW TESTAMENT

In the New Testament the terms 'repent' (*metanoeō*) and 'repentance' (*metanoia*) refer basically to a change of mind. It is all-important to note this signification. For repentance consists in a radical transformation of thought, attitude, outlook, and direction. In accordance with the pervasive Old Testament emphasis and with what appears also in the New Testament, repentance is a turning from sin unto God and His service. The co-ordination of turning (*epistrephō*) with repentance places this fact in relief (*cf.* Acts iii. 19, xxvi. 20) as well as the frequency with which turning from sin unto God occurs as the virtual synonym of repentance (*cf.* Lk. i. 16; Acts ix. 35, xi. 21, xiv. 15, xv. 19, xxvi. 18; 1 Thes. i. 9; 1 Pet. ii. 25). Repentance is a revolution in that which is most determinative in human personality and is the reflex in consciousness of the radical change wrought by the Holy Spirit in regeneration.

It is a mistake, however, to underrate the place of grief and hatred for sin and turning from it unto God. It is true that there can be a morbid and morose sorrow which has no affinity with repentance. It is the sorrow of the world which works death (2 Cor. vii. 10), exemplified in Judas (Mt. xxvii. 3–5) and Esau (Heb. xii. 17). But there is a godly sorrow that works repentance unto salvation (2 Cor. vii. 9, 10), and it is an indispensable ingredient in evangelical repentance. This grief is signally manifest in the examples of repentance which the Bible provides (*cf.* Jb. xlii. 5, 6; Ps. li. 1–17; Lk. xxii. 62). It could not be otherwise. Nothing is more relevant to our situation in relation to God than our sin, and the salvation to which repentance is directed is salvation from sin.

The necessity of repentance as a condition of salvation is clearly inscribed on the biblical witness. Our Lord began His public ministry with the message, 'Repent: for the kingdom of heaven is at hand' (Mt. iv. 17). One of His final announcements before the ascension was that 'repentance unto remission of sins should be preached in his name unto all nations' (Lk. xxiv. 47, *cf.* xiii. 3, 5). In the carrying out of this commission no word is more significant than that of Peter on the day of Pentecost (Acts ii. 38). To the same effect is Paul's declaration that the change in God's administration of grace to the world, resulting from Jesus' death and resurrection, is signalized by the command to men that 'they should all everywhere repent' (Acts xvii. 30). And Paul sums up his witness to both Jews and Greeks as that which consists in 'repentance toward God, and faith toward our Lord Jesus Christ' (Acts xx. 21).

The demand for repentance in the witness of Jesus and of the apostles as well as the fact that repentance is unto the remission of sins and eternal life (*cf.* Lk. xxiv. 47; Acts ii. 38, iii. 19, v. 31, xi. 18; 2 Cor. vii. 10) show that there is no salvation apart from repentance. This does not interfere with the complementary truth that we are saved through faith. Faith alone is the instrument of justification. But justification is not the whole of salvation, and faith is not the only condition. Faith dissociated from repentance would not be the faith that is unto salvation. The specific character of faith is trust, commitment to Christ, but it always exists in a context. Repentance is integral to that context. It is vain to ask, Which is prior, faith or repentance? They are always concurrently in exercise and are mutually conditioning. Faith is directed to Christ for salvation from sin unto holiness and life. But this involves hatred of sin and turning from it. Repentance is turning from sin unto God. But this implies the apprehension of the mercy of God in Christ.

BIBLIOGRAPHY. J. Calvin, *Institutes of the Christian Religion*, III, iii–v; J. Taylor, *The Doctrine and Practice of Repentance*, *Works*, IX, 1822; W. D. Chamberlain, *The Meaning of Repentance*, 1943. J.M.

REPHAIM (*r^e^pā'îm*). One of the pre-Israelite peoples of Palestine mentioned, together with the Zuzim and Emim, in the time of Abraham as having been defeated by Chedorlaomer (Gn. xiv. 5). They are also listed among the inhabitants of the land God promised to Abraham's seed (Gn. xv. 20). At the time of the conquest the Rephaim seem to have inhabited a wide area, but were known by different local names. In Moab the Moabites, who succeeded them there, called them Emim (*q.v.*) (Dt. ii. 11), and likewise in Ammon, where they preceded the Ammonites, they were known as Zamzummim (*q.v.*) (Dt. ii. 20, 21).

They were a formidable people, being compared in stature with the Anakim (see ANAK) (Dt. ii. 21), and LXX renders the name by *gigas*, 'giant' in Gn. xiv. 5; Jos. xii. 4, xiii. 12, and 1 Ch. xi. 15, xiv. 9, xx. 4, a rendering adopted by AV in Dt. ii. 11, 20, iii. 11, 13; Jos. xii. 4, xiii. 12, xv. 8, xvii. 15, xviii. 16; 1 Ch. xx. 4. (LXX translates it *Titanes* in 2 Sa. v. 18, 22.) It may be that the forms *rāpā'* and *rāpâ* (2 Sa. xxi. 16, 18, 20, 22; 1 Ch. xx. 6, 8), which are rendered 'giant' in EVV (LXX *gigas* in 2 Sa. xxi. 22; 1 Ch. xx. 6), are variant forms of the name *r^e^pā'îm*, but the context of these occurrences, in connection with a Philistine, is perhaps better suited by the meaning 'giant' (*q.v.*). The name is unknown in an ethnic sense outside the Bible.

In Ps. lxxxviii. 11 (verse 10, RV); Pr. ii. 18, ix. 18, xxi. 16; Jb. xxvi. 5; Is. xiv. 9, xxvi. 14, 19, the word *r^e^pā'îm* occurs in the sense of 'ghosts of the dead', and it is suggested by some that the name Rephaim was applied by the Israelites to the early inhabitants of the land as persons long since dead. The word occurs in Ugaritic (*rpùm*), perhaps referring to a class of minor gods or a sacred guild, though the meaning is uncertain, and in Phoenician tomb inscriptions (*rp'm*) in the sense of 'ghost'.

BIBLIOGRAPHY. J. Gray, 'The Rephaim', *PEQ*, LXXXI, 1949, pp. 127–139, and LXXXIV, 1952, pp. 39–41; H. W. F. Saggs, *Faith and Thought*, XC, 1958, pp. 170–172. T.C.M.

REPHIDIM. The last stopping-place of the Israelites on the Exodus from Egypt, before they reached Mt. Sinai (Ex. xvii. 1, xix. 2; Nu. xxxiii. 14, 15). Here the Israelites under Joshua fought against Amalek, and the successful outcome of the battle depended on Moses' holding up his hands, which he did with the support of Aaron and Hur (Ex. xvii. 8–16). After the battle, Jethro, Moses' father-in-law, persuaded Moses to give up judging the people entirely himself, and to appoint deputies for this purpose (Ex. xviii). The site of Rephidim is uncertain, the usual suggestion being the Wadi Refayid in SW Sinai.

BIBLIOGRAPHY. B. Rothenberg, *God's Wilderness*, 1961, pp. 143, 168. T.C.M.

REPROBATE. Isaiah, Jeremiah, and Ezekiel compare the sin of Israel to impurity in metal (Is. i. 22; Je. vi. 30; Ezk. xxii. 19, 20). In Je. vi. 30, 'Reprobate silver shall men call them', the Heb. verb *mā'as* is rendered 'reprobate' (AVmg, RV 'refuse'), *i.e.* 'tested and rejected by Yahweh because of ineradicable sin', this being the only occurrence of 'reprobate' in the Old Testament. However, in Is. i. 22 LXX renders Heb. *sîḡîm*, 'dross' (in 'thy silver is become dross'), by the adjective *adokimos*, which occurs eight times in the New Testament (seven of men, once of soil) with the meaning 'rejected after a searching test'.

In Rom. i. 28, the Greek puns *dokimazein* with *adokimos*, and may be rendered 'since they did not see fit to retain God in their mind' [lit. 'knowledge'] He handed them over to an unfit mind', where 'unfit' (AV 'reprobate', AVmg 'a mind void of judgment') means 'unfit to pass judgment', in the active or passive sense, because of unrighteousness, fornication, *etc.* (verses 29, 30).

In 1 Cor. ix. 27 Paul concludes 'an exhortation to self-denial and exertion' (Hodge), given in athletic metaphors, by attributing his personal bodily discipline to fear of disqualification, 'lest I . . . be a castaway (*adokimos*)'. But from what? Salvation or reward? The context favours ministerial reward (*cf.* iii. 10–15) and stresses the need of ceaseless vigilance against sin (*cf.* x. 12). The remaining occurrences are in 2 Cor. xiii. 5, 6, 7, where the test proposed is 'whether ye be in the faith', and the context implies that faith has empirical proofs, lacking which the Corinthians are 'reprobates', and even Paul himself would be 'as a reprobate', since he would be unable to demonstrate his apostolic authority; in 2 Tim. iii. 8 and in Tit. i. 16, where 'reprobate' means 'proved to be morally worthless'; and in Heb. vi. 8, where 'barren' (*adokimos*) soil illustrates the condition of hardened backsliders. None of these occurrences necessarily implies judicial abandonment to perdition (*q.v.*), yet all are consonant with such a doctrine: in each case the rejection follows demonstrable fault; in some God, in others man, makes the test. The human verdict anticipates the divine.

BIBLIOGRAPHY. *Arndt* (*s.v.* '*adokimos*'); J. Denney in *HDB* for full bibliography; E. K. Simpson, *Words Worth Weighing in the Greek New Testament*, 1946, pp. 17 f. M.R.W.F.

RESEN (Gk. *Dasen*). The city located between Nineveh and Calah founded by Nimrod or Ashur (so AV) and with them part of a great populated area (Gn. x. 12). *Rēš-êni* ('fountain-head') designated a number of places in Assyria. The sites of this name on the Ḫabur and Khosr Rivers do not, however, fit the geographical situation given in Gn. x. Also the proposed equation with Selamiyeh (2 miles north of Calah) is based on the false identification of this place with Larissa (Xenophon, *Anabasis* iii. 4), whereas it is now known to be the Greek name for Calah itself. A possible site for Resen is the early ruins of Hamam Ali with its adjacent sulphur springs on the right bank of the river Tigris about 8 miles south of Nineveh. D.J.W.

REST. The non-theological sense of 'rest' is prominent in the Bible. *E.g.* the Lord rests from activity (Gn. ii. 2 f.); the sabbath is to be a day of rest (Ex. xxxi. 15); the land of promise was to have rest every seventh year (Lv. xxv. 4 f.); and the Temple was the Lord's resting-place among His people (Ps. cxxxii. 8, 14).

In its theological sense 'rest' is even more prominent in the Bible. Israel was promised rest by the Lord in the land of Canaan (Dt. iii. 20), and to this rest the exiles would return from Babylon (Je. xlvi. 27). Rest and felicity were to be David's great gifts to Israel (1 Ch. xxii. 7–10). Alas, this great ideal of rest remained unfulfilled in Israel's experience (Heb. iii. 7–iv. 10) because of unbelief and disobedience (Ps. xcv. 8–11).

However, although rest in the Old Testament remains in the sphere of promise, in the New Testament there is fulfilment. Christians, by faith in Christ, have entered into rest (Heb. xii. 22–24). He is their peace. To all who come to Him He gives rest, rest that is relief, release and satisfaction to the soul (Mt. xi. 28–30).

But 'rest' in Scripture has also an eschatological content. 'There remaineth a rest' for the Christian as for Israel (Heb. iv. 9). The celestial city and the heavenly country (Heb. xi. 10, 16) are still in the future. Today there is the task (1 Cor. iii. 9), the good fight of faith (Eph. vi. 10–20), the pilgrimage (Heb. xi. 13–16). And even the rest to which death is the prelude (Rev. xiv. 13) is not fulness of rest (Rev. vi. 9–11). But those who have entered into the rest of faith, by casting anchor within the veil where Christ has gone, know that the final state of rest is secure.

J.G.S.S.T.

RESTITUTION. See CRIME AND PUNISHMENT.

RESTORATION. The noun *apokatastasis* is found only in Acts iii. 21, while the corresponding verb is used three times in the sense of a final restoration.

The idea goes back to the great prophets of the Old Testament. They foresaw the Exile, but they also prophesied that God would restore His people to their own land (Je. xxvii. 22; Dn. ix. 25, *etc.*). When this took place conditions in Judah were far from ideal, and thus men looked and longed for a further restoration, a restoration of prosperity and bliss.

In time this came to be associated with the Messiah. The Jews as a whole understood this restoration in terms of material prosperity, but Jesus saw it in the work of John the Baptist, who fulfilled the prophecy of Malachi (Mt. xvii. 11; Mk. ix. 12). Here, as elsewhere, He reinterpreted the messianic category which had become distorted among the Jews.

In the full sense the restoration is yet future. Though they had Jesus' interpretation of the prophecy of Malachi, the disciples could ask on the eve of the ascension, 'Lord, wilt thou at this time restore again the kingdom to Israel?' (Acts i. 6). Jesus' answer discourages them from speculation about matters which do not concern them, but it does not deny that there will be a restoration. The fullest reference comes in Acts iii. 19 ff. Here Peter looks for 'times of refreshing' which he associates with the return of the Lord Jesus Christ (verse 20), who is in heaven 'until the times of restitution (*i.e.* restoration) of all things'. From one point of view the restoration awaits the return of the Lord, and Peter sees this as a subject of prophecy from the very first. It is legitimate to infer that the restoration points to some such state as that of pre-fallen man, though there is no biblical passage which says this in so many words. Some have reasoned from the expression 'restitution of all things' to the thought of universal salvation. This is more than the expression will bear. That question must be determined by the teaching of Scripture as a whole. L.M.

RESURRECTION. The most startling characteristic of the first Christian preaching is its emphasis on the resurrection. The first preachers were sure that Christ had risen, and sure, in consequence, that believers would in due course rise also. This set them off from all the other teachers of the ancient world. There are resurrections elsewhere, but none of them is like that of Christ. They are mostly mythological tales connected with the change of the season and the annual miracle of spring. The Gospels tell of an individual who truly died but overcame death by rising again. And if it is true that Christ's resurrection bears no resemblance to anything in paganism it is also true that the attitude of believers to their own resurrection, the corollary of their Lord's, is radically different from anything in the heathen world. Nothing is more characteristic of even the best thought of the day than its hopelessness in the face of death. Clearly the resurrection is of the very first importance for the Christian faith.

The Christian idea of resurrection is to be distinguished from both Greek and Jewish ideas. The Greeks thought of the body as a hindrance to true life and they looked for the time when the soul would be free from its shackles. They conceived of life after death in terms of the immortality of the soul, but they firmly rejected all ideas of resurrection (*cf.* the mockery of Paul's preaching in Acts xvii. 32). The Jews were firmly persuaded of the values of the body, and thought these would not be lost. They thus looked for the body to be raised. But they thought it would be exactly the same body (*Apoc. Bar.* 1. 2). The Christians thought of the body as being raised, but also transformed so as to be a suitable vehicle for the very different life of the age to come (1 Cor. xv. 42 ff.). The Christian idea is thus distinctive.

I. RESURRECTION IN THE OLD TESTAMENT

There is little about resurrection in the Old Testament. That is not to say that it is not there. It is. But it is not prominent. The men of the Old Testament were very practical men, concentrating on the task of living out the present life in the service of God, and they had little time to spare for speculation about the next. Moreover, it must not be forgotten that they lived on the other side of Christ's resurrection, and it is this which gives the doctrine its basis. Sometimes they used the idea of resurrection to express the national hope of the re-birth of the nation (*e.g.* Ezk. xxxvii). The plainest statement on the resurrection of the individual is undoubtedly that in Dn. xii. 2, 'many of them that sleep in the dust of the earth shall awake, some to everlasting life, and some to shame and everlasting contempt'. This clearly envisages a resurrection both of the righteous and of the wicked, and it sees also eternal consequences of men's actions. There are other passages which look for resurrection, chiefly some in the Psalms (*e.g.* Pss. xvi. 10 f., xlix. 14 f.). The precise meaning of Job's great affirmation (Jb. xix. 25–27) is disputed, but it is difficult to think that there is no thought of resurrection here. Sometimes the prophets also give utterance to this thought (*e.g.* Is. xxvi. 19). But on the whole the Old Testament says little about it. This may, perhaps, be due to the fact that some doctrine of resurrection was found among such peoples as the Egyptians and Babylonians. At a time when syncretism was a grave danger this would have discouraged the Hebrews from taking too great an interest in it.

During the period between the two Testaments, when that danger was not so pressing, the idea is more prominent. No uniformity was reached, and even in New Testament times the Sadducees still denied that there was a resurrection. But by then most Jews accepted some idea of resurrection. Usually they thought that these same bodies would be brought back to life just as they are.

II. THE RESURRECTION OF CHRIST

On three occasions Christ brought back people from the dead (the daughter of Jairus, the son of the widow of Nain, and Lazarus). These, however, are not to be thought of as resurrection so much as resuscitation. There is no indication that any of these people did other than come back to the life that they had left. And Paul tells us explicitly that Christ is 'the firstfruits of them that slept' (1 Cor. xv. 20). But these miracles show us Christ as the master of death. This comes out again in the fact that He prophesied that He would rise three days after He was crucified (Mk. viii. 31, ix. 31, x. 34, *etc.*). This point is important. It shows Christ as supremely the master of the situation. And it also means that the resurrection is of the very first importance, for the veracity of our Lord is involved.

The Gospels tell us that Jesus was crucified and died. They tell us also that on the third day the tomb in which He was placed was empty, that angels told certain women that Jesus was risen, and that over a period of some weeks the Lord appeared to His followers. Sometimes it is denied that Jesus rose, but it is difficult to see how this can be maintained if we have regard to the evidence. There is first of all the fact of the empty tomb. The Gospels agree on this, and denials have the appearance of special pleading. Thus, it has been suggested that the disciples went to the wrong tomb, where a young man in white said, 'He is not here', meaning 'He is in another tomb'. But this in the first place is pure speculation, and in the second raises all sorts of questions. It is impossible to hold that the right tomb was completely forgotten by all, friend and foe alike. When the first preaching laid such stress on the resurrection we can be sure that the authorities would have spared no effort in the attempt to find the body.

But if the tomb was empty it would seem that there are only three possibilities: that friends took the body away, that foes took the body away, or that Jesus rose. The first hypothesis is more than difficult to maintain. All our evidence goes to show that there was no thought of resurrection in the minds of the disciples, and that they were men without hope on the evening of the first Good Friday. They were dispirited, beaten men, hiding away for fear of the Jews. Moreover, Matthew tells us that a guard was set over the tomb, so that they could not have stolen the body even had they wanted to do so. But the crowning improbability is that they would have suffered for preaching the resurrection as Acts tells us they did. Some were imprisoned, and James was executed. Men do not suffer such penalties for upholding what they know to be a lie. It must also be borne in mind that when the Christian sect was troublesome enough for the authorities to persecute it the chief priests would have been very ready to have paid for information as to the stealing of the body, and the case of Judas is sufficient to show that a traitor could be found in the ranks. All in all, it is impossible to hold that Christians stole away the body of Christ.

It is just as difficult to maintain that His foes removed the body. Why should they? There seems no conceivable motive. To have done so would have been to start the very rumours of a resurrection that the evidence shows they were so anxious to prevent. Moreover, the guard over the tomb would have been just as big an obstacle to them as to the friends of the Lord. But the absolutely decisive objection is their failure to produce the body when the first preaching began. Peter and his allies put great emphasis on the resurrection of their Lord. Clearly it had gripped their imagination. In this situation, had their enemies produced the body of Jesus, the Christian Church must have dissolved in a gale of laughter. The silence of the Jews, as someone has put it, is just as significant as the speech of the Christians. The failure of the enemies of Jesus to produce the body is conclusive evidence that they could not do so.

Since it seems impossible to hold either that friends or foes removed the body, and since the tomb was empty, it seems that we are shut up to the hypothesis of the resurrection. This is confirmed also by the resurrection appearances. Altogether there are ten different appearances recorded in our five accounts (the four Gospels and 1 Cor. xv). These accounts are not easy to harmonize (though this is not impossible, as is often asserted; the attempt made in the *Scofield Reference Bible*, for example, may or may not be the right one, but it certainly shows that harmonization is possible). But the difficulties show only that the accounts are independent. There is no stereotyped repetition of an official story. And there is impressive agreement on the main facts. There is great variety in the witnesses. Sometimes one or two saw the Lord, sometimes a larger number, as the eleven, once as many as five hundred. Men as well as women are included in the number. Mostly the appearances were to believers, but possibly that to James was to one who had not believed up till that point. Specially important is Paul. He was not credulous, but an educated man who was bitterly hostile to the Christians. And he is emphatic that he saw Jesus after He had risen from the dead. Indeed, so sure was he of this that he based the whole of the rest of his life on the certainty. Canon Kennett puts this point trenchantly. He speaks of Paul as having been converted within five years of the crucifixion and says, 'within a very few years of the time of the crucifixion of Jesus, the evidence for the resurrection of Jesus was in the mind of at least one man of education absolutely irrefutable' (*Interpreter*, V, 1908–9, p. 267).

We should not overlook the transformation of the disciples in all this. As noted before, they were beaten and dispirited men at the crucifixion, but they were ready to go to prison and even to die for the sake of Jesus shortly afterwards. Why the change? Men do not run such risks unless they are very sure of themselves. The disciples were completely convinced. We should perhaps add that their certainty is reflected in their worship. They were Jews, and Jews have a tenacity in clinging to their religious customs. Yet these men observed the Lord's day, a weekly memorial of the resurrection, instead of the sabbath. On that Lord's day they celebrated the holy communion, which was not a commemoration of a dead Christ, but a thankful remembrance of the blessings conveyed by a living and triumphant Lord. Their other sacrament, baptism, was a reminder that believers were buried with Christ and raised with Him (Col. ii. 12). The resurrection gave significance to all that they did.

Sometimes attempts are made to explain away all this. Thus, it is said that Christ did not really die, but swooned. Then in the coolness of the tomb He revived. This raises all sorts of questions. How did He get out of the tomb? What happened to Him? Why do we hear no more? When did He die? Questions multiply and the answers do not appear. Some have thought the disciples to have been the victims of hallucination. But the resurrection appearances cannot be so explained. Hallucinations come to those who are in some sense looking for them, and there is no evidence of this among the disciples. Once started they tend to continue, whereas these stop abruptly. Hallucinations are individual affairs, whereas in this case we have as many as five hundred people at once seeing the Lord. There seems no point in exchanging a miracle on the physical level for one on the psychological level, which is what this view demands. Probably the favourite idea today with those who deny the resurrection is that of vision. God sent to His servants visions which assured them that though Jesus was dead He still lived. Death is not the end, either for Him or for them. We are asked to accept the Easter faith, while rejecting the Easter message on which that faith is based. The big difficulty here is the moral one. There is no question but that the disciples believed that Jesus had risen. It was this which formed the main burden of their preaching and gave them their inspiration. If we adopt the vision theory it is hard to acquit God of deluding the disciples, an unthinkable conclusion. Moreover, such views ignore the empty tomb. This is a stubborn fact. Perhaps it is worth adding also that these views are quite modern (though occasionally there have been forerunners, *cf.* 2 Tim. ii. 17 f.). They form no part of historic Christianity, and if they are correct nearly all Christians have at all times been in serious error concerning a cardinal doctrine of the faith.

III. THE RESURRECTION OF BELIEVERS

Not only did Jesus rise, but one day all men too will rise. Jesus refuted the scepticism of the Sadducees on this point with an interesting argument from Scripture (Mt. xxii. 31, 32). The general New Testament position is that the resurrection of Christ carries with it the resurrection of believers. Jesus said, 'I am the resurrection, and the life: he that believeth in me, though he were dead, yet shall he live' (Jn. xi. 25). Several times He spoke of raising believers up at the last day (Jn. vi. 39, 40, 44, 54). The Sadducees were grieved because the apostles 'preached through Jesus the resurrection from the dead' (Acts iv. 2). Paul tells us that 'since by man came death, by man came also the resurrection of the dead. For as in Adam all die, even so in Christ shall all be made alive' (1 Cor. xv. 21 f.; *cf.* 1 Thes. iv. 14). Likewise Peter says that God 'hath begotten us again unto a lively hope by the resurrection of Jesus Christ from the dead' (1 Pet. i. 3). It is plain enough that the New Testament writers did not think of Christ's resurrection as an isolated phenomenon. It was a great divine act, and one fraught with consequence for men. Because God raised Christ He set His seal on the atoning work wrought out on the cross. He demonstrated His divine power in the face of sin and death, and at the same time His will to save men. Thus, the resurrection of believers follows immediately from that of their Saviour. So characteristic of them is resurrection that Jesus could speak of them as 'the children of God, being the children of the resurrection' (Lk. xx. 36).

This does not mean that all who rise rise to blessing. Jesus speaks of 'the resurrection of life' but also of 'the resurrection of damnation (*i.e.* judgment)' (Jn. v. 29). The plain New Testament teaching is that all will rise, but that those who have rejected Christ will find the resurrection a serious matter indeed. For believers the fact that their resurrection is connected with that of the Lord transforms the situation. In the light of His atoning work for them they face resurrection with calmness and joy.

Of the nature of the resurrection body Scripture says little. Paul can speak of it as 'a spiritual body' (1 Cor. xv. 44), which appears to mean a body which meets the needs of the spirit. He expressly differentiates it from the 'natural body' which we now have, and we infer that a 'body' answering to the needs of the spirit is in some respects different from that which we now know. The spiritual body has the qualities of incorruptibility, glory, and power (1 Cor. xv. 42 f.). Our Lord has taught us that there will be no marriage after the resurrection, and thus no sexual function (Mk. xii. 25).

Perhaps we can gain some help by thinking of the resurrection body of Christ, for John tells us that 'we shall be like him' (1 Jn. iii. 2), and Paul that 'our vile body' is to be fashioned 'like unto his glorious body' (Phil. iii. 21). Our Lord's risen body appears to have been in some sense like the natural body and in some sense different. Thus on some occasions He was recognized immediately (Mt. xxviii. 9; Jn. xx. 19 f.), but on others He was not (notably the walk to Emmaus, Lk. xxiv. 16; *cf.* Jn. xxi). He appeared suddenly in the midst of the disciples, who were gathered with the doors shut (Jn. xx. 19), while contrariwise He disappeared from the sight of the two at Emmaus (Lk. xxiv. 31). He spoke of having 'flesh and bones' (Lk. xxiv. 39). On occasion He ate food

(Lk. xxiv. 41–43), though we cannot hold that physical food is a necessity for life beyond death (*cf.* 1 Cor. vi. 13). It would seem that the risen Lord could conform to the limitations of this physical life or not as He chose, and this may indicate that when we rise we shall have a similar power.

IV. DOCTRINAL IMPLICATIONS OF THE RESURRECTION

The Christological significance of the resurrection is considerable. The fact that Jesus prophesied that He would rise from the dead on the third day has important implications for His Person. One who could do this is greater than the sons of men. Paul clearly regards the resurrection of Christ as of cardinal importance. 'If Christ be not risen,' he says, 'then is our preaching vain, and your faith is also vain. . . . And if Christ be not raised, your faith is vain; ye are yet in your sins' (1 Cor. xv. 14, 17). The point is that Christianity is a gospel, it is good news about how God sent His Son to be our Saviour. But if Christ did not really rise, then we have no assurance that our salvation has been accomplished. The reality of the resurrection of Christ is thus of deep significance. The resurrection of believers is also important. Paul's view is that if the dead do not rise we may as well adopt the motto 'let us eat and drink; for tomorrow we die' (1 Cor. xv. 32). Believers are not men for whom this life is all. Their hope lies elsewhere (1 Cor. xv. 19). This gives them perspective and makes for depth in living.

The resurrection of Christ is connected with our salvation, as when Paul says that He 'was delivered for our offences, and was raised again for our justification' (Rom. iv. 25, *cf.* viii. 33 f.). There is no need here to go into the precise significance of the two uses of 'for'. That is a task for the commentaries. We content ourselves with noting that the resurrection of Christ is connected with the central act whereby we are saved. Salvation is not something that takes place apart from the resurrection.

Nor does it stop there. Paul speaks of his desire to know Christ 'and the power of his resurrection' (Phil. iii. 10), and he exhorts the Colossians, 'If ye then be risen with Christ, seek those things which are above . . .' (Col. iii. 1). He has already reminded them that they were buried with Christ in baptism, and in the same sacrament were raised with Him (Col. ii. 12). In other words, the apostle sees the same power that brought Christ back from the dead as operative within those who are Christ's. The resurrection is an ongoing thing.

BIBLIOGRAPHY. W. Milligan, *The Resurrection of Our Lord*², 1883; J. Orr, *The Resurrection of Jesus*, 1909; W. J. Sparrow-Simpson, *The Resurrection and Modern Thought*, 1911; P. Gardner-Smith, *The Narratives of the Resurrection*, 1926; K. Barth, *The Resurrection of the Dead*, E.T., 1933; A. M. Ramsey, *The Resurrection of Christ*, 1946; G. Vos in *PTR*, XXVII, 1929, pp. 1–35, 193–226.

L.M.

REUBEN (*MT Re'ûḇēn*; LXX *Roubēn*; Pesh. *Roubîl*; Jos. *Roubēlos*; Arab. *Ra'ûbîn*; Lat. *Rubin*). **1.** The firstborn of Jacob by Leah (Gn. xxix. 32), whose choice of name is connected with the phrase, 'the Lord *has looked upon my affliction*' (Heb. *rā'â . . . be'onyî*). That this meaning was attached to the name is clear from the other names in this section: 'Simeon (Heard) . . . the Lord has *heard*', 'Levi (Attached) . . . my husband . . . will be *attached*', 'Judah (Praise) . . . I will *praise* the Lord', 'Dan (Judge) . . . God has *judged* me', *etc.* Attempts have been made to give the desired meaning, 'He has looked upon my affliction', to the Hebrew consonants for 'Reuben', which in our present text appears to mean, 'Behold a son'. Possibly the vocalization of the name is at fault.

Reuben had some admirable qualities in his character; unfortunately, they were offset by his incestuous act with Bilhah, his father's concubine (Gn. xxxv. 22). It was Reuben who advised his brothers not to kill Joseph, and returned to the pit to release him (Gn. xxxvii. 21, 29). Later he accused them of bringing calamity upon themselves, when they were held in the Egyptian court as suspected spies (Gn. xlii. 22). Again, it was Reuben who offered his own two sons as sufficient guarantee for the safety of Benjamin (Gn. xlii. 37).

In the blessing of the sons of Jacob, Reuben is recognized legally as the firstborn, although in actual fact the double-portion which went with the birthright (Dt. xxi. 17) was symbolically bequeathed to Joseph, through his two sons, Ephraim and Manasseh. However, after a eulogy of Reuben, no doubt sincerely meant, there is added a significant and prophetic utterance by the Patriarch: 'Unstable as water, you shall not have pre-eminence . . .' (Gn. xlix. 4, RSV). This legal recognition as firstborn is upheld in 1 Ch. v. 1, where we are told that the birthright belonged to Joseph *de facto* but not *de jure*, for 'he [Joseph] is not to be enrolled in the genealogy according to the birthright' (*cf.* Gesenius, *Heb. Gram.*²⁸, p. 349, § 114k). So it is that in Gn. xlvi. 8; Ex. vi. 14; Nu. xxvi. 5, Reuben retains his status as firstborn. Reuben had four sons before the descent into Egypt.

2. The tribe of Reuben was involved in the rebellion in the wilderness (Nu. xvi. 1). The tribe was linked with Gad and occupied territory east of Jordan. In the north it was contiguous with Gad, in the south it was bounded by the Arnon. The tribe's pursuits would be mainly pastoral, but those to the west of Jordan were mainly agricultural. This may have led to a separation of interests, for Reuben took no part in repelling the attack of Sisera (Jdg. v. 15 f.). In the time of Saul they united with Gad and Manasseh in an attack on the Hagarites, apparently a nomad people (1 Ch. v. 10, 19 f.).

Though there is mention of Gad on the Moabite Stone, there is none of Reuben, and thus it appears that at that time, *c.* 830 BC, they had lost their importance as warriors. However, they were never forgotten by their brethren; a place is reserved for the tribe of Reuben in Ezekiel's reconstructed Israel (Ezk. xlviii. 7, 31), and they are numbered among the hundred and forty and four thousand, sealed out of every tribe of the children of Israel, in the Apocalypse of John (Rev. vii. 5). R.J.A.S.

REUEL. 1. A son of Esau (Gn. xxxvi. 4, 10, 17; 1 Ch. i. 35). **2.** A Midianite priest, who received Moses when he fled from Egypt, and gave him his daughter Zipporah (Ex. ii. 18; Nu. x. 29). Also called Jethro (*q.v.*). **3.** Father of Eliasaph of Gad, who had command under Moses (Nu. i. 14, ii. 14, vii. 42, 47, x. 20). **4.** A Benjamite chief living at Jerusalem under Solomon (1 Ch. ix. 8).

The Greek spelling is 'Raguel' in all the above texts, the second Hebrew letter being *'ayin*. The name appears to mean 'friend of God'.

J.P.U.L.

REVELATION.

I. THE IDEA OF REVELATION

The English word 'reveal', from Lat. *revelo*, is the regular AV rendering of the Heb. *gālâ* and the Gk. *apokalyptō* (noun, *apokalypsis*), which corresponds to *gālâ* in the LXX and New Testament. *gālâ*, *apokalyptō*, and *revelo* all express the same idea—that of unveiling something hidden, so that it may be seen and known for what it is. Accordingly, when the Bible speaks of revelation, the thought intended is of God the Creator actively disclosing to men His power and glory, His nature and character, His will, ways, and plans—in short, Himself—in order that men may know Him. The revelation vocabulary in both Testaments is a wide one, covering the ideas of making obscure things clear, bringing hidden things to light, showing signs, speaking words, and causing the persons addressed to see, hear, perceive, understand, and know. None of the Old Testament words is a specifically theological term—each one has its profane usage—but in the New Testament *apokalyptō* and *apokalypsis* are used only in theological contexts, and the ordinary profane use of them does not appear, even where one might have expected it (*cf.* 2 Cor. iii. 13 ff.); which suggests that for the New Testament writers both terms possessed quasi-technical status.

Other New Testament words expressing the idea of revelation are *phaneroō*, 'manifest, make clear'; *epiphainō*, 'show forth' (noun, *epiphaineia*, 'manifestation'); *deiknuō*, 'show'; *exēgeomai*, 'unfold, explain, by narration', *cf.* Jn. i. 18; *chrēmatizō*, 'instruct, admonish, warn' (used in secular Greek of divine oracles, *cf. Arndt*, *MM*, *s.v.*; noun, *chrēmatismos*, 'answer of God', Rom. xi. 4).

From the standpoint of its contents, divine revelation is both indicative and imperative, and in each respect normative. God's disclosures are always made in the context of a demand for trust in, and obedience to, what is revealed—a response, that is, which is wholly determined and controlled by the contents of the revelation itself. In other words, God's revelation comes to man, not as information without obligation, but as a mandatory rule of faith and conduct. Man's life must be governed, not by private whims and fancies, nor by guesses as to divine things unrevealed, but by reverent belief of as much as God has told him, leading to conscientious compliance with as many imperatives as the revelation proves to contain (Dt. xxix. 29).

Revelation has two focal points: (1) God's purposes; (2) His person.

1. On the one hand, God tells men about Himself—who He is, what He has done, and is doing, and will do, and what He requires them to do. Thus, He took Noah, Abraham, and Moses, into His confidence, telling them what He had planned and what their part in His plan was to be (Gn. vi. 13–21, xii. 1 ff., xv. 13–21, xvii. 15–21, xviii. 17 ff.; Ex. iii. 7–22). Again, He declared to Israel the laws and promises of His covenant (Ex. xx–xxiii, *etc.*; Dt. iv. 13 f., xxviii, *etc.*; Pss. lxxviii. 5 ff., cxlvii. 19). He disclosed His purposes to the prophets (Am. iii. 7). Christ told His disciples 'all things that I heard of my Father' (Jn. xv. 15, RV), and promised them the Holy Spirit to complete His work of instructing them (Jn. xvi. 12 ff.). God revealed to Paul the 'mystery' of His eternal purpose in Christ (Eph. i. 9 ff., iii. 3–11). Christ revealed to John 'the things which must shortly come to pass' (Rev. i. 1, RV). From this standpoint, as God's own precise disclosure of His saving purpose and work, Paul calls the gospel 'the truth', in contrast with error and falsehood (2 Thes. ii. 11–13; 2 Tim. ii. 18; *etc.*). Hence the use of the phrase 'revealed truth' in Christian theology to denote what God has told men about Himself.

2. On the other hand, when God sends men His word, He also confronts them with Himself. The Bible does not think of revelation as a mere broadcasting of information, divinely guaranteed, but as God's personal coming to individuals to make Himself known to them (*cf.* Gn. xxxv. 7; Ex. vi. 3; Nu. xii. 6–8; Gal. i. 15 f.). This is the lesson to be learned from the theophanies of the Old Testament (*cf.* Ex. iii. 2 ff., xix. 11–20; Ezk. i; *etc.*), and from the part played by the enigmatic 'angel (messenger) of Yahweh', who is so evidently a manifestation of Yahweh Himself (*cf.* Gn. xvi. 10; Ex. iii. 2 ff.; Jdg. xiii. 9–23): the lesson, namely, that God is not only the author and subject of His messages to men but He is also His own messenger. When a man meets God's word, however casual and accidental the meeting may seem to be, God meets that man, addressing the word to him personally and calling for a personal response to Himself as its Author.

Speaking generally, the older Protestant theologians analysed revelation in terms entirely of God's communicating truths about Himself. They knew, of course, that God ordered biblical history and that He now enlightens men to accept the biblical message, but they dealt with the former under the heading of providence and the latter under the heading of illumination, and did not formally relate their concept of revelation to either. The focal centre of their doctrine of revelation was the Bible; they viewed Holy Scripture as revealed truth in writing, and revelation as the divine activity that led to its production. They correlated revelation with inspiration, defining the former as God's communication to the biblical writers of otherwise inaccessible truth about Himself, and the latter as His enabling them to write it all down truly, according to His will. (This formulation evidently has its roots in the book of Daniel: *cf.* Dn. ii. 19, 22, 28 ff., 47, vii. 1, x. 1, xii. 4.)

Many modern theologians, reacting against this view under pressure of a supposed need to abandon the notion of Scripture as revealed truth, speak of revelation wholly in terms of God's directing biblical history and making individuals aware of His presence, activity, and claims. The focal centre of the doctrine of revelation is thus shifted to the redemptive history which the Bible records. With this commonly goes the assertion that there is, properly speaking, no such thing as communicated truth ('propositional revelation') from God; revelation is essentially non-verbal in character. But this is to say in effect that the biblical idea of God *speaking* (the commonest and most fundamental revelatory act which Scripture ascribes to Him) is only a misleading metaphor; which seems unplausible. On these grounds, it is further held that the Bible is not, properly speaking, revelation, but a human response to revelation. This, however, seems unbiblical, since the New Testament uniformly quotes Old Testament statements—prophetic, poetic, legal, historical, factual, and admonitory —as authoritative utterances of God (*cf.* Mt. xix. 4 f.; Acts iv. 25 f.; Heb. i. 5 ff., iii. 7 ff.; *etc.*). The biblical view is that God reveals Himself by both deeds and words: first by ordering redemptive history, then by inspiring a written explanatory record of that history to make later generations 'wise unto salvation' (*cf.* 2 Tim. iii. 15 ff.; 1 Cor. x. 11; Rom. xv. 4), and finally by enlightening men in every age to discern the significance and acknowledge the authority of the revelation thus given and recorded (*cf.* Mt. xvi. 17; 2 Cor. iv. 6). Thus, the positive emphases in the two sets of ideas contrasted above are complementary rather than contradictory; both must be combined in order to cover the full range of the biblical concept of revelation.

II. THE NECESSITY OF REVELATION

The Bible assumes throughout that God must first disclose Himself before men can know Him. The Aristotelian idea of an inactive God whom man can discover by following out an argument is quite unbiblical. A revelatory initiative is needed, first, because *God is transcendent*. He is so far from man in His mode of being that man cannot see Him (Jn. i. 18; 1 Tim. vi. 16; *cf.* Ex. xxxiii. 20), nor find Him out by searching (*cf.* Jb. xi. 7, xxiii. 3–9), nor read His thoughts by shrewd guesswork (Is. lv. 8 f.). Even if man had not sinned, therefore, he could not have known God without revelation. In fact, we read of God speaking to unfallen Adam in Eden (Gn. ii. 16). Now, however, there is a second reason why man's knowledge of God must depend on God's revelatory initiative. *Man is sinful*. His powers of perception in the realm of divine things have been so dulled by Satan (2 Cor. iv. 4) and sin (*cf.* 1 Cor. ii. 14), and his mind is so prepossessed by his own fancied 'wisdom', which runs contrary to the true knowledge of God (Rom. i. 21 ff.; 1 Cor. i. 21), that it is beyond his natural powers to apprehend God, however presented to him. In fact, according to Paul, God presents Himself constantly to every man through His works of creation and providence (Rom. i. 19 ff.; Acts xiv. 17; *cf.* Ps. xix. 1 ff.), and the spontaneous operations of natural conscience (Rom. ii. 12–15, *cf.* i. 32); yet He is not recognized or known. The pressure of this continual self-disclosure on God's part produces idolatry, as the fallen mind in its perversity seeks to quench the light by turning it into darkness (Rom. i. 23 ff.; *cf.* Jn. i. 5), but it does not lead to knowledge of God, or to godliness of life. God's 'general revelation' (as it is usually called) of His eternity, power, and glory (Rom. i. 20; *cf.* Ps. xix. 1), His kindness to men (Acts xiv. 17), His moral law (Rom. ii. 12 ff.), His demand for worship and obedience (Rom. i. 21), and His wrath against sin (Rom. i. 18, 32), thus serve only to render men 'without excuse' for their 'ungodliness and unrighteousness' (Rom. i. 18–20).

This shows that fallen man's need of revelation goes beyond Adam's in two respects. First, he needs a revelation of God as a redeemer and restorer, One who shows mercy to sinners. God's revelation through creation and conscience speaks of law and judgment (Rom. ii. 14 f., i. 32), but not of forgiveness. Second, supposing that God grants such a revelation (the Bible is one long proclamation that He does), fallen man still needs spiritual enlightenment before he can grasp it; otherwise he will pervert it, as he has perverted natural revelation. The Jews had a revelation of mercy in the Old Testament, which pointed them to Christ, but on most of their hearts there was a veil which kept them from understanding it (2 Cor. iii. 14 ff.), and so they fell victim to a legalistic misconception of it (Rom. ix. 31–x. 4). Even Paul, who calls attention to these facts, had himself known the Christian gospel before his conversion—and tried to stamp it out; not till 'it pleased God . . . to reveal his Son in me'—*in*, by inward enlightenment—did Paul recognize it as the word of God. The need of divine enlightening to reveal to individuals the reality, authority, and meaning of revelation objectively given, and to conform their lives to it, is occasionally indicated in the Old Testament (Ps. cxix. 12, 27, *etc.*; Je. xxxi. 33 f.); in the New Testament, it is stressed most by Paul and in the recorded teaching of Christ (Mt. xi. 25, xiii. 11–17; Jn. iii. 3 ff., vi. 44 f., 63 ff., viii. 43–47, x. 26 ff., *cf.* xii. 37 ff.).

III. THE CONTENT OF REVELATION

a. Old Testament

The foundation and framework of Israel's religious outlook was the covenant which God announced between Himself and Abraham's seed (Gn. xvii. 1 ff.). A covenant (*q.v.*) is a defined relationship of promise and obligation binding two parties together. This covenant was a royal imposition whereby God pledged Himself to Abraham's clan as *their* God, thus authorizing them to invoke Him as *our* God and *my* God. The fact that God made known His name (Yahweh) to Israel (Ex. iii. 11–15, vi. 2 ff.; on the exegesis, *cf.* J. A. Motyer, *The Revelation of the Divine Name*, 1960) was a witness to this relationship. The 'name' stands for all that a person is, and for God to tell the Israelites His name was a sign that, such as He was, in all His power and glory, He was pledging Himself to them for their welfare. The goal of His relationship with Israel was the perfecting of the relationship itself: that is, that God should bless Abraham's seed with the fulness of His gifts, and that Abraham's seed should perfectly bless God by a perfect worship and obedience. Hence God continued to reveal Himself to the covenant community by His words of law and promise, and by His redemptive deeds as Lord of history for the realizing of this covenant eschatology.

God made the royal character of His covenant more explicit at Sinai, where, having dramatically shown His saving power in the Exodus from Egypt, He was formally acknowledged as Israel's Sovereign (Ex. xix. 3–8; Dt. xxxiii. 4 f.), and through the mouth of Moses, the archetypal prophet (*cf.* Dt. xviii. 15), promulgated the laws of the covenant, making it clear that enjoyment of covenant blessing was conditional upon obedience to them (Ex. xix. 5; *cf.* Lv. xxvi. 3 ff.; Dt. xxviii). These laws were committed to writing, the Decalogue in the first instance by God Himself (Ex. xxiv. 12, xxxi. 18, xxxii. 15 f.), the whole code eventually by Moses, as, in effect, God's amanuensis (Ex. xxxiv. 27 f.; Dt. xxxi. 9 ff., 24 ff.; *cf.* Ex. xxiv. 7). It is noteworthy that God through Hosea later spoke of the entire work of writing the law as His own work, though tradition was unanimous that Moses did it (Ho. viii. 12); here are some of the roots of the idea of biblical inspiration (*q.v.*). The law, once written, was regarded as a definitive and permanently valid disclosure of God's will for His people's life, and the priests were made permanently responsible for teaching it (Dt. xxxi. 9 ff.; *cf.* Ne. viii. 1 ff.; Hg. ii. 11 f.; Mal. ii. 7 f.).

God forbade Israelites to practise sorcery and divination for day-to-day guidance, as the Canaanites did (Dt. xviii. 9 ff.); they were to seek guidance from Him only (Is. viii. 19). He promised them a succession of prophets, men in whose mouths He would put His own words (Dt. xviii. 18; *cf.* Je. i. 9, v. 14; Ezk. ii. 7–iii. 11; Nu. xxii. 35, 38, xxiii. 5), to give His people such periodic direction as they needed (Dt. xviii. 15 ff.). Prophets in Israel fulfilled a vital ministry. The great prophets, at Yahweh's bidding, spoke God's words and interpreted His mind to kings and to the nation; they expounded and applied His law, pleading for repentance and threatening judgment in His name, and they declared what He would do, both in judgment and also in fulfilling the covenant eschatology by bringing in His kingdom after the judgment was over. And prophets may also have had a place in the cult as seers, men who could give answers from God to individuals who asked particular questions about guidance and the future (*cf.* 1 Sa. ix. 6 ff., xxviii. 6–20; 1 Ki. xxii. 5 ff.; see A. R. Johnson, *The Cultic Prophet in Ancient Israel*, 1944). A further means of guidance in pre-exilic Israel was the sacred lot, Urim and Thummim (*q.v.*), manipulated by the priests (Dt. xxxiii. 8 ff.; *cf.* 1 Sa. xiv. 36–42, xxviii. 6). Divine guidance for life of a more general sort was supplied also by the maxims of the 'wise men', whose wisdom was held to be from God (*cf.* Pr. i. 20, viii).

In addition to these arrangements for verbal or quasi-verbal communication from God, Israel knew certain theophanic and experimental manifestations which betokened the nearness of God: the 'glory' (*cf.* Ex. xvi. 10, xl. 34; Nu. xvi. 19; 1 Ki. viii. 10 f.; Ezk. i, *etc.*; see GLORY); the thunderstorm (Ps. xviii. 6–15, xxix); the sight of His 'face' and the joyful awareness of His 'presence' to which faithful worshippers aspired (Pss. xi. 7, xvi. 11, xvii. 15, li. 11 f.).

The chief emphases in the Old Testament revelation of God are upon: (*a*) God's uniqueness, as the Maker and Ruler of all things; (*b*) His holiness, *i.e.* the conjunction of awesome characteristics which set Him apart from men—majesty and greatness and strength, on the one hand, and purity and love of righteousness and hatred of wrongdoing, on the other; (*c*) His covenant faithfulness and patience and mercy, and His loyalty to His own gracious purposes towards the covenant people.

b. New Testament

In the New Testament Christ and the apostles are organs of new revelation, corresponding to Moses and the prophets in the Old. The fulfilment of Old Testament covenant eschatology is found in the kingdom of Christ and the Christian hope of glory. The one God of the Old Testament is revealed as Triune, by the coming first of Christ and then of the Spirit, and the disclosing of the divine redemptive purpose as one in which all three Persons of the Godhead work together (*cf.* Eph. i. 3–14; Rom. viii). Two events which will bring God's plan of human history to its climax are spoken of as acts of revelation still to come (the appearing of antichrist, 2 Thes. ii. 3, 6, 8, and of Christ, 1 Cor. i. 7, RV; 2 Thes. i. 7–10; 1 Pet. i. 7, RV, 13). The New Testament claims that the revelation of the Old Testament has been augmented along two chief lines.

(i) *The revelation of God in Christ.* The New Testament proclaims that 'God . . . hath at the end of these days spoken unto us in his Son' (Heb. i. 1 f., RV). This is God's crowning and final revelation, His last word to man. By His words and works, and by the over-all character of His life and ministry, Jesus Christ perfectly revealed God (Jn. i. 18, xiv. 7–11). His personal life was a perfect revelation of the character of God; for the Son is the image of God (2 Cor. iv. 4; Col. i. 15; Heb. i. 3), His *logos* (word, regarded as expressing His mind, Jn. i. 1 ff.), in whom, as incarnate, all the divine fulness dwelt (Col. i. 19, ii. 9). Equally, His messianic work revealed perfectly the saving purposes of God; for Christ is the wisdom of God (1 Cor. i. 24), through whom, as Mediator (1 Tim. ii. 5), all God's saving purposes are worked out and all the wisdom that man needs for his salvation may be found (Col. ii. 3; 1 Cor. i. 30, ii. 6 f.). The revelation of the Father by the Son, whom the Jews condemned as an impostor and blasphemer for declaring His Sonship, is a major theme of John's Gospel.

(ii) *The revelation of God's plan through Christ.* Paul declares that the 'mystery' (secret) of God's 'good pleasure' for the saving of the Church and the restoring of the cosmos through Christ is now revealed, after having been kept hidden up to the time of the incarnation (Rom. xvi. 25 f.; 1 Cor. ii. 7–10; Eph. i. 9 ff., iii. 3–11; Col. i. 19 ff.). He shows how this revelation abolishes the old wall of partition between Jew and Gentile (Rom. iii. 29 ff., ix–xi; Gal. ii. 15–iii. 29; Eph. ii. 11–iii. 6); similarly, the writer to the Hebrews shows how it abolishes the old priestly and sacrificial Jewish cultus (Heb. vii–x).

IV. THE NATURE OF REVELATION

It is clear from the foregoing that the Bible conceives of revelation as primarily and fundamentally verbal communication—God's *tôrâ* (teaching, instruction, law), or *d^{e}ḇārim* (words), in the Old Testament, and His *logos* or *rhēma*, 'word, utterance', in the New. The thought of God as revealed in His actions is secondary, and depends for its validity on the presupposition of verbal revelation. For men can only 'know that He is Yahweh' from seeing His works in history if He speaks to make it clear that they are His works, and to explain what they mean. Equally, men could never have guessed or deduced who and what Jesus of Nazareth was apart from God's statements about Him in the Old Testament, and Jesus' own self-testimony (*cf.* Jn. v. 37–39, viii. 13–18).

See INSPIRATION, PROPHECY.

BIBLIOGRAPHY. *Arndt*; A. Oepke in *TWNT*, III, pp. 565–597; B. B. Warfield, *The Inspiration and Authority of the Bible*, 1951; H. H. Rowley, *The Faith of Israel*, 1956; L. Köhler, *Old Testament Theology*, E.T., 1953; H. W. Robinson, *Inspiration and Revelation in the Old Testament*, 1946; E. F. Scott, *Revelation in the New Testament*, 1935; J. Orr, *Revelation and Inspiration*, 1910; B. Ramm, *Special Revelation and the Bible*, 1961. J.I.P.

REVELATION, BOOK OF. The last book of the Bible is, for most Christians, one of the least read and most difficult. A few passages from it are well known and well loved (*e.g.* vii. 9–17); but for the most part modern readers find the book unintelligible. This is largely because the book abounds in symbolism of a type that we do not use and to which we no longer possess the key. Yet this kind of imagery was readily comprehensible to the men of the day. Indeed, this partly accounts for our difficulties. The author could assume that his readers would detect his allusions, and therefore he felt no need to make explanations.

Revelation belongs to the class of literature known as apocalyptic (*q.v.*). It is the only book of this type in the New Testament, though there are apocalyptic passages in other books (*e.g.* Mt. xxiv), and the visions of Daniel belong to the same class. Characteristic of apocalyptic is the thought that God is sovereign, and that ultimately He will intervene in catastrophic fashion to bring to pass His good and perfect will. He is opposed by powerful and varied forces of evil, and these are usually referred to symbolically, as beasts, horns, *etc.* There are visions; angels speak; there is the clash of mighty forces; and ultimately the persecuted saints are vindicated. Much of this is conventional (which is why the first readers of Revelation would have understood it quite easily), but in the hands of many enthusiasts it led to turgid and grotesque phantasies. Biblical apocalyptic is much more restrained. Another difference between Revelation and the usual run of apocalyptic is that the author's name is given, whereas apocalypses were usually pseudonymous. The writers took names from the great ones of the past and ascribed their works to them. For our present purpose it is important to notice that in this book the Holy Spirit has made use of a recognized literary form, but that the book is not simply a conventional apocalypse. It has features of its own, and is a genuine prophecy, as the first three verses indicate.

I. OUTLINE OF CONTENTS

The book begins with a vision of the risen Lord, who gives messages to seven churches, those in Ephesus, Smyrna, Pergamos, Thyatira, Sardis, Philadelphia, and Laodicea, a group of cities in the Roman province of Asia (i. 1–iii. 22). The messages rebuke these churches where they have failed and encourage them on the path of Christian service. Then come visions of God and of the Lamb (iv. 1–v. 14), after which we read of the seven seals. As each seal is opened there is a vision recorded (vi. 1–17, viii. 1). This leads on to the seven trumpets, with a vision recorded after each trumpet is sounded (viii. 2–ix. 21, xi. 15–19). Between the sixth and seventh seals there is an interlude (vii. 1–17), and another between the sixth and seventh trumpets (x. 1–xi. 14). John then records various wonders in heaven, a woman bringing forth a man child, and opposed by Satan (xii. 1–17), beasts opposing themselves to God (xiii. 1–18), the Lamb on Mount Zion and His followers (xiv. 1–20). Next the seven last plagues are recounted. John sees seven angels with bowls, and as each pours out his bowl upon the earth one of the plagues follows (xv. 1–xvi. 21). Further judgments are then denounced on the scarlet woman, and on Babylon (xvii. 1–xix. 21), and the book concludes with visions of the millennium, of the new heavens and the new earth (xx. 1–xxii. 21).

It is uncertain how much of the book duplicates other sections. The recurrence of the number seven makes it fairly clear that some, at least, of the series are described in more than one way. What is certain is that the book envisages terrific opposition to God and the people of God, but that in the end God will triumph over every evil thing.

II. AUTHORSHIP AND DATE

The author tells us that his name was John, and he describes himself as God's 'servant' (Rev. i. 1), as one of the 'prophets' (Rev. xxii. 9), and as 'your brother, and companion in tribulation' (Rev. i. 9). Tradition has affirmed this John to be identical with John the apostle, and further, that he was the author of the Fourth Gospel and of the three Johannine Epistles. The view that the author was John the apostle goes back to Justin Martyr (*c.* AD 140), and is supported by Irenaeus and many others. The principal objection is the style of Revelation. The Greek is in many respects unlike that of the other Johannine writings. It is so unusual and sometimes shows such scant respect for the rules of Greek grammar that it is felt that it cannot come from the same pen as do the Gospel and the Epistles. (Charles speaks of it as 'unlike any Greek that was ever penned by mortal man'.) The question is too intricate to be discussed fully here. Suffice to say that, whereas most scholars today deny the apostolic authorship, there are some who find it best to think of all five Johannine writings as from one author, and that author the apostle John (*e.g.* E. Stauffer).

The book was obviously written at a time when the Church was undergoing persecution and difficulty. During the possible time for the composition of the book the two most important periods when this was so were during the reigns of Nero and of Domitian. The principal argument for the former date is Rev. xvii. 9 f., 'here is the mind which hath wisdom. The seven heads are seven mountains, on which the woman sitteth. And there are seven kings: five are fallen, and one is, and the other is not yet come.' If this refers to the emperors of Rome, then Nero was the fifth, and the writing would date from shortly after his reign. This is strengthened by the prophecy that 'the beast that was, and is not, even he is the eighth, and is of the seven' (Rev. xvii. 11). This appears to refer to the 'Nero-redivivus myth', the idea that Nero, though dead, would appear once more on this earth. Support is adduced from Rev. xiii. 18, which gives 'the number of the beast' as 666. Numbers were written in the 1st century, not with our convenient notation, but with letters of the alphabet. Each letter had a numerical value. By taking the numerical values of the letters making up 'Nero Caesar' in Hebrew we get 666. But it is difficult to see why it should be in Hebrew (when the book is in Greek), and anyway to get the desired result a variant spelling has to be adopted.

The later date is attested by a number of ancient authors, such as Irenaeus and Eusebius, who state categorically that the book was written in the time of Domitian. This is supported by certain indications of a general type within the book, though not by specific allusions to identifiable events. Thus the book speaks of certain groups of Christians as complacent and declining in spirituality. In Nero's reign the Church was still very young and vigorous. By the time of Domitian there is much more possibility of development and of degeneration. Most scholars today are agreed that the later date is to be preferred.

III. INTERPRETATION

How are we to understand all this? Four chief ways of looking at the book have emerged in the Christian Church.

a. The preterist view

This takes the book to describe past events. It sees all the visions as arising out of conditions in the Roman Empire of the 1st century AD. The seer was appalled at the possibilities for evil inherent in the Roman Empire and he used symbolic imagery to protest against it, and to record his conviction that God would intervene to bring about what pleased Him. In general, liberal scholars endorse this point of view. It enables them to understand the book without finding much place for predictive prophecy, and at the same time to see in Revelation a much-needed assertion of the truth of God's moral government of the world. Such a view roots the book in the circumstances of the writer's own day, which is surely right. But it overlooks the fact that the book calls itself a 'prophecy' (Rev. i. 3), and that some at any rate of its predictions refer to what is still future (*e.g.* chapters xxi, xxii).

b. The historicist view

This regards the book as setting forth in one grand sweep a panoramic view of history from the 1st century to the second coming of Christ. The writer's own day is mentioned, and so is the final time, but there is no indication of a break anywhere. Therefore, upholders of such views reason, the book must be held to give a continuous story of the whole period. Such views were held by most of the Reformers, who identified papal Rome with the beast. But the difficulties seem insuperable, and it is significant that, while stoutly maintaining that all history is here set forth, historicists have not been able to agree among themselves as to the precise episodes in history which the various visions symbolize. In nineteen hundred years one thinks that at least the main outlines should have emerged with clarity. It is also difficult to see why the outline of history should confine itself to Western Europe, especially since in earlier days at least much of the expansion of Christianity was in Eastern lands.

c. The futurist view

This maintains that from chapter iv onwards Revelation deals with events at the end-time. The book is not concerned with the prophet's own day, nor with later historical events, but with those happenings that will take place in connection with the second coming of the Lord. This view takes seriously the predictive element in the book (Rev. i. 19, iv. 1). And it has in its favour the fact that Revelation undeniably leads up to the final establishment of the rule of God, so that some of the book must refer to the last days. The principal objection is that this view tends to remove the book entirely from its historical setting. It is not easy to see what meaning it would have had for its first readers if this is the way it is to be understood.

d. The idealist or the poetic view

This insists that the main thrust of the book is concerned with inspiring persecuted and suffering Christians to endure to the end. To bring about this aim the writer has employed symbolic language, not meaning it to be taken for anything other than a series of imaginative descriptions of the triumph of God. Such views can be linked with other views, and are often found, for example, in combination with preterist ideas. The difficulty is that the seer does claim to be prophesying of later days.

None of the views has proved completely satisfying, and it is probable that a true view would combine elements from more than one of them. The outstanding merit of preterist views is that they give the book meaning for the men of the day in which it was written, and, whatever else we may say of the book, this insight must be retained. Historicist views similarly see the book as giving light on the Church throughout its history, and this cannot be surrendered. Futurist views take with the greatest seriousness the language of the book about the end-time. The book does emphasize the ultimate triumph of God and the events associated with it. Nor can the idealist view be abandoned, for the book does bring before us a stirring challenge to live for God in days when the opposition is fierce. Moreover, the Christian must always welcome the assurance that God's triumph is sure.

BIBLIOGRAPHY. Commentaries by H. B. Swete, 1906; R. H. Charles, *ICC*, 1920; M. Kiddle, *MNT*, 1940; N. B. Stonehouse, *The Apocalypse in the Ancient Church*, 1929; W. M. Ramsay, *Letters to the Seven Churches in Asia*, 1909; A. S. Peake, *The Revelation of John*, 1919; E. A. McDowell, *Meaning and Message of Revelation*, 1951; W. Hendriksen, *More than Conquerors*, 1939; M. C. Tenney, *Interpreting Revelation*, 1957. The literature is enormous; most of the books here listed have extensive bibliographies.

L.M.

REVENGE. See AVENGER OF BLOOD.

REVISED STANDARD VERSION. See ENGLISH VERSIONS.

REVISED VERSION. See ENGLISH VERSIONS.

REWARD. Thirteen Hebrew roots, of which *śāḵār* and *šōḥaḏ* are the chief, lie behind Old Testament expressions of 'reward'. In Greek the verb *apodidōmi* and noun *misthos* are used. All convey the meaning of payment, hire, or wages, and there are instances of 'reward' as pay for honest work done (1 Tim. v. 18) and dishonest gain, *i.e.* bribe (Mi. iii. 11).

1. Any reward depends for its significance upon the character of its bestower, and God's rewards, with which the biblical writers are chiefly concerned, both as blessings and as punishments, are manifestations of His justice (*e.g.* Ps. lviii. 11) and inseparable from the covenant (Dt. vii. 10) to which His commands are annexed. Thus the second commandment relates the penalty of disobedience to the jealousy of God, and the reward of obedience to His mercy (Ex. xx. 5). Dt. xxviii explains Israel's well-being in terms of submission to the covenant, a theme developed by the later prophets (*e.g.* Is. lxv. 6, 7, lxvi. 6). That obedience to God will bring visible temporal rewards is rightly expected throughout the Bible, but two false conclusions were also drawn from such teaching as Dt. xxviii, namely (i) that righteousness is automatically rewarded materially, and (ii) that suffering is a certain sign of sin (Job; Pss. xxxvii, lxxiii, all reflect the tension created by these false deductions, and Ec. viii. 14 marks an extreme cynicism). Yet it must be noted that in the Old Testament God Himself and His salvation is already known to be the supreme reward (Is. lxii. 10–12; Ps. lxiii. 3).

2. Jesus promised rewards to His disciples (Mk. ix. 41, x. 29; Mt. v. 3–12), so coupled with self-denial and suffering for the gospel's sake as to prevent a mercenary attitude. He slew the Pharisaic notion of meritorious service (Lk. xvii. 10) and discouraged desire for human reward (Mt. vi. 1), since God is the disciple's best reward. Jesus shows that reward is inseparable from Himself and from God, and the apostles laboured to establish the complete dependence of man's obedience and faith upon mercy and grace (Rom. iv. 4, vi. 23). Work, and therefore reward, is certainly looked for, but simply as an index of living faith (Jas. ii. 14–16), not as a basis of claim

upon God. The reward of salvation in Christ begins in time (2 Cor. v. 5) and its fulfilment is looked for after judgment (final rewards and punishments) when the covenant people enter into full enjoyment of the vision of God which is their enduring reward (Rev. xxi. 3).

BIBLIOGRAPHY. *Arndt* (*s.v.* '*misthos*'); J.-J. von Allmen, *Vocabulary of the Bible*, 1958 (*s.v.* 'reward'); A. Richardson, *A Theological Word Book*, 1950 (*s.v.* 'reward'); K. E. Kirk, *The Vision of God* (abridged version), 1934, pp. 69–76.

M.R.W.F.

REZEPH. A town destroyed by the Assyrians and mentioned by the Rabshakeh official of Sennacherib as a warning to Jerusalem of the fate of those cities who resisted their demands for surrender (2 Ki. xix. 12 = Is. xxxvii. 12). The details of any revolt or sack of this place (Assyr. *Raṣapa*) are not known, though the town is mentioned in Assyrian texts, where several governors are named in the years 839–673 BC. This important caravan-centre on the route from the Euphrates to Hamath was identified by Ptolemy (v. 16; Gk. *Rhēsapha*) and is the modern *Resāfa*, about 130 miles east-north-east of Hama, Syria.

D.J.W.

REZON. The son of Eliadah, who fled with a band of followers when David attacked Hadadezer of Zobah (1 Ki. xi. 23, 24). He occupied Damascus and became its ruler, opposing Israel during the reign of Solomon in alliance with Hadad of Edom (verse 25). He later 'reigned over Syria', and is thus thought to have outlived the united Hebrew monarchy and to be identified with Hezion (*Ḥadyân* of the Ben-hadad stele), father of Tab-Rimmon and grandfather of Ben-hadad I (*q.v.*), the king of Damascus with whom Asa of Judah made an alliance (1 Ki. xv. 18). If this is correct Rezon was the founder of the Dynasty of Aram (*q.v.*) who opposed Israel. Rezon (and Rezin) may be a title meaning 'prince' (*cf.* Pr. xiv. 28). See also DAMASCUS.

BIBLIOGRAPHY. M. F. Unger, *Israel and the Aramaeans of Damascus*, 1957.

D.J.W.

RHEGIUM. The modern Reggio di Calabria, a port-city on the Italian shore of the Strait of Messina, in southern Italy. An old Greek colony, Rhegium owed its importance under the Roman Empire to its position in relation to the navigation of the Strait and the Italian west coast. With the whirlpool of Charybdis and the rock of Scylla endangering navigation through the Strait, it was important to attempt the passage only with the most favourable sailing wind, and shipping moving north would wait at Rhegium for a south wind. This was done by the master of the ship which was taking Paul to Rome (Acts xxviii. 13).

J.H.P.

RHODA (Gk. *rhodē*, 'rose'). A maiden in the house of John Mark's mother who announced Peter's arrival (Acts xii. 13 ff.) after the angel had released him from prison. See W. M. Ramsay, *The Bearing of Recent Discovery . . .*, 1920, pp. 209 ff.

RHODES. The large island extending towards Crete from the south-western extremity of Asia Minor, and thus lying across the main sea route between the Aegean and the Phoenician ports. It was partitioned among three Greek states, of Dorian stock, early federated and sharing a common capital at the north-eastern point of the island. It was this city, also called Rhodes, that Paul touched at on his last journey to Palestine (Acts xxi. 1). After Alexander's conquests, and the establishment of the Macedonian kingdoms and many hellenized states throughout the eastern periphery of the Mediterranean, Rhodes grew to be the leading Greek republic, outstripping those of the old homeland. This was not only because she was now the natural clearing-house for the greatly increased east–west traffic, but because her position gave her an effective diplomatic leverage against the pressures of the rival kingdoms who disputed the hegemony of the strategic Aegean islands. As the champion of the old autonomy principle, she took the lead in calling for Roman intervention to protect it. Rhodes fell from favour with the Romans, however, who deliberately advanced Delos to destroy her ascendancy. By Paul's time her importance was gone, except as a resort of mellow distinction in learning and leisure.

BIBLIOGRAPHY. M. Rostovtzeff, *CAH*, VIII, pp. 619–642.

E.A.J.

RIBLAH, RIBLATH. 1. The name of a place in the district of Hamath, on the river Orontes, on the right bank of which are ruins near a modern village, Ribleh, 35 miles north-east of Baalbek and south of Hama. The site is easily defended and commands the main route from Egypt to the Euphrates as well as the neighbouring forests and valleys, from which ample supplies of food or fuel are obtained. For such reasons Riblah was chosen by Necho II as the Egyptian headquarters, following his defeat of Josiah at Megiddo and the sack of Kadesh in 609 BC. Here he deposed Jehoahaz, imposed tribute on Judah, and appointed Jehoiakim its king (2 Ki. xxiii. 31–35). When Nebuchadrezzar II defeated the Egyptians at Carchemish and Hamath in 605 BC he likewise chose Riblah as his military base for the subjugation of Palestine. From it he directed operations against Jerusalem in 589–587 BC, and here was brought the rebel Zedekiah to be blinded after watching the death of his sons (2 Ki. xxv. 6, 20, 21; Je. xxxix. 5–7, lii. 9–27). Diblath (RV 'Diblah') of Ezk. vi. 14 may be the same place, since an otherwise unknown situation is unlikely in the context.

2. Riblath at the north-east corner of the ideal boundary of Israel (Nu. xxxiv. 11) might be the same place as (1), though the border is generally considered to lie farther south (*cf.* Ezk. xlvii. 15–18). The suggestion commonly adopted, that this is to be read 'to Harbel' (LXX), modern Harmel in the Beqa', helps little in evaluating the border, since this place lies only 8 miles south-west of Riblah (1) itself. D.J.W.

RIDDLES. See GAMES.

RIE, RYE. See SPELT.

RIGHTEOUSNESS. Righteousness is a characteristic demand of the Old Testament. Right action and fair dealing between man and man was insisted upon by the prophets. 'Let judgment run down as waters, and righteousness as a mighty stream' (Am. v. 24). The ground for this insistence is that God requires righteousness in men (Mi. vi. 8; Ps. xv. 2). Those who judge are particularly required to exercise their office righteously (Lv. xix. 15). Pre-eminently God is the righteous Judge. That God will judge with the strictest justice every man according to his works is a sentiment found throughout Scripture. In the Old Testament this was often a source of comfort to the afflicted believer. But there is also in the Old Testament the recognition that our righteousness is insufficient for God's standard.

This last sentiment is central in Paul's concept of righteousness. He distinguishes between the righteousness of moral effort, which he calls 'the righteousness of the law' or 'my own righteousness' (Phil. iii. 9, 6; Rom. x. 1–6), and the righteousness of God. This latter righteousness has God as its source (Phil. iii. 9), and is received as a gift, 'the gift of righteousness' (Rom. v. 17). This gift from God is based on the work of Christ (Rom. v. 17). More particularly, it is based on the propitiation of Christ's death (Rom. iii. 19–26). It consists of the righteousness which Christ Himself achieved in His perfect obedience to His Father's will in life and death, in which He bore the curse of separation from God, which our breaches of God's law entail. Salvation is achieved by a judicial exchange between the sinner and the Saviour; the sinner receiving Christ's righteousness, the latter being made sin (2 Cor. v. 21; *cf.* 1 Cor. i. 30; 2 Pet. i. 1, where it is said that we share in the righteousness of Jesus Christ).

This gift of Christ's righteousness is made by God to all who believe (Rom. iii. 22), and it is the basis of God's verdict of justification (Rom. v. 18). Those clothed with this righteousness are justly acquitted and accepted as righteous at God's judgment bar (Rom. iii. 26).

The fact that God has provided this righteousness for sinners is the central fact of the gospel (Rom. i. 17). It is a righteousness which is independent of the degree to which we are able to conform to the law of God (Rom. iii. 21), for it is based on Christ's perfect conformity to the law and will of God.

Though the gift of righteousness in Christ to all who believe is the theme of the gospel, it was not a novel doctrine, but was testified to by the Old Testament (Rom. iii. 21). Paul quotes Habakkuk (Rom. i. 17) and speaks at length of Abraham, whose faith God took account of (Rom. iv. 3; *cf.* iv. 6).

Righteousness is conformity to law, especially to the law, mind, and will of God, which is the norm of righteousness. Christ fulfilled this righteousness, both by conformity to the precepts of God in life, and by conformity to the righteous judgment of God on sin in His death. His resurrection and exaltation is the vindication and reward of His righteousness (Heb. ii. 9; *cf.* Rom. ii. 7).

The word righteousness may be applied to well-doing of a less complete sort (*e.g.* Lk. i. 6), and in the Jewish vocabulary of the day it was applied to the particular act of well-doing in giving of alms (Mt. vi. 1, 2). See JUSTIFICATION.

BIBLIOGRAPHY. G. Quell and G. Schrenk, 'Righteousness', *Bible Key Words*, 1951.

D.B.K.

RIMMON. 1. The Syrian deity, a local representation of Hadad, the god of storm and war, in whose temple at Damascus the army-commander Naaman worshipped (2 Ki. v. 18). In gratitude for his cure from leprosy by Elisha he requested two mule loads of earth from Israel for the foundation of an altar he proposed to erect on his return home (2 Ki. v. 17). See NAAMAN. Rimmon, 'the Thunderer', was the Damascus Baal, and the temple was probably sited beneath the present Ummayid mosque in that city, which was itself built over an older temple dedicated to Zeus, whose symbol, like that of Rimmon, Hadad, and Baal, was a thunderbolt. See HADAD, HADAD-RIMMON.

2. A Benjamite from Beeroth, father of Baanah and Rechab, who assassinated Ishbosheth (2 Sa. iv. 2, 9). This personal name, like the similar place-names, if not an abbreviation of a form including the divine element Rimmon, is probably to be derived from the Heb. *rimmôn*, 'pomegranate'. See RIMMON below. D.J.W.

RIMMON (Heb. *rimmôn*, 'pomegranate'). **1.** A rocky place where 600 Benjamite survivors from Gibeah took refuge for four months (Jdg. xx. 45–47, xxi. 13). Robinson (*RB*, I, p. 440) identifies this with Rummūn, a village upon a hill 6 miles north-north-east of Jeba' (Gibeah) and 4 miles east of Bethel.

2. A town in the Negeb, by the border of Edom, belonging to Judah (Jos. xv. 32) and Simeon (Jos. xix. 7; 1 Ch. iv. 32, AV 'Remmon'). In the extreme south of Judah (Zc. xiv. 10) this place is probably the post-exilic En-Rimmon (Ne. xi. 29), and by a few is identified with the Rimmon-perez between Hazeroth and Moseroth where the Israelites camped (Nu. xxxiii. 19, 20).

3. A village in Zebulun (Jos. xix. 13, AV 'Remmon-methoar'). Some Hebrew MSS read *Dimnāh* (*cf.* 'Rimmon' in 1 Ch. vi. 77). A levitical place (Jos. xxi. 35), perhaps the modern Rummāneh, about 12 miles west of Tiberias (Galilee). D.J.W.

RING. See ORNAMENTS.

RIVER. Hebrew has a good many different words often rendered 'river', although this is not always an accurate translation of the original term.

The Hebrew word *naḥal* is common, meaning a wadi or torrent-valley; in summer a dry river-bed or ravine, but a raging torrent in the rainy season. The Jabbok was such a wadi (Dt. ii. 37), as were all the streams mentioned in the Elijah stories. Because these river-beds could suddenly become raging torrents, they often symbolize the pride of nations (Is. lxvi. 12), the strength of the invader (Je. xlvii. 2), and the power of the foe (Ps. cxxiv. 4). In his vision it was a *naḥal* that Ezekiel saw issuing from the Temple (xlvii. 5–12).

The second term, *nāhār*, is the regular word for 'river' in Hebrew. It is used of particular rivers: *e.g.* the rivers of Eden (Gn. ii. 10, 13, 14), the Euphrates (Dt. i. 7), and the rivers of Ethiopia (Is. xviii. 1), Damascus (2 Ki. v. 12), *etc.* In Ex. vii. 19, Ps. cxxxvii. 1, the word should almost certainly be rendered 'canals'. The waters from the rock struck by Moses formed a *nāhār* (Ps. cv. 41).

The word used most frequently of the Nile is *y*e*'ôr*. The term is also found in Coptic, and was probably an Egyptian loan-word (*BDB*): see, *e.g.*, Gn. xli. 1; Ex. i. 22. It is used by Jeremiah (xlvi. 7 f.) as a similitude of Egyptian invasion.

Other Hebrew terms for 'river' are *peleḡ*, irrigating canals (Pss. i. 3, lxv. 9); *'āp̄îq*, channel or river-bed (Ps. xlii. 1; Is. viii. 7); and *yûḇāl* or *'ûḇāl*, a stream or watercourse (Is. xxx. 25; Dn. viii. 2, 3, 6). In the New Testament the word for 'river' is *potamos*. It is used of the Euphrates (Rev. xvi. 12) and the Jordan (Mk. i. 5); of the river issuing from God's throne (Rev. xxii. 1 f.); and of the Holy Spirit under the figure of living water (Jn. vii. 38 f.). J.G.S.S.T.

RIVER OF EGYPT. See EGYPT, RIVER OF.

RIZPAH (Heb. *riṣpâ*, 'a hot stone', 'a live coal'). A daughter of a certain Aiah, and a concubine of Saul. On Saul's death, Abner, no doubt wishing to gain some advantage, and following the custom of those who occupied a throne after a king's death, took Rizpah himself (2 Sa. iii. 7). When rebuked by Ishbosheth, he reminded the king's son that he had stayed to support him rather than desert to David, and Ishbosheth was silenced (2 Sa. iii. 8–11).

Rizpah gave two sons to Saul, Mephibosheth and Armoni (2 Sa. xxi. 8). In later years king David learned that a severe famine in the land was a judgment on the people for the bloody deeds of Saul among the Gibeonites (2 Sa. xxi. 1). When he learned that the Gibeonites required the death of seven of Saul's sons as an atonement, he surrendered the two sons of Rizpah along with the sons of Michal (2 Sa. xxi. 1 ff.). All were hanged, and the grief-stricken Rizpah watched over the bodies for several months. This devotion led David to undertake the proper burial of the bones of Jonathan and Saul along with those of the men who had been hanged. J.A.T.

ROADS. See TRADE AND COMMERCE.

ROBE. See DRESS.

ROCK. In the Old Testament rock (*sela'*; *ṣûr*) symbolizes the security and defence of a steep and inaccessible refuge (*cf.* Is. xxxii. 2, xxxiii. 16). Similarly, it is used of an immovable foundation (*cf.* Ps. xl. 2): to remove 'the rock' is equivalent to shaking the world (*cf.* Jb. xviii. 4). In an interplay of these symbols it is not surprising to find God spoken of as a rock who gives security and safety to His people (*cf.* 2 Sa. xxii. 32). In Is. viii. 14 *ṣûr* is used of the messianic stone (see CORNERSTONE) rejected by the Jewish 'temple builders'. Together with Ps. cxviii. 22 and Is. xxviii. 16 it becomes important for New Testament typology: Jesus Christ, the rejected 'rock of offence', becomes the cornerstone of God's true Temple, the Christian Ecclesia (Rom. ix. 33; 1 Pet. ii. 6 ff.; *cf.* Ellis, pp. 88 ff.). In Paul the typology is extended to the identification of Christ with the rock whose nourishing water followed the Israelites in the wilderness (1 Cor. x. 1 ff.; *cf.* Ellis, pp. 66–70). The relation (and probable identification) of Peter (*q.v.*) with the rock in Mt. xvi. 18 is the subject of continuing discussion (*cf.* Cullmann, pp. 155–212).

BIBLIOGRAPHY. 'Cornerstone', *Baker's Dictionary of Theology*, 1959; O. Cullmann, *Peter: Disciple, Apostle, Martyr*, 1953; E. E. Ellis, *Paul's Use of the Old Testament*, 1957; *TWNT*, VI, 1959, pp. 94–112. E.E.E.

ROCK BADGER. See CONEY.

ROD. A word which has a great variety of meanings. 1. A stem, branch (Gn. xxx. 37; Ezk. xix. 11). 2. A support carried by travellers (Gn. xxxii. 10; Mk. vi. 8), shepherds (Ex. iv. 2; Ps. xxiii. 4, 'staff'), old men (Zc. viii. 4; Heb. xi. 21) and men of rank (Gn. xxxviii. 18); figurative in Is. iii. 1. 3. An instrument of punishment (Pr. *passim*; 1 Cor. iv. 21). 4. A club (Mk. xiv. 43) carried by soldiers (1 Sa. xiv. 27; 2 Sa. xxiii. 21) and shepherds (1 Sa. xvii. 40; *cf.* Ps. xxiii. 4, where it is used figuratively of divine guidance and protection). 5. A symbol of authority, both human (Jdg. v. 14, RV), *e.g.* a sceptre (Gn. xlix. 10, RV; Je. xlviii. 17), and divine, like Moses' rod (Ex. iv. 20) and Aaron's which confirmed the levitical priesthood (Nu. xvii; Heb. ix. 4). 6. A pole upon which ring-shaped loaves were hung. Breaking it is figurative of famine (Lv. xxvi. 26; Ps. cv. 16). 7. The wooden shaft of a spear (1 Sa. xvii. 7; 2 Sa. xxi. 19). 8. A pole used to transport sacred furniture, *e.g.* the ark (Ex. xxv. 13, xxvii. 6). 9. A magician's or diviner's wand (Ex. vii. 12; Ho. iv. 12). 10. A pike (Ezk. xxxix. 9); apparently a spear in Hab. iii. 14. 11. A carrying frame (Nu. xiii. 23). 12. A threshing-stick (Is. xxviii. 27).

In 2 Sa. iii. 29 *peleḵ* is the whorl of a spindle (AV, RV 'staff' after LXX); 'who holds a spindle'

(RSV) denotes effeminacy. In Ezk. vii. 10 probably read 'injustice', revocalizing *MT hummaṭṭeh* as *hammuṭṭeh*. Render 'tribe' in Ps. lxxiv. 2; Je. x. 16, li. 19; Mi. vi. 9 (see RSV): *maṭṭeh* and *šēḇeṭ* can mean 'rod' or 'tribe'.

BIBLIOGRAPHY. *BDB*; *Arndt*, *s.v.*; L. Koehler, *Lexicon in Veteris Testamenti Libros*, 1953.

L.C.A.

ROE, ROEBUCK. See GAZELLE.

ROLL. See WRITING.

ROMAN EMPIRE. The term in its modern usage is neither biblical nor even classical, and does not do justice to the delicacy and complexity of Roman methods of controlling the peoples of the Mediterranean. The word *imperium* signified primarily the sovereign authority entrusted by the Roman people to its elected magistrates by special act (the *lex curiata*). The *imperium* was always complete, embracing every form of executive power, religious, military, judicial, legislative, and electoral. Its exercise was confined by the collegiality of the magistracies, and also by the customary or legal restriction of its operation to a particular *provincia*, or sphere of duty. With the extension of Roman interests abroad, the province became more and more often a geographical one, until the systematic use of the magisterial *imperium* for controlling an 'empire' made possible the use of the term to describe a geographical and administrative entity. In New Testament times, however, the system was still far from being as complete or rigid as this implies.

I. THE NATURE OF ROMAN IMPERIALISM

The creation of a Roman province, generally speaking, neither suspended existing governments nor added to the Roman state. The 'governor' (there was no such generic term, the appropriate magisterial title being used) worked in association with friendly powers in the area to preserve Rome's military security, and if there was no actual warfare his work was mainly diplomatic. He was more like the regional commander of one of the modern treaty organizations which serve the interests of a major power than the modern colonial governor with his monarchical authority. The solidarity of the 'empire' was a product of the sheer preponderance of Roman might rather than of direct centralized administration. It embraced many hundreds of satellite states, each linked bilaterally with Rome, and each enjoying its individually negotiated rights and privileges. While the Romans obviously had it in their power to cut their way clean through the web of pacts and traditions, this suited neither their inclination nor their interest, and we find them even struggling to persuade dispirited allies to enjoy their subordinate liberties. At the same time there was going on a process of piecemeal assimilation through individual and community grants of Roman citizenship which bought out the loyalty of local notabilities in favour of the patronal power.

II. GROWTH OF THE PROVINCIAL SYSTEM

The art of diplomatic imperialism as explained above was developed during Rome's early dealings with her neighbours in Italy. Its genius has been variously located in the principles of the fetial priesthood, which enforced a strict respect for boundaries and allowed no other grounds for war, in the generous reciprocity of early Roman treaties, and in the Roman ideals of patronage, which required strict loyalty from friends and clients in return for protection. For whatever reason, Rome soon acquired the leadership of the league of Latin cities, and then over several centuries, under the impact of the sporadic Gallic and German invasions, and the struggles with overseas powers such as the Carthaginians and certain of the Hellenistic monarchs, built up treaty relations with all of the Italian states south of the Po valley. Yet it was not until 89 BC that these peoples were offered Roman citizenship and thus became municipalities of the republic. Meanwhile a similar process was taking place throughout the Mediterranean. At the end of the first Punic War Sicily was made a province (241 BC), and the Carthaginian peril led to further such steps in Sardinia and Corsica (231 BC), Hither and Further Spain (197 BC), and finally to the creation of a province of Africa itself after the destruction of Carthage in 146 BC. By contrast the Romans at first hesitated to impose themselves on the Hellenistic states of the east, until after the repeated failure of free negotiation provinces were created for Macedonia (148 BC) and Achaia (146 BC). In spite of a certain amount of violence, such as the destruction of both Carthage and Corinth in 146 BC, the advantages of the Roman provincial system soon became recognized abroad, as is made clear by the passing of three states to Rome by their rulers' bequest, leading to the provinces of Asia (133 BC), Bithynia, and Cyrene (74 BC). The Romans had been busy tidying up on their own account, and the threat to communications caused by piracy had by this time led to the creation of provinces for Narbonese Gaul, Illyricum, and Cilicia.

The careerism of Roman generals now began to play a prominent part. Pompey added Pontus to Bithynia and created the major new province of Syria as a result of his Mithridatic command of 66 BC, and in the next decade Caesar opened up the whole of Gaul, leaving the Romans established on the Rhine from the Alps to the North Sea. The last of the great Hellenistic states, Egypt, became a province after Augustus' defeat of Antony and Cleopatra in 31 BC. From this time onwards the policy was one of consolidation rather than expansion. Augustus pushed the frontier up to the Danube, creating the provinces of Raetia, Noricum, Pannonia, and Moesia. In the next generation local dynasties were succeeded by Roman governors in a number of areas. Galatia (25 BC) was followed by Cappadocia, Judaea, Britain, Mauretania, and Thrace (AD 46).

The New Testament thus stands at the point where the series of provinces has been completed and the whole Mediterranean has for the first time been provided with a uniform supervisory authority. At the same time the pre-existing governments still flourished in many cases, though with little prospect of future progress. The process of direct incorporation into the Roman republic went ahead until Caracalla in AD 212 extended citizenship to all free residents of the Mediterranean. From this time onwards the provinces are imperial territories in the modern sense. See map 15. See also PROVINCE.

III. THE ADMINISTRATION OF THE PROVINCES

Until the 1st century BC the provinces had fallen to the Roman magistrates either for their year of office itself or for the immediately subsequent year, when they continued to exercise the *imperium* as pro-magistrate. For all the high sense of responsibility of the Roman aristocrat, and his life-long training in politics and law, it was inevitable that his province was governed with a single eye to his next step in the capital. The first standing court at Rome was established for the trial of provincial governors for extortion. So long as the competition for office remained unrestrained, the creation of three-, five-, and ten-year commands only worsened the position. They became the basis for outright attempts at military usurpation. The satellite states were left in a hopeless plight. They had been accustomed to protect their interests against capricious governors by seeking the patronage of powerful houses in the senate, and justice was done in the long run. Now during the twenty years of civil war that followed the crossing of the Rubicon (49 BC) they were compelled to take sides and risk their wealth and liberty in an unpredictable conflict. Three times over the great resources of the East were mustered for an invasion of Italy itself, but in each case the invasion was abortive. It then fell to the victor, Augustus, during forty-five years of unchallenged power to restore the damage. He first accepted a province for himself embracing most of the regions where a major garrison was still needed, notably Gaul, Spain, Syria, and Egypt. This grant was renewed periodically until the end of his life, and the custom was maintained in favour of his successors. Regional commanders were appointed by his delegation, and thus a professional class of administrators was established, and consistent long-term planning was possible for the first time. The remaining provinces were still allotted to those engaged in the regular magisterial career, but the possibilities of using the position improperly were ruled out by the overwhelming strength of the Caesars, and inexperience tended to defer to them in any case, so that the Caesarian standard of administration was widely maintained. If it came to the worst a maladministered province could be transferred to the Caesarian allotment, as happened in the case of Bithynia in Pliny's day.

Three of the main responsibilities of the governors are well illustrated in the New Testament. The first was military security and public order. Fear of Roman intervention on this ground led to the betrayal of Jesus (Jn. xi. 48–50), and Paul was arrested by the Romans on the assumption that he was an agitator (Acts xxi. 31–38). The governments at Thessalonica (Acts xvii. 6–9) and at Ephesus (Acts xix. 40) demonstrate the paralysis that had crept in through fear of intervention. On the other hand, among the Phoenician states (Acts xii. 20) and at Lystra (Acts xiv. 19) there are violent proceedings with no sign of Roman control. The second major concern was with the revenues. The Caesars straightened out the taxation system and placed it on an equitable census basis (Lk. ii. 1). Jesus (Lk. xx. 22–25) and Paul (Rom. xiii. 6, 7) both defended their rights in this matter. The third and most onerous of their duties was jurisdiction. Both by reference from the local authorities (Acts xix. 38) and by appeal against them (Acts xxv. 9, 10) litigation was concentrated around the Roman tribunals. Long delays ensued as the cost and complexity of procedure mounted up. Hard-pressed governors struggled to force the onus back on to local shoulders (Lk. xxiii. 7; Acts xviii. 15). Christians, however, freely joined in the chorus of praise for Roman justice (Acts xxiv. 10; Rom. xiii. 4).

IV. THE ROMAN EMPIRE IN NEW TESTAMENT THOUGHT

While the intricate relations of governors, dynasts, and republics are everywhere apparent in the New Testament and familiar to its writers, the truly imperial atmosphere of the Caesarian ascendancy pervades it all. Caesar's decree summons Joseph to Bethlehem (Lk. ii. 4). He is the antithesis of God in Jesus' dictum (Lk. xx. 25). His distant envy seals Jesus' death warrant (Jn. xix. 12). Caesar commands the perjured loyalty of the Jews (Jn. xix. 15), the spurious allegiance of the Greeks (Acts xvii. 7), the fond confidence of the apostle (Acts xxv. 11). He is the supreme 'king' to whom Christian obedience is due (1 Pet. ii. 13). Yet his very exaltation was fatal to Christian loyalty. There was more than a grain of truth in the repeated insinuation (Jn. xix. 12; Acts xvii. 7, xxv. 8). In the last resort the Christians will defy him. It was the hands of 'wicked' men that crucified Jesus (Acts ii. 23). The vaunted justice is to be spurned by the saints (1 Cor. vi. 1). When Caesar retaliated (Rev. xvii. 6) the blasphemy of his claims revealed his doom at the hand of the Lord of lords and King of kings (Rev. xvii. 14). Thus, while Roman imperial peace opened the way for the gospel, Roman imperial arrogance flung down a mortal challenge.

BIBLIOGRAPHY. *CAH*, IX, X, XI; G. H. Stevenson, *Roman Provincial Administration*, 1949; R. Syme, *The Roman Revolution*, 1939; A. N.

Sherwin-White, *The Roman Citizenship*, 1939; F. E. Adcock, *Roman Political Ideas and Practice*, 1959; A. H. M. Jones, *Studies in Roman Government and Law*, 1960; H. Mattingly, *Roman Imperial Civilization*, 1957; M. Rostovtzeff, *The Social and Economic History of the Roman Empire*[2], 1957; E. A. Judge, *The Social Pattern of the Christian Groups in the First Century*, 1960.

E.A.J.

ROMANS, EPISTLE TO THE.

I. OUTLINE OF CONTENTS

a. Introduction (i. 1–15)

The apostle gives a long greeting followed by his reasons for his desire to visit the Roman church.

b. Doctrinal exposition (i. 16–viii. 39)

The major theme is the righteousness of God.

(i) Both Gentiles and Jews are equally guilty in face of God's righteousness (i. 18–iii. 20). This is in spite of the many privileges of the Jews.

(ii) God has nevertheless dealt with this situation. He has provided a propitiatory sacrifice in Christ (iii. 21–26). Since the benefits of this are appropriated by faith, the way is open for both Jews and Gentiles (iii. 27–31). The example of Abraham shows justification to be by faith and not works (iv. 1–25). Many blessings attend the believer's justification (v. 1–11). As sin is universal through Adam, so life comes through Christ (v. 12–21).

(iii) Righteousness must have an application to life. This is achieved through union with Christ, for as the believer has died with Him so he now lives in Him (vi. 1–14). This new life involves a new type of service, for the believer, although freed from the law, has become a slave of God (vi. 15–vii. 6). Law is no help towards sanctification, since it produces inner conflict (vii. 7–25). But life in the Spirit brings victory to the believer, for sin is robbed of its power and a new status of sonship replaces the bondage of sin (viii. 1–17). The believer has great hope for the future, which is even shared by the material creation (viii. 18–25). The present life is strengthened by the Spirit's intercession and by the security provided by God's love (viii. 26–39).

c. The problem of Israel (ix. 1–xi. 36)

The theme of God's righteousness is now treated historically in answer to its apparent conflict with the rejection of Israel.

(i) God's actions are sovereign and just. No creature has the right to question the Creator's decisions (ix. 1–29).

(ii) Israel's rejection is not arbitrary but due to their own fault, for they have had ample opportunity to repent (ix. 30–x. 21).

(iii) Nevertheless Israel may hope for restoration. God has always preserved a remnant (xi. 1–6). Israel's own failing has led to the inclusion of the Gentiles (xi. 7–12). The Gentiles will be the means of Israel's restoration (the olive-tree analogy) (xi. 13–24). The final state of Israel is in the hands of God in whom is inscrutable wisdom (xi. 25–36).

d. Practical exhortations (xii. 1–xv. 13)

(i) Duties resulting from dedicated lives of a personal and general character (xii. 1–21).

(ii) Duties affecting society as a whole, such as the duty of civic obedience, neighbourliness and sober conduct (xiii. 1–14).

(iii) The need for toleration among Christians. This is worked out in relation to the special problem of foods (xiv. 1–xv. 13).

e. Conclusion (xv. 14–xvi. 27)

(i) The writer states his motive in writing (xv. 14–21).

(ii) His future plans are then mentioned (xv. 22–29).

(iii) He asks for prayer support for his Jerusalem visit (xv. 30–33).

(iv) Many Christians are greeted by name (xvi. 1–16).

(v) Warnings are given about false teachers (xvi. 17–19).

(vi) Further personal greetings, a benediction, and doxology close the Epistle (xvi. 20–27).

II. THE CHRISTIAN CHURCH AT ROME

In the world of Paul's day the name of Rome meant much and was not without its strong fascination for the apostle himself, since he expresses a strong desire to preach the gospel there. As a missionary strategist he recognized the immense importance of the Christian church at the centre of the empire, and this may well have influenced the form of the Epistle which he addressed to it. Of the origin of this important church we know little, and it is perhaps useless to conjecture. It may have been founded by converts from the day of Pentecost who returned to their Roman homes rejoicing in their new-found faith, but, although some Romans are mentioned in Acts ii, there is no indication whether any of these were converted to Christianity on that day. But travel between Rome and her provinces was relatively easy in those days, and many Christians must have been among the travellers along the imperial highways. All that is certainly known is that by the time Paul writes to them the church was not only established but of considerable proportions. If the expulsion of Jews from Rome under the Emperor Claudius had anything to do with the Christian Church, as seems most probable from the reference to 'Chrestus' in the report of Suetonius, it is evident that it was of sufficient dimensions for such drastic action to be taken. And certainly under the Neronian persecutions not many years after this Epistle was written the Christians numbered a considerable multitude.

The question of Peter's connection with Rome cannot be answered with any conciseness, although any claims that Peter was founder of the church there may at once be dismissed. The apostle was still in Jerusalem at the time of the edict of Claudius, and the church must have been started many years before this. Moreover, Paul makes no mention of Peter in this Epistle, which would be hard to explain if Peter were in fact the head of the church at Rome at this time, as well as being directly opposed to his statement in xv. 20. Nevertheless, tradition strongly supports the view that Peter and Paul both suffered martyrdom in Rome, since so early a witness as Clement of Rome attests to this.

There has been some discussion regarding the composition of the Roman church, but it would seem most probable that it consisted of both Gentiles and Jews, with the former in the majority. Such a composition is to be expected in a cosmopolitan city with a strong Jewish colony, and is supported by an analysis of the Epistle itself. In some parts of his argument Paul seems to be addressing Jews, as, for instance, when he appeals to Abraham as 'our father' (iv. 1) and his direct address to a Jewish questioner in chapter ii; in other parts he turns his thought exclusively towards Gentiles (*cf.* i. 5 ff., xi. 13, 28–31). It is an interesting question from what source the Christian tradition within this church had been mainly derived, but there is little indication that it had been derived from the narrower Jewish–Christian stream and it is most natural to suppose that these Christians maintained an outlook similar to that of Paul himself. There is no evidence of the tension of the Jewish–Gentile controversy so apparent in the Galatian Epistle.

III. DATE AND PLACE OF WRITING

Such indications as are given in this Epistle about Paul's present location all point to the period of his stay in Greece at the close of his third missionary journey (Acts xx. 2). His face is now definitely turned towards the west, for he plans not only soon to visit Rome but to proceed with further missionary work in Spain (Rom. xv. 24, 28). His eastern travels are therefore at an end, and this would well fit his situation in Acts xx. Moreover, he is there on his way to Jerusalem, and in Rom. xv. 25 he says that his present plans are to go to Jerusalem with the contributions which many churches have made for the support of poverty-stricken Christians there. No doubt can exist, therefore, that the apostle writes this letter just before the final part of his third journey.

In confirmation of this conclusion there are certain indications in chapter xvi which point to Corinth as the place of despatch, although not all scholars are prepared to appeal to this chapter in support, since some believe it was sent to Ephesus and not Rome (see below). But leaving this aside, it is significant that Phebe (*q.v.*) is commended, and she was a deaconess of the church at Cenchrea, one of the two ports of Corinth. There is also a passing reference to a certain Gaius who was Paul's host at the time of writing, and it is possible that he is the Christian mentioned in 1 Cor. i. 14 (see GAIUS). Possibly the Erastus referred to in Rom. xvi. 23 is the Erastus mentioned in 2 Tim. iv. 20 as being left at Corinth, but this is by no means certain. More significant is the mention of Timothy and Sopater (Sosipater) (Rom. xvi. 21), both of whom accompanied Paul on his visit to Jerusalem (Acts xx. 4).

The Epistle may therefore be dated with relative accuracy, although the problems of New Testament chronology (*q.v.*) in general and Pauline chronology in particular forbid any absolute dating. A date between AD 57 and 59 would fit all the known data.

IV. THE PURPOSE OF THE EPISTLE

Certain immediate circumstances suggest themselves as the occasion which prompted the production of this Epistle. Paul's intention to do further missionary work in Spain caused him to appeal to the Christians at Rome to support him in this venture (*cf.* Rom. xv. 24). As he contemplates his visit to the Roman church he realizes that he may have a spiritual gift to impart to them and that he as well as they may be mutually encouraged (i. 11, 12).

The apostle may have heard of some practical difficulties which the Christians were experiencing, and he intends to correct in the ethical part of his letter (especially in chapter xiv) any wrong emphases. There is an allusion to false teachers in xvi. 17–19, where the Christians are told to avoid them, but this cannot be considered as part of the primary purpose of the letter, since it is appended almost as an afterthought. Clearly an anti-heretical purpose does not dominate the Epistle.

But the incidental purposes so far considered do not account for the theological form of the main part of the letter. What prompted the apostle to give such a prolonged theological exposition? He scarcely needed to have done this in order (on his approaching visit) to encourage interest in his western missionary plans. He must obviously have had some other dominating purpose. The first eleven chapters after the introductory portion (i. 1–15) read more like a treatise than a letter, and it is important to consider the reason for this.

The view that Paul wished to deposit with the Roman church a full statement of his doctrinal position has much to commend it. Here are enshrined for posterity some of the noblest concepts of Christianity which have rightly been accorded an honoured place in Christian theology. But a clear distinction must be made between the basic use that Christians have made of this Epistle and the purpose for which Paul originally intended it. It cannot be maintained that he envisaged laying the foundations of Pauline theology in this way. Moreover, there are some aspects of this theology which find no part in the argument of this Epistle, such as eschatology and the doctrine of the Church. It is not possible, therefore, to regard this Epistle as a full statement of Paul's doctrine. Nevertheless, it provides a well-reasoned presentation of some of his most dominant concepts, and it may well be that it was Paul's intention to inform the Roman church of these so that when he visits them the Christians will be intelligently acquainted with his teaching.

It is most probable that the apostle is deeply conscious that he has now reached the turning-point of his missionary career and his mind dwells upon some of the major concepts which have formed part of his continuing teaching work. In this case the inclusion of his matured reflections in a letter addressed to Rome may have been no more than an accident of circumstances in that at the time his face was turned Romeward. But it seems better to attach some importance to Paul's own esteem for the strategic importance of this church and to suppose that consciousness of this played some part in the character of his letter.

A more precise problem relating to the dogmatic purpose of the letter is the relative importance of the section dealing with the Jews' position (chapters ix–xi). Some of the earlier critical scholars (*i.e.* of the Tübingen school) regarded this portion as the kernel of the letter, in which case the purpose was supposed to be an endeavour to reconcile opposing Jewish and Gentile elements. But this theory is now wholly discounted. It is more in harmony with the facts to maintain that this section naturally follows on the earlier, more theological, debate. The problem in these chapters is the difficulty of reconciling the righteousness of God, the theme of the earlier chapters, with the apparent non-fulfilment of the ancient promises in the rejection of Israel. This theme must have been a burning one for all Jewish Christians, and would have been relevant in an address to any church with a group of such Christians.

V. THE INTEGRITY OF THE EPISTLE

Few scholars have had the temerity to question the authenticity of this Epistle, and the arguments of those who have done so are now recognized as wholly unfounded and subjective. But there are many scholars who question the concluding chapter, not on grounds disputing Pauline authorship but on the grounds that it does not belong to this Epistle. This opinion is based on several considerations: the large number of personal greetings which are supposed to be improbable to a church which Paul had never visited; the fact that three people, Aquila, Priscilla, and Epaenetus, had connections with Asia rather than Rome (although the first two originally came from Rome); the commendation of Phebe, which is considered less appropriate when addressed to a church where Paul was unknown; the unexpectedness of the allusions to the false teachings in verses 17–19; and the suitability of xv. 33 as an ending to the Epistle. But these considerations are not conclusive and can be otherwise explained. It was not Paul's practice to single out individuals in churches where he was known, and in view of travel facilities it is not surprising that he knew many at Rome or that some last heard of in Asia were then at Rome. Since Paul was well enough known at Rome to write them an Epistle, the commendation of Phebe presents no difficulty, while the warnings regarding false teachers may have been abruptly introduced either because Paul's notice had just been drawn to them or else because he purposely left the matter to the end so as not to emphasize it disproportionately. The ending xv. 33 may be possible as an ending, but is unparalleled in Paul's other Epistles. On the internal evidence from the Epistle there would seem to be insufficient grounds for regarding the chapter as originally detached and as sent to a quite different destination, either Ephesus or anywhere else.

Something must be said about the textual evidence for the ending of this Epistle, although this is not the place for a full discussion. It is sufficient to mention that there are different streams of textual evidence for the position of the benediction and the doxology, and some variations in the reference to Rome in i. 7, 15. There are even some indications that in some quarters the Epistle circulated without its two concluding chapters. This seems to have been particularly associated with Marcion. It is by no means easy to find a theory which accounts for all the variations in the textual evidence, and many different hypotheses have been proposed, some regarding chapters i–xiv as original, some i–xv, and others i–xvi. It is probable that the Epistle is original as it now stands, but that Marcion shortened it. In that case his text would have been responsible for the various textual traditions.

VI. THE LEADING THEMES OF THE EPISTLE

a. The righteousness of God

At the commencement of the doctrinal part of the Epistle Paul introduces the theme of God's righteousness, which he claims is now revealed to the believer (i. 17). To understand the development of Paul's argument as a whole it is necessary to consider in what ways Paul uses the concept of righteousness (*dikaiosynē*). Sanday and Headlam, in their excellent article on the righteousness of God (*A Critical and Exegetical Commentary on the Epistle to the Romans*, 1895, pp. 34–39), point out four different aspects of the manifestation of divine righteousness in this Epistle. The first is fidelity; for the promises of God must be fulfilled to accord with the divine nature (iii. 3, 4). The second is wrath, a particular aspect of righteousness in its abhorrence of all sin, and not as is sometimes supposed a quality opposed to righteousness (*cf.* i. 17 f., ii. 5). Righteousness and wrath are, in fact, indivisible, and it is a false exegesis which can treat of God's righteousness without allowing for the operation of God's wrath. The third is the manifestation of righteousness in the death of Christ, of which the classic statement is found in iii. 25 f. More will be said of this later, but for the present purpose it is necessary to note that in some way God's gift of Christ as a propitiatory sacrifice manifests His righteousness. It is not considered arbitrary or capricious, but is pre-eminently right and just. Only so could it reveal righteousness. The fourth aspect is the linking of righteousness with faith. It may be said to be characteristic of Pauline theology that the righteousness of God which has been manifested can also be appropriated by faith. God's righteousness is therefore considered as being active as well as passive, and in its active rôle it declares as righteous those who by nature are at enmity with God (see v. 10). This is the meaning of justification; not that men are actually made righteous but that they are accounted as righteous. The whole Epistle is in reality an exposition of this theme, and it has become basic not only to Pauline theology but to the subsequent Reformed theology which draws so much from it.

b. The goodness of God

In case anyone should think that Paul's conception of God was mainly influenced by His righteousness irrespective of His other attributes, it is well to be reminded that in this Epistle Paul has much to say about the loving character of God. The mere fact that God's righteousness is conceived of as active in man's salvation points to a motive of love linked with holiness. But Paul specifically draws attention to God's kindness and forbearance and patience (ii. 4). He points out that the supreme manifestation of God's love is in the amazing fact that Christ died for us while we were still sinners (v. 8). And the classic statement of the enduring quality of that love is found in viii. 35 ff., where Paul can think of nothing, either circumstantial or spiritual, which could possibly separate us from God's love.

When dealing with the problem of the rejection of Israel, Paul makes much of God's mercy and flatly refuses to acknowledge the possibility of His injustice (ix. 15). He quotes approvingly the statement of Isaiah that all day long God had stretched out His hands to the disobedient people of Israel (x. 21). Even when the apostle is obliged to speak of the severity of God, he at once reminds his readers of God's kindness to those who continue to abide in Him (xi. 22). It is the great prerogative of God to have mercy (xi. 32). Even in the practical part of the Epistle, Paul frequently thinks of the gracious character of God. His will is good, acceptable, and perfect (xii. 2). He receives both the weak and the strong, and this is cited as a reason why the one should not judge the other. He is called the God of steadfastness and encouragement (*tēs hypomonēs kai tēs paraklēseōs*, xv. 5), and this forms the basis of an exhortation to develop similar qualities in ourselves. Similarly, because God is a God of hope (xv. 13), Christians by the power of the Spirit are to abound in hope. Throughout the Epistle, in fact, Paul's thought is dominated by his conception of God. But one other aspect demands a brief comment on its own.

c. The sovereignty of God

It is mainly in chapters ix–xi that God's sovereignty comes into focus. In chapter ix Paul illustrates the theme by an appeal to the potter's power over the clay and, while the analogy may not be exact, it does illustrate the sovereignty of God's choice. But Paul is careful to link this more with mercy than with judgment. His thoughts on this important theme are wonderfully summed up in his amazement at the wisdom of God, which he describes as unsearchable and inscrutable (xi. 33 f.). This for him is a sufficient anchorage when faced with the most baffling theological problems.

d. The grace of God

No account can be given of God's grace until full appreciation has been made of man's sin, and this is well illustrated in this Epistle. The first three chapters are designed to show man's failure to attain to God's righteousness. Not only does Paul give a startling inventory of Gentile sins (chapter i) but he points out Israel's culpability in spite of their privileges. As his argument develops, Paul lays stress on the sinful nature of man under the terminology of flesh (*sarx*), by which he means moral rather than physical sinfulness. When speaking of Christ Paul is careful to differentiate His flesh, which was only in the likeness of sinful flesh, and man's flesh. It is clear that Christ had to become man to redeem man, for that is basic to Paul's doctrine of the two Adams (v. 12 ff.). In his description of his own struggles with sin (chapter vii) Paul has an acute sense of the power of sin. It is almost a personal enemy which does its utmost to destroy the soul. It takes advantage of the flesh. It brings all the members into bondage to its principles, which Paul calls the law of sin (vii. 23). It reduces man to the utmost wretchedness, from which only God through Christ can deliver.

This leads to a consideration of the saving activity of God in Christ. There has been much discussion over the significance of the word *hilastērion* (propitiatory) in iii. 25, and this is not the place to discuss its meaning. But it is important to remember that the most significant aspect of Paul's statement is that God took the initiative. This is in line with Paul's whole approach to the processes of redemption in this Epistle. The work of Christ on the cross is seen as an objective sacrifice provided by God on the basis of which sins may be remitted.

Paul deals in chapter vi with the operation of God's grace and shows that the superabundance of that grace must never be regarded as an occasion to greater sin. This is impossible because of the believer's close union with Christ, a doctrine which has an important place in Paul's thought. The illustration of baptism is used to show the character of the transformation which has been effected. Sin no longer has dominion because we are now under grace (vi. 14). Nevertheless, grace has made us slaves of God, so that a new obligation has replaced the old (vi. 20 f.).

e. The law of God

That the apostle had a high regard for the Jewish law is made clear by his statement that the commandment is holy, just, and good (vii. 12). He also recognizes the useful function of the law in manifesting the character of sin (vii. 7). Yet he is convinced by bitter experience that the law is completely ineffective as a means of salvation, not because of any inherent deficiencies in the law, for man's better self delights in the law (vii. 22), but because of man's own deficiencies.

Yet as he considers the law of God, the apostle at once perceives that for the Christian this comprises more than the mere letter of the Mosaic law. It involves what he calls the law of the Spirit (viii. 2), and his doctrine of the Holy Spirit, especially in His work of sanctification (in chapter viii), ought not to be divorced from its close connection with the law of God. Under the new covenant the commandments were to be written on the heart, and this is effected only through the indwelling Spirit. He introduces a new way of looking at God's requirements, for these become the laws of a Father under an entirely new relationship.

The Spirit of God is set over against the flesh (viii. 4 f.), gives life in place of death (viii. 11), bears witness to the Christian's sonship (viii. 14 f.), and intercedes for them in accordance with God's will (viii. 26 f.). Christian life is, therefore, not a matter of submission to a legal code, but a life controlled by the Spirit on the basis of a new law which involves such qualities as righteousness, peace, joy, hope, and love (*cf.* v. 3 f., xii. 11, xiv. 17, xv. 13, 30).

Bibliography. Commentaries by R. Haldane, 1874, reprinted 1958; C. Hodge, 1886, reprinted 1951; H. C. G. Moule, *EB*, 1893; J. Denney, *EGT*, 1900; W. Sanday and A. C. Headlam, *ICC*, 1902; C. H. Dodd, *MNT*, 1932; K. Barth, E.T., 1933; O. Michel, *MK*, 1957; C. K. Barrett, 1957; J. Murray, *NLC*, 1959; F. J. A. Hort, *Prolegomena to Romans and Ephesians*, 1895; T. W. Manson, 'St. Paul's Letter to the Romans —and Others', *BJRL*, XXXI, 1947–8, pp. 224 ff.; D. Guthrie, *New Testament Introduction: The Pauline Epistles*, 1961, pp. 21 ff. D.G.

ROME. Founded traditionally in 753 BC on its seven hills (the bluffs formed where the Latin plain falls away into the Tiber bed at the first easy crossing up from the mouth), Rome, as the excavations have shown, was in origin a meeting-place and a melting-pot, rather than the home of a pre-existing people. The process of accretion, stimulated at an early stage by the strategic requirements of the Etruscan states to the north and south, acquired its own momentum, and by a liberal policy of enfranchisement unique in antiquity Rome attracted to herself men and ideas from all over the Mediterranean, until nearly one thousand years from her beginning she had incorporated every other civilized community from Britain to Arabia. Rome was cosmopolitan and all the world was Roman. Yet this very comprehensiveness destroyed the uniqueness of the city, and the strategic centrality that had dictated her growth was lost with the opening up of the Danube and the Rhine, leaving Rome in the Middle Ages little more than a provincial city of Italy.

In New Testament times Rome was in the full flush of her growth. Multi-storey tenement blocks housed a proletariat of over a million, drawn from every quarter. The aristocracy, becoming just as international through the domestic favours of the Caesars, lavished the profits of three continents on suburban villas and country estates. The Caesars themselves had furnished the heart of the city with an array of public buildings perhaps never equalled in any capital. The same concentration of wealth provided the overcrowded masses with generous economic subsidies and entertainment. It also attracted literary and artistic talent from foreign parts. As the seat of the senate and of the Caesarian administration Rome maintained diplomatic contact with every other state in the Mediterranean, and the traffic in foodstuffs and luxury goods fortified the links.

I. ROME IN NEW TESTAMENT THOUGHT

The Acts of the Apostles has often been supposed to be an apostolic odyssey set between Jerusalem and Rome as the symbols of Jew and Gentile. The opposite pole to Jerusalem is, however, given as the 'uttermost part of the earth' (Acts i. 8), and, while the narrative certainly concludes at Rome, no great emphasis is laid on that. Attention is concentrated on the legal struggle between Paul and his Jewish opponents, and the journey to Rome serves as the resolution of this, culminating in Paul's denunciation of the Jews there and the unhindered preaching to the Gentiles. The theme of the book seems to be the release of the gospel from its Jewish matrix, and Rome provides a clear-cut terminal point in this process.

In the Revelation, however, Rome acquires a positively sinister significance. 'That great city, which reigneth over the kings of the earth' (Rev. xvii. 18), seated upon seven mountains (verse 9), and upon 'the waters' which are 'peoples, and multitudes, and nations, and tongues' (verse 15), is unmistakably the imperial capital. The seer, writing in Asia Minor, the greatest centre of industrial wealth in antiquity, discloses the feelings of those who suffered through the consortium with Rome. He scorns the famous compromise with 'the kings of the earth' who 'lived deliciously with her' (Rev. xviii. 9), and catalogues the sumptuous traffic (verses 12, 13) of the 'merchants of the earth' who have 'waxed rich through the abundance of her delicacies' (verse 3). He stigmatizes the artistic brilliance of the city (verse 22). How widespread such hatred was we do not know. In this case the reason is plain. Rome has already drunk the 'blood of the martyrs of Jesus' (Rev. xvii. 6).

II. THE ORIGIN OF CHRISTIANITY AT ROME

So far as the New Testament goes, it is not clear how the circle of Christians was established in Rome, nor even whether they constituted a church in the regular way. There is no unequivocal reference to any meeting or activity of the church as such, let alone to bishops or sacraments. The church of Rome simply fails to appear in our documents. Let it be said at once that this need not mean that it was not yet formed. It may merely be the case that it was not intimately connected with Paul, with whom most of our information is concerned.

Paul's first known link with Rome was when he met Aquila and Priscilla (*q.v.*) at Corinth (Acts xviii. 2). They had left the city as a result of Claudius' expulsion of the Jews. Since it is not stated that they were already Christians, the question must be left open. Suetonius says (*Claudius*, 25) that the trouble in Rome was caused by a certain Chrestus. Since this could be a variant of Christus, it has often been argued that Christianity had already reached Rome. Suetonius, however, knew about Christianity, and, even if he did make a mistake, agitation over Christus could be caused by any Jewish messianic movement, and not necessarily by Christianity alone. There is no hint in the Epistle to the Romans that there had been any conflict between Jews and Christians at Rome, and when Paul himself reached Rome the Jewish leaders professed personal ignorance of the sect (Acts xxviii. 22). This not only makes it unlikely that there had been a clash, but sharpens the question of the nature of the Christian organization at Rome, since we know that by this stage there was a considerable community there.

Some few years after meeting Aquila and Priscilla Paul decided that he 'must also see Rome' (Acts xix. 21). When he wrote the Epistle shortly afterwards his plan was to visit his friends in the city on the way to Spain (Rom. xv. 24). A considerable circle of these is named (chapter

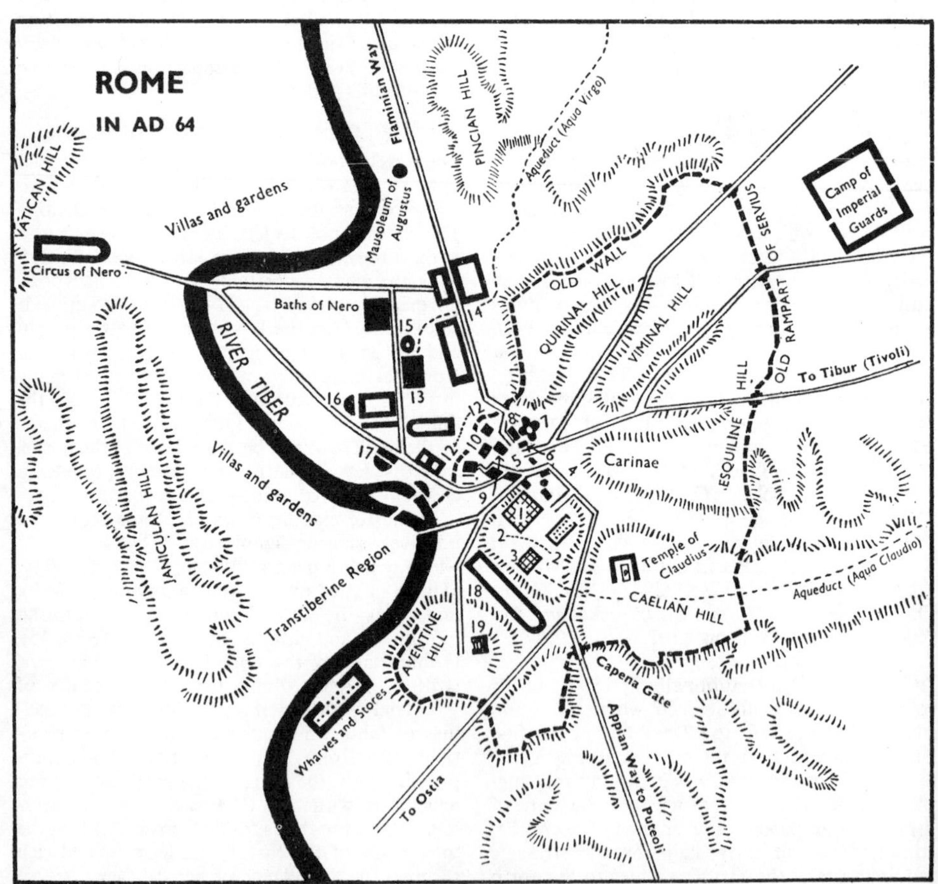

Fig. 175. Rome in AD 64. *Key:* 1. Palaces of Tiberius and Caligula; 2–2. Palatine Hill; 3. Palace of Augustus; 4. Sacred Way; 5. Forum; 6. Senate House; 7. Forum of Augustus; 8. Forum of Julius; 9. Temple of Concord; 10. Record Office; 11. Temple of Jupiter; 12–12. Capitoline Hill; 13. Baths of Agrippa; 14. Arch of Claudius; 15. Pantheon; 16. Theatre of Pompey; 17. Theatre of Balbus; 18. Circus of Maximus; 19. Temple of Diana.

xvi), they had been there 'many years' (Rom. xv. 23), and were well known in Christian circles abroad (Rom. i. 8). Paul's reference to his not building 'upon another man's foundation' (Rom. xv. 20) does not necessarily refer to the situation in Rome; it need only mean that this was the reason why his work abroad had been so lengthy (Rom. xv. 22, 23); indeed, the authority he assumes in the Epistle leaves little room for an alternative leader. The most natural assumption, on the internal evidence, is that Paul is writing to a group of persons who have collected in Rome over the years after having had some contact with him in the various churches of his foundation. A number of them are described as his 'kinsmen', others have worked with him in the past. He introduces a new arrival to them (Rom. xvi. 1). Although some bear Roman names, we must assume that they are recently enfranchised foreigners, or at least that the majority of them are not Romans, since Paul's references to the government allude to its capital and taxation powers over non-Romans in particular (Rom. xiii. 4, 7). Although some are Jews, the group seems to have a life of its own apart from the Jewish community (chapter xii). The reference in at least five cases to household units (Rom. xvi. 5, 10, 11, 14, 15) suggests that this may have been the basis of their association.

When Paul finally reached Rome several years later, he had been met on the way by 'the brethren' (Acts xxviii. 15). They do not appear again, however, either in connection with Paul's dealings with the Jewish authorities or, so far as the brief notice goes, during his two years' imprisonment. The seven letters that are supposed to belong to this period do sometimes contain greetings from 'the brethren', though they are mainly concerned with personal messages. The reference to rival preachers (Phil. i. 15) is the nearest we come to any positive New Testament evidence for a non-Pauline contribution to Roman Christianity. On the other hand, the assumption of a church organized independently of Paul might explain the amorphous character of Roman Christianity in his writings.

III. WAS PETER EVER IN ROME?

In the late 2nd century AD the tradition appears that Peter had worked in Rome and died there as a martyr, and in the 4th century the claim that he was first bishop of the Roman church appears. These traditions were never disputed in antiquity and are not inconsistent with the New Testament evidence. On the other hand, nothing in the New Testament positively supports them. Most students assume that 'Babylon' (1 Pet. v. 13) is a cryptic designation for Rome, but, although there are parallels for this in apocalyptic literature, it is difficult to see what the need for secrecy was in a letter, nor who was likely to be deceived in this case when the meaning was supposed to be plain to so wide a circle of readers. The so-called *First Epistle of Clement*, written when the memory of the apostles was still preserved by living members of the church at Rome, refers to both Peter and Paul in terms which imply that they both died martyrs' deaths there. The tantalizing fact that this is not positively asserted may, of course, simply mean that it was taken for granted. From about a century later comes the information that there were 'trophies' of Peter on the Vatican hill and of Paul on the road to Ostia. On the assumption that these were tombs, the two churches bearing the apostolic names were erected over them at later times. The recent Vatican excavations have revealed a monument which could well be the 2nd-century 'trophy' of Peter. It is associated with a burial-ground that was used in the late 1st century. We still lack any positive trace of Peter in Rome, however. The excavations strengthen the literary tradition, of course, and in default of further evidence we must allow the distinct possibility that Peter died in Rome. That he founded the church there and ruled it for any length of time has much feebler support in tradition, and faces the almost insuperable obstacle of the silence of Paul's Epistles.

The tradition of the martyrdom of the apostles is supplied with a lurid occasion by the massacre of AD 64 (see NERO). The account by Tacitus (*Annals* xv. 44) and the shorter notice by Suetonius (*Nero* xvi) supply us with several surprising points about the Christian community at Rome. Its numbers are described as very numerous. Its connection with Jesus is clearly understood, and yet it is distinguished from Judaism. It is an object of popular fear and disgust for reasons which are not explained, apart from a reference to 'hatred of the human race'. Thus Nero's mad atrocities merely highlight the revulsion with which the Christians were received in the metropolis of the world.

BIBLIOGRAPHY. See under ROMAN EMPIRE and also J. Carcopino, *Daily Life in Ancient Rome, the People and the City at the Height of the Empire*, 1941; O. Cullmann, *Peter: Disciple, Apostle, Martyr*, 1953. E.A.J.

ROOF. See HOUSE.

ROOM. See HOUSE.

ROPE. See CORD.

ROSE. See PLANTS.

ROSH. 1. In the RV this word occurs in the title of Gog who is described as 'prince of Rosh' (Ezk. xxxviii. 2, 3, xxxix. 1). AV and RVmg interpret as a title itself, 'chief', 'prince'. However, the name of a northerly people or country such as Meshech and Tubal is more probable. Gesenius suggested Russia, but this name is not attested in the area, and a very distant people named thus early is unlikely in the context. Most follow Delitzsch in identifying Rosh with Assyr. *Rašu* on the north-west border of Elam (*i.e.* in Media).

2. The name of one of the sons of Benjamin (Gn. xlvi. 21). D.J.W.

RUBY. See JEWELS AND PRECIOUS STONES.

RUDDER. See SHIPS AND BOATS.

RUE. See PLANTS.

RUFUS ('red'). A name of Italic rather than Latin origin, found twice in the New Testament (Mk. xv. 21; Rom. xvi. 13), probably referring to the same man. In Mk. xv. 21 Simon of Cyrene is identified for the benefit of a later generation as the father of Alexander and Rufus, brothers who were presumably known in Rome when Mark's Gospel was published there. The Roman Rufus who is greeted by Paul (on the assumption that Rom. xvi was sent to Rome) can hardly have been a different man. Paul describes him as a choice Christian. His mother had shown herself a mother to Paul (perhaps in Antioch, if we may further identify Simon of Cyrene with Simeon of Acts xiii. 1). F.F.B.

RUHAMAH (*ruḥāmâ*, 'pitied'). A symbolic name of Israel (Ho. ii. 1; *cf.* Rom. ix. 25, 26; 1 Pet. ii. 10) used to indicate the return of God's mercy. A play on words is involved, for the second child of Gomer, Hosea's wife, was called Lo-ruhamah ('unpitied'), denoting a time when God had turned His back on Israel because of her apostasy. See HOSEA, BOOK OF. J.D.D.

RULE. See ARTS AND CRAFTS.

RULER OF THE FEAST. See GOVERNOR.

RULERS OF THE CITY. The senior board of magistrates, five in number and later six, at Thessalonica. Their title (*politarchai*) is epigraphically attested for a number of Macedonian states (E. D. Burton, *American Journal of Theology*, II, 1898, pp. 598–632). As is nicely illustrated by the Acts (xvii. 6–9), they controlled the republic under Roman supervision. E.A.J.

RUMAH. Mentioned in 2 Ki. xxiii. 36 only. Josephus, in a parallel account, calls it 'Abouma', and probably means 'Arumah', a place mentioned in Jdg. ix. 41, in the vicinity of Shechem. But the name Rumah is quite possible. Eusebius refers to such a town, identifying it with Arimathaea. D.F.P.

RUSH, RUSHES. In AV this word corresponds to two Hebrew terms, *'ağmōn* and *gōme'*. The former is a general word, 'rushes', 'reed' (*q.v.*), related to *'ᵃgammîm*, 'reed-marsh' (Je. li. 32). For her unfaithfulness to God, Israel is stripped even of such ordinary basic raw materials as 'palm branch and reed' (Is. ix. 14), while these, for all their utility, will not avail Egypt in her troubles (Is. xix. 15). Rushes could be woven into rope, or used as fuel (Jb. xli. 2, 20, RV (and mg), RSV). The head bowed in outward penitence is like the bent-over tip of the rush (Is. lviii. 5, RV, RSV).

The term *gōme'* may signify the papyrus-plant (for which see PAPYRI AND OSTRACA, 'Egypt'), or else reeds generally; either meaning suits the biblical references to *gōme'*, which is depicted growing in the mire (Jb. viii. 11), symbolizing swampy growth (Is. xxxv. 7), used for papyrus skiffs in Egypt and Ethiopia (Is. xviii. 2) and Moses' ark of bulrushes (Ex. ii. 3). Heb. *gōme*, is probably the same as Egyp. *gmy* and *ḳmy*, 'reeds', 'rushes', attested from the 13th century BC onwards, and *kam* in Coptic.

BIBLIOGRAPHY. R. A. Caminos, *Late-Egyptian Miscellanies*, 1954, pp. 167, 168, 412; *cf.* W. Spiegelberg, *Koptische Etymologien*, 1920, pp. 4–6; T. O. Lambdin, *JAOS*, LXXIII, 1953, p. 149. K.A.K.

RUTH (Heb. *rûṯ*, perhaps contracted from *rᵉ'ûṯ*, 'female companion'). Ruth is the heroine of the book which bears her name (see next article). She was a Moabitess who lived in the time of the Judges.

In her own land Ruth had married Mahlon (Ru. iv. 10), the elder son of Elimelech and Naomi, Israelites from Bethlehem-judah who came to Moab during a famine. Naomi was widowed and then her two sons died without heirs. She determined to return to her native country, whereupon Ruth announced that she intended to accompany her, adopting both her nation and her God. Only by death would they be separated (Ru. i. 17).

During the barley harvest in Bethlehem Ruth went to glean in the fields of Boaz, a wealthy relative of Elimelech. Boaz noticed her and gave her his protection in acknowledgment of her loyalty to Naomi. She was invited to eat with the reapers, and was favoured throughout the barley harvest and the wheat harvest.

When all was harvested and the threshing had begun, acting on Naomi's instructions Ruth went to the threshing-floor at night and claimed Boaz's protection by appealing to his chivalry. He sent her back home as soon as it was light, with a present of six measures of barley, and the undertaking that, if her near kinsman was not prepared to marry her under the levirate marriage law, he would act as her kinsman-redeemer (*cf.* Lv. xxv. 25, 47–49).

With ten elders of the city as witnesses, he appealed to Naomi's kinsman to redeem a plot of land which had belonged to Elimelech, and which was a sacred trust that must not pass out of the family (*cf.* Lv. xxv. 23). To this he added the obligation of levirate marriage to Ruth (Ru. iv. 5). The kinsman could not afford this and renounced his right in favour of Boaz.

Ruth was married to Boaz, and their first child Obed was given to Naomi to continue the names of Elimelech, Mahlon, and Chilion. He was the grandfather of David (1 Ch. ii. 12; Mt. i. 5). M.G.

RUTH, BOOK OF. In the Hebrew Bible Ruth is one of the five *Megilloth* or 'rolls', included in the 'Writings', the third division of the Canon. It is read annually by the Jews at the Feast of Weeks. In the LXX, Vulg., and most modern versions it comes immediately after Judges; Josephus (*Contra Apionem* i. 8) apparently reckons it to be an appendix to Judges and does not count it separately in enumerating the total number of books in the Canon.

For the plot of the book, see RUTH.

I. OUTLINE OF CONTENTS

a. Naomi, widowed and bereft of her sons, returns from Moab to her native Bethlehem with her Moabite daughter-in-law Ruth (i. 1–22).

b. Ruth gleans in the field of Naomi's wealthy kinsman Boaz (ii. 1–23).

c. Ruth appeals to Boaz to perform the part of a kinsman-redeemer (iii. 1–18).

d. Ruth is married to Boaz and gives birth to Obed (iv. 1–17).

e. Genealogy from Perez to David (iv. 18–22).

II. AUTHORSHIP, DATE, AND PURPOSE

The Book of Ruth is fraught with difficulties for the critic, because, like Job, it contains no clue to its authorship. Tradition alone ascribes this idyllic pastoral to the last of the Judges, the prophet-priest Samuel.

The setting is that of the period of the Judges (Ru. i. 1), but its writing belongs to a later date. This is indicated when the author explains former customs (Ru. iv. 1–12). A very wide range of dating is offered for its actual composition, ranging from early pre-exilic times to a late post-exilic date.

The classical style and language do point to an early date, as does the attitude to foreign marriages, for under the Deuteronomic law a Moabite could not enter the congregation (Dt. xxiii. 3). The late dating is based on the antiquarian interest displayed in the book, and on its supposed connection with the reforms of Ezra and Nehemiah. One school of thought sees evidence of both early and late work in the book, supposing that the genealogy of David (Ru. iv. 18–22) and the explanations of early customs belong to a much later date than the book itself.

Many suggestions as to the purpose of the book have been put forward, among them the following. It was intended to supply a family tree for the greatest of the kings of Hebrew history, David, because this was omitted from the books of Samuel. It was a political pamphlet, an anti-separatist tract, written to counteract the stringency of Ezra and Nehemiah on the subject of mixed marriages. It was a humanitarian plea on behalf of the childless widow so that the next of kin would assume responsibility for her. It was designed to depict an overruling providence. It was to present a case for racial tolerance. Perhaps there was no ulterior motive at all, but it was a tale that had to be told. It certainly presents a most pleasing contrast with the narratives at the end of Judges, which belong to the same general period (Jdg. xvii–xxi).

BIBLIOGRAPHY. H. H. Rowley, 'The Marriage of Ruth', *HTR*, XL, 1947, pp. 77 ff., reprinted in *The Servant of the Lord and other Old Testament Essays*, 1952, pp. 161 ff.; E. Robertson, 'The Plot of the Book of Ruth', *BJRL*, XXXII, 1949–50, pp. 207 ff.

M.G.

S

SABAEANS. See Sheba (7).

SABAOTH. See God, Names of, iv*h*.

SABBATH (Heb. *šabbāṯ*, from the root *šāḇaṯ*, 'to cease', 'to desist'). In the Bible the principle is laid down that one day in seven is to be observed as a day holy to God. From the reason given for keeping the sabbath day in the Ten Commandments we learn that the example for the sabbath rest had been set by God Himself in the creation. The sabbath therefore is a creation ordinance (Ex. xx. 8–11).

In the account of creation the actual word 'sabbath' is not found, but the root from which the word is derived does occur (Gn. ii. 2). The work of creation had occupied six days; on the seventh God rested (lit. 'ceased') from His labour. Thus there appears the distinction between the six days of labour and the one of rest. This is true, even if the six days of labour be construed as periods of time longer than twenty-four hours. The language is anthropomorphic, for God is not a weary workman in need of rest. Nevertheless, the pattern is here set for man to follow. Ex. xx. 11 states that God 'rested' (Heb. *wayyānaḥ*) on the seventh day, and Ex. xxxi. 17 says that He ceased from His work and 'was refreshed' (*wayyinnāpaš*). The language is purposely strong so that man may learn the necessity of regarding the sabbath as a day on which he himself is to rest from his daily labours.

It has been held in contradistinction to what has been stated above that the institution of the sabbath derived from Babylonia. It is true that the Babylonian word *šabbatum* is related to the corresponding Hebrew word, but the force of the words is quite different. For one thing the Babylonians had a five-day week. Examination of contract tablets reveals that the days designated *šabbatum* were not days of cessation from labour. Contracts from Mari (Tell el-Harîrî) show that work was performed, sometimes over a period of several days, without any interruption every seventh day. The Bible clearly attributes the origin of the sabbath to the divine example.

The fourth commandment enjoins observance of the sabbath. In Genesis there is no mention of the sabbath apart from the creation account. There is, however, mention of periods of seven days (*cf.* Gn. vii. 4, 10, viii. 10, 12, xxix. 27 ff.). We may also note the narrative in Job that the seven sons celebrated a feast each on his day, and this was followed by the prayers and sacrifices of Job for the benefit of his children (Jb. i. 4, 5). This was not a single round, but was regularly practised. It may be that here is an intimation of worship on the first day of the cycle. At least the principle that one day in seven is holy to the Lord appears to be recognized here.

In Ex. xvi. 21–30 explicit mention is made of the sabbath in connection with the giving of manna. The sabbath is here represented as a gift of God (verse 29), to be for the rest and benefit of the people (verse 30). It was not necessary to work on the sabbath (*i.e.* to gather manna), for a double portion had been provided on the sixth day.

The sabbath was therefore known to Israel, and the injunction to remember it was one that would be understood. In the Decalogue it is made clear that the sabbath belongs to the Lord. It is therefore primarily His day, and the basic reason for observing it is that it is a day which belongs to Him. It is a day that He has blessed and that He has set apart for observance. This is not contradicted by the Decalogue given in Dt. v. 12 ff. In this latter passage the people are commanded to keep the sabbath in the manner in which the Lord has already commanded them (the reference is to Ex. xx. 8–11), and the fact that the sabbath belongs to the Lord is again stated (verse 14). An additional reason, however, is given for the observance of the command. This reason is merely additional; it does not conflict with those already given. Israel is commanded to observe the sabbath day, in order 'that thy manservant and thy maidservant may rest as well as thou'. Here is a humanitarian emphasis; but here also is emphasis upon the fact that the sabbath was made for man. Israel had been a slave in Egypt and had been delivered; so Israel must show the mercy of the sabbath towards those in her own midst who were slaves.

Throughout the remainder of the Pentateuch the sabbath legislation is found. It is interesting to note that there is a reference to the sabbath in each of the four last books of the Pentateuch. Genesis presents the divine rest; the four remaining books emphasize the sabbatical legislation. This shows the importance of the institution. Sabbath legislation, it may be said, is integral and essential to the basic law of the Old Testament, the Pentateuch (*cf.* Ex. xxxi. 13–16, xxxiv. 21, xxxv. 2 ff.; Lv. xix. 3, 30, xxiii. 3, 38).

In this connection the significance of the sabbatical legislation appears in the severe punishment that is meted out upon a sabbath-breaker. A man had been gathering sticks upon the sabbath day. For this act a special revelation from God decreed that he should be put to death. This man had denied the basic principle of the sabbath, namely, that the day belonged to the Lord, and therefore was to be observed only as the Lord had commanded (*cf.* Nu. xv. 32–36).

Upon the Pentateuchal legislation the prophets build; their utterances are in accordance with what had been revealed in the Pentateuch. The 'sabbaths' are often linked together with the 'new moons' (2 Ki. iv. 23; Am. viii. 5; Ho. ii. 11; Is. i. 13; Ezk. xlvi. 3). The older critical school, associated with the name of Wellhausen, believed that the prophets were condemning the sabbath as such, and that they thus stood in flat opposition to the law, which had not yet been written. In other words, the Pentateuchal 'sabbath' legislation was not yet in existence, or the prophets would not have dared to speak so vigorously against it. But even those who do not adopt a conservative attitude to Scripture are more and more coming to see that this was a misinterpretation. The prophets were not condemning the sabbath as such; they were condemning a misuse of the sabbath and of the other Pentateuchal institutions.

On the other hand, the prophets do point out the blessings that will follow from a proper observance of the sabbath. There were those who polluted the sabbath and did evil on that day (Is. lvi. 2–4), and it was necessary to turn from such things. In a classic passage (Is. lviii. 13) Isaiah sets forth the blessings that will come from a true observance of the day. It is not a day in which man is to do what pleases him, but rather one on which he is to do the will of God. God, not man, must determine how the sabbath is to be observed. Recognizing that the day is holy to the Lord will bring the true enjoyment of the promises.

During the Persian period emphasis was again laid upon observance of the sabbath day (Ne. x. 31, xiii. 15–22). During the period between the Testaments, however, a change gradually crept in with respect to the understanding of the purpose of the sabbath. In the synagogues the law was studied on the sabbath. Gradually oral tradition made its growth among the Jews, and attention was paid to the minutiae of observance. Two tractates of the Mishnah, *Shabbath* and *'Erubin*, are devoted to a consideration of how the sabbath was to be observed in detail. It was against this burdening of the commands of God with human tradition that our Lord inveighed. His remarks were not directed against the institution of the sabbath as such and not against the Old Testament teaching. But He did oppose the Pharisees who had made the Word of God of none effect with their burdensome oral tradition. Christ identified Himself as the Lord of the sabbath (Mk. ii. 28). In so speaking, He was not depreciating the importance and significance of the sabbath nor in any way contravening the Old Testament legislation. He was simply pointing out the true significance of the sabbath with respect to man and indicating His right to speak, inasmuch as He Himself was the Lord of the sabbath.

Although He was Lord of the sabbath, Jesus Christ went to the synagogue on the sabbath day, as was His custom (Lk. iv. 16). His observance of the sabbath was in accord with the Old Testament prescription to regard the day as holy to the Lord.

In His disagreement with the Pharisees (Mt. xii. 1–14; Mk. ii. 23–28; Lk. vi. 1–11) our Lord pointed out to the Jews their complete misunderstanding of the Old Testament commands. They had sought to make the observance of the sabbath more rigorous than God had commanded. It was not wrong to eat on the sabbath, even if the food must be obtained by plucking corn from the ears. Nor was it wrong to do good on the sabbath day. To heal was a work of mercy, and the Lord of the sabbath is merciful (*cf.* also Jn. v. 1–18; Lk. xiii. 10–17, xiv. 1–6).

On the first day of the week the Lord rose from the dead, and the Christians began to assemble on that day for worship of the risen Christ. This day is the Lord's Day, and as such is the sabbath which God had instituted at creation. The commands regarding it have never been abrogated. It belongs to God, not to the pleasure of man; it is for the benefit and blessing of man, and that blessing is obtained by a resting on the sabbath from all one's regular secular toil.

BIBLIOGRAPHY. J. Orr, *The Sabbath Scripturally and Practically Considered*, 1886; N. H. Snaith, *The Jewish New Year Festival*, 1947; J. Murray, *Principles of Conduct*, 1957, pp. 30–35. E.J.Y.

SABBATH DAY'S JOURNEY. See WEIGHTS AND MEASURES.

SABBATICAL YEAR. This term refers to the provision made concerning the land. Lv. xxv. 2 has *w^{e}šāḇ^{e}ṯâ hā'āreṣ šabbāṯ*, 'then shall the land keep a sabbath'. It is also called 'sabbath of rest' and 'year of rest' (Lv. xxv. 4, 5). After six years of sowing, pruning, and gathering, the land lay fallow for one year. The unattended growth of the field was for the poor to glean and what remained was for the beasts (Ex. xxiii. 11; Dt. xv. 2–18). To quiet fears of privation the Israelites were assured by the Lord that the sixth year would provide enough for three years (Lv. xxv. 20 f.). From the time of its institution this year of rest was observed in Israel (Ne. x. 31; 1 Macc. vi. 49, 53; *cf.* Jos., *Ant.* xii. 9. 5, xiv. 10. 6). Lv. xxvi. 34–43; 2 Ch. xxxvi. 21; Je. xxxiv. 14–22 refer to God's anger concerning the violation of this ordinance.

The culmination of the sabbatical years was reached each fiftieth year. This was a jubilee (Heb. *yôḇēl*, 'ram', thence 'trumpet' (ram's horn) by which the year was heralded). The sanctions of the sabbatical year were enforced. In addition, property reverted to its original owners, debts were remitted, and Hebrews who had been enslaved for debt were released. It was a time of thanksgiving and an occasion for the exercise of faith that God would provide food (Lv. xxv. 8, *etc.*).

The significance of rest for the land every seventh year does not lie merely in principles of soil chemistry. Neither does it follow the Canaanite pattern of a seven-year cycle without a harvest followed by seven years of plenty. In the text the land lies fallow for one year. (See C. H. Gordon, *Ugaritic Literature*, 1949, pp. 5 f.) The underlying reason for this arrangement lies in the disclosure that the seventh year of rest is a sabbath of rest both for the land and for the Lord (Lv. xxv. 2, 4). There is evident here a relation to the sabbath institution which is grounded in God's creative activity (see SABBATH). In accord with this disclosure other elements may be observed, namely that man is not the sole owner of the soil, and he does not hold property in perpetuity but possesses it in trust under God (Lv. xxv. 23). The Israelite was also to remember he possessed nothing by inherent right, for he was a slave in Egypt (Dt. xv. 15). Generosity is motivated by gratitude. D.F.

SABTA, SABTAH. The third son of Cush (Gn. x. 7, *sabtâ*; 1 Ch. i. 9, *sabtā'*) whose name also applied to his descendants. From the fact that among the other descendants of Cush (*q.v.*) there are names later associated with S Arabia, it is probable that Sabta refers to a tribe in this area. Some scholars identify the name with Shabwa, ancient capital of Ḥaḍramaut, but this is not certain. See ARABIA.

BIBLIOGRAPHY. J. A. Montgomery, *Arabia and the Bible*, 1934, p. 42. T.C.M.

SABTECA. The fifth son of Cush (Gn. x. 7 = 1 Ch. i. 9) whose name also referred to his descendants. The other descendants of Cush include names later associated with S Arabian tribes, indicating that the descendants of Sabteca probably later lived in this area. The name is otherwise unknown. T.C.M.

SACKBUT. See MUSIC AND MUSICAL INSTRUMENTS, II*a* (iii).

SACKCLOTH. A coarse cloth (Heb. *śaq*, Gk. *sakkos*, from which the English word is derived), usually made of goats' hair (*Siphra* 53b) and black in colour (Rev. vi. 12). The same Hebrew word sometimes means 'sack' (*e.g.* Gn. xlii. 27), which was evidently made of this material.

Sackcloth was worn as a sign of mourning for the dead (Gn. xxxvii. 34; 2 Sa. iii. 31; Joel i. 8; Judith viii. 5), or of mourning for personal or national disaster (Jb. xvi. 15; La. ii. 10; Est. iv. 1; 1 Macc. ii. 14), or of penitence for sins (1 Ki. xxi. 27; Ne. ix. 1; Jon. iii. 5; Mt. xi. 21), or of special prayer for deliverance (2 Ki. xix. 1, 2; Dn. ix. 3; Judith iv. 10; Baruch iv. 20; 1 Macc. iii. 47).

The form of the symbolic sackcloth was often a band or kilt tied around the waist (1 Ki. xx. 31, 32; Is. iii. 24, xx. 2; 2 Macc. x. 25). It was usually worn next to the skin (2 Ki. vi. 30; Jb. xvi. 15; 2 Macc. iii. 19), and was sometimes kept on all night (1 Ki. xxi. 27; Joel i. 13). In one case it replaces a robe, presumably over other clothes (Jon. iii. 6). Sometimes the sackcloth was spread out to lie on (2 Sa. xxi. 10; Is. lviii. 5), or spread out before the altar or on the altar (Judith iv. 11).

Palestinian shepherds wore sackcloth because it was cheap and durable (TB, *Shabbath* 64a). Prophets sometimes wore it as a symbol of the repentance which they preached (Is. xx. 2; Rev. xi. 3). According to Jon. iii. 8 and Judith iv. 10 even animals were clothed in sackcloth as a sign of national supplication. Wearing sackcloth for mourning and penitence was practised not only in Israel but also in Damascus (1 Ki. xx. 31), Moab (Is. xv. 3), Ammon (Je. xlix. 3), Tyre (Ezk. xxvii. 31), and Nineveh (Jon. iii. 5).

Clothing with sackcloth is used figuratively of the darkening of the heavenly bodies in Is. l. 3.

BIBLIOGRAPHY. G. Dalman, *Arbeit und Sitte*, V, 1939, pp. 18, 165, 176, 202; H. F. Lutz, *Textiles and Costumes among the Peoples of the Ancient Near East*, 1923, pp. 25, 26, 176, 177; P. Heinisch, 'Die Trauergebräuche bei den Israeliten', *Biblische Zeitfragen*, XIII, 7–8, pp. 16, 17. J.T.

SACRAMENTS. The word 'sacrament' (Lat. *sacramentum*) in its technical theological sense, when used to describe certain rites of the Christian faith, belongs to the period of the elaboration of doctrine much later than the New Testament. The Vulgate in some places thus renders Gk. *mystērion* (Eph. v. 32; Col. i. 27; 1 Tim. iii. 16; Rev. i. 20, xvii. 7), which was, however, more commonly rendered *mysterium* (see MYSTERY). In early ecclesiastical usage *sacramentum* was used in a wide sense of any ritual observance or sacred thing.

In everyday usage the word had been applied in two ways: (1) as a pledge or security deposited in public keeping by the parties in a lawsuit and forfeited to a sacred purpose; (2) as the oath taken by a Roman soldier to the emperor, and thence to any oath. These ideas later combined to produce the concept of a sacred rite which was a pledge or token, the receipt of which involved an oath of loyalty, and this led in time to the limitation of the word 'sacrament' to the two major rites of divine institution, baptism and the Lord's Supper. The wider use continued for many centuries. Hugo of St. Victor (12th century) can speak of as many as thirty sacraments, but Peter Lombard in the same period estimated seven as the number. The latter estimation is officially accepted by the Roman Church.

The common definition of a sacrament accepted by the Reformed and Roman Churches is that of an outward and visible sign, ordained by Christ, setting forth and pledging an inward and spiritual blessing. The definition owes much to the teaching and language of Augustine, who wrote of the visible form which bore some likeness to the thing invisible. When to this 'element', or visible form, the word of Christ's institution was added, a sacrament was made, so that the sacrament could be spoken of as 'the visible word' (see Augustine, *John Tract.* 80, *Epis.* 98, *Con. Faustum* 19. 16, *Serm.* 272).

Does the New Testament teach the obligation of sacramental rites on all Christians? What spiritual benefit is there in their reception, and how is it conveyed?

The obligation to continue sacramental rites depends on: (1) their institution by Christ; (2) His express command for their continuance; (3) their essential use as symbols of divine acts integral to the gospel revelation. There are only two rites obligatory in these ways on all Christians. There is no scriptural warrant for giving the other so-called sacramental rites (*i.e.* Confirmation, Orders, Matrimony, Penance, Extreme Unction) the same status as baptism and the Lord's Supper, which from the beginning are together associated with the proclamation of the gospel and the life of the Church (Acts ii. 41, 42; *cf.* 1 Cor. x. 1–4). They are linked with circumcision and the Passover, the obligatory rites of the Old Testament (Col. ii. 11; 1 Cor. v. 7, xi. 26). The Christian life is associated in its beginning and in its continuance with sacramental observance (Acts ii. 38; 1 Cor. xi. 26). Some of the deepest lessons of holiness and perfection are implicit in what Scripture says regarding the Christian's sacramental obligations (Rom. vi. 1–3; 1 Cor. xii. 13; Eph. iv. 5). References to the sacraments may underlie many passages where there is no explicit mention of them (*e.g.* Jn. iii, vi; Heb. x. 22; Jn. xix. 34). The risen Lord's great commission to the disciples to go to all nations with the gospel specifically commands the administration of baptism and clearly implies observance of the Lord's Supper (Mt. xxviii. 19, 20). Christ promises to be with His servants until the end of time. The work to which He has called them, including the observance of the sacraments, will not be completed before then. Paul also has no doubt that the Lord's Supper is to be continued, as a showing forth of the death of Christ, till He comes again (1 Cor. xi. 26). It is true that Matthew and Mark do not record the command 'this do in remembrance of me', but the evidence of the practice of the early Church (Acts ii. 42, xx. 7; 1 Cor. x. 16, xi. 26) more than compensates for this.

The efficacy of the sacraments depends on the institution and command of Christ. The elements in themselves have no power; it is their faithful use that matters. For through them men are brought into communion with Christ in His death and resurrection (Rom. vi. 3; 1 Cor. x. 16). Forgiveness (Acts ii. 38), cleansing (Acts xxii. 16; *cf.* Eph. v. 26), and spiritual quickening (Col. ii. 12) are associated with baptism. Participation in the body and blood of Christ is realized through Holy Communion (1 Cor. x. 16, xi. 27). Baptism and the Cup are linked together in the teaching of our Lord when He speaks of His death, and in the mind of the Church when it remembers its solemn obligations (Mk. x. 38, 39; 1 Cor. x. 1–5).

The sacraments are covenant rites: 'This cup is the new covenant' (Lk. xxii. 20, RV; 1 Cor. xi. 25). We are baptized 'into the name' (Mt. xxviii. 19). The new covenant was initiated by the sacrifice of the death of Christ (*cf.* Ex. xxiv. 8; Je. xxxi. 31, 32). Its blessings are conveyed by God through His word and promise in the gospel and its sacraments. There is clear evidence that many in apostolic days received blessing through the administration of the sacraments accompanied by the preaching of the word (Acts ii. 38 ff.). It was the gospel word or promise accompanying administration which gave meaning and efficacy to the rite. Those who had received only John's baptism were baptized again 'in the name of the Lord Jesus' (Acts xix. 1–7). It is apparent also that some received the sacraments without spiritual benefit (Acts viii. 12, 21; 1 Cor. xi. 27, x. 5–12). In the case of Cornelius and his household (Acts x. 44–48) we have an example of some who received the gifts which baptism seals, before they received the sacrament. Nevertheless, they still received the sacrament as bestowing benefit and as an obligation.

In the New Testament there is no conflict suggested between the use of sacraments and spirituality. When they are rightly received the sacraments do convey blessings to the believer. But these blessings are not confined to the use of the sacraments, nor when they are conveyed through the sacraments does their bestowal conflict in any way with the strong, scriptural emphasis on faith and godliness. The sacraments, when administered in accordance with the principles laid down in Scripture, recall us continually to the great ground of our salvation, Christ in His death and resurrection, and remind us of the obligations we have to walk worthily of the calling wherewith we are called. See BAPTISM, LORD'S SUPPER, THE.

BIBLIOGRAPHY. J. C. Lambert, *The Sacraments in the New Testament*, 1903; O. C. Quick, *The Christian Sacraments*, 1932; J. K. Mozley, *The Gospel Sacraments*, 1933; D. M. Baillie, *The Theology of the Sacraments*, 1957, pp. 37–124; Calvin, *Institutes*, IV. 14; G. Bornkamm in *TWNT*, IV, 1942, *s.v. mystērion.* R.J.C.

SACRIFICE AND OFFERING.

1. In the Old Testament.

I. TERMS

The Old Testament has no general word for 'sacrifice', except the rather sparsely used *qorbān*, 'that which is brought near' (*qrb*), which is practically confined to the levitical literature. (AV renders this term 'Corban' in the single New Testament reference of Mk. vii. 11.) *'Iššê* may also serve this purpose in the laws, but it is debated whether it should not be limited to 'fire-offerings' (*'ēš*) (but *cf.* Lv. xxiv. 9). The other frequently used words describe particular kinds of sacrifice, and are derived either from the mode of sacrifice, as *zeḇaḥ* (sacrifice), 'that which is slain' (*zāḇaḥ*), and *'ôlâ* (burnt-offering), 'that which goes up', or from its purpose, as *'āšām* (guilt-offering), 'for guilt' ('*āšām*), and *ḥaṭṭā'ṯ* (sin-offering), 'for sin' (*ḥaṭṭā'ṯ*). These may be distinguished in part by the disposal of the victim, whether wholly burnt ('*ôlâ*, Lv. i), or eaten by priests and worshippers together (*zeḇaḥ*, Lv. iii), or eaten by the priests alone (*ḥaṭṭā'ṯ* and '*āšām*, Lv. iv–v). For the distinction of '*ôlâ* and *zeḇaḥ*, see Dt. xii. 27 (*cf.* Je. vii. 21, where the prophet ironically suggests an obliteration of the distinction).

Also included under *qorbān* were the non-blood offerings 'offering, oblation', the cereal-offering (*minḥâ*, Lv. ii), the firstfruits (*rē'šîṯ*, *bikkûrîm*), the sheaf of 16 Nisan, the dough of the Feast of Weeks, and the tithes.

II. THEORIES OF THE BEGINNINGS

Sacrifice was not confined to Israel among the nations of antiquity (*cf.* Jdg. xvi. 23; 1 Sa. vi. 4; 2 Ki. iii. 27, v. 17), and many parallels from surrounding nations have been adduced in explanation of Israelite sacrifice. W. R. Smith ('Sacrifice', *EBr*[9], XXI, 1886, pp. 132–138; *The Religion of the Semites*[2], 1894) constructed, from the pre-Islamic nomadic Arabs, a hypothetical 'Semite', to whom the sacrificial meal was the earliest form, and the communion of the worshippers and the deity the controlling idea. The Pan-Babylonian movement (H. Winckler, A. Jeremias, from *c.* 1900 onwards) looked to the higher civilization of Mesopotamia, and to the developed ritual of propitiatory sacrifice practised there.

R. Dussaud preferred a Canaanite background, and found parallels first in the Carthaginian sacrificial tariffs (*Le sacrifice en Israel et chez les Phéniciens*, 1914, *Les origines cananéennes du sacrifice israélite*, 1921), and later in the Ras Shamra texts (*Les découvertes de Ras Shamra et l'Ancien Testament*, 1937). Here the materials of ancient Ugarit (*c.* 1400 BC) indicated a developed ritual of sacrifices bearing names similar to those of the Old Testament. The *šrp* was a burnt-offering, the *dbḥ*, a slain-offering for a meal, the *šlm*, possibly a propitiatory sacrifice, and the '*aṯm*, the equivalent of the Hebrew '*āšām*. (These were not Dussaud's identifications.) The myth and ritual school (S. H. Hooke, *The Origins of Early Semitic Ritual*, 1938; I. Engnell, *Studies in Divine Kingship in the Ancient Near East*, 1943) stressed this sedentary background and laid weight on the substitutionary rôle of the suffering king in the cult. This was not convincing to A. Alt, who had earlier claimed (*Der Gott der Väter*, 1929) that the real antecedents of Israelite faith were to be sought rather among the nomad Patriarchs, who had practised a form of religion centring in the god of the head of the clan (the 'God of Abraham', the 'God of Isaac', the 'God of Jacob'). V. Maag ('Der Hirte Israels', *Schweizerische Theologische Umschau*, XXVIII, 1958, pp. 2–28) took this further by noticing the dominance of the shepherd metaphor in the descriptions of this God, and from a background of the migrant shepherd cultures of the Asiatic steppes, suggested that their sacrifice was the fellowship meal in which the god took over the responsibility of the shed blood, which would otherwise have exacted vengeance (*cf.* A. E. Jensen, 'Über das Töten als kulturgeschichtliche Erscheinung', *Paideuma*, IV, 1950, pp. 23–38; H. Baumann, 'Nyama, die Rachemacht', *ibid.*, pp. 191–230). Israelite religion, as it appears in the Old Testament, is a syncretism in which the nomadic *zeḇaḥ* sacrifice exists alongside of gift sacrifices of the '*ôlâ* type, which come in from the sedentary Canaanite side (V. Maag, *VT*, VI, 1956, pp. 10–18).

Such a view finds place for both the sedentary and nomadic aspects, but becomes subjective when applied to particular Old Testament narratives. The Old Testament depicts early Israel less as nomadic than as a people in process of sedentarization. The Patriarchs already have the larger bovines and engage in some agriculture, and it may well be that a closer parallel to Hebrew sacrifice may be found among a tribe such as the African Nuer, whose sacrifice, as described by E. Evans-Pritchard (*Nuer Religion*, 1956) involved the offering of an ox in substitution for sin. The Wellhausen school, which traced an evolution from a joyous sacrificial meal in the earlier time to sin-offerings and guilt-offerings only in the post-exilic period (J. Wellhausen, *Prolegomena to the History of Israel*, 1885; W. R. Smith, *op. cit.*), regarded the connection of sacrifice with sin as the latest element. But this is no longer probable (*cf.* the writer's *Penitence and Sacrifice in Early Israel*, typescript, Zürich, 1960), as the following historical sketch will show.

III. THE DEVELOPMENT IN THE HISTORY

a. Patriarchal

It is significant that the first sacrifices mentioned in the book of Genesis were not *zᵉḇāḥîm* meals, but the gift-offerings of Cain and Abel (*minḥâ*, Gn. iv. 3, 4), and the burnt-offering of Noah ('*ôlâ*, Gn. viii. 20; we have here the first reference to an altar). Patriarchal altars are often described (*e.g.* Gn. xii. 6–8), but unfortunately details as to the type of sacrifice are lacking. Maag thinks of the *zeḇaḥ* communion meal, but T. C. Vriezen (*An Outline of Old Testament Theology*, 1958, p. 26) thinks the '*ôlâ* more typical. Gn. xxii gives some support to the latter position. Isaac knows that Abraham is in the habit of offering '*ôlâ* and that a lamb is the likely victim (verse 7). Sacrificial meals do, however, seal covenants (Gn. xxxi. 54, first use of *zeḇaḥ*), but not all covenants are of this type. Gn. xv. 9–11 is best understood as a purificatory ritual like that of the Hittite text translated by O. Masson (*RHR*, CXXXVII, 1950, pp. 5–25; *cf.* O. R. Gurney, *The Hittites*, 1952, p. 151).

As to the motives of sacrifice in this period, honouring of God and thanksgiving for His goodness were prominent, but more solemn thoughts cannot be ruled out. Noah's offering is to be seen, not simply as a thank-offering for deliverance, but as an expiation or atonement. When Jacob goes to Egypt (Gn. xlvi. 1), he pauses to seek God's will, and offers sacrifices (*zeḇaḥ*), which were possibly expiatory (*cf.* L. Rost, *VTSuppl.*, VII, 1960, p. 354; *ZDPV*, LXVI, 1943, pp. 205–216). In Egypt Israel is called to a solemn sacrifice in the wilderness (Ex. v. 3, *zeḇaḥ*), which required animal victims (Ex. x. 25, 26) and was distinguished from any offered by the Egyptians (Ex. viii. 26).

b. Amphictyonic

The recognition of early Israel as a tribal organization of the amphictyonic type is one of the gains of modern study. Noth thinks of this as coming into being only on the soil of Palestine in the time of the judges (*cf. The History of Israel*, 1958), but the strong biblical tradition takes it back to an earlier time and associates it with the name of Moses. Chief among amphictyonic occasions were the three festivals, at which sacrifice was to be offered: 'none shall appear before me empty' (Ex. xxiii. 15). The sacrifices we know best were those of the Passover and the covenant. The Passover combined the elements of sacrifice as an apotropaic and sacrifice as a communion meal. Secure in the knowledge that the blood had been shed to ward off evil, the members of each family could sit down to joyful fellowship (Ex. xii; Jos. v. 5–12; see PASSOVER). Similar elements probably entered into the covenant sacrifice and its renewals (Ex. xxiv. 1–8; Dt. xxvii. 1 ff.; Jos. viii. 30 ff., xxiv; *cf.* Ps. l. 5). The blood sprinkling purified the covenant and the eating of the meal marked its consummation (see COVENANT).

In addition, many other sacrifices both national and local were held. Typical of national sacrifices were those in times of disaster or war (Jdg. xx. 26, xxi. 4; 1 Sa. vii. 9), when penitence seems to have been the main note (*cf.* Jdg. ii. 1–5). Dedications and new beginnings were marked by sacrifice (Jdg. vi. 28; Ex. xxxii. 6; 1 Sa. vi. 14, xi. 15; 2 Sa. vi. 17), as were individual occasions of celebration (1 Sa. i. 3), intercession (Nu. xxiii. 1 ff.), and perhaps hospitality (Ex. xviii. 12).

c. Monarchic

The building of the Temple by Solomon provided opportunity for initiatory (1 Ki. viii. 62 ff.) and regular sacrifices (1 Ki. ix. 25), but as the sources are books of 'kings' they speak rather of royal participation (*cf.* 2 Ki. xvi. 10 ff.) than of that of the people. That the everyday cult was in progress, however, is attested by such a verse as 2 Ki. xii. 16, and by the frequent mention of sacrifice in the prophets and psalms. The many favourable references in the latter show that the condemnations of the former are not to be taken in an absolute sense, as if prophet and priest were opposed. The prophets object less to the cult itself than to the magic-working ideas borrowed from the fertility cults (Am. iv. 4, 5; Is. i. 11–16), and to such innovations as idolatry and child sacrifice introduced by apostatizing rulers (Je. xix. 4; Ezk. xvi. 21). An Isaiah can receive his call in the Temple (Is. vi), and a Jeremiah or an Ezekiel can find a place for a purified cult in the future (Je. xvii. 26; Ezk. xl–xlviii). This is also the predominant feeling of the psalmists, who constantly speak of their sacrifices of thanksgiving in payment of their vows (*e.g.* Ps. lxvi. 13–15). Expressions of penitence and the joy of forgiveness are also present (Pss. xxxii, li), and, although sacrifice is not often mentioned in these contexts, it is probably to be assumed from the fact that forgiveness is experienced in the Temple (Ps. lxv. 1–5). While there is no need to make all such references post-exilic, the prophets' complaint that penitence did not often enough accompany sacrifice in the late kingdom period should also be remembered.

d. Post-exilic

The disaster of the Exile is usually seen as resulting in a deeper sense of sin, and no doubt this is true (*cf.* 2 Ki. xvii. 7 ff.; Ne. ix), but not in the sense of Wellhausen that only then could the expiatory note of Lv. i–vii and Lv. xvi have entered Israelite religion. References to sacrifice in the non-levitical writings before and after the Exile, although usually too fragmentary to decide the issue, give little support to such an evolution. Joy, as well as penitence, continues to characterize sacrifice (Ezr. vi. 16–18; Ne. viii. 9 ff.). Temple and cult are valued (Hg. i–ii; Joel ii. 14, and especially Chronicles), but only as they are the vehicles of sincere worship (Mal. i. 6 ff., iii. 3 ff.). Apocalyptic and Wisdom literature take the cult for granted (Dn. ix. 21, 27; Ec. v. 4, ix. 2) and also continue the prophetic moral emphasis (Ec. v. 1; Pr. xv. 8).

IV. THE REGULATIONS OF THE LAWS

Laws for sacrifice are scattered through all the codes (Ex. xx. 24 ff., xxxiv. 25 ff.; Lv. xvii, xix. 5 ff.; Nu. xv; Dt. xii, *etc.*), but the sacrificial 'torah' *par excellence* is Lv. i–vii. Chapters i–v deal in turn with the burnt-offering (*'ôlâ*), cereal-offering (*minḥâ*), peace-offering (*zeḇaḥ*), sin-offering (*ḥaṭṭā't*), and guilt-offering (*'āšām*), while chapters vi, vii give additional regulations for all five—vi. 8–13 (burnt), vi. 14–18 (cereal), vi. 24–30 (sin), vii. 1–10 (guilt), vii. 11 ff. (peace). From these and other references the following synthetic account is compiled.

a. The materials

The sacrificial victim had to be taken from the clean animals and birds (Gn. viii. 20), and could be bullock, goat, sheep, dove, or pigeon (*cf.* Gn. xv. 9), but not camel or ass (Ex. xiii. 13) (see CLEAN AND UNCLEAN). These provisions are not to be traced to the idea of sacrifice as 'food for the gods' (*viz.* that the gods ate what man ate)—as might be suggested by Lv. iii. 11, xxi. 6; Ezk. xliv. 7—for fish (Lv. xi. 9) and wild animals (Dt. xii. 22) could be eaten but not sacrificed. The principle seems rather to have been that of property (*cf.* 2 Sa. xxiv. 24), the wild animals being regarded as in some sense already God's (Ps. l. 9 ff.; *cf.* Is. xl. 16), while the domestic animals had become man's by his labours (Gn. xxii. 13 is only apparently an exception), and were in a kind of 'biotic rapport' with him. This was even more clearly the case with the non-blood offerings, which had been produced by 'the sweat of his brow' (cereals, flour, oil, wine, *etc.*), and were also staple articles of the kitchen. Property unlawfully acquired was not acceptable (Dt. xxiii. 18).

The principle of 'the best for God' was observed throughout—as to sex, males being preferred to females (Lv. i. 3; but *cf.* Lv. iii. 1; Gn. xv. 9; 1 Sa. vi. 14, xvi. 2); as to age, maturity being especially valuable (1 Sa. i. 24, RSV); as to physical perfection, 'without blemish' being constantly emphasized (Lv. i. 3, iii. 1; Dt. xv. 21, xvii. 1; Lv. xxii. 17–25; *cf.* Mal. i. 6 ff., but note the exception for free-will offerings Lv. xxii. 23); and in some cases as to colour, red being chosen (Nu. xix. 2), perhaps as representing blood (*cf.* prehistoric cave paintings of animals). The difference between Israel and her neighbours is clearly seen in the rejection of the extension of this principle to what might be thought its logical climax in the human first-born. The child sacrifice, which was present in the late kingdom (2 Ki. xxi. 6), and the human sacrifices occasionally reported of earlier times (Jdg. xi. 29 ff.), were from outside influences, and were condemned by prophet (Je. vii. 31 ff.), precept (Lv. xx. 4), and example (Gn. xxii). Ex. xxii. 29b is clearly to be interpreted by Ex. xxxiv. 19, 20 and Ex. xiii. 12–16. The principle of substitution is present, not only in this replacing of the human first-born by an animal victim but in the provision given to the poor to offer the cheaper doves for a sin-offering (Lv. v. 7) and, if even this was too much, a cereal-offering (Lv. v. 11). The words 'such as he is able to get' (Lv. xiv. 22, *etc.*) are significant here.

Libations of oil (Gn. xxviii. 18), wine (Gn. xxxv. 14), and water (?1 Sa. vii. 6) seem to have had a place in the cult, but only the wine-offerings are referred to in the basic laws (Nu. xxviii. 7, *etc.*). The prohibition of leaven and honey (with some exceptions), and possibly also of milk, is probably to be put down to their liability to putrefaction. For the opposite reason salt was probably added to the sacrifices, because of its well-known preservative qualities (mentioned only in Lv. ii. 13 and Ezk. xliii. 24, but *cf.* Mk. ix. 49). Incense (*l^eḇônâ, q^eṭōreṯ*) played a considerable rôle, both as an independent offering (Ex. xxx. 7, *cf.* the instructions for its making in verses 34–38) and as an accompaniment of the cereal-offering (Lv. ii). Many scholars, doubting its early use on the ground that it was neither edible nor home-grown property (Je. vi. 20), think *q^eṭōreṯ* in the historical books describes the burning of the fat (*qṭr*) rather than incense, but this is not certain. (See N. H. Snaith, *IB*, III, 1954, p. 40, and J. A. Montgomery, *ICC*, *Kings*, 1952, p. 104, also *VT*, X, 1960, pp. 113–129; see also ALTAR.)

b. The occasions

The regulations cover both national and individual offerings, and daily and festival occasions. The first public sacrifices with good attestation are the seasonal ones, the Feast of Unleavened Bread, Firstfruits or Weeks, and Ingathering or Tabernacles (Ex. xxiii. 14–17, xxxiv. 18–23; Dt. xvi). With the first the Passover was early connected (Jos. v. 10–12), and with the last, in all probability, covenant renewal ceremonies (*cf.* Ex. xxiv; Dt. xxxi. 10 ff.; Jos. xxiv) and possibly new year and atoning rites (*cf.* Lv. xxiii. 27 ff.) (see also PENTECOST, PASSOVER, TABERNACLES, FEAST OF). A full tariff of sacrifices for these, and for additional observances, monthly (new moon), weekly (sabbath),

	Bullocks	*Rams*	*Lambs*	*Goats*
Daily (Morning and Evening)			2	
Sabbaths (additional)			2	
New Moons	2	1	7	1
Unleavened Bread (each day)	2	1	7	1
Total for seven days	14	7	49	7
Weeks (Firstfruits)	2	1	7	1
First day of 7th month	1	1	7	1
Day of Atonement	1	1	7	1
Tabernacles 1st day	13	2	14	1
,, 2nd day	12	2	14	1
,, 3rd day	11	2	14	1
,, 4th day	10	2	14	1
,, 5th day	9	2	14	1
,, 6th day	8	2	14	1
,, 7th day	7	2	14	1
,, 8th day	1	1	7	1
Total for eight days	71	15	105	8

and daily (morning and evening), is found in Nu. xxviii, xxix, and may be set out in tabular form as on p. 1116 (taken from A. R. S. Kennedy, *Leviticus and Numbers*, *Century Bible*, 1910, p. 349).

The date of the beginning of the twice-daily burnt-offering is controverted, and certainty is difficult to arrive at, because of the ambiguous nature of *minḥâ* for both cereal- and burnt-offerings. The chief references are—

	MORNING		EVENING	
	'Ôlâ	*Minḥâ*	*'Ôlâ*	*Minḥâ*
1 Ki. xviii. 29				x
2 Ki. iii. 20		x		
2 Ki. xvi. 15	x			x
Ezk. xlvi. 13, 14	x	x		
Ex. xxix. 38–42	x	x	x	x
Nu. xxviii. 3–8	x	x	x	x

'*Ōlâ* and *minḥâ* are also referred to without time notes in 1 Sa. iii. 14; Je. xiv. 12; and Ps. xx. 3, and continual '*ōlôṯ* and *minḥôṯ* in Ezr. iii. 3 ff. and Ne. x. 33.

Sacrifices of a more private nature were the Passover, for which the unit was the family (Ex. xii; *cf.* 1 Sa. xx. 6, but this was a new moon, not a full moon), and individual sacrifices, such as those in fulfilment of a vow (1 Sa. i. 3, *cf.* verse 21; 2 Sa. xv. 7 ff.), or in confirmation of a treaty (Gn. xxxi. 54), veneration of God (Jdg. xiii. 19), personal dedication (1 Ki. iii. 4), consecration (1 Sa. xvi. 3), or expiation (2 Sa. xxiv. 17 ff.). Whether the extending of hospitality to a guest was always regarded as a sacrificial occasion is not clear (Gn. xviii; Nu. xxii. 40; 1 Sa. xxviii. 24 may not have involved altar rites, but *cf.* 1 Sa. ix). Additional occasions mentioned in the laws are the cleansing of the leper (Lv. xiv), purification after child-birth (Lv. xii), the consecration of a priest (Lv. viii, ix) or a Levite (Nu. viii), and the release of a Nazirite from his vows (Nu. vi). Less frequent sacrifices were those of sanctuary dedication (2 Sa. vi. 13; 1 Ki. viii. 5 ff.; Ezk. xliii. 18 ff.; Ezr. iii. 2 ff.), royal coronations (1 Sa. xi. 15; 1 Ki. i. 9), and days of national penitence (Jdg. xx. 26; 1 Sa. vii) or preparation for battle (1 Sa. xiii. 8 ff.; Ps. xx).

Among seasonal offerings brought annually in recognition of God's share in productivity were firstlings and firstfruits (Ex. xiii, xxiii. 19; Dt. xv. 19 ff., xviii. 4, xxvi; Nu. xviii; *cf.* Gn. iv. 3, 4; 1 Sa. x. 3; 2 Ki. iv. 42), tithes (*q.v.*), and the offerings of the first sheaf (Lv. xxiii. 9 ff.) and the first dough (Nu. xv. 18–21; Ezk. xliv. 30; *cf.* Lv. xxiii. 15 ff.). Their purpose was probably not to consecrate the rest of the crop, but to deconsecrate it. All was God's until the first portion had been offered and accepted in lieu of the whole. Only then was the restriction on the human use of the remainder removed (Lv. xxiii. 14, *cf.* xix. 23–25). Even the portion brought was usually presented only in token at the altar, and afterwards taken away for the use of the priests or for a sacrificial meal. This was also the final fate of the weekly showbread (*q.v.*).

c. The ritual

The major altar sacrifices of Lv. i–v are described in a framework of a stereotyped ritual comprising six acts, of which three belong to the worshipper and three to the priest. They may be illustrated from the '*ôlâ* and the *zeḇaḥ* (*cf.* R. Rendtorff, *Die Gesetze in der Priesterschrift*, 1954).

Hebrew Term	'*Ōlâ* (Lv. i)		*Zeḇaḥ* (Lv. iii)		
	a 1–9	*b* 10–13	*a* 1–5	*b* 6–11	*c* 12–17
1. *hiqrîḇ*	3	10b	1b	6b	12b
2. *sāmaḵ*	4		2a	8a	13a
3. *šāḥaṭ*	5a	11a	2a	8a	13a
4. *zāraq*	5b	11b	2b	8b	13b
5. *hiqṭîr*	9b	13b	5	11	16
6. *'āḵal*					

The provisions for the sin-offering, several times repeated for various classes (Lv. iv. 1–12, 13–21, 22–26, 27–31), follow the same scheme, except in minor details. The burnt-offering of a bird (Lv. i. 14–17) and the cereal-offering (Lv. ii) of necessity present greater variations, but are not entirely dissimilar. A similar formula for the guilt-offering is not given (*cf.*, however, vii. 1–7), but it may be understood as coming under the law of the sin-offering (Lv. vii. 7).

1. The worshipper brings near (*hiqrîḇ*) his offering (also *hēḇî'*, '*āśâ*). The place of the sacrifice is the Tabernacle forecourt on the north side of the altar (for burnt-, sin-, and guilt-offerings, but not for the more numerous peace-offerings), although in earlier times it may have been the door of the tabernacle (Lv. xvii. 4), or local sanctuary (1 Sa. ii. 12 ff.), or a rough altar of stone or earth (Ex. xx. 24 ff.) or a rock (1 Sa. vi. 14) or pillar (Gn. xxviii. 18). Killing *on* the altar, although implied by Gn. xxii. 9 and Ex. xx. 24 (Ps. cxviii. 27 is corrupt), is not normal in the cult.

2. He lays his hands (*sāmaḵ*), or in the biblical period more probably one hand (*cf.* Nu. xxvii. 18), upon the victim, and possibly confesses his sin. This latter is mentioned, however, only in connection with the scapegoat, where the blood was not shed (Lv. xvi. 21) and with some sin-offerings (Lv. v. 5) and guilt-offerings (Nu. v. 7) (*cf.*, however, Dt. xxvi. 3; Jos. vii. 19, 20), so that the *s*ᵉ*mîḵâ* cannot certainly be claimed as a transferring of sin. On the other hand, it seems inadequate to regard it simply as an identification by the owner of his property, for such an identification is not made with the non-blood

sacrifices, where it would have been equally appropriate. Representation, if not transference, seems to be clearly involved (*cf.* the use of the same word for the commissioning of Joshua (Nu. xxvii. 18) and the Levites (Nu. viii. 10) and the stoning of a blasphemer (Lv. xxiv. 13 f.)). See P. Volz, *ZAW*, XXI, 1901, pp. 93–100, and for an opposite view J. C. Matthes, *ibid.*, XXIII, 1903, pp. 97–119.

3. The slaughtering (*šāḥaṭ*) is performed by the worshipper, except for the national offerings (Lv. xvi. 11; 2 Ch. xxix. 24). In the non-levitical literature the verb *zāḇaḥ* is used, but this may have referred to the subsequent cutting up of the sacrifice, and the laying of the parts on the altar (*mizbēaḥ*, not *mišḥaṭ*) (so K. Galling, *Der Altar*, 1925, pp. 56 ff.). For this, however, *ntḥ* is normally used (1 Ki. xviii. 23; Lv. i. 6), and *zāḇaḥ* describes rather the *zᵉḇāḥîm* sacrifices, except for a few passages (Ex. xx. 24; 1 Ki. iii. 4; *cf.* 2 Ki. x. 18 ff.) where it occurs with *'ōlôṯ*. These are perhaps to be put down to a loose use of the verb, which in the cognate languages can even be used of vegetable offerings, and in the Pi'el in Hebrew seems to be used quite generally for the whole round of the (usually apostate) cult. It is not certain, then, that every use of *zeḇaḥ* was sacrificial, or that meat could be eaten only on occasions of sacrifice, although this was often the case in antiquity (*cf.* the problem of the idol-meat at Corinth).

4. The manipulation (*zāraq*) of the blood is in the hands of the priest, who collects it in a basin and dashes it against the north-east and south-west corners of the altar in such a way that all four sides are spattered. This takes place with the animal burnt-offerings (Lv. i), peace-offerings (Lv. iii), and guilt-offerings (Lv. vii. 2), but not with the burnt-offering of birds (Lv. i. 15), where the quantity of blood was insufficient, and so was drained out on the side of the altar. The sin-offering (Lv. iv) uses a different set of verbs, *hizzâ* ('sprinkle') or *nāṯan* ('put') according to whether the offering is of primary or secondary rank (see below). The remainder of the blood is then poured out (*šāp̄aḵ*) at the base of the altar. The blood rite is referred to in the historical books only in 2 Ki. xvi. 15 (but *cf.* 1 Sa. xiv. 31–35; Ex. xxiv. 6–8).

5. Some burning (*hiqṭîr*) took place with all the sacrifices. Not only the blood but also the fat belonged to God, and this was first burnt (Gn. iv. 4; 1 Sa. ii. 16). This was not the fat in general, but specifically the fat of the kidneys, liver, and intestines. From the peace-, sin-, and guilt-offerings only this was burnt, from the cereal-offerings a portion called the *'azkārâ* was separated off and burnt, but the burnt-offering was wholly burnt except for the skin, which became the perquisite of the priests (Lv. vii. 8). A different kind of burning (*śārap̄*) away from the altar was the fate of the primary rank sin-offerings. In this burning the skin was also included.

6. The remaining portions of the sacrifice were eaten (*'āḵal*) in a sacrificial meal, either by the priests and worshippers together (peace-offering), or by the priests and their families, or by the priests alone. Priestly food was classified as either holy or most holy. The former included the peace-offerings (Lv. x. 14, xxii. 10 ff.) and firstfruits and tithes (Nu. xviii. 13), and could be eaten by the priest's family in any clean place, but the latter included the sin-offerings (Lv. vi. 26), guilt-offerings (Lv. vii. 6), cereal-offerings (Lv. vi. 16), and showbread (Lv. xxiv. 9), and could be

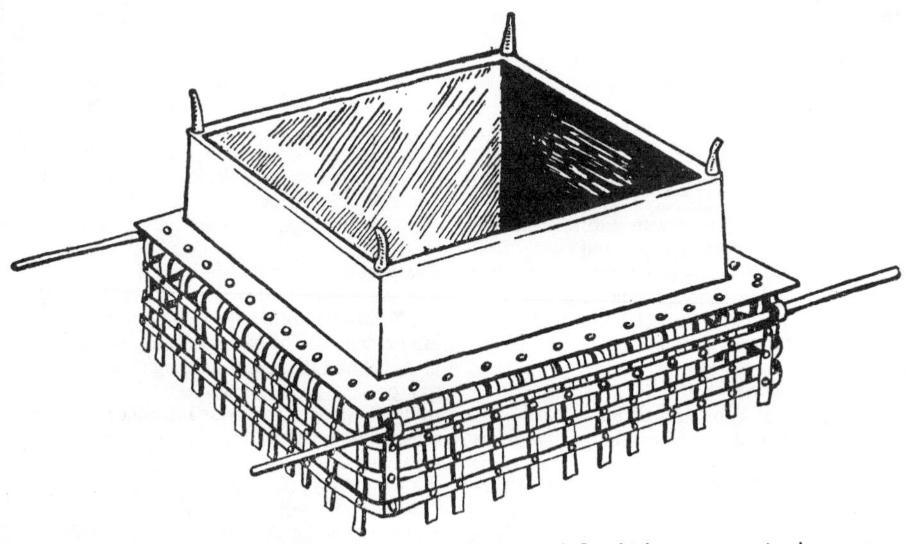

Fig. 176. A reconstruction of the altar described in Lv. xxvii. 1–8, which was set up in the courtyard of the Tabernacle.

eaten only by the priests themselves, and within the Temple precincts. The people's sacrificial meal from the peace-offering was the popular accompaniment of local worship in early times (1 Sa. i, ix), but with the centralization of the cult in Jerusalem (*cf.* Dt. xii) tended to recede before the more formal aspects of worship. As late as Ezk. xlvi. 21–24, however, provision continued to be made for it.

d. The kinds

(i) *'Ôlâ.* The burnt-offering seems to have a better claim to be regarded as the typical Hebrew sacrifice than the *zeḇaḥ* favoured by the Wellhausen school. It is present from the beginning (?Gn. iv, viii. 20, xxii. 2; Ex. x. 25, xviii. 12; Jdg. vi. 26, xiii. 16), early became a regular rite (1 Ki. ix. 25, *cf.* 1 Ki. x. 5, RSV), was never omitted on great occasions (1 Ki. iii. 4; Jos. viii. 31), and retained its dominant rôle to the latest times (Ezk. xliii. 18; Ezr. iii. 2–4) (see R. Rendtorff, *Studien zur Geschichte des Opfers im alten Israel*, typescript, Göttingen, 1953). Whatever may be said for Robertson Smith's view of a primary peace-offering, from which the burnt-offering later developed, as far as the Old Testament is concerned it is from the *'ôlâ* that the *minḥâ, 'āšām, ḥaṭṭā'ṯ*, and even *šelāmîm* seem to have arisen. The *kālîl* referred to five times (1 Sa. vii. 9; Ps. li. 19; Dt. xxxiii. 10; *cf.* Dt. xiii. 16 and Lv. vi. 22, 23) is also another name for the *'ôlâ*, although apparently differing somewhat in the Carthage and Marseilles tariffs.

While there is truth in Rost's view that the incidence of the *'ôlâ* is confined to Greece and the region 'bordered by the Taurus in the north, the Mediterranean in the west, and the desert in the east and south' ('Erwägungen zum israelitischen Brandopfer', *Von Ugarit nach Qumran* (Eissfeldt Festschrift), 1958, pp. 177–183), it does not follow that its origins in Israel are in human sacrifice (2 Ki. iii. 27) or rites of aversion of the Greek kind. Its undoubted gift character is apparent from the sublimation of the elements into a form in which they can be transported to God (Jdg. vi. 21, xiii. 20; *cf.* Dt. xxxiii. 10), but this does not say anything about the purpose of the gift, which may have been of homage and thanksgiving, or to expiate sin. The latter note is present in Jb. i. 5, xlii. 8 and many early passages, and is given as the reason for the sacrifice in Lv. i. 4 (*cf.* the Ugaritic Text IX: 7, where the burnt-offering (*šrp*) is connected to forgiveness of soul (*slḥ npš*)). When the sin-offering came to take precedence as the first of the series of sacrifices (Mishnah, *Zebahim* x. 2) it tended to take over this function, but this was not originally the case (*cf.* Nu. xxviii, xxix, and *cf.* Nu. vi. 14 with vi. 11).

(ii) *Minḥâ* ('meal-offering', 'meat-offering', AV, 'cereal-offering', RSV). It is somewhat confusing that this term is used in three different ways in the Old Testament. Thirty-four times it simply means 'present' or 'tribute' (*cf.* Jdg. iii. 15; 1 Ki. iv. 21—the root is probably *mānaḥ*, 'to give', *cf.* the peculiar form of the plural in the *MT* of Ps. xx. 3), ninety-seven times in the levitical literature it is the cereal-offering (*e.g.* in Lv. ii), and an indeterminate number of the remaining instances also have this meaning (*e.g.* Is. xliii. 23, lxvi. 20), but in the others it refers to sacrifice generally (1 Sa. xxvi. 19, ii. 29, and probably in Malachi), and to animal sacrifice in particular (1 Sa. ii. 12–17; Gn. iv. 3, 4; but see N. H. Snaith, *VT*, VII, 1957, pp. 314–316). S. R. Driver rightly defines *minḥâ* as not merely expressing the neutral idea of gift, but as denoting 'a present made to secure or retain good-will' (*HDB*, III, 1900, p. 587; *cf.* Gn. xxxiii. 10), and this propitiatory sense is to the fore also in such sacrificial references as 1 Sa. iii. 10–14, xxvi. 19.

In these references the *minḥâ* is an independent sacrifice, whereas in the laws it is the accompaniment of burnt-offerings and peace-offerings (Nu. xv. 1–16), except in Nu. v. 15, 25; Lv. v. 11–13, vi. 19–23. According to Lv. ii, it is to consist of either flour (ii. 1–3), baked cakes (ii. 4–10), or raw grain (ii. 14–16), together with oil and frankincense (*leḇônâ*). With this '*minḥâ* of the forecourt' may be compared what Kurtz called the '*minḥâ* of the holy place'—the altar of incense, the showbread on the table, and the oil in the lamp (*The Sacrificial Worship of the Old Testament*, 1865). Other ingredients might be salt (Lv. ii. 13) and wine (Lv. xxiii. 13). None of these offerings were eaten by the worshippers (but ?Lv. vii. 11–18). They went to the priests, but only after a 'memorial portion' (Lv. ii. 2) had been burnt on the altar. This RSV translation implies a derivation of *'azkārâ* from *zāḵar*, but G. R. Driver has suggested the meaning 'token', a part for the whole (*JSS*, I, 1956, pp. 97–105), and this would be yet another instance of the principle of substitution in the sacrifices.

(iii) *Zeḇaḥ* and *šelāmîm*. Again there is a variety of usage, in which *zeḇaḥ* and *šelāmîm* are sometimes interchangeable (Lv. vii. 11–21; 2 Ki. xvi. 13, 15), sometimes distinguished (Jos. xxii. 27; *cf.* Ex. xxiv. 5; 1 Sa. xi. 15), sometimes independent (2 Sa. vi. 17, 18; Ex. xxxii. 6), and sometimes combined into a compound expression *zeḇaḥ šelāmîm* or *ziḇeḥê šelāmîm* (so usually in the levitical law). It is doubtful if all these uses are to be understood as referring simply to the *zeḇaḥ* sacrificial meal. *Šelāmîm*, when used alone, was possibly not a meal at all (*cf.*, however, 2 Sa. vi. 19), but a solemn expiatory offering akin to the *'ôlâ* (so R. Rendtorff, *Studien zur Geschichte des Opfers*), and in conjunction with other sacrifices may still have retained this meaning. A *šlm* of a propitiatory kind seems to have been known at Ugarit (D. M. L. Urie, 'Sacrifice among the West Semites', *PEQ*, LXXXI, 1949, pp. 75–77) and is reflected in such passages as Jdg. xx. 26; 1 Sa. xiii. 9; 2 Sa. xxiv. 25. It is in no way inconsistent that a joyous meal followed, if the joy was the joy of forgiveness, for the *zeḇaḥ* covenant meal also usually marked a reconciliation after estrangement (Gn. xxxi. 54; *cf.* S. I. Curtiss, 'The Semitic Sacrifice of Reconciliation',

The Expositor, sixth series, VI, 1902, pp. 454–462).

Either of the proposed derivations of *šelem*—from *šālôm*, 'peace', so 'to make peace', or from *šillēm*, 'compensate', so 'to pay off, expiate'—would be in keeping and preferable to the reduction of the peace-offering to what were in fact only segments 'vow-offering' or 'thank-offering'. These two, together with the freewill-offering, made up three classes within the peace-offering proper, and the regulations governing them (Lv. vii. 11 ff.) are a supplement to those of Lv. iii. All three were thank-offerings, but the vow-offering, which discharged an earlier promise at the time of its accomplishment, was no longer optional, while the others were. Possibly it was for this reason that the vow reverted to the stricter regulation of a victim without blemish (Lv. xxii. 19; *cf.* Mal. i. 14, where it is added that it should be a male), while this requirement was relaxed for the freewill-offering (Lv. xxii. 23). Lv. vii also adds the rules for the sacrificial meal, which had been missing in Lv. iii—*viz.* that the thank-offering was to be eaten the same day, and the vow and freewill-offering not later than the next. The priests' portions are defined (Lv. vii. 32 ff.) as the 'wave' breast and the 'heave' shoulder (thigh). G. R. Driver (*op. cit.*) suggests some such meaning as 'contribution' for the terms 'wave' (*tᵉnûpâ*) and 'heave' (*tᵉrûmâ*), and this seems better than the older suggestion of horizontal and vertical motions at the altar, which are scarcely appropriate when rams, he-goats, and Levites are the objects of the actions (Nu. viii. 11).

(iv) *'Āšām and Ḥaṭṭā't.* The names of these offerings, guilt-offering (trespass-offering) and sin-offering, are the names of the offences for which they are to atone, *'āšām* ('guilt') and *ḥaṭṭā't* ('sin'). In a cultic context these terms refer, not so much to moral offences, as to those which are ceremonially defiling, although the moral aspect is by no means ruled out. Of the former kind are the sin-offerings of the leper (Lv. xiv; *cf.* Mk. i. 44) and the mother after childbirth (Lv. xii; *cf.* Lk. ii. 24), and of the latter, those of deception and misappropriation in Lv. vi. 1–7, and passion in Lv. xix. 20–22. These examples can have been but little more than random specimens to illustrate the laws, and should not be regarded as giving a full account of sacrifice for sin in these laws, much less in the cult as a whole. In the history, for example, these sacrifices scarcely figure at all. They are not mentioned in Deuteronomy (*cf.* Dt. xii), and are probably not to be understood in Ho. iv. 8. But this is to be put down less to their post-exilic origin as Wellhausen argued—for they are well known to Ezekiel (*cf.* xl. 39, xlii. 13) and may be hinted at in Ps. xl. 6; 2 Ki. xii. 16; 1 Sa. vi. 3 (unless these are only monetary)—than to their individual nature (this might explain the silence concerning the *'āšām*, which was not a festival sacrifice), and the fragmentary character of the records. They are equally silent for the post-exilic period (*'āšām* is mentioned, doubtfully, only in Ezr. x. 19 and *ḥaṭṭā't* in Ne. x. 33 and what appears a formula of the Chronicler in Ezr. vi. 17, viii. 35 and 2 Ch. xxix. 21 ff.).

Equally obscure is the relation between the two offerings (*e.g.* they are used synonymously in Lv. v. 6). All that can certainly be said is that sins against the neighbour are more prominent in the *'āšām* and those against God in the *ḥaṭṭā't*. The *'āšām* therefore requires a monetary compensation in addition to the sacrifice. The value of the misappropriation plus a fifth is to be repaid to the wronged neighbour (Lv. vi. 5) or, if he or his representative is not available, to the priest (Nu. v. 8). The sacrificial victim in the guilt-offering, usually a ram, also became the priest's, and after the regular blood and fat ritual could be eaten by the priests as 'most holy' (Lv. vii. 1–7). The same provision applies (Lv. vi. 24–29) to the sin-offerings of the ruler (Lv. iv. 22–26) and the common man (Lv. iv. 27–31), but in these cases the blood is put on the horns of the altar.

The sin-offerings of the high priest (Lv. iv. 1–12) and the whole community (Lv. iv. 13–21) follow a still more solemn ritual, in which the blood is sprinkled (*hizzâ*, not *zāraq*) before the veil of the sanctuary, and the bodies of the victims are not eaten but burned (*śārap̄*, not *hiqṭîr*) outside the camp (Lv. vi. 30; *cf.* Heb. xiii. 11). In addition to these four classes provisions are made for substitute offerings from the poor (Lv. v. 7–13). Chapters iv and v thus contain a graduated scale of victims: bull (high priest and congregation, but *cf.* Nu. xv. 24; Lv. ix. 15, xvi. 5), he-goat (ruler), she-goat or lamb (common man), turtle-doves or pigeons (poor), flour (very poor). The following principles may be remarked: everyone must bring some sin-offering, no-one may eat of his own sin-offering, and the more propitiatory the rite the nearer the blood must come to God. On the Day of Atonement the veil itself was penetrated and the blood sprinkled on the ark.

e. The meaning

The oft-stated purpose of the sacrifices in Leviticus is 'to atone' (*kipper*, Lv. i. 4, *etc.*). This verb may be explained in one of three ways: 'to cover', from the Arab. *kafara*; 'to wipe away', from the Akkadian *kuppuru*; 'to ransom by a substitute', from the Heb. noun *kōp̄er*. The last seems most in keeping with the theory of sacrifice given in Lv. xvii. 11, 'the life of the flesh is in the blood . . . it is the blood that maketh an atonement for the soul' (but *cf.* RSV), and with the principle at work in many of the practices encountered above: the choice of offering material in 'biotic rapport'; their designation by the laying on of the hand; the burning of a token such as the fat or the *'azkārâ*; the offering of a first portion and the redemption of the first-born (*cf.* S. H. Hooke, 'The Theory and Practice of Substitution', *VT*, II, 1952, pp. 1–17, and for an opposite view A. Metzinger's articles, *Bib*, XXI, 1940). To these might be added the ritual of the heifer in Dt. xxi and the scapegoat in Lv. xvi, which, although not blood sacrifices, reflect ideas which must *a fortiori* have been true of blood sacrifices. It was in this light that Lv. xvi was understood in the Jewish tradition (*e.g.* Mishnah, *Yoma*, vi. 4, 'bear our sins and be gone').

Such passages are a warning against confining the atonement to a single act, as if it were the death alone, or the presentation of the blood, or the disposal of the victim, which atoned. The death was important—the live goat is only half of the ritual in Lv. xvi (*cf.* verse 15 with xiv. 4–7, v. 7–11). The blood manipulation was also important—in 2 Ch. xxix. 24 it seems to make atonement subsequent to the killing. The final disposal of the victim by fire or eating or to Azazel also had its place—in Lv. x. 16–20 the priestly eating of the sin-offering is more than just declaratory. The view that the death of the victim was only to release the life that was in the blood, and that the atonement consisted only of the latter, is as one-sided as that which sees the death as a quantitative penal satisfaction. To the latter view it has been objected that the sins for which sacrifice was offered were not those meriting death, that sin-offerings did not always require death (*cf.* Lv. v. 11–13), and that the killing could not have been central or it would have been in the hands of the priest, not the layman. These objections tell only against extreme forms of the substitution theory, not against the principle of substitution itself.

The real advantage of the substitution theory is that it retains the categories of personal relationships, where other views tend to descend to sub-personal dynamistic categories, in which the blood itself is thought of as effecting mystic union or revitalizing in a semi-magical way (*cf.* the theories of H. Hubert and M. Mauss, 'Essai sur la nature et la fonction du sacrifice', *L'Année Sociologique*, II, 1897–8, pp. 29–138; A. Loisy, *RHLR*, NS, I, 1910, pp. 1–30, and *Essai historique sur le sacrifice*, 1920; S. G. Gayford, *Sacrifice and Priesthood*, 1924; A. Bertholet, *JBL*, XLIX, 1930, pp. 218–233, and *Der Sinn des kultischen Opfers*, 1942; E. O. James, *The Origins of Sacrifice*, 1933).

A weightier objection to the substitution theory is that which finds difficulty in the description of the sin-offering after the sacrifice as 'most holy', and as fit for priestly food. If a transfer of sin had taken place, would it not be unclean and fit only for destructive burning (*śārap̄*)? This was in fact the case with the primary rank sin-offerings. In the other cases the priestly eating is perhaps to be similarly interpreted, as if the power of superior 'holiness' in the priests through their anointing absorbed the uncleanness of the offering (*cf.* Lv. x. 16–20 and the article 'Sin-Eating', *ERE*, XI, 1920, pp. 572–576 (Hartland)). That we are dealing here with categories of 'holiness', which are not ours, is evident from the instruction to break the earthen vessels in which the sin-offering has been boiled (Lv. vi. 28; *cf.* CLEAN AND UNCLEAN). Alternatively, the death of the victim could be understood as neutralizing the infection of sin, so that the fat and blood could come unimpeded to the altar as an offering to God.

Whether other views of sacrifice such as 'homage' and 'communion' are possible alongside that outlined here, as favoured by most recent scholars (A. Wendel, *Das Opfer in der altisraelitischen Religion*, 1927; W. O. E. Oesterley, *Sacrifices in Ancient Israel*, 1937; H. H. Rowley, *The Meaning of Sacrifice*, 1950), or whether certain types of sacrifice express one of these aspects more than another (*e.g.* burnt-offering, homage, and peace-offering, communion) is best left an open question. But in the laws at least the burnt-offering, the cereal-offering, and even the peace-offering (but only rarely; *cf.* Ex. xxix. 33; Ezk. xlv. 15), as well as the sin- and guilt-offerings, are said to atone. And what is true of the laws seems to be true also of the history.

The question as to whether the offering was both an expiation (*i.e.* of sins) and a propitiation (*i.e.* of wrath) or only an expiation is also difficult to answer. *Kipper* undoubtedly means propitiation in some instances (Nu. xvi. 41–50; Ex. xxxii. 30), and this is supported by the use of the expression *rēaḥ nîḥōaḥ*, 'sweet-smelling savour', throughout the laws (*cf.* also Gn. viii. 21, and LXX of Dt. xxxiii. 10). *Rēaḥ nîḥōaḥ* may, however, have a weakened sense (G. B. Gray, *Sacrifice in the Old Testament*, 1925, pp. 77–81, points out that it is used where we should hardly expect it, with cereal and *zeḇaḥ* offerings, but not where we do expect it with sin- and guilt-offerings), and this is even more evidently the case with *kipper* when it is used in connection with such material things as the tabernacle furniture (Ex. xxix. 37; Ezk. xliii. 20, xlv. 19), and must be rendered simply 'cleanse'.

Of importance to the discussion here is the recognition that God Himself gave the ritual to sinful man (Lv. xvii. 11, 'the blood . . . I have given it to you upon the altar to make an atonement for your souls'). The sacrifices are to be seen as operating within the sphere of the covenant and covenanting grace. They were not 'man's expedient for his own redemption' as Köhler (*Old Testament Theology*, 1957) suggests, but were 'the fruit of grace, not its root' (A. C. Knudson, *The Religious Teaching of the Old Testament*, 1918, p. 295). The question as to whether within this context propitiation has a place is similar to the New Testament one, and will depend on the view taken of sin, and law and the nature of God (see ATONEMENT; also L. Morris, *The Apostolic Preaching of the Cross*, 1955).

It remains to be said that within the Old Testament itself there is much to suggest that its system was not a final one. No sacrifices availed, for example, for breach of covenant (*cf.* Ex. xxxii. 30 ff.)—it is in this light that the prophetic rejection of sacrifice is to be understood—or for sins of a 'high hand' that put man outside the covenant (Nu. xv. 30), though perhaps idolatry and apostasy would be illustrations here. While not accepting the view, on the one hand, that the efficacy of sacrifice was limited to inadvertent sins, which were no real sins at all, or, on the other, that prophets and pious psalmists saw no value in sacrifice whatsoever, it remains true that the cult was liable to abuse, when the inward tie between worshipper and means of worship was loosed, and prophetic religion became necessary to emphasize the priority of a personal relation to God. It is no accident, however, that when priestly and prophetic religion meet in the figure of the Servant of the Lord in Is. liii the highest point of Old Testament religion is reached, as all that is valuable in cult is taken up into a person, who both makes a sacrificial atonement (*hizzâ*, 'lamb', 'guilt-offering') and calls for the love and personal allegiance of the human heart.

BIBLIOGRAPHY. The works referred to throughout the article: articles on sacrifice in *EB*, *HDB*, *HDB* (one vol.), *ERE*, *ISBE*; S. I. Curtiss, *Primitive Semitic Religion Today*, 1902; articles in *The Expositor*, sixth series, 1902–5; O. Schmitz, *Die Opferanschauung des späteren Judentums*, 1910; F. C. N. Hicks, *The Fulness of Sacrifice*[3], 1946; F. D. Kidner, *Sacrifice in the Old Testament*, 1952; R. K. Yerkes, *Sacrifice in Greek and Roman Religions and Early Judaism*, 1952; K. Koch, *Die israelitischen Sühneanschauung und ihre historischen Wandlungen*, typescript, Erlangen, 1956; L. Moraldi, *Espiazione sacrificale e riti espiatori nell' ambiente biblico e nell' Antico Testamento*, 1956; F. Blome, *Die Opfermaterie in Babylonien und Israel*, 1934; T. C. Vriezen, 'The Term Hizza: Lustration and Consecration', *OTS*, VII, 1950, pp. 201–235; W. B. Stevenson, 'Hebrew '*Olah* and *Zebach* Sacrifices', *Festschrift Alfred Bertholet*, 1950, pp. 488–497; D. Schötz, *Schuld- und Sündopfer im Alten Testament*, 1930; L. Morris, 'Asham', *EQ*, XXX, 1958, pp. 196–210.

R.J.T.

2. In the New Testament.

The Greek words used are *thysia*, *dōron*, *prosphora* and their cognates, and *anapherō*, translated 'sacrifice, gift, offering, offer' (*thysia* in Mk. xii. 33 probably means 'meal-offering'); *holokautōma*, 'whole burnt offering'; *thymiama*, 'incense'; *spendō*, 'pour out as a drink-offering'. All were adopted, with the other terms given below, from LXX.

I. OLD TESTAMENT SACRIFICES IN THE NEW

The Old Testament sacrifices (see previous article) were still being offered during practically the whole period of the composition of the New, and it is not surprising, therefore, that even their literal significance comes in for some illuminating comment. Important maxims are to be found in Mt. v. 23, 24, xii. 3–5 and parallels, xvii. 24–27, xxiii. 16–20; 1 Cor. ix. 13, 14. It is noteworthy that our Lord has sacrifice offered for Him or offers it Himself at His presentation in the Temple, at His last Passover, and presumably on those other occasions when He went up to Jerusalem for the feasts. The practice of the apostles in Acts removes all ground from the opinion that after the sacrifice of Christ the worship of the Jewish Temple is to be regarded as an abomination to God. We find them frequenting the Temple, and Paul himself goes up to Jerusalem for Pentecost, and on that occasion offers the sacrifices (which included sin-offerings) for the interruption of vows (Acts xxi; *cf.* Nu. vi. 10–12). However, in principle these sacrifices were now unnecessary, for the old covenant was becoming 'old' and 'ready to vanish away' (Heb. viii. 13), so that when the Romans destroyed the Temple even the non-Christian Jews ceased to offer the sacrifices.

The Epistle to the Hebrews contains the fullest treatment of the Old Testament sacrifices. The teaching of this writer has its positive side (xi. 4), but his great concern is to point out their inadequacy except as types. The fact that they cannot gain for men entrance into the Holy of holies proves that they cannot free the conscience from guilt, but are simply carnal ordinances, imposed until a time of reformation (ix. 6–10). Their inadequacy to atone is shown also by the fact that mere animals are offered (x. 4), and by the very fact of their repetition (x. 1, 2). They are not so much remedies for sin as reminders of it (x. 3).

II. 'SPIRITUAL SACRIFICES'

'Spiritual sacrifices' (1 Pet. ii. 5; *cf.* Jn. iv. 23, 24; Rom. xii. 1) are the New Testament substitute for carnal ordinances, and appear frequently (Rom. xii. 1, xv. 16, 17; Phil. ii. 17, iv. 18; 2 Tim. iv. 6; Heb. xiii. 15, 16; Rev. vi. 9, viii. 3, 4). Even in the Old Testament, however, the psalmists and prophets sometimes use the language of sacrifice metaphorically (*e.g.* Ps. l. 13, 14, li. 16, 17; Is. lxvi. 20), and the usage is continued in the inter-testamental literature (Ecclus. xxxv. 1–3; *Testament of Levi*, iii. 6; *Manual of Discipline*, viii, ix; Philo, *De Somniis* ii. 183). The attempt of F. C. N. Hicks (*The Fulness of Sacrifice*, 1930) to refer such passages to literal sacrifices must be reckoned on the whole a failure. The sacrifices mentioned in these passages are not always immaterial, and sometimes involve death: the sense in which they are 'spiritual' is that they belong properly to the age of the Holy Spirit (Jn. iv. 23, 24; Rom. xv. 16). But sometimes they are immaterial, and they never have a prescribed ritual. It appears, in fact, that every act of the Spirit-filled man can be reckoned as a spiritual sacrifice, and the sense in which it is a sacrifice is that it is acceptable to God. It does not, of course atone. The antitype of atoning sacrifice is to be sought not here but in the sacrifice of Christ without which spiritual sacrifices would not be acceptable (Heb. xiii. 15; 1 Pet. ii. 5).

III. THE SACRIFICE OF CHRIST

The sacrifice of Christ is one of the chief themes of the New Testament. His saving work is sometimes spoken of in ethical, sometimes in penal but often also in sacrificial terms. He is spoken of as the slain lamb of God, whose precious blood takes away the sin of the world (Jn. i. 29, 36; 1 Pet. i. 18, 19; Rev. v. 6–10, xiii. 8)—a lamb being an animal used in various sacrifices. More specifically, He is spoken of as the true passover lamb (*pascha*, 1 Cor. v. 6–8), as a sin-offering (*peri hamartias*, Rom. viii. 3, *cf.* LXX Lv. v. 6, 7, 11, ix. 2, 3; Ps. xl. 6, *etc.*), and in Heb. ix–x as the fulfilment of the covenant sacrifices of Ex. xxiv, the red heifer of Nu. xix, and the Day of Atonement offerings. The New Testament constantly identifies our Lord with the suffering Servant of Is. lii, liii, who is a guilt-offering (Is. liii. 10), and with the Messiah (Christ) of Dn. ix, who is to atone for iniquity (verse 24). The New Testament uses the terms 'propitiate' and 'ransom' (see PROPITIATION, REDEEMER) of Christ in a sacrificial sense, and the idea of being cleansed by His blood (1 Jn. i. 7; Heb. *passim*) is sacrificial (see also CLEAN AND UNCLEAN, SANCTIFICATION).

The doctrine is most fully worked out in the Epistle to the Hebrews. The writer stresses the importance, in Christ's sacrifice, of His death (ii. 9, 14, ix. 15–17, 22, 25–28, xiii. 12, 20), and the fact that His sacrifice is over (i. 3, ix. 12, 25–28, x. 10, 12–14, 18), but his other statements have led some Anglo-Catholics (*e.g.* S. C. Gayford, *Sacrifice and Priesthood*, 1924) and the Presbyterian W. Milligan (*The Ascension and Heavenly Priesthood of our Lord*, 1892), to suppose, on the contrary, that the death is not the important element in Christ's sacrifice, and that His sacrifice goes on for ever. It is quite true that the Epistle confines Christ's priesthood and sanctuary to heaven (viii. 1–5, ix. 11), but it emphatically does not confine His sacrifice there. It states indeed that He offered there (viii. 3), but 'offer' is a word used equally of the donor who brings and kills a sacrifice outside the sanctuary and of the priest who presents it, either there on the altar or within. The reference here is doubtless to the sprinkling or 'offering' of blood in the Holy of holies on the Day of Atonement by the high priest (ix. 7, 21–24), a typical action fulfilled by Christ. All that was costly in the sacrifice—the part of the donor and the victim—took place at the cross: there remained only the priestly part—the presentation to God by an acceptable mediator—and this Christ performed by entering into His Father's presence at the ascension. There is no call to think of any *literal* presentation of Himself or of His blood at the ascension: it is enough that He entered as the Priest of the sacrifice slain at the cross, was at once welcomed, and sat down in glory, His work complete (see also PRIESTS AND LEVITES).

It is a mistake to view Christ's sacrifice as being any more a literal sacrifice than the spiritual sacrifices are. Both transcend their Old Testament types, and neither is ritual. The contention of Owen and others that Christ's sacrifice was a real sacrifice was directed against the Socinian view that Christ's death does not fulfil what the Old Testament sacrifices set out to do, and failed to do—the view which denied that Christ's death makes propitiation. But apart from the slaying (and this is not performed, as in Old Testament ritual, by the donor), everything in His sacrifice is spiritualized. For the blood of an animal we have the blood of the God-man (Heb. ix. 14). For spotlessness, we have sinlessness (Heb. ix. 14; 1 Pet. i. 19). For a sweet smell, we have true acceptableness (Eph. v. 2). For the sprinkling of our bodies with blood, we have forgiveness (Heb. ix. 13, 14, 19–22). For symbolical atonement, we have real atonement (Heb. x. 1–10).

IV. SACRIFICE AND THE LORD'S SUPPER

Sacrifice and the Lord's Supper are indissolubly connected—not indeed in the way that Romanists, Non-jurors, and Tractarians have wished to connect them, by making the eucharist an act of oblation, but as complementary to each other. To give 'do' and 'remembrance' (Lk. xxii. 19; 1 Cor. xi. 24, 25) a technical sacrificial sense is merely an afterthought of those who have already accepted the eucharistic sacrifice on non-scriptural grounds. The same is true of the attempt to exclude a future meaning from the participles 'given' and 'shed' (Mt. xxvi. 28; Mk. xiv. 24; Lk. xxii. 19, 20). And to correlate the eucharist with the eternal sacrifice of Christ in heaven is impossible if the eternal sacrifice is disproved. But to regard the eucharist as a *feast* upon Christ's sacrifice is demanded by the argument of 1 Cor. x. 14–22, in which it is made to correspond with Jewish and Gentile sacrificial meals; by the allusion to Ex. xxiv. 8 in Mt. xxvi. 28 and Mk. xiv. 24; and by the traditional interpretation of Heb. xiii. 10. Since the sacrifice of Christ is in so many points to be spiritualized, the language about the feast on His sacrifice is doubtless to be spiritualized also, but it is not to be bereft of its meaning. The meaning of the sacrificial meal was not the appropriation of atonement, but a feast with God upon the victim. We do not partake of a merely physical Christ any more than God accepted a merely physical Christ. But the God-man whom God received, we, in such sort as we may, receive also, and the mode in which Christ is available for our participation on earth today is presumably as divine Spirit (see also LORD'S SUPPER).

BIBLIOGRAPHY. Commentaries on the Epistle to the Hebrews; V. Taylor, *Jesus and His Sacrifice*, 1943; B. B. Warfield, *The Person and Work of Christ*, 1950, pp. 391–426; A. Richardson (ed.), *A Theological Word Book of the Bible*, 1950, pp. 213 f.; N. Dimock, *The Doctrine of the Death of Christ*, 1903; A. Cave, *The Scriptural Doctrine of Sacrifice and Atonement*, 1890; G. Vos, *The Teaching of the Epistle to the Hebrews* (ed. and rewritten by J. G. Vos), 1956; R. Cudworth, *The True Notion of the Lord's Supper*, 1642.

R.T.B.

SADDUCEES. Our sources are all hostile and inadequate for an accurate picture. They are: (1) Josephus, *BJ* ii. 8. 14; *Ant.* xiii. 5. 9, 10. 6,

xviii. 1. 4, xx. 9. 1; (2) the Mishnah, '*Erubin* vi. 2, *Ḥagigah* ii. 4, *Makkoth* i. 6, *Parah* iii. 3, 7, *Niddah* iv. 2, *Yadaim* iv. 6–8; (3) the New Testament, Mt. iii. 7, xvi. 1, 6, 11, 12, xxii. 23–34; Mk. xii. 18–27; Lk. xx. 27–38; Acts iv. 1, 2, v. 17, xxiii. 6–8.

The name and origins of the party are alike disputed. The name has been derived from Zadok, either Solomon's contemporary whose descendants were regarded as the pure priestly line (*cf.* Ezk. xliv. 15 f., xlviii. 11) or a hypothetical founder or early leader of the party (the statement in *Aboth of Rabbi Nathan* v that Antigonos of Socoh had two disciples, Zadok and Boëthus, who lapsed into heresy, has probably little historical basis). But the ruling Hasmonaean high-priestly family was not Zadokite (1 Macc. ii. 1, xiv. 29), and the double 'd' in both the Hebrew and Greek forms of the name is difficult to account for if it is derived from Zadok. T. W. Manson suggests a derivation from the Gk. *syndikoi*, 'fiscal controllers' (the double 'd' being accounted for by the assimilation of the 'n'). The connection with the word *ṣaddîq*, 'righteous', may have been a later assonance.

Four theories of the origin of the Sadducees may be briefly outlined. M. H. Segal, following Wellhausen, thought that they were mainly a political party, derived ultimately from the Judaean Hellenists. G. H. Box, following Geiger, thought that they were a religious party, and that some of the scribes in the Gospels were Sadducee scribes. L. Finkelstein thought that they were originally a rural aristocratic body, as opposed to the urban Pharisees. T. W. Manson thought that they were originally state officials (*cf.* above).

In manner the Sadducees were rather boorish, being rude to their peers as to aliens, and counting it a virtue to dispute with their teachers. They had no following among the populace, but were restricted to the well-to-do. They were more severe in judgment than other Jews. Many, but not all, priests were Sadducees; nearly all Sadducees, however, appear to have been priests, especially of the most powerful priestly families. Under the early Hasmonaeans some Sadducees held office in the *gerousia* ('senate' or Sanhedrin). John Hyrcanus, taking offence at the request of Eleazar, member of a Pharisaic deputation, that he resign the high-priesthood, transferred his allegiance from the Pharisees to the Sadducees. The Sadducees enjoyed the favour of the Hasmonaean rulers until the reign of Salome Alexandra (76–67 BC), who preferred the Pharisees. Under the Herods and Romans the Sadducees predominated in the Sanhedrin. The party died out with the destruction of the Temple in AD 70. Josephus says that, even when in power, the Sadducees were compelled for fear of the people to concur with the Pharisees.

In religion the Sadducees are marked for their conservatism. They denied the permanent validity of any but the written laws of the Pentateuch. They rejected the later doctrines of the soul and its after-life, the resurrection, rewards and retributions, angels and demons. They believed that there was no fate, men having a free choice of good and evil, prosperity and adversity being the outcome of their own course of action.

BIBLIOGRAPHY. E. Schürer, *HJP*, II, ii, pp. 1–10; M. H. Segal, *Expositor*, 8th series, XIII, 1917, pp. 81 ff.; G. H. Box, *Expositor*, XV, 1918, pp. 19 ff., 401 ff., and XVI, 1918, pp. 55 ff.; L. Finkelstein, *HTR*, XXII, 1929, pp. 185 ff.; T. W. Manson, *BJRL*, XXII, 1938, pp. 144 ff.; J. Z. Lauterbach, in *Studies in Jewish Literature in honour of Prof. K. Köhler*, 1913, pp. 180–190; J. W. Lightley, *Jewish Sects and Parties in the Time of Jesus*, 1923, pp. 5–178; J. Klausner, *Jesus of Nazareth*, tr. H. Danby, 1925, pp. 219–221 for ritual and legal differences from the Pharisees. See also L. Finkelstein, *The Pharisees*, 1938.

A.G.

SAFFRON. See PLANTS.

SAHIDIC VERSION. See TEXT AND VERSIONS.

SAINTS. See HOLINESS.

SALAMIS. A town on the east coast of the central plain of Cyprus, not to be confused with the famous island off the coast of Attica. It rivalled in importance Paphos, the Roman capital of the whole island, and eventually superseded it. The harbour which made Salamis a great commercial centre is now completely silted up. In the 1st century AD the Jewish community there was large enough to have more than one synagogue (Acts xiii. 5). Destroyed by earthquakes, the town was rebuilt in the 4th century AD as Constantia. Its ruins are 3 miles from Famagusta.

K.L.McK.

SALECAH, SALCAH. A place in the extreme east of Bashan (*q.v.*; Dt. iii. 10; Jos. xii. 5, xiii. 11). Though Bashan fell to the lot of Manasseh, the area occupied by Gad included Salecah (1 Ch. v. 11). It probably lay within the area conquered by David, but after Solomon's time it lay outside Israelite territory. The site is possibly the modern Salḫad (Nabataean *ṣlḫd*) on a southern spur of the Hauran, though this identification is not universally accepted. See *GTT*, pp. 13, 122, 128.

T.C.M.

SALEM. The place where Melchizedek ruled (Gn. xiv. 18; Heb. vii. 1, 8) near the valley of Shaveh (Gn. xiv. 17; AV 'king's dale'). It is mentioned in parallel with Zion (Ps. lxxvi. 2). Following Jos. (*Ant.* i. 10. 2), it is usually identified with the ancient site of Jerusalem, the city of Salem, *Uru-salem*, *uru-salimmu* of the cuneiform inscriptions (see JERUSALEM). This would suit the route probably taken by Abraham on his return from Damascus to Hebron when he encountered Melchizedek. Those who assume his return down the Jordan valley look for a more easterly location (see SALIM). The Samaritans link Salem with Salim east of Nablus, but this may be due to their ancient rivalry with Judah, where a 'Valley of Salem' is known as late as Maccabean times (Judith iv. 4). In Je. xli. 5 the LXX (B) reads Salem for Shiloh.

The name *šālēm* (Gk. *Salem*) means 'safe, at peace', though Jerusalem has been interpreted as 'Salem founded' implying a divine name Salem. For the early occurrence of this name form, *cf.* *šillēm* (Gn. xlvi. 24; Nu. xxvi. 49). D.J.W.

SALIM. A well-known place (Gk. *Saleim*) near Aenon on the river Jordan where John baptized (Jn. iii. 23). Of the many identifications proposed, the Salim (Salumias) about 8 miles south of Beisan (Bethshan-Scythopolis) is the most likely. The ruins of Tell Ridgha or Tell Sheikh Selim, as it is also called after the local shrine, lie near several springs which might have been called Aenon (Arab. *'ain*, 'spring'). This site would be under the control of Scythopolis (see DECAPOLIS). The Salim east of Nablus with which the Samaritans identify the Salem of Gn. xiv. 18 lies in the heart of Samaria. The land of Salim (AV 'Shaalim') is a region in hilly Ephraim, possibly between Aijalon and Ramah (1 Sa. ix. 4). *Cf.* W. F. Albright, *The Archaeology of Palestine*, 1960, p. 247; *id.*, in *The Background of the New Testament and its Eschatology* (ed. W. D. Davies and D. Daube), 1956, p. 159. See SALEM, SHAALBIM. D.J.W.

SALMON, SALMA. 1. Of Judah's line (Mt. i. 4, 5; Lk. iii. 32). The son of Nahshon, the father of Boaz the husband of Ruth and the great-grandfather of David the son of Jesse (Ru. iv. 20; 1 Ch. ii. 11). According to Mt. i. 5 he married Rahab (of Jericho).

2. Also of Judah's line. A son of Caleb (not to be confused with Caleb, son of Jephunneh), and father of the Bethlehemites, Netophathites, and other groups associated with the Kenites (1 Ch. ii. 51–54). C.H.D.

SALMONE. A promontory at the extreme eastern end of Crete, now known as Cape Sidero. On his way to Rome Paul's ship was prevented by a north-west wind from proceeding from off Cnidus along the north coast of Crete, and, tacking past Salmone, sheltered in the lee of the island (Acts xxvii. 7). K.L.McK.

SALOME (Heb. *šālôm*, 'peace', with Gk. suffix). **1.** According to Mk. xv. 40 and xvi. 1, of three women who saw the crucifixion and went to the tomb on Easter morning two were called Mary and one Salome. Mt. xxvii. 56 names two women called Mary, and the mother of the sons of Zebedee, who is probably to be identified with Salome. Jn. xix. 25 refers to two women called Mary, plus the mother of Jesus and His mother's sister, who stood near the cross. If His mother's sister is identified with Salome, then James and John, the sons of Zebedee, would be cousins of Jesus. It is equally possible, however, that John has made a different selection of names out of the 'many other women' who, according to Mk. xv. 41, were present at the crucifixion.

2. The daughter of Herodias, by her first husband Herod Philip. Though not named in the gospel accounts, she is usually identified with the girl who danced before Herod (Mk. vi. 22; Mt. xiv. 6). She married her grand-uncle Philip the tetrarch. D.R.H.

SALT. Whereas the Phoenicians obtained quantities of salt from the Mediterranean by evaporation in salt-pans, the Hebrews had access to an unlimited supply on the shores of the Dead Sea (Zp. ii. 9) and in the hill of Salt (Jebel Usdum), a 15-square-mile elevation located at the south-west corner of the Dead Sea. This area was traditionally associated with the fate of Lot's wife (Gn. xix. 26).

Such salt was of the rock or fossil variety, and, because of impurities and the occurrence of chemical changes, the outer layer was generally lacking in flavour. The reference in Mt. v. 13 is to this latter, much of which was discarded as worthless. Salt was valued as a preservative and for seasoning food (Mt. v. 13; Mk. ix. 50; Col. iv. 6). It was often used among Oriental peoples for ratifying agreements, so that salt became the symbol of fidelity and constancy. In the levitical cereal offerings (Lv. ii. 13) salt was used as a preservative to typify the eternal nature of the 'covenant of salt' existing between God and Israel (Nu. xviii. 19; 2 Ch. xiii. 5).

The effect of salt on vegetation was to produce a burned-up waste-land (Dt. xxix. 23). Thus the 'parched places in the wilderness' (Je. xvii. 6) were synonymous with a barren salt land (Jb. xxxix. 6). Abimelech followed an ancient custom in sowing ruined Shechem with salt (Jdg. ix. 45) as a token of perpetual desolation. Elisha used salt to sweeten the brackish waters of the Jericho spring (2 Ki. ii. 19–22). New-born infants were normally rubbed with salt prior to swaddling (Ezk. xvi. 4). Under Antiochus Epiphanes Syria imposed a tax upon salt, which was paid to Rome. R.K.H.

SALT, CITY OF (Heb. *'îr hammelaḥ*). In Jos. xv. 62 one of the frontier posts of the tribal territory of Judah 'in the wilderness', south of Middin, Secacah, and Nibshan (now identifiable, on the basis of recent excavation, with the Buqei'a Iron Age II settlements at Khirbet Abū Ṭabaq, Khirbet es-Samrah, and Khirbet el-Maqāri), and north of En-gedi. Its identification with Khirbet Qumrān, first suggested by M. Noth (*Josua*, 1938, p. 72), has been confirmed by the discovery of an Iron Age II fortress beneath the Qumran community settlement (*cf.* R. de Vaux, *RB*, LXI, 1954, p. 567; F. M. Cross Jr. and J. T. Milik, *BASOR*, 142, April 1956, pp. 5 ff.). See QUMRAN. F.F.B.

SALT SEA. See DEAD SEA.

SALT, VALLEY OF. Saline encrustations in steppe and desert lands are common. Some are of climatic origin; in other cases the climate has preserved geological salinity in the rocks. It is not possible to identify one topographic location from the biblical references. David and his lieutenant Abishai had memorable victories over the Edomites in the Valley of Salt (2 Sa. viii. 13; 1 Ch. xviii. 12). Later Amaziah had a similar victory (2 Ki. xiv. 7; 2 Ch. xxv. 11). Traditionally the site has been accepted as the plain south-south-west of the Dead Sea, opposite the oasis of the Zered delta, where a plain 6–8 miles long is overlooked by the salt range of Jebel Usdum, 5 miles long and 650 feet high. This plain passes imperceptibly into the glistening lowland of the Sebkha to the south-east, a soft, impassable waste of salt marsh, where an army could well be routed in confusion. But, equally well, the site could be Wadi el-Milh (salt), east of Beersheba, also overlooked by a rocky hill, Tell el-Milh. All that the more precise reference of 2 Ch. xxv. 11 suggests is that the plain was overlooked by a rocky hill, somewhere between Judah and Edom, presumably in the Arabah. J.M.H.

SALTWORT. See PLANTS.

SALUTATION. The AV terms 'salute', 'salutation' have changed somewhat in English usage; 'greet', 'greeting' are more congenial today. The following meanings of the word may be distinguished.

1. An epistolary message of greeting, involving no personal encounter. Paul occasionally uses the noun *aspasmos*, more frequently the cognate verb *aspazomai*, a customary formula in contemporary Greek correspondence, as the papyri prove (see *MM*). The greeting may be in the name of the writer, or of some other person specified by him (see Rom. xvi and elsewhere).

2. A formal greeting with obeisance from subject to monarch, invoking, with Oriental exaggeration, eternal life for him (*cf.* Ne. ii. 3, *etc.*, Hebrew; Dn. ii. 4, *etc.*, Aramaic).

3. A face-to-face greeting, formal, verbal, perhaps with hand gesture, but without physical contact. The Greek descriptive terms are the same as Paul's (Mt. x. 12; Mk. xii. 38, *etc.*). Note the mock homage to Jesus in Mk. xv. 18. The uttered word was frequently the imperative *chaire*, plural *chairete*, 'rejoice ', AV 'Hail!' (Mt. xxvii. 29, *etc.*). The infinitive *chairein* is also used (*cf.* 2 Jn. 11; 1 Macc. x. 18, 25). The commonest Hebrew terms are connected with blessing (root *bāraḵ*, 2 Ki. iv. 29, *etc.*), or with the invoking of peace (*šā'al lešālôm*, 1 Sa. xvii. 22, *etc.*). Modern Hebrew and Arabic greetings are based on these (*šālôm*, *salaam*).

4. A formal cheek kiss, Heb. *nāšaq* and cognate noun; Gk. *philēma* (*cf.* 1 Sa. x. 1; Rom. xvi. 16, *etc.*). The double-cheek kiss is still daily exchanged between males in the Orient. 5. The affectionate kiss, normally on the mouth, implying greater intimacy (same words, Gn. xxix. 11; Ct. i. 2). 6. The deceitful kiss (same words, Pr. xxvii. 6; the kiss of Judas, Mt. xxvi. 48, *etc.*).

Greetings might be forbidden through urgency (2 Ki. iv. 29; Lk. x. 4) or to prevent association with error (2 Jn. 11). R.A.S.

SALVATION. The English term used in AV is derived from Lat. *salvare*, 'to save', and *salus*, 'health', 'help', and translates Heb. *yešû'â* and cognates ('breadth', 'ease', 'safety') and Gk. *sōtēria* and cognates ('cure', 'recovery', 'redemption', 'remedy', 'rescue', 'welfare'). It means the action or result of deliverance or preservation from danger or disease, implying safety, health, and prosperity. The movement in Scripture is from the more physical aspects towards moral and spiritual deliverance. Thus, the earlier parts of the Old Testament lay stress on ways of escape for God's individual servants from the hands of their enemies, the emancipation of His people from bondage and their establishment in a land of plenty; the later parts lay greater emphasis upon the moral and religious conditions and qualities of blessedness and extend its amenities beyond the nation's confines. The New Testament indicates clearly man's thraldom to sin, its danger and potency, and the deliverance from it to be found exclusively in Christ. The Bible gives an unfolding account of how God provides the basis for salvation, presents it, and is Himself man's salvation.

I. IN THE OLD TESTAMENT

Old Testament salvation has both man-ward and God-ward aspects; man is in danger from disease, physical calamity, persecution from his foes, and death; in the community of God's chosen people captivity is the experience from which deliverance is needed, and the ideals of salvation are mainly eudaemonistic and earthbound. The deeper danger is the one in which individuals and communities stand before God, whose will they have transgressed and whose ill-favour they have incurred. Means of salvation, direct and indirect, are provided in this context through Patriarch, judge, lawgiver, priest, king, and prophet. The law, moral and ritualistic, while incapable, because of the nature of man's sin, of procuring a full salvation, indicated the character and claims of God and the conditions of man's well-being and put the brake in some degree on men's iniquities; its misuse, however, as a moral code produced a twofold legalism in which stringent, external adherence to regulations was devoid of inner spiritual reality, and man's attainments were paraded before God in a self-righteous claim for salvation.

Ceremonial rigidity was fraught with similar dangers, but while the high point of ritual observance—the Day of Atonement—accomplished only the remission of inadvertent sins, its elaborate paraphernalia pointed forward to the substance of true salvation. The prophetic emphasis on the need of inward transformation underlined the radical nature of man's wrongdoing and led to the foretelling of an apocalyptic, messianic salvation when God, according to His covenant promise, would, as a just God and a Saviour, Himself come in salvation (Is. lxv. 17; Dn. vii. 13 f.). The Old Testament doctrine of salvation reaches its zenith in the portrayal of the suffering Servant (*e.g.* Is. liii); in this respect the Old Testament sets the scene for, and adumbrates, the New Testament salvation.

II. IN THE NEW TESTAMENT

a. The Synoptic Gospels

The word salvation is mentioned by Jesus only once (Lk. xix. 9), where it may refer either to Himself as the embodiment of salvation imparting pardon to Zacchaeus, or to that which is evidenced by the transformed conduct of the publican. Our Lord, however, used 'save' and kindred terms to indicate first what He came to do (by implication, Mk. iii. 4; and by direct statement, Lk. iv. 18; Mt. xviii. 11; Lk. ix. 56; Mt. xx. 28), and secondly, what is demanded of man (Mk. viii. 35; Lk. vii. 50, viii. 12, xiii. 24; Mt. x. 22). Lk. xviii. 26, and context, shows that salvation calls for a contrite heart, childlike, receptive helplessness, and the renunciation of all for Christ—conditions it is impossible for man unaided to fulfil.

The testimony of others to our Lord's saving activity is both indirect (Mk. xv. 31) and direct (Mt. viii. 17). There is also the witness of His own name (Mt. i. 21, 23). All these varied usages suggest that salvation was present in the person and ministry of Christ and especially in His death.

b. The Fourth Gospel

This double truth is underlined in the Fourth Gospel, in which each chapter suggests different aspects of salvation. Thus in i. 12 f. men are born as sons of God by trusting in Christ; in ii. 5 the situation is remedied by doing 'whatsoever he saith unto you'; in iii. 5 new birth from the Spirit is essential for entering the kingdom, but iii. 14, 17 makes it clear that this new life is not possible apart from trust in the death of Christ, without which men are already under condemnation (iii. 18); in iv. 22 salvation is of the Jews—by revelation historically channelled through God's people—and is a gift inwardly transforming and equipping men for worship.

In v. 14 the one made whole must sin no more lest a worse thing come; in v. 39 the Scriptures testify of life (= salvation) in the Son, to whom life and judgment are committed; in v. 24 believers have already passed from death to life; in vi. 35 Jesus declares Himself the bread of life, to whom alone men should go (vi. 68) for the quickening words of eternal life; in vii. 39 water is the symbol of the saving life of the Spirit who was to come after Jesus had been glorified.

In viii. 12 the Evangelist shows the safety of the guidance of light and in verses 32, 36 the liberty through truth in the Son; in ix. 25, 37, 39 salvation is spiritual sight; in x. 10 entrance into the safety and abundant life of the fold and of the Father is through Christ; in xi. 25 f. resurrection-life belongs to the believer; in xi. 50 (*cf.* xviii. 14) the saving purpose of His death is unwittingly described; in xii. 32 Christ, lifted up in death, draws men to Him; in xiii. 10 His initial washing signifies salvation ('clean every whit'); in xiv. 6 He is the true and living way to the Father's abode; in xv. 5 abiding in Him, the Vine, is the secret of life's resources; in xvi. 7–15 for His sake the Spirit will deal with the obstacles to salvation and prepare for its realization; in xvii. 2, 3, 12 He keeps safely those who have knowledge of the true God and of Himself; in xix. 30 salvation is accomplished; in xx. 21–23 the words of peace and pardon accompany His gift of the Spirit; in xxi. 15–18 His healing love reinstils love in His follower and reinstates him for service.

c. The Acts

Acts traces the proclamation (*cf.* xvi. 17) of salvation in its impact first upon the crowds which are exhorted to be 'saved . . . from this untoward generation' (ii. 40) by repentance (itself a gift and part of salvation, xi. 18), remission of sins, and receiving the Holy Ghost; then upon a sick individual, ignorant of his true need, who is healed by the name of Jesus, the only name whereby we must be saved; and thirdly, upon the household of him who asked 'What must I do to be saved?' (xvi. 30 ff.).

d. The Pauline Epistles

Paul claims that the Scriptures make men 'wise unto salvation through faith which is in Christ Jesus' (2 Tim. iii. 15 ff.) and provide the ingredients essential for the enjoyment of a full-orbed salvation. Enlarging and applying the Old Testament concept of the righteousness of God, which itself had adumbrations of the saving righteousness of the New Testament, Paul shows how there is no salvation by means of the law, since it could only indicate the presence and excite the reactionary activity of sin and stop men's mouths in their guilt before God (Rom. iii. 19; Gal. ii. 16). Salvation is provided as the free gift of the righteous God acting in grace towards the undeserving sinner who, by the gift of faith, trusts in the righteousness of Christ who has redeemed him by His death and justified him by His resurrection. God, for Christ's sake, justifies the unmeriting sinner (*i.e.* reckons to him the perfect righteousness of Christ and regards him as if he had not sinned), forgives his sin, reconciles him to Himself in and through Christ who has 'made peace through the blood of his cross' (2 Cor. v. 18; Rom. v. 11; Col. i. 20), adopts him into His family (Gal. iv. 5 f.; Eph. i. 13; 2 Cor. i. 22), giving him the seal, earnest, and firstfruits of His Spirit in his heart, and so making him a new creation. By the same Spirit the subsequent resources of salvation enable him to walk in newness of life, mortifying the deeds of the body increasingly (Rom. viii. 13) until ultimately he is conformed to Christ (Rom. viii. 29) and his salvation is consummated in glory (Phil. iii. 21).

e. The Epistle to the Hebrews

The 'great' salvation of the Epistle to the Hebrews transcends the Old Testament adumbrations of salvation. The New Testament salvation is described in the language of sacrifice; the oft-repeated offerings of the Old Testament ritual that dealt mainly with unwitting sins and provided only a superficial salvation are replaced by the one sacrifice of Christ, Himself both saving Priest and Offering (Heb. ix. 26, x. 12). The outpouring of His life-blood in death effects atonement, so that henceforth man with a cleansed conscience can enter the presence of God in terms of the new covenant ratified by God through His Mediator (Heb. ix. 15, xii. 24). Hebrews, which lays such stress on Christ's dealing with sin by His suffering and death to provide eternal salvation, anticipates His second appearing, not then to deal with sin, but to consummate His people's salvation and, presumably, their attendant glory (ix. 28).

f. The Epistle of James

James teaches that salvation is not by 'faith' only but also by 'works' (ii. 24). His concern is to disillusion anyone who relies for his salvation on a mere intellectual acknowledgment of the existence of God without a change in heart resulting in works of righteousness. He does not discount true faith, but urges that its presence be shown by a conduct that in turn indicates the saving energies of true religion at work through the ingrafted Word of God. He is as concerned as any to bring back the sinner from the error of his way and save his soul from death (v. 20).

g. 1 and 2 Peter

1 Peter strikes a similar note to Hebrews about the costly salvation (i. 19) which was searched for and foretold by the prophets but is now a present reality to those who, like straying sheep, have returned to the Shepherd of their souls (ii. 24 f.). Its future aspect is known by those 'who are kept . . . unto salvation ready to be revealed' (1 Pet. i. 5).

In 2 Peter salvation involves escaping the corruption that is in the world through lust by being partakers of the divine nature (i. 4). In the context of sin the believer yearns for the new heavens and the new earth wherein dwells righteousness, but recognizes that the postponement of the parousia is due to the longsuffering of his Lord, which is itself an aspect of salvation (iii. 13, 15).

h. 1, 2, and 3 John

For 1 John the sacrificial language of Hebrews is congenial. Christ is our salvation by being the propitiation for our sins, as the outcome of God's love. It is God in His love in Christ's outpoured life-blood who covers our sins and cleanses us. As in the Fourth Gospel, salvation is conceived in terms of being born of God, knowing God, possessing eternal life in Christ, living in the light and truth of God, dwelling in God and knowing His dwelling in us through love by His Spirit (iii. 9, iv. 6, 13, v. 11). 3 John has a significant prayer for general prosperity and bodily health (natural well-being) to accompany prosperity of soul (verse 2).

i. The Epistle of Jude

Jude 3, in referring to the 'common salvation', has in mind something akin to the 'common faith' of Tit. i. 4, and allies it to the 'faith' (*cf.* Eph. iv. 5) for which believers are to contend. This salvation comprises the saving truths, privileges, demands, and experiences common to the variety of his readers. In verses 22 f. he would urgently present this salvation to various groups in doubt, danger, and degradation.

j. The Revelation

Revelation reiterates the theme (of 1 Jn.) of salvation as liberation or cleansing from sin by virtue of the blood of Christ and its constitution of believers as royal priests (i. 5 f.). In a manner reminiscent of the psalmist, the seer, in adoration, ascribes salvation in its comprehensiveness to God (vii. 10). The closing chapters of the book depict salvation in terms of the leaves of the tree of life which are for the healing of the nations, to which tree, as to the city of salvation, admission is given only to those whose names are written in the book of life.

III. THE WAY OF SALVATION

The presupposition of the Bible is that, since the fall, man—as an individual and in society—is in need of help, of salvation. He is in a vicious circle, in a dangerous position and condition, guilty, and impotent. His guilt disqualifies him from meriting the only resources which can deliver him from his position. No human power can solve the problem from within the circle. God must take the initiative if man is to be saved. There are various descriptions of man's predicament—failure, falling short, emptiness, alienation, bondage, rebellion, disease, corruption, pollution, death. Just as various are the futile attempts at remedy—intellectual enlightenment of ignorance, moral reform, aesthetic enhancement, medical or psychological treatment, social amelioration by the use of technological advancement, economic and political strategy, and above all, man-initiated religious techniques. Early in his story man had to see, as he still must see, that he cannot produce his own salvation because of the radical nature of his sin and self-centredness; his attempts to save himself are the worst affront to God and incur His judgment.

The Bible portrays God in holy love as conceiving and unfolding a 'plan of salvation'. Scripture references to what happened before or at 'the foundation of the world' have raised questions as to when, and in what order, God planned salvation (*cf.* Mt. xiii. 35, xxv. 34; Jn. xvii. 24; Eph. i. 4; Heb. iv. 3; 1 Pet. i. 20; Rev. xiii. 8, xvii. 8). However, it belongs more to speculative theology than to our purpose here to discuss in which chronological order to set the four terms creation, fall, election, salvation.

The means of salvation are more clearly delineated. It is evident that Father, Son, and Spirit are involved (the traditional wording is that the Father decrees, the Son procures, the Spirit applies salvation). The 'crux' of salvation is in the cross of Christ (Rom. i. 16; 1 Cor. i. 18). According due place to His life and resurrection, biblical theologians agree that it is in the death of His Son that God performs the focal act of salvation for man. Throughout, it is God Himself, in holy love, who provides the salvation. The portrayals are varied, but the composite picture is of the majesty, mystery, might, and mercy of God in action: the sin which is an affront to God's holiness is removed in Christ; legitimate peace-terms with God are ratified by Him who made peace through His cross and atonement between alienated man and his Maker; a ransom is paid to redeem or release the slave from bondage; an acquittal is given at the bar of justice, since God in His Son bears the judgment incurred by man, by identifying Himself with human sin; the honour of God is satisfied by Christ's perfection being submitted in obedience; Christ unites humanity in Himself and takes it in His sacrifice to the Father; Christ is supremely Victor in His death. The emphasis here is on the salvation which God in Christ has prepared *for* man and, while there is no separation between them, it is important to indicate how He works salvation *in* man.

It is by the Holy Spirit (*q.v.*) that salvation is made real to man. Man's experience of salvation has a threefold temporal aspect. It can be described in terms of past, present, and future; possessively, progressively, and prospectively; he is saved, is being saved, and will be saved (Eph. ii. 8; 1 Cor. i. 18; Mt. x. 22; Rom. v. 9, 10, viii. 24).

a. Possessively

Man by faith wrought in him by the Spirit is given a new status in Christ; he is already justified and acquitted for Christ's sake. Just as in his pre-justified status he could not deserve salvation, so after being justified (through no righteousness of his own) he cannot un-merit salvation or unjustify himself in the sense of undoing what God has done for him. He *is* redeemed, reconciled, forgiven, cleansed (Jn. xiii. 10), has passed from death to life, and is given the assurance by the Spirit's witnessing with his own spirit that he is a child of God (Rom. viii. 16), a co-heir with Christ, possessing a life which is eternal in its quality and duration and which shatters the bondage of the fear of death (Heb. ii. 15).

b. Progressively

The salvation-bearing grace of God (Tit. ii. 11), which is the power imparted by the preaching of the cross to those who are 'being saved' (1 Cor. i. 18, RSV), teaches the need for the sanctifying operation of the Spirit, the working out of the salvation which God has wrought for man (Phil. ii. 12), evidencing the denial of ungodliness and worldly lusts, and producing sober, righteous, and godly living in this present world. As faith is the operative fact in salvation conceived possessively, so is love in the outworking of salvation. By the love implanted by the Spirit man's life is conserved, he attains true selfhood in reflecting anew the image of God, and is truly present in his person to others who are in need of salvation.

c. Prospectively

Salvation in its fulness is to be realized in the future. Man is saved by hope. The believer is appointed to obtain salvation (1 Thes. v. 9; 2 Thes. ii. 13; 2 Tim. ii. 10; Heb. i. 14). Salvation is ready to be revealed in the last time (1 Pet. i. 5). This salvation is 'nearer than when we believed' (Rom. xiii. 11). To those who look for Christ He will appear the second time, not to deal with sin but 'unto salvation' (Heb. ix. 28). At the ultimate defeat of evil the heavenly voice will utter 'Now is come salvation'.

IV. PRIVILEGES AND RESPONSIBILITIES OF SALVATION

Recipients of salvation are nowhere encouraged to presume upon God. Even the elect are warned to make their calling and election sure (2 Pet. i. 10) and to work out their salvation with fear and trembling (Phil. ii. 13). The saved community of believers, the Church, is the custodian of salvation and the words *extra ecclesiam nulla salus* have real meaning when its solemn trusteeship of the *kērygma* and *didachē* of salvation is realized. It is to be the 'fellowship of the concerned', a saving as well as a saved people.

If salvation is truly working in believers their own fellowship (*koinōnia*) in the Spirit will increase and the 'vertical' downworking of God's saving power will constrain them to realize the 'horizontal' repercussions on society of the possession of salvation. Those who possess salvation are to be lights in the world, the salt of the earth, cities upon the hills. The story of the Church shows how it has learnt and must still learn to witness to its salvation prophetically in every age.

V. CONSUMMATION OF SALVATION

The Bible shows but little trace of a gradual saving of the whole of mankind, either in the sense of preparing them all for glory or transforming society by continued progress through the application of 'saving' principles. It does, however, promise the ultimate destruction of evil apocalyptically or eschatologically, the deliverance of the now groaning creation from the bondage of corruption into the glorious liberty of the children of God (Rom. viii. 21 ff.) at the 'adoption', the 'redemption of the body', the 'regeneration' (Mt. xix. 28), and the creation of 'new heavens and a new earth, wherein dwelleth righteousness', where God will be seen face to face.

See ATONEMENT, ELECTION, FORGIVENESS,

HOLY SPIRIT, JUSTIFICATION, RECONCILIATION, REDEEMER, REGENERATION, SANCTIFICATION.

BIBLIOGRAPHY. E. Brunner, *The Mediator*, 1947; R. W. Dale, *The Atonement*[20], 1899; J. Denney, *The Death of Christ*, reprinted 1951; P. T. Forsyth, *The Cruciality of the Cross*[2], 1948; L. Morris, *The Apostolic Preaching of the Cross*, 1955; J. Murray, *Redemption Accomplished and Applied*, 1955; L. Newbigin, *Sin and Salvation*, 1956; G. B. Stevens, *The Christian Doctrine of Salvation*, 1905. G.W.

SAMARIA. The name of the northern Israelite capital and of the territory surrounding it.

I. HISTORY

After reigning six years at Tirzah, Omri built a new capital for the northern kingdom on a hill 7 miles north-west of Shechem commanding the main trade routes through the Esdraelon plain. He purchased the site for two talents of silver and named it after its owner Shemer (1 Ki. xvi. 24). The place is otherwise unknown unless it is to be identified with Shamir, the home of Tola (Jdg. x. 1; Abel, *Géographie de la Palestine*, II, p. 444). The hill, which is 300 feet high and commands a view over the plain, was impregnable except by siege (2 Ki. vi. 24), and the name (*šōmerôn*) may be connected with the Heb. 'watch-post'.

Omri allowed the Syrians of Damascus to set up bazaars (AV 'streets') in his new city (1 Ki. xx. 34). For six years he worked on the construction of Samaria, and this was continued by Ahab, who built a house decorated or panelled with ivory (1 Ki. xxii. 39). In a temple for Baal of Sidon (Melqart), the deity whose worship Jezebel encouraged (1 Ki. xviii. 22), Ahab set up a pillar (*'ăšerâ*) near the altar which Jehoram later removed (2 Ki. iii. 2). Other shrines and buildings used by the idolatrous priests must have been in use from this time until the reform undertaken by Jehu (2 Ki. x. 19). Samaria itself was long considered by the prophets a centre of idolatry (Is. viii. 4, ix. 9; Je. xxiii. 13; Ezk. xxiii. 4; Ho. vii. 1; Mi. i. 6).

Ben-hadad II of Syria besieged Samaria, at first unsuccessfully (1 Ki. xx. 1–21), but later the Syrians reduced it to dire famine (2 Ki. vi. 25). It was relieved only by the panic and sudden withdrawal of the besiegers, which was discovered and reported by the lepers (2 Ki. vii). Ahab was buried in the city, as were a number of Israelite kings who made it their residence (1 Ki. xxii. 37; 2 Ki. xiii. 9, 13, xiv. 16). His descendants were slain there (2 Ki. x. 1), including Ahaziah, who hid in vain in the crowded city (2 Ch. xxii. 9). Samaria was again besieged in the time of Elisha and miraculously delivered (2 Ki. vi. 8 ff.).

During Menahem's ten-year reign he bought off the Assyrians by paying tribute, exacted as poll-tax, to Tiglath-pileser III (2 Ki. xv. 17–20). His son Pekah, however, drew the Assyrian army back again by his opposition to Judah, who appealed for help. Pekah heeded the plea of the prophet Oded to return the spoil and the Judaean captives whom he had brought to Samaria (2 Ch. xxviii. 8–15). The city, called *Samerina* or *Bit-Ḫumri* ('House of Omri') in the Assyrian Annals, was besieged by Shalmaneser V of Assyria in 725–722 BC (2 Ki. xvii. 3 ff.), though the final capture is claimed by his successor Sargon II (see SARGON). The citizens, incited by Iau-bi'di of Hamath, refused to pay the tax imposed on them, and in the following year (721 BC) Sargon initiated a scheme of mass deportation for the whole area. According to his annals, Sargon carried off 27,270 or 27,290 captives, and the effect was to terminate the existence of the northern kingdom of Israel as a homogeneous and independent state. The exiles were despatched to places in Syria, Assyria, and Babylonia and their place was taken by colonists from other disturbed parts of the Assyrian Empire (2 Ki. xvii. 24). The resultant failure to cultivate the outlying districts led to an increase in the incursions of lions (verse 25). Some Israelites, called Samaritans (verse 29), still inhabited part of the city and continued to worship at Jerusalem (Je. xli. 5). The town, according to a cuneiform inscription (*HES*, 247), was under an Assyrian governor and both Esarhaddon (Ezr. iv. 2) and Ashurbanipal (Ezr. iv. 9, 10) brought in additional peoples from Babylonia and Elam. The contention between Samaria and Judah, of earlier origin, gradually increased in intensity (see SAMARITANS), though Samaria itself declined in importance.

The city was colonized by the Greeks after its capture by Alexander in 331 BC, but little is known of it afterwards until the Roman occupation. It was, however, besieged by John Hyrcanus, and the surrounding countryside was devastated *c.* 111–107 BC. Pompey and Gabinius began to rebuild (Jos., *Ant.* xiv. 4. 4), but it was left to Herod to embellish the city, which he renamed Sebaste (Augusta) in honour of his emperor. In it he housed 6,000 veterans, including Greeks. On his death, Samaria became part of the territory of Archelaus and later a Roman colony under Septimus Severus. Despite the mutual antagonism between Judah and Samaria, Jesus Christ took the shorter route through Samaria to Galilee (Lk. xvii. 11), resting at Sychar near Shechem, a Samaritan city (Jn. iv. 4). Philip preached in Samaria, but perhaps the district rather than the city is intended, since the definite article is absent in Acts viii. 5.

II. ARCHAEOLOGY

The hill of Samaria (modern Sebastiyeh) was unoccupied from the Early Bronze Age until the Israelite kingdom (*RB*, LIII, 1946, pp. 589 ff.). Sixteen levels of occupation have been uncovered by the Harvard (1908–10) and, later, joint Harvard–Hebrew University–British School of Archaeology in Jerusalem expeditions (1931–5). The site is difficult to work because of the dense and continuous habitation, with constant rebuilding. Of the periods of occupation unearthed seven have been assigned to the Israelites:

Levels I–II = Omri–Ahab (twenty-eight years). The inner (5 feet thick) and outer (19½ feet thick) fortification wall, completed by the latter king, enclosed the summit. A main gateway seems to have had a columned entrance court. The palace, which was later adapted by Jeroboam II, had a wide court in which lay a reservoir or pool (33½ × 17 feet), probably the one in which Ahab's bloodstained chariot was washed down (1 Ki. xxii. 38). In an adjacent storeroom more than 200 plaques or fragments of ivories were discovered. These show Phoenician and pseudo-Egyptian styles and influences and may well have been inlays for furniture (see IVORY; *cf.* fig. 56, pl. V*a*). Sixty-five ostraca, inscribed in Old Hebrew, noted the capacity and original owners of the wine-jars, with the date of their contents (*DOTT*, pp. 204–208; *IEJ*, IX, 1959, pp. 184–187). These are probably to be assigned to the reign of Jeroboam II.

Level III marks the period of Jehu with adaptations of earlier buildings. Then, after an interval, come levels IV–VI, the Israelite period covering Jeroboam and the 8th century BC. The city was repaired in the last decades before its fall to the Assyrians in 722 BC, which is marked by the destruction level VII.

The remains of the Hellenistic buildings are well preserved, with a round tower standing nineteen courses of stone high, a fortress, the city wall (near the West Gate), coins, stamped jar-handles, and Greek pottery remaining. Some of these architectural features should perhaps be assigned to Perdiccas (*c.* 322 BC), Soter (312 BC), or Demetrius (296 BC).

The Roman city of Herod is notable for the great temple dedicated to Augustus, built over the Israelite palaces. Other remains include the enclosure wall, and West Gate, with three round towers, a 900-yard long colonnaded street bordered by porticos and shops, the temple of Isis rededicated to Kore, a basilica (74 × 35 yards), divided into three naves by Corinthian columns, a forum, a stadium, and an aqueduct. Many of the modern ruins are probably to be dated to later restorers, especially Septimius Severus (AD 193–211).

BIBLIOGRAPHY. A. Parrot, *Samaria*, 1958; J. W. Crowfoot, K. Kenyon, *etc.*, *Samaria*, I, *The Buildings at Samaria*, 1943; *Samaria*, II, *Early Ivories at Samaria*, 1938; *Samaria—Sebaste* III, *The Objects from Samaria*, 1957. D.J.W.

SAMARITANS. The fall of Samaria in 722 BC marked a new era in the history of the northern kingdom. The leading citizens were deported by Sargon, while exiles from other parts of the Assyrian Empire were imported by Sargon, Esarhaddon, and Ashurbanipal. The Israelites who were left formed the core of the new community and, despite the introduction of various cults, guaranteed the continuity of the worship of Yahweh. Closer relations were maintained with Judah before and after the fall of Jerusalem in 586 BC (*cf.* 2 Ch. xxx. 1 ff.; 2 Ki. xxiii. 19, 20; Je. xli. 4 ff.).

In the early Persian period, when the Jews were allowed to return to Jerusalem, they tried to rebuild the Temple and the city walls. At once they met with opposition from the ruling classes in

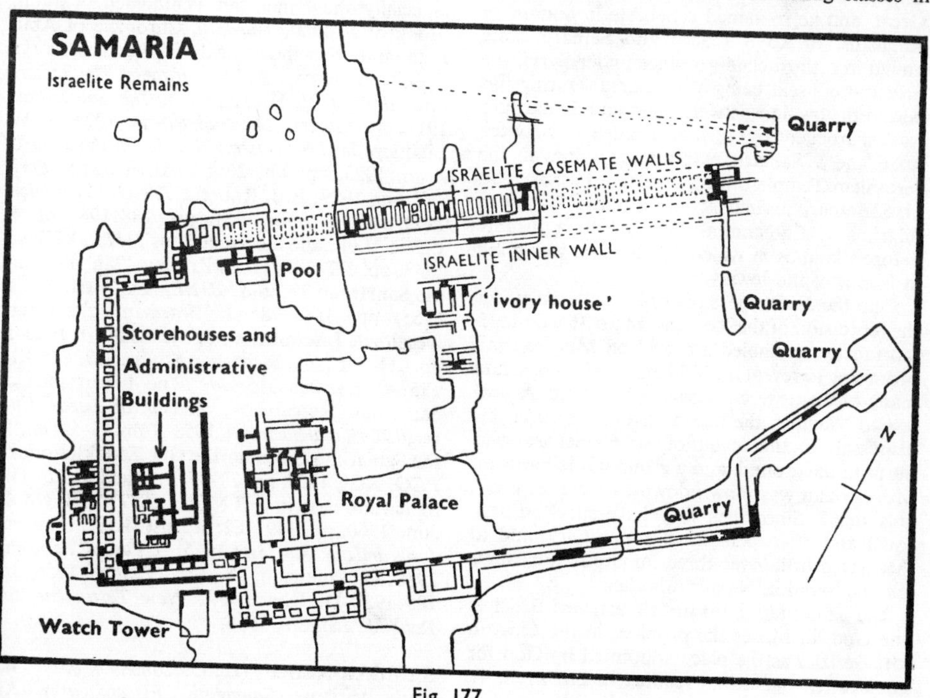

Fig. 177.

Samaria. There is no reason to think that this opposition was more than political, since as late as the end of the 5th century BC the Jews at Elephantine could write for help in rebuilding their temple to the authorities of both Jerusalem and Samaria.

With the advent of Ezra and Nehemiah the tension grew deeper. The new zeal for the purity of the race, which was imported from the Babylonian Jewish community, fastened on the mixed ancestry of the Samaritans. When the high priest's grandson married Sanballat's daughter, Nehemiah expelled him. Josephus recounts a similar incident, which he dates in the following century, and it is difficult to relate the two narratives. They may record quite distinct events, or Josephus may have confused some of his details. He connects the building of the Samaritan temple on Mt. Gerizim with this incident, and in dating the temple he is probably right.

The final breach between Jews and Samaritans must have occurred by *c.* 200 BC, when Ben Sira wrote Ecclus. i. 25, 26. The Samaritans possess the Law but not the Prophets, and this may also suggest a breach about this time. At the time of the Maccabean revolt, the Samaritans bowed before the storm, and their temple on Mt. Gerizim was dedicated to Zeus Xenios. The Hasmonaeans, however, acquired a growing ascendancy over Samaria, and *c.* 128 BC Hyrcanus captured Shechem and destroyed the Gerizim temple.

In 63 BC Pompey detached Samaria and annexed it to the new Province of Syria. The city of Samaria became a favourite seat of Herod the Great, and he re-named it Sebaste in honour of Augustus. In AD 6 Judaea and Samaria were united in a third-class province under Syria, the procurator's seat being at Caesarea. During this period the friction between Jews and Samaritans was sharpened by several incidents. Between AD 6 and 9 Samaritans scattered bones in the Jerusalem Temple during a certain Passover. In AD 52 Samaritans massacred a group of Galilaean pilgrims at En-gannim. This led to a dispute before Claudius in which the decision was given in favour of the Jews.

Like the Jews, the Samaritans suffered under the repression of the Romans. In AD 36 a Samaritan fanatic assembled a crowd on Mt. Gerizim, promising to reveal the hidden sacred vessels, and many of them were massacred by Pilate. A protest to Vitellius, the legate of Syria, secured his dismissal. In the revolt of AD 66 Sebaste was burnt to the ground, and a group of die-hards on Mt. Gerizim was mown down by Cerealis probably in 67. Since then they have survived as a small and often persecuted community, and to this day a little over three hundred Samaritans may be found in Nablus (Shechem).

The Samaritan creed has six articles: Belief in one God, in Moses the prophet, in the Law, in Mt. Gerizim as the place appointed by God for sacrifice (*cf.* Samaritan reading of Dt. xxvii. 4), in the day of judgment and recompense, and in the return of Moses as Taheb, or restorer (something akin to the Messiah). Their belief in the resurrection is problematical. The Jews regarded Samaritans as schismatics rather than Gentiles, and trusted them, *e.g.*, over tithes and uncleanness arising from a grave. The main bone of contention was the Gerizim temple. The Samaritan Pentateuch, despite theological modifications, is a very important witness to the original text.

John tells how Jesus spent two days in Shechem, where many believed on Him. During His ministry He regarded His mission as being primarily to Israel, but after His resurrection He commissioned the apostles to preach in Samaria, and the mission to Samaria was carried out specially by the Hellenists after Stephen's martyrdom.

Our sources for the history of the Samaritans are as follows: The Old Testament, especially 2 Kings xvii, Ezra and Nehemiah; Ecclus. l. 25, 26; 2 Macc. vi. 2; *Testament of Levi* vii. 2; the Prism of Sargon in the Assyrian Annals; the Elephantine Papyri (see A. E. Cowley, *Aramaic Papyri of the Fifth Century BC*, No. 30); the Mishnah (*Berakoth* vii. 1, viii. 8; *Demai* iii. 4, v. 9, vi. 1, vii. 4; *Shebiith* viii. 10; *Terumoth* iii. 9; *Shekalim* i. 5; *Rosh ha-Shanah* ii. 2; *Ketuboth* iii. 1; *Nedarim* iii. 10; *Gittin* i. 5; *Kiddushin* iv. 3; *Oholoth* xvii. 3; *Niddah* iv. 1, 2, vii. 4, 5); the Babylonian Talmud (*Masseket Kutim*); the New Testament (Mt. x. 5; Lk. ix. 52, x. 33, xvii. 16; Jn. iv. 7–42, viii. 48; Acts i. 8, viii. 1, 5–25, ix. 31, xv. 3); Josephus, especially *BJ* ii. 12. 3–7, *Ant.* ix. 14. 3, xi. 7. 2, 8. 2–7, xiii. 9. 1, xviii. 2. 2, 4. 1, 2, xx. 6. 1, 2; and Samaritan literature generally, especially the Samaritan Pentateuch, Targum, 'Book of Joshua', *Toledoth*, Chronicle of Abu'l Fath, and other theological and liturgical works.

BIBLIOGRAPHY. J. A. Montgomery, *The Samaritans*, 1907; J. E. H. Thomson, *The Samaritans*, 1919; M. Gaster, *The Samaritans*, 1923; J. W. Lightley, *Jewish Sects and Parties in the Time of Jesus*, 1925, pp. 179–265; L. E. Browne, *Early Judaism*, 1929; B. J. Roberts, *The Old Testament Text and Versions*, 1951, pp. 188–194; M. S. Enslin, 'Luke and the Samaritans', *HTR*, XXXVI, 1943, pp. 277–297; H. H. Rowley, 'Sanballat and the Samaritan Temple', *BJRL*, XXXVIII, No. 1, 1955, pp. 166–198; J. Bowman, 'Samaritan Decalogue Inscriptions', *BJRL*, XXXIII, 1950–1, pp. 211–236; *id.*, 'Samaritan Studies', *BJRL*, XL, 1957–8, pp. 298–315; *id.*, 'The Importance of Samaritan Researches', *Annual of Leeds University Oriental Society*, I, 1958–9, pp. 43–54; *id.*, 'Is the Samaritan Calendar the Old Zadokite one?', *PEQ*, XCI, 1959, pp. 23–37; J. Macdonald, 'The Samaritan Doctrine of Moses', *SJT*, XIII, No. 2, June 1960, pp. 149–162; see also T. W. Manson, *Jesus and the Non-Jews*, 1955; A. Parrot, *Samaria*, 1958; O. Cullmann, *The Early Church*, 1956, pp. 185–192; D. Daube, *The New Testament and Rabbinic Judaism*, 1956. A.G.

SAMGAR-NEBO (Heb. *samgar-n^{e}ḇô*; Gk. many variants *Samagoth*, *Eissamagath*). An officer of Nebuchadrezzar who sat with other Babylonian officials in the middle gate of Jerusalem after its capture in 587 BC (Je. xxxix. 3). It is uncertain whether this is a personal name (a rare Bab. Šumgir-Nabu has been suggested) or the title of Nergal-sharezer, the Rab-mag (*q.v.*). Many emendations to the text have been proposed, some with the object of making the three offices identical with those mentioned in verse 13, by taking Nebo with Sarsechim to be the same as Nebuchasban. This, however, is very doubtful. It is possible that *šamgar* may be the transliteration of the Babylonian title of an official of Nabu. See SARSECHIM, NEBO, NERGAL-SHAREZER.

D.J.W.

SAMOS. One of the larger islands in the Aegean Sea, off the coast of Asia Minor south-west of Ephesus. An Ionian settlement, it had been an important maritime state. Under the Romans it was part of the province of Asia until Augustus made it a free state in 17 BC. On his way home from his third missionary journey Paul sailed between Samos and the mainland (Acts xx. 15).

K.L.McK.

SAMOTHRACE (modern Samothraki). A small mountainous island in the north of the Aegean off the coast of Thrace, with a town of the same name on the north side. One of its peaks rises to some 5,500 feet, forming a conspicuous landmark. Sailing north-west from Troas on his way to Neapolis, Paul must have had a favourable wind to reach Samos in one day and Neapolis in one more (Acts xvi. 11, *cf.* xx. 6).

Samothrace was renowned as a centre of the mystery cult of the Kabeiroi, ancient fertility deities who were supposed to protect those in danger, especially at sea. K.L.McK.

SAMSON. The last of the Spirit-led judges of Israel before Samuel (see JUDGES). Samson's name, *šimšôn*, from Heb. *šemeš*, 'sun', probably meaning 'little sun' or 'sun-one', was given by his parents in anticipation of his heroic, sun-like strength and miraculous energy (*cf.* Jdg. v. 31; Ps. xix. 5, lxxxiv. 11).

I. CHARACTER

Before birth Samson was dedicated to God to be a life-long Nazirite (see NAZARITE). He trusted in God more often than not (Heb. xi. 32), and was mightily empowered by the Spirit of Yahweh (Jdg. xiii. 25, xiv. 6, 19, xv. 14) to perform prodigious feats of physical strength. By treating his Nazirite vows loosely, however, Samson was careless about honouring God at all times. Early in manhood he specifically disobeyed the prohibitions against approaching a dead body (xiv. 8) and drinking wine when he provided a feast or drinking bout (*mišteh*, xiv. 10); and he violated the Nazirite principle of being holy to Yahweh by his immoral intercourse with the Gaza harlot and with Delilah. He intensely hated the Philistines when co-existence was more popular. He was witty and had a grim sense of humour. But he was foolhardy, and his sensual passions made him so headstrong that he dissipated his God-given strength until the Lord forsook him.

II. HISTORICAL BACKGROUND

Born at the beginning of the forty-year-long Philistine oppression around 1090 BC (Jdg. xiii. 1), Samson probably began his career soon after the terrible battle near Aphek about 1070 BC when the Philistines captured the ark and burned Shiloh (1 Sa. iv; see SHILOH). The disheartened Israelites submitted to the Philistine yoke so that there was no national repentance or desire for a deliverer during Samson's twenty-year ministry (Jdg. xv. 11 f.; 1 Sa. vii. 2).

III. PERSONAL HISTORY

a. His birth and growth, Jdg. xiii

Like Isaac, Samuel, and John the Baptist, Samson was born to a previously barren woman. The angel of Yahweh promised Manoah and his wife a son who would *begin* to deliver Israel (xiii. 5). Samson was reared with spiritual training; as a result, the Spirit began to impel him against the Philistines (xiii. 25, xiv. 4; see PHILISTINES).

b. His attempted marriage and revenge, xiv. 1–xv. 8

Samson saw a Philistine woman in Timnath whom he was convinced he must marry in order to incite a quarrel with her people. His parents having arranged a betrothal, he returned after grape-harvest to marry her. At the seven-day wedding feast (*cf.* Gn. xxix. 27) he entertained his guests with a riddle, wagering that if they guessed it he would give them thirty sets of festal clothing. They could not solve his riddle about honey in the skeleton of a lion he had killed, so they threatened his already curious bride to secure the answer for them. Samson yielded to her entreaties, and, to keep his bargain, he went to Ashkelon and slew thirty Philistines to get the promised garments. Angry with the whole crowd, he went home and his bride was given to his 'best man' (xiv. 1–20). When he returned to visit his wife next spring her father refused him entrance. Now with ample justification, he cleverly caught 300 jackals, tied firebrands to their tails, and turned them loose in the grainfields and orchards of his enemies. Although he could not muster even 300 faithful men such as Gideon had he thus caused widespread havoc quickly and efficiently. In retaliation the Philistines burned his wife and father-in-law; he avenged this with a great slaughter (xv. 1–8).

c. His escape and victory at Lehi, xv. 9–19

Hiding out in the cliff of Etam, Samson was arrested by 3,000 men of Judah, which was suffering from Philistine reprisals. He let himself be bound with two new ropes, and was taken up to the Philistines at Lehi. When he heard their victory-cry the Spirit of Yahweh 'came mightily upon him' and he snapped his fetters, picked up a fresh jawbone of an ass, and smote with it a thousand humiliated foes. Tossing away his improvised weapon, he called the name of the place Ramath-lehi, 'Jawbone Hill'. When he called on the Lord for water and acknowledged the source of his triumph, God caused a stream to flow from a rock at Lehi with mortar-cup-holes for grinding grain (*maḵtēš*; *cf.* Pr. xxvii. 22; N. Glueck, *Rivers in the Desert*, 1959, p. 84).

d. His judgeship, xv. 20

Having thus established his charismatic authority, Samson settled local problems for Dan and Judah, and perhaps resided in Hebron, the chief city of Judah (*cf.* xvi. 3), while Samuel judged in Mizpeh (Tell en-Nasbeh, 1 Sa. vii. 6). Endued by the Spirit, Samson seems to have acted rather wisely for nearly twenty years. But he never could gather an army to fight the Philistines.

e. His downfall and death, Jdg. xvi

Like Solomon, however, Samson was ruined by the eventual debauching of love into lust. Self-confidently Samson strode into Gaza (see GAZA), perhaps seeking combat with a giant (*cf.* Jos. xi. 22; 2 Sa. xxi. 15–22). Noticing a harlot, he succumbed. When the Philistines heard of it, they surrounded the city all night. But Samson arose at midnight and laid hold of the gate doors, door posts, and bar and carried them off towards Hebron. This was the worst humiliation he could have inflicted on his enemies, because city gates symbolized national strength (xvi. 1–3). After this, Samson became infatuated with Delilah, a woman near his home (see SOREK, VALLEY OF). She collaborated with the Philistine princes to learn the secret of his tremendous strength. Their extravagant bribe may indicate Delilah was not a Philistine herself. Three times Samson evaded her bewitching and seductive wiles, but he did not flee as did Joseph (*cf.* Gn. xxxix. 12). Eventually, teased to distraction, he explained he was a Nazirite and that his unshorn locks were the key to his strength. By disclosing this secret he broke his covenant vow completely, and the Lord forsook him (xvi. 4–20). Blinded and put to humiliating labour, 'eyeless in Gaza, at the mill with slaves', Samson at last was led out of Gaza's prison to the forecourt of the temple of Dagon (see DAGON) to clown before the festive crowd. Meanwhile Samson's hair (together with his repentance) had grown, and his strength with his hair. Calling upon Yahweh, Samson braced himself against two wooden pillars which supported the roof of the portico in which the Philistine nobles were watching; above were 3,000 spectators. He pulled the columns off their stone pedestals and brought down the house, killing himself and more Philistines than the total he had slain during his life. This catastrophe decimated the Philistines, probably contributing to Israel's victory in the battle of Ebenezer soon afterwards (1 Sa. vii).

BIBLIOGRAPHY. C. F. Keil and F. Delitzsch, *Joshua, Judges, Ruth*, reprinted 1950, pp. 398–426; Samuel Ridout, *Lectures on the Book of Judges*, pp. 184–226; G. L. Robinson, 'Samson', *ISBE*, pp. 2675 ff.; C. F. Burney, *The Book of Judges*, 1920, pp. 335 ff.; J. Garstang, *Joshua-Judges*, 1931, pp. 334 ff.; F. F. Bruce, 'Judges', *NBC*, pp. 251–254.

J.R.

SAMUEL. Samuel, the last and greatest of the judges (Acts xiii. 20) and the first of the prophets (Acts iii. 24), was evidently considered in Old Testament times the greatest figure since Moses (Je. xv. 1). He was also Eli's successor in the priesthood, and 1 Sa. xiii. 13 implies that he alone was entitled to offer sacrifices.

He was a son of Elkanah, a pious Ephraimite, and of his wife, Hannah. Hannah, who had long been childless, made a vow that if God granted her a son he would be dedicated to the service of the sanctuary. His father was of Levite descent but not of the Aaronic line (1 Ch. vi. 33 f.). Samuel belonged to the province of Ramah, but it is nowhere stated that its chief town, Ramah, which gave its name to the province, was his birthplace or that he made his home there. In fact, the Hebrew wording in 1 Sa. xxviii. 3 implies that his city was other than Ramah; had this not been the case, the wording would simply have been: 'in the city of Ramah'. The phrase 'to come to Ramah' is used of the province (*cf.* 1 Sa. xix. 22). His name is sometimes associated with one of the smaller towns (1 Sa. xix. 18, 19), or 'daughters' as they were called in Hebrew (*cf., e.g.*, Jdg. xi. 26). His name means 'name of God', or 'a godly name'. It was probably part of a sentence spoken by Hannah at his birth. The full sentence would have been in some such form as: 'I asked for him *a godly name*'.

When Samuel was weaned, probably at the age of two or three, his mother brought him to Shiloh and formally dedicated him and left him with Eli. Her magnificent song of praise is recorded in 1 Sa. ii. 1–10, ending on the prophetic note of the messianic King.

Samuel, while still a lad, was favoured with a divine revelation (iii. 1–21). It concerned the downfall of the house of Eli, and it was only with reluctance that he communicated it to Eli. He grew in stature in the eyes of the people, and all the land knew that Samuel had been entrusted with a prophet's office by the Lord (iii. 20).

The tragic defeat of Israel and the loss of the ark, used as a talisman against the Philistines, with Eli's two sons among the slain, spelt the end of Eli's succession, and the rejection of the Aaronic priesthood. Although it is not explicitly stated, Samuel, the only person who came in question, took over the reins from the deceased Eli (*cf.* iv. 1).

When we next meet him, after a long interval, he is calling the people to national repentance, and to a re-dedication (vii. 3). The reference to 'judging' in vii. 6 is probably in regard to religious matters. Knowing only too well the shortness of the human memory, he erects a permanent reminder of their vows (vii. 12). As head of secular affairs, he made a circuit to judge Israel (vii. 16).

Samuel's sons were no better than Eli's. Their wickedness caused grave discontent with the hierarchical system and brought about a demand for its alternative—a monarchy, the common form of rule in neighbouring nations. God tells him to acquiesce, but he is allowed to give them a warning of the price they will have to pay in conscription, taxation, and serfdom (viii. 11–18).

An interesting sidelight is thrown on the private life of Samuel in ix. 1–24. It is hard to believe that there are some to whom it does not seem axiomatic that all men, great and small, have private as well as public lives. One has only to think of the place that religion had in the private lives of, say, W. E. Gladstone and Michael Faraday, which was unknown to many of their contemporaries. The theory that professes to detect here a primitive document lacks all objective support, as well as outraging the canons of common sense. The picture we have of Samuel is of a man deeply exercised spiritually, holding a retreat, doubtless for the purpose of inculcating true religion, which is always a personal thing involving the necessity of the leader making himself accessible to those whom he hopes to influence. He is at the same time deeply involved in the affairs of state, to the extent of being entrusted with the anointing of a national head. This event is the humble seed from which sprang the tree of the Monarchy. There are many parallels in history. An incident that turns a man into a 'kingmaker' could never be considered irrelevant.

Saul's inability to discern between the material and the spiritual was a source of great grief to Samuel. He arrogated to himself priestly privileges by offering sacrifices (xiii. 9) and was severely rebuked by Samuel. After the defeat of the Amalekites, Saul disobeyed the divine instructions, and Samuel treated him as a reprobate (xv. 10 ff.), and made no more official visits to him. See SAUL.

Samuel is now commissioned to initiate proceedings for the anointing of Saul's successor, and is sent to the family of David. The reaction of the elders of Bethlehem to his coming indicates unmistakably the greatness of the power wielded by him. Again when David sought refuge with Samuel, even Saul knew better than to exercise force against the prophet; he merely sent messengers (xix. 20).

We hear nothing more of Samuel until his death, but the national lamentation (xxviii. 3) indicates that he had not suffered eclipse. How much Saul had leaned upon him is brought out by his pathetic attempt to consult Samuel with the aid of the medium of Endor.

Samuel died before he saw the boy whom he had anointed become Israel's greatest king. In fact, at the time of his death David was being hunted by Saul in the wilderness of En-gedi. Samuel is one of the key figures in Israel's history, and his name is enshrined among the heroes of the faith in Heb. xi.

BIBLIOGRAPHY. E. Robertson, 'Samuel and Saul', *BJRL*, XXVIII, 1944, pp. 175 ff.; A. H. Edelkoort, *De Profeet Samuel*, 1955; see also bibliography under SAUL. W.J.M.

SAMUEL, BOOKS OF. The Books of Samuel record Israel's transition from a theocracy to a monarchy, the reign of Saul, and the active reign of David. The lives and acts of Samuel, of Saul, and of David provide a rough threefold division. The period covered is approximately one hundred years, from *c.* 1050 to 950 BC.

The Books of Samuel were treated by the Hebrew scribes as one book, as is shown by the marginal note to 1 Sa. xxviii. 24, which states that it is 'half of the book'.

I. AUTHORSHIP

The authorship or authors of the books are not implicitly mentioned. Samuel may well have been joint author with Nathan and Gad, as the statement in 1 Ch. xxix. 29 seems to imply: 'And the matters of David the king, the first and the last, they are written in the records of Samuel the seer, and of Nathan the prophet, and of Gad the prophet-seer.' It is explicitly said that Samuel himself made written records (1 Sa. x. 25).

II. CONTENTS OF 1 SAMUEL

The book begins with an account of the birth of Samuel. The collateral information about his family background throws interesting light on the practice and state of religion at this period, as does also the account of Eli, the high priest.

a. The career of Samuel

In the first chapter we have a description of a family embittered by domestic strife, so deep rooted that even the solemn religious exercises cannot temporarily eradicate it. The glimpse we are given of the depravity of the priesthood (ii. 12 ff.) is no less unsavoury. Elkanah himself was a gracious and affectionate husband, and Hannah was a gifted woman of deep piety. When her faith was rewarded by the gift of a son she gave expression to one of the great songs of the Old Testament (ii. 1–10).

God sent Eli two warnings, one by the mouth of a man of God (ii. 27 ff.), and the other by a special revelation to Samuel (iii. 4 ff.). Samuel, under pressure from Eli, revealed the contents of the message, and Eli received it without any show of resentment. Eli's failure to restrain his dissolute sons (iii. 13) was the cause of God's rejection of his house. The defeat of Israel by the Philistines and the loss of the ark as well as the death of his two sons brought about the old man's death (iv. 17 f.).

The Philistines placed the ark in the temple of Dagon, but the divine retributions that followed made its presence highly unwelcome, and they decided to return it. The ark was placed on a cart drawn by two cows deprived of their calves, but despite this they made straight for Beth-shemesh. The association of tumours with what was probably a species of rat seems to indicate an outburst of the bubonic plague (vi. 10 ff.). See EMERODS. When the ark arrived in Israel it was eventually deposited in the house of Abinadab, where it remained until removed by David (2 Sa. vi. 4).

Samuel was now not only head of the state but also supreme in spiritual matters. He saw it, therefore, as his first duty to recall the people to God. His secular duties involved him in making a yearly circuit of three centres, where he judged the people. When Samuel became old (or elderly) he shared his judicial responsibilities with his two sons, appointing them judges in the district of Beersheba. Their dishonest practices raised a storm of protest from the elders of Israel, followed by a demand for a king. In answer to his prayer, God bade Samuel acquiesce, but at the same time to warn the people of the heavy price involved (viii. 9 ff.). The people, however, were not to be dissuaded from their demand; the hierarchy had been a failure.

b. Anointing and accession of Saul

Samuel was in his own native district (country of Zuph) conducting what was probably a religious retreat when God apprised him of the visit of the man who was to be king. While the assembly was a provincial one, it is abundantly clear that Samuel's action with regard to Saul was not that of a local seer, as the young ass-breeder, with his mercenary background, supposed him to be. When Saul and Samuel met, seemingly by accident, Samuel invited him to his feast and made him chief guest. On the next morning, he anointed Saul as a token of the divine choice. Later the divine choice was demonstrated publicly when Saul was identified, probably by lot (x. 20 f.). He soon vindicated his choice by defeating the Ammonites (xi. 11). Samuel gathered the people at Gilgal and the people acclaimed Saul as their king (xi. 14).

Samuel, in preparation for his retirement from secular affairs, made a speech in which he recounted the great acts of God on behalf of Israel. His claim to have served the people faithfully and honestly was confirmed by them. Finally, he assured them of his continued prayer for them. He encouraged them to serve God and warned them of the tragic consequences of wickedness (xii. 1 ff.).

Saul was now king, but he made the fatal mistake of interfering in religious matters. He first gave offence by undertaking priestly duties (xiii. 9). Samuel arrived at the critical moment and rebuked him for his folly, which was to have as a consequence the rejection of his house.

His second offence was the flagrant disobedience of the divine command to exterminate the Amalekites (xv. 3). Samuel censured him and reminded him that obedience is better than ritual. Right ritual is no substitute for a right heart. He was again told that God had rejected him. Samuel agreed to Saul's request to keep up public appearances, an indication of Saul's preoccupation with externals (xv. 30). Samuel put or had Agag put to death. The translation 'to hew in pieces' has nothing to justify it. Samuel now broke off relations with Saul and he paid him no more visits. (The verb 'to see' in verse 35 is often used in the sense of 'to visit', *cf.* 2 Sa. xiii. 5.)

God's answer to Samuel's subsequent depression was to commission him to anoint the man who would ultimately be Saul's successor. God often subjected His future servants to prolonged preparation.

David was brought to the notice of Saul (xvi. 18), possibly through one of Samuel's friends. xvi. 22 is probably resumptive: 'Now Saul *had* sent to Jesse'. The expression 'to stand before' means to be in 'someone's service'; it does not mean 'to remain'. David was made *an* armour-bearer, possibly an honorary title.

c. David and Goliath

The Philistines and the Israelites were in a state of war, and the armies had taken up their positions. David, probably no longer required by a restored Saul, was back home. To his other duties was added that of supplying his brothers with rations as they waited in readiness. The expression 'going and returning *from* Saul' indicates that he was habitually at home. 'Saul' here simply means 'Saul's army'.

Goliath, a giant over 9 feet tall, carrying 125 lb. of armour, appeared in the intervening space between the two armies, challenging the Israelites to settle the matter by single combat (xvii. 1 ff.). David saw him on one of his visits and offered to accept the challenge. Saul, of course, had to give his approval (xvii. 37). David relied on his dexterity with a sling. He was probably accustomed to using stones about 1 lb. in weight. With a speed of 100–150 miles an hour, a stone from a sling was a lethal weapon. His accuracy was probably not a whit behind that of the men of Gibeah, who could sling at a hair and not miss (Jdg. xx. 16). His very first stone struck Goliath's forehead, and he fell either unconscious or dead. David made sure of his victim by using the giant's sword to cut off his head.

David, hitherto one among hundreds of similar youths about the camp, was now the centre of attention. Saul's failure to recognize David may have been due to the nature of his mental illness, or to the fact that there must always have been great numbers of young men milling about the court. The interval, too, between their two meetings may have been fairly long, and David's appearance might have changed considerably. The fact is that David, hitherto one of many, was now the great national hero. A public proclamation would have to be made, and David would have to be properly acclaimed. He had also become Saul's potential son-in-law. Knowing as we do the subsequent career of David, it is hard for us to realize that he was once an unknown country lad. To be fair to any event in history, we must try to recover the synchronic view.

A more significant triumph than the defeat of Goliath was the winning of the friendship of Jonathan (xviii. 1–4). It was made possible by the unjealous nature of the king's son.

d. David and Saul

David was given a great public ovation, and the women expressed themselves in song. Saul was displeased when he heard greater exploits being ascribed to David than to himself. This caused a recurrence of the old trouble. By now, he or his courtiers would have learned from David that he had already attended on the king. Once again David was asked to play to him. Saul twice in fits of mad jealousy tried to spear David. It was probably attributed to the strain of battle. These periods of mental trouble were in all probability intermittent, and only his most intimate associates would know about them (xviii. 8–11).

Saul gave David his daughter Michal (xviii. 27). When Saul subsequently again tried to kill David he fled, and, with the co-operation of his wife, eluded the men sent in pursuit. In connection with the subterfuge adopted by Michal to delay David's pursuers by representing to them that David was ill in bed, the object she used to take the place of David's body is called *teraphim*. In this context it would seem that a single object about the size of a man was used. Elsewhere it seems to indicate a number of small images (xix. 12 ff.).

David fled to Samuel, who, as the spiritual head and father of the people, was immune from Saul's attacks (xix. 18–24). Samuel was in Naioth, a provincial town in Ramah. Here he seemed to be acting as head of a college for prophets, whose main duty probably was to maintain the spiritual life of the nation. Similar institutions for the training of scribes had existed in the ancient Semitic East from earliest times. Saul did not use force against Samuel and had to content himself with sending messengers. Three delegations in all were sent, and each in turn was overpowered with the spirit of prophecy. Finally, when Saul himself went, he too began to prophesy. The saying that had become proverbial (x. 12) was now again on the lips of the spectators. The expression 'they were saying' implies that it was being repeated on all sides. It is here taken for granted that it was already well known. The 'therefore' must refer to Saul's behaviour on this occasion as the cause of the recollection, not of the origin, of the proverb (xix. 24).

David enlisted the help of Jonathan to find out the real intentions of his father. Jonathan discovered that Saul was determined to destroy David (xx. 1–24). Jonathan reported to David the facts, but encouraged David by expressing the conviction that he would ultimately win.

e. David's wanderings

David was compelled to become a fugitive (xxi. 1 ff.). He visited Ahimelech, the priest at Nob, and obtained from him bread and the sword of Goliath. This friendly help cost Ahimelech and his house, with the exception of Abiathar, one of his sons, their lives at the hands of Saul (xxii. 6–23).

David made his headquarters at Adullam, and was joined by his father's house as well as a band of fugitives and malcontents (xxii. 1–5). Realizing that the situation might be prolonged indefinitely, David placed his parents with the king of Moab. On the advice of Gad, the prophet, David himself moved to Judah (xxii. 5).

David had now sufficiently organized and trained his men so that he could take the offensive even against Philistine raiders. He delivered Keilah from their hands, but they, far from grateful, were later prepared to betray him to Saul (xxiii. 1–14).

David withdrew to the wilderness of Ziph (xxiii. 14). The Ziphites informed Saul (xxiii. 19), and later again revealed David's whereabouts to him (xxvi. 1 f.). David must have learned of their first betrayal, and as long as he was at large the Ziphites were exposed to his vengeance. The accounts of the two incidents of David's brushes with Saul have in common only the persons of the informers (xxiv. 1–23, xxvi. 1–25). The places are different: En-gedi (xxiv. 1) and the hill or hills of Hachilah in the wilderness of Ziph (xxvi. 1 f.). In the first David cut off Saul's skirt (xxiv. 4), and in the second he removed spear and water-jar (xxvi. 11). On the first occasion David was deferential (xxiv. 8), on the second defiant (xxvi. 14). As a consequence of the first, David's spirit was unbroken (xxiv. 22); after the second he was despondent (xxvii. 1). To effect such a change in a man of David's temperament would require a long period. There was probably, therefore, an interval of several years between the two incidents. Repetition of similar incidents is not unknown to history. The two escapes of Charles II in the vicinity of Boscobel House provide one instance.

The disheartened David now took the drastic step of seeking asylum with Achish, the Philistine king of Gath, who allowed him to reside in Ziklag (xxvii. 1–12). Even from here David found opportunities of helping his own people by raiding those hostile to them. He gained the confidence of Achish but not of his commanders, and when a major attack was planned against Israel they objected to the presence of David (xxix. 1–11). David, who had already started out with them, returned to find Ziklag pillaged by Amalekites, and the inhabitants, including his own two wives, carried off. He caught up with the raiders and destroyed them, recovered all that was lost and took much spoil, some of which he sent to the elders of Judah (xxx. 1–31).

f. Death of Saul

In xxviii. 1–25 we have the account of the distracted Saul seeking by means of the medium of Endor the help of the deceased Samuel. The apparition announced defeat for Israel and death for Saul and his sons. This disaster overtook Saul in the battle with the Philistines on Mt. Gilboa (xxxi. 1–13).

III. CONTENTS OF 2 SAMUEL

David now becomes the central figure, and, as the book is mainly concerned with his doings, the unity of the narrative is seldom interrupted by digressions.

It opens with the arrival of an Amalekite, who claims to have come straight from the battlefield of Mt. Gilboa and to have killed Saul at his own request (2 Sa. i. 1–16). If this story is true, then 1 Sa. xxxi. 5 should be translated 'When the armour-bearer saw that Saul was dying', which is possible. For Saul, the man entrusted with the task of exterminating the Amalekites, to receive his death-blow from an Amalekite would add the final touch to his tragedy. We have now no means of confirming whether the Amalekite's story was true or not, but that does not affect the truth of the record of it. David's treatment of the Amalekite was probably dictated by his view of the inviolability of the person of the one in authority.

The pathos of David's lament for Saul and Jonathan is deeply moving (i. 17–27). Verse 18 is probably an archival reference (*cf.* Jos. x. 13).

David transferred his residence from Ziklag to Hebron, where the men of Judah anointed him king over Judah (ii. 1–4). Abner, Saul's commander, put Ishbosheth, Saul's son, on the throne of Israel (ii. 8 f.).

A fateful meeting later took place at Gibeon between Abner and Joab, David's nephew and later his commander. In the bloody strife that ensued, Abner, in self-defence, killed Asahel, Joab's younger brother (ii. 12–32). When later Abner quarrelled with Ishbosheth, he determined to give his allegiance to David and to bring Israel with him. On returning from negotiations with David, he was pursued and murdered by Joab (iii. 6–29).

After Abner's death, two men, probably thinking to ingratiate themselves with David, murdered Ishbosheth. When they came to tell David he had them put to death (iv. 1–12).

The Israelites came to Hebron and invited David to become their leader (v. 1–5). David's next exploit was the capture of Jerusalem (v. 6–10). David became great and embarked on a building programme. In this he was helped by Hiram, king of Tyre (v. 10–12). When Israel's old enemies, the Philistines, decided to attack, David routed them (v. 17–25).

David then turned to the restoration of the religious life of his people. He had the ark brought from the house of Abinadab (1 Sa. vii. 1) to Jerusalem (vi. 1–23). He then proposed to proceed with the building of a house for God, but God informed him through Nathan that this work was reserved for his son (vii. 1–29).

A résumé of David's chief conquests, including the defeat of the Aramaeans of Zobah, is given in viii. 1–14.

David honoured his covenant with Jonathan by seeking out Mephibosheth, his one surviving son. David restored to him the family estates and treated him as one of his own sons (ix. 1–13).

David's success brought with it leisure and inactivity. In an idle hour he spied Bathsheba, the wife of Uriah, one of his faithful officers, and she visited him in her husband's absence. He added to his sin by having Uriah put in a position that resulted in his death. Over and above, Joab, his cruel and unprincipled commander, had to be enlisted as an accomplice. He was the sort of man who would exploit such a situation to the very utmost of his ability. Nathan, by means of a parable, brought David to see how reprehensible his behaviour had been (xi. 1–xii. 14). The child of the illicit union died. The next child born to Bathsheba was Solomon (xii. 24, 25).

Joab defeated the Ammonites and sent for David to accept the capitulation of Rabbah (modern Amman). The inhabitants were subjected to the most arduous forms of toil (xii. 26–31). In 1 Ch. xx. 1–3, where the incident is referred to, the verb 'to put', through the loss of part of the final letter, has become 'to saw'.

Absalom, David's son, after he had murdered his brother Amnon, fled (xiii. 1–19). Joab tried to effect a reconciliation between him and his father (xiv. 1–24). The seed of rebellion, however, had been sown in Absalom's heart, and by a trick he succeeded in getting two hundred of David's leading men to Hebron, and, while there, proclaimed his rebellion (xv. 7–12).

David abandoned Jerusalem. Few episodes in history are so fully recorded as this flight (xv. 13–xvi. 14). One of David's most trusted counsellors, Ahithophel, went over to Absalom. Hushai, another counsellor, though with Absalom, remained faithful to David and rendered Ahithophel's work ineffective (xvi. 15–xvii. 23).

David took the field against Absalom and defeated him near the forest of Ephraim. Joab killed Absalom, contrary to the king's express command. David's great grief made it impossible for him to celebrate the victory (xviii. 1–33).

David returned to Jerusalem. Soon he had to deal with the rebellion of Sheba, a Benjamite. The rebellion collapsed when Sheba was beheaded by some of his own followers (xx. 1–26).

In xxi. 15–22 we have a brief account of the repercussions of the blood-feud that inevitably followed David's slaying of Goliath. The incidents mentioned are probably only the most notable attempts made by Goliath's kin to avenge his ignominious death. Although these clashes seem to have taken place in times of war, a blood-feud goes on incessantly. If the reading omitting 'the brother of' in verse 19 (*cf.* 1 Ch. xx. 5, where it is present) is the right one, it would not be at all surprising to find one of the connection called after such a mighty kinsman.

David's song of deliverance (xxii. 1–51) has been included in the Psalter (Ps. xviii). The minor differences between them could be due either to transcriptional errors or to changes made by David himself.

The last words of David are found in xxiii. 1–7. Then follows a list of his mighty men with a brief mention of some of their exploits. This side-light on the mettle of his men helps to explain his great military successes (xxiii. 8–39).

David decided to take a census, and discovered that he had at his disposal 800,000 men. This may have given him a false confidence in his own resources. David became conscious of his guilt. He was given the choice of three kinds of punishment. David cast himself upon the mercy of the Lord who sent the pestilence, the briefest of the three. David set up an altar at the threshing-floor of Araunah, where the destroying angel had stood. The threshing-floor was on Mt. Moriah (2 Ch. iii. 1), the spot where God had provided a substitute for Isaac (Gn. xxii. 8), and not far from this spot stood the cross.

IV. CONCLUSION

The Books of Samuel cover one of the most formative periods in Israel's development. It is history at its best. Here we have the portrait of David, the great king and psalmist, a portrait that is unsurpassed in any history. While there is much in these books that reflects the low standards of the age, there are also great ethical peaks. Stress now begins to be laid on the distinction between the visible forms of worship and the realities behind them.

BIBLIOGRAPHY. Commentaries by H. P. Smith, *ICC*, 1912; R. de Vaux, *Bible de Jérusalem*, 1953; G. B. Caird, *IB*, II, 1953; H. W. Hertzberg, *Das Alte Testament Deutsch*, 1956; A. van den Born, 1956; with S. R. Driver, *Notes on the Hebrew Text and Topography of the Books of Samuel*, 1913; P. A. H. de Boer, *Research into the Text of 1 Samuel i–xvi*, 1938; *id.*, '1 Samuel xvii', *Oudtestamentische Studiën*, I, 1942, and '1 Samuel xviii–xxxi', *ibid.*, VI, 1949. W.J.M.

SANBALLAT. The name is Babylonian, *Sin-uballiṭ*, *i.e.* 'Sin (the moon-god) has given life'. In Ne. ii. 10, 19, xiii. 28 he is called the Horonite, probably denoting that he came from Beth-horon, about 18 miles north-west of Jerusalem (*cf.* Jos. x. 10, *etc.*). He was one of the chief opponents of Nehemiah. The Elephantine Papyri show that in 407 BC he was governor of Samaria. If when Nehemiah came in 445 BC he was either governor or hoping to be governor, he doubtless wanted to have control of Judaea also. The Elephantine Papyri speak of his two sons, Delaiah and Shelemiah, and these names may show that Sanballat was a worshipper of Yahweh. This means that he was descended either from an Israelite family which had not gone into captivity in 721 BC or from one of the peoples whom the Assyrian kings had imported into Palestine. In either case his religion was probably syncretistic (2 Ki. xvii. 33), though he put Yahweh first, and so won sympathy even from the high priest's family, into which his daughter married (Ne. xiii. 28). Josephus (*Ant.* xi. 7. 2) makes Sanballat responsible for the building of the Samaritan temple, which he dates about 330 BC. If the story is true, Josephus has confused the date; though there could have been a second governor with the same name.

BIBLIOGRAPHY. H. H. Rowley, 'Sanballat and the Samaritan Temple', *BJRL*, XXXVIII, 1955–6, pp. 166 ff. J.S.W.

SANCTIFICATION, SANCTIFY. This noun and verb, derived from Lat. *sanctus*, 'holy', and *facere*, 'to make', translate Heb. *qdš* and Gk. *hagiasmos*, *hagiazō*.

The basic sense of the Heb. root *qdš* is variously given as (i) 'set apart', (ii) 'brightness'. The former may underlie holiness or sanctification in terms of position, status, relationship, where the words are translated 'cut off', 'separated', 'set apart for exclusive use', 'dedicated', or 'consecrated', 'regarded as sacred or holy in contrast to common, profane, or secular'. The latter may underlie those usages which relate to condition, state, or process, leading on in the New Testament to the thought of an inward transformation gradually taking place, resulting in purity, moral rectitude, and holy, spiritual thoughts expressing themselves in an outward life of goodness and godliness. In this connection it should be noted that, while the verb 'sanctify' is used in the AV of the Old Testament, the noun 'holiness' is used rather than 'sanctification'.

I. IN THE OLD TESTAMENT

The two sets of meanings outlined above may be roughly designated the priestly and the prophetic, but they are not mutually exclusive. The primary reference of both is Godward.

a. God is depicted as holy in majesty, mysterious in His numinous otherness, loftily removed from man, sin, and earth (*cf.* Ex. iii. 5; Is. vi. 3 ff.).

The people are exhorted to sanctify the Lord of hosts (Is. viii. 13), and God says He will sanctify Himself and be sanctified in or by them, *i.e.* recognized in His sovereign claims (similarly He will be glorified, *i.e.* His sublimity will be acknowledged through His people's attitude and relationship to Him).

Any thing or person sanctified is recognized as set apart by God as well as by man (*e.g.* sabbath, Gn. ii. 3; altar, Ex. xxix. 37; tabernacle, Ex. xxix. 44; garments, Lv. viii. 30; fast, Joel i. 14; house, Lv. xxvii. 14; field, Lv. xxvii. 17; people, Ex. xix. 14; congregation, Joel ii. 16; priests, Ex. xxviii. 41). This does not necessarily involve an inward change. The ceremonial ritual of the law made provision for the infringements of which the people of God, who were set apart by God to belong exclusively to Him to be used as His instruments, were guilty.

b. While these were primarily external and ritual instances of sanctification, they were sometimes accompanied by the deeper, inward reality. God's exhortation, 'Be ye holy, for I am holy', required a moral and spiritual response from the people, a reflection of His moral excellences of righteousness, purity, hatred of moral evil, loving concern for the welfare of others in obedience to His will; for the Holy One of Israel was actively engaged for the good of His people (Ex. xix. 4) as well as being separated from evil. His holiness was both transcendent and immanent (Dt. iv. 7; Ps. lxxiii. 28), and theirs was to be correspondingly characterized. The prophets were alert to the dangers of a merely outward sanctification, and so they exhorted the people to reverence the Lord; they even went so far as to disparage the external, 'holy' observances when they were not accompanied by practical holiness (Is. i. 4, 11, viii. 13). The children of Israel were derogating from the holiness of God by their unholy lives among the nations. They were failing to observe the law of holiness (Lv. xvii–xxvi) which combined admirably both the moral and ritual aspects.

II. IN THE NEW TESTAMENT

There are five references to sanctification (*hagiasmos*) and another five instances in which the same word is translated 'holiness' in AV. Five other Gk. terms are translated 'holiness' (*hagiotēs, hagiōsynē, eusebeia, hosiotēs, hieroprepēs*). As in the Old Testament, we find a twofold usage of sanctification, but there are significant differences. The two synoptic usages of the verb 'sanctify' are ceremonial or ritual. Our Lord speaks of the Temple that sanctifies the gold and the altar that sanctifies the gift (Mt. xxiii. 17, 19). Here the primary meaning is consecration; the gold and gift are dedicated, set apart, and reckoned as especially sacred and valuable by their relation to the already holy Temple and altar. In a parallel use of this concept, but one more exalted and more directly spiritual since it has to do with the personal realm, Christ sanctifies or consecrates Himself for His sacrificial work, the Father sanctifies Him, and He bids His followers 'hallow' (regard with sacred reverence, devote a unique position to) the Father (Jn. xvii. 19, x. 36; Mt. vi. 9). A further extension of the thought comes in Christ's sanctifying of the people with His own blood (Heb. xiii. 12) and possibly in Jn. xvii. 17 the Father's sanctifying of the believers through the word of truth.

Concerning the latter and kindred texts the word 'possibly' is used advisedly because the idea of 'sanctification' here widens its meaning in the direction of a moral and spiritual change. The Epistle to the Hebrews forms a bridge between the external and internal meanings of sanctification. Christ by His sacrifice sanctifies His brethren not only in the sense of setting them apart but also in that of equipping them for the worship and service of God. This He does by making propitiation for their sins (Heb. ii. 17) and cleansing their consciences from dead works (Heb. ix. 13 ff.). This sanctification, however, is not conceived of primarily as a process but as an accomplished fact, for 'by one offering he hath perfected for ever them that are sanctified' (Heb x. 10, 14). At the same time the exhortation t grow in sanctification is not absent (*cf.* Heb. xi 14, where holiness is more of a state than status).

While 'sanctification' in Hebrews is somewha akin to 'justification' in such Epistles as Roman and Galatians, the distinction between the usage of 'sanctification' in these writings must not b overdrawn. Paul uses the term in two senses also In some cases he regards it as a status conferre upon believers who are in Christ for sanctification as for justification. The derived word 'saint refers primarily to their status in Christ ('sanctified in Christ Jesus', 1 Cor. i. 2; *cf.* 1 Pet. i. 2) A vicarious sanctification is the privilege of th non-Christian partner and children when on parent is a believer; this again is status-sanctification (1 Cor. vii. 14).

The second meaning of sanctification in Pau concerns the moral and spiritual transformatio of the justified believer who is regenerated, give new life, by God. The will of God is our sanctification (1 Thes. iv. 3), and to be sanctifie wholly is to be conformed to the image of Chris and so to realize in experience what it is to be i the image of God. Christ is the content and norm of the sanctified life: it is His risen life that i reproduced in the believer as he grows in grac and reflects the glory of his Lord. In this progressive experience of liberation from the lette of the law, man's spirit is set free by the Lord th Spirit (2 Cor. iii. 17, 18). The Holy Spirit is th operator in man's sanctification, but He work through the word of truth and the prayer o faith, and through the fellowship of believer (Eph. v. 26) as they test themselves in the light o the ideal of the love of the Spirit and the indispensability of holiness (Heb. xii. 14). Faith itself produced by the Spirit, lays hold of th sanctifying resources.

As justification implies deliverance from th penalty of sin, so sanctification implies deliverance from the pollutions, privations, and potenc of sin. As to the intensity and extensiveness an steps of this latter deliverance, however, there i much discussion. The prayer that God wi sanctify the believers wholly so that their whol spirit, soul, and body be preserved blameles unto the coming of Christ is followed by th assertion that 'faithful is he that calleth you, wh also will do it' (1 Thes. v. 23, 24). This raise three important questions.

a. Will God do it all at once?

Does sanctification by faith mean that comple sanctification is received as a gift in the sam manner as justification, so that the believer instantaneously made holy and enters once fo all into actual, practical holiness as a state? Som would urge that at a crisis-experience, subseque to conversion, the old man is crucified once fo all, and the root of sin extracted or the princip of sin eradicated. Some would go further an would stress the need for the reception and th exercise of the gifts of the Spirit (notably the gift of tongues) as evidence of such a work of the Spirit. Others consider that New Testament teaching is definitely opposed to this view and that the very existence of the Epistles with their reasoned statements of doctrine, arguments, appeals, and exhortations, contradicts it. See also below.

b. Will God do it all within the believer's lifetime? Among both those who emphasize the crisis-character of the experience of sanctification and those who see it rather as a process are some who claim for themselves very high attainments of sanctified living. Underlining such injunctions as 'Be ye therefore perfect' (Mt. v. 48), and not interpreting 'perfection' here as meaning 'maturity', they maintain that perfect love is achievable in this life. High claims in the direction of 'sinless perfection', however, usually minimize both the description of sin and the standard of moral living required. Sin is defined as 'the voluntary transgression of a known law' (Wesley) rather than as 'any want of conformity unto, or transgression of, the law of God' (*Westminster Shorter Catechism*), the latter being a definition which covers our sinful state and sins of omission as well as sins openly and deliberately committed. Others, agreeing that unbroken holiness and unblemished perfection may not be possible, claim that it is possible nevertheless to have the perfect possession of the perfect motive of love.

A minimizing of the standard occurs in C. G. Finney's claim that the Bible 'expressly limits obligation by ability'. 'The very language of the law', he writes, 'is such as to level its claims to the capacity of the subject however great or small that subject may be. "Thou shalt love the Lord thy God with all thy heart, with all thy soul, with all thy mind, and with all thy strength." Here then it is plain, that all the law demands, is the exercise of whatever strength we have, in the service of God. Now as entire sanctification consists in perfect obedience to the law of God, and as the law requires nothing more than the right use of whatever strength we have, it is, of course, forever settled, that a state of entire sanctification is attainable in this life, on the ground of natural ability' (*Systematic Theology*, 1851, p. 407). This is based on a lamentable misunderstanding of Dt. vi. 5.

c. Will God do it all without the believer's activity? Those who minimize sin and the standard of holiness God requires are in danger of placing undue stress on human enterprise in sanctification. There is, however, an opposite extreme which lays the entire onus of sanctification on God. He is expected to produce a saint instantaneously, or gradually to infuse a Christian with grace or the Spirit. This is to reduce man to a mere robot with no moral fibre and thus virtually to produce an immoral sanctification—which is a contradiction in terms. Those who are concerned for the intrinsic character of human spirit deny such impersonal operations of the Holy Spirit. They are also dubious of the claims that the Spirit works directly upon the unconscious, rather than through the conscious, processes of man's mind.

The believer is to have no illusions about the intensity of the struggle with sin (Rom. vii, viii; Gal. v), but should realize also that sanctification does not occur in instalments merely by his own endeavours to counteract his own evil tendencies. There is a progression of moral accomplishment but there is also a mysterious, sanctifying work within him. Moreover, it is not merely a synergism whereby the Spirit and the believer each contribute something. The action is attributable both to the Spirit and to the believer in the paradox of grace. God the Spirit works through the faithful recognition of the law of truth and the believer's response of love, and the net result is spiritual maturity expressed in the fulfilling of the law of love to one's neighbour. The consummation of sanctification to the believer who, by gracious faith in the work of Christ, by the Spirit 'purifieth himself' (1 Jn. iii. 3), is indicated by the assurance: 'we know that, when he shall appear, we shall be like him; for we shall see him as he is' (1 Jn. iii. 2). See HOLY SPIRIT, SALVATION.

BIBLIOGRAPHY. W. Marshall, *The Gospel Mystery of Sanctification*, 1692, reprinted 1955; J. Wesley, *A Plain Account of Christian Perfection*, reprinted 1952; C. Hodge, *Systematic Theology*, 1871–3, III; J. C. Ryle, *Holiness*, reprinted 1952; B. B. Warfield, *Perfectionism*, 2 vols., 1931; R. E. D. Clark, *Conscious and Unconscious Sin*, 1934; N. H. Snaith, *The Distinctive Ideas of the Old Testament*, 1944; D. M. Lloyd-Jones, *Christ our Sanctification*, 1948; G. C. Berkouwer, *Faith and Sanctification*, 1952; W. E. Sangster, *The Path to Perfection*[5], 1957. G.W.

SANCTUARY. The Hebrew words *miqdāš*, and its correlative *qōḏeš*, define a place set apart for the worship of God or gods. Whereas the Bible uses these words almost entirely of the place where Yahweh was worshipped, a study of cognate languages such as Canaanite shows that the same terms were used for the worship of the earlier inhabitants of Palestine. Excavation has revealed a wide variety of sanctuaries extending back to the fourth millennium BC. The most complete range of these at present known was excavated at Megiddo. A considerable variety of cult images and tools is now available for study.

Israel's earliest sanctuary was the movable tent known as the tabernacle (*q.v.*), where the ark containing the tables of the covenant was housed (Ex. xxv. 8, *etc.*). Detailed descriptions of the various parts of this structure occur in Ex. xxv–xxxi and xxxvi–xl, and the elaborate ritual associated with it is detailed in Leviticus.

With the settlement of Israel in the land, David planned, and Solomon completed, a permanent place of worship (1 Ch. xxii. 19, xxviii. 10, *etc.*).

Apostasy during the days of the kings brought foreign cult-practices into the Temple. Ezekiel and Zephaniah reproached God's people for defiling His sanctuary (Ezk. v. 11, xxiii. 39, xxviii. 18, *etc.*; Zp. iii. 4).

Israel's early sanctuaries were set up in the places where God appeared to His people or 'caused his name to dwell'. Finally Jerusalem became the official centre of worship. (See HIGH PLACE, TEMPLE.) J.A.T.

SAND (Heb. *ḥôl*; Gk. *ammos*). The Hebrew word derives from the verb *ḥûl* ('to whirl, dance'), doubtless a reference to the ease with which the light particles of silex, mica, felspar, *etc.*, are lifted and whirled by the wind. Sand is found extensively along the Mediterranean shores of S Palestine and Egypt, and in desert regions, thus providing a striking symbol of countless multitude (*e.g.* Gn. xxii. 17; Is. x. 22; Rev. xx. 8). It is used also to convey an idea of weight (Jb. vi. 3) and instability (Mt. vii. 26). A somewhat obscure allusion (Dt. xxxiii. 19, RSV) speaks of 'the hidden treasures of the sand', perhaps a reference to the manufacture of glass from sand (*cf.* Jos., *BJ* ii. 10. 2; Pliny, *Natural History* v. 17, xxxvi. 65). In Jb. xxix. 18, for 'sand' we should probably read 'phoenix' (so RVmg), but see full discussion by S. R. Driver and G. B. Gray in *ICC*, *Job*, 1921, pp. 201–204. J.D.D.

SANDAL. See DRESS.

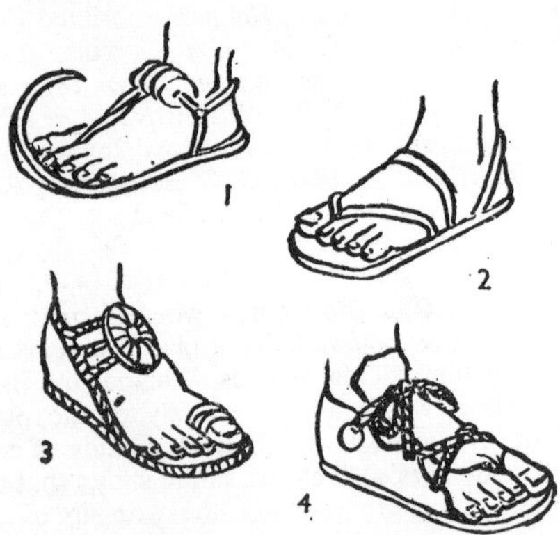

Fig. 178. Types of sandal: 1. Egyptian; 2. Greek; 3. Babylonian; 4. Roman.

SANHEDRIN, the transcription used in the Talmud for Gk. *synedrion* (from which Heb. *sanhedrîn* is a loan-word). Both before and at the time of Christ, it was the name for the highest tribunal of the Jews which met in Jerusalem and also for various lesser tribunals. In EVV the term is often translated 'council'. There are parallels in classical writings to similar courts in Greece and Rome. Josephus used the word for the council that governed the five districts into which the Roman Gabinius, proconsul of Syria 57–55 BC, divided Judaea (*Ant.* xiv. 5. 4, *BJ* i. 8. 5). Josephus first uses it of the Jews when referring to the summoning of the young Herod before it for alleged misdemeanours (*Ant.* xiv. 9. 3–5). In the New Testament the term refers either to the supreme Jewish court (Mt. xxvi. 59; Mk. xiv. 55; Lk. xxii. 66; Jn. xi. 47; Acts iv. 15, v. 21 ff., vi. 12 ff., xxii. 30, xxiii. 1 ff., xxiv. 20) or simply to any court of justice (Mt. v. 22). In a few cases other words are substituted for *synedrion, e.g. presbyterion*, 'body of elders' (Lk. xxii. 66; Acts xxii. 5), and *gerousia*, 'senate' (Acts v. 21).

I. HISTORY

The history of the Sanhedrin is not clear at all points. Traditionally it originated with the seventy elders who assisted Moses (Nu. xi. 16–24). Ezra is supposed to have reorganized this body after the Exile. The Persians gave authority to the Jews in local affairs (Ezr. vii. 25, 26, x. 14), and it is possible that the elders of Ezr. v. 5, 9, vi. 7, 14, x. 8, and the rulers of Ne. ii. 16, iv. 14, 19, v. 7, vii. 5, made up a body which resembled the later Sanhedrin. Later, the Greeks permitted a body known as the *gerousia* ('senate') which was made up of elders and represented the nation (Jos., *Ant.* xii. 3. 3; 1 Macc. xii. 3, 6, xiv. 20). In the days of the Seleucids this *gerousia* had dealings with such rulers as Antiochus the Great in 208 BC and with Antiochus V (Jos., *Ant.* xii. 3. 3), and was then apparently composed of elders drawn from the aristocracy (Jos., *Ant.* xiii. 5. 8; 1 Macc. xii. 6; 2 Macc. i. 10, iv. 44, xi. 27). In the days of the Maccabean revolt it was this council that united with Jonathan, the high priest and leader of the people, to make an alliance with Sparta (1 Macc. xii. 5 ff.), and it was they who advised him about building fortresses in Judaea (1 Macc. xii. 35; *cf.* xiii. 36, xiv. 20, 28, 47). It would appear that the high priest presided over this body.

Under the Romans, except for a short period under Gabinius, this body had wide powers. The term used for the district councils was subsequently adopted for the more powerful *gerousia* at Jerusalem, and by the close of the 1st century BC this council was known as the *synedrion*, though other terms such as *gerousia* and *boulē* ('council') were also used at times. It was Julius Caesar who reversed the plan of Gabinius and extended the power of the Sanhedrin once again over all Judaea (Jos., *Ant.* xiv. 9. 3–5, *BJ* i. 10. 7). Under the procurators (AD 6–66) the powers of the Sanhedrin were extensive, the internal government of the country being in its hands (Jos., *Ant.* xx. 10), and it was recognized even among the *diaspora* (Acts ix. 2, xxii. 5, xxvi. 12) in some ways. From the days of Archelaus, son of Herod the Great, its direct powers were, however, limited to Judaea, since it had no power over Jesus while He was in Galilee. In Judaea there were, of course, the local authorities who tried cases locally but reported certain cases to the central authority. The councils (*synedria*) of Mt. v. 22, x. 17; Mk. xiii. 9, and the *boulai* of Jos., *Ant.* iv. 8. 14, *etc.* were local courts of at least seven elders, and in large towns up to twenty-three elders.

After AD 70 the Sanhedrin was abolished and replaced by the Beth Din (Court of Judgment) which met at Jabneh (AD 68–70), Usah (80–116), Shafran (140–63), Sepphoris (163–93), and Tiberias (193–220). Though regarded in the Talmud as continuous with the Sanhedrin, it was essentially different, being composed of scribes whose decisions had only theoretical value.

II. CONSTITUTION AND COMPOSITION

The constitution of the Sanhedrin was modified during the years. Originally composed basically of the predominantly Sadducean priestly aristocracy, its membership changed from the days of Queen Alexandra (76–67 BC) when Pharisees (*q.v.*) were included, as well as scribes (*q.v.*). The method of appointment is not clear, but the aristocratic origin of the body suggests direct appointment of members of ancient families, to which were added secular rulers. Under Herod, who favoured the Pharisees and desired to restrict the Sadducees (*q.v.*) and the influence of the old nobility, the Sadducean element became less prominent, and the Pharisaic element, which had been growing in strength since the days of Queen Alexandra, became more influential. In New Testament times the Great Sanhedrin in Jerusalem comprised the high priests (that is the acting high priest and those who had been high priest), members of the privileged families from which the high priests were taken, the elders (tribal and family heads of the people and the priesthood), and the scribes, that is, the legal experts. The whole comprised both Sadducees and Pharisees (Mt. xxvi. 3, 57, 59; Mk. xiv. 53, xv. 1; Lk. xxii. 66; Acts iv. 1, 5 ff., v. 17, 21, 34, xxii. 30, xxiii. 6). The members were councillors (*bouleutēs*, Mk. xv. 43; Lk. xxiii. 50), as, for example, Joseph of Arimathaea.

According to Josephus and the New Testament, the high priest at the time was president (Jos., *Ant*. iv. 8. 17, xx. 10; Mt. xxvi. 57; Acts v. 17 ff., vii. 1, ix. 1 ff., xxii. 5, xxiv. 1). Thus, Caiaphas was president at the trial of Jesus, and Ananias at the trial of Paul (Acts xxiii. 2). It would seem that in earlier times the high priest had supreme authority, but this was curbed somewhat later. The appointment was no longer hereditary, but political, and ex-high priests made up the 'rulers' (Jn. vii. 26; Acts iv. 5–8, *etc*.).

III. EXTENT OF JURISDICTION

The jurisdiction was wide at the time of Christ. It exercised not only civil jurisdiction according to Jewish law but also criminal jurisdiction in some degree. It had administrative authority and could order arrests by its own officers of justice (Mt. xxvi. 47; Mk. xiv. 43; Acts iv. 1 ff., v. 17 ff., ix. 2). It was empowered to judge cases which did not involve capital punishment (Acts iv, v). Capital cases required the confirmation of the Roman procurator (Jn. xviii. 31), though the procurator's judgment was normally in accordance with the demands of the Sanhedrin, which in Jewish law had the power of life and death (Jos., *Ant*. xiv. 9. 3, 4; Mt. xxvi. 66). In the special case where a Gentile passed the barrier which divided the inner court of the Temple from that of the Gentiles the Sanhedrin was granted the power of death by Roman administrators (Acts xxi. 28 ff.). The only case of capital punishment in connection with the Sanhedrin in the New Testament is that of our Lord. The case of Stephen, it would seem, was an illegal mob act.

A study of the New Testament will give a cross-section of the kinds of matters that came before the Sanhedrin. Thus, Jesus was charged with blasphemy (Mt. xxvi. 57 ff.; Jn. xix. 7), Peter and John were charged with teaching the people false doctrine (Acts iv), Paul with transgressing the Mosaic law (Acts xxii–xxiv). These, of course, were religious matters. But at times the collection of revenue was the responsibility of the Sanhedrin, as in the time of Florus (Jos., *BJ* ii. 17. 1). There was, however, always a theoretical check on the powers of the Sanhedrin, for the Romans reserved the right to interfere in any area whatever, if necessary independently of the Jewish court. Paul's arrest in Acts xxiii is a case in point. It is probably best to regard the Sanhedrin as having two main areas of responsibility, political (administrative and judicial) and religious. It is not always clear how these two were carried out, and some writers have even suggested two different bodies, each known as the Sanhedrin. This is probably not necessary, but is suggested because of our lack of clear knowledge of procedures.

IV. PROCEDURE

There were correct times and places for meeting. Local courts met on the second and fifth days of the week, and the Sanhedrin in Jerusalem at definite (though unknown to us) times. They did not meet on festival days and on Sabbaths.

There were proper procedures. The Sanhedrin sat in a semicircle and had two clerks of court, one to record votes of acquittal and the other votes of condemnation. Disciples attended the courts and sat in front. Prisoners attended dressed in humble fashion. In capital cases the arguments for acquittal were presented, then those for conviction. If one spoke for acquittal he could not reverse his opinion, but if he spoke for condemnation he could later change his vote. Students could speak in favour of acquittal but not for condemnation. Acquittal might be declared on the day of the trial, but condemnation must wait till the day following. In voting, members stood, beginning with the youngest. For acquittal a simple majority sufficed, for condemnation a two-thirds majority was required. If twelve of the twenty-three judges necessary for a quorum voted for acquittal, and eleven for conviction, the prisoner was discharged. If twelve voted for conviction, and eleven against, the number of judges had to be increased by two, and this was repeated up to a total of seventy-one, or until an acquittal was achieved. The benefit of the doubt was allowed to persons where the case was as doubtful as this. Indeed, always, the benefit lay with the accused (Mishnah, *Sanhedrin* v. 5).

In this regard, the legality of the trial of Christ has been discussed by many writers, and it is fairly clear that there are elements about it which point in the direction of a miscarriage of justice.

BIBLIOGRAPHY. E. Schürer, *HJP*, 1901, II. i, pp. 163–195; J. Z. Lauterbach, *Jewish Encyclopaedia*, XI, 1905, pp. 41–44; I. Abrahams, *Encyclopaedia of Religion and Ethics*, II, 1920, pp. 184, 185; H. Danby, *The Mishnah*, E.T., 1933, tractate *Sanhedrin*, pp. 382–400; *id.*, 'The Trial of Jesus', *JTS*, XXI, 1919, pp. 51–76; J. Blinzler, *The Trial of Jesus*, 1959. J.A.T.

SAPHIR (RV 'Shaphir'). A town in the Philistine plain against which Micah prophesied (Mi. i. 11). The exact site is uncertain, but may be one of the three hut settlements es-Sūāfir near Ashdod. The identification of Shaphir with Shamir (Jos. xv. 48; Jdg. x. 1, 2) is tenuous. R.J.W.

SAPPHIRA (Gk. *sappheira*, transliteration of Aram. *šappîrâ*, fem. sing., 'beautiful'). In Acts v. 1 ff. wife of Ananias, a member of the primitive Jerusalem church. The name, in Greek and Aramaic, was found on an ossuary in Jerusalem in 1923, but J. Klausner's theory (*From Jesus to Paul*, 1944, pp. 289 f.) that the Sapphira of Acts is intended requires confirmation. See ANANIAS (1). F.F.B.

SAPPHIRE. See JEWELS AND PRECIOUS STONES.

SARAH, SARAI (Heb. *śārâ*, 'princess'). The principal wife of Abram, and also his half-sister on his father Terah's side (Gn. xx. 12). She went with him from Ur of the Chaldees, through Harran, to the land of Canaan. Famine caused them to turn aside to Egypt, and as Abram feared that her outstanding beauty might endanger his life Sarai posed as his sister. Pharaoh was attracted by her and took her into his harem. Then he suspected the truth, and husband and wife were sent away.

She posed as Abraham's sister on a second occasion, at the court of Abimelech, king of Gerar, in accordance with her husband's instructions: 'This is thy kindness which thou shalt shew unto me; at every place whither we shall come, say of me, He is my brother' (Gn. xx. 13)—words which suggest a settled policy. This incident further increased Abraham's wealth, for gifts were given him as compensation to an injured husband (Gn. xx. 14).

Her barrenness was a continual reproach to Sarai, and she gave her handmaiden, the Egyptian Hagar (*q.v.*), to her husband as his concubine. Hagar's pregnancy aroused her jealousy, and she ill-treated her to such an extent that Hagar ran away for a time. On her return Ishmael was born.

At the age of ninety, Sarai's name was changed to Sarah, and her husband's from Abram to Abraham. Yahweh blessed her and said she would bear a son, and become the 'mother of nations'.

When Abraham was granted a theophany, Sarah was asked to make cakes for the divine visitors. She overheard the prophecy about her son, and laughed; then, afraid, she denied her derision in face of the words, 'Is anything too hard for the Lord?' (Gn. xviii. 14). On the birth of Isaac, Sarah's reproach was removed. She was so incensed by Ishmael's derision at the feast to celebrate Isaac's weaning that she asked for Hagar and her son to be cast out.

Aged one hundred and twenty-seven, she died in Kiriath-arba (*q.v.*) and was buried in the cave of the field of Machpelah (Gn. xxiii. 1 ff.) (see HEBRON).

Sarah is named in Is. li. 2 as an example of trust in Yahweh. In the New Testament Paul mentions both Abraham and Sarah among those whose faith was counted for righteousness (Rom. iv. 19), and he writes of Sarah as the mother of the children of promise (Rom. ix. 9). The writer of the Epistle to the Hebrews includes Sarah in the list of the faithful (xi. 11). She is named also as an example of a wife's proper regard for her husband (1 Pet. iii. 6). M.G.

SARDIS. A city in the Roman province of Asia, in the west of what is now Asiatic Turkey. It was the capital of the ancient kingdom of Lydia, the greatest of the foreign powers encountered by the Greeks during their early colonization of Asia Minor. Its early prosperity, especially under Croesus, became a byword for wealth; its riches are said to have derived in part from the gold won from the Pactolus, a stream which flowed through the city. The original city was an almost impregnable fortress-citadel, towering above the broad valley of the Hermus, and nearly surrounded by precipitous cliffs of treacherously loose rock. Its position as the centre of Lydian supremacy under Croesus was ended abruptly when the Persian king Cyrus besieged the city and took the citadel (549 BC), apparently by scaling the cliffs and entering by a weakly defended point under cover of darkness. The same tactics again led to the fall of the city in 214 BC, when it was captured by Antiochus the Great. Though it lay on an important trade route down the Hermus valley, it never regained under Roman rule the spectacular prominence it had had in earlier centuries. In AD 26 its claim for the honour of building an imperial temple was rejected in favour of its rival Smyrna. There is now only a small village (Sart) near the site of the ancient city.

The letter to 'the angel of the church in Sardis' (Rev. iii. 1–6) suggests that the early Christian community there was imbued with the same spirit as the city, resting on its past reputation and without any present achievement, and failing, as the city had twice failed, to learn from its past and be vigilant. The symbol of 'garments' may be in part an allusion to the chief trade of the city, which was the making and dyeing of oollen garments. (See W. M. Ramsay, *The etters to the Seven Churches of Asia*, 1904, hapters xxv, xxvi.) E.M.B.G.

ARDIUS. See JEWELS AND PRECIOUS STONES.

ARDONYX. See JEWELS AND PRECIOUS STONES.

AREPTA. See ZAREPHATH.

ARGON. Sargon (Heb. *sargōn*; LXX *Arna*; ssyr. *Šarru-ūkîn*, '(the god) has established the ing(ship)' ruled Assyria 722–705 BC. His reign known in much detail from inscriptions at his alace at Khorsabad built in 717–707 BC, and rom historical texts and letters found at Nineveh nd Nimrud. Although he is named only once n the Old Testament (Is. xx. 1), his campaigns in yro-Palestine are of importance in understanding the historical background of the prophecies of saiah.

Sargon claimed the capture of Samaria, which ad been besieged by his predecessor Shalnaneser V for three years (2 Ki. xvii. 5, 6) until is death on 20 December 722 BC or 18 January 21 BC. It is probable that Sargon completed this peration and hurried back to Assyria to claim he throne. Although he bore the same royal ame as the heroic Sargon I of Agade (*c.* 2350 BC; ee ACCAD, NIMROD), there is some evidence that e was the legal successor to the throne and not a surper.

During the first months of his reign he faced a najor domestic crisis which was settled only by he grant of privileges to the citizens of Assur. In he spring of 720 BC he moved south against the Chaldean Marduk-apla-iddina II (see MERODACH-BALADAN), who had seized the Babylonian hrone. An indecisive battle at Der arrested the dvance of the supporting Elamites and Arabian ribes, but disturbances in the west rendered it expedient for Sargon to leave Marduk-apla-iddina as king in Babylon (721–710 BC).

In the west Yaubi'di of Hamath led Damascus, Arpad, Simirra, Samaria, and possibly Hatarikka, in an anti-Assyrian coalition. Late in 720 BC Sargon marched to defeat these allies in a battle near Qarqar, N Syria, and, reducing the participating cities once more to vassalage, he moved to destroy Raphia and thus cut off the rebel Hanun of Gaza from an Egyptian force, under its commander, which was defeated. This interpretation follows the identification of So or Sib'e (2 Ki. xvii. 4) as a Hebrew rendering of the term for leader (*re'e*) and not as the proper name of an unidentified Egyptian king (*JNES*, XIX, 1960, pp. 49–53).

During these operations Isaiah warned Judah of the inadvisability of participating, or of trusting, in Egyptian help, illustrating his message by the fate of Carchemish, Hamath, Arpad, Samaria, and Damascus (Is. x. 9). On his return from the Egyptian border Sargon deported a large part of the population of Samaria, which he began to rebuild as the capital of a new Assyrian province of Samaria. The process of repopulating the city with foreigners took several years and appears to have continued in the reign of Esarhaddon (Ezr. iv. 2).

In 716 BC Sargon sent his army commander (*turtan*; see TARTAN) to war against the Arabs in Sinai. This led to the reception of tribute from the pharaoh Shilkanni (Osorkon IV) of Egypt and from Samsi, queen of the Arabs. Despite these Assyrian successes, the people of Ashdod displaced their Assyrian-nominated ruler, Ahimetu, by a usurper Iadna (or Iamani) who initiated yet another Syro-Palestinian league against Assyria, doubtless relying on Egyptian help. In 712 BC the same *turtan* was sent to conquer Ashdod (Is. xx. 1), which was reduced to the status of an Assyrian province. Since Azaqa ('Azeqah or Tell es-Zakariye) on the Judaean border near Lachish surrendered in this campaign, it will be seen how narrowly independent Judah escaped a further invasion. Iamani fled to Nubia for refuge, only to be extradited to Nineveh by the ruler Shabaka.

On other fronts Sargon fought many battles, defeating the Mannaeans and Rusas of Urarṭu in 719–714 BC, and incorporating the defeated Carchemish as a provincial centre. In 710 and 707 BC, following raids into Media to neutralize the hill tribes, Sargon once more advanced against Merodach-baladan, who fled to Elam. Sargon's latter years were spent in suppressing rebellions in Kummukh and Tabal (where he was killed in action). He was succeeded by his son Sennacherib on 12 Ab, 705 BC. That he was 'not buried in his house' was later attributed to his sin in adopting a pro-Babylonian policy following his 'taking the hands of the god Bel (Marduk)' as king there in 709 BC.

BIBLIOGRAPHY. H. Tadmor, 'The Campaigns of Sargon II of Assur', *JCS*, XII, 1958, pp. 22–40, 77–100; H. W. F. Saggs, in *Iraq*, XVII, 1955, pp. 146–149; D. J. Wiseman, *DOTT*, pp. 58–63.

D.J.W.

SARID. A town on the southern boundary of Zebulun, mentioned in Jos. xix. 10, 12. *GTT* (p. 180) follows the ancient versions in reading 'Sadud' and, like most scholars, identifying it with Tell Shaddua, 4½ miles south-west of Nazareth.

SARSECHIM. The name of a Babylonian official present in Jerusalem after their capture of the city in 587 BC (Je. xxxix. 3). The name is as yet unidentified. It has been proposed to identify him with Nebushasban the Rab-saris (verse 13). Although the Gk. variants *Nabonsachar*, *Nabonsarach* include the previous Nebo, it would require considerable emendation of the text to bring *sarsᵉḵîm* into line with Nabu-sezibanni (*nᵉḇô-šaziḇôn*?). See RAB-SARIS. D.J.W.

SATAN. The name of the prince of evil, Heb. *śāṭān*, Gk. *Satanas*, means basically 'adversary' (the word is so rendered, *e.g.*, in Nu. xxii. 22). In the first two chapters of Job we read of 'the

Satan' as presenting himself before God among 'the sons of God'. It is sometimes said that in such passages Satan is not thought of as especially evil, but as simply one among the heavenly hosts. Admittedly we have not yet the fully developed doctrine, but the activities of 'the Satan' are certainly inimical to Job. The Old Testament references to Satan are few, but he is consistently engaged in activities against the best interests of men. He moves David to number the people (1 Ch. xxi. 1). He stands at the right hand of Joshua the high priest 'to resist him', thus drawing down the Lord's rebuke (Zc. iii. 1 f.). The psalmist thinks it a calamity to have Satan stand at one's right hand (Ps. cix. 6, AV, but *cf.* RV 'an adversary', RSV 'an accuser'). John tells us that 'the devil sinneth from the beginning' (1 Jn. iii. 8), and the Old Testament references to him bear this out.

Most of our information, however, comes from the New Testament, where the supremely evil being is referred to as Satan or as 'the devil' (*ho diabolos*) indifferently, with Beelzebub (or Beelzeboul, or Beezeboul) also employed on occasion (Mt. x. 25, xii. 24, 27). Other expressions, such as 'the prince of this world' (Jn. xiv. 30) or 'the prince of the power of the air' (Eph. ii. 2), also occur. He is always depicted as hostile to God, and as working to overthrow the purposes of God. Matthew and Luke tell us that at the beginning of His ministry Jesus had a severe time of testing when Satan tempted Him to go about His work in the wrong spirit (Mt. iv; Lk. iv; see also Mk. i. 13). When this period was completed the devil left Him 'for a season', which implies that the contest was later resumed. This is clear also from the statement that He 'was in all points tempted like as we are' (Heb. iv. 15). This conflict is not incidental. The express purpose of the coming of Jesus into the world was 'that he might destroy the works of the devil' (1 Jn. iii. 8; *cf.* Heb. ii. 14). Everywhere the New Testament sees a great conflict between the forces of God and of good, on the one hand, and those of evil led by Satan, on the other. This is not the conception of one writer or another, but is common ground.

There is no doubting the severity of the conflict. Peter stresses the ferocious opposition by saying that the devil 'as a roaring lion, walketh about, seeking whom he may devour' (1 Pet. v. 8). Paul thinks rather of the cunning employed by the evil one. 'Satan himself is transformed into an angel of light' (2 Cor. xi. 14), so that it is small wonder if his minions appear in an attractive guise. The Ephesians are exhorted to put on 'the whole armour of God, that ye may be able to stand against the wiles of the devil' (Eph. vi. 11), and there are references to 'the snare of the devil' (1 Tim. iii. 7; 2 Tim. ii. 26). The effect of such passages is to emphasize that Christians (and even archangels, Jude 9) are engaged in a conflict that is both relentlessly and cunningly waged. They are not in a position to retire from the conflict. Nor can they simply assume that evil will always be obviously evil. There is need for the exercise of discrimination as well as stout heartedness. But determined opposition wi always succeed. Peter exhorts us to resist th devil 'stedfast in the faith' (1 Pet. v. 9), and Jame says, 'Resist the devil, and he will flee from you (Jas. iv. 7). Paul exhorts not to 'give place [*i.e.* a opportunity, through indulgence in unrestraine anger] to the devil' (Eph. iv. 27), and the implica tion of putting on the whole armour of God i that thereby the believer will be able to resis anything the evil one does (Eph. vi. 11, 13) Paul puts his trust in the faithfulness of God 'God is faithful, who will not suffer you to b tempted above that ye are able; but will with th temptation also make a way to escape' (1 Cor. x 13). He is well aware of the resourcefulness o Satan, and that he is always seeking to 'get a advantage of us'. But he can add 'we are no ignorant of his devices' (or, as F. J. Rae trans lates, 'I am up to his tricks') (2 Cor. ii. 11).

Satan is continually opposed to the gospel, as we see throughout the Lord's ministry. He worked through Jesus' followers, as when Peter rejected the thought of the cross and was me with the rebuke 'Get thee behind me, Satan' (Mt. xvi. 23). Satan had further designs on Peter, but the Lord prayed for him (Lk. xxii. 31 f.). He worked also in the enemies of Jesus, for Jesus could speak of those who opposed Him as being 'of your father the devil' (Jn. viii. 44). All this comes to a climax in the passion. The work of Judas is ascribed to the activity of the evil one. Satan 'entered into' Judas (Lk. xxii. 3; Jn. xiii. 27). He 'put into the heart of Judas Iscariot, Simon's son, to betray him' (Jn. xiii. 2). With the cross in prospect Jesus can say 'the prince of this world cometh' (Jn. xiv. 30).

Satan continues to tempt men (1 Cor. vii. 5). We read of him at work in a professed believer, Ananias ('why hath Satan filled thine heart . . .?', Acts v. 3), and in an avowed opponent of the Christian way, Elymas ('thou child of the devil', Acts xiii. 10). The general principle is given in 1 Jn. iii. 8, 'He that committeth sin is of the devil'. Men may so give themselves over to Satan that they in effect belong to him. They become his 'children' (1 Jn. iii. 10). Thus we read of 'the synagogue of Satan' (Rev. ii. 9, iii. 9), and of men who dwell 'where Satan's seat is' (Rev. ii. 13). Satan hinders the work of missionaries (1 Thes. ii. 18). He takes away the good seed sown in the hearts of men (Mk. iv. 15). He sows 'the children of the wicked one' in the field that is the world (Mt. xiii. 38 f.). His activity may produce physical effects (Lk. xiii. 16). Always he is pictured as resourceful and active.

But the New Testament is sure of his limitations and defeat. His power is derivative (Lk. iv. 6). He can exercise his activity only within the limits that God lays down (Jb. i. 12, ii. 6; 1 Cor. x. 13; Rev. xx. 2, 7). He may even be used to set forward the cause of right (1 Cor. v. 5; *cf.* 2 Cor. xii. 7). Jesus saw a preliminary victory in the mission of the Seventy (Lk. x. 18). Our Lord thought of 'everlasting fire' as 'prepared for the devil and his angels' (Mt. xxv. 41), and John sees this come to pass (Rev. xx. 10). We have already noticed that the conflict with Satan comes to a head in the passion. There Jesus speaks of him as 'cast out' (Jn. xii. 31), and as 'judged' (Jn. xvi. 11). The victory is explicitly alluded to in Heb. ii. 14; 1 Jn. iii. 8. The work of preachers is 'to turn' men 'from the power of Satan unto God' (Acts xxvi. 18). Paul can say confidently, 'the God of peace shall bruise Satan under your feet shortly' (Rom. xvi. 20).

The witness of the New Testament then is clear. Satan is a malignant reality, always hostile to God and to God's people. But he has already been defeated in Christ's life and death and resurrection, and this defeat will become obvious and complete in the end of the age. See also ANTICHRIST, DEVIL, EVIL SPIRITS.

BIBLIOGRAPHY. F. J. Rae, *ExpT*, LXVI, 1954–5, pp. 212–215; J. M. Ross, *ExpT*, LXVI, 1954–5, pp. 58–61; W. O. E. Oesterley in *DCG*; E. Langton, *Essentials of Demonology*, 1949; W. Robinson, *The Devil and God*, 1945. L.M.

SATRAP. Heb. *'aḥašdarpᵉnîm* or its Aramaic equivalent occurs thirteen times in the Old Testament and in the AV is translated 'princes' in Daniel, 'lieutenants' in Ezra and Esther, but is always translated 'satraps' in the RV and RSV. It is from the Old Persian *khshathrapâvan*, 'the protector of the realm'. In Is. xli. 25 Delitzsch (*Commentary on Isaiah*, 1890) translates Heb. *sāḡān* by 'satrap' (*cf.* Is. x. 8, where he suggests the same rendering for Heb. *śar*). The satraps were viceroys invested with considerable power, having their own courts. Darius I was probably the first king to organize the Persian Empire into satrapies, twenty in all. J.A.B.

SATYR (*śā'îr*, 'hairy one', 'he-goat'). The Heb. plural (*śᵉ'îrîm*) is rendered 'satyrs' in RVmg of Lv. xvii. 7 and of 2 Ch. xi. 15 (AV 'devils', RV 'he-goats'). A similar meaning may be intended in 2 Ki. xxiii. 8 if Heb. *šᵉ'ārîm* ('gates'), which seems meaningless in the context, be regarded as a slip for *śᵉ'îrîm*. The precise nature of these 'hairy ones' is obscure. They may have been he-goats in the ordinary sense, or gods having the appearance of goats. Sacrifices were made to them in high places, with special priests performing the ritual.

From goat to demon in Semitic belief was an easy transition (*cf.* AZAZEL). AV speaks of satyrs, apparently demonic creatures, who danced on the ruins of Babylon (Is. xiii. 21), and figured also in the picture of the desolation of Edom (Is. xxxiv. 14), where the satyr is mentioned with the screech-owl (see LILITH), to which it evidently bears some resemblance.

BIBLIOGRAPHY. Oesterley and Robinson, *Hebrew Religion*, 1930, pp. 13, 64 ff.; *EBi* (*s.v.* 'satyr'). J.D.D.

SAUL (*šā'ûl*, 'asked', *i.e.* of God). **1.** King of ancient Edom, from Rehoboth (Gn. xxxvi. 37).

2. A son of Simeon (Gn. xlvi. 10; Ex. vi. 15; Nu. xxvi. 13).

3. First king of Israel, son of Kish, of the tribe of Benjamin. The story of Saul occupies most of 1 Samuel (chapters ix–xxxi) and depicts one of the most pathetic of all God's chosen servants.

Head and shoulders above his brethren, a man whose personal courage matched his physique, kingly to his friends and generous to his foes, Saul was the man chosen by God to institute the monarchy, to represent within himself the royal rule of Yahweh over His people. Yet three times over he was declared to have disqualified himself from the task to which he had been appointed, and even in that appointment there was a hint of the character of the man whom God, in His sovereignty, chose to be king.

Under the pressure of the Philistine suzerainty, the Israelites came to think that only a visible warrior-leader could bring about their deliverance. Rejecting the spiritual leadership of Yahweh, mediated through the prophetic ministry of Samuel, they demanded a king (1 Sa. viii). After warning them of the evils of such government—a warning which they did not heed—Samuel was instructed by God to grant the people's wish, and was guided to choose Saul, whom he anointed secretly in the land of Zuph (1 Sa. x. 1), confirming the appointment later by a public ceremony at Mizpeh (x. 17–25). Almost immediately Saul had the opportunity of showing his mettle. Nahash the Ammonite besieged Jabesh-gilead and offered cruel terms of surrender to its inhabitants, who sent for help to Saul, who was on the other side of the Jordan. Saul summoned the people by means of an object-lesson typical of his race and age, and with the army thus raised won a great victory (xi. 1–11). It is an evidence of his finer instincts that he refused at this time to acquiesce in the desire of his followers to punish those who had been unwilling to pay him homage (x. 27, xi. 12, 13).

Following this, a religious ceremony at Gilgal confirmed the appointment of Saul as king, which had obviously received divine approval in the defeat of the Ammonites. With a parting exhortation to the people to be assiduous in their obedience to God, which was accompanied by a miraculous sign, Samuel left the new king to the government of his nation. On three occasions only, one of them posthumously, was the old prophet to emerge from the background. Each time it was to remonstrate with Saul for disobeying the terms of his appointment, terms involving utter obedience to the slightest command of God. The first occasion was when Saul, through impatience, arrogated to himself the priestly office, offering sacrifice at Gilgal (xiii. 7–10). For this sacrilege his rejection from kingship was prophesied by Samuel, and Saul received the first hint that there was already, in the mind of God, the 'man after his heart' whom the Lord had selected to replace him.

The second occasion was when Saul's disobedience brought forth the prophet's well-known dictum that 'to obey is better than sacrifice, and to hearken than the fat of rams' (xv. 22). Again Saul's rejection from rule over Israel is declared and symbolically shown, and Samuel severs all contact with the fallen monarch. It is from the grave that Samuel emerges to rebuke Saul for the third and last time, and, whatever problems are raised by the story of the witch of Endor (chapter xxviii), it is clear that God permitted this supernatural interview with the unhappy king in order to fill Saul's cup of iniquity and to foretell his imminent doom.

For the long conflict between Saul and David, see the article DAVID, which deals with other aspects of Saul's character. It is significant that when the public anointing of David was made in Bethlehem, Samuel rejected Eliab, David's most manly brother, and was warned against assuming that natural and spiritual power necessarily went together (xvi. 7).

Saul is an object-lesson in the essential difference between the carnal and the spiritual man, as his New Testament namesake was to distinguish the two (1 Cor. iii, *etc.*). Living in a day when the Holy Spirit came upon men for a special time and purpose, rather than indwelling the children of God permanently, Saul was peculiarly susceptible to moodiness and uncertainty within himself (see also DISEASE AND HEALING). Yet his disobedience is inexcusable, for he had, as we have, access to the Word of God, as it was then ministered to him through Samuel.

His downfall was the more tragic because he was a public and representative figure among the people of God.

4. The Jewish name of the apostle Paul (*q.v.*; Acts xiii. 9).

BIBLIOGRAPHY. J. C. Gregory, 'The Life and Character of Saul', *ExpT*, XIX, 1907–8, pp. 510–513; A. C. Welch, *Kings and Prophets of Israel*, 1952, pp. 63–79; E. Robertson, *The Old Testament Problem*, 1946, pp. 105–136; J. Bright, *A History of Israel*, 1960, pp. 163–174. T.H.J.

SAVIOUR. See SALVATION.

SAVOUR. With one exception (Joel ii. 20) the word is used of a sweet or acceptable smell. It is characteristic of sacrifice; and in this connection it is used pointedly of the effect of the Christian's life on his fellows (2 Cor. ii. 15, 16). In Eph. v. 2 it is used of the sacrifice of Christ.

Two other references, referring to a loss of savour (Mt. v. 13; Lk. xiv. 34), connect this with insipidity or foolishness.

Common to all is the implicit association of cost, or distinctiveness, or strength with savour. Something is missing from God's people or the worship of God when there is no 'savour'.

In Mt. xvi. 23; Mk. viii. 33, AV 'savour' renders Gk. *phronein*, 'to set the mind on' (*cf.* RV, RSV). C.H.D.

SAW. See ARTS AND CRAFTS, II and IIc.

SCAB. Skin diseases are rife in the East, and it is often difficult both to identify precisely those mentioned in Scripture and to distinguish one from another. 'Scab', *e.g.*, represents four different Heb. words.

1. *gārāḇ*, Dt. xxviii. 27 ('scurvy', Lv. xxi. 20, xxii. 22; LXX, *psōra*; Vulg. *scabies*). Included among the curses that should overtake the disobedient, this was evidently not the true scurvy, but a chronic disease which formed a thick crust on the head and sometimes spread over the whole body. It was regarded as incurable.

2. *yallep̄eṯ*, 'scabbed' (LXX *leichēn*). One of the afflictions that rendered men unfit for the priesthood (Lv. xxi. 20) and animals unsuitable for sacrifices (Lv. xxii. 22), it may be another form of (1) above. 3. *sappaḥaṯ*, Lv. xiii. 2, xiv. 56. 4. *mispaḥaṯ*, Lv. xiii. 6–8.

A verbal form (*śippaḥ*) is employed in Is. iii. 17, 'smite with a scab'. See also DISEASE AND HEALING. J.D.D.

SCALING-LADDER. See FORTIFICATION AND SIEGECRAFT, IIa.

SCALL (*neṯeq*, Lv. xiii. 30–37, xiv. 54). Probably a general name for skin eruptions. Old and Middle English used it to denote scabbiness of the head. See also SCAB, DISEASE AND HEALING.

SCAPEGOAT. See AZAZEL.

SCARLET. See COLOURS.

SCEPTRE (Heb. *šēḇeṭ*, *šarᵉḇîṭ*; Gk. *rhabdos*). A staff or rod (*q.v.*), often very ornate, borne as a symbol of personal sovereignty or authority, normally by kings, but the same word is used of the rod of office of others (Gn. xxxviii. 18; Lv. xxvii. 32; Ps. xxiii. 4; Mi. vii. 14; Is. xxviii. 27). The term *šarᵉḇîṭ* (Akkadian *sabittu*) is used only of the sceptre of Persian rulers (Est. iv. 11, v. 2, viii. 4). See fig. 64.

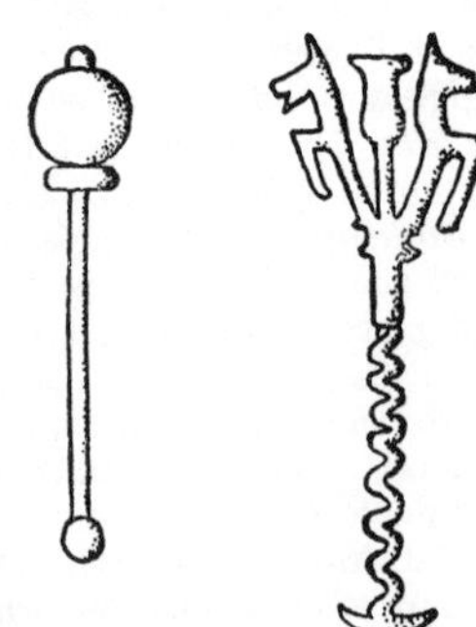

Fig. 179. *Left*, a royal mace; *right*, an elaborate sceptre held by the goddess Ishtar. See also fig. 64.

The term *šēḇeṭ* is used for the sceptre of the rulers of Egypt (Zc. x. 11), the Aramaean state of Bit Adini (Am. i. 5), Ashkelon (Am. i. 8), Babylon (Is. xiv. 5), and of the rulers of Israel (Ezk. xix. 11, 14).

In Gn. xlix. 10 and Nu. xxiv. 17 the term refers to Israel's future rulers. Both of these passages came to have messianic significance. The same word occurs in Ps. xlv. 6, a verse which was used in the New Testament to describe Christ as Son (Heb. i. 8), the sceptre of whose kingdom is a sceptre of righteousness.

The reed placed in our Lord's hand (Mt. xxvii. 29) was a symbol of sovereignty used in mockery. J.A.T.

SCEVA. Actual or putative father of a group of magical practitioners who, endeavouring to imitate Paul in Ephesus, used a spell with the name of Jesus for exorcism, were repudiated by the demon and set upon by the demoniac: an incident which deeply impressed Jew and Gentile alike (Acts xix. 13 ff.). The story was doubtless valued as a demonstration that the 'name' was no magical formula with automatic effect.

Sceva is described as a 'Jewish high priest' (*cf.* RV). Though this could denote a member of the senior priestly families, it is probably here a self-adopted title for advertisement—rather as a modern conjuror styles himself 'Professor'. 'The Sons of the High Priest Sceva' may have been the collective designation for this 'firm' of itinerant mountebanks (*cf.* verse 13); a Jewish high priest would, in the eyes of superstitious pagans, be an impressive source of esoteric knowledge.

There were seven 'sons' (verse 14), so that RV in verse 16, 'mastered *both* of them', while representing a better text than AV, is a little awkward. Several explanations have been offered: that *amphoterōn* in verse 16 means, not 'both', but 'all' (see examples in *MM*, *s.v. amphoteroi*); that Luke has shortened a written source and omitted intermediate parts of the story; that the number 'seven' has been accidentally introduced by translating Sceva's name as 'seven' (Heb. *šeḇa'*); or that the form of the story reflects the vivid recollection of an eyewitness that, while seven attempted the exorcism, only two were beaten up. The first suggestion implies a vulgarism unusual for Luke, the second less than his customary care, the third an exceedingly intricate textual history.

The MSS show many variants in detail.

A.F.W.

SCHISM. See HERESY.

SCHOOL.

I. IN THE OLD TESTAMENT

From the earliest times in the Ancient Near East schools attached to local temples were used for regular instruction in reading and writing. Among the Hebrews Moses, trained in Egypt (Acts vii. 22), was commanded to teach the people the law (Dt. iv. 10) and statutes (Lv. x. 11). This was done by repetition and example (Dt. xi. 19), public reading (Dt. xxxi. 10–13), and the use of specially composed songs (verse 19). Parents were responsible for their children's education (Gn. xviii. 19; Dt. vi. 7).

With the establishment of local sanctuaries and the Temple, young men were doubtless taught by the prophets (1 Sa. x. 11–13; 2 Ki. iv. 1), and among other instruction reading and writing was given (Jdg. viii. 14; Is. x. 19). The alphabet was learned by repetition (Is. xxviii. 10, AV 'precept upon precept . . .' being literally '*ṣ* after *ṣ*, *q* after *q* . . .'), but most subjects were imparted orally by question and answer (Mal. ii. 12, AV 'master and scholar', lit. 'he who rouses and he who answers', may, however, refer to watchmen).

The pupils (*limmûḏîm*, AV 'disciples') were taught by the prophets (Is. viii. 16, l. 4, liv. 13), as were kings (*e.g.* 2 Sa. xii. 1–7). There are no direct references in the Old Testament to special school buildings, but the introduction *c.* 75 BC in Judah by Simon ben-Sheṭaḥ of compulsory elementary education for boys six to sixteen years of age indicates the prior existence of such schools from the time of the second Temple. 1 Ch. xxv. 8 refers to scholars (*talmîḏ*) at the time of the first Temple. See also EDUCATION. For schools in the second millennium BC, see S. N. Kramer, *History Begins at Sumer*, 1958.

D.J.W.

II. IN THE NEW TESTAMENT

There is no trace whatever in the New Testament of schools for Hebrew children. It seems that the home was the place of elementary instruction. The synagogue was the centre of religious instruction with teaching in the hands of the scribes (Mt. vii. 29; Lk. iv. 16–32; Acts xix. 9). The word 'school' occurs in only one New Testament context (Acts xix. 9). There is nothing to indicate whether 'the school of Tyrannus' was devoted to elementary teaching (six to fourteen years) or to the advanced subjects of the Greek curriculum, philosophy, literature, and rhetoric (fourteen to eighteen years). A 'Western' addition to Acts xix. 9 runs: 'from the fifth to the tenth hour'. Tyrannus' accommodation was available for hire from 11 a.m. onwards. Instruction began at dawn simultaneously with the obligations of Paul's own calling (Acts xviii. 3). He used the afternoon for teaching in the hired school-house. See also EDUCATION. E.M.B.

SCHOOLMASTER. AV thus renders the Greek *paidagōgos* in Gal. iii. 24, 25. (RV reads 'tutor', as also in 1 Cor. iv. 15.) There is no satisfactory rendering, for the word has passed into a derivative of quite dissimilar meaning, and the office it signified passed with the social conditions which devised it. The Greek and Roman pedagogue was a trusted male attendant, commonly a slave, who had the general supervision of the boy, and saw him safely to and from school. This is the point of Paul's metaphor. E.M.B.

SCORPION (Heb. *'aqrāḇ*; Gk. *skorpios*). This arthropod order is most varied and plentiful in hot, dry countries, and there are a dozen kinds in Palestine. The venom of some is more powerful than that of the most dangerous desert vipers, but the sting of others is almost without effect on humans. Scorpions are largely nocturnal, spending the day hidden under stones: they feed entirely on small live animals. Several references in both Old and New Testaments are in proverbial form: *e.g.* 1 Ki. xii. 11, 'I will chastise you with

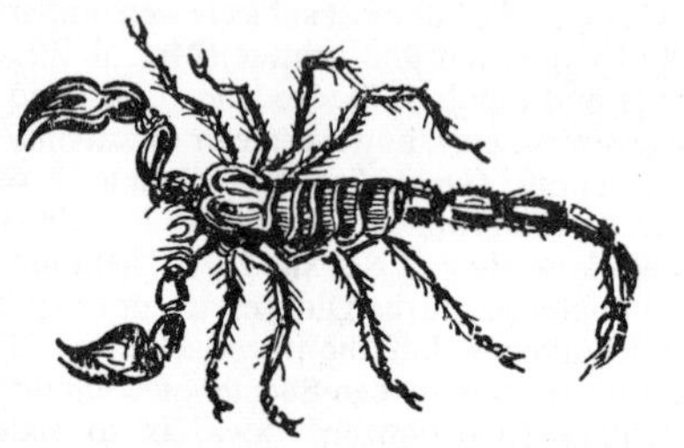

Fig. 180. A scorpion of a kind found in Palestine.

scorpions', possibly has reference to a many-tailed whip, loaded with hooked knobs of metal, and known as the scorpion (*cf.* 1 Macc. vi. 51). Our Lord strikingly contrasts a scorpion with an egg in Lk. xi. 12. G.C.

SCOURGING, SCOURGE. The English translation of several Hebrew and Greek words. 1. Heb. *biqqōreṯ* (Lv. xix. 20) is used in the context (AV), 'she shall be scourged'; or (AVmg), 'there shall be a scourging'. The Hebrew term, however, expresses the idea of investigation, conveyed by RSV, 'an inquiry shall be held'.

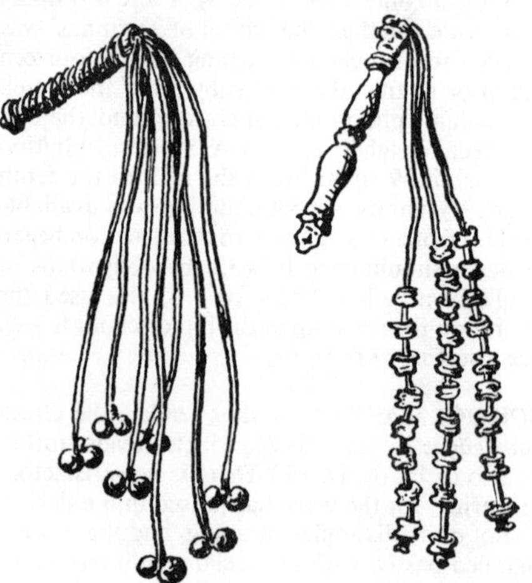

Fig. 181. Roman scourges, armed with lumps of lead and pieces of bone.

2. Heb. *šôṭ* (Jb. v. 21; Is. x. 26, *etc.*), *šōṭēṭ* (Jos. xxiii. 13), 'a scourge', but generally used in a metaphorical sense.

3. Gk. *mastigoō* (Mt. x. 17; Jn. xix. 1, *etc.*), *mastizō* (Acts xxii. 25), 'to whip', 'to scourge'; *phragelloō* (Mt. xxvii. 26; Mk. xv. 15). See CRUCIFIXION, II. See also fig. 181. J.D.D.

SCREECH OWL. See LILITH.

SCRIBE. In ancient Israel, as in all Near Eastern countries in antiquity, few knew the art of reading and writing, so the profession of scribe was held in high esteem. The words for 'scribe' in Hebrew (*sôpēr*, from *sāpar*, 'to count, tell'; Pi'el, 'to recount'), Ugaritic (*spr*) and Akkadian (*šapāru*, 'to send', 'write') cover the main duties of this highly skilled trade. Many scribes were employed by the public as secretaries to transcribe necessary legal contracts (Je. xxxii. 12), write letters, or keep accounts or records, usually from dictation (Je. xxxvi. 26). Others, known as 'the king's scribes' (2 Ch. xxiv. 11), were employed in public administration and were attached to the royal household, where the Chief Scribe acted as 'Secretary of State' and ranked before the Chronicler (*mazkîr*), who kept the state records (2 Sa. viii. 16; 1 Ki. iv. 3). As a high official the

Fig. 182. Part of a relief from Nimrud showing scribes recording booty taken by Tiglath-pileser III, one in the cuneiform script on a clay tablet or writing-board (*left*), the other in Aramaic on a papyrus or leather scroll, c. 740 BC.

Chief Scribe was one of the royal advisers (1 Ch. xxvii. 32). Thus Shebna the scribe, who later rose to be 'over the household' (*i.e.* Prime Minister), was sent by Hezekiah with the Prime Minister and elders to parley with the Assyrians besieging Jerusalem (2 Ki. xviii. 18, xix. 2; Is. xxxvi. 3). Some scribes were especially employed for military duties, which included the compilation of a list of those called out for war (Jdg. v. 14) or of the booty won, their senior official being designated 'principal scribe of the host' (2 Ki. xxv. 19; Je. lii. 25). Although other scribes were allotted to tasks in the Temple involving the collection of revenues (2 Ki. xii. 10), the scribal profession was, until the Exile, separate from the priesthood, who had their own literate officials. Senior scribes had their own rooms in the palace (Je. xxxvi. 12–21) or Temple (Je. xxxvi. 10).

Shaphan the scribe was given the newly discovered scroll of the law to read before the king (2 Ki. xxii. 8), but it was only in the post-exilic period that the scribes assumed the rôle of copyists, preservers, and interpreters of the law (Ezr. vii. 6). Ezra was both priest and scribe (vii. 11) and may well have acted as adviser on Jewish affairs to the Babylonian court, in the same way as did the specialist scribes of Assyria and Babylonia (see EZRA). By the 2nd century BC the majority of scribes were priests (1 Macc. vii. 12) and were the prototypes of the religious scribes of the New Testament day (see SCRIBES).

The scribe, as a person of education and means, was able to wear fine garments with a pen-case or 'inkhorn' hanging from his girdle (Ezk. ix. 2). His equipment included reed-pens (Je. viii. 8); a small knife for erasures and cutting papyrus (Je. xxxvi. 23), and, in some cases, styli for writing in the cuneiform script (see WRITING). The profession was often followed by whole families (1 Ch. ii. 55), and several sons are named as following their fathers in office.

BIBLIOGRAPHY. A. S. Diamond, *The Earliest Hebrew Scribes*, 1960; B. M. Metzger, 'When did Scribes begin to use Writing Desks?', *Akten der XI internationalen Byzantinisten-Kongress*, 1960, pp. 356 ff. D.J.W.

SCRIBES (Heb. *sōpᵉrîm*; Gk. *grammateis, nomikoi* (lawyers), and *nomodidaskaloi* (teachers of the law)). Scribes were experts in the study of the law of Moses (*Torah*). At first this occupation belonged to the priests. Ezra was priest and scribe (Ne. viii. 9). The offices were not necessarily separate. The chief activity of the scribe was undistracted study (Ecclus. xxxviii. 24). The rise of the scribes may be dated after the Babylonian Exile. 1 Ch. ii. 55 would suggest that the scribes were banded together into families and guilds. They were probably not a distinct political party in the time of Ben Sira (beginning of the 2nd century BC), but became one by the repressive measures of Antiochus Epiphanes. Scribes were found in Rome in the later imperial period, and in Babylonia in the 5th and 6th centuries AD. Not until about AD 70 are there detailed facts concerning individual scribes. They were mainly influential in Judaea up to AD 70, but they were to be found in Galilee (Lk. v. 17) and among the Dispersion.

The scribes were the originators of the synagogue service. Some of them sat as members of the Sanhedrin (Mt. xvi. 21, xxvi. 3). After AD 70 the importance of the scribes was enhanced. They preserved in written form the oral law and faithfully handed down the Hebrew Scriptures. They expected of their pupils a reverence beyond that given to parents (*Aboth* iv. 12).

The function of the scribes was threefold.

1. They preserved the law. They were the professional students of the law, and its defenders, especially in the Hellenistic period, when the priesthood had become corrupt. They transmitted unwritten legal decisions which had come into existence in their efforts to apply the Mosaic law to daily life. They claimed this oral law was more important than the written law (Mk. vii. 5 ff.). By their efforts religion was liable to be reduced to heartless formalism.

2. They gathered around them many pupils to instruct them in the law. The pupils were expected to retain the material taught and to transmit it without variation. They lectured in the Temple (Lk. ii. 46; Jn. xviii. 20). Their teaching was supposed to be free of charge (so Rabbi Zadok, Hillel, and others), but they were probably paid (Mt. x. 10; 1 Cor. ix. 3–18, for Paul's statement of his right), and even took advantage of their honoured status (Mk. xii. 40; Lk. xx. 47).

3. They were referred to as 'lawyers' and 'teachers of the law', because they were entrusted with the administration of the law as judges in the Sanhedrin (*cf.* Mt. xxii. 35; Mk. xiv. 43, 53; Lk. xxii. 66; Acts iv. 5; Jos., *Ant.* xviii. 1. 4). 'Lawyer' and 'scribe' are synonymous, and thus the two words are never joined in the New Testament. For their services in the Sanhedrin they were not paid. They were therefore obliged to earn their living by other means if they had no private wealth.

The Old Testament Apocrypha and Pseudepigrapha are sources for the origin of the scribal party. The books of Ezra, Nehemiah, Daniel, Chronicles, and Esther also indicate something of the beginnings of the movement, whereas Josephus and the New Testament speak of this group in a more advanced stage of development. There is no mention of the scribes in the Fourth Gospel. They belonged mainly to the party of the Pharisees, but as a body were distinct from them. On the matter of the resurrection they sided with Paul against the Sadducees (Acts xxiii. 9). They clashed with Christ, for He taught with authority (Mt. vii. 28, 29), and He condemned external formalism which they fostered. They persecuted Peter and John (Acts iv. 5), and had a part in Stephen's martyrdom (Acts vi. 12). However, although the majority opposed Christ (Mt. xxi. 15), some believed (Mt. viii. 19).

BIBLIOGRAPHY. G. F. Moore, *Judaism*, I, 1927, pp. 37–47; G. H. Box in *EBr*, 1948 edn.; J. D. Prince in *EBi*; D. Eaton in *HDB*; E. Schürer, *HJP*, II, i, 1901, pp. 306–379; W. Robertson Smith, *The Old Testament in the Jewish Church*, 1892, pp. 42–72 (with bibliography on p. 42).

C.L.F.

SCRIP. See BAG.

SCRIPTURE, SCRIPTURES.

I. VOCABULARY

Two Greek words are translated 'Scripture(s)' in EVV. *Gramma*, originally 'an alphabetical character' is used in the New Testament for 'document' (Lk. xvi. 6; Acts xxviii. 21), in a special sense by Paul for the law (Rom. ii. 27, 29, vii. 6; 2 Cor. iii. 6), and in the plural for the 'writings' of Moses (Jn. v. 47); for 'learning', sacred or profane (Jn.

vii. 15; Acts xxvi. 24), and only once in the phrase *ta hiera grammata*, 'the holy scriptures' (2 Tim. iii. 15). *Graphē*, on the other hand, which in secular Greek meant simply 'a writing' (though sometimes an authoritative writing in particular), is in the New Testament appropriated to 'the Scriptures' in a technical sense some fifty times, in most cases unmistakably the Old Testament. Associated with *graphē* is the formula *gegraptai*, 'it is written', occurring some sixty times in the New Testament, and found in Greek usage for legal pronouncements (*cf.* Deissmann, *BS*, pp. 112 ff.). Analogous forms occur in the Mishnah, but the Rabbis more often used formulae like 'It is said . . .'. The term 'the Scripture' (*ha-kāṯûḇ*) is also employed. (See B. M. Metzger, *JBL*, LXX, 1951, pp. 297 ff., for quotation formulae in rabbinic and New Testament documents.)

II. SIGNIFICANCE

Gegraptai meant 'It stands written in the Scriptures', and all Christians or Hellenistic Jews recognized that these comprised (Lk. xxiv. 44) 'the law, . . . the prophets, and . . . the psalms' (*i.e.* the *Keṯuḇim*, or Writings, see CANON OF THE OLD TESTAMENT). Though the AV, RSV translation of 2 Tim. iii. 16 ('every (all) scripture is inspired . . .') is probably preferable to that of RV, NEB, no contemporary would doubt the extent of 'every inspired scripture'. It was what Christians called the Old Testament, in which the gospel was rooted, of which Christ was the fulfilment, which was through faith in Christ able to lead a man to salvation, and was used in the primitive Church for all the purposes outlined in 2 Tim. iii. 15–17.

The question arises, however, at what date and in what sense Christians began to use the term 'Scriptures' for *Christian* writings. It has sometimes been suggested that 'according to the scriptures' in 1 Cor. xv. 3 f. refers to Christian testimony books or early Gospels, since no Old Testament passage specifies the resurrection on the third day. This is unacceptable: Paul means the Old Testament, as the groundwork of Christian preaching (see GOSPEL), and probably relates simply the fact of resurrection, not its occurrence on the third day, to prophecy (*cf.* B. M. Metzger, *JTS* (NS), VIII, 1957, pp. 118 ff.). Still less acceptable is Selwyn's suggestion that the anarthrous *en graphēi* in 1 Pet. ii. 6 means 'in writing' (*e.g.* in a hymn), for the passage quoted is from the Old Testament. Nevertheless, there were undoubtedly collections of authoritative sayings of the Lord in the apostolic Church (*cf.* O. Cullmann, *SJT*, III, 1950, pp. 180 ff., and see TRADITION), and 1 Tim. v. 18 seems to represent a quotation from such a collection, linked with an Old Testament citation, the two together being described as 'scripture'. Again, Paul in 1 Cor. ii. 9 cites by *gegraptai* a passage which, unless it is an extremely free rendering of Is. lxiv. 4, is unidentifiable. It occurs in various forms elsewhere in early literature, however, and now as Logion 17 of the *Gospel of Thomas* (see NEW TESTAMENT APOCRYPHA). It is perhaps worth considering whether Paul is quoting a saying of the Lord not recorded in our Gospels (as in Acts xx. 35) and citing it as he would 'scripture'.

If indeed the tradition of the Lord's words was so early called 'Scripture' it would be an easy step so to describe apostolic letters read in church; and, despite many dogmatic statements to the contrary, there would be no reason why this should not have occurred in apostolic times, as 2 Pet. iii. 16, as usually translated, represents: though perhaps we should translate 'they wrote the Scriptures *as well*' (*cf.* C. Bigg, *St. Peter and St. Jude*[2], *ICC*, 1901, *in loc.*).

We have, however, reached a dark place in New Testament history, though one where we may hope for future light. (See also BIBLE, CANON, INSPIRATION.)

BIBLIOGRAPHY. G. Schrenk, in *TWNT* (*s.v.* *graphē* and cognates); B. B. Warfield, *DCG* (= *Inspiration and Authority of the Bible*, 1948, pp. 229–241); E. E. Ellis, *Paul's Use of the Old Testament*, 1957. A.F.W.

SCROLL. See WRITING.

SCULPTURE. See ART, Ic(iv).

SCURVY. See SCAB.

SCYTHIANS. A tribe of horse-riding nomads and warriors from W Siberia inhabiting the Black Sea–Caspian area from about 2000 BC (see fig. 183). In the late 8th century BC they moved into N Persia and Urarṭu, driving the Cimmerians westwards (see GOMER). Their initial advances south-west were checked by Sargon II of Assyria (727–705 BC), but according to Herodotus the Scythians dominated W Persia for twenty-eight years through a number of military ventures. They assisted Assyria against the Medes, relieving Nineveh *c.* 630 BC, though later they attacked Harran and raided Palestine, to be

Fig. 183. Scythian horseman. Detail from a painted wall-hanging from Pazirik (S Russia, 5th century BC).

stopped from raiding Egypt only when Psammetichus I bought them off. Some scholars consider this to be the historical background of a prophecy by Jeremiah (xlvii; *IEJ*, I, 1950, pp. 154–159), but there are few references to the Scythians (Umman-manda) in contemporary texts. A group are believed to have settled at Beth-shean, called Scythopolis (so Jdg. i. 27, LXX).

The Scythians under Scylurus established their capital at Neapolis, in the Crimea, in 110 BC, their control of the steppes making them an intermediary in trade from Russia, especially in grain and slaves. The latter were called by the Pontic Greeks 'Scythians', though these were often their prisoners rather than their fellow nomadic freemen. Paul may use 'Scythian' in the latter sense (Col. iii. 11).

BIBLIOGRAPHY. T. Talbot Rice, *The Scythians*, 1957. D.J.W.

SEA (Heb. *yām*; Gk. *thalassa* and *pelagos*: this latter term, meaning 'open sea', occurs only once, Acts xxvii. 5).

The predominating sea in the Old Testament is, of course, the Mediterranean. Indeed, the word *yām* also means 'west', 'westward', *i.e.* 'seaward', from the geographical position of the Mediterranean with reference to Palestine. The Mediterranean is termed 'the great sea' (Jos. i. 4), 'the uttermost sea' (Dt. xi. 24), and 'the sea of the Philistines' (Ex. xxiii. 31).

Other seas mentioned in the Old Testament are the Red Sea, lit. 'sea of reeds' (Ex. xiii. 18); the Dead Sea, lit. 'sea of salt' (Gn. xiv. 3); the Sea of Galilee, lit. 'sea of *kinneret*' (Nu. xxxiv. 11). The word *yām* was also used of a particularly broad river, such as the Euphrates (Je. li. 35 f.) and the Nile (Na. iii. 8). It is used with reference to the great basin in the Temple court (1 Ki. vii. 23).

As one would expect, the New Testament *thalassa* is used with reference to the same seas as are mentioned in the Old Testament.

The Hebrews betrayed little interest in, or enthusiasm for, the sea. Probably their fear of the ocean stemmed from the ancient Semitic belief that the deep personified the power that fought against the deity. But for Israel the Lord was its Creator (Gn. i. 9 f.), and therefore its Controller (Ps. civ. 7–9; Acts iv. 24). He compels it to contribute to man's good (Gn. xlix. 25; Dt. xxxiii. 13) and to utter His praise (Ps. cxlviii. 7). In the figurative language of Isaiah (xvii. 12) and Jeremiah (vi. 23) the sea is completely under God's command. Many of the manifestations of the Lord's miraculous power were against the sea (Ex. xiv, xv; Ps. lxxvii. 16; Jon. i, ii). So also Christ's walking on the sea and stilling the storm (Mt. xiv. 25–33). God's final triumph will witness the disappearance of the sea in the world to come (Rev. xxi. 1). J.G.S.S.T.

SEA OF GLASS. Twice John saw in heaven 'as it were a sea of glass' (*hōs thalassa hyalinē*), 'before the throne' of God 'like unto crystal' (Rev. iv. 6) and later 'mingled with fire' (Rev. xv. 2). The picture of a sea in heaven may be traced through the apocalyptic literature (*e.g. Testament of Levi* ii. 7; *2 Enoch* iii. 3) back to 'the waters which were above the firmament' of Gn. i. 7; Pss. civ. 3, cxlviii. 4. The likeness to crystal stands in contrast with the semi-opacity of most ancient glass (*q.v.*) and speaks of the holy purity of heaven; the mingling with fire suggests the wrath of God (*cf.* Gn. vii. 11; *1 Enoch* liv. 7, 8). Beside or on the sea stand the victors over the beast: their song (Rev. xv. 3) recalls that of the Israelites beside the Red Sea (Ex. xv. 1 ff.).

M.H.C.

SEAH. See WEIGHTS AND MEASURES.

SEAL, SEALING.

I. IN THE OLD TESTAMENT

In the Near East, from which many thousands of individual seals have been recovered, engraved seals were common in ancient times, the Hebrews using a general term which did not specify the form of the seal itself (*ḥōtām*; Egyp. *htm*). The varied uses of such seals were much the same as in modern times.

a. Uses

(i) As a mark of authenticity and authority. Thus pharaoh handed a seal to Joseph his deputy (Gn. xli. 42) and Ahasuerus sealed royal edicts (Est. iii. 10, viii. 8–10). The action describes the passing of the master's word to his disciples (Is. viii. 16) and Yahweh granting authority to Zerubbabel (Hg. ii. 23; *cf.* Je. xxii. 24). For a non-biblical example of delegated seals on a covenant, see *Iraq*, XXI, 1958.

(ii) To witness a document. The seal was impressed on the clay or wax (see WRITING). Thus, his friends witnessed Jeremiah's deed of purchase (Je. xxxii. 11–14) and Nehemiah and his contemporaries attested the covenant (Ne. ix. 38, x. 1) and Daniel a prophecy (Dn. ix. 24).

(iii) To secure by affixing a seal. Thus, a clay document within its envelope or other receptacle, or a scroll tied by a cord to which was attached a lump of clay bearing a seal impression, could be examined and read only when the seal had been broken by an authorized person (*cf.* Rev. v. 1 f.). A sealed prophecy (Dn. xii. 9) or book (Is. xxix. 11) was thus a symbol for something as yet unrevealed.

To prevent unauthorized entry doors would be sealed by a cord or clay, with the sealing stretched across the gap between the door and its lock. This was done to the lions' den at Babylon (Dn. vi. 17; Bel and the Dragon 14) and to tombs (Herodotus, ii. 121; *cf.* Mt. xxvii. 66). The close-knit scales of a crocodile were likened to a sealed object (Jb. xli. 15).

Metaphorically the seal stood for what is securely held, as are the sins of man before God (Dt. xxxii. 34; Jb. xiv. 17), who alone has the authority to open and to seal (Jb. xxxiii. 16). He sets His seal as a token of completion (Ezk. xxviii. 12). The metaphor in Ct. iv. 12 is probably of chastity.

b. Form

With the invention of writing in the fourth millennium BC seals were used in large numbers. The cylinder-seal was the most common and was

Fig. 184. A Canaanite cylinder seal and impression. From Hazor, 14th century BC.

rolled on clay, though stamp seals are also found in contemporary use. In Palestine, under both Mesopotamian (often through Syrian and Phoenician) and Egyptian influences, cylinder-seals and scarabs were in use in the Canaanite period. The latter predominated for use on wax or clay lumps appended to papyrus. With the monarchy, stamp seals, 'button', conoid, or scaraboid, prevail (see figs. 184–6).

Fig. 185. A typical conoid stamp seal with engraving on the base. Assyrian, 8th–7th centuries BC.

The seal was pierced longitudinally so that it could be worn on a cord round the neck (Gn. xxxviii. 18; Je. xxii. 24; Ct. viii. 6) or on a pin, traces of which sometimes remain, for attachment to the dress. The scaraboid seals or seal stones were set in a ring to be worn on the hand or arm (Est. iii. 12). See fig. 187.

c. Materials

Poor persons could purchase roughly engraved seals made of local terracotta, bitumen, limestone, or frit. The majority of seals, however, were specially engraved by a skilled seal-cutter who used copper gravers, a cutting wheel, and sometimes a small bow-drill, perhaps 'the pen of iron, and with the point of a diamond' (Je. xvii. 1), to work the hard semi-precious stones (see ARTS AND CRAFTS). In Palestine, as elsewhere, carnelian, chalcedony, agate, jasper, rock crystal, and haematite were imported and frequently used. Imported Egyptian scarabs were of glazed steatite, and, later, glazed composition.

Engraved stones (Ex. xxviii. 11–23, xxxix. 8) were used as insets in the high priest's breast ornament. The fine stones and workmanship led to these seal stones or signet-rings (Heb. *ṭabba'aṯ*: Akkad. *ṭimbu'u*) being used as ornaments (Is. iii 21), votive offerings, or for sacred purposes (Ex xxxv. 22; Nu. xxxi. 50), like the group of seals in the Canaanite shrine at Hazor, or as amulets (*q.v.*). The Heb. *ṭabba'aṯ* is used also of rings in general (Ex. xxv. 12).

d. Designs

Before the monarchy cylinder seals followed the Phoenician or Syrian style, showing patterns well-filled designs, rows of men, or designs characteristic of the different fashions prevailing at various periods in Mesopotamia. The later Palestinian seals, usually oval, bear representations of lions (see *IBA*, fig. 52), winged human-headed lions or sphinxes (cherubim), griffins or the winged uraeus-snake. Egyptian motifs, with the lotus flower, the *ankh*-symbol of life, or the Horus-child, frequently occur. Scenes of worship seated deities, and animals and birds seem to show that this art did not offend Hebrew

Fig. 186. A scarab seal (Egyptian type). From Jericho, 15th century BC.

religious feeling. After the 7th century BC, however, the majority of seals bear only a two-line inscription (see fig. 76).

e. Inscriptions

Apart from the imported scarabs bearing Egyptian royal names which are useful for chronological purposes, the 150 seals inscribed with personal names in Hebrew provide the bulk of inscribed seals. These give the name of the owner and of his overlord, and sometimes his profession or office, or are simply inscribed with the personal name, and are thus of considerable historical and epigraphical interest. Of those seals found in excavations the jasper seal 'Belonging to Shema', servant of Jeroboam' (*lšm' 'bd yrb'm*) from Megiddo (with the design of a lion) is perhaps typical. Another, with a similar name, inscribed 'servant of the king', may refer to the same man (*cf.* 2 Ki. xxii. 12). The seal of Jaazaniah (see fig. 115) shows a cock on a black-and-white onyx seal dated *c.* 600 BC. The inscription reads 'Belonging to Yaazanyah, servant of the king' and may indicate as owner the Yaazanyahu of 2 Ki. xxv. 23 or a contemporary of the same name (Je. xxxv. 3, xl. 8; *cf.* Ezk. xi. 1). The seal of Gedaliah found at Lachish bears a tit

('He who is over the household', *cf.* 2 Ki. xviii. 18; see SHEBNA) and may be that of the governor of Judah (2 Ki. xxv. 22–25). The reverse shows the marks of the papyrus to which it was originally affixed. A seal impression from a papyrus scroll inscribed 'Belonging to Gealyahu, son of the king' (from Beth-zur) has been thought to be that of Igal, a descendant of Jehoiakim (1 Ch. iii. 22). The seal of Jotham, probably the king of that name (2 Ki. xv. 30 ff.), still bears its copper ring (design: a ram, found at Ezion-geber). Seal-impressions from the same seal have been found at Tell Beit Mirsim and Beth-shemesh inscribed

Fig. 187. An engraved ring seal in gold. Earlier signet-rings usually had the seal-stone inset. From Persia, 5th–4th centuries BC.

'Belonging to Eliakim, steward (*na'ar*) of Yaukin (Jehoiachin)'. Other biblical names (not necessarily to be identified with the persons mentioned in the Old Testament) found on seals include Hananiah, Azariah, Menahem, Nehemiah, Micaiah, and Shub'el.

c. Stamped jar-handles

Excavations in Palestine have produced more than six hundred jar-handles bearing seal impressions. Some appear to be royal pottery marks (*cf.* 1 Ch. iv. 23) giving the place of manufacture. The impressions are usually of four-winged scarabeus, a flying scroll with a single line inscription naming Hebron, Ziph, Socoh, Gibeon, and *mmšt*. Others bear personal names (perhaps of the potter), *e.g.* Shebnaiah, Azariah, Yopiah. Such stamped jar-handles have been found in quantity at Megiddo, Lachish, and Gibeon. A group of fiscal stamp impressions inscribed in Aramaic *yhd* (Judah) dated 400–200 BC are of special interest (see MONEY, also *BASOR*, 147, Oct. 1957, pp. 37–39, 148, Dec. 1957, pp. 28–30; *IEJ*, VII, 1957, pp. 146–153).

BIBLIOGRAPHY. (1) Palestinian seals: A. Rowe, *Catalogue of Egyptian Scarabs in the Palestine Archaeological Museum*, 1936; B. Parker, 'Cylinder Seals of Palestine', *Iraq*, XI, 1949; J. Nougayrol, *Cylindres sceaux et empreintes . . . trouvés en Palestine au cours des fouilles régulières*, 1939; A. Reifenberg, *Ancient Hebrew Seals*, 1950; D. Diringer, in *DOTT*, pp. 218–226. (2) For other Near Eastern seals: H. Frankfort, *Cylinder Seals*, 1939; D. J. Wiseman, *Cylinder Seals of Western Asia*, 1958. D.J.W.

II. IN THE NEW TESTAMENT

a. Literal use

The verb *sphragizō* (noun *sphragis*) is occasionally used in the New Testament in a literal sense, *e.g.* of the sealing of the tomb of Christ after His burial (Mt. xxvii. 66; *cf. Ev. Petr.* viii. 33), the sealing of Satan in the abyss (Rev. xx. 3), and the sealing of the apocalyptic roll against unauthorized scrutiny (Rev. v–viii. 1, *passim*). The practice of 'sealing' mentioned in this latter context would have been as familiar to Jews as to Romans (*cf.* Rev. xxii. 10, where the *logoi* are not 'sealed' because 'the time is at hand', and they are to be imminently used; contrast Dn. xii. 4, 9).

b. Figurative use

(i) In Rom. xv. 28 Paul refers to his intention of delivering a contribution (*koinōnia*) of the Gentiles to the saints in Jerusalem, and so of having 'sealed' (*sphragisamenos*) their offering. This may possibly imply a guarantee of his honesty ('under my own seal', NEB), but it will in any case denote Paul's *approval* of the Gentile action (so Theodore of Mopsuestia; *cf.* Jn. iii. 33, where *esphragisen* is used of man's 'approval' of the truth of God, and Jn. vi. 27, where precisely the same form of the verb is used with reference to God's attestation of the Christ).

(ii) An unusual use of the word *sphragis*, which carries still the sense of 'authentication', occurs in 1 Cor. ix. 2, when Paul describes his converts in the church at Corinth as the 'seal' affixed by Christ to his work; the vindication, indeed, of his apostolate.

(iii) In the discussion of Abraham's exemplary faith in Rom. iv, Paul mentions the *sēmeion* of circumcision as the confirming 'seal' (NEB 'hall-mark') of a righteousness which existed, by faith, before the rite itself was instituted. This use of the term 'seal' compares with that in the Apocalypse (Rev. vii. 2–8, ix. 4), where the servants of God are described as being 'sealed' with 'the seal of the living God' (vii. 2 f.; *cf.* Ezk. ix. 4; Rev. xiv. 1), as a safeguard as well as a mark of possession. A. G. Hebert suggests ('Seal', in *A Theological Word Book of the Bible*, ed. A. Richardson, 1950, p. 222) that these passages 'readily fall into a baptismal context'.

III. SEALING BY THE SPIRIT

One important New Testament image associates *sphragis* with *pneuma*. The Pauline characterization of the Christian inheritance in Eph. i, for example, proceeds against a background filled with Christian hope. In verse 13, accordingly, the Ephesian Christians are described as 'sealed with the promised Holy Spirit' (RSV); they have received in time, that is to say, an earnest of what they will become in eternity. Once more this use of 'sealing' includes the concept of 'possession' (*cf.* 2 Tim. ii. 19; Gal. vi. 17). Similarly, mention of the Holy Spirit in Eph. iv. 30, during a piece of practical exhortation to Christ-like behaviour, is followed by the qualifying phrase, 'in whom (*en hō*) you were sealed for the day of redemption' (RSV); while in 2 Cor. i. 21 f. believers are described as 'anointed' by God, who has 'put his seal' upon them, and given them the Holy Spirit as an eternal guarantee. We have to consider the nature of this 'seal', as well as the moment and results of the 'sealing'.

a. The nature of the seal. Considerable discussion has taken place on this point. R. E. O. White, for example (*The Biblical Doctrine of Initiation*, 1960, p. 203 and n.), takes the aorists of *sphragizō* in Eph. i. 13, iv. 30; 2 Cor. i. 22 to refer to the gift of the Spirit, acting as a 'divine seal upon baptism'. He discovers in support of this suggestion a 'regular' New Testament use of the aorist tense in connection with the reception of the Spirit by the believer in baptism. W. F. Flemington, on the other hand (*The New Testament Doctrine of Baptism*, 1953, pp. 66 f.), proposes baptism itself as the seal, and relates this to the word *sphragis* used in connection with the Jewish rite of circumcision. (So also O. Cullmann, in *Baptism in the New Testament*, E.T., 1950, p. 46.)

Clearly the Hebrew background to the theology of baptism, and to the notion of 'seal' itself, cannot be discounted; and Gregory Dix has tried to indicate the extent to which the early Fathers were indebted to their Jewish antecedents in this respect (' "The Seal" in the Second Century', *Theology*, LI, 1948, pp. 7 ff.). At the same time, as Dix also points out, it is not necessarily the New Testament which justifies any later connection made between 'baptism' and 'seal'; even the *Didachē* does not call water baptism a 'sealing', or connect the sacrament in any way with the gift of the Holy Spirit.

b. The moment of sealing. These considerations will suggest the doubt that also exists about the precise moment of the believer's 'sealing'. If we are right to associate the gift of the Holy Spirit with baptism (which is a frequent but not altogether regular pattern in the New Testament, *cf.* Acts viii. 36 ff., x. 44), we may consider that this 'sealing' by the Spirit takes place at baptism, or more precisely, perhaps, at the moment of commitment that finds its focus and expression in the sacrament of baptism. So G. W. H. Lampe, for example (*The Seal of the Spirit*, 1951), has carefully examined the origin and meaning of the cognate New Testament terms *sphragis* and *chrisma*, associated with the 'chrism' of Christ Himself in whom the Spirit of God was actively present, and shown that (in Pauline language) incorporation into the body of Christ is effected by baptism (rather than by any equivalent of 'confirmation', incidentally), and 'sealed' by the gift of the Holy Spirit (*op. cit.*, pp. 6, 61 f. For a summary of the arguments involved, and their proponents, see further R. E. O. White, *op. cit.*, Additional Note 8, pp. 352 ff.).

c. The results of sealing. It has become clear from 1st-century papyri that the language of 'sealing' came to acquire in the East the extended and important meaning, particularly in legal circles, of giving validity to documents, guaranteeing the genuineness of articles and so on. (The possible parallels that exist between *sphragizō* and initiation into Greek mystery cults are less likely to be significant.) It is easy as a result to see how the word *sphragis* and its cognates fit naturally into New Testament contexts which presuppose the theology of the covenant, and denote, in terms of the gift of the Holy Spirit, authentication as well as ownership. We have already noticed these to be aspects of the meaning of the term in other passages of the New Testament. Here again we are not far from further ideas suggested by the antecedent use of similar terms. The 'mark' of initiation administered by John the Baptist, for instance, was an entirely eschatological rite (Lk. iii. 3 ff.; note the reaction of the people to John's identity in verse 15); and in line with normative Jewish apocalyptic his baptism signified an 'earmarking' for salvation in view of coming judgment comparable to certain parts of the Psalms of Solomon (*e.g.* xv. 6 f., 8; *cf.* 2 Esdras vi. 5), and of the New Testament itself (2 Tim. ii. 19; and *cf.* the thought of 'sealing for security' already noticed in Rev. vii. 2 ff., *etc.*; see R. E. O. White, *op. cit.*, p. 88).

In the New Testament uses of the term 'seal' we have considered, the ideas of ownership, authentication, and security predominate. The three Pauline passages reviewed together (Eph. i. 13, iv. 30; 2 Cor. i. 22) indicate that the *arrabōn* of the Holy Spirit given to the believer, incorporated *en Christōi* by baptism through faith, is a 'token and pledge of final redemption' (G. W. H. Lampe, *op. cit.*, p. 61). In this way the gift of the Spirit is equivalent to 'putting on' Christ, sharing His *chrisma*, and becoming members of His body, the true Israel of God (*ibid.*; *cf.* 1 Cor. xii. 13). The gift of the Holy Spirit, in fact, confirms the covenant in which believers are 'sealed' as God's own.

Bibliography. The standard English work on this subject (New Testament) is G. W. H. Lampe, *The Seal of the Spirit*, 1951 (especially Part I). For the history of the idea, see also G. Dix, ' "The Seal" in the Second Century', *Theology*, LI, 1948, pp. 7 ff. For a fuller discussion of the relevant texts, see the major works on baptism in the New Testament, notably O. Cullmann, *Baptism in the New Testament*, tr. J. K. S. Reid, 1950; W. F. Flemington, *The New Testament Doctrine of Baptism*, 1953; P.-Ch. Marcel, *The Biblical Doctrine of Infant Baptism* tr. P. E. Hughes, 1953; and R. E. O. White, *The Biblical Doctrine of Initiation*, 1960. S.S.S.

SEA-MONSTER (*tannîn*) occurs in the AV in La. iv. 3 only. The LXX *drakontes*, 'dragons' identified the word with that translated 'serpent' in Ex. vii. 9, 10, 12, and elsewhere rendered 'dragon'. It should, however, be taken as the plural of the Hebrew *tan*, which is used eight times in Isaiah and Jeremiah of an animal frequenting desolate places, certainly the 'jackal'. It is rendered thus by RV and RSV. The context of La. iv. 3 indicates a mammal. The Hebrew word is usually identified with a root meaning 't mourn or howl'. The distinctive cry of the jackal is alluded to in Mi. i. 8; Jb. xxx. 29; Is. xiii. 22. See also DRAGON, SERPENT. D.G.S.

SEBA. 1. Son of Cush, classed under Ham (Gn. x. 7; 1 Ch. i. 9). **2.** Land and people in S Arabia, apparently closely related to the land and people of Sheba (*q.v.*); in fact, *s^e^bā'* (Seba) and *š^e^bā'* (Sheba) are commonly held to be simply the Old Arabian and Hebrew forms of the one name of a people, *i.e.* the well-known kingdom of Sheba. In a psalm (lxxii. 10) dedicated to Solomon, he is promised gifts from 'the kings of Sheba and (or: "yea") Seba'. In Isaiah's prophecies, Israel's ransom would take the wealth of Egypt, Ethiopia (Cush) and Seba (Is. xliii. 3), and the tall Sabaeans were to acknowledge Israel's God (Is. xlv. 14), first fulfilled in the wide spread of Judaism and first impact of Christianity there during the first five centuries AD. The close association of Seba/Sheba with Africa (Egypt and Cush) may just possibly reflect connections across the Red Sea between S Arabia and Africa from the 10th century BC onwards; for slender indications of this, see W. F. Albright, *BASOR*, 128, 1952, p. 45 with nn. 26, 27. Strabo (xvi. 4. 8–10) names a town Sabai and harbour Saba on the west or Red Sea coast of Arabia. K.A.K.

SEBAT. See CALENDAR.

SECACAH. A settlement in the plain of Judah (Jos. xv. 61); probably Khirbet es-Samrah, a site measuring 76 yards × 44 yards, including double walls (casemate on the east side) and a cistern. Irrigation works are found in the vicinity. The single level of occupation is dated 9th century BC or later (*BASOR*, 142). J.P.U.L.

SECHU (AV), **SECU** (RV and RSV). The Hebrew name, perhaps meaning 'outlook', of a place near Ramah, which Saul visited when seeking David and Samuel (1 Sa. xix. 22). A possible but uncertain identification is Khirbet Shuweikeh, about 3 miles north of el-Râm (biblical Ramah). Some MSS of the LXX read the unknown town Sephi, which represents, according to some scholars, Heb. *š^e^pî*, 'bare hill'; and the Pesh. similarly renders *sûpâ*, 'the end'; but other Gk. MSS and the Vulgate support the Massoretic Hebrew.

BIBLIOGRAPHY. F. M. Abel, *Géographie de la Palestine*, II, 1938, p. 453; C. R. Conder and H. H. Kitchener, *The Survey of Western Palestine*, III, 1883, p. 52. J.T.

SECOND COMING. See ESCHATOLOGY, IV.

SECT. See HERESY.

SECUNDUS. A Thessalonian Christian accompanying Paul (Acts xx. 4), probably as a delegate, with Aristarchus, of his church, to bring the collection for Jerusalem (*cf.* 1 Cor. xvi. 1 ff.). Agreement on the precise significance of Acts xx. 4 is incomplete, but Secundus seems included among those who awaited Paul at Troas. Zahn (*INT*, 1909, I, p. 213) conjectured that Secundus was another name of the Macedonian Gaius (mentioned with Aristarchus in Acts xix. 29), distinguished here from his companion Gaius of Derbe (see GAIUS).

The name is Latin, and attested in Thessalonian inscriptions. A.F.W.

SEED. The essential plant organism which enables the species to perpetuate itself. Seed-bearing plants are of great antiquity (Gn. i. 11), some excellent specimens of ferns being preserved from the Carboniferous period. They are uniformly much more highly developed than present-day ferns and lycopods.

The progeny of the species *Homo sapiens* was also regarded as 'seed' (Gn. iii. 15, xiii. 15). Thus the seed of Abraham constituted Isaac and his descendants (Gn. xxi. 12, xxviii. 14). The relationship between God and His people provided a perpetual establishment for the seed of Israel (Ps. lxxxix. 4), who would be ruled over by a descendant of the house of David (Acts ii. 30), interpreted by the early Christians in terms of Christ the Messiah (2 Tim. ii. 8).

The idea of the seed as the unit of reproduction of plant life found expression in several of Christ's parables. The spiritual significance of the seed varied with the differing circumstances under which the parables were narrated. In that of the seeds and the sower (Mt. xiii. 3–23; Lk. viii. 5–15), the seed was interpreted in Matthew as the 'word of the kingdom', while in Mark (iv. 3–20) and Luke it was the 'word of God'. In the parable of the seed and the tares (Mt. xiii. 24–30), the 'good seed' represented the children of the kingdom, while in the parable of the mustard seed (Mt. xiii. 31, 32; Mk. iv. 30–32) the seed represented the kingdom of heaven. In Mk. iv. 26–29 the mystery surrounding the development of the divine kingdom was likened to that connected with the germination and growth of a seed.

The Pauline doctrine of the resurrection body (1 Cor. xv. 35 ff.) reflected the thought of Christ concerning the necessity of wheat-grains dying before they could produce abundantly (Jn. xii. 24). The resurrection body of the believer will be significantly different in kind and degree from that laid to rest in the grave, bearing a relationship to it similar to that existing between an acorn and the mature oak. R.K.H.

SEIR. 1. The word *śē'îr* defines a mountain (Gn. xiv. 6; Ezk. xxxv. 15), a land (Gn. xxxii. 3, xxxvi. 21; Nu. xxiv. 18), and a people (Ezk. xxv. 8) in the general area of old Edom. Esau went to live there (Gn. xxxii. 3), and his descendants overcame the original inhabitants, the Horites (Gn. xiv. 6, xxxvi. 20; Dt. ii. 12; Jos. xxiv. 4). The Simeonites later destroyed some Amalekites who took refuge there (1 Ch. iv. 42, 43).

2. A landmark on the boundary of Judah (Jos. xv. 10). J.A.T.

SELA. Etymologically the word *sela'* or *has-sela'* means 'rock' or 'cliff' and may be used of any rocky place. There is, however, a specific Sela in the Bible which may now be identified with the massive rocky plateau, Umm el-Biyara, which towers 1,000 feet above the level of Petra (the Greek translation of Sela), and 3,700 feet above sea level. N. Glueck in 1933, and W. H. Morton in 1955, demonstrated the existence of an Iron Age Edomite settlement here. It was finally taken about 300 BC by the Nabataeans (*q.v.*), who converted the great valley to the north, some 4,500 feet long and 740–1,500 feet across, quite enclosed by mountain walls, into the amazing rock-cut city of Petra—the 'rose-red city half as old as time'.

The first reference in the Bible is in 2 Ki. xiv. 7, where we learn that Amaziah, king of Judah, captured Sela and renamed it Joktheel. Isaiah, referring to the coming judgment on Moab, spoke of fugitive Moabites sending tribute to Judah from distant Sela (Is. xvi. 1) and Obadiah, in condemning Edom, refers to those who dwell in the clefts of the rock (Sela, Ob. 3). Other references to 'the rock', in Jdg. i. 36, 2 Ch. xxv. 12, and Is. xlii. 11, almost certainly refer to the same place.

BIBLIOGRAPHY. F. M. Abel, *Géographie de la Palestine*, II, 1933, p. 407; N. Glueck, *AASOR*, XIV, 1933–4, pp. 77 f.; W. H. Morton, *Umm el Biyara*, *BA*, XIX, 1956, pp. 26 ff. J.A.T.

SELAH. An isolated word occurring seventy-one times in the Psalms and three times in Habakkuk (iii. 3, 9, 13; 'the minor Psalter'). Since all of these, except Pss. xli, lxxxi, name the kind of melody or psalmody in the title, it is generally agreed that Selah must be a musical or liturgical sign, though its precise import is not known. The following are the main suggestions:

1. A musical direction to the singers and/or orchestra to 'lift up', *i.e.* to sing or play *forte*. Thus LXX has *diapsalma* in each instance, perhaps a musical rather than a doxological interlude.

2. A liturgical mark (*sālal*, 'to lift up'; *cf.* Akkad. *sullu*, 'prayer'), perhaps to lift up the voice or the hands in prayer. It may have come into use, possibly in the exilic period, in connection with psalms used in public worship to denote those places at which the priest should pronounce a benediction. Some take it to mean 'to lift up' the eyes, for the purpose of repeating the verse, thus the equivalent of '*da capo*'. Others would derive it from an Aramaic root *sl*, 'to bow', and so interpret it as directing the worshipper at this point to prostrate himself.

3. The Targ. Aquila and Vulgate render Selah by phrases implying an ejaculation 'for ever', and make it a cry of worship like 'Amen' and 'Hallelujah' (Ps. xlvi. 3) at the close of the liturgy or at specified points within it (Ps. iii. 2, 4, *etc.*). D.J.W.

SELEUCIA. The former port of Antioch in Syria (1 Macc. xi. 8) which lay 5 miles north of the mouth of the Orontes river and 16 miles away from Antioch. Seleucia (*Seleukeia*) was founded by Seleucus Nicator in 301 BC, eleven years after he had founded the Seleucid kingdom. The city lay at the foot of Mt. Rhosus, to the north, and was itself in the north-east corner of a beautiful fertile plain still noted for its beauty. It was fortified on the south and west and surrounded by walls, but, although regarded as impregnable, it was taken by the Ptolemy Euergetes (1 Macc. xi. 8) in the Ptolemaic–Seleucid wars and remained in the hands of the Ptolemies till 219 BC, when Antiochus the Great recaptured it. He greatly beautified it, and, although it was lost again for a short time to Ptolemy Philometor in 146 BC, Seleucia was soon retaken. The Romans under Pompey made it a free city in 64 BC, and from then on it flourished until it began to decay fairly early in the Christian era. It is known in the Bible only in Acts xiii. 4, as the port of embarkation of Paul and Barnabas after they had been commissioned by the church in Antioch. From Seleucia they set sail for Cyprus on their first missionary journey. It is probably the port inferred in Acts xiv. 26, xv. 30, 39, though it is not named.

Seleucia today is an extensive ruin inviting serious archaeological investigation. The city area can be traced, and evidence of buildings, gates, walls, the amphitheatre, the inner harbour, and the great water conduit built by Constantius in AD 338 in solid rock to carry off the mountain torrent from the city are all to be seen. The channel which connected the inner harbour to the sea has, however, long since been silted up.

J.A.T.

SELEUCUS. One of Alexander's lesser generals, who took control of the far eastern satrapies after his death, and became a leading advocate of partition. After the battle of Ipsus in 301 BC he founded the port of Seleucia (in Pieria) (Acts xiii. 4) to serve his new western capital of Antioch, and the Seleucid domains were later extended over most of Asia Minor. The dynasty, many of whose kings bore the names of Seleucus or Antiochus, ruled from Syria for two and a half centuries, until suspended by the Romans. The vast and heterogeneous population called for a policy of active hellenization if their power was to be established. This and the fact that Palestine was the disputed frontier with the Ptolemies of Egypt caused trouble for the Jews. The Maccabaean revolt, with its legacy of petty kingdoms and principalities, and the religious sects of Jesus' time, was the result of the Seleucid attempt to secure Palestine.

BIBLIOGRAPHY. E. R. Bevan, *The House of Seleucus*, 1902; V. Tcherikover, *Hellenistic Civilization and the Jews*, 1959. E.A.J.

SEMITIC LANGUAGES. See LANGUAGE OF THE OLD TESTAMENT.

SENAAH. In the list of exiles who returned with Zerubbabel there are 3,630 (Ezr. ii. 35) or 3,930 (Ne. vii. 38) belonging to the town of Senaah. In Ne. iii. 3 the name of the town occurs again with the definite article. Since in both passages Jericho is mentioned in close proximity, Senaah may have been near Jericho. J.S.W.

SENATE, SENATOR. 1. The AV translation in Ps. cv. 22 (Heb. *z^e^qēnîm*; LXX *presbyteroi*), where RV has 'elders'. See ELDER. 2. Gk. *gerousia*, 'assembly of elders', Acts v. 21. See SANHEDRIN.

SENEH ('pointed rock') and **BOZEZ** ('height') were two sharp rocks between which Jonathan and his armour-bearer entered the garrison of the Philistines (1 Sa. xiv. 4 ff.). See MICHMASH. No precise identification of their location has been made, but see *GTT*, p. 317.

SENIR. The Amorite name for Mt. Hermon (*ś^e^nîr*; Assyr. *Saniru*; AV 'Shenir'), identified in Dt. iii. 9 but distinguished in Ct. iv. 8. Hermon is the southern peak of the Anti-Lebanon range, and Senir was probably a separate part of the mountain-ridge, the name being sometimes loosely applied to the whole. Early in the second millennium BC it seems to have been an Amorite cult-place. The Manassites expanded north to Senir at the expense of the Aramaeans (1 Ch. v. 23). Senir supplied fir-planks for Tyrian vessels (Ezk. xxvii. 5). J.W.C.

SENNACHERIB. Sennacherib (Heb. *sanḥērîb*; Assyr. *Sin-aḫḫē-eriba*, 'Sin has increased the brothers') ruled Assyria 705–681 BC. When his father, whom he had served as governor of the northern frontier, was assassinated, Sennacherib first marched to Babylonia, where Marduk-apla-iddina II (see MERODACH-BALADAN) was in revolt. He had ousted a local nominee Marduk-zakir-šum in 703 BC and was rallying support against Assyria. It was probably about this time that Merodach-baladan sent envoys to Hezekiah of Judah (2 Ki. xx. 12–19; Is. xxxix). Late in 702 BC Sennacherib defeated the Chaldean and his Elamite and Arab allies in battles at Cutha and Kish. He was then welcomed in Babylon, where he set Bel-ibni on the throne. The Assyrians ravaged Bît-Yakin and returned to Nineveh with many prisoners, Merodach-baladan himself having escaped to Elam.

Sennacherib had little difficulty in controlling his northern frontier, an area well known to him while crown prince. After a series of raids against the hill peoples in the East he moved against the West, where an anti-Assyrian coalition, backed by Egypt, was gaining power. The leader, Hezekiah of Judah, had seized Padi, the pro-Assyrian ruler of Ekron (2 Ki. xviii. 8), strengthened the fortifications and improved the water supplies at Jerusalem (2 Ki. xx. 20; see SILOAM), and called for help from Egypt (Is. xxx. 1–4).

Sennacherib's third campaign in Hezekiah's fourteenth year (701 BC) was directed against this coalition. He first marched down the Phoenician coast, capturing Great and Little Sidon, Zarephath, Mahalliba (see AHLAB), Ushu, Akzib, and Acco, but not attempting to lay siege to Tyre. He replaced Luli (Elulaeus), king of Sidon, who fled and died in exile, by Ethba'al (Tuba'al). The kings of Sidon, Arvad, Byblos, Beth-ammon, Moab, and Edom submitted, but Ashkelon refused and, with its neighbouring towns, including Beth-dagon and Joppa, was despoiled. Sennacherib claims to have marched to Eltekeh, where he defeated an Egyptian army. He then slew the nobles of Ekron for handing over Padi to Hezekiah, and sent detachments to destroy forty-six walled towns and many villages in Judah, from which he took 200,150 people and much spoil. He himself took part in the siege and capture of Lachish, and is depicted on his palace reliefs reviewing the spoil (see LACHISH). From here he sent officers to demand the surrender of Jerusalem (2 Ch. xxxii. 9).

Fig. 188. The design on the royal seal of Sennacherib, king of Assyria, 705–681 BC. The king stands between the god Ashur and the goddess Ninlil.

Sennacherib's own account of this campaign claims tribute from Hezekiah (Annals) and describes how he besieged 'Hezekiah the Jew . . . I shut him up like a caged bird within his royal capital, Jerusalem. I put watch-posts closely round the city and turned back to his fate anyone who came out of the city gate' (Taylor Prism, BM). Hezekiah paid the Assyrians tribute (2 Ki. xviii. 13–16; Is. xxxvi. 1 f.) which was later sent to Nineveh (Taylor Prism, dated 691 BC) and freed Padi, to whom some of the former Judaean territories were now given.

Sennacherib's account makes no mention of any conclusion of the siege (*cf.* 2 Ki. xix. 32–34) or of the defeat of the Assyrian army by the hand of the Lord, perhaps by a plague (verse 35) described by Herodotus (ii. 141) as 'a multitude of field mice which by night devoured all the quivers and bows of the enemy, and all the straps by which they held their shields . . . next morning they commenced their fight and great numbers fell as they had no arms with which to defend themselves'.

The majority of scholars hold that the mention of the approach of the Egyptian forces under Tirhakah (2 Ki. xix. 9; Is. xxxvii. 9) is an anachronism (see TIRHAKAH). Moreover, they consider 2 Ki. xix. 37 implies that the death of Sennacherib occurred soon after his return to Nineveh. They therefore postulate a second, and unsuccessful, Assyrian campaign against Jerusalem, perhaps following the attack on the Arabs 689–686 BC. Neither the extant Assyrian annals nor Babylonian chronicles mention such a campaign, and verses 36 f. do not necessarily state the length of time between Sennacherib's return from Palestine and his death in 681 BC, and this must have been some years on any interpretation. Thus the theory of a single campaign in 701 BC can still reasonably be held.

In 700 BC the Assyrians once more marched to Babylonia, where Bel-ibni had rebelled. Sennacherib placed his own son, Aššur-nadin-šum, on the throne, and he held sway until captured by the Elamites. In the series of campaigns which followed, Sennacherib fought the Elamites, and in 694 mounted a naval expedition across the Persian Gulf directed against those who had harboured Merodach-baladan. Erech was captured and, finally, Babylon sacked in 689 BC. On other frontiers Sennacherib invaded Cilicia and captured Tarsus, as well as raiding the Arabs south and east of Damascus.

At home Sennacherib was aided by his energetic West Semitic wife, Naqi'a-Zakutu, in the reconstruction of Nineveh, where he built a 'palace without a rival', an armoury, new city walls and gates. By providing a new source of water supply from the river Gomel (Bavian) led by an aqueduct (Jerwan) down to a dam (Ajeila) east of the metropolis he was able to irrigate parks and large tracts of land as well as to improve the natural defences of Nineveh formed by the rivers Tigris and Khosr.

He also built extensively at Assur and Kakzi and introduced many technological advances.

Sennacherib was assassinated by his sons while worshipping in the temple of Nisroch (2 Ki. xix. 37). The flight of the sons (see ADRAMMELECH, SHAREZER) may be reflected in an account of the disturbances following his death in December 681 BC given by his younger son Esarḥaddon, who had been elected crown prince in 687 BC, and now succeeded to the throne (verse 37). There is little support for the theory that Esarhaddon was the unnamed 'son' mentioned as assassin by the Babylonian Chronicle, or that the death took place in Babylon.

BIBLIOGRAPHY. D. D. Luckenbill, *The Annals of Sennacherib*, 1924; D. J. Wiseman in *DOTT*, pp. 64–73. D.J.W.

SEPHAR. The name of a 'mountain of the east' (*har haq-qeḏem*), mentioned in the Table of Nations (see NATIONS, TABLE OF) in defining the boundary of the territory of the sons of Joktan (Gn. x. 30). Judging from the names of other sons of Joktan, a mountain or promontory in S Arabia seems likely, and the coastal town of Ẓafār in the E Hadramaut has been suggested. In view, however, of the lack of precision in the Bible statement, and the discrepancy in the sibilants, there can be no certainty.

See J. A. Montgomery, *Arabia and the Bible*, 1934, p. 41. T.C.M.

SEPHARAD. The place in which captives from Jerusalem were exiled (Ob. 20). The location is as yet unidentified. Of many conjectures, the most plausible is the country of Saparda, named in the Assyrian Annals of Sargon and Esarhaddon as a country to the east allied to the Medes. It is probably the same as the Persian Sparda and lies south of Urmia and adjacent to Media. The Targum of Jonathan interpreted it as Spain, hence the term Sephardim for Spanish Jews (see also ASHKENAZ). A location in Anatolia is favoured by the Vulgate (*in Bosphoro*). D.J.W.

SEPHARVAIM. A city captured by the Assyrians (2 Ki. xvii. 24, 31, xviii. 34, xix. 13; Is. xxxvi. 19, xxxvii. 13). The context implies that it lies in Syria or adjacent territory and this is supported by the name of its deities (see ADRAMMELECH, ANAMMELECH). The place is unidentified, though Halévy's suggestion that it is the same as the later Sibraim near Damascus (Ezk. xlvii. 16) is possible. It cannot be the same as the Šab/mara'in of the Babylonian Chronicle, as this is Samaria. The usual interpretation of Sepharvaim as the twin cities of Sippar (of Šamaš and Anunitum) in Babylonia is unsupported from cuneiform sources, as Sippar had no independent king (*cf.* 2 Ki. xix. 13). D.J.W.

SEPTUAGINT. See TEXT AND VERSIONS.

SEPULCHRE. See BURIAL AND MOURNING.

SEPULCHRE OF THE KINGS, SEPULCHRE OF DAVID. It would appear from the Bible that the kings were buried in a special area near Jerusalem. The custom may go back to David's time (1 Ki. ii. 10). When Nehemiah was building the wall of Jerusalem one of his parties worked 'over against the sepulchres of David', not far from the 'pool of Siloah' (Ne. iii. 15, 16).

Most of the kings from David to Hezekiah were buried in the city of David, though some kings had their own private sepulchres, *e.g.* Asa (2 Ch. xvi. 14), and possibly Hezekiah (2 Ch. xxxii. 33), Manasseh (2 Ki. xxi. 18), Amon (2 Ki. xxi. 26), and Josiah (2 Ki. xxiii. 30; 2 Ch. xxxv. 24). Several kings died outside the bounds of Palestine: Jehoahaz in Egypt, Jehoiachin and Zedekiah in Babylon. Possibly Jehoiakim was not buried at all (Je. xxii. 19), and Jehoram, Joash, Uzziah, and Ahaz were not admitted to the royal sepulchre (2 Ch. xxi. 20, xxiv. 25, xxvi. 23, xxviii. 27).

In the New Testament the sepulchre of David was still remembered (Acts ii. 29), and Josephus (*BJ* v. 4. 2) speaks of the third wall passing by the sepulchral caverns of the kings. The exact site is not known today. Monuments in the Kedron Valley are late, both architecture and epigraphy pointing to the time of Herod the Great. The so-called 'tombs of the Kings' some distance to the north of the modern wall are post-Christian. J.A.T.

SERAIAH (*śᵉrāyâ, śᵉrāyāhû*, 'Yahweh hath prevailed'). **1.** David's scribe (2 Sa. viii. 17, RVmg 'secretary'), called also 'Sheva' (2 Sa. xx. 25), 'Shisha' (1 Ki. iv. 3), and 'Shavsha' (1 Ch. xviii. 16).

2. Son of Azariah and a chief priest in the time of Zedekiah. He was put to death by the king of Babylon at Riblah (2 Ki. xxv. 18 = Je. lii. 24). **3.** A son of Tanhumeth the Netophathite, and a captain who was among those whom Gedaliah, governor of Judaea, advised to submit to the Chaldeans (2 Ki. xxv. 23 = Je. xl. 8). **4.** A son of Kenaz (1 Ch. iv. 13, 14). **5.** A Simeonite, son of Asiel (1 Ch. iv. 35). **6.** A priest who returned with Zerubbabel to Jerusalem (Ezr. ii. 2; Ne. xii. 1, 12). **7.** One who sealed the covenant (Ne. x. 2), perhaps the same as (6) above. **8.** A priest, son of Hilkiah (Ne. xi. 11) and 'ruler of the house of God' in post-exilic Jerusalem. **9.** One of the officers of King Jehoiakim, ordered by him to arrest Baruch and Jeremiah (Je. xxxvi. 26). **10.** A prince of Judah who accompanied King Zedekiah to Babylon in the fourth year of his reign. Seraiah carried Jeremiah's prophecy against Babylon (Je. li. 59, 61). Some would associate him with (3) above. J.D.D.

SERAPHIM. The only mention of these celestial beings in Scripture is in the early vision of Isaiah (Is. vi). The seraphim (incorrectly rendered in AV as 'seraphims') were associated with cherubim and ophanim in the task of guarding the divine throne. The heavenly beings seen by Isaiah were human in form, but had six wings. With one pair they shielded their faces, with another they concealed their feet, and with the remaining pair they flew. The seraphim of the vision were stationed above the throne of God, and appear to have been leaders in divine worship. One of these creatures chanted a refrain which Isaiah recorded in the words, 'Holy, holy, holy is the Lord of hosts; the whole earth is full of his glory.'

So vigorous was this act of worship that the thresholds of the divine Temple shook, and the holy place was filled with smoke. The prophet lay in self-abasement before God and confessed his iniquity. Then one of the seraphim flew to him with a burning coal taken from the altar, and in an act of purification announced to Isaiah that his sin had been forgiven and his guilt removed.

From the foregoing it would appear that for Isaiah the seraphim constituted an order of angelic beings responsible for certain functions of guardianship and worship. However, they appear to have been distinct moral creatures, not just projections of the imagination or personifications of animals. Their moral qualities were employed exclusively in the service of God, and their position was such that they were privileged to exercise an atoning ministry while at the same time extolling the ethical and moral character of God.

The precise origin and meaning of the Hebrew term are uncertain. The *śārāp̄* of Nu. xxi. 6; Dt. viii. 15 was a venomous serpent which bit the Israelites in the desert, while Is. xiv. 29, xxx. 6 referred to a reptile popular in folklore. Some Jewish writers have attempted to derive the term from a cognate Heb. root *śārap̄*, 'to burn', holding that the seraphim were bright or shining angels. However, the root means 'to consume with fire' rather than 'to shine' or 'reflect', thus making the seraphim agents of purification by fire, as Isaiah indicated.

Archaeological investigation of a XIIth Dynasty tomb at Beni-hasan revealed two winged griffins, known in Demotic Egyptian by the name *seref*, guarding a grave. From Mesopotamia an artefact depicting a six-winged seraph was uncovered at Tell Halaf. The creature had a human body as opposed to the eagle–lion combination of Egypt, with four wings distributed below the waist and the remaining two between the shoulders. The face bore traces of late Hittite influence, and the artefact was dated about 1000 BC.

BIBLIOGRAPHY. J. Strachan in *HDB*; H. S. Nash in *SHERK* (*s.v.* 'angel'); H. Heppe, *Reformed Dogmatics*, E.T., 1950, pp. 210 ff.

R.K.H.

SERGIUS PAULUS. See PAULUS, SERGIUS.

SERJEANTS. A Roman magistrate was attended by a staff of lictors (the number depending on his rank) who carried bundles of rods (hence Gk. *rhabdouchoi*, 'rod-bearers', Acts xvi. 35) and axes symbolizing his capital powers. There being no regular police force, these 'serjeants' carried out police duties as well as escorting the magistrate. They occur at Philippi because it was a Roman colony. E.A.J.

SERMON ON THE MOUNT. The Sermon on the Mount is the title commonly given to the teachings of Jesus recorded in Mt. v–vii. Whether the name can be properly used for the somewhat parallel portion in Luke (vi. 20–49) depends upon one's interpretation of the literary relationship between the two. The latter is often called the Sermon on the Plain because it is said to have been delivered on 'a level place' (Lk. vi. 17, RSV) rather than 'on the mountain' (Mt. v. 1, RSV). But both expressions probably denote the same place approached from two different directions; see W. M. Christie, *Palestine Calling*, 1939, pp. 35 f.

Canon Liddon, in his Bampton Lectures, refers to the Sermon as 'that original draught of essential Christianity'. If this be interpreted to mean that the Sermon on the Mount is Christianity's message to the pagan world, we must counter with the reminder that it is manifestly *didachē*, not *kerygma*. By no stretch of the imagination can it be considered 'good news' to one depending upon fulfilment of its demands for entrance into the kingdom. (Imagine a man outside of Christ, without the empowering aid of the Holy Spirit, trying to exceed the righteousness of the scribes and Pharisees.) It is rather a character sketch of those who have already entered the kingdom and a description of the quality of ethical life which is now expected of them. In this sense, it is true, it is 'essential Christianity'.

I. COMPOSITION

In times past it was taken for granted that the Sermon on the Mount was a single discourse delivered by Jesus on a specific occasion. Certainly this is what appears to be the case as it is reported in Matthew. The disciples sat down (verse 1), Jesus opened His mouth and taught them (verse 2), and when it was over the crowds were astonished at His teaching (vii. 28). However, most scholars are of the opinion that the Sermon is really a compilation of sayings of the Lord—'a kind of epitome of all the sermons that Jesus ever preached' (W. Barclay, *The Gospel of Matthew*, I, p. 79). It is argued that: (1) There is far too much concentrated material here for one sermon. The disciples, not noted for acute spiritual perception, could never have assimilated such a wealth of ethical teaching. (2) The wide range of topics (description of kingdom blessedness, counsel on divorce, admonition concerning anxiety) is inconsistent with the unity of a single discourse. (3) The abruptness with which certain sections emerge in the Sermon (*e.g.* the teaching on prayer in Mt. vi. 1–11) is very noticeable. (4) Thirty-four verses occur in other, and often more suitable, contexts throughout Luke (*e.g.* the Lord's Prayer in Luke is introduced by a request from His disciples that He teach them to pray (Lk. xi. 1); the saying about the narrow gate comes in response to the question, 'Will those who are saved be few?' Lk. xiii. 23), and it is more likely that Matthew transposed sayings of Jesus into the Sermon than that Luke found them there and then scattered them throughout his Gospel. (5) It is characteristic of Matthew to gather together teaching material under certain headings and insert them into the narrative of Jesus' life (*cf.* B. W. Bacon, *Studies in Matthew*, 1930, pp. 269–325), and that the Sermon on the Mount is therefore simply the first of these didactic sections. (Others deal with the themes of discipleship (ix. 35–x. 42), the kingdom of heaven (xiii), true greatness (xviii), and the end of the age (xxiv, xxv).)

These considerations, however, do not force one to view the entire Sermon as an arbitrary composition. The historical setting in Mt. iv. 23–v. 1 leads us to expect an important discourse delivered on a specific occasion. Within the Sermon itself are various sequences which appear to be 'sermonettes' of Jesus and not topical collections of separate *logia*. A comparison with Luke's Sermon shows enough points of similarity (both begin with Beatitudes, close with the parable of the builders, and the intervening Lucan material —on loving one's enemies (vi. 27–36) and judging (vi. 37–42)—follows in the same sequence in Matthew) to suggest that behind both accounts there was a common source. Before either evangelist wrote there was in all probability a primitive framework which corresponded to an actual discourse delivered on a definite occasion. Such questions as whether the Sermon as it occurs in Matthew is closer to the original than the Lucan version, or whether Matthew followed a framework supplied by an earlier source, are still matters of scholarly debate. For our purpose it is enough to conclude that Matthew took a primitive sermon source and expanded it for his particular purpose by the introduction of relevant material.

II. LANGUAGE OF THE SERMON

In the last generation Aramaic scholarship has taught us much about 'The Poetry of Our Lord' —to borrow the title of C. F. Burney's book (1925). Even in translation we can recognize the various types of parallelism, which are the distinguishing feature of Semitic poetry. Mt. vii. 6, for example, is a fine illustration of 'synonymous' parallelism:

'Give not that which is holy unto the dogs,
Neither cast ye your pearls before swine.'

It appears that the Lord's Prayer is a poem of two stanzas, each of which has three lines of four beats apiece (*cf.* Burney, *op. cit.*, pp. 112 f.). The practical value of recognizing poetry where it occurs is that we are not so likely to interpret the text with such an inflexible literalism as we might employ in interpreting prose. How tragic if someone should (and history records that some have) literally 'pluck out his eye' or 'cut off his hand' in an attempt to do away with the passion of lust. A. M. Hunter notes that 'proverbs indeed are principles stated in extremes'. We must always avoid interpreting paradox with a crude literalism, but rather seek the principle that underlies the proverb (*Design for Life*, pp. 19, 20).

In this connection let us consider the quality of absoluteness in Jesus' moral imperatives. Verses like Mt. v. 48, 'Be ye therefore perfect even as your Father which is in heaven is perfect', have long troubled men. Part of the answer lies in the fact that these are not 'new laws' but broad principles set forth in terms of action. They fall into the category of prophetic injunction, which was always deeper and demanded more than the mere letter of the law. And they were ethics of the new age, designed for those who partook of a new power (*cf.* A. N. Wilder, 'The Sermon on the Mount', *IB*, VII, 1951, p. 163).

III. CIRCUMSTANCES

Both Matthew and Luke place the Sermon in the first year of Jesus' public ministry; Matthew a little earlier than Luke, who locates it immediately after the choosing of the Twelve and implies that it should be understood as somewhat of an 'ordination sermon'. In either case, it came in that period before the religious teachers could muster their opposition, and yet late enough for Jesus' fame to have spread through the land. The first months of His Galilaean ministry were spent in synagogue preaching, but soon the enthusiasm of His crowds necessitated some sort of outdoor preaching. A corresponding change can be seen in the character of His message. The early proclamation, 'Repent: for the kingdom of heaven is at hand' (Mt. iv. 17), has given way to exposition on the nature of the kingdom for those who seriously desired to learn.

Since the Sermon falls within the Galilaean ministry of Jesus, it is natural to assume that the scene of the Sermon would be one of the foothills which surrounded the northern plain. As Jesus entered Capernaum soon after (Mt. viii. 5), it was perhaps located in that general area. A Latin tradition, dating from about the 13th century, names a two-peaked hill, Karn Hattin, which lies a bit farther to the south, but only guides and tourists seem to take this identification with any degree of seriousness.

The Sermon is addressed primarily to disciples. This is the apparent meaning of both Mt. v. 1, 2 and Lk. vi. 20. Luke's use of the second person in the Beatitudes, in sayings like 'Ye are the salt of the earth' (Mt. v. 13), and the exalted ethic of the Sermon as a whole, can only mean that it was designed for those who had deserted paganism for life in the kingdom. Yet at the close of each account (Mt. vii. 28, 29; Lk. vii. 1) we learn of the presence of others. The solution seems to be that the crowd was there and heard Jesus as He taught, but that the discourse itself was directed primarily to the circle of disciples. Occasional utterances, such as the 'woes' of Lk. vi. 24–26, unless rhetorical devices, seem to be 'asides' to some who might be listening in and who needed such admonition.

IV. ANALYSIS

Regardless of whether one sees the Sermon as the summary of an actual discourse or as a mosaic of ethical sayings arranged by Matthew, there is little doubt that Mt. v–vii has a real unity marked by the logical development of a basic theme. This theme is presented in the Beatitudes and can be expressed as 'the quality and conduct of life in the kingdom'. The following is a descriptive analysis of the content of the Sermon.

a. The blessedness of those in the kingdom, v. 3–16

(i) The Beatitudes (v. 3–10).

(ii) An expansion of the final Beatitude and a digression to show the rôle of the disciple in an unbelieving world (v. 11–16).

b. The relationship of the message of Jesus to the old order, v. 17–48

(i) The thesis stated (v. 17). Jesus' message 'fulfils' the law by penetrating behind the letter and clarifying its underlying principle, thus bringing it to its ideal completion.

(ii) The thesis enlarged (v. 18–20).

(iii) The thesis illustrated (v. 21–48).

1. In the command not to kill, anger is the culpable element (v. 21–26).
2. Adultery is the fruit of an evil heart nourished on impure desire (v. 27–32).
3. Kingdom righteousness demands an honesty so transparent that oaths are unnecessary (v. 33–37).
4. *Lex talionis* must give way to a spirit of non-retaliation (v. 38–42).
5. Love is universal in application (v. 43–48).

c. Practical instructions for kingdom conduct, vi. 1–vii. 12

(i) Guard against false piety (vi. 1–18).

1. In almsgiving (vi. 1–4).
2. In prayer (vi. 5–15).
3. In fasting (vi. 16–18).

(ii) Dispel anxiety with simple trust (vi. 19–34).

(iii) Live in love (vii. 1–12).

d. Challenge to dedicated living, vii. 13–29

(i) The way is narrow (vii. 13, 14).

(ii) A good tree bears good fruit (vii. 15–20).

(iii) The kingdom is for those who hear and *do* (vii. 21–27).

V. INTERPRETATION

The Sermon on the Mount has had a long and varied history of interpretation. For Augustine, who wrote a treatise on the Sermon while still a bishop at Hippo (AD 393–396), it was the 'perfect rule or pattern of Christian life'—a new law in contrast with the old. Monastic orders interpreted it as a 'counsel of perfection' designed not for the populace but for the chosen few. The Reformers held it to be the 'uncompromising expression of divine righteousness directed towards all'. Tolstoy, the Russian novelist and (in later life) social reformer, resolved it into five commandments (suppression of all anger, chastity, no oaths, non-resistance, unreserved love of enemies), which if literally obeyed would do away with the existing evils and usher in a Utopian kingdom. Weiss and Schweitzer held that the demands were too radical for all times, and thus declared them 'interim ethics' for the early Christians, who believed that the end of all things was at hand. Still others, making great allowance for figurative language, understood the Sermon as the expression of a noble way of thinking—teaching which dealt with what man should *be* rather than with what he should *do*.

Thus the 20th-century interpreter is presented with a bewildering number of 'keys' with which to unlock the essential meaning of the Sermon on the Mount. With Kittel he can take the demands as purposely exaggerated so as to drive man to a sense of failure (and hence to repent and believe), or with Windisch he can differentiate between historical and theological exegesis and defend the practicability of the demands. With Dibelius he can interpret the great moral imperatives as the absolute ethic of the inbreaking kingdom, or with the Dispensationalists he can relegate the entire sermon to a future millennial reign of Christ.

How, then, shall we interpret the Sermon? The following will at least give us our guide lines: (1) Although couched in poetry and symbol, the Sermon still demands a quality of ethical conduct which is breathtaking in its dimensions. (2) Jesus is not laying down a new code of legal regulations but stating great ethical principles and how they affect the lives of those within the kingdom. (3) The Sermon is not a programme for the direct improvement of the world, but is directed to those who have denied the world in order to enter the kingdom. (4) It is neither an impractical ideal nor a fully attainable possibility. In the words of S. M. Gilmour, it is 'the ethic of that transcendental order which broke into history in Jesus Christ, has built itself into history in the church, but whose full realization lies beyond history when God will be "all in all" ' (*Journal of Religion*, XXI, July 1941, No. 3, p. 263).

BIBLIOGRAPHY. In addition to the extensive literature cited in other Bible dictionaries (see, *e.g.*, Votaw's article in *HDB*, extra vol., pp. 1–45), see H. K. McArthur, *Understanding the Sermon on the Mount*, 1960; J. W. Bowman and R. W. Tapp, *The Gospel from the Mount*, 1957; M. Dibelius, *The Sermon on the Mount*, 1940; A. M. Hunter, *Design for Life*, 1953; A. D. Lindsay, *The Moral Teaching of Jesus*, 1937; D. M. Lloyd-Jones, *Studies in the Sermon on the Mount*, I, 1959, II, 1960; A. N. Wilder's article in *IB*, VII, 1951, pp. 155–164; H. Windisch, *The Meaning of the Sermon on the Mount*, 1951, translation of revised edition of *Der Sinn der Bergpredigt*, 1st edn., 1929. R.H.M.

SERPENT.

I. GENERAL

Serpents or snakes are reptiles that have head, body, and tail but no limbs, and move over the ground on their belly, so that with their flickering tongue they are often described as licking or eating the dust (Gn. iii. 14; *cf.* Is. lxv. 25; Mi. vii. 17; and implicitly, Pr. xxx. 19). In simile, compare the nations creeping like snakes, to acknowledge Israel's God (Mi. vii. 17) and Egypt's flight from battle like a hissing snake down its bolt-hole (Je. xlvi. 22, RSV, in contrast to the Egyptian concept of the sacred uraeus-snake on a pharaoh's brow leading him to victory). The ability of various snakes to inject deadly poison into a wound when they bite or strike (Gn. xlix. 17; Ec. x. 8, 11; implicitly, Mt. vii. 10; Lk. xi. 11) enters into many biblical similes. Subjects of such similes include the harmfulness of the wicked (Dt. xxxii. 33 (rebellious Hebrews); Pss. lviii. 4, cxl. 3) or of overmuch wine (Pr. xxiii. 32), the Day of the Lord (Am. v. 19), and in metaphor foreign oppressors (Is. xiv. 29). Like war, famine, *etc.*, snake-bite could feature among divine judgments and punishments (Nu. xxi. 4–6; Je. viii. 17; Am. ix. 3), and deliverance from this harm could be granted to God's servants (Mk. xvi. 18; Lk. x. 19; *cf.* Acts xxviii. 3–6). Some snakes could be charmed (Ec. x. 11), others were considered 'deaf' to the charmer's techniques (Ps. lviii. 4, 5; Je. viii. 17). Snake-charmers may possibly be represented on Egyptian scarab-amulets (P. Montet, *L'Égypte et la Bible*, 1959, pp. 90–94, fig. 17). On snake-charming in Egypt, ancient and modern, *cf.* L. Keimer, *Histoires de Serpents dans l'Égypte Ancienne et Moderne*, 1947, and for Mesopotamia, see N. L. Corkill, 'Snake Specialists in Iraq', *Iraq*, VI, 1939, pp. 45–52.

Besides the general word *nāḥāš*, 'snake, serpent', and *śārāp̄*, 'burning' (see II below), Hebrew possesses several other words for serpents. The old word *peṯen* (Dt. xxxii. 33; Jb. xx. 14, 16; Pss. lviii. 4, xci. 13; Is. xi. 8; AV 'adder, asp') occurs as *bṯn* in the Ugaritic texts of the 14th century BC. This is often considered to be the Egyptian cobra (Arab. *naja haje*; and the related *naja nigricollis*, M. A. Murray, *JEA*, XXXIV, 1948, pp. 117, 118), and is the 'asp' of classical writers. The cobra gave rise to two Egyptian hieroglyphs. This venomous beast gave point to passages like Dt. xxxii. 33 and Jb. xx. 14, 16. The word *'ep̄'eh* (Jb. xx. 16; Is. xxx. 6, lix. 5; AV 'viper') is identical with Arab. *afa'â*, and like that word appears to be a further general term for serpents and sometimes more specifically for vipers (*cf.* L. Keimer, *Études d'Égyptologie*, VII, 1945, pp. 38, 39, 48, 49). In Gn. xlix. 17 (AV 'adder'), Heb. *šᵉp̄îp̄ôn* is often thought to represent the *cerastes* vipers: either or both the 'horned viper', *Cerastes cornutus*, and the hornless one, *Vipera cerastes*. In Egypt and Palestine these have been familiar from ancient times, and in Egypt became the hieroglyph for 'f', from the onomatopoeic words *fy*, *fyt*, 'cerastes-viper' (Keimer, *Études d'Égyptologie*, VII, 1945; P. E. Newberry, *JEA*, XXXIV, 1948, p. 118). The identification of *'akšûḇ* in Ps. cxl. 3 is uncertain; in Rom. iii. 13 it is rendered by Gk. *aspis*, 'asp'. The word *ṣip̄'ônî* is rendered by AV as 'adder' in Pr. xxiii. 32, and, like *ṣep̄a'* in Is. xiv. 29, as 'cockatrice' in Is. xi. 8, lix. 5; Je. viii. 17; these words certainly denote snakes of some kind. The animal that fastened on Paul's hand in Acts xxviii. 3 is often considered to be the common viper of the Mediterranean region; the same Greek word (*echidna*) is used in the powerful metaphors of Mt. iii. 7, xii. 34, xxiii. 33; Lk. iii. 7.

II. SPECIFIC

a. The first serpent in Scripture is the subtle creature of Gn. iii, used by Satan to alienate man from God (Rom. xvi. 20; 2 Cor. xi. 3), controlled by the devil like the demons in men and swine in New Testament days. For its part, the serpent was put under a curse that it would never rise above its (already customary) creeping posture (Gn. iii. 14). The serpent thus remained a biblical symbol of deceit (Mt. xxiii. 33), and the arch-deceiver himself is 'that old serpent' (Rev. xii. 9, 14, 15, xx. 2); Christians should match the serpent in his fabled wisdom if in no other respect (Mt. x. 16).

b. A sign performed by Moses before Israel (Ex. iv. 2–5, 28–30) and by Moses and Aaron before pharaoh (Ex. vii. 8–12) was to cast down his rod so that it become a serpent and take it up again as a rod, having on the latter occasion swallowed up the serpent-rods of the Egyptian magicians (for which see MAGIC AND SORCERY: Egyptian Magic and the Old Testament).

Fig. 189. A cobra in a reed basket. A conventional Egyptian rendering to convey the nature of the powerful goddess (who protected the king), of whom it was a symbol. From a painting in the tomb of Rekhonirē', Thebes, *c.* 1450 BC.

c. In the wilderness rebellious Israel was once punished by the onset of 'fiery serpents' (*nāḥāš śārāp̄*), whose venom was fatal (Nu. xxi. 4–9; *cf.* Dt. viii. 15). When Israel sought deliverance God commanded Moses to set up a bronze figure of a serpent on a pole, that those bitten might look to it, trusting in God's healing power, and live (see SERPENT, BRAZEN). The term *śārāp̄*, 'burning', or 'fiery', may refer to the effect of the venom or poison of the snakes concerned; it recurs in Is. xiv. 29 and xxx. 6 (where 'flying' might refer to the speed with which such reptiles may strike, as though 'winged'—so, modern Arab usage; for this and other explanations, see Keimer, *Histoires de Serpents*, p. 10, n. 2).

d. Some Hebrew references to 'serpents' apply not so much to snakes as to other fearful creatures, or are metaphorical of certain great military powers in the biblical world. Thus, the 'serpent' of Am. ix. 3 is probably some large denizen of the deep rather than a snake. In Is. xxvii. 1 the sword to be raised against 'Leviathan the fleeing (or, swift) serpent, Leviathan the twisting (or, winding) serpent, and . . . the dragon that is in the sea' (*cf.* RSV) most probably expressed coming judgment upon Assyria (land of the swift Tigris), Babylonia (of the winding Euphrates), and Egypt (*tannîn*, 'dragon, monster', as in Ezk. xxix. 3, xxxii. 2) respectively. Isaiah may here be announcing God's judgment on these pagan lands in terms of the ancient Canaanite myth of Baal's destruction of Lôtan or Leviathan and the many Mesopotamian tales of slaying dragons and serpents (Labbu, Zu, *etc.*), not to mention the Egyptian overthrowing of 'Apep, condemning them under their own popular imagery. In Jb. xxvi. 13 the identity of the 'fleeing serpent' (RSV) as associated with the sky is uncertain. Since the serpent can stand for Satan (*cf.* (*a*), above, and Rev. xii. 7–10, 14, 15, xx. 2) one may possibly compare here his alternative (?) designation of fallen Day Star (AV 'Lucifer'), to whom the king of Babylon is likened in Is. xiv. 12, 15; see also Jude 6 and 2 Pet. ii. 4.

In no case does any of these passages, biblical or non-biblical, refer to a creation-struggle of deity and monster, as all the serpent-slaying in them is done within an already created world. Furthermore, the Babylonian Ti'amat, whose death at Marduk's hands *is* associated with creation, was *not* a serpent or dragon, and therefore gives no support for assuming a struggle of deity and serpent/dragon at creation either (*cf.* A. Heidel, *The Babylonian Genesis*, 1951, pp. 83–88, 102–114). See also DRAGON, LEVIATHAN, RAHAB.

In Canaanite, Mesopotamian, Anatolian, and Egyptian mythology and cults, serpent deities are known (see fig. 65), and serpents in various contexts are symbols of protection (Egyptian uraeus), of evil (*e.g.* Egyptian 'Apep or Apopis), of fecundity (Egypto-Canaanite goddesses of sex; *ANEP*, figs. 471–4), or of continuing life (symbolized by repeated shedding of its skin, *cf.* A. Heidel, *The Gilgamesh Epic and Old Testament Parallels*, 1949, p. 92, n. 212). For Canaanite altar-stands with serpents modelled on them, see *ANEP*, figs. 585, 590. In the Canaanite texts from Ugarit note the prescribed sacrifice of 'a head of small cattle (for) 'Anat-Lôtan' (Gordon, *Ugaritic Literature*, 1949, pp. 114, 107, n. 1).

K.A.K.

SERPENT, BRAZEN. On the borders of Edom, rebellious Israel suffered deadly snakebite as a punishment and besought Moses to intercede with God for them, to save them from the serpents. God then commanded Moses to make a bronze figure of a serpent and set it up on a pole, so that anyone bitten by a serpent need only look at the bronze serpent-figure and he would live (Nu. xxi. 4–9; 1 Cor. x. 9, 11). By this means God granted the people deliverance and enforced the lesson of dependence upon Himself both for that deliverance and as a general principle. Centuries later, during his purge of idolatrous objects and customs, King Hezekiah of Judah destroyed the bronze serpent because the people had turned it into an idol, burning incense to it (2 Ki. xviii. 4). The following phrase *wayyiqrā' lô neḥuštān* may mean either 'he (= Hezekiah) called it Nehushtan' (*i.e.* 'only a bit of bronze'), or 'it was called Nehushtan' (*i.e.* by the people from of old). In either case it is a pun on the phrase *nāḥāš-nᵉḥōšeṯ*, 'serpent of bronze', two very similar-sounding words in Hebrew. The significance of serpents in surrounding paganism made Hezekiah's action especially imperative (*cf.* SERPENT, end of section II*d*; see also H. H. Rowley, 'Zadok and Nehushtan', *JBL*, LVIII, 1939, pp. 113 ff.). A bronze serpent was found at Gezer (see R. A. S. Macalister, *The Excavation of Gezer*, II, 1912, pp. 398, 399 and fig.; or I. Benzinger, *Hebräische Archäologie*³, 1927, p. 327, fig. 418), and a serpent standard at Hazor.

When speaking of His coming crucifixion, Jesus Christ used the incident of the serpent, which was lifted up that man might look in faith and live, in order to illustrate the significance of that impending event. Those who put faith in Him, uplifted on the cross for their sins, would have life eternal (Jn. iii. 14). K.A.K.

SERVANT. See SLAVE, SERVANT OF THE LORD.

SERVANT OF THE LORD.

I. IN THE OLD TESTAMENT

Heb. *'eḇeḏ*, 'servant', means a person at the disposal of another (G. A. Smith). He is the worker who belongs to a master (Zimmerli). *'Eḇeḏ* occurs 807 times in the *MT*. In secular usage the title was used of the slave; the servant in the service of the king; the politically subject; as a humble self-description; and of the sanctuary servants (Zimmerli). In religious usage it appears as the humble man's description of himself in the presence of his God (*e.g.* Ex. iv. 10; Pss. cxix. 17, cxliii. 12). Thus used, it acknowledges the lowly status of the speaker, the total claim of God upon a member of the people He has elected, and a corresponding confidence in commitment to God, who will vindicate His servant. In the plural, it denotes the pious *en masse* (Ps. cxxxv. 14). In the singular, it becomes also a description of Israel (Is. xli. 8). Here the title is given to the nation by God Himself, a use characteristic of the second part of Isaiah, and it expresses 'the idea of belonging utterly to Yahweh by grace' (Zimmerli). The title describes also certain specially distinguished servants of the Lord: the Patriarchs; Moses; kings, especially David; prophets; and also Job (Zimmerli).

In Is. xl ff. certain passages descriptive of a Servant of the Lord are distinguishable (although not detachable) from the rest of the prophecy. Known as the Servant Songs, they are delineated as: Is. xlii. 1–4 (5–7?), xlix. 1–6, l. 4–9, lii. 13–liii. 12. Their significance and interpretation have been much debated (North). Conservative students, who believe the prophecy points unmistakably to Jesus Christ, need not fear this debate. Prophets do not work in a vacuum. The attempt to equate the Servant of the Songs with Israel, or a historical figure (king or prophet), or the prophet himself (*cf.* Acts viii. 34), or a corporate personality oscillating between the prophet, the pious, and Israel as a whole, or to see the Songs in the light of the Tammuz myth or the ritual of the New Year Festival—may be viewed as attempts to place the thought of the prophet within the experience of his people. It is helpful to study the sources of this composite picture, and to discern its contemporary references. But these do not exhaust the message of the Songs. We are given 'a picture of the true servant of Yahweh which far transcends the personal experience of the prophet. Thus it is not by chance or by ineptitude that Is. liii has again and again been understood as alluding to the figure of the one that is to come' (Zimmerli). The Servant is a soteriological messianic figure (North), but the conception retains a certain fluidity between the thought of Israel as the Servant and the thought of an individual Servant *par excellence* (Rowley). Christ will both fulfil the servant mission of the old Israel and beget a new servant Israel.

In the description of the Servant there is progress, an individuation, as we pass from the first to the following songs. The personification becomes a Person (G. A. Smith). 'The figure that had stood half glimpsed in the shadows, as Jehovah was introducing His witnesses, hardly distinguishable from Israel, steps forward into the light and builds the bridge between the realities of human failure and the apparently inaccessible heights of the Divine will' (Ellison).

II. IN THE NEW TESTAMENT

This figure finds its fulfilment in Jesus Christ. That the early Church thought so is clear, but the question whether *Jesus* consciously applied the Isaianic Servant concept to Himself, and especially its theme of vicarious, atoning suffering, has been hotly debated. It is a strange phenomenon of critical scholarship that while some scholars (*e.g.* Cullmann, *Christology*) see the suffering Servant theme as central to the thinking and way of Jesus, others can find little trace of an influence of this kind (so Morna Hooker). The negative view helps to guard us against eisegesis; but it cannot stand. It depends overmuch on critical excision (*e.g.* Lk. xxii. 37 is dubbed 'obscure' and its meaning and genuineness 'extremely doubtful'). It takes no account of the delicate and creative use of Scripture by our Lord. (Of Lk. xxii. 37, James Denney said: 'It is surely improbable that He applied to Himself the most wonderful expression in Is. liii in a shallow verbal fashion, and put from Him the great meanings of which the chapter is full, and which the New Testament writers embrace with one accord.') It is right to claim that Is. liii is not the only passage that influenced Jesus' thought on His sufferings; but it is wrong to deny the uniqueness of that chapter among those scriptures that tell of the Christ's death for sin, His burial, and His resurrection. Furthermore, it should be recognized that Jesus' use of Scripture cannot be reduced to the level of His contemporaries' usage and judged by that; and that connections of thought may exist without exɔlicit linguistic parallels duly certified in some 'ewish school.

Jesus left no more than hints as to the meaning ɔf His death. Theological explication was to ollow: we must not 'rob Jesus of Paul' (P. T. Forsyth). But the hints (*e.g.* the 'many' of Mk. x. 45, xiv. 24) as good as say, 'See Isaiah liii—you'll ind the clue there'—and the early Church did. The early Church also maintained that the risen Christ had interpreted to them in all the Scrip- ures the things concerning Himself (Lk. xxiv). When they then went on to produce a Servant Christology and soteriology (Acts, 1 Peter, the nnotations in the Gospels) it seems clear nough, first, that the Isaianic Servant Songs nust have been prominent among the inter- reted Scriptures, and, secondly, that Jesus Him- elf must have found them significant for His nission.

Paul built upon this foundation (1 Cor. xv. 3,), and wove the suffering Servant theology into is own (2 Cor. v. 21; Rom. iv. 25, viii. 3, 4, 2–34). He shared vitally in the theological xtension of the Servant motif to the life of the nessianic people (2 Cor. iv. 5; Col. i. 24, 25) nd in the consequent reflection of this usage ack upon Christology (Phil. ii) (Mudge). Through the narrow channel of the title *pais heou* as applied to Jesus (Acts iii, iv), the Servant notif burst forth and broadened out (by many nguistic streams) to fertilize the life and thinking f the Body of Christ in its world mission. The attern of God's redemptive revelation is 'the orm of a servant'—elected, witnessing, suffering, lessing—and this becomes therefore the only uthentic pattern of the Church's life (Dillistone).

BIBLIOGRAPHY. G. A. Smith, *The Book of saiah*, II, *The Expositor's Bible*, 1907; H. W. Robinson, *The Cross in the Old Testament* (*The Cross of the Servant*, 1926); C. R. North, *The Suffering Servant in Deutero-Isaiah*[2], 1956; W. immerli and J. Jeremias, *The Servant of God*, .T., 1957; H. H. Rowley, *The Servant of the ord and Other Essays*, 1952; H. L. Ellison, *The ervant of Jehovah*, 1953; M. D. Hooker, *Jesus nd the Servant*, 1959; L. S. Mudge, 'The Servant ord and His Servant People', *SJT*, XII, 1959, p. 113 ff.; F. W. Dillistone, *Revelation and vangelism*, 1948. J.H.

ETH. 1. The third son of Adam and Eve, born fter the murder of Abel, and called Seth (*šēṯ*) ecause, Eve said, 'God has appointed (*šāṯ*) me nother seed instead of Abel' (Gn. iv. 25). It was rough Seth that the genealogy of Noah passed Gn. v. 3, 4; 1 Ch. i. 1; Lk. iii. 38). His son nosh was born when he was 105 years old (*MT* nd Samaritan Pentateuch; LXX reads 205) and e lived to the great age of 912 years (*MT*, amaritan Pentateuch, and LXX agree; Gn. iv. 26, . 6–8). The individual in the Sumerian King ist, Alalgar, who corresponds to Seth is credited ith a reign of 36,000 years.

2. An unknown individual whose name is ndered Sheth (Nu. xxiv. 17, AV and RSV; RV gives 'tumult'), the ancestor of a people men- tioned by Balaam as enemies of Israel. T.C.M.

SEVEN. See NUMBER.

SEVEN WORDS, THE. The first of the words spoken by our Lord from the cross (Lk. xxiii. 34) reveals a love that is utterly unexpected and utterly undeserved. He prayed for the Roman soldiers and even, as Peter suggests (Acts iii. 17), for the religious guides of the nation. How many more may be included within the scope of this prayer is known only to the Son and to the Father, to whom it was offered.

The second word was spoken to the penitent brigand (Lk. xxiii. 43), who, beyond the cross, saw the crown and the coming glory, and who said to Jesus, 'Remember me when thou comest in thy kingdom' (verse 42, RV). To him Jesus said in effect, 'Not far down the ages, but before the sun sets, thou shalt be with me in the bliss of Paradise'. There was to be no purgatory even for a sinner like that.

The third word (Jn. xix. 25–27) proves that we have in Jesus the supreme example of a 'heart at leisure from itself, to soothe and sympathize'. Though suffering severe physical pain and en- during far more awful agony of soul, He thought of His mother and made provision for her future. The sword was piercing her heart (Lk. ii. 35), but the tender words of her Son must have brought to her deep comfort and healing.

The first three words were spoken during the bright morning hours before noon. The fourth awe-inspiring word (Mt. xxvii. 46; Mk. xv. 34) was probably spoken by Jesus as the mysterious, supernatural three hours' darkness was lifting. 'Dumb darkness wrapped His soul a space', and into all the secrets of His 'unknown sufferings' we cannot enter; we can only think of Him in hushed reverence, as He endures to the uttermost the penalty our sin deserved. (See ELOI, ELOI, LAMA SABACHTHANI.)

The fifth word (Jn. xix. 28) followed close upon the fourth. It is the only word that speaks of physical suffering, and one recalls Alexander's striking words: 'The Fountain waileth out, "I thirst."' Jesus had refused a drugged drink (Mk. xv. 23), but He accepted another kind of drink, in order to moisten His parched throat and lips, so that, with a loud voice, He might make the declaration contained in the sixth word.

That word (Jn. xix. 30) consists of one com- prehensive Greek verb, *tetelestai*, 'It is finished'. It is a sigh of infinite relief because the pain and agony are past. It is also the cry, not of a vanquished victim but of a Victor, who has finished the work He had to do, has fulfilled all the Old Testament prophecies and types, and has once for all offered the one final sacrifice for sin (Heb. x. 12).

In the final word (Lk. xxiii. 46) Jesus quoted Ps. xxxi. 5. The redeemed are so really brothers of the Redeemer (Heb. ii. 11–13) that, in the moment of dying, they can use the same language, as they commend their souls into the hands of the Father—His Father, and their Father in Him. Many Christians have died with such language on their lips.

BIBLIOGRAPHY. V. Taylor, *Jesus and His Sacrifice*, 1937, pp. 157 ff., 197 ff.; R. G. Turnbull, *The Seven Words from the Cross*, 1956.

A.R.

SEVENEH. The RV, ASV rendering of the *MT* *s^ewēnēh* (Egyp. *Swn*, 'place of barter', 'market', Coptic *Suan*, Arab. *'Aswân*) in Ezk. xxix. 10, xxx. 6, where AV, RSV retain the classical form, Syene. Located on the first cataract of the Nile, Syene (modern 'Aswân) marked the boundary between Egypt and Ethiopia. 'From Migdol ('tower' in AV, RV) to Syene' means 'the length of Egypt from north to south'. *MT s^ewēnēh* should be read *s^ewēnâ* or *s^ewānâ*, the *â* signifying direction: 'to Syene' (RSV). A border fortress and a base for expeditions up the Nile, a terminus for river traffic and a source of red granite for Egyptian monuments (syenite), Syene was of special importance to the Jews because of its proximity to the island of Elephantine, which housed a colony of Jews who sought refuge in Egypt after Jerusalem fell (587 BC). The Qumran MS of Isaiah suggests that 'Syenites' should replace *sînîm* (Is. xlix. 12); LXX reads *Syene* for *Sin* in Ezk. xxx. 16.

BIBLIOGRAPHY. E. G. Kraeling, 'New Light on the Elephantine Colony', *BA*, XV, 1952, pp. 50–68.

D.A.H.

SEVENTY. See NUMBER.

SHAALBIM. A village inhabited by Amorites near Mt. Heres and Aijalon when they withstood the Danites. Later the Amorites were subjugated by the house of Joseph (Jdg. i. 35). With Makaz, Beth-shemesh and Elon-beth-Hanan, Shaalbim formed part of Solomon's second administrative district (1 Ki. iv. 9). It is almost certainly the same as Shaalabin, included with Aijalon in the list of Dan's territory (Jos. xix. 42), and Shaalbon, the house of Eliahba, one of David's warriors (2 Sa. xxiii. 32; 1 Ch. xi. 33). Because of the similar area covered it has been suggested that Shaalim of Jdg. i. 35; Jos. xix. 42 may also be the same place. The position of modern Selbīṭ, 3 miles north-west of Aijalon and 8 miles north of Beth-shemesh, suits all these contexts well, though the name is philologically different. Shaalbim, *etc.*, may mean 'haunt of foxes'.

D.J.W.

SHAARAIM. 1. On the line of the Philistine flight from Azekah, before the parting of the ways to Gath and Ekron (1 Sa. xvii. 52). This agrees with Jos. xv. 36; Abel, following LXX 'Ascalon' for Ekron, accepts a location at Tar'in (Tosephta Ohol. 18), much farther west.

2. In 1 Ch. iv. 31 Shaaraim is used for Sharuhen (*q.v.*).

J.P.U.L.

SHADDAI. See GOD, NAMES OF.

SHADOW (Heb. *ṣēl*, 'shadow', 'shade', 'defence'; Gk. *skia*, 'a shade', 'a shadow'; both words with derivative forms). The representation made by any solid body interposing between the sun or light and another body. As a shadow is constantly varying till at last, perhaps suddenly, it ceases to be, so are our days unsubstantial and fleeting, our death sudden (1 Ch. xxix. 15; Jb xiv. 2, xvii. 7). Darkness and gloominess are associated with shadows, and thus with 'the shadow of death' (Jb. iii. 5, xvi. 16, xxiv. 17; Ps. xxiii. 4), though this common interpretation of Heb. *ṣalmûṯ* is strictly inaccurate and should be rendered 'deep darkness'.

As a man can find welcome relief in the shade from the scorching heat (*cf.* Jon. iv. 5, 6), so the rule and shelter of the Almighty are called a shadow (La. iv. 20; Ezk. xxxi. 6; Ps. xci. 1; Is xxv. 4; *cf.* Ct. ii. 3). The servant's eagerly anticipated time for stopping work is called the 'shadow' (Jb. vii. 2). In contrast to the signs of approaching desolation and ruin, the 'shadows of the evening' (Je. vi. 4), the day of everlasting glory is when 'the shadows flee away' (Ct. ii. 17).

The ancient ceremonies are called a 'shadow of good things to come' (Heb. x. 1). The unchangeableness of God is contrasted with the 'play of passing shadows' (Jas. i. 17, NEB). In Heb. ix. 5 'shadowing' comes from *kataskiazō* 'to (cause a) shadow' or 'to shade fully' (*cf* Heb. *ṣālal*).

J.D.D.

SHADRACH. See HANANIAH (4).

SHALEM. A word treated by AV as the name of a place near Shechem, which was visited by Jacob (Gn. xxxiii. 18). RV ('in peace') and RSV ('safely'), however, prefer to take it in an adverbial sense from the verb *šālēm*, 'to be complete, sound', and this appears to make better sense. The word *šālēm*, identical in form, does occur as a place name in connection with Melchizedek, but is given as Salem (*q.v.*) in EVV.

T.C.M.

SHALISHAH. The district reached by Saul after passing through the hills of Ephraim and before reaching the land of Shaalim (see SALIM, SHAALBIM) in pursuit of his father's lost asses (1 Sa. ix. 4). The place seems to have had its own deity or shrine, Baal-shalishah (2 Ki. iv. 42). Since the places in conjunction with which Shalishah is cited are of uncertain location, its own situation is not known. Conder proposed the ruins of Khirbet Kefr Thilth, 19 miles north-east of Jaffa.

D.J.W.

SHALLUM (*šallûm* and *šallum*). This name is borne by fifteen individuals in the Old Testament, of whom the chief are: **1.** King of Israel *c.* 745 BC (2 Ki. xv. 10–15). He was the leader of a conspiracy that overthrew the dynasty of Jehu and thus fulfilled the century-old prophecy of 2 Ki. x. 30. He assassinated the son of Jeroboam II, Zechariah, when the latter had been reigning fo ix months. He himself reigned for only one month before becoming in turn the victim of a urther *coup d'état* by Menahem.

2. King of Judah *c.* 609 BC (see JEHOAHAZ). The son of Josiah, he reigned for only three months. He is referred to by this name in 1 Ch. ii. 15 and Je. xxii. 11. **3.** A Levite of the family f Korah who was a gate-keeper of the sanctuary n the time of David (1 Ch. ix. 17, 19). **4.** A high riest of the middle period of the monarchy 1 Ch. vi. 12, 13) and ancestor of Ezra (Ezr. vii.). **5.** The husband of Huldah the prophetess 2 Ki. xxii. 14; 2 Ch. xxxiv. 22) and 'keeper of the vardrobe'. He may well have been the uncle of eremiah (Je. xxxii. 7, *cf.* Je. xxxv. 4). **6.** A conemporary of Nehemiah, the son of Hallohesh, who administered a district in Jerusalem (Ne. iii. 2).

BIBLIOGRAPHY. D. Winton Thomas (ed.), *DOTT*, pp. 214 f.; H. Torczyner, *The Lachish Letters*, 1937, pp. 27 ff. J.C.J.W.

SHALMAN. The person who sacked Beth-arbel Ho. x. 14). This action was sufficiently well nown to serve as a warning to Israel. It is enerally assumed that this could be a reference o Shalmaneser V, the Assyrian king who beieged Samaria in 725–723 BC. In this event Arbel night Arbela, be west of Galilee (1 Macc. ix. 2). But against this, Shalmaneser's name is elsewhere written fully (see SHALMANESER) and the Galilee area fell to Tiglath-pileser III in 734–732 C (see ASSYRIA). Thus Shalman may refer to alamanu, king of Moab, mentioned in the nnals of Tiglath-pileser. Identification remains ncertain. D.J.W.

SHALMANESER (Heb. *šalman'eser*; Gk. *Salmennasar*; Assyr. *Šulmanu-ašaridu*, 'the god ulman is chief').

Shalmaneser was the name borne by several ulers of Assyria. The king of Assyria to whom Hoshea of Israel became subject (2 Ki. xvii. 3) was Shalmaneser V (727–722 BC), son of Tiglathileser III. When Hoshea failed to pay tribute in is seventh regnal year Shalmaneser began a hree-year siege of the Israelite capital Samaria. There are no annals of this king extant, but the ssyrian Eponym List records the siege and the abylonian Chronicle says that Shalmaneser broke (the resistance of) the city of Shamara'in' ee SAMARIA). It is likely that the 'king of ssyria' to whom the city fell (2 Ki. xvii. 6) was his same Shalmaneser, though the final capture f the city is claimed by his successor Sargon II 722/1 BC. It is possible that Sargon usurped the hrone during the siege and continued the camaign (*DOTT*, pp. 58–63).

Shalmaneser III, king of Assyria 859–824 BC, equently raided the west, and the first recorded ssyrian contact with the Israelites is found in is Annals. In 853 BC he fought a coalition of yrian kings under Irhuleni of Hamath and Hadadezer of Damascus at Qarqar. Among their lies was 'Ahab the Israelite', who, according to the Assyrians, provided 2,000 chariots and 10,000 men as his contribution. The Assyrian advance was temporary and Shalmaneser did not return for three years (1 Ki. xvi. 29, xx. 20, xxii. 1).

In his account of operations against Syria in 841 BC, inscribed on his black obelisk at Nimrud (see CALAH), Shalmaneser III claims to have defeated Hazael of Damascus (see 1 Ki. xix. 15). He did not, however, capture the city and moved *via* the Hauran to the Lebanon, where he received tribute from 'Jehu, son of Omri', an event not mentioned in the Old Testament but portrayed on the black obelisk (see plate VII*a*). See ASSYRIA, JEHU. D.J.W.

SHAMBLES (Gk. *makellon*, 1 Cor. x. 25; Lat. *macellum*). The meat-market (so RSV, NEB) at Corinth. See *JBL*, LXXX, 1934, pp. 134–141. Jewish law forbade dealing in such markets, which sold the flesh of ritually unclean animals. In this verse Paul is counselling his readers to avoid what in a later age was known as scrupulosity. J.D.D.

SHAME. The English word and its cognates appear 233 times (of which forty-six are in the New Testament) in the AV and 241 times (of which forty-six are in the New Testament) in the RSV. These occurrences are translations of original forms representing at least ten different Hebrew and seven different Greek roots and a considerably larger number of individual Hebrew and Greek words.

Two main meanings can be distinguished: descriptions of states of mind, and descriptions of physical states. The states of mind may be classified into three broad categories: first, those where an individual is or might be the object of contempt, derision, or humiliation; second, those where he feels bashfulness or shyness; third, those where he feels respect or awe. The physical states involve a degree of exposure or nudity, or the words are used as euphemisms for the sexual organs.

The most frequent usage by far involves the ideas connected with contempt, derision, and humiliation. Shame follows when the law of God is disregarded or forgotten (Ho. iv. 6, 7). God sends it upon the enemies of His people (Ps. cxxxii. 18). It is the result of sin and is removed in the day of liberty and restoration (Is. lxi. 7). It appears at times to be a punishment (Ps. xliv. 7, 9, 15). In contrast, it is also sometimes a positive preventive manifestation of the grace of God (Ezk. xliii. 10). It may induce positive action (Jdg. iii. 25). False shame at that which is not shameful, *viz.* allegiance to Christ, is to be avoided (Mk. viii. 38). There is also a figurative use of the term, as in Is. xxiv. 23 and in Jude 13.

The usage representing shyness or bashfulness is not as important, since it occurs infrequently. A clear example is the statement concerning the man and his wife before the fall in Gn. ii. 25. The usage which represents awe or respect is also rare. An Old Testament instance is Ezr. ix. 6; and there is the apostolic injunction of 1 Tim. ii. 9. In the former instance the common Hebrew root *bôš*, which appears on over ninety other occasions in the Old Testament text in the Qal stem alone, is used; whereas 1 Tim. ii. 9 is the only passage where *aidōs* occurs in the New Testament.

The uses of the words with a physical reference are concerned with nakedness. These occurrences are not frequent.

The biblical concept of shame is basically that of the mental state of humiliation due to sin, and to departure from the law of God, which brings obloquy and rejection by both God and man. The development of the concept is most extensive in the prophets and in the Pauline Epistles. The references to matters connected with sex are illustrative or figurative, and do not indicate that there is any more basic connection between shame and sexual functions than between shame and other functions which may occasion embarrassment by sinful use.

BIBLIOGRAPHY. G. Kittel, *TWNT*, 1933– , *s.v.* αἰδώς, αἰσχύνω; R. C. Trench, *Synonyms of the New Testament*, 1894, *s.v.* αἰσχύνη, αἰδώς, ἐντροπή.

P.W.

SHAMGAR (Heb. *šamgar*, probably from Hurrian *šimiqari*). A personal name repeatedly attested in Nuzian texts (*cf.* R. H. Pfeiffer and E. A. Speiser, *AASOR*, XVI, 1936, p. 161), called 'the son of Anath' (Jdg. iii. 31, v. 6), *i.e.* a native of Beth-anath (presumably a southern Beth-anath; *cf.* Jos. xv. 59). His killing of six hundred Philistines must belong to the earliest period of Philistine settlement in Canaan, since the reference to him in the Song of Deborah (Jdg. v. 6) indicates that he flourished before the battle of Kishon (*c.* 1125 BC). The ox-goad (Heb. *malmāḏ*) with which he wrought such havoc would have a metal tip which was sharpened as required (see GOAD). He is not described as a judge of Israel—indeed, he may well have been a Canaanite—but his exploit afforded the neighbouring Israelites some relief. Some LXX and other recensions repeat Jdg. iii. 31 at the end of chapter xvi, in a more 'Philistine' context. J. Garstang's surmise that Shamgar is identical with Ben-anath, a Syrian sea-captain and son-in-law of Rameses II (*c.* 1260 BC) is not convincing (*Joshua–Judges*, 1931, pp. 63 f., 284 ff.); still less so is Sir C. Marston's suggestion that 'The Ox-goad' was the name of his ship (*The Bible is True*, 1934, pp. 247 ff.).

BIBLIOGRAPHY. G. F. Moore, 'Shamgar and Sisera', *JAOS*, IX, 1898, pp. 159 f.; C. F. Burney, *Judges*, 1918, pp. 75 ff.; B. Maisler, 'Shamgar ben Anath', *PEQ*, LXVI, 1934, pp. 192 ff.; J. M. Myers, *IB*, II, 1953, pp. 683, 711.

F.F.B.

SHAMMAH. 1. A duke, or tribal chieftain (Heb. *'allûp̄*), of Edom, descended from Esau (Gn. xxxvi. 17). **2.** A brother of King David, and son of Jesse (1 Sa. xvi. 9). The name appears also as Shimea, with variant spellings Shimeah and Shimma in AV and RV. **3.** One of the outstanding three of David's warriors (2 Sa. xxiii. 11), described as a Hararite. The text of 2 Sa. xxiii. 32 f. should almost certainly be emended to read 'Jonathan *the son of* Shammah the Hararite'; otherwise a different Shammah must be intended. **4.** Another of David's warriors, a Harodite (2 Sa. xxiii. 25). 1 Ch. xi. 27 renders his name as Shammoth (a plural form of the name), and the Shamhuth of 1 Ch. xxvii. 8 may well be the same man.

D.F.P.

SHAPHAN. 1. The son of Azaliah who was state secretary (AV 'scribe') to Josiah. Hilkiah reported to him the discovery of the book of the law in the Temple (2 Ki. xxii. 3; 2 Ch. xxxiv. 8–24). He read from this book before Josiah who sent him to the prophetess Huldah. Shaphan was father of at least three sons. (i) Ahikam who assisted the prophet Jeremiah (2 Ki. xxii. 12; 2 Ch. xxxiv. 20; Je. xxvi. 24); (ii) Elasah who, with another man, was entrusted by Jeremiah with a letter to the exiles in Babylonia (Je. xxix. 3); (iii) Gemariah who tried to prevent Jehoiakim from burning the scroll containing Jeremiah's prophecies (Je. xxxvi. 10–12, 25). Shaphan had as grandsons Micaiah (Je. xxxvi. 11, 13) and Gedaliah, the governor of Judah after the Babylonian invasions of 589–587 BC, who helped Jeremiah (Je. xxxix. 14).

2. The father of Jaazaniah, seen sacrificing to idols in Ezekiel's vision (Ezk. viii. 11).

Even if the name is to be connected with Heb. *šāpān*, 'rock-badger', there is no evidence that it betokens totem worship (as G. B. Gray, *Hebrew Proper Names*, 1896, p. 103).

D.J.W.

SHAREZER. 1. A brother of Adrammelech who with him murdered their father Sennacherib in 681 BC (2 Ki. xix. 37; Is. xxxvii. 38). His name is known only from this reference and is probably an abbreviation from the Assyr.–Bab. *šar-uṣur*, 'He has protected the king', normally prefixed by the name of a deity. By reference to *Nergilus* in the account by Abydenus of the same event Nergal-sharezer has been proposed. Johns, however, considers the name a corruption of Šar-eṭir-Aššur, the known name of a son of Sennacherib.

2. A contemporary of Zechariah who inquired concerning the propriety of continuing the fast celebrating the anniversary of the destruction of the Temple (Zc. vii. 2). Because the text is difficult (see RVmg) it has been suggested that 'they of Bethel' may imply that the full name was the common Bab. Bel-šar-uṣur (see BELSHAZZAR).

D.J.W.

SHARON (Heb. *šārôn*; in AV of New Testament 'Saron', Acts ix. 35) means a level place or plain. It comprises the largest of the coastal plains in northern Palestine. Lying between the extensive marshes of the lower Crocodile river (Nahr es Zerka) and the valley of Aijalon and Joppa in the south, it runs some 50 miles from north to south and is 9–10 miles wide (see fig. 159). Its features have been largely determined by the Pleistocene shorelines and deposits. Inland from the belt of recent sand-dunes which divert and choke some of the coastal rivers, rises a zone of Mousterian red sands to about 180 feet, forming in the north a continuous belt of some 20 miles. Formerly, this zone was thickly forested with oaks, probably *Quercus infectoria*, and today this is one of the richest agricultural districts of Israel, planted with citrus groves. Inland from the belt of Mousterian sands, the streams have partially excavated a longitudinal trough along the foothills of an earlier Pleistocene shoreline. The river valleys, especially in the north of this trough, tended to be marshy until modern drainage developments. In the past, only in the southern border of Sharon was the land more favourable for settlement, and it is clear that most of Sharon was never colonized by the Israelites. In the north, Socoh, a district centre under Solomon (1 Ki. iv. 10), and Gilgal, seat of the petty kings defeated by Joshua (Jos. xii. 23), lay in the Samaritan foothills east of the plain. References to Lod and Ono in the south, both fortified outposts (1 Ch. viii. 12; Ezr. ii. 33; Ne. vii. 37), and 'the valley of craftsmen' separating them (Ne. xi. 35; *cf.* 1 Sa. xiii. 19, 20) appear to indicate they were settled by the returning exiles.

The 'excellency' of Sharon (Is. xxxv. 2), like the 'pride' of Jordan (Je. xii. 5, RV, xlix. 19), would suggest the dense vegetation cover rather than the fertility which Sharon has subsequently proved to possess in its Pleistocene sands, now under orange groves. For settlement it has long remained a 'waste' (Is. xxxiii. 9), and was used only for pasturage (1 Ch. v. 16; Is. lxv. 10). It was here that Shitrai supervised King David's flocks (1 Ch. xxvii. 29). The 'rose of Sharon' (Ct. ii. 1–3) suggests the flowers of the dense undergrowth. Four red flowers still follow each other in quick succession, an anemone (*Anemone coronaria*), a buttercup (*Ranunculus asiaticus*), a tulip (*Tulipa montana*), and a poppy (*Papaver* sp.). J.M.H.

SHARUHEN. A Simeonite settlement (Jos. xix. 6). Egyptian sources mention *Šrḥon*, a Hyksos fortress which resisted Ahmose for three years c. 1570 BC, barring his way to further conquests; usually identified with Tell el-Far'a, 15 miles south of Gaza (Albright, *BASOR*, 33, February 1929; Abel, *Géographie*, II, p. 451). Petrie's brief excavation revealed a strong Philistine occupation. See ARCHAEOLOGY. The Joshua context suits Tell el-Huweilfeh, a mile north of Khirbet Rammamein (Ain Rimmon?), proposed earlier by Albright, *JPOS*, IV, 1924, p. 135. See also Alt, *JPOS*, XV, 1935, pp. 311 ff. J.P.U.L.

SHAUL (*šā'ûl*, 'asked for'). In Hebrew exactly the same as 'Saul' (*q.v.*). **1.** A king of Edom (1 Ch. i. 48, 49; *cf.* Gn. xxxvi. 37, 38), belonging to Rehoboth. **2.** A son of Simeon by a Canaanitess (Gn. xlvi. 10), from whom the Shaulites took their name (Nu. xxvi. 13). **3.** A son of Kohath (1 Ch. vi. 24), called 'Joel' in 1 Ch. vi. 36. G.W.G.

SHAVEH, VALLEY OF. A valley near Salem (Gn. xiv. 17 f.), also known as 'the king's dale', where Absalom raised his memorial pillar (2 Sa. xviii. 18). If Salem is Jerusalem, the site may be at the top of the Valley of Hinnom. But an ancient Jewish tradition reads *ś-r-h*, another word meaning 'king', for *š-w-h* ('Shaveh'). (This involves only one slight consonantal change.) D.F.P.

SHAVSHA. The name of a secretary of state under David (2 Sa. viii. 17, where he is called Seraiah). He is called Shisha in 1 Ki. iv. 3, Shavsha in 1 Ch. xviii. 16, and Sheva in 2 Sa. xx. 25. Following de Vaux, Grollenberg (*Atlas of the Bible*) suggests that the form which must underlie these names indicates that the official was an Egyptian. His eldest son's name, Elihoreph, could mean 'my god is the Nile (god)', or in its LXX form Elihaph, 'my god is Apis'. If so, then the Egyptian father gave his son a hybrid name, the first element being Hebrew but the second expressing his allegiance to the religion of his Egyptian ancestors. This would further suggest that David brought in Egyptians to fill offices in his kingdom, organizing it at least in part on Egyptian models. But both of these names (and their bearers) may in fact be Semitic; if so, the evidence for Egyptian influence in the organization of David's kingdom is then much less.

BIBLIOGRAPHY. *RB*, XLVIII, 1939, pp. 398–400; H. Ranke, *Ägyptische Personennamen*, 1935, II, p. 318, No. 9; *KB*, p. 958 (*s.v.* 'Shavsha'); C. H. Gordon, *Ugaritic Manual*, 1955, III, Vocabulary, No. 2089; C. Virolleaud, *Palais Royal d'Ugarit*, II, 1957, glossaire p. 225 to Text 82: 7. R.A.H.G. K.A.K.

SHEARING-HOUSE, THE (*bêṯ 'ēqeḏ hā-rō'îm*, 'house of binding of the shepherds', 2 Ki. x. 12–14). The place where Jehu, bent on wiping out the house of Ahab, met and killed forty-two of the 'brethren' of Ahaziah. A suggested identification is with Beit Kad, about 16 miles north-east of Samaria. See *GTT*, p. 363.

SHEAR-JASHUB. A symbolical name ('a remnant will return') given to one of Isaiah's sons to express the truth that out of the judgment God would save a remnant (*e.g* Is. i. 9). When Isaiah went to Ahaz, Shear-jashub accompanied him as a reminder to the king that the nation, even at that dark time, would not completely perish (Is. vii. 3). E.J.Y.

SHEATH. See ARMOUR AND WEAPONS, II*a*.

SHEBA. 1. A city (*šeḇa'*) in the territory allotted to Simeon in S Palestine near Beersheba and Moladah (Jos. xix. 2; *MT* at 1 Ch. iv. 28 omits it in the parallel list, but LXX has 'Sama'). LXX reads 'Samaa' in MS B (*cf.* Jos. xv. 26) and 'Sabee' in MS A.

2. A Benjamite (*šeḇa'*) who revolted unsuccessfully against David after Absalom's death

(2 Sa. xx. 1, 2, 6, 7, 10, 21, 22). **3.** A leader (*šeḇa‘*) of the tribe of Gad (1 Ch. v. 13). **4.** A descendant (*šeḇā’*) of Cush through Raamah (Gn. x. 7; 1 Ch. i. 9); brother of Dedan (*q.v.*). **5.** A descendant (*šeḇā’*) of Shem through Joktan (Gn. x. 28; 1 Ch. i. 22). **6.** Son of Jokshan (*šeḇā’*) and grandson of Abraham and Keturah (Gn. xxv. 3; 1 Ch. i. 32); brother of Dedan.

7. The land (*šeḇā’*) whose queen (see SHEBA, QUEEN OF) visited Solomon (1 Ki. x. 1 ff.; 2 Ch. ix. 1 ff.) was in all probability the home of the Sabaeans in SW Arabia. J. A. Montgomery (*ICC*, *Kings*, 1951, pp. 215 f.) contends that the Sabaeans were still in N Arabia although they controlled the trade routes from S Arabia. On the other hand, J. Bright (*History of Israel*, 1960, p. 194), while recognizing that the Sabaeans were originally nomads, affirms, with greater probability, that by Solomon's time they had settled in the eastern area of what is modern Yemen.

The relationship between the Sabaeans and the three Shebas mentioned in Genesis is by no means clear. They may be distinct tribes, but the similarities among the groupings are striking: Raamah's sons (Gn. x. 7), Hamites, bear the same names as Abraham's grandsons—Sheba and Dedan (xxv. 3); both Cush, the Hamite (x. 7), and Joktan, the Semite, have descendants named Sheba and Havilah (x. 28, 29). The Table of Nations in Gn. x may reflect both the Semitic origin of the Sabaeans and also the fact that they settled in close proximity to Hamitic groups, *i.e.* Egyptians and Ethiopians. Indeed, classical Abyssinian culture testifies to a blending of Hamitic and Semitic elements, and the rôle that S Arabians who crossed the Bab el-Mandeb as traders and colonists played in shaping this culture is impressive.

It is as traders or raiders (Jb. i. 15) that the Old Testament most frequently speaks of the people of Sheba. Gold (1 Ki. x. 2; Ps. lxxii. 15; Is. lx. 6), frankincense (Is. lx. 6; Je. vi. 20), spices and jewels (1 Ki. x. 2; Ezk. xxvii. 22) were brought to northern markets in their caravans (Jb. vi. 19). Commercial opportunists, they were not above engaging in slave trade according to Joel iii. 8 (where less preferably LXX reads 'into captivity' for 'to the Sabaeans'). This extensive trading activity apparently led the Sabaeans to found colonies at various oases in N Arabia. These served as caravan bases and probably gave the colonists a degree of control over the northern area. Testimony to intercourse between Sheba and Canaan is found in a S Arabian clay stamp (*c.* 9th century BC) unearthed at Bethel (*BASOR*, 151, October 1958, pp. 9–16).

The most prominent of the Arab states during the first half of the first millennium BC, Sheba was ruled by *mukarribs*, priest-kings, who supervised both the political affairs and the polytheistic worship of the sun, moon, and star gods. Recent explorations by the University of Louvain (1951–2) and the American Foundation for the Study of Man (1950–3) have brought to light outstanding examples of Sabaean art and architecture, especially the temple of the moon-god at Marib the capital, which dates from the 8th century BC

BIBLIOGRAPHY. R. L. Bowen, Jr., and F. P Albright, *Archaeological Discoveries in Sout Arabia*, 1958; *GTT*; S. Moscati, *Ancient Semiti Civilizations*, 1957, pp. 181–194; G. Ryckmans *Les religions arabes préislamiques*^{2}, 1951; J Ryckmans, *L'institution monarchique en Arabi méridionale avant l'Islam*, 1951; G. W. Van Bee in *BA*, XV, 1952, pp. 2–18. D.A.H.

SHEBA, QUEEN OF. An unnamed Sabaea (see SHEBA) monarch who journeyed to Jerusaler to test Solomon's wisdom (1 Ki. x. 1–10, 13 2 Ch. ix. 1–9, 12). A major purpose of her costl (1 Ki. x. 10) yet successful (1 Ki. x. 13) visit ma have been to negotiate a trade-agreement wit Solomon, whose control of the trade route jeopardized the income which the Sabaeans wer accustomed to receive from the caravans whic crossed their territory.

Both Assyrian and S Arabian inscription testify to the presence of queens in Arabia a early as the 8th century BC. (See N. Abbott, 'Pre Islamic Arab Queens', *AJSL*, LVIII, 1941 pp. 1–22.) The widespread domestication of th camel a century or so before Solomon's tim made the Queen of Sheba's trip of about 1,20 miles feasible (1 Ki. x. 2). Her willingness t make this arduous journey is contrasted b Christ with the Jews' complacency in Mt. xii. 42 where she is called 'Queen of the South', a titl which reflects a Semitic construction like *malk šeḇā’* or *malkaṯ yāmîn*, Queen of Sheba or Yemei

This queen is enshrined in Ethiopian legend particularly the *Kebra Nagast* ('Glory of th Kings'), as the Queen of Ethiopia who bore b Solomon the first king of Ethiopia. This legen reflects the close tie which existed in antiquit between S Arabia and E Africa, which Josephu also notes when he calls this ruler 'Queen c Egypt and Ethiopia' (*Ant.* viii. 6. 5, 6; *cf.* als Gregory of Nyssa, *In Cant. Hom.* VII). Arabia legends remember her as Bilqis, although she not so named in the Qur'an (xxvii. 15–45).

D.A.H.

SHEBAM. See SIBMAH.

SHEBNA. A high official under Hezekiah. He variously designated minister ('which is over tl house', Is. xxii. 15), secretary (*sōp̄ēr*, 'scribe 2 Ki. xviii. 18, xix. 2; Is. xxxvi. 3), and sta official (*sōḵēn*, 'treasurer', Is. xxii. 15). A man wealth and high position, he was rebuked b Isaiah for preparing a conspicuously mon mental rock-hewn tomb and his downfall pr dicted (Is. xxii. 15–19). Part of the inscribed lint from this tomb has been recovered (N. Aviga *IEJ*, III, 1953, pp. 137–152; D. J. Wisema *IBA*, 1958, p. 59). The full name of Shebna ma be Shebanyah(u), a name which occurs in co temporary inscriptions and which may be con pared with that later borne by levitical pries (Ne. ix. 4, 5, x. 10; 1 Ch. xv. 24). D.J.W.

SHECHEM. 1. The son of Hamor, the Hivite, prince of Shechem (Gn. xxxiv; Jos. xxiv. 32; Jdg. ix. 28) who defiled Jacob's daughter Dinah. **2.** A descendant of Joseph's son Manasseh (Nu. xxvi. 31), founder of a family (Jos. xvii. 2). **3.** Son of Shemidah, of the tribe of Manasseh (1 Ch. vii. 19).

4. An important town in central Palestine with a long history and many historical associations. Normally it appears in the Bible as Shechem (*šeḵem*), but also once as Sichem (Gn. xii. 6, AV) and twice as Sychem (Acts vii. 16, AV). It was situated in the hill country of Ephraim (Jos. xx. 7), in the neighbourhood of Mt. Gerizim (Jdg. ix. 7). The original site is today represented by Tell Balāṭa, which lies at the east end of the valley running between Mt. Ebal on the north and Mt. Gerizim on the south, about 31 miles north of Jerusalem and 5½ miles south-east of Samaria.

Shechem (Sichem) is the first Palestinian site mentioned in Genesis. Abram encamped there at the 'oak of Moreh' (Gn. xii. 6, RSV). The 'Canaanite was then in the land', but the Lord revealed Himself to Abram and renewed His covenant promise. Abram thereupon built an altar to the Lord (Gn. xii. 7).

Abram's grandson, Jacob, on his return from Harran, came to Shalem, a city of Shechem, and pitched his tent (Gn. xxxiii. 18, 19) on a parcel of ground which he bought from Hamor, the Hivite prince of the region (Gn. xxxiii. 18, 19, xxxiv. 2). When Shechem, the son of Hamor, defiled Dinah, Simeon and Levi killed the men of the region (Gn. xxxiv. 25, 26), and the other sons of Jacob pillaged the town (verses 27–29), though Jacob condemned the action (Gn. xxxiv. 30, xlix. 5–7).

Here Jacob buried the 'strange gods' under the oak (Gn. xxxv. 1–4) and raised an altar to El-elohe-Israel ('God, the God of Israel', Gn. xxxiii. 20; see GOD, NAMES OF). Joseph later sought his brothers near the rich pasture lands round Shechem (Gn. xxxvii. 12 ff.).

In the 15th century BC the town fell into the hands of the Habiru as we learn from the Tell el-Amarna letters (*ANET*, pp. 477, 485–487, 489, 490). The name probably occurs earlier in Egyptian records dating back to the 19th–18th centuries BC (*ANET*, pp. 230, 329).

After the Israelite conquest of Palestine Joshua called for a renewal of the covenant at Shechem. Various features of the typical covenant pattern well known in the East in the centuries 1500–700 BC may be identified in Jos. viii. 30–35 (see COVENANT). Before his death, Joshua gathered the elders again to Shechem, reiterated the covenant, and received the oath of allegiance to God, the King (Jos. xxiv). Many modern scholars see in these assemblies a strong suggestion of an amphictyonic league centred at Shechem (*cf.* M. Noth, *The History of Israel*, 1958).

The boundary between Ephraim and Manasseh passed near the town (Jos. xvii. 7), which was one of the cities of refuge, and a levitical city assigned to the Kohathite Levites (Jos. xx. 7, xxi. 21; 1 Ch. vi. 67). The town lay in Ephraim (1 Ch. vii. 28). Here the Israelites buried the bones of Joseph which they had brought from Egypt (Gn. l. 25; Jos. xxiv. 32).

In the time of the judges, Shechem was still a centre of Canaanite worship and the temple of Baal-berith ('the lord of the covenant') features in the story of Gideon's son Abimelech (Jdg. ix. 4), whose mother was a Shechemite woman. Abimelech persuaded the men of the city to make him king (Jdg. ix. 6, *cf.* viii. 22, 23). He proceeded to slay the royal seed, but Jotham, one son who escaped the bloody purge, spoke a parable about the trees as he stood on Mt. Gerizim (Jdg. ix. 8–15), appealing to the citizens of Shechem to forsake Abimelech. This they did after three years (verses 22, 23), but Abimelech destroyed Shechem (verse 45) and then attacked the stronghold of the temple of Baal-berith and burned it over the heads of those who sought refuge there (verses 46–49).

After Solomon's death the assembly of Israel rejected Rehoboam at Shechem and made Jeroboam king (1 Ki. xii. 1–19; 2 Ch. x. 1–11). Jeroboam restored the town and made it his capital for a time (1 Ki. xii. 25), but later moved the capital to Penuel, and then to Tirzah. The town declined in importance thereafter, but continued in existence long after the fall of Samaria in 722 BC, for men from Shechem came with offerings to Jerusalem as late as 586 BC (Je. xli. 5).

In post-exilic times Shechem became the chief city of the Samaritans (Ecclus. l. 26; Jos., *Ant.* xi. 8. 6), who built a temple here. In 128 BC John Hyrcanus captured the town (Jos., *Ant.* xiii. 9. 1). In the time of the first Jewish revolt Vespasian camped near Shechem, and after the war the town was rebuilt and named Flavia Neapolis in honour of the Emperor Flavius Vespasianus (hence the modern Nablus).

Important excavations conducted at Tell Balāṭa by Carl Watzinger (1907–9), Ernst Sellin and his colleagues (between 1913 and 1934), and more recently by G. E. Wright (1956–8), have revealed the story of this site from the mid-fourth millennium BC down to *c.* 100 BC, when the Hellenistic city came to an end. The height of its prosperity was in the days of the Hyksos rulers (*c.* 1700–1550 BC), though it was an important town until the 9th–8th century BC, when it began to deteriorate. During the 4th century BC, however, it had new life, probably as a Samaritan centre. The question of whether Shechem is the same as the Sychar of Jn. iv. 5 is not clear (see SYCHAR).

BIBLIOGRAPHY. G. E. Wright in *BASOR*, 144, December 1956, and 148, December 1957; E. Sellin, *ZDPV*, 1926, 1927, 1928; E. Sellin and H. Steckeweh, *ZDPV*, 1941; M. Noth, *The History of Israel*, 1958, pp. 91 ff.; E. F. Campbell, R. J. Bull and G. R. H. Wright in *BA*, XXIV, December 1960.

J.A.T.

SHEEP. Heb. *ṣō'n*, the commonest word, is used both literally and metaphorically; *keḇeś* or *keśeḇ*, usually a lamb, is used only literally. There are other Hebrew terms, and *probaton* is used throughout the Greek New Testament and LXX. Etymology, however, is not important here.

The sheep is a clean, domesticated animal and has been known to man from remote antiquity. The kind familiar in Palestine has a very wide tail replete with valuable fat, ten or more pounds of it. It was suitable, from the eighth day of its life, for various kinds of sacrifice (Lv. xxii. 19, 27, *etc.*), and for food (Dt. xiv. 4, *etc.*), including the food of luxury (Is. xxii. 13). The wool or hide provided clothing (Jb. xxxi. 20; Heb. xi. 37). Abnormal fertility of the flock was a sign of human prosperity (Ps. cxliv. 13). The animal was customarily regarded as docile and responsive to affection (2 Sa. xii. 3), but greatly inferior in status and value to a human being (Mt. xii. 12). Nowhere in Scripture are actual sheep introduced more dramatically than in the bleating which was the audible witness of Saul's disobedience (1 Sa. xv. 14). But the metaphorical usages are of greater importance than the literal ones.

Despite their harmlessness, sheep suffer from a lack of initiative amounting to weakness so that, like many human beings, they are easily lost or led astray (Je. l. 6 and Mt. x. 6; Is. liii. 6 and 1 Pet. ii. 25; the parable of Mt. xviii. 12 f., *etc.*). Without a shepherd, it is a helpless creature (Nu. xxvii. 17; Mt. ix. 36, *etc.*; *cf.* Is. xiii. 14, and, more strongly, Zc. xiii. 7). God's human servants are very frequently likened to sheep (Ps. c. 3; Ezk. xxxiv. 31; Jn. xxi. 16 f., *etc.*). This idea is elaborated with much beauty and richness in Jn. x. The animal's utter defencelessness before those who would steal its coat (Is. liii. 7) or demand its life for their own ends (Is. liii. 7 and Acts viii. 32; Ps. xliv. 22 and Rom. viii. 36; Je. xii. 3, *etc.*) is pathetic. This is a fitting symbol of man's own mortality (Ps. xlix. 14). False prophets are said to parade in sheep's clothing because the sheep is symbolic of innocence (Mt. vii. 15). Sheep among wolves would normally be helpless, but Christ's followers are suitably protected (Mt. x. 16–19).

In Mt. xxv. 33 there is no difficulty about the significance of the right hand, which was considered to be both lucky and the place of honour. The precise differentiation between the sheep and the goats is more controversial. It might be based on colour-contrast—white and black are common hues of the respective species—or on the gentler nature of the sheep. Or the animals may be merely exclusive classes, with no additional symbolic implication.

Ct. iv. 2 (= vi. 6) begins by saying that the beloved's teeth are like a flock of ewes, newly shorn and washed and therefore gleaming white. There are strong arguments for claiming that the next phrase does not mean that each ewe bears twins—which would make the metaphor strangely mixed!—but that each tooth has its counterpart in the other jaw (*cf.* RVmg, Moffatt, and Midrash Rabbah on Ct. iv. 2). Or the word might be, not *maṭ'îmôṯ*, but *maṭmîmôṯ*, 'perfected' (J. J. Slotki, translator of Midrash Rabbah on Numbers, Soncino edn., 1939, p. 855, note 2). The last clause then means that no tooth is missing. The entire compliment is acceptable to Oriental, though not to Western, tastes.

The ram is slightly more aggressive than his spouse, and is easily distinguished from her by his long curved horns, which were used by the priests as trumpets (Jos. vi. 4) and for the storing of oil (1 Sa. xvi. 1). The skins of rams, dyed red, were used in the construction of the tabernacle (Ex. xxxvi. 19). Rams were used more frequently for sacrifice, though not to the entire exclusion of ewes. R.A.S.

SHEEP GATE. See JERUSALEM.

SHEET. 1. Heb. *sāḏîn*, 'linen garments' (Jdg. xiv. 12, 13). See reference to 'shirt' in DRESS. 2. Gk. *othonē*, 'a piece of linen', 'a linen sheet', used in describing Peter's vision at Joppa (Acts x. 11, xi. 5). See also LINEN.

SHEKEL. See MONEY, WEIGHTS AND MEASURES.

SHEKINAH. The Shekinah (*š^{e}ḵînâ*), the radiance, glory, or presence of God, 'dwelling' in the midst of His people, is used by Targumist and Rabbi to signify God Himself, obviating biblical anthropomorphisms and anthropopathisms distasteful to legal Judaism. Yet the God conceived in purified human terms inspired the noblest prophetic utterances, whereas the legalist God became cold, abstract, aloof. The Shekinah, the nearest Jewish equivalent to the Holy Spirit, became, with other Old Testament ideas or derivatives, Word, Wisdom, Spirit, *etc.*, a bridge between man's corporeality and God's transcendence. If the term is late, the concept saturates both Testaments. It underlies the notion of God dwelling in His sanctuary (Ex. xxv. 8, *etc.*) or among His people (Ex. xxix. 45 f., *etc.*). These and cognate passages use the root verb *shāḵan*, 'to dwell', from which Shekinah, the abiding presence, is derived.

The glory of God—*kāḇôḏ* in the Hebrew Bible, *doxa* in LXX and New Testament—is another name for the Shekinah. The Hebrew and Greek words may be applied to the glory of mere human beings, such as Jacob (Gn. xxxi. 1) o Solomon (Mt. vi. 29), but it is clear enoug when they refer to God. Thunder, lightning, an cloud may be outward concomitants of God' glory (Ex. xix. 16, xxiv. 15 ff.; Pss. xxix, xcvi Ezk. i. 4), or it may be specially associated wit the tent of meeting (Ex. xl. 34–38) or with th Temple (Ezk. xliii. 2, 4); but it is manifest also i creation (Ps. xix), and possesses elements mor numinous and mysterious than any of these (E xxxiii. 18–23). In fact, the glory of God regular becomes more glorious when it is deliberatel divorced from Temple or mercy-seat.

In the New Testament as in the Old, glory ma be predicated of God (Lk. ii. 9; Acts vii. 5

Cor. iii. 18) or ascribed to Him (Lk. ii. 14; ;om. xi. 36; Phil. iv. 20; Rev. vii. 12, *etc.*). The iving of this glory is mentioned as a human uty, fulfilled (Rom. iv. 20) or unfulfilled (Acts ii. 23; Rev. xvi. 9). It is present in a special 'ay in the heavenly temple (Rev. xv. 8) and in ıe heavenly city (Rev. xxi. 23).

The New Testament freely ascribes comparable lory to Christ. The question has been raised as ɔ whether this glory begins *before* or *after* Easter. 'he Synoptists are reticent about ascribing it to ıe earthly Jesus, except in reference to the arousia (*cf.* Mk. viii. 38, x. 37, xiii. 26; and arallels) or to Christ transfigured (Lk. ix. 32). 'et John does this freely (i. 14, ii. 11, xi. 4), evertheless distinguishing a fuller or final evelation as subsequent to the earthly ministry vii. 39, xii. 16, *etc.*). This seeming fluctuation is ot unnatural—the view of the earthly Jesus and he heavenly Christ would sometimes become ɔreshortened after the passion. The cognate verb *'oxazō* frequently replaces the noun (Jn. xii, vii, *etc.*).

Other passages worthy of special study include: Tim. iii. 16; Tit. ii. 13; Heb. xiii. 21; Jas. ii. 1; Pet. i. 11, 21, iv. 13, v. 1; Rev. v. 12 f.

BIBLIOGRAPHY. See *HDB* (*s.v.* 'Shekinah'); *ewE* (*s.v.* 'Anthropomorphism', 'Shekinah'); *'WNT*, II, pp. 236–257; R. A. Stewart, *Rabbinic 'heology*, 1961, pp. 40–42. R.A.S.

;HELAH. 1. Son of Arpachshad of the family of hem, and father of Eber (Gn. x. 24, xi. 12–15; Ch. i. 18, 24). **2.** Youngest son of Judah by hua (Gn. xxxviii. 5, xlvi. 12), promised by udah to his daughter-in-law Tamar after Er and)nan had died (Gn. xxxviii. 11, 14, 26). Father of he Shelanites (Nu. xxvi. 20). **3.** In Ne. iii. 15 RV) the name of the pool better known as iloam. AV gives 'Siloah'. J.G.G.N.

;HEM. The eldest son of Noah (Gn. v. 32, i. 10; 1 Ch. i. 4), and the ancestor of many lescendants (Gn. x). He was one of the eight eople to escape the flood in the ark (Gn. vii. 13), nd after it, when Noah was drunk, he and apheth covered their father's nakedness (Gn. x. 18, 23, 26, 27). Two years after the flood, /hen Shem was 100 years old, he became father f Arpachshad (Gn. xi. 10), through whom assed the line of descent to the Messiah (Lk. iii. 6), and it may be in reference to this fact that Joah made his prophetic statement in Gn. ix. 26. ince among the descendants of Shem listed in Gn. x. 21–31 a number are identified with eoples who are known to have spoken related anguages in antiquity, the term 'Semitic' has een applied for convenience to this group by nodern philologists. This is a modern use of the erm, however, and does not imply that all the lescendants of Shem spoke Semitic languages. t is stated that Shem lived for 500 years after he birth of Arpachshad (Gn. xi. 11), giving him life of 600 years. All the major versions agree on hese figures. An early theory (Poebel) has been recently revived (Kramer), to the effect that the name *šem* is derived, through various phonetic changes, from *šumer*, written *ki.en.gi* by the Sumerians, the Akkadian name of this people who formed an important element in the early population of Mesopotamia. This theory has not been widely accepted.

BIBLIOGRAPHY. S. N. Kramer, *Analecta Biblica*, XII, 1959, pp. 203, 204. T.C.M.

SHEMUEL (Heb. *šemû'ēl*, '(?) name of God'; *cf.* Samuel). **1.** The son of Ammihud, leader of the tribe of Simeon, appointed to assist in the division of Canaan (Nu. xxxiv. 20). In Nu. i. 6, ii. 12, vii. 36, 41, x. 19 the leader of the tribe is called Shelumiel, the son of Zurishaddai, and the LXX gives the name Salamiēl in all these instances. **2.** A grandson of Issachar (1 Ch. vii. 2). R.A.H.G.

SHEOL. See HELL.

SHEPHELAH (Heb. *šepēlâ*), a geographical term for the low hill tract between the coastal plain of Palestine and the high central ranges (see PALESTINE and fig. 159). The term is used only in the AV of 1 Macc. xii. 38, although the district is frequently referred to in the Old Testament. The RV rendering 'lowland' would give a truer picture if used in the plural form, to indicate its rolling relief of both hills and valleys. But its root-meaning ('to humble' or 'make low') suggests more accurately a district of relatively low relief at the foot of the central mountains. It occurs some twenty times (see Dt. i. 7; Jos. ix. 1, x. 40, xi. 2, 16, xii. 8, xv. 33; Jdg. i. 9; 1 Ki. x. 27; 1 Ch. xxvii. 28; 2 Ch. i. 15, ix. 27, xxvi. 10, xxviii. 18; Je. xvii. 26, xxxii. 44, xxxiii. 13; Ob. 19; Zc. vii. 7). Passages such as 2 Ch. xxvi. 10 and xxviii. 18 clearly distinguish it from the coastal plain. The location of the 'Shephelah' of Jos. xi. 2, 16 is distinct. There it refers to the hills around the town of Carmel (verse 2). 'Israelite Shephelah' in verse 16, according to G. A. Smith, may mean the land between Carmel and Samaria, a structural continuation of the true Shephelah farther south. J.M.H.

SHEPHERD. There are two kinds of biblical shepherd—those who have care of sheep, and those, divine or mortal, who have care of human beings. On the human level, very similar words of praise or censure may be applied to each type. The Hebrew term is the participial form *rō'eh*, the Greek *poimēn*. The care exercised over fellow-mortals may be political or spiritual. Homer and other secular writers frequently called kings and governors shepherds (*Iliad*, I, 263, II, 243, *etc.*). This usage is reflected, in deeper metaphors, in Ezk. xxxiv.

The literal shepherd pursued, and still pursues, an exacting calling, and one as old as Abel (Gn. iv. 2). He must find grass and water in a dry and stony land (Ps. xxiii. 2), protect his charges from the weather and from fiercer creatures (Am. iii.

12), and retrieve any strayed animal (Ezk. xxxiv. 8; Mt. xviii. 12, *etc.*). When his duties carried him far from human haunts a bag held his immediate necessities (1 Sa. xvii. 40, 49), and a tent might be his dwelling (Ct. i. 8). He might use dogs to assist him, like his modern counterpart (Jb. xxx. 1). When shepherds and flocks take up their more permanent abode in any city, this is a mark of depopulation and disaster through divine judgment (Je. vi. 3, xxxiii. 12; Zp. ii. 13–15). The shepherd on duty was liable to make restitution for any sheep lost (Gn. xxxi. 39), unless he could effectively plead circumstances beyond his foresight or control (Ex. xxii. 10–13). Ideally, the shepherd should be strong, devoted, and selfless, as many of them were. But ruffians were sometimes to be found in an honourable profession (Ex. ii. 17, 19), and some shepherds inevitably failed in their duty (Zc. xi, *passim*; Na. iii. 18; Is. lvi. 11, *etc.*).

Such is the honour of the calling that the Old Testament frequently delineates God as the Shepherd of Israel (Gn. xlix. 24; Pss. xxiii. 1, lxxx. 1), tender in His solicitude (Is. xl. 11), who may sometimes scatter the flock in wrath, then gather it again in forgiveness (Je. xxxi. 10). Sometimes the note is predominantly one of judgment, when human shepherd and sheep alike stand condemned and punished (Je. l. 6, li. 23; Zc. xiii. 7; and gospel applications). Such a shepherd may well tremble to stand before the Lord (Je. xlix. 19, l. 44). Sometimes there is a note of pity when the sheep are deserted by those responsible for them (Nu. xxvii. 17; 1 Ki. xxii. 17; Mk. vi. 34, *etc.*). Two shepherds mentioned with special approval are Moses (Is. lxiii. 11) and, surprisingly enough, a heathen executor of God's purposes, Cyrus (Is. xliv. 28). Scripture earnestly stresses the serious responsibility of human leaders to those who follow them. One of the most solemn chapters in the Old Testament is the denunciation of the faithless shepherds in Ezk. xxxiv (*cf.* Je. xxiii. 1–4, and even more sternly Je. xxv. 32–38). These, for their belly's sake, have fed themselves and not their sheep; they have killed and scattered their charges for their own profit; they have utterly neglected their proper pastoral care; therefore God will regather the sheep and judge the shepherds. He will in fact appoint one shepherd (Ezk. xxxiv. 23). This is critically interpreted as signifying the union of the northern and southern kingdoms, but it could very well look forward to Christ. In the New Testament it is Christ's mission to be Shepherd, even Chief Shepherd (Heb. xiii. 20 and 1 Pet. ii. 25; also 1 Pet. v. 4). This is worked out in detail in Jn. x, which merits detailed comparison with Ezk. xxxiv. The main points in John are: the iniquity of those who 'creep, and intrude and climb into the fold'; the using of the door as a mark of the true shepherd; the familiarity of the sheep with the voice of their appointed leader—modern shepherds in the East use precisely the same methods; the teachings regarding the Person of Christ, who is likened to the door and to the good shepherd, but con trasted with the worthless hireling; the relation ship of Christ, His followers, and God; the bring ing into the 'one flock' of the 'other sheep' (vers 16); and the rejection of those who are not th true sheep of Christ. (*Cf.* Milton, *Lycidas* especially lines 113–131.) R.A.S.

SHERAH (AV), **SHEERAH** (RV and RSV). Th Hebrew name, meaning 'a female relative', of a daughter of Ephraim, or of his son, Berial (1 Ch. vii. 24). She built or rebuilt three towns i the territory assigned to Ephraim, Beth-horon th nether and the upper, and Uzzen-sheerah. This i the only example in the Bible of a woman builde of towns. Codex Vaticanus of the LXX takes thi name as a common noun, 'those remaining', an the Pesh. translates the name as a verb, 'she wa left', but other Gk. MSS and the Vulg. support th interpretation as a proper name. J.T.

SHESHACH. An artificial word (Je. xxv. 26 li. 41), formed by the device known as Athbash The English equivalent would be to replace *a* by *z* *b* by *y*, *c* by *x*, *etc.* The Hebrew consonants *š-š-k* then, really represent *b-b-l*, *i.e.* *bāḇel*, 'Babylon' The vowels have no value. The device is her word-play, not cipher, since Je. li. 41 later men tions Babylon explicitly. D.F.P.

SHESHBAZZAR. A prince of Judah (Ezr. i. 8) whom Cyrus made governor of Judah and t whom he entrusted the Temple vessels, formerl captured by Nebuchadrezzar, for return t Jerusalem (Ezr. v. 14, 15). He laid the founda tions of the new Temple (Ezr. v. 16; *cf.* 1 Esdra vi. 18–20), which was completed by Zerubbabel his successor as governor, by 520 BC (Hg. i. 1 14). It is probably Sheshbazzar who is entitle 'Tirshatha' (*q.v.*) in Ezr. ii. 63; Ne. vii. 65, 70. A tempting, but unsupported, theory equate Sheshbazzar with Shenazzar, son of Jehoiachin and uncle of Zerubbabel (1 Ch. iii. 18).

His name (*šešbaṣṣar*) may represent the Bab. Šamaš-apal-uṣur ('Šamaš has guarded the son ship'), and some Greek versions have *sasab(al) assar*. As with the Babylonian names given t other Jews, there may be a deliberate alteration to avoid including the names of heathen deitie (see, *e.g.*, ABEDNEGO).

R. D. Wilson suggested that the full name might have been Šamaš-bān-zer-babili-uṣur, and thus he would be the same person as Zerubbabel (*ISBE*), a view formerly held by several scholar (*HDB*). D.J.W.

SHEVA. See SHAVSHA.

SHEWBREAD. See SHOWBREAD.

SHIBAH. The name of a well dug by Isaac' servants and named Shibah (*šiḇ'â*), or Shebah (Gn. xxvi. 33, AV), because of a covenant wit Abimelech. The word itself means 'seven' o 'oath'. Already, before Isaac's time, Abrahan had encountered trouble with Abimelech king c

Gerar and had finally entered into a covenant (Gn. xxi. 22–34). Seven ewe lambs were presented to Abimelech as a witness to the fact, and Abraham preserved the memory of this covenant by calling the place Beersheba ('well of seven', 'well of an oath'). Isaac revived the old name, using the feminine form *šiḇ'â* of the word *šeḇā'*. J.A.T.

SHIBBOLETH. A test-word by which the Gileadites under Jephthah detected the defeated Ephraimites who tried to escape across the Jordan after the battle (Jdg. xii. 5, 6). Since in the Ephraim local Semitic dialect initial *sh* became *s*, their true identity was disclosed when they pronounced *šibbōleṯ* as *sibbōleṯ*. Both words mean 'a stream in flood' (*cf.* Ps. lxix. 2; Is. xxvii. 12), though the former is also apt to be confused with *šibbōleṯ*, 'an ear of corn'. Those Ephraimites who were thus discovered were slain immediately (verse 6). In modern usage the word stands for the catchword or mark of a sect or party, often used disparagingly. D.J.W.

SHIELD. See ARMOUR AND WEAPONS.

SHIGGAION. See PSALMS.

SHIHOR. See RED SEA.

SHIHOR-LIBNATH. A small river forming part of the southern boundary of the tribe of Asher (Jos. xix. 26). Probably the modern Nahr ez-Zerqa, which runs to the south of Mt. Carmel (see RED SEA). See *GTT*, p. 190, n. 78; L. H. Grollenberg, *Atlas of the Bible*, 1957, pp. 58, 59. T.C.M.

SHILOAH. See SILOAM.

SHILOH. According to Jdg. xxi. 19, Shiloh is situated 'on the north side of Beth-el, on the east side of the highway that goeth up from Beth-el to Shechem, and on the south of Lebonah'. This identifies it as the modern Seilūn, a ruined site on a hill about 9 miles north of Bethel (Beitīn) and 3 miles south-east of el-Lubbān. The site was excavated by Danish expeditions in 1926–9 and 1932, and the results suggest that Shiloh was destroyed about 1050 BC and left desolate for many centuries until reoccupied in Hellenistic times.

It was at Shiloh that the tent of meeting was set up in the early days of the conquest (Jos. xviii. 1), and it was the principal sanctuary of the Israelites during the time of the Judges (Jdg. xviii. 31). It was the site of a local annual festival of dancing in the vineyards, perhaps at the Feast of Ingathering (Ex. xxiii. 16), which once provided the men of Benjamin with an opportunity to seize the maidens for wives (Jdg. xxi. 19 ff.), and this festival probably developed into the annual pilgrimage in which Samuel's parents were later to take part (1 Sa. i. 3). By the time of Eli and his sons the sanctuary had become a well-established structure for centralized worship, and the tent of Joshua had been replaced by a temple (*hêḵāl*) with door and door-posts (1 Sa. i. 9). Although Scripture does not refer directly to its destruction the archaeological evidence fits in well with the references to Shiloh as an example of God's judgment upon His people's wickedness (Ps. lxxviii. 60; Je. vii. 12, 14, xxvi. 6, 9). On the other hand, Ahijah the Shilonite is mentioned in 1 Ki. xi. 29, xiv. 2, and other inhabitants of Shiloh in Je. xli. 5. Some limited habitation must have continued after 1050 BC, but the priesthood transferred to Nob (1 Sa. xxii. 11, *cf.* xiv. 3) and Shiloh ceased to be a religious centre.

A reference of peculiar difficulty comes in Gn. xlix. 10, 'the sceptre shall not depart from Judah, nor the ruler's staff from between his feet, until Shiloh come' (RV). The Heb. *'aḏ kî-yāḇō' šîlōh* can be rendered in several ways. (i) As RV, taking Shiloh as a messianic title. (ii) As RVmg 'till he come to Shiloh', with the subject as Judah and the fulfilment in the assembling of Israel to Shiloh in Jos. xviii. 1, when the tribe of Judah nobly relinquished the pre-eminence it had formerly enjoyed. (iii) By emending *šîlōh* to *šellōh* and translating with the LXX 'until that which is his shall come', *i.e.* 'the things reserved for him', a vaguely messianic hope. (iv) Following a variant reading in LXX, 'until he come whose it is' whatever 'it' may be (Onkelos says it means the kingdom).

The last of these was generally favoured by the Fathers while the first does not seem to have been put forward seriously until the 16th century except in one doubtful passage in the Talmud. Against (i) is its uniqueness: nowhere else is Shiloh used as a title for the Messiah and the New Testament does not recognize it as a prophecy. If it were taken as a title it would have to mean something like 'the peace-giver', but this is not very natural linguistically. (ii) is plausible, but it scarcely fits in with what we know of the subsequent history of Judah; nor is it usual for a patriarchal blessing to have such a time-limit. A variant to get round that objection is the translation 'as long as people come to Shiloh', *i.e.* 'for ever', but it strains the Hebrew. (iii) and (iv) involve a minor emendation, and the renderings leave much to the imagination, but Ezk. xxi. 27 (verse 32 in Hebrew) shows that a similar construction can stand; indeed, Ezk. xxi. 27 is probably a deliberate echo and interpretation of Gn. xlix. 10. The use of *še-* for the relative particle is however normally regarded as late (but *cf.* Jdg. v. 7).

For reviews of the possible interpretations, see especially the commentaries of J. Skinner and S. R. Driver, also *HDB*; an interesting theory by J. Lindblom is found in the *VT* Congress Volume, 1953. For archaeological information, see W. F. Albright in *BASOR*, 9, February 1923, pp. 10 f.; and H. Kjaer in *JPOS*, X, 1930. pp. 87–114. J.B.Tr.

SHIMEATH. In 2 Ki. xii. 21 an Ammonitess, the mother of Jozacar (called Zabad in 2 Ch. xxiv. 26), one of the murderers of Joash.

SHIMEI, SHIMI, SHIMHI (Heb. *šim'î*, (?) abridged from *š*[e]*ma'yāhû*, 'Yahweh has heard'). The Old Testament records nineteen men named Shimei. The best known of these is Shimei the son of Gera, a Benjamite, and a kinsman of Saul, who cursed David for being a man of blood (2 Sa. xvi. 5 ff.). He proclaimed that Absalom's rebellion, which would bring an end to David's reign, was a just recompense for the blood of Saul's house which had been shed before the union of Judah and Israel; though in fact David had not been responsible for the killings (2 Sa. iii. 1–6, 27, iv. 8). David seems to have accepted this meekly, believing that Shimei spoke an admonition from the Lord (2 Sa. xvi. 11, 12), as if acknowledging that he was at all events the occasion of the killings. However, later in his life David concluded that Shimei had sowed dissension, and was not therefore a guiltless man (1 Ki. ii. 9).

Solomon showed clemency to Shimei, giving him a place in Jerusalem; but had him slain after three years, using his (wrongly) suspected complicity with Gath (1 Ki. ii. 36–46) to avenge his (Shimei's) bitterness towards David. C.H.D.

SHIMEITES, SHIMITES. This family came from a Shimei who was a son of Gershon, who was a son of Levi (Nu. iii. 21). This levitical family had part of the responsibility for the maintenance of the tent of meeting, as their sacred charge (Nu. iii. 25, 26).

SHIMRON-MERON. A Canaanite city whose king was allied with Hazor (Jos. xi. 1, simply 'Shimron') and so defeated by Joshua in his Galilaean war (Jos. xii. 20); probably identical with Shimron in the territory assigned to Zebulun, in the Bethlehem district (Jos. xix. 15). If so, it is possibly the present Tell es-Semuniyeh, about 3 miles SSE of Bethlehem, but this is disputed. Merom (*q.v.*) in 'Waters of Merom' is quite distinct from Shimron-meron. Whether Shimron should be identified with the *Šmw'nw*/*Šm'n* of the Egyptian lists of the 18th and 15th centuries BC (the Šamḫuna of the El-Amarna letters) through the LXX form *Symoōn* is highly doubtful. K.A.K.

SHINAR. The land in which were situated the great cities of Babylon, Erech, and Akkad (Gn. x. 10). It lay in a plain to which early migrants came to found the city and tower of Babel (Gn. xi. 2) and was a place of exile for the Jews (Is. xi. 11; Dn. i. 2). The LXX interprets it as 'Babylonia' (Is. xi. 11) or the 'land of Babylon' (Zc. v. 11), and this accords with the location implied in Gn. x. 10 (see ACCAD). Although the Syr. *Sen'ar* denotes the country round Baghdad, no earlier name for Babylonia corresponding with Shinar (Heb. *Šin'ār*) is yet known, the equation with Sumer (S Babylonia) being unlikely. For this reason some believe Shinar to be the W Semitic Sangar (Akkad. *Šanḫar* (Tell el-Amarna letter 5); Egyp. *Sangar*) in Syria (W. F. Albright, *AJSL*, XL, 1923, pp. 125 ff.). See also CALNEH. This northern location might apply to the land of which Amraphel was king (Gn. xiv. 2, 9). See HAMMURABI. D.J.W.

SHIPS AND BOATS.

I. IN THE OLD TESTAMENT

The Hebrews were not a seafaring people, and throughout their history had few ports, the coastline being held by alien maritime peoples (see PHOENICIANS, PHILISTINES). The districts of the tribes of Zebulun and Issachar bordered the Mediterranean (Gn. xlix. 13; Dt. xxxiii. 19), as for a time did those of Dan and Asher (see Jdg. v. 17). The Israelites were, of course, acquainted with sea-going vessels, and references to ships are thus often found in the Old Testament. A ship in time of storm (Pss. xlviii. 7, cvii. 23–30) wallowing like a drunkard (Pr. xxiii. 34) or safely brought into harbour (Ps. cvii. 30) called forth acknowledgment of the power and deliverance of God. The ability of a vessel to sail the ocean was a wonder (Pr. xxx. 19), and life itself was compared to the passing of a ship (Jb. ix. 26; Wisdom v. 10).

a. The development and use of shipping

From *c.* 3500 BC sailing ships with a square sail and forked stern (to hold a steering-paddle) were depicted in Egyptian paintings or modelled for use in tombs. The craft in general use, however, was a papyrus reed or wooden structure employed on the river Nile, where the sail may have first appeared in common use to take advantage of the constant north wind. By the Middle Kingdom (*c.* 2130–1780 BC) large ships, 180 feet long with a 60-foot beam, undertook the trade-run to Byblos in Syria (so Dt. xxviii. 68; *cf.* Pr. xxxi. 14). These may have been Phoenician vessels, for fleets of ships by this period traded with Cyprus and the Greek coast (Nu. xxiv. 24).

By the Amarna age the Egyptian naval dockyard of Tuthmosis III (1490–1437) and Amenophis III (1390–1353 BC) at Sakkara certainly employed Asiatics. Large masted sailing-vessels, some with centre keels, were made for Hatshepsut's expedition to Punt (Somaliland). Large vessels were also built in the Aegean equipped with both sails and oars. See fig. 190, no. 3.

When David's dynasty made a commercia[l] alliance with Hiram of Tyre (2 Sa. v. 11 ff.) i[t] was left to the Phoenicians to float cedar log[s] down the rivers from the Lebanon Mountain[s] and along the coast to Joppa. Lashed rafts o[f] logs (1 Ki. v. 9, *dōḇ*[e]*rôṯ*) or open 'duck-boards (?) (2 Ch. ii. 16, *rap̄sōḏôṯ*) were used for support. This method and route was also used for bringin[g] in supplies for the second Temple (Ezr. iii. 7). Joppa was first developed as a port capable o[f] receiving large vessels by Simon Maccabaeus (1 Macc. xiv. 5).

Solomon built his own port at Ezion-geber o[n] the Gulf of Aqabah and here built his sea-goin[g] ('Tarshish') ships (1 Ki. ix. 26–28). Jehoshapha[t]

ig. 190. Shipping in the ancient Near East. 1. Assyrian barge, *c.* 3200 BC. From a cylinder seal. 2. Model f a canoe in silver. From Ur, *c.* 2500 BC. 3. An Egyptian ocean-going vessel, *c.* 1480 BC. 4. Sennacherib's oldiers attack a flat-bottomed reed boat in the Babylonian marshes, *c.* 710 BC. 5. A Phoenician warship, . 700 BC. 6. An Assyrian river-raft supported on inflated goats' skins, *c.* 700 BC. 7. A Sidonian vessel vith a ram's-head prow as it appears on a 5th-century BC coin. 8. An Egyptian long-distance 'round' vessel, as used in the Mediterranean until Hellenistic times. See also figs. 45, 83.

did the same (1 Ki. xxii. 48). These ships, in co-operation with the Phoenician fleet, imported gold and rare goods from distant places and made voyages involving an absence of one to three years (see OPHIR).

In later times the shipping-routes were controlled by the Phoenicians under Tyre, which city was compared by the prophet Ezekiel to a ship (Ezk. xxvii).

b. Types of vessels

1. The commonest Heb. word for 'ship', *'ᵒniyyâ* (*e.g.* Jon. i. 3), is found in the Amarna texts as 'Canaanite' *'anayi* (a word which may be derived from the Indo-European *naus, navis*). The plural *'ᵒniyyôṯ* and the collective *'ᵒnî*, 'fleet', also occur frequently but do not distinguish the type of vessel employed. They were manned by 'seamen', *'anšê 'ᵒniyyôṯ* (1 Ki. ix. 27; *cf.* Gk. *nautai*, Acts xxvii. 27).

2. The 'ship of Tarshish' was a large ocean-going vessel carrying a heavy cargo (Ezk. xxvii. 25). Fleets of such ships were in use (1 Ki. ix. 26, x. 22). From the name they have been variously described as vessels in use as ore carriers for the refinery trade (W. F. Albright, *BASOR*, 83, October 1941, pp. 21 ff.) or as capable of reaching Tartessus in Sardinia (*cf.* 2 Ch. xx. 36). It is more likely that Tarshish refers to the well-known port of Tarsus in Cilicia and is in some way connected with the Gk. *tarsos*, 'oar'. Barnett considers the 'Tarshish ship' to be the sea-going Mycenaean ship so adapted that 30–60 double-banked oars could be used when becalmed. These ships, with rounded bows for merchantmen and 'long' protruding prows for warships, are shown on the sculptures of Sennacherib depicting his attack on the Phoenician fleet of Luli of Tyre in 700 BC. Similar ships are to be seen in ancient models and on later coins. The heavy hurricane superstructure deck (Gk. *katastrōma*), the screen (see IVORY) on which shields were hung, and the square sail on one yard, can be seen. See fig. 190, no. 5.

Another common Phoenician type of vessel is not specifically named in the Old Testament. It is the Gk. *hippos*, with a horse's head at the prow.

3. The *ṣî*-boat. This is a loan-word from Egyp. *t'ai*, and therefore perhaps a strong reed vessel used on rivers (Is. xxxiii. 21) or for the sea-crossing to Cush (Ezk. xxx. 9), to Cyprus, or up the Syrian coast (Nu. xxiv. 24). Such vessels, as all types of ships, could be fitted with a mast supported by ropes (Is. xxxiii. 21 ff.).

4. The *sᵉp̄înâ*, a large vessel with a deck, is mentioned only in Jonah (i. 5), though it may be similar to other covered ships (as some interpret *ṣilṣal*, Is. xviii. 1). It was manned by 'sailors' (*mallāḥîm*, Jon. i. 5) and had a 'pilot' (*ḥōḇēl*, Jon. i. 6; Ezk. xxvii. 8, 27–29).

5. The rowing-boat, *'ᵒnî šayiṭ* (Is. xxxiii. 21), could be either a small or a large vessel (thus AV 'galley') manned by many oarsmen (*šāṭîm*, Ezk. xxvii. 8; see 2 above).

6. *'ᵃḇārâ* (2 Sa. xix. 18) may denote a 'ferry-boat', a flat-bottomed skiff used to cross such rivers as the Jordan.

BIBLIOGRAPHY. R. D. Barnett, 'Early Shipping in the Near East', *Antiquity*, XXII, 1958, pp. 220–230; S. Smith, 'The Ship Tyre', *PEQ*, LXXXV, 1953, pp. 97 ff. D.J.W.

II. IN THE NEW TESTAMENT

a. On the Sea of Galilee

The Galilaean boats were used mainly for fishing (*e.g.* Mt. iv. 21 f.; Mk. i. 19 f.; Jn. xxi. 3 ff.; see FISH), but also generally for communications across the lake (*e.g.* Mt. viii. 23 ff., ix. 1, xiv. 13 ff.; Mk. viii. 10 ff.). Our Lord sometimes preached from a boat so that His voice might not be restricted by the crowd's pressing too close (Mk. iv. 1; Lk. v. 2 f.).

These vessels were not large: one could accommodate Jesus and His disciples (*e.g.* Mk. viii. 10), but an unusually large catch of fish enclosed by a single net was enough to overload two of them (Lk. v. 7). While they were no doubt fitted with sails, they were regularly equipped with oars to enable them to progress in calm weather and in the heavy storms which occasionally sweep across the lake (Mk. vi. 48; Jn. vi. 19).

b. On the Mediterranean

The main characteristics of Mediterranean ships had changed little over several centuries. Warships ('long ships', their length being about eight times their width) were regularly propelled by oars and rarely went far from the coast. Most of them carried between 15 and 75 tons. Merchant ships ('round ships', their length being three or four times their width) relied on sails, but often carried up to twenty oars for emergencies. They also generally remained reasonably close to land, but under favourable conditions would cross the open sea (see PATARA). A ship of 10,000 talents (about 250 tons) was considered large, although Pliny mentions one of apparently 1,300 tons.

Most of Paul's missionary voyages were probably undertaken in small coastal vessels, but on his journey to Rome he sailed in two of the great grain ships plying between Egypt and Italy, which might easily carry a complement of 276 crew and passengers (Acts xxvii. 37). About the same period Josephus travelled in a ship carrying 600 (*Vita* 3). Lucian (*Navigium* 1 ff.) gives a description of a large grain ship of AD 150; and in recent years a merchant ship of the 2nd century BC, wrecked off Marseilles with a cargo of wine and pottery, has been excavated by archaeologists. From these and other evidences we can get some idea of Paul's 'Castor and Pollux' (*q.v.*).

Such a ship would have a central mast with long yard-arms carrying a large square mainsail and possibly a small topsail, and a small foremast sloping forward almost like a bowsprit with a foresail (Gk. *artemōn*) which might be used to head the ship round and check drifting in a storm (possibly Acts xxvii. 17 ff., but see

F. F. Bruce *ad loc.*; see WIND, EUROCLYDON, QUICKSANDS) and to give the ship steerage way when it was not desired to take full advantage of the wind (Acts xxvii. 40, RV). By bracing the sails these ships could sail within about seven degrees of the wind.

The bows were swept up to a carved or painted figure to represent the name of the ship (Acts xxviii. 11), and on the stern, which was also raised, generally into a swan-neck shape, was a statue of the patron deity of the vessel's home port. Two large oars in the stern served as rudders, either operated separately or rotated together by means of ropes attached to a central piece of gear. These could be lashed in position in bad weather (*cf.* Acts xxvii. 40).

Anchors normally had a wooden stock with lead arms, and had small marker-buoys attached. A specimen found near Cyrene weighs about 12½ cwt. There would be three or more on board, and when anchoring off a beach one or two of them would be let down from the bows, mooring cables from the stern being attached to the shore. For manoeuvring or riding out a gale, however, anchors might be let out from the stern (Acts xxvii. 29). A sounding-lead was used to check the depth when near shallows (Acts xxvii. 28), and might be greased to bring up samples of the bottom.

A dinghy was towed astern in good weather, but hoisted on board in a storm (Acts xxvii. 16, 17) to prevent its being swamped or smashed. In the absence of lifeboats other than this dinghy survivors of a shipwreck would have to rely on spars. Paul had been shipwrecked three times before his journey to Rome (2 Cor. xi. 25).

The risks of any voyage were great, but so were the profits if it was successful (*cf.* Rev. xviii. 19). The owner often commanded his ship, perhaps with the assistance of a professional steersman or navigator; but on a vessel under contract to the Roman government an army officer might take precedence (Acts xxvii. 11). There might be as many as three decks on a large merchantman, and some luxuriously fitted cabins.

Ships were normally dismasted and laid up to avoid the winter storms from mid-November to mid-February (Acts xx. 3, 6, xxviii. 11; 1 Cor. xvi. 6 ff.; 2 Tim. iv. 21; Tit. iii. 12), and periods of about a month before and after this season were considered dangerous (Acts xxvii. 9). The main difficulty seems to have been the obscuring of the sky by storm clouds, thus making navigation by the sun and stars impossible. Delays due to weather were common. According to Josephus (*BJ* ii. 10. 5) one letter from the Emperor Gaius in Rome to Petronius in Judaea took three months to get there. See SAMOTHRACE.

There is some doubt about the meaning of 'undergirding the ship' in Acts xxvii. 17. The traditional view, which is not unlikely, is that ropes were passed under the ship, from side to side, to hold its timbers firm; but it may be the use of horizontal strengthening cables (so Smith) or of a hogging truss (so Cadbury), although this last is less likely in a large ship with decks to strengthen it.

c. Figurative use

Nautical metaphors are rare in the New Testament. In Heb. vi. 19 hope is called 'an anchor of the soul'; and Jas. iii. 4, 5 compares the tongue with a ship's rudder.

BIBLIOGRAPHY. J. Smith, *The Voyage and Shipwreck of St. Paul*[4], 1880; C. Storr, *Ancient Ships*, 1895; F. F. Bruce, *Acts*, 1951, pp. 452 ff.; *BC*, IV, pp. 326 ff.; H. J. Cadbury in *BC*, V, pp. 345 ff.

K.L.McK.

SHISHA. See SHAVSHA.

SHISHAK. Libyan prince who founded Egypt's XXIInd Dynasty as the Pharaoh Sheshonq I. He reigned for 21 years, *c.* 945–924 BC. He harboured Jeroboam as a fugitive from Solomon, after Ahijah's prophecy of Jeroboam's future kingship (1 Ki. xi. 29–40). Late in his reign, Shishak invaded Palestine in the fifth year of Rehoboam, 925 BC. He subdued Judah, taking the treasures of Jerusalem as tribute (1 Ki. xiv. 25, 26; 2 Ch. xii. 2–12), and also asserted his dominion over Israel, as is evidenced by a broken stele of his from Megiddo. At the temple of Amūn in Thebes, Shishak left a triumphal relief-scene, naming many Palestinian towns; see *ANEP*, p. 118, fig. 349, p. 290. See also LUBIM, SUKKIIM. For Shishak's invasion, see B. Maisler-Mazar, *VT Supplement Vol.*, IV, 1957, pp. 57–66; and *ARE*, IV, §§ 709–722. K.A.K.

SHITTIM. 'The acacia trees', called 'Abel-Shittim' ('field of acacias') in Nu. xxxiii. 49, where it is mentioned as one extremity of the Israelite camp before Jericho. Buhl, *Geography*, pp. 116, 265, suggested its identification with Tell Kefren, an area 8 miles wide and 15 miles long, east of the Jordan, on the plains of Moab opposite Jericho; others have proposed Tell el-Hammam.

The Israelites pitched their last camp there before entering Canaan, and after they had conquered Sihon and Og. Nu. xxii–xxxvi records the Israelites' stay in the area and Nu. xxv narrates the idolatry and immorality committed there. Joshua subsequently despatched spies from Shittim to view Jericho and the land of Canaan (Jos. ii. 1).

Joel iii. 18 mentioned 'the valley of Shittim' which will receive life-giving water in the Day of the Lord. The Wadi es-Sant has been proposed as a possible location for this valley (*cf.* J. A. Bewer, *Joel*, *ICC*, 1912, p. 142); others have identified it with the Kidron ravine (modern Wadi en-Nar). R.A.H.G.

SHOA. Ezekiel (xxiii. 23) prophesies that this people, together with other dwellers in Mesopotamia, will attack Jerusalem. Shoa has been identified with the people called *Sutu* or *Su* in Akkadian sources, though some now question this identification. According to the Amarna letters, they were Semitic nomads living in the Syrian desert in the 14th century BC. Later they migrated to the area east of Baghdad, and Assyrian records often mention them with the *Ḳutu*, called Koa in Ezk. xxiii. 23, as warring against Assyria. Some scholars (*e.g.* O. Procksch) take the word usually translated 'crying' in Is. xxii. 5 to be this proper name Shoa.

BIBLIOGRAPHY. F. Delitzsch, *Wo lag das Paradies?*, 1881, pp. 233–237; G. A. Cooke in *ICC*, 1936, on Ezk. xxiii. 23; R. T. O'Callaghan, *Aram Naharaim, Analecta Orientalia*, XXVI, 1948, pp. 88, 92–98, 101. J.T.

SHOBACH. The Aramaean general in command of the forces of Hadadezer, king of Aram, at the time of the war with Ammon (2 Sa. x. 16–18). He is not mentioned in the earlier operations at Rabbah when Joab and Abishai routed the Syrian army (verses 10–14), but this could be due to the presence of the king himself in command. It is therefore assumed that he held office after the event and is named (*šôḇaḵ*; Gk. *sōbak*; *cf.* *šôp̄aḵ*, 1 Ch. xix. 16–18) as the leader of the combined forces from Syria and east of the Euphrates in the battle at Helam, east of Jordan. Shobach was fatally wounded and the Aramaeans routed by David. D.J.W.

SHOBAL. 1. The son of Seir, an Edomite (Gn. xxxvi. 20), father of a clan (verse 23) and a Horite leader (verse 29 = 1 Ch. i. 38, 40). **2.** A son of Caleb and 'father' (founder) of Kiriath-jearim (1 Ch. ii. 50, 52), also a Judaean (1 Ch. iv. 1, 2). It is probable that (1) and (2) are related persons. D.J.W.

SHOBI (2 Sa. xvii. 27–29). An Ammonite, a prince of Rabbah, whose father Nahash (perhaps the son of the Nahash referred to in 1 Sa. xi. 1) had shown kindness to David (2 Sa. x. 2; 1 Ch. xix. 2), apparently when he was a fugitive.

When David came to the height of his power he, in his turn, showed kindness to the house of Nahash. This kindness was appreciated by Shobi, so that when David was retreating to Mahanaim before Absalom, Shobi was one of those who provided rest and refreshment for David's company. C.H.D.

Fig. 191. Shishak (Sheshonq I), attended by his son, the high priest Iuput, receives symbols of a long life and prosperous reign from the god Amen-Rē. From a relief at Karnak, *c.* 940 BC.

SHOCK. A wrap or stook of cut corn awaiting threshing (Ex. xxii. 6, 'stack'; Jdg. xv. 5; Jb. v. 26). The Hebrew word (*gāḏîš*) is used also of a burial cairn (Jb. xxi. 32). See also AGRICULTURE.

SHOE. Usually when this word occurs in the Bible it signifies 'sandal' (*q.v.* under DRESS). See also fig. 178.

SHOSHANNIM. See PSALMS.

SHOVEL (Heb. *yā'*). Bronze shovels were made for clearing ashes from off the altar of burnt-offering (Ex. xxvii. 3) and later by Hiram for Solomon's Temple (1 Ki. vii. 40, 45). Some Canaanite shovels have been discovered, *e.g.* at Megiddo (*BA*, IV, 1941, p. 29 and fig. 9).

Heb. *raḥaṯ* is mentioned in Is. xxx. 24; it was probably wooden. See FAN, AGRICULTURE.

A.R.M.

SHOWBREAD. Heb. *leḥem happānîm*, lit. 'bread of the face', *i.e.* bread set before the face or presence of God (Ex. xxv. 30, xxxv. 13, xxxix. 36, *etc.*) or *leḥem hamma'ᵃreḵeṯ*, lit. 'bread of ordering' (1 Ch. ix. 32, *etc.*). After Moses had received divine instructions concerning the making of a table, dishes, spoons, covers, and bowls for the 'holy place' of the tabernacle, he was directed to place 'showbread' on the table. This arrangement was never to cease (Ex. xxv. 30). The showbread consisted of twelve baked cakes, made of fine flour, each containing two-tenths of an ephah (see WEIGHTS AND MEASURES). These were set in two rows, six to a row (*ma'ᵃreḵeṯ*, Lv. xxiv. 6). Upon each row (lit. 'the row', Lv. xxiv. 7) of cakes frankincense was placed 'for a memorial' (*lᵉ'azkārâ*) and was offered by fire to the Lord (Lx. xxiv. 7). It was the duty of the priest each sabbath day to place fresh or hot bread on the table (1 Sa. xxi. 6). The old cakes then became the perquisite of Aaron and his sons who ate them in the holy place because they were 'most holy' (Lv. xxiv. 5–9). It was these loaves that David requested of Ahimelech, the priest, for himself and his men (1 Sa. xxi. 1–6; *cf.* Mt. xii. 4; Mk. ii. 26; Lk. vi. 4).

The position of the table upon which the showbread was placed was in the holy place on the north side of the tabernacle opposite the candlestick (Ex. xxvi. 35). The table was made of acacia wood overlaid with gold and bordered with a golden crown. It had a ring at each corner for the rods by which it was carried (Ex. xxv. 23–28). According to the original commandment it never failed to appear in the appointed place of God's worship (2 Ch. iv. 19, xiii. 11). The Kohathites had charge of the showbread (1 Ch. ix. 32).

The passages referred to do not themselves indicate the significance of the showbread, but it is possible to infer from these data that God is man's Provider and Sustainer, and that man lives constantly in the presence of God. This truth makes it obligatory for man to offer his life to God (Rom. xii. 1). D.F.

SHRINE. See DIANA.

SHUAH. 1. Shua (*šû'ā'*) the daughter of Heber of the tribe of Asher (1 Ch. vii. 32). **2.** Shua (*šûa'*) a Canaanite of Adullam whose daughter, Bath-shua (1 Ch. ii. 3), Judah took to wife (Gn. xxxviii. 2, 12). **3.** Shuah (*šûaḥ*) a son of Abraham by his wife Keturah (Gn. xxv. 2; 1 Ch. i. 32). **4.** Shuah (*šûḥâ*) a descendant of Judah and brother of Chelub father of Mehir (1 Ch. iv. 11). T.C.M.

SHUAL, LAND OF. A district in Benjamin mentioned as lying in the path of a company of plundering Philistines, as they moved from Michmash to Ophrah (1 Sa. xiii. 17). Unknown outside the Bible, but probably near Michmash.

T.C.M.

SHULAMMITE. A feminine noun (*šûlammîṯ*) applied to the heroine in Ct. vi. 13, 'Shulammite' has been a formidable problem to scholars. Some (*e.g.* Koehler's *Lexicon*) have connected it with an unknown town, Shulam; some (*e.g. ISBE*) classify it as a variant of Shunammite (*q.v.*); others (*e.g.* L. Waterman and H. Torczyner) identify the Shulammite with Abishag (*q.v.*) the Shunammite. E. J. Goodspeed (*AJSL*, L, 1934, pp. 102 ff.) and H. H. Rowley (*AJSL*, LVI, 1939, pp. 84–91) deny any connection with Shunem but view the word as a feminine counterpart of Solomon, 'the Solomoness'. Attempts have been made to derive the names Solomon and Shulammite from the god Shelem. See H. H. Rowley, *The Servant of the Lord*, 1952, p. 223. D.A.H.

SHUNEM, SHUNAMMITE. A town (probably modern Solem) in the territory of Issachar near Jezreel (Jos. xix. 18), Shunem (*šûnēm*) was the site of the Philistine camp before the battle of Gilboa (1 Sa. xxviii. 4). There Elisha sojourned frequently in the home of a generous woman (called the Shunammite, a feminine adjective derived from Shunem) whose son, born according to Elisha's prediction, was miraculously raised up by the prophet after being smitten with sun-stroke (2 Ki. iv. 8 ff.). It is this woman whose property was restored at Gehazi's behest after she had temporarily abandoned it to seek relief from famine in Philistia (2 Ki. viii. 1–6). From Shunem also David's men brought the beautiful Abishag (*q.v.*) to comfort their aged king (1 Ki. i. 3, 15). Adonijah's request for her hand in marriage cost him his life (1 Ki. ii. 17, 21, 22). See SHULAMMITE. D.A.H.

SHUR. A wilderness-region in the north-west part of the Sinai isthmus, south of the Mediterranean coastline and the 'way of the land of the Philistines', between the present line of the Suez Canal on its west and the 'River of Egypt' (*q.v.*; Wadi el-'Arish) on its east. Abraham and Sarah's handmaid Hagar fled to a well past Kadesh on the way to Shur (Gn. xvi. 7). For a time Abraham 'dwelled between Kadesh and Shur' and then sojourned at Gerar (Gn. xx. 1); Ishmael's descendants ranged over an area that reached as far as 'Shur, that is before [*i.e.* east of] Egypt' (Gn. xxv. 18). After passing through the sea (see RED SEA), Israel entered the wilderness of Shur before going south into Sinai (Ex. xv. 22). Shur lay on the direct route to Egypt from southern Palestine (1 Sa. xv. 7 and, most explicitly, xxvii. 8). K.A.K.

SHUSHAN. Susa, the ruins of which lie near the river Karun (see ULAI), SW Persia, was occupied almost continuously from prehistoric times until it was abandoned by the Seleucids. Here was the capital of Elam (*q.v.*), whose royal inscriptions of the second millennium have been recovered. It maintained its importance under the Kassites and its independence until sacked in 640 BC by Ashurbanipal, who sent men of Susa (Shushanites) to exile in Samaria (Ezr. iv. 9). Under the Achaemenids Susa flourished as one of the three royal cities (Dn. viii. 2; Ne. i. 1). Darius I built his palace here, the ruins of which, restored by Artaxerxes I (Longimanus) and II (Mnemon),

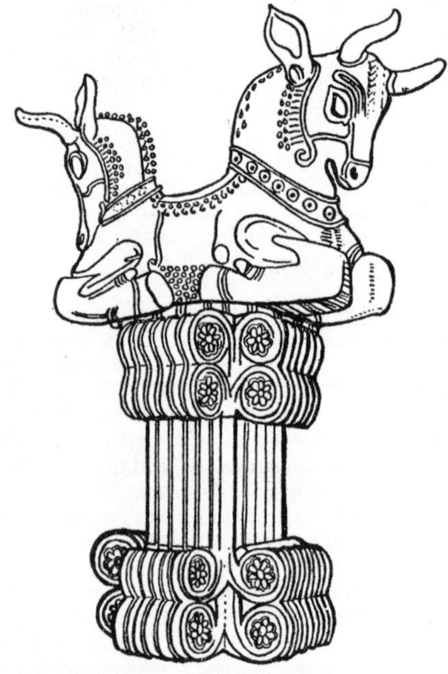

Fig. 192. Column-capital of a double bull supported on volutes. From the Apadana or audience hall at Susa, 4th century BC.

remain, with the Apadana, one of the outstanding Persian architectural features of the 5th century BC. This palace figures prominently in the book of Esther (i. 2, 5, ii. 3, iii. 15, *etc.*). See XERXES, ESTHER. The site was first excavated by Loftus in 1851, and subsequently extensive operations have been undertaken there by the French.

BIBLIOGRAPHY. R. Ghirshman, *Iran*, 1954.

D.J.W.

SHUSHAN-EDUTH. See PSALMS.

SHUTTLE. See SPINNING AND WEAVING.

SIBBOLETH. See SHIBBOLETH.

SIBMAH. A town wrested from Sihon king of the Amorites and allotted by Moses to the tribe of Reuben (*śibmâ*, Jos. xiii. 19, 21). It is identical with Sebam ('Shebam', AV); possibly its name was changed when it was rebuilt (Nu. xxxii. 3, 38). By the time of Isaiah and Jeremiah, who bewailed its devastation, it had reverted to the Moabites (Is. xvi. 8, 9; Je. xlviii. 32). Originally a land for cattle (Nu. xxxii. 4), it became famous for its vines and summer fruit. Jerome (*Comm. in Is.* 5) placed it about 500 paces from Heshbon: Khirbet qam el-qibsh, 3 miles WSW, is a feasible site.

J.W.C.

SICKNESS. See DISEASE AND HEALING.

SICKLE. See AGRICULTURE.

SIDDIM, VALE OF (Heb. *siddîm*, perhaps derived from Hittite *siyantas*, 'salt'). In Gn. xiv. 3, 10 a valley identified with the 'Salt Sea' and described as 'full of slimepits' (RSV 'bitumen pits'). Here the kings of the Jordan pentapolis were defeated by Chedorlaomer and his allies from the east. It was probably a fertile, well-watered region south of the Lisan peninsula, later submerged by the southward extension of the Dead Sea through earthquake action and consequent faulting of the rock-formation. From the bituminous products of the Dead Sea (still in evidence) the Greeks called it *Asphaltitis*.

BIBLIOGRAPHY. J. P. Harland, 'Sodom and Gomorrah', *BA*, V, 1942, pp. 17 ff., VI, 1943, pp. 41 ff.

F.F.B.

SIDON (Heb. *ṣîḏôn*, *ṣîḏōn*). The ancient Phoenician walled city and port in the Lebanon. Sidon (AV also 'Zidon'; modern Saida) had twin harbours and was divided into Greater Sidon (Jos. xi. 8) and Lesser Sidon.

According to tradition, Sidon was the first Phoenician city to be founded (see PHOENICIA) and became a principal Canaanite stronghold (Gn. x. 19; 1 Ch. i. 13). For some centuries the harbour was subordinate to the Egyptian XVIIIth–XIXth Dynasties. With declining Egyptian military control the city ruler Zimri-ada committed defection *c.* 1390 BC (so Amarna tablets). It is possible that the attempt to include Dor in Sidonian territory led to war with the Philistines, who *c.* 1150 BC plundered Sidon, whose inhabitants fled to Tyre. The city was, however, strong enough to oppose Israel (Jdg. x. 12), and during a period of active colonization apparently made an unsuccessful attempt to settle at Laish in the Upper Jordan (Jdg. xviii. 7, 27). Opposition to Phoenician expansion came also from the Assyrians, who under Tiglath-pileser I *c.* 1110 BC began to exact tribute from the ports, including Sidon. Ashurnasirpal II (*c.* 880 BC) claimed the city as a vassal, and in 841 BC Shalmaneser III marched to the Dog river to receive the tribute of Tyre, Sidon, and Israel (see JEHU), and depicted this on the temple gates at Balawat (now in BM). The Assyrian demands increased and the Sidonians rebelled. Tiglath-pileser III captured Tyre and perhaps Sidon in 739–738 (H. Tadmor, *Scripta Hierosolymitana*, VIII, 1961, p. 269, makes Zc. ix. 2 refer to this time). When Sennacherib marched in an attack foretold by Isaiah (xxiii. 2–12), Luli fled and died in exile and was replaced by Ethba'al (Tuba'lu) when Great and Little Sidon had been captured.

On Sennacherib's death Sidon once more revolted and Esarhaddon invaded Sidon, killed the ruler Abdi-milkutti, sacked the port and moved its inhabitants to Kar-Esarhaddon, and brought prisoners from Elam and Babylonia to replace the depleted population.

Sidon recovered its independence with the decline of the Assyrians, only to be besieged again and captured by Nebuchadrezzar *c.* 587 BC as foretold by Jeremiah (xxv. 22, xxvii. 3, xlvii. 4). Under the Persians it provided the majority of the Persian fleet (*cf.* Zc. ix. 2). About 350 BC, under Tabnit II (Tannes), Sidon led the rebellion of Phoenicia and Cyprus against Artaxerxes III (Ochus). The city was betrayed and 40,000 perished, the survivors burning the city and fleet. The fortifications were never rebuilt. The city under Strato II yielded to Alexander the Great without opposition and helped his siege of Tyre.

Under Antiochus III Sidon was a prosperous part of the kingdom of Ptolemy and later passed to the Seleucids and then to the Romans, who granted it local autonomy. Through all its history the principal temple was that of Eshmun, the god of healing. It is therefore significant that it was in the region of Sidon that Jesus Christ healed the Syro-Phoenician woman (Mk. vii. 24–31; *cf.* Mt. xi. 21). Many Sidonians listened to His teaching (Mk. iii. 8; Lk. vi. 17, x. 13, 14). Herod Agrippa I received a delegation from Sidon at Caesarea (Acts xii. 20) and Paul visited friends in the city on his way to Rome (Acts xxvii. 3). The inhabitants of Sidon, which was renowned as a centre of philosophical learning, were mainly Greek (*cf.* Mk. vii. 26). Many coins bear inscriptions of Sidonian rulers, and among the discoveries in the area have been the inscribed sarcophagus of Eshmunazar (*c.* 300 BC) and buildings in the port area of New Testament times (A. Poidebard and J. Lauffray, *Sidon*, 1951). See also PHOENICIA. For Phoenician inscriptions from Sidon, see G. A. Cooke, *North Semitic Inscriptions*, 1903, pp. 26–43, 401–403.

D.J.W.

SIEGE. See FORTIFICATION AND SIEGECRAFT.

SIEVE. The AV translation of two Hebrew words —*kᵉḇārâ* (Am. ix. 9) and *nāp̄â* (Is. xxx. 28). It was used to separate the grain from grit and dirt after threshing. See also AGRICULTURE.

SIGN.

I. IN THE OLD TESTAMENT

The word *'ōṯ* is used with several shades of meaning.

1. An outward mark or object intended to convey a distinctive message, *e.g.* tribal standards (Nu. ii. 2); circumcision (Gn. xvii. 11); stones from the Jordan (Jos. iv. 6).

2. Weather conditions indicating the will of God, *e.g.* sun and moon (Gn. i. 14); the rainbow (Gn. ix. 12).

3. Omens named by prophets as pledges of their predictions, *e.g.* the death of Samuel's sons (1 Sa. ii. 34); gifts of the Spirit to Saul (1 Sa. x. 7); the virgin with child (Is. vii. 11). (See also 2 Ki. xix. 29; Je. xliv. 29.)

4. Works of God. When the word 'sign' is used in the plural together with 'wonders' (*mōp̄ēṯ*) the events are understood to be the works of God, or attestations of His active presence among His people. This is seen in the account of the Exodus, where the plagues are described as signs (Ex. iv. 28, vii. 3, viii. 23); the Exodus itself, with the deaths of the Egyptian first-born, the crossing of the Red Sea, and the destruction of the Egyptian army, provides the supreme example of such signs and wonders (Dt. iv. 34, vi. 22, vii. 19). This conviction is found throughout the Old Testament (*e.g.* Jos. xxiv. 17; Ps. lxxviii. 43; Je. xxxii. 21; Ne. ix. 10), and Israel was assured that when God revealed Himself again it would be with 'signs and wonders' to herald His coming (Joel ii. 30).

II. IN THE NEW TESTAMENT

The word *sēmeion* also shows similar shades of meaning.

1. A meaningful God-given token, indicating what God has done (Rom. iv. 11) or is doing (Mt. xvi. 3) or is about to do (Mt. xxiv. 3, 30).

2. A miraculous authentication of a messenger from God. The power to work miracles or produce authenticating 'signs' was expected in the ancient world from those who claimed to be messengers of God. The people of Galilee asked for such as proof of the claims of Jesus; 'Master, we would see a sign' (Mt. xii. 38). Many times Jesus refused to perform miracles to satisfy this popular demand or to ratify His claims to be the Son of God; 'an evil and adulterous generation seeketh after a sign' (Mt. xii. 39, xvi. 4). John, however, realized that the miracles of Jesus Christ were purposive acts which demonstrated the power of God present and triumphant in this world, and he described them as 'signs' (Jn. ii. 11, iv. 54, xii. 18, RSV).

3. An indication of the presence of God acting in grace or judgment. The disciples expected demonstrations of power and outward manifestations, 'miracles, signs and wonders', to be the experience of the early Church, in confirmation of the power of the gospel (Acts ii. 43, iv. 30; 2 Cor. xii. 12). The final judgment of the world will also be heralded by dramatic portents— 'great signs' (Lk. xxi. 11, 25).

See also MIRACLES (and Bibliography there given).

A.A.J.

SIGNET. See SEAL, SEALING.

SIHON. An Amorite king (13th century BC), whose capital was Heshbon. According to Nu. xxi. 26–30 and Je. xlviii. 45, Sihon conquered the

Moabites and took their territory as far south as the river Arnon. Five Midianite princes were among his vassals (Jos. xiii. 21). His domain included the area from the Arnon on the south to the Jabbok on the north, and from the Jordan on the west to the desert on the east (Nu. xxi. 24; Jdg. xi. 22), and Jos. xii. 3 and xiii. 27 seem to extend his control north of the Jabbok to the Sea of Chinnereth. Moses sent an embassy to Sihon asking permission for the Israelites to pass through his kingdom (Nu. xxi. 21, 22; Dt. ii. 26–28). When Sihon refused, the Israelites defeated and killed him at Jahaz and occupied his territory (Nu. xxi. 21–32). This area was assigned to the tribes of Reuben and Gad (Nu. xxxii. 33–38; Jos. xiii. 10). The victory over Sihon is often recalled in the subsequent history of Israel (Dt. xxxi. 4, by Moses; Jos. ii. 10, by Rahab; Jos. ix. 10, by the Gibeonites; Jdg. xi. 19–21, by Jephthah; Ne. ix. 22, by Levites in a prayer of confession; and Pss. cxxxv. 11, cxxxvi. 19). The name Jebel Šîḥân for the mountain south of Ḏîbân (biblical Dibon) preserves in Arabic form the name of this king in the area which he once ruled. The Babylonian Talmud (*Niddah* 61a) records a tradition not found in the Bible that Sihon was the brother of King Og (also an Amorite), and a son of Ahijah, son of the legendary fallen angel Shamhazai.

BIBLIOGRAPHY. G. A. Smith, *The Historical Geography of the Holy Land*[25], 1931, pp. 588–591, 691–693; A. Musil, *Arabia Petraea, I, Moab*, 1907, pp. 375, 376. J.T.

SIKKUTH, SICCUTH. The word *sikkûṯ* as such does not occur in the Bible, but is translated 'tabernacle', in Am. v. 26, AV—a verse which refers to Israel's adoption of Assyrian gods. In this verse the unvocalized consonants are *skkt mlkkm*, which are better translated, 'Sakkuth your king', than by AV and LXX, 'the tabernacle of your Moloch'. The consonants *skkt* were vocalized to read *sikkûṯ*, 'tabernacle', probably by using the vowels of *šiqqûṣ*, 'an abominable thing'. However, the verse makes good sense if we read Sakkuth instead of 'tabernacle'. Sakkuth was the name of the god of war, and of sun and light, Adar-malek or Saturn (*cf.* 2 Ki. xvii. 31, Adrammelech), otherwise known as Ninurta (SAG.KUT). Kaimanu or Kaiwanu are alternative names for the planet. Hence Am. v. 26 should be translated, as in RSV, 'You shall take up Sakkuth your king, and Kaiwan your star-god, your images, which you made for yourselves . . .' (Others, however, regard this astral interpretation as improbable, and follow LXX in seeing in *Sikkuth* a reference to tent-shrines, while translating *Kaiwan* as 'pedestal(s)'—an interpretation attested as early as the *Zadokite Work* of the 1st century BC.) See REMPHAN. J.A.T.

SILAS. A leading member of the church at Jerusalem who also had prophetic gifts (Acts xv. 22, 32). Silas may be a Semitic name, possibly *šᵉʾîlāʾ*, the Aramaic form of Saul. There is little doubt that he is to be identified with 'Silvanus' (2 Cor. i. 19; 1 Thes. i. 1; 2 Thes. i. 1; 1 Pet. v. 12), which is probably the Latinized form of 'Silas', though it may be a separate *cognomen* chosen for its similarity.

In Acts Silas was sent by the church a. Jerusalem to welcome into fellowship the Gentiles converted through the church of Antioch (Acts xv. 22–35). When Paul and Barnabas quarrelled about John Mark, Barnabas went off with Mark and Paul took Silas as his companion on his second missionary journey (xv. 36–41). The fact of his Roman citizenship (xvi. 37–39) may have been one of the reasons for the choice, and his membership of the Jerusalem church would have been helpful to Paul. His rôle seems to have been to replace Mark rather than Barnabas. Nowhere is he referred to in a general way as an 'apostle' (contrast Barnabas in Acts xiv. 14) and his position seems to be subordinate. Mark was the 'minister' (*hypēretēs*) of the apostles before (xiii. 5), and that may indicate that he had some function similar to the synagogue attendants (Lk. iv. 20) in looking after the Scriptures and possibly catechetical scrolls later developed into his Gospel. If the function of Silas was similar we can more readily see how he could have the literary rôle assigned to Silvanus in the Epistles. He accompanied Paul through Syria, Asia Minor, Macedonia, and Thessalonica. When Paul left for Athens Silas stayed at Beroea and then joined Paul at Corinth (Acts xvi–xviii). Paul mentions his work there in 2 Cor. i. 19. He was associated with Paul in the letters written from Corinth (1 Thes. i. 1; 2 Thes. i. 1) and is not named again until the reference to him in 1 Peter.

Peter says that he is writing *dia Silouanou* (1 Pet. v. 12). This implies a literary function with probably a good amount of freedom. This could account for some of the resemblances in wording between 1 Peter, 1 and 2 Thessalonians, and the apostolic decree of Acts xv. R.E.N.

SILK. The AV rendering of three biblical words. 1. Heb. *mešî* (Ezk. xvi. 10, 13), perhaps 'silken thread', but the sense is obscure. LXX has *trichaptos*, 'woven of hair'; variants occur in other versions. 2. Heb. *šēš* (Pr. xxxi. 22 and mg of Gn. xli. 42 and Ex. xxv. 4), 'fine white linen'. See LINEN. 3. Gk. *sērikon* (Rev. xviii. 12), 'silk', 'silken', listed among the precious wares sold in the markets of Babylon the Great. J.D.D.

SILOAM. One of the principal sources of water supply to Jerusalem was the intermittent pool of Gihon ('Virgin's Fountain') below the Fountain Gate (Ne. iii. 15) and ESE of the city. This fed water along an open canal, which flowed slowly along the south-eastern slopes, called *Šilôaḥ* ('Sender'; LXX *Silōam*, Is. viii. 6). It followed the line of the later 'second aqueduct' (Wilson) which fell only ¼ inch in 300 yards, discharging into the Lower or Old Pool (mod. *Birket el-Ḥamra*) at the end of the central valley between the walls of the south-eastern and south-western hills (see fig. 193). It thus ran below 'the wall of the pool of Shiloah' (Ne. iii. 15) and watered the 'king's garden' on the adjacent slopes.

This Old Pool was probably the 'Pool of Siloam' in use in New Testament times for sick

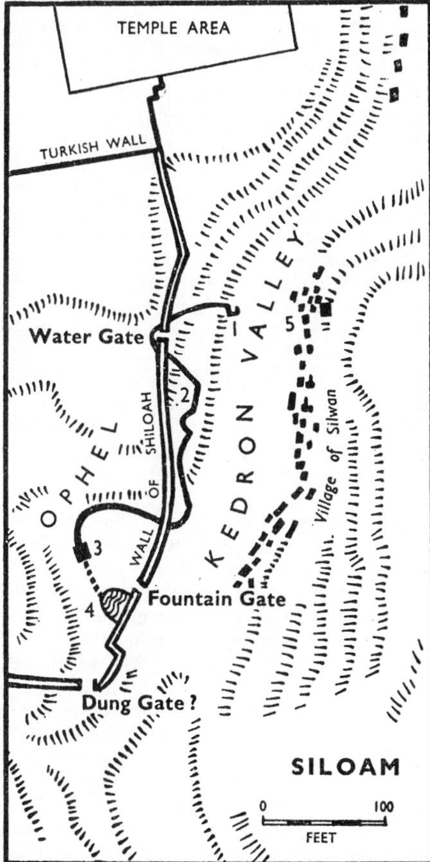

Fig. 193. Siloam. *Key:* 1. Gihon; 2. Hezekiah's tunnel; 3. Upper Pool (Birket Silwan); 4. Lower or Old Pool (Birket el-Hamra); 5. Steward's tomb. See also plates XVc, XVI.

persons and others to wash (Jn. ix. 7–11). The 'Tower of Siloam' which fell and killed eighteen persons—a disaster well known in our Lord's day (Lk. xiii. 4)—was probably sited on the Ophel ridge above the pool which, according to Josephus (*BJ* v. 4. 1), was near the bend of the old wall below Ophlas (Ophel). According to the Talmud (*Sukkoth* iv. 9), water was drawn from Siloam's pool in a golden vessel to be carried in procession to the Temple on the Feast of Tabernacles. Though there are traces of a Herodian bath and open reservoir (about 58 feet × 18 feet, originally 71 feet × 71 feet with steps on the west side), there can be no certainty that this was the actual pool in question. It has been suggested that the part of the city round the Upper Pool (*'Ain Silwān*) 100 yards above was called 'Siloam', the Lower being the King's Pool (Ne. ii. 14) or Lower Gihon.

When Hezekiah was faced with the threat of invasion by the Assyrian army under Sennacherib he 'stopped all the fountains', that is, all the rivulets and subsidiary canals leading down into the Kedron 'brook that ran through the midst of the land' (2 Ch. xxxii. 4). Traces of canals blocked at about this time were found by the Parker Mission. The king then diverted the upper Gihon waters through a 'conduit' or tunnel into an upper cistern or pool (the normal method of storing water) on the west side of the city of David (2 Ki. xx. 20). Ben Sira tells how 'Hezekiah fortified his city and brought the water into its midst; he pierced the rock with iron and enclosed the pool with mountains' (Ecclus. xlviii. 17–19). Hezekiah clearly defended the new source of supply with a rampart (2 Ch. xxxii. 30). The digging of the reservoir may be referred to by Isaiah (xxii. 11).

In 1880 bathers in the upper pool (also called *birket silwān*) found the entrance to a tunnel and about 15 feet inside a cursive Hebrew inscription, now in Istanbul (see WRITING), which reads: '. . . was being dug out. It was cut in the following manner . . . axes, each man towards his fellow, and while there were still three cubits to be cut through, the voice of one man calling to the other was heard, showing that he was deviating to the right. When the tunnel was driven through, the excavators met man to man, axe to axe, and the water flowed for 1,200 cubits from the spring to the reservoir. The height of the rock above the heads of the excavators was 100 cubits' (D. J. Wiseman, *IBA*, pp. 61–64).

When this remarkable Judaean engineering feat was excavated the marks of the picks and deviations to effect a junction midway were traced. The tunnel traverses 1,777 feet (others 1,749 feet), twisting to avoid constructions or rock faults or to follow a fissure, to cover a direct line of 1,090 feet. It is about 6 feet high and in parts only 20 inches wide. It has been suggested that this or a similar tunnel was the gutter (*ṣinnôr*) up which David's men climbed to capture the Jebusite city (2 Sa. v. 8). Modern buildings prevent any archaeological check that the upper pool is the 'reservoir' (*b^e^rēḵâ*) of Hezekiah or that from this the waters overflowed direct to the lower pool.

Below the modern village of Siloam (Silwān, first mentioned in 1697) on the eastern escarpment opposite the hill of Ophel are a number of rock-cut tombs. One of these bore a Hebrew inscription, the epitaph of a royal steward, probably the Shebna who was rebuked by Isaiah (xxii. 15, 16). See SHEBNA (also *IBA*, p. 59; *IEJ*, III, 1953, pp. 137–152). See fig. 193, and plate XVc.

BIBLIOGRAPHY. J. Simons, *Jerusalem in the Old Testament*, 1952. D.J.W.

SILVANUS. See SILAS.

SILVER. See MINING AND METALS, II*b*.

SILVERLING. Silver was often the basis in Old Testament times for comparative values of common commodities—thus Is. vii. 23, 'a thousand vines at a thousand (shekels of) silver' (Heb. *kesep̄*, AV 'silverling'). See also MONEY.

SIMEON. 1. The second son of Jacob by Leah (Gn. xxix. 33). Heb. *šim'ôn* was derived from *šāma'* ('to hear'), and its significance is given in Gn. xxix. 33. Simeon took part with Levi in the massacre of the men of Shechem for dishonouring their sister Dinah (Gn. xxxiv). He also played a prominent part in the affair of Joseph and his brothers, being given as a hostage so that they should return with Benjamin. Simeon may have been chosen by Joseph because he played a leading part in selling him to Egypt, or it may be because he was second to Reuben, who had acted more responsibly than the others (Gn. xxxvii. 21, 22, xlii. 22). In the blessing of Jacob, Simeon and Levi were rebuked for their violent nature, and they were to be divided and scattered (Gn. xlix. 5–7). The sons of Simeon were Jemuel, Jamin, Ohad, Jachin, Zohar, and Shaul, the son of a Canaanite woman (Gn. xlvi. 10; Ex. vi. 15).

2. The tribe of Simeon. The number of the tribe is given as 59,300 in Nu. i. 22, 23 and 22,200 'families' in Nu. xxvi. 14. They were to camp next to Reuben (Nu. ii. 12, 13). The tribe of Simeon was among those to be set on Mt. Gerizim and blessed (Dt. xxvii. 12), but it was not named (along with Issachar) in the blessing of Moses in Dt. xxxiii. In the promised land it was given a portion at the southern extremity and it came almost to be absorbed into the territory of Judah (Jos. xix. 1–9). The towns of the area were reckoned to belong to Judah in Jos. xv. 26–32, 42 and elsewhere. Judah and Simeon joined forces at the beginning of the conquest of Canaan (Jdg. i. 3, 17), but Judah was clearly the more powerful tribe. The sons of Simeon, despite keeping a genealogical record, did not multiply as fast as Judah (1 Ch. iv. 24–33). They did, however, win a victory over the Amalekites under Hezekiah (1 Ch. iv. 41–43), and they provided more men for David than did Judah (1 Ch. xii. 24, 25). The Chronicler seems to imply that Simeon belonged to the northern kingdom, but numbers of Simeonites joined Asa in restoring the worship of Yahweh (2 Ch. xv. 9). The tribe is not mentioned after the Exile, and the only other reference to it is among those sealed in Rev. vii. 7, where it comes seventh in the list.

3. An ancestor of Jesus (Lk. iii. 30).

4. A man in Jerusalem who was righteous and devout and who was looking for 'the consolation of Israel' (Lk. ii. 25–35). He is not to be identified with Rabbi Simon ben Hillel. He was one of the remnant who were longing for the coming of the Messiah, and had received a direct revelation that he would not die before seeing the Messiah with his own eyes. When the presentation of Jesus was about to take place he was guided by the Spirit to come into the Temple. On seeing Jesus he uttered the hymn of praise now known as the *Nunc Dimittis*. He saw that the Messiah would vindicate Israel in the eyes of the Gentiles. Simeon went on to speak to the astonished Mary of the rôle of Christ within Israel. He was to be like a stone causing some to fall and some to rise. He was to be a sign which would not be heeded but spoken against (34). Her own suffering as she watched His life and death was to be acute and He was to reveal the inmost thoughts of men (35). Having given his testimony to the Christ, Simeon fades silently from the picture.

5. A disciple at Antioch, with prophetic and teaching gifts, who was one of those who ordained Barnabas and Saul for their first missionary journey (Acts xiii. 1, 2). He was surnamed Niger, which suggests that he was an African, but he has not been proved to be the same person as Simon of Cyrene (Lk. xxiii. 26, *etc.*). Here RV and RSV read 'Symeon', which is the more normal rendering of the Greek but not of the Hebrew.

6. The archaic version of the name of Simon Peter used by James in his speech to the Council of Jerusalem (Acts xv. 14). RV and RSV render 'Symeon'. Some good MSS read *Symeon* also in 2 Pet. i. 1 (*cf.* RVmg, NEB). R.E.N.

SIMON. A later form of the Old Testament name of Simeon (see Acts xv. 14, where James uses the older form; also 2 Pet. i. 1, RVmg, NEB).

1. The chief disciple and apostle of Jesus, who was the son of Jonas (or John) and the brother of Andrew. Jesus gave him the name of Peter (*q.v.*).

2. The 'Canaanite' (Mt. x. 4; Mk. iii. 18, AV). 'Canaanite' here cannot mean an inhabitant of Canaan, nor can it represent one who dwells at Cana. Rather it should be rendered Cananaean (RV, RSV), an adherent of the party later known as the Zealots and rendered so by Luke (Lk. vi. 15; Acts i. 13). Whether Simon was a zealot in the political sense or the religious sense is a matter of some debate (see CANANAEAN, ZEALOT).

3. One of the brothers of our Lord (Mt. xiii. 55; Mk. vi. 3). **4.** A leper in Bethany in whose house the head of Jesus was anointed with oil (Mt. xxvi. 6; Mk. xiv. 3), probably related to Martha, Mary, and Lazarus (*qq.v.*). **5.** A man of Cyrene who was compelled to carry the cross of Jesus (Mk. xv. 21), possibly the Simeon of Acts xiii. 1 (see RUFUS). **6.** A Pharisee in whose house the feet of Jesus were washed with tears and anointed (Lk. vii. 40). Some scholars equate this Simon with (4) above and regard the stories as doublets; but they are strikingly different in their details (see MARY). **7.** Simon Iscariot, the father of Judas Iscariot (*q.v.*) (Jn. vi. 71, xii. 4, xiii. 2). **8.** Simon Magus (*q.v.*). **9.** A tanner at Joppa in whose house Peter lodged (Acts ix. 43).

F.S.F.

SIMON MAGUS. In the New Testament we meet Simon in 'the city of Samaria' (Sebaste?—

Acts viii. 9–24), where he has 'swept the Samaritans off their feet with his magical arts' (NEB, verse 9). Luke does not suggest that Simon was himself a Samaritan. In essence a Levantine mountebank, Simon cultivated the legend that he was a divine emanation—'that Power of God which is called the Great Power'. The concept and the title were pagan enough (*cf.* for analogies Ramsay, *BRD*, p. 117; Deissmann, *BS*, p. 336 n.), but the Samaritans would by 'God' intend 'Yahweh', and Simon must have acclimatized himself to his religious surroundings. He already represents, then, a significant syncretism of magical, Hellenistic, and erratic Jewish elements.

In the mass movement attending Philip's preaching Simon professed conversion and was baptized. Luke uses his regular expression 'believed', and there is no reason to doubt Simon's sincerity thus far. The sequel, however, shows that his basic attitudes were still those of the magician. So impressed is he with the visible manifestations of the Holy Spirit following the apostles' laying on of hands, that he applies to them, as to higher proficients in the same trade, for the formula at an appropriate price. Peter's crushing rebuke evidently terrified him, for he begged the apostles' intercession to avert the threatened peril. Simon is obsessed with the idea of *power*: throughout he conceives of it as residing in the apostles as super-magicians.

Here, rather abruptly, Luke leaves Simon; but a tangle of traditions about his later career survive in primitive Christian literature. If they include incongruities and legends there is no need, with de Faye, to discount the patristic descriptions, or to deny a connection between the Simon of Acts and the Simonian sect. Even Lucian's rascally oracle-monger Alexander discoursed on the errors of Epicurus: and there is nothing incredible in Simon, with striking ability and personality, and real psychic powers, and perhaps some education, combining the charlatan and the heresiarch.

Justin (*Apology* xxvi, *cf.* lvi, and *Trypho* cxx), himself from Samaria, says that Simon was born in the village of Gitta; that his companion Helen, a former prostitute, was widely regarded as his first divine 'idea', while he himself was acclaimed by multitudes in Samaria and Rome as a divinity. Indeed, Roman adulation had erected a statue inscribed *Simoni Deo Sancto*, 'to Simon the Holy God'. (This statue may actually have been erected to the Sabine deity Semo Sancus, but the Simonians, who worshipped at statues, perhaps saw opportunities in this one.)

Irenaeus (*Adv. Haer.* i. 16, Harvey), Hippolytus (*Philos.* vi. 7 ff.) and Epiphanius (*Panar.* xxi. 2 ff.) describe Simonian doctrine, the two latter employing publications which they allege, perhaps erroneously in Hippolytus's case, to emanate from the sect of Simon. He seems to have developed his old theme of 'the Great Power of God' into a Trinitarian scheme: Simon appeared to the Samaritans as the Father, to the Jews as the Son (he only *seemed* to suffer) and to the world at large as the Holy Spirit. He had a Redemption myth in which he rescued Helen ('the lost sheep') from the bondage of successive transmigrations in various female bodies; and he preached salvation by grace, requiring faith in Helen and himself, but allowing unrestrained liberty in morals afterwards. But Simon also borrowed heavily from Greek paganism and Greek philosophy, and some concepts appear which recur in more sophisticated Christian Gnosticism (*q.v.*). Irenaeus and the others regard him as the first major heretic, the initiator of a long chain of interrelated errors. The modern association of Gnostic origins with heretical forms of Judaism may suggest that their instinct was not far wrong.

Literature such as the Clementine romance and the *Acts* of Peter has many imaginative stories of encounters between Simon and Peter in Rome. (The once-popular idea that in the Clementines Simon is a cipher for Paul need no longer be taken seriously.) According to Hippolytus, his final exhibition misfired. He was buried alive, promising to reappear in three days; but he did not, for, in Hippolytus' laconic phrase, 'he was not the Christ'.

BIBLIOGRAPHY. R. P. Casey in *BC*, V, 1933, pp. 151 ff.; E. de Faye, *Gnostiques et Gnosticisme*[2], 1925, pp. 413 ff.; R. M. Grant, *Gnosticism and Early Christianity*, 1960, chapter 3. A.F.W.

SIN.

I. DEFINITION

The biblical terms for sin are varied. In Hebrew the most common are *ḥaṭṭā'ṯ* (in several forms of the same root), *'āwôn, peša', ra'*, and in the Greek *hamartia, hamartēma, parabasis, paraptōma, ponēria, anomia, adikia.* There are distinctions expressed in these terms; they reflect the different aspects from which sin may be viewed. Sin is failure, error, iniquity, transgression, trespass, lawlessness, unrighteousness. It is an unmitigated evil. But the definition of sin is not to be derived simply from the terms used in Scripture to denote it. The most characteristic feature of sin in all of its aspects is that it is directed against God. David expressed this in his confession, 'Against thee, thee only, have I sinned' (Ps. li. 4), and Paul in his indictment, 'the carnal mind is enmity against God' (Rom. viii. 7). This orientation must be kept in view when we consider the different terms. Any conception of sin which does not have in the forefront the contradiction which it offers to God is a deviation from the biblical representation. The common notion that sin is selfishness betrays a false assessment of its nature and gravity. From the outset and throughout its development sin is directed against God, and this analysis alone accounts for the diversity of its forms and activities. When the Scripture says that 'sin is the transgression of the law' (1 Jn. iii. 4) it is to this same concept that our attention is drawn. Law is the transcript of God's perfection; it is His holiness coming to expression for the regulation of thought and action consonant with that perfection. Transgression is violation of that which God's glory demands of us and is, therefore, in its essence the contradiction of God.

II. ORIGIN

Sin was present in the universe before the fall of Adam and Eve. This is evident from the presence and allegations of the tempter in Eden. It was upon the occasion of temptation that our first parents fell. But it is the origin of sin in the human family which concerns us. The Bible provides information on this subject, but no data bearing upon the fall of the devil and his angels.

Gn. iii describes for us the process, and 1 Tim. ii. 14 is the inspired comment (*cf.* Jas. i. 13, 14). When we read: 'And when the woman saw that the tree was good for food, and that it was pleasant to the eyes, and a tree to be desired to make one wise' (Gn. iii. 6) we are not justified in inferring that sin began with sensuous lust or even with the lust of the eyes. This fails to appreciate the genius of the tempter's assault and of the deception by which Eve had been ensnared. Satan's attack was directed against the integrity and veracity of God (*cf.* Gn. iii. 4), and the allegation by which he seduced the woman was that she and her husband would be as God, knowing good and evil (*cf.* Gn. iii. 5). It is to this godless aspiration that the attention of the woman was drawn, and it is particularly in her reaction indicated by the words 'a tree to be desired to make one wise' that we find the movement of defection and apostasy in Eve's heart and mind. This reaction shows that the tempter had gained her confidence, that she had acceded to his assault upon God's veracity, and that she desired that which the tempter averred, to be as God knowing good and evil. It is, therefore, to this type of lust that the narrative traces the origin of sin. She gave to the tempter the place that belonged to God only; she accepted the most blasphemous assault upon the integrity of God; she coveted for herself divine prerogatives. In her willingness to parley with the tempter, in her failure to react with horror against his suggestions, and in her acquiescence there is disclosed the process that preceded the act of eating the forbidden fruit. Here we have the origin of sin and we are pointed to its true character. Sin does not originate in overt action; it proceeds from the heart and mind. Depravity of heart registered itself in the transgression of the commandment; Adam and Eve became first estranged from God and then they committed actual transgression. They were drawn away of their own lust and enticed. How this could happen in their case is the mystery of the origin of sin.

The gravity of the first sin appears in the fact that the command violated was the summary exhibition of the authority, goodness, wisdom, justice, faithfulness, and grace of God. Transgression meant the repudiation of His authority, doubt of His goodness, dispute with His wisdom, rejection of His justice, contradiction of His veracity, and the spurning of His grace. Along the whole line of God's perfections sin was the contradiction. And this ever continues to be the character of sin.

III. CONSEQUENCES

The sin of Adam and Eve was not an isolated event. The consequences for them, for posterity, and for the world are immediately apparent.

a. Man's attitude to God

The changed attitude to God on the part of Adam and Eve evinces the revolution that took place in their minds. They 'hid themselves from the presence of the Lord God amongst the trees of the garden' (Gn. iii. 8), and the covering of themselves with aprons (Gn. iii. 7) is no doubt to be associated with the same complex of emotion. Made for the presence and fellowship of God, they now dreaded encounter with Him (*cf.* Jn. iii. 20). Shame and fear were now the dominant emotions (*cf.* Gn. ii. 25, iii. 7, 10), indicating the disruption that had taken place.

b. God's attitude to man

Not only was there a change in our first parents' attitude to God but also in God's attitude to them. Reproof, condemnation, curse, expulsion from the garden are all indicative of this revolution in God's relation to them. Sin is one-sided, but its consequences are not. Aspects of the divine character are turned towards Adam and Eve of which there is no intimation prior to their disobedience. Sin elicits God's wrath and displeasure, and necessarily so, because it is the contradiction of what He is. For God to be complacent towards sin is an impossibility. He cannot deny Himself.

c. Consequences for the human race

The unfolding history of man furnishes the catalogue of vices (Gn. iv. 8, 19, 23, 24, vi. 2, 3, 5). The sequel of abounding iniquity finds its issue in the destruction of mankind with the exception of eight persons (Gn. vi. 7, 13, vii. 21–24). The fall had abiding effect not only upon Adam and Eve but upon all who descended from them; there is racial solidarity in sin and evil.

d. Consequences for creation

The effects of the fall extend to the physical cosmos. 'Cursed is the ground for thy sake' (Gn. iii. 17; *cf.* Rom. viii. 20). Man is the crown of creation, made in God's image and, therefore, God's vicegerent (Gn. i. 26). The catastrophe of man's fall brought the catastrophe of curse upon that of which he was the crown and over which he was given dominion. Sin was an event in the realm of the human spirit, but it has its repercussions in the whole of creation.

e. The appearance of death

Death is the epitome of sin's penalty. This was the warning attached to the prohibition of Eden

(Gn. ii. 17), and it is the infliction that emanates from the curse (Gn. iii. 19). Death in the phenomenal realm consists in the separation of the integral elements of man's being. This dissolution exemplifies the principle of death, namely, separation, and it comes to its most extreme expression in separation from God, illustrated at the beginning in expulsion from the garden (Gn. iii. 23, 24), Eden being the symbol of God's presence and favour.

IV. IMPUTATION

The first sin of Adam had unique significance for the whole human race (Rom. v. 12, 14–19; 1 Cor. xv. 22). Here there is sustained emphasis upon the one trespass of the one man as that by which sin, condemnation, and death came to reign over the whole of mankind. The sin is identified as 'the transgression of Adam', 'the trespass of the one', 'one trespass', 'the disobedience of the one', and there can be no doubt but that the first trespass of Adam is intended. Hence the clause in Rom. v. 12, 'for that all have sinned', cannot refer to the actual sins of all men, far less to the hereditary depravity with which all are afflicted, but to the sin of all in the sin of Adam. For in verse 12 the clause in question clearly states the reason why 'death passed upon all men', and in the succeeding verses 'the one trespass' is stated to be the reason for the universal reign of death. If the same sin were not intended, Paul would be affirming two different things with reference to the same subject in the same context. This we cannot suppose. The only explanation of the two forms of statement is that all sinned in the sin of Adam. The same inference is to be drawn from 1 Cor. xv. 22, 'in Adam all die'. Death is the wages of sin and only of sin (Rom. vi. 23). If all die in Adam, it is because all sinned in Adam.

According to Scripture, the kind of solidarity with Adam which explains this participation of all in Adam's sin is the kind of solidarity which Christ sustains to those united to Him. The parallel in Rom. v. 12–19; 1 Cor. xv. 22, 45–49 between Adam and Christ indicates the same type of relationship in both cases, and we have no need or warrant to posit anything more ultimate in the case of Adam and the human race than we find in the case of Christ and His people. In the latter it is representative headship, and this is all that is necessary to ground the solidarity of all in the sin of Adam. Adam sinned, therefore all sinned. To say that the sin of Adam is imputed to all is but to say that all were involved in his sin by reason of his representative headship.

There are good reasons for insisting that this imputation of Adam's sin was immediate. When Paul reiterates that it was by the trespass and disobedience of the one that the many were made sinners, that the judgment of condemnation was pronounced upon all, and that the sentence of death passed upon all, there is immediate conjunction of the trespass of Adam, on the one hand, and the sin, condemnation, and death of all, on the other. We may not intrude any other sin between the sin of Adam and the sin of all as the reason for the involvement of all in Adam's sin and its consequences. The only ground is the union established between Adam and his posterity. The sin of Adam sustains as direct a relation to the condemnation and death of all as it sustained to Adam's own condemnation and death. This is the import of Rom. v. 12, 15–19; 1 Cor. xv. 22.

Rejection of this doctrine betrays not only failure to accept the witness of the relevant passages but also failure to appreciate the close relation which exists between the principle which governs our relation to Adam and the governing principle of the economy of salvation. The parallel between Adam as the first man and Christ as the last Adam shows that the accomplishment of salvation in Christ is based on the same operating principle as that by which we have become sinners and the heirs of death. The history of mankind is subsumed under two complexes, sin–condemnation–death and righteousness–justification–life. The former arises from our union with Adam, the latter from union with Christ. These are the only two orbits within which we live and move. God's government of men is directed in terms of these relationships. If we do not reckon with Adam we are thereby excluded from a proper understanding of Christ. All who die die in Adam; all who are made alive are made alive in Christ.

V. DEPRAVITY

Sin never consists merely in a voluntary act of transgression. Every volition proceeds from something that is more deep-seated than the volition itself, and so it is with sinful volition. A sinful act is the expression of a depraved heart (*cf.* Mk. vii. 20–23; Pr. iv. 23, xxiii. 7). Sin must always include, therefore, the perversity of heart, mind, disposition, and will. This was true, as we found, in the case of the first sin, and it applies to all sin. The imputation to posterity of the sin of Adam must, therefore, carry with it involvement in the perversity apart from which Adam's sin would be meaningless and its imputation an impossible abstraction. Paul says that 'by one man's disobedience many were made sinners' (Rom. v. 19). The depravity which sin entails and with which all men come into the world is for this reason a direct implicate of our solidarity with Adam in his sin. We come to be as individuals by natural generation, and as individuals we never exist apart from the sin of Adam reckoned as ours. Therefore David said, 'Behold, I was shapen in iniquity; and in sin did my mother conceive me' (Ps. li. 5), and our Lord, 'That which is born of the flesh is flesh' (Jn. iii. 6).

The witness of Scripture to the pervasiveness and totality of this depravity is explicit. Gn. vi. 5, viii. 21 provide a closed case. There is the *intensity*—'the wickedness of man was great in the earth'; there is the *inwardness*—the 'imagination of the thoughts of his heart', an expression unsurpassed in the usage of Scripture to indicate that the most rudimentary movement of thought was evil; there is the *totality*—'every imagination'; there is the *constancy*—'continually'; there is the *exclusiveness*—'only evil'; there is the *early manifestation*—'from his youth'. That the indictment of Gn. vi. 5 was not restricted to the period before the flood is shown by Gn. viii. 21. It is a permanent condition that no external catastrophe can remedy. There is no escape from the implications of this witness inscribed on the early pages of divine revelation. It leaves no loophole for any other verdict than that this depravity is total both intensively and extensively. It extends to the deepest movements of the human heart and characterizes all mankind.

Later assessments of our sinful condition are to the same effect. The Lord searches the heart and tries the reins (*cf.* Je. xvii. 10), and His judgment is, 'The heart is deceitful above all things, and desperately wicked: who can know it?' (Je. xvii. 9). In Rom. iii. 10–18 Paul reproduces various Old Testament passages drawn particularly from Pss. xiv and liii, in which the severest indictments are brought against men. That there is no exception appears both from the context and from the indictments themselves. In Rom. iii. 9 it is clear that the verses which follow are adduced to support the proposition that all, both Jews and Greeks, are under sin and to demonstrate what this sin involves. In terms of negation the charges are that 'there is none righteous, no, not one: there is none that understandeth, there is none that seeketh after God . . . there is none that doeth good, no, not one . . . there is no fear of God before their eyes'. From whatever angle man is viewed there is the total absence of that which is good and well-pleasing to God. Considered more positively, all have turned aside from God's way, they have all together become corrupted, and the bodily members are the instruments of iniquity. Thus the wide range of human function and activity is covered and the most determinative exercises of the human personality instanced in order to show the complete absence of good and the total presence of evil. Nothing else than the judgment of total depravity is the sum of this passage. In Rom. viii. 5–7 Paul speaks of the mind of the flesh, and flesh, when used ethically as is obvious here, means human nature directed and governed by sin. That flesh thus characterized belongs to all who are naturally procreated is the pronouncement of our Lord: 'That which is born of the flesh is flesh' (Jn. iii. 6). Hence when Paul says that 'the carnal mind is enmity against God' (Rom. viii. 7) he is characterizing 'the mind' that belongs to all men by nature; it is enmity against God. No stronger condemnatory judgment could be made, for it means that the thinking of the natural man is conditioned and governed by enmity directed against God; not only this—it is identified with this enmity. This is its native and characteristic exercise. At the point where the demands of God's glory are most manifest, at that point its hostility is most violent.

There are no degrees of depravity. There are, however, degrees of cultivation and expression. Depravity is not registered in actual transgression to an equal extent in all. There are multiple restraining factors. God does not give over all men to uncleanness, to vile affections, and to a reprobate mind in the way of which Paul speaks in Rom. i. 24, 26, 28. Total depravity is not incompatible with the exercise of the natural virtues and the promotion of civil righteousness. Unregenerate men are still endowed with conscience, and the work of the law is written upon their hearts so that they do the things of the law (Rom. ii. 14, 15). These 'works done by unregenerate men' are 'of good use both to themselves and others' (*Westminster Confession of Faith*, xvi. 7). Failure to do these things involves greater sin (Ps. xiv. 4; Mt. xxiii. 23). But the doctrine of depravity means that these works, though formally in accord with what God commands, are not good and well-pleasing to God in terms of the only criteria by which God's judgment of the good, the holy, and the pure is determined. These criteria are love to God as the animating motive, the law of God as the directing principle, and the glory of God as the controlling purpose. Although depraved men may do the things of the law, yet they are not subject to the law of God, and enmity against God rather than love governs their hearts (Rom. viii. 7; 1 Cor. ii. 14; *cf.* Mt. vi. 2, 5, 16; Mk. vii. 6, 7; Rom. xiii. 4; 1 Cor. x. 31, xiii. 3; Tit. i. 15, iii. 5; Heb. xi. 4, 6).

VI. INABILITY

Inability is concerned with the incapacity arising from the nature of depravity. If depravity is total, then inability for what is good and well-pleasing to God is complete. We are not able to change our character or act differently from it. The witness of Scripture is clear to this effect. In the matter of understanding the natural man cannot know the things of the Spirit of God because they are spiritually discerned (1 Cor. ii. 14). In respect of obedience to the law of God he is not only not subject to the law of God but he cannot be (Rom. viii. 7). They who are in the flesh cannot please God (Rom. viii. 8). A corrupt tree cannot bring forth good fruit (Mt. vii. 18). The impossibility in each case is undeniable. It is our Lord who affirms that even faith in Him is an impossibility apart from the gift and efficacious drawing of the Father (Jn. vi. 44, 45, 65). This witness on His part is to the same effect as His insistence that apart from the supernatural birth of water and of the Spirit no one can have intelligent appreciation of or entrance into the kingdom of God (Jn. iii. 3, 5, 6, 8; *cf.* Jn. i. 13; 1 Jn. ii. 29, iii. 9, iv. 7, v. 1, 4, 18). The necessity of so radical and momentous a transformation and re-creation as regeneration is proof of the hopelessness of our sinful condition. The upshot of the whole witness of Scripture to the bondage of sin is that it is a psychological, moral, and spiritual impossibility for the natural man to receive the things of the Spirit of God, to love God and do what is well-pleasing to Him, or to believe in Christ to the salvation of his soul. It is this enslavement that is the premise of the gospel, and the glory of the gospel is that it provides for release from the bonds of our servitude. It is the gospel of grace and power for the helpless.

VII. LIABILITY

Since sin is against God, He cannot be complacent towards it or indifferent to it. He must react against it. This reaction is specifically and pre-eminently His wrath. The frequency with which Scripture mentions the wrath of God compels us to take account of its reality and meaning. Various terms are used in the Old Testament. In Hebrew *'ap̄* in the sense of anger, and intensified in the form *ḥarôn 'ap̄* to express the fierceness of God's anger, is very common (*cf.* Ex. iv. 14, xxxii. 12; Nu. xi. 10, xxii. 22; Jos. vii. 1; Jb. xlii. 7; Ps. xxi. 9; Is. x. 5; Na. i. 6; Zp. ii. 2); *ḥēmâ* is likewise frequent (*cf.* Dt. xxix. 23; Pss. vi. 1, lxxix. 6, xc. 7; Je. vii. 20; Na. i. 2); *'eḇrâ* (*cf.* Ps. lxxviii. 49; Is. ix. 19, x. 6; Ezk. vii. 19; Ho. v. 10) and *qeṣep̄* (*cf.* Dt. xxix. 28; Ps. xxxviii. 1; Je. xxxii. 37, l. 13; Zc. i. 2) are used with sufficient frequency to be worthy of mention; *za'am* is also characteristic and expresses the thought of indignation (*cf.* Pss. xxxviii. 3, lxix. 24, lxxviii. 49; Is. x. 5; Ezk. xxii. 31; Na. i. 6). It is apparent that the Old Testament is permeated with references to the wrath of God. Often more than one of these terms appear together in order to strengthen and confirm the thought expressed. There is intensity in the terms themselves and in the constructions in which they occur to convey the notions of hot displeasure, fiery indignation, and holy vengeance.

The Greek terms are *orgē* and *thymos*, the former frequently predicated of God in the New Testament (*cf.* Jn. iii. 36; Rom. i. 18, ii. 5, 8, iii. 5, v. 9, ix. 22; Eph. ii. 3, v. 6; 1 Thes. i. 10; Heb. iii. 11; Rev. vi. 17) and the latter less frequently (*cf.* Rom. ii. 8; Rev. xiv. 10, 19, xvi. 1, 19, xix. 15; see *zēlos* in Heb. x. 27).

The wrath of God is, therefore, a reality, and the language and teaching of Scripture are calculated to impress upon us the severity by which it is characterized. There are three observations which particularly require mention. First, the wrath of God must not be interpreted in terms of the fitful passion so commonly associated with anger in us. It is the deliberate, resolute displeasure which the contradiction of His holiness demands. Secondly, it is not to be construed as vindictiveness but as holy indignation; nothing of the nature of malice attaches to it. It is not malignant hatred but righteous detestation. Thirdly, we may not reduce the wrath of God to His will to punish. Wrath is a positive outgoing of dissatisfaction as surely as that which is pleasing to God involves complacency. We must not eliminate from God what we call emotion. The wrath of God finds its parallel in the human heart, exemplified in a perfect way in Jesus Himself (*cf.* Mk. iii. 5, x. 14).

The epitome of sin's liability is, therefore, the holy wrath of God. Since sin is never impersonal, but exists in and is committed by persons, the wrath of God consists in the displeasure to which we are subjected; we are the objects. The penal inflictions which we suffer are the expressions of God's wrath. The sense of guilt and torment of conscience are the reflections in our consciousness of the displeasure of God. The essence of final perdition for the reprobate will consist in the unrestrained infliction of God's indignation (*cf.* Is. xxx. 33, lxvi. 24; Dn. xii. 2; Mk. ix. 43, 45, 48).

BIBLIOGRAPHY. J. Müller, *The Christian Doctrine of Sin*, 1877; J. S. Candlish, *The Biblical Doctrine of Sin*, 1896; *TWNT*, I, pp. 267–339 (E.T. by J. R. Coates, *Bible Key Words*, 1951); C. R. Smith, *The Bible Doctrine of Sin*, 1953; J. Orr, *Sin as a Problem of Today*, 1910; F. R. Tennant, *The Concept of Sin*, 1912; J. Owen, *Temptation and Sin*, 1958; J. Tulloch, *The Christian Doctrine of Sin*, 1876; J. Murray, *The Imputation of Adam's Sin*, 1959. J.M.

SIN. The Egyp. *sînw*, *swn*, 'fortress', is connected later with Egyp. *sîn*, 'clay, mud', hence its Greek name Pelusium, 'mud-city'. A fortress-city, it is now Tell Farama, on the seashore about 20 miles south-east of Port Said; an Egyptian key defence-post against invasion from the East through Palestine. Emendation in Ezk. xxx. 15, 16 to Seven(eh) (= Aswan) is unnecessary. On the name Sin, see Gardiner, *JEA*, V, 1918, pp. 253, 254. K.A.K.

SIN, WILDERNESS OF. A wilderness through which the Israelites passed between Elim and Mt. Sinai (Ex. xvi. 1, xvii. 1; Nu. xxxiii. 11, 12). It is usually identified with Debbet er-Ramleh, a sandy tract below Jebel et-Tih in the south-west of the Sinai peninsula; but another suggested location is on the coastal plain of el-Markhah. As its position depends on the fixing of Mt. Sinai, which is uncertain (see following article), it is impossible to determine the exact site. J.M.H.

SINAI, MOUNT.

I. SITUATION

The location of this mountain is uncertain. The following mountains are regarded by various scholars as Mt. Sinai: Ğebel Mûsa, Ras eṣ-ṣafṣafeh, Ğebel Serbāl and a mountain near al-Hrob. The tradition in favour of Ğebel Serbāl can be traced back as far as Eusebius; the tradition in favour of Ğebel Mûsa only as far as Justinian. The situation of Ğebel Serbāl, *e.g.* the fact that there is no wilderness at its foot, makes it improbable as the mountain of the covenant. The once widely accepted view of A. Musil that the volcanic mountain near al-Hrob is to be identified with Mt. Sinai is no longer popular with scholars, because it makes the reconstruction of the route of the Exodus impossible and it reads too much into Ex. xix. This leaves two possibilities: Ǧebel Mûsa and Ras eṣ-ṣafṣafeh. These two mountains are situated on a short ridge of granite of about 2 miles stretching from north-west to south-east. Ras eṣ-ṣafṣafeh (6,540 feet) is situated at the northern edge and Ǧebel Mûsa (7,363 feet) at the southern one. Tradition and most of the modern scholars accept Ǧebel Mûsa as Mt. Sinai. There is, none the less, a strong preference among certain scholars for Ras eṣ-ṣafṣafeh as the mountain of the covenant because of the considerable plain at its foot which would have been spacious enough for the large body of Israelites (*cf.* Ex. xx. 18: 'and stood afar off'). However, tradition in favour of Ǧebel Mûsa is so ancient (about 1,500 years) and the granite formations so imposing that it is quite probably Mt. Sinai. Furthermore, a few stations *en route* to the mountain point to the same conclusion.

II. MOUNT SINAI IN THE OLD TESTAMENT

Mount Sinai is also called Horeb in the Old Testament. Travelling past Marah and Elim, the Israelites reached Sinai in the third month after their departure from Egypt (Ex. xix. 1), and camped at its foot on a plain from which the top was visible (Ex. xix. 16, 18, 20). The Lord revealed Himself to Moses on this mountain and gave the Ten Commandments and other laws. The covenant made here between God and the people played a major rôle in binding the tribes together and moulding them into one nation serving one God. Although the authenticity of this account is rejected by certain modern schools, it is clear from Jdg. v. 5 that the Sinai tradition is an ancient part of Israelite belief. The prominent rôle of Mt. Sinai in the Old Testament and the strong tradition attached to it provide ample evidence in support of the historicity of the account. (See EXODUS.)

At the foot of Ǧebel Mûsa is the monastery of St. Catherine. It was here that Tischendorf discovered the famous 4th-century uncial MS of the Greek Bible called Codex Sinaiticus. The library of St. Catherine has ancient MSS in Greek, Arabic, Ethiopic, and Syriac (many of which have recently been made generally available on microfilm).

BIBLIOGRAPHY. B. Rothenberg, *God's Wilderness*, 1961. F.C.F.

SINEW. Heb. *gîḏ* (with which *cf.* Assyr. root *gâdu*, 'to bind'), the sinew viewed as that which bound the bones together (Ezk. xxxvii. 6; Jb. x. 11, RV).

The custom mentioned in Gn. xxxii. 32 is obscure. C. A. Simpson in *IB* quotes Robertson Smith as explaining it from the idea that the thigh was sacred as the seat of life, and Wellhausen as calling attention to a trace of it in ancient Arabia. The application of the custom involves the removing of the sinew in the thigh-joint before the flesh is cooked.

The passage in Jb. xxx. 17 uses a different Hebrew word and is better translated as in RV.

The term is not found in the New Testament. B.O.B.

SINGERS. See MUSIC AND MUSICAL INSTRUMENTS, I.

SINIM, SINITES. 1. Heb. *sînîm*. A distant land from which peoples will return (Is. xlix. 12). The context may imply a place, as yet unidentified, in the far south or east (so perhaps LXX, *gē Persōn*). Many scholars look for a connection with the classical Sinae (China), but it is unlikely that many Jews had travelled so far east by this period, though Phoenicians traded with India. For this reason others propose the more southerly Sin (Pelusium, Ezk. xxx. 15), Syene (Ezk. xxix. 10, xxx. 6), or Sin in Sinai (Ex. xvi. 1).

2. Sinites (Heb. *sînî*) were a Canaanite people (Gn. x. 17; 1 Ch. i. 15), probably to be identified with a region, near Arqā, on the Lebanon coast. The name survives in Nahr as-Sinn and Sinn addarb and may be the Phoenician *Usnu*, Assyrian *Usana* or *Sianu*, Ugaritic *'sn*. D.J.W.

SIN-OFFERING. See SACRIFICE AND OFFERING.

SION. A synonym for, or part of, Mt. Hermon (Dt. iv. 48). It is probably another form of 'Sirion' (Dt. iii. 9); indeed, Pesh. reads 'Sirion' here. A different word from 'Zion' (*q.v.*).

SIRA, JOSHUA BEN. See APOCRYPHA.

SIRAH, WELL OF. The place from which Joab secretly recalled Abner, former captain of Saul's armies, following his visit to David to discuss the surrender of Israel. Unknown to David, Joab slew Abner (2 Sa. iii. 26). Probably the modern Ain Sarah, 1½ miles north-west of Hebron. J.A.T.

SIRION (*śiryōn*). The Canaanite name for Mt. Hermon (*q.v.*) as used in the Bible by the Sidonians (Dt. iii. 9; *cf.* Ps. xxix. 6) and found in the form *šryn* in the Ugaritic texts. See C. H. Gordon, *Ugaritic Handbook*, 1947, p. 274. See also SION. T.C.M.

SISERA. 1. A Canaanite general who commanded Jabin's army (Jdg. iv. 2 f.) in the war against Deborah and Barak, and who was slain by Jael (*q.v.*) (Jdg. iv. 21, v. 26) after his army had been defeated. For suggested discrepancies in the narrative here, see C. F. Burney, *The Book of Judges*, 1930, pp. 79 ff. There is also conflicting evidence about his status, and some basis for suggesting that Sisera was an independent king of superior standing to Jabin king of Hazor, who was overthrown by Joshua (Jos. xi. 1–9; *cf.* Jdg. v. 28, 30). A full treatment of the different accounts is given in C. A. Simpson, *The*

Composition of the Book of Judges, 1957, pp. 12–24. See also DEBORAH.

2. The family-name of a class of Nethinim (foreign temple-slaves) who returned from exile with Zerubbabel (Ezr. ii. 53; Ne. vii. 55).

J.D.D.

SITNAH (*śiṭnâ*, 'hatred', 'contention'). A name given to a well which Isaac's servants dug in Gerar (Gn. xxvi. 21) and which was seized by the servants of Abimelech. For general location, see GERAR.

SIVAN. See CALENDAR (*Sîwān*).

SKIRT. The AV translation of three Heb. words. 1. *kānāp̄*, 'wing', 'extremity', is the usual term (Ruth iii. 9; 1 Sa. xxiv. 4; *etc.*). 2. *šûl* (Je. xiii. 22, 26; La. i. 9; Na. iii. 5) means 'hem', and is so rendered elsewhere in AV. 3. *peh* (Ps. cxxxiii. 2) is the common word for 'mouth', and the context is clearer if we follow RVmg, which in the verse concerned renders the Hebrew as 'collar'.

SKULL, PLACE OF A. See CALVARY.

SLANDER. See TALEBEARING.

SLAVE, SLAVERY.

I. IN THE OLD TESTAMENT

a. Introduction

Under the influence of Roman law, a slave is usually considered to be a person (male or female) owned by another, without rights, and—like any other form of personal property—to be used and disposed of in whatever way the owner may wish. In the ancient biblical East, however, slaves could and did acquire various rights before the law or by custom, and these included ownership (even of other slaves) and the power to conduct business while they were yet under their masters' control. Slavery is attested from the earliest times throughout the Ancient Near East, and owed its existence and perpetuation primarily to economic factors.

b. Sources of slaves

(i) *By capture.* Captives, especially prisoners of war, were commonly reduced to slavery (Gn. xiv. 21, claimed by the king of Sodom; Nu. xxxi. 9; Dt. xx. 14, xxi. 10 ff.; Jdg. v. 30; 1 Sa. iv. 9 (*cf.* RSV); 2 Ki. v. 2; 2 Ch. xxviii. 8, 10 ff.) a custom that goes back as far as written documents themselves, to roughly 3000 BC and probably further (references in I. Mendelsohn, *Slavery in the Ancient Near East*, 1949, pp. 1–3).

(ii) *By purchase.* Slaves could readily be bought from other owners or general merchants (*cf.* Gn. xvii. 12, 13, 27; Ec. ii. 7). The law allowed Hebrews to buy foreign slaves from foreigners at home or abroad (Lv. xxv. 44 f.). In antiquity, slaves were sold among all kinds of other merchandise and from country to country. Thus, the Midianites and Ishmaelites (see JOSEPH) sold Joseph to an Egyptian high official (Gn. xxxvii. 36, xxxix. 1), and Phoenician Tyre imported slaves and bronzeware from Asia Minor (Ezk. xxvii. 13) and sold Jews to the Ionians, thereby incurring a threat of like treatment of her own nationals (Joel iii. 4–8). For evidence of the large numbers of Semitic slaves that reached Egypt in Joseph's general period, probably mainly by trade, see references in JOSEPH or in Bibliography below. For Babylonian merchant-enterprise in slave-trading abroad in places such as Tyre, see Mendelsohn, *op. cit.*, pp. 3–5.

(iii) *By birth.* Children 'born in the house' of slave-parents became 'house-born slaves'; such are mentioned in Scripture from patriarchal times onward (Gn. xv. 3, xvii. 12, 13, 27; Ec. ii. 7; Je. ii. 14), and equally early in Mesopotamian documents (Mendelsohn, pp. 57, 58).

(iv) *As restitution.* If a convicted thief could not make restitution and pay his fines and damages, funds towards this could be raised by selling him as a slave (Ex. xxii. 3; *cf.* a similar provision in Hammurabi's Code, §§ 53–54: *ANET*, p. 168).

(v) *By default on debts.* Debtors who went bankrupt were often forced to sell their children as slaves, or their children would be confiscated as slaves by the creditor (2 Ki. iv. 1; Ne. v. 5, 8). The insolvent debtor himself, as well as his wife and family, commonly became the slave of his creditor and gave him his labour for three years to work off the debt and then go free, in Hammurabi's Code (§ 117: *DOTT*, p. 30, or *ANET*, pp. 170, 171). This seems to be the background to the Mosaic law in Ex. xxi. 2–6 (and 7–11), and in Dt. xv. 12–18, where a Hebrew slave must work six years, explicitly a 'double' period of time (Dt. xv. 18, AV, RV) compared with Hammurabi's three years (*cf.* Mendelsohn, pp. 32, 33), but on release he was to be granted stock to start up on his own again (see also *d*(i)1 below). Insolvency was a major cause of reduction to slave status in the biblical East (Mendelsohn, pp. 23, 26–29).

(vi) *Self-sale.* Selling oneself voluntarily into slavery, *i.e.* dependence on another, to escape poverty, was widely known (Mendelsohn, pp. 14–19, for data). Lv. xxv. 39–43, 47 ff., recognized this, but provided for redemption at (or with foreign owners, even before) Jubilee year.

(vii) *Abduction.* To steal a person, and to reduce a kidnapped person to slavery, was an offence punishable by death in the laws of both Hammurabi (§ 14: *DOTT*, p. 30; *ANET*, p. 166) and Moses (Ex. xxi. 16; Dt. xxiv. 7). Joseph's brothers were guilty of essentially such an offence (Gn. xxxvii. 27, 28 with xlv. 4; see JOSEPH), and might well be 'dismayed' and need reassurance not to be 'distressed' (Gn. xlv. 3, 5 RSV, and *cf.* Gn. l. 15).

c. Price of slaves

The price of slaves naturally varied somewhat according to circumstances and the sex, age, and condition of slaves, but the average price of slaves gradually rose like that of other commodities during the course of history; the female of child-bearing age being always more valuable than the male slave. In the late third millennium BC in Mesopotamia (Akkad and IIIrd Ur Dynasties) the average price of a slave was 10–15 shekels of silver (references in Mendelsohn, pp. 117–155). About 1700 BC Joseph was sold to the Ishmaelites for 20 shekels of silver (Gn. xxxvii. 28), precisely the current price for the patriarchal period, where ⅓ of a mina is 20 shekels (§§ 116, 214, 252: *DOTT*, p. 35; *ANET*, pp. 170, 175, 176), in (*e.g.*) Hammurabi's Code (*c.* 1750 BC), in contemporary Old Babylonian tablets (*cf.* Mendelsohn, *loc. cit.*), and at Mari (G. Boyer, *Archives Royales de Mari*, VIII, 1958, p. 23, No. 10, lines 1–4). By about the 15th century BC the average price was 30 shekels at Nuzi, and could be 20, 30, or 40 shekels at Ugarit in N Syria (Mendelsohn, pp. 118–155; J. Nougayrol, *Palais Royal d'Ugarit*, III, 1955, p. 228: 2 with refs., p. 23 n. 1) in the 14th/13th centuries BC, comparing well with the contemporary price of 30 shekels reflected in Ex. xxi. 32. In later days the average price for a male slave rose steadily under the Assyrian, Babylonian, and Persian Empires, to about 50–60 shekels, 50 shekels, and 90–120 shekels respectively (refs., Mendelsohn, pp. 117–118, 155). For 50 shekels in Assyrian times, *cf.* 2 Ki. xv. 20, where the Israelite notables under Menahem had to pay their value as slaves, presumably as ransom to avoid deportation to Assyria (D. J. Wiseman, *Iraq*, XV, 1953, p. 135, and *JTVI*, LXXXVII, 1955, p. 28). The successive and identical rises in average price for slaves in both the biblical and external records strongly suggest that the former are based directly on accurate traditions from the specific periods in question, *i.e.* the early and late second millennium and early first millennium BC, and are not at these points the elaboration of later traditionists or of over-statistical priestly redactors.

d. Privately owned slaves in Israel

(i) *Hebrew slaves.* 1. The law sought (like Hammurabi's Code five centuries earlier) to avoid the risk of wholesale population-drift into slavery and serfdom under economic pressure on small farmers, by limiting the length of service that insolvent debtors (see *b*(v) above) had to give to six years, their release to be accompanied by the provision of sufficient assets to make a new start (Ex. xxi. 2–6; Dt. xv. 12–18). A man already married when thus enslaved took his wife with him at release, but if he was formerly single and was given a wife by his master, that wife and any children remained the master's. Hence, those who wished to stay in service and keep their family could do so permanently (Ex. xxi. 6; Dt. xv. 16 f.); at Jubilee he would be released in any case (Lv. xxv. 40) in connection with the restoration of inheritance then (Lv. xxv. 28), even if he chose to stay on with his master permanently. Insolvent debtors in temporary enslavement similar to that of Ex. xxi. 2 ff. are probably the subject of Ex. xxi. 26, 27, the permanent loss of a member cancelling the debt and so bringing immediate release from the creditor/master (Mendelsohn, *op. cit.*, pp. 87, 88). In Jeremiah's day the king and the wealthy flagrantly abused the law of seventh-year release by freeing their slaves only to seize them again, and were duly condemned for this very sharp practice (Je. xxxiv. 8–17).

2. A Hebrew who voluntarily sold himself into slavery to escape from poverty was to serve his master until Jubilee year, when he would go free (Lv. xxv. 39–43) and receive back his inheritance (Lv. xxv. 28). But if his master was a foreigner he had the option of purchasing his freedom or being redeemed by a relative at any time before Jubilee (Lv. xxv. 47–55).

3. Female slaves were the subject of further specific law and custom. That a chief wife's servant-maids might bear children to their master for the childless wife is attested both in the patriarchal narrative (Gn. xvi) and in cuneiform documents, contemporary from Ur (Wiseman, *JTVI*, LXXXVIII, 1956, p. 124) and slightly later from Nuzi (C. H. Gordon, *BA*, III, 1940, p. 3; Wiseman, *IBA*, p. 27). Under the law, if a Hebrew girl was sold as a slave (Ex. xxi. 7–11) her marital status was carefully safeguarded: she might marry her master (and be redeemed if rejected), or his son, or become a properly maintained concubine, but would go free if the master failed to implement whichever of the three possibilities he had agreed to. In Mesopotamia such contracts were usually harsher, often having no safeguards whatever (*cf.* Mendelsohn, pp. 10 ff., 87).

(ii) *Foreign Slaves.* 1. Unlike Hebrew slaves, these could be enslaved permanently and handed on with other family property (Lv. xxv. 44–46). However, they were included in the commonwealth of Israel on patriarchal precedent (circumcision, Gn. xvii. 10–14, 27) and shared in festivals (Ex. xii. 44, Passover; Dt. xvi. 11, 14) and sabbath-rest (Ex. xx. 10, xxiii. 12).

2. A woman captured in war could be taken as full wife by a Hebrew, and would thereby cease to have slave status; thus, if she was subsequently divorced she went free and did not become a slave (Dt. xxi. 10–14).

(iii) *General conditions.* 1. The treatment accorded to slaves depended directly on the personality of their masters. It could be a relationship of trust (*cf.* Gn. xxiv, xxxix. 1–6) and affection (Dt. xv. 16), but discipline might be harsh, even fatal (*cf.* Ex. xxi. 21), though to kill a slave outright carried a penalty (Ex. xxi. 20), doubtless death (Lv. xxiv. 17, 22). It is just possible that Hebrew slaves, like some Babylonians, sometimes carried an outward token of their servitude (Mendelsohn, p. 49), though this remains uncertain. In some circumstances slaves could claim justice (Jb. xxxi. 13) or go to law (Mendelsohn, pp. 65, 70, 72), but—like the Egyptian spared by David—could be abandoned by callous masters when ill (1 Sa. xxx. 13). In patriarchal times a childless master could adopt a house-slave and make him his heir, as is recorded of Abraham and Eliezer before the births of Ishmael and Isaac (Gn. xv. 3), and of various people in cuneiform documents (Ur, *cf.* Wiseman, *JTVI*, LXXXVIII, 1956, p. 124; Nuzi, *cf.* Gordon, *BA*, III, 1940, pp. 2, 3).

2. Throughout ancient history, the available documents bear witness to the large numbers of people who tried to escape from slavery by running away, and those who in any way aided and abetted them could expect punishment, especially in early times (Mendelsohn, pp. 58 ff.). However, slaves that fled from one country to another came under a different category. States sometimes had mutual extradition clauses in their treaties; this may explain how Shimei so easily recovered two runaway slaves of his from King Achish of Gath in Philistia (1 Ki. ii. 39, 40; *cf.* Wiseman, *op. cit.*, p. 123). However, some states also at times decreed that if any nationals of theirs enslaved abroad returned to their homeland they would be set free and not be extradited. This was stipulated by Hammurabi of Babylon (Code, § 280: *DOTT*, p. 35; *ANET*, p. 177; *cf.* Mendelsohn, pp. 63, 64, 75, 77, 78), and is probably the meaning of Dt. xxiii. 15 f. (Mendelsohn, pp. 63, 64).

(iv) *Manumission.* In the Hebrew laws an enslaved debtor was to be released after six years (Ex. xxi. 2; Dt. xv. 12, 18), or as compensation for injury (Ex. xxi. 26, 27), and a girl could be redeemed or set free if repudiated, or if conditions of service were not honoured (Ex. xxi. 8, 11; see *d*(i)3 above). A Hebrew who sold himself into slavery was to be freed at Jubilee, or could be redeemed by purchase at any time from a foreign master (Lv. xxv. 39–43, 47–55; *d*(i)2 above). On Dt. xxiii. 15 f., see preceding section. A female captive could become a freedwoman by marriage (Dt. xxi. 10–14).

In 1 Ch. ii. 34 f. a Hebrew Sheshan had no sons, and so married his daughter to his Egyptian slave Jarha in order to continue his family line; it is most probable that Jarha would be made free in these circumstances (Mendelsohn, p. 57), and likewise Eliezer of Damascus (Gn. xv. 3), if he had not been replaced as heir to Abraham by Ishmael and then Isaac.

In Hebrew the term which denotes that a person is 'free', not (or no longer) a slave (*e.g.* Ex. xxi. 2, 5, 26, 27; Dt. xv. 12, 13, 18; Jb. iii. 19; Je. xxxiv. 9–11, 14, 16; *etc.*), is *ḥopšî*, which has a long history in the Ancient East, occurring as *ḫupšu* in cuneiform texts from the 18th to the 7th centuries BC, and usually referring to freedmen who are small landholders, tenant farmers, or hired labourers. When a Hebrew was freed this is the class he would be in. He would become a small landholder if he regained his inheritance (as at Jubilee) or a tenant or labourer on land held by others. On manumission in the Ancient East, see Mendelsohn, pp. 74–91; on *ḥopšî*, see Bibliography below.

e. State and Temple slavery

(i) *State slavery in Israel.* This was practised on a restricted scale. David caused the conquered Ammonites to do forced labour (2 Sa. xii. 31, RVmg, RSV), and Solomon conscripted the surviving descendants of the peoples of Canaan into his *mas-'ōḇēḏ*, permanent state labour-levy, but not true Israelites (see 1 Ki. ix. 15, 21, 22; burden-bearers and quarriers, verse 15 and 2 Ch. ii. 18). The Israelites served on temporary corvée (*mas*) in Lebanon only, by rota (1 Ki. v. 13 f.). There is no contradiction whatever between 1 Ki. v and ix on the corvées; *cf.* M. Haran, *VT*, XI, 1961, pp. 162–164, following and partly correcting Mendelsohn, pp. 96–98. The famous coppermines and foundry of Ezion-geber (see ELATH) were most likely worked with Canaanite and Ammonite/Edomite slave-labour (N. Glueck, *BASOR*, 79, 1940, pp. 4, 5; Mendelsohn, p. 95; Haran, *op. cit.*, p. 162). Such use of war-captives was common throughout the Near East, and in other countries outside Israel their less fortunate nationals and ordinary slaves could sometimes be taken over by the state (Mendelsohn, pp. 92–99).

(ii) *Temple slaves in Israel.* After the war with Midian, Moses levied from the warriors and Israel at large one in 500 and one in fifty respectively of their spoils in persons and goods, for service with the high priest and Levites at the tabernacle, obviously as menials (Nu. xxxi. 28, 30, 47). Then there were added to these the Gibeonites spared by Joshua, who became 'hewers of wood and drawers of water' for the house and altar of the Lord (Jos. ix. 3–27), *i.e.* menials for the tabernacle and its personnel. Also, David and his officers had dedicated foreigners (Nethinim) for similar service with the Levites who served the Temple, some of their descendants returning from captivity with Ezra (viii. 20); to these were added 'Solomon's servants' (Ezr. ii. 58). Ezekiel (xliv. 6–9) possibly warned against allowing these uncircumcised menials to usurp a place in the worship of a Temple that was not theirs. Under Nehemiah (iii. 26, 31) some of these lived in Jerusalem and helped repair its walls.

f. Conclusion: general trends

Generally, a more humane spirit breathes through the Old Testament laws and customs on slavery, as illustrated by the repeated injunctions in God's name not to rule over a brother Israelite harshly (*e.g.* Lv. xxv. 43, 46, 53, 55; Dt. xv. 14 f.). Even when Hebrew law and custom on slaves shares in the common heritage of the ancient Semitic world, there is this unique care in God's name for these people who by status were not people, something absent from the law codes of Babylon or Assyria. It should, moreover, be remembered that, by and large, the economy of the Ancient Near East was never one substantially or mainly based on slave-labour as in 'classical' and later Greece or above all in Imperial Rome (*cf.* Mendelsohn, pp. 111, 112, 116, 117, 121). And Job (xxxi. 13–15) heralds the concept of the equality of all men, of whatever station, before their creator God.

BIBLIOGRAPHY. A fundamental work which makes frequent reference to the Old Testament data is I. Mendelsohn, *Slavery in the Ancient Near East*, 1949, following up earlier studies, and supplemented by *IEJ*, V, 1955, pp. 65–72. The biblical data are summarized and evaluated by A. G. Barrois, *Manuel d'Archéologie Biblique*, II, 1953, pp. 38, 114, 211–215, and by R. de Vaux, *Les Institutions de l'Ancien Testament*, I, 1958, pp. 125–140, 328, 329 (in English as *Ancient Israel: its Life and Institutions*, 1961). On Temple slaves in Israel, *cf.* M. Haran, *VT*, XI, 1961, pp. 159–169. On *ḥopšî*, 'free(dman)', see Mendelsohn, *BASOR*, 83, 1941, pp. 36–39, and *ibid.*, No. 139, 1955, pp. 9–11; E. R. Lacheman, *ibid.*, No. 86, 1942, pp. 36, 37; D. J. Wiseman, *The Alalakh Tablets*, 1953, p. 10. For the Egyptian data on slavery, see the monograph by A. M. Bakir, *Slavery in Pharaonic Egypt*, 1952, supplemented for Joseph's period by W. C. Hayes, *A Papyrus of the Late Middle Kingdom in the Brooklyn Museum*, 1955, pp. 92–94, 98, 99, 133, 134, and especially G. Posener, *Syria*, XXXIV, 1957, pp. 147, 150–161. K.A.K.

II. IN THE NEW TESTAMENT

a. Systems of slavery in New Testament times

Jewish slavery, to judge by the Talmud, remained governed as always by the tight national unity of the people. There was a sharp distinction between Jewish and Gentile slaves. The former were subject to the sabbath-year manumission, and the onus fell upon Jewish communities everywhere to ransom their nationals held in slavery to Gentiles. Thus no fundamental division into bond and free was recognized. At the same time the whole people might be thought of as the servants of Yahweh.

By contrast, Greek slavery was justified in classical theory by the assumption of a natural order of slaves. Since only the citizen class were, strictly speaking, human, slaves were merely chattels. While this idea was carried into practice only in the rare cases where common sense and humanity broke down, the fact remains that throughout classical antiquity the institution of slavery was simply taken for granted, even by those who worked for its amelioration.

There was a very great diversity at different times and places in the extent and uses of slavery. Modern sentiment is dominated by the horrors of the mass agricultural slavery in Italy and Sicily during the two centuries between the Punic wars and Augustus, which were dramatized by a series of heroic slave-revolts. This was a by-product of the rapid Roman conquest of the Mediterranean, the main source of the glut of slaves being war prisoners. In New Testament times, however, there was very little warfare, and in any case the slave ranches were a peculiarly Roman method of farming. In Egypt, for instance, there was practically no agricultural slavery, the land being worked by a free peasantry under bureaucratic supervision. In Asia Minor and Syria there were great temple estates whose tenant farmers were in a kind of serfdom. In Palestine, to judge by the parables of Jesus, slaves were employed on country estates more in administrative positions, the labour being recruited on a casual basis.

Domestic and public slavery were the most widespread forms. In the former case the slaves were purchased and employed as an index of wealth. Where only one or two were owned, they worked beside their master at the same occupations. At Athens they were indistinguishable in the streets from free men, and the familiarity of slaves towards their owners was a stock theme of comedy. At Rome the great houses employed scores of slaves for sheer luxury. Their work was highly specialized and often largely effortless. In the case of public slaves, their status conferred a good deal of independence and respect. They performed all sorts of duties in the absence of a civil service, including even police services in some cases. Professions such as medicine or education were commonly filled by slaves.

The main sources of slavery were: (1) birth, depending on the law of the particular state concerning the various degrees of servile parentage; (2) the widespread practice of exposing unwanted children, who were then available for the use of anyone who cared to rear them; (3) the sale of one's own children into slavery; (4) voluntary slavery as a solution to problems such as debt; (5) penal slavery; (6) kidnapping and piracy; (7) the traffic across the Roman frontiers. Not all these sources were open in one place at any one time: there was a great deal of variation in local law and sentiment. The degree of slavery also varied greatly, and is impossible to calculate. It may have reached one-third of the population in Rome and the great metropolitan cities of the east. In areas where there was a peasant economy, however, it was reduced to a small fraction of that.

Manumission could be readily arranged at any time if owners wished. In Rome it was most commonly performed by testament, and limits had to be placed on the generosity of owners to prevent the too rapid dilution of the citizen body with persons of foreign extraction. In Greek states two common forms were a type of self-purchase, in which the legal incompetence of the slave was overcome by the ownership technically passing to a god, and manumission in return for a contract of services which simply meant that the slave continued in the same employment though legally free.

The condition of slavery was everywhere being steadily mitigated in New Testament times. Although slaves had no legal personality, owners recognized that they worked better the more their condition approximated to freedom, and the owning of property and contracting of marriages were normally allowed. Cruelty was condemned by the growing sentiment of common humanity, and in some cases legally controlled; in Egypt, for instance, the death of a slave was subject to a coroner's inquest. While in Greek states emancipated slaves became resident aliens of their former master's city, at Rome they automatically became citizens. Thus the vast flow of slaves into Italy, especially during the last two centuries before Christ, had the effect of internationalizing the Roman republic, anticipating the government's own policy of steadily broadening membership.

The New Testament attitude to slavery

The twelve disciples of Jesus apparently had no part in the system of slavery. They included neither slaves nor owners. The institution figures frequently in the parables, however (*e.g.* Mt. xxi. 34, xxii. 3), because the regal and baronial households to which it belonged afforded a nice analogy for the kingdom of God. Jesus repeatedly spoke of the relation of the disciples to Himself as that of servants to their lord (*e.g.* Mt. x. 24; Jn. xiii. 16). At the same time He stressed the inadequacy of this figure. The disciples were emancipated, as it were, and admitted to higher privileges of intimacy (Jn. xv. 15). Or again, to their acute embarrassment, Jesus Himself adopted the servile rôle (Jn. xiii. 4–17), with the object of encouraging them to mutual service.

Outside Palestine, however, where the churches were often established on a household basis, the membership included both masters and servants. Slavery was one of the human divisions that became meaningless in the new community in Christ (1 Cor. vii. 22; Gal. iii. 28). This apparently led to a desire for emancipation (1 Cor. vii. 20) and perhaps even to the active encouragement of it by some (1 Tim. vi. 3-5). Paul was not opposed to manumission if the opportunity was offered (1 Cor. vii. 21), but studiously refrained from putting pressure on owners, even where personal sentiment might have led him to do so (Phm. 8, 14). Not only was there the practical reason of not laying the churches open to criticism (1 Tim. vi. 1 f.), but the point of principle that all human stations are allotted by God (1 Cor. vii. 20). Slaves should therefore aim to please God by their service (Eph. vi. 5–8; Col. iii. 22). The fraternal bond with a believing master should be an added reason for serving him well (1 Tim. vi. 2). A master, on the other hand, might well let the fraternal sentiment prevail (Phm. 16), and certainly must treat his slaves with restraint (Eph. vi. 9) and strict equity (Col. iv. 1).

The fact that household slavery, which is the only kind referred to in the New Testament, was generally governed by feelings of goodwill and affection, is implied by its figurative use in the 'household of God' (Eph. ii. 19). The apostles are regularly God's stewards (1 Cor. iv. 1; Tit. i. 7; 1 Pet. iv. 10) and even plain servants (Rom. i. 1; Phil. i. 1). The legal character of 'the yoke of bondage' (Gal. v. 1) was not forgotten, however, and the idea of manumission and adoption into the family itself was a proud conclusion to this train of thought (Rom. viii. 15–17; Gal. iv. 5–7). Thus, whether in practice or by analogy, the apostles clearly branded the institution as part of the order that was passing away. In the last resort the fraternity of the sons of God would see all its members free of their bonds.

BIBLIOGRAPHY. W. W. Buckland, *The Roman Law of Slavery*, 1908; R. H. Barrow, *Slavery in the Roman Empire*, 1928; W. L. Westermann, *The Slave Systems of Greek and Roman Antiquity*, 1955 (with full bibliography); P. A. Brunt, review of the above, *Journal of Roman Studies*, XLVII, 1958, pp. 164–170; J. Murray, *Principles of Conduct*, 1957, chapter IV. E.A.J.

SLEEP. The Old Testament uses several words for 'sleep', the New Testament has fewer; but no particular significance attaches to them. They signify sleep in the sense of physical rest and recuperation.

As might be expected, 'sleep' is used in a figurative sense in both Testaments. In Pr. xix. 15, *etc.*, it describes mental torpor, and in Pr. xxiv. 33 it refers to physical sloth and laziness. Paul uses the figure to describe the state of spiritual torpor of the non-Christians (Eph. v. 14), which unmans them and renders them unprepared for Christ's second advent (Mt. xxv. 22). By contrast, the Christian has awakened from this spiritual torpor, but he is challenged to remain awake (1 Thes. v. 4–8; Rom. xiii. 11 f.; Mt. xxv. 13, xxvi. 41).

Sleep is also a synonym for physical death (Jb. xiv. 12; Jn. xi. 11–14; 1 Cor. xv. 18). This signifies that death, like sleep, is neither a permanent state, nor does it 'destroy the identity of the sleeper' (Lk. xxiv. 39 f.), in spite of the change to be effected at the resurrection (1 Cor. xv. 13 ff.).

'Deep sleep', *tardēmâ*, was supernaturally induced (Gn. ii. 21; 1 Sa. xxvi. 12), and was equivalent almost to a 'trance' (Gn. xv. 12), in which visions were granted (Jb. iv. 13; Dn. viii. 18). Its New Testament equivalent is *hypnos* (Acts xx. 9). But visions also came in the course of 'ordinary' sleep (Gn. xxviii. 10 ff.; 1 Sa. iii. 2 ff.). J.G.S.S.T.

SLEIGHT (Gk. *kybeia*, 'dice-playing', Eph. iv. 14; *cf. kybeuō*, 'to deceive', in Epictetus ii. 19, iii. 21). NEB approaches the Greek differently from AV, and renders the last part of the verse 'dupes of crafty rogues and their deceitful schemes'. Paul is warning against instability and against those whose slick dealings present a plausible mixture of truth and error. J.D.D.

SLIME. See BITUMEN.

SLING. See ARMOUR AND WEAPONS, II*d*.

SMITH. See ARTS AND CRAFTS, III*e*.

SMYRNA. A city in the Roman province of Asia, on the Aegean shore of what is now Asiatic Turkey (see fig. 26). There was a Greek colony near by from very early times, but it was captured and destroyed by the Lydians about the end of the 7th century BC and virtually ceased to exist until it was refounded on its present site by Lysimachus in the early 3rd century BC. It grew

Fig. 194. Assyrian (*left*) and Egyptian (*right*) slingers. The Assyrian has the egg-shaped stones in a pile before him, while the Egyptian carries sling-stones in a net hung round his neck.

to be one of the most prosperous cities in Asia Minor. It was the natural port for the ancient trade route through the Hermus valley, and its immediate hinterland was very fertile. Smyrna was a faithful ally of Rome long before the Roman power became supreme in the eastern Mediterranean. Under the Empire it was famous for its beauty and for the magnificence of its public buildings. It is now (called Izmir) the largest city in Asiatic Turkey.

The gospel probably reached Smyrna at an early date, presumably from Ephesus (Acts xix. 10). The 'angel of the church in Smyrna' is the recipient of the second (Rev. ii. 8–11) of the letters to the 'seven churches . . . in Asia'. As in other commercial cities, the church encountered opposition from the Jews (Rev. ii. 9, *cf.* iii. 9). The description of the Christ as the one who was dead and lived again (verse 8) may allude to the resurgence of the city to new prosperity after a long period in obscurity. The 'crown of life' (verse 10) may be used to contrast with the victor's crown at the games, or possibly with the hilltop cluster of fine buildings which was known as the 'crown of Smyrna'. The call to faithfulness (verse 10) is a call to the church to fulfil in the deepest way the historic reputation of the city. It was exemplified in the courage with which the aged bishop Polycarp refused to recant; he was martyred there *c.* AD 155/156. (See W. M. Ramsay, *The Letters to the Seven Churches of Asia*, 1904, chapters xix, xx.) E.M.B.G.

SNAIL. There is nothing to confirm the translation of *ḥōmeṭ* as 'snail' in the list of forbidden meats in Lv. xi. 30. RSV renders it 'sand lizard'. *Šaḇlûl* (Ps. lviii. 8) is accurately translated 'snail': 'as a snail which melteth' (AV); 'like the snail which dissolves into slime' (RSV). This reflects an ancient belief that in leaving a visible trail behind it the snail was gradually melting away.

G.C.

SNARES. Mechanical devices, often with a bait, for catching birds or animals. AV uses 'snare' for seven Hebrew and two Greek words, but RSV translates more accurately by other words in Jb. xviii. 8, 10; La. iii. 47; 1 Cor. vii. 35. Heb. *paḥ* (*cf.* Egyp. *pḫ'*) is translated 'snare' twenty-two times in AV; literally it is used of bird traps only (see Ps. cxxiv. 7; Pr. vii. 23; Ec. ix. 12; Am. iii. 5). The last passage mentions two kinds of traps used by fowlers, one which pins the bird to the ground and one with a noose which catches the bird around the neck and springs up. In the majority of cases *paḥ* is used figuratively, for example in Jos. xxiii. 13; Jb. xxii. 10; Ps. cxix. 110. Heb. *môqēš*, perhaps meaning 'striker', is translated 'snare' in AV twenty times, literally only in Jb. xl. 24, which implies that a snare cannot take the behemoth or hippopotamus. Examples of the figurative use of *môqēš* are Ex. x. 7; Is. viii. 14; Ps. lxiv. 5; 2 Sa. xxii. 6; Ex. xxiii. 33; Pr. xx. 25, xxii. 25. Other Hebrew words translated 'snare' in a figurative sense are *māṣôḏ*, 'means of hunting' (Ec. vii. 26) and the related *m*ᵉ*ṣûḏâ* (Ezk. xii. 13, xvii. 20).

In the Apocrypha 'snare' (Gk. *pagis*) is used in reference to a gazelle (Ecclus. xxvii. 20) and also figuratively (Ecclus. ix. 3, 13, xxvii. 26, 29).

In the New Testament Gk. *pagis* is translated 'snare' in a literal sense only in Lk. xxi. 35, which compares the suddenness of the Lord's coming to the springing of a trap. The figurative uses of *pagis* are Rom. xi. 9; 1 Tim. iii. 7, vi. 9; 2 Tim. ii. 26.

In Egypt today the following kinds of snares, some with ancient counterparts, are used: a clap-net, a clap-board over a hole, a clap-box, a springing noose, a trap with two jaws which close on the neck of the victim, and a cage with a sliding or springing door.

BIBLIOGRAPHY. G. Dalman, *Arbeit und Sitte*, VI, 1939, pp. 321–340; H. S. Gehman, 'Notes on *Môqēš*', *JBL*, LVIII, 1939, pp. 277–281; G. R. Driver, 'Reflections on Recent Articles, II. Heb. *môqēš*, "striker",' *JBL*, LXXIII, 1954, pp. 131–136. J.T.

SNOW (Heb. *šeleḡ*). The few references to it indicate its rarity in Palestine, where it is scarcely ever found south of Hebron and is unknown along the sea coast and Jordan valley. Only twice is a snowfall recorded (in 2 Sa. xxiii. 20 (= 1 Ch. xi. 22) and in 1 Macc. xiii. 22). But the snow cover of Lebanon, 'the white mountain', is proverbial (Je. xviii. 14), and lower down in the Hauran it is not infrequent (Ps. lxviii. 14). Elsewhere it is a rare feature, as the biblical incident of Benaiah would suggest (2 Sa. xxiii. 20).

Snow as a symbol is variously employed. It is God-given and controlled (Jb. xxxviii. 22), one of the wonders of God's power (Jb. xxxvii. 6; Ps. cxlvii. 16), and given for fertility (Is. lv. 10 f.) and to accomplish moral ends (Jb. xxxviii. 22, 23). It expresses whiteness (Ex. iv. 6; Nu. xii. 10; 2 Ki. v. 27; La. iv. 7; Dn. vii. 9), and therefore moral purity (Dn. vii. 9; Mk. ix. 3; Mt. xxviii. 3; Rev. i. 14). It describes the complete acceptance of the penitent sinner (Ps. li. 7; Is. i. 18). J.M.H.

SNUFFERS, SNUFF DISHES. The AV translations of *melqāḥayim*, 'tongs', and *meẓammerôt*, 'trimmers', both used for adjusting and trimming lamp-wicks (Ex. xxxvii. 23; 1 Ki. vii. 50, *etc*.; thus perhaps to be vocalized *mazmērôt*, 'pruning-knives'). Tongs, trimming-knives, and pans have been found at a number of Palestinian sites (G. E. Wright, *Biblical Archaeology*, 1957, pp. 141 f.). AV 'snuff dishes' also translates Heb. *maḥtôt*, '(gold)

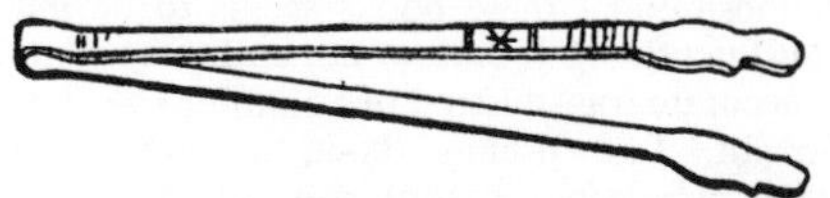

Fig. 195. A pair of bronze tongs with ends shaped like human hands. From el-Amarna, Egypt, c. 1350 BC.

pans', which were used for removing the trimmings from the lamps (Ex. xxv. 38; Nu. iv. 9). These are to be distinguished from the copper firepans and censers, likewise called *maḥtôt* (Ex. xxvii. 3; Nu. xvi. 6). D.W.G.

SO. By conspiring with 'So king of Egypt' *c*. 726/25 BC (2 Ki. xvii. 4), Hoshea brought down Assyrian retribution upon Israel. If So is the proper name of an Egyptian king he must be either the last shadowy Libyan pharaoh, Osorkon IV (Aa-kheper-rēʿ) *c*. 727–716 BC, or the *de facto* West-Delta ruler Tefnakht, *c*. 727–720 BC, or some lesser and unidentified East-Delta kinglet. No mere kinglet could have helped Hoshea, nor can *Sô'* derive from Tefnakht's name; it is barely possible that *Sô'* could be an abbreviation for Osorkon (IV), as Egyp. *Sese* for Rameses (II).

Some identify So, vocalized *Siwe*' or *Sewe*', with the Ethiopian Pharaoh Shabako (omitting formative *-ko*) who acted as army commander in Egypt before his accession. This is impossible in 726/25 BC, because the Ethiopians' West-Delta rivals, Tefnakht and Bekenranef (Bocchoris), held Lower Egypt until 716 BC. Others identify So/Siwe with 'Sib'e the *turtan* (army commander) of Egypt' whom Sargon II of Assyria defeated at Raphia in 720 BC. But So cannot be a king in 726/25 BC and then simply army commander in 720 BC, unless he were throughout a petty Delta kinglet acting as commander for Osorkon IV (or Tefnakht and Bekenranef). Therefore, if So is an Egyptian ruler's name, he would be either Osorkon IV abbreviated (but *not* Sib'e the *turtan*) or else a lesser kinglet and army commander under Osorkon IV, Tefnakht, or Bekenranef.

However, in *VT*, II, 1952, pp. 164–168, S. Yeivin suggests that *Sô'* is not a proper name but merely a transcription of Egyp. *ṯ*', 'vizier'; then *sô' melek miṣrayim* = 'the vizier of the king of Egypt'. Hoshea's fellow-conspirator would then be Osorkon IV's vizier, commanding such Egyptian forces as were available. As the cuneiform name of the Egyptian commander of 720 BC, hitherto read as Sib'e, must now almost certainly be read as Re'e (R. Borger, *JNES*, XIX, 1960, pp. 49–53), this name cannot be identified with So as a proper name. It is possible that Re'e could be the name of the Egyptian vizier if *sô'* does stand for *ṯ*', 'vizier', but there is at present no evidence to warrant any such assumption. K.A.K.

SOAP. 'Soap' is the rendering in the EVV of Heb. *bōrîṯ* (Mal. iii. 2; Je. ii. 22), a word derived from *bārar*, 'to purify'. It probably means 'lye', a solution of potash (potassium carbonate) and soda (sodium carbonate) in water, which acts as a simple detergent. This is obtained by filtering water through vegetable ash, various alkaline salts being produced, of which potash is the principal. The Hebrew term *bōr* is also best rendered 'lye' in Is. i. 25 and Jb. ix. 30 (RVmg, RSV), though this is not observed by AV. See also ARTS AND CRAFTS, Section III*h*.

BIBLIOGRAPHY. R. Campbell Thompson, *A Dictionary of Assyrian Chemistry and Geology*, 1936, p. 14; M. Levey, *Chemistry and Chemical Technology in Ancient Mesopotamia*, 1959, p. 122. T.C.M.

SOCOH, SOCO. 1. A town south-east of Azekah in the Shephelah, the scene of the Philistine defeat (1 Sa. xvii; see G. A. Smith, pp. 223 f., for tactical description). The name is preserved in Khirbet Suweike (Roman and Byzantine); slightly farther west, the Early Iron fortification Khirbet Abbad commands the Wadi es-Sunt (Vale of Elah) from the south. Here the Wadi es-Sur from the south is joined by wadis coming down from the hills west of Bethlehem. Either this or (2) below was fortified by Rehoboam and later taken by the Philistines (2 Ch. xi. 7, xxviii. 18).

2. A place in the highlands near Debir; Khirbet Suweike, 2 miles east of Dhahiriya (1 Ch. iv. 18 probably refers to this place). **3.** A town in Solomon's tribute-area of Hepher (1 Ki. iv. 10); probably the Bronze Age–Byzantine site Tell er-Ras by Suweike, north of Tulkarm in the plain of Sharon, and 15 miles north-west of Shechem (Tuthmosis III list no. 67). J.P.U.L.

SODOM. See PLAIN (CITIES OF).

SOJOURNER. See STRANGER.

SOLDIER. See ARMY.

SOLEMN ASSEMBLY. See CONGREGATION.

SOLOMON. The third king of Israel (*c*. 971–931 BC), son of David and Bathsheba (2 Sa. xii. 24); also named Jedidiah ('beloved of the Lord') by Nathan the prophet (2 Sa. xii. 25). Solomon (*šelōmōh*, probably 'peaceful') does not figure in the biblical narrative until the last days of David (1 Ki. i. 10 ff.) despite the fact that he was born (in Jerusalem; 2 Sa. v. 14) early in his father's reign.

I. THE RISE TO POWER

Solomon's path to the throne was far from smooth. Absalom's opposition was carried on by David's oldest surviving son, Adonijah (2 Sa. iii. 4), who made a strong bid for the throne during his father's last days (1 Ki. i. 5 ff.). Supported by David's deposed general, Joab, who had slain Absalom (2 Sa. xviii. 14, 15), and the influential priest, Abiathar, Adonijah rallied support and actually held a coronation feast at Enrogel. But Solomon was not without allies. Benaiah, the son of Jehoiada, had his eye on the generalship; Zadok coveted a prominent priestly position. Their spokesman was Nathan the prophet, a confidant of David and Bathsheba (1 Ki. i. 11 ff.). After Nathan and Bathsheba reminded David of his unexecuted promise concerning Solomon, the king gave instructions for Solomon's accession and sealed them with an oath (1 Ki. i. 28 ff.).

The news of Solomon's coronation broke up Adonijah's festivities (1 Ki. i. 41 ff.) but not his stratagems to control the kingdom. He implored Bathsheba to influence Solomon to give him Abishag, David's handmaiden (1 Ki. i. 3, 4), as wife (1 Ki. ii. 13 ff.). Solomon, apparently fearing that such a marriage would give Adonijah leverage with which to prise him from the throne, refused. Adonijah paid with his life for his rash proposal (1 Ki. ii. 25); when Abiathar the priest was banished from office (1 Ki. ii. 26, 27) and Joab vengefully slain before the altar (1 Ki. ii. 28 ff.), Solomon reigned without a rival. The prominent rôle of the queen-mother in this whole intrigue is noteworthy. Bathsheba seems to have blazed the trail for other queen-mothers in Judah, for the author of Kings faithfully records the name of each king's mother (*e.g.* 1 Ki. xv. 2, 10, *etc.*).

II. THE MASTER SAGE

Solomon was Israel's first *dynastic* ruler. Saul and David, like the judges, were chosen because God had given them a special measure of power: they were *charismatic* rulers. Although Solomon took office without God's *charisma*, he received it during his vision at Gibeon, when the Lord offered him his choice of gifts (1 Ki. iii. 5 ff.). Realizing the enormity of his task, Solomon chose an 'understanding heart' (verse 9). The story of the harlots' dispute over the baby (1 Ki. iii. 16 ff.) has become a classic display of Solomon's royal wisdom.

Surpassing his contemporaries in Egypt, Arabia, Canaan, and Edom in wisdom (1 Ki. iv. 29 ff.), Solomon became the great patron of Israel's Wisdom literature (*q.v.*). No other period of the monarchy provided the combination of international contacts, wealth, and relief from war necessary for literary productivity. Solomon took the lead in this movement, collecting and composing thousands of proverbs and songs (1 Ki. iv. 32). The statement that he spoke of trees, beasts, *etc.* (1 Ki. iv. 33) probably refers to his use of plants and animals in his proverbs rather than to accomplishments in botany and zoology, although close observation of these creatures would be necessary before he could use them in his sayings (*cf.* Pr. xxx. 24–31).

Two extensive collections in Proverbs (x. 1–xxii. 16, xxv. 1–xxix. 27) are credited to him, and the entire collection bears his name as the chief contributor (i. 1). Canticles and Ecclesiastes suggest that he is their author, although the latter does not mention his name. Though the final composition of these books seems to be much later than the 10th century BC, both may contain an accurate transmission of Solomon's work and thought. Two psalms (lxxii, a royal psalm; cxxvii, a wisdom psalm) complete the list of canonical writings attributed to him. The relationship of *corporate personality* (the view that members of a clan are so inter-related that when one member acts the others may be viewed as taking part in the act) to problems of authorship is not clear: it is possible that some of the Solomonic writings are products of sages who felt their kinship with their intellectual father so strongly that they credited him with their work.

No hero of antiquity (with the possible exception of Alexander the Great) is so widely celebrated in folk literature. The Jewish, Arabian, and Ethiopian tales about Solomon's intellectual prowess and magical powers are legion. (For collections of post-biblical tales about Solomon, see G. Salzberger, *Die Salomo-Sage*, 1907, and St. J. Seymour, *Tales of King Solomon*, 1924.)

III. THE IRON RULER

Solomon's task was to maintain and control the expanse of territory bequeathed him by David. Further, he had to effect as smooth a transition as possible from the tribal confederacy which had characterized pre-Davidic political life to the strong central government which alone could maintain Israel's empire.

The traditional tribal boundaries were replaced by administrative districts: twelve in Israel (1 Ki. iv. 7 ff.) and perhaps one in Judah; *cf.* the problematic iv. 19 in RSV. (See J. Bright, *A History of Israel*, 1960, p. 200, for the view that Jos. xv. 20–62 contains the list of the twelve districts of Judah.) Each of these tax districts was obligated to provide support for the court for a month during the year (1 Ki. iv. 7), which would appear an onerous task according to the list in 1 Ki. iv. 22, 23. (See FOOD, I*d* (iii).)

In addition to this, Solomon began recruiting labourers from among the Israelites, a measure unpalatable to a people who relished freedom. There is an apparent contradiction between 1 Ki. v. 13 ff. and ix. 22, the former stating that Solomon used 30,000 Israelites in forced labour and the latter affirming that Israelites held positions in the army but were not slaves. It may be that v. 13 ff. deals with events subsequent to the summary given in ix. 15 ff. When Canaanite labour proved insufficient for Solomon's enormous construction enterprises he was compelled to draft labourers from Israel. Further, there may be a technical difference between forced labour (*mas* in v. 13) and slave labour (*mas 'ôḇēḏ* in ix. 21). The unpopularity of Solomon's policy is evidenced in the assassination of Adoniram, the superintendent of the labour crews (1 Ki. iv. 6, v. 14, xii. 18) and in the request for redress of grievances, the denial of which by Rehoboam led to the secession of the northern kingdom (1 Ki. xii. 4 ff.).

Resentment was also engendered, in all probability, by Solomon's pledging of twenty Galilaean cities to Hiram in return for financial aid (1 Ki. ix. 10 ff.). The fact that Hiram may have returned these later (as 2 Ch. viii. 1, 2 seems to hint) would not have completely relieved the resentment. Solomon had accomplished monumental tasks, including the building of the Temple (*q.v.*), but at an exorbitant price: the good-will and loyalty of his people.

IV. THE ENTERPRISING MERCHANT

Trading was Solomon's forte. Knowing full well the significance of Israel's strategic control of the land-bridge between Egypt and Asia, he set out to exploit his position by controlling the major north–south caravan routes. His ties with Hiram of Tyre placed at his disposal fleets which enabled him to monopolize sea lanes as well.

Ezion-geber (*q.v.*), his manufacturing centre and sea-port on the Gulf of Aqabah, was a main base of his trading activities. From here his fleet manned by Phoenicians (the Israelites apparently had neither love for nor knowledge of the sea) sailed to Ophir (*q.v.*) carrying smelted copper. The phrase 'ships of Tarshish' is probably to be translated 'refinery ships', *i.e.* ships equipped to carry smelted ore (see TARSHISH). In return, these ships brought back splendid cargo: gold, silver, hardwood, jewels, ivory, and varieties of apes (1 Ki. ix. 26–28, x. 11, 12, 22; *peacocks* in verse 22 should probably be translated *baboons*).

The visit of the Queen of Sheba (1 Ki. x. 1–13) may have had a commercial purpose. Solomon's control of the trade routes and his sea ventures in the south made him a serious financial threat to the Sabaeans, whose strategic position in SW Arabia enabled them to control trade in incense and spice. The queen's journey was successful, but she probably had to share her profits with Solomon, as did other Arabian monarchs (x. 13–15).

Solomon's business acumen took advantage of Israel's location when he became the exclusive agent through whom the Hittites and Aramaeans had to negotiate in order to buy horses from Kue (Cilicia) or chariots from Egypt (1 Ki. x. 28, 29). These and other enterprises made silver as common as stone and cedar as sycamore in Jerusalem, where the king lived in Oriental splendour, in marked contrast to Saul's rustic simplicity in Gibeah. Although Israel's standard of living was undoubtedly raised, Israelites did not profit uniformly. The tendency towards centralization of wealth which brought the censure of the 8th-century prophets began during Solomon's golden reign.

V. THE PEACEFUL EMPEROR

Solomon, who had inherited a large empire from his father, apparently conducted no major military campaigns. His task was to maintain Israel's extensive boundaries and to exploit his position of strength during the power-vacuum created by the temporary eclipse of Egypt and Assyria. The two main pillars of Solomon's foreign policy were friendly alliances, sometimes sealed by marriage, and the maintenance of a formidable army.

Among his wives Solomon numbered pharaoh's daughter, an accomplishment almost unprecedented among ancient Oriental monarchs. Because of her high station, Solomon built a special wing on his palace for her (1 Ki. iii. 1, vii. 8). This alliance was profitable for Solomon, for pharaoh (probably one of the last members of the impotent Dynasty XXI) gave him the frontier city of Gezer as a dowry (1 Ki. ix. 16; see J. Bright, *op. cit.*, p. 191, n. 63, for the view that 'Gerar' is a preferable reading to 'Gezer'). In view of Solomon's numerous foreign marriages (1 Ki. xi. 1–3), it is not surprising that Arabian, Jewish, and especially Ethiopian traditions describe his amorous relations with the Queen of Sheba, who according to the Ethiopians bore him a son, Menelik I, the traditional founder of their royal house (see SHEBA, QUEEN OF).

Solomon made the most of his alliance with Hiram (*c.* 969–936 BC) of Tyre (1 Ki. v. 1–12). The Phoenicians, just entering their colonial heyday, supplied the architectural skill and many of the materials, especially the fine Lebanese woods, for Solomon's Temple and palaces; they designed and manned his ships; they provided a market for the Palestinian crops of wheat and olive oil. On at least one occasion Hiram came to Solomon's aid with a substantial loan (1 Ki. ix. 11).

The backbone of Solomon's military defence was a ring of cities strategically located near the borders of Israel and manned by companies of charioteers (1 Ki. ix. 15–19). His militia included 4,000 stalls for horses (40,000 in 1 Ki. iv. 26 is apparently a scribal error; *cf.* 2 Ch. ix. 25), 1,400 chariots, and 12,000 horsemen (1 Ki. x. 26). Several cities have yielded Solomonic remains in recent years, *e.g.* Hazor, Eglon, Gezer, and especially Megiddo (*q.v.*), where 450 stalls with elaborate systems for feeding and watering the horses were discovered. Y. Yadin ('New Light on Solomon's Megiddo', *BA*, XXIII, 1960, pp. 62–68) has disputed the customary crediting of these stables to Solomon. Having found a construction which resembles the Solomonic walls at Hazor and Gezer but differs from the stables, he attributes the latter to Ahab. Results of Yadin's find are still being evaluated.

Solomon's era of peace was marred by two recorded incidents, both of which are interpreted by the author of Kings in terms of divine judgment (1 Ki. xi. 14 ff., 23 ff.). Hadad, an Edomite prince, who had taken refuge in the court of Egypt during Joab's massacre of the Edomite males, returned to his homeland and apparently harassed Israel's southern flank (1 Ki. xi. 14–22, 25). Hadad's activities may have been confined to scattered skirmishes, for there is no indication that he posed a major threat to Solomon's southern port, Ezion-geber. The zest with which the pharaoh courted Hadad's favour is further indication of the Egyptians' *penchant* for forming beneficial alliances during this period.

Solomon's second antagonist was Rezon, who wrested Damascus from Israel and set up an independent kingdom in the city which had been David's northern headquarters (2 Sa. viii. 6). Solomon's loss of this strategically located, commercially important Aramaean city greatly weakened his control of northern and central Syria. The monolithic empire, which at the outset of Solomon's reign had stretched from the Gulf of Aqabah to the Orontes and Euphrates and from the Mediterranean coast to the Transjordan (*cf.* 1 Ki. iv. 24), was in danger of crumbling. (See M. Unger, *Israel and the Aramaeans of Damascus*, 1957, pp. 47–57.)

VI. THE FATAL FLAW

Marrying foreign wives was expedient politically, but not spiritually. The historian does not chide Solomon for sensuality but for disobedience to Israel's monotheistic ideal. Foreign marriages brought foreign religions, and the king compromised the convictions which he had expressed in his dedicatory prayer for the Temple (1 Ki. viii. 23, 27) by engaging in syncretistic worship to placate his wives. This violent breach of Israel's covenant could not go unpunished. Though judgment was stayed during Solomon's lifetime for David's sake, the seeds of dissatisfaction sown among the people by Solomon's harsh policies of taxation and *corvée* were to bear bitter fruit during the reign of his son and successor, Rehoboam (1 Ki. xi. 1–13).

BIBLIOGRAPHY. C. H. Gordon, *The World of the Old Testament*, 1958, pp. 180–189; A. Malamat, 'The Kingdom of David and Solomon in its Contact with Egypt and Aram Naharaim', *BA*, XXI, 1958, pp. 96–102; J. Montgomery, *ICC, Kings*, 1951, pp. 67–248; M. Noth, *The History of Israel*, 1958, pp. 201–223. D.A.H.

SOLOMON'S PORCH. See TEMPLE.

SON. See FAMILY.

SON OF GOD, SON OF MAN. See JESUS CHRIST (TEACHING OF).

SONG OF SOLOMON. 'Song of Songs' (*šîr haššîrîm*, i. 1) is a superlative denoting the best of songs. LXX *Asma Asmatōn* and Vulg. *Canticum Canticorum* (whence the alternative title 'Canticles') are literal translations of the Hebrew. The first of the five scrolls read at Jewish feasts, the Song is used at the Passover. Since analysis must depend on the particular theory of interpretation adopted (see below), no outline of contents is attempted here.

I. CANONICITY

The Mishnah (*Yadaim* iii. 5) seems to indicate that the Song was not accepted without dispute. Following an affirmative verdict by Rabbi Judah and a negative opinion by Rabbi Jose, Rabbi Aqiba affirms the canonicity of the Song in superlatives: 'the whole world is not worth the day on which the Song of Songs was given to Israel; all the Writings are holy, and the Song of Songs is the holy of holies'. His strong denial of any dispute may well serve as evidence for one.

Undoubtedly the opposition to canonizing the Song stemmed from its erotic nature. This objection was outweighed by the traditional Solomonic authorship and by rabbinic and Christian allegorical interpretations which lifted the poems above a sensual level.

II. AUTHORSHIP AND DATE

The traditional attribution to Solomon is based on the references to him (i. 5, iii. 7, 9, 11, viii. 11), especially the title verse (i. 1). The phrase *lišlômôh* probably intimates authorship but can mean 'for Solomon'. Solomon's prowess as a song writer is attested in 1 Ki. iv. 32 (*cf.* Pss. lxxii, cxxvii). The opinion expressed in *Baba Bathra* 15a that Hezekiah and his scribes wrote the Song of Songs is probably based on Pr. xxv. 1.

The presence of what seem to be Persian (*pardēs*, 'orchard', iv. 13) or Greek (*'appiryôn* from *phoreion*, AV 'chariot', better RSV 'palanquin', iii. 9) loan-words, a consistent (except for i. 1) use of *š* as the relative pronoun, and numerous words and phrases akin to Aramaic (see S. R. Driver, *Literature of the Old Testament*, p. 448) combine to suggest that the final redaction of the book, if not its actual composition, took place after Solomon's time. It seems unnecessary, however, to date the composition as late as the Greek period (*c.* 300 BC) in view of the evidences for intercourse between Canaan and Ionia from the Solomonic period onwards. S. R. Driver (*op. cit.*, p. 449) notes that the linguistic evidence, together with a number of geographical allusions (*e.g.* Sharon, ii. 1; Lebanon, iii. 9, iv. 8, 11, 15, *etc.*; Amana, Senir, Hermon, iv. 8; Tirzah, vi. 4; Damascus, vii. 4; Carmel, vii. 5), points to a *northern* origin. But there is no provincialism here. The author is acquainted with the geography of Palestine and Syria from Engedi, by the Dead Sea (i. 14), to the mountains of Lebanon.

III. LITERARY QUALITIES

The intensely personal speeches of Canticles take two main forms: dialogue (*e.g.* i. 9 ff.) and soliloquy (*e.g.* ii. 8–iii. 5). It is not easy to identify the participants in the conversation apart from the two lovers. Daughters of Jerusalem are men-oned (i. 5, ii. 7, iii. 5, *etc.*), and brief responses ave been credited to them (i. 8, v. 9, vi. 1, *etc.*). tatements have been attributed to citizens of erusalem (iii. 6–11) and Shulem (viii. 5). In ighly figurative lyrical poetry it is possible that ne central figures are reconstructing the re-ponses of others (*e.g.* the Shulammite seems to uote her brothers in viii. 8, 9).

The power of the poetry lies in the intensity of ove and devotion expressed and especially in the ich imagery which permeates the descriptions of ne lovers and their love. If these descriptions are oo intimately detailed to suit Western tastes we nust remember that they are the product of a istant time and place. If some of the similes ound less than complimentary (*e.g.* teeth like wes, neck like the tower of David, iv. 2 ff.), . Bentzen's reminder is apposite: 'Orientals fix ne eye on one single striking point, which ccording to our conceptions is perhaps not haracteristic' (*Introduction to the Old Testament*, p. 130). L. Waterman's opinion that the com-liments are back-handed (*JBL*, XLIV, 1925, p. 179 ff.) has not gained scholarly support. The astoral qualities of the imagery have been oted frequently. The poems abound in refer-nces to animals and especially plants. This fact as not gone unnoticed by those who find the ource of the Song in pagan fertility rites (see elow).

IV. THEORIES OF INTERPRETATION

nterpretations of the Song have been legion, and nere is little agreement among scholars as to its rigin, meaning, and purpose. The vividly de-ailed, erotic lyrics, the virtual absence of overt eligious themes, and the vagueness of its plot nake it a challenge to scholarship and a tempta-on to imaginative ingenuity. Indispensable to ne study of the varieties of interpretation is I. H. Rowley's essay 'The Interpretation of the ong of Songs' in *The Servant of the Lord, and ther Essays on the Old Testament*, 1952.

The problem of accepting a group of love oems into the Canon was solved for Rabbis and hurch Fathers by an *allegorical* method of inter-retation. Traces of this method are found in the lishnah and Talmud, while the Targum of the ong sees in the love-story a clear picture of iod's gracious dealings with Israel throughout er history. Once the allegorical trail had been lazed, the Rabbis vied with one another in ttempts to expand and redirect it. Allusions to srael's history were squeezed from the most un-kely parts of the Song. The Church Fathers and nany subsequent Christian interpreters baptized ne Song into Christ, finding within it an allegory f Christ's love for the Church or the believer. n the beauty and purity of the Shulammite *.v.*), Roman Catholic scholars (*e.g.* Ambrose) ave found descriptions of the Virgin Mary. hristian interpreters have yielded nothing to the abbis in imaginative interpretation of details. he allegorical approach has been predominant Protestant thought until recently, and includes as its advocates such stalwarts as Hengstenberg and Keil.

Closely related is the *typical* method which preserves the literal sense of the poem but also discerns a higher, more spiritual meaning. Avoid-ing the excesses in detailed interpretation of the allegorical method, typology stresses the major themes of love and devotion and finds in the story a picture of the love relationship between Christ and His believers. This approach has been justified by analogies from Arabic love-poems which may have esoteric meanings, by Christ's use of the story of Jonah (Mt. xii. 40) or the serpent in the wilderness (Jn. iii. 14), and by biblical analogies of spiritual marriage, *e.g.* Ho. i–iii; Je. ii. 2, iii. 1 ff.; Ezk. xvi. 6 ff., xxiii; Eph. v. 22 ff. Not a few modern conservatives have espoused the *typical* view, *e.g.* J. H. Raven (*Old Testament Introduction*, 1910), M. F. Unger (*Introductory Guide to the Old Testament*², 1956), W. J. Cameron (*NBC*).

Though Jews and Christians have found devo-tional benefits in allegorical or typical approaches to the Song, the exegetical basis of these ap-proaches is questionable. Both the abundance of details and the absence of clues as to deeper spiritual significance within the book itself speak against the finding of allegory or type in the Song.

The *dramatic* interpretation of Canticles, sug-gested by both Origen and Milton, was developed in the 19th century in two major forms. F. Delitzsch found two main characters, Solomon and the Shulammite girl. Taking her from her village home to Jerusalem, Solomon learned to love her as his wife with an affection that rose above physical attraction. H. Ewald formulated an interpretation based on three main characters: Solomon, the Shulammite, and her shepherd lover to whom she remains true despite the king's desperate efforts to win her. While Ewald's ap-proach (called the *shepherd hypothesis*), which was accepted by S. R. Driver and refined by other scholars, avoids some of the difficulties of Delitzsch's view by explaining why the lover is pictured as a shepherd (i. 7, 8) and why the poem ends in a northern pastoral setting, it has its own difficulties, *e.g.* the absence of dramatic instruc-tions, the complexities involved in the dialogues when Solomon describes the Shulammite's beauty while she responds in terms of her shepherd lover. Dramatic interpretations face another difficulty: the scarcity of evidence for dramatic literature among the Semites, especially the Hebrews.

J. G. Wetzstein's study of Syrian marriage customs prompted K. Budde to interpret the Song as a collection of *nuptial songs* akin to those used in the week-long marriage feast in which the bride and groom are crowned as king and queen. Critics of this view have pointed out the danger of using modern Syrian customs to illustrate ancient Palestinian practices. Also, the Shulammite is not called 'queen' anywhere in the Song.

The view of T. J. Meek that the Song is derived from the *liturgical rites* of the Tammuz (*q.v.*) cult (*cf.* Ezk. viii. 14) has gained widespread attention. But it is unlikely that a pagan liturgy with overtones of immorality would be incorporated in the Canon without a thorough revision in terms of Israel's faith, and the Song bears the marks of no such redaction.

Leroy Waterman, who had originally supported Meek's theory (*JBL*, XLIV, 1925), has recently returned to a historical basis for the Song. This he finds in the story of Abishag, David's Shunammite (*q.v.*) maiden (1 Ki. i. 3), who allegedly refused Solomon's overtures in favour of her shepherd lover. This interpretation hangs on the conjectural connection between Shunammite and Shulammite (*q.v.*).

An increasing number of scholars have viewed Canticles as a collection of *love-poems* not necessarily connected with wedding festivities or any other specific occasion. Attempts to assign the various sections to different authors (*e.g.* W. O. E. Oesterley divided the Song into twenty-eight distinct poems and emphatically denied the unity of the book; *Song of Songs*, 1936, p. 6b) have been resisted by a number of scholars, especially H. H. Rowley: 'The repetitions that occur leave the impression of a single hand . . .' (*op. cit.*, p. 212).

V. PURPOSE

If the Song is not an allegory or type conveying a spiritual message, what place does it have in the Canon? It serves as an object-lesson, an extended *māšāl* (see PROVERB), illustrating the rich wonders of human love. As biblical teaching concerning physical love has been emancipated from sub-Christian asceticism, the beauty and purity of marital love have been more fully appreciated. The Song, though expressed in language too bold for Western taste, provides a wholesome balance between the extremes of sexual excess or perversion and an ascetic denial of the essential goodness of physical love. E. J. Young carries the purpose one step further: 'Not only does it speak of the purity of human love, but by its very inclusion in the Canon it reminds us of a love that is purer than our own' (*Introduction to the Old Testament*, 1949, p. 327).

BIBLIOGRAPHY. W. Baumgartner, in *OTMS*, pp. 230–235; D. Buzy, *Le Cantique des Cantiques*, 1949; R. Gordis, *The Song of Songs*, 1954; W. Pouget and J. Guitton, *Canticle of Canticles*, tr. J. L. Lilly, 1948; L. Waterman, *The Song of Songs*, 1948. D.A.H.

SONG OF THE THREE HOLY CHILDREN.
See APOCRYPHA.

SONS (CHILDREN) OF GOD.

I. IN THE OLD TESTAMENT

a. Individuals of the class 'god'

This usage is probably non-Israelite in origin and may belong to the language of myth; if so it has been more or less assimilated to Old Test ment theology. The *bᵉnê-hā'ᵉlōhîm* in Gn. vi. 1, are contrasted with 'men' (*hā'āḏām*), the Adam race, which seems to preclude their identificatio with the line of Cain. Were they supernatur creatures, or some non-Adamic 'man'? In Jb. 6, ii. 1, xxxviii. 7; Ps. xxix. 1, lxxxix. 6, 'the so of God' form Yahweh's heavenly train or su ordinates. The term means 'gods' or 'migh ones' rather than 'sons of (the) God (Yahweh though the LXX translators of Job called them 't *angeloi* of God'. *Cf.* Dt. xxxii. 8, LXX, when RSV 'according to the number of the sons of Go (now confirmed by a Hebrew text from Qumrar as against *MT* '. . . sons (children) of Israe The 'son of the gods' in Dn. iii. 25 (RV) is call the 'angel' of the Jews' God (iii. 28).

b. Men who by divine appointment exercise God prerogative of judgment

The 'gods' ('ᵉlōhîm) of Ps. lxxxii. 6, called al 'children of the Most High' (*bᵉnê-'elyôn*), a apparently Israelite judges, so described becau they exercise God's power of life and death (2 Ch. xix. 6).

c. Those who are related to Yahweh by covenan

Sonship of God chiefly denotes relationship covenant (see COVENANT) and is used (i) of Isra as a whole ('Israel is my son, even my firstbor Ex. iv. 22; *cf.* Ho. xi. 1); (ii) of the Israelit generally ('Ye are the children of the Lord yo God', Dt. xiv. 1; *cf.* Ho. i. 10—of an individu Israelite in later Judaism, *e.g.* Wisdom ii. 18 (iii) of the Davidic king, Yahweh's anointed, wh will rule His people for ever ('Thou art my So this day have I begotten thee', Ps. ii. 7). Th relationship is not biological, though metapho of birth, infancy, and growth are sometimes us (Ho. xi. 1; Dt. xxxii. 6; Is. i. 2, lxiii. 8) and co formity to the Father's character expected. B basically sonship is established by God throu His covenant. Dt. xiv. 1, 2 well illustrates t covenantal context of Israel's sonship. T Messiah-King, though called (like Israel wi whom He is so closely identified) 'my firstbor (Ps. lxxxix. 27) and 'begotten' of Yahweh (P ii. 7), no less owes His status to God's covena with Him (Ps. lxxxix. 28; 2 Sa. xxiii. 5). T terms of this covenant ('I will be his father, a he shall be my son', 2 Sa. vii. 14) are parallel the terms of the covenant with Israel ('I . . . w be their God, and they shall be my peopl Je. xxxi. 33).

The word translated 'son', 'sons', 'children' Heb. *bēn* (except for Aram. *bar* in Dn. iii. 2 though other terms are employed when t metaphor is extended. The LXX mostly transla *bēn* by Gk. *hyios*; occasionally by *teknon* (witho obvious difference in sense) and in Job a Daniel by *angelos*.

II. IN THE NEW TESTAMENT

The three Old Testament uses are all to so degree represented in the New Testament.

Lk. xx. 36, RV

this verse 'sons of the resurrection'—a ebraism for 'those who attain to the world to me'—are called 'sons of God' because like the gels they live in God's presence. They have ased to be 'sons of this world', *i.e.* men subject the ordinances of earthly life. The application the term in this sense to *men* is due to the hope resurrection and links it with the sense of *c* low.

Jn. x. 34–36

these verses Ps. lxxxii. 6 is discussed by Jesus, no is arguing for His own sonship *a minori ad ius.* If Scripture calls them 'gods', by virtue of e Word of God which came to them, can He no works the work of God (especially 'judgent' and 'giving life') be less than they? (Jesus es not here say how much more, or in what ller sense, He is 'Son of God'.) In the Sermon the Mount the 'sons of God (the Most High)' e so called because they perform the work of od, peace-making, impartiality, *etc.* (Mt. v. 9, ; Lk. vi. 35, RV).

Rom. ix. 2 ff.; *Heb. ii. 10–17*

ne collective sonship of Israel is alluded to in om. ix. 4 ('the adoption') and elsewhere in so : as it is represented and fulfilled in Christ.). xi. 1 is applied to Jesus in Mt. ii. 15, and the nptation narrative, turning, as it does, on the ords 'If thou be the Son of God . . .', seems recapitulate the experience of Israel in the lderness. (Luke's account may also imply comparison with the temptation of Adam e son of God', Jesus' descent from whom has interposed between the baptism and temptation.) In the baptism and temptation rratives Jesus seems to fulfil both the rôle Messiah-King as 'son of God' and the rôle Israel as 'son of God'. (See JESUS CHRIST, E OF.)

The plural 'sons of God', however, often rels, without a direct connection with the sonp of Christ, the Old Testament application of term to God's covenant people who are to lect His holiness. Eph. v. 1 ('as dear children') y be little more than metaphorical, but Phil. 15 is based on the song of Moses (Dt. xxxii. 5, 18–20), 2 Cor. vi. 18 is based on a number of venantal passages (Lv. xxvi. 12; Is. xliii. 6, lii. ; Dt. xxxii. 19), and Jn. xi. 52 is based on such ophecies as those of Ezk. xxxiv, xxxvii, where reuniting of God's covenant people is in view. is not certain that John is here applying ildren of God' more widely than to the lost ep of the house of Israel.

The sonship of God's people is, however, ked with the unique sonship of Christ in Heb. 10–17. Here, Christ's sonship is that of the ssiah-King. The 'many sons' are the seed of raham and children of God by election even ore Christ's incarnation. But the means ereby they are brought as sons *to glory* is the Son's participation in their 'flesh and blood' and His death in respect to that.

d. The idea of 'adoption'

Paul accepted the description of Israelites as 'sons of God', but with the vital qualification that 'not the children of the flesh . . . but the children of the promise' were 'the children of God' and true partakers of the privilege (Rom. ix. 8, RV). By this canon, Gentiles as well as Jews might be sons of God if they believed (Gal. iii. 26), since all who had faith were 'one man in Christ'. Rom. viii expounds the doctrine of sonship. Here Paul invokes the idea of *hyiothesia,* 'adoption'. Legal adoption of children was common in Paul's day, and the term is frequent in inscriptions and papyri (see *MM, s.v.*). Nevertheless, the meaning of the term for Paul was primarily determined by God's calling of Israel, which he describes as its *hyiothesia* in Rom. ix. 4. The status of sonship conferred by God's covenant, not the negative idea of a second-class relationship often connoted by adoption in our usage, is meant. Israel's *hyiothesia* was not inconsistent with being called God's 'firstborn', and the positive content of the term is virtually identical with what is conveyed by the idea of spiritual generation. This sonship is indissolubly linked with the sonship of Christ (viii. 17), is attested and controlled by the Spirit (viii. 14, 16), and its ultimate nature will be disclosed when His sonship is disclosed and when God's elect are seen as conformed to that perfect 'image' of sonship, 'that he might be the firstborn among many brethren' (viii. 19, 29).

Paul uses both *hyios* and *teknon,* but with no discernible distinction.

e. John's use of 'children of God'

John's conception of 'children of God' differs only in emphasis from that of Paul, although he uses *hyios* exclusively of Christ and *teknon* of others. Westcott holds that John deliberately avoided *hyios,* 'the name of definite dignity and privilege', to describe the relation of Christians to God, since 'he regards their position not as the result of an "adoption" (*hyiothesia*), but as the result of a new life which advances from the vital germ to full maturity'. But this goes too far (and can hardly account for the use of *teknon* in Jn. xi. 52).

While John undoubtedly exploits the figure of natural birth, *e.g.* in regard to 'community of nature' (1 Jn. iii. 9), he is also conscious of the Old Testament background of usage in respect of Israel's sonship by calling. 'Children of God' may be interpreted in Jn. i. 12 of those to whom the Word of God came prior to the incarnation (see verse 14) and who received it. These believers were 'born of God', but their status was also a privilege conferred on them ('to them gave he the right to become children of God', Jn. i. 12, RV). Again in 1 Jn. iii, iv believers are described as 'born of God', with special reference to their reproducing God's character of love and righteousness; but the title 'children of God' is also a privilege bestowed (of God's love) through 'calling' (iii. 1). Though 'manifest' as children of God now by their behaviour (iii. 10), they await their perfect manifestation in the day when He is manifested and they fully reflect the image of their Father (iii. 2), which image is in the Son.

BIBLIOGRAPHY. B. F. Westcott, *The Epistles of St. John*, 1883, pp. 94, 119 ff.; *Arndt, s.v.* '*hyios*', '*teknon*'; A. Richardson, *An Introduction to the Theology of the New Testament*, 1958, pp. 147 ff., 263 ff. D.W.B.R.

SOOTHSAYER. See DIVINATION.

SOP. See LORD'S SUPPER, THE.

SOPATER, SOSIPATER. Sopater, a believer from Beroea in Macedonia (Acts xx. 4), was one of the missionary party which waited for Paul at Troas, and then accompanied him to Asia on his way to Syria. Sosipater is called, in Rom. xvi. 21, a kinsman (*syngenēs*) of Paul. His greeting was sent to the church at Rome.

Some consider that the references are to the same man. Perhaps Sopater was a fruit of Paul's preaching in Macedonia, and was therefore Paul's kinsman in Christ. In that event he had remained with Paul, and had grown into sufficient stature in the Church to be one who would greet other churches. C.H.D.

SORCERY. See MAGIC AND SORCERY.

SOREK, VALLEY OF. The home of Delilah (Jdg. xvi. 4). There is little doubt that this may be equated with the Wadi al-Sarar, a large valley lying between Jerusalem—starting some 13 miles from it—and the Mediterranean. It must always have offered a convenient route inland (it is today followed by the railway line). There is a ruin near the valley called Khirbet Surik, preserving the biblical name. Eusebius and Jerome made the same identification. D.F.P.

SOSTHENES. The chief ruler of the synagogue at Corinth, and successor (or possibly colleague) of the converted Crispus (*q.v.*). He was assaulted in court after Gallio disallowed a Jewish prosecution of Paul (Acts xviii. 17), either in an anti-Semitic demonstration by Greeks (as Western Text) or in Jewish spite against an unsuccessful or lukewarm spokesman.

The latter might indicate pro-Christian sympathy: did 'Paul sow, Apollos water' (*cf.* 1 Cor. iii. 6)? 'Sosthenes the brother' is co-sender of 1 Corinthians (i. 1), and Sosthenes is not the commonest of Greek names. Paul's tact and modesty, in approaching a sensitive church in association with the ex-archisynagogue, then at Ephesus, best explain the allusion. Joint-authorship is not implied.

Sosthenes' inclusion in the Seventy (Clem. Alex. *Hyp.* v, in Eus. *EH* i. 12. 1–2) doubtless reflects his assumed participation in a canonical letter. A.F.W.

SOUL. 1. The usual Heb. word *nepeš* (*n*ᵉ*šām*
Is. lvii. 16, is an exception) occurs 754 times i
the Old Testament. As is clear from Gn. ii.
the primary meaning is 'possessing life'. Thus it
frequently used of animals (Gn. i. 20, 24, 3
ix. 12, 15, 16; Ezk. xlvii. 9). Sometimes it
identified with the blood, as something which
essential to physical existence (Gn. ix. 4; L
xvii. 10–14; Dt. xii. 22–24). In many cases
indicates the life-principle. This sense is commo
in the Book of Psalms, though by no means co
fined to it.

The numerous occurrences with a psychic
reference cover various states of consciousnes
(*a*) where *nepeš* is the seat of physical appeti
(Nu. xxi. 5; Dt. xii. 15, 20, 21, xxiii. 24; J
xxxiii. 20; Pss. lxxviii. 18, cvii. 18; Ec. ii. 24; M
vii. 1); (*b*) where it is the source of emotion (J
xxx. 25; Pss. lxxxvi. 4, cvii. 26; Ct. i. 7; Is. i. 14
(*c*) where it is associated with the will and mor
action (Gn. xlix. 6; Dt. iv. 29; Jb. vii. 15; Ps
xxiv. 4, xxv. 1, cxix. 129, 167). In addition t
these uses there are others where *nepeš* designat
an individual or person (*e.g.* Lv. vii. 21, xvii. 1
Ezk. xviii. 4), or is employed with a pronomin
suffix to denote self (*e.g.* Jdg. xvi. 16; Ps. cxx.
Ezk. iv. 14). A remarkable extension of the latt
sense is the application of *nepeš* to a dead bod
(*e.g.* Lv. xix. 28; Nu. vi. 6; Hg. ii. 13). Usual
the *nepeš* is regarded as departing at death (*e.*
Gn. xxxv. 18), but the word is never used to mea
the spirit of the dead. Since Hebrew psycholog
lacked precise terminology, there is some ove
lapping in the uses of *nepeš*, *lēḇ* (*lēḇāḇ*), an
rûaḥ (see HEART, SPIRIT).

2. *Psychē*, the corresponding term to *nepeš* i
the New Testament, occurs in the Gospels wi
similar meanings, but there are eleven cases
the Synoptic Gospels where the reference is
life after death. In all four Gospels *pneuma*, t
equivalent of *rûaḥ*, sometimes denotes the pri
ciple of life, although at other times it stands f
the higher level of psychical life. *Kardia* corr
sponding to *lēḇ* (*lēḇāḇ*) also occurs in psychic
senses.

Paul uses *psychē* only twelve times. In six cas
the meaning is life (Rom. xi. 3, xvi. 4; 1 Cor. x
45; 2 Cor. i. 23; Phil. ii. 30; 1 Thes. ii. 8). Of fo
psychical uses three indicate desire (Eph. vi.
Phil. i. 27; Col. iii. 23) and one emotion (1 The
v. 23). The two remaining examples are person
(Rom. ii. 9, xiii. 1). For the higher aspects
ordinary human life, and especially for t
higher nature of a Christian, he uses *pneuma*.
line with this is his use of the adjectives *psychik*
and *pneumatikos* to distinguish human nature
apart from divine grace and possessing it (1 Co
ii. 14, 15). When he employs *psychē* along wi
pneuma in 1 Thes. v. 23 he is merely describi
the same immaterial part of man in its lower a
higher aspects.

Peter's usage is different. He applies *psychē*
the whole personality of man, including
higher aspects. On the other hand, he reser
pneuma, in its human reference, for that part

an which survives death. Thus one of the main fferences between Old Testament and New stament usage is the application of both *ychē* and *pneuma* to human existence beyond ath.

See also SPIRIT.

BIBLIOGRAPHY. A. R. Johnson, *The Vitality of e Individual in the Thought of Ancient Israel*, 949; E. White, 'A Preface to Biblical Psychogy', *JTVI*, LXXXIII, 1951, pp. 51 ff.; *id.*, 'The sychology of St. Paul's Epistles', *JTVI*, XXXVII, 1955, pp. 1 ff.; J. Laidlaw, *The Bible octrine of Man*, 1879, pp. 49–96, 179–220; . W. Robinson, *The Christian Doctrine of lan*[3], 1926, pp. 11–27, 104–111. W.J.C.

OWER, SOWING. See AGRICULTURE.

PAIN. For the discussion of possible Old estament references to Spain, see TARSHISH. A ries of Greek commercial colonies founded om Massilia (Marseilles) introduced Spain into orld history, and in the 3rd century BC it ecame a theatre for the long struggle between arthage and Rome. By 197 BC, the Carthaginans being dispossessed, two Roman provinces, lispania Citerior and Hispania Ulterior, were et up; but the forcible reconciliation of the panish tribes to Roman rule took almost two enturies more. Later, however, Spain developed, conomically and culturally, perhaps faster than ny other part of the empire. Augustus reorganized the peninsula into three provinces, lispania Tarraconensis, Baetica, and Lusitania: espasian extended Latin status to all the panish municipalities. The Senecas, Lucan, Quintilian, Martial, and other prominent Latin vriters of that age, as well as the emperors Trajan and Hadrian, were of Spanish birth.

These things show how forward-looking was aul's plan to travel beyond Rome to Spain Rom. xv. 24, 28), a project in which he clearly xpects the co-operation of the Roman Christians. Even if his first object was the Hellenized owns, 'it marks the beginning of an entirely new nterprise; behind it lies Gaul and perhaps Germany and Britain. He is about to pass over from the Greek into the distinctly Roman half of he civilised world' (J. Weiss, *History of Primitive Christianity*, E.T., I, p. 359).

Whether Paul achieved his ambition remains uncertain. The silence of the Pastorals may indicate a change of plan. Clement of Rome, c. AD 95, says that Paul reached 'the boundary of the West' (*1 Clem.* v)—most naturally interpreted, not of Rome, but of the Pillars of Hercules. The 2nd-century *Acts of Peter* and the Muratorian Fragment are more explicit, but may reflect assumptions based on Rom. xv. The earliest surviving Spanish traditions are too late to help, and later Roman theory was interested in proving that all Western churches were founded by Peter's lieutenants (Innocent, *Ep.* xxv. 2, AD 416). See further PAUL; Zahn, *An Introduction to the New Testament*, 1909, II, pp. 61 ff., 73 ff.; P. N. Harrison, *Problem of the Pastoral Epistles*, 1921, pp. 102 ff.

BIBLIOGRAPHY. Strabo, III; C. H. V. Sutherland, *The Romans in Spain 217 BC–AD 117*, 1939. A.F.W.

SPAN. See WEIGHTS AND MEASURES.

SPARROW. See BIRDS OF THE BIBLE.

SPEAR. See ARMOUR AND WEAPONS.

SPELT (*kussemeṯ*, Ex. ix. 32, RV; Is. xxviii. 25, AVmg). Translated 'rie' in AV, the Hebrew word denotes an inferior kind of wheat, the seed of *Triticum spelta*. In Egypt, where it came up after barley, it was used in the making of bread (Herodotus, ii. 36).

SPICES. Aromatic vegetable substances, highly esteemed by Ancient Near Eastern peoples. Spice caravans pioneered the trading routes from northern India to Sumeria, Akkad, and Egypt at a very early period, and subsequently these routes became an important factor in cultural exchanges. While many spices were brought to Palestine from Mesopotamia and India, a number of those in common use were the product of the country itself. In Old Testament times the Palestinian spice trade was carefully protected. Solomon derived considerable revenue by exacting tolls of the caravans passing through his realm.

Spices such as cummin, dill, cinnamon, and mint were employed in the preparation of food (Ezk. xxiv. 10) and the flavouring of wines (Ct. viii. 2). The manufacture of the sacred incense necessitated the use of frankincense, stacte, galbanum, onycha, and sweet cane (Ex. xxx. 34), while substances such as cassia, aloes, and spikenard (*qq.v.*) were used as unguents for cosmetic purposes (Est. ii. 12; Ct. iv. 14; Mk. xiv. 3; Jn. xii. 3). See fig. 196.

When bodies were being prepared for burial it was customary for spices to be placed in the graveclothes as a form of embalming. They included mixtures of myrrh and aloes (Jn. xix. 39) or, more generally, 'spices and ointments' (Lk. xxiii. 56). While they did not significantly inhibit putrefaction, they served as deodorants and disinfectants. See also PLANTS.

BIBLIOGRAPHY. H. N. and A. L. Moldenke, *Plants of the Bible*, 1952, pp. 75 ff., 82 ff., 177 ff. R.K.H.

SPIDER. Palestine has a large range of true spiders, and the web-spinners are clearly referred to in Jb. viii. 14; Is. lix. 5, 6 (*'akkāḇîš*). *Śᵉmāmîṯ* is also translated 'spider' in Pr. xxx. 28, 'The spider taketh hold with her hands'. A much more likely translation is gecko (see LIZARD): several members of this family of lizards, some of which live in buildings, are found in the Middle East. Their specially modified feet enable them to cling to smooth walls and even ceilings. G.C.

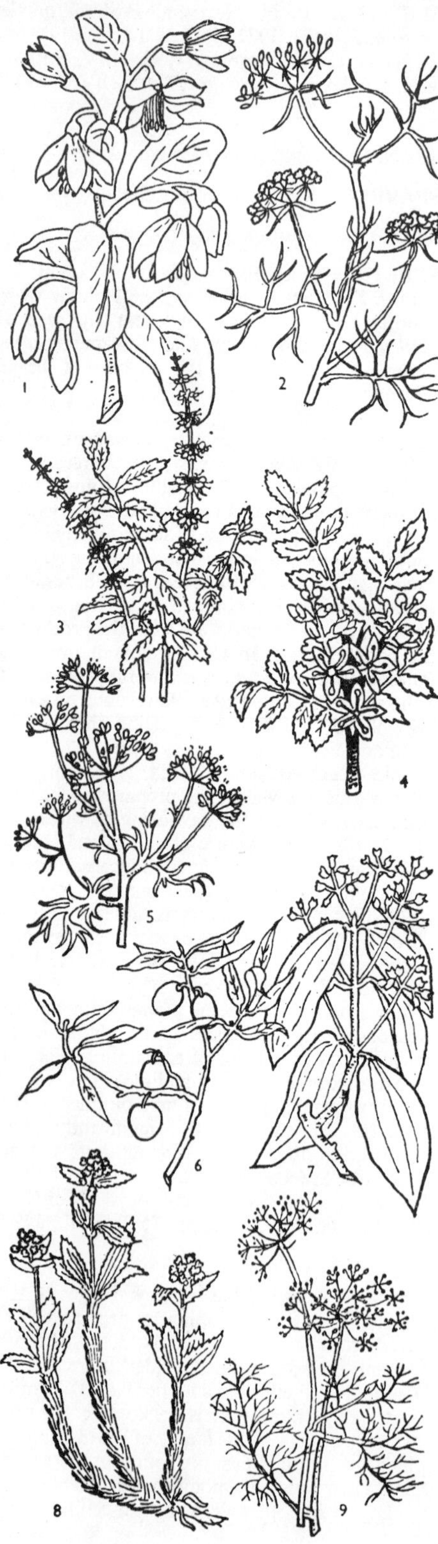

SPIKENARD (Heb. *nērd*; Gk. *nardos*). T fragrant essential oil obtained from the *Nard stachys jatamansi*, a perennial related to valeri but having more pleasantly scented roots. It is native of N India, where it is still used as perfume for the hair. In biblical times spikena was imported in sealed alabaster boxes whi were opened only on special occasions (Mk. xi 3; Jn. xii. 3). In Ct. i. 12, iv. 13 f. it is referr to as a perfume. New Testament spikenard w described as 'pistic', an obscure term probab meaning 'genuine'. R.K.H.

SPINDLE. See SPINNING AND WEAVING.

SPINNING AND WEAVING. Spinning (He *ṭāwâ*; Gk. *nēthō*) is the production of yarn fro short fibres by means of the spindle (*pele* cognate to Arab. *falkat*, 'whirl of spindle'; A 'distaff', Pr. xxxi. 19). This implement consiste of a wooden shank 9 to 12 inches long, hooke at one end to hold the yarn. Momentum wa given to the rotating spindle by a disc or whorl o stone, clay, or similarly heavy material part o the way down the shank. As the fingers an thumb of the right hand operated the spindle, th left arm held the distaff (*kîšôr*), on which the yo unspun fibres were wound. The spun yarn wa twisted on the spindle shank. Yarn was pro duced in linen and wool (Lv. xiii. 47), and i byssus, fine Egyptian linen (Pr. xxxi. 22), in goat hair (Ex. xxxv. 26), and in camels' hair (Mt. ii 4). Any mingling of two kinds of yarn wa expressly forbidden (Lv. xix. 19). Among th Hebrews spinning was the occupation of wome (Ex. xxxv. 25 f.), whereas in Egypt men also wer spinners.

Spinning was the necessary prelude to weavin (Heb. *'āraḡ*; Gk. *hyphainō*). In this process tw series of threads are involved, the longitudinal known as the warp (*šᵉṯî*), and the transverse o woof (*'ēreḇ*, Lv. xiii. 48). The horizontal loom was common in Egypt (see fig. 197). The form o the Hebrew loom is uncertain, but it is probabl that both horizontal and upright looms were i use. A. R. S. Kennedy expresses the view tha Delilah's loom (Jdg. xvi. 13) was probably hori zontal, assuming that this would be the easie type on which to deal with the hair of a sleepin person. In the upright loom the two vertica stakes were fastened at the top by a crossbeam from which the warp threads were suspended held taut by small weights of stone or clay. The beam (*mānôr*) probably provided the roller o which the woven cloth was wound (*HDB*). On the other hand, it may have been the means o carrying the heddles or loops by which the threads of the warp were raised and lowered to allow for the passage of the woof thread (*BDB*)

That weaving was a feature of the everyday life of the Hebrews is evident from the similes derived

Fig. 196. Spices known in biblical times: 1. Stacte 2. Cummin; 3. Mint; 4. Frankincense; 5. Galbanum; 6. Olives; 7. Cassia; 8. Spikenard; 9. Dill.

from it. The shaft of the giant Goliath's mighty spear was like a weaver's beam (1 Sa. xvii. 7; 2 Sa. xxi. 19). Job laments that his days are swifter than a loom (Jb. vii. 6), referring to the speed of the shuttle by which the thread of the woof was carried from one edge of the cloth to the other between the threads of the warp. The woof threads were then beaten together with the reed or stick (*yāṯēḏ*, Jdg. xvi. 14) to produce a firm cloth. Hezekiah describes premature death in terms of finished cloth rolled up and cut from the loom (Is. xxxviii. 12), leaving the ends of the warp threads or thrums (*dallâ*) still attached to the loom.

rûaḥ is to be regarded as the animating principle in relation to which *nep̄eš* is the living being. See Soul.

In many places *rûaḥ* is the 'wind', which is frequently thought of as powerful or even destructive (*e.g.* Ex. x. 13, xiv. 21; Jb. xxi. 18; Pss. i. 4, xxxv. 5, cvii. 25; Ezk. i. 4; 1 Ki. xix. 11). But it is always under God's control and effects His will (*cf.* Am. iv. 13; Jb. xxviii. 25; Pr. xxx. 4; Pss. civ. 3, cxxxv. 7, cxlviii. 8). Ezk. xxxvii. 1–14 provides examples of various uses of the word in close proximity. In verse 9 it means 'wind', in verses 5, 6, 8, 10, 'breath', and in verse 14, 'spirit'.

Fig. 197. Egyptian tomb model of women spinning and weaving.

Weaving provided an occupation for both men (Ex. xxxv. 35) and women (2 Ki. xxiii. 7). Priscilla, no less than Aquila and Paul, was a tentmaker (Acts xviii. 3). Weavers produced the hangings of the tabernacle in linen and goats' hair (Ex. xxvi. 1, 7), the hangings of pagan shrines (2 Ki. xxiii. 7), priestly robes (Ex. xxxix. 1), and Christ's seamless robe (*araphos*, 'unsewn', Jn. xix. 23).

The skill of Babylonian weavers is evident from the value Achan set on a Babylonian cloak (Jos. vii. 21). The Egyptians are mentioned as combing flax and weaving white cloth (*ḥôrāy*, Is. xix. 9).

The beginning of a guild of weavers may be traced back at least to the days of the Chronicler (1 Ch. iv. 21). G.I.E.

SPIRIT. 1. *Rûaḥ* occurs 378 times in the Old Testament. Of these the larger number of instances have a physical, physiological, or psychical connotation, but a considerable number have a supernatural reference. The noun derives from a verb meaning to breathe out through the nose with violence. Sometimes it stands for the 'life centre' and is virtually a synonym for *nep̄eš*, but such cases are comparatively few, and generally

As a psychological term *rûaḥ* is the 'dominant impulse or disposition' (*e.g.* Gn. xxvi. 35; Nu. v. 14, xiv. 24; Jb. xx. 3; Pss. xxxii. 2, li. 10; 2 Ki. xix. 7). Many instances occur where the state of *rûaḥ* in a man leads to a particular course of action (*cf.* Pr. xvi. 32, xxv. 28; Hg. i. 14).

Several times an evil spirit is indicated (*e.g.* 1 Sa. xvi. 16, xviii. 10; Nu. v. 14; Ho. iv. 12, v. 4) and 1 Ki. xxii. 19–25 appears to show that a personal spirit is intended. On the other hand, many uses imply a beneficent supernatural influence (*e.g.* Ex. xxviii. 3; Dt. xxxiv. 9; Is. xxviii. 6; Zc. xii. 10). The immanence of God is made evident when His will is effected everywhere by His Spirit (*cf.* Pss. civ, cxxxix). The earliest appearance of the word in this connection is in Gn. i. 2 (*cf.* Jb. xxxii. 8, xxxiii. 4). Specially noteworthy is the connection of the Spirit with the divine covenant with Israel (Hg. ii. 5) and the equipping of various officials for the service of God (Nu. xi. 25; 1 Sa. xi. 6, xvi. 13; Mi. iii. 8; Is. xi. 2, 3, lxi. 1). In three instances the expression 'holy spirit' occurs (Ps. li. 11; Is. lxiii. 10, 11). Whereas many phrases used of the Spirit of God are impersonal, the activity, knowledge, and character elsewhere attributed to this Spirit point in the direction of personality and deity.

2. *Pneuma*, the corresponding Greek term, appears 220 times in the New Testament. No fewer than ninety-one of these, with or without qualification as to character or source, stand for the Holy Spirit (*q.v.*). The general meanings of *pneuma* are similar to those of *rûaḥ*, but there is a noticeable change of emphasis, especially in the Pauline letters, where it is seldom used to denote the life-principle or breath, and is much more common with higher associations.

'Wind' is the correct translation in Jn. iii. 8, but elsewhere the word for wind is *anemos*. The meaning 'breath' is relevant in 2 Thes. ii. 8. A further meaning of *pneuma* is the immaterial part of man's constitution. Along with *sarx* it denotes the whole human personality (2 Cor. vii. 1; Col. ii. 5). The same idea is brought out by its combination with *sōma* (1 Cor. v. 3–5, vii. 34). Closely linked with this usage is that where the word means the part of man which survives death (Mt. xxvii. 50; Lk. viii. 55, xxiii. 46; Jn. xix. 30; Acts vii. 59; Heb. xii. 23; 1 Pet. iii. 18, 19; Rev. xi. 11).

As a psychological term *pneuma* represents the seat of perception, feeling, will, a state of mind, or may be equivalent to the *ego* (Mk. ii. 8; Lk. i. 47; Jn. xi. 33, xiii. 21; Acts xvii. 16, xviii. 25, xix. 21; Mt. xxvi. 41; 1 Cor. iv. 21; Gal. vi. 1; 1 Pet. iii. 4; Rom. viii. 16; 1 Cor. xvi. 18; Gal. vi. 18).

Many instances in the Synoptic Gospels and a few in Acts refer to evil spirits, but the most distinctive use in the New Testament is seen in the cases where the divine Spirit is indicated, and especially where He is directly connected with Christ, as the source from which He comes or the One whom He represents. Sometimes He is described as 'of God' (*e.g.* 1 Cor. ii. 11, 14), at other times as 'of the Lord' (*e.g.* Acts viii. 39, where Christ is meant) or 'of Christ' (*e.g.* Acts xvi. 7; 1 Pet. i. 11; Phil. i. 19). Several passages have the expression 'Holy Ghost' (*e.g.* Mt. xii. 32; Mk. iii. 29; Lk. xii. 10). In two places the Spirit is set alongside the Father and the Son in a context implying deity and equality (Mt. xxviii. 19; 2 Cor. xiii. 14; *cf.* 1 Pet. i. 2). See HOLY SPIRIT.

Neither Old Testament nor New Testament usage justifies the conception of the human constitution as a trichotomy.

BIBLIOGRAPHY. Works listed under SOUL; also A. McCaig, 'Thoughts on the Tripartite Theory of Human Nature', *EQ*, III, 1931, pp. 121 ff.; W. P. Dickson, *St. Paul's Use of the Terms Flesh and Spirit*, 1883, pp. 193 ff.; N. H. Snaith, *The Distinctive Ideas of the Old Testament*, 1944, pp. 141–158, 179–180. W.J.C.

SPIRITS IN PRISON. The single explicit reference is 1 Pet. iii. 19, with a possible hint in iv. 6. The patristic exegesis of iii. 19 f. regarded the 'disobedient' of Noah's day as typical of sinners who before the incarnation had no chance of hearing the gospel and repenting. The interval between the death and resurrection of Christ came later to be regarded (and especially in the Eastern Church) as the occasion when Jesus, by His descent into their 'prison', offered these 'spirits' life. Another suggestion for the meaning of this phrase refers to the proclamation of Christ's victory after His passion (with or without His offer of life) to the *angels* who fell (*cf.* 2 Pet. ii. 4 f.; Jude 6), and this is supported by the unqualified use of *pneumata*, 'spirits', which is used elsewhere in the Bible only of supernatural beings, never of departed human beings.

See the essay on 1 Pet. iii. 18–iv. 6 in E. G. Selwyn, *The First Epistle of St. Peter*, 1946, pp. 314–362; see also DESCENT INTO HADES.

S.S.S.

SPIRITUAL GIFTS.

I. NAME AND NATURE

The term 'spiritual gifts' represents the common rendering in English of the Greek neuter plural noun *charismata*, formed from *charizesthai* (to show favour, give freely), which is related to the noun *charis* (grace). The *charismata* may therefore be more accurately termed 'grace-gifts'. The singular form is found in Rom. i. 11, v. 15, 16, vi. 23; 1 Cor. i. 7, vii. 7; 2 Cor. i. 11; 1 Tim. iv. 14; 2 Tim. i. 6; 1 Pet. iv. 10; and the plural in Rom. xi. 29, xii. 6; 1 Cor. xii. 4, 9, 28, 30, 31. The plural form is used chiefly in a technical sense to denote the extraordinary gifts of the Holy Spirit bestowed on Christians for special service, though in a few instances the singular form is employed in a distributive or semi-collective sense with a similar technical signification (*cf.* 1 Tim. iv. 14; 2 Tim. i. 6; 1 Pet. iv. 10).

A general diffusion of the gifts of the Holy Spirit marking the new dispensation, was foretold by the prophet Joel (Joel ii. 28), and confirmed by the promises of Christ to His disciples (Mk. xvi. 17 f.; Jn. xiv. 12; Acts i. 8; *cf.* Mt. x. 1, 8 and parallels). On the day of Pentecost these promises and prophecies were fulfilled (Acts ii. 1–21, 33). Later, numerous spiritual gifts are frequently mentioned by Luke (Acts iii. 6 ff., v. 12–16, viii. 13, 18, ix. 33–41, x. 45 f., *etc.*), by Peter (1 Pet. iv. 10), and by Paul (Rom. xii. 6–8; 1 Cor. xii–xiv), who also describes them as 'spiritual things' (Gk. *pneumatika*, 1 Cor. xii. 1, xiv. 1), and 'spirits', that is, different manifestations of the Spirit (Gk. *pneumata*, 1 Cor. xiv. 12). The gifts are distributed by the Holy Spirit according to His sovereign will (1 Cor. xii. 11), and an individual believer may receive one or more of them (1 Cor. xii. 8 f., xiv. 5, 13).

II. PURPOSE AND DURATION

The purpose of these charismatic gifts is primarily the edification of the whole Church (1 Cor. xii. 4–7, xiv. 12), and, secondarily, the conviction and conversion of unbelievers (1 Cor. xiv. 21–25, *cf.* Acts ii. 12). Attempts to define this purpose more precisely have led to a number of different answers to the vexed question of the cessation of the *charismata*. Those who regard them as bestowed permanently on the Church attribute their early disappearance to a decline of faith and spirituality, and claim that they have been rediscovered in later times, especially during religious revivals. Those who regard them as a temporary endowment disagree about the time and cause of their withdrawal.

The popular view, that the *charismata* were given for the founding of the Church and ceased during the 4th century when it became strong enough to continue without their assistance (see B. B. Warfield, *Miracles: Yesterday and Today*, 1953, pp. 6–21), is contrary to historical evidence. Warfield himself held the view that the *charismata* were given for the authentication of the apostles as messengers of God, one of the signs of an apostle being the possession of those gifts and the power to confer them on other believers. The gifts gradually ceased with the death of those on whom the apostles had conferred them (*op. cit.*, pp. 3, 21 ff.). W. H. Griffith Thomas saw the *charismata* as a testimony to Israel of the Messiahship of Jesus, becoming inoperative after the end of Acts when Israel had refused the gospel (*The Holy Spirit of God*, 1913, pp. 48 f.). It may be possible to reconcile these views by distinguishing between those supernatural manifestations described as 'signs' (*sēmeia*) which accompanied the new dispensation and were closely associated with the apostolic circle and the evangelization of the Jews and Samaritans (Mk. xvi. 17 f.; Acts ii. 19, 43, iv. 16, 22, 30, v. 12, vi. 8, viii. 6, 13, xiv. 3; Rom. xv. 19; 2 Cor. xii. 12; Heb. ii. 3 f.), and those gifts which abide until 'that which is perfect is come' (1 Cor. xiii. 8–10).

III. INDIVIDUAL GIFTS

The lists of *charismata* in the New Testament (Rom. xii. 6–8; 1 Cor. xii. 4–11, 28–30; *cf.* Eph. iv. 7–12) are clearly incomplete. Various classifications of the gifts have been attempted, but they fall most simply into two main categories—those which qualify their possessors for the ministry of the word and those which equip them for practical service.

a. Gifts of utterance

(i) *Apostle* (Gk. *apostolos*, lit. 'one sent forth', envoy, missionary, 1 Cor. xii. 28 f.; *cf.* Eph. iv. 11). The title of 'apostle' was originally the exclusive privilege of the Twelve (Mt. x. 2; Lk. vi. 13; Acts i. 25 f.), but was later claimed by Paul (Rom. i. 1; 1 Cor. ix. 1 f., *etc.*), and applied in a less restricted sense to Barnabas (Acts xiv. 4, 14), Andronicus and Junias (Rom. xvi. 7), and possibly to Apollos (1 Cor. iv. 6, 9), Silvanus and Timothy (1 Thes. i. 1, ii. 6), and James the Lord's brother (1 Cor. xv. 7; Gal. i. 19). The special function of an apostle was, as its meaning suggests, to proclaim the gospel to the unbelieving world (Gal. ii. 7–9). (See APOSTLE.)

(ii) *Prophecy* (Gk. *prophēteia*, Rom. xii. 6; 1 Cor. xii. 10, 28, 29; *cf.* Eph. iv. 11). The chief function of the New Testament prophet was to convey divine revelations of temporary significance which proclaimed to the Church what it had to know and do in special circumstances. His message was one of edification, exhortation (Gk. *paraklēsis*), and consolation (1 Cor. xiv. 3; *cf.* Rom. xii. 8), and included occasional authoritative declarations of God's will in particular cases (Acts xiii. 1 f.), and rare predictions of future events (Acts xi. 28, xxi. 10 f.). His ministry was primarily directed to the Church (1 Cor. xiv. 4, 22). Some prophets were itinerant (Acts xi. 27 f., xxi. 10), but there were probably several attached to every church (Acts xiii. 1), as at Corinth, and a few of them are named (Acts xi. 28, xiii. 1, xv. 32, xxi. 9 f.). (See PROPHECY.)

The gift of the 'discernings of spirits' (Gk. *diakriseis pneumatōn*, 1 Cor. xii. 10, *cf.* xiv. 29) was complementary to that of prophecy, and enabled the hearers to judge claims to prophetic inspiration (1 Cor. xiv. 29), to prove successfully what utterances were of divine origin (1 Thes. v. 20 f.; 1 Jn. iv. 1–6), and to distinguish the genuine prophet from the false.

(iii) *Teaching* (Gk. *didaskalia*, Rom. xii. 7; 1 Cor. xii. 28 f.; *cf.* Eph. iv. 11). In contrast to the prophet, the teacher did not utter fresh revelations, but expounded and applied established Christian doctrine, and his ministry was probably confined to the local church (Acts xiii. 1; *cf.* Eph. iv. 11). The 'word of knowledge' (Gk. *logos gnōseōs*, 1 Cor. xii. 8), implying research and intellectual appreciation, is related to teaching; but the 'word of wisdom' (Gk. *logos sophias*, 1 Cor. xii. 8), expressing spiritual insight, may be related rather to the apostles or to the prophets.

(iv) *Kinds of tongues* (Gk. *genē glōssōn*, 1 Cor. xii. 10, 28 ff.) and the *interpretation of tongues* (Gk. *hermēneia glōssōn*, 1 Cor. xii. 10, 30). (See TONGUES, GIFT OF.)

b. Gifts for practical service

(i) *Gifts of power*. 1. Faith (Gk. *pistis*, 1 Cor. xii. 9) is not saving faith, but a higher measure of faith by which special, wonderful deeds are accomplished (Mt. xvii. 19 f.; 1 Cor. xiii. 2; Heb. xi. 33–40). 2. Gifts of healings (Gk. *charismata iamatōn*, 1 Cor. xii. 9, 28, 30) are given to perform miracles of restoration to health (Acts iii. 6, v. 15 f., viii. 7, xix. 12, *etc.*). 3. Working of miracles (Gk. *energēmata dynameōn*, 1 Cor. xii. 10, 28 f.), lit. 'of powers'. This gift conferred the ability to perform other miracles of varied kinds (Acts ix. 36 f., xiii. 11, xx. 9).

(ii) *Gifts of sympathy*. 1. Helps (Gk. *antilēpseis*, 1 Cor. xii. 28) denotes the succour given to the weak by the strong (see LXX of Pss. xxii. 19, lxxxix. 19; verb occurs in Acts xx. 35), and refers to special gifts to care for the sick and needy. It probably includes (2) the liberal almsgiver (Gk. *ho metadidous*, Rom. xii. 8) and (3) the one who performs works of mercy (Gk. *ho eleōn*, Rom. xii. 8). 4. The ministry (Gk. *diakonia*, Rom. xii. 7; *cf.* Acts vi. 1) of the deacon is doubtless in view (Phil. i. 1; 1 Tim. iii. 1–13).

(iii) *Gifts of administration*. 1. Governments

(Gk. *kybernēseis*, 1 Cor. xii. 28) are the gifts and authority to govern possessed by the ruling elders (1 Tim. v. 17). 2. The man who rules (Gk. *ho proistamenos*, Rom. xii. 8) shares the same gift and office (the Gk. word recurs in 1 Thes. v. 12; 1 Tim. v. 17). (See MINISTRY.)

BIBLIOGRAPHY. E. G. Selwyn, *The Christian Prophets*, 1900; H. A. Guy, *New Testament Prophecy: its Origin and Significance*, 1947; M. Barnett, *The Living Flame*, 1953; B. B. Warfield, *Miracles: Yesterday and Today*, 1953. W.G.P.

SPITTING. From early times the Oriental gesture of spitting upon or in the face of a person conveyed deep enmity (Nu. xii. 14). Christ submitted to this indignity as the suffering Servant (Is. l. 6; Mt. xxvi. 67).

The Essenes punished spitting in their assembly with a thirty-day penance (Jos., *BJ* ii. 8. 9, and the Qumran *Manual of Discipline*, vii. 13).

'Saliva', *ptysma*, was used by Christ to cure the blind (Mk. viii. 23; Jn. ix. 6) and a deaf mute (Mk. vii. 33). It was probably placed in the mouth to facilitate speech in the latter case. Its use with clay in Jn. ix. 6 was said by Irenaeus to be creative. The healing technique was common to both Jews and Greeks. Suetonius says Vespasian cured a blind man by spittle. The Rabbis condemned its use when accompanied with incantations. The usage persisted with the word *ephphatha* in baptismal rites in Rome and Milan. See A. E. J. Rawlinson, *The Gospel according to St. Mark*[5], 1942, p. 102. D.H.T.

SPOONS. See TABERNACLE, II.

SPRINGS. See FOUNTAIN.

SPY. See WAR.

STACHYS. A friend of Paul (Rom. xvi. 9) with an uncommon Greek name (but see instances in *Arndt*). Lightfoot (*Philippians*, p. 174) finds one Stachys a *medicus* attached to the Imperial household near this time. See AMPLIAS.

A.F.W.

STACTE (Heb. *nāṭāp̄*; Gk. *staktē*). One of the ingredients of the holy anointing oil (Ex. xxx. 34), it has been identified variously with *Liquidambar styracifolia*, *L. orientale* and *Commiphora opobalsamum*. Most probably stacte was the same as the 'sweet storax' of Ecclus. xxiv. 15. This shrub, *Styrax officinalis* L., is distributed plentifully throughout Palestine, and attains a maximum height of 20 feet. In antiquity the balsamic gummy exudate was highly prized as a perfume, and was obtained by making incisions in the branches and stems of the shrub.

It has been suggested that the 'spicery' or 'spices' mentioned in Gn. xxxvii. 25, xliii. 11; Ct. v. 1, 13, vi. 2 was storax or stacte. This identification has been questioned by most modern authorities, who prefer species of the Astragalus such as gum-tragacanth. See SPICES.

R.K.H.

STAFF. See ROD.

STALL. See MANGER.

STANDARD. See BANNER.

STARS.

I. GENERAL USE OF THE TERM

Stars (Heb. *kôḵāḇîm*; Gk. (LXX and New Testament) *asteres*) are nowhere in the Bible the subject of scientific curiosity. The term is used generally of any luminous non-terrestrial body, other than sun and moon. The great number of the stars is symbolic of God's prodigality (Ex. xxxii. 13; Dt. i. 10, x. 22, xxviii. 62; 1 Ch. xxvii. 23; Ne. ix. 23; Heb. xi. 12). God promises Abram that his seed shall be numerous as the stars (Gn. xv. 5, xxii. 17, xxvi. 4).

They are seen poetically as a majestic manifestation of God's 'otherness' in relation to men. He alone makes, controls, numbers them. Man's arrogant pride sometimes endeavours to usurp this authority (Gn. i. 16; Pss. viii. 3, cxxxvi. 9, cxlvii. 4; Am. v. 8; Jb. ix. 7; Je. xxxi. 35; Is. xiv. 13; Ob. 4; Na. iii. 16; *cf.* Gn. xxxvii. 9). A constant temptation was to worship stellar deities; but the stars are insignificant compared with Yahweh Himself (Dt. iv. 19; Je. vii. 18; Am. v. 26; Acts vii. 43). He is at the zenith of the heavens (Jb. xxii. 12).

God's final acts of redemption and judgment are foreshadowed by astronomical signs. The prophets and our Lord foretell such signs; and in Revelation they are prominent (Is. xiii. 10; Ezk. xxxii. 7; Dn. viii. 10; Joel ii. 10, iii. 15; Mt. xxiv. 29; Mk. xiii. 25; Lk. xxi. 25; Rev. vi. 13, viii. 10–12, ix. 1).

The word 'star' is also used metaphorically without astronomical reference, usually to imply dignity, either innate or usurped (Jb. xxxviii. 7; Dn. xii. 3; Rev. i. 16, 20, ii. 1, iii. 1, xii. 1, xxii. 16).

II. NAMED CONSTELLATIONS

A few constellations are mentioned in the Bible by name.

a. Arcturus (Jb. ix. 9, xxxviii. 32). Not the first magnitude star of that name in Boötes, but the prominent circumpolar constellation Ursa Major (RSV 'Bear'). Hence, 'with his sons'—the seven main stars of the group.

b. Mazzaroth (Jb. xxxviii. 32). Meaning obscure. Possibly the (twelve) zodiacal signs, or the southern ones only. (Aram. *Mazzaloth*, 'girdling stars', *i.e.* the Zodiacal circle.)

c. Orion (Jb. ix. 9, xxxviii. 31; Am. v. 8). 'The Hunter'—an outstanding southern constellation, containing the first magnitude stars Betelguese (top left, red) and Rigel (bottom right, blue). The range of colour and brightness of these and adjacent stars is an interesting illustration of 1 Cor. xv. 41.

d. Pleiades (Jb. ix. 9, xxxviii. 31); also the 'seven stars' of Am. v. 8. A compact cluster of seven faint stars in Taurus, constituting a connected system enveloped in nebulous material about 300 light-years from the sun. The Pleiades are visible just before sunrise in spring; the 'sweet influences' may be their supposed effect on the burgeoning of spring, while Orion, prominent in autumn, is thought of as ushering in winter by his harsh influence, which is, however, restrained until the proper time. An attractive but probably unacceptable alternative is that the 'binding' of the Pleiades by their mutual attraction, or (poetically) by the nebulosity surrounding them, is contrasted with the 'loosing' of Orion, the stars of which are physically unconnected, and associated for us only by our line of sight.

e. Chambers of the south (Jb. ix. 9). Obscure; possibly the constellations which appear over the horizon as one travels south along the trade route to Arabia.

The 'wicked' of Jb. xxxviii. 15 may be the 'dog-stars' (Canis major and Canis minor); the 'high arm' is probably the 'Navigator's Line', consisting of Sirius, Procyon, and Gemini.

III. THE STAR OF BETHLEHEM

The star heralding the birth of Jesus is mentioned in Mt. ii only, though seemingly foretold in Nu. xxiv. 17; Is. lx. 3. It has been explained in three ways.

a. It may have been Halley's Comet (11 BC) or another comet visible in 4 BC. This would have moved against the stars, and astrologers would have thought it significant. But would it have been visible long enough? And can the chronology be fitted in with the probable date of our Lord's birth?

b. It may have been a planetary conjunction. An interesting conjunction of Jupiter, Saturn, and Venus took place early in 7 BC. Astrologers would certainly have noted this; but its duration would be brief, and such a phenomenon could not naturally be referred to as 'a star'.

c. It may have been a supernova. Novae occur regularly; a faint star becomes suddenly brighter, then slowly fades. Probably all stars do this at some stage of development. Supernovae, however, are very rare; there has not been one in our galaxy since telescopes were invented. Novae are not usually visible to the naked eye, but a supernova in our galaxy might temporarily dominate the night sky, and produce more light than all the other stars together. Novae and supernovae are entirely unpredictable. The phrase *en tē anatolē*, 'at its rising' (Mt. ii. 2), may possibly reflect the awe of the wise men at the first rising of this new star. Its position would convey to them an immediate astrological meaning. It is not unfitting that a billion times the light of the sun should be poured out to herald the birth of the Saviour of the world.

IV. ASTRONOMY

There is no real 'astronomy' in the Bible; but a view of the universe is assumed which is not inconsistent with modern scientific cosmology. It is, of course, easy to find references to a primitive and unacceptable world-view comparable, for example, with the Babylonian creation myths. But to judge the Bible only by these is as uncritical as to judge our modern knowledge of the universe by our use of such terms as 'sunrise' and 'the canopy of heaven'. (See CREATION.)

We live in a gigantic star-system composed of perhaps a thousand million stars like the sun, arranged in a disc 60,000 light-years across. This is our 'universe'. But there are tens of millions of similar 'universes' or 'galaxies' visible up to a thousand million light-years away—the limit of present telescopes. The contrast between this cosmos and the three-decker universe of Semitic mythology is striking. The Bible is often closer to the former than the latter in spirit. For the universe of the biblical writers is rational, and of awe-inspiring immensity. Ps. civ, for example, speaks of a world which is completely rational, and depends entirely on God's laws; this is typical of the outlook of the biblical writers. In the promise to Abram, God couples the number of stars with the number of grains of sand. Only a few thousand stars could ever be visible to the naked eye, so on the face of it this is a feeble comparison. But the total number of stars in the galaxy *is* comparable with the number of grains of sand in all the world! The Bible is full of such implications of vastness quite beyond the knowledge of its day.

We assert, then, that the Bible consistently assumes a universe which is fully rational, and vast in size, in contrast to the typical contemporary world-view, in which the universe was not rational, and no larger than could actually be proved by the unaided senses. Careful astronomical observations were recorded by the Babylonians, who, by the 4th century BC, were able to predict such occurrences as the first appearance of the new moon, eclipses, *etc.*

BIBLIOGRAPHY. O. Neugebauer, *The Exact Sciences in Antiquity*, 1958; E. A. Milne, *Modern Cosmology and the Christian Idea of God*, 1952.

M.T.F.

STATER. See MONEY.

STEEL. See MINING AND METALS.

STEPHANAS. A Corinthian, whose family, one of the few baptized by Paul himself (1 Cor. i. 16), was known for its exertions in voluntary Christian service; Paul, perhaps thinking of the Corinthian factions, bespeaks recognition of such leadership (1 Cor. xvi. 15 ff.). The phrase 'the firstfruits of Achaia' (*cf.* Rom. xvi. 5) has been taken to indicate an Athenian origin (Acts xvii. 34), but it may rather indicate the first Christian *family* in the province, and thus the earnest of the church there (*cf.* Ramsay, *BRD*, pp. 385 ff.). The link sometimes made with the apostolic ordination of their 'firstfruits' in *1 Clement* xlii is purely verbal.

Stephanas, with Fortunatus and Achaicus (*q.v.*), delighted Paul with a visit at Ephesus

(1 Cor. xvi. 17): no doubt they carried the Corinthians' letter and returned with 1 Corinthians. No connection with the 'household of Chloe' (*q.v.*) is likely.

The name is a pet-form (from *Stephanēphoros?*). Two late MSS of Acts xvi. 27 identify him with the Philippian jailor. A.F.W.

STEPHEN (Gk. *stephanos*, 'crown'). Stephen was one of the seven men chosen by the disciples soon after the resurrection to look after the distribution of assistance to the widows of the Church, so that the apostles themselves should be free for their spiritual tasks (Acts vi. 1–6). All seven had Greek names, which suggests that they were Hellenistic Jews (one of them indeed, Nicolas of Antioch, was a proselyte). Stephen is recorded as standing out from the others in faith, grace, spiritual power, and wisdom (vi. 5, 8, 10). He had time to do more than the special work assigned to him, for he was among those foremost in working miracles and preaching the gospel.

He soon fell foul of the Hellenistic synagogue, which brought him before the Sanhedrin on charges of blasphemy (vi. 9–14). Stephen, with angelic face, replied to the charges with a survey of the history of Israel and an attack upon the Jews for continuing in the tradition of their fathers and killing the Messiah (vi. 15–vii. 53). This brought upon him the fury of the council, and when he claimed to see Jesus standing at the right hand of God (probably as his advocate or witness in his defence) he was seized and stoned to death (vii. 54–60). He met his end courageously, as did his Master, on accusations by false witnesses of seeking to overthrow the Temple and law (*cf.* Mt. xxvi. 59–61). He prayed as Jesus had done (Lk. xxiii. 34) for his persecutors' forgiveness, and he committed his soul into Christ's keeping (*cf.* Lk. xxiii. 46). Whether it was a legal execution or not, it seems that Pilate, who normally lived in Caesarea, turned a blind eye to it all.

There were striking consequences arising from Stephen's death. The persecution which followed (viii. 1) led to a more widespread preaching of the gospel (viii. 4, xi. 19). Stephen's death was also undoubtedly a factor in bringing Saul of Tarsus to Christ (vii. 58, viii. 1, 3, xxii. 20). But above all, Stephen's speech was the beginning of a theological revolution in the early Church, as the principles of the universal mission were clearly stated for the first time. Luke records it at great length, and this surely indicates the importance he attached to it.

Stephen's theme in reviewing the history of Israel was that God's presence cannot be localized, and that the people have always rebelled against the will of God. He showed first of all that Abraham lived a pilgrim life, not inheriting the land promised to him (vii. 2–8). Then he demonstrated how Joseph likewise left Canaan, sold by his brothers through jealousy (9–16). A long section deals with Moses, against whom Stephen was alleged to have spoken (verses 17–43). Moses also was shown to have been rejected by his brethren when he came to deliver them. Yet God vindicated him by sending him back to Egypt to bring His people out. Again they turned aside to idolatry in the wilderness and refused to obey Moses. This idolatry continued until the Babylonian Exile owing to their desire to have visible gods.

The next section (verses 44–50) deals with the tabernacle and the Temple. The tabernacle was mobile and went with God's people on their pilgrimage. The Temple was static and too easily gave rise to a localized view of God. But the Most High does not dwell in manufactured houses (*cf.* Mk. xiv. 58). The Jewish religion had become static and failed to move on towards the new Temple, the body of Christ.

The references to the tabernacle and the whole idea of the real but invisible Christian cultus is developed in the Epistle to the Hebrews, which has been seen to have close affinities with this speech. It is certain that Paul, too, worked out the principles stated by Christ and developed here by Stephen. When these principles were understood by the Church there ensued a break with the old Temple worship (Acts ii. 46). The Christians saw in practice that they were not just a sect of the old Israel. They were the new people of God, with the true temple, altar, and sacrifice, living the truly pilgrim life, and rejected, as the prophets and as Jesus had been, by the Jews.

BIBLIOGRAPHY. M. Simon, *St. Stephen and the Hellenists in the Primitive Church*, 1956; A. Cole, *The New Temple*, 1950; W. Manson, *The Epistle to the Hebrews*, 1951, pp. 25 ff. R.E.N.

STEWARD. In the Old Testament a steward is a man who is 'over a house' (Gn. xliii. 19, xliv. 4; Is. xxii. 15, *etc.*). In the New Testament there are two words translated steward: *epitropos* (Mt. xx. 8; Gal. iv. 2), *i.e.* one to whose care or honour one has been entrusted, a curator, a guardian; and *oikonomos* (Lk. xvi. 2, 3; 1 Cor. iv. 1, 2; Tit. i. 7; 1 Pet. iv. 10), *i.e.* a manager, a superintendent—from *oikos* ('house') and *nemō* ('to dispense' or 'to manage'). The word is used to describe the function of delegated responsibility, as in the parables of the labourers, and the unjust steward.

More profoundly, it is used of the Christian's responsibility, delegated to him under 'Christ's kingly government of His own house'. All things are Christ's, and Christians are His executors or stewards. Christians are admitted to the responsibilities of Christ's overruling of His world; so that stewardship (*oikonomia*) can be referred to similarly as a dispensation (1 Cor. ix. 17; Eph. iii. 2; Col. i. 25). C.H.D.

STOCKS (Heb. *mahpeḵeṯ*, 'pillory'; *saḏ*, 'fetters'; *ṣînōq*, 'a collar'). Referred to in later Old Testament passages only, this instrument of punishment comprised two large pieces of wood into which were inserted the feet, and sometimes also the hands and neck, of the prisoner. The prophets Jeremiah (Je. xx. 2, 3, *cf.* xxix. 26) and Hanani (2 Ch. xvi. 10, RVmg) were subjected to it, and Job uses the idea figuratively in mourning his affliction (Jb. xiii. 27, xxxiii. 11).

In the New Testament Gk. *xylon*, 'wood', 'tree', is used in describing the Philippian incident when Paul and Silas were put in the stocks (Acts xvi. 24). See PRISON. J.D.D.

STOICS. The Stoic school of philosophy derived its name from the Stoa Poikile, the portico in Athens where Zeno of Citium (335–263 BC) first taught its characteristic doctrines. His teaching was systematized and extended by Chrysippus (*c.* 280–207 BC), the 'second founder' of Stoicism. By the time when Paul encountered Stoics at Athens (Acts xvii. 18) their general attitude had been modified by elements taken from Platonism; of this more syncretist Stoicism Posidonius was a leading exponent.

Grappling with that same uncertainty of life which led the Epicureans to seek happiness in serene detachment, the Stoics sought salvation in aligning the will with the inherent Reason of the universe (see LOGOS). Man is happy when he does not want things to be any other than they are; let him, then, seek clear knowledge of the cycle of nature and cultivate a willing acceptance of it. Though a man must play his part willy-nilly in the outworking of universal Reason, for his own peace of mind it is essential that he do so consciously and willingly; he must seek out the things which befit his place in the natural order (*ta kathēkonta*) and pursue them not with desire, which might be disappointed, but with disinterested virtue. His fellow men he must serve not from love, which would make him suffer if service failed to help them, but from a pure recognition that the life of service is the 'natural' life for man. The universal Reason is God; traditional mythologies were given a symbolic interpretation in this sense.

All this seems very formal and austere, but individual Stoics, including the Roman emperor Marcus Aurelius, set a high standard of personal conduct. The form could, moreover, in part be adapted to receive a Christian content; much of Paul's language in the apologetic discourse on Mars' Hill is drawn from that of Stoicism (see AREOPAGUS).

BIBLIOGRAPHY. H. von Arnim, *Stoicorum Veterum Fragmenta*, 1903–5; E. Bevan, *Stoics and Sceptics*, 1913. M.H.C.

STOMACH, BELLY. Principally, Heb. *beṭen* *mē'îm*; Gk. *koilia*. Indistinguishable from bowels or womb (*qq.v.*) in the Old and New Testaments, these words being translated by 'belly' in AV generally when referring to eating, swelling, or wounding (Nu. v. 21; Jdg. iii. 21; Jn. i. 17; Lk. xv. 16).

Once in the New Testament the word *stomachos* is used (1 Tim. v. 23) of the stomach. In early Greek usage it referred to an opening, or the mouth (*cf.* MOUTH, *stoma*), later the opening of the stomach, so having a more precise physiological reference than in the Old Testament. B.O.B.

STOMACHER. The somewhat misleading AV translation of Heb. *p^e^ṯîḡîl*, a word of uncertain meaning which occurs only in Is. iii. 24 as an antithesis for 'a girding of sackcloth'. RSV 'a rich robe' seems to fit this requirement.

STONE. The chief biblical words are Heb. *'eḇen* and Gk. *lithos* and *akrogōniaios* ('cornerstone').

The common word 'stone' is used in the Bible with a variety of reference. Small stones made a convenient weapon (1 Sa. xvii. 40), were a means of attack and even execution (Nu. xxxv. 17; *cf.* Jn. viii. 59; Acts vii. 58 f.), formed a handy measure of weight (Lv. xix. 36, where *'eḇen* is so translated), and were used, when sharpened, as knives (Ex. iv. 25). Larger stones were used to cover wells (Gn. xxix. 2), to close the mouth of caves (Jos. x. 18) and of tombs (Mt. xxvii. 60), to serve as a landmark (2 Sa. xx. 8), as a memorial (Jos. iv. 20 ff.), and as a pillar or altar which had specifically religious associations (Gn. xxviii. 18; Dt. xxvii. 5). Stones were also, of course, a primary building material. J. C. Lambert (in *DCG*, II, pp. 678 f.) examines the association existing in the Gospels between 'stones' and the Person and teaching of Christ.

In all the Synoptic Gospels the record of our Lord's parable of the vineyard, which carries a number of Christological overtones, is followed by His citation of Ps. cxviii. 22, obviously applied to Himself (Mk. xii. 10 = Mt. xxi. 42 = Lk. xx. 17). This is an important clue to Christ's own understanding of His Person. The meaning of 'head stone' (LXX, *eis kephalēn gōnias*) in this psalm is 'top stone' or 'coping stone', that is, the carefully chosen and perfectly made stone which completes a building (*cf.* Zc. iv. 7). Probably the immediate reference here was to Israel herself, rejected by men but chosen by God. The real significance of the passage in its New Testament setting is made abundantly clear from Peter's quotation of Ps. cxviii. 22 with reference to Jesus, during his speech before the Jewish court in Jerusalem (Acts iv. 11). God has vindicated Him whom the Jews cast out, and exalted Him to the headship of the new Israel. In the *Epistle of Barnabas* (vi. 4) these words are quoted directly from the LXX (Ps. cxvii), and also applied to Christ.

The only Old Testament occurrences of the phrase 'corner stone' are Jb. xxxviii. 6 (LXX *lithos gōniaios*) and Is. xxviii. 16 (LXX *akrogōniaios*), and these are both figurative (*cf.* Ps. cxliv. 12). But unlike 'head of the corner', the stone referred to here would appear to be part of the foundation of a building, and to bear its weight. This is evidently the meaning of *akrogōniaios* in 1 Pet. ii. 6, where the writer quotes Is. xxviii. 16

itself. Christ is now the corner-stone of the Church, the location of which is the heavenly Zion (*cf.* Eph. ii. 20, where the same Greek word is used, and 1 Cor. iii. 11). In verse 7 of the same passage, however, Peter goes on to quote the same psalmic reference we have noted (cxviii. 22, echoed in verse 4), and he thus gives us the complementary truth that Christ is also the *head* of the Church, exalted by God the Father to that position of vindication. It is in this exaltation, moreover, that believers will share.

The writer's use of *lithos* in verse 8 with reference to stumbling suggests a confusion of images, although it is possible, as J. Y. Campbell points out ('Cornerstone', *A Theological Word Book of the Bible*, ed. A. Richardson, 1950, p. 53), that a stone at the corner of the foundation of a building might also form a stumbling-stone (*cf.* also Rom. ix. 32 f.). Christ is described in the same passage (verse 4) as a 'living stone' (*lithon zōnta*), alive and giving life to those who as believers are incorporated into Him, and built up as *lithoi zōntes* into the spiritual building of His Church for purposes of worship (verse 5) and witness (verse 9).

BIBLIOGRAPHY. J. R. Harris, *Testimonies*, I, 1916, pp. 26 ff.; S. H. Hooke, 'The Corner-stone of Scripture', *The Siege Perilous*, 1956, pp. 235–249; J. Y. Campbell, 'Cornerstone' in *A Theological Word Book of the Bible*, ed. A. Richardson, 1950, pp. 53 ff. S.S.S.

STONES, PRECIOUS. See JEWELS AND PRECIOUS STONES.

STONE-SQUARERS. The AV translation of Heb. *haggiblîm* in 1 Ki. v. 18, a word similarly explained by Targum and Syriac Peshitta. RV and RSV 'men of Gebal', a town in Phoenicia, is undoubtedly correct (*cf.* AVmg; so also LXX and Vulg.). For examples of Israelite masonry showing Phoenician influence, see W. F. Albright, *The Archaeology of Palestine*, 1949, pp. 125 ff. with pl. 21. It was common practice in Syria and Anatolia to reinforce masonry with wooden beams (*cf.* buildings at Hazor and Ras Shamra), and to use wooden beams as bearers for panelling. See WALLS. A.R.M.

STONING (Heb. *sāqal*, 'to stone', 'to be stoned'; Heb. *rāḡam*, 'to collect or cast stones'; Gk. *katalithazō*, 'to stone (thoroughly)'; Gk. *lithazō*, 'to stone'; Gk. *lithoboleō*, 'to cast stones'). Stoning was the usual Hebrew form of execution (Ex. xix. 13; Lv. xx. 27; Lk. xx. 6; Acts vii. 58, *etc.*). The prosecution witnesses (the law required at least two such) had to cast the first stone (Dt. xiii. 9 f.; *cf.* Jn. viii. 7), and afterwards if the victim still lived the spectators carried out the sentence, and the body was suspended until sunset (Dt. xxi. 23).

For an excellent summary of offences for which stoning was prescribed, and further details of the execution, see W. Corswant, *A Dictionary of Life in Bible Times*, E.T., 1960, p. 261. J.D.D.

STOOL. See MIDWIFE.

STORAX. See SPICES, STACTE.

STORE-CITIES. Towns (Heb. *'arê-miskenôṯ*) where provisions, often revenue paid in kind (grain, oil, wine, *etc.*), and weapons were laid up in magazines or storehouses by the central government, for maintaining frontier and defence forces, and as reserve supplies, *etc.* The Hebrews had to labour on Pharaoh's store-cities Pithom and Ra'amses on the eve of the Exodus (Ex. i. 11). The Delta-residence Ra'amses (Egyp. *Pi-Ramessē*) was frequently boasted of in Egyptian texts as being in a region of plenty, with stores and treasuries abundantly filled (*ANET*, 1955, pp. 470, 471; *JEA*, V, 1918, pp. 186 f., 192, 194 f.). Solomon had store-cities and depots in Israel and Hamath (1 Ki. ix. 19; 2 Ch. viii. 4–6). When summoned against Baasha of Israel by Asa of Judah, Ben-hadad I of Aram-Damascus smote stores in ('of') cities of Naphtali (2 Ch. xvi. 4). Jehoshaphat built store-cities in Judah (2 Ch. xvii. 12), and Hezekiah was proud of his well-filled storage-magazines for revenue in grain, wine, and oil (2 Ch. xxxii. 28). And likewise some of his contemporaries: Asitawanda king of Cilicia (*c.* 725 BC) 'filled the storehouses (or, depots) of (the city) Pa'ar' (*ANET*, p. 499; *cf.* Dupont-Sommer, *Oriens*, I, 1948, pp. 196, 197). Remains, possibly those of government storehouses, have been excavated in Palestine. For remains at Beth-shemesh and Lachish, *cf.* Wright, *Biblical Archaeology*, 1957, p. 130. For Hazor and Samaria, *cf.* K. M. Kenyon, *Archaeology in the Holy Land*, 1960, pp. 271, 272, 279, and Y. Yadin, *Hazor*, BM Exhibition Guide, 1958, p. 17 and fig. 30. K.A.K.

STOREY, STORY. See HOUSE.

STORK. See BIRDS OF THE BIBLE.

STORM. The more violent activities of nature are usually associated with rain- and hail-storms. Generally the incidence of violent rain-storms and cloud-bursts occurs at the commencement of the rainy season, or at the beginning of each renewed spell of rain during the cooler months. At Haifa, for example, on 9 December, 1921 11 inches fell in 24 hours. Thunder-storms are most frequent in November and December and occur most commonly in the Jordan Valley. Hail not infrequently accompanies thunder between December and March. Scripture vividly describes its disastrous effects upon the growing crops (Ps. lxxviii. 47; Is. xxviii. 2; Ezk. xiii. 1[illegible] 14; Hg. ii. 17). The wind-storms that sweep down upon the Sea of Galilee are vividly recorded in the events of Mk. iv. 37 ff., and perhaps in the parable of the badly founded house sited in some dried-up water-bed, when 'the rain descended and the floods came, and the winds blew, and beat upon that house' (Mt. vii. 27).

God spoke in the thunder-storm (Ex. ix. 2[illegible] xix. 16, 19; 1 Sa. vii. 10, xii. 18; Jb. xxxvii. 1–

?ss. xviii. 13, xxix. 3–9, civ. 7), as He judged in he earthquake (Je. iv. 24–26; Na. i. 5). The Hebrews in conceiving how 'thy glory went hrough four gates of fire, and earthquake, wind ınd cold' (2 Esdras iii. 19) had to learn, however, hat Yahweh was more revelatory to them in the Exodus than in storm and earthquake. This ertainly was the experience of Elijah, who had he consciousness of 'the still small voice' as nore expressive of the divine presence and power han earthquake, wind, and fire (1 Ki. xix. 11–13).
 See also EUROCLYDON, RAIN, THUNDER, WHIRLWIND, WIND. J.M.H.

STRANGER. In the AV this term is used rather ndiscriminately to translate a variety of words. The resultant confusion makes it difficult to listinguish the various classes described. These ıre the stranger, the foreigner, and the sojourner.

. The stranger

A stranger is essentially one who does not belong o the house or community in which he finds nimself. The word *zār* is from the root *zûr*, 'to urn aside' or 'to depart'. Thus it can be used imply of an outsider (1 Ki. iii. 18). It can there-ore mean one who usurps a position to which he ıas no right. The 'strange woman' in Proverbs is uch an interloper. A further extension of the vord makes it equivalent to alien or foreigner, .*e.* one who does not belong to the nation, and o virtually equates it with an enemy (Is. i. 7; 'e. v. 19, li. 51; Ezk. vii. 21, xxviii. 7, 10; Ob. 11).

. The foreigner

Foreigner' is the rendering of *nokrî*, which is, ıowever, more frequently translated in the AV by stranger'. The word can refer simply to one of ınother race; but it also acquires a religious onnotation because of the association of other ıations with idolatry. Therefore the Israelites vere forbidden to intermarry with the Canaan-tes (Dt. vii. 1–6). One of the indictments of Solomon is that he loved many strange (*i.e.* oreign) women who turned him aside from Yahweh (1 Ki. xi. 1 ff.). The Exile in Babylon was een as a judgment on this decline, which was videspread in the nation. As a result the return rom the Exile is marked by a vigorous enforce-nent of the prohibition of mixed marriages. This mphasis by Ezra on national purity (Ezr. ix, x) vas perverted in later Judaism into the hard xclusiveness which in the Judaizing movement ı the early Church proved such a hindrance to he free access of Gentile converts.

. The sojourner

A sojourner is one who dwells among another eople, in contrast to the foreigner, whose stay is emporary. The word thus rendered is *gēr* from e root *gûr*, 'to sojourn', though the alternative *šāḇ* is sometimes used in the simple sense of a ettler. The Israelites themselves were sojourners Egypt (Gn. xv. 13; Ex. xxii. 21; Dt. x. 19, xiii. 7). Indeed, this fact was to govern their attitude to the sojourners in Israel. These might comprise a whole tribe such as the Gibeonites (Jos. ix) or the remnants of the Canaanite tribes after the conquest. Their number was quite considerable, as may be seen in Solomon's census of them (2 Ch. ii. 17).

The sojourner had many privileges. The Israelites must not oppress him (Ex. xxii. 21, xxiii. 9; Lv. xix. 33, 34). Indeed, they are to go further and love him (Dt. x. 19). One reason given for the observance of the Sabbath is that the sojourner may be refreshed (Ex. xxiii. 12). The gleanings of the vineyard and the harvest field are to be left for him (Lv. xix. 10, xxiii. 22; Dt. xxiv. 19–21). He is included in the provision made in the cities of refuge (Nu. xxxv. 15; Jos. xx. 9). He is ranked with the fatherless and widow as being defenceless; and so God is his defence and will judge his oppressor (Pss. xciv. 6, cxlvi. 9; Je. vii. 6, xxii. 3; Ezk. xxii. 7, 29; Zc. vii. 10; Mal. iii. 5). The chief drawback of his position is that, if he is a bond-servant, he is not included in the general liberation in the year of Jubilee (Lv. xxv. 45, 46).

As far as religious life is concerned he is bound by the law which forbids leaven during the Feast of Unleavened Bread (Ex. xii. 19). He must abstain from work on the sabbath and on the Day of Atonement (Ex. xx. 10; Lv. xvi. 29). He shares the prohibitions on eating blood (Lv. xvii. 10, 13), immorality (Lv. xviii. 26), idolatry (Lv. xx. 2), and blasphemy (Lv. xxiv. 16). He might, however, eat unclean meat (Dt. xiv. 21). He is not compelled to keep the Passover, but if he wishes to do so he must be circumcised (Ex. xii. 48). He is indeed virtually on a level with the Israelite (Lv. xxiv. 22), and in Ezekiel's vision of the messianic age he is to share the inheritance of Israel (Ezk. xlvii. 22, 23).

In the New Testament the term 'stranger' is not generally used in this specialized sense but simply describes a foreigner or one away from home. The Old Testament usage is recalled in Eph. ii. 19 and 1 Pet. ii. 11. See PILGRIMAGE.

BIBLIOGRAPHY. *EBi* and *DAC* (*s.v.* 'stranger'); J. Pedersen, *Israel*, III–IV, 1940, pp. 272 ff., 585.
H.M.C.

STRANGLED (THINGS). Gk. *pnikta* (Acts xv. 20, 29, xxi. 25) refers to animals killed without shedding their blood, to eat which was repugnant to Jews (*cf.* Lv. xvii. 13; Dt. xii. 16, 23). For general principles involved, see IDOLS, MEATS OFFERED TO.

STRAW (Heb. *teḇen*; Arab. *tibn*). The stalk of wheat or barley. Chaff (*q.v.*) is the wind-scattered husk of the threshed grain, stubble the remains after harvesting. Chopped straw mixed with more solid foodstuffs contributed to the provender of horses, asses, and camels (Gn. xxiv. 32; Jdg. xix. 19; 1 Ki. iv. 28). In Egypt straw was and is mixed with clay to make the familiar mud bricks of the poorer houses (see plate III*b*). When the Israelite brickmakers, already overworked, had to collect their own stubble, their burdens were almost intolerably increased (Ex. v). Straw is also still used in certain kinds of hand-moulded pottery, later burnt by fire. Such was the strength of leviathan that he could bend iron like straw (Jb. xli. 27). In the peace of the messianic age the lion will cease to devour flesh, and eat straw (Is. xi. 7, lxv. 25). The final fate of Moab is pictured as straw trampled down among dung (Is. xxv. 10). In the Bible stubble (Heb. *qaš*, 'dried up') is used to typify worthless inflammable substances (Ex. xv. 7; Jb. xiii. 25, xli. 28, 29; Ps. lxxxiii. 13; Is. v. 24; so Gk. *kalamē* in 1 Cor. iii. 12).

BIBLIOGRAPHY. C. F. Nims, 'Bricks without Straw', *BA*, XIII, 1950, pp. 22 ff. R.A.S.

STRIPES. The AV rendering of several Hebrew and Greek words, only one of which (Gk. *plēgē*) occurs more than twice. The Deuteronomic law limited to forty the number of blows which a judge could prescribe (Dt. xxv. 2, 3). The punishment was generally carried out by a three-thonged scourge (see fig. 181), and the executioner himself was punished if the stipulated number were exceeded. Thus, what Paul describes in his 'foolish boasting' (2 Cor. xi. 24) was in fact the maximum penalty—*i.e.* thirteen strokes of three. Stripes can be a symbol of salutary correction (Ps. lxxxix. 32; *cf.* Pr. xiii. 24) and a reminder of the Lord's sacrifice (Is. liii. 5; 1 Pet. ii. 24). See also SCOURGING. J.D.D.

STRONG DRINK. See WINE AND STRONG DRINK.

STRONGHOLD. See FORTIFICATION AND SIEGECRAFT.

STUBBLE. See STRAW.

STUMBLING-BLOCK. In the Old Testament the Heb. root *kāšal*, 'to stagger', 'to stumble', forms the basis of *miḵšôl*, *maḵšēlâ*, 'that against which anyone stumbles' (Lv. xix. 14). It is used figuratively of idols (Is. lvii. 14; Ezk. vii. 19, xiv. 3, 4; Zp. i. 3).

In the New Testament two Greek words are used. *Proskomma* (*tou lithou*), 'stone of stumbling' (Rom. ix. 32, 33, xiv. 13; 1 Cor. viii. 9; 1 Pet. ii. 8), is used of any form of barrier. *Skandalon* (Rom. xi. 9; 1 Cor. i. 23; Rev. ii. 14), originally the trigger stick of a trap, is used in LXX to translate Heb. *miḵšôl*, but also of *môqēš*, 'a snare', 'a trap' (*cf.* Pss. lxix. 22, cxl. 5). *Cf.* also Mt. xvi. 23, 'thou art an offence (*skandalon*) unto me'. See W. Barclay, *New Testament Wordbook*, 1955 (*s.v.* '*skandalon*', '*skandalizein*'). D.O.S.

SUBURB. In AV and RV most commonly the equivalent of Heb. *migrāš*, more accurately rendered 'pasture lands' in RVmg and 'common land' in RSV in Lv. xxv. 34. It is used specially, but not exclusively, with regard to the uncultivated land, suitable for the pasturing of cattle, surrounding the levitical cities; its alienation from levitical ownership was forbidden (Lv. xxv. 34, *etc.*). In 2 Ki. xxiii. 11, AV, 'suburbs' is the rendering of Heb. *parwārîm* (RV and RSV 'precincts'), a word of doubtful origin and meaning, but possibly derived, like 'Parbar' (*q.v.*) in 1 Ch. xxvi. 18, from Old Persian *frabada*, 'forecourt'. F.F.B.

SUCCOTH. 1. First site on the journey of the Israelites during the Exodus, possibly equivalent to the Old Egyp. *ṯkw* (Pithom), which was in the eastern part of Wadi Tumilat (Ex. xii. 37, xiii. 20; Nu. xxxiii. 5, 6). This was the normal way in or out of Egypt for displaced persons. We find it mentioned in the Story of Sinuhe in Papyrus Anastasi V (19. 5–20. 6; 18. 6–19. 1) and in VI (5. 1). See ENCAMPMENT BY THE SEA, PITHOM.

2. City of the tribe of Gad (Jos. xiii. 27) in the Jordan Valley not far from a water passage (Jdg. viii. 5, 16) and from Zarethan (1 Ki. vii. 46). It is the modern Tell Akhsâs or Tell Dêr Allah. The name is explained in Gn. xxxiii. 17, where it is connected with 'booths', since Jacob established himself there. C.D.W.

SUCCOTH-BENOTH. The name of an object made by Babylonians while exiles in Samaria *c.* 722 BC and named among the pagan deities worshipped there (2 Ki. xvii. 30). The MT *sukkôṯ-b^{e}nôṯ* implies an interpretation as 'booths of daughters' (*cf.* Gk. *sokchōthbenithei*). This has been explained as either places of prostitution or as shrines in which were carried images of female deities, *e.g.* Banitu (an epithet of the Babylonian goddess Ishtar).

The parallelism with Nergal of Cutha seems to require the name of a deity here also. Following Rawlinson, Zēr-bānīt (Zarpanitum) the consort of Marduk (see MERODACH) has been proposed but this is very doubtful. D.J.W.

SUFFERING. In the Bible suffering is regarde as an intrusion into this created world. Creatio was made good, and free from pain (Gn. i. 31) When sin entered, suffering also entered in th form of conflict, pain, corruption, drudgery, an death (Gn. iii. 15–19). In the new heaven an earth suffering has been finally abolished (Re xxi. 4; Is. lxv. 17 ff.). The work of Christ is t deliver man from suffering, corruption, and deat (Rom. viii. 21; 1 Cor. xv. 26), as well as from si (Mt. i. 21). Though Satan is regarded as havir power to make men suffer (2 Cor. xii. 7; Jb. i. 1 ii. 6), they suffer only in the hand of God, an it is God who controls and sends suffering (Ar iii. 6; Is. xlv. 7; Mt. xxvi. 39; Acts ii. 23).

The burden of suffering was always keenly fe by God's people (Gn. xlvii. 9; 2 Sa. xiv. 14). I presence often became a problem, since it w regarded as sent by God (Ps. xxxix. 9), and th had to be related to the fact of God's love a righteousness (Ps. lxxiii). Therefore, in the mic of suffering, man was forced to decide how far could live by faith, and resist the demand for rational explanation. The problem was not acute at times when the sense of solidarity within the community was strong, and the individual, as a responsible member of his tribe or family in all circumstances, was able to accept the judgment and suffering that fell on his people as his own responsibility (Jos. vii). But the problem became more urgent as the responsible relation of each individual to God was emphasized (Je. xxxi. 29; Ezk. xviii. 2–4).

True faith, wrestling with the problem and burden of suffering, does not require an immediate and complete justification of God. It can wait in the darkness (Hab. ii. 2–4). It finds in the reality of God's presence and goodness a more decisive factor in the present situation than even the bitterness of pain (Ps. lxxiii. 21–23), and is willing to set against the distorted shape of things present the perfect new order of things in the kingdom of God, of which it has already received a foretaste (Ps. lxxiii. 24–26; Rom. viii. 18; 2 Cor. iv. 16–18). But the man of faith is not insensitive to the baffling nature of the problem. The book of Job shows him experiencing in an extreme degree the bitterness and perplexity of unexplained suffering, refusing to acquiesce in rational theories that make God's ways subject to simple human calculation, temporarily losing his balance, but able ultimately to recover, and finally, through an overwhelming vision of God Himself, reaching a certainty in which he can triumph over all his difficulties even though he is not yet, and knows he never will be, able to provide a rational explanation for all circumstances.

Though it is thus asserted that such solutions are inadequate when applied generally, yet sometimes definite understandable reasons are given for instances of suffering (*cf.* Ps. xxxvii), and several lines of thought on the problem appear and converge. Suffering can be the harvest of sin (Ho. viii. 7; Lk. xiii. 1–5; Gal. vi. 8), both for the individual (Ps. i) and for the community and nation (Am. i, ii). It can be regarded at times as a punishment administered by God, or a chastisement designed to correct the ways of His people (Pr. iii. 12; Jdg. ii. 22–iii. 6), or a means whereby men are tested or purified (Ps. lxvi. 10; Jas. i. 3, 12; 1 Pet. i. 7; Rom. v. 3) or brought closer to God in a new relationship of dependence and fellowship (Ps. cxix. 67; Rom. viii. 35–37). Thus suffering can be for good (Rom. viii. 28 f.), or it can have the opposite effect (Mt. xiii. 21).

In bearing their witness to the sufferings of the coming Messiah (1 Pet. i. 10–12) the Old Testament writers are taught how God can give a new meaning to suffering. Their own experience of serving God in His redemptive purposes in Israel taught them that the love of God must involve itself in sharing the affliction and shame of, and in bearing reproach from, those He was seeking to redeem (Ho. i–iii; Je. ix. 1, 2, xx. 7–10; Is. lxiii. 9). Therefore His true Servant, who will perfectly fulfil His redeeming will, will be a *Suffering Servant*. Such suffering will not simply arise as a result of faithfulness to God in pursuing His vocation, but will indeed constitute the very vocation He must fulfil (Is. liii). A new vicarious meaning and purpose is now seen in such unique suffering in which One can suffer in the place of, and as the inclusive representative of, all.

Suffering can have a new meaning for those who are members of the body of Christ. They can share in the sufferings of Christ (2 Cor. i. 5 ff.; Mk. x. 39; Rom. viii. 17), and regard themselves as pledged to a career or vocation of suffering (Phil. i. 29; 1 Pet. iv. 1, 2), since the members of the body must be conformed to the Head in this respect (Phil. iii. 10; Rom. viii. 29) as well as in respect of His glory. Whatever form the suffering of a Christian takes it can be regarded as a cross which may be taken up in following Christ in the way of His cross (Mt. xvi. 24; Rom. viii. 28, 29). Such suffering is indeed the inevitable way that leads to resurrection and glory (Rom. viii. 18; Heb. xii. 1, 2; Mt. v. 10; 2 Cor. iv. 17 f.). It is by tribulation that men enter the kingdom of God (Acts xiv. 22; Jn. xvi. 21). The coming of the new age is preceded by birth pangs on earth, in which the Church has its decisive share (Mt. xxiv. 21, 22; Rev. xii. 1, 2, 13–17; *cf., e.g.*, Dn. xii. 1; Mi. iv. 9, 10, v. 2–4). Since the sufferings of Christ are sufficient in themselves to set all men free (Is. liii. 4–6; Heb. x. 14), it is entirely by grace, and not in any way by necessity, that the sufferings in which His people participate with Him can be spoken of as filling up what is lacking in His affliction (Col. i. 24), and as giving fellowship in His vicarious and redemptive suffering.

BIBLIOGRAPHY. A. S. Peake, *The Problem of Suffering in the Old Testament*, 1904; S. R. Driver and G. B. Gray, *ICC*, *Job*, 1921; *ERE*; C. S. Lewis, *The Problem of Pain*, 1940; H. E. Hopkins, *The Mystery of Suffering*, 1959; W. Eichrodt, *Man in the Old Testament*, 1951; J.-J. von Allmen, *Vocabulary of the Bible*, 1958. R.S.W.

SUKKIIM (Egyp. *ṯktn, ṯk*). Libyan auxiliaries in the Egyptian army when Shishak (*q.v.*) invaded Palestine (2 Ch. xii. 3). They were employed as scouts from 13th to 12th centuries BC. See references in R. A. Caminos, *Late-Egyptian Miscellanies*, 1954, pp. 176, 177, 180. K.A.K.

SUMER, SUMERIANS. There are no direct biblical references to Sumer or the Sumerians, but the historic framework of Genesis rests upon the Sumerian civilization. There are several Sumerian loan-words in the Bible (*cf., e.g., hêḵāl*, 'palace', 'temple', from *é-gal*, 'palace'; lit. 'great house').

Sumer was a designation for the southern half of Iraq, roughly from Baghdad southwards, as opposed to the north, which was known as Akkad. It was written ideographically as *ki.en.gi(r)* but pronounced in one Sumerian dialect (*eme-sal*) as *keñir* and in another (*eme-ku*) as *sumer*. It was roughly equivalent to the area in the Bible called Shinar (*šin'ar*) (*q.v.*).

The Sumerians are an enigma in Mesopotamian history. They arrived at the head of the Persian Gulf from an unknown homeland in the latter half of the third millennium BC, speaking a language for which there are no known relatives, ancient or modern. They then applied the catalyst of their own peculiar genius, uniting the various cultural elements already in the land into a cohesive Mesopotamian culture, which in its essentials outlasted the later incursion of Amorites, Kassites, Assyrians, Persians, and many other ethnic groups to serve as the basic framework of Near Eastern civilization down to the present day. In fact, there are elements of Sumerian or early Mesopotamian culture which have been adopted by and adapted to our own general western European culture. Examples of these are the sexagesimal number system, familiar to us in telling time and measuring angles, some fundamentals of mathematics and geometry once thought to have originated with the Greeks, the basic principles of equality under law, and even some elements of artistic design and architecture. Therefore, we may well feel a sense of kinship with these amazing people of long ago.

I. ORIGIN

Following the remarkably homogeneous Obeid period of prehistoric Mesopotamia with its scores of large cities and towns characterized by a highly developed style of religious architecture, a period of division and decline set in. At about this time the Sumerians appeared at the mouth of the two great rivers and settled in the lower alluvial valley. No-one knows whence they came or in what numbers. But they probably came by sea and from the east. Unlike the periodic immigration of Semites into Mesopotamia, the stream of Sumerians soon ceased. After about a thousand years they were completely absorbed by the indigenous population and Sumerian became a dead language.

II. WRITING

The simplest and handiest criterion of different ethnic groups is language. But ancient languages can be known today only through inscriptions. Therefore, the origin of writing opens the door to more precise definition of cultural differences and provides a deeper insight into their character and nature. The close of the fourth millennium, then, marks a major milestone in the cultural history of Mesopotamia, for it was at this time that man took his earliest steps in writing. Some of these first tablets were found at the site of ancient Uruk (biblical Erech) and were inscribed in the Sumerian language. At first the script was pictographic, but it soon became stylized and the signs composed of groups of wedges, hence the name cuneiform. Evidently the Sumerians developed a system of writing because their concept of individual personal property rights under law required a means of recording all manner of legal transactions between individual owners of property. The script soon became sufficiently flexible to record all manner of material, including virtually every type of literature known to the ancient world. It thus permits us to examine all phases of Sumerian life as they themselves saw it.

III. HISTORY

The history of the Sumerians falls into three periods: (*a*) Early Sumerian, 3000–2700 BC; (*b*) Classic Sumerian, 2700–2250 BC; (*c*) Neo-Sumerian, 2100–1960 BC. It is reconstructed in each of these respective periods chiefly from epic poems, scattered historic records, and hundreds of thousands of business documents.

Fig. 198. A seated Sumerian prince. A detail from the mosaic standard found in the Royal Graves at Ur, *c.* 2600 BC.

a. The first period was dominated by three major cities: Uruk, Aratta, and Kish. The three leading figures, all rulers of Uruk, were Enmerkar, Lugalbanda, and especially Gilgamesh, who is the most famous hero of all Sumerian history. Since the historical figures and events were recovered not from contemporaneous records but from later literary compositions, it is difficult to assign the events to a given archaeological level of any of the cities mentioned (Aratta has not even been located yet). Furthermore, very little of this period has been uncovered in either Kish or Uruk. The epoch is a shadowy one, from which come faint echoes of lusty deeds performed by a young and vigorous people.

b. The classic period centres chiefly around four cities: Ur, Kish, Umma, and Lagash. The best-known rulers are Eannatum, Urukagina and Gudea of Lagash and Lugalzaggisi of Umma. By this time contemporaneous documents are extant bearing the names and recording some of the exploits of these rulers. We can therefore frequently identify many of the cities and even buildings to which reference is made in the documents. Rather more is known archaeologically than historically of Ur at this time. The names of the kings are known without reference to significant events. But the greatest treasure of all time from Mesopotamia belongs to this period—the fabulously rich 'royal tombs'. The first true historic document of any length also comes from this period and deals with strife between Umma and Lagash. Inscribed about 2400 BC at the time of Entemena of Lagash, it contains much economic and social data as well as history. But a later governor of Lagash, Gudea, is more widely known today, since scores of inscribed statues of him are extant, witnessing to the skill of sculpture in hard stone at this time. His inscriptions yield abundant data on economic and religious life. Lugalzaggisi, the last Sumerian king of the period, fell prey to the famous Semitic dynast Sargon of Agade.

c. Nearly two centuries later the Neo-Sumerian epoch with its capital at Ur rose on the ruins of the Akkadian dynasty. But Sumerian blood had thinned drastically as a result of widespread immigration of other peoples, chiefly Amorites. Only the first two of Ur's five kings actually bore Sumerian names. Nevertheless, even after all Sumerians disappeared and the language was no longer spoken it was still the language of religion, science, business, and law for many more centuries.

IV. CULTURE

Sumerian society appears at its beginning to have consisted of a collection of towns and villages clustered around a larger city which was ruled by a bicameral council of 'senators' and young arms-bearing men, both under the leadership of a 'lord' (*en*). All major decisions had to be referred to these councils, since government by representation was basic to Sumerian society. Later the term 'king' (*lugal*; lit. 'big man') was used. Possibly the concept was borrowed from neighbours, or the office itself developed with further centralizing of power. In time the power and influence of the temple and priests grew to such a degree that serious rivalry developed between palace and temple. In most cities the temple, through its vast ownership of land and its employment of skilled craftsmen, exercised considerable control over the local economy and received much revenue through rents and interest. Eventually the palace won the struggle, as the kings concentrated power under the crown by military conquest.

V. RELIGION

The difficulty in accurately describing Sumerian religion is the problem of separating theory from practice in the literary documents which purport to relate religious concepts. The highly complex pantheon with several echelons of deities, each with his particular sphere of activity, and the high-flown myths of origins are certainly creations of later speculative scribes and do not reflect common belief and daily practice. An aid in solving the problem is the large number of business documents which list actual sacrifices and gifts to the gods at the various temples, and describe ceremonies performed.

From these we learn that each city had its own special tutelary deity (Nanna of Ur, An of Uruk, Enki of Eridu, Enlil of Nippur, *etc.*), even though there were temples to several other gods in the same city. The four most prominent gods in song and worship were An (heaven-god), Enlil (air-god), Enki (water-god and god of wisdom), and Ninhursag (mother-goddess). An may have been at the head of the pantheon in very early days, but as far back as present records go (*c.* 2500 BC) Enlil is the chief of all the gods. Therefore Nippur, his city, became the chief cult centre of all Sumer, and kings of all periods even down to late Assyrian times visited the Ekur temple, Enlil's shrine in Nippur, to assure success for their reigns. In fact, the concept of 'lordship' (*namenlilla* in Sumerian) was so closely identified with the god Enlil that it became a Babylonian loan-word *ellelūlu*.

The behaviour of the gods was very human. They had fits of pique, jealousy, anger, and lust. They lied to each other, deceived one another, and committed every conceivable kind of violence. They became drunk, sick, sleepy, and even dead upon occasion. In fact, it was not so much the character but the magnitude of their powers and deeds that distinguished Sumerian gods from men.

VI. GOVERNMENT

The pattern of human government was seen as paralleled among the gods. Rulers in both spheres referred major decisions to councils of their peers. For both gods and men there were clearly defined levels of authority and delegated responsibility.

A noteworthy characteristic of Mesopotamian political theory was the concept that the earthly monarch, whether local governor or universal despot, held his kingdom under the appointment and sponsorship of the chief god, to whom he must give an account of his rulership. Originating with the Sumerians, this concept continued right down into the Neo-Assyrian Empire, in theory if not in practice. It is in direct contrast to the Egyptian idea of the absolute unquestioned authority of the divine pharaoh.

BIBLIOGRAPHY. S. N. Kramer, *History Begins at Sumer*, 1958; *id.*, *Mythologies of the Ancient World*, 1961; A. Falkenstein, *Das Sumerische*, 1959; A. Parrot, *Sumer*, 1961.

F.R.S.

SUN (Heb. *šemeš*, Gk. *hēlios*). In addition to many references which merely indicate the time of day, the Bible mentions natural effects of the sun, such as causing the fruits of the earth to grow (Dt. xxxiii. 14; 2 Sa. xxiii. 4), withering growth that is insufficiently rooted (Mt. xiii. 6), producing physical injury (Ps. cxxi. 6; Is. xlix. 10; Jon. iv. 8; Rev. vii. 16, xvi. 8, *etc.*), and inspiring the desire for life (Ec. xi. 7). The expression 'under the sun', occurring more than a score of times in the book of Ecclesiastes, may imply poetically that the sun is a witness of human conduct. Other poetical allusions, 'a tabernacle for the sun' (Ps. xix. 4) and the 'habitation' of the sun (Hab. iii. 11) may have been suggested by the Hebrew term for the setting of the sun, *bô'*, meaning literally 'to go in'. A parallel idea finds expression on certain Babylonian seals, which represent the sun issuing from a gate. Sun-worship assumed various forms in Judah (2 Ki. xxiii. 11; Ezk. viii. 16, 17).

In the Book of Psalms the sun is thrice mentioned as an emblem of constancy (Pss. lxxii. 5, 17, lxxxix. 36) and God Himself is said to be a sun (Ps. lxxxiv. 11), implying that He is the source of spiritual light and gladness. The face of Jesus at the time of the transfiguration is compared to the shining sun (Mt. xvii. 2), and it appeared to John in Patmos 'as the sun shineth in his strength' (Rev. i. 16). On the other hand, the glory of God and of Christ is declared to be greater and more enduring than sunlight (Is. xxiv. 23, lx. 19; Acts xxvi. 13; Rev. xxi. 23, xxii. 5). Malachi foretells that in 'the day of the Lord' the 'Sun of righteousness' will arise with healing in His rays for them that fear God. In its context this means that not only will the wicked be punished but the justice of God will be vindicated and the desire for righteousness of person and environment fully met (Mal. iv. 2). The Fathers understood the expression as referring to Christ, and the objection that *šemeš* is feminine cannot be pressed in view of its use in Ps. lxxxiv. 11 (see above). Part of the imagery associated with 'the day of the Lord' in Scripture is an eclipse of the sun (see Is. xiii. 10; Joel ii. 10, iii. 15; Am. viii. 9; Mt. xxiv. 29; Rev. vi. 12), while in the Apocalypse partial restriction of sunlight follows the sounding of the fourth trumpet (Rev. viii. 12). W.J.C.

SUPERSCRIPTION (Lat. *superscriptio*, 'a writing on or above', = Gk. *epigraphē*, which it translates). The word is used on two occasions in the New Testament.

1. In Mt. xxii. 20 (Mk. xii. 16; Lk. xx. 24) it is used with the word *eikōn* to refer to the head of the emperor and accompanying inscription on the obverse of a silver *denarius* (see MONEY). The *denarius* then in circulation bore the *eikōn* of the head of Tiberius and the *epigraphē* TI. CAESAR DIVI AUG. F. AUGUSTUS ('Tiberius Caesar Augustus, son of the divine Augustus').

2. In Mk. xv. 26 (Lk. xxiii. 38) the superscription is the placard, consisting of a board smeared with white gypsum and bearing in black letters the name of a condemned criminal and the offence for which he was being executed. Hence Mt. xxvii. 37 calls it an *aitia* (accusation): Jn. xix. 19, 20 uses the official Roman word *titulus*, calling it a *titlos*. This was usually hung about the criminal's neck on the way to execution, and subsequently affixed to the cross over his head. The superscription written by Pilate for Jesus in Hebrew, Greek, and Latin was 'This is Jesus of Nazareth, the King of the Jews'. D.H.W.

SUPERSTITION. See MAGIC AND SORCERY, DIVINATION.

SUPH. In Dt. i. 1 this may be a place-name (so in RV, RSV, 'over against Suph') whose location is quite uncertain (*cf. GTT*, § 431, p. 255, n. 223). In rendering 'over against the Red Sea', AV understands Suph as standing for *yam-sûp̄*, referring to the Gulf of Aqabah, which is also possible (see RED SEA). In Nu. xxi. 14 (RV, RSV), Suph(ah), 'storm'(?), is perhaps an area in which Waheb is located, in the brief quotation from the book of the wars of the Lord. Its relation to Suph in Dt. i. 1 is uncertain. Musil suggested it might be Khirbet Sufah, some 4 miles south-south-east of Madaba (*GTT*, § 441, pp. 261/2, n. 229 end). On Suph and Suphah, *cf.* also E. G. Kraeling, *JNES*, VII, 1948, p. 201. K.A.K.

SUPPER. See MEALS, LORD'S SUPPER, THE.

SURETY. A surety is a person who undertakes responsibility for a debt, or the fulfilment of an engagement by another. The word is also used to describe a pledge deposited as a security against loss or damage. It means also 'certainty'. In the latter sense we find the word used in Gn. xv. 13, xviii. 13, xxvi. 9; Acts xii. 11 (AV) (RV 'of a truth').

Scripture counsels extreme caution in standing surety (Pr. xi. 15, xvii. 18, xxii. 26, 27). The phrase 'to strike hands' is equivalent to being surety (Pr. vi. 1, 2, xvii. 18).

Judah undertook to be a personal surety for Benjamin's safety (Gn. xliii. 9, xliv. 32). The giving of hostages (2 Ki. xviii. 23; Is. xxxvi. 8) is a similar idea. The word is used of our Lord (Heb. vii. 22; *cf.* Ps. cxix. 122). M.R.G.

SUSANNA. See APOCRYPHA.

SWALLOW. See BIRDS OF THE BIBLE.

SWAN. See BIRDS OF THE BIBLE.

SWEARING. See OATHS.

SWEET CANE (Heb. *qāneh*, Is. xliii. 24; Je. vi. 20). The sweet or sugar cane (*Saccharum officinarum*) was known from ancient times to China India and Arabia, and by way of North Africa was carried by traders to the Holy Land. See COSMETICS AND PERFUMERY, V.

SWINE. The domestic swine of Palestine wa probably derived from *Sus scrofa*, the Europea wild boar. The children of Israel were divinel prohibited from eating swine (Lv. xi. 7; Dt. xi 8). It is important to note that swine are th alternate host for the parasitic tape-worm in ma contamination arises from eating infected mea

The worm develops rapidly in the alimentary canal from a small organism, living on the host's food and producing noxious effects.

The Pentateuchal prohibition grew into a national loathing with the Jews, becoming descriptive of what is despicable and hated. Thus in Pr. xi. 22 a woman of doubtful character is associated with a swine. To Jewish minds the prodigal son had reached the utter limits of paganism when feeding the swine of a Gentile (Lk. xv. 15). That there were herds of swine in the Gentile communities of Palestine and Transjordan in New Testament times is evident from Mt. viii. 30 ff.; Mk. v. 11 ff.; Lk. viii. 32 ff. The demons' plea to be sent into a nearby herd of swine would not appear strange to a Jew, who considered swine and demons of the same order. Similarly in Mt. vii. 6 Jesus warns His followers not to throw pearls before swine. The author of 2 Pet. ii. 22 regards false teachers as those who will return to their (swinish) pagan nature.

D.C.

SWORD. See ARMOUR AND WEAPONS.

SYCAMINE. See TREES.

SYCHAR. A town of Samaria, mentioned only once in the Bible under that name (Jn. iv. 5). Jesus met the woman of Samaria near Jacob's well, which lay in the neighbourhood of Sychar, and taught her the nature of spiritual worship. W. F. Albright would identify the place with ancient Shechem. The Old Syriac gospels read Shechem, which would point to an original Sychem (*cf.* Acts vii. 16), but the recent excavations of G. E. Wright at Shechem suggest that this town ceased to exist by about 100 BC. An alternative identification may be the village of Askar on the eastern slope of Mt. Ebal, about half a mile to the north of Jacob's well. There is still some doubt about the exact site (see SHECHEM).

See W. F. Albright, *The Archaeology of Palestine*, 1954, p. 247. J.A.T.

SYCOMORE. See TREES.

SYENE. See SEVENEH.

SYMBOL. This word is not found in the Bible, but the use of symbols is common to all religions. The Greek word *symbolon* had several uses, *e.g.* as a sign, pledge, token, and its importance derived from the fact that it was a representative object which guaranteed the reality of that which it symbolized. The *Oxford Dictionary* defines a symbol as 'a thing regarded by general consent as naturally typifying or representing or recalling something by possession of analogous qualities, or by association in fact or in thought'. This clear distinction between object and symbol is inevitable in analytical philosophy, but is not found in primitive thought. Malinowski emphasized that symbolism is founded, not in a relationship between an object and a sign, but in the influence that a sign or action has upon a receptive organism (*A Scientific Theory of Culture*, 1944). It is important to remember this when examining symbolism in the Bible.

I. IN THE OLD TESTAMENT

Old Testament symbols will be considered under the headings, *Personal, Objective,* and *Acted.*

a. Personal symbols

In early Israelite thought the clan or the family was the fundamental unit, not the individual. The life (*nep̄eš*) of the individuals made up the life of the group; the life of the group was extended through all the individuals. This psychological conception has been termed corporate personality (Wheeler Robinson) or group consciousness (Radcliffe Brown), and helps to explain how one person could symbolize a group of people (2 Sa. xviii. 3) or the presence of God (Ex. vii. 1).

There is an expression, *'îš hā'ĕlōhîm,* used more than seventy times and translated 'man of God', which could be translated 'divine man'. Twenty-seven times it refers to Elisha, and in the remaining instances to prophets such as Elijah and Samuel, or Moses and David. Elisha is credited with divine powers, such as restoring life (2 Ki. iv. 35) and mind reading (2 Ki. v. 26). He stands in the place of God, does the works of God, and is the symbol of God's presence. Similarly, Moses was as God to Aaron (Ex. iv. 15) and to pharaoh (Ex. vii. 1), in word and deed (Ex. xiv. 16, xvii. 9). All the prophets spoke the word of God, and when the Israelites heard them they heard God Himself; consequently, the person of the prophet was immune from harm. There is little evidence to show that the Israelite monarchy was regarded as divine, but it is possible that Solomon set himself up as a symbol of God.

b. Objective symbols

External objects were also used to symbolize the presence of God, in representative or conventional manner. The rainbow was accepted as the assurance that God's wrath had passed and that He would remember His covenant (Gn. ix. 13). Moses made a bronze serpent, symbolizing the wisdom and healing power of God (Nu. xxi. 9); golden calves were made to symbolize the great power of God (Ex. xxxii and 1 Ki. xii). More frequently objects were made without representing particular characteristics of God, one important example being the altar. The Hebrew word *mizbēaḥ*, from the root *zbḥ* ('slaughter'), suggests the place where the animal was prepared for sacrifice. One should note, however, that in the earliest accounts the Patriarchs erected altars after an appearance by God, to mark the site and claim it for Him for ever. In Israelite worship the altar symbolized the meeting-place of God with man, while the ark symbolized the presence of God because it contained the tablets of the Decalogue, and where the Word of the Lord was, there was the Lord Himself.

When the Temple was built it symbolized the

universal power of God. The Temple itself was a symbol of the earth, the brazen laver a symbol of the sea, and the golden candlestick a symbol of the sun. It was necessary that a priest should be properly vested when he entered the tabernacle or Temple, and the vestments were clearly symbolic. They were made of linen (Ex. xxviii. 39), which was regarded as having protective qualities (Lv. vi. 8–12). Two reasons are possible. As the sacrifices were animal, the flax as vegetable conferred an immunity which would not have been found in woollen or leather garments. But it is more likely that, as in many folk stories, flax was regarded as the symbol of immortality or indestructibility. Jewish scholars have suggested symbolic meanings for the colours of the vestments, and for each separate item. The ephod and breastplate symbolized the twelve tribes and judgment, and as the priest put them on they gave him power of judgment in the name of the Lord. His robe was decorated with pomegranates and bells—symbols of fertility and warnings to evil spirits. On his head was a mitre engraved with the words 'Holy to the Lord' (Ex. xxviii. 36, RSV), which made the priest himself the extension of the presence of God—His symbol.

c. Acted symbols

These symbols were actions that were illustrative or purposive beyond their immediate context. They demonstrated or introduced new circumstances. They must be distinguished from magic, which was designed to compel a particular action from God. When an Israelite slave preferred to surrender himself to permanent slavery rather than accept his freedom the owner pierced the slave's ear and fastened him to the doorpost to signify that the slave was from then on part of the household (Ex. xxi. 6). Other symbolic actions of a domestic nature were the surrender of a shoe to symbolize the surrender of all personal rights of inheritance (Ru. iv. 7) and the cutting of hair to symbolize the offering of the mourner's life to a dead relative (Is. xxii. 12).

Among religious symbolic actions, circumcision (*q.v.*) has always been a significant rite; originally connected with marriage, it was performed to avert the evil intentions of spirits that watch over the bridal chamber, but in Israel it was pushed back into childhood and then into infancy, and represents the dedication of the reproductive powers to divine guidance, and the incorporation of the child into the community.

The ceremony of the scapegoat by which the sins of the people were transferred to a goat on the Day of Atonement was a ritual of a type well known in many countries; it has been described as a clear instance of the principle of vicarious solidarity, here between priest, people, and goat (C. Lattey, *VT*, I, 1951, p. 272).

Other instances of transference by symbolic action are the red heifer (Nu. xix), which transferred uncleanness, and anointing, which transferred spiritual power (*e.g.* 1 Sa. xvi. 13).

Special attention should be paid to the importance of the symbolic actions of the prophets. These men not only proclaimed their message but performed actions to demonstrate what God would do, and thereby helped to bring about the result. They did not perform these actions to influence the will of God, but to prepare the way for that which He had decreed. Thus, Isaiah went about naked as a sign that God would bring poverty and exile upon Israel (Is. xx. 2). Jeremiah buried a new girdle in damp earth and later dug it up, spoiled, to show how Israel, once so close to God, had now been rejected and would be despoiled (Je. xiii). Ezekiel drew a city on a tile and set model siege engines round it to demonstrate the destruction of Jerusalem which God had already decided (Ezk. iv. 1–3). Other examples are in 1 Sa. xv. 27; Je. xix. 11, xxviii. 11.

II. IN THE NEW TESTAMENT

Here the situation is quite different. There are no symbolic persons; Jesus Christ was not a symbol of God, for He *was* God, as He claimed in the words, 'I and my Father are one' (Jn. x. 30). Neither could one describe the disciples as symbols, because they were servants under discipline, not representatives.

But Jesus performed symbolic actions and approved them for the Church. His healing miracles were not merely deeds of sympathy, but symbols or signs demonstrating the approach of the kingdom of God. Similarly, when He took the bread and the wine and gave them to the disciples, saying, 'Do this in remembrance of me', He was not simply exhorting them to good fellowship, but giving them a rite by which they could symbolize His presence eternally with His Church. So the Church has accepted the symbolism of the sacraments. In the bread and the wine the worshipper receives by faith the true body and blood of the Lord. In the waters of baptism sin is symbolically washed away and the person made a member of Christ's flock. In these actions the Church symbolizes its faith; the sacraments are not only illustrations but the appointed channels of divine grace. See SACRAMENTS.

In addition to the sacramental symbols, the Church has used the symbol of the cross. This is a true symbol in that it is a pictorial representation of a historical fact, a visual summary of certain essential features of the Christian faith, and at the same time a means of grace to the worshipper. In the history of Christian art there have crystallized accepted pictorial symbols of the twelve apostles, *e.g.* the keys for St. Peter, and the symbols of the four evangelists. At one time the fish was a popular symbol of the Christian faith as the letters of the Greek word for fish, *ichthys*, formed the initials of words meaning, 'Jesus Christ, son of God, Saviour'. The Christian Church has never forbidden the use of symbols, because they are rooted in the nature and experience of man, but it has not encouraged them, lest in stressing the symbol the Christian should lose the Lord Jesus Christ Himself.

BIBLIOGRAPHY. T. W. Dillistone, *Christianity and Symbolism*, 1955; E. Jenni, *Die symbolischen Handlungen der Propheten*, 1953; G. Cope, *Symbolism in the Bible and the Church*, 1958.

A.A.J.

SYMEON. See SIMEON.

SYMMACHUS' VERSION. See TEXT AND VERSIONS.

SYNAGOGUE. In the Old Testament 'synagogue' occurs only in Ps. lxxiv. 8, where it is a translation of *mô'ēḏ*. It is not definite that the reference has its present connotation. The Greek term *synagōgē* is used frequently in the LXX for the assembly of Israel, and occurs fifty-six times in the New Testament. The basic sense is a place of meeting, and thus it came to denote a Jewish place of worship. The Hebrew equivalent of the Greek noun is *k^e^nēseṯ*, a gathering of any persons or things for any purpose. In the Scriptures it is a gathering of individuals of a locality for worship or common action (Lk. xii. 11, xxi. 12). It came to refer to the building in which such meetings were held.

I. ITS SIGNIFICANCE

The importance of the synagogue for Judaism cannot be over-estimated. More than any other institution it gave character to the Jewish faith. Here Judaism learned its interpretation of the law. Ezk. xi. 16, 'Yet will I be to them as a little sanctuary', was interpreted by Jewish authorities to mean that in world-wide dispersion Israel would have the synagogue as a sanctuary in miniature to replace the loss of the Temple. Unlike the Temple, it was located in all parts of the land, and brought the people in touch with their religious leaders. A. Menes states: 'On the Sabbaths and holy days the loss of the Temple and the absence of the solemn sacrificial celebrations were keenly felt by the exiles . . . the synagogue . . . served as a substitute for the Temple. In the synagogue there was no altar, and prayer and the reading of the Torah took the place of the sacrifice. In addition the prayer house performed an important social function . . . it was a gathering point and a meeting place where the people could congregate whenever it was necessary to take counsel over important community affairs. The synagogue became the cradle of an entirely new type of social and religious life and established the foundation for a religious community of universal scope. For the first time Jewish monotheism emancipated itself in religious practice from its bonds to a specific and designated site. God was now brought to the people wherever they dwelt' ('The History of the Jews in Ancient Times', *The Jewish People*, I, pp. 78–152). Today the synagogue is still one of the dominant institutions of Judaism, and the centre of the religious life of the Jewish community. The book of Acts indicates the significant rôle the synagogue played in the propagation of the new messianic faith.

II. ITS ORIGIN

Neither the Old nor the New Testament furnishes any definite information as to the origin of the synagogue. The situation is not altered by extra-biblical sources, for there is no reference to the institution in the Apocrypha. The Apocryphal books do not even mention the burning of the synagogues of the land during the persecutions of Antiochus Epiphanes in the 2nd century BC (although a reference to this has been seen in Ps. lxxiv. 8). Before the Babylonian captivity worship was centred at the Temple in Jerusalem.

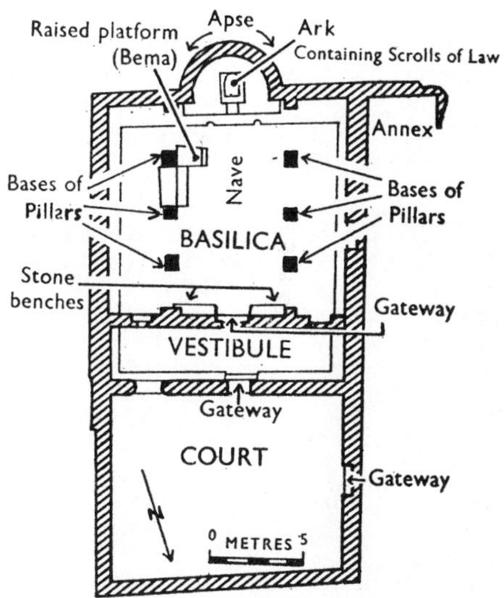

Fig. 199. A ground plan showing the design of the 3rd-century AD synagogue at Beth-Alpha.

During the Exile, when worship at Jerusalem was an impossibility, the synagogue arose as a place for instruction in the Scriptures and prayer. Such is the general opinion. R. W. Moss maintains, however, that 'the Exile marks not the first stage in the origin of the synagogue, but an important modification of its functions, worship becoming thenceforward the principal though far from the sole occupation, and the administrative functions falling for a time into abeyance' ('Synagogue' in *DCG*). In any event a probable basis for the origin of the institution is to be found in Ezk. xiv. 1: 'Then came certain of the elders of Israel unto me, and sat before me' (*cf.* Ezk. xx. 1). Levertoff asserts without equivocation, 'It must have come into being during the Bab. exile' ('Synagogue' in *ISBE*).

III. GENERAL DESCRIPTION

In the 1st century AD synagogues existed wherever Jews lived. *Cf.* Acts xiii. 5 (Salamis in Cyprus); xiii. 14 (Antioch in Pisidia); xiv. 1 (Iconium); xvii. 10 (Berea). Large cities, such as Jerusalem and Alexandria, had numerous synagogues. One legend has it that there were 394 synagogues in Jerusalem when Titus destroyed the city in AD 70; another sets the number at 480.

The Gospels speak of the synagogues of Nazareth (Mt. xiii. 54; Lk. iv. 16) and Capernaum (Mk. i. 21; Jn. vi. 59) as places where our Lord ministered. The apostle Paul found them wherever he went in Palestine, Asia Minor, and Greece. According to the Talmud (*Shabbath* 11a), it was required that synagogues be built on high ground or above surrounding houses. Archaeological evidence does not confirm such a practice for Palestine. In all probability the synagogues were constructed on the model of the Temple in Jerusalem. A. Edersheim states that the interior plan 'is generally that of two double colonnades, which seem to have formed the body of the Synagogue, the aisles east and west being probably used as passages. The intercolumnar distance is very small, never greater than 9½ feet' (*The Life and Times of Jesus the Messiah*, I, p. 435).

There was a portable ark in which the scrolls of the Law and the Prophets were kept (*Meḡillah* 3, 1). It faced the entrance of the building. On fast days the ark was carried in a procession. Before the ark and facing the worshippers were the 'chief seats' (Mt. xxiii. 6) for the religious and governing leaders of the synagogue. The Law was read from a *bēmâ* or platform (*Meḡillah* 3, 1). Ruins of such buildings can be seen at Tell Ḥum (probably the site of Capernaum), Nebartim, and other sites. The remains show the influence of a Graeco-Roman style. Synagogue ornaments were vine leaves, the seven-branched candlestick, the paschal lamb, and the pot of manna. The seats near the reading-desk were the more honourable (Mt. xxiii. 6; Jas. ii. 2, 3). Maimonides said, 'They put a platform in the middle of the house, so that he who reads from the Law, or he who speaks words of exhortation to the people, may stand upon it, and all may hear him.' Men and women were seated apart.

The Great Synagogue of tradition may have been organized by Nehemiah about 400 BC. It is said to have consisted of 120 members (*Pirqe Aboth* i. 1), who occupied themselves with the study of the law of Moses and transmitted it. The Sanhedrin succeeded it (*Aboth* x. 1). There is doubt as to the existence of the Great Synagogue, because neither the Apocrypha, nor Josephus, nor Philo mentions the body. Such silence, however, is not conclusive against the existence of such a council.

IV. ITS PURPOSE AND PRACTICE

The synagogue served a threefold purpose of worship, education, and government of the civil life of the community. Subject to the law of the land, the synagogue had its own government (Jos., *Ant.* xix. 5. 3). The congregation was governed by elders who were empowered to exercise discipline and punish members. Punishment was by scourging and excommunication. The chief officer was the ruler of the synagogue (*cf.* Mk. v. 22; Acts xiii. 15, xviii. 8). He supervised the service to see that it was carried on in accord with tradition. The attendant (Lk. iv. 20) brought the scrolls of Scripture for reading, replaced them in the ark, punished offending members by scourging, and instructed children to read. Peritz has shown that 'the primary function of the synagogue assemblies was the popular instruction in the law' ('Synagogue' in *EBi*). The dispenser of alms received the alms from the synagogue and distributed them. Finally, a competent interpreter was required to paraphrase the Law and the Prophets into the vernacular Aramaic.

Those qualified were permitted to conduct the services (Christ, Lk. iv. 16; Mt. iv. 23; Paul, Acts xiii. 15). The Sabbath was the appointed day for public worship (Acts xv. 21). The Mishnah (*Meḡillah* iv. 3) indicates that the service consisted of five parts. First, the *Shema*' was read. This prayer covers Dt. vi. 4–9, xi. 13–21; Nu. xv. 37–41. Then synagogical prayers were recited, the most ancient and best known being the eighteen petitions and benedictions.

As examples of the 'Eighteen Benedictions' these are chosen. The first reads: 'Blessed art Thou, the Lord our God, and the God of our fathers, the God of Abraham, the God of Isaac, and the God of Jacob: the great, the mighty and the terrible God, the most high God Who showest mercy and kindness, Who createst all things, Who rememberest the pious deeds of the patriarchs, and wilt in love bring a redeemer to their children's children for Thy Name's sake; O King, Helper, Saviour and Shield! Blessed art Thou, O Lord, the Shield of Abraham.' Another prayer is: 'And to Jerusalem, Thy city, Thou wilt return in mercy and wilt dwell in her midst, as Thou hast said. And do Thou build her soon in our days an eternal building, and the throne of David Thou wilt speedily establish in the midst of her.' The restoration of Israel to the land of their fathers, the return of the Shekinah glory to the Temple and rebuilt city of Jerusalem, and the re-establishment of the Davidic dynasty are recurring themes in the prayers.

These were followed by the reading of the Law. The Pentateuch, which is now read in the synagogues in annual cycles, was originally covered in three years. After the reading from the first portion of the Old Testament Canon a selection from the Prophets was read. In the time of Christ this portion was not yet fixed, but the reader was permitted to make his own choice (Lk. iv. 16 ff.). The reading of Scripture was central. The portion of the Prophets was expounded, and an exhortation drawn from it. The benediction concluded the service. Later additions were the translation and exposition of the Scripture portions read. To conduct public worship in the synagogue ten adult males were required.

'Synagogue of the Libertines' (*libertinoi*, from Lat. *libertini*, 'freedmen') was the name given to worshippers in a synagogue in Jerusalem who disputed with Stephen (Acts vi. 9). They were

:ws who had been captured in Pompey's cam-aign, then were freed later by their masters. hus the privileges of Roman citizenship were :corded them.

Reference is made in Rev. ii. 9 and iii. 9 to the ynagogue of Satan'. Since the citations are :neral in character, it is impossible with certainty) identify those who are meant by the apostle ohn. A heretical party within the infant Church ould seem to be indicated.

BIBLIOGRAPHY. Articles in *JewE, HDB, EBi*; . F. Moore, *Judaism*, I, 1927, pp. 281–307; Abrahams, *Studies in Pharisaism and the ospels*, I, 1917; A. E. Guilding, *The Fourth 'ospel and Jewish Worship*, 1960. C.L.F.

YNOPTICS. See GOSPELS.

YNTYCHE. See EUODIA.

YNZYGUS. Gk. *synzygos* (*syzygos*), 'yoke-llow', Phil. iv. 3, is treated as a personal name y *WH* margin and others, as though Paul meant 'okefellow by name and yokefellow by nature'. he word, however, is certainly to be taken as a ommon noun, the person addressed being (not ydia, supposed by S. Baring-Gould and others have been Paul's wife, but) very probably uke, who seems to have stayed in Philippi for e seven years separating the first 'we' section of cts (ending xvi. 17) from the second (beginning . 5). F.F.B.

YRACUSE. A city with a large harbour on the st coast of Sicily. Founded in 734 BC by orinthian colonists, it had by the end of the h century BC become the most important city, olitically and commercially, in Sicily, especially nder the tyrants Gelon and Dionysius I. With s allies it was strong enough to defeat the great thenian expedition to Sicily in 415–412 BC. he Romans captured it in 212 BC, in spite of a efence strengthened by the inventions of the eat mathematician Archimedes, and made it e seat of government of the province of Sicily. continued to flourish down to the 3rd century .

On the last stage of his journey to Rome Paul's ip stayed there for three days (Acts xxviii. 12), esumably waiting for a suitable wind, if, like e one that was wrecked, it was a grain ship, r Sicily as well as Africa supplied grain to ome. K.L.McK.

YRIA, SYRIANS. 1. In the English Old Testa-ent this merely denotes Aramaeans (*q.v.*).

2. The geographical entity Syria is compre-ended within the bounds set by the Taurus ountains in the north, the western bend of the uphrates river and the Arabian desert-edge from ere to the Dead Sea in the east, the Mediter-nean Sea on the west, and the Sinai isthmus at e extreme south (R. Dussaud, *Topographie istorique de la Syrie Antique et Médiévale*, 1927, . 1, 2, *etc.*; see this work generally).

3. 'Syria' is a Greek term; Nöldeke derived it from *Assyrios*, 'Assyria(n)', and this suggestion is open to the least objection. *Cf.* F. Rosenthal, *Die Aramaitische Forschung*, 1939, p. 3, n. 1.

4. Historically, ancient Syria existed as a political *unit* only during the period of the Hellenistic Seleucid monarchy, founded by Seleucus I (312–281 BC), who ruled over a realm that stretched from E Asia Minor and N Syria across Babylonia into Persia to the border of India; in 198 BC all 'Syria' belonged to this kingdom when Antiochus III finally gained Palestine from Ptolemy V of Egypt. But from 129 BC, with the

Fig. 200. Wooden handle for a spoon carved to depict a Syrian dressed in a long robe, and carrying a large double-handled jar. Second half of the second millennium BC, from Egypt.

Fig. 201. Part of a fresco from the tomb of Sebekhetep showing a group of emissaries from Syria bringing gifts of Phoenician workmanship. They wear white garments edged in blue and red which are wound below the waist. From Thebes, 15th century BC.

death of Antiochus VII, everything east of the Euphrates was lost, and the Seleucids held Syria only. After this, internal dynastic strife disrupted the shrinking state until Pompey annexed the region for Rome in 64 BC. Syria as defined in (2) above constituted the Roman province of Syria, with which Cilicia was closely associated (Judaea being separate from AD 70). See ANTIOCH (Syrian), ANTIOCHUS, ARCHAEOLOGY (Ras Shamra, Alalaẖ, *etc.*), and also *CAH*.

K.A.K.

SYRIAC VERSIONS. See TEXT AND VERSIONS.

SYROPHOENICIAN. An inhabitant of Phoenicia, which in New Testament times was part of the Roman province of Cilicia and Syria. It was a Syrophoenician woman (*syrophoinikissa*), a Greek from the region of Tyre and Sidon, who pleaded with Jesus to heal her daughter (Mk. vii. 26; *cf.* Mt. xv. 21–28).

J.A.T.

SYRTIS. See QUICKSANDS.

T

TAANACH. Modern Tell Ta'annak on the southern edge of the valley of Jezreel, guarding a pass across Mt. Carmel following the Wadi Abdullah.

Thothmes III mentions Taanach in the account of his conquest of Western Palestine (*c.* 1465 BC; *ANET*, pp. 234 ff.), as does Shishak (*q.v.*). Amarna letter 248 complains of a raid by men of Taanach on Megiddo, which was loyal to Egypt. The Israelites defeated the king of this city, but the tribe to which it was allotted, Manasseh, was unable to take possession of it (Jos. xii. 21, xvii. 11; Jdg. i. 27). It was one of the levitical cities (Jos. xxi. 25) and was also occupied by Issachar (1 Ch. vii. 29). Taanach and Megiddo are closely associated in Solomon's administrative division of Israel (1 Ki. iv. 12) and in the Song of Deborah, where 'Taanach by the waters of Megiddo' (Jdg. v. 19) is the site of the Canaanite defeat. Megiddo was, perhaps, of less importance at this time (see W. F. Albright, *The Archaeology of Palestine*, 1960, p. 117). Excavations in 1901–4 revealed a strong Late Bronze Age defensive system and some later occupation. Finds included twelve cuneiform tablets (*c.* 1450 BC) and an earthenware incense-altar of the Iron Age.

BIBLIOGRAPHY. E. Sellin, *Tell Ta'annek*, 1904; W. F. Albright, *BASOR*, 94, 1944, pp. 12–27.

A.R.M.

TABERNACLE. 1. Tabernacle (RV, more properly, 'Tent') of congregation: a provisional meeting-place of God and His people (Ex. xxxiii. 7–11).

2. The portable sanctuary in which God dwelt among the Israelites in the desert. It was used long after entry into Canaan. Under the Judges it was at Shiloh (Jos. xviii. 1), in Saul's reign at Nob (1 Sa. xxi; Mk. ii. 25, 26), and later at Gibeon (1 Ch. xvi. 39). Eventually Solomon laid it up in the Temple (1 Ki. viii. 4). It was called *miškān* = 'dwelling' (EVV 'tabernacle'), *'ōhel* = 'tent', the tabernacle of testimony (*'ēḏûṯ* = 'covenant terms') because it housed the covenant tablets, the tent (AV 'tabernacle') of meeting (*mô'ēḏ*: AV 'congregation') as the appointed meeting-place between God and His people, and the house of Jehovah (Ex. xxxiv. 26; Jos. vi. 24).

The materials used in its construction are listed at Ex. xxv. 3–7, xxxv. 5–9. The metal translated by the EVV as 'brass' was in fact copper. It was used to cover the altar, the fires of which would have melted brass. 'Blue, purple, and scarlet' refer to linen yarn or cloth dyed these colours. For a possible reconstruction, see plate XIV*a*.

I. THE CURTAINS AND COVERINGS

The term tabernacle, in its stricter sense, refers to ten linen curtains with figures of cherubim woven into the blue, purple, and scarlet tapestry work (Ex. xxvi. 1–6, xxxvi. 8–13). They each measured 28 cubits by 4, and were sewn along their length into two sets of five. Along one side of each set fifty loops of blue stuff were sewn and fifty gold clasps (AV 'taches', *q.v.*) passing through these loops joined the two sets together (see Ex. xxvi. 6, RV). The tabernacle was covered by eleven goats' hair curtains, called in strict terminology the tent (Ex. xxvi. 7–13, xxxvi. 14–18). These curtains each measured 30 cubits by 4.

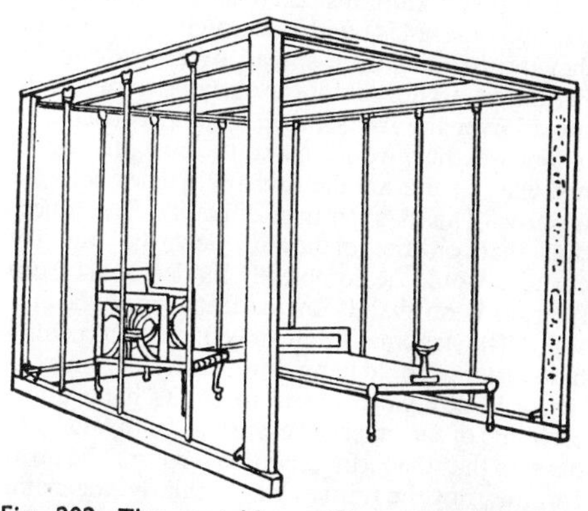

Fig. 202. The portable pavilion of Hetep-heres shown without its coverings but with chair, bed and head-rest placed within. From Giza, Egypt, c. 2600 BC.

They were sewn together along their length into two sets, one of five and the other of six, and then coupled together in the same way as the tabernacle; only here the clasps were copper and the loops presumably of goats' hair. Over the tent went two weatherproof coverings, one of rams' skins dyed red, the other of the skin of an animal which was probably the dugong (AV 'badger', RV 'seal'; Ex. xxvi. 14, xxxvi. 19).

These curtains and coverings were then draped round a framework to form the top, back, and two sides of the dwelling. The framework (Ex. xxvi. 15–30, xxxvi. 20–34) consisted of upright supports, 10 cubits high and 1½ cubits wide, each standing in two silver sockets, a talent each in weight. EVV call these supports 'boards' (*qᵉrāšîm*), but A. R. S. Kennedy (*HDB*, IV, pp. 659–662) has convincingly demonstrated that they were not solid planks but frames composed of two uprights (*yāḏôṯ*: EVV, wrongly, 'tenons') joined by cross-rails somewhat like a ladder. Frames would have three advantages over solid planks: they were much lighter, less liable to whip, and instead of hiding the tapestry curtains would form a panelling through which the curtains could be seen from the inside. Twenty frames, standing side by side, formed the south side, twenty the north, and six the west end. The two western corners were buttressed in some way by two additional frames. To keep the frames in alignment five poles (EVV 'bars') ran along both sides and the back, through gold rings attached to the cross-rails of each frame. The middle pole ran the whole length, the other four only part of the way. The frames and poles were of acacia wood overlaid with gold. The silver for the sockets was obtained from the census tax (Ex. xxx. 11–16, xxxviii. 25–27).

There are two main views as to how the curtains were draped around the framework: one, the older and more generally accepted, that the curtains were simply spread over the frames as a pall over a coffin, and the other, championed by J. Fergusson (Smith's *Dictionary of the Bible*, III, pp. 1452–1454) and since revived by others, that the curtains were spread over a ridge-pole. Fergusson argues that if the curtains were merely spread over the frames their weight, particularly in wet weather, would make the curtains sag, if not tear, in the middle and the frames collapse inwards. This is a genuine difficulty. The objection that on the orthodox view the tapestry curtains would be completely hidden apart from the roof is not valid, for the framework was not solid. The argument that only 1 cubit of goats'-hair curtain should hang down each side, whereas the orthodox view makes 10 cubits hang down each side of the tabernacle, springs from failure to observe that the term 'tabernacle' means the linen curtains, not the framework. Similarly, the claim that at the western end there was an overhanging awning called *miškān*, as distinct from the *'ōhel* (= the whole structure), is based on a misunderstanding of these technical terms (see above). There are, moreover, serious difficulties in the ridge-pole theory itself. Nowhere in the instructions is a ridge-pole mentioned. Fergusson claims the 'middle bar' of Ex. xxvi. 28 as a ridge-pole, but the natural interpretation is that the 'middle bar' was one of the five bars mentioned in the previous verse. Again, a ridge-pole would require that one of the door pillars and one of the veil pillars should be higher than the others to support the pole and there would have to be a pillar at the back of similar height. None of these things is mentioned in the directions. Then, the word used for arranging the curtains is not the normal word for pitching a tent, *nāṭâ*, but *pāraś*, which means 'to spread' (it is used for wrapping cloths round the furniture). But above all, since the back and sides are composed of open frames, the ridge-pole arrangement would leave the holy and most holy places exposed to view. Therefc the older view must be retained.

As the linen curtains (the tabernacle) we 28 cubits in length, and the goats'-hair curtai (the tent over the tabernacle) were 30 cub in length, the goats'-hair curtains would extenc cubit beyond the tabernacle at each side, ar being eleven in number, would have an ext 4 cubits over the tabernacle from front to bac The directions for the use of this extra pie read: '. . . and shalt double over the sixth curta in the forefront of the tent' (Ex. xxvi. 9b, R and again: 'And the overhanging part th remaineth of the curtains of the tent, the h curtain that remaineth, shall hang over the ba of the tabernacle' (Ex. xxvi. 12, RV). Obvious the tent was meant to cover the tabernacle at t back and front as on the two sides. At the ba the extra 2 cubits were allowed just to fall, b at the front the goats' hair was doubled over an presumably, tucked under the tabernacle curtai all the way along the top and sides, so protecti what otherwise would have been an open edge tabernacle curtain. There is no need to think w Kennedy that verse 12b is a late gloss, nor th the doubled curtain hung vertically down t front, for what would be done with the h curtain down the two sides?

II. THE INTERIOR

The interior of the dwelling was divided into t compartments by a veil hung under the cla that joined the tabernacle (Ex. xxvi. 31–3 Hence we know that the first compartment w 20 cubits deep, the second 10. The height of t frames, 10 cubits, gives us the second dimensi and in all probability the breadth of both co partments was 10 cubits likewise: for while t six frames at the back give a total breadth 9 cubits, allowance must be made for the thi ness of the frames and bars on each side. T first compartment is called 'the holy place', second 'the holy of holies', *i.e.* the most h place, or simply 'the holy place' (Lv. xvi. 2, Heb. ix. 12, x. 19, RV, *etc.*). Again, the fi compartment is sometimes called 'the first tab nacle' and the second 'the second taberna (Heb. ix. 6, 7). The dividing veil (*pārōḵeṯ*: a te used of no other hanging), made of the sa material, colours, and design as the taberna curtains, was hung by gold hooks on four acac wood pillars overlaid with gold and standing silver sockets. The pillars had no capitals. At door (= doorway) was a linen screen e broidered in blue, purple, and scarlet. It hung gold hooks on five acacia-wood pillars overl with gold standing in copper sockets. Th pillars did have capitals and were overlaid w gold, as were their fillets (Ex. xxvi. 36, 37, xx 37, 38). To distinguish the *pārōḵeṯ* from t screen the *pārōḵeṯ* is sometimes called the *sec* veil.

In the most holy place stood the ark (Ex. x 10–22, xxxvii. 1–8; see ARK OF THE COVENAN A slab (EVV 'mercy seat') of pure gold wit erub at each end rested on top. The name of is slab, *kappōreṯ*, is the subject of some contro-ersy. Some, taking its root *kpr* = to cover, anslate *kappōreṯ* as 'lid'. But whatever the iginal meaning of *kpr* was, in levitical ritual it eant 'propitiate', and on the Day of Atonement ood was sprinkled on the *kappōreṯ*. Hence it is r more likely that *kappōreṯ* meant 'propitiatory' o LXX and New Testament *hilastērion*). Accord-g to the *MT* the rings for the carrying poles ere placed by the 'feet' of the ark, but these are where described and some have felt that 'foot' *a'am*) is a mistake for 'corner' (*pē'â*). The AV so nders it. Regarding the poles there seems to be discrepancy between Ex. xxv. 15 and Nu. iv. 6; ssibly the poles normally remained in their ngs, but were temporarily removed to facilitate e covering of the ark for transport.

In the holy place in front of the veil was the cense altar (Ex. xxx. 1–10, xxxvii. 25–28). Made acacia wood and overlaid with pure gold—nce its other name, 'the golden altar'—it was a bit square and 2 cubits high, with horns pro-cting at the four corners and an ornamental ld moulding round the top. For transport, two les were shot through gold rings attached just der the moulding. The altar stood directly posite the ark (note the emphasis of xxx. 6), d so was regarded as 'belonging to' the most ly place (*cf.* 1 Ki. vi. 22 and Heb. ix. 4, where olden altar of incense' and not 'censer' seems be the right translation).

Somewhere along the north side stood a table r the presence-bread (Ex. xxv. 23–30, xxxvii.)–16; see TABLE and SHOWBREAD). In its ser-ce were used three kinds of pure gold vessels. hese are called in RV: (1) dishes, *i.e.* flat plates, ed probably to convey the bread to and from e table, and perhaps also to contain the bread hile on the table; (2) spoons, or perhaps cups, obably for incense (Lv. xxiv. 7); (3) flagons and wls, perhaps for wine; but the Old Testament es not connect wine with the presence-bread, d this accounts for the AV translation 'to cover ithal' instead of 'to pour out withal'.

On the south side stood the lampstand (EVV andlestick'; Ex. xxv. 31–40, xxxvii. 17–24, xl.). See LAMP. The table and lampstand from erod's Temple are both represented on Titus' rch at Rome. Some doubt is cast, however, on e accuracy of these sculptures, since on the mpstand's base various non-Jewish figures pear.

III. LOCATION AND SURROUNDINGS

he tabernacle stood in the western half of a urtyard, 100 × 50 cubits, the long sides run-ng north and south (Ex. xxvii. 9–19, xxxviii. -20). The tabernacle door faced east. The court-rd was bounded by a linen screen (EVV angings') 5 cubits high hung on pillars. There as an opening for a gate, 20 cubits wide, set ntrally in the east end. The gate screen was en, embroidered in blue, purple, and scarlet. e pillars were apparently made of acacia wood (they are not mentioned in the list of copper articles, Ex. xxxviii. 29–31), and stood in copper sockets. They were stabilized by guy ropes and pegs, and had capitals overlaid with silver and silver bands, called fillets, round the neck. Two main methods are advocated for spacing the pillars: (1) On the assumption that there was one pillar per 5 cubits of hanging, and that no pillar was counted twice, sixty pillars in all are placed to make twenty spaces along the two long sides and ten spaces along the two ends. The gate screen then hangs on four of its own pillars and one of the others, thus:

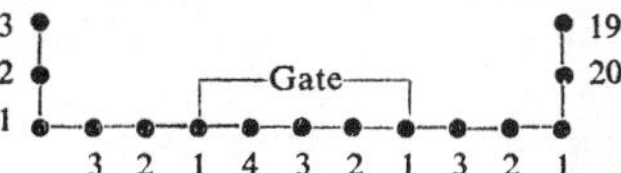

It is questionable whether this satisfies the direction for the 20 cubits of gate-screen '. . . *their pillars four* . . .' (2) Abandoning the assumption that the pillars were necessarily spaced 5 cubits apart, we may suppose that the corner pillars were counted twice as belonging, from the observer's viewpoint, to both end and side. This gives a total of only fifty-six pillars, but the text does not explicitly state that the total was sixty. The gate could then be recessed to give entrance at the sides and to allow the screen to hang constantly in place, thus:

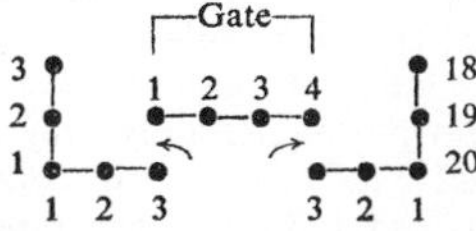

But this system gives very awkward measurements for the spaces between the pillars.

In the eastern half of the court stood first an altar, called the copper altar from its covering material, and the altar of burnt-offering from the chief sacrifice offered on it (Ex. xxvii. 1–8, xxxviii. 1–7). See fig. 176. It was a hollow framework of acacia wood, 5 cubits square and 3 high, with projecting horns at the top corners. The whole was overlaid with copper. Halfway up the altar, on the outside, was a horizontal ledge (AV 'compass') running all round. Running vertically all round, and reaching from the ground up to the ledge, was copper grating work, on the four corners of which were rings through which went acacia-wood poles overlaid with copper for transport purposes. The purpose of the ledge is not stated, nor is the function of the grating. The latter may have been designed to prevent the priests from treading in the blood poured at the base of the altar (Lv. iv. 7). Apparently the altar had no top, for none is mentioned, whereas with the golden altar the top is specifically mentioned. Consequently, some assume that the hollow framework was filled up with earth. The alternative is to suppose that the sacrifice was burned on the ground inside the framework, which would then act as a kind of incinerator. In the service of the altar the following copper vessels were used: (1) pots and shovels, to remove the ashes; (2) basins, presumably for the blood; (3) fleshhooks; (4) fire-pans, in which the fire may have been carried on the march.

Between the altar and the tabernacle door stood the laver (Ex. xxx. 17–21, xxxviii. 8, xl. 29–32). It was a copper basin, standing on a copper 'foot', and was made from the mirrors of the serving women. It held water for the priests' ablutions. Nothing is told us of its size, shape, ornamentation, or transport. In fact, the laver is missing from the instructions set out in the *MT* of Nu. iv, but it is mentioned in the LXX version, and its omission from the *MT* may be accidental. For all the other parts of the tabernacle detailed instructions for transport are given.

In camp the tabernacle was surrounded by two ranks of tents. In the first were the Levites, in the second the twelve tribes, three camping on each side (Nu. ii, iii. 1–39).

IV. PROBLEMS ARISING

The literary and historical problems surrounding the tabernacle are so bound up with the larger problem of the Old Testament that it would be idle to attempt a discussion, let alone a solution, of them here, but a few observations may be made on the prominent features.

1. It is alleged that the instructions are in parts impracticable and evidently the work of an idealist. But here much will depend on what view is held of God's purpose in including these records in Scripture. Certainly they are not the fully detailed blue-prints from which Moses' workmen worked, but rather general records 'for our learning'. Hence many practical details are omitted. At the same time portable shrines, employing practically the same constructional techniques as the tabernacle, are now known to have been in use in Egypt before the time of Moses; see K. A. Kitchen, *Tyndale House Bulletin*, 5, 6, 1960, pp. 7–13.

2. In the *MT* the altar of incense and laver come in Ex. xxx and not as expected in Ex. xxv and xxvii respectively. The liberal explanation is that Ex. xxx is a later addition to the already late P writings. On the other hand, there is much to be said for the present order being deliberate and original: see A. H. Finn, 'The Tabernacle Chapters', *JTS*, XVI, 1915, pp. 449–482, and *WDB* (*s.v.* 'Tabernacle').

3. From the wide divergence of the LXX from the *MT* it has been thought that the last chapters of Exodus in Hebrew had not yet reached their final form when the LXX was translated; and that the LXX followed in part a Hebrew tradition which knew of no incense altar. These conclusions have been proved unjustified: see the present writer's monograph *The Account of the Tabernacle*, 1959.

4. It is said that in the Pentateuch, as we now have it, there is conflict and discrepancy between the primitive 'tent of meeting' of the older E source and the elaborate, unhistorical tabernacle of the later P sources. But here again the existen of the conflict is a matter not of fact but interpretation: see J. Orr, *The Problem of the O Testament*, 1906, pp. 165–173, and A. H. Fin *The Unity of the Pentateuch*, 1917, pp. 255–28

V. CONCLUSION

It follows from the fact that the tabernacle w built to God's design that it had symbol significance for its own times. How far symbols were also types of spiritual realiti revealed to us is disputed. Doubtless, the extr vagant interpretations that from the ear centuries have been placed upon the subject ha brought it into disrepute. But the New Testame explicitly says that the tabernacle was 'a co and shadow of heavenly things', 'a parable', 'li in pattern to the true (tabernacle)' (Heb. viii. ix. 9, 24). Particular pieces of the furniture a quoted in the New Testament evidently with su significance attached to them, *e.g.* the veil a most holy place (Heb. vi. 19, x. 19, 20), incen altar and ark (Rev. viii. 3, xi. 19), and perha also mercy-seat (Rom. iii. 25, AV 'propitiation' and the implication of Heb. ix. 5 is that the writ could have given such an interpretation of all t tabernacle furniture.

BIBLIOGRAPHY. A. R. S. Kennedy, *HDB*, I pp. 653–668; this article is still definitive for mo reconstructional problems and contains refe ences to all the ancient sources and comment tors; K. A. Kitchen, 'Some Egyptian Bac ground to the Old Testament', *Tyndale Hou Bulletin*, 5, 6, 1960. D.W.G.

TABERNACLES, FEAST OF. Heb. *ḥag̃ ha sukkôṯ*, 'festival of booths' (Lv. xxiii. 34; Dt. x 13), or *ḥag̃ hā'āsîp̄*, 'festival of ingathering' (E xxiii. 16, xxxiv. 22). This was one of the thr great pilgrimage-festivals of the Jewish year; was kept for seven days from the fifteenth to t twenty-second day of the seventh month. It ca at the end of the year when the labours of the fie were gathered in, and was one of the three annu festivals at which every male was required appear (Ex. xxiii. 14–17, xxxiv. 23; Dt. xvi. 1 It was a time of rejoicing (Dt. xvi. 14). T designation 'feast of booths (tabernacles)' com from the requirement for everyone born Israelite to live in booths made of boughs trees and branches of palm trees for the sev days of the feast (Lv. xxiii. 42). Sacrifices we offered on the seven days, beginning with thirte bullocks and other animals on the first day a diminishing by one bullock each day until on t seventh seven bullocks were offered. On t eighth day there was a solemn assembly when o bullock, one ram, and seven lambs were offer (Nu. xxix. 36). This is the last day, 'that great d of the feast', which is probably alluded to in J vii. 37. As a feast, divinely instituted, it was nev forgotten in Israel. It was observed in the time Solomon (2 Ch. viii. 13), Hezekiah (2 Ch. xx 22), and after the Exile (Ezr. iii. 4; Zc. xiv. 16, 19). The ceremony of water-pouring, associat with this festival in post-exilic times and reflected in Jesus' proclamation in Jn. vii. 37 f., is not prescribed in the Pentateuch. Its recognition of rain as a gift from God, necessary to produce fruitful harvests, is implied in Zc. xiv. 17 (*cf.* 1 Sa. vii. 6).

This feast had a historical reference to the Exodus from Egypt and reminded the Jews of their wandering and dwelling in booths in the wilderness (Lv. xxiii. 43). However, this is not evidence of the conversion of the agricultural festival to a historical one. Rather it points to the truth that Israel's life rested upon redemption which in its ultimate meaning is the forgiveness of sin (2 Ch. xxx. 22). This fact separates this feast from the harvest festivals of the neighbouring nations whose roots lay in the mythological activity of the gods.

BIBLIOGRAPHY. T. H. Gaster, *Thespis*, 1950, pp. 317–336; C. H. Gordon, *Ugaritic Literature*, 1949, pp. 5 f., 57–63. D.F.

TABITHA. See DORCAS.

TABLE. This word is used in AV as a translation of the Lat. *tabula* in its various uses.

1. A writing-tablet or board of wood or ivory inlaid with a wax surface on which writing was impressed with a stylus (Heb. *lûaḥ*; Assyr. *lê'u*). Such boards were in use from at least the 8th century BC as an alternative to other writing material (Is. xxx. 8; Hab. ii. 2). *Cf.* Lk. i. 63, where Zacharias makes use of a *pinakidion*, which is the diminutive of *pinax*, the common Greek word for a writing-tablet. *Cf.* also 1 Macc. viii. 22 (Gk. *deltos*). See WRITING.

2. A flat, usually rectangular, surface either of stone or metal prepared for writing. In this sense 'table' is commonly used of the stone tablets bearing the Decalogue (Ex. xxiv. 12; *cf.* Heb. ix. 4) and figuratively of the prepared heart (Pr. iii. 3, vii. 3; Je. xvii. 1; *cf.* 2 Cor. iii. 3). In both the New Testament references the Greek word used is *plax*, meaning a flat stone. Heb. *lûaḥ* is also used of a plank used in the construction of the altar (Ex. xxvii. 8), a ship (Ezk. xxvii. 5), a door (Ct. viii. 9), and the metal plates at the base of Solomon's lavers (1 Ki. vii. 36). All these were potential surfaces for inscriptions.

3. A table as an article of furniture (Heb. *šulḥān*; Gk. *trapeza*). The table in the steppe, or wilderness (Pss. xxiii. 5, lxxviii. 19), was a prepared area or skin laid out on the ground (Heb. *šlḥ*). Elsewhere the word is used, as its modern counterpart, for the table made of wood or metal which was a common item of furniture (2 Ki. iv. 10). To eat 'at the king's table' was a signal honour (2 Sa. ix. 7; *cf.* Lk. xxii. 21), while to eat at 'one's own table', as well as having its literal meaning, denoted living at one's own expense (1 Ki. xviii. 19; Ne. v. 17). 'The table of the Lord' (Mal. i. 7, 12; Ezk. xli. 22, xliv. 16; 1 Cor. x. 21) implies that at which He is the host (see ALTAR). Ps. lxix. 22 is of uncertain meaning. D.J.W.

TABLET. See TABLE, WRITING.

TABOR. If Jos. xix. 22; Jdg. viii. 18; and 1 Ch. vi. 77 refer to the same place, Tabor was on the Zebulun–Issachar border; and it was presumably on or near Mt. Tabor. The 'oak', or 'terebinth' (RVmg), of 1 Sa. x. 3 must have been at a different Tabor, in Benjamite territory. D.F.P.

TABOR, MOUNT. A notable mountain rising from the Plain of Jezreel to 1,843 feet above sea-level. Its slopes are steep, and the views from the summit magnificent; hence it was considered worthy of comparison with Mt. Hermon, in spite of the latter's much greater bulk and height. An idolatrous shrine was set up on it in Hosea's day (*cf.* Ho. v. 1). In later times there was a town on the summit, which was taken and then fortified by Antiochus III in 218 BC. In 53 BC it was the scene of a battle between the Romans and Alexander the son of Aristobulus. Josephus, in his rôle as Jewish general, gave the town on the summit a defensive rampart in AD 66; remains of this wall can still be seen. The mountain also figured in the events of Crusader times.

Since the 4th century AD, and perhaps earlier, tradition has held that Mt. Tabor was the scene of the transfiguration. This is not very likely, especially in view of the town that was on the summit in New Testament days.

The Arabs called the mountain Jabal al-Tur; the Israelis have given it its old Hebrew name, *Har Tāḇôr*. D.F.P.

TABRET. See MUSIC AND MUSICAL INSTRUMENTS.

TACHES (Heb. *qᵉrāsîm*). Hooks, or clasps (so RV; LXX *krikoi* is inexact), used in the tabernacle (Ex. xxvi. 6, 11, 33, *etc.*). Fifty gold taches coupled the linen curtains, and fifty copper ones the goats'-hair curtains. See TABERNACLE, I. D.W.G.

TADMOR. This place-name occurs twice in AV (1 Ki. ix. 18; 2 Ch. viii. 4), and poses problems. Tadmor in AV in 1 Ki. ix. 18 is based on *qᵉrē'* and the ancient versions. The *kᵉṯîḇ* is *tāmār*. The ancient versions have 'Palmyra' (Gk. for 'palm tree' = Heb. *tāmār*). The problem is whether the Tamar of 1 Ki. ix. 18 (RV, RSV) is identical with the Tadmor of 2 Ch. viii. 4. The following solutions are proposed: 1. Later in the time of the Chronicler, when the government of Solomon was idealized, the unimportant Tamar of the Judaean desert was changed to the then well-known, illustrious Tadmor in the Syrian desert. 2. *Qᵉrē'* and the ancient versions are to be followed in identifying the place in 1 Ki. ix. 18 with Tadmor, the later Palmyra in the Syrian desert. 3. Tamar of 1 Ki. ix. 18 and Tadmor of 2 Ch. viii. 4 are different places. Tamar, the modern *Kurnub*, called *Thamara* in the *Onomasticon* of Eusebius, was situated on the route between Elath and Hebron. This city was fortified to protect the trade with S Arabia and the seaport Elath. Tadmor was the famous trading-centre north-east of Damascus and could have been brought under Solomon's rule with the operations against the Syrian Hamath and Zobah.

The third solution is acceptable, because Tamar in 1 Ki. ix. 18 is expressly called 'in the land' and thus in Israelite territory (*cf.* also Ezk. xlvii. 19, xlviii. 28). F.C.F.

TAHPANHES. An important Egyptian settlement in the E Delta, named with Migdol, Noph (Memphis), *etc.* (Je. ii. 16, xliv. 1, xlvi. 14; Ezk. xxx. 18 as Tehaphnehes), to which certain Jews fled *c.* 586 BC, taking thither the prophet Jeremiah (Je. xliii). The same consonantal spelling *Tḥpnḥs* recurs in a Phoenician papyrus letter of the 6th century BC found in Egypt (*cf.* A. Dupont-Sommer, *PEQ*, LXXXI, 1949, pp. 52–57). The LXX form Taphnas, Taphnais, probably equates Tahpanhes with the Pelusian Daphnai of Herodotus (ii. 30, 107) where the XXVIth Dynasty pharaoh Psammetichus I (664–610 BC) established a garrison of Greek mercenaries. On grounds of geographical location, the equivalence of Arabic Defneh with Daphnai, and the excavation at Defneh of Greek pottery and other objects, Tahpanhes-Daphnai is located at modern Tell Defneh ('Defenneh'), about 27 miles SSW of Port Said. The Egyptian for Tahpanhes is not inscriptionally attested, but may be **T'-ḥ(wt)-p'-nḥsy*, 'mansion of the Nubian', names compounded with *nḥsy*, 'Nubian', being known elsewhere in Egypt (so Spiegelberg).

'Pharaoh's house in Tahpanhes' and the 'brickwork' (RV) at its entry in which Jeremiah hid stones to presage Nebuchadrezzar's visitation there (Je. xliii. 9) may just possibly be the fortress of Psammetichus I, with traces of a brick platform on its north-west side, excavated by Petrie (*Nebesheh* (*Am*) *and Defenneh* (*Tahpanhes*) bound with *Tanis II*, 1888). K.A.K.

TAHPENES. An Egyptian queen whose sister the pharaoh married off to Hadad of Edom, 1 Ki. xi. 19, 20 (see PHARAOH, II 6). B. Grdseloff (*Revue de l'Histoire Juive en Égypte*, No. 1, 1947, pp. 88–90) takes Heb. *tḥpns* as a transcription of the Egyptian title *t(')-ḥ(mt)-p(')-ns(w)*, 'Royal Wife'. W. F. Albright (*BASOR*, 140, 1955, p. 32) postulates an Egyptian name **T(')-ḥ(nt)-p(')-* (or *pr-*) *-ns(w)*, for which partial parallels exist. K.A.K.

TAHTIM-HODSHI. In 2 Sa. xxiv. 6 a place in the north of David's realm, near the frontier with the kingdom of Hamath, mentioned in his census record. On the basis of LXX, *MT 'ereṣ taḥtîm ḥoḏšî* (AV 'the land of Tahtim-hodshi') has been very plausibly emended to *qāḏēš 'ereṣ ha-ḥittîm* (RSV 'Kadesh in the land of the Hittites'). See HITTITES, KADESH. F.F.B.

TALE. The AV rendering of four Hebrew words, each of which is thus translated once only. Three of them mean 'number': *mispār* (1 Ch. ix. 28); *maṯkōneṯ*, 'measure', 'proper quantity' (Ex. v. 8); and *tōḵen*, 'a weight', 'measure' (Ex. v. 18).

In the fourth occurrence the Hebrew word is *hegeh*, which could mean 'meditation' or 'utterance' and is found in the phrase 'as a tale that is told' (Ps. xc. 9), a rendering much disputed. LXX and Vulg. read 'as a spider's web'. The literal translation is 'like a sigh', and this is retained by RSV. See also TALEBEARING. J.D.D.

TALEBEARING, SLANDER. These words translate, in the Old Testament, expressions implying secrecy (Pr. xviii. 8, RSV 'whisperer'), evil report (Nu. xiv. 36, RSV), the giving out (Ps. l. 20) or carrying (Pr. xi. 13) of slander, or the (wrong) use of tongue (Ps. ci. 5) or feet (2 Sa. xix. 27). In the New Testament the words translate accusation (1 Tim. iii. 11, *diabolos*), speaking against (2 Cor. xii. 20; 1 Pet. ii. 1, *katalalia*) or defaming (Rom. iii. 8, *etc.*, *blasphēmeō*). All talebearing, whether false (*cf.* Mt. v. 11) or not (*cf.* Dn. iii. 8), malicious (Ps. xxxi. 13; Ezk. xxii. 9) or foolish (Pr. x. 18; *cf.* xviii. 8 = xxvi. 22; Mt. xii. 36), especially between neighbours (Je. ix. 4) or brothers (Jas. iv. 11), is condemned (Lv. xix. 16) and punished (Ps. ci. 5) by God, and causes quarrelling (Pr. xxvi. 20). Slander springs from the heart (Mk. vii. 22) of the natural man (Rom. i. 30), excludes from God's presence (Ps. xv. 3), and must be banished from the Christian community (2 Cor. xii. 20; Eph. iv. 31; Col. iii. 8; 1 Pet. ii. 1; *cf.* (of women) 1 Tim. iii. 11; Tit. ii. 3), which itself suffers slander (Mt. v. 11; *cf.* Rom. iii. 8). P.E.

TALENT. See WEIGHTS AND MEASURES, MONEY.

TALITHA CUMI. 'Damsel, arise'. Mk. v. 41 records these words spoken by Jesus in a Galilaean Aramaic dialect to the daughter of Jairus, the Jewish leader. The word used for damsel comes from a root meaning 'lamb' and is an affectionate term, like the English 'lambkin'. MSS א, B, C read *koum* for *koumi*. This is due to the fact that the final letter is not pronounced in some dialects. R.A.H.G.

TALMAI. 1. A descendant of 'Anaq (see ANAK) resident in Hebron at the time of the conquest (Nu. xiii. 22) but driven out by Caleb (Jos. xv. 14). He is described as a Canaanite in Jdg. i. 10 which records his death.

2. The son of Ammihud and ruler of Geshur. David married his daughter Maacah, who bore Absalom (2 Sa. iii. 3; 1 Ch. iii. 2). After the assassination of Amnon Absalom fled for refuge with Talmai in Geshur (2 Sa. xiii. 37). See GESHUR. The (Hurrian?) name Talmai occurs in Syrian texts (Alalaḫ) of the 14th century BC. D.J.W.

TALMUD AND MIDRASH.

I. TALMUD

Because much ignorance exists on the subject of the Talmud and its related literature, it will ell to define terms. As to form, the Talmud is mposed of the *Mishnah*, the oral law which as in existence by the end of the 2nd century), and was collected by Rabbi Judah the ince; and the *Gemara*, the comments of the abbis from AD 200 to 500 on the Mishnah. As contents the Talmud contains *Halakhah*, legal actments and precepts with the elaborate dis-ssions whereby decisions were reached; and *aggadah*, non-legal interpretations. The Talmud the source from which Jewish law is derived. is binding for faith and life on orthodox Jews. iberal Jews do not consider it authoritative, ough interesting and venerable. It is important r our knowledge of how the Jews interpreted e Old Testament. It also throws light on rtions of the New Testament.

The position is taken that the law of Moses d to be adapted to changing conditions in rael. The claim is made that the 'Great Syna-gue' (120 men) had such authority, but there is proof to support the assertion. Rabbi Akiba . AD 110–35) or an earlier scholar made a mprehensive collection of traditional laws. abbi Judah the Prince utilized this material ong with other portions in his edition of the ishnah. The earliest collection of Mishnah may assigned to the time of the noted schools of illel and Shammai, who flourished at the time the second Temple.

The Mishnah is divided on three principles:) subject-matter; (2) biblical order; and (3) arti-ial devices, such as numbers. The Mishnah is und in six orders or main divisions (called *dārîm*), which contain the material of sixty eatises. The main categories are subdivided into actates, chapters, and paragraphs. The first der (Seeds) treats of agricultural laws and ligious duties relating to cultivation of the nd, including commandments concerning the ibute of agricultural products to be given to the riest, the Levite, and the poor. The second ivision (Feasts) sets forth the various festivals f the religious calendar, including the observ-nce of the sabbath, with the ceremonies and crifices to be brought on those days. The third rder (Women) deals with the laws of marriage, ivorce, the levirate marriage, adultery, and gulations for the Nazirite.

The fourth division of the Mishnah (Fines) andles civil legislation, commercial transactions f different kinds, legal procedures, and a collec-on of the ethical maxims of the Rabbis. Sacred hings, the fifth order of the Mishnah, presents gislation concerning sacrifices, the first-born, ean and unclean animals, together with a escription of Herod's Temple. The sixth part of e Mishnah (Purifications) lays down the laws ouching levitical cleanness and uncleanness, ean and unclean persons and objects, and urifications. In all these portions it was the aim f Rabbi Judah to differentiate between current nd obsolete law, and between civil and religious ractices.

The Mishnah is marked by brevity, clarity, and comprehensiveness, and was employed as a text-book in rabbinical academies. After the editing of the Mishnah, it soon became the official standard of the Academies of Palestine (Tiberias, Caesarea, Sepphoris, and Lydda) and Babylonia (Sura, Pumbedita, and Nehardea), resulting in the Palestinian Talmud and the Babylonian Talmud respectively. Discussion in these seats of learning became the nucleus for the study of the law, which became known as the Talmud.

The greater part of the discussions in the Talmud is in dialogue form. The dialogue intro-duces questions and seeks after causes and origins. There are numerous lengthy digressions into the Haggadah. This is actually a literary device to relieve the complexity and monotony of legal discussions. The extant Talmud is a com-mentary on only two-thirds of the Mishnah. It contains rejected as well as accepted decisions of the law. The observation of A. Darmesteter is amply justified: 'The Talmud, exclusive of the vast Rabbinic literature attached to it, represents the uninterrupted work of Judaism from Ezra to the sixth century of the common era, the resul-tant of all the living forces and of the whole religious activity of a nation. If we consider that it is the faithful mirror of the manners, the institu-tions, the knowledge of the Jews, in a word of the whole of their civilization in Judea and Baby-lonia during the prolific centuries preceding and following the advent of Christianity, we shall understand the importance of a work, unique of its kind, in which a whole people has deposited its feelings, its beliefs, its soul' (*The Talmud*, p. 7).

II. MIDRASH

The term *midrash* derives from the Hebrew root *dāraš*, 'to search out, investigate', that is, to dis-cover a thought not seen on the surface. It has reference, then, to a didactic or homiletic ex-position. It occurs twice in the Old Testament, in 2 Ch. xiii. 22, where the 'story' (AV) or 'com-mentary' (RV) of the prophet Iddo is spoken of, and in 2 Ch. xxiv. 27, where the 'story' (RV 'commentary') of the book of the Kings is re-ferred to. 'They were probably didactic develop-ments of the historical narratives we possess, making use of these narratives to emphasize some religious truth; but nothing is known of them beyond their titles' (*HDB*, I, p. 459).

Our term has received its widest usage in extra-biblical context. Midrash is sometimes used in contrast to Mishnah, in which case it denotes that branch of rabbinic learning which has especially to do with the rules of traditional law. It is impossible at this stage of our study to state which is the older method of study, Midrash or Mishnah. (See G. F. Moore, *Judaism*, I, pp. 150 ff.) Suffice it to say, after the return of the Jews from Babylon with the activity of Ezra and his school on behalf of the law, exposition and commentary for the congregation became a necessity. The oral form of these commentaries was later crystallized into writing. Since the greater portion of the important works is no longer extant in the original composition, the date of compilation is almost impossible to ascertain. Midrashic activity came to an end soon after the completion of the Babylonian Talmud. In time the Midrash was displaced by the disciplines of history, grammar, and theology.

Midrashim are divided into expositional and homiletical. The former comment on the text of Scripture according to their present order, or join to them tales, parables, and the like (H. L. Strack, *Introduction to Talmud and Midrash*, pp. 201–205). The latter deal with individual texts, mostly from the beginnings of Scriptural lections. Midrashim exist on the Pentateuch, the Five Rolls, Lamentations, the Psalms, Proverbs, and other books.

BIBLIOGRAPHY. *HDB* (*s.v.* 'Commentary'); B. Cohen, 'Talmudic and Rabbinical Literature', *The Jewish People*, III, pp. 54–79; G. F. Moore, *Judaism*, 3 vols., 1927–30; H. L. Strack, *Introduction to Talmud and Midrash*, 1931; *JewE* (*s.v.* 'Midrash'). C.L.F.

TAMAR (*tāmār*, 'palm'). **1.** The wife, first of Er the eldest son of Judah, then of Onan (Gn. xxxviii. 6 ff.). After Onan's death his father Judah, not recognizing Tamar, became by her the father of twins, Perez and Zerah. The story of Tamar reveals something of the marriage customs in early Israel. See ONAN and MARRIAGE, IV.

2. Daughter of David, violated by Amnon her half-brother, and avenged by Absalom (2 Sa. xiii. 1 ff.; 1 Ch. iii. 9). **3.** A daughter of Absalom (2 Sa. xiv. 27). **4.** A city in south-east Judah (Ezk. xlvii. 19, xlviii. 28), near the Dead Sea. For discussion of location, see TADMOR. J.D.D.

TAMARISK. See TREES.

TAMMUZ. Ezekiel, in a vision, saw women sitting in the north gate of the Temple in Jerusalem weeping for 'the Tammuz' (Ezk. viii. 14). This mourning for the god Tammuz took place on the second day of the fourth month (June/July), which was named after this event (see CALENDAR). It commemorated the legendary death of the Sumerian deity Dumu.zi ('true son'), the prediluvian shepherd and husband of Ishtar. On his death, Ishtar mourned and called on all to do so. When she entered the underworld all birth, life, and joy ceased. It is now known that Tammuz did not rise to life with Ishtar's return, for he later appears as a god of the underworld. Those who see him as a dying and rising vegetation-deity take this to typify the disappearance of vegetation in the summer and its revival in the following spring rains. The cult figures little in Assyrian and Babylonian religion except for the Tammuz-liturgies, which support the myth. It seems to have become popular, however, in Syria and Phoenicia, where a similar legend is told of Adonis and Aphrodite. A reference to the planting of gardens to these deities is possibly given in Is. xvii. 10. The temple of Aphrodite in Gebal, Syria, was a principal centre of this cul also known in Egypt, where Adonis was identifie with Osiris.

BIBLIOGRAPHY. S. H. Hooke, *Babylonian a Assyrian Religion*, 1953, pp. 36–46. D.J.W.

TANNING, TANNER. See ARTS AND CRAFTS.

TAPPUAH ('apple-tree'). **1.** A Canaanite tow south of Shechem in Ephraim, near the border Manasseh (Jos. xvi. 8), whose king was defeat by Joshua (xii. 17). Probably modern Tell Sheik Abu Zarad, near Jasuf. Also called En-Tappua 'spring of Tappuah' (Jos. xvii. 7); *cf.* the 'Tip sah' of 2 Ki. xv. 16, which is probably to equated with Tappuah.

2. A town of Judah, in the lowlands east Azekah (Jos. xv. 34); *cf.* Beth-tappuah, 'hou of Tappuah', in the mountains west of Hebro connected with the sons of Caleb (Jos. xv. 53 and probably the modern Taffuh.

3. The name of one of the sons of Hebr (1 Ch. ii. 43). B.F.H.

TARES (Gk. *zizania*, Arab. *zuwān*; RVmg, N 'darnel'; RSV 'weeds'). A general word used denote any kind of vetch, but in Mt. xiii. 25 referring probably to the bearded darnel (*Loliu temulentum*). In the blade these tares resemb wheat, but if the biblical counsel be followed an both are allowed to grow together till harve (Mt. xiii. 30) the weed is clearly distinguishe and usually to women and children falls t tedious manual task of separation. The tares a often used as chicken food. Sowing tares in field for purposes of revenge (*cf.* Mt. xiii. 25 was a crime under Roman legislation. J.D.D.

TARGET. See ARMOUR AND WEAPONS, I*a*.

TARGUMS. The word *targum* is Hebre although not found in the Old Testament. means an Aramaic paraphrase, or interpretati translation, of some part of the Old Testamen After the Babylonian captivity, Arama gradually came to replace Hebrew as the nati tongue of the Jewish people, and so their rea understanding of the Hebrew Scriptur diminished. As Scripture, especially the Pent teuch, grew more and more important in Jewis eyes, and was considered a guide to faith and everyday life as well, so it became necessary translate it for the man in the street to unde stand. So in the synagogue began the practice following the reading of the Law with an or Aramaic translation of it.

The development of the synagogue and ritual was slow, and it is therefore impossible establish a certain date for the start of th practice. It is possible, however, that we find beginnings in Ne. viii. 8, where the word 'clearl may well mean 'with interpretation' (RSV, foo note). At any rate, the custom was established the synagogue well before the birth of Chris Mishnah *Megillah* iv. 4 lists the rules for the u of Targums. The translator was called 'methurgeman', his paraphrase a 'targum'. It should be stressed that the Targums were oral in their origins; had it been read out to him, the uninformed worshipper might have invested the translation with the same authority as Scripture itself, it was felt. But it need not be doubted that there were fairly fixed traditions; and when at length they were committed to writing there must have been plenty of traditional material to be utilized.

We know of written targums, of an unofficial character, of considerable antiquity; one of the Book of Job is known to have existed in the 1st Christian century, possibly the same as that recently found in Cave XI at Qumran. Otherwise the earliest targums we possess seem to have been committed to writing by the 5th century AD. Targums are extant covering all the Old Testament between them, except for Daniel, Ezra, and Nehemiah. We have several of the Pentateuch, not all of them complete, notably Targum Onkelos and two 'Jerusalem' or Palestinian Targums. (A complete text of the Palestinian Targum of the Pentateuch was recently identified in the Vatican Library.) On the Prophets (this section of the Hebrew Bible includes Joshua, Judges, Samuel, and Kings) we have Targum Jonathan ben Uzziel. And there are several on various parts of the Hagiographa; we do not know anything of their authors. Onkelos is claimed by TB (*Megillah* iii. 1) to have been a proselyte of the 1st century AD; but clearly TJ (*Megillah* i. 11) confuses him with Aquila, who is well known as the author of a Greek version of the Old Testament. Jonathan ben Uzziel lived in the 1st century BC. One of the Jerusalem Targums on the Pentateuch was erroneously given the name of Jonathan ben Uzziel during the 14th century; and it is still often referred to as 'Pseudo-Jonathan'.

Targum Onkelos is very conservative, and keeps close to the original, Targum Jonathan is much more interpretative, while 'Pseudo-Jonathan' uses the original merely as a vehicle for the popular stories that had grown up around biblical persons and events. But the same trends are to be found in them all. There is some bringing up to date of biblical names; thus Shinar (Gn. xi. 2) becomes Babel (*i.e.* Babylon). Figurative language is usually explained, with explanatory additions where necessary. Anthropomorphisms are strictly weeded out; so that man was created in the image of angels, not of God (Gn. i. 26); and actions on God's part are attributed to the 'Word of God', or the 'Glory of God', or some other circumlocution.

The Targums are useful for the light they throw upon Jewish traditional interpretations and, indeed, methods of interpretation. One particularly interesting passage is the paraphrase of Is. lii. 13–liii. 12 in Targum Jonathan. The suffering Servant' there is specifically called the Messiah, but with a single (possible) exception the sufferings are either removed altogether or else transferred to the people of Israel or to her enemies. Thus the identification is the same that Jesus made, but to Him the sufferings were an integral part of the Servant's, and therefore of the Messiah's, mission and ministry.

BIBLIOGRAPHY. J. F. Stenning, *The Targum of Isaiah*, 1949; B. J. Roberts, *The Old Testament Text and Versions*, 1951, chapter 14; F. F. Bruce, *The Books and the Parchments*, 1950, chapter 11.

D.F.P.

TARSHISH. See JEWELS AND PRECIOUS STONES (under Beryl).

TARSHISH. 1. A grandson of Benjamin, son of Bilhan (1 Ch. vii. 10). **2.** One of the seven notable princes of Ahasuerus, ruler of Persia (Est. i. 14).

3. The son of Javan, grandson of Noah (Gn. x. 4; 1 Ch. i. 7). The name Tarshish (*taršîš*), which occurs four times in AV as Tharshish (1 Ki. x. 22 (twice), xxii. 48; 1 Ch. vii. 10), refers both to the descendants and to the land.

Several of the references in the Old Testament are concerned with ships and suggest that Tarshish was a land bordering on the sea. Thus Jonah boarded a ship going to Tarshish (Jon. i. 3, iv. 2) from Joppa in order to flee to a distant land (Is. lxvi. 19). The land was rich in such metals as silver (Je. x. 9), iron, tin, lead (Ezk. xxvii. 12), which were exported to places like Joppa and Tyre (Ezk. xxvii). A land in the western Mediterranean where there are good deposits of mineral seems a likely identification, and many have thought of Tartessus in Spain (Herodotus, iv. 152). Certainly the mineral wealth of Spain attracted the Phoenicians, who founded colonies there. Interesting evidence comes from Sardinia, where monumental inscriptions erected by the Phoenicians in the 9th century BC bear the name Tarshish. W. F. Albright has suggested that the very word Tarshish suggests the idea of mining or smelting, and that in a sense any mineral-bearing land may be called Tarshish, although it would seem most likely that Spain is the land intended. An old Semitic root found in Akkadian *rašāšu* means 'to melt', 'to be smelted'. A derived noun *taršīšu* may be used to define a smelting-plant or refinery (Arab. *ršš*, 'to trickle', *etc.*, of liquid). Hence any place where mining and smelting were carried on could be called Tarshish.

What such a place looked like may be judged by the excavations of N. Glueck at Ezion-geber on the Gulf of Aqabah, where a copper refinery existed in the days of Solomon and on into the 9th century. Copper ore was mined in the area to the north in the Arabah region and refined at the port of Ezion-geber. It was precisely at this place that Solomon had his navy of Tarshish (1 Ki. x. 22, xxii. 48; 2 Ch. ix. 21). The expression *'onî taršîš*, navy of Tarshish or Tarshish fleet, may refer to the ships which carried the smelted metal either to distant lands from Ezion-geber or to Phoenicia from the W Mediterranean. For the view that Tarshish vessels were deep-sea-going vessels named after the port of Tarsus, or Gk. *tarsos*, 'oar', see SHIPS AND BOATS.

These ships symbolized wealth and power. A vivid picture of the day of divine judgment was to portray their destruction in that day (Ps. xlviii. 7; Is. ii. 16, xxiii. 1, 14).

BIBLIOGRAPHY. W. F. Albright, 'New Light on the Early History of Phoenician Colonization', *BASOR*, 83, 1941, pp. 14 ff.; N. Glueck, *The Other Side of Jordan*, 1940, pp. 93 ff.; *id*., 'Excavations at Ezion Geber', *BASOR*, 79, 1940, pp. 3 ff.; *GTT*, pp. 88 f. J.A.T.

TARSUS. Modern Tersous, a city on the Cilician plain, watered by the Cydnus, and some 10 miles inland after the fashion of most cities on the Asia Minor coast. To judge from the extent of its remains, Tarsus must have housed a population of no less than half a million in Roman times. The lower Cydnus was navigable, and a port had been skilfully engineered. North, a major highway led to the Cilician Gates, the famous pass through the Taurus range some 30 miles distant.

Nothing is known of the foundation of Tarsus. It was probably a native Cilician town, penetrated at a very early date by Greek colonists. The name of Mopsus is traditionally associated with Greek settlement in Cilicia, and may indicate, as Ramsay believed (*The Cities of St. Paul*, 1907, pp. 116 f.), early Ionian settlement. Gn. x. 4, 'The sons of Javan, Elishah and Tarshish . . .' may support this theory. Josephus' identification of Tarshish with Tarsus in this passage does not preclude a different interpretation in other contexts. The antiquity of Gn. x is a graver objection, but the words may be evidence of Ionian intrusion of very remote date.

Tarsus appears sporadically in history. It is mentioned in the Black Obelisk of Shalmaneser as one of the cities overrun by the Assyrians in the middle of the 9th century BC. Median and Persian rule followed, with that typically loose organization which permitted the rule of a Cilician subject-king. Xenophon, passing through in 401 BC, found Tarsus the royal seat of one Syennesis, ruling in such capacity. This petty king may have been deposed for his association with Cyrus' revolt which brought Xenophon and the Ten Thousand to Cilicia, for Alexander, in 334 BC, found the area in the hands of a Persian satrap. The coinage of the period suggests a mingling of Greek and Oriental influence, and gives no indication of autonomy. Ramsay professes to trace a decline of Greek influence under the Persian rule.

Nor did the Seleucid kings, who ruled after Alexander, promote the influence of the Greeks in Tarsus. Their general policy, here as elsewhere, was to discourage the Greek urge to city autonomy and its attendant liberalism. It is possible that the shock of the Roman defeat of Antiochus the Great and the peace of 189 BC, reversed the process. The settlement limited the Syrian domain to the Taurus, and Cilicia became a frontier region. The fact seems to have prompted Syria to some reorganization, a the granting of a form of autonomy to Tars The Tarsus of Paul, with its synthesis of E and West, Greek and Oriental, dates from t time.

A story in 2 Macc. iv. 30–36 reveals the ra growth of independence, and the reorganizati of the city which a Tarsian protest won fr Antiochus Epiphanes in 171 BC. The formati of a 'tribe' of Jewish citizens after the Alexandri fashion may date from this time. (Antioch anti-semitism was against metropolitan rec citrance.) Tarsian history in the rest of the 2 century BC is obscure. The 1st century BC better known. Roman penetration of Cili began in 104 BC, but Roman and Greek influer were both overwhelmed in Asia by the Orien reaction under Mithridates (83 BC). Pompe settlement in 65–64 BC reconstituted Cilicia as 'sphere of duty', which is the basic meaning 'province', rather than a geographical entity, a the governors, Cicero among them (51 BC), h a roving commission to pacify the pirate co and hinterlands and to protect Roman interest

In spite of Roman experimentation with t land at large, Tarsus flourished, played so part in the civil wars, was visited by Antony, a favoured by Augustus as the home town Athenodorus, his teacher at Apollonia and li long friend. The Roman citizenship of t Tarsian Jews dates probably from Pompe settlement. E.M.B.

TARTAK. The name of an idol or deity (*tart* worshipped by the men of Avva who were settl in Samaria after its capture by the Assyrians 722 BC (2 Ki. xvii. 31). The identification m remain open until the location of Avva itself sure. TB (*Sanhedrin* 63b) ascribes the form of ass to Tartak, but this is probably conjecture. D.J.W.

TARTAN. The title of a high Assyrian offic Two are mentioned in the Old Testament. T first was sent by Sargon II to besiege and captu Ashdod in 711 BC (Is. xx. 1). The second w sent by Sennacherib with other officials (s RAB-SARIS, RAB-SHAKEH) and a military force demand the surrender of Jerusalem in 701 (2 Ki. xviii. 17). In neither case is the person name of the officer given. The Assyr. *turtanu* listed in the Assyrian Eponym texts as the ne highest official after the king. He was also titul head of the province of which Harran was t capital. D.J.W.

TATNAI (Heb. *tattenai*; RV 'Tattenai'; *cf*. G *Sisinnes*, 1 Esdras vi. 3, vii. 1). The Persi governor, successor of Rehum, of the Samar district during the reign of Darius Hystaspes a Zerubbabel (Ezr. v. 3, 6, vi. 6, 13). He inves gated and reported in a sympathetic manner complaints made from Jerusalem against Jews his district. He is called 'Tattani, of the Distr across the River' (as Ezr. v. 6) in a cuneifo inscription from Babylon, dated 5 June 502 BC (*JNES*, III, 1944, p. 46). D.J.W.

TAVERNS, THE THREE (Lat. *Tres Tabernae*). This was a station about 30 miles from Rome on the Via Appia, which led south-eastwards from the city. It is mentioned by Cicero in his correspondence with Atticus. When the apostle Paul and his company were on their way from Puteoli to Rome Christians came out of the city and met him here (Acts xxviii. 15). B.F.C.A.

TAXES. See TRIBUTE.

TEACHER. See EDUCATION.

TEBETH. See CALENDAR.

TEKOA. 1. A town in Judah, about 6 miles south of Bethlehem, the home of Amos (Am. i. 1). When Joab 'perceived that the king's heart was toward Absalom' he sent to Tekoa for a wise woman who might reconcile David and Absalom (2 Sa. xiv. 1 f.). Rehoboam later fortified the town (2 Ch. xi. 6). Later, when Jehoshaphat was faced by Ammonites and Moabites, he consulted with the people in 'the wilderness of Tekoa' (2 Ch. xx. 20). Jeremiah called for the blowing of a trumpet in Tekoa in the face of the advancing enemy (Je. vi. 1). After the Exile the town was re-inhabited (Ne. iii. 5, 27). In Maccabean and Roman times the place was known, and the name lingers today as Khirbet Taqû'a, a ruined village of some 5 acres, which has not been excavated.

2. A descendant of Hezron, the grandson of Judah, belonging to the general Calebite stock (1 Ch. ii. 24, iv. 5).

BIBLIOGRAPHY. F. M. Abel, *Géographie de la Palestine*, II, 1933, p. 478. J.A.T.

TELAIM. The place where Saul gathered his army before his attack on the Amalekites (1 Sa. xv. 4). The incident described in 1 Sa. xv, in which Saul disobeyed God's word given by the prophet Samuel, provoked the severe rebuke of 1 Sa. xv. 22, 23, 'to obey is better than sacrifice'. Telaim (*ṭ^{e}lā'îm*) is identified by some with Telem (Jos. xv. 24), in the Negeb. Some MSS of LXX allow of an occurrence of the word in 1 Sa. xxvii. 8, and read 'they of Telaim' for 'of old'. J.A.T.

TELASSAR. A place inhabited by the 'children (sons) of Eden' and cited by Sennacherib's messengers to Hezekiah as an example of a town destroyed in previous Assyrian attacks (see also GOZAN, HARAN, REZEPH). The name *t^{e}la'śśār* (2 Ki. xix. 12) or *t^{e}laśśār* (Is. xxxvii. 12) represents Tell Assur ('mound of Assur'). The *b^{e}nê 'eḏen* probably lived in the area between the Euphrates and Baliḫ rivers, called in Assyrian Bît-Adini (Beth-Eden), but no Til-Assur has been found in this region, although the area does suit the context. A Til-Aššur named in the annals of Tiglath-pileser III and Esarhaddon appears to lie near the Assyrian border with Elam. The common form of the place-name means that it may yet be identified. There is no need to emend to Tell Bassar (Basher), south-east of Raqqa on the Euphrates (as L. Grollenberg, *Atlas of the Bible*, 1956, p. 164). D.J.W.

TELL EL-AMARNA. The capital of Egypt under Amenophis IV (Akhenaten), *c.* 1361–1345 BC. Its importance for biblical studies lies in the series of letters written in cuneiform on clay tablets which were discovered there by chance in 1887. See ARCHAEOLOGY, VIII*b*.

TEMA. The name (*tēmā'*) of the son and descendants of Ishmael (Gn. xxv. 15; 1 Ch. i. 30) and of the district they inhabited (Jb. vi. 19). It is mentioned, with Dedan and Buz, as a remote place (Je. xxv. 23) and as an oasis in the desert on a main trade route through Arabia (Is. xxi. 14). An Aramaic stele of the 6th century BC was found in the ruins of Taima about 250 miles NNW of Medina in NW Arabia. The city (Bab. *Tema'*) is also named in documents recording its occupation by Nabonidus during his exile (*AS*, VIII, 1958, p. 80). See BELSHAZZAR. D.J.W.

TEMAN. The grandson of Esau (Gn. xxxvi. 11; 1 Ch. i. 36), who may have given his name to the district, town, or tribe of that name in the northern part of Edom (Je. xlix. 20; Ezk. xxv. 13; Am. i. 12). The inhabitants were renowned for wisdom (Je. xlix. 7; Ob. 8 f.). Eliphaz the Temanite was one of Job's comforters (Jb. ii. 11, *etc.*). A duke (*'allûp̄*) of Teman (*têmān*) is named among the chiefs of Edom (Gn. xxxvi. 15, 42; 1 Ch. i. 53), and Husham was one of the early rulers (Gn. xxxvi. 34). The prophets include Teman among Edomite towns to be destroyed (Je. xlix. 20; Ezk. xxv. 13; Am. i. 12; Ob. 9). Habakkuk in his great vision saw God the Holy One coming from Teman (Hab. iii. 3).

N. Glueck (*The Other Side of Jordan*, 1940, pp. 25, 26) identifies it with Tawilan. J.A.T.

TEMPERANCE translates in AV the Gk. *enkrateia*, which occurs in three New Testament verses and means power or control over oneself. The corresponding adjective *enkratēs* and verb *enkrateuomai* are used both positively and negatively. Another word translated 'temperate', *nēphalios*, sometimes carries a restricted reference to drinking, such as is often read into the modern word 'temperance'.

The verb *enkrateuomai* is first used in the LXX in Gn. xliii. 31 to describe Joseph's control of his affectionate impulses towards his brothers. It refers also to the false self-restraint of Saul in 1 Sa. xiii. 12, and of Haman in Est. v. 10. According to Josephus, the Essenes exercised 'perpetual sobriety' (*BJ* ii. 8. 5), and some of them rejected marriage as incompatible with continence. The Greeks held temperance to be a cardinal virtue.

Christ made only a negative reference to temperance when He accused the Pharisees of *akrasia* (excess) in Mt. xxiii. 25. The context seems to indicate over-indulgence in food and drink.

A very significant use of *enkrateia* is found in Acts xxiv. 25. Since an adulteress sat beside Felix while Paul discussed self-control, its bearing on unchastity is easily apparent, and the verse compares naturally with 1 Cor. vii. 9. This restricted reference to chastity often features in later literature. The Encratites enjoined complete abstinence from marriage; and some Christian clergy today cannot marry. This distorted interpretation of 'temperance' is called demonic in 1 Tim. iv. 2, 3, and the qualification 'temperate' (*enkratēs*) is confidently applied to the married bishop in Tit. i. 8 (*cf.* 1 Pet. iii. 2).

Fig. 203. Carvings in bas-relief depicting Amenophis IV (*left*), the founder of Tell el-Amarna, and his wife Nefertiti.

The association of *enkrateia* with righteousness in Acts xxiv. 25 is parallel to other contexts where it is listed in catalogues of graces. In Gal. v. 22, 23 it is the last of nine virtues, and seems to be opposed to drunkenness and carousing in the corresponding list of vices. In 2 Pet. i. 6 it forms a midway stage in a distinct moral progress of the believer, which commences in faith and culminates in love. (The form of the passage recalls expositions of Stoic moral *prokopē*.) The related words *nēphalios* and *sōphrōn* (sober-minded) appear in a list of virtues demanded of older Christian men in Tit. ii. 2, 12.

The precise reference of *nēphalios* is to drunkenness, and the word is actually opposed to 'drunkard' in 1 Tim. iii. 2, 3. It can broaden out, however, to include other forms of self-control, as in Tit. ii. 2 and 1 Tim. iii. 11. This extended application should be recollected when rendering the verb *nēphō*, which in RV is always translated 'to be sober', but which usually means 'to be vigilant' in contexts like 1 Thes. v. 6 and 1 Pet. i. 13, iv. 7, v. 8. In 1 Cor. ix. 25 the widest possible reference is given to *enkrateuomai* when the Christian athlete is said to exercise self-control in all things.

Temperance in the New Testament is essentially a 'fruit of the Spirit' (Gal. v. 22, 23). A deliberate antithesis between spiritual life and carnal drunkenness is introduced into several passages describing prophetic inspiration (*e.g.* Acts ii. 15–17 and Eph. v. 18). Believers who 'drink of the Spirit' (1 Cor. xii. 13) are thought by the world to be 'intoxicated'; and indeed so they are, not with wine, but with zeal for the Christian warfare. This passion to be good soldiers of Christ expresses itself not in excess but in sober discipline; it is the true imitation of a Master, whose life, as Bernard says, was the 'mirror of temperance'.

BIBLIOGRAPHY. R. L. Ottley in *ERE* (*s.v.* 'Temperance'); *Arndt*; H. Rashdall, *Theory of Good and Evil*, 1907. D.H.T.

TEMPEST. See STORM, WHIRLWIND.

TEMPLE.

I. HISTORICAL BACKGROUND

Some of the earliest structures built by man were temples or shrines where he could worship his god in his 'house' (see K. M. Kenyon, *Archaeology in the Holy Land*, pp. 41, 51, for the Meso hic and Neolithic shrines at Jericho). The ›wer of Babel is the first structure mentioned the Bible which implies the existence of a nple (Gn. xi. 4; see BABEL). Although this ›ms to have been intended as a place where an might meet God, it symbolized the self-nfidence of man attempting to climb up to aven, and for such pride it was doomed.

In Mesopotamia, which Abraham left, each :y had a temple dedicated to its patron deity. ıe god was looked upon as the owner of the nd, and if it was not blessed by him it would be ıproductive, resulting in poor revenues for his mple. The local king or ruler acted as steward r the god.

There was no purpose in the semi-nomadic atriarchs building one particular shrine for their iod. He revealed Himself as and where He leased. Such occasions were sometimes the :ene of a sacrificial altar. They might be com-ıemorated by a pillar (Gn. xxii. 9, xxviii. 22; see ILLAR).

After Israel had grown into nationhood a entral shrine became a necessity, as a gathering-oint for all the people, a symbol of their unity ı the worship of their God. This need was ıpplied by the tabernacle (*q.v.*) during the trek hrough the wilderness and by recognized shrines uring the period of the judges (*e.g.* Shechem, os. viii. 30 ff., xxiv. 1 ff.; Shiloh, 1 Sa. i. 3).

The nations of Canaan had their own temples, imply called 'Dagon's house' or the house of ›hoever the patron deity was (Heb. *bêṯ dāḡôn*, Sa. v. 5; *bêṯ 'aštārôṯ*, 1 Sa. xxxi. 10; *cf. bêṯ hwh*, Ex. xxiii. 19).

The lack of a shrine of Yahweh appeared in-›idious when David had consolidated his power ınd built a permanent palace for himself. The :ing said, 'I dwell in a house of cedar, but the ark of God dwelleth within curtains' (2 Sa. vii. 2). It was not given to him to build the Temple because he was stained with the blood of his enemies, but he collected materials, gathered treasure, and bought the site (1 Ch. xxii. 8, 3; 2 Sa. xxiv. 18–25). Solomon began the actual construction in his fourth year, and the Temple was completed seven years later (see fig. 206; on the date, see CHRONOLOGY OF THE OLD TESTAMENT).

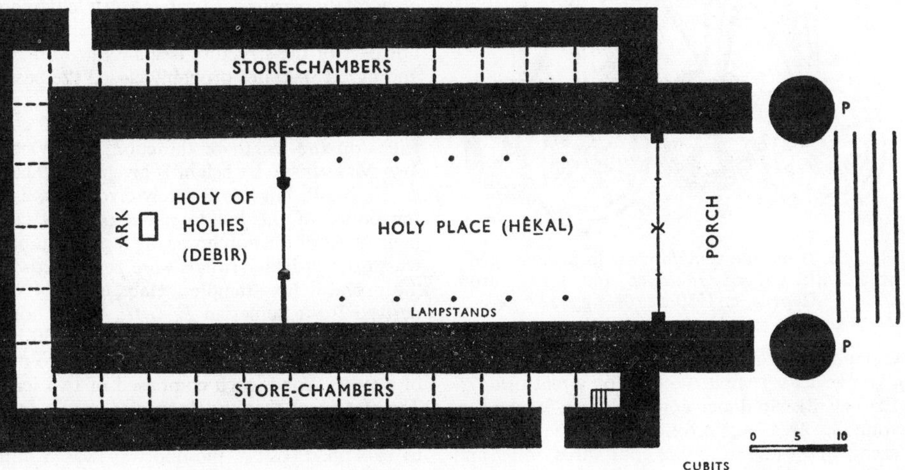

g. 204. Plan of Solomon's Temple showing the two pillars (P), Jachin and Boaz, and the steps leading ɔ to the Porch. See fig. 206 below and *cf.* the plan of Ezekiel's Temple (fig. 81), and that of the Temple at Tell Tainat (fig. 13).

II. SOLOMON'S TEMPLE

a. The site

That it stood within the area now called 'Haram esh-Sherif' at the east side of the 'Old City' of Jerusalem (*q.v.*) is undisputed. The precise location within the vast enclosure is less certain. The highest part of the rock (now covered by the mosque known as 'The Dome of the Rock') may have been the site of the innermost sanctuary or of the altar of burnt-offering outside (2 Ch. iii. 1). This rock was presumably part of the threshing-floor of Araunah (*q.v.*), bought by David for a sum given as fifty silver shekels (2 Sa. xxiv. 24) or 600 goldshekels (1 Ch. xxi. 25). See plate XVI.

Nothing of Solomon's structure remains above ground, nor were any definite traces found in the diggings sponsored by the Palestine Exploration Fund. Indeed, it is likely that the work of levelling the rock and building up the great retaining walls for the courtyard of Herod's Temple obliterated any earlier constructions.

b. Description

The passages 1 Ki. vi–vii and 2 Ch. iii–iv must be the bases of any reconstruction of Solomon's Temple. These accounts, while detailed, do not cover every feature, are not entirely understood, and contain some apparent discrepancies (*e.g.*

1 Ki. vi. 2 and 16 f.). They may be supplemented by incidental references and by the description of Ezekiel's Temple, an elaborated version of Solomon's building (Ezk. xl–xliii; see fig. 81). The Temple proper was an oblong, orientated

Fig. 205. A mobile temple laver in bronze decorated with winged sphinxes and birds. From Cyprus, *c.* 1150 BC. *Cf.* fig. 132.

east and west. It is reasonable to assume that, like Ezekiel's Temple, it stood on a platform (*cf.* Ezk. xli. 8). No dimensions are given for the surrounding area. Again following Ezekiel's plan, it seems that there were two courtyards, inner and

(AV 'molten' or 'brazen sea', 1 Ki. vii. 23–26). Tl great basin, 10 cubits in diameter, rested up four groups of four bronze oxen orientated to t four compass-points. These were removed l Ahaz (2 Ki. xvi. 17).

At the dedication of the Temple, Solom stood on a bronze 'scaffold' (2 Ch. vi. 12 f., He *kîyyôr*, the word used for 'laver' elsewhere, E xxx. 18, *etc.*; here it probably denotes a fram work), which has parallels in Syrian and Egypti sculptures and possibly in Akkadian (see W. Albright, *Archaeology and the Religion of Israe* 1953, pp. 152–154).

A flight of steps would have led up from tl inner court to the porch (Heb. *'ûlām*; see PORCI The entrance was flanked by two pillars wi elaborately ornamented capitals (AV 'chapiters Their purpose remains indeterminate; they we not part of the structure (see JACHIN AND BO and fig. 116). Gates probably closed the passa (*cf.* Ezk. xl. 48).

The porch was 10 cubits long and 20 cub wide (on the length of the cubit, see WEIGH AND MEASURES). Its height is given as 120 cub (2 Ch. iii. 4), but this is surely erroneous, as tl remainder of the building was only 30 cub high. West of the porch was the large chamber which the ordinary rituals were performed. Th 'holy place' (AV 'temple'; Heb. *hêḵāl*, a wo derived from Sumerian *É. GAL*, 'great hous was 40 cubits long, 20 in breadth, and 30 hig It was shut off from the porch by double doo of cypress wood, each composed of two leav The statement that the doorposts were a four (Heb. *mᵉzûzôṯ mē'ēṯ rᵉḇî'îṯ*, 1 Ki. vi. 33) is diffic to explain. Possibly the doorway was 5 cub

Fig. 206. Steven's reconstruction of Solomon's Temple, showing the twin pillars (Jachin and Boaz, *q.v.* the vestibule porch and side storage chambers. For a plan of the Temple see fig. 204.

outer; a suggestion supported by 1 Ki. vi. 36, vii. 12; 2 Ki. xxiii. 12; 2 Ch. iv. 9.

The bronze altar for burnt-offerings stood in the inner court (1 Ki. viii. 22, 64, ix. 25). It was 20 cubits square and 10 cubits high (2 Ch. iv. 1). Between this and the porch was the bronze laver

wide, *i.e.* one-quarter of the width of the dividin wall.

Latticed windows near the ceiling lighted th holy place (1 Ki. vi. 4). Here stood the golde incense-altar, the table for showbread, and fiv pairs of lampstands, together with the instru ments of sacrifice (see the respective articles). The double doors of cypress leading to the inner sanctuary (Heb. *d^{e}ḇîr*, 'innermost place'; AV 'oracle' is an unlikely rendering) were rarely opened, probably only for the high priest at the atonement ceremony. The doorposts and lintel are said to have been a fifth (Heb. *hā'ayil m^{e}zûzôṯ ḥ^{a}miššîṯ*, 1 Ki. vi. 31). As with the *hêḵāl*, this may be explained as one-fifth of the dividing wall, 4 cubits.

The inner sanctuary was a perfect cube of 20 cubits. Although it might be expected that the floor was raised above the *hêḵāl*, there is no hint of this. Within stood two wooden figures side by side, 10 cubits high. Two of their wings met in the centre above the ark of the covenant (*q.v.*), and the other wing of each touched the north and south walls respectively (1 Ki. vi. 23–28; see CHERUBIM). In this most holy place the presence of God was shown by a cloud (1 Ki. viii. 10 f.).

Each room was panelled with cedar wood and the floor planked with cypress (or pine, Heb. *b^{e}rôš*; see TREES). The walls and doors were carved with flowers, palm trees, and cherubim and overlaid with gold. No stonework was visible.

The outer walls of the inner sanctuary and the holy place were built with two offsets of 1 cubit to support the joists of three storeys of small chambers all around. Thus the ground-floor chambers were 5 cubits wide, those above 6, and the uppermost 7. A door in the south side gave access to a spiral staircase serving the upper floors. These rooms doubtless housed various stores and vestments, provided accommodation, maybe, for the priests in course, and sheltered the offerings of money and goods made by the worshippers.

Much has been made of the proximity of the royal palace to the Temple and the inference drawn that it was the 'Chapel Royal'. While admitting such a relationship (emphasized by the passage connecting the two buildings, 2 Ki. xvi. 18), it should be remembered that it was appropriate for the viceroy of Yahweh to reside near to the house of God; entry was not restricted to the king.

Solomon hired a Tyrian to take charge of the work and used Phoenician craftsmen (1 Ki. v. 10, 18, vii. 13, 14). It is not surprising to find parallels to the design of the Temple and its decoration in surviving examples of Phoenician or Canaanite handiwork. The ground plan is very similar to that of a small shrine of the 9th century BC excavated at Tell Tainat on the Orontes (see fig. 13). This shows the three rooms, an altar in the innermost and two columns in the porch, but supporting the roof (*AJA*, XLI, 1937, p. 9; *BA*, IV, 1941, pp. 20, 21). At Hazor a Late Bronze Age shrine is also tripartite and was constructed with timbers between the stone-courses (*BA*, XXII, 1959, pp. 3–8; *cf.* 1 Ki. v. 18, vi. 36; see STONE-SQUARERS). Numerous carved ivory panels (from the walls or furnishings of palaces) found throughout the Ancient East are Phoenician work, often with Egyptian themes. Among the common subjects are flowers, palms, and winged sphinxes, undoubtedly comparable with the carvings in the Temple. As with the Temple's panelling, these carvings were overlaid with gold and set with coloured stones.

c. Later history

Ancient temples generally served as state treasuries, emptied to pay tribute and filled with booty according to the power of the land. If, for some reason, a ruler paid little attention to the temple it would lose its revenue and rapidly fall into disrepair (*cf.* 2 Ki. xii. 4–15). Solomon's Temple was no exception. The treasures which he had gathered in the Temple were raided in the reign of his son, Rehoboam, by Shishak of Egypt (1 Ki. xiv. 26). Later kings, including even Hezekiah, who had adorned the Temple (2 Ki. xviii. 15 f.), used the treasure to purchase allies (Asa, 1 Ki. xv. 18) or to pay tribute and buy off an invader (Ahaz, 2 Ki. xvi. 8). The idolatrous kings added the appurtenances of a Canaanite shrine, including the symbols of pagan deities (2 Ki. xxi. 4, xxiii. 1–12), while Ahaz introduced an altar of an Assyrian type, displacing the laver, as token of his submission to Tiglath-pileser III (2 Ki. xvi. 17). By the time of Josiah (*c.* 640 BC), three centuries after its construction, the Temple was in need of considerable repair, which had to be financed by the contributions of the worshippers (2 Ki. xxii. 4). In 587 BC it was looted by Nebuchadrezzar and sacked (2 Ki. xxv. 9, 13–17). Even after the destruction men came to sacrifice there (Je. xli. 5).

III. EZEKIEL'S TEMPLE

The exiles were heartened in their grief (Ps. cxxxvii) by the vision of a new Temple granted to Ezekiel (Ezk. xl–xliii, *c.* 571 BC). More details are given of this than of Solomon's structure, although it was never built. For a reconstructed plan based on the biblical data, see fig. 81. The actual shrine was different in little other than its size (porch 20 cubits wide, 12 long; holy place 20 cubits wide and 40 long; inner sanctuary 20 cubits each way). The walls were again panelled and carved with palms and cherubim. The building was set on a platform mounted by ten steps which were flanked by two bronze pillars. Three tiers of rooms enfolded the inner sanctuary and the holy place. The vision gives a description of the surrounding area, something lacking from the account of the first Temple. An area of 500 cubits square was enclosed by a wall pierced by a single gateway on each of the north, east, and south sides. Three more gates, opposite the former, led to an inner courtyard, where the altar of sacrifice stood before the shrine. All these gates were well fortified to prevent the entry of any but Israelites. There were various buildings in the courtyards for storage and for the use of the priests.

IV. THE SECOND TEMPLE

This stood for almost 500 years, longer than either the first or Herod's Temple. Yet it is only vaguely known from incidental references. The exiles who returned (*c.* 537 BC) took with them the vessels looted by Nebuchadrezzar, and the authorization of Cyrus for the rebuilding of the Temple. Apparently the site was cleared of rubble and an altar built and the laying of the foundations commenced (Ezr. i, iii. 2, 3, 8–10). When eventually finished it was 60 cubits long and 60 cubits high, but even the foundations showed that it would be inferior to Solomon's Temple (Ezr. iii. 12). Around the shrine were store-places and priests' rooms. From some of these Nehemiah expelled the Ammonite Tobiah (Ne. xiii. 4–9). From 1 Macc. i. 21, iv. 49–51 comes some information about the furnishings. The ark had disappeared at the time of the Exile and was never recovered or replaced. Instead of Solomon's ten lampstands, one seven-branched candelabrum stood in the holy place with the table for showbread and the incense altar. These were taken as spoil by the Seleucid king of Syria, Antiochus IV Epiphanes (*c.* 175–163 BC), who set up the 'abomination of desolation' (a pagan altar or statue) on 15 December 167 BC (1 Macc. i. 54). The triumphant Maccabees (*q.v.*) cleansed the Temple from this pollution and replaced the furniture late in 164 BC (1 Macc. iv. 36–59). They also turned the enclosure into a fortress so strong that it resisted the siege of Pompey for three months (63 BC).

V. HEROD'S TEMPLE

The building of Herod's Temple, commenced early in 19 BC, was an attempt to reconcile the Jews to their Idumaean king rather than to glorify God. Great care was taken to respect the sacred area during the work, even to the training of a thousand priests as masons to build the shrine. Although the main structure was finished within ten years (*c.* 9 BC), work continued until AD 64. For a reconstruction, see fig. 15 and plate XIV*b*. See also plate XVI.

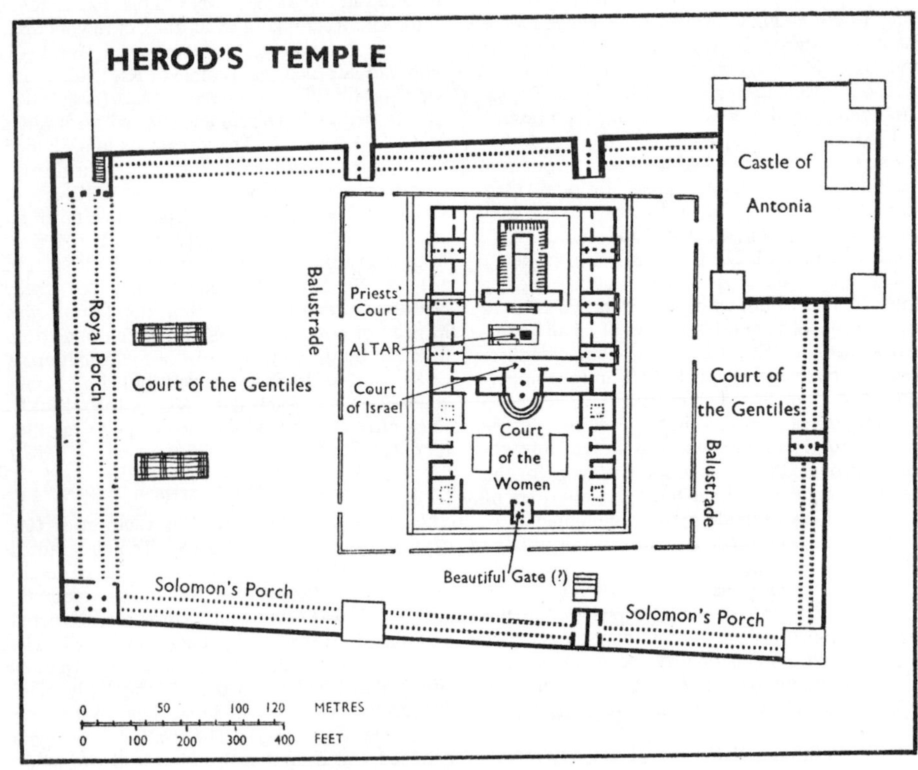

Fig. 207. Ground plan of Herod's Temple.

As a basis for the Temple buildings and to provide a gathering-place, an area about 500 yards from north to south and about 325 yards from east to west was made level. In places the rock surface was cut away, but a large part was built up with rubble and the whole enclosed by a wall of massive stone blocks (normally about 4 feet high and up to 15 feet long; *cf.* Mk. xiii. 1). At the south-east corner, overlooking the Kidron ravine, the inner courtyard was about 150 feet above the rock. Perhaps the parapet above this corner was the pinnacle of the Temple (Mt. iv. 5). Stretches of this wall still stand. One gateway pierced the northern wall (Tadi Gate), but was apparently never used, and one led through the wall on the east (under the present Golden Gate). Traces of the two Herodian gates on the south side are still visible beneath the Mosque of el-Aqsa. Ramps led upwards from these to the level of the court. Four gates faced the city on the west. They were approached by viaducts across the Tyropoeon valley (see JERUSALEM). At the north-west corner the fortress of Antonia dominated the enclosure. This was the residence of the procurators when in Jerusalem, and its garrison was always at hand to subdue any unrest in the Temple (*cf.* Lk. xiii. 1; Acts xxi. 31–35). The high priest's robes were stored therein as a token of subjection.

The outer court of the Temple was surrounded by a portico, inside the walls. As described by Josephus (*Ant.* xv. 410–416), the south porch had four rows of columns and was called the Royal Porch. The porticos of the other sides each had two rows. Solomon's Porch stretched along the east side (Jn. x. 23; Acts iii. 11, v. 12). In these colonnades the scribes held their schools and debates (*cf.* Lk. ii. 46, xix. 47; Mk. xi. 27) and the merchants and money-changers had their stalls (Jn. ii. 14–16; Lk. xix. 45, 46). The inner area was raised slightly above the court of the Gentiles and surrounded by a balustrade. Notices in Greek and Latin warned that no responsibility could be taken for the probable death of any Gentile who ventured within. Two of these inscriptions have been found (see plate XV*a*). Four gates gave access on the north and south sides and one on the east. This last had doors of Corinthian bronze-work and may have been the Beautiful Gate of Acts iii. 2.

The first court inside (Women's Court) contained the chests for gifts towards the expenses of the services (Mk. xii. 41–44). Men were allowed into the Court of Israel, raised above the Court of the Women, and at the time of the Feast of Tabernacles could enter the innermost (Priests') Court to circumambulate the altar. This was built of unhewn stone, 22 cubits away from the porch (*cf.* Mt. xxiii. 35; see ALTAR). The plan of the shrine copied Solomon's. The porch was 100 cubits wide and 100 cubits high. A doorway 20 cubits wide and 40 high gave entry, and one half that size led into the holy place. This was 40 cubits long and 20 cubits wide. A curtain divided the holy place from the inner sanctuary (the veil, Mt. xxvii. 51; Mk. xv. 38; *cf.* 2 Ch. iii. 14). The inner sanctuary was 20 cubits square and, like the holy place, 40 cubits high. An empty room above the holy place and the inner sanctuary rose to the height of the porch, 100 cubits, thus making a level roof. Three storeys of chambers surrounded the north, south, and west sides to a height of 40 cubits. Golden spikes were fixed on the roof to prevent birds from perching there.

The magnificent structure of cream stone and gold was barely finished (AD 64) before it was destroyed by the Roman soldiery (AD 70). The golden candelabrum, the table of showbread, and other objects were carried in triumph to Rome.

BIBLIOGRAPHY. The best summary is A. Parrot, *The Temple of Jerusalem*, 1957, with a comprehensive bibliography. For a detailed survey, see L. H. Vincent, *Jérusalem de l'Ancien Testament*, I and II, 1954; J. Simons, *Jerusalem in the Old Testament*, 1952. For reconstructions of Solomon's Temple, see G. E. Wright, *BA*, XVIII, 1955, pp. 41–44.

A.R.M.

VI. 'TEMPLE' IN THE NEW TESTAMENT

Two Greek words, *hieron* and *naos*, are translated 'temple'. The former refers to the collection of buildings which comprised the Temple at Jerusalem, the latter refers more specifically to the sanctuary. Commentators are in the habit of drawing attention to the fact that the word preferred by the New Testament writers to describe the Church as the Temple of God is *naos*. But the use of *naos* in Mt. xxvii. 5 and Jn. ii. 20 prevents one from making much of this fact. In the case of Mt. xxvii. 5 the term is almost certainly to be understood in the sense of *hieron*, otherwise we have the formidable difficulty of explaining how Judas penetrated the area which was closed to all except priests. As for Jesus' statement in Jn. ii. 20 that forty-six years were spent in building the *naos*, it is unlikely that only the sanctuary was in mind. The use of *naos* as a synonym for *hieron* is also present in Herodotus (ii. 170) and Jos. (*BJ* v. 207–211.

With the literal use of 'temple' in the New Testament, *cf.* 'house' (*oikos*), and 'place' (*topos*). For a description of the Temple of Jerusalem in the time of our Lord, see section v above. The metaphorical use of 'temple' should be compared with the metaphorical use of 'house', 'building' (*oikodomē*), 'tent' (*skēnē*), 'habitation' (*katoikētērion*; RSV 'dwelling place').

a. 'Temple' in the Gospels

The attitude of Jesus to the Temple of Jerusalem contains two opposing features. On the one hand, Jesus greatly respected it; on the other hand, He attached relatively little importance to it. Thus, He called it the 'house of God' (Mt. xii. 4; *cf.* Jn. ii. 16). Everything in it was holy, He taught, because it was sanctified by God who dwelt in it (Mt. xxiii. 17, 21). Zeal for His Father's house inspired Him to cleanse it (Jn. ii. 17), and thought of the impending doom of the holy city caused Him to weep (Lk. xix. 41 ff.). In contrast are those passages in which Jesus relegated the Temple to a very subordinate position. He was greater than the Temple (Mt. xii. 6). It had become a cover for the spiritual barrenness of Israel (Mk. xi. 12–26 and parallels). Soon it would perish, for a terrible desecration would render it unfit to exist (Mk. xiii. 1 f., 14 ff.). See also Mk. xiv. 57 f., xv. 29 f. and parallels. These differing attitudes are not, however, without explanation.

At the beginning of His ministry Jesus addressed Himself to the Jews and summoned all

Israel to repentance. In spite of mounting opposition, we find Him appealing to Jerusalem (Mk. xi. 1 ff. and parallels). The Temple was cleansed with a view to reforming the existing order (xi. 15 ff. and parallels). But the messianic implications of this action (Mal. iii. 1 ff.; *cf.* Psalms of Solomon xvii. 32 ff.; Mk. xi. 27 ff.) engendered still greater hostility on the part of the religious leaders, and Judaism, persistently obdurate and unreformable, was in the end judged as unworthy of the divine presence (Mk. xii. 1–12). So Jesus, who began by venerating the Temple, finally announced that His rejection and death would issue in its destruction. The accusation produced at the trial which asserted that Jesus had taught, 'I will destroy this temple that is made with hands, and within three days I will build another made without hands' (Mk. xiv. 58; *cf.* xv. 29) would therefore be a fitting peroration to the appeal of our Lord to Jewry. Mark attributes the saying, however, to false witnesses, and what constituted the falsity of the witness is a matter of conjecture among scholars. It is probably wisest to understand the charge as an unscrupulous combination of the prediction of Jesus that the Temple of Jerusalem would be destroyed (Mk. xiii. 2 and parallels) and the logion that the Son of man would be destroyed and rise again on the third day (Mk. viii. 31, ix. 31, x. 34 and parallels). That is to say, the falsity lay in misrepresentation of what Jesus actually had taught. One reason why Mark did not trouble to correct the misrepresentation may be due to the fact that the accusation was true in a deeper sense than the witnesses had in mind. The death of Jesus did in fact result in the supersession of the Temple of Jerusalem, and His resurrection put another in its place. The new Temple was the eschatological congregation of Jesus Messiah (Mt. xviii. 20; *cf.* Jn. xiv. 23). Luke and John, therefore, made no reference to the false witness because when they wrote their Gospels the accusation was no longer seen to be groundless.

b. 'Temple' in the Acts of the Apostles

Some time elapsed, however, before the full ramifications of the work of Christ became apparent, and in the Acts we find the apostles continuing to worship at the Temple of Jerusalem (Acts ii. 46, iii. 1 ff., v. 12, 20 f., 42; *cf.* Lk. xxiv. 52). It appears that the Hellenistic-Jewish party represented by Stephen was the first to discover that belief in Jesus as Messiah meant the abrogation of the order symbolized by the Jerusalem Temple (Acts vi. 11 ff.). Accordingly, Stephen's defence became an attack on the Temple, or, more correctly, on the attitude of mind to which the Temple gave rise (Acts vii). But whether it is justifiable to find in Stephen's denunciation of the Temple a hint of the new Temple made without hands, as some commentators do, is not at all certain. We are on firmer ground in Acts xv. 13–18. The 'tabernacle of David' of Am. ix. 11, to be sure, has the primary sense of dynasty or kingdom, but the use of this Old Testament text in the eschatology of the Covenanters of Qumran to support their novel conception of a spiritual temple (*CDC*, iii. 9) permits us to see here an adumbration of the doctrine of the Church as God's new Temple which is so common a feature of the Epistles.

c. 'Temple' in the Epistles

The doctrine of the Church as the realization of the messianic Temple of Old Testament and inter-testamental eschatology is most prominent in the writings of Paul. See 1 Cor. iii. 16–17, vi. 19; 2 Cor. vi. 16–vii. 1; Eph. ii. 19–22. The appeal to prophecy is particularly strong in the case of 2 Cor. vi. 16 ff., where we have an Old Testament couplet (Lv. xxvi. 12; Ezk. xxxvii. 27) which was already in use in Jewish eschatology on the messianic Temple (Jubilees i. 17). Also characteristic of the Temple image in 1 and 2 Corinthians is its hortatory and admonitory application. Since Christians are the realization of the long-cherished hope of the glorious Temple, they ought to live holy lives (2 Cor. vii. 1; *cf.* 1 Cor. vi. 18 ff.). Unity is likewise enjoined upon them. Since God is one, there is only one habitation in which He can dwell. Schism is tantamount to profanation of the Temple, and merits the same terrible penalty of death (1 Cor. iii. 5–17). In Ephesians the figure of the Temple is employed in the interests of doctrinal instruction. Uppermost in the mind of the writer is the inter-racial character of the Church. The language of the context of ii. 19–22 makes it plain that the apostle borrowed liberally from the Old Testament hope of the ingathering of Israel and the nations to the eschatological Temple at Jerusalem. For example, the words 'far' and 'nigh' of verses 13 and 17 (*cf.* Is. lvii. 19; Dn. ix. 7) were a rabbinic *terminus technicus* for the Gentiles and the Jews (*Numbers Rabbah* viii. 4). Similarly, the 'peace' mentioned in verses 14 and 17 is an allusion to the eschatological peace which was to prevail when Israel and the peoples were united in the one cult at Zion (Is. ii. 2 ff.; Mi. iv. 1 ff.; Enoch xc. 29 ff.). Paul undoubtedly regarded the fruits of his Gentile mission as the fulfilment of Jewish faith at its widest and most generous expression. He spiritualized the ancient hope of a reunited mankind, and represented Jews and Gentiles as the two walls of one building, joined by and resting upon Christ, the foremost cornerstone (Eph. ii. 19–22). The statement that the building 'grows' (*auxein*) into a 'temple' introduces a different figure, *viz.* that of the body, and reveals a certain fusion of images. 'Temple' and 'body' are largely coterminous ideas of the Church. Note the juxtaposition of the two conceptions in Eph. iv. 12, 16.

Parallels for Paul's use of the metaphor in 1 and 2 Corinthians are frequently sought in the writings of Philo and the Stoics, where the individual is called a 'temple'. The practice is scarcely justifiable, however. 1 Cor. vi. 19, 20 does indeed have the individual in mind, but only s a member of the community which corporately omprises the temple of God. Philo and the raeco-Roman humanists spiritualized the word emple' for the sake of anthropology, whereas aul was occupied with ecclesiology and eschato-gy and had only a very secondary interest in nthropology. If comparisons are desired one ay look for them with greater justification in e writings of the Covenanters of Qumran CDC, v. 6, viii. 4–10, ix. 5, 6).

With 'temple' in the Pauline Corpus *cf.* 'house' 1 Pet. ii. 4–10, where it is manifest that the umerous allusions in the New Testament to the iestly and sacrificial character of Christian life em from the conception of the Church as God's nctuary. See also 'house' in Heb. iii. 1–6.

'Temple' in Hebrews and Revelation

he idea of a heavenly Temple, which was com-on among the Semites and which helped to stain Jewish hope when the exigencies of the ter-testamental period made it appear that the mple of Jerusalem would never become e metropolis of the world, was adopted by the rly Christians. Allusions to it are present in . i. 51, xiv. 2 f.; Gal. iv. 21 ff.; and possibly in il. iii. 20. The 'building of God . . . eternal in e heavens' in the notoriously difficult passage Cor. v. 1–5 may also bear some connection th the idea. The conception is, of course, most veloped in the Epistle to the Hebrews and the ok of Revelation.

According to the writer to the Hebrews the nctuary in heaven is the pattern (*typos*), *i.e.* e original (*cf.* Ex. xxv. 8 f.), and the one on rth used by Jewry is a 'copy and shadow' eb. viii. 5, RSV). The heavenly sanctuary is erefore the true sanctuary (Heb. ix. 24). It longs to the people of the new covenant (Heb. 19, 20). Moreover, the fact that Christ our gh Priest is in this sanctuary means that we, hough still on earth, already participate in its rship (x. 19 ff., xii. 22 ff.). What is this mple? The writer supplies a clue when he says at the heavenly sanctuary was cleansed (ix. 23), made fit for use (*cf.* Nu. vii. 1). The assembly the firstborn (Heb. xii. 23), that is to say, the urch triumphant, is the heavenly Temple. See BERNACLE.

The celestial Temple in the book of Revelation part of the grand scheme of spiritualization dertaken by the author, and note should also taken of the celestial Mt. Zion (xiv. 1, xxi. 10) d the new Jerusalem (iii. 12, xxi. 2 ff.). In int of fact the prophet of Patmos was shown o Temples, one in heaven and the other on th. The latter is in mind in xi. 1 ff. The rassed militant Church is depicted under the ise of the Temple of Jerusalem, or, more urately, the sanctuary of the Temple of usalem, for the forecourt, that is, the luke-rm who are on the fringe of the Church, is luded from the measurement. The imagery es something to Zc. ii. 5, and appears to have same meaning as the sealing of the 144,000 in vii. 1–8. Those measured, alias the numbered, are the elect whom God protects.

Similar spiritualizing is evident in the author's vision of the Temple in heaven. On the top of Mt. Zion he sees not a magnificent edifice, but the company of the redeemed (xiv. 1, *cf.* xiii. 6). That John intends his readers to regard the martyr-host as taking the place of a temple is hinted at in iii. 12: 'Him that overcometh will I make a pillar in the temple of my God.' The heavenly Temple thus 'grows', like its earthly counterpart (see above on Eph. ii. 21 f.), as each of the faithful seals his testimony with martyr-dom. The building will eventually be completed when the decreed number of the elect is made up (vi. 11). It is from this Temple of living beings that God sends out His judgment upon im-penitent nations (xi. 19, xiv. 15 ff., xv. 5–xvi. 1), just as He once directed the destinies of the nations from the Temple of Jerusalem (Is. lxvi. 6; Mi. i. 2; Hab. ii. 20).

The new Jerusalem has no Temple (xxi. 22). In a document like Revelation which follows the traditional images and motifs so closely the idea of a Jerusalem without a Temple is surely novel. John's statement that he 'saw no temple therein' has been taken to mean that the whole city was a Temple; note that the shape of the city is cubical (xxi. 16), like the holy of holies in Solomon's Temple (1 Ki. vi. 20). But that is not what John says. He states plainly that God and the Lamb is the Temple. What he very likely means is that in the place of the Temple is God and His Son. Such indeed would appear to be the grand dénouement for which the writer prepares his readers. First he dramatically announces that the Temple in heaven is opened and its contents laid bare for human eyes to see (xi. 19). Later he drops the hint that the divine dwelling may be none other than God Himself (xxi. 3; note the play on the words *skēnē* and *skēnōsei*). Finally, he states quite simply that the Temple is the Lord God Almighty and the Lamb. One after another the barriers separating man from God are removed until nothing remains to hide God from His people. 'His servants . . . shall see his face' (xxii. 3 f.; *cf.* Is. xxv. 6 ff.). This is the glorious privilege of all who enter the new Jerusalem.

The use made of the ancient motif of the in-gathering and reunion of Israel and the nations at the eschatological Temple by the author of Revelation is thus different from, although com-plementary to, that of Paul. Paul, as we noted above, applied it to the terrestrial Church; John projects it into the heavenly realm and into the world to come. The difference is another illustra-tion of the flexibility of the Temple image.

BIBLIOGRAPHY. P. Bonnard, *Jésus-Christ édi-fiant son Église*, 1948; A. Cole, *The New Temple*, 1950; Y. M. J. Congar, *Le Mystère du Temple*, 1958; M. Fraeyman, 'La Spiritualisation de l'Idée du Temple dans les Épîtres pauliniennes,' *Ephemerides Theologicae Lovanienses*, XXIII, 1947, pp. 378–412; G. Kittel, *TWNT*, *s.v.* '*hieron*', '*naos*', '*oikodomē*', '*oikos*'; M. Simon,

'Le discours de Jésus sur la ruine du temple', *RB*, LVI, 1949, pp. 70–75; P. Vielhauer, *Oikodomē*, dissertation, 1939; H. Wenschkewitz, 'Die Spiritualisierung der Kultusbegriffe Tempel, Priester und Opfer im Neuen Testament', *Angelos*, IV, 1932, pp. 77–230. R.J.McK.

TEMPTATION. The biblical idea of temptation is not primarily of seduction, as in modern usage, but of making trial of a person, or putting him to the test; which may be done for the benevolent purpose of proving or improving his quality, as well as with the malicious aim of showing up his weaknesses or trapping him into wrong action. 'Tempt' in AV means 'test' in this unrestricted sense, in accordance with older English usage. It is only since the 17th century that the word's connotation has been limited to testing with evil intent.

The Hebrew noun is *massâ* (AV 'temptation'); the Hebrew verbs are *māsâ* (AV usually 'tempt') and *bāḥan* (AV usually 'prove' or 'try': a metaphor from metal refining). The LXX and New Testament use as equivalents the noun *peirasmos* and the verbs *(ek)peirazō* and *dokimazō*, the latter corresponding in meaning to *bāḥan*.

The idea of testing a person appears in various connections throughout the Bible.

1. Men test their fellow human beings, as one tests armour (1 Ki. x. 1; *cf.* 1 Sa. xvii. 39: *māsâ* both times), to explore and measure their capacities. The Gospels tell of Jewish opponents, with resentful scepticism, 'tempting' Christ ('trying him out', we might say) to see if they could make Him prove, or try to prove, His Messiahship to them on their terms (Mk. viii. 11); to see if His doctrine was defective or unorthodox (Lk. x. 25); and to see if they could trap Him into self-incriminating assertions (Mk. xii. 15).

2. Men should test themselves before the Lord's Supper (1 Cor. xi. 28: *dokimazō*), and at other times too (2 Cor. xiii. 5: *peirazō*), lest they become presumptuous and deluded about their spiritual state. The Christian needs to test his 'work' (*i.e.* what he is making of his life), lest he go astray and forfeit his reward (Gal. vi. 4). Sober self-knowledge, arising from disciplined self-scrutiny, is a basic element in biblical piety.

3. Men test God by behaviour which constitutes in effect a defiant challenge to Him to prove the truth of His words and the goodness and justice of His ways (Ex. xvii. 2; Nu. xiv. 22; Pss. lxxviii. 18, 41, 56, xcv. 9, cvi. 14; Mal. iii. 15; Acts v. 9, xv. 10). The place-name Massah was a permanent memorial of one such temptation (Ex. xvii. 7; Dt. vi. 16). Thus to goad God betrays extreme irreverence, and God Himself forbids it (Dt. vi. 16; *cf.* Mt. iv. 7; 1 Cor. x. 9 ff.). In all distresses God's people should wait on Him in quiet patience, confident that in due time He will meet their need according to His promise (*cf.* Pss. xxvii. 7–14, xxxvii. 7, xl, cxxx. 5 ff.; La. iii. 25 ff.; Phil. iv. 19).

4. God tests His people by putting them in situations which reveal the quality of their fait[h] and devotion, so that all can see what is in thei[r] hearts (Gn. xxii. 1; Ex. xvi. 4, xx. 20; Dt. viii. 2 16, xiii. 3; Jdg. ii. 22; 2 Ch. xxxii. 31). By thu[s] making trial of them, He purifies them, as meta[l] is purified in the refiner's crucible (Ps. lxvi. 10 Is. xlviii. 10; Zc. xiii. 9; 1 Pet. i. 6 f.; *cf.* Ps. cxix 67, 71); He strengthens their patience an[d] matures their Christian character (Jas. i. 2 ff., 12 *cf.* 1 Pet. v. 10); and He leads them into an en larged assurance of His love for them (*cf.* Gn xxii. 15 ff.; Rom. v. 3 ff.). Through faithfulness i[n] times of trial men become *dokimoi*, 'approved' in God's sight (Jas. i. 12; 1 Cor. xi. 19).

5. Satan tests God's people by manipulatin[g] circumstances, within the limits that God allow[s] him (*cf.* Jb. i. 12, ii. 6; 1 Cor. x. 13), in a[n] attempt to make them desert God's will. Th[e] New Testament knows him as 'the tempter' (*h peirazōn*, Mt. iv. 3; 1 Thes. iii. 5), the implacabl[e] foe of both God and men (1 Pet. v. 8; Rev. xii Christians must constantly be watchful (Mk. xiv 38; Gal. vi. 1; 2 Cor. ii. 11) and active (Eph. v 10 ff.; Jas. iv. 7; 1 Pet. v. 9) against the devil, fo[r] he is always at work trying to make them fal[l] whether by crushing them under the weight [of] hardship or pain (Jb. i. 11–ii. 7; 1 Pet. v. 9; Re[v.] ii. 10, *cf.* iii. 10; Heb. ii. 18), or by urging the[m] to a wrong fulfilment of natural desires (Mt. i[v.] 3 f.; 1 Cor. vii. 5), or by making them con placent, careless, and self-assertive (Gal. vi. Eph. iv. 27), or by misrepresenting God to the[m] and engendering false ideas of His truth and H[is] will (Gn. iii. 1–5; *cf.* 2 Cor. xi. 3; Mt. iv. 5 ff 2 Cor. xi. 14; Eph. vi. 11). Mt. iv. 5 f. shows th[at] Satan can even quote (and misapply) Scriptu[re] for this purpose. But God promises that a way [of] deliverance will always be open when He allo[ws] Satan to tempt Christians (1 Cor. x. 13; 2 Pe[t.] ii. 9; *cf.* 2 Cor. xii. 7–10).

The New Testament philosophy of temptati[on] is reached by combining these last two lines [of] thought. 'Temptations' (Lk. xxii. 28; Acts xx. 1 Jas. i. 2; 1 Pet. i. 6; 2 Pet. ii. 9) are the work [of] both God and the devil. They are testing situ tions in which the servant of God faces ne possibilities of both good and evil, and is expose[d] to various inducements to prefer the latter. Fro[m] this standpoint, temptations are Satan's wor[k] but Satan is God's tool as well as His foe (*cf.* J i. 11 f., ii. 5 f.), and it is ultimately God Himse[lf] who leads His servants into temptation (Mt. iv. vi. 13), permitting Satan to try to seduce them f[or] beneficent purposes of His own. However, thou[gh] temptations do not overtake men apart fro[m] God's will, the actual prompting to do wrong not of God, nor does it express His comma[nd] (Jas. i. 12 f.). The desire which impels to sin is n[ot] God's, but one's own, and it is fatal to yield to (Jas. i. 14 ff.). Christ taught His disciples to a[sk] God not to expose them to temptation (Mt. 13), and to watch and pray, lest they shou[ld] 'enter into' temptation (*i.e.* yield to its pressu[re]) when at any time God saw fit to try them by (Mt. xxvi. 41).

Temptation is not sin, for Christ was tempted as we are, yet remained sinless (Heb. iv. 15; *cf.* Mt. iv. 1 ff.; Lk. xxii. 28). Temptation becomes sin only when and as the suggestion of evil is accepted and yielded to.

BIBLIOGRAPHY. *Arndt*; H. Seeseman in *TWNT*, VI, 23–37; M. Dods in *DCG*; Trench, *Synonyms*[10], pp. 267 ff.

J.I.P.

TEN COMMANDMENTS. The 'ten words' (*d^{e}ḇārîm*; *cf.* Ex. xxxiv. 28; Dt. iv. 13, x. 4) were originally uttered by the divine voice from Sinai in the hearing of all Israel (Ex. xix. 16–xx. 17). Afterwards, in the presence of Moses on Sinai, they were twice written by the finger of God on the obverse and reverse of two stone 'tables' or tablets (Ex. xxxi. 18, xxxii. 15, 16, xxxiv. 1, 28; *cf.* Dt. x. 4). The first pair were shattered by Moses in angry symbolization of the significance of Israel's sin of the golden calf (Ex. xxxii. 19). The second pair were deposited in the ark (Ex. xxv. 16, xl. 20). Later, Moses republished the Ten Commandments in slightly modified form (Dt. v. 6–21).

The common designation of the contents of the two tablets as 'the Decalogue', though it enjoys biblical precedent, has tended to restrict unduly the Church's conception of that revelation. It is, indeed, a comprehensive summary of the law of God, the permanent validity of which is evident from the nature of its contents and the New Testament attitude towards it (*cf.*, *e.g.*, Mt. xix. 17–19, xxii. 37–40) and is further marked by its awesome promulgation, its durable physical form, and its location under God's throne in the sanctuary. Nevertheless, it is not adequately classified as law; it belongs to the broader category of covenant. The terminology 'covenant' (*b^{e}rîṯ*; Dt. iv. 13) and 'the words of the covenant' (Ex. xxxiv. 28; *cf.* Dt. xxix. 1, 9) is applied to it. It is also identified as the 'testimony' (*'ēḏûṯ*; Ex. xxv. 16, 21, xl. 20; *cf.* 2 Ki. xvii. 15), which describes the covenant order of life as one solemnly imposed and sworn to so that *'ēḏûṯ* becomes practically synonymous with *b^{e}rîṯ*. The two tablets are called 'the tables of the covenant' (Dt. ix. 9, 11, 15) and 'the tables of the testimony' (Ex. xxxi. 18, xxxii. 15, xxxiv. 29). The ark as the depository of the tablets is called 'the ark of the covenant' or 'of the testimony'; and the tabernacle where the ark was located, 'the tabernacle of the testimony'.

The historical occasion of the original giving of this revelation was the establishment of the theocratic covenant. The principles of Ex. xx. 1–17 as elaborated and applied in casuistic form in the book of the covenant (Ex. xx. 22–xxiii. 33) served as a legal instrument in the ratification of that covenant (Ex. xxiv. 1–8). The later, Deuteronomic, version is part of a document of covenant renewal.

When, therefore, the Scripture designates the revelation of the two tablets as 'the ten words', it clearly does so as *pars pro toto*. At the same time, this terminology and the preponderance of law content which it reflects indicates that the type of covenant involved is essentially the establishment of an authoritative order of life as a declaration of the Covenant-giver's lordship over His servants.

The covenantal character of the Decalogue is illuminated and corroborated by ancient international treaties of the type used to formalize the relationship of a suzerain and vassal. Suzerainty treaties begin with a preamble identifying the covenant lord, the speaker (*cf.* Ex. xx. 2a), and an historical prologue recounting especially the benefits previously bestowed on the vassal through the favour and might of the lord (*cf.* Ex. xx. 2b). The obligations imposed on the vassal, the longest section, follow. The foremost stipulation is the requirement of loyalty to the covenant lord or negatively the proscription of all alien alliances (*cf.* Ex. xx. 3–17, the first and great principle of which is whole-hearted love of Yahweh, who is a jealous God). Another section enunciated the curses and blessings which the gods of the covenant oath would visit on the vassals in accordance with their transgressions or fidelity (*cf.* Ex. xx. 5b, 6, 7b, 12b). Among other parallels are the 'I–thou' style, the practice of placing a copy of the covenant in the sanctuaries of the two parties, and the administrative policy of renewing the covenant with the successive generations of the vassal kingdom. In covenant renewal documents, modification of the stipulations, and particularly modernization, was customary. That explains the various differences between the Ex. xx and Dt. v forms of the Decalogue. For example, Dt. v. 21 adds 'his field' because of the relevance of land ownership to Israel's now imminent inheritance of Canaan.

In brief, the two tablets contained the quintessence of the Mosaic administration of the covenant of grace. Yahweh, Creator of heaven, earth, sea, and all that is in them, is presented as covenant Suzerain. The theocratic covenant relationship is traced to Yahweh's redemptive election and deliverance, and its continuance to the thousandth generation is attributed to His faithful mercies. The covenant way of life is sovereignly dictated in ten commandments, the standard of Israel's consecration to her Lord.

The very fact that the law is embedded in divine covenant disclosure points to the religious principle of personal devotion to God as the heart of true fulfilment of the law. But there is no incompatibility between the divine demand communicated in concrete imperatives and the call of God to personal commitment to Him in love. Yahweh describes the beneficiaries of His covenant mercy as 'them that love me, and keep my commandments' (Ex. xx. 6; *cf.* Jn. xiv. 15). The biblical ethic is rooted in biblical religion, and biblical religion is not shapeless mysticism but structured truth.

The revelation of the law in the context of redemptive covenant action indicates that conformity to the law is a soteric achievement of the grace of Yahweh who delivers from bondage. In this context even the preponderantly negative form of the Decalogue serves to magnify the grace of God who, though obliged to protest negatively against the sin of fallen man, offers His protest not as a final condemnation but as the standard of life within a restored covenant communion. The negative form thus becomes a divine promise to the redeemed servants of perfect ultimate triumph over the demonic power within and without, which would enslave them in the hell of endless alienation from God. An ethic rooted in such religion possesses the dynamic of faith, hope, and love.

Since the administration of the covenant of grace is an historically progressive development and the Decalogue appears as an integral element in the organic unfolding of covenant revelation, it is natural that the Decalogue's abiding principles are formulated in terms appropriate to the Mosaic age. For example, the specific form of the sabbath law reflects the Old Testament eschatological perspective and the promise appended to the fifth word (and elsewhere related to the entire law, *cf.* Dt. v. 33–vi. 3) employs the imagery of the contemporary, typical manifestation of God's kingdom. This does not detract from the Decalogue's authority as a permanent norm, but does require that the specific application at any given time reckon with the realities of redemptive history as an eschatologically decisive movement. The unbeliever, for example, is the believer's 'neighbour' until the judgment, but not after that.

As for the division into ten words, the Decalogue's parallelism with the suzerainty treaty structure shows the error of regarding the preamble and historical prologue as a commandment. Also, the variant forms of the prohibition of covetousness in Ex. xx. 17 and Dt. v. 21 contradict the division of it into two commandments, and that obviates the associated error of combining into one what most Protestants, following the oldest tradition, have regarded as the first and second commandments. The customary division of the Decalogue into 'two tables' stems from a mistaken conception of the nature of the two tables, which were actually duplicates (*cf.* M. G. Kline, 'The Two Tables of the Covenant', *WTJ*, XXII, 2, 1960, pp. 133–146).

BIBLIOGRAPHY. C. Hodge, *Systematic Theology*, III, 1940, pp. 271–465; G. Vos, *Biblical Theology*, 1954, pp. 145–159.

M.G.K.

TENT. A collapsible structure of cloth or skins supported on poles, and often held firm by cords stretched from the poles to pegs or stakes fixed in the ground all round. Compare Is. liv. 2, which mentions the curtains, cords, stakes, or tent-pegs (but not the poles); the tent-cloth was often dark in colour (Ct. i. 5). Tents were among the earliest habitations made by man himself (Gn. iv. 20, ix. 21). They were the normal dwelling of both nomadic and semi-nomadic people. The Hebrew Patriarchs lived in tents (Gn. xviii. 1, 6, 9, 10, *etc.*); and the womenfolk sometimes had their own tents (Sarah, Gn. xxiv. 67; Jacob, Leah, the maids, Rachel, Gn. xxxi. 33), doubtless adjoining those of their husbands. On their journeyings from Egypt to Canaan, Israel lived in tents (Ex. xvi. 16, xxxiii. 8, 10; Nu. xvi. 26, xix. 14), taking up more permanent dwellings when occupying Canaan. In the days of Jeremiah, the Rechabite sect held to the nomadic ideal of dwelling in tents and scorned the ways of sedentary life (Je. xxxv. 7), but even the romantic ideal of independent tent-nomadism was not to be treasured above devotion to God (Ps. lxxxiv. 10). Death is compared to packing up the tent in Jb. iv. 21 (RV, RSV); *cf.* 2 Cor. v. 1.

Fig. 208. An Assyrian army officer in his tent in which his servant prepares his bed. From a relief in the palace of Ashurbanipal, Nineveh, *c.* 650 BC.

Among other peoples, Scripture mentions the tents of the Midianites (Jdg. vi. 5, vii. 13), of Kedar (Ct. i. 5), and Cushan (Hab. iii. 7, also of Midian), all dwellers in the desert fringes of Transjordania and NW Arabia. Tents had specific uses in settled nations. Besides the peaceful shepherd tenting in his pastures (Ct. i. 8; Is. xxxviii. 12), kings and armies camped in tents in the field, *cf.* 1 Sa. xvii. 54 (David); 2 Ki. vii. 7, 8 (Aramaeans). Finally, 'tent' in ordinary speech came to be used of any kind of dwelling (not only literally; *cf.* 1 Ki. viii. 66; 2 Ki. xiii. 5, both rendered 'homes' in RSV), perhaps because the tent was largely used in the summer by many town and village dwellers. The external data on tents illustrate that in Scripture. In the patriarchal period the Egyptian Sinuhe in Canaan had a tent and encampment and plundered that of his adversary (*ANET*, p. 20b, line 145). In the period following Israel's Exodus and initial settlement Rameses III (*c.* 1192–1161 BC) records that he 'devastated Se'ir (*i.e.* Edom) among the nomad tribes, and pillaged their tents (*'hr*, from Heb. *'ōhel*) of people and goods' (*ANET*, 262a). Cf. Midian, Cushan, or Kedar. For pictures of Assyrian military tents (round, supported on poles and sticks), see *ANEP*, figs. 170, 171, 3… (royal war-tent). See also TABERNACLE.

K.A.K.

TERAH. 1. The father of Abram, Nahor, and Haran (Gn. xi. 27; AV 'Thara', Lk. iii. 34). Heb. *teraḥ* is usually taken as connected with …

moon-god and compared with Turaḫi, a place near Harran. Terah emigrated from Ur of the Chaldees and settled in Harran, where he died long after Abram's departure (Acts vii. 4 is an oral slip). In Jos. xxiv. 2 he is described as an idolater.

2. An unidentified Israelite encampment in the wilderness between Tahath and Mithkah (Nu. xxxiii. 27, 28; AV 'Tarah'). J.W.C.

TERAPHIM. These objects are mentioned in every period of the Old Testament: the Patriarchs (Gn. xxxi. 19); the judges (Jdg. xvii. 5–xviii. 30); early and late monarchy (1 Sa. xv. 23, xix. 13–16; 2 Ki. xxiii. 24; Ho. iii. 4; Ezk. xxi. 21); and post-exile (Zc. x. 2). When mentioned in Israelite contexts they are almost always condemned, directly (1 Sa. xv. 23; 2 Ki. xxiii. 24) or indirectly (Jdg. xvii. 6; Zc. x. 2). In their use, they are mostly associated with divination: note the pairing of ephod and teraphim in the idolatrous religion of Micah (Jdg. xvii. 5, *etc.*); the association with divination by arrows and hepatoscopy (Ezk. xxi. 21), and with spiritist practices (2 Ki. xxiii. 24). Nowhere are we told how they were consulted, nor even what their appearance was. While Gn. xxxi. 34 suggests that they were small objects, 1 Sa. xix. 13–16 suggests a life-size figure, or at least a life-size bust. However, it is possible that Michal placed the teraphim 'beside' rather than 'in' the bed, and that they were considered to have some prophylactic or curative propensity.

Fig. 209. A clay plaque of the intercessory goddess Lama from the chapel of Ḫendursag, Ur (c. 2000 BC). Such figurines may have been the teraphim of Old Testament times. See also fig. 112.

These last two references (also Jdg. xvii. 5 ff.) associate teraphim with the home, and Laban, at least, considered them as household gods (Gn. xxxi. 30). Archaeology has explained why the materialistic Laban (Gn. xxiv. 30, 31) should be so anxious about his gods: 'In (Nuzu) law the possession of such idols by the woman's husband ensured for him the succession to the father-in-law's property' (H. H. Rowley, *The Servant of the Lord*, 1952, p. 302). When Laban could not recover the teraphim he made haste to secure the rights of his sons by a fresh agreement with Jacob (Gn. xxxi. 48–55). Household gods found in Nuzi sites are of the figurine type (see G. E. Wright, *Biblical Archaeology*, 1957, p. 44).

The word 'teraphim' is the same type of plural as 'elohim'. Its derivation is uncertain: it may possibly come from *rāpā'*, 'to heal'; *tārāp̄*, 'to decay' ('decaying ones'); *r^epā'îm*, 'ghosts' (*cf.* the suggestion, for which, however, there is no contemporary evidence, that teraphim were originally mummified human heads; see *WC*; H. L. Ellison on Ezk. xxi. 21 in *Ezekiel: The Man and His Message*, 1956); or late Heb. *tōrep̄*, 'filth', a 'substitution word' like *bōšeṯ* for *ba'al*.

J.A.M.

TEREBINTH. See TREES.

TERTIUS. The amanuensis who wrote Romans at Paul's dictation (Rom. xvi. 22); on the process, see B. M. Metzger, 'Stenography and Church History', in *TCERK*, II, pp. 1060 f., and references there. He appends his own greetings, perhaps at the point where he resumes his pen after Paul has written some personal greetings in autograph (*cf.* Gal. vi. 11; Col. iv. 18; 2 Thes. iii. 17). This may suggest that he had Roman connections himself. The name is Latin and appears in a 1st-century inscription in the Roman cemetery of S. Priscilla (cited in *MM*). A.F.W.

TERTULLUS. A fairly common Roman name, in origin a diminutive of Tertius. Nothing is known of the orator Tertullus who accused Paul before Felix except what can be deduced from Acts xxiv. 1 ff.

From his use of the first person in verses 3, 4, 6, and 7 (although found only in the Western Text, verse 7 is undoubtedly genuine) it seems probable that Tertullus was a Jew. The words 'this nation' (verse 2) and 'the Jews' (verse 5) are not inconsistent with this deduction. It was not uncommon for Jews at this period to have Gentile names, and it was possible for a good Jew to be also a Roman citizen, with a Roman name (see PAUL).

The fulsome flattery (see FELIX) of Tertullus' opening sentences is in accordance with the rhetorical fashion of the period, but the rest of the speech is unimpressive. Even in his précis Luke makes it clear that Tertullus was trying to cover up a weak case with rhetorical padding. In addition to the real charge that Paul had attempted 'to profane the temple', Tertullus tries to represent him as one of the sedition-mongers and messianist politicians who were so often a problem to the Roman rulers of Palestine. K.L.McK.

TESTAMENT. See COVENANT.

TESTAMENTS OF THE TWELVE PATRIARCHS. See APOCALYPTIC, PSEUDEPIGRAPHA, I.

TESTIMONY. See ARK OF THE COVENANT, TABERNACLE, WITNESS.

TETRARCH. This title (Gk. *tetrarchos*) was used in classical Greek to denote the ruler of a fourth part of a region, and especially applied to the rulers of the four regions of Thessaly. The Romans gave it to any ruler of part of an Oriental province. When Herod the Great, who ruled Palestine as a client-king under the

Romans, died in 4 BC, his sons disputed their father's will. Appeal on their part to Augustus Caesar led to the division of the territory among three sons: Archelaus being appointed ethnarch of Judaea, Samaria, and Idumaea; Antipas tetrarch of Galilee and Peraea; and Philip tetrarch of Batanea, Trachonitis, Ituraea, Gaulanitis, and Auranitis, areas north-east of the Sea of Galilee. In the New Testament the word is used solely in reference to Herod Antipas (Mt. xiv. 1; Lk. iii. 19, ix. 7; Acts xiii. 1), though in Lk. iii. 1 the cognate verb is applied to Antipas, Philip, and Lysanias, tetrarch of Abilene (*qq.v.*).

BIBLIOGRAPHY. E. Schürer, *HJP*, 1898, I, ii, sections 16, 17. D.H.W.

TEXT AND VERSIONS.

1. Of the Old Testament

Texts and versions provide the raw materials for the discipline known as textual criticism. The ultimate aim is to provide a text in the form intended by its author. Generally speaking, the greater the age of a document, the greater is its authority. There may be cases, however, where this does not hold; for instance, of two MSS, the older may have been copied from a recent and poor exemplar, while the other goes back to a very much earlier and better one. The history of a document must be taken into consideration before a verdict can be given on readings.

Documents are exposed to the ravages of time and the frailty of human nature. It is the latter that gives rise to most of our problems. The errors of scribes, however, seem to run in well-defined channels. Among the common errors are: haplography (failure to repeat a letter or word); dittography (repeating what occurs only once); false recollection (of a similar passage or of another MS); homoeoteleuton (omission of a passage between identical words); line omission (sometimes through homoeoteleuton); confusion of letters of similar form; insertion into body of text of marginal notes. The comparative study of texts can help towards the elimination of corruptions. Here numerical preponderance is not decisive: several representatives of the same archetype count as only one witness. The form of textual transmission is best depicted as a genealogical tree, and the facts of the genealogical relations can be applied to the assessment of evidence for any given reading. The documentary evidence for the text of the Old Testament consists of Hebrew MSS from the 3rd century BC to the 12th century AD, and ancient versions in Aramaic, Greek, Syriac, and Latin.

From earliest times the Jews had at their disposal the means of producing written records. The North Semitic script (alphabetic) was in existence long before the time of Moses (see WRITING). The oldest example known to us is from the period of the Hyksos (*c.* 1700 BC) (see Gressmann, *Altorientalische Bilder zum Alten Testament*, 1926, plate cclix). Moses must have been familiar with Egyptian writing and literary methods. He may, too, have been acquainted with cuneiform, for Akkadian was already in use from the 15th century BC onwards as a diplomatic language in Egypt, as is shown by the El-Amarna letters. If the Bible did not expressly state that Moses was literate (Nu. xxxiii. 2 and *passim*), we should be compelled to infer it from collateral evidence. There is, therefore, no need to postulate a period of oral tradition. Analogies drawn from peoples of disparate culture, even if contemporary, are irrelevant. The fact is, that the peoples of the same cultural background as the Hebrews were literate from the fourth millennium BC onwards, and from the second millennium men were being trained not merely as scribes but as expert copyists. It is unlikely that under Moses the Hebrews were less advanced than their contemporaries or that they were less scrupulous in the transmission of their texts than the Egyptians and Assyrians (*cf.* W. J. Martin, *Dead Sea Scroll of Isaiah*, 1954, pp. 18 f.).

Before embarking on a description of the sources at our disposal for the restoration of the text of the Old Testament, it is important to recall the attitude of the Jews to their Scriptures. It can best be summed up in the statement by Josephus: 'We have given practical proof of our reverence for our own Scriptures. For, although such long ages have now passed, no one has ventured either to add, or to remove, or to alter a syllable; and it is an instinct with every Jew, from the day of his birth, to regard them as the decrees of God, to abide by them, and, if need be, cheerfully to die for them. Time and again ere now the sight has been witnessed of prisoners enduring tortures and death in every form in the theatres, rather than utter a single word against the laws and the allied documents' (*Against Apion*, I, pp. 179 f., Loeb Edition).

That Josephus is merely expressing the attitude of the biblical writers themselves is clear from such passages as Dt. iv. 2 ('Not shall you add to the word which I am commanding you, and not shall you take away from it, in order to keep the commandments of the Lord your God which I am commanding you') or Je. xxvi. 2 ('. . . all the words which I have commanded you to speak unto them; thou shalt not take away a word'). There is no reason to suppose that the Jews ever abandoned these principles. The theory, for long prevalent, that the Jews undertook a recension of the text of the Old Testament about AD 100 would now be hard to defend in view of the substantial agreement between the texts of the biblical scrolls from Qumran and the Massoretic text. Many of the divergences in texts may be due to the practice of employing the same scribe to copy both biblical texts and Targums. As the latter are frequently paraphrastic in their treatment of the text, this laxity could subconsciously easily affect the copyists.

I. THE TRANSMISSION OF THE TEXT

Measures for the preservation of the text must have already been in use in the pre-Christian era for in the Dead Sea Scroll of Isaiah (*e.g.* plate XXIX, lines 3 and 10) dots are used over doubtful words, just as is done later by the Massoretes. In New Testament times the scribes are too well established to be a recent innovation. It was doubtless due to their activity that terms such as 'jot' and 'tittle' (*q.v.*) owed their currency. The fact that 'jot' was then the smallest letter indicates that the 'square' characters were in use. The Talmud states that these scribes were called *sopherim* because they counted the letters in the Torah (*Qiddushin* 30a). Since their intensive preoccupation with the text of Scripture qualified them as exegetes and educationalists, the transmission of the text ceased to be regarded as their prime responsibility.

II. THE MASSORETES

The writing of the consonants only was sufficient as long as Hebrew remained a spoken language. Where a word might be ambiguous 'vowel-letters' could be used to make the reading clear. These 'vowel-indicators' were in origin residual: they arose through 'waw' and 'yod' amalgamating with a preceding vowel and losing their consonantal identity, but they continued to be written, and in time came to be treated as representing vowels. Their use was then extended to other words, where etymologically they were intrusive. Their insertion or omission was largely discretionary. Consequent variants have no significance. It was not until about the 7th century of our era that the Massoretes introduced a complete system of vowel-signs.

The Massoretes (lit. 'transmitters') succeeded the old scribes (*sopherim*) as the custodians of the sacred text. They were active from about AD 500 to 1000. The textual apparatus introduced by them is probably the most complete of its kind ever to be used. Long before their time, of course, others had given much thought to the preservation of the purity of the text. Rabbi Akiba, who died about AD 135, was credited with the saying 'The (accurate) transmission is a fence for the Torah.' He stressed the importance of preserving even the smallest letter. In this he was by no means the first, as the statement in Mt. v. 18 shows: 'Till heaven and earth pass, one jot or one tittle shall in no wise pass from the law, till all be fulfilled.'

The Massoretes introduced vowel-signs and punctuation or accentual marks into the consonantal text. Three systems of vocalization had been developed: two supralinear (Babylonian and Palestinian) and one infralinear, except for one sign. This system, called the Tiberian, supplanted the other two, and is the one now used in Hebrew texts.

As it was the resolute purpose of the Massoretes to hand on the text as they had received it, they left the consonantal text unchanged. Where they felt that corrections or improvements should be made, they placed these in the margin. Here the word preferred and which they intended to be read (called the *Q^e^rē'*, 'that which is to be read') was placed in the margin, but its vowels were placed under the consonants of the word in the inviolable text (called the *K^e^tîḇ*, 'the written'). It is possible that the form given in the margin (*Q^e^rē'*) was a variant reading. The view held in some quarters that the scribes or Massoretes boggled at giving variant readings, and in fact deliberately suppressed them, is contrary to what we know of the actual practice of the copyists.

The Massoretes retained, for instance, certain marks of the earlier scribes relating to doubtful words and listed certain of their conjectures (*s^e^ḇîrîn*). They used every imaginable safeguard, no matter how cumbersome or laborious, to ensure the accurate transmission of the text. The number of letters in a book was counted and its middle letter was given. Similarly with the words, and again the middle word of the book was noted.

ישראל על־כל־אשר עשו נאם־יהוה: הנה ימים
נאם־יהוה ונבנתה העיר ליהוה ממגדל חננאל שער הפנה:
ויצא עוד קוה המדה נגדו על גבעת גרב ונסב געתה: וכל־ מ
העמק הפגרים ׀ והדשן וכל־השרמות עד־נחל קדרון
עד־פנת שער הסוסים מזרחה קדש ליהוה לא־ינתש ולא־
יהרס עוד לעולם:

Fig. 210. The Massoretic text of Je. xxxi. 38–40. In verse 40 is a scribal error (*haššārēmôṯ* for *haššāḏēmôṯ*) which is corrected by a marginal note (Q^e^rē'). *Cf.* fig. 214.

They collected any peculiarities in spelling or in the forms or positions of letters. They recorded the number of times a particular word or phrase occurred. Among the many lists they drew up is one containing the words that occur only twice in the Old Testament. Their lists finally included all orthographic peculiarities of the text.

The textual notes supplied by the Massoretes are called the Massorah. The shorter notes placed in the margin of the codices are referred to as the *Massorah Parva*. They were later enlarged and arranged into lists and placed at the top or bottom of the page. In this form they were called *Massorah Magna*. This fuller form may give, for instance, the references to the passages where a certain form occurs, whereas the shorter would give only the number of the occurrences. The notes provide the results of their analysis of textual peculiarities. They give variant readings from recognized codices, such as the Mugah and Hilleli (both now lost).

Among the names of Massoretes known to us is that of Aaron ben Asher, who was active in the first half of the 10th century AD. Five generations of his family seem to have worked on the Hebrew text, and under Aaron the work reached a definitive stage. The best codex of this school is thought to be the one formerly in Aleppo, now in Israel. No facsimile of it has yet been produced. Another noted family of Massoretes was that of ben Naphtali, one of whom was apparently contemporary with Aaron ben Asher. The differences between them in their treatment of the text was largely confined to matters of vocalization. The 'Reuchlin' codex in Karlsruhe is a representative of the ben Naphtali approach.

The text edited by Jacob ben Chayyim for the second rabbinic Bible published by Daniel Bomberg in Venice in 1524–5 came to be accepted practically as a standard text. The text was eclectic in character, and scholars have been aware for some 250 years that it could be improved. It is significant, however, that M. D. Cassuto, a scholar who probably had a finer sense for Hebrew than any other in this field, and who had an unrivalled knowledge at first hand of the Aleppo Ben Asher codex, evidently saw no reason for preferring this to the Ben Chayyim text, which he has retained for his fine edition of the Hebrew Bible (Jerusalem, 1953). The non-expert might easily be misled by the somewhat hyperbolic language used of the extent of the differences to be found in the various MSS. They relate mostly to matters of vocalization, a not altogether indispensable aid in Semitic languages. Linguistically considered they are largely irrelevant minutiae, at the most of diachronistic interest. Belief in the golden age of the phoneme dies hard. It ranks with the naïveté that believes 'honour' is a better spelling than 'honor'. Vocalization in a Semitic language belongs primarily to orthography and grammar, and to exegesis, and only to a limited extent to textual criticism. There never was an original *vocalized* text to restore.

III. THE DEAD SEA SCROLLS

The sensational discovery in 1947 of the biblical MSS, in caves around Wadi Qumran to the north-west of the Dead Sea, has revolutionized the approach to the Old Testament text by going some 800 years behind the Massoretic apparatus. It has also been a salutary reminder that the purpose of the discipline is the restoration of a consonantal text. The fortuitous find of MSS by an Arab shepherd in one of the caves in this region led to a systematic exploration of other caves, resulting in the discovery of large quantities of biblical and non-biblical material. The original find included one complete MS of Isaiah and another containing about one-third of the book. The later discoveries brought to light fragments of every book of the Bible, with the exception of Esther, as well as Bible commentaries, and works of a religious nature. Some of the biblical fragments show differences from the standard text more in the nature of variant readings. However, with fragments it is difficult to evaluate the significance of such alterations: they could be due to inferior copying. In the absence of extensive samples of a scribe's work, it is impossible to pass judgment on his capabilities. Where the material is sufficiently copious, as in the case of the Isaiah scrolls, the divergences from the Massoretic text are not substantial. On the other hand, a promiscuous collection of biblical, semi-biblical, and non-biblical MSS bristles with so many difficulties in sorting and reconstructing that mistakes are inevitable. Already claims are being made for evidence of different recensions, but with fragments the evidence must remain tenuous. As there were translations of the LXX into Aramaic, there is no *a priori* reason why the same could not have been done for current Hebrew. It is all a little reminiscent of the controversy over the Samaritan Pentateuch when it first became known.

The Dead Sea biblical MSS gave us for the first time examples of Hebrew texts from pre-Christian times, some thousand years earlier than our oldest MSS; thus they take us behind the alleged suppression of all divergent texts in AD 100. According to the Talmud, an attempt was made to provide a standard text with the help of three Scrolls formerly belonging to the Temple, by taking in cases of disagreement the reading that had the support of two (TJ, *Ta'anith* IV, 2; *Sopherim* VI, 4; *Siphre* 356). The finds have helped to relegate questions of vocalization to their proper sphere, that of orthography and grammar, and have deprived of much of its pertinency the work done in the field of Massoretic studies by providing us with MSS much older than any hitherto at our disposal.

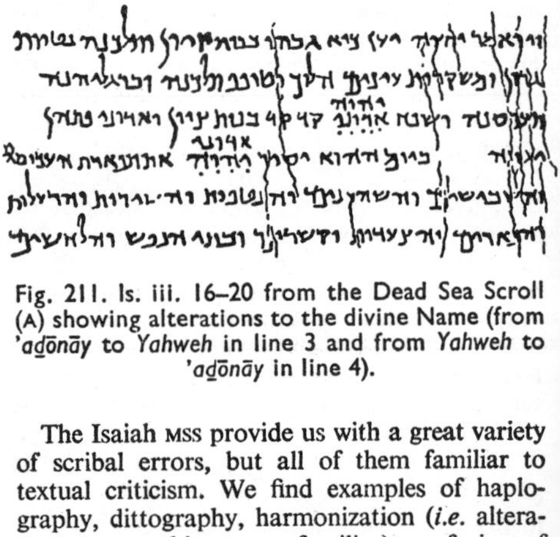

Fig. 211. Is. iii. 16–20 from the Dead Sea Scroll (A) showing alterations to the divine Name (from *'adōnāy* to *Yahweh* in line 3 and from *Yahweh* to *'adōnāy* in line 4).

The Isaiah MSS provide us with a great variety of scribal errors, but all of them familiar to textual criticism. We find examples of haplography, dittography, harmonization (*i.e.* alteration to something more familiar), confusion of letters, homoeoteleuton, line omission, and introduction into the text of marginal notes.

The great significance of these MSS is that they constitute an independent witness to the reliability of the transmission of our accepted text. There is no reason whatever to believe that the Qumran community would collaborate with the leaders in Jerusalem in adhering to any particular recension. They carry us back to an earlier point on the line of transmission, to the common ancestor of the great Temple scrolls and the unsophisticated scrolls from Qumran. See DEAD SEA SCROLLS.

IV. THE CAIRO GENIZAH

The MSS discovered from 1890 onwards in the Genizah of the Old Synagogue in Cairo are o considerable importance for the vocalized text. (A Genizah was the depository for scrolls no longer considered fit for use.) The lack of uniformity in vocalization and the virtual absence of variations from the consonantal text show that the vocalization was considered of secondary importance. Among the fragments of biblical MSS from this Genizah are some with supralinear vowel-signs. In the collection were also quantities of fragments of Targum and of rabbinic literature. Some of the MSS may be older than the 9th century.

V. THE HEBREW PENTATEUCH OF THE SAMARITANS

The Hebrew Pentateuch preserved by the Samaritans is unquestionably derived from a very ancient text. The Samaritans, probably the descendants of the mixed population of Samaria, the result of a partial deportation of Jews followed by the plantation of foreigners by Sargon in 721 BC (*cf.* 2 Ki. xvii. 24, xxiv. 15–16), were refused a share in the rebuilding of the Temple by the Jews returning under Ezra and Nehemiah. The breach which followed (probably in the time of Nehemiah, *c.* 445 BC) led to the establishment of a separate Samaritan cultic centre at Mt. Gerizim, near Shechem (now Nablus). Therewith all official and religious contacts between the two communities virtually

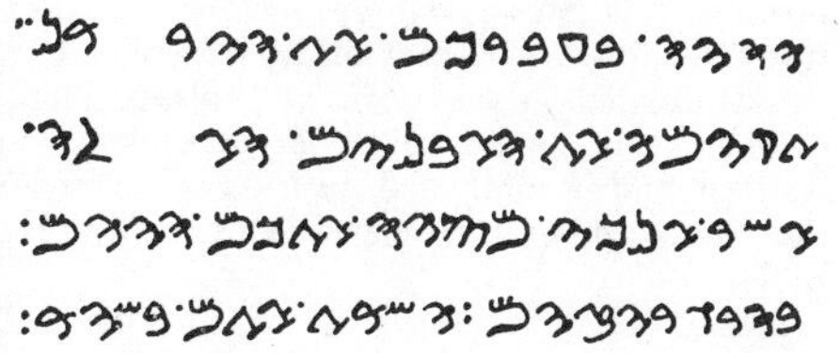

Fig. 212. Dt. xxvii. 4 from the Samaritan Pentateuch. Mount Gerizim is substituted for Mount Ebal at the beginning of line 4.

ceased, and the Hebrew text of the Pentateuch, in their hands when this occurred, was henceforth transmitted without interference from or collaboration with Jewish scribes. The copies of this Pentateuch, therefore, are descended from an archetype not later than the 5th century BC, and thus provide an independent check on the trustworthiness of the Hebrew transmission.

The oldest MS is in all probability the one accredited to Abishua, the great-grandson of Aaron (1 Ch. vi. 3 f.). This claim, of course, lacks substantiation. The MS itself, written on thin vellum, is not uniformly old; the oldest part seems to be that from the end of Numbers onwards. The script is archaic, similar to that found on Maccabean coins, but the occasional confusion of letters such as *d* and *r*, which should not normally be confused in this script, may well indicate that the script is not really archaic but only archaistic. Expert opinion would assign this scroll to the 13th century AD, or not much earlier than its alleged discovery by the high priest Phinehas in 1355.

The first copy of the Samaritan Pentateuch reached Europe in 1616 through Pietro della Valle, and in 1628 an account of it was published by J. Morinus, who claimed it to be far superior to the Massoretic text. This seems to be the case with every new discovery of documents, prompted either by a preference for the LXX or an innate hostility to the traditional Jewish text. There was in this instance another motive at work: the desire on the part of certain scholars to weaken the position of the Reformers in their stand for the authority of the Bible. Gesenius, probably Germany's greatest Hebrew scholar, brought this barren controversy to an end and demonstrated the superiority of the Massoretic text. We are witnessing in our day an attempt to reinstate the Samaritan Pentateuch. Some of its protagonists betray by their faith in the trustworthiness of the Samaritan transmission an ingenuousness never surpassed by the most extreme conservatives. It is true that in some 1,600 places the Samaritan agrees with the LXX, but the disagreements are equally numerous. It is not easy to account for the agreements; one possibility is that when corrections had to be made in the Samaritan Hebrew Pentateuch an Aramaic targum was used (the Samaritan dialect and Aramaic are practically identical, and the Samaritan version, that is, the translation of the Pentateuch into Samaritan, in places agrees *verbatim* with the Targum of Onkelos). There are numerous traces of the influence of the Aramaic targums in the LXX. See TARGUMS.

For many of the variants a simple explanation can be given: the attempt to show that God had chosen Gerizim. After the Ten Commandments in Ex. xx and in Dt. v, the Samaritan inserts the passage Dt. xxvii. 2–7 with 'Mount Ebal' replaced by 'Mount Gerizim', and Dt. xi. 30 changes 'over against Gilgal' into 'over against Shechem'.

Many of the variants are due to a misunderstanding of grammatical forms or syntactical constructions. Others consist of gratuitous additions from parallel passages. Some stem from dialect influence. Many arise from their effort to remove all anthropomorphic expressions.

There is no evidence that the Samaritans ever had a body of trained scribes, and the absence of any proper collations of MSS, as attested by the numerous variations, is not compatible with any serious textual knowledge. Neither do the deliberate changes or superfluous additions distinguish them as conscientious custodians of the sacred text. Therefore, its variants must be treated with extreme caution.

VI. TARGUMS

See separate article on this subject, and also 3 below (the Syriac Version). In addition it should be noted that an important Targum on the

Pentateuch is the Palestinian Targum (in the Palestinian dialect of Aramaic), formerly known only in fragmentary form, but recently identified in its completeness in a Vatican MS.

ועינ׳ עמעם דלמן יחזון
בעינהון ובאדניהון
ישמעון ובלבהון יסתכלו
ויתיבון וישתבק להון

Fig. 213. Targum Jonathan (Is. vi. 10) ending '. . . and they turn and it should be forgiven them', as in Mk. iv. 12, whereas *MT* has '. . . and be healed'.

VII. THE HEXAPLA

When Origen about AD 240 undertook to provide a more reliable Greek translation of the Old Testament, he produced the Hexapla, a six-column work, of which the first gave the Hebrew text and the second its transliteration into Greek characters. The fragments of this work which have come down to us are of considerable importance for the study of the text of the Old Testament

VIII. THE SYRIAC TRANSLATIONS

See section **3** below on the Syriac Version.

IX. OTHER VERSIONS

Of the other translations of the Old Testament the Coptic is based on the LXX. It was probably made in the 3rd century AD. There are two versions: one in Bohairic, the dialect of Lower Egypt; the other and older in Sahidic, the dialect of Thebes.

The Ethiopic translation, apparently made from the LXX, is too late to be of any real value.

The best-known Arabic translation is that of Saadia ha-Gaon (892–942). It would be surprising if this was the first translation into such an important language as Arabic. A midrashic reference to an Arabic translation of the Torah may have been prompted by an existing one. Arabic translations known to us are all too late to provide material for the textual criticism of the Old Testament.

BIBLIOGRAPHY. C. D. Ginsburg, *Hebrew Bible*, 1926–; R. Kittel, *Biblia Hebraica*, 1952; C. D. Ginsburg, *Introduction to the Massoretico-Critical Edition of the Hebrew Bible*, 1897; F. Buhl, *Kanon und Text*, 1891; F. Delitzsch, *Die Lese- und Schreibfehler im Alten Testament*, 1920; O. Eissfeldt, *Einleitung in das Alte Testament*, 1956; P. E. Kahle, *The Cairo Geniza*², 1959; F. G. Kenyon, *Our Bible and the Ancient Manuscripts*, 1939 (new edn., 1958); B. J. Roberts, *The Old Testament Text and Versions*, 1951; E. Würthwein, *Der Text des Alten Testaments*, 1952; M. Burrows, *Dead Sea Scrolls of St. Mark's Monastery*, 1950; W. J. Martin, *Dead Sea Scroll of Isaiah*, 1954; F. M. Cross, *The Ancient Library of Qumran and Modern Biblical Studies*, 1958.

W.J.M.

2. The Septuagint

Commonly denoted by 'LXX', the Septuagint is the most important Greek translation of the Old Testament, and the oldest known influential translation in any language.

I. ORIGINS

Its precise origins are still debated. A letter, purporting to be written by a certain Aristeas to his brother Philocrates in the reign of Ptolemy Philadelphus (285–246 BC), relates how Philadelphus, persuaded by his librarian to get a translation of the Hebrew scriptures for his royal library, appealed to the high priest at Jerusalem, who sent seventy-two elders to Alexandria with an official copy of the Law. There in seventy-two days they made a translation which was read before the Jewish community amid great applause, and then presented to the king. From the number of the translators it became known (somewhat inaccurately) as the Septuagint. The same story is told with variations by Josephus, but later writers embellish it with miraculous details. A Jewish priest Aristobulus, who lived in the 2nd century BC, is quoted by Clement of Alexandria and Eusebius as stating that while portions relating to Hebrew history had been translated into Greek previously, the entire Law was translated in the reign of Ptolemy Philadelphus; but Aristobulus is dependent on Aristeas and is motivated by a desire to prove that Plato, and even Homer, borrowed from the Bible!

Aristeas' letter belongs in fact to the 2nd century BC. Many of its details are exaggerated and even legendary, but it seems fairly certain that a translation of the Law only was made in Egypt (in the time of Ptolemy Philadelphus), primarily for the benefit of the Greek-speaking Jews there. This was the original Septuagint. The remaining books were translated piecemeal later: the canonical books some time before 117 BC (reference is made to them by the grandson of Sira in the prologue), the Apocrypha down to the beginning of the Christian era. Subsequently the name Septuagint was extended to cover all these translations. The apocryphal books are interspersed among the canonical books roughly according to their character; some items are inserted in the canonical books to which their subject-matter refers (see APOCRYPHA).

II. LANGUAGE

The Greek of the LXX is not straightfoward *koinē* Greek. At its most idiomatic, it abounds with Hebraisms; at its worst it is little more than Hebrew in disguise. But with these reservations the Pentateuch can be classed as fairly idiomatic and consistent, though there are traces of it eing the work of more than one translator. Outside the Pentateuch some books, it seems, were livided between two translators working simulaneously, while others were translated piecemeal t different times by different men using widely lifferent methods and vocabulary. Consequently he style varies from fairly good *koinē* Greek, as n Isaiah, part of Joshua, and 1 Maccabees, to ndifferent Greek, as in Chronicles, Psalms, ira, Judith, the Minor Prophets, Jeremiah, zekiel, and parts of Kings, to literal and someimes unintelligible versions as in Judges, Ruth, ong of Solomon, Lamentations, and other parts f Kings.

ΛΙΘΩΝ ΚΑΙ ΠΑΝ
ΤΕϹϹΑΡΗΜΩΘ
ΕΩϹΝΑΧΑΛΚΕ
ΔΡΩΝΕΩϹΓΩΝΙ

ig. 214. The LXX of Je. xxxviii. 40 (in *MT* Je. xxxi. 0) from the Codex Sinaiticus. The translators ave copied into Greek letters a Hebrew word vhich they did not understand because of a scribal error in the Hebrew MS. *Cf.* fig. 210.

Quality of translation judged by success in endering the Hebrew does not always coincide vith quality of Greek style. The Pentateuch again anks high. It is generally competent and faithful, hough it occasionally paraphrases anthroponorphisms offensive to Alexandrian Jews, disegards consistency in religious technical terms, nd shows its impatience with the repetitive echnical descriptions in Exodus by mistakes, bbreviations, and wholesale omissions. Comaratively few books attain to the standard of the entateuch; most are of medium quality, some re very poor. Isaiah as a translation is bad; sther, Job, Proverbs, and 1 Esdras are free araphrastic renderings. The original version of ob was much shorter than the Hebrew; it was ubsequently filled in with interpolations from heodotion. The Greek Proverbs contains things ot in the *MT* at all, and Hebrew sentiments are eely altered to suit the Greek outlook. The LXX endering of Daniel was so paraphrastic that it as replaced early, perhaps in the 1st century AD, y a later translation (generally attributed to heodotion, but differing from his principles and ntedating him), and the LXX rendering is nowdays to be found in only two MSS and the yriac. One of the translators of Jeremiah somemes rendered Hebrew words by Greek words hat conveyed similar sound but utterly dismilar meaning. Other books resemble Theootion in style, both in their over-literalness and their occasional use of transliteration instead f translation. Of the apocryphal books, some re not translations at all but free Greek comositions.

III. TRANSLATIONS AND REVISIONS

Throughout the Old Testament the MSS themselves differ in the degree of faithfulness to the Hebrew which their texts display. This is largely because they contain the results of revisions aimed at conforming the LXX more closely to the Hebrew of their times. Some, however, believe that many such differences spring not from revisions of one original translation, but from a mixture of originally independent rival translations. Their theory, proposed and developed largely by Paul Kahle, is that the LXX had its origin in numerous oral, and subsequently written, translations for use in the services after the reading of the Hebrew original. Later an official standardized version of the Law was made, but did not entirely replace the older versions, while for the rest of the books there never was a standard Jewish translation, but only a variety of versions. Eventually, the Christians took over the authorized Pentateuch, adopted one or other of the translations of the other books and extended the name Septuagint to cover the whole, which thereafter was regarded as the canonical text. Dr. Kahle would claim as survivals of these originally independent translations: (1) the Quinta and Sexta columns of Origen's Hexapla (see below); (2) Ur-Theodotion, *i.e.* a translation said to be quoted once or twice in the New Testament and later attributed to Theodotion simply because he revised it; (3) Ur-Lucian, *i.e.* another old translation which it is claimed appears in writings before Lucian's time, and bears his name because made the basis of his revision; (4) certain quotations in the New Testament that differ from the LXX; (5) the rival texts of the great uncial MSS of some books, *e.g.* Judges. He would regard as futile any attempt to work back through the layers of variant readings in our MSS to an 'original' LXX; all we could hope to uncover would be traces of rival versions, themselves largely fragmentary, though useful as independent witnesses to the several stages and states of the Hebrew text.

This theory, however, founded largely on analogy with other versions, such as the Aramaic Targums, the Vulgate, and the AV, has not been generally accepted by scholars actively working on the actual text of the LXX. They maintain that essential disagreements between the LXX MSS are relatively few; the portions where they are identical are overwhelmingly large; the variants, to which Dr. Kahle appeals, can with more likelihood be accounted for as revisions of a basic LXX text than as survivals of rival translations, or even as back-readings from the New Testament; the New Testament quotations can equally well be explained as coming from Aramaic sources or as the writers' private translations; non-LXX translations in early writers like Philo are frequently due to the substitution of contaminated texts by later revisers; and there is no positive evidence that the early Christians ever 'canonized' any particular Greek Old Testament text.

Of the revisions of the Greek Old Testament the greatest and easiest to trace is Origen's. He completed by about AD 245 an enormous edition containing in six parallel columns (hence the name *Hexapla*): (1) the Hebrew text; (2) the Hebrew text transliterated into Greek letters; (3) Aquila's translation; (4) Symmachus' translation; (5) the LXX as revised by himself; (6) Theodotion's translation. In the Psalms he gave also the versions which he called Quinta, Sexta, and Septima, and in other books the first two of these. His method of revision was to choose from the Greek MSS available to him the readings nearest to the Hebrew text current in his time. Where his text lacked something compared with the Hebrew, he inserted appropriate words, marked by critical signs, mostly from Theodotion's translation; and where his text contained readings absent from the Hebrew, he retained them but enclosed them in other critical signs. Finally, the order of the Greek text was changed, where necessary, to agree with the Hebrew. The Milan palimpsest of the Psalms discovered in 1896 preserves a copy of five columns of the Hexapla (*Psalterii Hexapli Reliquiae*. Cura et Studio Iohannis Card. Mercati editae. Pars Prima. Codex Rescriptus Bybliothecae Ambrosianae O 39 SVP. Phototypice Expressus et Transcriptus. In Bybliotheca Vaticana MCMLVIII). For the rest of the Old Testament Origen's great work has perished, except for column five, which was published separately by the historian Eusebius and Pamphilus, and is nowadays represented with greater or less faithfulness by a number of MSS.

Another edition, produced by Lucian of Samosata (martyred 311), is said to be characterized by the combination of variants into conflate readings, the substitution of synonyms for words in the LXX, lucidity of style, and the use of Atticisms. The result, however, is very unequal. In the Prophets Lucian's text is mostly of poor quality; in the Pentateuch his variants are generally unimportant, but in the historical books his text is most valuable, being often based on a Hebrew text superior to the *MT*. Whether Lucian himself had access to this Hebrew text, or whether he culled his readings from an earlier non-LXX translation, is, as was indicated above, a debated point.

Jerome (in the *Prologus galeatus*) mentions a third revision by Hesychius (also probably martyred in AD 311) of Alexandria. Little is known about him or the principles of his revision, which cannot be identified with any certainty.

Prof. A. Rahlfs found two more recensions (*R* and *C*) in Ruth, Judges, and Kingdoms, and Dr. P. Katz found one resembling *R* in other books. Besides these more or less well-defined recensions, evidence has accumulated in recent times that the kind of revision which Origen did thoroughly was done partially by others in the centuries before him.

IV. PROBLEMS ARISING

Well-intentioned as all this revisory work was it has introduced multitudinous readings whic have laboriously to be eliminated to reconstruc the earlier stages of the LXX text. The later cursiv MSS are, of course, generally more affected tha the early uncials and papyri; but even the grea uncials (Codex Vaticanus (B), Codex Alexan drinus (A), and Codex Sinaiticus (א)) are no immune from pre-Origen revision. Moreover early codices containing the whole Bible wer originally compiled from scrolls containin single books; consequently, the quality of text i codices tends to vary from book to book Vaticanus, for instance, is hexaplaric in Isaiah while in Judges it represents a 4th-century AI revision. Generally, however, it is a copy (a poo one, as its numerous omissions show) of a tex critically revised according to the best evidenc available early in the Christian era. Hence i sometimes presents a text purer than that of th still earlier papyri, which remarkably enoug show numerous agreements with later cursives Alexandrinus has suffered far more from re vision. Sinaiticus, generally speaking, holds position mid-way between B and A. Of the earl sizable papyri, none as yet presents a text tha is not basically LXX. Now, laborious as is th work of eliminating revisers' readings, it is o practical importance. The expositor who, t illumine the New Testament, appeals to some LX word or phrase must be sure that that word o phrase was not introduced by a reviser after Nev Testament times.

But in numerous places the unrevised LXX tex disagrees substantially with the *MT* in meaning order, and content; and this is important, sinc the LXX was, until recently, the earliest witnes to the Old Testament text. No Hebrew MS, unt the discovery of the Dead Sea Scrolls, was earlie than the late 9th century AD. Moreover, thes Hebrew MSS all contained the text as edited b the Massoretes, whereas the LXX (*i.e.* before th main revisions) witnesses to a pre-Massoreti text. Where it differs from the *MT*, the LXX is i some places evidently inferior, in other place just as clearly superior; sometimes it is supporte by the Samaritan text or one of the Dead Se Scrolls. These latter occasionally agree with th LXX, where formerly we thought that the LX was merely a loose paraphrase, unauthorized b any Hebrew, though again the readings of th early scrolls are not necessarily good reading any more than readings of the early New Testa ment MSS are invariably better than those of th later uncials. In yet other places the difference between the *MT* and the LXX remain undecided but it is becoming increasingly evident that th older method of comparing individual reading of the LXX with individual readings of the *MT* ha led to an exaggerated view of the LXX's wort The present trend is first to study carefully eac book of the LXX as a whole, and to assess th translator's attitude towards his Hebrew and hi ranslation technique, before appealing to any ne part of his translation to settle a disputed Iebrew reading. And such study has, on the whole, tended to diminish preference for the LXX.

V. SIGNIFICANCE

'aluable as a monument of Hellenistic Greek, he LXX occasionally preserves meanings of Iebrew words that were current when the LXX ranslation was made, but which were subequently lost. It acts also as a linguistic and heological bridgehead between the Hebrew of he Old Testament and the Greek of the New; or it served as 'Bible' to generations of Greekpeaking Jews in many countries, and it is often uoted in the New Testament. (Luke and the vriter to the Hebrews use it most, Matthew east. The New Testament quotations which do ot agree with the LXX can be attributed to inxact quotation from memory, the writer's own ranslation, translation of Aramaic sources, ranslation of Hebrew texts different from the *AT*, perhaps to other Greek translations, perhaps lso to deliberate adaptation of the Hebrew nder the Holy Spirit's guidance.) Consequently, he great psychological and theological terms of he New Testament must be understood, not ierely (often not at all) in their pagan sense, but n the light of the Hebrew words which they epresent in the LXX.

Moreover, the LXX was taken everywhere by he Christian missionaries and was retained by he churches, even when the Jews rejected it in avour of more accurate versions. Eventually, it ame to stand alongside the Greek New Testanent to form one whole Bible. It was translated nto Coptic, Ethiopic, Gothic, Armenian, Arabic, Georgian, Slavonic, and Old Latin, establishing he faith of converts by making available to them he messianic prophecies and influencing the hought of the early theologians. To this day it emains the official version of the Greek Orthoox Church.

BIBLIOGRAPHY. P. Katz, 'Septuagintal Studies n the Mid-century', in *The Background of the Vew Testament and its Eschatology*, ed. W. D. Davies and D. Daube, 1956; F. G. Kenyon, *Our Bible and the Ancient Manuscripts* (revised edn.), 958; B. J. Roberts, *The Old Testament Text and Versions*, 1951; numerous articles by H. M. Orlinsky and J. Ziegler, and the latter's introuctions to his Göttingen editions of the LXX.

D.W.G.

. The Syriac Version

After the LXX, the oldest and most important ranslation of the Hebrew Scriptures is the Syriac 'ersion. This translation, used by the Syriac Church, was described since the 9th century as he Peshitta (Syr. *pšiṭṭâ*) or 'simple' translation.

I. ORIGINS

Despite scholarly research into the origin of the ersion, we have no direct information of the uthor(s) or the date of the translation, and as early as Theodore of Mopsuestia (died 428) details concerning its provenance were unknown.

Internal evidence, however, enables us to arrive at some conclusions as to its probable origin. Linguistic affinities have been noted between the Palestinian Aramaic Targum and the Syriac translation of the Pentateuch, whereas Syriac (the name usually given to Christian Aramaic) is an E Aramaic language, and an explanation of this phenomenon which has been offered by P. Kahle throws some light on the possible origin of the version.

These linguistic traces of W Aramaic in a version which is otherwise in E Aramaic dialect reveal some acquaintance with a Palestinian Targum to the Pentateuch. Similarly, A. Baumstark has shown the direct agreement of the Peshitta text of Gn. xxix. 17 with a Genizah text and the Palestinian Targum as against Targum Onkelos and Pseudo-Jonathan ('Neue orientalische Probleme biblischer Textgeschichte', *ZDMG*, XIV, 1935, pp. 89–118). These facts suggest that the Peshitta Pentateuch originated in an E Aramaic district which had some relationship with Jerusalem.

The ruling house of Adiabene, a kingdom situated between the two rivers Zab, east of the Tigris, was converted to Judaism about AD 40. Royal children were sent to Jerusalem for their education, and some members of the royal house were buried there. Judaism spread among the people of Adiabene, and they needed the Hebrew Scriptures in a language they could understand—*i.e.* Syriac, so it is probable that parts of the Syriac Old Testament, and at first the Pentateuch, were introduced into the kingdom in the middle of the 1st century. The Palestinian Targum composed in the W Aramaic dialect of Judaea was in current use at that time in Palestine, and we must suppose that this was transposed into the Aramaic dialect spoken in Adiabene.

This, however, is not a complete solution, as Baumstark has shown that the original text of the Syriac version goes back even farther than the Palestinian Targum. The Palestinian Targum contains haggadic explanations which in general are not found in the Syriac Bible. On the other hand, the oldest preserved fragment of this Targum containing part of Ex. xxi and xxii does not possess any haggadic explanation, while the Syriac version of Ex. xxii. 4, 5 follows the usual Jewish interpretation. Hence it is supposed that this fragment represents an older type of the Targum than that which might have been sent to Adiabene.

Further examination of MSS of the Peshitta Pentateuch has revealed that at an early period there existed two texts, one a more literal translation of the Hebrew and the other a rendering, as has been described above, closely related to the Palestinian Targum. Many scholars think that the literal translation is the earlier on the ground that the Syriac Church Fathers Aphrahat and Ephraem used a text which followed the Hebrew more closely than did the text in common use in the 6th century.

The question remains how this translation came to be recognized as the official Old Testament Scriptures of the Syriac Church. If we regard the literal translation as the work of Jewish translators, made for the Jewish community, it would seem that this translation was taken over by the Syriac Church, improved in style, and this text was accepted as standard about the 5th century AD. This Syriac Church had taken root in the district of Arbela, the capital of Adiabene, before the end of the 1st century, and in the course of the 2nd century Edessa, east of the Upper Euphrates, was the centre of Mesopotamian Christianity.

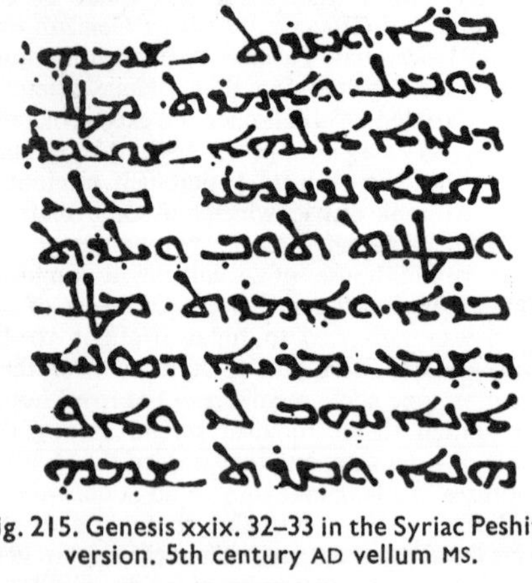

Fig. 215. Genesis xxix. 32–33 in the Syriac Peshitta version. 5th century AD vellum MS.

When at the beginning of the 4th century the Christian faith was declared the official religion of the Roman Empire, codices of the LXX were produced, and B. J. Roberts writes (*The Old Testament Text and Versions*, 1951, p. 222), 'it is reasonable to suppose that a similar development was taken with the Peshitta version. Thus it is held that an attempt was made to revise the Syriac version in order to bring it more into harmony with the LXX. It took place shortly after the New Testament Peshitta was revised, but it is obvious that the recension was not carried out in the same way for all the sacred books. Thus the Psalter and the Prophetic books, because of their relatively greater importance for the New Testament, were more carefully collated with the Greek version. Job and Proverbs, on the other hand, were scarcely touched and the same may be said to be true, but to a lesser degree, of Genesis.'

A reference must be made here to an alternative view concerning the origin of the Syriac version. R. H. Pfeiffer (*Introduction to the Old Testament*, 1941, p. 120), quotes F. Buhl (*Kanon und Text des Alten Testaments*, 1890, p. 187) that 'the Peshitta owed its origin to Christian efforts: in part older individual Jewish translations were utilized, in part the remainder was commissioned to Jewish Christians for translation'. Such a view is possible, as the Syriac Christians included large Jewish element and came possibly from a originally Jewish congregation.

Concerning the influence of the LXX on th Peshitta, the conclusion of W. E. Barnes may als be quoted (*JTS*, II, 1901, p. 197): 'The influenc of the Septuagint is for the most part *sporadi* affecting the translation of a word here and of word there. The Syriac translators must indee have known that their knowledge of Hebrew wa far in advance of the knowledge possessed by th Septuagint, and yet the stress of Greek fashio had its way now and again. The Syriac trar scribers on the contrary were ignorant Hebrew and ready to introduce readings foun in a Greek version or recommended by a Gree Father. So the Peshitta in its later text has mo of the Septuagint than in its earlier form. It only in the Psalter (so it seems to me at th present stage of my work) that any general Gree influence bringing in a new characteristic is to b found. That characteristic is a dread of anthropo morphisms from which the Syriac translators the Pentateuch were free.'

II. LANGUAGE AND TRANSLATION

An examination of the character of the Syria translation in the various books of the Ol Testament shows there is no uniformity of ren dering between the various books, and this im plies a variety of authors. Of the Peshitta Samuel S. R. Driver has written (*Notes on th Hebrew Text and the Topography of the Books Samuel*[2], 1913, p. lxxi): 'The Hebrew text pre supposed by the Peshitta deviates less from th Massoretic text than that which underlies th LXX, though it does not approach it so closely a that on which the Targums are based. It is wort observing that passages not infrequently occu in which Peshitta agrees with the text of *Lucia* where both deviate from the Massoretic text. I the translation of the books of Samuel the Jewis element alluded to above is not so strongl marked as in that of the Pentateuch; but it nevertheless present, and may be traced i certain characteristic expressions, which woul hardly be met with beyond the reach of Jewis influence. . . .'

For the character of the translation in othe books we may quote B. J. Roberts (*The Ol Testament Text and Versions*, 1951, pp. 221 f. 'The book of Psalms, for example, is a fre translation showing considerable influence of th Septuagint; Proverbs and Ezekiel closely re semble the Targumim. Isaiah and the Minc Prophets, for the most part, are again fairl freely translated. The book of Job, although servile translation, is in parts unintelligible, du partly to textual corruption and partly to th influence of other translations. The Song of Song is a literal translation, Ruth a paraphras Chronicles more than any other book is para phrastic, containing Midrashic elements an exhibiting many of the characters of a Targun This book did not originally belong to the Syria 'anon, and it is conjectured that the Syriac ersion was composed by Jews in Edessa in the aird century AD. Christian tendencies, perhaps nanating from an early Christian re-editing, are be observed in the translation of many pasages, prominent among them being Gn. xlvii. 31; . ix. 5, liii. 8, lvii. 15; Je. xxxi. 31; Ho. xiii. 14; c. xii. 10. Many Psalms evidently derive their iperscriptions from Christian origins, although places they also embody some Jewish tradiions. How far, however, these may be due to ter redactoral activity cannot be determined.'

III. LATER HISTORY OF THE PESHITTA TEXT

t the end of the first quarter of the 5th century a hism took place in the Syriac Church, with the sult that Nestorius and his followers withdrew astwards. Nestorius was expelled from the ishopric of Constantinople in 431 and he took ith him the Peshitta Bible. Following the estruction of their school at Edessa in 489, the estorians fled to Persia and established a new hool at Nisibis. The two branches of the hurch kept their own Bible texts, and from the me of Bar-Hebraeus in the 13th century others ave been distinctive Eastern and Western. The astern, Nestorian, texts have undergone fewer evisions based on Hebrew and Greek versions n account of the more isolated location of this hurch.

IV. OTHER TRANSLATIONS

ther Syriac translations were made at an early ate, but there remains no complete MS evidence. ragments exist of a Christian Palestinian Syriac erusalem) translation, a version of the Old and lew Testaments dating from the 4th to the 6th enturies. This was made from the LXX and innded for the religious worship of the Melchite alestinian-Syriac) Church. It is written in yriac characters, and the language is Palestinian ramaic.

Philoxenus of Mabbug commissioned the anslation of the whole Bible from Greek (*c.* AD)8); of this only a few fragments remain, giving ortions of the New Testament and Psalter. aumstark states that the extant remains are onfined to fragments which are based on a ucianic recension of the text of Isaiah. These elong to the early 6th century AD.

Another Syriac version of the Old Testament 'as made by Paul, Bishop of Tella in Mesopomia, in 617 and 618. This follows the text of the ireek and also keeps the Hexaplaric signs in arginal notes. Readings are given from Aquila, ymmachus, and Theodotion. As this is really a yriac version of the LXX column of Origen's lexapla, it is known as the Syro-Hexaplaric text, nd it is a valuable witness to the Hexaplar text f the LXX.

V. THE MANUSCRIPTS AND EDITIONS OF THE PESHITTA

he oldest *dated* biblical MS yet known, British luseum MS Add. 11425, dated AD 464, contains the Pentateuch except the book of Leviticus (MS 'D'). Other extant MSS of Isaiah and Psalms date to the 6th century. The important West Syriac Codex Ambrosianus in Milan of the 6th or 7th century has been published photolithographically by A. M. Ceriani (*Translatio Syra Pescitto Veteris Testamenti*, 1867). This consists of the whole of the Old Testament and is close to the *MT*.

The writings of the Syriac Church Fathers, *e.g.* Ephraem Syrus (died AD 373) and Aphrahat (letters dated 337–345), contain quotations from the Old Testament, giving textual readings of an early date. The commentaries of Philoxenus, Bishop of Mabbug 485–519, give Jacobite readings. The most valuable authority for the text is the *'Auṣar Raze* of Bar-Hebraeus, composed in 1278.

No complete critical edition of the Syriac Old Testament yet exists. The *editio princeps* of the Peshitta was prepared by a Maronite, Gabriel Sionita, for inclusion in the Paris Polyglot of 1645. He used as his main source the MS *Codex Syriaque* b in the Bibliothèque Nationale in Paris. This is an erratic 17th-century MS.

The Peshitta text in Brian Walton's Polyglot of 1657 is that of the Paris Polyglot; S. Lee's *Vetus Testamentum Syriace*, 1823, is essentially a reprint of the texts of the Paris and Walton Polyglots, although Lee had access to Codex B (the Buchanan Bible, 12th century) and three MSS, p, u, and e, West Syriac MSS of the 17th century.

The Urmia edition was published in 1852, and in many places follows the readings of Nestorian MSS. In 1887–91 the Dominican monks at Mosul published both Old and New Testaments, also depending upon an East Syriac tradition.

There also exist critical editions of individual books.

BIBLIOGRAPHY. See end of section **4. Aramaic,** below.

4. Aramaic

I. ARAMAIC TEXT OF THE OLD TESTAMENT

For this, see LANGUAGE OF THE OLD TESTAMENT, section II.

II. ARAMAIC IN THE NEW TESTAMENT

From the time of the Exile Aramaic spread as the vernacular language in Palestine, and it was the commonly spoken language in the country in New Testament times, probably more so than Greek, which had been introduced at the time of the conquests of Alexander the Great.

The Gospels record Christ's words in Aramaic on three different occasions: Mk. v. 41—*Talitha cumi*; Mk. vii. 34—*ephphatha*, representing a dialect form of *'itpattaḥ*; and His cry upon the cross, Mk. xv. 34—*Eloi, Eloi, lama sabachthani?* (*q.v.*; *cf.* Mt. xxvii. 46). We read also that when Jesus prayed in the Garden of Gethsemane He addressed God the Father as *'Abbā'*, an Aramaic word for 'father'.

In Rom. viii. 15 and Gal. iv. 6 Paul also uses

this intimate form '*Abba*, Father', as an intimation that God has sent the Spirit of His Son into the hearts of believers in Christ when they pray, '*Abba*, Father'. Another Aramaism current in early churches, *Maranatha* (*maranā ṯā*'), 'Our Lord, come!' is recorded by Paul in 1 Cor. xvi. 22. Other Aramaic words found in the New Testament are *Akeldama* ('field of blood', Acts i. 19), and several place-names and personal names.

In addition, it is mentioned in Acts xxvi. 14 that Paul heard the risen Christ speaking to him 'in the Hebrew tongue', for which we should undoubtedly understand Aramaic (see F. F. Bruce, *The Book of the Acts*, 1954, p. 491, n. 18), as we should also in Acts xxii. 2, where it is stated that Paul addressed the mob at Jerusalem in this tongue, giving an indication that the people were more familiar with Aramaic than with Greek. See also LANGUAGE OF THE NEW TESTAMENT.

BIBLIOGRAPHY. F. F. Bruce, *The Books and the Parchments*, 1950, pp. 54 ff., 181 ff. and bibliography on p. 230; P. Kahle, *The Cairo Geniza*, 1947, pp. 129 ff., 179–197; R. H. Pfeiffer, *Introduction to the Old Testament*, 1941, pp. 120 f.; B. J. Roberts, *The Old Testament Text and Versions*, 1951, pp. 214–228 and detailed bibliography on pp. 309 f.; T. H. Robinson, 'The Syriac Bible', in *Ancient and English Versions of the Bible* (ed. H. Wheeler Robinson), 1940; E. R. Rowlands, 'The Targum and the Peshitta Version of the Book of Isaiah', *VT*, IX, 1959, pp. 178 ff.; H. H. Rowley (ed.), *OTMS*, pp. 257 f.; E. Würthwein, *The Text of the Old Testament*, 1957, pp. 59 ff. and bibliography on p. 172; M. Black, *An Aramaic Approach to the Gospels and Acts*, 1946; G. H. Dalman, *The Words of Jesus*, 1902; *id.*, *Jesus–Jeshua*, 1929; C. C. Torrey, *Documents of the Primitive Church*, 1941; G. M. Lamsa (tr.), *The Holy Bible from Ancient Eastern Manuscripts*, 1957. R.A.H.G.

5. The New Testament

The New Testament has been handed down amidst many hazards encountered by all the literature of antiquity. The mistakes of the scribe and the corrections of the redactor have left their mark upon all the sources from which we derive our knowledge of its text (or wording). Before we may ascertain the original text we have to apply to the prolific mass of material a series of disciplines, *viz.* (i) Diplomatic—the study of ancient documents, necessarily associated with palaeography—the science of ancient writing. (ii) 'Recensio'—the study of the inter-relation of the documents by which the *stemmata* or 'family-trees' may be ascertained and, in ideal conditions, an archetypal text established. (iii) 'Examinatio'—the process of choice between the variants of the documents where these differ uncompromisingly and cannot be explained in terms of simple error. (iv) 'Emendatio'—the resolution of the remaining insoluble difficulties by conjectural emendation. In the text of the Ne Testament there is much still to be done in sta (i); on the basis of previous work of this kin great stress has been laid in the last century c stage (ii) and its possibilities; at present mo stress is laid than hitherto on stage (iii) and th criteria by which variants may be distinguishe but subtle and difficult as these three stages ma be, there appears to be little need here to reso to stage (iv).

This arises from the wealth of source materi at our disposal. The standard list of Greek Ne Testament MSS was begun by C. R. Gregory (*D griechischen HSS. des NTs*, 1908), continue by E. von Dobschuetz (*ZNW*, XXIII, XX XXVII, XXXII) and K. Aland (*ibid.*, XL XLVIII). In this there now appear sixty-eig papyri, 241 uncial MSS, 2,533 minuscule MSS, an 1,838 lectionary MSS. Here indeed is *embarras richesse*. Moreover, besides sources in the origin Greek, recourse may be had to the ancie translations (usually termed 'versions') in th languages of Christian antiquity and to the cit tions made by Christian writers from the Scri tures. Both these prove to be sources of the mo important evidence for the establishment of th text and its history.

I. MANUSCRIPTS

Our primary source is in Greek MSS, which a found in a number of different materials. Th first of these is *papyrus* (*q.v.*); this is a durab writing material made from reeds. It was use throughout the ancient world, but has been pr served mainly in the sands of Egypt. Among th most significant of the sixty-eight listed papy of the New Testament (indicated in the list Gregory–von Dobschuetz–Aland by a 'p' Gothic style, followed by a numeral) are th following.

(i) *Of the Gospels*. p45 (Chester Beatty papyr of the Gospels, Dublin) *c.* AD 250 contains c seventeen extant pages (out of thirty) large par of Luke and Mark, somewhat less of Matthe and John; p52 (John Rylands Library, Ma chester) *c.* AD 100–150 is our earliest fragment the New Testament; p66 (Bodmer papyrus John, Geneva) *c.* AD 200 contains the Gospel John, with some gaps in chapters xiv–xxi.

(ii) *Of the Acts of the Apostles*. p38 (Michiga pap. 1571, Ann Arbor), dated by some in th 3rd century, by some in the 4th, contains Ac xviii. 27–xix. 6: xix. 12–16; p45 (Chester Beatt as above) thirteen pages containing parts Acts v. 30–xvii. 17; p48 (Florence) from the 3 century, a single leaf containing Acts xxiii. 11–2

(iii) *Of the Pauline Epistles*. p46 (Chest Beatty papyrus of the Epistles, Dublin) *c.* AD 2 contains on ninety leaves considerable parts Romans, Hebrews, 1 and 2 Corinthians, Gal tians, Ephesians, Philippians, Colossians, 1 The salonians, in this order.

(iv) *Of the Revelation*. p47 (Chester Beat papyrus of Revelation, Dublin) ten leaves co taining Rev. ix. 10–xvii. 2.

All these papyri make significant contributions our knowledge of the text. It should be par-cularly noted, however, that it is the age of ese MSS, not their material or place of origin, hich accords such significance to them. A late apyrus need not of necessity have any great nportance.

The second material of which Greek MSS were ade is *parchment*. This was the skin of sheep nd goats dried and polished with pumice; it ade a durable writing material resistant to all imates. It was used from antiquity till the late Iiddle Ages, when paper began to replace it.

ig. 216. A small papyrus fragment of the Gospel f John (p52), c. AD 125 (Jn. xviii. 31–33, 37, 38). See also plates XIII*b*, *c*.

he form of the manuscript book was originally e scroll, but few Christian writings survive in is form. The Christian book was usually the odex, *i.e.* the form of binding and pagination miliar to us. (See WRITING, Section IV.) Many archment codices survive (the papyri are also in is form) and some are works of great beauty. ome were even 'de luxe' editions coloured with urple and written in gold or silver ink. At ertain periods, however, parchment became carce and the writing on old MSS would be rased and the parchment re-used. Such re-used ss are called *palimpsests*: it is often the erased riting which is of importance to modern cholarship, in which case the use of chemical re-gents, photography, and other modern tech-ical methods is often required before it can be eciphered.

The parchment MSS of the New Testament ogether with the relatively few paper MSS of the 5th and 16th centuries) are divided by a three-old classification. The first main demarcation is at between MSS containing continuous texts and ose arranged according to the lections for daily ervices and church festivals. The latter are rmed lectionaries or *evangelistaria*; they are ndicated in the Gregory–von Dobschuetz–Aland st by the letter 'l' followed by a numeral ('l' lone indicates a gospel lectionary; 'l^{a}' indicates lectionary of the Epistles; 'l + ^{a}', a lectionary ontaining both Gospels and Epistles). This roup of MSS has been too little studied in any systematic way: the series *Studies in the Lectionary Text of the Greek New Testament* (1933 onwards) is slowly redressing the balance. The former group is further divided into two sub-groups distinguished by the style of writing employed in their execution and roughly consecutive in point of time. The relatively older group is that of the *Uncials*, *i.e.* MSS written in capital letters: the relatively younger group is that of the *Minuscules* or *Cursives*, *i.e.* MSS written in the stylized form of the lower case perfected by Theodore the Studite and other scribes of the 10th century and thereabouts.

As in the case of the papyri it should be noted that an uncial MS is not *ipso facto* a better representative of the New Testament text than a minuscule. Some older uncials rightly occupy a chief place in critical apparatus; some younger are comparatively worthless. Similarly, minuscules, though later in date, may prove to be faithful copies of early MSS; such then have as great importance as uncials.

Uncials are indicated in the Gregory–von Dobschuetz–Aland list by capital letters of the Latin and Greek alphabets or by a numeral preceded by a zero. Important among the uncials are the following: (i) Codex Sinaiticus (א or 01), a 4th-century MS of the Old and New Testaments; in addition to its intrinsically important text it contains a series of corrections made in the 6th century and probably to be connected with the critical work of Pamphilus of Caesarea, scholar and martyr. (ii) Codex Vaticanus (B or 03), a MS of similar content, but lacking the latter part of the New Testament from chapter ix, verse 14 of Hebrews to the end of the Revelation. Both these MSS are probably of Egyptian origin. (iii) Codex Alexandrinus (A or 02), a 5th-century MS containing Old and New Testaments, probably of Constantinopolitan origin. (iv) Codex Ephraemi Rescriptus (C or 04), a 5th-century MS of Old and New Testaments re-used in the 13th century for the works of Ephraem the Syrian in Greek translation. (v) Codex Bezae (Cantabrigiensis) (D or 05), 4th or 5th century in date and of uncertain provenance—suggestions range from Gaul to Jerusalem; it presents a Greek text on the left page, a Latin on the right, and contains an incomplete text of the Gospels and Acts with a few verses of 1 John. (vi) Codex Washingtonianus (the Freer Codex) (W or 032), probably

ETRESPONDENSDIXITILLIS IHS
UIDETEHASMAGNASSTRUCTURAS
AMENDICOUOBIS
QUIANONRELINQUETURHICLAPIS
SUPERLAPIDEMQUINONDESTRUATUR
ETPOSTTERTIUMDIEM
ALIUTRESUSCITETURSINEMANIBUS

Fig. 217. The Latin text of Mk. xiii. 2 with the addition 'and after three days another shall be raised up without hands'. From the Codex Bezae (D).

a 4th-century MS, containing the Gospels of which the text-type varies considerably from place to place. (vii) Codex Koridethianus (Θ or 038), which it is impossible to date, since it was apparently written by a scribe unaccustomed to Greek, probably a Georgian; the MS copied by him was apparently a late uncial of the 10th century. (viii) Codex Laudianus (E^{a} or 08), a 6th- or 7th-century Graeco-Latin MS of the Acts. (ix, x, xi) Codices Claromontanus, Boernerianus, Augiensis (D^{paul} or 06; G^{paul} or 012; F^{paul} or 010), a group of Graeco-Latin MSS, the former of the 6th, the two latter of the 9th century, containing the Pauline Epistles. (xii) Codex Euthalianus, (H^{paul} or 015), 6th-century MS much fragmented and scattered, containing the Pauline Epistles connected, according to a colophon (*i.e.* appended note), with a MS in the library of Pamphilus of Caesarea.

These MSS give the varying text-types existing in the 4th century; it is around these that debate has centred in the last hundred years and on these MSS that critical texts have been based. As an exploratory investigation this is justifiable, but, as more recent discoveries have shown, the complexity of the data is greater than this procedure would imply.

The researches of Lake, Ferrar, Bousset, Rendel Harris, von Soden, Valentine-Richards, and many others have made it abundantly plain that a fair proportion of minuscules of all dates contain in larger or smaller measure important ancient texts or traces of such texts: to give then even an approximate indication of all important minuscules is virtually impossible. The following remarks only adumbrate the significance of this material. Two MSS numbered 33 and 579 in Gregory's list are very closely allied to the text of B; 579 has even been described as presenting a text older than B itself. The text of Θ, otherwise unknown in the uncials save in part of W, is also found in 565, 700, and some others; as such a text was known to Origen, these are of great significance. Closely allied texts are found in the minuscule families known as family 1 and family 13 and in MSS 21, 22, and 28. In the Acts some of the peculiarities of D and E are attested by various minuscules, pre-eminent among which are 383, 614, and 2147. In the Pauline Epistles the minuscule evidence has not been so thoroughly sifted yet, save in the unsatisfactory work of von Soden. However, 1739 has attracted much study, and with its congeners 6, 424, 1908, and the late uncials erroneously placed together as M^{paul}, proves to attest a text of equal antiquity and comparable significance to that of p46 and B. In the Revelation, 2344 is an ally of A and C, the best witnesses to the original text of that book.

II. VERSIONS

By the mid-3rd century parts at least of the New Testament had been translated from the Greek original into three of the languages of the ancient world—Latin, Syriac, and Coptic. From that time on, these versions were revised and e panded: and in their turn became the basis other translations. Especially in the East, Bit translation became an integral part of the m sionary work of both Greek-speaking a Syriac-speaking Christians. As churches d veloped and theology flourished, versions wou be revised to the standard of the Greek text th prevalent. So, both by reason of their ultima antiquity and by their contacts with the Gre at various historical points, the versions pr serve much significant material for textu criticism.

From this outline it will be plain that ea version has a history. There is need, then, f internal textual criticism of any version before can be used in the determination of the Gre text; and in scarcely any case may we speak 'such and such a version' but need to speak such MSS or such a form or stage of the version question. This, already observed for the Lat and Syriac versions, should become the gener rule.

In tracing the internal history of a version v have the advantage of the phenomenon 'rendering' to aid us, which is not to be found dealing with the Greek text. In the Greek, tex types can be differentiated by variant readin alone: in any version even the same reading m be found differently rendered in particular MS Where this is so, different stages in the evoluti of the version may be traced.

Difficulties are to be met, however, in the u of any version for the criticism of the Gree text. These arise because no language can r produce any other with complete exactness. Th is so even in the case of cognates of Greek such Latin or Armenian; it is more strikingly true languages of other linguistic type such as Copt or Georgian. Particles essential to the one a found to have no equivalent or no necessa equivalent in the other; verbs have no equivale conjugation; nuances and idioms are lost. Som times a pedantic translator will maltreat his ov language in order to give a literal rendering of t Greek; in such a case we may have an almo verbatim report of the Greek model. But in t earliest versions pedantry has no place and v encounter the difficulties of racy idiom and som times paraphrase. Nevertheless, the evidence the versions needs to be mastered in the quest f the original text.

An important factor in the history of most the versions is the *Diatessaron*, a harmony of t four Gospels and some apocryphal source ma *c.* AD 180 by Tatian, an Assyrian Christian co verted in Rome and a disciple of Justin Mart (see CANON OF THE NEW TESTAMENT). Unfo tunately for research, no unequivocal evidence it has been available, until very recently, i Syriac, its probable original language. The mo important witnesses to it are a commentary upc it by Ephraem the Syrian preserved in Armenia (a considerable portion of the Syriac original this commentary came to light in 1957); a transl on into Arabic extant in several MSS, but aparently much influenced before its translation y the text of the Syriac Peshitta; the Latin odex Fuldensis, similarly influenced by the atin Vulgate; and a fragment in Greek found at ura-Europos. Its widespread vogue and inuence are shown by the existence of harmonies ased upon it in Old High German, Middle High erman, mediaeval Dutch, Middle English, the uscan and Venetian dialects of mediaeval Italian, ersian, and Turkish. It is quite clear that a *iatessaron* lies beneath the oldest stratum of the yriac and Armenian versions and that it played inconsiderable part in the history of the Latin. hese matters are still an area for research and bate.

The three basic versions made directly from reek are the Latin, Syriac, and Coptic. Of none these is the earliest stage certainly known. The arcionites early translated the Marcionite ospels and the Pauline letters into Latin; the *iatessaron* was probably translated into Latin; d Tertullian already uses a rendering of all ur Gospels besides translating directly from the reek. Our MS evidence for the pre-Vulgate stage the Latin consists of about thirty fragmentary ss. These show a somewhat bewildering richness variants well meriting the *bon mot* of Jerome, *ot sunt paene (exemplaria) quot codices*'. Scholars ually distinguish two or three main types of xt (*viz.* 'African', 'European', and sometimes talian') in the various parts of the New Testaent before Jerome.

But in the Gospels at least there is more internnection between types than is usually thought: d even in the 'African' Latin of MSS k and e ere may be discerned more than one stage of anslation and revision. Jerome undertook a vision of the Latin Bible (normally known as e Vulgate) at the request of the Pope Damasus out AD 382. It is uncertain how far his revision tually extended. The latter books of the New estament are probably very little revised. In the urse of time this revision itself became corrupt d a number of attempts at purification figure in history, most notably those of Cassiodorus, lcuin, and Theodulph.

The Syriac Church, after using an apocryphal ospel, was first introduced to the canonical ospels in the form of the *Diatessaron*: this mained long in vogue, but was gradually supanted by the separated Gospels in the form own to us in the Curetonian and Sinaitic MSS d in citations. This retained much of Tatian's nguage in a four-Gospel form. We have no MSS a parallel version of the Acts and Epistles, but e citations made by Ephraem indicate its istence. Towards the end of the 4th century a vision was made of an Old Syriac base to a reek standard akin to Codex B of the Greek; is was the Peshitta, which in course of time came the 'Authorized Version' of all the riac churches. Its author is unknown: more an one hand has been at work. The version mprises in the New Testament the canonical books apart from 2 Peter, 2 and 3 John, Jude, and Revelation. Later scholarly revisions—by Polycarp, at the command of Mar Xenaia (Philoxenus) of Mabbug (AD 508) and by Thomas of Harkel (AD 616) made good the omission. Few MSS of either remain, and the existence of a separate Harklean version (as distinct from the addition of scholarly marginal apparatus to the Philoxenian) is still a matter of debate. The version in the quite distinct Palestinian Syriac dialect is generally thought to be unconnected with this stream of translation, but otherwise its origins are at present obscure. Much of the New Testament is extant in lectionary form.

Biblical remains are found in several dialects of Coptic: the entire New Testament in Bohairic, the dialect of Lower Egypt and the Delta; almost the whole in Sahidic, the dialect of Upper Egypt; considerable fragments in Fayyumic and Achmimic; and the Gospel of John in sub-Achmimic. To trace in detail the history of the versions in these dialects and in the various parts of the New Testament is still an unaccomplished task: neither the dates of the versions nor the interrelations between them, if any, have yet been elucidated from the abundant materials to hand. The Sahidic is usually in the 3rd or 4th century, while for the Bohairic dates as diverse as the 3rd century and the 7th have been proposed. In the main these versions agree with the Greek text-types found in Egypt: the Diatessaric element so evident in the Latin and Syriac texts is scarcely present here, and it may be concluded that, whatever the internal relations of the versions in the different dialects, the Coptic as a whole stands in a direct relation to the Greek text.

The majority of other versions are dependent on these. From the Latin come mediaeval versions in a number of W European languages: while these mainly reflect the Vulgate, traces of Old Latin readings are to be found. Thus, Provençal and Bohemian versions preserve an important text of the Acts. The Syriac versions served as base for a number of others, the most important eing the Armenian (from which the Georgian was in its turn translated), and the Ethiopic. These have complex internal history, their ultimate form conformed to the Greek, but their earlier stages less so. Persian and Sogdian versions derive from the Syriac, while the many Arabic versions and the fragmentarily preserved Nubian have both Syriac and Coptic ancestry. The Gothic and the Slavonic are direct translations from the Greek in the 4th and 10th centuries respectively.

III. PATRISTIC CITATIONS

For dating different text-types and for establishing their geographical location, we rely on the data provided by scriptural citations in early Christian writings. Much significant work has been done in this field, the most important results being in respect of Origen, Chrysostom, and Photius among Greek writers, of Cyprian, Lucifer of Cagliari, and Novatian among the Latins, and of Ephraem and Aphrahat among the Syrians. About the effects of the work of Marcion and Tatian on the New Testament text and concerning the text attested by Irenaeus—all matters of great importance—we are still in some uncertainty.

The whole field is much complicated by the vagaries of human memory and customs of citation. We also find instances where the writer on changing his domicile changed his MSS or on the contrary took a particular text-type with him. For these reasons few would accept a reading attested in citation alone; yet Friedrich Blass and, more recently, M.-E. Boismard have dared to do this in works on the text of the Gospel of John.

IV. ANALYSIS

In many cases of classical literature it is found that the material available for the establishment of the text may be analysed into one *stemma* or line of descent, leading down from the archetype which may be adequately reconstructed even where a careful transcript is not to be discovered among the MSS, as is often the case. The New Testament material is not patient of such analysis in spite of the efforts of a number of scholars to apply a genealogical method to it. Westcott and Hort used the criterion of conflate readings as the primary stage in such an analysis. In this way they established the inferiority of the text of the mass of the late MSS, a conclusion corroborated by their second criterion, the evidence of patristic citation. They were then faced, however, with two main types of text, *viz.* that attested by B ℵ and that attested by D lat. Between these texts of equal antiquity they were unable to decide by these two objective criteria, and so fell back on a third, inevitably somewhat subjective, namely, that of intrinsic probability. By this means they were enabled to follow the B ℵ text in most cases and to reject the D lat text.

Hermann von Soden's analysis of the same material arrived at a system of three recensions, all dating in his view from the 4th century: by a simple arithmetical procedure he thought himself able to arrive at a pre-recensional text, always allowing for the factor of harmonization which he considered all-pervasive (and due in the Gospels to the corrupting influence of the *Diatessaron*). Neither scheme has met with the approval of more recent scholarship. Hort's scheme fails partly because subsequent discovery reveals in the earlier centuries not two texts, one pure, one corrupt, but a complex of so-called 'mixed texts', *i.e.* in which features and readings of both are found combined; and partly because of the probable bias of his Attic-trained judgment against the harsh Greek of the Codex Bezae and its allies. Von Soden's scheme fails likewise both because of the at times artificial rigidity of his triple pattern and because of his errors in respect of the *Diatessaron*. To establish the text and the history of its corruption and preservation we need the analysis of text-types and recensions, which—at least in certain periods—exist: but purely genealogical method will by itself establi the text. Our earliest MSS and other data prese texts in which readings good and bad a mingled; in every part of the New Testament t textual critic must resort to the practice of reasoned eclecticism, *i.e.* the practice of scienti judgment by intrinsic probability. A number objective criteria may be established for th purpose.

V. CRITERIA

In this matter stylistic and linguistic standar play a large part. In every part of the Ne Testament enough remains without serio variation to enable studies of the characteris style and usage of individual writers to be mad In cases of textual doubt we may use such kno ledge of the accustomed style of the book question. Furthermore, we shall in the Gosp prefer variants where the influence of paral Synoptic passages is absent; or those in which strongly Aramaic cast in the Greek reveals t underlying original tradition. Throughout, shall avoid constructions of Attic or Attici Greek, preferring those of the Hellenis vernacular. In other places, factors from a wid sphere may be discerned. Palaeography can elu date variants which derive from primitive erro in the MS tradition. The history or economics the 1st century AD can sometimes show us t choice between variants by providing informati on technical terms, value of currency, *etc.* Chur history and the history of doctrine may reve where variants show accommodation to lat doctrinal trends.

It will be plain from the fact that su criteria can be applied that in spite of the pr fusion of material the text of the New Testame is fairly well and accurately preserved, w enough at least for us to make stylistic judgme about, *e.g.*, Paul or John, or to judge in wh cases doctrine has transformed the text. The te is in no instance so insecure as to necessitate t alteration of the basic gospel. But those wh love the Word of God will desire the great accuracy in the most minute details, knowing t nuances of meaning made possible by wo order, tense, change of particle, *etc.*

VI. HISTORY OF THE TEXT

In brief outline we may thus sketch the history the New Testament text. Many of the facto earliest at work are those described in the histo of the growth of the Canon of the New Tes ment (*q.v.*). The circulation of separate Gospe but of the Pauline letters as a Corpus; t chequered history of the Acts and the book Revelation; the overshadowing of the Catho Epistles by the rest; all these are reflected in t textual data for the several books. During t period of the establishment of the Canon number of factors were at work. There was tendency as early as we can trace to atten emendation of the Greek according to prevaili fashions or even scribal whim; in the case of the Gospels a close verbal identity was sought, often at the expense of Mark. In some cases, 'floating tradition' was added; or items were taken away from the written word. Such heretical teachers as Marcion and Tatian left the mark of tendentious correction upon their editions of the text, and doubtless their opponents were not blameless in this. In the Acts, alterations were made perhaps for purely literary or popularizing motives. So, by the early 3rd century, there resulted that mixture of good and bad which we find attested in our MSS, versions, and patristic evidence.

At some time in the late 3rd or early 4th century it would seem that some attempts at recension took place, but it is a curiosity of history that little direct evidence of this is to be found. The names of Hesychius and Lucian are given by Jerome in his letter to Damasus; but we have no further information about the work of these men, or of Pamphilus, whose activity has also been conjectured. Yet at all events we find the text-types of Alexandrian, Caesaraean, and Byzantine clearly marked in the Gospels; while the triple scheme is not found so clearly in the Epistles, the Alexandrian and Byzantine strains are to be found, and the absence of a Caesaraean may be due to a failure in research, not to fact; in Revelation there is a quite distinct fourfold pattern. The material of the so-called 'Western Text' is earlier than these texts, and it is uncertain whether it may be termed a recension in the strict sense. What principles guided these recensions is to be deduced only from the text itself. The general sobriety of the Alexandrian is clear in the Pauline Epistles, but is not uniform throughout the New Testament as Hort and others have thought: few present-day critics would follow it in its entirety or any one text-type, much less term a text so constituted the 'original' Greek.

In the Middle Ages the Alexandrian text seems to have suffered eclipse. Various forms of Caesaraean and Byzantine wrestled for supremacy till about the 10th century. After this, the Byzantine text may be said to have been supreme in the sense that many MSS of nearly identical type were produced and have been preserved. But variants from even the earliest times are recrudescent in late MSS, and important MSS of other recensions and even of pre-recensional type come from very late dates, while some late MSS in fact change their allegiance in a bewildering fashion from text-type to text-type.

VII. CONCLUSION

Thus the task of New Testament textual criticism is vast and unfinished. Certainly, advances have been made since the material began to be collected and examined in the 17th century. Both Hort and von Soden present texts better than the printed texts of the Renaissance, and provide a sound basis upon which satisfactory exegesis may proceed. It is evident that some of the principles behind the Alexandrian text were sound. But it must be constantly borne in mind that it is at such a recensional form and not at the original that these scholars had arrived. The textual critic will be as the scribe discipled in the kingdom of heaven; bringing forth from his treasures things new and old. The busy textual projects of these post-war years will bring us nearer to the apostolic *ipsissima verba* than previous generations were favoured to come; yet we cannot but build on other men's foundations.

BIBLIOGRAPHY. P. Maas, *Textkritik*[2], 1950 (E.T., 1958); G. Pasquali, *Storia della Tradizione e Critica del Testo*[2], 1952; C. Tischendorf, *Novum Testamentum Graece*, 8a Editio Maior, 1869–72; H. von Soden, *Die Schriften des neuen Testaments in ihrer aeltesten erreichbaren Textgestalt*, 1911–13; C. R. Gregory, *Textkritik des neuen Testaments*, 1900–09; *id.*, *Canon and Text of the New Testament*, 1907; F. H. A. Scrivener, *Introduction to the Criticism of the New Testament*[4], 1894; A. Vööbus, *Early Versions of the New Testament*, 1954; B. F. Westcott and F. J. A. Hort, *The New Testament in the Original Greek*, 1881; K. Lake, *The Text of the New Testament*[6], 1928; M-J. Lagrange, *Critique Textuelle*, II: *La Critique Rationelle*[2], 1935; G. D. Kilpatrick, 'Western Text and Original Text in the Gospels and Acts', *JTS*, XLIV, 1943, pp. 24–36, and 'Western Text and Original Text in the Epistles', *JTS*, XLV, 1944, pp. 60–65; G. Zuntz, *The Text of the Epistles*, 1953; M. M. Parvis and A. P. Wikgren (eds.), *New Testament Manuscript Studies*, 1950; A. J. F. Klijn, *A Survey of the Researches into the Western Text of the Gospels and Acts*, 1949; J. Schmid, *Studien zur Geschichte des griechischen Apokalypse-Textes*, 1955; A. Souter, *Text and Canon of the New Testament*[2], 1954; L. Leloir, 'L'originale syriaque du commentaire de S. Éphrem sur le Diatessaron', *Studia Biblica et Orientalia*, II, 1959, pp. 391 ff.

Editions with select apparatus: *Novum Testamentum Graece et Latine* . . . edidit Augustinus Merk[8], 1958; *Novum Testamentum Graece* . . . curavit E. Nestle[23], 1957; Η ΚΑΙΝΗ ΔΙΑΘΗΚΗ (ed. G. D. Kilpatrick), British and Foreign Bible Society, 1958.

J.N.B.

THADDAEUS. This name occurs only in the list of the twelve apostles (Mt. x. 3; Mk. iii. 18). The equivalent in Lk. vi. 16 is 'Judas the brother of James' (*cf.* also Acts i. 13). AV in Mt. x. 3 reads 'Lebbaeus, whose surname was Thaddaeus'. Most textual critics now read simply 'Thaddaeus' and treat 'Lebbaeus' as an intrusion from the Western Text, though some have suggested 'Lebbaeus' to be correct and 'Thaddaeus' to have been introduced from Mk. iii. 18. 'Thaddaeus' is probably derived from Aramaic *taḏ*, meaning the female breast, and suggests warmth of character and almost feminine devotedness. 'Lebbaeus' comes from Heb. *lēḇ*, 'heart', and it may therefore be an explanation of the other name. Attempts have been made to derive 'Thaddaeus' from 'Judah' and 'Lebbaeus' from 'Levi'.

There seems little doubt that Thaddaeus is to be identified with 'Judas of James' (see F. F. Bruce, *The Acts of the Apostles*, 1951, p. 73). The name 'Judas' would not be popular with the deed of Judas Iscariot in mind, and this may be why it is not used in Matthew and Mark. The post-canonical literature does not help us to obtain a clear picture, but Jerome says that Thaddaeus was also called 'Lebbaeus' and 'Judas of James', and that he was sent on a mission to Abgar, king of Edessa. Eusebius, on the other hand, reckoned him to be one of the Seventy. The mention of the Gospel of Thaddaeus in some MSS of the *Decretum Gelasii* is thought to be due to a scribal error. R.E.N.

THANK-OFFERING. See SACRIFICE AND OFFERING (Old Testament), IV*d*.

THEATRE. Greek theatres were usually cut in some naturally concave hillside such as might be afforded by the acropolis of the town concerned.

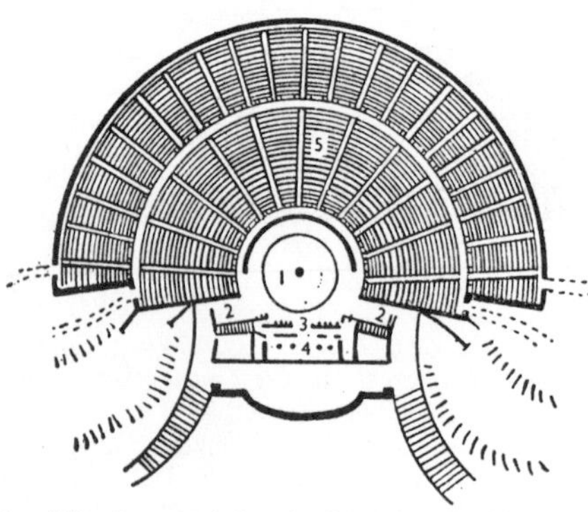

Fig. 218. A typical Greek theatre at Epidaurus in the Peloponnese (4th century BC). *Key:* 1. Orchestra; 2. *Parodoi, i.e.* entrances to the theatre for the spectators and to the orchestra for the chorus; 3. Stage; 4. *Skēnē*, the permanent background to the action; 5. Auditorium.

There was thus no limit to size, provided the acoustic properties were adequate, and some theatres seated many thousands of persons. The seats rose precipitously in a single tier around the *orchēstra*, or dancing space. Behind this the theatre was enclosed by a raised stage, the *skēnē*. Together with the gymnasium, the theatre was the centre of cultural affairs, and might be used as a place for official assemblies, as at Ephesus (Acts xix. 29). This particular theatre stood facing down the main thoroughfare of the city towards the docks, and as in most Greek states remains the most substantial relic of the past. E.A.J.

THEBES. See No.

THEBEZ (*tēḇēṣ*, 'brightness'). A fortified city in Mt. Ephraim, in the course of capturing which Abimelech (*q.v.*) was mortally wounded by a millstone hurled down on him by a woman (Jdg. ix. 50 ff.; 2 Sa. xi. 21). Thebez is the modern Tūbās, about 10 miles north of Nablus, and north-east of Shechem on the road to Beth-shan.

THEFT. See CRIME AND PUNISHMENT.

THEODOTION. See TEXT AND VERSIONS.

THEOPHILUS (Gk. *theophilos*, 'dear to God', 'friend of God'), the man to whom both parts of Luke's history were dedicated (Lk. i. 3; Acts i. 1). Some have thought that the name indicates generally 'the Christian reader', others that it conceals a well-known figure, such as Titus Flavius Clemens, the Emperor Vespasian's nephew (so B. H. Streeter, *The Four Gospels*, 1924, pp. 534 ff.). But it is most probably a real name. The title 'most excellent' given to him in Lk. i. 3 may denote a member of the equestrian order (possibly in some official position) or may be a courtesy title (*cf.* Acts xxiii. 26, xxiv. 3, xxvi. 25). Theophilus had acquired some information about Christianity, but Luke decided to supply him with a more orderly and reliable account. He may have been a representative of that class of Roman society which Luke wished to influence in favour of the gospel, but scarcely the advocate briefed for Paul's defence before Nero (so J. I. Still, *St. Paul on Trial*, 1923, pp. 84 ff.). F.F.B.

THESSALONIANS, EPISTLES TO THE.

I. OUTLINE OF CONTENTS

1 Thessalonians

a. Greeting (i. 1).

b. Thanksgiving for the Thessalonian Christians' faith and steadfastness (i. 2–10).

c. Paul's explanation of his recent conduct (ii. 1–16).

d. Narrative of events since he left Thessalonica (ii. 17–iii. 10).

e. His prayer for an early reunion with them (iii. 11–13).

f. Encouragement to holy living and brotherly love (iv. 1–12).

g. Concerning the parousia (iv. 13–v. 11).

h. General exhortations (v. 12–22).

i. Prayer, final greeting, and benediction (v. 23–28).

2 Thessalonians

a. Greeting (i. 1–2).

b. Thanksgiving and encouragement (i. 3–12).

c. Events which must precede the day of the Lord (ii. 1–12).

d. Further thanksgiving and encouragement (ii. 13–iii. 5).

e. The need for discipline (iii. 6–15).

f. Prayer, final greeting, and benediction (iii. 16–18).

II. AUTHORSHIP

Both the Epistles to the Thessalonians are superscribed with the names of Paul, Silvanus,

= Silas), and Timothy; but in both Paul is the eal author, although he associates with himself is two companions who had recently shared his issionary work in Thessalonica. In 1 Thessalonians Paul speaks by name in the first person ingular (ii. 18) and refers to Timothy in the third erson (iii. 2, 6); in 2 Thessalonians he appends is personal signature (iii. 17) and is therefore to e identified with the 'I' of ii. 5. His use of 'we' nd 'us' when he is referring to himself alone is as vident in these Epistles as in others, especially so 1 1 Thes. iii. 1: 'we thought it good to be left at thens alone' (*cf.* Acts xvii. 15 f.).

There has been little difficulty about the auline authorship of 1 Thessalonians; F. C. aur's ascription of it to a disciple of Paul's who rote after AD 70 to revive interest in the parousia but a curiosity in the history of criticism.

Greater difficulty has been felt with 2 Thessalonians. Its style is said to be formal as comared with that of the first Epistle; this judgment, ased on such expressions as 'we are bound' and t is meet' in i. 3, is not of great moment; it ertainly needs no such explanation as that ffered by M. Dibelius—that this Epistle was ritten to be read in church—for the same is true f the first Epistle (*cf.* 1 Thes. v. 27). More erious is the argument that the eschatology of Thessalonians contradicts that of 1 Thessalonians. The first Epistle stresses the unxpectedness with which the day of the Lord will rrive, 'as a thief in the night' (1 Thes. v. 2), hereas the second Epistle stresses that certain vents will intervene before its arrival (2 Thes. . 1 ff.), and does so in a passage whose apocayptic character is unparalleled in the Pauline iterature.

A. Harnack accounted for the difference with he suggestion that 1 Thessalonians was written o the Gentile section of the church of Thessalonica, and 2 Thessalonians to the Jewish ection. This is not only rendered improbable by he direction of 1 Thes. v. 27 that that Epistle be ead to 'all the holy brethren' but is incredible in he light of Paul's fundamental insistence on the neness of Gentile and Jewish believers in hrist. Equally unconvincing is F. C. Burkitt's upplement to Harnack's theory—that both pistles were drafted by Silvanus and approved y Paul, who added 1 Thes. ii. 18 ('even I Paul') nd 2 Thes. iii. 17 in his own hand.

Alternative suggestions to the Pauline authorhip of both letters raise greater difficulties than he Pauline authorship does. If 2 Thessalonians is seudonymous, it was an unbelievable refinement f subtlety on the writer's part to warn the eaders against letters forged in Paul's name (ii.); the salutation in 2 Thes. iii. 17 is intelligible nly as Paul's safeguard against the danger of uch forged letters. The difficulties raised by the auline authorship can best be accounted for y considering the occasion and relation of he two letters. Both letters were included in he earliest ascertainable edition of the Pauline orpus.

III. OCCASION

a. The First Epistle

Paul and his companions had to leave Thessalonica hastily in the early summer of AD 50, after making a number of converts and planting a church in the city (*cf.* Acts xvii. 1–10, and see THESSALONICA). The circumstances of their departure meant that their converts would inevitably be exposed to persecution, for which they were imperfectly prepared, because Paul had not had time to give them all the basic teaching which he thought they required. At the earliest opportunity he sent Timothy back to see how the Thessalonian Christians were faring. When Timothy returned to him in Corinth (*cf.* Acts xviii. 5) he brought good news of their steadfastness and zeal in propagating the gospel, but reported that they had certain problems, some ethical (with special reference to sexual relations) and some eschatological (in particular, they were concerned lest at the parousia those of their number who had died should be at a disadvantage as compared with those who were still alive). Paul wrote to them immediately, expressing his joy at Timothy's good news, protesting that his recent abrupt departure from them was through no choice of his own (as his detractors urged), stressing the importance of chastity and diligence in daily work, and assuring them that believers who died before the parousia would suffer no disadvantage but would be raised to rejoin their living brethren and 'meet the Lord in the air' at His coming.

b. The Second Epistle

Before long, however, further news reached Paul which indicated that there were still some misapprehensions to be removed. He suspected that some of these misapprehensions might be due to misrepresentations of his teaching to the Thessalonian church. Some members of the church had inferred that the parousia was so imminent that there was no point in going on working. Paul explains that certain events must take place before the parousia; in particular, there will be a world-wide rebellion against God, led by one who will incarnate the forces of lawlessness and anarchy, which at present are being held in check by a power which he need not name in writing, since his readers know what he means. (The allusiveness of his reference to this power makes it likely that he had in mind the Roman Empire, whose maintenance of law and order gave him cause for gratitude several times in the course of his apostolic service.) As for those who were disinclined to work, he speaks to them even more sharply than in the former Epistle; to live at the expense of others is unworthy of able-bodied Christians, who had seen an example of the worthier course in the conduct of Paul himself and his colleagues. Spongers and slackers must be treated by their fellow-Christians in a way that will bring them to their senses.

An attempt has sometimes been made to relieve the difficulties felt in relating the two Epistles to each other by supposing that 2 Thessalonians was written first. But 2 Thessalonians does presuppose some previous correspondence from Paul (ii. 15), while the language of 1 Thes. ii. 17–iii. 10 certainly implies that 1 Thessalonians was Paul's first letter to the Thessalonian Christians after his enforced departure from them.

IV. TEACHING

With the possible exception of Galatians (*q.v.*), the two Thessalonian letters are Paul's earliest surviving writings. They give us an illuminating, and in some ways a surprising, impression of certain phases of Christian faith and life twenty years after the death and resurrection of Christ. The main lines have already been laid down; the Thessalonian Christians (formerly pagan idolaters for the most part) were converted through hearing and accepting the apostolic preaching (1 Thes. i. 9 f.); Jesus, in whom they had put their trust, is the Son of God who can be freely and spontaneously spoken of in terms which assume rather than assert His equality with the Father (*cf.* 1 Thes. i. 1, iii. 11; 2 Thes. i. 1, ii. 16); the gospel which has brought them salvation carries with it healthy practical implications for everyday life. The living and true God is holy, and He desires His people to be holy too; this holiness extends to such matters as relations with the other sex (1 Thes. iv. 3) and the honest earning of their daily bread (1 Thes. iv. 11 f.; 2 Thes. iii. 10–12). The apostles themselves had set an example in these and other matters (1 Thes. ii. 5 ff.; 2 Thes. iii. 7 ff.).

Both Epistles reflect the intense eschatological awareness of those years, and the unhealthy excesses to which it tended to give rise. Paul does not discourage this awareness (indeed, eschatology had evidently been prominent in his preaching at Thessalonica), but he teaches the Thessalonians not to confuse the suddenness of the parousia with its immediacy, and he impresses on them the ethical corollaries of Christian eschatology. He himself did not know then whether he would still be alive at the parousia; he hoped he would be, but he had received no assurance on the point. His prime concern was to discharge his appointed work so faithfully that the day would not find him unprepared and ashamed. So to his converts he presents the parousia as a comfort and hope for the bereaved and distressed, a warning to the careless and unruly, and for all a stimulus to holy living. The parousia will effect the ultimate conquest of evil; it will provide the universal manifestation of that triumph which is already guaranteed by the saving work of Christ.

BIBLIOGRAPHY. Commentaries on the Greek text by G. G. Findlay, *CGT*, 1904; G. Milligan, 1908; J. Moffatt, *EGT*, 1910; J. E. Frame, *ICC*, 1913; B. Rigaux, *Études Bibliques*, 1956; on the English text by J. Denney, *The Expositor's Bible*, 1892; C. F. Hogg and W. E. Vine, 1914; E. J. Bicknell, *WC*, 1932; W. Neil, *MNT*, 1950; *id.*, *Torch Commentaries*, 1957; W. Hendriksen, 1955; J. W. Bailey, *IB*, XI, 1955; L. Morris, *TNTC*, 1956; *id.*, *NLC*, 1959; also J. B. Lightfoot, *Biblical Essays*, 1893, pp. 235 ff.; *id.*, *Notes on the Epistles of St. Paul*, 1895, pp. 1 ff.; K. Lake, *Earlier Epistles of St. Paul*, 1911, pp. 61 ff.; T. W. Manson, 'St. Paul in Greece', *BJRL*, XXXV, 1952–3, pp. 428 ff. F.F.B.

THESSALONICA. Founded after the triumph of Macedonia to grace her new position in world affairs, the city rapidly outstripped its older neighbours and became the principal metropolis of Macedonia. Situated at the junction of the main land route from Italy to the East with the main route from the Aegean to the Danube, her position under the Romans was assured, and she has remained a major city to this day. Thessalonica was the first place where Paul's preaching achieved a numerous and socially prominent following (Acts xvii. 4). His opponents, lacking their hitherto customary influence in high places, resorted to mob agitation to force the government's hand. The authorities, neatly trapped by the imputation of disloyalty towards the imperial power, took the minimum action to move Paul on without hardship to him. In spite of his success, Paul made a point of not placing himself in debt to his followers (Phil. iv. 16 f.; 1 Thes. ii. 9). Not that they were themselves without generosity (1 Thes. iv. 10); Paul was apparently afraid that the flourishing condition of the church would encourage parasites unless he himself set the strictest example of self-support (2 Thes. iii. 8–12). The two Epistles, written soon after his departure, reflect also his anxiety to conserve his gains from rival teachers (2 Thes. ii. 2) and from disillusionment in the face of further agitation (1 Thes. iii. 3). He need not have feared. Thessalonica remained a triumphant crown to his efforts (1 Thes. i. 8). See THESSALONIANS, EPISTLES TO THE.

BIBLIOGRAPHY. E. Oberhummer, *RE*, *s.v.* 'Thessalonika'. E.A.J.

THEUDAS. 1. In Acts v. 36 an impostor (possibly a messianic pretender) who some time before AD 6 gathered a band of 400 men, but he was killed and his followers dispersed. His activity was probably one of the innumerable disorders which broke out in Judaea after Herod's death in 4 BC. Origen (*Contra Celsum*, i. 57) says he arose 'before the birth of Jesus', but that may simply be an inference from this passage, where Gamaliel speaks of his rising as having preceded that of Judas (*q.v.*).

2. In Jos., *Ant.* xx. 5. 1 a magician who led many followers to the Jordan, promising that the river would be divided at his command, so that they could cross it dry-shod. They were attacked by cavalry sent against them by the procurator Fadus (*c.* 46–44 BC), and Theudas's head was brought to Jerusalem. F.F.B.

HIGH. Heb. *yārēḵ*, also translated 'side' in AV, f altar or tabernacle (2 Ki. xvi. 14; Nu. iii. 29). 'he variant form *yar^{e}ḵâ* is always used of objects r places generally, apparently in the dual, *i.e.* erived from the thought of the two thighs. The ther word translated 'thigh' in AV (Is. xlvii. 2) efers to the leg, see RV. The Gk. *mēros* is used nce (Rev. xix. 16), where it probably refers to ie locality of the inscription on the garment. See relevant comment in *NBC*.)

The Hebrew word is found in similar usage to *ıoṯnayim* or *h^{a}lāṣayim* and Gk. *osphys*, 'loins', ı respect of the parts of the body usually clothed Ex. xxviii. 42; *cf.* Is. xxxii. 11), and especially f the position where a sword is worn (Ps. xlv. 3); lso of the locality of the genital organs, and so y figure of speech to one's offspring (Gn. xlvi. 6; *cf.* Gn. xxxv. 11; Acts ii. 30; *moṯnayim* is not sed in this sense). The custom of making an ath by placing the hand under another's thigh Gn. xxiv. 2 f., xlvii. 29 ff.) signifies the associa- on of the peculiar power of these parts, perhaps vith the idea of invoking the support of the erson's descendants to enforce the oath. For ssociation in a particular form of oath, see Ju. v. 21 ff.

Smiting upon the thigh is a sign of anguish Je. xxxi. 19). For a discussion of the custom of ot eating the sinew of the thigh joint (Gn. xxxii. 2), see SINEW. B.O.B.

HISTLES. See THORNS.

HOMAS. One of the twelve apostles. In the sts of the Twelve which are arranged in three roups of four each, Thomas occurs in the second roup (Mt. x. 2–4; Mk. iii. 16–19; Lk. vi. 14–16; Acts i. 13). He is linked with Matthew in Mt. x. 3 nd with Philip in Acts i. 13. The name comes om Aram. *t^{e}'ômā'*, meaning 'twin'; John three imes uses the Gk. version of it, 'Didymus' (xi. 6, xx. 24, xxi. 2). The question whose twin he vas cannot be answered with certainty. Various raditions (Syriac and Egyptian) suggest that his ersonal name was Judas.

It is only in the Fourth Gospel that there are ny personal references to Thomas. He was pre- ared to go with Jesus to the tomb of Lazarus nd to possible death at the hands of the Jews Jn. xi. 16). He confessed himself unable to under- tand where Jesus was going when He warned the 'welve of His impending departure (Jn. xiv. 5). 'he chief incident for which he has always been emembered, and for which he has been called Doubting Thomas', is his disbelief in the resur- ection. He missed the appearance of Christ to he other apostles (Jn. xx. 24) and said that he eeded visual and tactual proof of the resur- ection (xx. 25). A week later Christ appeared gain to the Eleven and He offered Thomas the pportunity to test the reality of His body. 'homas' confession of faith, 'My Lord and my God' (xx. 28), marks the climax of the Fourth Gospel; blessing is promised to those who can ome to faith without the aid of sight. R.E.N.

THORNS. A good deal of difference exists among botanists about the identity of the thorns and briers mentioned in Scripture, owing to the fact that over twenty different words are em- ployed to describe spiny or thorny plants.

In general, thorns expressed the concept of fruitlessness or vexatious endeavour (Gn. iii. 18; Nu. xxxiii. 55; Jos. xxiii. 13). They were evidence of divine judgment on the ungodly (Na. i. 10), or of sheer misfortune (Ezk. ii. 6). If allowed to grow unchecked in orchards or vineyards they made serious inroads on the productivity of the trees and vines (Pr. xxiv. 31; Is. xxxiv. 13; Je. xii. 13), but when kept in control and arranged in the form of hedges they served as effective barriers to wild animals (Pr. xv. 19; Ho. ii. 6). Thorns were a popular quick-burning fuel in Old Testament times, as among the modern Bedouin Arabs (Ps. lviii. 9; Is. ix. 18, x. 17). The destructive nature of thorns was expressed graphically in the Gospel parables (Mt. xiii. 7; Mk. iv. 7; Lk. viii. 7), as was their essential fruit- lessness (Mt. vii. 16).

Some of the biblical references to 'thorns' are undoubtedly to the Palestinian bramble, *Rubus sanctus*, and the elmleaf bramble, *R. ulmifolius* Schott. The reference in Ps. lviii. 9 has been interpreted in terms of the species *R. sanctus*, but some modern botanists prefer the Palestinian buckthorn, *Rhamnus palaestina* Boiss. This shrub grows throughout the Holy Land and is found in the Sinai peninsula also. The 'thorns' of Pr. xv. 19 and Ho. ii. 6 may perhaps be the prickly Jericho balsam (*Balanites aegyptiaca*) or the box- thorn (*Lycium europaeum* L.), while the 'thorns of the wilderness' (Jdg. viii. 7) may be species of *Astragalus*, *Acacia*, or *Zizyphus*. The references in Is. xxxiv. 13 and Ho. ix. 6 are probably to the *Xanthium spinosum* L., a weedy plant producing prickly, bur-like fruits.

BIBLIOGRAPHY. H. N. and A. L. Moldenke, *Plants of the Bible*, 1952, pp. 202 ff., 241 ff.

R.K.H.

THORNS, CROWN OF. This was made by the Roman soldiers and placed on the head of Christ when He was mocked before the crucifixion (Mt. xxvii. 29; Mk. xv. 17; Jn. xix. 2). It was, with the sceptre of reed and the purple robe, symbolic of the fact that He had been said to be King of the Jews. The superscription on the cross likewise proclaimed this in mockery. Yet Christians have seen the life of Jesus as a royal road from the manger of Bethlehem to the cross of Calvary, and the very incidents in which He least seemed to be a king have won their allegiance more than any- thing else. For John especially the moment of Christ's humiliation is the moment of His glory (xii. 31–33; *cf.* Heb. ii. 9).

It is uncertain exactly what plant is signified by *akantha*. There are a number of plants with sharp spines which grow in Palestine. Christians have seen the thorns as symbolic of the effects of sin (Gn. iii. 18; Nu. xxxiii. 55; Pr. xxii. 5; Mt. vii. 16, xiii. 7; Heb. vi. 8).

H. St. J. Hart (*JTS*, NS, III, 1952) suggests that the crown was made from palm leaves, which would be readily available. *Phoenix dactylifera* has sharp spines. The crown might thus have been intended to resemble the 'radiate crown' of a divine ruler, so that Christ was being mocked as 'God' as well as 'king'. R.E.N.

THOUSAND. See ARMY, NUMBER.

THRACE. A tribally organized region lying between Macedonia and the Greek states of the Bosporus coast. It had always maintained a sturdy independence of Greek control, and the Romans left it as an isolated enclave under its own dynasties until AD 44, when it was incorporated into the Caesarean province under a low-ranking procurator. Republican institutions were not widely developed before the 2nd century AD. There is no record of Christianity there in New Testament times.

BIBLIOGRAPHY. A. H. M. Jones, *Cities of the Eastern Roman Provinces*, 1937; J. Keil, *CAH*, XI, 1936, pp. 570–573. E.A.J.

THREE HOLY CHILDREN, SONG OF THE. See APOCRYPHA.

THRESHING, -FLOOR. See AGRICULTURE.

THRESHOLD. See HOUSE.

THRONE. The word *kissē'* may refer to any seat or to one of special importance (1 Ki. ii. 19). Its root (*kāsâ*, 'to cover') suggests a canopied construction, hence a throne (*e.g.* Ex. xi. 5; Ezk. xxvi. 16). The throne symbolizes dignity and authority (Gn. xli. 40; 2 Sa. iii. 10), which may extend beyond the immediate occupant (2 Sa. vii. 13–16). Since the king is Yahweh's representative, his throne is 'the throne of the kingdom of the Lord over Israel' (1 Ch. xxviii. 5); it typifies Yahweh's throne in the heavens (1 Ki. xxii. 10, 19; *cf.* Is. vi. 1). Righteousness and justice are therefore enjoined upon its occupants (Pr. xvi. 12, xx. 28; *cf.* Is. ix. 7; 2 Sa. xiv. 9). Although Yahweh's throne is transcendent (Is. lxvi. 1; *cf.* Mt. v. 34), He graciously condescends to sit enthroned upon the cherubim (*e.g.* 1 Sa. iv. 4). In the messianic age 'Jerusalem shall be called the throne of the Lord' (Je. iii. 17, RSV; *cf.* Ezk. xliii. 7). The thrones of judgment in Dn. vii. 9 ff. form a good introduction to the usual sense of the word in the New Testament.

Jesus receives 'the throne of his father David' (Lk. i. 32; *cf.* Acts ii. 30; Heb. i. 5–9, all of which allude to 2 Sa. vii. 12–16. *Cf.* also Heb. viii. 1, xii. 2). As Son of man, He will judge from His throne (Mt. xxv. 31 ff.). In the world to come the disciples will have thrones and assist the Son of man (Mt. xix. 28; *cf.* Lk. xxii. 30). The faithful are promised a seat on the throne of the Lamb (Rev. iii. 21), and the pre-millennial judgment appears to be committed to them (xx. 4; *cf.* Dn. vii. 9, 22). In the post-millennial judgment, however, there is only the great white throne (xx. 11).

Fig. 219. Types of farming implements used in Palestine. *Right*, a board studded with nails which was drawn across the threshing-floor to separate the wheat from the chaff. *Left*, a disc harrow.

The disparity is more apparent than real, for Dn. vii forms the background of each vision. Similarly, the vision of the august throne of God and the Lamb in Rev. xxii. 3 compares with Mt. xix. 28 and Lk. xxii. 30, because John, in adding 'and they shall *reign* . . .' (xxii. 5), undoubtedly has in mind the thrones of the faithful. See also 'throne of grace' (Heb. iv. 16). R.J.McK.

THRUM. See SPINNING AND WEAVING.

THUMB. Heb. *bōhen*, in the Old Testament, equally and always together, of the thumb and big toe, differentiated by the designation, 'of the hand' or 'of the foot'. The root is related to an Arabic word meaning 'to cover' or 'shut', hence of that member which closes or covers the hand.

The practice of placing blood from the sacrificial beast upon the right thumb, great toe, and also ear of the priests probably indicated the dedication of the prominent organs of hearing, doing, and walking, symbolizing the securing of the whole man (see EAR) (Ex. xxix. 20; Lv. viii.

3, *etc.*). Similarly, the practice of cutting off the umbs and great toes of a defeated enemy prob-bly symbolized his being rendered powerless 'dg. i. 6 f.), and also ceremonially incompetent discharge any sacral duties. B.O.B.

HUMMIM. See URIM AND THUMMIM.

HUNDER. Most frequent during the winter ason, thunder is vividly described in Jb. xxxvii nd Ps. xxix. The few rainstorms of summer are sually associated with thunder (*e.g.* 1 Sa. xii. 17); e coincidence of this event with Samuel's essage helped to deepen the warning to Israel hen they desired a king. A desert thunderstorm ems the most plausible explanation for the arrative of 2 Ki. iii. 4–27, when 'the country was lled with water', presumably as a result of a esert thunderstorm on the plateau east of the ered valley. In another military campaign a understorm decided the result of the battle etween Israel and the Philistines (1 Sa. vii. 10).

Thunder is frequently associated with the voice f God and is spoken of as a voice in Pss. lxxvii. 8, civ. 7. The creative voice of God which bade e waters go to their appointed place (Gn. i. 9) identified with thunder (Ps. civ. 7). It was ssociated with the giving of the law at Sinai Ex. xix. 16, xx. 18), and the voice out of heaven hich answered Christ (Jn. xii. 28 f.) was identi-ed by those present as a thunder-peal. Voices ke thunder are referred to in the Apocalypse Rev. vi. 1, xiv. 2, xix. 6), where they are even iven articulate meaning (Rev. x. 3 f.).

See also PLAGUES OF EGYPT. J.M.H.

HYATIRA. A city in the Roman province of sia, in the west of what is now Asiatic Turkey. t occupied an important position in a low-lying orridor' connecting the Hermus and Caicus alleys. It was a frontier garrison, first on the estern frontier of the territory of Seleucus I of yria (who founded it in the 4th century BC), and ter, after changing hands, on the eastern ontier of the kingdom of Pergamum. With that ingdom, it passed under Roman rule in 133 BC. ut it remained an important point in the oman road-system, for it lay on the road from ergamum, the provincial capital, to Laodicea, nd thence to the eastern provinces. It was also n important centre of manufacture; dyeing, arment-making, pottery, and brass-working are mong the trades known to have existed there. A rge town (Akhisar) still stands on the same site.

The Thyatiran woman Lydia, the 'seller of urple' whom Paul met at Philippi (Acts xvi. 14), as probably the overseas agent of a Thyatiran anufacturer; she was probably arranging the ale of dyed woollen goods which were known imply by the name of the dye. The Thyatiran hurch was the fourth (Rev. i. 11) of the 'seven hurches of Asia'. Some of the symbols in the tter to the church (Rev. ii. 18–29) seem to llude to the circumstances of the city. The escription of the Christ (verse 18) is appropriate for a city renowned for its brass-working (*chalkolibanos*, translated 'fine brass', may be a technical term for some local type of brassware). The terms of the promise (verses 26, 27) may reflect the long military history of the city. 'Jezebel' (the name is probably symbolic) was evidently a woman who was accepted within the fellowship of the church (verse 20). Her teaching probably advocated a measure of compromise with some activity which was implicitly pagan. This is likely to have been membership of the social clubs or 'guilds' into which the trades were organized. These bodies fulfilled many admirable functions, and pursuance of a trade was almost impossible without belonging to the guild; yet their meetings were inextricably bound up with acts of pagan worship and immorality. (See W. M. Ramsay, *The Letters to the Seven Churches of Asia*, 1904, chapters xxiii, xxiv.) M.J.S.R.

THYINE WOOD. See TREES.

TIBERIAS. A city on the west shore of the Sea of Galilee (see GALILEE, SEA OF) which subsequently gave its name to the lake. It was founded by Herod Antipas about AD 20 and named after the Emperor Tiberius. The principal factors influencing Herod's choice of site seem to have been: (1) a defensive position represented by a rocky projection above the lake; (2) proximity to some already-famous warm springs which lay just to the south. Otherwise, the site offered little, and the beautiful buildings of the city (which became Herod's capital) rose on ground that included a former graveyard, and so rendered the city unclean in Jewish eyes.

Tiberias is mentioned only once in the Gospels (Jn. vi. 23; 'sea of Tiberias' appears in Jn. vi. 1, xxi. 1), and there is no record of Christ ever visiting it. It was a thoroughly Gentile city, and He seems to have avoided it in favour of the numerous Jewish towns of the lake shore. By a curious reversal, however, after the destruction of Jerusalem it became the chief seat of Jewish learning, and both the Mishnah and the Palestinian Talmud were compiled there, in the 3rd and 5th centuries respectively.

Of the towns which surrounded the Sea of Galilee in New Testament times, Tiberias is the only one which remains of any size at the present day. J.H.P.

TIBERIUS. The stepson of Augustus Caesar, reluctantly adopted as his heir when all other hope of a direct succession was lost. On Augustus' death in AD 14, Tiberius at fifty-six years of age had a lifetime's experience of government behind him. It was nevertheless a momentous decision when the Senate transferred Augustus' powers bodily to him, thus recognizing that the *de facto* ascendancy of Augustus was now an indispensable instrument of the Roman state. For twenty-three years Tiberius loyally and unimaginatively continued Augustus' policies. His dourness gradually lost him the confidence of the nation, and he withdrew to a disgruntled retirement on Capri until his death. In his absence treason trials and the intervention of the praetorian guard set dangerous new precedents in Roman politics. He is referred to in Lk. iii. 1 and indirectly wherever 'Caesar' is mentioned in the Gospels.

Fig. 220. A silver denarius of Tiberius, Roman emperor AD 14–37. See also plate XV*b*.

BIBLIOGRAPHY. F. B. Marsh, *The Reign of Tiberius*, 1931; M. P. Charlesworth, *CAH*, X, 1934, chapter xix. E.A.J.

TIBHATH. A town in the Aramaean kingdom of Zobah (*Ṣôḇâ*). After David defeated a composite force of Aramaeans, including men from Zobah and Damascus, he pressed on to the towns of Tibhath (*Ṭiḇḥaṯ*) and Chun, from which he took booty (1 Ch. xviii. 8). J.A.T.

TIDAL. 'Tidal (*Tiḏ'āl*) king of nations (*gōyîm*)' was one of the four kings (Gn. xiv. 1, 9) headed by Chedorlaomer of Elam who subdued the five kings of the cities of the plain (Sodom, Gomorrah, *etc.*) and then, when these latter rebelled thirteen years later, swept through Transjordan and vanquished the forces of Sodom and Gomorrah. Abraham then pursued and defeated the four kings in order to recover his nephew Lot, captured by them in the defeat of Sodom and Gomorrah.

The name Tid'al is almost certainly identical with the Hittite name Tudḫalia; Asiatic *ḫ* (like Akkadian *ḫ*) can transcribe, and be transcribed by, a West Semitic '*ayin*. However, the individual concerned cannot be certainly identified at present. Of the four or five Hittite kings named Tudḫalia, all except the first one date to *c.* 1400–1200 BC, and therefore lived long after Abraham (*c.* 19th century BC; see CHRONOLOGY OF THE OLD TESTAMENT). Tudḫalia I lived about 1740 BC, still not early enough. However, in the early second millennium BC, Asia Minor and N Syria were not political unities but divided among various small states and groups. Tidal may well have been an early Tudḫalia ruling a federation of Indo-European (Hittite and Luvian) groups—hence Heb. *gōyîm*, 'nations'—on the borders of SE Asia Minor and N Syria in about the 19th century BC.

BIBLIOGRAPHY. F. M. Th. Böhl, *King Hammurabi of Babylon in the Setting of his Time*, 1946; F. F. Bruce, *The Hittites and the Old Testament*, 1947, especially pp. 19–23; K. A. Kitchen, *Hittite Hieroglyphs, Aramaeans and Hebrew Traditions*, forthcoming. K.A.K.

TIGLATH-PILESER, TILGATH-PILNESER. This king of Assyria is known by more than on[e] name. *Tiḡlaṯ-pil'eser* (2 Ki. xv. 29, xvi. 7–10) i[s] close to Assyr. *Tukulti-apil-Ešarra* ('My trust is i[n] the son of Ešarra') and the Aram. *tgltplsr* (Zinjir[li] Stele). The variant late Heb. *tilgaṯ-piln'ese[r]* (1 Ch. v. 6; 2 Ch. xxviii. 20; LXX *Algathphellasar*) may reflect a later Aramaic form. The king['s] native name Pul is given in both the Old Testa[ment] (2 Ki. xv. 19; 1 Ch. v. 26) and the Babylonian Chronicle (*Pulu*).

Tiglath-pileser III (745–727 BC) was a son o[f] Adad-nirari III (*Archiv für Orientforschung*, III, 1926, p. 1, n. 2). The history of his reign is imperfectly known owing to the fragmentary nature o[f] the extant inscriptions, mainly found at Nimru[d] (see CALAH), but the primary events are listed i[n] the Assyrian Eponym canon.

The first campaign was directed against th[e] Aramaeans in Babylonia, where Pul 'took th[e] hands of Bel' and regained control until th[e] rebellion of Ukīn-zēr in 731 and the siege o[f] Sapia, following which the Chaldean chie[f] Marduk-apla-iddina submitted to the Assyrian (see MERODACH-BALADAN). Other campaign[s] were directed against the Medes and Urartian[s] (Armenia).

In 743 BC Tiglath-pileser marched to subdu[e] the N Syrian city states which were unde[r] Urartian domination. During the three-yea[r] siege of Arpad he received tribute from Carchemish, Hamath, Tyre, Byblos, Rezin o[f] Damascus, and other rulers. Among those listed Menahem (*Menuhimme*) of Samaria, who was t[o] die soon afterwards, raised his contribution b[y] collecting 1 mina (50 shekels) from each of th[e] 60,000 men of military age 'so that his hand (*i.e.* Tiglath-pileser's) would be with him t[o] confirm the kingdom in his hands' (2 Ki. xv. 19[–]20).

While Tiglath-pileser himself was fightin[g] Sarduri of Urarṭu, a revolt was instigated b[y] 'Azriyau of Yaudi' (Annals). It would seem tha[t] when the Urartians imposed control on Carchemish, Bît-Adini (see EDEN) and Cilicia th[e] weakened Aramaean states in S Syria came unde[r] the leadership of Azariah of Judah, who at thi[s] time was stronger than Israel. Azariah-Uzzia[h] (the names '*zr* and '*zz* are variants; G. Brin, *Leshonenu*, XXIV, 1960, pp. 8–14), however, die[d] soon afterwards (2 Ki. xv. 7), and 'Judaeans' ar[e] named among captives settled in Ullubu (nea[r] Bitlis). N Syria was organized into an Assyria[n] province (Unqi) under local governors.

When opposition to Assyria continued, Tiglath-pileser marched again to the west in 734. The Phoenician seaports were plundered an[d] heavy tribute imposed on Ashkelon and on Gaza whose ruler Hanun fled to Egypt. Statues of th[e] Assyrian king were set up in their temples. Th[e] army which had marched through the wester[n] border of Israel (Bıt-Humri; the earlier readin[g] of the names Galilee and Naphtali in thes[e] Annals is now disproved) turned back at th[e] 'River of Egypt' (*naḥal-muṣur*). Rezin of Damas[-] cus, Ammon, Edom, Moab, and (Jeho)ahaz of Judah (*Iauḫazi* (*mat*)*Iaudaia*) paid tribute (2 Ch. xxviii. 19–21).

Ahaz, however, received no immediate help from Assyria against the combined attacks of Rezin and Pekah of Israel, who, with Edomites and Philistines, raided Judah (2 Ch. xxviii. 17, 18). Jerusalem itself was besieged (2 Ki. xvi. 5, 6) and relieved only by the Assyrian march on Damascus late in 733 BC. When Damascus fell in 732 BC, Metenna of Tyre also capitulated and Israel, including Ijon, Abel-beth-Maachah, Janoah, Kadesh, Hazor, Gilead, Galilee, and all Naphtali, was despoiled and captives were taken (verse 9). A destruction level at Hazor (*q.v.*) is attributed to this period. Tiglath-pileser claims to have replaced Pekah (*Paqaḫa*) on the throne of Israel by Hoshea (*Ausi'*) and may well have plotted the murder of the former as described in 2 Ki. xv. 30.

Fig. 221. Tiglath-pileser III, king of Assyria 745–727 BC. From a relief.

Ahaz paid for Assyrian help by becoming a vassal, which probably required certain religious concessions and practices to be observed (*cf.* 2 Ki. xvi. 7–16). Tiglath-pileser extended his control to include Samsi, queen of Aribi (Arabia), Sabaeans, and Idiba'il (Adbeel of Gn. xxv. 13). With captive labour Tiglath-pileser III built himself a palace at Calah, from which have been recovered reliefs depicting the king himself and his campaigns. Although Tiglath-pileser I (1115–1077 BC) invaded Phoenicia, there is no reference to him in the Old Testament. See also ASSYRIA.

BIBLIOGRAPHY. D. J. Wiseman in *Iraq*, XIII, 1951, pp. 21–24; *ib.*, XVIII, 1956, pp. 117–129; H. W. F. Saggs in *Iraq*, XIX, 1957, pp. 114–154; H. Tadmor, 'Azriyau of Yaudi' in *Scripta Hierosolymitana*, VIII, 1961, pp. 232–271; S. Smith, *CAH*, III, 1925, pp. 32–42. D.J.W.

TIGRIS. The Greek name for one of the four rivers marking the location of Eden (Gn. ii. 14). It rises in the Armenian Mountains and runs south-east for 1,146 miles via Diabekhr through the Mesopotamian plain to join the river Euphrates 40 miles north of the Persian Gulf, into which it flows. It is a wide river as it meanders through Babylonia (Dn. x. 4) and is fed by tributaries from the Persian hills, the Greater and Lesser Zab, Adhem and Diyala rivers. When the snows melt the river floods in March–May and October–November. Nineveh, Calah, and Assur are among the ancient cities which lay on its banks. See EUPHRATES. D.J.W.

TILE, TILING. Ezekiel was commanded to scratch a representation of Jerusalem on a sun-dried brick (iv. 1; Heb. *l^e^ḇēnâ*, AV 'tile'). Plans engraved on clay tablets have been found (*e.g.* *ANEP*, no. 260). When Moses and the elders were given a vision of the God of Israel (Ex. xxiv. 10) there was beneath Him 'as it were a paved work of a sapphire stone'. This may well be a comparison with the contemporary dais built for Rameses II at Qantir which was covered with blue glazed tiles; *cf.* 'Sapphire' under JEWELS AND PRECIOUS STONES and W. C. Hayes, *Glazed Tiles from a Palace of Rameses II at Kantir*, 1937. Roof tiles were not used in ancient Palestine, so far as is known, so in Lk. v. 19 Gk. *keramos* should be translated more generally 'roofing'. See HOUSE. A.R.M.

TILGATH-PILNESER. See TIGLATH-PILESER.

TIMBREL. See MUSIC AND MUSICAL INSTRUMENTS.

TIME.

I. TIMES AND SEASONS

It is a striking feature of Old Testament thought that, although the Hebrews had ways of measuring the passing of time (see CALENDAR), they had no word for chronological time in the abstract. Hebrew does, however, provide a number of words for time and season in the sense of an appointed time, the right time, the opportunity for some event or action. The most common word is *'ēṯ* (*cf.* Ec. iii. 1 ff. for a characteristic use); *z^e^mān* has the same meaning. *Mô'ēḏ* comes from a root meaning 'appoint' and is used of natural periods such as the new moon (*e.g.* Ps. civ. 19) and of appointed festivals (*e.g.* Nu. ix. 2). In particular, all these words are used to refer to the times appointed by God, the opportunities given by Him (*e.g.* Dt. xi. 14; Ps. cxlv. 15; Is. xlix. 8; Je. xviii. 23). This usage is carried on in the New Testament by the Gk. *kairos* (*cf.* Lk. xix. 44; Acts xvii. 26; Tit. i. 3; 1 Pet. i. 11).

The Bible thus stresses not the abstract continuity of time but rather the God-given content of certain moments of history. This view of time may be called 'linear', in contrast with the cyclical view of time common in the ancient world; God's purpose moves to a consummation; things do not just go on or return to the point whence they began. But calling the biblical view of time 'linear' must not be allowed to suggest that time and history flow on in an inevitable succession of events; rather the Bible stresses 'times', the points at which God Himself advances His purposes in the world (see also DAY OF THE LORD).

God is sovereign in appointing these times, and so not even the Son during His earthly ministry knew the day and hour of the consummation (Mk. xiii. 32; Acts i. 7). God's sovereignty extends also to the times of an individual life (Ps. xxxi. 15).

In the Aramaic of the Book of Daniel the word *'iddān* refers to chronological periods of time (*e.g.* ii. 9, iii. 15), often apparently a year (*e.g.* iv. 16, vii. 25, though not all interpreters agree that years are meant). God's sovereignty is still stressed (ii. 21).

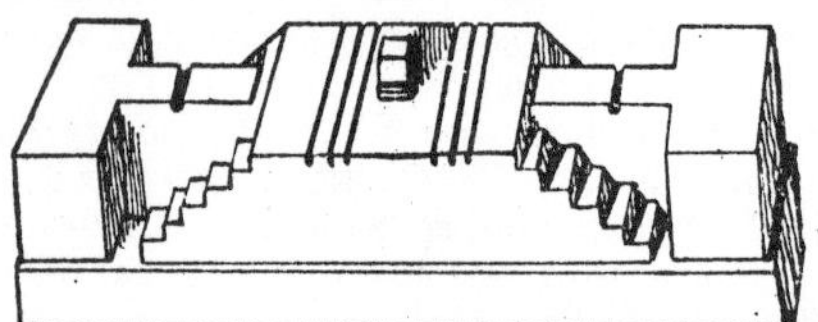

Fig. 222. An Egyptian model shadow clock. The time was calculated from the position of the shadow cast from the central block across the graduated lines on the upper surface, the steps, and the inclined plane (*behind*). Limestone, Graeco-Roman period.

The word *chronos* sometimes refers in the New Testament, as in secular Greek, simply to the passing of time (*e.g.* Lk. xx. 9; Acts xiv. 28). The context may give it the sense of 'delay', 'time of tarrying or waiting' (*e.g.* Acts xviii. 20, 23); this is probably the meaning of Rev. x. 6 rather than that 'time shall have an end'. Acts i. 7 may mean that God gives the times of opportunity and decision (*kairoi*) and also decides when they shall begin and end (*chronoi*); *cf.* Acts vii. 17; Gal. iv. 4.

II. ETERNITY

Hebrew has the words *'aḏ* and *'ôlām* for any period whose limit, at any rate in one direction, is not fixed, such as the unknown length of a man's life (*cf.* 1 Sa. i. 22, 28) or the age of the hills (Gn. xlix. 26). Above all, these words are applied to God, whose being is unlimited by any bound of time (Ps. xc. 2). This absence of temporal limit also belongs to all God's attributes and to His grace towards His people (*cf.* Je. xxxi. 3, xxxii. 40; Ho. ii. 19). To express more intensely the conviction that God is not limited to any fixed span Hebrew uses a poetic intensive plural (*e.g.* Ps. cxlv. 13; Dn. ix. 24) or a double form (*e.g.* Ps. cxxxii. 14).

The New Testament usage of *aiōn* is similar; it can be used of a lifetime (1 Cor. viii. 13, Phillips) or of an indefinite time in the past (Lk. i. 70) or future (Mk. xi. 14). It is intensively used in phrases such as *eis tous aiōnas tōn aiōnōn* (*e.g.* Gal. i. 5); that such uses are intensive rather than true plurals envisaging a series of world periods, 'ages of ages', is suggested by Heb. i. 8, where the genitive is in the singular; these phrases do, however, refer particularly to the time since creation, for God is described as active *pro tōn aiōnōn*, 'before the ages' (1 Cor. ii. 7, RSV).

The adjective *aiōnios* corresponds to the use of *aiōn* with reference to God, and therefore adds to its temporal sense of 'everlasting' a qualitative overtone of 'divine/immortal'. This tendency is helped by the fact that in late Heb. *'ôlām* is used in the spatial sense of 'the world'; *cf.* the AV translation of *aiōn* in *e.g.* Mk. x. 30; Eph. i. 21.

III. THE TWO AGES

The New Testament picks out one of the times appointed by God as decisive. The first note of Jesus' preaching was 'The time is fulfilled' (Mk. i. 15). The life and work of Jesus mark the crisis of God's purposes (Eph. i. 10). This is the great opportunity (2 Cor. vi. 2) which Christians must fully seize (Eph. v. 16; Col. iv. 5). Within the period of Jesus' earthly ministry there is a further narrowing of attention to the time of His death and resurrection (*cf.* Mt. xxvi. 18; Jn. vii. 6).

It is the fact that this decisive time is in the past which makes the difference between the Jewish and Christian hopes for the future: the Jew looks for the decisive intervention of God in the future; the Christian can have an even keener expectation of the consummation of all things because he knows that the decisive moment is past 'once for all'. The last times are with us already (Acts ii. 17; Heb. i. 2; 1 Jn. ii. 18; 1 Pet. i. 20).

The New Testament makes a striking modification of the contemporary Jewish division of time into the present age and the age to come. There is still a point of transition in the future between 'this time' and 'the world to come' (Mk. x. 30; Eph. i. 21; Tit. ii. 12, 13), but there is an anticipation of the consummation, because in Jesus God's purpose has been decisively fulfilled. The gift of the Spirit is the mark of this anticipation, this tasting of the powers of the world to come (Eph. i. 14; Heb. vi. 4–6; *cf.* Rom. viii. 18–23; Gal. i. 4). Hence John consistently stresses that we now have eternal life, *zōē aiōnios* (*e.g.* Jn. iii. 36). It is not simply that *aiōnios* has qualitative overtones; rather John is urging the fact that Christians now have the life into which they will fully enter by resurrection (Jn. xi. 23–25). This 'overlapping' of the two ages is possibly what Paul has in mind in 1 Cor. x. 11.

IV. TIME AND ETERNITY

Philosophical discussion of the relationship between time and eternity does not arise within the pages of Scripture. The expressions used to denote the unlimited character of God's Being are themselves temporal.

Many Christian philosophers have maintained that the intensive time language of the Bibl oints to aspects of the Being of God which in hilosophy can best be expressed in terms of an ternity in some way qualitatively different from me.

Others have held that any talk of God's Being s timeless is unscriptural; that our language is ecessarily time-referring and that we cannot alk about timeless being without the risk of so bstracting it from the world that it cannot be ought to influence the world's life directly at ll. Thus if the Christian view of God as active n history is to be preserved we must adhere to e biblical language rather than use any Platonist rminology which contrasts the world of time ere' with a world of eternity 'there'. Neverthe-ss, the New Testament goes beyond a simple ntithesis of this world and the next, 'now' and hen', by its doctrine of anticipation.

Whatever the outcome of the philosophical ebate, Scripture roundly asserts that God is not mited by time as we are, that He is 'the king of ges' (1 Tim. i. 17, RSV; *cf.* 2 Pet. iii. 8).

BIBLIOGRAPHY. F. H. Brabant, *Time and ternity in Christian Thought*, 1937; O. Cullmann, *hrist and Time*, 1951; J. Marsh, *The Fulness of ime*, 1952; H. Sasse, art. *aiōn* in *TWNT*.

M.H.C.

IMNA. 1. A concubine of Eliphaz the son of sau, mother of Amalek (Gn. xxxvi. 12). **2.** A aughter of Seir and sister of Lotan (Gn. xxxvi. 2). **3.** A chief of Edom (1 Ch. i. 51; wrongly alled 'Timnah' in Gn. xxxvi. 40).

IMNAH. 1. Khirbet Tibneh, 4 miles south-west Zorah across the Vale of Sorek, showing Early on remains. On the northern boundary of udah (Jos. xv. 10) and formerly counted as anite (Jos. xix. 43), it changed hands more than nce between Israelites and Philistines (Jdg. xiv. 2 Ch. xxviii. 18). Samson's first wife lived ere.

2. A place south of Hebron (Jos. xv. 57 and rhaps Gn. xxxviii. 12). J.P.U.L.

IMNATH-HERES, TIMNATH-SERAH. The rsonal inheritance of Joshua, where he was ried (Jos. xix. 50, xxiv. 30; Jdg. ii. 9). The maritans claimed Kafr Haris, 10 miles south-st of Shechem, as the site; V. Guérin (*Samaria*, , 1938, pp. 84–104) proposed Khirbet Tibneh, a te Bronze–Early Iron site 17 miles from rusalem and from Shechem, commanding from e south a deep ravine, with the traditional mb of Joshua (mentioned by Eusebius) among hers in the side of the valley on the east.

Ḥeres is a rare word for 'sun' (*cf.* Jdg. i. 35, i. 13, *MT*; Jb. ix. 7; Is. xix. 18, LXX (B), mmachus, *et al.* for *MT ḥeres*); if it had olatrous implications the variant *seraḥ*, con-ting 'extra', was perhaps intended to avoid em (Moore, *Judges*, *ICC*, 1895, *ad* ii. 9); but is leaves unexplained the retention of *ḥeres* in g. ii. 9 and *šemeš* elsewhere; see Burney, *dges*, 1918, p. 32. J.P.U.L.

TIMOTHEUS. The AV form of Timothy (*q.v.*) in all but five occurrences of the name (2 Cor. i. 1; 1 Tim. i. 2; 2 Tim. i. 2; Phm. 1; Heb. xiii. 23).

TIMOTHY. The son of a mixed marriage; his mother, who evidently instructed him in the Scriptures, was a Jewess and his father a Greek (Acts xvi. 1; 2 Tim. i. 5). He was a native of Lystra (Acts xvi. 1) and was highly esteemed by his Christian brethren both there and in Iconium (Acts xvi. 2). When he became a Christian is not specifically stated but it is a reasonable inference that he was a convert of Paul's first missionary journey, which included Lystra in its itinerary, and that on that occasion he witnessed Paul's sufferings (2 Tim. iii. 11). By the time of Paul's second missionary journey through the same region Timothy's mother also was a Christian.

The apostle was strongly attracted to the young man and although he had only recently replaced Barnabas by Silas as his travelling companion he added Timothy to his party, perhaps as a substitute for John Mark whom he had refused to take (Acts xv. 36 f.). This choice appears to have had other endorsement, for Paul later refers to prophetic utterances which confirmed Timothy's being set apart for this work (*cf.* 1 Tim. i. 18, iv. 14). He had received at this time a special endowment for his mission, communicated through the laying on of the hands of the elders and of Paul (1 Tim. iv. 14; 2 Tim. i. 6). To allay any needless opposition from local Jews, Timothy was circumcised before setting out on his journeys.

He was first entrusted with a special commission to Thessalonica to encourage the persecuted Christians. He is associated with Paul and Silvanus in the greetings of both Epistles directed to that church, and was present with Paul during his preaching work at Corinth (2 Cor. i. 19). He is next heard of during the apostle's Ephesian ministry, when he was sent with Erastus on another important mission to Macedonia, whence he was to proceed to Corinth (1 Cor. iv. 17). The young man was evidently of a timid disposition, for Paul urges the Corinthians to set him at ease and not to despise him (1 Cor. xvi. 10, 11, *cf.* iv. 17 ff.). From the situation which resulted in Corinth (see 2 Corinthians) Timothy's mission was not successful, and it is significant that, although his name was associated with Paul's in the greeting to this Epistle, it is Titus and not Timothy who has become the apostolic delegate. He accompanied Paul on his next visit to Corinth, for he was with him as a fellow-worker when the Epistle to the Romans was written (Rom. xvi. 21).

Timothy also went with Paul on the journey to Jerusalem with the collection (Acts xx. 4, 5) and is next heard of when Paul, then a prisoner, wrote Colossians, Philemon, and Philippians. In the latter Epistle he is warmly commended and Paul intends soon to send him to them in order to ascertain their welfare. When the apostle was released from his imprisonment and engaged in further activity in the east as the Pastoral Epistles indicate, it would seem that Paul left Timothy at Ephesus (1 Tim. i. 3) and commissioned him to deal with false teachers and supervise public worship and the appointment of church officials. Although Paul evidently hoped to rejoin Timothy, the fear that he might be delayed occasioned the writing of the first letter to him and this was followed by another when Paul was not only re-arrested but on trial for his life. Timothy was urged to hasten to him, but whether he arrived in time cannot be ascertained. Later Timothy himself became a prisoner as Heb. xiii. 23 shows, but no details are given, and of his subsequent history nothing definite is known.

He was affectionate (2 Tim. i. 4) but very fearful (2 Tim. i. 7 ff.), needing not a few personal admonitions from his father in the faith; he is warned not to give way to youthful lusts (2 Tim. ii. 22) and not to be ashamed of the gospel (2 Tim. i. 8). Yet no other of Paul's companions is so warmly commended for his loyalty (1 Cor. xvi. 10; Phil. ii. 19 ff.; 2 Tim. iii. 10 ff.). It is fitting that the apostle's concluding letter should be addressed so affectionately to this almost reluctant successor, whose weaknesses are as apparent as his virtues. D.G.

TIMOTHY AND TITUS, EPISTLES TO. The two Epistles to Timothy and one to Titus, commonly grouped together as the Pastoral Epistles, belong to the period at the close of Paul's life and provide valuable information about the great missionary apostle's thoughts as he prepared to pass on his tasks to others. They are addressed to two of his closest associates, and for that reason introduce a different kind of Pauline correspondence from the earlier church Epistles.

I. OUTLINE OF CONTENTS

1 Timothy

a. Paul and Timothy (i. 1–20)

The need for Timothy to refute false teaching at Ephesus (i. 3–11); Paul's experience of God's mercy (i. 12–17); a special commission for Timothy (i. 18–20).

b. Worship and order in the Church (ii. 1–iv. 16)

Public prayer (ii. 1–8); the position of women (ii. 9–15); the qualifications of bishops and deacons (iii. 1–13); the Church: its character and its adversaries (iii. 14–iv. 5); the Church: Timothy's personal responsibilities (iv. 6–16).

c. Discipline within the Church (v. 1–25)

A discussion of the treatment suitable for various groups, especially widows and elders (v. 1–25).

d. Miscellaneous injunctions (vi. 1–19)

About servants and masters (vi. 1, 2); about false teachers (vi. 3–5); about wealth (vi. 6–10); about the aims of a man of God (vi. 11–16); more about wealth (vi. 17–19).

e. Concluding admonitions to Timothy (vi. 20, 2

2 Timothy

a. Paul's special regard for Timothy (i. 1–14)

Greeting and thanksgiving (i. 1–5); exhortation and encouragements to Timothy (i. 6–14).

b. Paul and his associates (i. 15–18)

The disloyal Asiatics and the helpful Onesiphorus (i. 15–18).

c. Special directions to Timothy (ii. 1–26)

Encouragements and exhortations (ii. 1–13); advice on the treatment of false teachers (ii. 14–26).

d. Predictions about the last days (iii. 1–9)

The times of moral deterioration to come (ii 1–9).

e. More advice to Timothy (iii. 10–17)

A reminder of Paul's early experiences of persecution (iii. 10–12); an exhortation to Timothy to continue as he had begun (iii. 13–17).

f. Paul's farewell message (iv. 1–22)

A final charge to Timothy (iv. 1–5); a confessio of faith (iv. 6–8); some personal requests an warnings (iv. 9–15); Paul's first defence and h future hope (iv. 16–18); greetings and benedictio (iv. 19–22).

Titus

a. Paul's greeting to Titus (i. 1–4)

The apostle's consciousness of his high callin (i. 1–4).

b. The kind of men Titus must appoint as elders (o bishops) (i. 5–9)

c. The Cretan false teachers (i. 10–16)

Their character and the need to rebuke them (10–16).

d. Christian behaviour (ii. 1–10)

Advice about the older and younger people an about slaves (ii. 1–10).

e. Christian teaching (ii. 11–iii. 7)

What the grace of God has done for Christian (ii. 11–15); what Christians ought to do in societ (iii. 1, 2); how Christianity contrasts wit paganism (iii. 3–7).

f. Closing admonitions to Titus (iii. 8–15)

About good works (iii. 8); about false teacher (iii. 9, 10); about Paul's companions and hi future plans (iii. 11–15).

II. THE HISTORICAL SITUATION

It is difficult to reconstruct this period of Paul' life, because there is no independent court c appeal such as the Acts supplies in the case of th earlier Epistles. But certain data may be ascer ained from the Epistles themselves. At the time f writing 1 Timothy and Titus, Paul is not in rison, but when 2 Timothy was written he is not nly a prisoner (i. 8, ii. 9), but appears to be on ial for his life, with the probability that an dverse verdict is imminent which will result in is execution (iv. 6–8). From 1 Tim. i. 3 it is clear hat Paul had recently been in the vicinity of phesus, where he had left Timothy to fulfil a pecific mission, mainly of administration. The pistle to Titus provides additional historical ata, for from i. 5 it may be inferred that Paul ad paid a recent visit to Crete, on which occa-ion he must have had opportunity to ascertain he condition of the churches and to give specific structions to Titus for rectifying any de-ciencies. At the conclusion of the letter (iii. 12) ne apostle urges Titus to join him at Nicopolis or the winter, and it is fairly safe to assume that his was the city situated in Epirus, in which case is the sole reference to Paul visiting that istrict. Titus is also instructed to help Zenas nd Apollos on their journey (iii. 13), but the recise point of this allusion is obscure.

2 Timothy is much more specific in historical nformation. In i. 16 Paul refers to Onesiphorus s having sought him out while in Rome, which uggests that the writer is still in Rome as a risoner. In iv. 16 he mentions an earlier trial hich is generally regarded as the preliminary xamination preparing for the official trial before ne Roman authorities. Paul makes an interesting equest in iv. 13 for a cloak which he had left ehind at the house of Carpus at Troas, which ould seem to imply that he had recently visited nere. In the same passage Paul mentions that he ecently left Trophimus sick at Miletus (iv. 20), hile Erastus, an associate of his, had stayed ehind at Corinth.

It is impossible to fit all these historical data as ey stand into the Acts history, and there is erefore no alternative if their authenticity is to e maintained (see later discussion) but to assume at Paul was released from the imprisonment entioned at the close of Acts, that he had a eriod of further activity in the East, and that he as rearrested, tried, and finally executed in ome by the imperial authorities. The data vailable from the Pastorals are insufficient to cilitate a reconstruction of Paul's itinerary, but urther activity in Greece, Crete, and Asia is at east certain. Some scholars, on the basis of Rom. v. 24, 28, have also fitted into this period a visit Spain, and if this assumption is correct this estern visit must have preceded Paul's return to e eastern churches. But if Colossians, Phile-on, and Philippians are assigned to the Roman nprisonment (see separate articles) it seems clear at Paul's face was turned towards the east and ot the west at the time of his release. See also HRONOLOGY OF THE NEW TESTAMENT.

III. PURPOSE

ssuming therefore that all three of these pistles were written within a comparatively short interval of time, it must next be noted that they have a common purpose. They are all designed to supply Paul's associates with exhortations and encouragements for both present and future responsibilities. There is a good deal of instruction about ecclesiastical administration, but it would be wrong to assume that such instruction wholly accounts for the underlying purpose of each. Of the three Epistles the motive for writing 2 Timothy is clearer than that of the others. The apostle is delivering his final charge to his timid successor, and in the course of it reminds Timothy of his early history (i. 5–7) and exhorts him to act worthily of his high calling. Many times throughout the Epistle solemn exhortations are directed to him (i. 6, 8, 13 f., ii. 1, 22, iii. 14, iv. 1 f.), which suggest that Paul was not too certain of his courage in face of the heavy responsibilities now falling upon him. The apostle yearns to see him again and twice urges him to come as soon as possible (iv. 9, 21), although the tone of the concluding part of the letter suggests that Paul is not convinced that circumstances will permit a reunion (*cf.* iv. 6). There are warnings about ungodly men who cause trouble to the Church both in the present and in the last days (iii. 1 f.), and Timothy is urged to avoid these. He is to entrust to worthy men the task of passing on the traditions already received (ii. 2).

The purpose behind the other two Epistles is less plain, for in both instances Paul has only recently left the recipients, and the need for such detailed instructions is not immediately apparent. It would seem probable that much of the subject-matter had already been communicated orally, for in both Epistles detailed qualifications are given for the main office-bearers of the Church, and it is inconceivable that until this time neither Timothy nor Titus had received any such instruction. In all probability the Epistles were intended to strengthen the hands of Paul's representatives in their respective tasks. Timothy appears to have had some difficulty in commanding respect (*cf.* 1 Tim. iv. 12 f.), while Titus had a particularly unenviable constituency in Crete according to Tit. i. 10 ff. Both men are to have sober concern for sound doctrine and right conduct and to teach it to others (1 Tim. iv. 11, vi. 2; Tit. ii. 1, 15, iii. 8).

It is not to be expected that in these letters the apostle would present to his closest friends anything in the nature of a theological treatise. There was no need to dwell on the great Christian doctrines, oral expositions of which both Timothy and Titus must often have heard from their master's lips. But they did need to be reminded of the futility of wasting time with certain groups of false teachers whose teachings were dominated by irrelevances and wordy combats which led nowhere (see 1 Tim. i. 4, iv. 1 f., vi. 3 f., 20). There does not appear to be any close connection between these heresies in the Ephesian and Cretan churches and that combated by Paul in his letter to Colossae, but they may have been different forms of the tendency which later developed into 2nd-century Gnosticism.

IV. AUTHENTICITY

Modern criticism has so much challenged the Pauline authorship of these Epistles that the attestation of the early Church is of prime importance in a fair examination of the whole question. There are few New Testament writings which have stronger attestation, for these Epistles were widely used from the time of Polycarp, and there are possible traces in the earlier works of Clement of Rome and Ignatius. The omission of the Epistles from Marcion's Canon (*c.* AD 140) has been thought by some to be evidence that they were not known in his time, but, in view of his propensity to cut out what did not appeal to him or disagreed with his doctrine, this line of evidence can hardly be taken seriously. The only other possible evidence for the omission of the Epistles is the Chester Beatty papyri, but since these are incomplete it is again precarious to base any positive hypothesis upon their evidence, especially in view of the fact that the Epistles were known and used in the East at an earlier period than the papyri represent.

Objections to authenticity must therefore be regarded as modern innovations contrary to the strong evidence from the early Church. These objections began seriously with Schleiermacher's attack on the genuineness of 1 Timothy (1807) and have been developed by many other scholars, among whom the most notable have been F. C. Baur, H. J. Holtzmann, P. N. Harrison, and M. Dibelius. They have been based on four main problems. At different periods of criticism different difficulties have been given prominence, but it is probably the cumulative effect which has persuaded some modern scholars that these Epistles cannot be by Paul.

a. The historical problem

As already mentioned, the historical situation cannot belong to the period of the Acts history and the consequent need for postulating a release theory has caused some scholars to suggest alternative theories. Either all the personal references are the invention of the author, or else some of them are genuine notes which have been incorporated into the author's own productions. There has never been anything approaching unanimity among the advocates of the latter alternative as to the identification of the 'notes', which in itself raises some suspicions against the theory. Moreover, the notion of a fiction writer producing personal notes of such verisimilitude is improbable, and neither theory is necessary if the perfectly reasonable supposition that Paul was released from his first Roman imprisonment is maintained.

b. The ecclesiastical problem

It has been claimed that the ecclesiastical situation reflects a 2nd-century state of affairs, but this line of criticism has been widely influenced by the assumption that: (i) 2nd-century Gnosticism is combated in the Epistles, and (ii) that the church organization was too developed for the primitive period. The force of the first assumption is reduced to nothing by the increasing modern recognition that Gnosticism had much earlier roots than was at one time imagined and that the form of heresy combated in these Epistles is far removed from developed Gnosticism. The second assumption is equally insecure in view of the fact that the church organization is certainly more primitive than in the time of Ignatius and betrays no anachronism with the period of the apostle.

c. The doctrinal problem

The absence of the great Pauline doctrinal discussions as found in the earlier letters and the presence of stereotyped expressions such as 'the faith' and 'sound doctrine', which suggest a stage of development when Christian doctrine had reached fixity as tradition, have given rise to further doubts about Pauline authorship. But the recognition of the mainly personal character of these communications and of the knowledge that both Timothy and Titus already had of Paul's main teaching is sufficient to account for the first objection, while the second may be annulled by the valid assumption that Paul as a far-sighted missionary pioneer, however creative and dynamic his earlier pronouncements may have been in his church Epistles, could not have been unmindful of the need for conservation of true doctrine, and the aptness of the terms used for this purpose must be admitted.

d. The linguistic problem

These Epistles contain an unusually large number of words used nowhere else in the New Testament and a number not found anywhere else in Paul's writings, and these indications are claimed to demonstrate their un-Pauline character, especially when supported by the absence of many pronouns, prepositions, and particles used by the apostle. But word-counts of this kind can be effective only if sufficient data exist to serve as a fair basis of comparison, and this cannot be maintained in the case of the Pauline Epistles, where the total vocabulary does not exceed 2,500 different words. There appears to be no valid reason why the differences of vocabulary and style could not have taken place in the writings of one man.

In conclusion, it may be stated that these objections, even when cumulatively considered, do not provide adequate reason for discarding the acknowledged and unchallenged conviction of the Christian Church until the 19th century that these three Epistles are genuine writings of the apostle Paul.

V. VALUE

Throughout the history of the Church these Epistles have been used to instruct the minister

›f Christ in their duties and demeanour, and have •een invaluable in providing a pattern of prac-ical behaviour. Yet their usefulness and appeal ıave not been restricted to this, for they contain nany gems of spiritual encouragement and heological insight which have greatly enriched he devotional life of the Church. Such passages ‸s 1 Tim. iii. 16 and Tit. ii. 12 ff., iii. 4 ff., among nany others, draw the reader's attention to some •f the great truths of the gospel, while the last hapter of 2 Timothy preserves the moving swan-ong of the great apostle.

BIBLIOGRAPHY. J. H. Bernard, *The Pastoral ;pistles*, 1899; M. Dibelius and H. Conzelmann, *)ie Pastoralbriefe*, 1955; B. S. Easton, *The 'astoral Epistles*, 1948; D. Guthrie, *The Pastoral ;pistles, TNTC*, 1957; *id., New Testament Intro-luction*, I, *The Pauline Epistles*, 1961; P. N. Iarrison, *The Problem of the Pastoral Epistles*, 921; J. Jeremias, *Die Briefe an Timotheus und 'itus, Das Neue Testament Deutsch*, 1953; W. Aichaelis, *Pastoralbriefe und Gefangenschafts-riefe*, 1930; E. K. Simpson, *The Pastoral ;pistles*, 1954; C. Spicq, *Les Épîtres Pastorales, ;tudes Bibliques*, 1948. D.G.

'IN. See MINING AND METALS.

'IPHSAH (*tip̄saḥ*, 'a ford', 'a passage'). **1.** Prob-bly Thapsacus, an important crossing on the vest bank of the Middle Euphrates. At the orth-east boundary of Solomon's territory 1 Ki. iv. 24), it was placed strategically on a reat east–west trade route. **2.** An unidentified own attacked by Menahem of Israel (2 Ki. xv. 6). Some identify with (1) above; others, in-luding RSV, follow the Lucian LXX and amend he name to Tappuah (*q.v.*), but this has little ritical support. J.D.D.

'IRAS (*tîrās*). One of the sons of Japheth, and a rother of Gomer, Madai, Javan, and Muški Gn. x. 2; 1 Ch. i. 5), all probably northern eoples (see NATIONS, TABLE OF). The name is ommonly identified with the Tursha (*Trš.w*) ıentioned among the northern invaders in the 3th century BC by Merenptah (see EGYPT). 'hese are in turn often equated with the *Tyrsēnoi* lialectal form of *Tyrrhēnoi*) of Greek literature, onnected by many with the Etruscans, though ıis identification is still questioned.

BIBLIOGRAPHY. A. H. Gardiner, *Ancient ;gyptian Onomastica*, Text, I, 1947, p. 196*; M. allottino, *The Etruscans*, 1955, pp. 55–56; see lso *AS*, IX, 1959, pp. 197 ff. T.C.M.

'IRE. See DRESS.

'IRHAKAH. The pharaoh Taharqa of Egypt's XVth ('Ethiopian') Dynasty; he reigned venty-six years, *c.* 690–664 BC. 2 Ki. xix. 9 = Is. xxxvii. 9) appears to indicate that Tirhakah ‹d those Egyptian forces which Sennacherib *.v.*) had to defeat at Eltekeh (*q.v.*) in 701 BC 'hile attacking Hezekiah of Judah. If so, Tir-akah was then only the army-commander, as he was not king until eleven years later. The epithet 'king of Ethiopia' is that of the source used in Isaiah and 2 Kings, and would date from 690 BC or after. An alternative view, namely that Sen-nacherib again invaded Palestine early in Tir-hakah's actual reign (*c.* 688 BC?), requires two major assumptions: a second Palestinian cam-paign by Sennacherib, otherwise unknown, and a conflation of the two campaigns into one by the Old Testament narrators; references in W. F. Albright, *BASOR*, 130, 1953, pp. 8, 9. The theory of M. F. L. Macadam (*Temples of Kawa*, I, 1949, pp. 18–20) that Tirhakah was born *c.* 709 BC, and so could not command troops in 701 BC, is unnecessary and open to other objec-tions; see J. Leclant and J. Yoyotte, *Bulletin de l'Institut Français d'Archéologie Orientale*, LI, 1952, pp. 17–27. K.A.K.

TIRSHATHA. A title used of the governor of Judaea under the Persian Empire (Ezr. ii. 63; Ne. vii. 65, 70, viii. 9, x. 1). It is probably a Persian form (*cf.* Avestan *taršta*, 'reverend') roughly equivalent to the English 'His Excel-lency'. The title puzzled the Greek translators, who either omit it or render it as a proper name, 'Athersastha', 'Attharates', or 'Atharias'.

J.S.W.

TIRZAH. **1.** The youngest daughter of Zelo-phehad (Nu. xxvi. 33, xxvii. 1; Jos. xvii. 3).

2. A Canaanite town noted for its beauty (Ct. vi. 4), and captured by Joshua (Jos. xii. 24). In later times Jeroboam lived there (1 Ki. xiv. 17). The place became the capital of Israel in the days of Baasha (1 Ki. xv. 21, 33, xvi. 6), Elah, and Zimri (1 Ki. xvi. 8, 9, 15). Zimri burned the palace over his own head when trapped there by Omri (1 Ki. xvi. 17, 18). After six years Omri transferred the capital to Samaria. Towards the end of Israel's life, Menahem, a resident of Tir-zah, was able to overthrow Shallum and usurp the throne (2 Ki. xv. 14, 16).

Père de Vaux believes the large mound of Tell el-Far'a, about 7 miles north-east of Nab-lus, where he has excavated for several years, is the site of Tirzah. Excavation reveals a city which flourished in the 9th century BC but later sank to the status of an ordinary provincial town. See R. de Vaux, articles on excavations at Tell el-Far'a in *RB*, 1947–52. J.A.T.

TISHBITE, THE (*hattišbî*). A name associated only with Elijah (1 Ki. xvii. 1, *etc.*), evidently denoting an inhabitant of Tishbeh or a place of some similar name in Naphtali or Gilead. N. Glueck renders 1 Ki. xvii. 1, 'Elijah the Jabeshite, from Jabesh-gilead', a place near and to the west of Abel-meholah (*q.v.*). This would suggest that the brook Cherith (1 Ki. xvii. 5) was a tributary of the Jabesh, which flows into the Jordan. See, however, E. König, 'Elijah the Tishbite', *ExpT*, XII, 1900–1, p. 383. J.D.D.

TISHRI. See CALENDAR.

TITHES. The custom of tithing did not originate with the Mosaic Law (Gn. xiv. 17–20), nor was it peculiar to the Hebrews. It was practised among other ancient peoples. There are three main questions to consider.

1. What were the Hebrews required to tithe? The Torah legislated that 'the seed of the land' (crops), 'the fruit of the tree', and 'the herd, or . . . the flock' (Lv. xxvii. 30–32) were to be tithed. The manner of tithing live-stock was as follows: the owner counted the animals as they passed out to pasture, and every tenth one was given to God. In this way there was no possibility of selecting inferior animals for the tithing of the flocks and herds (Lv. xxvii. 32 f.). If a Hebrew preferred to dedicate the tenth of his cereal and fruit yields in the form of their monetary value he was free to do so, but a fifth of that sum had to be added to it. He was not allowed to redeem the tenth of his flocks and herds in this way (Lv. xxvii. 31, 33).

2. To whom were the tithes paid? They were to be given to the Levites (Nu. xviii. 21 ff.). But in Heb. vii. 5 it is said to be the sons of Levi 'who receive the office of the priesthood' who are to be the recipients of the tithes. This departure from the Law may have been due to the Levites' unwillingness to fulfil their duties in Jerusalem after the return under Ezra (Ezr. viii. 15 ff.). The Levites, because of the nature of their status and functions in the community, had no means of income, livelihood, or inheritance to ensure their support; therefore, and in return 'for their service which they serve, even the service of the tabernacle', they were to receive 'all the tenth in Israel' (Nu. xviii. 21, 24). This passage in Nu. xviii mentions only the tithing of cereal and fruit crops (verse 27). The Levites, however, were not allowed to keep the whole of the tenth. They were directed to 'offer up an heave offering' which was to be taken out of the tenth, which represented 'a tenth part of the tithe' (Nu. xviii. 26). This 'tithe of the tithe' was to be 'of all the best thereof' (verse 29) and was to be given to the priests (verse 28; Ne. x. 39).

3. Where were the Hebrews to offer their tithes? They were to bring them 'unto the place which the Lord your God shall choose out of all your tribes, to put his name there' (Dt. xii. 5 f., 17 f.); *i.e.* Jerusalem. And the offering of the tithes was to take the form of a ritual meal, in which the Levite was to share (Dt. xii. 7, 12). If Jerusalem was a long way off from a man's village the transporting of the tithe of his crops might create a problem, but he could always take his tithe in the form of money (Dt. xiv. 22–27). Every third year the tithe was to be offered in each man's own locality (Dt. xiv. 28 f.), although on these occasions he was still obligated to go up to Jerusalem to worship after the offering of his tithes in his home community (Dt. xxvi. 12 ff.).

To these comparatively simple laws in the Pentateuch governing tithing there were added a host of minutiae which turned a beautiful religious principle into a grievous burden. These complex additions are recorded in the Mishnaic and Talmudic literature. This unfortunate tendency in Israel undoubtedly contributed to the conviction that acceptance with God could be merited through such ritual observances as tithing (Lk. xi. 42), without submitting to the moral law of justice, mercy, and faith (Mt. xxiii. 23 f.).

The tithes paid by Abraham, the ancestor of Israel and, therefore, of the Aaronic priesthood, to Melchizedek (Gn. xiv. 20), and his receiving the blessing of this priest-king (Gn. xiv. 19) signifies in Hebrews vii. 1 ff. that Melchizedek's priesthood was infinitely superior to the Aaronic or levitical priesthood. Why Abraham paid tithes to Melchizedek is not explained in Gn. xiv. 18–20.

The New Testament reference to the tithing of 'mint, anise, and cummin' (Mt. xxiii. 23; Lk. xi. 42) illustrates a Talmudic extension of the Mosaic law, ensuring that 'everything that is eaten . . . and that grows out of the earth' must be tithed.

J.G.S.S.T.

TITLE. See SUPERSCRIPTION.

TITTLE. See JOT AND TITTLE.

TITUS. Although not mentioned in Acts, Titus was one of Paul's companions in whom he placed a considerable amount of trust. He is first heard of at the time of the Gentile controversy when he accompanied Paul and Barnabas to Jerusalem (Gal. ii. 1). He provided a test case since he was a Gentile, but he was apparently not compelled to be circumcised (Gal. ii. 3). Titus probably accompanied Paul on his subsequent journeys, but no definite information of his work is available until the time of the Corinthian crisis. He had evidently been acting as Paul's representative at Corinth during the year preceding the writing of 2 Corinthians (*cf.* viii. 1 with a special commission to organize the collection scheme there. The task was unfinished, for Titus is later urged by Paul to return to Corinth to see its completion (2 Cor. viii. 6).

A more delicate task was the smoothing over of the tense situation which had arisen between Paul and the Corinthians, a task which clearly demanded a man of great tact and force of character. He appears to have been a stronger personality than Timothy (*cf.* 1 Cor. xvi. 10; 2 Cor. vii. 15) and possessed ability as an administrator. A comparison of 2 Cor. ii and vii suggests that he carried a letter from Paul to the Corinthians which has since been lost (the 'severe letter') and in which the apostle took them to task with much anguish of heart for their high-handed attitude. Titus eventually rejoined Paul in Macedonia (2 Cor. vii. 6) with good news, and as a result 2 Corinthians was written and was willingly carried by Titus (2 Cor. viii. 16 f.), who seems to have possessed a particular affection and serious concern for the Corinthians. He is described by the apostle as his 'partner and fellow-helper' (viii. 23), who would not think of taking advantage of those entrusted to his care (xii. 18).

From the Epistle addressed to him it may be

rmised that Titus accompanied Paul to Crete bsequent to the latter's release from the Roman prisonment and was left there to consolidate e work (Tit. i. 5 f.). The letter urges the use of thority in establishing a worthy ministry, in ercoming opposition, and in the teaching of und doctrine. He was summoned to rejoin Paul Nicopolis when relieved by either Artemas or ychicus (Tit. iii. 12), and may possibly have en further commissioned at Nicopolis for an angelistic mission to Dalmatia on which he as engaged at the time when Paul wrote Timothy (2 Tim. iv. 10). Later tradition, how-er, assumed his return to Crete and described m as bishop there until his old age (Eus., *EH* . 4. 6). For the possibility that he was Luke's other (which might explain the absence of his me from Acts), see W. M. Ramsay, *St. Paul e Traveller and Roman Citizen*[14], 1920, p. 390.

D.G.

ITUS, EPISTLE TO. See TIMOTHY AND TUS, EPISTLES TO.

OB. The name of an Aramaean principality uated east of the Jordan and north of Gilead, entioned in connection with Jephthah and avid (Jdg. xi. 3; 2 Sa. x. 6, RV). The district of ıbias of 1 Macc. v. 13 is probably identical. equates it with Susitha, or Hippos, a city of e Decapolis on the south-east of the Sea of alilee. However, al-Taiyiba, 10 miles south of adara, has also been proposed; this name eserves the Arabic form of Heb. *ṭôḇ*, 'good', t al-Taiyiba itself is a common place-name.

D.F.P.

OBIAH. A name borne by several men in the d Testament. The most important was one of e opponents of Nehemiah. In Ne. ii. 10 he is lled 'the servant, the Ammonite'. He may have en a freed slave who rose to a position of fluence in Ammon, perhaps even governor of e province. He was probably the ancestor of e Tobiads who governed Ammon for genera-ons after his time, as attested in the 3rd-century- Zeno papyri and by palace and tomb remains 'Araq el-Emir in Jordan. If Ezr. iv. 7–23 is ted shortly before the coming of Nehemiah e EZRA, BOOK OF) Tobiah may well be identi-d with Tabeel of Ezr. iv. 7. Tobiah is Hebrew r 'Yahweh is good' and *Ṭabeel* is Aramaic for od is good'.

For a full discussion of the Tobiad family ith bibliography) from the days of the second mple, see B. Mazar, *IEJ*, VII, 1957, pp. 137–5, 229–238. The inscription at 'Araq el-Emir ove the family burial site (see fig. 14) is prob-ly to be dated to the time of the Tobiah who eceded Nehemiah (Zc. vi. 10).

J.S.W.

OBIT, BOOK OF. See APOCRYPHA.

OGARMAH. The third son of Gomer, grand-n of Japheth and brother of Ashkenaz and phath (Gn. x. 3; 1 Ch. i. 6). (Beth-)Togarmah, with Tubal, Javan, and Mesech (*q.v.*) supplied horses and mules to Tyre (Ezk. xxvii. 14) and soldiers to Gog (Lydia?; Ezk. xxxviii. 6). In the 14th century BC Tegarama is described as lying between Carchemish and Harran (Mursilis II), on a main trade route through SW Armenia. It was called Til-garimanu in Assyrian times (Sargon and Sennacherib Annals) and was the capital of Kammanu on the border of Tabal. This identification, first proposed by F. Delitzsch, is supported by E. Bilgiç (*A.f.O.*, XV, p. 29) and W. F. Albright (*Recent Discoveries in Bible Lands*, 1955, p. 71) but denied by Poebel (*AJSL*, LV, p. 294, n. 47).

D.J.W.

TOLA. 1. A family name in the leading clan of Issachar (Gn. xlvi. 13; Nu. xxvi. 23; 1 Ch. vii. 1, 2). **2.** Tola ben Puah of Shamir, an unknown village on Mt. Ephraim, a national judge after Abimelech's reign for twenty-three years. Puah was also a family name in Issachar.

J.P.U.L.

TOLL. See TRIBUTE.

TOMB. See BURIAL AND MOURNING.

TONGS. See SNUFFERS.

TONGUE. Heb. *lāšôn*, Gk. *glōssa*, both of the tongue of man and, by extension, of man's language. The Hebrew is also used of the tongue of animals (Ex. xi. 7), and reptiles (Jb. xx. 16), with the still common misapprehension that the poison of a snake lies in its tongue. It is also used of tongue-shaped objects, or phenomena, *e.g.* a wedge of gold (Jos. vii. 21) or a bay of the sea (Jos. xv. 2).

It was apparently believed in biblical times that dumbness was due to some paralysis or binding of the tongue or its cleaving to the palate (Ps. cxxxvii. 6; Mk. vii. 35; Lk. i. 64) (see BODY for a statement on the apparent belief among the Hebrews that the organs functioned semi-independently).

The tongue is used in parallel with or interchangeably for lip and mouth, as the instruments of speech or related concepts (see LIP, MOUTH) and is spoken of as good or evil (Ps. cxx. 2; Pr. vi. 17, x. 20), learned (Is. l. 4), singing (Ps. li. 14) and speaking (Ps. lxxi. 24). As the mouth can be said to contain something, so wickedness can be hidden under the tongue (Jb. xx. 12), or the tongue can be filled with singing (Ps. cxxvi. 2).

The metaphor of a sharp tongue was used in Old Testament times. The tongue was spoken of as being whetted like a sword (Ps. lxiv. 3; *cf.* Ps. cxl. 3 and Heb. iv. 12; Rev. i. 16) and the simile of a bow and arrow is also used (Je. ix. 3, 8). The tremendous influence of words for good or ill is expressed by attributing power to the tongue (Pr. xviii. 21; Jas. iii. 5, 6).

Famine and thirst are described as causing the tongue to cleave to the palate (La. iv. 4), and it withers through disease (Zc. xiv. 12).

Destroying the power of an enemy by dividing their tongues (Ps. lv. 9) may conceivably refer literally to a practice similar to the putting out of their eyes (2 Ki. xxv. 7); but it is more likely figurative, referring to the confusion of language as at Babel (Gn. xi. 1 ff., where the word for language is lip, *śāpâ*; *cf.* Is. xix. 18). The alienation of man from man due to the gulf created by language difference, cutting, as it does, across the whole area of instinctive feelings, common interests, and co-operation, is attributed in the Genesis passage to the sinful pride of man, bringing upon them this form of visitation by God.

The word 'tongue' is thus used to describe the different nations, or tribes, which generally have distinctive languages (Is. lxvi. 18; Rev. v. 9). The word is found in AV, not in the Greek or RV, to designate Hebrew as a language (Jn. v. 2; Rev. ix. 11, xvi. 16).

See also TONGUES, GIFT OF. B.O.B.

TONGUES, CONFUSION OF. See BABEL.

TONGUES, GIFT OF. Speaking with tongues, or *glossolalia* (Gk. *glōssolalia*), is a spiritual gift (see SPIRITUAL GIFTS) mentioned in Mk. xvi. 17; Acts x. 44–46, xix. 6, and described in Acts ii. 1–13; 1 Cor. xii–xiv.

When the assembled disciples were filled with the Holy Spirit on the day of Pentecost they began 'to speak with other tongues (*lalein heterais glōssais*), as the Spirit gave them utterance' (Acts ii. 4), so that many Jews of the Dispersion were astonished to hear the praises of God in the languages (*glōssa*, verse 11) and dialects (*dialektos*, verses 6, 8) of their native lands (verses 9 ff.). Although by general agreement Luke clearly intended the phrase 'to speak with other tongues' to signify that the disciples spoke in foreign languages, this explanation has not been universally accepted. From the days of the early Fathers some have seen in verse 8 evidence for a miracle of hearing wrought on the audience. Gregory Nazianzen (*Orat.* XLI, x, *In Pentecosten*) rejected this view on the ground that it transfers the miracle from the disciples to the unconverted multitude, and it also overlooks the fact that speaking with tongues began before there was any audience (verse 4, *cf.* verse 6).

In the opinion of many modern scholars the *glossolalia* of Acts ii. 1–13 was similar to that described in 1 Cor. xii–xiv, and consisted of unintelligible ecstatic utterances. It is held that the original account of Pentecost (Acts ii. 1–6a, 12 f., without *heterais*, verse 4) mentioned only ecstatic utterances, and Luke interpolated the reference to foreign languages (Acts ii. 6b–11, and *heterais*) either as a more favourable explanation when *glossolalia* had fallen into disrepute (H. Weinel, *Die Wirkungen des Geistes und der Geister*, 1899, pp. 74 ff.) or as a symbolic interpretation influenced by the conception of Pentecost as a reversal of the curse of Babel (Gn. xi. 1–9), or as a parallel to the giving of the law at Sinai in the seventy languages of mankind (Midrash *Tanchuma* 26c; see F. J. Foakes-Jackson and K. Lake, *The Beginnings of Chri tianity*, 1920–33, V, pp. 114 ff.). Since there is n MS evidence for this theory and Luke is unlike to have misunderstood the nature of *glossolali* the parallels clearly in his mind must have bee suggested by the fact that the disciples actual spoke in foreign languages. To what extent the did so is uncertain, for most of their heare probably knew Greek or Aramaic, but the Galilaean speech was at least delivered from i peculiarities and made intelligible to the polygl multitude (verse 7; *cf.* Mk. xiv. 70).

Speaking 'with new tongues' (*glōssais kainai* is mentioned in Mk. xvi. 17 (not an original pa of the Gospel) as a sign following faith in Chris It accompanied the outpouring of the Ho Spirit upon the first Gentile converts (Acts x. 44 46, xi. 15), and was doubtless one of the visib manifestations among the earliest Samarita believers (Acts viii. 18). The isolated group disciples at Ephesus, who may have been ear believers in Christ unaware of Pentecost (N. Stonehouse, 'Repentance, Baptism and the Gi of the Holy Spirit', *WTJ*, XIII, 1950–5 pp. 11 ff.), also spoke in tongues when the Ho Spirit came on them (Acts xix. 6). In each ca general spontaneous *glossolalia* was sensib evidence of the repetition of the initial bestow of the Spirit at Pentecost, and apparently serve to endorse the inclusion of new classes believers into the cautious Jewish–Christia Church (*cf.* Acts x. 47, xi. 17, 18; see W. Scroggie, *The Baptism of the Spirit and Speaki with Tongues*, p. 16).

Corinthian *glossolalia* differed in some respec from that described in Acts. In Jerusaler as also in Caesarea and Ephesus, whole com panies on whom the Spirit fell immediately bro into tongues, whereas at Corinth not all possesse the coveted gift (1 Cor. xii. 10, 30). *Glossolalia* Acts appears to have been an irresistible ar temporary initial experience, but at Corinth was a continuing gift under the control of th speaker (1 Cor. xiv. 27, 28). At Pentecost th 'tongues' were readily understood by the heare but at Corinth the additional gift of interpret tion was necessary to make them intelligib (verses 5, 13, 27). Only at Pentecost is speaking foreign languages explicitly mentioned. On th other hand, *glossolalia* is everywhere represente as consisting of articulate, significant utteranc inspired by the Holy Spirit and employ primarily for worship (Acts ii. 11, x. 46; 1 Co xiv. 2, 14–17, 28).

Tongues varied in character (1 Cor. xii. 10 At Corinth they were apparently not forei languages, which Paul denotes by a differe word (*phōnē*, xiv. 10, 11), because a special gi not linguistic proficiency, was necessary understand them; nor were they meaningle ecstatic sounds, though the mind was inacti (verse 14) and the utterances, without interpre tion, unintelligible even to the speaker (verse 1 because words (verse 19) and contents (vers 14–17) were recognized, and interpreted tongu ere equivalent to prophecy (verse 5). A definite nguistic form is suggested by the Greek words or 'to interpret', which, elsewhere in the New estament, except in Lk. xxiv. 27, always mean o translate' (*cf.* J. G. Davies, 'Pentecost and lossolalia', *JTS*, NS, III, 1952, pp. 228 ff.), and ongues are probably best regarded as special anguages' not having ordinary human characeristics, inspired by the Holy Spirit for worship, or a sign to unbelievers (xiv. 22), and, when nterpreted, for the edification of believers. The orinthians so overrated and abused *glossolalia* hat Paul strictly limited its exercise in public verses 27, 28) and emphasized the superior value f prophecy for the whole church (verses 1, 5). t is uncertain how far later manifestations of *lossolalia* resemble the New Testament phenoenon.

BIBLIOGRAPHY. E. Lombard, *De la Glossolalie hez les Premiers Chrétiens*, 1910; E. Mosiman, *Das Zungenreden*, 1911; A. Mackie, *The Gift of ongues*, 1921; G. B. Cutten, *Speaking with ongues*, 1947; M. Barnett, *The Living Flame*, 953. W.G.P.

OOLS. See ARTS AND CRAFTS.

OPAZ. See JEWELS AND PRECIOUS STONES.

OPHEL. Mentioned only in Dt. i. 1. It has een identified with Tafile, a site 16 miles southast of the Dead Sea, but the identification is oubtful.

OPHETH, TOPHET. This was a 'high place' n the valley of Hinnom (*q.v.*) just outside erusalem, where child sacrifices were made to a eity Molech. Josiah defiled this idolatrous hrine, and Jeremiah prophesied that the place ould be used as a cemetery (Je. vii. 32 f.). The eaning and etymology of the word are unertain. The generally accepted derivation is from n Aramaic root *tpt*; it will then mean 'fireplace'. his accords well with the fact that the sacrifices o Molech were made by fire (*cf.* 2 Ki. xxiii. 10). D.F.P.

ORAH. See LAW.

ORCH. The word occurs only four times in AV. n the Old Testament it twice renders *lappîḏ* Na. ii. 3; Zc. xii. 6), the traditional torch conisting of a long pole with rags soaked in oil rapped round the top of it. It also erroneously enders *pᵉlāḏâ*, probably meaning 'steel fitting', n Na. ii. 4. In the New Testament it stands for *ampas* in Jn. xviii. 3. It is possible that *lampas* hould be rendered 'torch' rather than 'lamp' *q.v.*) on other occasions too. R.E.N.

ORTOISE. Tortoises are found in all countries f the Middle East. It is possible that the tortoise referred to as *ṣāḇ* in Lv. xi. 29, for it is a reptile hat would be seen from time to time, but other uthorities translate it 'lizard', and the identity ust be considered doubtful. Tortoises were known in ancient Assyria (*allutu*), hence a curse runs 'may you be turned upside down like a tortoise (and die)' (*Iraq*, XX, 1958, p. 76). G.C.

TOWER. See FORTIFICATION AND SIEGECRAFT.

TOWER OF BABEL. See BABEL.

TOWN. See CITY.

TOWN CLERK. The *grammateus* (Acts xix. 35) was frequently the secretary of a board of magistrates, responsible for the accurate recording of official decisions. At Ephesus he was clearly the president of the assembly. His punctilious regard for legal niceties, and anxiety about Roman intervention, mark him as a member of the Romanized aristocracy, among whom Paul found support (verse 31). His speech has been much admired as a little masterpiece of political *savoir faire*. E.A.J.

TRACHONITIS. The only biblical reference is Lk. iii. 1, where, linked with Ituraea (*q.v.*), it is called the tetrarchy of Philip (the brother of Herod, tetrarch of Galilee). Trachonitis must have been the district around Trachon (Josephus uses both names); Trachon corresponds with the modern al-Laja', a pear-shaped area of petrified volcanic rock some 350 square miles in area, to the east of Galilee and south of Damascus. It is on the whole extremely unproductive, but here and there are patches of fertile ground, with a spring or two. The cracked and broken nature of its terrain made it ideal for outlaws and brigands. Among others Varro (governor of Syria under Augustus), Herod the Great, and Herod Agrippa I endeavoured to civilize the area, with varying success. Later on a Roman road was built through it. Targum Jonathan identifies the Old Testament Argob with Trachonitis. D.F.P.

TRADE AND COMMERCE.

I. IN THE OLD TESTAMENT

Palestine has always been the only natural bridge between Europe and Asia on the north and Africa on the south. This accounts for the fact that, although she was a poor country, she was constantly enriched by the trade and commerce that went through her land. Ezk. xxvii. 12–25 presents a cross-section of the world commerce that passed through her territory. (See PALESTINE.)

Palestine's major contributions to commerce in Old Testament times were agricultural products and metals. Phoenicia just to the north was a manufacturing area forced to import food. Israel supplied her with grain, oil, and wine. Egypt to the south had a surplus of grain, but was short of olive oil and wine. As the desert peoples to the east became more influential after David's day they too absorbed Palestine's agricultural products.

Iron, which had been earlier introduced by the Philistines, appeared in such quantity after

David's wide conquests in Syria that it could also be passed on to iron-hungry Egypt. Just how much iron Palestine itself smelted is still uncertain. Solomon erected the largest smelter yet found in ancient times, but he concentrated on copper, selling it down the Red Sea to the backward peoples of Arabia and Africa. These lands in return sent precious incense, spices, and gold to the Mediterranean *via* Palestine as well as Egypt. This Arabian commerce in Palestine was at its peak in Nabataean times. During the inter-testamental period the asphalt traffic from the Dead Sea was so important that this body of water was called the Asphalt Sea, and it entered into international politics. Perfumes and spices were always items of exchange, some varieties moving out of the country and others moving in. Both were more important in ancient times than today. Spices, for example, were a common method of varying a rather monotonous menu.

Palestine's flocks produced a surplus of wool, which was probably exported both in bulk and as manufactured goods. Moab was a major wool producer. The excavations at Kiriath-sepher have shown that this was a manufacturing city devoted exclusively to weaving and dyeing of cloth. Flax was also used for clothing. If it was exported, then it was sent to Phoenicia, since Egypt was a heavy producer of linen. The wide distribution of expensive garments is shown by the finding of a Babylonian garment at the time of Joshua's conquest of Jericho, although that city was of minor importance. The value of good raiment is seen in the fact that it was commonly included in the list of booty taken in war.

Egypt (*q.v.*) was the outstanding manufacturing nation along the Mediterranean in early days, but Phoenicia began to cut into her trade much as Japan did into world commerce in our time. Phoenicia imitated and modified Egyptian craftsmanship. With Phoenicia's expanding manufacturing and shipping trade, Israel had a constantly increasing market for her agricultural products. Palestine itself entered the manufacturing field about the time of the written prophets. Indeed, much of their social criticism deals with the inevitable economic crises which come when any agricultural people shifts into full-scale manufacturing. An early date to Pentateuchal laws is demonstrated by the absence of any manufacturing code. Palestine used modern assembly-line techniques and standardization of forms and sizes. Their mass-production material was of good quality, although they were often using poorer materials and cheaper labour. Their manufactured goods, however, seemed to have been primarily for local consumption. Trade guilds came in at this time, and trade marks were used by the pottery manufacturers. See ARTS AND CRAFTS. In Old Testament times agricultural taxes were largely paid in kind, and the government had its own potteries making official government standardized containers with the government seal stamped on the handles.

Coined money came into Palestine towards the close of Old Testament times. Previously gol and silver in ingots, bars, and rings were weighe out. Jewels offered a more convenient and fairl safe method of investing and transporting large sums than would be convenient in bullion. Afte Alexander the Great, coined money was commo (see MONEY). During the inter-testamental period Jewish bankers came into prominence, and th synagogues of Asia Minor in New Testamen times are in part due to Jewish influence i banking and commerce. During this same perio Alexandria, which had become probably th greatest manufacturing city of the world attracted a heavy Jewish population.

Only in the days of Solomon and Jehoshapha did sea commerce play an important part i Palestinian trade, and both ventures were short lived. Sea commerce was predominantly in th hands of foreigners, first Philistines and other se peoples, then later Phoenicians and Greeks.

For land travel the ass was the beast of burde until about David's day, when the camel, pre viously used primarily for war, also becam available for the caravan trade. Part of Pale stine's commercial wealth came from thes caravans, which purchased necessary supplie from farmers and craftsmen as they move through the country. At the local market-plac the population absorbed foreign news, and th efficacy of this news medium can be seen in th sermons of Amos, with their broad picture c world affairs. Ishmaelites and Midianite handled much of the early commerce on th desert fringe. Later the Ammonites took ove from them and became the dominant camel owning people before the Nabataeans, wh brought desert commerce to its financial peak.

Ben-hadad and the Omri dynasty had busines depots in each other's capital city, and this wa probably common practice between adjacen nations. Israel and Phoenicia were normally o far better terms with each other than Israel an Syria. A good source of income for the goverr ment was the tax on commerce entering th country. This source of wealth, of course, was a its peak in the days of David and Solomon. Bu there was a second peak of prosperity unde Jeroboam II in Israel and Uzziah in Judah.

The major trade routes of Palestine ran nort and south. The most important came out c Egypt, crossed the Philistine plain, continue along the eastern edge of the plain of Sharo crossed the Carmel ridge at Megiddo, and the went on to Dan either *via* Hazor of Galilee or *vi* Beth-shan and the upland road just north of th Yarmuq river. The high ridge road *via* Beersheb Hebron, Jerusalem, Shechem, and Beth-sha handled more local traffic than through com merce. East of the Jordan valley was the king highway coming out of the Gulf of Aqabah an touching the key cities of Kir, Dibon, Medeb *etc.*, along the centre of the populated areas. second road followed a parallel track to the ea of the king's highway and just inside the dese fringe. Today a modern highway follows th former and the railway the latter. These routes picked up the Arabian trade at such points as Petra, Amman, and Edrei.

East and west roads were less profitable, except the most southern one, where Arabian commerce came *via* Nabataean Petra to Gaza. Commerce also came out of the caravan city of Amman, down the Jabbok valley, up to Shechem, and over to the Mediterranean. More commerce, however, probably came through the Hauran down to Beth-shan and up the plain of Esdraelon to the Mediterranean. The great grain fields of the Hauran sold their wheat down this route. A shorter road cut across Galilee from the Sea of Galilee to Accho. The major seaports used in Old Testament times were Joppa, Dor, and Accho. Ashkelon was the Philistine seaport, and Gaza was the Mediterranean outlet for the Nabataean trade.

BIBLIOGRAPHY. D. Baly, *The Geography of the Bible*, 1957.

J.L.K.

II. IN THE NEW TESTAMENT

Trade and commerce have no large place in the New Testament. The coast of Palestine is harbourless and swept with surf, and no natural port formed a cross-road for trade. The sea in Hebrew metaphor is a barrier, not a pathway, and such an attitude was natural in a land which fronted the unbroken border of the waters. The ruins of artificial harbours are common enough, and suggest rather the futility than the success of man's attempts to tame the eastern end of the Mediterranean (see G. A. Smith, *The Historical Geography of the Holy Land*[25], 1931, pp. 127–144).

Caravan routes, on the other hand, naturally onverged on Palestine, and the New Testament s aware of the activities of the trader. Such arables as those of the talents and the merchant vho found 'a pearl of great price' were obviously neant to be understood by the audience to which hey were addressed. But this was the petty trade f a small, poor, and under-privileged land.

Major activities in trade and commerce, all hrough New Testament times, were in the hands f the Romans and Italians. State interference ith the processes of trade, which became a ombre feature of late Imperial times, was lready visible in the 1st century. The legal achinery by which a 'mark in hand or head' ould prevent the non-conformist from buying nd selling (Rev. xiii. 16, 17) was early apparent. he foreign trade of the Empire was extensive nd varied. There is also evidence that it was nbalanced, for the hoards of Roman coins und commonly in India are clear indication of perilous leakage of bullion, and one cause of the eeping paralysis of inflation.

Latin and Greek words in early Irish, German, anian, Indian, and even Mongolian tongues are idence of the wide influence of Roman trade. chaeology, especially on the S Indian coast, s a similar word to say. A recent excavation at ndicherry has established the fact of a large Roman trade with India in the 1st century. Roman merchants, indeed, were ubiquitous. There was a Roman market, the remains of which may still be seen, outside the sacred precincts at Delphi. Trade was no doubt brisk in amulets and souvenirs, and may have been typical of petty Italian enterprise abroad wherever crowds were gathered. Similar activity in the Temple of Jerusalem had been cannily kept in the hands of the Sadducean priests.

From the 2nd century before Christ a Roman city stood on Delos, the Aegean centre of the slave-trade, and when Mithridates in 88 BC massacred the Italian residents of Asia Minor and the Aegean islands, 25,000 fell in Delos alone out of a total of 100,000 victims. They must have been mostly traders and the agents of commerce. The capital itself, whose population in the 1st century was something like one million, was a vast market, and a grim, satiric chapter in the Apocalypse (Rev. xviii), constructed after the fashion of an Old Testament 'taunt-song', and in imitation of Ezekiel xxvii, speaks of the wealth and volume of Rome's luxury trade, and the economic disruption sure to follow the loss of a market so rich.

Roman trade extended far beyond the boundaries of the Empire. The 'far country' of Mt. xxv. 14 is quite literal. Merchants from Italy carried their foods into unsubdued Germany, along the 'amber route' to the Baltic, to India, and perhaps China. All this activity sprang from Rome's dominance, the peace which she policed, and above all from the absence of political frontiers over significant areas of the world. Petronius' Trimalchio, the *nouveau riche* of the *Satiricon*, could make fortunes and lose them, and make them again. Of Augustus the merchants said that 'through him they sailed the seas in safety, through him they could make their wealth, through him they were happy'.

The account of the last journey of Paul to Rome, so ably told by Luke, first in a ship of Adramyttium of Asia Minor, and then in an Alexandrian freighter, probably under charter to the Roman government for the transport of Egyptian corn, gives a vivid picture of the hazards of trade and navigation.

Apart from the list of Rev. xviii, which may have been deliberately selected in accordance with the polemic and satirical purpose of the passage, the commodities of export trade are not widely known. No cargo lists survive. Oysters came from Britain to Rome in barrels of sea-water. Cornish tin, no doubt, came down the same sea-route. Northern Gaul seems to have had the rudiments of an exporting textile industry, and Gaul certainly exported cheap Samian pottery. Underwater archaeology on wrecked ships has revealed that large cargoes of wine were carried. A monogram device of a double S in a trident seems to indicate that one such freighter, wrecked near Marseilles, was the property of one Severus Sestius, who occupied 'the House of the Trident' on Delos.

On the subject of mass production for such trade there is little information, and none on the business organization necessarily involved. Certain localities, however, became famous for special products, and the resultant commerce would have been in the control of specialist traders who would create and operate their own markets. A striking example is Lydia, 'a seller of purple, of the city of Thyatira' in Asia Minor (Acts xvi. 14), whom Paul's party met at Philippi in Macedonia. Corinthian bronze, in ornaments and mirrors (1 Cor. xiii. 12), and the *cilicium* or goats'-hair cloth, which was either the product or the raw-material of Paul's 'tent-making' (Acts xviii. 3), were probably distributed by similar private enterprise. The imagery of John's letter to Laodicea (Rev. iii. 14–18) is partly derived from the trade and commerce of the town. Ramsay has established the existence of a Laodicean trade in valuable black woollen garments. Laodicea and Colossae produced black fleeces, the evidence of which is still genetically apparent, it is said, in the sheep of the area today. There was also a Laodicean eye-salve, based probably on the kaolin of the thermal area at Hierapolis, 6 miles away. Hence the taunt about 'white garments' and 'eye-salve' (see W. M. Ramsay, *The Letters to the Seven Churches of Asia*, chapters xxix and xxx).

Thyatira, of the earlier letter, was also a centre of trade and commerce, though probably without Laodicea's export emphasis. Lydia has already been mentioned, and archaeological evidence speaks of wool- and linen-workers, dyers, leather-workers, tanners, potters, slave-traders, and bronze-smiths. The dyers, and Lydia was probably one of them, dealt in a purple dye made from the madder root, which undercut the expensive sea-dye from the murex shell.

It is curious to note that, in writing to Thyatira, John uses the figure of Jezebel, sign and symbol of Israel's compromising trade partnership with Phoenicia, to describe a local 'Nicolaitan'. 'Jezebel' of Thyatira had no doubt taught some form of compromise with the surrounding pagan world. In a town of brisk trade activity some such adjustment would appear more urgently necessary because of the power of the trade guilds.

These organizations were a source of major difficulty to Christians, who sought, in their daily converse with the pagan world around, to keep a clear conscience. The trade guilds or *collegia* appear in Acts xix as a force of organized opposition to Christianity. An important trade commodity of Ephesus, now that the harbour was silting, and commerce was passing to Smyrna, was the manufacture of silver souvenirs and cult objects of Artemis, for sale to the pilgrims who visited the famous shrine. Ephesus saw the guilds concerned exercise sufficient pressure to end Paul's ministry. A famous letter of Pliny (*Ep.* x. 96), which vividly describes the suppression of a vigorous church in Bithynia in AD 112, is also a clear indication of such influence. The guild of the butchers, alarmed at the falling sales of sacrificial meat, successfully stirred up offici action against the church. It was difficult f Christians, whose trade depended upon measure of goodwill, to carry on their dai activities if they obviously abstained fro fellowship with their colleagues. On the oth hand, since all the callings of trade and con merce were under the patronage of pagan deitie fellowship, and indeed membership of a trac *collegium*, involved the compromising act libation or sacrifice at the guild dinner. Recor exist of a considerable number of such organiz tions, and the strictures of Jude, Peter, and Joh against the 'Nicolaitans', the 'followers Balaam' and 'Jezebel', suggest that the simp functions of trade and commerce may hav proved a source of deep division in the ear Church.

BIBLIOGRAPHY. G. A. Smith in *EBi* (s. 'Trade'); F. J. Foakes-Jackson and K. Lak (eds.), *The Beginnings of Christianity*, I, 1920, p 218 ff. E.M.B.

TRADES. See ARTS AND CRAFTS.

TRADITION. That which is handed down, pa ticularly teaching handed down from a teacher his disciples. The Gk. noun *paradosis* is used fo times of Christian tradition, and the verb *par didōmi*, usually translated 'deliver', occurs s times in the same connection, but the concept often present without any mention of the wor The references in the Gospels occur in Mt. and Mk. vii, and are all concerned with Jewi tradition, which is here considered first.

I. JEWISH TRADITION

The word does not occur in the Old Testamer but between the Testaments much teaching elaboration and explanation of the Old Test ment was added by the Rabbis. This was hand down from teacher to pupil, and by our Lord day had assumed a place alongside Scripture importance. This equation of human comme tary with the divine revelation was condemned our Lord. By such tradition the Word of G was 'transgressed', 'made of none effect', la aside, and rejected (Mt. xv. 3, 6; Mk. vii. 8, 13). The doctrines taught by it were 'the co mandments of men' (Mt. xv. 9; Mk. vii. 6, and the effect in practice was unreality a hypocrisy (Mt. xv. 8, 9; Mk. vii. 6, 7). M could not add to the Word of God witho adulterating the truth.

II. CHRISTIAN TRADITION

Although the word 'tradition' is used in t Gospels only of Jewish tradition, the concept present in our Lord's own teaching. He plac His own teaching alongside the Word of God an authoritative commentary, which He hand down to His disciples. Thus in the Sermon on t Mount Jesus quotes from the law, and again a again puts beside it His own words, prefaci His comment with 'but I say unto you' (Mt.

2, 28, 32, 34, 39, 44, *cf.* vi. 25). He claimed that y so doing He was not abrogating the law as the harisees had done, but fulfilling it (Mt. v. 17–9). His justification for so doing is found in His erson. As the Spirit-anointed Messiah, to whom iod had not given the Spirit by measure, He lone could make a valid and authoritative comientary on the Spirit-inspired Word of God to be laced alongside it.

A similar emphasis on the Person of Christ is ound in relevant passages in the Epistles. In Col. . 8 Paul warns 'lest any man spoil you through hilosophy and vain deceit, after the tradition of ien . . . and not after Christ'. The contrast to uman tradition is Christ. So in Gal. i. 14, 16 aul shows that he abandoned the tradition of ie elders when God revealed His Son in him; hrist not only creates the true tradition but onstitutes it as well. Christian tradition in the lew Testament therefore consists of the followig three elements: (*a*) the facts of Christ (1 Cor. . 23, xv. 3; Lk. i. 2, where 'delivered' translates *iredosan*); (*b*) the theological interpretation of iose facts; see, *e.g.*, the whole argument of Cor. xv; (*c*) the manner of life which flows om them (1 Cor. xi. 2; 2 Thes. ii. 15, iii. 6, 7). Jude 3 the 'faith . . . once for all delivered' sv) covers all three elements (*cf.* Rom. vi. 17).

Christ was made known by the apostolic stimony to Him; the apostles therefore claimed iat their tradition was to be received as authori.tive (1 Cor. xi. 2; 2 Thes. ii. 15, iii. 6). See also ph. iv. 20, 21, where the readers had not heard hrist in the flesh but had heard the apostolic stimony to Him. Christ had told the apostles iat they would bear witness of Him because they id been with Him from the beginning; in the .me context He promised the gift of the Spirit ho would lead them into all truth (Jn. xv. 26, ', xvi. 13). This combination of eyewitness stimony and Spirit-guided witness produced a radition' that was a true and valid complement the Old Testament Scriptures. So 1 Tim. v. 18 id 2 Pet. iii. 16 place apostolic tradition along.le Scripture and describe it as such, and 2 Pet. 16, 19 founds Christian belief on eyewitness stimony and the more sure word of prophecy the Old Testament.

The apostolic office was limited to eye.tnesses, and, as only eyewitnesses could bear a ithful witness to Christ as He lived and died id rose again, true tradition must also be ostolic. This was recognized by the Church in ter years when the Canon of the New Testaent was eventually produced on the basis of the ostolic nature of the books concerned. postolic tradition was at one time oral, but for it is crystallized in the apostolic writings conining the Spirit-guided witness to the Christ of od. Other teaching, while it may be instructive id useful and worthy of serious consideration, innot claim to be placed alongside the Old and ew Testaments as authoritative without manisting the same defects as condemned Jewish idition in the eyes of our Lord.

BIBLIOGRAPHY. O. Cullmann, 'The Tradition', in *The Early Church*, 1956, pp. 59 ff. D.J.V.L.

TRANCE. The word 'trance' occurs five times in the AV. In Nu. xxiv. 4, 16 the Hebrew simply says that Balaam 'fell down' (*nāpal*): the words 'into a trance' are an addition (LXX *en hypnō*). In Acts x. 10, xi. 5, xxii. 17 'trance' is the rendering of *ekstasis*, whence 'ecstasy'; in Mk. v. 42, xvi. 8; Lk. v. 26; Acts iii. 10, 'amazement' or 'astonishment'. In a trance-state self-control and self-consciousness are at a minimum, but in this ecstatic state revelatory visions were received.

J.G.S.S.T.

TRANSFIGURATION. The transfiguration is recorded in Mt. xvii. 1–8; Mk. ix. 2–8; Lk. ix. 28–36. Its absence from John is usually accounted for on the ground that the whole of Christ's life was a manifestation of the divine glory (Jn. i. 14, ii. 11, *etc.*). There is also a reference to it in 2 Pet. i. 16–18.

In the Synoptic Gospels the event takes place about a week after Peter's confession of the Messiahship of Jesus. He took His three closest disciples, Peter, James, and John, up to a mountain (probably Hermon, which rises to a height of 9,000 feet above sea-level). There He was transformed (rather than changed in appearance) and His garments shone with heavenly brightness. Moses and Elijah then appeared and talked to Him, and Peter suggested making three tents for them. A voice then came from a cloud declaring Christ's Sonship and His authority, after which the vision ended. The narrative suggests that the whole event was objective, though many modern scholars have sought to describe it in terms of a subjective experience of Jesus or of Peter.

The transfiguration marks an important stage in the revelation of Jesus as the Christ and the Son of God. It is an experience similar to His baptism (Mt. iii. 13–17; Mk. i. 9–11; Lk. iii. 21 f.). Here His glory is revealed not just through His deeds, but in a more personal way. The glory denotes the royal presence, for the kingdom of God is in the midst of His people.

There are many features about the account which derive significance from the Old Testament. Moses and Elijah represent the Law and the Prophets witnessing to the Messiah and being fulfilled and superseded by Him. Each of them had had a vision of the glory of God on a mountain, Moses on Sinai (Ex. xxiv. 15) and Elijah on Horeb (1 Ki. xix. 8). Each of them left no known grave (Dt. xxxiv. 6; 2 Ki. ii. 11). The law of Moses and the coming of Elijah are mentioned together in the last verses of the Old Testament (Mal. iv. 4–6). The two men at the empty tomb (Lk. xxiv. 4; Jn. xx. 12) and at the ascension (Acts i. 10) and the 'two witnesses' (Rev. xi. 3) are sometimes also identified with Moses and Elijah. The heavenly voice, 'This is my beloved Son; hear him' (Mk. ix. 7), marks Jesus out not only as the Messiah but also as the Prophet of Dt. xviii. 15 ff.

The cloud symbolizes the covering of the divine presence (Ex. xxiv. 15–18; Ps. xcvii. 2). There is a cloud to receive Christ out of His disciples' sight at the ascension (Acts i. 9). The return of Christ will be with clouds (Rev. i. 7).

In Luke we are told that the subject of their conversation was the *exodos* which He was to accomplish at Jerusalem. This seems to mean not simply His death but the great facts of His death and resurrection as the means of redemption of His people typified by the Old Testament Exodus from Egypt.

The transfiguration is therefore a focal point in the revelation of the kingdom of God, for it looks back to the Old Testament and shows how Christ fulfils it, and it looks on to the great events of the cross, resurrection, ascension, and parousia. Peter was wrong in trying to make the experience permanent. What was needed was the presence of Jesus alone and attention to His voice.

BIBLIOGRAPHY. G. H. Boobyer, *St. Mark and the Transfiguration Story*, 1942; A. M. Ramsey, *The Glory of God and the Transfiguration of Christ*, 1949. R.E.N.

TRANSGRESSION. See SIN.

TRAVAIL. Seventeenth-century English made no distinction between the words 'travel' and 'travail', the two spellings being employed indiscriminately for the two ideas in the earlier editions of the AV. Later editions have, on the whole, conformed to the changing usage. The English word translates a number of Hebrew and Greek words, all of which are normally connected with childbirth. The word is sometimes employed metaphorically, notably in Rom. viii. 22 and Gal. iv. 19, and in simile as in Ps. xlviii. 6 and Mi. iv. 9, 10. G.W.G.

TREASURE, TREASURY. 'Treasure' usually refers to valuables, such as silver or gold. 'Treasures of darkness' (Is. xlv. 3) are hoarded riches; 'treasures of wickedness' (Pr. x. 2; Mi. vi. 10) are ill-gotten gains. RV and RSV often replace 'treasure' by 'treasury' in the Old Testament. In Mt. ii. 11 'treasures' are boxes containing valuables.

'Treasury' and 'treasure house' frequently signify a place where treasure is stored, generally attached to a sanctuary (Jos. vi. 19, 24; 1 Ki. vii. 51, RV; Dn. i. 2) or belonging to a king (2 Ki. xii. 18, RSV; Est. iii. 9). In Ezr. ii. 69, RV; Ne. vii. 70 f., RV, 'treasury' is a fund for rebuilding the Temple. In Mk. xii. 41; Lk. xxi. 1 it refers to the thirteen trumpet-shaped offertory boxes placed in the Court of the Women in the Temple; it is apparently used of the vicinity of these boxes in Jn. viii. 20.

'Treasure' also has the wider meaning of a store (Ex. i. 11), *e.g.* provisions (Je. xli. 8). In Mt. xiii. 52 it is a store-room. 'Treasury' can be a storage place in the Temple (Ne. x. 38, xii. 44, xiii. 12) or in the palace (2 Ki. xx. 13, 15; Je. xxxviii. 11). In Ezr. v. 17 'treasure house' refe to the Babylonian 'archives' (RSV) where doc ments were stored.

The Bible uses 'treasure' and 'treasury' met phorically too. Yahweh keeps sin in His memory treasuries (Dt. xxxii. 34, RSV) and has punis ment in store for the wicked (Ps. xvii. 14, RS *cf.* Rom. ii. 5). Awe of Yahweh is Zion's treasu (Is. xxxiii. 6). The sky is Yahweh's 'goc treasury' containing rain (Dt. xxviii. 12, RVm RSV); in poetry, snow, hail (Jb. xxxviii. 22, RV and the wind (Ps. cxxxv. 7; Je. x. 13, RV, li. 1 RV) also have treasuries or 'storehouses' (RSV).

In the Synoptic Gospels Jesus often us 'treasure' figuratively. Since God rewards whol hearted service in the hereafter, it is termed layi up treasure in heaven, which is contrasted wi money-making in Mt. vi. 19 f.; Mk. x. 21 ar parallels; Lk. xii. 33. As the storehouse of eith good or evil the heart controls conduct (Mt. x 35; Lk. vi. 45). A man's heart is where h treasure is (Mt. vi. 21; Lk. xii. 34), *i.e.* his i terests are determined by what he values most

Paul's phrase 'treasure in earthen vessel (2 Cor. iv. 7) contrasts the glory of the divi gospel with the weakness of its human ministe Wisdom and knowledge are treasures to be fou only in Christ (Col. ii. 3).

'Peculiar treasure' is the AV and RV renderi of *sᵉgullâ* in Ex. xix. 5; Ps. cxxxv. 4; Ec. ii. 8. T RV also translates it thus in Mal. iii. 17 ('jewels'). The Hebrew word occurs with 'peopl in Dt. vii. 6, xiv. 2, xxvi. 18. It means 'person property'. Apart from 1 Ch. xxix. 3; Ec. ii. where it is used literally of kings' possessio *sᵉgullâ* is applied to Israel as Yahweh's very ov people. Tit. ii. 14; 1 Pet. ii. 9, and possibly Eph. 14 use the LXX equivalents of the new Israel.

BIBLIOGRAPHY. *Arndt*; L. Koehler, *Lexicon Veteris Testamenti Libros*, 1953. L.C.A.

TREES.

a. Algum (Heb. *'algûmmîm*, 2 Ch. ii. 8, ix. 10, 1

Apparently a tree native to Lebanon, and pc sibly the coniferous tree called the eastern sav or Grecian juniper, *Juniperus excelsa* Bieb. T evergreen cypress, *Cupressus sempervirens* Gord., has also been suggested. A doubt suggestion is that the algum is identical with t almug tree of Ophir and that it was re-export to Judah from Lebanon and thought by t Chronicler to be native there. The reference 'algum trees' in 2 Ch. ix. 10, 11 appears to be example of metathesis, or it may be simply alternative form.

b. Almug (Heb. *'almûggîm*, 1 Ki. x. 11, 12)

Imported into Judah with gold from Ophir. T location of Ophir (*q.v.*) remains a matter conjecture, and the identity of the tree is u certain. The most convincing identification with the red sandal-wood, *Pterocarpus santalir* L.f., a large leguminous tree native to India a Ceylon.

c. Ash (Heb. *'ōren*, Is. xliv. 14)

May be *Fraxinus ornus* L., or possibly *F. parvifolia* Lam. or *F. syriaca* Boiss., but as they occur no farther south than Lebanon they are unlikely to be the tree intended. Other versions translate *'ōren* as pine-tree, bay-tree, fir-tree, or cedar, and most of these are more suitable than ash.

d. Bay-tree (Heb. *'ezrāḥ*, Ps. xxxvii. 35)

Laurus nobilis L., a tree 40–60 feet high with evergreen, fragrant leaves, infrequent in Palestine, but well known and used as a spice and garland. Other versions render 'cedar of Lebanon'; but *'ezrāḥ* elsewhere in the Old Testament means 'native', and a plant indigenous to Palestine is indicated here. The cedar is not a native of Palestine.

e. Box-tree (Heb. *te'aššûr*, Is. xli. 19, lx. 13)

Buxus longifolia Boiss., a small tree up to 20 feet high with small evergreen leaves. The wood is extremely hard and fine-grained. At the Feast of Tabernacles booths were made of branches of box.

f. Cedar (Heb. *'erez*, Gk. *kedros*)

Cedrus libani Loud., the cedar of Lebanon, a stately coniferous tree now rare and protected in Lebanon. The wood was highly esteemed for its durability, and was used, for example, for building David's house (2 Sa. v. 11 *etc.*), Solomon's Temple (1 Ki. v. 6–10, *etc.*) and the new Temple built after the Babylonian Exile (Ezr. iii. 7). Solomon had chariots, or more probably sedans (Heb. *'appiryôn*), made of cedar (Ct. iii. 9). Cedars can attain 120 feet in height, and Old Testament writers used them as a figure of stature in man (Ezk. xxxi. 3; Am. ii. 9). The cedar wood burnt by a priest during levitical cleansing (Lv. xiv. 4–6, 49–52; Nu. xix. 6) would not have been the cedar of Lebanon but a well-known plant of the Sinai desert, probably the brown-berried cedar, *Juniperus oxycedrus* L., or the Phoenician juniper, *Juniperus phoenicia* L., both of which are fragrant when burnt.

g. Chestnut (Heb. *'armôn*, Gn. xxx. 37; Ezk. xxxi. 8)

'Chesnut' (AV) is a better translation than 'plane-tree', *Platanus orientalis* L. (*q.v.*), of other versions, since the sweet chestnut (*Castanea*) is not native to Palestine.

h. Cypress (Heb. *tirzâ*)

In Is. xliv. 14 cypress wood is used in making a heathen idol. Other versions render 'holm-oak' or (RSV) 'holm tree' (*Quercus ilex* L.), or 'plane-tree' (*Platanus orientalis* L.); but cypress (*Cupressus sempervirens* L.) may well be correct, since it is well known in Palestine. Its fine habit is indicated in Ecclus. xxiv. 13 and l. 10.

i. Fig (see separate article FIG).

j. Fir (Heb. *berôš*, *berôtîm*).

The fir, fir-tree, and pine are botanically in the genus *Pinus*, and in the Bible probably refer to two species, *P. brutia* Tenore and *P. halepensis* Mill. These are evergreen coniferous trees native to the hills of Palestine and Lebanon. In Is. xli. 19 and lv. 13 the fir is used symbolically to indicate that the desert shall become fertile. The wood is excellent for building construction; it was used in building Solomon's Temple (1 Ki. v. 8, 10, *etc.*) and for ship boards (Ezk. xxvii. 5) and also for musical instruments (2 Sa. vi. 5). (Other versions translate the Hebrew as 'cypress'.) The reference to a green fir-tree in Ho. xiv. 8 continues with a mention of its fruit, which is presumably edible. This is probably *Pinus pinea* L., the stone pine, which has edible seeds.

k. Heath (Heb. *'ar'ār*, Je. xvii. 6; *'arô'ēr*, Je. xlviii. 6)

Unlikely to be a species of *Erica* to which the name heath usually refers. It is most likely to be the brown-berried cedar, *Juniperus oxycedrus* L., a heathy shrub growing in rocky parts of the desert and on rock cliffs. *Tamarix mannifera* (Ehrenb.) Bunge, a shrub of the Palestinian deserts, has also been suggested.

l. Mulberry-tree

The translation of Heb. *bekā'îm* as 'mulberry trees' (2 Sa. v. 23, 24; 1 Ch. xiv. 14, 15) is not now accepted. Mulberry leaves do not rustle in the breeze, as is demanded by the context. Species of poplar (*q.v.*) are well known for this, and the most likely species here is the Euphrates aspen, or balsam tree of RSV (*Populus euphratica* Oliv.), a tree native to the Palestine area. The true mulberry (*Morus nigra* L.) is the 'sycamine' (see below) of the New Testament.

m. Oak (Heb. *'allâ*, *'allôn*, *'ēlâ*)

Species of the genus *Quercus*. There are about twenty-four kinds of oak in Palestine, and it is difficult to determine which species is meant by any of the Hebrew words used. Some Palestinian species are evergreen (*Q. ilex* L., *Q. coccifera* L., *Q. palaestina* Kotschy), but most are deciduous (*e.g. Q. sessiliflora* Salisb., *Q. lusitanica* Lam., *Q. aegilops* L., *Q. cerris* L.); *cf.* Is. vi. 13. Oaks are sturdy, hardwood trees which live to a great age, and the fruit, or acorn, is set in a cup.

Heb. *'ašērâ* is translated in AV (following LXX *alsos*) as an idolatrous 'grove' or a 'high place' (Ex. xxxiv. 13; Dt. xvi. 21; 2 Ki. xvii. 16, *etc.*), since it was thought to refer to clumps of oaks. But recent scholarship holds that the reference is not to trees but to an image or cult-pole of the Canaanite goddess Asherah (*q.v.*), consort of El.

An oak was a favourite tree under which to sit (1 Ki. xiii. 14), or to bury the dead (Gn. xxxv. 8; 1 Ch. x. 12). The wood, though hard, is seldom mentioned. It was used for oars (Ezk. xxvii. 6) and graven images (Is. xliv. 14). Bashan was renowned for its oaks (Is. ii. 13; Ezk. xxvii. 6;

Zc. xi. 2), and to this day there are many finely grown trees of *Q. aegilops* L. in that region. The scarlet or crimson dye, used in Hebrew rites (Ex. xxv. 4, xxvi. 1; Heb. ix. 19, *etc.*), was obtained from a scale-insect that covered branchlets of the kermes oak (*Q. coccifera* L.). Absalom was caught in an oak (2 Sa. xviii. 9, 10); the suggestion that this was a terebinth is unlikely, since the terebinth is usually a small tree.

n. Oil-tree (Heb. *'eṣ šāmen,* Is. xli. 19)

The narrow-leaved oleaster, *Elaeagnus angustifolia* L., a small tree frequent in Palestine. Like the true olive (*q.v.*), to which it is unrelated, it yields an oil, but it is poor and the fruits are small.

o. Palm-tree (Heb. *tāmār*)

The date palm, *Phoenix dactylifera* L., a tall, slender, unbranched tree with a tuft of leaves 6–9 feet long at its crown. The male and female flowers are borne on separate trees in clusters among the leaves. The palm is frequent in Palestine, and appears, from the numerous references, to have been abundant in biblical times. It often gave its name to the place where it grew, *e.g.* Tamar (Ezk. xlvii. 19, xlviii. 28); Hazezon-tamar (Gn. xiv. 7, *etc.*). The palm typified grace, elegance, and uprightness (Ps. xcii. 12; Je. x. 5), and Tamar was used as a woman's name (2 Sa. xiii. 1). It was also a symbol of victory and rejoicing, and the use of palm leaves ('branches') during Jesus' entry into Jerusalem (Jn. xii. 13) was significant (*cf.* Rev. vii. 9). The form of the palm was used in architectural ornamentation (1 Ki. vi. 29, 32; Ezk. xl. 31).

p. Pine (see Fir above).

q. Poplar (Heb. *liḇneh*)

Rods of poplar were peeled by Jacob in his deception of Laban (Gn. xxx. 37). This may be the white poplar, *Populus alba* L., a fair-sized tree with the leaves white underneath and with fast-growing shoots. The tree gives a dense shade, and when planted in groves would well suit the pagan rites mentioned in Ho. iv. 13. The phrase in Ho. xiv. 5, 'cast forth his roots as Lebanon' (AV) is rendered 'strike root as the poplar' in Moffatt and RSV. The 'mulberry trees' (*q.v.*) of AV are probably *Populus euphratica* Oliv., as also the 'willows of the brook' (Lv. xxiii. 40) and the 'willows' on which the Hebrews hung their harps (Ps. cxxxvii. 2).

r. Sycamine (Gk. *sykaminos,* Lk. xvii. 6)

The black mulberry (*Morus nigra* L.), a small, sturdy tree with blood-red, edible fruits, cultivated in Palestine. Mulberry is the food of the silkworm, and silk was used in Palestine at least from the time of Ezekiel (Ezk. xvi. 10, 13).

s. Sycomore (Heb. *šiqmâ,* Gk. *sykomōraia*)

The sycomore-fig (sycamore, RSV), *Ficus sycomorus* L., a sturdy tree 30–40 feet high, with a short trunk, widely spreading branches, and evergreen leaves. It was, and still is, abundant in Egypt and the lowlands of Palestine (1 Ki. x. 27; 2 Ch. i. 15, ix. 27). The fruits are edible and were sufficiently important for King David to appoint an overseer to look after the olive-trees and sycomore-trees (1 Ch. xxvii. 28) and for the psalmist to regard the destruction of the sycomores by frost as a calamity for the Egyptians comparable with the destruction of their vines (Ps. lxxviii. 47). In Am. vii. 14 the AV translation, 'a gatherer of sycomore fruit', is incorrect, since the Hebrew means a dresser or tender of the fruit. This is the operation of cutting the top of each fig to ensure its ripening. Zacchaeus climbed a sycomore to see Jesus pass (Lk. xix. 4). This fig-tree should not be confused with the European sycamore (*Acer pseudoplatanus* L.) or the North American plane (*Platanus*) also known as sycamore.

t. Tamarisk

AV does not mention this tree but later versions use it in place of the words 'shrubs' (Heb. *śîḥim*) in Gn. xxi. 15, and 'grove' and 'tree' (Heb. *'ēšel*) in Gn. xxi. 33; 1 Sa. xxii. 6, xxxi. 13. It is a stunted bush or gnarled tree of desert regions with very small scale-like leaves and usually pink flowers. Three species of tamarisk (*Tamarix articulata* Vahl, *T. pentandra* Pall., *T. tetragyna* Ehrenb.) occur in the desert areas of S Palestine and Beersheba.

u. Terebinth

AV renders the Heb. word *'ēlâ,* Is. vi. 13 and Ho. iv. 13, as 'teil tree' and 'elm' respectively, but later versions generally agree that the tree referred to is the Palestine terebinth, *Pistacia terebinthus* var. *palaestina* (Boiss.) Post. This is a spreading tree, usually less than 25 feet high, which occurs very frequently in warm, dry, and hilly places in the Palestine area.

v. Thyine-wood (Gk. *thyinos,* Rev. xviii. 12)

Apparently wood from the sanderac-tree, *Tetraclinis articulata* (Vahl) Masters, a small coniferous tree native to N Africa. The wood is dark, hard, and fragrant, and was valued by the Greeks and Romans for use in cabinet-making. Another name for it is citron wood (botanically unrelated to *Citrus*), and some versions use that name here; others have identified it with wood from the almug-tree (*q.v.* above).

w. Willow (Heb. *'ᵃrāḇîm, ṣapṣāpâ*)

Species of *Salix* (*S. acmophylla* Boiss., *S. alba* L., *S. fragilis* L., *S. subserrata* Willd.) are commonly found beside streams in Palestine, and in the biblical references are usually linked with their habitat (Jb. xl. 22; Is. xv. 7, xliv. 4; Ezk. xvii. 5). The Palestinian willows are shrubs or small trees often forming thickets about water. The 'willows of the brook' (Lv. xxiii. 40) and the 'willows' of Babylon (Ps. cxxxvii. 2) are now usually regarded as being a species of poplar (*q.v.* above) and are certainly not the Chinese weeping 'illows with which they have been erroneously lentified. The 'green withs' that were used by)elilah to bind Samson would be twigs of willow.

BIBLIOGRAPHY. H. N. and A. L. Moldenke, *'lants of the Bible*, 1952; W. Walker, *All the lants of the Bible*, 1958. F.N.H.

'RESPASS-OFFERING. See SACRIFICE AND)FFERING (Old Testament), IV*d* (iv).

'RIAL OF JESUS. The arrest of our Lord in ıe garden is followed, in the Synoptic tradition, y His removal to a meeting of the Jewish leaders Mk. xiv. 53). Jn. xviii. 12, 13 preserves an ıdependent account of a preliminary examina- on before Annas, the father-in-law of the high riest Caiaphas. There follows an interrogation oncerning His disciples and His teaching, which inconclusive because Jesus refuses to answer irect questions put by the high priest (Jn. xviii. 9). He is abused (Jn. xviii. 22), and sent as a risoner to Caiaphas (Jn. xviii. 24).

The reference to 'the high priest' in Jn. xviii. 9 has raised a difficulty. If the Lord is ques- oned by Caiaphas in xviii. 19, why does Annas ɜmit Him to the same person in xviii. 24? It is ɜmpting to see in this preliminary investigation ıe first of the two Jewish 'trials' which are escribed in Mark. 'The high priest' in Jn. xviii. 9 will then be Caiaphas, but the enquiry will be f an informal character. Its chronological lacing will be the evening of the arrest. Jn. xviii. 4, which records the official appearance before 'aiaphas and the full Sanhedrin, will be dated the ıllowing morning (*cf.* Jn. xviii. 28) and be arallel with the consultation of Mk. xv. 1.

John, however, makes no mention of the issues hich are so prominent in the Synoptic report of ıe first 'trial': the question of Jesus' Messiahship ıd the accusation of blasphemy.

Mk. xiv. 53–65 describes an appearance of the risoner before an assembly of 'all the chief riests and the elders and the scribes' (Mk. xiv. 3), under the presidency of the high priest. The ravamen of the charge is the witnesses' state- ıent that Jesus had prophesied the destruction the Jerusalem sanctuary (*cf.* Mk. xiii. 2; Acts . 13, 14) and the establishment of a new Temple. he claim to be the builder of a new Temple ɜems to be the equivalent to the claim to lessiahship, according to contemporary Jewish ɔpectation. But it was the new Temple of His ɔdy, the Church (Jn. ii. 19; 1 Cor. iii. 16; Eph. 21), that He had in view.

The incriminating challenge of the high priest, .rt thou the Christ, the Son of the Blessed?' ew from Him the reply, 'You said that I am', ɔcording to important MS evidence of Mk. xiv. 2. Further, His use of the title 'the Son of man' ıd His quotation of Ps. cx. 1 and Dn. vii. 13 e an unmistakable claim to His unique status ıd destiny, which Caiaphas was quick to grasp ıd interpret as overt blasphemy. 'It was not asphemy to claim to be the Messiah, but to eak with assurance of sharing the throne of God and of the fulfilment of Daniel's vision in himself and his community was blasphemy in- deed' (Vincent Taylor).

The symbolic action of the high priest's tearing of his clothes, as laid down in the Mishnah, is the prelude to the verdict, 'guilty of death' (Mk. xiv. 64), and the horseplay of the officers (xiv. 65).

A second meeting of the Sanhedrin the follow- ing morning was necessary if, with Vincent Tay- lor, we take Mk. xiv. 64 to record a condemna- tion of Jesus as deserving of death but not the judicial verdict which was required to be passed by 'the whole council' (xv. 1). The Prisoner is then led away to the Roman governor Pilate for the sentence of death to be pronounced. Whether the Jewish council had the power to pronounce and carry out the death sentence on religious grounds (as Juster and Lietzmann believe) or not (so Jn. xviii. 31: see Barrett's full note) is a com- plicated question. There is evidence for the view that the Jewish leaders had the power to carry out death sentences at this time. For example, in the Mishnah the tractate *Sanhedrin* gives a variety of regulations for the different types of execution. The warning inscription on Herod's Temple, promising death to any foreigner who is caught inside the barrier and fence around the sanctuary, does not read like an idle threat. Stephen is put to death following a session of the Jewish San- hedrin. These pieces of evidence seem hardly to harmonize with the admission of Jn. xviii. 31: 'It is not lawful for us to put any man to death'. E. C. Hoskyns in his commentary (pp. 616 f.) sees in the use of the verb 'put to death' (*apok- teinai*) a veiled and subtle reference to death by crucifixion as distinct from the customary method of capital punishment for blasphemy, *viz.* stoning. The Jewish admission, then, that they cannot carry out a judicial sentence by crucifixion is recorded by the evangelist who means his readers to see in it (verse 32) the way in which it fulfilled unconsciously yet provi- dentially God's age-old plan adumbrated in such verses as Dt. xxi. 23; Ex. xii. 46; Nu. ix. 12; *cf.* Jn. xix. 36. See G. D. Kilpatrick's brochure, *The Trial of Jesus*, 1953; and T. A. Burkill in *VC*, X, 1956, and XII, 1958.

Before Pilate the allegation turns on Jesus' claim to kingship (Mk. xv. 2; Lk. xxiii. 2) which the Jews would wish Pilate to construe in a political sense. Thus the main charge preferred is one of *majestas* or treason against the Roman imperial authority. See Jn. xix. 12. Pilate, how- ever, from the first, is suspicious of these charges and sees through the accusers' motives (Mk. xv. 4, 10). He tries to extricate himself in three separate ways from the task of sentencing Jesus to death. He tries to pass the responsibility to Herod (Lk. xxiii. 7 ff.); then to offer to punish Jesus by flogging and release Him (Lk. xxiii. 16, 22); finally to release Jesus as an act of clemency at the feast (Mk. xv. 6; Jn. xviii. 39). All these expedients fail. Herod sends Him back; the fickle and disappointed crowd will not be con- tent with any punishment less than the death sentence (Lk. xxiii. 18, 23); and Jesus Barabbas, a condemned murderer, is preferred to Jesus the Christ. And, in spite of the repeatedly confessed innocence of the Prisoner (Lk. xxiii. 14, 15, 22), He is sentenced to the death of the cross by the judgment of the procurator (Mk. xv. 15), and as the Lord Himself had foreseen (Jn. xii. 33, xviii. 32).

BIBLIOGRAPHY. J. Blinzler, *The Trial of Jesus*, 1960; P. Winter, *On the Trial of Jesus*, 1961.

R.P.M.

TRIBES OF ISRAEL. When the Israelites entered Canaan they entered as twelve tribes, and portions of the land were assigned to each of the twelve (*cf.* Jos. xiii. 1 ff., and see map 4). These twelve tribes were descended from the twelve sons of Jacob who had gathered themselves about their father and heard his prophecies uttered concerning them and their future (Gn. xlix).

According to certain modern theories the biblical picture of the origin of the tribes cannot be accepted. The Bible states that the entire nation was in Egypt, but some of these theories hold that not all of the tribes had been in Egypt. Basic to these theories is the idea that there was a dualism or separation between the Leah and the Rachel tribes, and that the Leah tribes had settled in the cultivated land earlier than had the tribes descended from Rachel. It is sometimes held that the cult of Yahweh was brought into the land by the Joseph tribes, and then adopted by the Leah tribes. In the worship of Yahweh there arose a religious amphictyony, somewhat akin to the amphictyonies of the old Greek states. It was thus the worship or cult of Yahweh which bound the tribes together.

It is clear that such modern theories as that just outlined fly in the face of express statements of Scripture, and presuppose that much of what the Bible has to say must be rejected. This rejection is often based upon a reconstruction of the authorship and contents of the biblical documents that seriously modifies or even reverses the picture of Israel's history which the Bible gives.

Moses had already made a division between tribes to inhabit the east and those to inhabit the west side of the Jordan river. On the east side portions were allotted to the tribes of Reuben and of Gad, together with the half-tribe of Manasseh. This last was to occupy the territory south of the Sea of Galilee, including the villages of Jair together with Ashtaroth and Edrei. Gad was to occupy the land immediately south of that of Manasseh extending approximately to the northern end of the Dead Sea, and south of this section was the territory of Reuben, which reached as far south as Aroer and the Arnon.

On the west side of the Jordan in Canaan proper the remainder of the tribes were to settle. Their inheritance was to be determined by lot, save that to the tribe of Levi no inheritance was to be given. Eventually the tribes became divided into northern and southern, represented respectively by Ephraim and Judah. The norther kingdom came to be designated by the terr Israel.

In the south territory was allotted to Simeor who appears to have occupied land in the Negel Above him was the allotment of Judah, includin the Judaean hill country and extending as fa north as to include Bethlehem and almost t the city of Jerusalem itself. Immediately above th territory of Judah and extending east to th Jordan was the territory of Benjamin. This sec tion reached to the north only a few miles an only as far west as the edge of the hill country To its west was the small section given to th tribe of Dan.

Above the two tribes of Dan and Benjami was the territory which had been allotted t Ephraim which reached as far north as the rive Kanah and Shechem. Then came the larg section assigned to the half-tribe of Manasseh comprising everything between the Mediter ranean and the Jordan river and extending nort to Megiddo. Above Manasseh was Issachar an Zebulun, and on the sea-coast, reaching nort from Carmel, the territory of Asher.

As time went on the tribe of Judah gained mor and more in significance, for it really embrace Benjamin, and Jerusalem became the capital. I the north the tribal distinctions seemed to becom less important than at first, and the norther kingdom as such became the enemy of Judah The northern tribes, Zebulun and Naphtali, wer first carried into captivity, and then in 722 B Samaria itself fell. Nebuchadrezzar finally cor quered Jerusalem in 587 BC, and the entire natic ceased its existence as such. Tribal distinction became of less and less significance, and prac tically disappeared after the Exile.

BIBLIOGRAPHY. J. Bright, *History of Israe* 1959, pp. 128 ff.

E.J.Y.

TRIBULATION. The English word 'tribulatio occurs four times in the Old Testament an twenty-one times in the New Testament. In th latter we find the clearest light that has eve shone upon the suffering and the sorrow of ma The Greek word, which has in it the idea o pressure, as of a heavy burden on the spirit, *thlipsis*, which is in other New Testament pa sages translated 'affliction', 'trouble', an 'anguish'. The English word is derived from La *tribulum*, the threshing instrument, or harrov by means of which the Roman husbandma separated the corn from the husks. Thoug tribulation may crush and bruise us, it separat our chaff from the wheat, so that we are prepare for the granary of heaven.

'Sorrow is hard to bear and doubt is slow t clear', but the New Testament is the most joyf book in the world because its writers have bee delivered from the doubt that paralyses the sou and they live in the sunshine of the love of Chris They know that their affliction (*thlipsis*) is wor ing out for them the glory that is to be (2 Co iv. 17, 18). They exult in hope of the glory o

God, and they are enabled to exult even in tribulations (*thlipsis*), because they know that tribulation will produce staying power and ripeness of character, so that the hope which was implanted in them at the beginning of their Christian experience is confirmed and intensified; this hope never disappoints, because the love of God has been poured out in its full flood-tide in their hearts (Rom. v. 1–5). That love is eternal and unchangeable, and it guides us, through many tribulations (Acts xiv. 22, RV), through great tribulation (Rev. vii. 14), to the eternal, unfading kingdom. While the tribulation lasts, comfort comes which the comforted ones must pass on to others (2 Cor. i. 3, 4).

The term is occasionally found with eschatological reference, as in Mk. xiii. 19 (Mt. xxiv. 21), echoing Dn. xii. 1; *cf.* 2 Thes. i. 6 ff.; Rev. vii. 14.

A.R.

TRIBUTE. Tribute in the sense of an impost paid by one state to another, as a mark of subjugation, is a common feature of international relationships in the ancient Semitic world. The tributary could be either a hostile state or an ally. Like deportation, its purpose was to weaken a hostile state. Deportation aimed at depleting the man-power; the aim of tribute was probably two-fold: to impoverish the subjugated state and at the same time to increase the conqueror's own revenues and to acquire commodities in short supply in his own country. As an instrument of administration it was one of the simplest ever devised: the subjugated country could be made responsible for the payment of a yearly tribute. Its non-arrival would be taken as a sign of rebellion, and an expedition would then be sent to deal with the recalcitrant. This was probably the explanation of the situation recorded in Gn. xiv.

There are already in Sumerian literature references to tribute, although a specific term does not yet seem to be in use. The scene on the reverse of the 'Standard' of Ur is in all probability a tribute scene, as the carriers are identical in appearance with the enemies depicted on the obverse (Woolley, *Ur Excavations*, II, pp. 266 ff.). In ancient Egypt, too, the payment of tribute is often referred to. For instance, in the inscriptions of the Theban tomb of *Tnn* we read: 'The bringing of imposts from *Rtnw* (Syria, *etc.*), and the deliveries of the northern lands: silver, gold, malachite, precious stones, of the land of the god, from the great ones of all lands, as they came to the good god (*i.e.* the king) to supplicate, and to ask for breath' (*Urkunden des äg. Altertums*, IV, 1007, 8 ff.). The Egyptian kings, however, are not above representing gifts as tribute. Tuthmosis reports having received tribute from the Assyrians, but we know that he made a reciprocal gift of 20 talents of gold to Ashur-nadin-ahi (EA 16, 21).

It is in Assyria that the rôle of tribute assumed its greatest importance. One of the earliest references to tribute is by Shamshi-Adad I in the 18th century BC. It continues to be mentioned down to Neo-Babylonian times. Cyrus claims that all the kings from the Mediterranean to the Persian Gulf brought him tribute.

Fig. 223. Israelites bearing tribute from Jehu, king of Israel, to Shalmaneser III, king of Assyria. It consists of silver, gold, vessels, buckets, a block of antimony, staves, and fruit. From the black obelisk, 841 BC. See also plate VII*a*.

From the Assyrian sources we learn that Israel, too, was compelled to pay tribute. Shalmaneser III (858–824 BC) exacted tribute of Jehu. On one of the panels of the black obelisk, Jehu is shown prostrating himself before the Assyrian king (see fig. 223 and also plate VII*a*). Adad-nirari (810–782) claims that Israel was among a number of states (Tyre, Sidon, Edom, and Philistia) from whom he received tribute (*DOTT*, p. 51). Tiglath-pileser III (745–727) received tribute from Menahem of Israel and from Ahaz (called by him Jehoahaz). He later states that he deposed Pekah, and put Hoshea on the throne (as a puppet king), and received tribute of gold and silver (*DOTT*, pp. 54 ff. and 2 Ki. xv. 17–30, xvi. 7–18). Sargon II (722–705) not only exacted tribute from Israel but deported part of the population of Samaria (2 Ki. xvii. 6, 24–34, xviii. 11). The most detailed list of a tribute payment is that given by Sennacherib (705–681). It consists not only of large quantities of gold and silver but also of rich inlaid furniture and even musicians (*DOTT*, p. 67). Manasseh, king of Judah, is mentioned as a tributary of Esarhaddon (681–669).

There are a number of terms in the Old Testament denoting taxes in general, but none seems to be confined exclusively to the meaning of tribute. *'eškār*, used only twice (Ps. lxxii. 10; Ezk. xxvii. 15), could have the meaning of tribute, at least in the Psalm. *mas* occurs twenty-two times, but seems generally to have the meaning of corvée (*cf.* Ex. i. 11 or 1 Ki. v. 13); in a passage like Esther x it would refer to tribute. *maśśā'* seems on two occasions to mean impost or tax (Ho. viii. 10 and 2 Ch. xvii. 11). *'ōneš* in 2 Ki. xxiii. 33, and possibly also in Pr. xix. 19, denotes tribute, but the verb from the same root can mean to impose a fine (*cf.* Ex. xxi. 22). *meḵes*, translated 'tribute' in the AV in Nu. xxxi. 28, 37–41, was a levy on the spoils of war. *belô* (Aramaic), as it is used of a group in the community, cannot refer to 'tribute' in the strict sense (Ezr. iv. 13, 20, vii. 24). *middâ*, used in both Hebrew and Aramaic contexts (Ezr. iv. 13, 20, vi. 8, vii. 24; Ne. v. 4), may refer to tribute.

That tribute is not given greater prominence in the Old Testament may be due to the fact that Israel, being a small nation, had few opportunities of imposing tribute. The gifts that Hiram, king of Tyre, brought to Solomon were the gifts of an ally and a friend, and it was probably taken for granted that Solomon would reciprocate (1 Ki. v. 10 and *passim*, ix. 11).

See also TEMPLE, MONEY, TREASURE, TREASURY.

BIBLIOGRAPHY. W. J. Martin, *Tribut und Tributleistungen bei den Assyrern*, 1936. W.J.M.

TRINITY. The word Trinity is not found in the Bible, and, though used by Tertullian in the last decade of the 2nd century, it did not find a place formally in the theology of the Church till the 4th century. It is, however, the distinctive and all-comprehensive doctrine of the Christian faith and 'gathers up into the seam of a single grand generalisation with respect to the being and activity of God all the major aspects of Christian truth' (Lowry). Theology seeks to define the subsistence of God by stating that God is one in His essential being, but that the divine essence exists in three modes or forms, each constituting a Person, yet in such a way that the divine essence is wholly in each Person.

I. DERIVATION

a. In the Old Testament

Though the doctrine is not developed in the Old Testament, it is implicit in the divine self-disclosure from the very beginning. But in accordance with the historical character of the divine revelation it is presented at first only in a very rudimentary form. This is found not only in isolated passages but interwoven in the entire organism of the Old Testament revelation. The earliest foreshadowing is contained in the narrative of the creation, where Elohim is seen to create by means of Word and Spirit (Gn. i. 3). Here we are for the first time introduced to the Word put forth as a personal creative power, and to the Spirit as the bringer of life and order to the creation. There is revealed thus early a threefold centre of activity. God as Creator thought out the universe, expressed His thought in a Word, and made His Spirit its animating principle, thus indicating that the universe was not to have a separate existence apart from God or opposed to Him. It is thought that Gn. i. 26 ('And God said, Let us make man in our image and after our likeness') implies that a revelation of the Triune God had been given to man when first created, inasmuch as he was to be given the divine fellowship, but that the consciousness was afterwards lost with the loss of his original righteousness. Both the creative activity of God and His government are at a later stage associated with the Word personified as Wisdom (Pr. viii. 22 ff.; Jb. xxviii. 23–27), and with the Spirit as the Dispenser of all blessings and the source of physical strength, courage, culture, and government (Ex. xxxi. 3; Nu. xi. 25; Jdg. iii. 10).

The threefold source revealed in creation became still more evident in the unfolding of redemption. The revelation of redemption was entrusted to the *mal'aḵ Yahweh*, the Messenger of Yahweh, sometimes referred to as the Angel of the covenant. We do not claim that in every Old Testament passage in which it appears the designation refers to a divine being, for it is clear that in such passages as 2 Sa. xxiv. 16; 1 Ki. xix. 5; 2 Ki. xix. 35, the reference is to a created angel invested with divine authority for the execution of a special mission. In other passages (*e.g.* Gn. xvi. 7, xxiv. 7, xlviii. 16) the Angel of Yahweh not only bears the divine name but has divine dignity and power, dispenses divine deliverance and accepts homage and adoration proper only to God. The Spirit of God is also given prominence in connection with revelation and redemption, and is assigned His office in the equipment of the Messiah for His work (Is. xi. 2, xlii. 1, lxi. 1) and of His people for the response of faith and obedience (Joel ii. 28; Is. xxxii. 15; Ezk. xxxvi. 26, 27). Thus the God who revealed Himself objectively through the Angel-Messenger revealed Himself subjectively in and through the Spirit, the Dispenser of all blessings and gifts within the sphere of redemption. The threefold Aaronic blessing (Nu. vi. 24) must also be noted as perhaps the prototype of the New Testament apostolic blessing.

b. In the inter-testamental period

In this period there was a definite, if vague and shadowy, preparation for the full revelation of the Trinity to be given in the New Testament. The transcendence and remoteness of God in

Jewish thought made men look for a mediator. Philo, under an apprehension of the absolute metaphysical contrast between God and the world, conceived of mediating entities who should mediate between God and the creation. This was recognized by many to be the office of the Messiah, but there was a strong tendency to ascribe the same remoteness and transcendence to the heavenly Messiah. It was felt, however, that when the Messiah should come to earth, the Holy Spirit also, who had left the prophetic scene since Malachi, would return in prophetic power. Though three Persons were vaguely thought of, the subject of their relationship was scarcely touched on and was left in complete obscurity.

c. In the New Testament

Preparatory to the advent of Christ, the Holy Spirit came into the consciousness of God-fearing men in a degree that was not known since the close of Malachi's ministry. John the Baptist, more especially, was conscious of the presence and calling of the Spirit, and it is probable that his preaching had a trinitarian reference: he called for repentance towards God, faith in the coming Messiah, and spoke of a baptism of the Holy Spirit, of which his baptism with water was a symbol. The agency of the Spirit in the incarnation is disclosed to Mary (Lk. i. 35), together with the intimation that the Son born of her would be called 'the Son of the Highest', and that 'the Lord God (would) give unto him the throne of his father David'. Thus the Father and the Spirit were disclosed as operating in the incarnation of the Son. At the baptism in the Jordan the three Persons can be distinguished: the Son being baptized, the Father speaking from heaven, and the Spirit descending in the objective symbol of a dove. Jesus, having thus received the witness of the Father and the Spirit, received authority to baptize with the Holy Spirit. John the Baptist would seem to have recognized very early that the Holy Spirit would come from the Messiah, and not merely with Him. The third Person was thus the Spirit of God and the Spirit of Christ.

In His public ministry, as well as in His private teaching of the Twelve, Jesus constantly directed attention to the Father as the One who sent Him on His mission and from whom He derived His authority (Jn. v. 19, 20). In His disputation with the Jews He claimed that His own Sonship was not simply from David, but from a source that made Him David's Lord, and that it had been so at the very time when David uttered the words (Mt. xxii. 43). This would indicate both His deity and pre-existence. Christ bore ever clearer testimony to the Person and office of the Spirit as His own ministry was drawing to a close (Jn. xv, xvi), and He designates Him as both the Spirit from the Father and the Spirit from Himself (Jn. xv. 26). This is the basis of Christian belief in the 'double procession' of the Spirit. The fellowship of the Father and the Spirit appears in the work of redemption as revealed by Christ, the Father sending the Son to undertake the work, and the Father and the Son sending the Spirit to apply the salvation which Christ wrought. It thus became evident why the God of the covenant was revealed as triune, since salvation was seen to rest upon each of the Persons in the Godhead. Christ's trinitarian teaching received its most clear and concise expression in the baptismal formula: baptizing into 'the name of the Father, and of the Son, and of the Holy Ghost' (Mt. xxviii. 19). Baptizing 'into the name' is a Hebrew form of expression, rather than a Greek, and it carries with it what would seem a complete break with Judaism in including under a singular name not only the Father, but the Son and the Holy Ghost.

The outpouring of the Spirit at Pentecost brought the personality of the Holy Spirit into greater prominence and at the same time shed new light from the Spirit upon the Son. The apostolic conception of the Holy Ghost and of His relation to the Father and the Son is clear from Acts. Peter, in explaining the phenomenon of Pentecost, represents it as the activity of the Trinity. 'This Jesus . . . being by the right hand of God exalted, and having received of the Father the promise of the Holy Ghost, he hath shed forth this, which ye now see and hear' (Acts ii. 32, 33). It is not too much to say that the apostolic Church was built upon faith in the Father, the Son, and the Holy Ghost. In the Epistles of Paul, Peter, John, James, and Jude, as well as in the Epistle to the Hebrews, redemption is uniformly traced to the threefold Source, and each Person appears as the object of worship and adoration. The apostolic benediction, 'The grace of the Lord Jesus Christ, and the love of God, and the communion of the Holy Ghost, be with you all' (2 Cor. xiii. 14), not only sums up the apostolic teaching, but it interprets the deeper meaning of the Trinity in Christian experience, the saving grace of the Son as that which gives access to the love of the Father and the communion of the Spirit.

II. FORMULATION

As already indicated, Scripture does not give us a fully formulated doctrine of the Trinity, but it contains all the elements out of which theology has constructed the doctrine. The teaching of Christ bears testimony to the true personality of each of the distinctions within the Godhead and also sheds light upon the relations existing between the three Persons. It was left to theology to formulate from this a doctrine of the Trinity. The necessity to formulate the doctrine was thrust upon the Church by forces from without, and it was, in particular, its faith in the deity of Christ, and the necessity to defend it, that first compelled the Church to face the duty of formulating a full doctrine of the Trinity for its rule of faith. Irenaeus and Origen share with Tertullian the responsibility for the formulation of the doctrine which is still, in the main, that of the Church catholic. Under the leadership of Athanasius the doctrine was proclaimed as the faith of the

Church at the Council of Nicea (AD 325), and at the hands of Augustine a century later it received a formulation, enshrined in the so-called Athanasian Creed, that is accepted by Trinitarian churches to this day. After it had received a further elucidation at the hands of John Calvin (for which, see B. B. Warfield, *Calvin and Augustine*, 1956, pp. 189–284) it passed into the body of the Reformed faith.

In most formularies the doctrine is stated by saying that God is One in His essential being, but that in this being there are three Persons, yet so as not to form separate and distinct individuals. They are three modes or forms in which the divine essence exists. 'Person' is, however, an imperfect expression of the truth inasmuch as the term denotes to us a separate rational and moral individual. But in the being of God there are not three individuals, but only three personal self-distinctions within the one divine essence. Then again, personality in man implies independence of will, actions, and feelings, leading to behaviour peculiar to the person. This cannot be thought of in connection with the Trinity: each Person is self-conscious and self-directing, yet never acting independently or in opposition. When we say that God is a Unity we mean that, though God is in Himself a threefold centre of life, His life is not split into three. He is one in essence, in personality, and in will. When we say that God is a Trinity in Unity we mean that there is unity in diversity, and that diversity manifests itself in Persons, in characteristics, and in operations. Moreover, the subsistence and operations of the three Persons are marked by a certain order, involving a certain subordination in relation, though not in nature. The Father as the fount of deity is First: He is said to originate. The Son, eternally begotten of the Father, is Second: He is said to reveal. The Spirit, eternally proceeding from the Father and the Son, is Third: He is said to execute. While this does not suggest priority in time or in dignity, since all three Persons are divine and eternal, it does suggest an order of precedence in operation and revelation. Thus we can say that creation is from the Father, through the Son, by the Holy Spirit.

III. IMPLICATIONS OF THE DOCTRINE

The implications of the doctrine are vitally important not only for theology but for Christian experience and life. As to the Godhead, it reveals that God is the truly living One. It removes Him far from any conception of stagnation or mere passivity. God in Trinity is fullness of life, living in eternal relationships, and in never-ceasing fellowship. This again makes intelligible the revelation and self-communication of God. As God can, in an absolute sense, communicate Himself inwards in an act of self-revelation among the three Persons, so He is able, in a relative sense, to impart Himself outwards in revelation and communication to His creation. As to the universe, the doctrine of the Trinity gives both unity and diversity, making the universe into a cosmos. Since all things hang on the good will of God, there can be no dualism at the heart of the universe. But there is room for boundless variety. If there is in God a diversity of life, may it not be reflected in His universe in the widely diversified forms in which life manifests itself? God's life can find many manifestations and this gives complexity and many-sidedness to the universe He has planned. Moreover, the fellowship that constitutes the Trinity is the basis of fellowship within the human family, within the home, within society, and more especially within the Church, where the Holy Spirit is the Agent and Medium of fellowship.

BIBLIOGRAPHY. J. R. Illingworth, *The Doctrine of the Trinity*, 1909; C. W. Lowry, *The Trinity and Christian Devotion*, 1946; A. E. Garvie, *The Christian Doctrine of the Godhead*, 1925; H. Bavinck, *The Doctrine of God*, 1951, pp. 255–334; B. B. Warfield in *ISBE* (*s.v.* 'Trinity'); R. S. Franks, *The Doctrine of the Trinity*, 1953; K. Barth, *Church Dogmatics*, E.T., 1936, I, pp. 339 ff.

R.A.F.

TROAS. Mentioned in Acts xvi. 8–11, xx. 5–12; 2 Cor. ii. 12. Troas was founded near the site of the old city of Troy by the successors of Alexander the Great, and named after him Alexandria Troas. It was made a Roman colony by Augustus. According to Suetonius, Julius Caesar toyed with the idea of transferring the government there from Rome, since, according to tradition, Aeneas the Trojan founded Rome, and his son Iulus was the ancestor of the Julian family. It was the main port of NW Asia Minor, and the port for travellers from Asia to Macedonia. The church at Troas is twice referred to by Ignatius. The word 'Troas' can refer either to the city or to the district round about it. D.R.H.

TROGYLLIUM (or Trogyllia). A promontory of the west coast of Asia Minor between Ephesus and Miletus, and reaching to within a mile of Samos. Paul's delay there (Acts xx. 15) was no doubt due to the difficulty of navigating a strait in darkness. The Alexandrian text omits reference to this delay at Trogyllium, but is almost certainly at fault here. K.L.McK.

TROPHIMUS. An Ephesian Christian who evidently accompanied Paul to Europe after the Ephesian riot, later re-crossing and awaiting Paul at Troas for the journey to Jerusalem—doubtless as one of the delegates of the Asian churches with the collection (Acts xx. 1–5; *cf.* 1 Cor. xvi. 1–4). In Jerusalem, however, Jewish pilgrims from Asia recognized him in Paul's company and afterwards, finding Paul in the Temple with four others, jumped to the false conclusion that he had introduced Trophimus there (Acts xxi. 27 ff.). Trespass beyond the Court of the Gentiles would for Trophimus be to risk the death penalty. The incident issued in a riot, and Paul's arrest.

2 Tim. iv. 20 states that Paul left Trophim[us]

sick at Miletus. This was near Trophimus' own city; but if Timothy was himself in the Ephesus area it may seem strange that he needed this information. The circumstances and intention of the verse are, however, uncertain: it may be connected with greetings, like the immediate context, or perhaps Paul's mind has reverted to the diminution of his band of helpers (*cf.* verses 10–12). P. N. Harrison (*Problem of the Pastoral Epistles*, 1921, pp. 118 ff.) argues that Paul was *en route* for Troas (*cf.* 2 Cor. ii. 12) when he left Trophimus; G. S. Duncan (*St. Paul's Ephesian Ministry*, 1929, pp. 191 ff.) that he was returning from Corinth to Asia (*cf.* 2 Cor. i. 8). Preferable to these intricate hypotheses is the view that Paul was heading westward, destined for his second Roman imprisonment. A.F.W.

TRUMPET. See MUSIC AND MUSICAL INSTRUMENTS.

TRUMPETS, FEAST OF. 'Day of blowing the trumpets' (*yôm t^erû'â*, Nu. xxix. 1) or 'memorial of blowing of trumpets' (Lv. xxiii. 24). The seventh month in the Jewish calendar, *Tišri*, was the beginning of the civil year. The first day of the month was to be 'a day of solemn rest' (RSV), in which 'no servile work' was to be done. The LXX of Nu. xxix. 1 renders the phrase *yôm t^erû'â* by *hēmera sēmasias*, 'a day of signalling', but the Mishnah and traditional Jewish practice have understood by this the use of the *šôpār*, usually, though not always, made of ram's horn. Tradition is not clear as to what precisely was meant by the blowing, which was accompanied by the reading of relevant passages of Scripture (H. G. Friedmann, *JQR*, I, 1888, pp. 62 ff.). T.H.J.

TRUTH. Truth, like its relation knowledge (*q.v.*), is used in the Old Testament in two senses: (1) the intellectual, of facts which may be ascertained to be true or false (Dt. xvii. 4; 1 Ki. x. 6); (2) far more commonly, the existential and moral, of truth as the attribute of a person. Joseph's brothers are detained in prison 'that your words may be proved, whether there be any truth in you' (Gn. xlii. 16), *i.e.* whether they are dependable, consistent, of reliable character. It is significant that of the Hebrew words translated 'truth' (*'^emet*, *'^emûnâ*), the latter is sometimes rendered by the EVV as 'faithfulness' (Dt. xxxii. 4, RSV; Ho. ii. 20) (see also AMEN). The Old Testament thinks much more of the basis of truth in a reliable person than of the mere facts of the case. This reliability is basically an attribute of God (Ps. xxxi. 5; Je. x. 10), whose truth 'reacheth unto the clouds' (Ps. cviii. 4), and who 'keepeth truth for ever' (Ps. cxlvi. 6). The God of the Bible is thus very far removed from the capricious pagan deities. He is true, *i.e.* consistent, both in His loving care for His children (Gn. xxxii. 9 f.) and in His implacable hostility against sin (Ps. liv. 5).

It is no far cry from truth as an attribute of God Himself to one of His activity. So He judges truly (Ps. xcvi. 13), and sends truth forth (Ps. lvii. 3). His word is true in the sense that it is permanently valid. 'As Thou art truth, so is Thy word truth, for it is written "Thy word, O God, stands fast in heaven" (Ps. cxix. 89)' (Exodus Rabbah on xxix. 1, cited *TWNT*, *s.v.* 'Truth'). Truth is demanded of man as his response to God in obedience to the law (Ps. cxix. 151) and in his inmost nature (Ps. li. 6), and is the bedrock of all human relationships (Ex. xx. 16; Dt. v. 20).

In Greek literature, however, the words for truth (*alētheia*, *alēthēs*, *alēthinos*) do not have the same personal and moral connotation. Rather, truth is intellectual. It is 'the *complete* or *real* state of affairs . . . As in forensic language *alētheia* is the state of affairs to be proved, over against the various assertions of the parties, so in the historians it is the historical state of affairs over against myth, and in the philosophers that which really *is*, in the absolute sense' (R. Bultmann, *TWNT*, quoted by C. H. Dodd, *The Interpretation of the Fourth Gospel*, 1953, p. 171).

In the New Testament these Greek words occur commonly, and bring with them both their Old Testament and their classical and Hellenistic Greek meanings, so that it is often an extremely delicate matter to decide which nuance predominates. It is possible, however, to distinguish three broad senses in which the words are used, even though these may overlap.

1. Dependability, truthfulness, uprightness of character (the Hebrew sense predominating). This applies to God (Rom. iii. 7, xv. 8) and to men (2 Cor. vii. 14; Eph. v. 9) alike. The use of the actual word 'truth' in this sense is not common, but the thought of a God who can be trusted to keep His word is implicit throughout the New Testament.

2. Truth in the absolute sense of that which is real and complete as opposed to what is false and wanting (Mk. v. 33; Eph. iv. 25). The Christian faith in particular is the truth (Gal. ii. 5; Eph. i. 13). Jesus claimed that He was truth personified (Jn. xiv. 6; *cf.* Eph. iv. 21). He mediates the truth (Jn. i. 17) and the Holy Spirit leads men into it (Jn. xvi. 13; *cf.* xiv. 17; 1 Jn. iv. 6), so that Jesus' disciples know it (Jn. viii. 32; 2 Jn. 1), do it (Jn. iii. 21), abide in it (Jn. viii. 44), and their new birth as God's children rests upon it (Jas. i. 18). This truth is more than a credal formula, it is God's active word which must be obeyed (Rom. ii. 8; Gal. v. 7).

3. The adjective *alēthinos* especially sometimes carries the 'Platonic' sense of something real as opposed to mere appearance or copy. The Christ is thus a minister of the true tabernacle (Heb. viii. 2) in contrast with the shadows of the levitical ritual (Heb. viii. 4 f.). In clear allusion to the words of institution of the Lord's Supper, Jesus declares that He is the true bread (Jn. vi. 32, 35) and the true vine (Jn. xv. 1), *i.e.* that He is the eternal reality symbolized by the bread and wine. Similarly, the true worshippers (Jn. iv. 23) are not so much sincere as real. Their worship is a real approach to God who is spirit, in contrast

to the ritual which restricts God to Jerusalem or Mt. Gerizim (Jn. iv. 21), and which can at best symbolize and at worst distort Him.

BIBLIOGRAPHY. R. Bultmann in *TWNT*; C. H. Dodd, *The Interpretation of the Fourth Gospel*, 1953, pp. 139 f., 170–178; D. J. Theron, '*Aletheia* in the Pauline Corpus', *EQ*, XXVI, 1954, pp. 3–18. F.H.P.

TRYPHENA AND TRYPHOSA. Two women, probably—from the manner of mentioning them and the similarity of their names—sisters, greeted in Rom. xvi. 12. Like other women addressed there (Mary, verse 6; Persis, verse 12), they were noted for 'labour'—the recurrence of this term may indicate some regular form of service (*cf.* W. Sanday and A. C. Headlam, *Romans*, *ICC*, p. xxxv). The names ('Delicate' and 'Dainty') were widely used, including in Rome, where Lightfoot (*Philippians*, pp. 175 f.) pointed to several examples in 'Caesar's household' in Paul's time. Another contemporary Tryphena was the daughter of Polemon I of Pontus, mother of three kings, who appears as the sympathetic queen in the *Acts of Paul and Thecla*. A.F.W.

TUBAL-CAIN. The son of Lamech by Zillah (Gn. iv. 22) and half-brother of Jabal and Jubal (*qq.v.*). In the words of AV he was 'an instructer of every artificer in brass and iron', but this could be as well translated 'a hammerer of every cutting tool of copper or iron', and could mean either that he was a metal-smith, the most commonly held view, or that he discovered the possibilities of cold forging native copper and meteoric iron, a practice attested archaeologically from prehistoric times. T.C.M.

TURTLE DOVE. See BIRDS OF THE BIBLE.

TWELVE. See NUMBER.

TWIN BROTHERS. See CASTOR AND POLLUX.

TYCHICUS. An Asian—the 'Western' Text says an Ephesian—who accompanied Paul to Jerusalem, doubtless as a delegate of his church with the collection (Acts xx. 4; *cf.* 1 Cor. xvi. 1–4). He was the apostle's personal representative—probably (taking 'sent' as an epistolary aorist) the bearer of the letters—to the Colossians (Col. iv. 7-9) and Ephesians (Eph. vi. 21, 22), and, should Ephesians (*q.v.*) be a circular letter, to other Asian churches as well. Paul seems to have considered him a possible relief for Titus in Crete (Tit. iii. 12), and to have sent him to Ephesus (bearing 2 Timothy?) just when Timothy was needed elsewhere (2 Tim. iv. 12). These commissions reflect that trustworthiness which Paul commends (Eph. vi. 21; Col. iv. 7). His designation as a 'minister' in these contexts probably relates to service to the Church, possibly to service to Paul, most improbably to the status of deacon (*q.v.*). Some who have questioned the authenticity of Ephesians have connected Tychicus with its origin (*cf.* W. L. Knox, *St. Paul and the Church of the Gentiles*, 1939, p. 203; C. L. Mitton, *Epistle to the Ephesians*, 1950, p. 268). A.F.W.

TYRANNUS. There is no known reference to Tyrannus apart from Acts xix. 9, in which Paul at Ephesus is said to have reasoned daily in the school of Tyrannus. The word 'school' (*q.v.*) means a group or place where lectures are given and discussed. It is not known whether Tyrannus was the founder of the school or its owner at the time of Paul's stay. The word translated 'one' in AV, which would support the latter view, is not in the best MSS. D.R.H.

TYRE, TYRUS. The principal seaport on the Phoenician coast, about 25 miles south of Sidon and 35 north of Carmel, Tyre (Heb. *Ṣôr*; Assyr. *Ṣur(r)u*; Egyp. *Ḏaru*; Gk. *Tyros*) comprised two harbours. One lay on an island, the other 'Old' port on the mainland may be the Uššu of Assyrian inscriptions. The city, which was watered by the river Litani, dominated the surrounding plain, in the north of which lay Sarepta (see ZAREPHATH).

I. HISTORY

According to Herodotus (ii. 44), Tyre was founded *c.* 2700 BC, though some see in its omission from the list of cities conquered by Tuthmosis III *c.* 1485 the implication that it had not yet been founded as a colony of Sidon. It is likely, however, that it took an early and active part in the sea-trade in trade and luxuries with Egypt which led to the Egyptian campaigns to control the Phoenician coast. During the Amarna period the local ruler of Tyre, Abimilki, remained loyal, writing to Amenophis III of the defection of surrounding towns and requesting aid against the Amorite Aziru and king of Sidon. When the Philistines plundered Sidon (*c.* 1200 BC) many of its inhabitants fled to Tyre, which now became the 'daughter of Sidon' (Is. xxiii. 12, RSV), the principal Phoenician port. By the late second millennium BC it was counted as a strongly defended city on the border of the land allocated to Asher (Jos. xix. 29), and this reputation continued (2 Sa. xxiv. 7; AV 'strong hold').

With the decline of Egypt Tyre was independent, its rulers dominating most of the Phoenician coastal cities, including the Lebanon hinterland. Hiram I was a friend of David and supplied materials for building the royal palace at Jerusalem (2 Sa. v. 11; 1 Ki. v. 1; 1 Ch. xiv. 1), a policy he continued during the reign of Solomon, when he sent wood and stone for the construction of the Temple (1 Ki. v. 1–12; 2 Ch. ii. 3–16) in return for food supplies and territorial advantages (1 Ki. ix. 10–14). Tyrians, including a bronze-caster also named Hiram, assisted in Solomon's projects (1 Ki. vii. 13, 14). During his reign Hiram I linked the mainland port with the island by an artificial causeway and built a temple dedicated to the deities Melqart and starte. As part of his policy of colonial expansion ıd trade he assisted Solomon's development of e Red Sea port of Ezion-geber for southern ›yages (1 Ki. ix. 27), his ships reaching distant aces (1 Ki. ix. 28; see OPHIR). From this time, 'ten called 'the golden age of Tyre', the people ›came the merchant princes of the E Mediter- .nean (Is. xxiii. 8), and were henceforth noted ›r their seafaring prowess (Ezk. xxvi. 17, ‹vii. 32). The primary trade was in their own anufactured glass (*q.v.*) and the special scarlet- ırple dyes, called 'Tyrian', made from the local *urex* (see ARTS AND CRAFTS, PHOENICIA).

The Canon of Ptolemy is still a primary source ›r the king list, though, despite correlations with ssyrian and Hebrew history, there remains a vergence of about ten years in the date of ıe earlier rulers. Thus Hiram I is dated *c.* 979– 45 BC (see CHRONOLOGY OF THE OLD TESTA- ENT; *cf.* Albright, *c.* 969–936 BC). His successor aal-(m)azzar I (= Balbazeros) was followed by bd-Ashtart, who was murdered by his brothers, ıe eldest of whom, Methus-Astartus, usurped ıe throne. Phelles, who succeeded Astharymus 897 BC, was overthrown by the high priest thbaal (Ithobal), whose daughter Jezebel was arried to Ahab of Israel to confirm the alliance ade between their countries (1 Ki. xvi. 31). thbaal was also a contemporary of Ben-hadad I. is success against Phelles may have been ›nnected with the invasion of Ashurnasirpal of Assyria, who took a heavy tribute from yre.

The port suffered another blow in 841 BC, hen, in his eighteenth regnal year, Shalmaneser I of Assyria received tribute from *Ba'alimanzar* the same time as Jehu paid him homage at the ahr-el-Kelb (*Sumer*, VII, 1951, 3–21). Baalezer was followed by Metten I (*c.* 829–821) and by ygmalion (Pu'm-yaton), in whose seventh year 25 BC; others 815 BC) Carthage was founded om Tyre.

Assyrian pressure on Phoenicia continued, and yre paid tribute to Adad-nirari III of Assyria in 03 BC and its king *Hirammu* (Hiram II) sent fts to Tiglath-pileser III, who claims that his bshakeh (*q.v.*) took 150 talents of gold from letenna (Metten II), the next king of Tyre (*i.e.* 730 BC). By such means the city retained a large easure of autonomy. According to Josephus, ıalmaneser V of Assyria (whose own records e wanting) laid siege to Tyre in 724, and the ty fell with Samaria into the hands of Sargon II 722 BC. Local Assyrian officials supervised the turn of taxes in kind to Nineveh, and con- derable unrest was fomented from Egypt, to hom the Tyrians turned for help. This led to ›nunciation of Tyre by the Hebrew prophets ho followed Isaiah, by Amos for handing over ebrew prisoners to Edom (i. 9) and by Joel i. 5, 6) for their selling them as slaves to the reeks. Tyre came under the domination of don, and when Sennacherib approached its ıler Luli (Elulaeus) fled and died in exile. This saved the city from assault, for the Assyrians installed their nominee Tuba'alu (Ethbaal III) in 701 BC.

Esarhaddon, who was keeping the route open to attack Egypt, executed Abdi-milkitti of Sidon (*c.* 677 BC) and set Ba'ali (I) on the throne, binding him by treaty to Assyria. However, Tyre, insti- gated by Tirhakah of Egypt, rebelled and Esar- haddon besieged the port, which did not, how- ever, fall until 664 BC to Ashurbanipal, who made Azi-Baal king, taking his sisters and many officials as hostages to Nineveh.

With the decline of Assyria at the end of the reign of Ashurbanipal (*c.* 636–627 BC), Tyre re- gained her autonomy and much of her former sea-trade. Nevertheless, Jeremiah prophesied Tyre's subjection to the Babylonians (xxv. 22, xxvii. 1–11), as did Ezekiel later (xxvi. 1–xxviii. 19, xxix. 18–20) and Zechariah (ix. 2 ff.). Nebu- chadrezzar II besieged Tyre for thirteen years *c.* 587–574 BC (Jos., *Life* i. 21; *JBL*, LI, 1932, pp. 94 ff.), but no contemporary record of this remains (*cf.* Ezk. xxix. 18–20). The city (under Ba'ali II) eventually recognized Babylonian suzerainty, and a number of Babylonian con- tracts confirm this and give the names of the local Babylonian officials. For a decade the city was ruled by 'judges' (*špṭ*).

In 332 BC Alexander the Great laid siege to the island port for seven months and captured it only by building a mole to the island fortress. Despite heavy losses, the port soon recovered under Seleucid patronage. Herod I rebuilt the main temple, which would have been standing when our Lord visited the district bordering Tyre and Sidon (Mt. xv. 21–28; Mk. vii. 24–31). People of Tyre heard Him speak (Mk. iii. 8; Lk. vi. 17), and He cited Tyre as a heathen city which would bear less responsibility than those Galilaean towns which constantly witnessed His ministry (Mt. xi. 21, 22; Lk. x. 13, 14). Christians were active in Tyre in the 1st century (Acts xxi. 3–6), and there the scholar Origen was buried (AD 254).

II. ARCHAEOLOGY

The main extant ruins date from the fall of the Crusader city in AD 1291, but excavations from 1921 (*Syria*, VI, 1922), and from 1937 in the harbour, have traced some of the earlier founda- tions. However, the many coins minted in Tyre from the 5th century BC onwards, found at many sites throughout the ancient Near East and Mediterranean, attest its greatness.

The 'ladder of Tyre' (Jos., *BJ* ii. 10. 2), which marked the division between Phoenicia and Palestine proper (1 Macc. xi. 59), is identified with the rocky promontory at Ras en-Naqara or Ras el-'Abyad.

BIBLIOGRAPHY. W. F. Albright, 'The New Assyro-Tyrian Synchronism and the Chronology of Tyre' in *Mélanges Isidore Lévy*, 1955, pp. 1–9; A. Poidebard and L. Cayeux, *Un grand Port disparu, Tyr*, 1939; and references to Tyre in ancient texts (*ANET*; *DOTT*). D.J.W.

U

UCAL. See ITHIEL.

UKNAZ. The reading of AVmg in 1 Ch. iv. 15, where AV gives 'even Kenaz', RV 'and Kenaz', RSV 'Kenaz', a son of Elah. As 'sons' are here attributed to Elah, it is conjectured that some names have fallen out of the text, which would then read, 'the sons of Elah . . . and Kenaz'.

R.A.H.G.

ULAI. The river flowing east of Susa in Elam (SW Persia) where Daniel heard a man's voice (Dn. viii. 16). The river (Heb. *'ûlāi*; Assyr. *Ulai*; classical *Eulaeus*) has changed its course in modern times, and the present Upper Kherkhah and Lower Karun (Pasitigris) rivers may then have been a single stream flowing into the delta at the north of the Persian Gulf. The river is illustrated in the Assyrian reliefs showing Ashurbanipal's attack on Susa in 640 BC (R. D. Barnett, *Assyrian Palace Reliefs*, 1960, plates 118–127).

D.J.W.

UNBELIEF. Expressed by two Greek words in the New Testament, *apistia* and *apeitheia*. According to *MM*, the word *apeitheia*, together with *apeitheō* and *apeithēs*, 'connotes invariably disobedience, rebellion, contumacy'. So Paul says that the Gentiles have obtained mercy through the rebellion of the Jews (Rom. xi. 30). See also Rom. xi. 32; Heb. iv. 6, 11. This disobedience springs from *apistia*, 'a want of faith and trust'. *Apistia* is a state of mind, and *apeitheia* an expression of it. Unbelief towards Himself was the prime sin of which Christ said that the Spirit would convict the world (Jn. xvi. 9). Unbelief in all its forms is a direct affront to the divine veracity (*cf.* 1 Jn. v. 10), which is why it is so heinous a sin. The children of Israel did not enter into God's rest for two reasons. They lacked faith (*apistia*, Heb. iii. 19), and they disobeyed (*apeitheia*, Heb. iv. 6). 'Unbelief finds its practical issue in disobedience' (Westcott on Heb. iii. 12).

D.O.S.

UNCHASTITY. See MARRIAGE.

UNCLEAN ANIMALS, -NESS. See CLEAN AND UNCLEAN.

UNCTION. In its three New Testament occurrences, *i.e.* 1 Jn. ii. 20, 27 (twice), AV renders Gk. *chrisma*, 'unction', and RV has 'anointing'. Verses 18–27 present a warning against deceivers (verse 26) and antichrists (verse 18). Christians who, by virtue of their 'unction' (verses 20, 27), are all able to discern schism (verse 19) and heresy (denial of the incarnation, verse 22) a[re] exhorted to adhere to the apostolic messa[ge] (verse 24), which led them to confess the Fath[er] and the Son. Grammatically, 'unction' must [be] either (*a*) 'that which is smeared on' (so B. [F.] Westcott, *The Epistles of John*, 1892); or ([*b*]) 'the act of anointing' (so A. E. Brooke, *IC[C]*, 1912); but in either case the word refers to t[he] gift of the Holy Spirit, of which baptism is t[he] outward sign. Others, less plausibly, urge a refe[r]ence to oil and laying on of hands, while C. [H.] Dodd, arguing from Hellenistic parallels (*MN[TC]*, 1946, pp. 58–64), suggests 'initiation', that i[s,] baptismal confession based upon the Word, an[d] this rendering appears in NEB. See also ANOINTIN[G].

M.R.W.F.

UNICORN. See WILD OX.

UNKNOWN GOD (Gk. *agnōstos theos*). In Ac[ts] xvii. 23 Paul refers to an Athenian altar-dedic[a]tion 'To the unknown God' which forms the te[xt] of his Areopagus address (see AREOPAGU[S]). Pausanias (*Description of Greece*, i. 1. 4) says th[at] in Athens there are 'altars of gods called u[n]known' and Philostratus (*Life of Apollonius [of] Tyana*, vi. 3. 5) similarly speaks of 'altars of u[n]known divinities' as set up there. They a[re] frequently associated with a story told by Di[o]genes Laertius (*Lives of Philosophers*, i. 11[0]) about the setting up of 'anonymous altars' in an[d] around Athens on one occasion to avert a pes[ti]lence. Similar dedications are attested elsewher[e] if the name of a local deity was uncertain or t[he] wording of an original dedication had become los[t].

BIBLIOGRAPHY. E. Norden, *Agnostos Theo[s]*, 1912; K. Lake, 'The Unknown God', in F. [J.] Foakes-Jackson and K. Lake, *The Beginnings [of] Christianity*, V, 1933, pp. 240–246.

F.F.B.

UNLEAVENED BREAD. See LEAVEN.

UPHARSIN. See MENE, MENE, TEKEL, U[PHARSIN].

UPHAZ. An unidentified location from whi[ch] came fine gold (Je. x. 9; Dn. x. 5). It may, how[]ever, be a technical term for 'refined gold' its[elf] (so 1 Ki. x. 18, *mūpāz*; *cf. mippāz*, Is. xiii. 1[2]) similar to the definition 'pure gold' (*zāh[āb] ṭāhôr*; 2 Ch. ix. 17). Others, with some suppo[rt] from vss, read *'ūpīr* (see OPHIR) for *'ūpaz* owi[ng] to the similarity of Heb. *z* and *r*.

D.J.W.

UPPER ROOM. See HOUSE.

UR OF THE CHALDEES. The city whi[ch] Terah and Abram left to go to Harran (Gn. [x]

28, 31, xv. 7; Ne. ix. 7). Considered by Stephen to be in Mesopotamia (Acts vii. 2, 4). An old identification of *'Ûr* with Urfa (Edessa), 20 miles north-west of Harran, is unlikely on philological grounds, and *Ura'* is the name of several places known in Asia Minor. Moreover, such an identification would require Abraham to retrace his steps eastwards before setting out west towards Canaan. This identification requires that the 'Chaldea' which identifies the location must be equated with the Indo-Aryan Ḫaldai (part of ancient Armenia). The Chaldeans were a Semitic people known in Babylonia from at least the end of the second millennium BC (see CHALDAEA), but there are no references to their presence in N Mesopotamia. LXX wrote 'the land (*chōra*) of the Chaldees', perhaps being unfamiliar with the site. However, Eupolemus (*c*. 150 BC) refers to Ur as a city in Babylonia called Camarina ('the moon') or Ouria. The Talmudic interpretation of Ur as Erech is unlikely since the latter is distinguished in Gn. x. 10.

The most generally accepted identification is with the ancient site of Ur (*Uri*), modern Tell el-Muqayyar, 9 miles west of Nasiriyeh on the river Euphrates in S Iraq. Excavations at this site in 1922–34 by the joint British Museum and University Museum, Philadelphia, expedition under Sir C. L. Woolley have traced the history of the site from the 'Al 'Ubaid period (fourth millennium BC) until it was abandoned about 300 BC. Many spectacular discoveries were made, especially in the royal cemeteries of the early Dynastic III period (*c*. 2500 BC). Beneath these a layer of water-laid clay is equated by the discoverer with the great flood of the Epic of Gilgamesh and the Bible. The ruins of the temple tower (*ziggurat*) built by Ur-Nammu, the founder of the prosperous Sumerian IIIrd Dynasty (*c*. 2150–2050 BC) still dominate the site (see fig. 29 and BABEL). The history and economy of the city is well known from thousands of inscribed tablets and the many buildings found at the site. The principal deity was Nannar (Semitic Sin or Su'en), who was also worshipped at Harran. The city was later ruled by the Neo-Babylonian (Chaldean) kings of Babylonia.

BIBLIOGRAPHY. C. L. Woolley, *Excavations at Ur*, 1954; H. W. F. Saggs, 'Ur of the Chaldees', *Iraq*, XXII, 1960. D.J.W.

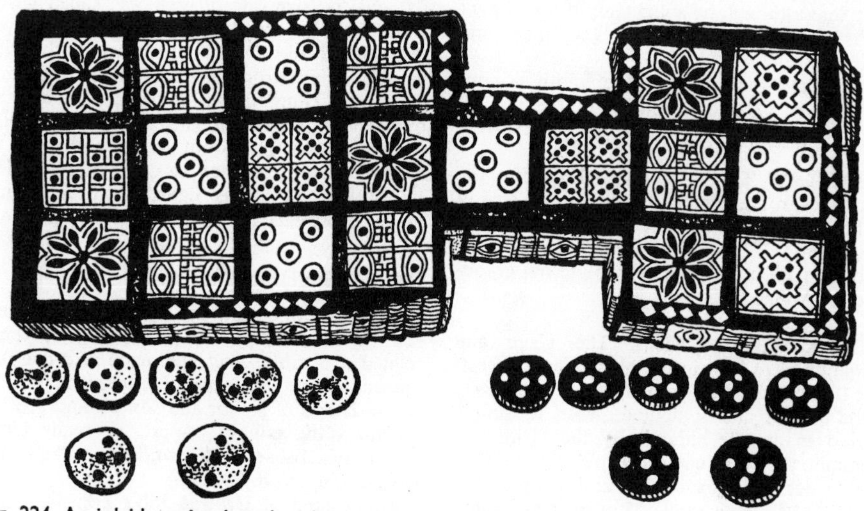

Fig. 224. An inlaid gaming board with counters from the royal graves at Ur. The method of play is uncertain, *c*. 2600 BC. See also plates Ib, c.

URBANE, URBANUS. Properly Urbanus (RV): Latin servile name (*cf*. Deissmann, *BS*, pp. 271 ff.) recurrent in inscriptions of the Imperial household (*e.g. CIL*, vi. 4237)—perhaps the Urbanus greeted in Rom. xvi. 9 belonged to it (*cf*. Phil. iv. 22; Lightfoot, *Philippians*, p. 174). 'Our fellow-worker' (so, correctly, RV) need not imply service with Paul personally. Paul, exact with pronouns, uses '*my* fellow-worker' for companions (*cf*. Rom. xvi. 3, 21). See also AMPLIAS. A.F.W.

URIAH, URIJAH (*'ûriyyâ, 'ûriyyāhû*, 'my light is Yahweh'). **1.** A Hittite and one of David's 'mighty men' (2 Sa. xxiii. 39; 1 Ch. xi. 41) who resided in Jerusalem. Both his name and his conduct suggest that he had espoused the Hebrew religion (*cf*. 2 Sa. xi. 11). He owes his prominence in Scripture primarily to David's adultery with Bathsheba, Uriah's Israelite wife, while her husband was serving with the army under Joab in the siege of the Ammonite capital, Rabbah (2 Sa. xi; *cf*. 1 Ki. xv. 5; Mt. i. 6). His strong sense of duty and single-minded loyalty to his comrades stand out in contrast to David's own temporary self-centredness and duplicity. Had he been less virtuous, David would have had no need to resort to the desperate expedient of murder by proxy (2 Sa. xi. 15).

2. High priest in the time of Ahaz. He is mentioned as one of the two 'faithful witnesses' taken by Isaiah to attest the cryptic prophecy concerning Maher-shalal-hash-baz (Is. viii. 2). That Uriah was chosen for this purpose simply implies that his testimony would carry weight with the people. He appears in an unfavourable light in the account of the reign of Ahaz in 2 Ki. xvi (inexplicably both AV and RV here give his name as Urijah). He complies without demur with the king's instructions regarding certain undesirable innovations in Temple worship (see AHAZ).

3. A prophet, a contemporary of Jeremiah, who like him faithfully declared the word of Yahweh (Je. xxvi. 20–24). He encountered extreme opposition from Jehoiakim and the court, and although he sought asylum in Egypt he was brought back by the king's command and put to death.

4. A priest, the father of Meremoth, a contemporary of Ezra (Ezr. viii. 33; *cf.* Ne. viii. 4).

J.C.J.W.

URIEL (*'ûrî'ēl*, 'God is my light'). **1.** Chief of the Kohathites in the reign of David. He assisted in the bringing up of the ark from the house of Obed-edom (1 Ch. xv. 5, 11). He is probably the same as in 1 Ch. vi. 24. **2.** The maternal grandfather of Abijah (2 Ch. xiii. 2). M.A.M.

URIM AND THUMMIM. The Urim and Thummim were kept in the high priest's breastplate (Ex. xxviii. 30; Lv. viii. 8), a pouch fastened to the ephod, and sometimes, with it, simply referred to as 'the ephod'. By the Urim and Thummim the priest could declare God's will to both leader (Nu. xxvii. 21) and people (Dt. xxxiii. 8, 10). Nu. xxvii. 21 also significantly places Urim and Thummim in the history of Israel. It has often been noted that Urim and Thummim are not mentioned between the early monarchy and post-exilic times. The existence of prophecy seems to make the Urim and Thummim superfluous. Moses, legislating in Nu. xxvii. 21 for the period immediately following his own death, commits the national leader to the guidance of Urim and Thummim; and when the age of prophecy is clearly past the national leaders desire a revival of this form of direction (Ezr. ii. 63; Ne. vii. 65).

We must now consider two passages which speak of the oracular use of the ephod. When Abiathar fled to David he brought with him an ephod (1 Sa. xxiii. 6). This must have been the high-priestly ephod with the breastplate of Urim and Thummim attached, for the customary priestly (linen) ephod (1 Sa. xxii. 18) would not need this special mention. When David requires guidance (1 Sa. xxiii. 9–12) he asks direct questions, eliciting a simple affirmative or negative. This suggests that the Urim and Thummim was a form of casting lots, whether tossed from the pouch (*cf.* Pr. xvi. 33) or ceremonially drawn out by the priest. 1 Sa. xiv presents similarities: *cf.* verses 3 and 41 with xxiii. 6 and 9; note the identical title of God, verse 41, xxiii. 10, indicating a customary formula. The Hebrew text of verse 41 presents oddities, and, if reconstructed with the help of LXX, could read, 'If this guilt is in me or in Jonathan my son, give Urim, and if it is in thy people Israel, give Thummim', a distinctly similar use of the sacred lot. However, man could not compel God to speak, for (1 Sa. xxviii. 6) 'The Lord answered him not . . . by Urim.' How did the method operate? Ex. xxviii. 30, implying objects placed in the pouch, rules out the ancient explanation that, in reply to a question, a supernatural light played in the gems of the breastplate and thus gave answer (Jos., *Ant.* viii. 9). It has been, however, plausibly suggested that the Urim and Thummim were two flat objects; one side of each was called Urim, from *'ārar*, 'to curse', and when both displayed this side the answer was negative; the other side was Thummim, from *tāmam*, 'to be perfect', and a complete Thummim meant 'yes'; one Urim and one Thummim meant 'no reply'. This must remain a hypothesis, but it has the merit of meeting such evidence as we possess. The translation of Urim as 'lights', from *'ôr*, 'light', makes a less effective contrast with Thummim.

J.A.M.

USURY. See DEBT, DEBTOR, *b*.

UZ. 1. Son of Aram and grandson of Shem (Gn. x. 23). In 1 Ch. i. 17 Uz (*'ûṣ*, perhaps related to Arabic *'Awḍ*, the name of a deity) is named among the sons, *i.e.* descendants, of Shem. **2.** Son of Nahor and Milcah and brother of Buz (Gn. xxii. 21, where AV reads Huz). **3.** Son of Dishan and grandson of Seir, the Horite (Gn. xxxvi. 28).

4. The land of Uz was Job's homeland (Jb. i. 1; *cf.* Je. xxv. 20 and La. iv. 21), the location of which is uncertain. Of the numerous suggestions (*e.g.* near Palmyra, near Antioch, or in N Mesopotamia) the two most likely are Hauran, south of Damascus, and the area between Edom and N Arabia. The former is supported by Josephus (*Ant.* i. 6. 4) and both Christian and Muslim traditions. On this view Uz is the land settled by the son of Aram.

Most modern scholars incline towards the more southerly location. Job's friends seem to have come from the vicinity of Edom, *e.g.* Eliphaz the Temanite (Jb. ii. 11). Uz appears to have been accessible both to Sabaean bedouin from Arabia and Chaldean marauders from Mesopotamia (Jb. i. 15, 17). The postscript to the LXX locates Uz 'in the regions of Idumaea and Arabia', but partly on the basis of a spurious identification of Job with Jobab (Gn. xxxvi. 33). Uz in Je. xxv. 20 is coupled with Philistia, Edom, Moab, and Ammon, while La. iv. 21 indicates that the Edomites were occupying the land of Uz. However, the LXX omits Uz in both of these passages, and the identity of this land of Uz wit[h] Job's is not certain. The fact that Job is numbere[d] ith the people of the east (i. 3; *cf.* Jdg. vi. 3, 33; s. xi. 14; Ezk. xxv. 4, 10) seems to substantiate a ocation in the area of Edom. D.A.H.

UZAL. 1. Heb. *'ûzāl* in Gn. x. 27 and 1 Ch. i. 21 ignifies an Arabian descendant of Joktan, peraps connected with 'Azal, given by Arab hisorians as the ancient name of San'a in Yemen.

2. Ezk. xxvii. 19, AV translates 'Dan also and avan going to and fro occupied in thy fairs' rom Heb. *w^e^dān w^e^yāwān m^e^'ûzzāl b^e^'izbônayik ātānû*, which RVmg renders 'Vedan and Javan raded from Uzal for thy wares', while RSV reads and wine from Uzal they exchanged for your vares' (following LXX). Uzal may be identified vith Izalla in north-east Syria, whence Nebuhadrezzar obtained wine (S. Langdon, *Neuabylonische Königsinschriften*, no. 9, I, l. 22; *cf.* . 23 'wine from *Ḫilbunim*' with Helbon of Ezk. xvii. 18. For location of Izalla, see D. J. Wisenan, *Chronicles of Chaldaean Kings*, pp. 18, 22, Map 2). The alteration of *w^e^yāwān* to *w^e^yayin*, and wine', is very slight. Although *w^e^dān* may be mitted as a scribal error due to the proximity f Dedan (verse 20), it might be a cognate of Assyrian *dannu*, 'a large jar or vat used for storing vine or beer'. This would lead to a translation, and vat(s) of wine from Uzal they exchanged for our wares'. A.R.M.

UZZA (*'uzzā'*). **1.** A descendant of Ehud, a Benjamite (1 Ch. viii. 7). **2.** A son of Merari 1 Ch. vi. 29). **3.** The head of a family of Nethiim who returned from the Exile (Ezr. ii. 49). **4.** A son of Abinadab, probably a Levite (*cf.* 1 Sa. vii. 1), who drove the new cart carrying the ark when it was removed from Kiriath-jearim 2 Sa. vi. 3). When the oxen stumbled he 'put orth his hand to the ark of God, and took hold of it', for which irreverent handling of the ark he was struck dead by God (2 Sa. vi. 6, 7). **5.** The otherwise unknown owner of a garden in which Manasseh and Amon were buried (2 Ki. xxi. 18, 26). M.A.M.

UZZI. A priest in the line of descent from Eleazar (1 Ch. vi. 5; Ezr. vii. 4), probably contemporary with Eli. See ELI, GERIZIM. For others of the same name, see 1 Ch. vii. 2, 7; Ne. xi. 22, xii. 19. G.T.M.

UZZIAH (*'uzziyyâ, 'uzziyyāhû*, 'Yahweh is my strength'. An alternative form Azariah—*'^a^zaryâ* or *'^a^zaryāhû*, 'Yahweh has helped'—is found in 2 Ki. xiv. 21, xv. 1, 6–8; 1 Ch. iii. 12). **1.** King of Judah *c.* 791–740 BC. His long reign of fifty-two years commenced when, as a lad of sixteen, he was freely chosen by the people (2 Ki. xiv. 21; 2 Ch. xxvi. 1) to succeed his father Amaziah, who had been assassinated (see AMAZIAH). The possibility that Uzziah was associated with his father on the throne some years before the latter's death cannot be discounted despite the silence of Scripture. A period of co-regency is almost demanded by the chronology (see CHRONOLOGY OF THE OLD TESTAMENT).

The author of Kings shows great reticence in dealing with his reign (2 Ki. xiv. 21, 22, xv. 1–7) and offers no explanation of the tragic circumstances which occasioned his leprosy and withdrawal from public life towards the end of his reign. The account in Chronicles is much fuller (2 Ch. xxvi) and reveals what an able and energetic monarch Uzziah was. Even here we find no reference to the severe earthquake that occurred during his reign (Am. i. 1), the memory of which persisted down to post-exilic times (Zc. xiv. 5). Josephus preserves the tradition that the earthquake coincided with Uzziah's act of sacrilege (*Ant.* ix. 10. 4).

The kingdom of Judah enjoyed great prosperity under Uzziah. This was partly due to the temporary decline in the power of Assyria (*q.v.*). He regained control of the port of Elath on the Gulf of Aqabah and rebuilt it (2 Ki. xiv. 22). He waged successful campaigns against the Philistines and Arabians, and the Ammonites paid tribute to him. The folly of his father had rendered his kingdom extremely vulnerable to attack. He therefore strengthened the fortifications of Jerusalem (2 Ch. xxvi. 9; *cf.* 2 Ki. xiv. 13), providing special armaments for its defence, maintained a large, well-equipped army, and constructed fortress cities in strategic locations. Extensive as were his power and influence, it is far from certain that he is to be identified with the Azariah mentioned in the annals of Tiglath-pileser III (see *ANET*, pp. 282 f.). Besides his military interests, Uzziah took a great delight in agriculture and cattle-farming.

2. A Kohathite Levite (1 Ch. vi. 24). **3.** A priest named among those who married foreign wives (Ezr. x. 21).

BIBLIOGRAPHY. *DOTT*, pp. 53–56; E. R. Thiele, *The Mysterious Numbers of the Hebrew Kings*, 1951, chapter V. J.C.J.W.

V

VAGABOND. 1. Heb. *nûḏ*, 'to move', 'to wander', is used in the description of Cain's condition after God's sentence on him (Gn. iv. 12, 14). See also NOD. 2. Heb. *nûa'*, 'to totter about' (like beggars), is used in an imprecatory psalm (Ps. cix. 10). 3. Gk. *perierchomai*, 'to come or go round about', is used to describe some Jewish exorcists (Acts xix. 13; RV, NEB 'strolling'; RSV 'itinerant'; *cf.* Lat. *vagari*, 'to wander').

J.D.D.

VALE, VALLEY. In Palestine, where rain falls only at a certain time of year, the landscape is cut by many narrow valleys and stream-beds (wadis), wet only in the rainy season (Heb. *naḥal*; Arab. *wadî*). Often water may be found below ground in such wadis during the dry months (*cf.* Gn. xxvi. 17, 19). Perennial rivers flow through wider valleys and plains (Heb. *'ēmeq*, *biq'â*) or cut narrow gorges through the rock. Heb. *šᵉpēlâ* denotes low ground, especially the coastal plain (see SHEPHELAH); *gay'* is simply a valley. For geographical details, see under proper names: HINNOM, JEHOSHAPHAT, SALT (VALLEY OF), *etc.*

A.R.M.

VANITY. The three main words for vanity are distributed broadly as follows: *heḇel*, Psalms, Ecclesiastes, Jeremiah; *šāw'*, Job, Ezekiel; *tōhû*, Isaiah. *Heḇel*, lit. 'a vapour', 'a breath' (*cf.* Pss. lxxviii. 33, xciv. 11; Is. lvii. 13, *etc.*), indicates the fruitlessness of human endeavours. Such is man's natural life (Jb. vii. 3; Ps. xxxix. 5, 6, *etc.*). Figuratively *heḇel* conveys the idea of unsubstantial, worthless, thus 'the vanity of idols' (*cf.* Je. x. 15, li. 18, *etc.*). The worship of such is consequently unprofitable (Dt. xxxii. 21; 1 Sa. xv. 23; Pss. iv. 2, xxiv. 4, *etc.*). Unprofitable, too, are those who practise such vanities (1 Sa. xii. 21; 2 Ki. xvii. 15; Is. xli. 29, xliv. 9). Idolatry is mere vanity by which God is provoked (Dt. xxxii. 21; 1 Ki. xvi. 13, 26, *etc.*), in contrast with the true worship of God (*cf.* Is. xxx. 7, xl, *etc.*). Because idols and their worship are vanities, worthless likewise must be the proclamation of false prophets (Je. xxiii. 16; Ezk. xiii. 1–23; Zc. x. 2). An 'oblation of vanity' (Is. i. 13, RVmg) is ritual without righteousness. Wealth got by vanity dwindles (Pr. xiii. 11; LXX, Vulg., 'in haste'; *cf.* xxi. 6). *Heḇel* has reference to man's human life: 'man at his best estate' (Heb. 'standing firm') is vanity (a 'breath'?) (Pss. xxxix. 5, *cf.* verse 11, lxii. 9, lxxviii. 33, *etc.*). This *heḇel* of all human existence is fully treated in the book of Ecclesiastes.

With *šāw'* the idea of 'foul', 'unseemly', 'evil' is introduced. Jb. xxxi. 5 illustrates this wit reference to behaviour; Pss. xii. 2, xli. 6; Ezk xiii. 8 to speech; Ezk. xiii. 6, 9 (*cf.* verse 23), xx 29, xxii. 28 to sight. The word *'āwen* meanin 'breath' is also translated 'vanity' (*e.g.* Jb. xv. 35 Ps. x. 7; Pr. xxii. 8; Is. xli. 29, lviii. 9; Zc. x. 2 It inclines, however, more to the idea of iniquit and is so translated in the RV in the above refe ences except Is. xli. 29; Zc. x. 2, where 'vanity' i retained. *Tōhû*, lit. 'a waste' (*cf.* Gn. i. 1; D xxxii. 10, *etc.*), then figuratively 'emptiness' 'uselessness'; so God the Lord regards the na tions (Is. xl. 17, *cf.* verse 23). Ps. iv. 2; Hab. ii. 1 have the word *rîq*, translated 'vanity' in EV lit. 'emptiness' (*cf.* Je. li. 34), in the figurativ sense a useless thing.

In the New Testament the word vanity occu three times only, where the purely biblical an ecclesiastical *mataiotēs* is used (LXX for *heḇe* and *šāw'*). (1) In Eph. iv. 17 it refers to behavio and there 'includes moral as well as intellectua worthlessness or fatuity. It is of all that is com prehended under the word *nous*, the understand ing of the heart, that this vanity is predicate Everything included in the following verse respecting the blindness and depravity of th heart is therefore comprehended in the wor vanity' (C. Hodge, *The Epistle to the Ephesian* 1856, *ad loc.*). (2) In 2 Pet. ii. 18 the reference is t speech with the idea of 'devoid of truth', 'in appropriate'. (3) In Rom. viii. 20 the thought i 'frailty', 'want of vigour' (*cf.* use of verb in Ron i. 21 'to make empty', 'foolish'). 'The idea is tha of looking for what one does not find—hence c futility, frustration, disappointment. Sin brough this doom on creation; it made a pessimistic vie of the universe inevitable. *Hypetagē*: the precis time denoted is that of the Fall, when God pro nounced the ground cursed for man's sake' (J Denney in *EGT*).

Heathen deities are vanities, vain things (Act xiv. 15; *cf.* Je. ii. 5, x. 3, *etc.*). Cognate with th word 'vanity' is 'vain', literally 'devoid of forc or purpose'. Our Lord pronounced Gentile wor ship and Pharisaic piety so (Mt. vi. 7, xv. 9; Mk vii. 7); so too Paul estimated pagan philosoph (Rom. i. 21; Eph. v. 6, *etc.*). It is possib through faithlessness in Christian service t become so (*cf.* 1 Cor. ix. 15; 2 Cor. vi. 1, ix. 3 Phil. ii. 16; 1 Thes. iii. 5). Where Christ's resu rection is denied, preaching is 'false' (1 Cor. x 14) and faith without force (1 Cor. xv. 17 Allegiance to the law robs faith of its wort (Rom. iv. 14), and Christ's death of its effe (Gal. ii. 21). Yet faith without works is as vain a works without faith (Jas. ii. 20).

H.D.MCD.

'ASHNI. According to AV, following the *MT* of Ch. vi. 28, Vashni was the elder son of Samuel. .v and RSV following the Syriac, and Lagarde's ecension of the LXX and the parallel text 1 Sa. iii. 2 supply Joel as the name of Samuel's elder on; the Hebrew letters of 'Vashni' are then re-ointed with 'the' inserted to give the meaning and the second' Ahijah. R.A.H.G.

'ASHTI. The wife of Ahasuerus (*q.v.*), who was leposed because she refused to appear at a anquet at which the king wished to show off her eauty. See ESTHER, BOOK OF.

'EDAN. See UZAL.

/EIL. See DRESS, TABERNACLE, TEMPLE.

'ERMILION (Heb. *šāšar*). A word of unknown tymology denoting a bright red colour, appro-riate to a luxuriously painted ceiling (Je. xxii. 4) and to the exotic clothing of the Chaldeans Ezk. xxiii. 14). In mosaics and frescoes the sraelites seem to have used a kind of paint, robably obtained from iron or lead oxide.

/ERSIONS. See ENGLISH VERSIONS, TEXT AND /ERSIONS.

'ESSELS. Before the invention of pottery during the sixth millennium BC) vessels were nan-made containers from skins, rushes, wood, and stone. These, made of perishable materials, ave seldom survived. The dry sands of Egypt ave preserved some leather and basketry (see ;. Cole, *The Neolithic Revolution*, BM (Natural Iistory), 1959, Plate XI). The peculiar geological conditions at Jericho have resulted in the pre-ervation of a quantity of wooden dishes and rays in tombs of the mid-second millennium BC *PEQ*, 1952, plate XXIII, 1953, plate XLIII). See ig. 118. Such wooden vessels, together with leather containers, baskets, and sacks, all widely used by he modern Palestinian peasants, were probably s important as pottery in daily life (*cf.* Lv. xi. 32). 3ottles for carrying both water and wine were imply skins sewn up tightly (Heb. *'ōḇ*, Jb. xxxii. 19; *ḥēmeṯ*, Gn. xxi. 14; *nᵉ'ōḏ*, Jos. ix. 4; *nēḇel*, Sa. i. 24; Gk. *askos*, Mt. ix. 17). Soft stones, imestone, alabaster, basalt, and even obsidian vere cut and ground into shape as bowls, jars, lishes, *etc.* After the introduction of metal tools see ARCHAEOLOGY) elaborately carved stone vessels were produced, and these often formed art of the equipment of a temple (*e.g.* at Hazor, ee Y. Yadin, *Hazor*, 1958, plates 21, 23). Large jars of stone or earthenware were used or storing liquids. The porous earthenware of which the vessels were made absorbed a little of he liquid, thus hindering evaporation and keep-ng the contents cool (Heb. *kaḏ*, 'pitcher', Gn. xxiv. 14; *cf.* 1 Ki. xvii. 12 ff., AV 'barrel'; Gk. *ithinai hydriai*, 'stone water-jars', Jn. ii. 6). The ich could afford vessels of metal, glass, and ivory Jb. xxviii. 17; Rev. xviii. 12). Metal vessels are arely found in Palestine, but bronze bowls of Phoenician workmanship found at Nimrud (H. Frankfort, *Art and Architecture of the Ancient Orient*, 1954, plates 141–143) show the type in use during the Monarchy. Gold and silver vessels were a convenient method of storing wealth before the introduction of coined money, and formed the bulk of temple and royal treasures and payments of tribute (see *DOTT*, p. 48, c). Some metal shapes were imitated in pottery (*e.g.* at Samaria, *BA*, XXII, 1959, fig. 18, top left). Glass and ivory were mainly used for small cosmetic flasks and toilet instruments (see figs. 42, 58; and *BA*, XX, 1957, fig. 4; *IEJ*, VI, 1956, plate 20B; see GLASS).

Fig. 225. Vessels from Megiddo. *Left:* a bronze vessel as restored (Iron Age). *Right:* a haematite jar with gold mounts (Late Bronze Age). For pottery see fig. 171.

Definition of the various Hebrew terms describing vessels is not usually possible. Many containers, although differently named, could serve the same purpose (1 Sa. ii. 14). For the types and proposed identifications of earthenware vessels, see POTTERY and fig. 171. The following terms seem to describe metal vessels only, mostly used in the Tabernacle and the Temple: 1. Heb. *'ᵃğarṭāl* (Ezr. i. 9), a large bowl; 2. *gullâ* (Zc. iv. 2; *cf.* 1 Ki. vii. 41), a round bowl for holding the oil in a lamp (see JACHIN AND BOAZ), in Ec. xii. 6 perhaps a hanging lamp; 3. *kap̄* (Nu. vii. 14), a shallow open dish for holding incense; 4. *kᵉp̄ôr* (1 Ch. xxviii. 17), a small bowl; 5. *mᵉnaqqiyyâ* (Ex. xxv. 29), the golden bowl from which libations were poured; 6. *merqāḥâ* (Jb. xli. 31), an apothecary's compounding jar, possibly pottery; 7. *mizrāq* (Ex. xxvii. 3), a large basin used at the altar of burnt-offering, probably to catch the blood, and also a large banqueting bowl (Am. vi. 6); 8. *ṣinṣeneṯ* (Ex. xvi. 33), the golden jar in which the specimen of manna was kept (*cf.* Heb. ix. 4); 9. *qᵉ'ārâ* (Ex. xxv. 29; Nu. vii. 13), a plate; 10. *qaśwâ* (Ex. xxv. 29), the golden pitcher containing wine for libations. For Heb. *dûḏ*, *sîr*, and *qallaḥaṯ* translated 'caldron', see POTTERY; in Jb.

xli. 20 Heb. *'ag̱môn* is not 'caldron' but possibly 'rushes' (*cf.* Is. lviii. 5 where *'ag̱môn* is 'rush').

The Gk. *chalkion* (Mk. vii. 4) is simply any bronze vessel. Heb. *k^eli*, Aram. *mā'n*, Gk. *skeuos* are general words for implements, equipment (1 Sa. viii. 12; Acts ix. 15) and hence, in many contexts, vessels both actual (1 Sa. ix. 7; Jn. xix. 29) and metaphorical (1 Pet. iii. 7).

Bibliography. J. L. Kelso, *The Ceramic Vocabulary of the Old Testament*, *BASOR*, Supplementary Studies, 5–6, 1948. A.R.M.

VESTURE. An archaic word denoting dress which AV uses to translate the following terms: Heb. *beg̱eḏ*, 'cloak', 'garment', 'covering' (Gn. xli. 42); Heb. *k^esûṯ*, 'a covering' (Dt. xxii. 12, see also Fringes); Heb. *l^eḇûš*, 'clothing', 'dress', 'attire' (Pss. xxii. 18, cii. 26); Gk. *himation*, 'an outer garment' (Rev. xix. 13, 16), possibly a large square piece of cloth which could be used as a shawl or as a cloak (so rendered in Mt. v. 40; 'raiment' in Lk. ix. 29); Gk. *himatismos*, 'dress', 'apparel' (Mt. xxvii. 35; Jn. xix. 24); Gk. *peribolaion*, 'what is thrown round one' (Heb. i. 12). See also Dress.

In 2 Ki. x. 22 there is a reference to the one who was over the 'vestry' (*meltāḥâ*; *cf.* 'keeper of the wardrobe', 2 Ki. xxii. 14), who cared for the 'vestments' (*malbûš*) or sacred dresses used by priests in the temple of Baal. J.D.D.

VIAL. 1. Heb. *paḵ*, 'a flask'. A vial of oil was used in anointing Saul (1 Sa. x. 1) and Jehu (2 Ki. ix. 1, 3, AV 'box', *q.v.*). 2. Gk. *phialē*, 'a bowl', 'a basin'. A broad shallow 'bowl' (thus RV) used for incense and drink offering. The word is found eight times in Revelation (Rev. v. 8, *etc.*), and nowhere else in the New Testament. See Pottery.

VICTORY. The primary biblical assertion is that victory belongs to God (Jon. ii. 9; 1 Cor. xv. 54–57; Rev. vii. 10). This is succinctly expressed in the phrase 'the battle is the Lord's' (1 Sa. xvii. 47), *i.e.* victory belongs exclusively to the Lord: it is His to bestow at will.

There are three special features of the Lord's victory which enable us to glimpse its inner character. In the first place, sometimes the Lord's victory is the defeat of His people (*e.g.* Jdg. ii. 14; Is. xlii. 24, 25; Je. xxv. 8, 9). The Lord's victory is the exercise of holy sovereignty in the course of history. 'Victory' is another way of saying that the government of the world rests in the hands of a holy God, who orders all things according to inflexible principles of morality, so that sometimes His holiness must be asserted against His people, and becomes 'his strange act' (Is. xxviii. 21).

Secondly, this holy government of the world will issue in the great victory of the eschatological 'Day of the Lord'. The power of victory is annexed to the holy rule of the only God. Therefore the issue of that conflict is not in doubt. Just as, at creation, there was no possibility of opposing the Creator's will, so, at the new creation, He will speak and it shall be done (Ezk. xxxviii, xxxix; Rev. xix).

Thirdly, the people of God enter upon victory by the obedience of faith: *i.e.* they experience victory in God's victory (Ex. xiv. 13, 14; Dt. xxviii. 1–14; Ps. xx; Eph. vi. 16; 1 Jn. v. 4, 5). As the Lord Jesus said, only the Son can set men free (Jn. viii. 36); those who abide in His word know the truth, and the truth sets them free (Jn. viii. 31, 32).

The Old Testament associates 'peace', 'righteousness', and 'salvation' with victory. The peace of the victor (*e.g.* 1 Ki. xxii. 28; Is. xli. 3, Hebrew text) is not simply cessation of hostilities—even the defeated have that! It is the enjoyment of total well-being which victory brings. Salvation is, positively, the personal enlargement, and negatively, the deliverance which victory effects (1 Sa. xiv. 45; Jdg. vi. 14). Righteousness is the personal quality which guarantees victory (Is. lix. 16, 17). All these cluster in a unique way round the cross of the Lord Jesus Christ, the supreme victory of God: peace (Eph. ii. 14 ff.), salvation (Tit. iii. 4–7), and righteousness (Rom. i. 17, iii. 21–27).

Bibliography. J. Pedersen, *Israel*, I–IV, 1926–40, Index *s.v.* 'Victory'; J.-J. von Allmen, *Vocabulary of the Bible*, 1958, *s.v.* 'Victory'. J.A.M.

VILLAGE. The AV rendering of eight Hebrew words and one Greek word. For *baṯ*, 'daughter' (Nu. xxi. 25, *etc.*), and *ḥāṣēr*, 'court', 'village' (Ex. viii. 13, *etc.*), see City and *cf.* Suburb. Villages were grouped around a fortified town into which the inhabitants could retreat in time of major war.

The regular term for a village is *kāp̄ār*, 'protected' (1 Ch. xxvii. 25; Ct. vii. 11), found also in the forms *kōp̄er* (1 Sa. vi. 18) and *k^ep̄îr* (Ne. vi. 2). Like Arab. *kefr*, the word is often found in place names (*e.g.* 'Capernaum').

Some speculation has arisen regarding the three remaining Hebrew words. In Hab. iii. 14 AV has *pārāz*, but RV and RSV render 'warriors'. In Est. ix. 19 *p^erāzôṯ*, 'the open country', is used to describe open towns (so RSV). In Jdg. v. 7, 11 *p^erāzîm* is rendered by AV '(the inhabitants of) the villages', but by RV 'rulers' (verse 7) and 'his rule' (verse 11). In the two latter words some scholars have tried to establish a link with 'Perizzites' (*q.v.*), but this is uncertain.

In the New Testament Gk. *kōmē* is the only word translated 'village' (Mt. ix. 35, *etc.*; *cf.* Lk. viii. 1 for a distinction between 'city' (*polis*) and 'village'). J.D.D.

VINE, VINEYARD. The common grape-vine, *Vitis vinifera* L., is a slender plant which trails on the ground or climbs supports by means of tendrils. It is mentioned throughout Scripture, frequently in a symbolic sense. First named in connection with Ararat (Gn. ix. 20), perhaps its original habitat, it was also cultivated in ancient Egypt. Paintings found on the walls of Egyptian

:ombs depicted the various stages of wine-naking, while inscriptions and sculptures ıttested to the importance of the vine.

Viticulture was practised in Canaan prior to he Hebrew invasion, as is indicated by the rovisions set out by Melchizedek (Gn. xiv. 18), he report of the spies (Nu. xiii. 20, 24) and the eferences of Moses to the promised land (Dt. i. 11). That Judah was already renowned for its viticulture may be inferred from the blessing of acob (Gn. xlix. 11). The valley of Eshcol 'grape-cluster') then as now was a particularly roductive locality, as was the valley of Sorek in he Philistine plain (Jdg. xiv. 5, xv. 5, xvi. 4). The En-gedi vineyards were also notable (Ct. i. 4), as were those of Sibmah (Je. xlviii. 32), for whose ruin Jeremiah lamented. Ezekiel recorded hat the wine of Helbon was exported to Tyre Ezk. xxvii. 18), while Hosea referred to the scent of the wine of Lebanon (Ho. xiv. 7). The ideal of he invading nomadic Israelite was realized when sedentary occupation made it possible for every man to sit 'under his vine and under his fig ree' (1 Ki. iv. 25).

The preparation of a vineyard involved the xcavating of a trench about a yard wide to en-compass the intended area of cultivation (Is. v. ff.). Upright posts were driven into the bottom of the ditch to provide firm support for the pro-ective hedgerow or fence (Mk. xii. 1), which often consisted of prickly shrubs or thorns. Some-imes large gaps in the fence were filled in by neans of earth or heaps of stones. The enclosed ırea of ground was next dug over carefully, and when the soil was friable the young vines were planted. Normally they were arranged in rows ıbout 8 feet apart, and when the fruit-bearing ranches developed they were raised above the ground on supports (Ezk. xvii. 6). The vines were pruned each spring (Lv. xxv. 3; Jn. xv. 2) by neans of pruning-hooks (Joel iii. 10). The vine-dressers, who pruned and cultivated the vines, ppear to have belonged to the poorer classes Is. lxi. 5). A covered wooden structure, the watchtower, was erected on an elevation over-looking the vineyard (Mk. xii. 1), where the householder and his family maintained a watch throughout the vintage period (Jb. xxvii. 18; Is. i. 8).

When the grapes had reached maturity they were gathered in baskets and taken to the wine-presses (Ho. ix. 2), which were hewn out of the solid rock. The grapes were trodden out by helpers (Am. ix. 13), who shouted and sang together (Is. xvi. 10; Je. xxv. 30). The fermenting wine was stored in strong new goatskin bags (Mt. ix. 17) or in large pottery containers. Tax-collectors claimed their share of the produce (*cf.* Is. iii. 14), and accumulated debts were often discharged in terms of wine (2 Ch. ii. 10). Exemption from military service was granted to men engaged in the vintage. No other plants were to be sown in a vineyard (Dt. xxii. 9), and the vines were allowed to lie fallow every seventh year (Ex. xxiii. 11; Lv. xxv. 3). When the harvest had been gathered in the poor were permitted to enter the vineyard to glean any remaining bunches (Lv. xix. 10; Dt. xxiv. 21). When a vine-yard had become completely unproductive it was abandoned (*cf.* Is. xvi. 8) and the dry vines used for fuel and making charcoal (Ezk. xv. 4; Jn. xv. 6).

ig. 226. Egyptians gathering grapes in an arbour, treading out the wine-juice in a press, and storing he wine in jars stoppered with clay and stamped with a seal. Painting, tomb of Nakht, Thebes, c. 1400 BC.

Apart from their use in the form of wine, grapes constituted an important item in the diet of the Hebrews, supplying iron and other essen-tial minerals. A certain proportion of the harvest was preserved in the form of raisin cakes (1 Sa. xxv. 18).

Used symbolically, the vine was the emblem of prosperity and peace among the ancient Hebrews. More particularly it symbolized the chosen people. They were the vine which God had taken out of Egypt (Ps. lxxx. 8–14; Is. v. 1–5) and planted in a particularly choice land. They had been given all the attention necessary for the production of outstanding fruit, but instead yielded only wild grapes. For this they were to be abandoned to the depredations of their enemies.

No fewer than five parables of Jesus related to vines and their culture. These were the fig in the vineyard (Lk. xiii. 6–9); labourers in the vineyard (Mt. xx. 1–6); new wine in old wineskins (Mt. ix. 17); the two sons (Mt. xxi. 28–32); and the wicked husbandmen (Mt. xxi. 33; Mk. xii. 1–11; Lk. xx. 9–18). Particularly significant was Christ's description of Himself as the true vine (Jn. xv. 1 ff.), with whom all true believers are in organic relationship. At the Last Supper the fruit of the vine symbolized Christ's atoning blood, becoming the sacramental wine of the Christian Communion service. In Christian art the fruitful vine has often symbolized the union of Christ with His followers.

BIBLIOGRAPHY. A. I. Perold, *Treatise on Viticulture*, 1927; H. N. and A. L. Moldenke, *Plants of the Bible*, 1952, pp. 28 ff., 239 f. R.K.H.

VINE OF SODOM. A variety of opinion exists regarding the nature of the allusions in the Song of Moses (Dt. xxxii. 32). There is a distinct possibility that the expression may be figurative, describing the bitterness of Israel's enemies. If a real plant, one which conceals a powdery substance underneath an attractive rind is indicated. The *Solanum sodomeum* L. or *Calotropis procera* has been suggested. More probably the phrase arose from association with the colocynth, *Citrullus colocynthis*, whose fruit is bitter and poisonous. R.K.H.

VINEGAR (Heb. *ḥōmeṣ*, Gk. *oxos*). A sour liquid resulting from acetous fermentation in wine or other strong drink. The acid nature of vinegar is indicated in Pr. x. 26, xxv. 20, while a reference in Ps. lxix. 21 not merely attests to its nauseous flavour but implies that it was used in punishment.

The vinegar of Ru. ii. 14 is typical of the fermented acid drinks enjoyed by labourers in wine-growing countries. The *posca* of the Romans was very similar in nature, and formed part of the soldiers' rations. It was this which was offered to the crucified Christ as refreshment (Mk. xv. 36; Jn. xix. 29, 30), and was different from the myrrh-flavoured anodyne which He had refused earlier (Mt. xxvii. 34; Mk. xv. 23). Wine or vinegar was prohibited to Nazirites (Nu. vi. 3), hence the gravity of the offence in Am. ii. 12. R.K.H.

VIOL. See MUSIC AND MUSICAL INSTRUMENTS.

VIPER. See SERPENT, and fig. 38.

VIRGIN. Two Hebrew words are translated 'virgin' by AV, *b*^{e}*ṯûlâ* and *'almâ*. The first of these comes from a root meaning 'to separate' and is the common word for a woman who has never had sexual intercourse (Gk. *parthenos*). Metaphorically it is used of nations and place-names, *e.g.* the virgin of Israel (Je. xviii. 13, xxxi. 4, 21; Am. v. 2); the virgin daughter of Zion (Is. xxxvii. 22); Judah (La. i. 15); Zidon (Is. xxiii. 12); Babylon (Is. xlvii. 1); Egypt (Je. xlvi. 11). The second is derived from a root meaning 'to be sexually mature', and refers to a woman of marriageable age who has not yet borne children, though she may be married. It occurs seven times and is translated 'virgin' (Gn. xxiv. 43; Ct. i. 3, vi. 8; Is. vii. 14), 'maid' (Ex. ii. 8; Pr. xxx. 19), and 'damsels' (Ps. lxviii. 25). The Greek equivalent is usually *neanis*, 'a young woman', but in Gn. xxiv. 43 (of Rebekah) and in Is. vii. 14 *parthenos* is used. As a result, the Isaiah passage has been regarded since early Christian times as a prophecy of the virgin birth of Christ (Mt. i. 23).

The primary meaning of Isaiah's sign to Ahaz is probably that in less than nine months (reading RSVmg 'with child and shall bear') the tide would turn in such a way that a child would be given the name of Immanuel, 'God is with us'. The messianic interpretation is based on the coincidence of the name Immanuel, which expressed so well the early Christians' belief in the deity of the Christ, and the LXX rendering 'the virgin (*hē parthenos*) shall be with child and shall bear a son', which is a legitimate translation of the Hebrew words but which imports into the sign to Ahaz the implication that the mother of Immanuel was a specific woman who was at the time of writing still a virgin (*i.e.* in at least nine months' time a son would be called Immanuel). The door is thus left open for Matthew and the early Church to see a remarkable verbal correspondence with what happened at the birth of Jesus Christ. For a fuller study of this passage, and a different viewpoint, see IMMANUEL.

On the various explanations of Paul's teaching on virgins in 1 Cor. vii. 25–38, see L. Morris, *I Corinthians*, *TNTC*, 1958. See also MARRIAGE. J.B.Tr.

VIRGIN BIRTH. See INCARNATION.

VIRTUE. The word used in the Old Testament is Heb. *ḥayil*, 'ability', 'efficiency', often involving moral worth, as in Ru. iii. 11; Pr. xii. 4, xxxi. 10 (*'ēšeṯ ḥayil*, 'a woman of worth', 'a virtuous woman'); *cf.* Pr. xxxi. 29 (*'āśâ ḥayil*, 'to do worthily').

In the New Testament AV renders two words as 'virtue'. 1. Gk. *aretē*, meaning any excellence of a person or thing (1 Pet. ii. 9; 2 Pet. i. 3, 5). In Homer the word is used especially of manly qualities (*cf.* Phil. iv. 8). In the LXX it is the equivalent of Heb. *hôḏ*, 'splendour', 'majesty' (of God, Hab. iii. 3), and *t*^{e}*hillâ*, 'praise' (Is. xlii. 12, xliii. 21, quoted in 1 Pet. ii. 9). 2. *Dynamis*, 'power', 'influence' (Mk. v. 30; Lk. vi. 19, viii. 46), is used of the healing influence proceeding from our Lord. The word is commonly translated 'strength' (*e.g.* 2 Cor. xii. 9; Heb. xi. 11). D.O.S.

VISION. The border line between vision and dream or trance is difficult, if not impossible, to determine. This is reflected in the biblical vocabulary of 'vision'.

Heb. *ḥāzôn* comes from a root used to describe

e beholding of a vision by the seer while in an static state (Is. i. 1; Ezk. xii. 27); while the ord *mar'â*, from the ordinary root 'to see', eans vision as a means of revelation (Nu. xii. 6; Sa. iii. 15). The New Testament uses two words this connection: *horama* (Acts ix. 10, 12, x. 3, ', 19) and *optasia* (Lk. i. 22; Acts xxvi. 19; Cor. xii. 1). They signify 'appearance' or ision'. The emphasis seems to be upon the static nature of the experience, and the velatory character of the knowledge, which me to the biblical prophets and seers. The perience points to a special awareness of God ared by saintly men (*e.g.* Je. i. 11; Dn. ii. 19; cts ix. 10, xvi. 9), and to God's readiness to veal Himself to men (Ps. lxxxix. 19; Acts x. 3).

The circumstances in which the revelatory sions came to the seers of the Bible are varied. ey came in men's waking hours (Dn. x. 7; cts ix. 7); by day (Acts x. 3) or by night (Gn. vi. 2). But the visions had close connections ith the dream-state (Nu. xii. 6; Jb. iv. 13).

In the Old Testament the recipients of revela- ry visions were the prophets, 'writing' (Is. i. 1; b. 1; Na. i. 1) and 'non-writing' (2 Sa. vii. 17; Ki. xxii. 17–19; 2 Ch. ix. 29). But the outstand- g examples were Ezekiel and Daniel. In the ew Testament Luke manifests greatest interest visions. He reports, *e.g.*, the visions of acharias (Lk. i. 22), Ananias (Acts ix. 10), ornelius (x. 3), Peter (x. 10 ff.), and Paul (xviii. ; although Paul treated visions with much serve (2 Cor. xii. 1 ff.). But obviously the blical 'visionaries' were men of action and out- anding intelligence.

Biblical visions concerned both immediate tuations (Gn. xv. 1 f.; Acts xii. 7) and the 'far- f divine event' of the kingdom of God, as the ritings of Isaiah, Daniel, and John testify. In is connection the passages in 1 Sa. iii. 1; Pr. ix. 18 are especially relevant. J.G.S.S.T.

OW. The idea of 'vow' in Semitic thought may ell have been derived from the name of a deity. so, it illustrates the fact that in biblical usage a ow is always used with reference to God and offers a new interpretation for such passages as Je. xxxii. 35: they must then be construed as the sacrificing of children, not 'unto Molech' (*mōleḵ*), but 'as a *mōleḵ*', *i.e.* a votive or 'vowed' offering. On Jdg. xi. 30 f., see JEPHTHAH. A vow may be either to perform (Gn. xxviii. 20 ff.) or abstain from (Ps. cxxxii. 2 ff.) an act in return for God's favour (Nu. xxi. 1–3) or as an expression of zeal or devotion towards God (Ps. xxii. 25). It is no sin to vow or not to vow, but, if made—pre- sumably uttered (Dt. xxiii. 23)—a vow is as sacredly binding as an oath (*q.v.*) (Dt. xxiii. 21–23). Therefore, a vow should not be made hastily (Pr. xx. 25); for the person vowing, *e.g.* to offer a sacrifice, then enters into 'the sphere of the offering' and is released only when the sacrifice is made (Pedersen). To have this fulfilment is the state of the happy man (Jb. xxii. 27), and the character of Israel's future blessedness (Na. i. 15). On the other hand, to substitute a blemished animal for the one vowed reveals a sin and brings God's curse (Mal. i. 14).

What is already the Lord's (*e.g.* firstlings, tithes (Lv. xxvii. 26)), or an abomination to the Lord (Dt. xxiii. 18), cannot be vowed or con- secrated; but since a firstborn child might be re- deemed (Lv. xxvii; Nu. iii. 44 ff.), it is proper for Hannah to give Samuel to the Lord as a Nazirite (*q.v.*) (1 Sa. i. 11). A vow has no virtue in itself (Ps. li. 16 ff.), and may be only the pious pretence of a treacherous (2 Sa. xv. 7 ff.) or immoral (Pr. vii. 14) person. Thus, in the New Testa- ment the religionist's vow of Corbān is condemned by Christ (Mk. vii. 11). Paul's (probably not Aquila's) vow (*euchē*) no doubt was a tem- porary Nazirite vow—a sincere and proper ex- pression of the ancient Hebrew faith (Acts xviii. 18, *cf.* xxi. 23). (See NAZARITE.)

BIBLIOGRAPHY. A. R. Johnson, *Sacral Kingship in Ancient Israel*, 1955, p. 40 n.; J. Pedersen, *Israel, Its Life and Culture*, 1959, IV, pp. 265 f., 324–330. E.E.E.

VULGATE. See TEXT AND VERSIONS.

VULTURE. See BIRDS OF THE BIBLE.

W

WAFER. Two Hebrew words are thus rendered in AV. *Ṣappîḥiṯ*, 'a cake', appears once only (Ex. xvi. 31; *cf.* 'cakes baked with oil', Nu. xi. 8, RSV, RVmg). The more usual word is *rāqîq*, 'thin cake', 'wafer', referring to home-made bread named from its thinness (Ex. xxix. 2; Nu. vi. 15, *etc.*; *cf.* Arab. *warak*, 'foliage', 'paper'). See also BREAD.

WAGES. Basically the payment made for services rendered. The frequency of the term in the Bible is somewhat obscured in that the Hebrew and Greek terms are sometimes translated 'reward' or 'hire'.

In Old Testament society the hired labourer was not common. The family worked the farm. The family group included slaves and relatives whose wages would be in kind, *e.g.* those of Jacob as he worked for Laban. But Moses' grandson received money as well as his keep for his service as family priest (Jdg. xvii. 10). And when Saul consulted Samuel, the seer, he first planned to pay the fee in kind, but finally resolved on a monetary fee (1 Sa. ix. 7, 8).

In primitive communities the employer had great power in fixing wages, and Jacob could complain that Laban had changed his wages ten times (Gn. xxxi. 41). But the Old Testament legislated to protect the wage-earner. Unscrupulous employers must not take advantage of his economic weakness. He must be given a fair wage, and paid promptly each day (Dt. xxiv. 14, 15).

Men working for wages meet us in the New Testament, both in actuality (Mk. i. 20) and in parable (Mt. xx. 1, 2; Lk. xv. 17, 19; Jn. x. 13, *etc.*). The principle is laid down in the maxim, 'the worker earns his pay' (Lk. x. 7, NEB). Paul makes use of this to lay bare the essential truth at the heart of the gospel. 'To him that worketh', he says, 'is the reward (*i.e.* wage, Gk. *misthos*) not reckoned of grace, but of debt' (Rom. iv. 4). Then he goes on to point out that men are saved, not by working for a heavenly wage but by believing 'on him that justifieth the ungodly' (Rom. iv. 5). By contrast the lost receive an exact if grim wage, for 'the wages of sin is death' (Rom. vi. 23; *cf.* 2 Pet. ii. 13, 15).

There is a sense in which the preachers of the gospel receive wages from those to whom they preach (*misthos* is used in this connection in Lk. x. 7; 2 Cor. xi. 8; 1 Tim. v. 18). Our Lord Himself enjoined the principle that 'they which preach the gospel should live of the gospel' (1 Cor. ix. 14). This must not be misinterpreted, however, for in both Old and New Testaments those who teach for the sake of money ar castigated (Mi. iii. 11; Tit. i. 7; 1 Pet. v. 2).

There are many passages which speak of Go as giving wages or reward for righteousness (*e.* Lk. vi. 23, 35; 1 Cor. iii. 14; 2 Jn. 8). The meta phor is striking, but Scripture makes it clear th we are not to think of any rewards that God ma give as merited in any strict sense. They are th acts of grace of a beneficent God who delights t give His people all things richly to enjoy. Th knowledge of these gratuitous rewards is given t us in order to strengthen our perseverance in th way of righteousness. D.B.K.

WAGON. See CART.

WAILING. See BURIAL AND MOURNING.

WALK. Of the very many occasions when th verb is used in the Old Testament and the Nev the vast majority have the strictly literal sense c moving along or making one's way. It was th normal activity of men, but where the ability t walk had been lost it was capable of bein restored by Christ. This outward healing corre sponded to an inward renewal which Jesu claimed to be able to effect (Mk. ii. 9). Jesus i further represented in the Gospels as walking an enabling others to walk under conditions nc normally given to men (Mk. vi. 48). Here agai as Matthew's Gospel makes clear, the physic act has a spiritual significance (Mt. xiv. 31 Walking can stand as representative of the who range of human activity to which an impoter man is restored (Acts iii. 6).

The term is used in an anthropomorphic sens of God who walks in the garden in the cool c the evening (Gn. iii. 8), and metaphorically it applied to the heart (Jb. xxxi. 7), to the moo (Jb. xxxi. 26), to the tongue of the wicked (P lxxiii. 9), and to the pestilence (Ps. xci. 6). Mo frequently it stands for the whole manner of man's life and conduct, and to the attitude whic God takes up towards him, so that God ca say: 'If ye . . . will walk contrary unto me; the will I also walk contrary unto you' (Lv. xxv 23, 24).

On occasion the term can be used in a mo limited sense, referring to specific laws an observances enjoined upon men (Acts xxi. 2 *cf.* Heb. *hᵃlāḵâ*, 'rule', lit. 'walk'), while in John' Gospel it sometimes assumes the connotation c unwearied activity (Jn. xi. 9), and sometimes c public appearance (Jn. vii. 1). The word *stoich* which appears once in Acts and four times in th Pauline Epistles, is used of the setting of plants i rows, and of soldiers walking in file. Met horically it denotes a somewhat more studied observance of the new rule of life, although the distinction is not always maintained. It is this sense which dominates the usage of all the forms in the Epistles, where there is a frequent contrasting of the walk which was characteristic of believers in their unregenerate days, and that to which they are called through faith in Christ. Baptism is to mark decisively the dividing-point between these two (Rom. vi. 4), which is as clear as the distinction between the life of Christ before and after His resurrection. This renewal of life can equally well be expressed as walking in the spirit in contrast to walking according to the flesh. F.S.F.

WALLS. To build his earliest houses, man used any available stone or lumps of unbaked mud, roughly shaped, *e.g.* Jarmo in eastern Iraq (*Antiquity*, XXLV, 1950, pp. 185–195), Jericho (*PEQ*, LXXXVIII, 1956, plates X, XI). In Palestine stone foundations were often surmounted by brick walls. The enormous city walls of the mid-second millennium BC consisted of a strong stone footing, the outer, battered, face smoothed over with plaster to keep horses at a distance, with thick brick walls, sometimes containing chambers inside them, rising above (for those at Jericho, see *ANEP*, no. 715; *PEQ*, LXXXIV, 1952, plate XVI. 1).

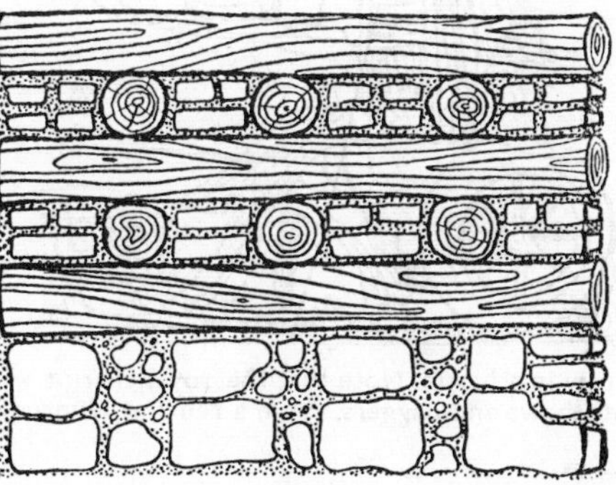

Fig. 227. The use of wood, mud-brick, and stone in wall construction. Reconstructed from excavations in Syria (Alalaḫ and Sinjirli). Second millennium BC.

Masonry was commonly bound together by a timber framework (see H. C. Thomson, 'A Row of Cedar Beams', *PEQ*, XCII, 1960, pp. 57 ff.). Fine examples of Israelite masonry have been found at Samaria. The blocks were carefully cut and laid with a simple bond. Those above ground were smoothed, the foundation courses drafted (*ANEP*, no. 718). The impressive effect of an Israelite walled city may be gauged from reconstructions of Lachish and Tell en-Nasbeh (possibly Mizpah). See also ARTS AND CRAFTS, BRICK, FORTIFICATION AND SIEGECRAFT, HOUSE. A.R.M.

WAR. Old Testament: *milḥāmâ*, 313 times, from *lāḥam*, 'to fight', *cf.* Arab. *laḥama*, 'fit close together', denoting the army in battle array (*BDB*); New Testament: *polemos*, 18 times.

I. STRATEGIC IMPORTANCE OF PALESTINE

Standing between the Euphrates and Tigris, on the one hand, and the Nile country, on the other, Palestine was in a position of great strategic importance and was the natural highway for trading caravans. Understandably, it was an area of constant conflict. Moreover, Israel, situated between the aggressive and often cruel nations of Assyria, Babylon, and Egypt, could not help being involved in foreign politics. The country was mountainous and lent itself mainly to the foray, so much so that Israel's enemies thought Jehovah was a god of the hills (1 Ki. xx. 23). The main battles were fought in the strategic plains of Esdraelon and Gilgal.

II. WAR AND RELIGION

Every department of Israel's existence, including her warfare, was bound up with her God. He is known as a 'man of war' (Ex. xv. 3; Is. xlii. 13). The name 'Lord of hosts' (more fully 'Yahweh, the God of hosts', a title first attested at the inter-tribal sanctuary of Shiloh) is not properly understood, though it may well mean 'Lord of the army', including both the heavenly and the earthly (*cf.* Ex. xii. 41; 1 Sa. xvii. 45). See *HDB*, V, 635 f., and E. Jacob, *Theology of the Old Testament*, 1958, pp. 54 f. One of the literary sources of the Old Testament history was the 'book of the wars of Yahweh' (*q.v.*; Nu. xxi. 14), which may have been a collection of war songs celebrating Israel's victories. The Lord, as Captain, headed the army (2 Ch. xiii. 12), as well as sending His people out to battle (2 Ch. vi. 34). He sets ambushes (2 Ch. xx. 22), and teaches the psalmist to fight (Ps. cxliv. 1). Sometimes He takes over the battle Himself while the army of Israel stands still (2 Ch. xx. 17). The presence of the ark was a pledge of the presence of the Lord (see ARK OF THE COVENANT). A war which was 'of God' was bound to succeed (1 Ch. v. 22), for He Himself would give the enemy into the people's hands (Dt. xx. 13), sometimes using natural forces to this end (Jdg. v. 4, 5). War and its preparation were thus sanctified (*qiddēš milḥāmâ*, 'to sanctify war', Je. vi. 4; Joel iii. 9), and were inaugurated by sacrifice, often the burnt-offering (Jdg. vi. 20, 26). The battle cry, used with great effect, had a religious significance, *e.g.* 'the sword of the Lord, and of Gideon' (Jdg. vii. 18, 20). It has been suggested that Saul's distribution of the sacrificial pieces was intended to unite the warriors in a holy league of war under Jehovah by a covenant. Thus, as far as Israel was concerned, war was in the will of God, commanded by Him, and accomplished through trust in Him. Israel's enemies were God's enemies. The necessity of survival of God's covenant people and the elimination of all extreme forms of immorality which might corrupt the life of the chosen people whom God was using as His saving instrument for the world may well help to explain the teaching of the ban involving complete destruction, Heb. *ḥērem*, originally meaning devoted, then 'devoted to destruction', 'thing hostile to theocracy' (*cf.* Jos. vi. 17, 24). God's plan must never be obstructed by idolatry (Dt. vii. 1–6) and drastic action was required to keep Israel in holy existence. On the other hand, war could be used as punishment against Israel (Hab. i. 6; Is. x. 5 f.; Je. xxv. 1–9; Ezk. xxi. 8–23). It is the false prophet who prophesies peace and security (Je. xxviii). War is a temporary expediency; David is not allowed to build the Temple because of bloodstained hands (1 Ki. v. 3) and the final consummation involves the transformation of weapons of war into implements of peace (Is. ii. 4; Mi. iv. 3). The promised Messiah is named the Prince of Peace (Is. ix. 6) who would, however, inaugurate His kingdom through final defeat of the enemies of Yahweh (Dn. vii, x; Zc. xiv; Ps. cx).

III. METHOD OF WARFARE

Other preliminaries, beside the religious (*cf. supra*), included the sending of spies (Jos. ii). For obvious reasons spring was the best season for war (2 Sa. xi. 1). The usual methods of warfare were adopted—unless peace could be obtained by negotiating (Jdg. xi. 12)—such as the foray (1 Sa. xiv), siege (1 Ki. xx. 1), and the ambush (Jos. viii). Sometimes combat was left to selected single persons (1 Sa. xvii). Weapons included slings (2 Ki. iii. 25), and battering-rams (Ezk. iv. 2). Music often accompanied the men of war (2 Ch. xx. 20–22). See further J. H. Kitchen, *Holy Field* 1955, pp. 90–104.

Fig. 228. King Ashurnasirpal II leading the Assyrian army in a battle. Note that the royal chariot wit three occupants is protected by soldiers armed with bows and daggers. From a relief at Nimrud.

IV. WAR IN THE NEW TESTAMENT

While in the Old Testament the kingdom of Gc was more or less co-extensive with a nation in th midst of other nations depending on all mean including war, for its existence and preservatio in the New Testament it loses its nation character and takes on a new form. It is th change which largely governs the New Test ment writers' attitude to war. The hearer of Joh the Baptist or the follower of Christ who is at th same time a soldier is neither commended n condemned (Lk. iii. 14, RSV; Acts x). Jesu accepted war as part of the present world ord and as inevitable (Mt. xxiv. 6), but warned th they that take the sword must perish by it (M xxvi. 52); and the government appointed by Go 'beareth not the sword in vain' (Rom. xiii. 4). Th Zealots (*q.v.*) were even represented among t disciples, though there their energies were cha nelled along non-political lines. Military men a commended in the gallery of heroes (Heb. x 32). It was later that men such as Tertullian ar Origen maintained that soldiering and th Christian faith were incompatible (*DAC*, II, 656 However, the kingdom of God itself must nev be advanced by physical force (Jn. xviii. 36), fo it is not of this world. Peter is rebuked for h aggressive action at the arrest (Mt. xxvi. 52–54 The New Testament fills out the teaching of th Old Testament by revealing the true nature the battle as heavenly and spiritual; the real aren of war is heaven (Rev. xii. 7). On yieldin llegiance to Christ the Christian enters a conflict, nd thus military metaphors are used prolifically. he Christian is a soldier (2 Tim. ii. 3) who has ɔ 'war a good warfare' (1 Tim. i. 18). See also Pet. ii. 11; 2 Cor. x. 3–4; Eph. vi. 10–20. As the ross has robbed the enemy of its power (Col. ii. 5), final victory is certain (Rev. xvii. 14) at the oming in power of the Messiah (2 Thes. ii. 8), ut not before a final battle has been engaged and on, the scene of which is apocalyptically de-cribed as Armageddon (*q.v.*) (Rev. xvi. 16). The eaning of this is uncertain, though most likely is based on the hill of Megiddon, near which any famous battles took place in the reigns of lecho and Josiah (2 Ch. xxxv. 22). There is little robability in C. C. Torrey's view that the lebrew *har moʻeḏ* ('mount of assembly', *sc.* of e gods) is meant. Still more unlikely is Zim-on's suggestion that it is grounded on the 'God ersus chaos' mythology (see RAHAB), the name eing derived from Hyesemigadon, a form ccurring in a magical Greek papyrus as the ame of the husband of the Babylonian goddess f the underworld. This final conflict of good and vil would thus fulfil the Old Testament's promise f eternal peace inaugurated by the coming in ower of the Messiah, the Lamb overcoming ith His own word, the 'breath of his mouth' Rev. xix. 21; *cf.* Is. xi. 4). The influence of Ps. cx felt throughout the New Testament, and the arly Christians lived in the hope of final con-uest. Indeed, in Christ they had already onquered (Jn. xvi. 33), the victory was given Cor. xv. 57), for the last enemy was overcome y resurrection (1 Cor. xv. 26). See also ARMOUR ND WEAPONS.

BIBLIOGRAPHY. G. von Rad, *Der heilige Krieg n alten Israel*, 1951; *id.*, *Studies in Deuteronomy*, 953, pp. 45–59; C. H. W. Brekelmans, *De Ḥerem het Oude Testament*, 1959; E. W. Heaton, *'veryday Life in Old Testament Times*, 1956, pp. 44–159. J.A.B.

VARS OF THE LORD, BOOK OF THE. A ocument mentioned and quoted in Nu. xxi. 14f. he quotation ends with the word 'Moab' (verse 5), but possibly fragments of poetry in verses 17, 8, and 27–30 come from the same source. The ork was evidently a collection of popular songs ommemorating the early battles of the Israelites. he name indicates that the Israelites viewed ahweh virtually as their commander-in-chief, nd credited Him with their victories. Another milar work was probably the Book of Jashar of Sa. i. 18; it is evident that this document was ompiled after the time of David, and probably e Book of the Wars of the Lord appeared at the ame period. A few scholars, following the LXX, ould emend the text of Nu. xxi. 14 to excise the eference to any such document. D.F.P.

'ASHPOT (Heb. *sîr raḥaṣ*). Used in triumphant orn of Moab's inferiority (Pss. lx. 8, cviii. 9). his may be identified with wide-mouthed bowls ound at ancient sites. See VESSELS. A.R.M.

WATCH. 1. The guard of soldiers (Gk. *koustōdia*) mentioned by Matthew as being deputed to watch over our Lord's tomb.

2. A measure of time into which the twelve hours of the night were divided. In Israelite times the division was threefold (Jdg. vii. 19). In New Testament times the Roman division into four watches seems to have been used (*cf.* Mk. vi. 48).

WATCHMAN, WATCH-TOWERS. Watchman is in Hebrew *ṣōpeh* and *šōmēr*, in Greek *phylax* and *tērōn*; watch-tower is in Hebrew *miṣpâ*, *miḡdāl*, and *baḥan*. Watch-towers were used for two different purposes in biblical times: (1) Towers were built from the earliest times (*cf.* Gn. xxxv. 21) in the pastures to protect cattle and sheep against wild animals and thieves (*cf.* 2 Ch. xxvi. 10; Mi. iv. 8). It is possible that towers were erected in vineyards and cornfields for protection against thieves (*cf.* Is. xxvii. 3). (2) Towers of a more complex structure were built in the defence works of larger cities. The oldest Israelite tower of this kind as yet known was excavated by W. F. Albright at Tell el-Ful, the citadel of Saul. It is a corner tower which forms part of a casemate wall.

Important is the discovery by Albright at Tell Beit Mirsim in S Palestine of a gate tower with a rectangular court. This court gives access to six paved rooms probably for guests (see ARCHITECTURE). Excavations at Tell en-Nasbeh show that towers were constructed in the city's defence wall at distances of about 33 yards apart and extending about 2 yards to the outside. Square towers were built in early Israelite times, but later round ones were favoured. Herod erected in Jerusalem three massive towers, called Hippicus, Phasael, and Mariamne. The ground structure of the so-called 'tower of David' is possibly that of Phasael ($8\frac{1}{2} \times 44\frac{1}{2}$ yards). The *miḡdāl* and *millôʼ* (Jdg. ix. 6, 20; 2 Sa. v. 9; 1 Ki. ix. 15) were citadels or a kind of acropolis in a walled city. This citadel was used as a final place of refuge after the city was conquered. A good example of a *miḡdāl* was excavated at Beth-shean (*cf.* C. Watzinger, *Denkmäler*, II, 1935, plates 19–21).

In the watch-towers were watchmen on the alert for hostile action against the city. They were also there to give word to the king of any person approaching the city wall (*e.g.* 2 Sa. xviii. 24–27; 2 Ki. ix. 17–20). In time of hostility the dangers of the night were especially feared and the watchmen eagerly looked forward to the break of day (Is. xxi. 11). See also FORTIFICATION AND SIEGECRAFT. F.C.F.

WATER (Heb. *mayim*, Gk. *hydōr*). In a part of the world where water is in short supply, it naturally features significantly in the lives of the people of the Bible. Nothing is more serious to them than absence of water (see 1 Ki. xvii. 1 ff.; Je. xiv. 3; Joel i. 20; Hg. i. 11), and conversely rainfall is a sign of God's favour and goodness. An equally serious menace to life is water that has been polluted or rendered undrinkable. This was one of the plagues of Egypt (Ex. vii. 17 ff.). The Israelites found the water at Marah bitter (Ex. xv. 23), and the well at Jericho was unpleasant in Elisha's day (2 Ki. ii. 19–22).

It was common practice in time of warfare for an invading army to cut off the water-supply of beleaguered cities, as did Jehoshaphat with the wells of Moab (2 Ki. iii. 19, 25), and Holofernes at Bethulia (Judith vii. 7 ff.). Hezekiah brilliantly averted this danger by the construction of the tunnel which exists to this day in Jerusalem, running from the Virgin's fountain (Gihon), outside the city walls of his day, to the Pool of Siloam (2 Ch. xxxii. 30, see SILOAM). Under conditions when water had to be rationed (La. v. 4; Ezk. iv. 11, 16), the phrase 'water of affliction' could fittingly be used (Is. xxx. 20), but the context usually suggests punishment (1 Ki. xxii. 27; 2 Ch. xviii. 26).

Frequently water is symbolical of God's blessing and of spiritual refreshment, as in Ps. xxiii. 2; Is. xxxii. 2, xxxv. 6, 7, xli. 18, *etc.*, and the longing for it indicates spiritual need (Pss. xlii. 1, lxiii. 1; Am. viii. 11). In Ezekiel's vision of God's house (xlvii. 1–11) the waters that poured out from under the threshold represented the unrestricted flow of Yahweh's blessings upon His people (*cf.* Zc. xiv. 8). Jeremiah describes Yahweh as 'the fountain of living waters' (ii. 13, xvii. 13), a phrase that is echoed in Jn. vii. 38 of the Holy Spirit. In the New Testament water is connected with eternal life as the supreme blessing that God gives (Jn. iv. 14; Rev. vii. 17, xxi. 6, xxii. 1, 17), but in Eph. v. 26; Heb. x. 22, the predominant idea is that of baptismal cleansing for forgiveness of sins.

The idea of cleansing comes next to that of refreshment. In the ceremonial system washing was a prominent feature. Priests were washed at their consecration (Ex. xxix. 4); Levites too were sprinkled with water (Nu. viii. 7). Special ablutions were demanded of the chief priest on the Day of Atonement (Lv. xvi. 4, 24, 26), of the priest in the 'water of separation' ritual (Nu. xix. 1–10), and of all men for the removal of ceremonial defilement (Lv. xi. 40, xv. 5 ff., xvii. 15, xxii. 6; Dt. xxiii. 11). The laver before the tabernacle was a constant reminder of the need for cleansing in the approach to God (Ex. xxx. 18–21). A developed form of this ritual ablution was practised by the Qumran sect and by a variety of Jewish baptist sects which flourished before and after the turn of the Christian era. These provide the background to John's baptism of repentance and to the Christian baptism of cleansing, initiation, and incorporation into Christ. (See BAPTISM.)

A third aspect is that of danger and death. The story of the flood, the drowning of the Egyptians in the Red Sea, and the general fear of the sea and deep waters expressed by the psalmist (xviii. 16, xxxii. 6, xlvi. 3, lxix. 1 ff., *etc.*) indicate that water could in Yahweh's hands be an instrument of judgment, although at the same time there was the thought of salvation through danger for th faithful people of God (*cf.* Is. xliii. 2, lix. 19). It is hard to say to what extent these ideas wer moulded by the Canaanite myths of the contest c Baal with the tyrannical waters of the sea, re counted in the Ras Shamra texts. Present-da Scandinavian scholars and Hooke's 'Myth an Ritual' school see in these Old Testamen references, especially in the Psalms, a clue to th existence in Israel of an annual kingly festival a which the victory of Yahweh, personified by th king, was re-enacted. That Hebrew thought an poetry echo the language of Near Eastern mytho logy is clear (*cf.* the references to Rahab Leviathan, the dragon, *etc.*), but to hold that th Canaanite rituals themselves or the doctrina beliefs underlying them were taken over by th religion of Israel goes beyond the evidence. Th views of Gunkel, Mowinckel, and others are we discussed by A. R. Johnson in the chapter on 'Th Psalms' in *The Old Testament and Modern Study* 1951.

BIBLIOGRAPHY. P. Reymond, *L'Eau, Sa Vi et Sa Signification dans l'Ancien Testament*, 195[illegible]

J.B.Tr.

WATERPOTS. See VESSELS.

WAVE-BREAST, WAVE-OFFERING. See SACRIFICE AND OFFERING (Old Testament, IV*d* (iii).

WAY. 1. Old Testament usage. Apart from th obvious literal uses, there are a number of closel linked metaphorical ones. They derive from th fact that one on a public path becomes know and his goal and purposes are revealed by th road he takes. Most important is the sense o God's purposes and will, *e.g.* Ex. xxxiii. 13; Jb xxi. 14, 31; Ps. lxvii. 2; Pr. viii. 22; Ezk. xviii. 25 There follows naturally the idea of God's com mandments, *cf.* especially Ps. cxix. 'Way' is use generally of man's conduct, good or bad, an even of that of animals, *e.g.* Ps. i. 1, 6; Pr. xx 19, 20.

2. New Testament usage. There are tw developments of Old Testament usage that ca for comment. In Mt. vii. 13, 14 (*cf.* Lk. xiii. 24 we have the two ways in which man can wal contrasted. The thought is common in rabbini literature and was developed in the *Didache*, th *Epistle of Barnabas*, and later patristic writing From Acts ix. 2, xix. 9, 23, xxii. 4, xxiv. 14, 22 w learn that 'the Way' was the oldest designatio of the Christian Church for itself. This is partl an extension of a use already found in the Ol Testament; *cf.* Is. xl. 3 with xl. 10, 11, whe God's people are seen being led along God's wa It can also be explained from Mt. vii. 14 as th Way to salvation. Probably Jn. xiv. 6 was mo influential of all, for here Christ claims to be th summing up of all 'the Way' means in relatio ship to God. H.L.E.

WAYMARK. A sign, usually made of a heap o stones, to mark a track (Je. xxxi. 21, plura v 'high heaps'). The meaning is clear from the ontext and parallelism: Heb. *ṣiyyûn*, *cf.* Arab. *uwwah*, 'guide-stone'; Syr. *ṣwāyâ*, 'stone-heap'. The same Hebrew word is used of a monument r pile of stones used to mark the burial place of he dead (Ezk. xxxix. 15, AV 'sign'; 2 Ki. xxiii. 17, v 'title'). D.J.W.

VEALTH. The view of the Old Testament and f the New Testament is that wealth is a blessing rom God. Abraham is a typical example of a vealthy God-fearing man (Gn. xiii. 2). The salmists celebrate material blessings. The godly nan flourishes 'like a tree planted by the rivers of vater' (Ps. i. 3). 'Wealth and riches' are in the ouse of the man that 'feareth the Lord' (Ps. xii. 1, 3). God is beneficent, and material wealth s a consequence of His bounty: 'God . . . giveth s richly all things to enjoy' (1 Tim. vi. 17).

The possession of wealth, however, brings with the duty of generous liberality towards those in eed (1 Tim. vi. 18; 2 Cor. viii and ix). See LMS. Such is Christ's own example, 'Though he vas rich, yet for your sakes he became poor, that e through his poverty might be rich' (2 Cor. iii. 9). Faithfulness in the use of riches brings piritual reward (Lk. xvi. 11); for true wealth nd true riches are the spiritual blessings which od gives, rather than His material blessings Lk. xii. 33, xvi. 11).

The Bible recognizes that the possession of aterial wealth brings with it great dangers. For xample, there is the danger of failing to acknow-dge that God is the Source of the blessing Dt. viii. 17, 18; Ho. ii. 8). There is the related anger of trusting in riches (Ps. lii. 7). This anger of trusting in riches is so great that our ord said that it was extremely difficult for a rich an to enter the kingdom of heaven, explaining e hard saying by the paraphrase 'they that trust riches'. The disciples rightly concluded that all en have this besetting sin; to which our Lord plied that God alone can change the heart Mk. x. 23, 27). Another spiritual danger ssociated with riches is materialism, that is, aking riches the centre of one's interest. This as the case of the wealthy farmer in Lk. xii. 21, ho was not rich towards God; and of the church f Laodicea (Rev. iii. 17). This temptation that ealth brings is described in the parable of the ower (Mt. xiii. 22), where the deceitfulness of ches chokes the word, so that it becomes un-uitful in the life. See MAMMON.

Covetousness, or the desire to be rich, is an vil against which the Scriptures frequently warn. he love of money is described as the root of all inds of evil (1 Tim. vi. 9, 10). Consequently a pirit of contentment with such things as God has iven is a virtue inculcated in both Testaments Ps. lxii. 10; 1 Tim. vi. 8; Heb. xiii. 5).

Because of the dangers of riches into which the ossessor so frequently falls, rich men are, as a lass, denounced in several passages of the Scrip-ures, *e.g.* Lk. vi. 24 f. and Jas. v. Blessings are, owever, pronounced on the poor (Lk. vi. 20 ff.); for poverty should quicken faith in God, which riches so frequently in practice deadens. D.B.K.

WEAPONS. See ARMOUR AND WEAPONS.

WEASEL. Mentioned only in Lv. xi. 29, translated from *ḥōleḏ*. Several members of the weasel tribe are found in Palestine, and also a mongoose, but there is nothing to confirm that *ḥōleḏ* refers to all or any of them. Its identity must therefore remain doubtful. G.C.

WEAVING. See SPINNING AND WEAVING.

WEDDING. See MARRIAGE.

WEDGE (OF GOLD). See MONEY.

WEEKS, FEAST OF. See PENTECOST (FEAST OF).

WEEPING. See BURIAL AND MOURNING.

WEIGHTS AND MEASURES.

1. In the Old Testament

Metrology, an exact science, requires legal sanction to enforce the authority granted to any particular system. In the Ancient Near East standards varied between districts and cities, and there is no evidence that Israel had or used an integrated system. David (2 Sa. xiv. 26) and Ezekiel (xlv. 10) pronounced certain basic

Fig. 229. An Egyptian weighing gold rings on a balance against weights in the shape of a bull's head and a cone. More such weights lie in a dish. He adjusts the plummet to obtain an exact balance. Thebes, tomb painting, *c.* 15th century BC.

standards of weight and measurements. Rabbinic tradition that standard measures were deposited in the Temple is unverified (*cf.* 1 Ch. xxiii. 29). The law, however, prescribed that the Hebrew keep a just weight, measure, and balance (Lv. xix. 35, 36; Ezk. xlv. 10). The prophets spoke against those merchants who, by increasing or decreasing their weights (Dt. xxv. 13), or using deceitful weights (Mi. vi. 11) or false balances (Pr. xi. 1, xx. 23), defrauded their fellows. Since

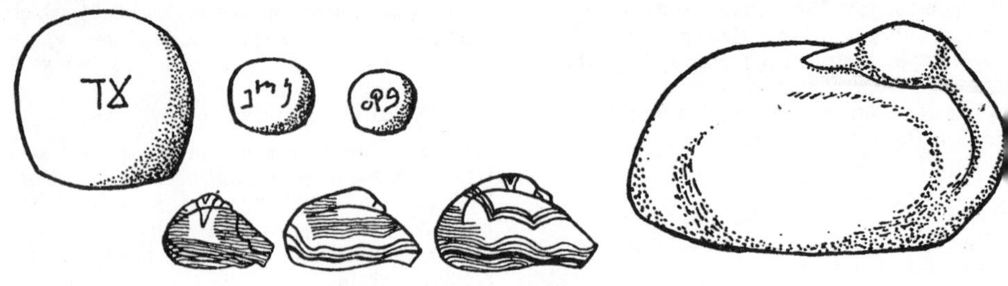

Fig. 230. *Upper left:* Hebrew stone weights—(i) 8 shekels (91·4 gm.); (ii) *'nṣp* = temple shekel; (ii *bq'* = half-shekel. From Lachish, 7th–6th centuries BC. *Lower centre:* Banded agate weights in the shap of ducks. *Right:* A stone duck-weight inscribed '2 talents' = 1 cwt. 21½ lb. From Lagadu, *c.* 2100 BC

ancient balances had a margin of error of up to 6% (*PEQ*, LXXIV, 1942, p. 86), and no two Hebrew weights yet found of the same inscribed denomination have proved to be of exactly identical weight, the importance of this exhortation can be seen. These, and other variants, mean that ancient weights and measures can be given only their approximate equivalent in modern terms.

I. WEIGHTS

Ancient weights were stones (Heb. *'eḇen*) carved in shapes, usually with a flat base, which made them easy to handle or recognize (*e.g.* turtles, ducks, lions). See figs. 230, 231. They were often inscribed with their weight and the standard followed, *e.g.* in Hebrew weights I: II: III: 7: T: 1, 2, 4, 8 and X = *lmlk*, 'royal' (Y. Yadin, *Studies in the Bible*, 1960, pp. 1–9). Weights were carried in a pouch or wallet (Dt. xxv. 13; Mi. vi. 11; Pr. xvi. 11) in order that the purchaser could check with the 'weights current among the merchants' at a given place (so Gn. xxiii. 16, RSV).

a. Talent (Heb. *kikkār*, 'a round'; Akkad. *biltu*, 'a burden'; Gk. *talanton*, 'a weight'). This was the largest unit, probably named after the characteristic shape in which large metal lumps were moulded, as in the lead cover of the ephah (Zc. v. 7). It was used to weigh gold (2 Sa. xii. 30, *etc.*), silver (1 Ki. xx. 39), iron (1 Ch. xxix. 7) and bronze (Ex. xxxviii. 29). 666 talents of gold were included in Solomon's annual revenue (1 Ki. x. 14).

The 30 talents of gold paid by Hezekiah as tribute (2 Ki. xviii. 14) corresponds with the amount Sennacherib claims to have received (Annals), implying a similar talent in use in Judah and Assyria at this time. This might be the 'light' talent of about 30 kg., as inscribed Babylonian duck-weights of this value range 29·76–30·27 kg. A weight found at Tell Beit Mirsim (4,565 gm.) has been interpreted as this talent of 30·43 kg. or, more likely, of 28·53 kg. (*i.e.* 8 minas of 570·6 gm. = 8 × 50 shekels of 11·41 gm.; see below).

Other Babylonian weights show that a 'heavy' or double standard talent was also in use, weighed examples ranging from 58·68 to 59·82, *i.e.* about 60 kg.

b. Mina, maneh (AV; Heb. *māneh*; Akkad. *manû*), was a weight used to measure gold (1 Ki x. 17), silver (Ezr. ii. 69; Ne. vii. 71, 72), an other commodities. The talent was subdivide into 60 minas of 50 shekels or 50 minas of 6 shekels. There is some evidence that in Palestine as at Ras Shamra, the 50-shekel mina was in us in pre-exilic times. The payment by 603,550 me of a poll-tax of ½ shekel (see *bekah*) produced 10 talents, 1,775 shekels, *i.e.* 3,000 shekels to th talent (as at Ras Shamra), but could be inter preted by either standard. However, multiple of 50 shekels (*e.g.* 400—Gn. xxiii. 15; 500—Ex xxx. 24; 5,000—1 Sa. xvii. 5; 16,750—Nu. xxxi 52) seem to be conclusive evidence for the use of 50-shekel mina.

Ezekiel's metrological reforms included the re definition of the mina to 60 shekels (xlv. 12, *MT* 20 + 25 + 15). Thus the new Hebrew mina a 20 (gerahs) × 60 (shekels) kept the value of th mina unchanged in relation to the Babylonian which comprised 24 (*girū*) × 50 (*šiqlu*) = 1,20 gerahs.

c. The *shekel* (Heb. *šeqel*; Akkad. *šiqlu*; Aram. Ugar. *tql*) was common to all Semitic metrologie and was the basic weight (*šāqal*, 'to weigh'). It value varied considerably at different times an areas:

(i) The royal shekel, set by 'the king's weight (2 Sa. xiv. 26), was a standard known also i Babylonia. This was probably the 'heavy sheke of Ras Shamra (*kbd*). Analysis of weights dis covered at Gibeon, Gezer, Megiddo, and Te en-Nasbeh show a 'heavy' shekel of 12·5–12·8 gm., *i.e.* about 13 gm. (0·457 oz.).

(ii) The common shekel was often used t weigh metal objects (1 Sa. xvii. 5; Goliath' armour of 5,000 shekels = 125 lb.), hair (2 Sa xiv. 26), food (Ezk. iv. 10), and commonly gol and silver, thus implying its use as a means c payment. The shekel was not recognized as coin until the reign of Darius I (see MONEY).

Seventeen inscribed weights of a shekel o multiples upwards show a variation 11·08–12·25 average 11·38 gm. This compares well wit calculations based on the inscribed weights c smaller denominations (see below), which con firm a possible devaluation in post-exilic time to about 11·7–11·4 gm. (0·401 oz.) for the sheke

(iii) The temple shekel or 'shekel of the sanc

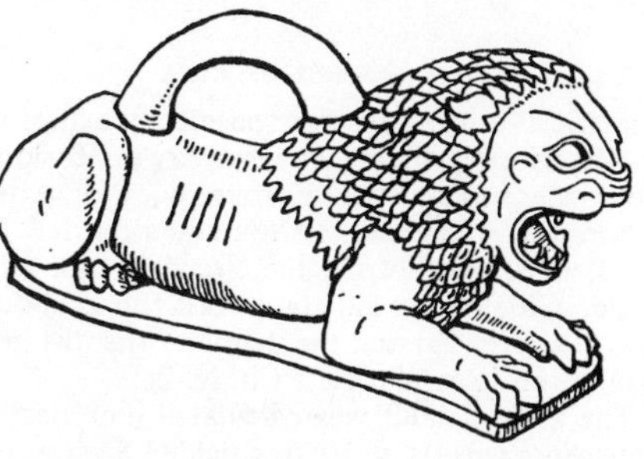

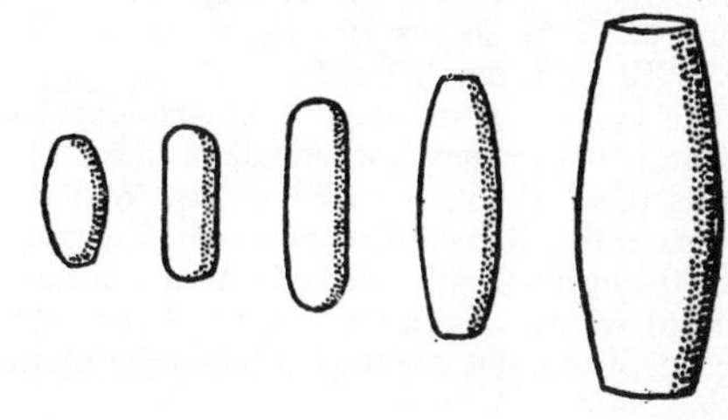

ig. 231. *Left:* Assyrian weight in the shape of a lion inscribed '5 (menas)', and on reverse 'Property of halmaneser' (845 BC). *Right:* A series of Babylonian polished haematite weights ranging from 25·57 to 83·70 gm. 18th century BC.

ıary' (Ex. xxx. 13; Lv. v. 15, *etc.*) was equivalent ɔ a *beqa'* or ½ shekel (Ex. xxxviii. 26) and 0 gerahs (Ezk. xlv. 12), though later with re-aluation it equalled ⅓ shekel (Ne. x. 32). This ıekel is believed to be the *nṣp* (see below), of ·hich examples have been discovered weighing ·28–10·5 gm., *i.e.* about 10 gm. (0·351 oz.) de-reciating to about 9·8 gm. (0·345 oz.).

d. nṣp or 'part' was five-sixths shekel. Thirteen xamples give it a weight of about 10 gm. (see bove).

e. pim (Heb. *pîm* or *payim*) is mentioned only 1 Sa. xiii. 21 (AV 'Yet they had a file (with ıouths)') which should be translated 'and the harge was a *pim* for the ploughshares . . .' (so sv). This weight was ⅔ of a unit (*cf.* Akkad. *šini)pu*), probably of the common shekel, since even inscribed *pim* weights (from Lachish, erusalem, Gezer, Tell en-Nasbeh) range 7·18–·13 gm., *i.e.* about ¼ oz.

f. bekah (Heb. *beqa'*, 'fraction, division') was sed for weighing gold (Gn. xxiv. 22) and for aying the poll-tax said to be the equivalent of ıalf a shekel, after the shekel of the sanctuary' Ex. xxxviii. 26). Since seven inscribed weights ıscribed *bq'* have been found (at Lachish, erusalem, Gezer, and Beth-zur), this enables a heck to be made of the value of the shekel. 'hese *bq'* have an average weight of 6·02 gm.

g. ḥmš, 'one-fifth' was inscribed on a turtle-haped weight from Samaria weighing 2·499 gm. 'his compares with another inscribed '¼ *nṣp šql*', implying a subdivision of the Ezekiel ıekel.

h. gerah (Heb. *gērâ*; Assyr. *girû*). This was efined as one-twentieth of a shekel (Ex. xxx. 13; 'zk. xlv. 12).

i. Other weights. The *peres* (Aram. pl. *parsin*) f Dn. v. 25, 28 was a subdivision of the shekel use at Babylon (*cf.* O. Bab. *paras*), and like the *arisu* (Alalaḫ) probably equal to ½ shekel. Thus ıe writing on the wall superficially implied a :atement of weight 'Mina, mina, shekel, half-ıekel'. The *qᵉśîṭâ* (Gn. xxxiii. 19; Jos. xxiv. 32; b. xlii. 11) appears to be a unit of as yet un-nown weight (see KESITAH; also fig. 140).

The table given on p. 1323 indicates the relation f these weights to each other and gives approxi-ıate modern equivalents, which should be used with caution owing to the varying standards in use in antiquity.

II. LINEAR MEASURES

Linear measures were based on the 'natural' units which could be easily applied.

a. The *reed* (*qāneh*), though often denoting a measuring instrument rather than a measure (see ARTS AND CRAFTS), was of 6 cubits length and exact enough to be reckoned as a unit of length (Ezk. xl. 5; *cf.* 'rod', Rev. xxi. 15, RSV).

Fig. 232. Assyrians weighing tribute in a balance. From the black basalt obelisk of Ashurnasirpal II. Nimrud, *c.* 880 BC.

b. The *cubit* (Heb. *'ammâ*; Akkad. *ammātu*; Lat. *cubitus*) was the distance from elbow to finger tip. This 'natural' cubit (AV 'cubit of a man', Dt. iii. 11) was used to indicate the general size of a person (4 cubits the height of a man; *cf.* 1 Sa. xvii. 4; 1 Ch. xi. 23) or object (Est. v. 14; Zc. v. 2). It described depth (Gn. vii. 20) or distance (Jn. xxi. 8).

A more precisely defined cubit was used for exact measurement. This *standard Hebrew cubit* was 17·5 inches, slightly shorter than the common Egyptian cubit of 17·6 inches. This generally accepted figure compares closely with the length given for the Siloam tunnel as '1,200 cubits', equivalent to a measured 1,749 feet (533·1 metres), giving a cubit of 17·49 inches. Excavated buildings at Megiddo, Lachish, Gezer, and Hazor (see fig. 102) reveal a plan based on multiples of this measure. Also Solomon's bronze laver of 1,000 *bath* capacity (*i.e.* 22,000 litres; 1 Ki. vii. 23–26; 2 Ch. iv. 2, 5), when calculated for the capacity of a sphere, gives a cubit of 17·51 inches (R. B. Y. Scott, *JBL*, LXXVII, 1958, pp. 210–212).

The *long* or 'royal' *cubit* was a handbreadth ('palm') longer than the standard cubit of 6 palms (Ezk. xl. 5), *i.e.* 20·4 inches. With this compare the Babylonian cubit of 19·8 inches (of 30 fingers length marked on a statue of Gudea) which was 'three fingers' shorter than the Egyptian cubit of 20·65 inches (Herodotus, *Hist.* i. 178).

c. The *gōmeḏ* (AV 'cubit') occurs only in Jdg. iii. 16, where it describes a weapon, probably a dagger rather than a sword, and has thus been interpreted as a subdivision (perhaps ⅔) of the cubit, or as the short cubit of 5 palms mentioned in the Mishnah.

d. The *span* (*zereṯ*), or outstretched hand from the thumb to the little finger (Vulg. wrongly *palmus*), was a half-cubit (1 Sa. xvii. 4; Ex. xxviii. 16; Ezk. xliii. 13), though 'half a cubit' could be expressed literally (Ex. xxv. 10).

e. The *palm* (*ṭep̄aḥ*; *ṭōp̄aḥ*) or 'handbreadth' was the width of the hand at the base of the four fingers (hence Vulg. *quattuor digitis*), *i.e.* 2·9 inches. Thus was measured the thickness of the bronze laver (1 Ki. vii. 26 = 2 Ch. iv. 5), the edge of the tabernacle table (Ex. xxv. 25, xxxvii. 12), and of that in Ezekiel's Temple (xl. 5, xliii. 13). A man's life is but (a few) handbreadths in length (Ps. xxxix. 5).

f. The *finger* or digit (*'eṣba'*) was a ¼ handbreadth (Je. lii. 21), and the smallest subdivision of the cubit in common use in Palestine, as in Egypt and Mesopotamia. It is generally taken to be 0·73 inch.

g. Distance, as opposed to the measurement of objects, was in pre-exilic times reckoned by equation with a known average. It is reckoned as a 'bowshot' (Gn. xxi. 16), the length of a ploughed furrow (1 Sa. xiv. 14), 'a day's journey' (Nu. xi. 31; 1 Ki. xix. 4), or 'a journey of three days' (Gn. xxx. 36; Ex. iii. 18; Jon. iii. 3). It is not proved that the latter is to be taken merely as general indication of 'a long distance' (*cf.* 'a seven days' journey', Gn. xxxi. 23), for exact standards were used by the Babylonians; *e.g. bēru*, 'double-hour' march of 10·692 km. (*AfO*, XVI, 1953, p. 20, n. 138).

The step (*peśa'*) in 1 Sa. xx. 3 was used metaphorically rather than in the exact manner of the contemporary Assyrian 'foot' (= 12·96 inches). Similarly the 'stretch of the ground' (*kiḇraṯ hā'āreṣ*, AV 'little way', Gn. xxxv. 16, xlviii. 7; 2 Ki. v. 19) was only a vague indication of distance.

In Maccabean times Hellenistic measures were introduced. Thus Beth-zur was about 5 *schoinoi* from Jerusalem (2 Macc. xi. 5), *i.e.* 30·5 km. at the Ptolemaic value of a *schoinos* of 6·1 km. The Alexandrian *stadion* of 184·9 metres was employed. Jerusalem to Scythopolis was 60 *stades* (2 Macc. xii. 29), which corresponds well with the known distance of 110 km. between these two cities.

III. MEASURES OF AREA

Superficial areas were not specifically expresse but described by giving the necessary dimensions Thus the square was of four sides of equa dimension (*m^e^rubbā'aṯ*, AV 'foursquare', 1 Ki. vii 31; Ezk. xl. 47, xlv. 2), the circumference of a circle 'a line of . . . did compass it round about (AV, 1 Ki. vii. 23) and the diameter the distanc 'from brim to brim' (AV, 2 Ch. iv. 2).

The area of land was calculated empirically Thus vineyards (Is. v. 10) or a field (1 Sa. xiv. 14 could be measured by the *ṣemeḏ* (AV 'acre'), *i.e* the area a pair of yoked animals could plough i a day (*cf.* Arab. *faddan*). In Babylonia this wa defined as 6,480 square cubits = two-fifths acre This in later times was the Lat. *jugum*, *jugerum* o 28,800 square Rom. feet = ⅝ acre. Anothe method was to estimate the area by the amoun of seed (*s^e'â*) required to sow it (Lv. xxvii. 16 1 Ki. xviii. 32). In the Hellenistic period this wa 3⅗ seahs to a *jugerum* of land, *i.e.* 0·173 acre pe seah or 5·19 acres per homer of 30 seahs (*JBL* LXIV, 1945, p. 372), which seems to have im proved to 0·193 and 5·79 acres respectively by th 2nd century AD.

The specific measurement of the pasture round the levitical cities (Nu. xxxv. 4, 5) present difficulties. It may have been an area 2,000 cubit square (verse 5), the centres of the sides of whic were also reckoned as at a radius of 1,000 cubit from the city walls (verse 4).

IV. DRY MEASURES OF CAPACITY

The terms used derive originally from the re ceptacles which contained an agreed amount an thus served as a measure.

a. Homer (Heb. *ḥōmer*; Akkad. *imēr*), 'a donkey load', was commonly used as a measur for cereals (Lv. xxvii. 16; Ezk. xlv. 13). Th collection of 10 homers of quails (Nu. xi. 32 implied gluttony, whereas the return of only a ephah of wheat from a homer of seed was a picture of failure (Is. v. 10), there being 10 ephah to the homer, which equalled about 220 litre (48·4 gallons).

b. Cor (Heb. *kōr*; Akkad. *gur*) was a large dr measure equal to the homer (Ezk. xlv. 14) use of fine flour (*sōleṯ*), meal (*qemaḥ*, 1 Ki. iv 22), wheat, and barley (2 Ch. ii. 10, xxvii. 5). I also appears as a liquid measure for oil (Ezk. xlv 14), though 2 Ch. ii. 10 and Gk. reads *bath* (*cf.* th parallel passage, 1 Ki. v. 11).

c. Half-homer (Heb. *leṯeḵ*) occurs only i Ho. iii. 2 as a measure for barley. As it i mentioned after the homer, Aq., Sym., and Vulg interpret as ½ *kōr* or ½ homer, but there is n confirmatory evidence for this. The *leṯeḵ* ma be a Phoenician measure.

d. Ephah (Heb. *'ēp̄â*; Egyp. *ipt*) is the nam of a vessel large enough to hold a person (Zc. v 6–10), and thence of an exact measure (Lv. xix 36). Used only of cereals, and with subdivision o one-sixth (Ezk. xlv. 13, xlvi. 14) or one-tent (Lv. v. 11), it was in common use from an earl eriod (Jdg. vi. 19). The ephah must never be minished (Am. viii. 5) but always be of equal ust) measure (Dt. xxv. 14; Pr. xx. 10). The hah was equal to the liquid measure *bath*, both ing one-tenth of a homer (Ezk. xlv. 11).

e. Seah (Heb. *sᵉâ*; Akkad. *sûtu*) was also a easure for flour and cereals (Gn. xviii. 6; 1 Ki. viii. 32).

equal to a tenth (one-tenth) of an ephah (Nu. xxviii. 5), and therefore equal to the omer.

h. Cab (Heb. *qab̲*; Akkad. *qa*), a measure of capacity which occurs only in 1 Ki. vi. 25, where among the inflated prices at the siege of Samaria ¼ *qab̲* of carob pods was sold for 5 (shekels) of silver. The cab = 4 log = one-fifth seah = one-sixth hin = about 2 litres.

OLD TESTAMENT WEIGHTS WITH MODERN EQUIVALENTS

AV TERM	RATIOS					APPROXIMATE EQUIVALENTS metric	lb.	oz.
Talent	1					30 kg.	66	2·2
Maneh	60	1				500 gm.	1	1·6
Shekel	3,000	50	1			11·4 gm.	—	0·4
„ (Ezekiel)	(3,600)	(60)	—			9·5 gm.	—	0·33
Bekah	6,000	100	2	1		6·02 gm.	—	0·212
Gerah	72,000	1,200	20	10	1	0·5 gm.	—	0·018

OLD TESTAMENT MEASURES WITH MODERN EQUIVALENTS

A. Linear

AV TERM	RATIOS					APPROXIMATE EQUIVALENTS metres, *etc.*	ft.	in.
Reed	1					2·67 m.	8	9
„ (Ezekiel)	(1)					3·1 m.	10	—
Cubit	6	1				46 cm.	1	6
„ (Ezekiel)	(7)					52 cm.	1	9
Span	12	2	1			223 mm.	—	7
Palm	—	6(7)	3	1		74 mm.	—	3
Finger	—	24	12	4	1	18·6 mm.	—	¾

B. Capacity

AV TERM	RATIOS								APPROXIMATE EQUIVALENTS litres, *etc.*	galls.	pts.
Homer = *cor**	1								220	48	3
Half-homer (*letek̲*)	2	1							110	24	1½
Ephah = *bath* †	10	5	1						22	4	6¾
Seah	30	15	3	1					7·3	1	5
Hin †	60	30	6	2	1				3·66	—	6½
Omer = *'iśśārôn*	100	50	10	—	—	1			2·2		4
Cab	180	90	18	6	3	—	1		1·2		2
Log †	720	36	72	24	12	—	4	1	0·3		½

* Dry and liquid measure. † Liquid measure only.

f. Omer (Heb. *'ōmer*, *cf.* Arab. *'umar*, 'a nall bowl') occurs only in the account of the llection of manna (Ex. xvi), being used both the measure itself (verses 18, 32, 33) and the amount measured (verses 16, 22). ne *'ōmer* was equal to one-tenth of an ephah erse 36).

g. A *'tenth* deal' (AV; Heb. *'iśśārôn*) was a easure used for flour (Ex. xxix. 40; Nu. xv. 4)

i. The 'measure' (AV; Heb. *šālîš*) of Ps. lxxx. 5; Is. xl. 12 is literally 'a third', but no unit is expressed, so that the measure of capacity is unknown.

It will be noted that these dry measures combine the Babylonian sexagesimal reckonings (1 *gur* = 30 *sutu* = 180 *qa*) with the decimal system (also employed by the Assyrians). See table above.

v. LIQUID MEASURES OF CAPACITY

a. Bath (Heb. *baṯ*; Gk. *batos*, Lk. xvi. 6 only) was the equivalent in liquid of the ephah (Ezk. xlv. 11, 14). It was used to measure water (1 Ki. vii. 26), wine (Is. v. 10), and oil (2 Ch. ii. 10; so also 1 Ki. v. 11). It was an exact and standard measure (Ezk. xlv. 10). For its modern equivalent (about 22 litres), see below.

b. Hin (Heb. *hîn*; Egyp. *hnw*, 'a pot') was used of the vessel employed as a measure (Lv. xix. 36) and of the measure of water (Ezk. iv. 11), oil (Ex. xxix. 40), or wine (Lv. xxiii. 13). According to Josephus (*Ant.* iii. 8. 3, 9. 4), the *hin* was equal to one-sixth of a *bath*.

c. Log (Heb. *lōḡ*) is used only in Lv. xiv. 10 as a measure of oil in the ceremony for the purification of the leper. According to the Talmud, this was equal to one-twelfth of a *bath*.

The values of these liquid measures depend upon that of the *bath*. This is uncertain, since the only inscribed vessels marked *bt* (Tell Beit Mirsim) and *bt lmlk* (Lachish) are fragmentary and cannot be reconstructed with certainty; thus the value of the *bath* has been variously calculated between 20·92 and 46·6 litres. On the assumptions that the *bath* measure was half the size of the 'royal *bath*' and that these inscriptions denoted the full capacity of the vessels, the proposal of 22 litres in biblical times (Albright) and 21·5 litres in Hellenistic times is usually adopted as a basis for calculation (see table p. 1323), since it receives some support from the comparison with the capacity of Solomon's laver, which held 1,000 *baths* = 22,000 litres (see table).

BIBLIOGRAPHY. R. B. Y. Scott, 'Weights and Measures of the Bible', *BA*, XXII, 1951, pp. 22–40; R. de Vaux, *Les Institutions de l'Ancien Testament*, I, 1958, pp. 297–317; A. E. Berriman, *Historical Metrology*, 1953; A. H. Gardiner, *Egyptian Grammar*[3], 1957, pp. 197–200 (for Egyptian metrology).

2. In the New Testament

I. WEIGHTS

Only two weights are mentioned in the New Testament. The *litra* of Jn. xii. 3, xix. 39 (*cf.* Lat. *libra*: AV 'pound'—from this weight we have our abbreviation *lb.* for pound) was a Roman measure of weight equivalent to 327·45 gm., or just under 12 oz. avoirdupois. In Rev. xvi. 21 the adjective *talantiaios*, 'weighing a talent', is used to describe hailstones: *Arndt* maintains that this talent equalled 125 librae, and so would be about 90 lb. in weight, but *HDB* calculates it as weighing about 45 lb.

II. LINEAR MEASURES

a. The *cubit*. As in Old Testament times, measurements were related to the parts of the body, and the basic unit was still the *pēchys* ('forearm') or cubit: under the Roman Empire the Jewish cubit measured 21·6 inches, and this is probably the length indicated in Jn. xxi. 8; Rev. xxi. 17. In M vi. 27; Lk. xii. 25 the term is also used.

b. The *orgyia* ('fathom', Acts xxvii. 28) wa the length of the outstretched arms, and so wa approximately 6 feet. This was a Greek unit c measure, derived from the verb *oregō*, 'I stretch Herodotus (ii. 149) says that it equalled 6 Gk feet or 4 Gk. cubits.

c. The *stadion* ('furlong', Lk. xxiv. 13; Jn. v 19, xi. 18; Rev. xiv. 20, xxi. 16) was 100 *orgyic* and equalled about 202 yards (606¾ feet or 184 metres). As the race-course at Olympia was sup posed to be exactly a stade long, the word wa used for an arena, as in 1 Cor. ix. 24—hence th English 'stadium'.

d. The *milion* ('mile'—Mt. v. 41) was a Gk transliteration of the Roman measurement *mil passuum*, 'a thousand paces'. This was 1,61 English yards (1,478·5 metres), or 8 stades, an was calculated on the basis of 5 Roman fee (each of 11·65 inches) to the pace (4 feet 10·2 inches).

e. The sabbath day's journey mentioned i Acts i. 12 was not a proper measurement, bu rather the product of rabbinical exegesis of Ex xvi. 29 and Nu. xxxv. 5 (*cf.* Lumby in *CGT a loc.*). It was fixed at 2,000 cubits (Talmu '*Erubin* 51a) and was called *tĕḥûm ha-šabbāṯ*- the limit of the sabbath.

III. MEASURES OF AREA

None are used in the New Testament, but th basic unit under the Roman Empire was th *jugerum*, or acre. This was calculated in terms the amount of land a yoke of oxen could ploug in a day, which was estimated at one *actus*, c furrow (120 feet), by two (240 feet), and so th *jugerum* was the equivalent of 2 square *actus*, c 28,800 square feet (3,200 square yards), abo two-thirds of an acre.

IV. DRY MEASURES OF CAPACITY

a. The *choinix* ('measure', Rev. vi. 6), commonl rendered 'quart', is variously estimated at 1½- pints, and the best calculation would be just ove 1 litre. It was a Greek measure, and Herodotu (vii. 187) narrates that it was the daily ration c grain per man in Xerxes' invasion army.

b. The *saton* (Aram. *sā'ṯâ*, Heb. *se'â*) was th *se'â* of Old Testament times: Jos. (*Ant.* ix. 4. rates this as equivalent to 1½ *modii* (see below It is the measure mentioned in Mt. xiii. 3 Lk. xiii. 21, where 3 *sata* of leaven are added the wheat-flour: each *saton* would be about pecks.

c. The *koros* of Lk. xvi. 7 (a 'measure of wheat was Heb. *kōr*. Josephus (*Ant.* xv. 9. 2) equates it 10 Attic *medimnoi*, and, as the *medimnos* co tained 48 *choinikes*, this would rate the *koros* 525 litres, or nearly 131 English, 157 America gallons. Since Ezk. xlv. 11 rates the *baton* as th tenth of a *koros*, it is generally regarded th Josephus here mistook the *medimnos* for t *metrētēs*, and that the *koros* contained 10 *metr tai*, about 86 gallons (just over 103 Americ llons). It was used for both dry and liquid easure.

d. The *modios* (AV 'bushel') of Mt. v. 15; Mk. . 21; Lk. xi. 33 was Lat. *modius*, and all three ferences use the word to denote the vessel used measure this amount. It was a grain measure ntaining 16 *sextarii*: 6 *modii* equalled the Gk. *edimnos* (Cornelius Nepos, *Attica* ii). Thus the *odius* contained 8 *choinikes* and was about 8·75 res, or roughly 1 peck, 2·3 American gallons.

V. LIQUID MEASURES OF CAPACITY

The *xestēs* of Mk. vii. 4, 8 is again a reference to e vessel used for measuring this capacity, and is ken by most scholars (but see Moulton and oward, *Grammar of New Testament Greek*, II, 29, p. 155) to be a corruption of the Latin *xtarius*. This was a liquid and dry measure the xteenth part of a *modius*, a little under 1 pint.

b. The *batos* ('measure' of oil in Lk. xvi. 6) is a k. form of Heb. *bat* (see above). According to sephus (*Ant.* viii. 2. 9), it contains 72 *sextarii* or *modii*—about 39½ litres, or about 8½ English, American, gallons.

c. The *metrētēs* mentioned in Jn. ii. 6 (rendered rkin') was a Gk. liquid measure approximately uivalent to the *bat*, and so containing about 8½ nglish gallons. Thus the stone water-pots used the wedding-feast at Cana held between 17 and gallons each (20–30 American gallons).

D.J.W.
D.H.W.

ELL. 1. An artificial shaft sunk to reach underound water, percolating or collected (Heb. *'ēr*; Arab. *bir*; Gk. *phrear*), whereas a spring

g. 233. A typical city well, based on those exvated at Calah (Nimrud) dated 879 BC. The pulley heel was made of mulberry wood and was probly set on some kind of wooden cross-bar now lost.

Ieb. and Arab. *'ayin*; Gk. *pēgē*) is the work of ture. AV confusion of terminology is due to the me confusion in 17th-century English, reflected so in Milton. Hebrew and Greek are unnbiguous.

2. An artificial shaft sunk to reach a natural underground spring—a fusion of concepts in which the terms could be interchanged correctly. There is a reasonable presumption that the well from which Rachel drew in Gn. xxiv was of this type—likewise Jacob's well at Shechem, where Jesus met the woman of Samaria in John iv. This would explain satisfactorily the puzzling alternation of words in these two chapters.

3. A cistern (*q.v.*) or pit, large or small, public or private, for collecting rain-water: Heb. *bôr*; Gk. *lakkos*. The well at Bethlehem (1 Ch. xi. 17, 18) was probably an example.

4. A shaft, dry or with miry clay, used as a dungeon for which the same Hebrew word is used (Gn. xxxvii. 24; Ps. xl. 2; Je. xxxviii. 6, *etc.*).

The praise of the well of living water in folksong is reflected in Nu. xxi. 17, 18.

In the arid parts of the East water (*q.v.*) may become as precious as gold. Wells were, and still remain, the subjects of fierce disputes and even strife. (*Cf.* Gn. xxi. 25, *etc.*) They became heritable, and were exploited by human monopolies at an earlier date than land. R.A.S.

WEN (Heb. *yabbeleṯ*, Lv. xxii. 22; *cf.* LXX *myrmēkiōnta*). Included in a list of blemishes which made animals an unacceptable sacrifice to the Lord. According to Jewish tradition, the Hebrew word applies to 'one suffering from warts'. RVmg reads 'having sores'; RSV, 'having a discharge'. See also DISEASE AND HEALING.

WHALE. This is the AV rendering of: 1. Gk. *kētos* (Mt. xii. 40; RV 'whale'; RVmg 'seamonster', *q.v.*) used by Homer and Herodotus for a seal, large fish, or sea-monster. The Hebrew of Jon. i. 17 (*dāḡ gāḏôl*) means 'great fish'. 2. Heb. *tannîn* (Gn. i. 21; Jb. vii. 12); RV 'sea-monster'.

3. Heb. *tannîm* (Ezk. xxxii. 2; AVmg, RV 'dragon') is the same as the plural of *tan*, 'jackals', by which it can sometimes be translated (for 'jackal', see FOX). Sperm whales and large sharks capable of swallowing a man have been identified in the E Mediterranean (*HDB*), and with porpoises and other large fish were hunted in antiquity. It is, however, not certain that the 'whale' is implied by any of these terms in Scripture. See also FISH. D.J.W.

WHEAT. A cereal grass of great antiquity and importance as a food of mankind. Belonging to the genus *Triticum*, the cultivated species may have originated from the wild small spelt wheat, *Triticum aegilopoides*. Owing to its physical and chemical qualities, it makes more palatable and better bread than any other cereal.

Wheat formed an important part of the diet of the children of Israel (Jdg. vi. 11; Ru. ii. 23; 2 Sa. iv. 6), and the wheat harvest is used as a calendar reference (Gn. xxx. 14; 1 Sa. vi. 13, xii. 17). Because of its importance as a food, it is a symbol of God's goodness and provision (Pss. lxxxi. 16, cxlvii. 14). It was used as a cereal offering in the Temple (Ezr. vi. 9, vii. 22) and forms part of the sacrifice made by David on Ornan's threshing-floor (1 Ch. xxi. 23).

Its botanical nature whereby one grain gives rise to several new ears of wheat, while the original grain is used up, is taken by Christ to show that spiritual fruitfulness has its origin in the death of self (Jn. xii. 24; *cf.* 1 Cor. xv. 36 ff.). As symbolic of the children of God, it is contrasted with the valueless chaff (Mt. iii. 12). Similarly, in Mt. xiii. 24–30 the tares (*q.v.*), *Lolium temulentum*, in their early stages of growth appear as grass-like as wheat, but can easily be distinguished at harvest-time. See also AGRICULTURE. D.C.

WHEEL. The earliest attested wheels (Heb. *galgal*, *'ôpān*) are clay models of chariot wheels and fragments of a potter's wheel (*cf.* Je. xviii. 3, Heb. *'obnayim*) of the fourth millennium BC (see C. L. Woolley, *Ur Excavations IV*, 1956, p. 28, plate 24). Early wheels were made from wooden planks pegged together (see fig. 54 and *ANEP*, nos. 163, 169, 303), but with the displacement of the ass by the horse around 1500 BC lighter spoked wheels came into use (see fig. 55 and *ANEP*, nos. 167, 168, 183, 184). The bronze stands made for Solomon's Temple were miniature chariot wheels, with axles, rims, spokes, and hubs (1 Ki. vii. 33). Daniel had a vision of the Ancient of days seated on a throne with wheels of fire (vii. 9), and Ezekiel describes the wheels in his visions of the chariot of God (i, x; see CHARIOT). The rumble of chariot wheels betokened the approach of an enemy (Je. xlvii. 3; Na. iii. 2), but all those hostile to God's people will be blown away like tumbleweed (Ps. lxxxiii. 13; Is. xvii. 13, RSV). In later Hebrew *galgal* is used *pars pro toto* for wagon (Ezk. xxiii. 24, xxvi. 10). Wheels were also used as part of the machinery for drawing water (Ec. xii. 6). On the wheel of birth (Jas. iii. 6, AV 'course of nature'), see R. V. G. Tasker, *James*, *TNTC*, 1956, pp. 75 f. A.R.M.

WHIRLWIND. The English translation of Heb. *sûpâ* applies loosely to any violent storm and is not restricted to a rotary movement of air (Jb. xxxvii. 9; Pr. i. 27, x. 25; Is. v. 28, xvii. 13, xxi. 1, lxvi. 15; Je. iv. 13; Am. i. 14; Na. i. 3). In AV it is translated 'storm' in other passages (Jb. xxi. 18; Ps. lxxxiii. 15; Is. xxix. 6). *Seʿārâ* is used synonymously, translated 'whirlwind' when it stands alone (*e.g.* 2 Ki. ii. 1; Jb. xxxviii. 1, xl. 6; Is. xl. 24, xli. 16) but sometimes 'storm' (Ps. cvii. 29; Is. xxix. 6). RV uses the expression only once in its technical sense (Je. xxiii. 19).

The whirlwind is used aptly as a figure for the sudden attack of the invader (Is. v. 28; Je. iv. 13; Dn. xi. 40; Am. i. 14 f.). It also symbolizes divine judgment because of its sudden motion (Ps. xviii. 10; Na. i. 3) and divine wrath (Ps. lviii. 9; Pr. x. 25; Is. xvii. 13, xxviii. 17, lxvi. 15; Ho. viii. 7). It is similarly used of the messianic wrath, described in Mt. vii. 24–27. See WIND. J.M.H.

WHITE. See COLOURS.

WHITE OF AN EGG (*rîr ḥallāmûṯ*, Jb. vi. 6 RVmg 'the juice of purslain'). Used as a symbo of something tasteless, perhaps the sap of som vegetable. D. J. Wiseman (*The Alalakh Tablets* 1953, p. 87), in outlining 18th-century BC ratio lists from Alalaḫ, notes a possible connectio between *ḫilimitu*, classed among the grains, an Syr. *ḥallâmûṯ* (*cf.* Hebrew form above). J.D.D.

WHORE. See PROSTITUTION.

WICKED. In the Old Testament, *rāšāʿ*, 'wicked ungodly', and *raʿ*, 'evil', are most common *ponēros*, 'bad, malignant', as contrasted wit *chrēstos*, is the usual New Testament word although *athesmos*, *anomos*, and *kakos* are als used. While the term is often used in the genera sense of 'wrong' (Ps. xviii. 21), it refers mor specifically to evil, not in its moral or judicia sense, but in its active form, *i.e.* mischief (Nu xvi. 26). As such, it denotes perversity of min (Pr. xv. 26; Rom. i. 29) by which the natural ma surrenders himself to evil impulses (Ps. x. 1–11) Wickedness has its seat in the heart (Je. xvii. 9 Mk. vii. 21–23), and is inspired by Satan (Mt xiii. 19; 1 Jn. iii. 12). It is progressive (Gn. vi. 5 and contagious (1 Sa. xxiv. 13) in its manifesta tion. The wicked man is utterly perverse, findin unholy delight in the infliction of injury (Pr. xxi 10). Jesus often characterized the sin of His con temporaries as wickedness (Mt. xvi. 4), whil Peter declares that wicked men crucified th Saviour (Acts ii. 23).

The Psalms frequently contrast the righteou and the wicked, raising the question of th prosperity of the wicked, and offering sug gestions which provide a partial answer (Pss xxxvii. 35, 36, ix. 15, *et passim*). But this questior which is part of the general problem of evil, i insoluble in the light of the Old Testament revela tion. Throughout the Scriptures there is a stron insistence on the certainty of punishment for a who are wicked (Ps. ix. 17; Je. xvi. 4; Mt. xii 49). It is significant to note that *ponēros* is neve applied to believers; in 1 Cor. v. 13 the referenc is to a nominal member of the Christian com munity. It is by wicked works that unbeliever are alienated from God (Col. i. 21), but thos who are progressing in faith have overcome 'th wicked one' (1 Jn. ii. 13), for the shield of fait is a sure defence against his attack (Eph. vi. 16 See SIN. A.F.

WIDOW.

I. IN THE OLD TESTAMENT

Hebrew legislation has always been solicitou for widows and, together with the fatherless an strangers, made special provision for them (*e.g* Ex. xxii. 21 f.; Dt. xiv. 29, xvi. 11, 14, xxiv. 17 *cf.* Je. vii. 6). Even in pre-Mosaic times there wa recognition of the predicament of the childles widow and arrangements made for her (G xxxviii; see MARRIAGE, section IV), and these were formally enjoined under Moses (Dt. xxv. 5 ff.; see also KIN, KINSMAN).

Since the bearing of children was accounted a great honour, and one still more enhanced later when the nation looked for Messiah (Is. xi. 1), widowhood in such as were not past the age of childbearing, as well as barrenness (*q.v.*), was reckoned a shame and a reproach (Is. iv. 1, liv. 4). The widows of kings, however, continued in their widowhood, and were the property, though not always the wives, of the new king. To ask any of them in marriage was tantamount to a claim to the kingdom (1 Ki. ii. 13 ff.).

As widows are often overlooked by men, God has a peculiar concern for them (Pss. lxviii. 5, cxlvi. 9; Pr. xv. 25), and kindness to them was commended as one of the marks of true religion (Jb. xxix. 13; Is. i. 17). The oppression and injury of widows, on the other hand, would incur dire punishment (Ps. xciv. 6; Mal. iii. 5). Jerusalem and Babylon are likened in their desolation to widows (La. i. 1; Is. xlvii. 8), and the effect of violent death compared to that of wives becoming widows (La. v. 3; Ezk. xxii. 25).

See also ORPHAN, STRANGER.

II. IN THE NEW TESTAMENT

The Christian Church inherited from Judaism the duty of providing for the widow. The Jewish-Christian author of James states categorically that to give assistance to widows in their distress is a mark of the kind of religion with which God can find no fault (i. 27). Even if widows were left comparatively well-off, they needed to be protected from the unscrupulous. One of the things that Jesus condemned in some Pharisees was that they 'devoured widows' houses' (Mk. xii. 40); and He was probably drawing an illustration from contemporary life when He told the story of the widow who by her persistence in demanding justice was wearing the judge out! (Lk. xviii. –5). More often widows were left in penury. One of the earliest good works that engaged the attention of the church at Jerusalem was an organized daily distribution of alms to widows in need; and seven men were appointed to see that the Greek-speaking widows were not overlooked in favour of those who spoke Aramaic (Acts vi. –4). Acts also gives a striking illustration of charity shown by one individual when, after the death of Tabitha, it records that 'all the widows' Joppa assembled to testify before Peter to the kindness she had shown to them (ix. 39).

Paul told the Corinthians that he thought it good that widows should not marry again, but was far from making this a rule. Remarriage, however, should be within the Christian fellow- (see 1 Cor. vii. 8, 9, 39). On the other hand, writing to Timothy, he expresses his desire that *young* widows should marry again; and urges that widows 'in the full sense', *i.e.* those who have relatives to support them, and who are regular their religious duties, should be given a special status and be a charge upon the Church. A roll should be kept of these, and only those should be placed upon it who were over sixty years of age and who had given evidence of their good works, by caring for children, by hospitality, or by rendering service to those of God's people who were in distress (1 Tim. v. 9, 10).

In Rev. xviii. 7 'widow' is used metaphorically of a city bereaved of its inhabitants and stricken by plague and famine. J.D.D.

R.V.G.T.

WIFE. See MARRIAGE.

WILDERNESS. In Scripture the words rendered 'wilderness' or 'desert' include not only the barren deserts of sand dunes or rock that colour the popular imagination of a desert but also steppe-lands and pasture lands suitable for grazing livestock.

The commonest Hebrew word is *midbār*, an ancient word already well-attested in Canaanite epics from Ugarit (14th century BC, going back to earlier origin) as *mdbr* (Gordon, *Ugaritic Manual*, III, 1955, p. 254, No. 458). This word can indicate grassy pastures (Ps. lxv. 12; Joel ii. 22), supporting sheep (*cf.* Ex. iii. 1), but sometimes burnt up by the summer droughts (Je. xxiii. 10; Joel i. 19, 20), as well as denoting desolate wastes of rock and sand (Dt. xxxii. 10; Jb. xxxviii. 26). The same applies to Gk. *erēmos* in the New Testament; note that the 'desert' of Mt. xiv. 15 does not lack 'much grass' (Jn. vi. 10).

The Heb. *y^ešîmôn*, sometimes rendered as a proper name 'Jeshimon' in AV, is used of relatively bare wildernesses in Judaea in 1 Sa. xxiii. 19, 24, xxvi. 1, 3. The wilderness viewed from Pisgah (Nu. xxi. 20, xxiii. 28; *cf.* Dt. xxxiv. 1 ff.) would doubtless include the marly waste lands on either side of the Jordan's channel before it entered the Dead Sea, the slopes of Pisgah and its range into the Jordan valley, and perhaps the edges of the Judaean wilderness opposite, behind Jericho and north and south of Qumran. For general references, *cf.* Dt. xxxii. 10; Ps. cvii. 4; Is. xliii. 19. Besides its use as a proper name for the long rift valley from the Dead Sea to the Gulf of Aqabah, the term *'^arābā* can be used as a common noun for steppe or scrubland where wild creatures must seek out their food (Jb. xxiv. 5; Je. xvii. 6) or else of barren desert (Jb. xxxix. 6 in parallel with saltflats). The words *ṣiyyâ*, 'dry lands' (Jb. xxx. 3; Ps. lxxviii. 17) and *tōhû*, 'empty waste' (Jb. vi. 18, xii. 24; Ps. cvii. 40) likewise refer to barren deserts. K.A.K.

WILDERNESS OF WANDERING.

I. LIMITS

After leaving Egypt by crossing the Sea of Reeds (Ex. xiv. 10–xv), and until they finally by-passed Edom and Moab to reach the Jordan (Nu. xx ff.), Israel spent long years in the intervening territory, comprising, first, the peninsula of Sinai flanked on west and east by the Gulfs of Suez and Aqabah and separated from the Mediterranean on the north by the dusty 'way of the land of the Philistines' that linked Egypt to Palestine, secondly, the long Arabah rift-valley extending south from the Dead Sea to the Gulf of Aqabah, and thirdly, the wilderness of Zin south of Beersheba. See fig. 80.

II. PHYSICAL FEATURES

The road from Egypt by 'the way of the land of the Philistines' to Raphia (Rafa) and Gaza, runs roughly parallel with the Mediterranean coast, passing through and along the northern fringes of a barren sandy desert—the wilderness of Shur (*q.v.*)—which lies between the line of the modern Suez Canal and the Wadi el-'Arish (River of Egypt, *q.v.*), and then through cultivable land which becomes more evident between El-'Arish and Gaza (see NEGEB; *cf.* A. H. Gardiner, *JEA*, VI, 1920, pp. 114, 115; C. S. Jarvis, *Yesterday and Today in Sinai*, 1931, p. 107); 20–40 miles south of the coast road runs the 'way of the wilderness of Shur', from Egypt to the region of Kadesh and north-east to Beersheba. South of this road there gradually rise the limestone hills and wadis of the limestone plateau of Et-Tih which, from a 'base-line' north of a line drawn between the heads of the Suez and Aqabah Gulfs, occupies a great semicircle projecting into the peninsula of Sinai. This plateau is fringed by sandstone outcrops. Across the plateau to Aqabah there ran an ancient trade-route, later to become a pilgrim-route for Mecca. South of the plateau the southern peninsula is occupied by a triangular-shaped area of granite, gneiss, and other hard, crystalline rocks forming mountain ranges, which include the traditional Mt. Sinai, several peaks rising to 6,000–7,000 feet. This region is separated at its north-west and north-east corners from the limestone plateau by sandstone hills containing deposits of copper ores and turquoise. In the east the limestone plateau of Et-Tih gives way to the jumbled rocks and wadis of the S Negeb, bounded by the Rift Valley of the Arabah between the Dead Sea and the Gulf of Aqabah.

Although the scenery of Sinai is characterized by a barren desolate grandeur, yet it is not merely or wholly an impassable desert. There are wells and springs at intervals of a day's journey all down the west coast from the Suez region to Merkhah; the water-table is usually close to the gravelly ground-surface. The wadis usually have some kind of scanty vegetation; where more permanent streams exist, notably in the broad Wadi Feiran (the finest oasis in Sinai), the vegetation flourishes accordingly. There is a 'rainy season' (up to twenty days) during winter, with mists, fogs, and dews. The nature of water-sources and vegetation amid the gaunt rocks of Sinai is best appreciated—short of actually going there—by comparing the successive reports of some of the principal travellers and residents in Sinai and adjoining areas.

In the past, there has been much and persistent wholesale destruction of tamarisk and acacia groves for firewood and charcoal, there being a steady export of the latter to Egypt in the 19th century (Stanley, *Sinai and Palestine*, 1905 edn., p. 25). Thus, in ancient times the Sinai peninsula may have had a little more vegetation in its wadis and consequently slightly better rains; but there has apparently been no fundamental climatic change since antiquity.

III. THE ROUTE OF THE JOURNEYINGS

The precise route taken by Israel from the Sea of Reeds (between Qantara and Suez, see RED SEA) to the edges of Moab is still a matter of conjecture, the more so as almost none of the names of Israelite stopping-places have survived in the late, fluid, and descriptive Arabic nomenclature of the peninsula of Sinai. A name like Feiran immediately suggests the Heb. Paran—but the geographical location of modern Feiran is virtually impossible for the Heb. Paran. Likewise, it is easy to compare Di-zahab and Hazeroth with modern Dhahab and Huderah on the eas side of the peninsula, but this in no way prove their topographical identity.

The nomenclature of the peninsula was pos sibly no more fixed in Moses' day than in mor recent times: various stopping-places were name by the Israelites in relation to events that oc curred on their travels, *e.g.* Kibroth-hattaavah 'graves of lusting' (Nu. xi. 34), and they left n sedentary population behind to perpetuate suc names on the spot. Furthermore, the tradition attaching to the present Mt. Sinai (Gebel Mus and environs) have not been traced back beyon the early Christian centuries; this does not itself prove those traditions wrong, but permi of no certainty. The traditional route ascribed t the Israelites is certainly a possible one (s fig. 80). From the wilderness of Shur (*q.v.*), th are usually considered to have passed sou along the western coast-strip of the Sinai peni sula, Marah and Elim often being placed at 'A Hawarah and Wadi Gharandel respective That the camp after Elim (Ex. xvi. 1) is 'by t *yam sûp*' (Heb. of Nu. xxxiii. 10), *i.e.* the Sea Reeds, or here by extension the Gulf of Suez (RED SEA), indicates clearly that Israel had kept the west side of the Sinai peninsula and not go north (the way of the Philistines). The Gulf Aqabah is too far away to be the *yam sûp* in t passage. Somewhat later, Israel encamped Dophkah. This name is sometimes considered mean 'smeltery' (G. E. Wright, *Biblical Archa logy*, 1957, p. 64; Wright and Filson, *Westmins Historical Atlas of the Bible*, 1957 edn., p. and so to be located at the Egyptian mini centre of Serabit el-Khadim. For copper a especially turquoise mining in that area, Lucas, *Ancient Egyptian Materials and Industr* 1948, pp. 231–235; J. Černý, A. H. Gardin and T. E. Peet, *Inscriptions of Sinai*, II, 19 pp. 5–8.

As Egyptian expeditions visited this regi only during January to March (just once ay), and did not live permanently at the mines f. Petrie, *Researches in Sinai*, 1906, p. 169), e Israelites would not meet them in that region, they left Egypt in the month Abib (Ex. xiii. 4), . about March (*cf.* PLAGUES OF EGYPT), and ft Elim a month later (Ex. xvi. 1), *i.e.* about pril. However, there is no direct evidence that ophkah must be Serabit el-Khadim; it could be y copper-mining spot in the metalliferous ndstone belt across south-central Sinai (which vours a southerly route for Israel in any case). ephidim is sometimes identified with Wadi eiran, sometimes with Wadi Refayid, and Mt. nai with the summits of Gebel Musa (or, less ely, Mt. Serbal near Feiran). See the works of obinson, Lepsius, Stanley, and Palmer cited in e Bibliography below. Beyond Mt. Sinai, hahab on the east coast might be Di-zahab (Dt. 1; so most recently, Y. Aharoni, *Antiquity and rvival*, II: 2/3, 1957, pp. 289, 290, fig. 7); if so, uderah on a different road is less likely to be e Hazeroth of Nu. xi. 35, xxxiii. 17, 18. The xt really fixed points are Kadesh-barnea .v.) on the borders of the wilderness(es) of Zin d Paran (Nu. xii. 16, xiii. 26) at 'Ain Qudeirat 'Ain Qudeis and the surrounding region, in- ding 'Ain Qudeirat, and Ezion-geber at the ad of the Gulf of Aqabah (Nu. xxxiii. 35 f.).

For the phenomenon of the earth swallowing Korah, Dathan, and Abiram (Nu. xvi), a most teresting explanation has been offered by G. ort, *Australian Biblical Review*, VII, 1959, . 2–26, especially 19–26. She would locate this cident in the Arabah Rift Valley between the ead Sea and the Gulf of Aqabah. Here are to found mudflats or lakes of mud known as *wirs*, in various stages of development. A hard ust of clayey mud overlying a layer of hard salt d one of half-dry mud, the whole about a foot ick, eventually forms over the deep mass of uid mud and ooze. When this crust is hard it y be walked on or crossed with impunity, but creased humidity (and especially rainstorms) ll break up the crust and turn the whole into ey mud. When Dathan, Abiram, and Korah's herents withdrew from the main camp they uld have moved their tents to one of these ceptively level, hard mudflats, unaware that y were driving their tent-pegs into simply a ck, hard crust and not true, solid ground. om his long years of experience in Sinai and dian (Ex. ii–iv), Moses had probably learned this phenomenon, but not so the Israelites. hen a storm approached he saw the danger and led the Israelites away from the tents of the els—a new thing would happen, the earth uld swallow them up. The crust broke up and rebels, their families, and their possessions re all swallowed up in the mud. Then the rm broke, and the 250 men with censers were uck by lightning—smitten down by the fire of Lord.

Miss Hort thought that this incident occurred Kadesh-barnea, and therefore that Kadesh uld be located in the Arabah. But there are possible reasons for locating Kadesh (*q.v.*) in the region of 'Ain Qudeis and 'Ain Qudeirat, and in fact Nu. xvi does *not* state that the revolt(s) of Korah, Dathan, and Abiram occurred at Kadesh. When the spies had returned from Canaan to Israel at Kadesh, and Israel's faith was found wanting (Nu. xiii f.), Israel was to go forth 'into the wilderness by the way of the Red Sea' (Nu. xiv. 25), *i.e.* into the Arabah towards the Gulf of Aqabah. And it is after this, while Israel were on their travels (*cf.* Nu. xv. 32–36: a camp-site in the wilderness, after leaving Kadesh), that this incident (Nu. xvi) occurred, *i.e.* in the Arabah as befits Miss Hort's explanation. It should be noted that it is the whole, unitary account of the twin rebellions in Nu. xvi and their awesome end that alone makes sense and fits the physical phenomena in question; the supposed sources obtained by conventional documentary literary analyses severally yield fragmentary pictures that correspond to no known realities.

The long list of names in Nu. xxxiii. 19–35 fall into the thirty-eight years of wandering, and cannot be located at present. The precise route past Edom (Nu. xx. 22 ff., xxi, xxxiii. 38–44) is also none too clear. Some of the incidents in these long journeys reflect the natural pheno- mena of the area. The repeated phenomenon of water coming from the smitten rock (Ex. xvii. 1–7; Nu. xx. 2–13) reflects the water-holding properties of Sinai limestone: an army N.C.O. once produced quite a good flow of water when he accidentally hit such a rock face with a spade! See Jarvis, *Yesterday and Today in Sinai*, 1931, pp. 174, 175. The digging of wells as recorded in Nu. xxi. 16–18 (*cf.* Gn. xxvi. 19) reflects the known occurrence of sub-surface water in various regions of Sinai, the Negeb, and S Transjordan (see references above, and N. Glueck, *Rivers in the Desert*, 1959, p. 22). The references to the catching of quail (Ex. xvi. 13; Nu. xi. 31–35) have been interpreted by some as requiring a northern route for the Exodus along the Mediterranean (*e.g.* Jarvis, *op. cit.*, pp. 169, 170; *cf.* J. Bright, *A History of Israel*, 1960, p. 114, after J. Gray, *VT*, IV, 1954, pp. 148–154; G. E. Wright, *Biblical Archaeology*, 1957, p. 65). But that route was explicitly forbidden to Israel (Ex. xiii. 17 f.), and in any case the quails land on the Medi- terranean coast of Sinai (from Europe) only in the *autumn* and at dawn, whereas Israel found them in the *spring* in the evening, in or following Abib, *i.e.* March (Ex. xvi. 13), and a year and a month later (Nu. x. 11, xi. 31). These two points exclude the Mediterranean coast from Israel's route on these two occasions, and directly favour the southern route by the Gulfs of Suez and Aqabah *via* 'Mt. Sinai'. The quail return to Europe in the spring—the season when Israel twice had them—across the upper ends of the Gulfs of Suez and Aqabah, and in the evening (Lucas, *The Route of the Exodus*, 1938, pp. 58–63 and refs., and p. 81, overstressing Aqabah at the expense of Suez). Thus, although nomencla- ture and excavation can do very little for the geography of Israel's journeyings through Sinai, the natural phenomena help to delimit the possibilities and make something like the traditional route possible if not in fact probable.

A minority view would make Israel cross the Sinai peninsula more directly to the head of the Gulf of Aqabah and locate Mt. Sinai in Midian. Among the best advocates of such a view is Lucas (*The Route of the Exodus*, 1938) who does not invoke non-existent active volcanoes as some of his predecessors had done. However, this view is no freer of topographical difficulties than any other, and fails entirely to account for the origin of the traditions of the Christian period that attached themselves to the peninsula now called Sinai and not to Midian.

For a good comparative table of the data on the route and stopping-places on Israel's wanderings in Exodus–Numbers, Nu. xxxiii, and Deuteronomy, see J. D. Davis and H. S. Gehman, *WDB*, pp. 638, 639.

IV. THE NUMBERS OF THE ISRAELITES

During the long period that Israel was in Egypt the descendants of Israel 'were fruitful, and increased abundantly, and multiplied . . . and the land was filled with them' (Ex. i. 7). When Israel left Egypt there went '600,000 men on foot' besides their families and the mixed multitude, while from a census of the men from the tribes other than Levi held at Sinai comes the total of 603,550 men over twenty who could bear arms (Nu. ii. 32). These figures are commonly held to imply a total number of Israelites—men, women, and children—of somewhat more than two million, on the basis of general population-statistics. That the slender resources of Sinai were of themselves insufficient to support such a multitude is indicated by the Bible itself (as well as suggested by exploration) in that Israel's chief sustenance came from God-given manna (*q.v.*; Ex. xvi, *cf.* verses 3, 4, 35). Israel never went wholly without (Dt. ii. 7), although the water-supply sometimes nearly failed them (*e.g.* at Rephidim, Ex. xvii. 1; Kadesh, Nu. xx. 2). In any case, they would soon learn to subsist on very little water per head indeed, as illustrated by Robinson's guide in Sinai, who was able to go without water for a fortnight by living on camel's milk, while sheep and goats as well as camels can sometimes go without water for three or four months if they have had fresh pasture (E. Robinson, *Biblical Researches*, I, 1841 edn., p. 221).

Furthermore, it is wholly misleading to imagine the Israelites marching in long 'columns of four' up and down Sinai, or trying to encamp all together *en masse* in some little wadi at each stop. They would be spread out in their tribal and family groups, occupying at any one time a variety of neighbouring wadis for all their scattered encampments; after they left Sinai with the ark and tabernacle (as baggage when on the move), the sites where these were successively lodged would be the focus of the various tribal camps, as in Nu. ii. In various parts of Sinai th water-table is not far below the ground-surfac as illustrated by numerous travellers' reports; th scattered Israelite encampments would thus ofte get the little they needed by digging small pi over an area. *Cf.* Robinson, *Biblical Researche* I, 1841, pp. 100 (general observations), 12 Lepsius, *Letters, etc.*, 1853, p. 306; Currelly i Petrie, *Researches in Sinai*, 1906, p. 249; Luca *The Route of the Exodus*, 1938, p. 68.

There have been many attempts down th years to interpret the census-lists in Nu. i an xxvi and related figures in Ex. xii. 37, xxxviii. 24 29, besides the levitical reckoning (Nu. iv. 21–4 and other figures (*e.g.* Nu. xvi. 49), in order t gain from the Hebrew text a more modest tot for the number of the people of Israel involved i the Exodus from Egypt through Sinai to Pal stine. For the two most recent attempts, se R. E. D. Clark, *JTVI*, LXXXVII, 1955, pp. 82–9 (taking *'lp* as 'officer' instead of '1000' in man cases), and G. E. Mendenhall, *JBL*, LXXVI 1958, pp. 52–66 (taking *'lp* as a tribal sub-un instead of '1000'), who refers to earlier trea ments. While none of these attempts accounts fo all the figures involved, they indicate sever possible clues to a better understanding o various apparently high figures in the Old Test ment. The fact is that these records must rest o some basis of ancient reality; the apparently hig figures are beyond absolute disproof, while n alternative interpretation has yet adequate accounted for all the data involved. See NUMBE

BIBLIOGRAPHY. E. Robinson, *Biblical R searches in Palestine, Mount Sinai and Arab Petraea*, I, 1841 edn., pp. 98–100, 129, 131, 17 C. R. Lepsius, *Letters from Egypt, Ethiopia a the Peninsula of Sinai*, 1853, pp. 306, 307; A. Stanley, *Sinai and Palestine*, 1905 edn., pp. 16–1 22, 24–27; E. H. Palmer, *The Desert of t Exodus*, I, 1871, pp. 22–26; W. M. F. Petrie an C. T. Currelly, *Researches in Sinai*, 1906, pp. 1 30, 247–250, 254–256 (Feiran), 269; C. Woolley and T. E. Lawrence, *Palestine Explor tion Fund Annual*, III, 1915, p. 33; C. S. Jarv *Yesterday and Today in Sinai*, 1931, p. 99; A. Lucas, *The Route of the Exodus*, 1938, pp. 19, 4 45, 68; W. F. Albright, *BASOR*, 109, 1948, p. (El-'Arish rains; scrub vegetation in north). F photographs of Sinai scenery, see G. E. Wrigh *Biblical Archaeology*, 1957, pp. 62–64, figs. 3 35; or L. H. Grollenberg, *Shorter Atlas of t Bible*, 1959, pp. 76, 77; Petrie, *Researches Sinai*, 1906, *passim*; B. Rothenberg, *God Wilderness*, 1961, *passim*. K.A.K.

WILD OX. Heb. *t*[e]*'ô* is probably the antelo (*Antilopus leucoryx*), living wild in the scru covered hill-country with the goats and gazel It was among the animals which the Israelit were permitted to eat (Dt. xiv. 5, AV 'wild ox Nets were set up forming an enclosure into whi the creatures were chased by dogs and th caught (Is. li. 20, AV 'wild bull'; see fig. 111).

A.R.M.

VILLOW. See TREES.

VIMPLE. From Old English *wimpel* meaning ıood' or 'veil'; it appears once in AV (Is. iii. 22) s translating Heb. *miṭpaḥaṯ* (RV 'shawl'), which ı Ru. iii. 15 is rendered 'vail' (RV, RSV 'mantle'). ʌs an item of feminine apparel it may signify a loak, but the precise meaning is obscure. See lso DRESS (*b*). *Cf.* the dress of Judaean women as hown on the Assyrian reliefs (fig. 70*b*, no. 3, and g. 127).

VIND (Heb. *rûaḥ*). 1. The Hebrews conceived of limate as influenced by the four winds from the ɔur corners of the earth (Je. xlix. 36; Dn. vii. 2; ᒑev. vii. 1). The wind may be a source of blessıg or a curse, according to its source. Its vast ower suggests the wind is the breath of God (s. xl. 7), controlled by Him (Ps. cvii. 25; Pr. xx. 4; Mk. iv. 41), created by Him (Am. iv. 13) nd creative for His purposes (Gn. i. 2; Ezk. xxvii. 9).

2. As compound names for winds are imossible in Hebrew, such as the north-east wind ee EUROCLYDON), the four cardinal points are sed freely to describe other directions (Ezk. xxvii. 9; Dn. viii. 8; Zc. ii. 6; Mt. xxiv. 31; Rev. ii. 1).

a. The north wind (*rûaḥ ṣāpôn*) is associated ith cold conditions, the north-east wind disersing the rain (Jb. xxxvii. 9, 22; Pr. xxv. 23).

b. The south wind (*rûaḥ dārôm*) is variable in s effects, whether tempestuous (Is. xxi. 1; Zc. :. 14) or gentle (Acts xxvii. 13). The sirocco, sually associated with the south wind, is parcularly hot and desiccating, a katabatic wind hich descends from the highlands of Sinai and rabia (Jb. xxxvii. 16, 17; Je. iv. 11; Ho. xii. 1; k. xii. 55). But the katabatic effects can be used wherever there is a sudden change of radient, so that its effects are also described s east winds (Is. xxvii. 8; Ezk. xvii. 10; Ho. ii. 15; Jon. iv. 8). It destroys the grass, and l vegetation wilts (Ps. ciii. 16; Is. xl. 6–8; Jas. 11).

c. The east wind (*rûaḥ qāḏîm*) is similarly escribed as a dry wind from the wilderness (Jb. 19; Je. iv. 11, xiii. 24), strong and gusty (Ex. v. 21; Jb. xxvii. 21, xxxviii. 24; Je. xviii. 17) and ith scorching heat (Am. iv. 9; Ho. xiii. 15), fecting the vegetation (Gn. xli. 6, 23, 27; Ezk. vii. 10, xix. 12).

d. The west wind (*rûaḥ yām*) is in Arabic escribed as 'the father of rain' (1 Ki. xviii. 44, 5; Lk. xii. 54). Distinction, however, should be ade between the diurnal sea breezes which are marked feature of the coast in summer, bringg down the high temperatures, and the westers which blow strongly in winter, exposing all ıchorages to NW gales. The wind is symbolic of othingness (Is. xli. 29) and of the transitoriness man (Ps. lxxviii. 39), and is used also in conection with the Spirit of God (Jn. iii. 8; Acts ii. ; see HOLY SPIRIT). J.M.H.

INDOW. See HOUSE.

WINE AND STRONG DRINK.

I. IN THE OLD TESTAMENT

Among a considerable number of synonyms used in the Old Testament the most common are *yayin* (usually translated 'wine') and *šēḵār* (usually translated 'strong drink'). These terms are frequently used together, and they are employed irrespective of whether the writer is commending wine and strong drink as desirable or warning against its dangers. A third word, *tîrôš*, sometimes translated 'new' or 'sweet wine', has often been regarded as unfermented and therefore unintoxicating wine, but an example such as Ho. iv. 11, together with the usage of the Talmud, makes clear that it is capable of being used in a bad sense equally with the others. Furthermore, while there are examples of the grapes being pressed into a cup and presumably used at once (Gn. xl. 11), it is significant that the term 'wine' is never applied to the resultant juice.

The term 'new wine' does not indicate wine which has not fermented, for in fact the process of fermentation sets in very rapidly, and unfermented wine could not be available many months after the harvest (Acts ii. 13). It represents rather wine made from the first drippings of the juice before the winepress was trodden. As such it would be particularly potent and would come immediately to mind as a probable explanation of what seemed to be a drunken state. Modern custom in Palestine, among a people who are traditionally conservative as far as religious feasts are concerned, also suggests that the wine used was fermented. It may be said, therefore, that the Bible in employing various synonyms makes no consistent distinction between them.

Naturally in a land and climate particularly suited to the cultivation of the vine, we find that wine was often associated with corn, and together they stand for a full and adequate supply of food and of the good gifts of life. They can be promised therefore as the tokens of the blessing of God (Gn. xxvii. 28), and they are acceptable to Him when offered back upon the altar (Ex. xxix. 40). As a discipline, however, they are on occasion to be dispensed with, as when a man engages in priestly service (Lv. x. 9), or in the case of a Nazirite during the course of his vow (Nu. vi. 3). The abstinence of the Rechabites falls within a different category, for it was in an attempt to preserve the nomadic life that they dwelt in tents, and their refusal of wine was not on account of the dangers of its abuse, but because they were associated with the planting of vineyards, the sowing of seed, and the building of houses (Je. xxxv. 7). Evidence is by no means lacking, however, that even to those who accepted the agricultural way of life the dangers of strong drink were apparent. The warnings of the book of Proverbs are clear, and in the time of Isaiah even the priests have fallen into the snare.

These two aspects of wine, its use and its

abuse, its benefits and its curse, its acceptance in God's sight and its abhorrence, are interwoven into the fabric of the Old Testament so that it may gladden the heart of man (Ps. civ. 15) or cause his mind to err (Is. xxviii. 7), it can be associated with merriment (Ec. x. 19) or with anger (Is. v. 11), it can be used to uncover the shame of Noah (Gn. ix. 21) or in the hands of Melchizedek to honour Abraham (Gn. xiv. 18).

In metaphorical usage the same characteristics are to be observed. Wine may represent that which God Himself has prepared (Pr. ix. 5), and which He offers to as many as will receive it from His hand (Is. lv. 1); yet, on the other hand, it may equally well represent the intoxicating influence of Babylonian supremacy which brings ruin.

II. IN THE NEW TESTAMENT

In the New Testament the common word is Gk. *oinos* (*cf.* Heb. *yayin*). Once we find *sikera*, 'strong drink' (Lk. i. 15), a loan-word from Semitic (*cf.* Heb. *šēḵār*), and once *gleukos*, 'new wine' (Acts ii. 13). This last word means literally 'sweet wine'; the vintage of the current year had not come round, but there were means of keeping wine sweet all the year round.

The references in the New Testament are very much fewer in number, but once more the good and the bad aspects are equally apparent, and many of the points which we noticed in the Old Testament have their counterpart in the New. John the Baptist is to abstain from wine in view of his special commission (Lk. i. 15), but this does not imply that of itself wine is evil, for Jesus is not only present at the wedding in Cana of Galilee, but when the wine fails He replenishes the supply in extraordinarily ample measure, and later His readiness to eat and drink with publicans and sinners draws forth the accusation that He is gluttonous and a wine-bibber. The refusal of Jesus to drink the wine offered to Him in accordance with Jewish custom at His crucifixion (Mk. xv. 23) was not based upon an objection to wine as such, but was due to a determination to die with an unclouded mind. Later He accepted the wine (vinegar) which was the ordinary drink of labourers in the field and of the lower class of soldiers.

On more than one occasion Jesus used wine to illustrate His teaching. Mk. ii. 22 points to the current practice of putting new wine into new skins and emphasizes the impossibility of doing otherwise. Commentators differ regarding the interpretation of this parable. For, while the new wine clearly points to the lively and powerful working of Christ's new teaching, the skins which are broken may equally well refer to certain conventional forms or to the whole Judaistic system or to the human heart, all of which need to be recast in accordance with the challenge of the new age which has arrived. Unfortunately the Pharisees were unwilling to face the changes which would have been involved, and obstinately clung to the system upon which their livelihood depended (Lk. v. 39).

Metaphorically in the New Testament the word 'wine' is again used both in a good and a bad sense. The latter is found several times in Revelation, where the inhabitants of the earth are depicted as having been made drunk by the fornication of Babylon (Rev. xvii. 2) while she herself is drunk with their blood (Rev. xvii. 6). On the other hand, Paul exhorts his readers to be filled with the Spirit (Eph. v. 18) in contrast with their being intoxicated with wine. There are, of course, certain similarities between the two conditions, a consideration which may well have led Paul to express himself in this way. Certainly on the day of Pentecost there were many who took the evidences of the Spirit to be nothing else than the result of strong drink. Strangely enough this same interpretation had been placed long ago upon the movement of the lips of Hannah as she prayed in the presence of Eli, a supposed fault which Eli was quicker to rebuke in her than in his own sons, of whom the fault was actually true.

Timothy is exhorted by Paul to take a little wine because of its medicinal properties (1 Tim. v. 23; *cf.* its application in a different form in the story of the good Samaritan), but in the Pastoral Epistles there is a recognition of the grave dangers of excess, and those who bear office or in any way give leadership within the Christian community, both men and women, are specifically warned against this fault, which would unfit them for their task (1 Tim. iii. 8; Tit. ii. 3). This abuse is particularly unfitting within the Church, for if it is true that drunkenness is in general a sign of heedlessness in spiritual matters, and a disregard of the imminent return of Christ (Rom. xiii. 13), how much more is it to be deplored at the Lord's table, where it reveals not only a spirit of complete indifference towards God but a spirit of utter thoughtlessness in regard to those who stand together within the Christian fellowship.

To sum up, then, it may be said that while wine is not condemned as being without usefulness, it brings in the hands of sinful men such dangers of becoming uncontrolled that even those who count themselves to be strong would be wise to abstain, if not for their own sake, yet for the sake of weaker brethren (Rom. xiv. 21). If it is argued that there are many other things which may be abused besides wine, the point may be immediately conceded, but wine has so often proved itself to be peculiarly fraught with danger that Paul names it specifically at the same time as he lays down the general principle. That this principle has application within the setting of modern life is beyond dispute among those who take their Christian responsibility seriously.

BIBLIOGRAPHY. C. Seltman, *Wine in the Ancient World*, 1957; J. P. Free, *Archaeology and Bible History*, 1950, Appendix II, pp. 351 ff.

F.S.F.

WINEFAT, PRESS VAT. See WINE AND STRONG DRINK.

WINNOW. See FAN, AGRICULTURE.

WISDOM.

I. IN THE OLD TESTAMENT

ike all Hebrew intellectual virtues, wisdom enerally *ḥoḵmâ*, though other words are used; *g.*: *bînâ*, 'understanding', Jb. xxxix. 26; Pr. xxiii. ; *t*[e]*ḇûnâ*, 'insight', Ps. cxxxvi. 5; *śeḵel* or *śēḵel*, rudence', Pr. xii. 8, xxiii. 9) is intensely praccal, not theoretical. Basically, wisdom is the art f being successful, of forming the correct plan gain the desired results. Its seat is the heart, e centre of moral and intellectual decision (*cf.* Ki. iii. 9, 12).

Those who possess technical skill are called ise: Bezaleel, chief artisan of the tabernacle (Ex. xxi. 3; RSV 'ability'); artificers of idols (Is. xl.); Je. x. 9); professional mourners (Je. ix. 17); avigators or shipwrights (Ezk. xxvii. 8, 9). ractical wisdom may take on a sinister aspect, in Jonadab's crafty advice (2 Sa. xiii. 3).

Kings and leaders were in special need of isdom. On them hung the responsibility for orrect decisions in political and social affairs. oshua (Dt. xxxiv. 9), David (2 Sa. xiv. 20), olomon (1 Ki. iii. 9, 12, iv. 29 ff.) were granted isdom to enable them to deal with their official uties. The messianic King predicted by Isaiah i. 2) was to be equipped with wisdom to judge npartially. 'Wonderful counsellor' (ix. 6) avers at His advice would be amazingly successful. ee N. W. Porteous, 'Royal Wisdom' in *Wisdom Israel and in the Ancient Near East.*

A special class of wise men (or women, *cf.* 2 Sa. v. 2) seems to have developed during the onarchy. By Jeremiah's time they had taken eir place beside prophets and priests as a major ligious and social influence. Their task was to rmulate workable plans, to prescribe advice for ccessful living (Je. xviii. 18). The wise man or unsellor stood in a parental relationship to ose whose well-being hinged on his advice: seph was a 'father' to pharaoh (Gn. xlv. 8); eborah, a 'mother' in Israel (Jdg. v. 7). See A. H. de Boer, 'The Counsellor' in *Wisdom in rael.*

Wisdom in the fullest sense belongs to God one (Jb. xii. 13 ff.; Is. xxxi. 2; Dn. ii. 20–23). is wisdom is not only completeness of knowdge pervading every realm of life (Jb. x. 4, vi. 6; Pr. v. 21, xv. 3) but also 'consists in his esistible fulfilment of what he has in his mind' . Pedersen, *Israel: Its Life and Culture*, I–II, 198). The universe (Pr. iii. 19 f., viii. 22–31; . x. 12) and man (Jb. x. 8 ff.; Ps. civ. 24; Pr. xiv. , xxii. 2) are products of His creative wisdom. atural (Is. xxviii. 23–29) and historical (Is. xxxi. processes are governed by His wisdom, which cludes an infallible discrimination between good d evil and is the basis for the just rewards and nishments which are the lot of the righteous d the wicked (Pss. i, xxxvii, lxxiii; Pr. x. 3, 4, xii. 2, *etc.*). Such wisdom is inscrutable b. xxviii. 12–21): God in His grace must reveal if man is going to grasp it at all (Jb. xxviii. 23, 28). Even wisdom derived from natural abilities or distilled from experience is a gracious gift, because God's creative activity makes such wisdom possible.

Biblical wisdom is both religious and practical. Stemming from the fear of the Lord (Jb. xxviii. 28; Ps. cxi. 10; Pr. i. 7, ix. 10), it branches out to touch all of life, as the extended commentary on wisdom in Proverbs indicates. Wisdom takes insights gleaned from the knowledge of God's ways and applies them in the daily walk. This combination of insight and obedience (and all insight must issue in obedience) relates wisdom to the prophetic emphasis on the knowledge (*i.e.* the cordial love and obedience) of God (*e.g.* Ho. ii. 20, iv. 1, 6, vi. 6; Je. iv. 22, ix. 3, 6; and especially Pr. ix. 10).

Pagan wisdom, though it, too, may be religious, has no anchor in the covenant-God and, therefore, is doomed to failure, as the prophets frequently point out (Is. xix. 11 ff.; Ezk. xxviii. 2 ff.; Ob. 8). When secularism, materialism, and disdain of the covenant-ideals squeezed the fear of God out of Israel's wisdom it became practical atheism, as vapid as its pagan counterpart, and drew Isaiah's fire: 'Woe unto them that are wise in their own eyes' (v. 21; *cf.* xxix. 14; Je. xviii. 18).

A special problem is the personification of wisdom in Pr. viii. 22 ff. Jb. xxviii anticipates this personification by depicting wisdom as a mystery inscrutable to men but apparent to God. In Pr. i. 20–33 wisdom is likened to a woman crying in the streets for men to turn from their foolish ways and to find instruction and security in her (*cf.* also Pr. iii. 15–20). The personification continues in Pr. viii and reaches its climax in verses 22 ff., where wisdom claims to be the first creation of God and, perhaps, an assistant in the work of creation (viii. 30, *cf.* iii. 19; the difficult *'āmôn*, 'as one brought up' in AV, should be translated 'master workman', as in RV, RSV; see W. F. Albright in *Wisdom in Israel*, p. 8). The purpose of wisdom's recitation of her credentials is to attract men to pay her rightful heed, as viii. 32–36 indicates. Therefore, caution must be exercised in reading into this passage a view of hypostatization, *i.e.* that wisdom is depicted as having an independent existence. The Hebrews' characteristic resistance to speculation and abstraction frequently led their poets to deal with inanimate objects or ideals as though they had personality. See H. W. Robinson, *Inspiration and Revelation in the Old Testament*, 1946, p. 260; H. Ringgren, *Word and Wisdom*, 1947. For the influence of the personification of wisdom on the Logos idea of the Fourth Gospel, see LOGOS.

II. IN THE NEW TESTAMENT

By and large New Testament wisdom (*sophia*) has the same intensely practical nature as in the Old. Seldom neutral (although *cf.* 'the wisdom of Egypt', Acts vii. 22), it is either God-given or God-opposing. If divorced from God's revelation it is impoverished and unproductive at best

(1 Cor. i. 17, ii. 4; 2 Cor. i. 12) and foolish or even devilish at worst (1 Cor. i. 19 ff.; Jas. iii. 15 ff.). Worldly wisdom is based on intuition and experience without revelation, and thus has severe limitations. The failure to recognize these limitations brings biblical condemnation on all (especially the Greeks) who haughtily attempt to cope with spiritual issues by human wisdom.

The truly wise are those to whom God has graciously imparted wisdom: Solomon (Mt. xii. 42; Lk. xi. 31), Stephen (Acts vi. 10), Paul (2 Pet. iii. 15), Joseph (Acts vii. 10). One of Christ's legacies to His disciples was the wisdom to say the right thing in times of persecution and examination (Lk. xxi. 15). A similar wisdom is necessary for understanding the apocalyptic oracles and enigmas (Rev. xiii. 18, xvii. 9). Wisdom is essential not only for leaders of the Church (Acts vi. 3) but for all believers that they may perceive God's purposes in redemption (Eph. i. 8, 9) and may walk worthily of God (Col. i. 9; Jas. i. 5, iii. 13–17) and discreetly before unbelievers (Col. iv. 5). As Paul has taught his hearers in all wisdom (Col. i. 28), so they who are mature enough to understand this spiritual wisdom (1 Cor. ii. 6, 7) are to instruct others in it (Col. iii. 16).

God's wisdom is clearly demonstrated in His provision of redemption (Rom. xi. 33), which is manifested in the Church (Eph. iii. 10). It is supremely revealed 'not in some esoteric doctrine . . . addressed to . . . initiates of some secret cult, but in action, God's supreme action in Christ on the Cross' (N. W. Porteous, *op. cit.*, p. 258). This wisdom, previously veiled to human minds, brooks no philosophical or practical rivals. The best attempts of men to untangle the problems of human existence are shown to be foolishness in the light of the cross.

The incarnate Christ grew in wisdom (Lk. ii. 40, 52) as a boy and astonished His audiences by His wisdom as a man (Mt. xiii. 54; Mk. vi. 2). His claims included wisdom (Mt. xii. 42) and a unique knowledge of God (Mt. xi. 25 ff.). Twice He personifies wisdom in a manner reminiscent of Proverbs: Mt. xi. 19 (= Lk. vii. 35) and Lk. xi. 49 (Mt. xxiii. 34 ff.). In both passages Christ may be alluding to Himself as 'Wisdom', although this is not certain, especially in the latter instance. (See *Arndt* for suggested interpretations.) Paul's *wisdom Christology* (1 Cor. i. 24, 30) was probably influenced both by Christ's claims and by the apostolic consciousness (grounded in Christ's teachings in Matthew) that Christ was the *new Torah*, the complete revelation of God's will, replacing the old law. Since the commandments and wisdom are linked in Dt. iv. 6, and especially in Jewish thought (*e.g.* Ecclus. xxiv. 23; *Apocalypse of Baruch* iii. 37 ff.), it is not unexpected that Paul would view Jesus, the *new Torah*, as the wisdom of God. That Paul saw in Christ the fulfilment of Pr. viii. 22 ff. seems apparent from Col. i. 15 ff., which strongly reflects the Old Testament description of wisdom.

Paul's wisdom Christology is a dynamic concept, as is shown by the emphasis on Christ's activity in creation in Col. i. 15 ff. and in redemption in 1 Cor. i. 24, 30. The latter verses affirm that in the crucifixion God made Jesus our wisdom, a wisdom further defined as embracing righteousness, sanctification, and redemption. As the slain yet exalted Lord of the Church, He is lauded for wisdom (Rev. v. 12). 'Receive' in this verse implies acknowledgment of attributes which are already Christ's; for in Him 'are hid all the treasures of wisdom' (Col. ii. 3).

BIBLIOGRAPHY. W. D. Davies, *Paul and Rabbinic Judaism*, 1948, pp. 147–176; E. Jacob and R. Mehl in *A Companion to the Bible*, ed. J.-J. von Allmen, 1958; M. Noth and D. W. Thomas (eds.), *Wisdom in Israel and in the Ancient Near East*, 1955; W. G. Lambert, *Babylonian Wisdom Literature*, 1960.

D.A.H.

WISDOM LITERATURE. A literary *genre* common in the Ancient Near East in which instructions for successful living are given or the perplexities of human existence are contemplated. There are two main types: proverbial (see PROVERB) wisdom—short, pithy sayings which state rules for personal happiness and welfare (*e.g.* Proverbs), and speculative wisdom—monologues (*e.g.* Ecclesiastes) or dialogues (*e.g.* Job) which attempt to delve into such problems as the meaning of existence and the relationship between God and man. This speculative wisdom is practical and empirical, not theoretical. Problems of human existence are discussed in terms of concrete examples: 'There was a man . . . whose name was Job.'

The roots of wisdom literature are probably to be found in short, crisp popular sayings which express rules for success or common observations concerning life. Old Testament examples are found in 1 Ki. xx. 11; Je. xxiii. 28, xxxi. 29, *inter al.* The transition from oral to literary wisdom took place in Egypt *c.* 2500 BC (*e.g* *Instruction of the Vizier Ptah-Hotep*) and i Sumeria shortly after. Throughout the Nea East, a class of scribes or wise men arose whos highly honoured task was to create or collect an polish sagacious sayings (Ec. xii. 9), usually unde the patronage of court or temple. Two of Israel' kings are credited with important contribution in this area: Solomon (1 Ki. iv. 29–34) an Hezekiah (Pr. xxv. 1). By the 7th century BC th wise man (*ḥāḵām*) had assumed sufficient pro minence in Judah to be classed with prophet c priest (Je. viii. 8, 9, xviii. 18). As the phenomeno of prophecy faded in the Persian and Gree periods, the wise men gained in stature, as th important apocryphal works, Ecclesiasticus an Wisdom of Solomon, and the Mishnaic tracta *Pirqe Aboth* (Sayings of the Fathers), show.

The wise men employed several literary devic as aids to memory. The most frequent device w the use of poetic parallelism of either a synthe (*e.g.* Pr. xviii. 10) or antithetic (*e.g.* Pr. x. type. Comparisons are common (*e.g.* Pr. xvii. as are numerical sequences (*e.g.* Pr. xxx. 15 ff

Alliteration and acrostic patterns (*e.g.* Ps. xxxvii; Pr. xxxi. 10–31) are employed occasionally. Riddles (Jdg. xiv. 12 ff.; *cf.* 1 Ki. x. 1), fables (*e.g.* Jdg. ix. 7–15; Ezk. xvii. 3 ff., xix. 1 ff.), parables, which are extensions of the comparisons mentioned above (*e.g.* 2 Sa. xii. 1–4; Is. xxviii. 4), and allegories (*e.g.* Is. v. 1–7) are part of the wise man's repertoire. This sampling testifies to the impact made by wisdom literature on historical and prophetic writings. H. Gunkel has categorized certain psalms as wisdom poetry: Pss. cxxvii, cxxxiii (simple proverbial type); Pss. i, xxxvii, xlix, lxxiii, cxii, cxxviii. S. Mowinckel has called these psalms examples of 'learned psalmography'. Amos has drawn frequently from wisdom motifs: the numerical patterns in Am. i, ii; the cause and effect questions in Am. iii. 3–8; the aphoristic questions in Am. vi. 12. Wisdom influence is detectable in the New Testament both in the teaching methods of Christ, who as the Master Sage employs parables and proverbs, and also in the Epistle of James (*e.g.* i. 5 ff., iii. 13 ff.).

Though an international phenomenon, as the Old Testament freely recognizes (Edom in 1 Ki. iv. 31; Ob. 8; Je. xlix. 7; and Egypt in Gn. xli. 8; 1 Ki. iv. 30; Is. xix. 11–15 were particularly renowned), wisdom literature has not escaped Israel's peculiar stamp. Israel's sages confessed that true wisdom stemmed from God (*cf.* Jb. xxviii). The impact of Israel's prophets upon her sages cannot be ignored. H. Wheeler Robinson (*Inspiration and Revelation in the Old Testament*, 1946, p. 241) goes so far as to define the wisdom movement as '*the discipline whereby was taught the application of prophetic truth to the individual life in the light of experience*'.

BIBLIOGRAPHY. W. Baumgartner, *Israelitische und altorientalische Weisheit*, 1933; J. Fichtner, 'Die altorientalische Weisheit in ihrer israelitisch-jüdischen Ausprägung', *BZAW*, LXII, 1933; M. Noth and D. W. Thomas (eds.), *Wisdom in Israel and in the Ancient Near East*, 1955; O. S. Rankin, *Israel's Wisdom Literature*, 1936; H. Ranston, *The Old Testament Wisdom Books and Their Teaching*, 1930; J. C. Rylaarsdam, *Revelation in Jewish Wisdom Literature*, 1946.

D.A.H.

WISDOM OF SOLOMON. See APOCRYPHA.

WISE MEN. See MAGI.

WITCH, WITCHCRAFT. See MAGIC AND SORCERY.

WITHERED HAND. Gk. *xēros* (Mt. xii. 10; Lk. vi. 6, 8), 'dry', 'withered', denotes a hand in which the muscles, and sometimes also the bones, are nerveless and shrunken, leaving the affected limb shorter and thinner than normal—a chronic condition in biblical times regarded as incurable. Some identify with the modern infantile paralysis. See also DISEASE AND HEALING. *Cf.* fig. 68.

WITNESS. In EVV 'to witness', 'to bear witness', a 'witness', 'to testify', 'testimony' (with a few minor additional renderings) represent a somewhat arbitrary and not always consistent rendering of the following Hebrew and Greek words. In the Old Testament: *'ānâ* (lit. 'to answer'), *'ûḏ* (verb), *'ēḏ*, *'ēḏâ*, *'ēḏûṯ*, *tᵉ'ûḏâ*; in the New Testament: *martyreō* (verb) and compounds, *martys, martyria, martyrion*. Though 'to witness' is used with a wide range of connotations, the forensic often being virtually forgotten, it is never used in the frequent modern English usage as a synonym of 'to see'.

'ēḏ and its rare synonym *'ēḏâ* always refer to the person or thing bearing witness, examples of the latter being Gn. xxxi. 48, 52; Jos. xxii. 27, 28, 34, xxiv. 27; Is. xix. 20. The New Testament equivalent, *martys*, is used only of persons, there being no example of a thing as bearer of witness.

Hebrew, disliking abstracts, rarely speaks of witness in the sense of evidence given. In the three cases it does (Ru. iv. 7; Is. viii. 16, 20) it uses *tᵉ'ûḏâ*. Greek uses the conception frequently, but distinguishes between *martyria*, the act of testifying or the testimony, and *martyrion*, that which may serve as evidence or proof or the fact established by evidence.

'ēḏûṯ, always rendered 'testimony' except in the AV of Nu. xvii. 7, 8, xviii. 2; 2 Ch. xxiv. 6, where it is 'witness', has lost its forensic meaning completely and is a technical religious term (see also COVENANT), rendered by *KB* 'monitory sign, reminder, exhortation'. The outstanding example of *'ēḏûṯ* is the tables of the Ten Commandments (Ex. xvi. 34, xxv. 16, 21, *etc.*). Hence the ark which contained them became 'the ark of the testimony' (Ex. xxv. 22, *etc.*), the tent which sheltered them 'the tent of the testimony' (Nu. xvii. 7, RV), and the veil dividing off the Holy of holies 'the vail of the testimony' (Lv. xxiv. 3). The term is then enlarged to cover the law as a whole, *e.g.* Pss. lxxviii. 5, cxix. 2 and frequently. The meaning in 2 Ki. xi. 12 is doubtful (see *ICC*, *ad loc.*).

AV translation 'martyr' in Acts xxii. 20; Rev. ii. 13, xvii. 6 (also RV, RSV) is hardly justified, though *martys* quickly developed this meaning; *cf. Arndt*, p. 495b.

H.L.E.

WIZARD. See MAGIC AND SORCERY.

WOE. The AV rendering of the Greek interjection *ouai*, meaning 'Alas for'. When Jesus says 'Woe unto you', He is not so much pronouncing a final judgment as describing the miserable condition in God's sight of those He is addressing. Their wretchedness lies not least in the fact that they are living in a fool's paradise, unaware of the misery that awaits them. The state of the materially-minded blinded by wealth to their spiritual needs, of the self-satisfied, of the impenitent and unsympathetic, and of those who are universally popular is declared by Jesus to be wretched (Lk. vi. 24–26). Similarly, the woeful condition of the Pharisees and scribes (Lk. 'lawyers') lies, Jesus tells them, in the hypocritical zeal, the lack of proportion, the love of display, and the self-complacency which disfigure their religion (Mt. xxiii. 13–33; Lk. xi. 42–52). When Jesus addresses the words 'Woe unto you' to the unrepentant cities Chorazin and Bethsaida, He follows them with a prophecy of the doom that awaits them (Mt. xi. 21) as they are in a woeful state for having refused the gospel. Paul says he would be in a woeful state if he failed to preach it (1 Cor. ix. 16). The seer in the Revelation uses the word *ouai* as an interjection in his dirge over fallen Babylon (Rev. xviii. 10–16), and as a noun to describe three 'woes', a comprehensive term covering various plagues and disasters which will herald the final judgment (Rev. ix. 12, xi. 14).

R.V.G.T.

WOLF. Heb. *zᵉʾēḇ* (Is. xi. 6, *etc.*) and Gk. *lykos* (Mt. vii. 15, *etc.*) undoubtedly refer to the SE Asiatic form of the wolf. Its range has been greatly reduced by the growth of population and modern methods of control, but up to New Testament times it was common enough to be a danger to livestock, if not to human lives. The potential danger of attack by wolves is implied in most of the passages, but it should be noted that the wolf is, in fact, mentioned only metaphorically throughout. The wolf of Palestine was similar to, though rather smaller than, the wolf of central and northern Europe. The Hebrew word could be translated 'jackal' (for which, see Fox), but it is never so rendered in AV. G.C.

WOMAN (Heb. *'iššâ*, Gk. *gynē*). Woman is introduced into the Old Testament narrative as a 'help meet' for man, as his partner (Gn. ii. 20). See EVE.

From the Hebrew laws we see that the mother was to be honoured (Ex. xx. 12), feared (Lv. xix. 3), and obeyed (Dt. xxi. 18 ff.). She was to be reckoned with in her household, naming the children, and being responsible for their early education. The same sacrifice was offered for cleansing, whether the new-born child was male or female (Lv. xii. 5 f.). She attended the religious gatherings for worship, and brought her offerings for sacrifice. The Nazirite vow was taken by her as she sought to dedicate herself specially to the worship of Yahweh (Nu. vi. 2).

The woman was exempt from sabbath labour (Ex. xx. 10), and if sold as a slave was freed like the man in the seventh year. If there were no male heirs, the woman could inherit and become a landowner in her own right.

Young men were exhorted to marry within the tribe lest their womenfolk wooed them away from their service of Yahweh.

Monogamy was regarded as the ideal state, although polygamy was common, and the relationship of Yahweh and Israel was often compared with that of a husband and wife.

There are many examples of women of stature playing their part in the life of the people, *e.g.* Miriam, Deborah, Huldah, and being in a direct personal relationship with Yahweh. On the other hand, one sees the tremendous influence wielded against Yahweh by women such as Jezebel an Maacah.

As time went on there was a tendency, unde rabbinical teaching, to make the man more prc minent, and to move away from the idea c Gn. ii. 20.

Of greatest importance in the New Testamen is our Lord's attitude to women and His teachin concerning them.

Mary (*q.v.*), the mother of Jesus, was describe as 'Blessed . . . among women' (Lk. i. 42) by he kinswoman Elisabeth. Anna, the prophetess a the Temple, recognized the baby's identity (Lk ii. 38). There was much concerning her Son tha Mary did not understand, but she 'kept all thes things, and pondered them in her heart' (Lk. i 19), until the time to make public the details c His birth and boyhood. As He was on the cros Jesus commended her to the care of a disciple.

The Gospel narratives abound with instance of Jesus' encounters with women. He forgav them, He healed them, He taught them, and the in their turn served Him by making provision fo His journeys, by giving hospitality, by deeds c love, by noting His tomb so that they could per form the last rites for Him, and by becoming eye witnesses of His resurrection.

Jesus included them in His teaching illustra tions, making it clear that His message involve them. By thus honouring them He put woma on an equality with man, demanding the sam standard from both the sexes and offering th same way of salvation.

After the resurrection the women joined 'i prayer and supplication' with the other follower of Jesus, in entire fellowship with them (Acts i 14). They helped to elect Matthias (Acts i. 15 26), and received the power and gifts of the Hol Spirit on the Day of Pentecost (Acts ii. 1–4, 18)

It was the home of Mary, the mother of Joh Mark, which became a centre of the church a Jerusalem (Acts xii. 12). Paul's first convert i Europe was the woman Lydia (Acts xvi. 14) Priscilla with her husband taught the grea Apollos the full truths of the gospel. The fou daughters of Philip 'did prophesy' (Acts xxi. 9) Many others, as, for example, Phebe, wer active Christians and wholly engaged in the ser vice of the gospel.

Paul dealt with the local situation in th churches by requiring that the conventions of th time be observed. Meanwhile he laid down th principle that 'God is no respecter of persons and that Christians 'are all one in Christ Jesus (Gal. iii. 28). M.G.

WOMB. Heb. *beṭen*, *mēʿîm* (Ru. i. 11 only), an *reḥem* or *raḥam*; Gk. *gastēr*, *koilia* or *mētra*, th former two in both cases being used also of th belly generally, indicating the Hebrew vaguenes about the internal physiology (see STOMACH BOWELS). The reference is generally to the plac or time of life's beginning (Jb. i. 21; Is. xlix. 1) and so figuratively of the origin of anything (Jb xxxviii. 29). The formation of the babe in th vomb is a wonderful mystery to the biblical vriters, who, understandably enough, attribute t to the direct action and care of God (Jb. xxxi. 15; Ec. xi. 5). The presence of the living babe in he womb some time before birth is mentioned in he New Testament (Lk. i. 41). Barrenness (*q.v.*) s attributed to the closing up of the womb, ometimes specifically stated to be done by God 1 Sa. i. 5). This is a great cause of sorrow and hame to the woman concerned (verse 6). The irstborn (*q.v.*), referred to as that which openeth he womb, is regarded as holy (Ex. xiii. 2; Lk. ii. 23). B.O.B.

VONDERS. See MIRACLES, SIGN.

VOOL. Fine wavy hair forming the fleece of the heep or goat. After spinning, it is woven into loth from which woollen garments are made. There was a Mosaic prohibition against wearing loth made of a mixture of wool and linen (Dt. xii. 11). Wool is sometimes used as an illustra-ion of whiteness and purity (Is. i. 18).

R.F.H.

VORD. In the Old Testament the word (*dāḇār*) f God is used 394 times of a divine com-nunication which comes from God to men in the orm of commandment, prophecy, warning, or ncouragement. The usual formula is 'the word f Yahweh came (lit. was) unto . . .' but some-imes the word is seen as a vision (Is. ii. 1; Je. ii. 1, xxxviii. 21). Yahweh's word is an extension f the divine personality, invested with divine uthority, and is to be heeded by angels and men Ps. ciii. 20; Dt. xii. 32); it stands for ever (Is. xl.), and once uttered it cannot return unfulfilled (s. lv. 11). It is used as a synonym for the law 'ôrâ) of God in Ps. cxix, where alone its refer-nce is to a written rather than a spoken message.

In the New Testament it translates two terms, *ogos* and *rhēma*, the former being supremely sed of the message of the Christian gospel (Mk. . 2; Acts vi. 2; Gal. vi. 6), though the latter also ears the same meaning (Rom. x. 8; Eph. vi. 17; Heb. vi. 5, *etc.*). Our Lord spoke of the word of God (in the parable of the sower, Lk. viii. 11; see lso Mk. vii. 13; Lk. xi. 28), but in the Synoptic ospels He always used the plural of His own nessage ('my words', Mt. xxiv. 35 and parallels; Mk. viii. 38; Lk. xxiv. 44). In the Fourth Gospel, owever, the singular is often found. To the early hurch the word was a message revealed from od in Christ, which was to be preached, ninistered, and obeyed. It was the word of life Phil. ii. 16), of truth (Eph. i. 13), of salvation Acts xiii. 26), of reconciliation (2 Cor. v. 19), of e cross (1 Cor. i. 18). See also LOGOS. J.B.Tr.

'ORK. The main words here are the Heb. *a'ᵃśeh* (181 times), 'an act', 'a doing' (*cf.* Gn. v. ; Ex. v. 4, *etc.*, and especially in the Psalms of od's act, see Pss. viii. 3, 6, xix. 1, *etc.*); *m^{e}lā'ḵâ* 17 times; *cf.* Gn. ii. 2, 3; Ex. xx. 9, *etc.*); *pō'al* 0 times), 'a deed' (*cf.* Dt. xxxii. 4, *etc.*). Gk. *ergon* (142 times) is found frequently in John, Hebrews, James, and Revelation. Less frequent is the abstract *energeia*, literally 'energy' (EVV 'working'). This is a specific Pauline word (Eph. i. 19, iii. 7, iv. 16; Phil. iii. 21; Col. i. 29; 2 Thes. ii. 9). Note should be taken also of the Heb. *y^{e}gî'â*, 'labour', 'weariness', and *'āmāl*, 'labour', 'misery'; *cf.* Gk. *kopiaō*, 'to labour', 'to be wearied out' (*cf.* Mt. xi. 28; Jn. iv. 38, *etc.*), and *ergatēs*, 'a worker' (Mt. ix. 37, 38, xx. 1, 2, 8; Lk. x. 2, 7; Jas. v. 4).

In classical Greek the verb *kopiaō* has reference to the weariness which labour produces (*cf. LSJ ad loc.*), but in the New Testament it signifies the toil itself (*cf.* Mt. vi. 28, xi. 28; Lk. v. 5, xii. 27; Jn. iv. 38). The word *ergatēs* has reference to the business or the trade by which men gain their subsistence (Acts xix. 24), and it is also used to denote the profit which results from their activity (Acts xvi. 16, 19) as well as the toil which the pursuit of their gain involves. *Ergasia* occurs in an ethical sense in Eph. iv. 19 and means literally 'to make a trade of'; *cf.* 'worker' (*ergatēs*) in Lk. xiii. 27; 2 Cor. xi. 13; Phil. iii. 2, and in a good sense Mt. x. 10; 2 Tim. ii. 15. Luke's usage of the Latinism *dos ergasian*, 'give diligence' (Lk. xii. 58), to emphasize Christ's warning concerning reconciliation with an adversary is thought by some to be derived from his medical studies, where the term had reference to the making of some mixture, the mixture itself, and the work of digestion, and of the lungs, *etc.* (*cf.* W. K. Hobart, *The Medical Language of St. Luke*, 1882, p. 243). The phrase, however, occurs in the LXX (*cf.* Wisdom xiii. 19) with which Luke was familiar.

I. THE GENERAL SENSE

It is clear from the interchangeable use of certain words to indicate God's activity and man's that work is itself a God-ordained thing. Work was from the beginning God's purpose for men, and is set forth in Ps. civ. 19–24 and Is. xxviii. 23–29 as a provision of the divine wisdom. Creation itself 'works' (*cf.* Pr. vi. 6–11). The fact of work as forming an integral part of the pattern of the divine purpose for man is implied in the fourth commandment. But the entrance of sin changed work from a joy to a toil (*cf.* Gn. iii. 16–19). Work has thus become a burden instead of a blessing, and, although not bad in itself, it has lost its true value. It has become an occasion for sin; idolatry results when it becomes an end in itself (*cf.* Ec. ii. 4–11, 20–23; Lk. xii. 16–22). By some it has become the means of exploitation and oppression (*cf.* Ex. i. 11–14, ii. 23; Jas. v. 4). But in redemption, work is again transformed into a means of blessing. From the beginning Christianity has condemned idleness even when this has been indulged in in the name of religion (*cf.* 1 Thes. iv. 11; also Eph. iv. 28; 1 Tim. v. 13). Our Lord, working as a carpenter (Mk. vi. 3), has sanctified common toil, and Paul set an example in honest labour (Acts xviii. 3). He virtually established a law of social economics in his announcement in 2 Thes. iii. 10: 'If any would not work, neither should he eat.' On the other side the principle proclaimed by our Lord remains the basis of society, 'the labourer is worthy of his hire' (Lk. x. 7).

In the experience of grace human tasks are given a new value and become more worth while. They are performed for the sake of the Name. And in their fulfilment in this context they are thrice blessed. The one who works is himself blessed in his reception of divine grace to carry through his labours for the glory of God; those who receive the results of such tasks done in a new spirit and with a new quality are benefited also; and in all God is Himself glorified. Such work is done 'in' and 'for' the Lord (*cf.* Rom. xiv. 7, 8; Eph. vi. 5–9; Col. iii. 23, 24). In this way man becomes a steward of God's riches (1 Cor. iv. 1, 2; *cf.* Mt. xxv. 14–30) and a servant of his neighbour (Mt. xxv. 40; Gal. v. 13; 1 Pet. iv. 10). The genuineness of man's faith is proved in the end by the quality of his works (*cf.* Mt. xvi. 27, *praxis*). Yet in the end the acceptance of the labourer will be an act of divine grace (*cf.* 1 Cor. iii. 8–15; note especially verse 10).

II. THE SPIRITUAL AND ETHICAL REFERENCE

The word 'work' is used with reference to God's act of creation and providence. In the Psalms this note is given special emphasis. God's work or works are great and manifold (*cf.* Pss. xcii. 5, civ. 24, cxi. 2, *etc.*). They give Him everlasting praise (*cf.* Ps. cxlv. 4, 9, 10), declare His righteousness (cxlv. 17) and bring Him joy (civ. 31). It 's the same in the New Testament (*cf.* Heb. iv. 10; Jn. i. 3; Acts xiii. 41; Rev. xv. 3). The term is used also for the work of salvation committed by the Father to the Son. This is specifically a Johannine idea. The Son has come to do the Father's work (*cf.* Jn. iv. 34, v. 36, ix. 4, x. 25, 37, *etc.*), which work He has finished (Jn. xv. 24, xvii. 4). This means that nothing can be added to the work He has done, since it is once and for all. Salvation is therefore not a matter of merit but of grace (see WORKS, GRACE, SALVATION, *etc.*). But the redeemed man will work and serve and labour and thus commend himself in the Lord. He will be fruitful in every good work (Col. i. 10; *cf.* Gal. vi. 4; 2 Thes. ii. 17; 2 Tim. ii. 21; *etc.*). Those who undertake special work for God are to be esteemed for their work's sake (*cf.* 1 Thes. v. 13; also Phil. ii. 29). Yet no work for God can be done apart from the inworking of His grace (*cf.* Eph. ii. 10, iii. 20; Phil. ii. 13; Col. i. 29, *etc.*). Such is the 'work of faith, and labour of love' (1 Thes. i. 3; *cf.* 2 Thes. i. 11).

BIBLIOGRAPHY. J. Calvin, *Institutes*, III, vii; A. Richardson, *The Biblical Doctrine of Work*, 1952; J. Murray, *Principles of Conduct*, 1957, pp. 82–106.

H.D.McD.

WORKS. The three main uses of this term, although distinct, are essentially related; the works of God, the works of Jesus Christ, and the works of man in relation to faith.

1. In the Old Testament the works of God ar presented as evidence of God's supreme power authority, wisdom, and benevolence. The Ol Testament defines the Deity not by abstrac terms such as omnipotence, but by His activity Moses adduced the works of God as evidence o His unique distinction from other gods (Dt. iii 24). In the Psalms the works of God are fre quently proclaimed as providing confidence i His power and authority and His sole right t receive worship. These works are His creativ activity (Ps. civ. 24) and His sovereign acts i relation to His redeemed people (Ps. lxxvii. 11-20) and to the nations (Ps. xlvi. 8–10).

2. It was by His works that Jesus revealed tha He was both Messiah and Son of God, exempli fied by His answer to John the Baptist (Mt. xi 2–5). John's Gospel records the significan activity of Jesus with set purpose to reveal Hi Messiahship and deity so as to induce faith i His Person (Jn. xx. 30, 31). Frequently Jesu pointed to His works as evidence that He wa sent by the Father (Jn. v. 36, x. 37, 38). Bein the very works of God (Jn. ix. 3, 4), His work are sufficient ground for faith in Him as bein uniquely related to the Father (Jn. x. 38, xiv. 10 11). It was through equating His work with tha of God that He was accused of blasphemy i identifying Himself with God (Jn. v. 17–23) His death completed that work (Jn. xvii. 4 xix. 30).

3. The believer also demonstrates by his goo works the divine activity within him (Mt. v. 16 Jn. vi. 28, xiv. 12). Conversely, the man who ha no faith demonstrates by his evil works hi separation from God (Jn. iii. 19; Col. i. 21 Eph. v. 11; 2 Pet. ii. 8, *etc.*). Good work are therefore the evidence of living faith, a James emphasizes in opposition to those wh claim to be saved by faith alone without work (Jas. ii. 14–26). James is in harmony with Paul who also repeatedly declared the necessity fo works, *i.e.* for behaviour appropriate to the ne life in Christ following our entry into it by fait alone (Eph. ii. 8–10; 1 Cor. vi. 9–11; Gal. v. 16 26, *etc.*). The works rejected by Paul are thos which men claim as earning God's favour an securing their discharge from the guilt of si (Rom. iv. 1–5; Eph. ii. 8, 9; Tit. iii. 5). Sinc salvation is given by God in grace, no degree c works can merit it. The good works of th heathen are therefore unavailing as a means c salvation, since the man himself relies on th flesh and not on the grace of God (Rom. vi 7, 8).

J.C.C.

WORLD. The Greek word *kosmos* means b derivation 'the *ordered* world'. It is used in th New Testament, but not in LXX, sometimes fc what we should call the 'universe', the create world, described in the Old Testament as 'a things' or 'heaven and earth' (Acts xvii. 24). Th 'world' in this sense was made by the Word (J i. 10); and it was this 'world' of which Jesus w speaking when He said it would not profit a ma anything if he gained the whole of it and lost his soul in the process (Mt. xvi. 26).

But, because mankind is the most important part of the universe, the word *kosmos* is more often used in the limited sense of human beings, being a synonym for *hē oikoumenē gē*, 'the inhabited earth', also translated in the New Testament by 'world'. It is into this 'world' that men are born, and in it they live till they die (Jn. xvi. 21). It was all the kingdoms of this world that the devil offered to give to Christ if He would worship him (Mt. iv. 8, 9). It was this world, the world of men and women of flesh and blood, that God loved (Jn. iii. 16), and into which Jesus came when He was born of a human mother (Jn. xi. 27).

It is, however, an axiom of the Bible that this world of human beings, the climax of the divine creation, the world that God made especially to reflect His glory, is now in rebellion against Him. Through the transgression of one man, sin has entered into it (Rom. v. 18) with universal consequences. It has become, as a result, a *disordered* world in the grip of the evil one (1 Jn. v. 19). And so, very frequently in the New Testament, and particularly in the Johannine writings, the word *kosmos* has a sinister significance. It is not the world as God intended it to be, but '*this* world' set over against God, following its own wisdom and living by the light of its own reason (1 Cor. i. 21), not recognizing the Source of all true life and illumination (Jn. i. 10). The two dominant characteristics of '*this* world' are *pride*, born of man's failure to accept his creaturely estate and his dependence on the Creator, which leads him to act as though he forsooth were the lord and giver of life; and *covetousness*, which causes him to desire and possess all that is attractive to his physical senses (1 Jn. ii. 16). And, as man tends in effect to worship what he covets, such covetousness is idolatry (Col. iii. 5). Accordingly, worldliness is the enthronement of something other than God as the supreme object of man's interests and affections. Pleasures and occupations, not necessarily wrong in themselves, become so when an all-absorbing attention is paid to them.

'*This* world' is pervaded by a spirit of its own, which has to be exorcized by the Spirit of God, if it is not to remain in control over human reason and understanding (1 Cor. ii. 12). Man is in bondage to the elements which comprise the world (Col. ii. 20) until he is emancipated from them by Christ. He cannot overcome it till he is himself 'born of God' (1 Jn. v. 4). Legalism, asceticism, and ritualism are this world's feeble and enfeebling substitutes for true religion (Gal. iv. 9, 10); and only a true knowledge of God as revealed by Christ can prevent men from relying upon them. It was because the Jews relied upon them that they did not recognize either the Christ in the days of His flesh (Jn. i. 11) or His followers (1 Jn. iii. 1). Similarly, false prophets who advocate such things, or antichrists who are antinomian in their teaching, will always be listened to by those who belong to this world (1 Jn. iv. 5).

Christ, whom the Father sent to be the Saviour of this world (1 Jn. iv. 14), and whose very presence in it was a judgment upon it (Jn. ix. 39), freed men from its sinister forces by Himself engaging in mortal combat with its 'prince', the perpetual instigator of the evil within it. The crisis of this world came when Jesus left the upper room and went forth to meet this prince (Jn. xiv. 30, 31). By voluntarily submitting to death, Jesus brought about the defeat of him who held men in the grip of death, but who had no claims upon Himself (Jn. xii. 31, 32, xiv. 30). On the cross, judgment was passed upon the prince of the world (Jn. xvi. 11); and faith in Christ as the Son of God, who offered the sacrifice which alone can cleanse men from the guilt and power of sin (a cleansing symbolized by the flow of water and blood from His stricken side, Jn. xix. 34), enables the believer to overcome the world (1 Jn. v. 4–6), and to endure the tribulations which the world inevitably brings upon him (Jn. xvi. 33). The love of a Christian for God, the Father of Jesus Christ His Redeemer, who is the propitiation for the sins of the whole world (1 Jn. ii. 2), acts with the expulsive power of a new affection; it makes it abhorrent to him to set his affections any longer upon 'this world', which, because it is severed from the true source of life, is transitory and contains within itself the seeds of its own decay (1 Jn. ii. 15–17). A man who has come to experience the *higher* love for God, and for Christ and His brethren, must abandon the lower love for all that is contaminated by the spirit of the world: friendship of the world is of necessity enmity with God (Jas. iv. 2).

Jesus, in His last prayer in the upper room, did not pray for the world, but for those whom His Father had given Him out of the world. By this 'gift', these men whom Jesus described as 'His own' ceased to have the characteristics of the world; and Jesus prayed that they might be kept safe from its evil influences (Jn. xvii. 9), for He knew that after His own departure they would have to bear the brunt of the world's hatred which had hitherto been directed almost entirely against Himself. As the risen and ascended Christ He still limits His intercessions to those who draw nigh to God through Him (Heb. vii. 25); and He continues to manifest Himself not to the world but to His own that are in the world (Jn. xiv. 22).

But it is very certain that Christ's disciples cannot and must not attempt to retreat from this world. It is into this world, *all* the world (Mk. xvi. 15), that He sends them. They are to be its light (Mt. v. 14); and the 'field' in which the Church is to do its work of witnessing to the truth as it is in Jesus is no less comprehensive than the world itself (Mt. xiii. 38). For the world is still God's world, even though at present it lies under the evil one. In the end, 'earth's true loveliness will be restored'; and, with all evil destroyed and the sons of God manifested, the whole creation will be 'delivered from the bondage of corruption into the glorious liberty of the children of God' (Rom. viii. 21). Then God will be 'all in all' (1 Cor. xv. 28); or, as that verse has recently been translated, 'present in a total manner in the universe' (so J. Héring, *Vocabulary of the New Testament*, 1958). The seer of Revelation envisages the day when great voices in heaven will proclaim: 'The kingdoms of this world are become the kingdoms of our Lord, and of his Christ; and he shall reign for ever and ever' (Rev. xi. 15). R.V.G.T.

WORM. The use of the word 'worm' is technically confined to several classes of invertebrate animals, but it is applied much more widely in popular language. Wire-worms and wood-worms are beetles, cutworms are caterpillars, slow worms are lizards, and so on. In ancient times and among less-developed people the usage is even more vague. Five Hebrew words are translated 'worm', and there is little doubt that in the popular sense the translation can be accepted. In most passages the use is figurative, and more precise identification is difficult.

In the well-known passage Jb. xix. 26, the AVmg or RSV should be followed: 'after my skin has been destroyed'. There is no word for 'worms' in the Hebrew text. G.C.

WORMWOOD (Heb. *laʿᵃnâ*, Gk. *apsinthos*). Many species of wormwood grow in Palestine, but the biblical references are either to *Artemisia herba-alba* or *A. judaica* L. All species have a strong, bitter taste, leading to the use of the plant as a symbol of bitterness, sorrow, and calamity (Pr. v. 4; La. iii. 15, 19; Am. v. 7, vi. 12 (AV 'hemlock'). Moses used it to show the perils of secret idolatry (Dt. xxix. 18), as did Jeremiah in warning of the punishment awaiting disobedient Israel (Je. ix. 15, xxiii. 15). R.K.H.

WORSHIP. The vocabulary of worship in the Bible is very extensive, but the essential concept in both the Old and New Testaments is 'service'. In both Testaments worship is Heb. *ʿᵃḇōḏâ* and Gk. *latreia*, each signifying originally the labour of slaves or hired servants. And in order to offer this 'worship' to God His servants must prostrate themselves—Heb. *hištaḥᵃwâ* or Gk. *proskyneō*—and thus manifest reverential fear and adoring awe and wonder.

In the Old Testament there are instances of individual worship (Gn. xxiv. 26 f.; Ex. xxxiii. 9–xxxiv. 8). But the emphasis is upon worship in the congregation (Ps. xlii. 4; 1 Ch. xxix. 20). In tabernacle and Temple worship ritual was prominent. Apart from the daily morning and evening sacrifices, the celebration of Passover and the observance of the Day of Atonement would be highlights in the Jewish Church calendar. The ritual acts of shedding of blood, presenting incense, pronouncing the priestly blessing, *etc.*, would tend to emphasize the ceremonial to the detriment of the spiritual aspects of worship, and even tend to introduce a sense of tension or conflict between the two attitudes (Pss. xl. 6, l. 7–15; Mi. vi. 6–8). But many in Israel would be able to take the public praise (*e.g.* Pss. xciii, xcv–c) and prayers (*e.g.* Pss. lx, lxxix, lxxx), and use them to express their love and gratitude to God (Dt. xi. 13) in a real act of inward spiritual worship.

This highly-developed public worship offered in the tabernacle and Temple is a far cry from earlier times when the Patriarchs believed that the Lord could be worshipped wherever He had chosen to reveal Himself. But that public worship in the Temple was a spiritual reality is clear from the fact that when the sanctuary was destroyed, and the exiles found themselves in Babylon, worship remained a necessity, and to meet this need the synagogue service, consisting of (1) the *Shemaʿ*, (2) prayers, (3) Scripture readings, and (4) exposition, was 'created'. But later in the second Temple the daily services, the sabbath, the annual festivals and fasts, and the praises of the hymn-book (Book of Psalms) of this second Temple ensured that worship remained a vital factor in Jewish national life.

In the New Testament Temple and synagogue worship are again found. Christ participated in both, but He always inculcated the worship that is the love of the heart towards a heavenly Father. In His teaching the approach to God through ritual and priestly mediation is not merely unimportant, it is now unnecessary. At last 'worship' is true *ʿᵃḇōḏâ* or *latreia*, a service offered to God not only in terms of temple worship but of service to one's fellows (Lk. x. 25 ff.; Mt. v. 23 f.; Jn. iv. 20–24; Jas. i. 27). At the beginning, however, the Church did not abandon temple worship; and probably Christians continued to attend the synagogue services too. And when the break between Judaism and the Church finally came Christian worship may have been modelled on the synagogue service.

The great contributory factor in the break away from the Jewish sabbath, Temple, ritual, *etc.*, was the bitter antagonism of the Jews against the Church. But so far as the New Testament is concerned our notions of Christian worship are very vague. Clearly the day of worship *par excellence* was the Lord's Day (Acts xx. 7), although we do hear of daily services at the beginning (Acts ii. 46). There is no mention of services commemorating the Lord's resurrection and the Spirit's coming at Pentecost. Worship would be conducted in believers' homes. In such circumstances official ministrants would be unnecessary. Simplicity would be the keynote of these house-church worship services, consisting for the most part of praise (Eph. v. 19; Col. iii. 16), prayer, reading from the Scriptures, and exposition. In the church at Corinth we hear of 'speaking in tongues' (1 Cor. xiv). The love-feast, followed by the Lord's Supper (1 Cor. xi. 23–28) were also common features of Christian worship. But the emphasis throughout would be upon the Spirit, and the inner love and devotion of the heart. See also PRAYER, PRAISE.

BIBLIOGRAPHY. J. V. Bartlett in *ERE*; R. Martin-
chard in J.-J. von Allmen (ed.), *Vocabulary of*
ie Bible, 1958, pp. 471–474; R. Abba, *Principles*
f Christian Worship, 1957. J.G.S.S.T.

VRATH. The permanent attitude of the holy nd just God when confronted by sin and evil is esignated His 'wrath'. It is inadequate to regard ais term merely as a description of 'the in-vitable process of cause and effect in a moral niverse' or as another way of speaking of the sults of sin. It is rather a personal quality, ithout which God would cease to be fully ghteous and His love would degenerate into entimentality. His wrath, however, even though ke His love it has to be described in human inguage, is not wayward, fitful, or spasmodic, as uman anger always is. It is as permanent and as onsistent an element in His nature as is His ove. This is well brought out in the treatise of actantius, *De ira Dei*.

The injustice and impiety of men, for which ley have no excuse, *must* be followed by mani-estations of the divine wrath in the lives both of idividuals and of nations (see Rom. i. 18–32); nd the Old Testament contains numerous lustrations of this, such as the destruction of odom and Gomorrah and the downfall of lineveh (see Dt. xxix. 23; Na. i. 2–6). But until ie final 'day of wrath', which is anticipated iroughout the Bible and portrayed very vividly the Revelation, God's wrath is always tem-ered with mercy, particularly in His dealings ith His chosen people (see, *e.g.*, Ho. xi. 8 ff.). or a sinner, however, to 'trade' upon this mercy to treasure 'up unto (himself) wrath against ie day of wrath and revelation of the righteous dgment of God' (Rom. ii. 5). Paul was con-nced that one of the main reasons why Israel iiled to arrest the process of moral decline lay in ieir wrong reaction to the forbearance of God, ho so often refrained from punishing them to ie extent they deserved. They despised 'the ches of his goodness and forbearance and long-ffering', and failed to see that it was intended lead them to repentance (Rom. ii. 4).

In their unredeemed state men's rebellion gainst God is, in fact, so persistent that they are evitably the objects of His wrath (Eph. ii. 3), id 'vessels of wrath fitted to destruction' (Rom. . 22). Nor does the Mosaic law rescue them om this position, for, as the apostle states in om. iv. 15, 'the law worketh wrath'. Because it quires perfect obedience to its commands, the enalties exacted for disobedience render the fender more subject to the divine wrath. It is, be sure, only by the merciful provision for nners made in the gospel that they can cease to the objects of this wrath and become the cipients of this grace. The love of God for nners expressed in the life and death of Jesus is e dominant theme of the New Testament, and is love is shown not least because Jesus ex-rienced on man's behalf and in his stead the isery, the afflictions, the punishment, and the death which are the lot of sinners subject to God's wrath. Consequently, Jesus can be de-scribed as 'the deliverer from the wrath to come' (see 1 Thes. i. 10); and Paul can write: 'Being now justified by his blood, we shall be saved from wrath through him' (Rom. v. 9). On the other hand, the wrath of God remains upon all who, seeking to thwart God's redemptive pur-pose, are disobedient to God's Son, through whom alone such justification is rendered possible.

BIBLIOGRAPHY. R. V. G. Tasker, *The Biblical Doctrine of the Wrath of God*, 1951; G. H. C. Macgregor, 'The Concept of the Wrath of God in the New Testament', *NTS*, VII, 1960–1, pp. 101 ff. R.V.G.T.

WRESTLING. See GAMES.

Fig. 234. Copper offering stand modelled as two men engaged in belt-wrestling. From Tell Agrab, Iraq, c. 2300 BC.

WRITING. Throughout the Ancient Near East, from at least *c.* 3100 BC onwards, writing was a hallmark of civilization and progress. In the second millennium BC there were several experi-ments which led to the development of the alphabet, with a consequent general increase in literacy. Although as yet few documents have been found in Palestine itself before the exilic period when compared to the many thousands from the neighbouring territories, it is reasonable to assume that its proximity to other cultural centres enabled it to share the art of writing throughout all periods also, as is indicated by the commonest words for writing (Heb. *kāṯaḇ*; Aram. *k*ᵉ*ṯaḇ*; Gk. *graphō*) occurring more than 450 times in the Old and New Testaments.

I. BIBLICAL REFERENCES

Moses is said to have written (Ex. xvii. 14) the Decalogue (Ex. xxiv. 12, xxxiv. 27), the words of

Yahweh (Ex. xxiv. 4), the Law (Torah, Jos. viii. 31), and spoken about a written copy of it (Dt. xxvii). He also wrote all the statutes (Dt. xxx. 10) and judgments (Ex. xxxiv. 27; *cf.* 2 Ki. xvii. 37), as well as legal enactments (Dt. xxiv. 1; Mk. x. 4), details of the journeys made by the Israelites (Nu. xxxiii. 2), and the words of the victory song (Dt. xxxi. 19, 22). In these he was helped by literate officials (*šōṭᵉrîm*, Nu. xi. 16, AV 'officers'; *cf.* Akkad. *šaṭāru*, 'to write') who, by reason of their ability to record decisions, were closely connected with the judiciary (Dt. xvi. 18; 1 Ch. xxiii. 4; Jos. viii. 33). During the Exodus wanderings priests also wrote down curses (Nu. v. 23) and names of objects (xvii. 3). Joshua wrote a copy of the Ten Commandments (Jos. viii. 32) and of the renewed covenant (xxiv. 26).

Samuel wrote down the charter of the newly created kingship of Saul (1 Sa. x. 25, AV 'manner'). David wrote letters to his commander Joab (2 Sa. xi. 14) and details of the Temple administration, as did his son Solomon (2 Ch. xxxv. 4), who corresponded with Hiram of Tyre in writing (2 Ch. ii. 11). As in all periods, court scribes were frequently employed to write lists of persons (1 Ch. iv. 41, xxiv. 6; see also Nu. xi. 26; Is. x. 19; Je. xxii. 30; Ne. xii. 22; SCRIBE).

Isaiah the prophet wrote (2 Ch. xxvi. 22; Is. viii. 1) and dictated to a scribe (xxx. 8). In his time Hezekiah both wrote letters (*'iggereṯ*) to Ephraim and Manasseh (2 Ch. xxx. 1; *cf.* Is. xxxviii. 9 entitled 'the writing (*miḵtāḇ*) of Hezekiah') and received them from the Assyrian king Sennacherib (Is. xxxvii. 14, xxxix. 1; 2 Ch. xxxii. 17). Jeremiah dictated to his amanuensis Baruch (Je. xxx. 2, xxxvi. 27, xlv. 1), as probably did Hosea (viii. 12) and Malachi (iii. 16), for the written word was an important part of prophecy (2 Ch. xxi. 12), its value being emphasized also by Job (xix. 23).

As is known from extant MSS, the Neo-Babylonian and Persian periods were marked by increasing literacy. Daniel and the Babylonian savants could read, and therefore presumably could themselves write, Aramaic (Dn. v. 24 f.). There was an active correspondence within the empire as in earlier periods (see POST, ASSYRIA, BABYLONIA). Nehemiah wrote down the covenant (Ne. ix. 38), while his opponents in Samaria wrote to the Persian king (Ezr. iv. 6, 7), as did other district-governors (Ezr. v. 7, vi. 2). Ezra himself was a scribe who wrote decrees or state documents in the local dialects (viii. 34), in the style of court officials, including Mordecai, on behalf of the king (Est. ix. 28 f.), who affixed his seal (Dn. vi. 25; see also SEAL).

Jesus Christ and His apostles made constant reference to the written Scriptures (*e.g.* 'it is written'—*gegraptai*—occurs 106 times). Our Lord Himself was literate (Jn. vii. 14, 15) and wrote publicly on at least one occasion (Jn. viii. 6). Zacharias the priest wrote on a wax-covered writing-board (Lk. i. 63), and the Roman governor Pilate had a trilingual inscription written to be placed on the cross (Jn. xix. 19, 22).

Fig. 235. 'I am Darius, the king' written in Old Persian, Elamite, and Babylonian cuneiform scripts. From the seal of Darius I (521–486 BC).

John (xxi. 24), Luke (i. 3; Acts i. 1), and Paul himself (Gal. vi. 11; Phm. 19; Rom. xv. 15), though often using an amanuensis such as Tertius (Rom. xvi. 22), wrote the historical records and letters which have come down to us. Through to Revelation there is constant reference to writing in its use for letters, legal evidence, and record (Rev. i. 11, xxi. 5). Since writing, by its nature, is a means of communication, declaration, and testimony, it is used to illustrate the impression, written in (*engraphō*, 2 Cor. iii. 2 f.) or upon (*epigraphō*, Heb. viii. 10, x. 16) the mind and heart (*cf.* Je. xxxi. 33; Pr. iii. 3) by the Holy Spirit (sometimes called 'inner writing').

II. MATERIALS

Almost any smooth surface was used for writing.

a. Stone

Inscriptions were carved on stone or rock surfaces (Jb. xix. 24), monumental texts being cut on prepared stele, obelisk, or cliff-face (*e.g.* Hebrew ɔmb inscription, see SHEBNA, *IBA*, fig. 53, *f.* 43, 48). The softer or more rugged surfaces ould be covered with a plaster coating, before ıscription, as in Egypt, and on the altar stones Jos. viii. 32; Dt. xxvii. 2 f.). Stone tablets were ıormally used for royal, commemorative, or eligious texts or public copies of legal edicts (see IAMMURABI). Such rectangular stone tablets, pparently no larger than 18 × 12 inches, were ısed for the Ten Commandments (Ex. xxxii. 16). 'hese tablets (*lûḥōṯ*: AV 'tables') were 'written vith the finger of God' or 'the writing of God' *miktāḇ 'ᵉlōhîm*), usually taken to be a clear well-vritten script in contrast to the mere scratches of nan (see fig. 49). The word 'tablet' (*lûaḥ*) prob-ıbly describes the (rectangular) form rather than he material, and there is no certainty that in the)ld Testament it denotes a clay tablet, though he use of these in Palestine in the second mil-ennium BC is known from finds (see III below).

. Writing-boards

The tablets used by Isaiah (xxx. 8) and Habakkuk ii. 2) may have been writing-boards made of vood or ivory with a recess to hold an inlaid wax ıurface (Akkad. *lē'u*). Such writing-boards, ısually hinged to form a diptych or polyptych, ould be used for writing in any script. The ndividual leaf was called a 'door', a term also ısed for a column of writing (Je. xxxvi. 23, AV leaves'). The earliest yet found, at Nimrud, Assyria, is inscribed with a long composition of ,000 lines dated *c.* 705 BC (*Iraq*, XVII, 1955, ɔp. 3–13) and is a type also shown on the sculp-ures in use by scribes for field notes (fig. 182; *'BA*, fig. 60). Similar writing-boards, the fore-unner of the school slate, were frequently used n Greek and Roman times (Lk. i. 63; *pinakidion*, ı small writing-tablet, AV 'table').

. Clay tablets (see also IV*a* below)

The 'brick' (*lᵉḇēnâ*) used by Ezekiel (iv. 1) was robably of clay similar to the tablets used for lans and surveys in Babylonia, though the word ould be used to describe any flat tile. The great tablet' on which Isaiah had to write with the pen of a man' (as opposed to that of a skilled ıcribe?) was a sheet or 'blank surface' of an un-ıpecified material (Is. viii. 1, *gillāyôn*).

l. Papyrus

This is not directly mentioned in the Old Testa-nent as a writing-material (Heb. *nᵉyār*; Akkad. *ııyāru*; Egyp. *nḏr*). It was, however, obtainable from Phoenicia, Lake Huleh, and the Jordan (see PAPYRI) in the 11th century and onwards, and its use is attested by the marks on the backs of seal impressions originally attached to this perishable substance (*e.g.* the reverse of the seal of GEDA-LIAH, *q.v.*). Papyrus (from which the English word 'paper' is derived) was also known to the Assyrians and Babylonians in the 7th century (R. P. Dougherty, 'Writing on Parchment and Papyrus among the Babylonians and the Assyrians', *JAOS*, XLVIII, 1928, pp. 109–135). Used extensively in Egypt in all periods, papyri were found among the Dead Sea Scrolls of the 2nd century BC–2nd century AD period (see DEAD SEA SCROLLS). Isaiah's 'paper reed' (xix. 7, *'ārôt*), though possibly an indirect reference to papyri, is better interpreted as 'bare place'. The 'paper' used by John (2 Jn. 12) was probably papyrus (Gk. *chartēs*).

e. Leather and parchment

This was in rarer use than papyrus in Egypt and Babylonia from early times and for scrolls from the 17th century BC onwards. Skins of goats and sheep would have been available to the Israelites, and their use for later copies of biblical texts, also attested among the Dead Sea Scrolls (*q.v.*), may well imply an earlier employment of this material.

Parchment is attested from *c.* 1288 BC in Egypt, and was with other leather scrolls much used from the Persian period onwards. Parchment (Lat., Gk. *membrana*), which consisted of specially pre-pared animal-skins, was more durable than papyrus and was used by Paul (2 Tim. iv. 13).

f. Ostraca

Potsherds or ostraca were another common writing material, since their low cost and avail-ability made them especially useful for the writing of short memoranda with pen or brush and ink. Sherds used for recording trade have been found at Samaria in the time of Jeroboam II, and letters written in the alphabetic script (see V*b* (ii) below) of the time of Jeremiah were found in the gateway of Lachish *c.* 590 BC (see LACHISH and fig. 161). Other inscribed sherds from the 7th century include a letter complaining about the confiscation of a cloak (*cf.* Ex. xxii. 26), found at Mezad Hashavyahu in Israel (*IEJ*, IX, 1960, pp. 129–139). See also PAPYRI AND OSTRACA.

Pottery sometimes had characters inscribed or stamped on it before firing (see fig. 96; see also PEKAH, fig. 163; SEAL, stamped jar impressions).

III. WRITING IMPLEMENTS

1. Metal chisels and gravers were readily available for inscribing stone, metal, ivory, or clay (see ARTS AND CRAFTS; SEAL). The 'stylus' (*ḥereṭ*) or 'pen' (*'ēṭ*) used by Isaiah with its 'iron' point has been interpreted either as used for writing with a soft 'nib' or as a hard (emery?) point for use on iron, lead, or other hard surface (Is. viii. 1, Vulg. *stylus*; see also Je. xvii. 1; Jb. xix. 24). None of the many pointed instruments so far excavated can be identified beyond question as used for writing a linear script. The 'pen of the scribes' (Je. viii. 8) used for writing with ink on ostraca, papyrus, or other smooth surfaces was a reed, split or cut to act as a brush. In ancient Egypt such pens were cut from rushes (*Juncus maritimus*) from 6 to 16 inches long, the end being cut to a flat chisel shape so that the thick or thin strokes might be made with the broad or narrow edges. In Graeco-Roman times reeds (*Phragmites communis*) were cut to a point and split like a

quill-pen (A. Lucas, *Ancient Egyptian Materials and Industries*, 1948, p. 417). This type of pen was the *kalamos* used in New Testament times (3 Jn. 13). The stylus used for writing the cuneiform script was a square-ended reed. For a discussion of the shape, method of use, and illustrations of scribes with pens, chisels, and styli, see G. R. Driver, *Semitic Writing*, 1948, pp. 17 ff.

2. Ink was usually a black carbon (charcoal) mixed with gum or oil for use on parchment or with a metallic substance for papyrus. It was kept as a dried cake on which the scribe would dip his moistened pen. The ink of the Lachish ostraca was a mixture of carbon and iron (as oak-galls or copperas). The Romans also used the juice of cuttle-fish (Persius, *Sat.* iii. 13), which, like most inks, could easily be erased by washing (Nu. v. 23) or by scratching with the 'penknife' (Je. xxxvi. 23, Heb. *ta'ar sōpēr*, 'scribe's knife') normally used for trimming or cutting pens or scrolls. It has been suggested that Heb. *d^eyô*, 'ink' (Je. xxxvi. 18), should be emended to *r^eyô* (= Egyp. *ryt*, 'ink'; T. Lamdin, *JAOS*, LXXIII, 1953, p. 154), but this is not certain. The ink used by Paul (2 Cor. iii. 3) and John (2 Jn. 12) is simply designated 'black' (*melan*).

The 'inkhorn' (Ezk. ix. 2, 3, 11; Heb. *qeseṯ*) may be the palette (Egyp. *gsti*), the narrow rectangular wooden board with a long groove to hold the rush pens and circular hollows for the cakes of black and red ink. For illustrations of these palettes, *etc.*, see W. C. Hayes, *The Sceptre of Egypt*, I, 1953, pp. 292–296; J. B. Pritchard, *The Ancient Near East*, 1958, figs. 52, 55; *IBA*, p. 32, fig. 27. Similar palettes were in use in Syria, being carried by the scribe 'by his side' (Ezk. ix. 2, 3, 11), as shown on the Aramaic stele of Bar-Rekub (*ANEP*, 460).

IV. FORMS OF DOCUMENTS

a. Tablets

The clay documents on which cuneiform script was inscribed vary in size (about $\frac{1}{4}$ inch square to 18 × 12 inches) according to the amount of space required for the text. The inscription from left to right ran in lines (rarely ruled) down the obverse (flat) side along the lower edge, then on down the reverse (convex) side, the upper, and left edges. Where more than one tablet was needed to complete a work each text in the series was linked by a catchline and colophon (see VI below) to indicate its correct place.

Contracts were often enclosed in a clay envelope on which the text was repeated and the seals of the witnesses impressed (see SEAL). Larger historical or commemorative inscriptions were written on clay prisms or barrel-shaped cylinders which were stored in the Temple or placed as foundation deposits. Wooden tablets or writing-boards varied both in size and in the number of leaves as required.

b. The roll

The usual form of the 'book' in Old and New Testament times was a roll or scroll (*m^egillâ*) of papyrus, leather, or parchment in which the te was written 'within' (recto) and, when necessar continued 'without' on the back (verso) a described by Ezekiel (ii. 10). This was sometime called the 'roll of a book' (*m^egillaṯ sēper*; Ps. x 8; Ezk. ii. 9); the LXX (B) of Je. xxxvi. 2, (*chartion biblion*) implies the use of papyrus. Th term for scroll (*cf.* Bab. *magillatu*) is not neces sarily a late one and it is likely that the Jewis tradition requiring copies of the law to be mad on a leather roll (*Sopherim* i. 1–3) reflects earlie practice, for leather was used in Egypt fron *c.* 1580 BC for writing out laws (*BA*, VI, 1943 pp. 74–75).

The Heb. *sēper*, usually translated 'book' in AV could also refer to a roll or scroll (so AV Is. xxxiv 4, correctly). It denotes any parchment o papyrus document (R. P. Dougherty, *op. cit.* p. 114) and means a 'writing, document, missive or book' (*cf.* Akkad. *šipru*). It is synonymou with the term for 'letter' (*'iggereṯ*, Est. ix. 25) being also used for a letter or order from th king (2 Sa. xi. 14; 2 Ki. v. 10, x. 1; Is. xxxvii. 14 or published decree (Est. i. 22).

Sēper, as a general term for writing, is use of the communication from a prophet (Je. xxv 13, xxix. 1; Dn. xii. 4); a legal certificate o divorce (Dt. xxiv. 1; Je. iii. 8; Is. l. 1); a contrac for the purchase of real estate (Je. xxxii. 11); or a indictment (Jb. xxxi. 35). It also denotes a genera register (Ne. vii. 5; Gn. v. 1), a covenant (Ex xxiv. 7) or law book (Dt. xxviii. 61; Jos. viii. 31 a book of poems (Nu. xxi. 14; Jos. x. 13) as we as collections of historical data (1 Ki. xi. 41, xiv 19; 1 Ch. xxvii. 24; 2 Ch. xvi. 11, xxv. 26). Onc 'the books' (plural *s^epārîm*) refers to the canonica scriptures of the time (Dn. ix. 2). It refers t the divine records (Pss. lxix. 28, cxxxix. 16 Mal. iii. 16; Ex. xxxii. 32; Dn. xii. 1) and onc to book-learning in general (Is. xxix. 11; *cf.* Dn i. 4).

The scroll, as the writing-boards and cla tablets, was inscribed in as many column (*d^elāṯôṯ*), and therefore of any length, as require (Je. xxxvi. 23).

In New Testament times the 'book' (*biblion* was a roll as used for the law (Mk. xii. 26; Lk iv. 17–20). It formed a scroll (Rev. vi. 14) mad up of sections of papyrus (*q.v.*), the inner bark o which (*byblos*) was used. Like the Heb. *sēper* the Gk. *biblion* could be used of any (or un specified) form of written document, includin registration lists (Phil. iv. 3; Rev. xiii. 8). 'Th books' (plural *ta biblia*; Jn. xxi. 25; 2 Tim. iv. 13 hence our 'Bible') came to be a term for th collected Scriptures. Where a small scroll was i mind *biblaridion* was used (Rev. x. 2–10).

c. The codex

About the 2nd century AD the roll began to b replaced by the codex, a collection of sheets o writing material folded and fastened together a one edge and often protected by covers. This wa an important step in the development of th modern 'book', and was based on the physica form of the writing-tablet. At first these papyrus or parchment notebooks were little used for pagan literature, but were used in Palestine (Mishnah, *Kelim* xx. iv. 7), and especially in Egypt, for biblical writings where the adaptation of 'the codex form to receive all texts both of the Old and New Testaments used in Christian communities . . . was complete, as far as our present evidence goes, before the end of the second century, if not earlier'. Outside Christian circles the codex form was generally accepted by the 4th century AD. It has even been suggested, but not proved, that this form was developed by the early Christian Church because of the ease of transport and reference. Certainly the *membranai* requested by Paul (2 Tim. iv. 13) could have been a papyrus notebook of his own addresses or other writings or, more likely, an early Christian writing, perhaps the second Gospel or the Book of Testimonies, an anthology of Old Testament passages used to support the Christian claim. These writings were a contrast to 'books' (*ta biblia*), in general probably rolls (of the LXX?). For the significance of the early codices in the history of the Canon of Scripture, see CANON. See C. H. Roberts, 'The Codex', *Proceedings of the British Academy*, XL, 1954, pp. 169–204.

V. SCRIPTS

a. Hieroglyphs

(i) *Egyptian.* The native script of pharaonic Egypt appears in three forms: hieroglyphic (Gk. *hieros*, 'sacred', and *glypho*, 'carving'), hieratic (Gk. *hieratikos*, 'priestly'), and demotic (Gk. *demotikos*, 'popular'). See fig. 236, col. 1.

1. The *hieroglyphic* system. The Egyptian hieroglyphs are pictorial signs, originally pictures to express the things they represent; many of them were soon used to express sounds—specifically the consonants of the Egyptian word for the thing represented by the picture-hieroglyph. Such a sign could then be used to stand for the same consonants in spelling out other words. Some of these phonetic signs came to stand for just one such consonant, becoming thus the world's first alphabetic signs. However, the Egyptians never isolated these as a separate alphabet as did their West Semitic neighbours. After most Egyptian words as spelt out by phonetic or sound signs, there comes a picture-sign or 'determinative' which signifies the general class into which the word falls. However, in very many cases it would be more accurate to say that the phonetic signs were actually added in front of the picture-sign (so-called 'determinative') as complements to determine the precise reading or sound of the latter, and thus its correct meaning, rather than that the picture-sign acted as classifier to the phonetically written word (*cf.* H. W. Fairman, *Annales du Service des Antiquités de l'Égypte*, XLIII, 1943, pp. 297, 298; *cf.* P. Lacau, *Sur le Système hiéroglyphique*, 1954, p. 108). Where a phonetic sign could have more than one sound-value, supplementary alphabetic signs could be added to show which reading was intended, though these were sometimes added even where no ambiguity existed. See fig. 165.

2. *Hieratic and demotic.* The other two Egyptian scripts, hieratic and demotic, are adaptations of the hieroglyphic script which retained its splendid pictorial shapes throughout Egyptian history. The hieratic script is a cursive form of hieroglyphic script, written with pen and ink on papyrus, reduced to formal symbols no longer pictorial, for ease of rapid writing. Hieratic is to hieroglyphs what our long-hand script is to printed characters. The hieroglyphs first appear in Egypt just before the foundation of the pharaonic monarchy (1st Dynasty) *c.* 3000 BC, and hieratic came into use soon after. The third form of Egyptian script, demotic, is simply an even more rapid and abbreviated form of hieratic handwriting that first appears about the 7th century BC, and like the other two scripts lasted until the 5th century AD.

3. *Decipherment.* The ancient scripts of Egypt finally passed out of use in the 4th (hieroglyphic) and the 5th (demotic) centuries AD, and remained a closed book for thirteen centuries until the discovery of the Rosetta Stone in 1799 during Napoleon's Egyptian expedition made possible the decipherment of Egypt's ancient scripts and language. The Rosetta Stone was a bilingual decree of Ptolemy V, 196 BC, in Greek and Egyptian, the latter in both hieroglyphic and demotic scripts. This and the Bankes obelisk eventually enabled the Frenchman, J. F. Champollion, to achieve the basic decipherment of the Egyptian hieroglyphs in 1822, showing that they were largely phonetic in use and that the Egyptian language was in fact simply the parent of Coptic, the language of the native Egyptian Church.

4. *Scope.* From the very beginning, the Egyptian hieroglyphs were used for all purposes: historical records, religious texts, and the mundane purposes of administration. They were accordingly drawn on papyrus or ostraca, carved on stone monuments, and engraved in wood or metal wherever inscriptions were required. However, from early in the third millennium, the more rapid cursive script—hieratic—became customary for writing on papyrus, and so for all the records of daily life and administration, while hieroglyphs continued in use for all formal texts, stone inscriptions, and monumental purposes. Eventually, from the 7th century BC, demotic largely replaced hieratic as the script of business and administration, and hieratic from the 10th century BC onwards became largely the script of religious papyri.

BIBLIOGRAPHY. On the Egyptian scripts, see A. H. Gardiner, *Egyptian Grammar*, 1957, pp. 5–8. On the hieroglyphs themselves as pictures, see N. M. Davies, *Picture Writing in Ancient Egypt*, 1958, illustrated in colour. On the origin and early development of the hieroglyphic system, see S. Schott, *Hieroglyphen: Untersuchungen zum Ursprung der Schrift*, 1950, and Lacau, *op. cit.* For the Rosetta Stone, see BM

EGYPTIAN HIEROGLYPH	SINAITIC (c. 1500 BC)	CANAANITE PSEUDO-HIER. (c. 2000 BC)	REPRESENTS	S. ARABIAN (c. 300 BC)	PHOENICIAN (c. 1000 BC)	EARLY HEBREW [SILOAM] (c. 710 BC)	EARLY HEBREW [LACHISH] (588 BC)
			ox				
			house				
			throw-stick				
			door				
			man with raised arms				
			prop				
			weapon?				
			twisted hank				
			palm of hand				
			staff				
			water				
			snake				
			fish				
			eye				
			mouth				
			grasshopper				
			monkey?				
			head				
			(papyrus) clump				
			cross				
1	2	3	4	5	6	7	8

Fig. 236. Some of the varying forms of the alphabet used in

ARAMAIC EPHANTINE h CENT. BC)	FORMAL HEBREW (2nd CENT. AD)	HEBREW NAME	PHONETIC VALUE	OLD GREEK (7th CENT. BC)	FORMAL GREEK (5th CENT. BC)	GREEK NAME	ROMAN
	א	'alep̄	'		Α	alpha	A
	ב	bêṯ	b		Β	beta	B
	ג	gîmel	g		Γ	gamma	G
	ד	dāleṯ	d		Δ	delta	D
	ה	hē	h		Ε	epsilon	E
	ו	waw	w		Υ	(digamma)	FY
	ז	zayin	z		Ζ	zeta	Z
	ח	ḥêṯ	ḥ		Η	eta	H
	ט	ṭêṯ	ṭ		Θ	theta	
	י	yôḏ	y		Ι	iota	I
	כ	kap̄	k		Κ	kappa	K
	ל	lāmeḏ	l		Λ	lambda	L
	מ	mēm	m		Μ	mu	M
	נ	nûn	n		Ν	nu	N
	ס	sāmek̲	s		Ξ	xi	
	ע	ʿayin	ʿ		Ο	omicron	O
	פ	pê'	p		Π	pi	P
	צ	ṣadê	s			(san)	
	ק	qôp̄	q		Ϙ	(koppa)	Q
	ר	rêš	r		Ρ	rho	R
	ש	šîn	š		Σ	sigma	S
	ת	taw	t		Τ	tau	T
9	10	11	12	13	14	15	16

development from early pictographs to the roman script.

brochure *The Rosetta Stone*, and, for its discoverer, W. R. Dawson, *JEA*, XLIII, 1957, p. 117, with *ib*., XLIV, 1958, p. 123. On the decipherment of the hieroglyphs, see F. Ll. Griffith, *JEA*, XXXVII, 1951, pp. 38–46, or Gardiner, *op. cit*., pp. 9–11; *Egypt of the Pharaohs*, 1961, pp. 11–14, 19–26.

(ii) *Hittite*. The system of hieroglyphs used by the Hittites in Anatolia and Syria, mainly in the latter half of the second millennium BC, was deciphered in 1946 by Bossert (see *AS*, III, 1953, pp. 53–95) and this script is now being studied in detail and used for comparison with the Hittite dialects written in the cuneiform script (E. Laroche, *Les Hiéroglyphes Hittites*, I, 1960).

b. Linear

(i) *Pictographic* (see Table, fig. 236, cols. 1–3). Written documents from early Babylonia (Sumer) *c*. 3000 BC, and soon thereafter from Egypt, employed simple and compound pictograms. Early signs, also pictographic, from Byblos show that from *c*. 2500 BC in Syria similar scripts were in use, though as yet not fully read. The early seal impressions from Byblos (Gebal) of *c*. 3100 BC would also imply that the first steps towards writing had been taken, although there is not complete agreement with E. Dhorme that these early signs were a form of Phoenician. Objects of the Egyptian Middle Kingdom dating from Byblos show that *c*. 2100–1700 BC pseudo-hieroglyphs were then in use.

(ii) *Proto-Phoenician* (see Table, cols. 2, 3). The Byblos alphabetic signs, like the potters' marks from Lebe'ah near Sidon, may show early forms of the later Phoenician alphabetic letters. The inscriptions from Serabit el-Khadim and valleys near Sinai found by Petrie in 1904 are now generally accepted as showing letters derived from Egyptian hieroglyphs (see v*a* above) to be dated *c*. 1500 BC. The number of different signs (20–33) indicates, however, a non-Egyptian alphabetic script which has been variously designated early Canaanite, Sinaitic, or proto-Phoenician (see Table). Potsherds bearing 'early Canaanite' signs found at Gezer, Tell el-Hesi, Lachish (also on a dagger), Beth-shemesh, and Hazor perhaps testify to a widespread use of this script in Palestine at this period.

Thus by 1500 BC the *alphabet* came into general use in Syria–Palestine, perhaps from the need to find a simpler form of writing than the more cumbrous Egyptian hieroglyphs and Babylonian cuneiform scripts for purposes of trade. In essence, certain Egyptian (or Byblian ?) hieroglyphic signs were used in an unusual way to represent foreign sounds by isolating their consonantal sound (*e.g*. Egyp. *r*', 'mouth', for letter-value *r*). These signs, given their Semitic names for the equivalent pictogram (*i.e*. Heb. *pe*, 'mouth'), were then used solely to represent the Semitic alphabetic letters (*i.e*. P̱). See also Table and Bibliography.

The order of the Phoenician alphabet is attested by the acrostic Heb. texts (Na. i. 2–14; Pss. ix, x, xxv, xxxiv, xxxvii, cxi, cxii, cxix (A also adds the Hebrew letters as sectional hea ings), cxlv, La. i–iv; Pr. xxxi. 10–31; Ecclus. 13, 29), and by Ugaritic lists of letters (see fig. 23 The early Greek alphabet maintained the san scheme, but the reason for the arrangement letters is much debated. It may well be due mnemonic needs and set out partly accordi to similarities in the meanings of the words us for the individual letters or to the nature of t sounds they express (Driver, *op. cit*., pp. 18 185).

(iii) *Phoenician–early Hebrew* (see Table, co 6–8). There are gaps in the present knowledge the development of the linear—so-called 'Phoe cian'—script. Then come the Byblian inscriptio (*c*. 1300 BC), the Shaphatbaal (*c*. 1200 BC) and t inscriptions on the tomb and sarcophagus Ahiram of Byblos, now generally dated *c*. 10 BC (*BASOR*, 134, 1954, p. 9). The evidence is t scattered chronologically and geographically f a detailed study of the epigraphy and palae graphy to be possible, though there is sufficie to show that the script changed so little over o thousand years that any literate person cou probably have read the script at any point in development, for the number, phonetic valu and basic form of the letters remained consta and the script was always written horizonta from right to left (*BA*, XIII, 1950, p. 84).

1. The major *monumental* inscriptions for t study of the epigraphy (see Table, col. 7) a (*a*) The agricultural calendar from Gez variously attributed to an archaic or unskil hand and dated to the 11th or 10th century (see fig. 49; GEZER; *DOTT*, 201–203). (*b*) T stele of Mesha', king of Moab (see plate X MOAB). This thirty-four-line inscription is imp tant both historically and as a good example the development of the monumental Hebr script in use in a remote place *c*. 850 BC. The w cut letters already show a tendency to beco cursive. This is further seen in (*c*) the Silo Inscription (see SILOAM; *IBA*, fig. 56), dati from the reign of Hezekiah, *c*. 710 BC, and (*d*) t Tomb inscription of the Royal Steward fr Siloam of about the same date (see SHEBN *IBA*, fig. 53). For the lapidary form of the scr on seals (*q.v.*), see fig. 115. (*e*) The final change monumental square Hebrew script is clearly se developing on the Uzziah plaque (*IBA*, fig. 1 and tomb inscription of the *Ḥēzîr* family Jerusalem (G. A. Cooke, *Text-book of No Semitic Inscriptions*, 148A), both of the 1st cent BC–AD period.

2. The *cursive* hand which the Old Testam writers would have originally employed is s in the inscribed arrow-heads and other sma writings of *c*. 1000 BC. The earliest body of tex seventy-five ostraca from Samaria assigned to reign of Jeroboam II (*c*. 760 BC; Y. Yad *Studies in the Bible*, 1960, pp. 9–17; *DO* pp. 204–208). These show a clear, flowing scr written by scribes long practised in the art. T unvocalized words are divided by small stro

or dots. A few scattered sherds from Jerusalem, Beth-shemesh, Tell el-Hesi, Megiddo, and Ezion-geber show that the script is close to that on the Siloam tunnel inscription and changed only a little in outward form by the time of the Lachish letters dated to *c.* 590–587 BC, which show a more advanced stage of the current hand (see fig. 161; Table, col. 8; LACHISH; *DOTT*, pp. 212–215).

(iv) *Aramaic* (see Table, col. 9). The individual development of Aramaic as opposed to the 'Phoenician' script goes back to *c.* 1000. By *c.* 850 the texts from Tell Halaf and Arslan Tash still show a close resemblance to the Phoenician linear script. From the same area (Buraij, near Aleppo) and period comes the Melqart stele, the earliest inscribed monument bearing the name of a king of Damascus (Ben-hadad, son of Tabrimmon, 1 Ki. xv. 18; see fig. 35; *DOTT*, pp. 239–241).

Almost a century later the forty-six-line inscription of Zakir, king of Hamath, with a relief of the weather-god (*DOTT*, pp. 242–250) and the treaty of Mati'el of Arpad with Bar-Ga'ayah *c.* 754 BC, show the extensive use of the script for Aramaean texts (A. Dupont-Sommer, *Les inscriptions araméennes de Sfiré*, 1958). The increasingly cursive style, already seen developing in Judah, is attested by the Bar-Rekub stele (*ANEP*, 460) and by a list of names on a sherd from Nimrud (Calah) in Assyria from the 7th century BC (*Iraq*, XIX, 1957, pp. 139–145). Similar Aramaic script is to be found on clay tablets found in this and the following century (J. Stevenson, *Assyrian and Babylonian Contracts with Aramaic Reference Notes*, 1902), and on a papyrus letter sent from Philistia to Egypt *c.* 604 (D. J. Wiseman, *Chronicles of Chaldaean Kings*, 1956, p. 28; *DOTT*, pp. 251–255). The latter shows a more archaic hand than the many 5th-century papyri from Elephantine in Egypt (see PAPYRI; *DOTT*, pp. 256–269) and other sites (G. R. Driver, *Documents of the Fifth Century BC*, 1951). One of the peculiarities of these texts is the occurrence of archaic and late Aramaic forms side by side (as in Je. x. 11). By this time the elegant cursive Persian 'chancellery hand' is found throughout the Ancient Near East.

(v) *Early Jewish Scripts*. The discoveries of MSS from the Wadi Qumran (see DEAD SEA SCROLLS), Judaean caves (especially the dated texts from Murabba'at), and inscribed ossuaries from the Jerusalem area has produced a wealth of material for the study of the formal and cursive Palaeo-Hebrew and early Jewish scripts from the 3rd century BC to the 2nd century AD. The fall of the Persian Empire and the displacement of the common Aramaic of the imperial court led to many local variations. See plate XII*a*.

1. The Archaic or proto-Jewish script of Judah, *c.* 250–150 BC, as reflected in the Qumran MSS, shows a formal hand derived from the Persian Aramaic which, by the late 3rd century, is a cross between the formal and cursive scripts and close to the common Aramaic scripts of Palmyra and Nabataea which also emerged at this time. While these national scripts cannot yet be more precisely dated, formal, semi-formal, and true cursive hands can sometimes be distinguished. This script is also to be seen on coins of the period.

2. The Hasmonean period (*c.* 150–30 BC) saw the development of the formal, squarer, and more angular hand seen in its first stages in the Nash Papyrus, now dated *c.* 150 BC.

3. The Herodian period (30 BC–AD 70) was a time of swift development, and texts can thus be closely dated.

4. The post-Herodian period (after AD 70) is now well known from dated commercial and legal documents. The cursive script is not a literary but highly involved hand. The development of all these Jewish hands is illustrated and discussed in detail by F. M. Cross (*The Bible and the Ancient Near East*, ed. G. E. Wright, 1961, pp. 133–202).

(vi) *Greek*. The Greek alphabet was by tradition attributed to a Phoenician trader Cadmus (Herodotus, *Hist.* v. 58, 59) and, by comparison between the early Greek alphabets at Athens, Crete, Thera, Corinth, and Naxos and dated Phoenician texts (see above), this view is justified. It would seem probable from the form of the letters that the Greeks had by the middle of the 9th century BC adapted the script to the needs of their Indo-European language. They used the Phoenician symbols for sounds which they did not possess (' h ḥ ' u̥ (w) y), for the vowel sounds they required (a e ē o y i respectively), and thus created the first true alphabet in which consonants and vowels were represented by distinct signs.

The abundance of monumental and manuscript evidence makes the study of Greek epigraphy and palaeography an important and exact science for the background of the biblical Greek texts. From W Greece the alphabet reached the Etruscans, and thus through the Roman script entered Europe (see Table, col. 16).

(vii) *Other scripts*. As well as the development of the Phoenician script for use in the Greek, and thence Roman, and subsequently European scripts (see Table), the Sinaitic type script was developed into both a formal and a cursive series of alphabetic letters for use in the south Semitic scripts (see Table, col. 5). The earliest example is the text of Balu'a in Moab (*c.* 1200–1100 BC), where the affinity to Sinaitic can still be seen, although divergent forms were already developing. Examples of these were found at Ezion-geber (Aqabah) and Ur (Babylonia) of the 8th–7th centuries BC. By this time, as evidenced by Babylonian seal impressions (W. F. Albright, *BASOR*, 128, 1952, pp. 39–45) and latterly cuneiform texts (*e.g.* B. Kienast, *Vorläufiger Bericht . . . Warka*, 1955/6), the impressive and formal S Arabian script with its local variations and cursive forms, best known from the 2nd century BC onwards, was in use.

c. Cuneiform scripts

(i) *Akkadian.* In Babylonia pictographs were used for writing on clay and stone from *c.* 3100 BC onwards. It was, however, soon found difficult to draw curved lines on clay, and the pictograph was gradually replaced by its representation made by a series of wedge-shaped incisions. A further change for convenience from writing down columns from right to left resulted in the classical script being written horizontally in columns, the lines running from left to right. The sign (a combination of wedges) which was at first used for a complete word (ideogram) became used for sounds or syllables (phonogram); certain signs being also used as determinatives placed before or after words of a distinct class (*e.g.* deities, personal and place-names, animals, wooden objects, *etc.*). By 2800 BC the cuneiform script had fully developed, though the forms of signs were modified at different periods (for a Table illustrating this development see *IBA*, fig. 22).

By the second millennium BC Akkadian cuneiform, using at least 500 different signs, was in use outside Mesopotamia (where it was employed for the Sumerian, Babylonian, and Assyrian languages) for writing in Palestine. The chief cities used it for diplomatic correspondence with Egypt (see ARCHAEOLOGY, VIII*b*), and in Palestine about twenty tablets in this script have been found—at Taanach (twelve), Tell el-Hesi, Gezer, Shechem (a letter) and Jericho dating from the 15th–14th centuries BC. The discovery of a copy of part of the Epic of Gilgamesh at Megiddo in 1955 (*'Atiqot*, II, 1959, pp. 121–128) shows that at this period the few scribes trained in this script had readily available the major Babylonian literary texts and reference works. Similarly, cuneiform was employed for writing the local Semitic and Hurrian dialects at Ras Shamra (Akkadian texts) and Alalaḫ in Syria (see also ARCHAEOLOGY) as well as in Anatolia (Hittite at Boghaz-Koi and Urarṭian texts from E Turkey). See R. Labat, *Manuel d'Épigraphie akkadienne*, 1948.

(ii) *Ugaritic.* At Ras Shamra scribes employed cuneiform Akkadian for international correspondence and some economic texts in the 15th–14th centuries BC. Parallel with this, however, a unique system of writing was developed. It combined the simplicity of the existing Canaanite (Phoenician) alphabet with the Mesopotamian system of writing with a stylus on clay, thus transcribing the consonantal alphabet by means of cuneiform writing. Since it was employed for both Semitic and non-Semitic (Hurrian) languages, thirty-one signs were developed (by the addition of a few wedges in a simple pattern bearing little or no relation to Akkadian) to represent the consonant and three *'ālep̄* signs with variant vowels ('a 'i 'u). A number of scribal practice tablets give the order of the alphabet which prefigured the later Hebrew letters (C. Virolleaud, *Palais royal d'Ugarit II*, 1957), see fig. 237.

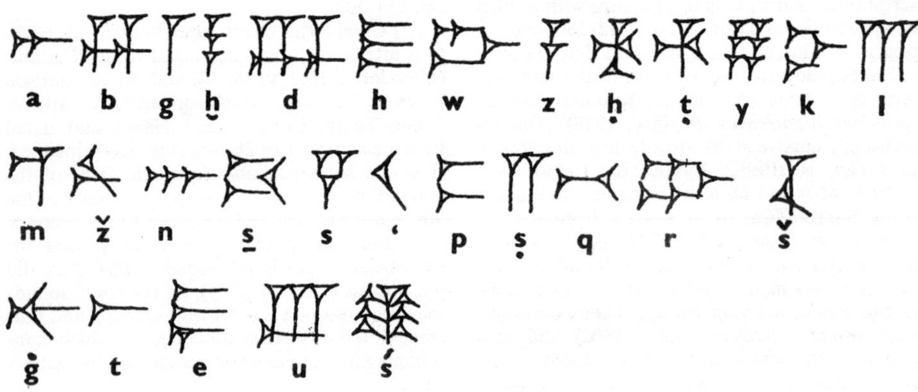

Fig. 237. The cuneiform alphabet of Ugarit. The letters were written in this order on several tablets found at Ras Shamra, probably copying the arrangement of the Phoenician-Canaanite alphabet with additional signs.

This script was used for both religious, literary (mythological), and administrative texts and for a few letters (see ARCHAEOLOGY). Although easier to learn than Akkadian, it does not appear to have been widely used, examples having been discovered only at Tabor and Beth-shemesh. The invention appears to have come too late to oust the already established and simplified Phoenician linear script. For a general survey, see C. H. Gordon, *Ugaritic Handbook*, 1947.

(iii) *Old Persian.* By the late 7th century BC the Aramaic alphabetic script had largely displaced the cuneiform script, except in a few traditional centres and types of temple documents for which, as at Babylon until AD 75, the Babylonian cuneiform script continued to be used.

Under the Achaemenid Persians a specia system, derived from the cuneiform of Baby lonia, was employed alongside the Aramaic script for their Indo-Iranian (Aryan) language

This simplified cuneiform is mainly known from historical texts of the reigns of Darius I and Xerxes. An inscription of the former written on a rock at Behistun in Old Persian, Babylonian, and Elamite provided the key to the decipherment of the cuneiform scripts, the Old Persian version being deciphered soon after Rawlinson's copy of 1845 had been published. This cuneiform script comprises 3 vowel signs, 33 consonantal signs with inherent vowel plus 8 ideograms and 2 word dividers (see fig. 235). A variant form of cuneiform script was used for the Elamite (SW Persia) language for more than 750 economic texts from Persepolis *c.* 492–460 BC (G. G. Cameron, *Persepolis Treasury Tablets*, 1948).

VI. LITERACY AND LITERARY METHODS

Evidence for the degree of literacy, which varied according to time and place, is small. Gideon was able to lay hands on a young man of Succoth in Jordan who wrote down a list of the city elders (Jdg. viii. 14; Heb., AVmg, RVmg 'write', AV, RV, unjustifiably 'describe'). Such ability among the young to write (Is. x. 19) was enhanced by the advent of the alphabet and by the establishment of schools for scribes attached to temples and shrines (see SCHOOL). Every Israelite householder had to write the words of the Law (Dt. vi. 9, xi. 20). Writing, though not so well attested in the West as in Babylonia, was certainly widespread in Syria and Palestine by the second millennium, when at least five scripts were in use, *viz.* Egyptian hieroglyphs, Sinaitic pictographs, Byblian alphabet, Akkadian cuneiform, and the Ugaritic alphabetic cuneiform (see v above).

Writing was generally undertaken by trained scribes (*q.v.*), who could be drawn from any class of the population (*contra* E. Nielsen, *Oral Tradition*, 1954, pp. 25, 28), though most higher officials in administration were literate. The mass of cuneiform tablets, ostraca, and papyri so far found shows the prominent place of the written word throughout the Ancient Near East. A percentage is difficult to estimate owing to the incompleteness of the records, but the six scribes to a population of about 2,000 at Alalaḫ in Syria in *c.* 1800–1500 BC is probably indicative of the literacy in important towns (D. J. Wiseman, *The Alalakh Tablets*, p. 13). Recent studies show that scribes may have learned their Akkadian at main 'university' centres such as Aleppo in Syria or Babylon itself.

Documents were stored in baskets, boxes, or jars (Je. xxxii. 14) and laid up in the local temple (1 Sa. x. 25; Ex. xvi. 34, *cf.* 2 Ki. xxii. 8) or special archive stores (Ezr. vi. 1). Specific reference books were held by scribes (as, *e.g.*, at Nippur, *c.* 1950 BC). Tiglath-pileser I (*c.* 1100 BC) at Assur and Ashurbanipal (*c.* 650 BC) at Nineveh collected copies of texts or had them written for their libraries. When copying texts a scribe would often quote the source, giving the condition of the document from which he copied, and stating whether the text had been checked with the original document, or only copied down from oral tradition, which was considered a less reliable method (J. Læssøe, 'Literacy and Oral Tradition in Ancient Mesopotamia', *Studia Orientalia Ioanni Pedersen*, 1953, pp. 205–218). Oral tradition was conceived as existing alongside the written word but not taking the place of primary authority. The colophon (both Akkadian and Egyptian) would also give the title or catchline which designated the work; but authorship was often, but not invariably, anonymous. It is likely that the Hebrew writers used similar methods.

BIBLIOGRAPHY. See references given in text above, also, for a full description, G. R. Driver, *Semitic Writing*[2], 1954; I. J. Gelb, *A Study of Writing*, 1952; D. Diringer, *The Alphabet*, 1948; J. Černý, *Paper and Books in Ancient Egypt*, 1952; F. G. Kenyon, *Books and Readers in Greece and Rome*[2], 1951.

D.J.W.

X

XERXES. See AHASUERUS.

Y

YAHWEH. See GOD, NAMES OF.

YARN. The 'linen yarn' in the AV of 1 Ki. x. 28 and 2 Ch. i. 16 is due to a misunderstanding of the Hebrew text. The correct translation, referring to a country called Kue (*i.e.* Cilicia, *q.v.*), is to be found in the RSV. The principal yarns referred to in the Scriptures are wool and linen.

Other yarns mentioned are goats' hair, camels' hair, cotton (Heb. *karpas*; Est. i. 6; *cf. EBi*, I, p. 915), and silk (Rev. xviii. 12). In Ezk. xvi. 10, 13 Heb. *mešî* is sometimes translated as 'silk' (*cf.* RSV), but since the word seems to be an Egyptian loan-word (mostly meaning linen in Egyptian), and silk was not introduced into Egypt until the Roman period, some doubt is cast on the identification. R.F.H.

YEAR. See CALENDAR.

YOKE. The AV rendering of several Hebrew and Greek words, used either literally for the wooden frame joining two animals (usually oxen), o metaphorically as describing one individual' subjection to another. The words are *môṭ* (Na. i 13) and *môṭâ* (Is. lviii. 6; Je. xxvii. 2, *etc.*), 'a bar' *'ōl* (Gn. xxvii. 40; La. i. 14, *etc.*), 'a yoke'; *ṣeme* (1 Sa. xi. 7; Jb. i. 3, *etc.*), 'yoke of oxen'; *zeugo* (Lk. xiv. 19), 'a pair'; *zygos* (Mt. xi. 29; 1 Tim vi. 1, *etc.*), 'a yoke', 'a balance'. See also AGRICULTURE.

In 2 Cor. vi. 14 Paul uses *heterozygeō*, 'to b yoked with one of another kind'. For the 'yoke fellow' of Phil. iv. 3 see SYNZYGUS. J.D.D.

YOKEFELLOW. See SYNZYGUS.

Z

ZAANAIM. (*Qᵉrē' Zaanannim, q.v.*) Heber pitched by a tree here (Jdg. iv. 11). Khan Leggun near Tell Abu Qudeis (= Kedesh), on a route through the hills opposite Tabor, is probable and suggests the name (*BDB*); but as 'terebinth' has no article, G. F. Moore (*ICC*, 1903, *ad loc.*) reads ***baṣᵉ'annîm*** '(the terebinth of) Baṣ'annim', in place of *MT bᵉṣa'anayim*, '(the terebinth in) Zaanaim' (*cf.* C. F. Burney, *Judges*, 1918, *ad loc.*); *cf.* LXX (B). J.P.U.L.

ZAANAN. A place mentioned in Mi. i. 11, the inhabitants of which remained in their city when invading forces passed through the land. It may be identical with Zenan in the Shephelah of Judah listed in Jos. xv. 37.

ZAANANNIM. The context (Jos. xix. 33) and probable meaning (*BDB*) indicate Khan et-Tuggar, a caravan stage and Late Bronze site.

ZABAD. 1. An Ephraimite (1 Ch. vii. 21). **2.** A man of Judah, of the lineage of Hezron (1 Ch. ii. 36 f.). **3.** One of David's mighty men (1 Ch. xi. 41), probably to be equated with (2); note the name Ahlai in the parentage of both. **4.** A conspirator against Joash (2 Ch. xxiv. 26). The correct form of the name is Jozacar (*q.v.*). *Cf.* 2 Ki. xii. 21. **5, 6, 7.** Three priests who put away their foreign wives, as directed by Ezra (Ezr. x. 27, 33, 43). D.F.P.

ZABBAI. Possibly a shortened form of *zāḇaḏyâ*, 'The Lord bestowed upon' (W. Rudolph). This name is found in Ezr. x. 28 and Ne. iii. 20. Zabbai was forced by Ezra, according to Ezr. x. 28, to put away his foreign wife. Zabbai in Ne. iii. 20 is problematic. He was the father of Baruch who helped with the rebuilding of the walls of Jerusalem. Either he is the same person as in Ezra, or a different person with the same name, or Zabbai must be replaced by Zakkai (*cf.* Ezr. ii. 9 and various MSS, Vulgate an Syriac). F.C.F.

ZABDI. 1. The grandfather of Achan who too some of the devoted spoil at Jericho (Jos. vii. 1 17, 18). He is also called Zimri (1 Ch. ii. 6) **2.** The name of a member of the tribe of, Benjamin (1 Ch. viii. 19). **3.** An officer of David' vineyards (1 Ch. xxvii. 27). **4.** A Levite (Ne. xi 17), also called Zichri (1 Ch. ix. 15). R.A.H.G.

ZACCHAEUS, from Heb. and Aram. *Zakkai*, reduced form of Zechariah. A chief tax-collecto at Jericho who became a disciple of Christ (Lk xix. 1–10). He was probably the general tax farmer of Jericho and undoubtedly had abuse his position on occasions to enrich himsel Being a small man, he climbed a tree to see Jesus who then asked to stay at his house. Zacchaeu welcomed Him and showed practical repentanc in giving half his goods to the poor and fourfol compensation to any whom he had defrauded Christ said that this showed him to be a true so of Abraham and declared that salvation ha come, not only to him, but to his house. The self righteous in the crowd were critical of Jesus action, but He declared His mission to be th seeking and saving of the lost. R.E.N.

ZACHARIAS. See ZECHARIAH.

ZADOK (Heb. *ṣāḏôq*, 'righteous'(?)). **1.** Son o Ahitub, who was, according to 1 Ch. vi. 1 ff. 50 ff., a descendant of Eleazar, third son o Aaron. He was priest at David's court along wit Abiathar (2 Sa. viii. 17) and had charge of the ar (2 Sa. xv. 24 f.); he took part in the anointing o Solomon as David's successor when Abiatha supported Adonijah (1 Ki. i. 7 ff.). He and hi descendants discharged the chief-priestly dutie in Solomon's Temple until its destruction i 587 BC. Ezekiel restricts the priestly privileges i his new commonwealth to the Zadokite family on the ground that they alone were innocent of apostasy under the monarchy (Ezk. xliv. 15 ff.). In the second Temple the Zadokites retained the high priesthood continuously until 171 BC, when it was transferred to Menelaus by Antiochus IV; even after that a Zadokite priesthood presided over the Jewish temple at Leontopolis in Egypt until Vespasian closed it soon after AD 70. The Qumran community remained loyal to the Zadokite priesthood and looked forward to its restoration.

2. A descendant of Zadok, grandfather of Hilkiah (1 Ch. vi. 12, ix. 11; Ne. xi. 11). **3.** Father-in-law of King Uzziah and grandfather of Jotham (2 Ki. xv. 33; 2 Ch. xxvii. 1). **4, 5.** Two builders of the wall under Nehemiah (Ne. iii. 4, 29); one or the other of these may be the same as Zadok, a signatory to the covenant (Ne. x. 21), and 'Zadok the scribe' (Ne. xiii. 13).

BIBLIOGRAPHY. H. H. Rowley, 'Zadok and Nehushtan', *JBL*, LVIII, 1939, pp. 113 ff.; *id.*, 'Melchizedek and Zadok' in *Festschrift für A. Bertholet* (ed. W. Baumgartner), 1950, pp. 461 ff.

F.F.B.

ZAIR. 2 Ki. viii. 21 records that King Joram passed over to Zair to crush a revolt of the Edomites, hence its probable location was on the border of Edom. Some MSS of the LXX read here Z(e)ior, and Zair may possibly be identical with Zior (*q.v.*), listed in Jos. xv. 54, in the Judaean hill-country. R.A.H.G.

ZALMON. 1. A personal name. One of David's mighty men, said to be an Ahohite (2 Sa. xxiii. (28. He is called Ilai in 1 Ch. xi. 29.

2. The name of a mountain in the vicinity of the tower of Shechem (Jdg. ix. 48). Its identification is far from certain, but the massif of Jabal al-Kabir has been proposed.

3. Another mountain, mentioned in Ps. lxviii. 14 (spelt Salmon in AV). Some have equated it with the foregoing, but this mountain would appear to have been to the east of the Jordan, possibly one of the highest peaks of Bashan.

D.F.P.

ZAMZUMMIM (*zamzummîm*, meaning uncertain; possibly 'whisperers', 'murmurers', from an Arabic root). One of the names given to the Rephaim in an archaeological note in Dt. ii. 20–23. They were a prehistoric race of giant stature who were the earlier inhabitants of Palestine, and who left traces of their presence (*e.g.* Dt. iii. 11; Jos. xv. 8; 2 Sa. xxi. 16, 18, 20, 22 (RVmg)). 'Zamzummim' was the name used for them by the Ammonites, who dispossessed them. *Cf.* the 'Zuzim' (*q.v.*) of Gn. xiv. 5. J.G.G.N.

ZANOAH. 1. A place in the Shephelah (Jos. xv. 34; Ne. iii. 13, xi. 30), identified with Khirbet Zanu', 2 miles south of Beth-shemesh, west of modern Zanoah (*BASOR*, 18, 1925).

2. A town in the hills near Juttah (Jos. xv. 56; 1 Ch. iv. 18), perhaps Khirbet Beit 'Amra, overlooking the Wadi el-Halil or Hevron, part of which was called Wadi Abu Zenah; or Khirbet Zanuta, south-west of Eshtemoa (W. Rudolph, *Chronikbücher*, 1955, *ad loc.*; Israeli Survey); or Khirbet Yaqin, 3 miles south-east of Hebron, reading 'Zanoah of Kain' (Noth, citing LXX; but the renderings are dubious). J.P.U.L.

ZAPHNATH-PAANEAH. An Egyptian name bestowed by pharaoh upon Joseph at his investiture (Gn. xli. 45); the search for its Egyptian original has produced many widely divergent suggestions. Steindorff's *Ḏ(d)-p'-nṯ(r)-Iw.f-'nḫ* is phonetically good, but is circumstantially inappropriate in meaning and of too late a date. Most other suggestions are either phonetically unacceptable or else lack any real Egyptian parallels. However, the Heb. consonantal form *Ṣ-p-n-t p-'-n-ḥ* may, with one slight change (for euphony in Hebrew) to *Ṣ-t-n-p p-'-n-ḥ*, stand for (*Yôsēp̄*)*ḏd-n.f 'Ip-'nḫ* '(Joseph), who is called 'Ip̄'ankh'; *ḏd-n.f* would be the well-known construction introducing a second name, the name itself being 'Ip-'ankh, a common name in the Middle Kingdom and Hyksos periods, *i.e.* in the patriarchal and Joseph's age. See Kitchen, *The Joseph Narrative and its Egyptian Background.*

K.A.K.

ZAPHON. A town referred to in Jos. xiii. 27, lying in Gadite territory in the Jordan valley. The name is the normal Hebrew word for 'north', and it is so translated in Jdg. xii. 1, where probably the proper name should be understood (*cf.* RVmg). TJ identifies it with the Amathus of Josephus, which is to be located at Tell 'Ammatah; but this is improbable. Other proposed locations for Zaphon are Tell al-Sa'idiya and Tell al-Qos. D.F.P.

ZAREPHATH. A small Phoenician town (mod. Sarafand) which originally belonged to Sidon. It passed into the possession of Tyre after 722 BC, following help given to Shalmaneser by the fleet of Sidon in his unsuccessful attempt to capture Tyre. Sennacherib included the town in the list of places captured during his invasion of Phoenicia in 701 BC.

It was situated about 8 miles south of Sidon on the road to Tyre and is mentioned in 1 Ki. xvii. 9 ff. as the place to which Elijah went during the drought in King Ahab's reign and where he restored life to the son of the widow with whom he lodged (see SIDON). Lk. iv. 26 refers to this incident, the town there being called by the Greek and Latin name, Sarepta.

Obadiah prophesied that in the Day of the Lord those of the children of Israel who were deported by Sargon after the fall of Samaria should possess Phoenicia as far as Zarephath.

R.A.H.G.

ZARETHAN. This town is spelt variously Zaretan, Zartanah, and Zarthan in AV; and the name appears as Zeredah (so RV; AV has Zeredathah) in 2 Ch. iv. 17. Zarethan is mentioned in connection with Beth-shean, Adam, and Succoth, and lay in the Jordan valley, near a ford over the river. Its exact site has been debated, but it almost certainly lay west of the Jordan. One suggested location, Qarn Sartaba, perhaps recalls the name Zarethan; this site, or its immediate vicinity, has been put forward recently by J. Simons (*GTT*, pp. 292 f.), while Tell al-Sa'idiya has been proposed by N. Glueck (*The River Jordan*, 1946, pp. 154 ff.). D.F.P.

ZEALOT (Gk. *zēlōtēs*). One of the twelve apostles is called Simon the Zealot (Lk. vi. 15; Acts i. 13), either because of his zealous temperament or because of some association with the party of the Zealots. (See also CANANAEAN.) Paul speaks of himself as having been a religious zealot (Acts xxii. 3; Gal. i. 14), and the many members of the church of Jerusalem are described as all 'zealots for the law' (Acts xxi. 20).

The party of the Zealots, described by Josephus as the 'fourth philosophy' among the Jews (*BJ* ii. 8. 1; *Ant*. xviii. 1. 1, 6), was founded by Judas the Galilaean (*q.v.*), who led a revolt against Rome in AD 6 (see CENSUS). They opposed the payment of tribute by Israel to a pagan emperor on the ground that this was treason to God, Israel's true King. They were called Zealots because they followed the example of Mattathias and his sons and followers, who manifested zeal for the law of God when Antiochus IV tried to suppress the Jewish religion (1 Macc. ii. 24–27), and the example of Phinehas, who showed comparable zeal in a time of apostasy in the wilderness (Nu. xxv. 11; Ps. cvi. 30 f.). When the revolt of AD 6 was crushed they kept its spirit alive for sixty years. Members of Judas's family were Zealot leaders; two of his sons were crucified by the procurator Alexander *c.* AD 46 (Jos., *Ant*. xx. 5. 2), and a third, Menahem, attempted to seize the leadership of the anti-Roman revolt in AD 66 (Jos., *BJ* ii. 17. 8 f.). Zealots were active throughout the war of AD 66–73; the last Zealot stronghold, Masada, fell in May AD 73, but even then the Zealot spirit was not completely quenched. See ASSASSINS.

BIBLIOGRAPHY. Jos., *BJ*, *passim*; F. J. Foakes-Jackson and K. Lake, 'The Zealots', in *The Beginnings of Christianity*, I, 1920, pp. 421 ff.; W. R. Farmer, *Maccabees, Zealots and Josephus*, 1956; C. Roth, 'The Zealots in the War of 66–73', *JSS*, IV, 1959, pp. 332 ff. F.F.B.

ZEBAH (Heb. *zeḇaḥ*, 'slaughter', 'sacrifice'). One of two kings of Midian who raided Palestine in the days of Gideon the judge. Some of Gideon's people had been slain in a Midianite raid (Jdg. viii. 18 f.). Gideon carefully selected 300 and pursued the raiders. The people of Succoth and Penuel refused to help him and were later punished. At Karkor (verse 10) Gideon captured the two chiefs Zebah and Zalmunna and slew them. Following this exploit, Gideon was invited to be king over Israel, but refused (Jdg. viii. 22, 23). This incident finds a place among the list of victories God gave His people in Ps. lxxxiii (verses 1–12). J.A.T.

ZEBEDEE (Gk. *Zebedaios* from Heb. *ziḇdî*, 'the gift of Yahweh'). The father of the apostles James and John (Mk. i. 19) and husband of Salome (Mt. xxvii. 56; Mk. xv. 40). A Galilaean fisherman, probably of some means (*cf.* Mk. i. 20); he evidently lived at or near Bethsaida.

ZEBOIIM, ZEBOIM. 1. A city of the plain, eventually destroyed with Sodom and Gomorrah (Dt. xxix. 23). Its king Shemeber was one of the confederates defeated by Chedorlaomer (Gn. xiv). The name is spelt Zeboiim in RV (Heb. *ṣ^{e}ḇōyîm*) throughout, and sometimes in AV. **2.** A valley near Michmash in Benjamite territory (1 Sa. xiii. 18), modern Wadi Abu Daba. The Hebrew phrase means 'ravine of hyenas' (*gê ṣ^{e}ḇō'îm*). **3.** A Benjamite town of post-exilic times, near Lydda (Ne. xi. 34, Heb. *ṣ^{e}ḇō'îm*). D.F.P.

ZEBUL (*z^{e}ḇûl*, 'elevation, height, lofty abode'. Possibly shortened from '(God's)-dwelling' or '(Baal)-zebul', after the Philistine god. 'Zebul' was a pre-Philistine god, meaning 'lord of the earth', frequently mentioned in the Ras Shamra texts. The lieutenant of Abimelech and governor of Shechem, who by his resourcefulness saved his master when the Shechemites under Gaal rebelled against Abimelech's despotic rule (Jdg. ix. 26–41). J.G.G.N.

ZEBULUN (Gk. *Zaboulon*). One of the twelve tribes, descendants of Jacob and Leah. The root may be connected with the Akkad. *zabalu*, 'carry', and appears also to mean 'exalt' (*KB* Suppl., p. 150; *JPOS*, XVI, 1936, pp. 17 f.; so LXX, Gn. xxx. 20), rather than 'dwell' as traditionally interpreted; *cf.* 1 Ki. viii. 13; Is. lxiii. 15. The name has been tentatively read in Ugaritic texts of the 14th century, but not necessarily as a proper noun (Albright, *BASOR*, 71, pp. 38 f., 'patricians'; *cf.* de Vaux, *RB*, 1948, pp. 326 f.).

Three clans are enumerated, of Sered, Elon, and Jahleel (Gn. xlvi. 14; Nu. xxvi. 26); Sered and Elon (Aijalon) are also place-names. The territory reached from the river before Jokneam (possibly the Kishon, but in Jos. xxi. 34 Jokneam is reckoned in Zebulun, so Wadi el-Milh may be meant) eastwards to the slopes of Tabor and northwards to Rimmon, probably Rummaneh, 6 miles north of Nazareth (1 Ch. vi. 77; Jos. xxi. 35, 'Dimnah'). To the east lay the towns of Kesulloth-on-Tabor and Daberath, in Issachar (Jos. xix. 12, 18, xxi. 28; 'Tabor' in 1 Ch. vi. 77 is probably a corruption, the text here being defective, *cf.* Jos. xxi. 34 f.). Near the southern boundary lay Sarid (so Jos. xix. 10 *MT* and LXX (A); perhaps Shadud, 4 miles south-west of Nazareth, *GTT*, p. 180, following Syriac). On the west, the boundary was with Asher up to th vale of Yiphtach-El ('God will open'), probably Sahl el-Battof. In this direction Nahalal (*q.v.*) and Qitron were infiltrated rather than occupied (Jdg. i. 30). Notwithstanding Gn. xlix. 13, Zebulun did not in the event reach the sea, but remained a Galilaean tribe (contrast Asher, Jdg. v. 17 f.); Dt. xxxiii. 19, speaking of Zebulun and Issachar, may refer to their position on a trade route (*cf.* Is. ix. 1), for Israel was never a seafaring people.

The land itself was fruitful (1 Ch. xii. 40; Jos., *BJ* iii. 3. 2); and the tribe had a high reputation in Israel for patriotism (Jdg. v. 14, 18, vi. 35; 1 Ch. xii. 33). In Hezekiah's time some of them came to the Passover (2 Ch. xxx. 11). The following towns mark Zebulun's contribution to successive phases of Israelite history: Aijalon, home of the judge Elon; Gath-hepher, home of Jonah; Nazareth, where Jesus spent His early years; Jotapata, defended by Josephus (*BJ* iii); Sepphoris, the Roman administrative centre.

BIBLIOGRAPHY. H. H. Rowley, *From Joseph to Joshua*, 1948, pp. 34 f., 112 f.; *GTT*, pp. 179 ff., 206 f.; A. Saarisalo, 'Topographical Researches', *JPOS*, VIII, 1928, and IX, 1929; J. Garstang, *Joshua-Judges*, 1931.

J.P.U.L.
A.S.

ZECHARIAH, ZACHARIAH, ZACHARIAS. Some twenty-eight men bear this name in the Bible, most of them mentioned only once or twice, including the last king of Jehu's line (spelt Zachariah) (2 Ki. xiv. 29, xv. 8, 11). The best known is the prophet, who is mentioned with Haggai in Ezr. v. 1, vi. 14, and whose prophecies are found in the book that bears his name. As these two prophets were enthusiasts for the rebuilding of the Temple in 520 BC, one must account for their silence during the period 536–520 BC, when the Temple building was neglected. Either their parents had brought them as infants in the return in 537 BC or they did not return until about 520 BC; in this case also they must have been infants in 537 BC, or their enthusiasm would have brought them back then. This means that Zechariah was a young man when he began to prophesy, and indeed it may be he, and not the man with the measuring line, who is referred to as 'this young man' in Zc. ii. 4. It is likely that the second part of his book belongs to his old age. (See ZECHARIAH, BOOK OF.)

In the New Testament Zacharias is the father of John the Baptist (Lk. i. 5, *etc.*). There is also a mention of 'Zacharias son of Barachias, whom ye slew between the temple and the altar' (Mt. xxiii. 35; *cf.* Lk. xi. 51). Since the prophet Zechariah was the son of Berechiah (Zc. i. 1), it is possible that he was martyred, although there is no independent record of this. Others suppose that the reference is to the martyrdom of Zechariah the son of Jehoiada in 2 Ch. xxiv. 20–22, and that the error of the father's name is due either to the evangelist, or, since it does not occur in the best MSS of Luke, to a copyist's addition. Since Chronicles is the last book in the Hebrew Bible, the naming of Abel and Zechariah in this verse would be the equivalent of our phrase 'from Genesis to Revelation'. There is also a Zechariah the son of Jeberechiah, who is called as a witness in Is. viii. 2, but there is no reason to suppose that he is the one referred to by Christ. J.S.W.

ZECHARIAH, BOOK OF.

I. OUTLINE OF CONTENTS

a. Prophecies dated between 520 *and* 518 BC, *during the rebuilding of the Temple*, i. 1–viii. 23

(i) Introduction. Zechariah in the line of the true prophets (i. 1–6).

(ii) First vision. Angelic riders are told that God will restore Jerusalem (i. 7–17).

(iii) Second vision. Four destroying horns are destroyed by four carpenters (RV, RSV 'smiths') (i. 18–21).

(iv) Third vision. The new Jerusalem cannot be contained by walls, but will be the home of Jews and Gentiles (ii. 1–13).

(v) Fourth vision. Joshua the high priest, accused by Satan, is vindicated by God, given access to His presence, and made a type of the Branch-Messiah (iii. 1–10).

(vi) Fifth vision. A seven-branched candlestick, or lamp, fed by two branches (probably Joshua and Zerubbabel), from two olive trees. A special word of encouragement to Zerubbabel (iv. 1–14).

(vii) Sixth vision. An immense flying scroll carries God's words of condemnation of sin (v. 1–4).

(viii) Seventh vision. A woman in an ephah measure, symbolizing sin, is removed to the unclean land of Babylon, the place of exile (v. 5–11).

(ix) Eighth vision. Four chariots go out through the earth as God's executives (vi. 1–8).

(x) Joshua is crowned as a symbol of the Branch-Messiah who builds the Temple, and who rules as Priest-King (vi. 9–15).

(xi) A question about observing fasts that had been instituted to commemorate the fall of Jerusalem in 587 BC. Fasts will become feasts, and all nations will share the blessing (vii. 1–viii. 23).

b. Undated prophecies, evidently from a later period in Zechariah's ministry, ix. 1–xiv. 21

(i) The judgment of Israel's enemies is seen in the light of the coming of the Prince of Peace (ix. 1–17).

(ii) Evil shepherds give place to God's Leader, who gathers in His people (x. 1–12).

(iii) The Good Shepherd confounds the evil shepherds, but is rejected by the flock, who consequently suffer under yet another evil shepherd (xi. 1–17).

(iv) Jerusalem in distress looks to the One whom her people have pierced, and repents with true sorrow (xii. 1–14).

(v) Jewish prophecy ceases when the Good Shepherd is smitten and opens the fountain that cleanses from sin (xiii. 1–9).

(vi) The distress of Jerusalem is followed by the blessings and judgments of God's kingdom (xiv. 1–21).

II. AUTHORSHIP AND UNITY

Throughout i–viii Zechariah is named as the author, and the period is that of Ezr. v, vi. This claim is generally accepted, though occasionally attempts have been made to distinguish the Zechariah of the prophecies from the Zechariah of the visions (*e.g.* by S. B. Frost, *Old Testament Apocalyptic*, 1952).

The problem of ix–xiv is more complicated, and many hold that these chapters are neither to be ascribed to Zechariah nor are a unity in themselves. A moderate view, adopted by, *e.g.*, H. L. Ellison in *Men Spake from God*, 1952, is that three anonymous prophecies have been added at the end of the Minor Prophets, each introduced by the phrase, 'The burden of the word of the Lord'. The three are Zc. ix. 1–xi. 17; Zc. xii. 1–xiv. 21; Mal. i. 1–iv. 6. Others (*e.g.* W. O. E. Oesterley and T. H. Robinson, *Introduction to the Books of the Old Testament*, 1934) find in these chapters fragments from various dates.

The main arguments against Zechariah's authorship are: (i) The difference of atmosphere between i–viii and ix–xiv. The former are full of hope and promise; the latter show bad leadership and threat of attack. There is no reference to the recent rebuilding of the Temple. (ii) There is a reference in ix. 13 to Greece as the dominant power, not Persia as in the days of Zechariah. (iii) The derogatory reference to prophecy in xiii and apocalyptic pictures in xiv are marks of a late date.

The first two contentions assume that, if the chapters are by Zechariah, they must belong to approximately the same period as i–viii. We have no means of knowing the length of Zechariah's prophetic ministry, but there are indications that he was a young man when he was first called to prophesy in 520 BC (see ZECHARIAH). Jeremiah prophesied for over forty years, and Isaiah for over fifty. If these chapters were uttered in Zechariah's old age they would be drawing near to the time of Malachi, Ezra, and Nehemiah, and perhaps Joel, when the atmosphere of first enthusiasm had given place to coldness, formality, poor leadership, and fear of attack.

The reference to Greece is not, then, a serious objection, even if one does not give any weight to belief in divine prediction, which is certainly present in the King and the Shepherd references in these chapters. Greece, or Javan, is named by Ezk. xxvii. 13, 19, and also by Is. lxvi. 19, as one of the places to which missionaries will go to declare God's glory. It is worth noting for the sake of the argument that many commentators would make 'Trito-Isaiah' (Is. lvi–lxvi) a contemporary of the actual Zechariah who wrote i–viii. It is probable that Zechariah had seen the vision of the chariots going 'toward the west country' (vi. 6, RSV), and in viii. 7 he foresees captives returning from the west. Later Joel iii. 6 refers to Jews who had been sold by the Phoenicians as slaves to the Greeks.

From about 520 BC onwards the Greeks in Asia Minor were a continual source of trouble to Darius, and in 500 BC a great Ionian revolt occurred. In 499 BC the Athenians burnt the Persian stronghold of Sardis, and in 490 BC and 480 BC, the Persians, in a full-scale invasion of Greece, were defeated at Marathon and Salamis. From a purely human point of view, Zechariah could have looked to Greece as a power that would harass the countries in the Persian Empire whose seaboard looked towards the west. Indeed there may already have been raids on the coasts of Palestine. It should, however, be noted that Javan is only one out of several powers who are dealt with in chapter ix.

The contention about the derogatory reference to prophecy in xiii reads too much into the passage. The writer cannot be belittling prophecy, since he is himself professing to be a prophet. In the context the thought is of the pierced Shepherd, whose death opens the fountain for sin, as being the climax of prophecy, so that true prophecy ceases, and any professed prophecy that remains is only false.

The contention about the later apocalyptic imagery of xiv is a subjective opinion. It should be realized that the dating of eschatological and apocalyptic passages in the Old Testament is based largely on opinion. Because there is much apocalyptic in the inter-testamental period, it is assumed that similar pictures in the prophets, *e.g.* Isaiah and Zechariah, must be given a late date.

From the positive standpoint, there are certain definite links between i–viii and ix–xiv; *e.g.* the need for repentance and cleansing (i. 4, iii. 3, 4, 9, v. 1–11, vii. 5–9, ix. 7, xii. 10, xiii. 1, 9); Jerusalem as the head (i. 16, 17, ii. 11, 12, xii. 6, xiv. 9 f.); the return of the nation (ii. 6, 10, viii. 7, 8, ix. 12, x. 6–12); Israel's enemies are to be subdued (i. 21, xii, xiv) and converted (ii. 11, viii. 20–23, ix. 7, xiv. 16–19). There are also some similarities of style: *e.g.* the fondness for the number 'two' (iv. 3, v. 9, vi. 1, xi. 7, xiii. 8); the vocatival address (ii. 7, 10, iii. 2, 8, iv. 7, ix. 9, 13, xi. 1, 2, xiii. 7); the phrase 'pass through nor return' occurs in vii. 14 and ix. 8, and nowhere else in the Old Testament.

It is not possible to prove the unity of the book, but one should not too readily abandon it. It is not necessary to look for contemporary figures in ix. 8, 16, 17 and xii. 10, though upholders of the later date suggest various priestly characters of the Maccabean age. If contemporary identifications were needed, the conservative commentator would be bound to say that we know nothing about the leaders in Judaea between 516 and 458 BC, and personal intrigues and assassinations were as likely then as in Maccabean times.

BIBLIOGRAPHY. H. G. Mitchell, *ICC*, 1912; C. H. H. Wright, *Zechariah and his Prophecies*, 1878; D. Baron, *Visions and Prophecies of Zechariah*, 1918; L. G. Rignell, *Die Nacht-*

esichte des Sacharja, 1950; F. F. Bruce, 'The Book of Zechariah and the Passion Narrative', BJRL, XLIII, 1960–61, pp. 336 ff. J.S.W.

ZEDAD. One of the sites on the northern border of the promised land (Nu. xxxiv. 8), mentioned also in Ezekiel's vision of the limits of restored Israel (Ezk. xlvii. 15). Fohrer identifies it with Sadad, south-east of Homs on the road from Riblah to Palmyra. The LXX reading of Saradak and the Samaritan Ṣrdh have led to another identification in Khirbet Ṣerādā (Van Kasteren, Buhl).

BIBLIOGRAPHY. G. B. Gray, *Numbers*, *ICC*, 1903, p. 459. R.A.H.G.

ZEDEKIAH (*ṣiḏqiyyāhû*—*ṣiḏqiyyâ*, only in 1 Ki. xxii. 11; Je. xxvii. 12, xxviii. 1, xxix. 3—'righteousness of Yahweh'). **1.** The last king of Judah c. 597–587 BC. He was the youngest son of Josiah and was placed on the throne by Nebuchadrezzar when his nephew Jehoiachin was deposed and deported to Babylon along with the cream of the Judaean kingdom. Both Jeremiah and Ezekiel seem to regard Jehoiachin as the last legitimate king of Judah. Zedekiah (his name was changed from Mattaniah—*mattanyâ*, 'gift of Yahweh'—by Nebuchadrezzar as a mark of vassalage) ruled over the moral dregs of the nation whom Yahweh had reserved to suffer the full weight of His wrath (*cf.* Je. xxiv, xxix. 16–19; Ezk. xi. 14–21).

The formal accounts of his reign (2 Ki. xxiv. 18–xxv. 7; 2 Ch. xxxvi. 10–21; Je. xxxix. 1–10, lii. 1–11) focus chief attention on his rebellion against Nebuchadrezzar which led to the invasion of Judah and the siege of Jerusalem by the Chaldeans in December 589 BC. After holding out for eighteen months, the city, reduced to extreme famine conditions, fell in July 587 BC. Zedekiah and the remnant of his army managed to escape under cover of darkness, but were pursued and captured in the Jordan valley near Jericho. The king was taken to Riblah on the Orontes, where he witnessed in Nebuchadrezzar's presence the execution of his sons before being deprived of his sight. Later he was removed to Babylon along with the majority of his subjects who survived the fearful carnage of Jerusalem's overthrow.

Much additional light is thrown on Zedekiah's character and the circumstances of his reign in the contemporary writings of Jeremiah and Ezekiel. The corrupt religion and the moral degeneracy of the last days of the Judaean kingdom are strikingly portrayed (Ezk. viii–xi, xxii). It appears that almost from the first Zedekiah was restive under the Babylonian yoke. Jeremiah warned him not to participate in a coalition of neighbouring states against his overlord (Je. xxvii). Possibly it was these activities which brought him under suspicion and necessitated his visit to Babylon in 593 BC (Je. li. 59). The pro-Egyptian party was in the ascendancy at the court. Under its influence Zedekiah openly rebelled. This was not merely an act of political suicide, it was a flagrant violation of the oath of loyalty to Nebuchadrezzar which the king had sworn in the name of Yahweh (Ezk. xvii).

The essential weakness of Zedekiah's character appears in his occasional consultations with Jeremiah during the course of the siege (Je. xxi. 1–7, xxxvii. 17–21, xxxviii. 14–28) and his treatment of the prophet (Je. xxxviii. 1–13). Granted that he was surrounded by a group of worthless advisers, Ezekiel's description of him as the 'deadly wounded wicked one, the prince (*nāśî'*) of Israel' (Ezk. xxi. 25, RV) is not over-severe when his perfidious conduct is remembered (Je. xxxiv. 8–22).

2. One of Ahab's four hundred court prophets and apparently the leader of the group (1 Ki. xxii. 11, 24; 2 Ch. xviii. 10, 23). **3.** A false prophet among the exiles in Babylon (Je. xxix. 21–23). **4.** A prince of Judah in the reign of Jehoiakim (Je. xxxvi. 12).

BIBLIOGRAPHY. *DOTT*, pp. 212–217.

J.C.J.W.

ZELOPHEHAD. The son of Hepher, grandson of Gilead of the tribe of Manasseh, father of five daughters (Nu. xxvi. 33; Jos. xvii. 3, 1 Ch. vii. 15). After his death, in the wilderness wanderings, because he was without male issue, his daughters successfully claimed the inheritance before Moses and Eleazar (Nu. xxvii. 1, 7). Thus originated the law whereby the property of a man without a male heir should pass first to his daughters (verse 8). The Gileadite chiefs later made the further request that the women should marry only within their own tribe to ensure the continuity of possession of such inheritances within the same tribe. This, being granted, also became Hebrew law (Nu. xxxvi. 2–9).

D.J.W.

ZELZAH. After Samuel had anointed Saul 'prince over his people Israel' (1 Sa. x. 1, RSV) one of the signs given to Saul was that he would meet 'two men by Rachel's tomb . . . at Zelzah' (1 Sa. x. 2). LXX translates Zelzah by 'leaping furiously' (from *ṣōlᵉḥîm*), and the Vulgate 'in the south'. There is, however, a village Beit Jala between Bethel and Bethlehem, to the west, which may be the location referred to in this verse. R.A.H.G.

ZEMARAIM. 1. A Benjamite town, listed with Beth-arabah and Bethel (Jos. xviii. 22). Proposed locations are Khirbet al-Samra and (more probably) Ras al-Zaimara.

2. A mountain in the hill country of Ephraim (2 Ch. xiii. 4). Bethel was presumably in the same general locality (*cf.* verse 19), so probably the mountain was near to, and named after, the town Zemaraim. D.F.P.

ZEMARITE, THE. A Canaanite tribe, mentioned in Gn. x. 18 and 1 Ch. i. 16. In both instances the name is listed between Arvadite and Hamathite. The tribe's home was the Ṣumur of the Tell el-Amarna letters, the Ṣimirra of Assyrian texts. Its modern name is Sumra, and it lies on the Mediterranean coast north of Tripoli. D.F.P.

ZENAS. Greek pet-name from Zenodorus (*cf.* Lightfoot on Col. iv. 15); a lawyer (*nomikos*), accompanying Apollos to an unknown destination: Titus was to provide them with supplies and a good send-off (Tit. iii. 13). They doubtless brought Titus Paul's letter (*cf.* Zahn, *INT*, II, p. 49). Only association with Apollos suggests that *nomikos* here has its usual New Testament sense of 'expert in Torah'. Zenas' proficiency was probably in Roman law: *nomikos* is used of eminent jurists like Mucius Scaevola (Plutarch, *Sulla* 36) or of humble notaries (*cf.* examples in *MM*).

An *Acts of Titus* (5th century) claims his authority, and menologies include him in the Seventy. A.F.W.

ZEPHANIAH. The only biographical reference to Zephaniah appears in the first verse of the book which bears his name. The genealogy of the prophet is carried back four generations to Hizkiah, or Hezekiah. Although this Hezekiah is not identified as the Judaean king of that name, the unusual form of Zephaniah's genealogy is best explained on that assumption.

The name of Zephaniah, 'Yahweh has hidden', may indicate that the prophet was born during the time of the atrocities perpetrated by Manasseh, who, tradition says, 'sawed asunder' the prophet Isaiah (*cf.* Heb. xi. 37).

Zephaniah prophesied during the reign of his kinsman, Josiah, the great-grandson of Hezekiah. Josiah came to the throne at the age of eight (640 BC) and was largely influenced by Hilkiah the high priest. It may be presumed that Zephaniah also had an influence for godliness on King Josiah. In his eighteenth year the young king ordered the renovation of the Temple during which the 'book of the law of Yahweh' was found. When read before the king and the people of Jerusalem, this Scripture brought about a reformation in the life of the nation.

Zephaniah probably ministered early in the reign of Josiah. He speaks of the 'remnant of Baal' in Jerusalem (Zp. i. 4), and other idolatrous customs which were abandoned after the discovery of the law (i. 5; *cf.* 2 Ki. xxii. 1–xxiii. 25; 2 Ch. xxxiv. 1–7).

Nahum, who prophesied the destruction of Nineveh, which took place in 612 BC, was probably a contemporary of Zephaniah, as was Jeremiah, who lived to see the destruction of Jerusalem (587 BC). The length of the ministry of Zephaniah is not known. C.F.P.

ZEPHANIAH, BOOK OF. This book is the ninth of the Minor Prophets. It is pre-eminently concerned with the Day of Yahweh, which had earlier appeared as a factor in the prophecies of Amos (Am. v. 18–20). Zephaniah, however, made the Day of Yahweh his central message. The visions of the Day of Yahweh subsequently played a conspicuous part in apocalyptic literature.

I. OUTLINE OF CONTENTS

a. Warning of the impending Day of Yahweh, i. 1–ii. 3

(i) Superscription (i. 1).
(ii) The destruction of all things (i. 2, 3).
(iii) Judgment on Judah and Jerusalem (i. 4–13).
(iv) Judgment described (i. 14–18).
(v) Judgment may be avoided (ii. 1–3).

b. Judgment on foreign nations, ii. 4–15

(i) Philistia (ii. 4–7).
(ii) Moab and Ammon (ii. 8–11).
(iii) Egypt (ii. 12).
(iv) Assyria (ii. 13–15).

c. Judgment on Jerusalem and subsequent blessing, iii. 1–20

(i) The sins of Jerusalem judged (iii. 1–8).
(ii) The remnant of Judah blessed (iii. 9–20).

II. HISTORICAL BACKGROUND

The religious state of the kingdom of Judah deteriorated markedly following the death of Hezekiah. Manasseh, his son, rebuilt the altars to Baal which Hezekiah had destroyed (2 Ch. xxxiii. 1–11). Religion was debased to the level of crass externalism. The revival of idolatrous worship, common in the days of Ahaz (2 Ki. xvi. 3, 4), was from the prophetic viewpoint a rejection of Israel's covenant with Yahweh.

Scythian invaders attacked Assyria in 632 BC. Josiah was able to carry out his reforms without fear of Assyrian interference. The Scythians moved into western Asia and reached the Egyptian border where they were bought off by Pharaoh Psammetichus I. They do not appear to have attacked Israel, although the ferocity of their assault provided a background against which Zephaniah pictured the wrath of Yahweh.

III. MESSAGE OF THE BOOK

Zephaniah's prophecies begin with a message of gloom. The prophet denounced the idolatry which he saw in Jerusalem, where there had been no spiritual revival since the days of Hezekiah. Zephaniah declared that God's judgment was imminent both on Judah's idolatrous neighbours (ii. 4–15) and on Judah and Jerusalem (i. 4–18, iii. 1–7).

The prophet, however, is not a pessimist. Beyond the impending doom he sees a better day. God must bring His people through the afflicting fires in order to prepare them to be a means of blessing to all mankind.

Some of the abuses denounced by Zephaniah were removed in Josiah's reformation (621 BC).

BIBLIOGRAPHY. J. M. P. Smith *et al.* in *ICC*, 1912; G. G. V. Stonehouse, *Zephaniah, Nahum and Habakkuk*, 1929. C.F.P.

ZEPHATH. See HORMAH.

ZEPHATHAH. 'The valley of Zephathah at (l^e) Mareshah' (2 Ch. xiv. 10); LXX apparently read *baggai' miṣṣāpôn* ('in the valley to the north') for *b^egê' ṣ^epāṯâ*. There are complex re-entrants in gently-sloping country both north and south of Mareshah. J.P.U.L.

ZER. A fortified city in the territory of Naphtali (Jos. xix. 35). It is not necessary to adopt the LXX reading *Tyros, i.e.* Tyre, which presupposes a Hebrew reading *ṣōr* instead of *MT ṣēr.*

ZERAH. From *zāraḥ*, 'to rise, shine/come forth', especially of the sun.

1. Son of Reuel son of Esau and Basemath (Gn. xxxvi. 4, 10, 13, 17; 1 Ch. i. 35, 37), who might be same as: **2.** Father of Jobab, second of the early kings of Edom (Gn. xxxvi. 33; 1 Ch. i. 44).

3. Son of Judah by Tamar, and twin of Perez (Gn. xxxviii. 29, 30; 1 Ch. ii. 4); progenitor of the Judaean clan of Zerahites (Nu. xxvi. 20), among whom was Achan who sinned at Jericho (Jos. vii. 1, 17–18, 24, xxii. 20; 1 Ch. ii. 6), besides others (1 Ch. ix. 6; Ne. xi. 24).

4. Son of Simeon and progenitor of a Simeonite clan of Zerahites (Nu. xxvi. 13; 1 Ch. iv. 24); the Zohar of Gn. xlvi. 10; Ex. vi. 15. **5.** Descendant of Levi through Gershom (1 Ch. vi. 21, 41).

6. An Ethiopian who invaded Judah with large Ethiopian and Libyan forces (2 Ch. xiv. 9–15, xvi. 8) and was routed in battle at Mareshah by Asa in his fourteenth year, *c.* 897 BC (*cf.* 2 Ch. xv, especially verse 10, and E. R. Thiele, *The Mysterious Numbers of the Hebrew Kings*, 1951, pp. 58–60, on 2 Ch. xv. 19, xvi. 1). Whether Zerah's starting-point was Egypt or Arabia is disputed. The only point favouring Arabia is the Semitic form of the name Zerah. His retreat by Gerar might hint, and the presence of Libyans in his forces strongly indicates, that Zerah had come from Egypt. Note that Zerah is *not* called king; hence he cannot be the Libyan pharaoh Osorkon I (*c.* 924–889 BC) in whose reign the battle occurred. The clear difference between Heb. *ḥ* and Egyp. *k* probably excludes identification of the names Zerah, *zrḥ*, and Osorkon, *(w)srk(n)*; no convincing Egyptian or Ethiopian original for Zerah's name is yet forthcoming. Zerah would therefore probably be an Ethiopian army-commander leading the Egyptian forces on behalf of Osorkon I, who was seeking to follow up the success of his father Shishak; Zerah's ignominious defeat is unlikely to appear in the scanty Egyptian records of the period. K.A.K.

ZERED, a mountain-torrent (Heb. *naḥal*) or wadi crossed by the Israelites on their journey round the frontiers of Edom and Moab (Nu. xxi. 12; Dt. ii. 13 f.). In Numbers it is mentioned as a camping-ground, which accords with the order to 'rise up' in Dt. ii. 13. Its identification is disputed; probably it is mod. Wadi el-Hesâ, which runs into the Dead Sea from the south-east. The comments which follow in Dt. ii. 14 ff. show that its crossing was regarded as an important stage in the journey. G.T.M.

ZERUBBABEL. The exact meaning of the name is uncertain; perhaps it is from Akkad. *zeru-Babili*, 'seed of Babylon'. He was the son of Shealtiel, or Salathiel, and thus grandson of King Jehoiachin (Ezr. iii. 2; Hg. i. 1; Mt. i. 12). In 1 Ch. iii. 19 the Hebrew, though not LXX, makes him the son of Pedaiah, Shealtiel's brother. If this is not a copyist's error, there may have been a levirate marriage. It is most unlikely that Zerubbabel is to be identified with Sheshbazzar (*q.v.*), since the account given in the letter sent to Darius (Ezr. v. 6–17) is hardly intelligible unless Sheshbazzar was dead at the time of the interview which it records, whereas Zerubbabel is actively building the Temple. Sheshbazzar may have been Zerubbabel's uncle, Shenazzar (1 Ch. iii. 18), but, whoever he was, he was more of a figurehead, while Zerubbabel and Joshua were the active leaders. Zerubbabel returned with the main party under Sheshbazzar in 537 BC, and laid the foundations of the Temple (Ezr. iii). Ezra records that the work was hindered until 520 BC, when a fresh beginning was made, with Zerubbabel and Joshua again in the lead (Ezr. v, vi; Hg. i, ii). In Hg. i. 1, ii. 2 Zerubbabel is called 'governor'.

The visions of Zechariah encourage both Joshua and Zerubbabel in their work, and Zc. iv. 6–10 promises that the mountain of opposition (probably that of Ezr. v) will be removed, and Zerubbabel will complete the work. It is often held that the crowning of Joshua in Zc. vi. 9–15 was really the crowning of Zerubbabel, but there is no MS evidence for this, and in iii. 8 it appears to be Joshua who is the type of the messianic Branch, as here. Since E. Sellin in 1898 it has been increasingly assumed, on the basis of the crowning and the promise of protection in Hg. ii. 20–23, that Haggai and Zechariah induced the Jews to crown Zerubbabel as king, though this act of rebellion was speedily crushed by Persia. There is no shred of evidence for or against this theory.

BIBLIOGRAPHY. L. E. Browne, *Early Judaism*, 1929; A. C. Welch, *Post-Exilic Judaism*, 1935; J. S. Wright, *The Building of the Second Temple*, 1958. J.S.W.

ZERUIAH (*ṣ^erûyâ, ṣ^eruyâ*; possibly from Arab. root, either (1) 'run blood, bleed', or (2) the name of an odoriferous tree, or its gum). The mother of Abishai, Joab, and Asahel, David's officers (1 Sa. xxvi. 6; 2 Sa. ii. 18, viii. 16, *etc.*). Her husband is never mentioned, for which there are several explanations. He may have died young, or she may have been the more significant character. It may reflect the ancient custom of tracing kinship through the female line, or she may have married a foreigner, remaining in her own clan, her children being reckoned as belonging to that clan. She was also David's sister (1 Ch. ii. 16), though 2 Sa. xvii. 25 may imply that she was strictly a step-sister, Jesse's wife being earlier married to Nahash. J.G.G.N.

ZEUS. See JUPITER.

ZIBA (*ṣîḇā'*, *ṣiḇā'*, 'a post'). A servant of Saul (2 Sa. ix. 2) who introduced Mephibosheth to David when he desired to honour Jonathan's memory. When Mephibosheth was given a place at court Ziba was appointed steward of Saul's estates bestowed on Mephibosheth (2 Sa. ix). When David was driven out by Absalom's rebellion Ziba brought him food and also falsely accused Mephibosheth of deserting the king, thereby gaining possession of the property (2 Sa. xvi. 1–4). On David's return, Ziba hastened to meet him (2 Sa. xix. 17), but later his treachery was revealed. The king, in a difficult position, divided the property between them, and Mephibosheth was seemingly content (2 Sa. xix. 24–30). J.G.G.N.

ZICHRI. 1, 2. Two Levites: (*a*) a grandson of Kohath (Ex. vi. 21); (*b*) a son of Eliezer (1 Ch. xxvi. 25). **3–6.** Four Benjamites: (*a*) 1 Ch. viii. 19; (*b*) verse 23; (*c*) verse 27; (*d*) Ne. xi. 9. **7.** A Reubenite (1 Ch. xxvii. 16). **8.** An Asaphite (1 Ch. ix. 15) called Zabdi (*q.v.*, Ne. xi. 17; see also Zaccur, 1 Ch. xxv. 2, 10; Ne. xii. 35). **9.** A Judahite, father of Amasiah, a captain of Jehoshaphat (2 Ch. xvii. 16) and perhaps identical with the father of Elishaphat, captain of Jehoiada, who took part in the overthrow of Queen Athaliah in favour of Joash (2 Ch. xxiii. 1). **10.** A warrior in the reign of Pekah (2 Ch. xxviii. 7). **11.** A priest (Ne. xii. 17). R.A.H.G.

ZIDON. See SIDON.

ZIF. See CALENDAR.

ZIKLAG. Ziklag appears in Jos. xv. 31 as being near the Edomite boundary, in the south of Judah. It was apportioned to the Simeonites, but later fell into Philistine hands. David, when a Philistine vassal, ruled it and was later able to retain and incorporate it in his own realm. It remained in the hands of Judah in both pre-exilic and post-exilic times. Tentative locations are Zuhailika and Tell al-Khuwailifa, the latter more favoured by modern scholars. D.F.P.

ZILPAH. The handmaid of Jacob's first wife Leah, given to Leah by her father Laban (Gn. xxix. 24). Leah later gave her to Jacob as a concubine, and she bore him Gad and Asher.

ZIMRAN (*zimrān*, meaning uncertain). Possibly derives from *zimrâ*, 'song, fame', thus 'the celebrated one', *i.e.* in song or fame. Alternatively, it may derive from *zemer*, 'mountain-sheep or goat'. A son of Abraham by the concubine Keturah (Gn. xxv. 2; 1 Ch. i. 32).

ZIMRI (*zimrî*). **1.** A Simeonite prince (Nu. xxv. 6–15) who was put to death by Phinehas, the grandson of Aaron, for his audacious wickedness in bringing a Midianitess into the camp in contempt of the general spirit of penitence among the Israelites for the apostasy of Baal-peor. (See BAAL.)

2. King of Israel *c.* 876 BC (1 Ki. xvi. 9–20). He reigned in Tirzah for only a week following his assassination of Elah in fulfilment of the prophecy against the dynasty of Baasha (1 Ki. xvi. 1–4). His *coup d'état* lacked popular support, the majority following Omri, who immediately laid siege to Tirzah. When the city fell, Zimri burned down the palace over his own head. J.C.J.W.

ZIN (Heb. *ṣin*). A name loosely applied to the Wilderness of Zin traversed by the Israelites in the Exodus, close to the borders of Canaan (Nu. xiii. 21). It refers to the extensive area between the camping-place of the Israelites at the oasis of Kadesh-barnea in NE Sinai, to the Ascent of Aqrabbim or Scorpion Pass constituting the limit between Edom and Judah (Jos. xv. 1–4; *cf.* Nu. xxxiv. 1–5). The wilderness of Paran lay to the south of it, though Kadesh appears to have been included in both territories, and the two wilderness districts occur within the still broader term 'Negeb' (*q.v.*).

BIBLIOGRAPHY. C. L. Woolley and T. E. Lawrence, *The Wilderness of Zin*, 1936. J.M.H.

ZION. See JERUSALEM.

ZIOR. A city listed in Jos. xv. 54 in the Judaean hill-country north-east of Hebron and allocated to the tribe of Judah; modern Si'ir (see ZAIR).

ZIPH. 1. A town in southern Judah, near the Edomite boundary (Jos. xv. 24), perhaps to be located at al-Zaifa. **2.** A town in the hill-country of Judah (Jos. xv. 55), associated with David and with Rehoboam, who fortified it. It is identified with Tell Zif, south-east of Hebron. **3.** A man of Judah (1 Ch. iv. 16). D.F.P.

ZIPPOR (*ṣippôr*, *ṣippōr*, 'bird', perhaps here 'sparrow'). Father of Balak, the Moabite king who sought Balaam's aid in withstanding the advance of the Israelites (Nu. xxii. 2, 4, 10, 16, xxiii. 18; Jos. xxiv. 9; Jdg. xi. 25). J.G.G.N.

ZIPPORAH. Daughter of Jethro priest of Midian and wife of Moses. She apparently opposed the circumcision of their second son Gershom, but felt compelled to perform the duty herself when Moses' life was endangered because of its omission (Ex. iv. 24–26). See MOSES. M.A.M.

ZIZ. The name of an ascent used by the Moabites and Ammonites in a campaign against Jehoshaphat of Judah (2 Ch. xx. 16). Their army lay previously at Engedi, on the west shore of the

Dead Sea; and they reached the wilderness of Tekoa. These details make the Wadi Hasasa, just north of Engedi, a virtually certain identification. D.F.P.

ZOAN. Ancient city, Egyp. *ḏ'n(t)* to which Heb. *ṣō'an* exactly corresponds. The Greek Tanis and modern site of Ṣan el-Ḥagar near the southern shore of Lake Menzaleh in NE Delta. The curious note in Nu. xiii. 22 that Hebron was built seven years before Zoan in Egypt may indicate a refounding of Zoan in the Middle Kingdom (*c.* 2000–1800 BC); or more probably by the Hyksos kings in the 18th century BC, whose northern capital Avaris Zoan may possibly be. For the era of Tanis, see CHRONOLOGY OF THE OLD TESTAMENT, IIIb). Ps. lxxviii. 12, 43 places the Exodus miracles in 'the field of Zoan', precisely the Egyp. *sḫt ḏ'(nt)*, 'field of Dja'(ne)', a term apparently applied to the region near Zoan; the possible identity of Zoan and Ra'amses (*q.v.*) is still uncertain. From 1100 BC until about 660 BC, Zoan was the effective capital of Egypt in the XXIst to XXIIIrd Dynasties, and the northern base of the Ethiopian XXVth Dynasty. Hence the prominence of Zoan as the seat of pharaoh's counsellors and princes (Is. xix. 11, 13, xxx. 4) and among Egypt's great cities in Ezekiel's (xxx. 14) word of judgment. On Zoan/Tanis, see A. H. Gardiner, *Ancient Egyptian Onomastica*, II, 1947, pp. 199*–201*, and P. Montet, *Les Énigmes de Tanis*, 1952, and the sources they cite. K.A.K.

ZOAR. See PLAIN, CITIES OF THE.

ZOBAH. An Aramaean kingdom which flourished during the early Hebrew monarchy, and which took the field against Saul and David. One of its kings was Hadadezer (2 Sa. viii. 3). It lay between Hamath, to its north, and Damascus to its south, and at its height its influence reached these cities. It is unnecessary to postulate two Zobahs, one of them south of Damascus, merely because it is listed with Beth-rehob and Maacah in 2 Sa. x. 6 (both of these cities were south of Damascus).

BIBLIOGRAPHY. J. Bright, *A History of Israel*, 1959, pp. 181–183. D.F.P.

ZOHELETH, STONE OF (*'eḇen hazzōḥeleṯ*). A stone near En-rogel, to the south-east of Jerusalem, the scene of the slaughtering of animals by Adonijah (1 Ki. i. 9). The meaning of *zōḥeleṯ* is uncertain, but it is usually connected with *zāḥal*, 'to withdraw, crawl away'. From this, some would interpret the phrase as 'the stone of slipping' and connect it with a steep and slippery rock slope, called by the Arabs *zaḥweileh*, or some neighbouring surface, near Siloam. Others would translate the phrase 'the serpent's stone', and link it with a possible identification of En-rogel (*q.v.*) with the dragon well (Ne. ii. 13). In the absence of sufficient data the identification remains doubtful.

BIBLIOGRAPHY. J. Simons, *Jerusalem in the Old Testament*, 1952, pp. 160–162. T.C.M.

ZOPHAR. The third of Job's friends was Zophar the Naamathite (Jb. ii. 11). We have no knowledge where his home was, except that it was presumably east of Jordan. He is distinguished by the brutality of his commonsense position. He speaks in chapters xi, xx, and possibly in xxvii. 13–23. (See JOB.) H.L.E.

ZOPHIM. This place-name comes from Heb. *ṣōp̄îm*, 'watchers'. The location of 'the field of the watchers' according to Nu. xxiii. 14 is difficult to determine. It must have been on a high part of the Pisgah Mts., from which Balaam could see the encampment of the Israelites at Shittim. Some propose to take the Heb. *śāḏeh* here in the meaning of the Akkadian *šadû*, 'mountain' ('the mountain of the watchers'). The word 'watcher' is sometimes used in the sense of prophet (*cf.* Is. lii. 8, lvi. 10) and is thus especially applicable to Balaam. F.C.F.

ZORAH. A town in the lowlands of Judah (Jos. xv. 33), closely connected with the Samson stories. Its site is Ṣar'a, on the north side of the Wadi al-Ṣarar, the biblical valley of Sorek. The Tell el-Amarna letters refer to it as Zarkha. It was fortified by Rehoboam (2 Ch. xi. 10) and re-occupied after the Babylonian Exile (Ne. xi. 29). The references to Hebron and Beersheba in these two passages, however, may suggest that there was another similarly named city a considerable distance south of Samson's territory. D.F.P.

ZUZIM (Heb. *zûzîm*; Gk. *ethnē ischyra*, 'strong peoples'). A people, conquered by Chedorlaomer, whose territory lay east of Jordan (Gn. xiv. 5). Their principal city, Ham, is probably to be identified with the modern village of the same name north-east of the Gilboa Mts. in N Jordan. Tristram (*Moab*, pp. 182 ff.) and others, however, have sought to identify them with the Moabite village of Ziza, between Bozra and Lejūn. Because the Zuzim are mentioned in parallel with the Rephaim and Emim, it may be that it is descriptive of the inhabitants (so LXX) rather than a tribal name. For this reason some equate them with Zamzummim who are identified with, or described as, Rephaim (Dt. ii. 20), whose territory was later overrun by Ammonites. D.J.W.

SOME ANCIENT WRITERS QUOTED OR REFERRED TO IN THE TEXT

(*Titles of writings have not normally been given if citations in the text of the Dictionary are self-evident. They are not in any case intended to form a complete list. Cross references set in small capital letters are to articles in the Dictionary.*)

Acts of Paul [and Thecla]: 2nd-century apocryphal work; see NEW TESTAMENT APOCRYPHA.

Acts of Pilate: embedded in the *Gospel of Nicodemus,* for which see NEW TESTAMENT APOCRYPHA.

Apocalypse of Peter: 2nd-century apocryphal work; see NEW TESTAMENT APOCRYPHA.

Apostolic Constitutions: (Arian?) church order and liturgy, *c.* AD 350 (?), but incorporating earlier material.

Appian: Greek historian; *floruit* early 2nd century AD.

Apuleius, Lucius: pagan romance writer; *Apology, Metamorphoses* (*The Golden Ass*); *floruit* mid-2nd century AD.

Aquila: Jewish proselyte, translator of the Old Testament; see TEXT AND VERSIONS.

Aristides: Christian apologist; *floruit* mid-2nd century AD.

Aristo of Pella: Jewish Christian writer; *floruit* mid-2nd century AD; fragments in Origen and Eusebius.

Aristotle: philosopher; 384–322 BC.

Augustine (Aurelius Augustinus): exegete and dogmatic and polemical theologian; AD 354–430.

Augustus (C. Iulius Caesar Octavianus): Emperor; 63 BC–AD 14. *Res Gestae Divi Augusti* is a brief account of Augustus' public life, often called the *Monumentum Ancyranum*, from its main text.

Aurelius (Marcus Aurelius Antoninus Pius): Emperor; AD 121–180. *Meditations.*

Barnabas, Epistle of: early 2nd-century homiletic work; see PATRISTIC LITERATURE.

Caesar, Gaius Julius: soldier and statesman; 102(?)–44 BC. Commentaries on the Gallic War (*De Bello Gallico*) and Civil War (*De Bello Civili*).

Cassius, Dio: see Dio Cassius below.

Celsus: 2nd-century anti-Christian propagandist; essence of *The True Word* preserved by Origen in *Contra Celsum.*

Cicero, Marcus Tullius: lawyer and philosophic writer; 116–43 BC.

Clementine Homilies and **Recognitions:** tendentious early Christian literature falsely attributed to Clement of Rome; see NEW TESTAMENT APOCRYPHA.

Clement of Alexandria: Christian philosopher and miscellaneous writer, *c.* AD 150–211; *Protrepticus* (or *Exhortation to the Greeks*), *Hypotyposeis* (lost: fragments in Eusebius), *Paedagogus, The Rich Man's Salvation* (*Quis dives salvetur?*), *Stromateis* (or, *Miscellanies*).

Clement of Rome: author of Christian letter, *c.* AD 95, often called *1 Clement;* reputed author of anonymous homily called *2 Clement;* see PATRISTIC LITERATURE.

Cyprian (Caecilianus Cyprianus Thascius): Latin ecclesiastical writer; died AD 258.

Demetrius: Greek rhetor and literary critic; *floruit* 1st century AD (?).

Diatessaron; see Tatian below.

Didache, or *Teaching of the Apostles*: liturgy and church order of uncertain 1st- or 2nd-century date; see PATRISTIC LITERATURE.

Didascalia (Apostolorum): 3rd-century church order.

Dio Cassius: Greek historian, *c.* AD 150–235. Parts of the history known only in the 11th-century *Epitome* by Xiphilinus.

Diodorus Siculus: Greek historian; *floruit* 1st century BC.

Dionysius of Halicarnassus: Greek rhetor and historian; died 8 BC.

Ephraem Syrus: Syrian Christian preacher and hymnodist; *c.* AD 306–373; *Commentary on the Gospel*, other commentaries, mostly fragmentary, *Carmina Nisibena.*

Epictetus: Stoic philosopher and moralist; *floruit* late 1st century AD. The *Discourses* and *Enchiridion* bearing his name are posthumous compilations.

Epicurus: Greek philosopher and founder of the Epicurean school; 342–270 BC.

Epiphanius: Christian anti-heretical writer; *c.* AD 315–403; *Panarion* (or *Adversus Haereses*).

Euripides: Greek dramatist; 485(?)–406 BC.

Eusebius (Pamphili, of Caesarea): Christian historian; AD 265–340; *Ecclesiastical History, The Martyrs of Palestine, Life of Constantine, Praeparatio Evangelica, Chronicle, Theophania.*

Galen (Claudius Galenus): Greek medical writer; AD 129–*c.* 200.

Gelasius: Bishop of Rome from AD 492 to 496. His relationship to the 'Gelasian Decree', a 6th-century (?) text on orthodox and unorthodox books, including much earlier material, is uncertain.

Gregory of Nazianzus: Christian rhetor, preacher, and poet; *c.* AD 330–390.

Gregory of Tours: Christian historian and hagiographer; AD 538–594.

Gregory the Great: Roman bishop and pastoral theologian; *c.* AD 540–604.

Hebrews, Gospel according to: early non-canonical Gospel; see NEW TESTAMENT APOCRYPHA.

Hegesippus: 2nd-century Jewish-Christian chronicler; fragments preserved in Eusebius and elsewhere.

Herakleon: Christian heretical commentator; *floruit* early 2nd century.

Hermas, The Shepherd of: 2nd-century Christian hortatory work; see PATRISTIC LITERATURE.

Hermetica: see HERMETIC LITERATURE.

Herodotus: Greek historian; *c.* 485–425 BC.

Hesychius: Greek grammarian and lexicographer; *floruit* 5th century AD (?).

Hippolytus: Christian exegete, polemical theologian and writer on liturgy; died AD 235; *Philosophumena* (or *Refutation of all Heresies*), *The Apostolic Tradition* (only in late revisions), *Chronicle*, and many commentaries on biblical books.

Horace (Q. Horatius Flaccus): Latin poet and literary critic; 65–8 BC.

Ignatius: alias Theophorus, Christian bishop; died *c.* AD 115; author of seven letters; see PATRISTIC LITERATURE.

Irenaeus: Christian theologian and anti-heretical writer; *c.* AD 140–202; *Adversus Haereses* (cited normally according to Harvey's edition), *Demonstration of the Apostolic Preaching.*

Isocrates: Athenian rhetor; 436–338 BC; twenty-one extant discourses; *Epistles.*

Jerome (Eusebius Hieronymus): Christian scholar, theologian and translator; AD 348(?)–420; *Epistles, De Viris illustribus, Chronicle,* various homilies and commentaries on biblical books; see also TEXT AND VERSIONS.

Josephus, Flavius: Jewish historian and apologist; AD 37–*c.* 100. *Antiquities of the Jewish Nation, Bellum Judaicum* (or *The Jewish War*), *Contra Apionem* (*Against Apion*, an anti-Semitic writer), *Life* (an autobiographical apologia).

Justin [Martyr]: Christian apologist; *floruit* mid-2nd century; *Apology* (the so-called 'First Apology' is referred to, unless otherwise stated), *Dialogue with Trypho.*

Juvenal (Decimus Junius Iuvenalis): Latin satirist; *floruit* AD 100–130.

Lactantius, L. Caecilius Firmianus: Christian apologist; *floruit* early 4th century; *De Opificio Dei; Divine Institutes; Epitome* of the Institutes.

Liber Pontificalis: Latin chronicle, various dates; cited from Duchesne's edition.

Livy (Titus Livius): Latin historian; 59(?) BC–AD 17.

Lucian: Greek rhetor, essayist and religious satirist; *floruit* late 2nd century AD.

Manetho: Egyptian historian; *floruit* 3rd century BC; his lost history was used by Josephus, Eusebius, and others.

Martial (M. Valerius Martialis): Latin poet and epigrammatist; *floruit* AD 64–100.

Nicolaus of Damascus: Greek historian; *floruit* late 1st century BC; works known only in fragments.

Numenius of Apamea: Greek pagan philosopher; *floruit* late 2nd century AD; works known only in fragments.

Origen (Origenes Adamantius): Christian scholar, exegete, and theologian; AD 185(?)–255; *Contra Celsum, De Principiis* (*First Principles*), *Exhortation to Martyrdom, On Prayer*, many homilies and commentaries on biblical books.

Papias: Christian bishop; *floruit* early 2nd century; *Expositions of the Oracles of the Lord* (lost: fragments and allusions in Irenaeus, Eusebius and later writers).

Pausanias: Greek geographer and traveller; *floruit* 2nd century AD; *Description of Greece.*

Philo: Alexandrine Jewish writer; *floruit* early 1st century AD. See PHILO.

Photius: Byzantine statesman, ecclesiastic and bibliophile; *c.* AD 820–891; *Bibliotheca* (or *Myriobiblion*).

Plato: Greek philosopher; 429/8–347 BC.

Pliny, the Elder (Gaius Plinius Secundus): Latin encyclopaedist; *c.* AD 23–79; *Natural History.*

Pliny, the Younger (Gaius Plinius Caecilius Secundus): nephew of the above; rhetor and statesman; *c.* AD 61–?; *Epistles, Panegyric.*

Plutarch: Greek biographer and essayist; *c.* AD 46–120; *Parallel Lives, Moralia.*

Poimandres: Hermetic tractate; see HERMETIC LITERATURE.

Polybius: Greek historian; *c.* 204–*c.* 122 BC.

Polycarp: Christian bishop; *floruit* late 1st and early 2nd century AD; see PATRISTIC LITERATURE: *The Martyrdom of Polycarp* is substantially a contemporary account.

Pomponius Mela: Latin geographer; *floruit* mid-1st century.

Porphyry: Neoplatonic philosopher and anti-Christian writer; AD 233–*c.* 304.

Ptolemy (Claudius Ptolemaeus): Alexandrine astronomer and geographer; *floruit* mid-2nd century AD.

Quintilian (M. Fabius Quintilianus): Latin writer on rhetoric; AD 30–96; *Institutio oratoria.*

Res Gestae Divi Augusti: see Augustus above.

Rufinus, Tyrannius (of Aquileia): Christian Latin writer and translator of Origen, Eusebius, *etc.*; *c.* AD 345–411.

Sallust (C. Sallustius Crispus): Latin historian; 86–35 BC; *Catiline, Jugurtha, Histories.*

Seneca, the Elder (L. Annaeus): Latin rhetor; *c.* 55 BC–*c.* AD 40.

Seneca, the Younger (L. Annaeus): son of the above; philosopher and Nero's tutor; *c.* 4 BC–AD 65.

Solomon, Odes of: Collection of Gnostic-Christian (?) hymns; date uncertain.

Sozomen: Greek church historian; *floruit c.* AD 400; *Ecclesiastical History.*

Statius, Publius Papinius: Latin poet; *floruit* late 1st century AD; *Silvae, Thebaid, Achilleis.*

Stobaeus, Joannes: anthologist; *floruit* late 5th century AD (?).

Strabo: geographer; *c.* 64 BC–AD 24(?); *Geography.*

(C) Suetonius Tranquillus: Latin historian; *floruit* early 2nd century; author of biographies of the Caesars, from Julius to Domitian.

Symmachus: Jewish Christian translator of the Old Testament; see TEXT AND VERSIONS.

Tacitus, Cornelius: Latin historian; *c.* AD 58–*c.* 120; *Agricola, Germania, Historiae, Annals.*

Tatian: Greek–Syrian Christian apologist and missionary; *floruit* mid-2nd century; *Oration to the Greeks, Diatessaron* (a harmony of the four Gospels); see TEXT AND VERSIONS (New Testament).

Tertullian (Q. Septimius Florens Tertullianus): Christian Latin apologist and practical and polemical theologian; *c.* AD 160–*c.* 230; *Apology, Adversus Marcionem, De Praescriptione Haereticorum, De Spectaculis, De Corona Militis, Ad Scapulam, Adversus Praxeam, etc.*

Theodore of Mopsuestia: Christian theologian and exegete; *c.* AD 350–428/9.

Theodotion: Jewish proselyte; translator of the Old Testament; see TEXT AND VERSIONS.

Thomas, Acts of [Judas]: 2nd-century apocryphal work; see NEW TESTAMENT APOCRYPHA.

Thomas, Gospel of: see NEW TESTAMENT APOCRYPHA.

Thucydides: Athenian historian; *c.* 457–*c.* 401 BC.

Truth, Gospel of: Gnostic work, attributed to Valentinus; see CHENOBOSKION, NEW TESTAMENT APOCRYPHA.

Valentinus: Christian heretical theologian; *floruit* mid-2nd century; *Gospel of Truth;* but see NEW TESTAMENT APOCRYPHA.

Varro, M. Terentius: Latin scholar; 116–27 BC; *De re rustica, De lingua Latina, Antiquities* (known only at secondhand).

Vergil (P. Vergilius Maro): Latin poet; 70–19 BC; *Aeneid, Eclogues* (or *Bucolics*), *Georgics.*

Xenophon: Athenian soldier and writer; *c.* 430–*c.* 340(?) BC; *The Anabasis, The Cyropaedia* (or *Education of Cyrus*).

ACKNOWLEDGMENTS

Most of the line drawings in the text have been specially drawn for this volume and may not be reproduced without permission. Where direct access to the objects themselves has not been possible use has been made of published photographs appearing in such volumes as R. D. Barnett, *Assyrian Palace Reliefs*, J. B. Pritchard, *The Ancient Near East in Pictures* (*ANEP*), and D. J. Wiseman, *Illustrations from Biblical Archaeology* (*IBA*). Some drawings have been copied from other published works, and permission to use this copyright material is gratefully acknowledged to the authors and publishers of the books concerned. Details of all sources are given in the Index.

Permission to reproduce the photographs used in plates I–XVI is gratefully acknowledged to the Trustees of the British Museum (all BM numbers) and to the other copyright owners listed in the Index.

In preparing the list of proposed articles for the Dictionary the Organizing Editor had access to a series of entries compiled for a projected (but unpublished) *Readers' Guide to Biblical Archaeology*, by the late W. W. Skeat, M.A., F.S.A., a former Guide Lecturer of the British Museum, and made available by courtesy of his executors.

INDEX OF LINE DRAWINGS

INDEX OF LINE DRAWINGS

INDEX OF HALF-TONE ILLUSTRATIONS

XV*b*. An inscribed stone from Caesarea bearing the name of Pilate. By courtesy of the Director of the Missione della Archaeologica Italiana a Caesarea.

XV*c*. The pool of Siloam as it is today. By courtesy of Mr. A. R. Millard.

XV*d*. The Areopagus and the Temple of Athena. By courtesy of the Greek Embassy, London.

XVI. An air photograph of Jerusalem with key. By courtesy of Elia Photo Service, Jerusalem, Jordan.

INDEX TO COLOURED MAPS

LIST OF MAPS

1. The Ancient Near East, *c.* 1800 BC.
2. Palestine and Syria in the Time of the Patriarchs.
3. The Hebrew Settlement of the Promised Land.
4. Palestine in the Time of the Judges.
5. Geography of the Books of Samuel.
6. The Kingdoms of Judah and Israel.
7. The Assyrian and Neo-Babylonian Empires.
8. Palestine in Old Testament Times.
9. The Persian Empire.
10. Palestine under Persian Rule.
11. Jerusalem in the Time of Nehemiah.
12. The province of Judah under Nehemiah.
13. The Hellenistic Empire.
14. Palestine under the Maccabees.
15. The Roman Empire.
16. Palestine in New Testament Times.
17. The Travels of St. Paul.

INDEX OF PLACE-NAMES

The bold figures refer to the numbers of the coloured maps. The following abbreviations have been employed: Kh.—Khirbet; Mt.—Mount; R.—River; T.—Tell; W.—Wadi. An asterisk indicates that there is an entry in the text of the Dictionary for the place so marked.

a. Egyptian jewellers in their workshop. The bow-drill is being used to pierce beads while another craftsman employs a graver or similar instrument. Note the sistrum in the upper right corner (*cf.* fig. 147). From the tomb of Sebek-hetep (No. 63), Thebes, *c.* 1420 BC.

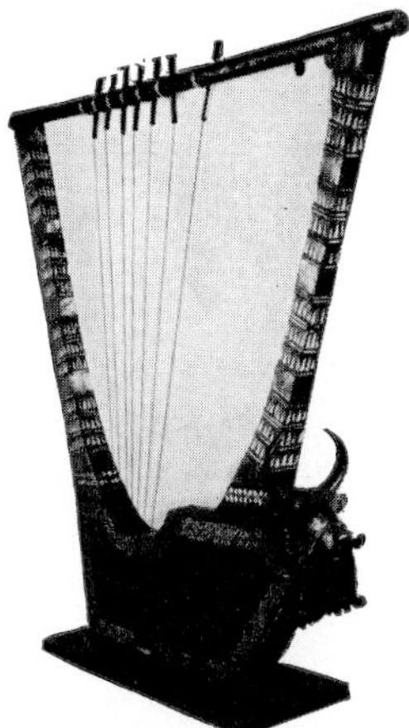

Lyre found at Ur, *c.* 2500 BC. The wooden frame .s decorated with shell, red limestone, and lapis- uli, and plated with gold. A golden bull's head ɔjects from the front of the sounding-box. See article ART, pp. 86 ff.

Court headdress from a tomb at Ur, *c.* 2500 BC. gold ribbon held the hair in place, strings of gold .ves hung across the forehead, while a gold, flower-headed pin was inserted at the back.

a. Wooden model of an Egyptian granary, *c.* 2350 BC. The grain was poured into bins around the walls through holes in the roof and removed through hatches in front. Inscriptions on each bin describe the type and the quantity of the grain. See article STORE-CITIES, p. 1218.

b. Alabaster head of a cow sacred to the goddess Hathor (see fig. 75), *c.* 1500 BC. Ex. xxxii. 1–6 relates how the Israelites in the wilderness caused Aaron, during Moses' absence, to make a golden calf to which they offered sacrifices, an action reflecting Egyptian practice.

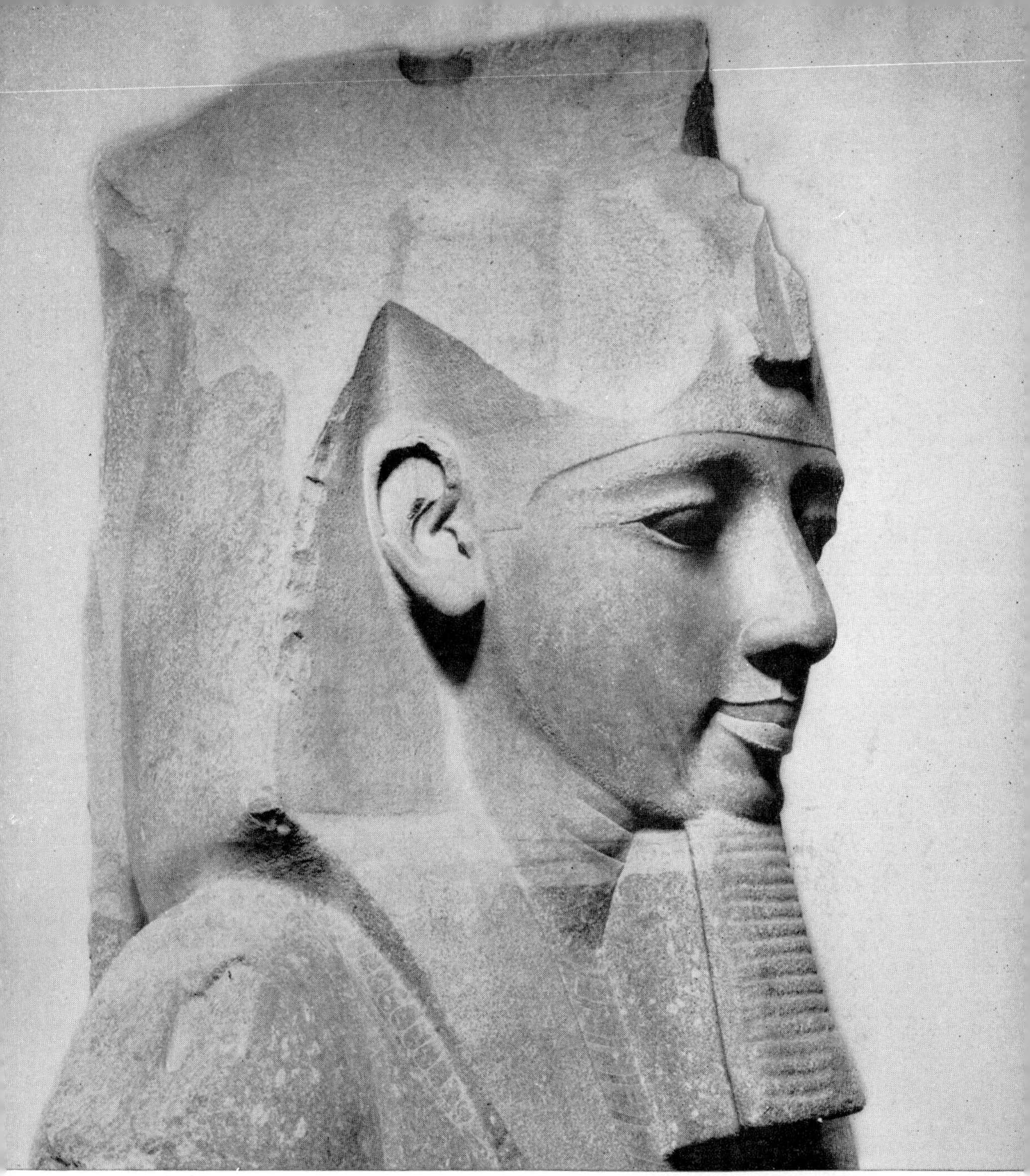

a. The head from a colossal statue of the Egyptian king Rameses I (*c.* 1290–1224 BC), who was probably the pharaoh at the time of Moses and the Exodus. Found at Thebes.

. An Egyptian brick made of sun-dried clay from the Nile ixed with chopped straw to bind it together, *c.* 1290 BC. It is amped with the name and title of Rameses II. For a tomb-inting showing Egyptians manufacturing this kind of brick see ;. 44. Kiln-baked bricks, which are much more durable, are rdly known in Egypt or Palestine before the Roman occupa-on. They were used in Mesopotamian lands, however, from earliest times.

a. The fine head of a lady in white stone of almost life size. Originally the eyes and eyebrows were inlaid with coloured stones and the head grooved to take an inset wig. The head, worked in the early third millennium BC, is a masterpiece of ancient Oriental art. From Warka (biblical Erech). Now in the Baghdad Museum.

b. Head of a woman carved in ivory, originally partially covered with gold leaf. Probably part of the decoration of palace furniture, and possibly of Phoenician workmanship (*cf.* fig. 114). This piece has been called the 'Mona Lisa' of ancient Iraq. From Nimrud, 8th century BC.

c. A limestone slab from a doorway in Senna-cherib's palace at Nineveh, *c.* 700 BC. The room were probably enriched with woven carpets, bu as these would be damaged by the heavy woode doors, similar designs were carved on the stone of the threshold.

Plate IV

n openwork plaque of ivory, 5½ inches high, d at Nimrud, but made in Syria or Phoenicia, taken to Assyria as tribute or booty during the century BC. The seated lion wearing a royal r and a cobra headdress is copied from an yptian original. See article, IVORY, pp. 590 f.

low Egyptian chair of acacia wood with feet ne form of lion's paws and a high back inlaid ivory and ebony. The seat is made of plaited ng (*cf*. fig. 118). From Thebes, New Kingdom, c. 1250 BC.

Plate V

a. The Assyrian king Ashurbanipal pouring a li
tion over lions killed in the hunt (see pl. VI
Before him are an altar, an incense stand, and t
musicians. From Nineveh, *c.* 650 BC. *Cf.* figs.
137.

b. A stele showing Esarhaddon, king of Ass
(681–669 BC). He holds by a leash Tirhakah, kin
Egypt and Ethiopia, and a bearded captive, poss
Ba'ali of Tyre. Above are the symbols of Assyr
gods. Diorite (10 feet 6 inches high). Fr
Zenjirli.

c, d. Impressions made from two stone cylin
seals. *Top:* A seal 'belonging to the scribe Adda'
2250 BC. It shows the sun-god rising between t
mountains, the god of the Deep standing on
left and Ishtar, goddess of War, on his rig
Below: A Persian king grasps a lion and a bear
man seizes a bull by its ear, *c.* 500 BC.

Plate VI

a. Panels from the black obelisk showing Jehu, king of Israel bowing before Shalmaneser III, king of Assyria. Behind him comes the tribute carried by Israelite porters. This limestone stele was originally set up in the central square at Nimrud, *c.* 850 BC. See also fig. 223.

b. Three registers from the lion-hunt sculptures from the palace of Ashurbanipal (*c.* 669–627 BC) at Nineveh. *Top:* the king heroically kills a lion with a short sword. *Centre:* He despatches another from horseback. *Below:* courtiers and attendants ride the field. *Cf.* figs. 25, 108, 134.

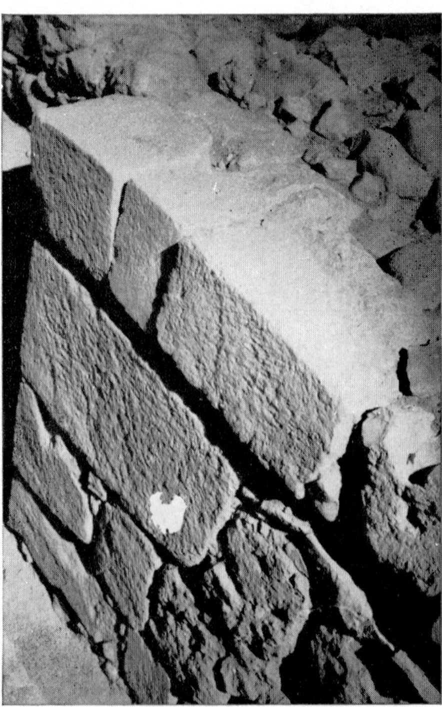

a. A general view of the ruins of Babylon showing the foundations of the Ishtar gateway and the ceremonial highway. The walls are decorated with bulls, lions, and composite creatures, symbols of the city's gods (see fig. 150). This part of the city was rebuilt by Nebuchadrezzar II, king of Babylonia 605–562 BC.

b. A corner-stone of well-trimmed building blocks strengthening walls of less skilfully set stone. Israelite masonry at Hazor, 8th century BC. See article CORNERSTONE, p. 258.

a. A model reconstruction of the Ishtar gateway at Babylon showing also the processional way. See article BABYLON, pp. 117 ff.

b. A boundary-stone (*kudurru*) delineating the property held by the official shown receiving his charter from Marduk-apla-iddina II (Merodach-baladan), king of Babylon, 722–711, 705–703 BC. Above the two figures are emblems of four deities upon pedestals. Nabu (Nebo), Ninḫursag, Ea and Marduk (spade symbol). Black marble, 18 inches high. Now in the Berlin State Museum.

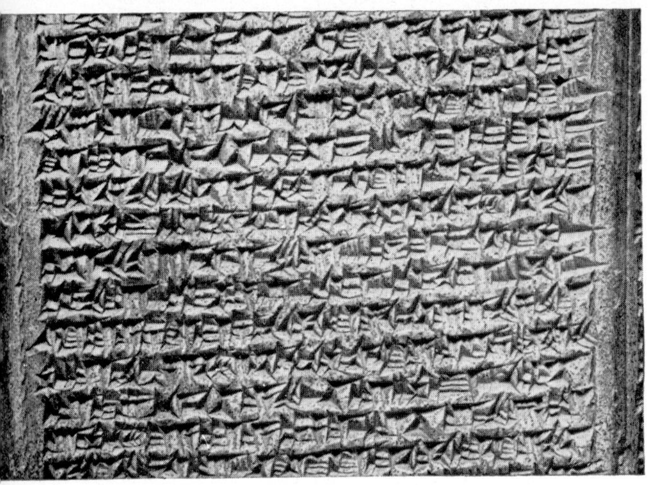

a. A six-sided clay prism inscribed in cuneiform with an account of the events of the early campaigns of the reign of Sennacherib (*c.* 705–681 BC). The section enlarged describes the siege of Hezekiah within Jerusalem in 701 BC. For a transcription see p. 524. From Nineveh, 15 inches high.

b. An inscription on black basalt, 3 feet 3 inches high, in which Mesha, king of Moab, records his successful revolt against Israel after Ahab's death (2 Ki. i. 1, iii. 4, 5) and lists the villages recovered. From Dhiban, *c.* 830 BC.

c. A limestone plaque, 15 inche square, found in Jerusalem. It bear an Aramaic inscription, 'Hither were brought the bones of Uzziah, king o Judah. Not to be opened,' and date probably from the 1st century AD a a time of reburial.

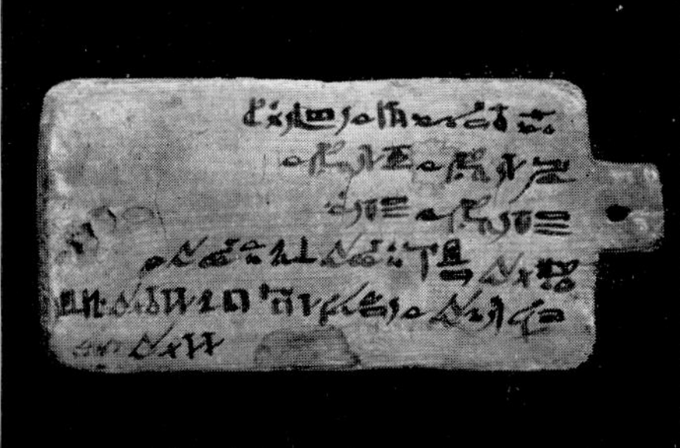

a. Wooden writing-board from an Egyptian school, *c.* 1000 BC. Lists of objects and names, in this case probably Cretan names, were written on these tablets as text-books.

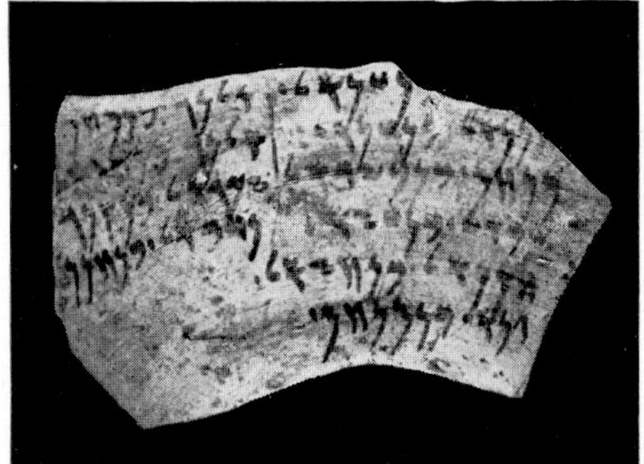

b. An ostracon found at Nimrud inscribed on both sides with lists of personal names. The writing is Aramaic, but the names (*e.g.* Menahem, Hananel, son of Hazael, 'Elisha' *etc.*) are probably those of Hebrew exiles. 8th century BC.

c. An alabaster vase found in the ruins of the Mausoleum at Halicarnassus (now Bodrum in Western Turkey). It was probably presented to a local ruler by Xerxes, king of Persia, whose name and titles are engraved upon it in Persian and Babylonian cuneiform and Egyptian hieroglyphs; *c.* 480 BC.

d. An Etruscan writing-board made of ivory. The inset panel was originally filled with wax and a resin to take the imprint of the stylus. An inscription along the edge has not been deciphered. When not in use it would be hung up on a nail. From Marsiliana, possibly an import from the Orient, *c.* 700 BC. See article WRITING, pp. 1341 ff.

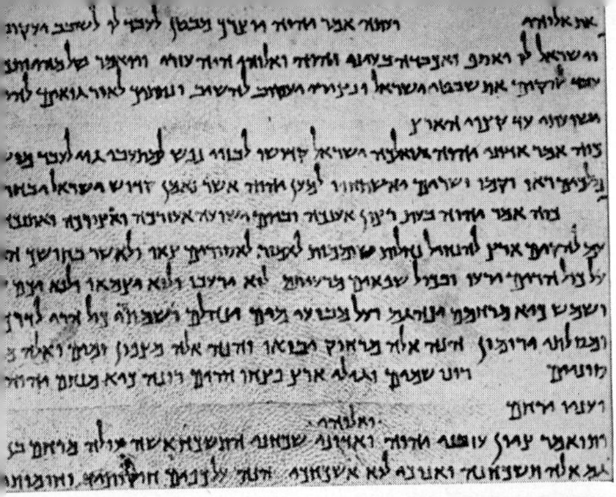

a. Isaiah xlix. 5–16, in the oldest known copy of a complete book of the Hebrew Old Testament. This leather scroll some 24 feet long and 10 inches high, found in a cave near the Dead Sea, must be very like the one used in the synagogue at Nazareth from which our Lord read (*cf.* Lk. iv. 17). See also pp. 299 ff., 1256.

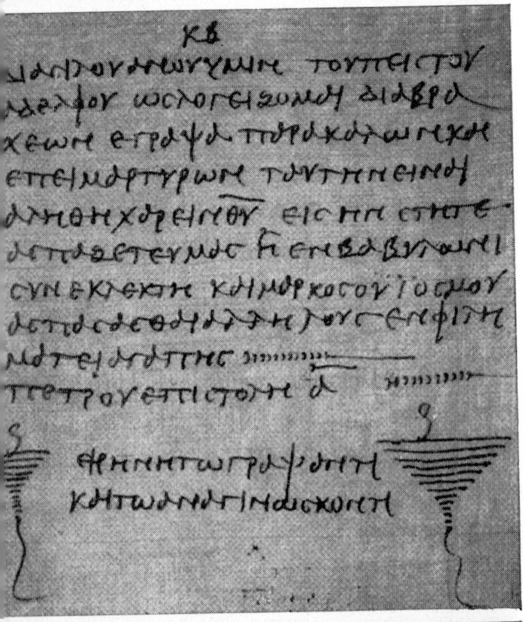

b. The closing verses of I Peter from the oldest known manuscript of this Epistle, a papyrus of *c.* AD 200 recently found in Egypt together with several other New Testament books, and now in the Bodmer Library, Geneva. See article TEXT AND VERSIONS, pp. 1264 ff.

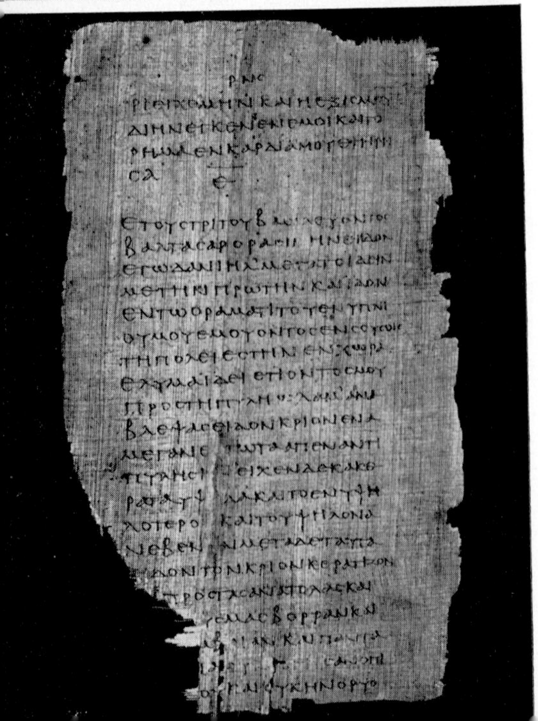

c. A papyrus manuscript of *c.* AD 250 originall
containing Ezekiel, Daniel, and Esther in the Sep
tuagint translation. This was one of eleven book
from an early Christian library found north o
Memphis in Egypt. The passage shown is Dn. vi
28–viii. 48. From the Chester-Beatty collection
Dublin.

Plate XII

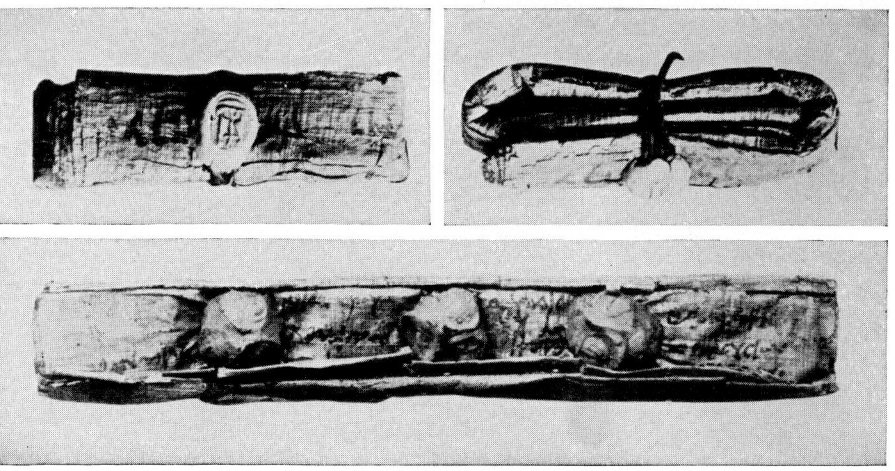

A papyrus found at Elephantine showing how such documents were rolled, folded, tied, and sealed hen despatched. Paul's letters may well have been carried to their destinations in this way. It may have een a scroll such as this 'written within and on the back' and 'sealed with seven seals' which John saw in his vision (Rev. v. 1).

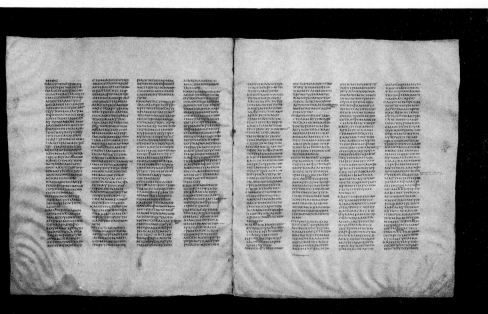

A double folio of the Codex Sinaiticus (Lk. xix. 30–xx. 34), an uncial manuscript of the 4th century), probably of Egyptian origin. It is one of the earliest and most important complete MSS of the whole ble. The Old Testament section reproduces the Septuagint Greek version (see fig. 214). The story of its scovery in a monastery library at the foot of Mt. Sinai and its subsequent purchase from Russia by the British Museum is well known.

a. A reconstruction, by Dr. D. W. Gooding, of the tabernacle based on the information given in Exodus. In this photograph some of the curtains have been removed to show the position of the ark of the covenant, the incense altar in front of the veil, the table for the show-bread, and the seven-branched candlestick. In the courtyard stood the laver (not described in detail), used by the priests in their ablutions, and the altar of burnt-offering (for a detailed drawing of which see fig. 176). In the model the wires connecting the court pillars are for convenience only and are not intended to represent the 'fillets'. For a full description see pp. 1231–1234.

b. Dr. C. Schick's reconstruction of Herod's Temple. In preparing an elaborate model of this kind much has to be assumed. Archaeological discoveries provide only basic information regarding dimensions and some general indications as to the architectural style employed and the kind of ornamentation which might be expected. The description given by Josephus also helps. This model should be compared with an earlier reconstruction shown on p. 79 and the ground plan given on p. 1246. Building commenced in 19 BC, and the main structure was completed in ten years. Work continued until AD 64, but six years later everything was demolished in the destruction of Jerusalem.

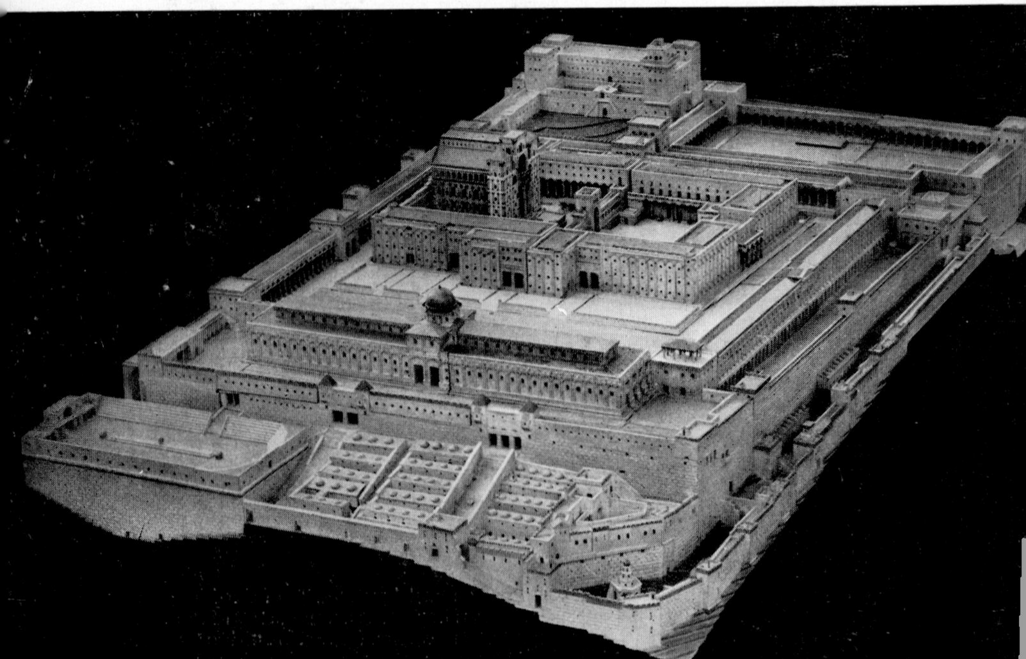

a. An inscribed stone discovered in Jerusalem and dating from New Testament times. It forbids Gentiles to enter the inner court of the Temple on pain of death and must have been built into the wall or balustrade separating the court of the Gentiles from the Temple precincts. See fig. 207.

b. A stone discovered during excavations in the theatre at Caesarea in 1961 and bearing the names of Pilate and Tiberius. This is the first time Pilate's name has been found on a stone inscription.

c. The Pool of Siloam in Jerusalem. The present enclosure occupies the central part of a Roman structure with porticoes surrounding the water. The opening of the tunnel made by Hezekiah to bring the water from the spring of Gihon (see fig. 193) can be seen at the top of the picture. See articles SILOAM, JERUSALEM.

d. A view of the citadel hill at Athens surmounted by the temple of Athena (the Parthenon), built *c.* 430 BC. Just below is the Areopagus or 'Mars Hill', the original meeting-place of the Council of the Areopagites.

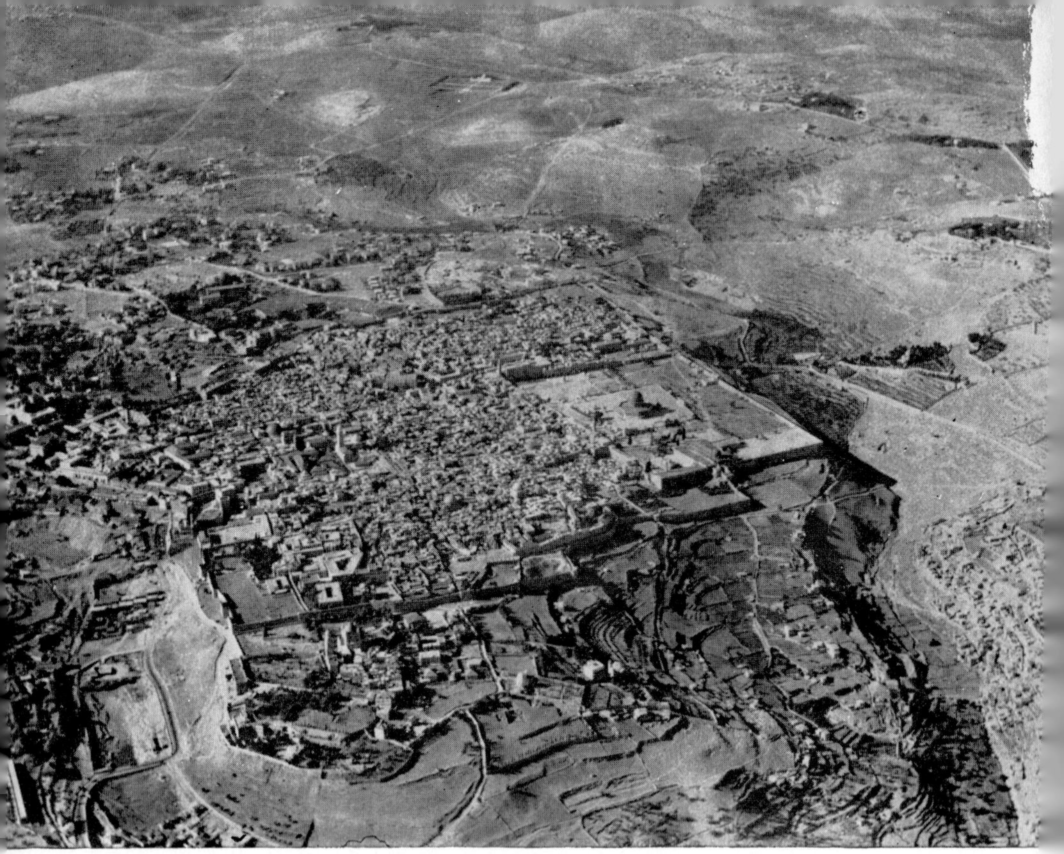

A recent air photograph of Jerusalem and its environs with (*below*) a key showing both ancient and modern sites. *Cf.* figs. 119, 120, 121.

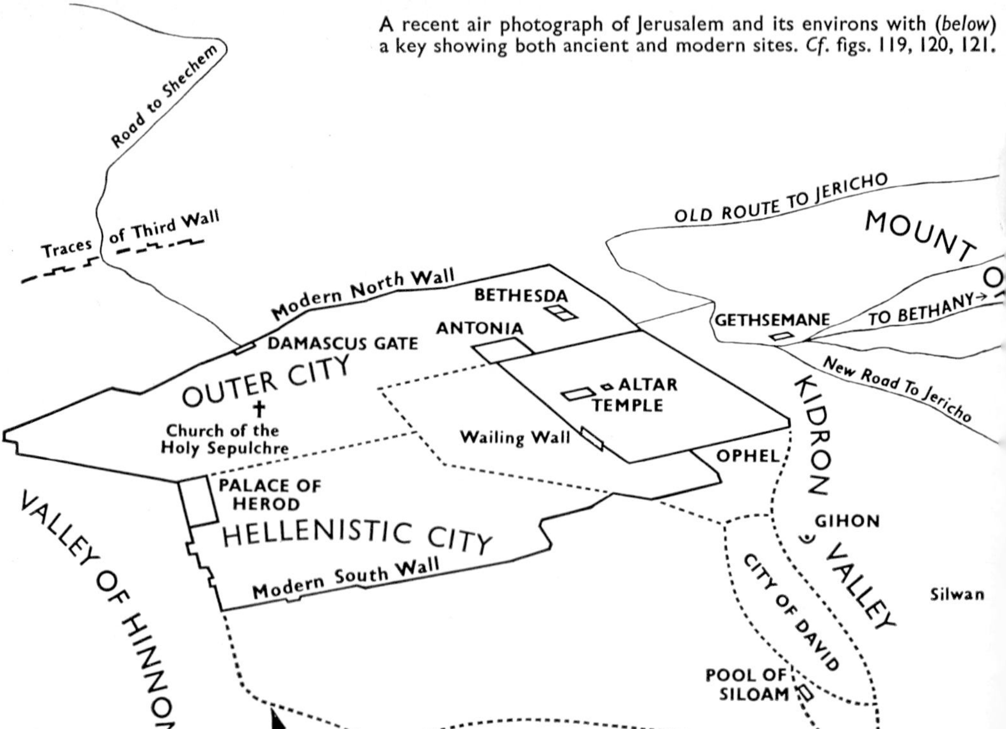

Road to Shechem
Traces of Third Wall
OLD ROUTE TO JERICHO
Modern North Wall
BETHESDA
ANTONIA
DAMASCUS GATE
GETHSEMANE
TO BETHANY→
New Road To Jericho
OUTER CITY
ALTAR
TEMPLE
Church of the Holy Sepulchre
Wailing Wall
KIDRON
OPHEL
PALACE OF HEROD
HELLENISTIC CITY
GIHON
VALLEY
VALLEY OF HINNOM
Modern South Wall
CITY OF DAVID
Silwan
POOL OF SILOAM
N

Plate XVI

Printed in Great Br

MAP I
TH
NEAR EAST
c. 1800 BC
0 50 100 150 Miles
0 50 100 150 200 Kms.
Main Patriarchal Route
Alternative Route
(BLACK SEA)
HITTITES
Troy
Hattusha
Kanish
Tarsus
Carchemish
Harran
PADAN-ARAM
Halab
AMURRU
Hamath
Tadmor
Mari
Euphrates
Tigris
(Hiddekel)
Nineveh
ASSYRIA
Assur
Arrapha
Nuzi
Eshnunna
Dêr
ELAM
Shushan
Accad
BABYLONIA
Cuth
Babylon
Kish
Nippur
Adab
Erech
Lagash
Larsa
Ur
Eridu
CAPHTOR
Knossos
ALASHIYA
THE GREAT SEA
Ugarit
Arvad
Gebal
Sidon
Tyre
Damascus
CANAAN
Hazor
Shechem
Jerusalem
Ashkelon
Mamre
Gerar
Beersheba
Zoan
On
Memphis
EGYPT
Beni-hasan
Abydos
PATHROS
RED SEA

MAP 2
PALESTINE AND SYRIA IN THE TIME OF THE PATRIARCHS
Over 3000 feet
1200–3000 ,,
600–1200 ,,
0– 600 ,,
Below Sea-level
0 25 50 75 Miles
0 25 50 75 100 Kms.
Taurus Mts.
Tarsus
Amanus Mts.
Carchemish
Harran
PADAN-ARAM
Pethor
Alalah
Halab
Ugarit
Enkomi
ALASHIYA
Hamath
Arvad
Qatna
Kadesh
Tadmor
THE GREAT SEA
Gebal
Lebanon
Sidon
Damascus
Tyre
Hermon
Dan
Hazor
Ashteroth-Karnaim
Carmel
Megiddo
Taanach
Dothan
Shechem
Succoth
Penuel
Jabbok
Mahanaim
Bethel
Ai
Jordan
CANAAN
Jerusalem
Adullam
Bethlehem
Mamre
Gerar
Hebron
PHILISTINES
Beersheba
NEGEB
Rehoboth
Vale of Siddim (now covered by Dead Sea)
Kadesh-barnea
SEIR

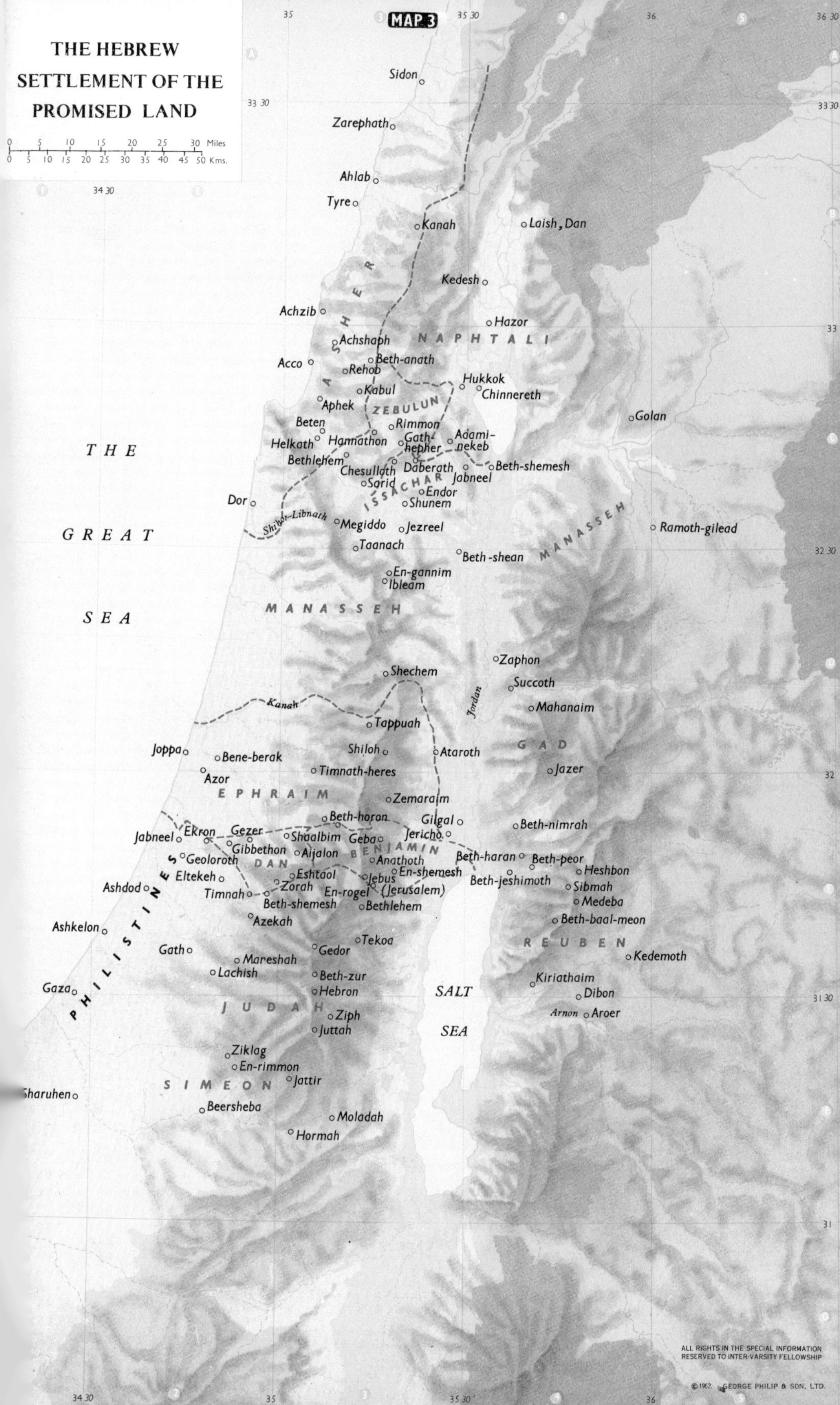
MAP 3
THE HEBREW SETTLEMENT OF THE PROMISED LAND
0 5 10 15 20 25 30 Miles
0 5 10 15 20 25 30 35 40 45 50 Kms.
THE GREAT SEA
SALT SEA
ASHER
NAPHTALI
ZEBULUN
ISSACHAR
MANASSEH
MANASSEH
EPHRAIM
GAD
BENJAMIN
DAN
PHILISTINES
JUDAH
REUBEN
SIMEON
Sidon
Zarephath
Ahlab
Tyre
Kanah
Laish, Dan
Kedesh
Achzib
Hazor
Achshaph
Acco
Beth-anath
Rehob
Hukkok
Chinnereth
Kabul
Aphek
Beten
Rimmon
Golan
Helkath
Hannathon
Gath-hepher
Adami-nekeb
Bethlehem
Chesulloth
Daberath
Beth-shemesh
Jabneel
Sorid
Endor
Shunem
Dor
Shihor-Libnath
Megiddo
Jezreel
Ramoth-gilead
Taanach
Beth-shean
En-gannim
Ibleam
Zaphon
Shechem
Succoth
Kanah
Jordan
Mahanaim
Tappuah
Shiloh
Ataroth
Joppa
Bene-berak
Timnath-heres
Jazer
Azor
Zemaraim
Beth-horon
Gilgal
Beth-nimrah
Jabneel
Ekron
Gezer
Shaalbim
Geba
Jericho
Gibbethon
Aijalon
Beth-haran
Beth-peor
Geoloroth
Anathoth
Heshbon
Eltekeh
Eshtaol
Jebus
En-shemesh
Beth-jeshimoth
Ashdod
Zorah
En-rogel
(Jerusalem)
Sibmah
Timnah
Beth-shemesh
Bethlehem
Medeba
Azekah
Beth-baal-meon
Ashkelon
Tekoa
Gath
Gedor
Kedemoth
Mareshah
Lachish
Beth-zur
Kiriathaim
Gaza
Hebron
Dibon
Arnon
Aroer
Ziph
Juttah
Ziklag
En-rimmon
Jattir
Sharuhen
Beersheba
Moladah
Hormah
ALL RIGHTS IN THE SPECIAL INFORMATION RESERVED TO INTER-VARSITY FELLOWSHIP
© 1962 GEORGE PHILIP & SON, LTD.

MAP 4
PALESTINE IN THE TIME OF THE JUDGES
0 5 10 15 20 25 30 Miles
0 5 10 15 20 25 30 35 40 45 50 Kms.
THE GREAT SEA
Sidon
PHOENICIANS
ASHER
Tyre
Dan
Misrephoth-maim
Kedesh-naphtali
NAPHTALI
Meroz
Hazor
Merom
Achshaph
Beth-anath
Rehob
Chinnereth
Aphek
Kishon
Carmel
Madôn
Bethlehem
Tabor
Harosheth
Shimron-meron
ISSACHAR
Jokneam
Moreh
Dor
Ophrah
HAVVOTH - JAIR
BASHAN
Megiddo
Zaanannim
Jezreel
Kedesh
Harod
Taanach
Beth-shean
MANASSEH
Jabesh-gilead
Thebez
Abel-meholah
Tirzah
Zaphon
Ebal
Shechem
Pirathon
Gerizim
Jordan
Succoth
Jabbok
Penuel
Tappuah
Adam
Mizpah
Aphek
Zarethan
Shiloh
GAD
EPHRAIM
Timnath-heres
Jogbehah
AMMON
Bethel
Rimmon
Beth-horon
Ai
Shaalbim
Mizpah
Ramah
Jericho
Gilgal
Ekron
Gezer
Gibeon
Geba
Aijalon
Gibeah
Minnith
DAN
Chephirah
BENJAMIN
Beth-jeshimoth
Heshbon
Eshtaol
Jerusalem
Zorah
Kiriath-jearim
Nebo
Ashdod
Timnah
Makkedah
Libnah
Jarmuth
Bethlehem
Azekah
Adullam
Etam
REUBEN
Ashkelon
Gath
Lachish
PHILISTINES
Gaza
Hebron
SALT SEA
JUDAH
Debir
MOAB
Beersheba
Hormah
Ascent of Akrabbim
EDOM
ALL RIGHTS IN THE SPECI
RESERVED TO INTER-VARS
© 1962 GEORGE PH

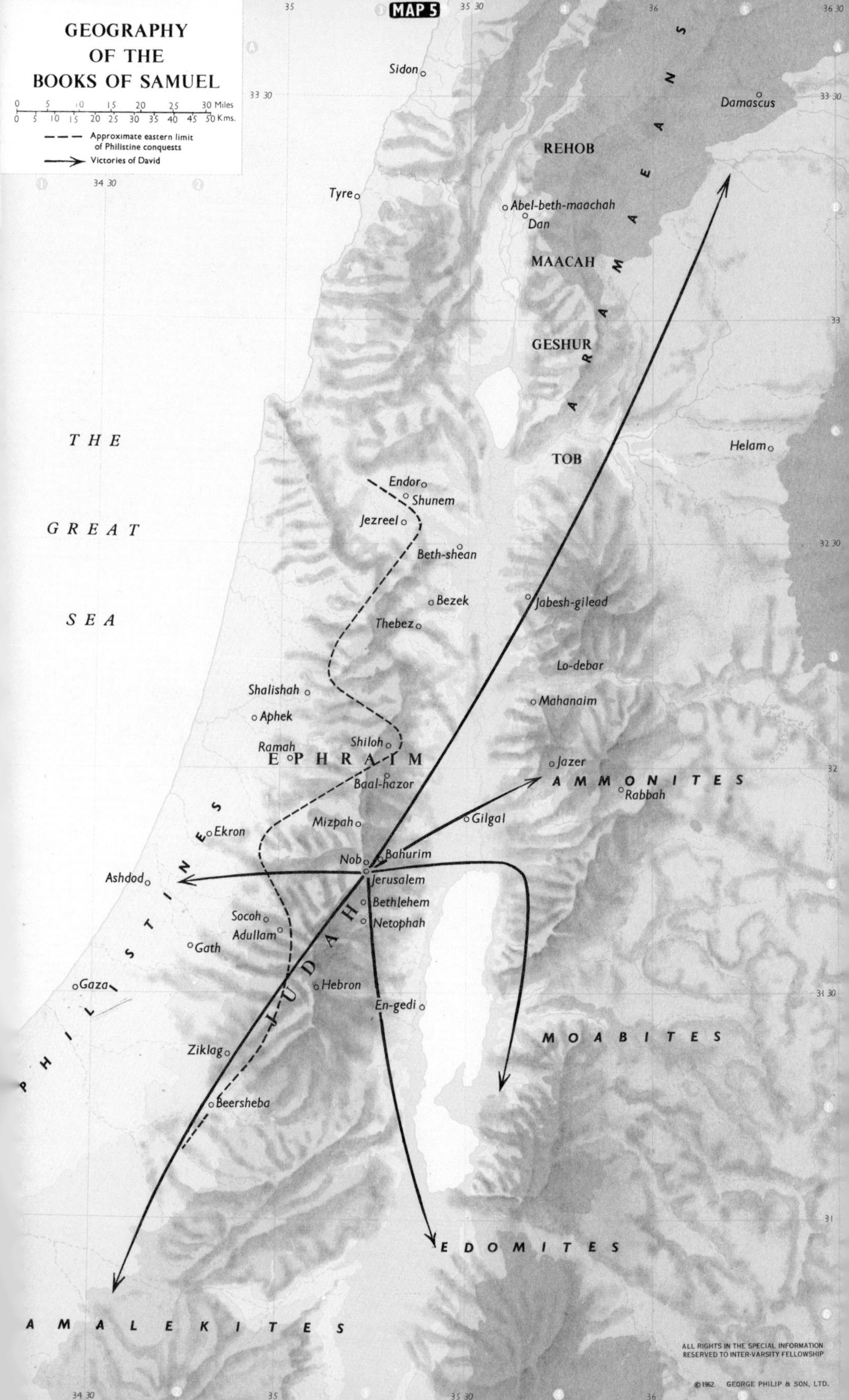
MAP 5
GEOGRAPHY OF THE BOOKS OF SAMUEL
0 5 10 15 20 25 30 Miles
0 5 10 15 20 25 30 35 40 45 50 Kms.
Approximate eastern limit of Philistine conquests
Victories of David
THE GREAT SEA
Sidon
Tyre
Damascus
REHOB
Abel-beth-maachah
Dan
MAACAH
GESHUR
TOB
ARAMAEANS
Helam
Endor
Shunem
Jezreel
Beth-shean
Bezek
Jabesh-gilead
Thebez
Lo-debar
Mahanaim
Shalishah
Aphek
Shiloh
Ramah
EPHRAIM
Jazer
AMMONITES
Rabbah
Baal-hazor
Gilgal
Mizpah
Ekron
Nob
Bahurim
Jerusalem
Ashdod
Bethlehem
Netophah
Socoh
Adullam
Gath
Gaza
Hebron
En-gedi
JUDAH
PHILISTINES
MOABITES
Ziklag
Beersheba
EDOMITES
AMALEKITES
34 30
35
35 30
36
36 30
33 30
33
32 30
32
31 30
31
ALL RIGHTS IN THE SPECIAL INFORMATION RESERVED TO INTER-VARSITY FELLOWSHIP
©1962. GEORGE PHILIP & SON, LTD.

MAP 6
THE KINGDOMS OF JUDAH AND ISRAEL
0 5 10 15 20 25 30 Miles
0 5 10 15 20 25 30 35 40 45 50 Kms.
Sidon
Zarephath
Tyre
PHOENICIA
Lebanon
Hermon
Abana
Damascus
Pharpar
Abel-beth-maachah
Dan
ARAM
Kedesh-naphtali
Hazor
Chinnereth
GALILEE
Carmel
Kishon
Gath-hepher
THE GREAT SEA
Jokneam
Dor
Shunem
Megiddo
Jezreel
Taanach
HAVVOTH-JAIR
Beth-arbel
Ramoth-gilead
Beth-shean
Ibleam
Dothan
Cherith
Tishbeh
Socoh
Abel-meholah
Tirzah
Samaria
ISRAEL
Shechem
Succoth
Jordan
Penuel
Mahanaim
AMMO
Tappuah
Zarethan
Joppa
Shiloh
Ephron
Zemaraim
Rabbath-ammon
Bethel
Beth-horon
Jericho
Gilgal
Ekron
Gezer
Jabneel
Mizpah
Shaalbim
Geba
Gibbethon
Gibeon
Ramah
Elealeh
Aijalon
Kiriath-jearim
Heshbon
Ashdod
Zorah
Jerusalem
JUDAH
Medeba
Bethlehem
Libnah
Azekah
Baal-meon
Etam
Socoh
Adullam
Tekoa
Maresheth-gath
Zaanan
Mareshah
Ataroth
Beth-zur
Lachish
SALT SEA
Shaphir
Hebron
Dibon
Adoraim
Ziph
En-gedi
PHILISTIA
Gerar
MOAB
Beersheba
Nimrim
Kir-hareseth
EDOM
33 30
33
32 30
32
31 30
31
34 30
35
35 30
36
ALL RIGHTS IN THE SPECI
RESERVED TO INTER-VARS
© 1962. GEORGE PHI

MAP 7
BABYLONIA
0 50 100 150 Miles
0 50 100 150 200 Kms.
Approximate boundary of Assyrian Empire c. 640 B C
Approximate boundary of Neo-Babylonian Empire c. 580 B C
(BLACK SEA)
LYDIA
Sardis
YAMAN
Pteria
MEDIAN EMPIRE
URARTU (ARARAT)
Tušpa
THE GREAT SEA
Harran
Gozan
Calno
Carchemish
Arpad
CHALDAEAN EMPIRE
Nineveh
Calah
Assur
Rezeph
Eden
Hamath
Ecbatana
Gebal
Riblah
Helbon
Damascus
Tyre
ELAM
Euphrates
Tigris
Dur Kurigalzu
Babylon
Nippur
Shushan
Samaria
Ashdod
Jerusalem
Sais
Tahpanhes
On
Memphis
Sela
Bozrah
Elath
Ur
Persepolis
Teima
Dedan
Nile
Thebes

MAP 8
PALESTINE IN OLD TESTAMENT TIMES
0 5 10 15 Miles
0 5 10 15 20 Kms.
Gibeon Ancient names
El-Jib Modern names
Aphek Other names
Excavated sites
33 30
34 30
35
35 30
36
36 30
33
32 30
Sidon
Zarephath
Damascus
Ijon?
Tyre
Abel-beth-maachah
(Abel-maim)
Laish, Dan
Baal-gad?
Janoah?
Kadesh
Iron
Misrephoth-maim
Achzib
Hazor
Tell el-Qedah
Merom
Ramah
Acco
Aphek
MT. CARMEL
Abu Hawan
Hannathon
Madon
SEA OF
CHINNERETH
—695ft.
Aphek
Golan
Karnaim
Ashtaroth
Harosheth?
Gath-hepher
Beth-yerah
Khirbet Kerak
Athlit
Shimron
Abila
THE
Jokneam
Endor
Dor
Megiddo
Tell el-Mutesellim
Shunem
Lo-debar
Edrei
Jezreel
Ramoth-gilead
Tob?
Taanach
Tell Ta'annak
GREAT
Arubboth?
Beth-haggan
Beth-shean
Scythopolis
Tell el-Husn
Pella
Ibleam
Sharon
Hadera
Dothan
Tell Dotha
Jabesh-gilead
Bezek
Tishbeh
Mahanaim

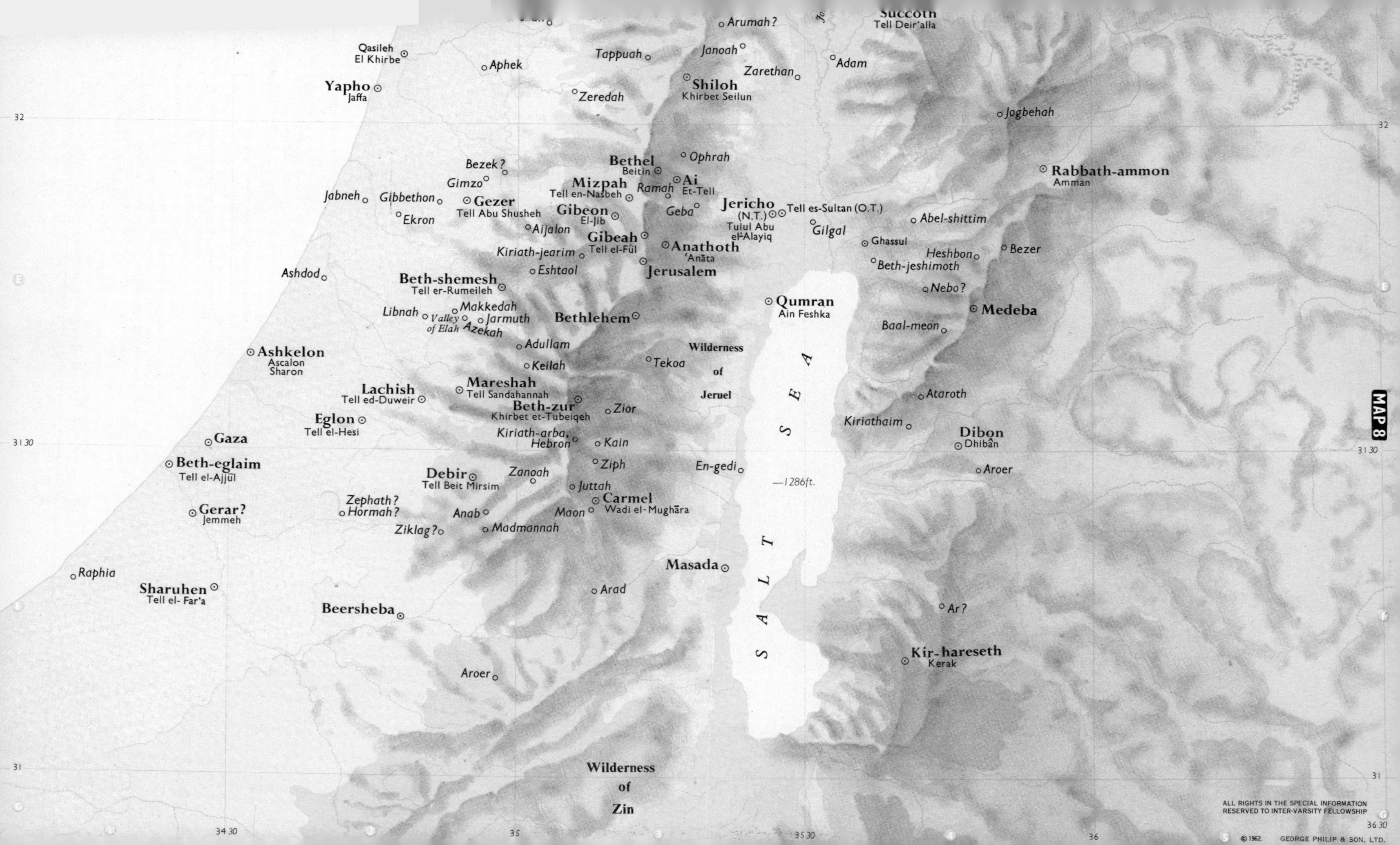
MAP 8
Succoth
Tell Deir'alla
Arumah?
Qasileh
El Khirbe
Aphek
Tappuah
Janoah
Adam
Zarethan
Shiloh
Khirbet Seilun
Yapho
Jaffa
Zeredah
Jogbehah
Bethel
Beitin
Ophrah
Bezek?
Gimzo
Rabbath-ammon
Amman
Ai
Et-Tell
Mizpah
Tell en-Nasbeh
Ramah
Jabneh
Gibbethon
Gezer
Tell Abu Shusheh
Gibeon
El-Jib
Geba
Jericho
(N.T.)
Tell es-Sultan (O.T.)
Tulul Abu el-Alayiq
Abel-shittim
Ekron
Aijalon
Gibeah
Tell el-Fûl
Gilgal
Ghassul
Kiriath-jearim
Anathoth
'Anāta
Heshbon
Bezer
Beth-jeshimoth
Ashdod
Eshtaol
Jerusalem
Beth-shemesh
Tell er-Rumeileh
Nebo?
Qumran
Ain Feshka
Medeba
Makkedah
Libnah
Valley of Elah
Jarmuth
Azekah
Bethlehem
Baal-meon
Ashkelon
Ascalon
Sharon
Adullam
Wilderness of Jeruel
Tekoa
Keilah
SALT SEA
Mareshah
Tell Sandahannah
Lachish
Tell ed-Duweir
Ataroth
Beth-zur
Khirbet et-Tubeiqeh
Zior
Eglon
Tell el-Hesi
Kiriathaim
Kiriath-arba,
Hebron
Dibon
Dhibân
Gaza
Kain
Beth-eglaim
Tell el-Ajjul
Ziph
En-gedi
Aroer
Debir
Tell Beit Mirsim
Zanoah
—1286ft.
Juttah
Carmel
Wadi el-Mughāra
Zephath?
Hormah?
Gerar?
Jemmeh
Anab
Maon
Ziklag?
Madmannah
Masada
Raphia
Sharuhen
Tell el-Far'a
Arad
Ar?
Beersheba
Kir-hareseth
Kerak
Aroer
Wilderness of Zin
32
31 30
31
34 30
35
35 30
36
36 30

MAP 9
THE PERSIAN EMPIRE
0 50 100 150 Miles
0 50 100 150 200 Kms.
Boundary of the Empire
(BLACK SEA)
HYRCANIAN SEA
PERSIAN GULF
RED
THE GREAT SEA
MACEDONIA
THESSALY
Thermopylae
Plataea
Salamis
Athens
GREECE (YAMAN)
Sparta
Byzantium
Sestus
LYDIA
Sardis
Miletus
CAPHTOR
Pteria
CAPPADOCIA
CILICIA
Tarsus
Issus
KITTIM
Citium
ARMENIA
ASSYRIA
Harran
Gozan
Halab
Tiphsah
Arbela
Euphrates
Tigris
Arvad
PHOENICIA
ABAR NAHARA
Sidon
Tyre
Damascus
Dor
Samaria
Ashdod
Jerusalem
Gaza
Hebron
LIBYA
Naucratis
Sais
Zoan
Tahpanhes
On
Memphis
EGYPT
Nile
ARABIA
Dumah
Sippar
Babylon
CHALDAEA
Nippur
Erech
Ur
MEDIA
Achmetha
Rages
HYRCANIA
PARTHIA
ANSHAN
Shushan
Ulai
PERSIA
Parsa-garda
Persepolis
ALL RIGHTS IN THE SPECIAL INFORMATION RESERVED TO INTER-VARSITY FELLOWSHIP

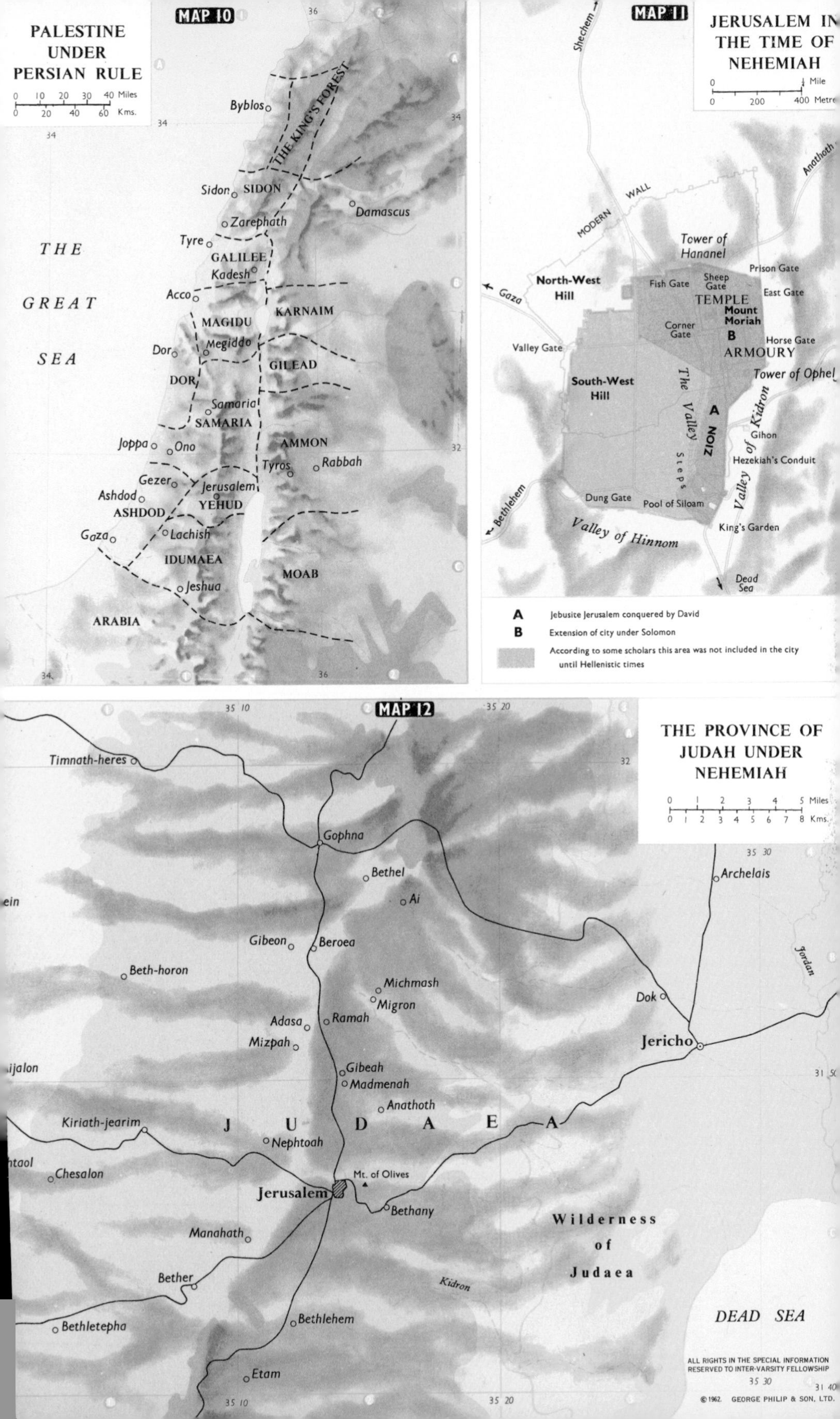
MAP 10
PALESTINE UNDER PERSIAN RULE
0 10 20 30 40 Miles
0 20 40 60 Kms.
THE GREAT SEA
Byblos
THE KING'S FOREST
Sidon
SIDON
Damascus
Zarephath
Tyre
GALILEE
Kadesh
Acco
KARNAIM
MAGIDU
Megiddo
Dor
GILEAD
DOR
Samaria
SAMARIA
Joppa
Ono
AMMON
Tyros
Rabbah
Gezer
Jerusalem
Ashdod
YEHUD
ASHDOD
Gaza
Lachish
IDUMAEA
MOAB
Jeshua
ARABIA
MAP 11
JERUSALEM IN THE TIME OF NEHEMIAH
0 Mile
0 200 400 Metre
Shechem
Anathoth
MODERN WALL
Tower of Hananel
Prison Gate
North-West Hill
Fish Gate
Sheep Gate
East Gate
Gaza
TEMPLE
Mount Moriah
Corner Gate
B
Horse Gate
Valley Gate
ARMOURY
Tower of Ophel
South-West Hill
The Valley
A
Valley of Kidron
ZION
Gihon
Steps
Hezekiah's Conduit
Bethlehem
Dung Gate
Pool of Siloam
Valley of Hinnom
King's Garden
Dead Sea
A Jebusite Jerusalem conquered by David
B Extension of city under Solomon
According to some scholars this area was not included in the city until Hellenistic times
MAP 12
THE PROVINCE OF JUDAH UNDER NEHEMIAH
0 1 2 3 4 5 Miles
0 1 2 3 4 5 6 7 8 Kms.
Timnath-heres
Gophna
Bethel
Archelais
Ai
Gibeon
Beroea
Beth-horon
Jordan
Michmash
Migron
Dok
Adasa
Ramah
Mizpah
Jericho
Gibeah
Madmenah
Anathoth
Kiriath-jearim
J U D A E A
Nephtoah
Chesalon
Mt. of Olives
Jerusalem
Bethany
Wilderness of Judaea
Manahath
Bether
Kidron
Bethletepha
Bethlehem
DEAD SEA
Etam

MAP 13
THE HELLENISTIC EMPIRE
0 50 100 150 Miles
0 50 100 150 200 Kms.
Boundary of the Empire of Alexander the Great
Boundaries of succession states after the battle of Ipsus, 301 BC
(BLACK SEA)
Caucasia
Thrace
Philippopolis
Macedonia
Pella
KINGDOM OF CASSANDER
Hellas
Athens
KINGDOM OF LYSIMACHUS
Mysia
Pergamum
Sardis
Lydia
Ephesus
Gordium
Ipsus
Phrygia
Pisidia
Cappadocia
Cilicia
Issus
Antioch
KINGDOM OF SELEUCUS
Armenia
Nisibis
Media
Rages
Parthia
Ecbatana
Mesopotamia
Syria
Arvad
Byblos
Palmyra
Tyre
Damascus
Coelesyria
Seleucia
Babylonia
Babylon
Shushan
Parsa-garda
Persepolis
MEDITERRANEAN SEA
Jerusalem
Gaza
Alexandria
KINGDOM OF PTOLEMY
Memphis
Egypt
Arabia
PERSIAN GULF

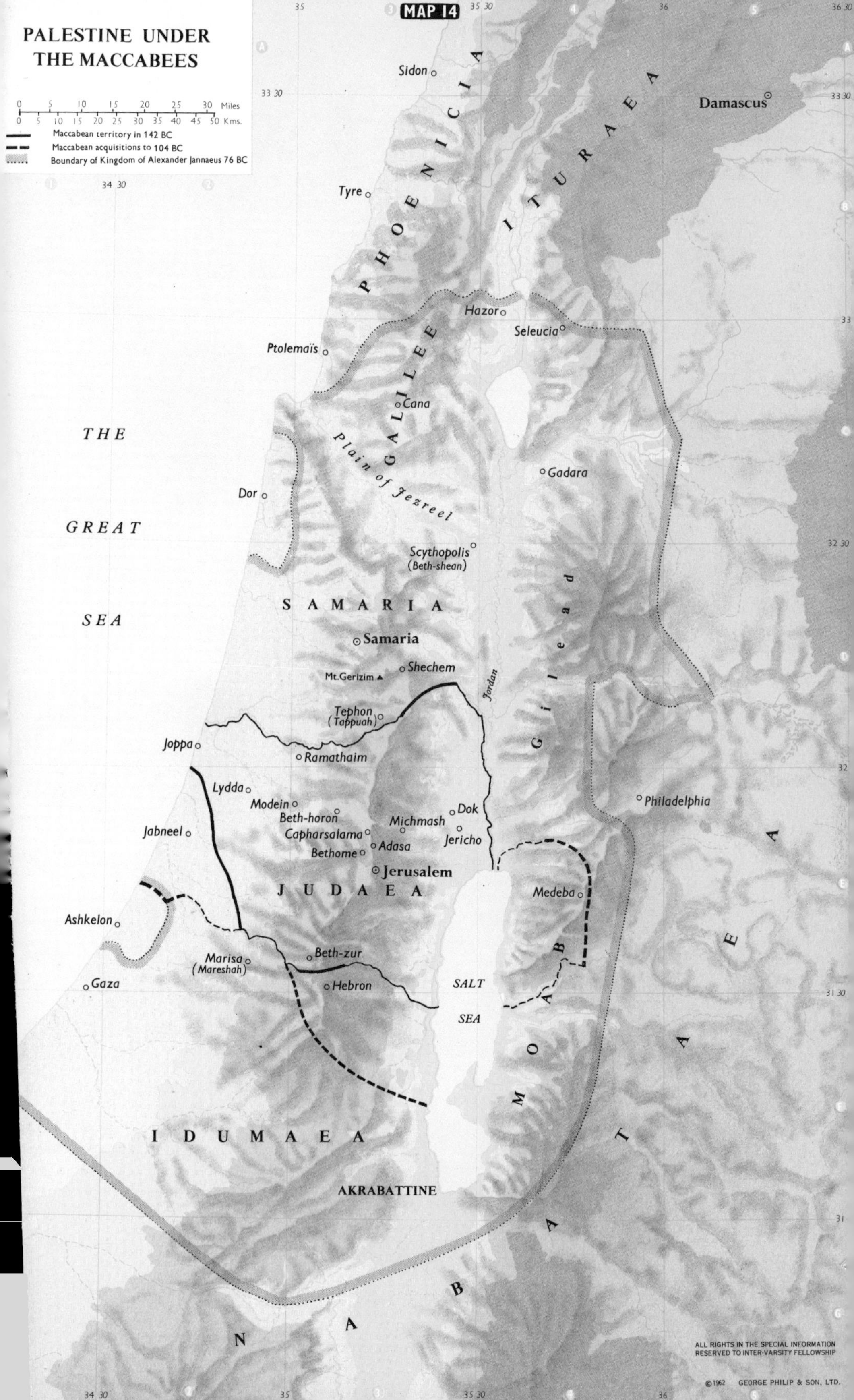
MAP 14
PALESTINE UNDER THE MACCABEES
0 5 10 15 20 25 30 Miles
0 5 10 15 20 25 30 35 40 45 50 Kms.
Maccabean territory in 142 BC
Maccabean acquisitions to 104 BC
Boundary of Kingdom of Alexander Jannaeus 76 BC
35
35 30
36
36 30
33 30
34 30
33
32 30
32
31 30
31
Sidon
PHOENICIA
ITURAEA
Damascus
Tyre
Hazor
Seleucia
Ptolemaïs
GALILEE
Cana
Plain of Jezreel
THE
GREAT
SEA
Dor
Gadara
Scythopolis
(Beth-shean)
SAMARIA
Samaria
Shechem
Mt.Gerizim
Jordan
Gilead
Tephon
(Tappuah)
Joppa
Ramathaim
Lydda
Modein
Beth-horon
Michmash
Dok
Jericho
Philadelphia
Jabneel
Capharsalama
Adasa
Bethome
Jerusalem
JUDAEA
Medeba
Ashkelon
Marisa
(Mareshah)
Beth-zur
Gaza
Hebron
SALT
SEA
MOAB
IDUMAEA
AKRABATTINE
NABATAEA
34 30
35
35 30
36
ALL RIGHTS IN THE SPECIAL INFORMATION RESERVED TO INTER-VARSITY FELLOWSHIP
©1962 GEORGE PHILIP & SON, LTD.

MAP 15
THE ROMAN EMPIRE
0 50 100 150 Miles
0 50 100 150 200 Kms.
Boundary of the Empire at the death of Augustus (AD 14)
PANNONIA
DACIA
REGNUM BOSPORI
PONTUS EUXINUS
Danuvius
DALMATIA
MOESIA
ITALIA
MARE ADRIATICUM
CORSICA
Roma
SARDINIA
THRACIA
MACEDONIA
Philippi
Thessalonica
Byzantium
BITHYNIA
PONTUS
GALATIA
CAPPADOCIA
MESOPOTAMIA
Euphrates
EPIRUS
Nicopolis
MYSIA
ASIA
LYDIA
Ephesus
PHRYGIA
PISIDIA
PAMPHYLIA
LYCIA
CILICIA
Tarsus
Antiochia
SYRIA
SICILIA
Carthago
Corinth
Athenae
ACHAIA
Sparta
RHODUS
CRETA
CYPRUS
MARE INTERNUM
Damascus
Tyrus
Bostra
Caesarea
Jerusalem
Gaza
NABATAEA
AFRICA
Cyrene
CYRENAICA
Alexandria
ALL RIGHTS IN THE SPECIAL INFORMATION

MAP 16
PALESTINE IN NEW TESTAMENT TIMES
0 5 10 15 20 25 30 Miles
0 5 10 15 20 25 30 35 40 45 50 Kms.
Provincial Frontiers
Main Roads
PHOENICIA
ABILENE
Damascus
Pharpar
Hermon
Tyre
Caesarea Philippi
ITURAEA
TRACHONITIS
Ptolemais
Chorazin
Capernaum
Bethsaida
GALILEE
Magdala
Lake of Gennesaret (Sea of Galilee)
Tiberias
Hippos
Cana
Nazareth
Nain
Gadara
Abila
THE GREAT SEA
Plain of Sharon
Caesarea
Scythopolis
DECAPOLIS
Pella
Aenon near Salim
SAMARIA
Sebaste
Gerasa
Sychar
Antipatris
Alexandrium
Joppa
Arimathaea
Jordan
Ephraim
Lydda
PERAEA
Philadelphia
Jamnia
Jericho
Bethany (Bethabara)
Jerusalem
Bethany
Azotus
Kh. Qumran
Bethlehem
Ashkelon
Herodium
JUDAEA
Gaza
Hebron
Machaerus
SALT SEA
Masada
Beersheba
IDUMAEA
NABATAEA
ALL RIGHTS IN THE SPECIAL INFORMATION RESERVED TO INTER-VARSITY FELLOWSHIP
© 1962. GEORGE PHILIP & SON, LTD.

MAP 17
TRAVELS OF ST. PAUL
0 50 100 150 Miles
0 50 100 150 200 Kms.
First Missionary Journey
Second Missionary Journey
Third Missionary Journey
Journey to Rome
The Seven Churches of Asia
PANNONIA
DACIA
ILLYRICUM
MOESIA
Danube
EUXINE SEA
ITALIA
Tiber
Rome
Appii Forum
Puteoli
SEA OF ADRIA
THRACIA
MACEDONIA
Philippi
Neapolis
Amphipolis
Thessalonica
Apollonia
Beroea
Samothrace
Byzantium
Nicomedia
BITHYNIA & PONTUS
KINGDOM OF POLEMON
GALATIA
CAPPADOCIA
Euphrates
ACHAIA
Athens
Corinth
Cenchreae
AEGEAN SEA
Troas
Assos
Adramyttium
Pergamum
Thyatira
Sardis
Mitylene
ASIA
Philadelphia
Smyrna
Laodicea
Colossae
Ephesus
Samos
Miletus
Patmos
Antioch in Pisidia
Iconium
Lystra
Derbe
KINGDOM OF ANTIOCHUS
CILICIA
Tarsus
Perga
Attalia
PAMPHYLIA
LYCIA
Patara
Myra
Cos
Cnidus
Rhodes
Seleucia
Antioch
SYRIA
SICILIA
Rhegium
Syracuse
Melita
CRETE
Phoenix
Lasea
Salmone
Fair Havens
Cauda
Salamis
CYPRUS
Paphos
MEDITERRANEAN SEA
COELESYRIA
Damascus
Sidon
Tyre
Ptolemais
KINGDOM OF HEROD AGRIPPA
Caesarea
Joppa
Antipatris
Jerusalem
Gaza
NABATAEA
Nile Delta
Alexandria
CYRENAICA

R
220.3 D74 C.
DOUGLAS
NEW BIBLE DICTIONARY
12.95